Trust Carol J. Buck and

to take you through the levels of coding success!

Step 4: Specialize

Step 3: Certify

Step 2: Practice

Step 1: Learn

With the resources you need for every level of coding success, **Carol J. Buck** and **Elsevier** are with you every step of your coding career. From beginning to advanced, from the classroom to the workplace, from application to certification, the Step Series products are your guides to greater opportunities and successful career advancement.

Keep climbing with the most trusted name in medical coding!

Author and Educator
Carol J. Buck, MS, CPC-I,
CPC, CPC-H, CCS-P

See the ad in the back of this book for details on the steps to coding success.

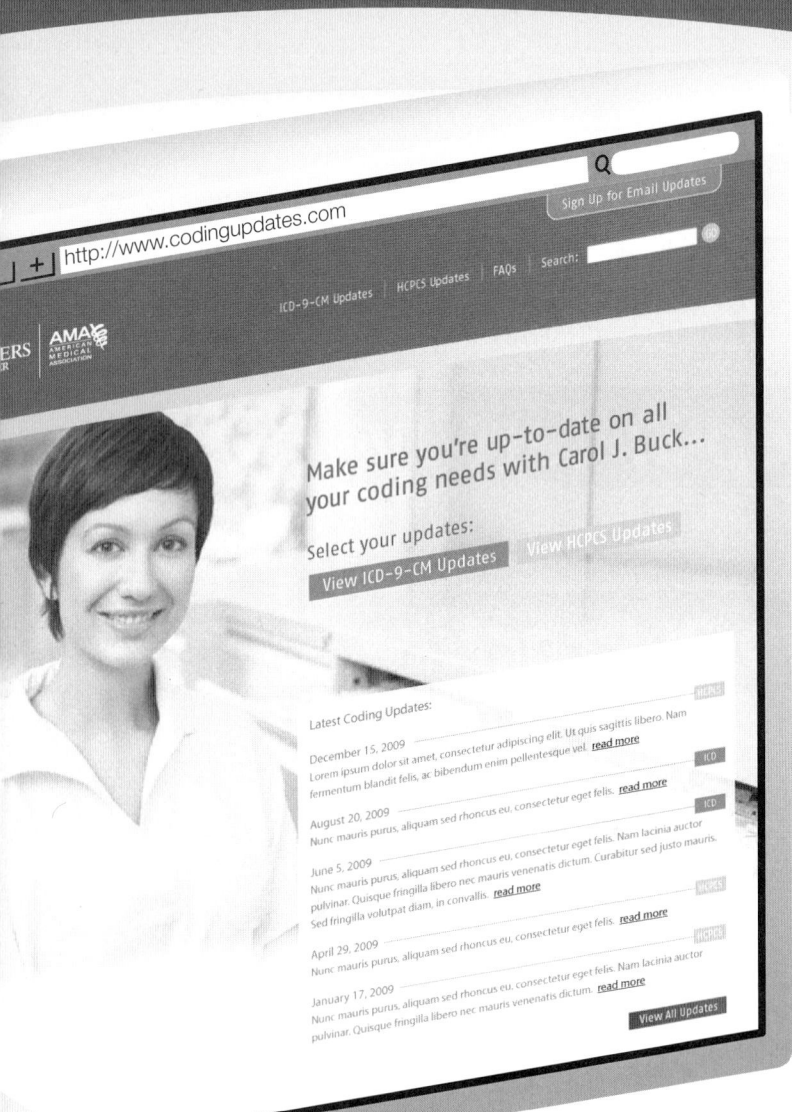

STANDARD EDITION

2010

ICD-10-CM

DRAFT

STANDARD EDITION

INCLUDES NETTER ANATOMY ART

2010

ICD-10-CM

DRAFT

Carol J. Buck
MS, CPC-I, CPC, CPC-H, CCS-P
Program Director, Retired
Medical Secretary Programs
Northwest Technical College
East Grand Forks, Minnesota

SAUNDERS
ELSEVIER

SAUNDERS
ELSEVIER

3251 Riverport Lane
St. Louis, Missouri 63043

2010 ICD-10-CM STANDARD EDITION DRAFT   ISBN: 978-1-4160-2567-2

Notices

Knowledge and best practice in this field are constantly changing. As new research and experience broaden our understanding, changes in research methods, professional practices, or medical treatment may become necessary.

Practitioners and researchers must always rely on their own experience and knowledge in evaluating and using any information, methods, compounds, or experiments described herein. In using such information or methods they should be mindful of their own safety and the safety of others, including parties for whom they have a professional responsibility.

With respect to any drug or pharmaceutical products identified, readers are advised to check the most current information provided (i) on procedures featured or (ii) by the manufacturer of each product to be administered, to verify the recommended dose or formula, the method and duration of administration, and contraindications. It is the responsibility of practitioners, relying on their own experience and knowledge of their patients, to make diagnoses, to determine dosages and the best treatment for each individual patient, and to take all appropriate safety precautions.

To the fullest extent of the law, neither the Publisher nor the authors, contributors, or editors, assume any liability for any injury and/or damage to persons or property as a matter of products liability, negligence or otherwise, or from any use or operation of any methods, products, instructions, or ideas contained in the material herein.

Library of Congress Cataloging-in-Publication Data

Buck, Carol J.
  2010 ICD-10-CM draft / Carol J. Buck. — Standard ed.
    p. ; cm.
  ISBN 978-1-4160-2567-2 (pbk. : alk. paper)
1. Nosology—Code numbers. 2. International classification of diseases, 10th revision, clinical modification. I. American Medical Association. II. Title.
  [DNLM: 1. International statistical classification of diseases and related health problems. 10th revision. Clinical modification. 2. Disease—classification. 3. Forms and Records Control—methods. 4. International Classification of Diseases. 5. Medical Records. WB 15 B922i 2010]
  RB115.B8255 2010
  616.001'2--dc22

                                                        2009053950

Publisher: Michael S. Ledbetter
Developmental Editor: Jenna Johnson
Publishing Services Manager: Pat Joiner-Myers

Printed in Canada

Last digit is the print number: 9 8 7 6 5 4 3 2 1

CONTENTS

ICD-10-CM

SYMBOLS AND CONVENTIONS

The ICD-10-CM, Volume 1, Tabular List contains illustrations, pictures, and items to assist you in understanding difficult terminology, diseases/conditions, or coding in a specific category. Items are always printed in ███████ ink so the added material is not mistaken for official notations or instructions. ███████ ink is used for other annotations in the text. Your ideas on what other descriptions or illustrations should be in future editions of this text are always appreciated.

ICD-10-CM, Volume 1, Tabular List Symbols

Throughout this text revisions and additions are indicated by the following symbols:

- ●   Use Additional Character(s): The colored dot cautions that the code requires additional digit(s) to ensure the greatest specificity.

- ■   Unspecified: The square before a code indicates that although the code is valid as a principal (first-listed) diagnosis, it is not as specific as other codes without the symbol.

- OGCR   The Official Guidelines for Coding and Reporting symbol includes the placement of a portion of a guideline as that guideline pertains to the code by which it is located. The complete OGCR are located in Part I.

- 🖤 🖤   Indicates complications and comorbidities and major complications and comorbidities according to the Inpatient Prospective Payment System (IPPS) rule published in the *Federal Register.*

- ❶   First Listed: The number 1 inside a circle appears before Z codes that are to be listed as the first code.

- ①/②   First Listed or Secondary: The 1/2 inside a circle appears before a Z code to indicate that the code may be the first listed code or a secondary code.

- ❷   Secondary Only: The number 2 inside a circle appears before Z codes that are to be listed as a secondary code. These codes may not be listed as the first code.

Includes

The word "Includes" appears immediately under certain categories to further define, or give examples of, the content of the category.

Excludes Notes

The ICD-10-CM has two types of excludes notes. Each note has a different definition for use, but they are both similar in that they indicate that codes excluded from each other are independent of each other.

Excludes1

A type 1 Excludes note is a pure excludes. It means "NOT CODED HERE!" An Excludes1 note indicates that the code excluded should never be used at the same time as the code above the Excludes1 note. An Excludes1 is for use for when two conditions cannot occur together, such as a congenital form versus an acquired form of the same condition.

Excludes2

A type 2 Excludes note represents "Not included here." An Excludes2 note indicates that the condition excluded is not part of the condition it is excluded from but a patient may have both conditions at the same time. When an Excludes2 note appears under a code, it is acceptable to use both the code and the excluded code together.

Code first / Use additional code notes (etiology/manifestation paired codes)

Certain conditions have both an underlying etiology and multiple body system manifestations due to the underlying etiology. For such conditions the ICD-10-CM has a coding convention that requires the underlying condition be sequenced first, followed by the manifestation. Wherever such a combination exists, there is a "Use additional code" note at the etiology code, and a "code first" note at the manifestation code. These instructional notes indicate the proper sequencing order of the codes, etiology followed by manifestation.

In most cases the manifestation codes will have in the code title, "in diseases classified elsewhere." Codes with this title are a component of the etiology/manifestation convention. The code title indicates that it is a manifestation code. "In diseases classified elsewhere" codes are never permitted to be used as first-listed or principle diagnosis codes. They must be used in conjunction with an underlying condition code and they must be listed following the underlying condition.

Code also

A "code also" note instructs that two codes may be required to fully describe a condition but the sequencing of the two codes is discretionary, depending on the severity of the conditions and the reason for the encounter.

7th characters and placeholder x for codes less than 6 characters that require a 7th character a placeholder x should be assigned for all characters less than 6. The 7th character must always be the 7th character of a code

ICD-10-CM, VOLUMES 1 AND 2 SYMBOLS

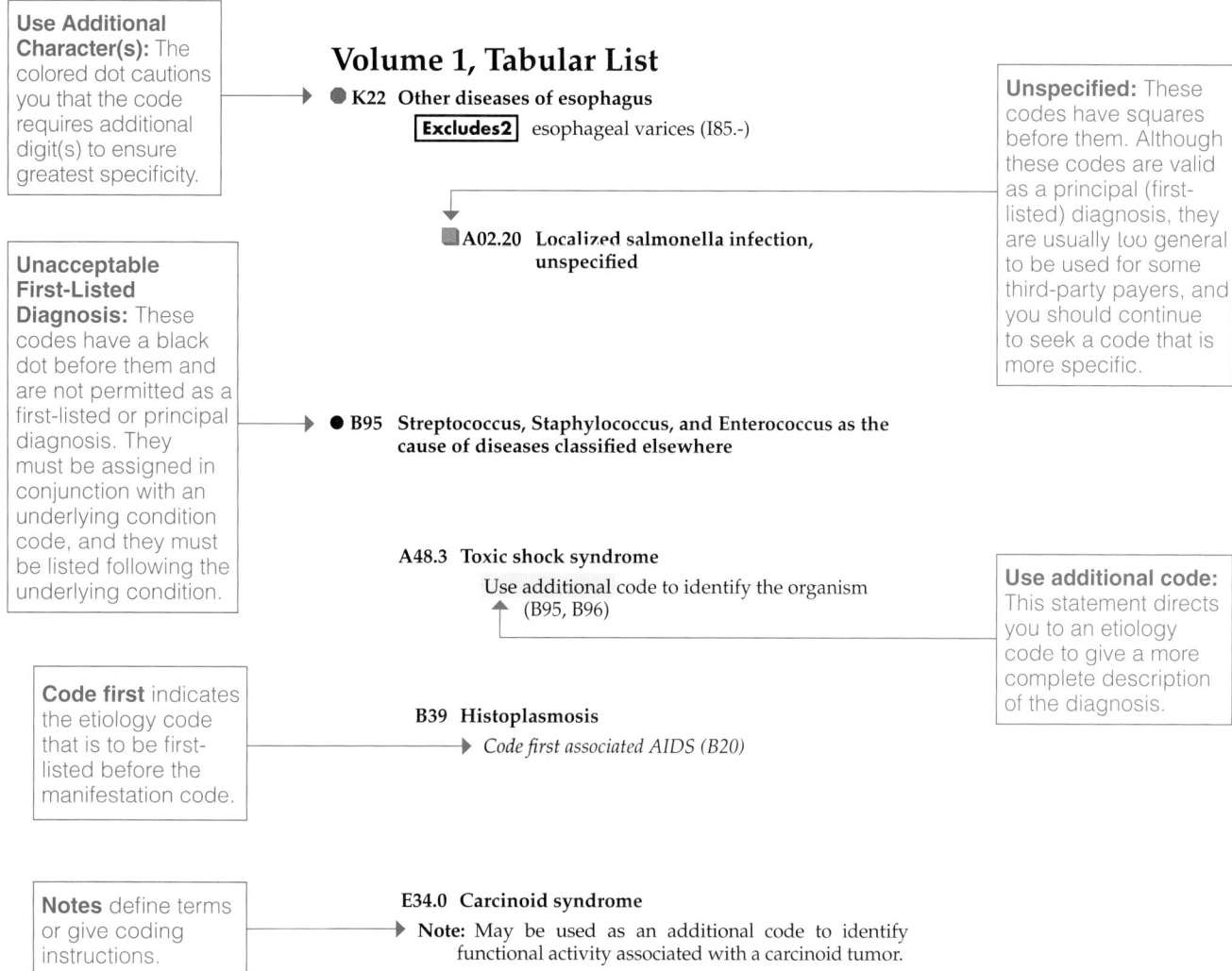

Use Additional Character(s): The colored dot cautions you that the code requires additional digit(s) to ensure greatest specificity.

Unacceptable First-Listed Diagnosis: These codes have a black dot before them and are not permitted as a first-listed or principal diagnosis. They must be assigned in conjunction with an underlying condition code, and they must be listed following the underlying condition.

Code first indicates the etiology code that is to be first-listed before the manifestation code.

Notes define terms or give coding instructions.

Volume 1, Tabular List

● **K22 Other diseases of esophagus**

   Excludes2 esophageal varices (I85.-)

■ **A02.20   Localized salmonella infection, unspecified**

● **B95   Streptococcus, Staphylococcus, and Enterococcus as the cause of diseases classified elsewhere**

A48.3   Toxic shock syndrome

   Use additional code to identify the organism
   (B95, B96)

B39   Histoplasmosis

   Code first associated AIDS (B20)

E34.0   Carcinoid syndrome

   Note: May be used as an additional code to identify functional activity associated with a carcinoid tumor.

Unspecified: These codes have squares before them. Although these codes are valid as a principal (first-listed) diagnosis, they are usually too general to be used for some third-party payers, and you should continue to seek a code that is more specific.

Use additional code: This statement directs you to an etiology code to give a more complete description of the diagnosis.

Codes or index entries are for purposes of illustration only and may not be current.

OGCR Section I.C.6.B.5.
Neoplasm Related Pain Code G89.3 is assigned to pain documented as being related, associated or due to cancer, primary or secondary malignancy, or tumor. This code is assigned regardless of whether the pain is acute or chronic.

OGCR: The Official Guidelines for Coding and Reporting are placed near the codes to which they refer and are highlighted.

First Listed: This symbol appears before Z codes that are acceptable as first-listed diagnoses.

❶ Z33.2 **Encounter for elective termination of pregnancy**
    Excludes1   early fetal death with retention of dead fetus (O02.1)
    late fetal death (O36.4)
    spontaneous abortion (O03)

First or Secondary: This symbol appears before Z codes that are acceptable as first or secondary diagnoses.

Z21 **Asymptomatic human immunodeficiency virus [HIV] infection status**

Secondary Only: This symbol appears before Z codes that are acceptable only as secondary diagnoses.

❷ Z33.1 **Pregnant state, incidental**

I70.2   **Atherosclerosis of native arteries of the extremities**
    Mönckeberg's (medial) sclerosis
    Use additional code, if applicable, to identify chronic total occlusion of artery of extremity (I70.92)

code, if applicable, directs the coder to other conditions that may be appropriate to report.

I74   **Arterial embolism and thrombosis**
    Includes   embolic infarction
    thrombotic infarction
    embolic occlusion
    thrombotic occlusion

The word "and" should be interpreted to mean either "and" or "or" when it appears in a title.

Codes or index entries are for purposes of illustration only and may not be current.

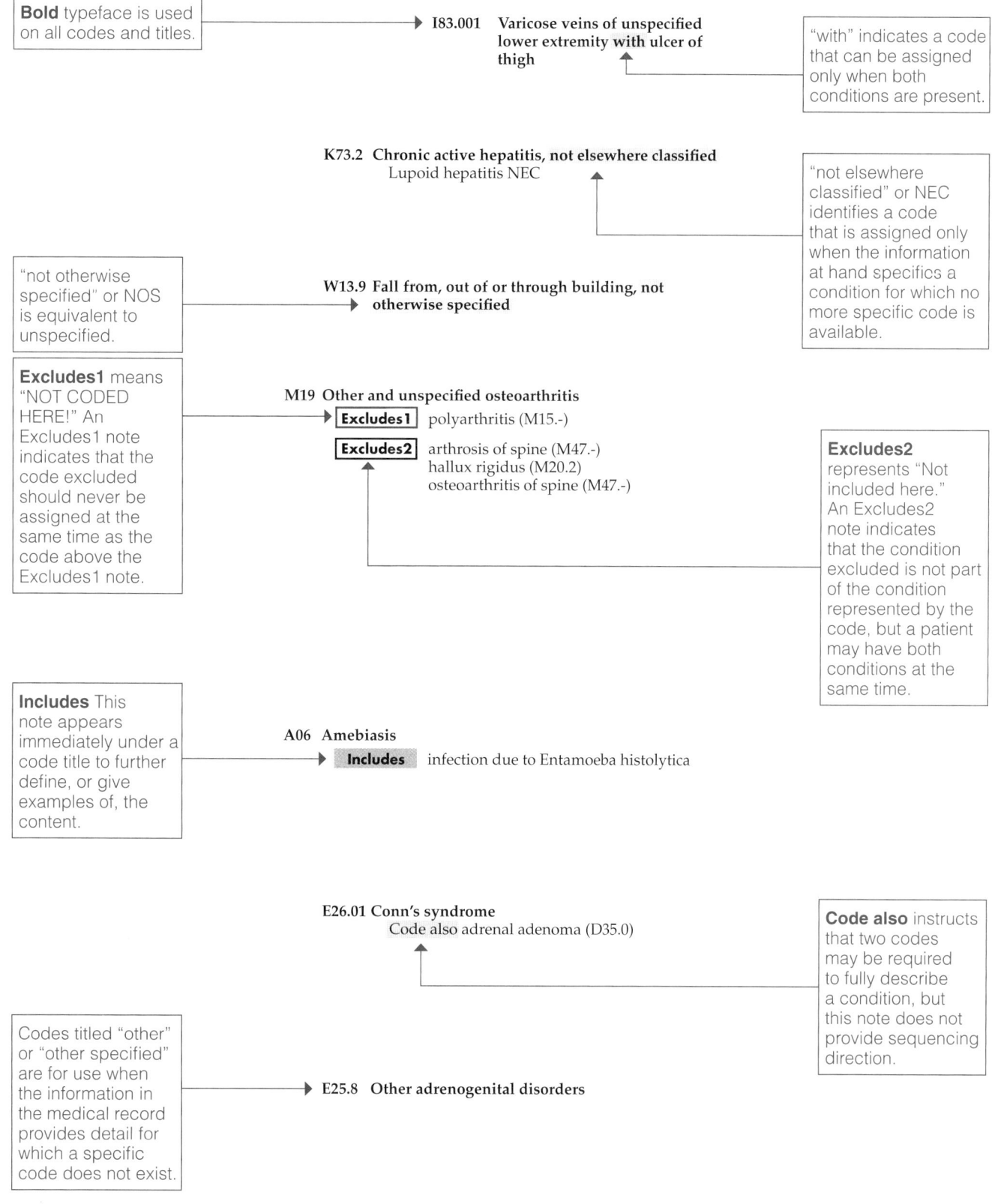

Bold typeface is used on all codes and titles.

I83.001 **Varicose veins of unspecified lower extremity with ulcer of thigh**

"with" indicates a code that can be assigned only when both conditions are present.

K73.2 **Chronic active hepatitis, not elsewhere classified**
Lupoid hepatitis NEC

"not elsewhere classified" or NEC identifies a code that is assigned only when the information at hand specifics a condition for which no more specific code is available.

"not otherwise specified" or NOS is equivalent to unspecified.

W13.9 **Fall from, out of or through building, not otherwise specified**

Excludes1 means "NOT CODED HERE!" An Excludes1 note indicates that the code excluded should never be assigned at the same time as the code above the Excludes1 note.

M19 **Other and unspecified osteoarthritis**
Excludes1 polyarthritis (M15.-)
Excludes2 arthrosis of spine (M47.-)
hallux rigidus (M20.2)
osteoarthritis of spine (M47.-)

Excludes2 represents "Not included here." An Excludes2 note indicates that the condition excluded is not part of the condition represented by the code, but a patient may have both conditions at the same time.

Includes This note appears immediately under a code title to further define, or give examples of, the content.

A06 **Amebiasis**
Includes infection due to Entamoeba histolytica

E26.01 **Conn's syndrome**
Code also adrenal adenoma (D35.0)

Code also instructs that two codes may be required to fully describe a condition, but this note does not provide sequencing direction.

Codes titled "other" or "other specified" are for use when the information in the medical record provides detail for which a specific code does not exist.

E25.8 **Other adrenogenital disorders**

Codes or index entries are for purposes of illustration only and may not be current.

Volume 2, Alphabetic Index

| Main terms are in **bold** typeface. | → | **Aberrant** (congenital) - *see also* Malposition, congenital
    adrenal gland Q89.1 |

STANDARD EDITION

2010

ICD-10-CM

DRAFT

PART I

Introduction

ICD-10-CM Official Guidelines for Coding and Reporting 2010

Narrative changes appear in bold text
Items underlined have been moved within the guidelines
since the 2009 version
Italics **are used to indicate revisions to heading changes**

The Centers for Medicare and Medicaid Services (CMS) and the National Center for Health Statistics (NCHS), two departments within the U.S. Federal Government's Department of Health and Human Services (DHHS) provide the following guidelines for coding and reporting using the International Classification of Diseases, 10th Revision, Clinical Modification (ICD-10-CM). These guidelines should be used as a companion document to the official version of the ICD-10-CM as published on the NCHS website. The ICD-10-CM is a morbidity classification published by the United States for classifying diagnoses and reason for visits in all health care settings. The ICD-10-CM is based on the ICD-10, the statistical classification of disease published by the World Health Organization (WHO).

These guidelines have been approved by the four organizations that make up the Cooperating Parties for the ICD-10-CM: the American Hospital Association (AHA), the American Health Information Management Association (AHIMA), CMS, and NCHS.

These guidelines are a set of rules that have been developed to accompany and complement the official conventions and instructions provided within the ICD-10-CM itself. **The instructions and conventions of the classification take precedence over guidelines.** These guidelines are based on the coding and sequencing instructions in Volumes I, and II of ICD-10-CM, but provide additional instruction. Adherence to these guidelines when assigning ICD-10-CM diagnosis codes is required under the Health Insurance Portability and Accountability Act (HIPAA). The diagnosis codes (Volumes 1-2) have been adopted under HIPAA for all healthcare settings. A joint effort between the healthcare provider and the coder is essential to achieve complete and accurate documentation, code assignment, and reporting of diagnoses and procedures. These guidelines have been developed to assist both the healthcare provider and the coder in identifying those diagnoses and procedures that are to be reported. The importance of consistent, complete documentation in the medical record cannot be overemphasized. Without such documentation accurate coding cannot be achieved. The entire record should be reviewed to determine the specific reason for the encounter and the conditions treated.

The term encounter is used for all settings, including hospital admissions. In the context of these guidelines, the term provider is used throughout the guidelines to mean physician or any qualified health care practitioner who is legally accountable for establishing the patient's diagnosis. Only this set of guidelines, approved by the Cooperating Parties, is official.

1

The guidelines are organized into sections. Section I includes the structure and conventions of the classification and general guidelines that apply to the entire classification, and chapter-specific guidelines that correspond to the chapters as they are arranged in the classification. Section II includes guidelines for selection of principal diagnosis for non-outpatient settings. Section III includes guidelines for reporting additional diagnoses in non-outpatient settings. Section IV is for outpatient coding and reporting. It is necessary to review all sections of the guidelines to fully understand all of the rules and instructions needed to code properly.

ICD-10-CM Official Guidelines for Coding and Reporting

Section I. Conventions, general coding guidelines and chapter specific guidelines

A. Conventions for the ICD-10-CM
1. The Alphabetic Index and Tabular List
2. Format and Structure:
3. Use of codes for reporting purposes
4. Placeholder character
5. 7th Characters
6. Abbreviations
    a. Index abbreviations
    b. Tabular abbreviations
7. Punctuation
8. Use of "and"
9. Other and Unspecified codes
    a. "Other" codes
    b. "Unspecified" codes
10. Includes Notes
11. Inclusion terms
12. Excludes Notes
    a. Excludes1
    b. Excludes2
13. Etiology/manifestation convention ("code first", "use additional code" and "in diseases classified elsewhere" notes)
14. "And"
15. "With"
16. "See" and "See Also"
17. "Code also note"
18. Default codes
19. **Syndromes**

B. General Coding Guidelines
1. Locating a code in the ICD-10-CM
2. Level of Detail in Coding
3. Code or codes from A00.0 through T88.9, Z00-Z99.8
4. Signs and symptoms
5. Conditions that are an integral part of a disease process
6. Conditions that are not an integral part of a disease process
7. Multiple coding for a single condition
8. Acute and Chronic Conditions
9. Combination Code
10. Late Effects (Sequela)
11. Impending or Threatened Condition
12. Reporting Same Diagnosis Code More than Once
13. Laterality
14. **Documentation for BMI and Pressure Ulcer Stages**

C. Chapter-Specific Coding Guidelines
1. Chapter 1: Certain Infectious and Parasitic Diseases (A00-B99)
    a. Human Immunodeficiency Virus (HIV) Infections
    b. Infectious agents as the cause of diseases classified to other chapters
    c. Infections resistant to antibiotics
    d. Sepsis, Severe Sepsis, and Septic Shock

2. Chapter 2: Neoplasms (C00-D49)
   a. Treatment directed at the malignancy
   b. Treatment of secondary site
   c. Coding and sequencing of complications
   d. Primary malignancy previously excised
   e. Admissions/Encounters involving chemotherapy, immunotherapy and radiation therapy
   f. Admission/encounter to determine extent of malignancy
   g. Symptoms, signs, and abnormal findings listed in Chapter 18 associated with neoplasms
   h. Admission/encounter for pain control/management
   i. Malignancy in two or more noncontiguous sites
   j. Disseminated malignant neoplasm, unspecified
   k. Malignant neoplasm without specification of site
   l. Sequencing of neoplasm codes
   m. Current malignancy versus personal history of malignancy
   n. Leukemia in remission versus personal history of leukemia
   o. Aftercare following surgery for neoplasm
   p. Follow-up care for completed treatment of a malignancy
   q. Prophylactic organ removal for prevention of malignancy
   r. Malignant neoplasm associated with transplanted organ
3. Chapter 3: Disease of the blood and blood-forming organs and certain disorders involving the immune mechanism (D50-D89)
4. Chapter 4: Endocrine, Nutritional, and Metabolic Diseases (E00-E89)
   a. Diabetes mellitus
5. Chapter 5: Mental and behavioral disorders (F01 – F99)
   a. Pain disorders related to psychological factors
6. Chapter 6: Diseases of Nervous System and Sense Organs (G00-G99)
   a. Dominant/nondominant side
   b. Pain - Category G89
7. Chapter 7: Diseases of Eye and Adnexa (H00-H59)
8. Chapter 8: Diseases of Ear and Mastoid Process (H60-H95)
9. Chapter 9: Diseases of Circulatory System (I00-I99)
   a. Hypertension
   b. Atherosclerotic coronary artery disease and angina
   c. Intraoperative and Postprocedural cerebrovascular accident
   d. Sequelae of Cerebrovascular Disease
   e. Acute myocardial infarction (AMI)
10. Chapter 10: Diseases of Respiratory System (J00-J99)
    a. Chronic Obstructive Pulmonary Disease [COPD] and Asthma
    b. Acute Respiratory Failure
    c. Influenza due to *certain identified influenza viruses*
11. Chapter 11: Diseases of Digestive System (K00-K94) Reserved for future guideline expansion
12. Chapter 12: Diseases of Skin and Subcutaneous Tissue (L00-L99)
    a. Pressure ulcer stage codes
13. Chapter 13: Diseases of the Musculoskeletal System and Connective Tissue (M00-M99)
    a. Site and laterality
    b. Acute traumatic versus chronic or recurrent musculoskeletal conditions
    c. Coding of Pathologic Fractures
    d. Osteoporosis
14. Chapter 14: Diseases of Genitourinary System (N00-N99)
    a. Chronic kidney disease
15. Chapter 15: Pregnancy, Childbirth, and the Puerperium (O00-O9A)
    a. General Rules for Obstetric Cases
    b. Selection of OB Principal or First-listed Diagnosis
    c. Pre-existing conditions versus conditions due to the pregnancy
    d. Pre-existing hypertension in pregnancy
    e. Fetal Conditions Affecting the Management of the Mother
    f. HIV Infection in Pregnancy, Childbirth and the Puerperium

h. Long term use of insulin

i. Gestational (pregnancy induced) diabetes

j. Sepsis and septic shock complicating abortion, pregnancy, childbirth and the puerperium

k. Puerperal sepsis

l. Alcohol and tobacco use during pregnancy, childbirth and the puerperium

m. Poisoning, toxic effects, adverse effects and underdosing in a pregnant patient

n. Normal Delivery, Code O80

o. The Peripartum and Postpartum Periods

p. Code O94, Sequelae of complication of pregnancy, childbirth, and the puerperium

q. Abortions

16. Chapter 16: Newborn (Perinatal) Guidelines (P00-P96)

    a. General Perinatal Rules

    b. Observation and Evaluation of Newborns for Suspected Conditions not Found

    c. Coding Additional Perinatal Diagnoses

    d. Prematurity and Fetal Growth Retardation

    e. Low birth weight and immaturity status

    f. Bacterial Sepsis of Newborn

    g. Stillbirth

17. Chapter 17: Congenital malformations, deformations, and chromosomal abnormalities (Q00-Q99)

18. Chapter 18: Symptoms, signs, and abnormal clinical and laboratory findings, not elsewhere classified (R00-R99)

    a. Use of symptom codes

    b. Use of a symptom code with a definitive diagnosis code

    c. Combination codes that include symptoms

    d. Repeated falls

    e. Glasgow coma scale

    f. Functional quadriplegia

    g. SIRS due to Non-Infectious Process

    g. Death NOS

19. Chapter 19: Injury, poisoning, and certain other consequences of external causes (S00-T88)

    a. Code Extensions

    b. Coding of Injuries

    c. Coding of Traumatic Fractures

    d. Coding of Burns and Corrosions

    e. Adverse Effects, Poisoning, Underdosing and Toxic Effects

    f. Adult and child abuse, neglect and other maltreatment

    g. Complications of care

20. Chapter 20: External Causes of Morbidity (V01-Y99)

    a. General External Cause Coding Guidelines

    b. Place of Occurrence Guideline

    c. Activity Code

    d. Place of Occurrence, Activity, *and Status* Codes Used with other External Cause Code

    e. If the Reporting Format Limits the Number of External Cause Codes

    f. Multiple External Cause Coding Guidelines

    g. Child and Adult Abuse Guideline

    h. Unknown or Undetermined Intent Guideline

    i. Late Effects of External Cause Guidelines

    j. Terrorism Guidelines

    k. External cause status

21. Chapter 21: Factors influencing health status and contact with health services (Z00-Z99)

    a. Use of Z codes in any healthcare setting

    b. Z Codes indicate a reason for an encounter

    c. Categories of Z Codes

Section II. Selection of Principal Diagnosis

A. Codes for symptoms, signs, and ill-defined conditions
B. Two or more interrelated conditions, each potentially meeting the definition for principal diagnosis
C. Two or more diagnoses that equally meet the definition for principal diagnosis
D. Two or more comparative or contrasting conditions
E. A symptom(s) followed by contrasting/comparative diagnoses
F. Original treatment plan not carried out
G. Complications of surgery and other medical care
H. Uncertain Diagnosis
 I. Admission from Observation Unit
    1. Admission Following Medical Observation
    2. Admission Following Post-Operative Observation
 J. Admission from Outpatient Surgery

Section III. Reporting Additional Diagnoses

A. Previous conditions
B. Abnormal findings
C. Uncertain Diagnosis

Section IV. Diagnostic Coding and Reporting Guidelines for Outpatient Services

A. Selection of first-listed condition
    1. Outpatient Surgery
    2. Observation Stay
B. Codes from A00.0 through T88.9, Z00-Z99
C. Accurate reporting of ICD-10-CM diagnosis codes
D. Codes that describe symptoms and signs
E. Encounters for circumstances other than a disease or injury
F. Level of Detail in Coding
    1. ICD-10-CM codes with 3, 4, or 5 digits
    2. Use of full number of digits required for a code
G. ICD-10-CM code for the diagnosis, condition, problem, or other reason for encounter/visit
H. Uncertain diagnosis
 I. Chronic diseases
 J. Code all documented conditions that coexist
K. Patients receiving diagnostic services only
L. Patients receiving therapeutic services only
M. Patients receiving preoperative evaluations only
N. Ambulatory surgery
O. Routine outpatient prenatal visits
P. Encounters for general medical examinations with abnormal findings
Q. Encounters for routine health screenings

Section I. Conventions, general coding guidelines and chapter specific guidelines

The conventions, general guidelines and chapter-specific guidelines are applicable to all health care settings unless otherwise indicated. **The conventions and instructions of the classification take precedence over guidelines.**

A. **Conventions for the ICD-10-CM**
<u>**The conventions for the ICD-10-CM are the general rules for use of the classification independent of the guidelines. These conventions are incorporated within the Index and Tabular of the ICD-10-CM as instructional notes.**</u>

  1. **The Alphabetic Index and Tabular List**
    The ICD-10-CM is divided into the Index, an alphabetical list of terms and their corresponding code, and the Tabular List, a chronological list of codes divided into chapters based on body system or condition. The Index is

divided into two parts, the Index to Diseases and Injury, and the Index to External Causes of Injury. Within the Index of Diseases and Injury there is a Neoplasm Table and a Table of Drugs and Chemicals.

See Section I.C2. General guidelines
See Section I.C.19. Adverse effects, poisoning, underdosing and toxic effects

2. **Format and Structure:**
   The ICD-10-CM Tabular List contains categories, subcategories and codes. Characters for categories, subcategories and codes may be either a letter or a number. All categories are 3 characters. A three-character category that has no further subdivision is equivalent to a code. Subcategories are either 4 or 5 characters. Codes may be 4, 5, 6 or 7 characters. That is, each level of subdivision after a category is a subcategory. The final level of subdivision is a code. All codes in the Tabular List of the official version of the ICD-10-CM are in bold. Codes that have applicable 7th characters are still referred to as codes, not subcategories. A code that has an applicable 7th character is considered invalid without the 7th character.

   The ICD-10-CM uses an indented format for ease in reference

3. **Use of codes for reporting purposes**
   For reporting purposes only codes are permissible, not categories or subcategories, and any applicable 7th character is required.

4. **Placeholder character**
   The ICD-10-CM utilizes a placeholder character "X". The "X" is used as a 5th character placeholder at certain 6 character codes to allow for future expansion. An example of this is at the poisoning, adverse effect and underdosing codes, categories T36-T50. Where a placeholder exists, the X must be used in order for the code to be considered a valid code.

5. **7th Characters**
   Certain ICD-10-CM categories have applicable 7th characters. The applicable 7th character is required for all codes within the category, or as the notes in the Tabular List instruct. The 7th character must always be the 7th character in the data field. If a code that requires a 7th character is not 6 characters, a placeholder X must be used to fill in the empty characters.

6. **Abbreviations**
   a. **Index abbreviations**
      NEC "Not elsewhere classifiable"
      This abbreviation in the Index represents "other specified". When a specific code is not available for a condition the Index directs the coder to the "other specified" code in the Tabular.

   b. **Tabular abbreviations**
      NEC "Not elsewhere classifiable"
      This abbreviation in the Tabular represents "other specified". When a specific code is not available for a condition, the Tabular includes an NEC entry under a code to identify the code as the "other specified" code.
      NOS "Not otherwise specified"
      This abbreviation is the equivalent of unspecified.

7. **Punctuation**
   [ ] Brackets are used in the tabular list to enclose synonyms, alternative wording or explanatory phrases. Brackets are used in the Index to identify manifestation codes.
   ( ) Parentheses are used in both the Index and Tabular to enclose supplementary words that may be present or absent in the statement of a disease or procedure without affecting the code number to which it is assigned. The terms within the parentheses are referred to as nonessential modifiers.
   : Colons are used in the Tabular List after an incomplete term which needs one or more of the modifiers following the colon to make it assignable to a given category.

8. **Use of "and"**
   When the term "and" is used in a narrative statement it represents and/or.

9. **Other and Unspecified codes**

   a. **"Other" codes**
   Codes titled "other" or "other specified" are for use when the information in the medical record provides detail for which a specific code does not exist. Index entries with NEC in the line designate "other" codes in the Tabular. These Index entries represent specific disease entities for which no specific code exists so the term is included within an "other" code.

   b. **"Unspecified" codes**
   Codes (usually a code with a 4th digit 9 or 5th digit 0 for diagnosis codes) titled "unspecified" are for use when the information in the medical record is insufficient to assign a more specific code. For those categories for which an unspecified code is not provided, the "other specified" code may represent both other and unspecified.

10. **Includes Notes**
    This note appears immediately under a three-digit code title to further define, or give examples of, the content of the category.

11. **Inclusion terms**
    List of terms is included under some codes. These terms are the conditions for which that code is to be used. The terms may be synonyms of the code title, or, in the case of "other specified" codes, the terms are a list of the various conditions assigned to that code. The inclusion terms are not necessarily exhaustive. Additional terms found only in the Index may also be assigned to a code.

12. **Excludes Notes**
    The ICD-10-CM has two types of excludes notes. Each type of note has a different definition for use but they are all similar in that they indicate that codes excluded from each other are independent of each other.

    a. **Excludes1**
    A type 1 Excludes note is a pure excludes note. It means "NOT CODED HERE!" An Excludes1 note indicates that the code excluded should never be used at the same time as the code above the Excludes1 note. An Excludes1 is used when two conditions cannot occur together, such as a congenital form versus an acquired form of the same condition.

    b. **Excludes2**
    A type 2 excludes note represents "Not included here". An excludes2 note indicates that the condition excluded is not part of the condition represented by the code, but a patient may have both conditions at the same time. When an Excludes2 note appears under a code, it is acceptable to use both the code and the excluded code together, when appropriate.

13. **Etiology/manifestation convention ("code first", "use additional code" and "in diseases classified elsewhere" notes)**
    Certain conditions have both an underlying etiology and multiple body system manifestations due to the underlying etiology. For such conditions, the ICD-10-CM has a coding convention that requires the underlying condition be sequenced first followed by the manifestation. Wherever such a combination exists, there is a "use additional code" note at the etiology code, and a "code first" note at the manifestation code. These instructional notes indicate the proper sequencing order of the codes, etiology followed by manifestation.

    In most cases the manifestation codes will have in the code title, "in diseases classified elsewhere." Codes with this title are a component of the etiology/manifestation convention. The code title indicates that it is a manifestation code. "In diseases classified elsewhere" codes are never permitted to be used as first listed or principal diagnosis codes. They must be used in conjunction with an underlying condition code and they must be listed following the underlying condition. See category F02, Dementia in other diseases classified elsewhere, for an example of this convention.

There are manifestation codes that do not have "in diseases classified elsewhere" in the title. For such codes a "use additional code" note will still be present and the rules for sequencing apply.

In addition to the notes in the Tabular, these conditions also have a specific Index entry structure. In the Index both conditions are listed together with the etiology code first followed by the manifestation codes in brackets. The code in brackets is always to be sequenced second.

An example of the etiology/manifestation convention is dementia in Parkinson's disease. In the index, code G20 is listed first, followed by code F02.80 or F02.81 in brackets. Code G20 represents the underlying etiology, Parkinson's disease, and must be sequenced first, whereas codes F02.80 and F02.81 represent the manifestation of dementia in diseases classified elsewhere, with or without behavioral disturbance.

"Code first" and "Use additional code" notes are also used as sequencing rules in the classification for certain codes that are not part of an etiology/ manifestation combination. *See Section I.B.7. Multiple coding for a single condition.*

14. **"And"**
The word "and" should be interpreted to mean either "and" or "or" when it appears in a title.

15. **"With"**
The word "with" in the Alphabetic Index is sequenced immediately following the main term, not in alphabetical order.

16. **"See" and "See Also"**
The "see" instruction following a main term in the Index indicates that another term should be referenced. It is necessary to go to the main term referenced with the "see" note to locate the correct code.

A "see also" instruction following a main term in the index instructs that there is another main term that may also be referenced that may provide additional index entries that may be useful. It is not necessary to follow the "see also" note when the original main term provides the necessary code.

17. **"Code also note"**
A "code also" note instructs that two codes may be required to fully describe a condition, but this note does not provide sequencing direction.

18. **Default codes**
A code listed next to a main term in the ICD-10-CM Index is referred to as a default code. The default code represents that condition that is most commonly associated with the main term, or is the unspecified code for the condition. If a condition is documented in a medical record (for example, appendicitis) without any additional information, such as acute or chronic, the default code should be assigned.

19. **Syndromes**
**Follow the Alphabetic Index guidance when coding syndromes.
In the absence of index guidance, assign codes for the documented manifestations of the syndrome.**

B. **General Coding Guidelines**

1. **Locating a code in the ICD-10-CM**
To select a code in the classification that corresponds to a diagnosis or reason for visit documented in a medical record, first locate the term in the Index, and then verify the code in the Tabular List. Read and be guided by instructional notations that appear in both the Index and the Tabular List.

It is essential to use both the Index and Tabular List when locating and assigning a code. The Index does not always provide the full code. Selection of the full code, including laterality and any applicable 7th character can only be done in the Tabular list. A dash (-) at the end of an Index entry indicates that additional characters are required. Even if a dash is not included at the Index entry, it is necessary to refer to the Tabular list to verify that no 7th character is required.

2. **Level of Detail in Coding**

   Diagnosis codes are to be used and reported at their highest number of digits available.

   ICD-10-CM diagnosis codes are composed of codes with 3, 4, 5, 6 or 7 digits. Codes with three digits are included in ICD-10-CM as the heading of a category of codes that may be further subdivided by the use of fourth and/or fifth digits, which provide greater detail.

   A three-digit code is to be used only if it is not further subdivided. A code is invalid if it has not been coded to the full number of characters required for that code, including the 7th character, if applicable.

3. **Code or codes from A00.0 through T88.9, Z00-Z99.8**

   The appropriate code or codes from A00.0 through T88.9, Z00-Z99.8 must be used to identify diagnoses, symptoms, conditions, problems, complaints or other reason(s) for the encounter/visit.

4. **Signs and symptoms**

   Codes that describe symptoms and signs, as opposed to diagnoses, are acceptable for reporting purposes when a related definitive diagnosis has not been established (confirmed) by the provider. Chapter 18 of ICD-10-CM, Symptoms, Signs, and Abnormal Clinical and Laboratory Findings, Not Elsewhere Classified (codes R00.0 - R99) contains many, but not all codes for symptoms.

5. **Conditions that are an integral part of a disease process**

   Signs and symptoms that are associated routinely with a disease process should not be assigned as additional codes, unless otherwise instructed by the classification.

6. **Conditions that are not an integral part of a disease process**

   Additional signs and symptoms that may not be associated routinely with a disease process should be coded when present.

7. **Multiple coding for a single condition**

   In addition to the etiology/manifestation convention that requires two codes to fully describe a single condition that affects multiple body systems, there are other single conditions that also require more than one code. "Use additional code" notes are found in the Tabular at codes that are not part of an etiology/manifestation pair where a secondary code is useful to fully describe a condition. The sequencing rule is the same as the etiology/ manifestation pair, "use additional code" indicates that a secondary code should be added.

   For example, for bacterial infections that are not included in chapter 1, a secondary code from category B95, Streptococcus, Staphylococcus, and Enterococcus, as the cause of diseases classified elsewhere, or B96, Other bacterial agents as the cause of diseases classified elsewhere, may be required to identify the bacterial organism causing the infection. A "use additional code" note will normally be found at the infectious disease code, indicating a need for the organism code to be added as a secondary code.

   "Code first" notes are also under certain codes that are not specifically manifestation codes but may be due to an underlying cause. When there is a "code first" note and an underlying condition is present, the underlying condition should be sequenced first.

   "Code, if applicable, any causal condition first", notes indicate that this code may be assigned as a principal diagnosis when the causal condition is unknown or not applicable. If a causal condition is known, then the code for that condition should be sequenced as the principal or first-listed diagnosis.

   Multiple codes may be needed for late effects, complication codes and obstetric codes to more fully describe a condition. See the specific guidelines for these conditions for further instruction.

8. **Acute and Chronic Conditions**

   If the same condition is described as both acute (subacute) and chronic, and separate subentries exist in the Alphabetic Index at the same indentation level, code both and sequence the acute (subacute) code first.

9. **Combination Code**
A combination code is a single code used to classify:
Two diagnoses, or
A diagnosis with an associated secondary process (manifestation)
A diagnosis with an associated complication
Combination codes are identified by referring to subterm entries in the Alphabetic Index and by reading the inclusion and exclusion notes in the Tabular List.

Assign only the combination code when that code fully identifies the diagnostic conditions involved or when the Alphabetic Index so directs. Multiple coding should not be used when the classification provides a combination code that clearly identifies all of the elements documented in the diagnosis. When the combination code lacks necessary specificity in describing the manifestation or complication, an additional code should be used as a secondary code.

10. **Late Effects (Sequela)**
A late effect is the residual effect (condition produced) after the acute phase of an illness or injury has terminated. There is no time limit on when a late effect code can be used. The residual may be apparent early, such as in cerebral infarction, or it may occur months or years later, such as that due to a previous injury. Coding of late effects generally requires two codes sequenced in the following order: The condition or nature of the late effect is sequenced first. The late effect code is sequenced second.

An exception to the above guidelines are those instances where the code for late effect is followed by a manifestation code identified in the Tabular List and title, or the late effect code has been expanded (at the fourth, fifth or sixth character levels) to include the manifestation(s). The code for the acute phase of an illness or injury that led to the late effect is never used with a code for the late effect.
See Section I.C.9. Sequelae of cerebrovascular disease
See Section I.C.15. Sequelae of complication of pregnancy, childbirth and the puerperium
See Section I.C.19. Code extensions

11. **Impending or Threatened Condition**
Code any condition described at the time of discharge as "impending" or "threatened" as follows:
If it did occur, code as confirmed diagnosis.
If it did not occur, reference the Alphabetic Index to determine if the condition has a subentry term for "impending" or "threatened" and also reference main term entries for "Impending" and for "Threatened."
If the subterms are listed, assign the given code.
If the subterms are not listed, code the existing underlying condition(s) and not the condition described as impending or threatened.

12. **Reporting Same Diagnosis Code More than Once**
Each unique ICD-10-CM diagnosis code may be reported only once for an encounter. This applies to bilateral conditions **when there are no distinct codes identifying laterality** or two different conditions classified to the same ICD-10-CM diagnosis code.

13. **Laterality**
For bilateral sites, the final character of the codes in the ICD-10-CM indicates laterality. An unspecified side code is also provided should the side not be identified in the medical record. If no bilateral code is provided and the condition is bilateral, assign separate codes for both the left and right side.

14. **Documentation for BMI and Pressure Ulcer Stages**
For the Body Mass Index (BMI) and pressure ulcer stage codes, code assignment may be based on medical record documentation from clinicians who are not the patient's provider (i.e., physician or other qualified healthcare practitioner legally accountable for establishing the patient's diagnosis), since this information is typically documented by other clinicians involved in the care of the patient (e.g., a dietitian often documents the BMI and nurses often documents the pressure ulcer

stages). However, the associated diagnosis (such as overweight, obesity, or pressure ulcer) must be documented by the patient's provider. If there is conflicting medical record documentation, either from the same clinician or different clinicians, the patient's attending provider should be queried for clarification.

The BMI codes should only be reported as secondary diagnoses. As with all other secondary diagnosis codes, the BMI codes should only be assigned when they meet the definition of a reportable additional diagnosis (see Section III, Reporting Additional Diagnoses).

C. Chapter-Specific Coding Guidelines

In addition to general coding guidelines, there are guidelines for specific diagnoses and/or conditions in the classification. Unless otherwise indicated, these guidelines apply to all health care settings. Please refer to Section II for guidelines on the selection of principal diagnosis.

1. Chapter 1: Certain Infectious and Parasitic Diseases (A00-B99)

a. Human Immunodeficiency Virus (HIV) Infections

1) Code only confirmed cases

Code only confirmed cases of HIV infection/illness. This is an exception to the hospital inpatient guideline Section II, H.

In this context, "confirmation" does not require documentation of positive serology or culture for HIV; the provider's diagnostic statement that the patient is HIV positive, or has an HIV-related illness is sufficient.

2) Selection and sequencing of HIV codes

(a) Patient admitted for HIV-related condition

If a patient is admitted for an HIV-related condition, the principal diagnosis should be B20, followed by additional diagnosis codes for all reported HIV-related conditions.

(b) Patient with HIV disease admitted for unrelated condition

If a patient with HIV disease is admitted for an unrelated condition (such as a traumatic injury), the code for the unrelated condition (e.g., the nature of injury code) should be the principal diagnosis. Other diagnoses would be B20 followed by additional diagnosis codes for all reported HIV-related conditions.

(c) Whether the patient is newly diagnosed

Whether the patient is newly diagnosed or has had previous admissions/ encounters for HIV conditions is irrelevant to the sequencing decision.

(d) Asymptomatic human immunodeficiency virus

Z21, Asymptomatic human immunodeficiency virus [HIV] infection status, is to be applied when the patient without any documentation of symptoms is listed as being "HIV positive," "known HIV," "HIV test positive," or similar terminology. Do not use this code if the term "AIDS" is used or if the patient is treated for any HIV-related illness or is described as having any condition(s) resulting from his/her HIV positive status; use B20 in these cases.

(e) Patients with inconclusive HIV serology

Patients with inconclusive HIV serology, but no definitive diagnosis or manifestations of the illness, may be assigned code R75, Inconclusive laboratory evidence of human immunodeficiency virus [HIV].

(f) Previously diagnosed HIV-related illness

Patients with any known prior diagnosis of an HIV-related illness should be coded to B20. Once a patient has developed an HIV-related illness, the patient should always be assigned code B20 on every subsequent admission/ encounter. Patients previously diagnosed with any HIV illness (B20) should never be assigned to R75 or Z21, Asymptomatic human immunodeficiency virus [HIV] infection status.

(g) HIV Infection in Pregnancy, Childbirth and the Puerperium

During pregnancy, childbirth or the puerperium, a patient admitted (or presenting for a health care encounter) because of an HIV-related illness should receive a principal diagnosis code of O98.7-, Human immunodeficiency [HIV] disease complicating pregnancy, childbirth and the puerperium, followed by B20 and the code(s) for the HIV-related illness(es). Codes from Chapter 15 always take sequencing priority.

Patients with asymptomatic HIV infection status admitted (or presenting for a health care encounter) during pregnancy, childbirth, or the puerperium should receive codes of O98.7- and Z21.

(h) Encounters for testing for HIV

If a patient is being seen to determine his/her HIV status, use code Z11.4, Encounter for screening for human immunodeficiency virus [HIV]. Use additional codes for any associated high risk behavior.

If a patient with signs or symptoms is being seen for HIV testing, code the signs and symptoms. An additional counseling code Z71.7, Human immunodeficiency virus [HIV] counseling, may be used if counseling is provided during the encounter for the test.

When a patient returns to be informed of his/her HIV test results and the test result is negative, use code Z71.7, Human immunodeficiency virus [HIV] counseling.

If the results are positive, see previous guidelines and assign codes as appropriate.

b. Infectious agents as the cause of diseases classified to other chapters

Certain infections are classified in chapters other than Chapter 1 and no organism is identified as part of the infection code. In these instances, it is necessary to use an additional code from Chapter 1 to identify the organism. A code from category B95, Streptococcus, Staphylococcus, and Enterococcus as the cause of diseases classified to other chapters, B96, Other bacterial agents as the cause of diseases classified to other chapters, or B97, Viral agents as the cause of diseases classified to other chapters, is to be used as an additional code to identify the organism. An instructional note will be found at the infection code advising that an additional organism code is required.

c. Infections resistant to antibiotics

Many bacterial infections are resistant to current antibiotics. It is necessary to identify all infections documented as antibiotic resistant. Assign code Z16, Infection with drug resistant microorganisms, following the infection code for these cases.

d. Sepsis, Severe Sepsis, and Septic Shock

1) Coding of Sepsis and Severe Sepsis

(a) Sepsis

For a diagnosis of sepsis, assign the appropriate code for the underlying systemic infection. If the type of infection or causal organism is not further specified, assign code A41.9, Sepsis, unspecified.

A code from subcategory R65.2, Severe sepsis, should not be assigned unless severe sepsis or an associated acute organ dysfunction is documented.

(i) Negative or inconclusive blood cultures and sepsis
Negative or inconclusive blood cultures do not preclude a diagnosis of sepsis in patients with clinical evidence of the condition, however, the provider should be queried.

(ii) Urosepsis
The term urosepsis is a nonspecific term. It is not to be considered synonymous with sepsis. It has no default code in the Alphabetic Index. Should a provider use this term, he/she must be queried for clarification.

(iii) Sepsis with organ dysfunction
If a patient has sepsis and associated acute organ dysfunction or multiple organ dysfunction (MOD), follow the instructions for coding severe sepsis.

(iv) Acute organ dysfunction that is not clearly associated with the sepsis
If a patient has sepsis and an acute organ dysfunction, but the medical record documentation indicates that the acute organ

dysfunction is related to a medical condition other than the sepsis, do not assign a code from subcategory R65.2, Severe sepsis. An acute organ dysfunction must be associated with the sepsis in order to assign the severe sepsis code. If the documentation is not clear as to whether an acute organ dysfunction is related to the sepsis or another medical condition, query the provider.

(b) Severe sepsis

The coding of severe sepsis requires a minimum of 2 codes: first a code for the underlying systemic infection, followed by a code from subcategory R65.2, Severe sepsis. If the causal organism is not documented, assign code A41.9, Sepsis, unspecified, for the infection. Additional code(s) for the associated acute organ dysfunction are also required.

Due to the complex nature of severe sepsis, some cases may require querying the provider prior to assignment of the codes.

2) Septic shock

Septic shock is circulatory failure associated with severe sepsis, and therefore, it represents a type of acute organ dysfunction. For all cases of septic shock, the code for the underlying systemic infection should be sequenced first, followed by code R65.21, Severe sepsis with septic shock. Any additional codes for the other acute organ dysfunctions should also be assigned.

Septic shock indicates the presence of severe sepsis. Code R65.21, Severe sepsis with septic shock, must be assigned if septic shock is documented in the medical record, even if the term severe sepsis is not documented.

3) Sequencing of severe sepsis

If severe sepsis is present on admission, and meets the definition of principal diagnosis, the underlying systemic infection should be assigned as principal diagnosis followed by the appropriate code from subcategory R65.2 as required by the sequencing rules in the Tabular List. A code from subcategory R65.2 can never be assigned as a principal diagnosis.

When severe sepsis develops during an encounter (it was not present on admission) the underlying systemic infection and the appropriate code from subcategory R65.2 should be assigned as secondary diagnoses.

Severe sepsis may be present on admission but the diagnosis may not be confirmed until sometime after admission. If the documentation is not clear whether severe sepsis was present on admission, the provider should be queried.

4) Sepsis and severe sepsis with a localized infection

If the reason for admission is both sepsis or severe sepsis and a localized infection, such as pneumonia or cellulitis, a code(s) for the underlying systemic infection should be assigned first and the code for the localized infection should be assigned as a secondary diagnosis. If the patient has severe sepsis, a code from subcategory R65.2 should also be assigned as a secondary diagnosis. If the patient is admitted with a localized infection, such as pneumonia, and sepsis/ severe sepsis doesn't develop until after admission, the localized infection should be assigned first, followed by the appropriate sepsis/severe sepsis codes.

5) Sepsis due to a postprocedural infection

Sepsis resulting from a postprocedural infection is a complication of medical care. For such cases, the postprocedural infection code, such as, T80.2, Infections following infusion, transfusion, and therapeutic injection, T81.4, Infection following a procedure, T88.0, Infection following immunization, or O86.0, Infection of obstetric surgical wound, should be coded first, followed by the code for the specific infection. If the patient has severe sepsis the appropriate code from subcategory R65.2 should also be assigned with the additional code(s) for any acute organ dysfunction.

6) Sepsis and severe sepsis associated with a noninfectious process (condition)

In some cases a noninfectious process (condition), such as trauma, may lead to an infection which can result in sepsis or severe sepsis. If sepsis or severe sepsis is documented as associated with a noninfectious condition, such as a burn or serious injury, and this condition meets the definition for principal diagnosis, the code for the noninfectious condition should be sequenced first, followed by the code for the resulting infection. If severe sepsis, is present a code from subcategory R65.2 should also be assigned with any associated organ dysfunction(s) codes. It is not necessary to assign a code from subcategory R65.1, Systemic inflammatory response syndrome (SIRS) of non-infectious origin, for these cases.

If the infection meets the definition of principal diagnosis it should be sequenced before the non-infectious condition. When both the associated non-infectious condition and the infection meet the definition of principal diagnosis either may be assigned as principal diagnosis.

Only one code from category R65, Symptoms and signs specifically associated with systemic inflammation and infection, should be assigned. Therefore, when a non-infectious condition leads to an infection resulting in severe sepsis, assign the appropriate code from subcategory R65.2, Severe sepsis. Do not additionally assign a code from subcategory R65.1, Systemic inflammatory response syndrome (SIRS) of non-infectious origin.

See Section I.C.18. SIRS due to non-infectious process

7) Sepsis and septic shock complicating abortion, pregnancy, childbirth, and the puerperium

See Section I.C.15. Sepsis and septic shock complicating abortion, pregnancy, childbirth and the puerperium

8) Newborn sepsis

See Section I.C.16. Newborn sepsis

2. Chapter 2: Neoplasms (C00-D49)

General guidelines

Chapter 2 of the ICD-10-CM contains the codes for most benign and all malignant neoplasms. Certain benign neoplasms, such as prostatic adenomas, may be found in the specific body system chapters. To properly code a neoplasm it is necessary to determine from the record if the neoplasm is benign, in-situ, malignant, or of uncertain histologic behavior. If malignant, any secondary (metastatic) sites should also be determined.

The neoplasm table in the Alphabetic Index should be referenced first. However, if the histological term is documented, that term should be referenced first, rather than going immediately to the Neoplasm Table, in order to determine which column in the Neoplasm Table is appropriate. For example, if the documentation indicates "adenoma," refer to the term in the Alphabetic Index to review the entries under this term and the instructional note to "see also neoplasm, by site, benign." The table provides the proper code based on the type of neoplasm and the site. It is important to select the proper column in the table that corresponds to the type of neoplasm. The Tabular should then be referenced to verify that the correct code has been selected from the table and that a more specific site code does not exist.

See Section I.C.21. Factors influencing health status and contact with health services, Status, for information regarding Z15.0, codes for genetic susceptibility to cancer.

a. Treatment directed at the malignancy

If the treatment is directed at the malignancy, designate the malignancy as the principal diagnosis.

The only exception to this guideline is if a patient admission/encounter is solely for the administration of chemotherapy, immunotherapy or radiation therapy, assign the appropriate Z51.— code as the first-listed or principal diagnosis, and the diagnosis or problem for which the service is being performed as a secondary diagnosis.

b. Treatment of secondary site

When a patient is admitted because of a primary neoplasm with metastasis and treatment is directed toward the secondary site only, the secondary neoplasm is designated as the principal diagnosis even though the primary malignancy is still present.

c. Coding and sequencing of complications

Coding and sequencing of complications associated with the malignancies or with the therapy thereof are subject to the following guidelines:

1) Anemia associated with malignancy

When admission/encounter is for management of an anemia associated with the malignancy, and the treatment is only for anemia, the appropriate code for the malignancy is sequenced as the principal or first-listed diagnosis followed by code D63.0, Anemia in neoplastic disease).

2) Anemia associated with chemotherapy, immunotherapy and radiation therapy

When the admission/encounter is for management of an anemia associated with **an adverse effect of** chemotherapy, immunotherapy or radiotherapy and the only treatment is for the anemia, **the appropriate adverse effect code should be sequenced first, followed by the appropriate codes for the anemia and neoplasm.**

3) Management of dehydration due to the malignancy

When the admission/encounter is for management of dehydration due to the malignancy or the therapy, or a combination of both, and only the dehydration is being treated (intravenous rehydration), the dehydration is sequenced first, followed by the code(s) for the malignancy.

4) Treatment of a complication resulting from a surgical procedure

When the admission/encounter is for treatment of a complication resulting from a surgical procedure, designate the complication as the principal or first-listed diagnosis if treatment is directed at resolving the complication.

d. Primary malignancy previously excised

When a primary malignancy has been previously excised or eradicated from its site and there is no further treatment directed to that site and there is no evidence of any existing primary malignancy, a code from category Z85, Personal history of primary and secondary malignant neoplasm, should be used to indicate the former site of the malignancy. Any mention of extension, invasion, or metastasis to another site is coded as a secondary malignant neoplasm to that site. The secondary site may be the principal or first-listed with the Z85 code used as a secondary code.

e. Admissions/Encounters involving chemotherapy, immunotherapy and radiation therapy

1) Episode of care involves surgical removal of neoplasm

When an episode of care involves the surgical removal of a neoplasm, primary or secondary site, followed by adjunct chemotherapy or radiation treatment during the same episode of care, the neoplasm code should be assigned as principal or first-listed diagnosis, using codes in the C00-D49 series or where appropriate in the C83-C90 series.

2) Patient admission/encounter solely for administration of chemotherapy, immunotherapy and radiation therapy

If a patient admission/encounter is solely for the administration of chemotherapy, immunotherapy or radiation therapy assign code Z51.0, Encounter for antineoplastic radiation therapy, or Z51.11, Encounter for antineoplastic chemotherapy, or Z51.12, Encounter for antineoplastic immunotherapy as the first-listed or principal diagnosis. If a patient receives more than one of these therapies during the same admission more than one of these codes may be assigned, in any sequence.

The malignancy for which the therapy is being administered should be assigned as a secondary diagnosis.

3) Patient admitted for radiation therapy, chemotherapy or immunotherapy and develops complications

When a patient is admitted for the purpose of radiotherapy, immunotherapy or chemotherapy and develops complications such as uncontrolled nausea and vomiting or dehydration, the principal or first-listed diagnosis is Z51.0, Encounter for antineoplastic radiation therapy, or Z51.11, Encounter for antineoplastic chemotherapy, or Z51.12, Encounter for antineoplastic immunotherapy followed by any codes for the complications.

f. Admission/encounter to determine extent of malignancy

When the reason for admission/encounter is to determine the extent of the malignancy, or for a procedure such as paracentesis or thoracentesis, the primary malignancy or appropriate metastatic site is designated as the principal or first-listed diagnosis, even though chemotherapy or radiotherapy is administered.

g. Symptoms, signs, and abnormal findings listed in Chapter 18 associated with neoplasms

Symptoms, signs, and ill-defined conditions listed in Chapter 18 characteristic of, or associated with, an existing primary or secondary site malignancy cannot be used to replace the malignancy as principal or first-listed diagnosis, regardless of the number of admissions or encounters for treatment and care of the neoplasm.

See section I.C.21. Factors influencing health status and contact with health services, Encounter for prophylactic organ removal.

h. Admission/encounter for pain control/management

See Section I.C.6. for information on coding admission/encounter for pain control/ management.

i. Malignancy in two or more noncontiguous sites

A patient may have more than one malignant tumor in the same organ. These tumors may represent different primaries or metastatic disease, depending on the site. Should the documentation be unclear, the provider should be queried as to the status of each tumor so that the correct codes can be assigned.

j. Disseminated malignant neoplasm, unspecified

Code C80.0, Disseminated malignant neoplasm, unspecified, is for use only in those cases where the patient has advanced metastatic disease and no known primary or secondary sites are specified. It should not be used in place of assigning codes for the primary site and all known secondary sites.

k. Malignant neoplasm without specification of site

Code C80.1, Malignant neoplasm, unspecified, equates to Cancer, unspecified. This code should only be used when no determination can be made as to the primary site of a malignancy. This code should rarely be used in the inpatient setting.

l. Sequencing of neoplasm codes

1) Encounter for treatment of primary malignancy

If the reason for the encounter is for treatment of a primary malignancy, assign the malignancy as the principal/first listed diagnosis. The primary site is to be sequenced first, followed by any metastatic sites.

2) Encounter for treatment of secondary malignancy

When an encounter is for a primary malignancy with metastasis and treatment is directed toward the metastatic (secondary) site(s) only, the metastatic site(s) is designated as the principal/first listed diagnosis. The primary malignancy is coded as an additional code.

3) Malignant neoplasm in a pregnant patient

Codes from chapter 15, Pregnancy, childbirth, and the puerperium, are always sequenced first on a medical record. A code from subcategory O94.1-, Malignant neoplasm complicating pregnancy, childbirth, and the puerperium, should be used first, followed by the appropriate code from Chapter 2 to indicate the type of neoplasm.

4) Encounter for complication associated with a neoplasm

When an encounter is for management of a complication associated with a neoplasm, such as dehydration, and the treatment is only for the complication, the complication is coded first, followed by the appropriate code(s) for the neoplasm.

The exception to this guideline is anemia. When the admission/encounter is for management of an anemia associated with the malignancy, and the

treatment is only for anemia, the appropriate code for the malignancy is sequenced as the principal or first-listed diagnosis followed by code D63.0, Anemia in neoplastic disease.

5) Complication from surgical procedure for treatment of a neoplasm
When an encounter is for treatment of a complication resulting from a surgical procedure performed for the treatment of the neoplasm, designate the complication as the principal/first listed diagnosis. See guideline regarding the coding of a current malignancy versus personal history to determine if the code for the neoplasm should also be assigned.

6) Pathologic fracture due to a neoplasm
When an encounter is for a pathological fracture due to a neoplasm, if the focus of treatment is the fracture, a code from subcategory M84.5, Pathological fracture in neoplastic disease, should be sequenced first, followed by the code for the neoplasm.

If the focus of treatment is the neoplasm with an associated pathological fracture, the neoplasm code should be sequenced first, followed by a code from M84.5 for the pathological fracture. The "code also" note at M84.5 provides this sequencing instruction.

m. Current malignancy versus personal history of malignancy
When a primary malignancy has been excised but further treatment, such as an additional surgery for the malignancy, radiation therapy or chemotherapy is directed to that site, the primary malignancy code should be used until treatment is completed.

When a primary malignancy has been previously excised or eradicated from its site, there is no further treatment (of the malignancy) directed to that site, and there is no evidence of any existing primary malignancy, a code from category Z85, Personal history of primary and secondary malignant neoplasm, should be used to indicate the former site of the malignancy.

See Section I.C.21. Factors influencing health status and contact with health services, History (of)

n. Leukemia in remission versus personal history of leukemia
The categories for leukemia, and category C90, Multiple myeloma, have codes for in remission. There are also codes Z85.6, Personal history of leukemia, and Z85.79, Personal history of other malignant neoplasms of lymphoid, hematopoietic and related tissues. If the documentation is unclear, as to whether the patient is in remission, the provider should be queried.

See Section I.C.21. Factors influencing health status and contact with health services, History (of)

o. Aftercare following surgery for neoplasm
See Section I.C.21. Factors influencing health status and contact with health services, Aftercare

p. Follow-up care for completed treatment of a malignancy
See Section I.C.21. Factors influencing health status and contact with health services, Follow-up

q. Prophylactic organ removal for prevention of malignancy
See Section I.C. 21, Factors influencing health status and contact with health services, Prophylactic organ removal

r. Malignant neoplasm associated with transplanted organ
A malignant neoplasm of a transplanted organ should be coded as a transplant complication. Assign first the appropriate code from category T86.-, Complications of transplanted organ, followed by code C80.2, Malignant neoplasm associated with transplanted organ. Use an additional code for the specific malignancy.

3. **Chapter 3: Disease of the blood and blood-forming organs and certain disorders involving the immune mechanism (D50-D89)**
Reserved for future guideline expansion

4. **Chapter 4: Endocrine, Nutritional, and Metabolic Diseases (E00-E89)**

a. **Diabetes mellitus**

The diabetes mellitus codes are combination codes that include the type of DM, the body system affected, and the complications affecting that body system. As many codes within a particular category as are necessary to describe all of the complications of the disease may be used. They should be sequenced based on the reason for a particular encounter. Assign as many codes from categories E08 – E13 as needed to identify all of the associated conditions that the patient has.

1) **Type of diabetes**

The age of a patient is not the sole determining factor, though most type 1 diabetics develop the condition before reaching puberty. For this reason type 1 diabetes mellitus is also referred to as juvenile diabetes.

2) **Type of diabetes mellitus not documented**

If the type of diabetes mellitus is not documented in the medical record the default is E11.-, Type 2 diabetes mellitus.

3) **Diabetes mellitus and the use of insulin**

If the documentation in a medical record does not indicate the type of diabetes but does indicate that the patient uses insulin, code E11, Type 2 diabetes mellitus, should be assigned for type 2 patients who routinely use insulin, code Z79.4, Long-term (current) use of insulin, should also **be assigned** to indicate that the patient uses insulin. Code Z79.4 should not be assigned if insulin is given temporarily to bring a type 2 patient's blood sugar under control during an encounter.

4) **Diabetes mellitus in pregnancy and gestational diabetes**

See Section I.C.15. Diabetes mellitus in pregnancy.
See Section I.C.15. Gestational (pregnancy induced) diabetes

5) **Complications due to insulin pump malfunction**

(a) **Underdose of insulin due insulin pump failure**

An underdose of insulin due to an insulin pump failure should be assigned to a code from subcategory T85.6, Mechanical complication of other specified internal and external prosthetic devices, implants and grafts, that specifies the type of pump malfunction, as the principal or first listed code, followed by code T38.3x6-, Underdosing of insulin and oral hypoglycemic [antidiabetic] drugs. Additional codes for the type of diabetes mellitus and any associated complications due to the underdosing should also be assigned.

(b) **Overdose of insulin due to insulin pump failure**

The principal or first listed code for an encounter due to an insulin pump malfunction resulting in an overdose of insulin, should also be T85.6-, Mechanical complication of other specified internal and external prosthetic devices, implants and grafts, followed by code T38.3x1-, Poisoning by insulin and oral hypoglycemic [antidiabetic] drugs, accidental (unintentional).

6) **Secondary Diabetes Mellitus**

Codes under category E08, Diabetes mellitus due to underlying condition, and E09, Drug or chemical induced diabetes mellitus, identify complications/manifestations associated with secondary diabetes mellitus. Secondary diabetes is always caused by another condition or event (e.g., cystic fibrosis, malignant neoplasm of pancreas, pancreatectomy, adverse effect of drug, or poisoning).

(a) **Secondary diabetes mellitus and the use of insulin**

For patients who routinely use insulin, code Z79.4, Long-term (current) use of insulin, should also be assigned. Code Z79.4 should not be assigned if insulin is given temporarily to bring a patient's blood sugar under control during an encounter.

(b) **Assigning and sequencing secondary diabetes codes and its causes**

The sequencing of the secondary diabetes codes in relationship to codes for the cause of the diabetes is based on the tabular instructions for categories E08

and E09. For example, for category E08, Diabetes mellitus due to underlying condition, code first the underlying condition; for category E09, Drug or chemical induced diabetes mellitus, code first the drug or chemical (T36-T65).

  (i) Secondary diabetes mellitus due to pancreatectomy
  For postpancreatectomy diabetes mellitus (lack of insulin due to the surgical removal of all or part of the pancreas), assign code E89.1, Postsurgical hypoinsulinemia. Assign a code from category E08 and code Z79.4, Other acquired absence of organ, as additional codes.

  (ii) Secondary diabetes due to drugs
  Secondary diabetes may be caused by an adverse effect of correctly administered medications, poisoning or late effect of poisoning.
  See section I.C.19.e for coding of adverse effects and poisoning, and section I.C.20 for external cause code reporting.

5. **Chapter 5: Mental and behavioral disorders (F01 – F99)**

  a. Pain disorders related to psychological factors
  Assign code F45.41, for pain that is exclusively psychological. Code F45.41, Pain disorder with related psychological factors, should be used following the appropriate code from category G89, Pain, not elsewhere classified, if there is documentation of a psychological component for a patient with acute or chronic pain.
  See Section I.C.6. Pain

6. **Chapter 6: Diseases of Nervous System and Sense Organs (G00-G99)**

  a. Dominant/nondominant side
  Codes from category G81, Hemiplegia and hemiparesis, and subcategories, G83.1, Monoplegia of lower limb, G83.2, Monoplegia of upper limb, and G83.3, Monoplegia, unspecified, identify whether the dominant or nondominant side is affected. Should this information not be available in the record, **and the classification system does not indicate a default,** the default should be dominant. For ambidextrous patients, the default should also be dominant.

  b. Pain - Category G89

  1) General coding information
  Codes in category G89, Pain, not elsewhere classified, may be used in conjunction with codes from other categories and chapters to provide more detail about acute or chronic pain and neoplasm-related pain, unless otherwise indicated below.

  If the pain is not specified as acute or chronic, post-thoracotomy, postprocedural, or neoplasm-related, do not assign codes from category G89.

  A code from category G89 should not be assigned if the underlying (definitive) diagnosis is known, unless the reason for the encounter is pain control/ management and not management of the underlying condition.

  When an admission or encounter is for a procedure aimed at treating the underlying condition (e.g., spinal fusion, kyphoplasty), a code for the underlying condition (e.g., vertebral fracture, spinal stenosis) should be assigned as the principal diagnosis. No code from category G89 should be assigned.

  (a) Category G89 Codes as Principal or First-Listed Diagnosis
  Category G89 codes are acceptable as principal diagnosis or the first-listed code:
  - When pain control or pain management is the reason for the admission/ encounter (e.g., a patient with displaced intervertebral disc, nerve impingement and severe back pain presents for injection of steroid into the spinal canal). The underlying cause of the pain should be reported as an additional diagnosis, if known.
  - When a patient is admitted for the insertion of a neurostimulator for pain control, assign the appropriate pain code as the principal or first listed diagnosis. When an admission or encounter is for a procedure aimed at treating the underlying condition and a neurostimulator

is inserted for pain control during the same admission/encounter, a code for the underlying condition should be assigned as the principal diagnosis and the appropriate pain code should be assigned as a secondary diagnosis.

(b) Use of Category G89 Codes in Conjunction with Site Specific Pain Codes

(i) Assigning Category G89 and Site-Specific Pain Codes

Codes from category G89 may be used in conjunction with codes that identify the site of pain (including codes from chapter 18) if the category G89 code provides additional information. For example, if the code describes the site of the pain, but does not fully describe whether the pain is acute or chronic, then both codes should be assigned.

(ii) Sequencing of Category G89 Codes with Site-Specific Pain Codes

The sequencing of category G89 codes with site-specific pain codes (including chapter 18 codes), is dependent on the circumstances of the encounter/admission as follows:

- If the encounter is for pain control or pain management, assign the code from category G89 followed by the code identifying the specific site of pain (e.g., encounter for pain management for acute neck pain from trauma is assigned code G89.11, Acute pain due to trauma, followed by code M54.2, Cervicalgia, to identify the site of pain).
- If the encounter is for any other reason except pain control or pain management, and a related definitive diagnosis has not been established (confirmed) by the provider, assign the code for the specific site of pain first, followed by the appropriate code from category G89.

2) Pain due to devices, implants and grafts
See Section I.C.19. Pain due to medical devices

3) Postoperative Pain
The provider's documentation should be used to guide the coding of postoperative pain, as well as Section III. Reporting Additional Diagnoses and Section IV. Diagnostic Coding and Reporting in the Outpatient Setting.

The default for post-thoracotomy and other postoperative pain not specified as acute or chronic is the code for the acute form.

Routine or expected postoperative pain immediately after surgery should not be coded.

(a) Postoperative pain not associated with specific postoperative complication
Postoperative pain not associated with a specific postoperative complication is assigned to the appropriate postoperative pain code in category G89.

(b) Postoperative pain associated with specific postoperative complication
Postoperative pain associated with a specific postoperative complication (such as painful wire sutures) is assigned to the appropriate code(s) found in Chapter 19, Injury, poisoning, and certain other consequences of external causes. If appropriate, use additional code(s) from category G89 to identify acute or chronic pain (G89.18 or G89.28).

4) Chronic pain
Chronic pain is classified to subcategory G89.2. There is no time frame defining when pain becomes chronic pain. The provider's documentation should be used to guide use of these codes.

5) Neoplasm Related Pain
Code G89.3 is assigned to pain documented as being related, associated or due to cancer, primary or secondary malignancy, or tumor. This code is assigned regardless of whether the pain is acute or chronic.

This code may be assigned as the principal or first-listed code when the stated reason for the admission/encounter is documented as pain control/pain management. The underlying neoplasm should be reported as an additional diagnosis.

When the reason for the admission/encounter is management of the neoplasm and the pain associated with the neoplasm is also documented, code G89.3 may be assigned as an additional diagnosis. It is not necessary to assign an additional code for the site of the pain.

See Section I.C.2 for instructions on the sequencing of neoplasms for all other stated reasons for the admission/encounter (except for pain control/pain management).

6) Chronic pain syndrome

Central pain syndrome (G89.0) and chronic pain syndrome (G89.4) are different than the term "chronic pain," and therefore codes should only be used when the provider has specifically documented this condition.

See Section I.C.5. Pain disorders related to psychological factors

7. Chapter 7: Diseases of Eye and Adnexa (H00-H59)
Reserved for future guideline expansion

8. Chapter 8: Diseases of Ear and Mastoid Process (H60-H95)
Reserved for future guideline expansion

9. Chapter 9: Diseases of Circulatory System (I00-I99)

a. Hypertension

1) Hypertension with Heart Disease

Heart conditions classified to I50.- or I51.4-I51.9, are assigned to, a code from category I11, Hypertensive heart disease, when a causal relationship is stated (due to hypertension) or implied (hypertensive). Use an additional code from category I50, Heart failure, to identify the type of heart failure in those patients with heart failure.

The same heart conditions (I50.-, I51.4-I51.9) with hypertension, but without a stated causal relationship, are coded separately. Sequence according to the circumstances of the admission/encounter.

2) Hypertensive Chronic Kidney Disease

Assign codes from category I12, Hypertensive chronic kidney disease, when both hypertension and a condition classifiable to category N18, Chronic kidney disease (CKD), are present. Unlike hypertension with heart disease, ICD-10-CM presumes a cause-and-effect relationship and classifies chronic kidney disease with hypertension as hypertensive chronic kidney disease.

The appropriate code from category N18 should be used as a secondary code with a code from category I12 to identify the stage of chronic kidney disease.

See Section I.C.14. Chronic kidney disease.

If a patient has hypertensive chronic kidney disease **and acute** renal failure, an additional code for the acute renal failure is required.

3) Hypertensive Heart and Chronic Kidney Disease

Assign codes from combination category I13, Hypertensive heart and chronic kidney disease, when both hypertensive kidney disease and hypertensive heart disease are stated in the diagnosis. Assume a relationship between the hypertension and the chronic kidney disease, whether or not the condition is so designated. If heart failure is present, assign an additional code from category I50 to identify the type of heart failure.

The appropriate code from category N18, Chronic kidney disease, should be used as a secondary code with a code from category I13 to identify the stage of chronic kidney disease.

See Section I.C.14. Chronic kidney disease.

The codes in category I13, Hypertensive heart and chronic kidney disease, are combination codes that include hypertension, heart disease and chronic kidney disease. The Includes note at I13 specifies that the conditions included at I11 and I12 are included together in I13. If a patient has hypertension, heart disease and chronic kidney disease then a code from I13 should be used, not individual codes for hypertension, heart disease and chronic kidney disease, or codes from I11 or I12.

For patients with both acute renal failure and chronic kidney disease an additional code for acute renal failure is required.

4) Hypertensive Cerebrovascular Disease

For hypertensive cerebrovascular disease, first assign the appropriate code from categories I60-I69, followed by the appropriate hypertension code.

5) Hypertensive Retinopathy

Code H35.0, Hypertensive retinopathy, should be used with code I10, Essential (primary) hypertension, to include the systemic hypertension. The sequencing is based on the reason for the encounter.

6) Hypertension, Secondary

Secondary hypertension is due to an underlying condition. Two codes are required: one to identify the underlying etiology and one from category I15 to identify the hypertension. Sequencing of codes is determined by the reason for admission/encounter.

7) Hypertension, Transient

Assign code R03.0, Elevated blood pressure reading without diagnosis of hypertension, unless patient has an established diagnosis of hypertension. Assign code O13.-, Gestational [pregnancy-induced] hypertension without significant proteinuria, or O14.-, Gestational [pregnancy-induced] hypertension with significant proteinuria, for transient hypertension of pregnancy.

8) Hypertension, Controlled

This diagnostic statement usually refers to an existing state of hypertension under control by therapy. Assign code I10.

9) Hypertension, Uncontrolled

Uncontrolled hypertension may refer to untreated hypertension or hypertension not responding to current therapeutic regimen. In either case, assign code I10.

b. Atherosclerotic coronary artery disease and angina

ICD-10-CM has combination codes for atherosclerotic heart disease with angina pectoris. The subcategories for these codes are I25.11, Atherosclerotic heart disease of native coronary artery with angina pectoris and I25.7, Atherosclerosis of coronary artery bypass graft(s) and coronary artery of transplanted heart with angina pectoris.

When using one of these combination codes it is not necessary to use an additional code for angina pectoris. A causal relationship can be assumed in a patient with both atherosclerosis and angina pectoris, unless the documentation indicates the angina is due to something other than the atherosclerosis.

If a patient with coronary artery disease is admitted due to an acute myocardial infarction (AMI), the AMI should be sequenced before the coronary artery disease.

See Section I.C.9. Acute myocardial infarction (AMI)

c. Intraoperative and Postprocedural cerebrovascular accident

Medical record documentation should clearly specify the cause-and-effect relationship between the medical intervention and the cerebrovascular accident in order to assign a code for intraoperative or postprocedural cerebrovascular accident.

Proper code assignment depends on whether it was an infarction or hemorrhage and whether it occurred intraoperatively or postoperatively. If it was a cerebral hemorrhage, code assignment depends on the type of procedure performed.

d. Sequelae of Cerebrovascular Disease

1) Category I69, Sequelae of Cerebrovascular disease

Category I69 is used to indicate conditions classifiable to categories I60-I67 as the causes of late effects (neurologic deficits), themselves classified elsewhere. These "late effects" include neurologic deficits that persist after initial onset of conditions classifiable to categories I60-I67. The neurologic deficits caused by cerebrovascular disease may be present from the onset or may arise at any time after the onset of the condition classifiable to categories I60-I67.

2) Codes from category I69 with codes from I60-I67

Codes from category I69 may be assigned on a health care record with codes from I60-I67, if the patient has a current cerebrovascular accident (CVA) and deficits from an old CVA.

3) Code Z86.73

Assign code Z86.73, Personal history of transient ischemic attack (TIA), and cerebral infarction without residual deficits (and not a code from category I69) as an additional code for history of cerebrovascular disease when no neurologic deficits are present.

e. Acute myocardial infarction (AMI)

1) ST elevation myocardial infarction (STEMI) and non ST elevation myocardial infarction (NSTEMI)

The ICD-10-CM codes for acute myocardial infarction (AMI) identify the site, such as anterolateral wall or true posterior wall. Subcategories I21.0-I21.2 and code I21.4 are used for ST elevation myocardial infarction (STEMI). Code I21.4, Non-ST elevation (NSTEMI) myocardial infarction, is used for non ST elevation myocardial infarction (NSTEMI) and nontransmural MIs.

2) Acute myocardial infarction, unspecified

Code I21.3, ST elevation (STEMI) myocardial infarction of unspecified site, is the default for the unspecified term acute myocardial infarction. If only STEMI or transmural MI without the site is documented, query the provider as to the site, or assign code I21.3.

3) AMI documented as nontransmural or subendocardial but site provided

If an AMI is documented as nontransmural or subendocardial, but the site is provided, it is still coded as a subendocardial AMI. If NSTEMI evolves to STEMI, assign the STEMI code. If STEMI converts to NSTEMI due to thrombolytic therapy, it is still coded as STEMI.

See Section I.C.21.3 for information on coding status post administration of tPA in a different facility within the last 24 hours.

4) Subsequent acute myocardial infarction

A code from category I22, Subsequent ST elevation (STEMI) and non ST elevation (NSTEMI) myocardial infarction, is to be used when a patient who has suffered an AMI has a new AMI within the 4 week time frame of the initial AMI. A code from category I22 must be used in conjunction with a code from category I21.

The sequencing of the I22 and I21 codes depends on the circumstances of the encounter. Should a patient who is in the hospital due to an AMI have a subsequent AMI while still in the hospital code I21 would be sequenced first as the reason for admission, with code I22 sequenced as a secondary code. Should a patient have a subsequent AMI after discharge for care of an initial AMI, and the reason for admission is the subsequent AMI, the I22 code should be sequenced first followed by the I21. An I21 code must accompany an I22 code to identify the site of the initial AMI, and to indicate that the patient is still within the 4 week time frame of healing from the initial AMI.

The guidelines for assigning the correct I22 code are the same as for the initial AMI.

10. Chapter 10: Diseases of Respiratory System (J00-J99)

a. Chronic Obstructive Pulmonary Disease [COPD] and Asthma

1) Acute exacerbation of chronic obstructive bronchitis and asthma

The codes in categories J44 and J45 distinguish between uncomplicated cases and those in acute exacerbation. An acute exacerbation is a worsening or a decompensation of a chronic condition. An acute exacerbation is not equivalent to an infection superimposed on a chronic condition, though an exacerbation may be triggered by an infection.

b. **Acute Respiratory Failure**

1) **Acute respiratory failure as principal diagnosis**

Code J96.0, Acute respiratory failure, or code J96.2, Acute and chronic respiratory failure, may be assigned as a principal diagnosis when it is the condition established after study to be chiefly responsible for occasioning the admission to the hospital, and the selection is supported by the Alphabetic Index and Tabular List. However, chapter-specific coding guidelines (such as obstetrics, poisoning, HIV, newborn) that provide sequencing direction take precedence.

2) **Acute respiratory failure as secondary diagnosis**

Respiratory failure may be listed as a secondary diagnosis if it occurs after admission, or if it is present on admission, but does not meet the definition of principal diagnosis.

3) **Sequencing of acute respiratory failure and another acute condition**

When a patient is admitted with respiratory failure and another acute condition, (e.g., myocardial infarction, cerebrovascular accident, aspiration pneumonia), the principal diagnosis will not be the same in every situation. This applies whether the other acute condition is a respiratory or nonrespiratory condition. Selection of the principal diagnosis will be dependent on the circumstances of admission. If both the respiratory failure and the other acute condition are equally responsible for occasioning the admission to the hospital, and there are no chapter-specific sequencing rules, the guideline regarding two or more diagnoses that equally meet the definition for principal diagnosis (*Section II, C.*) may be applied in these situations.

If the documentation is not clear as to whether acute respiratory failure and another condition are equally responsible for occasioning the admission, query the provider for clarification.

c. **Influenza due to** *certain identified influenza viruses*

Code only confirmed cases of avian influenza **(code J09.0-, Influenza due to identified avian influenza virus) or novel H1N1 or swine flu, code J09.1-**. This is an exception to the hospital inpatient guideline Section II, H. (Uncertain Diagnosis).

In this context, "confirmation" does not require documentation of positive laboratory testing specific for avian **or novel H1N1 (H1N1 or swine flu)** influenza. However, coding should be based on the provider's diagnostic statement that the patient has avian influenza.

If the provider records "suspected or possible or probable avian influenza," the appropriate influenza code from category J10, Influenza due to other influenza virus, should be assigned. **A code from category** J09, Influenza due to **certain identified** influenza viruses, should not be assigned.

11. **Chapter 11: Diseases of Digestive System (K00-K94)**
    Reserved for future guideline expansion

12. **Chapter 12: Diseases of Skin and Subcutaneous Tissue (L00-L99)**

    a. **Pressure ulcer stage codes**

    1) **Pressure ulcer stages**
    Codes from category L89, Pressure ulcer, are combination codes that identify the site of the pressure ulcer as well as the stage of the ulcer.
    The ICD-10-CM classifies pressure ulcer stages based on severity, which is designated by stages 1-4, unspecified stage and unstageable.
    Assign as many codes from category L89 as needed to identify all the pressure ulcers the patient has, if applicable.

    2) **Unstageable pressure ulcers**
    Assignment of the code for unstageable pressure ulcer (L89.--0) should be based on the clinical documentation. These codes are used for pressure ulcers whose stage cannot be clinically determined (e.g., the ulcer is covered by eschar or has been treated with a skin or muscle graft) and pressure ulcers that are documented as deep tissue injury but not documented as due

to trauma. This code should not be confused with the codes for unspecified stage (L89.--9). When there is no documentation regarding the stage of the pressure ulcer, assign the appropriate code for unspecified stage (L89.--9).

3) Documented pressure ulcer stage

Assignment of the pressure ulcer stage code should be guided by clinical documentation of the stage or documentation of the terms found in the index. For clinical terms describing the stage that are not found in the index, and there is no documentation of the stage, the provider should be queried.

4) Patients admitted with pressure ulcers documented as healed

No code is assigned if the documentation states that the pressure ulcer is completely healed.

5) Patients admitted with pressure ulcers documented as healing

Pressure ulcers described as healing should be assigned the appropriate pressure ulcer stage code based on the documentation in the medical record. If the documentation does not provide information about the stage of the healing pressure ulcer, assign the appropriate code for unspecified stage.

If the documentation is unclear as to whether the patient has a current (new) pressure ulcer or if the patient is being treated for a healing pressure ulcer, query the provider.

6) Patient admitted with pressure ulcer evolving into another stage during the admission

If a patient is admitted with a pressure ulcer at one stage and it progresses to a higher stage, assign the code for the highest stage reported for that site.

13. Chapter 13: Diseases of the Musculoskeletal System and Connective Tissue (M00-M99)

a. Site and laterality

Most of the codes within Chapter 13 have site and laterality designations. The site represents either the bone, joint or the muscle involved. For some conditions where more than one bone, joint or muscle is usually involved, such as osteoarthritis, there is a "multiple sites" code available. For categories where no multiple site code is provided and more than one bone, joint or muscle is involved, multiple codes should be used to indicate the different sites involved.

1) Bone versus joint

For certain conditions, the bone may be affected at the upper or lower end, (e.g., avascular necrosis of bone, M87, Osteoporosis, M80, M81). Though the portion of the bone affected may be at the joint, the site designation will be the bone, not the joint.

b. Acute traumatic versus chronic or recurrent musculoskeletal conditions

Many musculoskeletal conditions are a result of previous injury or trauma to a site, or are recurrent conditions. Bone, joint or muscle conditions that are the result of a healed injury are usually found in chapter 13. Recurrent bone, joint or muscle conditions are also usually found in chapter 13. Any current, acute injury should be coded to the appropriate injury code from chapter 19. Chronic or recurrent conditions should generally be coded with a code from chapter 13. If it is difficult to determine from the documentation in the record which code is best to describe a condition, query the provider.

c. Coding of Pathologic Fractures

7th character A is for use as long as the patient is receiving active treatment for the fracture. Examples of active treatment are: surgical treatment, emergency department encounter, evaluation and treatment by a new physician. 7th character, D is to be used for encounters after the patient has completed active treatment. The other 7th characters, listed under each subcategory in the Tabular List, are to be used for subsequent encounters for treatment of problems associated with the healing, such as malunions, nonunions, and sequelae.

Care for complications of surgical treatment for fracture repairs during the healing or recovery phase should be coded with the appropriate complication codes.

See Section I.C.19. Coding of traumatic fractures.

d. Osteoporosis

Osteoporosis is a systemic condition, meaning that all bones of the musculoskeletal system are affected. Therefore, site is not a component of the codes under category M81, Osteoporosis without current pathological fracture. The site codes under category M80, Osteoporosis with current pathological fracture, identify the site of the fracture, not the osteoporosis.

1) Osteoporosis without pathological fracture

Category M81, Osteoporosis without current pathological fracture, is for use for patients with osteoporosis who do not currently have a pathologic fracture due to the osteoporosis, even if they have had a fracture in the past. For patients with a history of osteoporosis fractures, status code Z87.31, Personal history of osteoporosis fracture, should follow the code from M81.

2) Osteoporosis with current pathological fracture

Category M80, Osteoporosis with current pathological fracture, is for patients who have a current pathologic fracture at the time of an encounter. The codes under M80 identify the site of the fracture. A code from category M80, not a traumatic fracture code, should be used for any patient with known osteoporosis who suffers a fracture, even if the patient had a minor fall or trauma, if that fall or trauma would not usually break a normal, healthy bone.

14. Chapter 14: Diseases of Genitourinary System (N00-N99)

a. Chronic kidney disease

1) Stages of chronic kidney disease (CKD)

The ICD-10-CM classifies CKD based on severity. The severity of CKD is designated by stages I-V. Stage II, code N18.2, equates to mild CKD; stage III, code N18.3, equates to moderate CKD; and stage IV, code N18.4, equates to severe CKD. Code N18.6, End stage renal disease (ESRD), is assigned when the provider has documented end-stage-renal disease (ESRD).

If both a stage of CKD and ESRD are documented, assign code N18.6 only.

2) Chronic kidney disease and kidney transplant status

Patients who have undergone kidney transplant may still have some form of **chronic kidney disease** CKD because the kidney transplant may not fully restore kidney function. Therefore, the presence of CKD alone does not constitute a transplant complication. Assign the appropriate N18 code for the patient's stage of CKD and code Z94.0, Kidney transplant status. If a transplant complication such as failure or rejection **or other transplant complication** is documented, see section I.C.19.g for information on coding complications of a kidney transplant. If the documentation is unclear as to whether the patient has a complication of the transplant, query the provider.

3) Chronic kidney disease with other conditions

Patients with CKD may also suffer from other serious conditions, most commonly diabetes mellitus and hypertension. The sequencing of the CKD code in relationship to codes for other contributing conditions is based on the conventions in the Tabular List.

See I.C.9. Hypertensive chronic kidney disease.
See I.C.19. Chronic kidney disease and kidney transplant complications.

15. Chapter 15: Pregnancy, Childbirth, and the Puerperium (O00-O9A)

a. General Rules for Obstetric Cases

1) Codes from chapter 15 and sequencing priority

Obstetric cases require codes from chapter 15, codes in the range O00-O9A, Pregnancy, Childbirth, and the Puerperium. Chapter 15 codes have sequencing priority over codes from other chapters. Additional codes from other chapters may be used in conjunction with chapter 15 codes to further specify conditions. Should the provider document that the pregnancy is incidental to the encounter, then code Z33.1, Pregnant state, incidental, should be used in place of any chapter 15 codes. It is the provider's responsibility to state that the condition being treated is not affecting the pregnancy.

2) Chapter 15 codes used only on the maternal record

Chapter 15 codes are to be used only on the maternal record, never on the record of the newborn.

3) Final character for trimester

The majority of codes in Chapter 15 have a final character indicating the trimester of pregnancy. The timeframes for the trimesters are indicated at the beginning of the chapter. If trimester is not a component of a code it is because the condition always occurs in a specific trimester, or the concept of trimester of pregnancy is not applicable. Certain codes have characters for only certain trimesters because the condition does not occur in all trimesters, but it may occur in more than just one.

Assignment of the final character for trimester should be based on the trimester for the current admission/encounter. This applies to the assignment of trimester for pre-existing conditions as well as those that develop during or are due to the pregnancy.

Whenever delivery occurs during the current admission, and there is an "in childbirth" option for the obstetric complication being coded, the "in childbirth" code should be assigned.

4) Selection of trimester for inpatient admissions *that encompass more than one trimesters*

In instances when a patient is admitted to a hospital for complications of pregnancy **during one trimester** and remains in the hospital **into a subsequent trimester, the trimester character for** the antepartum complication code should be assigned on the basis of the trimester when the complication developed, **not the trimester of the discharge. If the condition developed prior to the current admission/encounter or represents a pre-existing condition, the trimester character for the trimester at the time of the admission/encounter should be assigned.**

5) Unspecified trimester

Each category that includes codes for trimester has a code for "unspecified trimester." The "unspecified trimester" code should rarely be used, such as when the documentation in the record is insufficient to determine the trimester and it is not possible to obtain clarification.

b. Selection of OB Principal or First-listed Diagnosis

1) Routine outpatient prenatal visits

For routine outpatient prenatal visits when no complications are present, a code from category Z34, Encounter for supervision of normal pregnancy, should be used as the first-listed diagnosis. These codes should not be used in conjunction with chapter 15 codes.

2) Prenatal outpatient visits for high-risk patients

For routine prenatal outpatient visits for patients with high-risk pregnancies, a code from category O09, Supervision of high-risk pregnancy, should be used as the first-listed diagnosis. Secondary chapter 15 codes may be used in conjunction with these codes if appropriate.

3) Episodes when no delivery occurs

In episodes when no delivery occurs, the principal diagnosis should correspond to the principal complication of the pregnancy which necessitated the encounter. Should more than one complication exist, all of which are treated or monitored, any of the complications codes may be sequenced first.

4) When a delivery occurs

When a delivery occurs, the principal diagnosis should correspond to the main circumstances or complication of the delivery. In cases of cesarean delivery, the selection of the principal **diagnosis should be the condition established after study that was responsible for the patient's admission. If the patient was admitted with a condition that resulted in the performance of a cesarean procedure, that condition should be selected as the principal diagnosis. If** the reason for **the** admission/encounter was unrelated to the condition resulting in the cesarean delivery, **the condition related to the** reason for the admission/encounter should be selected as the principal diagnosis, even if a cesarean was performed.

5) Outcome of delivery

A code from category Z37, Outcome of delivery, should be included on every maternal record when a delivery has occurred. These codes are not to be used on subsequent records or on the newborn record.

c. Pre-existing conditions versus conditions due to the pregnancy

Certain categories in Chapter 15 distinguish between conditions of the mother that existed prior to pregnancy (pre-existing) and those that are a direct result of pregnancy. When assigning codes from Chapter 15, it is important to assess if a condition was pre-existing prior to pregnancy or developed during or due to the pregnancy in order to assign the correct code.

Categories that do not distinguish between pre-existing and pregnancy-related conditions may be used for either. It is acceptable to use codes specifically for the puerperium with codes complicating pregnancy and childbirth if a condition arises postpartum during the delivery encounter.

d. Pre-existing hypertension in pregnancy

Category O10, Pre-existing hypertension complicating pregnancy, childbirth and the puerperium, includes codes for hypertensive heart and hypertensive chronic kidney disease. When assigning one of the O10 codes that includes hypertensive heart disease or hypertensive chronic kidney disease, it is necessary to add a secondary code from the appropriate hypertension category to specify the type of heart failure or chronic kidney disease.

See Section I.C.9. Hypertension.

e. Fetal Conditions Affecting the Management of the Mother

1) Codes from categories O35 and O36

Codes from categories O35, Maternal care for known or suspected fetal abnormality and damage, and O36, Maternal care for other fetal problems, are assigned only when the fetal condition is actually responsible for modifying the management of the mother, i.e., by requiring diagnostic studies, additional observation, special care, or termination of pregnancy. The fact that the fetal condition exists does not justify assigning a code from this series to the mother's record.

2) In utero surgery

In cases when surgery is performed on the fetus, a diagnosis code from category O35, Maternal care for known or suspected fetal abnormality and damage, should be assigned identifying the fetal condition. Assign the appropriate procedure code for the procedure performed.

No code from Chapter 16, the perinatal codes, should be used on the mother's record to identify fetal conditions. Surgery performed in utero on a fetus is still to be coded as an obstetric encounter.

f. HIV Infection in Pregnancy, Childbirth and the Puerperium

During pregnancy, childbirth or the puerperium, a patient admitted because of an HIV-related illness should receive a principal diagnosis from subcategory O98.7-, Human immunodeficiency [HIV] disease complicating pregnancy, childbirth and the puerperium, followed by the code(s) for the HIV-related illness(es).

Patients with asymptomatic HIV infection status admitted during pregnancy, childbirth, or the puerperium should receive codes of O98.7- and Z21, Asymptomatic human immunodeficiency virus [HIV] infection status.

g. Diabetes mellitus in pregnancy

Diabetes mellitus is a significant complicating factor in pregnancy. Pregnant women who are diabetic should be assigned a code O24, Diabetes mellitus in pregnancy, childbirth, and the puerperium, first, followed by the appropriate diabetes code(s) (E08-E13) from Chapter 4.

h. Long term use of insulin

Code Z79.4, Long-term (current) use of insulin, should also be assigned if the diabetes mellitus is being treated with insulin.

i. Gestational (pregnancy induced) diabetes

Gestational (pregnancy induced) diabetes can occur during the second and third trimester of pregnancy in women who were not diabetic prior to pregnancy. Gestational diabetes can cause complications in the pregnancy similar to those of pre-existing diabetes mellitus. It also puts the woman at greater risk of developing diabetes after the pregnancy. Codes for gestational diabetes are in subcategory O24.4, Gestational diabetes mellitus. No other code from category O24, Diabetes mellitus in pregnancy, childbirth, and the puerperium, should be used with a code from O24.4.

The codes under subcategory O24.4 include diet controlled and insulin controlled. If a patient with gestational diabetes is treated with both diet and insulin, only the code for insulin-controlled is required.

Code **Z79.4**, Long-term (current) use of insulin, should **not** be assigned **with codes from subcategory O24.4.**

An abnormal glucose tolerance in pregnancy is assigned a code from subcategory O99.81, Abnormal glucose complicating pregnancy, childbirth, and the puerperium.

j. Sepsis and septic shock complicating abortion, pregnancy, childbirth and the puerperium

When assigning a chapter 15 code for sepsis complicating abortion, pregnancy, childbirth, and the puerperium, a code for the specific type of infection should be assigned as an additional diagnosis. If severe sepsis is present, a code from subcategory R65.2, Severe sepsis, and code(s) for associated organ dysfunction(s) should also be assigned as additional diagnoses.

k. Puerperal sepsis

Code O85, Puerperal sepsis, should be assigned with a secondary code to identify the causal organism (e.g., for a bacterial infection, assign a code from category B95-B96, Bacterial infections in conditions classified elsewhere). A code from category A40, Streptococcal sepsis, or A41, Other sepsis, should not be used for puerperal sepsis. If applicable, use additional codes to identify severe sepsis (R65.2-) and any associated acute organ dysfunction.

l. Alcohol and tobacco use during pregnancy, childbirth and the puerperium

1) Alcohol use during pregnancy, childbirth and the puerperium

Codes under subcategory O99.31, Alcohol use complicating pregnancy, childbirth, and the puerperium, should be assigned for any pregnancy case when a mother uses alcohol during the pregnancy or postpartum. A secondary code from category F10, Alcohol related disorders, should also be assigned.

2) Tobacco use during pregnancy, childbirth and the puerperium

Codes under subcategory O99.33, Smoking (tobacco) complicating pregnancy, childbirth, and the puerperium, should be assigned for any pregnancy case when a mother uses any type of tobacco product during the pregnancy or postpartum. A secondary code from category F17, Nicotine dependence, or code Z72.0, Tobacco use, should also be assigned.

m. Poisoning, toxic effects, adverse effects and underdosing in a pregnant patient

A code from subcategory O9A.2, Injury, poisoning and certain other consequences of external causes complicating pregnancy, childbirth, and the puerperium, should be sequenced first, followed by the appropriate poisoning, toxic effect, adverse effect or underdosing code, and then the additional code(s) that specifies the condition caused by the poisoning, toxic effect, adverse effect or underdosing.

See Section I.C.19. Adverse effects, poisoning, underdosing and toxic effects.

n. Normal Delivery, Code O80

1) Encounter for full term uncomplicated delivery

Code O80 should be assigned when a woman is admitted for a full-term normal delivery and delivers a single, healthy infant without any complications antepartum, during the delivery, or postpartum during the delivery episode. Code O80 is always a principal diagnosis. It is not to be used if any other code from chapter 15 is needed to describe a current complication of the antenatal, delivery, or perinatal period. Additional codes from other chapters may be used with code O80 if they are not related to or are in any way complicating the pregnancy.

2) Uncomplicated delivery with resolved antepartum complication

Code O80 may be used if the patient had a complication at some point during the pregnancy, but the complication is not present at the time of the admission for delivery.

3) Outcome of delivery for O80

Z37.0, Single live birth, is the only outcome of delivery code appropriate for use with O80.

o. The Peripartum and Postpartum Periods

1) Peripartum and Postpartum periods

The postpartum period begins immediately after delivery and continues for six weeks following delivery. The peripartum period is defined as the last month of pregnancy to five months postpartum.

2) Peripartum and postpartum complication

A postpartum complication is any complication occurring within the six-week period.

3) Pregnancy-related complications after 6 week period

Chapter 15 codes may also be used to describe pregnancy-related complications after the peripartum or postpartum period if the provider documents that a condition is pregnancy related.

4) Admission for routine postpartum care following delivery outside hospital

When the mother delivers outside the hospital prior to admission and is admitted for routine postpartum care and no complications are noted, code Z39.0, Encounter for care and examination of mother immediately after delivery, should be assigned as the principal diagnosis.

5) Pregnancy associated cardiomyopathy

Pregnancy associated cardiomyopathy, code O90.3, is unique in that it may be diagnosed in the third trimester of pregnancy but may continue to progress months after delivery. For this reason, it is referred to as peripartum cardiomyopathy. Code O90.3 is only for use when the cardiomyopathy develops as a result of pregnancy in a woman who did not have pre-existing heart disease.

p. Code O94, Sequelae of complication of pregnancy, childbirth, and the puerperium

1) Code O94

Code O94, Sequelae of complication of pregnancy, childbirth, and the puerperium, is for use in those cases when an initial complication of a pregnancy develops a sequelae requiring care or treatment at a future date.

2) After the initial postpartum period

This code may be used at any time after the initial postpartum period.

3) Sequencing of Code O94

This code, like all late effect codes, is to be sequenced following the code describing the sequelae of the complication.

q. Abortions

1) Abortion with Liveborn Fetus

When an attempted termination of pregnancy results in a liveborn fetus assign a code from subcategory O60.1, Preterm labor with preterm delivery,

and a code from category Z37, Outcome of Delivery. The procedure code for the attempted termination of pregnancy should also be assigned.

2) Retained Products of Conception following an abortion
Subsequent encounters for retained products of conception following a spontaneous abortion or elective termination of pregnancy are assigned the appropriate code from category O03, Spontaneous abortion, or code Z33.2, Encounter for elective termination of pregnancy. This advice is appropriate even when the patient was discharged previously with a discharge diagnosis of complete abortion.

16. Chapter 16: Newborn (Perinatal) Guidelines (P00-P96)
For coding and reporting purposes the perinatal period is defined as before birth through the 28th day following birth. The following guidelines are provided for reporting purposes

a. General Perinatal Rules

1) Use of Chapter 16 Codes
Codes in this chapter are <u>never</u> for use on the maternal record. Codes from Chapter 15, the obstetric chapter, are never permitted on the newborn record. Chapter 16 code may be used throughout the life of the patient if the condition is still present.

2) Principal Diagnosis for Birth Record
When coding the birth episode in a newborn record, assign a code from category Z38, Liveborn according to place of birth and type of delivery, as the principal diagnosis. A code from category Z38 is assigned only once, to a newborn at the time of birth. If a newborn is transferred to another institution, a code from category Z38 should not be used at the receiving hospital.
A code from category Z38 is used only on the newborn record, not on the mother's record.

3) Use of Codes from other Chapters with Codes from Chapter 16
Codes from other chapters may be used with codes from chapter 16 if the codes from the other chapters provide more specific detail. Codes for signs and symptoms may be assigned when a definitive diagnosis has not been established. If the reason for the encounter is a perinatal condition, the code from chapter 16 should be sequenced first.

4) Use of Chapter 16 Codes after the Perinatal Period
Should a condition originate in the perinatal period, and continue throughout the life of the patient, the perinatal code should continue to be used regardless of the patient's age.

5) Birth process or community acquired conditions
If a newborn has a condition that may be either due to the birth process or community acquired and the documentation does not indicate which it is, the default is due to the birth process and the code from Chapter 16 should be used. If the condition is community-acquired, a code from Chapter 16 should not be assigned.

6) Code all clinically significant conditions
All clinically significant conditions noted on routine newborn examination should be coded. A condition is clinically significant if it requires:
- clinical evaluation; or
- therapeutic treatment; or
- diagnostic procedures; or
- extended length of hospital stay; or
- increased nursing care and/or monitoring; or
- has implications for future health care needs

Note: The perinatal guidelines listed above are the same as the general coding guidelines for "additional diagnoses", except for the final point regarding implications for future health care needs. Codes should be assigned for conditions that have been specified by the provider as having implications for future health care needs.

b. Observation and Evaluation of Newborns for Suspected Conditions not Found

Assign a code from categories P00-P04 to identify those instances when a healthy newborn is evaluated for a suspected condition that is determined after study not to be present. Do not use a code from categories P00-P04 when the patient has identified signs or symptoms of a suspected problem; in such cases, code the sign or symptom.

c. Coding Additional Perinatal Diagnoses

1) Assigning codes for conditions that require treatment

Assign codes for conditions that require treatment or further investigation, prolong the length of stay, or require resource utilization.

2) Codes for conditions specified as having implications for future health care needs

Assign codes for conditions that have been specified by the provider as having implications for future health care needs.

Note: This guideline should not be used for adult patients.

d. Prematurity and Fetal Growth Retardation

Providers utilize different criteria in determining prematurity. A code for prematurity should not be assigned unless it is documented. Assignment of codes in categories P05, Disorders of newborn related to slow fetal growth and fetal malnutrition, and P07, Disorders of newborn related to short gestation and low birth weight, not elsewhere classified, should be based on the recorded birth weight and estimated gestational age. Codes from category P05 should not be assigned with codes from category P07.

When both birth weight and gestational age are available, two codes from category P07 should be assigned, with the code for birth weight sequenced before the code for gestational age.

e. Low birth weight and immaturity status

Codes from subcategory Z91.7, Low birth weight and immaturity status, are for use as personal status codes for a child or adult who was premature or had a low birth weight as a newborn and this is affecting the patient's current health status.

See Section I.C.21. Factors influencing health status and contact with health services, Status.

f. Bacterial Sepsis of Newborn

Category P36, Bacterial sepsis of newborn, includes congenital sepsis. If a perinate is documented as having sepsis without documentation of congenital or community acquired, the default is congenital and a code from category P36 should be assigned. If the P36 code includes the causal organism, an additional code from category B95, Streptococcus, Staphylococcus, and Enterococcus as the cause of diseases classified elsewhere, or B96, Other bacterial agents as the cause of diseases classified elsewhere, should **not** be assigned. If the P36 code does not include the causal organism, assign an additional code from category B96. If applicable, use additional codes to identify severe sepsis (R65.2-) and any associated acute organ dysfunction.

g. Stillbirth

Code P95, Stillbirth, is only for use in institutions that maintain separate records for stillbirths. No other code should be used with P95. Code P95 should not be used on the mother's record.

17. Chapter 17: Congenital malformations, deformations, and chromosomal abnormalities (Q00-Q99)

Assign an appropriate code(s) from categories Q00-Q99, Congenital malformations, deformations, and chromosomal abnormalities when a malformation/deformation or chromosomal abnormality is documented. A malformation/deformation/or chromosomal abnormality may be the principal/first listed diagnosis on a record or a secondary diagnosis.

When a malformation/deformation/or chromosomal abnormality does not have a unique code assignment, assign additional code(s) for any manifestations that may be present.

When the code assignment specifically identifies the malformation/ deformation/or chromosomal abnormality, manifestations that are an inherent component of the anomaly should not be coded separately. Additional codes should be assigned for manifestations that are not an inherent component.

Codes from Chapter 17 may be used throughout the life of the patient. If a congenital malformation or deformity has been corrected, a personal history code should be used to identify the history of the malformation or deformity. Although present at birth, malformation/deformation/or chromosomal abnormality may not be identified until later in life. Whenever the condition is diagnosed by the physician, it is appropriate to assign a code from codes Q00-Q89.

For the birth admission, the appropriate code from category Z38, Liveborn infants, according to place of birth and type of delivery, should be sequenced as the principal diagnosis, followed by any congenital anomaly codes, Q00-Q89.

18. **Chapter 18: Symptoms, signs, and abnormal clinical and laboratory findings, not elsewhere classified (R00-R99)**
Chapter 18 includes symptoms, signs, abnormal results of clinical or other investigative procedures, and ill-defined conditions regarding which no diagnosis classifiable elsewhere is recorded. Signs and symptoms that point to a **specific** diagnosis have been assigned to a category in other chapters of the classification.

a. Use of symptom codes
Codes that describe symptoms and signs are acceptable for reporting purposes when a related definitive diagnosis has not been established (confirmed) by the provider.

b. Use of a symptom code with a definitive diagnosis code
Codes for signs and symptoms may be reported in addition to a related definitive diagnosis when the sign or symptom is not routinely associated with that diagnosis, such as the various signs and symptoms associated with complex syndromes. The definitive diagnosis code should be sequenced before the symptom code.

Signs or symptoms that are associated routinely with a disease process should not be assigned as additional codes, unless otherwise instructed by the classification.

c. Combination codes that include symptoms
ICD-10-CM contains a number of combination codes that identify both the definitive diagnosis and common symptoms of that diagnosis. When using one of these combination codes, an additional code should not be assigned for the symptom.

d. Repeated falls
Code R29.6, Repeated falls, is for use for encounters when a patient has recently fallen and the reason for the fall is being investigated.

Code Z91.81, History of falling, is for use when a patient has fallen in the past and is at risk for future falls. When appropriate, both codes R29.6 and Z91.81 may be assigned together.

e. Glasgow coma scale
The Glasgow coma scale codes (R40.2-) can be used in conjunction with traumatic brain injury codes or sequelae of cerebrovascular accident codes. These codes are primarily for use by trauma registries, but they may be used in any setting where this information is collected. The coma scale codes should be sequenced after the diagnosis code(s).

These codes, one from each subcategory, are needed to complete the scale. The 7th character indicates when the scale was recorded. The 7th character should match for all three codes.

At a minimum, report the initial score documented on presentation at your facility. This may be a score from the emergency medicine technician (EMT) or in the emergency department. If desired, a facility may choose to capture multiple Glasgow coma scale scores.

f. Functional quadriplegia

Functional quadriplegia (code R53.2) is the lack of ability to use one's limbs or to ambulate due to extreme debility. It is not associated with neurologic deficit or injury, and code R53.2 should not be used for cases of neurologic quadriplegia. It should only be assigned if functional quadriplegia is specifically documented in the medical record.

g. SIRS due to Non-Infectious Process

The systemic inflammatory response syndrome (SIRS) can develop as a result of certain non-infectious disease processes, such as trauma, malignant neoplasm, or pancreatitis. When SIRS is documented with a noninfectious condition, and no subsequent infection is documented, the code for the underlying condition, such as an injury, should be assigned, followed by code R65.10, Systemic inflammatory response syndrome (SIRS) of non-infectious origin without acute organ dysfunction, or code R65.11, Systemic inflammatory response syndrome (SIRS) of non-infectious origin with acute organ dysfunction. If an associated acute organ dysfunction is documented, the appropriate code(s) for the specific type of organ dysfunction(s) should be assigned in addition to code R65.11. If acute organ dysfunction is documented, but it cannot be determined if the acute organ dysfunction is associated with SIRS or due to another condition (e.g., directly due to the trauma), the provider should be queried.

g. Death NOS

Code R99, Ill-defined and unknown cause of mortality, is only for use in the very limited circumstance when a patient who has already died is brought into an emergency department or other healthcare facility and is pronounced dead upon arrival. It does not represent the discharge disposition of death.

19. Chapter 19: Injury, poisoning, and certain other consequences of external causes (S00-T88)

a. Code Extensions

Most categories in chapter 19 have 7th character extensions that are required for each applicable code. Most categories in this chapter have three extensions (with the exception of fractures): A, initial encounter, D, subsequent encounter and S, sequela.

Extension "A", initial encounter is used while the patient is receiving active treatment for the injury. Examples of active treatment are: surgical treatment, emergency department encounter, and evaluation and treatment by a new physician.

Extension "D" subsequent encounter is used for encounters after the patient has received active treatment of the injury and is receiving routine care for the injury during the healing or recovery phase. Examples of subsequent care are: cast change or removal, removal of external **or** internal fixation device, medication adjustment, other aftercare and follow up visits following injury treatment.

The aftercare Z codes should not be used for aftercare for injuries. For aftercare of an injury, assign the acute injury code with the 7th character "D" (subsequent encounter).

Extension "S", sequela, is for use for complications or conditions that arise as a direct result of an injury, such as scar formation after a burn. The scars are sequelae of the burn. When using extension "S", it is necessary to use both the injury code that precipitated the sequela and the code for the sequela itself. The "S" is added only to the injury code, not the sequela code. The "S" extension identifies the injury responsible for the sequela. The specific type of sequela (e.g. scar) is sequenced first, followed by the injury code.

b. Coding of Injuries

When coding injuries, assign separate codes for each injury unless a combination code is provided, in which case the combination code is assigned. Multiple injury codes are provided in ICD-10-CM, but should not be assigned unless information for a more specific code is not available. These **traumatic injury** codes (S00-T14.9) are not to be used for normal, healing surgical wounds or to identify complications of surgical wounds.

GUIDELINES (ICD-10-CM)

34

The code for the most serious injury, as determined by the provider and the focus of treatment, is sequenced first.

1) Superficial injuries
Superficial injuries such as abrasions or contusions are not coded when associated with more severe injuries of the same site.

2) Primary injury with damage to nerves/blood vessels
When a primary injury results in minor damage to peripheral nerves or blood vessels, the primary injury is sequenced first with additional code(s) for injuries to nerves and spinal cord (such as category S04), and/or injury to blood vessels (such as category S15). When the primary injury is to the blood vessels or nerves, that injury should be sequenced first.

c. Coding of Traumatic Fractures
The principles of multiple coding of injuries should be followed in coding fractures. Fractures of specified sites are coded individually by site in accordance with both the provisions within categories S02, S12, S22, S32, S42, **S49,** S52, **S59,** S62, S72, **S79,** S82, **S89,** S92 and the level of detail furnished by medical record content.

A fracture not indicated as open or closed should be coded to closed. A fracture not indicated whether displaced or not displaced should be coded to displaced.

More specific guidelines are as follows:

1) Initial vs. Subsequent Encounter for Fractures
Traumatic fractures are coded using the appropriate 7th character extension for initial encounter (A, B, C) while the patient is receiving active treatment for the fracture. Examples of active treatment are: surgical treatment, emergency department encounter, and evaluation and treatment by a new physician.

Fractures are coded using the appropriate 7th character extension for subsequent care for encounters after the patient has completed active treatment of the fracture and is receiving routine care for the fracture during the healing or recovery phase. Examples of fracture aftercare are: cast change or removal, removal of external or internal fixation device, medication adjustment, and follow-up visits following fracture treatment.

Care for complications of surgical treatment for fracture repairs during the healing or recovery phase should be coded with the appropriate complication codes.

Care of complications of fractures, such as malunion and nonunion, should be reported with the appropriate 7th character extensions for subsequent care with nonunion (K, M, N,) or subsequent care with malunion (P, Q, R).

A code from category M80, not a traumatic fracture code, should be used for any patient with known osteoporosis who suffers a fracture, **even if the patient had a minor fall or trauma, if that fall or trauma would not usually break a normal, healthy bone**.

See Section I.C.13. Osteoporosis.

The aftercare Z codes should not be used for aftercare for injuries. For aftercare of an injury, assign the acute injury code with the 7th character "D" (subsequent encounter).

2) Multiple fractures sequencing
Multiple fractures are sequenced in accordance with the severity of the fracture. The provider should be asked to list the fracture diagnoses in the order of severity.

d. Coding of Burns and Corrosions
The ICD-10-CM distinguishes between burns and corrosions. The burn codes are for thermal burns, except sunburns, that come from a heat source, such as a fire or hot appliance. The burn codes are also for burns resulting from electricity and radiation. Corrosions are burns due to chemicals. The guidelines are the same for burns and corrosions.

Current burns (T20-T25) are classified by depth, extent and by agent (X code). Burns are classified by depth as first degree (erythema), second degree (blistering), and third degree (full-thickness involvement). Burns of the eye and internal organs (T26-T28) are classified by site, but not by degree.

1) Sequencing of burn and related condition codes

Sequence first the code that reflects the highest degree of burn when more than one burn is present.

a. When the reason for the admission or encounter is for treatment of external multiple burns, sequence first the code that reflects the burn of the highest degree.

b. When a patient has both internal and external burns, the circumstances of admission govern the selection of the principal diagnosis or first-listed diagnosis.

c. When a patient is admitted for burn injuries and other related conditions such as smoke inhalation and/or respiratory failure, the circumstances of admission govern the selection of the principal or first-listed diagnosis.

2) Burns of the same local site

Classify burns of the same local site (three-digit category level, T20-T28) but of different degrees to the subcategory identifying the highest degree recorded in the diagnosis.

3) Non-healing burns

Non-healing burns are coded as acute burns.
Necrosis of burned skin should be coded as a non-healed burn.

4) Infected Burn

For any documented infected burn site, use an additional code for the infection.

5) Assign separate codes for each burn site

When coding burns, assign separate codes for each burn site. Category T30, Burn and corrosion, body region unspecified is extremely vague and should rarely be used.

6) Burns and Corrosions Classified According to Extent of Body Surface Involved

Assign codes from category T31, Burns classified according to extent of body surface involved, or T32, Corrosions classified according to extent of body surface involved, when the site of the burn is not specified or when there is a need for additional data. It is advisable to use category T31 as additional coding when needed to provide data for evaluating burn mortality, such as that needed by burn units. It is also advisable to use category T31 as an additional code for reporting purposes when there is mention of a third-degree burn involving 20 percent or more of the body surface.

Categories T31 and T32 are based on the classic "rule of nines" in estimating body surface involved: head and neck are assigned nine percent, each arm nine percent, each leg 18 percent, the anterior trunk 18 percent, posterior trunk 18 percent, and genitalia one percent. Providers may change these percentage assignments where necessary to accommodate infants and children who have proportionately larger heads than adults, and patients who have large buttocks, thighs, or abdomen that involve burns.

7) Encounters for treatment of late effects of burns

Encounters for the treatment of the late effects of burns or corrosions (i.e., scars or joint contractures) should be coded with a burn or corrosion code with the 7th character "S" or sequela.

8) Sequelae with a late effect code and current burn

When appropriate, both a code for a current burn or corrosion with 7th character extension "A" or "D" and a burn or corrosion code with extension "S" may be assigned on the same record (when both a current burn and sequelae of an old burn exist). Burns and corrosions do not heal at the same rate and a current healing wound may still exist with sequela of a healed burn or corrosion.

9) Use of an external cause code with burns and corrosions

An external cause code should be used with burns and corrosions to identify the source and intent of the burn, as well as the place where it occurred.

e. Adverse Effects, Poisoning , Underdosing and Toxic Effects

Codes in categories T36-T65 are combination codes that include the substances related to adverse effects, poisonings, toxic effects and underdosing, as well as the external cause. No additional external cause code is required for poisonings, toxic effects, adverse effects and underdosing codes.

A code from categories T36-T65 is sequenced first, followed by the code(s) that specify the nature of the adverse effect, poisoning, or toxic effect. **Note: This sequencing instruction does not apply to underdosing codes (fifth or sixth character "6", for example T36.0x6-).**

1) Do not code directly from the Table of Drugs

Do not code directly from the Table of Drugs and Chemicals. Always refer back to the Tabular List.

2) Use as many codes as necessary to describe

Use as many codes as necessary to describe completely all drugs, medicinal or biological substances.

3) If the same code would describe the causative agent

If the same code would describe the causative agent for more than one adverse reaction, poisoning, toxic effect or underdosing, assign the code only once.

4) If two or more drugs, medicinal or biological substances

If two or more drugs, medicinal or biological substances are reported, code each individually unless the combination code is listed in the Table of Drugs and Chemicals.

5) The occurrence of drug toxicity is classified in ICD-10-CM as follows:

(a) Adverse Effect

Assign the appropriate code for adverse effect (for example, T36.0x5-) when the drug was correctly prescribed and properly administered. Use additional code(s) for all manifestations of adverse effects. Examples of manifestations are tachycardia, delirium, gastrointestinal hemorrhaging, vomiting, hypokalemia, hepatitis, renal failure, or respiratory failure.

(b) Poisoning

When coding a poisoning or reaction to the improper use of a medication (e.g., overdose, wrong substance given or taken in error, wrong route of administration), assign the appropriate code from categories T36-T50. Poisoning codes have an associated intent: accidental, intentional self-harm, assault and undetermined. Use additional code(s) for all manifestations of poisonings.

If there is also a diagnosis of drug abuse or dependence **on** the substance, the abuse or dependence is coded as an additional code.

Examples of poisoning include:

(i) Error was made in drug prescription Errors made in drug prescription or in the administration of the drug by provider, nurse, patient, or other person.

(ii) Overdose of a drug intentionally taken If an overdose of a drug was intentionally taken or administered and resulted in drug toxicity, it would be coded as a poisoning.

(iii) Nonprescribed drug taken with correctly prescribed and properly administered drug.
If a nonprescribed drug or medicinal agent was taken in combination with a correctly prescribed and properly administered drug, any drug toxicity or other reaction resulting from the interaction of the two drugs would be classified as a poisoning.

(iv) Interaction of drug(s) and alcohol.
When a reaction results from the interaction of a drug(s) and alcohol, this would be classified as poisoning.
See Section I.C.4. if poisoning is the result of insulin pump malfunctions.

(c) Underdosing

Underdosing refers to taking less of a medication than is prescribed by a **provider** or a manufacturer's instruction. For underdosing, assign the code from categories T36-T50 **(fifth or sixth character "6")**.

Codes for underdosing should never be assigned as principal or first-listed codes. If a patient has a relapse or exacerbation of the medical condition for which the drug is prescribed because of the reduction in dose, then the medical condition itself should be coded.

Noncompliance (Z91.12-, Z91.13-) or complication of care (Y63.61, Y63.8-Y63.9) codes are to be used with an underdosing code to indicate intent, if known.

(d) Toxic Effects

When a harmful substance is ingested or comes in contact with a person, this is classified as a toxic effect. The toxic effect codes are in categories T51-T65.

Toxic effect codes have an associated intent: accidental, intentional self-harm, assault and undetermined.

f. Adult and child abuse, neglect and other maltreatment

Sequence first the appropriate code from categories T74.- or T76.- for abuse, neglect and other maltreatment, followed by any accompanying mental health or injury code(s).

If the documentation in the medical record states abuse or neglect it is coded as confirmed. It is coded as suspected if it is documented as suspected.

For cases of confirmed abuse or neglect an external cause code from the assault section (X92-Y08) should be added to identify the cause of any physical injuries. A perpetrator code (Y07) should be added when the perpetrator of the abuse is known. For suspected cases of abuse or neglect, do not report external cause or perpetrator code.

If a suspected case of abuse, neglect or mistreatment is ruled out during an encounter code Z04.71, Suspected adult physical and sexual abuse, ruled out, or code Z04.72, Suspected child physical and sexual abuse, ruled out, should be used, not a code from T76.

g. Complications of care

1) Complications of care

(a) Documentation of complications of care

As with all procedural or postprocedural complications, code assignment is based on the provider's documentation of the relationship between the condition and the procedure.

2) Pain due to medical devices

Pain associated with devices, implants or grafts left in a surgical site (for example painful hip prosthesis) is assigned to the appropriate code(s) found in Chapter 19, Injury, poisoning, and certain other consequences of external causes. Specific codes for pain due to medical devices are found in the T code section of the ICD-10-CM. Use additional code(s) from category G89 to identify acute or chronic pain due to presence of the device, implant or graft (G89.18 or G89.28).

3) Transplant complications

(a) Transplant complications other than kidney

Codes under category T86, Complications of transplanted organs and tissues, are for use for both complications and rejection of transplanted organs. A transplant complication code is only assigned if the complication affects the function of the transplanted organ. Two codes are required to fully describe a transplant complication: the appropriate code from category T86 and a secondary code that identifies the complication.

Pre-existing conditions or conditions that develop after the transplant are not coded as complications unless they affect the function of the transplanted organs.

See I.C.21.c.3 for transplant organ removal status
See I.C.2.r for malignant neoplasm associated with transplanted organ.

(b) Chronic kidney disease and kidney transplant complications
Patients who have undergone kidney transplant may still have some form of chronic kidney disease (CKD) because the kidney transplant may not fully restore kidney function. Code T86.1- should be assigned for documented complications of a kidney transplant, such as transplant failure or rejection or other transplant complication. Code T86.1- should not be assigned for post kidney transplant patients who have chronic kidney (CKD) unless a transplant complication such as transplant failure or rejection is documented. If the documentation is unclear as to whether the patient has a complication of the transplant, query the provider.

For patients with CKD following a kidney transplant, but who do not have a complication such as failure or rejection, *see section I.C.14. Chronic kidney disease and kidney transplant status.*

4) Complication codes that include the external cause
As with certain other T codes, some of the complications of care codes have the external cause included in the code. The code includes the nature of the complication as well as the type of procedure that caused the complication. No external cause code indicating the type of procedure is necessary for these codes.

5) Complications of care codes within the body system chapters
Intraoperative and postprocedural complication codes are found within the body system chapters with codes specific to the organs and structures of that body system. These codes should be sequenced first, followed by a code(s) for the specific complication, if applicable.

6) Ventilator associated pneumonia

(a) Documentation of Ventilator associated Pneumonia
As with all procedural or postprocedural complications, code assignment is based on the provider's documentation of the relationship between the condition and the procedure.

Code J95.851, Ventilator associated pneumonia, should be assigned only when the provider has documented ventilator associated pneumonia (VAP). An additional code to identify the organism (e.g., Pseudomonas aeruginosa, code B96.5) should also be assigned. Do not assign an additional code from categories J12-J18 to identify the type of pneumonia.

Code J95.851 should not be assigned for cases where the patient has pneumonia and is on a mechanical ventilator but the provider has not specifically stated that the pneumonia is ventilator-associated pneumonia.

If the documentation is unclear as to whether the patient has a pneumonia that is a complication attributable to the mechanical ventilator, query the provider.

(b) Patient admitted with pneumonia and develops VAP
A patient may be admitted with one type of pneumonia (e.g., code J13, Pneumonia due to Streptococcus pneumonia) and subsequently develop VAP. In this instance, the principal diagnosis would be the appropriate code from categories J12-J18 for the pneumonia diagnosed at the time of admission. Code J95.851, Ventilator associated pneumonia, would be assigned as an additional diagnosis when the provider has also documented the presence of ventilator associated pneumonia.

20. **Chapter 20: External Causes of Morbidity (V01-Y99)**
Introduction: These guidelines are provided for the reporting of external causes of morbidity codes in order that there will be standardization in the process. These codes are secondary codes for use in any health care setting.

External cause codes are intended to provide data for injury research and evaluation of injury prevention strategies. These codes capture how the injury or health condition happened (cause), the intent (unintentional or accidental; or intentional, such as suicide or assault), the place where the event occurred the activity of the patient at the time of the event, **and the person's status (e.g., civilian, military).**

a. General External Cause Coding Guidelines

1) Used with any code in the range of A00.0-T88.9, Z00-Z99

An external cause code may be used with any code in the range of A00.0-T88.9, Z00-Z99, classification that is a health condition due to an external cause. Though they are most applicable to injuries, they are also valid for use with such things as infections or diseases due to an external source, and other health conditions, such as a heart attack that occurs during strenuous physical activity.

2) External cause code used for length of treatment

Assign the external cause code, with the appropriate 7th character (initial encounter, subsequent encounter or sequela) for each encounter for which the injury or condition is being treated.

3) Use the full range of external cause codes

Use the full range of external cause codes to completely describe the cause, the intent, the place of occurrence **and** if applicable, the activity of the patient at the time of the event, **and the patient's status,** for all injuries, and other health conditions due to an external cause.

4) Assign as many external cause codes as necessary

Assign as many external cause codes as necessary to fully explain each cause. If only one external code can be recorded, assign the code most related to the principal diagnosis.

5) The selection of the appropriate external cause code

The selection of the appropriate external cause code is guided by the Index to External Causes, which is located after the Alphabetical Index to diseases and by Inclusion and Exclusion notes in the Tabular List.

6) External cause code can never be a principal diagnosis

An external cause code can never be a principal (first listed) diagnosis.

7) Combination external cause codes

Certain of the external cause codes are combination codes that identify sequential events that result in an injury, such as a fall which results in striking against an object. The injury may be due to either event or both. The combination external cause code used should correspond to the sequence of events regardless of which caused the most serious injury.

8) No external cause code needed in certain circumstances

No external cause code from Chapter 20 is needed if the external cause and intent are included in a code from another chapter (e.g. T360x1- Poisoning by penicillins, accidental (unintentional)).

b. Place of Occurrence Guideline

Codes from category Y92, Place of occurrence of the external cause, are secondary codes for use after other external cause codes to identify the location of the patient at the time of injury or other condition.

A place of occurrence code is used only once, at the initial encounter for treatment. No 7th characters are used for Y92. Only one code from Y92 should be recorded on a medical record. A place of occurrence code should be used in conjunction with an activity code, Y93.

Do not use place of occurrence code Y92.9 if the place is not stated or is not applicable.

c. Activity Code

Assign a code from category Y93, Activity code, **to describe** the activity of the patient at the time the injury **or other health condition occurred**.

An activity code is used only once, at the initial encounter for treatment. Only one code from Y93 should be recorded on a medical record. An activity code should be used in conjunction with a place of occurrence code, Y92.

If a patient is a student but is injured while performing an activity for income, use 7th character "2", work related activity.

A work related activity is any activity for which payment or income is received.
The activity codes are not applicable to poisonings, adverse effects, misadventures or late effects.
Do not assign Y93.9, Unspecified activity, if the activity is not stated.

d. Place of Occurrence, Activity, *and Status* **Codes Used with other External Cause Code**

When applicable, place of occurrence, activity, **and external cause status codes** are sequenced after the main external cause code(s). Regardless of the number of external cause codes assigned, there should be only one place of occurrence code, one activity, **and one external cause status** code assigned to an encounter.

e. If the Reporting Format Limits the Number of External Cause Codes

If the reporting format limits the number of external cause codes that can be used in reporting clinical data, **report the code for the cause/intent** most related to the principal diagnosis. **If the format permits capture of additional external cause codes, the cause/intent, including medical misadventures, of the additional events should be reported rather than the codes for place, activity, or external status.**

f. Multiple External Cause Coding Guidelines

More than one external cause code is required to fully describe the external cause of an illness, injury or poisoning. The assignment of external cause codes should be sequenced in the following priority:

If two or more events cause separate injuries, an external cause code should be assigned for each cause. The first listed external cause code will be selected in the following order:

External cause codes for child and adult abuse take priority over all other external cause codes.

See Section I.C.19., Child and Adult abuse guidelines.

External cause codes for terrorism events take priority over all other external cause codes except child and adult abuse.

External cause codes for cataclysmic events take priority over all other external cause codes except child and adult abuse and terrorism.

External cause codes for transport accidents take priority over all other external cause codes except cataclysmic events, child and adult abuse and terrorism.

Activity and external cause status codes are assigned following all causal (intent) external cause codes.

The first-listed external cause code should correspond to the cause of the most serious diagnosis due to an assault, accident, or self-harm, following the order of hierarchy listed above.

g. Child and Adult Abuse Guideline

Adult and child abuse, neglect and maltreatment are classified as assault. Any of the assault codes may be used to indicate the external cause of any injury resulting from the confirmed abuse.

For confirmed cases of abuse, neglect and maltreatment, when the perpetrator is known, a code from Y07, Perpetrator of maltreatment and neglect, should accompany any other assault codes.

See Section I.C.19. Adult and child abuse, neglect and other maltreatment

h. Unknown or Undetermined Intent Guideline

If the intent (accident, self-harm, assault) of the cause of an injury or other condition is unknown or unspecified, code the intent as accidental intent. All transport accident categories assume accidental intent.

1) Use of undetermined intent

External cause codes for events of undetermined intent are only for use if the documentation in the record specifies that the intent cannot be determined

i. Late Effects of External Cause Guidelines

1) Late effect external cause codes

Late effects are reported using the external cause code with the 7th character extension "S" for sequela. These codes should be used with any report of a late effect or sequela resulting from a previous injury.

2) Late effect external cause code with a related current injury
A late effect external cause code should never be used with a related current nature of injury code.

3) Use of late effect external cause codes for subsequent visits
Use a late effect external cause code for subsequent visits when a late effect of the initial injury is being treated. Do not use a late effect external cause code for subsequent visits for follow-up care (e.g., to assess healing, to receive rehabilitative therapy) of the injury or poisoning when no late effect of the injury has been documented.

j. Terrorism Guidelines

1) Cause of injury identified by the Federal Government (FBI) as terrorism
When the cause of an injury is identified by the Federal Government (FBI) as terrorism, the first-listed external cause code should be a code from category Y38, Terrorism. The definition of terrorism employed by the FBI is found at the inclusion note at the beginning of category Y38. Use additional code for place of occurrence (Y92.-). More than one Y38 code may be assigned if the injury is the result of more than one mechanism of terrorism.

2) Cause of an injury is suspected to be the result of terrorism
When the cause of an injury is suspected to be the result of terrorism a code from category Y38 should not be assigned. Suspected cases should be classified as assault.

3) Code Y38.9, Terrorism, secondary effects
Assign code Y38.9, Terrorism, secondary effects, for conditions occurring subsequent to the terrorist event. This code should not be assigned for conditions that are due to the initial terrorist act.

It is acceptable to assign code Y38.9 with another code from Y38 if there is an injury due to the initial terrorist event and an injury that is a subsequent result of the terrorist event.

k. External cause status
A code from category Y99, External cause status, should be assigned whenever any other external cause code is assigned for an encounter, including an Activity code, except for the events noted below. Assign a code from category Y99, External cause status, to indicate the work status of the person at the time the event occurred. The status code indicates whether the event occurred during military activity, whether a non-military person was at work, whether an individual including a student or volunteer was involved in a non-work activity at the time of the causal event.

A code from Y99, External cause status, should be assigned, when applicable, with other external cause codes, such as transport accidents and falls. The external cause status codes are not applicable to poisonings, adverse effects, misadventures or late effects.

Do not assign a code from category Y99 if no other external cause codes (cause, activity) are applicable for the encounter.

Do not assign code Y99.9, Unspecified external cause status, if the status is not stated.

21. **Chapter 21: Factors influencing health status and contact with health services (Z00-Z99)**
Note: The chapter specific guidelines provide additional information about the use of Z codes for specified encounters.

a. Use of Z codes in any healthcare setting
Z codes are for use in any healthcare setting. Z codes may be used as either a first listed (principal diagnosis code in the inpatient setting) or secondary code, depending on the circumstances of the encounter. Certain Z codes may only be used as first listed or principal diagnosis.

b. Z Codes indicate a reason for an encounter
Z codes are not procedure codes. A corresponding procedure code must accompany a Z code to describe the procedure performed.

c. Categories of Z Codes

1) Contact/Exposure

Category Z20 indicates contact with, **and suspected** exposure to, communicable diseases. These codes are for patients who do not show any sign or symptom of a disease but **are suspected to** have been exposed to it by close personal contact with an infected individual or are in an area where a disease is epidemic.

Category Z77, indicates contact with and suspected exposures hazardous to health.

Contact/exposure codes may be used as a first listed code to explain an encounter for testing, or, more commonly, as a secondary code to identify a potential risk.

2) Inoculations and vaccinations

Code Z23 is for encounters for inoculations and vaccinations. It indicates that a patient is being seen to receive a prophylactic inoculation against a disease. Procedure codes are required to identify the actual administration of the injection and the type(s) of immunizations given. Code Z23 may be used as a secondary code if the inoculation is given as a routine part of preventive health care, such as a well-baby visit.

3) Status

Status codes indicate that a patient is either a carrier of a disease or has the sequelae or residual of a past disease or condition. This includes such things as the presence of prosthetic or mechanical devices resulting from past treatment. A status code is informative, because the status may affect the course of treatment and its outcome. A status code is distinct from a history code. The history code indicates that the patient no longer has the condition.

A status code should not be used with a diagnosis code from one of the body system chapters, if the diagnosis code includes the information provided by the status code. For example, code Z94.1, Heart transplant status, should not be used with a code from subcategory T86.2, Complications of heart transplant. The status code does not provide additional information. The complication code indicates that the patient is a heart transplant patient.

For encounters for weaning from a mechanical ventilator, assign code J96.1, Chronic respiratory failure, followed by code Z99.11, Dependence on respirator [ventilator] status.

The status Z codes/categories are:

Z14   Genetic carrier
        Genetic carrier status indicates that a person carries a gene, associated with a particular disease, which may be passed to offspring who may develop that disease. The person does not have the disease and is not at risk of developing the disease.

Z15   Genetic susceptibility to disease
        Genetic susceptibility indicates that a person has a gene that increases the risk of that person developing the disease.

Codes from category Z15 should not be used as principal or first-listed codes. If the patient has the condition to which he/she is susceptible, and that condition is the reason for the encounter, the code for the current condition should be sequenced first. If the patient is being seen for follow-up after completed treatment for this condition, and the condition no longer exists, a follow-up code should be sequenced first, followed by the appropriate personal history and genetic susceptibility codes. If the purpose of the encounter is genetic counseling associated with procreative management, code Z31.5, Encounter for genetic counseling, should be assigned as the first-listed code, followed by a code from category Z15. Additional codes should be assigned for any applicable family or personal history.

Z16   Infection with drug-resistant microorganisms
        This code indicates that a patient has an infection that is resistant to drug treatment. Sequence the infection code first.

Z17   Estrogen receptor status

Z21   Asymptomatic HIV infection status
This code indicates that a patient has tested positive for HIV but has manifested no signs or symptoms of the disease.

Z22   Carrier of infectious disease
Carrier status indicates that a person harbors the specific organisms of a disease without manifest symptoms and is capable of transmitting the infection.

Z28.3   Underimmunization status

Z33.1   Pregnant state, incidental
This code is a secondary code only for use when the pregnancy is in no way complicating the reason for visit. Otherwise, a code from the obstetric chapter is required.

Z66   Do not resuscitate

Z67   Blood type

Z68   Body mass index (BMI)

Z74.01   Bed confinement status

Z76.82   Awaiting organ transplant status

Z78   Other specified health status

Z79   Long-term (current) drug therapy

Codes from this category indicate a patient's continuous use of a prescribed drug (including such things as aspirin therapy) for the long-term treatment of a condition or for prophylactic use. It is not for use for patients who have addictions to drugs. This subcategory is not for use of medications for detoxification or maintenance programs to prevent withdrawal symptoms in patients with drug dependence (e.g., methadone maintenance for opiate dependence). Assign the appropriate code for the drug dependence instead.

Assign a code from Z79 if the patient is receiving a medication for an extended period as a prophylactic measure (such as for the prevention of deep vein thrombosis) or as treatment of a chronic condition (such as arthritis) or a disease requiring a lengthy course of treatment (such as cancer). Do not assign a code from category Z79 for medication being administered for a brief period of time to treat an acute illness or injury (such as a course of antibiotics to treat acute bronchitis).

Z88   Allergy status to drugs, medicaments and biological substances
Except: Z88.9, Allergy status to unspecified drugs, medicaments and biological substances status

Z89   Acquired absence of limb

Z90   Acquired absence of organs, not elsewhere classified

Z91.0-   Allergy status, other than to drugs and biological substances

Z92.82   Status post administration of tPA (rtPA) in a different facility within the last 24 hours prior to admission to a current facility
Assign code Z92.82, Status post administration of tPA (rtPA) in a different facility within the last 24 hours prior to admission to current facility, as a secondary diagnosis when a patient is received by transfer into a facility and documentation indicates they were administered tissue plasminogen activator (tPA) within the last 24 hours prior to admission to the current facility. This guideline applies even if the patient is still receiving the tPA at the time they are received into the current facility.
The appropriate code for the condition for which the tPA was administered (such as cerebrovascular disease or myocardial infarction) should be assigned first.
Code Z92.82 is only applicable to the receiving facility record and not to the transferring facility record.

Z93   Artificial opening status

Z94   Transplanted organ and tissue status

Z95   Presence of cardiac and vascular implants and grafts

Z96   Presence of other functional implants

Z97   Presence of other devices

Z98   Other postprocedural states

Assign code Z98.85, Transplanted organ removal status, to indicate that a transplanted organ has been previously removed. This code should not be assigned for the encounter in which the transplanted organ is removed. The complication necessitating removal of the transplant organ should be assigned for that encounter.

See section I.C.19.g.3. for information on the coding of organ transplant complications.

Z99   Dependence on enabling machines and devices, not elsewhere classified

Note: Categories Z89-Z90 and Z93-Z99 are for use only if there are no complications or malfunctions of the organ or tissue replaced, the amputation site or the equipment on which the patient is dependent.

4) History (of)

There are two types of history Z codes, personal and family. Personal history codes explain a patient's past medical condition that no longer exists and is not receiving any treatment, but that has the potential for recurrence, and therefore may require continued monitoring.

Family history codes are for use when a patient has a family member(s) who has had a particular disease that causes the patient to be at higher risk of also contracting the disease.

Personal history codes may be used in conjunction with follow-up codes and family history codes may be used in conjunction with screening codes to explain the need for a test or procedure. History codes are also acceptable on any medical record regardless of the reason for visit. A history of an illness, even if no longer present, is important information that may alter the type of treatment ordered.

The history Z code categories are:

Z80   Family history of primary malignant neoplasm
Z81   Family history of mental and behavioral disorders
Z82   Family history of certain disabilities and chronic diseases (leading to disablement)
Z83   Family history of other specific disorders
Z84   Family history of other conditions
Z85   Personal history of malignant neoplasm
Z86   Personal history of certain other diseases
Z87   Personal history of other diseases and conditions
Z91.4- Personal history of psychological trauma, not elsewhere classified
Z91.5 Personal history of self-harm
Z91.8- Other specified personal risk factors, not elsewhere classified
Z92   Personal history of medical treatment
Except: Z92.0, Personal history of contraception
Except: Z92.82, Status post administration of tPA (rtPA) in a different facility within the last 24 hours prior to admission to a current facility

5) Screening

Screening is the testing for disease or disease precursors in seemingly well individuals so that early detection and treatment can be provided for those who test positive for the disease (e.g., screening mammogram).

The testing of a person to rule out or confirm a suspected diagnosis because the patient has some sign or symptom is a diagnostic examination, not a screening. In these cases, the sign or symptom is used to explain the reason for the test.

A screening code may be a first listed code if the reason for the visit is specifically the screening exam. It may also be used as an additional code if the screening is done during an office visit for other health problems. A screening code is not necessary if the screening is inherent to a routine examination, such as a pap smear done during a routine pelvic examination.

Should a condition be discovered during the screening then the code for the condition may be assigned as an additional diagnosis.

The Z code indicates that a screening exam is planned. A procedure code is required to confirm that the screening was performed.

The screening Z codes/categories:

Z11	Encounter for screening for infectious and parasitic diseases
Z12	Encounter for screening for malignant neoplasms
Z13	Encounter for screening for other diseases and disorders
	Except: Z13.9, Encounter for screening, unspecified
Z36	Encounter for antenatal screening for mother

6) Observation

There are two observation Z code categories. They are for use in very limited circumstances when a person is being observed for a suspected condition that is ruled out. The observation codes are not for use if an injury or illness or any signs or symptoms related to the suspected condition are present. In such cases the diagnosis/symptom code is used with the corresponding external cause code.

The observation codes are to be used as principal diagnosis only. Additional codes may be used in addition to the observation code but only if they are unrelated to the suspected condition being observed.

Codes from subcategory Z03.7 Encounter for suspected maternal and fetal conditions ruled out, may either be used as a first listed or as an additional code assignment depending on the case. They are for use in very limited circumstances on a maternal record when an encounter is for a suspected maternal or fetal condition that is ruled out during that encounter (for example, a maternal or fetal condition may be suspected due to an abnormal test result). These codes should not be used when the condition is confirmed. In those cases, the confirmed condition should be coded. In addition, these codes are not for use if an illness or any signs or symptoms related to the suspected condition or problem are present. In such cases the diagnosis/symptom code is used.

Additional codes may be used in addition to the code from subcategory Z03.7, but only if they are unrelated to the suspected condition being evaluated.

Codes from subcategory Z03.7 may not be used for encounters for antenatal screening of mother. *See Section I.C.21.c.5, Screening.*

For encounters for suspected fetal condition that are inconclusive following testing and evaluation, assign the appropriate code from category O35, O36, O40 or O41.

The observation Z code categories:

Z03	Encounter for medical observation for suspected diseases and conditions ruled out
Z04	Encounter for examination and observation for other reasons
	Except: Z04.9, Encounter for examination and observation for unspecified reason

7) Aftercare

Aftercare visit codes cover situations when the initial treatment of a disease has been performed and the patient requires continued care during the healing or recovery phase, or for the long-term consequences of the disease. The aftercare Z code should not be used if treatment is directed at a current, acute disease. The diagnosis code is to be used in these cases.

Exceptions to this rule are codes Z51.0, Encounter for antineoplastic radiation therapy, and codes from subcategory Z51.1, Encounter for antineoplastic chemotherapy and immunotherapy. These codes are to be first listed, followed by the diagnosis code when a patient's encounter is solely to receive radiation therapy, chemotherapy, **or immunotherapy** for the treatment of a neoplasm. If the reason for the encounter is more than one type of antineoplastic therapy, code Z51.0 and a code from subcategory Z51.1 may be assigned together, in which case one of these codes would be reported as a secondary diagnosis.

The aftercare Z codes should also not be used for aftercare for injuries. For aftercare of an injury, assign the acute injury code with the 7th character "D" (subsequent encounter).

The aftercare codes are generally first listed to explain the specific reason for the encounter. An aftercare code may be used as an additional code when some type of aftercare is provided in addition to the reason for admission and no diagnosis code is applicable. An example of this would be the closure of a colostomy during an encounter for treatment of another condition.

Aftercare codes should be used in conjunction with other aftercare codes or diagnosis codes to provide better detail on the specifics of an aftercare encounter visit, unless otherwise directed by the classification. Should a patient receive multiple types of antineoplastic therapy during the same encounter, code Z51.0, Encounter for antineoplastic radiation therapy, and codes from subcategory Z51.1, Encounter for antineoplastic chemotherapy and immunotherapy, may be used together on a record.
The sequencing of multiple aftercare codes **depends on the circumstances of the encounter.**

Certain aftercare Z code categories need a secondary diagnosis code to describe the resolving condition or sequelae. For others, the condition is **included** in the code title.

Additional Z code aftercare category terms include fitting and adjustment, and attention to artificial openings.

Status Z codes may be used with aftercare Z codes to indicate the nature of the aftercare. For example code Z95.1, Presence of aortocoronary bypass graft, may be used with code Z48.812, Encounter for surgical aftercare following surgery on the circulatory system, to indicate the surgery for which the aftercare is being performed. A status code should not be used when the aftercare code indicates the type of status, such as using Z43.0, Encounter for attention to tracheostomy, with Z93.0, Tracheostomy status.

The aftercare Z category/codes:
- **Z42** **Encounter for plastic and reconstructive surgery following medical procedure or healed injury**
- Z43 Encounter for attention to artificial openings
- Z44 Encounter for fitting and adjustment of external prosthetic device
- Z45 Encounter for adjustment and management of implanted device
- Z46 Encounter for fitting and adjustment of other devices
- Z47 Orthopedic aftercare
- Z48 Encounter for other postprocedural aftercare
- Z49 Encounter for care involving renal dialysis
- Z51 Encounter for other aftercare

8) Follow-up
The follow-up codes are used to explain continuing surveillance following completed treatment of a disease, condition, or injury. They imply that the condition has been fully treated and no longer exists. They should not be confused with aftercare codes, or injury codes with 7th character "D," that explain ongoing care of a healing condition or its sequelae. Follow-up codes may be used in conjunction with history codes to provide the full picture of the healed condition and its treatment. The follow-up code is sequenced first, followed by the history code.

A follow-up code may be used to explain **multiple** visits. Should a condition be found to have recurred on the follow-up visit, then the code for the condition should be assigned as an additional diagnosis.

The follow-up Z code categories:
- Z08 Encounter for follow-up examination after completed treatment for malignant neoplasm
- Z09 Encounter for follow-up examination after completed treatment for conditions other than malignant neoplasm
- Z39 Encounter for maternal postpartum care and examination

9) Donor
Codes in category Z52, Donors of organs and tissues, are used for living individuals who are donating blood or other body tissue. These codes are only for individuals donating for others, not for self-donations. They are not used to identify cadaveric donations.

10) Counseling

Counseling Z codes are used when a patient or family member receives assistance in the aftermath of an illness or injury, or when support is required in coping with family or social problems. They are not used in conjunction with a diagnosis code when the counseling component of care is considered integral to standard treatment.

The counseling Z codes/categories:

Z30.0- Encounter for general counseling and advice on contraception
Z31.5 Encounter for genetic counseling
Z31.6- Encounter for general counseling and advice on procreation
Z32.2 Encounter for childbirth instruction
Z32.3 Encounter for childcare instruction
Z69 Encounter for mental health services for victim and perpetrator of abuse
Z70 Counseling related to sexual attitude, behavior and orientation
Z71 Persons encountering health services for other counseling and medical advice, not elsewhere classified
Z76.81 Expectant mother prebirth pediatrician visit

11) Encounters for Obstetrical and Reproductive Services

See Section I.C.15. Pregnancy, Childbirth, and the Puerperium, for further instruction on the use of these codes.

Z codes for pregnancy are for use in those circumstances when none of the problems or complications included in the codes from the Obstetrics chapter exist (a routine prenatal visit or postpartum care). Codes in category Z34, Encounter for supervision of normal pregnancy, are always first listed and are not to be used with any other code from the OB chapter.

The outcome of delivery, category Z37, should be included on all maternal delivery records. It is always a secondary code. Codes in category Z37 should not be used on the newborn record.

Z codes for family planning (contraceptive) or procreative management and counseling should be included on an obstetric record either during the pregnancy or the postpartum stage, if applicable.

Z codes/categories for obstetrical and reproductive services:

Z30 Encounter for contraceptive management
Z31 Encounter for procreative management
Z32.2 Encounter for childbirth instruction
Z32.3 Encounter for childcare instruction
Z33 Pregnant state
Z34 Encounter for supervision of normal pregnancy
Z36 Encounter for antenatal screening of mother
Z37 Outcome of delivery
Z39 Encounter for maternal postpartum care and examination
Z76.81 Expectant mother prebirth pediatrician visit

12) Newborns and Infants

See Section I.C.16. Newborn (Perinatal) Guidelines, for further instruction on the use of these codes.

Newborn Z codes/categories:

Z76.1 Encounter for health supervision and care of foundling
Z00.1- Encounter for routine child health examination
Z38 Liveborn infants according to place of birth and type of delivery

13) Routine and administrative examinations

The Z codes allow for the description of encounters for routine examinations, such as, a general check-up, or, examinations for administrative purposes, such as, a pre-employment physical. The codes are not to be used if the examination is for diagnosis of a suspected condition or for treatment purposes. In such cases the diagnosis code is used. During a routine exam, should a diagnosis or condition be discovered, it should be coded as an additional code. Pre-existing and chronic conditions and history codes may also be included as additional codes as long as the examination is for administrative purposes and not focused on any particular condition.

Some of the codes for routine health examinations distinguish between "with" and "without" abnormal findings. Code assignment depends on the information that is known at the time the encounter is being coded. For example, if no abnormal findings were found during the examination, but the encounter is being coded before test results are back, it is acceptable to assign the code for "without abnormal findings." When assigning a code for "with abnormal findings," additional code(s) should be assigned to identify the specific abnormal finding(s).

Pre-operative examination **and pre-procedural laboratory examination** Z codes are for use only in those situations when a patient is being cleared for **a procedure or** surgery and no treatment is given.

The Z codes/categories for routine and administrative examinations:

Z00   Encounter for general examination without complaint, suspected or reported diagnosis
Z01   Encounter for other special examination without complaint, suspected or reported diagnosis
Z02   Encounter for administrative examination
       Except: Z02.9, Encounter for administrative examinations, unspecified
Z32.0- Encounter for pregnancy test

14) Miscellaneous Z codes

The miscellaneous Z codes capture a number of other health care encounters that do not fall into one of the other categories. Certain of these codes identify the reason for the encounter; others are for use as additional codes that provide useful information on circumstances that may affect a patient's care and treatment.

Prophylactic Organ Removal

For encounters specifically for prophylactic removal of an organ (such as prophylactic removal of breasts due to a genetic susceptibility to cancer or a family history of cancer), the principal or first listed code should be a code from category Z40, Encounter for prophylactic surgery, followed by the appropriate codes to identify the associated risk factor (such as genetic susceptibility or family history).

If the patient has a malignancy of one site and is having prophylactic removal at another site to prevent either a new primary malignancy or metastatic disease, a code for the malignancy should also be assigned in addition to a code from subcategory Z40.0, Encounter for prophylactic surgery for risk factors related to malignant neoplasms. A Z40.0 code should not be assigned if the patient is having organ removal for treatment of a malignancy, such as the removal of the testes for the treatment of prostate cancer.

Miscellaneous Z codes/categories:

Z28   Immunization not carried out
       Except: Z28.3, Underimmunization status
Z40   Encounter for prophylactic surgery
Z41   Encounter for procedures for purposes other than remedying health state
       Except: Z41.9, Encounter for procedure for purposes other than remedying health state, unspecified
Z53   Persons encountering health services for specific procedures and treatment, not carried out
Z55   Problems related to education and literacy
Z56   Problems related to employment and unemployment
Z57   Occupational exposure to risk factors
Z58   Problems related to physical environment
Z59   Problems related to housing and economic circumstances
Z60   Problems related to social environment
Z62   Other problems related to upbringing
Z63   Other problems related to primary support group, including family circumstances
Z64   Problems related to certain psychosocial circumstances

Z65	Problems related to other psychosocial circumstances
Z72	Problems related to lifestyle
Z73	Problems related to life management difficulty
Z74	Problems related to care provider dependency
	Except: Z74.01, Bed confinement status
Z75	Problems related to medical facilities and other health care
Z76.0	Encounter for issue of repeat prescription
Z76.3	Healthy person accompanying sick person
Z76.4	Other boarder to healthcare facility
Z76.5	Malingerer [conscious simulation]
Z76.89	Persons encountering health services in other specified circumstances
Z91.1-	Patient's noncompliance with medical treatment and regimen
Z91.89	Other specified personal risk factors, not elsewhere classified

15) Nonspecific Z codes

Certain Z codes are so non-specific, or potentially redundant with other codes in the classification, that there can be little justification for their use in the inpatient setting. Their use in the outpatient setting should be limited to those instances when there is no further documentation to permit more precise coding. Otherwise, any sign or symptom or any other reason for visit that is captured in another code should be used.

Nonspecific Z codes/categories:

Z02.9	Encounter for administrative examinations, unspecified
Z04.9	Encounter for examination and observation for unspecified reason
Z13.9	Encounter for screening, unspecified
Z41.9	Encounter for procedure for purposes other than remedying health state, unspecified
Z52.9	Donor of unspecified organ or tissue
Z88.9	Allergy status to unspecified drugs, medicaments and biological substances status
Z92.0	Personal history of contraception

16) Z Codes That May Only be Principal/First-Listed Diagnosis

The following Z codes/categories may only be reported as the principal/first-listed diagnosis, except when there are multiple encounters on the same day and the medical records for the encounters are combined:

Z00	Encounter for general examination without complaint, suspected or reported diagnosis
Z01	Encounter for other special examination without complaint, suspected or reported diagnosis
Z02	Encounter for administrative examination
Z03	Encounter for medical observation for suspected diseases and conditions ruled out
Z33.2	Encounter for elective termination of pregnancy
Z31.81	Encounter for male factor infertility in female patient
Z31.82	Encounter for Rh incompatibility status
Z31.83	Encounter for assisted reproductive fertility procedure cycle
Z31.84	**Encounter for fertility preservation procedure**
Z34	Encounter for supervision of normal pregnancy
Z39	Encounter for maternal postpartum care and examination
Z38	Liveborn infants according to place of birth and type of delivery
Z42	**Encounter for plastic and reconstructive surgery following medical procedure or healed injury**
Z51.0	Encounter for antineoplastic radiation therapy
Z51.1-	Encounter for antineoplastic chemotherapy and immunotherapy
Z52	Donors of organs and tissues
	Except: Z52.9, Donor of unspecified organ or tissue
Z76.1	Encounter for health supervision and care of foundling
Z76.2	Encounter for health supervision and care of other healthy infant and child
Z99.12	Encounter for respirator [ventilator] dependence during power failure

Section II. Selection of Principal Diagnosis

The circumstances of inpatient admission always govern the selection of principal diagnosis. The principal diagnosis is defined in the Uniform Hospital Discharge Data Set (UHDDS) as "that condition established after study to be chiefly responsible for occasioning the admission of the patient to the hospital for care."

The UHDDS definitions are used by hospitals to report inpatient data elements in a standardized manner. These data elements and their definitions can be found in the July 31, 1985, Federal Register (Vol. 50, No, 147), pp. 31038-40.

Since that time the application of the UHDDS definitions has been expanded to include all non-outpatient settings (acute care, short term, long term care and psychiatric hospitals; home health agencies; rehab facilities; nursing homes, etc).

In determining principal diagnosis the coding conventions in the ICD-10-CM, Volumes I and II take precedence over these official coding guidelines.
(See Section I.A., Conventions for the ICD-10-CM)

The importance of consistent, complete documentation in the medical record cannot be overemphasized. Without such documentation the application of all coding guidelines is a difficult, if not impossible, task.

A. **Codes for symptoms, signs, and ill-defined conditions**
Codes for symptoms, signs, and ill-defined conditions from Chapter 18 are not to be used as principal diagnosis when a related definitive diagnosis has been established.

B. **Two or more interrelated conditions, each potentially meeting the definition for principal diagnosis.**
When there are two or more interrelated conditions (such as diseases in the same ICD-10-CM chapter or manifestations characteristically associated with a certain disease) potentially meeting the definition of principal diagnosis, either condition may be sequenced first, unless the circumstances of the admission, the therapy provided, the Tabular List, or the Alphabetic Index indicate otherwise.

C. **Two or more diagnoses that equally meet the definition for principal diagnosis**
In the unusual instance when two or more diagnoses equally meet the criteria for principal diagnosis as determined by the circumstances of admission, diagnostic workup and/or therapy provided, and the Alphabetic Index, Tabular List, or another coding guidelines does not provide sequencing direction, any one of the diagnoses may be sequenced first.

D. **Two or more comparative or contrasting conditions.**
In those rare instances when two or more contrasting or comparative diagnoses are documented as "either/or" (or similar terminology), they are coded as if the diagnoses were confirmed and the diagnoses are sequenced according to the circumstances of the admission. If no further determination can be made as to which diagnosis should be principal, either diagnosis may be sequenced first.

E. **A symptom(s) followed by contrasting/comparative diagnoses**
When a symptom(s) is followed by contrasting/comparative diagnoses, the symptom code is sequenced first. All the contrasting/comparative diagnoses should be coded as additional diagnoses.

F. **Original treatment plan not carried out**
Sequence as the principal diagnosis the condition, which after study occasioned the admission to the hospital, even though treatment may not have been carried out due to unforeseen circumstances.

G. **Complications of surgery and other medical care**
When the admission is for treatment of a complication resulting from surgery or other medical care, the complication code is sequenced as the principal diagnosis. If the complication is classified to the T80-T88 series and the code lacks the necessary specificity in describing the complication, an additional code for the specific complication should be assigned.

H. Uncertain Diagnosis

If the diagnosis documented at the time of discharge is qualified as "probable", "suspected", "likely", "questionable", "possible", or "still to be ruled out", or other similar terms indicating uncertainty, code the condition as if it existed or was established. The bases for these guidelines are the diagnostic workup, arrangements for further workup or observation, and initial therapeutic approach that correspond most closely with the established diagnosis.

Note: This guideline is applicable only to inpatient admissions to short-term, acute, long-term care and psychiatric hospitals.

I. Admission from Observation Unit

1. Admission Following Medical Observation

When a patient is admitted to an observation unit for a medical condition, which either worsens or does not improve, and is subsequently admitted as an inpatient of the same hospital for this same medical condition, the principal diagnosis would be the medical condition which led to the hospital admission.

2. Admission Following Post-Operative Observation

When a patient is admitted to an observation unit to monitor a condition (or complication) that develops following outpatient surgery, and then is subsequently admitted as an inpatient of the same hospital, hospitals should apply the Uniform Hospital Discharge Data Set (UHDDS) definition of principal diagnosis as "that condition established after study to be chiefly responsible for occasioning the admission of the patient to the hospital for care."

J. Admission from Outpatient Surgery

When a patient receives surgery in the hospital's outpatient surgery department and is subsequently admitted for continuing inpatient care at the same hospital, the following guidelines should be followed in selecting the principal diagnosis for the inpatient admission:

- If the reason for the inpatient admission is a complication, assign the complication as the principal diagnosis.
- If no complication, or other condition, is documented as the reason for the inpatient admission, assign the reason for the outpatient surgery as the principal diagnosis.
- If the reason for the inpatient admission is another condition unrelated to the surgery, assign the unrelated condition as the principal diagnosis.

Section III. Reporting Additional Diagnoses

GENERAL RULES FOR OTHER (ADDITIONAL) DIAGNOSES
For reporting purposes the definition for "other diagnoses" is interpreted as additional conditions that affect patient care in terms of requiring:

clinical evaluation; or
therapeutic treatment; or
diagnostic procedures; or
extended length of hospital stay; or
increased nursing care and/or monitoring.

The UHDDS item #11-b defines Other Diagnoses as "all conditions that coexist at the time of admission, that develop subsequently, or that affect the treatment received and/or the length of stay. Diagnoses that relate to an earlier episode which have no bearing on the current hospital stay are to be excluded." UHDDS definitions apply to inpatients in acute care, short-term, long term care and psychiatric hospital setting. The UHDDS definitions are used by acute care short-term hospitals to report inpatient data elements in a standardized manner. These data elements and their definitions can be found in the July 31, 1985, Federal Register (Vol. 50, No, 147), pp. 31038-40.

Since that time the application of the UHDDS definitions has been expanded to include all non-outpatient settings (acute care, short term, long term care and psychiatric hospitals; home health agencies; rehab facilities; nursing homes, etc).

The following guidelines are to be applied in designating "other diagnoses" when neither the Alphabetic Index nor the Tabular List in ICD-10-CM provide direction. The listing of the diagnoses in the patient record is the responsibility of the attending provider.

A. Previous conditions

If the provider has included a diagnosis in the final diagnostic statement, such as the discharge summary or the face sheet, it should ordinarily be coded. Some providers include in the diagnostic statement resolved conditions or diagnoses and status-post procedures from previous admission that have no bearing on the current stay. Such conditions are not to be reported and are coded only if required by hospital policy.

However, history codes (categories Z80-Z87) may be used as secondary codes if the historical condition or family history has an impact on current care or influences treatment.

B. Abnormal findings

Abnormal findings (laboratory, x-ray, pathologic, and other diagnostic results) are not coded and reported unless the provider indicates their clinical significance. If the findings are outside the normal range and the attending provider has ordered other tests to evaluate the condition or prescribed treatment, it is appropriate to ask the provider whether the abnormal finding should be added.

Please note: This differs from the coding practices in the outpatient setting for coding encounters for diagnostic tests that have been interpreted by a provider.

C. Uncertain Diagnosis

If the diagnosis documented at the time of discharge is qualified as "probable", "suspected", "likely", "questionable", "possible", or "still to be ruled out" or other similar terms indicating uncertainty, code the condition as if it existed or was established. The bases for these guidelines are the diagnostic workup, arrangements for further workup or observation, and initial therapeutic approach that correspond most closely with the established diagnosis.

Note: This guideline is applicable only to inpatient admissions to short-term, acute, long-term care and psychiatric hospitals.

Section IV. Diagnostic Coding and Reporting Guidelines for Outpatient Services

These coding guidelines for outpatient diagnoses have been approved for use by hospitals/ providers in coding and reporting hospital-based outpatient services and provider-based office visits.

Information about the use of certain abbreviations, punctuation, symbols, and other conventions used in the ICD-10-CM Tabular List (code numbers and titles), can be found in Section IA of these guidelines, under "Conventions Used in the Tabular List." Information about the correct sequence to use in finding a code is also described in Section I.

The terms encounter and visit are often used interchangeably in describing outpatient service contacts and, therefore, appear together in these guidelines without distinguishing one from the other.

Though the conventions and general guidelines apply to all settings, coding guidelines for outpatient and provider reporting of diagnoses will vary in a number of instances from those for inpatient diagnoses, recognizing that:

The Uniform Hospital Discharge Data Set (UHDDS) definition of principal diagnosis applies only to inpatients in acute, short-term, long-term care and psychiatric hospitals.

Coding guidelines for inconclusive diagnoses (probable, suspected, rule out, etc.) were developed for inpatient reporting and do not apply to outpatients.

A. Selection of first-listed condition

In the outpatient setting, the term first-listed diagnosis is used in lieu of principal diagnosis.

In determining the first-listed diagnosis the coding conventions of ICD-10-CM, as well as the general and disease specific guidelines take precedence over the outpatient guidelines.

Diagnoses often are not established at the time of the initial encounter/visit. It may take two or more visits before the diagnosis is confirmed.

The most critical rule involves beginning the search for the correct code assignment through the Alphabetic Index. Never begin searching initially in the Tabular List as this will lead to coding errors.

1. Outpatient Surgery
When a patient presents for outpatient surgery (same day surgery), code the reason for the surgery as the first-listed diagnosis (reason for the encounter), even if the surgery is not performed due to a contraindication.

2. Observation Stay
When a patient is admitted for observation for a medical condition, assign a code for the medical condition as the first-listed diagnosis.

When a patient presents for outpatient surgery and develops complications requiring admission to observation, code the reason for the surgery as the first reported diagnosis (reason for the encounter), followed by codes for the complications as secondary diagnoses.

B. Codes from A00.0 through T88.9, Z00-Z99
The appropriate code(s) from A00.0 through T88.9, Z00-Z99 must be used to identify diagnoses, symptoms, conditions, problems, complaints, or other reason(s) for the encounter/visit.

C. Accurate reporting of ICD-10-CM diagnosis codes
For accurate reporting of ICD-10-CM diagnosis codes, the documentation should describe the patient's condition, using terminology which includes specific diagnoses as well as symptoms, problems, or reasons for the encounter. There are ICD-10-CM codes to describe all of these.

D. Codes that describe symptoms and signs
Codes that describe symptoms and signs, as opposed to diagnoses, are acceptable for reporting purposes when a diagnosis has not been established (confirmed) by the provider. Chapter 18 of ICD-10-CM, Symptoms, Signs, and Abnormal Clinical and Laboratory Findings Not Elsewhere Classified (codes R00-R99) contain many, but not all codes for symptoms.

E. Encounters for circumstances other than a disease or injury
ICD-10-CM provides codes to deal with encounters for circumstances other than a disease or injury. The Factors Influencing Health Status and Contact with Health Services codes (Z00-99) is provided to deal with occasions when circumstances other than a disease or injury are recorded as diagnosis or problems.

See Section I.C.21. Factors influencing health status and contact with health services.

F. Level of Detail in Coding

1. ICD-10-CM codes with 3, 4, or 5 digits
ICD-10-CM is composed of codes with either 3, 4, 5, 6 or 7 digits. Codes with three digits are included in ICD-10-CM as the heading of a category of codes that may be further subdivided by the use of fourth fifth digits, sixth or seventh digits which provide greater specificity.

2. Use of full number of digits required for a code
A three-digit code is to be used only if it is not further subdivided. A code is invalid if it has not been coded to the full number of characters required for that code, including the 7th character extension, if applicable.

G. ICD-10-CM code for the diagnosis, condition, problem, or other reason for encounter/visit
List first the ICD-10-CM code for the diagnosis, condition, problem, or other reason for encounter/visit shown in the medical record to be chiefly responsible for the services provided. List additional codes that describe any coexisting conditions. In some cases the first-listed diagnosis may be a symptom when a diagnosis has not been established (confirmed) by the physician.

H. Uncertain diagnosis

Do not code diagnoses documented as "probable", "suspected," "questionable," "rule out," or "working diagnosis" or other similar terms indicating uncertainty. Rather, code the condition(s) to the highest degree of certainty for that encounter/visit, such as symptoms, signs, abnormal test results, or other reason for the visit.

   Please note: This differs from the coding practices used by short-term, acute care, long-term care and psychiatric hospitals.

I. Chronic diseases

Chronic diseases treated on an ongoing basis may be coded and reported as many times as the patient receives treatment and care for the condition(s)

J. Code all documented conditions that coexist

Code all documented conditions that coexist at the time of the encounter/visit, and require or affect patient care treatment or management. Do not code conditions that were previously treated and no longer exist. However, history codes (categories Z80-Z87) may be used as secondary codes if the historical condition or family history has an impact on current care or influences treatment.

K. Patients receiving diagnostic services only

For patients receiving diagnostic services only during an encounter/visit, sequence first the diagnosis, condition, problem, or other reason for encounter/visit shown in the medical record to be chiefly responsible for the outpatient services provided during the encounter/visit. Codes for other diagnoses (e.g., chronic conditions) may be sequenced as additional diagnoses.

   For encounters for routine laboratory/radiology testing in the absence of any signs, symptoms, or associated diagnosis, assign Z01.89, Encounter for other specified special examinations. If routine testing is performed during the same encounter as a test to evaluate a sign, symptom, or diagnosis, it is appropriate to assign both the V code and the code describing the reason for the non-routine test.

   For outpatient encounters for diagnostic tests that have been interpreted by a physician, and the final report is available at the time of coding, code any confirmed or definitive diagnosis(es) documented in the interpretation. Do not code related signs and symptoms as additional diagnoses.

   Please note: This differs from the coding practice in the hospital inpatient setting regarding abnormal findings on test results.

L. Patients receiving therapeutic services only

For patients receiving therapeutic services only during an encounter/visit, sequence first the diagnosis, condition, problem, or other reason for encounter/visit shown in the medical record to be chiefly responsible for the outpatient services provided during the encounter/visit. Codes for other diagnoses (e.g., chronic conditions) may be sequenced as additional diagnoses.

   The only exception to this rule is that when the primary reason for the admission/encounter is chemotherapy or radiation therapy, the appropriate Z code for the service is listed first, and the diagnosis or problem for which the service is being performed listed second.

M. Patients receiving preoperative evaluations only

For patients receiving preoperative evaluations only, sequence first a code from subcategory Z01.81, Encounter for pre-procedural examinations, to describe the pre-op consultations. Assign a code for the condition to describe the reason for the surgery as an additional diagnosis. Code also any findings related to the pre-op evaluation.

N. Ambulatory surgery

For ambulatory surgery, code the diagnosis for which the surgery was performed. If the postoperative diagnosis is known to be different from the preoperative diagnosis at the time the diagnosis is confirmed, select the postoperative diagnosis for coding, since it is the most definitive.

O. Routine outpatient prenatal visits
See Section I.C.15. Routine outpatient prenatal visits.

P. Encounters for general medical examinations with abnormal findings
The subcategories for encounters for general medical examinations, Z00.0-, provide codes for with and without abnormal findings. Should a general medical examination result in an abnormal finding, the code for general medical examination with abnormal finding should be assigned as the first listed diagnosis. A secondary code for the abnormal finding should also be coded.

Q. Encounters for routine health screenings
See Section I.C.21. Factors influencing health status and contact with health services, Screening

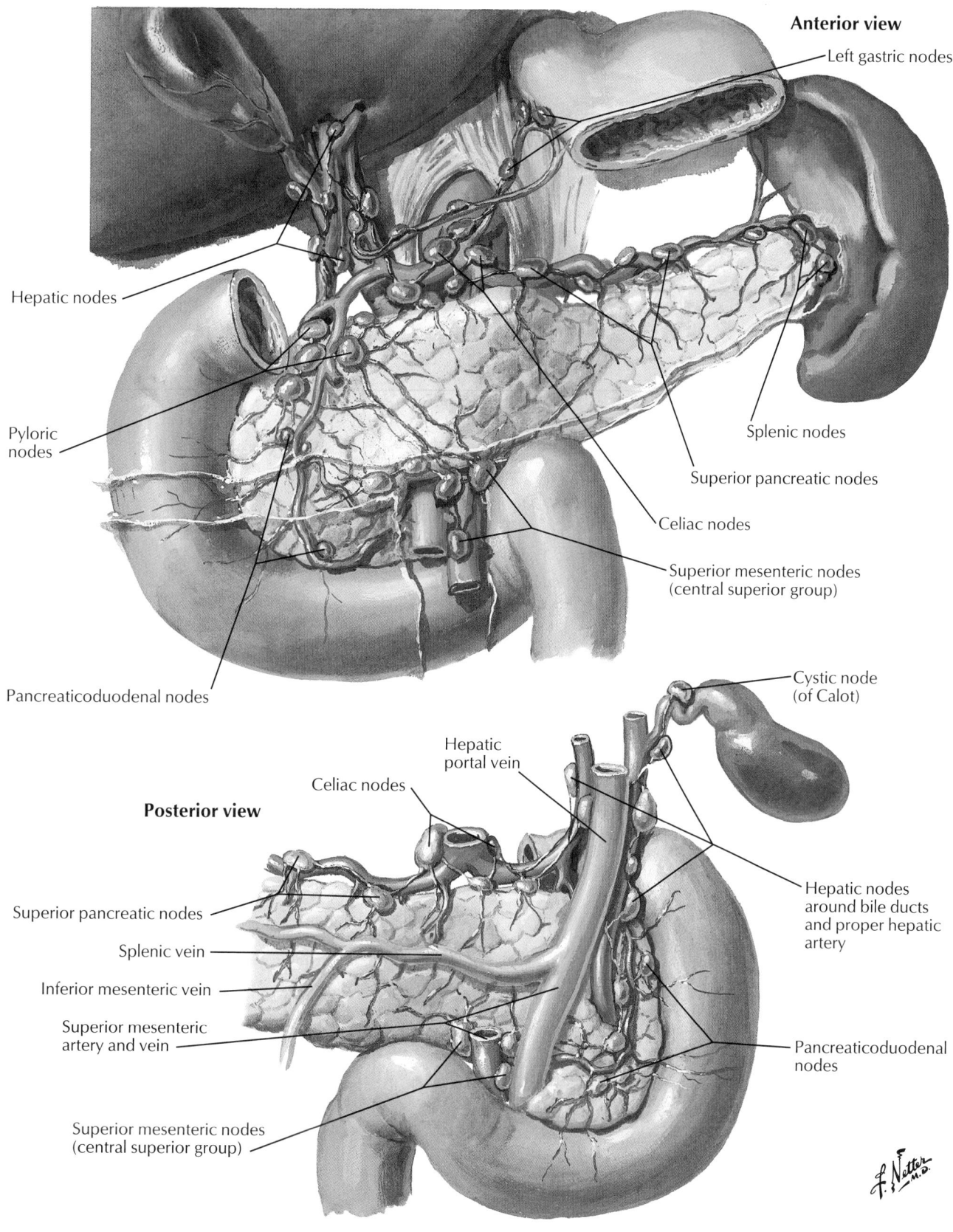

Anterior view

Left gastric nodes

Hepatic nodes

Pyloric nodes

Pancreaticoduodenal nodes

Splenic nodes

Superior pancreatic nodes

Celiac nodes

Superior mesenteric nodes (central superior group)

Cystic node (of Calot)

Hepatic portal vein

Celiac nodes

Posterior view

Superior pancreatic nodes

Splenic vein

Inferior mesenteric vein

Superior mesenteric artery and vein

Superior mesenteric nodes (central superior group)

Hepatic nodes around bile ducts and proper hepatic artery

Pancreaticoduodenal nodes

Plate 315   Lymph Vessels and Nodes of Pancreas. (Netter: Atlas of Human Anatomy, 4 ed, 2006, Saunders.)

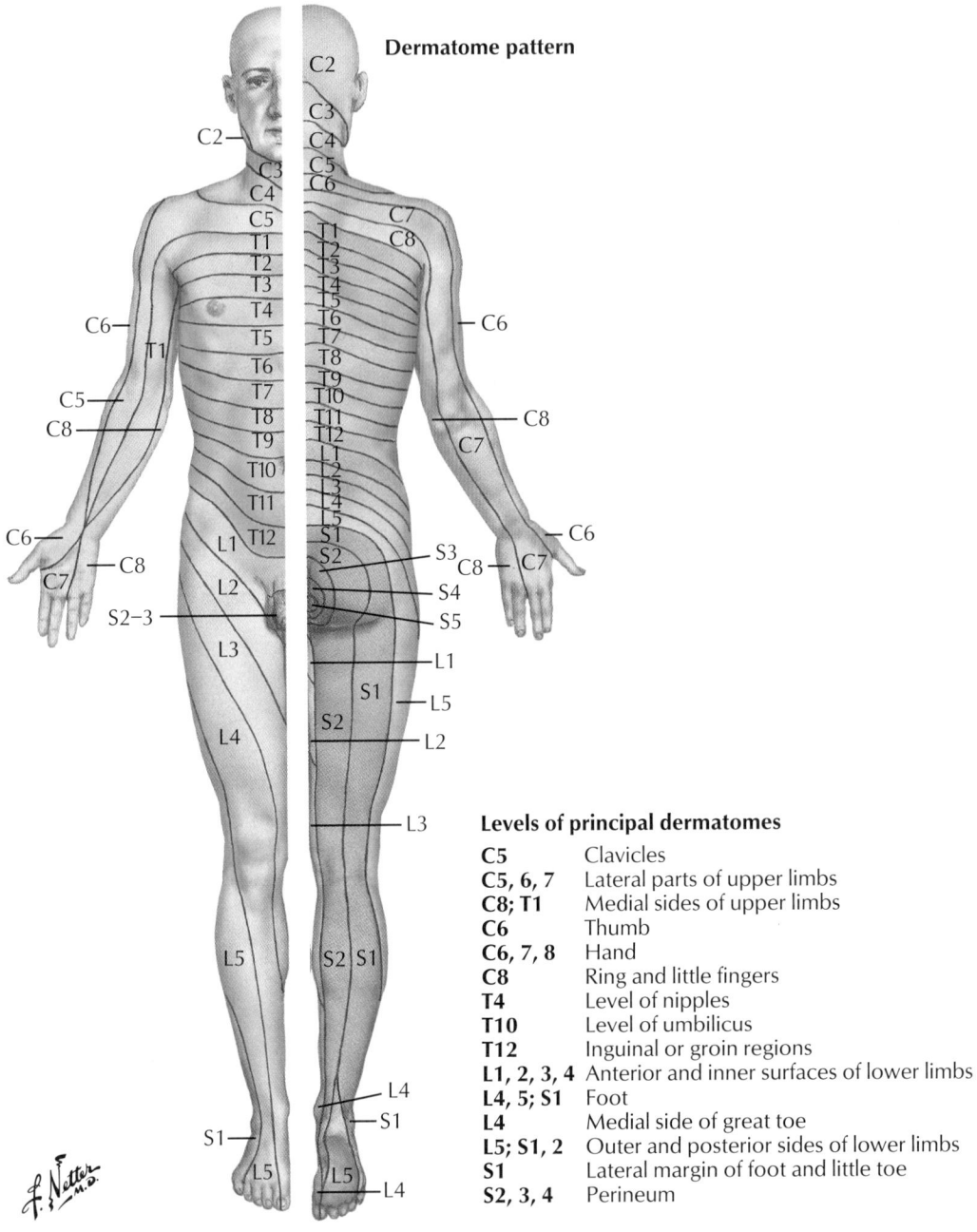

Dermatome pattern

Levels of principal dermatomes

C5	Clavicles
C5, 6, 7	Lateral parts of upper limbs
C8; T1	Medial sides of upper limbs
C6	Thumb
C6, 7, 8	Hand
C8	Ring and little fingers
T4	Level of nipples
T10	Level of umbilicus
T12	Inguinal or groin regions
L1, 2, 3, 4	Anterior and inner surfaces of lower limbs
L4, 5; S1	Foot
L4	Medial side of great toe
L5; S1, 2	Outer and posterior sides of lower limbs
S1	Lateral margin of foot and little toe
S2, 3, 4	Perineum

Plate 164 Dermatomes. (Netter: Atlas of Human Anatomy, 4 ed, 2006, Saunders.)

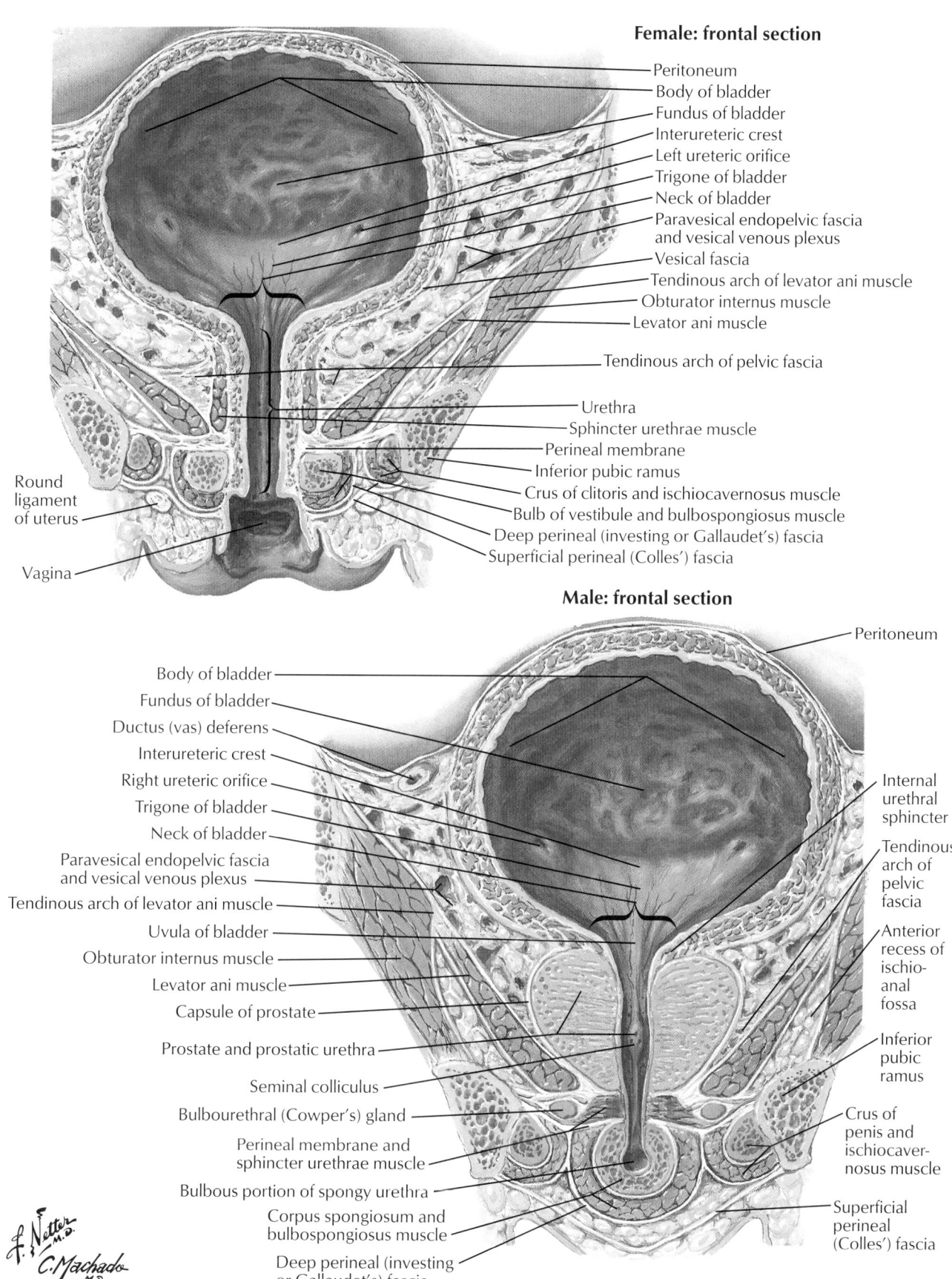

Female: frontal section

Peritoneum
Body of bladder
Fundus of bladder
Interureteric crest
Left ureteric orifice
Trigone of bladder
Neck of bladder
Paravesical endopelvic fascia and vesical venous plexus
Vesical fascia
Tendinous arch of levator ani muscle
Obturator internus muscle
Levator ani muscle

Tendinous arch of pelvic fascia

Urethra
Sphincter urethrae muscle
Perineal membrane
Inferior pubic ramus
Crus of clitoris and ischiocavernosus muscle
Bulb of vestibule and bulbospongiosus muscle
Deep perineal (investing or Gallaudet's) fascia
Superficial perineal (Colles') fascia

Round ligament of uterus

Vagina

Male: frontal section

Peritoneum

Body of bladder
Fundus of bladder
Ductus (vas) deferens
Interureteric crest
Right ureteric orifice
Trigone of bladder
Neck of bladder
Paravesical endopelvic fascia and vesical venous plexus
Tendinous arch of levator ani muscle
Uvula of bladder
Obturator internus muscle
Levator ani muscle
Capsule of prostate
Prostate and prostatic urethra
Seminal colliculus
Bulbourethral (Cowper's) gland
Perineal membrane and sphincter urethrae muscle
Bulbous portion of spongy urethra
Corpus spongiosum and bulbospongiosus muscle
Deep perineal (investing or Gallaudet's) fascia

Internal urethral sphincter
Tendinous arch of pelvic fascia
Anterior recess of ischio-anal fossa
Inferior pubic ramus
Crus of penis and ischiocavernosus muscle
Superficial perineal (Colles') fascia

Plate 366 Urinary Bladder: Female and Male. (Netter: Atlas of Human Anatomy, 4 ed, 2006, Saunders.)

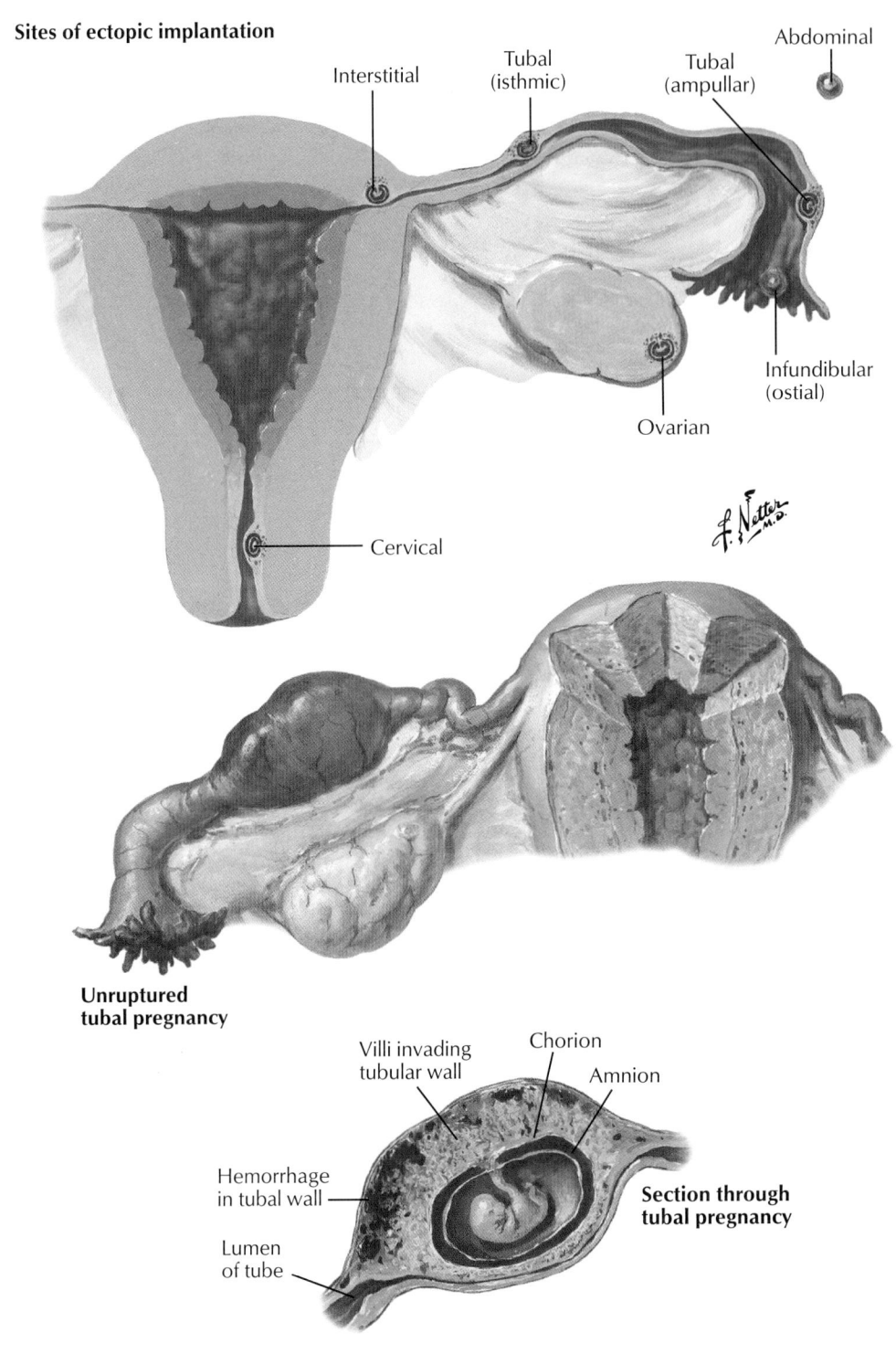

Sites of ectopic implantation

Interstitial Tubal (isthmic) Tubal (ampullar) Abdominal

Infundibular (ostial)

Ovarian

Cervical

Unruptured tubal pregnancy

Villi invading tubular wall Chorion Amnion

Hemorrhage in tubal wall

Section through tubal pregnancy

Lumen of tube

Plate 375 Ectopic Pregnancy. (Netter: Atlas of Human Anatomy, 4 ed, 2006, Saunders.)

NAP-4

NETTER ANATOMY PLATE

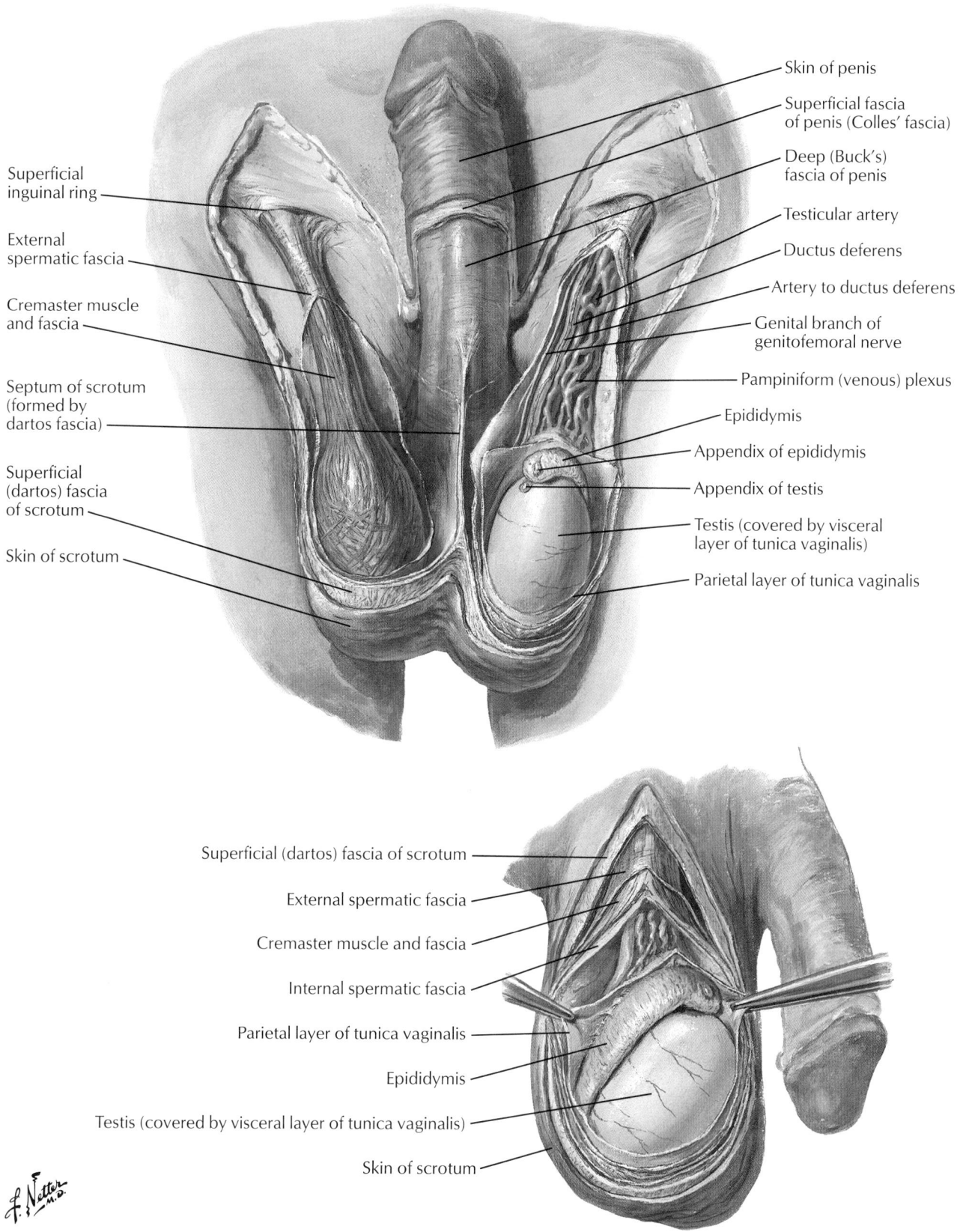

Skin of penis

Superficial fascia of penis (Colles' fascia)

Deep (Buck's) fascia of penis

Testicular artery

Ductus deferens

Artery to ductus deferens

Genital branch of genitofemoral nerve

Pampiniform (venous) plexus

Epididymis

Appendix of epididymis

Appendix of testis

Testis (covered by visceral layer of tunica vaginalis)

Parietal layer of tunica vaginalis

Superficial inguinal ring

External spermatic fascia

Cremaster muscle and fascia

Septum of scrotum (formed by dartos fascia)

Superficial (dartos) fascia of scrotum

Skin of scrotum

Superficial (dartos) fascia of scrotum

External spermatic fascia

Cremaster muscle and fascia

Internal spermatic fascia

Parietal layer of tunica vaginalis

Epididymis

Testis (covered by visceral layer of tunica vaginalis)

Skin of scrotum

Plate 387   Scrotum and Contents. (Netter: Atlas of Human Anatomy, 4 ed, 2006, Saunders.)

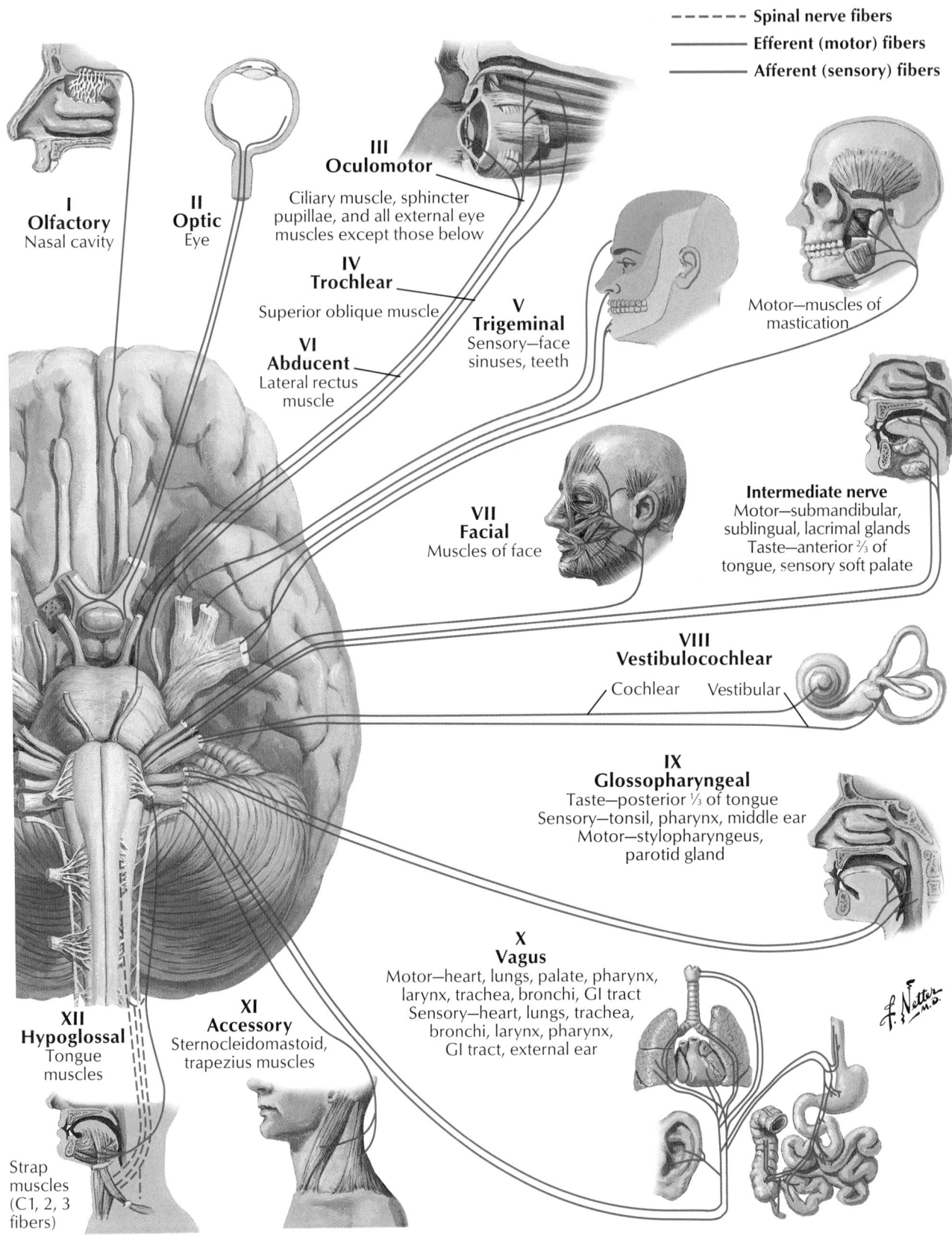

Spinal nerve fibers
Efferent (motor) fibers
Afferent (sensory) fibers

I Olfactory
Nasal cavity

II Optic
Eye

III Oculomotor
Ciliary muscle, sphincter pupillae, and all external eye muscles except those below

IV Trochlear
Superior oblique muscle

V Trigeminal
Sensory—face sinuses, teeth

VI Abducent
Lateral rectus muscle

Motor—muscles of mastication

VII Facial
Muscles of face

Intermediate nerve
Motor—submandibular, sublingual, lacrimal glands
Taste—anterior ⅔ of tongue, sensory soft palate

VIII Vestibulocochlear
Cochlear   Vestibular

IX Glossopharyngeal
Taste—posterior ⅓ of tongue
Sensory—tonsil, pharynx, middle ear
Motor—stylopharyngeus, parotid gland

X Vagus
Motor—heart, lungs, palate, pharynx, larynx, trachea, bronchi, GI tract
Sensory—heart, lungs, trachea, bronchi, larynx, pharynx, GI tract, external ear

XII Hypoglossal
Tongue muscles

XI Accessory
Sternocleidomastoid, trapezius muscles

Strap muscles (C1, 2, 3 fibers)

Plate 118 Cranial Nerves (Motor and Sensory Distribution): Schema. (Netter: Atlas of Human Anatomy, 4 ed, 2006, Saunders.)

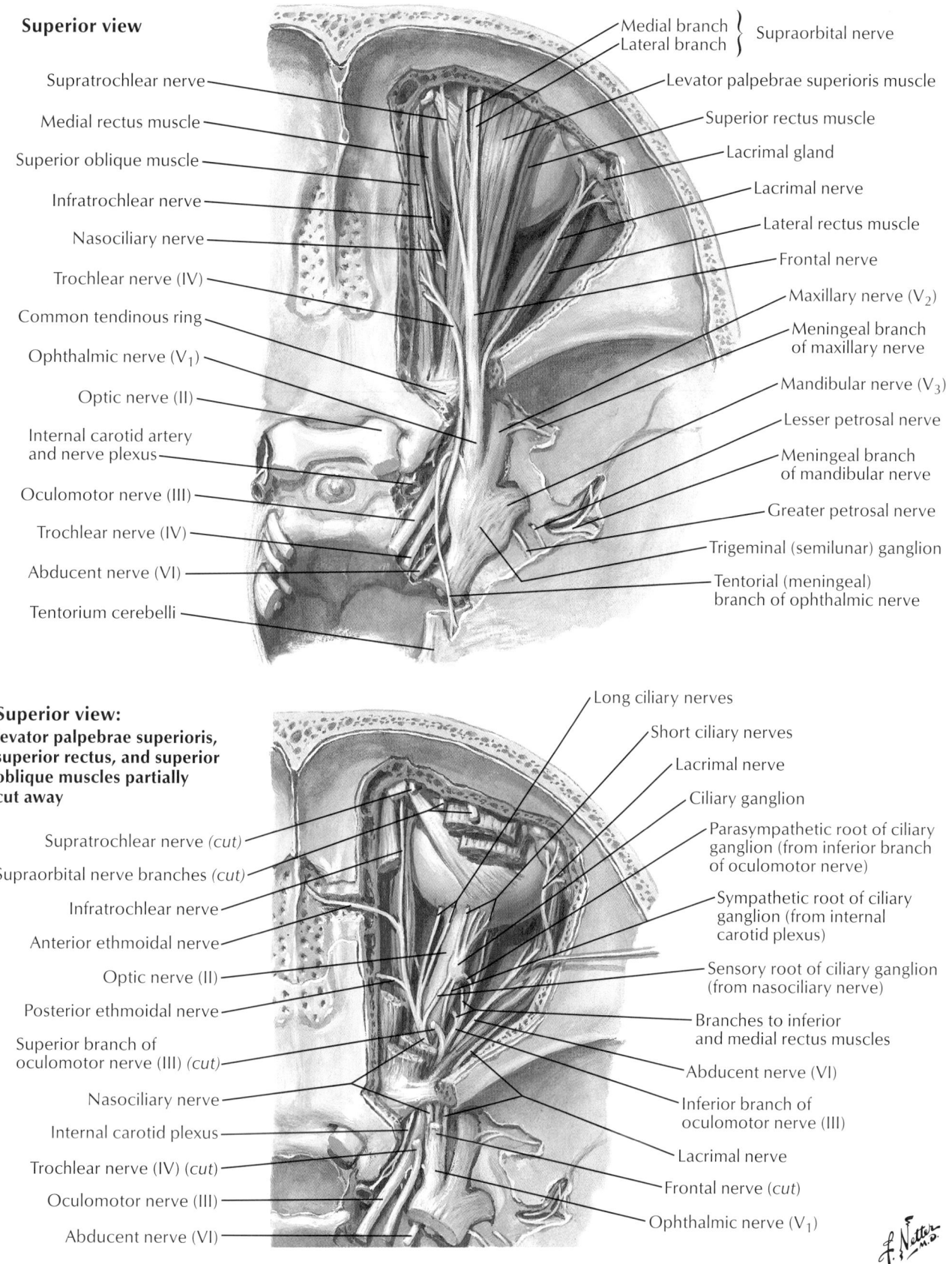

Superior view

Supratrochlear nerve

Medial rectus muscle

Superior oblique muscle

Infratrochlear nerve

Nasociliary nerve

Trochlear nerve (IV)

Common tendinous ring

Ophthalmic nerve (V₁)

Optic nerve (II)

Internal carotid artery and nerve plexus

Oculomotor nerve (III)

Trochlear nerve (IV)

Abducent nerve (VI)

Tentorium cerebelli

Medial branch } Supraorbital nerve
Lateral branch

Levator palpebrae superioris muscle

Superior rectus muscle

Lacrimal gland

Lacrimal nerve

Lateral rectus muscle

Frontal nerve

Maxillary nerve (V₂)

Meningeal branch of maxillary nerve

Mandibular nerve (V₃)

Lesser petrosal nerve

Meningeal branch of mandibular nerve

Greater petrosal nerve

Trigeminal (semilunar) ganglion

Tentorial (meningeal) branch of ophthalmic nerve

Superior view:
levator palpebrae superioris, superior rectus, and superior oblique muscles partially cut away

Supratrochlear nerve *(cut)*

Supraorbital nerve branches *(cut)*

Infratrochlear nerve

Anterior ethmoidal nerve

Optic nerve (II)

Posterior ethmoidal nerve

Superior branch of oculomotor nerve (III) *(cut)*

Nasociliary nerve

Internal carotid plexus

Trochlear nerve (IV) *(cut)*

Oculomotor nerve (III)

Abducent nerve (VI)

Long ciliary nerves

Short ciliary nerves

Lacrimal nerve

Ciliary ganglion

Parasympathetic root of ciliary ganglion (from inferior branch of oculomotor nerve)

Sympathetic root of ciliary ganglion (from internal carotid plexus)

Sensory root of ciliary ganglion (from nasociliary nerve)

Branches to inferior and medial rectus muscles

Abducent nerve (VI)

Inferior branch of oculomotor nerve (III)

Lacrimal nerve

Frontal nerve *(cut)*

Ophthalmic nerve (V₁)

Plate 86 Nerves of Orbit. (Netter: Atlas of Human Anatomy, 4 ed, 2006, Saunders.)

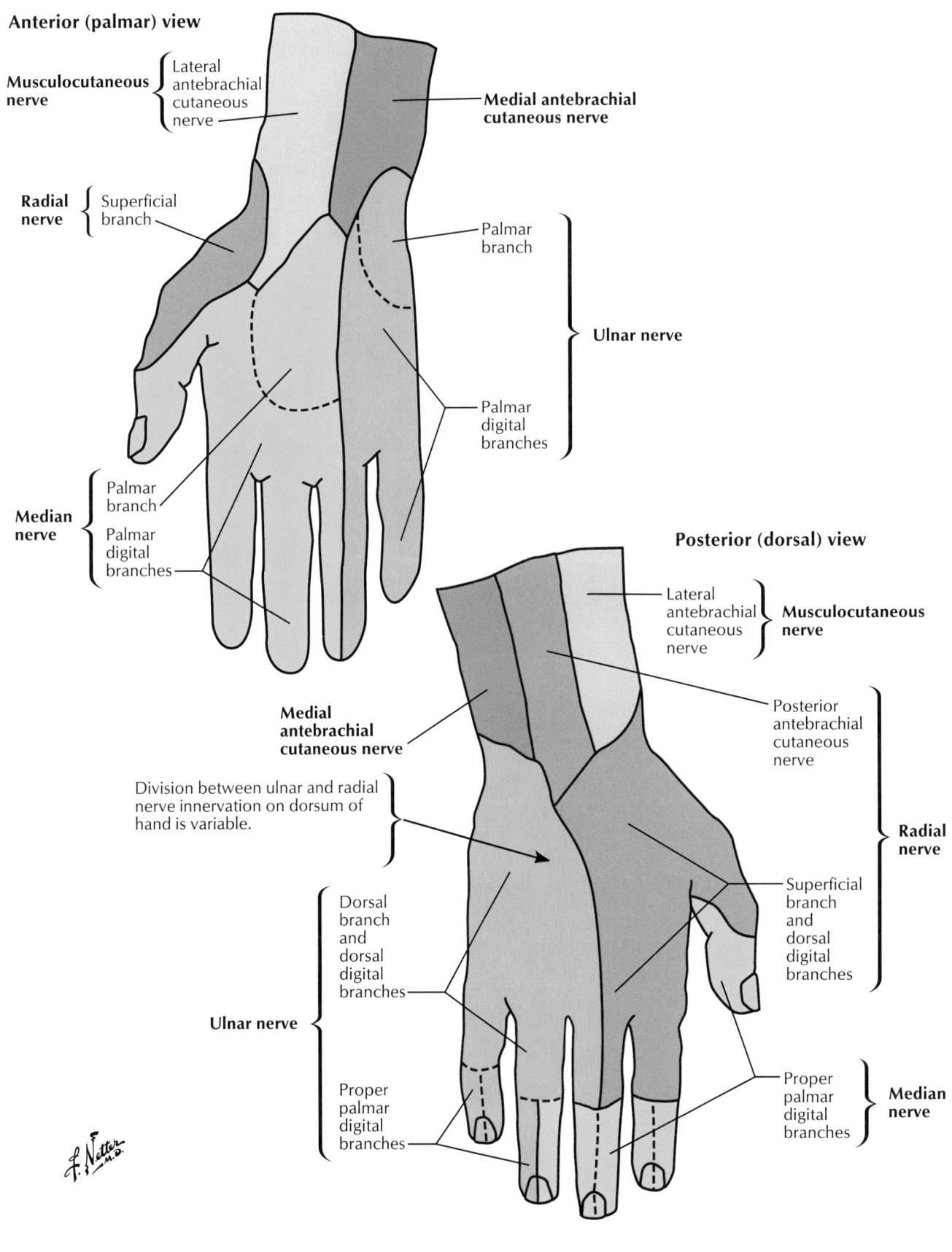

Anterior (palmar) view

Musculocutaneous nerve { Lateral antebrachial cutaneous nerve

Medial antebrachial cutaneous nerve

Radial nerve { Superficial branch

Palmar branch

Ulnar nerve

Palmar digital branches

Median nerve { Palmar branch / Palmar digital branches

Posterior (dorsal) view

Lateral antebrachial cutaneous nerve } **Musculocutaneous nerve**

Medial antebrachial cutaneous nerve

Posterior antebrachial cutaneous nerve

Radial nerve

Division between ulnar and radial nerve innervation on dorsum of hand is variable.

Superficial branch and dorsal digital branches

Ulnar nerve { Dorsal branch and dorsal digital branches

Proper palmar digital branches

Proper palmar digital branches } **Median nerve**

Plate 472   Cutaneous Innervation of Wrist and Hand. (Netter: Atlas of Human Anatomy, 4 ed, 2006, Saunders.)

NAP-8

Anterior view

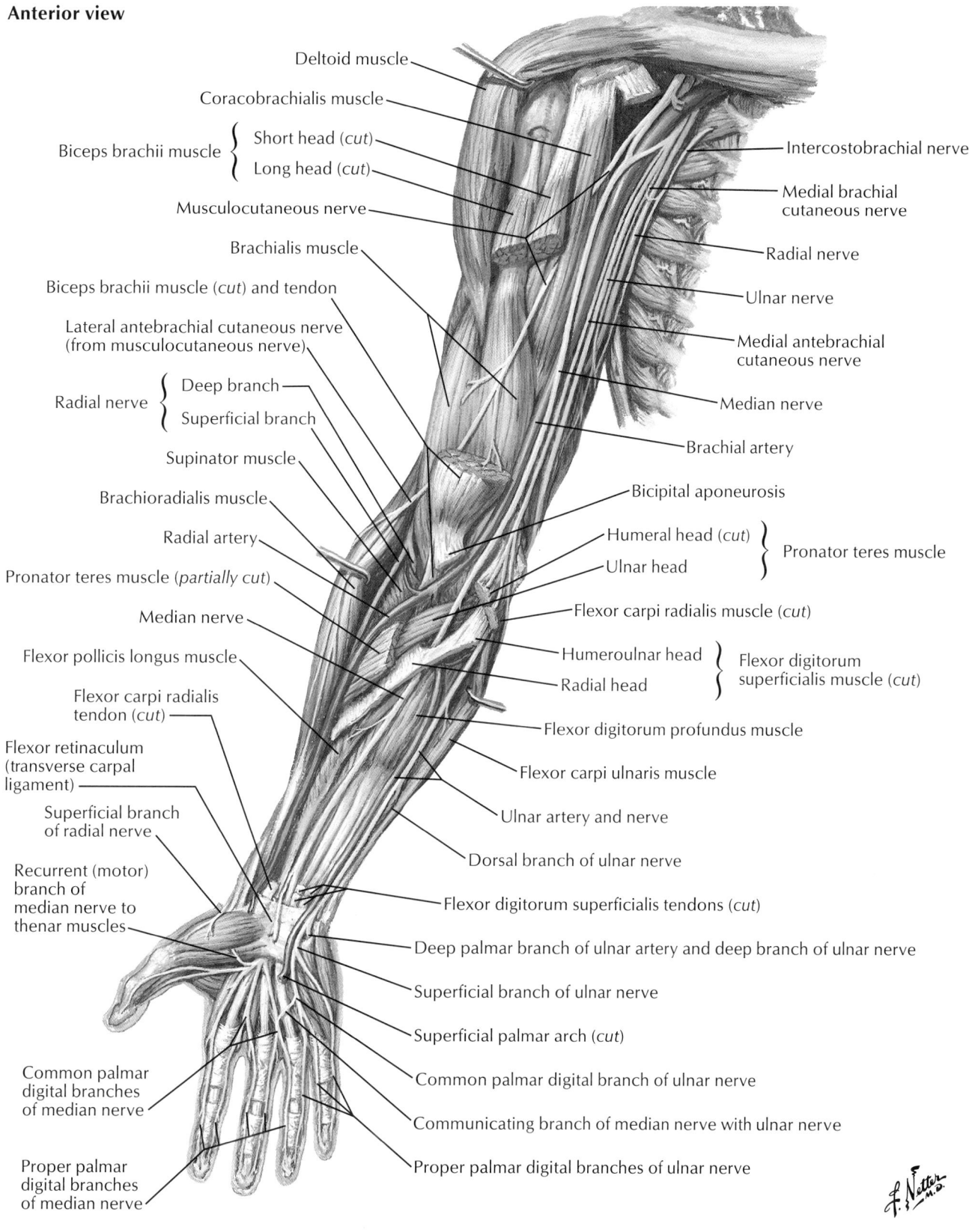

Deltoid muscle

Coracobrachialis muscle

Biceps brachii muscle {
Short head (*cut*)
Long head (*cut*)

Musculocutaneous nerve

Brachialis muscle

Biceps brachii muscle (*cut*) and tendon

Lateral antebrachial cutaneous nerve (from musculocutaneous nerve)

Radial nerve {
Deep branch
Superficial branch

Supinator muscle

Brachioradialis muscle

Radial artery

Pronator teres muscle (*partially cut*)

Median nerve

Flexor pollicis longus muscle

Flexor carpi radialis tendon (*cut*)

Flexor retinaculum (transverse carpal ligament)

Superficial branch of radial nerve

Recurrent (motor) branch of median nerve to thenar muscles

Common palmar digital branches of median nerve

Proper palmar digital branches of median nerve

Intercostobrachial nerve

Medial brachial cutaneous nerve

Radial nerve

Ulnar nerve

Medial antebrachial cutaneous nerve

Median nerve

Brachial artery

Bicipital aponeurosis

Humeral head (*cut*)
Ulnar head
} Pronator teres muscle

Flexor carpi radialis muscle (*cut*)

Humeroulnar head
Radial head
} Flexor digitorum superficialis muscle (*cut*)

Flexor digitorum profundus muscle

Flexor carpi ulnaris muscle

Ulnar artery and nerve

Dorsal branch of ulnar nerve

Flexor digitorum superficialis tendons (*cut*)

Deep palmar branch of ulnar artery and deep branch of ulnar nerve

Superficial branch of ulnar nerve

Superficial palmar arch (*cut*)

Common palmar digital branch of ulnar nerve

Communicating branch of median nerve with ulnar nerve

Proper palmar digital branches of ulnar nerve

Plate 473 Arteries and Nerves of Upper Limb. (Netter: Atlas of Human Anatomy, 4 ed, 2006, Saunders.)

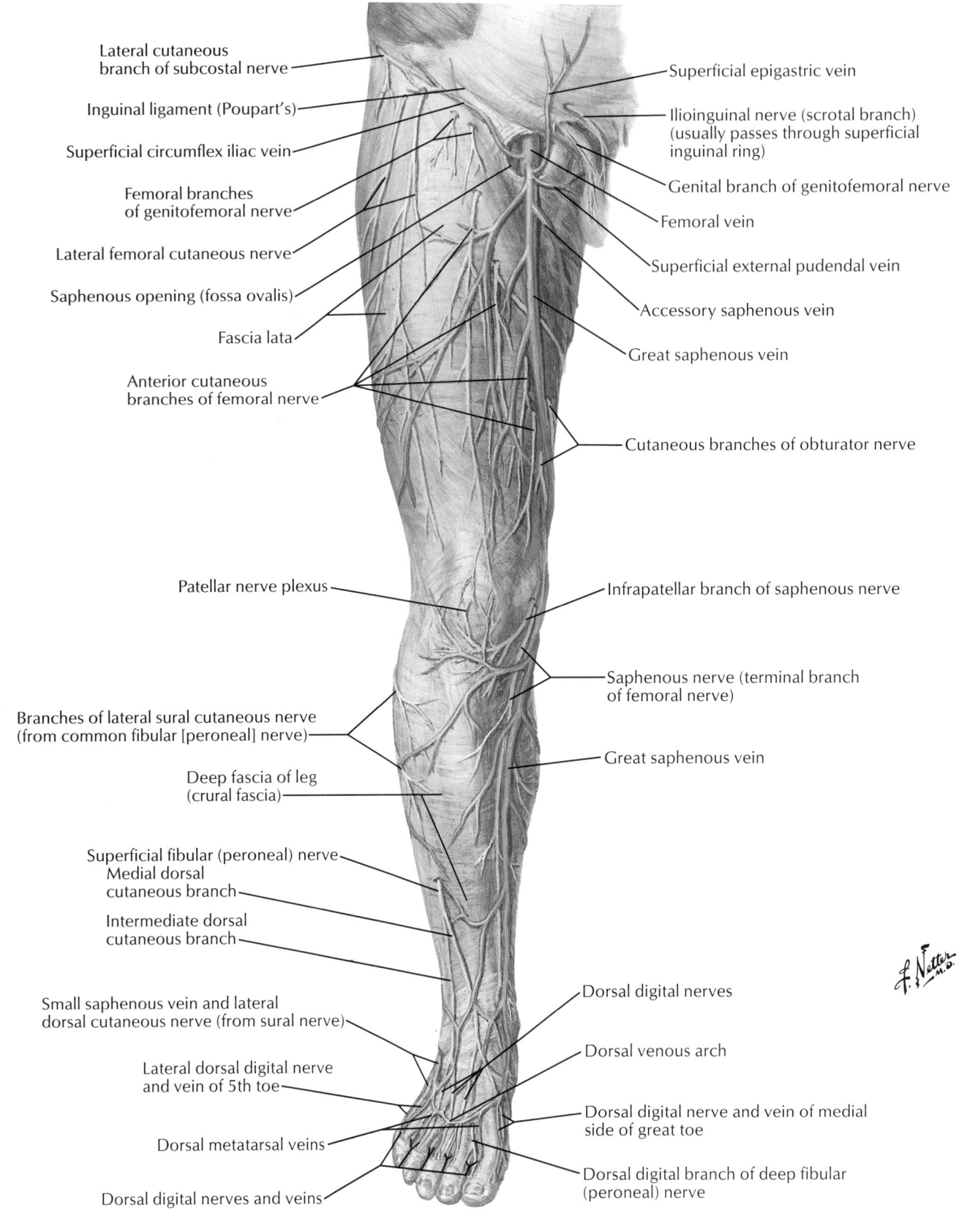

Lateral cutaneous branch of subcostal nerve

Inguinal ligament (Poupart's)

Superficial circumflex iliac vein

Femoral branches of genitofemoral nerve

Lateral femoral cutaneous nerve

Saphenous opening (fossa ovalis)

Fascia lata

Anterior cutaneous branches of femoral nerve

Patellar nerve plexus

Branches of lateral sural cutaneous nerve (from common fibular [peroneal] nerve)

Deep fascia of leg (crural fascia)

Superficial fibular (peroneal) nerve Medial dorsal cutaneous branch

Intermediate dorsal cutaneous branch

Small saphenous vein and lateral dorsal cutaneous nerve (from sural nerve)

Lateral dorsal digital nerve and vein of 5th toe

Dorsal metatarsal veins

Dorsal digital nerves and veins

Superficial epigastric vein

Ilioinguinal nerve (scrotal branch) (usually passes through superficial inguinal ring)

Genital branch of genitofemoral nerve

Femoral vein

Superficial external pudendal vein

Accessory saphenous vein

Great saphenous vein

Cutaneous branches of obturator nerve

Infrapatellar branch of saphenous nerve

Saphenous nerve (terminal branch of femoral nerve)

Great saphenous vein

Dorsal digital nerves

Dorsal venous arch

Dorsal digital nerve and vein of medial side of great toe

Dorsal digital branch of deep fibular (peroneal) nerve

Plate 544   Superficial Nerves and Veins of Lower Limb: Anterior View. (Netter: Atlas of Human Anatomy, 4 ed, 2006, Saunders.)

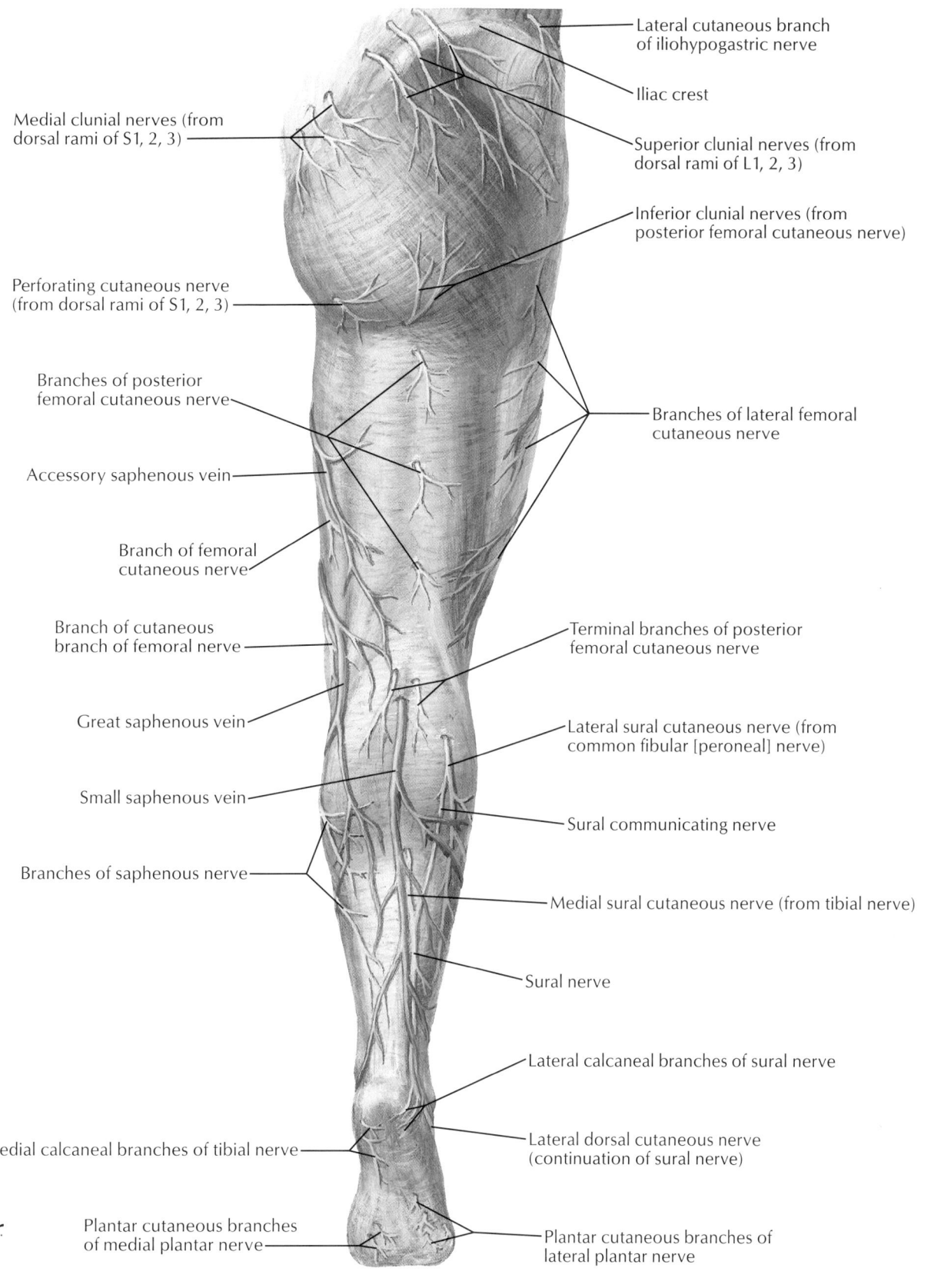

Lateral cutaneous branch
of iliohypogastric nerve

Iliac crest

Medial clunial nerves (from
dorsal rami of S1, 2, 3)

Superior clunial nerves (from
dorsal rami of L1, 2, 3)

Inferior clunial nerves (from
posterior femoral cutaneous nerve)

Perforating cutaneous nerve
(from dorsal rami of S1, 2, 3)

Branches of posterior
femoral cutaneous nerve

Branches of lateral femoral
cutaneous nerve

Accessory saphenous vein

Branch of femoral
cutaneous nerve

Branch of cutaneous
branch of femoral nerve

Terminal branches of posterior
femoral cutaneous nerve

Great saphenous vein

Lateral sural cutaneous nerve (from
common fibular [peroneal] nerve)

Small saphenous vein

Sural communicating nerve

Branches of saphenous nerve

Medial sural cutaneous nerve (from tibial nerve)

Sural nerve

Lateral calcaneal branches of sural nerve

Medial calcaneal branches of tibial nerve

Lateral dorsal cutaneous nerve
(continuation of sural nerve)

Plantar cutaneous branches
of medial plantar nerve

Plantar cutaneous branches of
lateral plantar nerve

Plate 545 Superficial Nerves and Veins of Lower Limb: Posterior View. (Netter: Atlas of Human Anatomy, 4 ed, 2006, Saunders.)

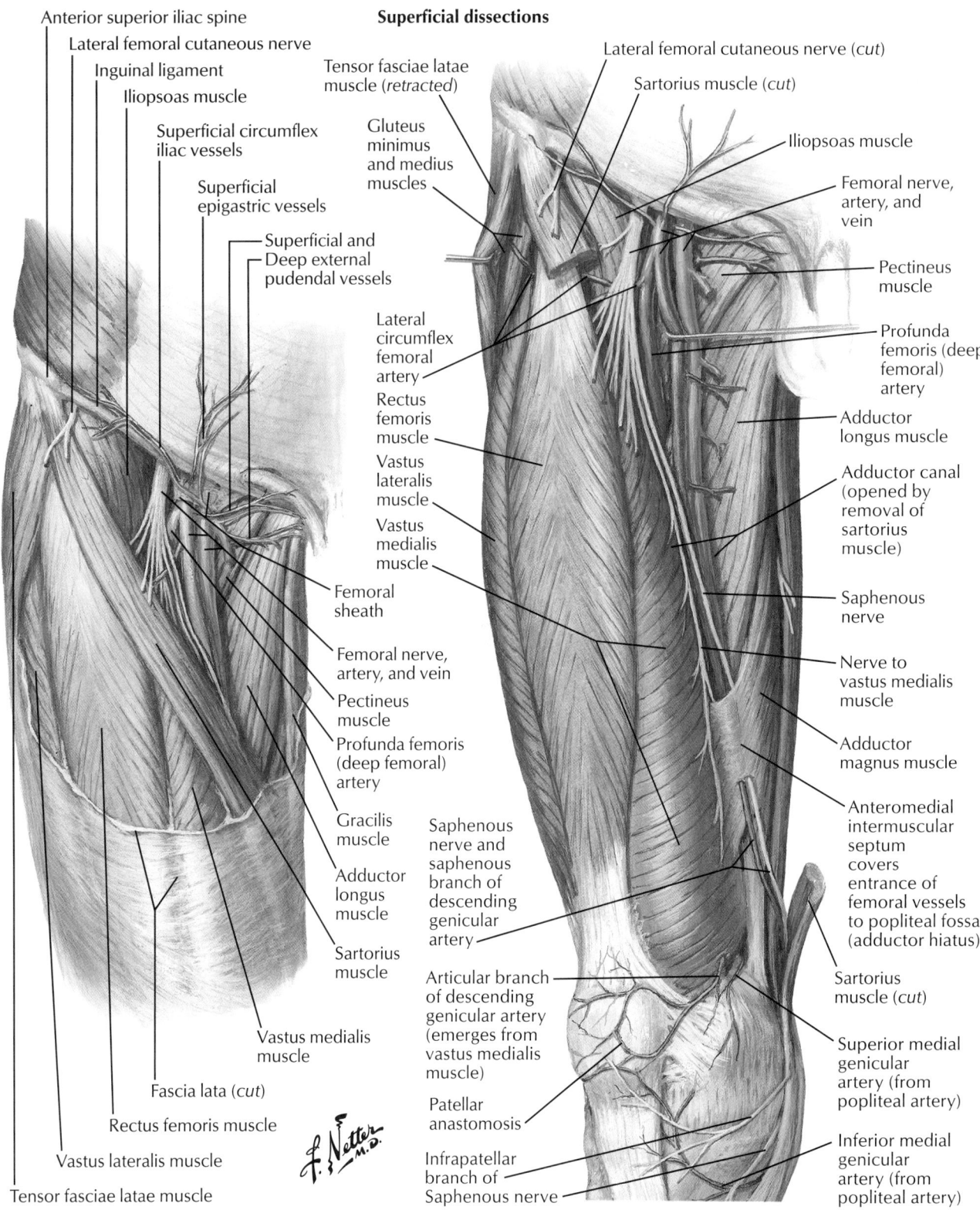

Superficial dissections

Anterior superior iliac spine
Lateral femoral cutaneous nerve
Inguinal ligament
Iliopsoas muscle
Superficial circumflex iliac vessels
Superficial epigastric vessels
Superficial and Deep external pudendal vessels

Tensor fasciae latae muscle (*retracted*)
Gluteus minimus and medius muscles
Lateral circumflex femoral artery
Rectus femoris muscle
Vastus lateralis muscle
Vastus medialis muscle
Femoral sheath
Femoral nerve, artery, and vein
Pectineus muscle
Profunda femoris (deep femoral) artery
Gracilis muscle
Adductor longus muscle
Sartorius muscle
Vastus medialis muscle
Fascia lata (*cut*)
Rectus femoris muscle
Vastus lateralis muscle
Tensor fasciae latae muscle

Lateral femoral cutaneous nerve (*cut*)
Sartorius muscle (*cut*)
Iliopsoas muscle
Femoral nerve, artery, and vein
Pectineus muscle
Profunda femoris (deep femoral) artery
Adductor longus muscle
Adductor canal (opened by removal of sartorius muscle)
Saphenous nerve
Nerve to vastus medialis muscle
Adductor magnus muscle
Anteromedial intermuscular septum covers entrance of femoral vessels to popliteal fossa (adductor hiatus)
Sartorius muscle (*cut*)
Superior medial genicular artery (from popliteal artery)
Inferior medial genicular artery (from popliteal artery)

Saphenous nerve and saphenous branch of descending genicular artery
Articular branch of descending genicular artery (emerges from vastus medialis muscle)
Patellar anastomosis
Infrapatellar branch of Saphenous nerve

Plate 500 Arteries and Nerves of Thigh: Anterior Views. (Netter: Atlas of Human Anatomy, 4 ed, 2006, Saunders.)

Deep dissection

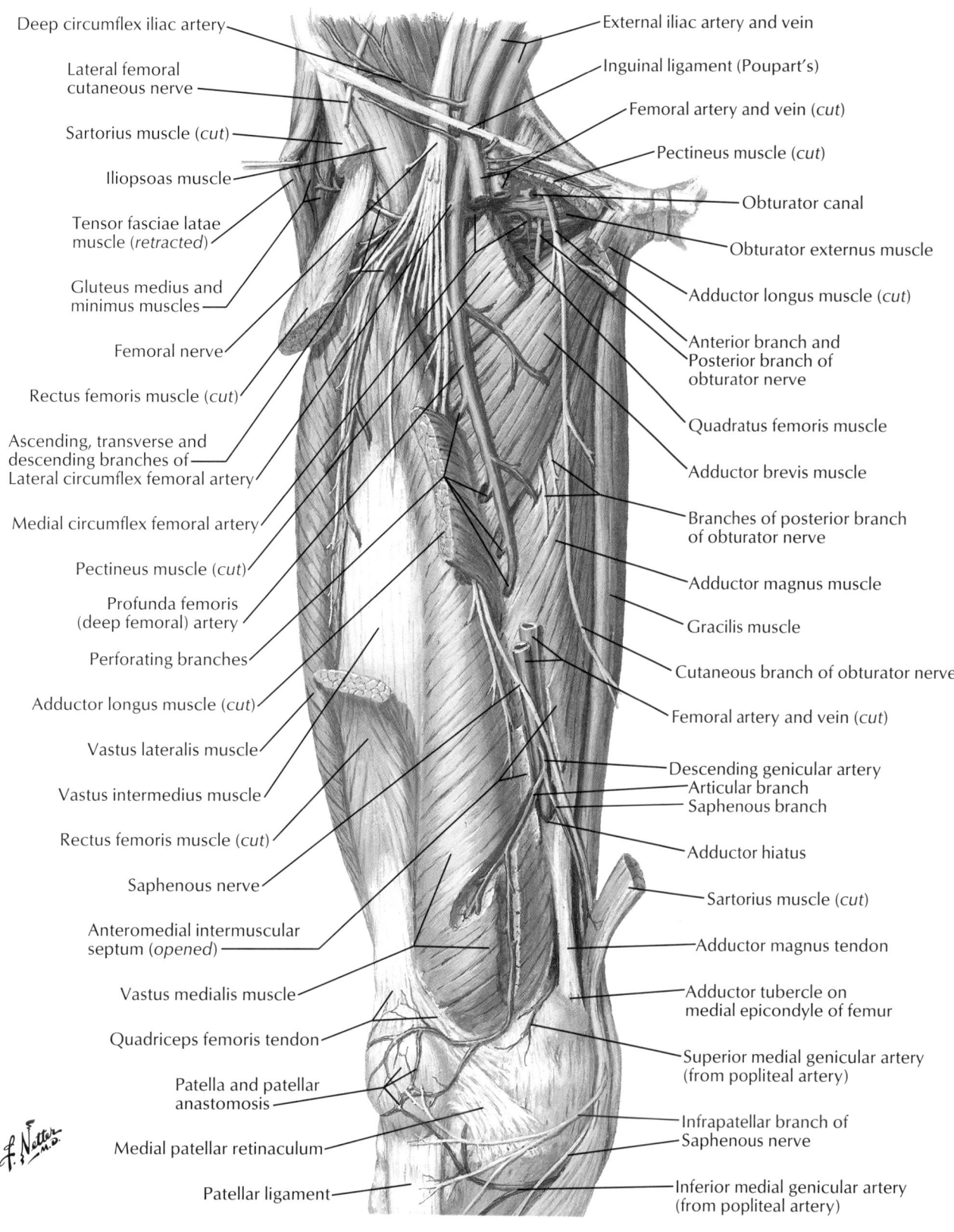

Deep circumflex iliac artery

Lateral femoral cutaneous nerve

Sartorius muscle (*cut*)

Iliopsoas muscle

Tensor fasciae latae muscle (*retracted*)

Gluteus medius and minimus muscles

Femoral nerve

Rectus femoris muscle (*cut*)

Ascending, transverse and descending branches of Lateral circumflex femoral artery

Medial circumflex femoral artery

Pectineus muscle (*cut*)

Profunda femoris (deep femoral) artery

Perforating branches

Adductor longus muscle (*cut*)

Vastus lateralis muscle

Vastus intermedius muscle

Rectus femoris muscle (*cut*)

Saphenous nerve

Anteromedial intermuscular septum (*opened*)

Vastus medialis muscle

Quadriceps femoris tendon

Patella and patellar anastomosis

Medial patellar retinaculum

Patellar ligament

External iliac artery and vein

Inguinal ligament (Poupart's)

Femoral artery and vein (*cut*)

Pectineus muscle (*cut*)

Obturator canal

Obturator externus muscle

Adductor longus muscle (*cut*)

Anterior branch and Posterior branch of obturator nerve

Quadratus femoris muscle

Adductor brevis muscle

Branches of posterior branch of obturator nerve

Adductor magnus muscle

Gracilis muscle

Cutaneous branch of obturator nerve

Femoral artery and vein (*cut*)

Descending genicular artery
Articular branch
Saphenous branch

Adductor hiatus

Sartorius muscle (*cut*)

Adductor magnus tendon

Adductor tubercle on medial epicondyle of femur

Superior medial genicular artery (from popliteal artery)

Infrapatellar branch of Saphenous nerve

Inferior medial genicular artery (from popliteal artery)

Plate 501   Arteries and Nerves of Thigh: Posterior View. (Netter: Atlas of Human Anatomy, 4 ed, 2006, Saunders.)

Deep dissection

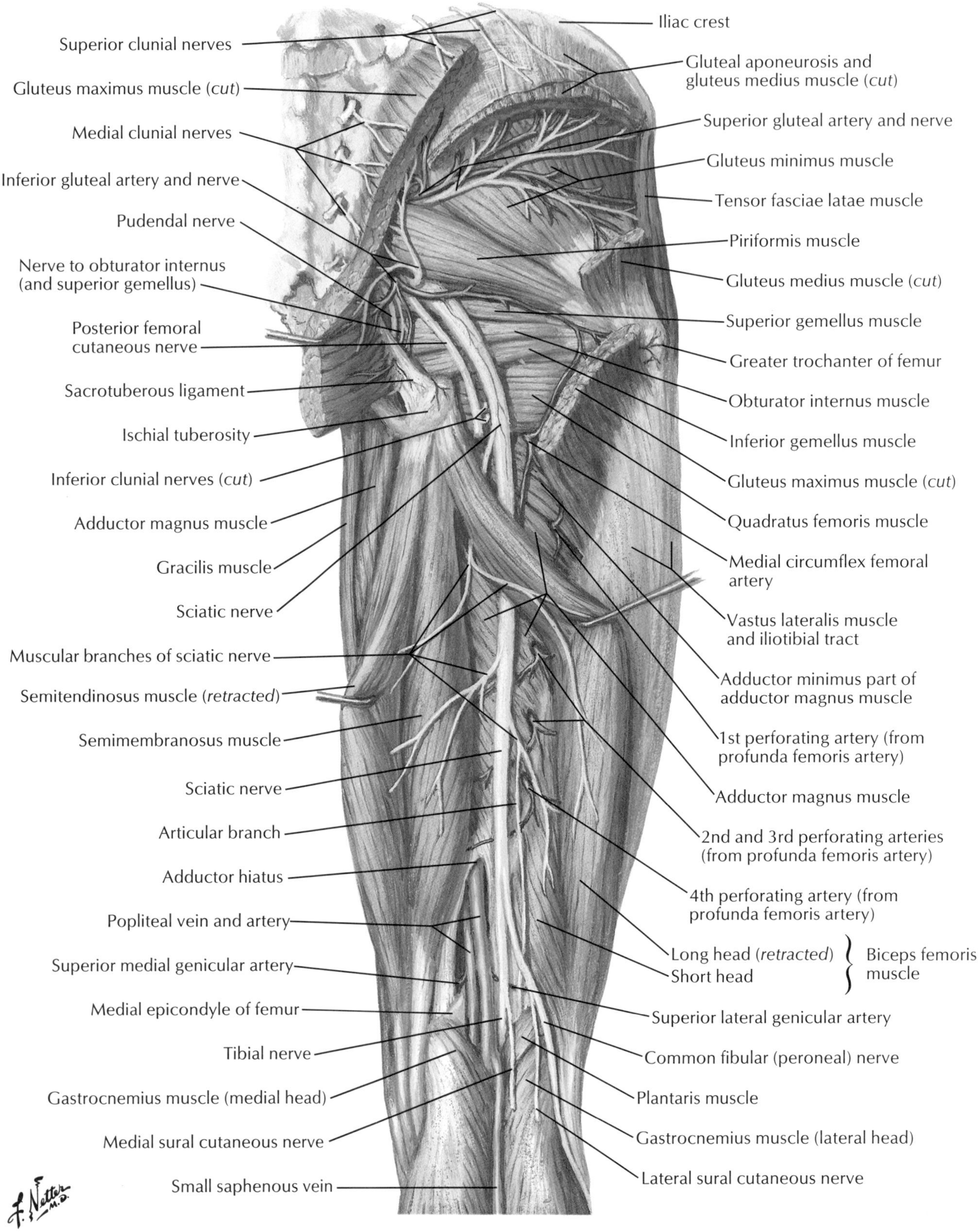

Superior clunial nerves

Gluteus maximus muscle (*cut*)

Medial clunial nerves

Inferior gluteal artery and nerve

Pudendal nerve

Nerve to obturator internus
(and superior gemellus)

Posterior femoral
cutaneous nerve

Sacrotuberous ligament

Ischial tuberosity

Inferior clunial nerves (*cut*)

Adductor magnus muscle

Gracilis muscle

Sciatic nerve

Muscular branches of sciatic nerve

Semitendinosus muscle (*retracted*)

Semimembranosus muscle

Sciatic nerve

Articular branch

Adductor hiatus

Popliteal vein and artery

Superior medial genicular artery

Medial epicondyle of femur

Tibial nerve

Gastrocnemius muscle (medial head)

Medial sural cutaneous nerve

Small saphenous vein

Iliac crest

Gluteal aponeurosis and
gluteus medius muscle (*cut*)

Superior gluteal artery and nerve

Gluteus minimus muscle

Tensor fasciae latae muscle

Piriformis muscle

Gluteus medius muscle (*cut*)

Superior gemellus muscle

Greater trochanter of femur

Obturator internus muscle

Inferior gemellus muscle

Gluteus maximus muscle (*cut*)

Quadratus femoris muscle

Medial circumflex femoral
artery

Vastus lateralis muscle
and iliotibial tract

Adductor minimus part of
adductor magnus muscle

1st perforating artery (from
profunda femoris artery)

Adductor magnus muscle

2nd and 3rd perforating arteries
(from profunda femoris artery)

4th perforating artery (from
profunda femoris artery)

Long head (*retracted*) ⎫ Biceps femoris
Short head   ⎭ muscle

Superior lateral genicular artery

Common fibular (peroneal) nerve

Plantaris muscle

Gastrocnemius muscle (lateral head)

Lateral sural cutaneous nerve

Plate 502 Arteries and Nerves of Thigh: Posterior View. (Netter: Atlas of Human Anatomy, 4 ed, 2006, Saunders.)

Horizontal section

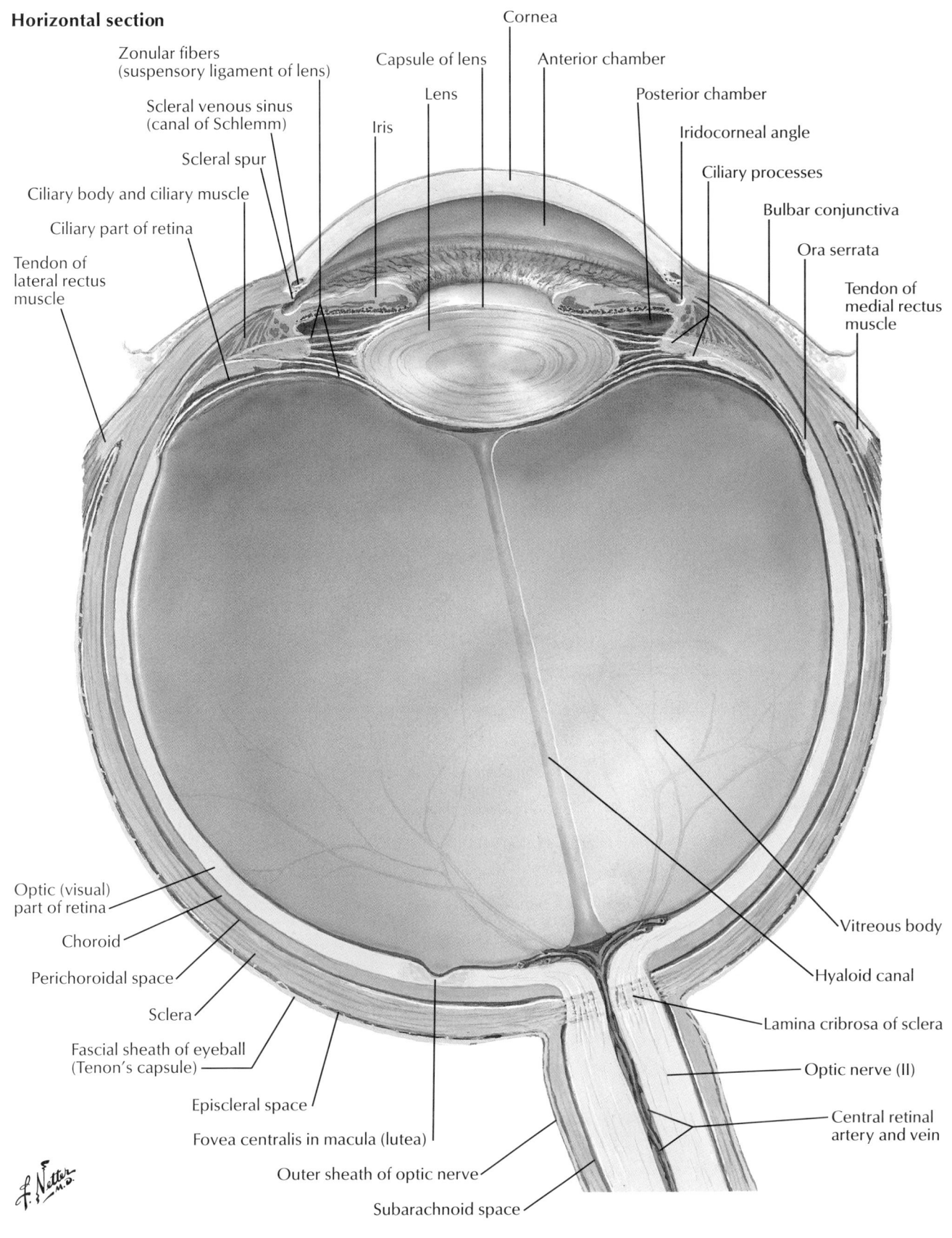

Zonular fibers (suspensory ligament of lens)

Scleral venous sinus (canal of Schlemm)

Scleral spur

Ciliary body and ciliary muscle

Ciliary part of retina

Tendon of lateral rectus muscle

Cornea

Capsule of lens

Lens

Iris

Anterior chamber

Posterior chamber

Iridocorneal angle

Ciliary processes

Bulbar conjunctiva

Ora serrata

Tendon of medial rectus muscle

Optic (visual) part of retina

Choroid

Perichoroidal space

Sclera

Fascial sheath of eyeball (Tenon's capsule)

Episcleral space

Fovea centralis in macula (lutea)

Outer sheath of optic nerve

Subarachnoid space

Vitreous body

Hyaloid canal

Lamina cribrosa of sclera

Optic nerve (II)

Central retinal artery and vein

Plate 87 Eyeball. (Netter: Atlas of Human Anatomy, 4 ed, 2006, Saunders.)

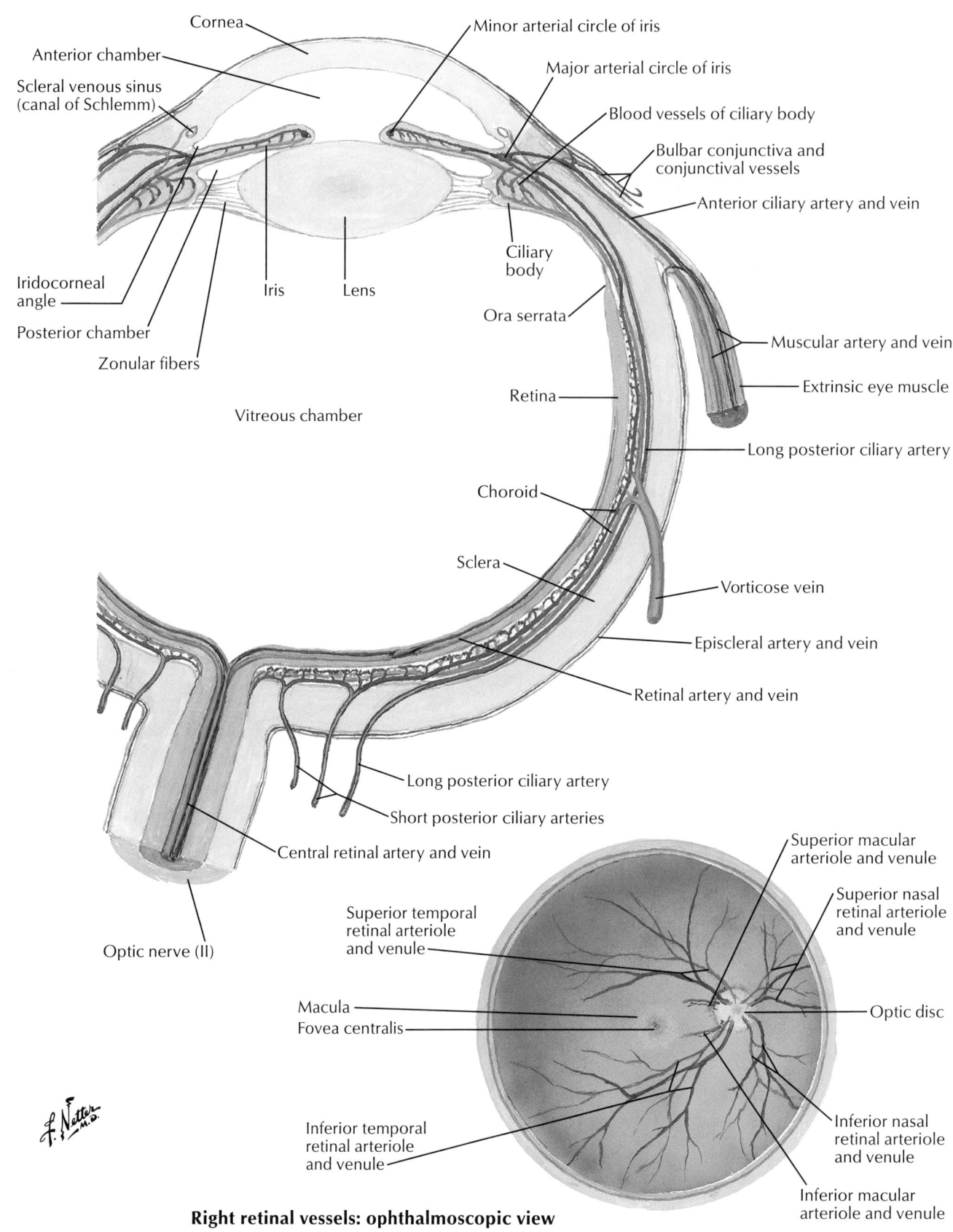

Cornea

Anterior chamber

Scleral venous sinus
(canal of Schlemm)

Minor arterial circle of iris

Major arterial circle of iris

Blood vessels of ciliary body

Bulbar conjunctiva and
conjunctival vessels

Anterior ciliary artery and vein

Iridocorneal
angle

Iris   Lens

Ciliary
body

Ora serrata

Muscular artery and vein

Posterior chamber

Extrinsic eye muscle

Zonular fibers

Retina

Long posterior ciliary artery

Vitreous chamber

Choroid

Sclera

Vorticose vein

Episcleral artery and vein

Retinal artery and vein

Long posterior ciliary artery

Short posterior ciliary arteries

Central retinal artery and vein

Optic nerve (II)

Superior macular
arteriole and venule

Superior temporal
retinal arteriole
and venule

Superior nasal
retinal arteriole
and venule

Macula

Fovea centralis

Optic disc

Inferior temporal
retinal arteriole
and venule

Inferior nasal
retinal arteriole
and venule

Inferior macular
arteriole and venule

Right retinal vessels: ophthalmoscopic view

Plate 90   Intrinsic Arteries and Veins of Eye. (Netter: Atlas of Human Anatomy, 4 ed, 2006, Saunders.)

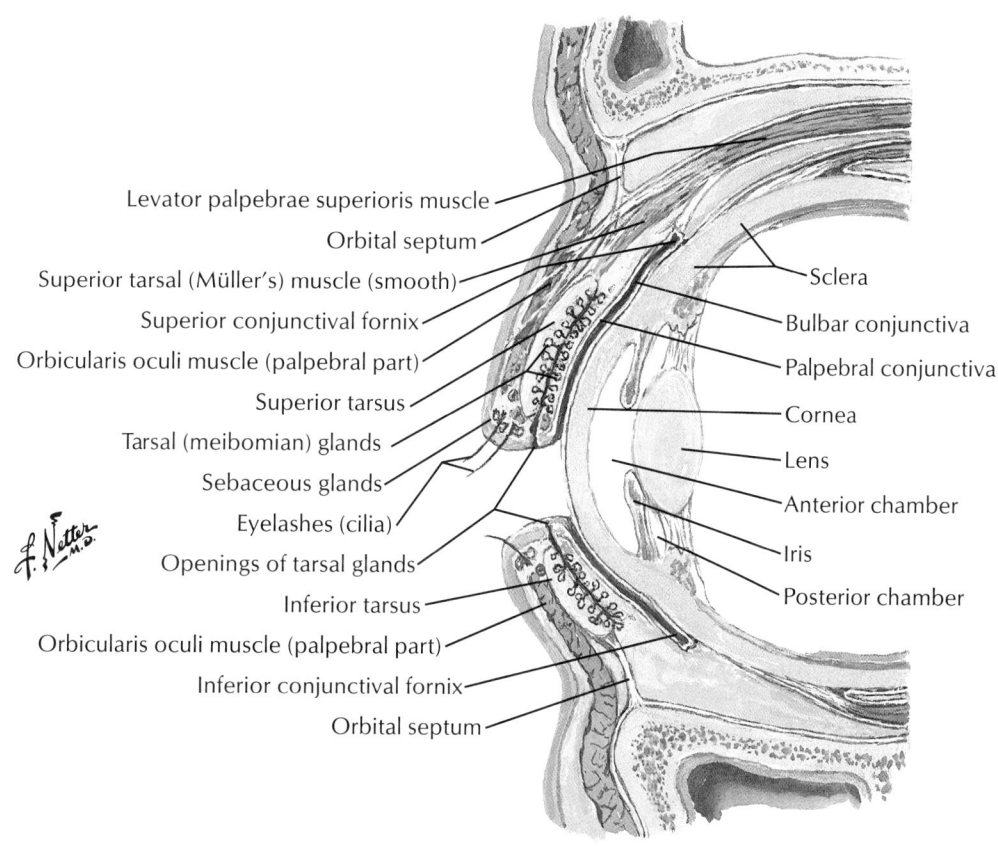

Levator palpebrae superioris muscle

Orbital septum

Superior tarsal (Müller's) muscle (smooth)

Superior conjunctival fornix

Orbicularis oculi muscle (palpebral part)

Superior tarsus

Tarsal (meibomian) glands

Sebaceous glands

Eyelashes (cilia)

Openings of tarsal glands

Inferior tarsus

Orbicularis oculi muscle (palpebral part)

Inferior conjunctival fornix

Orbital septum

Sclera

Bulbar conjunctiva

Palpebral conjunctiva

Cornea

Lens

Anterior chamber

Iris

Posterior chamber

Plate 81, Middle   Eyelids. (Netter: Atlas of Human Anatomy, 4 ed, 2006, Saunders.)

Superior palpebral conjunctiva: tarsal (meibomian) glands shining through

Seen through cornea { Pupil / Iris

Corneoscleral junction (corneal limbus)

Bulbar conjunctiva over sclera

Inferior conjunctival fornix

Inferior palpebral conjunctiva: tarsal glands shining through

Superior lacrimal papilla and punctum

Plica semilunaris

Lacrimal caruncle in lacrimal lake (lacus lacrimalis)

Inferior lacrimal papilla and punctum

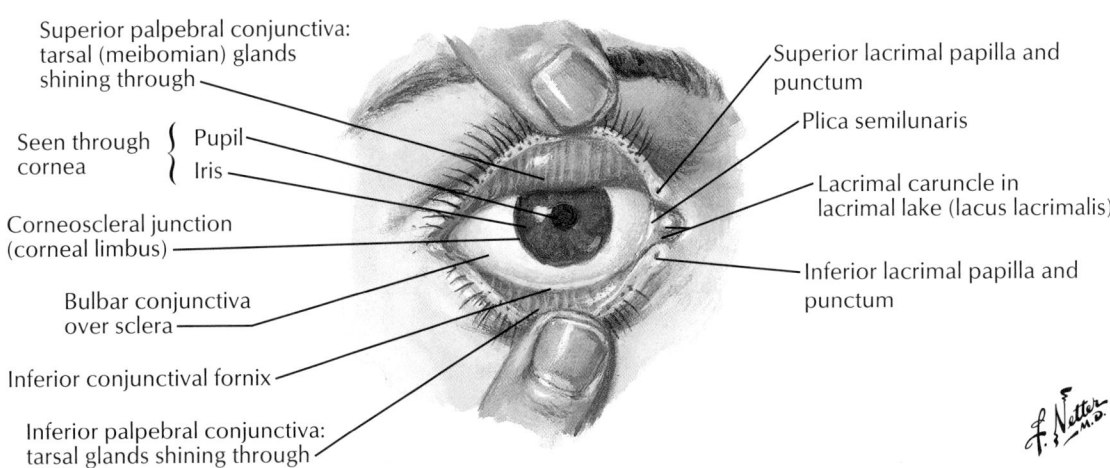

Plate 81, Upper Eyelid. (Netter: Atlas of Human Anatomy, 4 ed, 2006, Saunders.)

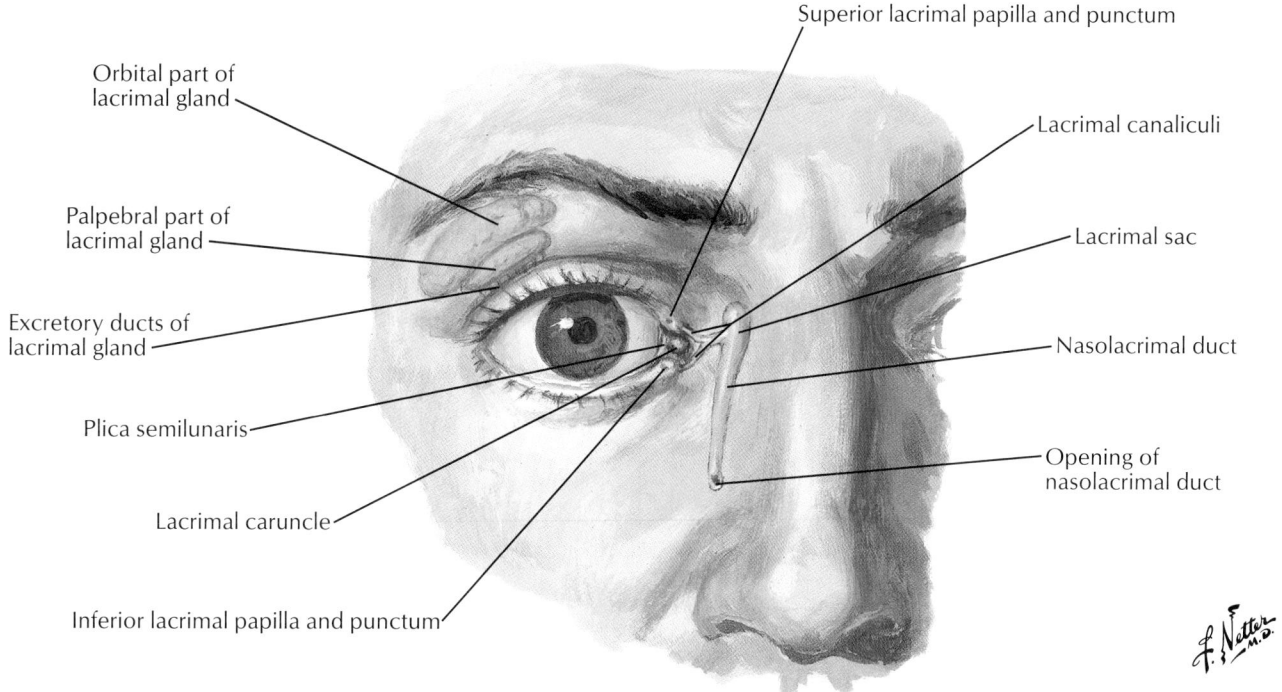

Orbital part of
lacrimal gland

Palpebral part of
lacrimal gland

Excretory ducts of
lacrimal gland

Plica semilunaris

Lacrimal caruncle

Inferior lacrimal papilla and punctum

Superior lacrimal papilla and punctum

Lacrimal canaliculi

Lacrimal sac

Nasolacrimal duct

Opening of
nasolacrimal duct

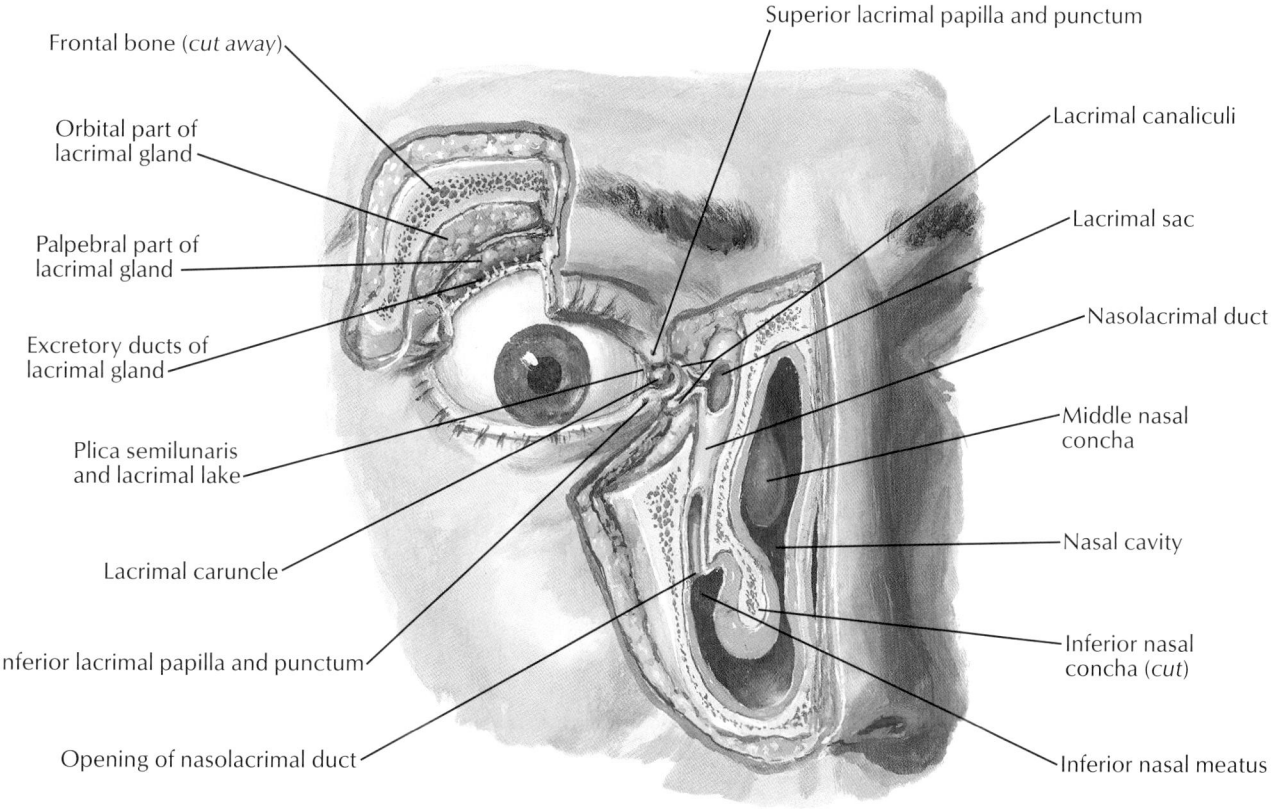

Frontal bone (cut away)

Orbital part of
lacrimal gland

Palpebral part of
lacrimal gland

Excretory ducts of
lacrimal gland

Plica semilunaris
and lacrimal lake

Lacrimal caruncle

Inferior lacrimal papilla and punctum

Opening of nasolacrimal duct

Superior lacrimal papilla and punctum

Lacrimal canaliculi

Lacrimal sac

Nasolacrimal duct

Middle nasal
concha

Nasal cavity

Inferior nasal
concha (cut)

Inferior nasal meatus

Plate 82   Lacrimal Apparatus. (Netter: Atlas of Human Anatomy, 4 ed, 2006, Saunders.)

Frontal section

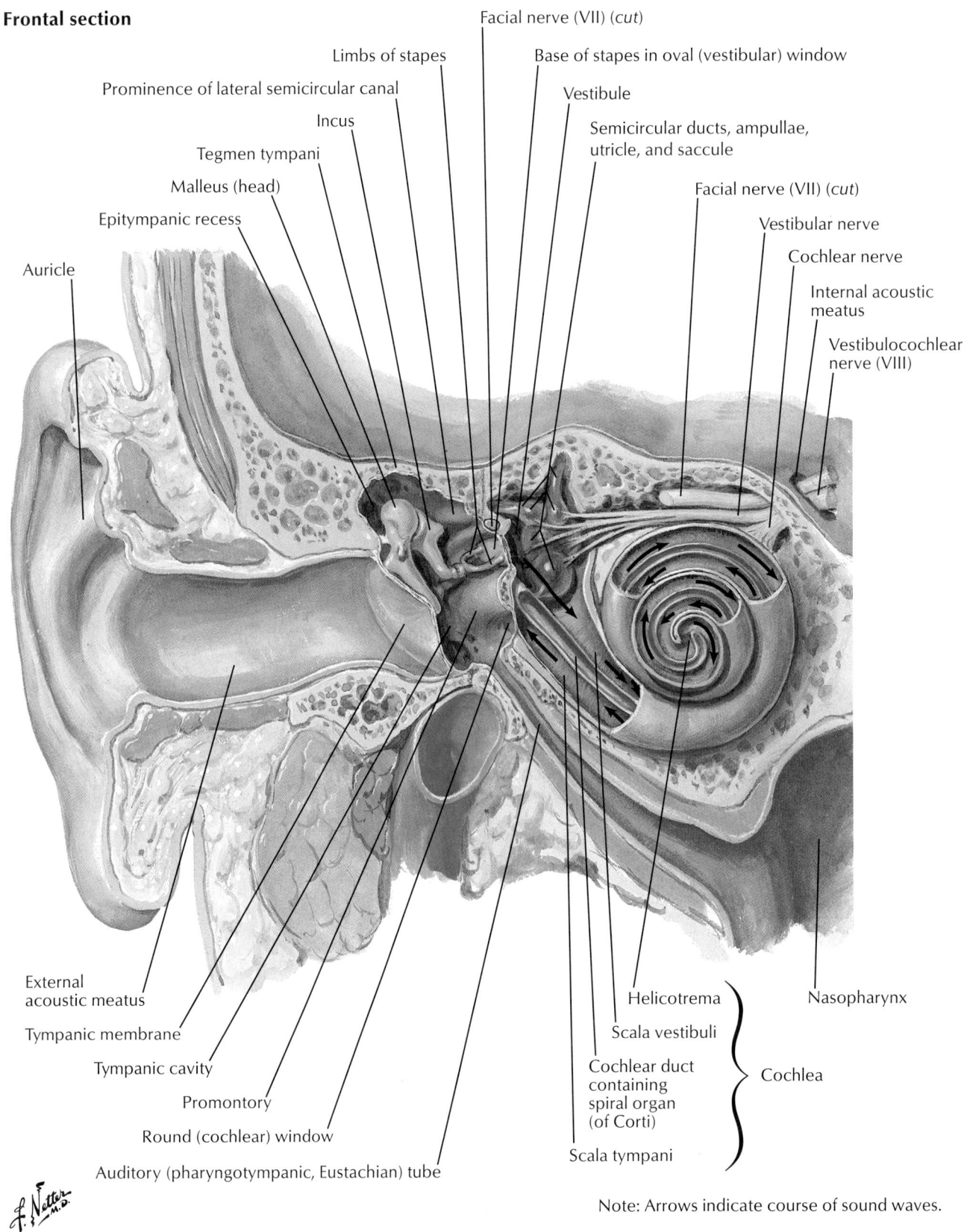

Facial nerve (VII) (*cut*)

Limbs of stapes

Base of stapes in oval (vestibular) window

Prominence of lateral semicircular canal

Vestibule

Incus

Semicircular ducts, ampullae, utricle, and saccule

Tegmen tympani

Malleus (head)

Facial nerve (VII) (*cut*)

Epitympanic recess

Vestibular nerve

Cochlear nerve

Internal acoustic meatus

Auricle

Vestibulocochlear nerve (VIII)

External acoustic meatus

Helicotrema

Nasopharynx

Tympanic membrane

Scala vestibuli

Tympanic cavity

Cochlear duct containing spiral organ (of Corti)

Cochlea

Promontory

Round (cochlear) window

Scala tympani

Auditory (pharyngotympanic, Eustachian) tube

Note: Arrows indicate course of sound waves.

Plate 92   Pathway of Sound Reception. (Netter: Atlas of Human Anatomy, 4 ed, 2006, Saunders.)

Medial wall of tympanic cavity: lateral view

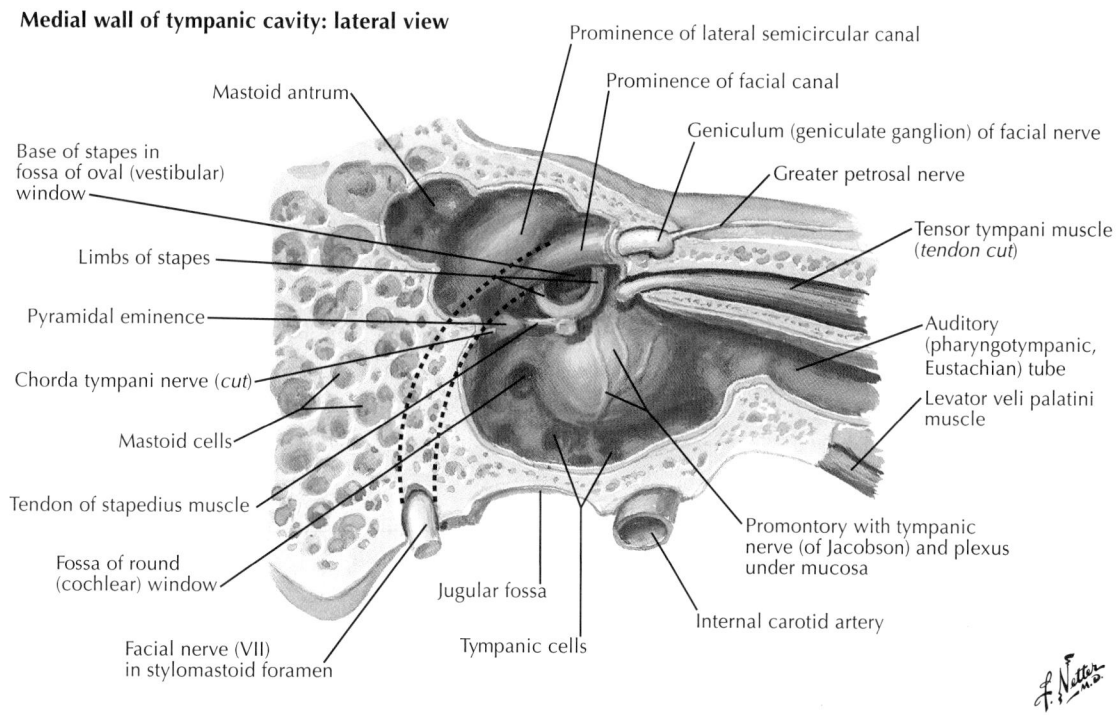

Mastoid antrum

Prominence of lateral semicircular canal

Prominence of facial canal

Geniculum (geniculate ganglion) of facial nerve

Greater petrosal nerve

Base of stapes in fossa of oval (vestibular) window

Tensor tympani muscle (*tendon cut*)

Limbs of stapes

Pyramidal eminence

Auditory (pharyngotympanic, Eustachian) tube

Chorda tympani nerve (*cut*)

Levator veli palatini muscle

Mastoid cells

Tendon of stapedius muscle

Promontory with tympanic nerve (of Jacobson) and plexus under mucosa

Fossa of round (cochlear) window

Jugular fossa

Tympanic cells

Internal carotid artery

Facial nerve (VII) in stylomastoid foramen

Plate 94 Tympanic Cavity. (Netter: Atlas of Human Anatomy, 4 ed, 2006, Saunders.)

Otoscopic view of right tympanic membrane

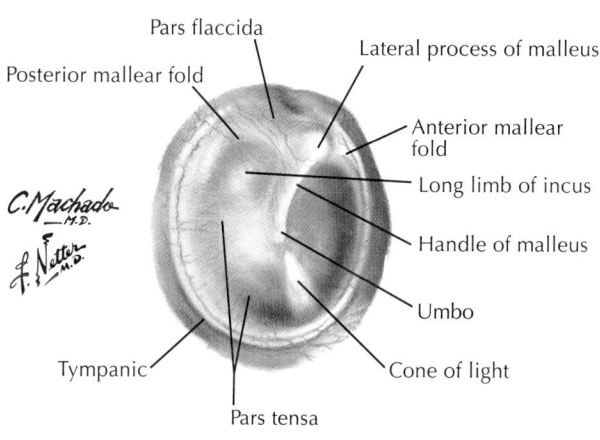

Pars flaccida

Posterior mallear fold

Lateral process of malleus

Anterior mallear fold

Long limb of incus

Handle of malleus

Umbo

Cone of light

Tympanic

Pars tensa

Plate 93 Tympanic Cavity. (Netter: Atlas of Human Anatomy, 4 ed, 2006, Saunders.)

Dissected right bony labyrinth (otic capsule): membranous labyrinth removed

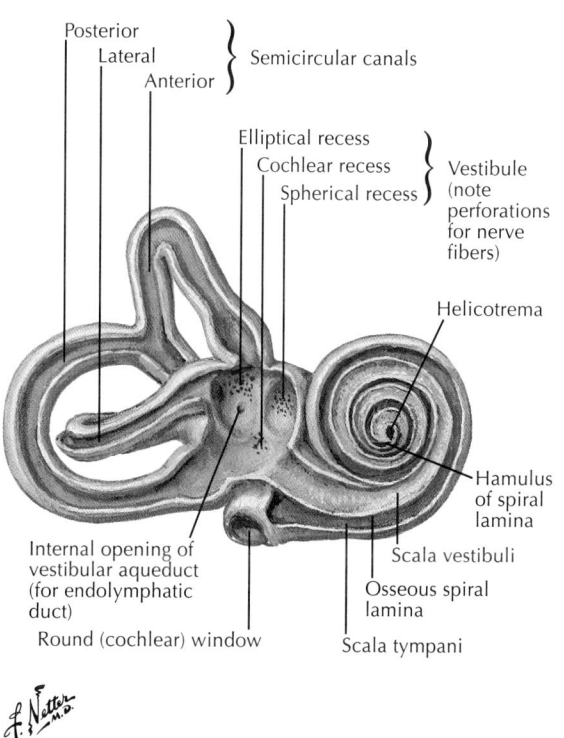

Posterior

Lateral

Anterior

Semicircular canals

Elliptical recess

Cochlear recess

Spherical recess

Vestibule (note perforations for nerve fibers)

Helicotrema

Hamulus of spiral lamina

Scala vestibuli

Osseous spiral lamina

Scala tympani

Internal opening of vestibular aqueduct (for endolymphatic duct)

Round (cochlear) window

Plate 95 Bony Membranous Labyrinth. (Netter: Atlas of Human Anatomy, 4 ed, 2006, Saunders.)

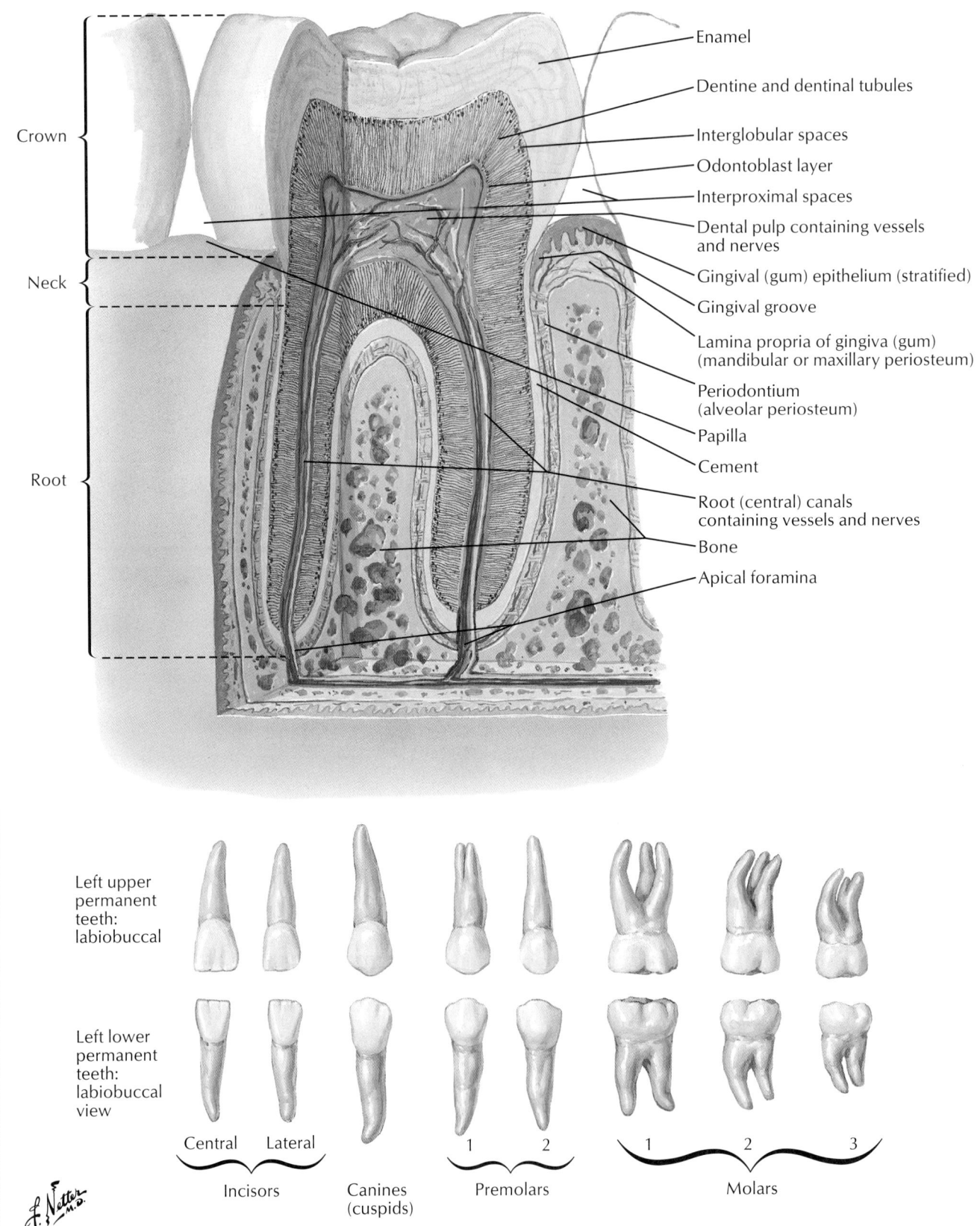

Crown

Neck

Root

Enamel

Dentine and dentinal tubules

Interglobular spaces

Odontoblast layer

Interproximal spaces

Dental pulp containing vessels and nerves

Gingival (gum) epithelium (stratified)

Gingival groove

Lamina propria of gingiva (gum) (mandibular or maxillary periosteum)

Periodontium (alveolar periosteum)

Papilla

Cement

Root (central) canals containing vessels and nerves

Bone

Apical foramina

Left upper permanent teeth: labiobuccal

Left lower permanent teeth: labiobuccal view

Central   Lateral

Incisors

Canines (cuspids)

1   2

Premolars

1   2   3

Molars

Plate 57 Teeth. (Netter: Atlas of Human Anatomy, 4 ed, 2006, Saunders.)

Tongue

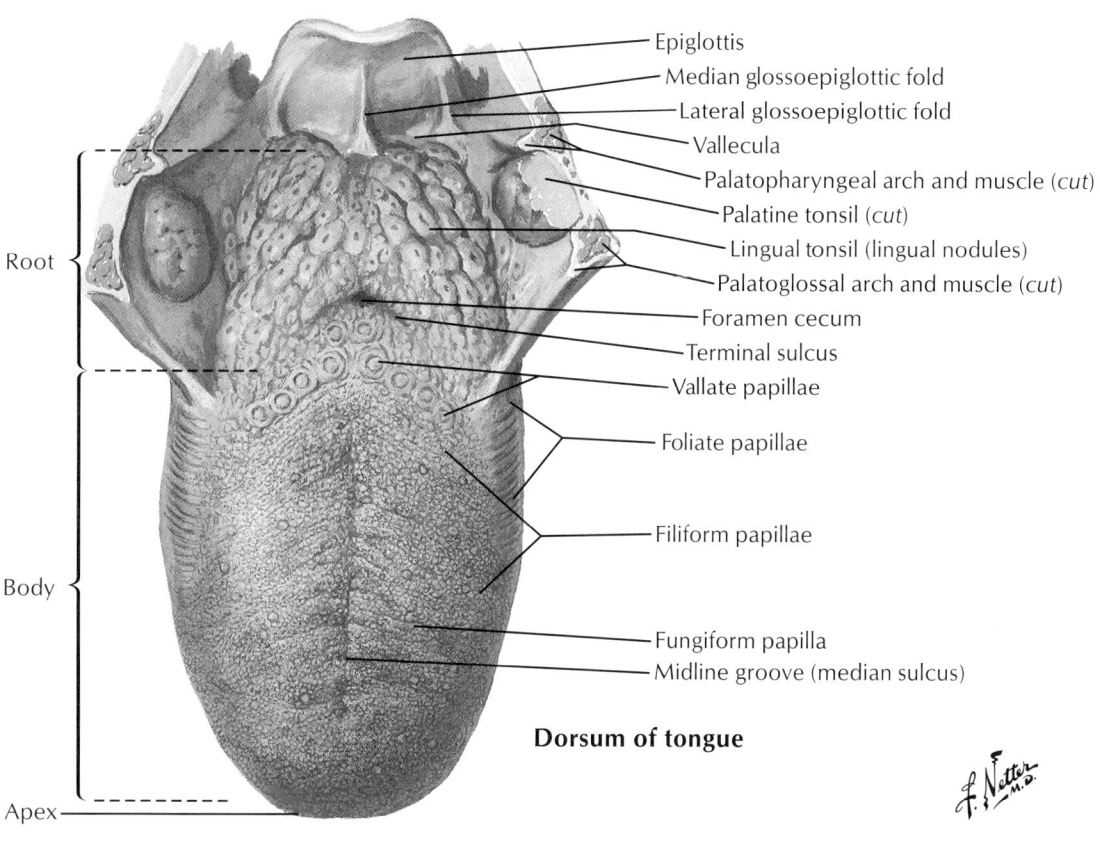

Epiglottis
Median glossoepiglottic fold
Lateral glossoepiglottic fold
Vallecula
Palatopharyngeal arch and muscle (*cut*)
Palatine tonsil (*cut*)
Lingual tonsil (lingual nodules)
Palatoglossal arch and muscle (*cut*)
Foramen cecum
Terminal sulcus
Vallate papillae

Foliate papillae

Filiform papillae

Fungiform papilla
Midline groove (median sulcus)

Root

Body

Apex

Dorsum of tongue

Plate 58 Tongue. (Netter: Atlas of Human Anatomy, 4 ed, 2006, Saunders.)

NAP-23

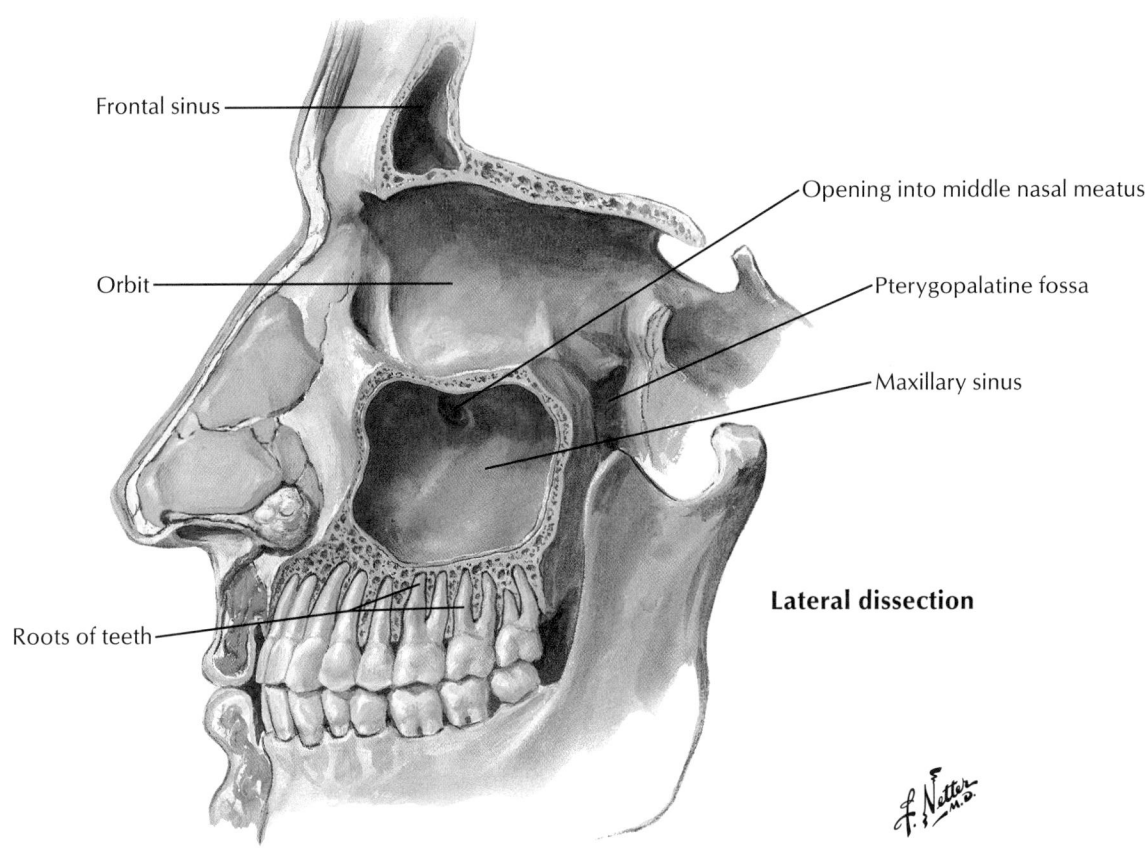

Frontal sinus

Orbit

Roots of teeth

Opening into middle nasal meatus

Pterygopalatine fossa

Maxillary sinus

Lemma dissection

Lateral dissection

Plate 49 Paranasal Sinuses. (Netter: Atlas of Human Anatomy, 4 ed, 2006, Saunders.)

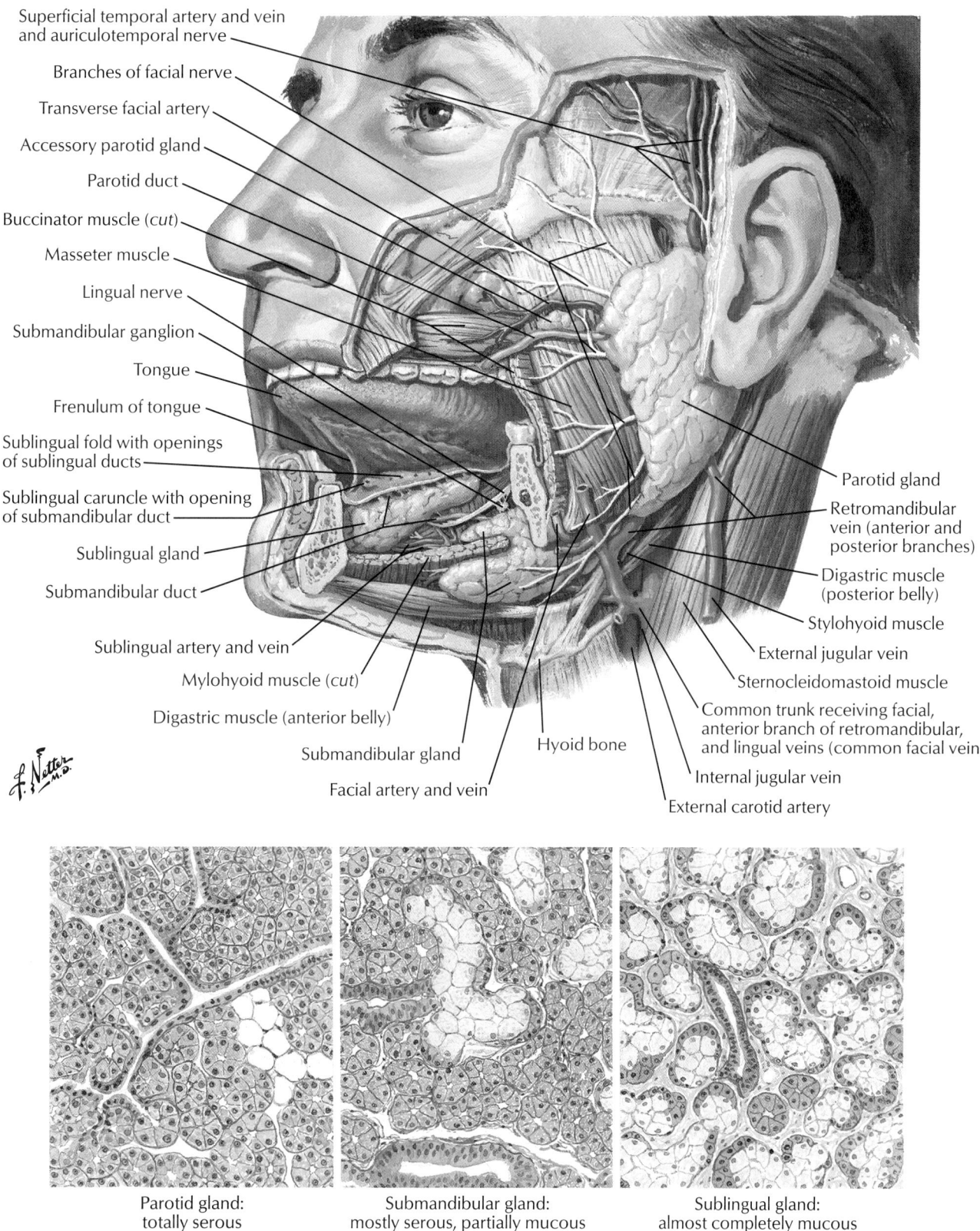

Superficial temporal artery and vein
and auriculotemporal nerve

Branches of facial nerve

Transverse facial artery

Accessory parotid gland

Parotid duct

Buccinator muscle (*cut*)

Masseter muscle

Lingual nerve

Submandibular ganglion

Tongue

Frenulum of tongue

Sublingual fold with openings
of sublingual ducts

Sublingual caruncle with opening
of submandibular duct

Sublingual gland

Submandibular duct

Sublingual artery and vein

Mylohyoid muscle (*cut*)

Digastric muscle (anterior belly)

Submandibular gland

Facial artery and vein

Hyoid bone

Parotid gland

Retromandibular
vein (anterior and
posterior branches)

Digastric muscle
(posterior belly)

Stylohyoid muscle

External jugular vein

Sternocleidomastoid muscle

Common trunk receiving facial,
anterior branch of retromandibular,
and lingual veins (common facial vein)

Internal jugular vein

External carotid artery

Parotid gland:
totally serous

Submandibular gland:
mostly serous, partially mucous

Sublingual gland:
almost completely mucous

Plate 61 Salivary Glands. (Netter: Atlas of Human Anatomy, 4 ed, 2006, Saunders.)

Coronary Arteries: Arteriographic Views

Right coronary artery: left anterior oblique view

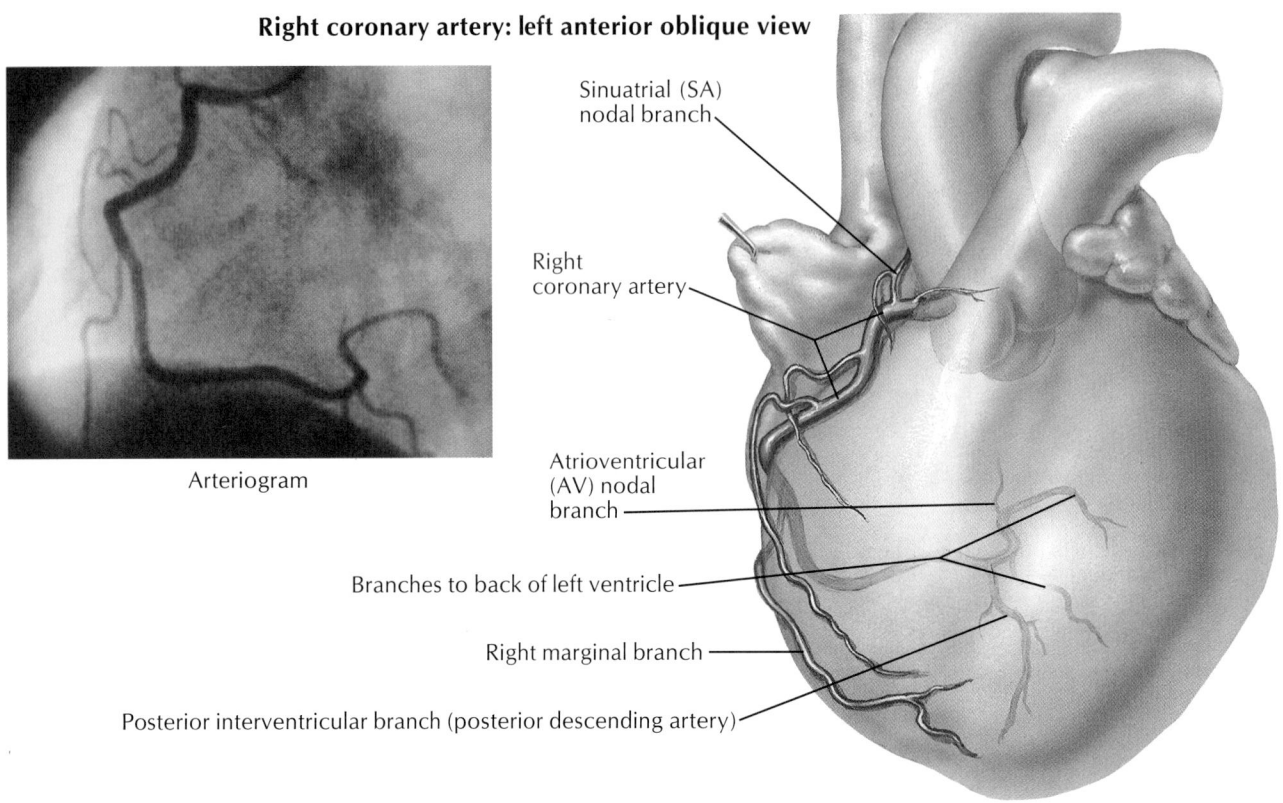

Arteriogram

Sinuatrial (SA) nodal branch

Right coronary artery

Atrioventricular (AV) nodal branch

Branches to back of left ventricle

Right marginal branch

Posterior interventricular branch (posterior descending artery)

Right coronary artery: right anterior oblique view

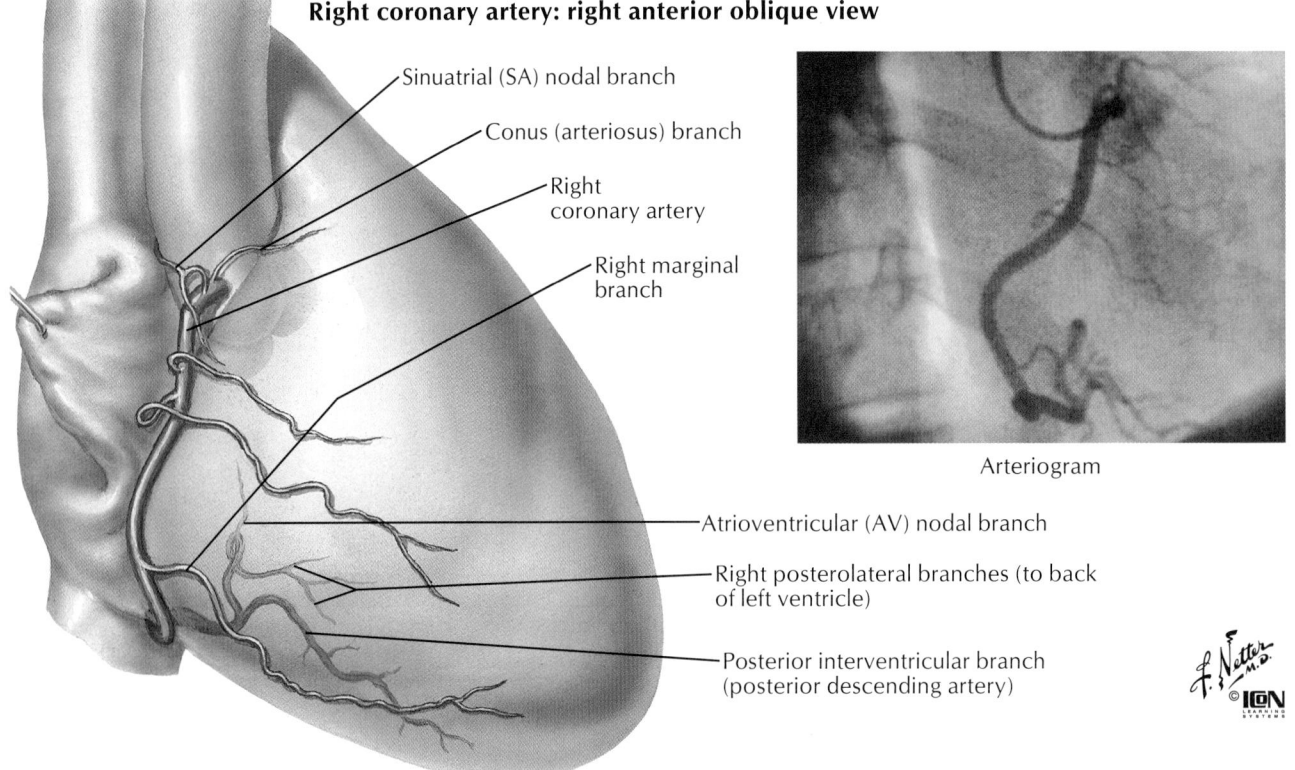

Sinuatrial (SA) nodal branch

Conus (arteriosus) branch

Right coronary artery

Right marginal branch

Arteriogram

Atrioventricular (AV) nodal branch

Right posterolateral branches (to back of left ventricle)

Posterior interventricular branch (posterior descending artery)

Plate 218   Coronary Arteries: Arteriographic Views. (Netter: Atlas of Human Anatomy, 4 ed, 2006, Saunders.)

Left coronary artery: left anterior oblique view

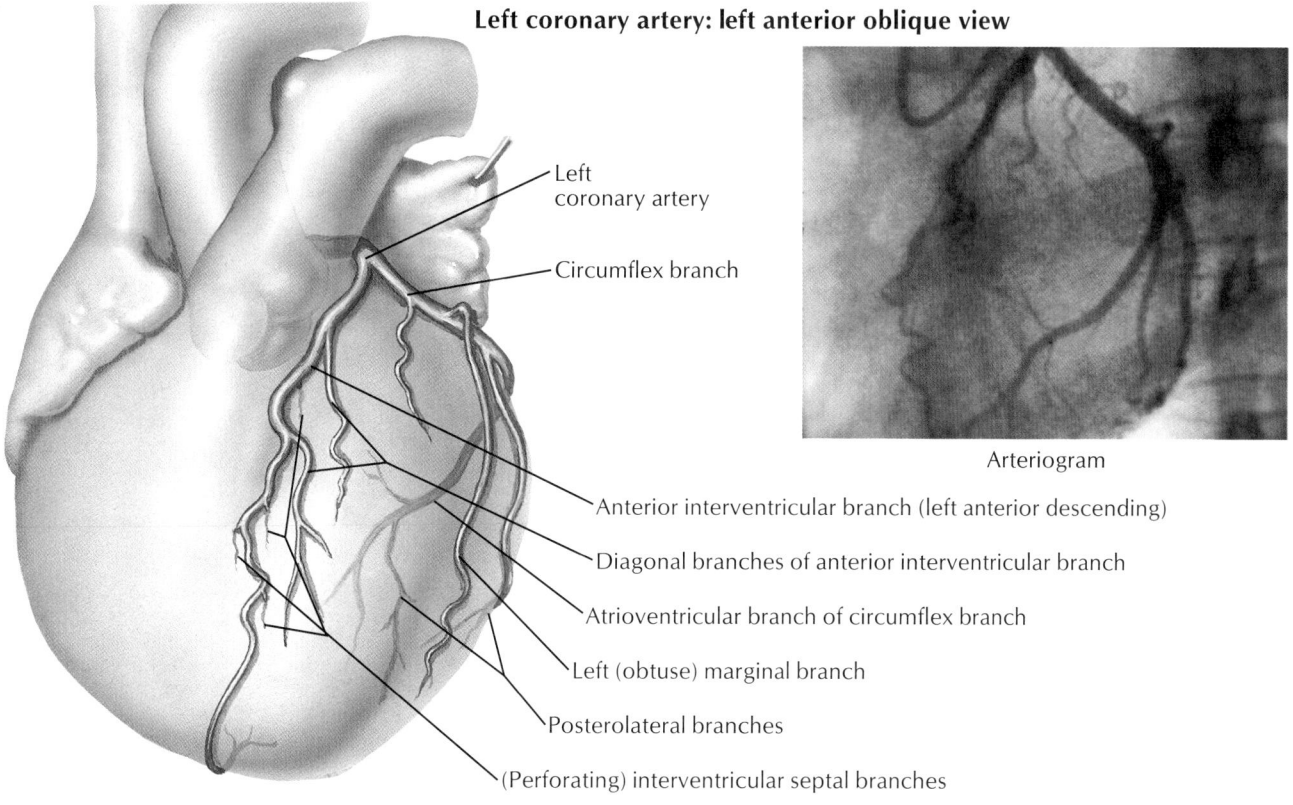

Left coronary artery

Circumflex branch

Arteriogram

Anterior interventricular branch (left anterior descending)

Diagonal branches of anterior interventricular branch

Atrioventricular branch of circumflex branch

Left (obtuse) marginal branch

Posterolateral branches

(Perforating) interventricular septal branches

Left coronary artery: right anterior oblique view

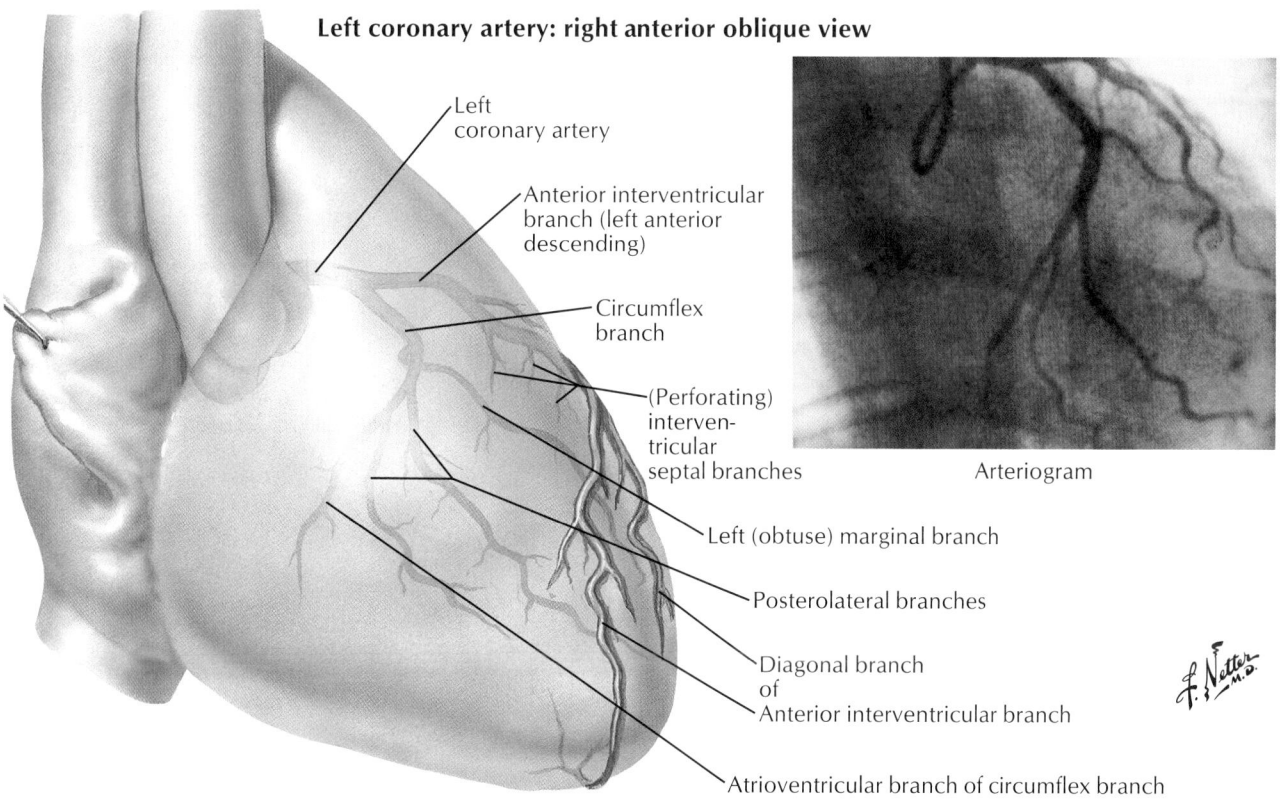

Left coronary artery

Anterior interventricular branch (left anterior descending)

Circumflex branch

(Perforating) interventricular septal branches

Arteriogram

Left (obtuse) marginal branch

Posterolateral branches

Diagonal branch of Anterior interventricular branch

Atrioventricular branch of circumflex branch

Plate 219 Coronary Arteries: Arteriographic Views. (Netter: Atlas of Human Anatomy, 4 ed, 2006, Saunders.)

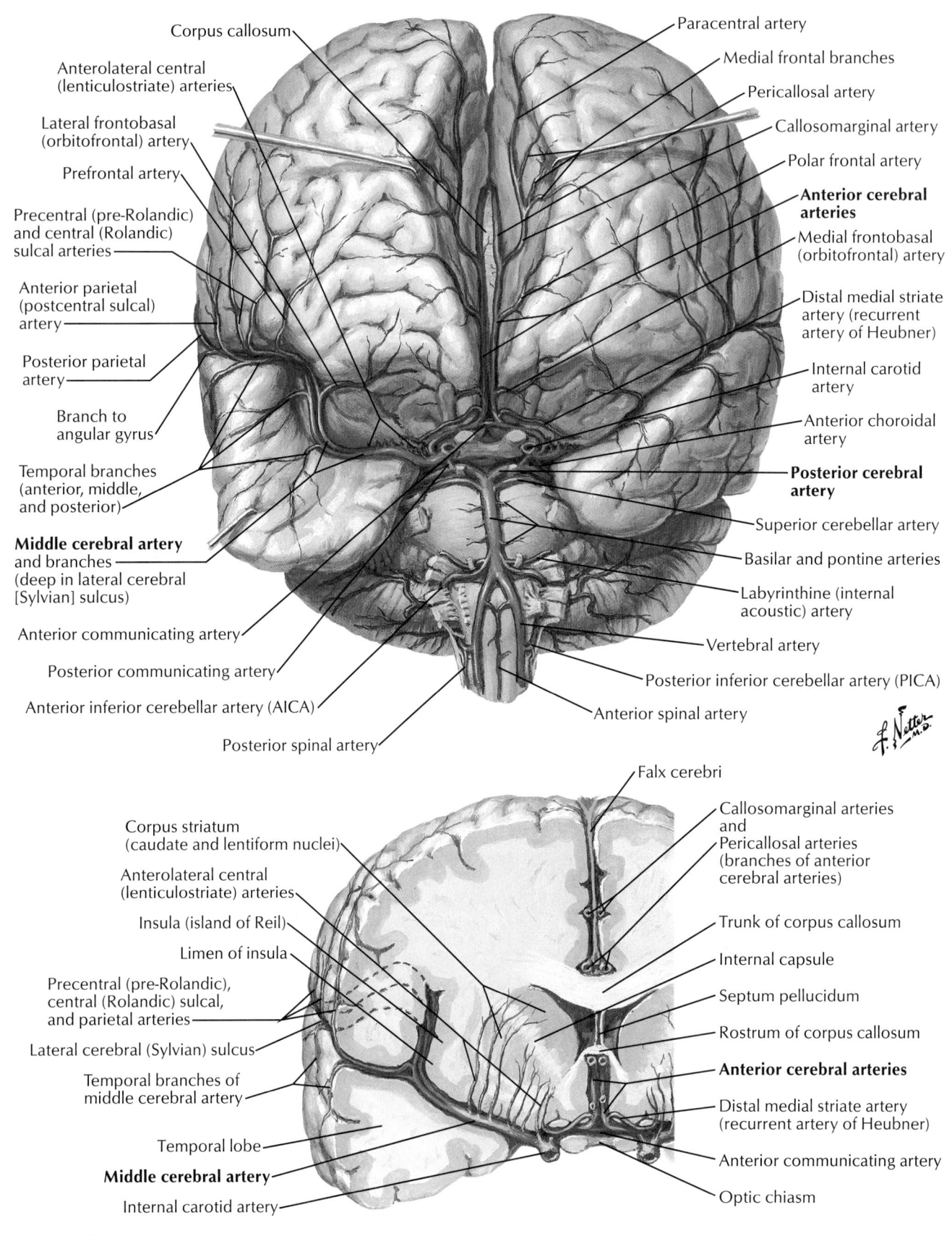

Corpus callosum

Anterolateral central (lenticulostriate) arteries

Lateral frontobasal (orbitofrontal) artery

Prefrontal artery

Precentral (pre-Rolandic) and central (Rolandic) sulcal arteries

Anterior parietal (postcentral sulcal) artery

Posterior parietal artery

Branch to angular gyrus

Temporal branches (anterior, middle, and posterior)

Middle cerebral artery and branches (deep in lateral cerebral [Sylvian] sulcus)

Anterior communicating artery

Posterior communicating artery

Anterior inferior cerebellar artery (AICA)

Posterior spinal artery

Paracentral artery

Medial frontal branches

Pericallosal artery

Callosomarginal artery

Polar frontal artery

Anterior cerebral arteries

Medial frontobasal (orbitofrontal) artery

Distal medial striate artery (recurrent artery of Heubner)

Internal carotid artery

Anterior choroidal artery

Posterior cerebral artery

Superior cerebellar artery

Basilar and pontine arteries

Labyrinthine (internal acoustic) artery

Vertebral artery

Posterior inferior cerebellar artery (PICA)

Anterior spinal artery

Corpus striatum (caudate and lentiform nuclei)

Anterolateral central (lenticulostriate) arteries

Insula (island of Reil)

Limen of insula

Precentral (pre-Rolandic), central (Rolandic) sulcal, and parietal arteries

Lateral cerebral (Sylvian) sulcus

Temporal branches of middle cerebral artery

Temporal lobe

Middle cerebral artery

Internal carotid artery

Falx cerebri

Callosomarginal arteries and Pericallosal arteries (branches of anterior cerebral arteries)

Trunk of corpus callosum

Internal capsule

Septum pellucidum

Rostrum of corpus callosum

Anterior cerebral arteries

Distal medial striate artery (recurrent artery of Heubner)

Anterior communicating artery

Optic chiasm

Plate 141   Arteries of Brain: Frontal View and Section. (Netter: Atlas of Human Anatomy, 4 ed, 2006, Saunders.)

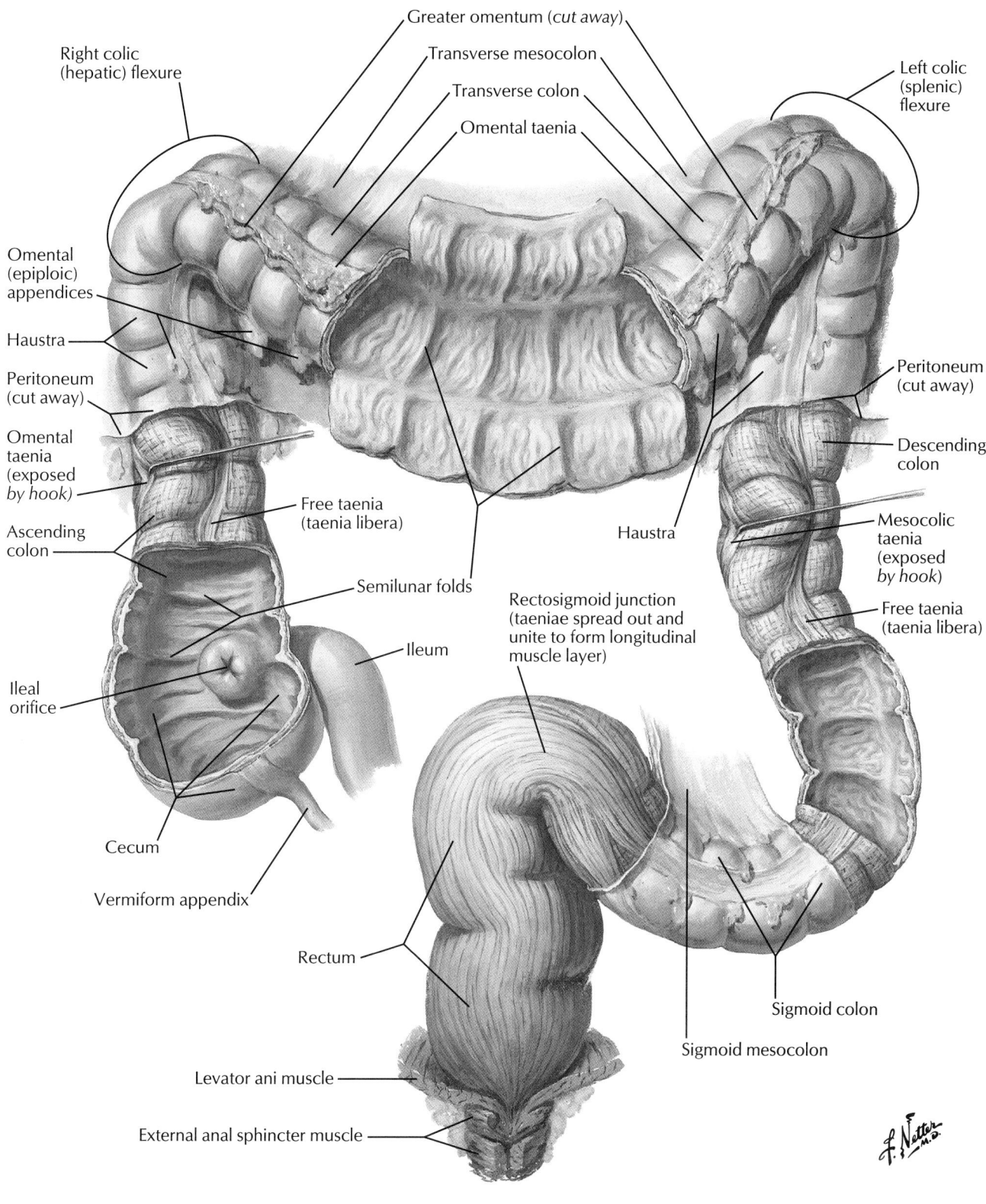

Right colic
(hepatic) flexure

Greater omentum (*cut away*)

Transverse mesocolon

Transverse colon

Omental taenia

Left colic
(splenic)
flexure

Omental
(epiploic)
appendices

Haustra

Peritoneum
(cut away)

Omental
taenia
(exposed
by hook)

Ascending
colon

Free taenia
(taenia libera)

Semilunar folds

Ileum

Haustra

Peritoneum
(cut away)

Descending
colon

Mesocolic
taenia
(exposed
by hook)

Free taenia
(taenia libera)

Ileal
orifice

Rectosigmoid junction
(taeniae spread out and
unite to form longitudinal
muscle layer)

Cecum

Vermiform appendix

Rectum

Sigmoid colon

Sigmoid mesocolon

Levator ani muscle

External anal sphincter muscle

Plate 284   Mucosa and Musculature of Large Intestine. (Netter: Atlas of Human Anatomy, 4 ed, 2006, Saunders.)

NAP-29

NETTER ANATOMY PLATE

Transverse Section: T3–4 Intervertebral Disc, Manubrium

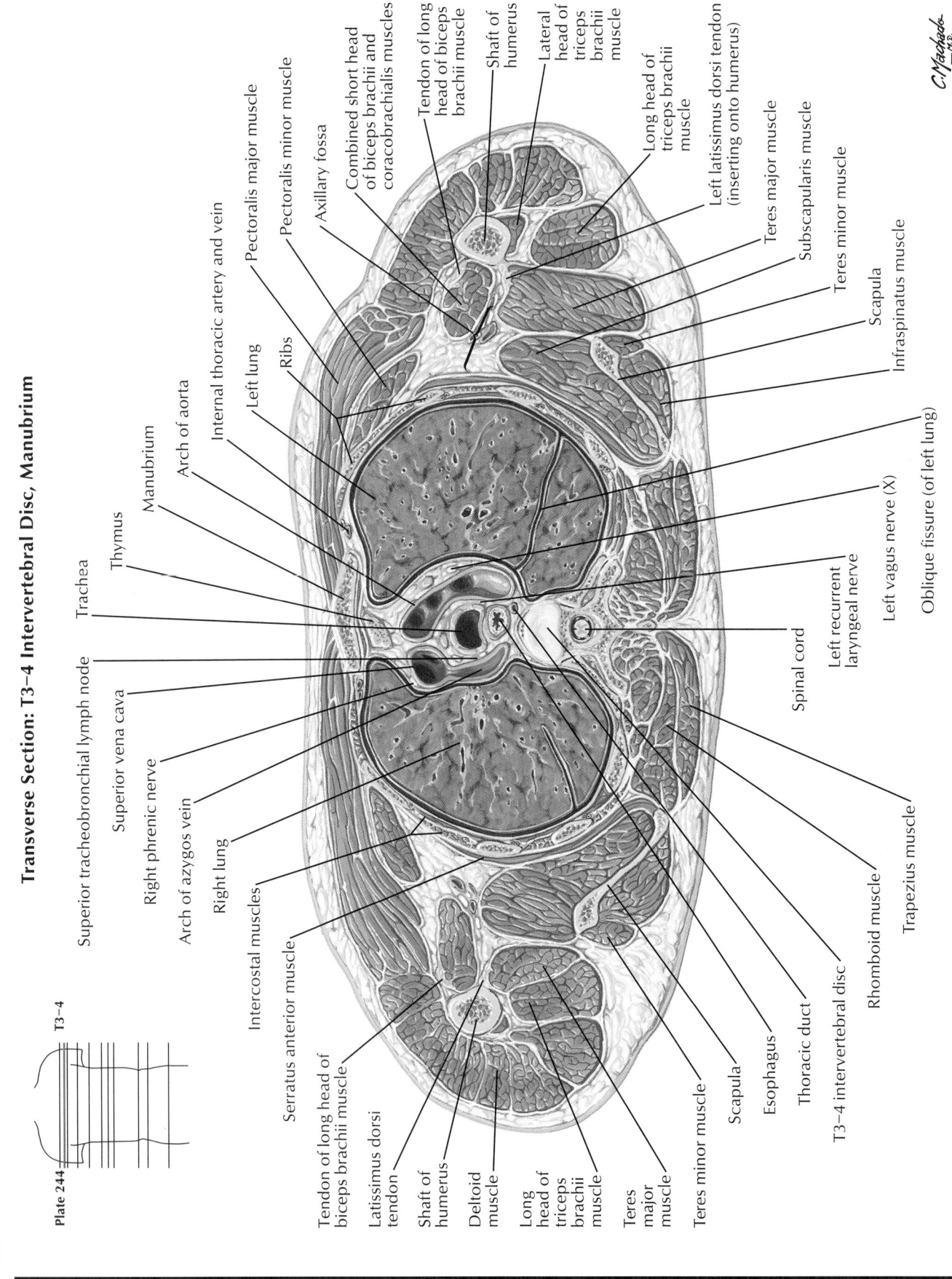

Plate 244

T3–4

Combined short head of biceps brachii and coracobrachialis muscles

Pectoralis minor muscle

Pectoralis major muscle

Tendon of long head of biceps brachii muscle

Shaft of humerus

Lateral head of triceps brachii muscle

Long head of triceps brachii muscle

Left latissimus dorsi tendon (inserting onto humerus)

Teres major muscle

Subscapularis muscle

Teres minor muscle

Scapula

Infraspinatus muscle

Axillary fossa

Internal thoracic artery and vein

Left lung

Ribs

Arch of aorta

Manubrium

Thymus

Trachea

Superior tracheobronchial lymph node

Superior vena cava

Right phrenic nerve

Arch of azygos vein

Right lung

Intercostal muscles

Serratus anterior muscle

Tendon of long head of biceps brachii muscle

Latissimus dorsi tendon

Shaft of humerus

Deltoid muscle

Long head of triceps brachii muscle

Teres major muscle

Teres minor muscle

Scapula

Esophagus

Thoracic duct

T3–4 intervertebral disc

Rhomboid muscle

Trapezius muscle

Spinal cord

Left recurrent laryngeal nerve

Left vagus nerve (X)

Oblique fissure (of left lung)

Plate 244 Cross Section of Thorax at T3-4 Disc Level. (Netter: Atlas of Human Anatomy, 4 ed, 2006, Saunders.)

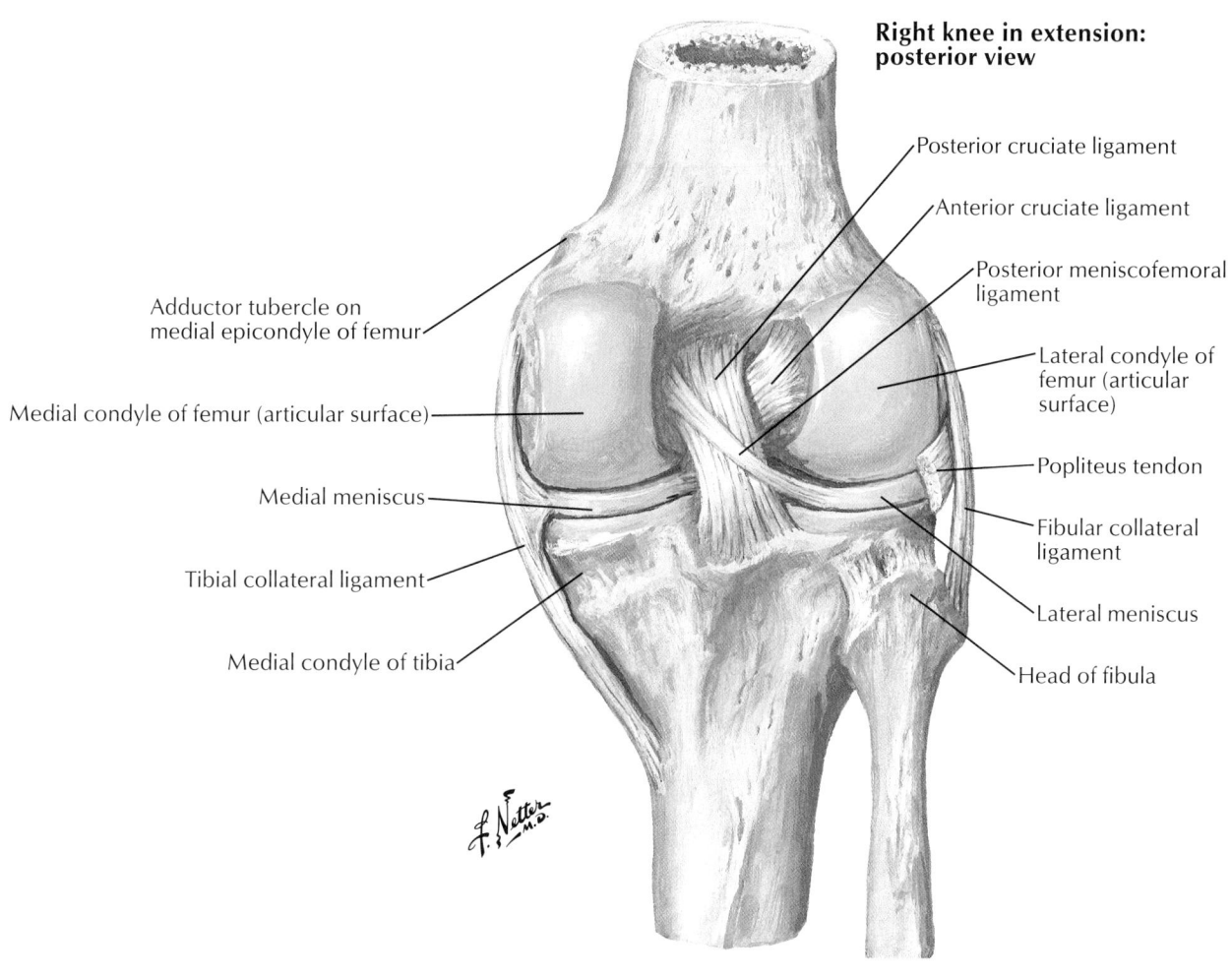

Right knee in extension: posterior view

Posterior cruciate ligament

Anterior cruciate ligament

Posterior meniscofemoral ligament

Adductor tubercle on medial epicondyle of femur

Lateral condyle of femur (articular surface)

Medial condyle of femur (articular surface)

Popliteus tendon

Medial meniscus

Fibular collateral ligament

Tibial collateral ligament

Lateral meniscus

Medial condyle of tibia

Head of fibula

Plate 509   Knee: Cruciate and Collateral Ligaments. (Netter: Atlas of Human Anatomy, 4 ed, 2006, Saunders.)

Paramedian (sagittal) dissection

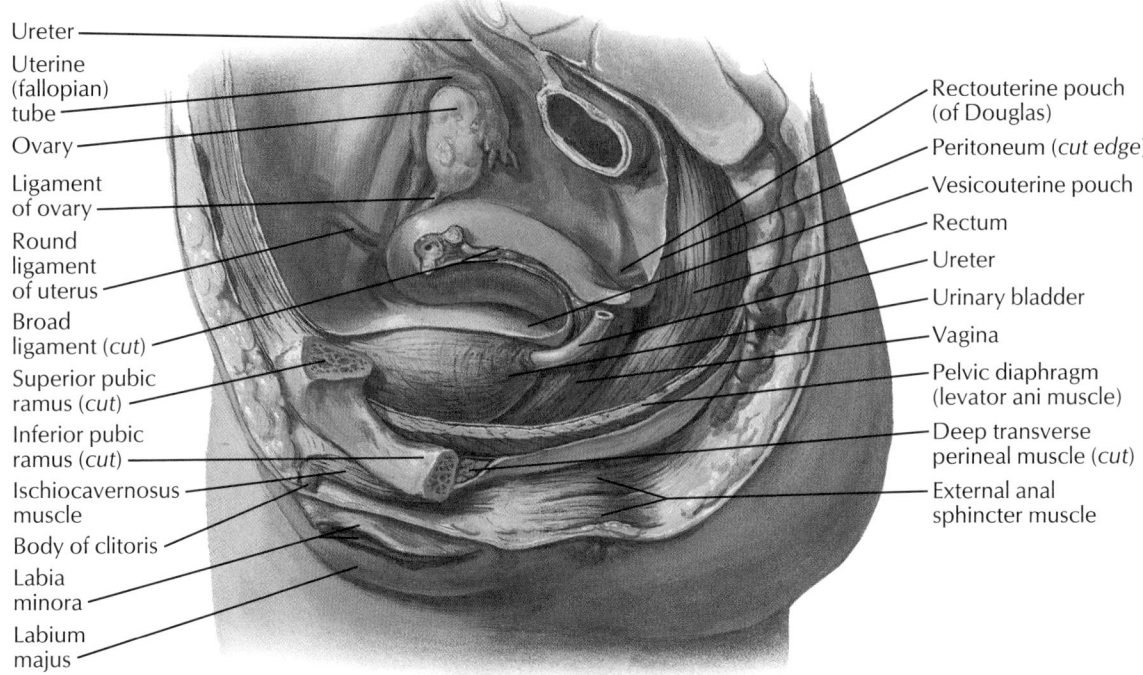

Ureter

Uterine (fallopian) tube

Ovary

Ligament of ovary

Round ligament of uterus

Broad ligament (*cut*)

Superior pubic ramus (*cut*)

Inferior pubic ramus (*cut*)

Ischiocavernosus muscle

Body of clitoris

Labia minora

Labium majus

Rectouterine pouch (of Douglas)

Peritoneum (*cut edge*)

Vesicouterine pouch

Rectum

Ureter

Urinary bladder

Vagina

Pelvic diaphragm (levator ani muscle)

Deep transverse perineal muscle (*cut*)

External anal sphincter muscle

Median (sagittal) section

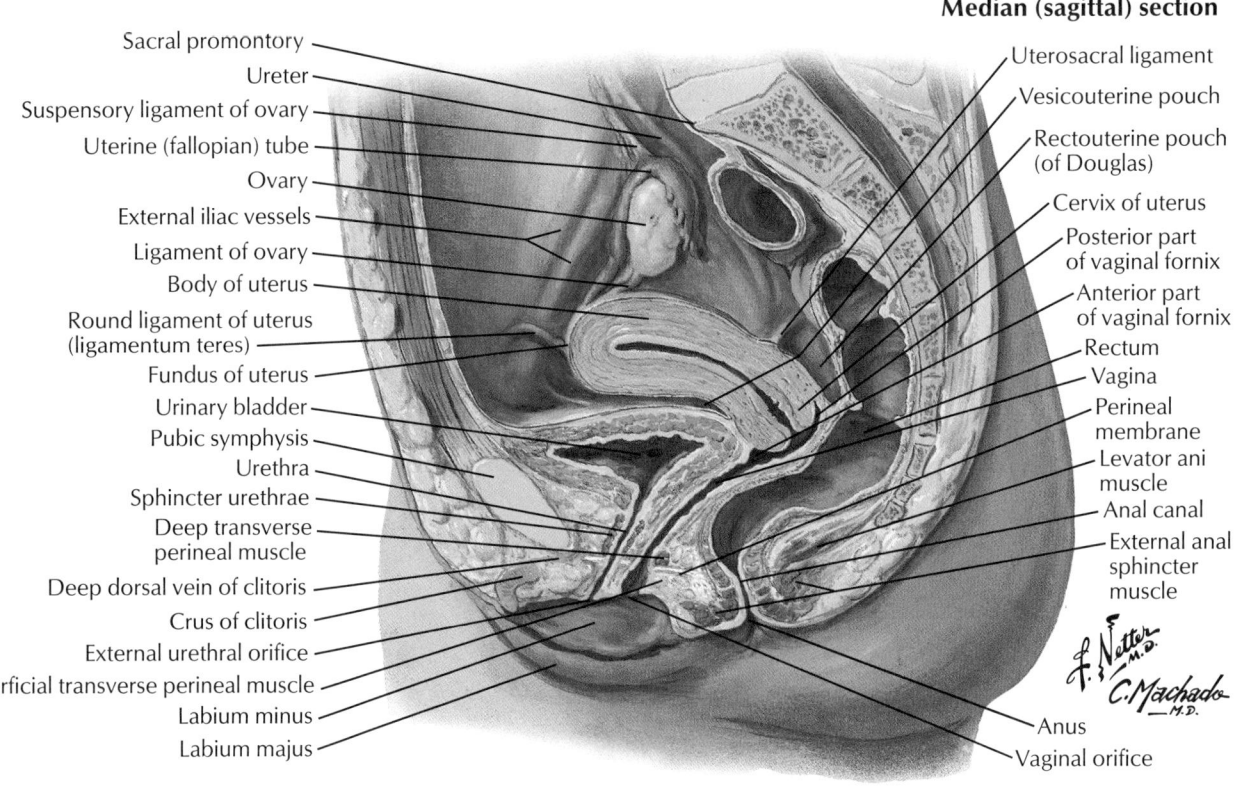

Sacral promontory

Ureter

Suspensory ligament of ovary

Uterine (fallopian) tube

Ovary

External iliac vessels

Ligament of ovary

Body of uterus

Round ligament of uterus (ligamentum teres)

Fundus of uterus

Urinary bladder

Pubic symphysis

Urethra

Sphincter urethrae

Deep transverse perineal muscle

Deep dorsal vein of clitoris

Crus of clitoris

External urethral orifice

Superficial transverse perineal muscle

Labium minus

Labium majus

Uterosacral ligament

Vesicouterine pouch

Rectouterine pouch (of Douglas)

Cervix of uterus

Posterior part of vaginal fornix

Anterior part of vaginal fornix

Rectum

Vagina

Perineal membrane

Levator ani muscle

Anal canal

External anal sphincter muscle

Anus

Vaginal orifice

Plate 360   Pelvic Viscera and Perineum: Female. (Netter: Atlas of Human Anatomy, 4 ed, 2006, Saunders.)

PART II

Alphabetic Index

A

Aarskog's syndrome Q87.1
Abandonment - *see* Maltreatment, abandonment
Abasia (-astasia) (hysterical) F44.4
Abderhalden-Kaufmann-Lignac syndrome (cystinosis) E72.04
Abdomen, abdominal - *see also* condition
  acute R10.0
  angina K55.1
  muscle deficiency syndrome Q79.4
Abdominalgia - *see* Pain, abdominal
Abduction contracture, hip or other joint - *see* Contraction, joint
Aberrant (congenital) - *see also* Malposition, congenital
  adrenal gland Q89.1
  artery (peripheral) Q27.8
    basilar NEC Q28.1
    cerebral Q28.3
    coronary Q24.5
    digestive system Q27.8
    eye Q15.8
    lower limb Q27.8
    precerebral Q28.1
    pulmonary Q25.7
    renal Q27.2
    retina Q14.1
    specified site NEC Q27.8
    subclavian Q27.8
    upper limb Q27.8
    vertebral Q28.1
  breast Q83.8
  endocrine gland NEC Q89.2
  hepatic duct Q44.5
  pancreas Q45.3
  parathyroid gland Q89.2
  pituitary gland Q89.2
  sebaceous glands, mucous membrane, mouth, congenital Q38.6
  spleen Q89.09
  subclavian artery Q27.8
  thymus (gland) Q89.2
  thyroid gland Q89.2
  vein (peripheral) NEC Q27.8
    cerebral Q28.3
    digestive system Q27.8
    lower limb Q27.8
    precerebral Q28.1
    specified site NEC Q27.8
    upper limb Q27.8
Aberration
  distantial - *see* Disturbance, visual
  mental F99
Abetalipoproteinemia E78.6
Abiotrophy R68.89
Ablatio, ablation
  retinae - *see* Detachment, retina
Ablepharia, ablepharon Q10.3
Abnormal, abnormality, abnormalities - *see also* Anomaly
  acid-base balance (mixed) E87.4
  albumin R77.0
  alphafetoprotein R77.2
  alveolar ridge K08.9
  anatomical relationship Q89.9
  apertures, congenital, diaphragm Q79.1
  auditory perception H93.29-
    diplacusis - *see* Diplacusis
    hyperacusis - *see* Hyperacusis
    recruitment - *see* Recruitment, auditory

Abnormal, abnormality, abnormalities *(Continued)*
  auditory perception *(Continued)*
    threshold shift - *see* Shift, auditory threshold
  autosomes Q99.9
    fragile site Q95.5
  basal metabolic rate R94.8
  biosynthesis, testicular androgen E29.1
  bleeding time R79.1
  blood-gas level R79.81
  blood level (of)
    cobalt R79.0
    copper R79.0
    iron R79.0
    lithium R78.89
    magnesium R79.0
    mineral NEC R79.0
    zinc R79.0
  blood pressure
    elevated R03.0
    low reading (nonspecific) R03.1
  blood sugar R73.09
  bowel sounds R19.15
    absent R19.11
    hyperactive R19.12
  brain scan R94.02
  breathing R06.9
  caloric test R94.138
  cerebrospinal fluid R83.9
    cytology R83.6
    drug level R83.2
    enzyme level R83.0
    hormones R83.1
    immunology R83.4
    microbiology R83.5
    nonmedicinal level R83.3
    specified type NEC R83.8
  chemistry, blood R79.9
    C-reactive protein R79.82
    drugs - *see* Findings, abnormal, in blood
    gas level R79.81
    minerals R79.0
    pancytopenia R79.1
    specified NEC R79.89
    PTT R79.1
    toxins - *see* Findings, abnormal, in blood
  chest sounds (friction) (rales) R09.89
  chromosome, chromosomal Q99.9
    with more than three X chromosomes, female Q97.1
    analysis result R89.8
      bronchial washings R84.8
      cerebrospinal fluid R83.8
      cervix uteri NEC R87.89
      nasal secretions R84.8
      nipple discharge R89.8
      peritoneal fluid R85.89
      pleural fluid R84.8
      prostatic secretions R86.8
      saliva R85.89
      seminal fluid R86.8
      sputum R84.8
      synovial fluid R89.8
      throat scrapings R84.8
      vagina R87.89
      vulva R87.89
      wound secretions R89.8
    dicentric replacement Q93.2
    ring replacement Q93.2

Abnormal, abnormality, abnormalities *(Continued)*
  chromosome, chromosomal *(Continued)*
    sex Q99.8
      female phenotype Q97.9
        specified NEC Q97.8
      male phenotype Q98.9
        specified NEC Q98.8
      structural male Q98.6
      specified NEC Q99.8
  clinical findings NEC R68.89
  coagulation D68.9
    newborn, transient P61.6
    profile R79.1
    time R79.1
  communication - *see* Fistula
  conjunctiva, vascular H11.41-
  coronary artery Q24.5
  cortisol-binding globulin E27.8
  course, eustachian tube Q17.8
  creatinine clearance R94.4
  cytology
    anus R85.619
      atypical squamous cells cannot exclude high grade squamous intraepithelial lesion (ASC-H) R85.611
      atypical squamous cells of undetermined significance (ASC-US) R85.610
      cytologic evidence of malignancy R85.614
      high grade squamous intraepithelial lesion (HGSIL) R85.613
      human papillomavirus (HPV) DNA test
        high risk positive R85.81
        low risk postive R85.82
      inadequate smear R85.615
      low grade squamous intraepithelial lesion (LGSIL) R85.612
      satisfactory cervical smear but lacking transformation zone R85.616
      specified NEC R85.618
      unsatisfactory smear R85.615
  dark adaptation curve H53.61
  dentofacial NEC - *see* Anomaly, dentofacial
  development, developmental Q89.9
    central nervous system Q07.9
  diagnostic imaging
    abdomen, abdominal region NEC R93.5
    biliary tract R93.2
    breast R92.8
    central nervous system NEC R90.89
    cerebrovascular NEC R90.89
    coronary circulation R93.1
    digestive tract NEC R93.3
    gastrointestinal (tract) R93.3
    genitourinary organs R93.8
    head R93.0
    heart R93.1
    intrathoracic organ NEC R93.8
    limbs R93.6
    liver R93.2
    lung (field) R91
    musculoskeletal system NEC R93.7
    retroperitoneum R93.5
    sites specified NEC R93.8
    skin and subcutaneous tissue R93.8
    skull R93.0
    urinary organs R93.4

Abnormal, abnormality, abnormalities
(Continued)
  direction, teeth, fully erupted M26.30
  ear ossicles, acquired NEC H74.39-
    ankylosis - *see* Ankylosis, ear ossicles
    discontinuity - *see* Discontinuity, ossicles, ear
    partial loss - *see* Loss, ossicles, ear (partial)
  Ebstein Q22.5
  echocardiogram R93.1
  echoencephalogram R90.81
  echogram - *see* Abnormal, diagnostic imaging
  electrocardiogram [ECG] [EKG] R94.31
  electroencephalogram [EEG] R94.01
  electrolyte - *see* Imbalance, electrolyte
  electromyogram [EMG] R94.131
  electro-oculogram [EOG] R94.110
  electrophysiological intracardiac studies R94.39
  electroretinogram [ERG] R94.111
  erythrocytes
    congenital, with perinatal jaundice D58.9
  feces (color) (contents) (mucus) R19.5
  finding - *see* Findings, abnormal, without diagnosis
  fluid
    amniotic – *see* Abnormal, specimen, specified
    cerebrospinal – *see* Abnormal, cerebrospinal fluid
    peritoneal – *see* Abnormal, specimen, digestive organs
    pleural – *see* Abnormal, specimen, respiratory organs
    synovial – *see* Abnormal, specimen, specified
    thorax (bronchial washings) (pleural fluid) – *see* Abnormal, specimen, respiratory organs
    vaginal – *see* Abnormal, specimen, female genital organs
  form
    teeth K00.2
    uterus - *see* Anomaly, uterus
  function studies
    auditory R94.120
    bladder R94.8
    brain R94.09
    cardiovascular R94.30
    ear R94.128
    endocrine NEC R94.7
    eye NEC R94.118
    kidney R94.4
    liver R94.5
    nervous system
      central NEC R94.09
      peripheral NEC R94.138
    pancreas R94.8
    placenta R94.8
    pulmonary R94.2
    special senses NEC R94.128
    spleen R94.8
    thyroid R94.6
    vestibular R94.121
  gait - *see* Gait
    hysterical F44.4
  gastrin secretion E16.4
  globulin R77.1
    cortisol-binding E27.8
    thyroid-binding E07.89

Abnormal, abnormality, abnormalities
(Continued)
  glomerular, minor (*see also* N00-N07 with fourth character .0) N05.0
  glucagon secretion E16.3
  glucose tolerance (test) (non-fasting) R73.09
  gravitational (G) forces or states (effect of) T75.81
  hair (color) (shaft) L67.9
    specified NEC L67.8
  hard tissue formation in pulp (dental) K04.3
  head movement R25.0
  heart
    rate R00.9
      specified NEC R00.8
    shadow R93.1
    sounds NEC R01.2
  hemoglobin (disease) (*see also* Disease, hemoglobin) D58.2
    trait - *see* Trait, hemoglobin, abnormal
  histology NEC R89.7
  immunological findings R89.4
    in serum R76.9
      specified NEC R76.8
  increase in appetite R63.2
  involuntary movement - *see* Abnormal, movement, involuntary
  jaw closure M26.51
  karyotype R89.8
  kidney function test R94.4
  knee jerk R29.2
  leukocyte (cell) (differential) NEC D72.9
  liver
  loss of
    height R29.890
    weight R63.4
  mammogram NEC R92.8
    calcification (calculus) R92.1
    microcalcification R92.0
  Mantoux test R76.1
  movement (disorder) - *see also* Disorder, movement
    head R25.0
    involuntary R25.9
      fasciculation R25.3
      of head R25.0
      spasm R25.2
      specified type NEC R25.8
      tremor R25.1
  myoglobin (Aberdeen) (Annapolis) R89.7
  neonatal screening P09
  oculomotor study R94.113
  palmar creases Q82.8
  Papanicolaou (smear)
    anus R85.619
      atypical squamous cells cannot exclude high grade squamous intraepithelial lesion (ASC-H) R85.611
      atypical squamous cells of undetermined significance (ASC-US) R85.610
      cytologic evidence of malignancy R85.614
      high grade squamous intraepithelial lesion (HGSIL) R85.613
      human papillomavirus (HPV) DNA test
        high risk positive R85.81
        low risk postive R85.82
      inadequate smear R85.615

Abnormal, abnormality, abnormalities
(Continued)
  Papanicolaou *(Continued)*
    anus *(Continued)*
      low grade squamous intraepithelial lesion (LGSIL) R85.612
      satisfactory cervical smear but lacking transformation zone R85.616
      specified NEC R85.618
      unsatisfactory smear R85.615
    bronchial washings R84.6
    cerebrospinal fluid R83.6
    cervix R87.619
      atypical squamous cells cannot exclude high grade squamous intraepithelial lesion (ASC-H) R87.611
      atypical squamous cells of undetermined significance (ASC-US) R87.610
      cytologic evidence of malignancy R87.614
      high grade squamous intraepithelial lesion (HGSIL) R87.613
      inadequate smear R87.615
      low grade squamous intraepithelial lesion (LGSIL) R87.612
      satisfactory cervical smear but lacking transformation zone R87.616
      specified NEC R87.618
      thin preparaton R87.619
      unsatisfactory smear R87.615
    nasal secretions R84.6
    nipple discharge R89.6
    peritoneal fluid R85.69
    pleural fluid R84.6
    prostatic secretions R86.6
    saliva R85.69
    seminal fluid R86.6
    sites NEC R89.6
    sputum R84.6
    synovial fluid R89.6
    throat scrapings R84.6
    vagina R87.629
      atypical squamous cells cannot exclude high grade squamous intraepithelial lesion (ASC-H) R87.621
      atypical squamous cells of undetermined significance (ASC-US) R87.620
      cytologic evidence of malignancy R87.624
      high grade squamous intraepithelial lesion (HGSIL) R87.623
      inadequate smear R87.625
      low grade squamous intraepithelial lesion (LGSIL) R87.622
      specified NEC R87.628
      thin preparation R87.629
      unsatisfactory smear R87.625
    vulva R87.69
    wound secretions R89.6
  partial thromboplastin time (PTT) R79.1
  plantar reflex R29.2
  pelvis (bony) - *see* Deformity, pelvis
  percussion, chest (tympany) R09.89
  periods (grossly) - *see* Menstruation
  phonocardiogram R94.39
  plasma
    protein R77.9
      specified NEC R77.8
    viscosity R70.1

59

Abnormal, abnormality, abnormalities
(Continued)
pleural (folds) Q34.0
posture R29.3
product of conception O02.9
    specified type NEC O02.8
prothrombin time (PT) R79.1
pulmonary
    artery, congenital Q25.7
    function, newborn P28.89
    test results R94.2
pulsations in neck R00.2
pupillary H21.56-
    function (reaction) (reflex) - see
        Anomaly, pupil, function
radiological examination - see Abnormal, diagnostic imaging
red blood cell(s) (morphology)
    (volume) R71.8
reflex - see Reflex
renal function test R94.4
response to nerve stimulation
    R94.130
retinal correspondence H53.31
retinal function study R94.111
rhythm, heart - see also Arrhythmia
saliva - see Abnormal, specimen, digestive organs
scan
    kidney R94.4
    liver R94.2
    thyroid R94.6
secretion
    gastrin E16.4
    glucagon E16.3
semen, seminal fluid - see Abnormal, specimen, male genital organs
serum level (of)
    acid phosphatase R74.8
    alkaline phosphatase R74.8
    amylase R74.8
    enzymes R74.9
        specified NEC R74.8
    lipase R74.8
    triacylglycerol lipase R74.8
shape
    gravid uterus - see Anomaly, uterus
sinus venosus Q21.1
size, tooth, teeth K00.2
spacing, tooth, teeth, fully erupted
    M26.30
specimen
    digestive organs (peritoneal fluid)
        (saliva) R85.9
        cytology R85.69
        drug level R85.2
        enzyme level R85.0
        histology R85.7
        hormones R85.1
        immunology R85.4
        microbiology R85.5
        nonmedicinal level R85.3
        specified type NEC R85.89
    female genital organs (secretions)
        (smears) R87.9
        cytology R87.60
            cervix R87.619
                inadequate (unsatisfactory)
                    smear R87.615
                human papillomavirus (HPV)
                    DNA test
                    high risk positive R87.810
                    low risk positive R87.820
                specified NEC R87.89

Abnormal, abnormality, abnormalities
(Continued)
specimen (Continued)
    female genital organs (Continued)
        cytology (Continued)
            vagina R87.629
                inadequate (unsatisfactory)
                    smear R87.625
                human papillomavirus (HPV)
                    DNA test
                    high risk positive R87.811
                    low risk positive R87.821
            vulva R87.69
        drug level R87.2
        enzyme level R87.0
        histological R87.7
        hormones R87.1
        immunology R87.4
        microbiology R87.5
        nonmedicinal level R87.3
        specified type NEC R87.89
    male genital organs (prostatic secretions) (semen) R86.9
        cytology R86.6
        drug level R86.2
        enzyme level R86.0
        histological R86.7
        hormones R86.1
        immunology R86.4
        microbiology R86.5
        nonmedicinal level R86.3
        specified type NEC R86.8
    nipple discharge - see Abnormal, specimen, specified
    respiratory organs (bronchial
        washings) (nasal secretions)
        (pleural fluid) (sputum)
        R84.9
        cytology R84.6
        drug level R84.2
        enzyme level R84.0
        histology R84.7
        hormones R84.1
        immunology R84.4
        microbiology R84.5
        nonmedicinal level R84.3
        specified type NEC R84.8
    specified fluid, organ, system and
        tissue NOS R89.9
        cytology R89.6
        drug level R89.2
        enzyme level R89.0
        histology R89.7
        hormones R89.1
        immunology R89.4
        microbiology R89.5
        nonmedicinal level R89.3
        specified type NEC R89.8
    synovial fluid - see Abnormal, specimen, specified
    thorax (bronchial washings) (pleural
        fluids) - see Abnormal, specimen, respiratory organs
    vagina (secretion) (smear) R87.629
    vulva (secretion) (smear) R87.69
    wound secretion - see Abnormal, specimen, specified
    spermatozoa - see Abnormal, specimen, male genital organs
    sputum (amount) (color) (odor) R09.3
    stool (color) (contents) (mucus) R19.5
        bloody K92.1
        guaiac positive R19.5
    synchondrosis Q78.8

Abnormal, abnormality, abnormalities
(Continued)
thermography - see Abnormal, diagnostic imaging
thyroid-binding globulin E07.89
tooth, teeth (form) (size) K00.2
toxicology (findings) R78.9
transport protein E88.09
tumor marker NEC R97.8
ultrasound results - see Abnormal, diagnostic imaging
umbilical cord complicating delivery
    O69.9
urination NEC R39.19
urine (constituents) R82.90
    bile R82.2
    cytological examination R82.8
    drugs R82.5
    fat R82.0
    glucose R81
    heavy metals R82.6
    hemoglobin R82.3
    histological examination R82.8
    ketones R82.4
    microbiological examination (culture)
        R82.7
    myoglobin R82.1
    positive culture R82.7
    protein – see Proteinuria
    specified substance NEC R82.99
        chromoabnormality NEC R82.91
    substances nonmedical R82.6
uterine hemorrhage – see Hemorrhage,
    uterus
vectorcardiogram R94.39
visually evoked potential (VEP)
    R94.112
white blood cells D72.9
    specified NEC D72.89
weight
    gain R63.5
    loss R63.4
X-ray examination - see Abnormal,
    diagnostic imaging
Abnormity (any organ or part) - see
    Anomaly
Abocclusion M26.29
    hemolytic disease (newborn) P55.1
    incompatibility reaction ABO T80.3
Abolition, language R48.8
Aborter, habitual or recurrent
    without current pregnancy N96
    care in current pregnancy O26.2-
Abortion (complete) (spontaneous)
    O03.9
    attempted (elective) (failed) O07.4
        complicated by
            afibrinogenemia O07.1
            cardiac arrest O07.36
            chemical damage of pelvic organ(s)
                O07.34
            circulatory collapse O07.31
            cystitis O07.38
            defibrination syndrome O07.1
            electrolyte imbalance O07.39
            embolism (air) (amniotic fluid)
                (blood clot) (fat) (pulmonary)
                (septic) (soap) O07.2
            endometritis O07.0
            genital tract and pelvic infection
                O07.0
            hemorrhage (delayed) (excessive)
                O07.1
            hemolysis O07.1

Abortion *(Continued)*
 attempted *(Continued)*
  complicated by *(Continued)*
   infection
    genital tract or pelvic O07.0
    urinary tract tract O07.38
   intravascular coagulation O07.1
   laceration of pelvic organ(s) O07.34
   metabolic disorder O07.33
   oliguria O07.32
   oophoritis O07.0
   parametritis O07.0
   pelvic peritonitis O07.0
   perforation of pelvic organ(s)
    O07.34
   renal failure or shutdown O07.32
   salpingitis or salpingo-oophoritis
    O07.0
   sepsis O07.37
   shock O07.31
   specified condition NEC O07.39
   tubular necrosis (renal) O07.32
   uremia O07.32
   urinary tract infection O07.38
   venous complication NEC
    O07.35
    embolism (air) (amniotic fluid)
     (blood clot) (fat) (pulmo-
     nary) (septic) (soap) O07.2
 complicated (by) (following) O03.80
  afibrinogenemia O03.6
  cardiac arrest O03.86
  chemical damage of pelvic organ(s)
   O03.84
  circulatory collapse O03.81
  cystitis O03.88
  defibrination syndrome O03.6
  electrolyte imbalance O03.89
  embolism (air) (amniotic fluid) (blood
   clot) (fat) (pulmonary) (septic)
   (soap) O03.7
  endometritis O03.5
  genital tract and pelvic infection
   O03.5
  hemolysis O03.6
  hemorrhage (delayed) (excessive)
   O03.6
  infection
   genital tract or pelvic O03.5
   urinary tract O03.88
  intravascular coagulation O03.6
  laceration of pelvic organ(s)
   O03.84
  metabolic disorder O03.83
  oliguria O03.82
  oophoritis O03.5
  parametritis O03.5
  pelvic peritonitis O03.5
  perforation of pelvic organ(s)
   O03.84
  renal failure or shutdown O03.82
  salpingitis or salpingo-oophoritis
   O03.5
  sepsis O03.87
  shock O03.81
  specified condition NEC O03.89
  tubular necrosis (renal) O03.82
  uremia O03.82
  urinary tract infection O03.88
  venous complication NEC O03.85
   embolism (air) (amniotic fluid)
    (blood clot) (fat) (pulmonary)
    (septic) (soap) O03.7
 failed - *see* Abortion, attempted

Abortion *(Continued)*
 habitual or recurrent N96
  with current abortion - *see* categories
   O03-O06
  without current pregnancy N96
  care in current pregnancy O26.2-
 incomplete (spontaneous) O03.4
  complicated (by) (following)
   O03.30
   afibrinogenemia O03.1
   cardiac arrest O03.36
   chemical damage of pelvic organ(s)
    O03.34
   circulatory collapse O03.31
   cystitis O03.38
   defibrination syndrome O03.1
   electrolyte imbalance O03.39
   embolism (air) (amniotic fluid)
    (blood clot) (fat) (pulmonary)
    (septic) (soap) O03.2
   endometritis O03.0
   genital tract and pelvic infection
    O03.0
   hemolysis O03.1
   hemorrhage (delayed) (excessive)
    O03.1
   infection
    genital tract or pelvic O03.0
    urinary tract O03.38
   intravascular coagulation O03.1
   laceration of pelvic organ(s)
    O03.34
   metabolic disorder O03.33
   oliguria O03.32
   oophoritis O03.0
   parametritis O03.0
   pelvic peritonitis O03.0
   perforation of pelvic organ(s)
    O03.34
   renal failure or shutdown O03.32
   salpingitis or salpingo-oophoritis
    O03.0
   sepsis O03.37
   shock O03.31
   specified condition NEC O03.39
   tubular necrosis (renal) O03.32
   uremia O03.32
   urinary infection O03.38
   venous complication NEC O03.35
    embolism (air) (amniotic fluid)
     (blood clot) (fat) (pulmo-
     nary) (septic) (soap) O03.2
 induced (encounter for) Z33.2
  complicated by O04.80
   afibrinogenemia O04.6
   cardiac arrest O04.86
   chemical damage of pelvic organ(s)
    O04.84
   circulatory collapse O04.81
   cystitis O04.88
   defibrination syndrome O04.6
   electrolyte imbalance O04.89
   embolism (air) (amniotic fluid)
    (blood clot) (fat) (pulmonary)
    (septic) (soap) O04.7
   endometritis O04.5
   genital tract and pelvic infection
    O04.5
   hemolysis O04.6
   hemorrhage (delayed) (excessive)
    O04.6
   infection
    genital tract or pelvic O04.5
    urinary tract O04.88

Abortion *(Continued)*
 induced *(Continued)*
  complicated by *(Continued)*
   intravascular coagulation O04.6
   laceration of pelvic organ(s)
    O04.84
   metabolic disorder O04.83
   oliguria O04.82
   oophoritis O04.5
   parametritis O04.5
   pelvic peritonitis O04.5
   perforation of pelvic organ(s)
    O04.84
   renal failure or shutdown O04.82
   salpingitis or salpingo-oophoritis
    O04.5
   sepsis O04.87
   shock O04.81
   specified condition NEC O04.89
   tubular necrosis (renal) O04.82
   uremia O04.82
   urinary tract infection O04.88
   venous complication NEC
    O04.85
    embolism (air) (amniotic fluid)
     (blood clot) (fat) (pulmo-
     nary) (septic) (soap) O04.7
  missed O02.1
  spontaneous - *see* Abortion (complete)
   (spontaneous)
  threatened O20.0
  threatened (spontaneous) O20.0
  tubal O00.1
  with retained products of conception
   – *see* Abortion, incomplete
Abortus fever A23.1
Aboulomania F60.7
Abrami's disease D59.8
Abramov-Fiedler myocarditis (acute
  isolated myocarditis) I40.1
Abrasion
 abdomen, abdominal (wall) S30.811
 alveolar process S00.512
 ankle S90.51-
 antecubital space - *see* Abrasion, elbow
 anus S30.817
 arm (upper) S40.81-
 auditory canal – *see* Abrasion, ear
 auricle – *see* Abrasion, ear
 axilla – *see* Abrasion, arm
 back, lower S30.810
 breast S20.11-
 brow S00.81
 buttock S30.810
 calf – *see* Abrasion, leg
 canthus – *see* Abrasion, eyelid
 cheek S00.81
  internal S00.512
 chest wall – *see* Abrasion, thorax
 chin S00.81
 clitoris S30.814
 cornea S05.0-
 costal region - *see* Abrasion, thorax
 dental K03.1
 digit(s)
  foot - *see* Abrasion, toe
  hand – *see* Abrasion, finger
 ear S00.41-
 elbow S50.31-
 epididymis S30.813
 epigastric region S30.811
 epiglottis S10.11
 esophagus (thoracic) S27.818
  cervical S10.11

Abrasion *(Continued)*
  eyebrow – *see* Abrasion, eyelid
  eyelid S00.21-
  face S00.81
  finger(s) S60.41-
    index S60.41-
    little S60.41-
    middle S60.41-
    ring S60.41-
  flank S30.811
  foot (except toe(s) alone) S90.81-
    toe – *see* Abrasion, toe
  forearm S50.81-
    elbow only – *see* Abrasion, elbow
  forehead S00.81
  genital organs, external
    female S30.816
    male S30.815
  groin S30.811
  gum S00.512
  hand S60.51-
  head S00.91
    ear - *see* Abrasion, ear
    eyelid - *see* Abrasion, eyelid
    lip S00.511
    nose S00.31
    oral cavity S00.512
    scalp S00.01
    specified site NEC S00.81
  heel – *see* Abrasion, foot
  hip S70.21-
  inguinal region S30.811
  interscapular region S20.419
  jaw S00.81
  knee S80.21-
  labium (majus) (minus) S30.814
  larynx S10.11
  leg (lower) S80.81-
    knee – *see* Abrasion, knee
    upper - *see* Abrasion, thigh
  lip S00.511
  lower back S30.810
  lumbar region S30.810
  malar region S00.81
  mammary – *see* Abrasion, breast
  mastoid region S00.81
  mouth S00.512
  nail
    finger – *see* Abrasion, finger
    toe – *see* Abrasion, toe
  nape S10.81
  nasal S00.31
  neck S10.91
    specified site NEC S10.81
    throat S10.11
  nose S00.31
  occipital region S00.01
  oral cavity S00.512
  orbital region – *see* Abrasion, eyelid
  palate S00.512
  palm – *see* Abrasion, hand
  parietal region S00.01
  pelvis S30.810
  penis S30.812
  perineum
    female S30.814
    male S30.810
  periocular area – *see* Abrasion, eyelid
  phalanges
    finger – *see* Abrasion, finger
    toe – *see* Abrasion, toe
  pharynx S10.11
  pinna – *see* Abrasion, ear
  popliteal space – *see* Abrasion, knee

Abrasion *(Continued)*
  prepuce S30.812
  pubic region S30.810
  pudendum
    female S30.816
    male S30.815
  sacral region S30.810
  scalp S00.01
  scapular region – *see* Abrasion, shoulder
  scrotum S30.813
  shin – *see* Abrasion, leg
  shoulder S40.21-
  sternal region S20.319
  submaxillary region S00.81
  submental region S00.81
  subungual
    finger(s) – *see* Abrasion, finger
    toe(s) – *see* Abrasion, toe
  supraclavicular fossa S10.81
  supraorbital S00.81
  temple S00.81
  temporal region S00.81
  testis S30.813
  thigh S70.31-
  thorax, thoracic (wall) S20.91
    back S20.41
    front S20.31-
  throat S10.11
  thumb S60.31-
  toe(s) (lesser) S90.416
    great S90.41-
  tongue S00.512
  tooth, teeth (dentifrice) (habitual)
    (hard tissues) (occupational)
    (ritual) (traditional) K03.1
  trachea S10.11
  tunica vaginalis S30.813
  tympanum, tympanic membrane – *see*
    Abrasion, ear
  uvula S00.512
  vagina S30.814
  vocal cords S10.11
  vulva S30.814
  wrist S60.81-
Abrism - *see* Poisoning, food, noxious, plant
Abruptio placentae O45.9-
  with
    afibrinogenemia O45.01-
    coagulation defect O45.00-
      specified NEC O45.09-
    disseminated intravascular coagula-
      tion O45.02-
    hypofibrinogenemia O45.01-
  specified NEC O45.8-
Abruption, placenta - *see* Abruptio
  placentae
Abscess (connective tissue) (embolic) (fistulous) (infective) (metastatic) (multiple)
  (pernicious) (pyogenic) (septic) L02.91
  with
    diverticular disease (intestine) K57.80
      with bleeding K57.81
      large intestine K57.20
        with
          bleeding K57.21
          small intestine K57.40
            with bleeding K57.41
      small intestine K57.00
        with
          bleeding K57.01
          large intestine K57.40
            with bleeding K57.41
    lymphangitis - code by site under
      Abscess

Abscess *(Continued)*
  abdomen, abdominal
    cavity K65.1
    wall L02.211
  abdominopelvic K65.1
  accessory sinus – *see* Sinusitis
  adrenal (capsule) (gland) E27.8
  alveolar K04.7
    with sinus K04.6
  amebic A06.4
    brain (and liver or lung abscess)
      A06.6
    genitourinary tract A06.82
    liver (without mention of brain or
      lung abscess) A06.4
    lung (and liver) (without mention of
      brain abscess) A06.5
    specified site NEC A06.89
    spleen A06.89
  anerobic A48.0
  ankle - *see* Abscess, lower limb
  anorectal K61.2
  antecubital space - *see* Abscess, upper
    limb
  antrum (chronic) (Highmore) - *see*
    Sinusitis, maxillary
  anus K61.0
  apical (tooth) K04.7
    with sinus (alveolar) K04.6
  appendix K35.1
  areola (acute) (chronic) (nonpuerperal)
    N61
    puerperal, postpartum or gestational
      - *see* Infection, nipple
  arm (any part) - *see* Abscess, upper limb
  artery (wall) I77.8
  atheromatous I77.2
  auricle, ear - *see* Abscess, ear, external
  axilla (region) L02.41-
    lymph gland or node L04.2
  back (any part, except buttock) L02.212
  Bartholin's gland N75.1
    with
      abortion – *see* Abortion, by type
        complicated by, sepsis
      ectopic or molar pregnancy O08.0
      following ectopic or molar pregnancy
        O08.0
  Bezold's – *see* Mastoiditis, acute
  bilharziasis B65.1
  bladder (wall) – *see* Cystitis, specified
    type NEC
  bone (subperiosteal) - *see also* Osteomy-
    elitis, specified type NEC
    accessory sinus (chronic) - *see*
      Sinusitis
    chronic or old - *see* Osteomyelitis,
      chronic
    jaw (lower) (upper) M27.2
    mastoid – *see* Mastoiditis, acute,
      subperiosteal
    petrous – *see* Petrositis
    spinal (tuberculous) A18.01
      nontuberculous - *see* Osteomyelitis,
        vertebra
  bowel K63.0
  brain (any part) (cystic) (otogenic)
    G06.0
    amebic (with abscess of any other
      site) A06.6
    gonococcal A54.82
    pheomycotic (chromomycotic) B43.1
    tuberculous A17.81

Abscess *(Continued)*
 breast (acute) (chronic) (nonpuerperal)
   N61
  newborn P39.0
  puerperal, postpartum, gestational
   - *see* Mastitis, obstetric, purulent
 broad ligament N73.2
  acute N73.0
  chronic N73.1
 Brodie's (localized) (chronic) M86.8x-
 bronchi J98.09
 buccal cavity K12.2
 bulbourethral gland N34.0
 bursa M71.00
  ankle M71.07-
  elbow M71.02-
  foot M71.07-
  hand M71.04-
  hip M71.05-
  knee M71.06-
  multiple sites M71.09
  pharyngeal J39.1
  shoulder M71.01-
  specified site NEC M71.08
  wrist M71.03-
 buttock L02.31
 canthus - *see* Blepharoconjunctivitis
 cartilage - *see* Disorder, cartilage, specified type NEC
 cecum K35.1
 cerebellum, cerebellar G06.0
  sequelae G09
 cerebral (embolic) G06.0
  sequelae G09
 cervical (meaning neck) L02.11
  lymph gland or node L04.0
 cervix (stump) (uteri) - *see* Cervicitis
 cheek (external) L02.01
  inner K12.2
 chest J86.9
  with fistula J86.0
  wall L02.213
 chin L02.01
 choroid - *see* Inflammation,
   chorioretinal
 circumtonsillar J36
 cold (lung) (tuberculous) - *see also* Tuberculosis, abscess, lung
  articular - *see* Tuberculosis, joint
 colon (wall) K63.0
 colostomy K94.02
 conjunctiva - *see* Conjunctivitis, acute
 cornea H16.31-
 corpus
  cavernosum N48.21
  luteum – *see* Oophoritis
 Cowper's gland N34.0
 cranium G06.0
 cul-de-sac (Douglas') (posterior) - *see*
   Peritonitis, pelvic, female
 cutaneous - *see* Abscess, by site
 dental K04.7
  with sinus (alveolar) K04.6
 dentoalveolar K04.7
  with sinus K04.6
 diaphragm, diaphragmatic K65.1
 Douglas' cul-de-sac or pouch - *see* Peritonitis, pelvic, female
 Dubois A50.59
 ear (middle) - *see also* Otitis, media,
   suppurative
  acute – *see* Otitis, media, suppurative,
   acute
  external H60.0-

Abscess *(Continued)*
 entamebic - *see* Abscess, amebic
 enterostomy K94.12
 epididymis N45.4
 epidural G06.2
  brain G06.0
  spinal cord G06.1
 epiglottis J38.7
 epiploon, epiploic K65.1
 erysipelatous - *see* Erysipelas
 esophagus K20.8
 ethmoid (bone) (chronic) (sinus) J32.2
 external auditory canal - *see* Abscess,
   ear, external
 extradural G06.2
  brain G06.0
   sequelae G09
  spinal cord G06.1
 extraperitoneal K68.19
 eye - *see* Endophthalmitis, purulent
 eyelid H00.03-
 face (any part, except ear, eye and nose)
   L02.01
 fallopian tube - *see* Salpingitis
 fascia M72.8
 fauces J39.1
 fecal K63.0
 femoral (region) - *see* Abscess, lower limb
 filaria, filarial - *see* Infestation, filarial
 finger (any) - *see also* Abscess, hand
  nail - *see* Cellulitis, finger
 foot L02.61-
 forehead L02.01
 frontal sinus (chronic) J32.1
 gallbladder K81.0
 genital organ or tract
  female (external) N76.4
  male N49.9
   multiple sites N49.8
   specified NEC N49.8
 gestational mammary O91.11-
 gestational subareolar O91.11-
 gingival K05.21
 gland, glandular (lymph) (acute) - *see*
   Lymphadenitis, acute
 gluteal (region) L02.31
 gonorrheal - *see* Gonococcus
 groin L02.214
 gum K05.21
 hand L02.51-
 head NEC L02.811
  face (any part, except ear, eye and
   nose) L02.01
 heart - *see* Carditis
 heel - *see* Abscess, foot
 helminthic - *see* Infestation, helminth
 hepatic (cholangitic) (hematogenic) (lymphogenic) (pylephlebitic) K75.0
  amebic A06.4
 hip (region) - *see* Abscess, lower limb
 ileocecal K35.1
 ileostomy (bud) K94.12
 iliac (region) L02.214
  fossa K35.1
 infraclavicular (fossa) - *see* Abscess,
   upper limb
 inguinal (region) L02.214
  lymph gland or node L04.1
 intestine, intestinal NEC K63.0
  rectal K61.1
 intra-abdominal - *see also* Abscess, peritoneum K65.1
  postoperative T81.4
   retroperitoneal K68.11

Abscess *(Continued)*
 intracranial G06.0
 intramammary - *see* Abscess, breast
 intraorbital - *see* Abscess, orbit
 intraperitoneal K65.1
 intrasphincteric (anus) K61.4
 intraspinal G06.1
 intratonsillar J36
 ischiorectal (fossa) K61.3
 jaw (bone) (lower) (upper) M27.2
 joint - *see* Arthritis, pyogenic or pyemic
  spine (tuberculous) A18.01
   nontuberculous - *see* Spondylopa-
    thy, infective
 kidney N15.1
  with calculus N20.0
   with hydronephrosis N13.6
  puerperal (postpartum) O86.21
 knee - *see also* Abscess, lower limb
  joint M00.9
 labium (majus) (minus) N76.4
 lacrimal
  caruncle - *see* Inflammation, lacrimal,
   passages, acute
  gland - *see* Dacryoadenitis
  passages (duct) (sac) - *see* Inflammation, lacrimal, passages, acute
 lacunar N34.0
 larynx J38.7
 lateral (alveolar) K04.7
  with sinus K04.6
 leg (any part) - *see* Abscess, lower limb
 lens H27.8
 lingual K14.0
  tonsil J36
 lip K13.0
 Littre's gland N34.0
 liver (cholangitic) (hematogenic)
   (lymphogenic) (pylephlebitic)
   (pyogenic) K75.0
  amebic (due to Entamoeba histolytica) (dysenteric) (tropical) A06.4
   with
    brain abscess (and liver or lung
     abscess) A06.6
    lung abscess A06.5
 loin (region) L02.211
 lower limb L02.41-
 lumbar (tuberculous) A18.01
  nontuberculous L02.212
 lung (miliary) (putrid) J85.2
  with pneumonia J85.1
   due to specified organism (*see*
    Pneumonia, in (due to))
  amebic (with liver abscess) A06.5
   with
    brain abscess A06.6
    pneumonia A06.5
 lymph, lymphatic, gland or node
   (acute) - *see also* Lymphadenitis,
   acute
 mesentery I88.0
 malar M27.2
 mammary gland - *see* Abscess, breast
 marginal, anus K61.0
 mastoid – *see* Mastoiditis, acute
 maxilla, maxillary M27.2
  molar (tooth) K04.7
   with sinus K04.6
  premolar K04.7
  sinus (chronic) J32.0
 mediastinum J85.3
 meibomian gland - *see* Hordeolum
 meninges G06.2

Abscess *(Continued)*
　mesentery, mesenteric K65.1
　mesosalpinx – *see* Salpingitis
　mons pubis L02.215
　mouth (floor) K12.2
　muscle - *see* Myositis, infective
　myocardium I40.0
　nabothian (follicle) - *see* Cervicitis
　nasal J32.9
　nasopharyngeal J39.1
　navel L02.216
　　newborn P38.9
　　　with mild hemorrhage P38.1
　　　without hemorrhage P38.9
　neck (region) L02.11
　　lymph gland or node L04.0
　nephritic - *see* Abscess, kidney
　nipple N61
　　associated with
　　　lactation - *see* Pregnancy, compli-
　　　　cated by,
　　　pregnancy - *see* Pregnancy, compli-
　　　　cated by
　nose (external) (fossa) (septum) J34.0
　　sinus (chronic) - *see* Sinusitis
　omentum K65.1
　operative wound T81.4
　orbit, orbital - *see* Cellulitis, orbit - oto-
　　genic G06.0
　ovary, ovarian (corpus luteum) – *see*
　　Oophoritis
　oviduct – *see* Oophoritis
　palate (soft) K12.2
　　hard M27.2
　palmar (space) - *see* Abscess, hand
　pancreas (duct) - *see* Pancreatitis, acute
　parafrenal N48.21
　parametric, parametrium N73.2
　　acute N73.0
　　chronic N73.1
　paranephric N15.1
　parapancreatic - *see* Pancreatitis, acute
　parapharyngeal J39.0
　pararectal K61.1
　parasinus - *see* Sinusitis
　parauterine (*see also* Disease, pelvis,
　　inflammatory) N73.2
　paravaginal - *see* Vaginitis
　parietal region (scalp) L02.811
　parodontal K05.21
　parotid (duct) (gland) K11.3
　　region K12.2
　pectoral (region) L02.213
　pelvis, pelvic
　　female - *see* Disease, pelvis,
　　　inflammatory
　　male, peritoneal K65.1
　penis N48.21
　　gonococcal (accessory gland) (peri-
　　　urethral) A54.1
　perianal K61.0
　periapical K04.7
　　with sinus (alveolar) K04.6
　periappendicular K35.1
　pericardial I30.1
　pericecal K35.1
　pericemental K05.21
　pericholecystic - *see* Cholecystitis, acute
　pericoronal K05.21
　peridental K05.21
　perimetric (*see also* Disease, pelvis,
　　inflammatory) N73.2
　perinephric, perinephritic - *see* Abscess,
　　kidney

Abscess *(Continued)*
　perineum, perineal (superficial) L02.215
　　urethra N34.0
　periodontal (parietal) K05.21
　　apical K04.7
　periosteum, periosteal - *see also* Osteo-
　　myelitis, specified type NEC
　　with osteomyelitis - *see also* Osteomy-
　　　elitis, specified type NEC
　　　acute - *see* Osteomyelitis, acute
　　　chronic - *see* Osteomyelitis, chronic
　peripharyngeal J39.0
　peripleuritic J86.9
　　with fistula J86.0
　periprostatic N41.2
　perirectal K61.1
　perirenal (tissue) - *see* Abscess, kidney
　perisinuous (nose) - *see* Sinusitis
　peritoneum, peritoneal (perforated)
　　(ruptured) K65.1
　　with appendicitis K35.1
　　pelvic
　　　female - *see* Peritonitis, pelvic,
　　　　female
　　　male K65.1
　　postoperative T81.4
　　puerperal, postpartum, childbirth
　　　O85
　　tuberculous A18.31
　peritonsillar J36
　perityphlic K35.1
　periureteral N28.89
　periurethral N34.0
　　gonococcal (accessory gland) (peri-
　　　urethral) A54.1
　periuterine (*see also* Disease, pelvis,
　　inflammatory) N73.2
　perivesical – *see* Cystitis, specified type
　　NEC
　petrous bone – *see* Petrositis
　phagedenic NOS L02.91
　　chancroid A57
　pharynx, pharyngeal (lateral) J39.1
　pilonidal L05.01
　pituitary (gland) E23.6
　pleura J86.9
　　with fistula J86.0
　popliteal - *see* Abscess, lower limb
　postcecal K35.1
　postlaryngeal J38.7
　postnasal J34.0
　postoperative (any site) T81.4
　　retroperitoneal K68.11
　postpharyngeal J39.0
　posttonsillar J36
　post-typhoid A01.09
　pouch of Douglas - *see* Peritonitis,
　　pelvic, female
　premammary - *see* Abscess, breast
　prepatellar - *see* Abscess, lower limb
　prostate N41.2
　　gonococcal (acute) (chronic) A54.23
　psoas muscle K68.12
　puerperal - code by site under Puer-
　　peral, abscess
　pulmonary - *see* Abscess, lung
　pulp, pulpal (dental) K04.0
　rectovaginal septum K63.0
　rectovesical – *see* Cystitis, specified type
　　NEC
　rectum K61.1
　renal - *see* Abscess, kidney
　retina - *see* Inflammation, chorioretinal
　retrobulbar - *see* Abscess, orbit

Abscess *(Continued)*
　retrocecal K65.1
　retrolaryngeal J38.7
　retromammary - *see* Abscess, breast
　retroperitoneal NEC K68.19
　　postprocedural K68.11
　retropharyngeal J39.0
　retrouterine - *see* Peritonitis, pelvic, female
　retrovesical – *see* Cystitis, specified type
　　NEC
　root, tooth K04.7
　　with sinus (alveolar) K04.6
　round ligament (*see also* Disease, pelvis,
　　inflammatory) N73.2
　rupture (spontaneous) NOS L02.91
　sacrum (tuberculous) A18.01
　　nontuberculous M46.28
　salivary (duct) (gland) K11.3
　scalp (any part) L02.811
　scapular - *see* Osteomyelitis, specified
　　type NEC
　sclera - *see* Scleritis
　scrofulous (tuberculous) A18.2
　scrotum N49.2
　seminal vesicle N49.0
　septal, dental K04.7
　　with sinus (alveolar) K04.6
　serous - *see* Periostitis
　shoulder (region) - *see* Abscess, upper
　　limb
　sigmoid K63.0
　sinus (accessory) (chronic) (nasal) - *see*
　　also Sinusitis
　　intracranial venous (any) G06.0
　Skene's duct or gland N34.0
　skin - *see* Abscess, by site
　specified site NEC L02.818
　spermatic cord N49.1
　sphenoidal (sinus) (chronic) J32.3
　spinal cord (any part) (staphylococcal)
　　G06.1
　　tuberculous A17.81
　spine (column) (tuberculous) A18.01
　　epidural G06.1
　　nontuberculous - *see* Osteomyelitis,
　　　vertebra
　spleen D73.3
　　amebic A06.89
　stitch T81.4
　subarachnoid G06.2
　　brain G06.0
　　spinal cord G06.1
　subareolar - *see* Abscess, breast
　subcecal K35.1
　subcutaneous - *see also* Abscess, by site
　　pheomycotic (chromomycotic)
　　　B43.2
　subdiaphragmatic K65.1
　subdural G06.2
　　brain G06.0
　　　sequelae G09
　　spinal cord G06.1
　subgaleal L02.811
　subhepatic K65.1
　sublingual K12.2
　　gland K11.3
　submammary - *see* Abscess, breast
　submandibular (region) (space) (tri-
　　angle) K12.2
　　gland K11.3
　submaxillary (region) L02.01
　　gland K11.3
　submental L02.01
　　gland K11.3

Abscess *(Continued)*
  subperiosteal - *see* Osteomyelitis, specified type NEC
  subphrenic K65.1
    postoperative T81.4
  suburethral N34.0
  sudoriparous L75.8
  supraclavicular (fossa) - *see* Abscess, upper limb
  suprapelvic, acute N73.0
  suprarenal (capsule) (gland) E27.8
  sweat gland L74.8
  tear duct - *see* Inflammation, lacrimal, passages, acute
  temple L02.01
  temporal region L02.01
  temporosphenoidal G06.0
  tendon (sheath) M65.00
    ankle M65.07-
    foot M65.07-
    forearm M65.03-
    hand M65.04-
    lower leg M65.06-
    pelvic region M65.05-
    shoulder region M65.01-
    specified site NEC M65.08
    thigh M65.05-
    upper arm M65.02-
  testis N45.4
  thigh - *see* Abscess, lower limb
  thorax J86.9
    with fistula J86.0
  throat J39.1
  thumb - *see also* Abscess, hand
    nail - *see* Cellulitis, finger
  thymus (gland) E32.1
  thyroid (gland) E06.0
  toe (any) - *see also* Abscess, foot
    nail - *see* Cellulitis, toe
  tongue (staphylococcal) K14.0
  tonsil(s) (lingual) J36
  tonsillopharyngeal J36
  tooth, teeth (root) K04.7
    with sinus (alveolar) K04.6
    supporting structures NEC K05.21
  trachea J39.8
  trunk L02.219
    abdominal wall L02.211
    back L02.212
    chest wall L02.213
    groin L02.214
    perineum L02.215
    umbilicus L02.216
  tubal - *see* Salpingitis
  tuberculous - *see* Tuberculosis, abscess
  tubo-ovarian - *see* Salpingo-oophoritis
  tunica vaginalis N49.1
  umbilicus L02.216
  upper
    limb L02.41-
    respiratory J39.8
  urethral (gland) N34.0
  urinary N34.0
  uterus, uterine (wall) - *see also* Endometritis
    ligament (*see also* Disease, pelvis, inflammatory) N73.2
    neck - *see* Cervicitis
  uvula K12.2
  vagina (wall) - *see* Vaginitis
  vaginorectal - *see* Vaginitis
  vas deferens N49.1
  vermiform appendix K35.1

Abscess *(Continued)*
  vertebra (column) (tuberculous) A18.01
    nontuberculous - *see* Osteomyelitis, vertebra
  vesical – *see* Cystitis, specified type NEC
  vesico-uterine pouch - *see* Peritonitis, pelvic, female
  vitreous (humor) - *see* Endophthalmitis, purulent
  vocal cord J38.3
  von Bezold's – *see* Mastoiditis, acute
  vulva N76.4
  vulvovaginal gland N75.1
  web space - *see* Abscess, hand
  wound T81.4
  wrist - *see* Abscess, upper limb
Absence (of) (organ or part) (complete or partial)
  adrenal (gland) (congenital) Q89.1
    acquired E89.6
  albumin in blood E88.09
  alimentary tract (congenital) Q45.8
    upper Q40.8
  alveolar process (acquired) - *see* Anomaly, alveolar
  ankle (acquired) Z89.44-
  anus (congenital) Q42.3
    with fistula Q42.2
  aorta (congenital) Q25.4
  appendix, congenital Q42.8
  arm (acquired) Z89.209
    above elbow Z89.22-
      congenital (with hand present) - *see* Agenesis, arm, with hand present
      and hand – *see* Agenesis, forearm, and hand
    below elbow Z89.21-
      congenital (with hand present) - *see* Agenesis, arm, with hand present
      and hand – *see* Agenesis, forearm, and hand
    congenital - *see* Defect, reduction, upper limb
    shoulder Z89.23-
      congenital (with hand present) - *see* Agenesis, arm, with hand present
  artery (congenital) (peripheral) Q27.8
    brain Q28.3
    coronary Q24.5
    pulmonary Q25.7
    specified NEC Q27.8
    umbilical Q27.0
  atrial septum (congenital) Q21.1
  auditory canal (congenital) (external) Q16.1
  auricle (ear), congenital Q16.0
  bile, biliary duct, congenital Q44.5
  bladder (acquired) Z90.6
    congenital Q64.5
  bowel sounds R19.11
  brain Q00.0
    part of Q04.3
  breast(s) (and nipple(s)) (acquired) Z90.1
    congenital Q83.8
  broad ligament Q50.6
  bronchus (congenital) Q32.4
  canaliculus lacrimalis, congenital Q10.4

Absence *(Continued)*
  cerebellum (vermis) Q04.3
  cervix (acquired) (with uterus) Z90.710
    with remaining uterus Z90.712
    congenital Q51.5
  chin, congenital Q18.8
  cilia (congenital) Q10.3
    acquired - *see* Madarosis
  clitoris (congenital) Q52.6
  coccyx, congenital Q76.49
  cold sense R20.8
  congenital
    lumen - *see* Atresia
    organ or site NEC - *see* Agenesis
    septum - *see* Imperfect, closure
  corpus callosum Q04.0
  cricoid cartilage, congenital Q31.8
  diaphragm (with hernia), congenital Q79.1
  digestive organ(s) or tract, congenital Q45.8
    acquired NEC Z90.4
    upper Q40.8
  ductus arteriosus Q28.8
  duodenum (acquired) Z90.4
    congenital Q41.0
  ear, congenital Q16.9
    acquired - *see* subcategory H93.8
    auricle Q16.0
    external Q16.0
    inner Q16.5
    lobe, lobule Q17.8
    middle, except ossicles Q16.4
      ossicles Q16.3
    ossicles Q16.3
  ejaculatory duct (congenital) Q55.4
  endocrine gland (congenital) NEC Q89.2
    acquired E89.89
  epididymis (congenital) Q55.4
    acquired Z90.79
  epiglottis, congenital Q31.8
  esophagus (congenital) Q39.8
    acquired (partial) Z90.4
  eustachian tube (congenital) Q16.2
  extremity (acquired) Z89.9
    congenital Q73.0
    lower (above knee) Z89.619
      below knee Z89.5-
    upper - *see* Absence, arm
  eye (acquired) Z90.01
    congenital Q11.1
    muscle (congenital) Q10.3
  eyeball (acquired) Z90.01
  eyelid (fold) (congenital) Q10.3
    acquired Z90.01
  face, specified part NEC Q18.8
  fallopian tube(s) (acquired) Z90.79
    congenital Q50.6
  family member (causing problem in home) NEC Z63.32 - *see also* Disruption, family
  femur, congenital – *see* Defect, reduction, lower limb, longitudinal, femur
  fibrinogen (congenital) D68.2
    acquired D65
  finger(s) (acquired) Z89.02-
    congenital – *see* Agenesis, hand
  foot (acquired) Z89.43-
    congenital – *see* Agenesis, foot

Absence *(Continued)*
  forearm (acquired) - *see* Absence, arm, below elbow
  gallbladder (acquired) Z90.4
    congenital Q44.0
  gamma globulin in blood D80.1
    hereditary D80.0
  genital organs
    acquired (female) (male) Z90.79
    female, congenital Q52.8
      external Q52.71
      internal NEC Q52.8
    male, congenital Q55.8
  genitourinary organs, congenital NEC
    female Q52.8
    male Q55.8
  globe (acquired) Z90.01
    congenital Q11.1
  glottis, congenital Q31.8
  hand and wrist (acquired) Z89.11-
    congenital – *see* Agenesis, hand
  head, part (acquired) NEC Z90.09
  heat sense R20.8
  hip Z89.62-
  hymen (congenital) Q52.4
  ileum (acquired) Z90.4
    congenital Q41.2
  immunoglobulin, isolated NEC D80.3
    IgA D80.2
    IgG D80.3
    IgM D80.4
  incus (acquired) - *see* Loss, ossicles, ear
    congenital Q16.3
  inner ear, congenital Q16.5
  intestine (acquired) (small) Z90.4
    congenital Q41.9
      specified NEC Q41.8
    large Z90.4
      congenital Q42.9
        specified NEC Q42.8
  iris, congenital Q13.1
  jejunum (acquired) Z90.4
    congenital Q41.1
  joint, congenital NEC Q74.8
  kidney(s) (acquired) Z90.5
    congenital Q60.2
      bilateral Q60.1
      unilateral Q60.0
  labyrinth, membranous Q16.5
  larynx (congenital) Q31.8
    acquired Z90.02
  leg (acquired) (above knee) Z89.61-
    below knee (acquired) Z89.5-
    congenital – *see* Defect, reduction, lower limb
  lens (acquired) - *see also* Aphakia
    congenital Q12.3
    post cataract extraction Z98.4-
  limb (acquired) - *see* Absence, extremity
  lip Q38.6
  liver (congenital) Q44.7
  lung (fissure) (lobe) (bilateral) (unilateral) (congenital) Q33.3
    acquired (any part) Z90.2
  menstruation - *see* Amenorrhea
  muscle (congenital) (pectoral) Q79.8
    ocular Q10.3
  neck, part Q18.8
  neutrophil - *see* Agranulocytosis
  nipple(s) (with breast(s)) (acquired) Z90.1-
    congenital Q83.2
  nose (congenital) Q30.1
    acquired Z90.09

Absence *(Continued)*
  organ
    of Corti, congenital Q16.5
    or site, congenital NEC Q89.8
      acquired NEC Z90.89
  osseous meatus (ear) Q16.4
  ovary (acquired)
    bilateral Z90.722
    congenital
      bilateral Q50.02
      unilateral Q50.01
    unilateral Z90.721
  oviduct (acquired)
    bilateral Z90.722
    congenital Q50.6
    unilateral Z90.721
  pancreas (congenital) Q45.0
    acquired Z90.4
  parathyroid gland (acquired) E89.2
    congenital Q89.2
  patella, congenital Q74.1
  penis (congenital) Q55.5
    acquired Z90.79
  pericardium (congenital) Q24.8
  pituitary gland (congenital) Q89.2
    acquired E89.3
  prostate (acquired) Z90.79
    congenital Q55.4
  pulmonary valve Q22.0
  punctum lacrimale (congenital) Q10.4
  radius, congenital - *see* Defect, reduction, upper limb, longitudinal, radius
  rectum (congenital) Q42.1
    with fistula Q42.0
    acquired Z90.4
  respiratory organ NOS Q34.9
  rib (acquired) Z90.89
    congenital Q76.6
  sacrum, congenital Q76.49
  salivary gland(s), congenital Q38.4
  scrotum, congenital Q55.29
  seminal vesicles (congenital) Q55.4
    acquired Z90.79
  septum
    atrial (congenital) Q21.1
    between aorta and pulmonary artery Q21.4
    ventricular (congenital) Q20.4
  sex chromosome
    female phenotype Q97.8
    male phenotype Q98.8
  skull bone (congenital) Q75.8
    with
      anencephaly Q00.0
      encephalocele - *see* Encephalocele
      hydrocephalus Q03.9
        with spina bifida - *see* Spina bifida, by site, with hydrocephalus
      microcephaly Q02
  spermatic cord, congenital Q55.4
  spine, congenital Q76.49
  spleen (congenital) Q89.01
    acquired Z90.81
  sternum, congenital Q76.7
  stomach (acquired) (partial) Z90.3
    congenital Q40.2
  superior vena cava, congenital Q26.8

Absence *(Continued)*
  teeth, tooth (congenital) K00.0
    acquired (complete) K08.109
      class I K08.101
      class II K08.102
      class III K08.103
      class IV K08.104
      due to
        caries K08.139
          class I K08.131
          class II K08.132
          class III K08.133
          class IV K08.134
        periodontal disease K08.129
          class I K08.121
          class II K08.122
          class III K08.123
          class IV K08.124
        specified NEC K08.199
          class I K08.191
          class II K08.192
          class III K08.193
          class IV K08.194
        trauma K08.119
          class I K08.111
          class II K08.112
          class III K08.113
          class IV K08.114
    partial K08.409
      class I K08.401
      class II K08.402
      class III K08.403
      class IV K08.404
      due to
        caries K08.439
          class I K08.431
          class II K08.432
          class III K08.433
          class IV K08.434
        periodontal disease K08.429
          class I K08.421
          class II K08.422
          class III K08.423
          class IV K08.424
        specified NEC K08.499
          class I K08.491
          class II K08.492
          class III K08.493
          class IV K08.494
        trauma K08.419
          class I K08.411
          class II K08.412
          class III K08.413
          class IV K08.414
  tendon (congenital) Q79.8
  testis (congenital) Q55.0
    acquired Z90.79
  thumb (acquired) Z89.01-
    congenital – *see* Agenesis, hand
  thymus gland Q89.2
  thyroid (gland) (acquired) E89.0
    cartilage, congenital Q31.8
    congenital E03.1
  toe(s) (acquired) Z89.42-
    with foot - *see* Absence, foot and ankle
    congenital – *see* Agenesis, foot
    great Z89.41-
  tongue, congenital Q38.3
  trachea (cartilage), congenital Q32.1

Absence *(Continued)*
  transverse aortic arch, congenital
    Q25.4
  tricuspid valve Q22.4
  umbilical artery, congenital Q27.0
  upper arm and forearm with hand
    present, congenital – *see* Agenesis,
    arm, with hand present
  ureter (congenital) Q62.4
    acquired Z90.6
  urethra, congenital Q64.5
  uterus (acquired) Z90.710
    with cervix Z90.710
    with remaining cervical stump
      Z90.711
    congenital Q51.0
  uvula, congenital Q38.5
  vagina, congenital Q52.0
  vas deferens (congenital) Q55.4
    acquired Z90.79
  vein (peripheral) congenital NEC
    Q27.8
    cerebral Q28.3
    digestive system Q27.8
    great Q26.8
    lower limb Q27.8
    portal Q26.5
    precerebral Q28.1
    specified site NEC Q27.8
    upper limb Q27.8
  vena cava (inferior) (superior), congenital Q26.8
  ventricular septum Q20.4
  vertebra, congenital Q76.49
  vulva, congenital Q52.71
  wrist (acquired) Z89.12-
Absorbent system disease I87.8
Absorption
  carbohydrate, disturbance K90.4
  chemical - *see* Table of drugs and
    chemicals
    through placenta (newborn) P04.9
      environmental substance P04.6
      nutritional substance P04.5
      obstetric anesthetic or analgesic
        drug P04.0
  drug NEC - *see* Table of drugs and
    chemicals
    addictive
      through placenta (newborn) P04.49
        cocaine P04.41
    medicinal
      through placenta (newborn) P04.1
    through placenta (newborn) P04.1
      obstetric anesthetic or analgesic
        drug P04.0
  fat, disturbance K90.4
    pancreatic K90.3
  noxious substance - *see* Table of drugs
    and chemicals
  protein, disturbance K90.4
  starch, disturbance K90.4
  toxic substance - *see* Table of drugs and
    chemicals
  uremic - *see* Uremia
Abstinence symptoms, syndrome
  alcohol F10.239
    with delirium F10.231
  cocaine F14.23
  neonatal P96.1
  nicotine - *see* Dependence, drug, nicotine, with, withdrawal
  opioid F11.93
    with dependence F11.23

Abstinence symptoms, syndrome
  (Continued)
  psychoactive NEC F19.939
    with
      delirium F19.931
      dependence F19.239
        with
          delirium F19.231
          perceptual disturbance
            F19.232
          uncomplicated F19.230
      perceptual disturbance F19.932
      uncomplicated F19.930
    sedative F13.939
      with
        delirium F13.931
        dependence F13.239
          with
            delirium F13.231
            perceptual disturbance
              F13.232
            uncomplicated F13.230
        perceptual disturbance F13.932
        uncomplicated F13.930
    stimulant NEC F15.93
      with dependence F15.23
Abulia R68.89
Abulomania F60.7
Abuse
  adult - *see* Maltreatment, adult
    as reason for
      couple seeking advice (including
        offender) Z63.0
  alcohol (non-dependent) F10.10
    with
      anxiety disorder F10.180
      intoxication F10.129
        with delirium F10.121
        uncomplicated F10.120
      mood disorder F10.14
      other specified disorder
        F10.188
      psychosis F10.159
        delusions F10.150
        hallucinations F10.151
      sexual dysfunction F10.181
      sleep disorder F10.182
      unspecified disorder F10.19
      counseling and surveillance
        Z71.41
  amphetamine (or related substance)
    - *see* Abuse, drug, stimulant
    NEC
  analgesics (non-prescribed) (over the
    counter) F55.8
  antacids F55.0
  antidepressants - *see* Abuse, drug, psychoactive NEC
  anxiolytic – *see* Abuse, drug, sedative
  barbiturates – *see* Abuse, drug,
    sedative
  caffeine - *see* Abuse, drug, stimulant
    NEC
  cannabis, cannabinoids – *see* Abuse,
    drug, cannabis
  child – *see* Maltreatment, child
  cocaine – *see* Abuse, drug, cocaine
  drug NEC (non-dependent) F19.10
    with sleep disorder F19.182
    amphetamine type - *see* Abuse, drug,
      stimulant NEC
    analgesics (non-prescribed) (over the
      counter) F55.8
    antacids F55.0

Abuse *(Continued)*
  drug NEC *(Continued)*
    antidepressants – *see* Abuse, drug,
      psychoactive NEC
    anxiolytics – *see* Abuse, drug,
      sedative
    barbiturates – *see* Abuse, drug,
      sedative
    caffeine - *see* Abuse, drug, stimulant
      NEC
    cannabis F12.10
      with
        anxiety disorder F12.180
        intoxication F12.129
          with
            delirium F12.121
            perceptual disturbance
              F12.122
          uncomplicated F12.120
        other specified disorder F12.188
        psychosis F12.159
          delusions F12.150
          hallucinations F12.151
        unspecified disorder F12.19
    cocaine F14.10
      with
        anxiety disorder F14.180
        intoxication F14.129
          with
            delirium F14.121
            perceptual disturbance
              F14.122
          uncomplicated F14.120
        mood disorder F14.14
        other specified disorder
          F14.188
        psychosis F14.159
          delusions F14.150
          hallucinations F14.151
        sexual dysfunction F14.181
        sleep disorder F14.182
        unspecified disorder F14.19
    counseling and surveillance Z71.51
    hallucinogen F16.10
      with
        anxiety disorder F16.180
        flashbacks F16.183
        intoxication F16.129
          with
            delirium F16.121
            perceptual disturbance
              F16.122
          uncomplicated F16.120
        mood disorder F16.14
        other specified disorder F16.188
        perception disorder, persisting
          F16.183
        psychosis F16.159
          delusions F16.150
          hallucinations F16.151
        unspecified disorder F16.19
    hashish – *see* Abuse, drug, cannabis
    herbal or folk remedies F55.1
    hormones F55.3
    hypnotics – *see* Abuse, drug, sedative
    inhalant F18.10
      with
        anxiety disorder F18.180
        dementia, persisting F18.17
        intoxication F18.129
          with delirium F18.121
          uncomplicated F18.120
        mood disorder F18.14
        other specified disorder F18.188

Abuse *(Continued)*
  drug NEC *(Continued)*
    inhalant *(Continued)*
      with *(Continued)*
        psychosis F18.159
          delusions F18.150
          hallucinations F18.151
        unspecified disorder F18.19
    laxatives F55.2
    LSD – *see* Abuse, drug, hallucinogen
    marihuana – *see* Abuse, drug, cannabis
    morphine type (opioids) – *see* Abuse, drug, opioid
    opioid F11.10
      with
        intoxication F11.129
          with
            delirium F11.121
            perceptual disturbance F11.122
          uncomplicated F11.120
        mood disorder F11.14
        other specified disorder F11.188
        psychosis F11.159
          delusions F11.150
          hallucinations F11.151
        sexual dysfunction F11.181
        sleep disorder F11.182
        unspecified disorder F11.19
    PCP (phencyclidine) (or related substance) - *see* Abuse, drug, psychoactive NEC
    psychoactive NEC F19.10
      with
        amnestic disorder F19.16
        anxiety disorder F19.180
        dementia F19.17
        intoxication F19.129
          with
            delirium F19.121
            perceptual disturbance F19.122
          uncomplicated F19.120
        mood disorder F19.14
        other specified disorder F19.188
        psychosis F19.159
          delusions F19.150
          hallucinations F19.151
        sexual dysfunction F19.181
        sleep disorder F19.182
        unspecified disorder F19.19
    sedative, hypnotic or anxiolytic F13.10
      with
        anxiety disorder F13.180
        intoxication F13.129
          with delirium F13.121
          uncomplicated F13.120
        mood disorder F13.14
        other specified disorder F13.188
        psychosis F13.159
          delusions F13.150
          hallucinations F13.151
        sexual dysfunction F13.181
        sleep disorder F13.182
        unspecified disorder F13.19
    solvent – *see* Abuse, drug, inhalant
    steroids F55.3

Abuse *(Continued)*
  drug NEC *(Continued)*
    stimulant NEC F15.10
      with
        anxiety disorder F15.180
        intoxication F15.129
          with
            delirium F15.121
            perceptual disturbance F15.122
          uncomplicated F15.120
        mood disorder F15.14
        other specified disorder F15.188
        psychosis F15.159
          delusions F15.150
          hallucinations F15.151
        sexual dysfunction F15.181
        sleep disorder F15.182
        unspecified disorder F15.19
    tranquilizers – *see* Abuse, drug, sedative
    vitamins F55.4
  hallucinogens – *see* Abuse, drug, hallucinogen
  hashish – *see* Abuse, drug, cannabis
  herbal or folk remedies F55.1
  hormones F55.3
  hypnotic – *see* Abuse, drug, sedative
  inhalant – *see* Abuse, drug, inhalant
  laxatives F55.2
  LSD – *see* Abuse, drug, hallucinogen
  marihuana – *see* Abuse, drug, cannabis
  morphine type (opioids) – *see* Abuse, drug, opioid
  non-psychoactive substance NEC F55.8
    antacids F55.0
    folk remedies F55.1
    herbal remedies F55.1
    hormones F55.3
    laxatives F55.2
    steroids F55.3
    vitamins F55.4
  opioids – *see* Abuse, drug, opioid
  PCP (phencyclidine) (or related substance) - *see* Abuse, drug, psychoactive NEC
  physical (adult) (child) – *see* Maltreatment, physical abuse
  psychoactive substance - *see* Abuse, drug, psychoactive NEC
  psychological (adult) (child) – *see* Maltreatment. psychological abuse
  sedative – *see* Abuse, drug, sedative
  sexual – *see* Maltreatment, sexual abuse
  solvent – *see* Abuse, drug, inhalant
  steroids F55.3
  vitamins F55.4
Acalculia R48.8
  developmental F81.2
Acanthamebiasis (with) B60.10
  conjunctiva B60.12
  keratoconjunctivitis B60.13
  meningoencephalitis B60.11
  other specified B60.19
Acanthocephaliasis B83.8
Acanthocheilonemiasis B74.4
Acanthocytosis E78.6
Acantholysis L11.9
Acanthosis (acquired) (nigricans) L83
  benign Q82.8
  congenital Q82.8
  seborrheic L82.1
    inflamed L82.0
  tongue K14.3

Acapnia E87.3
Acarbia E87.2
Acardia, acardius Q89.8
Acardiacus amorphus Q89.8
Acardiotrophia I51.4
Acariasis B88.0
  scabies B86
Acarodermatitis (urticarioides) B88.0
Acarophobia F40.218
Acatalasemia, acatalasia E80.3
Acathisia (drug induced) G25.71
Accelerated atrioventricular conduction I45.6
Accentuation of personality traits (type A) Z73.1
Accessory (congenital)
  adrenal gland Q89.1
  anus Q43.4
  appendix Q43.4
  atrioventricular conduction I45.6
  auditory ossicles Q16.3
  auricle (ear) Q17.0
  biliary duct or passage Q44.5
  bladder Q64.79
  blood vessels NEC Q27.9
    coronary Q24.5
  bone NEC Q79.8
  breast tissue, axilla Q83.1
  carpal bones Q74.0
  cecum Q43.4
  chromosome(s) NEC (nonsex) Q92.9
    with complex rearrangements NEC Q92.5
      seen only at prometaphase Q92.8
    partial Q92.9
    sex
      female phenotype Q97.8
    13 - *see* Trisomy, 13
    18 - *see* Trisomy, 18
    21 - *see* Trisomy, 21
  coronary artery Q24.5
  cusp(s), heart valve NEC Q24.8
    pulmonary Q22.3
  cystic duct Q44.5
  digit(s) Q69.9
  ear (auricle) (lobe) Q17.0
  endocrine gland NEC Q89.2
  eye muscle Q10.3
  eyelid Q10.3
  face bone(s) Q75.8
  fallopian tube (fimbria) (ostium) Q50.6
  finger(s) Q69.0
  foreskin N47.8
  frontonasal process Q75.8
  gallbladder Q44.1
  genital organ(s)
    female Q52.8
      external Q52.79
      internal NEC Q52.8
    male Q55.8
  genitourinary organs NEC Q89.8
    female Q52.8
    male Q55.8
  hallux Q69.2
  heart Q24.8
    valve NEC Q24.8
      pulmonary Q22.3
  hepatic ducts Q44.5
  hymen Q52.4
  intestine (large) (small) Q43.4
  kidney Q63.0
  lacrimal canal Q10.6
  leaflet, heart valve NEC Q24.8

Accessory *(Continued)*
ligament, broad Q50.6
liver Q44.7
duct Q44.5
lobule (ear) Q17.0
lung (lobe) Q33.1
muscle Q79.8
navicular of carpus Q74.0
nervous system, part NEC Q07.8
nipple Q83.3
nose Q30.8 - organ or site not listed - *see*
Anomaly, by site
ovary Q50.31
oviduct Q50.6
pancreas Q45.3
parathyroid gland Q89.2
parotid gland (and duct) Q38.4
pituitary gland Q89.2
preauricular appendage Q17.0
prepuce N47.8
renal arteries (multiple) Q27.2
rib Q76.6
cervical Q76.5
roots (teeth) K00.2
salivary gland Q38.4
sesamoid bones Q74.8
foot Q74.2
hand Q74.0
skin tags Q82.8
spleen Q89.09
sternum Q76.7
submaxillary gland Q38.4
tarsal bones Q74.2
teeth, tooth K00.1
tendon Q79.8
thumb Q69.1
thymus gland Q89.2
thyroid gland Q89.2
toes Q69.2
tongue Q38.3
tooth, teeth K00.1
tragus Q17.0
ureter Q62.5
urethra Q64.79
urinary organ or tract NEC Q64.8
uterus Q51.2
vagina Q52.1
valve, heart NEC Q24.8
pulmonary Q22.2
vertebra Q76.49
vocal cords Q31.8
vulva Q52.79
Accident
birth - *see* Birth, injury
cardiac - *see* Infarct, myocardium
cerebral I63.9
cerebrovascular (embolic) (ischemic)
(thrombotic) I63.9
aborted I63.9
hemorrhagic - *see* Hemorrhage, intracranial, intracerebral
old (without sequelae) Z86.73
with sequelae (of) - *see* Sequelae, disease, cerebrovascular disease
coronary - *see* Infarct, myocardium
craniovascular I63.9
vascular, brain I63.9
Accidental - *see* condition
Accommodation (disorder) *(see also*
condition)
hysterical paralysis of F44.89
insufficiency of H52.4
paresis - *see* Paresis, of accommodation
spasm - *see* Spasm, of accommodation

Accouchement - *see* Delivery
Accreta placenta O43.21-
without hemorrhage O73.0
Accretio cordis (nonrheumatic) I31.0
Accretions, tooth, teeth K03.6
Acculturation difficulty Z60.3
Accumulation secretion, prostate
N42.89
Acephalia, acephalism, acephalus,
acephaly Q00.0
Acephalobrachia monster Q89.8
Acephalochirus monster Q89.8
Acephalogaster Q89.8
Acephalostomus monster Q89.8
Acephalothorax Q89.8
Acerophobia F40.298
Acetonemia R79.89
in Type 1 diabetes E10.10
with coma E10.11
Acetonuria R82.4
Achalasia (cardia) (esophagus) K22.0
congenital Q39.5
pylorus Q40.0
sphincteral NEC K59.8
Ache(s) - *see* Pain
Acheilia Q38.6
Achillobursitis - *see* Tendinitis, Achilles
Achillodynia - *see* Tendinitis, Achilles
Achlorhydria, achlorhydric (neurogenic)
K31.83
anemia D50.8
diarrhea K31.83
psychogenic F45.8
secondary to vagotomy K91.1
Achluophobia F40.228
Acholia K82.8
Acholuric jaundice (familial) (splenomegalic) - *see also* Spherocytosis
acquired D59.8
Achondrogenesis Q77.0
Achondroplasia (osteosclerosis
congenita) Q77.4
Achroma, cutis L80
Achromat(ism), achromatopsia
(acquired) (congenital) H53.51
Achromia, congenital - *see* Albinism
Achromia parasitica B36.0
Achylia gastrica K31.89
psychogenic F45.8
Acid
burn - *see* Corrosion
deficiency
amide nicotinic E52
ascorbic E54
folic E53.8
nicotinic E52
pantothenic E53.8
intoxication E87.2
peptic disease K30
phosphatase deficiency E83.39
stomach K30
psychogenic F45.8
Acidemia E87.2
argininosuccinic E72.22
isovaleric E71.110
metabolic (newborn) P19.9
first noted before onset of labor P19.0
first noted during labor P19.1
noted at birth P19.2
methylmalonic E71.120
pipecolic E72.3
propionic E71.121
Acidity, gastric (high) K30
psychogenic F45.8

Acidocytopenia - *see* Agranulocytosis
Acidocytosis D72.1
Acidopenia - *see* Agranulocytosis
Acidosis (lactic) (respiratory) E87.2
in Type 1 diabetes E10.10
with coma E10.11
kidney, tubular N25.89
lactic E87.2
metabolic NEC E87.2
with respiratory acidosis E87.4
late, of newborn P74.0
mixed metabolic and respiratory,
newborn P84
newborn P84
renal (hyperchloremic) (tubular)
N25.89
respiratory E87.2
complicated by
metabolic
acidosis E87.4
alkalosis E87.4
Aciduria
argininosuccinic E72.22
glutaric (type I) E72.3
type II E71.313
type III E71.5-
orotic (congenital) (hereditary) (pyrimidine deficiency) E79.8
anemia D53.0
Acladiosis (skin) B36.0
Aclasis, diaphyseal Q78.6
Acleistocardia Q21.1
Aclusion - *see* Anomaly, dentofacial,
malocclusion
Acne L70.9
artificialis L70.8
atrophica L70.2
cachecticorum (Hebra) L70.8
conglobata L70.1
cystic L70.0
decalvans L66.2
excoriée des jeunes filles L70.5
frontalis L70.2
indurata L70.0
infantile L70.4
keloid L73.0
lupoid L70.2
necrotic, necrotica (miliaris) L70.2
neonatal L70.4
nodular L70.0
occupational L70.8
picker's L70.5
pustular L70.0
rodens L70.2
rosacea L71.9
specified NEC L70.8
tropica L70.3
varioliformis L70.2
vulgaris L70.0
Acnitis (primary) A18.4
Acosta's disease T70.29
Acoustic - *see* condition
Acousticophobia F40.298
Acquired (*see also* condition)
immunodeficiency syndrome
(AIDS) B20
Acrania Q00.0
Acroasphyxia, chronic I73.89
Acrobystitis N47.7
Acrocephalopolysyndactyly Q87.0
Acrocephalosyndactyly Q87.0
Acrocephaly Q75.0
Acrochondrohyperplasia - *see* Syndrome,
Marfan's

69

Acrocyanosis I73.8
  newborn P28.2
    meaning transient blue hands and
      feet - omit code
Acrodermatitis L30.8
  atrophicans (chronica) L90.4
  continua (Hallopeau) L40.2
  enteropathica (hereditary) E83.2
  Hallopeau's L40.2
  infantile papular L44.4
  perstans L40.2
  pustulosa continua L40.2
  recalcitrant pustular L40.2
Acrodynia – *see* Poisoning, mercury
Acromegaly, acromegalia E22.0
Acromelalgia I73.98
Acromicria, acromikria Q79.8
Acronyx L60.0
Acropachy, thyroid—*see* Thyrotoxicosis
Acroparesthesia (simple) (vasomotor)
  I73.89
Acropathy, thyroid – *see* Thyrotoxicosis
Acrophobia F40.241
Acroposthitis N47.7
Acroscleriasis, acroscleroderma,
  acrosclerosis - *see* Sclerosis,
  systemic
Acrosphacelus I96
Acrospiroma, eccrine – *see* Neoplasm,
  skin, benign
Acrostealgia - *see* Osteochondropathy
Acrotrophodynia - *see* Immersion
ACTH ectopic syndrome E24.3
Actinic - *see* condition
Actinobacillosis, actinobacillus A28.8
  mallei A24.0
  muris A25.1
Actinomyces israelii (infection) – *see*
  Actinomycosis
Actinomycetoma (foot) B47.1
Actinomycosis, actinomycotic A42.9
  with pneumonia A42.0
  abdominal A42.1
  cervicofacial A42.2
  cutaneous A42.89
  gastrointestinal A42.1
  pulmonary A42.0
  sepsis A42.7
  specified site NEC A42.89
Actinoneuritis G62.8
Action, heart
  disorder I49.9
  irregular I49.9
    psychogenic F45.8
Active - *see* condition
Activated protein C resistance D68.51
Activity (involving) Y93.9
  aerobic and step exercise (class) Y93.a3
  alpine skiing Y93.23
  animal care NEC Y93.k9
  arts and handcrafts NEC Y93.d9
  athletics NEC Y93.79
  athletics played as a team or group
    NEC Y93.69
  athletics played individually NEC
    Y93.59
  baking Y93.g3
  ballet Y93.41
  barbells Y93.b3
  BASE (Building, Antenna, Span, Earth)
    jumping Y93.33
  baseball Y93.64
  basketball Y93.67
  bathing (personal) Y93.e1

Activity *(Continued)*
  beach volleyball Y93.68
  bike riding Y93.55
  boogie boarding Y93.18
  bowling Y93.54
  boxing Y93.71
  brass instrument playing Y93.j4
  building construction Y93.h3
  bungee jumping Y93.34
  calisthenics Y93.a2
  canoeing (in calm and turbulent water)
    Y93.16
  capture the flag Y93.68
  cardiorespiratory exercise NEC Y93.a9
  caregiving (providing) NEC Y93.f9
    bathing Y93.f1
    lifting Y93.f2
  cellular
    communication device Y93.c2
    telephone Y93.c2
  challenge course Y93.a5
  cheerleading Y93.45
  circuit training Y93.a4
  cleaning
    floor Y93.e5
  limbing NEC Y93.39
    mountain Y93.31
    rock Y93.31
    wall Y93.31
  cool down exercises Y93.a2
  combatives Y93.75
  computer
    keyboarding Y93.c1
    technology NEC Y93.c9
  computer keyboarding Y93.c1
  computer technology NEC Y93.c9
  confidence course Y93.a5
  construction (building) Y93.h3
  cooking and baking Y93.g3
  cricket Y93.69
  crocheting Y93.d1
  cross country skiing Y93.24
  dancing (all types) Y93.41
  digging
    dirt Y93.h1
  dirt digging Y93.h1
  dishwashing Y93.g1
  diving (platform) (springboard) Y93.12
    underwater Y93.15
  dodge ball Y93.68
  downhill skiing Y93.23
  drum playing Y93.j2
  dumbbells Y93.b3
  electronic
    devices NEC Y93.c9
      hand held interactive Y93.c2
    game playing (using) (with)
      keyboard or other stationary device
        Y93.c1
      interactive device Y93.c2
  elliptical machine Y93.a1
  exercise(s)
    machines ((primarily) for)
      cardiorespiratory conditioning
        Y93.a1
      muscle strengthening Y93.b1
    muscle strengthening (non-machine)
      NEC Y93.b9
  external motion NEC Y93.i9
    rollercoaster Y93.i1
  field hockey Y93.65
  figure skating (pairs) (singles) Y93.21
  flag football Y93.62
  floor mopping and cleaning Y93.e5

Activity *(Continued)*
  food preparation and clean up Y93.g1
  football (American) NOS Y93.61
    flag Y93.62
    tackle Y93.61
    touch Y93.62
  four square Y93.68
  free weights Y93.b3
  frisbee (ultimate) Y93.74
  furniture
    building Y93.d3
    finishing Y93.d3
    repair Y93.d3
  game playing (electronic)
    using keyboard or other stationary
      device Y93.c1
    using interactive device Y93.c2
  gardening Y93.h2
  golf Y93.53
  grass drills Y93.a6
  grilling and smoking food Y93.g2
  grooming and shearing an animal
    Y93.k3
  guerilla drills Y93.a6
  gymnastics (rhythmic) Y93.43
  handball Y93.73
  handcrafts NEC Y93.d9
  hand held interactive electronic device
    Y93.c2
  hang gliding Y93.35
  hiking (on level or elevated terrain)
    Y93.01
  hockey (ice) Y93.22
    field Y93.65
  horseback riding Y93.52
  household maintenance NEC Y93.e9
  ice NEC Y93.29
    dancing Y93.21
    hockey Y93.22
    skating Y93.21
  inline roller skating Y93.51
  ironing Y93.e4
  judo Y93.75
  jumping (off) NEC Y93.39
    BASE (Building, Antenna, Span,
      Earth) Y93.33
    bungee Y93.34
    jacks Y93.a2
    rope Y93.56
  jumping jacks Y93.a2
  jumping rope Y93.56
  karate Y93.75
  kayaking (in calm and turbulent water)
    Y93.16
  keyboarding (computer) Y93.c1
  kickball Y93.68
  knitting Y93.d1
  lacrosse Y93.65
  land maintenance NEC Y93.h9
  landscaping Y93.h2
  laundry Y93.e2
  machines (exercise)
    primarily for cardiorespiratory
      conditioning Y93.a1
    primarily for muscle strengthening
      Y93.b1
  maintenance
    building NEC Y93.h9
    household NEC Y93.e9
    land Y93.h9
    property Y93.h9
  marching (on level or elevated terrain)
    Y93.01
  martial arts Y93.75

Activity *(Continued)*
  microwave oven Y93.g3
  mopping (floor) Y93.e5
  mountain climbing Y93.31
  milking an animal Y93.k2
  muscle strengthening
      exercises (non-machine) NEC Y93.b9
      machines Y93.b1
  musical keyboard (electronic) playing
      Y93.j1
  nordic skiing Y93.24
  obstacle course Y93.a5
  oven (microwave) Y93.g3
  packing up and unpacking in moving
      to a new residence Y93.e6
  parasailing Y93.19
  percussion instrument playing NEC Y93.j2
  personal
      bathing and showering Y93.e1
      hygiene NEC Y93.e8
      showering Y93.e1
  physical games generally associated
      with school recess, summer camp
      and children Y93.68
  physical training NEC Y93.a9
  piano playing Y93.j1
  pilates Y93.b4
  platform diving Y93.12
  playing musical instrument
      brass instrument Y93.j4
      drum Y93.j2
      musical keyboard (electronic) Y93.j1
      percussion instrument NEC Y93.j2
      piano Y93.j1
      string instrument Y93.j3
      winds instrument Y93.j4
  property maintenance NE Y93.h9
  pruning (garden and lawn) Y93.h2
  pull-ups Y93.b2
  push-ups Y93.b2
  racquetball Y93.73
  rafting (in calm and turbulent water)
      Y93.16
  raking (leaves) Y93.h1
  rappelling Y93.32
  refereeing a sports activity Y93.81
  residential relocation Y93.e6
  rhythmic gymnastics Y93.43
  rhythmic movement NEC Y93.49
  riding
      horseback Y93.52
      rollercoaster Y93.i1
  rock climbing Y93.31
  rollercoaster riding Y93.i1
  roller skating (inline) Y93.51
  rough housing and horseplay Y93.83
  rowing (in calm and turbulent water)
      Y93.16
  rugby Y93.63
  running Y93.02
  SCUBA diving Y93.15
  sewing Y93.d2
  shoveling Y93.h1
      dirt Y93.h1
      snow Y93.h1
  showering (personal) Y93.e1
  sit-ups Y93.b2
  skateboarding Y93.51
  skating (ice) Y93.21
      roller Y93.51
  skiing (alpine) (downhill) Y93.23
      cross country Y93.24
      nordic Y93.24
      water Y93.17

Activity *(Continued)*
  sledding (snow) Y93.23
  sleeping (sleep) Y93.84
  smoking and grilling food Y93.g2
  snorkeling Y93.15
  snow NEC Y93.29
      shoveling Y93.h1
      sledding Y93.23
      tubing Y93.23
  soccer Y93.66
  softball Y93.64
  specified NEC Y93.89
  spectator at an event Y93.82
  sports NEC Y93.79
      sports played as a team or group
          NEC Y93.69
      sports played individually NEC
          Y93.59
  springboard diving Y93.12
  squash Y93.73
  stationary bike Y93.a1
  step (stepping) exercise (class) Y93.a3
  stepper machine Y93.a1
  stove Y93.g3
  string instrument playing Y93.j3
  surfing Y93.18
      wind Y93.18
  swimming Y93.11
  tackle football Y93.61
  tap dancing Y93.41
  tennis Y93.73
  tobogganing Y93.23
  touch football Y93.62
  track and field events (non-running)
      Y93.57
  running Y93.02
  trampoline Y93.44
  treadmill Y93.a1
  trimming shrubs Y93.h2
  tubing (in calm and turbulent water)
      Y93.16
      snow Y93.23
  ultimate frisbee Y93.74
  underwater diving Y93.15
  unpacking in moving to a new
      residence Y93.e6
  use of stove, oven and microwave oven
      Y93.g3
  vacuuming Y93.e3
  volleyball (beach) (court) Y93.68
  wake boarding Y93.17
  walking an animal Y93.k1
  walking (on level or elevated terrain)
      Y93.01
      an animal Y93.k1
  wall climbing Y93.31
  warm up and cool down exercises
      Y93.a2
  water NEC Y93.19
      aerobics Y93.14
      craft NEC Y93.19
      exercise Y93.14
      polo Y93.13
      skiing Y93.17
      sliding Y93.18
      survival training and testing Y93.19
  weeding (garden and lawn) Y93.h2
  wind instrument playing Y93.j4
  windsurfing Y93.18
  wrestling Y93.72
  yoga Y93.42
Acute - *see also* condition
  abdomen R10.0
  gallbladder - *see* Cholecystitis, acute

Acyanotic heart disease (congenital)
    Q24.9
Acystia Q64.5
Adair-Dighton syndrome (brittle bones
    and blue sclera, deafness) Q78.0
Adamantinoblastoma - *see*
    Ameloblastoma
Adamantinoma - *see* Cyst, calcifying
    odontogenic
  long bones C40.90
      lower limb C40.2-
      upper limb C40.0-
  malignant C41.1
      jaw (bone) (lower) C41.1
          upper C41.0
  tibial C40.2-
Adamantoblastoma – *see* Ameloblastoma
Adams-Stokes(-Morgagni) disease or
    syndrome I45.9
Adaption reaction - *see* Disorder,
    adjustment
Addiction (*see also* Dependence)
    F19.20
  alcohol, alcoholic (ethyl) (methyl)
      (wood) (without remission)
      F10.20
      with remission F10.21
  drug – *see* Dependence, drug
  ethyl alcohol (without remission)
      F10.20
      with remission F10.21
  heroin – *see* Dependence, drug, opioid
  methyl alcohol (without remission)
      F10.20
      with remission F10.21
  methylated spirit (without remission)
      F10.20
      with remission F10.21
  morphine(-like substances) – *see* Depen-
      dence, drug, opioid
  nicotine - *see* Dependence, drug,
      nicotine
  opium and opioids – *see* Dependence,
      drug, opioid
  tobacco - *see* Dependence, drug,
      nicotine
Addisonian crisis E27.2
Addison's
  anemia (pernicious) D51.0
  disease (bronze) or syndrome E27.1
      tuberculous A18.7
  keloid L94.0
Addison-Biermer anemia (pernicious)
    D51.0
Addison-Schilder complex E71.428
Additional - *see also* Accessory
  chromosome(s) Q99.8
      sex - *see* Abnormal, chromosome, sex
      21 - *see* Trisomy, 21
Adduction contracture, hip or other joint
    - *see* Contraction, joint
Adenitis - *see also* Lymphadenitis
  acute, unspecified site L04.9
  axillary I88.9
      acute L04.2
      chronic or subacute I88.1
  Bartholin's gland N75.8
  bulbourethral gland - *see* Urethritis
  cervical I88.9
      acute L04.0
      chronic or subacute I88.1
  chancroid (Hemophilus ducreyi) A57
  chronic, unspecified site I88.1
  Cowper's gland - *see* Urethritis

71

Adenitis (*Continued*)
  due to Pasteurella multocida (p. septica) A28.0
  epidemic, acute B27.09
  gangrenous L04.9
  gonorrheal NEC A54.89
  groin I88.9
    acute L04.1
    chronic or subacute I88.1
  infectious (acute) (epidemic) B27.09
  inguinal I88.9
    acute L04.1
    chronic or subacute I88.1
  lymph gland or node, except mesenteric I88.9
    acute - *see* Lymphadenitis, acute
    chronic or subacute I88.1
  mesenteric (acute) (chronic) (nonspecific) (subacute) I88.0
  parotid gland (suppurative) - *see* Sialoadenitis
  salivary gland (any) (suppurative) - *see* Sialoadenitis
  scrofulous (tuberculous) A18.2
  Skene's duct or gland - *see* Urethritis
  strumous, tuberculous A18.2
  subacute, unspecified site I88.1
  sublingual gland (suppurative) - *see* Sialoadenitis
  submandibular gland (suppurative) - *see* Sialoadenitis
  submaxillary gland (suppurative) - *see* Sialoadenitis
  tuberculous - *see* Tuberculosis, lymph gland
  urethral gland - *see* Urethritis
  Wharton's duct (suppurative) - *see* Sialoadenitis
Adenoacanthoma - *see* Neoplasm, malignant
Adenoameloblastoma - *see* Cyst, calcifying odontogenic
Adenocarcinoid (tumor) - *see* Neoplasm, malignant
Adenocarcinoma - *see also* Neoplasm, malignant
  with
    acidophil
      specified site - *see* Neoplasm, malignant
      unspecified site C75.1
  adrenal cortical C74.0-
  alveolar - *see* Neoplasm, lung, malignant
  apocrine
    breast - *see* Neoplasm, breast, malignant
    in situ
      breast D05.7-
      specified site NEC - *see* Neoplasm, skin, in situ
      unspecified site D04.9
    specified site NEC - *see* Neoplasm, skin, malignant
    unspecified site C44.9
  basal cell
    specified site - *see* Neoplasm, skin, malignant
  basophil
    specified site - *see* Neoplasm, malignant
    unspecified site C75.1
  bile duct type C22.1
    liver C22.1
    specified site NEC - *see* Neoplasm, malignant
    unspecified site C22.1

Adenocarcinoma (*Continued*)
  bronchiolar - *see* Neoplasm, lung, malignant
  bronchioloalveolar - *see* Neoplasm, lung, malignant
  ceruminous C44.2-
  cervix, in situ D06.9 *see also* Carcinoma, cervix uteri, in situ
  chromophobe
    specified site - *see* Neoplasm, malignant
    unspecified site C75.1
  diffuse type (M8145/3)
    specified site - *see* Neoplasm, malignant
    unspecified site C16.9
  duct
    infiltrating
      with Paget's disease – *see* Neoplasm, breast, malignant
      specified site - *see* Neoplasm, malignant
      unspecified site (female) C50.91- male C50.92-
    specified site - *see* Neoplasm, malignant
    unspecified site
      female C56.9
      male C61
  eosinophil
    specified site - *see* Neoplasm, malignant
    unspecified site C75.1
  follicular
    with papillary C73
    moderately differentiated C73
    specified site - *see* Neoplasm, malignant
    trabecular C73
    unspecified site C73
    well differentiated C73
  Hurthle cell C73
  in
    adenomatous
      polyposis coli C18.9
  infiltrating duct
    with Paget's disease – *see* Neoplasm, breast, malignant
    specified site - *see* Neoplasm, malignant
    unspecified site (female) C50.91- male C50.92-
  inflammatory
    specified site - *see* Neoplasm, malignant
    unspecified site (female) C50.91- male C50.92-
  intestinal type
    specified site - *see* Neoplasm, malignant
    unspecified site C16.9
  intracystic papillary
  intraductal
    breast D05.1-
    noninfiltrating
      breast D05.1-
      papillary
        with invasion
          specified site - *see* Neoplasm, malignant
          unspecified site (female) C50.91- male C50.92-
        breast D05.1-

Adenocarcinoma (*Continued*)
  intraductal (*Continued*)
    noninfiltrating (*Continued*)
      papillary (*Continued*)
        specified site NEC - *see* Neoplasm, in situ
        unspecified site D05.1-
      specified site NEC - *see* Neoplasm, in situ
      unspecified site D05.1-
    papillary
      with invasion
        specified site - *see* Neoplasm, malignant
        unspecified site (female) C50.91- male C50.92-
        breast D05.1-
      specified site - *see* Neoplasm, in situ
      unspecified site D05.1-
    specified site NEC - *see* Neoplasm, in situ
    unspecified site D05.1-
  islet cell
    with exocrine, mixed
      specified site - *see* Neoplasm, malignant
      unspecified site C25.9
    pancreas C25.4
    specified site NEC - *see* Neoplasm, malignant
    unspecified site C25.4
  lobular
    in situ
      breast D05.0-
      specified site NEC - *see* Neoplasm, in situ
      unspecified site D05.0-
    specified site - *see* Neoplasm, malignant
    unspecified site (female) C50.91- male C50.92-
  mucoid - *see also* Neoplasm, malignant
    cell
      specified site - *see* Neoplasm, malignant
      unspecified site C75.1
  nonencapsulated sclerosing C73
    with follicular C73
    follicular variant C73
    intraductal (noninfiltrating)
      with invasion
        specified site - *see* Neoplasm, malignant
        unspecified site (female) C50.91- male C50.92
      breast D05.1-
      specified site NEC - *see* Neoplasm, in situ
      unspecified site D05.1-
  serous
    specified site - *see* Neoplasm, malignant
    unspecified site C56.9
  papillocystic
    specified site - *see* Neoplasm, malignant
    unspecified site C56.9
  pseudomucinous
    specified site - *see* Neoplasm, malignant
    unspecified site C56.9
  renal cell C64.-
  sebaceous - *see* Neoplasm, skin, malignant

Adenocarcinoma *(Continued)*
  serous - *see also* Neoplasm, malignant
    papillary
      specified site - *see* Neoplasm,
        malignant
      unspecified site C56.9
    sweat gland - *see* Neoplasm, skin,
      malignant
    water-clear cell C75.0
Adenocarcinoma-in-situ – *see also*
    Neoplasm, in situ
  breast D05.9-
Adenofibroma
  clear cell - *see* Neoplasm, benign
  endometrioid D27.9
    borderline malignancy D39.10
    malignant C56.-
  mucinous
    specified site - *see* Neoplasm, benign
    unspecified site D27.9
  papillary
    specified site - *see* Neoplasm, benign
    unspecified site D27.9
  prostate - *see* Enlargement, enlarged,
      prostate
  serous
    specified site - *see* Neoplasm, benign
    unspecified site D27.9
  specified site - *see* Neoplasm, benign
  unspecified site D27.9
Adenofibrosis
  breast - *see* Fibroadenosis, breast
  endometrioid N80.0
Adenoiditis (chronic) J35.02
  with tonsillitis J35.03
  acute J03.90
    recurrent J03.91
    specified organism NEC J03.80
      recurrent J03.81
    staphylococcal J03.80
      recurrent J03.81
    streptococcal J03.00
      recurrent J03.01
Adenoids - *see* condition
Adenolipoma - *see* Neoplasm, benign
Adenolipomatosis, Launois-Bensaude
    E88.89
Adenolymphoma
  specified site - *see* Neoplasm, benign
  unspecified site D11.9
Adenoma - *see also* Neoplasm, benign
  acidophil
    specified site - *see* Neoplasm, benign
    unspecified site D35.2
  acidophil-basophil, mixed
    specified site - *see* Neoplasm, benign
    unspecified site D35.2
  acinar (cell)
  acinic cell
  adrenal (cortical) D35.00
    clear cell D35.00
    compact cell D35.00
    glomerulosa cell D35.00
    heavily pigmented variant D35.00
    mixed cell D35.00
  alpha-cell
    pancreas D13.7
    specified site NEC - *see* Neoplasm,
      benign
    unspecified site D13.7
  alveolar D14.30
  apocrine
    breast (female) D24.0-
      male D24.1-

Adenoma *(Continued)*
  apocrine *(Continued)*
    specified site NEC - *see* Neoplasm,
      skin, benign
    unspecified site D23.9
  basal cell D11.9
  basophil
    specified site - *see* Neoplasm, benign
    unspecified site D35.2
  basophil-acidophil, mixed
    specified site - *see* Neoplasm, benign
    unspecified site D35.2
  beta-cell
    pancreas D13.7
    specified site NEC - *see* Neoplasm,
      benign
    unspecified site D13.7
  bile duct D13.4
    common D13.5
    extrahepatic D13.5
    intrahepatic D13.4
    specified site NEC - *see* Neoplasm,
      benign
    unspecified site D13.4
  black D35.00
  bronchial D38.1
    cylindroid type – *see* Neoplasm, lung,
      malignant
  ceruminous D23.2-
  chief cell D35.1
  chromophobe
    specified site - *see* Neoplasm, benign
    unspecified site D35.2
  colloid
    specified site - *see* Neoplasm, benign
    unspecified site D34
  duct
  eccrine, papillary – *see* Neoplasm, skin,
    benign
  endocrine, multiple
    single specified site - *see* Neoplasm,
      uncertain behavior
    two or more specified sites D44.8
    unspecified site D44.8
  endometrioid - *see also* Neoplasm, benign
    borderline malignancy - *see*
      Neoplasm, uncertain behavior
  eosinophil
    specified site - *see* Neoplasm, benign
    unspecified site D35.2
  fetal
    specified site - *see* Neoplasm, benign
    unspecified site D34
  follicular
    specified site - *see* Neoplasm, benign
    unspecified site D34
  hepatocellular D13.4
  Hurthle cell D34
  islet cell
    pancreas D13.7
    specified site NEC - *see* Neoplasm, benign
    unspecified site D13.7
  liver cell D13.4
  macrofollicular
    specified site - *see* Neoplasm, benign
    unspecified site D34
  malignant, malignum - *see* Neoplasm,
    malignant
  mesonephric
  microcystic
    pancreas D13.7
    specified site NEC - *see* Neoplasm,
      benign
    unspecified site D13.7

Adenoma *(Continued)*
  microfollicular
    specified site - *see* Neoplasm, benign
    unspecified site D34
  mucoid cell
    specified site - *see* Neoplasm, benign
    unspecified site D35.2
  multiple endocrine
    single specified site - *see* Neoplasm,
      uncertain behavior
    two or more specified sites D44.8
    unspecified site D44.8
  nipple (female) D24.0-
    male D24.1-
  papillary - *see also* Neoplasm, benign
    eccrine - *see* Neoplasm, skin, benign
  Pick's tubular
    specified site - *see* Neoplasm, benign
    unspecified site
      female D27.9
      male D29.20
  pleomorphic
    carcinoma in - *see* Neoplasm, salivary
      gland, malignant
    specified site - *see* Neoplasm,
      malignant
    unspecified site C08.9
  polypoid - *see also* Neoplasm, benign
    adenocarcinoma in - *see* Neoplasm,
      malignant
    adenocarcinoma in situ - *see*
      Neoplasm, in situ
  prostate - *see* Neoplasm, benign, prostate
  rete cell D29.20
  sebaceous - *see* Neoplasm,
    skin, benign
  Sertoli cell
    specified site - *see* Neoplasm, benign
    unspecified site
      female D27.9
      male D29.20
  skin appendage - *see* Neoplasm, skin,
    benign
  sudoriferous gland - *see* Neoplasm,
    skin, benign
  sweat gland - *see* Neoplasm, skin,
    benign
  testicular
    specified site - *see* Neoplasm, benign
    unspecified site
      female D27.9
      male D29.20
  tubular - *see also* Neoplasm, benign
    adenocarcinoma in - *see* Neoplasm,
      malignant
    adenocarcinoma in situ - *see*
      Neoplasm, in situ
  Pick's
    specified site - *see* Neoplasm, benign
    unspecified site
      female D27.9
      male D29.20
  tubulovillous - *see also* Neoplasm, benign
    adenocarcinoma in - *see* Neoplasm,
      malignant
    adenocarcinoma in situ - *see*
      Neoplasm, in situ
  villous - *see* Neoplasm, uncertain
    behavior
    adenocarcinoma in - *see* Neoplasm,
      malignant
    adenocarcinoma in situ - *see*
      Neoplasm, in situ
  water-clear cell D35.1

Adenomatosis
  endocrine (multiple) E31.20
    single specified site - *see* Neoplasm,
      uncertain behavior
  erosive of nipple (female) D24.0-
    male D24.1-
  pluriendocrine - *see* Adenomatosis,
    endocrine
  pulmonary D38.1
    malignant - *see* Neoplasm, lung,
      malignant
  specified site - *see* Neoplasm, benign
  unspecified site D12.6
Adenomatous
  goiter (nontoxic) E04.9
    with hyperthyroidism – *see* Hyper-
      thyroidism, with, goiter, nodular
    toxic – *see* Hyperthyroidism, with,
      goiter, nodular
Adenomyoma - *see also* Neoplasm, benign
  prostate – *see* Enlarged, prostate
Adenomyometritis N80.0
Adenomyosis N80.0
Adenopathy (lymph gland) R59.9
  generalized R59.1
  inguinal R59.0
  localized R59.0
  mediastinal R59.0
  mesentery R59.0
  syphilitic (secondary) A51.49
  tracheobronchial R59.0
    tuberculous A15.4
      primary (progressive) A15.7
  tuberculous - *see also* Tuberculosis,
    lymph gland
    tracheobronchial A15.4
      primary (progressive) A15.7
Adenosalpingitis - *see* Salpingitis
Adenosarcoma - *see* Neoplasm, malignant
Adenosclerosis I88.8
Adenosis (sclerosing) **breast** - *see* Fibroadenosis, breast
Adenovirus, as cause of disease classi-
  fied elsewhere B97.0
Adentia (complete) (partial) - *see* Absence,
  teeth
Adherent - *see also* Adhesions
  labia (minora) N90.8
  pericardium (nonrheumatic) I31.0
    rheumatic I09.2
  placenta (with hemorrhage) O72.0
    without hemorrhage O73.0
  prepuce, newborn N47.0
  scar (skin) L90.5
  tendon in scar L90.5
Adhesions, adhesive (postinfective)
  K66.0
  with intestinal obstruction K56.5
  abdominal (wall) - *see* Adhesions,
    peritoneum
  appendix K38.8
  bile duct (common) (hepatic) K83.8
  bladder (sphincter) N32.89
  bowel - *see* Adhesions, peritoneum
  cardiac I31.0
    rheumatic I09.2
  cecum - *see* Adhesions, peritoneum
  cervicovaginal N88.1
    congenital Q52.8
    postpartal O90.89
      old N88.1
  cervix N88.1
  ciliary body NEC - *see* Adhesions, iris
  clitoris N90.8

Adhesions, adhesive *(Continued)*
  colon - *see* Adhesions, peritoneum
  common duct K83.8
  congenital - *see also* Anomaly, by site
    fingers – *see* Syndactylism, complex,
      fingers
    omental, anomalous Q43.3
    peritoneal Q43.3
    toes Q70.2
    tongue (to gum or roof of mouth)
      Q38.3
  conjunctiva (acquired) H11.21-
    congenital Q15.8
  cystic duct K82.8
  diaphragm - *see* Adhesions, peritoneum
  due to foreign body - *see* Foreign body
  duodenum - *see* Adhesions, peritoneum
  epididymis N50.8
  epidural - *see* Adhesions, meninges
  epiglottis J38.7
  eyelid H02.59
  female pelvis N73.6
  gallbladder K82.8
  globe H44.89
  heart I31.0
    rheumatic I09.2
  ileocecal (coil) - *see* Adhesions,
    peritoneum
  ileum - *see* Adhesions, peritoneum
  intestine - *see also* Adhesions,
    peritoneum
    with obstruction K56.5
  intra-abdominal - *see* Adhesions,
    peritoneum
  iris H21.509
    anterior H21.51-
    goniosynechiae H21.52-
    posterior H21.54-
    to corneal graft T85.89
  joint - *see* Ankylosis
    knee M23.8x
    temporomandibular M26.61
  labium (majus) (minus), congenital
    Q52.5
  liver - *see* Adhesions, peritoneum
  lung J98.4
  mediastinum J98.5
  meninges (cerebral) (spinal) G96.12
    congenital Q07.8
    tuberculous (cerebral) (spinal) A17.0
  mesenteric - *see* Adhesions, peritoneum
  nasal (septum) (to turbinates) J34.89
  ocular muscle - *see* Strabismus,
    mechanical
  omentum - *see* Adhesions, peritoneum
  ovary N73.6
    congenital (to cecum, kidney or
      omentum) Q50.39
  paraovarian N73.6
  pelvic (peritoneal)
    female N73.6
      postprocedural N99.4
    male - *see* Adhesions, peritoneum
    postpartal (old) N73.6
    tuberculous A18.17
  penis to scrotum (congenital) Q55.8
  periappendiceal - *see also* Adhesions,
    peritoneum
  pericardium (nonrheumatic) I31.0
    focal I31.8
    rheumatic I09.2
    tuberculous A18.84
  pericholecystic K82.8
  perigastric - *see* Adhesions, peritoneum

Adhesions, adhesive *(Continued)*
  periovarian N73.6
  periprostatic N42.89
  perirectal - *see* Adhesions, peritoneum
  perirenal N28.89
  peritoneum, peritoneal (postinfective)
    (postprocedural) K66.0
    with obstruction (intestinal) K56.5
    congenital Q43.3
    pelvic, female N73.6
      postprocedural N99.4
    postpartal, pelvic N73.6
    to uterus N73.6
  peritubal N73.6
  periureteral N28.89
  periuterine N73.6
  perivesical N32.89
  perivesicular (seminal vesicle) N50.8
  pleura, pleuritic J94.8
    tuberculous NEC A15.6
  pleuropericardial J94.8
  postoperative (gastrointestinal tract)
    K66.0
    with obstruction K91.3
    due to foreign body accidentally
      left in wound – *see* Foreign
      body, accidentally left during a
      procedure
    pelvic peritoneal N99.4
    urethra - *see* Stricture, urethra,
      postprocedural
    vagina N99.2
  postpartal, old (vulva or perineum)
    N90.8
  preputial, prepuce N47.5
  pulmonary J98.4
  pylorus - *see* Adhesions, peritoneum
  sciatic nerve - *see* Lesion, nerve, sciatic
  seminal vesicle N50.8
  shoulder (joint) - *see* Capsulitis,
    adhesive
  sigmoid flexure - *see* Adhesions,
    peritoneum
  spermatic cord (acquired) N50.8
    congenital Q55.4
  spinal canal G96.12
  stomach - *see* Adhesions, peritoneum
  subscapular - *see* Capsulitis, adhesive
  temporomandibular M26.61
  tendinitis - *see also* Tenosynovitis, speci-
    fied type NEC
    shoulder - *see* Capsulitis, adhesive
  testis N44.8
  tongue, congenital (to gum or roof of
    mouth) Q38.3
    acquired K14.8
  trachea J39.8
  tubo-ovarian N73.6
  tunica vaginalis N44.8
  uterus N73.6
    internal N85.6
    to abdominal wall N73.6
  vagina (chronic) N89.5
    postoperative N99.2
  vitreous H43.89
  vulva N90.8
Adiaspiromycosis B48.8
Adie(-Holmes) pupil or syndrome - *see*
  Anomaly, pupil, function, tonic
  pupil
Adiponecrosis neonatorum P83.8
Adiposis - *see also* Obesity
  cerebralis E23.6
  dolorosa E88.2

A

Adiposity - *see also* Obesity
  heart - *see* Degeneration, myocardial
    localized E65
Adiposogenital dystrophy E23.6
Adjustment
  disorder – *see* Disorder, adjustment
  implanted device - *see* Encounter (for),
    adjustment (of)
  prosthesis, external - *see* Fitting
  reaction – *see* Disorder, adjustment
Administration of tPA (rtPA) in a
    different facility within the last
    24 hours prior to admission to
    current facility Z92.82
Admission (for) - *see also* Encounter (for)
  adjustment (of)
    artificial
      arm Z44.00-
        complete Z44.01-
        partial Z44.02-
      eye Z44.2
      leg Z44.10-
        complete Z44.11-
        partial Z44.12-
    brain neuropacemaker Z46.2
      implanted Z45.42
    breast
      implant Z41.81
      prosthesis (external) Z44.3
    colostomy belt Z46.89
    contact lenses Z46.0
    cystostomy device Z46.6
    dental prosthesis Z46.3
    device NEC
      abdominal Z46.89
      implanted Z45.9
        cardiac Z45.09
          defibrillator Z45.02
          pacemaker Z45.018
            pulse generator Z45.010
        hearing device Z45.328
          bone conduction Z45.320
          cochlear Z45.321
        infusion pump Z45.1
        nervous system Z45.49
          CSF drainage Z45.41
          hearing device - *see* Admission, adjustment, device, implanted, hearing device
          neuropacemaker Z45.42
          visual substitution Z45.31
        specified NEC Z45.89
        vascular access Z45.2
        visual substitution Z45.31
      nervous system Z46.2
        implanted - *see* Admission, adjustment, device, implanted, nervous system
      orthodontic Z46.4
      prosthetic Z44.9
        arm - *see* Admission, adjustment, artificial, arm
        breast Z44.3
        dental Z46.3
        eye Z44.2
        leg - *see* Admission, adjustment, artificial, leg
        specified type NEC Z44.8
      substitution
        auditory Z46.2
          implanted - *see* Admission, adjustment, device, implanted, hearing device

Admission (Continued)
  adjustment (Continued)
    device NEC (Continued)
      substitution (Continued)
        nervous system Z46.2
          implanted - *see* Admission, adjustment, device, implanted, nervous system
        visual Z46.2
          implanted Z45.31
      urinary Z46.6
    hearing aid Z46.1
      implanted - *see* Admission, adjustment, device, implanted, hearing device
    ileostomy device Z46.89
    intestinal appliance or device NEC Z46.89
    neuropacemaker (brain) (peripheral nerve) (spinal cord) Z46.2
      implanted Z45.42
    orthodontic device Z46.4
    orthopedic (brace) (cast) (device) (shoes) Z46.89
    pacemaker
      cardiac Z45.018
        pulse generator Z45.010
      nervous system Z46.2
        implanted Z45.42
    portacath (port-a-cath) Z45.2
    prosthesis Z44.9
      arm - *see* Admission, adjustment, artificial, arm
      breast Z44.3
      dental Z46.3
      eye Z44.2
      leg - *see* Admission, adjustment, artificial, leg
      specified NEC Z44.8
    spectacles Z46.0
  aftercare (*see also* Aftercare) Z51.89
    postpartum
      immediately after delivery Z39.0
      routine follow-up Z39.2
    radiation therapy (antineoplastic) Z51.0
  attention to artificial opening (of) Z43.9
    artificial vagina Z43.7
    colostomy Z43.3
    cystostomy Z43.5
    enterostomy Z43.4
    gastrostomy Z43.1
    ileostomy Z43.2
    jejunostomy Z43.4
    nephrostomy Z43.6
    specified site NEC Z43.8
      intestinal tract Z43.4
      urinary tract Z43.6
    tracheostomy Z43.0
    ureterostomy Z43.6
    urethrostomy Z43.6
  breast augmentation or reduction Z41.1
  breast reconstruction following mastectomy Z42.1
  change of
    dressing (nonsurgical) Z48.00
    neuropacemaker device (brain) (peripheral nerve) (spinal cord) Z46.2
      implanted Z45.42
    surgical dressing Z48.01
  circumcision, ritual or routine (in absence of diagnosis) Z41.2
  clinical research investigation Z00.6

Admission (Continued)
  contraceptive management Z30.9
  cosmetic surgery NEC Z41.1
  counseling (*see also* Counseling)
    dietary Z71.3
    HIV Z71.7
    human immunodeficiency virus Z71.7
    nonattending third party Z71.0
    procreative management NEC Z31.69
  delivery, full-term, uncomplicated O80
    cesarean, without indication O82
  dietary surveillance and counseling Z71.3
  ear piercing Z41.3
  examination (*see also* Examination) at health care facility (adult) Z00.00
    with abnormal findings Z00.01
    clinical research investigation Z00.6
    dental Z01.20
      with abnormal findings Z01.21
    donor (potential) Z00.5
    ear Z01.10
      with abnormal findings NEC Z01.118
    eye Z01.00
      with abnormal findings Z01.01
    general, specified reason NEC Z00.5
    hearing Z01.10
      with abnormal findings NEC Z01.118
    postpartum checkup Z39.2
    psychiatric (general) Z00.8
      requested by authority Z04.6
    vision Z01.00
      with abnormal findings Z01.01
  fitting (of)
    artificial
      arm - *see* Admission, adjustment, artificial, arm
      eye Z44.2
      leg - *see* Admission, adjustment, artificial, leg
    brain neuropacemaker Z46.2
      implanted Z45.42
    breast prosthesis (external) Z44.3
    colostomy belt Z46.89
    contact lenses Z46.0
    cystostomy device Z46.6
    dental prosthesis Z46.3
    dentures Z46.3
    device NEC
      abdominal Z46.89
      nervous system Z46.2
        implanted - *see* Admission, adjustment, device, implanted, nervous system
      orthodontic Z46.4
      prosthetic Z44.9
        breast Z44.3
        dental Z46.3
        eye Z44.2
      substitution
        auditory Z46.2
          implanted - *see* Admission, adjustment, device, implanted, hearing device
        nervous system Z46.2
          implanted - *see* Admission, adjustment, device, implanted, nervous system
        visual Z46.2
          implanted Z45.31

75

Admission (*Continued*)
fitting (*Continued*)
hearing aid Z46.1
ileostomy device Z46.89
intestinal appliance or device NEC
Z46.89
neuropacemaker (brain) (peripheral
nerve) (spinal cord) Z46.2
implanted Z45.42
orthodontic device Z46.4
orthopedic device (brace) (cast)
(shoes) Z46.89
prosthesis Z44.9
arm - *see* Admission, adjustment,
artificial, arm
breast Z44.3
dental Z46.3
eye Z44.2
leg - *see* Admission, adjustment,
artificial, leg
specified type NEC Z44.8
spectacles Z46.0
follow-up examination Z09
intrauterine device management
Z30.43
initial prescription Z30.014
mental health evaluation Z00.8
requested by authority Z04.6
observation - *see* Observation
Papanicolaou smear, cervix Z12.4
for suspected malignant neoplasm
Z12.4
plastic surgery, cosmetic NEC Z41.1
postpartum observation
immediately after delivery Z39.0
routine follow-up Z39.2
poststerilization (for restoration)
Z31.0
aftercare Z31.42
plastic and reconstructive surgery
following medical procedure or
healed injury NEC Z42.8
procreative management Z31.9
prophylactic (measure)
organ removal Z40.00
breast Z40.01
ovary Z40.02
specified organ NEC Z40.09
testes Z40.09
vaccination Z23
psychiatric examination (general)
Z00.8
requested by authority Z04.6
radiation therapy (antineoplastic)
Z51.0
reconstructive surgery following
medical procedure or healed
injury NEC Z42.8
removal of
cystostomy catheter Z43.5
device
intrauterine contraceptive
Z30.43
drains Z48.03
dressing (nonsurgical) Z48.00
intrauterine contraceptive device
Z30.43
neuropacemaker (brain) (peripheral
nerve) (spinal cord) Z46.2
implanted Z45.42
staples Z48.02
surgical dressing Z48.01
sutures Z48.02
ureteral stent Z46.6

Admission (*Continued*)
respirator/ventilator use during power
failure (Z99.12)
restoration of organ continuity
(poststerilization) Z31.0
aftercare Z31.42
sensitivity test—*see also* Test, skin
allergy NEC Z01.82
Mantoux Z11.1
tuboplasty following previous sterilization Z31.0
aftercare Z31.42
vasoplasty following previous sterilization Z31.0
aftercare Z31.42
vision examination Z01.00
with abnormal findings Z01.01
waiting period for admission to other
facility Z75.1
Adnexitis (suppurative) - *see*
Salpingo-oophoritis
Adolescent X-linked adrenoleuko-
dystrophy E71.421
Adrenal (gland) - *see* condition
Adrenalism, tuberculous A18.7
Adrenalitis, adrenitis E27.8
autoimmune E27.1
meningococcal, hemorrhagic A39.1
Adrenarche, premature E27.0
Adrenocortical syndrome - *see* Cushing's
syndrome
Adrenogenital syndrome E25.9
acquired E25.8
congenital E25.0
salt loss E25.0
Adrenogenitalism, congenital E25.0
Adrenoleukodystrophy E71.529
neonatal E71.511
X-linked E71.529
Addison only phenotype E71.528
Addison-Schilder E71.528
adolescent E71.521
adrenomyeloneuropathy E71.522
childhood cerebral E71.520
other specified E71.528
Adrenomyeloneuropathy E71.522
Adventitious bursa - *see* Bursopathy,
specified type NEC
Adverse effect - *see* Table of drugs and
chemicals, categories T36-T50, with
6th character 5
Advice - *see* Counseling
Adynamia (episodica) (hereditary)
(periodic) G72.3
Aeration lung imperfect, newborn - *see*
Atelectasis
Aerobullosis T70.3
Aerocele - *see* Embolism, air
Aerodermectasia
subcutaneous (traumatic) T79.7
Aerodontalgia T70.29
Aeroembolism T70.3
Aerogenes capsulatus infection
A48.0
Aero-otitis media T70.0
Aerophagy, aerophagia (psychogenic)
F45.8
Aerophobia F40.228
Aerosinusitis T70.1
Aerotitis T70.0
Affection - *see* Disease
Afibrinogenemia (*see also* Defect,
coagulation) D68.8
acquired D65

Afibrinogenemia (*Continued*)
congenital D68.2
in abortion – *see* Abortion, by type,
complicated by, afibrinogenemia
puerperal O72.3
African
sleeping sickness B56.9
tick fever A68.1
trypanosomiasis B56.9
gambian B56.0
rhodesian B56.1
Aftercare (*see also* Care) Z51.89
following surgery (for) (on)
amputation Z47.81
attention to
drains Z48.03
dressings (nonsurgical) Z48.00
surgical Z48.01
sutures Z48.02
circulatory system Z48.812
delayed (planned) wound closure Z48.1
digestive system Z48.815
genitourinary system Z48.816
joint replacement Z47.1
neoplasm Z48.3
nervous system Z48.811
oral cavity Z48.814
organ transplant
bone marrow Z48.290
heart Z48.21
heart-lung Z48.280
kidney Z48.22
liver Z48.23
lung Z48.24
multiple organs NEC Z48.288
specified NEC Z48.298
orthopedic NEC Z47.89
planned wound closure Z48.1
removal of internal fixation device Z47.2
respiratory system Z48.813
scoliosis Z47.82
sense organs Z48.810
skin and subcutaneous tissue Z48.817
specified body system
circulatory Z48.812
digestive Z48.815
genitourinary Z48.816
nervous Z48.811
oral cavity Z48.814
respiratory Z48.813
sense organs Z48.810
skin and subcutaneous tissue
Z48.817
teeth Z48.814
specified NEC Z48.89
spinal - *see* Aftercare, following surgery (for) (on), specified body
system
teeth Z48.814
fracture - code to fracture with extension d
involving
removal of
drains Z48.03
dressings (nonsurgical) Z48.00
staples Z48.02
surgical dressings Z48.01
sutures Z48.02
neuropacemaker (brain) (peripheral
nerve) (spinal cord) Z46.2
implanted Z45.42
orthopedic NEC Z47.89
postprocedural - *see* Aftercare, following surgery

After-cataract - *see* Cataract, secondary
Agalactia (primary) O92.3
   elective, secondary or therapeutic
      O92.5
Agammaglobulinemia (acquired (second-
     ary)) (nonfamilial) D80.1
   with
      immunoglobulin-bearing B-lympho-
        cytes D80.1
      lymphopenia D81.9
   autosomal recessive (Swiss type) D80.0
   Bruton's X-linked D80.0
   common variable (CVAgamma) D80.1
   congenital sex-linked D80.0
   hereditary D80.0
   lymphopenic D81.9
   Swiss type (autosomal recessive)
      D80.0
   X-linked (with growth hormone
      deficiency)(Bruton) D80.0
Aganglionosis (bowel) (colon) Q43.1
Age (old) - *see* Senility
Agenesis
   adrenal (gland) Q89.1
   alimentary tract (complete) (partial)
      NEC Q45.8
     upper Q40.8
   anus, anal (canal) Q42.3
     with fistula Q42.2
   aorta Q25.4
   appendix Q42.8
   arm (complete) Q71.0-
     with hand present Q71.1-
   artery (peripheral) Q27.9
     brain Q28.3
     coronary Q24.5
     pulmonary Q25.7
     specified NEC Q27.8
     umbilical Q27.0
   auditory (canal) (external) Q16.1
   auricle (ear) Q16.0
   bile duct or passage Q44.5
   bladder Q64.5
   bone Q79.9
   brain Q00.0
     part of Q04.3
   breast (with nipple present) Q83.8
     with absent nipple Q83.0
   bronchus Q32.4
   canaliculus lacrimalis Q10.4
   carpus – *see* Agenesis, hand
   cartilage Q79.9
   cecum Q42.8
   cerebellum Q04.3
   cervix Q51.5
   chin Q18.8
   cilia Q10.3
   circulatory system, part NOS Q28.9
   clavicle Q74.0
   clitoris Q52.6
   coccyx Q76.49
   colon Q42.9
     specified NEC Q42.8
   corpus callosum Q04.0
   cricoid cartilage Q31.8
   diaphragm (with hernia) Q79.1
   digestive organ(s) or tract (complete)
      (partial) NEC Q45.8
     upper Q40.8
   ductus arteriosus Q28.8
   duodenum Q41.0
   ear Q16.9
     auricle Q16.0
     lobe Q17.8

Agenesis *(Continued)*
   ejaculatory duct Q55.4
   endocrine (gland) NEC Q89.2
   epiglottis Q31.8
   esophagus Q39.8
   eustachian tube Q16.2
   eye Q11.1
     adnexa Q15.8
   eyelid (fold) Q10.3
   face
     bones NEC Q75.8
     specified part NEC Q18.8
   fallopian tube Q50.6
   femur – *see* Defect, reduction, lower
      limb, longitudinal, femur
   fibula – *see* Defect, reduction, lower
      limb, longitudinal, fibula
   finger (complete) (partial) – *see* Agen-
      esis, hand
   foot (and toes) (complete) (partial)
      Q72.3-
   forearm (with hand present) - *see* Agen-
      esis, arm, with hand present
     and hand Q71.2-
   gallbladder Q44.0
   gastric Q40.2
   genitalia, genital (organ(s))
     female Q52.8
      external Q52.71
      internal NEC Q52.8
     male Q55.8
   glottis Q31.8
   hair Q84.0
   hand (and fingers) (complete) (partial)
      Q71.3-
   heart Q24.8
     valve NEC Q24.8
      pulmonary Q22.0
   hepatic Q44.7
   humerus - *see* Defect, reduction, upper
     limb
   hymen Q52.4
   ileum Q41.2
   incus Q16.3
   intestine (small) Q41.9
     large Q42.9
      specified NEC Q42.8
   iris (dilator fibers) Q13.1
   jaw M26.09
   jejunum Q41.1
   kidney(s) (partial) Q60.2
     bilateral Q60.1
     unilateral Q60.0
   labium (majus) (minus) Q52.71
   labyrinth, membranous Q16.5
   lacrimal apparatus Q10.4
   larynx Q31.8
   leg (complete) Q72.0-
     with foot present Q72.1-
     lower leg (with foot present) – *see*
       Agenesis, leg, with foot
       present
     and foot Q72.2-
   lens Q12.3
   limb (complete) Q73.0
     lower – *see* Agenesis, leg
     upper – *see* Agenesis, arm
   lip Q38.0
   liver Q44.7
   lung (fissure) (lobe) (bilateral) (unilat-
     eral) Q33.3
   mandible, maxilla M26.09
   metacarpus – *see* Agenesis, hand
   metatarsus – *see* Agenesis, foot

Agenesis *(Continued)*
   muscle Q79.8
     eyelid Q10.3
     ocular Q15.8
   musculoskeletal system NEC Q79.8
   nail(s) Q84.3
   neck, part Q18.8
   nerve Q07.8
   nervous system, part NEC Q07.8
   nipple Q83.2
   nose Q30.1
   nuclear Q07.8
   oesophagus Q39.8
   organ
     of Corti Q16.5
     or site not listed - *see* Anomaly,
       by site
   osseous meatus (ear) Q16.1
   ovary
     bilateral Q50.02
     unilateral Q50.01
   oviduct Q50.6
   pancreas Q45.0
   parathyroid (gland) Q89.2
   parotid gland(s) Q38.4
   patella Q74.1
   pelvic girdle (complete) (partial) Q74.2
   penis Q55.5
   pericardium Q24.8
   pituitary (gland) Q89.2
   prostate Q55.4
   punctum lacrimale Q10.4
   radioulnar - *see* Defect, reduction, upper
     limb
   radius - *see* Defect, reduction, upper
     limb, longitudinal, radius
   rectum Q42.1
     with fistula Q42.0
   renal Q60.2
     bilateral Q60.1
     unilateral Q60.0
   respiratory organ NEC Q34.8
   rib Q76.6
   roof of orbit Q75.8
   round ligament Q52.8
   sacrum Q76.49
   salivary gland Q38.4
   scapula Q74.0
   scrotum Q55.29
   seminal vesicles Q55.4
   septum
     atrial Q21.1
     between aorta and pulmonary artery
      Q21.4
     ventricular Q20.4
   shoulder girdle (complete) (partial)
      Q74.0
   skull (bone) Q75.8
     with
      anencephaly Q00.0
      encephalocele - *see* Encephalocele
      hydrocephalus Q03.9
       with spina bifida - *see* Spina
        bifida, by site, with
        hydrocephalus
      microcephaly Q02
   spermatic cord Q55.4
   spinal cord Q06.0
   spine Q76.49
   spleen Q89.01
   sternum Q76.7
   stomach Q40.2
   submaxillary gland(s) (congenital)
      Q38.4

Agenesis *(Continued)*
  tarsus – *see* Agenesis, foot
  tendon Q79.8
  testicle Q55.0
  thymus (gland) Q89.2
  thyroid (gland) E03.1
    cartilage Q31.8
  tibia – *see* Defect, reduction, lower limb, longitudinal, tibia
  tibiofibular – *see* Defect, reduction, lower limb, specified type NEC
  toe (and foot) (complete) (partial) – *see* Agenesis, foot
  tongue Q38.3
  trachea (cartilage) Q32.1
  ulna - *see* Defect, reduction, upper limb, longitudinal, ulna
  upper limb – *see* Agenesis, arm
  ureter Q62.4
  urethra Q64.5
  urinary tract NEC Q64.8
  uterus Q51.0
  uvula Q38.5
  vagina Q52.0
  vas deferens Q55.4
  vein(s) (peripheral) Q27.9
    brain Q28.3
    great NEC Q26.8
    portal Q26.5
  vena cava (inferior) (superior) Q26.8
  vermis of cerebellum Q04.3
  vertebra Q76.49
  vulva Q52.71
Ageusia R43.2
Agitated - *see* condition
Agitation R45.1
Aglossia (congenital) Q38.3
Aglossia-adactylia syndrome Q87.0
Aglycogenosis E74.00
Agnosia (body image) (other senses) (tactile) (visual) R48.1
  developmental F88
  verbal R48.1
    auditory R48.1
      developmental F80.2
    developmental F80.2
  visual object H53.16
Agoraphobia F40.00
  with panic disorder F40.01
  without panic disorder F40.02
Agrammatism R48.8
Agranulocytopenia – *see* Agranulocytosis
Agranulocytosis (chronic) (cyclical) (genetic) (infantile) (periodic) (pernicious) D70.9 - *see also* Neutropenia
  congenital D70.0
  cytoreductive cancer chemotherapy sequela D70.1
  drug-induced D70.2
    due to cytoreductive cancer chemotherapy D70.1
  due to infection D70.3
  secondary D70.8
    drug-induced D70.2
      due to cytoreductive cancer chemotherapy D70.1
Agraphia (absolute) R48.8
  with alexia R48.0
  developmental F81.81
Ague (dumb) - *see* Malaria
Agyria Q04.3
Ahumada-del Castillo syndrome E23.0
Aichomophobia F40.298

AIDS (related complex) B20
Ailment heart - *see* Disease, heart
Ailurophobia F40.218
Ainhum (disease) L94.6
Air
  anterior mediastinum J98.2
  compressed, disease T70.3
  conditioner lung or pneumonitis J67.7
  embolism (artery) (cerebral) (any site) T79.0
    with ectopic or molar pregnancy O08.2
    due to implanted device NEC - *see* Complications, by site and type, specified NEC
    following
      ectopic or molar pregnancy O08.2
      infusion, therapeutic injection or transfusion T80.0
    in pregnancy, childbirth or puerperium - *see* Embolism, obstetric
    traumatic T79.0
  hunger, psychogenic F45.8
  rarefied, effects of - *see* Effect, adverse, high altitude
  sickness T75.3
Airplane sickness T75.3
Akathisia (drug-induced) (treatment-induced) G25.71
  neuroleptic induced (acute) G25.71
Akinesia R29.898
Akinetic mutism R41.89
Akureyri's disease G93.3
Alactasia, congenital E73.0
Alagille's syndrome Q44.7
Alastrim B03
Albers-Schönberg syndrome Q78.2
Albert's syndrome - *see* Tendinitis, Achilles
Albinism, albino E70.30
  with hematologic abnormality E70.339
    Chédiak-Higashi syndrome E70.330
    Hermansky-Pudlak syndrome E70.331
    other specified E70.338
  I E70.320
  II E70.321
  ocular E70.319
    autosomal recessive E70.311
    other specified E70.318
    X-linked E70.310
  oculocutaneous E70.329
    other specified E70.328
    tyrosinase (ty) negative E70.320
    tyrosinase (ty) positive E70.321
  other specified E70.39
Albinismus E70.30
Albright(-McCune)(-Sternberg) syndrome Q78.1
Albuminous - *see* condition
Albuminuria, albuminuric (acute) (chronic) (subacute) (- *see also* Proteinuria) R80.9
  complicating pregnancy – *see* Proteinuria, gestational
  with
    gestational hypertension – *see* Pre-eclampsia
    pre-existing hypertension – *see* Hypertension, complicating pregnancy, pre-existing with proteinuria

Albuminuria, albuminuric *(Continued)*
  gestational – *see* Proteinuria, gestational
  with
    gestational hypertension – *see* Pre-eclampsia
    pre-existing hypertension – *see* Hypertension, complicating pregnancy, pre-existing with proteinuria
  orthostatic R80.2
  postural R80.2
  pre-eclamptic - *see* Pre-eclampsia
  scarlatinal A38.8
Albuminurophobia F40.298
Alcaptonuria E70.29
Alcohol, alcoholic, alcohol-induced
  addiction (without remission) F10.20
    with remission F10.21
  amnestic disorder, persisting F10.96
    with dependence F10.26
  brain syndrome, chronic F10.97
    with dependence F10.27
  cardiopathy I42.6
  counseling and surveillance Z71.41
    family member Z71.42
  delirium (acute) (tremens) (withdrawal) F10.231
    with intoxication F10.921
    in
      abuse F10.121
      dependence F10.221
  dementia F10.97
    with dependence F10.27
  deterioration F10.97
    with dependence F10.27
  hallucinosis (acute) F10.951
    in
      abuse F10.151
      dependence F10.251
  insanity F10.959
  intoxication (acute) (without dependence) F10.129
    with
      delirium F10.121
      dependence F10.229
        with delirium F10.221
        uncomplicated F10.220
      uncomplicated F10.120
  jealousy F10.959
  Korsakoff's, Korsakov's, Korsakow's F10.26
  liver K70.9
    acute - *see* Disease, liver, alcoholic, hepatitis
  mania (acute) (chronic) F10.959
  paranoia, paranoid (type) psychosis F10.950
  pellagra E52
  poisoning, accidental (acute) NEC - *see* Table of drugs and chemicals, alcohol, poisoning
  psychosis - *see* Psychosis, alcoholic
  withdrawal (without convulsions) F10.239
    with delirium F10.231
Alcoholism (chronic) (without remission) F10.20
  with
    psychosis - *see* Psychosis, alcoholic
    remission F10.21
  Korsakov's F10.96
    with dependence F10.26

Alder (-Reilly) anomaly or syndrome (leukocyte granulation) D72.0
Aldosteronism E26.9
  familial (type I) E26.02
  glucocorticoid-remediable E26.02
  primary (due to (bilateral) adrenal hyperplasia) E26.09
  primary NEC E26.09
  secondary E26.1
  specified NEC E26.89
Aldosteronoma D44.10
Aldrich(-Wiskott) syndrome (eczema-thrombocytopenia) D82.0
Alektorophobia F40.218
Aleppo boil B55.1
Aleukemic - *see* condition Aleukia
  congenital D70.0
  hemorrhagica D61.9
    congenital D61.09
  splenica D73.1
Alexia R48.0
  developmental F81.0
  secondary to organic lesion R48.0
Algoneurodystrophy M89.00
  ankle M89.07-
  foot M89.07-
  forearm M89.03-
  hand M89.04-
  lower leg M89.06-
  multiple sites M89.0-
  shoulder M89.01-
  specified site NEC M89.08
  thigh M89.05-
  upper arm M89.02-
Algophobia F40.298
Alienation, mental - *see* Psychosis
Alkalemia E87.3
Alkalosis E87.3
  metabolic E87.3
    with respiratory acidosis E87.4
  respiratory E87.3
Alkaptonuria E70.29
Allen-Masters syndrome N83.8
Allergy, allergic (reaction) (to) T78.40
  air-borne substance NEC (rhinitis) J30.89
  alveolitis (extrinsic) J67.9
    due to
      Aspergillus clavatus J67.4
      Cryptostroma corticale J67.5
      organisms (fungal, thermophilic actinomycete) growing in ventilation (air conditioning) systems J67.7
    specified type NEC J67.8
  anaphylactic shock T78.2
  angioneurotic edema T78.3
  animal (dander) (epidermal) (hair) (rhinitis) J30.81
  bee sting (anaphylactic shock) - *see* Toxicity, venom, arthropod, bee
  biological - *see* Allergy, drug
  colitis K52.2
  dander (animal) (rhinitis) J30.81
  dandruff (rhinitis) J30.81
  dental restorative material (existing) K08.55
  dermatitis - *see* Dermatitis, contact, allergic
  diathesis - *see* History, allergy
  drug, medicament & biological (any) (external) (internal) T78.40
    correct substance properly administered - *see* Table of drugs and chemicals, by drug, adverse effect

Allergy, allergic *(Continued)*
  drug, medicament & biological *(Continued)*
    wrong substance given or taken NEC (by accident) - *see* Table of drugs and chemicals, by drug, poisoning
  due to pollen J30.1
  dust (house) (stock) (rhinitis) J30.89
    with asthma - *see* Asthma, allergic extrinsic
  eczema - *see* Dermatitis, contact, allergic
  epidermal (animal) (rhinitis) J30.81
  feathers (rhinitis) J30.89
  food (any) (ingested) NEC T78.1
    anaphylactic shock - *see* Shock, anaphylactic, food
    dermatitis - *see* Dermatitis, due to, food
    dietary counseling and surveillance Z71.3
    in contact with skin L23.6
    rhinitis J30.5
    status (without reaction) Z91.018
      eggs Z91.012
      milk products Z91.011
      peanuts Z91.010
      seafood Z91.013
      specified NEC Z91.018
  gastrointestinal K52.2
  grain J30.1
  grass (hay fever) (pollen) J30.1
    asthma - *see* Asthma, allergic extrinsic
  hair (animal) (rhinitis) J30.81
  history (of) - *see* History, allergy
  horse serum - *see* Allergy, serum
  inhalant (rhinitis) J30.89
    pollen J30.1
  kapok (rhinitis) J30.89
  medicine - *see* Allergy, drug
  milk protein K52.2
  nasal, seasonal due to pollen J30.1
  pneumonia J82
  pollen (any) (hay fever) J30.1
    asthma - *see* Asthma, allergic extrinsic
  primrose J30.1
  primula J30.1
  purpura D69.0
  ragweed (hay fever) (pollen) J30.1
    asthma - *see* Asthma, allergic extrinsic
  rose (pollen) J30.1
  seasonal NEC J30.2
  Senecio jacobae (pollen) J30.1
  serum (prophylactic) (therapeutic) T80.6
    anaphylactic shock T80.5
  shock (anaphylactic) T78.2
    due to
      adverse effect of correct medicinal substance properly administered T88.6
      serum or immunization T80.5
        anaphylactic T80.5
  specific NEC T78.49
  tree (any) (hay fever) (pollen) J30.1
    asthma - *see* Asthma, allergic extrinsic
  upper respiratory J30.9
  urticaria L50.0
  vaccine - *see* Allergy, serum
Allescheriasis B48.2
Alligator skin disease Q80.9
Allocheiria, allochiria R20.8

Almeida's disease - *see* Paracoccidioidomycosis
Alopecia (hereditaria) (prematura) (seborrheica) L65.9
  androgenic L64.9
    drug-induced L64.0
    specified NEC L64.8
  areata L63.9
    ophiasis L63.2
    specified NEC L63.8
    totalis L63.0
    universalis L63.1
  cicatricial L66.9
    specified NEC L66.8
  circumscripta L63.9
  congenital, congenitalis Q84.0
  due to cytotoxic drugs NEC L65.8
  mucinosa L65.2
  postinfective NEC L65.8
  postpartum L65.0
  premature L64.8
  specific (syphilitic) A51.32
  specified NEC L65.8
  syphilitic (secondary) A51.32
  totalis (capitis) L63.0
  universalis (entire body) L63.1
  X-ray L58.1
Alpers' disease G31.81
Alpine sickness T70.29
Alport syndrome Q87.81
ALTE (apparent life threatening event in infant and newborn) R68.13
Alteration (of), Altered
  awareness, transient R40.4
  mental status R41.82
  pattern of family relationships affecting child Z62.898
  sensation
    following
      cerebrovascular disease I69.998
        specified NEC I69.898
      cerebral infarction I69.398
      intracerebral hemorrhage I69.198
      nontraumatic intracranial hemorrhage NEC I69.298
      specified disease NEC I69.898
      subarachnoid hemorrhage I69.098
Alternating - *see* condition
Altitude, high (effects) - *see* Effect, adverse, high altitude
Aluminosis (of lung) J63.0
Alveolitis
  allergic (extrinsic) - *see* Pneumonitis, hypersensitivity
  due to
    Aspergillus clavatus J67.4
    Cryptostroma corticale J67.6
  fibrosing (cryptogenic) (idiopathic) J84.1
  jaw M27.3
  sicca dolorosa M27.3
Alveolus, alveolar - *see* condition
Alymphocytosis D72.820
  thymic (with immunodeficiency) D82.1
Alymphoplasia, thymic D82.1
Alzheimer's disease or sclerosis - *see* Disease, Alzheimer's
Amastia (with nipple present) Q83.8
  with absent nipple Q83.0
Amathophobia F40.228
Amaurosis (acquired) (congenital) - *see also* Blindness
  fugax G45.3
  hysterical F44.6

Amputation *(Continued)*
　traumatic *(Continued)*
　　testes (complete) S38.231
　　　partial S38.232
　　thigh – *see* Amputation, traumatic, hip
　　thorax, part of S28.1
　　　breast - *see* Amputation, traumatic,
　　　　breast
　　thumb (complete) (metacarpophalan-
　　　geal) S68.01-
　　　partial S68.02-
　　　transphalangeal (complete)
　　　　S68.51-
　　　　partial S68.52-
　　toe (lesser) S98.13-
　　　great S98.11-
　　　　partial S98.12-
　　　more than one S98.21-
　　　　partial S98.22-
　　　partial S98.14-
　　vulva (complete) S38.211
　　　partial S38.212
Amputee (bilateral) (old) Z89.9
Amsterdam dwarfism Q87.1
Amusia R48.8
　developmental F80.8
Amyelencephalus, amyelencephaly
　Q00.0
Amyelia Q06.0
Amygdalitis - *see* Tonsillitis
Amygdalolith J35.8
Amyloid heart (disease) E85.4 *[I43]*
Amyloidosis (generalized) (primary)
　E85.9
　with lung involvement E85.4 *[J99]*
　familial E85.2
　genetic E85.2
　heart E85.4 *[I43]*
　hemodialysis-associated E85.3
　liver E85.4 *[K77]*
　localized E85.4
　neuropathic heredofamilial E85.1
　non-neuropathic heredofamilial
　　E85.0
　organ limited E85.4
　Portuguese E85.1
　pulmonary E85.4 *[J99]*
　secondary systemic E85.3
　skin (lichen) (macular) E85.4 *[L99]*
　specified NEC E85.8
　subglottic E85.4 *[J99]*
Amylopectinosis (brancher enzyme
　deficiency) E74.03
Amylophagia - *see* Pica
Amyoplasia congenita Q79.8
Amyotonia M62.89
　congenita G70.2
Amyotrophia, amyotrophy, amyotrophic
　G71.8
　congenita Q79.8
　diabetic – *see* Diabetes, amyotrophy
　lateral sclerosis G12.21
　neuralgic G54.5
　spinal progressive G12.21
Anacidity, gastric K31.83
　psychogenic F45.8
Anaerosis of newborn P28.89
Analbuminemia E88.09
Analgesia - *see* Anesthesia
Analphalipoproteinemia E78.6
Anaphylactic
　purpura D69.0
　shock or reaction - *see* Shock,
　　anaphylactic

Anaphylactoid shock or reaction – *see*
　Shock, anaphylactic
Anaphylactoid syndrome of pregnancy
　O88.01-
Anaphylaxis – *see* Shock, anaphylactic
Anaplasia cervix N87.9 - *see also* Dyspla-
　sia, cervix
Anarthria R47.1
Anasarca R60.1
　cardiac - *see* Failure, heart, congestive
　lung J18.2
　newborn P83.2
　nutritional E43
　pulmonary J18.2
　renal N04.9
Anastomosis
　aneurysmal - *see* Aneurysm
　arteriovenous ruptured brain
　　I60.8
　intestinal K63.89
　　complicated NEC K91.89
　　　involving urinary tract N99.89
　retinal and choroidal vessels (congeni-
　　tal) Q14.8
Anatomical narrow angle H40.0
Ancylostoma, ancylostomiasis (bra-
　ziliense) (caninum) (ceylanicum)
　(duodenale) B76.0
　Necator americanus B76.1
Andersen's disease (glycogen storage)
　E74.09
Anderson-Fabry disease E75.21
Andes disease T70.29
Andrews' disease (bacterid) L08.0
Androblastoma
　benign
　　specified site - *see* Neoplasm, benign
　　unspecified site
　　　female D27.9
　　　male D29.20
　malignant
　　specified site - *see* Neoplasm,
　　　malignant
　　unspecified site
　　　female C56.9
　　　male C62.90
　specified site - *see* Neoplasm, uncertain
　　behavior
　tubular
　　with lipid storage
　　　specified site - *see* Neoplasm,
　　　　benign
　　　unspecified site
　　　　female D27.9
　　　　male D29.20
　　specified site - *see* Neoplasm, benign
　　unspecified site
　　　female D27.9
　　　male D29.20
　unspecified site
　　female D39.10
　　male D40.10
Androgen insensitivity syndrome
　E34.50 - *see also* Syndrome, androgen
　insensitivity
Androgen resistance syndrome E34.50
　- *see also* Syndrome, androgen
　insensitivity
Android pelvis Q74.2
　with disproportion (fetopelvic) O33.3
　　causing obstructed labor O65.3
Androphobia F40.290
Anectasis, pulmonary (newborn) - *see*
　Atelectasis

Anemia (essential) (general) (hemoglo-
　bin deficiency) (infantile) (primary)
　(profound) D64.9
　with (due to) (in)
　　disorder of
　　　anaerobic glycolysis D55.2
　　　　pentose phosphate pathway D55.1
　　　koilonychia D50.9
　　achlorhydric D50.8
　　achrestic D53.1
　　Addison(-Biermer) (pernicious) D51.0
　　agranulocytic – *see* Agranulocytosis
　　amino-acid-deficiency D53.0
　　aplastic D61.9
　　　congenital D61.09
　　　drug-induced D61.1
　　　due to
　　　　drugs D61.1
　　　　external agents NEC D61.2
　　　　infection D61.2
　　　　radiation D61.2
　　　idiopathic D61.3
　　　red cell (pure) D60.9
　　　　chronic D60.0
　　　　congenital D61.01
　　　　specified type NEC D60.8
　　　　transient D60.1
　　　specified type NEC D61.89
　　　toxic D61.2
　　aregenerative
　　　congenital D61.09
　　asiderotic D50.9
　　atypical (primary) D64.9
　　Baghdad spring D55.0
　　Balantidium coli A07.0
　　Biermer's (pernicious) D51.0
　　blood loss (chronic) D50.0
　　　acute D62
　　bothriocephalus B70.0 *[D63.8]*
　　brickmaker's B76.9 *[D63.8]*
　　cerebral I67.8
　　childhood D58.9
　　chlorotic D50.8
　　chronic simple D53.9
　　chronica congenita aregenerativa
　　　D61.09
　　combined system disease NEC D51.0
　　　[G32.0]
　　　due to dietary vitamin B12 deficiency
　　　　D51.3 *[G32.0]*
　　complicating pregnancy, childbirth or
　　　puerperium – *see* Pregnancy, com-
　　　plicated by (management affected
　　　by), anemia
　　congenital P61.4
　　　aplastic D61.09
　　　due to isoimmunization NOS P55.9
　　　dyserythropoietic, dyshematopoietic
　　　　D64.4
　　　following fetal blood loss P61.3
　　　Heinz body D58.2
　　　hereditary hemolytic NOS D58.9
　　　pernicious D51.0
　　　spherocytic D58.0
　　Cooley's (erythroblastic) D56.1
　　cytogenic D51.0
　　deficiency D53.9
　　　2, 3 diphosphoglycurate mutase
　　　　D55.2
　　　2, 3 PG D55.2
　　　6 phosphogluconate dehydrogenase
　　　　D55.1
　　　6-PGD D55.1
　　　amino-acid D53.0

Anemia *(Continued)*
  deficiency *(Continued)*
    combined B12 and folate D53.1
    enzyme D55.9
      drug-induced (hemolytic) D59.2
      glucose-6-phosphate dehydroge-
        nase (G6PD) D55.0
      glycolytic D55.2
      nucleotide metabolism D55.3
      related to hexose monophosphate
        (HMP) shunt pathway NEC
        D55.1
      specified type NEC D55.8
    erythrocytic glutathione D55.1
    folate D52.9
      dietary D52.0
      drug-induced D52.1
    folic acid D52.9
      dietary D52.0
      drug-induced D52.1
    G SH D55.1
    GGS-R D55.1
    glucose-6-phosphate dehydrogenase
      D55.0
    glutathione reductase D55.1
    glyceraldehyde phosphate dehydro-
      genase D55.2
    G6PD D55.0
    hexokinase D55.2
    iron D50.9
      secondary to blood loss (chronic)
        D50.0
    nutritional D53.9
      with
        poor iron absorption D50.8
        specified deficiency NEC
          D53.8
    phosphofructo-aldolase D55.2
    phosphoglycerate kinase D55.2
    PK D55.2
    protein D53.0
    pyruvate kinase D55.2
    transcobalamin II D51.2
    triose-phosphate isomerase D55.2
    vitamin B12 NOS D51.9
      dietary D51.3
      due to
        intrinsic factor deficiency D51.0
        selective vitamin B12 malabsorp-
          tion with proteinuria D51.1
      pernicious D51.0
      specified type NEC D51.8
  Diamond-Blackfan (congenital hypo-
    plastic) D61.01
  dibothriocephalus B70.0 *[D63.8]*
  dimorphic D53.1
  diphasic D53.1
  Diphyllobothrium (Dibothriocephalus)
    B70.0 *[D63.8]*
  due to (in) (with)
    antineoplastic chemotherapy D64.81
    blood loss (chronic) D50.0
      acute D62
    chemotherapy, antineoplastic D64.81
    chronic disease classified elsewhere
      NEC D63.8
    chronic kidney disease D63.1
    deficiency
      amino-acid D53.0
      copper D53.8
      folate (folic acid) D52.9
        dietary D52.0
        drug-induced D52.1
      molybdenum D53.8

Anemia *(Continued)*
  due to *(Continued)*
    deficiency *(Continued)*
      protein D53.0
      zinc D53.8
    dietary vitamin B12 deficiency D51.3
    disorder of
      glutathione metabolism D55.1
      nucleotide metabolism D55.3
    drug - *see* Anemia, by type (*see also*
      Table of Drugs and Chemicals)
    end stage renal disease D63.1
    enzyme disorder D55.9
    fetal blood loss P61.3
    fish tapeworm (D latum) infestation
      B70.0 *[D63.8]*
    hemorrhage (chronic) D50.0
      acute D62
    impaired absorption D50.9
    loss of blood (chronic) D50.0
      acute D62
    myxedema E03.9 *[D63.8]*
    Necator americanus B76.1 *[D63.8]*
    prematurity P61.2
    selective vitamin B12 malabsorption
      with proteinuria D51.1
    transcobalamin II deficiency D51.2
  Dyke-Young type (secondary) (symp-
    tomatic) D59.1
  dyserythropoietic (congenital) D64.4
  dyshematopoietic (congenital) D64.4
  Egyptian B76.9 *[D63.8]*
  elliptocytosis - *see* Elliptocytosis
  enzyme-deficiency, drug-induced D59.2
  epidemic (*see also* Ancylostomiasis)
    B76.9 *[D63.8]*
  erythroblastic
    familial D56.1
    newborn (*see also* Disease, hemolytic)
      P55.9
    of childhood D56.1
  erythrocytic glutathione deficiency
    D55.1
  erythropoietin-resistant anemia (EPO
    resistant anemia) D63.1
  Faber's (achlorhydric anemia) D50.9
  factitious (self-induced blood letting)
    D50.0
  familial erythroblastic D56.1
  Fanconi's (congenital pancytopenia)
    D61.09
  favism D55.0
  fish tapeworm (D. latum) infestation
    B70.0 *[D63.8]*
  folate (folic acid) deficiency D52.9
  glucose-6-phosphate dehydrogenase
    (G6PD) deficiency D55.0
  glutathione-reductase deficiency D55.1
  goat's milk D52.0
  granulocytic – *see* Agranulocytosis
  Heinz body, congenital D58.2
  hemolytic D58.9
    acquired D59.9
      with hemoglobinuria NEC D59.6
      autoimmune NEC D59.1
      infectious D59.4
      specified type NEC D59.8
      toxic D59.4
    acute D59.9
      due to enzyme deficiency specified
        type NEC D55.8
      Lederer's D59.1
    autoimmune D59.1
      drug-induced D59.0

Anemia *(Continued)*
  hemolytic *(Continued)*
    chronic D58.9
      idiopathic D59.9
    cold type (secondary) (symptomatic)
      D59.1
    congenital (spherocytic) - *see*
      Spherocytosis
    due to
      cardiac conditions D59.4
      drugs (nonautoimmune) D59.2
        autoimmune D59.0
      enzyme disorder D55.9
        drug-induced D59.2
      presence of shunt or other internal
        prosthetic device D59.4
    familial D58.9
    hereditary D58.9
      due to enzyme disorder D55.9
        specified type NEC D55.8
      specified type NEC D58.8
    idiopathic (chronic) D59.9
    mechanical D59.4
    microangiopathic D59.4
    nonautoimmune D59.4
      drug-induced D59.2
    nonspherocytic
      congenital or hereditary NEC
        D55.8
        glucose-6-phosphate dehydroge-
          nase deficiency D55.0
        pyruvate kinase deficiency
          D55.2
      type
        I D55.1
        II D55.2
    type
      I D55.1
      II D55.2
    secondary D59.4
      autoimmune D59.1
    specified (hereditary) type NEC
      D58.8
    Stransky-Regala type (*see also* Hemo-
      globinopathy) D58.8
    symptomatic D59.4
      autoimmune D59.1
    toxic D59.4
    warm type (secondary) (symptom-
      atic) D59.1
  hemorrhagic (chronic) D50.0
    acute D62
  Herrick's D57.1
  hexokinase deficiency D55.2
  hookworm B76.9 *[D63.8]*
  hypochromic (idiopathic) (microcytic)
    (normoblastic) D50.9
    due to blood loss (chronic) D50.0
      acute D62
    familial sex-linked D64.0
    pyridoxine-responsive D64.3
    sideroblastic, sex-linked D64.0
  hypoplasia, red blood cells D61.9
    congenital or familial D61.09
  hypoplastic (idiopathic) D61.9
    congenital or familial (of childhood)
      D61.09
  hypoproliferative (refractive) D61.9
  idiopathic D64.9
    aplastic D61.3
    hemolytic, chronic D59.9
  in (due to) (with)
    chronic kidney disease D63.1
    end stage renal disease D63.1

Anemia *(Continued)*
  in *(Continued)*
    failure, kidney (renal) D63.1
    neoplastic disease *(see also* Neoplasm)
      D63.0
    intertropical *(see also* Ancylostomiasis)
      D63.8
    iron deficiency D50.9
      secondary to blood loss (chronic)
        D50.0
        acute D62
      specified type NEC D50.8
    Joseph-Diamond-Blackfan (congenital
      hypoplastic) D61.01
    Lederer's (hemolytic) D59.1
    leukoerythroblastic D61.82
    macrocytic D53.9
      nutritional D52.0
      tropical D52.8
    malarial *(see also* Malaria) B54
      [D63.8]
    malignant (progressive) D51.0
    malnutrition D53.9
    marsh *(see also* Malaria) B54 *[D63.8]*
    Mediterranean D56.9
    megaloblastic D53.1
      combined B12 and folate deficiency
        D53.1
      hereditary D51.1
      nutritional D52.0
      orotic aciduria D53.0
      refractory D53.1
      specified type NEC D53.1
    megalocytic D53.1
    microcytic (hypochromic) D50.9
      due to blood loss (chronic) D50.0
        acute D62
      familial D56.8
    microelliptopoikilocytic (Rietti-Greppi-
      Micheli) D56.9
    miner's B76.9 *[D63.8]*
    myelodysplastic D46.9
    myelofibrosis D75.81
    myelogenous D64.89
    myelopathic D64.89
    myelophthisic D61.82
    myeloproliferative D47.z9
    newborn P61.4
      due to
        ABO (antibodies, isoimmunization,
          maternal/fetal incompatibil-
          ity) P55.1
        Rh (antibodies, isoimmunization,
          maternal/fetal incompatibil-
          ity) P55.0
      following fetal blood loss P61.3
      posthemorrhagic (fetal) P61.3
    nonspherocytic hemolytic - *see* Anemia,
      hemolytic, nonspherocytic
    normocytic (infectional) D64.9
      due to blood loss (chronic) D50.0
        acute D62
      myelophthisic D61.82
    nutritional (deficiency) D53.9
      with
        poor iron absorption D50.8
        specified deficiency NEC D53.8
      megaloblastic D52.0
    of prematurity P61.2
    orotaciduric (congenital) (hereditary)
      D53.0
    osteosclerotic D64.89
    ovalocytosis (hereditary) – *see*
      Elliptocytosis

Anemia *(Continued)*
  paludal *(see also* Malaria) B54 *[D63.8]*
  pernicious (congenital) (malignant)
    (progressive) D51.0
  pleochromic D64.89
    of sprue D52.8
  posthemorrhagic (chronic) D50.0
    acute D62
    newborn P61.3
  postoperative (postprocedural)
    due to (acute) blood loss D62
      chronic blood loss D50.0
    specified NEC D64.9
  postpartum O90.81
  pressure D64.89
  progressive D64.9
    malignant D51.0
    pernicious D51.0
  protein-deficiency D53.0
  pseudoleukemica infantum D64.89
  pure red cell D60.9
    congenital D61.01
  pyridoxine-responsive D64.3
  pyruvate kinase deficiency D55.2
  refractory D46.4
    with
      excess of blasts D46.20
        1 (RAEB 1) D46.21
        2 (RAEB 2) D46.22
        in transformation (RAEB T)
          - *see* Leukemia, acute
          myeloblastic
      hemochromatosis D46.1
      sideroblasts (ringed) (RARS) D46.1
    megaloblastic D53.1
    sideroblastic D46.1
    sideropenic D50.8
    without ring sideroblasts, so stated
      D46.0
    without sideroblasts without excess
      of blasts D46.0
  Rietti-Greppi-Micheli D56.9
  scorbutic D53.2
  secondary to
    blood loss (chronic) D50.0
      acute D62
    hemorrhage (chronic) D50.0
      acute D62
  semiplastic D61.89
  sickle-cell - *see* Disease, sickle-cell
  sideroblastic D64.3
    hereditary D64.0
    hypochromic, sex-linked D64.0
    pyridoxine-responsive NEC D64.3
    refractory D46.1
    secondary (due to)
      disease D64.1
      drugs and toxins D64.2
    specified type NEC D64.3
  sideropenic (refractory) D50.9
    due to blood loss (chronic) D50.0
      acute D62
  simple chronic D53.9
  specified type NEC D64.89
  spherocytic (hereditary) - *see*
    Spherocytosis
  splenic D64.89
  splenomegalic D64.89
  stomatocytosis D58.8
  syphilitic (acquired) (late) A52.79
    [D63.8]
  target cell D64.89
  thalassemia D56.9

Anemia *(Continued)*
  thrombocytopenic - *see*
    Thrombocytopenia
  toxic D61.2
  tropical B76.9 *[D63.8]*
    macrocytic D52.8
  tuberculous A18.89 *[D63.8]*
  vegan D51.3
  vitamin
    B$_6$-responsive D64.3
    B$_{12}$ deficiency (dietary) pernicious
      D51.0
  von Jaksch's D64.89
  Witts' (achlorhydric anemia) D50.8
Anencephalus, anencephaly Q00.0
Anemophobia F40.228
Anergasia - *see* Psychosis, organic
Anesthesia, anesthetic (of skin) R20.0
  complication or reaction NEC *(see also*
    Complications, anesthesia) T88.59
  due to
    correct substance properly admin-
      istered - *see* Table of drugs and
      chemicals, by drug, adverse
      effect
    overdose or wrong substance
      given - *see* Table of drugs
      and chemicals, by drug,
      poisoning
  cornea H18.81-
  dissociative F44.6
  functional (hysterical) F44.6
  hyperesthetic, thalamic G89.0
  hysterical F44.6
  local skin lesion R20.0
  sexual (psychogenic) F52.1
  shock (due to) T88.2
  skin R20.0
  testicular N50.9
Anetoderma (maculosum) (of) L90.8
  Jadassohn-Pellizzari L90.2
  Schweniger-Buzzi L90.1
Aneurin deficiency E51.9
Aneurysm (anastomotic) (artery) (cirsoid)
    (diffuse) (false) (fusiform) (multiple)
    (saccular) I72.9
  abdominal (aorta) I71.4
    ruptured I71.3
    syphilitic A52.01
  aorta, aortic (nonsyphilitic) I71.9
    abdominal I71.4
      ruptured I71.3
    arch I71.2
      ruptured I71.1
    arteriosclerotic I71.9
      ruptured I71.8
    ascending I71.2
      ruptured I71.1
    congenital Q25.4
    descending I71.9
      abdominal I71.4
        ruptured I71.3
        ruptured I71.8
      thoracic I71.2
        ruptured I71.1
    ruptured I71.8
    sinus, congenital Q25.4
    syphilitic A52.01
    thoracic I71.2
      ruptured I71.1
    thoracoabdominal I71.6
      ruptured I71.5
    thorax, thoracic (arch) I71.2
      ruptured I71.1

Aneurysm *(Continued)*
  aorta, aortic *(Continued)*
    transverse I71.2
      ruptured I71.1
    valve (heart) *(see also* Endocarditis,
      aortic) I35.8
  arteriosclerotic I72.9
    cerebral I67.1
      ruptured - *see* Hemorrhage, intra-
        cranial, subarachnoid
  arteriovenous (congenital) (periph-
    eral) - *see also* Malformation,
    arteriovenous
    acquired I77.0
      brain I67.1
      coronary I25.41
      pulmonary I28.0
    brain Q28.2
      ruptured I60.8
    peripheral - *see* Malformation, arterio-
      venous, peripheral
    precerebral vessels Q28.0
    specified site NEC - *see also* Malfor-
      mation, arteriovenous
      acquired I77.0
  basal - *see* Aneurysm, brain
  berry (congenital) (nonruptured) I67.1
    ruptured I60.7
  brain I67.1
    arteriosclerotic I67.1
      ruptured - *see* Hemorrhage, intra-
        cranial, subarachnoid
    arteriovenous (congenital) (nonrup-
      tured) Q28.2
      acquired I67.1
        ruptured I60.8
      ruptured I60.8
    berry (congenital) (nonruptured)
      I67.1
      ruptured *(see also* Hemorrhage,
        intracranial, subarachnoid)
        I60.7
    congenital Q28.3
      ruptured I60.7
    meninges I67.1
      ruptured I60.8
    miliary (congenital) (nonruptured)
      I67.1
      ruptured *(see also* Hemorrhage, in-
        tracranial, subarachnoid) I60.7
    mycotic I33.0
    ruptured - *see* Hemorrhage, intracra-
      nial, subarachnoid
    syphilitic (hemorrhage) A52.05
  cardiac (false) *(see also* Aneurysm, heart)
    I25.3
  carotid artery (common) (external) I72.0
    internal (intracranial) I67.1
      extracranial portion I72.0
      ruptured into brain I60.0-
    syphilitic A52.09
      intracranial A52.05
  cavernous sinus I67.1
    arteriovenous (congenital) (nonrup-
      tured) Q28.3
      ruptured I60.8
  central nervous system, syphilitic
    A52.05
  cerebral - *see* Aneurysm, brain
  chest - *see* Aneurysm, thorax
  circle of Willis I67.1
    congenital Q28.3
      ruptured I60.6
    ruptured I60.6

Aneurysm *(Continued)*
  common iliac artery I72.3
  congenital (peripheral) Q27.8
    brain Q28.3
      ruptured I60.7
    coronary Q24.5
    digestive system Q27.8
    lower limb Q27.8
    pulmonary Q25.7
    retina Q14.1
    specified site NEC Q27.8
    upper limb Q27.8
  conjunctiva - *see* Abnormality, conjunc-
    tiva, vascular
  conus arteriosus - *see* Aneurysm, heart
  coronary (arteriosclerotic) (artery)
    I25.41
    arteriovenous, congenital Q24.5
    congenital Q24.5
    ruptured - *see* Infarct, myocardium
    syphilitic A52.06
    vein I25.89
  cylindroid (aorta) I71.9
    ruptured I71.8
    syphilitic A52.01
  ductus arteriosus Q25.0
  endocardial, infective (any valve) I33.0
  femoral (artery) (ruptured) I72.4
  heart (wall) (chronic or with a stated
    duration of over 4 weeks) I25.3
    valve - *see* Endocarditis
  iliac (common) (artery) (ruptured) I72.3
  infective I72.9
    endocardial (any valve) I33.0
  innominate (nonsyphilitic) I72.8
    syphilitic A52.09
  interauricular septum - *see* Aneurysm,
    heart
  interventricular septum - *see* Aneurysm,
    heart
  intrathoracic (nonsyphilitic) I71.2
    ruptured I71.1
    syphilitic A52.01
  lower limb I72.4
  lung (pulmonary artery) I28.1
  mediastinal (nonsyphilitic) I72.8
    syphilitic A52.09
  miliary (congenital) I67.1
    ruptured - *see* Hemorrhage, intracere-
      bral, subarachnoid, intracranial
  mitral (heart) (valve) I34.8
  mural - *see* Aneurysm, heart
  mycotic I72.9
    endocardial (any valve) I33.0
    ruptured, brain - *see* Hemorrhage,
      intracerebral, subarachnoid
  myocardium - *see* Aneurysm, heart
  neck I72.0
  patent ductus arteriosus Q25.0
  peripheral NEC I72.8
    congenital Q27.8
      digestive system Q27.8
      lower limb Q27.8
      specified site NEC Q27.8
      upper limb Q27.8
  popliteal (artery) (ruptured) I72.4
  precerebral, congenital (nonruptured)
    Q28.1
  pulmonary I28.1
    arteriovenous Q25.7
      acquired I28.0
    syphilitic A52.09
    valve (heart) - *see* Endocarditis,
      pulmonary

Aneurysm *(Continued)*
  racemose (peripheral) I72.9
    congenital - *see* Aneurysm, congenital
  radial I72.1
  Rasmussen NEC A15.0
  renal (artery) I72.2
  retina - *see also* Disorder, retina,
    microaneurysms
    congenital Q14.1
    diabetic - *see* Diabetes, microaneu-
      rysms, retinal
  sinus of Valsalva Q25.4
  spinal (cord) I72.8
    syphilitic (hemorrhage) A52.09
  splenic I72.8
  subclavian (artery) (ruptured) I72.8
    syphilitic A52.09
  syphilitic (aorta) A52.01
    central nervous system A52.05
    congenital (late) A50.54 *[I79.0]*
    spine, spinal A52.09
  thoracoabdominal (aorta) I71.6
    ruptured I71.5
    syphilitic A52.01
  thorax, thoracic (aorta) (arch) (non-
    syphilitic) I71.2
    ruptured I71.1
    syphilitic A52.01
  traumatic (complication) (early), speci-
    fied site - *see* Injury, blood vessel
  tricuspid (heart) (valve) I07.8
  ulnar I72.1
  upper limb (ruptured) I72.1
  valve, valvular - *see* Endocarditis
  venous - *see also* Varix I86.8
    congenital Q27.8
      digestive system Q27.8
      lower limb Q27.8
      specified site NEC Q27.8
      upper limb Q27.8
  ventricle - *see* Aneurysm, heart
Angelman syndrome Q93.5
Anger R45.4
Angiectasis, angiectopia I99.8
Angiitis I77.6
  allergic granulomatous M30.1
  hypersensitivity M31.0
  necrotizing M31.9
    specified NEC M31.8
  nervous system, granulomatous I67.7
Angina (attack) (cardiac) (chest) (heart)
  (pectoris) (syndrome) (vasomotor)
  I20.9
  with
    atherosclerotic heart disease
      - *see* Arteriosclerosis, coronary
      (artery),
    documented spasm I20.1
  abdominal K55.1
  accelerated - *see* Angina, unstable
  agranulocytic - *see* Agranulocytosis
  angiospastic - *see* Angina, with docu-
    mented spasm
  aphthous B08.5
  crescendo - *see* Angina, unstable
  croupous J05.0
  cruris I73.9
  de novo effort - *see* Angina, unstable
  diphtheritic, membranous A36.0
  equivalent I20.8
  exudative, chronic J37.0
  following acute myocardial infarction
    I23.7
  gangrenous diphtheritic A36.0

Angina *(Continued)*
　intestinal K55.1
　Ludovici K12.2
　Ludwig's K12.2
　malignant diphtheritic A36.0
　membranous J05.0
　　diphtheritic A36.0
　　Vincent's A69.1
　mesenteric K55.1
　monocytic - *see* Mononucleosis,
　　infectious
　of effort - *see* Angina, specified NEC
　phlegmonous J36
　　diphtheritic A36.0
　post-infarctional I23.7
　pre-infarctional - *see* Angina, unstable
　Prinzmetal - *see* Angina, with docu-
　　mented spasm
　progressive - *see* Angina, unstable
　pseudomembranous A69.1
　pultaceous, diphtheritic A36.0
　spasm-induced - *see* Angina, with docu-
　　mented spasm
　specified NEC I20.8
　stable I20.9
　stenocardia - *see* Angina, specified NEC
　stridulous, diphtheritic A36.2
　tonsil J36
　trachealis J05.0
　unstable I20.0
　variant - *see* Angina, with documented
　　spasm
　Vincent's A69.1
　worsening effort - *see* Angina, unstable
Angioblastoma - *see* Neoplasm, connec-
　tive tissue, uncertain behavior
Angiocholecystitis - *see* Cholecystitis,
　acute
Angiocholitis - *see* Cholecystitis, acute
Angiodysgenesis spinalis G95.19
Angiodysplasia (cecum) (colon) K55.20
　with bleeding K55.21
　duodenum (and stomach) K31.819
　　with bleeding K31.811
　stomach (and duodenum) K31.819
　　with bleeding K31.811
Angioedema (allergic) (any site) (with
　urticaria) T78.3
　hereditary D84.1
Angioendothelioma - *see* Neoplasm,
　uncertain behavior
　benign D18.00
　　intra-abdominal D18.03
　　intracranial D18.02
　　skin D18.01
　　specified site NEC D18.09
　bone - *see* Neoplasm, bone, malignant
　Ewing's - *see* Neoplasm, bone,
　　malignant
Angioendotheliomatosis C85.70
Angiofibroma - *see also* Neoplasm, benign
　juvenile
　　specified site - *see* Neoplasm, benign
　　unspecified site D10.6
Angiohemophilia (A) (B) D68.0
Angioid streaks (choroid) (macula)
　(retina) H35.33
Angiokeratoma - *see* Neoplasm, skin,
　benign
　corporis diffusum E75.21
Angioleiomyoma - *see* Neoplasm,
　connective tissue, benign
Angiolipoma - *see also* Lipoma
　infiltrating - *see* Lipoma

Angioma - *see also* Hemangioma,
　by site
　capillary I78.1
　hemorrhagicum hereditaria I78.0
　intra-abdominal D18.03
　intracranial D18.02
　malignant - *see* Neoplasm, connective
　　tissue, malignant
　plexiform D18.00
　　intra-abdominal D18.03
　　intracranial D18.02
　　skin D18.01
　　specified site NEC D18.09
　senile I78.1
　serpiginosum L81.7
　skin D18.01
　specified site NEC D18.09
　spider I78.1
　stellate I78.1
Angiomatosis Q82.8
　bacillary A79.89
　encephalotrigeminal Q85.8
　hemorrhagic familial I78.0
　hereditary familial I78.0
　liver K76.4
Angiomyolipoma - *see* Lipoma
Angiomyoliposarcoma - *see* Neoplasm,
　connective tissue, malignant
Angiomyoma - *see* Neoplasm, connective
　tissue, benign
Angiomyosarcoma - *see* Neoplasm,
　connective tissue, malignant
Angiomyxoma - *see* Neoplasm, connective
　tissue, uncertain behavior
Angioneurosis F45.8
Angioneurotic edema (allergic) (any site)
　(with urticaria) T78.3
　hereditary D84.1
Angiopathia, angiopathy I99.9
　cerebral I67.9
　　amyloid E85.4 *[I68.1]*
　diabetic (peripheral) - *see* Diabetes,
　　angiopathy
　peripheral I73.9
　　diabetic - *see* Diabetes, angiopathy
　　specified type NEC I73.89
　retinae syphilitica A52.05
　retinalis (juvenilis)
　　diabetic - *see* Diabetes, retinopathy
　　proliferative - *see* Retinopathy,
　　　proliferative
Angiosarcoma - *see also* Neoplasm,
　connective tissue, malignant
　liver C22.3
Angiosclerosis - *see* Arteriosclerosis
Angiospasm (peripheral) (traumatic)
　(vessel) I73.9
　brachial plexus G54.0
　cerebral G45.9
　cervical plexus G54.2
　nerve
　　arm - *see* Mononeuropathy, upper
　　　limb
　　　axillary G54.0
　　　median - *see* Lesion, nerve,
　　　　median
　　　ulnar - *see* Lesion, nerve, ulnar
　　axillary G54.0
　　leg - *see* Mononeuropathy, lower
　　　limb
　　median – *see* Lesion, nerve, median
　　plantar – *see* Lesion, nerve, plantar
　　ulnar - *see* Lesion, nerve, ulnar
Angiospastic disease or edema I73.9

Angiostrongyliasis
　due to
　　Parastrongylus
　　　cantonensis B83.2
　　　costaricensis B81.3
　intestinal B81.3
Anguillulosis - *see* Strongyloidiasis
Angulation
　cecum - *see* Obstruction, intestine
　coccyx (acquired) - *see also* subcategory
　　M43.8
　　congenital NEC Q76.49
　femur (acquired) - *see also* Deformity,
　　limb, specified type NEC, thigh
　　congenital Q74.2
　intestine (large) (small) - *see* Obstruc-
　　tion, intestine
　sacrum (acquired) - *see also* subcategory
　　M43.8
　　congenital NEC Q76.49
　sigmoid (flexure) - *see* Obstruction,
　　intestine
　spine - *see* Dorsopathy, deforming,
　　specified NEC
　tibia (acquired) - *see also* Deformity,
　　limb, specified type NEC, lower
　　leg
　　congenital Q74.2
　ureter N13.5
　　with infection N13.6
　wrist (acquired) - *see also* Deformity,
　　limb, specified type NEC,
　　forearm
　　congenital Q74.0
Angulus infectiosus (lips) K13.0
Anhedonia R45.84
Anhidrosis L74.4
Anhydration, anhydremia E86.0
　with
　　hypernatremia E87.0
　　hyponatremia E87.1
Anhydremia E86.0
　with
　　hypernatremia E87.0
　　hyponatremia E87.1
Anidrosis L74.4
Anisakiasis (infection) (infestation)
　B81.0
Anisakis larvae infestation B81.0
Aniseikonia H52.32
Anisocoria (pupil) H57.09
　congenital Q13.2
Anisocytosis R71.8
Anisometropia (congenital) H52.31
Ankle - *see* condition
Ankyloblepharon (eyelid) (acquired) -
　see also Blepharophimosis
　filiforme (adnatum) (congenital)
　　Q10.3
　total Q10.3
Ankyloglossia Q38.1
Ankylosis (fibrous) (osseous) (joint)
　M24.60
　ankle M24.67-
　arthrodesis status Z98.1
　cricoarytenoid (cartilage) (joint) (larynx)
　　J38.7
　dental K03.5
　ear ossicles H74.31-
　elbow M24.62-
　foot M24.67-
　hand M24.64-
　hip M24.65-

Ankylosis *(Continued)*
  incostapedial joint (infectional) - *see*
    Ankylosis, ear ossicles
  jaw (temporomandibular) M26.61
  knee M24.66-
  lumbosacral (joint) M43.27
  postoperative (status) Z98.1
  produced by surgical fusion, status
    Z98.1
  sacro-iliac (joint) M43.28
  shoulder M24.61-
  spine (joint) - *see also* Fusion, spine
    spondylitic - *see* Spondylitis,
      ankylosing
  surgical Z98.1
  temporomandibular M26.61
  tooth, teeth (hard tissues) K03.5
  wrist M24.63-
Ankylostoma - *see* Ancylostoma
Ankylostomiasis - *see* Ancylostomiasis
Ankylurethria - *see* Stricture, urethra
Annular - *see also* condition
  detachment, cervix N88.8
  organ or site, congenital NEC - *see*
    Distortion
  pancreas (congenital) Q45.1
Anodontia (complete) (partial) (vera)
  K00.0
  acquired K08.10
Anomaly, anomalous (congenital)
  (unspecified type) Q89.9
  abdominal wall NEC Q79.59
  acoustic nerve Q07.8
  adrenal (gland) Q89.1
  Alder (-Reilly) (leukocyte granulation)
    D72.0
  alimentary tract Q45.9
    upper Q40.9
  alveolar M26.70
    hyperplasia M26.79
      mandibular M26.72
      maxillary M26.71
    hypoplasia M26.79
      mandibular M26.74
      maxillary M26.73
    ridge (process) M26.79
    specified NEC M26.79
  ankle (joint) Q74.2
  anus Q43.9
  aorta (arch) NEC Q25.4
    coarctation (preductal) (postductal)
      Q25.1
  aortic cusp or valve Q23.9
  appendix Q43.8
  apple peel syndrome Q41.1
  aqueduct of Sylvius Q03.0
    with spina bifida - *see* Spina bifida,
      with hydrocephalus
  arm Q74.0
  arteriovenous NEC
    coronary Q24.5
    gastrointestinal Q27.33
      acquired - *see* Angiodysplasia
  artery (peripheral) Q27.9
    basilar NEC Q28.1
    cerebral Q28.3
    coronary Q24.5
    digestive system Q27.8
    eye Q15.8
    great Q25.9
      specified NEC Q25.8
    lower limb Q27.8
    peripheral Q27.9
      specified NEC Q27.8

Anomaly, anomalous *(Continued)*
  artery *(Continued)*
    pulmonary NEC Q25.7
    renal Q27.2
    retina Q14.1
    specified site NEC Q27.8
    subclavian Q27.8
    umbilical Q27.0
    upper limb Q27.8
    vertebral NEC Q28.1
  aryteno-epiglottic folds Q31.8
  atrial
    bands or folds Q20.8
    septa Q21.1
  atrioventricular
    excitation I45.6
    septum Q21.0
  auditory canal Q17.8
  auricle
    ear Q17.8
      causing impairment of hearing
        Q16.9
    heart Q20.8
  Axenfeld's Q15.0
  back Q89.9
  band
    atrial Q20.8
    heart Q24.8
    ventricular Q24.8
  Bartholin's duct Q38.4
  biliary duct or passage Q44.5
  bladder Q64.70
    absence Q64.5
    diverticulum Q64.6
    exstrophy Q64.10
      cloacal Q64.12
      extroversion Q64.19
      specified type NEC Q64.19
      supravesical fissure Q64.11
    neck obstruction Q64.31
    specified type NEC Q64.79
  bone Q79.9
    arm Q74.0
    face Q75.9
    leg Q74.2
    pelvic girdle Q74.2
    shoulder girdle Q74.0
    skull Q75.9
      with
        anencephaly Q00.0
        encephalocele - *see*
          Encephalocele
        hydrocephalus Q03.9
          with spina bifida - *see* Spina
            bifida, by site, with
            hydrocephalus
        microcephaly Q02
  brain (multiple) Q04.9
    vessel Q28.3
  breast Q83.9
  broad ligament Q50.6
  bronchus Q32.4
  bulbus cordis Q21.9
  bursa Q79.9
  canal of Nuck Q52.4
  canthus Q10.3
  capillary Q27.9
  cardiac Q24.9
    chambers Q20.9
      specified NEC Q20.8
    septal closure Q21.9
      specified NEC Q21.8
    valve NEC Q24.8
      pulmonary Q22.3

Anomaly, anomalous *(Continued)*
  cardiovascular system Q28.8
  carpus Q74.0
  caruncle, lacrimal Q10.6
  cascade stomach Q40.2
  cauda equina Q06.3
  cecum Q43.9
  cerebral Q04.9
    vessels Q28.3
  cervix Q51.9
  Chédiak-Higashi(-Steinbrinck) (con-
    genital gigantism of peroxidase
    granules) E70.330
  cheek Q18.9
  chest wall Q67.8
    bones Q76.9
  chin Q18.9
  chordae tendineae Q24.8
  choroid Q14.3
    plexus Q07.8
  chromosomes, chromosomal Q99.9
    D(1) - *see* condition, chromosome 13
    E(3) - *see* condition, chromosome 18
    G - *see* condition, chromosome 21
    sex
      female phenotype Q97.8
      gonadal dysgenesis (pure)
        Q99.1
      Klinefelter's Q98.4
      male phenotype Q98.9
      Turner's Q96.9
    specified NEC Q99.8
  cilia Q10.3
  circulatory system Q28.9
  clavicle Q74.0
  clitoris Q52.6
  coccyx Q76.49
  colon Q43.9
  common duct Q44.5
  communication
    coronary artery Q24.5
    left ventricle with right atrium Q21.0
  concha (ear) Q17.3
  connection
    portal vein Q26.5
    pulmonary venous Q26.4
      partial Q26.3
      total Q26.2
    renal artery with kidney Q27.2
  cornea (shape) Q13.4
  coronary artery or vein Q24.5
  cranium - *see* Anomaly, skull
  cricoid cartilage Q31.8
  cystic duct Q44.5
  dental
    alveolar - *see* Anomaly, alveolar
    arch relationship M26.20
      specified NEC M26.29
  dentofacial M26.9
    alveolar - *see* Anomaly, alveolar
    dental arch relationship M26.20
      specified NEC M26.29
    functional M26.50
      specified NEC M26.59
    jaw-cranial base relationship
      M26.10
      asymmetry M26.12
        maxillary M26.11
      specified type NEC M26.19
    jaw size M26.00
      macrogenia M26.05
      mandibular
        hyperplasia M26.03
        hypoplasia M26.04

Anomaly, anomalous *(Continued)*
 dentofacial *(Continued)*
  jaw size *(Continued)*
   maxillary
    hyperplasia M26.01
    hypoplasia M26.02
   microgenia M26.06
   specified type NEC M26.09
  malocclusion M26.4
   dental arch relationship NEC M26.29
   jaw-cranial base relationship – *see*
    Anomaly, dentofacial,
    jaw-cranial base relationship
   jaw size - *see* Anomaly, dentofacial,
    jaw size
   specified type NEC M26.89
   temporomandibular joint M26.60
    adhesions M26.61
    ankylosis M26.61
    arthralgia M26.62
    articular disc M26.63
    specified type NEC M26.69
   tooth position, fully erupted
    M26.30
    specified NEC M26.39
 dermatoglyphic Q82.8
 diaphragm (apertures) NEC Q79.1
 digestive organ(s) or tract Q45.9
  lower Q43.9
  upper Q40.9
 distance, interarch (excessive) (inadequate) M26.25
 distribution, coronary artery Q24.5
 ductus
  arteriosus Q25.0
  botalli Q25.0
 duodenum Q43.9
 dura (brain) Q04.9
  spinal cord Q06.9
 ear (external) Q17.9
  causing impairment of hearing Q16.9
  inner Q16.5
  middle (causing impairment of hearing) Q16.4
  ossicles Q16.3
 Ebstein's (heart) (tricuspid valve) Q22.5
 ectodermal Q82.9
 Eisenmenger's (ventricular septal
  defect) Q21.8
 ejaculatory duct Q55.4
 elbow Q74.0
 endocrine gland NEC Q89.2
 epididymis Q55.4
 epiglottis Q31.8
 esophagus Q39.9
 eustachian tube Q17.8
 eye Q15.9
  anterior segment Q13.9
  posterior segment Q14.9
  ptosis (eyelid) Q10.0
  specified NEC Q15.8
 eyebrow Q18.8
 eyelid Q10.3
  ptosis Q10.0
 face Q18.9
  bone(s) Q75.9
 fallopian tube Q50.6
 fascia Q79.9
 femur NEC Q74.2
 fibula NEC Q74.2
 finger Q74.0
 fixation, intestine Q43.3
 flexion (joint) NOS Q74.9
  hip or thigh Q65.8

Anomaly, anomalous *(Continued)*
 foot NEC Q74.2
  varus (congenital) Q66.3
 foramen
  Botalli Q21.1
  ovale Q21.1
 forearm Q74.0
 forehead Q75.8
 form, teeth K00.2
 fovea centralis Q14.1
 frontal bone - *see* Anomaly, skull
 gallbladder (position) (shape) (size)
  Q44.1
 Gartner's duct Q52.4
 gastrointestinal tract Q45.9
 genitalia, genital organ(s) or system
  female Q52.9
   external Q52.70
   internal NOS Q52.9
  male Q55.9
   hydrocele P83.5
   specified NEC Q55.8
 genitourinary NEC
  female Q52.9
  male Q55.9
 Gerbode Q21.0
 glottis Q31.8
 granulation or granulocyte, genetic
  (constitutional) (leukocyte)
  D72.0
 gum Q38.6
 gyri Q07.9
 hair Q84.2
 hand Q74.0
 hard tissue formation in pulp
  K04.3
 head - *see* Anomaly, skull
 heart Q24.9
  auricle Q20.8
  bands or folds Q24.8
  fibroelastosis cordis I42.4
  obstructive NEC Q22.6
  patent ductus arteriosus (Botalli)
   Q25.0
  septum Q21.9
   auricular Q21.1
   interatrial Q21.1
   interventricular Q21.0
    with pulmonary stenosis or
     atresia, dextraposition
     of aorta and hypertrophy
     of right ventricle Q21.3
   specified NEC Q21.8
   ventricular Q21.0
    with pulmonary stenosis or
     atresia, dextraposition
     of aorta and hypertrophy
     of right ventricle Q21.3
  tetralogy of Fallot Q21.3
  valve NEC Q24.8
   aortic
    bicuspid valve Q23.1
    insufficiency Q23.1
    stenosis Q23.0
     subaortic Q24.2
   mitral
    insufficiency Q23.3
    stenosis Q23.2
   pulmonary Q22.3
    atresia Q22.0
    insufficiency Q22.2
    stenosis Q22.1
     infundibular Q24.3
     subvalvular Q24.3

Anomaly, anomalous *(Continued)*
 heart *(Continued)*
  valve NEC *(Continued)*
   tricuspid
    atresia Q22.4
    stenosis Q22.4
   ventricle Q20.8
 heel NEC Q74.2
 Hegglin's D72.0
 hemianencephaly Q00.0
 hemicephaly Q00.0
 hemicrania Q00.0
 hepatic duct Q44.5
 hip NEC Q74.2
 hourglass stomach Q40.2
 humerus Q74.0
 hydatid of Morgagni
  female Q50.5
  male (epididymal) Q55.4
   testicular Q55.29
 hymen Q52.4
 hypersegmentation of neutrophils,
  hereditary D72.0
 hypophyseal Q89.2
 ileocecal (coil) (valve) Q43.9
 ileum Q43.9
 ilium NEC Q74.2
 integument Q84.9
  specified NEC Q84.8
 interarch distance (excessive) (inadequate) M26.25
 intervertebral cartilage or disc
  Q76.49
 intestine (large) (small) Q43.9
  with anomalous adhesions, fixation
   or malrotation Q43.3
 iris Q13.2
 ischium NEC Q74.2
 jaw – *see* Anomaly, dentofacial
  alveolar - *see* Anomaly, alveolar
 jaw-cranial base relationship – *see*
  Anomaly, dentofacial, jaw-cranial
  base relationship
 jejunum Q43.8
 joint Q74.9
  specified NEC Q74.8
 Jordan's D72.0
 kidney(s) (calyx) (pelvis) Q63.9
  artery Q27.2
  specified NEC Q63.8
 Klippel-Feil (brevicollis) Q76.1
 knee Q74.1
 labium (majus) (minus) Q52.70
 labyrinth, membranous Q16.5
 lacrimal apparatus or duct Q10.6
 larynx, laryngeal (muscle) Q31.9
  web(bed) Q31.0
 lens Q12.9
 leucocytes, genetic D72.0
  granulation (constitutional)
   D72.0
 lid (fold) Q10.3
 ligament Q79.9
  broad Q50.6
  round Q52.8
 limb Q74.9
  lower NEC Q74.2
   reduction deformity – *see* Defect,
    reduction, lower limb
  upper Q74.0
 lip Q38.0
 liver Q44.7
  duct Q44.5
 lower limb NEC Q74.2

Anomaly, anomalous *(Continued)*
lumbosacral (joint) (region) Q76.49
  kyphosis - *see* Kyphosis,
    congenital
  lordosis - *see* Lordosis, congenital
lung (fissure) (lobe) Q33.9
mandible - *see* Anomaly, dentofacial
maxilla - *see* Anomaly, dentofacial
May (-Hegglin) D72.0
meatus urinarius NEC Q64.79
meningeal bands or folds Q07.9
  constriction of Q07.8
  spinal Q06.9
meninges Q07.9
  cerebral Q04.8
  spinal Q06.9
meningocele Q05.9
mesentery Q45.9
metacarpus Q74.0
metatarsus NEC Q74.2
middle ear Q16.4
  ossicles Q16.3
mitral (leaflets) (valve) Q23.9
  insufficiency Q23.3
  specified NEC Q23.8
  stenosis Q23.2
mouth Q38.6
multiple NEC Q89.7
muscle Q79.9
  eyelid Q10.3
musculoskeletal system, except limbs
  Q79.9
myocardium Q24.8
nail Q84.6
narrowness, eyelid Q10.3
nasal sinus (wall) Q30.9
neck (any part) Q18.9
nerve Q07.9
  acoustic Q07.8
  optic Q07.8
nervous system (central) Q07.9
nipple Q83.9
nose, nasal (bones) (cartilage) (septum)
  (sinus) Q30.9
  specified NEC Q30.8
ocular muscle Q15.8
omphalomesenteric duct Q43.0
opening, pulmonary veins Q26.4
optic
  disc Q14.2
  nerve Q07.8
opticociliary vessels Q13.2
orbit (eye) Q10.7
organ Q89.9
  of Corti Q16.5
origin
  artery
    innominate Q25.8
    pulmonary Q25.7
    renal Q27.2
    subclavian Q25.8
osseous meatus (ear) Q16.1
ovary Q50.39
oviduct Q50.6
palate (hard) (soft) NEC Q38.5
pancreas or pancreatic duct
  Q45.3
papillary muscles Q24.8
parathyroid gland Q89.2
paraurethral ducts Q64.79
parotid (gland) Q38.4
patella Q74.1
Pelger-Huët (hereditary hyposegmentation) D72.0

Anomaly, anomalous *(Continued)*
pelvic girdle NEC Q74.2
pelvis (bony) NEC Q74.2
  rachitic E64.3
penis (glans) Q55.69
pericardium Q24.8
peripheral vascular system Q27.9
Peter's Q13.4
pharynx Q38.8
pigmentation L81.9
  congenital Q82.8
pituitary (gland) Q89.2
pleural (folds) Q34.0
portal vein Q26.5
  connection Q26.5
position, tooth, teeth, fully erupted
  M26.30
  specified NEC M26.39
precerebral vessel Q28.1
prepuce Q55.69
prostate Q55.4
pulmonary Q33.9
  artery NEC Q25.7
  valve Q22.3
    atresia Q22.0
    insufficiency Q22.2
    specified type NEC Q22.2
    stenosis Q22.1
      infundibular Q24.3
      subvalvular Q24.3
  venous connection Q26.4
    partial Q26.3
    total Q26.2
pupil Q13.2
  function H57.00
    anisocoria H57.02
    Argyll Robertson pupil H57.01
    miosis H57.03
    mydriasis H57.04
    specified type NEC H57.09
    tonic pupil H57.05-
pylorus Q40.3
radius Q74.0
rectum Q43.9
reduction (extremity) (limb)
  femur (longitudinal) - *see* Defect,
    reduction, lower limb, longitudi-
    nal, femur
  fibula (longitudinal) - *see* Defect,
    reduction, lower limb, longitudi-
    nal, fibula
  lower limb - *see* Defect, reduction,
    lower limb
  radius (longitudinal) - *see* Defect,
    reduction, upper limb, longitu-
    dinal, radius
  tibia (longitudinal) - *see* Defect,
    reduction, lower limb, longitu-
    dinal, tibia
  ulna (longitudinal) - *see* Defect,
    reduction, upper limb, longitu-
    dinal, ulna
  upper limb - *see* Defect, reduction,
    upper limb
refraction - *see* Disorder, refraction
renal Q63.9
  artery Q27.2
  pelvis Q63.9
    specified NEC Q63.8
respiratory system Q34.9
  specified NEC Q34.8
retina Q14.1
rib Q76.6
  cervical Q76.5

Anomaly, anomalous *(Continued)*
Rieger's Q13.81
rotation - *see* Malrotation
  hip or thigh Q65.8
round ligament Q52.8
sacroiliac (joint) NEC Q74.2
sacrum NEC Q76.49
  kyphosis - *see* Kyphosis, congenital
  lordosis - *see* Lordosis, congenital
saddle nose, syphilitic A50.57
salivary duct or gland Q38.4
scapula Q74.0
scrotum - *see* Malformation, testis and
  scrotum
sebaceous gland Q82.9
seminal vesicles Q55.4
sense organs NEC Q07.8
sex chromosomes NEC - *see also*
  Anomaly, chromosomes
  female phenotype Q97.8
  male phenotype Q98.9
shoulder (girdle) (joint) Q74.0
sigmoid (flexure) Q43.9
simian crease Q82.8
sinus of Valsalva Q25.4
skeleton generalized Q78.9
skin (appendage) Q82.9
skull Q75.9
  with
    anencephaly Q00.0
    encephalocele - *see* Encephalocele
    hydrocephalus Q03.9
      with spina bifida - *see* Spina
        bifida, by site, with
        hydrocephalus
    microcephaly Q02
specified organ or site NEC Q89.8
spermatic cord Q55.4
spine, spinal NEC Q76.49
  column NEC Q76.49
    kyphosis - *see* Kyphosis,
      congenital
    lordosis - *see* Lordosis,
      congenital
  cord Q06.9
  nerve root Q07.8
spleen Q89.09
  agenesis Q89.01
stenonian duct Q38.4
sternum NEC Q76.7
stomach Q40.3
submaxillary gland Q38.4
tarsus NEC Q74.2
tendon Q79.9
testis - *see* Malformation, testis and
  scrotum
thigh NEC Q74.2
thorax (wall) Q67.8
  bony Q76.9
throat Q38.8
thumb Q74.0
thymus gland Q89.2
thyroid (gland) Q89.2
  cartilage Q31.8
tibia NEC Q74.2
  saber A50.56
toe Q74.2
tongue Q38.3
tooth, teeth K00.9
  eruption K00.6
  position, fully erupted M26.30
  spacing, fully erupted M26.30
trachea (cartilage) Q32.1
tragus Q17.9

Anomaly, anomalous *(Continued)*
 tricuspid (leaflet) (valve) Q22.9
  atresia or stenosis Q22.4
  Ebstein's Q22.5
 Uhl's (hypoplasia of myocardium, right ventricle) Q24.8
 ulna Q74.0
 umbilical artery Q27.0
 union
  cricoid cartilage and thyroid cartilage Q31.8
  thyroid cartilage and hyoid bone Q31.8
  trachea with larynx Q31.8
 upper limb Q74.0
 urachus Q64.4
 ureter Q62.8
  obstructive NEC Q62.39
   cecoureterocele Q62.32
   orthotopic ureterocele Q62.31
 urethra Q64.70
  absence Q64.5
  double Q64.74
  fistula to rectum Q64.73
  obstructive Q64.39
   stricture Q64.32
  prolapse Q64.71
  specified type NEC Q64.79
 urinary tract Q64.9
 uterus Q51.9
  with only one functioning horn Q51.8
 uvula Q38.5
 vagina Q52.4
 valleculae Q31.8
 valve (heart) NEC Q24.8
  coronary sinus Q24.5
  inferior vena cava Q24.8
  pulmonary Q22.3
  sinus coronario Q24.5
  venae cavae inferioris Q24.8
 vas deferens Q55.4
 vascular Q27.9
  brain Q28.3
  ring Q25.4
 vein(s) (peripheral) Q27.9
  brain Q28.3
  cerebral Q28.3
  coronary Q24.5
  great Q26.9
   specified NEC Q26.8
 vena cava (inferior) (superior) Q26.9
 venous - *see* Anomaly, vein(s)
 venous return Q26.8
 ventricular
  bands or folds Q24.8
  septa Q21.0
 vertebra Q76.49
  kyphosis - *see* Kyphosis, congenital
  lordosis - *see* Lordosis, congenital
 vesicourethral orifice Q64.79
 vessel(s) Q27.9
  optic papilla Q14.2
  precerebral Q28.1
 vitelline duct Q43.0
 vitreous body or humor Q14.0
 vulva Q52.70
 wrist (joint) Q74.0
Anomia R48.8
Anonychia (congenital) Q84.3
 acquired L60.8
Anophthalmos, anophthalmus (congenital) (globe) Q11.1
 acquired Z90.01
Anopia, anopsia H53.46-
 quadrant H53.46-

Anorchia, anorchism, anorchidism Q55.0
Anorexia R63.0
 hysterical F44.89
 nervosa F50.00
  atypical F50.9
  binge-eating type F50.2
   with purging F50.02
  restricting type F50.01
Anorgasmy, psychogenic (female) F52.31
 male F52.32
Anosmia R43.0
 hysterical F44.6
 postinfectional J39.8
Anosognosia R41.89
Anosteoplasia Q78.9
Anovulatory cycle N97.0
Anoxemia R09.02
 newborn P84
Anoxia (pathological) R09.01
 altitude T70.20
 cerebral G93.1
  complicating
   anesthesia (general) (local) or other sedation T88.59
    in labor and delivery O74.3
    in pregnancy O29.21-
    postpartum, puerperal O89.2
   delivery (cesarean) (instrumental) O75.4
  during a procedure G97.81
  newborn P84
  resulting from a procedure G97.82
 due to
  drowning T75.1
  high altitude T70.20
 heart - *see* Insufficiency, coronary
 intrauterine P84
 myocardial - *see* Insufficiency, coronary
 newborn P84
 spinal cord G95.11
 systemic (by suffocation) (low content in atmosphere) - *see* Asphyxia, traumatic
Anteflexion - *see* Anteversion
Antenatal
 care (normal pregnancy) Z34.90
 screening (encounter for) of mother Z36
Antepartum - *see* condition
Anterior - *see* condition
Antero-occlusion M26.220
Anteversion
 cervix - *see* Anteversion, uterus
 femur (neck), congenital Q65.8
 uterus, uterine (cervix) (postinfectional) (postpartal, old) N85.4
  congenital Q51.8
  in pregnancy or childbirth - *see* Pregnancy, complicated by
Anthophobia F40.228
Anthracosilicosis J60
Anthracosis (lung) (occupational) J60
 lingua K14.3
Anthrax A22.9
 with pneumonia A22.1
 cerebral A22.8
 colitis A22.2
 cutaneous A22.0
 gastrointestinal A22.2
 inhalation A22.1
 intestinal A22.2
 meningitis A22.8
 pulmonary A22.1

Anthrax *(Continued)*
 respiratory A22.1
 sepsis A22.7
 specified manifestation NEC A22.8
Anthropoid pelvis Q74.2
 with disproportion (fetopelvic) O33.0
Anthropophobia F40.10
 generalized F40.11
Antibodies, maternal (blood group) - *see* Isoimmunization, affecting management of pregnancy
 anti-D - *see* Isoimmunization, affecting management of pregnancy, Rh
 newborn P55.0
Anticardiolipin syndrome D68.61
Anticoagulant, circulating (intrinsic) D68.31
 drug-induced (extrinsic) D68.32
Antidiuretic hormone syndrome E22.2
Antimonial cholera – *see* Poisoning, antimony
Antiphospholipid syndrome D68.61
Antisocial personality F60.2
Antithrombinemia - *see* Circulating anticoagulants
Antithromboplastinemia - *see* Circulating anticoagulants
Antithromboplastinogenemia - *see* Circulating anticoagulants
Antitoxin complication or reaction - *see* Complications, vaccination
Antlophobia F40.228
Antritis J32.0
 maxilla J32.0
  acute J01.00
   recurrent J01.01
 stomach K29.60
  with bleeding K29.61
Antrum, antral - *see* condition
Anuria R34
 calculus (impacted) (recurrent) - *see* Calculus, urinary
 following ectopic or molar pregnancy O08.4
 newborn P96.0
 postprocedural N99.0
 postrenal N13.8
 traumatic (following crushing) T79.5
Anus, anal - *see* condition
Anusitis K62.8
Anxiety F41.9
 depression F41.8
 episodic paroxysmal F41.0
 generalized F41.1
 hysteria F41.8
 neurosis F41.1
 panic type F41.0
 reaction F41.1
 separation, abnormal (of childhood) F93.0
 specified NEC F41.8
 state F41.1
Aorta, aortic - *see* condition
Aortectasia I71.9
Aortitis (nonsyphilitic) (calcific) I77.6
 arteriosclerotic I70.0
 Doehle-Heller A52.02
 luetic A52.02
 rheumatic - *see* Endocarditis, acute, rheumatic
 specific (syphilitic) A52.02
 syphilitic A52.02
  congenital A50.54 *[I79.1]*

Apathetic thyroid storm – *see*
  Thyrotoxicosis
Apathy R45.3
Apeirophobia F40.228
Apepsia K30
  psychogenic F45.8
Aperistalsis, esophagus K22.0
Apertognathia M26.29
Apert's syndrome Q87.0
Aphagia R13.0
  psychogenic F50.9
Aphakia (acquired) (postoperative)
  H27.0-
  congenital Q12.3
Aphasia (amnestic) (global) (nominal)
  (semantic) (syntactic) R47.01
  acquired, with epilepsy (Landau-
    Kleffner syndrome) F80.3
  auditory (developmental) F80.2
  developmental (receptive type) F80.2
    expressive type F80.1
    Wernicke's F80.2
  following
    cerebrovascular disease I69.920
      cerebral infarction I69.320
      intracerebral hemorrhage
        I69.120
      nontraumatic intracranial hemor-
        rhage NEC I69.220
      specified disease NEC I69.820
      subarachnoid hemorrhage
        I69.020
  progressive isolated G31.01 [F02.80]
    with behavioral disturbance G31.01
      [F02.81]
  sensory F80.2
  syphilis, tertiary A52.19
  Wernicke's (developmental) F80.2
Aphonia (organic) R49.1
  hysterical F44.4
  psychogenic F44.4
Aphthae, aphthous - *see also* condition
  Bednar's K12.0
  cachectic K14.0
  epizootic B08.8
  oral K12.0
  stomatitis K12.0
  ulcer (oral) (recurrent) K12.0
  fever B08.8
  oral (recurrent) K12.0
  stomatitis (major) (minor) K12.0
  thrush B37.0
  ulcer (oral) (recurrent) K12.0
    genital organ(s) NEC
      female N76.6
      male N50.8
    larynx J38.7
Apical - *see* condition
Apiphobia F40.218
Aplasia - *see also* Agenesis
  abdominal muscle syndrome Q79.4
  alveolar process (acquired) – *see*
    Anomaly, alveolar
    congenital Q38.6
  aorta (congenital) Q25.4
  axialis extracorticalis (congenita)
    E75.29
  bone marrow (myeloid) D61.9
    congenital D61.01
  brain Q00.0
    part of Q04.3
  bronchus Q32.4
  cementum K00.4
  cerebellum Q04.3

Aplasia *(Continued)*
  cervix (congenital) Q51.5
  congenital pure red cell D61.01
  corpus callosum Q04.0
  cutis congenita Q84.8
  erythrocyte congenital D61.01
  extracortical axial E75.29
  eye Q11.1
  fovea centralis (congenital) Q14.1
  gallbladder, congenital Q44.0
  iris Q13.1
  labyrinth, membranous Q16.5
  limb (congenital) Q73.8
    lower – *see* Defect, reduction, lower limb
    upper – *see* Agenesis, arm
  lung, congenital (bilateral) (unilateral)
    Q33.3
  pancreas Q45.0
  parathyroid-thymic D82.1
  Pelizaeus-Merzbacher E75.29
  penis Q55.5
  prostate Q55.4
  red cell (pure) (with thymoma) D60.9
    chronic D60.0
    congenital D61.01
    constitutional D61.01
    hereditary D61.01
    of infants D61.01
    primary D61.01
    specified type NEC D60.8
    transient D60.1
  round ligament Q52.8
  skin Q84.8
  spermatic cord Q55.4
  spleen Q89.01
  testicle Q55.0
  thymic, with immunodeficiency D82.1
  thyroid (congenital) (with myxedema)
    E03.1
  uterus Q51.0
  ventral horn cell Q06.1
Apnea, apneic (spells) R06.81
  newborn NEC P28.4
    sleep (primary) P28.3
  sleep G47.30
    central (primary) G47.31
      in conditions classified elsewhere
        G47.37
    obstructive (adult) (pediatric) G47.33
    primary central G47.31
    specified NEC G47.39
Apneumatosis, newborn P28.0
Apocrine metaplasia (breast) – *see* Dysplasia, mammary, specified type NEC
Apophysitis (bone) – *see also*
  Osteochondropathy
  calcaneus M92.8
  juvenile M92.9
Apoplectiform convulsions (cerebral
  ischemia) I67.8
Apoplexia, apoplexy, apoplectic
  adrenal A39.1
  heart (auricle) (ventricle) - *see* Infarct,
    myocardium
  heat T67.0
  hemorrhagic (stroke) - *see* Hemorrhage,
    intracranial
  meninges, hemorrhagic - *see* Hemor-
    rhage, intracranial, subarachnoid
  uremic N18.9 [I68.8]
Appearance
  bizarre R46.1
  specified NEC R46.89
  very low level of personal hygiene R46.0

Appendage
  epididymal (organ of Morgagni) Q55.4
  intestine (epiploic) Q43.8
  preauricular Q17.0
  testicular (organ of Morgagni) Q55.29
Appendicitis (pneumococcal) (retrocecal)
  K37
  with
    perforation or rupture K35.2
    peritoneal abscess K35.3
      with peritonitis K35.2
    peritonitis K35.2
      with perforation or rupture K35.2
      localized K35.3
      generalized K35.2
  acute (catarrhal) (fulminating) (gan-
    grenous) (obstructive) (retrocecal)
    (suppurative) K35.80
    with
      perforation or rupture K35.2
      peritoneal abscess K35.3
        with peritonitis K35.2
      peritonitis K35.2
        with perforation or rupture K35.2
        localized K35.3
        generalized K35.2
    specified NEC K35.89
  amebic A06.89
  chronic (recurrent) K36
  exacerbation - *see* Appendicitis, acute
  gangrenous - *see* Appendicitis, acute
  healed (obliterative) K36
  interval K36
  neurogenic K36
  obstructive K36
  recurrent K36
  relapsing K36
  subacute (adhesive) K36
  subsiding K36
  suppurative - *see* Appendicitis, acute
  tuberculous A18.32
Appendix, appendicular - *see also* condition
  epididymus Q55.4
  Morgagni
    female Q50.5
    male (epididymal) Q55.4
    testicular Q55.29
  testis Q55.29
Appendicopathia oxyurica B80
Appetite
  depraved – *see* Pica
  excessive R63.2
  lack or loss (*see also* Anorexia) R63.0
    nonorganic origin – *see* Disorder,
      eating
    psychogenic F50.8
  perverted (hysterical) – *see* Pica
Apple peel syndrome Q41.1
Apprehension state F41.1
Apprehensiveness, abnormal F41.9
Approximal wear K03.0
Apraxia (classic) (ideational) (ideokinetic)
  (ideomotor) (motor) (verbal) R48.2
  following
    cerebrovascular disease I69.990
      specified NEC I69.890
      cerebral infarction I69.390
      intracerebral hemorrhage I69.190
      nontraumatic intracranial hemor-
        rhage NEC I69.290
      specified disease NEC I69.890
      subarachnoid hemorrhage
        I69.090
  oculomotor, congenital H51.8

Aptyalism K11.7
Apudoma - *see* Neoplasm, uncertain behavior
Aqueous misdirection H40.83-
Arabicum elephantiasis - *see* Infestation, filarial
Arachnitis - *see* Meningitis
Arachnodactyly - *see* Syndrome, Marfan's
Arachnoiditis (acute) (adhesive) (basal) (brain) (cerebrospinal) - *see* Meningitis
Arachnophobia F40.210
Arboencephalitis, Australian A83.4
Arborization block (heart) I45.5
ARC (AIDS-related complex) B20
Arches - *see* condition
Arcuatus uterus Q51.8
Arcus (cornea) senilis - *see* Degeneration, cornea, senile
Arc-welder's lung J63.4
Areflexia R29.2
Areola - *see* condition
Argentaffinoma - *see also* Neoplasm, uncertain behavior
  malignant - *see* Neoplasm, malignant
  syndrome E34.0
Argininemia E72.21
Arginosuccinic aciduria E72.22
Argyll Robertson phenomenon, pupil or syndrome (syphilitic) A52.19
  atypical H57.09
  nonsyphilitic H57.09
Argyria, argyriasis
  conjunctival - *see* Deposit, conjunctiva
  from drug or medicament - *see* Table of drugs and chemicals, by substance
Argyrosis, conjunctival - *see* Deposit, conjunctiva
Arhinencephaly Q04.1
Ariboflavinosis E53.0
Arm - *see* condition
Arnold-Chiari disease, obstruction or syndrome (type II) Q07.00
  with
    hydrocephalus Q07.02
      with spina bifida Q07.03
    spina bifida Q07.01
      with hydrocephalus Q07.03
  type III – *see* Encephalocele
  type IV Q04.8
Aromatic amino-acid metabolism disorder E70.9
  specified NEC E70.8
Arousals, confusional G47.51
Arrest, arrested
  cardiac I46.9
    complicating
      abortion - see Abortion, by type, complicated by, cardiac arrest
      anesthesia (general) (local) or other sedation - see Table of drugs and chemicals, by drug,
        in labor and delivery O74.2
        in pregnancy O29.11-
        postpartum, puerperal O89.1
      delivery (cesarean) (instrumental) O75.4
    due to
      cardiac condition I46.2
      specified condition NEC I46.8
    intraoperative I97.71-
    newborn P29.81

Arrest, arrested *(Continued)*
  cardiac *(Continued)*
    postprocedural I97.12-
      obstetric procedure O75.4
    cardiorespiratory - *see* Arrest, cardiac
    circulatory - *see* Arrest, cardiac
    deep transverse O64.0
    development or growth
      bone - see Disorder, bone, development or growth
      child R62.50
      tracheal rings Q32.1
    epiphyseal
      complete
        femur M89.15-
        humerus M89.12-
        tibia M89.16-
        ulna M89.13-
      forearm M89.13-
        specified NEC M89.13-
        ulna - see Arrest, epiphyseal, by type, ulna
      lower leg M89.16-
        specified NEC M89.168
        tibia - see Arrest, epiphyseal, by type, tibia
      partial
        femur M89.15-
        humerus M89.12-
        tibia M89.16-
        ulna M89.13-
      specified NEC M89.18
    granulopoiesis – *see* Agranulocytosis
    growth plate - *see* Arrest, epiphyseal
    heart - *see* Arrest, cardiac
    legal, anxiety concerning Z65.3
    physeal - *see* Arrest, epiphyseal
    respiratory R09.2
      newborn P28.81
    sinus I45.5
    spermatogenesis (complete) - *see* Azoospermia
      incomplete - see Oligospermia
    transverse (deep) O64.0
Arrhenoblastoma
  benign
    specified site - see Neoplasm, benign
    unspecified site
      female D27.9
      male D29.20
  malignant
    specified site - see Neoplasm, malignant
    unspecified site
      female C56.9
      male C62.90
  specified site - *see* Neoplasm, uncertain behavior
  unspecified site
    female D39.10
    male D40.10
Arrhythmia (auricle)(cardiac)(juvenile) (nodal) (reflex)(sinus)(supraventricular)(transitory)(ventricle) I49.9
  block I45.9
  extrasystolic I49.49
  newborn
    bradycardia P29.12
    tachycardia P29.11
    occurring before birth P03.819
      before onset of labor P03.810
      during labor P03.811

Arrhythmia *(Continued)*
  psychogenic F45.8
  specified NEC I49.8
  vagal R55
  ventricular re-entry I47.0
Arrillaga-Ayerza syndrome (pulmonary sclerosis with pulmonary hypertension) I27.0
Arsenical pigmentation L81.8
  from drug or medicament - *see* Table of drugs and medicaments
Arsenism - *see* Poisoning, arsenic
Arterial - *see* condition
Arteriofibrosis - *see* Arteriosclerosis
Arteriolar sclerosis - *see* Arteriosclerosis
Arteriolith - *see* Arteriosclerosis
Arteriolitis I77.6
  necrotizing, kidney I77.5
  renal - *see* Hypertension, kidney
Arteriolosclerosis - *see* Arteriosclerosis
Arterionephrosclerosis - *see* Hypertension, kidney
Arteriopathy I77.9
Arteriosclerosis, arteriosclerotic (diffuse) (obliterans) (of) (senile) (with calcification) I70.90
  aorta I70.0
  arteries of extremities - *see* Arteriosclerosis, extremities
  brain I67.2
    extremities - *see* Arteriosclerosis, extremities, bypass graft
  cardiac – *see* Disease, heart, ischemic, atherosclerotic
  cardiopathy - *see* Disease, heart, ischemic, atherosclerotic
  cardiorenal - *see* Hypertension, cardiorenal
  cardiovascular – *see* Disease, heart, ischemic, atherosclerotic
  central nervous system I67.2
  cerebral I67.2
  cerebrovascular I67.2
  coronary (artery) I25.10
    due to lipid rich plaque I25.83
    native vessel
      with
        angina pectoris I25.119
          specified type NEC I25.118
          unstable I25.110
            with documented spasm I25.111
        ischemic chest pain I25.119
    bypass graft I25.810
      with
        angina pectoris I25.709
          specified type NEC I25.708
          unstable I25.700
            with documented spasm I25.701
        ischemic chest pain I25.709
      autologous artery I25.810
        with
          angina pectoris I25.729
            specified type I25.728
            unstable I25.720
              with documented spasm I25.721
          ischemic chest pain I25.729

Arteriosclerosis, arteriosclerotic
  (Continued)
 coronary *(Continued)*
  bypass graft *(Continued)*
   autologous vein I25.810
    with
     angina pectoris I25.719
      specified type I25.718
      unstable I25.710
      with documented spasm
       I25.711
     ischemic chest pain
      I25.719
   nonautologous biological
    I25.810
    with
     angina pectoris I25.739
      specified type I25.738
      unstable I25.730
      with documented spasm
       I25.731
     ischemic chest pain I25.739
   specified type NEC I25.810
    with
     angina pectoris I25.799
      specified type I25.798
      unstable I25.790
      with documented spasm
       I25.791
     ischemic chest pain I25.799
  transplanted heart I25.811
   native coronary artery I25.811
    with
     angina pectoris I25.759
      specified type I25.758
      unstable I25.750
      with documented spasm
       I25.751
     ischemic chest pain I25.759
    bypass graft I25.812
     with
      angina pectoris I25.769
       specified type I25.768
       unstable I25.760
       with documented spasm
        I25.761
      ischemic chest pain
       I25.769
 extremities (native arteries)
  I70.209
  bypass graft I70.309
   autologous vein graft I70.409
    leg I70.409
     with
      gangrene (and intermittent
       claudication, rest pain
       and ulcer) I70.469
      intermittent claudication
       I70.419
      rest pain (and intermittent
       claudication) I70.429
     bilateral I70.403
      with
       gangrene (and intermit-
        tent claudication,
        rest pain and ulcer)
        I70.463
       intermittent claudication
        I70.413
       rest pain (and intermittent
        claudication)
        I70.423
      specified type NEC
       I70.493

Arteriosclerosis, arteriosclerotic
  (Continued)
 extremities *(Continued)*
  bypass graft *(Continued)*
   autologous vein graft *(Continued)*
    leg *(Continued)*
     left I70.402
      with
       gangrene (and intermit-
        tent claudication,
        rest pain and ulcer)
        I70.462
       intermittent claudication
        I70.412
       rest pain (and intermittent
        claudication)
        I70.422
       ulceration (and intermit-
        tent claudication
        and rest pain)
        I70.449
        ankle I70.443
        calf I70.442
        foot site NEC I70.445
        heel I70.444
        lower leg NEC I70.448
        midfoot I70.444
        thigh I70.441
      specified type NEC I70.492
     right I70.401
      with
       gangrene (and intermit-
        tent claudication,
        rest pain and ulcer)
        I70.461
       intermittent claudication
        I70.411
       rest pain (and intermittent
        claudication)
        I70.421
       ulceration (and intermit-
        tent claudication and
        rest pain) I70.439
        ankle I70.433
        calf I70.432
        foot site NEC I70.435
        heel I70.434
        lower leg NEC I70.438
        midfoot I70.434
        thigh I70.431
      specified type NEC I70.491
     specified type NEC I70.499
    specified NEC I70.408
     with
      gangrene (and intermittent
       claudication, rest pain
       and ulcer) I70.468
      intermittent claudication
       I70.418
      rest pain (and intermittent
       claudication) I70.428
      ulceration (and intermittent
       claudication and rest
       pain) I70.45
     specified type NEC I70.498
    leg I70.309
     with
      gangrene (and intermittent
       claudication, rest pain
       and ulcer) I70.369
      intermittent claudication
       I70.319
      rest pain (and intermittent
       claudication) I70.329

Arteriosclerosis, arteriosclerotic
  (Continued)
 extremities *(Continued)*
  bypass graft *(Continued)*
   leg *(Continued)*
    bilateral I70.303
     with
      gangrene (and intermittent
       claudication, rest
       pain and ulcer)
       I70.363
      intermittent claudication
       I70.313
      rest pain (and intermittent
       claudication)
       I70.323
     specified type NEC
      I70.393
    left I70.302
     with
      gangrene (and intermittent
       claudication, rest
       pain and ulcer)
       I70.362
      intermittent claudication
       I70.312
      rest pain (and intermittent
       claudication)
       I70.322
      ulceration (and intermittent
       claudication and rest
       pain) I70.349
       ankle I70.343
       calf I70.342
       foot site NEC I70.345
       heel I70.344
       lower leg NEC I70.348
       midfoot I70.344
       thigh I70.341
     specified type NEC I70.392
    right I70.301
     with
      gangrene (and intermittent
       claudication, rest
       pain and ulcer)
       I70.361
      intermittent claudication
       I70.311
      rest pain (and intermittent
       claudication)
       I70.321
      ulceration (and intermittent
       claudication and rest
       pain) I70.339
       ankle I70.333
       calf I70.332
       foot site NEC I70.335
       heel I70.334
       lower leg NEC I70.338
       midfoot I70.334
       thigh I70.331
     specified type NEC I70.391
    specified type NEC I70.399
   nonautologous biological graft
    I70.509
    leg I70.509
     with
      gangrene (and intermittent
       claudication, rest pain
       and ulcer) I70.569
      intermittent claudication
       I70.519
      rest pain (and intermittent
       claudication) I70.529

Arteriosclerosis, arteriosclerotic
  (Continued)
 extremities *(Continued)*
  bypass graft *(Continued)*
   nonautologous biological graft
    (Continued)
    leg *(Continued)*
     bilateral I70.503
      with
       gangrene (and intermit-
        tent claudication,
        rest pain and ulcer)
        I70.563
       intermittent claudication
        I70.513
       rest pain (and intermittent
        claudication)
        I70.523
       specified type NEC I70.593
     left I70.502
      with
       gangrene (and intermit-
        tent claudication,
        rest pain and ulcer)
        I70.562
       intermittent claudication
        I70.512
       rest pain (and intermittent
        claudication)
        I70.522
       ulceration (and intermit-
        tent claudication and
        rest pain) I70.549
        ankle I70.543
        calf I70.542
        foot site NEC I70.545
        heel I70.544
        lower leg NEC I70.548
        midfoot I70.544
        thigh I70.541
       specified type NEC I70.592
     right I70.501
      with
       gangrene (and intermit-
        tent claudication,
        rest pain and ulcer)
        I70.561
       intermittent claudication
        I70.511
       rest pain (and intermittent
        claudication)
        I70.521
       ulceration (and intermit-
        tent claudication and
        rest pain) I70.539
        ankle I70.533
        calf I70.532
        foot site NEC I70.535
        heel I70.534
        lower leg NEC I70.538
        midfoot I70.534
        thigh I70.531
       specified type NEC I70.591
    specified type NEC I70.599
   specified NEC I70.508
    with
     gangrene (and intermittent
      claudication, rest pain
      and ulcer) I70.568
     intermittent claudication
      I70.518
     rest pain (and intermittent
      claudication) I70.528

Arteriosclerosis, arteriosclerotic
  (Continued)
 extremities *(Continued)*
  bypass graft *(Continued)*
   nonautologous biological graft
    (Continued)
    specified NEC *(Continued)*
     with *(Continued)*
      ulceration (and intermittent
       claudication and rest
       pain) I70.55
     specified type NEC I70.598
   nonbiological graft I70.609
    leg I70.609
     with
      gangrene (and intermittent
       claudication, rest pain
       and ulcer) I70.669
      intermittent claudication
       I70.619
      rest pain (and intermittent
       claudication) I70.629
     bilateral I70.603
      with
       gangrene (and intermit-
        tent claudication,
        rest pain and ulcer)
        I70.663
       intermittent claudication
        I70.613
       rest pain (and intermittent
        claudication)
        I70.623
       specified type NEC I70.693
     left I70.602
      with
       gangrene (and intermit-
        tent claudication,
        rest pain and ulcer)
        I70.662
       intermittent claudication
        I70.612
       rest pain (and intermittent
        claudication)
        I70.622
       ulceration (and intermit-
        tent claudication and
        rest pain) I70.649
        ankle I70.643
        calf I70.642
        foot site NEC I70.645
        heel I70.644
        lower leg NEC I70.648
        midfoot I70.644
        thigh I70.641
       specified type NEC I70.692
     right I70.601
      with
       gangrene (and intermit-
        tent claudication,
        rest pain and ulcer)
        I70.661
       intermittent claudication
        I70.611
       rest pain (and intermittent
        claudication)
        I70.621
       ulceration (and intermit-
        tent claudication and
        rest pain) I70.639
        ankle I70.633
        calf I70.632
        foot site NEC I70.635
        heel I70.634

Arteriosclerosis, arteriosclerotic
  (Continued)
 extremities *(Continued)*
  bypass graft *(Continued)*
   nonbiological graft *(Continued)*
    leg *(Continued)*
     right *(Continued)*
      with *(Continued)*
       ulceration *(Continued)*
        lower leg NEC
         I70.638
        midfoot I70.634
        thigh I70.631
        specified type NEC
         I70.691
      specified type NEC I70.699
    specified NEC I70.608
     with
      gangrene (and intermittent
       claudication, rest
       pain and ulcer)
       I70.668
      intermittent claudication
       I70.618
      rest pain (and intermittent
       claudication)
       I70.628
      ulceration (and intermittent
       claudication and rest
       pain) I70.65
     specified type NEC I70.698
   specified graft NEC I70.709
    leg I70.709
     with
      gangrene (and intermittent
       claudication, rest
       pain and ulcer)
       I70.769
      intermittent claudication
       I70.719
      rest pain (and intermittent
       claudication) I70.729
     bilateral I70.703
      with
       gangrene (and intermit-
        tent claudication,
        rest pain and ulcer)
        I70.763
       intermittent claudication
        I70.713
       rest pain (and intermittent
        claudication) I70.723
       specified type NEC I70.793
     left I70.702
      with
       gangrene (and intermit-
        tent claudication,
        rest pain and ulcer)
        I70.762
       intermittent claudication
        I70.712
       rest pain (and intermittent
        claudication) I70.722
       ulceration (and intermit-
        tent claudication and
        rest pain) I70.749
        ankle I70.743
        calf I70.742
        foot site NEC I70.745
        heel I70.744
        lower leg NEC I70.748
        midfoot I70.744
        thigh I70.741
       specified type NEC I70.792

Arteriosclerosis, arteriosclerotic
(Continued)
extremities (Continued)
bypass graft (Continued)
specified graft NEC (Continued)
leg (Continued)
right I70.701
with
gangrene (and intermittent claudication, rest pain and ulcer) I70.761
intermittent claudication I70.711
rest pain (and intermittent claudication) I70.721
ulceration (and intermittent claudication and rest pain) I70.739
ankle I70.733
calf I70.732
foot site NEC I70.735
heel I70.734
lower leg NEC I70.738
midfoot I70.734
thigh I70.731
specified type NEC I70.791
specified type NEC I70.799
specified NEC I70.708
with
gangrene (and intermittent claudication, rest pain and ulcer) I70.768
intermittent claudication I70.718
rest pain (and intermittent claudication) I70.728
ulceration (and intermittent claudication and rest pain) I70.75
specified type NEC I70.798
specified NEC I70.308
with
gangrene (and intermittent claudication, rest pain and ulcer) I70.368
intermittent claudication I70.318
rest pain (and intermittent claudication) I70.328
ulceration (and intermittent claudication and rest pain) I70.35
specified type NEC I70.398
leg I70.209
with
gangrene (and intermittent claudication, rest pain and ulcer) I70.269
intermittent claudication I70.219
rest pain (and intermittent claudication) I70.229
bilateral I70.203
with
gangrene (and intermittent claudication, rest pain and ulcer) I70.263
intermittent claudication I70.213
rest pain (and intermittent claudication) I70.223
specified type NEC I70.293

Arteriosclerosis, arteriosclerotic
(Continued)
extremities (Continued)
leg (Continued)
left I70.202
with
gangrene (and intermittent claudication, rest pain and ulcer) I70.262
intermittent claudication I70.212
rest pain (and intermittent claudication) I70.222
ulceration (and intermittent claudication and rest pain) I70.249
ankle I70.243
calf I70.242
foot site NEC I70.245
heel I70.244
lower leg NEC I70.248
midfoot I70.244
thigh I70.241
specified type NEC I70.292
right I70.201
with
gangrene (and intermittent claudication, rest pain and ulcer) I70.261
intermittent claudication I70.211
rest pain (and intermittent claudication) I70.221
ulceration (and intermittent claudication and rest pain) I70.239
ankle I70.233
calf I70.232
foot site NEC I70.235
heel I70.234
lower leg NEC I70.238
midfoot I70.234
thigh I70.231
specified type NEC I70.291
specified type NEC I70.299
specified site NEC I70.208
with
gangrene (and intermittent claudication, rest pain and ulcer) I70.268
intermittent claudication I70.218
rest pain (and intermittent claudication) I70.228
ulceration (and intermittent claudication and rest pain) I70.25
specified type NEC I70.298
generalized I70.91
heart (disease) – see Arteriosclerosis, coronary (artery),
kidney - see Hypertension, kidney
medial - see Arteriosclerosis, extremities
mesenteric (artery) K55.1
Mönckeberg's - see Arteriosclerosis, extremities
myocarditis I51.4
peripheral (of extremities) - see Arteriosclerosis, extremities
pulmonary (idiopathic) I27.0
renal (arterioles) - see also Hypertension, kidney
artery I70.1
retina (vascular) I70.8
specified artery NEC I70.8
spinal (cord) G95.19
vertebral (artery) I67.2

Arteriospasm I73.9
Arteriovenous - see condition
Arteritis I77.6
allergic M31.0
aorta (nonsyphilitic) I77.6
syphilitic A52.02
aortic arch M31.4
brachiocephalic M31.4
brain I67.7
syphilitic A52.04
cerebral I67.7
in systemic lupus erythematosus M32.19
listerial A32.89
syphilitic A52.04
tuberculous A18.89
coronary (artery) I25.89
rheumatic I01.8
chronic I09.89
syphilitic A52.06
cranial (left) (right), giant cell M31.6
deformans - see Arteriosclerosis
giant cell NEC M31.6
with polymyalgia rheumatica M31.5
necrosing or necrotizing M31.9
specified NEC M31.8
nodosa M30.0
obliterans - see Arteriosclerosis
pulmonary I28.8
rheumatic - see Fever, rheumatic
senile - see Arteriosclerosis
suppurative I77.2
syphilitic (general) A52.09
brain A52.04
coronary A52.06
spinal A52.09
temporal, giant cell M31.6
young female aortic arch syndrome M31.4
Artery, arterial - see also condition
abscess I77.8
single umbilical Q27.0
Arthralgia (allergic) - see also Pain, joint
in caisson disease T70.3
temporomandibular M26.62
Arthritis, arthritic (acute) (chronic) (non-pyogenic) (subacute) M19.90
meaning osteoarthritis - see Osteoarthritis
allergic - see Arthritis, specified form NEC
ankylosing (crippling) (spine) - see also Spondylitis, ankylosing
sites other than spine - see Arthritis, specified form NEC
atrophic - see Osteoarthritis
spine - see Spondylitis, ankylosing
back - see Spondylopathy, inflammatory
blennorrhagic (gonococcal) A54.42
Charcot's - see Arthropathy, neuropathic
diabetic - see Diabetes, arthropathy, neuropathic
syringomyelic G95.0
chylous (filarial) B74.9 (see also category M01)
climacteric (any site) NEC - see Arthritis, specified form NEC
crystal(-induced) - see Arthritis, in, crystals
deformans - see Osteoarthritis
degenerative - see Osteoarthritis
due to or associated with
acromegaly E22.0
brucellosis - see Brucellosis

Arthritis, arthritic *(Continued)*
  due to or associated with *(Continued)*
    caisson disease T70.3
    diabetes - *see* Diabetes, arthropathy
    dracontiasis B72 *(see also* category
      M01)
    enteritis NEC
      regional - *see* Enteritis, regional
    erysipelas A46
    erythema
      epidemic A25.1
      nodosum L52
    filariasis NOS B74.9
    glanders A24.0
    helminthiasis *(see also* category M01)
      B83.9
    hemophilia D66
    Henoch (-Schölein) purpura D69.0
    human parvovirus *(see also* category
      M01) B97.6
    infectious disease NEC - *see* category
      M01
    leprosy *(see also* Leprosy) A30.9
    Lyme disease A69.23
    mycobacteria A31.8
    parasitic disease NEC B89 *(see also*
      category M01)
    paratyphoid fever *(see also* Fever,
      paratyphoid) A01.4 *(see also*
      category M01)
    rat bite fever A25.1
    regional enteritis – *see* Enteritis,
      regional
    respiratory disorder NOS J98.9
    serum sickness T80.6
    syringomyelia G95.0
    typhoid fever A01.04
  epidemic erythema A25.1
  febrile - *see* Fever, rheumatic
  gonococcal A54.42
  gouty (acute) - *see* Gout, idiopathic
  in (due to)
    acromegaly *(see also* subcategory
      M14.8-) E22.0
    amyloidosis *(see also* subcategory
      M14.8-) E85.4
    bacterial disease *(see also* subcategory
      M01) A49.9
    Behçet's syndrome M35.2
    caisson disease *(see also* subcategory
      M14.8-) T70.3
    coliform bacilli (Escherichia coli) - *see*
      Arthritis, in, pyogenic organism
      NEC
    crystals M11.9
      dicalcium phosphate - *see* Arthritis,
        in, crystals, specified type NEC
      hydroxyapatite M11.0-
      pyrophosphate - *see* Arthritis, in,
        crystals, specified type NEC
      specified type NEC M11.80
        ankle M11.87-
        elbow M11.82-
        foot joint M11.87-
        hand joint M11.84-
        hip M11.85-
        knee M11.86-
        multiple site M11.8-
        shoulder M11.81-
        specified joint NEC M11.88
        wrist M11.83-
    dermatoarthritis, lipoid E78.81
    dracontiasis (dracunculiasis) B72 *(see
      also* category M01)

Arthritis, arthritic *(Continued)*
  in *(Continued)*
    endocrine disorder NEC *(see also*
      subcategory M14.8-) E34.9
    enteritis, infectious NEC A09 *(see also*
      category M01)
      specified organism NEC A08.8 *(see
        also* category M01)
    erythema
      multiforme *(see also* subcategory
        M14.8-) L51.9
      nodosum *(see also* subcategory
        M14.8-) L52
    gout - *see* Gout, idiopathic
    Hemophilus influenzae B96.3
      [M00.80]
    helminthiasis NEC B83.9 *(see also*
      category M01)
    hemochromatosis *(see also* subcat-
      egory M14.8-) E83.11
    hemoglobinopathy NEC D58.2
      [M36.3]
    hemophilia NEC D66 *[M36.2]*
    Henoch(-Schönlein) purpura D69.0
      [M36.4]
    hyperparathyroidism NEC *(see also*
      subcategory M14.8-) E21.3
    hypersensitivity reaction NEC T78.49
      [M36.4]
    hypogammaglobulinemia *(see also*
      subcategory M14.8-) D80.1
    hypothyroidism NEC *(see also* subcat-
      egory M14.8-) E03.9
    infection - *see* Arthritis, pyogenic or
      pyemic
      spine - *see* Spondylopathy, infective
    infectious disease NEC *(see also*
      category M01) B99
    leprosy A30.9 *(see also* category M01)
    leukemia NEC C95.90 *[M36.1]*
    lipoid dermatoarthritis E78.81
    Lyme disease A69.23
    Mediterranean fever, familial *(see also*
      subcategory M14.8-) E85.0
    Meningococcus A39.83
    metabolic disorder NEC *(see also*
      subcategory M14.8-) E88.9
    multiple myelomatosis C90.00
      [M36.1]
    mumps B26.85
    mycosis NEC B49 *(see also* category
      M01)
    myelomatosis (multiple) C90.00
      [M36.1]
    neurological disorder NEC G98.0
    ochronosis *(see also* subcategory
      M14.8-) E70.29
    O'nyong-nyong A92.1 *(see also* cat-
      egory M01)
    parasitic disease NEC B89 *(see also*
      category M01)
    paratyphoid fever A01.4 *(see also*
      category M01)
    Pseudomonas - *see* Arthritis, pyo-
      genic, bacterial NEC
    psoriasis L40.50
    pyogenic organism NEC - *see* Arthri-
      tis, pyogenic, bacterial NEC
    Reiter's disease - *see* Reiter's disease
    respiratory disorder NEC *(see also*
      subcategory M14.8-) J98.9
    reticulosis, malignant *(see also*
      subcategory M14.8-) C85.70
    rubella B06.82

Arthritis, arthritic *(Continued)*
  in *(Continued)*
    Salmonella (arizonae) (cholerae-suis)
      (enteritidis) (typhimurium)
      A02.23
    sarcoidosis D86.86
    specified bacteria NEC - *see* Arthritis,
      pyogenic, bacterial NEC
    sporotrichosis B42.82
    syringomyelia G95.0
    thalassemia NEC D56.9 *[M36.3]*
    tuberculosis - *see* Tuberculosis,
      arthritis
    typhoid fever A01.04
    urethritis, Reiter's - *see* Reiter's
      disease
    viral disease NEC B34.9 *(see also*
      category M01)
  infectious or infective - *see also* Arthritis,
    pyogenic or pyemic
    spine - *see* Spondylopathy, infective
  juvenile M08.90
    with systemic onset - *see* Still's
      disease
    ankle M08.97-
    elbow M08.92-
    foot joint M08.97-
    hand joint M08.94-
    hip M08.95-
    knee M08.96-
    multiple site M08.99
    pauciarticular M08.40
      ankle M08.47-
      elbow M08.42-
      foot joint M08.47-
      hand joint M08.44-
      hip M08.45-
      knee M08.46-
      shoulder M08.41-
      specified joint NEC M08.48
      wrist M08.43-
    psoriatic L40.54
    rheumatoid - *see* Arthritis, rheuma-
      toid, juvenile
    shoulder M08.91-
    vertebra M08.98
    specified type NEC M08.80
      ankle M08.87-
      elbow M08.82-
      foot joint M08.87-
      hand joint M08.84-
      hip M08.85-
      knee M08.86-
      multiple site M08.89
      shoulder M08.81-
      specified joint NEC M08.88
      wrist M08.83-
    wrist M08.93-
  meningococcal A39.83
  menopausal (any site) NEC - *see* Arthri-
    tis, specified form NEC
  mutilans (psoriatic) L40.52
  mycotic NEC B49 *(see also* category
    M01)
  neuropathic (Charcot) - *see* Arthropathy,
    neuropathic
    diabetic - *see* Diabetes, arthropathy,
      neuropathic
    nonsyphilitic NEC G98.0
    syringomyelic G95.0
  ochronotic *(see also* subcategory M14.8-)
    E70.29
  palindromic (any site) *see* Rheumatism,
    palindromic

Arthritis, arthritic *(Continued)*
  pneumococcal M00.10
    ankle M00.17-
    elbow M00.12-
    foot joint - *see* Arthritis, pneumococcal, ankle
    hand joint M00.14-
    hip M00.15-
    knee M00.16-
    multiple site M00.19
    shoulder M00.11-
    vertebra M00.18
    wrist M00.13-
  postdysenteric - *see* Arthropathy, postdysenteric
  postmeningococcal A39.84
  postrheumatic, chronic - *see* Arthropathy, postrheumatic, chronic
  primary progressive - *see also* Arthritis, specified form NEC
    spine - *see* Spondylitis, ankylosing
  psoriatic L40.50
  purulent (any site except spine) - *see* Arthritis, pyogenic or pyemic
    spine - *see* Spondylopathy, infective
  pyogenic or pyemic (any site except spine) M00.9
    bacterial NEC M00.80
      ankle M00.87-
      elbow M00.82-
      foot joint - *see* Arthritis, bacterial NEC, ankle
      hand joint M00.84-
      hip M00.85-
      knee M00.86-
      multiple site M00.89
      shoulder M00.81-
      vertebra M00.88
      wrist M00.83-
    pneumococcal - *see* Arthritis, pneumococcal
    spine - *see* Spondylopathy, infective
    staphylococcal - *see* Arthritis, staphylococcal
    streptococcal - *see* Arthritis, streptococcal NEC
      pneumococcal - *see* Arthritis, pneumococcal
  rheumatic - *see also* Arthritis, rheumatoid
    acute or subacute - *see* Fever, rheumatic
  rheumatoid M06.9
    with
      carditis - *see* Rheumatoid, carditis
      endocarditis - *see* Rheumatoid, carditis
      heart involvement NEC - *see* Rheumatoid, carditis
      lung involvement - *see* Rheumatoid, lung
      myocarditis - *see* Rheumatoid, carditis
      myopathy - *see* Rheumatoid, myopathy
      pericarditis - *see* Rheumatoid, carditis
      polyneuropathy - *see* Rheumatoid, polyneuropathy
      rheumatoid factor - *see* Arthritis, rheumatoid, seropositive

Arthritis, arthritic *(Continued)*
  rheumatoid *(Continued)*
    with *(Continued)*
      splenoadenomegaly and leukopenia - *see* Felty's syndrome
      vasculitis - *see* Rheumatoid, vasculitis
      visceral involvement NEC - *see* Rheumatoid, arthritis, with involvement of organs NEC
    juvenile (with or without rheumatoid factor) M08.00
      ankle M08.07-
      elbow M08.02-
      foot joint M08.07-
      hand joint M08.04-
      hip M08.05-
      knee M08.06-
      multiple site M08.09
      shoulder M08.01-
      vertebra M08.08
      wrist M08.03-
    seronegative M06.00
      ankle M06.07-
      elbow M06.02-
      foot joint M06.07-
      hand joint M06.04-
      hip M06.05-
      knee M06.06-
      multiple site M06.09
      shoulder M06.01-
      vertebra M06.08
      wrist M06.03-
    seropositive M05.9
      without organ involvement M05.70
        ankle M05.77-
        elbow M05.72-
        foot joint M05.77-
        hand joint M05.74-
        hip M05.75-
        knee M05.76-
        multiple site M05.79
        shoulder M05.71-
        vertebra - *see* Spondylitis, ankylosing
        wrist M05.73-
      specified type NEC M06.80
        ankle M06.87-
        elbow M06.82-
        foot joint M06.87-
        hand joint M06.84-
        hip M06.85-
        knee M06.86-
        multiple site M06.89
        shoulder M06.81-
        vertebra M06.88
        wrist M06.83-
      spine - *see* Spondylitis, ankylosing
    rubella B06.82
    scorbutic (*see also* subcategory M14.8-) E54
    senile or senescent - *see* Osteoarthritis
    septic (any site except spine) - *see* Arthritis, pyogenic or pyemic
      spine - *see* Spondylopathy, infective
    serum (nontherapeutic) (therapeutic) - *see* Arthropathy, postimmunization
    specified form NEC M13.80
      ankle M13.87-
      elbow M13.82-
      foot joint M13.87-
      hand joint M13.84-
      hip M13.85-
      knee M13.86-

Arthritis, arthritic *(Continued)*
  specified form NEC *(Continued)*
    multiple site M13.89
    shoulder M13.81-
    specified joint NEC M13.88
    wrist M13.83-
  spine - *see also* Spondylopathy, inflammatory
    infectious or infective NEC - *see* Spondylopathy, infective
    Marie-Strümpell - *see* Spondylitis, ankylosing
    pyogenic - *see* Spondylopathy, infective
    rheumatoid - *see* Spondylitis, ankylosing
    traumatic (old) - *see* Spondylopathy, traumatic
    tuberculous A18.01
  staphylococcal M00.00
    ankle M00.07-
    elbow M00.02-
    foot joint - *see* Arthritis, staphylococcal, ankle
    hand joint M00.04-
    hip M00.05-
    knee M00.06-
    multiple site M00.09
    shoulder M00.01-
    vertebra M00.08
    wrist M00.03-
  streptococcal NEC M00.20
    ankle M00.27-
    elbow M00.22-
    foot joint - *see* Arthritis, streptococcal, ankle
    hand joint M00.24-
    hip M00.25-
    knee M00.26-
    multiple site M00.29
    shoulder M00.21-
    vertebra M00.28
    wrist M00.23-
  suppurative - *see* Arthritis, pyogenic or pyemic
  syphilitic (late) A52.16
    congenital A50.55 *[M12.80]*
  syphilitica deformans (Charcot) A52.16
  temporomandibular M26.69
  toxic of menopause (any site) - *see* Arthritis, specified form NEC
  transient - *see* Arthropathy, specified form NEC
  traumatic (chronic) - *see* Arthropathy, traumatic
  tuberculous A18.02
    spine A18.01
  uratic - *see* Gout, idiopathic
  urethritica (Reiter's) - *see* Reiter's disease
  vertebral - *see* Spondylopathy, inflammatory
  villous (any site) - *see* Arthropathy, specified form NEC
Arthrocele - *see* Effusion, joint
Arthrodesis status Z98.1
Arthrodynia - *see also* Pain, joint
Arthrofibrosis, joint - *see* Ankylosis
Arthrodysplasia Q74.9
Arthrogryposis (congenital) Q68.8
  multiplex congenita Q74.3
Arthrokatadysis M24.7

Arthropathy (*see also* Arthritis) M12.9
  Charcot's - *see* Arthropathy, neuropathic
  diabetic - see Diabetes, arthropathy,
    neuropathic
    syringomyelic G95.0
  cricoarytenoid J38.7
  crystal(-induced) - *see* Arthritis, in,
    crystals
  diabetic NEC - *see* Diabetes, arthropathy
  distal interphalangeal, psoriatic L40.51
  enteropathic M07.60
    ankle M07.67-
    elbow M07.62-
    foot joint M07.67-
    hand joint M07.64-
    hip M07.65-
    knee M07.66-
    multiple site M07.69
    shoulder M07.61-
    vertebra M07.68
    wrist M07.63-
  following intestinal bypass M02.00
    ankle M02.07-
    elbow M02.02-
    foot joint M02.07-
    hand joint M02.04-
    hip M02.05-
    knee M02.06-
    multiple site M02.09
    shoulder M02.01-
    vertebra M02.08
    wrist M02.03-
  gouty - *see also* Gout, idiopathic
    in (due to)
      Lesch-Nyhan syndrome E79.1
        [M14.8-]
      sickle-cell disorders D57.- *[M14.8-]*
  hemophilic NEC D66 *[M36.2]*
    in (due to)
      hyperparathyroidism NEC E21.3
        [M14.8-]
      metabolic disease NOS E88.9
        [M14.8-]
  in (due to)
    acromegaly E22.0 *[M14.8-]*
    amyloidosis E85.4 *[M14.8-]*
    blood disorder NOS D75.9 *[M36.3]*
    diabetes - see Diabetes, arthropathy
    endocrine disease NOS E34.9
      [M14.8-]
    erythema
      multiforme L51.9 *[M14.8-]*
      nodosum L52 *[M14.8-]*
    hemochromatosis E83.11 *[M14.8-]*
      hemoglobinopathy NEC D58.2
        [M36.3]
      hemophilia NEC D66 *[M36.2]*
      Henoch-Schönlein purpura D69.0
        [M36.4]
    hyperthyroidism E05.90 *[M14.8-]*
    hypothyroidism E03.9 *[M14.8-]*
    infective endocarditis I33.0 *[M12.80]*
    leukemia NEC C95.90 *[M36.1]*
    malignant histiocytosis C96.1 *[M36.1]*
    metabolic disease NOS E88.9 *[M14.8-]*
    multiple myeloma C90.00 *[M36.1]*
    neoplastic disease NOS (see also
      Neoplasm) D49.9 *[M36.1]*
    nutritional deficiency (see also sub-
      category M14.8-) E63.9
    psoriasis NOS L40.50
    sarcoidosis D86.86
    syphilis (late) A52.77
      congenital A50.55 *[M12.80]*

Arthropathy (*Continued*)
  hemochromatosis (*Continued*)
    thyrotoxicosis (see also subcategory
      M14.8-) E05.90
    ulcerative colitis K51.90 *[M07.60]*
    viral hepatitis (postinfectious) NEC
      B19.9 *[M12.80]*
    Whipple's disease (see also subcat-
      egory M14.8-) K90.81
  Jaccoud - *see* Arthropathy, postrheu-
    matic, chronic
  juvenile - *see* Arthritis, juvenile
    psoriatic L40.54
  mutilans (psoriatic) L40.52
  neuropathic (Charcot) M14.60
    ankle M14.67-
    diabetic - *see* Diabetes, arthropathy,
      neuropathic
    elbow M14.62-
    foot joint M14.67-
    hand joint M14.64-
    hip M14.65-
    knee M14.66-
    multiple site M14.69
    nonsyphilitic NEC G98.0
    shoulder M14.61-
    syringomyelic G95.0
    vertebra M14.68
    wrist M14.63-
  osteopulmonary - *see* Osteoarthropathy,
    hypertrophic, specified NEC
  postdysenteric M02.10
    ankle M02.17-
    elbow M02.12-
    foot joint M02.17-
    hand joint M02.14-
    hip M02.15-
    knee M02.16-
    multiple site M02.19
    shoulder M02.11-
    vertebra M02.18
    wrist M02.13-
  postimmunization M02.20
    ankle M02.27-
    elbow M02.22-
    foot joint M02.27-
    hand joint M02.24-
    hip M02.25-
    knee M02.26-
    multiple site M02.29
    shoulder M02.21-
    vertebra M02.28
    wrist M02.23-
  postinfectious NEC B99 *[M12.80]*
    in (due to)
      enteritis due to Yersinia enteroco-
        litica A04.6 *[M12.80]*
      syphilis A52.77
      viral hepatitis NEC B19.9
        [M12.80]
  postrheumatic, chronic (Jaccoud)
    M12.00
    ankle M12.07-
    elbow M12.02-
    foot joint M12.07-
    hand joint M12.04-
    hip M12.05-
    knee M12.06-
    multiple site M12.09
    shoulder M12.01-
    specified joint NEC M12.08
    wrist M12.03-
  psoriatic NEC L40.59
    interphalangeal, distal L40.51

Arthropathy (*Continued*)
  reactive M02.9
    in (due to)
      infective endocarditis I33.0 *[M02.9]*
    specified type NEC M02.80
      ankle M02.87-
      elbow M02.82-
      foot joint M02.87-
      hand joint M02.84-
      hip M02.85-
      knee M02.86-
      multiple site M02.89
      shoulder M02.81-
      vertebra M02.88
      wrist M02.83-
  specified form NEC M12.80
    ankle M12.87-
    elbow M12.82-
    foot joint M12.87-
    hand joint M12.84-
    hip M12.85-
    knee M12.86-
    multiple site M12.89
    shoulder M12.81-
    specified joint NEC M12.88
    wrist M12.83-
  syringomyelic G95.0
  tabes dorsalis A52.16
  tabetic A52.16
  transient – *see* Arthropathy, specified
    form NEC
  traumatic M12.50
    ankle M12.57-
    elbow M12.52-
    foot joint M12.57-
    hand joint M12.54-
    hip M12.55-
    knee M12.56-
    multiple site M12.59
    shoulder M12.51-
    specified joint NEC M12.58
    wrist M12.53-
Arthropyosis - *see* Arthritis, pyogenic or
  pyemic
Arthrosis (deformans) (degenerative) (localized) M19.90 - *see also*
  Osteoarthritis
  spine - *see* Spondylosis
Arthus' phenomenon or reaction
  T78.41
  due to
    drug - see Table of drugs and chemi-
      cals, by drug
Articular - *see* condition
Articulation, reverse (teeth) M26.24
Artificial
  insemination complication - see
    Complications, artificial,
    fertilization
  opening status (functioning) (without
    complication) Z43.9
    anus (colostomy) Z93.3
    colostomy Z93.3
    cystostomy Z93.50
      appendico-vesicostomy Z93.52
      cutaneous Z93.51
      specified NEC Z93.59
    enterostomy Z93.4
    gastrostomy Z93.1
    ileostomy Z93.2
    intestinal tract NEC Z93.4
    jejunostomy Z93.4
    nephrostomy Z93.6
    specified site NEC Z93.8

Artificial *(Continued)*
  opening status *(Continued)*
    tracheostomy Z93.0
    ureterostomy Z93.6
    urethrostomy Z93.6
    urinary tract NEC Z93.6
    vagina Z93.8
    vagina status Z93.8
Arytenoid - *see* condition
Asbestosis (occupational) J61
ASC-H (atypical squamous cells cannot
    exclude high grade squamous
    intraepithelial lesion on cytologic
    smear)
  anus R85.611
  cervix R87.611
  vagina R87.621
ASC-US (atypical squamous cells of
    undetermined significance on cyto-
    logic smear)
  anus R85.610
  cervix R87.610
  vagina R87.620
Ascariasis B77.9
  with
    complications NEC B77.89
    intestinal complications B77.0
    pneumonia, pneumonitis B77.81
Ascaridosis, ascaridiasis - *see* Ascariasis
Ascaris (infection) (infestation) (lumbri-
    coides) - *see* Ascariasis
Ascending - *see* condition
Aschoff's bodies - *see* Myocarditis,
    rheumatic
Ascites (abdominal) R18.8
  cardiac I50.9
  chylous (nonfilarial) I89.8
    filarial - *see* Infestation, filarial
  due to
    cirrhosis, alcoholic K70.31
    hepatitis
      alcoholic K70.11
      chronic active K71.51
    S. japonicum B65.2
  heart I50.9
  malignant R18.0
  pseudochylous R18.8
  syphilitic A52.74
  tuberculous A18.31
Aseptic - *see* condition
Asherman's syndrome N85.6
Asialia K11.7
Asiatic cholera - *see* Cholera
Askin's tumor - *see* Neoplasm, connective
    tissue, malignant
Asocial personality F60.2
Asomatognosia R41.4
Aspartylglucosaminuria E77.1
Asperger's disease or syndrome
    F84.5
Aspergilloma - *see* Aspergillosis
Aspergillosis (with pneumonia)
    B44.9
  bronchopulmonary, allergic B44.81
  disseminated B44.7
  generalized B44.7
  pulmonary NEC B44.1
    allergic B44.81
    invasive B44.0
  specified NEC B44.89
  tonsillar B44.2
Aspergillus (flavus) (fumigatus) (infec-
    tion) (terreus) - *see* Aspergillosis
Aspermatogenesis - *see* Azoospermia

Aspermia (testis) - *see* Azoospermia
Asphyxia, asphyxiation (by) R09.01
  antenatal P84
  birth P84
  bunny bag - *see* Asphyxia, due to,
    mechanical threat to breathing,
    trapped in bed clothes
  carbon monoxide – *see* Table of drugs
    and chemicals
  crushing S28.0
  drowning T75.1
  gas, fumes, or vapor - *see* Table of drugs
    and chemicals
  inhalation - *see* Inhalation
  intrauterine P84
  local I73.00
    with gangrene I73.01
  mucus - *see also* Foreign body, respira-
    tory tract, causing asphyxia
  newborn P84
  pathological R09.01
  postnatal P84
    mechanical - *see* Asphyxia, due
      to, mechanical threat to
      breathing
  prenatal P84
  reticularis R23.1
  strangulation - *see* Asphyxia, due
    to, mechanical threat to
    breathing
  submersion T75.1
  traumatic T71.9
    due to
      crushed chest S28.0
      foreign body (in) - *see* Foreign body,
        respiratory tract, causing
        asphyxia
      low oxygen content of ambient air
        T71.20
      due to
        being trapped in
          low oxygen environment
            T71.29
          in car trunk T71.221
            circumstances undeter-
              mined T71.224
            done with intent to
              harm by
              another person
                T71.223
            self T71.222
          in refrigerator T71.231
            circumstances
              undetermined
              T71.234
            done with intent to
              harm by
              another person
                T71.233
            self T71.232
        cave-in T71.21
      mechanical threat to breathing
        (accidental) T71.191
        circumstances undetermined
          T71.194
        done with intent to harm by
          another person T71.193
        self T71.192
      hanging T71.161
        circumstances undetermined
          T71.164
        done with intent to harm by
          another person T71.163
        self T71.162

Asphyxia, asphyxiation *(Continued)*
  traumatic T71.9 *(Continued)*
    due to *(Continued)*
      mechanical threat to breathing
        (Continued)
        plastic bag T71.121
          circumstances undetermined
            T71.124
          done with intent to harm by
            another person T71.123
          self T71.122
        smothering
          in furniture T71.151
            circumstances undeter-
              mined T71.154
            done with intent to harm by
              another person T71.153
            self T71.152
          under
            another person's body
              T71.141
              circumstances undeter-
                mined T71.144
              done with intent to harm
                T71.143
            pillow T71.111
              circumstances undeter-
                mined T71.114
              done with intent to harm
                by
                  another person T71.113
                  self T71.112
        trapped in bed clothes T71.131
          circumstances undetermined
            T71.134
          done with intent to harm by
            another person T71.133
          self T71.132
  vomiting, vomitus - *see* Foreign body,
    respiratory tract, causing asphyxia
Aspiration
  amniotic (clear) fluid (newborn) P24.10
    with
      pneumonia (pneumonitis) P24.11
      respiratory symptoms P24.11
  blood
    newborn (without respiratory symp-
      toms) P24.20
      with
        pneumonia (pneumonitis)
          P24.21
        respiratory symptoms P24.21
    specified age NEC - *see* Foreign body,
      respiratory tract
  bronchitis J69.0
  food or foreign body (with asphyxia-
    tion) - *see* Asphyxia, food
  liquor (amnii) (newborn) P24.10
    with
      pneumonia (pneumonitis) P24.11
      respiratory symptoms P24.11
  meconium (newborn) (without respira-
    tory symptoms) P24.00
    with
      pneumonitis (pneumonitis) P24.01
      respiratory symptoms P24.01
  milk (newborn) (without respiratory
    symptoms) P24.30
    with
      pneumonia (pneumonitis) P24.31
      respiratory symptoms P24.31
    specified age NEC – *see* Foreign body,
      respiratory tract

Aspiration *(Continued)*
mucus - *see also* Foreign body, by site,
causing asphyxia
newborn P24.10
with
pneumonia (pneumonitis)
P24.11
respiratory symptoms P24.11
neonatal P24.9
specific NEC (without respiratory
symptoms) P24.80
with
pneumonia (pneumonitis)
P24.81
respiratory symptoms P24.81
newborn P24.9
specific NEC (without respiratory
symptoms) P24.80
with
pneumonia (pneumonitis)
P24.81
respiratory symptoms P24.81
pneumonia J69.0
pneumonitis J69.0
syndrome of newborn - *see* Aspiration,
by substance, with pneumonia
vernix caseosa (newborn) P24.80
with
pneumonia (pneumonitis) P24.81
respiratory symptoms P24.81
vomitus – *see also* Foreign body, respiratory tract
newborn (without respiratory symptoms) P24.30
with
pneumonia (pneumonitis)
P24.31
respiratory symptoms P24.31
Asplenia (congenital) Q89.01
postsurgical D73.0
Assam fever B55.0
Assault, sexual - *see* Maltreatment
Assmann's focus NEC A15.0
Astasia(-abasia) (hysterical) F44.4
Asteatosis cutis L85.3
Astereognosia, astereognosis R48.1
Asterixis R27.8
in liver disease K71.3
Asteroid hyalitis - *see* Deposit, crystalline
Asthenia, asthenic R53.1
cardiac (*see also* Failure, heart) I50.9
psychogenic F45.8
cardiovascular (*see also* Failure, heart)
I50.9
psychogenic F45.8
heart (*see also* Failure, heart) I50.9
psychogenic F45.8
hysterical F44.4
myocardial (*see also* Failure, heart) I50.9
psychogenic F45.8
nervous F48.8
neurocirculatory F45.8
neurotic F48.8
psychogenic F48.8
psychoneurotic F48.8
psychophysiologic F48.8
reaction (psychophysiologic) F48.8
senile R54
Asthenopia - *see also* Discomfort, visual
hysterical F44.6
psychogenic F44.6
Asthenospermia – *see* Abnormal, specimen, male genital organs

Asthma, asthmatic (bronchial) (catarrh)
(spasmodic) J45.909
with
chronic obstructive bronchitis J44.9
with
acute lower respiratory infection
J44.0
exacerbation (acute) J44.1
chronic obstructive pulmonary disease J44.9
with
acute lower respiratory infection
J44.0
exacerbation (acute) J44.1
exacerbation (acute) J45.901
hay fever – *see* Asthma, allergic
extrinsic
rhinitis, allergic – *see* Asthma, allergic
extrinsic
status asthmaticus J45.902
allergic extrinsic J45.909
with
exacerbation (acute) J45.901
status asthmaticus J45.902
atopic – *see* Asthma, allergic
extrinsic
cardiac - *see* Failure, ventricular, left
cardiobronchial I50.1
childhood J45.909
with
exacerbation (acute) J45.901
status asthmaticus J45.902
chronic obstructive J44.9
with
acute lower respiratory infection
J44.0
exacerbation (acute) J44.1
collier's J60
cough variant J45.991
detergent J69.8
due to
detergent J69.8
inhalation of fumes J68.3
eosinophilic J82
extrinsic, allergic – *see* Asthma, allergic
extrinsic
grinder's J62.8
hay – *see* Asthma, allergic extrinsic
heart I50.1
idiosyncratic – *see* Asthma,
nonallergic
intermittent (mild) J45.20
with
exacerbation (acute) J45.21
status asthmaticus J45.22
intrinsic, nonallergic – *see* Asthma,
nonallergic
Kopp's E32.8
late-onset - *see* Asthma, by type
mild intermittent J45.20
with
exacerbation (acute) J45.21
status asthmaticus J45.22
mild persistent J45.30
with
exacerbation (acute) J45.31
status asthmaticus J45.32
Millar's (laryngismus stridulus)
J38.5
miner's J60
mixed J45.909
with
exacerbation (acute) J45.901
status asthmaticus J45.902

Asthma, asthmatic *(Continued)*
moderate persistent J45.40
with
exacerbation (acute) J45.41
status asthmaticus J45.42
nervous – *see* Asthma, nonallergic
nonallergic (intrinsic) J45.909
with
exacerbation (acute) J45.901
status asthmaticus J45.902
persistent
mild J45.30
with
exacerbation (acute) J45.31
status asthmaticus J45.32
moderate J45.40
with
exacerbation (acute) J45.41
status asthmaticus J45.42
severe J45.50
with
exacerbation (acute) J45.51
status asthmaticus J45.52
platinum J45.998
pneumoconiotic NEC J64
potter's J62.8
predominantly allergic J45.909
psychogenic F54
pulmonary eosinophilic J82
red cedar J67.8
Rostan's I50.1
sandblaster's J62.8
sequoiosis J67.8
severe persistent J45.50
with
exacerbation (acute) J45.51
status asthmaticus J45.52
specified NEC J45.998
stonemason's J62.8
thymic E32.8
tuberculous - *see* Tuberculosis,
pulmonary
Wichmann's (laryngismus stridulus)
J38.5
wood J67.8
Astigmatism (compound) (congenital)
H52.20-
irregular H52.21-
regular H52.22-
Astraphobia F40.220
Astroblastoma
specified site - *see* Neoplasm, malignant
unspecified site C71.9
Astrocytoma (cystic)
anaplastic
specified site - *see* Neoplasm,
malignant
unspecified site C71.9
fibrillary
specified site - *see* Neoplasm,
malignant
unspecified site C71.9
fibrous
specified site - *see* Neoplasm,
malignant
unspecified site C71.9
gemistocytic
specified site - *see* Neoplasm,
malignant
unspecified site C71.9
juvenile
specified site - *see* Neoplasm,
malignant
unspecified site C71.9

Astrocytoma (Continued)
  pilocytic
    specified site - see Neoplasm,
        malignant
    unspecified site C71.9
  piloid
    specified site - see Neoplasm,
        malignant
    unspecified site C71.9
  protoplasmic
    specified site - see Neoplasm,
        malignant
    unspecified site C71.9
  specified site NEC - see Neoplasm,
        malignant
  subependymal D43.2
    giant cell
      specified site - see Neoplasm,
          uncertain behavior -
          unspecified site D43.2
      specified site - see Neoplasm, uncer-
          tain behavior
          unspecified site D43.2
  unspecified site C71.9
Astroglioma
  specified site - see Neoplasm,
      malignant
  unspecified site C71.9
Asymbolia R48.8
Asymmetry - see also Distortion
  between native and reconstructed
      breast N65.1
  face Q67.0
  jaw (lower) – see Anomaly, dentofacial,
      jaw-cranial base relationship,
      asymmetry
Asynergia, asynergy R27.8
  ventricular I51.89
Asystole (heart) - see Arrest, cardiac
At risk
  for falling Z91.81
Ataxia, ataxy, ataxic R27.0
  acute R27.8
  brain (hereditary) G11.9
  cerebellar (hereditary) G11.9
    with defective DNA repair G11.3
    alcoholic G31.2
    early-onset G11.1
    in
      alcoholism G31.2
      myxedema E03.9 [G13.8]
      neoplastic disease (see also
          Neoplasm) D49.9
          [G13.1]
    late-onset (Marie's) G11.2
  cerebral (hereditary) G11.9
  congenital nonprogressive G11.0
  family, familial - see Ataxia,
      hereditary
  following
    cerebrovascular disease I69.993
      specified NEC I69.893
      cerebral infarction I69.393
      intracerebral hemorrhage
          I69.193
      nontraumatic intracranial hemor-
          rhage NEC I69.293
      specified disease NEC I69.893
          subarachnoid hemorrhage
              I69.093
  Friedreich's (heredofamilial) (cerebel-
      lar) (spinal) G11.1

Ataxia, ataxy, ataxic (Continued)
  gait R26.0
    hysterical F44.4
  general R27.8
  hereditary G11.9
    with neuropathy G60.2
    cerebellar - see Ataxia, cerebellar
    spastic G11.4
    specified NEC G11.8
    spinal (Friedreich's) G11.1
  heredofamilial - see Ataxia, hereditary
  Hunt's G11.1
  hysterical F44.4
  locomotor (progressive) (syphilitic)
      (partial) (spastic) A52.11
    diabetic – see Diabetes, ataxia
  Marie's (cerebellar) (heredofamilial)
      (late- onset) G11.2
  nonorganic origin F44.4
  nonprogressive, congenital G11.0
  psychogenic F44.4
  Roussy-Lévy G60.0
  Sanger-Brown's (hereditary) G11.2
  spastic hereditary G11.4
  spinal
    hereditary (Friedreich's) G11.1
    progressive (syphilitic) A52.11
  spinocerebellar, X-linked recessive
      G11.1
  telangiectasia (Louis-Bar) G11.3
Ataxia-telangiectasia (Louis-Bar)
    G11.3
Atelectasis (massive) (partial) (pressure)
    (pulmonary) J98.11
  newborn P28.10
    due to resorption P28.11
    partial P28.19
    primary P28.0
    secondary P28.19
  primary (newborn) P28.0
  tuberculous - see Tuberculosis,
      pulmonary
Atelocardia Q24.9
Atelomyelia Q06.1
Atheroembolism
  of
    extremities
      lower I75.02-
      upper I75.01-
    kidney I75.81
    specified NEC I75.89
Atheroma, atheromatous (see also Arterio-
    sclerosis) I70.90
  aorta, aortic I70.0
    valve (see also Endocarditis, aortic)
        I35.8
  aorto-iliac I70.0
  artery - see Arteriosclerosis
  basilar (artery) I67.2
  carotid (artery) (common) (internal)
      I67.2
  cerebral (arteries) I67.2
  coronary (artery) I25.10
    with angina pectoris - see Arterio-
        sclerosis, coronary (artery),
    degeneration - see Arteriosclerosis
  heart, cardiac – see Disease, heart, isch-
      emic, atherosclerotic
  mitral (valve) I34.8
  myocardium, myocardial – see Disease,
      heart, ischemic, atherosclerotic

Atheroma, atheromatous (Continued)
  pulmonary valve (heart) (see also
      Endocarditis, pulmonary)
      I37.8
  tricuspid (heart) (valve) I36.8
  valve, valvular - see Endocarditis
  vertebral (artery) I67.2
Atheromatosis - see Arteriosclerosis
Atherosclerosis - see also Arteriosclerosis
  coronary artery I25.10
    with angina pectoris - see Arterio-
        sclerosis, coronary (artery),
    coronary, due to lipid rich plaque I25.83
  transplanted heart I25.810
    native coronary artery I25.811
      with angina pectoris - see Arterio-
          sclerosis, coronary (artery),
    bypass graft I25.812
      with angina pectoris - see Arterio-
          sclerosis, coronary (artery),
Athetosis (acquired) R25.8
  bilateral (congenital) G80.3
  congenital (bilateral) (double) G80.3
  double (congenital) G80.3
  unilateral R25.8
Athlete's
  foot B35.3
  heart I51.7
Athrepsia E41
Athyrea (acquired) - see also
    Hypothyroidism
  congenital E03.1
Atonia, atony, atonic
  bladder (sphincter) (neurogenic) N31.2
  capillary I78.8
  cecum K59.8
    psychogenic F45.8
  colon - see Atony, intestine
  congenital P94.2
  esophagus K22.8
  intestine K59.8
    psychogenic F45.8
  stomach K31.89
    neurotic or psychogenic F45.8
  uterus (during labor) O62.2
    with hemorrhage (postpartum) O72.1
    postpartum (with hemorrhage) O72.1
    without hemorrhage O75.89
Atopy - see History, allergy
Atransferrinemia, congenital E88.09
Atresia, atretic
  alimentary organ or tract NEC Q45.8
    upper Q40.8
  ani, anus, anal (canal) Q42.3
    with fistula Q42.2
  aorta (arch) (ring) Q25.2
  aortic (orifice) (valve) Q23.0
    arch Q25.2
    congenital with hypoplasia of
        ascending aorta and defective
        development of left ventricle
        (with mitral stenosis) Q23.4
    in hypoplastic left heart syndrome
        Q23.4
  aqueduct of Sylvius Q03.0
    with spina bifida - see Spina bifida,
        with hydrocephalus
  artery NEC Q27.8
    cerebral Q28.3
    coronary Q24.5
    digestive system Q27.8
    eye Q15.8

Atresia, atretic (Continued)
  artery NEC (Continued)
    lower limb Q27.8
    pulmonary Q25.5
    specified site NEC Q27.8
    umbilical Q27.0
    upper limb Q27.8
  auditory canal (external) Q16.1
  bile duct (common) (congenital) (hepatic) Q44.2
    acquired - see Obstruction, bile duct
  bladder (neck) Q64.39
    obstruction Q64.31
  bronchus Q32.4
  cecum Q42.8
  cervix (acquired) N88.2
    congenital Q51.8
    in pregnancy or childbirth – see
        Anomaly, cervix, in pregnancy
        or childbirth
      causing obstructed labor O65.5
  choana Q30.0
  colon Q42.9
    specified NEC Q42.8
  common duct Q44.2
  cricoid cartilage Q31.8
  cystic duct Q44.2
    acquired K82.8
      with obstruction K82.0
  digestive organs NEC Q45.8
  duodenum Q41.0
  ear canal Q16.1
  ejaculatory duct Q55.4
  epiglottis Q31.8
  esophagus Q39.0
    with tracheoesophageal fistula Q39.1
  eustachian tube Q17.8
  fallopian tube (congenital) Q50.6
    acquired N97.1
  follicular cyst N83.0
  foramen of
    Luschka Q03.1
      with spina bifida - see Spina bifida,
          with hydrocephalus
    Magendie Q03.1
      with spina bifida - see Spina bifida,
          with hydrocephalus
  gallbladder Q44.1
  genital organ
    external
      female Q52.79
      male Q55.8
    internal
      female Q52.8
      male Q55.8
  glottis Q31.8
  gullet Q39.0
    with tracheoesophageal fistula
        Q39.1
  heart valve NEC Q24.8
    pulmonary Q22.0
    tricuspid Q22.4
  hymen Q52.3
    acquired (postinfective) N89.6
  ileum Q41.2
  intestine (small) Q41.9
    large Q42.9
      specified NEC Q42.8
  iris, filtration angle Q15.0
  jejunum Q41.1
  lacrimal apparatus Q10.4
  larynx Q31.8

Atresia, atretic (Continued)
  meatus urinarius Q64.33
  mitral valve Q23.2
    in hypoplastic left heart syndrome
        Q23.4
  nares (anterior) (posterior) Q30.0
  nasopharynx Q34.8
  nose, nostril Q30.0
    acquired J34.89
  oesophagus Q39.0
    with tracheoesophageal fistula
        Q39.1
  organ or site NEC Q89.8
  osseous meatus (ear) Q16.1
  oviduct (congenital) Q50.6
    acquired N97.1
  parotid duct Q38.4
    acquired K11.8
  pulmonary (artery) Q25.5
    valve Q22.0
  pulmonic Q22.0
  pupil Q13.2
  rectum Q42.1
    with fistula Q42.0
  salivary duct Q38.4
    acquired K11.8
  sublingual duct Q38.4
    acquired K11.8
  submandibular duct Q38.4
    acquired K11.8
  submaxillary duct Q38.4
    acquired K11.8
  thyroid cartilage Q31.8
  trachea Q32.1
  tricuspid valve Q22.4
  ureter Q62.10
    pelvic junction Q62.11
    vesical orifice Q62.12
  ureteropelvic junction Q62.11
  ureterovesical orifice Q62.12
  urethra (valvular) Q64.39
    stricture Q64.32
  urinary tract NEC Q64.8
  uterus Q51.8
    acquired N85.8
  vagina (congenital) Q52.4
    acquired (postinfectional) (senile)
        N89.5
  vas deferens Q55.3
  vascular NEC Q27.8
    cerebral Q28.3
    digestive system Q27.8
    lower limb Q27.8
    specified site NEC Q27.8
    upper limb Q27.8
  vein NEC Q27.8
    digestive system Q27.8
    great Q26.8
    lower limb Q27.8
    portal Q26.5
    pulmonary Q26.3
    specified site NEC Q27.8
    upper limb Q27.8
  vena cava (inferior) (superior) Q26.8
  vesicourethral orifice Q64.31
  vulva Q52.79
    acquired N90.5
Atrichia, atrichosis - see Alopecia
Atrophia - see also Atrophy
  cutis senilis L90.8
    due to radiation L57.8
  gyrata of choroid and retina H31.23

Atrophia (Continued)
  senilis R54
    dermatological L90.8
      due to radiation (nonionizing)
          (solar) L57.8
  unguium L60.3
    congenita Q84.6
Atrophie blanche (en plaque) (de Milian)
    L95.0
Atrophoderma, atrophodermia (of)
    L90.9
  diffusum (idiopathic) L90.4
  maculatum L90.8
    et striatum L90.8
      due to syphilis A52.79
    syphilitic A51.39
  neuriticum L90.8
  Pasini and Pierini L90.3
  pigmentosum Q82.1
  reticulatum symmetricum faciei
      L66.4
  senile L90.8
    due to radiation (nonionizing) (solar)
        L57.8
  vermiculata (cheeks) L66.4
Atrophy, atrophic (of)
  adrenal (capsule) (gland) E27.49
    primary (autoimmune) E27.1
  alveolar process or ridge (edentulous)
      K08.20
  anal sphincter (disuse) N81.84
  appendix K38.8
  arteriosclerotic - see Arteriosclerosis
  bile duct (common) (hepatic) K83.8
  bladder N32.89
    neurogenic N31.8
  blanche (en plaque) (of Milian) L95.0
  bone (senile) NEC - see also Disorder,
      bone, specified type NEC
    due to
      tabes dorsalis (neurogenic) A52.11
  brain (cortex) (progressive) G31.9
    circumscribed G31.01 [F02.80]
      with behavioral disturbance G31.01
          [F02.81]
    senile NEC G31.1
  breast N64.2
    obstetric - see Disorder, breast, speci-
        fied type NEC
  buccal cavity K13.79
  cardiac - see Degeneration, myocardial
  cartilage (infectional) (joint) - see Disor-
      der, cartilage, specified NEC
  cerebellar - see Atrophy, brain
  cerebral - see Atrophy, brain
  cervix (mucosa) (senile) (uteri) N88.8
    menopausal N95.8
  Charcot-Marie-Tooth G60.0
  choroid (central) (macular) (myopic)
      (retina) H31.10-
    diffuse secondary H31.12-
    gyrate H31.23
    senile H31.11-
  ciliary body - see Atrophy, iris
  conjunctiva (senile) H11.89
  corpus cavernosum N48.89
  cortical - see Atrophy, brain
  cystic duct K82.8
  Déjérine-Thomas G23.8
  disuse NEC - see Atrophy, muscle
  Duchenne-Aran G12.21
  ear - see subcategory H93.8

Atrophy, atrophic *(Continued)*
  edentulous alveolar ridge K08.20
  endometrium (senile) N85.8
    cervix N88.8
  enteric K63.89
  epididymis N50.8
  eyeball - *see* Disorder, globe, degener-
      ated condition, atrophy
  eyelid (senile) - *see* Disorder, eyelid,
      degenerative
  facial (skin) L90.9
  fallopian tube (senile) N83.32
    with ovary N83.33
  fascioscapulohumeral (Landouzy-
      Déjérine) G71.0
  fatty, thymus (gland) E32.8
  gallbladder K82.8
  gastric K29.40
    with bleeding K29.41
  gastrointestinal K63.89
  glandular I89.8
  globe H44.52-
  gum K06.0
  hair L67.8
  heart (brown) - *see* Degeneration,
      myocardial
  hemifacial Q67.4
    Romberg G51.8
  infantile E41
    paralysis, acute - *see* Poliomyelitis,
        paralytic
  intestine K63.89
  iris (essential) (progressive) H21.26-
    specified NEC H21.29
  kidney (senile) (terminal) (*see also* Scle-
      rosis, renal) N26.1
    with hypertension - *see* Hypertension,
        kidney
    congenital or infantile Q60.5
      bilateral Q60.4
      unilateral Q60.3
    hydronephrotic - *see* Hydronephrosis
  lacrimal gland (primary) H04.14-
    secondary H04.15-
  Landouzy-Déjérine G71.0
  laryngitis, infective J37.0
  larynx J38.7
  Leber's optic (hereditary) H47.22
  lip K13.0
  liver (yellow) K72.90
    with coma K72.91
    acute, subacute K72.00
      with coma K72.01
    chronic K72.10
      with coma K72.11
  lung (senile) J98.4
  macular (dermatological) L90.8
    syphilitic, skin A51.39
      striated A52.79
  mandible (edentulous) K08.20
    minimal K08.21
    moderate K08.22
    severe K08.23
  maxilla K08.20
    minimal K08.24
    moderate K08.25
    severe K08.26
  muscle, muscular (diffuse) (general) (id-
      iopathic) (primary) M62.50
    ankle M62.57-
    Duchenne-Aran G12.21
    foot M62.57-

Atrophy, atrophic *(Continued)*
  muscle, muscular *(Continued)*
    forearm M62.53-
    hand M62.54-
    infantile spinal G12.0
    lower leg M62.56-
    multiple sites M62.59
    myelopathic - *see* Atrophy, muscle,
        spinal
    myotonic G71.11
    neuritic G58.9
    neuropathic (peroneal) (progressive)
        G60.0
    pelvic (disuse) N81.84
    peroneal G60.0
    progressive (bulbar) G12.21
      adult G12.1
      infantile (spinal) G12.0
      spinal G12.9
        adult G12.1
        infantile G12.0
    pseudohypertrophic G71.0
    shoulder region M62.51-
    specified site NEC M62.58
    spinal G12.9
      Aran-Duchenne G12.9
      adult form G12.1
      childhood form, type II G12.1
      distal G12.1
      hereditary NEC G12.1
      infantile, type I (Werdnig-
          Hoffmann) G12.0
      juvenile form, type III (Kugelberg-
          Welander) G12.1
      progressive G12.21
      scapuloperoneal form G12.1
      specified NEC G12.8
    syphilitic A52.78
    thigh M62.55-
    upper arm M62.52-
  myocardium - *see* Degeneration,
      myocardial
  myometrium (senile) N85.8
    cervix N88.8
  myopathic NEC - *see* Atrophy, muscle
  myotonia G71.11
  nail L60.3
  nasopharynx J31.1
  nerve - *see also* Disorder, nerve
    abducens - *see* Strabismus, paralytic,
        sixth nerve
    accessory G52.8
    acoustic or auditory - *see* subcategory
        H93.3
    cranial G52.9
      eighth (auditory) - *see* subcategory
          H93.3
      eleventh (accessory) G52.8
      fifth (trigeminal) G50.8
      first (olfactory) G52.0
      fourth (trochlear) - *see* Strabismus,
          paralytic, fourth nerve
      second (optic) H47.20
      sixth (abducens) - *see* Strabismus,
          paralytic, sixth nerve
      tenth (pneumogastric) (vagus) G52.2
      third (oculomotor) - *see* Strabismus,
          paralytic, third nerve
      twelfth (hypoglossal) G52.3
    hypoglossal G52.3
    oculomotor - *see* Strabismus, para-
        lytic, third nerve

Atrophy, atrophic *(Continued)*
  nerve *(Continued)*
    olfactory G52.0
    optic (papillomacular bundle)
      syphilitic (late) A52.15
        congenital A50.44
    pneumogastric G52.2
    trigeminal G50.8
    trochlear - *see* Strabismus, paralytic,
        fourth nerve
    vagus (pneumogastric) G52.2
  neurogenic, bone, tabetic A52.11
  nutritional E41
  old age R54
  olivopontocerebellar G23.8
  optic (nerve) H47.20
    glaucomatous H47.23-
    hereditary H47.22
    syphilitic (late) A52.15
      congenital A50.44
    primary H47.21-
    specified type NEC H47.29-
  orbit H05.31-
  ovary (senile) N83.31
    with fallopian tube N83.33
  oviduct (senile) – *see* Atrophy, fallopian
      tube
  palsy, diffuse (progressive) G12.22
  pancreas (duct) (senile) K86.8
  parotid gland K11.0
  pelvic muscle N81.84
  penis N48.89
  pharynx J39.2
  pluriglandular E31.8
    autoimmune E31.0
  polyarthritis M15.9
  prostate N42.89
  pseudohypertrophic (muscle) G71.0
  renal (*see also* Sclerosis, renal) N26.1
  retina, retinal (postinfectional)
      H35.89
  rhinitis J31.0
  salivary gland K11.0
  scar L90.5
  sclerosis, lobar (of brain) G31.09
      [F02.80]
    with behavioral disturbance G31.09
        [F02.81]
  scrotum N50.8
  seminal vesicle N50.8
  senile R54
    due to radiation (nonionizing) (solar)
        L57.8
  skin (patches) (spots) L90.9
    degenerative (senile) L90.8
    due to radiation (nonionizing) (solar)
        L57.8
    senile L90.8
  spermatic cord N50.8
  spinal (acute) (cord) G95.89
    muscular - *see* Atrophy, muscle,
        spinal
    paralysis G12.20
      acute - *see* Poliomyelitis,
          paralytic
      meaning progressive muscular
          atrophy G12.21
  spine (column) - *see* Spondylopathy,
      specified NEC
  spleen (senile) D73.0
  stomach K29.40
    with bleeding K29.41

Atrophy, atrophic *(Continued)*
striate (skin) L90.6
syphilitic A52.79
subcutaneous L90.9
sublingual gland K11.0
submandibular gland K11.0
submaxillary gland K11.0
Sudeck's - *see* Algoneurodystrophy
suprarenal (capsule) (gland) E27.49
primary E27.1
systemic affecting central nervous
system
in
myxedema E03.9 *[G13.8]*
neoplastic disease (see also Neoplasm) D49.9 *[G13.1]*
tarso-orbital fascia, congenital Q10.3
testis N50.0
thenar, partial – *see* Syndrome, carpal
tunnel
thymus (fatty) E32.8
thyroid (gland) (acquired) E03.4
with cretinism E03.1
congenital (with myxedema) E03.1
tongue (senile) K14.8
papillae K14.4
trachea J39.8
tunica vaginalis N50.8
turbinate J34.89
tympanic membrane (nonflaccid)
H73.82-
flaccid H73.81-
upper respiratory tract J39.8
uterus, uterine (senile)
N85.8
cervix N88.8
due to radiation (intended effect)
N85.8
adverse effect or misadventure
N99.89
vagina (senile) N95.2
vas deferens N50.8
vascular I99.8
vertebra (senile) - *see* Spondylopathy,
specified NEC
vulva (senile) N90.5
Werdnig-Hoffmann G12.0
yellow - *see* Failure, hepatic
Attack, attacks
with alteration of consciousness
(with automatisms) - *see*
Epilepsy, localization-related,
symptomatic, with complex
partial seizures
Adams-Stokes I45.9
akinetic – *see* Epilepsy, generalized,
idiopathic
angina - *see* Angina
atonic – *see* Epilepsy, generalized,
idiopathic
cataleptic - *see* Catalepsy
coronary - *see* Infarct, myocardium
cyanotic, newborn P28.2
drop NEC R55
epileptic - *see* Epilepsy
heart - *see* infarct, myocardium
hysterical F44.9
jacksonian – *see* Epilepsy, localization-
related, symptomatic, with simple
partial seizures
myocardium, myocardial - *see* Infarct,
myocardium

Attack, attacks *(Continued)*
myoclonic - *see* Epilepsy, generalized,
idiopathic
panic F41.0
psychomotor – *see* Epilepsy,
localization-related,
symptomatic, with complex
partial seizures
salaam – *see* Epilepsy, generalized,
specified NEC
schizophreniform, brief F23
Stokes-Adams I45.9
syncope R55
transient ischemic (TIA)
G45.9
specified NEC G45.8
unconsciousness R55
hysterical F44.89
vasomotor R55
vasovagal (paroxysmal) (idiopathic) R55
without alteration of consciousness
- *see* Epilepsy, localization-related,
symptomatic, with simple partial
seizures
Attention (to)
artificial
opening (of) Z43.9
digestive tract NEC Z43.4
colon Z43.3
ilium Z43.2
stomach Z43.1
specified NEC Z43.8
trachea Z43.0
urinary tract NEC Z43.6
cystostomy Z43.5
nephrostomy Z43.6
ureterostomy Z43.6
urethrostomy Z43.6
vagina Z43.7
colostomy Z43.3
cystostomy Z43.5
deficit disorder or syndrome F98.8
with hyperactivity - *see* Disorder,
attention-deficit
hyperactivity
gastrostomy Z43.1
ileostomy Z43.2
jejunostomy Z43.4
nephrostomy Z43.6
surgical dressings Z48.01
sutures Z48.02
tracheostomy Z43.0
ureterostomy Z43.6
urethrostomy Z43.6
Attrition
gum K06.0
tooth, teeth (excessive) (hard tissues)
K03.0
Atypical, atypism - *see also* condition
cells (on cytolgocial smear) (endocervical) (endometrial) (glandular)
cervix R87.619
vagina R87.629
cervical N87.9
endometrium N85.9
hyperplasia N85.00
parenting situation Z62.9
Auditory - *see* condition
Aujeszky's disease B33.8
Aurantiasis, cutis E67.1
Auricle, auricular - *see also* condition
cervical Q18.2

Auriculotemporal syndrome G50.8
Austin Flint murmur (aortic insuffi-
ciency) I35.1
Australian
Q fever A78
X disease A83.4
Autism, autistic (childhood) (infantile)
F84.0
atypical F84.9
Autodigestion R68.89
Autoerythrocyte sensitization (syn-
drome) D69.2
Autographism L50.3
Autoimmune
disease (systemic) M35.9
lymphoproliferative syndrome [ALPS]
D89.82
thyroiditis E06.3
Autointoxication R68.89
Automatism G93.89
epileptic – *see* Epilepsy, localization-
related, symptomatic, with
complex partial seizures
paroxysmal, idiopathic – *see* Epilepsy,
localization-related, symptomatic,
with complex partial seizures
Autonomic, autonomous
bladder (neurogenic) N31.2
hysteria seizure F44.5
Autosensitivity, erythrocyte D69.2
Autosensitization, cutaneous L30.2
Autosome - *see* condition by chromosome
involved
Autotopagnosia R48.1
Autotoxemia R68.89
Autumn - *see* condition
Avellis' syndrome G46.8
Aversion, sexual F52.1
Aviator's
disease or sickness - *see* Effect, adverse,
high altitude
ear T70.0
Avitaminosis (multiple) (*see also* Deficiency, vitamin) E56.9
B E53.9
with
beriberi E51.11
pellagra E52
B2 E53.0
B6 E53.1
B12 E53.8
D E55.9
with rickets E55.0
G E53.0
K E56.1
nicotinic acid E52
Avulsion (traumatic)
blood vessel - *see* Injury, blood vessel
bone - *see* Fracture, by site
cartilage - *see also* Dislocation, by site
symphyseal (inner), complicating
delivery O71.6
external site other than limb - *see*
Wound, open, by site
eye S05.7-
head (intracranial)
external site NEC S08.89
scalp S08.0
internal organ or site - *see* Injury,
by site
joint - *see also* Dislocation, by site
capsule - *see* Sprain, by site

Avulsion *(Continued)*
  kidney S37.06-
  ligament - *see* Sprain, by site
  limb - *see also* Amputation, traumatic,
      by site
    skin and subcutaneous tissue - *see*
        Wound, open, by site
  muscle - *see* Injury, muscle
  nerve (root) - *see* Injury, nerve
  scalp S08.0
  skin and subcutaneous tissue - *see*
      Wound, open, by site
  spleen S36.032
  symphyseal cartilage (inner),
      complicating delivery O71.6
  tendon - *see* Injury, muscle
  tooth S03.2

Awareness of heart beat R00.2
Axenfeld's
  anomaly or syndrome Q15.0
  degeneration (calcareous) Q13.4
Axilla, axillary - *see also* condition
  breast Q83.1
Axonotmesis - *see* Injury, nerve
Ayerza's disease or syndrome
    (pulmonary artery sclerosis
    with pulmonary hypertension)
    I27.0
Azoospermia (organic) N46.01
  due to
    drug therapy N46.021
    efferent duct obstruction
        N46.023

Azoospermia *(Continued)*
  due to *(Continued)*
    infection N46.022
    radiation N46.024
    specified cause NEC N46.029
    systemic disease N46.025
Azotemia R79.89
  meaning uremia N19
Aztec ear Q17.3
Azygos
  continuation inferior vena cava
      Q26.8
  lobe (lung) Q33.1

B

Baastrup's disease - *see* Kissing spine
Babesiosis B60.0
Babington's disease (familial hemor-
rhagic telangiectasia) I78.0
Babinski's syndrome A52.79
Baby
  crying constantly R68.11
  floppy (syndrome) P94.2
Bacillary - *see* condition
Bacilluria N39.0
Bacillus - *see also* Infection, bacillus
  abortus infection A23.1
  anthracis infection A22.9
  coli infection B96.2
  Flexner's A03.1
  mallei infection A24.0
  Shiga's A03.0
  suipestifer infection – *see* Infection,
    salmonella
Back - *see* condition
Backache (postural) M54.9
  sacroiliac M53.3
  specified NEC M54.89
Backflow - *see* Reflux
Backward reading (dyslexia) F81.0
Bacteremia R78.81
  with sepsis - *see* Sepsis
Bactericholia – *see* Cholecystitis, acute
Bacterid, bacteride (pustular) L40.3
Bacterium, bacteria, bacterial
  agent NEC, as cause of disease classi-
    fied elsewhere B96.89
  in blood - *see* Bacteremia
  in urine - *see* Bacteriuria
Bacteriuria, bacteruria N39.0
  asymptomatic N39.0
Bacteroides
  fragilis, as cause of disease classified
    elsewhere B96.6
Bad
  heart - *see* Disease, heart
  trip
    due to drug abuse - *see* Abuse, drug,
      hallucinogen
    due to drug dependence - *see* Depen-
      dence, drug, hallucinogen
Baelz's disease (cheilitis glandularis apos-
  tematosa) K13.0
Baerensprung's disease (eczema marginatum) B35.6
Bagasse disease or pneumonitis J67.1
Bagassosis J67.1
Baker's cyst - *see* Cyst, Baker's
Bakwin-Krida syndrome (craniometaphyseal dysplasia) Q78.5
Balancing side interference M26.56
Balanitis (circinata) (erosiva) (gangrenosa)
  (phagedenic) (vulgaris) N48.1
  amebic A06.82
  candidal B37.42
  due to Haemophilus ducreyi A57
  gonococcal (acute) (chronic) A54.09
  xerotica obliterans N48.0
Balanoposthitis N47.6
  gonococcal (acute) (chronic) A54.09
  ulcerative (specific) A63.8
Balanorrhagia - *see* Balanitis
Balantidiasis, balantidiosis A07.0
Bald tongue K14.4
Baldness - *see also* Alopecia
  male-pattern - *see* Alopecia, androgenic
Balkan grippe A78

Balloon disease - *see* Effect, adverse, high
  altitude
Balo's disease (concentric sclerosis) G37.5
Bamberger-Marie disease - *see* Osteoarthropathy, hypertrophic, specified
  type NEC
Bancroft's filariasis B74.0
Band(s)
  adhesive - *see* Adhesions, peritoneum
  anomalous or congenital - *see also*
    Anomaly, by site
    heart (atrial) (ventricular) Q24.8
    intestine Q43.3
    omentum Q43.3
  cervix N88.1
  constricting, congenital Q79.8
  gallbladder (congenital) Q44.1
  intestinal (adhesive) - *see* Adhesions,
    peritoneum
  obstructive
    intestine K56.5
    peritoneum K56.5
  periappendiceal, congenital Q43.3
  peritoneal (adhesive) - *see* Adhesions,
    peritoneum
  uterus N73.6
    internal N85.6
  vagina N89.5
Bandemia D72.825
Bandl's ring (contraction), complicating
  delivery O62.4
Bangkok hemorrhagic fever A91
Bang's disease (brucella abortus) A23.1
Bankruptcy, anxiety concerning Z59.8
Bannister's disease T78.3
  hereditary D84.1
Banti's disease or syndrome (with cirrho-
  sis) (with portal hypertension) K76.6
Bar, median, prostate - *see* Enlargement,
  enlarged, prostate
Barcoo disease or rot - *see* Ulcer, skin
Barlow's disease E54
Barodontalgia T70.29
Baron Münchausen syndrome - *see* Disor-
  der, factitious
Barosinusitis T70.1
Barotitis T70.0
Barotrauma T70.29
  odontalgia T70.29
  otitic T70.0
  sinus T70.1
Barraquer(-Simons) disease or syndrome
  (progressive lipodystrophy) E88.1
Barré-Guillain disease or syndrome
  G61.0
Barré-Liéou syndrome (posterior cervical
  sympathetic) M53.0
Barrel chest M95.4
Barrett's
  disease - *see* Barrett's, esophagus
  esophagus K22.70
    with dysplasia K22.719
      high grade K22.711
      low grade K22.710
    without dysplasia K22.70
  syndrome - *see* Barrett's, esophagus
  ulcer K22.10
    with bleeding K22.11
    without bleeding K22.10
Bársony (-Polgár) (-Teschendorf) syndrome
  (corkscrew esophagus) K22.4
Bartholinitis (suppurating) N75.8
  gonococcal (acute) (chronic) (with
    abscess) A54.1

Barth syndrome E78.71
Bartonellosis A44.9
  cutaneous A44.1
  mucocutaneous A44.1
  specified NEC A44.8
  systemic A44.0
Barton's fracture S52.56-
Bartter's syndrome E26.81
Basal - *see* condition
Basan's (hidrotic) ectodermal dysplasia
  Q82.4
Baseball finger – *see* Dislocation, finger
Basedow's disease (exophthalmic goiter)
  – *see* Hyperthyroidism, with, goiter
Basic - *see* condition
Basilar - *see* condition
Bason's (hidrotic) ectodermal dysplasia
  Q82.4
Basopenia - *see* Agranulocytosis
Basophilia D72.824
Basophilism (cortico-adrenal) (Cushing's)
  (pituitary) E24.0
Bassen-Kornzweig disease or syndrome
  E78.6
Bat ear Q17.5
Bateman's
  disease B08.1
  purpura (senile) D69.2
Bathing cramp T75.1
Bathophobia F40.248
Batten(-Mayou) disease E75.4
  retina E75.4 *[H36]*
Batten-Steiner syndrome G71.11
Battered – *see* Maltreatment
Battey Mycobacterium infection A31.0
Battle exhaustion F43.0
Battledore placenta O43.19-
Baumgarten-Cruveilhier cirrhosis,
  disease or syndrome K74.69
Bauxite fibrosis (of lung) J63.1
Bayle's disease (general paresis) A52.17
Bazin's disease (primary) (tuberculous)
  A18.4
Beach ear - *see* Swimmer's, ear
Beaded hair (congenital) Q84.1
Béal conjunctivitis or syndrome B30.2
Beard's disease (neurasthenia) F48.8
Beat(s)
  atrial, premature I49.1
  ectopic I49.49
  elbow - *see* Bursitis, elbow
  escaped, heart I49.49
  hand - *see* Bursitis, hand
  knee - *see* Bursitis, knee
  premature I49.40
    atrial I49.1
    auricular I49.1
    supraventricular I49.1
Beau's
  disease or syndrome - *see* Degeneration,
    myocardial
  lines (transverse furrows on fingernails)
    L60.4
Bechterev's syndrome - *see* Spondylitis,
  ankylosing
Beck's syndrome (anterior spinal artery
  occlusion) I65.8
Becker's
  cardiomyopathy I42.8
  disease
    idiopathic mural endomyocardial
      disease I42.3
    myotonia congenita, recessive form
      G71.12

Becker's *(continued)*
  dystrophy G71.0
  pigmented hairy nevus D22.5
Beckwith-Wiedemann syndrome Q87.3
Bed confinement status Z74.01
Bed sore- *see* Ulcer, pressure, by site
Bedbug bite(s) - *see* Bite(s), by site, superficial, insect
Bedclothes, asphyxiation or suffocation by - *see* Asphyxia, traumatic, due to, mechanical, trapped
Bednar's
  aphthae K12.0
  tumor - *see* Neoplasm, malignant, by site
Bedridden Z74.01
Bedsore - *see* Ulcer, pressure, by site
Bedwetting - *see* Enuresis
Bee sting (with allergic or anaphylactic shock) - *see* Toxicity, venom, arthropod, bee
Begbie's disease (exophthalmic goiter) – *see* Hyperthyroidism, with, goiter
Beer drinker's heart (disease) I42.6
Behavior
  antisocial
    adult Z72.811
    child or adolescent Z72.810
  disorder, disturbance - *see* Disorder, conduct
  disruptive - *see* Disorder, conduct
  drug *see*king Z72.89
  inexplicable R46.2
  marked evasiveness R46.5
  obsessive-compulsive R46.81
  overactivity R46.3
  poor responsiveness R46.4
  self-damaging (life-style) Z72.89
  sleep-incompatible Z72.821
  slowness R46.4
  specified NEC R46.89
  strange (and inexplicable) R46.2
  suspiciousness R46.5
  type A pattern Z73.1
  undue concern or preoccupation with stressful events R46.6
  verbosity and circumstantial detail obscuring reason for contact R46.7
Behcet's disease or syndrome M35.2
Behr's disease - *see* Degeneration, macula
Beigel's disease or morbus (white piedra) B36.2
Bejel A65
Bekhterev's syndrome - *see* Spondylitis, ankylosing
Belching - *see* Eructation
Bell's
  mania F30.8
  palsy, paralysis G51.0
    infant or newborn P11.3
  spasm G51.3
Bence Jones albuminuria or proteinuria NEC R80.3
Bends T70.3
Benedikt's paralysis or syndrome G46.3
Benign (see also condition)
  prostatic hyperplasia – *see* Hyperplasia, prostate
Bennett's fracture (displaced) S62.21-
Benson's disease - *see* Deposit, crystalline

Bent
  back (hysterical) F44.4
  nose M95.0
    congenital Q67.4
Bereavement (uncomplicated) Z63.4
Bergeron's disease (hysterical chorea) F44.4
Berger's disease - *see* Nephropathy, IgA
Beriberi (dry) E51.11
  heart (disease) E51.12
  polyneuropathy E51.11
  wet E51.12
    involving circulatory system E51.11
Berlin's disease or edema (traumatic) S05.8x-
Berlock (berloque) **dermatitis** L56.2
Bernard-Horner syndrome G90.2
Bernard-Soulier disease or thrombopathia D69.1
Bernhardt(-Roth) disease - *see* Mononeuropathy, lower limb, meralgia paresthetica
Bernheim's syndrome - *see* Failure, heart, congestive
Bertielliasis B71.8
Berylliosis (lung) J63.2
Besnier-Boeck(-Schaumann) disease - *see* Sarcoidosis
Besnier's
  lupus pernio D86.3
  prurigo L20.0
Bestiality F65.89
Best's disease H35.50
Beta-mercaptolactate-cysteine disulfiduria E72.09
Betalipoproteinemia, broad or floating E78.2
Betting and gambling Z72.6
  pathological (compulsive) F63.0
Bezoar T18.9
  intestine T18.3
  stomach T18.2
Bezold's abscess – *see* Mastoiditis, acute
Bianchi's syndrome R48.8
Bicornate or bicornis uterus Q51.3
  in pregnancy or childbirth O34.59-
    causing obstructed labor O65.5
Bicuspid aortic valve Q23.1
Biedl-Bardet syndrome Q87.89
Bielschowsky(-Jansky) disease E75.4
Biermer's (pernicious) anemia or disease D51.0
Biett's disease L93.0
Bifid (congenital)
  apex, heart Q24.8
  clitoris Q52.6
  kidney Q63.8
  nose Q30.2
  patella Q74.1
  scrotum Q55.29
  toe NEC Q74.2
  tongue Q38.3
  ureter Q62.8
  uterus Q51.3
  uvula Q35.7
Biforis uterus (suprasimplex) Q51.3
Bifurcation (congenital)
  gallbladder Q44.1
  kidney pelvis Q63.8
  renal pelvis Q63.8
  rib Q76.6
  tongue, congenital Q38.3
  trachea Q32.1
  ureter Q62.8
  urethra Q64.74
  vertebra Q76.49

Big spleen syndrome D73.1
Bigeminal pulse R00.8
Bilateral - *see* condition
Bile
  duct - *see* condition
  pigments in urine R82.2
Bilharziasis - *see also* Schistosomiasis
  chyluria B65.0
  cutaneous B65.3
  galacturia B65.0
  hematochyluria B65.0
  intestinal B65.1
  lipemia B65.9
  lipuria B65.0
  oriental B65.2
  piarhemia B65.9
  pulmonary NOS B65.9 [J99]
    pneumonia B65.9 [J17]
  tropical hematuria B65.0
  vesical B65.0
Biliary - *see* condition
Bilirubin metabolism disorder E80.7
  specified NEC E80.6
Bilirubinemia, familial nonhemolytic E80.4
Bilirubinuria R82.2
Biliuria R82.2
Bilocular stomach K31.2
Binswanger's disease I67.3
Biparta, bipartite
  carpal scaphoid Q74.0
  patella Q74.1
  vagina Q52.1
Bird
  face Q75.8
  fancier's disease or lung J67.2
Birt-Hogg-Dube syndrome Q87.89
Birth
  complications in mother - *see* Delivery, complicated
  compression during NOS P15.9
  defect - *see* Anomaly
  immature (less than 37 completed weeks) - *see* Preterm infant, newborn
    extremely (less than 28 completed weeks) - *see* Immaturity, extreme
  inattention, at or after – *see* Maltreatment, child, neglect
  injury NOS P15.9
    basal ganglia P11.1
    brachial plexus NEC P14.3
    brain (compression) (pressure) P11.2
    central nervous system NOS P11.9
    cerebellum P11.1
    cerebral hemorrhage P10.1
    external genitalia P15.5
    eye P15.3
    face P15.4
    fracture
      bone P13.9
        specified NEC P13.8
      clavicle P13.4
      femur P13.2
      humerus P13.3
      long bone, except femur P13.3
      radius and ulna P13.3
      skull P13.0
      spine P11.5
      tibia and fibula P13.3
    intracranial P11.2
      laceration or hemorrhage P10.9
        specified NEC P10.8

Birth *(Continued)*
  injury NOS *(Continued)*
    intraventricular hemorrhage P10.2
    laceration
      brain P10.1
      by scalpel P15.8
      peripheral nerve P14.9
    liver P15.0
    meninges
      brain P11.1
      spinal cord P11.5
    nerve
      brachial plexus P14.3
      cranial NEC (except facial)
        P11.4
      facial P11.3
      peripheral P14.9
      phrenic (paralysis) P14.2
    paralysis
      facial nerve P11.3
      spinal P11.5
    penis P15.5
    rupture
      spinal cord P11.5
    scalp P12.9
    scalpel wound P15.8
    scrotum P15.5
    skull NEC P13.1
      fracture P13.0
    specified type NEC P15.8
    spinal cord P11.5
    spine P11.5
    spleen P15.1
    sternomastoid (hematoma)
      P15.2
    subarachnoid hemorrhage P10.3
    subcutaneous fat necrosis P15.6
    subdural hemorrhage P10.0
    tentorial tear P10.4
    testes P15.5
    vulva P15.5
  lack of care, at or after – *see* Maltreatment, child, neglect
  neglect, at or after – *see* Maltreatment, child, neglect
  palsy or paralysis, newborn, NOS (birth injury) P14.9
  premature (infant) - *see* Preterm infant, newborn
  shock, newborn P96.89
  trauma - *see* Birth, injury
  weight
    low (2499 grams or less) - *see* Low, birthweight
      extremely (999 grams or less) - *see* Low, birthweight, extreme
    4000 grams to 4499 grams P08.1
    4500 grams or more P08.0
Birthmark Q82.5
Bisalbuminemia E88.09
Biskra's button B55.1
Bite(s) (animal) (human)
  abdomen, abdominal
    wall S31.159
      with penetration into peritoneal cavity S31.659
      epigastric region S31.152
        with penetration into peritoneal cavity S31.652
      left
        lower quadrant S31.154
          with penetration into peritoneal cavity S31.654

Bite(s) *(Continued)*
  abdomen, abdominal *(Continued)*
    wall *(Continued)*
      left *(Continued)*
        upper quadrant S31.151
          with penetration into peritoneal cavity S31.651
        periumbilic region S31.155
          with penetration into peritoneal cavity S31.655
      right
        lower quadrant S31.153
          with penetration into peritoneal cavity S31.653
        upper quadrant S31.150
          with penetration into peritoneal cavity S31.650
      superficial NEC S30.871
        insect S30.861
  alveolar (process) - *see* Bite, oral cavity
  amphibian (venomous) – *see* Venom, bite, amphibian
  animal – *see also* Bite, by site
    venomous – *see* Venom
  ankle S91.05-
    superficial NEC S90.57-
      insect S90.56-
  antecubital space – *see* Bite, elbow
  anus S31.835
    superficial NEC S30.877
      insect S30.867
  arm (upper) S41.15-
    lower – *see* Bite, forearm
    superficial NEC S40.87-
      insect S40.86-
  arthropod NEC – *see* Venom, bite, arthropod
  auditory canal (external) (meatus) – *see* Bite, ear
  auricle, ear – *see* Bite, ear
  axilla – *see* Bite, arm
  back - *see also* Bite, thorax, back
    lower S31.050
      with penetration into retroperitoneal space S31.051
    superficial NEC S30.870
      insect S30.860
  bedbug - *see* Bite(s), by site, superficial, insect
  breast S21.05-
    superficial NEC S20.17
      insect S20.16-
  brow - *see* Bite, head, specified site NEC
  buttock S31.805
    superficial NEC S30.870
      insect S30.860
  calf – *see* Bite, leg
  canaliculus lacrimalis – *see* Bite, eyelid
  canthus, eye – *see* Bite, eyelid
  centipede - *see* Toxicity, venom, arthropod, centipede
  cheek (external) S101.45-
    superficial NEC S00.87
      insect S00.86
    internal - *see* Bite, oral cavity
  chest wall – *see* Bite, thorax
  chigger B88.0
  chin – *see* Bite, head, specified site NEC
  clitoris - *see* Bite, vulva
  costal region - *see* Bite, thorax
  digit(s)
    hand – *see* Bite, finger
    toe - *see* Bite, toe

Bite(s) *(Continued)*
  ear (canal) (external) S01.35-
    superficial NEC S00.479
      insect S00.46-
  elbow S51.05-
    superficial NEC S50.37-
      insect S50.36-
  epididymis - *see* Bite, testis
  epigastric region - *see* Bite, abdomen
  epiglottis - *see* Bite, neck, specified site NEC
  esophagus, cervical S11.25
    superficial NEC S10.17
      insect S10.16
  eyebrow – *see* Bite, eyelid
  eyelid S01.15-
    superficial NEC S00.27-
      insect S00.26-
  face NEC – *see* Bite, head, specified site NEC
  finger(s) S61.259
    with
      damage to nail S61.359
    index S61.258
      with
        damage to nail S61.358
      left S61.251
        with
          damage to nail S61.351
      right S61.250
        with
          damage to nail S61.350
      superficial NEC S60.478
        insect S60.46-
    little S61.25-
      with
        damage to nail S61.35-
      superficial NEC S60.47-
        insect S60.46-
    middle S61.25-
      with
        damage to nail S61.35-
      superficial NEC S60.47-
        insect S60.46-
    ring S61.25-
      with
        damage to nail S61.35-
      superficial NEC S60.47-
        insect S60.46-
    superficial NEC S60.479
      insect S60.469
    thumb - *see* Bite, thumb
  flank - *see* Bite, abdomen, wall
  flea - *see* Bite, insect, by site
  foot (except toe(s) alone) S91.35-
    superficial NEC S90.87-
      insect S90.86-
    toe - *see* Bite, toe
  forearm S51.85-
    elbow only – *see* Bite, elbow
    superficial NEC S50.87-
      insect S50.86-
  forehead – *see* Bite, head, specified site NEC
  genital organs, external
    female S31.552
      superficial NEC S30.876
        insect S30.866
      vagina and vulva - *see* Bite, vulva
    male S31.551
      penis - *see* Bite, penis
      scrotum - *see* Bite, scrotum
      superficial NEC S30.875
        insect S30.865
      testes - *see* Bite, testis

Bite(s) *(Continued)*
  groin - *see* Bite, abdomen, wall
  gum - *see* Bite, oral cavity
  hand S61.45-
    finger - *see* Bite, finger
    superficial NEC S60.57-
      insect S60.56-
    thumb - *see* Bite, thumb
  head S01.95
    cheek – *see* Bite, cheek
    ear – *see* Bite, ear
    eyelid – *see* Bite, eyelid
    lip - *see* Bite, lip
    nose - *see* Bite, nose
    oral cavity - *see* Bite, oral cavity
    scalp - *see* Bite, scalp
    specified site NEC S01.85
      superficial NEC S00.87
        insect S00.86
    superficial NEC S00.97
      insect S00.96
    temporomandibular area – *see* Bite, cheek
  heel – *see* Bite, foot
  hip S71.05-
    superficial NEC S70.27-
      insect S70.26-
  hymen S31.45
  hypochondrium - *see* Bite, abdomen, wall
  hypogastric region - *see* Bite, abdomen, wall
  inguinal region - *see* Bite, abdomen, wall
  insect - *see* Bite, insect, by site
  instep – *see* Bite, foot
  interscapular region - *see* Bite, thorax, back
  jaw – *see* Bite, head, specified site NEC
  knee S81.05-
    superficial NEC S80.27-
      insect S80.26-
  labium (majus) (minus) - *see* Bite, vulva
  lacrimal duct – *see* Bite, eyelid
  larynx S11.015
    superficial NEC S10.17
      insect S10.16
  leg (lower) S81.85-
    ankle – *see* Bite, ankle
    foot – *see* Bite, foot
    knee – *see* Bite, knee
    superficial NEC S80.87-
      insect S80.86-
    toe – *see* Bite, toe
    upper – *see* Bite, thigh
  lip S01.551
    superficial NEC S00.571
      insect S00.561
  lizard (venomous) – *see* Venom, bite, reptile
  loin - *see* Bite, abdomen, wall
  lower back - *see* Bite, back, lower
  lumbar region - *see* Bite, back, lower
  malar region – *see* Bite, head, specified site NEC
  mammary – *see* Bite, breast
  marine animals (venomous) - *see* Toxicity, venom, marine animal
  mastoid region – *see* Bite, head, specified site NEC
  mouth - *see* Bite, oral cavity
  nail
    finger – *see* Bite, finger
    toe – *see* Bite, toe
  nape - *see* Bite, neck, specified site NEC
  nasal (septum) (sinus) - *see* Bite, nose

Bite(s) *(Continued)*
  nasopharynx – *see* Bite, head, specified site NEC
  neck S11.95
    involving
      cervical esophagus - *see* Bite, esophagus, cervical
      larynx - *see* Bite, larynx
      pharynx - *see* Bite, pharynx
      thyroid gland S11.15
      trachea - *see* Bite, trachea
    specified site NEC S11.85
      superficial NEC S10.87
        insect S10.86
    superficial NEC S10.97
      insect S10.96
    throat S11.85
      superficial NEC S10.17
        insect S10.16
  nose (septum) (sinus) S01.25
    superficial NEC S00.37
      insect S00.36
  occipital region - *see* Bite, scalp
  oral cavity S01.552
    superficial NEC S00.572
      insect S00.562
  orbital region - *see* Bite, eyelid
  palate - *see* Bite, oral cavity
  palm – *see* Bite, hand
  parietal region - *see* Bite, scalp
  pelvis S31.050
    with penetration into retroperitoneal space S31.051
    superficial NEC S30.870
      insect S30.860
  penis S31.25
    superficial NEC S30.872
      insect S30.862
  perineum
    female - *see* Bite, vulva
    male - *see* Bite, pelvis
  periocular area (with or without lacrimal passages) - *see* Bite, eyelid
  phalanges
    finger – *see* Bite, finger
    toe – *see* Bite, toe
  pharynx S11.25
    superficial NEC S10.17
      insect S10.16
  pinna – *see* Bite, ear
  poisonous – *see* Venom
  popliteal space – *see* Bite, knee
  prepuce - *see* Bite, penis
  pubic region - *see* Bite, abdomen, wall
  pudendum
    female - *see* Bite, vulva
    male - *see* Bite, pelvis
  rectovaginal septum - *see* Bite, vulva
  red bug B88.0
  reptile NEC – *see also* Venom, bite, reptile
    nonvenomous - *see* Bite, by site
    snake – *see* Venom, bite, snake
  sacral region - *see* Bite, back, lower
  sacroiliac region - *see* Bite, back, lower
  salivary gland - *see* Bite, oral cavity
  scalp S01.05
    superficial NEC S00.07
      insect S00.06
  scapular region – *see* Bite, shoulder
  scrotum S31.35
    superficial NEC S30.873
      insect S30.863
  sea-snake (venomous) - *see* Toxicity, venom, snake, sea snake

Bite(s) *(Continued)*
  shin – *see* Bite, leg
  shoulder S41.05-
    superficial NEC S40.27-
      insect S40.26-
  snake – *see also* Venom, bite, snake
    nonvenomous - *see* Bite, by site
  spermatic cord - *see* Bite, testis
  spider (venomous) – *see* Toxicity, venom, spider
    nonvenomous - *see* Bite, insect, by site
  sternal region - *see* Bite, thorax, front
  submaxillary region – *see* Bite, head, specified site NEC
  submental region – *see* Bite, head, specified site NEC
  subungual
    finger(s) – *see* Bite, finger
    toe – *see* Bite, toe
  superficial - *see* Bite, superficial, by site
  supraclavicular fossa S11.85
  supraorbital - *see* Bite, head, specified site NEC
  temple, temporal region – *see* Bite, head, specified site NEC
  temporomandibular area – *see* Bite, cheek
  testis S31.35
    superficial NEC S30.873
      insect S30.863
  thigh S71.15-
    superficial NEC S70.37-
      insect S70.36-
  thorax, thoracic (wall) S21.95
    back S21.25-
    breast – *see* Bite, breast
    front S21.15-
    superficial NEC S20.97
      back S20.47-
      front S20.37-
      insect S20.96
        back S20.46-
        front S20.36-
  throat – *see* Bite, neck, throat
  thumb S61.05-
    with
      damage to nail S61.15-
    superficial NEC S60.37-
      insect S60.36-
  thyroid S11.15
    superficial NEC S10.87
      insect S10.86
  toe(s) S91.15-
    with
      damage to nail S91.25-
    great S91.15-
      with
        damage to nail S91.25-
    lesser S91.15-
      with
        damage to nail S91.25-
    superficial NEC S90.47-
      great S90.47-
      insect S90.46-
        great S90.46-
  tongue S01.552
  trachea S11.025
    superficial NEC S10.17
      insect S10.16
  tunica vaginalis - *see* Bite, testis
  tympanum, tympanic membrane - *see* Bite, ear
  umbilical region S31.155
  uvula - *see* Bite, oral cavity
  vagina - *see* Bite, vulva

Bite(s) (Continued)
  venomous – see Venom
  vocal cords S11.035
    superficial NEC S10.17
      insect S10.16
  vulva S31.45
    superficial NEC S30.874
      insect S30.864
  wrist S61.55-
    superficial NEC S60.87-
      insect S60.86-
Biting, cheek or lip K13.1
Biventricular failure (heart) I50.9
Björck (-Thorson) syndrome (malignant carcinoid) E34.0
Black
  death A20.9
  eye S00.1-
  hairy tongue K14.3
  heel (foot) S90.3-
  lung (disease) J60
  palm (hand) S60.22-
Blackfan-Diamond (congenital hypoplastic) anemia or syndrome D61.01
Blackhead L70.0
Blackout R55
Bladder - see condition
Blast (air) (hydraulic) (immersion) (underwater)
  blindness S05.8x-
  injury
    abdomen or thorax - see Injury, by site
    ear (acoustic nerve trauma) - see
      Injury, nerve, acoustic, specified type NEC
  syndrome NEC T70.8
Blastoma - see Neoplasm, malignant
  pulmonary - see Neoplasm, lung, malignant
Blastomycosis, blastomycotic B40.9
  Brazilian - see Paracoccidioidomycosis
  cutaneous B40.3
  disseminated B40.7
  European - see Cryptococcosis
  generalized B40.7
  keloidal B48.0
  North American B40.9
  primary pulmonary B40.0
  pulmonary B40.2
    acute B40.0
    chronic B40.1
  skin B40.3
  South American - see Paracoccidioidomycosis
  specified NEC B40.89
Bleb(s) R23.8
  emphysematous (lung) (solitary) J43.9
  endophthalmitis H59.43
  filtering (vitreous), after glaucoma surgery Z98.83
  inflamed (infected), postprocedural H59.40
    stage 1 H59.41
    stage 2 H59.42
    stage 3 H59.43
  lung (ruptured) J43.9
    congenital - see Atelectasis
    newborn P25.8
  subpleural (emphysematous) J43.9
Blebitis, postprocedural H59.40
  stage 1 H59.41
  stage 2 H59.42
  stage 3 H59.43

Bleeder (familial) (hereditary) – see Hemophilia
Bleeding – see also Hemorrhage
  anal K62.5
  anovulatory N97.0
  atonic, following delivery O72.1
  capillary I78.8
    puerperal O72.2
  contact (postcoital) N93.0
  due to uterine subinvolution N85.3
  ear - see Otorrhagia
  excessive, associated with menopausal onset N92.4
  familial - see Defect, coagulation
  following intercourse N93.0
  gastrointestinal K92.2
  hemorrhoids NEC - see Hemorrhoids, by type, bleeding
  intermenstrual (regular) N92.3
    irregular N92.1
  intraoperative - see Complication, intraoperative, hemorrhage
  irregular N92.6
  menopausal N92.4
  newborn, intraventricular - see Newborn, affected by, hemorrhage, intraventricular
  nipple N64.59
  nose R04.0
  ovulation N92.3
  postclimacteric N95.0
  postcoital N93.0
  postmenopausal N95.0
  postoperative – see Hemorrhage, postoperative
  preclimacteric N92.4
  puberty (excessive, with onset of menstrual periods) N92.2
  rectum, rectal K62.5
    newborn P54.2
  tendencies - see Defect, coagulation
  throat R04.1
  tooth socket (post-extraction) K91.840
  umbilical stump P51.9
  uterus, uterine NEC N93.9
    climacteric N92.4
    dysfunctional of functional N93.8
    menopausal N92.4
    preclimacteric or premenopausal N92.4
    unrelated to menstrual cycle N93.9
  vagina, vaginal (abnormal) N93.9
    dysfunctional or functional N93.8
    newborn P54.6
  vicarious N94.89
Blennorrhagia, blennorrhagic - see Gonorrhea
Blennorrhea (acute) (chronic) - see also Gonorrhea
  inclusion (neonatal) (newborn) P39.1
  lower genitourinary tract (gonococcal) A54.00
  neonatorum (gonococcal ophthalmia) A54.31
Blepharelosis - see Entropion
Blepharitis (angularis) (ciliaris) (eyelid) (marginal) (nonulcerative) H01.009
  herpes zoster B02.39
  left H01.006
    lower H01.005
    upper H01.004
  right H01.003
    lower H01.002
    upper H01.001

Blepharitis (Continued)
  squamous H01.029
    left H01.026
      lower H01.025
      upper H01.024
    right H01.023
      lower H01.022
      upper H01.021
  ulcerative H01.019
    left H01.016
      lower H01.015
      upper H01.014
    right H01.013
      lower H01.012
      upper H01.011
Blepharochalasis H02.30
  congenital Q10.0
  left H02.36
    lower H02.35
    upper H02.34
  right H02.33
    lower H02.32
    upper H02.31
Blepharoclonus H02.59
Blepharoconjunctivitis H10.50-
  angular H10.52-
  contact H10.53-
  ligneous H10.51-
Blepharophimosis (eyelid) H02.529
  congenital Q10.3
  left H02.526
    lower H02.525
    upper H02.524
  right H02.523
    lower H02.522
    upper H02.521
Blepharoptosis H02.40-
  congenital Q10.0
  mechanical H02.41-
  myogenic H02.42-
  neurogenic H02.43-
  paralytic H02.43-
Blepharopyorrhea, gonococcal A54.39
Blepharospasm G24.5
  drug induced G24.01
Blighted ovum O02.0
Blind - see also Blindness
  bronchus (congenital) Q32.4
  loop syndrome K90.2
    congenital Q43.8
  sac, fallopian tube (congenital) Q50.6
  spot, enlarged - see Defect, visual field, localized, scotoma, blind spot area
  tract or tube, congenital NEC - see Atresia, by site
Blindness (acquired) (congenital) (both eyes) H54.0
  blast S05.8x-
  color - see Deficiency, color vision
  concussion S05.8x-
  cortical H47.619
    left brain H47.612
    right brain H47.611
  day H53.11
  due to injury (current episode) S05.9-
    sequelae — code to injury with extension s
  eclipse (total) - see Retinopathy, solar
  emotional (hysterical) F44.6
  face H53.16
  hysterical F44.6
  legal (both eyes) (USA definition) H54.8
  mind R48.8

Blindness *(Continued)*
- night H53.60
  - abnormal dark adaptation curve H53.61
  - acquired H53.62
  - congenital H53.63
  - specified type NEC H53.69
  - vitamin A deficiency E50.5
- one eye (other eye normal) H54.40
  - left (normal vision on right) H54.42
    - low vision on right H54.12
    - low vision, other eye H54.10
  - right (normal vision on left) H54.41
    - low vision on left H54.11
- psychic R48.8
- river B73.01
- snow - *see* Photokeratitis
- sun, solar - *see* Retinopathy, solar
- transient - *see* Disturbance, vision, subjective, loss, transient
- traumatic (current episode) S05.9-
- word (developmental) F81.0
  - acquired R48.0
  - secondary to organic lesion R48.0

Blister (nonthermal)
- abdominal wall S30.821
- alveolar process S00.522
- ankle S90.52-
- antecubital space – *see* Blister, elbow
- anus S30.827
- arm (upper) S40.82-
- auditory canal – *see* Blister, ear
- auricle – *see* Blister, ear
- axilla – *see* Blister, arm
- back, lower S30.820
- beetle dermatitis L24.89
- breast S20.12-
- brow S00.82
- calf – *see* Blister, leg
- canthus – *see* Blister, eyelid
- cheek S00.82
  - internal S00.522
- chest wall – *see* Blister, thorax
- chin S00.82
- costal region - *see* Blister, thorax
- digit(s)
  - foot - *see* Blister, toe
  - hand – *see* Blister, finger
- due to burn - *see* Burn, by site, second degree
- ear S00.42-
- elbow S50.32-
- epiglottis S10.12
- esophagus, cervical S10.12
- eyebrow – *see* Blister, eyelid
- eyelid S00.22-
- face S00.82
- fever B00.1
- finger(s) S60.429
  - index S60.42-
  - little S60.42-
  - middle S60.42-
  - ring S60.42-
- foot (except toe(s) alone) S90.82-
  - toe – *see* Blister, toe
- forearm S50.82-
  - elbow only – *see* Blister, elbow
- forehead S00.82
- genital organ
  - female S30.826
  - male S30.825
- gum S00.522
- hand S60.52-

Blister *(Continued)*
- head S00.92
  - ear - *see* Blister, ear
  - eyelid - *see* Blister, eyelid
  - lip S00.521
  - nose S00.32
  - oral cavity S00.522
  - scalp S00.02
  - specified site NEC S00.82
- heel – *see* Blister, foot
- hip S70.22-
- interscapular region S20.429
- jaw S00.82
- knee S80.22-
- larynx S10.12
- leg (lower) S80.82-
  - knee – *see* Blister, knee
  - upper - *see* Blister, thigh
- lip S00.521
- malar region S00.82
- mammary – *see* Blister, breast
- mastoid region S00.82
- mouth S00.522
- multiple, skin, nontraumatic R23.8
- nail
  - finger – *see* Blister, finger
  - toe – *see* Blister, toe
- nasal S00.32
- neck S10.92
  - specified site NEC S10.82
  - throat S10.12
- nose S00.32
- occipital region S00.02
- oral cavity S00.522
- orbital region – *see* Blister, eyelid
- palate S00.522
- palm – *see* Blister, hand
- parietal region S00.02
- pelvis S30.820
- penis S30.822
- periocular area – *see* Blister, eyelid
- phalanges
  - finger – *see* Blister, finger
  - toe – *see* Blister, toe
- pharynx S10.12
- pinna – *see* Blister, ear
- popliteal space – *see* Blister, knee
- scalp S00.02
- scapular region – *see* Blister, shoulder
- scrotum S30.823
- shin – *see* Blister, leg
- shoulder S40.22-
- sternal region S20.329
- submaxillary region S00.82
- submental region S00.82
- subungual
  - finger(s) – *see* Blister, finger
  - toe(s) – *see* Blister, toe
- supraclavicular fossa S10.82
- supraorbital S00.82
- temple S00.82
- temporal region S00.82
- testis S30.823
- thermal - *see* Burn, second degree, by site
- thigh S70.32-
- thorax, thoracic (wall) S20.92
  - back S20.42-
  - front S20.32-
- throat S10.12
- thumb S60.32-
- toe(s) S90.42-
  - great S90.42-
- tongue S00.522

Blister *(Continued)*
- trachea S10.12
- tympanum, tympanic membrane – *see* Blister, ear
- upper arm - *see* Blister, arm (upper)
- uvula S00.522
- vagina S30.824
- vocal cords S10.12
- vulva S30.824
- wrist S60.82-

Bloating R14.0

Bloch-Sulzberger disease or syndrome Q82.3

Block(ed)
- alveolocapillary J84.1
- arborization (heart) I45.5
- arrhythmic I45.9
- atrioventricular (incomplete) (partial) I44.30
  - with atrioventricular dissociation I44.2
  - complete I44.2
    - congenital Q24.6
  - congenital Q24.6
  - first degree I44.0
  - second degree (types I and II) I44.1
  - specified NEC I44.39
  - third degree I44.2
  - types I and II I44.1
- auriculoventricular - *see* Block, atrioventricular
- bifascicular (cardiac) I45.2
- bundle-branch (complete) (false) (incomplete) I45.4
  - bilateral I45.2
  - left I44.7
    - with right bundle branch block I45.2
    - hemiblock I44.60
      - anterior I44.4
      - posterior I44.5
    - incomplete I44.7
      - with right bundle branch block I45.2
  - right I45.10
    - with
      - left bundle branch block I45.2
      - left fascicular block I45.2
    - specified NEC I45.19
    - Wilson's type I45.19
- cardiac I45.9
- conduction I45.9
  - complete I44.2
- fascicular (left) I44.60
  - anterior I44.4
  - posterior I44.5
  - right I45.0
  - specified NEC I44.69
- foramen Magendie (acquired) G91.1
  - congenital Q03.1
    - with spina bifida - *see* Spina bifida, by site, with hydrocephalus
- heart I45.9
  - bundle branch I45.4
    - bilateral I45.2
  - complete (atrioventricular) I44.2
  - congenital Q24.6
  - first degree (atrioventricular) I44.0
  - second degree (atrioventricular) I44.1
  - specified type NEC I45.5
  - third degree (atrioventricular) I44.2
- hepatic vein I82.0

Block(ed) *(Continued)*
  intraventricular (nonspecific) I45.4
    bundle branch
      bilateral I45.2
  kidney N28.9
    postcystoscopic or postprocedural N99.0
  Mobitz (types I and II) I44.1
  myocardial - *see* Block, heart
  nodal I45.5
  organ or site, congenital NEC - *see* Atresia, by site
  portal (vein) I81
  second degree (types I and II) I44.1
  sinoatrial I45.5
  sinoauricular I45.5
  third degree I44.2
  trifascicular I45.3
  tubal N97.1
  vein NOS I82.90
  Wenckebach (types I and II) I44.1
Blockage - *see* Obstruction
Blocq's disease F44.4
Blood
  constituents, abnormal R78.9
  disease D75.9
  donor - *see* Donor, blood
  dyscrasia D75.9
    with
      abortion - *see* Abortion, by type
        with excessive hemorrhage
      ectopic pregnancy O08.1
      molar pregnancy O08.1
      following ectopic or molar pregnancy O08.1
      newborn P61.9
      puerperal, postpartum O72.3
  flukes NEC - *see* Schistosomiasis
  in
    feces K92.1
      occult R19.5
    urine - *see* Hematuria
  mole O02.0
  occult in feces R19.5
  pressure
    decreased, due to shock following injury T79.4
    examination only Z01.30
    fluctuating I99.8
    high - *see* Hypertension
      incidental reading, without diagnosis of hypertension R03.0
    low - *see also* Hypotension
      incidental reading, without diagnosis of hypotension R03.1
  spitting - *see* Hemoptysis
  staining cornea - *see* Pigmentation, cornea, stromal
  transfusion
    reaction or complication - *see* Complications, transfusion
  type
    A (Rh positive) Z67.10
      Rh negative Z67.11
    AB (Rh positive) Z67.30
      Rh negative Z67.31
    B (Rh positive) Z67.20
      Rh negative Z67.21
    O (Rh positive) Z67.40
      Rh negative Z67.41
    Rh (positive) Z67.90
      negative Z67.91
  vessel rupture - *see* Hemorrhage
  vomiting - *see* Hematemesis

Blood-forming organs, disease D75.9
Bloodgood's disease – *see* Mastopathy, cystic
Bloom(-Machacek)(-Torre) syndrome Q82.8
Blount's disease or osteochondrosis - *see* Osteochondrosis, juvenile, tibia
Blue
  baby Q24.9
  diaper syndrome E72.09
  dome cyst (breast) – *see* Cyst, breast
  dot cataract Q12.0
  nevus D22.9
  sclera Q13.5
    with fragility of bone and deafness Q78.0
  toe syndrome I75.02-
Blueness - *see* Cyanosis
Blues, postpartal O90.6
  baby O90.6
Blurring, visual H53.8
Blushing (abnormal) (excessive) R23.2
BMI - *see* Body, mass index
Boarder, hospital NEC Z76.4
  accompanying sick person Z76.3
  healthy infant or child Z76.2
    foundling Z76.1
Bockhart's impetigo L01.02
Bodechtel-Guttman disease (subacute sclerosing panencephalitis) A81.1
Boder-Sedgwick syndrome (ataxia-telangiectasia) G11.3
Body, bodies
  Aschoff's - *see* Myocarditis, rheumatic
  asteroid, vitreous - *see* Deposit, crystalline
  cytoid (retina) - *see* Occlusion, artery, retina
  drusen (degenerative) (macula) (retinal) - *see also* Degeneration, macula, drusen
    optic disc - *see* Drusen, optic disc
  foreign - *see* Foreign body
  loose
    joint, except knee - *see* Loose, body, joint
      knee M23.4-
    sheath, tendon – *see* Disorder, tendon, specified type NEC
  mass index (BMI)
    adult
      19 or less Z68.1
      20.0-20.9 Z68.20
      21.0-21.9 Z68.21
      22.0-22.9 Z68.22
      23.0-23.9 Z68.23
      24.0-24.9 Z68.24
      25.0-25.9 Z68.25
      26.0-26.9 Z68.26
      27.0-27.9 Z68.27
      28.0-28.9 Z68.28
      29.0-29.9 Z68.29
      30.0-30.9 Z68.30
      31.0-31.9 Z68.31
      32.0-32.9 Z68.32
      33.0-33.9 Z68.33
      34.0-34.9 Z68.34
      35.0-35.9 Z68.35
      36.0-36.9 Z68.36
      37.0-37.9 Z68.37
      38.0-38.9 Z68.38
      39.0-39.9 Z68.39
      40 or greater Z68.4

Body, bodies *(Continued)*
  mass index *(Continued)*
    pediatric
      5th percentile to less than 85th percentile for age Z68.52
      85th percentile to less than 95th percentile for age Z68.53
      greater than or equal to ninety-fifth percentile for age Z68.54
      less than fifth percentile for age Z68.51
  Mooser's A75.2
  rice - *see also* Loose, body, joint
    knee M23.4-
  rocking F98.4
Boeck's
  disease or sarcoid - *see* Sarcoidosis
  lupoid (miliary) D86.3
Boerhaave's syndrome (spontaneous esophageal rupture) K22.3
Boggy
  cervix N88.8
  uterus N85.8
Boil - *see also* Furuncle, by site
  Aleppo B55.1
  Baghdad B55.1
  Delhi B55.1
  lacrimal
    gland - *see* Dacryoadenitis
    passages (duct) (sac) - *see* Inflammation, lacrimal, passages, acute
  Natal B55.1
  orbit, orbital - *see* Abscess, orbit
  tropical B55.1
Bold hives - *see* Urticaria
Bombé, iris - *see* Membrane, pupillary
Bone - *see* condition
Bonnevie-Ullrich syndrome Q87.1
Bonnier's syndrome - *see* subcategory H81.8
Bonvale dam fever T73.3
Bony block of joint - *see* Ankylosis
BOOP (bronchiolitis obliterans organized pneumonia) J84.8
Borderline
  osteopenia M85.8-
  pelvis, with obstruction during labor O65.1
  personality F60.3
Borna disease A83.9
Bornholm disease B33.0
Boston exanthem A88.0
Botalli, ductus (patent) (persistent) Q25.0
Bothriocephalus latus infestation B70.0
Botulism (foodborne intoxication) A05.1
  infant A48.51
  non-foodborne A48.52
  wound A48.52
Bouba - *see* Yaws
Bouchard's nodes (with arthropathy) M15.2
Bouffée délirante F23
Bouillaud's disease or syndrome (rheumatic heart disease) I01.9
Bourneville's disease Q85.1
Boutonniere deformity (finger) - *see* Deformity, finger, boutonniere
Bouveret(-Hoffmann) syndrome (paroxysmal tachycardia) I47.9
Bovine heart - *see* Hypertrophy, cardiac
Bowel - *see* condition
Bowen's
  dermatosis (precancerous) - *see* Neoplasm, skin, in situ

Bowen's (Continued)
  disease - see Neoplasm, skin, in situ
  epithelioma - see Neoplasm, skin, in situ
  type
    epidermoid carcinoma-in-situ - see
      Neoplasm, skin, in situ
    intraepidermal squamous cell
      carcinoma - see Neoplasm, skin,
      in situ
Bowing
  femur - see also Deformity, limb, speci-
    fied type NEC, thigh
    congenital Q68.3
  fibula - see also Deformity, limb, speci-
    fied type NEC, lower leg
    congenital Q68.4
  forearm - see Deformity, limb, specified
    type NEC, forearm
  leg(s), long bones, congenital Q68.5
  radius - see Deformity, limb, specified
    type NEC, forearm
  tibia - see also Deformity, limb, specified
    type NEC, lower leg
    congenital Q68.4
Bowleg(s) (acquired) M21.16-
  congenital Q68.5
  rachitic E64.3
Boyd's dysentery A03.2
Brachial - see condition
Brachycardia R00.1
Brachycephaly Q75.0
Bradley's disease A08.19
Bradyarrhythmia, cardiac I49.8
Bradycardia (sinoatrial) (sinus) (vagal)
  R00.1
  neonatal P29.12
  reflex G90.09
  tachycardia syndrome I49.5
Bradykinesia R25.8
Bradypnea R06.89
Bradytachycardia I49.5
Brailsford's disease or osteochondrosis -
  see Osteochondrosis, juvenile, radius
Brain - see also condition
  death G93.89
  syndrome - see Syndrome, brain
Branched-chain amino-acid disorder E71.2
Branchial - see condition
  cartilage, congenital Q18.2
Branchiogenic remnant (in neck) Q18.0
Brash (water) R12
Bravais-jacksonian epilepsy – see Epilepsy, localization-related, symptomatic, with simple partial seizures
Braxton Hicks contractions - see False,
  labor
Brazilian leishmaniasis B55.2
Break, retina (without detachment)
  H33.30-
  with retinal detachment - see Detach-
    ment, retina
  horseshoe tear H33.31-
  multiple H33.33-
  round hole H33.32-
Breakage, prosthetic joint - see Complications..., joint prosthesis, mechanical,
  breakdown, by site
Breakdown
  device, graft or implant (see also
    Complications, by site and type,
    mechanical) T85.618
    arterial graft NEC - see Complication,
      cardiovascular device, mechani-
      cal, vascular

Breakdown (Continued)
  device, graft or implant (Continued)
    breast (implant) T85.41
    catheter NEC T85.618
      cystostomy T83.010
      dialysis (renal) T82.41
        intraperitoneal T85.611
      infusion NEC T82.514
        spinal (epidural) (subdural)
          T85.610
      urinary (indwelling) T83.018
    electronic (electrode) (pulse genera-
      tor) (stimulator)
      bone T84.310
      cardiac T82.119
        electrode T82.110
        pulse generator T82.111
        specified type NEC T82.118
      nervous system - see Complication,
        prosthetic device, mechani-
        cal, electronic nervous system
        stimulator
      urinary - see Complication,
        genitourinary, device, urinary,
        mechanical
    fixation, internal (orthopedic) NEC
      - see Complication, fixation
      device, mechanical
    gastrointestinal - see Complications,
      prosthetic device, mechanical,
      gastrointestinal device
    genital NEC T83.418
      intrauterine contraceptive device
        T83.31
      penile prosthesis T83.410
    heart NEC - see Complication, cardio-
      vascular device, mechanical
    joint prosthesis – see Complications...,
      joint prosthesis,internal, me-
      chanical, by site
    ocular NEC - see Complications,
      prosthetic device, mechanical,
      ocular device
    orthopedic NEC - see Complication,
      orthopedic, device, mechanical
    specified NEC T85.618
    sutures, permanent T85.612
      used in bone repair - see Complica-
        tions, fixation device, internal
        (orthopedic), mechanical
    urinary NEC - see also Complication,
      genitourinary, device, urinary,
      mechanical
      graft T83.21
    vascular NEC - see Complication,
      cardiovascular device,
      mechanical
    ventricular intracranial shunt T85.01
  nervous F48.8
  perineum O90.1
  respirator J95.850
    specified NEC J95.859
  ventilator J95.850
    specified NEC J95.859
Breast - see also condition
  buds E30.1
    in newborn P96.89
  dense R92.2
  nodule N63
Breath
  foul R19.6
  holder, child R06.89
  holding spell R06.89
  shortness R06.02

Breathing
  labored - see Hyperventilation
  mouth R06.5
    causing malocclusion M26.5
  periodic R06.3
    high altitude G47.32
Breathlessness R06.81
Breda's disease - see Yaws
Breech presentation (mother) O32.1
  causing obstructed labor O64.1
  footling O32.8
    causing obstructed labor O64.8
  incomplete O32.8
    causing obstructed labor O64.8
Breisky's disease N90.4
Brennemann's syndrome I88.0
Brenner
  tumor (benign) D27.9
    borderline malignancy D39.1
    malignant C56
    proliferating D39.1
Bretonneau's disease or angina A36.0
Breus' mole O02.0
Brevicollis Q76.49
Brickmakers' anemia B76.9
Bridge, myocardial Q24.5
BRBPR K62.5
Bright red blood per rectum (BRBPR)
  K62.5
Bright's disease - see also Nephritis
  arteriosclerotic - see Hypertension,
    kidney
Brill(-Zinsser) disease (recrudescent
  typhus) A75.1
  flea-borne A75.2
  louse-borne A75.1
Brill-Symmers' disease C82.90
Brion-Kayser disease - see Fever,
  parathyroid
Briquet's disorder or syndrome F45.0
Brissaud's
  infantilism or dwarfism E23.0
  motor-verbal tic F95.2
Brittle
  Bones disease Q78.0
  nails L60.3
    congenital Q84.6
Broad - see also condition
  beta disease E78.2
  ligament laceration syndrome
    N83.8
Broad- or floating-betalipoproteinemia
  E78.2
Brock's syndrome (atelectasis due
  to enlarged lymph nodes)
  J98.19
Brocq-Duhring disease (dermatitis herpetiformis) L13.0
Brodie's abscess or disease M86.8x-
Broken
  arches - see also Deformity, limb,
    flat foot
  arm (meaning upper limb) - see Frac-
    ture, arm
  back - see Fracture, vertebra
  bone - see Fracture
  implant or internal device - see
    Complications, by site and type,
    mechanical
  leg (meaning lower limb) - see Fracture,
    leg
  nose S02.2
  tooth, teeth - see Fracture, tooth
Bromhidrosis, bromidrosis L75.0

Bromidism, bromism G92
  due to
    correct substance properly admin-
      istered - *see* Table of drugs and
      chemicals, by drug, adverse effect
    overdose or wrong substance given
      or taken - *see* Table of drugs and
      chemicals, by drug, poisoning
  chronic (dependence) F13.20
Bromidrosiphobia F40.298
Bronchi, bronchial - *see* condition
Bronchiectasis (cylindrical) (diffuse) (fusiform) (localized) (saccular) J47.9
  with
    acute lower respiratory infection J47.0
    exacerbation (acute) J47.1
  congenital Q33.4
  tuberculous NEC - *see* Tuberculosis,
    pulmonary
Bronchiolectasis - *see* Bronchiectasis
Bronchiolitis (acute) (infective) (subacute)
  J21.9
  with
    bronchospasm or obstruction J21.9
    influenza, flu or grippe - *see*
      Influenza, with, respiratory
      manifestations
  chemical (chronic) J68.4
    acute J68.0
  chronic (fibrosing) (obliterative) J44.9
  due to
    external agent - *see* Bronchitis, acute,
      due to
    human metapneumovirus J21.1
    respiratory syncytial virus J21.0
    specified organism NEC J21.8
  fibrosa obliterans J44.9
  influenzal - *see* Influenza, with, respira-
    tory manifestations
  obliterans J42
    with organizing pneumonia (BOOP)
      J84.8
  obliterative (chronic) (subacute) J44.9
    due to fumes or vapors J68.4
    due to chemicals, gases, fumes or
      vapors (inhalation) J68.4
Bronchitis (diffuse) (fibrinous) (hypostatic) (infective) (membranous)
  (with tracheitis) J40
  with
    influenza, flu or grippe - *see*
      Influenza, with, respiratory
      manifestations
    obstruction (airway) (lung) J44.9
    tracheitis (15 years of age and above)
      J40
      acute or subacute J20.9
      chronic J42
      under 15 years of age J20.9
  acute or subacute (with bronchospasm
    or obstruction) J20.9
    with
      bronchiectasis J47.1
      chronic obstructive pulmonary
        disease J44.0
      chemical (due to gases, fumes or
        vapors) J68.0
      due to
        fumes or vapors J68.0
        Haemophilus influenzae J20.1
        Mycoplasma pneumoniae J20.0
        radiation J70.0
        specified organism NEC J20.8
        Streptococcus J20.2

Bronchitis (*Continued*)
  acute or subacute (*Continued*)
    due to (*Continued*)
      virus
        coxsackie J20.3
        echovirus J20.7
        parainfluenzae J20.4
        respiratory syncytial J20.5
        rhinovirus J20.6
    viral NEC J20.8
  allergic (acute) J45.900
    with
      exacerbation (acute) J45.901
      status asthmaticus J45.902
  arachidic T17.528
  aspiration (due to fumes or vapors) J68.0
  asthmatic J45.9
    chronic J44.9
      with
        acute lower respiratory infection
          J44.0
        exacerbation (acute) J44.1
  capillary - *see* Pneumonia, broncho
  caseous (tuberculous) A15.5
  castellani's A69.8
  catarrhal (15 years of age and above) J40
    acute - *see* Bronchitis, acute
    chronic J41.0
    under 15 years of age J20.9
  chemical (acute) (subacute) J68.0
    chronic J68.4
    due to fumes or vapors J68.0
      chronic J68.4
  chronic J42
    with
      airways obstruction J44.9
      tracheitis (chronic) J42
    asthmatic (obstructive) J44.9
    catarrhal J41.0
    chemical (due to fumes or vapors) J68.4
    due to
      chemicals, gases, fumes or vapors
        (inhalation) J68.4
      radiation J70.1
      tobacco smoking J41.0
    emphysematous J44.9
    mucopurulent J41.1
    non-obstructive J41.0
    obliterans J44.9
    obstructive J44.9
    purulent J41.1
    simple J41.0
  croupous - *see* Bronchitis, acute
  due to gases, fumes or vapors (chemi-
    cal) J68.0
  emphysematous (obstructive) J44.9
  exudative - *see* Bronchitis, acute
  fetid J41.1
  grippal - *see* Influenza, with, respiratory
    manifestations
  in those under 15 years age - *see* Bron-
    chitis, acute
    chronic - *see* Bronchitis, chronic
  influenzal - *see* Influenza, with, respira-
    tory manifestations
  mixed simple and mucopurulent J41.8
  moulder's J62.8
  mucopurulent (chronic) (recurrent) J41.1
    acute or subacute J20.9
    simple (mixed) J41.8
  obliterans (chronic) J44.9
  obstructive (chronic) (diffuse) J44.9
  pituitous J41.1
  pneumococcal, acute or subacute J20.2

Bronchitis (*Continued*)
  pseudomembranous, acute or subacute
    - *see* Bronchitis, acute
  purulent (chronic) (recurrent) J41.1
    acute or subacute - *see* Bronchitis, acute
  putrid J41.1
  senile (chronic) J42
  simple and mucopurulent (mixed) J41.8
  smokers' J41.0
  spirochetal NEC A69.8
  subacute - *see* Bronchitis, acute
  suppurative (chronic) J41.1
    acute or subacute - *see* Bronchitis, acute
  tuberculous A15.5
  under 15 years of age - *see* Bronchitis,
    acute
    chronic - *see* Bronchitis, chronic
  viral NEC, acute or subacute (see also
    Bronchitis, acute) J20.8
Bronchoalveolitis J18.0
Bronchoaspergillosis B44.1
Bronchocele meaning goiter E04.0
Broncholithiasis J98.09
  tuberculous NEC A15.5
Bronchomalacia J98.09
  congenital Q32.2
Bronchomycosis NOS B49 *[J99]*
  candidal B37.1
Bronchopleuropneumonia - *see* Pneumonia, broncho
Bronchopneumonia - *see* Pneumonia,
  broncho
Bronchopneumonitis - *see* Pneumonia,
  broncho
Bronchopulmonary - *see* condition
Bronchopulmonitis - *see* Pneumonia,
  broncho
Bronchorrhagia (see Hemoptysis)
Bronchorrhea J98.09
  acute J20.9
  chronic (infective) (purulent) J42
Bronchospasm (acute) J98.01
  with
    bronchiolitis, acute J21.9
    bronchitis, acute (conditions in J20)
      - *see* Bronchitis, acute
  due to external agent - *see* condition,
    respiratory, acute, due to
  exercise induced J45.990
Bronchospirochetosis A69.8
  castellani A69.8
Bronchostenosis J98.09
Bronchus - *see* condition
Brontophobia F40.220
Bronze baby syndrome P83.8
Brooke's tumor - *see* Neoplasm, skin,
  benign
Brown enamel of teeth (hereditary) K00.5
Brown's sheath syndrome H50.61-
Brown-Séquard disease, paralysis or
  syndrome G83.81
Bruce sepsis A23.0
Brucellosis (infection) A23.9
  abortus A23.1
  canis A23.3
  dermatitis A23.9
  melitensis A23.0
  mixed A23.8
  sepsis A23.9
    melitensis A23.0
    specified NEC A23.8
  suis A23.2
Bruck-de Lange disease Q87.1
Bruck's disease - *see* Deformity, limb

Brugsch's syndrome Q82.8
Bruise (skin surface intact) - *see also*
    Contusion
  with
    open wound - *see* Wound, open
  internal organ - *see* Injury, by site
  newborn P54.5
  scalp, due to birth injury, newborn P12.3
  umbilical cord O69.5
Bruit (arterial) R09.89
  cardiac R01.1
Brush burn - *see* Abrasion, by site
Bruton's X-linked agammaglobulinemia
    D80.0
Bruxism
  psychogenic F45.8
  sleep related G47.63
Bubbly lung syndrome P27.0
Bubo I88.8
  blennorrhagic (gonococcal) A54.89
  chancroidal A57
  climatic A55
  due to Haemophilus ducreyi A57
  gonococcal A54.89
  indolent (nonspecific) I88.8
  inguinal (nonspecific) I88.8
    chancroidal A57
    climatic A55
    due to H. ducreyi A57
    infective I88.8
  scrofulous (tuberculous) A18.2
  soft chancre A57
  suppurating - *see* Lymphadenitis, acute
  syphilitic (primary) A51.0
    congenital A50.07
  tropical A55
  virulent (chancroidal) A57
Bubonic plague A20.0
Bubonocele - *see* Hernia, inguinal
Buccal - *see* condition
Buchanan's disease or osteochondrosis
    M91.0
Buchem's syndrome (hyperostosis corti-
    calis) M85.2
Bucket-handle fracture or tear (semilunar
    cartilage) - *see* Tear, meniscus
Budd-Chiari syndrome (hepatic vein
    thrombosis) I82.0
Budgerigar fancier's disease or lung J67.2
Buds
  breast E30.1
    in newborn P96.89
Buerger's disease (thromboangiitis oblit-
    erans) I73.1
Bulbar - *see* condition
Bulbus cordis (left ventricle) (persistent)
    Q21.8
Bulimia (nervosa) F50.2
  atypical F50.9
  normal weight F50.9
Bulky
  stools R19.5
  uterus N85.2
Bulla(e) R23.8
  lung (emphysematous) (solitary) J43.9
    newborn P25.8
Bullet wound - *see also* Wound, open
  fracture - code as Fracture, by site
  internal organ - *see* Injury, by site
Bundle
  branch block (complete) (false) (incom-
    plete) - *see* Block, bundle-branch
  of His - *see* condition
Bunion - *see* Deformity, toe, hallux valgus

Buphthalmia, buphthalmos (congenital)
    Q15.0
Burdwan fever B55.0
Bürger-Grütz disease or syndrome E78.3
Buried roots K08.3
Burke's syndrome K86.8
Burkitt
  cell leukemia C91.0-
  lymphoma (malignant) C83.7-
    small noncleaved, diffuse C83.70
    spleen C83.77
    undifferentiated C83.70
  tumor C83.70
  type
    acute lymphoblastic leukemia C91.0-
    undifferentiated C83.70
Burn (electricity) (flame) (hot gas, liquid
    or hot object) (radiation) (steam)
    (thermal) T30.0
  abdomen, abdominal (muscle) (wall)
    T21.02
    first degree T21.12
    second degree T21.22
    third degree T21.32
  above elbow T22.039
    first degree T22.139
    left T22.032
      first degree T22.132
      second degree T22.232
      third degree T22.332
    right T22.031
      first degree T22.131
      second degree T22.231
      third degree T22.331
    second degree T22.238
    third degree T22.339
  acid (caustic) (external) (internal) - *see*
    Corrosion, by site
  alimentary tract NEC T28.2
    esophagus T28.1
    mouth T28.0
    pharynx T28.0
  alkaline (caustic) (external) (internal)
    - *see* Corrosion, by site
  ankle T25.019
    first degree T25.119
    left T25.012
      first degree T25.112
      second degree T25.212
      third degree T25.312
    multiple with foot - *see* Burn,
      lower, limb, multiple, ankle
      and foot
    right T25.011
      first degree T25.111
      second degree T25.211
      third degree T25.311
    second degree T25.219
    third degree T25.319
  anus – *see* Burn, buttock
  arm (lower) (upper) - *see* Burn, upper,
    limb
  axilla T22.049
    first degree T22.149
    left T22.042
      first degree T22.142
      second degree T22.242
      third degree T22.342
    right T22.041
      first degree T22.141
      second degree T22.241
      third degree T22.341
    second degree T22.249
    third degree T22.349

Burn *(Continued)*
  back (lower) T21.04
    first degree T21.14
    second degree T21.24
    third degree T21.34
    upper T21.03
      first degree T21.13
      second degree T21.23
      third degree T21.33
  blisters - code as Burn, second degree,
    by site
  breast(s) – *see* Burn, chest wall
  buttock(s) T21.05
    first degree T21.15
    second degree T21.25
    third degree T21.35
  calf T24.039
    first degree T24.139
    left T24.032
      first degree T24.132
      second degree T24.232
      third degree T24.332
    right T24.031
      first degree T24.131
      second degree T24.231
      third degree T24.331
    second degree T24.239
    third degree T24.339
  canthus (eye) – *see* Burn, eyelid
  caustic acid or alkaline - *see* Corrosion,
    by site
  cervix T28.3
  cheek T20.06
    first degree T20.16
    second degree T20.26
    third degree T20.36
  chemical (acids) (alkalines)
    (caustics) (external) (internal) -
    see Corrosion, by site
  chest wall T21.01
    first degree T21.11
    second degree T21.21
    third degree T21.31
  chin T20.03
    first degree T20.13
    second degree T20.23
    third degree T20.33
  colon T28.2
  conjunctiva (and cornea) – *see* Burn,
    cornea
  cornea (and conjunctiva) T26.1-
    chemical – *see* Corrosion, cornea
  corrosion (external) (internal) - *see*
    Corrosion, by site
  deep necrosis of underlying tissue -
    code as Burn, third degree, by site
  dorsum of hand T23.069
    first degree T23.169
    left T23.062
      first degree T23.162
      second degree T23.262
      third degree T23.362
    right T23.061
      first degree T23.161
      second degree T23.261
      third degree T23.361
    second degree T23.269
    third degree T23.369
  due to ingested chemical agent - *see*
    Corrosion, by site
  ear (auricle) (external) (canal) T20.01
    first degree T20.11
    second degree T20.21
    third degree T20.31

Burn *(Continued)*
  elbow T22.029
    first degree T22.129
    left T22.022
      first degree T22.122
      second degree T22.222
      third degree T22.322
    right T22.021
      first degree T22.121
      second degree T22.221
      third degree T22.321
    second degree T22.229
    third degree T22.329
  epidermal loss - code as Burn, second
      degree, by site
  erythema, erythematous - code as Burn,
      first degree, by site
  esophagus T28.1
  extent (percentage of body surface)
    less than 10 percent T31.0
    10-19 percent T31.10
      with 0-9 percent third degree burns
          T31.10
      with 10-19 percent third degree
          burns T31.11
    20-29 percent T31.20
      with 0-9 percent third degree burns
          T31.20
      with 10-19 percent third degree
          burns T31.21
      with 20-29 percent third degree
          burns T31.22
    30-39 percent T31.30
      with 0-9 percent third degree burns
          T31.30
      with 10-19 percent third degree
          burns T31.31
      with 20-29 percent third degree
          burns T31.32
      with 30-39 percent third degree
          burns T31.33
    40-49 percent T31.40
      with 0-9 percent third degree burns
          T31.40
      with 10-19 percent third degree
          burns T31.41
      with 20-29 percent third degree
          burns T31.42
      with 30-39 percent third degree
          burns T31.43
      with 40-49 percent third degree
          burns T31.44
    50-59 percent T31.50
      with 0-9 percent third degree burns
          T31.50
      with 10-19 percent third degree
          burns T31.51
      with 20-29 percent third degree
          burns T31.52
      with 30-39 percent third degree
          burns T31.53
      with 40-49 percent third degree
          burns T31.54
      with 50-59 percent third degree
          burns T31.55
    60-69 percent T31.60
      with 0-9 percent third degree burns
          T31.60
      with 10-19 percent third degree
          burns T31.61
      with 20-29 percent third degree
          burns T31.62
      with 30-39 percent third degree
          burns T31.63

Burn *(Continued)*
  extent *(Continued)*
    60-69 percent *(Continued)*
      with 40-49 percent third degree
          burns T31.64
      with 50-59 percent third degree
          burns T31.65
      with 60-69 percent third degree
          burns T31.66
    70-79 percent T31.70
      with 0-9 percent third degree burns
          T31.70
      with 10-19 percent third degree
          burns T31.71
      with 20-29 percent third degree
          burns T31.72
      with 30-39 percent third degree
          burns T31.73
      with 40-49 percent third degree
          burns T31.74
      with 50-59 percent third degree
          burns T31.75
      with 60-69 percent third degree
          burns T31.76
      with 70-79 percent third degree
          burns T31.77
    80-89 percent T31.80
      with 0-9 percent third degree burns
          T31.80
      with 10-19 percent third degree
          burns T31.81
      with 20-29 percent third degree
          burns T31.82
      with 30-39 percent third degree
          burns T31.83
      with 40-49 percent third degree
          burns T31.84
      with 50-59 percent third degree
          burns T31.85
      with 60-69 percent third degree
          burns T31.86
      with 70-79 percent third degree
          burns T31.87
      with 80-89 percent third degree
          burns T31.88
    90 percent or more T31.90
      with 0-9 percent third degree burns
          T31.90
      with 10-19 percent third degree
          burns T31.91
      with 20-29 percent third degree
          burns T31.92
      with 30-39 percent third degree
          burns T31.93
      with 40-49 percent third degree
          burns T31.94
      with 50-59 percent third degree
          burns T31.95
      with 60-69 percent third degree
          burns T31.96
      with 70-79 percent third degree
          burns T31.97
      with 80-89 percent third degree
          burns T31.98
      with 90 percent or more third
          degree burns T31.99
  extremity - *see* Burn, limb
  eye(s) and adnexa T26.4-
    with resulting rupture and
        destruction of eyeball
        T26.2-
    conjunctival sac – *see* Burn, cornea
    cornea – *see* Burn, cornea
    lid – *see* Burn, eyelid

Burn *(Continued)*
  eye(s) and adnexa *(Continued)*
    periocular area – *see* Burn
        eyelid
    specified site NEC T26.3-
  eyeball - *see* Burn, eye
  eyelid(s) T26.0-
    chemical – *see* Corrosion, eyelid
  face – *see* Burn, head
  finger T23.029
    first degree T23.129
    left T23.022
      first degree T23.122
      second degree T23.222
      third degree T23.322
    multiple sites (without thumb)
        T23.039
      with thumb T23.049
        first degree T23.149
        left T23.042
          first degree T23.142
          second degree T23.242
          third degree T23.342
        right T23.041
          first degree T23.141
          second degree T23.241
          third degree T23.341
        second degree T23.249
        third degree T23.349
      first degree T23.139
      left T23.032
        first degree T23.132
        second degree T23.232
        third degree T23.332
      right T23.031
        first degree T23.131
        second degree T23.231
        third degree T23.331
      second degree T23.239
      third degree T23.339
    right T23.021
      first degree T23.121
      second degree T23.221
      third degree T23.321
    second degree T23.229
    third degree T23.329
  flank – *see* Burn, abdominal wall
  foot T25.029
    first degree T25.129
    left T25.022
      first degree T25.122
      second degree T25.222
      third degree T25.322
    multiple with ankle - *see* Burn,
        lower, limb, multiple, ankle
        and foot
    right T25.021
      first degree T25.121
      second degree T25.221
      third degree T25.321
    second degree T25.229
    third degree T25.329
  forearm T22.019
    first degree T22.119
    left T22.012
      first degree T22.112
      second degree T22.212
      third degree T22.312
    right T22.011
      first degree T22.111
      second degree T22.211
      third degree T22.311
    second degree T22.219
    third degree T22.319

Burn (*Continued*)
forehead T20.06
  first degree T20.16
  second degree T20.26
  third degree T20.36
fourth degree - code as Burn, third
  degree, by site
friction - *see* Burn, by site
from swallowing caustic or corrosive
  substance NEC - *see* Corrosion,
  by site
full thickness skin loss - code as Burn,
  third degree, by site
gastrointestinal tract NEC T28.2
  from swallowing caustic or
    corrosive substance
    T28.7
genital organs
  external
    female T21.07
      first degree T21.17
      second degree T21.27
      third degree T21.37
    male T21.06
      first degree T21.16
      second degree T21.26
      third degree T21.36
  internal T28.3
    from caustic or corrosive substance
    T28.8
groin – *see* Burn, abdominal wall
hand(s) T23.009
  back - *see* Burn, dorsum of hand
  finger - *see* Burn, finger
  first degree T23.109
  left T23.002
    first degree T23.102
    second degree T23.202
    third degree T23.302
  multiple sites with wrist T23.099
    first degree T23.199
    left T23.092
      first degree T23.192
      second degree T23.292
      third degree T23.392
    right T23.091
      first degree T23.191
      second degree T23.291
      third degree T23.391
    second degree T23.299
    third degree T23.399
  palm - *see* Burn, palm
  right T23.001
    first degree T23.101
    second degree T23.201
    third degree T23.301
  second degree T23.209
  third degree T23.309
  thumb - *see* Burn, thumb
head (and face) (and neck) T20.00
  cheek - *see* Burn, cheek
  chin - *see* Burn, chin
  ear - *see* Burn, ear
  eye(s) only - *see* Burn, eye
  first degree T20.10
  forehead - *see* Burn, forehead
  lip - *see* Burn, lip
  multiple sites T20.09
    first degree T20.19
    second degree T20.29
    third degree T20.39
  neck - *see* Burn, neck
  nose - *see* Burn, nose
  scalp - *see* Burn, scalp

Burn (*Continued*)
head (*Continued*)
  second degree T20.20
  third degree T20.30
hip(s) – *see* Burn, lower, limb
inhalation – *see* Burn, respiratory
  tract
  caustic or corrosive substance
    (fumes) - *see* Corrosion, respira-
    tory tract
internal organ(s) T28.40
  alimentary tract T28.2
    esophagus T28.1
  eardrum T28.41
  esophagus T28.1
  from caustic or corrosive substance
    (swallowing) NEC - *see* Corro-
    sion, by site
  genitourinary T28.3
  mouth T28.0
  pharynx T28.0
  respiratory tract - *see* Burn, respira-
    tory tract
  specified organ NEC T28.49
interscapular region – *see* Burn, back,
  upper
intestine (large) (small) T28.2
knee T24.029
  first degree T24.129
  left T24.022
    first degree T24.122
    second degree T24.222
    third degree T24.322
  right T24.021
    first degree T24.121
    second degree T24.221
    third degree T24.321
  second degree T24.229
  third degree T24.329
labium (majus) (minus) – *see* Burn,
  genital organs, external,
  female
lacrimal apparatus, duct, gland or
  sac – *see* Burn, eye, specified site
  NEC
larynx T27.0
  with lung T27.1
leg(s) (lower) (upper) - *see* Burn, lower,
  limb
lightning - *see* Burn, by site
limb(s)
  lower (except ankle or foot alone)
    – *see* Burn, lower, limb
  upper – *see* Burn, upper limb
lip(s) T20.02
  first degree T20.12
  second degree T20.22
  third degree T20.32
lower
  back – *see* Burn, back
  limb T24.009
    ankle - *see* Burn, ankle
    calf - *see* Burn, calf
    first degree T24.109
    foot – *see* Burn, foot
    knee - *see* Burn, knee
    left T24.002
      first degree T24.102
      second degree T24.202
      third degree T24.302
    multiple sites, except ankle and
      foot T24.099
    ankle and foot T25.099
      first degree T25.199

Burn (*Continued*)
lower (*Continued*)
  limb (*Continued*)
    multiple sites, except ankle and
      foot (*Continued*)
    ankle and foot (*Continued*)
      left T25.092
        first degree T25.192
        second degree T25.292
        third degree T25.392
      right T25.091
        first degree T25.191
        second degree T25.291
        third degree T25.391
      second degree T25.299
      third degree T25.399
    first degree T24.199
    left T24.092
      first degree T24.192
      second degree T24.292
      third degree T24.392
    right T24.091
      first degree T24.191
      second degree T24.291
      third degree T24.391
    second degree T24.299
    third degree T24.399
    right T24.001
      first degree T24.101
      second degree T24.201
      third degree T24.301
    second degree T24.209
    hip – *see* Burn, thigh
    thigh - *see* Burn, thigh
    third degree T24.309
    toe - *see* Burn, toe
lung (with larynx and trachea)
  T27.1
mouth T28.0
neck T20.07
  first degree T20.17
  second degree T20.27
  third degree T20.37
nose (septum) T20.04
  first degree T20.14
  second degree T20.24
  third degree T20.34
ocular adnexa – *see* Burn, eye
orbit region - *see* Burn, eyelid
palm T23.059
  first degree T23.159
  left T23.052
    first degree T23.152
    second degree T23.252
    third degree T23.352
  right T23.051
    first degree T23.151
    second degree T23.251
    third degree T23.351
  second degree T23.259
  third degree T23.359
partial thickness - code as Burn,
  unspecified degree, by site
pelvis – *see* Burn, trunk
penis – *see* Burn, genital organs,
  external, male
perineum
  female – *see* Burn, genital organs,
    external, female
  male – *see* Burn, genital organs,
    external, male
periocular area – *see* Burn, eyelid
pharynx T28.0
rectum T28.2

Burn *(Continued)*
  unspecified site with extent of
      body surface involved
      specified *(Continued)*
    90 percent or more *(Continued)*
      with *(Continued)*
        80-89 percent third degree
          T31.98
        90-99 percent third degree
          T31.99
  upper limb T22.00
    above elbow - *see* Burn, above elbow
    axilla - *see* Burn, axilla
    elbow - *see* Burn, elbow
    first degree T22.10
    forearm - *see* Burn, forearm
    hand – *see* Burn, hand
    interscapular region – *see* Burn, back,
      upper
    multiple sites T22.099
      first degree T22.199
      left T22.092
        first degree T22.192
        second degree T22.292
        third degree T22.392
      right T22.091
        first degree T22.191
        second degree T22.291
        third degree T22.391
      second degree T22.299
      third degree T22.399
    second degree T22.20
    scapular region - *see* Burn, scapular
      region
    shoulder – *see* Burn, shoulder
    third degree T22.30
    wrist - *see* Burn, wrist
  uterus T28.3
  vagina T28.3
  vulva – *see* Burn, genital organs, exter-
    nal, female
  wrist T23.079
    first degree T23.179
    left T23.072
      first degree T23.172
      second degree T23.272
      third degree T23.372
    multiple sites with hand T23.099
      first degree T23.199
      left T23.092
        first degree T23.192
        second degree T23.292
        third degree T23.392
      right T23.091
        first degree T23.191
        second degree T23.291
        third degree T23.391
      second degree T23.299
      third degree T23.399
    right T23.071
      first degree T23.171
      second degree T23.271
      third degree T23.371
    second degree T23.279
    third degree T23.379
Burnett's syndrome E83.52

Burning
  feet syndrome E53.9
  sensation R20.8
  tongue K14.6
Burn-out (state) Z73.0
Burns' disease or osteochondrosis - *see*
    Osteochondrosis, juvenile, ulna
Bursa - *see* condition
Bursitis M71.9
  Achilles - *see* Tendinitis, Achilles
  adhesive - *see* Bursitis, specified NEC
  ankle - *see* Enthesopathy, lower limb,
    ankle, specified type NEC
  calcaneal - *see* Enthesopathy, foot, speci-
    fied type NEC
  collateral ligament, tibial - *see* Bursitis,
    tibial collateral
  due to use, overuse, pressure - *see also*
    Disorder, soft tissue, due to use,
    specified type NEC
  specified NEC - *see* Disorder, soft tissue,
    due to use, specified NEC
  Duplay's M75.0
  elbow NEC M70.3-
    olecranon M70.2-
  finger - *see* Disorder, soft tissue, due to
    use, specified type NEC, hand
  foot - *see* Enthesopathy, foot, specified
    type NEC
  gonococcal A54.49
  gouty - *see* Gout, idiopathic
  hand M70.1-
  hip NEC M70.7-
    trochanteric M70.6-
  infective NEC M71.10
    abscess - *see* Abscess, bursa
    ankle M71.17-
    elbow M71.12-
    foot M71.17-
    hand M71.14-
    hip M71.15-
    knee M71.16-
    multiple sites M71.19
    shoulder M71.11-
    specified site NEC M71.18
    wrist M71.13-
  ischial - *see* Bursitis, hip
  knee NEC M70.5-
    prepatellar M70.4-
  occupational NEC - *see also* Disorder,
    soft tissue, due to, use
  olecranon - *see* Bursitis, elbow,
    olecranon
  pharyngeal J39.1
  popliteal - *see* Bursitis, knee
  prepatellar M70.4-
  radiohumeral M77.8
  rheumatoid M06.20
    ankle M06.27-
    elbow M06.22-
    foot joint M06.27-
    hand joint M06.24-
    hip M06.25-
    knee M06.26-
    multiple site M06.29
    shoulder M06.21-

Bursitis *(Continued)*
  rheumatoid *(Continued)*
    vertebra M06.28
    wrist M06.23-
  scapulohumeral - *see* Bursitis, shoulder
  semimembranous muscle (knee) - *see*
    Bursitis, knee
  shoulder M75.5-
    adhesive - *see* Capsulitis, adhesive
  specified NEC M71.50
    ankle M71.57-
    due to use, overuse or pressure - *see*
      Disorder, soft tissue, due to, use
    elbow M71.52-
    foot M71.57-
    hand M71.54-
    hip M71.55-
    knee M71.56-
    shoulder - *see* Bursitis, shoulder
    specified site NEC M71.58
    tibial collateral M76.4-
    wrist M71.53-
  subacromial - *see* Bursitis, shoulder
  subcoracoid - *see* Bursitis, shoulder
  subdeltoid - *see* Bursitis, shoulder
  syphilitic A52.78
  Thornwaldt, Tornwaldt J39.2
  tibial collateral - *see* Bursitis, tibial
    collateral
  toe - *see* Enthesopathy, foot, specified
    type NEC
  trochanteric (area) - *see* Bursitis, hip,
    trochanteric
  wrist - *see* Bursitis, hand
Bursopathy M71.9
  specified type NEC M71.80
    ankle M71.87-
    elbow M71.82-
    foot M71.87-
    hand M71.84-
    hip M71.85-
    knee M71.86-
    multiple sites M71.89
    shoulder M71.81-
    specified site NEC M71.88
    wrist M71.83-
Burst stitches or sutures (complication of
    surgery) T81.31
  external operation wound T81.31
  internal operation wound T81.32
Buruli ulcer A31.1
Bury's disease L95.1
Buschke's
  disease B45.3
  scleredema - *see* Sclerosis, systemic
Busse-Buschke disease B45.3
Buttock - *see* condition
Button
  Biskra B55.1
  Delhi B55.1
  oriental B55.1
Buttonhole deformity (finger) - *see* Defor-
    mity, finger, boutonniere
Bwamba fever A92.8
Byssinosis J66.0
Bywaters' syndrome T79.5

C

Cachexia R64
 cancerous R64
 cardiac - *see* Disease, heart
 dehydration E86.0
  with
   hypernatremia E87.0
   hyponatremia E87.1
 due to malnutrition R64
 exophthalmic – *see* Hyperthyroidism
 heart - *see* Disease, heart
 hypophyseal E23.0
 hypopituitary E23.0
 lead – *see* Poisoning, lead
 malignant R64
 marsh - *see* Malaria
 nervous F48.8
 old age R54
 paludal - *see* Malaria
 pituitary E23.0
 renal N28.9
 saturnine – *see* Poisoning, lead
 senile R54
 Simmonds' E23.0
 splenica D73.0
 strumipriva E03.4
 tuberculous NEC - *see* Tuberculosis
Café au lait spots L81.3
Caffey's syndrome Q78.8
Caisson disease T70.3
Cake kidney Q63.1
Caked breast (puerperal, postpartum) O92.79
Calabar swelling B74.3
Calcaneal spur - *see* Spur, bone, calcaneal
Calcaneo-apophysitis M92.8
Calcareous - *see* condition
Calcicosis J62.8
Calciferol (vitamin D) deficiency E55.9
 with rickets E55.0
Calcification
 adrenal (capsule) (gland) E27.1
  tuberculous B90.8 *[E35]*
 aorta I70.0
 artery (annular) - *see* Arteriosclerosis
 auricle (ear) - *see* Disorder, pinna, specified type NEC
 basal ganglia G23.8
 bladder N32.89
  due to Schistosoma hematobium B65.0
 brain (cortex) - *see* Calcification, cerebral
 bronchus J98.09
 bursa M71.40
  ankle M71.47-
  elbow M71.42-
  foot M71.47-
  hand M71.44-
  hip M71.45-
  knee M71.46-
  multiple sites M71.49
  shoulder M75.3-
  specified site NEC M71.48
  wrist M71.43-
 cardiac - *see* Degeneration, myocardial
 cerebral (cortex) G93.89
  artery I67.2
 cervix (uteri) N88.8
 choroid plexus G93.89
 conjunctiva - *see* Concretion, conjunctiva

Calcification *(Continued)*
 corpora cavernosa (penis) N48.89
 cortex (brain) - *see* Calcification, cerebral
 dental pulp (nodular) K04.2
 dentinal papilla K00.4
 fallopian tube N83.8
 falx cerebri G96.19
 gallbladder K82.8
 general E83.59
 heart - *see also* Degeneration, myocardial
  valve - *see* Endocarditis
 intervertebral cartilage or disc (postinfective) - *see* Disorder, disc, specified NEC
 intracranial - *see* Calcification, cerebral
 joint - *see* Disorder, joint, specified type NEC
 kidney N28.89
  tuberculous B90.1 *[N29]*
 larynx (senile) J38.7
 lens - *see* Cataract, specified NEC
 lung (active) (postinfectional) J98.4
  tuberculous B90.9
 lymph gland or node (postinfectional) I89.8
  tuberculous (see also Tuberculosis, lymph gland) B90.8
 mammographic R92.1
 massive (paraplegic) - *see* Myositis, ossificans, in, quadriplegia
 medial – *see* Arteriosclerosis, extremities
 meninges (cerebral) (spinal) G96.19
 metastatic E83.59
 Mönckeberg's - *see* Arteriosclerosis, extremities
 muscle M61.9
  due to burns - *see* Myositis, ossificans, in, burns
  paralytic - *see* Myositis, ossificans, in, quadriplegia
  specified type NEC M61.40
   ankle M61.47-
   foot M61.47-
   forearm M61.43-
   hand M61.44-
   lower leg M61.46-
   multiple sites M61.49
   pelvic region M61.45-
   shoulder region M61.41-
   specified site NEC M61.48
   thigh M61.45-
   upper arm M61.42-
 myocardium, myocardial - *see* Degeneration, myocardial
 ovary N83.8
 pancreas K86.8
 penis N48.89
 periarticular - *see* Disorder, joint, specified type NEC
 pericardium (see also Pericarditis) I31.1
 pineal gland E34.8
 pleura J94.8
  postinfectional J94.8
  tuberculous NEC B90.9
 pulpal (dental) (nodular) K04.2
 sclera H15.89
 spleen D73.89
 subcutaneous L94.2
 suprarenal (capsule) (gland) E27.49
 tendon (sheath) - *see also* Tenosynovitis, specified type NEC
  with bursitis, synovitis or tenosynovitis *see* Tendinitis, calcific

Calcification *(Continued)*
 uterus N85.8
 trachea J39.8
 ureter N28.89
 uterus N85.8
 vitreous - *see* Deposit, crystalline
Calcified - *see* Calcification
Calcinosis (interstitial) (tumoral) (universalis) E83.59
 with Raynaud's phenomenon, esophageal dysfunction, sclerodactyly, telangiectasia (CREST syndrome) M34.1
 circumscripta (skin) L94.2
 cutis L94.2
Calciphylaxis (see also Calcification, by site) E83.59
Calcium
 deposits - *see* Calcification, by site
 metabolism disorder E83.50
 salts or soaps in vitreous - *see* Deposit, crystalline
Calciuria R82.99
Calculi - *see* Calculus
Calculosis, intrahepatic – *see* Calculus, bile duct
Calculus, calculi, calculous
 ampulla of Vater - *see* Calculus, bile duct
 anuria (impacted) (recurrent) N20.0
 appendix K38.1
 bile duct (common) (hepatic) K80.50
  with
   calculus of gallbladder – *see* Calculus, gallbladder and bile duct
   cholangitis K80.30
    with
     cholecystitis – *see* Calculus, bile duct, with cholecystitis
     obstruction K80.31
    acute K80.32
     with
      chronic cholangitis K80.36
       with obstruction K80.37
      obstruction K80.33
    chronic K80.34
     with
      acute cholangitis K80.36
       with obstruction K80.37
      obstruction K80.35
   cholecystitis (with cholangitis) K80.40
    with obstruction K80.41
    acute K80.42
     with
      chronic cholecystitis K80.46
       with obstruction K80.47
      obstruction K80.43
    chronic K80.44
     with
      acute cholecystitis K80.46
       with obstruction K80.47
      obstruction K80.45
   obstruction K80.51
  biliary - *see also* Calculus, gallbladder
   specified NEC K80.80
    with obstruction K80.81
  bilirubin, multiple - *see* Calculus, gallbladder
  bladder (encysted) (impacted) (urinary) (diverticulum) N21.0
  bronchus J98.09

Calculus, calculi, calculous *(Continued)*
  calyx (kidney) (renal) - *see* Calculus, kidney
  cholesterol (pure) (solitary) - *see* Calculus, gallbladder
  common duct (bile) - *see* Calculus, bile duct
  conjunctiva - *see* Concretion, conjunctiva
  cystic N21.0
    duct - *see* Calculus, gallbladder
  dental (subgingival) (supragingival) K03.6
  diverticulum
    bladder N21.0
    kidney N20.0
  epididymis N50.8
  gallbladder K80.20
    with
      bile duct calculus – *see* Calculus, gallbladder and bile duct
      cholecystitis K80.10
        with obstruction K80.11
        acute K80.00
          with
            chronic cholecystitis K80.12
              with obstruction K80.13
            obstruction K80.01
        chronic K80.10
          with
            acute cholecystitis K80.12
              with obstruction K80.13
            obstruction K80.11
        specified NEC K80.18
          with obstruction K80.19
      obstruction K80.21
  gallbladder and bile duct K80.70
    with
      cholecystitis K80.60
        with obstruction K80.61
        acute K80.62
          with
            chronic cholecystitis K80.66
              with obstruction K80.67
            obstruction K80.63
        chronic K80.64
          with
            acute cholecystitis K80.66
              with obstruction K80.67
            obstruction K80.65
      obstruction K80.71
  hepatic (duct) - *see* Calculus, bile duct
  ileal conduit N21.8
  intestinal (impaction) (obstruction) K56.4
  kidney (impacted) (multiple) (pelvis) (recurrent) (staghorn) N20.0
    with calculus, ureter N20.2
    congenital Q63.8
  lacrimal passages - *see* Dacryolith
  liver (impacted) - *see* Calculus, bile duct
  lung J98.4
  mammographic R92.1
  nephritic (impacted) (recurrent) - *see* Calculus, kidney
  nose J34.89
  pancreas (duct) K86.8
  parotid duct or gland K11.5
  pelvis, encysted - *see* Calculus, kidney
  prostate N42.0
  pulmonary J98.4
  pyelitis (impacted) (recurrent) N20.0
    with hydronephrosis N13.2

Calculus, calculi, calculous *(Continued)*
  pyelonephritis (impacted) (recurrent) - *see* category N20
    with hydronephrosis N13.2
  renal (impacted) (recurrent) - *see* Calculus, kidney
  salivary (duct) (gland) K11.5
  seminal vesicle N50.8
  staghorn - *see* Calculus, kidney
  Stensen's duct K11.5
  stomach K31.89
  sublingual duct or gland K11.5
    congenital Q38.4
  submandibular duct, gland or region K11.5
  submaxillary duct, gland or region K11.5
  suburethral N21.8
  tonsil J35.8
  tooth, teeth (subgingival) (supra-gingival) K03.6
  tunica vaginalis N50.8
  ureter (impacted) (recurrent) N20.1
    with calculus, kidney N20.2
      with hydronephrosis N13.2
        with infection N13.6
  urethra (impacted) N21.1
  urinary (duct) (impacted) (passage) (tract) N20.9
    with hydronephrosis N13.2
      with infection N13.6
    in (due to)
    lower N21.9
      specified NEC N21.8
  vagina N89.8
  vesical (impacted) N21.0
  Wharton's duct K11.5
  xanthine E79.8 *[N22]*
Calicectasis N28.89
Caliectasis N28.89
California
  disease B38.9
  encephalitis A83.5
Caligo cornea - *see* Opacity, cornea, central
Callositas, callosity (infected) L84
Callus (infected) L84
  bone - *see* Osteophyte
  excessive, following fracture - code as Sequelae of fracture
Calorie deficiency or malnutrition (see also Malnutrition) E46
Calvé-Perthes disease - *see* Legg-Calve-Perthes disease
Calvé's disease - *see* Osteochondrosis, juvenile, spine
Calvities - *see* Alopecia, androgenic
Cameroon fever - *see* Malaria
Camptocormia (hysterical) F44.4
Camurati-Engelmann syndrome Q78.3
Canal - *see also* condition
  atrioventricular common Q21.2
Canaliculitis (lacrimal) (acute) (subacute) H04.33-
  Actinomyces A42.89
  chronic H04.42-
Canavan's disease E75.29
Canceled procedure (surgical) Z53.9
  because of
    contraindication Z53.09
      smoking Z53.01
    left against medical advice (AMA) Z53.21

Canceled procedure *(Continued)*
  because of *(Continued)*
    patient's decision Z53.20
      for reasons of belief or group pressure Z53.1
      specified reason NEC Z53.29
    specified reason NEC Z53.8
Cancer - *see also* Neoplasm, malignant
  bile duct type, liver C22.1
  blood - *see* Leukemia
  hepatocellular C22.0
  unspecified site (primary) (secondary) C80.1
Cancer(o)phobia F45.29
Cancerous - *see* Neoplasm, malignant
Cancrum oris A69.0
Candidiasis, candidal B37.9
  balanitis B37.42
  bronchitis B37.1
  cheilitis B37.83
  congenital P37.5
  cystitis B37.41
  disseminated B37.7
  endocarditis B37.6
  enteritis B37.82
  esophagitis B37.81
  intertrigo B37.2
  lung B37.1
  meningitis B37.5
  mouth B37.0
  nails B37.2
  neonatal P37.5
  onychia B37.2
  oral B37.0
  osteomyelitis B37.89
  otitis externa B37.84
  paronychia B37.2
  perionyxis B37.2
  pneumonia B37.1
  proctitis B37.82
  pulmonary B37.1
  pyelonephritis B37.49
  sepsis B37.7
  skin B37.2
  specified site NEC B37.89
  stomatitis B37.0
  systemic B37.7
  urethritis B37.41
  urogenital site NEC B37.49
  vagina B37.3
  vulva B37.3
  vulvovaginitis B37.3
Candidid L30.2
Candidosis - *see* Candidiasis
Candiru infection or infestation B88.8
Canities (premature) L67.1
  congenital Q84.2
Canker (mouth) (sore) K12.0
  rash A38.9
Cannabinosis J66.2
Canton fever A75.9
Cantrell's syndrome Q87.89
Capillariasis (intestinal) B81.1
  hepatic B83.8
Capillary - *see* condition
Caplan's syndrome - *see* Rheumatoid, lung
Capsule - *see* condition
Capsulitis (joint) - *see also* Enthesopathy
  adhesive (shoulder) M75.0-
  hepatic K65.8
  labyrinthine - *see* Otosclerosis, specified NEC
  thyroid E06.9

Caput
  crepitus Q75.8
  medusae I86.8
  succedaneum P12.81
Car sickness T75.3
Carapata (disease) A68.0
Carate - *see* Pinta
Carbon lung J60
Carboxyhemoglobinemia – *see* Table of
    drugs and chemicals
Carbuncle L02.93
  abdominal wall L02.231
  anus K61.0
  auditory canal, external - *see* Table of
      drugs and chemicals
  auricle ear - *see* Abscess, ear, external
  axilla L02.43-
  back (any part) L02.232
  breast N61
  buttock L02.33
  cheek (external) L02.03
  chest wall L02.233
  chin L02.03
  corpus cavernosum N48.21
  ear (any part) (external) (middle) - *see*
      Abscess, ear, external
  external auditory canal - *see* Abscess,
      ear, external
  eyelid - *see* Abscess, eyelid
  face NEC L02.03
  femoral (region) - *see* Carbuncle, lower
      limb
  finger - *see* Carbuncle, hand
  flank L02.231
  foot L02.63-
  forehead L02.03
  genital – *see* Abscess, genital
  gluteal (region) L02.33
  groin L02.234
  hand L02.53-
  head NEC L02.831
  heel - *see* Carbuncle, foot
  hip - *see* Carbuncle, lower limb
  kidney - *see* Abscess, kidney
  knee - *see* Carbuncle, lower limb
  labium (majus) (minus) N76.4
  lacrimal
      gland - *see* Dacryoadenitis
      passages (duct) (sac) - *see*
          Inflammation, lacrimal,
          passages, acute
  leg - *see* Carbuncle, lower limb
  lower limb L02.43-
  malignant A22.0
  multiple sites L02.93
  navel L02.236
  neck L02.13
  nose (external) (septum) J34.0
  orbit, orbital - *see* Abscess, orbit
  palmar (space) - *see* Carbuncle,
      hand
  partes posteriores L02.33
  pectoral region L02.233
  penis N48.21
  perineum L02.235
  pinna - *see* Abscess, ear, external
  popliteal - *see* Carbuncle, lower limb
  scalp L02.831
  seminal vesicle N49.0
  shoulder - *see* Carbuncle, upper limb
  specified site NEC L02.838
  temple (region) L02.03
  thumb - *see* Carbuncle, hand
  toe - *see* Carbuncle, foot

Carbuncle *(Continued)*
  trunk L02.239
    abdominal wall L02.231
    back L02.232
    chest wall L02.233
    groin L02.234
    perineum L02.235
    umbilicus L02.236
  umbilicus L02.236
  upper limb L02.43-
  urethra N34.0
  vulva N76.4
Carbunculus – *see* Carbuncle
Carcinoid (tumor) - *see* Tumor,
    carcinoid
Carcinoidosis E34.0
Carcinoma (malignant) - *see also*
    Neoplasm
  acidophil
    specified site - *see* Neoplasm,
        malignant
    unspecified site C75.1
  acidophil-basophil, mixed
    specified site - *see* Neoplasm,
        malignant
    unspecified site C75.1
  adnexal (skin) - *see* Neoplasm, skin,
      malignant
  adrenal cortical C74.0-
  alveolar - *see* Neoplasm, lung,
      malignant
    cell - *see* Neoplasm, lung, malignant
  ameloblastic C41.1
    upper jaw (bone) C41.0
  apocrine
    breast - *see* Neoplasm, breast,
        malignant
    specified site NEC - *see* Neoplasm,
        skin, malignant
    unspecified site C44.9
  basal cell (pigmented) - *see also* Neo-
      plasm, skin, malignant
    fibro-epithelial - *see* Neoplasm, skin,
        malignant
    morphea - *see* Neoplasm, skin,
        malignant
    multicentric - *see* Neoplasm, skin,
        malignant
  basaloid
  basal-squamous cell, mixed - *see* Neo-
      plasm, skin, malignant
  basophil
    specified site - *see* Neoplasm,
        malignant
    unspecified site C75.1
  basophil-acidophil, mixed
    specified site - *see* Neoplasm,
        malignant
    unspecified site C75.1
  basosquamous - *see* Neoplasm, skin,
      malignant
  bile duct
    with hepatocellular, mixed C22.0
    liver C22.1
    specified site NEC - *see* Neoplasm,
        malignant
    unspecified site C22.1
  branchial or branchiogenic C10.4
  bronchial or bronchogenic - *see* Neo-
      plasm, lung, malignant
  bronchiolar - *see* Neoplasm, lung,
      malignant
  bronchioloalveolar - *see* Neoplasm,
      lung, malignant

Carcinoma *(Continued)*
  C cell
    specified site - *see* Neoplasm,
        malignant
    unspecified site C73
  ceruminous C44.2-
  cervix uteri
    in situ D06.9
      endocervix D06.0
      exocervix D06.1
      specified site NEC D06.7
  chorionic
    specified site - *see* Neoplasm,
        malignant
    unspecified site
      female C58
      male C62.90
  chromophobe
    specified site - *see* Neoplasm,
        malignant
    unspecified site C75.1
  cloacogenic
    specified site - *see* Neoplasm,
        malignant
    unspecified site C21.2
  diffuse type
    specified site - *see* Neoplasm,
        malignant
    unspecified site C16.9
  duct (cell)
    with Paget's disease - *see* Neoplasm,
        breast, malignant
    infiltrating
      with lobular carcinoma (in situ)
        specified site - *see* Neoplasm,
            malignant
        unspecified site (female)
            C50.91-
          male C50.92-
      specified site - *see* Neoplasm,
          malignant
      unspecified site (female) C50.91-
        male C50.92-
  ductal
    with lobular
      specified site - *see* Neoplasm,
          malignant
      unspecified site (female) C50.91-
        male C50.92-
  ductular, infiltrating
    specified site - *see* Neoplasm,
        malignant
    unspecified site (female) C50.91-
      male C50.92-
  embryonal
    liver C22.7
  endometrioid
    specified site - *see* Neoplasm,
        malignant
    unspecified site
      female C56.9
      male C61
  eosinophil
    specified site - *see* Neoplasm,
        malignant
    unspecified site C75.1
  epidermoid - *see also* Carcinoma, squa-
      mous cell
    in situ, Bowen's type - *see* Neoplasm,
        skin, in situ
  fibroepithelial, basal cell - *see* Neo-
      plasm, skin, malignant
  follicular
    with papillary (mixed) C73

Carcinoma *(Continued)*
  follicular *(Continued)*
    moderately differentiated C73
    pure follicle C73
    specified site - *see* Neoplasm,
      malignant
    trabecular C73
    unspecified site C73
    well differentiated C73
  generalized, with unspecified primary
    site C80.0
  glycogen-rich - *see* Neoplasm, breast,
    malignant
  granulosa cell C56.-
  hepatic cell C22.0
  hepatocellular C22.0
    with bile duct, mixed C22.0
    fibrolamellar C22.0
  hepatocholangiolitic C22.0
  Hurthle cell C73
  in
    adenomatous
      polyposis coli C18.9
    pleomorphic adenoma - *see* Neoplasm,
      salivary glands, malignant
    situ - *see* Carcinoma-in-situ
  infiltrating
    duct
      with lobular
        specified site - *see* Neoplasm,
          malignant
        unspecified site (female) C50.91-
          male C50.92-
      with Paget's disease - *see* Neo-
        plasm, breast, malignant
      specified site - *see* Neoplasm,
        malignant
      unspecified site (female) C50.91-
        male C50.92-
    ductural
      specified site - *see* Neoplasm,
        malignant
      unspecified site (female) C50.91-
        male C50.92-
    lobular
      specified site - *see* Neoplasm,
        malignant
      unspecified site (female) C50.91-
        male C50.92-
  inflammatory
    specified site - *see* Neoplasm,
      malignant
    unspecified site (female) C50.91-
      male C50.92-
  intestinal type
    specified site - *see* Neoplasm,
      malignant
    unspecified site C16.9
  intracystic
    noninfiltrating - *see* Neoplasm, in situ
  intraductal (noninfiltrating)
    with Paget's disease - *see* Neoplasm,
      breast, malignant
    breast D05.1-
    papillary
      with invasion
        specified site - *see* Neoplasm,
          malignant
        unspecified site (female) C50.91-
          male C50.92-
      breast D05.1-
      specified site NEC - *see* Neoplasm,
        in situ
      unspecified site (female) D05.1-

Carcinoma *(Continued)*
  intraductal *(Continued)*
    specified site NEC - *see* Neoplasm,
      in situ
    unspecified site (female) D05.1-
  intraepidermal - *see* Neoplasm, in situ
    squamous cell, Bowen's type - *see*
      Neoplasm, skin, in situ
  intraepithelial - *see* Neoplasm, in situ
    squamous cell - *see* Neoplasm, in situ
  intraosseous C41.1
    upper jaw (bone) C41.0
  islet cell
    with exocrine, mixed
      specified site - *see* Neoplasm,
        malignant
      unspecified site C25.9
    pancreas C25.4
    specified site NEC - *see* Neoplasm,
      malignant
    unspecified site C25.4
  juvenile, breast - *see* Neoplasm, breast,
    malignant
  large cell
    small cell
      specified site - *see* Neoplasm,
        malignant
      unspecified site C34.90
  Leydig cell (testis)
    specified site - *see* Neoplasm, malignant
    unspecified site
      female C56.9
      male C62.90
  lipid-rich (female) C50.91-
    male C50.92-
  liver cell C22.0
  lobular (infiltrating)
    with intraductal
      specified site - *see* Neoplasm,
        malignant
      unspecified site (female)
        C50.91-
        male C50.92-
    noninfiltrating
      breast D05.0-
      specified site NEC - *see* Neoplasm,
        in situ
      unspecified site D05.0-
    specified site - *see* Neoplasm,
      malignant
    unspecified site (female) C50.91-
      male C50.92-
  medullary
    with
      amyloid stroma
        specified site - *see* Neoplasm,
          malignant
        unspecified site C73
      lymphoid stroma
        specified site - *see* Neoplasm,
          malignant
        unspecified site (female)
          C50.91-
          male C50.92-
  Merkel cell C4a.9
    anal margin C4a.51
    anal skin C4a.51
    canthus C4a.1-
    ear and external auricular canal
      C4a.2-
    external auricular canal C4a.2-
    eyelid, including canthus C4a.1-
    face C4a.30
      specified NEC C4a.39

Carcinoma *(Continued)*
  Merkel cell *(Continued)*
    hip C4a.7-
    lip C4a.0
    lower limb, including hip C4a.7-
    neck C4a.4
    nodal presentation C7b.1
    nose C4a.31
    overlapping sites C4a.8
    perianal skin C4a.51
    scalp C4a.4
    secondary C7b.1
    shoulder C4a.6-
    skin of breast C4a.52
    trunk NEC C4a.59
    upper limb, including shoulder C4a.6-
    visceral metastatic C7b.1
  metastatic - *see* Neoplasm, secondary
  metatypical - *see* Neoplasm, skin,
    malignant
  morphea, basal cell - *see* Neoplasm,
    skin, malignant
  mucoid
    cell
      specified site - *see* Neoplasm,
        malignant
      unspecified site C75.1
  neuroendocrine - *see also* Tumor,
    neuroendocrine
    high grade, any site C7a.1
    poorly differentiated, any site C7a.1
  nonencapsulated sclerosing C73
  noninfiltrating
    intracystic - *see* Neoplasm, in situ
    intraducta
      breast D05.1-
      papillary
        breast D05.1-
        specified site NEC - *see* Neoplasm,
          in situ
        unspecified site D05.1-
      specified site - *see* Neoplasm, in situ
      unspecified site D05.1-
    lobular
      breast D05.0-
      specified site NEC - *see* Neoplasm,
        in situ
      unspecified site (female) D05.1-
  oat cell
    specified site - *see* Neoplasm, malignant
    unspecified site C34.90
  odontogenic C41.1
    upper jaw (bone) C41.0
  papillary
    with follicular (mixed) C73
    follicular variant C73
    intraductal (noninfiltrating)
      with invasion
        specified site - *see* Neoplasm,
          malignant
        unspecified site (female) C50.91-
          male C50.92-
      breast D05.1-
      specified site NEC - *see* Neoplasm,
        in situ
      unspecified site D05.1-
    serous
      specified site - *see* Neoplasm,
        malignant
      surface
        specified site - *see* Neoplasm,
          malignant
        unspecified site C56.9
      unspecified site C56.9

Carcinoma *(Continued)*
papillocystic
specified site - *see* Neoplasm,
malignant
unspecified site C56.9
parafollicular cell
specified site - *see* Neoplasm,
malignant
unspecified site C73
pilomatrix - *see* Neoplasm, skin,
malignant
pseudomucinous
specified site - *see* Neoplasm,
malignant
unspecified site C56.9
renal cell C64.-
Schmincke - *see* Neoplasm, nasopharynx, malignant
Schneiderian
specified site - *see* Neoplasm,
malignant
unspecified site C30.0
sebaceous - *see* Neoplasm, skin,
malignant
secondary - *see also* Neoplasm,
secondary
Merkel cell C7b.1
secretory, breast - *see* Neoplasm, breast,
malignant
serous
papillary
specified site - *see* Neoplasm,
malignant
unspecified site C56.9
surface, papillary
specified site - *see* Neoplasm,
malignant
unspecified site C56.9
Sertoli cell
specified site - *see* Neoplasm,
malignant
unspecified site C62.90
female C56.9
male C62.90
skin appendage - *see* Neoplasm, skin,
malignant
small cell
fusiform cell
specified site - *see* Neoplasm, malignant
unspecified site C34.90
intermediate cell
specified site - *see* Neoplasm,
malignant
unspecified site C34.90
large cell
specified site - *see* Neoplasm,
malignant
unspecified site C34.90
solid
with amyloid stroma
specified site - *see* Neoplasm,
malignant
unspecified site C73
microinvasive
specified site - *see* Neoplasm,
malignant
unspecified site C53.9
sweat gland - *see* Neoplasm, skin,
malignant
theca cell C56.-
thymic C37
unspecified site (primary) (secondary)
C80.1
water-clear cell C75.0

Carcinoma-in-situ - *see also* Neoplasm,
in situ
breast NOS D05.9-
specified type NEC D05.7-
epidermoid - *see also* Neoplasm, in situ
with questionable stromal invasion
cervix D06.9
specified site NEC - *see* Neoplasm,
in situ
unspecified site D06.9
Bowen's type - *see* Neoplasm, skin,
in situ
intraductal
breast D05.1-
specified site NEC - *see* Neoplasm,
in situ
unspecified site D05.1-
lobular
with
infiltrating duct
breast (female) C50.91-
male C50.92-
specified site NEC - *see* Neoplasm, malignant
unspecified site (female) C50.91-
male C50.92-
intraductal
breast D05.7-
specified site NEC - *see* Neoplasm, in situ
unspecified site (female) D05.7-
breast D05.0-
specified site NEC - *see* Neoplasm,
in situ
unspecified site D05.0-
squamous cell - *see also* Neoplasm, in
situ
with questionable stromal invasion
cervix D06.9
specified site NEC - *see* Neoplasm,
in situ
unspecified site D06.9
Carcinomaphobia F45.29
Carcinomatosis C80.0
peritonei C78.6
unspecified site (primary) (secondary)
C80.0
Carcinosarcoma - *see* Neoplasm,
malignant, by site
embryonal - *see* Neoplasm, malignant,
by site
Cardia, cardial - *see* condition
Cardiac - *see also* condition
death, sudden – *see* Arrest, cardiac
pacemaker
in situ Z95.0
management or adjustment
Z45.018
tamponade I31.4
Cardialgia - *see* Pain, precordial
Cardiectasis - *see* Hypertrophy, cardiac
Cardiochalasia K21.9
Cardiomalacia I51.5
Cardiomegalia glycogenica diffusa
E74.02 *[I43]*
Cardiomegaly - *see also* Hypertrophy,
cardiac
congenital Q24.8
glycogen E74.02 *[I43]*
idiopathic I51.7
Cardiomyoliposis I51.5
Cardiomyopathy (familial) (idiopathic)
I42.9
alcoholic I42.6

Cardiomyopathy *(Continued)*
amyloid E85.4 *[I43]*
arteriosclerotic – *see* Disease, heart,
ischemic, atherosclerotic
beriberi E51.12
cobalt-beer I42.6
congenital I42.4
congestive I42.0
constrictive NOS I42.5
dilated I42.0
due to
alcohol I42.6
beriberi E51.12
cardiac glycogenosis E74.02 *[I43]*
drugs I42.7
Friedreich's ataxia G11.1
external agents NEC I42.7
myotonia atrophica G71.19 *[I43]*
progressive muscular dystrophy
G71.0
glycogen storage E74.02 *[I43]*
hypertensive - *see* Hypertension, heart
hypertrophic (nonobstructive) I42.2
obstructive I42.1
congenital Q24.8
in
Chagas' disease (chronic) B57.2
acute B57.0
sarcoidosis D86.85
ischemic I25.5
metabolic E88.9 *[I43]*
thyrotoxic E05.90 *[I43]*
with thyroid storm E05.91 *[I43]*
newborn I42.8
congenital I42.4
nutritional E63.9 *[I43]*
beriberi E51.12
obscure of Africa I42.8
peripartum O90.3
postpartum O90.3
restrictive NEC I42.5
rheumatic I09.0
secondary I42.9
stress induced I51.81
takotsubo I51.81
thyrotoxic E05.90 *[I43]*
with thyroid storm E05.91 *[I43]*
toxic NEC I42.7
tuberculous A18.84
viral B33.24
Cardionephritis - *see* Hypertension,
cardiorenal
Cardionephropathy - *see* Hypertension,
cardiorenal
Cardionephrosis - *see* Hypertension,
cardiorenal
Cardiopathia nigra I27.0
Cardiopathy (see also Disease, heart)
I51.9
idiopathic I42.9
mucopolysaccharidosis E76.3 *[I52]*
Cardiopericarditis - *see* Pericarditis
Cardiophobia F45.29
Cardiorenal - *see* condition
Cardiorrhexis - *see* Infarct, myocardium
Cardiosclerosis – *see* Disease, heart, isch-
emic, atherosclerotic
Cardiosis - *see* Disease, heart
Cardiospasm (esophagus) (reflex) (stom-
ach) K22.0
congenital Q39.5
with megaesophagus Q39.5
Cardiostenosis - *see* Disease, heart
Cardiosymphysis I31.0

Cardiovascular - *see* condition
Carditis (acute) (bacterial) (chronic) (subacute) I51.89
  meningococcal A39.50
  rheumatic - *see* Disease, heart, rheumatic
  rheumatoid - *see* Rheumatoid, carditis
  viral B33.20
Care (of) (for) (following)
  child (routine) Z76.2
  family member (handicapped) (sick)
    creating problem for family Z63.6
    provided away from home for holi-
      day relief Z75.5
    unavailable, due to
      absence (person rendering care)
        (sufferer) Z74.2
      inability (any reason) of person
        rendering care Z74.2
  foundling Z76.1
  holiday relief Z75.5
  improper – *see* Maltreatment
  lack of (at or after birth) (infant) – *see*
    Maltreatment, child, neglect
  lactating mother Z39.1
  palliative Z51.5
  postpartum
    immediately after delivery Z39.0
    routine follow-up Z39.2
  respite Z75.5
  unavailable, due to
    absence of person rendering care Z74.2
    inability (any reason) of person ren-
      dering care Z74.2
  well-baby Z76.2
Caries
  bone NEC A18.03
  dental K02.9
    arrested (coronal) (root) K02.3
    chewing surface
      limited to enamel K02.51
      penetrating into dentin K02.52
      penetrating into pulp K02.53
    coronal surface
      chewing surface
        limited to enamel K02.51
        penetrating into dentin K02.52
        penetrating into pulp K02.53
      pit and fissure surface
        limited to enamel K02.51
        penetrating into dentin K02.52
        penetrating into pulp K02.53
      smooth surface
        limited to enamel K02.61
        penetrating into dentin K02.62
        penetrating into pulp K02.63
    pit and fissure surface
      limited to enamel K02.51
      penetrating into dentin K02.52
      penetrating into pulp K02.53
    smooth surface
      limited to enamel K02.61
      penetrating into dentin K02.62
      penetrating into pulp K02.63
    root K02.7
  external meatus - *see* Disorder, ear,
    external, specified type NEC
  hip (tuberculous) A18.02
  initial (tooth)
    chewing surface K02.51
    pit and fissure surface K02.51
    smooth surface K02.61
  knee (tuberculous) A18.02
  labyrinth - *see* subcategory H83.8
  limb NEC (tuberculous) A18.03

Caries *(Continued)*
  mastoid process (chronic) – *see* Mastoid-
    itis, chronic
    tuberculous A18.03
  middle ear - *see* subcategory H74.8
  nose (tuberculous) A18.03
  orbit (tuberculous) A18.03
  ossicles, ear - *see* Abnormal, ear ossicles
  petrous bone – *see* Petrositis
  root (dental) (tooth) K02.7
  sacrum (tuberculous) A18.01
  spine, spinal (column) (tuberculous)
    A18.01
  syphilitic A52.77
    congenital (early) A50.02 *[M90.80]*
  tooth, teeth - *see* Caries, dental
  tuberculous A18.03
  vertebra (column) (tuberculous) A18.01
Carious teeth - *see* Caries, dental
Carneous mole O02.0
Carnitine insufficiency E71.40
Carotid body or sinus syndrome G90.01
Carotidynia G90.01
Carotinemia (dietary) E67.1
Carotinosis (cutis) (skin) E67.1
Carpal tunnel syndrome – *see* Syndrome,
  carpal tunnel
Carpenter's syndrome Q87.0
Carpopedal spasm - *see* Tetany
Carr-Barr-Plunkett syndrome Q97.1
Carrier (suspected) of
  amebiasis Z22.1
  bacterial disease NEC Z22.39
    diphtheria Z22.2
    intestinal infectious NEC Z22.1
      typhoid Z22.0
    meningococcal Z22.31
    sexually transmitted Z22.4
    specified NEC Z22.39
    staphylococcal Z22.32
    streptococcal Z22.338
      group B Z22.330
    typhoid Z22.0
  cholera Z22.1
  diphtheria Z22.2
  gastrointestinal pathogens NEC Z22.1
  genetic Z14.8
    cystic fibrosis Z14.1
    hemophilia A (asymptomatic) Z14.01
      symptomatic Z14.02
  gonorrhea Z22.4
  HAA (hepatitis Australian-antigen)
    Z22.59
  HB(c)(s)-AG Z22.51
  hepatitis (viral) Z22.50
    Australia-antigen (HAA) Z22.59
    B surface antigen (HBsAg) Z22.51
      with acute delta-(super)infection
        B17.0
    C Z22.52
    specified NEC Z22.59
  human T-cell lymphotropic virus type-1
    (HTLV-1) infection Z22.6
  infectious organism Z22.9
    specified NEC Z22.8
  meningococci Z22.31
  Salmonella typhosa Z22.0
  serum hepatitis – *see* Carrier, hepatitis
  staphylococci Z22.32
  streptococci Z22.338
    group B Z22.330
  syphilis Z22.4
  typhoid Z22.0
  venereal disease NEC Z22.4

Carrion's disease A44.0
Carter's relapsing fever (Asiatic) A68.1
Cartilage - *see* condition
Caruncle (inflamed)
  conjunctiva (acute) - *see* Conjunctivitis,
    acute
  labium (majus) (minus) N90.8
  lacrimal - *see* Inflammation, lacrimal,
    passages
  myrtiform N89.8
  urethral (benign) N36.2
Cascade stomach K31.2
Caseation lymphatic gland (tuberculous)
  A18.2
Cassidy (-Scholte) syndrome (malignant
  carcinoid) E34.0
Castellani's disease A69.8
Castration, traumatic, male S38.231
Casts in urine R82.99
Cat
  cry syndrome Q93.4
  ear Q17.3
Catabolism, senile R54
Catalepsy (hysterical) F44.2
  schizophrenic F20.2
Cataplexy (idiopathic) *see* - Narcolepsy
Cataract (cortical) (immature) (incipient)
  H26.9
  with
    neovascularization – *see* Cataract,
      complicated
  age-related - *see* Cataract, senile
  anterior
    and posterior axial embryonal Q12.0
    pyramidal Q12.0
  associated with
    galactosemia E74.21 *[H28]*
    myotonic disorders G71.19 *[H28]*
  blue Q12.0
  central Q12.0
  cerulean Q12.0
  complicated H26.20
    with
      neovascularization H26.21-
      ocular disorder H26.22-
      glaucomatous flecks H26.23-
  congenital Q12.0
  coraliform Q12.0
  coronary Q12.0
  crystalline Q12.0
  diabetic – *see* Diabetes, cataract
  drug-induced H26.3-
  due to
    ocular disorder – *see* Cataract,
      complicated
    radiation H26.8
  electric H26.8
  extraction status Z98.4-
  glass-blower's H26.8
  heat ray H26.8
  heterochromic - *see* Cataract,
    complicated
  hypermature - *see* Cataract, senile,
    morgagnian type
  in (due to)
    chronic iridocyclitis - *see* Cataract,
      complicated
    diabetes – *see* Diabetes, cataract
    endocrine disease E34.9 *[H28]*
    eye disease - *see* Cataract,
      complicated
    hypoparathyroidism E20.9 *[H28]*
    malnutrition-dehydration E46 *[H28]*
    metabolic disease E88.9 *[H28]*

Cataract *(Continued)*
  chronic iridocyclitis *(Continued)*
    myotonic disorders G71.19 *[H28]*
    nutritional disease E63.9 *[H28]*
  infantile - *see* Cataract, presenile
  irradiational - *see* Cataract, specified
      NEC
  juvenile - *see* Cataract, presenile
  malnutrition-dehydration E46 *[H28]*
  morgagnian - *see* Cataract, senile, mor-
      gagnian type
  myotonic G71.19 *[H28]*
  myxedema E03.9 *[H28]*
  nuclear
    embryonal Q12.0
    sclerosis - *see* Cataract, senile, nuclear
  presenile H26.00-
    combined forms H26.06-
    cortical H26.01-
    lamellar - *see* Cataract, presenile,
        cortical
    nuclear H26.03-
    specified NEC H26.09
    subcapsular polar (anterior) H26.04-
      posterior H26.05-
      zonular - *see* Cataract, presenile,
          cortical
  secondary H26.40
    Soemmering's ring H26.41-
    specified NEC H26.49-
    to eye disease - *see* Cataract,
        complicated
  senile H25.9
    brunescens - *see* Cataract, senile,
        nuclear
    combined forms H25.81-
    coronary - *see* Cataract, senile,
        incipient
    cortical H25.01-
    hypermature - *see* Cataract, senile,
        morgagnian type
    incipient (mature) (total) H25.09-
      cortical - *see* Cataract, senile,
          cortical
      subcapsular - *see* Cataract, senile,
          subcapsular
    morgagnian type (hypermature)
        H25.2-
    nuclear (sclerosis) H25.1-
    polar subcapsular (anterior) (pos-
        terior) - *see* Cataract, senile,
        incipient
    punctate - *see* Cataract, senile,
        incipient
    specified NEC H25.89
    subcapsular polar (anterior) H25.03-
      posterior H25.04-
  snowflake – *see* Diabetes, cataract
  specified NEC H26.8
  toxic - *see* Cataract, drug-induced
  traumatic H26.10-
    localized H26.11-
    partially resolved H26.12-
    total H26.13-
  zonular (perinuclear) Q12.0
Cataracta - *see also* Cataract
  brunescens - *see* Cataract, senile,
      nuclear
  centralis pulverulenta Q12.0
  cerulea Q12.0
  complicata - *see* Cataract, complicated
  congenita Q12.0
  coralliformis Q12.0
  coronaria Q12.0

Cataracta *(Continued)*
  diabetic – *see* Diabetes, cataract
  membranacea
    accreta - *see* Cataract, secondary
    congenita Q12.0
  nigra – *see* Cataract, senile, nuclear
  sunflower - *see* Cataract, complicated
Catarrh, catarrhal (acute) (febrile) (infec-
    tious) (inflammation) (see also
    condition) J00
  bronchial - *see* Bronchitis
  chest – *see* Bronchitis
  chronic J31.0
  due to congenital syphilis A50.03
  enteric - *see* Enteritis
  eustachian H68.009
  fauces - *see* Pharyngitis
  gastrointestinal - *see* Enteritis
  gingivitis K05.00
    plaque induced K05.00
    nonplaque induced K05.01
  hay - *see* Fever, hay
  intestinal - *see* Enteritis
  larynx, chronic J37.0
  liver B15.9
    with hepatic coma B15.0
  lung – *see* Bronchitis
  middle ear, chronic - *see* Otitis, media,
      nonsuppurative, chronic, serous
  mouth K12.1
  nasal (chronic) - *see* Rhinitis
  nasobronchial J31.1
  nasopharyngeal (chronic) J31.1
    acute J00
  pulmonary – *see* Bronchitis
  spring (eye) (vernal) - *see* Conjunctivitis,
      acute, atopic
  summer (hay) - *see* Fever, hay
  throat J31.2
  tubotympanal - *see also* Otitis, media,
      nonsuppurative
    chronic - *see* Otitis, media, nonsuppu-
        rative, chronic, serous
Catatonia (schizophrenic) F20.2
Catatonic
  disorder due to known physiologic
      condition F06.1
  schizophrenia F20.2
  stupor R40.1
Cat-scratch - *see also* Abrasion
  disease or fever A28.1
Cauda equina - *see* condition
Cauliflower ear M95.1-
Causalgia (upper limb) G56.4-
  lower limb G57.7-
Cause
  external, general effects T75.89
  not stated (morbidity) R69
  unknown (morbidity) R69
Caustic burn - *see* Corrosion, by site
Cavare's disease (familial periodic paraly-
    sis) G72.3
Cave-in, injury
  crushing (severe) - *see* Crush
  suffocation - *see* Asphyxia, traumatic,
      due to low oxygen, due to
      cave-in
Cavernitis (penis) N48.29
Cavernositis N48.29
Cavernous - *see* condition
Cavitation of lung - *see also* Tuberculosis,
    pulmonary
  nontuberculous J98.4
Cavities, dental - *see* Caries, dental

Cavity
  lung - *see* Cavitation of lung
  optic papilla Q14.2
  pulmonary - *see* Cavitation of lung
Cavovarus foot, congenital Q66.1
Cavus foot (congenital) Q66.7
  acquired - *see* Deformity, limb, foot,
      specified NEC
Cazenave's disease L10.2
Cecitis K52.9
  with perforation, peritonitis, or rupture
      K65.8
Cecum - *see* condition
Celiac
  artery compression syndrome I77.4
  disease K90.0
  infantilism K90.0
Cell(s), cellular - *see also* condition
  in urine R82.99
Cellulitis (diffuse) (phlegmonous) (septic)
    (suppurative) L03.90
  abdominal wall L03.311
  anaerobic A48.0
  ankle - *see* Cellulitis, lower limb
  anus K61.0
  arm - *see* Cellulitis, upper limb
  auricle (ear) - *see* Cellulitis, ear
  axilla L03.11-
  back (any part) L03.312
  broad ligament
    acute N73.0
  buttock L03.317
  cervical (meaning neck) L03.221
  cervix (uteri) - *see* Cervicitis
  cheek (external) L03.211
    internal K12.2
  chest wall L03.313
  chronic L03.90
  clostridial A48.0
  corpus cavernosum N48.22
  digit
    finger - *see* Cellulitis, finger
    toe - *see* Cellulitis, toe
  Douglas' cul-de-sac or pouch
    acute N73.0
  drainage site (following operation)
      T81.4
  ear (external) H60.1-
  eosinophilic (granulomatous) L98.3
  erysipelatous - *see* Erysipelas
  external auditory canal - *see* Cellulitis,
      ear
  eyelid - *see* Abscess, eyelid
  face NEC L03.211
  finger (intrathecal) (periosteal) (subcu-
      taneous) (subcuticular) L03.01-
  foot - *see* Cellulitis, lower limb
  gangrenous - *see* Gangrene
  genital organ NEC
    female (external) N76.4
    male N49.9
      multiple sites N49.8
      specified NEC N49.8
  gluteal (region) L03.317
  gonococcal A54.89
  groin L03.314
  hand - *see* Cellulitis, upper limb
  head NEC L03.811
    face (any part, except ear, eye and
        nose) L03.211
  heel - *see* Cellulitis, lower limb
  hip - *see* Cellulitis, lower limb
  jaw (region) L03.211
  knee - *see* Cellulitis, lower limb

Cellulitis (Continued)
labium (majus) (minus) - see Vulvitis
lacrimal passages - see Inflammation,
  lacrimal, passages
larynx J38.7
leg - see Cellulitis, lower limb
lip K13.0
lower limb L03.11-
  toe - see Cellulitis, toe
mouth (floor) K12.2
multiple sites, so stated L03.90
nasopharynx J39.1
navel L03.316
  newborn P38.9
    with mild hemorrhage P38.1
    without hemorrhage P38.9
neck (region) L03.221
nose (septum) (external) J34.0
orbit, orbital H05.01-
palate (soft) K12.2
pectoral (region) L03.313
pelvis, pelvic (chronic)
  female (see also Disease, pelvis,
    inflammatory) N73.2
    acute N73.0
  following ectopic or molar
    pregnancy O08.0
  male K65.0
penis N48.22
perineal, perineum L03.315
perirectal K61.1
peritonsillar J36
periurethral N34.0
periuterine (see also Disease, pelvis,
  inflammatory) N73.2
    acute N73.0
pharynx J39.1
rectum K61.1
retroperitoneal K68.9
round ligament
  acute N73.0
scalp (any part) L03.811
scrotum N49.2
seminal vesicle N49.0
shoulder - see Cellulitis, upper limb
specified site NEC L03.818
submandibular (region) (space)
    (triangle) K12.2
  gland K11.3
submaxillary (region) K12.2
  gland K11.3
thigh - see Cellulitis, lower limb
thumb (intrathecal) (periosteal)
    (subcutaneous) (subcuticular) -
    see Cellulitis, finger
toe (intrathecal) (periosteal) (subcutane-
    ous) (subcuticular) L03.03-
tonsil J36
trunk L03.319
  abdominal wall L03.311
  back (any part) L03.312
  buttock L03.317
  chest wall L03.313
  groin L03.314
  perineal, perineum L03.315
  umbilicus L03.316
tuberculous (primary) A18.4
umbilicus L03.316
upper limb L03.11-
  axilla - see Cellulitis, axilla
  finger - see Cellulitis, finger
  thumb - see Cellulitis, finger
vaccinal T88.0
vocal cord J38.3

Cellulitis (Continued)
vulva - see Vulvitis
wrist - see Cellulitis, upper limb
Cementoblastoma, benign - see Cyst,
  calcifying odontogenic
Cementoma - see Cyst, calcifying
  odontogenic
Cementoperiostitis - see Periodontitis
Cementosis K03.4
Central auditory processing disorder
  H93.25
Central pain syndrome G89.0
Cephalematocele, cephal(o)hematocele
  newborn P52.8
    birth injury P10.8
  traumatic – see Hematoma, brain
Cephalematoma, cephalhematoma
    (calcified)
  newborn (birth injury) P12.0
  traumatic – see Hematoma, brain
Cephalgia, cephalalgia - see also Headache
  histamine G44.009
    intractable G44.001
    not intractable G44.009
  trigeminal autonomic (TAC) NEC
    G44.099
    intractable G44.091
    not intractable G44.099
Cephalic - see condition
Cephalitis - see Encephalitis
Cephalocele - see Encephalocele
Cephalomenia N94.89
Cephalopelvic - see condition
Cerclage (with cervical incompetence)
    in pregnancy –see Incompetence,
    cervix, in pregnancy
Cerebellitis - see Encephalitis
Cerebellum, cerebellar - see condition
Cerebral - see condition
Cerebritis - see Encephalitis
Cerebro-hepato-renal syndrome Q87.89
Cerebromalacia - see Softening, brain
Cerebroside lipidosis E75.22
Cerebrospasticity (congenital) G80.1
Cerebrospinal - see condition
Cerebrum - see condition
Ceroid-lipofuscinosis, neuronal E75.4
Cerumen (accumulation) (impacted)
  H61.2-
Cervical - see also condition
  auricle Q18.2
  dysplasia in pregnancy – see Abnormal,
    cervix, in pregnancy or childbirth
  erosion in pregnancy – see Abnormal,
    cervix, in pregnancy or childbirth
  fibrosis in pregnancy – see Abnormal,
    cervix, in pregnancy or childbirth
  fusion syndrome Q76.1
  rib Q76.5
  shortening (complicating pregnancy)
    O26.87-
Cervicalgia M54.2
Cervicitis (acute) (chronic) (nonvenereal)
    (senile (atrophic)) (subacute) (with
    ulceration) N72
  with
    abortion – see Abortion, by type
      complicated by genital tract and
      pelvic infection
    ectopic pregnancy O08.0
    molar pregnancy O08.0
  chlamydial A56.09
  gonococcal A54.03
  herpesviral A60.03

Cervicitis (Continued)
puerperal (postpartum) O86.11
syphilitic A52.76
trichomonal A59.09
tuberculous A18.16
Cervicocolpitis (emphysematosa) (see
  also Cervicitis) N72
Cervix - see condition
Cesarean delivery, previous, affecting
  management of pregnancy O34.21
Céstan(-Chenais) paralysis or syndrome
  G46.3
Céstan-Raymond syndrome I65.8
Cestode infestation B71.9
  specified type NEC B71.8
Cestodiasis B71.9
Chabert's disease A22.9
Chacaleh E53.8
Chafing L30.4
Chagas' (-Mazza) disease (chronic) B57.2
  with
    cardiovascular involvement NEC
      B57.2
    digestive system involvement B57.30
      megacolon B57.32
      megaesophagus B57.31
      other specified B57.39
    megacolon B57.32
    megaesophagus B57.31
    myocarditis B57.2
    nervous system involvement B57.40
      meningitis B57.41
      meningoencephalitis B57.42
      other specified B57.49
    specified organ involvement NEC
      B57.5
  acute (with) B57.1
    cardiovascular NEC B57.0
    myocarditis B57.0
Chagres fever B50.9
Chairridden Z74.09
Chalasia (cardiac sphincter) K21.9
Chalazion H00.19
  left H00.16
    lower H00.15
    upper H00.14
  right H00.13
    lower H00.12
    upper H00.11
Chalcosis - see also Disorder, globe, degen-
    erative, chalcosis
  cornea - see Deposit, cornea
  crystalline lens - see Cataract,
    complicated
  retina H35.89
Chalicosis (pulmonum) J62.8
Chancre (any genital site) (hard)
    (hunterian) (mixed) (primary) (sero-
    negative) (seropositive) (syphilitic)
    A51.0
  congenital A50.07
  conjunctiva NEC A51.2
  Ducrey's A57
  extragenital A51.2
  eyelid A51.2
  lip A51.2
  nipple A51.2
  Nisbet's A57
  of
    carate A67.0
    pinta A67.0
    yaws A66.0
  palate, soft A51.2
  phagedenic A57

Chancre *(Continued)*
  simple A57
  soft A57
    bubo A57
    palate A51.2
  urethra A51.0
  yaws A66.0
Chancroid (anus) (genital) (penis)
    (perineum) (rectum) (urethra)
    (vulva) A57
Chandler's disease (osteochondritis dis-
    secans, hip) - *see* Osteochondritis,
    dissecans, hip
Change(s) (in) (of) - *see also* Removal
  arteriosclerotic - *see* Arteriosclerosis
  bone - *see also* Disorder, bone
    diabetic – *see* Diabetes, bone change
  bowel habit R19.4
  cardiorenal (vascular) - *see* Hyperten-
    sion, cardiorenal
  cardiovascular - *see* Disease,
    cardiovascular
  circulatory I99.9
  cognitive (mild) (organic) R41.89
  color, tooth, teeth
    during formation K00.8
    posteruptive K03.7
  contraceptive device Z30.43
  corneal membrane H18.30
    Bowman's membrane fold or rupture
      H18.31-
    Descemet's membrane
      fold H18.32-
      rupture H18.33-
  coronary - *see* Disease, heart, ischemic
  degenerative, spine or vertebra - *see*
    Spondylosis
  dental pulp, regressive K04.2
  dressing (nonsurgical) Z48.00
    surgical Z48.01
  heart - *see* Disease, heart
  hip joint - *see* Derangement, joint, hip
  hyperplastic larynx J38.7
  hypertrophic
    nasal sinus J34.89
    turbinate, nasal J34.3
    upper respiratory tract J39.8
  indwelling catheter Z46.6
  inflammatory - *see also* Inflammation
    sacroiliac M46.1
  job, anxiety concerning Z56.1
  joint – *see* Derangement, joint
  life – *see* Menopause
  mental status R41.82
  minimal (glomerular) (see also
    N00-N07 with fourth character .0)
    N05.0
  myocardium, myocardial - *see* Degen-
    eration, myocardial - of life - *see*
    Menopause
  pacemaker Z45.018
    pulse generator Z45.010
  personality (enduring) F68.8
    due to (secondary to)
      general medical condition F07.0
      secondary (nonspecific) F60.89
  regressive, dental pulp K04.2
  renal - *see* Disease, renal
  retina H35.9
    myopic - *see* Disorder, globe, degen-
      erative, myopia
  sacroiliac joint M53.3
  senile (see also condition) R54
  sensory R20.8

Change(s) *(Continued)*
  skin R23.9
    acute, due to ultraviolet radiation
      L56.9
      specified NEC L56.8
    chronic, due to nonionizing radiation
      L57.9
      specified NEC L57.8
    cyanosis R23.0
    flushing R23.2
    pallor R23.1
    petechiae R23.3
    specified change NEC R23.8
    swelling - *see* Mass, localized
    texture R23.4
  trophic
    arm – *see* Mononeuropathy, upper
      limb
    leg – *see* Mononeuropathy, lower limb
  vascular I99.9
  vasomotor I73.9
  voice R49.9
    psychogenic F44.4
    specified NEC R49.8
Changing sleep-work schedule, affecting
    sleep G47.26
Changuinola fever A93.1
Chapping skin T69.8
Charcot-Marie-Tooth disease, paralysis
    or syndrome G60.0
Charcot's
  arthropathy - *see* Arthropathy,
    neuropathic
  cirrhosis K74.3
  disease (tabetic arthropathy) A52.16
  joint (disease) (tabetic) A52.16
    diabetic – *see* Diabetes, with,
      arthropathy
    syringomyelic G95.0
  syndrome (intermittent claudication)
    I73.9
CHARGE association Q89.8
Charley-horse (quadriceps) M62.831
  traumatic (quadriceps) S76.11-
Charlouis' disease - *see* Yaws
Cheadle's disease E54
Checking (of)
  cardiac pacemaker (battery)
    (electrode(s)) Z45.018
    pulse generator Z45.010
  device
    contraceptive Z30.43
Check-up - *see* Examination
Chédiak-Higashi(-Steinbrinck) syndrome
    (congenital gigantism of peroxidase
    granules) E70.330
Cheek - *see* condition
Cheese itch B88.0
Cheese-washer's lung J67.8
Cheese-worker's lung J67.8
Cheilitis (acute) (angular) (catarrhal)
    (chronic) (exfoliative) (gangrenous)
    (glandular) (infectional) (suppura-
    tive) (ulcerative) (vesicular) K13.0
  actinic (due to sun) L56.8
    other than from sun L59.8
  candidal B37.83
Cheilodynia K13.0
Cheiloschisis - *see* Cleft, lip
Cheilosis (angular) K13.0
  with pellagra E52
  due to
    vitamin B$_2$ (riboflavin) deficiency
      E53.0

Cheiromegaly M79.89
Cheiropompholyx L30.1
Cheloid - *see* Keloid
Chemical burn - *see* Corrosion, by site
Chemodectoma - *see* Paraganglioma,
    nonchromaffin
Chemosis, conjunctiva - *see* Edema,
    conjunctiva
Chemotherapy (session) (for)
  cancer Z51.11
  neoplasm Z51.11
Cherubism M27.8
Chest - *see* condition
Cheyne-Stokes breathing (respiration)
    R06.3
Chiari's
  disease or syndrome (hepatic vein
    thrombosis) I82.0
  malformation
    type I G93.5
    type II – *see* Spina bifida
  net Q24.8
Chicago disease B40.9
Chickenpox - *see* Varicella
Chiclero ulcer or sore B55.1
Chigger (infestation) B88.0
Chignon (disease) B36.8
  newborn (from vacuum extraction)
    (birth injury) P12.1
Chilaiditi's syndrome (subphrenic
    displacement, colon)
    Q43.3
Chilblain(s) (lupus) T69.1
Child
  custody dispute Z65.3
Childbirth - *see* Delivery
Childhood
  cerebral X-linked adrenoleukodystro-
    phy E71.420
  period of rapid growth Z00.2
Chill(s) R68.83
  with fever R50.9
  congestive in malarial regions B54
  without fever R68.83
Chilomastigiasis A07.8
Chimera 46,XX/46,XY Q99.0
Chin - *see* condition
Chinese dysentery A03.9
Chionophobia F40.228
Chitral fever A93.1
Chlamydia, chlamydial A74.9
  cervicitis A56.09
  conjunctivitis A74.0
  cystitis A56.01
  endometritis A56.11
  epididymitis A56.19
  female
    pelvic inflammatory disease
      A56.11
    pelviperitonitis A56.11
  orchitis A56.19
  peritonitis A74.81
  pharyngitis A56.4
  proctitis A56.3
  psittaci (infection) A70
  salpingitis A56.11
  sexually-transmitted infection NEC
    A56.8
  specified NEC A74.89
  urethritis A56.01
  vulvovaginitis A56.02
Chlamydiosis - *see* Chlamydia
Chloasma (skin) (idiopathic) (symptom-
    atic) L81.1

Chloasma *(Continued)*
  eyelid H02.719
    hyperthyroid E05.90 *[H02.719]*
      with thyroid storm E05.91
        [H02.719]
    left H02.716
      lower H02.715
      upper H02.714
    right H02.713
      lower H02.712
      upper H02.711
Chloroma C92.3-
Chlorosis D50.9
  Egyptian B76.9 *[D63.8]*
  miner's B76.9 *[D63.8]*
Chlorotic anemia D50.9
Chocolate cyst (ovary) N80.1
Choked
  disc or disk - *see* Papilledema
  on food, phlegm, or vomitus NOS - *see* Asphyxia, food
  while vomiting NOS - *see* Asphyxia, food
Chokes (resulting from bends) T70.3
Choking sensation R09.89
Cholangiectasis K83.8
Cholangiocarcinoma
  with hepatocellular carcinoma, combined C22.0
  liver C22.1
  specified site NEC - *see* Neoplasm, malignant
  unspecified site C22.1
Cholangiohepatitis K83.8
  due to fluke infestation B66.1
Cholangiohepatoma C22.0
Cholangiolitis (acute) (chronic) (extrahepatic) (gangrenous) (intrahepatic) K83.0
  paratyphoidal - *see* Fever, paratyphoid
  typhoidal A01.09
Cholangioma D13.4
  malignant - *see* Cholangiocarcinoma
Cholangitis (ascending) (primary) (recurrent) (sclerosing) (secondary) (stenosing) (suppurative) K83.0
  with calculus, bile duct - *see* Calculus, bile duct, with cholangitis
  chronic nonsuppurative destructive K74.3
Cholecystectasia K82.8
Cholecystitis K81.9
  with
    calculus, stones in
      bile duct (common) (hepatic) - *see* Calculus, bile duct, with cholecystitis
      cystic duct – *see* Calculus, gallbladder, with cholecystitis
      gallbladder – *see* Calculus, gallbladder, with cholecystitis
      choledocholithiasis - *see* Calculus, bile duct, with cholecystitis
      cholelithiasis – *see* Calculus, gallbladder, with cholecystitis
    acute (emphysematous) (gangrenous) (suppurative) K81.0
      with
        calculus, stones in
          cystic duct – *see* Calculus, gallbladder, with cholecystitis, acute

Cholecystitis *(Continued)*
  acute *(Continued)*
    with *(Continued)*
      calculus, stones in *(Continued)*
        gallbladder – *see* Calculus, gallbladder, with cholecystitis, acute
        choledocholithiasis - *see* Calculus, bile duct, with cholecystitis, acute
        cholelithiasis – *see* Calculus, gallbladder, with cholecystitis, acute
  chronic cholecystitis K81.2
    with gallbladder calculus K80.12
      with obstruction K80.13
  chronic K81.1
    with acute cholecystitis K81.2
      with gallbladder calculus K80.12
        with obstruction K80.13
  emphysematous (acute) - *see* Cholecystitis, acute
  gangrenous - *see* Cholecystitis, acute
  paratyphoidal, current A01.4
  suppurative - *see* Cholecystitis, acute
  typhoidal A01.09
Cholecystolithiasis - *see* Calculus, gallbladder
Choledochitis (suppurative) K83.0
Choledocholith - *see* Calculus, bile duct
Choledocholithiasis (common duct) (hepatic duct) - *see* Calculus, bile duct
  cystic - *see* Calculus, gallbladder
  typhoidal A01.09
Cholelithiasis (cystic duct) (gallbladder) (impacted) (multiple) - *see* Calculus, gallbladder
  bile duct (common) (hepatic) - *see* Calculus, bile duct
  hepatic duct - *see* Calculus, bile duct
  specified NEC K80.80
    with obstruction K80.81
Cholemia - *see also* Jaundice
  familial (simple) (congenital) E80.4
  Gilbert's E80.4
Choleperitoneum, choleperitonitis K65.3
Cholera (Asiatic) (epidemic) (malignant) A00.9
  antimonial – *see* Poisoning, antimony
  classical A00.0
  due to Vibrio cholerae 01 A00.9
    biovar cholerae A00.0
    biovar eltor A00.1
    el tor A00.1
  el tor A00.1
Cholerine - *see* Cholera
Cholestasis NEC K83.1
  due to total parenteral nutrition (TPN) K76.8
  with hepatocyte injury K71.0
  pure K71.0
Cholesteatoma (ear) (middle) (with reaction) H71.9-
  attic H71.0-
  external ear (canal) H60.4-
  mastoid H71.2-
  postmastoidectomy cavity (recurrent) - *see* Complications, postmastoidectomy, recurrent cholesteatoma
  recurrent (postmastoidectomy) - *see* Complications, postmastoidectomy, recurrent cholesteatoma
  tympanum H71.1-

Cholesteatosis, diffuse H71.3-
Cholesteremia E78.0
Cholesterin in vitreous - *see* Deposit, crystalline
Cholesterol
  deposit
    retina H35.89
    vitreous - *see* Deposit, crystalline
  elevated (high) E78.0
    with elevated (high) triglycerides E78.2
    screening for Z13.220
  imbibition of gallbladder K82.4
Cholesterolemia (essential) (familial) (hereditary) (pure) E78.0
Cholesterolosis, cholesterosis (gallbladder) K82.4
  cerebrotendinous E75.5
Cholocolic fistula K82.3
Choluria R82.2
Chondritis M94.8x9
  auricular H61.03-
  costal (Tietze's) M94.0
  external ear H61.03-
  patella, posttraumatic - *see* Chondromalacia, patella
  pinna H61.03-
  purulent M94.8x
  tuberculous NEC A18.02
    intervertebral A18.01
Chondroblastoma - *see also* Neoplasm, bone, benign
  malignant - *see* Neoplasm, bone, malignant
Chondrocalcinosis M11.20
  ankle M11.27-
  elbow M11.22-
  familial M11.10
    ankle M11.17-
    elbow M11.12-
    foot joint M11.17-
    hand joint M11.14-
    hip M11.15-
    knee M11.16-
    multiple site M11.19
    shoulder M11.11-
    specified joint NEC M11.18
    wrist M11.13-
  foot joint M11.27-
  hand joint M11.24-
  hip M11.25-
  knee M11.26-
  multiple site M11.29
  shoulder M11.21-
  specified joint NEC M11.28
  specified type NEC M11.20
    ankle M11.27-
    elbow M11.22-
    foot joint M11.27-
    hand joint M11.24-
    hip M11.25-
    knee M11.26-
    multiple site M11.29
    shoulder M11.21-
    specified joint NEC M11.28
    wrist M11.23-
  wrist M11.23-
Chondrodermatitis nodularis helicis or anthelicis - *see* Perichondritis, ear
Chondrodysplasia Q78.9
  with hemangioma Q78.4
  calcificans congenita Q77.3
  fetalis Q77.4

Chondrodysplasia *(Continued)*
  metaphyseal (Jansen's) (McKusick's)
    (Schmid's) Q78.5
  punctata Q77.3
Chondrodystrophy, chondrodystrophia
  (familial) (fetalis) (hypoplastic) Q78.9
  calcificans congenita Q77.3
  myotonic (congenital) G71.13
  punctata Q77.3
Chondroectodermal dysplasia Q77.6
Chondrogenesis imperfecta Q77.4
Chondrolysis M94.35-
Chondroma - *see also* Neoplasm, cartilage,
  benign
  juxtacortical - *see* Neoplasm, bone,
    benign
  periosteal - *see* Neoplasm, bone, benign
Chondromalacia (systemic) M94.20
  acromioclavicular joint M94.21-
  ankle M94.27-
  elbow M94.22-
  foot joint M94.27-
  glenohumeral joint M94.21-
  hand joint M94.24-
  hip M94.25-
  knee M94.26-
    patella M22.4-
  multiple sites M94.29
  patella M22.4-
  rib M94.28
  sacroiliac joint M94.259
  shoulder M94.21-
  sternoclavicular joint M94.21-
  vertebral joint M94.28
  wrist M94.23-
Chondromatosis - *see also* Neoplasm,
  cartilage, uncertain behavior
  internal Q78.4
Chondromyxosarcoma – *see* Neoplasm,
  cartilage, malignant
Chondro-osteodysplasia (Morquio-Brailsford type) E76.219
Chondro-osteodystrophy E76.29
Chondro-osteoma – *see* Neoplasm, bone,
  benign
Chondropathia tuberosa M94.0
Chondrosarcoma – *see* Neoplasm, cartilage, malignant
  juxtacortical - *see* Neoplasm, bone,
    malignant
  mesenchymal - *see* Neoplasm, connec-
    tive tissue, malignant
  myxoid - *see* Neoplasm, cartilage,
    malignant
Chordee (nonvenereal) N48.89
  congenital Q54.4
  gonococcal A54.09
Chorditis (fibrinous) (nodosa) (tuberosa)
  J38.2
Chordoma - *see* Neoplasm, malignant
Chorea (chronic) (gravis) (posthemiplegic) (senile) (spasmodic) G25.5
  with
    heart involvement I02.0
      active or acute (conditions in I01-)
        I02.0
      rheumatic I02.9
        with valvular disorder I02.0
      rheumatic heart disease (chronic)
        (inactive)(quiescent) - code
        to rheumatic heart condition
        involved
  drug-induced G25.4
  habit F95.8

Chorea *(Continued)*
  hereditary G10
  Huntington's G10
  hysterical F44.4
  minor I02.9
    with heart involvement I02.0
  progressive G25.5
    hereditary G10
  rheumatic (chronic) I02.9
    with heart involvement I02.0
  Sydenham's I02.9
    with heart involvement - *see* Chorea,
      with rheumatic heart disease
    nonrheumatic G25.5
Choreoathetosis (paroxysmal) G25.5
Chorioadenoma (destruens) D39.2
Chorioamnionitis O41.12-
Chorioangioma D26.7
Choriocarcinoma - *see* Neoplasm,
  malignant
  combined with
    embryonal carcinoma – *see*
      Neoplasm, malignant
    other germ cell elements – *see*
      Neoplasm, malignant
    teratoma - *see* Neoplasm,
      malignant
  specified site - *see* Neoplasm,
    malignant
  unspecified site
    female C58
    male C62.90
Chorioencephalitis (acute) (lymphocytic)
  (serous) A87.2
Chorioepithelioma - *see* Choriocarcinoma
Choriomeningitis (acute) (lymphocytic)
  (serous) A87.2
Chorionepithelioma – *see* Choriocarcinoma
Chorioretinitis - *see also* Inflammation,
  chorioretinal
  disseminated - *see also* Inflammation,
    chorioretinal, disseminated
    in neurosyphilis A52.19
  focal - *see also* Inflammation, chorioreti-
    nal, focal
  Egyptian B76.9 *[D63.8]*
  histoplasmic B39.9 *[H32]*
  in (due to)
    histoplasmosis B39.9 *[H32]*
    syphilis (secondary) A51.43
      late A52.71
    toxoplasmosis (acquired) B58.01
      congenital (active) P37.1 *[H32]*
    tuberculosis A18.53
  juxtapapillary, juxtapapillaris - *see*
    Inflammation, chorioretinal, focal,
    juxtapapillary
  leprous A30.9 *[H32]*
  miner's B76.9 *[D63.8]*
  progressive myopia (degeneration) - *see*
    Disorder, globe, degenerative,
    myopia
  syphilitic (secondary) A51.43
    congenital (early) A50.01 *[H32]*
    late A50.32
    late A52.71
  tuberculous A18.53
Chorioretinopathy, central serous
  H35.71-
Choroid - *see* condition
Choroideremia H31.21
Choroiditis - *see* Chorioretinitis
Choroidopathy - *see* Disorder,
  choroid

Choroidoretinitis - *see* Chorioretinitis
Choroidoretinopathy, central serous - *see*
  Chorioretinopathy, central serous
Christian-Weber disease M35.6
Christmas disease D67
Chromaffinoma - *see also* Neoplasm,
  benign
  malignant - *see* Neoplasm, malignant
Chromatopsia - *see* Deficiency, color
  vision
Chromhidrosis, chromidrosis L75.1
Chromoblastomycosis - *see*
  Chromomycosis
Chromoconversion R82.91
Chromomycosis B43.9
  brain abscess B43.1
  cerebral B43.1
  cutaneous B43.0
  skin B43.0
  specified NEC B43.8
  subcutaneous abscess or cyst B43.0
Chromophytosis B36.0
Chromosome - *see* condition by chromo-
  some involved
  D(1) - *see* condition, chromosome 13
  E(3) - *see* condition, chromosome 18
  G - *see* condition, chromosome 21
Chromotrichomycosis B36.8
Chronic - *see* condition
  fracture - *see* Fracture, pathological
Churg-Strauss syndrome M30.1
Chyle cyst, mesentery I89.8
Chylocele (nonfilarial) I89.8
  filarial (see also Infestation, filarial)
    B74.9 *[N51]*
  tunica vaginalis N50.8
    filarial (see also Infestation, filarial)
      B74.9 *[N51]*
Chylomicronemia (fasting) (with hyper-
  prebetalipoproteinemia) E78.3
Chylopericardium I31.3
  acute I30.9
Chylothorax (nonfilarial) I89.8
  filarial (see also Infestation, filarial)
    B74.9 *[J91.8]*
Chylous - *see* condition
Chyluria (nonfilarial) R82.0
  due to
    bilharziasis B65.0
    Brugia (malayi) B74.1
      timori B74.2
    schistosomiasis (bilharziasis) B65.0
    Wuchereria (bancrofti) B74.0
  filarial - *see* Infestation, filarial
Cicatricial (deformity) - *see* Cicatrix
Cicatrix (adherent) (contracted) (painful)
  (vicious) (see also Scar) L90.5
  adenoid (and tonsil) J35.8
  alveolar process M26.79
  anus K62.8
  auricle - *see* Disorder, pinna, specified
    type NEC
  bile duct (common) (hepatic) K83.8
  bladder N32.89
  bone - *see* Disorder, bone, specified type
    NEC
  brain G93.89
  cervix (postoperative) (postpartal) N88.1
  common duct K83.8
  cornea H17.9
    tuberculous A18.59
  duodenum (bulb), obstructive K31.5
  esophagus K22.2
  eyelid - *see* Disorder, eyelid function

Cicatrix *(Continued)*
  hypopharynx J39.2
  lacrimal passages - *see* Obstruction,
     lacrimal
  larynx J38.7
  lung J98.4
  middle ear - *see* subcategory H74.8
  mouth K13.79
  muscle M62.89
    with contracture *see* Contraction,
      muscle NEC
  nasopharynx J39.2
  palate (soft) K13.79
  penis N48.89
  pharynx J39.2
  prostate N42.89
  rectum K62.8
  retina - *see* Scar, chorioretinal
  semilunar cartilage - *see* Derangement,
     meniscus
  seminal vesicle N50.8
  skin L90.5
    infected L08.89
    postinfective L90.5
    tuberculous B90.8
  specified site NEC L90.5
  throat J39.2
  tongue K14.8
  tonsil (and adenoid) J35.8
  trachea J39.8
  tuberculous NEC B90.9
  urethra N36.8
  uterus N85.8
  vagina N89.8
    postoperative N99.2
  vocal cord J38.3
  wrist, constricting (annular) L90.5
CIDP (chronic inflammatory demyelinat-
    ing polyneuropathy) G61.81
CIN - *see* Neoplasia, intraepithelial, cervix
Cinchonism - *see* Deafness, ototoxic
  correct substance properly admin-
     istered - *see* Table of drugs and
     chemicals, by drug, adverse effect
  overdose or wrong substance given
     or taken - *see* Table of drugs and
     chemicals, by drug, poisoning
Circle of Willis - *see* condition
Circular - *see* condition
Circulating anticoagulants D68.31
  due to drugs D68.32
  following childbirth O72.3
Circulation
  collateral, any site I99.8
  defective (lower extremity) I99.8
    congenital Q28.9
  embryonic Q28.9
  failure (peripheral) R57.9
    newborn P29.89
  fetal, persistent P29.3
  heart, incomplete Q28.9
Circulatory system - *see* condition
Circulus senilis (cornea) - *see* Degenera-
    tion, cornea, senile
Circumcision (in absence of medical
    indication) (ritual) (routine)
    Z41.2
Circumscribed - *see* condition
Circumvallate placenta O43.11-
Cirrhosis, cirrhotic (hepatic) (liver)
    K74.60
  alcoholic K70.30
    with ascites K70.31
  atrophic - *see* Cirrhosis, liver

Cirrhosis, cirrhotic *(Continued)*
  Baumgarten-Cruveilhier K74.69
  biliary (cholangiolitic) (cholangitic)
    (hypertrophic) (obstructive)
    (pericholangiolitic) K74.5
    due to
      Clonorchiasis B66.1
      flukes B66.3
    primary K74.3
    secondary K74.4
  cardiac (of liver) K76.1
  Charcot's K74.3
  cholangiolitic, cholangitic, cholostatic
    (primary) K74.3
  congestive K76.1
  Cruveilhier-Baumgarten K74.69
  cryptogenic (liver) K74.69
  due to
    hepatolenticular degeneration
      E83.01
    Wilson's disease E83.01
    xanthomatosis E78.2
  fatty K76.0
    alcoholic K70.0
  Hanot's (hypertrophic) K74.3
  hepatic - *see* Cirrhosis, liver
  hypertrophic K74.3
  Indian childhood K74.69
  kidney - *see* Sclerosis, renal
  Laennec's K70.30
    with ascites K70.31
    alcoholic K70.30
      with ascites K70.31
    nonalcoholic K74.69
  liver K74.60
    alcoholic K70.30
      with ascites K70.31
      fatty K70.0
    congenital P78.81
    syphilitic A52.74
  lung (chronic) - *see* Fibrosis, lung
  macronodular K74.69
    alcoholic K70.30
      with ascites K70.31
  micronodular K74.69
    alcoholic K70.30
      with ascites K70.31
  mixed type K74.69
  monolobular K74.3
  nephritis – *see* Sclerosis, renal
  nutritional K74.69
    alcoholic K70.30
      with ascites K70.31
  obstructive - *see* Cirrhosis, biliary
  ovarian N83.8
  pancreas (duct) K86.8
  portal K74.69
    alcoholic K70.30
      with ascites K70.31
  postnecrotic K74.69
    alcoholic K70.30
      with ascites K70.31
  pulmonary - *see* Fibrosis, lung
  renal - *see* Sclerosis, renal
  spleen D73.2
  stasis K76.1
  Todd's K74.3
  unilobar K74.3
  xanthomatous (biliary) K74.5
    due to xanthomatosis (familial)
      (metabolic) (primary) E78.2
Cistern, subarachnoid R93.0
Citrullinemia E72.23
Citrullinuria E72.23

Civatte's disease or poikiloderma L57.3
Clam diggers' itch B65.3
Clammy skin R23.1
Clap - *see* Gonorrhea
Clarke-Hadfield syndrome (pancreatic
    infantilism) K86.8
Clark's paralysis G80.9
Clastothrix L67.8
Claude Bernard-Horner syndrome G90.2
  traumatic – *see* Injury, nerve, cervical
    sympathetic
Claude's disease or syndrome G46.3
Claudication, intermittent I73.9
  cerebral (artery) G45.9
  spinal cord (arteriosclerotic) G95.19
    syphilitic A52.09
  venous (axillary) I87.8
Claudicatio venosa intermittens I87.8
Claustrophobia F40.240
Clavus (infected) L84
Clawfoot (congenital) Q66.8
  acquired - *see* Deformity, limb, clawfoot
Clawhand (acquired) - *see also* Deformity,
    limb, clawhand
  congenital Q68.1
Clawtoe (congenital) Q66.8
  acquired - *see* Deformity, toe, specified
    NEC
Clay eating – *see* Pica
Cleansing of artificial opening – *see*
    Attention to, artificial, opening
Cleft (congenital) - *see also* Imperfect,
    closure
  alveolar process M26.79
  branchial (cyst) (persistent) Q18.2
  cricoid cartilage, posterior Q31.8
  lip (unilateral) Q36.9
    with cleft palate Q37.9
      hard Q37.1
        with soft Q37.5
      soft Q37.3
        with hard Q37.5
    bilateral Q36.0
      with cleft palate Q37.8
      hard Q37.0
        with soft Q37.4
      soft Q37.2
        with hard Q37.4
    median Q36.1
  nose Q30.2
  palate Q35.9
    with cleft lip (unilateral) Q37.9
      bilateral Q37.8
    hard Q35.1
      with
        cleft lip (unilateral) Q37.1
          bilateral Q37.0
        soft Q35.5
          with cleft lip (unilateral) Q37.5
            bilateral Q37.4
    medial Q35.5
    soft Q35.3
      with
        cleft lip (unilateral) Q37.3
          bilateral Q37.2
        hard Q35.5
          with cleft lip (unilateral) Q37.5
            bilateral Q37.4
  penis Q55.69
  scrotum Q55.29
  thyroid cartilage Q31.8
  uvula Q35.7
Cleidocranial dysostosis Q74.0
Cleptomania F63.2

Clicking hip (newborn) R29.4
Climacteric (female) - *see also* Menopause
  arthritis (any site) NEC - *see* Arthritis, specified form NEC
  depression (single episode) F32.8
  male (symptoms) (syndrome) NEC N50.8
  paranoid state F22
  polyarthritis NEC - *see* Arthritis, specified form NEC
  symptoms (female) N95.11
Clinical research investigation (clinical trial) (control subject) Z00.6
Clitoris - *see* condition Cloaca (persistent) Q43.7
Clonorchiasis, clonorchis infection (liver) B66.1
Clonus R25.8
Closed bite M26.29
Clostridium (C.) perfringens, as cause of disease classified elsewhere B96.7
Closure
  congenital, nose Q30.0
  cranial sutures, premature Q75.0
  defective or imperfect NEC - *see* Imperfect, closure
  fistula, delayed - *see* Fistula
  foramen ovale, imperfect Q21.1
  hymen N89.6
  interauricular septum, defective Q21.1
  interventricular septum, defective Q21.0
  lacrimal duct - *see also* Stenosis, lacrimal, duct
    congenital Q10.5
  nose (congenital) Q30.0
    acquired M95.0
  of artificial opening - *see* Attention to, artificial, opening
  vagina N89.5
  valve - *see* Endocarditis
  vulva N90.5
Clot (blood) - *see also* Embolism
  atrial appendage I57.89
  artery (obstruction) (occlusion) - *see* Embolism
  bladder N32.89
  brain (intradural or extradural) - *see* Occlusion, artery, cerebral
  circulation I74.9
  heart - *see also* Infarct, myocardium
    not resulting in infarction I24.0
  vein - *see* Thrombosis
Clouded state R40.1
  epileptic – *see* Epilepsy, specified NEC
  paroxysmal – *see* Epilepsy, specified NEC
Cloudy antrum, antra J32.0
Clouston's (hidrotic) ectodermal dysplasia Q82.4
Clubbed nail pachydermoperiostosis M89.40 [L62]
Clubbing of finger(s) (nails) R68.3
Clubfinger R68.3
  congenital Q68.1
Clubfoot (congenital) Q66.8
  acquired - *see* Deformity, limb, clubfoot
  equinovarus Q66.0
  paralytic - *see* Deformity, limb, clubfoot
Clubhand (congenital) (radial) - *see* Defect, reduction, upper limb, longitudinal, radius
  acquired - *see* Deformity, limb, clubhand
Clubnail R68.3
  congenital Q84.6

Clump, kidney Q63.1
Clumsiness, clumsy child syndrome F82
Cluttering F98.8
Clutton's joints A50.51 [M12.80]
Coagulation, intravascular (diffuse) (disseminated) - *see also* Defibrination syndrome
  complicating abortion – *see* Abortion, by type, complicated by, intravascular coagulation
Coagulopathy - *see also* Defect, coagulation
  consumption D65
  intravascular D65
  newborn P60
Coalminer's
  elbow - *see* Bursitis, elbow, olecranon
  lung or pneumoconiosis J60
Coalition
  calcaneo-scaphoid Q66.8
  tarsal Q66.8
Coalworker's lung or pneumoconiosis J60
Coarctation of aorta (preductal) (postductal) Q25.1
Coated tongue K14.3
Coats' disease (exudative retinopathy) - *see* Retinopathy, exudative
Cocainism - *see* Dependence, drug, cocaine
Coccidioidomycosis B38.9
  cutaneous B38.3
  disseminated B38.7
  generalized B38.7
  meninges B38.4
  prostate B38.81
  pulmonary B38.2
    acute B38.0
    chronic B38.1
  skin B38.3
  specified NEC B38.89
Coccidioidosis - *see* Coccidioidomycosis
Coccidiosis (intestinal) A07.3
Coccydynia, coccygodynia M53.3
Coccyx - *see* condition
Cochin-China diarrhea K90.1
Cockayne's syndrome Q87.1
Cocked up toe - *see* Deformity, toe, specified NEC
Cock's peculiar tumor L72.1
Codman's tumor - *see* Neoplasm, bone, benign
Coenurosis B71.8
Coffee-worker's lung J67.8
Cogan's syndrome - *see also* Keratitis, interstitial, specified type NEC
  oculomotor apraxia H51.8
Coitus, painful (female) N94.1
  male N53.12
  psychogenic F52.6
Cold J00
  with influenza, flu, or grippe - *see* Influenza, with, respiratory manifestations
  agglutinin disease or hemoglobinuria (chronic) D59.1
  bronchial - *see* Bronchitis
  chest – *see* Bronchitis
  common (head) J00
  effects of T69.9
    specified effect NEC T69.8
  excessive, effects of T69.9
    specified effect NEC T69.8
  exhaustion from T69.8

Cold *(Continued)*
  exposure to T69.9
    specified effect NEC T69.8
  head J00
  injury syndrome (newborn) P80.0
  on lung - *see* Bronchitis
  rose J30.1
  sensitivity, auto-immune D59.1
  virus J00
Coldsore B00.1
Colibacillosis A49.8
  as the cause of other disease B96.2
  generalized A41.50
Colic (bilious) (infantile) (intestinal) (recurrent) (spasmodic) R10.83
  abdomen R10.83
    psychogenic F45.8
  appendix, appendicular K38.8
  bile duct - *see* Calculus, bile duct
  biliary - *see* Calculus, bile duct
  common duct - *see* Calculus, bile duct
  cystic duct - *see* Calculus, gallbladder
  Devonshire NEC – *see* Poisoning, lead
  gallbladder - *see* Calculus, gallbladder
  gallstone - *see* Calculus, gallbladder
    gallbladder or cystic duct - *see* Calculus, gallbladder
  hepatic (duct) - *see* Calculus, bile duct
  hysterical F45.8
  kidney N23
  lead NEC – *see* Poisoning, lead
  mucous K58.9
    with diarrhea K58.0
    psychogenic F54
  nephritic N23
  painter's NEC – *see* Poisoning, lead
  pancreas K86.8
  psychogenic F45.8
  renal N23
  saturnine NEC – *see* Poisoning, lead
  ureter N23
  urethral N36.8
    due to calculus N21.1
  uterus NEC N94.89
    menstrual - *see* Dysmenorrhea
  worm NOS B83.9
Colicystitis – *see* Cystitis
Colitis (acute) (catarrhal) (chronic) (noninfective) (hemorrhagic) - *see also* Enteritis K52.9
  allergic K52.2
  amebic (acute) (see also Amebiasis) A06.0
    nondysenteric A06.2
  anthrax A22.2
  bacillary - *see* Infection, Shigella
  balantidial A07.0
  Clostridium difficile A04.7
  coccidial A07.3
  collagenous K52.89
  cystica superficialis K52.89
  dietary counseling and surveillance (for) Z71.3
  dietetic K52.2
  due to radiation K52.0
  eosinophilic K52.82
  food hypersensitivity K52.2
  giardial A07.1
  granulomatous – *see* Enteritis, regional, large intestine
  infectious - *see* Enteritis, infectious
  ischemic K55.9
    acute (fulminant) (subacute) K55.0
    chronic K55.1

131

Colitis (Continued)
  ischemic (Continued)
    due to mesenteric artery insufficiency K55.1
    fulminant (acute) K55.0
  left sided K51.50
    with
      complication K51.519
        specified NEC K51.518
      abscess K51.514
      fistula K51.513
      obstruction K51.512
      rectal bleeding K51.511
  lymphocytic K52.89
  membranous
    psychogenic F54
  microscopic (collagenous) (lymphocytic) K52.89
  mucous - see Syndrome, irritable, bowel
    psychogenic F54
  noninfective K52.9
    specified NEC K52.89
  polyposa – see Polyps, colon, inflammatory
  protozoal A07.9
  pseudomembranous A04.7
  pseudomucinous - see Syndrome, irritable, bowel
  regional – see Enteritis, regional, large intestine
  segmental – see Enteritis, regional, large intestine
  septic - see Enteritis, infectious
  spastic K58.9
    with diarrhea K58.0
    psychogenic F54
  staphylococcal A04.8
    foodborne A05.0
  subacute ischemic K55.0
  thromboulcerative K55.0
  toxic K52.1
  transmural – see Enteritis, regional, large intestine
  trichomonal A07.8
  tuberculous (ulcerative) A18.32
  ulcerative (chronic) K51.90
    with
      complication K51.919
        abscess K51.914
        fistula K51.913
        obstruction K51.912
        rectal bleeding K51.911
        specified complication NEC K51.918
    enterocolitis - see Enterocolitis, ulcerative
    ileocolitis - see Ileocolitis, ulcerative
    mucosal proctocolitis – see Proctocolitis, mucosal
    proctitis - see Proctitis, ulcerative
    pseudopolyposis – see Polyps, colon, inflammatory
    psychogenic F54
    rectosigmoiditis - see Rectosigmoiditis, ulcerative
    specified type NEC K51.80
      with
        complication K51.819
          abscess K51.814
          fistula K51.813
          obstruction K51.812
          rectal bleeding K51.811
          specified complication NEC K51.818

Collagenosis, collagen disease (nonvascular) (vascular) M35.9
  cardiovascular I42.8
  reactive perforating L87.1
  specified NEC M35.8
Collapse R55
  adrenal E27.2
  cardiorespiratory R57.0
  cardiovascular R57.0
    newborn P29.89
  circulatory (peripheral) R57.9
    during or after labor and delivery O75.1
    following ectopic or molar pregnancy O08.3
    newborn P29.89
  during or after labor and delivery O75.1
  external ear canal - see Stenosis, external ear canal
  general R55
  heart - see Disease, heart
  heat T67.1
  hysterical F44.89
  labyrinth, membranous (congenital) Q16.5
  lung (massive) (see also Atelectasis) J98.19
    pressure due to anesthesia (general) (local) or other sedation T88.2
      during labor and delivery O74.1
      in pregnancy O29.02-
      postpartum, puerperal O89.09
  myocardial - see Disease, heart
  nervous F48.8
  neurocirculatory F45.8
  nose M95.0
  postoperative (cardiovascular) T81.1
  pulmonary (see also Atelectasis) J98.19
    newborn - see Atelectasis
  trachea J39.8
  tracheobronchial J98.09
  valvular - see Endocarditis
  vascular (peripheral) R57.9
    during or after labor and delivery O75.1
    following ectopic or molar pregnancy O08.3
    newborn P29.89
  vertebra M48.50-
    cervical region M48.52-
    cervicothoracic region M48.53-
    in (due to)
      metastasis - see Collapse, vertebra, in, specified disease NEC
      osteoporosis (see also Osteoporosis) M80.88
        cervical region M80.88
        cervicothoracic region M80.88
        lumbar region M80.88
        lumbosacral region M80.88
        multiple sites M80.88
        occipito-atlanto-axial region M80.88
        sacrococcygeal region M80.88
        thoracic region M80.88
        thoracolumbar region M80.88
      specified disease NEC M48.50-
        cervical region M48.52-
        cervicothoracic region M48.53-
        lumbar region M48.56-
        lumbosacral region M48.57-
        occipito-atlanto-axial region M48.51-
        sacrococcygeal region M48.58-
        thoracic region M48.54-
        thoracolumbar region M48.55-

Collapse (Continued)
  vertebra (Continued)
    lumbar region M48.56-
    lumbosacral region M48.57-
    occipito-atlanto-axial region M48.51-
    sacrococcygeal region M48.58-
    thoracic region M48.54-
    thoracolumbar region M48.55-
Collateral – see also condition
  circulation (venous) I87.8
  dilation, veins I87.8
Colles' fracture S52.53-
Collet(-Sicard) syndrome G52.7
Collier's asthma or lung J60
Collodion baby Q80.2
Colloid nodule (of thyroid) (cystic) E04.1
Coloboma (iris) Q13.0
  eyelid Q10.3
  fundus Q14.8
  lens Q12.2
  optic disc (congenital) Q14.2
    acquired H47.31-
Coloenteritis - see Enteritis
Colon - see condition
Colonization status - see Carrier (suspected) of
Coloptosis K63.4
Color blindness - see Deficiency, color vision
Colostomy
  attention to Z43.3
  fitting or adjustment Z46.89
  malfunctioning K94.03
  status Z93.3
Colpitis (acute) - see Vaginitis
Colpocele N81.5
Colpocystitis - see Vaginitis
Colpospasm N94.2
Column, spinal, vertebral - see condition
Coma R40.20
  with
    motor response (none) R40.231
      abnormal R40.233
      extension R40.232
      flexion withdrawal R40.234
      localizes pain R40.235
      obeys commands R40.236
    opening of eyes (never) R40.211
      in response to
        pain R40.212
        sound R40.213
      spontaneous R40.214
    verbal response (none) R40.221
      confused conversation R40.224
      inappropriate words R40.223
      incomprehensible words R40.222
      oriented R40.225
  eclamptic - see Eclampsia
  epileptic – see Epilepsy
  hepatic - see Failure, hepatic, by type, with coma
  hyperglycemic (diabetic) - see Diabetes, coma
  hyperosmolar (diabetic) - see Diabetes, coma
  hypoglycemic (diabetic) - see Diabetes, coma, hypoglycemic
  nondiabetic E15
  in diabetes - see Diabetes, coma
  insulin-induced - see Coma, hypoglycemic
  myxedematous E03.5
  newborn P91.5

Coma *(Continued)*
persistent vegetative state R40.3
prediabetic – *see* Diabetes, hyperosmolarity
Comatose - *see* Coma
Combat fatigue F43.0
Combined - *see* condition
Comedo, comedones (giant) L70.0
Comedocarcinoma - *see also* Neoplasm, breast, malignant
noninfiltrating
breast D05.7-
specified site - *see* Neoplasm, in situ
unspecified site D05.7-
Comedomastitis – *see* Ectasia, mammary duct
Comminuted fracture - code as Fracture, closed
Common
arterial trunk Q20.0
atrioventricular canal Q21.2
atrium Q21.1
cold (head) J00
truncus (arteriosus) Q20.0
variable immunodeficiency - *see* Immunodeficiency, common variable
ventricle Q20.4
Commotio, commotion (current)
brain – *see* Injury, intracranial, concussion
cerebri – *see* Injury, intracranial, concussion
retinae S05.8x-
spinal cord - *see* Injury, spinal cord, by region
spinalis – *see* Injury, spinal cord, by region
Communication
between
base of aorta and pulmonary artery Q21.4
left ventricle and right atrium Q20.5
pericardial sac and pleural sac Q34.8
pulmonary artery and pulmonary vein, congenital Q25.7
congenital between uterus and digestive or urinary tract Q51.7
Compartment syndrome (deep) (posterior) (traumatic) T79.A0
abdomen T79.A3
lower extremity (hip, buttock, thigh, leg, foot, toes) T79.A2
nontraumatic
abdomen M79.A3
lower extremity (hip, buttock, thigh, leg, foot, toes) M79.A2-
specified site NEC M79.A9
upper extremity (shoulder, arm, forearm, wrist, hand, fingers) M79.A1-
specified site NEC T79.A9
upper extremity (shoulder, arm, forearm, wrist, hand, fingers) T79.A1
Compensation
failure - *see* Disease, heart
neurosis, psychoneurosis – *see* Disorder, factitious
Complaint - *see also* Disease
bowel, functional K59.9
psychogenic F45.8
intestine, functional K59.9
psychogenic F45.8
kidney - *see* Disease, renal
miners' J60

Complete - *see* condition
Complex
Addison-Schilder E71.428
cardiorenal - *see* Hypertension, cardiorenal
Costen's M26.69
disseminated mycobacterium avium-intracellulare (DMAC) A31.2
Eisenmenger's (ventricular septal defect) I27.89
hypersexual F52.8
jumped process, spine - *see* Dislocation, vertebra
primary, tuberculous A15.7
Schilder-Addison E71.428
subluxation (vertebral) M99.19
abdomen M99.19
acromioclavicular M99.17
cervical region M99.11
cervicothoracic M99.11
costochondral M99.18
costovertebral M99.18
head region M99.10
hip M99.15
lower extremity M99.16
lumbar region M99.13
lumbosacral M99.13
occipitocervical M99.10
pelvic region M99.15
pubic M99.15
rib cage M99.18
sacral region M99.14
sacrococcygeal M99.14
sacroiliac M99.14
specified NEC M99.19
sternochondral M99.18
sternoclavicular M99.17
thoracic region M99.12
thoracolumbar M99.12
upper extremity M99.17
Taussig-Bing (transposition, aorta and overriding pulmonary artery) Q20.1
Complication(s) (from) (of)
accidental puncture or laceration during a procedure (of) - *see* Complications, intraoperative (intraprocedural), puncture or laceration
amputation stump (surgical) (late) NEC T87.9
infection or inflammation T87.40
lower limb T87.4-
upper limb T87.2-
necrosis T87.50
lower limb T87.5-
upper limb T87.5-
neuroma T87.30
lower limb T87.3-
upper limb T87.3-
specified type NEC T87.8
anastomosis (and bypass) – *see also* Complications, prosthetic device or implant
intestinal (internal) NEC K91.89
involving urinary tract N99.89
urinary tract (involving intestinal tract) N99.89
vascular – *see* Complications, cardiovascular device or implant
anesthesia, anesthetic (see also Anesthesia, complication) T88.59
brain, postpartum, puerperal O89.2

Complication(s) *(Continued)*
anesthesia, anesthetic *(Continued)*
cardiac
in
labor and delivery O74.2
pregnancy O29.19-
postpartum, puerperal O89.1
central nervous system
in
labor and delivery O74.3
pregnancy O29.29-
postpartum, puerperal O89.2
difficult or failed intubation T88.4
in pregnancy O29.6-
failed sedation (conscious) (moderate) during procedure T88.52
hyperthermia, malignant T88.3
hypothermia T88.51
intubation failure T88.4
malignant hyperthermia T88.3
pulmonary
in
labor and delivery O74.1
pregnancy NEC O29.09-
postpartum, puerperal O89.09
shock T88.2
spinal and epidural
in
labor and delivery NEC O74.6
headache O74.5
pregnancy NEC O29.5x-
postpartum, puerperal NEC O89.5
headache O89.4
anti-reflux device - *see* Complications, esophageal anti-reflux device
aortic (bifurcation) graft - *see* Complications, graft, vascular
aortocoronary (bypass) graft - *see* Complications, coronary artery (bypass) graft
aortofemoral (bypass) graft - *see* Complications, extremity artery (bypass) graft
arteriovenous
fistula, surgically created T82.9
embolism T82.818
fibrosis T82.828
hemorrhage T82.838
infection or inflammation T82.7
mechanical
breakdown T82.510
displacement T82.520
leakage T82.530
malposition T82.520
obstruction T82.590
perforation T82.590
protrusion T82.590
pain T82.848
specified type NEC T82.898
stenosis T82.858
thrombosis T82.868
shunt, surgically created T82.9
embolism T82.818
fibrosis T82.828
hemorrhage T82.838
infection or inflammation T82.7
mechanical
breakdown T82.511
displacement T82.521
leakage T82.531
malposition T82.521
obstruction T82.591
perforation T82.591
protrusion T82.591

133

Complication(s) *(Continued)*
  arteriovenous *(Continued)*
    shunt, surgically created *(Continued)*
      pain T82.848
      specified type NEC T82.898
      stenosis T82.858
      thrombosis T82.868
  arthroplasty – *see* Complications, joint
    prosthesis
  artificial
    fertilization or insemination N98.9
      attempted introduction (of)
        embryo in embryo transfer
          N98.3
        ovum following in vitro fertiliza-
          tion N98.2
      hyperstimulation of ovaries N98.1
      infection N98.0
      specified NEC N98.8
    heart T82.9
      embolism T82.817
      fibrosis T82.827
      hemorrhage T82.837
      infection or inflammation T82.7
      mechanical
        breakdown T82.512
        displacement T82.522
        leakage T82.532
        malposition T82.522
        obstruction T82.592
        perforation T82.592
        protrusion T82.592
      pain T82.847
      specified type NEC T82.897
      stenosis T82.857
      thrombosis T82.867
  opening
    cecostomy – *see* Complications,
      colostomy
    colostomy – *see* Complications,
      colostomy
    cystostomy - *see* Complications,
      cystostomy
    enterostomy – *see* Complications,
      enterostomy
    gastrostomy – *see* Complications,
      gastrostomy
    ileostomy – *see* Complications,
      enterostomy
    jejunostomy – *see* Complications,
      enterostomy
    nephrostomy - *see* Complications,
      stoma, urinary tract
    tracheostomy - *see* Complications,
      tracheostomy
    ureterostomy - *see* Complications,
      stoma, urinary tract
    urethrostomy - *see* Complications,
      stoma, urinary tract
  balloon implant or device
    gastrointestinal T85.89
      embolism T85.81
      fibrosis T85.82
      hemorrhage T85.83
      infection and inflammation T85.79
      pain T85.84
      specified type NEC T85.89
      stenosis T85.85
      thrombosis T85.86
    vascular (counterpulsation) T82.9
      embolism T82.818
      fibrosis T82.828
      hemorrhage T82.838
      infection or inflammation T82.7

Complication(s) *(Continued)*
  balloon implant or device *(Continued)*
    vascular *(Continued)*
      mechanical
        breakdown T82.513
        displacement T82.523
        leakage T82.533
        malposition T82.523
        obstruction T82.593
        perforation T82.593
        protrusion T82.593
      pain T82.848
      specified type NEC T82.898
      stenosis T82.858
      thrombosis T82.868
  bile duct implant (prosthetic) T85.89
    embolism T85.81
    fibrosis T85.82
    hemorrhage T85.83
    infection and inflammation T85.79
    mechanical
      breakdown T85.510
      displacement T85.520
      malfunction T85.510
      malposition T85.520
      obstruction T85.590
      perforation T85.590
      protrusion T85.590
      specified NEC T85.590
    pain T85.84
    specified type NEC T85.89
    stenosis T85.85
    thrombosis T85.86
  bladder device (auxiliary) – *see* Compli-
    cations, genitourinary, device or
    implant, urinary system
  bleeding (postoperative) - *see* Complica-
    tion, postoperative, hemorrhage
    intraoperative – *see* Complication,
      intraoperative, hemorrhage
  blood vessel graft – *see* Complications,
    graft, vascular
  bone
    device NEC T84.9
      embolism T84.81
      fibrosis T84.82
      hemorrhage T84.83
      infection or inflammation T84.7
      mechanical
        breakdown T84.318
        displacement T84.328
        malposition T84.328
        obstruction T84.398
        perforation T84.398
        protrusion T84.398
      pain T84.84
      specified type NEC T84.89
      stenosis T84.85
      thrombosis T84.86
    graft – *see* Complications, graft,
      bone
    growth stimulator (electrode) - *see*
      Complications, electronic stimu-
      lator device, bone
    marrow transplant – *see* Complica-
      tions, transplant, bone, marrow
  brain neurostimulator (electrode) – *see*
    Complications, electronic stimula-
    tor device, brain
  breast implant (prosthetic) T85.89
    capsular contracture T85.44
    embolism T85.81
    fibrosis T85.82
    hemorrhage T85.83

Complication(s) *(Continued)*
  breast implant *(Continued)*
    infection and inflammation T85.79
    mechanical
      breakdown T85.41
      displacement T85.42
      leakage T85.43
      malposition T85.42
      obstruction T85.49
      perforation T85.49
      protrusion T85.49
      specified NEC T85.49
    pain T85.84
    specified type NEC T85.89
    stenosis T85.85
    thrombosis T85.86
  bypass - *see also* Complications, pros-
    thetic device or implant
    aortocoronary - *see* Complications,
      coronary artery (bypass) graft
    arterial - *see also* Complications, graft,
      vascular
      extremity - *see* Complications, ex-
        tremity artery (bypass) graft
  cardiac - *see also* Disease, heart
    device, implant or graft T82.9
      embolism T82.817
      fibrosis T82.827
      hemorrhage T82.837
      infection or inflammation T82.7
        valve prosthesis T82.6
      mechanical
        breakdown T82.519
          specified device NEC T82.518
        displacement T82.529
          specified device NEC T82.528
        leakage T82.539
          specified device NEC T82.538
        malposition T82.529
          specified device NEC T82.528
        obstruction T82.599
          specified device NEC T82.598
        perforation T82.599
          specified device NEC T82.598
        protrusion T82.599
          specified device NEC T82.598
      pain T82.847
      specified type NEC T82.897
      stenosis T82.857
      thrombosis T82.867
  cardiovascular device, graft or implant
    T82.9
    arteriovenous
      fistula, artificial - *see* Complication,
        arteriovenous, fistula, surgi-
        cally created
      shunt - *see* Complication, arterio-
        venous, shunt, surgically
        created
    aortic graft - *see* Complications, graft,
      vascular
    artificial heart - *see* Complication,
      artificial, heart
    balloon (counterpulsation) device
      - *see* Complication, balloon
      implant, vascular
    carotid artery graft - *see* Complica-
      tions, graft, vascular
    coronary bypass graft - *see* Complica-
      tion, coronary artery (bypass)
      graft
    dialysis catheter (vascular) - *see*
      Complication, catheter,
      dialysis

Complication(s) *(Continued)*
cardiovascular device, graft or implant *(Continued)*
electronic T82.9
electrode T82.9
embolism T82.817
fibrosis T82.827
hemorrhage T82.837
infection T82.7
mechanical
breakdown T82.110
displacement T82.120
leakage T82.190
obstruction T82.190
perforation T82.190
protrusion T82.190
specified type NEC T82.190
pain T82.847
specified NEC T82.897
stenosis T82.857
thrombosis T82.867
embolism T82.817
fibrosis T82.827
hemorrhage T82.837
infection T82.7
mechanical
breakdown T82.119
displacement T82.129
leakage T82.199
obstruction T82.199
perforation T82.199
protrusion T82.199
specified type NEC T82.199
pain T82.847
pulse generator T82.9
embolism T82.817
fibrosis T82.827
hemorrhage T82.837
infection T82.7
mechanical
breakdown T82.111
displacement T82.121
leakage T82.191
obstruction T82.191
perforation T82.191
protrusion T82.191
specified type NEC T82.191
pain T82.847
specified NEC T82.897
stenosis T82.857
thrombosis T82.867
specified condition NEC T82.897
specified device NEC T82.9
embolism T82.817
fibrosis T82.827
hemorrhage T82.837
infection T82.7
mechanical
breakdown T82.118
displacement T82.128
leakage T82.198
obstruction T82.198
perforation T82.198
protrusion T82.198
specified type NEC T82.198
pain T82.847
specified NEC T82.897
stenosis T82.857
thrombosis T82.867
stenosis T82.857
thrombosis T82.867
extremity artery graft - *see* Complication, extremity artery (bypass) graft

Complication(s) *(Continued)*
cardiovascular device, graft or implant *(Continued)*
femoral artery graft - *see* Complication, extremity artery (bypass) graft
heart-lung transplant - *see* Complication, transplant, heart, with lung
heart
transplant - *see* Complication, transplant, heart
valve - *see* Complication, prosthetic device, heart valve
graft - *see* Complication, heart, valve, graft
infection or inflammation T82.7
umbrella device - *see* Complication, umbrella device, vascular
vascular graft (or anastomosis) - *see* Complication, graft, vascular
carotid artery (bypass) graft - *see* Complications, graft, vascular
catheter (device) NEC – *see also* Complications, prosthetic device or implant
cystostomy T83.89
embolism T83.81
fibrosis T83.82
hemorrhage T83.83
infection and inflammation T83.59
mechanical
breakdown T83.010
displacement T83.020
leakage T83.030
malposition T83.020
obstruction T83.090
perforation T83.090
protrusion T83.090
specified NEC T83.090
pain T83.84
specified type NEC T83.89
stenosis T83.85
thrombosis T83.86
dialysis (vascular) T82.9
embolism T82.818
fibrosis T82.828
hemorrhage T82.838
infection and inflammation T82.7
intraperitoneal - *see* Complications, catheter, intraperitoneal
mechanical
breakdown T82.41
displacement T82.42
leakage T82.43
malposition T82.42
obstruction T82.49
perforation T82.49
protrusion T82.49
pain T82.848
specified type NEC T82.898
stenosis T82.858
thrombosis T82.868
epidural infusion T85.89
embolism T85.81
fibrosis T85.82
hemorrhage T85.83
infection and inflammation T85.79
mechanical
breakdown T85.610
displacement T85.620
leakage T85.630
malfunction T85.610
malposition T85.620
obstruction T85.690

Complication(s) *(Continued)*
catheter (device) NEC *(Continued)*
epidural infusion *(Continued)*
mechanical *(Continued)*
perforation T85.690
protrusion T85.690
specified NEC T85.690
pain T85.84
specified type NEC T85.89
stenosis T85.85
thrombosis T85.86
intraperitoneal dialysis T85.89
embolism T85.81
fibrosis T85.82
hemorrhage T85.83
infection and inflammation T85.71
mechanical
breakdown T85.611
displacement T85.621
leakage T85.631
malfunction T85.611
malposition T85.621
obstruction T85.691
perforation T85.691
protrusion T85.691
specified NEC T85.691
pain T85.84
specified type NEC T85.89
stenosis T85.85
thrombosis T85.86
intravenous infusion T82.9
embolism T82.818
fibrosis T82.828
hemorrhage T82.838
infection or inflammation T82.7
mechanical
breakdown T82.514
displacement T82.524
leakage T82.534
malposition T82.524
obstruction T82.594
perforation T82.594
protrusion T82.594
pain T82.848
specified type NEC T82.898
stenosis T82.858
thrombosis T82.868
subdural infusion T85.89
embolism T85.81
fibrosis T85.82
hemorrhage T85.83
infection and inflammation T85.79
mechanical
breakdown T85.610
displacement T85.620
leakage T85.630
malfunction T85.610
malposition T85.620
obstruction T85.690
perforation T85.690
protrusion T85.690
specified NEC T85.690
pain T85.84
specified type NEC T85.89
stenosis T85.85
thrombosis T85.86
urethral, indwelling T83.89
embolism T83.81
fibrosis T83.82
hemorrhage T83.83
infection and inflammation T83.51
mechanical
breakdown T83.018
pain T83.84

Complication(s) *(Continued)*
  catheter (device) NEC *(Continued)*
    urethral, indwelling *(Continued)*
      specified type NEC T83.89
      stenosis T83.85
      thrombosis T83.86
    urinary (indwelling) – *see* Complications, catheter, urethral, indwelling
  cecostomy (stoma) – *see* Complications, colostomy
  cesarean delivery wound NEC O90.89
    disruption O90.0
    hematoma O90.2
    infection (following delivery) O86.0
  chemotherapy (antineoplastic) NEC T88.7 This code not for use in the inpatient setting
  chin implant (prosthetic) - *see* Complication, prosthetic device or implant, specified NEC
  circulatory system I99.8
    intraoperative I97.88
    postprocedural I97.89
      following cardiac surgery I97.19-
        postcardiotomy syndrome I97.0
      lymphedema after mastectomy I97.2
      hypertension I97.3
      specified NEC I97.89
  colostomy (stoma) K94.00
    hemorrhage K94.01
    infection K94.02
    malfunction K94.03
    mechanical K94.03
    specified complication NEC K94.09
  contraceptive device, intrauterine – *see* Complications, intrauterine, contraceptive device
  cord (umbilical) - *see* Complications, umbilical cord
  corneal graft – *see* Complications, graft, cornea
  coronary artery (bypass) graft T82.9
    atherosclerosis - *see* Arteriosclerosis, coronary (artery),
    embolism T82.818
    fibrosis T82.828
    hemorrhage T82.838
    infection and inflammation T82.7
    mechanical
      breakdown T82.211
      displacement T82.212
      leakage T82.213
      malposition T82.212
      obstruction T82.218
      perforation T82.218
      protrusion T82.218
      specified NEC T82.218
    pain T82.848
    specified type NEC T82.897
    stenosis T82.858
    thrombosis T82.868
  counterpulsation device (balloon), intra- aortic – *see* Complications, balloon implant, vascular
  cystostomy (stoma) N99.518
    catheter - *see* Complications, catheter, cystostomy
    hemorrhage N99.510
    infection N99.511
    malfunction N99.512
    specified type NEC N99.518

Complication(s) *(Continued)*
  delivery (see also Complications, obstetric) O75.9
    procedure (instrumental) (manual) (surgical) O75.4
    specified NEC O75.89
  dialysis (peritoneal) (renal) - *see also* Complications, infusion
    catheter (vascular) - *see* Complication, catheter, dialysis
    peritoneal, intraperitoneal – *see* Complications, catheter, intraperitoneal
  dorsal column (spinal) neurostimulator – *see* Complications, electronic stimulator device, spinal cord
  drug NEC T88.7 This code not for use in the inpatient setting
  ear procedure - *see also* Disorder, ear
    intraoperative H95.88-
      hematoma - *see* Complications..., intraoperative..., hemorrhage (hematoma) (of), ear
      hemorrhage - *see* Complications..., intraoperative..., hemorrhage (hematoma) (of), ear
      laceration - *see* Complications..., intraoperative..., puncture or laceration..., ear specified NEC H95.88-
    postoperative H95.89-
      external ear canal stenosis H95.81-
      hematoma - *see* Complications..., postprocedural..., hemorrhage (hematoma) (of), ear
      hemorrhage - *see* Complications..., postprocedural..., hemorrhage (hematoma) (of), ear
      postmastoidectomy - *see* Complications, postmastoidectomy
      specified NEC H95.89-
  ectopic pregnancy O08.9
    damage to pelvic organs O08.6
    embolism O08.2
    genital infection O08.0
    hemorrhage (delayed) (excessive) O08.1
    metabolic disorder O08.5
    renal failure O08.4
    shock O08.3
    specified type NEC O08.0
    venous complication NEC O08.7
  electronic stimulator device
    bladder (urinary) – *see* Complications, electronic stimulator device, urinary
    bone T84.89
      breakdown T84.310
      displacement T84.320
      embolism T84.81
      fibrosis T84.82
      hemorrhage T84.83
      infection or inflammation T84.7
      malfunction T84.310
      malposition T84.320
      mechanical NEC T84.390
      obstruction T84.390
      pain T84.84
      perforation T84.390
      protrusion T84.390
      specified type NEC T84.89
      stenosis T84.85
      thrombosis T84.86

Complication(s) *(Continued)*
  electronic stimulator device *(Continued)*
    brain T85.89
      embolism T85.81
      fibrosis T85.82
      hemorrhage T85.83
      infection and inflammation T85.79
      mechanical
        breakdown T85.110
        displacement T85.120
        leakage T85.190
        malposition T85.120
        obstruction T85.190
        perforation T85.190
        protrusion T85.190
        specified NEC T85.190
      pain T85.84
      specified type NEC T85.89
      stenosis T85.85
      thrombosis T85.86
    cardiac (defibrillator) (pacemaker) – *see* Complications, cardiovascular device or implant, electronic
    muscle T84.89
      breakdown T84.418
      displacement T84.428
      embolism T84.81
      fibrosis T84.82
      hemorrhage T84.83
      infection or inflammation T84.7
      mechanical NEC T84.498
      pain T84.84
      specified type NEC T84.89
      stenosis T84.85
      thrombosis T84.86
    nervous system T85.9
      brain – *see* Complications, electronic stimulator device, brain
      embolism T85.81
      fibrosis T85.82
      hemorrhage T85.83
      infection and inflammation T85.79
      mechanical
        breakdown T85.118
        displacement T85.128
        leakage T85.199
        malposition T85.128
        obstruction T85.199
        perforation T85.199
        protrusion T85.199
        specified NEC T85.199
      pain T85.84
      peripheral nerve – *see* Complications, electronic stimulator device, peripheral nerve
      specified type NEC T85.89
      spinal cord – *see* Complications, electronic stimulator device, spinal cord
      stenosis T85.85
      thrombosis T85.86
    peripheral nerve T85.89
      embolism T85.81
      fibrosis T85.82
      hemorrhage T85.83
      infection and inflammation T85.79
      mechanical
        breakdown T85.111
        displacement T85.121
        leakage T85.191
        malposition T85.121
        obstruction T85.191
        perforation T85.191

Complication(s) *(Continued)*
  electronic stimulator device *(Continued)*
    peripheral nerve *(Continued)*
      mechanical *(Continued)*
        protrusion T85.191
          specified NEC T85.191
      pain T85.84
      specified type NEC T85.89
      stenosis T85.85
      thrombosis T85.86
    spinal cord T85.89
      embolism T85.81
      fibrosis T85.82
      hemorrhage T85.83
      infection and inflammation
          T85.79
      mechanical
        breakdown T85.112
        displacement T85.122
        leakage T85.192
        malposition T85.122
        obstruction T85.192
        perforation T85.192
        protrusion T85.192
        specified NEC T85.192
      pain T85.84
      specified type NEC T85.89
      stenosis T85.85
      thrombosis T85.86
    urinary T83.9
      embolism T83.81
      fibrosis T83.82
      hemorrhage T83.83
      infection and inflammation
          T83.59
      mechanical
        breakdown T83.110
        displacement T83.120
        malposition T83.120
        perforation T83.190
        protrusion T83.190
        specified NEC T83.190
      pain T83.84
      specified type NEC T83.89
      stenosis T83.85
      thrombosis T83.86
  electroshock therapy T88.9
    specified NEC T88.8
  endocrine E34.9
    postprocedural
      adrenal hypofunction E89.6
      hypoinsulinemia E89.1
      hypoparathyroidism E89.2
      hypopituitarism E89.3
      hypothyroidism E89.0
      ovarian failure E89.40
        asymptomatic E89.40
        symptomatic E89.41
      specified NEC E89.89
      testicular hypofunction E89.5
  endodontic treatment NEC M27.59
  enterostomy (stoma) K94.10
    hemorrhage K94.11
    infection K94.12
    malfunction K94.13
    mechanical K94.13
    specified complication NEC
        K94.19
  episiotomy, disruption O90.1
  esophageal anti-reflux device T85.89
    embolism T85.81
    fibrosis T85.82
    hemorrhage T85.83
    infection and inflammation T85.79

Complication(s) *(Continued)*
  esophageal anti-reflux device *(Continued)*
    mechanical
      breakdown T85.511
      displacement T85.521
      malfunction T85.511
      malposition T85.521
      obstruction T85.591
      perforation T85.591
      protrusion T85.591
      specified NEC T85.591
    pain T85.84
    specified type NEC T85.89
    stenosis T85.85
    thrombosis T85.86
  esophagostomy K94.30
    hemorrhage K94.31
    infection K94.32
    malfunction K94.33
    mechanical K94.33
    specified complication NEC K94.39
  extracorporeal circulation T80.9
  extremity artery (bypass) graft T82.9
    arteriosclerosis - *see* Arteriosclerosis,
        extremities, bypass graft
    embolism T82.818
    fibrosis T82.828
    hemorrhage T82.838
    infection and inflammation T82.7
    mechanical
      breakdown T82.318
        femoral artery T82.312
      displacement T82.328
        femoral artery T82.322
      leakage T82.338
        femoral artery T82.332
      malposition T82.328
        femoral artery T82.322
      obstruction T82.398
        femoral artery T82.392
      perforation T82.398
        femoral artery T82.392
      protrusion T82.398
        femoral artery T82.392
    pain T82.848
    specified type NEC T82.898
    stenosis T82.858
    thrombosis T82.868
  eye H57.9
    corneal graft - *see* Complications,
        graft, cornea
    implant (prosthetic) T85.89
      embolism T85.81
      fibrosis T85.82
      hemorrhage T85.83
      infection and inflammation
          T85.79
      mechanical
        breakdown T85.318
        displacement T85.328
        leakage T85.398
        malposition T85.328
        obstruction T85.398
        perforation T85.398
        protrusion T85.398
        specified NEC T85.398
      pain T85.84
      specified type NEC T85.89
      stenosis T85.85
      thrombosis T85.86
    intraocular lens - *see* Complications,
        intraocular lens
    orbital prosthesis - *see* Complications,
        orbital prosthesis

Complication(s) *(Continued)*
  female genital N94.9
    device, implant or graft NEC –
        see Complications, genitouri-
        nary, device or implant, genital
        tract
  femoral artery (bypass) graft - *see*
      Complication, extremity artery
      (bypass) graft
  fixation device, internal (orthopedic)
      T84.9
    infection and inflammation
        T84.60
      arm T84.61-
        humerus T84.61-
        radius T84.61-
        ulna T84.61-
      leg T84.629
        femur T84.62-
        fibula T84.62-
        tibia T84.62-
      specified site NEC T84.69
      spine T84.63
    mechanical
      breakdown
        limb T84.119
          carpal T84.210
          femur T84.11-
          fibula T84.11-
          humerus T84.11-
          metacarpal T84.210
          metatarsal T84.213
          phalanx
            foot T84.213
            hand T84.210
          radius T84.11-
          tarsal T84.213
          ulna T84.11-
          tibia T84.11-
        specified bone NEC T84.218
        spine T84.216
      displacement
        limb T84.129
          carpal T84.220
          femur T84.12-
          fibula T84.12-
          humerus T84.12-
          metacarpal T84.220
          metatarsal T84.223
          phalanx
            foot T84.223
            hand T84.220
          radius T84.12-
          tarsal T84.223
          ulna T84.12-
          tibia T84.12-
        specified bone NEC T84.228
        spine T84.226
      malposition - *see* Complications,
          fixation device, internal,
          mechanical, displacement
      obstruction - *see* Complications,
          fixation device, internal,
          mechanical, specified
          type NEC
      perforation - *see* Complications,
          fixation device, internal,
          mechanical, specified
          type NEC
      protrusion - *see* Complications,
          fixation device, internal,
          mechanical, specified
          type NEC
      specified type NEC

137

Complication(s) (Continued)
  fixation device, internal (Continued)
    mechanical (Continued)
      limb T84.199
        carpal T84.290
        femur T84.19-
        fibula T84.19-
        humerus T84.19-
        metacarpal T84.290
        metatarsal T84.293
        phalanx
          foot T84.293
          hand T84.290
        radius T84.19-
        tarsal T84.293
        tibia T84.19-
        ulna T84.19-
      specified bone NEC T84.298
      vertebra T84.296
    specified type NEC T84.89
    embolism T84.81
    fibrosis T84.82
    hemorrhage T84.83
    pain T84.84
    specified complication NEC T84.89
    stenosis T84.85
    thrombosis T84.86
  following
    acute myocardial infarction NEC I23.8
    aneurysm (false) (of cardiac wall)
      (of heart wall) (ruptured)
      I23.3
    angina I23.7
    atrial
      septal defect I23.1
      thrombosis I23.6
    cardiac wall rupture I23.3
    chordae tendinae rupture I23.4
    defect
      septal
        atrial (heart) I23.1
        ventricular (heart) I23.2
    hemopericardium I23.0
    papillary muscle rupture I23.5
    rupture
      cardiac wall I23.3
        with hemopericardium I23.0
      chordae tendineae I23.4
      papillary muscle I23.5
    specified NEC I23.8
    thrombosis
      atrium I23.6
      auricular appendage I23.6
      ventricle (heart) I23.6
    ventricular
      septal defect I23.2
      thrombosis I23.6
  ectopic or molar pregnancy O08.9
    cardiac arrest O08.81
    sepsis O08.82
    specified type NEC O08.89
    urinary tract infection O08.83
  gastrointestinal K92.9
    bile duct prosthesis - see Complica-
      tions, bile duct implant
    esophageal anti-reflux device - see
      Complications, esophageal anti-
      reflux device
    postoperative
      colostomy – see Complications,
        colostomy
      dumping syndrome K91.1
      enterostomy – see Complications,
        enterostomy

Complication(s) (Continued)
  gastrointestinal (Continued)
    postoperative (Continued)
      gastrostomy – see Complications,
        gastrostomy
      malabsorption NEC K91.2
      obstruction K91.3
      postcholecystectomy syndrome
        K91.5
      specified NEC K91.89
      vomiting after GI surgery K91.0
    prosthetic device or implant
      bile duct prosthesis - see Complica-
        tions, bile duct implant
      esophageal anti-reflux device - see
        Complications, esophageal
        anti-reflux device
      specified type NEC
      embolism T85.81
        fibrosis T85.82
        hemorrhage T85.83
        mechanical
          breakdown T85.518
          displacement T85.528
          malfunction T85.518
          malposition T85.528
          obstruction T85.598
          perforation T85.598
          protrusion T85.598
          specified NEC T85.598
        pain T85.84
        specified complication NEC
          T85.89
        stenosis T85.85
        thrombosis T85.86
  gastrostomy (stoma) K94.20
    hemorrhage K94.21
    infection K94.22
    malfunction K94.23
    mechanical K94.23
    specified complication NEC K94.29
  genitourinary
    device or implant T83.9
      genital tract T83.9
        infection or inflammation T83.6
        intrauterine contraceptive device
          - see Complications, intra-
          uterine, contraceptive device
        mechanical - see Complications,
          by device, mechanical
        penile prosthesis - see Complica-
          tions, prosthetic device,
          penile
        specified type NEC T83.89
          embolism T83.81
          fibrosis T83.82
          hemorrhage T83.83
          pain T83.84
          specified complication NEC
            T83.89
          stenosis T83.85
          thrombosis T83.86
      urinary system T83.9
        cystostomy catheter - see Compli-
          cation, catheter, cystostomy
        electronic stimulator – see
          Complications, electronic
          stimulator device, urinary
        indwelling urethral catheter - see
          Complications, catheter,
          urethral, indwelling
        infection or inflammation T83.59
          indwelling urinary catheter
            T83.51

Complication(s) (Continued)
  genitourinary (Continued)
    device or implant (Continued)
      urinary system (Continued)
        kidney transplant - see
          Complication, transplant,
          kidney
        organ graft - see Complication,
          graft, urinary organ
        specified type NEC T83.89
          embolism T83.81
          fibrosis T83.82
          hemorrhage T83.83
          mechanical T83.198
            breakdown T83.118
            displacement T83.128
            malfunction T83.118
            malposition T83.128
            obstruction T83.198
            perforation T83.198
            protrusion T83.198
            specified NEC T83.198
          pain T83.84
          specified complication NEC
            T83.89
          stenosis T83.85
          thrombosis T83.86
        sphincter implant - see Compli-
          cations, implant, urinary
          sphincter
    postprocedural
      pelvic peritoneal adhesions
        N99.4
      renal failure N99.0
      specified NEC N99.89
      stoma - see Complications, stoma,
        urinary tract
      urethral stricture – see Stricture,
        urethra, postprocedural
      vaginal
        adhesions N99.2
        vault prolapse N99.3
  graft (bypass) (patch) – see also Com-
    plications, prosthetic device or
    implant
    aorta - see Complications, graft,
      vascular
    arterial - see Complication, graft,
      vascular
    bone T86.839
      failure T86.831
      infection T86.832
      mechanical T84.318
        breakdown T84.318
        displacement T84.328
        protrusion T84.398
        specified type NEC T84.398
      rejection T86.830
      specified type NEC T86.838
    carotid artery - see Complications,
      graft, vascular
    cornea T86.849
      failure T86.841
      infection T86.842
      mechanical T85.318
        breakdown T85.318
        displacement T85.328
        protrusion T85.398
        specified type NEC T85.398
      rejection T86.840
      specified type NEC T86.848
    femoral artery (bypass) - see Compli-
      cation, extremity artery (bypass)
      graft

Complication(s) *(Continued)*
  graft *(Continued)*
    genital organ or tract – *see* Complica-
      tions, genitourinary, device or
      implant, genital tract
    muscle T84.9
      breakdown T84.410
      displacement T84.420
      embolism T84.81
      fibrosis T84.82
      hemorrhage T84.83
      infection and inflammation T84.7
      mechanical NEC T84.490
      pain T84.84
      specified type NEC T84.89
      stenosis T84.85
      thrombosis T84.86
    nerve - *see* Complication, prosthetic
      device or implant, specified
      NEC
    skin – *see* Complications, prosthetic
      device or implant, skin graft
    tendon T84.89
      breakdown T84.410
      displacement T84.420
      embolism T84.81
      fibrosis T84.82
      hemorrhage T84.83
      infection and inflammation T84.7
      mechanical NEC T84.490
      pain T84.84
      specified type NEC T84.89
      stenosis T84.85
      thrombosis T84.86
    urinary organ T83.89
      embolism T83.81
      fibrosis T83.82
      hemorrhage T83.83
      infection and inflammation
        T83.59
        indwelling urinary catheter
          T83.51
      mechanical
        breakdown T83.21
        displacement T83.22
        leakage T83.23
        malposition T83.22
        obstruction T83.29
        perforation T83.29
        protrusion T83.29
        specified NEC T83.29
      pain T83.84
      specified type NEC T83.89
      stenosis T83.85
      thrombosis T83.86
    vascular T82.9
      embolism T82.818
      femoral artery - *see* Complication,
        extremity artery (bypass) graft
      fibrosis T82.828
      hemorrhage T82.838
      mechanical
        breakdown T82.319
          aorta (bifurcation) T82.310
          carotid artery T82.311
          specified vessel NEC T82.318
        displacement T82.329
          aorta (bifurcation) T82.320
          carotid artery T82.321
          specified vessel NEC T82.328
        leakage T82.339
          aorta (bifurcation) T82.330
          carotid artery T82.331
          specified vessel NEC T82.338

Complication(s) *(Continued)*
  graft *(Continued)*
    vascular *(Continued)*
      mechanical *(Continued)*
        malposition T82.329
          aorta (bifurcation) T82.320
          carotid artery T82.321
          specified vessel NEC T82.328
        obstruction T82.399
          aorta (bifurcation) T82.390
          carotid artery T82.391
          specified vessel NEC T82.398
        perforation T82.399
          aorta (bifurcation) T82.390
          carotid artery T82.391
          specified vessel NEC T82.398
        protrusion T82.399
          aorta (bifurcation) T82.390
          carotid artery T82.391
          specified vessel NEC T82.398
      pain T82.848
      specified complication NEC T82.898
      stenosis T82.858
      thrombosis T82.868
  heart I51.9
    assist device
      infection and inflammation
        T82.7
    following acute myocardial infarction
      - *see* Complications, following,
      acute myocardial infarction
    postoperative - *see* Complications,
      circulatory system
    transplant - *see* Complication, trans-
      plant, heart
      and lung(s) – *see* Complications,
        transplant, heart, with lung
    valve
      graft (biological) T82.9
        embolism T82.817
        fibrosis T82.827
        hemorrhage T82.837
        infection and inflammation T82.7
        mechanical T82.228
          breakdown T82.221
          displacement T82.222
          leakage T82.223
          malposition T82.222
          obstruction T82.218
          perforation T82.228
          protrusion T82.228
        pain T82.847
        specified type NEC T82.897
        stenosis T82.857
        thrombosis T82.867
      prosthesis T82.09
        embolism T82.817
        fibrosis T82.827
        hemorrhage T82.837
        infection or inflammation
          T82.6
        mechanical T82.01
          breakdown T82.01
          displacement T82.02
          leakage T82.03
          malposition T82.02
          obstruction T82.09
          perforation T82.09
          protrusion T82.09
        pain T82.847
        specified type NEC T82.897
          mechanical T82.09
        stenosis T82.857
        thrombosis T82.867

Complication(s) *(Continued)*
  hematoma - *see* Complication
  hemodialysis - *see* Complications,
    dialysis
  hemorrhage
  ileostomy (stoma) – *see* Complications,
    enterostomy
  immunization (procedure) - *see* Compli-
    cations, vaccination
  implant - *see also* Complications, by site
    and type
    urinary sphincter T83.9
      embolism T83.81
      fibrosis T83.82
      hemorrhage T83.83
      infection and inflammation T83.59
      mechanical
        breakdown T83.111
        displacement T83.121
        leakage T83.191
        malposition T83.121
        obstruction T83.191
        perforation T83.191
        protrusion T83.191
        specified NEC T83.191
      pain T83.84
      specified type NEC T83.89
      stenosis T83.85
      thrombosis T83.86
  infusion (procedure) T80.9
    air embolism T80.0
    blood - *see* Complications, transfusion
    catheter - *see* Complications, catheter
    infection T80.29
    phlebitis T80.1
    pump - *see* Complications, cardio-
      vascular, device or implant
    sepsis T80.29
    serum reaction T80.6
      anaphylactic shock T80.5
    specified type NEC T80.89
  inhalation therapy NEC T81.81
  injection (procedure) T80.9
    drug reaction - *see* Reaction, drug
    infection T80.29
    sepsis T80.29
    serum (prophylactic) (therapeutic)
      - *see* Complications, vaccination
    specified type NEC T80.89
    vaccine (any) - *see* Complications,
      vaccination
  inoculation (any) - *see* Complications,
    vaccination
  insulin pump
    infection and inflammation T85.72
    mechanical
      breakdown T85.614
      displacement T85.624
      leakage T85.633
      malposition T85.624
      obstruction T85.694
      perforation T85.694
      protrusion T85.694
      specified NEC T84.694
  intestinal pouch NEC K91.858
  intraocular lens (prosthetic) T85.89
    embolism T85.81
    fibrosis T85.82
    hemorrhage T85.83
    infection and inflammation T85.79
    mechanical
      breakdown T85.21
      displacement T85.22
      malposition T85.22

Complication(s) *(Continued)*
  intraocular lens *(Continued)*
    mechanical *(Continued)*
      obstruction T85.29
      perforation T85.29
      protrusion T85.29
      specified NEC T85.29
    pain T85.84
    specified type NEC T85.89
    stenosis T85.85
    thrombosis T85.86
  intraoperative (intraprocedural)
    cardiac arrest
      during cardiac surgery I97.710
      during other surgery I97.711
    cardiac functional disturbance NEC
      during cardiac surgery I97.790
      during other surgery I97.791
    hemorrhage (hematoma) (of)
      circulatory system organ or
        structure
        during cardiac bypass I97.411
        during cardiac catheterization
          I97.410
        during other circulatory system
          procedure I97.418
        during other procedure I97.42
      digestive system organ
        during procedure on digestive
          system K91.61
        during procedure on other organ
          K91.62
      ear
        during procedure on ear and
          mastoid process H95.21
        during procedure on other organ
          H95.22
      endocrine system organ or structure
        during procedure on endocrine
          system organ or structure
          E36.01
        during procedure on other organ
          E36.02
      eye and adnexa
        during ophthalmic procedure
          H59.11-
        during other procedure H59.12-
      genitourinary organ or structure
        during procedure on genito-
          urinary organ or structure
          N99.61
        during procedure on other organ
          N99.62
      mastoid process
        during procedure on ear and
          mastoid process H95.21
        during procedure on other organ
          H95.22
      musculoskeletal structure
        during musculoskeletal surgery
          M96.810
        during non-orthopedic surgery
          M96.811
        during orthopedic surgery
          M96.810
      nervous system
        during a nervous system proce-
          dure G97.31
        during other procedure G97.32
      respiratory system
        during procedure on respiratory
          system organ or structure
          J95.61
        during other procedure J95.62

Complication(s) *(Continued)*
  intraoperative *(Continued)*
    hemorrhage *(Continued)*
      skin and subcutaneous tissue
        during a dermatologic procedure
          L76.01
        during a procedure on other
          organ L76.02
      spleen
        during a procedure on the spleen
          D78.01
        during a procedure on other
          organ D78.02
    puncture or laceration (accidental)
      (unintentional) (of)
      brain
        during a nervous system proce-
          dure G97.48
        during other procedure
          G97.49
      circulatory system organ or
        structure
        during circulatory system proce-
          dure I97.51
        during other procedure I97.52
      digestive system
        during procedure on digestive
          system K91.71
        during procedure on other organ
          K91.72
      ear
        during procedure on ear and
          mastoid process H95.31
        during procedure on other organ
          H95.32
      endocrine system organ or
        structure
        during procedure on endocrine
          system organ or structure
          E36.11
        during procedure on other organ
          E36.12
      eye and adnexa
        during ophthalmic procedure
          H59.21-
        during other procedure
          H59.22-
      genitourinary organ or structure
        during procedure on genito-
          urinary organ or structure
          N99.71
        during procedure on other organ
          N99.72
      mastoid process
        during procedure on ear and
          mastoid process H95.31
        during procedure on other organ
          H95.32
      musculoskeletal structure
        during musculoskeletal surgery
          M96.820
        during non-orthopedic surgery
          M96.821
        during orthopedic surgery
          M96.820
      nervous system
        during a nervous system proce-
          dure G97.48
        during other procedure G97.49
      respiratory system
        during procedure on respiratory
          system organ or structure
          J95.71
        during other procedure J95.72

Complication(s) *(Continued)*
  intraoperative *(Continued)*
    puncture or laceration *(Continued)*
      skin and subcutaneous tissue
        during a dermatologic procedure
          L76.11
        during a procedure on other
          organ L76.12
      spleen
        during a procedure on the spleen
          D78.11
        during a procedure on other
          organ D78.12
    specified NEC
    circulatory system I97.88
      digestive system K91.81
      ear H95.88
      endocrine system E36.8
      eye and adnexa H59.88
      genitourinary system N99.81
      mastoid process H95.88
      musculoskeletal structure
        H96.89
      nervous system G97.81
      respiratory system J95.88
      skin and subcutaneous tissue
        L76.81
      spleen D78.81
  intraperitoneal catheter (dialysis)
    (infusion) – *see* Complications,
    catheter, intraperitoneal
  intrauterine
    contraceptive device
      embolism T83.81
      fibrosis T83.82
      hemorrhage T83.83
      infection and inflammation
        T83.6
      mechanical
        breakdown T83.31
        displacement T83.32
        malposition T83.32
        obstruction T83.39
        perforation T83.39
        protrusion T83.39
        specified NEC T83.39
      pain T83.84
      specified type NEC T83.89
      stenosis T83.85
      thrombosis T83.86
    procedure (fetal), to newborn
      P96.5
  jejunostomy (stoma) – *see* Complica-
    tions, enterostomy
  joint prosthesis, internal T84.9
    breakage (fracture) T84.01-
    dislocation T84.02-
    fracture T84.01-
    instability T84.02-
    subluxation T84.02-
    infection or inflammation
      T84.50
      hip T84.5-
      knee T84.5-
      specified joint NEC T84.59
    malposition - *see* Complications,
      joint prosthesis, mechanical,
      displacement
    mechanical
      breakage, broken T84.01-
      dislocation T84.02-
      fracture T84.01-
      instability T84.02-
      subluxation T84.02-

Complication(s) *(Continued)*
  joint prosthesis, internal *(Continued)*
    mechanical *(Continued)*
      leakage - *see* Complications, joint
        prosthesis, mechanical,
        specified NEC
      loosening T84.039
        hip T84.03-
        knee T84.03-
        specified joint NEC T84.038
      obstruction - *see* Complications,
        joint prosthesis, mechanical,
        specified NEC
      perforation - *see* Complications,
        joint prosthesis, mechanical,
        specified NEC
      periprosthetic
        osteolysis T84.059
          hip T84.05-
          knee T84.05-
          other specified joint T84.058
        fracture T84.049
          hip T84.04-
          knee T84.04-
          other specified joint T84.048
      protrusion - *see* Complications,
        joint prosthesis, mechanical,
        specified NEC
      specified complication NEC
        T84.099
        hip T84.09-
        knee T84.09-
        other specified joint T84.098
      wear of articular bearing surface
        T84.069
        hip T84.06-
        knee T84.06-
        other specified joint T84.068
    specified joint NEC T84.89
    embolism T84.81
    fibrosis T84.82
    hemorrhage T84.83
    pain T84.84
    specified complication NEC T84.89
    stenosis T84.85
    thrombosis T84.86
  kidney transplant – *see* Complications,
    transplant, kidney
  labor O75.9
    specified NEC O75.89
  liver transplant (immune or nonim-
    mune) – *see* Complications, trans-
    plant, liver
  lumbar puncture G97.1
    cerebrospinal fluid leak G97.0
    headache or reaction G97.1
  lung transplant – *see* Complications,
    transplant, lung
    and heart – *see* Complications, trans-
    plant, lung, with heart
  male genital N50.9
    device, implant or graft – *see*
      Complications, genitourinary,
      device or implant, genital tract
    postprocedural or postoperative – *see*
      Complications, genitourinary,
      postprocedural
    specified NEC N99.89
  mastoid (process) procedure
    intraoperative H95.88-
      hematoma - *see* Complications...,
        intraoperative..., hemorrhage
        (hematoma) (of), mastoid
        process

Complication(s) *(Continued)*
  mastoid *(Continued)*
    intraoperative *(Continued)*
      hemorrhage - *see* Complications...,
        intraoperative..., hemorrhage
        (hematoma) (of), mastoid
        process
      laceration - *see* Complications,...
        intraoperative..., puncture or
        laceration..., mastoid process
      specified NEC H95.88-
    postmastoidectomy - *see* Complica-
      tions, postmastoidectomy
    postoperative H95.89-
      external ear canal stenosis H95.81-
      hematoma - *see* Complications...,
        postprocedural, hemorrhage
        (hematoma) (of), mastoid
        process
      hemorrhage - *see* Complications...,
        postprocedural, hemorrhage
        (hematoma) (of), mastoid
        process
      postmastoidectomy - *see* Complica-
        tions, postmastoidectomy
      specified NEC H95.89-
    mastoidectomy cavity - *see* Complica-
      tions, postmastoidectomy
  mechanical - *see* Complications, by site
    and type, mechanical
  medical procedures T88.9 - *see also*
    Complication, intraoperative
  metabolic E88.9
    postoperative E89.89
      specified NEC E89.89
  molar pregnancy NOS O08.9
    damage to pelvic organs O08.6
    embolism O08.2
    genital infection O08.0
    hemorrhage (delayed) (excessive)
      O08.1
    metabolic disorder O08.5
    renal failure O08.4
    shock O08.3
    specified type NEC O08.0
    venous complication NEC O08.7
  musculoskeletal system - *see also* Com-
    plication, intraoperative (intrapro-
    cedural), by site
    device, implant or graft NEC – *see*
      Complications, orthopedic,
      device or implant
    internal fixation (nail) (plate) (rod)
      – *see* Complications, fixation
      device, internal
    joint prosthesis – *see* Complications,
      joint prosthesis
    postoperative (postprocedural)
      M96.89
      with osteoporosis – *see*
        Osteoporosis
      fracture following insertion of
        device - *see* Fracture, follow-
        ing insertion of orthopedic
        implant, joint prosthesis or
        bone plate
      joint instability after prosthesis
        removal M96.89
      lordosis M96.4
      postlaminectomy syndrome NEC
        M96.1
        kyphosis M96.3
      pseudarthrosis M96.0
      specified complication NEC M96.89

Complication(s) *(Continued)*
  musculoskeletal system *(Continued)*
    post radiation M96.89
      kyphosis M96.3
      scoliosis M96.5
      specified complication NEC M96.89
  nephrostomy (stoma) – *see* Complica-
    tions, stoma, urinary tract, external
    NEC
  nervous system G98.8
    central G96.9
    device, implant or graft - *see also*
      Complication, prosthetic device
      or implant, specified NEC
      electronic stimulator (electrode(s))
        – *see* Complications, electronic
        stimulator device
      ventricular shunt - *see* Complica-
        tions, ventricular shunt
    electronic stimulator (electrode(s))
      – *see* Complications, electronic
      stimulator device
    postprocedural G97.82
      intracranial hypotension G97.2
      specified NEC G97.82
      spinal fluid leak G97.0
  newborn, due to intrauterine (fetal)
    procedure P96.5
  nonabsorbable (permanent) sutures -
    see Complication, sutures,
    permanent
  obstetric O75.9
    procedure (instrumental) (manual)
      (surgical) specified NEC O75.4
    specified NEC O75.89
    surgical wound NEC O90.89
      hematoma O90.2
      infection O86.0
  ocular lens implant – *see* Complications,
    intraocular lens
  ophthalmologic
    postprocedural bleb - *see* Blebitis
  orbital prosthesis T85.89
    embolism T85.81
    fibrosis T85.82
    hemorrhage T85.83
    infection and inflammation T85.79
    mechanical
      breakdown T85.31-
      displacement T85.32-
      malposition T85.32-
      obstruction T85.39-
      perforation T85.39-
      protrusion T85.39-
      specified NEC T85.39-
    pain T85.84
    specified type NEC T85.89
    stenosis T85.85
    thrombosis T85.86
  organ or tissue transplant (partial) (to-
    tal) - *see* Complications, transplant
  orthopedic - *see also* Disorder, soft tissue
    device or implant T84.9
      bone
        device or implant - *see* Complica-
          tion, bone, device NEC
        graft - *see* Complication, graft,
          bone
      breakdown T84.418
      displacement T84.428
      electronic bone stimulator - *see*
        Complications, electronic
        stimulator device, bone
      embolism T84.81

Complication(s) *(Continued)*
  orthopedic *(Continued)*
    device or implant *(Continued)*
      fibrosis T84.82
      fixation device - *see* Complication, fixation device, internal
      hemorrhage T84.83
      infection or inflammation T84.7
      joint prosthesis - *see* Complication, joint prosthesis, internal
      malfunction T84.418
      malposition T84.428
      mechanical NEC T84.498
      muscle graft - *see* Complications, graft, muscle
      obstruction T84.498
      pain T84.84
      perforation T84.498
      protrusion T84.498
      specified complication NEC T84.89
      stenosis T84.85
      tendon graft - *see* Complications, graft, tendon
      thrombosis T84.86
    fracture (following insertion of device) - *see* Fracture, following insertion of orthopedic implant, joint prosthesis or bone plate
    postprocedural M96.89
      fracture - *see* Fracture, following insertion of orthopedic implant, joint prosthesis or bone plate
      postlaminectomy syndrome NEC M96.1
        kyphosis M96.3
        lordosis M96.4
      postradiation
        kyphosis M96.2
        scoliosis M96.5
      pseudarthrosis post-fusion M96.0
      specified type NEC M96.89
  pacemaker (cardiac) – *see* Complications, cardiovascular device or implant, electronic
  pancreas transplant - *see* Complications, transplant, pancreas
  penile prosthesis (implant) – *see* Complications, prosthetic device, penile
  perfusion NEC T80.9
  perineal repair (obstetrical) NEC O90.89
    disruption O90.1
    hematoma O90.2
    infection (following delivery) O86.0
  phototherapy T88.9
    specified NEC T88.8
  postmastoidectomy NEC H95.19-
    cyst, mucosal H95.13-
    granulation H95.12-
    inflammation, chronic H95.11-
    recurrent cholesteatoma H95.0-
  postoperative - *see* Complications, postprocedural
    circulatory – *see* Complications, circulatory system
    ear – *see* Complications, ear
    endocrine – *see* Complications, endocrine
    eye – *see* Complications, eye
    lumbar puncture G97.1
      cerebrospinal fluid leak G97.0

Complication(s) *(Continued)*
  postoperative *(Continued)*
    nervous system (central) (peripheral) – *see* Complications, nervous system
    respiratory system – *see* Complications, respiratory system
  postprocedural – *see also* Complications, surgical procedure
    cardiac arrest
      following cardiac surgery I97.120
      following other surgery I97.121
    cardiac functional disturbance NEC
    following cardiac surgery I97.190
    following other surgery I97.191
    cardiac insufficiency
      following cardiac surgery I97.110
      following other surgery I97.111
    chorioretinal scars following retinal surgery H59.81-
    following cataract surgery
      cataract (lens) fragments H59.02-
      cystoid macular edema H59.03-
      specified NEC H59.09-
      vitreous (touch) syndrome H59.01-
    heart failure
      following cardiac surgery I97.130
      following other surgery I97.131
    hemorrhage (hematoma) (of)
      circulatory system organ or structure
        following a cardiac bypass I97.611
        following a cardiac catheterization I97.610
        following other circulatory system procedure I97.618
        following other procedure I97.62
      digestive system
        following procedure on digestive system K91.840
        following procedure on other organ K91.841
      ear
        following procedure on ear and mastoid process H95.41
        following other procedure H95.42
      endocrine system
        following endocrine system procedure E89.810
        following other procedure E89.811
      eye and adnexa
        following ophthalmic procedure H59.31-
        following other procedure H59.32-
      genitourinary organ or structure
        following procedure on genitourinary organ or structure N99.820
        following procedure on other organ N99.821
      mastoid process
        following procedure on ear and mastoid process H95.41
        following other procedure H95.42
      musculoskeletal structure
        following musculoskeletal surgery M96.830
        following non-orthopedic surgery M96.831
        following orthopedic surgery M96.830

Complication(s) *(Continued)*
  postprocedural *(Continued)*
    hemorrhage *(Continued)*
      nervous system
        during a nervous system procedure G97.51
        during other procedure G97.52
      respiratory system
        during procedure on respiratory system organ or structure J95.830
        during other procedure J95.831
      skin and subcutaneous tissue
        following a dermatologic procedure L76.21
        following a procedure on other organ L76.22
      spleen
        following procedure on the spleen D78.21
        following procedure on other organ D78.22
    specified NEC
      circulatory system I97.89
      digestive K91.89
      ear H95.89
      endocrine E89.89
      eye and adnexa H59.89
      genitourinary N99.89
      mastoid process H95.89
      metabolic E89.89
      musculoskeletal structure M96.89
      nervous system G97.82
      respiratory system J95.89
      skin and subcutaneous tissue L76.82
      spleen D78.89
  pregnancy NEC - *see* Pregnancy, complicated by
  prosthetic device or implant T85.9
    bile duct - *see* Complications, bile duct implant
    breast - *see* Complications, breast implant
    cardiac and vascular NEC – *see* Complications, cardiovascular device or implant
    corneal transplant - *see* Complications, graft, cornea
    electronic nervous system stimulator - *see* Complications, electronic stimulator device
    epidural infusion catheter - *see* Complications, catheter, epidural
    esophageal anti-reflux device - *see* Complications, esophageal anti-reflux device
    genital organ or tract – *see* Complications, genitourinary, device or implant, genital tract
    heart valve - *see* Complications, heart, valve, prosthesis
    infection or inflammation T85.79
      intestine transplant T86.892
      liver transplant T86.43
      lung transplant T86.812
      pancreas transplant T86.892
      skin graft T86.822
    intraocular lens - *see* Complications, intraocular lens
    intraperitoneal (dialysis) catheter - *see* Complications, catheter, intraperitoneal

Complication(s) *(Continued)*
  prosthetic device or implant *(Continued)*
    joint – *see* Complications, joint pros-
      thesis, internal
    mechanical NEC T85.698
      dialysis catheter (vascular) - *see*
        also Complication, catheter,
        dialysis, mechanical
        peritoneal - *see* Complication,
          catheter, intraperitoneal,
          mechanical
      gastrointestinal device T85.598
      ocular device T85.398
      subdural (infusion) catheter T85.690
      suture, permanent T85.692
        that for bone repair - *see* Com-
          plications, fixation device,
          internal (orthopedic),
          mechanical
      ventricular shunt
        breakdown T85.01
        displacement T85.02
        leakage T85.03
        malposition T85.02
        obstruction T85.09
        perforation T85.09
        protrusion T85.09
        specified NEC T85.09
  orbital - *see* Complications, orbital
    prosthesis
  penile T83.89
    embolism T83.81
    fibrosis T83.82
    hemorrhage T83.83
    infection and inflammation
      T83.6
    mechanical
      breakdown T83.410
      displacement T83.420
      leakage T83.490
      malposition T83.420
      obstruction T83.490
      perforation T83.490
      protrusion T83.490
      specified NEC T83.490
    pain T83.84
    specified type NEC T83.89
    stenosis T83.85
    thrombosis T83.86
  skin graft T86.829
    artificial skin or decellularized
      allodermis
      embolism T85.81
      fibrosis T85.82
      hemorrhage T85.83
      infection and inflammation
        T85.79
      mechanical
        breakdown T85.613
        displacement T85.623
        malfunction T85.613
        malposition T85.623
        obstruction T85.693
        perforation T85.693
        protrusion T85.693
        specified NEC T85.693
      pain T85.84
      specified type NEC T85.89
      stenosis T85.85
      thrombosis T85.86
    failure T86.821
    infection T86.822
    rejection T86.820
    specified NEC T86.828

Complication(s) *(Continued)*
  prosthetic device or implant *(Continued)*
    specified NEC T85.89
      embolism T85.81
      fibrosis T85.82
      hemorrhage T85.83
      infection and inflammation
        T85.79
      mechanical
        breakdown T85.618
        displacement T85.628
        leakage T85.638
        malfunction T85.618
        malposition T85.628
        obstruction T85.698
        perforation T85.698
        protrusion T85.698
        specified NEC T85.698
      pain T85.84
      specified type NEC T85.89
      stenosis T85.85
      thrombosis T85.86
    subdural infusion catheter - *see*
      Complications, catheter,
      subdural
    sutures - *see* Complications, sutures
    urinary organ or tract NEC – *see*
      Complications, genitourinary,
      device or implant, urinary
      system
    vascular – *see* Complications, cardio-
      vascular device or implant
    ventricular shunt - *see* Complications,
      ventricular shunt (device)
  puerperium - *see* Puerperal
  puncture, spinal G97.1
    cerebrospinal fluid leak G97.0
    headache or reaction G97.1
  pyelogram N99.89
  radiation
    kyphosis M96.2
    scoliosis M96.5
  reattached
    extremity (infection) (rejection)
      lower T87.1x-
      upper T87.0x-
    specified body part NEC T87.2
  reconstructed breast
    asymmetry between native and
      reconstructed breast N65.1
    deformity N65.0
    disproportion between native and
      reconstructed breast N65.1
    excess tissue N65.0
    misshappen N65.0
  reimplant NEC – *see also* Complications,
    prosthetic device or implant
    limb (infection) (rejection) – *see* Com-
      plications, reattached, extremity
    organ (partial) (total) - *see* Complica-
      tions, transplant
    prosthetic device NEC - *see* Complica-
      tions, prosthetic device
  renal N28.9
    allograft – *see* Complications, trans-
      plant, kidney
    dialysis - *see* Complications, dialysis
  respirator
    mechanical J95.850
      specified NEC J95.859
  respiratory system J98.9
    device, implant or graft - *see* Com-
      plication, prosthetic device or
      implant, specified NEC

Complication(s) *(Continued)*
  respiratory system *(Continued)*
    lung transplant – *see* Complications,
      prosthetic device or implant,
      lung transplant
    postoperative J95.9
      Mendelson's syndrome (chemical
        pneumonitis) J95.4
      pneumothorax J95.81
      pulmonary insufficiency (acute)
        (after nonthoracic surgery)
        J95.2
        chronic J95.3
        following thoracic surgery J95.1
      respiratory failure J95.82
      specified NEC J95.89
      subglottic stenosis J95.5
      tracheostomy complication - *see*
        Complications, tracheostomy
    therapy T81.89
  sedation during labor and delivery
    O74.9
    cardiac O74.2
    central nervous system O74.3
    pulmonary NEC O74.1
  shunt – *see also* Complications, pros-
    thetic device or implant
    arteriovenous – *see* Complications,
      arteriovenous, shunt
    ventricular (communicating) – *see*
      Complications, ventricular
      shunt
  skin
    graft T86.829
      failure T86.821
      infection T86.822
      rejection T86.820
      specified type NEC T86.828
  spinal
    anesthesia - *see* Complications, anes-
      thesia, spinal
    catheter (epidural) (subdural) – *see*
      Complications, catheter
    puncture or tap G97.1
      cerebrospinal fluid leak G97.0
      headache or reaction G97.1
  stent
    bile duct - *see* Complications, bile
      duct prosthesis
    urinary T83.89
      embolism T83.81
      fibrosis T83.82
      hemorrhage T83.83
      infection and inflammation
        T83.59
      mechanical
        breakdown T83.112
        displacement T83.122
        leakage T83.192
        malposition T83.122
        obstruction T83.192
        perforation T83.192
        protrusion T83.192
        specified NEC T83.192
      pain T83.84
      specified type NEC T83.89
      stenosis T83.85
      thrombosis T83.86
  stoma
    digestive tract
      colostomy – *see* Complications,
        colostomy
      enterostomy – *see* Complications,
        enterostomy

Complication(s) *(Continued)*
  stoma *(Continued)*
    digestive tract *(Continued)*
      esophagostomy - *see* Complications, esophagostomy
      gastrostomy – *see* Complications, gastrostomy
    urinary tract N99.538
      cystostomy – *see* Complications, cystostomy
      external NOS N99.528
        hemorrhage N99.520
        infection N99.521
        malfunction N99.522
        specified type NEC N99.528
      hemorrhage N99.530
      infection N99.531
      malfunction N99.532
      specified type NEC N99.538
  surgical material, nonabsorbable - *see* Complication, suture, permanent
  surgical procedure (on) T81.9
    amputation stump (late) – *see* Complications, amputation stump
    cardiac - *see* Complications, circulatory system
    cholesteatoma, recurrent - *see* Complications, postmastoidectomy, recurrent cholesteatoma
    circulatory (early) – *see* Complications, circulatory system
    digestive system – *see* Complications, gastrointestinal
    dumping syndrome (postgastrectomy) K91.1
    ear – *see* Complications, ear
    elephantiasis or lymphedema I97.89
      postmastectomy I97.2
    emphysema (surgical) T81.82
    endocrine – *see* Complications, endocrine
    eye – *see* Complications, eye
    fistula (persistent postoperative) T81.83
    foreign body inadvertently left in wound (sponge) (suture) (swab) – *see* Foreign body, accidentally left during a procedure
    gastrointestinal – *see* Complications, gastrointestinal
    genitourinary NEC N99.89
    hematoma - *see* Complications, hematoma
    hemorrhage – *see* Complications, hemorrhage associated with procedure
    hepatic failure K91.82
    hyperglycemia (postpancreatectomy) E89.1
    hypoinsulinemia (postpancreatectomy) E89.1
    hypoparathyroidism (postparathyroidectomy) E89.2
    hypopituitarism (posthypophysectomy) E89.3
    hypothyroidism (post-thyroidectomy) E89.0
    intestinal obstruction K91.3
    intracranial hypotension following ventricular shunting (ventriculostomy) G97.2
    lymphedema I97.89
      postmastectomy I97.2

Complication(s) *(Continued)*
  surgical procedure *(Continued)*
    malabsorption (postsurgical) NEC K91.2
      osteoporosis - *see* Osteoporosis, postsurgical malabsorption
    mastoidectomy cavity NEC - *see* Complications, postmastoidectomy
    metabolic E89.89
      specified NEC E89.89
    musculoskeletal – *see* Complications, musculoskeletal system
    nervous system (central) (peripheral) – *see* Complications, nervous system
    ovarian failure E89.40
      asymptomatic E89.40
      symptomatic E89.41
    peripheral vascular - *see* Complications, surgical procedure, vascular
    postcardiotomy syndrome I97.0
    postcholecystectomy syndrome K91.5
    postcommissurotomy syndrome I97.0
    postgastrectomy dumping syndrome K91.1
    postlaminectomy syndrome NEC M96.1
      kyphosis M96.3
    postmastectomy lymphedema syndrome I97.2
    postmastoidectomy cholesteatoma - *see* Complications, postmastoidectomy, recurrent cholesteatoma
    postvagotomy syndrome K91.1
    postvalvulotomy syndrome I97.0
    pulmonary insufficiency (acute) J95.2
      chronic J95.3
      following thoracic surgery J95.1
    reattached body part – *see* Complications, reattached
    respiratory – *see* Complications, respiratory system
    shock (hypovolemic) T81.1
    spleen (postoperative) D78.89
      intraoperative D78.81
    stitch abscess T81.4
    subglottic stenosis (postsurgical) J95.5
    testicular hypofunction E89.5
    transplant - *see* Complications, organ or tissue transplant
    urinary NEC N99.89
    vaginal vault prolapse (posthysterectomy) N99.3
    vascular (peripheral)
      artery T81.719
        mesenteric T81.710
        renal T81.711
        specified NEC T81.718
      vein T81.72
    wound infection T81.4
  suture, permanent (wire) NEC T85.89
    with repair of bone - *see* Complications, fixation device, internal
    embolism T85.81
    fibrosis T85.82
    hemorrhage T85.83
    infection and inflammation T85.79

Complication(s) *(Continued)*
  suture, permanent (wire) NEC *(Continued)*
    mechanical
      breakdown T85.612
      displacement T85.622
      malfunction T85.612
      malposition T85.622
      obstruction T85.692
      perforation T85.692
      protrusion T85.692
      specified NEC T85.692
    pain T85.84
    specified type NEC T85.89
    stenosis T85.85
    thrombosis T85.86
  tracheostomy J95.00
    granuloma J95.09
    hemorrhage J95.01
    infection J95.02
    malfunction J95.03
    mechanical J95.03
    obstruction J95.03
    specified type NEC J95.09
    tracheo-esophageal fistula J95.04
  transfusion (blood) (lymphocytes) (plasma) T80.9
    embolism T80.1
      air T80.0
    hemolysis T80.89
    incompatibility reaction (ABO) (blood group) T80.3
      minor blood group (Duffy) (E) (K(ell)) (Kidd) (Lewis) (M) (N) (P) (S) T80.89
      Rh (factor) T80.4
    infection T80.29
    reaction NEC T80.89
    sepsis T80.29
    shock T80.89
    thromboembolism, thrombus T80.1
  transplant T86.90
    bone T86.839
      failure T86.831
      infection T86.832
      rejection T86.830
      specified type NEC T86.839
    bone marrow T86.00
      specified type NEC T86.09
    cornea T86.849
      failure T86.841
      infection T86.842
      rejection T86.840
      specified type NEC T86.848
    failure T86.92
    heart T86.20
      with lung T86.30
      cardiac allograft vasculopathy T86.290
        failure T86.32
        infection T86.33
        rejection T86.31
        specified type NEC T86.39
      failure T86.22
      infection T86.23
      rejection T86.21
      specified type NEC T86.298
    infection T86.93
    intestine T86.859
      failure T86.851
      infection T86.852
      rejection T86.850
      specified type NEC T86.858

Complication(s) *(Continued)*
  transplant *(Continued)*
    kidney T86.10
      failure T86.12
      infection T86.13
      rejection T86.11
      specified type NEC T86.19
    liver T86.40
      failure T86.42
      infection T86.43
      rejection T86.41
      specified type NEC T86.49
    lung T86.819
      with heart T86.30
        failure T86.32
        infection T86.33
        rejection T86.31
        specified type NEC T86.39
      failure T86.811
      infection T86.812
      rejection T86.810
      specified type NEC T86.818
    malignant neoplasm C80.2
    pancreas T86.899
      failure T86.891
      infection T86.892
      rejection T86.890
      specified type NEC T86.898
    post-transplant lymphoproliferative
        disorder (PTLD) D47.z1
    rejection T86.91
    skin T86.829
      failure T86.821
      infection T86.822
      rejection T86.820
      specified type NEC T86.828
    specified
      tissue T86.899
        failure T86.891
        infection T86.892
        rejection T86.890
        specified type NEC T86.898
      type NEC T86.99
  trauma (early) T79.9
    specified NEC T79.8
  ultrasound therapy NEC T88.9
  umbilical cord NEC
    complicating delivery O69.9
      specified NEC O69.89
  umbrella device, vascular T82.9
    embolism T82.818
    fibrosis T82.828
    hemorrhage T82.838
    infection or inflammation
        T82.7
    mechanical
      breakdown T82.515
      displacement T82.525
      leakage T82.535
      malposition T82.525
      obstruction T82.595
      perforation T82.595
      protrusion T82.595
    pain T82.848
    specified type NEC T82.898
    stenosis T82.858
    thrombosis T82.868
  urethral catheter - *see* Complications,
    catheter, urethral,
    indwelling
  vaccination T88.1
    anaphylaxis NEC T80.5
    arthropathy - *see* Arthropathy,
      postimmunization

Complication(s) *(Continued)*
  vaccination *(Continued)*
    cellulitis T88.0
    encephalitis or encephalomyelitis G04.01
    infection (general) (local) NEC T88.0
    meningitis G03.8
    myelitis G04.89
    protein sickness T80.6
    rash T88.1
    reaction (allergic) T88.1
      Herxheimer's T88.6
      serum T80.6
    sepsis T88.0
    serum intoxication, sickness, rash, or
        other serum reaction NEC T80.6
    anaphylactic shock T80.5
    shock (allergic) (anaphylactic) T80.5
    vaccinia (generalized) (localized)
        T88.1
  vas deferens device or implant – *see*
    Complications, genitourinary,
    device or implant, genital tract
  vascular I99.9
    device or implant T82.9
      embolism T82.818
      fibrosis T82.828
      hemorrhage T82.838
      infection or inflammation T82.7
      mechanical
        breakdown T82.519
          specified device NEC T82.518
        displacement T82.529
          specified device NEC T82.528
        leakage T82.539
          specified device NEC T82.538
        malposition T82.529
          specified device NEC T82.528
        obstruction T82.599
          specified device NEC T82.598
        perforation T82.599
          specified device NEC T82.598
        protrusion T82.599
          specified device NEC T82.598
      pain T82.848
      specified type NEC T82.898
      stenosis T82.858
      thrombosis T82.868
    dialysis catheter - *see* Complication,
      catheter, dialysis
    graft T82.9
      embolism T82.818
      fibrosis T82.828
      hemorrhage T82.838
      mechanical
        breakdown T82.319
          aorta (bifurcation) T82.310
          carotid artery T82.311
          specified vessel NEC T82.318
        displacement T82.329
          aorta (bifurcation) T82.320
          carotid artery T82.321
          specified vessel NEC T82.328
        leakage T82.339
          aorta (bifurcation) T82.330
          carotid artery T82.331
          specified vessel NEC T82.338
        malposition T82.329
          aorta (bifurcation) T82.320
          carotid artery T82.321
          specified vessel NEC T82.328
        obstruction T82.399
          aorta (bifurcation) T82.390
          carotid artery T82.391
          specified vessel NEC T82.398

Complication(s) *(Continued)*
  vascular *(Continued)*
    graft *(Continued)*
      mechanical *(Continued)*
        perforation T82.399
          aorta (bifurcation) T82.390
          carotid artery T82.391
          specified vessel NEC T82.398
        protrusion T82.399
          aorta (bifurcation) T82.390
          carotid artery T82.391
          specified vessel NEC T82.398
      pain T82.848
      specified complication NEC
          T82.898
      stenosis T82.858
      thrombosis T82.868
    following infusion, therapeutic
        injection or transfusion
        T80.1
    postoperative - *see* Complications,
      postoperative, circulatory
  vena cava device (filter) (sieve)
      (umbrella) – *see* Complications,
      umbrella device, vascular
  ventilation therapy NEC T81.81
  ventilator
    mechanical J95.850
      specified NEC J95.859
  ventricular (communicating) shunt
      (device) T85.89
    embolism T85.81
    fibrosis T85.82
    hemorrhage T85.83
    infection and inflammation
        T85.79
    mechanical
      breakdown T85.01
      displacement T85.02
      leakage T85.03
      malposition T85.02
      obstruction T85.09
      perforation T85.09
      protrusion T85.09
      specified NEC T85.09
    pain T85.84
    specified type NEC T85.89
    stenosis T85.85
    thrombosis T85.86
  wire suture, permanent (implanted)
      - *see* Complications, suture,
      permanent
Compressed air disease T70.3
Compression
  with injury - code by Nature of
      injury
  artery I77.1
    celiac, syndrome I77.4
  brachial plexus G54.0
  brain (stem) G93.5
    due to
      contusion (diffuse) – *see* Injury,
        intracranial, diffuse
      focal – *see* Injury, intracranial,
        focal
      injury NEC – *see* Injury, intracra-
        nial, diffuse
      traumatic – *see* Injury, intracranial,
        diffuse
  bronchus J98.09
  cauda equina G83.4
  celiac (artery) (axis) I77.4
  cerebral - *see* Compression, brain
  cervical plexus G54.2

Compression (*Continued*)
  cord
    spinal – *see* Compression, spinal
    umbilical - *see* Compression, umbilical cord
  cranial nerve G52.9
    eighth - *see* subcategory H93.3
    eleventh G52.8
    fifth G50.8
    first G52.0
    fourth - *see* Strabismus, paralytic, fourth nerve
    ninth G52.1
    second - *see* Disorder, nerve, optic
    seventh G52.8
    sixth - *see* Strabismus, paralytic, sixth nerve
    tenth G52.2
    third G52.8
    twelfth G52.3
  diver's squeeze T70.3
  during birth (newborn) P15.9
  esophagus K22.2
  eustachian tube – *see* Obstruction, eustachian tube, cartilaginous
  facies Q67.1
  fracture - *see* Fracture
  heart - *see* Disease, heart
  intestine - *see* Obstruction, intestine
  laryngeal nerve, recurrent G52.2
    with paralysis of vocal cords and larynx J38.00
      bilateral J38.02
      unilateral J38.01
  lumbosacral plexus G54.1
  lung J98.4
  lymphatic vessel I89.0
  medulla - *see* Compression, brain
  nerve (see also Disorder, nerve) G58.9
    arm NEC - *see* Mononeuropathy, upper limb
    axillary G54.0
    cranial – *see* Compression, cranial nerve
    leg NEC - *see* Mononeuropathy, lower limb
    median (in carpal tunnel) – *see* Syndrome, carpal tunnel
    optic - *see* Disorder, nerve, optic
    plantar - *see* Lesion, nerve, plantar
    posterior tibial (in tarsal tunnel) – *see* Syndrome, tarsal tunnel
    root or plexus NOS (in) G54.9
      intervertebral disc disorder NEC - *see* Disorder, disc, with, radiculopathy
      with myelopathy - *see* Disorder, disc, with, myelopathy
      neoplastic disease (see also Neoplasm) D49.9 [G55]
      spondylosis - *see* Spondylosis, with radiculopathy
    sciatic (acute) – *see* Lesion, nerve, sciatic
    sympathetic G90.8
    traumatic - *see* Injury, nerve
    ulnar – *see* Lesion, nerve, ulnar
    upper extremity NEC – *see* Mononeuropathy, upper limb
  spinal (cord) G95.20
    by displacement of intervertebral disc NEC - *see also* Disorder, disc, with, myelopathy

Compression (*Continued*)
  spinal (*Continued*)
    nerve root NOS G54.9
      due to displacement of intervertebral disc NEC - *see* Disorder, disc, with, radiculopathy
      with myelopathy - *see* Disorder, disc, with, myelopathy
    specified NEC G95.29
    spondylogenic (cervical) (lumbar, lumbosacral) (thoracic) - *see* Spondylosis, with myelopathy NEC
    anterior - *see* Syndrome, anterior, spinal artery, compression
    traumatic -*see* Injury, spinal cord, by region
  subcostal nerve (syndrome) - *see* Mononeuropathy, upper limb, specified NEC
  sympathetic nerve NEC G90.8
  syndrome T79.5
  trachea J39.8
  ulnar nerve (by scar tissue) - *see* Lesion, nerve, ulnar
  umbilical cord
    complicating delivery O69.2
      cord around neck O69.1
      prolapse O69.0
      specified NEC O69.2
  ureter N13.5
  vein I87.1
  vena cava (inferior) (superior) I87.1
Compulsion, compulsive
  gambling F63.0
  neurosis F42
  personality F60.5
  states F42
  swearing F42
    in Gilles de la Tourette's syndrome F95.2
  tics and spasms F95.9
Concato's disease (pericardial polyserositis) A19.9
  nontubercular I31.1
  pleural - *see* Pleurisy, with effusion
Concavity chest wall M95.4
Concealed penis Q55.69
Concern (normal) **about sick person in family** Z63.6
Concrescence (teeth) K00.2
Concretio cordis I31.1
  rheumatic I09.2
Concretion - *see also* Calculus
  appendicular K38.1
  canaliculus - *see* Dacryolith
  clitoris N90.8
  conjunctiva H11.12-
  eyelid - *see* Disorder, eyelid, specified type NEC
  lacrimal passages - *see* Dacryolith
  prepuce (male) N47.8
  salivary gland (any) K11.5
  seminal vesicle N50.8
  tonsil J35.8
Concussion (brain) (cerebral) (current) S06.0x-
  blast (air) (hydraulic) (immersion) (underwater)
    abdomen or thorax - *see* Injury, blast, by site
    ear with acoustic nerve injury - *see* Injury, nerve, acoustic, specified type NEC

Concussion (*Continued*)
  cauda equina S34.3
  conus medullaris S34.139
  ocular S05.8x-
  spinal (cord)
    cervical S14.0
    lumbar S34.01
    sacral S34.02
    thoracic S24.0
  syndrome F07.81
Condition - *see* Disease
Conditions arising in the perinatal period - *see* Newborn, affected by
Conduct disorder - *see* Disorder, conduct
Condyloma A63.0
  acuminatum A63.0
  gonorrheal A54.09
  latum A51.31
  syphilitic A51.31
    congenital A50.07
  venereal, syphilitic A51.31
Conflagration - *see also* Burn
  asphyxia (by inhalation of smoke, gases, fumes or vapors) - *see* Table of drugs and chemicals
Conflict (with) - *see also* Discord
  family Z73.9
  marital Z63.0
    involving divorce or estrangement Z63.5
  parent-child Z62.820
    parent-adopted child Z62.821
    parent-biological child Z62.820
    parent-foster child Z62.822
  social role NEC Z73.5
Confluent - *see* condition
Confusion, confused R41.0
  epileptic F05
  mental state (psychogenic) F44.89
  psychogenic F44.89
  reactive (from emotional stress, psychological trauma) F44.89
Confusional arousals G47.51
Congelation T69.9
Congenital - *see also* condition
  aortic septum Q25.4
  intrinsic factor deficiency D51.0
  malformation - *see* Anomaly
Congestion, congestive
  bladder N32.89
  bowel K63.89
  brain G93.89
  breast N64.59
  bronchial J98.09
  catarrhal J31.0
  chest R09.89
  chill, malarial - *see* Malaria
  circulatory NEC I99.8
  duodenum K31.89
  eye - *see* Hyperemia, conjunctiva
  facial, due to birth injury P15.4
  general R68.89
  glottis J37.0
  heart - *see* Failure, heart, congestive
  hepatic K76.1
  hypostatic (lung) – *see* Edema, lung
  intestine K63.89
  kidney N28.89
  labyrinth - *see* subcategory H83.8
  larynx J37.0
  liver K76.1
  lung R09.89
    active or acute - *see* Pneumonia
  malaria, malarial - *see* Malaria

Congestion, congestive (Continued)
    nasal R09.81
    nose R09.81
    orbit, orbital - see also Exophthalmos
        inflammatory (chronic) - see Inflam-
            mation, orbit
    ovary N83.8
    pancreas K86.8
    pelvic, female N94.89
    pleural J94.8
    prostate (active) N42.1
    pulmonary - see Congestion, lung
    renal N28.89
    retina H35.81
    seminal vesicle N50.1
    spinal cord G95.19
    spleen (chronic) D73.2
    stomach K31.89
    trachea - see Tracheitis
    urethra N36.8
    uterus N85.8
        with subinvolution N85.3
    venous (passive) I87.8
    viscera R68.89
Congestive - see Congestion
Conical
    cervix (hypertrophic elongation) N88.4
    cornea - see Keratoconus
    teeth K00.2
Conjoined twins Q89.4
Conjugal maladjustment Z63.0
    involving divorce or estrangement
        Z63.5
Conjunctiva - see condition
Conjunctivitis (staphylococcal) (strepto-
    coccal) NOS H10.9
    Acanthamoeba B60.12
    acute H10.3-
        chemical H10.21- - see also Corrosion,
            cornea
        atopic H10.1-
        mucopurulent H10.02-
            follicular H10.01-
        pseudomembranous H10.22-
        serous except viral H10.23-
            viral - see Conjunctivitis, viral
        toxic H10.21-
    adenoviral (acute) (follicular) B30.1
    allergic (acute) - see Conjunctivitis,
        acute, atopic
        chronic H10.45
            vernal H10.44
    anaphylactic - see Conjunctivitis, acute,
        atopic
    Apollo B30.3
    atopic (acute) - see Conjunctivitis, acute,
        atopic
    Béal's B30.2
    blennorrhagic (gonococcal) (neonato-
        rum) A54.31
    chemical (acute) H10.21- - see also
        Corrosion, cornea
    chlamydial A74.0
        due to trachoma A07.0
        neonatal P39.1
    chronic (nodosa) (petrificans) (phlycte-
        nular) H10.40-
        allergic H10.45
            vernal H10.44
        follicular H10.43-
        giant papillary H10.41-
        simple H10.42-
        vernal H10.44
    coxsackievirus 24 B30.3

Conjunctivitis (Continued)
    diphtheritic A36.86
    due to
        dust - see Conjunctivitis, acute, atopic
        filariasis B74.3
        mucocutaneous leishmaniasis B55.2
    enterovirus type 70 (hemorrhagic) B30.3
    epidemic (viral) B30.9
        hemorrhagic B30.3
    gonococcal (neonatorum) A54.31
    granular (trachomatous) A71.1
        sequelae (late effect) B94.0
    hemorrhagic (acute) (epidemic) B30.3
    herpes zoster B02.31
    in (due to)
        Acanthamoeba B60.12
        adenovirus (acute) (follicular) B30.1
        Chlamydia A74.0
        coxsackievirus 24 B30.3
        diphtheria A36.86
        enterovirus type 70 (hemorrhagic) B30.3
        filariasis B74.9
        gonococci A54.31
        herpes (simplex) virus B00.53
            zoster B02.31
        infectious disease NEC B99
        meningococci A39.89
        mucocutaneous leishmaniasis B55.2
        rosacea L71.9
        syphilis (late) A52.71
        zoster B02.31
    inclusion A74.0
    infantile P39.1
        gonococcal A54.31
    Koch-Weeks' - see Conjunctivitis, acute,
        mucopurulent
    light - see Conjunctivitis, acute, atopic
    ligneous - see Blepharoconjunctivitis,
        ligneous
    meningococcal A39.89
    mucopurulent - see Conjunctivitis,
        acute, mucopurulent
    neonatal P39.1
        gonococcal A54.31
    Newcastle B30.8
    of Béal B30.2
    parasitic
        filariasis B74.9
        mucocutaneous leishmaniasis B55.2
    Parinaud's H10.89
    petrificans H10.89
    rosacea L71.9
    specified NEC H10.89
    swimming-pool B30.1
    trachomatous A71.1
        acute A71.0
        sequelae (late effect) B94.0
    traumatic NEC H10.89
    tuberculous A18.59
    tularemic A21.1
    tularensis A21.1
    viral B30.9
        due to
            adenovirus B30.1
            enterovirus B30.3
        specified NEC B30.8
Conjunctivochalasis H11.82-
Connective tissue - see condition
Conn's syndrome E26.01
Conradi(-Hunermann) **disease** Q77.3
Consanguinity Z84.3
    counseling Z71.89
Conscious simulation (of illness) Z76.5
Consecutive - see condition

Consolidation lung (base) - see Pneumo-
    nia, lobar
Constipation (atonic) (neurogenic)
    (simple) (spastic) K59.00
    drug-induced - see Table of drugs and
        chemicals
    outlet dysfunction K59.02
    psychogenic F45.8
    slow transit K59.01
    specified NEC K59.09
Constitutional - see also condition
    substandard F60.7
Constitutionally substandard F60.7
Constriction - see also Stricture
    auditory canal - see Stenosis, external
        ear canal
    bronchial J98.09
    duodenum K31.5
    esophagus K22.2
    external
        abdomen, abdominal (wall) S30.841
        alveolar process S00.542
        ankle S90.54-
        antecubital space – see Constriction,
            external, forearm
        arm (upper) S40.84-
        auricle – see Constriction, external,
            ear
        axilla – see Constriction, external, arm
        back, lower S30.840
        breast S20.14-
        brow S00.84
        buttock S30.840
        calf – see Constriction, external, leg
        canthus – see Constriction, external,
            eyelid
        cheek S00.84
            internal S00.542
        chest wall – see Constriction, external,
            thorax
        chin S00.84
        clitoris S30.844
        costal region - see Constriction, exter-
            nal, thorax
        digit(s)
            hand – see Constriction, external,
                finger
            foot - see Constriction, external, toe
        ear S00.44-
        elbow S50.34-
        epididymis S30.843
        epigastric region S30.841
        esophagus, cervical S10.14
        eyebrow – see Constriction, external,
            eyelid
        eyelid S00.24-
        face S00.84
        finger(s) S60.44-
            index S60.44-
            little S60.44-
            middle S60.44-
            ring S60.44-
        flank S30.841
        foot (except toe(s) alone) S90.84-
            toe – see Constriction, external, toe
        forearm S50.84-
            elbow only – see Constriction,
                external, elbow
        forehead S00.84
        genital organs, external
            female S30.846
            male S30.845
        groin S30.841
        gum S00.542

Constriction *(Continued)*
  external *(Continued)*
    hand S60.54-
    head S00.94
      ear - *see* Constriction, external, ear
      eyelid - *see* Constriction, external, eyelid
      lip S00.541
      nose S00.34
      oral cavity S00.542
      scalp S00.04
      specified site NEC S00.84
    heel – *see* Constriction, external, foot
    hip S70.24-
    inguinal region S30.841
    interscapular region S20.449
    jaw S00.84
    knee S80.24-
    labium (majus) (minus) S30.844
    larynx S10.14
    leg (lower) S80.84-
      knee – *see* Constriction, external, knee
      upper - *see* Constriction, external, thigh
    lip S00.541
    lower back S30.840
    lumbar region S30.840
    malar region S00.84
    mammary – *see* Constriction, external, breast
    mastoid region S00.84
    mouth S00.542
    nail
      finger – *see* Constriction, external, finger
      toe – *see* Constriction, external, toe
    nasal S00.34
    neck S10.94
      specified site NEC S10.84
      throat S10.14
    nose S00.34
    occipital region S00.04
    oral cavity S00.542
    orbital region – *see* Constriction, external, eyelid
    palate S00.542
    palm – *see* Constriction, external, hand
    parietal region S00.04
    pelvis S30.840
    penis S30.842
    perineum
      female S30.844
      male S30.840
    periocular area – *see* Constriction, external, eyelid
    phalanges
      finger – *see* Constriction, external, finger
      toe – *see* Constriction, external, toe
    pharynx S10.14
    pinna – *see* Constriction, external, ear
    popliteal space – *see* Constriction, external, knee
    prepuce S30.842
    pubic region S30.840
    pudendum
      female S30.846
      male S30.845
    sacral region S30.840
    scalp S00.04
    scapular region – *see* Constriction, external, shoulder

Constriction *(Continued)*
  external *(Continued)*
    scrotum S30.843
    shin – *see* Constriction, external, leg
    shoulder S40.24-
    sternal region S20.349
    submaxillary region S00.84
    submental region S00.84
    subungual
      finger(s) – *see* Constriction, external, finger
      toe(s) – *see* Constriction, external, toe
    supraclavicular fossa S10.84
    supraorbital S00.84
    temple S00.84
    temporal region S00.84
    testis S30.843
    thigh S70.34-
    thorax, thoracic (wall) S20.94
      back S20.44-
      front S20.34-
    throat S10.14
    thumb S60.34-
    toe(s) (lesser) S90.44-
      great S90.44-
    tongue S00.542
    trachea S10.14
    tunica vaginalis S30.843
    uvula S00.542
    vagina S30.844
    vulva S30.844
    wrist S60.84-
  gallbladder - *see* Obstruction, gallbladder
  intestine - *see* Obstruction, intestine
  larynx J38.6
    congenital Q31.8
      specified NEC Q31.8
      subglottic Q31.1
  organ or site, congenital NEC - *see* Atresia, by site
  prepuce (acquired) (congenital) N47.1
  pylorus (adult hypertrophic) K31.1
    congenital or infantile Q40.0
    newborn Q40.0
  ring dystocia (uterus) O62.4
  spastic - *see also* Spasm
    ureter N13.5
  ureter N13.5
    with infection N13.6
  urethra - *see* Stricture, urethra
  visual field (peripheral) (functional) - *see* Defect, visual field
Constrictive - *see* condition
Consultation
  medical - *see* Counseling, medical
  religious Z71.81
  specified reason NEC Z71.89
  spiritual Z71.81
  without complaint or sickness Z71.9
    feared complaint unfounded Z71.1
    specified reason NEC Z71.89
Consumption - *see* Tuberculosis
Contact (with) (*see also* Exposure (to))
  acariasis Z20.7
  AIDS virus Z20.6
  air pollution Z77.110
  algae and algae toxins Z77.121
  algae bloom Z77.121
  anthrax Z20.810
  aromatic amines Z77.020
  aromatic (hazardous) compounds NEC Z77.028

Contact *(Continued)*
  aromatic dyes NOS Z77.028
  arsenic Z77.010
  asbestos Z77.090
  bacterial disease NEC Z20.818
  benzene Z77.021
  blue-green algae bloom Z77.121
  body fluids (potentially hazardous) Z77.21
  brown tide Z77.121
  chemicals (chiefly nonmedicinal) (hazardous) NEC Z77.098
  chromium compounds Z77.018
  cholera Z20.09
  communicable disease Z20.9
    bacterial NEC Z20.818
    specified NEC Z20.89
    viral NEC Z20.828
  cyanobacteria bloom Z77.121
  dyes Z77.098
  Escherichia coli (E. coli) Z20.01
  fiberglass - *see* Table of drugs and chemicals, fiberglass
  German measles Z20.4
  gonorrhea Z20.2
  hazardous metals NEC Z77.018
  hazardous substances NEC Z77.29
  hazards in the physical environment NEC Z77.128
  hazards to health NEC Z77.9
  HIV Z20.6
  HTLV-III/LAV Z20.6
  human immunodeficiency virus (HIV) Z20.6
  infection Z20.9
    specified NEC Z20.89
  infestation (parasitic) NEC Z20.7
  intestinal infectious disease NEC Z20.09
    Escherichia coli (E. coli) Z20.01
  lead Z77.011
  meningococcus Z20.811
  mold (toxic) Z77.120
  nickel dust Z77.018
  noise Z77.122
  parasitic disease Z20.7
  pediculosis Z20.7
  pfiesteria piscicida Z77.121
  poliomyelitis Z20.89
  pollution
    air Z77.110
    environmental NEC Z77.118
    soil Z77.112
    water Z77.111
  polycyclic aromatic hydrocarbons Z77.028
  rabies Z20.3
  radiation, naturally occurring NEC Z77.123
  radon Z77.123
  red tide (Florida) Z77.121
  rubella Z20.4
  sexually-transmitted disease Z20.2
  smallpox (laboratory) Z20.89
  syphilis Z20.2
  tuberculosis Z20.1
  varicella Z20.820
  venereal disease Z20.2
  viral disease NEC Z20.828
  viral hepatitis Z20.5
  water pollution Z77.111
Contamination, food - *see* Intoxication, foodborne

Contraception, contraceptive
  advice Z30.09
  counseling Z30.09
  device (intrauterine) (in situ) Z97.5
    causing menorrhagia T83.83
    checking Z30.43
    complications - *see* Complications,
      intrauterine, contraceptive
      device
    in place Z97.5
    initial prescription Z30.014
    reinsertion Z30.43
    removal Z30.43
  emergency (postcoital) Z30.012
  initial prescription Z30.019
    injectable Z30.013
    intrauterine device Z30.014
    pills Z30.011
    postcoital (emergency) Z30.012
    specified type NEC Z30.018
    subdermal implantable Z30.019
  maintenance Z30.40
    examination Z30.8
    injectable Z30.42
    intrauterine device Z30.43
    pills Z30.41
    specified type NEC Z30.49
    subdermal implantable Z30.49
  management Z30.9
    specified NEC Z30.8
  postcoital (emergency) Z30.012
  prescription Z30.019
    repeat Z30.40
  sterilization Z30.2
  surveillance (drug) – *see* Contraception,
    maintenance
Contraction(s), contracture, contracted
  Achilles tendon - *see also* Short, tendon,
    Achilles
    congenital Q66.8
  amputation stump (surgical) (flexion)
    (late) T87.8
  anus K59.8
  bile duct (common) (hepatic) K83.8
  bladder N32.89
    neck or sphincter N32.0
  bowel, cecum, colon or intestine, any
    part - *see* Obstruction, intestine
  Braxton Hicks - *see* False, labor
  breast implant, capsular T85.44
  bronchial J98.09
  burn (old) - *see* Cicatrix
  cervix - *see* Stricture, cervix
  cicatricial - *see* Cicatrix
  conjunctiva, trachomatous, active A71.1
    sequelae (late effect) B94.0
  Dupuytren's M72.0
  eyelid - *see* Disorder, eyelid function
  fascia (lata) (postural) M72.8
    Dupuytren's M72.0
    palmar M72.0
    plantar M72.2
  finger NEC - *see also* Deformity, finger
    congenital Q68.1
    joint - *see* Contraction, joint, hand
  flaccid - *see* Contraction, paralytic
  gallbladder K82.0
  heart valve - *see* Endocarditis
  hip - *see* Contraction, joint, hip
  hourglass
    bladder N32.89
      congenital Q64.79
    gallbladder K82.0
      congenital Q44.1

Contraction(s), contracture, contracted
(Continued)
  hourglass *(Continued)*
    stomach K31.89
      congenital Q40.2
      psychogenic F45.8
    uterus (complicating delivery) O62.4
  hysterical F44.4
  internal os - *see* Stricture, cervix
  joint (abduction) (acquired) (adduction)
    (flexion) (rotation) M24.50
    ankle M24.57-
    congenital NEC Q68.8
      hip Q65.8
    elbow M24.52-
    foot joint M24.57-
    hand joint M24.54-
    hip M24.55-
      congenital Q65.8
    hysterical F44.4
    knee M24.56-
    shoulder M24.51-
    wrist M24.53-
  kidney (granular) (secondary) N26.9
    congenital Q63.8
    hydronephritic - *see* Hydronephrosis
      Page N26.2
    pyelonephritic - *see* Pyelitis, chronic
    tuberculous A18.11
  ligament - *see also* Disorder, ligament
    congenital Q79.8
  muscle (postinfective) (postural) NEC
    M62.40
    with contracture of joint - *see* Contrac-
      tion, joint
    ankle M62.47-
    congenital Q79.8
      sternocleidomastoid Q68.0
    extraocular - *see* Strabismus
    eye (extrinsic) - *see* Strabismus
    foot M62.47-
    forearm M62.43-
    hand M62.44-
    hysterical F44.4
    ischemic (Volkmann's) T79.6
    lower leg M62.46-
    multiple sites M62.49
    pelvic region M62.45-
    posttraumatic – *see* Strabismus,
      paralytic
    psychogenic F45.8
      conversion reaction F44.4
    shoulder region M62.41-
    specified site NEC M62.48
    thigh M62.45-
    upper arm M62.42-
  neck – *see* Torticollis
  ocular muscle - *see* Strabismus
  organ or site, congenital NEC - *see*
    Atresia, by site
  outlet (pelvis) - *see* Contraction, pelvis
  palmar fascia M72.0
  paralytic
    joint - *see* Contraction, joint
    muscle - *see also* Contraction, muscle
      NEC
      ocular – *see* Strabismus, paralytic
  pelvis (acquired) (general) M95.5
    with disproportion (fetopelvic) O33.1
      causing obstructed labor O65.1
    inlet O33.2
    mid-cavity O33.3
    outlet O33.3
  plantar fascia M72.2

Contraction(s), contracture, contracted
(Continued)
  premature
    atrium I49.1
    auriculoventricular I49.49
    heart I49.49
    junctional I49.2
    supraventricular I49.1
    ventricular I49.3
  prostate N42.89
  pylorus NEC - *see also* Pylorospasm
    psychogenic F45.8
  rectum, rectal (sphincter) K59.8
  ring (Bandl's) (complicating delivery)
    O62.4
  scar - *see* Cicatrix
  spine - *see* Dorsopathy, deforming
  sternocleidomastoid (muscle), congeni-
    tal Q68.0
  stomach K31.89
    hourglass K31.89
      congenital Q40.2
      psychogenic F45.8
    psychogenic F45.8
  tendon (sheath) M62.40
    with contracture of joint - *see* Contrac-
      tion, joint
    Achilles - *see* Short, tendon, Achilles
    ankle M62.47-
      Achilles - *see* Short, tendon,
        Achilles
    foot M62.47-
    forearm M62.43-
    hand M62.44-
    lower leg M62.46-
    multiple sites M62.49
    neck M62.48
    pelvic region M62.45-
    shoulder region M62.41-
    specified site NEC M62.48
    thigh M62.45-
    thorax M62.48
    trunk M62.48
    upper arm M62.42-
  toe - *see* Deformity, toe, specified NEC
  ureterovesical orifice (postinfectional)
    N13.5
    with infection N13.6
  urethra - *see also* Stricture, urethra
    orifice N32.0
  uterus N85.8
    abnormal NEC O62.9
    clonic (complicating delivery)
      O62.4
    dyscoordinate (complicating deliv-
      ery) O62.4
    hourglass (complicating delivery)
      O62.4
    hypertonic O62.4
    hypotonic NEC O62.2
    inadequate
      primary O62.0
      secondary O62.1
    incoordinate (complicating delivery)
      O62.4
    poor O62.2
    tetanic (complicating delivery)
      O62.4
  vagina (outlet) N89.5
  vesical N32.89
    neck or urethral orifice N32.0
  visual field - *see* Defect, visual field,
    generalized
  Volkmann's (ischemic) T79.6

Contusion (skin surface intact)
 abdomen, abdominal (muscle) (wall)
   S30.1
 adnexa, eye NEC S05.8x-
 adrenal gland S37.812
 alveolar process S00.532
 ankle S90.0-
 antecubital space – *see* Contusion, forearm
 anus S30.3
 arm (upper) S40.02-
   lower (with elbow) – *see* Contusion,
     forearm
 auditory canal – *see* Contusion, ear
 auricle – *see* Contusion, ear
 axilla – *see* Contusion, arm, upper
 back - *see also* Contusion, thorax, back
   lower S30.0
 bile duct S36.13
 bladder S37.22
 bone NEC T14.8
 brain (diffuse) – *see* Injury, intracranial,
     diffuse
   focal – *see* Injury, intracranial, focal
 brainstem S06.38-
 breast S20.0-
 broad ligament S37.892
 brow S00.83
 buttock S30.0
 canthus, eye S00.1-
 cauda equina (spine) S34.3
 cerebellar, traumatic S06.37-
 cerebral S06.33-
   left side S06.32-
   right side S06.31-
 cheek S00.83
   internal S00.532
 chest (wall) – *see* Contusion, thorax
 chin S00.83
 clitoris S30.23
 colon - *see* Injury, intestine, large,
     contusion
 common bile duct S36.13
 conjunctiva S05.1-
   with foreign body (in conjunctival
     sac) - *see* Foreign body, conjunc-
     tival sac
 conus medullaris (spine) S34.139
 cornea – *see* Contusion, eyeball
   with foreign body – *see* Foreign body,
     cornea
 corpus cavernosum S30.21
 cortex (brain) (cerebral) – *see* Injury,
     intracranial, diffuse
   focal – *see* Injury, intracranial, focal
 costal region – *see* Contusion, thorax
 cystic duct S36.13
 diaphragm S27.802
 duodenum S36.420
 ear S00.43-
 elbow S50.0-
   with forearm – *see* Contusion,
     forearm
 epididymis S30.22
 epigastric region S30.1
 epiglottis S10.0
 esophagus (thoracic) S27.812
   cervical S10.0
 eyeball S05.1-
 eyebrow S00.1-
 eyelid (and periocular area) S00.1-
 face NEC S00.83
 fallopian tube S37.529
   bilateral S37.522
   unilateral S37.521

Contusion *(Continued)*
 femoral triangle S30.1
 finger(s) S60.00
   with damage to nail (matrix) S60.10
   index S60.02-
     with damage to nail S60.12-
   little S60.05-
     with damage to nail S60.15-
   middle S60.03-
     with damage to nail S60.13-
   ring S60.04-
     with damage to nail S60.14-
   thumb – *see* Contusion, thumb
 flank S30.1
 foot (except toe(s) alone) S90.3-
   toe – *see* Contusion, toe
 forearm S50.1-
   elbow only – *see* Contusion, elbow
 forehead S00.83
 gallbladder S36.122
 genital organs, external
   female S30.202
   male S30.201
 globe (eye) – *see* Contusion, eyeball
 groin S30.1
 gum S00.532
 hand S60.22-
   finger(s) – *see* Contusion, finger
   wrist – *see* Contusion, wrist
 head S00.93
   ear - *see* Contusion, ear
   eyelid - *see* Contusion, eyelid
   lip S00.531
   nose S00.33
   oral cavity S00.532
   scalp S00.03
   specified part NEC S00.83
 heel – *see* Contusion, foot
 hepatic duct S36.13
 hip S70.0-
 ileum S36.428
 iliac region S30.1
 inguinal region S30.1
 interscapular region S20.229
 intra-abdominal organ S36.92
   colon - *see* Injury, intestine, large,
     contusion
   liver S36.112
   pancreas - *see* Contusion, pancreas
   rectum S36.62
   small intestine - *see* Injury, intestine,
     small, contusion
   specified organ NEC S36.892
   spleen - *see* Contusion, spleen
   stomach S36.32
 iris (eye) – *see* Contusion, eyeball
 jaw S00.83
 jejunum S36.428
 kidney - *see* Injury, kidney, contusion
 knee S80.0-
 labium (majus) (minus) S30.23
 lacrimal apparatus, gland or sac S05.8x-
 larynx S10.0
 leg (lower) S80.1-
   knee – *see* Contusion, knee
 lens – *see* Contusion, eyeball
 lip S00.531
 liver S36.112
 lower back S30.0
 lumbar region S30.0
 lung S27.329
   bilateral S27.322
   unilateral S27.321
 malar region S00.83

Contusion *(Continued)*
 mastoid region S00.83
 membrane, brain – *see* Injury, intracra-
     nial, diffuse
   focal – *see* Injury, intracranial, focal
 mesentery S36.892
 mesosalpinx S37.529
   bilateral S37.522
   unilateral S37.521
 mouth S00.532
 muscle - *see* Contusion, by site
 nail
   finger – *see* Contusion, finger, with
     damage to nail
   toe – *see* Contusion, toe, with damage
     to nail
 nasal S00.33
 neck S10.93
   specified site NEC S10.83
   throat S10.0
 newborn P54.5
 nerve - *see* Injury, nerve
 nose S00.33
 occipital
   lobe (brain) – *see* Injury, intracranial,
     diffuse
   focal – *see* Injury, intracranial, focal
   region (scalp) S00.03
 orbit (region) (tissues) S05.1-
 ovary S37.429
   bilateral S37.422
   unilateral S37.421
 palate S00.532
 pancreas S36.229
   body S36.221
   head S36.220
   tail S36.222
 parietal
   lobe (brain) – *see* Injury, intracranial,
     diffuse
   focal – *see* Injury, intracranial, focal
   region (scalp) S00.03
 pelvic organ S37.92
   adrenal gland S37.812
   bladder S37.22
   fallopian tube - *see* Contusion, fal-
     lopian tube
   kidney - *see* Contusion, kidney
   ovary - *see* Contusion, ovary
   prostate S37.823
   specified organ NEC S37.892
   ureter S37.12
   urethra S37.32
   uterus S37.62
 pelvis S30.0
 penis S30.21
 perineum
   female S30.23
   male S30.0
 periocular area S00.1-
 peritoneum S36.81
 periurethral tissue – *see* Contusion,
     urethra
 pharynx S10.0
 pinna – *see* Contusion, ear
 popliteal space – *see* Contusion, knee
 prepuce S30.21
 prostate S37.822
 pubic region S30.1
 pudendum
   female S30.202
   male S30.201
 quadriceps femoris – *see* Contusion,
     thigh

Contusion *(Continued)*
  rectum S36.62
  retroperitoneum S36.892
  round ligament S37.892
  sacral region S30.0
  scalp S00.03
    due to birth injury P12.3
  scapular region – *see* Contusion, shoulder
  sclera – *see* Contusion, eyeball
  scrotum S30.22
  seminal vesicle S37.892
  shoulder S40.01-
  skin NEC T14.8
  small intestine - *see* Injury, intestine,
    small, contusion
  spermatic cord S30.22
  spinal cord - *see* Injury, spinal cord, by
    region
    cauda equina S34.3
    conus medullaris S34.139
  spleen S36.029
    major S36.021
    minor S36.020
  sternal region S20.219
  stomach S36.32
  subconjunctival S05.1-
  subcutaneous NEC T14.8
  submaxillary region S00.83
  submental region S00.83
  subperiosteal NEC T14.8
  subungual
    finger – *see* Contusion, finger, with
      damage to nail
    toe – *see* Contusion, toe, with damage
      to nail
  supraclavicular fossa S10.83
  supraorbital S00.83
  suprarenal gland S37.812
  temple (region) S00.83
  temporal
    lobe (brain) – *see* Injury, intracranial,
      diffuse
    focal – *see* Injury, intracranial, focal
    region S00.83
  testis S30.22
  thigh S70.1-
  thorax (wall) S20.20
    back S20.22-
    front S20.21-
  throat S10.0
  thumb S60.01-
    with damage to nail S60.11-
  toe(s) (lesser) S90.12-
    with damage to nail S90.22-
    great S90.11-
      with damage to nail S90.21-
      specified type NEC S90.221
  tongue S00.532
  trachea (cervical) S10.0
    thoracic S27.52
  tunica vaginalis S30.22
  tympanum, tympanic membrane – *see*
    Contusion, ear
  ureter S37.12
  urethra S37.32
  urinary organ NEC S37.892
  uterus S37.62
  uvula S00.532
  vagina S30.23
  vas deferens S37.892
  vesical S37.22
  vocal cord(s) S10.0
  vulva S30.23
  wrist S60.21-

Conus (congenital) (any type) Q14.8
  cornea - *see* Keratoconus
  medullaris syndrome G95.81
Conversion hysteria, neurosis or reaction
  F44.9
Converter, tuberculosis (test reaction) R76.1
Conviction (legal), anxiety concerning
  Z65.0
  with imprisonment Z65.1
Convulsions (idiopathic) (see also
  Seizure(s)) R56.9
  apoplectiform (cerebral ischemia) I67.8
  benign neonatal (familial) - *see* Epilepsy,
    generalized, idiopathic
  dissociative F44.5
  epileptic - *see* Epilepsy
  epileptiform, epileptoid - *see* Seizure,
    epileptiform
  ether (anesthetic) - *see* Table of drugs
    and chemicals, by drug
  febrile R56.00
    with status epilepticus G40.901
    complex R56.01
      with status epilepticus G40.901
    simple R56.00
  hysterical F44.5
  infantile P90
    epilepsy - *see* Epilepsy
  jacksonian – *see* Epilepsy, localization-
    related, symptomatic, with simple
    partial seizures
  myoclonic G25.3
  neonatal, benign (familial) - *see* Epi-
    lepsy, generalized, idiopathic
  newborn P90
  obstetrical (nephritic) (uremic) - *see*
    Eclampsia
  paretic A52.17
  psychomotor – *see* Epilepsy, localiza-
    tion-related, symptomatic, with
    complex partial seizures
  recurrent R56.9
  reflex R25.8
  scarlatinal A38.8
  tetanus, tetanic - *see* Tetanus
  thymic E32.8
Convulsive - *see also* Convulsions
Cooley's anemia D56.1
Coolie itch B76.9
Cooper's
  disease – *see* Mastopathy, cystic
  hernia - *see* Hernia, abdomen, specified
    site NEC
Copra itch B88.0
Coprolith or coprostasis K56.4
Coprophagy F50.8
Coprophobia F40.298
Coproporphyria, hereditary E80.29
Cor
  biloculare Q20.8
  bovis, bovinum - *see* Hypertrophy, cardiac
  pulmonale (chronic) I27.81
    acute I26.09
  triatriatum, triatrium Q24.2
  triloculare Q20.8
    biatrium Q20.4
    biventriculare Q21.1
Corbus' disease (gangrenous balanitis)
  N48.1
Cord - *see also* condition
  around neck (tightly) (with compression)
    complicating delivery O69.1
  bladder G95.89
    tabetic A52.19

Cordis ectopia Q24.8
Corditis (spermatic) N49.1
Corectopia Q13.2
Cori's disease (glycogen storage) E74.03
Corkhandler's disease or lung J67.3
Corkscrew esophagus K22.4
Corkworker's disease or lung J67.3
Corn (infected) L84
Cornea - *see also* condition
  donor Z52.5
  plana Q13.4
Cornelia de Lange syndrome Q87.1
Cornu cutaneum L85.8
Cornual gestation or pregnancy O00.8
Coronary (artery) - *see* condition
Coronavirus, as cause of disease classi-
  fied elsewhere B97.29
  SARS-associated B97.21
Corpora - *see also* condition
  amylacea, prostate N42.89
  cavernosa - *see* condition
Corpulence - *see* Obesity
Corpus - *see* condition
Corrected transposition Q20.5
Corrosion (injury) (acid) (caustic) (chemi-
  cal) (lime) (external) (internal) T30.4
  abdomen, abdominal (muscle) (wall)
    T21.42
    first degree T21.52
    second degree T21.62
    third degree T21.72
  above elbow T22.439
    first degree T22.539
    left T22.432
      first degree T22.532
      second degree T22.632
      third degree T22.732
    right T22.431
      first degree T22.531
      second degree T22.631
      third degree T22.731
    second degree T22.639
    third degree T22.739
  alimentary tract NEC T28.7
  ankle T25.419
    first degree T25.519
    left T25.412
      first degree T25.512
      second degree T25.612
      third degree T25.712
    multiple with foot - *see* Corrosion,
      lower, limb, multiple, ankle and
      foot
    right T25.411
      first degree T25.511
      second degree T25.611
      third degree T25.711
    second degree T25.619
    third degree T25.719
  anus – *see* Corrosion, buttock
  arm(s) (meaning upper limb(s)) - *see*
    Corrosion, upper limb
  axilla T22.449
    first degree T22.549
    left T22.442
      first degree T22.542
      second degree T22.642
      third degree T22.742
    right T22.441
      first degree T22.541
      second degree T22.641
      third degree T22.741
    second degree T22.649
    third degree T22.749

Corrosion *(Continued)*
  foot *(Continued)*
    left *(Continued)*
      second degree T25.622
      third degree T25.722
      multiple with ankle - *see* Corrosion,
        lower, limb, multiple, ankle and
        foot
      right T25.421
        first degree T25.521
        second degree T25.621
        third degree T25.721
      second degree T25.629
      third degree T25.729
  forearm T22.419
    first degree T22.519
    left T22.412
      first degree T22.512
      second degree T22.612
      third degree T22.712
    right T22.411
      first degree T22.511
      second degree T22.611
      third degree T22.711
    second degree T22.619
    third degree T22.719
  forehead T20.46
    first degree T20.56
    second degree T20.66
    third degree T20.76
  fourth degree - code as Corrosion, third
    degree, by site
  full thickness skin loss - code as Corro-
    sion, third degree, by site
  gastrointestinal tract NEC T28.7
  genital organs
    external
      female T21.47
        first degree T21.57
        second degree T21.67
        third degree T21.77
      male T21.46
        first degree T21.56
        second degree T21.66
        third degree T21.76
    internal T28.7
      from caustic or corrosive substance
        T28.8
  groin – *see* Corrosion, abdominal wall
  hand(s) T23.409
    back - *see* Corrosion, dorsum of hand
    finger - *see* Corrosion, finger
    first degree T23.509
    left T23.402
      first degree T23.502
      second degree T23.602
      third degree T23.702
    multiple sites with wrist T23.499
      first degree T23.599
      left T23.492
        first degree T23.592
        second degree T23.692
        third degree T23.792
      right T23.491
        first degree T23.591
        second degree T23.691
        third degree T23.791
      second degree T23.699
      third degree T23.799
    palm - *see* Corrosion, palm
    right T23.401
      first degree T23.501
      second degree T23.601
      third degree T23.701

Corrosion *(Continued)*
  hand(s) *(Continued)*
    second degree T23.609
    third degree T23.709
    thumb - *see* Corrosion, thumb
  head (and face) (and neck) T20.40
    cheek - *see* Corrosion, cheek
    chin - *see* Corrosion, chin
    ear - *see* Corrosion, ear
    eye(s) only - *see* Corrosion, eye
    first degree T20.50
    forehead - *see* Corrosion, forehead
    lip - *see* Corrosion, lip
    multiple sites T20.49
      first degree T20.59
      second degree T20.69
      third degree T20.79
    neck - *see* Corrosion, neck
    nose - *see* Corrosion, nose
    scalp - *see* Corrosion, scalp
    second degree T20.60
    third degree T20.70
  hip(s) – *see* Corrosion, lower, limb
  inhalation - *see* Corrosion, respiratory
    tract
  internal organ(s) T28.90
    alimentary tract T28.7
      esophagus T28.6
    esophagus T28.6
    from caustic or corrosive substance
      (swallowing) NEC - *see* Corro-
      sion, by site
    genitourinary T28.8
    mouth T28.5
    pharynx T28.5
    specified organ NEC T28.99
  interscapular region – *see* Corrosion,
    back, upper
  intestine (large) (small) T28.7
  knee T24.429
    first degree T24.529
    left T24.422
      first degree T24.522
      second degree T24.622
      third degree T24.722
    right T24.421
      first degree T24.521
      second degree T24.621
      third degree T24.721
    second degree T24.629
    third degree T24.729
  labium (majus) (minus) – *see*
    Corrosion, genital organs,
    external, female
  lacrimal apparatus, duct, gland or
    sac – *see* Corrosion, eye, specified
    site NEC
  larynx T27.4
    with lung T27.5
  leg(s) (meaning lower limb(s)) - *see*
    Corrosion, lower limb
  limb(s)
    lower – *see* Corrosion, lower, limb
    upper – *see* Corrosion, upper
      limb
  lip(s) T20.42
    first degree T20.52
    second degree T20.62
    third degree T20.72
  lower
    back – *see* Corrosion, back
    limb T24.409
      ankle - *see* Corrosion, ankle
      calf - *see* Corrosion, calf

Corrosion *(Continued)*
  lower *(Continued)*
    limb *(Continued)*
      first degree T24.509
      foot – *see* Corrosion, foot
      knee – *see* Corrosion, knee
      left T24.402
        first degree T24.502
        second degree T24.602
        third degree T24.702
      multiple sites, except ankle and
        foot T24.499
        ankle and foot T25.499
          first degree T25.599
          left T25.492
            first degree T25.592
            second degree T25.692
            third degree T25.792
          right T25.491
            first degree T25.591
            second degree T25.691
            third degree T25.791
          second degree T25.699
          third degree T25.799
        first degree T24.599
        left T24.492
          first degree T24.592
          second degree T24.692
          third degree T24.792
        right T24.491
          first degree T24.591
          second degree T24.691
          third degree T24.791
        second degree T24.699
        third degree T24.799
      right T24.401
        first degree T24.501
        second degree T24.601
        third degree T24.701
      second degree T24.609
      hip – *see* Corrosion, thigh
      thigh - *see* Corrosion, thigh
      third degree T24.709
    lung (with larynx and trachea)
      T27.5
    mouth T28.5
    neck T20.47
      first degree T20.57
      second degree T20.67
      third degree T20.77
    nose (septum) T20.44
      first degree T20.54
      second degree T20.64
      third degree T20.74
    ocular adnexa – *see* Corrosion, eye
    orbit region - *see* Corrosion, eyelid
    palm T23.459
      first degree T23.559
      left T23.452
        first degree T23.552
        second degree T23.652
        third degree T23.752
      right T23.451
        first degree T23.551
        second degree T23.651
        third degree T23.751
      second degree T23.659
      third degree T23.759
    partial thickness - code as
      Corrosion, unspecified degree,
      by site
    pelvis – *see* Corrosion, trunk
    penis – *see* Corrosion, genital organs,
      external, male

Corrosion *(Continued)*
  perineum
    female – *see* Corrosion, genital or-
      gans, external, female
    male – *see* Corrosion, genital organs,
      external, male
  periocular area – *see* Corrosion, eyelid
  pharynx T28.5
  rectum T28.7
  respiratory tract T27.7
    larynx – *see* Corrosion, larynx
    specified part NEC T27.6
    trachea – *see* Corrosion, larynx
  sac, lacrimal – *see* Corrosion, eye, speci-
    fied site NEC
  scalp T20.45
    first degree T20.55
    second degree T20.65
    third degree T20.75
  scapular region T22.469
    first degree T22.569
    left T22.462
      first degree T22.562
      second degree T22.662
      third degree T22.762
    right T22.461
      first degree T22.561
      second degree T22.661
      third degree T22.761
    second degree T22.669
    third degree T22.769
  sclera – *see* Corrosion, eye, specified site
    NEC
  scrotum – *see* Corrosion, genital organs,
    external, male
  shoulder T22.459
    first degree T22.559
    left T22.452
      first degree T22.552
      second degree T22.652
      third degree T22.752
    right T22.451
      first degree T22.551
      second degree T22.651
      third degree T22.751
    second degree T22.659
    third degree T22.759
  stomach T28.7
  temple – *see* Corrosion, head
  testis – *see* Corrosion, genital organs,
    external, male
  thigh T24.419
    first degree T24.519
    left T24.412
      first degree T24.512
      second degree T24.612
      third degree T24.712
    right T24.411
      first degree T24.511
      second degree T24.611
      third degree T24.711
    second degree T24.619
    third degree T24.719
  thorax (external) – *see* Corrosion,
    trunk
  throat (meaning pharynx) T28.5
  thumb(s) T23.419
    first degree T23.519
    left T23.412
      first degree T23.512
      second degree T23.612
      third degree T23.712
    multiple sites with fingers T23.449
      first degree T23.549

Corrosion *(Continued)*
  thumb(s) *(Continued)*
    multiple sites with fingers *(Continued)*
      left T23.442
        first degree T23.542
        second degree T23.642
        third degree T23.742
      right T23.441
        first degree T23.541
        second degree T23.641
        third degree T23.741
      second degree T23.649
      third degree T23.749
    right T23.411
      first degree T23.511
      second degree T23.611
      third degree T23.711
    second degree T23.619
    third degree T23.719
  toe T25.439
    first degree T25.539
    left T25.432
      first degree T25.532
      second degree T25.632
      third degree T25.732
    right T25.431
      first degree T25.531
      second degree T25.631
      third degree T25.731
    second degree T25.639
    third degree T25.739
  tongue T28.5
  tonsil(s) T28.5
  total body - *see* Corrosion, multiple
    body regions
  trachea T27.4
    with lung T27.5
  trunk T21.40
    abdominal wall – *see* Corrosion,
      abdominal wall
    anus – *see* Corrosion, buttock
    axilla – *see* Corrosion, upper limb
    back – *see* Corrosion, back
    breast – *see* Corrosion, chest wall
    buttock – *see* Corrosion, buttock
    chest wall – *see* Corrosion, chest wall
    first degree T21.50
    flank – *see* Corrosion, abdominal wall
    genital
      female – *see* Corrosion, genital
        organs, external, female
      male – *see* Corrosion, genital or-
        gans, external, male
    groin – *see* Corrosion, abdominal
      wall
    interscapular region – *see* Corrosion,
      back, upper
    labia – *see* Corrosion, genital organs,
      external, female
    lower back – *see* Corrosion, back
    penis – *see* Corrosion, genital organs,
      external, male
    perineum
      female – *see* Corrosion, genital
        organs, external, female
      male – *see* Corrosion, genital
        organs, external, male
    scapular region – *see* Corrosion,
      upper limb
    scrotum – *see* Corrosion, genital
      organs, external, male
    shoulder – *see* Corrosion, upper
      limb
    second degree T21.60

Corrosion *(Continued)*
  trunk *(Continued)*
    specified site NEC T21.49
      first degree T21.59
      second degree T21.69
      third degree T21.79
    testes – *see* Corrosion, genital organs,
      external, male
    third degree T21.70
    upper back – *see* Corrosion, back,
      upper
    vagina T28.8
    vulva – *see* Corrosion, genital organs,
      external, female
  unspecified site with extent of body
    surface involved specified
  less than 10 percent T32.0
  10-19 percent (0-9 percent third
    degree) T32.10
    with 10-19 percent third degree
      T32.11
  20-29 percent (0-9 percent third
    degree) T32.20
    with
      10-19 percent third degree T32.21
      20-29 percent third degree T32.22
  30-39 percent (0-9 percent third
    degree) T32.30
    with
      10-19 percent third degree T32.31
      20-29 percent third degree T32.32
      30-39 percent third degree T32.33
  40-49 percent (0-9 percent third
    degree) T32.40
    with
      10-19 percent third degree T32.41
      20-29 percent third degree T32.42
      30-39 percent third degree T32.43
      40-49 percent third degree T32.44
  50-59 percent (0-9 percent third
    degree) T32.50
    with
      10-19 percent third degree T32.51
      20-29 percent third degree T32.52
      30-39 percent third degree T32.53
      40-49 percent third degree T32.54
      50-59 percent third degree T32.55
  60-69 percent (0-9 percent third
    degree) T32.60
    with
      10-19 percent third degree T32.61
      20-29 percent third degree T32.62
      30-39 percent third degree T32.63
      40-49 percent third degree T32.64
      50-59 percent third degree T32.65
      60-69 percent third degree T32.66
  70-79 percent (0-9 percent third
    degree) T32.70
    with
      10-19 percent third degree T32.71
      20-29 percent third degree T32.72
      30-39 percent third degree T32.73
      40-49 percent third degree T32.74
      50-59 percent third degree T32.75
      60-69 percent third degree T32.76
      70-79 percent third degree T32.77
  80-89 percent (0-9 percent third
    degree) T32.80
    with
      10-19 percent third degree T32.81
      20-29 percent third degree T32.82
      30-39 percent third degree T32.83
      40-49 percent third degree T32.84
      50-59 percent third degree T32.85

Corrosion *(Continued)*
  unspecified site with extent of body sur-
    face involved specified *(Continued)*
    80-89 percent *(Continued)*
      with *(Continued)*
        60-69 percent third degree T32.86
        70-79 percent third degree T32.87
        80-89 percent third degree T32.88
    90 percent or more (0-9 percent third
      degree) T32.90
      with
        10-19 percent third degree T32.91
        20-29 percent third degree T32.92
        30-39 percent third degree T32.93
        40-49 percent third degree T32.94
        50-59 percent third degree T32.95
        60-69 percent third degree T32.96
        70-79 percent third degree T32.97
        80-89 percent third degree T32.98
        90-99 percent third degree T32.99
  upper limb (axilla) (scapular region) T22.40
    above elbow - *see* Corrosion, above
      elbow
    axilla - *see* Corrosion, axilla
    elbow - *see* Corrosion, elbow
    first degree T22.50
    forearm - *see* Corrosion, forearm
    hand – *see* Corrosion, hand
    interscapular region – *see* Corrosion,
      back, upper
    multiple sites T22.499
      first degree T22.599
      left T22.492
        first degree T22.592
        second degree T22.692
        third degree T22.792
      right T22.491
        first degree T22.591
        second degree T22.691
        third degree T22.791
      second degree T22.699
      third degree T22.799
    scapular region - *see* Corrosion,
      scapular region
    second degree T22.60
    shoulder – *see* Corrosion, shoulder
    third degree T22.70
    wrist - *see* Corrosion, hand
  uterus T28.8
  vagina T28.8
  vulva – *see* Corrosion, genital organs,
    external, female
  wrist T23.479
    first degree T23.579
    left T23.472
      first degree T23.572
      second degree T23.672
      third degree T23.772
    multiple sites with hand T23.499
      first degree T23.599
      left T23.492
        first degree T23.592
        second degree T23.692
        third degree T23.792
      right T23.491
        first degree T23.591
        second degree T23.691
        third degree T23.791
      second degree T23.699
      third degree T23.799
    right T23.471
      first degree T23.571
      second degree T23.671
      third degree T23.771

Corrosion *(Continued)*
  wrist *(Continued)*
    second degree T23.679
    third degree T23.779
Corrosive burn - *see* Corrosion
Corsican fever - *see* Malaria
Cortical - *see* condition
Cortico-adrenal - *see* condition
Coryza (acute) J00
  with grippe or influenza - *see* Influenza,
    with, respiratory manifestations
  syphilitic
    congenital (chronic) A50.05
Costen's syndrome or complex
  M26.69
Costiveness - *see* Constipation
Costochondritis M94.0
Cotard's syndrome F22
Cot death R99
Cotia virus B08.8
Cotton wool spots (retinal) H35.81
Cotungo's disease - *see* Sciatica
Cough (affected) (chronic) (epidemic)
  (nervous) R05
  with hemorrhage - *see* Hemoptysis
  bronchial R05
    with grippe or influenza - *see*
      Influenza, with, respiratory
      manifestations
  functional F45.8
  hysterical F45.8
  laryngeal, spasmodic R05
  psychogenic F45.8
  smokers' J41.0
  tea taster's B49
Counseling (for) Z71.9
  abuse NEC
    perpetrator Z69.82
    victim Z69.81
  alcohol abuser Z71.41
    family Z71.42
  child abuse
    nonparental
      perpetrator Z69.021
      victim Z69.020
    parental
      perpetrator Z69.011
      victim Z69.010
  consanguinity Z71.89
  contraceptive Z30.09
  dietary Z71.3
  drug abuser Z71.51
    family member Z71.52
  family Z71.89
  fertility preservation (prior to cancer
    therapy) (prior to removal of
    gonads) Z31.62
  for non-attending third party
    Z71.0
    related to sexual behavior or
      orientation Z70.2
  genetic NEC Z31.5
  health (advice) (education)
    (instruction) - *see* Counseling,
    medical
  human immunodeficiency virus (HIV)
    Z71.7
  impotence Z70.1
  insulin pump use Z71.82
  medical (for) Z71.9
    boarding school resident Z59.3
    consanguinity Z71.89
    feared complaint and no disease
      found Z71.1

Counseling *(Continued)*
  medical *(Continued)*
    human immunodeficiency virus
      (HIV) Z71.7
    institutional resident Z59.3
    on behalf of another Z71.0
      related to sexual behavior or
        orientation Z70.2
    person living alone Z60.2
    specified reason NEC Z71.89
  natural family planning
    procreative Z31.61
    to avoid pregnancy Z30.02
  perpetrator (of)
    abuse NEC Z69.82
    child abuse
      non-parental Z69.021
      parental Z69.011
    spousal abuse Z69.12
    rape NEC Z69.82
  procreative NEC Z30.69
    fertility preservation (prior to cancer
      therapy) (prior to removal of
      gonads) Z31.62
    using natural family planning Z30.61
  promiscuity Z70.1
  rape victim Z69.81
  religious Z71.81
  sex, sexual (related to) Z70.9
    attitude(s) Z70.0
    behavior or orientation Z70.1
    combined concerns Z70.3
    non-responsiveness Z70.1
    on behalf of third party Z70.2
    specified reason NEC Z70.8
  specified reason NEC Z71.89
  spiritual Z71.81
  spousal abuse (perpetrator)
    Z69.12
    victim Z69.11
  substance abuse Z71.89
    alcohol Z71.41
    drug Z71.51
    tobacco Z71.6
  tobacco use Z71.6
  use (of)
    insulin pump Z71.82
  victim (of)
    abuse Z69.81
    child abuse
      by parent Z69.010
      non-parental Z69.020
    rape NEC Z69.81
Coupled rhythm R00.8
Couvelaire syndrome or uterus (complicating delivery) O45.8x-
Cowperitis - *see* Urethritis
Cowper's gland - *see* condition
Cowpox B08.010
  due to vaccination T88.1
Coxa
  magna M91.4-
  plana M91.2-
  valga (acquired) - *see also* Deformity,
    limb, specified type NEC, thigh
    congenital Q65.8
    sequelae (late effect) of rickets E64.3
  vara (acquired) - *see also* Deformity,
    limb, specified type NEC, thigh
    congenital Q65.8
    sequelae (late effect) of rickets E64.3
Coxalgia, coxalgic (nontuberculous) - *see*
  also Pain, joint, hip
  tuberculous A18.02

Coxitis - *see* Monoarthritis, hip
Coxsackie (virus) (infection) B34.1
   as cause of disease classified elsewhere
      B97.11
   carditis B33.20
   central nervous system NEC A88.8
   endocarditis B33.21
   enteritis A08.3
   meningitis (aseptic) A87.0
   myocarditis B33.22
   pericarditis B33.23
   pharyngitis B08.5
   pleurodynia B33.0
   specific disease NEC B33.8
Crabs, meaning pubic lice B85.3
Crack baby P04.41
Cracked nipple N64.0
   associated with
      lactation O92.13
      pregnancy O92.11-
Cracked tooth K03.81
Cradle cap L21.0
Craft neurosis F48.8
Cramp(s) R25.2
   abdominal - *see* Pain, abdominal
   bathing T75.1
   colic R10.83
      psychogenic F45.8
   due to immersion T75.1
   fireman T67.2
   heat T67.2
   immersion T75.1
   intestinal - *see* Pain, abdominal
      psychogenic F45.8
   leg, sleep related G47.62
   limb (lower) (upper) NEC R25.2
      sleep related G47.62
   linotypist's F48.8
      organic G25.89
   muscle (limb) (general) R25.2
      due to immersion T75.1
      psychogenic F45.8
   occupational (hand) F48.8
      organic G25.89
   salt-depletion E87.1
   sleep related, leg G47.62
   stoker's T67.2
   swimmer's T75.1
   telegrapher's F48.8
      organic G25.89
   typist's F48.8
      organic G25.89
   uterus N94.89
      menstrual - *see* Dysmenorrhea
   writer's F48.8
      organic G25.89
Cranial - *see* condition
Craniocleidodysostosis Q74.0
Craniofenestria (skull) Q75.8
Craniolacunia (skull) Q75.8
Craniopagus Q89.4
Craniopathy, metabolic M85.2
Craniopharyngeal - *see* condition
Craniopharyngioma D44.4
Craniorachischisis (totalis) Q00.1
Cranioschisis Q75.8
Craniostenosis Q75.0
Craniosynostosis Q75.0
Craniotabes (cause unknown) M83.8
   neonatal P96.3
   rachitic E64.3
   syphilitic A50.56
Cranium - *see* condition
Craw-craw - *see* Onchocerciasis

Creaking joint - *see* Derangement, joint,
   specified type NEC
Creeping
   eruption B76.9
   palsy or paralysis G12.22
Crenated tongue K14.8
Creotoxism A05.9
Crepitus
   caput Q75.8
   joint - *see* Derangement, joint, specified
      type NEC
Crescent or conus choroid, congenital
   Q14.3
CREST syndrome M34.1
Cretin, cretinism (congenital) (endemic)
   (nongoitrous) (sporadic) E00.9
   pelvis
      with disproportion (fetopelvic) O33.0
         causing obstructed labor O65.0
   type
      hypothyroid E00.1
      mixed E00.2
      myxedematous E00.1
      neurological E00.0
Creutzfeldt-Jakob disease or syndrome
   (with dementia) A81.00
   familial A81.09
   iatrogenic A81.09
   specified NEC A81.09
   sporadic A81.09
   variant (vCJD) A81.01
Crib death R99
Cribriform hymen Q52.3
Cri-du-chat syndrome Q93.4
Crigler-Najjar disease or syndrome
   E80.5
Crime, victim of Z65.4
Crimean hemorrhagic fever A98.0
Criminalism F60.2
Crisis
   abdomen R10.0
   acute reaction F43.0
   addisonian E27.2
   adrenal (cortical) E27.2
   celiac K90.0
   Dietl's N13.8
   emotional – *see also* Disorder,
      adjustment
      acute reaction to stress F43.0
      specific to childhood and adolescence
         F93.8
   glaucomatocyclitic - *see* Glaucoma,
      secondary, inflammation
   heart - *see* Failure, heart
   nitritoid I95.2
      correct substance properly admin-
         istered - *see* Table of drugs and
         chemicals, by drug, adverse
         effect
      overdose or wrong substance given
         or taken - *see* Table of drugs
         and chemicals, by drug,
         poisoning
   oculogyric H51.8
      psychogenic F45.8
   Pel's (tabetic) A52.11
   psychosexual identity F64.2
   renal N28.0
   sickle-cell D57.00
      with
         acute chest syndrome D57.01
         splenic sequestration D57.02
   state (acute reaction) F43.0
   tabetic A52.11

Crisis *(Continued)*
   thyroid - *see* Thyrotoxicosis with
      thyroid storm
   thyrotoxic - *see* Thyrotoxicosis with
      thyroid storm
Crocq's disease (acrocyanosis) I73.89
Crohn's disease – *see* Enteritis, regional
Crooked septum, nasal J34.2
Cross syndrome E70.328
Crossbite (anterior) (posterior) M26.24
Cross-eye - *see* Strabismus
Croup, croupous (catarrhal) (infectious)
   (inflammatory) (nondiphtheritic) J05.0
   bronchial J20.9
   diphtheritic A36.2
   false J38.5
   spasmodic J38.5
      diphtheritic A36.2
   stridulous J38.5
      diphtheritic A36.2
Crouzon's disease Q75.1
Crowding, tooth, teeth, fully erupted
   M26.31
CRST syndrome M34.1
Cruchet's disease A85.8
Cruelty in children - *see also* Disorder,
   conduct
Crural ulcer – *see* Ulcer, lower limb
Crush, crushed, crushing
   abdomen S38.1
   ankle S97.0-
   arm (upper) (and shoulder) S47.-
   axilla – *see* Crush, arm
   back, lower S38.1
   buttock S38.1
   cheek S07.0
   chest S28.0
   cranium S07.1
   ear S07.0
   elbow S57.0-
   extremity
      lower
         ankle - *see* Crush, ankle
         below knee - *see* Crush, leg
         foot - *see* Crush, foot
         hip - *see* Crush, hip
         knee - *see* Crush, knee
         thigh - *see* Crush, thigh
         toe - *see* Crush, toe
      upper
         below elbow S67.9-
         elbow - *see* Crush, elbow
         finger - *see* Crush, finger
         forearm - *see* Crush, forearm
         hand - *see* Crush, hand
         thumb - *see* Crush, thumb
         upper arm - *see* Crush, arm
         wrist - *see* Crush, wrist
   face S07.0
   finger(s) S67.1-
      with hand (and wrist) – *see* Crush,
         hand, specified site NEC
      index S67.19-
      little S67.19-
      middle S67.19-
      ring S67.19-
      thumb – *see* Crush, thumb
   foot S97.8-
      toe – *see* Crush, toe
   forearm S57.8-
   genitalia, external
      female S38.002
         vagina S38.03
         vulva S38.03

Crush, crushed, crushing (Continued)
  genitalia, external (Continued)
    male S38.001
      penis S38.01
      scrotum S38.02
      testis S38.02
  hand (except fingers alone) S67.2-
    with wrist S67.4-
  head S07.9
    specified NEC S07.8
  heel - see Crush, foot
  hip S77.0-
    with thigh S77.2-
  internal organ (abdomen, chest, or
      pelvis) NEC T14.8
  knee S87.0-
  labium (majus) (minus) S38.03
  larynx S17.0
  leg (lower) S87.8-
    knee – see Crush, knee
  lip S07.0
  lower
    back S38.1
    leg – see Crush, leg
  neck S17.9
  nerve - see Injury, nerve
  nose S07.0
  pelvis S38.1
  penis S38.01
  scalp S07.8
  scapular region – see Crush, arm
  scrotum S38.02
  severe, unspecified site T14.8
  shoulder (and upper arm) – see Crush,
      arm
  skull S07.1
  syndrome (complication of trauma)
      T79.5
  testis S38.02
  thigh S77.1-
    with hip S77.2-
  throat S17.8
  thumb S67.0-
    with hand (and wrist) – see Crush,
        hand, specified site NEC
  toe(s) S97.10-
    great S97.11-
    lesser S97.12-
  trachea S17.0
  vagina S38.03
  vulva S38.03
  wrist S67.3-
    with hand S67.4-
Crusta lactea L21.0
Crusts R23.4
Crutch paralysis - see Injury, brachial
    plexus
Cruveilhier-Baumgarten cirrhosis,
    disease or syndrome K74.69
Cruveilhier's atrophy or disease
    G12.8
Crying (constant) (continuous)
    (excessive)
  child, adolescent, or adult R45.83
  infant (baby) (newborn) R68.11
Cryofibrinogenemia D89.2
Cryoglobulinemia (essential)
    (idiopathic) (mixed) (primary)
    (purpura) (secondary) (vasculitis)
    D89.1
  with lung involvement D89.1
    [J99]
Cryptitis (anal) (rectal) K62.8

Cryptococcosis, cryptococcus (infection)
    (neoformans) B45.9
  bone B45.3
  cerebral B45.1
  cutaneous B45.2
  disseminated B45.7
  generalized B45.7
  meningitis B45.1
  meningocerebralis B45.1
  osseous B45.3
  pulmonary B45.0
  skin B45.2
  specified NEC B45.8
Cryptopapillitis (anus) K62.8
Cryptophthalmos Q11.2
  syndrome Q87.0
Cryptorchid, cryptorchism, cryptorchi-
    dism Q53.9
  bilateral Q53.20
    abdominal Q53.21
    perineal Q53.22
  unilateral Q53.10
    abdominal Q53.11
    perineal Q53.12
Cryptosporidiosis A07.2
  hepatobiliary B88.8
  respiratory B88.8
Cryptostromosis J67.6
Crystalluria R82.99
Cubitus
  congenital Q68.8
  valgus (acquired) M21.0-
    congenital Q68.8
    sequelae (late effect) of rickets
        E64.3
  varus (acquired) M21.1-
    congenital Q68.8
    sequelae (late effect) of rickets
        E64.3
Cultural deprivation or shock Z60.3
Curling esophagus K22.4
Curling's ulcer - see Ulcer, peptic, acute
Curschmann (-Batten) (-Steinert) disease
    or syndrome G71.11
Curse, Ondine's – see Apnea, sleep
Curvature
  organ or site, congenital NEC - see
      Distortion
  penis (lateral) Q55.61
  Pott's (spinal) A18.01
  radius, idiopathic, progressive (con-
      genital) Q74.0
  spine (acquired) (angular) (idiopathic)
      (incorrect) (postural) - see Dorsopa-
      thy, deforming
    congenital Q67.5
    due to or associated with
      Charcot-Marie-Tooth disease (see
          also subcategory M49.8) G60.0
      osteitis
        deformans M88.88
        fibrosa cystica (see also subcat-
            egory M49.8) E21.0
      tuberculosis (Pott's curvature)
          A18.01
    sequelae (late effect) of rickets E64.3
    tuberculous A18.01
Cushingoid due to steroid therapy E24.2
  correct substance properly admin-
      istered - see Table of drugs and
      chemicals, by drug, adverse effect
  overdose or wrong substance given
      or taken - see Table of drugs and
      chemicals, by drug, poisoning

Cushing's
  syndrome or disease E24.9
    drug-induced E24.2
    iatrogenic E24.2
    pituitary-dependent E24.0
    specified NEC E24.8
  ulcer - see Ulcer, peptic, acute
Cusp, Carabelli - omit code
Cut (external) - see also Laceration
  muscle - see Injury, muscle
Cutaneous - see also condition
  hemorrhage R23.3
  larva migrans B76.9
Cutis - see also condition
  hyperelastica Q82.8
    acquired L57.4
  laxa (hyperelastica) - see Dermatolysis
  marmorata R23.8
  osteosis L94.2
  pendula - see Dermatolysis
  rhomboidalis nuchae L57.2
  verticis gyrata Q82.8
    acquired L91.8
Cyanosis R23.0
  due to
    patent foramen botalli Q21.1
    persistent foramen ovale Q21.1
  enterogenous D74.8
  paroxysmal digital –see Raynaud's
      disease
    with gangrene I73.01
  retina, retinal H35.89
Cyanotic heart disease I24.9
  congenital Q24.9
Cycle
  anovulatory N97.0
  menstrual, irregular N92.6
Cyclencephaly Q04.9
Cyclical vomiting G43.a09 - see also
      Vomiting, cyclical
  psychogenic F50.8
Cyclitis (see also Iridocyclitis) H20.9
  chronic - see Iridocyclitis, chronic
  Fuchs' heterochromic H20.81-
  granulomatous - see Iridocyclitis, chronic
  lens-induced - see Iridocyclitis,
      lens-induced
  posterior H30.2-
Cycloid personality F34.0
Cyclophoria H50.54
Cyclopia, cyclops Q87.0
Cyclopism Q87.0
Cyclosporiasis A07.4
Cyclothymia F34.0
Cyclothymic personality F34.0
Cyclotropia H50.41-
Cylindroma - see also Neoplasm,
      malignant
  eccrine dermal - see Neoplasm, skin,
      benign
  skin - see Neoplasm, skin, benign
Cylindruria R82.99
Cynanche
  diphtheritic A36.2
  tonsillaris J36
Cynophobia F40.218
Cynorexia R63.2
Cyphosis - see Kyphosis
Cyprus fever - see Brucellosis
Cyst (colloid) (mucous) (simple)
    (retention)
  adenoid (infected) J35.8
  adrenal gland E27.8
    congenital Q89.1

Cyst (Continued)
  air, lung J98.4
  allantoic Q64.4
  alveolar process (jaw bone) M27.40
  amnion, amniotic O41.8x-
  anterior
    chamber (eye) - see Cyst, iris
    nasopalatine K09.1
  antrum J34.1
  anus K62.8
  apical (tooth) (periodontal) K04.8
  appendix K38.8
  arachnoid, brain (acquired) G93.0
    congenital Q04.6
  arytenoid J38.7
  Baker's M71.2-
    ruptured M66.0
    tuberculous A18.02
  Bartholin's gland N75.0
  bile duct (common) (hepatic) K83.5
  bladder (multiple) (trigone) N32.89
  blue dome (breast) – see Cyst, breast
  bone (local) NEC M85.60
    aneurysmal M85.50
      ankle M85.57-
      foot M85.57-
      forearm M85.53-
      hand M85.54-
      jaw M27.49
      lower leg M85.56-
      multiple site M85.59
      neck M85.58
      rib M85.58
      shoulder M85.51-
      skull M85.58
      specified site NEC M85.58
      thigh M85.55-
      toe M85.57-
      upper arm M85.52-
      vertebra M85.58
    solitary M85.40
      ankle M85.47-
      fibula M85.46-
      foot M85.47-
      hand M85.44-
      humerus M85.42-
      jaw M27.49
      neck M85.48
      pelvis M85.45-
      radius M85.43-
      rib M85.48
      shoulder M85.41-
      skull M85.48
      specified site NEC M85.48
      tibia M85.46-
      toe M85.47-
      ulna M85.43-
      vertebra M85.48
    specified type NEC M85.60
      ankle M85.67-
      foot M85.67-
      forearm M85.63-
      hand M85.64-
      jaw M27.40
        developmental (nonodontogenic)
          K09.1
        odontogenic K09.0
        latent M27.0
      lower leg M85.66-
      multiple site M85.69
      neck M85.68
      rib M85.68
      shoulder M85.61-
      skull M85.68

Cyst (Continued)
  bone (local) NEC (Continued)
    specified type NEC (Continued)
      specified site NEC M85.68
      thigh M85.65-
      toe M85.67-
      upper arm M85.62-
      vertebra M85.68
  brain (acquired) G93.0
    congenital Q04.6
    hydatid B67.99 [G94]
    third ventricle (colloid), congenital
      Q04.6
  branchial (cleft) Q18.0
  branchiogenic Q18.0
  breast (benign) (blue dome) (peduncu-
    lated) (solitary) N60.0-
    involution – see Dysplasia, mammary,
      specified type NEC
    sebaceous – see Dysplasia, mammary,
      specified type NEC
  broad ligament (benign) N83.8
  bronchogenic (mediastinal) (sequestra-
    tion) J98.4
    congenital Q33.0
  buccal K09.8
  bulbourethral gland N36.8
  bursa, bursal NEC M71.30
    with rupture - see Rupture, synovium
    ankle M71.37-
    elbow M71.32-
    foot M71.37-
    hand M71.34-
    hip M71.35-
    multiple sites M71.39
    pharyngeal J39.2
    popliteal space - see Cyst, Baker's
    shoulder M71.31-
    specified site NEC M71.38
    wrist M71.33-
  calcifying odontogenic (M9301/0)
    D16.5
    upper jaw (bone) (maxilla) D16.4
  canal of Nuck (female) N94.89
    congenital Q52.4
  canthus - see Cyst, conjunctiva
  carcinomatous - see Neoplasm,
    malignant
  cauda equina G95.89
  cavum septi pellucidi - see Cyst, brain
  celomic (pericardium) Q24.8
  cerebellopontine (angle) - see Cyst,
    brain
  cerebellum - see Cyst, brain
  cerebral - see Cyst, brain
  cervical lateral Q18.1
  cervix NEC N88.8
    embryonic Q51.6
    nabothian N88.8
  chiasmal optic NEC - see Disorder,
    optic, chiasm
  chocolate (ovary) N80.1
  choledochus, congenital Q44.4
  chorion O41.8x-
  choroid plexus G93.0
  ciliary body - see Cyst, iris
  clitoris N90.7
  colon K63.89
  common (bile) duct K83.5
  congenital NEC Q89.8
    adrenal gland Q89.1
    epiglottis Q31.8
    esophagus Q39.8
    fallopian tube Q50.4

Cyst (Continued)
  congenital NEC (Continued)
    kidney Q61.00
      more than one (multiple) Q61.02
        specified as polycystic Q61.3
          adult type Q61.2
          infantile type NEC Q61.19
            collecting duct dilation
              Q61.11
      solitary Q61.01
    larynx Q31.8
    liver Q44.6
    lung Q33.0
    mediastinum Q34.1
    ovary Q50.1
    oviduct Q50.4
    periurethral (tissue) Q64.79
    prepuce Q55.69
    salivary gland (any) Q38.4
    sublingual Q38.6
    submaxillary gland Q38.6
    thymus (gland) Q89.2
    tongue Q38.3
    ureterovesical orifice Q62.8
    vulva Q52.79
  conjunctiva H11.44-
  cornea H18.89-
  corpora quadrigemina G93.0
  corpus
    albicans N83.29
    luteum (hemorrhagic) (ruptured)
      N83.1
  Cowper's gland (benign) (infected)
    N36.8
  cranial meninges G93.0
  craniobuccal pouch E23.6
  craniopharyngeal pouch E23.6
  cystic duct K82.8
  Cysticercus - see Cysticercosis
  Dandy-Walker Q03.1
    with spina bifida – see Spina bifida
  dental (root) K04.8
    developmental K09.0
    eruption K09.0
    primordial K09.0
  dentigerous (mandible) (maxilla)
    K09.0
  dermoid - see Neoplasm, benign, by site
    with malignant transformation C56.-
    implantation
      external area or site (skin) NEC
        L72.0
      iris - see Cyst, iris, implantation
      vagina N89.8
      vulva N90.7
    mouth K09.8
    oral soft tissue K09.8
    sacrococcygeal - see Cyst, pilonidal
  developmental K09.1
    odontogenic K09.0
    oral region (nonodontogenic) K09.1
    ovary, ovarian Q50.1
  dura (cerebral) G93.0
    spinal G96.19
  ear (external) Q18.1
  echinococcal - see Echinococcus
  embryonic
    cervix uteri Q51.6
    fallopian tube Q50.4
    vagina Q51.6
  endometrium, endometrial (uterus)
    N85.8
    ectopic - see Endometriosis
  enterogenous Q43.8

Cyst *(Continued)*
  epidermal, epidermoid (inclusion) (see
        also Cyst, skin) L72.0
    mouth K09.8
      oral soft tissue K09.8
  epididymis N50.8
  epiglottis J38.7
  epiphysis cerebri E34.8
  epithelial (inclusion) L72.0
  epoophoron Q50.5
  eruption K09.0
  esophagus K22.8
  ethmoid sinus J34.1
  external female genital organs NEC
        N90.7
  eye NEC H57.8
    congenital Q15.8
  eyelid (sebaceous) H02.829
    infected - *see* Hordeolum
    left H02.826
      lower H02.825
      upper H02.824
    right H02.823
      lower H02.822
      upper H02.821
  fallopian tube N83.8
    congenital Q50.4
  fimbrial (twisted) Q50.4
  fissural (oral region) K09.1
  follicle (graafian) (hemorrhagic) N83.0
    nabothian N88.8
  follicular (atretic) (hemorrhagic) (ovar-
        ian) N83.0
    dentigerous K09.0
    odontogenic K09.0
    skin L72.9
      specified NEC L72.8
  frontal sinus J34.1
  gallbladder K82.8
  ganglion – *see* Ganglion
  Gartner's duct Q52.4
  gingiva K09.0
  gland of Moll - *see* Cyst, eyelid
  globulomaxillary K09.1
  graafian follicle (hemorrhagic) N83.0
  granulosal lutein (hemorrhagic) N83.1
  hemangiomatous D18.00
    intra-abdominal D18.03
    intracranial D18.02
    skin D18.01
    specified site NEC D18.09
  hydatid (see also Echinococcus) B67.90
    brain B67.99 *[G94]*
    liver (see also Cyst, liver, hydatid)
          B67.8
    lung NEC B67.99 *[J99]*
    Morgagni
      female Q50.5
      male (epididymal) Q55.4
        testicular Q55.29
    specified site NEC B67.99
  hymen N89.8
    embryonic Q52.4
  hypopharynx J39.2
  hypophysis, hypophyseal (duct) (recur-
        rent) E23.6
    cerebri E23.6
  implantation (dermoid)
    external area or site (skin) NEC
          L72.0
    iris - *see* Cyst, iris, implantation
    vagina N89.8
    vulva N90.7
  incisive canal K09.1

Cyst *(Continued)*
  inclusion (epidermal) (epithelial) (epi-
        dermoid) (squamous) L72.0
    not of skin - code under Cyst, by site
  intestine (large) (small) K63.89
  intracranial - *see* Cyst, brain
  intraligamentous - *see also* Disorder,
        ligament
    knee - *see* Derangement, knee
  intrasellar E23.6
  iris H21.309
    exudative H21.31-
    idiopathic H21.30-
    implantation H21.32-
    parasitic H21.33-
    pars plana (primary) H21.34-
      exudative H21.35-
  jaw (bone) (aneurysmal) (hemorrhagic)
        (traumatic) M27.40
    developmental (odontogenic) K09.0
    fissural K09.1
  joint NEC - *see* Disorder, joint, specified
        type NEC
  kidney (acquired) N28.1
    calyceal - *see* Hydronephrosis
    congenital Q61.00
    more than one (multiple) Q61.02
      specified as polycystic Q61.3
        adult type (autosomal dominant)
              Q61.2
        infantile type (autosomal reces-
              sive) NEC Q61.19
          collecting duct dilation Q61.11
    pyelogenic - *see* Hydronephrosis
    simple N28.1
    solitary (single) Q61.01
      acquired N28.1
  labium (majus) (minus) N90.7
    sebaceous N90.7
  lacrimal - *see also* Disorder, lacrimal
        system, specified NEC
    gland H04.13-
    passages or sac - *see* Disorder, lacrimal
          system, specified NEC
  larynx J38.7
  lateral periodontal K09.0
  lens H27.8
    congenital Q12.8
  lip (gland) K13.0
  liver (idiopathic) K76.8
    congenital Q44.6
    hydatid B67.8
      granulosus B67.0
      multilocularis B67.5
  lung J98.4
    congenital Q33.0
    giant bullous J43.9
  lutein N83.1
  lymphangiomatous D18.1
  lymphoepithelial, oral soft tissue K09.8
  macula - *see* Degeneration, macula,
        hole
  malignant - *see* Neoplasm, malignant
  mammary gland - *see* Cyst, breast
  mandible M27.40
    dentigerous K09.0
    radicular K04.8
  maxilla M27.40
    dentigerous K09.0
    radicular K04.8
  medial, face and neck Q18.8
  median
    anterior maxillary K09.1
    palatal K09.1

Cyst *(Continued)*
  mediastinum, congenital Q34.1
  meibomian (gland) - *see* Chalazion
    infected - *see* Hordeolum
  membrane, brain G93.0
  meninges (cerebral) G93.0
    spinal G96.19
  meniscus, knee - *see* Derangement,
        knee, meniscus, cystic
  mesentery, mesenteric K66.8
    chyle I89.8
  mesonephric duct
    female Q50.5
    male Q55.4
  milk N64.89
  Morgagni (hydatid)
    female Q50.5
    male (epididymal) Q55.4
      testicular Q55.29
  mouth K09.8
  Müllerian duct Q50.4
    appendix testis Q55.29
    cervix Q51.6
    fallopian tube Q50.4
    female Q50.4
    male Q55.29
    prostatic utricle Q55.4
    vagina (embryonal) Q52.4
  multilocular (ovary) D39.10
    benign - *see* Neoplasm, benign
  myometrium N85.8
  nabothian (follicle) (ruptured)
        N88.8
  nasoalveolar K09.8
  nasolabial K09.8
  nasopalatine (anterior) (duct) K09.1
  nasopharynx J39.2
  neoplastic - *see* Neoplasm, uncertain
        behavior
    benign - *see* Neoplasm, benign
  nervous system NEC G96.8
  neuroenteric (congenital) Q06.8
  nipple – *see* Cyst, breast
  nose (turbinates) J34.1
    sinus J34.1
  odontogenic, developmental K09.0
  omentum (lesser) K66.8
    congenital Q45.8
  ora serrata - *see* Cyst, retina, ora serrata
  oral
    region K09.9
      developmental (nonodontogenic)
            K09.1
      specified NEC K09.8
    soft tissue K09.9
      specified NEC K09.8
  orbit H05.81-
  ovary, ovarian (twisted) N83.20
    adherent N83.20
    chocolate N80.1
    corpus
      albicans N83.29
      luteum (hemorrhagic) N83.1
    dermoid D27.9
    developmental Q50.1
    due to failure of involution NEC
          N83.20
    endometrial N80.1
    follicular (graafian) (hemorrhagic)
          N83.0
    hemorrhagic N83.20
    in pregnancy or childbirth O34.8-
      with obstructed labor O65.5
    multilocular D39.10

159

Cyst *(Continued)*
    ovary, ovarian *(Continued)*
        pseudomucinous D27.9
        retention N83.29
        serous N83.20
        specified NEC N83.29
        theca lutein (hemorrhagic) N83.1
        tuberculous A18.18
    oviduct N83.8
    palate (median) (fissural) K09.1
    palatine papilla (jaw) K09.1
    pancreas, pancreatic (hemorrhagic)
            (true) K86.2
        congenital Q45.2
        false K86.3
    paralabral
        hip M24.85-
        shoulder S43.43-
    paramesonephric duct Q50.4
        female Q50.4
        male Q55.29
    paranephric N28.1
    paraphysis, cerebri, congenital Q04.6
    parasitic B89
    parathyroid (gland) E21.4
    paratubal N83.8
    paraurethral duct N36.8
    paroophoron Q50.5
    parotid gland K11.6
    parovarian Q50.5
    pelvis, female N94.89
        in pregnancy or childbirth O34.8-
            causing obstructed labor O65.5
    penis (sebaceous) N48.89
    periapical K04.8
    pericardial, congenital Q24.8
        acquired (secondary) I31.8
    pericoronal K09.0
    periodontal K04.8
        lateral K09.0
    peripelvic (lymphatic) N28.1
    peritoneum K66.8
        chylous I89.8
    periventricular, acquired, newborn
            P91.1
    pharynx (wall) J39.2
    pilar L72.1
    pilonidal (infected) (rectum) L05.91
        with abscess L05.01
        malignant C44.59
    pituitary (duct) (gland) E23.6
    placenta O43.19-
    pleura J94.8
    popliteal - *see* Cyst, Baker's
    porencephalic Q04.6
        acquired G93.0
    postanal (infected) - *see* Cyst,
            pilonidal
    postmastoidectomy cavity (muco-
            sal) - *see* Complications, post-
            mastoidectomy, cyst
    preauricular Q18.1
    prepuce N47.4
        congenital Q55.69
    primordial (jaw) K09.0
    prostate N42.89
    pseudomucinous (ovary) D27.9
    pupillary, miotic H21.27-
    radicular (residual) K04.8
    radiculodental K04.8
    ranular K11.8
    Rathke's pouch E23.6
    rectum (epithelium) (mucous) K62.8
    renal – *see* Cyst, kidney

Cyst *(Continued)*
    residual (radicular) K04.8
    retention (ovary) N83.29
        salivary gland K11.6
    retina H33.19-
        ora serrata H33.11-
        parasitic H33.12-
    retroperitoneal K68.9
    sacrococcygeal (dermoid) - *see* Cyst,
            pilonidal
    salivary gland or duct (mucous
            extravasation or retention)
            K11.6
    Sampson's N80.1
    sclera H15.89
    scrotum L72.9
        sebaceous L72.1
    sebaceous (duct) (gland) L72.1
        breast – *see* Dysplasia, mammary,
                specified type NEC
        eyelid - *see* Cyst, eyelid
        genital organ NEC
            female N94.89
            male N50.8
        scrotum L72.1
    semilunar cartilage (knee) (multiple)
            - *see* Derangement, knee, meniscus,
            cystic
    seminal vesicle N50.8
    serous (ovary) N83.20
    sinus (accessory) (nasal) J34.1
    Skene's gland N36.8
    skin L72.9
        breast – *see* Dysplasia, mammary,
                specified type NEC
        epidermal, epidermoid L72.0
        epithelial L72.0
        eyelid - *see* Cyst, eyelid
        genital organ NEC
            female N90.7
            male N50.8
        inclusion L72.0
        scrotum L72.9
        sebaceous L72.1
        sweat gland or duct L74.8
    solitary
        bone - *see* Cyst, bone, solitary
        jaw M27.40
        kidney N28.1
    spermatic cord N50.8
    sphenoid sinus J34.1
    spinal meninges G96.19
    spleen NEC D73.4
        congenital Q89.09
        hydatid (see also Echinococcus)
                B67.99 *[D77]*
    Stafne's M27.0
    subarachnoid intrasellar R93.0
    subcutaneous, pheomycotic (chromo-
            mycotic) B43.2
    subdural (cerebral) G93.0
        spinal cord G96.19
    sublingual gland K11.6
    submandibular gland K11.6
    submaxillary gland K11.6
    suburethral N36.8
    suprarenal gland E27.8
    suprasellar - *see* Cyst, brain
    sweat gland or duct L74.8
    synovial - *see also* Cyst, bursa
        ruptured *see* Rupture, synovium
    tarsal - *see* Chalazion
    tendon (sheath) – *see* Disorder, tendon,
            specified type NEC

Cyst *(Continued)*
    testis N44.2
        tunica albuginea N44.1
    theca lutein (ovary) N83.1
    Thornwaldt's J39.2
    thymus (gland) E32.8
    thyroglossal duct (infected) (persistent)
            Q89.2
    thyrolingual duct (infected) (persistent)
            Q89.2
    thyroid (gland) E04.1
    tongue K14.8
    tonsil J35.8
    tooth - *see* Cyst, dental
    Tornwaldt's J39.2
    trichilemmal L72.1
    trichodermal L72.1
    tubal (fallopian) N83.8
        inflammatory – *see* Salpingitis, chronic
    tubo-ovarian N83.8
        inflammatory N70.13
    tunica
        albuginea testis N44.1
        vaginalis N50.8
    turbinate (nose) J34.1
    Tyson's gland N48.89
    urachus, congenital Q64.4
    ureter N28.89
    ureterovesical orifice N28.89
    urethra, urethral (gland) N36.8
    uterine ligament N83.8
    uterus (body) (corpus) (recurrent)
            N85.8
        embryonic Q51.8
            cervix Q51.6
    vagina, vaginal (implantation) (inclu-
            sion) (squamous cell) (wall)
            N89.8
        embryonic Q52.4
    vallecula, vallecular (epiglottis)
            J38.7
    vesical (orifice) N32.89
    vitreous body H43.89
    vulva (implantation) (inclusion)
            N90.7
        congenital Q52.79
        sebaceous gland N90.7
    vulvovaginal gland N90.7
    wolffian
        female Q50.5
        male Q55.4
Cystadenocarcinoma - *see* Neoplasm,
            malignant
    bile duct C22.1
        specified site - *see* Neoplasm,
                malignant
        unspecified site
            female C56.9
            male C61
            specified site - *see* Neoplasm,
                    malignant
            unspecified site C56.9
        specified site - *see* Neoplasm,
                malignant
        unspecified site C56.9
            specified site - *see* Neoplasm,
                    malignant
            unspecified site C56.9
Cystadenofibroma
    clear cell - *see* Neoplasm, benign
    endometrioid D27.9
        borderline malignancy D39.1-
        malignant C56.-

Cystadenofibroma (Continued)
  endometrioid (Continued)
    specified site - see Neoplasm,
        benign
    unspecified site D27.9
    specified site - see Neoplasm,
        benign
    unspecified site D27.9
  specified site - see Neoplasm, benign
  unspecified site D27.9
Cystadenoma - see also Neoplasm,
    benign
  bile duct D13.4
  endometrioid - see Neoplasm,
      benign
    borderline malignancy - see Neo-
        plasm, uncertain behavior
  malignant - see Neoplasm, malignant
  mucinous
    borderline malignancy
      ovary C56.-
      specified site NEC - see Neoplasm,
          uncertain behavior
      unspecified site C56.9
    papillary
      borderline malignancy
        ovary C56.-
        specified site NEC - see Neo-
            plasm, uncertain behavior
        unspecified site C56.9
      specified site - see Neoplasm,
          benign
      unspecified site D27.9
    specified site - see Neoplasm, benign
    unspecified site D27.9
  papillary
    borderline malignancy
      ovary C56.-
      specified site NEC - see Neoplasm,
          uncertain behavior
      unspecified site C56.9
    lymphomatosum
      specified site - see Neoplasm,
          benign
      unspecified site D11.9
    mucinous
      borderline malignancy
        ovary C56.-
        specified site NEC - see Neo-
            plasm, uncertain behavior
        unspecified site C56.9
      specified site - see Neoplasm,
          benign
      unspecified site D27.9
    pseudomucinous
      borderline malignancy
        ovary C56.-
        specified site NEC - see Neo-
            plasm, uncertain behavior
        unspecified site C56.9
      specified site - see Neoplasm,
          benign
      unspecified site D27.9
    serous
      borderline malignancy
        ovary C56.-
        specified site NEC - see Neo-
            plasm, uncertain behavior
        unspecified site C56.9
      specified site - see Neoplasm,
          benign
      unspecified site D27.9
    specified site - see Neoplasm, benign
    unspecified site D27.9

Cystadenoma (Continued)
  pseudomucinous
    borderline malignancy
      ovary C56.-
      specified site NEC - see Neoplasm,
          uncertain behavior
      unspecified site C56.9
    papillary
      borderline malignancy
        ovary C56.-
        specified site NEC - see Neo-
            plasm, uncertain behavior
        unspecified site C56.9
      specified site - see Neoplasm,
          benign
      unspecified site D27.9
    specified site - see Neoplasm, benign
    unspecified site D27.9
  serous
    borderline malignancy
      ovary C56.-
      specified site NEC - see Neoplasm,
          uncertain behavior
      unspecified site C56.9
    papillary
      borderline malignancy
        ovary C56.-
        specified site NEC - see Neo-
            plasm, uncertain behavior
        unspecified site C56.9
      specified site - see Neoplasm,
          benign
      unspecified site D27.9
    specified site - see Neoplasm, benign
    unspecified site D27.9
Cystathionine synthase deficiency
    E72.11
Cystathioninemia E72.19
Cystathioninuria E72.19
Cystic - see also condition
  breast (chronic) – see Mastopathy,
      cystic
  corpora lutea (hemorrhagic)
      N83.1
  duct - see condition
  eyeball (congenital) Q11.0
  fibrosis - see Fibrosis, cystic
  kidney (congenital) Q61.3
    adult type Q61.2
    infantile type NEC Q61.19
      collecting duct dilatation
          Q61.11
    medullary Q61.5
  liver, congenital Q44.6
  lung disease J98.4
    congenital Q33.0
  mastitis, chronic - see Mastopathy, cystic
  medullary, kidney Q61.5
  meniscus - see Derangement, knee,
      meniscus, cystic
  ovary N83.20
Cysticercosis, cysticerciasis B69.9
  with
    epileptiform fits B69.0
    myositis B69.81
  brain B69.0
  central nervous system B69.0
  cerebral B69.0
  ocular B69.1
  specified NEC B69.89
Cysticercus cellulose infestation – see
    Cysticercosis
Cystinosis (malignant) E72.04
Cystinuria E72.01

Cystitis (exudative) (hemorrhagic) (sep-
    tic) (suppurative) N30.90
  with
    fibrosis – see Cystitis, chronic,
        interstitial
    hematuria N30.91
    leukoplakia – see Cystitis, chronic,
        interstitial
    malakoplakia – see Cystitis, chronic,
        interstitial
    metaplasia – see Cystitis, chronic,
        interstitial
    prostatitis N41.3
  acute N30.00
    with hematuria N30.01
    of trigone N30.30
      with hematuria N30.31
  allergic – see Cystitis, specified type NEC
  amebic A06.81
  bilharzial B65.9
  blennorrhagic (gonococcal) A54.01
  bullous – see Cystitis, specified type NEC
  calculous N21.0
  chlamydial A56.01
  chronic N30.20
    with hematuria N30.21
    interstitial N30.10
      with hematuria N30.11
    of trigone N30.30
      with hematuria N30.31
    specified NEC N30.20
      with hematuria N30.21
  cystic(a) – see Cystitis, specified type
      NEC
  diphtheritic A36.85
  echinococcal
    granulosus B67.2
    multilocularis B67.69
  emphysematous – see Cystitis, specified
      type NEC
  encysted – see Cystitis, specified type
      NEC
  eosinophilic – see Cystitis, specified
      type NEC
  follicular - see Cystitis, of trigone
  gangrenous – see Cystitis, specified type
      NEC
  glandularis – see Cystitis, specified type
      NEC
  gonococcal A54.01
  incrusted – see Cystitis, specified type
      NEC
  interstitial (chronic) – see Cystitis,
      chronic, interstitial
  irradiation N30.40
    with hematuria N30.41
  irritation – see Cystitis, specified type
      NEC
  malignant – see Cystitis, specified type
      NEC
  of trigone N30.30
    with hematuria N30.31
  panmural – see Cystitis, chronic,
      interstitial
  polyposa – see Cystitis, specified type
      NEC
  prostatic N41.3
  puerperal (postpartum) O86.22
  radiation – see Cystitis, irradiation
  specified type NEC N30.80
    with hematuria N30.81
  subacute – see Cystitis, chronic
  submucous – see Cystitis, chronic,
      interstitial

Cystitis *(Continued)*
    syphilitic (late) A52.76
    trichomonal A59.03
    tuberculous A18.12
    ulcerative – *see* Cystitis, chronic,
        interstitial
Cystocele(-urethrocele)
    female N81.10
        with prolapse of uterus - *see* Prolapse,
            uterus
        lateral N81.12
        midline N81.11
        paravaginal N81.12
    in pregnancy or childbirth O34.8-
        causing obstructed labor O65.5
    male N32.89
Cystolithiasis N21.0
Cystoma - *see also* Neoplasm, benign
    endometrial, ovary N80.1
        specified site - *see* Neoplasm, benign
        unspecified site D27.9
    simple (ovary) N83.29

Cystoplegia N31.2
Cystoptosis N32.89
Cystopyelitis - *see* Pyelonephritis
Cystorrhagia N32.89
Cystosarcoma phyllodes (female) D48.61-
    benign (female) D24.0-
        male D24.1-
    male D48.62-
    malignant - *see* Neoplasm, breast, malignant
Cystostomy
    attention to Z43.5
    complication - *see* Complications,
        cystostomy
    status Z93.50
        appendico-vesicostomy Z93.52
        cutaneous Z93.51
        specified NEC Z93.59
Cystourethritis - *see* Urethritis
Cystourethrocele - *see also* Cystocele
    female N81.10
        with uterine prolapse – *see* Prolapse,
            uterus

Cystourethrocele *(Continued)*
    female *(Continued)*
        lateral N81.12
        midline N81.11
        paravaginal N81.12
    male N32.89
Cytomegalic inclusion disease
    congenital P35.1
Cytomegalovirus infection B25.9
Cytomycosis (reticuloendothelial) B39.4
Cytopenia D75.9
    refractory
        with multilineage dysplasia D46.a
           and ringed sideroblasts
               (RCMD RS) D46.b
Czerny's disease (periodic hydrarthrosis
    of the knee) - *see* Effusion, joint,
    knee

D

Daae (-Finsen) disease (epidemic pleurodynia) B33.0
Da Costa's syndrome F45.8
Dabney's grip B33.0
Dacryoadenitis, dacryadenitis H04.00-
acute H04.01-
chronic H04.02-
Dacryocystitis H04.30-
acute H04.32-
chronic H04.41-
neonatal P39.1
phlegmonous H04.31-
syphilitic A52.71
congenital (early) A50.01
trachomatous, active A71.1
sequelae (late effect) B94.0
Dacryocystoblenorrhea - *see* Inflammation, lacrimal, passages, chronic
Dacryocystocele - *see* Disorder, lacrimal system, changes
Dacryolith, dacryolithiasis H04.51-
Dacryoma - *see* Disorder, lacrimal system, changes
Dacryopericystitis - *see* Dacryocystitis
Dacryops H04.11-
Dacryostenosis - *see also* Stenosis, lacrimal
congenital Q10.5
Dactylitis
bone - *see* Osteomyelitis
sickle cell D57.00
Hb C D57.219
Hb SS D57.00
specified NEC D57.819
skin L08.9
syphilitic A52.77
tuberculous A18.03
Dactylolysis spontanea (ainhum) L94.6
Dactylosymphysis Q70.9
fingers – *see* Syndactylism, complex, fingers
toes Q70.2
Damage
arteriosclerotic - *see* Arteriosclerosis
brain (nontraumatic) G93.9
anoxic, hypoxic G93.1
resulting from a procedure G97.82
child NOS G80.9
due to birth injury P11.2
cardiorenal (vascular) - *see* Hypertension, cardiorenal
cerebral NEC - *see* Damage, brain
coccyx, complicating delivery O71.6
coronary - *see* Disease, heart, ischemic
eye, birth injury P15.3
liver (nontraumatic) K76.9
alcoholic K70.9
due to drugs - *see* Disease, liver, toxic
toxic - *see* Disease, liver, toxic
medication T88.7 This code not for use in the inpatient setting
pelvic
joint or ligament, during delivery O71.6
organ NEC
during delivery O71.5
following ectopic or molar pregnancy O08.6
renal - *see* Disease, renal
subendocardium, subendocardial - *see* Degeneration, myocardial
vascular I99.9

Dana-Putnam syndrome (subacute combined sclerosis with pernicious anemia) - *see* Degeneration, combined
Danbolt (-Closs) syndrome (acrodermatitis enteropathica) L08.89
Dandruff L21.0
Dandy-Walker syndrome Q03.1
with spina bifida – *see* Spina bifida
Danlos' syndrome Q79.6
Darier(-White) disease (congenital) Q82.8
meaning erythema annulare centrifugum L53.1
Darier-Roussy sarcoid D86.3
Darling's disease or histoplasmosis B39.4
Darwin's tubercle Q17.8
Dawson's (inclusion body) encephalitis A81.1
De Beurmann(-Gougerot) disease B42.1
De la Tourette's syndrome F95.2
De Lange's syndrome Q87.1
De Morgan's spots (senile angiomas) I78.1
De Quervain's
disease (tendon sheath) M65.4
syndrome E34.51
thyroiditis (subacute granulomatous thyroiditis) E06.1
De Toni-Fanconi(-Debré) syndrome E72.09
with cystinosis E72.04
Dead
fetus, retained (mother) O36.4
early pregnancy O02.1
labyrinth - *see* subcategory H83.2
ovum, retained O02.0
Deaf nonspeaking NEC H91.3
Deafmutism (acquired) (congenital) NEC H91.3
hysterical F44.6
syphilitic, congenital (*see also* subcategory H94.8) A50.09
Deafness (acquired) (complete) (hereditary) (partial) H91.9-
with blue sclera and fragility of bone Q78.0
auditory fatigue - *see* Deafness, specified type NEC
aviation T70.0
nerve injury - *see* Injury, nerve, acoustic, specified type NEC
boilermaker's - *see* subcategory H83.3
central - *see* Deafness, sensorineural
conductive H90.2
and sensorineural, mixed H90.8
bilateral H90.6
bilateral H90.0
unilateral H90.1-
congenital H90.5
with blue sclera and fragility of bone Q78.0
due to toxic agents - *see* Deafness, ototoxic
emotional (hysterical) F44.6
functional (hysterical) F44.6
high frequency H91.9-
hysterical F44.6
low frequency H91.9-
mental R48.8
mixed conductive and sensorineural H90.8
bilateral H90.6
unilateral H90.7-
nerve - *see* Deafness, sensorineural
neural - *see* Deafness, sensorineural

Deafness *(Continued)*
noise-induced - *see also* subcategory H83.3
nerve injury - *see* Injury, nerve, acoustic, specified type NEC
nonspeaking H91.3
ototoxic - *see* subcategory H91.0
perceptive - *see* Deafness, sensorineural
psychogenic (hysterical) F44.6
sensorineural H90.5
and conductive, mixed H90.8
bilateral H90.6
bilateral H90.3
unilateral H90.4-
sensory - *see* Deafness, sensorineural
specified type NEC - *see* subcategory H91.8
sudden (idiopathic) H91.2-
syphilitic A52.15
transient ischemic H93.01-
traumatic - *see* Injury, nerve, acoustic, specified type NEC
word (developmental) H93.25
Death (cause unknown) (of) (unexplained) (unspecified cause) R99
cardiac (sudden) (with successful resuscitation) code to underlying disease
family history of Z82.41
personal history of Z86.74
family member (assumed) Z63.4
Debility (chronic) (general) (nervous) R53.81
congenital or neonatal NOS P96.9
old age R54
nervous R53.81
senile R54
Débove's disease (splenomegaly) R16.1
Decalcification
bone - *see* Osteoporosis
teeth K03.89
Decapsulation, kidney N28.89
Decay
dental - *see* Caries, dental
senile R54
tooth, teeth - *see* Caries, dental
Deciduitis (acute)
following ectopic or molar pregnancy O08.0
Decline (general) - *see* Debility
cognitive, age-associated R41.81
Decompensation
cardiac (acute) (chronic) - *see* Disease, heart
cardiovascular - *see* Disease, cardiovascular
heart - *see* Disease, heart
hepatic - *see* Failure, hepatic
myocardial (acute) (chronic) - *see* Disease, heart
respiratory J98.8
Decompression sickness T70.3
Decrease(d)
absolute neutrophile count - *see* Neutropenia
blood
platelets - *see* Thrombocytopenia
pressure R03.1
due to shock following
injury T79.4
operation T81.1
estrogen E28.39
postablative E89.40
asymptomatic E89.40
symptomatic E89.41

Decrease(d) *(Continued)*
  fragility of erythrocytes D58.8
  function
    lipase (pancreatic) K90.3
    ovary in hypopituitarism E23.0
    parenchyma of pancreas K86.8
    pituitary (gland) (anterior) (lobe) E23.0
      posterior (lobe) E23.0
  functional activity R68.89
  glucose R73.09
  hematocrit R71.0
  hemoglobin R71.0
  leukocytes D72.819
    specified NEC D72.818
  libido R68.82
  lymphocytes D72.810
  platelets D69.6
  respiration, due to shock following
      injury T79.4
  sexual desire R68.82
  tear secretion NEC - *see* Syndrome, dry
      eye
  tolerance
    fat K90.4
    glucose R73.09
    pancreatic K90.3
    salt and water E87.8
  vision NEC H54.7
  white blood cell count D72.819
    specified NEC D72.818
Decubitus (ulcer) - see Ulcer, pressure,
    by site
  cervix N86
Deepening acetabulum - *see* Derange-
    ment, joint, specified type NEC, hip
Defect, defective Q89.9
  3-(hydroxysteroid dehydrogenase
      E25.0
  11 hydroxylase E25.0
  21 hydroxylase E25.0
  abdominal wall, congenital Q79.59
  antibody immunodeficiency D80.9
  aorticopulmonary septum Q21.4
  atrial septal (ostium secundum type)
      Q21.1
    following acute myocardial infarction
        (current complication) I23.1
    ostium primum type Q21.2
  atrioventricular
    canal Q21.2
    septum Q21.2
  auricular septal Q21.1
  bilirubin excretion NEC E80.6
  biosynthesis, androgen (testicular)
      E29.1
  bulbar septum Q21.0
  catalase E80.3
  cell membrane receptor complex (CR3)
      D71
  circulation I99.9
    congenital Q28.9
    newborn Q28.9
  coagulation (factor) (*see also* Deficiency,
      factor) D68.9
    with
      ectopic pregnancy O08.1
      molar pregnancy O08.1
    acquired D68.4
    antepartum with hemorrhage – *see*
        Hemorrhage, antepartum, with
        coagulation defect
    due to
      liver disease D68.4
      vitamin K deficiency D68.4

Defect, defective *(Continued)*
  coagulation *(Continued)*
    hereditary NEC D68.2
    intrapartum O67.0
    newborn, transient P61.6
    postpartum O72.3
    specified type NEC D68.8
  complement system D84.1
  conduction (heart) I45.9
    bone - *see* Deafness, conductive
  congenital, organ or site not listed - *see*
      Anomaly, by site
  coronary sinus Q21.1
  cushion, endocardial Q21.2
  degradation, glycoprotein E77.1
  dental bridge, crown, fillings - *see*
      Defect, dental restoration
  dental restoration K08.50
    specified NEC K08.59
  dentin (hereditary) K00.5
  Descemet's membrane, congenital
      Q13.89
  developmental - *see also* Anomaly
    cauda equina Q06.3
  diaphragm
    with elevation, eventration or hernia
        see Hernia, diaphragm
    congenital Q79.1
      with hernia Q79.0
      gross (with hernia) Q79.0
  ectodermal, congenital Q82.9
  Eisenmenger's Q21.8
  enzyme
    catalase E80.3
    peroxidase E80.3
  esophagus, congenital Q39.9
  extensor retinaculum M62.89
  fibrin polymerization D68.2
  filling
    bladder R93.4
    kidney R93.4
    stomach R93.3
    ureter R93.4
  Gerbode Q21.0
  glycoprotein degradation E77.1
  Hageman (factor) D68.2
  hearing - *see* Deafness
  high grade F70
  interatrial septal Q21.1
  interauricular septal Q21.1
  interventricular septal Q21.0
    with dextroposition of aorta, pulmo-
        nary stenosis and hypertrophy
        of right ventricle Q21.3
    in tetralogy of Fallot Q21.3
  learning (specific) – *see* Disorder,
      learning
  lymphocyte function antigen-1 (LFA-1)
      D84.0
  lysosomal enzyme, post-translational
      modification E77.0
  major osseous M89.70
    ankle M89.77-
    carpus M89.74-
    clavicle M89.71-
    femur M89.75-
    fibula M89.76-
    fingers M89.74-
    foot M89.77-
    forearm M89.73-
    hand M89.74-
    humerous M89.72-
    lower leg M89.76-
    metacarpus M89.74-

Defect, defective *(Continued)*
  major osseous *(Continued)*
    metatarsus M89.77-
    multiple sites M89.9
    pelvic region M89.75-
    pelvis M89.75-
    radius M89.73-
    scapula M89.71-
    shoulder region M89.71-
    specified NEC M89.78
    tarsus M89.77-
    thigh M89.75-
    tibia M89.76-
    toes M89.77-
    ulna M89.73-
  mental - *see* Retardation, mental
  modification, lysosomal enzymes, post-
      translational E77.0
  obstructive, congenital
    renal pelvis Q62.39
    ureter Q62.39
      atresia – *see* Atresia, ureter
      cecoureterocele Q62.32
      megaureter Q62.2
      orthotopic ureterocele Q62.31
  osseous, major M89.70
    ankle M89.77-
    carpus M89.74-
    clavicle M89.71-
    femur M89.75-
    fibula M89.76-
    fingers M89.74-
    foot M89.77-
    forearm M89.73-
    hand M89.74-
    humerous M89.72-
    lower leg M89.76-
    metacarpus M89.74-
    metatarsus M89.77-
    multiple sites M89.9
    pelvic region M89.75-
    pelvis M89.75-
    radius M89.73-
    scapula M89.71-
    shoulder region M89.71-
    specified NEC M89.78
    tarsus M89.77-
    thigh M89.75-
    tibia M89.76-
    toes M89.77-
    ulna M89.73-
  osteochondral NEC M95.8 - *see also*
      Deformity
  ostium
    primum Q21.2
    secundum Q21.1
  peroxidase E80.3
  placental blood supply - *see* Insuffi-
      ciency, placental
  platelets, qualitative D69.1
    constitutional D68.0
  postural NEC, spine - *see* Dorsopathy,
      deforming
  reduction
    limb Q73.8
      lower Q72.9-
        absence – *see* Agenesis, leg
        foot – *see* Agenesis, foot
        split foot Q72.7-
        longitudinal
          femur Q72.4-
          fibula Q72.6-
          tibia Q72.5-
        specified type NEC Q72.8-

Defect, defective (Continued)
  reduction (Continued)
    limb (Continued)
      specified type NEC Q73.8
      upper Q71.9-
        absence – see Agenesis, arm
          forearm – see Agenesis, forearm
          hand – see Agenesis, hand
        lobster-claw hand Q71.6-
        longitudinal
          radius Q71.4-
          ulna Q71.5-
        specified type NEC Q71.8-
  renal pelvis Q63.8
    obstructive Q62.39
  respiratory system, congenital Q34.9
  restoration, dental K08.50
    specified NEC K08.59
  retinal nerve bundle fibers H35.89
  septal (heart) NOS Q21.9
    acquired (atrial) (auricular) (ventricular) (old) I51.0
    atrial Q21.1
      concurrent with acute myocardial infarction - see Infarct, myocardium
      following acute myocardial infarction (current complication) I23.1
      ventricular - see also Defect, ventricular septal Q21.0
    sinus venosus Q21.1
  speech R47.9
    developmental F80.9
    specified NEC R47.89
  Taussig-Bing (aortic transposition and overriding pulmonary artery) Q20.1
  teeth, wedge K03.1
  vascular (local) I99.9
    congenital Q27.9
  ventricular septal Q21.0
    concurrent with acute myocardial infarction - see Infarct, myocardium
    following acute myocardial infarction (current complication) I23.2
    in tetralogy of Fallot Q21.3
  vision NEC H54.7
  visual field H53.40
    bilateral
      heteronymous H53.47
      homonymous H53.46-
    generalized contraction H53.48-
    localized
      arcuate H53.43-
      scotoma (central area) H53.41-
        blind spot area H53.42-
      sector H53.43-
      specified type NEC H53.45-
  voice R49.9
    specified NEC R49.8
  wedge, tooth, teeth (abrasion) K03.1
Deferentitis N49.1
  gonorrheal (acute) (chronic) A54.23
Defibrination (syndrome) D65
  antepartum – see Hemorrhage, antepartum, with coagulation defect, disseminated intravascular coagulation
  following ectopic or molar pregnancy O08.1
  intrapartum O67.0

Defibrination (Continued)
  newborn P60
  postpartum O72.3
Deficiency, deficient
  3B hydroxysteroid dehydrogenase E25.0
  5-alpha reductase (with male pseudohermaphroditism) E29.1
  11 hydroxylase E25.0
  21 hydroxylase E25.0
  abdominal muscle syndrome Q79.4
  accelerator globulin (Ac G) (blood) D68.2
  AC globulin (congenital) (hereditary) D68.2
    acquired D68.4
  acid phosphatase E83.39
  activating factor (blood) D68.2
  adenosine deaminase (ADA) D81.3
  aldolase (hereditary) E74.19
  alpha-1-antitrypsin E88.01
  amino-acids E72.9
  anemia - see Anemia
  aneurin E51.9
  antibody with
    hyperimmunoglobulinemia D80.6
    near-normal immunoglobins D80.6
  antidiuretic hormone E23.2
  anti-hemophilic
    factor (A) D66
      B D67
      C D68.1
    globulin (AHG) NEC D66
  antithrombin (antithrombin III) D68.59
  ascorbic acid E54
  attention (disorder) (syndrome) F98.8
    with hyperactivity - see Disorder, attention-deficit hyperactivity
  autoprothrombin
    I D68.2
    II D67
    C D68.2
  beta-glucuronidase E76.29
  biotin E53.8
  biotin-dependent carboxylase D81.819
  biotinidase D81.810
  brancher enzyme (amylopectinosis) E74.03
  calciferol E55.9
    with
      adult osteomalacia M83.8
      rickets - see Rickets
  calcium (dietary) E58
  calorie, severe E43
    with marasmus E41
      and kwashiorkor E42
  cardiac - see Insufficiency, myocardial
  carnitine E71.40
    due to
      hemodialysis E71.43
      inborn errors of metabolism E71.42
      Valproic acid therapy E71.43
    iatrogenic E71.43
    muscle palmityltransferase E71.314
    primary E71.41
    secondary E71.448
  carotene E50.9
  central nervous system G96.8
  ceruloplasmin (Wilson) E83.01
  choline E53.8
  Christmas factor D67
  chromium E61.4
  clotting (blood) (see also Deficiency, coagulation factor) D68.9

Deficiency, deficient (Continued)
  clotting factor NEC (hereditary) (see also Deficiency, factor) D68.2
  coagulation NOS D68.9
    with
      ectopic pregnancy O08.1
      molar pregnancy O08.1
    acquired (any) D68.4
    antepartum hemorrhage – see Hemorrhage, antepartum, with coagulation defect
    clotting factor NEC (see also Deficiency, factor) D68.2
    due to
      hyperprothrombinemia D68.4
      liver disease D68.4
      vitamin K deficiency D68.4
    newborn, transient P61.6
    postpartum O72.3
    specified NEC D68.8
  cognitive F09
  color vision H53.50
    achromatopsia H53.51
    acquired H53.52
    deuteranomaly H53.53
    protanomaly H53.54
    specified type NEC H53.59
    tritanomaly H53.55
  combined glucocorticoid and mineralocorticoid E27.49
  contact factor D68.2
  copper (nutritional) E61.0
  corticoadrenal E27.40
    primary E27.1
  craniofacial axis Q75.0
  cyanocobalamin E53.8
  C1 esterase inhibitor (C1-INH) D84.1
  debrancher enzyme (limit dextrinosis) E74.03
  dehydrogenase
    long chain/very long chain acyl CoA E71.310
    medium chain acyl CoA E71.311
    short chain acyl CoA E71.312
  diet E63.9
  disaccharidase E73.9
  edema - see Malnutrition, severe
  endocrine E34.9
  energy-supply - see Malnutrition
  enzymes, circulating NEC E88.09
  ergosterol E55.9
    with
      adult osteomalacia M83.8
      rickets - see Rickets
  essential fatty acid (EFA) E63.0
  factor - see also Deficiency, coagulation
    Hageman D68.2
    I (congenital) (hereditary) D68.2
    II (congenital) (hereditary) D68.2
    IX (congenital) (functional) (hereditary) (with functional defect) D67
    multiple (congenital) D68.8
      acquired D68.4
    V (congenital) (hereditary) D68.2
    VII (congenital) (hereditary) D68.2
    VIII (congenital) (functional) (hereditary) (with functional defect) D66
      with vascular defect D68.0
    X (congenital) (hereditary) D68.2
    XI (congenital) (hereditary) D68.1
    XII (congenital) (hereditary) D68.2
    XIII (congenital) (hereditary) D68.2

165

Deficiency, deficient *(Continued)*
  femoral, proximal focal (congenital)
    – *see* Defect, reduction, lower limb,
    longitudinal, femur
  fibrin-stabilizing factor (congenital)
    (hereditary) D68.2
    acquired D68.4
  fibrinase D68.2
  fibrinogen (congenital) (hereditary)
    D68.2
    acquired D65
  folate E53.8
  folic acid E53.8
  foreskin N47.3
  fructokinase E74.11
  fructose 1,6-diphosphatase E74.19
  fructose-1-phosphate aldolase E74.19
  galactokinase E74.29
  galactose-1-phosphate uridyl transfer-
    ase E74.29
  gammaglobulin in blood D80.1
    hereditary D80.0
  glass factor D68.2
  glucocorticoid E27.49
    mineralocorticoid E27.49
  glucose-6-phosphatase E74.01
  glucose-6-phosphate dehydrogenase
    anemia D55.0
  glucuronyl transferase E80.5
  glycogen synthetase E74.09
  gonadotropin (isolated) E23.0
  growth hormone (idiopathic) (isolated)
    E23.0
  Hageman factor D68.2
  hemoglobin D64.9
  hepatophosphorylase E74.09
  homogentisate 1,2-dioxygenase E70.29
  hormone
    anterior pituitary (partial) NEC
      E23.0
      growth E23.0
    growth (isolated) E23.0
    pituitary E23.0
    testicular E29.1
  hypoxanthine-(guanine)-phosphori-
    bosyltransferase (HGPRT) (total
    H-PRT) E79.1
  immunity D84.9
    cell-mediated D84.8
      with thrombocytopenia and ec-
        zema D82.0
    combined D81.9
    humoral D80.9
    IgA (secretory) D80.2
    IgG D80.3
    IgM D80.4
  immuno - *see* Immunodeficiency
  immunoglobulin, selective
    A (IgA) D80.2
    G (IgG) (subclasses) D80.3
    M (IgM) D80.4
  inositol (B complex) E53.8
  intrinsic
    factor (congenital) D51.0
    sphincter N36.42
      with urethral hypermobility
        N36.43
  iodine E61.8
    congenital syndrome - *see* Syndrome,
      iodine-deficiency, congenital
  iron E61.1
    anemia D50.9
  kalium E87.6
  kappa-light chain D80.8

Deficiency, deficient *(Continued)*
  labile factor (congenital) (hereditary)
    D68.2
    acquired D68.4
  lacrimal fluid (acquired) - *see also* Syn-
    drome, dry eye
    congenital Q10.6
  lactase
    congenital E73.0
    secondary E73.1
  Laki-Lorand factor D68.2
  lecithin cholesterol acyltransferase
    E78.6
  lipocaic K86.8
  lipoprotein (familial) (high density)
    E78.6
  liver phosphorylase E74.09
  lysosomal (-1, 4 glucosidase E74.02
  magnesium E61.2
  major histocompatibility complex
    class I D81.6
    class II D81.7
  manganese E61.3
  menadione (vitamin K) E56.1
    newborn P53
  mental (familial) (hereditary) - *see*
    Retardation, mental
  methylenetetrahydrofolate reductase
    (MTHFR) E72.12
  mineral NEC E61.8
  mineralocorticoid E27.49
    with glucocorticoid E27.49
  molybdenum (nutritional) E61.5
  moral F60.2
  multiple nutrient elements E61.7
  muscle
    carnitine (palmityltransferase)
      E71.314
    phosphofructokinase E74.09
  myoadenylate deaminase E79.2
  myocardial - *see* Insufficiency,
    myocardial
  myophosphorylase E74.04
  NADH diaphorase or reductase (con-
    genital) D74.0
  NADH-methemoglobin reductase (con-
    genital) D74.0
  natrium E87.1
  niacin (amide) (-tryptophan) E52
  nicotinamide E52
  nicotinic acid E52
  number of teeth - *see* Anodontia
  nutrient element E61.9
    multiple E61.7
    specified NEC E61.8
  nutrition, nutritional E63.9
    sequelae - *see* Sequelae, nutritional
      deficiency
    specified NEC E63.8
  ornithine transcarbamylase E72.4
  ovarian E28.39
  oxygen - *see* Anoxia
  pantothenic acid E53.8
  parathyroid (gland) E20.9
  perineum (female) N81.89
  phenylalanine hydroxylase E70.1
  phosphoenolpyruvate carboxykinase
    E74.4
  phosphofructokinase E74.19
  phosphomannomutase E74.8
  phosphomannose isomerase E74.8
  phosphomannosyl mutase E74.8
  phosphorylase kinase, liver E74.09
  pituitary hormone (isolated) E23.0

Deficiency, deficient *(Continued)*
  plasma thromboplastin
    antecedent (PTA) D68.1
    component (PTC) D67
  platelet NEC D69.1
    constitutional D68.0
  polyglandular E31.8
    autoimmune E31.0
  potassium (K) E87.6
  prepuce N47.3
  proaccelerin (congenital) (hereditary)
    D68.2
    acquired D68.4
  proconvertin factor (congenital) (he-
    reditary) D68.2
    acquired D68.4
  protein (*see also* Malnutrition) E46
    anemia D53.0
    C D68.59
    S D68.59
  prothrombin (congenital) (heredItary)
    D68.2
    acquired D68.4
  Prower factor D68.2
  pseudocholinesterase E88.09
  PTA (plasma thromboplastin anteced-
    ent) D68.1
  PTC (plasma thromboplastin compo-
    nent) D67
  purine nucleoside phosphorylase (PNP)
    D81.5
  pyracin (alpha) (beta) E53.1
  pyridoxal E53.1
  pyridoxamine E53.1
  pyridoxine (derivatives) E53.1
  pyruvate
    carboxylase E74.4
    dehydrogenase E74.4
  riboflavin (vitamin B2) E53.0
  salt E87.1
  secretion
    ovary E28.39
    salivary gland (any) K11.7
    urine R34
  selenium (dietary) E59
  serum antitrypsin, familial E88.01
  short stature homeobox gene (SHOX)
    with
      dyschondrosteosis Q78.8
      short stature (idiopathic) E34.3
      Turner's syndrome Q96.9
  sodium (Na) E87.1
  SPCA (factor VII) D68.2
  sphincter, intrinsic N36.42
    with urethral hypermobility N36.43
  stable factor (congenital) (hereditary)
    D68.2
    acquired D68.4
  Stuart-Prower (factor X) D68.2
  sucrase E74.39
  sulfatase E75.29
  sulfite oxidase E72.19
  thiamin, thiaminic (chloride) E51.9
    beriberi (dry) E51.11
      wet E51.12
  thrombokinase D68.2
    newborn P53
  thyroid (gland) - *see* Hypothyroidism
  tocopherol E56.0
  tooth bud K00.0
  transcobalamine II (anemia) D51.2
  vanadium E61.6
  vascular I99.9
  vasopressin E23.2

Deficiency, deficient (*Continued*)
  viosterol – *see* Deficiency, calciferol
  vitamin (multiple) NOS E56.9
    A E50.9
      with
        Bitot's spot (corneal) E50.1
        follicular keratosis E50.8
        keratomalacia E50.4
        manifestations NEC E50.8
        night blindness E50.5
        scar of cornea, xerophthalmic
          E50.6
        xeroderma E50.8
        xerophthalmia E50.7
        xerosis
          conjunctival E50.0
            and Bitot's spot E50.1
          cornea E50.2
            and ulceration E50.3
      sequelae E64.1
    B (complex) NOS E53.9
      with
        beriberi (dry) E51.11
          wet E51.12
        pellagra E52
    B1 NOS E51.9
      beriberi (dry) E51.11
        with circulatory system manifes-
          tations E51.11
        wet E51.12
    B12 E53.8
    B2 (riboflavin) E53.0
    B6 E53.1
    C E54
      sequelae E64.2
    D E55.9
      with
        adult osteomalacia M83.8
        rickets - *see* Rickets
        25-hydroxylase E83.32
    E E56.0
    folic acid E53.8
    G E53.0
    group B E53.9
      specified NEC E53.8
    H (biotin) E53.8
    K E56.1
      of newborn P53
    nicotinic E52
    P E56.8
    PP (pellagra-preventing) E52
    specified NEC E56.8
    thiamin E51.9
      beriberi - *see* Beriberi
  zinc, dietary E60
Deficit - *see also* Deficiency
  cognitive
    following
      cerebrovascular disease I69.91
        cerebral infarction I69.31
        intracerebral hemorrhage I69.11
        nontraumatic intracranial hem-
          orrhage NEC I69.21
        specified disease NEC I69.81
        subarachnoid hemorrhage
          I69.01
  neurologic NEC R29.818
    ischemic
      reversible (RIND) I63.9
        prolonged (PRIND) I63.9
  oxygen R09.02
  prolonged reversible ischemic neuro-
    logic (PRIND) I63.9
Deficit attention - *see* Attention, deficit

Deflection
  radius - *see* Deformity, limb, specified
    type NEC, forearm
  septum (acquired) (nasal) (nose) J34.2
  spine - *see* Curvature, spine
  turbinate (nose) J34.2
Defluvium
  capillorum - *see* Alopecia
  ciliorum - *see* Madarosis
  unguium L60.8
Deformity Q89.9
  abdomen, congenital Q89.9
  abdominal wall
    acquired M95.8
    congenital Q79.59
  acquired (unspecified site) M95.9
  adrenal gland Q89.1
  alimentary tract, congenital Q45.9
    upper Q40.9
  ankle (joint) (acquired) - *see also* Defor-
    mity, limb, lower leg
    abduction - *see* Contraction, joint,
      ankle
    congenital Q68.8
    contraction - *see* Contraction, joint,
      ankle
    specified type NEC - *see* Deformity,
      limb, foot, specified NEC
  anus (acquired) K62.8
    congenital Q43.9
  aorta (arch) (congenital) Q25.4
    acquired I77.8
  aortic
    arch, acquired I77.8
    cusp or valve (congenital) Q23.8
      acquired (*see also* Endocarditis,
        aortic) I35.8
  arm (acquired) (upper) - *see also* Defor-
    mity, limb, upper arm
    congenital Q68.8
    forearm - *see* Deformity, limb, forearm
  artery (congenital) (peripheral) NOS
    Q27.9
    acquired I77.8
    coronary (acquired) I25.9
      congenital Q24.5
    umbilical Q27.0
  atrial septal Q21.1
  auditory canal (external) (congeni-
    tal) – *see also* Malformation, ear,
    external
    acquired - *see* Disorder, ear, external,
      specified type NEC
  auricle
    ear (congenital) – *see also* Malforma-
      tion, ear, external
      acquired - *see* Disorder, pinna,
        deformity
  back - *see* Dorsopathy, deforming
  bile duct (common) (congenital) (he-
    patic) Q44.5
    acquired K83.8
  biliary duct or passage (congenital)
    Q44.5
    acquired K83.8
  bladder (neck) (trigone) (sphincter)
    (acquired) N32.89
    congenital Q64.79
  bone (acquired) NOS M95.9
    congenital Q79.9
    turbinate M95.0
  brain (congenital) Q04.9
    acquired G93.89
    reduction Q04.3

Deformity (*Continued*)
  breast (acquired) N64.89
    congenital Q83.9
    reconstructed N65.0
  bronchus (congenital) Q32.4
    acquired NEC J98.09
  bursa, congenital Q79.9
  canaliculi (lacrimalis) (acquired) - *see also*
    Disorder, lacrimal system, changes
    congenital Q10.6
  canthus, acquired - *see* Disorder, eyelid,
    specified type NEC
  capillary (acquired) I78.8
  cardiovascular system, congenital Q28.9
  caruncle, lacrimal (acquired) - *see also*
    Disorder, lacrimal system, changes
    congenital Q10.6
  cascade, stomach K31.2
  cecum (congenital) Q43.9
    acquired K63.89
  cerebral, acquired G93.89
    congenital Q04.9
  cervix (uterus) (acquired) NEC N88.8
    congenital Q51.9
  cheek (acquired) M95.2
    congenital Q18.9
  chest (acquired) (wall) M95.4
    congenital Q67.8
    sequelae (late effect) of rickets E64.3
  chin (acquired) M95.2
    congenital Q18.9
  choroid (congenital) Q14.3
    acquired H31.8
    plexus Q07.8
      acquired G96.19
  cicatricial - *see* Cicatrix
  cilia, acquired - *see* Disorder, eyelid,
    specified type NEC
  clavicle (acquired) M95.8
    congenital Q68.8
  clitoris (congenital) Q52.6
    acquired N90.8
  clubfoot - *see* Clubfoot
  coccyx (acquired) - *see* subcategory
    M43.8
  colon (congenital) Q43.9
    acquired K63.89
  concha (ear), congenital – *see also* Mal-
    formation, ear, external
    acquired - *see* Disorder, pinna,
      deformity
  cornea (acquired) H18.70
    congenital Q13.4
    descemetocele - *see* Descemetocele
    ectasia - *see* Ectasia, cornea
    specified NEC H18.79-
    staphyloma - *see* Staphyloma, cornea
  coronary artery (acquired) I25.9
    congenital Q24.5
  cranium (acquired) – *see* Deformity,
    skull
  cricoid cartilage (congenital) Q31.8
    acquired J38.7
  cystic duct (congenital) Q44.5
    acquired K82.8
  Dandy-Walker Q03.1
    with spina bifida – *see* Spina bifida
  diaphragm (congenital) Q79.1
    acquired J98.6
  digestive organ NOS Q45.9
  ductus arteriosus Q25.0
  duodenal bulb K31.89
  duodenum (congenital) Q43.9
    acquired K31.89

Deformity *(Continued)*
  dura - *see* Deformity, meninges
  ear (acquired) - *see also* Disorder, pinna, deformity
    congenital (external) Q17.9
      internal Q16.5
      middle Q16.4
        ossicles Q16.3
      ossicles Q16.3
  ectodermal (congenital) NEC Q84.9
  ejaculatory duct (congenital) Q55.4
    acquired N50.8
  elbow (joint) (acquired) - *see also* Deformity, limb, upper arm
    congenital Q68.8
    contraction - *see* Contraction, joint, elbow
  endocrine gland NEC Q89.2
  epididymis (congenital) Q55.4
    acquired N50.8
  epiglottis (congenital) Q31.8
    acquired J38.7
  esophagus (congenital) Q39.9
    acquired K22.8
  eustachian tube (congenital) NEC Q17.8
  eye, congenital Q15.9
  eyebrow (congenital) Q18.8
  eyelid (acquired) - *see also* Disorder, eyelid, specified type NEC
    congenital Q10.3
  face (acquired) M95.2
    congenital Q18.9
  fallopian tube, acquired N83.8
  femur (acquired) - *see* Deformity, limb, specified type NEC, thigh
  fetal
    with fetopelvic disproportion O33.7
      causing obstructed labor O66.3
  finger (acquired) M20.00-
    boutonniere M20.02-
    congenital Q68.1
    flexion contracture - *see* Contraction, joint, hand
    mallet finger M20.01-
    specified NEC M20.09-
    swan-neck M20.03-
  flexion (joint) (acquired) M21.20 - *see also* Deformity, limb, flexion
    congenital NOS Q74.9
      hip Q65.8
  foot (acquired) - *see also* Deformity, limb, lower leg
    cavovarus (congenital) Q66.1
    congenital NOS Q66.9
      specified type NEC Q66.8
    specified type NEC - *see* Deformity, limb, foot, specified NEC
    valgus (congenital) Q66.6
      acquired - *see* Deformity, valgus, ankle
    varus (congenital) NEC Q66.3
      acquired - *see* Deformity, varus, ankle
  forearm (acquired) - *see also* Deformity, limb, forearm
    congenital Q68.8
  forehead (acquired) M95.2
    congenital Q75.8
  frontal bone (acquired) M95.2
    congenital Q75.8
  gallbladder (congenital) Q44.1
    acquired K82.8

Deformity *(Continued)*
  gastrointestinal tract (congenital) NOS Q45.9
    acquired K63.89
  genitalia, genital organ(s) or system NEC
    female (congenital) Q52.9
      acquired N94.89
      external Q52.70
    male (congenital) Q55.9
      acquired N50.8
  globe (eye) (congenital) Q15.8
    acquired H44.89
  gum, acquired NEC K06.8
  hand (acquired) - *see* Deformity, limb, forearm
    congenital Q68.1
  head (acquired) M95.2
    congenital Q75.8
  heart (congenital) Q24.9
    septum Q21.9
      auricular Q21.1
      ventricular Q21.0
    valve (congenital) NEC Q24.8
      acquired - *see* Endocarditis
  heel (acquired) – *see* Deformity, foot
  hepatic duct (congenital) Q44.5
    acquired K83.8
  hip (joint) (acquired) - *see also* Deformity, limb, thigh
    congenital Q65.9
    due to (previous) juvenile osteochondrosis - *see* Coxa, plana
    flexion - *see* Contraction, joint, hip
    hourglass - *see* Contraction, hourglass
  humerus (acquired) M21.82-
    congenital Q74.0
  hypophyseal (congenital) Q89.2
  ileocecal (coil) (valve) (acquired) K63.89
    congenital Q43.9
  ileum (congenital) Q43.9
    acquired K63.89
  ilium (acquired) M95.5
    congenital Q74.2
  integument (congenital) Q84.9
  intervertebral cartilage or disc (acquired) *see* Disorder, disc, specified NEC
  intestine (large) (small) (congenital) NOS Q43.9
    acquired K63.89
  intrinsic minus or plus (hand) - *see* Deformity, limb, specified type NEC, forearm
  iris (acquired) H21.89
    congenital Q13.2
  ischium (acquired) M95.5
    congenital Q74.2
  jaw (acquired) (congenital) M26.9
  joint (acquired) NEC M21.90
    congenital Q68.8
    elbow M21.92-
    hand M21.94-
    hip M21.95-
    knee N21.96-
    shoulder M21.92-
    wrist N21.93-
  kidney(s) (calyx) (pelvis) (congenital) Q63.9
    acquired N28.89
    artery (congenital) Q27.2
      acquired I77.8
  Klippel-Feil (brevicollis) Q76.1

Deformity *(Continued)*
  knee (acquired) NEC - *see also* Deformity, limb, lower leg
    congenital Q68.2
  labium (majus) (minus) (congenital) Q52.79
    acquired N90.8
  lacrimal passages or duct (congenital) NEC Q10.6
    acquired - *see* Disorder, lacrimal system, changes
  larynx (muscle) (congenital) Q31.8
    acquired J38.7
    web (glottic) Q31.0
  leg (upper) (acquired) NEC - *see also* Deformity, limb, thigh
    congenital Q68.8
    lower leg - *see* Deformity, limb, lower leg
  lens (acquired) H27.8
    congenital Q12.9
  lid (fold) (acquired) - *see also* Disorder, eyelid, specified type NEC
    congenital Q10.3
  ligament (acquired) - *see* Disorder, ligament
    congenital Q79.9
  limb (acquired) M21.90
    clawfoot M21.53-
    clawhand M21.51-
    clubfoot M21.54-
    clubhand M21.52-
    congenital, except reduction deformity Q74.9
    flat foot M21.4-
    flexion M21.20
      ankle M21.27-
      elbow M21.22-
      finger M21.24-
      hip M21.25-
      knee M21.26-
      shoulder M21.21-
      toe M21.27-
      wrist M21.23-
    foot
      claw - *see* Deformity, limb, clawfoot
      club - *see* Deformity, limb, clubfoot
      drop M21.37-
      flat - *see* Deformity, limb, flat foot
      specified NEC M21.6x-
    forearm M21.93-
    hand M21.94-
    lower leg M21.96-
    specified type NEC M21.80
      forearm M21.83-
      lower leg M21.86-
      thigh M21.85-
      upper arm M21.82-
    thigh M21.95-
    unequal length M21.70
      short site is
        femur M21.75-
        fibula M21.76-
        humerus M21.72-
        radius M21.73-
        tibia M21.76-
        ulna M21.73-
      upper arm M21.92-
    valgus - *see* Deformity, valgus
    varus - *see* Deformity, varus
    wrist drop M21.33-
  lip (acquired) NEC K13.0
    congenital Q38.0

Deformity *(Continued)*
  liver (congenital) Q44.7
    acquired K76.8
  lumbosacral (congenital) (joint) (region)
      Q76.49
    acquired - *see* subcategory M43.8
    kyphosis - *see* Kyphosis, congenital
    lordosis - *see* Lordosis, congenital
  lung (congenital) Q33.9
    acquired J98.4
  lymphatic system, congenital Q89.9
  Madelung's (radius) Q74.0
  mandible (acquired) (congenital) M26.9
  maxilla (acquired) (congenital) M26.9
  meninges or membrane (congenital)
      Q07.9
    cerebral Q04.8
      acquired G96.19
    spinal cord (congenital) G96.19
      acquired G96.19
  metacarpus (acquired) - *see* Deformity,
      limb, forearm
    congenital Q74.0
  metatarsus (acquired) – *see* Deformity,
      foot
    congenital Q66.9
  middle ear (congenital) Q16.4
    ossicles Q16.3
  mitral (leaflets) (valve) I05.8
    parachute Q23.2
    stenosis, congenital Q23.2
  mouth (acquired) K13.79
    congenital Q38.6
  multiple, congenital NEC Q89.7
  muscle (acquired) M62.89
    congenital Q79.9
      sternocleidomastoid Q68.0
  musculoskeletal system (acquired)
      M95.9
    congenital Q79.9
    specified NEC M95.8
  nail (acquired) L60.8
    congenital Q84.6
  nasal - *see* Deformity, nose
  neck (acquired) M95.3
    congenital Q18.9
      sternocleidomastoid Q68.0
  nervous system (congenital) Q07.9
  nipple (congenital) Q83.9
    acquired N64.89
  nose (acquired) (cartilage) M95.0
    bone (turbinate) M95.0
    congenital Q30.9
      bent or squashed Q67.4
    saddle M95.0
      syphilitic A50.57
    septum (acquired) J34.2
      congenital Q30.8
    sinus (wall) (congenital) Q30.8
      acquired M95.0
    syphilitic (congenital) A50.57
      late A52.73
  ocular muscle (congenital) Q10.3
    acquired - *see* Strabismus, mechanical
  opticociliary vessels (congenital) Q13.2
  orbit (eye) (acquired) H05.30
    atrophy - *see* Atrophy, orbit
    congenital Q10.7
    due to
      bone disease NEC H05.32-
      trauma or surgery H05.33-
    enlargement - *see* Enlargement, orbit
    exostosis - *see* Exostosis, orbit
  organ of Corti (congenital) Q16.5

Deformity *(Continued)*
  ovary (congenital) Q50.39
    acquired N83.8
  oviduct, acquired N83.8
  palate (congenital) Q38.5
    acquired M27.8
    cleft (congenital) - *see* Cleft, palate
  pancreas (congenital) Q45.3
    acquired K86.8
  parathyroid (gland) Q89.2
  parotid (gland) (congenital) Q38.4
    acquired K11.8
  patella (acquired) (congenital) - *see* Disorder, patella,
      specified NEC
  pelvis, pelvic (acquired) (bony) M95.5
    with disproportion (fetopelvic)
        O33.0
      causing obstructed labor O65.0
    congenital Q74.2
    rachitic sequelae (late effect) E64.3
  penis (glans) (congenital) Q55.69
    acquired N48.89
  pericardium (congenital) Q24.8
    acquired - *see* Pericarditis
  pharynx (congenital) Q38.8
    acquired J39.2
  pinna, acquired - *see also* Disorder,
      pinna, deformity
    congenital Q17.9
  pituitary (congenital) Q89.2
  posture - *see* Dorsopathy, deforming
  prepuce (congenital) Q55.69
    acquired N47.8
  prostate (congenital) Q55.4
    acquired N42.89
  pupil (congenital) Q13.2
    acquired - *see* Abnormality, pupillary
  pylorus (congenital) Q40.3
    acquired K31.89
  rachitic (acquired), old or healed E64.3
  radius (acquired) - *see also* Deformity,
      limb, forearm
    congenital Q68.8
  rectum (congenital) Q43.9
    acquired K62.8
  reduction (extremity) (limb), congenital
      (*see also* condition and site) Q73.8
    brain Q04.3
    lower – *see* Defect, reduction, lower
        limb
    upper - *see* Defect, reduction, upper
        limb
  renal - *see* Deformity, kidney
  respiratory system (congenital) Q34.9
  rib (acquired) M95.4
    congenital Q76.6
    cervical Q76.5
  rotation (joint) (acquired) *see* Deformity,
      limb, specified site NEC
    congenital Q74.9
    hip - *see* Deformity, limb, specified
        type NEC, thigh
    congenital Q65.8
  sacroiliac joint (congenital) Q74.2
    acquired - *see* subcategory M43.8
  sacrum (acquired) - *see* subcategory
      M43.8
  saddle
    back - *see* Lordosis
    nose M95.0
      syphilitic A50.57
  salivary gland or duct (congenital)
      Q38.4
    acquired K11.8

Deformity *(Continued)*
  scapula (acquired) M95.8
    congenital Q68.8
  scrotum (congenital) - *see also* Malfor-
      mation, testis and scrotum
    acquired N50.8
  seminal vesicles (congenital) Q55.4
    acquired N50.8
  septum, nasal (acquired) J34.2
  shoulder (joint) (acquired) - *see* Defor-
      mity, limb, upper arm
    congenital Q74.0
    contraction - *see* Contraction, joint,
        shoulder
  sigmoid (flexure) (congenital) Q43.9
    acquired K63.89
  skin (congenital) Q82.9
  skull (acquired) M95.2
    congenital Q75.8
      with
        anencephaly Q00.0
        encephalocele - *see* Encephalocele
        hydrocephalus Q03.9
          with spina bifida - *see* Spina
              bifida, by site, with
              hydrocephalus
        microcephaly Q02
  soft parts, organs or tissues (of pelvis)
      in pregnancy or childbirth NEC
      O34.8-
      causing obstructed labor O65.5
  spermatic cord (congenital) Q55.4
    acquired N50.8
      torsion – *see* Torsion, spermatic
          cord
  spinal - *see* Dorsopathy, deforming
    column (acquired) - *see* Dorsopathy,
        deforming
    congenital Q67.5
    cord (congenital) Q06.9
      acquired G95.89
    nerve root (congenital) Q07.9
  spine (acquired) - *see also* Dorsopathy,
      deforming
    congenital Q67.5
    rachitic E64.3
    specified NEC - *see* Dorsopathy,
        deforming, specified NEC
  spleen
    acquired D73.89
    congenital Q89.09
  Sprengel's (congenital) Q74.0
  sternocleidomastoid (muscle), congeni-
      tal Q68.0
  sternum (acquired) M95.4
    congenital NEC Q76.7
  stomach (congenital) Q40.3
    acquired K31.89
  submandibular gland (congenital)
      Q38.4
  submaxillary gland (congenital)
      Q38.4
    acquired K11.8
  talipes - *see* Talipes
  testis (congenital) - *see also* Malforma-
      tion, testis and scrotum
    acquired N44.8
      torsion – *see* Torsion, testis
  thigh (acquired) - *see also* Deformity,
      limb, thigh
    congenital NEC Q68.8
  thorax (acquired) (wall) M95.4
    congenital Q67.8
    sequelae of rickets E64.3

Deformity *(Continued)*
 thumb (acquired) - *see also* Deformity, finger
  congenital NEC Q68.1
 thymus (tissue) (congenital) Q89.2
 thyroid (gland) (congenital) Q89.2
  cartilage Q31.8
   acquired J38.7
 tibia (acquired) - *see also* Deformity, limb, specified type NEC, lower leg
  congenital NEC Q68.8
  saber (syphilitic) A50.56 [M90.80]
 toe (acquired) M20.60-
  congenital Q66.9
  hallux rigidus M20.2-
  hallux valgus M20.1-
  hallux varus M20.3-
  hammer toe M20.4-
  specified NEC M20.5x-
 tongue (congenital) Q38.3
  acquired K14.8
 tooth, teeth K00.2
 trachea (rings) (congenital) Q32.1
  acquired J39.8
 transverse aortic arch (congenital) Q25.4
 tricuspid (leaflets) (valve) I07.8
  atresia or stenosis Q22.4
  Ebstein's Q22.5
 trunk (acquired) M95.8
  congenital Q89.9
 ulna (acquired) - *see also* Deformity, limb, forearm
  congenital NEC Q68.8
 urachus, congenital Q64.4
 ureter (opening) (congenital) Q62.8
  acquired N28.89
 urethra (congenital) Q64.79
  acquired N36.8
 urinary tract (congenital) Q64.9
  urachus Q64.4
 uterus (congenital) Q51.9
  acquired N85.8
 uvula (congenital) Q38.5
 vagina (acquired) N89.8
  congenital Q52.4
 valgus NEC M21.00
  ankle M21.07-
  elbow M21.02-
  knee M21.06-
 valve, valvular (congenital) (heart) Q24.8
  acquired - *see* Endocarditis
 varus NEC M21.10
  ankle M21.17-
  elbow M21.12-
  knee M21.16-
  tibia - *see* Osteochondrosis, juvenile, tibia
 vas deferens (congenital) Q55.4
  acquired N50.8
 vein (congenital) Q27.9
  great Q26.9
 vertebra - *see* Dorsopathy, deforming
 vesicourethral orifice (acquired) N32.89
  congenital NEC Q64.79
 vessels of optic papilla (congenital) Q14.2
 visual field (contraction) - *see* Defect, visual field
 vitreous body, acquired H43.89
 vulva (congenital) Q52.79
  acquired N90.8

Deformity *(Continued)*
 wrist (joint) (acquired) - *see also* Deformity, limb, forearm
  congenital Q68.8
  contraction - *see* Contraction, joint, wrist
Degeneration, degenerative
 adrenal (capsule) (fatty) (gland) (hyaline) (infectional) E27.8
 amyloid (*see also* Amyloidosis) E85.9
 anterior cornua, spinal cord G12.29
 anterior labral S43.49-
 aorta, aortic I70.0
  fatty I77.8
 aortic valve (heart) - *see* Endocarditis, aortic
 arteriovascular - *see* Arteriosclerosis
 artery, arterial (atheromatous) (calcareous) - *see also* Arteriosclerosis
  cerebral, amyloid E85.4 [I68.1]
  medial - *see* Arteriosclerosis, extremities
 articular cartilage NEC - *see* Derangement, joint, articular cartilage, by site
 atheromatous - *see* Arteriosclerosis
 basal nuclei or ganglia G23.9
  specified NEC G23.8
 bone NEC - *see* Disorder, bone, specified type NEC
 brachial plexus G54.0
 brain (cortical) (progressive) G31.9
  alcoholic G31.2
  arteriosclerotic I67.2
  childhood G31.9
   specified NEC G31.89
  cystic G31.89
   congenital Q04.6
  in
   alcoholism G31.2
   beriberi E51.2
   cerebrovascular disease I67.9
   congenital hydrocephalus Q03.9
    with spina bifida – *see also* Spina bifida
   Fabry-Anderson disease E75.21
   Gaucher's disease E75.22
   Hunter's syndrome E76.1
   lipidosis
    cerebral E75.4
    generalized E75.6
   mucopolysaccharidosis - *see* Mucopolysaccharidosis
   myxedema E03.9 [G32.8]
   neoplastic disease (*see also* Neoplasm) D49.6 [G32.8]
   Niemann-Pick disease E75.249 [G32.8]
   sphingolipidosis E75.3 [G32.8]
   vitamin B_{12} deficiency E53.8 [G32.8]
  senile NEC G31.1
 breast N64.89
 Bruch's membrane - *see* Degeneration, choroid
 capillaries (fatty) I78.8
  amyloid E85.8 [I79.8]
 cardiac - *see also* Degeneration, myocardial
  valve, valvular - *see* Endocarditis
 cardiorenal - *see* Hypertension, cardiorenal
 cardiovascular - *see also* Disease, cardiovascular
  renal - *see* Hypertension, cardiorenal

Degeneration, degenerative *(Continued)*
 cerebellar NOS G31.9
  alcoholic G31.2
  primary (hereditary) (sporadic) G11.9
 cerebral - *see* Degeneration, brain
 cerebrovascular I67.9
  due to hypertension I67.4
 cervical plexus G54.2
 cervix N88.8
  due to radiation (intended effect) N88.8
   adverse effect or misadventure N99.89
 chamber angle H21.21-
 changes, spine or vertebra - *see* Spondylosis
 chorioretinal - *see also* Degeneration, choroid
  hereditary H31.20
 choroid (colloid) (drusen) H31.11-
  atrophy - *see* Atrophy, choroidal
  hereditary - *see* Dystrophy, choroidal, hereditary
 ciliary body H21.22-
 cochlear - *see* subcategory H83.8
 combined (spinal cord) (subacute) E53.8 [G32.0]
  with anemia (pernicious) D51.0 [G32.0]
   due to dietary vitamin B12 deficiency D51.3 [G32.0]
  in (due to)
   vitamin B12 deficiency E53.8 [G32.0]
    anemia D51.9 [G32.0]
 conjunctiva H11.10
  concretions - *see* Concretion, conjunctiva
  deposits - *see* Deposit, conjunctiva
  pigmentations - *see* Pigmentation, conjunctiva
  pinguecula - *see* Pinguecula
  xerosis - *see* Xerosis, conjunctiva
 cornea H18.40
  calcerous H18.43
   band keratopathy H18.42-
  familial, hereditary - *see* Dystrophy, cornea
  hyaline (of old scars) H18.49
  keratomalacia - *see* Keratomalacia
  nodular H18.45-
  peripheral H18.46-
  senile H18.41-
  specified type NEC H18.49
 cortical (cerebellar) (parenchymatous) G31.89
  alcoholic G31.2
  diffuse, due to arteriopathy I67.2
 cutis L98.8
  amyloid E85.4 [L99]
 dental pulp K04.2
 disc disease - *see* Degeneration, intervertebral disc NEC
 dorsolateral (spinal cord) - *see* Degeneration, combined
 extrapyramidal G25.9
 eye, macular - *see also* Degeneration, macula
  congenital or hereditary - *see* Dystrophy, retina
 facet joints - *see* Spondylosis
 fatty
  liver NEC K76.0
   alcoholic K70.0

Degeneration, degenerative *(Continued)*
  grey matter (brain) (Alpers') G31.81
  heart - *see also* Degeneration,
    myocardial
    amyloid E85.4 [I43]
    atheromatous – *see* Disease, heart,
      ischemic, atherosclerotic
    ischemic – *see* Disease, heart,
      ischemic
  hepatolenticular (Wilson's) E83.01
  hepatorenal K76.7
  hyaline (diffuse) (generalized)
    localized - *see* Degeneration, by site
  infrapatellar fat pad M79.4
  intervertebral disc NOS
    with
      myelopathy - *see* Disorder, disc,
        with, myelopathy
      radiculitis or radiculopathy
        - *see* Disorder, disc, with,
        radiculopathy
    cervical, cervicothoracic - *see*
      Disorder, disc, cervical,
      degeneration
      with
        myelopathy - *see* Disorder,
          disc, cervical, with
          myelopathy
        neuritis, radiculitis or radicu-
          lopathy - *see* Disorder, disc,
          cervical, with neuritis
    lumbar region M51.36
      with
        myelopathy M51.06
        neuritis, radiculitis, radiculopa-
          thy or sciatica M51.16
    lumbosacral region M51.37
      with
        myelopathy M51.07
        neuritis, radiculitis, radicu-
          lopathy or sciatica
          M51.17
    sacrococcygeal region M53.3
    thoracic region M51.34
      with
        myelopathy M51.04
        neuritis, radiculitis, radiculopa-
          thy M51.14
    thoracolumbar region M51.35
      with
        myelopathy M51.05
        neuritis, radiculitis, radiculopa-
          thy M51.15
  intestine, amyloid E85.4
  iris (pigmentary) H21.23-
  ischemic - *see* Ischemia
  joint disease – *see* Osteoarthritis
  kidney N28.89
    amyloid E85.4 [N29]
    cystic, congenital Q61.9
    fatty N28.89
    polycystic Q61.3
      adult type (autosomal dominant)
        Q61.2
      infantile type (autosomal recessive)
        NEC Q61.19
        collecting duct dilatation
          Q61.11
  Kuhnt-Junius - *see* Degeneration,
    macula
  lens – *see* Cataract
  lenticular (familial) (progressive)
    (Wilson's) (with cirrhosis of liver)
    E83.01

Degeneration, degenerative *(Continued)*
  liver (diffuse) NEC K76.8
    amyloid E85.4 [K77]
    cystic K76.8
      congenital Q44.6
    fatty NEC K76.0
      alcoholic K70.0
    hypertrophic K76.8
    parenchymatous, acute or subacute
      K72.00
      with coma K72.01
    pigmentary K76.8
    toxic (acute) K71.9
  lung J98.4
  lymph gland I89.8
    hyaline I89.8
  macula, macular (acquired) (atrophic)
    (exudative) (senile) H35.30
    angioid streaks H35.33
    congenital or hereditary - *see* Dystro-
      phy, retina
    cystoid H35.35-
    drusen H35.36-
    exudative H35.31
    hole H35.34-
    nonexudative H35.32
    puckering H35.37-
    toxic H35.38-
  membranous labyrinth, congenital
    (causing impairment of hearing)
    Q16.5
  meniscus - *see* Derangement, meniscus
  mitral - *see* Insufficiency, mitral
  Mönckeberg's - *see* Arteriosclerosis,
    extremities
  motor centers, senile G31.1
  multi-system G90.3
  mural - *see* Degeneration, myocardial
  muscle (fatty) (fibrous) (hyaline) (pro-
    gressive) M62.89
    heart - *see* Degeneration, myocardial
  myelin, central nervous system G37.9
  myocardial, myocardium (fatty) (hya-
    line) (senile) I51.5
    with rheumatic fever (conditions in
      I00) I09.0
      active, acute or subacute I01.2
        with chorea I02.0
      inactive or quiescent (with chorea)
        I09.0
    hypertensive - *see* Hypertension,
      heart
    rheumatic - *see* Degeneration, myo-
      cardial, with rheumatic fever
    syphilitic A52.06
  nasal sinus (mucosa) J32.9
    frontal J32.1
    maxillary J32.0
  nerve - *see* Disorder, nerve
  nervous system G31.9
    alcoholic G31.2
    amyloid E85.4 [G99.8]
    autonomic G90.9
    fatty G31.89
    specified NEC G31.89
  nipple N64.89
  olivopontocerebellar (hereditary) (fa-
    milial) G23.8
  osseous labyrinth - *see* subcategory
    H83.8
  ovary N83.8
    cystic N83.20
    microcystic N83.20
  pallidal pigmentary (progressive) G23.0

Degeneration, degenerative *(Continued)*
  pancreas K86.8
    tuberculous A18.83
  penis N48.89
  pigmentary (diffuse) (general)
    localized - *see* Degeneration, by site
    pallidal (progressive) G23.0
  pineal gland E34.8
  pituitary (gland) E23.6
  popliteal fat pad M79.4
  posterolateral (spinal cord) - *see* Degen-
    eration, combined
  pulmonary valve (heart) I37.8
  pulp (tooth) K04.2
  pupillary margin H21.24-
  renal – *see* Degeneration, kidney
  retina H35.9
    hereditary (cerebroretinal) (con-
      genital) (juvenile) (macula)
      (peripheral) (pigmentary) - *see*
      Dystrophy, retina
    Kuhnt-Junius - *see* Degeneration,
      macula, hole
    macula (cystic) (exudative) (hole)
      (nonexudative) (pseudohole)
      (senile) (toxic) - *see* Degenera-
      tion, macula
    peripheral H35.40
      lattice H35.41-
      microcystoid H35.42-
      paving stone H35.43-
      secondary
        pigmentary H35.45-
        vitreoretinal H35.46-
      senile reticular H35.44-
    pigmentary (primary) - *see also* Dys-
      trophy, retina
    secondary - *see* Degeneration,
      retina, peripheral, secondary
    posterior pole - *see* Degeneration,
      macula
  saccule, congenital (causing impairment
    of hearing) Q16.5
  senile R54
    brain G31.1
    cardiac, heart or myocardium - *see*
      Degeneration, myocardial
    motor centers G31.1
    vascular - *see* Arteriosclerosis
  sinus (cystic) - *see also* Sinusitis
    polypoid J33.1
  skin L98.8
    amyloid E85.4 [L99]
    colloid L98.8
  spinal (cord) G31.89
    amyloid E85.4 [G32.8]
    combined (subacute) - *see* Degenera-
      tion, combined
    dorsolateral - *see* Degeneration,
      combined
    familial NEC G31.89
    fatty G31.89
    funicular - *see* Degeneration,
      combined
    posterolateral - *see* Degeneration,
      combined
    subacute combined - *see* Degenera-
      tion, combined
    tuberculous A17.81
  spleen D73.0
    amyloid E85.4 [D77]
  stomach K31.89
  striatonigral G23.2
  suprarenal (capsule) (gland) E27.8

Degeneration, degenerative *(Continued)*
  synovial membrane (pulpy) – *see* Disorder, synovium, specified type NEC
  tapetoretinal - *see* Dystrophy, retina
  thymus (gland) E32.8
    fatty E32.8
  thyroid (gland) E07.89
  tricuspid (heart) (valve) I07.9
  tuberculous NEC - *see* Tuberculosis
  turbinate J34.89
  uterus (cystic) N85.8
  vascular (senile) - *see* Arteriosclerosis
    hypertensive - *see* Hypertension
  vitreoretinal, secondary - *see* Degeneration, retina, peripheral, secondary, vitreoretinal
  vitreous (body) H43.81-
  Wallerian - *see* Disorder, nerve
  Wilson's hepatolenticular E83.01
Deglutition
  paralysis R13.0
    hysterical F44.4
  pneumonia J69.0
Degos' disease I77.8
Dehiscence (of)
  cesarean wound O90.0
  closure of
    cornea T81.31
    craniotomy T81.32
    fascia (muscular) (superficial) T81.32
    internal organ or tissue T81.32
    laceration (external) (internal) T81.33
    ligament T81.32
    mucosa T81.31
    muscle or muscle flap T81.32
    ribs or rib cage T81.32
    skin and subcutaneous tissue (full-thickness) (superficial) T81.31
    skull T81.32
    sternum (sternotomy) T81.32
    tendon T81.32
    traumatic laceration (external) (internal) T81.33
  episiotomy O90.1
  operation wound NEC T81.31
    external operation wound (superficial) T81.31
    internal operation wound (deep) T81.32
  perineal wound (postpartum) O90.1
  traumatic injury wound repair T81.33
  wound T81.30
    traumatic repair T81.33
Dehydration E86.0
  hypertonic E87.0
  hypotonic E87.1
  newborn P74.1
Déjérine-Roussy syndrome G93.89
Déjérine-Sottas disease or neuropathy (hypertrophic) G60.0
Déjérine-Thomas atrophy G23.8
Delay, delayed
  any plane in pelvis
    complicating delivery O66.9
  birth or delivery NOS O63.9
  closure, ductus arteriosus (Botalli) P29.3
  coagulation - *see* Defect, coagulation
  conduction (cardiac) (ventricular) I45.9
  delivery, second twin, triplet, etc O63.2
  development R62.50
    global F88
    intellectual (specific) F81.9
    language F80.9
      due to hearing loss F80.4

Delay, delayed *(Continued)*
  development *(Continued)*
    learning F81.9
    pervasive F84.9
    physiological R62.50
      specified stage NEC R62.0
    reading F81.0
    sexual E30.0
    speech F80.9
      due to hearing loss F80.4
    spelling F81.81
  gastric emptying K30
  menarche E28.39
  menstruation (cause unknown) N91.0
  milestone R62.0
  passage of meconium (newborn) P76.0
  primary respiration P28.9
  puberty (constitutional) E30.0
  separation of umbilical cord P96.82
  sexual maturation, female E30.0
  sleep phase syndrome G47.21
  union, fracture - *see* Fracture, by site
  vaccination Z28.9
Deletion(s)
  autosome Q93.9
    identified by fluorescence in situ hybridization (FISH) Q93.89
    identified by in situ hybridization (ISH) Q93.89
  chromosome
    with complex rearrangements NEC Q93.7
    part of NEC Q93.5
    seen only at prometaphase Q93.89
    short arm
      4 Q93.3
      5p Q93.4
      22q11.2 Q93.81
    specified NEC Q93.89
  long arm chromosome 18 or 21 Q93.89
    with complex rearrangements NEC Q93.7
  microdeletions NEC Q93.88
Delhi boil or button B55.1
Delinquency (juvenile) (neurotic) F91.8
  group Z72.810
Delinquent immunization status Z28.3
Delirium, delirious (acute or subacute) (not alcoholor drug-induced) (with dementia) R41.0
  alcoholic (acute) (tremens) (withdrawal) F10.921
    with intoxication F10.921
      in
        abuse F10.121
        dependence F10.221
  due to (secondary to)
    alcohol
      intoxication F10.921
        in
          abuse F10.121
          dependence F10.221
      withdrawal F10.231
    amphetamine intoxication F15.921
      in
        abuse F15.121
        dependence F15.221
    anxiolytic
      intoxication F13.921
        in
          abuse F13.121
          dependence F13.221
      withdrawal F13.231

Delirium, delirious *(Continued)*
  due to *(Continued)*
    cannabis intoxication (acute) F12.921
      in
        abuse F12.121
        dependence F12.221
    cocaine intoxication (acute) F14.921
      in
        abuse F14.121
        dependence F14.221
    general medical condition F05
    hallucinogen intoxication F16.921
      in
        abuse F16.121
        dependence F16.221
    hypnotic
      intoxication F13.921
        in
          abuse F13.121
          dependence F13.221
      withdrawal F13.231
    inhalant intoxication (acute) F18.921
      in
        abuse F18.121
        dependence F18.221
    multiple etiologies F05
    opioid intoxication (acute) F11.921
      in
        abuse F11.121
        dependence F11.221
    phencyclidine intoxication (acute) F19.921
      in
        abuse F19.121
        dependence F19.221
    psychoactive substance NEC intoxication (acute) F19.921
      in
        abuse F19.121
        dependence F19.221
    sedative
      intoxication F13.921
        in
          abuse F13.121
          dependence F13.221
      withdrawal F13.231
    unknown etiology F05
  exhaustion F43.0
  hysterical F44.89
  postprocedural (postoperative) F05
  puerperal F05
  thyroid - *see* Thyrotoxicosis with thyroid storm
  traumatic - *see* Injury, intracranial
  tremens (alcohol-induced) F10.231
    sedative-induced F13.231
Delivery (childbirth) (labor)
  arrested active phase O62.1
  cesarean (for)
    abnormal
      pelvis (bony) (deformity) (major) NEC with disproportion (fetopelvic) O33.0
        with obstructed labor O65.0
      presentation or position O32.9
    abruptio placentae O45.*see also* Abruptio placentae
    acromion presentation O32.2
    atony, uterus O62.2
    breech presentation O32.1
      incomplete O32.8
    brow presentation O32.3
    cephalopelvic disproportion O33.9
    cerclage O34.3-

Delivery *(Continued)*
  cesarean *(Continued)*
    chin presentation O32.3
    cicatrix of cervix O34.4-
    contracted pelvis (general)
      inlet O33.2
      outlet O33.3
    cord presentation or prolapse
        O69.0
    cystocele O34.8-
    deformity (acquired) (congenital)
      pelvic organs or tissues NEC
          O34.8-
      pelvis (bony) NEC O33.0
    disproportion NOS O33.9
    eclampsia - *see* Eclampsia
    face presentation O32.3
    failed
      forceps O66.5
      induction of labor O61.9
        instrumental O61.1
        mechanical O61.1
        medical O61.0
        specified NEC O61.8
        surgical O61.1
      trial of labor NOS O66.40
        following previous cesarean
            delivery O66.41
      vacuum extraction O66.5
      ventouse O66.5
    fetal-maternal hemorrhage O43.01-
    hemorrhage (intrapartum) O67.9
      with coagulation defect O67.0
      specified cause NEC O67.8
    high head at term O32.4
    hydrocephalic fetus O33.6
    incarceration of uterus O34.51-
    incoordinate uterine action O62.4
    increased size, fetus O33.5
    inertia, uterus O62.2
      primary O62.0
      secondary O62.1
    lateroversion, uterus O34.59-
    mal lie O32.9
    malposition
      fetus O32.9
      pelvic organs or tissues NEC
          O34.8-
      uterus NEC O34.59-
    malpresentation NOS O32.9
    oblique presentation O32.2
    oversize fetus O33.5
    pelvic tumor NEC O34.8-
    placenta previa O44.1-
      without hemorrhage O44.0-
    placental insufficiency O36.51-
    polyp, cervix O34.4-
      causing obstructed labor O65.5
    poor dilatation, cervix O62.0
    pre-eclampsia O14.9-
      mild O14.0-
      severe (H.E.L.L.P.) O14.1-
    previous
      cesarean delivery O34.21
      surgery (to)
        cervix O34.4-
        gynecological NEC O34.8-
        rectum O34.7-
        uterus O34.29
        vagina O34.6-
    prolapse
      arm or hand O32.2
      uterus O34.52-
    prolonged labor NOS O63.9

Delivery *(Continued)*
  cesarean *(Continued)*
    rectocele O34.8-
    retroversion
      uterus O34.59-
    rigid
      cervix O34.4-
      pelvic floor O34.8-
      perineum O34.7-
      vagina O34.6-
      vulva O34.7-
    sacculation, pregnant uterus O34.59-
    scar(s)
      cervix O34.4-
      cesarean delivery O34.21
      uterus O34.29
    Shirodkar suture in situ O34.3-
    shoulder presentation O32.2
    stenosis or stricture, cervix O34.4-
    streptococcus B carrier state O99.824
    transverse presentation or lie O32.2
    tumor, pelvic organs or tissues NEC
        O34.8-
      cervix O34.4-
    umbilical cord presentation or pro-
        lapse O69.0
    without indication O82
  completely normal case O80
  complicated O75.9
    by
      abnormal, abnormality (of)
        forces of labor O62.9
          specified type NEC O62.8
        glucose O99.814
        uterine contractions NOS O62.9
      abruptio placentae O45.9-
      abuse
        physical O9A.32
        psychological O9A.52
        sexual O9A.42
      adherent placenta O72.0
        without hemorrhage O73.0
      alcohol use O99.314
      anemia (pre-existing) O99.02
      anesthetic death O74.8
      annular detachment of cervix O71.3
      atony, uterus O62.2
      attempted vacuum extraction and
          forceps O66.5
      Bandl's ring O62.4
      bariatric surgery status O99.844
      bleeding - *see* Delivery, complicated
          by, hemorrhage
      blood disorder NEC O99.12
      cervical dystocia (hypotonic) O62.2
        primary O62.0
        secondary O62.1
      circulatory system disorder O99.42
      compression of cord (umbilical)
          NEC O69.2
      condition NEC O99.89
      contraction, contracted ring O62.4
      cord (umbilical)
        around neck
          with compression O69.1
          without compression O69.81
        bruising O69.5
        complication O69.9
          specified NEC O69.89
        compression NEC O69.2
        entanglement O69.2
          without compression O69.82
        hematoma O69.5
        presentation O69.0

Delivery *(Continued)*
  complicated *(Continued)*
    by *(Continued)*
      cord *(Continued)*
        prolapse O69.0
        short O69.3
        thrombosis (vessels) O69.5
        vascular lesion O69.5
      Couvelaire uterus O45.8x-
      delay following rupture of
          membranes (spontaneous)
          – *see* Pregnancy, complicated
          by, premature rupture of
          membranes
      depressed fetal heart tones O76
      diabetes O24.92
        gestational O24.429
          diet controlled O24.420
          insulin controlled O24.421
        pre-existing O24.32
          specified NEC O24.82
          type 1 O24.02
          type 2 O24.12
      diastasis recti (abdominis) O71.89
      dilatation
        bladder O66.8
        cervix incomplete, poor or slow
            O62.0
      disease NEC O99.89
      disruptio uteri - *see* Delivery,
          complicated by, rupture,
          uterus
      drug use O99.324
      dysfunction, uterus NOS O62.9
        hypertonic O62.4
        hypotonic O62.2
          primary O62.0
          secondary O62.1
        incoordinate O62.4
      eclampsia O15.1
      embolism (pulmonary) - *see*
          Embolism, obstetric
      endocrine, nutritional or metabolic
          disease NEC O99.284
      failed
        attempted vaginal birth after
            previous cesarean delivery
            O66.41
        induction of labor O61.9
          instrumental O61.1
          mechanical O61.1
          medical O61.0
          specified NEC O61.8
          surgical O61.1
        trial of labor O66.40
      female genital mutilation O65.5
      fetal
        abnormal acid-base balance
            O68
        acidemia O68
        acidosis O68
        alkalosis O68
        death, early O02.1
        deformity O66.3
        heart rate or rhythm (abnormal)
            (non-reassuring) O76
        hypoxia O77.8
        stress O77.9
          due to drug administration
              O77.1
          electrocardiographic evidence
              of O77.8
          ultrasound evidence of O77.8
          specified NEC O77.8

173

Delivery *(Continued)*
  complicated *(Continued)*
    by *(Continued)*
      fever during labor O75.2
      gastric banding status O99.844
      gastric bypass status O99.844
      gastrointestinal disease NEC O99.62
      gestational diabetes O24.429
        diet controlled O24.420
        insulin (and diet) controlled O24.421
      gonorrhea O98.22
      hematoma O71.7
        ischial spine O71.7
        pelvic O71.7
        vagina O71.7
        vulva or perineum O71.7
      hemorrhage (uterine) O67.9
        associated with
          afibrinogenemia O67.0
          coagulation defect O67.0
          hyperfibrinolysis O67.0
          hypofibrinogenemia O67.0
        due to
          low-lying placenta O44.1-
            without hemorrhage O44.0-
          placenta previa O44.1-
            without hemorrhage O44.0-
          premature separation of
            placenta (normally
            implanted) O45.—*See also*
            Abruptio placentae
          retained placenta O72.0
          uterine leiomyoma O67.8
        placenta NEC O67.8
        postpartum NEC (atonic) (immediate) O72.1
          with retained or trapped placenta O72.0
          delayed O72.2
          secondary O72.2
          third stage O72.0
      hourglass contraction, uterus O62.4
      hypertension, hypertensive (preexisting) - *see* Hypertension, complicated by, childbirth (labor)
      hypotension O26.5-
      incomplete dilatation (cervix) O62.0
      incoordinate uterus contractions O62.4
      inertia, uterus O62.2
        during latent phase of labor O62.0
        primary O62.0
        secondary O62.1
      infection (maternal) O98.92
        carrier state NEC O99.834
        gonorrhea O98.22
        human immunodeficiency [HIV] O98.72
        sexually transmitted NEC O98.32
        specified NEC O98.82
        syphilis O98.12
        tuberculosis O98.02
        viral hepatitis O98.42
        viral NEC O98.52
      injury (to mother) O71.9
        nonobstetric O9A.22
          caused by abuse - *see* Delivery, complicated by, abuse

      intrauterine fetal death, early O02.1
      inversion, uterus O71.2
      laceration (perineal) O70.9
        anus (sphincter) O70.4
          with third degree laceration O70.2
            with mucosa O70.3
          without third degree laceration O70.4
        bladder (urinary) O71.5
        bowel O71.5
        cervix (uteri) O71.3
        fourchette O70.0
        hymen O70.0
        labia O70.0
        pelvic
          floor O70.1
          organ NEC O71.5
        perineum, perineal O70.9
          first degree O70.0
          fourth degree O70.3
          muscles O70.1
          second degree O70.1
          skin O70.0
          slight O70.0
          third degree O70.2
        peritoneum O71.5
        rectovaginal (septum) (without perineal laceration) O71.4
          with perineum O70.2
            with anal or rectal mucosa O70.3
        specified NEC O71.89
        sphincter ani - *see* Delivery, complicated, by, laceration, anus (sphincter)
        urethra O71.5
        uterus O71.81
          before labor O71.81
        vagina, vaginal (deep) (high) (without perineal laceration) O71.4
          with perineum O70.0
          muscles, with perineum O70.1
        vulva O70.0
      liver disorder O26.62
      malignancy O9A.12
      malnutrition O25.2
      malposition, malpresentation
        placenta (with hemorrhage) O44.1-
        uterus or cervix O65.5
        without obstruction O32.9 - *see also* Delivery, complicated by, obstruction
          breech O32.1
          compound O32.6
          face (brow) (chin) O32.3
          footling O38.8
          high head O32.4
          oblique O32.2
          specified NEC O32.8
          transverse O32.2
          unstable lie O32.0
      meconium in amniotic fluid O77.0
      mental disorder NEC O99.344
      metrorrhexis - *see* Delivery, complicated by, rupture, uterus
      nervous system disorder O99.354
      obesity (pre-exisitng) O99.214
      obesity surgery status O99.844

      obstetric trauma O71.9
        specified NEC O71.89
      obstruction
        due to
          breech (complete) (frank)
            presentation O64.1
            incomplete O64.8
          brow presenation O64.3
          buttock presentation O64.1
          chin presentation O64.2
          compound presentation O64.5
          contracted pelvis O65.1
          deep transverse arrest O64.0
          deformed pelvis O65.0
          dystocia (fetal) O66.9
            due to
              conjoined twins O66.3
              fetal
                abnormality NEC O66.3
                ascites O66.3
                hydrops O66.3
                meningomyelocele O66.3
                sacral teratoma O66.3
                tumor O66.3
             hydrocephalic fetus O66.3
          shoulder O66.0
          face presentation O64.2
          fetopelvic disproportion O65.4
          footling presentation O64.8
          impacted shoulders O66.0
          incomplete rotation of fetal head O64.0
          large fetus O66.2
          locked twins O66.1
          malposition O64.9
            specified NEC O64.8
          malpresentation O64.9
            specified NEC O64.8
          multiple fetuses NEC O66.6
          pelvic
            abnormality (maternal) O65.9
              organ O65.5
              specified NEC O65.8
            contraction
              inlet O65.2
              mid-cavity O65.3
              outlet O65.3
          persistent (position)
            occipitoiliac O64.0
            occipitoposterior O64.0
            occipitosacral O64.0
            occipitotransverse O64.0
          prolapsed arm O64.4
          shoulder presentation O64.4
         specified NEC O66.8
      pathological retraction ring, uterus O62.4
      penetration, pregnant uterus by instrument O71.1
      perforation - *see* Delivery, complicated by, laceration
      placenta, placental
        ablatio O45.9-
        abnormality O43.9-
          specified NEC O43.89-
        abruptio O45.9-
        accreta O43.21-
        adherent (with hemorrhage) O72.0
          without hemorrhage O73.0
        detachment (premature) O45.9-
        disorder O43.9-

Delivery *(Continued)*
complicated *(Continued)*
by *(Continued)*
placenta, placental *(Continued)*
hemorrhage NEC O67.8
increta (with hemorrhage) O43.22-
low (implantation) O44.1-
without hemorrhage O44.0-
malformation O43.10-
malposition O44.1-
without hemorrhage O44.0-
percreta O43.23-
previa (central) (lateral) (low)
(marginal) (partial) (total)
O44.1-
retained (with hemorrhage) O72.0
without hemorrhage O73.0
separation (premature) O45.9-
specified NEC O45.8x-
vicious insertion O44.1-
precipitate labor O62.3
premature rupture, membranes
O42.90 - *see also* Pregnancy,
complicated by, premature
rupture of membranes
prolapse
arm or hand O32.8
cord (umbilical) O69.0
foot or leg O32.8
uterus O34.52-
prolonged labor O63.9
first stage O63.0
second stage O63.1
protozoal disease (maternal) O98.62
respiratory disease NEC O99.52
retained membranes or portions of
placenta O72.2
without hemorrhage O73.1
retarded birth O63.9
retention of secundines (with hemorrhage) O72.0
without hemorrhage O73.0
partial O72.2
without hemorrhage O73.1
rupture
bladder (urinary) O71.5
cervix O71.3
pelvic organ NEC O71.5
urethra O71.5
uterus (during or after labor)
O71.1
before labor O71.0-
separation, pubic bone (symphysis
pubis) O71.6
shock O75.1
shoulder presentation O64.4
skin disorder NEC O99.72
spasm, cervix O62.4
stenosis or stricture, cervix O65.5
streptococcus B carrier state O99.824
subluxation of symphysis (pubis)
O26.72
syphilis (maternal) O98.12
tear - *see* Delivery, complicated by,
laceration
tetanic uterus O62.4
trauma (obstetrical) O71.9
non-obstetric O9A.22
tuberculosis (maternal) O98.02
tumor, pelvic organs or tissues
NEC O65.5
umbilical cord around neck
with compression O69.1
without compression O69.81

Delivery *(Continued)*
complicated *(Continued)*
by *(Continued)*
uterine inertia O62.2
during latent phase of labor
O62.0
primary O62.0
secondary O62.1
vasa previa O69.4
velamentous insertion of cord
O43.12-
specified complication NEC O75.89
delayed NOS O63.9
following rupture of membranes
artificial O75.5
second twin, triplet, etc. O63.2
forceps, low following failed vacuum
extraction O66.5
missed (at or near term) O36.4
normal O80
obstructed - *see* Delivery, complicated
by, obstruction
precipitate O62.3
preterm *(see also* Pregnancy, complicated by, preterm labor) O60.10
spontaneous O80
term pregnancy NOS O80
uncomplicated O80
vaginal, following previous cesarean
delivery O34.21
Delusions (paranoid) - *see* Disorder,
delusional
Dementia (degenerative (primary)) (old
age) (persisting) F03
with
Lewy bodies G31.83 [F02.80]
with behavioral disturbance G31.83
[F02.81]
Parkinsonism G31.83 [F02.80]
with behavioral disturbance G31.83
[F02.81]
alcoholic F10.97
with dependence F10.27
Alzheimer's type – *see* Disease,
Alzheimer's
arteriosclerotic - *see* Dementia, vascular
atypical, Alzheimer's type – *see* Disease,
Alzheimer's, specified NEC
congenital - *see* Retardation, mental
frontal (lobe) G31.09 [F02.80]
with behavioral disturbance G31.09
[F02.81]
frontotemporal G31.09 [F02.80]
with behavioral disturbance G31.09
[F02.81]
specified NEC G31.09 [F02.80]
with behavioral disturbance G31.09
[F02.81]
in (due to)
alcohol F10.97
with dependence F10.27
Alzheimer's disease – *see* Disease,
Alzheimer's
arteriosclerotic brain disease - *see*
Dementia, vascular
cerebral lipidoses E75.-[F02.80]
with behavioral disturbance
E75.-[F02.81]
Creutzfeldt-Jakob disease *(see also*
Creutzfeldt-Jakob disease or syndrome (with dementia)) A81.00
epilepsy G40.-[F02.80]
with behavioral disturbance
G40.-[F02.81]

Dementia *(Continued)*
in *(Continued)*
hepatolenticular degeneration E83.01
[F02.80]
with behavioral disturbance E83.01
[F02.81]
human immunodeficiency virus
(HIV) disease B20 [F02.80]
with behavioral disturbance B20
[F02.81]
Huntington's disease or chorea
G10
hypercalcemia E83.52 [F02.80]
with behavioral disturbance E83.52
[F02.81]
hypothyroidism, acquired E03.9
[F02.80]
with behavioral disturbance E03.9
[F02.81]
due to iodine deficiency E01.8
[F02.80]
with behavioral disturbance
E01.8 [F02.81]
inhalants F18.97
with dependence F18.27
multiple
etiologies F03
sclerosis G35 [F02.80]
with behavioral disturbance G35
[F02.81]
neurosyphilis A52.17 [F02.80]
with behavioral disturbance A52.17
[F02.81]
juvenile A50.49 [F02.80]
with behavioral disturbance
A50.49 [F02.81]
niacin deficiency E52 [F02.80]
with behavioral disturbance E52
[F02.81]
paralysis agitans G20 [F02.80]
with behavioral disturbance G20
[F02.81]
Parkinson's disease (parkinsonism)
G20 [F02.80]
with behavioral disturbance G20
[F02.81]
pellagra E52 [F02.80]
with behavioral disturbance E52
[F02.81]
Pick's G31.01 [F02.80]
with behavioral disturbance G31.01
[F02.81]
polyarteritis nodosa M30.0 [F02.80]
with behavioral disturbance M30.0
[F02.81]
psychoactive drug F19.97
with dependence F19.27
inhalants F18.97
with dependence F18.27
sedatives, hypnotics or anxiolytics
F13.97
with dependence F13.27
sedatives, hypnotics or anxiolytics
F13.97
with dependence F13.27
systemic lupus erythematosus
M32.-[F02.80]
with behavioral disturbance
M32.-[F02.81]
trypanosomiasis
African B56.9 [F02.80]
with behavioral disturbance
B56.9 [F02.81]
unknown etiology F03

Dementia *(Continued)*
  in *(Continued)*
    vitamin B12 deficiency E53.8 [F02.80]
      with behavioral disturbance E53.8
        [F02.81]
    volatile solvents F18.97
      with dependence F18.27
      with behavioral disturbance G31.83
        [F02.81]
    infantile, infantilis F84.3
    Lewy body G31.83 [F02.80]
    multi-infarct - *see* Dementia, vascular
    paralytica, paralytic (syphilitic) A52.17
        [F02.80]
      with behavioral disturbance A52.17
        [F02.81]
      juvenilis A50.45 [F02.80]
        with behavioral disturbance
            A50.45 [F02.81]
    paretic A52.17
    praecox - *see* Schizophrenia
    presenile F03
      Alzheimer's type – *see* Disease,
          Alzheimer's, early onset
    primary degenerative F03
    progressive, syphilitic A52.17
    senile F03
      with acute confusional state F05
      Alzheimer's type – *see* Disease,
          Alzheimer's, late onset
      depressed or paranoid type F03
    vascular (acute onset) (mixed)
        (multi-infarct) (subcortical)
        F01.50
      with behavioral disturbance F01.51
Demineralization, bone - *see*
    Osteoporosis
Demodex folliculorum (infestation)
    B88.0
Demophobia F40.248
Demoralization R45.3
Demyelination, demyelinization
  central nervous system G37.9
    specified NEC G37.8
  corpus callosum (central) G37.1
  disseminated, acute G36.9
    specified NEC G36.8
  global G35
  in optic neuritis G36.0
Dengue (classical) (fever) A90
  hemorrhagic A91
  sandfly A93.1
Dennie-Marfan syphilitic syndrome
    A50.45
Dens evaginatus, in dente or invaginatus
    K00.2
Dense breasts R92.2
Density
  increased, bone (disseminated) (gen-
      eralized) (spotted) - *see* Disorder,
      bone, density and structure,
      specified type NEC
  lung (nodular) J98.4
Dental - *see also* condition
  examination Z01.20
    with abnormal findings Z01.21
  restoration
    aesthetically inadequate or displeas-
        ing K08.56
    defective K08.50
      specified NEC K08.59
    failure of marginal integrity K08.51
    failure of periodontal anatomical
        integrity K08.54

Dentia praecox K00.6
Denticles (pulp) K04.2
Dentigerous cyst K09.0
Dentin
  irregular (in pulp) K04.3
  opalescent K00.5
  secondary (in pulp) K04.3
  sensitive K03.89
Dentinogenesis imperfecta K00.5
Dentinoma - *see* Cyst, calcifying
    odontogenic
Dentition (syndrome) K00.7
  delayed K00.6
  difficult K00.7
  precocious K00.6
  premature K00.6
  retarded K00.6
Dependence (on) (syndrome) F19.20
  with remission F19.21
  alcohol (ethyl) (methyl) (without remis-
      sion) F10.20
    with
      amnestic disorder, persisting F10.26
      anxiety disorder F10.280
      dementia, persisting F10.27
      intoxication F10.229
        with delirium F10.221
        uncomplicated F10.220
      mood disorder F10.24
      psychotic disorder F10.259
        with
          delusions F10.250
          hallucinations F10.251
      remission F10.21
      sexual dysfunction F10.281
      sleep disorder F10.282
      specified disorder NEC F10.288
      withdrawal F10.239
        with
          delirium F10.231
          perceptual disturbance F10.232
        uncomplicated F10.230
    counseling and surveillance Z71.41
  amobarbital – *see* Dependence, drug,
      sedative
  amphetamine(s) (type) – *see* Depen-
      dence, drug, stimulant NEC
  amytal (sodium) – *see* Dependence,
      drug, sedative
  analgesic NEC F55.8
  anesthetic (agent) (gas) (general) (local)
      NEC – *see* Dependence, drug,
      psychoactive NEC
  anxiolytic NEC – *see* Dependence, drug,
      sedative
  barbital(s) – *see* Dependence, drug,
      sedative
  barbiturate(s) (compounds) (drugs
      classifiable to T42.30-T42.33) – *see*
      Dependence, drug, sedative
  benzedrine – *see* Dependence, drug,
      stimulant NEC
  bhang – *see* Dependence, drug, cannabis
  bromide(s) NEC – *see* Dependence,
      drug, sedative
  caffeine – *see* Dependence, drug, stimu-
      lant NEC
  cannabis (sativa) (indica) (resin) (de-
      rivatives) (type) – *see* Dependence,
      drug, cannabis
  chloral (betaine) (hydrate) – *see* Depen-
      dence, drug, sedative
  chlordiazepoxide – *see* Dependence,
      drug, sedative

Dependence *(Continued)*
  coca (leaf) (derivatives) – *see* Depen-
      dence, drug, cocaine
  cocaine – *see* Dependence, drug, cocaine
  codeine – *see* Dependence, drug, opioid
  combinations of drugs F19.20
  dagga – *see* Dependence, drug, cannabis
  demerol – *see* Dependence, drug, opioid
  dexamphetamine – *see* Dependence,
      drug, stimulant NEC
  dexedrine – *see* Dependence, drug,
      stimulant NEC
  dextromethorphan – *see* Dependence,
      drug, opioid
  dextromoramide – *see* Dependence,
      drug, opioid
  dextro-nor-pseudo-ephedrine– *see* De-
      pendence, drug, stimulant NEC
  dextrorphan – *see* Dependence, drug,
      opioid
  diazepam – *see* Dependence, drug,
      sedative
  dilaudid – *see* Dependence, drug,
      opioid
  D-lysergic acid diethylamide – *see* De-
      pendence, drug, hallucinogen
  drug NEC F19.20
    with sleep disorder F19.282
    cannabis F12.20
      with
        anxiety disorder F12.280
        intoxication F12.229
          with
            delirium F12.221
            perceptual disturbance
                F12.222
          uncomplicated F12.220
        other specified disorder F12.288
        psychosis F12.259
          delusions F12.250
          hallucinations F12.251
        unspecified disorder F12.29
      in remission F12.21
    cocaine F14.20
      with
        anxiety disorder F14.280
        intoxication F14.229
          with
            delirium F14.221
            perceptual disturbance
                F14.222
          uncomplicated F14.220
        mood disorder F14.24
        other specified disorder F14.288
        psychosis F14.259
          delusions F14.250
          hallucinations F14.251
        sexual dysfunction F14.281
        sleep disorder F14.282
        unspecified disorder F14.29
        withdrawal F14.23
      in remission F14.21
      withdrawal symptoms in newborn
          P96.1
    counseling and surveillance Z71.51
    hallucinogen F16.20
      with
        anxiety disorder F16.280
        flashbacks F16.283
        intoxication F16.229
          with delirium F16.221
          uncomplicated F16.220
        mood disorder F16.24
        other specified disorder F16.288

Dependence *(Continued)*
  drug NEC *(Continued)*
    hallucinogen *(Continued)*
      with *(Continued)*
        perception disorder, persisting F16.283
        psychosis F16.259
          delusions F16.250
          hallucinations F16.251
        unspecified disorder F16.29
      in remission F16.21
    in remission F19.21
    inhalant F18.20
      with
        amnestic disorder F13.26
        anxiety disorder F18.280
        dementia, persisting F18.27
        intoxication F18.229
          with delirium F18.221
          uncomplicated F18.220
        mood disorder F18.24
        other specified disorder F18.288
        psychosis F18.259
          delusions F18.250
          hallucinations F18.251
        sexual dysfunction F13.281
        unspecified disorder F18.29
        withdrawal F13.239
          with
            delirium F13.231
            perceptual disturbance F13.232
            uncomplicated F13.230
      in remission F18.21
    nicotine F17.200
      with disorder F17.299
        remission F17.211
        specified disorder NEC F17.298
        withdrawal F17.203
      chewing tobacco F17.220
        with disorder F17.229
        remission F17.221
        specified disorder NEC F17.228
        withdrawal F17.223
      cigarettes F17.210
        with disorder F17.219
        remission F17.211
        specified disorder NEC F17.218
        withdrawal F17.213
      specified product NEC F17.290
        with disorder F17.299
        remission F17.291
        specified disorder NEC F17.298
        withdrawal F17.292
    opioid F11.20
      with
        intoxication F11.229
          with
            delirium F11.221
            perceptual disturbance F11.222
          uncomplicated F11.220
        mood disorder F11.24
        other specified disorder F11.288
        psychosis F11.259
          delusions F11.250
          hallucinations F11.251
        sexual dysfunction F11.281
        sleep disorder F11.282
        unspecified disorder F11.29
        withdrawal F11.23
      in remission F11.21

Dependence *(Continued)*
  drug NEC *(Continued)*
    psychoactive NEC F19.20
      with
        amnestic disorder F19.26
        anxiety disorder F19.280
        dementia F19.27
        intoxication F19.229
          with
            delirium F19.221
            perceptual disturbance F19.222
          uncomplicated F19.220
        mood disorder F19.24
        other specified disorder F19.288
        psychosis F19.259
          delusions F19.250
          hallucinations F19.251
        sexual dysfunction F19.281
        sleep disorder F19.282
        unspecified disorder F19.29
        withdrawal F19.239
          with
            delirium F19.231
            perceptual disturbance F19.232
          uncomplicated F19.230
    sedative, hypnotic or anxiolytic F13.20
      with
        amnestic disorder F13.26
        anxiety disorder F13.280
        dementia, persisting F13.27
        intoxication F13.229
          with delirium F13.221
          uncomplicated F13.220
        mood disorder F13.24
        other specified disorder F13.288
        psychosis F13.259
          delusions F13.250
          hallucinations F13.251
        sexual dysfunction F13.281
        sleep disorder F13.282
        unspecified disorder F13.29
        withdrawal F13.239
          with
            delirium F13.231
            perceptual disturbance F13.232
          uncomplicated F13.230
      in remission F13.21
    stimulant NEC F15.20
      with
        anxiety disorder F15.280
        intoxication F15.229
          with
            delirium F15.221
            perceptual disturbance F15.222
          uncomplicated F15.220
        mood disorder F15.24
        other specified disorder F15.288
        psychosis F15.259
          delusions F15.250
          hallucinations F15.251
        sexual dysfunction F15.281
        sleep disorder F15.282
        unspecified disorder F15.29
        withdrawal F15.23
      in remission F15.21
  ethyl
    alcohol (without remission) F10.20
      with remission F10.21
    bromide – *see* Dependence, drug, sedative

Dependence *(Continued)*
  ethyl *(Continued)*
    carbamate F19.20
    chloride F19.20
    morphine – *see* Dependence, drug, opioid
  ganja – *see* Dependence, drug, cannabis
  glue (airplane) (sniffing) – *see* Dependence, drug, inhalant
  glutethimide – *see* Dependence, drug, sedative
  hallucinogenics – *see* Dependence, drug, hallucinogen
  hashish – *see* Dependence, drug, cannabis
  hemp – *see* Dependence, drug, cannabis
  heroin (salt) (any) – *see* Dependence, drug, opioid
  hypnotic NEC – *see* Dependence, drug, sedative
  Indian hemp – *see* Dependence, drug, cannabis
  inhalants – *see* Dependence, drug, inhalant
  khat – *see* Dependence, drug, stimulant NEC
  laudanum – *see* Dependence, drug, opioid
  LSD(-25) (derivatives) – *see* Dependence, drug, hallucinogen
  luminal – *see* Dependence, drug, sedative
  lysergic acid – *see* Dependence, drug, hallucinogen
  maconha – *see* Dependence, drug, cannabis
  marihuana – *see* Dependence, drug, cannabis
  meprobamate – *see* Dependence, drug, sedative
  mescaline – *see* Dependence, drug, hallucinogen
  methadone – *see* Dependence, drug, opioid
  methamphetamine(s) – *see* Dependence, drug, stimulant NEC
  methaqualone – *see* Dependence, drug, sedative
  methyl
    alcohol (without remission) F10.20
      with remission F10.21
    bromide – *see* Dependence, drug, sedative
    morphine – *see* Dependence, drug, opioid
    phenidate – *see* Dependence, drug, stimulant NEC
    sulfonal – *see* Dependence, drug, sedative
  morphine (sulfate) (sulfite) (type) – *see* Dependence, drug, opioid
  narcotic (drug) NEC – *see* Dependence, drug, opioid
  nembutal – *see* Dependence, drug, sedative
  neraval – *see* Dependence, drug, sedative
  neravan – *see* Dependence, drug, sedative
  neurobarb – *see* Dependence, drug, sedative
  nicotine – *see* Dependence, drug, nicotine
  nitrous oxide F19.20
  nonbarbiturate sedatives and tranquilizers with similar effect – *see* Dependence, drug, sedative

Dependence *(Continued)*
on
aspirator Z99.0
care provider (because of) Z74.9
impaired mobility Z74.09
need for
assistance with personal care
Z74.1
continuous supervision Z74.3
no other household member able
to render care Z74.2
specified reason NEC Z74.8
machine Z99.89
enabling NEC Z99.89
specified type NEC Z99.89
renal dialysis (hemodialysis) (peritoneal) Z99.2
respirator Z99.11
ventilator Z99.11
wheelchair Z99.3
opiate – *see* Dependence, drug, opioid
opioids – *see* Dependence, drug,
opioid
opium (alkaloids) (derivatives) (tinc-
ture) – *see* Dependence, drug,
opioid
oxygen (long-term) (supplemental)
Z99.81
paraldehyde – *see* Dependence, drug,
sedative
paregoric – *see* Dependence, drug,
opioid
PCP (phencyclidine) F19.20
pentobarbital – *see* Dependence, drug,
sedative
pentobarbitone (sodium) – *see* Dependence, drug, sedative
pentothal – *see* Dependence, drug,
sedative
peyote – *see* Dependence, drug,
hallucinogen
phencyclidine (PCP) (and related substances) F19.20
phenmetrazine– *see* Dependence, drug,
stimulant NEC
phenobarbital – *see* Dependence, drug,
sedative
polysubstance F19.20
psilocibin, psilocin, psilocyn, psilo-
cyline – *see* Dependence, drug,
hallucinogen
psychostimulant NEC– *see* Dependence,
drug, stimulant NEC
secobarbital – *see* Dependence, drug,
sedative
seconal – *see* Dependence, drug,
sedative
sedative NEC – *see* Dependence, drug,
sedative
specified drug NEC – *see* Dependence,
drug
stimulant NEC– *see* Dependence, drug,
stimulant NEC
substance NEC – *see* Dependence,
drug
supplemental oxygen Z99.81
tobacco – *see* Dependence, drug,
nicotine
counseling and surveillance Z71.6
tranquilizer NEC – *see* Dependence,
drug, sedative
vitamin B6 E53.1
volatile solvents – *see* Dependence,
drug, inhalant

Dependency
care-provider Z74.9
passive F60.7
reactions (persistent) F60.7
Depersonalization (in neurotic state)
(neurotic) (syndrome) F48.1
Depletion
extracellular fluid E86.9
plasma E86.1
potassium E87.6
nephropathy N25.89
salt or sodium E87.1
causing heat exhaustion or prostration T67.4
nephropathy N28.9
volume NOS E86.9
Deployment (current) (military) status
Z56.82
in theater or in support of military war,
peacekeeping and humanitarian
operations Z56.82
personal history of Z91.82
military war, peacekeeping and
humanitarian deployment
(current or past conflict) Z91.82
returned from Z91.82
Depolarization, premature I49.40
atrial I49.1
junctional I49.2
specified NEC I49.49
ventricular I49.3
Deposit
bone in Boeck's sarcoid D86.89
calcareous, calcium - *see* Calcification
cholesterol
retina H35.89
vitreous (body) (humor) - *see* Deposit,
crystalline
conjunctiva H11.11-
cornea H18.00-
argentous H18.02-
due to metabolic disorder H18.03-
Kayser-Fleischer ring H18.04-
pigmentation - *see* Pigmentation,
cornea
crystalline, vitreous (body) (humor)
H43.2-
hemosiderin in old scars of cornea - *see*
Pigmentation, cornea, stromal
metallic in lens - *see* Cataract, specified
NEC
skin R23.8
tooth, teeth (betel) (black) (green) (materia alba) (orange) (tobacco) K03.6
urate, kidney - *see* Calculus, kidney
Depraved appetite – *see* Pica
Depressed
HDL cholesterol E78.6
Depression (acute) (mental) F32.9
agitated (single episode) F32.2
anaclitic – *see* Disorder, adjustment
anxiety F41.8
persistent F34.1
arches - *see also* Deformity, limb, flat
foot
atypical (single episode) F32.8
basal metabolic rate R94.8
bone marrow D75.89
central nervous system R09.2
cerebral R29.81
newborn P91.4
cerebrovascular I67.9
chest wall M95.4
climacteric (single episode) F32.8

Depression *(Continued)*
endogenous (without psychotic symptoms) F33.2
with psychotic symptoms F33.3
functional activity R68.89
hysterical F44.89
involutional (single episode) F32.8
major F32.9
with psychotic symptoms F32.3
major (recurrent) - *see* Disorder, depressive, recurrent
manic-depressive - *see* Disorder, depressive, recurrent
masked (single episode) F32.8
medullary G93.89
menopausal (single episode) F32.8
metatarsus - *see* Depression, arches
monopolar F33.9
nervous F34.1
neurotic F34.1
nose M95.0
postnatal F53
postpartum F53
post-psychotic of schizophrenia F32.8
post-schizophrenic F32.8
psychogenic (reactive) (single episode)
F32.9
psychoneurotic F34.1
psychotic (single episode) F32.3
recurrent F33.3
reactive (psychogenic) (single episode)
F32.9
psychotic (single episode) F32.3
recurrent - *see* Disorder, depressive,
recurrent
respiratory center G93.89
seasonal - *see* Disorder, depressive,
recurrent
senile F03
severe, single episode F32.2
situational F43.21
skull Q67.4
specified NEC (single episode) F32.8
sternum M95.4
visual field - *see* Defect, visual field
vital (recurrent) (without psychotic
symptoms) F33.2
with psychotic symptoms F33.3
single episode F32.2
Deprivation
cultural Z60.3
effects NOS T73.9
specified NEC T73.8
emotional NEC Z65.8
affecting infant or child – *see* Maltreatment, child, psychological
food T73.0
protein - *see* Malnutrition
sleep Z72.820
social Z60.4
affecting infant or child – *see* Maltreatment, child, psychological
specified NEC T73.8
vitamins - *see* Deficiency, vitamin
water T73.1
Derangement
ankle (internal) - *see* Derangement,
joint, ankle
cartilage (articular) NEC - *see* Derangement, joint, articular cartilage, by
site
recurrent - *see* Dislocation, recurrent
cruciate ligament, anterior, current injury
- *see* Sprain, knee, cruciate, anterior

Derangement *(Continued)*
  elbow (internal) - *see* Derangement, joint, elbow
  hip (joint) (internal) (old) - *see* Derangement, joint, hip
  joint (internal) M24.9
    ankylosis - *see* Ankylosis
    articular cartilage M24.10
      ankle M24.17-
      elbow M24.12-
      foot M24.17-
      hand M24.14-
      hip M24.15-
      knee NEC M23.9-
      loose body - *see* Loose, body
      shoulder M24.11-
      wrist M24.13-
    contracture - *see* Contraction, joint
    current injury - *see also* Dislocation
      knee, meniscus or cartilage - *see* Tear, meniscus
    dislocation
      pathological - *see* Dislocation, pathological
      recurrent - *see* Dislocation, recurrent
    knee – *see* Derangement, knee
    ligament - *see* Disorder, ligament
    loose body - *see* Loose, body
    recurrent - *see* Dislocation, recurrent
    specified type NEC M24.80
      ankle M24.87-
      elbow M24.82-
      foot joint M24.87-
      hand joint M24.84-
      hip M24.85-
      shoulder M24.81-
      wrist M24.83-
    temporomandibular M26.69
  knee (recurrent) M23.9-
    ligament disruption, spontaneous M23.609
      anterior cruciate M23.61-
      capsular M23.67-
      instability, chronic M23.5-
      lateral collateral M23.64-
      medial collateral M23.63-
      posterior cruciate M23.62-
    loose body M23.4-
    meniscus M23.30-
      cystic M23.00-
        lateral M23.02-
          anterior horn M23.04-
          posterior horn M23.05-
          specified NEC M23.06-
        medial M23.00-
          anterior horn M23.01-
          posterior horn M23.02-
          specified NEC M23.03-
      degenerate - *see* Derangement, knee, meniscus, specified NEC
      detached - *see* Derangement, knee, meniscus, specified NEC
      due to old tear or injury M23.20-
        lateral M23.20-
          anterior horn M23.24-
          posterior horn M23.25-
          specified NEC M23.26-
        medial M23.20-
          anterior horn M23.21-
          posterior horn M23.22-
          specified NEC M23.23-
      retained - *see* Derangement, knee, meniscus, specified NEC

Derangement *(Continued)*
  knee *(Continued)*
    meniscus *(Continued)*
      specified NEC M23.30-
        lateral M23.30-
          anterior horn M23.34-
          posterior horn M23.35-
          specified NEC M23.36-
        medial M23.30-
          anterior horn M23.31-
          posterior horn M23.32-
          specified NEC M23.33-
      old M23.8x-
      specified NEC - *see* subcategory M23.8
    low back NEC - *see* Dorsopathy, specified NEC
    meniscus - *see* Derangement, knee, meniscus
    mental - *see* Psychosis
    patella, specified NEC - *see* Disorder, patella, derangement NEC
    semilunar cartilage (knee) - *see* Derangement, knee, meniscus, specified NEC
    shoulder (internal) - *see* Derangement, joint, shoulder
Dercum's disease E88.2
Derealization (neurotic) F48.1
Dermal - *see* condition
Dermaphytid - *see* Dermatophytosis
Dermatitis (eczematous) L30.9
  ab igne L59.0
  acarine B88.0
  actinic (due to sun) L57.8
    other than from sun L59.8
  allergic – *see* Dermatitis, contact, allergic
  ambustionis, due to burn or scald - *see* Burn
  amebic A06.7
  ammonia L22
  arsenical (ingested) L27.8
  artefacta L98.1
    psychogenic F54
  atopic L20.9
    psychogenic F54
    specified NEC L20.89
  autoimmune progesterone L30.8
  berlock, berloque L56.2
  blastomycotic B40.3
  blister beetle L24.89
  bullous, bullosa L13.9
    mucosynechial, atrophic L12.1
    seasonal L30.8
    specified NEC L13.8
  calorica L59.0
    due to burn or scald - *see* Burn
  caterpillar L24.89
  cercarial B65.3
  combustionis L59.0
    due to burn or scald - *see* Burn
  congelationis T69.1
  contact (occupational) L25.9
    allergic L23.9
      due to
        adhesives L23.1
        cement L23.5
        chemical products NEC L23.5
        chromium L23.0
        cosmetics L23.2
        dander (cat) (dog) L23.81
        drugs in contact with skin L23.3
        dyes L23.4
        food in contact with skin L23.6
        hair (cat) (dog) L23.81

Dermatitis *(Continued)*
  contact *(Continued)*
    allergic *(Continued)*
      due to *(Continued)*
        insecticide L23.5
        metals L23.0
        nickel L23.0
        plants, non-food L23.7
        plastic L23.5
        rubber L23.5
        specified agent NEC L23.89
      due to
        chemical products NEC L25.3
        cosmetics L25.0
        dander (cat) (dog) L23.81
        drugs in contact with skin L25.1
        dyes L25.2
        food in contact with skin L25.4
        hair (cat) (dog) L23.81
        plants, non-food L25.5
        specified agent NEC L25.8
      irritant L24.9
        due to
          chemical products NEC L24.5
          cosmetics L24.3
          detergents L24.0
          drugs in contact with skin L24.4
          food in contact with skin L24.6
          oils and greases L24.1
          plants, non-food L24.7
          solvents L24.2
          specified agent NEC L24.89
    contusiformis L52
    diabetic - *see* E09-E13 with .63
    diaper L22
    diphtheritica A36.3
    dry skin L85.3
    due to
      acetone (contact) (irritant) L24.2
      acids (contact) (irritant) L24.5
      adhesive(s) (allergic) (contact) (plaster) L23.1
        irritant L24.5
      alcohol (irritant) (skin contact) (substances in T51.00-T51.93) L24.2
        taken internally L27.8
      alkalis (contact) (irritant) L24.5
      arsenic (ingested) L27.8
      carbon disulfide (contact) (irritant) L24.2
      caustics (contact) (irritant) L24.5
      cement (contact) L24.5
      cereal (ingested) L27.2
      chemical(s) NEC L24.5
        taken internally L27.8
      chlorocompounds L24.2
      chromium (contact) (irritant) L24.81
      coffee (ingested) L27.2
      cold weather L30.8
      cosmetics (contact) L25.0
        allergic L23.2
        irritant L24.3
      cyclohexanes L24.2
      dander (cat) (dog) L23.81
      Demodex species B88.0
      Dermanyssus gallinae B88.0
      detergents (contact) (irritant) L24.0
      dichromate L24.81
      drugs and medicaments (generalized) (internal use) L27.0
        external - *see* Dermatitis, due to, drugs, in contact with skin

Dermatitis *(Continued)*
  due to *(Continued)*
    drugs and medicaments *(Continued)*
      in contact with skin L25.1
        allergic L23.3
        irritant L24.4
      localized skin eruption L27.1
      specified substance - *see* Table of
        drugs and chemicals
    dyes (contact) L25.2
      allergic L23.4
      irritant L24.89
    epidermophytosis - *see*
      Dermatophytosis
    esters L24.2
    external irritant NEC L24.9
    fish (ingested) L27.2
    flour (ingested) L27.2
    food (ingested) L27.2
      in contact with skin L23.6
    fruit (ingested) L27.2
    furs (allergic) (contact) L23.81
    glues - *see* Dermatitis, due to, adhesives
    glycols L24.2
    greases NEC (contact) (irritant) L24.1
    hair (cat) (dog) L23.81
    hot
      objects and materials - *see* Burn
      weather or places L59.0
    hydrocarbons L24.2
    infrared rays L59.8
    ingestion, ingested substance L27.9
      chemical NEC L27.8
      drugs and medicaments - *see* Der-
        matitis, due to, drugs
      food L27.2
      specified NEC L27.8
    insecticide in contact with skin L24.5
    internal agent L27.9
      drugs and medicaments (general-
        ized) - *see* Dermatitis, due to,
        drugs
      food L27.2
    irradiation - *see* Dermatitis, due to,
      radioactive substance
    ketones L24.2
    lacquer tree (allergic) (contact) L23.7
    light (sun) NEC L57.8
      acute L56.8
      other L59.8
    Liponyssoides sanguineus B88.0
    low temperature L30.8
    meat (ingested) L27.2
    metals, metal salts (contact) (irritant)
      L24.81
    milk (ingested) L27.2
    nickel (contact) (irritant) L24.81
    nylon (contact) (irritant) L24.5
    oils NEC (contact) (irritant) L24.1
    paint solvent (contact) (irritant) L24.2
    petroleum products (contact) (ir-
      ritant) (substances in T52.00-
      T52.93) L24.2
    plants NEC (contact) L25.5
      allergic L23.7
      irritant L24.7
    plasters (adhesive) (any) (allergic)
      (contact) L23.1
      irritant L24.5
    plastic (contact) L24.5
    preservatives (contact) - *see* Dermati-
      tis, due to, chemical, in contact
      with skin
    primrose (allergic) (contact) L23.7

Dermatitis *(Continued)*
  due to *(Continued)*
    primula (allergic) (contact) L23.7
    radiation L59.8
      nonionizing (chronic exposure)
        L57.8
      sun NEC L57.8
        acute L56.8
    radioactive substance L58.9
      acute L58.0
      chronic L58.1
    radium L58.9
      acute L58.0
      chronic L58.1
    ragweed (allergic) (contact) L23.7
    Rhus (allergic) (contact) (diversiloba)
      (radicans) (toxicodendron) (ven-
      enata) (verniciflua) L23.7
    rubber (contact) L24.5
    Senecio jacobaea (allergic) (contact)
      L23.7
    solvents (contact) (irritant) (sub-
      stances in T52.00-T53.93) L24.2
    specified agent NEC (contact) L25.8
      allergic L23.89
      irritant L24.89
    sunshine NEC L57.8
      acute L56.8
    tetrachlorethylene (contact) (irritant)
      L24.2
    toluene (contact) (irritant) L24.2
    turpentine (contact) L24.2
    ultraviolet rays (sun NEC) (chronic
      exposure) L57.8
      acute L56.8
    vaccine or vaccination L27.0
      specified substance - *see* Table of
        drugs and chemicals
    varicose veins - *see* Varix, leg, with,
      inflammation
    X-rays L58.9
      acute L58.0
      chronic L58.1
  dyshydrotic L30.1
  dysmenorrheica N94.6
  escharotica - *see* Burn
  exfoliative, exfoliativa (generalized) L26
    neonatorum L00
  eyelid - *see also* Dermatosis, eyelid
    allergic H01.119
      left H01.116
        lower H01.115
        upper H01.114
      right H01.113
        lower H01.112
        upper H01.111
    contact - *see* Dermatitis, eyelid, allergic
    due to
      Demodex species B88.0
      herpes (zoster) B02.39
        simplex B00.59
    eczematous H01.139
      left H01.136
        lower H01.135
        upper H01.134
      right H01.133
        lower H01.132
        upper H01.131
  facta, factitia, factitial L98.1
    psychogenic F54
  flexural NEC L20.82
  friction L30.4
  fungus B36.9
    specified type NEC B36.8

Dermatitis *(Continued)*
  gangrenosa, gangrenous infantum L08.0
  harvest mite B88.0
  heat L59.0
  herpesviral, vesicular (ear) (lip) B00.1
  herpetiformis (bullous) (erythematous)
    (pustular) (vesicular) L13.0
    juvenile L12.2
    senile L12.0
  hiemalis L30.8
  hypostatic, hypostatica - *see* Varix, leg,
    with, inflammation
  infectious eczematoid L30.3
  infective L30.3
  irritant – *see* Dermatitis, contact, irritant
  Jacquet's (diaper dermatitis) L22
  Leptus B88.0
  lichenified NEC L28.0
  medicamentosa (generalized) (internal
    use) - *see* Dermatitis, due to drugs
  mite B88.0
  multiformis L13.0
    juvenile L12.2
  napkin L22
  neurotica L13.0
  nummular L30.0
  papillaris capillitii L73.0
  pellagrous E52
  perioral L71.0
  photocontact L56.2
  polymorpha dolorosa L13.0
  pruriginosa L13.0
  pruritic NEC L30.8
  psychogenic F54
  purulent L08.0
  pustular
    contagious B08.02
    subcorneal L13.1
  pyococcal L08.0
  pyogenica L08.0
  repens L40.2
  Ritter's (exfoliativa) L00
  Schamberg's L81.7
  schistosome B65.3
  seasonal bullous L30.8
  seborrheic L21.9
    infantile L21.1
    specified NEC L21.8
  sensitization NOS L23.9
  septic L08.0
  solare L57.8
  specified NEC L30.8
  stasis I87.2
    with varicose ulcer - *see* Varix, leg,
      with ulcer, with inflammation
    due to postthrombotic syndrome - *see*
      Syndrome, postthrombotic
  suppurative L08.0
  traumatic NEC L30.4
  trophoneurotica L13.0
  ultraviolet (sun) (chronic exposure) L57.8
    acute L56.8
  varicose - *see* Varix, leg, with, inflammation
  vegetans L10.1
  verrucosa B43.0
  vesicular, herpesviral B00.1
Dermatoarthritis, lipoid E78.81
Dermatochalasis, eyelid H02.839
  left H02.836
    lower H02.835
    upper H02.834
  right H02.833
    lower H02.832
    upper H02.831

Dermatofibroma (lenticulare) - *see* Neoplasm, skin, benign
protuberans - *see* Neoplasm, skin, uncertain behavior
Dermatofibrosarcoma - *see* Neoplasm, skin, malignant
protuberans - *see* Neoplasm, skin, malignant
pigmented C80.1
Dermatographia L50.3
Dermatolysis (exfoliativa) (congenital) Q82.8
acquired L57.4
eyelids - *see* Blepharochalasis
palpebrarum - *see* Blepharochalasis
senile L57.4
Dermatomegaly NEC Q82.8
Dermatomucosomyositis M33.10
with
myopathy M33.12
respiratory involvement M33.11
specified organ involvement NEC M33.19
Dermatomycosis B36.9
furfuracea B36.0
specified type NEC B36.8
Dermatomyositis (acute) (chronic) - *see also* Dermatopolymyositis
in (due to) neoplastic disease (*see also* Neoplasm) D49.9 [M36.0]
Dermatoneuritis of children – *see* Poisoning, mercury
Dermatophilosis A48.8
Dermatophytid L30.2
Dermatophytide - *see* Dermatophytosis
Dermatophytosis (epidermophyton) (infection) (Microsporum) (tinea) (Trichophyton) B35.9
beard B35.0
body B35.4
capitis B35.0
corporis B35.4
deep-seated B35.8
disseminated B35.8
foot B35.3
granulomatous B35.8
groin B35.6
hand B35.2
nail B35.1
perianal (area) B35.6
scalp B35.0
specified NEC B35.8
Dermatopolymyositis M33.90
with
myopathy M33.92
respiratory involvement M33.91
specified organ involvement NEC M33.99
in neoplastic disease (*see also* Neoplasm) D49.9 [M36.0]
juvenile M33.00
with
myopathy M33.02
respiratory involvement M33.01
specified organ involvement NEC M33.09
specified NEC M33.10
myopathy M33.12
respiratory involvement M33.11
specified organ involvement NEC M33.19
Dermatopolyneuritis – *see* Poisoning, mercury
Dermatorrhexis Q79.6
acquired L57.4

Dermatosclerosis - *see also* Scleroderma
localized L94.0
Dermatosis L98.9
Andrews' L08.89
Bowen's - *see* Neoplasm, skin, in situ
bullous L13.9
specified NEC L13.8
exfoliativa L26
eyelid (noninfectious)
dermatitis - *see* Dermatitis, eyelid
discoid lupus erythematosus - *see* Lupus, erythematosus, eyelid
xeroderma - *see* Xeroderma, acquired, eyelid
factitial L98.1
febrile neutrophilic L98.2
gonococcal A54.89
herpetiformis L13.0
juvenile L12.2
linear IgA L13.8
menstrual NEC L98.8
neutrophilic, febrile L98.2
occupational – *see* Dermatitis, contact
papulosa nigra L82.1
pigmentary L81.9
progressive L81.7
Schamberg's L81.7
psychogenic F54
purpuric, pigmented L81.7
pustular, subcorneal L13.1
transient acantholytic L11.1
Dermographia, dermographism L50.3
Dermoid (cyst) - *see also* Neoplasm, benign
with malignant transformation C56.-
due to radiation (nonionizing) L57.8
Dermopathy
infiltrative with thyrotoxicosis - *see* Thyrotoxicosis
nephrogenic fibrosing L90.8
Dermophytosis - *see* Dermatophytosis
Descemetocele H18.73-
Descemet's membrane - *see* condition
Descending - *see* condition
Descensus uteri - *see* Prolapse, uterus
Desert
rheumatism B38.0
sore - *see* Ulcer, skin
Desertion (newborn) – *see* Maltreatment, abandonment
Desmoid (extra-abdominal) (tumor) - *see* Neoplasm, connective tissue, uncertain behavior
abdominal D48.1
Despondency F32.9
Desquamation, skin R23.4
Destruction, destructive - *see also* Damage
articular facet - *see also* Derangement, joint, specified type NEC
knee M23.8x-
vertebra - *see* Spondylosis
bone - *see also* Disorder, bone, specified type NEC
syphilitic A52.77
joint - *see also* Derangement, joint, specified type NEC
sacroiliac M53.3
rectal sphincter K62.8
septum (nasal) J34.89
tuberculous NEC - *see* Tuberculosis
tympanum, tympanic membrane (nontraumatic) - *see* Disorder, tympanic membrane, specified NEC
vertebral disc - *see* Degeneration, intervertebral disc

Destructiveness - *see also* Disorder, conduct
adjustment reaction – *see* Disorder, adjustment
Desultory labor O62.2
Detachment
cartilage - *see* Sprain
cervix, annular N88.8
complicating delivery O71.3
choroid (old) (postinfectional) (simple) (spontaneous) H31.40-
hemorrhagic H31.41-
serous H31.42-
ligament - *see* Sprain
meniscus (knee) - *see also* Derangement, knee, meniscus, specified NEC
current injury - *see* Tear, meniscus
due to old tear or injury - *see* Derangement, knee, meniscus, due to old tear
retina (without retinal break) (serous) H33.2-
with retinal:
break H33.00-
giant H33.03-
multiple H33.02-
single H33.01-
dialysis H33.04-
pigment epithelium - *see* Degeneration, retina, separation of layers, pigment epithelium detachment
rhegmatogenous - *see* Detachment, retina, with retinal, break
specified NEC H33.8
total H33.05-
traction H33.4-
vitreous (body) H43.89
Detergent asthma J69.8
Deterioration
epileptic F06.8
general physical R53.81
heart, cardiac - *see* Degeneration, myocardial
mental - *see* Psychosis
myocardial, myocardium - *see* Degeneration, myocardial
senile (simple) R54
Deuteranomaly (anomalous trichromat) H53.53
Deuteranopia (complete) (incomplete) H53.53
Development
abnormal, bone Q79.9
arrested R62.50
bone - *see* Arrest, development or growth, bone
child R62.50
due to malnutrition E45
defective, congenital - *see also* Anomaly, by site
cauda equina Q06.3
left ventricle Q24.8
in hypoplastic left heart syndrome Q23.4
valve Q24.8
pulmonary Q22.2
delayed (*see also* Delay, development) R62.50
arithmetical skills F81.2
language (skills) (expressive) F80.1
learning skill F81.9
mixed skills F88
motor coordination F82
reading F81.0

Development *(Continued)*
  delayed *(Continued)*
    specified learning skill NEC F81.89
    speech F80.9
    spelling F81.81
    written expression F81.81
  imperfect, congenital - *see also* Anomaly,
    by site
    heart Q24.9
    lungs Q33.6
  incomplete
    bronchial tree Q32.4
    organ or site not listed - *see* Hypopla-
      sia, by site
    respiratory system Q34.9
  sexual, precocious NEC E30.1
  tardy, mental *(see also* Retardation,
    mental) F79
Developmental - *see* condition
  testing, child - *see* Examination, child
Devergie's disease (pityriasis rubra
  pilaris) L44.0
Deviation (in)
  conjugate palsy (eye) (spastic) H51.0
  esophagus (acquired) K22.8
  eye, skew H51.8
  midline (jaw) (teeth) (dental arch) M26.29
    specified site NEC - *see* Malposition
  nasal septum J34.2
    congenital Q67.4
  opening and closing of the mandible
    M26.53
  organ or site, congenital NEC - *see* Mal-
    position, congenital
  septum (nasal) (acquired) J34.2
    congenital Q67.4
  sexual F65.9
    bestiality F65.89
    erotomania F52.8
    exhibitionism F65.2
    fetishism, fetishistic F65.0
      transvestism F65.1
    frotteurism F65.81
    masochism F65.51
    multiple F65.89
    necrophilia F65.89
    nymphomania F52.8
    pederosis F65.4
    pedophilia F65.4
    sadism, sadomasochism F65.52
    satyriasis F52.8
    specified type NEC F65.89
    transvestism F64.1
    voyeurism F65.3
  teeth, midline M26.29
  trachea J39.8
  ureter, congenital Q62.61
Device
  cerebral ventricle (communicating) in
    situ Z98.2
  contraceptive - *see* Contraceptive,
    device
  drainage, cerebrospinal fluid, in situ
    Z98.2
Devic's disease G36.0
Devil's
  grip B33.0
  pinches (purpura simplex) D69.2
Devitalized tooth K04.99
Devonshire colic – *see* Poisoning, lead
Dextraposition, aorta Q20.3
  in tetralogy of Fallot Q21.3
Dextrinosis, limit (debrancher enzyme
  deficiency) E74.03

Dextrocardia (true) Q24.0
  with
    complete transposition of viscera
      Q89.3
    situs inversus Q89.3
Dextrotransposition, aorta Q20.3
d-glycericacidemia E72.59
Dhat syndrome F48.8
Dhobi itch B35.6
Di George's syndrome D82.1
Di Guglielmo's disease C94.0-
Diabetes, diabetic (mellitus) (sugar)
  E11.9
  with
    amyotrophy E11.44
    arthropathy NEC E11.618
    autonomic (poly)neuropathy E11.43
    cataract E11.36
    Charcot's joints E11.610
    chronic kidney disease E11.22
    circulatory complication NEC
      E11.59
    complication E11.8
      specified NEC E11.69
    dermatitis E11.620
    foot ulcer E11.621
    gangrene E11.52
    gastroparesis E11.43
    glomerulonephrosis, intracapillary
      E11.21
    glomerulosclerosis, intercapillary
      E11.21
    hyperglycemia E11.65
    hyperosmolarity E11.00
      with coma E11.01
    hypoglycemia E11.640
      with coma E11.641
    kidney complications NEC E11.29
    Kimmelstiel-Wilson disease E11.21
    mononeuropathy E11.41
    myasthenia E11.44
    necrobiosis lipoidica E11.620
    nephropathy E11.21
    neuralgia E11.42
    neurologic complication NEC E11.49
    neuropathic arthropathy E11.6100
    neuropathy E11.40
    ophthalmic complication NEC
      E11.39
    oral complication NEC E11.638
    periodontal disease E11.630
    peripheral angiopathy E11.51
      with gangrene E11.52
    polyneuropathy E11.42
    renal complication NEC E11.29
    renal tubular degeneration E11.29
    retinopathy E11.319
      with macular edema E11.311
      nonproliferative E11.329
        with macular edema E11.321
        mild E11.329
          with macular edema E11.321
        moderate E11.339
          with macular edema E11.331
        severe E11.349
          with macular edema E11.341
      proliferative E11.359
        with macular edema E11.351
    skin complication NEC E11.628
    skin ulcer NEC E11.622
    complicating pregnancy - *see* Pregnancy,
      complicated by, diabetes
  dietary counseling and surveillance
    Z71.3

Diabetes, diabetic *(Continued)*
  due to drug or chemical E09.9
  with
    amyotrophy E09.44
    arthropathy NEC E09.618
    autonomic (poly)neuropathy
      E09.43
    cataract E09.36
    Charcot's joints E09.610
    chronic kidney disease E09.22
    circulatory complication NEC
      E09.59
    complication E09.8
      specified NEC E09.69
    dermatitis E09.620
    foot ulcer E09.621
    gangrene E09.52
    gastroparesis E09.43
    glomerulonephrosis, intracapillary
      E09.21
    glomerulosclerosis, intercapillary
      E09.21
    hyperglycemia E09.65
    hyperosmolarity E09.00
      with coma E09.01
    hypoglycemia E09.640
      with coma E09.641
    ketoacidosis E09.10
      with coma E09.11
    kidney complications NEC E09.29
    Kimmelsteil-Wilson disease E09.21
    mononeuropathy E09.41
    myasthenia E09.44
    necrobiosis lipoidica E09.620
    nephropathy E09.21
    neuralgia E09.42
    neurologic complication NEC
      E09.49
    neuropathic arthropathy E09.610
    neuropathy E09.40
    ophthalmic complication NEC
      E09.39
    oral complication NEC E09.638
    periodontal disease E09.630
    peripheral angiopathy E09.51
      with gangrene E09.52
    polyneuropathy E09.42
    renal complication NEC E09.29
    renal tubular degeneration E09.29
    retinopathy E09.319
      with macular edema E09.311
      nonproliferative E09.329
        with macular edema E09.321
        mild E09.329
          with macular edema E09.321
        moderate E09.339
          with macular edema E09.331
        severe E09.349
          with macular edema E09.341
      proliferative E09.359
        with macular edema E09.351
    skin complication NEC E09.628
    skin ulcer NEC E09.622
  due to underlying condition E08.9
  with
    amyotrophy E08.44
    arthropathy NEC E08.618
    autonomic (poly)neuropathy
      E08.43
    cataract E08.36
    Charcot's joints E08.610
    chronic kidney disease E08.22
    circulatory complication NEC
      E08.59

Diabetes, diabetic (Continued)
  due to underlying condition (Continued)
    with (Continued)
      complication E08.8
        specified NEC E08.69
      dermatitis E08.620
      foot ulcer E08.621
      gangrene E08.52
      gastroparesis E08.43
      glomerulonephrosis, intracapillary
        E08.21
      glomerulosclerosis, intercapillary
        E08.21
      hyperglycemia E08.65
      hyperosmolarity E08.00
        with coma E08.01
      hypoglycemia E08.640
        with coma E08.641
      ketoacidosis E08.10
        with coma E08.11
      kidney complications NEC E08.29
      Kimmelsteil-WIlson disease E08.21
      mononeuropathy E08.41
      myasthenia E08.44
      necrobiosis lipoidica E08.620
      nephropathy E08.21
      neuralgia E08.42
      neurologic complication NEC
        E08.49
      neuropathic arthropathy E08.610
      neuropathy E08.40
      ophthalmic complication NEC
        E08.39
      oral complication NEC E08.638
      periodontal disease E08.630
      peripheral angiopathy E08.51
        with gangrene E08.52
      polyneuropathy E08.42
      renal complication NEC E08.29
      renal tubular degeneration E08.29
      retinopathy E08.319
        with macular edema E08.311
        nonproliferative E08.329
          with macular edema E08.321
          mild E08.329
            with macular edema E08.321
          moderate E08.339
            with macular edema E08.331
          severe E08.349
            with macular edema E08.341
        proliferative E08.359
          with macular edema E08.351
      skin complication NEC E08.628
      skin ulcer NEC E08.622
  gestational (in pregnancy) O24.419
    affecting newborn P70.0
    diet-controlled O24.410
    in childbirth O24.429
      diet-controlled O24.420
      insulin (and diet) controlled O24.421
    insulin (and diet) controlled O24.411
    puerperal O24.439
      diet-controlled O24.430
      insulin (and diet) controlled O24.431
  inadequately controlled - code to Diabe-
    tes, by type, with hyperglycemia
  insipidus E23.2
    nephrogenic N25.1
    pituitary E23.2
    vasopressin resistant N25.1
  insulin dependent code to type of
    diabetes
  juvenile-onset - see Diabetes, type 1
  ketosis-prone - see Diabetes, type 1

Diabetes, diabetic (Continued)
  latent R73.09
  neonatal (transient) P70.2
  non-insulin dependent code to type of
    diabetes
  out of control - code to Diabetes, by
    type, with hyperglycemia
  phosphate E83.39
  poorly controlled - code to Diabetes, by
    type, with hyperglycemia
  specified type NEC E13.9
    with
      amyotrophy E13.44
      arthropathy NEC E13.618
      autonomic (poly)neuropathy E13.43
      cataract E13.36
      Charcot's joints E13.610
      chronic kidney disease E13.22
      circulatory complication NEC E13.59
      complication E13.8
        specified NEC E13.69
      dermatitis E13.620
      foot ulcer E13.621
      gangrene E13.52
      gastroparesis E13.43
      glomerulonephrosis, intracapillary
        E13.21
      glomerulosclerosis, intercapillary
        E13.21
      hyperglycemia E13.65
      hyperosmolarity E13.00
        with coma E13.01
      hypoglycemia E13.640
        with coma E13.641
      ketoacidosis E13.10
        with coma E13.11
      kidney complications NEC E13.29
      Kimmelsteil-Wilson disease E13.21
      mononeuropathy E13.41
      myasthenia E13.44
      necrobiosis lipoidica E13.620
      nephropathy E13.21
      neuralgia E13.42
      neurologic complication NEC E13.49
      neuropathic arthropathy E13.610
      neuropathy E13.40
      ophthalmic complication NEC E13.39
      oral complication NEC E13.638
      periodontal disease E13.630
      peripheral angiopathy E13.51
        with gangrene E13.52
      polyneuropathy E13.42
      renal complication NEC E13.29
      renal tubular degeneration E13.29
      retinopathy E13.319
        with macular edema E13.311
        nonproliferative E13.329
          with macular edema E13.321
          mild E13.329
            with macular edema E13.321
          moderate E13.339
            with macular edema E13.331
          severe E13.349
            with macular edema E13.341
        proliferative E13.359
          with macular edema E13.351
      skin complication NEC E13.628
      skin ulcer NEC E13.622
  steroid-induced - see Diabetes, due to,
    drug or chemical
  type 1 E10.9
    with
      amyotrophy E10.44
      arthropathy NEC E10.618

Diabetes, diabetic (Continued)
  type 1 (Continued)
    with (Continued)
      autonomic (poly)neuropathy
        E10.43
      cataract E10.36
      Charcot's joints E10.610
      chronic kidney disease E10.22
      circulatory complication NEC
        E10.59
      complication E10.8
        specified NEC E10.69
      dermatitis E10.620
      foot ulcer E10.621
      gangrene E10.52
      gastroparesis E10.43
      glomerulonephrosis, intracapillary
        E10.21
      glomerulosclerosis, intercapillary
        E10.21
      hyperglycemia E10.65
      hyperosmolarity E10.00
        with coma E10.01
      hypoglycemia E10.640
        with coma E10.641
      ketoacidosis E10.10
        with coma E10.11
      kidney complications NEC E10.29
      Kimmelsteil-Wilson disease E10.21
      mononeuropathy E10.41
      myasthenia E10.44
      necrobiosis lipoidica E10.620
      nephropathy E10.21
      neuralgia E10.42
      neurologic complication NEC
        E10.49
      neuropathic arthropathy E10.610
      neuropathy E10.40
      ophthalmic complication NEC
        E10.39
      oral complication NEC E10.638
      periodontal disease E10.630
      peripheral angiopathy E10.51
        with gangrene E10.52
      polyneuropathy E10.42
      renal complication NEC E10.29
      renal tubular degeneration E10.29
      retinopathy E10.319
        with macular edema E10.311
        nonproliferative E10.329
          with macular edema E10.321
          mild E10.329
            with macular edema E10.321
          moderate E10.339
            with macular edema E10.331
          severe E10.349
            with macular edema E10.341
        proliferative E10.359
          with macular edema E10.351
      skin complication NEC E10.628
      skin ulcer NEC E10.622
  type 2 E11.9
    with
      amyotrophy E11.44
      arthropathy NEC E11.618
      autonomic (poly)neuropathy
        E11.43
      cataract E11.36
      Charcot's joints E11.610
      chronic kidney disease E11.22
      circulatory complication NEC
        E11.59
      complication E11.8
        specified NEC E11.69

Diabetes, diabetic *(Continued)*
  type 2 *(Continued)*
    with *(Continued)*
      dermatitis E11.620
      foot ulcer E11.621
      gangrene E11.52
      gastroparesis E11.43
      glomerulonephrosis, intracapillary E11.21
      glomerulosclerosis, intercapillary E11.21
      hyperglycemia E11.65
      hyperosmolarity E11.00
        with coma E11.01
      hypoglycemia E11.640
        with coma E11.641
      kidney complications NEC E11.29
      Kimmelstiel-Wilson disease E11.21
      ketoacidosis E11.10
        with coma E11.11
      mononeuropathy E11.41
      myasthenia E11.44
      necrobiosis lipoidica E11.620
      nephropathy E11.21
      neuralgia E11.42
      neurologic complication NEC E11.49
      neuropathic arthropathy E11.610
      neuropathy E11.40
      ophthalmic complication NEC E11.39
      oral complication NEC E11.638
      periodontal disease E11.630
      peripheral angiopathy E11.51
        with gangrene E11.52
      polyneuropathy E11.42
      renal complication NEC E11.29
      renal tubular degeneration E11.29
      retinopathy E11.319
        with macular edema E11.311
        nonproliferative E11.329
          with macular edema E11.321
          mild E11.329
            with macular edema E11.321
          moderate E11.339
            with macular edema E11.331
          severe E11.349
            with macular edema E11.341
        proliferative E11.359
          with macular edema E11.351
      skin complication NEC E11.628
      skin ulcer NEC E11.622
Diacyclothrombopathia D69.1
Diagnosis deferred R69
Dialysis (intermittent) (treatment)
  noncompliance (with) Z91.15
  renal (hemodialysis) (peritoneal), status Z99.2
  retina, retinal - *see* Detachment, retina, with retinal, dialysis
Diamond-Blackfan anemia (congenital hypoplastic) D61.01
Diamond-Gardener syndrome (auto-erythrocyte sensitization) D69.2
Diaper rash L22
Diaphoresis (excessive) R61
Diaphragm - *see* condition
Diaphragmalgia R07.1
Diaphragmatitis, diaphragmitis J98.6
Diaphysial aclasis Q78.6
Diaphysitis - *see* Osteomyelitis, specified type NEC
Diarrhea, diarrheal (disease) (infantile) (inflammatory) R19.7
  achlorhydric K31.83

Diarrhea, diarrheal *(Continued)*
  allergic K52.2
  amebic (*see also* Amebiasis) A06.0
    with abscess - *see* Abscess, amebic
    acute A06.0
    chronic A06.1
    nondysenteric A06.2
  bacillary - *see* Dysentery, bacillary
  balantidial A07.0
  cachectic NEC K52.89
  Chilomastix A07.8
  choleriformis A00.1
  chronic (noninfectious) K52.9
  coccidial A07.3
  Cochin-China K90.1
    strongyloidiasis B78.0
  Dientamoeba A07.8
  dietetic K52.2
  due to
    bacteria A04.9
      specified NEC A04.8
    Campylobacter A04.5
    Capillaria philippinensis B81.1
    Clostridium difficile A04.7
    Clostridium perfringens (C) (F) A04.8
    Cryptosporidium A07.2
    Escherichia coli A04.4
      enteroaggregative A04.4
      enterohemorrhagic A04.3
      enteroinvasive A04.2
      enteropathogenic A04.0
      enterotoxigenic A04.1
      specified NEC A04.4
    food hypersensitivity K52.2
    Necator americanus B76.1
    S. japonicum B65.2
    specified organism NEC A08.8
      bacterial A04.8
      viral A08.3
    Staphylococcus A04.8
    Trichuris trichiura B79
    virus - *see* Enteritis, viral
    Yersinia enterocolitica A04.6
  dysenteric A09
  endemic A09
  epidemic A09
  flagellate A07.9
  Flexner's (ulcerative) A03.1
  functional K59.1
    following gastrointestinal surgery K91.89
    psychogenic F45.8
  Giardia lamblia A07.1
  giardial A07.1
  hill K90.1
  infectious A09
  malarial – *see* Malaria
  mite B88.0
  mycotic NEC B49
  neonatal (noninfectious) P78.3
  nervous F45.8
  neurogenic K59.1
  noninfectious K52.9
  postgastrectomy K91.1
  postvagotomy K91.1
  protozoal A07.9
    specified NEC A07.8
  psychogenic F45.8
  specified
    bacterium NEC A04.8
    virus NEC A08.3
  strongyloidiasis B78.0
  toxic K52.1

Diarrhea, diarrheal *(Continued)*
  trichomonal A07.8
  tropical K90.1
  tuberculous A18.32
  viral - *see* Enteritis, viral
Diastasis
  cranial bones M84.88
    congenital NEC Q75.8
  joint (traumatic) - *see* Dislocation
  muscle M62.00
    ankle M62.07-
    congenital Q79.8
    foot M62.07-
    forearm M62.03-
    hand M62.04-
    lower leg M62.06-
    pelvic region M62.05-
    shoulder region M62.01-
    specified site NEC M62.08
    thigh M62.05-
    upper arm M62.02-
  recti (abdomen)
    complicating delivery O71.89
    congenital Q79.59
Diastema, tooth, teeth, fully erupted M26.32
Diastematomyelia Q06.2
Diataxia, cerebral G80.4
Diathesis
  allergic - *see* History, allergy
  bleeding (familial) D69.9
  cystine (familial) E72.00
  gouty - *see* Gout
  hemorrhagic (familial) D69.9
    newborn NEC P53
  spasmophilic R29.0
Diaz's disease or osteochondrosis (juvenile) (talus) - *see* Osteochondrosis, juvenile, tarsus
Dibothriocephalus, dibothriocephaliasis (latus) (infection) (infestation) B70.0
  larval B70.1
Dicephalus, dicephaly Q89.4
Dichotomy, teeth K00.2
Dichromat, dichromatopsia (congenital) - *see* Deficiency, color vision
Dichuchwa A65
Dicroceliasis B66.2
Didelphia, didelphys - *see* Double uterus
Didymytis N45.1
  with orchitis N45.3
Dietary
  inadequacy or deficiency E63.9
  surveillance and counseling Z71.3
Dietl's crisis N13.8
Dieulafoy lesion (hemorrhagic)
  duodenum K31.82
  esophagus K22.8
  intestine (colon) K63.81
  stomach K31.82
Difficult, difficulty (in)
  acculturation Z60.3
  feeding R63.3
    newborn P92.9
      breast P92.5
      specified NEC P92.8
    nonorganic (infant or child) F98.29
  intubation, in anesthesia T88.4
  mechanical, gastroduodenal stoma K91.89
    causing obstruction K91.3
  reading (developmental) F81.0
    secondary to emotional disorders F93.9

Difficult, difficulty (in) *(Continued)*
  spelling (specific) F81.81
    with reading disorder F81.89
    due to inadequate teaching
      Z55.8
  swallowing - *see* Dysphagia
  walking R26.2
  work
    conditions NEC Z56.5
    schedule Z56.3
Diffuse - *see* condition
DiGeorge's syndrome (thymic hypoplasia) D82.1
Digestive - *see* condition
Diktyoma - *see* Neoplasm, malignant
Dilaceration, tooth K00.4
Dilatation
  anus K59.8
    venule - *see* Hemorrhoids
  aorta (focal) (general) - *see* Aneurysm, aorta
  artery - *see* Aneurysm
  bladder (sphincter) N32.89
    congenital Q64.79
  blood vessel I99.8
  bronchial J47.9
    with
      exacerbation (acute) J47.1
      lower respiratory infection
        J47.0
  calyx (due to obstruction) - *see*
    Hydronephrosis
  capillaries I78.8
  cardiac (acute) (chronic) - *see also*
    Hypertrophy, cardiac
    congenital Q24.8
      valve NEC Q24.8
        pulmonary Q22.2
    valve - *see* Endocarditis
  cavum septi pellucidi Q06.8
  cervix (uteri) - *see also* Incompetency, cervix
    incomplete, poor, slow complicating
      delivery O62.0
  colon K59.3
    congenital Q43.1
    psychogenic F45.8
  common duct (acquired) K83.8
    congenital Q44.5
  cystic duct (acquired) K82.8
    congenital Q44.5
  duct, mammary – *see* Ectasia, mammary duct
  duodenum K59.8
  esophagus K22.8
    congenital Q39.5
    due to achalasia K22.0
  eustachian tube, congenital Q17.8
  gallbladder K82.8
  gastric - *see* Dilatation, stomach
  heart (acute) (chronic) - *see also* Hypertrophy, cardiac
    congenital Q24.8
    valve - *see* Endocarditis
  ileum K59.8
    psychogenic F45.8
  jejunum K59.8
    psychogenic F45.8
  kidney (calyx) (collecting structures) (cystic) (parenchyma) (pelvis) (idiopathic) N28.89
  lacrimal passages or duct - *see* Disorder, lacrimal system, changes
  lymphatic vessel I89.0

Dilatation *(Continued)*
  mammary duct – *see* Ectasia, mammary duct
  Meckel's diverticulum (congenital) Q43.0
  myocardium (acute) (chronic) - *see* Hypertrophy, cardiac organ or site, congenital NEC - *see* Distortion
  pancreatic duct K86.8
  pericardium - *see* Pericarditis
  pharynx J39.2
  prostate N42.89
  pulmonary
    artery (idiopathic) I28.8
    valve, congenital Q22.2
  pupil H57.04
  rectum K59.3
  saccule, congenital Q16.5
  salivary gland (duct) K11.8
  sphincter ani K62.8
  stomach K31.89
    acute K31.0
    psychogenic F45.8
  submaxillary duct K11.8
  trachea, congenital Q32.1
  ureter (idiopathic) N28.82
    congenital Q62.2
    due to obstruction N13.4
  urethra (acquired) N36.8
  vasomotor I73.9
  vein I86.8
  ventricular, ventricle (acute) (chronic)
    - *see also* Hypertrophy, cardiac
    cerebral, congenital Q04.8
  venule NEC I86.8
  vesical orifice N32.89
Dilated, dilation - *see* Dilatation
Diminished, diminution
  hearing (acuity) - *see* Deafness
  sense or sensation (cold) (heat) (tactile) (vibratory) R20.8
  vision NEC H54.7
  vital capacity R94.2
Diminuta taenia B71.0
Dimitri-Sturge-Weber disease Q85.8
Dimple
  parasacral, pilonidal or postanal - *see* Cyst, pilonidal
Dioctophyme renalis (infection) (infestation) B83.8
Dipetalonemiasis B74.4
Diphallus Q55.69
Diphtheria, diphtheritic (gangrenous) (hemorrhagic) A36.9
  carrier (suspected) Z22.2
  cutaneous A36.3
  faucial A36.0
  infection of wound A36.3
  laryngeal A36.2
  myocarditis A36.81
  nasal, anterior A36.89
  nasopharyngeal A36.1
  neurological complication A36.89
  pharyngeal A36.0
  specified site NEC A36.89
  tonsillar A36.0
Diphyllobothriasis (intestine) B70.0
  larval B70.1
Diplacusis H93.22-
Diplegia (upper limbs) G83.0
  congenital (cerebral) G80.8
  facial G51.0
  lower limbs G82.20
  spastic G80.1

Diplococcus, diplococcal - *see* condition
Diplopia H53.2
Dipsomania F10.20
  with
    psychosis -*see* Psychosis, alcoholic
    remission F10.21
Dipylidiasis B71.1
Direction, teeth, abnormal, fully erupted M26.30
Dirofilariasis B74.8
Dirt-eating child F98.3
Disability
  heart - *see* Disease, heart
  knowledge acquisition F81.9
  learning F81.9
  limiting activities Z73.6
  spelling, specific F81.81
Disappearance of family member Z63.4
Disarticulation - *see* Amputation
  meaning traumatic amputation - *see* Amputation, traumatic
Discharge (from)
  abnormal finding in - *see* Abnormal, specimen
  breast (female) (male) N64.52
  diencephalic autonomic idiopathic – *see* Epilepsy, specified NEC
  ear - *see also* Otorrhea
    blood - *see* Otorrhagia
  excessive urine R35.8
  nipple N64.52
  penile R36.9
  postnasal R09.82
  prison, anxiety concerning Z65.2
  urethral R36.9
    without blood R36.0
    hematospermia R36.1
  vaginal N89.8
Discitis, diskitis M46.40
  cervical region M46.42
  cervicothoracic region M46.43
  lumbar region M46.46
  lumbosacral region M46.47
  multiple sites M46.49
  occipito-atlanto-axial region M46.41
  pyogenic - *see* Infection, intervertebral disc, pyogenic
  sacrococcygeal region M46.48
  thoracic region M46.44
  thoracolumbar region M46.45
Discoid
  meniscus (congenital) Q68.6
  semilunar cartilage (congenital) - *see* Derangement, knee, meniscus, specified NEC
Discoloration
  nails L60.8
  teeth (posteruptive) K03.7
    during formation K00.8
Discomfort
  chest R07.89
  visual H53.14-
Discontinuity, ossicles, ear H74.2-
Discord (with)
  boss Z56.4
  classmates Z55.4
  counselor Z64.4
  employer Z56.4
  family Z63.8
  fellow employees Z56.4
  in-laws Z63.1
  landlord Z59.2
  lodgers Z59.2
  neighbors Z59.2

Discord (with) (*Continued*)
  probation officer Z64.4
  social worker Z64.4
  teachers Z55.4
  workmates Z56.4
Discordant connection
  atrioventricular (congenital) Q20.5
  ventriculoarterial Q20.3
Discrepancy
  centric occlusion maximum intercuspa-
      tion M26.55
  leg length (acquired) - *see* Deformity,
      limb, unequal length
    congenital – *see* Defect, reduction,
        lower limb
  uterine size date O26.84-
Discrimination
  ethnic Z60.5
  political Z60.5
  racial Z60.5
  religious Z60.5
  sex Z60.5
Disease, diseased - *see also* Syndrome
  absorbent system I87.8
  acid-peptic K30
  Acosta's T70.29
  Adams-Stokes (-Morgagni) (syncope
      with heart block) I45.9
  Addison's anemia (pernicious) D51.0
  adenoids (and tonsils) J35.9
  adrenal (capsule) (cortex) (gland) (med-
      ullary) E27.9
    hyperfunction E27.0
    specified NEC E27.8
  ainhum L94.6
  airway
    obstructive, chronic J44.9
      due to
        cotton dust J66.0
        specific organic dusts NEC J66.8
    reactive - *see* Asthma
  akamushi (scrub typhus) A75.3
  Albers-Schönberg's (marble bones)
      Q78.2
  Albert's - *see* Tendinitis, Achilles
  alimentary canal K63.9
  alligator-skin Q80.9
    acquired L85.0
  alpha heavy chain C88.3
  alpine T70.29
  altitude T70.20
  alveolar ridge
    edentulous K06.9
      specified NEC K06.8
  alveoli, teeth K08.9
  Alzheimer's G30.9 [F02.80]
    with behavioral disturbance G30.9
        [F02.81]
    early onset G30.0 [F02.80]
      with behavioral disturbance G30.0
          [F02.81]
    late onset G30.1 [F02.80]
      with behavioral disturbance G30.1
          [F02.81]
    specified NEC G30.8 [F02.80]
      with behavioral disturbance G30.8
          [F02.81]
  amyloid - *see* Amyloidosis
  Andersen's (glycogenosis IV) E74.09
  Andes T70.29
  Andrews' (bacterid) L08.89
  angiospastic I73.9
    cerebral G45.9
    vein I87.8

Disease, diseased (*Continued*)
  anterior
    chamber H21.9
    horn cell G12.29
  antiglomerular basement membrane
      (antiGBM) antibody M31.0
    tubulo-interstitial nephritis N12
  antral – *see* Sinusitis, maxillary
  anus K62.9
    specified NEC K62.8
  aorta (nonsyphilitic) I77.9
    syphilitic NEC A52.02
  aortic (heart) (valve) I35.9
    rheumatic I06.9
  Apollo B30.3
  aponeuroses - *see* Enthesopathy
  appendix K38.9
    specified NEC K38.8
  aqueous (chamber) H21.9
  Arnold-Chiari - *see* Arnold-Chiari
      disease
  arterial I77.9
    occlusive – *see* Occlusion, by site
      due to stricture or stenosis I77.1
  arteriocardiorenal - *see* Hypertension,
      cardiorenal
  arteriolar (generalized) (obliterative)
      I77.9
  arteriorenal - *see* Hypertension, kidney
  arteriosclerotic - *see also* Arteriosclerosis
    cardiovascular – *see* Disease, heart,
        ischemic, atherosclerotic
    coronary (artery) – *see* Disease, heart,
        ischemic, atherosclerotic
    heart – *see* Disease, heart, ischemic,
        atherosclerotic
  artery I77.9
    cerebral I67.9
    coronary I25.10
      with angina pectoris - *see* Arterio-
          sclerosis, coronary (artery),
  arthropod-borne NOS (viral) A94
    specified type NEC A93.8
  atticoantral, chronic H66.20
    left H66.22
      with right H66.23
    right H66.21
      with left H66.23
  auditory canal - *see* Disorder, ear,
      external
  auricle, ear NEC - *see* Disorder, pinna
  Australian X A83.4
  autoimmune (systemic) NOS M35.9
    hemolytic (cold type) (warm type)
        D59.1
      drug-induced D59.0
    thyroid E06.3
  aviator's - *see* Effect, adverse, high
      altitude
  Ayala's Q78.5
  Ayerza's (pulmonary artery sclerosis
      with pulmonary hypertension)
      I27.0
  Babington's (familial hemorrhagic
      telangiectasia) I78.0
  bacterial A49.9
    specified NEC A48.8
    zoonotic A28.9
      specified type NEC A28.8
  Baelz's (cheilitis glandularis apostema-
      tosa) K13.0
  bagasse J67.1
  balloon - *see* Effect, adverse, high
      altitude

Disease, diseased (*Continued*)
  Bang's (brucella abortus) A23.1
  Bannister's T78.3
  barometer makers' – *see* Poisoning,
      mercury
  Barraquer (-Simons') (progressive lipo-
      dystrophy) E88.1
  Barrett's - *see* Barrett's, esophagus
  Bartholin's gland N75.9
  basal ganglia G25.9
    degenerative G23.9
      specified NEC G23.8
    specified NEC G25.89
  Basedow's (exophthalmic goiter) - *see*
      Hyperthyroidism, with, goiter
      (diffuse)
  Bateman's B08.1
  Batten-Steinert G71.11
  Battey A31.0
  Beard's (neurasthenia) F48.8
  Becker
    idiopathic mural endomyocardial
        I42.3
    myotonia congenita G71.12
  Begbie's (exophthalmic goiter) - *see*
      Hyperthyroidism, with, goiter
      (diffuse)
  Beigel's (white piedra) B36.2
  behavioral, organic F07.9
  Benson's - *see* Deposit, crystalline
  Bernard-Soulier (thrombopathy) D69.1
  Bernhardt (-Roth) - *see* Mononeu-
      ropathy, lower limb, meralgia
      paresthetica
  Biermer's (pernicious anemia) D51.0
  bile duct (common) (hepatic) K83.9
    with calculus, stones - *see* Calculus,
        bile duct
    specified NEC K83.8
  biliary (tract) K83.9
    specified NEC K83.8
  Billroth's – *see* Spina bifida
  bird fancier's J67.2
  black lung J60
  bladder N32.9
    in (due to)
      schistosomiasis (bilharziasis) B65.0
          [N33]
    specified NEC N32.89
  bleeder's D66
  blood D75.9
    forming organs D75.9
    vessel I99.9
  Bloodgood's - *see* Mastopathy, cystic
  Bodechtel-Guttmann (subacute scleros-
      ing panencephalitis) A81.1
  bone - *see also* Disorder, bone
    aluminum M83.4
    fibrocystic NEC
      jaw M27.49
  bone-marrow D75.9
  Borna A83.9
  Bornholm (epidemic pleurodynia) B33.0
  Bouchard's (myopathic dilatation of the
      stomach) K31.0
  Bouillaud's (rheumatic heart disease)
      I01.9
  Bourneville (-Brissaud) (tuberous scle-
      rosis) Q85.1
  Bouveret (-Hoffmann) (paroxysmal
      tachycardia) I47.9
  bowel K63.9
    functional K59.9
      psychogenic F45.8

Disease, diseased *(Continued)*
  brain G93.9
    arterial, artery I67.9
    arteriosclerotic I67.2
    congenital Q04.9
    degenerative - *see* Degeneration,
      brain
    inflammatory - *see* Encephalitis
    organic G93.9
      arteriosclerotic I67.2
    parasitic NEC B71.9 [G94]
    senile NEC G31.1
    specified NEC G93.89
  breast *(see also* Disorder, breast) N64.9
    cystic (chronic) – *see* Mastopathy,
      cystic
    fibrocystic – *see* Mastopathy, cystic
    Paget's
      female, unspecified side C50.91-
      male, unspecified side C50.92-
    specified NEC N64.89
  Breda's – *see* Yaws
  Bretonneau's (diphtheritic malignant
    angina) A36.0
  Bright's – *see* Nephritis
    arteriosclerotic - *see* Hypertension,
      kidney
  Brill's (recrudescent typhus) A75.1
  Brill-Zinsser (recrudescent typhus)
    A75.1
  Brion-Kayser – *see* Fever, paratyphoid
  broad
    beta E78.2
    ligament (noninflammatory) N83.9
      inflammatory - *see* Disease, pelvis,
        inflammatory
      specified NEC N83.8
  Brocq-Duhring (dermatitis herpetifor-
    mis) L13.0
  Brocq's
    meaning
      dermatitis herpetiformis L13.0
      prurigo L28.2
  bronchopulmonary J98.4
  bronchus NEC J98.09
  bronze Addison's E27.1
    tuberculous A18.7
  budgerigar fancier's J67.2
  bullous L13.9
    chronic of childhood L12.2
    specified NEC L13.8
  Buerger's (thromboangiitis obliterans)
    I73.1
  Bürger-Grüütz (essential familial hyper-
    lipemia) E78.3
  bursa - *see* Bursopathy
  caisson T70.3
  California - *see* Coccidioidomycosis
  capillaries I78.9
    specified NEC I78.8
  Carapata A68.0
  cardiac - *see* Disease, heart
  cardiopulmonary, chronic I27.9
  cardiorenal (hepatic) (hypertensive)
    (vascular) - *see* Hypertension,
    cardiorenal
  cardiovascular (atherosclerotic) I25.10
    with angina pectoris - *see* Arterioscle-
      rosis, coronary (artery),
    congenital Q28.9
    newborn P29.9
      specified NEC P29.89
    hypertensive - *see* Hypertension,
      heart

Disease, diseased *(Continued)*
  cardiovascular *(Continued)*
    renal (hypertensive) - *see* Hyperten-
      sion, cardiorenal
    syphilitic (asymptomatic) A52.00
  cartilage - *see* Disorder, cartilage
  Castellani's A69.8
  cat-scratch A28.1
  Cavare's (familial periodic paralysis)
    G72.3
  cecum K63.9
  celiac (adult) (infantile) K90.0
  cellular tissue L98.9
  central core G71.2
  cerebellar, cerebellum - *see* Disease,
    brain
  cerebral - *see also* Disease, brain
    degenerative - *see* Degeneration,
      brain
  cerebrospinal G96.9
  cerebrovascular I67.9
    acute I67.8
      embolic I63.4-
      thrombotic I63.3-
    arteriosclerotic I67.2
    specified NEC I67.8
  cervix (uteri) (noninflammatory) N88.9
    inflammatory - *see* Cervicitis
    specified NEC N88.8
  Chabert's A22.9
  Chandler's (osteochondritis dissecans,
    hip) - *see* Osteochondritis, dis-
    secans, hip
  Charlouis – *see* Yaws
  Chédiak-Steinbrinck (-Higashi) (con-
    genital gigantism of peroxidase
    granules) D72.0
  chest J98.9
  Chiari's (hepatic vein thrombosis) I82.0
  Chicago B40.9
  Chignon (white piedra) B36.2
  chigo, chigoe B88.1
  childhood granulomatous D71
  Chinese liver fluke B66.1
  chlamydial A74.9
    specified NEC A74.89
  cholecystic K82.9
  choroid H31.9
    specified NEC H31.8
  Christmas D67
  chronic bullous of childhood L12.2
  chylomicron retention E78.3
  ciliary body H21.9
    specified NEC H21.89
  circulatory (system) NEC I99.8
    newborn P29.9
    syphilitic A52.00
      congenital A50.54
  coagulation factor deficiency (congeni-
    tal) - *see* Defect, coagulation
  coccidioidal - *see* Coccidioidomycosis
  cold
    agglutinin or hemoglobinuria D59.1
      paroxysmal D59.6
    hemagglutinin (chronic) D59.1
  collagen NOS (nonvascular) (vascular)
    M35.9
    specified NEC M35.8
  colon K63.9
    functional K59.9
      congenital Q43.2
    ischemic K55.0
  combined system - *see* Degeneration,
    combined

Disease, diseased *(Continued)*
  compressed air T70.3
  Concato's (pericardial polyserositis)
    I31.1
    pleural - *see* Pleurisy, with effusion
  conjunctiva H11.9
    chlamydial A74.0
    specified NEC H11.89
    viral B30.9
      specified NEC B30.8
  connective tissue, systemic (diffuse)
    M35.9
    in (due to)
      hypogammaglobulinemia D80.1
        [M36.8]
      ochronosis E70.29 [M36.8]
    specified NEC M35.8
  Conor and Bruch's (boutonneuse fever)
    A77.1
  Cooper's – *see* Mastopathy, cystic
  Cori's (glycogenosis III) E74.03
  corkhandler's or corkworker's J67.3
  cornea H18.9
    specified NEC H18.89-
  coronary (artery) – *see* Disease, heart,
    ischemic, atherosclerotic
    congenital Q24.5
    ostial, syphilitic (aortic) (mitral) (pul-
      monary) A52.03
  corpus cavernosum N48.9
    specified NEC N48.89
  Cotugno's - *see* Sciatica
  coxsackie (virus) NEC B34.1
  cranial nerve NOS G52.9
  Creutzfeldt-Jakob - *see* Creutzfeldt-
    Jakob disease or syndrome
  Crocq's (acrocyanosis) I73.89
  Crohn's – *see* Enteritis, regional
  Curschmann's G71.19
  cystic
    breast (chronic) – *see* Mastopathy,
      cystic
    kidney, congenital Q61.9
    liver, congenital Q44.6
    lung J98.4
      congenital Q33.0
  cytomegalic inclusion (generalized)
    B25.9
    with pneumonia B25.0
    congenital P35.1
  cytomegaloviral B25.9
    specified NEC B25.8
  Czerny's (periodic hydrarthrosis of the
    knee) - *see* Effusion, joint, knee
  Daae (-Finsen) (epidemic pleurodynia)
    B33.0
  Darling's – *see* Histoplasmosis capsulati
  Débove's (splenomegaly) R16.1
  deer fly – *see* Tularemia
  Degos' I77.8
  demyelinating, demyelinizating (ner-
    vous system) G37.9
    multiple sclerosis G35
    specified NEC G37.8
  dense deposit *(see also* N00-N07 with
    fourth character .6) N05.6
  deposition, hydroxyapatite - *see* Dis-
    ease, hydroxyapatite deposition
  de Quervain's (tendon sheath) M65.4
    thyroid (subacute granulomatous
      thyroiditis) E06.1
  Devergie's (pityriasis rubra pilaris) L44.0
  Devic's G36.0
  diaphorase deficiency D74.0

Disease, diseased *(Continued)*
  diaphragm J98.6
  diarrheal, infectious NEC A09
  digestive system K92.9
    specified NEC K92.89
  disc, degenerative - *see* Degeneration, intervertebral disc
  discogenic - *see also* Displacement, intervertebral disc NEC
    with myelopathy - *see* Disorder, disc, with, myelopathy
  diverticular - *see* Diverticula
  Dubois (thymus) A50.59
  Duchenne-Griesinger G71.0
  Duchenne's
    muscular dystrophy G71.0
    pseudohypertrophy, muscles G71.0
  ductless glands E34.9
  Duhring's (dermatitis herpetiformis) L13.0
  duodenum K31.9
    specified NEC K31.89
  Dupré's (meningism) R29.1
  Dupuytren's (muscle contracture) M72.0
  Durand-Nicholas-Favre (climatic bubo) A55
  Duroziez's (congenital mitral stenosis) Q23.2
  ear - *see* Disorder, ear
  Eberth's – *see* Fever, typhoid
  Ebola (virus) A98.4
  Ebstein's heart Q22.5
  Echinococcus - *see* Echinococcus
  echovirus NEC B34.1
  Eddowes' (brittle bones and blue sclera) Q78.0
  edentulous (alveolar) ridge K06.9
    specified NEC K06.8
  Edsall's T67.2
  Eichstedt's (pityriasis versicolor) B36.0
  Ellis-van Creveld (chondroectodermal dysplasia) Q77.6
  end stage renal (ESRD) N18.6
    due to hypertension I12.0
  endocrine glands or system NEC E34.9
  endomyocardial (eosinophilic) I42.3
  English (rickets) E55.0
  enteroviral, enterovirus NEC B34.1
    central nervous system NEC A88.8
  epidemic B99.9
    specified NEC B99.8
  epididymis N50.9
  Erb (-Landouzy) G71.0
  esophagus K22.9
    functional K22.4
    psychogenic F45.8
    specified NEC K22.8
  Erdheim-Chester (ECD) E88.89
  Eulenburg's (congenital paramyotonia) G71.19
  eustachian tube – *see* Disorder, eustachian tube
  external
    auditory canal - *see* Disorder, ear, external
    ear - *see* Disorder, ear, external
  extrapyramidal G25.9
    specified NEC G25.89
  eye H57.9
    anterior chamber H21.9
    inflammatory NEC H57.8
    muscle (external) - *see* Strabismus
    specified NEC H57.8
    syphilitic - *see* Oculopathy, syphilitic

Disease, diseased *(Continued)*
  eyeball H44.9
    specified NEC H44.89
  eyelid - *see* Disorder, eyelid
    specified NEC - *see* Disorder, eyelid, specified type NEC
  eyeworm of Africa B74.3
  facial nerve (seventh) G51.9
    newborn (birth injury) P11.3
  Fahr (of brain) G23.8
  Fahr Volhard (of kidney) I12.-
  fallopian tube (noninflammatory) N83.9
    inflammatory - *see* Salpingo-oophoritis
    specified NEC N83.8
  familial periodic paralysis G72.3
  Fanconi's (congenital pancytopenia) D61.09
  fascia NEC *see also* Disorder, muscle
    inflammatory - *see* Myositis
    specified NEC M62.89
  Fauchard's (periodontitis) - *see* Periodontitis
  Favre-Durand-Nicolas (climatic bubo) A55
  Fede's K14.0
  Feer's – *see* Poisoning, mercury
  female pelvic inflammatory (*see also* Disease, pelvis, inflammatory) N73.9
    syphilitic (secondary) A51.42
    tuberculous A18.17
  Fernels' (aortic aneurysm) I71.9
  fibrocaseous of lung - *see* Tuberculosis, pulmonary
  fibrocystic - *see* Fibrocystic disease
  Fiedler's (leptospiral jaundice) A27.0
  fifth B08.3
  file-cutter's – *see* Poisoning, lead
  fish-skin Q80.9
    acquired L85.0
  Flajani (-Basedow) (exophthalmic goiter) - *see* Hyperthyroidism, with, goiter (diffuse)
  flax-dresser's J66.1
  fluke – *see* Infestation, fluke
  foot and mouth B08.8
  foot process - *see* Nephrosis
  Forbes' (glycogenosis III) E74.03
  Fordyce-Fox (apocrine miliaria) L75.2
  Fordyce's (ectopic sebaceous glands) (mouth) Q38.6
  Forestier's (rhizomelic pseudopolyarthritis) M35.3
    meaning ankylosing hyperostosis - *see* Hyperostosis, ankylosing
  Fothergill's
    neuralgia – *see* Neuralgia, trigeminal
    scarlatina anginosa A38.9
  Fournier's N49.3
  fourth B08.8
  Fox (-Fordyce) (apocrine miliaria) L75.2
  Francis' – *see* Tularemia
  Franklin's C88.2
  Frei's (climatic bubo) A55
  Friedreich's
    combined systemic or ataxia G11.1
    myoclonia G25.3
  frontal sinus – *see* Sinusitis, frontal
  fungus NEC B49
  Gaisböck's (polycythemia hypertonica) D75.1
  gallbladder K82.9
    calculus – *see* Calculus, gallbladder
    cholecystitis – *see* Cholecystitis
    cholesterolosis K82.4

Disease, diseased *(Continued)*
  gallbladder *(Continued)*
    fistula – *see* Fistula, gallbladder
    hydrops K82.1
    obstruction – *see* Obstruction, gallbladder
    perforation K82.2
    specified NEC K82.8
  gamma heavy chain C88.2
  Gamna's (siderotic splenomegaly) D73.2
  Gamstorp's (adynamia episodica hereditaria) G72.3
  Gandy-Nanta (siderotic splenomegaly) D73.2
  ganister J62.8
  gastric - *see* Disease, stomach
  gastroesophageal reflux (GERD) K21.9
    with esophagitis K21.0
  gastrointestinal (tract) K92.9
    amyloid E85.4
    functional K59.9
      psychogenic F45.8
    specified NEC K92.89
  Gee (-Herter) (-Heubner) (-Thaysen) (nontropical sprue) K90.0
  genital organs
    female N94.9
    male N50.9
  Gerhardt's (erythromelalgia) I73.81
  Gibert's (pityriasis rosea) L42
  Gierke's (glycogenosis I) E74.01
  Gilles de la Tourette's (motor-verbal tic) F95.2
  gingiva K06.9
    specified NEC K06.8
  gland (lymph) I89.9
  Glanzmann's (hereditary hemorrhagic thrombasthenia) D69.1
  glass-blower's (cataract) - *see* Cataract, specified NEC
    salivary gland hypertrophy K11.1
  Glisson's – *see* Rickets
  globe H44.9
    specified NEC H44.89
  glomerular - *see also* Glomerulonephritis
    with edema - *see* Nephrosis
    acute – *see* Nephritis, acute
    chronic - *see* Nephritis, chronic
    minimal change N05.0
    rapidly progressive N01.9
  glycogen storage E74.00
    Andersen's E74.09
    Cori's E74.03
    Forbes' E74.03
    generalized E74.00
    glucose-6-phosphatase deficiency E74.01
    heart E74.02 [I43]
    hepatorenal E74.09
    Hers' E74.09
    liver and kidney E74.01
    McArdle's E74.04
    muscle phosphofructokinase E74.09
    myocardium E74.02 [I43]
    Pompe's E74.02
    Tauri's E74.09
    type 0 E74.09
    type I E74.01
    type II E74.02
    type III E74.03
    type IV E74.09
    type V E74.04
    type VI-XI E74.09
    Von Gierke's E74.01

Disease, diseased *(Continued)*
  Goldstein's (familial hemorrhagic telangiectasia) I78.0
  gonococcal NOS A54.9
  graft-versus-host (GVH) D89.813
    acute D89.810
    acute on chronic D89.812
    chronic D89.811
  grainhandler's J67.8
  granulomatous (childhood) (chronic) D71
  Graves' (exophthalmic goiter) - *see* Hyperthyroidism, with, goiter (diffuse)
  Griesinger's - *see* Ancylostomiasis
  Grisel's M43.6
  Gruby's (tinea tonsurans) B35.0
  Guillain-Barré G61.0
  Guinon's (motor-verbal tic) F95.2
  gum K06.9
  gynecological N94.9
  H (Hartnup's) E72.02
  Haff - *see* Poisoning, mercury
  Hageman (congenital factor XII deficiency) D68.2
  hair (color) (shaft) L67.9
    follicles L73.9
      specified NEC L73.8
  Hamman's (spontaneous mediastinal emphysema) J98.2
  hand, foot and mouth B08.4
  Hansen's - *see* Leprosy
  Hantavirus, with pulmonary manifestations B33.4
    with renal manifestations A98.5
  Harada's H30.81-
  Hartnup (pellagra-cerebellar ataxia-renal aminoaciduria) E72.02
  Hart's (pellagra-cerebellar ataxia-renal aminoaciduria) E72.02
  Hashimoto's (struma lymphomatosa) E06.3
  Hb - *see* Disease, hemoglobin
  heart (organic) I51.9
    with
      pulmonary edema (acute) (*see also* Failure, ventricular, left) I50.1
      rheumatic fever (conditions in I00)
        active I01.9
          with chorea I02.0
          specified NEC I01.8
        inactive or quiescent (with chorea) I09.9
          specified NEC I09.89
    amyloid E85.4 [I43]
    aortic (valve) I35.9
    arteriosclerotic or sclerotic (senile) - *see* Disease, heart, ischemic, atherosclerotic
    artery, arterial - *see* Disease, heart, ischemic, atherosclerotic
    beer drinkers' I42.6
    beriberi (wet) E51.12
    black I27.0
    congenital Q24.9
      cyanotic Q24.9
      specified NEC Q24.8
    coronary - *see* Disease, heart, ischemic
    cryptogenic I51.9
    fibroid - *see* Myocarditis
    functional I51.89
      psychogenic F45.8
    glycogen storage E74.02 [I43]
    gonococcal A54.83
    hypertensive - *see* Hypertension, heart

Disease, diseased *(Continued)*
  heart *(Continued)*
    hyperthyroid (*see also* Hyperthyroidism) E05.90 [I43]
      with thyroid storm E05.91 [I43]
    ischemic (chronic or with a stated duration of over 4 weeks) I25.9
      atherosclerotic (of) I25.10
        with angina pectoris - *see* Arteriosclerosis, coronary (artery)
        coronary artery bypass graft - *see* Arteriosclerosis, coronary (artery),
      cardiomyopathy I25.5
      diagnosed on ECG or other special investigation, but currently presenting no symptoms I25.6
      silent I25.6
      specified form NEC I25.89
    kyphoscoliotic I27.1
    meningococcal A39.50
      endocarditis A39.51
      myocarditis A39.52
      pericarditis A39.53
    mitral I05.9
      specified NEC I05.8
    muscular - *see* Degeneration, myocardial
    psychogenic (functional) F45.8
    pulmonary (chronic) I27.9
      in schistosomiasis B65.9 [I52]
      specified NEC I27.89
    rheumatic (chronic) (inactive) (old) (quiescent) (with chorea) I09.9
      active or acute I01.9
        with chorea (acute) (rheumatic) (Sydenham's) I02.0
      specified NEC I09.89
    senile - *see* Myocarditis
    syphilitic A52.06
      aortic A52.03
        aneurysm A52.01
      congenital A50.54 [I52]
    thyrotoxic (*see also* Thyrotoxicosis) E05.90 [I43]
      with thyroid storm E05.91 [I43]
    valve, valvular (obstructive) (regurgitant) - *see also* Endocarditis
      congenital NEC Q24.8
        pulmonary Q22.3
    vascular - *see* Disease, cardiovascular
  heavy chain NEC C88.2
    alpha C88.3
    gamma C88.2
    mu C88.2
  Hebra's
    pityriasis
      maculata et circinata L42
      rubra pilaris L44.0
    prurigo L28.2
  hematopoietic organs D75.9
  hemoglobin or Hb
    abnormal (mixed) NEC D58.2
      with thalassemia D56.9
    AS genotype D57.3
    Bart's D56.8
    C (Hb-C) D58.2
      with other abnormal hemoglobin NEC D58.2
      elliptocytosis D58.1
      Hb-S D57.2-
      sickle-cell D57.2-
    thalassemia D56.9
    D (Hb-D) D58.2

Disease, diseased *(Continued)*
  hemoglobin or Hb *(Continued)*
    E (Hb-E) D58.2
      elliptocytosis D58.1
    H (Hb-H) (thalassemia) D56.0
      with other abnormal hemoglobin NEC D56.9
    I thalassemia D56.9
    M D74.0
    S or SS D57.1
    SC D57.2-
    SD D57.8-
    SE D57.8-
    spherocytosis D58.0
    unstable, hemolytic D58.2
  hemolytic (newborn) P55.9
    autoimmune (cold type) (warm type) D59.1
    drug-induced D59.0
    due to or with
      incompatibility
        ABO (blood group) P55.1
        blood (group) (Duffy) (K(ell)) (Kidd) (Lewis) (M) (S) NEC P55.8
        Rh (blood group) (factor) P55.0
      Rh negative mother P55.0
    specified type NEC P55.8
    unstable hemoglobin D58.2
  hemorrhagic D69.9
    newborn P53
  Henoch (-Schönlein) (purpura nervosa) D69.0
  hepatic - *see* Disease, liver
  hepatolenticular E83.01
  heredodegenerative NEC
    spinal cord G95.89
  herpesviral, disseminated B00.7
  Hers' (glycogenosis VI) E74.09
  Herter (-Gee) (-Heubner) (nontropical sprue) K90.0
  Heubner-Herter (nontropical sprue) K90.0
  high fetal gene or hemoglobin thalassemia D56.9
  Hildenbrand's - *see* Typhus
  hip (joint) M25.9
    congenital Q65.8
    suppurative M00.9
    tuberculous A18.02
  His (-Werner) (trench fever) A79.0
  Hodgson's I71.9
    ruptured I71.8
  Holla - *see* Spherocytosis
  hookworm B76.9
    specified NEC B76.8
  host-versus-graft D89.813
    acute D89.810
    acute on chronic D89.812
    chronic D89.811
  human immunodeficiency virus (HIV) B20
  Huntington's G10
  Hutchinson's (cheiropompholyx) L30.1
  hyaline (diffuse) (generalized)
    membrane (lung) (newborn) P22.0
      adult J80
  hydatid - *see* Echinococcus
  hydroxyapatite deposition M11.00
    ankle M11.07-
    elbow M11.02-
    foot joint M11.07-
    hand joint M11.04-

Disease, diseased *(Continued)*
  hydroxyapatite deposition *(Continued)*
    hip M11.05-
    knee M11.06-
    multiple site M11.09
    shoulder M11.01-
    vertebra M11.08
    wrist M11.03-
  hyperkinetic - *see* Hyperkinesia
  hypertensive - *see* Hypertension
  hypophysis E23.7
  Iceland G93.3
  I-cell E77.0
  immune D89.9
  immunoproliferative (malignant) C88.9
    small intestinal C88.3
    specified NEC C88.8
  inclusion B25.9
    salivary gland B25.9
  infectious, infective B99.9
    congenital P37.9
      specified NEC P37.8
    viral
    specified NEC B99.8
  inflammatory
    penis N48.29
      abscess N48.21
      cellulitis N48.22
    prepuce N47.7
      balanoposthitis N47.6
    tubo-ovarian – *see*
      Salpingo-oophoritis
  intervertebral disc - *see also* Disorder, disc
    with myelopathy - *see* Disorder, disc, with, myelopathy
    cervical, cervicothoracic - *see* Disorder, disc, cervical
    with
      myelopathy - *see* Disorder, disc, cervical, with myelopathy
      neuritis, radiculitis or radiculopathy - *see* Disorder, disc, cervical, with neuritis
      specified NEC - *see* Disorder, disc, cervical, specified type NEC
    lumbar (with)
      myelopathy M51.06
      neuritis, radiculitis, radiculopathy or sciatica M51.16
      specified NEC M51.86
    lumbosacral (with)
      myelopathy M51.07
      neuritis, radiculitis, radiculopathy or sciatica M51.17
      specified NEC M51.87
    specified NEC - *see* Disorder, disc, specified NEC
    thoracic (with)
      myelopathy M51.04
      neuritis, radiculitis or radiculopathy M51.14
      specified NEC M51.84
    thoracolumbar (with)
      myelopathy M51.05
      neuritis, radiculitis or radiculopathy M51.15
      specified NEC M51.85
  intestine K63.9
    functional K59.9
      psychogenic F45.8
      specified NEC K59.8
    organic K63.9

Disease, diseased *(Continued)*
  intestine *(Continued)*
    protozoal A07.9
    specified NEC K63.89
  iris H21.9
    specified NEC H21.89
  iron metabolism or storage E83.10
  island (scrub typhus) A75.3
  itai-itai – *see* Poisoning, cadmium
  Jakob-Creutzfeldt - *see* Creutzfeldt-Jakob disease or syndrome
  jaw M27.9
    fibrocystic M27.49
    specified NEC M27.8
  jigger B88.1
  joint - *see also* Disorder, joint
    Charcot's - *see* Arthropathy, neuropathic (Charcot)
    degenerative - *see* Osteoarthritis
      multiple M15.9
      spine - *see* Spondylosis
    hypertrophic – *see* Osteoarthritis
    sacroiliac M53.3
    specified NEC - *see* Disorder, joint, specified type NEC
    spine NEC - *see* Dorsopathy
    suppurative - *see* Arthritis, pyogenic or pyemic
  Jourdain's (acute gingivitis) K05.00
    plaque induced K05.00
    nonplaque induced K05.01
  Kaschin-Beck (endemic polyarthritis) M12.10
    ankle M12.17-
    elbow M12.12-
    foot joint M12.17-
    hand joint M12.14-
    hip M12.15-
    knee M12.16-
    multiple site M12.19
    shoulder M12.11-
    vertebra M12.18
    wrist M12.13-
  Katayama B65.2
  Kedani (scrub typhus) A75.3
  Keshan E59
  kidney (functional) (pelvis) N28.9
    chronic N18.9
      hypertensive - *see* Hypertension, kidney
      stage 1 N18.1
      stage 2 (mild) N18.2
      stage 3 (moderate) N18.3
      stage 4 (severe) N18.4
      stage 5 N18.5
    cystic (congenital) Q61.9
    fibrocystic (congenital) Q61.8
    hypertensive - *see* Hypertension, kidney
    in (due to)
      schistosomiasis (bilharziasis) B65.9 [N29]
    multicystic Q61.4
    polycystic Q61.3
      adult type Q61.2
      childhood type NEC Q61.19
        collecting duct dilatation Q61.11
  Kimmelstiel (-Wilson) (intercapillary polycystic (congenital) glomerulosclerosis) – *see* E09-E13 with .21
  Kinnier Wilson's (hepatolenticular degeneration) E83.01
  kissing - *see* Mononucleosis, infectious
  Klebs' (*see also* Glomerulonephritis) N05.-

Disease, diseased *(Continued)*
  Klippel-Feil (brevicollis) Q76.1
  Köhler-Pellegrini-Stieda (calcification, knee joint) - *see* Bursitis, tibial collateral
  Kok Q89.8
  König's (osteochondritis dissecans) – *see* Osteochondritis, dissecans
  Korsakoff's (nonalcoholic) F04
    alcoholic F10.96
      with dependence F10.26
  Kostmann's (infantile genetic agranulocytosis) D70.0
  kuru A81.81
  Kyasanur Forest A98.2
  labyrinth, ear - *see* Disorder, ear, inner
  lacrimal system - *see* Disorder, lacrimal system
  Lafora's G25.3
  Lancereaux-Mathieu (leptospiral jaundice) A27.0
  Landry's G61.0
  Larrey-Weil (leptospiral jaundice) A27.0
  larynx J38.7
  legionnaire's A48.1
    nonpneumonic A48.2
  Lenegre's I44.2
  lens H27.9
    specified NEC H27.8
  Lev's (acquired complete heart block) I44.2
  Lewy body (dementia) G31.83 [F02.80]
    with behavioral disturbance G31.83 [F02.81]
  Lichtheim's (subacute combined sclerosis with pernicious anemia) D51.0
  Lightwood's (renal tubular acidosis) N25.89
  Lignac's (cystinosis) E72.04
  lip K13.0
  lipid-storage E75.6
    specified NEC E75.5
  Lipschütz's N76.6
  liver (chronic) (organic) K76.9
    alcoholic (chronic) K70.9
      acute – *see* Disease, liver, alcoholic, hepatitis
      cirrhosis K70.30
        with ascites K70.31
      failure K70.40
        with coma K70.41
      fatty liver K70.0
      fibrosis K70.2
      hepatitis K70.10
        with ascites K70.11
      sclerosis K70.2
    cystic, congenital Q44.6
    drug-induced (idiosyncratic) (toxic) (predictable) (unpredictable) - *see* Disease, liver, toxic
    end stage K72.90
      due to hepatitis - *see* Hepatitis
    fatty, nonalcoholic (NAFLD) K76.0
      alcoholic K70.0
    fibrocystic (congenital) Q44.6
    fluke
      Chinese B66.1
      oriental B66.1
      sheep B66.3
    glycogen storage E74.09 [K77]
    in (due to)
      schistosomiasis (bilharziasis) B65.9 [K77]

Disease, diseased *(Continued)*
  liver *(Continued)*
    inflammatory K75.9
      alcoholic K70.1
      specified NEC K75.89
    polycystic (congenital) Q44.6
    toxic K71.9
      with
        cholestasis K71.0
        cirrhosis (liver) K71.7
        fibrosis (liver) K71.7
        focal nodular hyperplasia K71.8
        hepatic granuloma K71.8
        hepatic necrosis K71.10
          with coma K71.11
        hepatitis NEC K71.6
          acute K71.2
          chronic
            active K71.50
              with ascites K71.51
            lobular K71.4
            persistent K71.3
          lupoid K71.50
            with ascites K71.51
        peliosis hepatis K71.8
        veno-occlusive disease (VOD) of liver K71.8
    veno-occlusive K76.5
  Lobo's (keloid blastomycosis) B48.0
  Lobstein's (brittle bones and blue sclera) Q78.0
  Ludwig's (submaxillary cellulitis) K12.2
  lumbosacral region M53.87
  lung J98.4
    black J60
    congenital Q33.9
    cystic J98.4
      congenital Q33.0
    fibroid (chronic) - *see* Fibrosis, lung
    fluke B66.4
      oriental B66.4
    in
      amyloidosis E85.4 [J99]
      sarcoidosis D86.0
      Sjögren's syndrome M35.02
      systemic
        lupus erythematosus M32.13
        sclerosis M34.81
    interstitial J84.9
      acute B59
      specified NEC J84.8
    obstructive (chronic) J44.9
      with
        acute
          bronchitis J44.0
          exacerbation NEC J44.1
          lower respiratory infection J44.0
        alveolitis, allergic J67.9
        asthma J44.9
        bronchiectasis J47.9
          with
            exacerbation (acute) J47.1
            lower respiratory infection J47.0
        bronchitis J44.9
          with
            exacerbation (acute) J44.1
            lower respiratory infection J44.0
        emphysema J44.9
        hypersensitivity pneumonitis J67.9
      decompensated J44.1
        with
          exacerbation (acute) J44.1

Disease, diseased *(Continued)*
  lung *(Continued)*
    polycystic J98.4
      congenital Q33.0
    rheumatoid (diffuse) (interstitial) - *see* Rheumatoid, lung
  Lutembacher's (atrial septal defect with mitral stenosis) Q21.1
  Lyme A69.20
  lymphatic (gland) (system) (channel) (vessel) I89.9
  lymphoproliferative D47.9
    specified NEC D47.z9
    T-gamma D47.z9
    X-linked D82.3
  Magitot's M27.2
  malarial - *see* Malaria
  malignant - *see also* Neoplasm, malignant
  Manson's B65.1
  maple bark J67.6
  maple-syrup-urine E71.0
  Marburg (virus) A98.3
  Marion's (bladder neck obstruction) N32.0
  Marsh's (exophthalmic goiter) - *see* Hyperthyroidism, with, goiter (diffuse)
  mastoid (process) - *see* Disorder, ear, middle
  Mathieu's (leptospiral jaundice) A27.0
  Maxcy's A75.2
  McArdle (-Schmid-Pearson) (glycogenosis V) E74.04
  mediastinum J98.5
  medullary center (idiopathic) (respiratory) G93.89
  Meige's (chronic hereditary edema) Q82.0
  meningococcal – *see* Infection, meningococcal
  mental F99
    organic F06.9
  mesenchymal M35.9
  mesenteric embolic K55.0
  metabolic, metabolism E88.9
    bilirubin E80.7
  metal-polisher's J62.8
  metastatic (*see also*- Metastasis) C79.9
  microvascular code to condition
  middle ear - *see* Disorder, ear, middle
  Mikulicz' (dryness of mouth, absent or decreased lacrimation) K11.8
  Milroy's (chronic hereditary edema) Q82.0
  Minamata – *see* Poisoning, mercury
  minicore G71.2
  Minor's G95.19
  Minot's (hemorrhagic disease, newborn) P53
  Minot-von Willebrand-Jüürgens (angiohemophilia) D68.0
  Mitchell's (erythromelalgia) I73.81
  mitral (valve) I05.9
    nonrheumatic I34.9
  mixed connective tissue M35.1
  Monge's T70.29
  Morgagni-Adams-Stokes (syncope with heart block) I45.9
  Morgagni's (syndrome) (hyperostosis frontalis interna) M85.2
  Morton's (with metatarsalgia) - *see* Lesion, nerve, plantar
  Morvan's G95.0

Disease, diseased *(Continued)*
  motor neuron (bulbar) (familial) (mixed type) (spinal) G12.20
    amyotrophic lateral sclerosis G12.21
    progressive bulbar palsy G12.22
    specified NEC G12.29
  moldy hay J67.0
  moyamoya I67.5
  mu heavy chain disease C88.2
  multicore G71.2
  muscle *see also* Disorder, muscle
    inflammatory - *see* Myositis
    ocular (external) - *see* Strabismus
  musculoskeletal system, soft tissue - *see also* Disorder, soft tissue
    specified NEC - *see* Disorder, soft tissue, specified type NEC
  mushroom workers' J67.5
  mycotic B49
  myelodysplastic, not classified C94.6
  myeloproliferative, not classified C94.6
    chronic D47.1
  myocardium, myocardial (*see also* Degeneration, myocardial) I51.5
    primary (idiopathic) I42.9
  myoneural G70.9
  Naegeli's D69.1
  nails L60.9
    specified NEC L60.8
  Nairobi (sheep virus) A93.8
  nasal J34.9
  nemaline body G71.2
  nerve - *see* Disorder, nerve
  nervous system G98.8
    autonomic G90.9
    central G96.9
      specified NEC G96.8
    congenital Q07.9
    parasympathetic G90.9
    specified NEC G98.8
    sympathetic G90.9
    vegetative G90.9
  neuromuscular system G70.9
  Newcastle B30.8
  Nicolas (-Durand)-Favre (climatic bubo) A55
  nipple N64.9
    Paget's C50.01-
      female C50.01-
      male C50.02-
  Nishimoto (-Takeuchi) I67.5
  nonarthropod-borne NOS (viral) B34.9
    enterovirus NEC B34.1
  nonautoimmune hemolytic D59.4
    drug-induced D59.2
  Nonne-Milroy-Meige (chronic hereditary edema) Q82.0
  nose J34.9
  nucleus pulposus - *see* Disorder, disc
  nutritional E63.9
  oast-house-urine E72.19
    ocular
      herpesviral B00.50
      zoster B02.30
  obliterative vascular I77.1
  Ohara's – *see* Tularemia
  Opitz's (congestive splenomegaly) D73.2
  Oppenheim-Urbach (necrobiosis lipoidica diabeticorum) – *see* E09-E13 with .63
  optic nerve NEC - *see* Disorder, nerve, optic orbit - *see* Disorder, orbit
  Oriental liver fluke B66.1
  Oriental lung fluke B66.4

Disease, diseased *(Continued)*
  Ormond's N13.5
  Oropouche virus A93.0
  Osler-Rendu (familial hemorrhagic
    telangiectasia) I78.0
  osteofibrocystic E21.0
  Otto's M24.7
  outer ear - *see* Disorder, ear, external
  ovary (noninflammatory) N83.9
    cystic N83.20
    inflammatory - *see* Salpingo-oophoritis
    polycystic E28.2
    specified NEC N83.8
  Owren's (congenital) – *see* Defect,
    coagulation
  pancreas K86.9
    cystic K86.2
    fibrocystic E84.9
    specified NEC K86.8
  panvalvular I08.9
    specified NEC I08.8
  parametrium (noninflammatory) N83.9
  parasitic B89
    cerebral NEC B71.9 [G94]
    intestinal NOS B82.9
    mouth B37.0
    skin NOS B88.9
    specified type - *see* Infestation
    tongue B37.0
  parathyroid (gland) E21.5
    specified NEC E21.4
  Parkinson's G20
  parodontal K05.6
  Parrot's (syphilitic osteochondritis)
    A50.02
  Parry's (exophthalmic goiter) - *see*
    Hyperthyroidism, with, goiter
    (diffuse)
  Parson's (exophthalmic goiter) - *see*
    Hyperthyroidism, with, goiter
    (diffuse)
  Paxton's (white piedra) B36.2
  pearl-worker's - *see* Osteomyelitis,
    specified type NEC
  Pellegrini-Stieda (calcification, knee
    joint) - *see* Bursitis, tibial collateral
  pelvis, pelvic
    female NOS N94.9
      specified NEC N94.89
    gonococcal (acute) (chronic) A54.24
    inflammatory (female) N73.9
      acute N73.0
      chronic N73.1
      specified NEC N73.8
      syphilitic (secondary) A51.42
        late A52.76
      tuberculous A18.17
    organ, female N94.9
    peritoneum, female NEC N94.89
  penis N48.9
    inflammatory N48.29
      abscess N48.21
      cellulitis N48.22
    specified NEC N48.89
  periapical tissues NOS K04.90
  periodontal K05.6
    specified NEC K05.5
  periosteum - *see* Disorder, bone, speci-
    fied type NEC
  peripheral
    arterial I73.9
    autonomic nervous system G90.9
    nerves - *see* Polyneuropathy
    vascular NOS I73.9

Disease, diseased *(Continued)*
  peritoneum K66.9
    pelvic, female NEC N94.89
    specified NEC K66.8
  persistent mucosal (middle ear) H66.20
    left H66.22
      with right H66.23
    right H66.21
      with left H66.23
  Petit's – *see* Hernia, abdomen, specified
    site NEC
  pharynx J39.2
    specified NEC J39.2
  Phocas' – *see* Mastopathy, cystic
  photochromogenic (acid-fast bacilli)
    (pulmonary) A31.0
    nonpulmonary A31.9
  Pick's G31.01 [F02.80]
    with behavioral disturbance G31.01
      [F02.81]
  pigeon fancier's J67.2
  pineal gland E34.8
  pink – *see* Poisoning, mercury
  Pinkus' (lichen nitidus) L44.1
  pinworm B80
  Piry virus A93.8
  pituitary (gland) E23.7
  pituitary-snuff-taker's J67.8
  pleura (cavity) J94.9
    specified NEC J94.8
  pneumatic drill (hammer) T75.21
  Pollitzer's (hidradenitis suppurativa)
    L73.2
  polycystic
    kidney or renal Q61.3
      adult type Q61.2
      childhood type NEC Q61.19
        collecting duct dilatation Q61.11
    liver or hepatic Q44.6
    lung or pulmonary J98.4
      congenital Q33.0
    ovary, ovaries E28.2
    spleen Q89.09
  Pompe's (glycogenosis II) E74.02
  Posada-Wernicke B38.9
  Potain's (pulmonary edema) J18.2
  prepuce N47.8
    inflammatory N47.7
      balanoposthitis N47.6
  Pringle's (tuberous sclerosis) Q85.1
  prion, central nervous system A81.9
    specified NEC A81.89
  prostate N42.9
    specified NEC N42.89
  protozoal B64
    acanthamebiasis – *see*
      Acanthamebiasis
    African trypanosomiasis – *see* African
      trypanosomiasis
    babesiosis B60.0
    Chagas disease – *see* Chagas disease
    intestine, intestinal A07.9
    leishmaniasis – *see* Leishmaniasis
    malaria – *see* Malaria
    naegleriasis B60.2
    pneumocystosis B59
    specified organism NEC B60.8
    toxoplasmosis – *see* Toxoplasmosis
  pseudo-Hurler's E77.0
  psychiatric F99
  psychotic - *see* Psychosis
  Puente's (simple glandular cheilitis)
    K13.0
  puerperal - *see* Puerperal

Disease, diseased *(Continued)*
  pulmonary - *see also* Disease, lung
    artery I28.9
    chronic obstructive J44.9
      with
        acute bronchitis J44.0
        exacerbation (acute) J44.1
        lower respiratory infection
          (acute) J44.0
      decompensated J44.1
        with
          exacerbation (acute) J44.1
    heart I27.9
      specified NEC I27.89
    hypertensive (vascular) I27.0
    valve I37.9
      rheumatic I09.89
  pulp (dental) NOS K04.90
  pulseless M31.4
  Putnam's (subacute combined sclerosis
    with pernicious anemia) D51.0
  Pyle (-Cohn) (craniometaphyseal dys-
    plasia) Q78.5
  ragpicker's or ragsorter's A22.1
  Raynaud's –*see* Raynaud's disease
  reactive airway - *see* Asthma
  Reclus' (cystic) – *see* Mastopathy, cystic
  rectum K62.9
    specified NEC K62.8
  Refsum's (heredopathia atactica poly-
    neuritiformis) G60.1
  renal (chronic) (functional) (pelvis) (*see*
    also Disease, kidney) N18.9
    with
      edema - *see* Nephrosis
      glomerular lesion - *see*
        Glomerulonephritis
        with edema - *see* Nephrosis
      interstitial nephritis N12
    acute N28.9
    cystic, congenital Q61.9
    diabetic – *see* E09-E13 with .22
    end-stage (failure) N18.6
      due to hypertension I12.0
    fibrocystic (congenital) Q61.8
    hypertensive - *see* Hypertension,
      kidney
    lupus M32.14
    phosphate-losing (tubular) N25.0
    polycystic (congenital) Q61.3
      adult type Q61.2
      childhood type NEC Q61.19
        collecting duct dilatation Q61.11
    rapidly progressive N01.9
    subacute N01.9
  Rendu-Osler-Weber (familial hemor-
    rhagic telangiectasia) I78.0
  renovascular (arteriosclerotic) - *see*
    Hypertension, kidney
  respiratory (tract) J98.9
    acute or subacute NOS J06.9
      due to
        chemicals, gases, fumes or va-
          pors (inhalation) J68.3
        external agent J70.9
          specified NEC J70.8
        radiation J70.0
      noninfectious J39.8
    chronic NOS J98.9
      due to
        chemicals, gases, fumes or va-
          pors J68.4
        external agent J70.9
          specified NEC J70.8

Disease, diseased *(Continued)*
  respiratory *(Continued)*
    chronic *(Continued)*
      due to *(Continued)*
        radiation J70.1
      newborn P27.9
        specified NEC P27.8
    due to
      chemicals, gases, fumes or vapors J68.9
        acute or subacute NEC J68.3
        chronic J68.4
      external agent J70.9
        specified NEC J70.8
    newborn P28.9
      specified type NEC P28.89
    upper J39.9
      acute or subacute J06.9
      noninfectious NEC J39.8
      specified NEC J39.8
      streptococcal J06.9
  retina, retinal H35.9
    Batten's or Batten-Mayou E75.4 [H36]
    specified NEC H35.89
  rheumatoid - *see* Arthritis, rheumatoid
  rickettsial NOS A79.9
    specified type NEC A79.89
  Riga (-Fede) (cachectic aphthae) K14.0
  Riggs' (compound periodontitis) - *see* Periodontitis
  Ritter's L00
  Rivalta's (cervicofacial actinomycosis) A42.2
  Robles' (onchocerciasis) B73.1
  Roger's (congenital interventricular septal defect) Q21.0
  Rosenthal's (factor XI deficiency) D68.1
  Rossbach's (hyperchlorhydria) K30
  Ross River B33.1
  Rotes Quérol - *see* Hyperostosis, ankylosing
  Roth (-Bernhardt) - *see* Mononeuropathy, lower limb, meralgia paresthetica
  Runeberg's (progressive pernicious anemia) D51.0
  sacroiliac NEC M53.3
  salivary gland or duct K11.9
    inclusion B25.9
    specified NEC K11.8
    virus B25.9
  sandworm B76.9
  Schimmelbusch's – *see* Mastopathy, cystic
  Schmorl's - *see* Schmorl's disease or nodes
  Schönlein (-Henoch) (purpura rheumatica) D69.0
  Schottmüller's –*see* Fever, paratyphoid
  Schultz's (agranulocytosis) – *see* Agranulocytosis
  Schwalbe-Ziehen-Oppenheim G24.1
  Schwartz-Jampel G71.13
  sclera H15.9
    specified NEC H15.89
  scrofulous (tuberculous) A18.2
  scrotum N50.9
  sebaceous glands L73.9
  semilunar cartilage, cystic - *see also* Derangement, knee, meniscus, cystic
  seminal vesicle N50.9
  serum NEC T80.6

Disease, diseased *(Continued)*
  sexually transmitted A64
    anogenital
      herpesviral infection – *see* Herpes, anogenital
      warts A63.0
    chancroid A57
    chlamydial infection – *see* Chlamydia
    gonorrhea – *see* Gonorrhea
    granuloma inguinale A58
    specified organism NEC A63.8
    syphilis – *see* Syphilis
    trichomoniasis – *see* Trichmoniasis
  Sézary C84.1-
  shimamushi (scrub typhus) A75.3
  shipyard B30.0
  sickle-cell D57.1
    with crisis (vasoocclusive pain) D57.00
      with
        acute chest syndrome D57.01
        splenic sequestration D57.02
    elliptocytosis D57.8-
    Hb-C D57.20
      with crisis (vasoocclusive pain) D57.219
      with
        acute chest syndrome D57.211
        splenic sequestration D57.212
      without crisis D57.20
    Hb-SD D57.80
      with crisis D57.819
      with
        acute chest syndrome D57.811
        splenic sequestration D57.812
    Hb-SE D57.80
      with crisis D57.819
      with
        acute chest syndrome D57.811
        splenic sequestration D57.812
    specified NEC D57.80
      with crisis D57.819
      with
        acute chest syndrome D57.811
        splenic sequestration D57.812
    spherocytosis D57.80
      with crisis D57.819
      with
        acute chest syndrome D57.811
        splenic sequestration D57.812
    thalassemia D57.40
      with crisis (vasoocclusive pain) D57.419
      with
        acute chest syndrome D57.411
        splenic sequestration D57.412
      without crisis D57.40
  silo-filler's J68.8
  simian B B00.4
  Simons' (progressive lipodystrophy) E88.1
  sin nombre virus B33.4
  sinus - *see* Sinusitis
  Sirkari's B55.0
  sixth B08.20
    due to human herpesvirus 6 B08.21
    due to human herpesvirus 7 B08.22
  skin L98.9
    due to metabolic disorder NEC E88.9 [L99]
    specified NEC L98.8
  slim (HIV) B20
  small vessel I73.9
  Sneddon-Wilkinson (subcorneal pustular dermatosis) L13.1

Disease, diseased *(Continued)*
  South African creeping B88.0
  spinal (cord) G95.9
    congenital Q06.9
    specified NEC G95.89
  spine - *see also* Spondylopathy
    joint - *see* Dorsopathy
    tuberculous A18.01
  spinocerebellar (hereditary) G11.9
    specified NEC G11.8
  spleen D73.9
    amyloid E85.4 [D77]
    organic D73.9
    polycystic Q89.09
    postinfectional D73.89
  sponge-diver's - *see* Toxicity, venom, marine animal, sea anemone
  Startle Q89.8
  Steinert's G71.11
  Sticker's (erythema infectiosum) B08.3
  Stieda's (calcification, knee joint) - *see* Bursitis, tibial collateral
  Stokes' (exophthalmic goiter) - *see* Hyperthyroidism, with, goiter (diffuse)
  Stokes-Adams (syncope with heart block) I45.9
  stomach K31.9
    functional, psychogenic F45.8
    specified NEC K31.89
  stonemason's J62.8
  storage
    glycogen - *see* Disease, glycogen storage
    mucopolysaccharide - *see* Mucopolysaccharidosis
  striatopallidal system NEC G25.89
  Stuart-Prower (congenital factor X deficiency) D68.2
  Stuart's (congenital factor X deficiency) D68.2
  subcutaneous tissue - *see* Disease, skin
  supporting structures of teeth K08.9
    specified NEC K08.8
  suprarenal (capsule) (gland) E27.9
    hyperfunction E27.0
    specified NEC E27.8
  sweat glands L74.9
    specified NEC L74.8
  Swift (-Feer) – *see* Poisoning, mercury
  swimming-pool granuloma A31.1
  Sylvest's (epidemic pleurodynia) B33.0
  sympathetic nervous system G90.9
  synovium – *see* Disorder, synovium
  syphilitic - *see* Syphilis
  systemic tissue mast cell C96.2
  tanapox (virus) B08.71
  Tangier E78.6
  Tarral-Besnier (pityriasis rubra pilaris) L44.0
  Tauri's E74.09
  tear duct - *see* Disorder, lacrimal system
  tendon, tendinous – *see also* Disorder, tendon
    nodular - *see* Trigger finger
  terminal vessel I73.9
  testis N50.9
  thalassemia Hb-S - *see* Disease, sickle cell, thalassemia
  Thaysen-Gee (nontropical sprue) K90.0
  Thomsen G71.12
  throat J39.2
    septic J02.0
  thromboembolic - *see* Embolism

Disease, diseased *(Continued)*
  thymus (gland) E32.9
    specified NEC E32.8
  thyroid (gland) E07.9
    heart *(see also* Hyperthyroidism)
      E05.90 [I43]
      with thyroid storm E05.91 [I43]
    specified NEC E07.89
  Tietze's M94.0
  tongue K14.9
    specified NEC K14.8
  tonsils, tonsillar (and adenoids) J35.9
  tooth, teeth K08.9
    hard tissues K03.9
      specified NEC K03.89
    pulp NEC K04.99
    specified NEC K08.8
  Tourette's F95.2
  trachea NEC J39.8
  tricuspid I07.9
    nonrheumatic I36.9
  triglyceride-storage E75.5
  trophoblastic - *see* Mole, hydatidiform
  tsutsugamushi A75.3
  tube (fallopian) (noninflammatory)
    N83.9
    inflammatory - *see* Salpingitis
    specified NEC N83.8
  tuberculous NEC - *see* Tuberculosis
  tubo-ovarian (noninflammatory) N83.9
    inflammatory - *see*
      Salpingo-oophoritis
    specified NEC N83.8
  tubotympanic, chronic - *see* Otitis, media,
    suppurative, chronic, tubotympanic
  tubulo-interstitial N15.9
    specified NEC N15.8
  tympanum - *see* Disorder, tympanic
    membrane
  Uhl's Q22.6
  Underwood's (sclerema neonatorum)
    P83.0
  Unverricht (-Lundborg) - *see* Epilepsy,
    generalized, idiopathic
  Urbach-Oppenheim (necrobiosis li-
    poidica diabeticorum) –*see* E09-E13
    with .63
  ureter N28.9
    in (due to)
      schistosomiasis (bilharziasis) B65.0
      [N29]
  urethra N36.9
    specified NEC N36.8
  urinary (tract) N39.9
    bladder N32.9
      specified NEC N32.89
    specified NEC N39.8
  uterus (noninflammatory) N85.9
    infective - *see* Endometritis
    inflammatory - *see* Endometritis
    specified NEC N85.8
  uveal tract (anterior) H21.9
    posterior H31.9
  vagabond's B85.1
  vagina, vaginal (noninflammatory)
    N89.9
    inflammatory NEC N76.89
    specified NEC N89.8
  valve, valvular I38
    multiple I08.9
      specified NEC I08.8
  van Creveld-von Gierke (glycogenosis
    I) E74.01
  vas deferens N50.9

Disease, diseased *(Continued)*
  vascular I99.9
    arteriosclerotic - *see* Arteriosclerosis
    ciliary body NEC - *see* Disorder, iris,
      vascular
    hypertensive - *see* Hypertension
    iris NEC - *see* Disorder, iris, vascular
    obliterative I77.1
      peripheral I73.9
    occlusive I99.8
    peripheral (occlusive) I73.9
      in diabetes mellitus – *see* E09-E13
      with .51
  vasomotor I73.9
  vasospastic I73.9
  vein I87.9
  venereal (*see also* Disease, sexually
    transmitted) A64
    chlamydial NEC A56.8
      anus A56.3
      genitourinary NOS A56.2
      pharynx A56.4
      rectum A56.3
    fifth A55
    sixth A55
    specified nature or type NEC A63.8
  vertebra, vertebral - *see also*
    Spondylopathy
    disc - *see* Disorder, disc
  vibration – *see* Vibration, adverse effects
  viral, virus (*see also* Disease, by type of
    virus) B34.9
    arbovirus NOS A94
    arthropod-borne NOS A94
    congenital P35.9
      specified NEC P35.8
    Hanta (with renal manifestations)
      (Dobrava) (Puumala) (Seoul)
      A98.5
      with pulmonary manifestations
        (Andes) (Bayou) (Bermejo)
        (Black Creek Canal) (Choclo)
        (Juquitiba) (Laguna negra)
        (Lechiguanas) (New York)
        (Oran) (Sin nombre) B33.4
    Hantaan (Korean hemorrhagic fever)
      A98.5
    human immunodeficiency (HIV) B20
    Kunjin A83.4
    nonarthropod-borne NOS B34.9
    Powassan A84.8
    Rocio (encephalitis) A83.6
    Sin nombre (Hantavirus (cardio)-
      pulmonary syndrome B33.4
    Tahyna B33.8
    vesicular stomatitis A93.8
  vitreous H43.9
    specified NEC H43.89
  vocal cord J38.3
  Volkmann's, acquired T79.6
  von Eulenburg's (congenital paramyo-
    tonia) G71.19
  von Gierke's (glycogenosis I) E74.01
  von Graefe's - *see* Strabismus, paralytic,
    ophthalmoplegia, progressive
  von Willebrand (-Jüürgens) (angiohe-
    mophilia) D68.0
  Vrolik's (osteogenesis imperfecta) Q78.0
  vulva (noninflammatory) N90.9
    inflammatory NEC N76.89
    specified NEC N90.8
  Wallgren's (obstruction of splenic vein
    with collateral circulation) I87.8
  Wassilieff's (leptospiral jaundice) A27.0

Disease, diseased *(Continued)*
  wasting NEC R64
    due to malnutrition E41
  Waterhouse-Friderichsen A39.1
  Wegner's (syphilitic osteochondritis)
    A50.02
  Weil's (leptospiral jaundice of lung)
    A27.0
  Weir Mitchell's (erythromelalgia) I73.81
  Werdnig-Hoffmann G12.0
  Wermer's E31.21
  Werner-His (trench fever) A79.0
  Werner-Schultz (neutropenic spleno-
    megaly) D73.81
  Wernicke-Posadas B38.9
  whipworm B79
  white blood cells D72.9
    specified NEC D72.89
  white matter R90.82
  white-spot, meaning lichen sclerosus et
    atrophicus L90.0
    penis N48.0
    vulva N90.4
  Wilkie's K55.1
  Wilkinson-Sneddon (subcorneal pustu-
    lar dermatosis) L13.1
  Willis' – *see* Diabetes
  Wilson's (hepatolenticular degenera-
    tion) E83.01
  woolsorter's A22.1
  yaba monkey tumor B08.72
  yaba pox (virus) B08.72
  zoonotic, bacterial A28.9
    specified type NEC A28.8
Disfigurement (due to scar) L90.5
Disgerminoma - *see* Dysgerminoma
DISH (diffuse idiopathic skeletal
  hyperostosis) - *see* Hyperostosis,
  ankylosing
Disinsertion, retina - *see* Detachment, retina
Dislocatable hip, congenital Q65.6
Dislocation (articular)
  with fracture - *see* Fracture
  acromioclavicular (joint) S43.10-
    with displacement
      100%-200% S43.12-
      more than 200% S43.13-
    inferior S43.14-
    posterior S43.15-
  ankle S93.0-
  astragalus – *see* Dislocation, ankle
  atlantoaxial S13.121
  atlantooccipital S13.111
  atloidooccipital S13.111
  breast bone S23.29
  capsule, joint code by site under
    Dislocation
  carpal (bone) – *see* Dislocation, wrist
  carpometacarpal (joint) NEC S63.05-
    thumb S63.04-
  cartilage (joint) code by site under
    Dislocation
  cervical spine (vertebra) - *see* Disloca-
    tion, vertebra, cervical
  chronic - *see* Dislocation, recurrent
  clavicle – *see* Dislocation, acromiocla-
    vicular joint
  coccyx S33.2
  congenital NEC Q68.8
  coracoid – *see* Dislocation, shoulder
  costal cartilage S23.29
  costochondral S23.29
  cricoarytenoid articulation S13.29
  cricothyroid articulation S13.29

Dislocation *(Continued)*
  dorsal vertebra - *see* Dislocation, vertebra, thoracic
  ear ossicle - *see* Discontinuity, ossicles, ear
  elbow S53.10-
    congenital Q68.8
    pathological - *see* Dislocation, pathological NEC, elbow
    radial head alone – *see* Dislocation, radial head
    recurrent - *see* Dislocation, recurrent, elbow
    traumatic S53.10-
      anterior S53.11-
      lateral S53.14-
      medial S53.13-
      posterior S53.12-
      specified type NEC S53.19-
  eye, nontraumatic - *see* Luxation, globe
  eyeball, nontraumatic - *see* Luxation, globe
  femur
    distal end – *see* Dislocation, knee
    proximal end – *see* Dislocation, hip
  fibula
    distal end – *see* Dislocation, ankle
    proximal end – *see* Dislocation, knee
  finger S63.25-
    index S63.25-
    interphalangeal S63.27-
      distal S63.29-
        index S63.29-
        little S63.29-
        middle S63.29-
        ring S63.29-
      index S63.27-
      little S63.27-
      middle S63.27-
      proximal S63.28-
        index S63.28-
        little S63.28-
        middle S63.28-
        ring S63.28-
      ring S63.27-
    little S63.25-
    metacarpophalangeal S63.26-
      index S63.26-
      little S63.26-
      middle S63.26-
      ring S63.26-
    middle S63.25-
    recurrent - *see* Dislocation, recurrent, finger
    ring S63.25-
    thumb – *see* Dislocation, thumb
  foot S93.30-
    recurrent - *see* Dislocation, recurrent, foot
    specified site NEC S93.33-
    tarsal joint S93.31-
    tarsometatarsal joint S93.32-
    toe – *see* Dislocation, toe
  fracture - *see* Fracture
  glenohumeral (joint) – *see* Dislocation, shoulder
  glenoid – *see* Dislocation, shoulder
  habitual - *see* Dislocation, recurrent
  hip S73.00-
    anterior S73.03-
      obturator S73.02-
    central S73.04-
    congenital (total) Q65.2
      bilateral Q65.1

Dislocation *(Continued)*
  hip *(Continued)*
    congenital *(Continued)*
      partial Q65.5
        bilateral Q65.4
        unilateral Q65.3-
      unilateral Q65.0-
    developmental M24.85-
    pathological - *see* Dislocation, pathological NEC, hip
    posterior S73.01-
    recurrent - *see* Dislocation, recurrent, hip
  humerus, proximal end – *see* Dislocation, shoulder
  incomplete - *see* Subluxation, by site
  incus - *see* Discontinuity, ossicles, ear
  infracoracoid – *see* Dislocation, shoulder
  innominate (pubic junction) (sacral junction) S33.39
    acetabulum – *see* Dislocation, hip
  interphalangeal (joint(s))
    finger S63.279
      distal S63.29-
        index S63.29-
        little S63.29-
        middle S63.29-
        ring S63.29-
      index S63.27-
      little S63.27-
      middle S63.27-
      proximal S63.28-
        index S63.28-
        little S63.28-
        middle S63.28-
        ring S63.28-
      ring S63.27-
    foot or toe – *see* Dislocation, toe
    thumb S63.12-
      distal joint S63.14-
      proximal joint S63.13-
  jaw (cartilage) (meniscus) S03.0
  joint prosthesis - *see* Complications, joint prosthesis, mechanical, displacement, by site
  knee S83.106
    cap – *see* Dislocation, patella
    congenital Q68.2
    old M23.8x-
    patella – *see* Dislocation, patella
    pathological - *see* Dislocation, pathological NEC, knee
    proximal tibia
      anteriorly S83.11-
      laterally S83.14-
      medially S83.13-
      posteriorly S83.12-
    recurrent – *see also* Derangement, knee, specified NEC
    specified type NEC S83.19-
  lacrimal gland H04.16-
  lens (complete) H27.1-
    anterior H27.12-
    congenital Q12.1
    ocular implant - *see* Complications, intraocular lens
    partial H27.11-
    posterior H27.13-
    traumatic S05.8x-
  ligament code by site under Dislocation
  lumbar (vertebra) - *see* Dislocation, vertebra, lumbar

Dislocation *(Continued)*
  lumbosacral (vertebra) - *see also* Dislocation, vertebra, lumbar
    congenital Q76.49
  mandible S03.0
  meniscus (knee) - *see* Tear, meniscus
    other sites code by site under Dislocation
  metacarpal (bone)
    distal end – *see* Dislocation, finger
    proximal end S63.06-
  metacarpophalangeal (joint)
    finger S63.26-
      index S63.26-
      little S63.26-
      middle S63.26-
      ring S63.26-
    thumb S63.11-
  metatarsal (bone) – *see* Dislocation, foot
  metatarsophalangeal (joint(s)) – *see* Dislocation, toe
  midcarpal (joint) S63.03-
  midtarsal (joint) – *see* Dislocation, foot
  neck S13.20
    specified site NEC S13.29
    vertebra - *see* Dislocation, vertebra, cervical
  nose (septal cartilage) S03.1
  occipitoatloid S13.111
  old - *see* Derangement, joint, specified type NEC
  ossicles, ear - *see* Discontinuity, ossicles, ear
  partial - *see* Subluxation, by site
  patella S83.006
    congenital Q74.1
    lateral S83.01-
    recurrent (nontraumatic) M22.0-
      incomplete M22.1-
    specified type NEC S83.09-
  pathological NEC M24.30
    ankle M24.37-
    elbow M24.32-
    foot joint M24.37-
    hand joint M24.34-
    hip M24.35-
    knee M24.36-
    lumbosacral joint - *see* subcategory M53.2
    pelvic region - *see* Dislocation, pathological, hip
    sacroiliac - *see* subcategory M53.2
    shoulder M24.31-
    wrist M24.33-
  pelvis NEC S33.30
    specified NEC S33.39
  phalanx
    finger or hand – *see* Dislocation, finger
    foot or toe – *see* Dislocation, toe
  prosthesis, internal - *see* Complications, prosthetic device, by site, mechanical
  radial head S53.006
    anterior S53.01-
    posterior S53.02-
    specified type NEC S53.09-
  radiocarpal (joint) S63.02-
  radiohumeral (joint) – *see* Dislocation, radial head
  radioulnar (joint)
    distal S63.01-
    proximal – *see* Dislocation, elbow

Disorder (Continued)
  alcohol-related (Continued)
    with (Continued)
      sexual dysfunction F10.981
      sleep disorder F10.988
  allergic - *see* Allergy
  alveolar NEC J84.0
  amino-acid
    cystathioninuria E72.19
    cystinosis E72.04
    cystinuria E72.01
    glycinuria E72.09
    homocystinuria E72.11
    metabolism - *see* Disturbance, metabolism, amino-acid
    specified NEC E72.8
    neonatal, transitory P74.8
    renal transport NEC E72.09
    transport NEC E72.09
  amnesic, amnestic
    alcohol-induced F10.96
      with dependence F10.26
    due to (secondary to) general medical condition F04
    psychoactive NEC-induced F19.96
      with
        abuse F19.16
        dependence F19.26
    sedative, hypnotic or anxiolytic-induced F13.96
      with dependence F13.26
  anaerobic glycolysis with anemia D55.2
  anxiety F41.9
    due to (secondary to)
      alcohol F10.980
      amphetamine F15.980
        in
          abuse F15.180
          dependence F15.280
      anxiolytic F13.980
        in
          abuse F13.180
          dependence F13.280
      caffeine F15.980
        in
          abuse F15.180
          dependence F15.280
      cannabis F12.980
        in
          abuse F12.180
          dependence F12.280
      cocaine F14.980
        in
          abuse F14.180
          dependence F14.180
      general medical condition F06.4
      hallucinogen F16.980
        in
          abuse F16.180
          dependence F16.280
      hypnotic F13.980
        in
          abuse F13.180
          dependence F13.280
      inhalant F18.980
        in
          abuse F18.180
          dependence F18.280
      phencyclidine F19.980
        in
          abuse F19.180
          dependence F19.280

Disorder (Continued)
  anxiety (Continued)
    due to (Continued)
      psychoactive substance NEC F19.980
        in
          abuse F19.180
          dependence F19.280
      sedative F13.980
        in
          abuse F13.180
          dependence F13.280
      volatile solvents F18.980
        in
          abuse F18.180
          dependence F18.280
    generalized F41.1
    mixed
      with depression (mild) F41.8
      specified NEC F41.3
    organic F06.4
    phobic F40.9
      of childhood F40.8
    specified NEC F41.8
  aortic valve – *see* Endocarditis, aortic
  aromatic amino-acid metabolism E70.9
    specified NEC E70.8
  arteriole NEC I77.8
  artery NEC I77.8
  articulation - *see* Disorder, joint
  attachment (childhood)
    disinhibited F94.2
    reactive F94.1
  attention-deficit hyperactivity (adolescent) (adult) (child) F90.9
    combined type F90.2
    hyperactive type F90.1
    inattentive type F90.0
    specified type NEC F90.8
  attention-deficit without hyperactivity (adolescent) (adult) (child) F90.0
  auditory processing (central) H93.25
  autistic F84.0
  autonomic nervous system G90.9
    specified NEC G90.8
  avoidant, child or adolescent F40.10
  balance
    acid-base E87.8
      mixed E87.4
    electrolyte E87.8
    fluid NEC E87.8
  behavioral (disruptive) - *see* Disorder, conduct
  beta-amino-acid metabolism E72.8
  bile acid and cholesterol metabolism E78.70
    Barth syndrome E78.71
    other specified E78.79
    Smith-Lemli-Opitz syndrome E78.72
  bilirubin excretion E80.6
  binocular
    movement H51.9
      convergence
        excess H51.12
        insufficiency H51.11
      internuclear ophthalmoplegia - *see* Ophthalmoplegia, internuclear
      palsy of conjugate gaze H51.0
      specified type NEC H51.8
    vision NEC - *see* Disorder, vision, binocular

Disorder (Continued)
  bipolar (I) F31.9
    current episode
      depressed F31.9
        with psychotic features F31.5
        without psychotic features F31.30
          mild F31.31
          moderate F31.32
          severe (without psychotic features) F31.4
            with psychotic features F31.5
      hypomanic F31.0
      manic F31.9
        with psychotic features F31.2
        without psychotic features F31.10
          mild F31.11
          moderate F31.12
          severe (without psychotic features) F31.13
            with psychotic features F31.2
      mixed F31.60
        mild F31.61
        moderate F31.62
        severe (without psychotic features) F31.63
        with psychotic features F31.64
      severe depression (without psychotic features) F31.4
        with psychotic features F31.5
    in remission (currently) F31.70
      in full remission
        most recent episode
          depressed F31.76
          hypomanic F31.72
          manic F31.74
          mixed F31.78
      in partial remission
        most recent episode
          depressed F31.75
          hypomanic F31.71
          manic F31.73
          mixed F31.77
    specified NEC F31.89
    II F31.81
    organic F06.30
    single manic episode F30.9
      mild F30.11
      moderate F30.12
      severe (without psychotic symptoms) F30.13
      with psychotic symptoms F30.2
  bladder N32.9
    functional NEC N31.9
    in schistosomiasis B65.0 [N33]
    specified NEC N32.89
  bleeding D68.9
  blood D75.9
    in congenital early syphilis A50.09 [D77]
  body dysmorphic F45.22
  bone M89.9
    continuity M84.9
      specified type NEC M84.80
        ankle M84.87-
        fibula M84.86-
        foot M84.87-
        hand M84.84-
        humerus M84.82-
        neck M84.88
        pelvis M84.859

Disorder *(Continued)*
  bone *(Continued)*
    continuity *(Continued)*
      specified type NEC *(Continued)*
        radius M84.83-
        rib M84.88
        shoulder M84.81-
        skull M84.88
        thigh M84.85-
        tibia M84.86-
        ulna M84.83-
        vertebra M84.88
    density and structure M85.9
      cyst - *see also* Cyst, bone, specified
          type NEC
        aneurysmal - *see* Cyst, bone,
            aneurysmal
        solitary - *see* Cyst, bone, solitary
      diffuse idiopathic skeletal hyper-
          ostosis - *see* Hyperostosis,
          ankylosing
      fibrous dysplasia (monostotic) - *see*
          Dysplasia, fibrous, bone
      fluorosis - *see* Fluorosis, skeletal
      hyperostosis of skull M85.2
      osteitis condensans - *see* Osteitis,
          condensans
      specified type NEC M85.8-
        ankle M85.87-
        foot M85.87-
        forearm M85.83-
        hand M85.84-
        lower leg M85.86-
        multiple sites M85.89
        neck M85.88
        rib M85.88
        shoulder M85.81-
        skull M85.88
        thigh M85.85-
        upper arm M85.82-
        vertebra M85.88
    development and growth NEC
        M89.20
      carpus M89.24-
      clavicle M89.21-
      femur M89.25-
      fibula M89.26-
      finger M89.24-
      humerus M89.22-
      ilium M89.259
      ischium M89.259
      metacarpus M89.24-
      metatarsus M89.27-
      multiple sites M89.29
      neck M89.28
      radius M89.23-
      rib M89.28
      scapula M89.21-
      skull M89.28
      tarsus M89.27-
      tibia M89.26-
      toe M89.27-
      ulna M89.23-
      vertebra M89.28
    specified type NEC M89.8x-
  brachial plexus G54.0
  branched-chain amino-acid metabolism
      E71.2
    specified NEC E71.19
  breast N64.9
    agalactia – *see* Agalactia
    associated with
      lactation O92.70
        specified NEC O92.79

Disorder *(Continued)*
  breast *(Continued)*
    associated with *(Continued)*
      pregnancy O92.20
        specified NEC O92.29
      puerperium O92.20
        specified NEC O92.29
    cracked nipple – *see* Cracked nipple
    galactorrhea – *see* Galactorrhea
    hypogalactia O92.4
    lactation disorder NEC O92.79
    mastitis – *see* Mastitis
    nipple infection – *see* Infection, nipple
    retracted nipple – *see* Retraction,
        nipple
    specified type NEC N64.89
  Briquet's F45.0
  cannabis use
    due to drug abuse - *see* Abuse, drug,
        cannabis
    due to drug dependence - *see* Depen-
        dend, drug, cannabis
  carbohydrate
    absorption, intestinal NEC E74.39
    metabolism (congenital) E74.9
      specified NEC E74.8
  cardiac, functional I51.89
  carnitine metabolism E71.40
  cartilage M94.9
    articular NEC - *see* Derangement,
        joint, articular cartilage
    chondrocalcinosis - *see*
        Chondrocalcinosis
    specified type NEC M94.8x-
      articular - *see* Derangement, joint,
          articular cartilage
      multiple sites M94.8x0
  catatonic
    due to (secondary to) known physi-
        ological condition F06.1
    organic F06.1
  central auditory processing H93.25
  cervical
    region NEC M53.82
    root (nerve) NEC G54.2
  character NEC F68.8
  childhood disintegrative NEC F84.3
  cholesterol and bile acid metabolism
      E78.70
    Barth syndrome E78.71
    other specified E78.79
    Smith-Lemli-Opitz syndrome
        E78.72
  choroid H31.9
    atrophy - *see* Atrophy, choroid
    degeneration - *see* Degeneration,
        choroid
    detachment - *see* Detachment,
        choroid
    dystrophy - *see* Dystrophy, choroid
    hemorrhage - *see* Hemorrhage,
        choroid
    rupture - *see* Rupture, choroid
    scar - *see* Scar, chorioretinal
    solar retinopathy - *see* Retinopathy,
        solar
    specified type NEC H31.8
  ciliary body - *see* Disorder, iris
    degeneration - *see* Degeneration, cili-
        ary body
  coagulation (factor) (*see also* Defect,
      coagulation) D68.9
    newborn, transient P61.6
  coccyx NEC M53.3

Disorder *(Continued)*
  cognitive F09
    due to (secondary to) general medical
        condition F06.9
    persisting R41.89
      due to
        alcohol F10.97
          with dependence F10.27
        anxiolytics F13.97
          with dependence F13.27
        hypnotics F13.97
          with dependence F13.27
        sedatives F13.97
          with dependence F13.27
        specified substance NEC F19.97
          with
            abuse F19.17
            dependence F19.27
  conduct (childhood) F91.9
    adjustment reaction – *see* Disorder,
        adjustment
    adolescent onset type F91.2
    childhood onset type F91.1
    compulsive F63.9
    confined to family context F91.0
    depressive F91.8
    group type F91.2
    hyperkinetic – *see* Disorder, attention-
        deficit hyperactivity
    oppositional defiance F91.3
    socialized F91.2
    solitary aggressive type F91.1
    specified NEC F91.8
    unsocialized (aggressive) F91.1
  conduction, heart I45.9
  congenital glycosylation (CDG) E74.8
  conjunctiva H11.9
    infection - *see* Conjunctivitis
  connective tissue, localized L94.9
    specified NEC L94.8
  conversion - *see* Disorder, dissociative
  convulsive (secondary) - *see*
      Convulsions
  cornea H18.9
    deformity - *see* Deformity, cornea
    degeneration - *see* Degeneration,
        cornea
    deposits - *see* Deposit, cornea
    due to contact lens H18.82-
      specified as edema - *see* Edema,
          cornea
    edema - *see* Edema, cornea
    keratitis - *see* Keratitis
    keratoconjunctivitis - *see*
        Keratoconjunctivitis
    membrane change - *see* Change,
        corneal membrane
    neovascularization - *see* Neovascular-
        ization, cornea
    scar - *see* Opacity, cornea
    specified type NEC H18.89-
    ulcer - *see* Ulcer, cornea
  corpus cavernosum N48.9
  cranial nerve - *see* Disorder, nerve,
      cranial
  cyclothymic F34.0
  defiant oppositional F91.3
  delusional (persistent) (systematized)
      F22
    induced F24
  depersonalization F48.1
  depressive F32.9
    major F32.9
      with psychotic symptoms F32.3

Disorder *(Continued)*
  depressive *(Continued)*
    major *(Continued)*
      in remission (full) F32.5
        partial F32.4
      recurrent F33.9
      single episode F32.9
        mild F32.0
        moderate F32.1
        severe (without psychotic symptoms) F32.2
          with psychotic symptoms F32.3
    organic F06.31
    recurrent F33.9
      current episode
        mild F33.0
        moderate F33.1
        severe (without psychotic symptoms) F33.2
          with psychotic symptoms F33.3
      in remission F33.40
        full F33.42
        partial F33.41
      specified NEC F33.8
    single episode - *see* Episode, depressive
  developmental F89
    arithmetical skills F81.2
    coordination (motor) F82
    expressive writing F81.81
    language (receptive type) F80.2
      expressive F80.1
    learning F81.9
      arithmetical F81.2
      reading F81.0
    mixed F88
    motor coordination or function F82
    pervasive F84.9
      specified NEC F84.8
    phonological F80.0
    reading F81.0
    scholastic skills - *see also* Disorder, learning
      mixed F81.89
    specified NEC F88
    speech F80.9
      and language disorder F80.9
      articulation F80.0
    written expression F81.81
  diaphragm J98.6
  digestive (system) K92.9
    newborn P78.9
      specified NEC P78.89
    postprocedural – *see* Complication, gastrointestinal
    psychogenic F45.8
  disc (intervertebral) M51.9
    with
      myelopathy
        cervical region M50.00
        cervicothoracic region M50.03
        lumbar region M51.06
        lumbosacral region M51.07
        mid-cervical region M50.02
        occipito-atlanto-axial region M50.01
        sacrococcygeal region M53.3
        thoracic region M51.04
        thoracolumbar region M51.05
      radiculopathy
        cervical region M50.10
        cervicothoracic region M50.13

Disorder *(Continued)*
  disc *(Continued)*
    with *(Continued)*
      radiculopathy *(Continued)*
        lumbar region M51.16
        lumbosacral region M51.17
        mid-cervical region M50.12
        occipito-atlanto-axial region M50.11
        sacrococcygeal region M53.3
        thoracic region M51.14
        thoracolumbar region M51.15
    cervical M50.90
      with
        myelopathy M50.00
          cervicothoracic region M50.03
          mid-cervical region M50.02
          occipito-atlanto-axial region M50.01
        neuritis, radiculitis or radiculopathy M50.10
          cervicothoracic region M50.13
          mid-cervical region M50.12
          occipito-atlanto-axial region M50.11
      cervicothoracic region M50.93
      degeneration M50.30
        cervicothoracic region M50.33
        mid-cervical region M50.32
        occipito-atlanto-axial region M50.31
      displacement M50.20
        cervicothoracic region M50.23
        mid-cervical region M50.22
        occipito-atlanto-axial region M50.21
      mid-cervical region M50.92
      occipito-atlanto-axial region M50.91
      specified type NEC M50.80
        cervicothoracic region M50.83
        mid-cervical region M50.82
        occipito-atlanto-axial region M50.81
    specified NEC
      lumbar region M51.86
      lumbosacral region M51.87
      sacrococcygeal region M53.3
      thoracic region M51.84
      thoracolumbar region M51.85
  disinhibited attachment (childhood) F94.2
  disintegrative, childhood NEC F84.3
  disruptive behavior F98.9
  dissocial personality F60.2
  dissociative F44.9
    affecting
      motor function F44.4
        and sensation F44.7
      sensation F44.6
        and motor function F44.7
    brief reactive F43.0
    due to (secondary to) general medical condition F06.8
    mixed F44.7
    organic F06.8
    other specified NEC F44.89
  double heterozygous sickling - *see* Disease, sickle-cell
  dream anxiety F51.5
  drug induced hemorrhagic D68.32
  drug related F19.99
    abuse - *see* Abuse, drug
    dependence - *see* Dependence, drug

Disorder *(Continued)*
  dysmorphic body F45.1
  dysthymic F34.1
  ear H93.9-
    bleeding - *see* Otorrhagia
    deafness - *see* Deafness
    degenerative H93.09-
    discharge - *see* Otorrhea
    external H61.9-
      auditory canal stenosis - *see* Stenosis, external ear canal
      exostosis - *see* Exostosis, external ear canal
      impacted cerumen - *see* Impaction, cerumen
      otitis - *see* Otitis, externa
      perichondritis - *see* Perichondritis, ear
      pinna - *see* Disorder, pinna
      specified type NEC H61.89-
    inner H83.9-
      vestibular dysfunction - *see* Disorder, vestibular function
    middle H74.9-
      ossicle - *see* Abnormal, ear ossicles
      polyp - *see* Polyp, ear (middle)
      postprocedural - *see* Complications, ear, procedure
  eating (adult) (psychogenic) F50.9
    anorexia – *see* Anorexia
    bulimia F50.2
    child F98.29
      pica F98.3
      rumination disorder F98.21
    pica F50.8
      childhood F98.3
  electrolyte (balance) NEC E87.8
    with
      abortion – *see* Abortion by type complicated by specified condition NEC
      ectopic pregnancy O08.5
      molar pregnancy O08.5
    acidosis (metabolic) (respiratory) E87.2
    alkalosis (metabolic) (respiratory) E87.3
  elimination, transepidermal L87.9
    specified NEC L87.8
  emotional (persistent) F34.9
    of childhood F93.9
    specified NEC F93.8
  endocrine E34.9
    postprocedural E89.89
      specified NEC E89.89
  erectile (male) (organic) N52.9 - *see also* Dysfunction, sexual, male, erectile
    nonorganic F52.21
  erythematous - *see* Erythema
  esophagus K22.9
    functional K22.4
    psychogenic F45.8
  eustachian tube H69.9-
    infection – *see* Salpingitis, eustachian
    obstruction – *see* Obstruction, eustachian tube
    patulous – *see* Patulous, eustachian tube
    specified NEC H69.8-
  extrapyramidal G25.9
    specified type NEC G25.89
  eye H57.9
    postprocedural *see* Complication, postprocedural, eye

Disorder *(Continued)*
  eyelid H02.9
    cyst - *see* Cyst, eyelid
    degenerative H02.70
      chloasma - *see* Chloasma, eyelid
      madarosis - *see* Madarosis
      specified type NEC H02.79
      vitiligo - *see* Vitiligo, eyelid
      xanthelasma - *see* Xanthelasma
    dermatochalasis - *see* Dermato-chalasis
    edema - *see* Edema, eyelid
    elephantiasis - *see* Elephantiasis, eyelid
    foreign body, retained - *see* Foreign
      body, retained, eyelid
    function H02.59
      abnormal innervation syndrome
        - *see* Syndrome, abnormal
        innervation
      blepharochalasis - *see*
        Blepharochalasis
      blepharoclonus - *see* Blepharoclonus
      blepharophimosis - *see*
        Blepharophimosis
      blepharoptosis - *see* Blepharoptosis
      lagophthalmos - *see* Lagophthalmos
      lid retraction - *see* Retraction, lid
    hypertrichosis - *see* Hypertrichosis,
      eyelid
    specified type NEC H02.89
    vascular H02.879
      left H02.876
        lower H02.875
        upper H02.874
      right H02.873
        lower H02.872
        upper H02.871
  factitious F68.10
    with predominantly
      psychological symptoms F68.11
        with physical symptoms F68.13
      physical symptoms F68.12
        with psychological symptoms
        F68.13
  factor, coagulation - *see* Defect,
    coagulation
  fatty acid
    metabolism E71.30
      specified NEC E71.39
    oxidation
      LCAD E71.310
      MCAD E71.311
      SCAD E71.312
      specified deficiency NEC E71.318
  feeding (infant or child) R63.3 – *see also*
    Disorder, eating
  feigned (with obvious motivation) Z76.5
    without obvious motivation – *see*
      Disorder, factitious
  female
    hypoactive sexual desire F52.0
    orgasmic F52.31
    sexual arousal F52.22
  fibroblastic M72.9
    specified NEC M72.8
  fluency
    following
      cerebral infarction I69.323
      cerebrovascular disease I69.923
        specified disease NEC I69.823
      intracerebral hemorrhage I69.123
      nontraumatic intracranial hemor-
        rhage NEC I69.223
      subarachnoid hemorrhage I69.023
  fluid balance E87.8

Disorder *(Continued)*
  follicular (skin) L73.9
    specified NEC L73.8
  fructose metabolism E74.10
    essential fructosuria E74.11
    fructokinase deficiency E74.11
    fructose-1, 6-diphosphatase defi-
      ciency E74.19
    hereditary fructose intolerance E74.12
    other specified E74.19
  functional polymorphonuclear neutro-
    phils D71
  gamma-glutamyl cycle E72.8
  gastric (functional) K31.9
    motility K30
    psychogenic F45.8
    secretion K30
  gastrointestinal (functional) NOS K92.9
    newborn P78.9
    psychogenic F45.8
  gender-identity or -role F64.9
    childhood F64.2
    effect on relationship F66
    of adolescence or adulthood (non-
      transsexual) F64.1
    specified NEC F64.8
    uncertainty F66
  genitourinary system
    female N94.9
    male N50.9
    psychogenic F45.8
  globe H44.9
    degenerated condition H44.50
      absolute glaucoma H44.51-
      atrophy H44.52-
      leucocoria H44.53-
    degenerative H44.30
      chalcosis H44.31-
      myopia H44.2-
      siderosis H44.32-
      specified type NEC H44.39-
    endophthalmitis - *see*
      Endophthalmitis
    foreign body, retained - *see* Foreign
      body, intraocular, old, retained
    hemophthalmos - *see* Hemophthalmos
    hypotony H44.40
      due to
        ocular fistula H44.42-
        specified disorder NEC H44.43-
      flat anterior chamber H44.41-
      primary H44.44-
    luxation - *see* Luxation, globe
    specified type NEC H44.89
  glomerular (in) N05.9
    amyloidosis E85.4 [N08]
    cryoglobulinemia D89.1 [N08]
    disseminated intravascular coagula-
      tion D65 [N08]
    Fabry's disease E75.21 [N08]
    familial lecithin cholesterol acyltrans-
      ferase deficiency E78.6 [N08]
    Goodpasture's syndrome M31.0
    hemolytic-uremic syndrome D59.3
    Henoch (-Schönlein) purpura D69.0
      [N08]
    malariae malaria B52.0
    microscopic polyangiitis M31.7 [N08]
    multiple myeloma C90.00 [N08]
    mumps B26.83
    schistosomiasis B65.9 [N08]
    sepsis NEC A41.9 [N08]
      streptococcal A40.9 [N08]
    sickle-cell disorders D57.- [N08]

Disorder *(Continued)*
  glomerular (in) *(Continued)*
    strongyloidiasis B78.9 [N08]
    subacute bacterial endocarditis
      I33.0 [N08]
    syphilis A52.75
    systemic lupus erythematosus
      M32.14
    thrombotic thrombocytopenic pur-
      pura M31.1 [N08]
    Waldenström macroglobulinemia
      C88.0 [N08]
    Wegener's granulomatosis M31.31
  gluconeogenesis E74.4
  glucosaminoglycan metabolism
    - *see* Disorder, metabolism,
    glucosaminoglycan
  glycine metabolism E72.50
    d-glycericacidemia E72.59
    hyperhydroxyprolinemia E72.59
    hyperoxaluria E72.53
    hyperprolinemia E72.59
    non-ketotic hyperglycinemia E72.51
    oxalosis E72.53
    oxaluria E72.53
    sarcosinemia E72.59
    trimethylaminuria E72.52
  glycoprotein metabolism E77.9
    specified NEC E77.8
  habit (and impulse) F63.9
    involving sexual behavior NEC
      F65.9
    specified NEC F63.89
  heart action I49.9
  hematological D75.9
    newborn (transient) P61.9
      specified NEC P61.8
  hematopoietic organs D75.9
  hemorrhagic NEC D69.9
    drug-induced D68.32
    due to extrinsic circulating anticoagu-
      lants D68.32
    due to intrinsic circulating anticoagu-
      lants D68.31
      following childbirth O72.3
  hemostasis - *see* Defect, coagulation
  histidine metabolism E70.40
    histidinemia E70.41
    other specified E70.49
  hyperkinetic – *see* Disorder, attention-
    deficit hyperactivity
  hyperleucine-isoleucinemia E71.19
  hypervalinemia E71.19
  hypoactive sexual desire F52.0
  hypochondriacal F45.20
    body dysmorphic F45.22
    neurosis F45.21
    other specified F45.29
  identity
    dissociative F44.81
    of childhood F93.8
  immune mechanism (immunity)
    D89.9
    specified type NEC D89.8
  impaired renal tubular function N25.9
    specified NEC N25.89
  impulse (control) F63.9
  inflammatory
    penis N48.29
      abscess N48.21
      cellulitis N48.22
  integument, newborn P83.9
    specified NEC P83.8
  intermittent explosive F63.81

Disorder *(Continued)*
  internal secretion pancreas - *see* Increased, secretion, pancreas, endocrine
  intestine, intestinal
    carbohydrate absorption NEC E74.39
      postoperative K91.2
    functional NEC K59.9
      postoperative K91.89
    psychogenic F45.8
    vascular K55.9
      chronic K55.1
      specified NEC K55.8
  intraoperative (intraprocedural) - *see* Complications, intraoperative
  involuntary emotional expression (IEED) F07.89
  iris H21.9
    adhesions - *see* Adhesions, iris
    atrophy - *see* Atrophy, iris
    chamber angle recession - *see* Recession, chamber angle
    cyst - *see* Cyst, iris
    degeneration - *see* Degeneration, iris
    iridodialysis - *see* Iridodialysis
    iridoschisis - *see* Iridoschisis
    miotic pupillary cyst - *see* Cyst, pupillary
    pupillary
      abnormality - *see* Abnormality, pupillary
      membrane - *see* Membrane, pupillary
    specified type NEC H21.89
    vascular NEC H21.1x-
  iron metabolism E83.10
    hemochromatosis E83.11
    other specified E83.19
  isovaleric acidemia E71.110
  jaw, developmental M27.0
    temporomandibular – *see* Anomaly, dentofacial, temporomandibular joint
  joint M25.9
    derangement - *see* Derangement, joint
    effusion - *see* Effusion, joint
    fistula - *see* Fistula, joint
    hemarthrosis - *see* Hemarthrosis
    instability - *see* Instability, joint
    osteophyte - *see* Osteophyte
    pain - *see* Pain, joint
    psychogenic F45.8
    specified type NEC M25.80
      ankle M25.87-
      elbow M25.82-
      foot joint M25.87-
      hand joint M25.84-
      hip M25.85-
      knee M25.86-
      shoulder M25.81-
      wrist M25.83-
    stiffness - *see* Stiffness, joint
  ketone metabolism E71.32
  kidney N28.9
    functional (tubular) N25.9
    in
      schistosomiasis B65.9 [N29]
    tubular function N25.9
      specified NEC N25.89
  lacrimal system H04.9
    changes H04.69
      fistula - *see* Fistula, lacrimal

Disorder *(Continued)*
  lacrimal system *(Continued)*
    gland H04.19
      atrophy - *see* Atrophy, lacrimal gland
      cyst - *see* Cyst, lacrimal, gland
      dacryops - *see* Dacryops
      dislocation - *see* Dislocation, lacrimal gland
      dry eye syndrome - *see* Syndrome, dry eye
      infection - *see* Dacryoadenitis
      granuloma - *see* Granuloma, lacrimal
      inflammation - *see* Inflammation, lacrimal
      obstruction - *see* Obstruction, lacrimal
      specified NEC H04.89
  lactation NEC O92.79
  language (developmental) F80.9
    expressive F80.1
    mixed receptive and expressive F80.2
    receptive F80.2
  late luteal phase dysphoric N94.89
  learning (specific) F81.9
    acalculia R48.8
    alexia R48.0
    mathematics F81.2
    reading F81.0
    specified NEC F81.89
    spelling F81.81
    written expression F81.81
  lens H27.9
    aphakia - *see* Aphakia
    cataract - *see* Cataract
    dislocation - *see* Dislocation, lens
    specified type NEC H27.8
  ligament M24.20
    ankle M24.27-
    attachment, spine – *see* Enthesopathy, spinal
    elbow M24.22-
    foot joint M24.27-
    hand joint M24.24-
    hip M24.25-
    knee - *see* Derangement, knee, specified NEC
    shoulder M24.21-
    vertebra M24.28
    wrist M24.23-
  ligamentous attachments - *see also* Enthesopathy
    spine - *see* Enthesopathy, spinal
  lipid
    metabolism, congenital E78.9
    storage E75.6
      specified NEC E75.5
  lipoprotein
    deficiency (familial) E78.6
    metabolism E78.9
      specified NEC E78.89
  liver K76.9
    malarial B54 [K77]
  low back - *see also* Dorsopathy, specified NEC
  lumbosacral
    plexus G54.1
    root (nerve) NEC G54.4
  lung, interstitial, drug-induced J70.4
    acute J70.2
    chronic J70.3
  lymphoproliferative, post-transplant (PTLD) D47.z1
  lysine and hydroxylysine metabolism E72.3

Disorder *(Continued)*
  male
    erectile (organic) N52.9 —*see also* Dysfunction, sexual, male, erectile
      nonorganic F52.21
    hypoactive sexual desire F52.0
    orgasmic F52.32
  manic F30.9
    organic F06.33
  mastoid - *see also* Disorder, ear, middle
    postprocedural - *see* Complications, ear, procedure
  meniscus - *see* Derangement, knee, meniscus
  menopausal N95.9
    specified NEC N95.8
  menstrual N92.6
    psychogenic F45.8
    specified NEC N92.5
  mental (or behavioral) (nonpsychotic) F99
    due to (secondary to)
      amphetamine
        due to drug abuse - *see* Abuse, drug, stimulant
        due to drug dependence - *see* Dependence, drug, stimulant
      brain disease, damage and dysfunction F06.9
      caffeine use
        due to drug abuse - *see* Abuse, drug, stimulant
        due to drug dependence - *see* Dependence, drug, stimulant
      cannabis use
        due to drug abuse - *see* Abuse, drug, cannabis
        due to drug dependence - *see* Dependence, drug, cannabis
      general medical condition F06.9
      sedative or hypnotic use
        due to drug abuse - *see* Abuse, drug, sedative
        due to drug dependence - *see* Dependence, drug, sedative
      tobacco (nicotine) use - *see* Dependence, drug, nicotine
    following organic brain damage F07.9
      frontal lobe syndrome F07.0
      personality change F07.0
      postconcussional syndrome F07.81
      specified NEC F07.89
    infancy, childhood or adolescence F98.9
    neurotic - *see* Neurosis
    organic or symptomatic F06.9
    presenile, psychotic F03
    problem NEC
    psychoneurotic - *see* Neurosis
    psychotic - *see* Psychosis
    puerperal F53
    senile, psychotic NEC F03
  metabolic, amino acid, transitory, newborn P74.8
  metabolism NOS E88.9
    amino-acid E72.9
      aromatic E70.9
        albinism – *see* Albinism
        histidine E70.40
          histidinemia E70.41
          other specified E70.49
        hyperphenylalaninemia EE70.1
          classical phenylketonuria E70.0

Disorder *(Continued)*
  metabolism *(Continued)*
   amino-acid *(Continued)*
    aromatic *(Continued)*
     other specified E70.8
     tryptophan E70.5
     tyrosine E70.20
      hypertyrosinemia E70.21
      other specified E70.29
    branched chain E71.2
     3-methylglutaconic aciduria
       E71.111
     hyperleucine-isoleucinemia
       E71.19
     hypervalinemia E71.19
     isovaleric acidemia E71.110
     maple syrup urine disease E71.0
     methylmalonic acidemia E71.120
     organic aciduria NEC E71.118
     other specified E71.19
     proprionate NEC E71.128
     proprionic acidemia E71.121
    glycine E72.50
     d-glycericacidemia E72.59
     hyperhydroxyprolinemia E72.59
     hyperoxaluria E72.53
     hyperprolinemia E72.59
     non-ketotic hyperglycinemia
       E72.51
     other specified E72.59
     sarcosinemia E72.59
     trimethylaminuria E72.52
    hydroxylysine E72.3
    lysine E72.3
    ornithine E72.4
    other specified E72.8
     beta-amino acid E72.8
     gamma-glutamyl cycle E72.8
    straight-chain E72.8
    sulfur-bearing E72.10
     homocystinuria E72.11
     methylenetetrahydrofolate re-
       ductase deficiency E72.12
     other specified E72.19
   bile acid and cholesterol metabolism
      E78.70
   bilirubin E80.7
    specified NEC E80.6
   calcium E83.50
    hypercalcemia E83.52
    hypocalcemia E83.51
    other specified E83.59
   carbohydrate E74.9
    specified NEC E74.8
   cholesterol and bile acid metabolism
      E78.70
   congenital E88.9
   copper E83.00
    Wilson's disease E83.01
    specified type NEC E83.09
   cystinuria E72.01
   fructose E74.10
   galactose E74.20
   glucosaminoglycan E76.9
    mucopolysaccharidosis - *see*
       Mucopolysaccharidosis
    specified NEC E76.8
   glutamine E72.8
   glycine E72.50
   glycogen storage (hepatorenal) E74.01
   glycoprotein E77.9
    specified NEC E77.8
   glycosaminoglycan E76.9
    specified NEC E76.8

Disorder *(Continued)*
  metabolism *(Continued)*
   in labor and delivery O75.89
   iron E83.10
   isoleucine E71.19
   leucine E71.19
   lipoid E78.9
   lipoprotein E78.9
    specified NEC E78.89
   magnesium E83.40
    hypermagnesemia E83.41
    hypomagnesemia E83.42
    other specified E83.49
   mineral E83.9
    specified NEC E83.89
   mitochondrial E88.40
    MELAS syndrome E88.41
    MERFF syndrome E88.42
    other specified E88.49
   ornithine E72.4
   phosphatases E83.30
   phosphorus E83.30
    acid phosphatase deficiency E83.39
    hypophosphatasia E83.39
    hypophosphatemia E83.39
     familial E83.31
    other specified E83.39
    pseudovitamin D deficiency E83.32
   plasma protein NEC E88.09
   porphyrin - *see* Porphyria
   postprocedural E89.89
    specified NEC E89.89
   purine E79.9
    specified NEC E79.8
   pyrimidine E79.9
    specified NEC E79.8
   pyruvate E74.4
   serine E72.8
   sodium E87.8
   specified NEC E88.89
   threonine E72.8
   valine E71.19
   zinc E83.2
  methylmalonic acidemia E71.120
  micturition NEC R39.19
   feeling of incomplete emptying
      R39.14
   hesitancy R39.11
   poor stream R39.12
   psychogenic F45.8
   split stream R39.13
   straining R39.16
   urgency R39.15
  mitochondrial metabolism E88.40
  mitral (valve) – *see* Endocarditis,
     mitral
  mixed
   anxiety and depressive F41.8
   of scholastic skills (developmental)
      F81.89
   receptive expressive language F80.2
  mood F39
   bipolar – *see* Disorder, bipolar
   depressive – *see* Disorder, depressive
   due to (secondary to)
    alcohol F10.959
    amphetamine F15.94
     in
      abuse F15.14
      dependence F15.24
    anxiolytic F13.94
     in
      abuse F13.14
      dependence F13.24

Disorder *(Continued)*
  mood *(Continued)*
   due to *(Continued)*
    cocaine F14.94
     in
      abuse F14.14
      dependence F14.24
    general medical condition F06.30
    hallucinogen F16.94
     in
      abuse F16.14
      dependence F16.24
    hypnotic F13.94
     in
      abuse F13.14
      dependence F13.24
    inhalant F18.94
     in
      abuse F18.14
      dependence F18.24
    opioid F11.94
     in
      abuse F11.14
      dependence F11.24
    phencyclidine (PCP) F19.94
     in
      abuse F19.14
      dependence F19.24
    physiological condition F06.30
     with
      depressive features F06.31
      major depressive-like episode
        F06.32
      manic features F06.33
      mixed features F06.34
    psychoactive substance NEC
       F19.94
     in
      abuse F19.14
      dependence F19.24
    sedative F13.94
     in
      abuse F13.14
      dependence F13.24
    volatile solvents F18.94
     in
      abuse F18.14
      dependence F18.24
   manic episode F30.9
    with psychotic symptoms F30.2
    in remission (full) F30.4
     partial F30.3
    specified type NEC F30.8
    without psychotic symptoms
       F30.10
     mild F30.11
     moderate F30.12
     severe F30.13
   organic F06.30
    right hemisphere F07.89
   persistent F34.9
    cyclothymia F34.0
    dysthymia F34.1
    specified type NEC F34.8
   recurrent F39
   right hemisphere organic F07.89
  movement G25.9
   drug-induced G25.70
    akathisia G25.71
    specified NEC G25.79
   hysterical F44.4
   periodic limb G47.61
    sleep related G47.61
   specified NEC G25.89

Disorder *(Continued)*
  movement *(Continued)*
    sleep related NEC G47.69
    stereotyped F98.4
    treatment-induced G25.9
  multiple personality F44.81
  muscle M62.9
    attachment, spine – *see* Enthesopathy, spinal
    in trichinellosis - *see* Trichinellosis, with muscle disorder
    psychogenic F45.8
    specified type NEC M62.89
    tone, newborn P94.9
      specified NEC P94.8
  muscular
    attachments - *see also* Enthesopathy
      spine - *see* Enthesopathy, spinal
    urethra N36.44
  musculoskeletal system, soft tissue - *see* Disorder, soft tissue
    postprocedural M96.89
    psychogenic F45.8
  myoneural G70.9
    due to lead G70.1
    specified NEC G70.8
    toxic G70.1
  myotonic NEC G71.19
  neck region NEC - *see* Dorsopathy, specified NEC
  nerve G58.9
    abducent NEC - *see* Strabismus, paralytic, sixth nerve
    accessory G52.8
    acoustic - *see* subcategory H93.3
    auditory - *see* subcategory H93.3
    auriculotemporal G50.8
    axillary G54.0
    cerebral - *see* Disorder, nerve, cranial
    cranial G52.9
      eighth - *see* subcategory H93.3
      eleventh G52.8
      fifth G50.9
      first G52.0
      fourth NEC - *see* Strabismus, paralytic, fourth nerve
      multiple G52.7
      ninth G52.1
      second NEC - *see* Disorder, nerve, optic
      seventh NEC G51.9
      sixth NEC - *see* Strabismus, paralytic, sixth nerve
      specified NEC G52.8
      tenth G52.2
      third NEC - *see* Strabismus, paralytic, third nerve
      twelfth G52.3
    entrapment - *see* Neuropathy, entrapment
    facial G51.9
      specified NEC G51.8
    femoral – *see* Lesion, nerve, femoral
    glossopharyngeal NEC G52.1
    hypoglossal G52.3
    intercostal G58.0
    lateral
      cutaneous of thigh - *see* Mononeuropathy, lower limb, meralgia paresthetica
      popliteal – *see* Lesion, nerve, popliteal
    lower limb – *see* Mononeuropathy, lower limb

Disorder *(Continued)*
  nerve *(Continued)*
    medial popliteal – *see* Lesion, nerve, popliteal, medial
    median NEC – *see* Lesion, nerve, median
    multiple G58.7
    oculomotor NEC - *see* Strabismus, paralytic, third nerve
    olfactory G52.0
    optic NEC H47.09-
      hemorrhage into sheath - *see* Hemorrhage, optic nerve
      ischemic H47.09-
    peroneal – *see* Lesion, nerve, popliteal
    phrenic G58.8
    plantar - *see* Lesion, nerve, plantar
    pneumogastric G52.2
    posterior tibial - *see* Syndrome, tarsal tunnel
    radial – *see* Lesion, nerve, radial
    recurrent laryngeal G52.2
    root G54.9
      cervical G54.2
      lumbosacral G54.1
      specified NEC G54.8
      thoracic G54.3
    sciatic NEC – *see* Lesion, nerve, sciatic
    specified NEC G58.8
      lower limb – *see* Mononeuropathy, lower limb, specified NEC
      upper limb – *see* Mononeuropathy, upper limb, specified NEC
    sympathetic G90.9
    tibial – *see* Lesion, nerve, popliteal, medial
    trigeminal G50.9
      specified NEC G50.8
    trochlear NEC - *see* Strabismus, paralytic, fourth nerve
    ulnar – *see* Lesion, nerve, ulnar
    upper limb – *see* Mononeuropathy, upper limb
    vagus G52.2
  nervous system G98.8
    autonomic (peripheral) G90.9
      specified NEC G90.8
    central G96.9
      specified NEC G96.8
    parasympathetic G90.9
    specified NEC G98.8
    sympathetic G90.9
    vegetative G90.9
  neurohypophysis NEC E23.3
  neurological NEC R29.81
  neuromuscular G70.9
    hereditary NEC G71.9
    specified NEC G70.8
    toxic G70.1
  neurotic F48.9
    specified NEC F48.8
  neutrophil, polymorphonuclear D71
  nicotine use – *see* Dependence, drug, nicotine
  nightmare F51.5
  nose J34.9
    specified NEC J34.89
  obsessive-compulsive F42
  odontogenesis NOS K00.9
  oesophagus - *see* Disorder, esophagus
  opioid use
    due to drug abuse - *see* Abuse, drug, opioid

Disorder *(Continued)*
  oesophagus *(Continued)*
    due to drug dependence - *see* Dependence, drug, opioid
  oppositional defiant F91.3
  optic
    chiasm H47.49
      due to
        inflammatory disorder H47.41
        neoplasm H47.42
        vascular disorder H47.43
    disc H47.39-
      coloboma - *see* Coloboma, optic disc
      drusen - *see* Drusen, optic disc
      pseudopapilledema - *see* Pseudopapilledema
    radiations - *see* Disorder, visual, pathway
    tracts - *see* Disorder, visual, pathway
  orbit H05.9
    cyst - *see* Cyst, orbit
    deformity - *see* Deformity, orbit
    edema - *see* Edema, orbit
    enophthalmos - *see* Enophthalmos
    exophthalmos - *see* Exophthalmos
    hemorrhage - *see* Hemorrhage, orbit
    inflammation - *see* Inflammation, orbit
    myopathy - *see* Myopathy, extraocular muscles
    retained foreign body - *see* Foreign body, orbit, old
    specified type NEC H05.89
  organic
    anxiety F06.4
    catatonic F06.1
    delusional F06.2
    dissociative F06.8
    emotionally labile (asthenic) F06.8
    mood (affective) F06.30
    schizophrenia-like F06.2
  orgasmic (female) F52.31
    male F52.32
  ornithine metabolism E72.4
  overanxious F41.1
    of childhood F93.8
  pain
    with related psychological factors F45.42
    exclusively related to psychological factors F45.41
    (secondary) due to a general medical condition R52.9
  pancreatic internal secretion E16.9
    specified NEC E16.8
  panic F41.0
    with agoraphobia F40.01
  papulosquamous L44.9
    specified NEC L44.8
  paranoid F22
    induced F24
    shared F24
  parathyroid (gland) E21.5
    specified NEC E21.4
  parietoalveolar NEC J84.0
  paroxysmal, mixed R56.9
  patella M22.90
    chondromalacia - *see* Chondromalacia, patella
    derangement NEC M22.3x-
    recurrent
      dislocation - *see* Dislocation, patella, recurrent

Disorder *(Continued)*
  patella *(Continued)*
    recurrent *(Continued)*
      subluxation - *see* Dislocation, patella, recurrent, incomplete
      specified NEC M22.8x-
    patellofemoral M22.2x-
  pentose phosphate pathway with anemia D55.1
  perception, due to hallucinogens F16.983
    in
      abuse F16.183
      dependence F16.283
  peripheral nervous system NEC G64
  peroxisomal E71.50
    biogenesis
      neonatal adrenoleukodystrophy E71.511
      specified disorder NEC E71.518
      Zellweger syndrome E71.510
    rhizomelic chondrodysplasia punctata E71.540
    specified form NEC E71.548
      group 1 E71.518
      group 2 E71.53
      group 3 E71.542
    X-linked adrenoleukodystrophy E71.529
      adolescent E71.521
      adrenomyeloneuropathy E71.522
      childhood E71.420
      specified form NEC E71.428
    Zellweger-like syndrome E71.541
  persistent
    (somatoform) pain F45.41
    affective (mood) F34.9
  personality *(see also* Personality) F60.9
    affective F34.0
    aggressive F60.3
    amoral F60.2
    anankastic F60.5
    antisocial F60.2
    anxious F60.6
    asocial F60.2
    asthenic F60.7
    avoidant F60.6
    borderline F60.3
    change (secondary) due to general medical condition F07.0
    compulsive F60.5
    cyclothymic F34.0
    dependent (passive) F60.7
    depressive F34.1
    dissocial F60.2
    emotional instability F60.3
    expansive paranoid F60.0
    explosive F60.3
    following organic brain damage F07.9
    histrionic F60.4
    hyperthymic F34.0
    hypothymic F34.1
    hysterical F60.4
    immature F60.89
    inadequate F60.7
    labile F60.3
    mixed (nonspecific) F60.89
    moral deficiency F60.2
    narcissistic F60.81
    negativistic F60.89
    obsessional F60.5
    obsessive(-compulsive) F60.5
    organic F07.9
    overconscientious F60.5

Disorder *(Continued)*
  personality *(Continued)*
    paranoid F60.0
    passive(-dependent) F60.7
    passive-aggressive F60.89
    pathological NEC F60.9
    pseudosocial F60.2
    psychopathic F60.2
    schizoid F60.1
    schizotypal F21
    self-defeating F60.7
    specified NEC F60.89
    type A F60.5
    unstable (emotional) F60.3
  pervasive, developmental F84.9
  phobic anxiety, childhood F40.8
  phosphate-losing tubular N25.0
  pigmentation L81.9
    choroid, congenital Q14.3
    diminished melanin formation L81.6
    iron L81.8
    specified NEC L81.8
  pinna (noninfective) H61.10-
    deformity, acquired H61.11-
    hematoma H61.12-
    perichondritis - *see* Perichondritis, ear
    specified type NEC H61.19-
  pituitary gland E23.7
    iatrogenic (postprocedural) E89.3
    specified NEC E23.6
  platelets D69.1
  plexus G54.9
    specified NEC G54.8
  polymorphonuclear neutrophils D71
  porphyrin metabolism - *see* Porphyria
  postconcussional F07.81
  posthallucinogen perception F16.983
    in
      abuse F16.183
      dependence F16.283
  postmenopausal N95.9
    specified NEC N95.8
  postprocedural (postoperative) - *see* Complications, postprocedural
  post-transplant lymphoproliferative D47.z1
  post-traumatic stress (PTSD) F43.10
    acute F43.0
    chronic F43.12
  premenstrual dysphoric (PMDD) N94.3
  prepuce N47.8
  propionic acidemia E71.121
  prostate N42.9
    specified NEC N42.89
  psychogenic NOS *(see also* condition) F45.9
    anxiety F41.8
    appetite F50.9
    asthenic F48.8
    cardiovascular (system) F45.8
    compulsive F42
    cutaneous F54
    depressive F32.9
    digestive (system) F45.8
    dysmenorrheic F45.8
    dyspneic F45.8
    endocrine (system) F54
    eye NEC F45.8
    feeding – *see* Disorder, eating
    functional NEC F45.8
    gastric F45.8
    gastrointestinal (system) F45.8
    genitourinary (system) F45.8
    heart (function) (rhythm) F45.8
    hyperventilatory F45.8

Disorder *(Continued)*
  psychogenic NOS *(Continued)*
    hypochondriacal – *see* Disorder, hypochondriacal
    intestinal F45.8
    joint F45.8
    learning F81.9
    limb F45.8
    lymphatic (system) F45.8
    menstrual F45.8
    micturition F45.8
    monoplegic NEC F44.4
    motor F44.4
    muscle F45.8
    musculoskeletal F45.8
    neurocirculatory F45.8
    obsessive F42
    occupational F48.8
    organ or part of body NEC F45.8
    paralytic NEC F44.4
    phobic F40.9
    physical NEC F45.8
    rectal F45.8
    respiratory (system) F45.8
    rheumatic F45.8
    sexual (function) F52.9
    skin (allergic) (eczematous) F54
    sleep F51.9
    specified part of body NEC F45.8
    stomach F45.8
  psychological F99
    associated with
      disease classified elsewhere F54
      sexual
        development F66
        relationship F66
        uncertainty about gender identity F66
  psychomotor NEC F44.4
    hysterical F44.4
  psychoneurotic - *see also* Neurosis
    mixed NEC F48.8
  psychophysiologic - *see* Disorder, somatoform
  psychosexual F65.9
    development F66
    identity of childhood F64.2
  psychosomatic NOS - *see* Disorder, somatoform
    multiple F45.0
    undifferentiated F45.1
  psychotic - *see* Psychosis
    transient (acute) F23
  puberty E30.9
    specified NEC E30.8
  pulmonary (valve) – *see* Endocarditis, pulmonary
  purine metabolism E79.9
  pyrimidine metabolism E79.9
  pyruvate metabolism E74.4
  reactive attachment (childhood) F94.1
  reading R48.0
    developmental (specific) F81.0
  receptive language F80.2
  receptor, hormonal, peripheral E34.50
    - *see also* Syndrome, androgen insensitivity
  recurrent brief depressive F33.8
  reflex R29.2
  refraction H52.7
    aniseikonia H52.32
    anisometropia H52.31
    astigmatism - *see* Astigmatism
    hypermetropia - *see* Hypermetropia

Disorder *(Continued)*
  refraction *(Continued)*
    myopia - *see* Myopia
    presbyopia H52.4
    specified NEC H52.6
  relationship F68.8
    due to sexual orientation F66
  REM sleep behavior G47.52
  renal function, impaired (tubular) N25.9
  resonance R49.9
    specified NEC R49.8
  respiratory function, impaired - *see also*
      Failure, respiration
    postprocedural – *see* Complication,
        postoperative, respiratory system
    psychogenic F45.8
  retina H35.9
    angioid streaks H35.33
    changes in vascular appearance H35.01-
    degeneration - *see* Degeneration, retina
    dystrophy (hereditary) - *see* Dystro-
        phy, retina
    edema H35.81
    hemorrhage - *see* Hemorrhage, retina
    ischemia H35.82
    macular degeneration - *see* Degenera-
        tion, macula
    microaneurysms H35.04-
    microvascular abnormality NEC H35.09
    neovascularization - *see* Neovascular-
        ization, retina
    retinopathy - *see* Retinopathy
    separation of layers H35.70
      central serous chorioretinopathy
          H35.71-
        pigment epithelium detachment
            (serous) H35.72-
          hemorrhagic H35.73-
    specified type NEC H35.89
    telangiectasis - *see* Telangiectasis, retina
    vasculitis - *see* Vasculitis, retina
  retroperitoneal K68.9
  right hemisphere organic affective F07.89
  rumination (infant or child) F98.21
  sacrum, sacrococcygeal NEC M53.3
  schizoaffective F25.9
    bipolar type F25.8
    depressive type F25.1
    manic type F25.0
    mixed type F25.8
    specified NEC F25.8
  schizoid of childhood F84.5
  schizophreniform F20.81
    brief F23
  schizotypal (personality) F21
  secretion, thyrocalcitonin E07.0
  seizure R56.9
    intractable G40.919
      with status epilepticus G40.911
  semantic pragmatic F80.8
    with autism F84.0
  sense of smell R43.1
    psychogenic F45.8
  separation anxiety, of childhood F93.0
  sexual
    arousal, female F52.22
    aversion F52.1
    function, psychogenic F52.9
    maturation F66
    nonorganic F52.9
    preference (*see also* Deviation, sexual)
        F65.9
      fetishistic transvestism F65.1
    relationship F66

Disorder *(Continued)*
  shyness, of childhood and adolescence
      F40.10
  sibling rivalry F93.8
  sickle-cell (sickling) (homozygous) *See*
      Disease, sickle-cell
    heterozygous D57.3
    specified type NEC D57.8-
    trait D57.3
  sinus (nasal) J34.9
    specified NEC J34.89
  skin L98.9
    atrophic L90.9
      specified NEC L90.8
    newborn P83.9
      specified NEC P83.8
    granulomatous L92.9
      specified NEC L92.8
    hypertrophic L91.9
      specified NEC L91.8
    infiltrative NEC L98.6
    psychogenic (allergic) (eczematous)
        F54
  sleep G47.9
    breathing-related – *see* Apnea, sleep
    circadian rhythm G47.20
      advance sleep phase type
          G47.22
      delayed sleep phase type
          G47.21
      due to
        alcohol
          abuse F10.182
          dependence F10.282
          use F10.982
        amphetamines
          abuse F15.182
          dependence F15.282
          use F15.982
        caffeine
          abuse F15.182
          dependence F15.282
          use F15.982
        cocaine
          abuse F14.182
          dependence F14.282
          use F14.982
        drug NEC
          abuse F19.182
          dependence F19.282
          use F19.982
        opioid
          abuse F11.182
          dependence F11.282
          use F11.982
        psychoactive substance NEC
          abuse F19.182
          dependence F19.282
          use F19.982
        sedative, hypnotic, or anxiolytic
          abuse F13.182
          dependence F13.282
          use F13.982
        stimulant NEC
          abuse F15.182
          dependence F15.282
          use F15.982
      free running type G47.24
      in conditions classified elsewhere
          G47.27
      irregular sleep wake type G47.23
      jet lag type G47.25
      shift work type G47.26
      specified NEC G47.29

Disorder *(Continued)*
  sleep *(Continued)*
    due to
      alcohol
        abuse F10.182
        dependence F10.282
        use F10.982
      amphetamine
        abuse F15.182
        dependence F15.282
        use F15.982
      anxiolytic
        abuse F13.182
        dependence F13.282
        use F13.982
      caffeine
        abuse F15.182
        dependence F15.282
        use F15.982
      cocaine
        abuse F14.182
        dependence F14.282
        use F14.982
      drug NEC
        abuse F19.182
        dependence F19.282
        use F19.982
      hypnotic
        abuse F13.182
        dependence F13.282
        use F13.982
      opioid
        abuse F11.182
        dependence F11.282
        use F11.982
      psychoactive substance NEC
        abuse F19.182
        dependence F19.282
        use F19.982
      sedative
        abuse F13.182
        dependence F13.282
        use F13.982
      stimulant NEC
        abuse F15.182
        dependence F15.282
        use F15.982
    emotional F51.9
    excessive somnolence - *see*
        Hypersomnia
    hypersomnia type - *see* Hypersomnia
    initiating or maintaining - *see*
        Insomnia
    nightmares F51.5
    nonorganic F51.9
      specified NEC F51.8
    parasomnia type G47.50
    specified NEC G47.8
    terrors F51.4
    walking F51.3
  sleep-wake pattern or schedule – *see*
      Disorder, sleep, circadian rhythm
  social
    anxiety of childhood F40.10
    functioning in childhood F94.9
      specified NEC F94.8
  soft tissue M79.9
    ankle M79.9
    due to use, overuse and pressure
        M70.90
      ankle M70.97-
      bursitis - *see* Bursitis
      foot M70.97-
      forearm M70.93-

Disorder *(Continued)*
  soft tissue *(Continued)*
    due to use, overuse and pressure
      (Continued)
      hand M70.94-
      lower leg M70.96-
      multiple sites M70.99
      pelvic region M70.95-
      shoulder region M70.91-
      specified site NEC M70.98
      specified type NEC M70.80
        ankle M70.87-
        foot M70.87-
        forearm M70.83-
        hand M70.84-
        lower leg M70.86-
        multiple sites M70.89
        pelvic region M70.85-
        shoulder region M70.81-
        specified site NEC M70.88
        thigh M70.85-
        upper arm M70.82-
      thigh M70.95-
      upper arm M70.92-
    foot M79.9
    forearm M79.9
    hand M79.9
    lower leg M79.9
    multiple sites M79.9
    occupational – *see* Disorder, soft
      tissue, due to use, overuse and
      pressure
    pelvic region M79.9
    shoulder region M79.9
    specified type NEC M79.89
    thigh M79.9
    upper arm M79.9
  somatization F45.0
  somatoform F45.9
    pain (persistent) F45.41
    somatization (multiple) (long-lasting)
      F45.0
    specified NEC F45.8
    undifferentiated F45.1
  somnolence, excessive G47.10
  specific
    arithmetical F81.2
    developmental, of motor F82
    reading F81.0
    speech and language F80.9
    spelling F81.81
    written expression F81.81
  speech R47.9
    articulation (functional) (specific)
      F80.0
    developmental F80.9
    specified NEC R47.89
  spelling (specific) F81.81
  spine - *see also* Dorsopathy
    ligamentous or muscular attach-
      ments, peripheral - *see* Enthe-
      sopathy, spinal
    specified NEC - *see* Dorsopathy,
      specified NEC
  stereotyped, habit or movement
    F98.4
  stomach (functional) - *see* Disorder,
    gastric
  stress F43.9
    post-traumatic F43.10
      acute F43.0
      chronic F43.12
  sulfur-bearing amino-acid metabolism
    E72.10

Disorder *(Continued)*
  sweat gland (eccrine) L74.9
    apocrine L75.9
      specified NEC L75.8
    specified NEC L74.8
  synovium M67.90
    acromioclavicular M67.91-
    ankle M67.97-
    elbow M67.92-
    foot M67.97-
    forearm M67.93-
    hand M67.94-
    hip M67.95-
    knee M67.96-
    multiple sites M67.99
    rupture – *see* Rupture, synovium
    shoulder M67.91-
    specified type NEC M67.80
      acromioclavicular M67.81-
      ankle M67.87-
      elbow M67.82-
      foot M67.87-
      hand M67.84-
      hip M67.85-
      knee M67.86-
      multiple sites M67.89
      wrist M67.83-
    synovitis – *see* Synovitis
    upper arm M67.92-
    wrist M67.93-
  temperature regulation, newborn
    P81.9
    specified NEC P81.8
  temporomandibular joint – *see* Anom-
    aly, dentofacial, temporomandibu-
    lar joint
  tendon M67.90
    acromioclavicular M67.91-
    ankle M67.97-
    contracture – *see* Contracture, tendon
    elbow M67.92-
    foot M67.97-
    forearm M67.93-
    hand M67.94-
    hip M67.95-
    knee M67.96-
    multiple sites M67.99
    rupture – *see* Rupture, tendon
    shoulder M67.91-
    specified type NEC M67.80
      acromioclavicular M67.81-
      ankle M67.87-
      elbow M67.82-
      foot M67.87-
      hand M67.84-
      hip M67.85-
      knee M67.86-
      multiple sites M67.89
      trunk M67.88
      wrist M67.83-
    synovitis – *see* Synovitis
    tendinitis – *see* Tendinitis
    tenosynovitis – *see* Tenosynovitis
    upper arm M67.92-
    trunk M67.98
    wrist M67.93-
  thoracic root (nerve) NEC G54.3
  thyrocalcitonin hypersecretion E07.0
  thyroid (gland) E07.9
    function NEC, neonatal, transitory
      P72.2
    iodine-deficiency related E01.8
    specified NEC E07.89
  tic - *see* Tic

Disorder *(Continued)*
  tooth K08.9
    development K00.9
      specified NEC K00.8
    eruption K00.6
  Tourette's F95.2
  trance and possession F44.89
  tricuspid (valve) – *see* Endocarditis,
    tricuspid
  tryptophan metabolism E70.5
  tubular, phosphate-losing N25.0
  tubulo-interstitial (in)
    brucellosis A23.9 [N16]
    cystinosis E72.04
    diphtheria A36.84
    glycogen storage disease E74.00
      [N16]
    leukemia NEC C95.90 [N16]
    lymphoma NEC C85.90 [N16]
    mixed cryoglobulinemia D89.1
      [N16]
    multiple myeloma C90.00 [N16]
    Salmonella infection A02.25
    sarcoidosis D86.84
    sepsis A41.9 [N16]
      streptococcal A40.9 [N16]
    systemic lupus erythematosus
      M32.15
    toxoplasmosis B58.83
    transplant rejection T86.91 [N16]
    Wilson's disease E83.01 [N16]
  tubulo-renal function, impaired
    N25.9
    specified NEC N25.89
  tympanic membrane H73.9-
    atrophy - *see* Atrophy, tympanic
      membrane
    infection - *see* Myringitis
    perforation - *see* Perforation,
      tympanum
    specified NEC H73.89-
  unsocialized aggressive F91.1
  urea cycle metabolism E72.20
    argininemia E72.21
    arginosuccinic aciduria E72.22
    citrullinemia E72.23
    ornithine transcarbamylase defi-
      ciency E72.4
    other specified E72.29
  ureter (in) N28.9
    schistosomiasis B65.0 [N29]
    tuberculosis A18.11
  urethra N36.9
    specified NEC N36.8
  urinary system N39.9
    specified NEC N39.8
  valve, heart
    aortic - *see* Endocarditis, aortic
    mitral – *see* Endocarditis, mitral
    pulmonary – *see* Endocarditis,
      pulmonary
    rheumatic
      aortic - *see* Endocarditis, aortic,
        rheumatic
      mitral – *see* Endocarditis, mitral
      pulmonary – *see* Endocarditis,
        pulmonary, rheumatic
      tricuspid – *see* Endocarditis,
        tricuspid
    tricuspid – *see* Endocarditis, tricuspid
  vestibular function H81.9-
    specified NEC - *see* subcategory
      H81.8
  vertigo - *see* Vertigo

Disorder *(Continued)*
  vision, binocular H53.30
    abnormal retinal correspondence
      H53.31
    diplopia H53.2
    fusion with defective stereopsis H53.32
    simultaneous perception H53.33
    suppression H53.34
  visual
    cortex
      blindness H47.619
        left brain H47.612
        right brain H47.611
      due to
        inflammatory disorder H47.629
          left brain H47.622
          right brain H47.621
        neoplasm H47.639
          left brain H47.632
          right brain H47.631
        vascular disorder H47.649
          left brain H47.642
          right brain H47.641
    pathway H47.9
      due to
        inflammatory disorder H47.51-
        neoplasm H47.52-
        vascular disorder H47.53-
    optic chiasm - *see* Disorder, optic,
      chiasm
  vitreous body H43.9
    crystalline deposits - *see* Deposit,
      crystalline
    degeneration - *see* Degeneration,
      vitreous
    hemorrhage - *see* Hemorrhage,
      vitreous
    opacities - *see* Opacity, vitreous
    prolapse - *see* Prolapse, vitreous
    specified type NEC H43.89
  voice R49.9
    specified type NEC R49.8
  volatile solvent use
    due to drug abuse - *see* Abuse, drug,
      inhalant
    due to drug dependence - *see* Depen-
      dence, drug, inhalant
  white blood cells D72.9
    specified NEC D72.89
  withdrawing, child or adolescent F40.10
Disorientation R41.0
Displacement, displaced
  acquired traumatic of bone, cartilage,
    joint, tendon NEC - *see* Dislocation
  adrenal gland (congenital) Q89.1
  appendix, retrocecal (congenital) Q43.8
  auricle (congenital) Q17.4
  bladder (acquired) N32.89
    congenital Q64.19
  brachial plexus (congenital) Q07.8
  brain stem, caudal (congenital) Q04.8
  canaliculus (lacrimalis), congenital
    Q10.6
  cardia through esophageal hiatus (con-
    genital) Q40.1
  cerebellum, caudal (congenital) Q04.8
  cervix - *see* Malposition, uterus
  colon (congenital) Q43.3
  device, implant or graft (*see also*
    Complications, by site and type,
    mechanical) T85.9
    arterial graft NEC - *see* Complication,
      cardiovascular device, mechani-
      cal, vascular

Displacement, displaced *(Continued)*
  device, implant or graft *(Continued)*
    breast (implant) T85.42
    catheter NEC T85.628
      dialysis (renal) T82.42
        intraperitoneal T85.621
      infusion NEC T82.524
        spinal (epidural) (subdural)
          T85.620
      urinary (indwelling)
        cystostomy T83.020
    electronic (electrode) (pulse genera-
      tor) (stimulator) - *see* Complica-
      tion, electronic stimulator
    fixation, internal (orthopedic) NEC
      - *see* Complication, fixation
      device, mechanical
    gastrointestinal - *see* Complications,
      prosthetic device, mechanical,
      gastrointestinal device
    genital NEC T83.428
      intrauterine contraceptive device
        T83.32
      penile prosthesis T83.420
    heart NEC - *see* Complication, cardio-
      vascular device, mechanical
    joint prosthesis – *see* Complications,
      joint prosthesis, mechanical
    ocular - *see* Complications, prosthetic
      device, mechanical, ocular
      device
    orthopedic NEC - *see* Complication,
      orthopedic, device or graft,
      mechanical
    specified NEC T85.628
    urinary NEC - *see also* Complication,
      genitourinary, device, urinary,
      mechanical
      graft T83.22
    vascular NEC - *see* Complica-
      tion, cardiovascular device,
      mechanical
    ventricular intracranial shunt T85.02
  electronic stimulator
    bone T84.320
    cardiac - *see* Complications, cardiac
      device, electronic
    nervous system - *see* Complication,
      prosthetic device, mechani-
      cal, electronic nervous system
      stimulator
    urinary - *see* Complications, electronic
      stimulator, urinary
  epithelium
    cuboidal, beyond limits of external
      os Q51.8
  esophageal mucosa into cardia of stom-
    ach, congenital Q39.8
  esophagus (acquired) K22.8
    congenital Q39.8
  eyeball (acquired) (lateral) (old) - *see*
    Displacement, globe
    congenital Q15.8
    current – *see* Avulsion, eye
  fallopian tube (acquired) N83.4
    congenital Q50.6
    opening (congenital) Q50.6
  gallbladder (congenital) Q44.1
  gastric mucosa (congenital) Q40.2
  globe (acquired) (old) (lateral) H05.21-
    current – *see* Avulsion, eye
  heart (congenital) Q24.8
    acquired I51.89
  hymen (upward) (congenital) Q52.4

Displacement, displaced *(Continued)*
  intervertebral disc NEC
    with myelopathy - *see* Disorder, disc,
      with, myelopathy
    cervical, cervicothoracic (with)
      M50.20
      myelopathy - *see* Disorder, disc,
        cervical, with myelopathy
      neuritis, radiculitis or radiculopa-
        thy - *see* Disorder, disc, cervi-
        cal, with neuritis
    due to trauma - *see* Dislocation,
      vertebra
    lumbar region M51.26
      with
        myelopathy M51.06
        neuritis, radiculitis, radiculopa-
          thy or sciatica M51.16
    lumbosacral region M51.27
      with
        myelopathy M51.07
        neuritis, radiculitis, radiculopa-
          thy or sciatica M51.17
    sacrococcygeal region M53.3
    thoracic region M51.24
      with
        myelopathy M51.04
        neuritis, radiculitis, radiculopa-
          thy M51.14
    thoracolumbar region M51.25
      with
        myelopathy M51.05
        neuritis, radiculitis, radiculopa-
          thy M51.15
  intrauterine device T83.32
  kidney (acquired) N28.83
    congenital Q63.2
  lachrymal, lacrimal apparatus or duct
    (congenital) Q10.6
  lens, congenital Q12.1
  macula (congenital) Q14.1
  Meckel's diverticulum Q43.0
  nail (congenital) Q84.6
    acquired L60.8
  oesophagus (acquired) - *see* Displace-
    ment, esophagus
  opening of Wharton's duct in mouth
    Q38.4
  organ or site, congenital NEC - *see* Mal-
    position, congenital
  ovary (acquired) N83.4
    congenital Q50.39
    free in peritoneal cavity (congenital)
      Q50.39
    into hernial sac N83.4
  oviduct (acquired) N83.4
    congenital Q50.6
  parathyroid (gland) E21.4
  parotid gland (congenital) Q38.4
  punctum lacrimale (congenital) Q10.6
  sacro-iliac (joint) (congenital) Q74.2
    current injury S33.2
    old - *see* subcategory M53.2
  salivary gland (any) (congenital) Q38.4
  spleen (congenital) Q89.09
  stomach, congenital Q40.2
  sublingual duct Q38.4
  tongue (downward) (congenital) Q38.3
  tooth, teeth, fully erupted M26.30
    horizontal M26.33
    vertical M26.34
  trachea (congenital) Q32.1
  ureter or ureteric opening or orifice
    (congenital) Q62.62

Displacement, displaced *(Continued)*
  uterine opening of oviducts or fallopian
      tubes Q50.6
  uterus, uterine - *see* Malposition, uterus
  ventricular septum Q21.0
      with rudimentary ventricle Q20.4
Disproportion
  between native and reconstructed
      breast N65.1
  fiber-type G71.2
Disruptio uteri - *see* Rupture, uterus
Disruption (of)
  ciliary body NEC H21.89
  closure of
      cornea T81.31
      craniotomy T81.32
      fascia (muscular) (superficial) T81.32
      internal organ or tissue T81.32
      laceration (external) (internal) T81.33
      ligament T81.32
      mucosa T81.31
      muscle or muscle flap T81.32
      ribs or rib cage T81.32
      skin and subcutaneous tissue (full-
          thickness) (superficial) T81.31
      skull T81.32
      sternum (sternotomy) T81.32
      tendon T81.32
      traumatic laceration (external) (inter-
          nal) T81.33
  family Z63.8
      due to
          absence of family member NEC
              Z63.32
          absence of family member due to
              military deployment Z63.31
          alcoholism and drug addiction in
              family Z63.72
          bereavement Z63.4
          death (assumed) or disappearance
              of family member Z63.4
          divorce or separation Z63.5
          drug addiction in family Z63.72
          return of family member from
              military deployment (current
              or past conflict) Z63.71
          stressful life events NEC Z63.7
  iris NEC H21.89
  ligament(s) - *see also* Sprain
      knee
          current injury - *see* Dislocation, knee
          old (chronic) - *see* Derangement,
              knee, instability
          spontaneous NEC - *see* Derange-
              ment, knee, disruption
              ligament
  ossicular chain - *see* Discontinuity, os-
      sicles, ear
  pelvic circle (stable) S32.810
      unstable S32.811
  wound T81.30
      episiotomy O90.1
      operation T81.31
          cesarean O90.0
          external operation wound
              (superficial) T81.31
          internal operation wound (deep)
              T81.32
      perineal (obstetric) O90.1
      traumatic injury repair T81.33
      traumatic injury wound repair T81.33
Dissatisfaction with
  employment Z56.9
  school environment Z55.4

Dissecting - *see* condition
Dissection
  aorta I71.00
      abdominal I71.02
      thoracic I71.01
      thoracoabdominal I71.03
  artery
      carotid I77.71
      cerebral (nonruptured) I67.0
          ruptured - *see* Hemorrhage, intra-
              cranial, subarachnoid
      coronary I25.42
      iliac I77.72
      renal I77.73
      specified NEC I77.79
      vertebral I77.74
  traumatic - *see* Wound, open, by site
  vascular I99.8
  wound - *see* Wound, open
Disseminated - *see* condition
Dissociation
  auriculoventricular or atrioventricular
      (AV) (any degree) (isorhythmic)
      I45.89
      with heart block I44.2
  interference I45.89
Dissociative reaction, state F44.9
Dissolution, vertebra - *see*
      Osteoporosis
Distension, distention
  abdomen R14.0
  bladder N32.89
  cecum K63.89
  colon K63.89
  gallbladder K82.8
  intestine K63.89
  kidney N28.89
  liver K76.8
  seminal vesicle N50.8
  stomach K31.89
      acute K31.0
      psychogenic F45.8
  ureter – *see* Dilatation, ureter
  uterus N85.8
Distoma hepaticum infestation
      B66.3
Distomiasis B66.9
  bile passages B66.3
  hemic B65.9
  hepatic B66.3
      due to Clonorchis sinensis B66.1
  intestinal B66.5
  liver B66.3
      due to Clonorchis sinensis B66.1
  lung B66.4
  pulmonary B66.4
Distomolar (fourth molar) K00.1
Disto-occlusion (Division I) (Division II)
      M26.212
Distortion(s) (congenital)
  adrenal (gland) Q89.1
  arm NEC Q68.8
  bile duct or passage Q44.5
  bladder Q64.79
  brain Q04.9
  cervix (uteri) Q51.9
  chest (wall) Q67.8
      bones Q76.8
  clavicle Q74.0
  clitoris Q52.6
  coccyx Q76.49
  common duct Q44.5
  coronary Q24.5
  cystic duct Q44.5

Distortion(s) *(Continued)*
  ear (auricle) (external) Q17.3
      inner Q16.5
      middle Q16.4
          ossicles Q16.3
  endocrine NEC Q89.2
  eustachian tube Q17.8
  eye (adnexa) Q15.8
  face bone(s) NEC Q75.8
  fallopian tube Q50.6
  femur NEC Q68.8
  fibula NEC Q68.8
  finger(s) Q68.1
  foot Q66.9
  genitalia, genital organ(s)
      female Q52.8
          external Q52.79
          internal NEC Q52.8
  gyri Q04.8
  hand bone(s) Q68.1
  heart (auricle) (ventricle) Q24.8
      valve (cusp) Q24.8
  hepatic duct Q44.5
  humerus NEC Q68.8
  hymen Q52.4
  intrafamilial communications Z63.8
  jaw NEC M26.89
  labium (majus) (minus) Q52.79
  leg NEC Q68.8
  lens Q12.8
  liver Q44.7
  lumbar spine Q76.49
      with disproportion O33.8
          causing obstructed labor O65.0
  lumbosacral (joint) (region) Q76.49
      kyphosis - *see* Kyphosis, congenital
      lordosis - *see* Lordosis, congenital
  nerve Q07.8
  nose Q30.8
  organ
      of Corti Q16.5
      or site not listed - *see* Anomaly, by site
          ossicles, ear Q16.3
  oviduct Q50.6
  pancreas Q45.3
  parathyroid (gland) Q89.2
  pituitary (gland) Q89.2
  radius NEC Q68.8
  sacroiliac joint Q74.2
  sacrum Q76.49
  scapula Q74.0
  shoulder girdle Q74.0
  skull bone(s) NEC Q75.8
      with
          anencephalus Q00.0
          encephalocele - *see* Encephalocele
          hydrocephalus Q03.9
              with spina bifida - *see* Spina
                  bifida, with hydrocephalus
          microcephaly Q02
  spinal cord Q06.8
  spine Q76.49
      kyphosis - *see* Kyphosis, congenital
      lordosis - *see* Lordosis, congenital
  spleen Q89.09
  sternum NEC Q76.7
  thorax (wall) Q67.8
      bony Q76.8
  thymus (gland) Q89.2
  thyroid (gland) Q89.2
  tibia NEC Q68.8
  toe(s) Q66.9
  tongue Q38.3
  trachea (cartilage) Q32.1

Distortion(s) *(Continued)*
ulna NEC Q68.8
ureter Q62.8
urethra Q64.79
  causing obstruction Q64.39
uterus Q51.9
vagina Q52.4
vertebra Q76.49
  kyphosis - *see* Kyphosis, congenital
  lordosis - *see* Lordosis, congenital
visual - *see also* Disturbance, vision
  shape and size H53.15
vulva Q52.79
wrist (bones) (joint) Q68.8
Distress
abdomen - *see* Pain, abdominal
acute respiratory (adult) (child) J80
epigastric R10.13
fetal P84
  complicating pregnancy - *see* Stress, fetal
gastrointestinal (functional) K30
  psychogenic F45.8
intestinal (functional) NOS K59.9
  psychogenic F45.8
maternal, during labor and delivery O75.0
respiratory R06.00
  adult J80
  child J80
  newborn P22.9
    specified NEC P22.8
  orthopnea R06.01
  psychogenic F45.8
  shortness of breath R06.02
  specified type NEC R06.09
Distribution vessel, atypical Q27.9
coronary artery Q24.5
precerebral Q28.1
Districhiasis L68.8
Disturbance(s) - *see also* Disease
absorption K90.9
  calcium E58
  carbohydrate K90.4
  fat K90.4
    pancreatic K90.3
  protein K90.4
  starch K90.4
  vitamin - *see* Deficiency, vitamin
acid-base equilibrium E87.8
  mixed E87.4
activity and attention (with hyperkinesis) – *see* Disorder, attention-deficit hyperactivity
amino acid transport E72.00
assimilation, food K90.9
auditory nerve, except deafness - *see* subcategory H93.3
behavior - *see* Disorder, conduct
blood clotting (mechanism) (*see also* Defect, coagulation) D68.9
cerebral
  nerve - *see* Disorder, nerve, cranial
  status, newborn P91.9
    specified NEC P91.8
circulatory I99.9
conduct (*see also* Disorder, conduct) F91.9
  adjustment reaction – *see* Disorder, adjustment
  compulsive F63.9
  disruptive F91.9
  hyperkinetic – *see* Disorder, attention-deficit hyperactivity

Disturbance(s) *(Continued)*
conduct *(Continued)*
  socialized F91.2
  specified NEC F91.8
  unsocialized F91.1
coordination R27.8
cranial nerve - *see* Disorder, nerve, cranial
deep sensibility - *see* Disturbance, sensation
digestive K30
  psychogenic F45.8
electrolyte - *see also* Imbalance, electrolyte
  newborn, transitory P74.4
    hyperammonemia P74.6
    potassium balance P74.3
    sodium balance P74.2
    specified type NEC P74.4
emotions specific to childhood and adolescence F93.9
  with
    anxiety and fearfulness NEC F93.8
    elective mutism F94.0
    oppositional disorder F91.3
    sensitivity (withdrawal) F40.10
    shyness F40.10
    social withdrawal F40.10
  involving relationship problems F93.8
  mixed F93.8
  specified NEC F93.8
endocrine (gland) E34.9
  neonatal, transitory P72.9
    specified NEC P72.8
equilibrium R42
fructose metabolism E74.10
gait – *see* Gait
  hysterical F44.4
  psychogenic F44.4
gastrointestinal (functional) K30
  psychogenic F45.8
habit, child F98.9
hearing, except deafness and tinnitus - *see* Abnormal, auditory perception
heart, functional (conditions in I44-I50)
  due to presence of (cardiac) prosthesis I97.19-
  postoperative I97.89
    cardiac surgery I97.19-
hormones E34.9
innervation uterus (parasympathetic) (sympathetic) N85.8
keratinization NEC
  gingiva K05.10
    plaque induced K05.10
    nonplaque induced K05.11
  lip K13.0
  oral (mucosa) (soft tissue) K13.29
  tongue K13.29
learning (specific) – *see* Disorder, learning
memory - *see* Amnesia
  mild, following organic brain damage F06.8
mental F99
  associated with diseases classified elsewhere F54
metabolism E88.9
  with
    abortion – *see* Abortion, by type with other specified complication
    ectopic pregnancy O08.5
    molar pregnancy O08.5

Disturbance(s) *(Continued)*
metabolism *(Continued)*
  amino-acid E72.9
    aromatic E70.9
    branched-chain E71.2
    straight-chain E72.8
    sulfur-bearing E72.10
  ammonia E72.20
  arginine E72.21
  arginosuccinic acid E72.22
  carbohydrate E74.9
  cholesterol E78.9
  citrulline E72.23
  cystathionine E72.19
  general E88.9
  glutamine E72.8
  histidine E70.40
  homocystine E72.19
  hydroxylysine E72.3
  in labor or delivery O75.89
  iron E83.10
  lipoid E78.9
  lysine E72.3
  methionine E72.19
  neonatal, transitory P74.9
    calcium and magnesium P71.9
      specified type NEC P71.8
    carbohydrate metabolism P70.9
      specified type NEC P70.8
    specified NEC P74.8
  ornithine E72.4
  phosphate E83.39
  sodium NEC E87.8
  threonine E72.8
  tryptophan E70.5
  tyrosine E70.20
  urea cycle E72.20
motor R29.2
nervous, functional R45.0
neuromuscular mechanism (eye), due to syphilis A52.15
nutritional E63.9
  nail L60.3
ocular motion H51.9
  psychogenic F45.8
oculogyric H51.8
  psychogenic F45.8
oculomotor H51.9
  psychogenic F45.8
olfactory nerve R43.1
optic nerve NEC - *see* Disorder, nerve, optic
oral epithelium, including tongue NEC K13.29
perceptual due to
  alcohol withdrawal F10.232
  amphetamine intoxication F15.922
    in
      abuse F15.122
      dependence F15.222
  anxiolytic withdrawal F13.232
  cannabis intoxication (acute) F12.922
    in
      abuse F12.122
      dependence F12.222
  cocaine intoxication (acute) F14.922
    in
      abuse F14.122
      dependence F14.222
  hypnotic withdrawal F13.232
  opioid intoxication (acute) F11.922
    in
      abuse F11.122
      dependence F11.222

209

Disturbance(s) *(Continued)*
  perceptual due to *(Continued)*
    phencyclidine intoxication (acute)
        F19.922
      in
        abuse F19.122
        dependence F19.222
    sedative withdrawal F13.232
  personality (pattern) (trait) *(see also*
      Disorder, personality) F60.9
    following organic brain damage F07.9
  polyglandular E31.9
    specified NEC E31.8
  potassium balance, newborn P74.3
  psychogenic F45.9
  psychomotor F44.4
  psychophysical visual H53.16
  pupillary - *see* Anomaly, pupil, function
  reflex R29.2
  rhythm, heart I49.9
  salivary secretion K11.7
  sensation (cold) (heat) (localization)
      (tactile discrimination) (texture)
      (vibratory) NEC R20.9
    hysterical F44.6
    skin R20.9
      anesthesia R20.0
      hyperesthesia R20.3
      hypoesthesia R20.1
      paresthesia R20.2
      specified type NEC R20.8
    smell R43.9
      and taste (mixed) R43.8
      anosmia R43.0
      parosmia R43.1
      specified NEC R43.8
    taste R43.9
      and smell (mixed) R43.8
      parageusia R43.2
      specified NEC R43.8
  sensory - *see* Disturbance, sensation
  situational (transient) – *see also* Disor-
      der, adjustment
    acute F43.0
  sleep G47.9
    nonorganic origin F51.9
  smell - *see* Disturbance, sensation, smell
  sociopathic F60.2
  sodium balance, newborn P74.2
  speech R47.9
    developmental F80.9
    specified NEC R47.89
  stomach (functional) K31.9
  sympathetic (nerve) G90.9
  taste - *see* Disturbance, sensation, taste
  temperature
    regulation, newborn P81.9
      specified NEC P81.8
    sense R20.8
      hysterical F44.6
  tooth
    eruption K00.6
    formation K00.4
    structure, hereditary NEC K00.5
  touch - *see* Disturbance, sensation
  vascular I99.9
    arteriosclerotic - *see* Arteriosclerosis
  vasomotor I73.9
  vasospastic I73.9
  vision, visual H53.9
    following
      cerebrovascular disease I69.998
        specified NEC I69.898
        cerebral infarction I69.398

Disturbance(s) *(Continued)*
  vision, visual *(Continued)*
    following *(Continued)*
      cerebrovascular disease *(Continued)*
        intracerebral hemorrhage I69.198
        nontraumatic intracranial hem-
            orrhage NEC I69.298
        specified disease NEC I69.898
        subarachnoid hemorrhage
            I69.098
    psychophysical H53.16
    specified NEC H53.8
    subjective H53.10
      day blindness H53.11
      discomfort H53.14-
      distortions of shape and size
          H53.18
      loss
        sudden H53.13-
        transient H53.12-
      specified type NEC H53.19
  voice R49.9
    psychogenic F44.4
    specified NEC R49.8
Diuresis R35.8
Diver's palsy, paralysis or squeeze
    T70.3
Diverticulitis (acute) K57.92
  bladder - *see* Cystitis
  ileum - *see* Diverticulitis, intestine,
      small
  intestine K57.92
    with
      abscess, perforation or peritonitis
          K57.80
        with bleeding K57.81
      bleeding K57.93
    congenital Q43.8
    large K57.32
      with
        abscess, perforation or peritonitis
            K57.20
          with bleeding K57.21
        bleeding K57.33
        small intestine K57.52
          with
            abscess, perforation or peri-
                tonitis K57.40
              with bleeding K57.41
            bleeding K57.53
    small K57.12
      with
        abscess, perforation or peritonitis
            K57.00
          with bleeding K57.01
        bleeding K57.13
        large intestine K57.52
          with
            abscess, perforation or peri-
                tonitis K57.40
              with bleeding K57.41
            bleeding K57.53
Diverticulosis K57.90
  with bleeding K57.91
  large intestine K57.30
    with
      bleeding K57.31
      small intestine K57.50
        with bleeding K57.51
  small intestine K57.10
    with
      bleeding K57.11
      large intestine K57.50
        with bleeding K57.51

Diverticulum, diverticula (multiple) K57.90
  appendix (noninflammatory) K38.2
  bladder (sphincter) N32.3
    congenital Q64.6
  bronchus (congenital) Q32.4
    acquired J98.09
  calyx, calyceal (kidney) N28.89
  cardia (stomach) K31.4
  cecum - *see* Diverticulosis, intestine, large
    congenital Q43.8
  colon - *see* Diverticulosis, intestine, large
    congenital Q43.8
  duodenum - *see* Diverticulosis, intestine,
      small
    congenital Q43.8
  epiphrenic (esophagus) K22.5
  esophagus (congenital) Q39.6
    acquired (epiphrenic) (pulsion) (trac-
        tion) K22.5
  eustachian tube – *see* Disorder, eusta-
      chian tube, specified NEC
  fallopian tube N83.8
  gastric K31.4
  heart (congenital) Q24.8
  ileum - *see* Diverticulosis, intestine, small
  jejunum - *see* Diverticulosis, intestine,
      small
  kidney (pelvis) (calyces) N28.89
    with calculus - *see* Calculus, kidney
  Meckel's (displaced) (hypertrophic) Q43.0
  midthoracic K22.5
  organ or site, congenital NEC - *see*
      Distortion
  pericardium (congenital) (cyst) Q24.8
    acquired I31.8
  pharyngoesophageal (congenital) Q39.6
    acquired K22.5
  pharynx (congenital) Q38.7
  rectosigmoid - *see* Diverticulosis, intes-
      tine, large
    congenital Q43.8
  rectum - *see* Diverticulosis, intestine, large
  Rokitansky's K22.5
  seminal vesicle N50.8
  sigmoid - *see* Diverticulosis, intestine, large
    congenital Q43.8
  stomach (acquired) K31.4
    congenital Q40.2
  trachea (acquired) J39.8
  ureter (acquired) N28.89
    congenital Q62.8
  ureterovesical orifice N28.89
  urethra (acquired) N36.1
    congenital Q64.79
  ventricle, left (congenital) Q24.8
  vesical N32.3
    congenital Q64.6
  Zenker's (esophagus) K22.5
Division
  cervix uteri (acquired) N88.8
  external os into two openings by frenum
      Q51.8
  glans penis Q55.69
  labia minora (congenital) Q52.79
  ligament (partial or complete) (current)
      - *see also* Sprain
    with open wound - *see* Wound, open
  muscle (partial or complete) (current)
      - *see also* Injury, muscle
    with open wound - *see* Wound, open
  nerve (traumatic) - *see* Injury, nerve
  spinal cord - *see* Injury, spinal cord, by
      region
  vein I87.8

Divorce, causing family disruption Z63.5
Dix-Hallpike neurolabyrinthitis - *see* Neuronitis, vestibular
Dizziness R42
  hysterical F44.89
  psychogenic F45.8
DMAC (disseminated mycobacterium aviumintracellulare complex) A31.2
DNR (do not resuscitate) Z66
Doan-Wiseman syndrome (primary splenic neutropenia) – *see* Agranulocytosis
Doehle-Heller aortitis A52.02
Dog bite - *see* Bite
Dohle body panmyelopathic syndrome D72.0
Dolichocephaly Q67.2
Dolichocolon Q43.8
Dolichostenomelia - *see* Syndrome, Marfan's
Donohue's syndrome E34.8
Donor (organ or tissue) Z52.9
  blood (whole) Z52.000
    autologous Z52.010
    specified donor NEC Z52.090
    specified component (lymphocytes) (platelets) NEC Z52.008
      autologous Z52.018
      specified donor NEC Z52.098
    stem cells Z52.001
      autologous Z52.011
      specified donor NEC Z52.091
  bone Z52.20
    autologous Z52.21
    marrow Z52.3
    specified type NEC Z52.29
  cornea Z52.5
  egg (Oocyte) Z52.819
    age 35 and over Z52.812
      anonymous recipient Z52.812
      designated recipient Z52.813
    under age 35 Z52.810
      anonymous recipient Z52.810
      designated recipient Z52.811
  kidney Z52.4
  liver Z52.6
  lung Z52.89
  lymphocyte *see* Donor, blood, specified components NEC
  Oocyte - *see* Donor, egg
  platelets Z52.008
  potential, examination of Z00.5
  semen Z52.89
  skin Z52.10
    autologous Z52.11
    specified type NEC Z52.19
  specified organ or tissue NEC Z52.89
  sperm Z52.89
Donovanosis A58
Dorsalgia M54.9
  psychogenic F45.41
  specified NEC M54.89
Dorsopathy M53.9
  deforming M43.9
    specified NEC - *see* subcategory M43.8
  specified NEC M53.80
    cervical region M53.82
    cervicothoracic region M53.83
    lumbar region M53.86
    lumbosacral region M53.87
    occipito-atlanto-axial region M53.81
    sacrococcygeal region M53.88
    thoracic region M53.84
    thoracolumbar region M53.85

Double
  albumin E88.09
  aortic arch Q25.4
  auditory canal Q17.8
  auricle (heart) Q20.8
  bladder Q64.79
  cervix Q51.8
    with doubling of uterus (and vagina) Q51.10
      with obstruction Q51.11
  external os Q51.8
  inlet ventricle Q20.4
  kidney with double pelvis (renal) Q63.0
  meatus urinarius Q64.75
  monster Q89.4
  outlet
    left ventricle Q20.2
    right ventricle Q20.1
  pelvis (renal) with double ureter Q62.5
  tongue Q38.3
  ureter (one or both sides) Q62.5
    with double pelvis (renal) Q62.5
  urethra Q64.74
  urinary meatus Q64.75
  uterus Q51.2
    with
      doubling of cervix (and vagina) Q51.10
        with obstruction Q51.11
      in pregnancy or childbirth O34.59-
        causing obstructed labor O65.5
  vagina Q52.1
    with doubling of uterus (and cervix) Q51.10
      with obstruction Q51.11
  vision H53.2
  vulva Q52.79
Douglas' pouch, cul-de-sac - *see* condition
Down syndrome Q90.0
  meiotic nondisjunction Q90.0
  mitotic nondisjunction Q90.1
  mosaicism Q90.1
  translocation Q90.2
Dracontiasis B72
Dracunculiasis, dracunculosis B72
Dream state, hysterical F44.89
Dreschlera (hawaiiensis) (infection) B43.8
Drepanocytic anemia - *see* Disease, sickle-cell
Dresbach's syndrome (elliptocytosis) D58.1
Dressler's syndrome I24.1
Drift, ulnar - *see* Deformity, limb, specified type NEC, forearm
Drinking (alcohol)
  excessive, to excess NEC (without dependence) F10.10
    habitual (continual) (without remission) F10.20
      with remission F10.21
Drip, postnasal (chronic) R09.82
  due to
    allergic rhinitis - *see* Rhinitis, allergic
    common cold J00
    gastroesophageal reflux - *see* Reflux, gastroesophageal
    nasopharyngitis - *see* Nasopharyngitis
    other know condition code to condition
    sinusitis - *see* Sinusitis

Droop
  facial R29.810
    cerebrovascular disease I69.992
      specified NEC I69.892
      cerebral infarction I69.392
      intracerebral hemorrhage I69.192
      nontraumatic intracranial hemorrhage NEC I69.292
      specified disease NEC I69.892
      subarachnoid hemorrhage I69.092
Drop (in)
  attack NEC R55
  finger - *see* Deformity, finger
  foot - *see* Deformity, limb, foot, drop
  hematocrit (precipitous) R71.0
  hemoglobin R71.0
  toe - *see* Deformity, toe, specified NEC
  wrist - *see* Deformity, limb, wrist drop
Dropped heart beats I45.9
Dropsy, dropsical - *see also* Hydrops
  abdomen R18.8
  brain - *see* Hydrocephalus
  cardiac, heart - *see* Failure, heart, congestive
  gangrenous - *see* Gangrene
  heart - *see* Failure, heart, congestive
  kidney – *see* Nephrosis
  lung - *see* Edema, lung
  newborn due to isoimmunization P56.0
  pericardium - *see* Pericarditis
Drowned, drowning (near) T75.1
Drowsiness R40.0
Drug
  abuse counseling and surveillance Z71.51
  addiction - *see* Dependence
  dependence - *see* Dependence
  habit - *see* Dependence
  harmful use - *see* Abuse, drug
  induced fever R50.2
  overdose - *see* Table of drugs and chemicals, by drug, poisoning
  poisoning - *see* Table of drugs and chemicals, by drug, poisoning
  resistant organism infection Z16
  wrong substance given or taken in error - *see* Table of drugs and chemicals, by drug, poisoning
Drunkenness (without dependence) F10.129
  acute in alcoholism F10.229
  chronic (without remission) F10.20
    with remission F10.21
  pathological (without dependence) F10.129
    with dependence F10.229
  sleep F51.9
Drusen
  macula (degenerative) (retina) - *see* Degeneration, macula, drusen
  optic disc H47.32-
Dry, dryness - *see also* condition
  larynx J38.7
  mouth R68.2
    due to dehydration E86.0
  nose J34.89
  socket (teeth) M27.3
  throat J39.2
DSAP L56.5
Duane's syndrome H50.81-
Dubin-Johnson disease or syndrome E80.6
Dubois' disease (thymus gland) A50.59 [E35]
Dubowitz' syndrome Q87.1

Duchenne-Aran muscular atrophy G12.21
Duchenne-Griesinger disease G71.0
Duchenne's
  disease or syndrome
    motor neuron disease G12.22
    muscular dystrophy G71.0
  locomotor ataxia (syphilitic) A52.11
  paralysis
    birth injury P14.0
    due to or associated with
      motor neuron disease G12.22
      muscular dystrophy G71.0
Ducrey's chancre A57
Duct, ductus - see condition
Duhring's disease (dermatitis herpetiformis) L13.0
Dullness, cardiac (decreased) (increased) R01.2
Dumb ague - see Malaria
Dumbness - see Aphasia
Dumdum fever B55.0
Dumping syndrome (postgastrectomy) K91.1
Duodenitis (nonspecific) (peptic) K29.80
  with bleeding K29.81
Duodenocholangitis - see Cholangitis
Duodenum, duodenal - see condition
Duplay's bursitis or periarthritis - see Tendinitis, calcific, shoulder
Duplication, duplex - see also Accessory
  alimentary tract Q45.8
  anus Q43.4
  appendix (and cecum) Q43.4
  biliary duct (any) Q44.5
  bladder Q64.79
  cecum (and appendix) Q43.4
  chromosome NEC
    with complex rearrangements NEC Q92.5
    seen only at prometaphase Q92.8
  cystic duct Q44.5
  digestive organs Q45.8
  esophagus Q39.8
  frontonasal process Q75.8
  intestine (large) (small) Q43.4
  kidney Q63.0
  liver Q44.7
  oesophagus Q39.8
  pancreas Q45.3
  penis Q55.69
  respiratory organs NEC Q34.8
  salivary duct Q38.4
  spinal cord (incomplete) Q06.2
  stomach Q40.2
Dupré's disease (meningism) R29.1
Dupuytren's contraction or disease M72.0
Durand-Nicolas-Favre disease A55
Durotomy (inadvertent) (incidental) G97.41
Duroziez's disease (congenital mitral stenosis) Q23.2
Dutton's relapsing fever (West African) A68.1
Dwarfism E34.3
  achondroplastic Q77.4
  congenital E34.3
  constitutional E34.3
  hypochondroplastic Q77.4
  hypophyseal E23.0
  infantile E34.3
  Laron-type E34.3
  Lorain(-Levi) type E23.0
  metatropic Q77.8

Dwarfism (Continued)
  nephrotic-glycosuric (with hypophosphatemic rickets) E72.09
  nutritional E45
  pancreatic K86.8
  pituitary E23.0
  renal N25.0
  thanatophoric Q77.1
Dyke-Young anemia (secondary) (symptomatic) D59.1
Dysacusis - see Abnormal, auditory perception
Dysadrenocortism E27.9
  hyperfunction E27.0
Dysarthria R47.1
  following
    cerebral infarction I69.322
    cerebrovascular disease I69.922
      specified disease NEC I69.822
    intracerebral hemorrhage I69.122
    nontraumatic intracranial hemorrhage NEC I69.222
    subarachnoid hemorrhage I69.022
Dysautonomia (familial) G90.1
Dysbarism T70.3
Dysbasia R26.2
  angiosclerotica intermittens I73.9
  hysterical F44.4
  lordotica (progressiva) G24.1
  nonorganic origin F44.4
  psychogenic F44.4
Dysbetalipoproteinemia (familial) E78.2
Dyscalculia R48.8
  developmental F81.2
Dyschezia K59.00
Dyschondroplasia (with hemangiomata) Q78.4
Dyschromia (skin) L81.9
Dyscollagenosis M35.9
Dyscranio-pygo-phalangy Q87.0
Dyscrasia
  blood (with) D75.9
    antepartum hemorrhage - see Hemorrhage, antepartum, with coagulation defect
    newborn P61.9
      specified type NEC P61.8
    intrapartum hemorrhage O67.0
    puerperal, postpartum O72.3
    polyglandular, pluriglandular E31.9
Dysendocrinism E34.9
Dysentery, dysenteric (catarrhal) (diarrhea) (epidemic) (hemorrhagic) (infectious) (sporadic) (tropical) A09
  abscess, liver A06.4
  amebic (see also Amebiasis) A06.0
    with abscess - see Abscess, amebic
    acute A06.0
    chronic A06.1
  arthritis A09 (see also category M01)
    bacillary A03.9 (see also category M01)
  bacillary A03.9
    arthritis A03.9 (see also category M01)
    Boyd A03.2
    Flexner A03.1
    Schmitz(-Stutzer) A03.0
    Shiga(-Kruse) A03.0
    Shigella A03.9
      boydii A03.2
      dysenteriae A03.0
      flexneri A03.1
      group A A03.0
      group B A03.1
      group C A03.2

Dysentery, dysenteric (Continued)
  bacillary (Continued)
    Shigella (Continued)
      group D A03.3
      sonnei A03.3
      specified type NEC A03.8
    Sonne A03.3
    specified type NEC A03.8
  balantidial A07.0
  Balantidium coli A07.0
  Boyd's A03.2
  candidal B37.82
  Chilomastix A07.8
  Chinese A03.9
  coccidial A07.3
  Dientamoeba (fragilis) A07.8
  Embadomonas A07.8
  Entamoeba, entambic - see Dysentery, amebic
  Flexner-Boyd A03.2
  Flexner's A03.1
  Giardia lamblia A07.1
  Hiss-Russell A03.1
  Lamblia A07.1
  leishmanial B55.0
  malarial – see Malaria
  metazoal B82.0
  monilial B37.82
  protozoal A07.9
  Salmonella A02.0
  schistosomal B65.1
  Schmitz(-Stutzer) A03.0
  Shiga(-Kruse) A03.0
  Shigella NOS - see Dysentery, bacillary
  Sonne A03.3
  strongyloidiasis B78.0
  trichomonal A07.8
  viral (see also Enteritis, viral) A08.4
Dysequilibrium R42
Dysesthesia R20.8
  hysterical F44.6
Dysfibrinogenemia (congenital) D68.2
Dysfunction
  adrenal E27.9
    hyperfunction E27.0
  autonomic
    due to alcohol G31.2
    somatoform F45.8
  bladder N31.9
    neurogenic NOS - see Dysfunction, bladder, neuromuscular
    neuromuscular NOS N31.9
      atonic (motor) (sensory) N31.2
      autonomous N31.2
      flaccid N31.2
      nonreflex N31.2
      reflex N31.1
      specified NEC N31.8
      uninhibited N31.0
    bleeding, uterus N93.8
  cerebral G93.89
  colon K59.9
    psychogenic F45.8
  colostomy K94.03
  cystic duct K82.8
  cystostomy (stoma) – see Complications, cystostomy
  ejaculatory N53.19
    anejaculatory orgasm N53.13
    painful N53.12
    premature F52.4
    retarded N53.11
  endocrine NOS E34.9
  endometrium N85.8

Dysfunction (Continued)
  enterostomy K94.13
  gallbladder K82.8
  gastrostomy (stoma) K94.23
  gland, glandular NOS E34.9
  heart I51.89
  hemoglobin D75.89
  hepatic K76.8
  hypophysis E23.3
  hypothalamic NEC E23.3
  ileostomy (stoma) K94.13
  jejunostomy (stoma) K94.13
  kidney - see Disease, renal
  labyrinthine - see subcategory H83.2
  left ventricular, following sudden
      emotional stress I51.81
  liver K76.8
  male – see Dysfunction, sexual, male
  orgasmic (female) F52.31
    male F52.32
  ovary E28.9
    specified NEC E28.8
  papillary muscle I51.89
  parathyroid E21.4
  physiological NEC R68.89
    psychogenic F59
  pineal gland E34.8
  pituitary (gland) E23.3
  platelets D69.1
  polyglandular E31.9
    specified NEC E31.8
  psychophysiologic F59
  psychosexual F52.9
    with
      dyspareunia F52.6
      premature ejaculation F52.4
      vaginismus F52.5
  pylorus K31.9
  rectum K59.9
    psychogenic F45.8
  reflex (sympathetic) - see Syndrome,
      pain, complex regional I
  segmental - see Dysfunction, somatic
  senile R54
  sexual (due to) R37
    alcohol F10.981
    amphetamine F15.981
      in
        abuse F15.181
        dependence F15.281
    anxiolytic F13.981
      in
        abuse F13.181
        dependence F13.281
    cocaine F14.981
      in
        abuse F14.181
        dependence F14.281
    excessive sexual drive F52.8
    failure of genital response (male)
        F52.21
      female F52.22
    female N94.9
      aversion F52.1
      dyspareunia N94.1
        psychogenic F52.6
      frigidity F52.22
      nymphomania F52.8
      orgasmic F52.31
      psychogenic F52.9
        aversion F52.1
        dyspareunia F52.6
        frigidity F52.22
        nymphomania F52.8

Dysfunction (Continued)
  sexual (Continued)
    female (Continued)
      psychogenic (Continued)
        orgasmic F52.31
        vaginismus F52.5
      vaginismus N94.2
        psychogenic F52.5
    hypnotic F13.981
      in
        abuse F13.181
        dependence F13.281
    inhibited orgasm (female) F52.31
      male F52.32
    lack
      of sexual enjoyment F52.1
      or loss of sexual desire F52.0
    male N53.9
      anejaculatory orgasm N53.13
      ejaculatory N53.19
        painful N53.12
        premature F52.4
        retarded N53.11
      erectile N52.9
        drug induced N52.2
        due to
          disease classified elsewhere
            N52.1
          drug N52.2
        postoperative (postprocedural)
          N52.39
        following
          prostatectomy N52.34
            radical N52.31
          radical cystectomy N52.32
          urethral surgery N52.33
        psychogenic F52.21
        specified cause NEC N52.8
        vasculogenic
          arterial insufficiency N52.01
            with corporo-venous occlu-
              sive N52.03
          corporo-venous occlusive
            N52.02
            with arterial insufficiency
              N52.03
      impotence – see Dysfunction, sexual,
          male, erectile
      psychogenic F52.9
        aversion F52.1
        erectile F52.21
        orgasmic F52.32
        premature ejaculation F52.4
        satyriasis F52.8
        specified type NEC F52.8
      specified type NEC N53.8
    nonorganic F52.9
      specified NEC F52.8
    opioid F11.981
      in
        abuse F11.181
        dependence F11.281
    orgasmic dysfunction (female) F52.31
      male F52.32
    premature ejaculation F52.4
    psychoactive substances NEC F19.981
      in
        abuse F19.181
        dependence F19.281
    psychogenic F52.9
    sedative F13.981
      in
        abuse F13.181
        dependence F13.281

Dysfunction (Continued)
  sexual (Continued)
    sexual aversion F52.1
    vaginismus (nonorganic) (psycho-
        genic) F52.5
  sinoatrial node I49.5
  somatic M99.09
    abdomen M99.09
    acromioclavicular M99.07
    cervical region M99.01
    cervicothoracic M99.01
    costochondral M99.08
    costovertebral M99.08
    head region M99.00
    hip M99.05
    lower extremity M99.06
    lumbar region M99.03
    lumbosacral M99.03
    occipitocervical M99.00
    pelvic region M99.05
    pubic M99.05
    rib cage M99.08
    sacral region M99.04
    sacrococcygeal M99.04
    sacroiliac M99.04
    specified NEC M99.09
    sternochondral M99.08
    sternoclavicular M99.07
    thoracic region M99.02
    thoracolumbar M99.02
    upper extremity M99.07
  somatoform autonomic F45.8
  stomach K31.89
    psychogenic F45.8
  suprarenal E27.9
    hyperfunction E27.0
  symbolic R48.9
    specified type NEC R48.8
  temporomandibular (joint) (joint-pain
      syndrome) M26.69
  testicular (endocrine) E29.9
    specified NEC E29.8
  thymus E32.9
  thyroid E07.9
  ureterostomy (stoma) – see Complica-
      tions, stoma, urinary tract
  urethrostomy (stoma) – see Complica-
      tions, stoma, urinary tract
  uterus, complicating delivery O62.9
    hypertonic O62.4
    hypotonic O62.2
      primary O62.0
      secondary O62.1
  ventricular I51.9
    with congestive heart failure I50.9
    left, reversible, following sudden
        emotional stress I51.81
Dysgenesis
  gonadal (due to chromosomal anomaly)
      Q96.9
    pure Q99.1
  renal Q60.5
    bilateral Q60.4
    unilateral Q60.3
  reticular D72.0
  tidal platelet D69.3
Dysgerminoma
  specified site - see Neoplasm,
      malignant
  unspecified site
    female C56.9
    male C62.90
Dysgeusia R43.2
Dysgraphia R27.8

Dyshidrosis, dysidrosis L30.1
Dyskaryotic cervical smear R87.619
Dyskeratosis L85.8
  cervix - *see* Dysplasia, cervix
  congenital Q82.8
  uterus NEC N85.8
Dyskinesia G24.9
  biliary (cystic duct or gallbladder)
      K82.8
  drug induced
      orofacial G24.01
  esophagus K22.4
  hysterical F44.4
  intestinal K59.8
  nonorganic origin F44.4
  orofacial (idiopathic) G24.4
      drug induced G24.01
  psychogenic F44.4
  subacute, drug induced G24.01
  tardive G24.01
      neuroleptic induced G24.01
  trachea J39.8
  tracheobronchial J98.09
Dyslalia (developmental) F80.0
Dyslexia R48.0
  developmental F81.0
Dyslipidemia E78.5
  depressed HDL cholesterol E78.6
  elevated fasting triglycerides E78.1
Dysmaturity - *see also* Light for dates
  pulmonary (newborn) (Wilson-Mikity)
      P27.0
Dysmenorrhea (essential) (exfoliative)
      N94.6
  congestive (syndrome) N94.6
  primary N94.4
  psychogenic F45.8
  secondary N94.5
Dysmetabolic syndrome X E88.81
Dysmetria R27.8
Dysmorphism (due to)
  alcohol Q86.0
  exogenous cause NEC Q86.8
  hydantoin Q86.1
  warfarin Q86.2
Dysmorphophobia (nondelusional)
      F45.22
  delusional F22
Dysnomia R47.01
Dysorexia R63.0
  psychogenic F50.8
Dysostosis
  cleidocranial, cleidocranialis
      Q74.0
  craniofacial Q75.1
  Fairbank's (idiopathic familial
      generalized osteophytosis)
      Q78.9
  mandibulofacial (incomplete)
      Q75.4
  multiplex E76.01
  oculomandibular Q75.5
Dyspareunia (female) N94.1
  male N53.12
  nonorganic F52.6
  psychogenic F52.6
  secondary N94.1
Dyspepsia (allergic) (atonic) (congenital)
      (functional) (gastrointestinal)
      (occupational) (reflex) K30
  intestinal K59.8
  nervous F45.8
  neurotic F45.8
  psychogenic F45.8

Dysphagia R13.10
  cervical R13.19
  following
      cerebrovascular disease I69.991
          specified NEC I69.891
          cerebral infarction I69.391
          intracerebral hemorrhage I69.191
          nontraumatic intracranial hemor-
              rhage NEC I69.291
          specified disease NEC I69.891
              subarachnoid hemorrhage
                  I69.091
  functional (hysterical) F45.8
  hysterical F45.8
  nervous (hysterical) F45.8
  neurogenic R13.19
  oral phase R13.11
  oropharyngeal phase R13.12
  pharyneal phase R13.13
  pharyngoesophageal phase
      R13.14
  psychogenic F45.8
  sideropenic D50.1
  spastica K22.4
  specified NEC R13.19
Dysphagocytosis, congenital
      D71
Dysphasia R47.02
  developmental
      expressive type F80.1
      receptive type F80.2
  following
      cerebrovascular disease I69.921
          cerebral infarction I69.321
          intracerebral hemorrhage
              I69.121
          nontraumatic intracranial hemor-
              rhage NEC I69.221
          specified disease NEC I69.821
          subarachnoid hemorrhage
              I69.021
Dysphonia R49.0
  functional F44.4
  hysterical F44.4
  psychogenic F44.4
  spastica J38.3
Dysphoria, postpartal O90.6
Dyspituitarism E23.3
Dysplasia - *see also* Anomaly
  acetabular, congenital Q65.8
  anus (histologically confirmed) (mild)
      (moderate) K62.82
      severe D01.3
  arrhythmogenic right ventricular
      I42.8
  arterial, fibromuscular I77.3
  asphyxiating thoracic (congenital)
      Q77.2
  brain Q07.9
  bronchopulmonary, perinatal
      P27.1
  cervix (uteri) N87.9
      mild N87.0
      moderate N87.1
      severe D06.9
  chondroectodermal Q77.6
  colon D12.6
  craniometaphyseal Q78.5
  dentinal K00.5
  diaphyseal, progressive Q78.3
  dystrophic Q77.5
  ectodermal (anhidrotic) (congenital)
      (hereditary) Q82.4
      hydrotic Q82.8

Dysplasia *(Continued)*
  epithelial, uterine cervix - *see* Dysplasia,
      cervix
  eye (congenital) Q11.2
  fibrous
      bone NEC (monostotic) M85.00
          ankle M85.07-
          foot M85.07-
          forearm M85.03-
          hand M85.04-
          lower leg M85.06-
          multiple site M85.09
          neck M85.08
          rib M85.08
          shoulder M85.01-
          skull M85.08
          specified site NEC M85.08
          thigh M85.05-
          toe M85.07-
          upper arm M85.02-
          vertebra M85.08
      diaphyseal, progressive Q78.3
      jaw M27.8
      polyostotic Q78.1
  florid osseous - *see also* Cyst, calcifying
      odontogenic
  high grade, focal D12.6
  hip, congenital Q65.8
  joint, congenital Q74.8
  kidney Q61.4
      multicystic Q61.4
  leg Q74.2
  lung, congenital (not associated with
      short gestation) Q33.6
  mammary (gland) (benign) N60.9-
      cyst (solitary) – *see* Cyst, breast
      cystic –*see* Mastopathy, cystic
      duct ectasia – *see* Ectasia, mammary
          duct
      fibroadenosis – *see* Fibroadenosis,
          breast
      fibrosclerosis – *see* Fibrosclerosis,
          breast
      specified type NEC N60.8-
  metaphyseal (Jansen's) (McKusick's)
      (Schmid's) Q78.5
  muscle Q79.8
  oculodentodigital Q87.0
  periapical (cemental) (cemento-osseous)
      - *see* Cyst, calcifying odontogenic
  periosteum - *see* Disorder, bone, speci-
      fied type NEC
  polyostotic fibrous Q78.1
  prostate (*see also* Neoplasia, intraepithe-
      lial, prostate) N42.3
  renal Q61.4
      multicystic Q61.4
  retinal, congenital Q14.1
  right ventricular, arrhythmogenic
      I42.8
  septo-optic Q04.4
  skin L98.8
  spinal cord Q06.1
  spondyloepiphyseal Q77.7
  thymic, with immunodeficiency
      D82.1
  vagina N89.3
      mild N89.0
      moderate N89.1
      severe NEC D07.2
  vulva N90.3
      mild N90.0
      moderate N90.1
      severe NEC D07.1

Dyspnea (nocturnal) (paroxysmal) R06.00
  asthmatic (bronchial) J45.909
    with
      exacerbation (acute) J45.901
      bronchitis J45.909
        with
          exacerbation (acute) J45.901
          status asthmaticus J45.902
        chronic J44.9
      status asthmaticus J45.902
    cardiac - see Failure, ventricular, left
    cardiac - see Failure, ventricular, left
  functional F45.8
  hyperventilation R06.4
  hysterical F45.8
  newborn orthopnea R06.01
  psychogenic F45.8
  shortness of breath R06.02
  specified type NEC R06.09
Dyspraxia R27.8
  developmental (syndrome) F82
Dysproteinemia E88.09
Dysreflexia, autonomic G90.4
Dysrhythmia
  cardiac I49.9
    newborn
      bradycardia P29.12
      tachycardia P29.11
      occurring before birth P03.819
        before onset of labor P03.810
        during labor P03.811
    postoperative I97.89
  cerebral or cortical - see Epilepsy
Dyssomnia - see Disorder, sleep
Dyssynergia
  biliary K83.8
  bladder sphincter N36.44
  cerebellaris myoclonica (Hunt's ataxia)
    G11.1
Dysthymia F34.1
Dysthyroidism E07.9
Dystocia O66.9
  affecting newborn P03.1
  cervical (hypotonic) O62.2
    affecting newborn P03.6
    primary O62.0
    secondary O62.1
  contraction ring O62.4
  fetal O66.9
    abnormality NEC O66.3
    conjoined twins O66.3
    oversize O66.2
  maternal O66.9
  positional O64.9
  shoulder (girdle) O66.0
    causing obstructed labor O66.0
  uterine NEC O62.4

Dystonia G24.9
  deformans progressiva G24.1
  drug induced NEC G24.09
    acute G24.02
    specified NEC G24.09
  familial G24.1
  idiopathic G24.1
    familial G24.1
    nonfamilial G24.2
    orofacial G24.4
  lenticularis G24.8
  musculorum deformans G24.1
  neuroleptic induced (acute) G24.02
  orofacial (idiopathic) G24.4
  oromandibular G24.4
    due to drug G24.01
  specified NEC G24.8
  torsion (familial) (idiopathic)
    G24.1
    acquired G24.8
    genetic G24.1
    symptomatic (nonfamilial)
      G24.2
Dystonic movements R25.8
Dystrophy, dystrophia
  adiposogenital E23.6
  Becker's type G71.0
  cervical sympathetic G90.2
  choroid (hereditary) H31.20
    central areolar H31.22
    choroideremia H31.21
    gyrate atrophy H31.23
    specified type NEC H31.29
  cornea (hereditary) H18.50
    endothelial H18.51
    epithelial H18.52
    granular H18.53
    lattice H18.54
    macular H18.55
    specified type NEC H18.59
  myotonic (myotonica) G71.11
  Duchenne's type G71.0
  due to malnutrition E45
  Erb's G71.0
  Fuchs' H18.52
  Gower's muscular G71.0
  hair L67.8
  infantile neuraxonal G31.89
  Landouzy-Déjérine G71.0
  Leyden-Möbius G71.0
  muscular G71.0
    benign (Becker type) G71.0
    congenital (hereditary) (progressive)
      G71.2
      myotonic G71.11
    distal G71.0
    Duchenne type G71.0

Dystrophy, dystrophia
  muscular (Continued)
    Emery-Dreifuss G71.0
    Erb type G71.0
    facioscapulohumeral G71.0
    Gower's G71.0
    hereditary (progressive) G71.0
    Landouzy-Déjérine type G71.0
    limb-girdle G71.0
    myotonic G71.11
    progressive (hereditary) G71.0
      Charcot-Marie(-Tooth) type
        G60.0
      pseudohypertrophic (infantile)
        G71.0
      severe (Duchenne type) G71.0
  myocardium, myocardial - see Degen-
    eration, myocardial
  myotonic, myotonica G71.11
  nail L60.3
    congenital Q84.6
  nutritional E45
  ocular G71.0
  oculocerebrorenal E72.03
  oculopharyngeal G71.0
  ovarian N83.8
  polyglandular E31.8
  reflex (neuromuscular) (sympathetic)
    - see Syndrome, pain, complex
    regional I
  retinal (hereditary) H35.50
    in
      lipid storage disorders E75.6
        [H36]
      systemic lipidoses E75.6 [H36]
    involving
      pigment epithelium H35.54
      sensory area H35.53
    pigmentary H35.52
    vitreoretinal H35.51
  Salzmann's nodular - see Degeneration,
    cornea, nodular
  scapuloperoneal G71.0
  skin NEC L98.8
  sympathetic (reflex) - see Syndrome,
    pain, complex regional I
    cervical G90.2
  tapetoretinal H35.54
  thoracic, asphyxiating Q77.2
  unguium L60.3
    congenital Q84.6
  vitreoretinal H35.51
  vulva N90.4
  yellow (liver) - see Failure, hepatic
Dysuria R30.0
  psychogenic F45.8

E

Eales' disease - *see* Vasculitis, retina
Ear - *see also* condition
  piercing Z41.3
  tropical B36.8
  wax (impacted) H61.20
    left H61.22
      with right H61.23
    right H61.21
      with left H61.23
Earache - *see* subcategory H92.0
Early satiety R68.81
Eaton-Lambert syndrome G73.1
  not associated with neoplasm G70.8
Eberth's disease (typhoid fever) A01.00
Ebola virus disease A98.4
Ebstein's anomaly or syndrome (heart) Q22.5
Eccentro-osteochondrodysplasia E76.29
Ecchondroma - *see* Neoplasm, bone, benign
Ecchondrosis D48.0
Ecchymosis R58
  conjunctiva - *see* Hemorrhage, conjunctiva
  eye (traumatic) – *see* Contusion, eyeball
  eyelid (traumatic) — *see* Contusion, eyelid
  newborn P54.5
  spontaneous R23.3
  traumatic - *see* Contusion
Echinococciasis - *see* Echinococcus
Echinococcosis - *see* Echinococcus
Echinococcus (infection) B67.90
  granulosus B67.4
    bone B67.2
    liver B67.0
    lung B67.1
    multiple sites B67.32
    specified site NEC B67.39
    thyroid B67.31 *[E35]*
  liver NOS B67.8
    granulosus B67.0
    multilocularis B67.5
  lung NEC B67.99
    granulosus B67.1
    multilocularis B67.69
  multilocularis B67.7
    liver B67.5
    multiple sites B67.61
    specified site NEC B67.69
  specified site NEC B67.99
    granulosus B67.39
    multilocularis B67.69
  thyroid NEC B67.99
    granulosus B67.31 *[E35]*
    multilocularis B67.69 *[E35]*
Echinorhynchiasis B83.8
Echinostomiasis B66.8
Echolalia R48.8
Echovirus, as cause of disease classified elsewhere B97.12
Eclampsia, eclamptic (coma) (convulsions) (delirium) (with hypertension) NEC O15.9
  during labor and delivery O15.1
  postpartum O15.2
  pregnancy O15.0-
  puerperal O15.2
Economic circumstances affecting care Z59.9
Economo's disease A85.8

Ectasia, ectasis
  aorta - *see* Aneurysm, aorta
  breast – *see* Ectasia, mammary duct
  capillary I78.8
  cornea H18.71-
  gastric antral vascular (GAVE) K31.819
    with hemorrhage K31.811
    without hemorrhage K31.819
  mammary duct N60.4-
  salivary gland (duct) K11.8
  sclera - *see* Sclerectasia
Ecthyma L08.0
  contagiosum B08.02
  gangrenosum L08.0
  infectiosum B08.02
Ectocardia Q24.8
Ectodermal dysplasia (anhidrotic) Q82.4
Ectodermosis erosiva pluriorificialis L51.1
Ectopic, ectopia (congenital)
  abdominal viscera Q45.8
    due to defect in anterior abdominal wall Q79.59
  ACTH syndrome E24.3
  adrenal gland Q89.1
  anus Q43.5
  atrial beats I49.1
  beats I49.49
    atrial I49.1
    ventricular I49.3
  bladder Q64.10
  bone and cartilage in lung Q33.5
  brain Q04.8
  breast tissue Q83.8
  cardiac Q24.8
  cerebral Q04.8
  cordis Q24.8
  endometrium - *see* Endometriosis
  gastric mucosa Q40.2
  gestation - *see* Pregnancy, by site
  heart Q24.8
  hormone secretion NEC E34.2
  kidney (crossed) (pelvis) Q63.2
  lens, lentis Q12.1
  mole - *see* Pregnancy, by site
  organ or site NEC - *see* Malposition, congenital
  pancreas Q45.3
  pregnancy - *see* Pregnancy, ectopic
  pupil - *see* Abnormality, pupillary
  renal Q63.2
  sebaceous glands of mouth Q38.6
  spleen Q89.09
  testis Q53.00
    bilateral Q53.02
    unilateral Q53.01
  thyroid Q89.2
  tissue in lung Q33.5
  ureter Q62.63
  ventricular beats I49.3
  vesicae Q64.10
Ectromelia Q73.8
  lower limb – *see* Defect, reduction, limb, lower, specified type NEC
  upper limb - *see* Defect, reduction, limb, upper, specified type NEC
Ectropion H02.109
  cervix N86
    with cervicitis N72
  congenital Q10.1
  eyelid (paralytic) H02.109
    cicatricial H02.119
      left H02.116
        lower H02.115
        upper H02.114

Ectropion *(Continued)*
  eyelid *(Continued)*
    cicatricial *(Continued)*
      right H02.113
        lower H02.112
        upper H02.111
    congenital Q10.1
    left H02.106
      lower H02.105
      upper H02.104
    mechanical H02.129
      left H02.126
        lower H02.125
        upper H02.124
      right H02.123
        lower H02.122
        upper H02.121
    right H02.103
      lower H02.102
      upper H02.101
    senile H02.139
      left H02.136
        lower H02.135
        upper H02.134
      right H02.133
        lower H02.132
        upper H02.131
    spastic H02.149
      left H02.146
        lower H02.145
        upper H02.144
      right H02.143
        lower H02.142
        upper H02.141
  iris H21.89
  lip (acquired) K13.0
    congenital Q38.0
  urethra N36.8
  uvea H21.89
Eczema (acute) (chronic) (erythematous) (fissum) (rubrum) (squamous) (*see also* Dermatitis) L30.9
  contact – *see* Dermatitis, contact
  dyshydrotic L30.1
  external ear - *see* Otitis, externa, acute, eczematoid
  flexural L20.82
  herpeticum B00.0
  hypertrophicum L28.0
  hypostatic - *see* Varix, leg, with, inflammation
  impetiginous L01.1
  infantile (due to any substance) L20.83
    intertriginous L21.1
    seborrheic L21.1
  intertriginous NEC L30.4
    infantile L21.1
  intrinsic (allergic) L20.84
  lichenified NEC L28.0
  marginatum (hebrae) B35.6
  pustular L30.3
  stasis - *see* Varix, leg, with, inflammation
  vaccination, vaccinatum T88.1
  varicose - *see* Varix, leg, with, inflammation
Eczematid L30.2
Eddowes(-Spurway) syndrome Q78.0
Edema, edematous (infectious) (pitting) (toxic) R60.9
  with nephritis - *see* Nephrosis
  allergic T78.3
  amputation stump (surgical) (sequelae (late effect)) T87.8

Edema, edematous *(Continued)*
  angioneurotic (allergic) (any site) (with urticaria) T78.3
    hereditary D84.1
  angiospastic I73.9
  Berlin's (traumatic) S05.8x-
  brain G93.6
    due to birth injury P11.0
    newborn (anoxia or hypoxia) P52.4
      birth injury P11.0
    traumatic – *see* Injury, intracranial, cerebral edema
  cardiac - *see* Failure, heart, congestive
  cardiovascular - *see* Failure, heart, congestive
  cerebral - *see* Edema, brain
  cerebrospinal - *see* Edema, brain
  cervix (uteri) (acute) N88.8
    puerperal, postpartum O90.89
  chronic hereditary Q82.0
  circumscribed, acute T78.3
    hereditary D84.1
  conjunctiva H11.42-
  cornea H18.2-
    idiopathic H18.22-
    secondary H18.23-
      due to contact lens H18.21-
  due to
    lymphatic obstruction I89.0
    salt retention E87.0
  epiglottis - *see* Edema, glottis
  essential, acute T78.3
    hereditary D84.1
  extremities, lower - *see* Edema, legs
  eyelid NEC H02.849
    left H02.846
      lower H02.845
      upper H02.844
    right H02.843
      lower H02.842
      upper H02.841
  familial, hereditary Q82.0
  famine - *see* Malnutrition, severe
  generalized R60.1
  glottis, glottic, glottidis (obstructive) (passive) J38.4
    allergic T78.3
      hereditary D84.1
  heart - *see* Failure, heart, congestive
  heat T67.7
  hereditary Q82.0
  inanition - *see* Malnutrition, severe
  intracranial G93.6
  iris H21.89
  joint - *see* Effusion, joint
  larynx - *see* Edema, glottis
  legs R60.0
    due to venous obstruction I87.1
    hereditary Q82.0
  localized R60.0
    due to venous obstruction I87.1
  lower limbs - *see* Edema, legs
  lung J81.1
    with heart condition or failure - *see* Failure, ventricular, left
    acute J81.0
    chemical (acute) J68.1
      chronic J68.1
    chronic J81.1
      due to
        chemicals, gases, fumes or vapors (inhalation) J68.1

Edema, edematous *(Continued)*
  lung *(Continued)*
    chronic *(Continued)*
      due to *(Continued)*
        external agent J70.9
          specified NEC J70.8
        radiation J70.1
    due to
      chemicals, fumes or vapors (inhalation) J68.1
      external agent J70.9
        specified NEC J70.8
      high altitude T70.29
      near drowning T75.1
      radiation J70.0
    meaning failure, left ventricle I50.1
  lymphatic I89.0
    due to mastectomy I97.2
  macula H35.81
    cystoid, following cataract surgery - *see* Complications, postprocedural, following cataract surgery
    diabetic – *see* Diabetes, macular edema
  malignant – *see* Gangrene, gas
  Milroy's Q82.0
  nasopharynx J39.2
  newborn P83.30
    hydrops fetalis - *see* Hydrops, fetalis
    specified NEC P83.39
  nutritional - *see also* Malnutrition, severe
    with dyspigmentation, skin and hair E40
  optic disc or nerve - *see* Papilledema
  orbit H05.22-
  pancreas K86.8
  papilla, optic - *see* Papilledema
  penis N48.89
  periodic T78.3
    hereditary D84.1
  pharynx J39.2
  pulmonary - *see* Edema, lung
  Quincke's T78.3
    hereditary D84.1
  renal – *see* Nephrosis
  retina H35.81
    diabetic – *see* Diabetes, macular edema
  salt E87.0
  scrotum N50.8
  seminal vesicle N50.8
  spermatic cord N50.8
  spinal (cord) (vascular) (nontraumatic) G95.19
  starvation - *see* Malnutrition, severe
  stasis - *see* Hypertension, venous, (chronic)
  subglottic - *see* Edema, glottis
  supraglottic - *see* Edema, glottis
  testis N44.8
  tunica vaginalis N50.8
  vas deferens N50.8
  vulva (acute) N90.8
Edentulism *see* Absence, teeth, acquired
Edsall's disease T67.2
Educational handicap Z55.9
  specified NEC Z55.8
Edward's syndrome — *see* Trisomy, 18
Effect, adverse
  abnormal gravitational (G) forces or states T75.81
  abuse – *see* Maltreatment
  air pressure T70.9
    specified NEC T70.8

Effect, adverse *(Continued)*
  altitude (high) - *see* Effect, adverse, high altitude
  anesthesia (*see also* Anesthesia) T88.59
    in labor and delivery O74.9
    in pregnancy NEC O29.3-
    local, toxic
      in labor and delivery O74.4-
      postpartum, puerperal O89.3
    postpartum, puerperal O89.9
    specified NEC T88.59
      in labor and delivery O74.8
      postpartum, puerperal O89.8
    spinal and epidural T88.59
      headache T88.59
        in labor and delivery O74.5
        postpartum, puerperal O89.4
      specified NEC
        in labor and delivery O74.6
        postpartum, puerperal O89.5
  antitoxin - *see* Complications, vaccination
  atmospheric pressure T70.9
    due to explosion T70.8
    high T70.3
    low - *see* Effect, adverse, high altitude
    specified effect NEC T70.8
  biological, correct substance properly administered - *see* Effect, adverse, drug
  blood (derivatives) (serum) (transfusion) - *see* Complications, transfusion
  chemical substance - *see* Table of drugs and chemicals
  cold (temperature) (weather) T69.9
    chilblains T69.1
    frostbite - *see* Frostbite
    specified effect NEC T69.8
  drugs and medicaments T88.7 This code not for use in the inpatient setting
    specified drug - *see* Table of drugs and chemicals, by drug, adverse effect
    specified effect - code to condition
  electric current, electricity (shock) T75.4
    burn - *see* Burn
  exertion (excessive) T73.3
  exposure - *see* Exposure
  external cause NEC T75.89
  foodstuffs T78.1
    allergic reaction - *see* Allergy, food
      causing anaphylaxis – *see* Shock, anaphylactic, food
    noxious – *see* Poisoning, food, noxious
  gases, fumes, or vapors - *see* Table of drugs and chemicals
  glue (airplane) sniffing
    due to drug abuse - *see* Abuse, drug, inhalant
    due to drug dependence - *see* Dependence, drug, inhalant
  heat - *see* Heat
  high altitude NEC T70.29
    anoxia T70.20
    on
      ears T70.0
      sinuses T70.1
    polycythemia D75.1
  high pressure fluids T70.8
  hot weather - *see* Heat
  hunger T73.0
  immersion, foot – *see* Immersion

217

Effect, adverse *(Continued)*
  immunization - *see* Complications, vaccination
  immunological agents - *see* Complications, vaccination
  infrared (radiation) (rays) NOS
    dermatitis or eczema L59.8
  infusion - *see* Complications, infusion
  lack of care of infants – *see* Maltreatment, child
  lightning - *see* Lightning
  medical care T88.9
    specified NEC T88.8
  medicinal substance, correct, properly administered - *see* Effect, adverse, drug
  motion T75.3
  noise, on inner ear - *see* subcategory H83.3
  overheated places - *see* Heat
  psychosocial, of work environment Z56.5
  radiation (diagnostic) (infrared) (natural source) (therapeutic) (ultraviolet) (X-ray) NOS
    dermatitis or eczema - *see* Dermatitis, due to, radiation
    fibrosis of lung J70.1
    pneumonitis J70.0
    pulmonary manifestations
      acute J70.0
      chronic J70.1
    skin L59.9
  radioactive substance NOS
    dermatitis or eczema - *see* Radiodermatitis
    dermatitis or eczema - *see* Radiodermatitis
  reduced temperature T69.9
    immersion foot or hand – *see* Immersion
    specified effect NEC T69.8
  serum (prophylactic) (therapeutic) NEC T80.6
  specified NEC T78.8
    external cause NEC T75.89
  strangulation - *see* Asphyxia, traumatic
  submersion T75.1
  thirst T73.1
  toxic - *see* Toxicity
  transfusion - *see* Complications, transfusion
  ultraviolet (radiation) (rays) NOS
    burn (*see* Burn)
    dermatitis or eczema - *see* Dermatitis, due to, ultraviolet rays
      acute L56.8
  vaccine (any) - *see* Complications, vaccination
  vibration - *see* Vibration, adverse effects
  water pressure NEC T70.9
    specified NEC T70.8
  weightlessness T75.82
  whole blood - *see* Complications, transfusion
  work environment Z56.5
Effect(s) (of) (from) - *see* Effect, adverse NEC
Effects, late - *see* Sequelae
Effluvium
  anagen L65.1
  telogen L65.0
Effort syndrome (psychogenic) F45.8

Effusion
  amniotic fluid - *see* Pregnancy, complicated by, prematue rupture of membranes
  brain (serous) G93.6
  bronchial – *see* Bronchitis
  cerebral G93.6
  cerebrospinal - *see also* Meningitis
    vessel G93.6
  chest - *see* Effusion, pleura
  chylous, chyliform (pleura) J94.0
  intracranial G93.6
  joint M25.40
    ankle M25.47-
    elbow M25.42-
    foot joint M25.47-
    hand joint M25.44-
    hip M25.45-
    knee M25.46-
    shoulder M25.41-
    specified joint NEC M25.48
    wrist M25.43-
  malignant pleural J91.0
  meninges - *see* Meningitis
  pericardium, pericardial (noninflammatory) I31.3
    acute - *see* Pericarditis, acute
  peritoneal (chronic) R18.8
  pleura, pleurisy, pleuritic, pleuroperi-cardial J90
    chylous, chyliform J94.0
    due to systemic lupus erythematosis M32.13
    influenzal - *see* Influenza, with, respiratory manifestations
    malignant J91.0
    newborn P28.89
    tuberculous NEC A15.6
      primary (progressive) A15.7
  spinal - *see* Meningitis
  thorax, thoracic - *see* Effusion, pleura
Egg shell nails L60.3
  congenital Q84.6
Egyptian splenomegaly B65.1
Ehrlichiosis A77.40
  due to
    E. chafeensis A77.41
    E. sennetsu A79.81
    specified organism NEC A77.49
Ehlers-Danlos syndrome Q79.6
Eichstedt's disease B36.0
Eisenmenger's
  complex or syndrome I27.89
  defect Q21.8
Ejaculation
  painful N53.12
  premature F52.4
  retarded N53.11
  retrograde N53.14
  semen, painful N53.12
    psychogenic F52.6
Ekbom's syndrome (restless legs) G25.81
Ekman's syndrome (brittle bones and blue sclera) Q78.0
Elastic skin Q82.8
  acquired L57.4
Elastofibroma - *see* Neoplasm, connective tissue, benign
Elastoma (juvenile) Q82.8
  Miescher's L87.2
Elastomyofibrosis I42.4
Elastosis
  actinic, solar L57.8
  atrophicans (senile) L57.4

Elastosis *(Continued)*
  perforans serpiginosa L87.2
  senilis L57.4
Elbow - *see* condition
Electric current, electricity, effects (concussion) (fatal) (nonfatal) (shock) T75.4
  burn - *see* Burn
Electric feet syndrome E53.8
Electrocution T75.4
  from electroshock gun (taser) T75.4
Electrolyte imbalance E87.8
  with
    abortion – *see* Abortion by type complicated by specified condition NEC
    ectopic pregnancy O08.5
    molar pregnancy O08.5
Elephantiasis (nonfilarial) I89.0
  arabicum – *see* Infestation, filarial
  bancroftian B74.0
  congenital (any site) (hereditary) Q82.0
  due to
    Brugia (malayi) B74.1
      timori B74.2
    mastectomy I97.2
    Wuchereria (bancrofti) B74.0
  eyelid H02.859
    left H02.856
      lower H02.855
      upper H02.854
    right H02.853
      lower H02.852
      upper H02.851
  filarial, filariensis - *see* Infestation, filarial
  glandular I89.0
  graecorum A30.9
  lymphangiectatic I89.0
  lymphatic vessel I89.0
    due to mastectomy I97.2
  scrotum (nonfilarial) I89.0
  streptococcal I89.0
  surgical I97.89
    postmastectomy I97.2
  telangiectodes I89.0
  vulva (nonfilarial) N90.8
Elevated, elevation
  antibody titer R76.0
  basal metabolic rate R94.8
  blood pressure - *see also* Hypertension
    reading (incidental) (isolated) (nonspecific), no diagnosis of hypertension R03.0
  blood sugar R73.09
  body temperature (of unknown origin) R50.9
  C-reactive protein (CRP) R79.82
  cancer antigen 125 [CA 125] R97.1
  carcinoembryonic antigen [CEA] R97.0
  cholesterol E78.0
    with high triglycerides E78.2
  conjugate, eye H51.0
  diaphragm, congenital Q79.1
  erythrocyte sedimentation rate R70.0
  fasting glucose R73.01
  fasting triglycerides E78.1
  finding on laboratory examination - *see* Findings, abnormal, inconclusive, without diagnosis, by type of exam
  GFR (glomerular filtration rate) - *see* Findings, abnormal, inconclusive, without diagnosis, by type of exam
  glucose tolerance (oral) R73.02
  immunoglobulin level R76.8
  indolacetic acid R82.5

Elevated, elevation (*Continued*)
  lactic acid dehydrogenase (LDH) level R74.0
  leukocytes D72.829
  lipoprotein a level E78.8
  liver function
    study R94.5
    test R79.89
      alkaline phosphatase R74.8
      aminotransferase R74.0
      bilirubin R17
      hepatic enzyme R74.8
      lactate dehydrogenase R74.0
  lymphocytes D72.820
  prostate specific antigen [PSA] R97.2
  Rh titer T80.4
  scapula, congenital Q74.0
  sedimentation rate R70.0
  SGOT R74.0
  SGPT R74.0
  transaminase level R74.0
  triglycerides E78.1
    with high cholesterol E78.2
  tumor associated antigens [TAA] NEC R97.8
  tumor specific antigens [TSA] NEC R97.8
  urine level of
    catecholamine R82.5
    indoleacetic acid R82.5
    17-ketosteroids R82.5
    steroids R82.5
    vanillylmandelic acid (VMA) R82.5
  venous pressure I87.8
  white blood cell count D72.829
  specified NEC D72.828
Elliptocytosis (congenital) (hereditary) D58.1
  Hb C (disease) D58.1
  hemoglobin disease D58.1
  sickle-cell (disease) D57.8-
    trait D57.3
Ellison-Zollinger syndrome E16.4
Ellis-van Creveld syndrome
  (chondroectodermal dysplasia) Q77.6
Elongated, elongation (congenital) - *see also* Distortion
  bone Q79.9
  cervix (uteri) Q51.8
    acquired N88.4
    hypertrophic N88.4
  colon Q43.8
  common bile duct Q44.5
  cystic duct Q44.5
  frenulum, penis Q55.69
  labia minora (acquired) N90.6
  ligamentum patellae Q74.1
  petiolus (epiglottidis) Q31.8
  tooth, teeth K00.2
  uvula Q38.6
Eltor cholera A00.1
Emaciation (due to malnutrition) E41
Embadomoniasis A07.8
Embedded tooth, teeth K01.0
  root only K08.3
Embolic - *see* condition
Embolism (multiple) (paradoxical) I74.9
  air (any site) (traumatic) T79.0
    following
      abortion - *see* Abortion by type complicated by embolism
      ectopic pregnancy O08.2
      infusion, therapeutic injection or transfusion T80.0
      molar pregnancy O08.2

Embolism (*Continued*)
  air (*Continued*)
    following (*Continued*)
      procedure NEC
        artery T81.719
          mesenteric T81.710
          renal T81.711
          specified NEC T81.718
        vein T81.72
    in pregnancy, childbirth or puerperium - *see* Embolism, obstetric
  amniotic fluid (pulmonary) - *see also* Embolism, obstetric
    following
      abortion - *see* Abortion by type complicated by embolism
      ectopic pregnancy O08.2
      molar pregnancy O08.2
  aorta, aortic I74.10
    abdominal I74.0
    bifurcation I74.0
    saddle I74.0
    thoracic I74.11
  artery I74.9
    auditory, internal I65.8
    basilar - *see* Occlusion, artery, basilar
    carotid (common) (internal) - *see* Occlusion, artery, carotid
    cerebellar (anterior inferior) (posterior inferior) (superior) I66.3
    cerebral - *see* Occlusion, artery, cerebral
    choroidal (anterior) I66.8
    communicating posterior I66.8
    coronary - *see also* Infarct, myocardium
      not resulting in infarction I24.0
    extremity I74.4
      lower I74.3
      upper I74.2
    hypophyseal I66.8
    iliac I74.5
    limb I74.4
      lower I74.3
      upper I74.2
    mesenteric (with gangrene) K55.0
    ophthalmic - *see* Occlusion, artery, retina
    peripheral I74.4
    pontine I66.8
    precerebral - *see* Occlusion, artery, precerebral
    pulmonary - *see* Embolism, pulmonary
    renal N28.0
    retinal - *see* Occlusion, artery, retina
    septic I76
    specified NEC I74.8
    vertebral - *see* Occlusion, artery, vertebral
  basilar (artery) I65.1
  blood clot
    following
      abortion - *see* Abortion by type complicated by embolism
      ectopic or molar pregnancy O08.2
      in pregnancy, childbirth or puerperium - *see* Embolism, obstetric
  brain - *see also* Occlusion, artery, cerebral
    following
      abortion - *see* Abortion by type complicated by embolism
      ectopic or molar pregnancy O08.2

Embolism (*Continued*)
  brain (*Continued*)
    puerperal, postpartum, childbirth - *see* Embolism, obstetric
  capillary I78.8
  cardiac - *see also* Infarct, myocardium
    not resulting in infarction I24.0
  carotid (artery) (common) (internal) - *see* Occlusion, artery, carotid
  cavernous sinus (venous) - *see* Embolism, intracranial venous sinus
  cerebral - *see* Occlusion, artery, cerebral
  cholesterol - *see* Atheroembolism
  coronary (artery or vein) (systemic) - *see* Occlusion, coronary
  due to device, implant or graft - *see also* Complications, by site and type, specified NEC
    arterial graft NEC T82.818
    breast (implant) T85.81
    catheter NEC T85.81
      dialysis (renal) T82.818
        intraperitoneal T85.81
      infusion NEC T82.818
        spinal (epidural) (subdural) T85.81
      urinary (indwelling) T83.81
    electronic (electrode) (pulse generator) (stimulator)
      bone T84.81
      cardiac T82.817
      nervous system (brain) (peripheral nerve) (spinal) T85.81
      urinary T83.81
    fixation, internal (orthopedic) NEC T84.81
    gastrointestinal (bile duct) (esophagus) T85.81
    genital NEC T83.81
    heart (graft) (valve) T82.817
    joint prosthesis T84.81
    ocular (corneal graft) (orbital implant) T85.81
    orthopedic (bone graft) NEC T86.838
    specified NEC T85.81
    urinary (graft) NEC T83.81
    vascular NEC T82.818
    ventricular intracranial shunt T85.81
  extremities
    lower - *see* Embolism, vein, lower extremity
      arterial I74.3
    upper I74.2
  eye H34.9
  fat (cerebral) (pulmonary) (systemic) T79.1
    following
      abortion - *see* Abortion by type complicated by embolism
      ectopic or molar pregnancy O08.2
      complicating delivery - *see* Embolism, obstetric
  following
    abortion - *see* Abortion by type complicated by embolism
    ectopic or molar pregnancy O08.2
    infusion, therapeutic injection or transfusion
      air T80.0
      thrombus T80.1
  heart (fatty) - *see also* Infarct, myocardium
    not resulting in infarction I24.0

Embolism *(Continued)*
  hepatic (vein) I82.0
  in pregnancy, childbirth or puerperium - *see* Embolism, obstetric
  intestine (artery) (vein) (with gangrene) K55.0
  intracranial - *see also* Occlusion, artery, cerebral
    venous sinus (any) G08
      nonpyogenic I67.6
  intraspinal venous sinuses or veins G08
    nonpyogenic G95.19
  kidney (artery) N28.0
  lateral sinus (venous) - *see* Embolism, intracranial, venous sinus
  leg - *see* Embolism, vein, lower extremity
    arterial I74.3
  longitudinal sinus (venous) - *see* Embolism, intracranial, venous sinus
  lung (massive) - *see* Embolism, pulmonary
  meninges I66.8
  mesenteric (artery) (vein) (with gangrene) K55.0
  obstetric (in) (pulmonary)
    childbirth O88.82
      air O88.02
      amniotic fluid O88.12
      blood clot O88.22
      fat O88.82
      pyemic O88.32
      septic O88.32
      specified type NEC O88.82
    pregnancy O88.81-
      air O88.01-
      amniotic fluid O88.11-
      blood clot O88.21-
      fat O88.81-
      pyemic O88.31-
      septic O88.31-
      specified type NEC O88.81-
    puerperal O88.83
      air O88.03
      blood clot O88.23
      fat O88.83
      pyemic O88.33
      septic O88.33
      specified type NEC O88.83
  ophthalmic - *see* Occlusion, artery, retina
  penis N48.81
  peripheral artery NEC I74.8
  pituitary E23.6
  popliteal (artery) I74.3
  portal (vein) I81
  postoperative, postprocedural
    artery T81.719
      mesenteric T81.710
      renal T81.711
      specified NEC T81.718
    vein T81.72
  precerebral artery - *see* Occlusion, artery, precerebral
  puerperal - *see* Embolism, obstetric
  pulmonary (acute) (artery) (vein) I26.99
    with acute cor pulmonale I26.09
    chronic I27.82
    healed or old Z86.71
    following
      abortion - *see* Abortion by type complicated by embolism
      ectopic or molar pregnancy O08.2
    in pregnancy, childbirth or puerperium - *see* Embolism, obstetric
    personal history of Z86.71

Embolism *(Continued)*
  pulmonary *(Continued)*
    septic I26.90
      with acute cor pulmonale I26.01
  pyemic (multiple) I76
    following
      abortion - *see* Abortion by type complicated by embolism
      ectopic or molar pregnancy O08.2
    Hemophilus influenzae A41.3
    pneumococcal A40.3
      with pneumonia J13
    puerperal, postpartum, childbirth (any organism) - *see* Embolism, obstetric
    specified organism NEC A41.89
    staphylococcal A41.2
    streptococcal A40.9
  renal (artery) N28.0
    vein I82.3
  retina, retinal - *see* Occlusion, artery, retina
  saddle (aorta) I74.0
  septic (arterial) I76
    complicating abortion – *see* Abortion, by type, complicated by, embolism
  sinus - *see* Embolism, intracranial, venous sinus
  soap complicating abortion – *see* Abortion, by type, complicated by, embolism
  spinal cord G95.19
    pyogenic origin G06.1
  spleen, splenic (artery) I74.8
  thrombus (thromboembolism) following infusion, therapeutic injection or transfusion T80.1
  upper extremity I74.2
  vein (acute) I82.90
    antecubital I82.61-
    axillary I82.a1-
    basilic I82.61-
    brachial I82.62-
    brachiocephalic (innominate) I82.290
    cephalic I82.61-
    cerebral I67.6
    chronic I82.91
      antecubital I82.71-
      axillary I82.a2-
      basilic I82.71-
      brachial I82.72-
      brachiocephalic (innominate) I82.291
      cephalic I82.71-
      innominate I82.291
      internal jugular I82.c2-
      radial I82.72-
      specified NEC I82.891
      subclavian I82.b2-
      thoracic NEC I82.291
      ulnar I82.72-
      upper extremity I82.70-
        deep I82.72-
        superficial I82.71-
    coronary - *see also* Infarct, myocardium
      not resulting in infarction I24.0
    deep vein (lower extremity) I82.40
      chronic I82.50
        femoral I82.51-
        iliac I82.52-
        popliteal I82.53-
        specified NEC I82.59-
        tibial I82.54-
      specified NEC I82.49-
    femoral I82.41-
    hepatic I82.0

Embolism *(Continued)*
  vein *(Continued)*
    iliac (iliofemoral) I82.42-
    innominate I82.290
    internal jugular I82.c1-
    lower extremity I82.40
      specified NEC I82.49-
      superficial vein I82.81-
    mesenteric (with gangrene) K55.0
    popliteal I82.43-
    portal I81
    pulmonary - *see* Embolism, pulmonary
    renal I82.3
    radial I82.62-
    saphenous (greater) (lesser) I82.81-
    subclavian I82.b1-
    specified NEC I82.890
    superficial (lower extremity) I82.81-
    tibial I82.44-
    thoracic NEC I82.290
    ulnar I82.62-
    upper extremity I82.60-
      deep I82.62-
      superficial I82.61-
    vena cava
      inferior (acute) I82.220
        chronic I82.221
      superior (acute) I82.210
        chronic I82.211
    venous sinus G08
    vessels of brain - *see* Occlusion, artery, cerebral
Embolus - *see* Embolism
Embryoma - *see also* Neoplasm, uncertain behavior
  benign - *see* Neoplasm, benign
  kidney C64.-
  liver C22.0
  malignant - *see also* Neoplasm, malignant
    kidney C64.
    liver C22.0
    testis C62.9-
      descended C62.1-
      undescended C62.0-
  testis C62.9-
    descended (scrotal) C62.1-
    undescended C62.0-
Embryonic
  circulation Q28.9
  heart Q28.9
  vas deferens Q55.4
Embryopathia NOS Q89.9
Embryotoxon Q13.4
Emesis - *see* Vomiting
Emotional lability R45.86
Emotionality, pathological F60.3
Emotogenic disease – *see* Disorder, psychogenic
Emphysema (atrophic) (bullous) (chronic) (interlobular) (lung) (obstructive) (pulmonary) (senile) (vesicular) J43.9
  cellular tissue (traumatic) T79.7
    surgical T81.82
  centrilobular J43.2
  compensatory J98.3
  congenital (interstitial) P25.0
  conjunctiva H11.89
  connective tissue (traumatic) T79.7
    surgical T81.82
  due to chemicals, gases, fumes or vapors J68.4

Emphysema *(Continued)*
  eyelid(s) - *see* Disorder, eyelid, specified type NEC
    surgical T81.82
    traumatic T79.7
  interstitial J98.2
    congenital P25.0
    perinatal period P25.0
  laminated tissue T79.7
    surgical T81.82
  mediastinal J98.2
    newborn P25.2
  orbit, orbital - *see* Disorder, orbit, specified type NEC
  panacinar J43.1
  panlobular J43.1
  specified NEC J43.8
  subcutaneous (traumatic) T79.7
    nontraumatic J98.2
    postprocedural T81.82
    surgical T81.82
  surgical T81.82
  thymus (gland) (congenital) E32.8
  traumatic (subcutaneous) T79.7
  unilateral J43.0
Empty nest syndrome Z60.0
Empyema (acute) (chest) (double) (pleura) (supradiaphragmatic) (thorax) J86.9
  with fistula J86.0
  accessory sinus (chronic) - *see* Sinusitis
  antrum (chronic) - *see* Sinusitis, maxillary
  brain (any part) - *see* Abscess, brain
  ethmoidal (chronic) (sinus) - *see* Sinusitis, ethmoidal
  extradural - *see* Abscess, extradural
  frontal (chronic) (sinus) - *see* Sinusitis, frontal
  gallbladder K81.0
  mastoid (process) (acute) – *see* Mastoiditis, acute
  maxilla, maxillary M27.2
    sinus (chronic) - *see* Sinusitis, maxillary
  nasal sinus (chronic) - *see* Sinusitis
  sinus (accessory) (chronic) (nasal) - *see* Sinusitis
  sphenoidal (sinus) (chronic) - *see* Sinusitis, sphenoidal
  subarachnoid - *see* Abscess, extradural
  subdural - *see* Abscess, subdural
  tuberculous A15.6
  ureter - *see* Ureteritis
  ventricular - *see* Abscess, brain
En coup de sabre lesion L94.1
Enamel pearls K00.2
Enameloma K00.2
Enanthema, viral B09
Encephalitis (chronic) (hemorrhagic) (idiopathic) (nonepidemic) (spurious) (subacute) G04.90
  acute - *see also* Encephalitis, viral A86
    disseminated G04.00
      infectious G04.00
      noninfectious G04.81
      postimmunization (postvaccination) G04.01
      postinfectious G04.00
    inclusion body A85.8
    necrotizing hemorrhagic (postinfectious) G04.30
      postimmunization G04.31
  arboviral, arbovirus NEC A85.2

Encephalitis *(Continued)*
  arthropod-borne NEC (viral) A85.2
  Australian A83.4
  California (virus) A83.5
  Central European (tick-borne) A84.1
  Czechoslovakian A84.1
  Dawson's (inclusion body) A81.1
  diffuse sclerosing A81.1
  disseminated, acute G04.00
  due to
    cat scratch disease A28.1
    malaria – *see* Malaria
    rickettsiosis – *see* Rickettsiosis
    smallpox inoculation G04.01
    typhus – *see* Typhus
  Eastern equine A83.2
  endemic (viral) A86
  epidemic NEC (viral) A86
  equine (acute) (infectious) (viral) A83.9
    Eastern A83.2
    Venezuelan A92.2
    Western A83.1
  Far Eastern (tick-borne) A84.0
  following vaccination or other immunization procedure G04.01
  herpes zoster B02.0
  herpesviral B00.4
    due to herpesvirus 6 B10.01
    due to herpesvirus 7 B10.09
    specified NEC B10.09
  Ilheus (virus) A83.8
  inclusion body A81.1
  in (due to)
    actinomycosis A42.82
    adenovirus A85.1
    African trypanosomiasis B56.9 *[G05.3]*
    Chagas' disease (chronic) B57.42
    cytomegalovirus B25.8
    enterovirus A85.0
    herpes (simplex) virus B00.4
      due to herpesvirus 6 B10.01
      due to herpesvirus 7 B10.09
      specified NEC B10.09
    infectious disease NEC B99 *[G05.3]*
    influenza - *see* Influenza, with, manifestations NEC
    listeriosis A32.12
    measles B05.0
    mumps B26.2
    naegleriasis B60.2
    parasitic disease NEC B89 *[G05.3]*
    poliovirus A80.9 *[G05.3]*
    rubella B06.01
    syphilis
      congenital A50.42
      late A52.14
    systemic lupus erythematosus M32.19
    toxoplasmosis (acquired) B58.2
      congenital P37.1
    tuberculosis A17.82
    zoster B02.0
  infectious (acute) (virus) NEC A86
  Japanese (B type) A83.0
  La Crosse A83.5
  lead – *see* Poisoning, lead
  lethargica (acute) (infectious) A85.8
  louping ill A84.8
  lupus erythematosus, systemic M32.19
  lymphatica A87.2
  Mengo A85.8
  meningococcal A39.81
  Murray Valley A83.4

Encephalitis *(Continued)*
  otitic NEC H66.40 *[G05.3]*
  parasitic NOS B71.9
  periaxial G37.0
  periaxialis (concentrica) (diffuse) G37.5
  postchickenpox B01.11
  postexanthematous NEC B09
  postimmunization G04.01
  postmeasles B05.0
  postvaccinal G04.01
  postvaricella B01.11
  postviral NEC A86
  Powassan A84.8
  Rasmussen G04.81
  Rio Bravo A85.8
  Russian
    autumnal A83.0
    spring-summer (taiga) A84.0
  saturnine – *see* Poisoning, lead
  specified NEC G04.81
  St. Louis A83.3
  subacute sclerosing A81.1
  summer A83.0
  suppurative G04.81
  tick-borne A84.9
  Torula, torular (cryptococcal) B45.1
  toxic NEC G92
  trichinosis B75 *[G05.3]*
  type
    B A83.0
    C A83.3
  van Bogaert's A81.1
  Venezuelan equine A92.2
  Vienna A85.8
  viral, virus A86
    arthropod-borne NEC A85.2
    mosquito-borne A83.9
      Australian X disease A83.4
      California virus A83.5
      Eastern equine A83.2
      Japanese (B type) A83.0
      Murray Valley A83.4
      specified NEC A83.8
      St. Louis A83.3
      type B A83.0
      type C A83.3
      Western equine A83.1
    tick-borne A84.9
      biundulant A84.1
      central European A84.1
      Czechoslovakian A84.1
      diphasic meningoencephalitis A84.1
      Far Eastern A84.0
      Russian spring-summer (taiga) A84.0
      specified NEC A84.8
    specified type NEC A85.8
  Western equine A83.1
Encephalocele Q01.9
  frontal Q01.0
  nasofrontal Q01.1
  occipital Q01.2
  specified NEC Q01.8
Encephalocystocele – *see* Encephalocele
Encephalomalacia (brain) (cerebellar) (cerebral) - *see* Softening, brain
Encephalomeningitis - *see* Meningoencephalitis
Encephalomeningocele - *see* Encephalocele
Encephalomeningomyelitis - *see* Meningoencephalitis

Encephalomyelitis (see also Encephalitis)
G04.90
  acute disseminated (postinfectious)
    G04.00
      infectious G04.00
      noninfectious G04.81
      postimmunization G04.01
  acute necrotizing hemorrhagic (postin-
    fectious) G04.30
      postimmunization G04.31
  benign myalgic G93.3
  equine A83.9
    Eastern A83.2
    Venezuelan A92.2
    Western A83.1
  in diseases classified elsewhere G05.3
  myalgic, benign G93.3
  postchickenpox B01.11
  postinfectious NEC G04.00
  postmeasles B05.0
  postvaccinal G04.01
  postvaricella B01.11
  rubella B06.01
  specified NEC G04.81
  Venezuelan equine A92.2
Encephalomyelocele - see Encephalocele
Encephalomyelomeningitis - see
  Meningoencephalitis
Encephalomyelopathy G96.9
Encephalomyeloradiculitis (acute) G61.0
Encephalomyeloradiculoneuritis (acute)
  (Guillain-Barré) G61.0
Encephalomyeloradiculopathy G96.9
Encephalopathia hyperbilirubinemica,
  newborn P57.9
  due to isoimmunization (conditions in
    P55) P57.0
Encephalopathy (acute) G93.40
  acute necrotizing hemorrhagic (postin-
    fectious) G04.30
      postimmunization G04.31
  alcoholic G31.2
  anoxic - see Damage, brain, anoxic
  arteriosclerotic I67.2
  centrolobar progressive (Schilder) G37.0
  congenital Q07.9
  demyelinating callosal G37.1
  hepatic - see Failure, hepatic
  hyperbilirubinemic, newborn P57.9
    due to isoimmunization (conditions
      in P55) P57.0
  hypertensive I67.4
  hypoglycemic E16.2
  hypoxic - see Damage, brain, anoxic
  hypoxic ischemic P91.60
    mild P91.61
    moderate P91.62
    severe P91.63
  in (due to)
    birth injury P11.1
    hyperinsulinism E16.1 [G94]
    influenza - see Influenza, with, mani-
      festations NEC
    lack of vitamin (see also Deficiency,
      vitamin) E56.9 [G32.8]
    neoplastic disease (see also Neoplasm)
      D49.9 [G13.1]
    serum (nontherapeutic) (therapeutic)
      T80.6
    syphilis A52.17
    trauma (postconcussional) F07.81
      current injury – see Injury,
        intracranial
    vaccination G04.01

Encephalopathy (Continued)
  lead – see Poisoning, lead
  metabolic G93.41
    toxic G92
  myoclonic, early, symptomatic – see
    Epilepsy, generalized, specified
    NEC
  necrotizing, subacute (Leigh) G31.82
  pellagrous E52 [G32.8]
  portosystemic - see Failure, hepatic
  postcontusional F07.81
    current injury – see Injury, intracra-
      nial, diffuse
  posthypoglycemic (coma) E16.1 [G94]
  postradiation G93.89
  saturnine – see Poisoning, lead
  septic G93.41
  specified NEC G93.49
  spongiform, subacute (viral) A81.00
  toxic G92
    metabolic G92
  traumatic (postconcussional) F07.81
    current injury – see Injury, intracranial
  vitamin B deficiency NEC E53.9 [G32.8]
    vitamin B1 E51.2
  Wernicke's E51.2
Encephalorrhagia – see Hemorrhage,
  intracranial, intracerebral
Encephalosis, posttraumatic F07.81
Enchondroma - see also Neoplasm, bone,
  benign
Enchondromatosis (cartilaginous) (multiple) Q78.4
Encopresis R15
  functional F98.1
  nonorganic origin F98.1
  psychogenic F98.1
Encounter (with health service) (for) Z76.89
  adjustment and management (of)
    breast implant Z45.81
    implanted device NEC Z45.89
    myringotomy device (stent) (tube)
      Z45.82
  administrative purpose only Z02.9
    examination for
      adoption Z02.82
      armed forces Z02.3
      disability determination Z02.71
      driving license Z02.4
      employment Z02.1
      insurance Z02.6
      medical certificate NEC Z02.79
      paternity testing Z02.81
      residential institution admission
        Z02.2
      school admission Z02.0
      sports Z02.5
      specified reason NEC Z02.89
  aftercare - see Aftercare
  antenatal screening Z36
  assisted reproductive fertility procedure
    cycle Z31.83
  blood typing Z01.83
    Rh typing Z01.83
  breast augmentation or reduction Z41.1
  breast implant exchange (different ma-
    terial) (different size) Z45.81
  breast reconstruction following mastec-
    tomy Z42.1
  check-up - see Examination
  chemotherapy for neoplasm Z51.11
  counseling - see Counseling
  delivery, full-term, uncomplicated O80
    cesarean, without indication O82

Encounter (Continued)
  examination - see Examination
  expectant parent(s) (adoptive) pre-birth
    pediatrician visit Z76.81
  fertility preservation procedure (prior
    to cancer therapy) (prior to re-
    moval of gonads) Z31.84
  fitting (of) - see also Fitting (and adjust-
    ment) (of)
  genetic
    counseling Z31.5
    testing - see Test, genetic
  hearing conservation and treatment
    Z01.12
  immunotherapy for neoplasm
    Z51.12
  in vitro fertilization cycle Z31.83
  instruction (in)
    childbirth Z32.2
    child care (postpartal) (prenatal)
      Z32.3
    natural family planning
      procreative Z31.61
      to avoid pregnancy Z30.02
  insulin pump titration Z46.81
  laboratory (as part of a general medical
    examination) Z00.00
    with abnormal findings Z00.01
  mental health services (for)
    abuse NEC
      perpetrator Z69.82
      victim Z69.81
    child abuse
      nonparental
        perpetrator Z69.021
        victim Z69.020
      parental
        perpetrator Z69.011
        victim Z69.010
    spousal or partner abuse
      perpetrator Z69.12
      victim Z69.11
  observation (for) (ruled out)
    exposure to (suspected)
      anthrax Z03.810
      biological agent NEC Z03.818
  pediatrician visit, by expectant parent(s)
    (adoptive) Z76.81
  plastic and reconstructive surgery
    following medical procedure or
    healed injury NEC Z42.8
  pregnancy
    supervision of - see Pregnancy, super-
      vision of
    test Z32.00
      result negative Z32.02
      result positive Z32.01
  radiation therapy (antineoplastic)
    Z51.0
  radiological (as part of a general medical
    examination) Z00.00
    with abnormal findings Z00.01
  reconstructive surgery following medi-
    cal procedure or healed injury
    NEC Z42.8
  removal (of) - see also Removal
    artificial
      arm Z44.00-
        complete Z44.01-
        partial Z44.02-
      eye Z44.2-
      leg Z44.10-
        complete Z44.11-
        partial Z44.12-

Encounter *(Continued)*
  removal *(Continued)*
    breast implant Z45.81
      tissue expander (without synchro-
        nous insertion of permanent
        implant) Z45.81
    device Z46.9
      specified NEC Z46.89
    external
      fixation device - code to fracture
        with extension d
    prosthesis, prosthetic device Z44.9
      breast Z44.3-
      specified NEC Z44.8
    implanted device NEC Z45.89
    internal fixation device Z47.2
    insulin pump Z46.81
    myringotomy device (stent) (tube)
      Z45.82
    nervous system device NEC Z46.2
      brain neuropacemaker Z46.2
      visual substitution device Z46.2
        implanted Z45.31
    non-vascular catheter Z46.82
    orthodontic device Z46.4
    stent
      ureteral Z46.6
    urinary device Z46.6
  repeat cervical smear to confirm
    findings of recent normal smear
    following initial abnormal smear
    Z01.42
  respirator/ventilator use during power
    failure (Z99.12)
  Rh typing Z01.83
  screening - *see* Screening
  specified NEC Z76.89
  sterilization Z30.2
  suspected condition, ruled out
    amniotic cavity and membrane
      Z03.71
    cervical shortening Z03.75
    fetal anomaly Z03.73
    fetal growth Z03.74
    maternal and fetal conditions NEC
      Z03.70
    oligohydramnios Z03.71
    placental problem Z03.72
    polyhydramnios Z03.71
  suspected exposure (to), ruled out
    anthrax Z03.810
    biological agents NEC Z03.818
  termination of pregnancy, elective
    Z33.2
  testing - *see* Test
  therapeutic drug level monitoring
    Z51.81
  titration, insulin pump Z46.81
  training
    insulin pump Z71.82
  X-ray of chest
    as part of a general medical examina-
      tion Z00.00
    with abnormal findings Z00.01
Encystment - *see* Cyst
Endarteritis (bacterial, subacute) (infective) I77.6
  brain I67.7
  cerebral or cerebrospinal I67.7
  deformans - *see* Arteriosclerosis
  embolic - *see* Embolism
  obliterans - *see also* Arteriosclerosis
    pulmonary I28.8
  pulmonary I28.8

Endarteritis *(Continued)*
  retina - *see* Vasculitis, retina
  senile - *see* Arteriosclerosis
  syphilitic A52.09
    brain or cerebral A52.04
    congenital A50.54 *[I79.8]*
  tuberculous A18.89
Endemic - *see* condition
Endocarditis (chronic) (marantic) (nonbacterial thrombotic) (valvular) I38
  with rheumatic fever (conditions in I00)
    active - *see* Endocarditis, acute,
      rheumatic
    inactive or quiescent (with chorea)
      I09.1
  acute or subacute I33.9
    infective I33.0
    rheumatic (aortic) (mitral) (pulmo-
      nary) (tricuspid) I01.1
      with chorea (acute) (rheumatic)
        (Sydenham's) I02.0
  aortic (heart) (nonrheumatic) (valve)
    I35.8
    with
      mitral disease I08.0
        with tricuspid (valve) disease
          I08.3
        active or acute I01.1
          with chorea (acute) (rheu-
            matic) (Sydenham's) I02.0
      rheumatic fever (conditions in I00)
        active - *see* Endocarditis, acute,
          rheumatic
        inactive or quiescent (with cho-
          rea) I06.9
      tricuspid (valve) disease I08.2
        with mitral (valve) disease I08.3
    acute or subacute I33.9
    arteriosclerotic I35.8
    rheumatic I06.9
      with mitral disease I08.0
        with tricuspid (valve) disease
          I08.3
        active or acute I01.1
          with chorea (acute) (rheu-
            matic) (Sydenham's) I02.0
      active or acute I01.1
        with chorea (acute) (rheumatic)
          (Sydenham's) I02.0
      specified NEC I06.8
    specified cause NEC I35.8
    syphilitic A52.03
  arteriosclerotic I38
  atypical verrucous (Libman-Sacks)
    M32.11
  bacterial (acute) (any valve) (subacute)
    I33.0
  candidal B37.6 *[I39]*
  congenital Q24.8
  constrictive I33.0
  Coxiella burnetii A78 *[I39]*
  Coxsackie B33.21
  due to
    prosthetic cardiac valve T82.6
    Q fever A78
    Serratia marcescens I33.0
    typhoid (fever) A01.02
  gonococcal A54.83
  infectious or infective (acute) (any
    valve) (subacute) I33.0
  lenta (acute) (any valve) (subacute)
    I33.0
  Libman-Sacks M32.11
  listerial A32.82

Endocarditis *(Continued)*
  Löffler's I42.3
  malignant (acute) (any valve) (sub-
    acute) I33.0
  meningococcal A39.51
  mitral (chronic) (double) (fibroid)
    (heart) (inactive) (valve) (with
    chorea) I05.9
    with
      aortic (valve) disease I08.0
        with tricuspid (valve) disease
          I08.3
        active or acute I01.1
          with chorea (acute) (rheu-
            matic) (Sydenham's) I02.0
      rheumatic fever (conditions in I00)
        active - *see* Endocarditis, acute,
          rheumatic
        inactive or quiescent (with cho-
          rea) I05.9
      tricuspid (valve) disease I08.1
        with aortic (valve) disease I08.3
    active or acute I01.1
      with chorea (acute) (rheumatic)
        (Sydenham's) I02.0
    bacterial I33.0
    arteriosclerotic I34.8
    nonrheumatic I34.8
      acute or subacute I33.9
    specified NEC I05.8
  monilial B37.6
  multiple valves I08.9
    specified disorders I08.8
  mycotic (acute) (any valve) (subacute)
    I33.0
  pneumococcal (acute) (any valve) (sub-
    acute) I33.0
  pulmonary (chronic) (heart) (valve)
    I37.8
    with rheumatic fever (conditions in
      I00)
      active - *see* Endocarditis, acute,
        rheumatic
      inactive or quiescent (with chorea)
        I09.89
        with aortic, mitral or tricuspid
          disease I08.8
    acute or subacute I33.9
      rheumatic I01.1
        with chorea (acute) (rheumatic)
          (Sydenham's) I02.0
    arteriosclerotic I37.8
    congenital Q22.2
    rheumatic (chronic) (inactive) (with
      chorea) I09.89
      active or acute I01.1
        with chorea (acute) (rheumatic)
          (Sydenham's) I02.0
    syphilitic A52.03
  purulent (acute) (any valve) (subacute)
    I33.0
  Q fever A78 *[I39]*
  rheumatic (chronic) (inactive) (with
    chorea) I09.1
    active or acute (aortic) (mitral) (pul-
      monary) (tricuspid) I01.1
      with chorea (acute) (rheumatic)
        (Sydenham's) I02.0
  rheumatoid - *see* Rheumatoid, carditis
  septic (acute) (any valve) (subacute)
    I33.0
  streptococcal (acute) (any valve) (sub-
    acute) I33.0
  subacute - *see* Endocarditis, acute

Endocarditis *(Continued)*
  suppurative (acute) (any valve) (subacute) I33.0
  syphilitic A52.03
  toxic I33.9
  tricuspid (chronic) (heart) (inactive) (rheumatic) (valve) (with chorea) I07.9
    with
      aortic (valve) disease I08.2
        mitral (valve) disease I08.3
      mitral (valve) disease I08.1
        aortic (valve) disease I08.3
      rheumatic fever (conditions in I00)
        active - *see* Endocarditis, acute, rheumatic
        inactive or quiescent (with chorea) I07.8
    active or acute I01.1
      with chorea (acute) (rheumatic) (Sydenham's) I02.0
    arteriosclerotic I36.8
    nonrheumatic I36.8
      acute or subacute I33.9
    specified cause, except rheumatic I36.8
  tuberculous - *see* Tuberculosis, endocarditis
  typhoid A01.02
  ulcerative (acute) (any valve) (subacute) I33.0
  vegetative (acute) (any valve) (subacute) I33.0
  verrucous (atypical) (nonbacterial) (nonrheumatic) M32.11
Endocardium, endocardial - *see also* condition
  cushion defect Q21.2
Endocervicitis - *see also* Cervicitis
  due to intrauterine (contraceptive) device T83.6
  hyperplastic N72
Endocrine - *see* condition
Endocrinopathy, pluriglandular E31.9
Endodontic
  overfill M27.52
  underfill M27.53
Endodontitis K04.0
Endomastoiditis - *see* Mastoiditis
Endometrioma N80.9
Endometriosis N80.9
  appendix N80.5
  bladder N80.8
  bowel N80.5
  broad ligament N80.3
  cervix N80.0
  colon N80.5
  cul-de-sac (Douglas') N80.3
  exocervix N80.0
  fallopian tube N80.2
  female genital organ NEC N80.8
  gallbladder N80.8
  in scar of skin N80.6
  internal N80.0
  intestine N80.5
  lung N80.8
  myometrium N80.0
  ovary N80.1
  parametrium N80.3
  pelvic peritoneum N80.3
  peritoneal (pelvic) N80.3
  rectovaginal septum N80.4
  rectum N80.5
  round ligament N80.3
  skin (scar) N80.6

Endometriosis *(Continued)*
  specified site NEC N80.8
  stromal (M8931/1) D39.0
  umbilicus N80.8
  uterus (internal) N80.0
  vagina N80.4
  vulva N80.8
Endometritis (decidual) (nonspecific) (purulent) (senile (atrophic) (suppurative) N71.9
  with ectopic pregnancy O08.0
  acute N71.0
  blenorrhagic (gonococcal) (acute) (chronic) A54.24
  cervix, cervical (with erosion or ectropion) - *see also* Cervicitis
    hyperplastic N72
  chlamydial A56.11
  chronic N71.1
  following
    abortion - *see* Abortion by type complicated by genital infection
    ectopic or molar pregnancy O08.0
  gonococcal, gonorrheal (acute) (chronic) A54.24
  hyperplastic N85.00 - *see also* Hyperplasia, endometrial
    cervix N72
  puerperal, postpartum, childbirth O86.12
  subacute N71.0
  tuberculous A18.17
Endometrium - *see* condition
Endomyocarditis - *see* Endocarditis
Endomyocardiopathy, South African I42.3
Endomyofibrosis I42.3
Endomyometritis - *see* Endometritis
Endopericarditis - *see* Endocarditis
Endoperineuritis - *see* Disorder, nerve
Endophlebitis - *see* Phlebitis
Endophthalmia - *see* Endophthalmitis, purulent
Endophthalmitis (acute) (infective) (metastatic) (subacute) H44.009
  bleb associated H59.4- - *see also* Bleb, inflamed (infected), postprocedural
  gonorrheal A54.39
  in (due to)
    cysticercosis B69.1
    onchocerciasis B73.01
    toxocariasis B83.0
  panuveitis - *see* Panuveitis
  parasitic H44.12-
  purulent H44.00-
    panophthalmitis - *see* Panophthalmitis
    vitreous abscess H44.02-
  specified NEC H44.19
  sympathetic - *see* Uveitis, sympathetic
Endosalpingioma D28.2
Endosalpingiosis N94.89
Endosteitis - *see* Osteomyelitis
Endothelioma, bone - *see* Neoplasm, bone, malignant
Endotheliosis (hemorrhagic infectional) D69.8
Endotoxemia - code to condition
Endotrachelitis - *see* Cervicitis
Engelmann(-Camurati) **syndrome** Q78.3
English disease – *see* Rickets
Engman's disease L30.3
Engorgement
  breast N64.59
    newborn P83.4
    puerperal, postpartum O92.79

Engorgement *(Continued)*
  lung (passive) - *see* Edema, lung
  pulmonary (passive) - *see* Edema, lung
  stomach K31.89
  venous, retina - *see* Occlusion, retina, vein, engorgement
Enlargement, enlarged - *see also* Hypertrophy
  adenoids J35.2
    with tonsils J35.3
  alveolar ridge K08.8
    congenital – *see* Anomaly, alveolar
  apertures of diaphragm (congenital) Q79.1
  gingival K06.1
  heart, cardiac - *see* Hypertrophy, cardiac
  lacrimal gland, chronic H04.03-
  liver - *see* Hypertrophy, liver
  lymph gland or node R59.9
    generalized R59.1
    localized R59.0
  orbit H05.34-
  organ or site, congenital NEC - *see* Anomaly, by site
  parathyroid (gland) E21.0
  pituitary fossa R93.0
  prostate N40.0
    with lower urinary tract symptoms (LUTS) N40.1
    without lower urinary tract symtpoms (LUTS) N40.0
  sella turcica R93.0
  spleen - *see* Splenomegaly
  thymus (gland) (congenital) E32.0
  thyroid (gland) - *see* Goiter
  tongue K14.8
  tonsils J35.1
    with adenoids J35.3
  uterus N85.2
Enophthalmos H05.40-
  due to
    orbital tissue atrophy H05.41-
    trauma or surgery H05.42-
Enostosis M27.8
Entamebic, entamebiasis - *see* Amebiasis
Entanglement
  umbilical cord(s) O69.2
    with compression O69.2
      without compression O69.82
    around neck (with compression) O69.1
      without compression O69.81
    of twins in monoamniotic sac O69.2
Enteralgia - *see* Pain, abdominal
Enteric - *see* condition
Enteritis (acute) (diarrheal) (hemorrhagic) (noninfective) (septic) K52.9
  aertrycke infection A02.0
  adenovirus A08.2
  allergic K52.2
  amebic (acute) A06.0
    with abscess - *see* Abscess, amebic
    chronic A06.1
      with abscess - *see* Abscess, amebic
      nondysenteric A06.2
    nondysenteric A06.2
  astrovirus A08.32
  bacillary NOS A03.9
  bacterial A04.9
    specified NEC A04.8
  calicivirus A08.31
  candidal B37.82
  Chilomastix A07.8
  choleriformis A00.1
  chronic (noninfectious) K52.9
    ulcerative – *see* Colitis, ulcerative

Enteritis *(Continued)*
  cicatrizing (chronic) – *see* Enteritis,
    regional, small intestine
  Clostridium
    botulinum (food poisoning) A05.1
    difficile A04.7
  coccidial A07.3
  coxsackie virus A08.39
  dietetic K52.2
  due to
    astrovirus A08.32
    calicivirus A08.31
    coxsackie virus A08.39
    echovirus A08.39
    enterovirus NEC A08.39
    food hypersensitivity K52.2
    infectious organism (bacterial) (viral)
        - *see* Enteritis, infectious
    torovirus A08.39
    Yersinia enterocolitica A04.6
  echovirus A08.39
  eltor A00.1
  enterovirus NEC A08.39
  eosinophilic K52.81
  epidemic (infectious) A09
  fulminant K55.0
  gangrenous - *see* Enteritis, infectious
  giardial A07.1
  infectious NOS A09
    due to
      adenovirus A08.2
      Aerobacter aerogenes A04.8
      Arizona (bacillus) A02.0
      bacteria NOS A04.9
        specified NEC A04.8
      Campylobacter A04.5
      Clostridium perfringens A04.8
      Enterobacter aerogenes A04.8
      enterovirus A08.3
      Escherichia coli A04.4
        enteroaggregative A04.4
        enterohemorrhagic A04.3
        enteroinvasive A04.2
        enteropathogenic A04.0
        enterotoxigenic A04.1
        specified NEC A04.4
      specified
        bacteria NEC A04.8
        virus NEC A08.3
      Staphylococcus A04.8
      virus NEC A08.4
        specified type NEC A08.3
      Yersinia enterocolitica A04.6
    specified organism NEC A08.8
  influenzal - *see* Influenza, with, diges-
      tive manifestations
  ischemic K55.9
    acute K55.0
    chronic K55.1
  microsporidial A07.8
  mucomembranous, myxomembranous -
      see Syndrome, irritable bowel
  mucous - *see* Syndrome, irritable bowel
  necroticans A05.2
  necrotizing of newborn - *see* Enterocoli-
      tis, necrotizing, in newborn
  neurogenic - *see* Syndrome, irritable bowel
  newborn necrotizing - *see* Enterocolitis,
      necrotizing, in newborn
  noninfectious K52.9
  norovirus A08.11
  parasitic NEC B82.9
  paratyphoid (fever) - *see* Fever, paratyphoid
  protozoal A07.9
    specified NEC A07.8

Enteritis *(Continued)*
  radiation K52.0
  regional (of) K50.90
    with
      complication K50.919
        abscess K50.914
        fistula K50.913
        intestinal obstruction K50.912
        rectal bleeding K50.911
        specified complication NEC
            K50.918
    colon - *see* Enteritis, regional, large
        intestine
    duodenum - *see* Enteritis, regional,
        small intestine
    ileum - *see* Enteritis, regional, small
        intestine
    jejunum - *see* Enteritis, regional, small
        intestine
    large bowel - *see* Enteritis, regional,
        large intestine
    large intestine (colon) (rectum)
        K50.10
      with
        complication K50.119
          abscess K50.114
          fistula K50.113
          intestinal obstruction K50.112
          rectal bleeding K50.111
          small intestine (duodenum)
              (ileum) (jejunum) in-
              volvement K50.819
            with
              complication K50.819
                abscess K50.814
                fistula K50.813
                intestinal obstruction
                    K50.812
                rectal bleeding K50.811
                specified complication
                    NEC K50.818
          specified complication NEC
              K50.118
    rectum - *see* Enteritis, regional, large
        intestine
    small intestine (duodenum) (ileum)
        (jejunum) K50.00
      with
        complication K50.019
          abscess K50.014
          fistula K50.013
          intestinal obstruction K50.012
          large intestine (colon) (rectum)
              involvement K50.819
            with
              complication K50.819
                abscess K50.814
                fistula K50.813
                intestinal obstruction
                    K50.812
                rectal bleeding K50.811
                specified complication
                    NEC K50.818
          rectal bleeding K50.011
          specified complication NEC
              K50.018
  rotaviral A08.0
  Salmonella, salmonellosis (arizonae)
      (cholerae-suis) (enteritidis)
      (typhimurium) A02.0
  segmental – *see* Enteritis, regional
  septic A09
  Shigella - *see* Infection, Shigella
  small round structured NEC A08.19

Enteritis *(Continued)*
  spasmodic, spastic - *see* Syndrome,
      irritable bowel
  staphylococcal A04.8
    due to food A05.0
  torovirus A08.39
  toxic K52.1
  trichomonal A07.8
  tuberculous A18.32
  typhosa A01.00
  ulcerative (chronic) – *see* Colitis, ulcerative
  viral A08.4
    adenovirus A08.2
    enterovirus A08.3
    Rotavirus A08.0
    small round structured NEC A08.19
    specified NEC A08.39
    virus specified NEC A08.3
Enterobiasis B80
Enterobius vermicularis (infection)
    (infestation) B80
Enterocele - *see also* Hernia, abdomen
  pelvic, pelvis (acquired) (congenital)
      N81.5
  vagina, vaginal (acquired) (congenital)
      NEC N81.5
Enterocolitis (*see also* Enteritis) K52.9
  due to Clostridium difficile A04.7
  fulminant ischemic K55.0
  granulomatous – *see* Enteritis, regional
  hemorrhagic (acute) K55.0
    chronic K55.1
  infectious NEC A09
  ischemic K55.9
  necrotizing
    due to Clostridium difficile A04.7
    in newborn P77.9
      stage 1 (without pneumatosis,
          without perforation) P77.1
      stage 2 (with pneumatosis, without
          perforation) P77.2
      stage 3 (with pneumatosis, with
          perforation) P77.3
  noninfectious K52.9
    newborn - *see* Enterocolitis, necrotiz-
        ing, in newborn
  pseudomembranous (newborn) A04.7
  radiation K52.0
    newborn - *see* Enterocolitis, necrotiz-
        ing, in newborn
  ulcerative (chronic) *see* Pancolitis, ulcer-
      ative (chronic)
Enterogastritis - *see* Enteritis
Enterolith, enterolithiasis (impaction) K56.4
Enteropathy K63.9
  gluten-sensitive K90.0
  hemorrhagic, terminal K55.0
  protein-losing K90.4
Enteroperitonitis – *see* Peritonitis
Enteroptosis K63.4
Enterorrhagia K92.2
Enterospasm - *see also* Syndrome, irritable,
    bowel
  psychogenic F45.8
Enterostenosis K56.69 - *see also* Obstruc-
    tion, intestine
Enterostomy
  complication – *see* Complication,
      enterostomy
  status Z93.4
Enterovirus, as cause of disease classified
    elsewhere B97.10
  coxsackievirus B97.11
  echovirus B97.12
  other specified B97.19

Enthesopathy (peripheral) M77.9
  Achilles tendinitis - *see* Tendinitis, Achilles
  ankle and tarsus M77.9
    specified type NEC - *see* Enthesopathy, foot, specified type NEC
  anterior tibial syndrome - *see* Enthesopathy, lower limb, lower leg, specified type NEC
  calcaneal spur - *see* Spur, bone, calcaneal
  elbow region M77.8
    lateral epicondylitis - *see* Epicondylitis, lateral
    medial epicondylitis - *see* Epicondylitis, medial
  foot NEC M77.9
    metatarsalgia - *see* Metatarsalgia
    specified type NEC M77.5-
  forearm M77.9
  gluteal tendinitis - *see* Tendinitis, gluteal
  hand M77.9
  hip - *see* Enthesopathy, lower limb, thigh, specified type NEC
  iliac crest spur - *see* Spur, bone, iliac crest
  iliotibial band syndrome - *see* Syndrome, iliotibial band
  knee - *see* Enthesopathy, lower limb, lower leg, specified type NEC
  lateral epicondylitis - *see* Epicondylitis, lateral
  lower limb M76.90
    Achilles tendinitis - *see* Tendinitis, Achilles
    anterior tibial syndrome - *see* Enthesopathy, lower limb, lower leg, specified type NEC
    gluteal tendinitis - *see* Tendinitis, gluteal
    iliac crest spur - *see* Spur, bone, iliac crest
    iliotibial band syndrome - *see* Syndrome, iliotibial band
    lower leg M76.96-
      specified type NEC M76.86-
    multiple sites M76.99
    patellar tendinitis - *see* Tendinitis, patellar
    pelvic region - *see* Enthesopathy, lower limb, thigh
    peroneal tendinitis - *see* Tendinitis, peroneal
    posterior tibial syndrome - *see* Enthesopathy, lower limb, lower leg, specified type NEC
    psoas tendinitis - *see* Tendinitis, psoas
    shoulder M77.9
    specified type NEC M76.80
      ankle - *see* Enthesopathy, lower limb, ankle, specified type NEC
      lower leg - *see* Enthesopathy, lower limb, lower leg, specified type NEC
      multiple sites M76.89
      pelvic region - *see* Enthesopathy, lower limb, thigh, specified type NEC
      thigh - *see* Enthesopathy, lower limb, thigh, specified type NEC
    thigh M76.95-
      specified type NEC M76.85-
    tibial collateral bursitis - *see* Bursitis, tibial collateral
  medial epicondylitis - *see* Epicondylitis, medialmetatarsalgia - *see* Metatarsalgia

Enthesopathy *(Continued)*
  multiple sites M77.9
  patellar tendinitis - *see* Tendinitis, patellar
  pelvis M77.9
  periarthritis of wrist - *see* Periarthritis, wrist
  peroneal tendinitis - *see* Tendinitis, peroneal
  posterior tibial syndrome - *see* Enthesopathy, lower limb, lower leg, specified type NEC
  psoas tendinitis - *see* Tendinitis, psoas
  shoulder region - *see* Lesion, shoulder
  specified site NEC M77.9
  specified type NEC M77.8
  spinal M46.00
    cervical region M46.02
    cervicothoracic region M46.03
    lumbar region M46.06
    lumbosacral region M46.07
    multiple sites M46.09
    occipito-atlanto-axial region M46.01
    sacrococcygeal region M46.08
    thoracic region M46.04
    thoracolumbar region M46.05
  tibial collateral bursitis - *see* Bursitis, tibial collateral
  upper arm M77.9
  wrist and carpus NEC M77.8
    calcaneal spur - *see* Spur, bone, calcaneal
    periarthritis of wrist - *see* Periarthritis, wrist
Entomophobia F40.218
Entomophthoromycosis B46.8
Entrance, air into vein - *see* Embolism, air
Entrapment, nerve - *see* Neuropathy, entrapment
Entropion (eyelid) (paralytic) H02.009
  cicatricial H02.019
    left H02.016
      lower H02.015
      upper H02.014
    right H02.013
      lower H02.012
      upper H02.011
  congenital Q10.2
  left H02.006
    lower H02.005
    upper H02.004
  mechanical H02.029
    left H02.026
      lower H02.025
      upper H02.024
    right H02.023
      lower H02.022
      upper H02.021
  right H02.003
    lower H02.002
    upper H02.001
  senile H02.039
    left H02.036
      lower H02.035
      upper H02.034
    right H02.033
      lower H02.032
      upper H02.031
  spastic H02.049
    left H02.046
      lower H02.045
      upper H02.044
    right H02.043
      lower H02.042
      upper H02.041

Enucleated eye (traumatic, current) S05.7-
Enuresis R32
  functional F98.0
  habit disturbance F98.0
  nocturnal R32
    psychogenic F98.0
  nonorganic origin F98.0
  psychogenic F98.0
Eosinopenia – *see* Agranulocytosis
Eosinophilia (allergic) (hereditary) (idiopathic) (secondary) D72.1
  infiltrative J82
  Löffler's J82
  pulmonary NEC J82
  tropical (pulmonary) J82
Eosinophilia-myalgia syndrome M35.8
Ependymitis (acute) (cerebral) (chronic) (granular) - *see* Encephalomyelitis
Ependymoblastoma
  specified site - *see* Neoplasm, malignant
  unspecified site C71.9
Ependymoma (epithelial) (malignant)
  anaplastic
    specified site - *see* Neoplasm, malignant
    unspecified site C71.9
  benign (M9391/0)
    specified site - *see* Neoplasm, benign
    unspecified site D33.2
  myxopapillary D43.2
    specified site - *see* Neoplasm, uncertain behavior
    unspecified site D43.2
  papillary D43.2
    specified site - *see* Neoplasm, uncertain behavior
    unspecified site D43.2
  specified site - *see* Neoplasm, malignant
  unspecified site C71.9
Ependymopathy G93.89
Ephelis, ephelides L81.2
Epiblepharon (congenital) Q10.3
Epicanthus, epicanthic fold (eyelid) (congenital) Q10.3
Epicondylitis (elbow)
  lateral M77.1-
  medial M77.0-
Epicystitis – *see* Cystitis
Epidemic - *see* condition
Epidermidalization, cervix - *see* Dysplasia, cervix
Epidermis, epidermal - *see* condition
Epidermodysplasia verruciformis B07.8
Epidermolysis
  bullosa (congenital) Q81.9
    acquired L12.30
      drug-induced L12.31
      specified cause NEC L12.35
    dystrophica Q81.2
    letalis Q81.1
    simplex Q81.0
    specified NEC Q81.8
  necroticans combustiformis L51.2
    due to drug - *see* Table of drugs and chemicals, by drug
Epidermophytid - *see* Dermatophytosis
Epidermophytosis (infected) - *see* Dermatophytosis
Epididymis - *see* condition
Epididymitis (acute) (nonvenereal) (recurrent) (residual) N45.1
  with orchitis N45.3
  blennorrhagic (gonococcal) A54.23
  caseous (tuberculous) A18.15

Epididymitis *(Continued)*
  chlamydial A56.19
  filarial B74.9
  gonococcal A54.23
  syphilitic A52.76
  tuberculous A18.15
Epididymo-orchitis *(see also* Epididymitis)
  N45.3
Epidural - *see* condition
Epigastrium, epigastric - *see* condition
Epigastrocele - *see* Hernia, ventral
Epiglottis - *see* condition
Epiglottitis, epiglottiditis (acute) J05.10
  with obstruction J05.11
  chronic J37.0
Epignathus Q89.4
Epilepsia partialis continua - *see* Epilepsy, syndromes, special
Epilepsy, epileptic, epilepsia (attack) (cerebral) (convulsion) (fit) (seizure) G40.909 Note: the following terms are to be considered equivalent to intractable: pharmacoresistant (pharmacologically resistant), treatment resistant, refractory (medically) and poorly controlled
  with
    complex partial seizures - *see* Epilepsy, localization-related, symptomatic, with complex partial seizures
    myoclonic absences – *see* Epilepsy, generalized, specified NEC
    myoclonic-astatic seizures – *see* Epilepsy, generalized, specified NEC
    simple partial seizures - *see* Epilepsy, localization-related, symptomatic, with simple partial seizures
  akinetic - *see* Epilepsy, generalized, idiopathic
  benign childhood with centrotemporal EEG spikes - *see* Epilepsy, localization-related, idiopathic
  benign myoclonic in infancy - *see* Epilepsy, generalized, idiopathic
  Bravais-jacksonian - *see* Epilepsy, localization-related, symptomatic, with simple partial seizures
  childhood with occipital EEG paroxysms - *see* Epilepsy, localization-related, idiopathic
  childhood absence - *see* Epilepsy, generalized, idiopathic
  climacteric - *see* Epilepsy, specified NEC
  cysticercosis B69.0
  deterioration (mental) F06.8
  due to syphilis A52.19
  focal - *see* Epilepsy, localization-related, symptomatic, with simple partial seizures
  generalized
    idiopathic G40.309
      intractable G40.319
        with status epilepticus G40.311
        without status epilepticus G40.319
      not intractable G40.309
        with status epilepticus G40.301
        without status epilepticus G40.309
    specified NEC
      intractable G40.419
        with status epilepticus G40.411
        without status epilepticus G40.419
      not intractable G40.409
        with status epilepticus G40.401
        without status epilepticus G40.409

Epilepsy, epileptic, epilepsia *(Continued)*
  impulsive petit mal - *see* Epilepsy, generalized, idiopathic
  intractable G40.919
    with status epilepticus G40.911
    without status epilepticus G40.919
  juvenile absence - *see* Epilepsy, generalized, idiopathic
  juvenile myoclonic - *see* Epilepsy, generalized, idiopathic
  localization-related (focal) (partial)
    idiopathic G40.009
      with seizures of localized onset G40.009
        intractable G40.019
          with status epilepticus G40.011
          without status epilepticus G40.019
        not intractable G40.009
          with status epilepticus G40.001
          without status epilepticus G40.009
    symptomatic
      with complex partial seizures G40.209
        intractable G40.219
          with status epilepticus G40.211
          without status epilepticus G40.219
        not intractable G40.209
          with status epilepticus G40.201
          without status epilepticus G40.209
      with simple partial seizures G40.109
        intractable G40.119
          with status epilepticus G40.111
          without status epilepticus G40.119
        not intractable G40.109
          with status epilepticus G40.101
          without status epilepticus G40.109
  myoclonus, myoclonic (progressive) - *see* Epilepsy, generalized, idiopathic
  not intractable G40.909
    with status epilepticus G40.901
    without status epilepticus G40.909
  on awakening - *see* Epilepsy, generalized, idiopathic
  parasitic NOS B71.9 *[G94]*
  partialis continua – *see* Epilepsy, syndromes, special
  peripheral - *see* Epilepsy, specified NEC
  procursiva - *see* Epilepsy, localization-related, symptomatic, with simple partial seizures
  progressive (familial) myoclonic - *see* Epilepsy, generalized, idiopathic
  reflex - *see* Epilepsy, specified NEC
  related to
    alcohol G40.509
      intractable G40.519
        with status epilepticus G40.511
        without status epliepticus G40.519
      not intractable G40.509
        with status epilepticus G40.501
        without status epliepticus G40.509
    drugs G40.509
      intractable G40.519
        with status epilepticus G40.511
        without status epliepticus G40.519
      not intractable G40.509
        with status epilepticus G40.501
        without status epliepticus G40.509

Epilepsy, epileptic, epilepsia *(Continued)*
  related to *(Continued)*
    hormonal changes G40.509
      intractable G40.519
        with status epilepticus G40.511
        without status epliepticus G40.519
      not intractable G40.509
        with status epilepticus G40.501
        without status epliepticus G40.509
    sleep deprivation G40.509
      intractable G40.519
        with status epilepticus G40.511
        without status epliepticus G40.519
      not intractable G40.509
        with status epilepticus G40.501
        without status epliepticus G40.509
    stress G40.509
      intractable G40.519
        with status epilepticus G40.511
        without status epliepticus G40.519
      not intractable G40.509
        with status epilepticus G40.501
        without status epliepticus G40.509
    somatomotor - *see* Epilepsy, localization-related, symptomatic, with simple partial seizures
    somatosensory - *see* Epilepsy, localization-related, symptomatic, with simple partial seizures
  specified NEC G40.809
    intractable G40.819
      with status epilepticus G40.811
      without status epilepticus G40.819
    not intractable G40.809
      with status epilepticus G40.801
      without status epilepticus G40.809
  syndromes
    generalized
      idiopathic G40.309
        intractable G40.319
          with status epilepticus G40.311
          without status epilepticus G40.319
        not intractable G40.309
          with status epilepticus G40.301
          without status epilepticus G40.309
      specified NEC G40.409
        intractable G40.419
          with status epilepticus G40.411
          without status epilepticus G40.419
        not intractable G40.409
          with status epilepticus G40.401
          without status epilepticus G40.409
    localization-related (focal) (partial)
      idiopathic G40.009
        with seizures of localized onset G40.009
          intractable G40.019
            with status epilepticus G40.011
            without status epilepticus G40.019

Epilepsy, epileptic, epilepsia (Continued)
  syndromes (Continued)
    localization-related (Continued)
      idiopathic (Continued)
        with seizures of localized onset
          (Continued)
          not intractable G40.009
            with status epilepticus
              G40.001
            without status epilepticus
              G40.009
      symptomatic
        with complex partial seizures
          G40.209
        intractable G40.219
          with status epilepticus
            G40.211
          without status epilepticus
            G40.219
        not intractable G40.209
          with status epilepticus
            G40.201
          without status epilepticus
            G40.209
        with simple partial seizures
          G40.109
        intractable G40.119
          with status epilepticus
            G40.111
          without status epilepticus
            G40.119
        not intractable G40.109
          with status epilepticus
            G40.101
          without status epilepticus
            G40.109
      special G40.509
        intractable G40.519
          with status epilepticus G40.511
          without status epilepticus
            G40.519
        not intractable G40.509
          with status epilepticus G40.501
          without status epilepticus
            G40.509
      specified NEC G40.809
        intractable G40.819
          with status epilepticus G40.811
          without status epilepticus
            G40.819
        not intractable G40.809
          with status epilepticus G40.801
          without status epilepticus
            G40.809
  tonic(-clonic) – see Epilepsy, general-
    ized, idiopathic
  twilight F05
  uncinate (gyrus) – see Epilepsy,
    localization-related, sympto-
    matic, with complex partial
    seizures
  Unverricht (-Lundborg) (familial myo-
    clonic) – see Epilepsy, generalized,
    idiopathic
  visceral – see Epilepsy, specified NEC
  visual – see Epilepsy, specified NEC
Epiloia Q85.1
Epimenorrhea N92.0
Epipharyngitis - see Nasopharyngitis
Epiphora H04.20-
  due to
    excess lacrimation H04.21-
    insufficient drainage H04.22-
Epiphyseal arrest – see Arrest, epiphyseal

Epiphyseolysis, epiphysiolysis – see
  Osteochondropathy
Epiphysitis – see also Osteochondropathy
  juvenile M92.9
  syphilitic (congenital) A50.02
Epiplocele - see Hernia, abdomen
Epiploitis - see Peritonitis
Epiplosarcomphalocele – see Hernia,
  umbilicus
Episcleritis (suppurative) H15.10-
  in (due to)
    syphilis A52.71
    tuberculosis A18.51
  nodular H15.12-
  periodica fugax H15.119
    angioneurotic - see Edema,
      angioneurotic
  syphilitic (late) A52.71
  tuberculous A18.51
Episode
  affective, mixed F39
  depersonalization (in neurotic state)
    F48.1
  depressive F32.9
    major F32.9
      mild F32.0
      moderate F32.1
      severe (without psychotic symp-
        toms) F32.2
        with psychotic symptoms
          F32.3
    recurrent F33.9
      brief F33.8
    specified NEC F32.8
  hypomanic F30.8
  manic F30.9
    with
      psychotic symptoms F30.2
      remission (full) F30.4
        partial F30.3
    other specified F30.8
    recurrent F31.89
    without psychotic symptoms F30.10
      mild F30.11
      moderate F30.12
      severe (without psychotic symp-
        toms) F30.13
      with psychotic symptoms
        F30.2
  psychotic F23
    organic F06.8
  schizophrenic (acute) NEC, brief F23
Epispadias (female) (male) Q64.0
Episplenitis D73.89
Epistaxis (multiple) R04.0
  hereditary I78.0
  vicarious menstruation N94.89
Epithelioma (malignant) - see also Neoplasm, malignant
  adenoides cysticum - see Neoplasm,
    skin, benign
  basal cell - see Neoplasm, skin,
    malignant
  benign - see Neoplasm, benign
  Bowen's - see Neoplasm, skin, in situ
  calcifying, of Malherbe - see Neoplasm,
    skin, benign
  external site - see Neoplasm, skin,
    malignant
  intraepidermal, Jadassohn - see Neo-
    plasm, skin, benign
  squamous cell - see Neoplasm, malig-
    nant, by site
Epitheliomatosis pigmented Q82.1

Epitheliopathy, multifocal placoid pig-
  ment H30.14-
Epithelium, epithelial - see condition
Epituberculosis (with atelectasis) (al-
  lergic) A15.7
Eponychia Q84.6
Epstein's
  nephrosis or syndrome - see Nephrosis
  pearl K09.8
Epulis (gingiva) (fibrous) (giant cell)
  K06.8
Equinia A24.0
Equinovarus (congenital) (talipes) Q66.0
  acquired - see Deformity, limb, clubfoot
Equivalent
  convulsive (abdominal) – see Epilepsy,
    specified NEC
  epileptic (psychic) – see Epilepsy,
    localization-related, symptomatic,
    with complex partial seizures
Erb(-Duchenne) paralysis (birth injury)
  (newborn) P14.0
Erb-Goldflam disease or syndrome
  G70.00
  with exacerbation (acute) G70.01
  in crisis G70.01
Erb's
  disease G71.0
  palsy, paralysis (brachial) (birth) (new-
    born) P14.0
  spinal (spastic) syphilitic A52.17
  pseudohypertrophic muscular dystro-
    phy G71.0
Erdheim's syndrome (acromegalic macrospondylitis) E22.0
Erection, painful (persistent) – see
  Priapism
Ergosterol deficiency (vitamin D) E55.9
  with
    adult osteomalacia M83.8
    rickets - see Rickets
Ergotism - see also Poisoning, food, noxious, plant
  from ergot used as drug (migraine
    therapy) - see Table of Drugs and
    Chemicals
Erosio interdigitalis blastomycetica B37.2
Erosion
  artery I77.2
    without rupture I77.8
  bone - see Disorder, bone, density and
    structure, specified NEC
  bronchus J98.09
  cartilage (joint) - see Disorder, cartilage,
    specified type NEC
  cervix (uteri) (acquired) (chronic) (con-
    genital) N86
    with cervicitis N72
  cornea (nontraumatic) - see Ulcer,
    cornea
    recurrent H18.83-
    traumatic – see Abrasion, cornea
  dental (idiopathic) (occupational) (due
    to diet, drugs or vomiting) K03.2
  duodenum, postpyloric - see Ulcer,
    duodenum
  esophagus K22.10
    with bleeding K22.11
  gastric - see Ulcer, stomach
  gastrojejunal - see Ulcer, gastrojejunal
  intestine K63.3
  lymphatic vessel I89.8
  pylorus, pyloric (ulcer) - see Ulcer,
    stomach

Erosion *(Continued)*
spine, aneurysmal A52.09
stomach - *see* Ulcer, stomach
teeth (idiopathic) (occupational) (due to diet, drugs or vomiting) K03.2
urethra N36.8
uterus N85.8
Erotomania F52.8
Error
metabolism, inborn — *se* Disorder, metabolism
refractive - *see* Disorder, refraction
Eructation R14.2
nervous or psychogenic F45.8
Eruption
creeping B76.9
drug (generalized) (taken internally) L27.0
fixed L27.1
in contact with skin - *see* Dermatitis, due to drugs
localized L27.1
Hutchinson, summer L56.4
Kaposi's varicelliform B00.0
napkin L22
polymorphous light (sun) L56.4
recalcitrant pustular L13.8
ringed R23.8
skin (nonspecific) R21
creeping (meaning hookworm) B76.9
due to inoculation/vaccination (generalized) (*see also* Dermatitis, due to, vaccine) L27.0
localized L27.1
erysipeloid A26.0
feigned L98.1
Kaposi's varicelliform B00.0
lichenoid L28.0
meaning dermatitis - *see* Dermatitis
toxic NEC L53.0
tooth, teeth, abnormal (incomplete) (late) (premature) (sequence) K00.6
vesicular R23.8
Erysipelas (gangrenous) (infantile) (newborn) (phlegmonous) (suppurative) A46
external ear A46 [H62.40]
puerperal, postpartum O86.89
Erysipeloid A26.9
cutaneous (Rosenbach's) A26.0
disseminated A26.8
sepsis A26.7
specified NEC A26.8
Erythema, erythematous (infectional) (inflammation) L53.9
ab igne L59.0
annulare (centrifugum) (rheumaticum) L53.1
arthriticum epidemicum A25.1
brucellum – *see* Brucellosis
chronic figurate NEC L53.3
chronicum migrans (Borrelia burgdorferi) A69.20
diaper L22
due to
chemical NEC L53.0
in contact with skin L24.5
drug (internal use) - *see* Dermatitis, due to, drugs
elevatum diutinum L95.1
endemic E52
epidemic, arthritic A25.1
figuratum perstans L53.3
gluteal L22

Erythema, erythematous *(Continued)*
heat - code by site under Burn, first degree
ichthyosiforme congenitum bullous Q80.3
induratum (nontuberculous) L52
tuberculous A18.4
infectiosum B08.3
intertrigo L30.4
iris L51.9
marginatum L53.2
in (due to) acute rheumatic fever I00
medicamentosum - *see* Dermatitis, due to, drugs
migrans A26.0
chronicum A69.20
tongue K14.1
multiforme (major) (minor) L51.9
bullous, bullosum L51.1
conjunctiva L51.1
nonbullous L51.0
pemphigoides L12.0
specified NEC L51.8
napkin L22
neonatorum P83.8
toxic P83.1
nodosum L52
tuberculous A18.4
palmar L53.8
pernio T69.1
rash, newborn P83.8
scarlatiniform (recurrent) (exfoliative) L53.8
solare L55.0
specified NEC L53.8
toxic, toxicum NEC L53.0
newborn P83.1
tuberculous (primary) A18.4
Erythematous, erythematosus - *see* condition
Erythermalgia (primary) I73.81
Erythralgia I73.81
Erythrasma L08.1
Erythredema (polyneuropathy) – *see* Poisoning, mercury
Erythremia (acute) C94.0-
chronic D45
secondary D75.1
Erythroblastopenia (*see also* Aplasia, red cell) D60.9
congenital D61.01
Erythroblastophthisis D61.09
Erythroblastosis (fetalis) (newborn) P55.9
due to
ABO (antibodies) (incompatibility) (isoimmunization) P55.1
Rh (antibodies) (incompatibility) (isoimmunization) P55.0
Erythrocyanosis (crurum) I73.89
Erythrocythemia - *see* Erythremia
Erythrocytosis (megalosplenic) (secondary) D75.1
familial D75.0
oval, hereditary - *see* Elliptocytosis
secondary D75.1
stress D75.1
Erythroderma (secondary) (*see also* Erythema) L53.9
bullous ichthyosiform, congenital Q80.3
desquamativum L21.1
ichthyosiform, congenital (bullous) Q80.3

Erythroderma *(Continued)*
neonatorum P83.8
psoriaticum L40.8
Erythrodysesthesia, palmar plantar (PPE) L27.1
Erythrogenesis imperfecta D61.09
Erythroleukemia C94.0-
Erythromelalgia I73.81
Erythrophagocytosis D75.89
Erythrophobia F40.298
Erythroplakia, oral epithelium, and tongue K13.29
Erythroplasia (Queyrat) D07.4
specified site - *see* Neoplasm, skin, in situ
unspecified site D07.4
Escherichia (E.) coli, as cause of disease classified elsewhere B96.2
Esophagismus K22.4
Esophagitis (acute) (alkaline) (chemical) (chronic) (infectional) (necrotic) (peptic) (postoperative) K20.9
candidal B37.81
due to gastrointestinal reflux disease K21.0
eosinophilic K20.0
reflux K21.0
specified NEC K20.8
tuberculous A18.83
ulcerative K22.10
with bleeding K22.11
Esophagocele K22.5
Esophagomalacia K22.8
Esophagospasm K22.4
Esophagostenosis K22.2
Esophagostomiasis B81.8
Esophagotracheal - *see* condition
Esophagus - *see* condition
Esophoria H50.51
convergence, excess H51.12
divergence, insufficiency H51.8
Esotropia - *see* Strabismus, convergent concomitant
Essential - *see* condition
Esthesioneuroblastoma C30.0
Esthesioneurocytoma C30.0
Esthesioneuroepithelioma C30.0
Esthiomene A55
Estivo-autumnal malaria (fever) B50.9
Estrangement (marital) Z63.5
parent-child NEC Z62.890
Estriasis - *see* Myiasis
Ethanolism - *see* Alcoholism
Etherism - *see* Dependence, drug, inhalant
Ethmoid, ethmoidal - *see* condition
Ethmoiditis (chronic) (purulent) (nonpurulent) - *see also* Sinusitis, ethmoidal
influenzal - *see* Influenza, with, respiratory manifestations
Woakes' J33.1
Ethylism - *see* Alcoholism
Eulenburg's disease (congenital paramyotonia) G71.19
Eumycetoma B47.0
Eunuchoidism E29.1
hypogonadotropic E23.0
European blastomycosis - *see* Cryptococcosis
Eustachian - *see* condition
Evaluation (for) (of)
development state
adolescent Z00.3

Evaluation (Continued)
  development state (Continued)
    period of
      delayed growth in childhood
        Z00.70
          with abnormal findings Z00.71
      rapid growth in childhood Z00.2
      puberty Z00.3
    growth and developmental state (pe-
      riod of rapid growth) Z00.2
      delayed growth Z00.70
        with abnormal findings Z00.71
    mental health (status) Z00.8
      requested by authority Z04.6
    period of
      delayed growth in childhood Z00.70
        with abnormal findings Z00.71
      rapid growth in childhood Z00.2
  suspected condition - see Observation
Evans syndrome D69.41
Eventration - see also Hernia, ventral
  colon into chest - see Hernia,
    diaphragm
  diaphragm (congenital) Q79.1
Eversion
  bladder N32.89
  cervix (uteri) N86
    with cervicitis N72
  foot NEC - see also Deformity, valgus,
    ankle
    congenital Q66.6
  punctum lacrimale (postinfectional)
    (senile) H04.52-
  ureter (meatus) N28.89
  urethra (meatus) N36.8
  uterus N81.4
Evidence
  cytologic
    of malignancy on anal smear
      R85.614
    of malignancy on cervical smear
      R87.614
    of malignancy on vaginal smear
      R87.624
Evisceration
  birth injury P15.8
  traumatic NEC
    eye – see Enucleated eye
Evulsion - see Avulsion
Ewing's sarcoma or tumor - see
  Neoplasm, bone, malignant
Examination (for) (following) (general)
  (of) (routine) Z00.00 - see also Test
  with abnormal findings Z00.01
  abuse, physical (alleged), ruled out
    adult Z04.71
    child Z04.72
  adolescent (development state) Z00.3
  alleged rape or sexual assault (victim),
    ruled out
    adult Z04.41
    child Z04.42
  allergy Z01.82
  annual (adult) (periodic) (physical)
    Z00.00
    with abnormal findings Z00.01
    gynecological Z01.419
      with abnormal findings Z01.411
  antibody response Z01.84
  blood - see Examination, laboratory
  blood pressure Z01.30
    with abnormal findings Z01.31
  cancer staging - see Neoplasm,
    malignant

Examination (Continued)
  cervical Papanicolaou smear Z12.4
    as part of routine gynecological
      examination Z01.419
      with abnormal findings Z01.411
  child (over 28 days old) Z00.129
    with abnormal findings Z00.121
    under 28 days old - see Newborn,
      examination
  clinical research control or normal com-
    parison Z00.6
  contraceptive (drug) maintenance
    (routine) Z30.8
    device (intrauterine) Z30.43
  dental Z01.20
    with abnormal findings Z01.21
  donor (potential) Z00.5
  ear Z01.10
    with abnormal findings NEC Z01.118
  eye Z01.00
    with abnormal findings Z01.01
  following
    accident NEC Z04.3
      transport Z04.1
      work Z04.2
    assault, alleged, ruled out
      adult Z04.71
      child Z04.72
    motor vehicle accident Z04.1
    treatment (for) Z09
      combined NEC Z09
        fracture Z09
        malignant neoplasm Z08
      malignant neoplasm Z08
      mental disorder Z09
      specified condition NEC Z09
  follow-up (routine) (following) Z09
    chemotherapy NEC Z09
      malignant neoplasm Z08
    fracture Z09
    malignant neoplasm Z08
    postpartum Z39.2
    psychotherapy Z09
    radiotherapy NEC Z09
      malignant neoplasm Z08
    surgery NEC Z09
      malignant neoplasm Z08
  gynecological Z01.419
    with abnormal findings Z01.411
    for contraceptive maintenance Z30.8
  health - see Examination, medical
  hearing Z01.10
    with abnormal findings NEC Z01.118
    following failed hearing screening
      Z01.110
  immunity status testing Z01.84
  laboratory (as part of a general medical
    examination) Z00.00
    with abnormal findings Z00.01
    preprocedural Z01.812
  lactating mother Z39.1
  medical (adult) (for) (of) Z00.00
    with abnormal findings Z00.01
    administrative purpose only Z02.9
      specified NEC Z02.89
    admission to
      armed forces Z02.3
      old age home Z02.2
      prison Z02.89
      residential institution Z02.2
      school Z02.0
        following illness or medical
          treatment Z02.0
      summer camp Z02.89

Examination (Continued)
  medical (Continued)
    adoption Z02.82
    blood alcohol or drug level Z02.83
    camp (summer) Z02.89
    clinical research, normal subject Z00.6
    control subject in clinical research Z00.6
    donor (potential) Z00.5
    driving license Z02.4
    general (adult) Z00.00
      with abnormal findings Z00.01
    immigration Z02.89
    insurance purposes Z02.6
    marriage Z02.89
    medicolegal reasons NEC Z04.8
    naturalization Z02.89
    participation in sport Z02.5
    paternity testing Z02.81
    population survey Z00.8
    pre-employment Z02.1
    pre-operative - see Examination,
      pre-procedural
    pre-procedural
      cardiovascular Z01.810
      respiratory Z01.811
      specified NEC Z01.818
    preschool children
      for admission to school Z02.0
    prisoners
      for entrance into prison Z02.89
    recruitment for armed forces Z02.3
    specified NEC Z00.8
    sport competition Z02.5
  medicolegal reason NEC Z04.8
  newborn - see Newborn, examination
  pelvic (annual) (periodic) Z01.419
    with abnormal findings Z01.411
  period of rapid growth in childhood
    Z00.2
  periodic (adult) (annual) (routine) Z00.00
    with abnormal findings Z00.01
  physical (adult) Z00.00 - see also Exami-
    nation, medical
    sports Z02.5
  postpartum
    immediately after delivery Z39.0
    routine follow-up Z39.2
  prenatal (normal pregnancy) - see
    Category O34
  pre-chemotherapy (antineoplastic)
    Z01.818
  pre-procedural (pre-operative)
    cardiovascular Z01.810
    laboratory Z01.812
    respiratory Z01.811
    specified NEC Z01.818
  prior to chemotherapy (antineoplastic)
    Z01.818
  psychiatric NEC Z00.8
    follow-up not needing further care
      Z09
    requested by authority Z04.6
  radiological (as part of a general medi-
    cal examination) Z00.00
    with abnormal findings Z00.01
  repeat cervical smear to confirm
    findings of recent normal smear
    following initial abnormal smear
      Z01.42
  skin (hypersensitivity) Z01.82
  special (see also Examination, by type)
    Z01.89
    specified type NEC Z01.89
  specified type or reason NEC Z04.8

Examination *(Continued)*
  teeth Z01.20
    with abnormal findings Z01.21
  urine - *see* Examination, laboratory
  vision Z01.00
    with abnormal findings Z01.01
Exanthem, exanthema - *see also* Rash
  with enteroviral vesicular stomatitis B08.4
  Boston A88.0
  epidemic with meningitis A88.0 *[G02]*
  subitum B08.20
    due to human herpesvirus 6 B08.21
    due to human herpesvirus 7 B08.22
  viral, virus B09
    specified type NEC B08.8
Excess, excessive, excessively
  alcohol level in blood R78.0
  androgen (ovarian) E28.1
  attrition, tooth, teeth K03.0
  carotene, carotin (dietary) E67.1
  cold, effects of T69.9
    specified effect NEC T69.8
  convergence H51.12
  crying
    in child, adolescent, or adult R45.83
    in infant R68.11
  development, breast N62
  divergence H51.8
  drinking (alcohol) NEC (without de-
      pendence) F10.10
    habitual (continual) (without remis-
        sion) F10.20
  eating R63.2
  estrogen E28.0
  fat - *see also* Obesity
    in heart - *see* Degeneration,
        myocardial
    localized E65
  foreskin N47.8
  gas R14.8
  glucagon E16.3
  heat - *see* Heat
  intermaxillary vertical dimension of
      fully erupted teeth M26.37
  interocclusal distance of fully erupted
      teeth M26.37
  kalium E87.5
  large
    colon K59.3
      congenital Q43.8
    infant P08.0
    organ or site, congenital NEC - *see*
        Anomaly, by site
  long
    organ or site, congenital NEC - *see*
        Anomaly, by site
  menstruation (with regular cycle) N92.0
    with irregular cycle N92.1
  napping Z72.821
  natrium E87.0
  number of teeth K00.1
  nutrient (dietary) NEC R63.2
  potassium (K) E87.5
  salivation K11.7
  secretion - *see also* Hypersecretion
    milk O92.6
    sputum R09.3
    sweat R61
  sexual drive F52.8
  short
    organ or site, congenital NEC - *see*
        Anomaly, by site
    umbilical cord in labor or delivery
        O69.3

Excess, excessive, excessively *(Continued)*
  skin, eyelid (acquired) - *see*
      Blepharochalasis
    congenital Q10.3
  sodium (Na) E87.0
  spacing of fully erupted teeth M26.32
  sputum R09.3
  sweating R61
  thirst R63.1
    due to deprivation of water T73.1
  tuberosity of jaw M26.07
  vitamin
    A (dietary) E67.0
      administered as drug (prolonged
          intake) - *see* Table of drugs
          and chemicals, vitamins,
          adverse effect
      overdose or wrong substance given
          or taken - *see* Table of drugs and
          chemicals, vitamins, poisoning
    D (dietary) E67.3
      administered as drug (prolonged
          intake) - *see* Table of drugs
          and chemicals, vitamins,
          adverse effect
      overdose or wrong substance given
          or taken - *see* Table of drugs and
          chemicals, vitamins, poisoning
  weight
    gain R63.5
    loss R63.4
Excitability, abnormal, under minor
    stress (personality disorder) F60.3
Excitation
  anomalous atrioventricular I45.6
  psychogenic F30.8
  reactive (from emotional stress, psycho-
      logical trauma) F30.8
Excitement
  hypomanic F30.8
  manic F30.9
  mental, reactive (from emotional stress,
      psychological trauma) F30.8
  state, reactive (from emotional stress,
      psychological trauma) F30.8
Excoriation (traumatic) - *see also* Abrasion
  neurotic L98.1
Exfoliation
  due to erythematous conditions
      according to extent of body
      surface involved L49.0
    10-19 percent of body surface L49.1
    20-29 percent of body surface L49.2
    30-39 percent of body surface L49.3
    40-49 percent of body surface L49.4
    50-59 percent of body surface L49.5
    60-69 percent of body surface L49.6
    70-79 percent of body surface L49.7
    80-89 percent of body surface L49.8
    90-99 percent of body surface L49.9
    less than 10 percent of body surface
        L49.0
  teeth, due to systemic causes K08.0
Exfoliative - *see* condition
Exhaustion, exhaustive (physical NEC)
    R53.83
  battle F43.0
  cardiac - *see* Failure, heart
  delirium F43.0
  due to
    cold T69.8
    excessive exertion T73.3
    exposure T73.2
    neurasthenia F48.8

Exhaustion, exhaustive *(Continued)*
  heart - *see* Failure, heart
  heat (*see also* Heat, exhaustion) T67.5
    due to
      salt depletion T67.4
      water depletion T67.3
  maternal, complicating delivery O75.81
  mental F48.8
  myocardium, myocardial - *see* Failure,
      heart
  nervous F48.8
  old age R54
  psychogenic F48.8
  psychosis F43.0
  senile R54
  vital NEC Z73.0
Exhibitionism F65.2
Exocervicitis - *see* Cervicitis
Exomphalos Q79.2
  meaning hernia - *see* Hernia, umbilicus
Exophoria H50.52
  convergence, insufficiency H51.11
  divergence, excess H51.8
Exophthalmos H05.2-
  congenital Q15.8
  constant NEC H05.24-
  displacement, globe - *see* Displacement,
      globe
  due to thyrotoxicosis (hyperthyroidism) -
      see Hyperthyroidism, with, goiter
      (diffuse)
  dysthyroid - *see* Hyperthyroidism, with,
      goiter (diffuse)
  goiter - *see* Hyperthyroidism, with,
      goiter (diffuse)
  intermittent NEC H05.25-
  malignant - *see* Hyperthyroidism, with,
      goiter (diffuse)
  orbital
    edema - *see* Edema, orbit
    hemorrhage - *see* Hemorrhage, orbit
  pulsating NEC H05.26-
  thyrotoxic, thyrotropic - *see* Hyperthy-
      roidism, with, goiter (diffuse)
Exostosis - *see also* Disorder, bone
  cartilaginous - *see* Neoplasm, bone,
      benign
  congenital (multiple) Q78.6
  external ear canal H61.81-
  gonococcal A54.49
  jaw (bone) M27.8
  multiple, congenital Q78.6
  orbit H05.35-
  osteocartilaginous - *see* Neoplasm,
      bone, benign
  syphilitic A52.77
Exotropia - *see* Strabismus, divergent
  concomitant
Explanation of
  investigation finding Z71.2
  medication Z71.89
Exposure (to) (*see also* Contact, with)
    T75.89
  acariasis Z20.7
  AIDS virus Z20.6
  air pollution Z77.110
  algae and algae toxins Z77.121
  algae bloom Z77.121
  anthrax Z20.810
  aromatic amines Z77.020
  aromatic (hazardous) compounds NEC
      Z77.028
  aromatic dyes NOS Z77.028
  arsenic Z77.010

Exposure (Continued)
  asbestos Z77.090
  bacterial disease NEC Z20.818
  benzene Z77.021
  blue-green algae bloom Z77.121
  body fluids (potentially hazardous)
      Z77.21
  brown tide Z77.121
  chemicals (chiefly nonmedicinal) (haz-
      ardous) NEC Z77.098
  cholera Z20.09
  chromium compounds Z77.018
  cold, effects of T69.9
      specified effect NEC T69.8
  communicable disease Z20.9
      bacterial NEC Z20.818
      specified NEC Z20.89
      viral NEC Z20.828
  cyanobacteria bloom Z77.121
  disaster Z65.5
  discrimination Z60.5
  dyes Z77.098
  Escherichia coli (E. coli) Z20.01
  effects of T73.9
  environmental tobacco smoke (acute)
      (chronic) Z77.22
  exhaustion due to T73.2
  fiberglass - see Table of drugs and
      chemicals, fiberglass
  German measles Z20.4
  gonorrhea Z20.2
  hazardous metals NEC Z77.018
  hazardous substances NEC Z77.29
  hazards in the physical environment
      NEC Z77.128
  hazards to health NEC Z77.9
  human immunodeficiency virus (HIV)
      Z20.6
  human T-lymphotropic virus type-1
      (HTLV-1) Z20.89
  industrial toxic agents (gases) (liquids)
      (solids) (vapors) Z57.5
      nonoccupational Z58.5
  infestation (parasitic) NEC Z20.7
  intestinal infectious disease NEC Z20.09
      Escherichia coli (E. coli) Z20.01
  lead Z77.011
  meningococcus Z20.811
  mold (toxic) Z77.120
  nickel dust Z77.018
  noise Z77.122
  occupational
      air contaminants NEC Z57.39
      dust Z57.2

Exposure (Continued)
  occupational (Continued)
      environmental tobacco smoke Z57.31
      extreme temperature Z57.6
      noise Z57.0
      radiation Z57.1
      risk factors Z57.9
          specified NEC Z57.8
      toxic agents (gases) (liquids) (solids)
          (vapors) in agriculture Z57.4
      toxic agents (gases) (liquids) (solids)
          (vapors) in industry NEC
          Z57.5
      vibration Z57.7
  parasitic disease NEC Z20.7
  pediculosis Z20.7
  persecution Z60.5
  pfiesteria piscicida Z77.121
  poliomyelitis Z20.89
  polycyclic aromatic hydrocarbons
      Z77.028
  pollution
      air Z77.110
      environmental NEC Z77.118
      soil Z77.112
      water Z77.111
  prenatal (drugs) (toxic chemicals) - see
      Newborn, affected by (suspected
      to be), noxious substances trans-
      mitted via placenta or breast milk
  rabies Z20.3
  radiation, naturally occurring NEC
      Z77.123
  radon Z77.123
  red tide (Florida) Z77.121
  rubella Z20.4
  second hand tobacco smoke (acute)
      (chronic) Z77.22
  sexually-transmitted disease Z20.2
  smallpox (laboratory) Z20.89
  syphilis Z20.2
  terrorism Z65.4
  torture Z65.4
  tuberculosis Z20.1
  varicella Z20.820
  venereal disease Z20.2
  viral disease NEC Z20.828
  war Z65.5
  water pollution Z77.110
Exsanguination - see Hemorrhage
Exstrophy
  abdominal contents Q45.8
  bladder Q64.10
      cloacal Q64.12

Exstrophy (Continued)
  bladder (Continued)
      specified type NEC Q64.19
      supravesical fissure Q64.11
Extensive - see condition
Extra - see also Accessory
  marker chromosomes (normal indi-
      vidual) Q92.61
      in abnormal individual Q92.62
  rib Q76.6
      cervical Q76.5
Extrasystoles (supraventricular) I49.49
  atrial I49.1
  auricular I49.1
  junctional I49.2
  ventricular I49.3
Extrauterine gestation or pregnancy - see
      Pregnancy, by site
Extravasation
  blood R58
  chyle into mesentery I89.8
  pelvicalyceal N13.8
  pyelosinus N13.8
  urine (from ureter) R39.0
  vesicant agent
      antineoplastic chemotherapy
          T80.810
      other agent NEC T80.818
Extremity - see condition, limb
Extrophy - see Exstrophy
Extroversion
  bladder Q64.19
  uterus N81.4
      complicating delivery O71.2
      postpartal (old) N81.4
Extruded tooth (teeth) M26.34
Extrusion
  breast implant (prosthetic) T85.42
  eye implant (globe) (ball) T85.328
  intervertebral disc - see Displacement,
      intervertebral disc
  ocular lens implant (prosthetic) - see
      Complications, intraocular
      lens
  vitreous - see Prolapse, vitreous
Exudate
  pleural - see Effusion, pleura
  retina H35.89
Exudative - see condition
Eye, eyeball, eyelid - see condition
Eyestrain - see Disturbance, vision,
      subjective
Eyeworm disease of Africa B74.3

F

Faber's syndrome (achlorhydric anemia) D50.9
Fabry(-Anderson) **disease** E75.21
Faciocephalalgia, autonomic (*see also* Neuropathy, peripheral, autonomic) G90.09
Factor(s)
　psychic, associated with diseases classified elsewhere F54
　psychological
　　affecting physical conditions F54
　　or behavioral
　　　affecting general medical condition F54
　　　associated with disorders or diseases classified elsewhere F54
Fahr disease (of brain) G23.8
Fahr Volhard disease (of kidney) I12.-
Failure, failed
　abortion – *see* Abortion, attempted
　aortic (valve) I35.8
　　rheumatic I06.8
　attempted abortion - *see* Abortion, attempted
　biventricular I50.9
　bone marrow – *see* Anemia, aplastic
　cardiac - *see* Failure, heart
　cardiorenal (chronic) I50.9
　　hypertensive I13.2
　cardiorespiratory (*see also* Failure, heart) R09.2
　cardiovascular (chronic) - *see* Failure, heart
　cerebrovascular I67.9
　cervical dilatation in labor O62.0
　circulation, circulatory (peripheral) R57.9
　compensation - *see* Disease, heart
　compliance with medical treatment or regimen – *see* Noncompliance
　congestive - *see* Failure, heart, congestive
　dental implant (endosseous) M27.69
　　due to
　　　failure of dental prosthesis M27.63
　　　lack of attached gingiva M27.62
　　　occlusal trauma (poor prosthetic design) M27.62
　　　parafunctional habits M27.62
　　　periodontal infection (peri-implantitis) M27.62
　　　poor oral hygiene M27.62
　　osseointegration M27.61
　　　due to
　　　　complications of systemic disease M27.61
　　　　poor bone quality M27.61
　　　iatrogenic M27.61
　　post-osseointegration
　　　biological M27.62
　　　due to complications of systemic disease M27.62
　　　iatrogenic M27.62
　　　mechanical M27.63
　　pre-integration M27.61
　　pre-osseointegration M27.61
　　specified NEC M27.69
　descent of head (at term) of pregnancy (mother) O32.4
　endosseous dental implant - *see* Failure, dental implant

Failure, failed (*Continued*)
　engagement of head (term of pregnancy) (mother) O32.4
　erection (penile) N52.9 - *see also* Dysfunction, sexual, male, erectile
　nonorgqanic F52.21
　examination(s), anxiety concerning Z55.2
　expansion terminal respiratory units (newborn) (primary) P28.0
　forceps NOS (with subsequent cesarean delivery) O66.5
　gain weight (child over 28 days old) R62.51
　　adult R62.7
　　newborn P92.6
　genital response (male) F52.21
　　female F52.22
　heart (acute) (senile) (sudden) I50.9
　　with
　　　acute pulmonary edema - *see* Failure, ventricular, left
　　　decompensation - *see* Failure, heart, congestive
　　　dilatation - *see* Disease, heart
　　arteriosclerotic I70.90
　　biventricular I50.9
　　combined left-right sided I50.9
　　compensated I50.9
　　complicating
　　　anesthesia (general) (local) or other sedation
　　　　in labor and delivery O74.2
　　　　in pregnancy O29.12-
　　　　postpartum, puerperal O89.1
　　　delivery (cesarean) (instrumental) O75.4
　　congestive (compensated) (decompensated) I50.9
　　　with rheumatic fever (conditions in I00)
　　　　active I01.8
　　　　inactive or quiescent (with chorea) I09.81
　　　newborn P29.0
　　　rheumatic (chronic) (inactive) (with chorea) I09.81
　　　　active or acute I01.8
　　　　　with chorea I02.0
　　decompensated I50.9
　　degenerative - *see* Degeneration, myocardial
　　diastolic (congestive) I50.30
　　　acute (congestive) I50.31
　　　　and (on) chronic (congestive) I50.33
　　　chronic (congestive) I50.32
　　　　and (on) acute (congestive) I50.33
　　　combined with systolic (congestive) I50.40
　　　　acute (congestive) I50.41
　　　　　and (on) chronic (congestive) I50.43
　　　　chronic (congestive) I50.42
　　　　　and (on) acute (congestive) I50.43
　　due to presence of cardiac prosthesis I97.13-
　　following cardiac surgery I97.13-
　　high output NOS I50.9
　　hypertensive - *see* Hypertension, heart
　　left (ventricular) - *see* Failure, ventricular, left

Failure, failed (*Continued*)
　heart (*Continued*)
　　low output (syndrome) NOS I50.9
　　newborn P29.0
　　organic - *see* Disease, heart
　　peripartum O90.3
　　postprocedural I97.13-
　　rheumatic (chronic) (inactive) I09.9
　　right (ventricular) (secondary to left heart failure) - *see* Failure, heart, congestive
　　systolic (congestive) I50.20
　　　acute (congestive) I50.21
　　　　and (on) chronic (congestive) I50.23
　　　chronic (congestive) I50.22
　　　　and (on) acute (congestive) I50.23
　　　combined with diastolic (congestive) I50.40
　　　　acute (congestive) I50.41
　　　　　and (on) chronic (congestive) I50.43
　　　　chronic (congestive) I50.42
　　　　　and (on) acute (congestive) I50.43
　　　thyrotoxic (*see also* Thyrotoxicosis) E05.90 [I43]
　　　　with thyroid storm E05.91 [I43]
　　valvular - *see* Endocarditis
　hepatic K72.90
　　with coma K72.91
　　acute or subacute K72.00
　　　with coma K72.01
　　　due to drugs K71.10
　　　　with coma K71.11
　　alcoholic (acute) (chronic) (subacute) K70.40
　　　with coma K70.41
　　chronic K72.10
　　　with coma K72.11
　　　due to drugs (acute) (subacute) (chronic) K71.10
　　　　with coma K71.11
　　due to drugs (acute) (subacute) (chronic) K71.10
　　　with coma K71.11
　　postprocedural K91.82
　hepatorenal K76.7
　induction (of labor) O61.9
　　abortion - *see* Abortion, attempted
　　by
　　　oxytocic drugs O61.0
　　　prostaglandins O61.0
　　instrumental O61.1
　　mechanical O61.1
　　medical O61.0
　　specified NEC O61.8
　　surgical O61.1
　intubation during anesthesia T88.4
　　in pregnancy O29.6-
　　labor and delivery O74.7
　　postpartum, puerperal O89.6
　involution, thymus (gland) E32.0
　kidney (*see also* Disease, kidney, chronic) N19
　　acute N17.9 - *see also* Failure, renal, acute
　lactation (complete) O92.3
　　partial O92.4
　Leydig's cell, adult E29.1
　liver - *see* Failure, hepatic
　menstruation at puberty N91.0
　mitral I05.8

Failure, failed (Continued)
  myocardial, myocardium (see also
      Failure, heart) I50.9
    chronic (see also Failure, heart,
        congestive) I50.9
    congestive (see also Failure, heart,
        congestive) I50.9
  orgasm (female) (psychogenic) F52.31
    male F52.32
  ovarian (primary) E28.39
    iatrogenic E89.40
      asymptomatic E89.40
      symptomatic E89.41
      postprocedural (postablative) (postir-
          radiation) (postsurgical) E89.40
        asymptomatic E89.40
        symptomatic E89.41
  ovulation causing infertility N97.0
  polyglandular, autoimmune E31.0
  prosthetic joint implant - see Complica-
      tions, joint prosthesis, mechanical,
      breakdown, by site
  renal N19
    tubular necrosis (acute) N17.0
    acute N17.9
      with
        cortical necrosis N17.1
        medullary necrosis N17.2
        tubular necrosis N17.0
      specified NEC N17.8
    chronic N18.9
      hypertensive - see Hypertension,
          kidney
    congenital P96.0
    end stage (chronic) N18.6
      due to hypertension I12.0
    following
      abortion - see Abortion by type
          complicated by specified
          condition NEC
      crushing T79.5
      ectopic or molar pregnancy
          O08.4
      labor and delivery (acute) O90.4
    hypertensive - see Hypertension,
        kidney
    postprocedural N99.0
  respiration, respiratory J96.9
    acute J96.0
      with chronic J96.2
    center G93.89
    chronic J96.1
      with acute J96.2
    newborn P28.5
    postprocedural J95.82
  rotation
    cecum Q43.3
    colon Q43.3
    intestine Q43.3
    kidney Q63.2
  sedation (conscious) (moderate) during
      procedure T88.52
    history of Z92.83
  segmentation - see also Fusion
    fingers – see Syndactylism, complex,
        fingers
    toes Q70.2
    vertebra Q76.49
      with scoliosis Q76.3
  seminiferous tubule, adult E29.1
  senile (general) R54
  sexual arousal (male) F52.21
    female F52.22
  testicular endocrine function E29.1

Failure, failed (Continued)
  to thrive (child over 28 days old) R62.51
    adult R62.7
    newborn P92.6
  transplant T86.92
    bone T86.831
      marrow T86.09
    cornea T86.841
    heart T86.22
      with lung(s) T86.32
    intestine T86.891
    kidney T86.12
    liver T86.42
    lung(s) T86.811
      with heart T86.32
    pancreas T86.891
    skin (allograft) (autograft) T86.821
    specified organ or tissue NEC T86.891
  trial of labor (with subsequent cesarean
      delivery) O66.40
    following previous cesarean delivery
        O66.41
  tubal ligation N99.89
  urinary - see Disease, kidney, chronic
  vacuum extraction NOS (with subse-
      quent cesarean delivery) O66.5
  vasectomy N99.89
  ventouse NOS (with subsequent cesar-
      ean delivery) O66.5
  ventricular (see also Failure, heart) I50.9
    left I50.1
      with rheumatic fever (conditions
          in I00)
        active I01.8
          with chorea I02.0
        inactive or quiescent (with cho-
            rea) I09.81
        rheumatic (chronic) (inactive) (with
            chorea) I09.81
        active or acute I01.8
          with chorea I02.0
    right (see also Failure, heart, conges-
        tive) I50.9
  vital centers, newborn P91.8
Fainting (fit) R55
Fallen arches - see Deformity, limb, flat
    foot
Falling, falls (repeated) R29.6
  any organ or part - see Prolapse
Fallopian
  insufflation Z31.41
  tube - see condition
Fallot's
  pentalogy Q21.3
  tetrad or tetralogy Q21.3
  triad or trilogy Q22.2
False - see also condition
  croup J38.5
  joint - see Nonunion, fracture
  labor (pains) O47.9
    at or after 37 completed weeks of
        gestation O47.1
    before 37 completed weeks of gesta-
        tion O47.0-
  passage, urethra (prostatic) N36.0
  pregnancy F45.8
Family, familial - see also condition
  disruption Z63.8
    involving divorce or separation Z63.5
  Li-Fraumeni (syndrome) Z15.01
  planning advice Z30.09
  problem Z63.9
    specified NEC Z63.8
  retinoblastoma C69.2-

Famine (effects of) T73.0
  edema - see Malnutrition, severe
Fanconi (-de Toni)(-Debré) syndrome
    E72.09
  with cystinosis E72.04
Fanconi's anemia (congenital pancytope-
    nia) D61.09
Farber's disease or syndrome E75.29
Farcy A24.0
Farmer's
  lung J67.0
  skin L57.8
Farsightedness - see Hypermetropia
Fascia - see condition
Fasciculation R25.3
Fasciitis M72.9
  diffuse (eosinophilic) M35.4
  infective M72.8
    necrotizing M72.6
  necrotizing M72.6
  nodular M72.4
  perirenal (with ureteral obstruction)
      N13.5
    with infection N13.6
  plantar M72.2
  specified NEC M72.8
  traumatic (old) M72.8
    current - code by site under Sprain
Fascioliasis B66.3
Fasciolopsis, fasciolopsiasis (intestinal)
    B66.5
Fascioscapulohumeral myopathy G71.0
Fast pulse R00.0
Fat
  embolism – see Embolism, fat
  excessive - see also Obesity
    in heart - see Degeneration,
        myocardial
  in stool R19.5
  localized (pad) E65
    heart - see Degeneration, myocardial
    knee M79.4
    retropatellar M79.4
  necrosis
    breast N64.1
    mesentery K65.4
    omentum K65.4
  pad E65
    knee M79.4
Fatigue R53.83
  auditory deafness – see Deafness
  chronic R53.82
  combat F43.0
  general R53.83
    psychogenic F48.8
  heat (transient) T67.6
  muscle M62.89
  myocardium - see Failure, heart
  neoplasm-related R53.0
  nervous, neurosis F48.8
  operational F48.8
  psychogenic (general) F48.8
  senile R54
  voice R49.8
Fatness - see Obesity
Fatty - see also condition
  apron E65
  degeneration - see Degeneration, fatty
  heart (enlarged) - see Degeneration,
      myocardial
  liver NEC K76.0
    alcoholic K70.0
    nonalcoholic K76.0
  necrosis - see Degeneration, fatty

Fauces - *see* condition
Fauchard's disease (periodontitis) - *see* Periodontitis
Faucitis J02.9
Favism (anemia) D55.0
Favus - *see* Dermatophytosis
Fazio-Londe disease or syndrome G12.1
Fear complex or reaction F40.9
Fear of - *see* Phobia
Feared complaint unfounded Z71.1
Febris, febrile - *see also* Fever
  flava (*see also* Fever, yellow) A95.9
  melitensis A23.0
  pestis - *see* Plague
  puerperalis O85
  recurrens - *see* Fever, relapsing
  rubra A38.9
Fecal - *see* condition
Fecalith (impaction) K56.4
  appendix K38.1
  congenital P76.8
Fede's disease K14.0
Feeble rapid pulse due to shock following injury T79.4
Feeble-minded F70
Feeding
  difficulties R63.3
  problem R63.3
    newborn P92.9
      specified NEC P92.8
    nonorganic (adult) - *see* Disorder, eating
Feeling (of)
  foreign body in throat R09.89
Feer's disease – *see* Poisoning, mercury
Feet - *see* condition
Feigned illness Z76.5
Feil-Klippel syndrome (brevicollis) Q76.1
Feinmesser's (hidrotic) ectodermal dysplasia Q82.4
Felinophobia F40.218
Felon - *see also* Cellulitis, digit
  with lymphangitis - *see* Lymphangitis, acute, digit
Felty's syndrome M05.00
  ankle M05.07-
  elbow M05.02-
  foot joint M05.07-
  hand joint M05.04-
  hip M05.05-
  knee M05.06-
  multiple site M05.09
  shoulder M05.01-
  vertebra - *see* Spondylitis, ankylosing
  wrist M05.03-
Female gential cutting status - *see* Female genital mutilation status (FGM)
Female genital mutilation status (FGM) N90.810
  specified NEC N90.818
  type I (clitorectomy status) N90.811
  type II (clitorectomy with excision of labia minora status) N90.812
  type III (infibulation status) N90.813
  type IV N90.818
Femur, femoral - *see* condition
Fenestration, fenestrated - *see also* Imperfect, closure
  aortico-pulmonary Q21.4
  cusps, heart valve NEC Q24.8
    pulmonary Q22.2
  pulmonic cusps Q22.2
Fernell's disease (aortic aneurysm) I71.9

Fertile eunuch syndrome E23.0
Fetalis uterus Q51.8
Fetid
  breath R19.6
  sweat L75.0
Fetishism F65.0
  transvestic F65.1
Fetus, fetal - *see also* condition
  alcohol syndrome (dysmorphic) Q86.0
  compressus O31.0-
  hydantoin syndrome Q86.1
  lung tissue P28.0
  papyraceous O31.0-
Fever (inanition) (of unknown origin) (persistent) (with chills) (with rigor) R50.9
  abortus A23.1
  Aden (dengue) A90
  African tick-borne A68.1
  American
    mountain (tick) A93.2
    spotted A77.0
  aphthous B08.8
  arbovirus, arboviral A94
    hemorrhagic A94
    specified NEC A93.8
  Argentinian hemorrhagic A96.0
  Assam B55.0
  Australian Q A78
  Bangkok hemorrhagic A91
  Barmah forest A92.8
  Bartonella A44.0
  bilious, hemoglobinuric B50.8
  blackwater B50.8
  blister B00.1
  Bolivian hemorrhagic A96.1
  Bonvale dam T73.3
  boutonneuse A77.1
  brain - *see* Encephalitis
  Brazilian purpuric A48.4
  breakbone A90
  Bullis A77.0
  Bunyamwera A92.8
  Burdwan B55.0
  Bwamba A92.8
  Cameroon - *see* Malaria
  Canton A75.9
  catarrhal (acute) J00
    chronic J31.0
  cat-scratch A28.1
  Central Asian hemorrhagic A98.0
  cerebral - *see* Encephalitis
  cerebrospinal meningococcal A39.0
  Chagres B50.9
  Chandipura A92.8
  Changuinola A93.1
  Charcot's (biliary) (hepatic) (intermittent) - *see* Calculus, bile duct
  Chikungunya (viral) (hemorrhagic) A92.0
  Chitral A93.1
  Colombo – *see* Fever, paratyphoid
  Colorado tick (virus) A93.2
  congestive (remittent) - *see* Malaria
  Congo virus A98.0
  continued malarial B50.9
  Corsican - *see* Malaria
  Crimean-Congo hemorrhagic A98.0
  Cyprus – *see* Brucellosis
  dandy A90
  deer fly - *see* Tularemia
  dengue (virus) A90
    hemorrhagic A91
    sandfly A93.1
  desert B38.0

Fever *(Continued)*
  drug induced R50.2
  due to heat T67.0
  due to conditions classified elsewhere R50.81
  enteric A01.00
  enteroviral exanthematous (Boston exanthem) A88.0
  ephemeral (of unknown origin) R50.9
  epidemic hemorrhagic A98.5
  erysipelatous - *see* Erysipelas
  estivo-autumnal (malarial) B50.9
  famine A75.0
  five day A79.0
  following delivery O86.4
  Fort Bragg A27.89
  gastroenteric A01.00
  gastromalarial - *see* Malaria
  Gibraltar – *see* Brucellosis
  glandular - *see* Mononucleosis, infectious
  Guama (viral) A92.8
  Haverhill A25.1
  hay (allergic) J30.1
    with asthma (bronchial) J45.909
    with
      exacerbation (acute) J45.901
      status asthmaticus J45.902
    due to
      allergen other than pollen J30.89
      pollen, any plant or tree J30.1
  heat (effects) T67.0
  hematuric, bilious B50.8
  hemoglobinuric (malarial) (bilious) B50.8
  hemorrhagic (arthropod-borne) NOS A94
    with renal syndrome A98.5
    arenaviral A96.9
      specified NEC A96.8
    Argentinian A96.0
    Bangkok A91
    Bolivian A96.1
    Central Asian A98.0
    Chikungunya A92.0
    Crimean-Congo A98.0
    dengue (virus) A91
    epidemic A98.5
    Junin (virus) A96.0
    Korean A98.5
    Kyasanur forest A98.2
    Machupo (virus) A96.1
    mite-borne A93.8
    mosquito-borne A92.8
    Omsk A98.1
    Philippine A91
    Russian A98.5
    Singapore A91
    Southeast Asia A91
    Thailand A91
    tick-borne NEC A93.8
    viral A99
      specified NEC A98.8
  hepatic – *see* Cholecystitis
  herpetic - *see* Herpes
  icterohemorrhagic A27.0
  Indiana A93.8
  infective B99.9
    specified NEC B99.8
  intermittent (bilious) - *see also* Malaria
    of unknown origin R50.9
    pernicious B50.9
  iodide R50.2
  Japanese river A75.3
  jungle - *see also* Malaria
    yellow A95.0

Fever *(Continued)*
 Junin (virus) hemorrhagic A96.0
 Katayama B65.2
 kedani A75.3
 Kenya (tick) A77.1
 Kew Garden A79.1
 Korean hemorrhagic A98.5
 Lassa A96.2
 Lone Star A77.0
 Machupo (virus) hemorrhagic A96.1
 malaria, malarial – *see* Malaria
 Malta A23.9
 Marseilles A77.1
 marsh - *see* Malaria
 Mayaro (viral) A92.8
 Mediterranean – *see* Brucellosis
  familial E85.0
  tick A77.1
 meningeal - *see* Meningitis
 Meuse A79.0
 Mexican A75.2
 mianeh A68.1
 miasmatic - *see* Malaria
 mosquito-borne (viral) A92.9
  hemorrhagic A92.8
 mountain – *see also* Brucellosis
  meaning Rocky Mountain spotted
   fever A77.0
  tick (American) (Colorado) (viral)
   A93.2
 Mucambo (viral) A92.8
 mud A27.9
 Neapolitan – *see* Brucellosis
 neutropenic D70.9
 newborn P81.9
  environmental P81.0
 Nine-Mile A78
 non-exanthematous tick A93.2
 North Asian tick-borne A77.2
 Omsk hemorrhagic A98.1
 O'nyong-nyong (viral) A92.1
 Oropouche (viral) A93.0
 Oroya A44.0
 paludal - *see* Malaria
 Panama (malarial) B50.9
 Pappataci A93.1
 paratyphoid A01.4
  A A01.1
  B A01.2
  C A01.3
 parrot A70
 periodic (Mediterranean) E85.0
 persistent (of unknown origin) R50.9
 petechial A39.0
 pharyngoconjunctival B30.2
 Philippine hemorrhagic A91
 phlebotomus A93.1
 Piry (virus) A93.8
 Pixuna (viral) A92.8
 Plasmodium ovale B53.0
 polioviral (nonparalytic) A80.4
 Pontiac A48.2
 postimmunization R50.83
 postoperative R50.82
  due to infection T81.4
 postvaccination R50.83
 presenting with conditions classified
  elsewhere R50.81
 pretibial A27.89
 puerperal O85
 Q A78
 quadrilateral A78
 quartan (malaria) B52.9
 Queensland (coastal) (tick) A77.3

Fever *(Continued)*
 quintan A79.0
 rabbit - *see* Tularemia
 rat-bite A25.9
  due to
   Spirillum A25.0
   Streptobacillus moniliformis A25.1
 recurrent - *see* Fever, relapsing
 relapsing (Borrelia) A68.9
  Carter's (Asiatic) A68.1
  Dutton's (West African) A68.1
  Koch's A68.9
  louse-borne A68.0
  Novy's
   louse-borne A68.0
   tick-borne A68.1
  Obermeyer's (European) A68.0
  tick-borne A68.1
 remittent (bilious) (congestive) (gastric) -
  see Malaria
 rheumatic (active) (acute) (chronic)
  (subacute) I00
  with central nervous system involvement I02.9
  active with heart involvement - *see*
   category I01
  inactive or quiescent with
   cardiac hypertrophy I09.89
   carditis I09.9
   endocarditis I09.1
    aortic (valve) I06.9
     with mitral (valve) disease
      I08.0
    mitral (valve) I05.9
     with aortic (valve) disease
      I08.0
    pulmonary (valve) I09.89
    tricuspid (valve) I07.8
   heart disease NEC I09.89
   heart failure (congestive) (condi-
    tions in I50.9) I09.81
   left ventricular failure (conditions
    in I50.1) I09.81
   myocarditis, myocardial degenera-
    tion (conditions in I51.4) I09.0
   pancarditis I09.9
   pericarditis I09.2
 Rift Valley (viral) A92.4
 Rocky Mountain spotted A77.0
 rose J30.1
 Ross River B33.1
 Russian hemorrhagic A98.5
 San Joaquin (Valley) B38.0
 sandfly A93.1
 Sao Paulo A77.0
 scarlet A38.9
 seven day (leptospirosis) (autumnal)
  (Japanese) A27.89
  dengue A90
 shin-bone A79.0
 Singapore hemorrhagic A91
 solar A90
 Songo A98.5
 sore B00.1
 South African tick-bite A68.1
 Southeast Asia hemorrhagic A91
 spinal - *see* Meningitis
 spirillary A25.0
 splenic – *see* Anthrax
 spotted A77.9
  American A77.0
  Brazilian A77.0
  cerebrospinal meningitis A39.0
  Colombian A77.0

Fever *(Continued)*
 spotted *(Continued)*
  due to Rickettsia
   australis A77.3
   conorii A77.1
   rickettsii A77.0
   sibirica A77.2
   specified type NEC A77.8
  Ehrlichiosis A77.40
   due to
    E. chafeensis A77.41
    specified organism NEC
     A77.49
  Rocky Mountain A77.0
 steroid R50.2
 streptobacillary A25.1
 subtertian B50.9
 Sumatran mite A75.3
 sun A90
 swamp A27.9
 swine A02.8
 sylvatic, yellow A95.0
 Tahyna A83.5
 tertian - *see* Malaria, tertian
 Thailand hemorrhagic A91
 thermic T67.0
 three-day A93.1
 tick
  American mountain A93.2
  Colorado A93.2
  Kemerovo A93.8
  Mediterranean A77.1
  mountain A93.2
  nonexanthematous A93.2
  Quaranfil A93.8
 tick-bite NEC A93.8
 tick-borne (hemorrhagic) NEC A93.8
 trench A79.0
 tsutsugamushi A75.3
 typhogastric A01.00
 typhoid (abortive) (hemorrhagic) (intermittent) (malignant) A01.00
  complicated by
   arthritis A01.04
   heart involvement A01.02
   meningitis A01.01
   osteomyelitis A01.05
   pneumonia A01.03
   specified NEC A01.09
 typhomalarial – *see* Malaria
 typhus - *see* Typhus (fever)
 undulant - *see* Brucellosis
 unknown origin R50.9
 uveoparotid D86.89
 valley B38.0
 Venezuelan equine A92.2
 vesicular stomatitis A93.8
 viral hemorrhagic - *see* Fever, hemorrhagic, by type of virus
 Volhynian A79.0
 Wesselsbron (viral) A92.8
 West
  African B50.8
  Nile (viral) A92.30
   with
    complications NEC A92.39
    cranial nerve disorders A92.32
    encephalitis A92.31
    encephalomyelitis A92.31
    neurologic manifestation NEC
     A92.32
    optic neuritis A92.32
    polyradiculitis A92.32
 Whitmore's - *see* Melioidosis

Fever *(Continued)*
  Wolhynian A79.0
  worm B83.9
  yellow A95.9
    jungle A95.0
    sylvatic A95.0
    urban A95.1
  Zika (viral) A92.8
Fibrillation
  atrial or auricular (established) I48.0
  cardiac I49.8
  heart I49.8
  muscular M62.89
  ventricular I49.01
Fibrin
  ball or bodies, pleural (sac) J94.1
  chamber, anterior (eye) (gelatinous exudate) - *see* Iridocyclitis, acute
Fibrinogenolysis - *see* Fibrinolysis
Fibrinogenopenia D68.8
  acquired D65
  congenital D68.2
Fibrinolysis (hemorrhagic) (acquired) D65
  antepartum hemorrhage – *see* Hemorrhage, antepartum, with coagulation defect
  following
    abortion - *see* Abortion by type complicated by hemorrhage
    ectopic or molar pregnancy O08.1
  intrapartum O67.0
  newborn, transient P60
  postpartum O72.3
Fibrinopenia (hereditary) D68.2
  acquired D68.4
Fibrinopurulent - *see* condition
Fibrinous - *see* condition
Fibroadenoma
  cellular intracanalicular (female) D24.0-
    male D24.1-
  giant (female) D24.0-
    male D24.1-
  intracanalicular
    cellular (female) D24.0-
      male D24.1-
    giant (female) D24.0-
      male D24.1-
    specified site - *see* Neoplasm, benign
    unspecified site (female) D24.0-
      male D24.1-
  juvenile (female) D24.0-
    male D24.1-
  pericanalicular
    specified site - *see* Neoplasm, benign
    unspecified site (female) D24.0-
      male D24.1-
  phyllodes (female) D24.0-
    male D24.1-
  prostate D29.1
  specified site NEC - *see* Neoplasm, benign
  unspecified site (female) D24.0-
    male D24.1-
Fibroadenosis, breast (chronic) (cystic) (diffuse) (periodic) (segmental) N60.2-
Fibroangioma - *see also* Neoplasm, benign
  juvenile (M9160/0)
    specified site - *see* Neoplasm, benign
    unspecified site D10.6

Fibrochondrosarcoma - *see* Neoplasm, cartilage, malignant
Fibrocystic
  disease - *see also* Fibrosis, cystic
    breast – *see* Mastopathy, cystic
    jaw M27.49
    kidney (congenital) Q61.8
    liver Q44.6
    pancreas E84.9
  kidney (congenital) Q61.8
Fibrodysplasia ossificans progressiva - *see* Myositis, ossificans, progressiva
Fibroelastosis (cordis) (endocardial) (endomyocardial) I42.4
Fibroid (tumor) - *see also* Neoplasm, connective tissue, benign
  disease, lung (chronic) - *see* Fibrosis, lung
  heart (disease) - *see* Myocarditis
  in pregnancy or childbirth O34.1-
    causing obstructed labor O65.5
  induration, lung (chronic) - *see* Fibrosis, lung
  lung - *see* Fibrosis, lung
  pneumonia (chronic) - *see* Fibrosis, lung
  uterus D25.9
Fibrolipoma - *see* Lipoma
Fibroliposarcoma - *see* Neoplasm, connective tissue, malignant
Fibroma - *see also* Neoplasm, connective tissue, benign
  ameloblastic - *see* Cyst, calcifying odontogenic
  bone (nonossifying) - *see* Disorder, bone, specified type NEC
    ossifying - *see* Neoplasm, bone, benign
  cementifying - *see* Neoplasm, bone, benign
  chondromyxoid - *see* Neoplasm, bone, benign
  desmoplastic - *see* Neoplasm, connective tissue, uncertain behavior
  durum - *see* Neoplasm, connective tissue, benign
  fascial - *see* Neoplasm, connective tissue, benign
  invasive - *see* Neoplasm, connective tissue, uncertain behavior
  molle - *see* Lipoma
  myxoid - *see* Neoplasm, connective tissue, benign
  nasopharynx, nasopharyngeal (juvenile) D10.6
  nonosteogenic (nonossifying) - *see* Dysplasia, fibrous
  odontogenic (central) - *see* Cyst, calcifying odontogenic
  ossifying - *see* Neoplasm, bone, benign
  periosteal - *see* Neoplasm, bone, benign
  soft - *see* Lipoma
Fibromatosis M72.9
  abdominal - *see* Neoplasm, connective tissue, uncertain behavior
  aggressive - *see* Neoplasm, connective tissue, uncertain behavior
  congenital generalized - *see* Neoplasm, connective tissue, uncertain behavior

Fibromatosis *(Continued)*
  Dupuytren's M72.0
  gingival K06.1
  palmar (fascial) M72.0
  plantar (fascial) M72.2
  pseudosarcomatous (proliferative) (subcutaneous) M72.4
  retroperitoneal D48.3
  specified NEC M72.8
Fibromyalgia M79.7
Fibromyoma - *see also* Neoplasm, connective tissue, benign
  uterus (corpus) - *see also* Leiomyoma, uterus
    in pregnancy or childbirth – *see* Fibroid, in pregnancy or childbirth
      causing obstructed labor O65.5
Fibromyositis M79.7
Fibromyxolipoma D17.9
Fibromyxoma - *see* Neoplasm, connective tissue, benign
Fibromyxosarcoma - *see* Neoplasm, connective tissue, malignant
Fibro-odontoma, ameloblastic - *see* Cyst, calcifying odontogenic
Fibro-osteoma - *see* Neoplasm, bone, benign
Fibroplasia, retrolental H35.17
Fibropurulent - *see* condition
Fibrosarcoma - *see also* Neoplasm, connective tissue, malignant
  ameloblastic C41.1
    upper jaw (bone) C41.0
  congenital - *see* Neoplasm, connective tissue, malignant
  fascial - *see* Neoplasm, connective tissue, malignant
  infantile - *see* Neoplasm, connective tissue, malignant
  odontogenic C41.1
    upper jaw (bone) C41.0
  periosteal - *see* Neoplasm, bone, malignant
Fibrosclerosis
  breast N60.3-
  multifocal M35.5
  penis (corpora cavernosa) N48.6
Fibrosis, fibrotic
  adrenal (gland) E27.8
  amnion O41.8x-
  anal papillae K62.8
  arteriocapillary - *see* Arteriosclerosis
  bladder N32.89
    interstitial – *see* Cystitis, chronic, interstitial
    localized submucosal – *see* Cystitis, chronic, interstitial
    panmural – *see* Cystitis, chronic, interstitial
  breast – *see* Fibrosclerosis, breast
  capillary - *see also* Arteriosclerosis I70.90
    lung (chronic) - *see* Fibrosis, lung
  cardiac - *see* Myocarditis
  cervix N88.8
  chorion O41.8x-
  corpus cavernosum (sclerosing) N48.6
  cystic (of pancreas) E84.9
    with
      distal intestinal obstruction syndrome E84.19
      fecal impaction E84.19
      intestinal manifestations NEC E84.19

Fibrosis, fibrotic (Continued)
  cystic (Continued)
    with (Continued)
      pulmonary manifestations E84.0
      specified manifestations NEC
        E84.8
  due to device, implant or graft (see also
    Complications, by site and type,
    specified NEC) T85.82
    arterial graft NEC T82.828
    breast (implant) T85.82
    catheter NEC T85.82
      dialysis (renal) T82.828
        intraperitoneal T85.82
      infusion NEC T82.828
        spinal (epidural) (subdural)
          T85.82
      urinary (indwelling) T83.82
    electronic (electrode) (pulse genera-
      tor) (stimulator)
      bone T84.82
      cardiac T82.827
      nervous system (brain) (peripheral
        nerve) (spinal) T85.82
      urinary T83.82
    fixation, internal (orthopedic) NEC
      T84.82
    gastrointestinal (bile duct) (esopha-
      gus) T85.82
    genital NEC T83.82
    heart NEC T82.827
    joint prosthesis T84.82
    ocular (corneal graft) (orbital im-
      plant) NEC T85.82
    orthopedic NEC T84.82
    specified NEC T85.82
    urinary NEC T83.82
    vascular NEC T82.828
    ventricular intracranial shunt
      T85.82
  ejaculatory duct N50.8
  endocardium - see Endocarditis
  endomyocardial (tropical) I42.3
  epididymis N50.8
  eye muscle - see Strabismus, mechanical
  heart - see Myocarditis
  hepatic - see Fibrosis, liver
  hepatolienal (portal hypertension)
    K76.6
  hepatosplenic (portal hypertension)
    K76.6
  infrapatellar fat pad M79.4
  intrascrotal N50.8
  kidney N26.9
  liver K74.0
    with sclerosis K74.2
    alcoholic K70.2
  lung (atrophic) (capillary) (chronic)
    (confluent) (massive) (perialveo-
    lar) (peribronchial) J84.1
    with
      anthracosilicosis J60
      anthracosis J60
      asbestosis J61
      bagassosis J67.1
      bauxite J63.1
      berylliosis J63.2
      byssinosis J66.0
      calcicosis J62.8
      chalicosis J62.8
      dust reticulation J64
      farmer's lung J67.0
      ganister disease J62.8
      graphite J63.3

Fibrosis, fibrotic (Continued)
  lung (Continued)
    with (Continued)
      pneumoconiosis NOS J64
      siderosis J63.4
      silicosis J62.8
    congenital P27.8
    diffuse (idiopathic) (interstitial)
      J84.1
      chemicals, gases, fumes or vapors
        (inhalation) J68.4
      talc J62.0
    following radiation J70.1
    idiopathic J84.1
    postinflammatory J84.1
    silicotic J62.8
    tuberculous - see Tuberculosis,
      pulmonary
  lymphatic gland I89.8
  median bar – see Hyperplasia,
    prostate
  mediastinum (idiopathic) J98.5
  meninges G96.19
  myocardium, myocardial - see
    Myocarditis
  ovary N83.8
  oviduct N83.8
  pancreas K86.8
  penis NEC N48.6
  pericardium I31.0
  perineum, in pregnancy or childbirth
    O34.7-
    causing obstructed labor O65.5
  pleura J94.1
  popliteal fat pad M79.4
  prostate (chronic) – see Hyperplasia,
    prostate
  pulmonary - see also Fibrosis, lung
    congenital P27.8
  rectal sphincter K62.8
  retroperitoneal, idiopathic (with ure-
    teral obstruction) N13.5
    with infection N13.6
  sclerosing mesenteric (idiopathic)
    K65.4
  scrotum N50.8
  seminal vesicle N50.8
  senile R54
  skin L90.5
  spermatic cord N50.8
  spleen D73.89
    in schistosomiasis (bilharziasis) B65.9
      [D77]
  subepidermal nodular - see Neoplasm,
    skin, benign
  submucous (oral) (tongue) K13.5
  testis N44.8
    chronic, due to syphilis A52.76
  thymus (gland) E32.8
  tongue, submucous K13.5
  tunica vaginalis N50.8
  uterus (non-neoplastic) N85.8
  vagina N89.8
  valve, heart - see Endocarditis
  vas deferens N50.8
  vein I87.8
Fibrositis (periarticular) M79.7
  nodular, chronic (Jaccoud's) (rheuma-
    toid) - see Arthropathy, postrheu-
    matic, chronic Fibrothorax
    J94.1
Fibrotic - see Fibrosis
Fibrous - see condition

Fibroxanthoma - see also Neoplasm, con-
    nective tissue, benign
  atypical - see Neoplasm, connective tis-
    sue, uncertain behavior
  malignant - see Neoplasm, connective
    tissue, malignant
Fibroxanthosarcoma - see Neoplasm, con-
    nective tissue, malignant
Fiedler's
  disease (icterohemorrhagic leptospiro-
    sis) A27.0
  myocarditis (acute) I40.1
Fifth disease B08.3
  venereal A55
Filaria, filarial, filariasis –see Infestation,
    filarial
Filatov's disease - see Mononucleosis,
    infectious
File-cutter's disease – see Poisoning,
    lead
Filling defect
  biliary tract R93.2
  bladder R93.4
  duodenum R93.3
  gallbladder R93.2
  gastrointestinal tract R93.3
  intestine R93.3
  kidney R93.4
  stomach R93.3
  ureter R93.4
Fimbrial cyst Q50.4
Financial problem affecting care NOS
    Z59.9
  bankruptcy Z59.8
  foreclosure on loan Z59.8
Findings, abnormal, inconclusive, with-
    out diagnosis - see also Abnormal
  17-ketosteroids, elevated R82.5
  acetonuria R82.4
  alcohol in blood R78.0
  antenatal screening of mother O28.9
    biochemical O28.1
    cytological O28.2
    chromosomal O28.5
    genetic O28.5
    hematological O28.0
    radiological O28.4
    specified NEC O28.8
    ultrasonic O28.3
  anisocytosis R71.8
  antibody titer, elevated R76.0
  bacteriuria N39.0
  bicarbonate E87.8
  bile in urine R82.2
  blood sugar (high) R73.09
    low (transient) E16.2
  casts, urine R82.99
  catecholamines R82.5
  cells, urine R82.99
  chloride E87.8
  cholesterol E78.9
    high E78.0
      with high triglycerides E78.2
  chyluria R82.0
  cloudy
    dialysis effluent R88.0
    urine R82.90
  creatinine clearance R94.4
  crystals, urine R82.99
  culture
    blood R78.81
    positive - see Positive, culture
  echocardiogram R93.1
  electrolyte level, urinary R82.99

Findings, abnormal, inconclusive, without diagnosis *(Continued)*
function study NEC R94.8
bladder R94.8
endocrine NEC R94.7
thyroid R94.6
kidney R94.4
liver R94.5
pancreas R94.8
placenta R94.8
pulmonary R94.2
spleen R94.8
gallbladder, nonvisualization R93.2
glucose (tolerance test) (non-fasting) R73.09
glycosuria R81
heart
shadow R93.1
sounds R01.2
hematinuria R82.3
hematocrit drop (precipitous) R71.0
hemoglobinuria R82.3
human papillomavirus (HPV) DNA test positive
cervix
high risk R87.810
low risk R87.820
vagina
high risk R87.811
low risk R87.821
in blood (of substance not normally found in blood) R78.9
addictive drug NEC R78.4
alcohol (excessive level) R78.0
cocaine R78.2
hallucinogen R78.3
heavy metals (abnormal level) R78.79
lead R78.71
lithium (abnormal level) R78.89
opiate drug R78.1
psychotropic drug R78.5
specified substance NEC R78.89
steroid agent R78.6
indolacetic acid, elevated R82.5
ketonuria R82.4
lactic acid dehydrogenase (LDH) R74.0
liver function test R79.89
mammogram NEC R92.8
calcification (calculus) R92.1
inconclusive result (due to dense breasts) R92.2
microcalcification R92.0
mediastinal shift R93.1
melanin, urine R82.99
myoglobinuria R82.1
neonatal screening P09
nonvisualization of gallbladder R93.2
odor of urine NOS R82.90
Papanicolaou cervix R87.619
pneumoencephalogram R93.0
poikilocytosis R71.8
potassium (deficiency) E87.6
excess E87.5
PPD R76.1
radiologic (X-ray) R93.8
abdomen R93.5
biliary tract R93.2
breast R92.8
gastrointestinal tract R93.3
genitourinary organs R93.4
head R93.0
inconclusive due to excess body fat of patient R93.9
intrathoracic organs NEC R93.1

Findings, abnormal, inconclusive, without diagnosis *(Continued)*
radiologic *(Continued)*
placenta R93.8
retroperitoneum R93.5
skin R93.8
skull R93.0
subcutaneous tissue R93.8
red blood cell (count) (morphology) (sickling) (volume) R71.8
scan NEC R94.8
bladder R94.8
bone R94.8
kidney R94.4
liver R93.2
lung R94.2
pancreas R94.8
placental R94.8
spleen R94.8
thyroid R94.6
sedimentation rate, elevated R70.0
SGOT R74.0
SGPT R74.0
sodium (deficiency) E87.1
excess E87.0
specified body fluid NEC R88.8
stress test R94.39
thyroid (function) (metabolic rate) (scan) (uptake) R94.6
transaminase (level) R74.0
triglycerides E78.9
high E78.1
with high cholesterol E78.2
tuberculin skin test (without active tuberculosis) R76.1
urine R82.90
acetone R82.4
bacteria N39.0
bile R82.2
casts or cells R82.99
chyle R82.0
culture positive R82.7
glucose R81
hemoglobin R82.3
ketone R82.4
sugar R81
vanillylmandelic acid (VMA), elevated R82.5
vectorcardiogram (VCG) R93.1
ventriculogram R93.0
white blood cell (count) (differential) (morphology) D72.9
xerography R92.8
Finger - *see* condition
Fire, Saint Anthony's - *see* Erysipelas
Fire-setting
pathological (compulsive) F63.1
Fish hook stomach K31.89
Fishmeal-worker's lung J67.8
Fissure, fissured
anus, anal K60.2
acute K60.0
chronic K60.1
congenital Q43.8
ear, lobule, congenital Q17.8
epiglottis (congenital) Q31.8
larynx J38.7
congenital Q31.8
lip K13.0
congenital – *see* Cleft, lip
nipple N64.0
associated with
lactation O92.13
pregnancy O92.11-
puerperium O92.12

Fissure, fissured *(Continued)*
nose Q30.2
palate (congenital) - *see* Cleft, palate
skin R23.4
spine (congenital) - *see also* Spina bifida
with hydrocephalus - *see* Spina bifida, by site, with hydrocephalus
tongue (acquired) K14.5
congenital Q38.3
Fistula (cutaneous) L98.8
abdomen (wall) K63.2
bladder N32.2
intestine NEC K63.2
ureter N28.89
uterus N82.5
abdominorectal K63.2
abdominosigmoidal K63.2
abdominothoracic J86.0
abdominouterine N82.5
congenital Q51.7
abdominovesical N32.2
accessory sinuses - *see* Sinusitis
actinomycotic - *see* Actinomycosis
alveolar antrum - *see* Sinusitis, maxillary
alveolar process K04.6
anorectal K60.5
antrobuccal - *see* Sinusitis, maxillary
antrum - *see* Sinusitis, maxillary
anus, anal (recurrent) (infectional) K60.3
congenital Q43.6
with absence, atresia and stenosis Q42.2
tuberculous A18.32
aorta-duodenal I77.2
appendix, appendicular K38.3
arteriovenous (acquired) (nonruptured) I77.0
brain I67.1
congenital Q28.2
ruptured I60.8
ruptured I60.8
cerebral – *see* Fistula, arteriovenous, brain
congenital (peripheral) - *see also* Malformation, arteriovenous
brain Q28.2
ruptured I60.8
coronary Q24.5
pulmonary Q25.7
coronary I25.41
congenital Q24.5
pulmonary I28.0
congenital Q25.7
surgically created (for dialysis) Z99.2
complication - *see* Complication, arteriovenous, fistula, surgically created
traumatic - *see* Injury, blood vessel
artery I77.2
aural (mastoid) – *see* Mastoiditis, chronic
auricle - *see also* Disorder, pinna, specified type NEC
congenital Q18.1
Bartholin's gland N82.8
bile duct (common) (hepatic) K83.3
with calculus, stones - *see* Calculus, bile duct
biliary (tract) - *see* Fistula, bile duct
bladder (sphincter) NEC (*see also* Fistula, vesico-) N32.2
into seminal vesicle N32.2

Fistula *(Continued)*
  bone - *see also* Disorder, bone, specified
      type NEC
    with osteomyelitis, chronic - *see*
        Osteomyelitis, chronic, with
        draining sinus
  brain G93.89
    arteriovenous (acquired) I67.1
      congenital Q28.2
  branchial (cleft) Q18.0
  branchiogenous Q18.0
  breast N61
    puerperal, postpartum or gestational,
        due to mastitis (purulent) - *see*
        Mastitis, obstetric, purulent
  bronchial J86.0
  bronchocutaneous, bronchomediastinal,
      bronchopleural, bronchopleurome-
      diastinal (infective) J86.0
    tuberculous NEC A15.5
  bronchoesophageal J86.0
    congenital Q39.2
      with atresia of esophagus Q39.1
  bronchovisceral J86.0
  buccal cavity (infective) K12.2
  cecosigmoidal K63.2
  cecum K63.2
  cerebrospinal (fluid) G96.0
  cervical, lateral Q18.1
  cervicoaural Q18.1
  cervicosigmoidal N82.4
  cervicovesical N82.1
  cervix N82.8
  chest (wall) J86.0
  cholecystenteric - *see* Fistula,
      gallbladder
  cholecystocolic - *see* Fistula, gallbladder
  cholecystocolonic - *see* Fistula,
      gallbladder
  cholecystoduodenal - *see* Fistula,
      gallbladder
  cholecystogastric - *see* Fistula,
      gallbladder
  cholecystointestinal - *see* Fistula,
      gallbladder
  choledochoduodenal - *see* Fistula, bile
      duct
  cholocolic K82.3
  coccyx - *see* Sinus, pilonidal
  colon K63.2
  colostomy K94.09
  common duct - *see* Fistula, bile duct
  congenital, site not listed - *see* Anomaly,
      by site
  coronary, arteriovenous I25.41
    congenital Q24.5
  costal region J86.0
  cul-de-sac, Douglas' N82.8
  cystic duct - *see also* Fistula, gallbladder
    congenital Q44.5
  dental K04.6
  diaphragm J86.0
  duodenum K31.6
  ear (external) (canal) - *see* Disorder, ear,
      external, specified type NEC
  enterocolic K63.2
  enterocutaneous K63.2
  enterouterine N82.4
    congenital Q51.7
  enterovaginal N82.4
    congenital Q52.2
    large intestine N82.3
    small intestine N82.2
  enterovesical N32.1

Fistula *(Continued)*
  epididymis N50.8
    tuberculous A18.15
  esophagobronchial J86.0
    congenital Q39.2
      with atresia of esophagus Q39.1
  esophagocutaneous K22.8
  esophagopleural-cutaneous J86.0
  esophagotracheal J86.0
    congenital Q39.2
      with atresia of esophagus Q39.1
  esophagus K22.8
    congenital Q39.2
      with atresia of esophagus Q39.1
  ethmoid - *see* Sinusitis, ethmoidal
  eyeball (cornea) (sclera) - *see* Disorder,
      globe, hypotony
  eyelid H01.8
  fallopian tube, external N82.5
  fecal K63.2
    congenital Q43.6
  from periapical abscess K04.6
  frontal sinus - *see* Sinusitis, frontal
  gallbladder K82.3
    with calculus, cholelithiasis, stones -
        see Calculus, gallbladder
  gastric K31.6
  gastrocolic K31.6
    congenital Q40.2
    tuberculous A18.32
  gastroenterocolic K31.6
  gastroesophageal K31.6
  gastrojejunal K31.6
  gastrojejunocolic K31.6
  genital tract (female) N82.9
    specified NEC N82.8
    to intestine NEC N82.4
    to skin N82.5
  hepatic artery-portal vein, congenital
      Q26.6
  hepatopleural J86.0
  hepatopulmonary J86.0
  ileorectal or ileosigmoidal K63.2
  ileovaginal N82.2
  ileovesical N32.1
  ileum K63.2
  in ano K60.3
    tuberculous A18.32
  inner ear (labyrinth) - *see* subcategory
      H83.1
  intestine NEC K63.2
  intestinocolonic (abdominal) K63.2
  intestinoureteral N28.89
  intestinouterine N82.4
  intestinovaginal N82.4
    large intestine N82.3
    small intestine N82.2
  intestinovesical N32.1
  ischiorectal (fossa) K61.3
  jejunum K63.2
  joint M25.10
    ankle M25.17-
    elbow M25.12-
    foot joint M25.17-
    hand joint M25.14-
    hip M25.15-
    knee M25.16-
    shoulder M25.11-
    specified joint NEC M25.18
    tuberculous - *see* Tuberculosis, joint
    wrist M25.13-
  kidney N28.89
  labium (majus) (minus) N82.8
  labyrinth - *see* subcategory H83.1

Fistula *(Continued)*
  lacrimal (gland) (sac) H04.61-
  lacrimonasal duct - *see* Fistula, lacrimal
  laryngotracheal, congenital Q34.8
  larynx J38.7
  lip K13.0
    congenital Q38.0
  lumbar, tuberculous A18.01
  lung J86.0
  lymphatic I89.8
  mammary (gland) N61
  mastoid (process) (region) – *see* Mas-
      toiditis, chronic
  maxillary J32.0
  medial, face and neck Q18.8
  mediastinal J86.0
  mediastinobronchial J86.0
  mediastinocutaneous J86.0
  middle ear - *see* subcategory H74.8
  mouth K12.2
  nasal J34.89
    sinus - *see* Sinusitis
  nasopharynx J39.2
  nipple N64.0
  nose J34.89
  oral (cutaneous) K12.2
    maxillary J32.0
    nasal (with cleft palate) - *see* Cleft,
        palate
  orbit, orbital - *see* Disorder, orbit, speci-
      fied type NEC
  oroantral J32.0
  oviduct, external N82.5
  palate (hard) M27.8
  pancreatic K86.8
  pancreaticoduodenal K86.8
  parotid (gland) K11.4
    region K12.2
  penis N48.89
  perianal K60.3
  pericardium (pleura) (sac) - *see*
      Pericarditis
  pericecal K63.2
  perineorectal K60.4
  perineosigmoidal K63.2
  perineum, perineal (with urethral
      involvement) NEC N36.0
    tuberculous A18.13
    ureter N28.89
  perirectal K60.4
    tuberculous A18.32
  peritoneum K65.9
  pharyngoesophageal J39.2
  pharynx J39.2
    branchial cleft (congenital) Q18.0
  pilonidal (infected) (rectum) - *see* Sinus,
      pilonidal
  pleura, pleural, pleurocutaneous, pleu-
      roperitoneal J86.0
    tuberculous NEC A15.6
  pleuropericardial I31.8
  portal vein-hepatic artery, congenital
      Q26.6
  postauricular H70.81-
  postoperative, persistent T81.83
    specified site - *see* Fistula, by site
  preauricular (congenital) Q18.1
  prostate N42.89
  pulmonary J86.0
    arteriovenous I28.0
      congenital Q25.7
    tuberculous - *see* Tuberculosis,
        pulmonary
  pulmonoperitoneal J86.0

Fistula (*Continued*)
rectolabial N82.4
rectosigmoid (intercommunicating) K63.2
rectoureteral N28.89
rectourethral N36.0
  congenital Q64.73
rectouterine N82.4
  congenital Q51.7
rectovaginal N82.3
  congenital Q52.2
  tuberculous A18.18
rectovesical N32.1
  congenital Q64.79
rectovesicovaginal N82.3
rectovulval N82.4
  congenital Q52.79
rectum (to skin) K60.4
  congenital Q43.6
    with absence, atresia and stenosis Q42.0
  tuberculous A18.32
renal N28.89
retroauricular – *see* Fistula, postauricular
salivary duct or gland (any) K11.4
  congenital Q38.4
scrotum (urinary) N50.8
  tuberculous A18.15
semicircular canals - *see* subcategory H83.1
sigmoid K63.2
  to bladder N32.1
sinus - *see* Sinusitis
skin L98.8
  to genital tract (female) N82.5
splenocolic D73.89
stercoral K63.2
stomach K31.6
sublingual gland K11.4
submandibular gland K11.4
submaxillary (gland) K11.4
  region K12.2
thoracic J86.0
  duct I89.8
thoracoabdominal J86.0
thoracogastric J86.0
thoracointestinal J86.0
thorax J86.0
thyroglossal duct Q89.2
thyroid E07.89
trachea, congenital (external) (internal) Q32.1
tracheoesophageal J86.0
  congenital Q39.2
    with atresia of esophagus Q39.1
  following tracheostomy J95.04
traumatic arteriovenous - *see* Injury, blood vessel, by site
tuberculous - code by site under Tuberculosis
typhoid A01.09
umbilicourinary Q64.8
urachus, congenital Q64.4
ureter (persistent) N28.89
ureteroabdominal N28.89
ureterorectal N28.89
ureterosigmoido-abdominal N28.89
ureterovaginal N82.1
ureterovesical N32.2
urethra N36.0
  congenital Q64.79
  tuberculous A18.13
urethroperineal N36.0

Fistula (*Continued*)
urethroperineovesical N32.2
urethrorectal N36.0
  congenital Q64.73
urethroscrotal N50.8
urethrovaginal N82.1
urethrovesical N32.2
urinary (tract) (persistent) (recurrent) N36.0
uteroabdominal N82.5
  congenital Q51.7
uteroenteric, uterointestinal N82.4
  congenital Q51.7
uterorectal N82.4
  congenital Q51.7
uteroureteric N82.1
uterourethral Q51.7
uterovaginal N82.8
uterovesical N82.1
  congenital Q51.7
uterus N82.8
vagina (postpartal) (wall) N82.8
vaginocutaneous (postpartal) N82.5
vaginointestinal NEC N82.4
  large intestine N82.3
  small intestine N82.2
vaginoperineal N82.5
vasocutaneous, congenital Q55.7
vesical NEC N32.2
vesicoabdominal N32.2
vesicocervicovaginal N82.1
vesicocolic N32.1
vesicocutaneous N32.2
vesicoenteric N32.1
vesicointestinal N32.1
vesicometrorectal N82.4
vesicoperineal N32.2
vesicorectal N32.1
  congenital Q64.79
vesicosigmoidal N32.1
vesicosigmoidovaginal N82.3
vesicoureteral N32.2
vesicoureterovaginal N82.1
vesicourethral N32.2
vesicourethrorectal N32.1
vesicouterine N82.1
  congenital Q51.7
vesicovaginal N82.0
vulvorectal N82.4
  congenital Q52.79
Fit R56.9
  epileptic - *see* Epilepsy
  fainting R55
  hysterical F44.5
  newborn P90
Fitting (and adjustment) (of)
  artificial
    arm - *see* Admission, adjustment, artificial, arm
    breast Z44.3
    eye Z44.2
    leg - *see* Admission, adjustment, artificial, leg
  brain neuropacemaker Z46.2
    implanted Z45.42
  catheter, non-vascular Z46.82
  colostomy belt Z46.89
  contact lenses Z46.0
  cystostomy device Z46.6
  dentures Z46.3
  device NOS Z46.9
    abdominal Z46.89
    gastrointestinal NEC Z46.59
    implanted NEC Z45.89

Fitting (*Continued*)
  device NOS (*Continued*)
    nervous system Z46.2
      implanted - *see* Admission, adjustment, device, implanted, nervous system
    orthodontic Z46.4
    orthoptic Z46.0
    orthotic Z46.89
    prosthetic (external) Z44.9
      breast Z44.3
      dental Z46.3
      eye Z44.2
      specified NEC Z44.8
    specified NEC Z46.89
    substitution
      auditory Z46.2
        implanted - *see* Admission, adjustment, device, implanted, hearing device
      nervous system Z46.2
        implanted - *see* Admission, adjustment, device, implanted, nervous system
      visual Z46.2
        implanted Z45.31
    urinary Z46.6
  gastric lap band Z46.51
  gastrointestinal appliance NEC Z46.59
  glasses (reading) Z46.0
  hearing aid Z46.1
  ileostomy device Z46.89
  insulin pump Z46.81
  intestinal appliance NEC Z46.89
  myringotomy device (stent) (tube) Z45.82
  neuropacemaker Z46.2
    implanted Z45.42
  non-vascular catheter Z46.82
  orthodontic device Z46.4
  orthopedic device (brace) (cast) (corset) (shoes) Z46.89
  pacemaker (cardiac) Z45.018
    nervous system (brain) (peripheral nerve) (spinal cord) Z46.2
      implanted Z45.42
    pulse generator Z45.010
  portacath (port-a-cath) Z45.2
  prosthesis (external) Z44.9
    arm - *see* Admission, adjustment, artificial, arm
    breast Z44.3
    dental Z46.3
    eye Z44.2
    leg - *see* Admission, adjustment, artificial, leg
    specified NEC Z44.8
  spectacles Z46.0
  wheelchair Z46.89
Fitzhugh-Curtis syndrome
  due to
    Chlamydia trachomatis A74.81
    Neisseria gonorrhorea (gonococcal peritonitis) A54.85
Fitz's syndrome (acute hemorrhagic pancreatitis) K85.8
Fixation
  joint - *see* Ankylosis
  larynx J38.7
  stapes - *see* Ankylosis, ear ossicles
    deafness - *see* Deafness, conductive
  uterus (acquired) - *see* Malposition, uterus
  vocal cord J38.3
Flabby ridge K06.8

Flaccid - *see also* condition
  palate, congenital Q38.5
Flail
  chest S22.5-
    newborn (birth injury) P13.8
  joint (paralytic) M25.20
    ankle M25.27-
    elbow M25.22-
    foot joint M25.27-
    hand joint M25.24-
    hip M25.25-
    knee M25.26-
    shoulder M25.21-
    specified joint NEC M25.28
    wrist M25.23-
Flajani's disease - *see* Hyperthyroidism,
    with, goiter (diffuse)
Flashbacks (residual to hallucinogen use)
    F16.283
Flap, liver K71.3
Flat
  chamber (eye) - *see* Disorder, globe,
      hypotony, flat anterior chamber
  chest, congenital Q67.8
  foot (acquired) (fixed type) (painful)
      (postural) - *see also* Deformity,
      limb, flat foot
    rachitic sequelae (late effect) E64.3
  organ or site, congenital NEC - *see*
      Anomaly, by site
  pelvis M95.5
    with disproportion (fetopelvic) O33.0
      causing obstructed labor O65.0
    congenital Q74.2
Flatau-Schilder disease G37.0
Flatback syndrome M40.30
  lumbar region M40.36
  lumbosacral region M40.37
  thoracolumbar region M40.35
Flattening
  head, femur M89.8x5
  hip - *see* Coxa, plana
  lip (congenital) Q18.8
  nose (congenital) Q67.4
    acquired M95.0
Flatulence R14.3
  psychogenic F45.8
Flatus R14.3
  vaginalis N89.8
Flax-dresser's disease J66.1
Flea bite - *see* Injury, bite, insect
Flecks, glaucomatous (subcapsular) - *see*
    Cataract, complicated
Fleischer(-Kayser) ring (cornea) H18.04-
Fleshy mole O02.0
Flexibilitas cerea - *see* Catalepsy
Flexion
  cervix - *see* Malposition, uterus
  contracture, joint - *see* Contraction, joint
  deformity, joint M21.20 - *see also* Defor-
      mity, limb, flexion
    hip, congenital Q65.8
  uterus - *see also* Malposition, uterus
    lateral - *see* Lateroversion, uterus
Flexner-Boyd dysentery A03.2
Flexner's dysentery A03.1
Flexure - *see* Flexion
Flint murmur (aortic insufficiency) I35.1
Floater, vitreous - *see* Opacity, vitreous
Floating
  cartilage (joint) - *see also* Loose, body,
      joint
    knee - *see* Derangement, knee, loose
        body

Floating *(Continued)*
  gallbladder, congenital Q44.1
  kidney N28.89
    congenital Q63.8
  spleen D73.89
Flooding N92.0
Floor - *see* condition
Floppy
  baby syndrome (nonspecific) P94.2
  iris syndrome (intraoperative) (IFIS)
      H21.81
  nonrheumatic mitral valve syndrome
      I34.1
Flu - *see also* Influenza
  avian - *see* Influenza, due to identified
      avian influenza virus
  bird - *see* Influenza, due to identified
      avian influenza virus
  intestinal NEC A08.4
  swine - *see* Influenza, due to identified
      novel H1N1 influenza virus
Fluctuating blood pressure I99.8
Fluid
  abdomen R18.8
  chest J94.8
  heart - *see* Failure, heart, congestive
  joint - *see* Effusion, joint
  loss (acute) E86.9
    with
      hypernatremia E87.0
      hyponatremia E87.1
  lung - *see* Edema, lung
  peritoneal cavity R18.8
  pleural cavity J94.8
  retention E87.7
Flukes NEC - *see also* Infestation, fluke
  blood NEC - *see* Schistosomiasis
  liver B66.3
Fluor (vaginalis) N89.8
  trichomonal or due to Trichomonas
      (vaginalis) A59.00
Fluorosis
  dental K00.3
  skeletal M85.10
    ankle M85.17-
    foot M85.17-
    forearm M85.13-
    hand M85.14-
    lower leg M85.16-
    multiple site M85.19
    neck M85.18
    rib M85.18
    shoulder M85.11-
    skull M85.18
    specified site NEC M85.18
    thigh M85.15-
    toe M85.17-
    upper arm M85.12-
    vertebra M85.18
Flush syndrome E34.0
Flushing R23.2
  menopausal N95.11
Flutter
  atrial or auricular I48.1
  heart I49.8
    atrial or auricular I48.1
    ventricular I49.02
  ventricular I49.02
Fochier's abscess - code by site under
    Abscess
Focus, Assmann's - *see* Tuberculosis,
    pulmonary
Fogo selvagem L10.3
Foix-Alajouanine syndrome G95.19

Fold, folds (anomalous) - *see also* Anom-
    aly, by site
  Descemet's membrane - *see* Change, cor-
      neal membrane, Descemet's, fold
  epicanthic Q10.3
  heart Q24.8
Folie à deux F24
Follicle
  cervix (nabothian) (ruptured) N88.8
  graafian, ruptured, with hemorrhage
      N83.0
  nabothian N88.8
Follicular - *see* condition
Folliculitis (superficial) L73.9
  abscedens et suffodiens L66.3
  cyst N83.0
  decalvans L66.2
  deep - *see* Furuncle, by site
  gonococcal (acute) (chronic) A54.01
  keloid, keloidalis L73.0
  pustular L01.02
  ulerythematosa reticulata L66.4
Folliculome lipidique
  specified site - *see* Neoplasm, benign
  unspecified site
    female D27.9
    male D29.20
Følling's disease E70.0
Follow-up - *see* Examination, follow-up
Fong's syndrome (hereditary osteo-
    onychodysplasia) Q78.5
Food
  allergy L27.2
  asphyxia (from aspiration or inhalation) -
      see Asphyxia, food
  choked on - *see* Asphyxia, food
  deprivation T73.0
    specified kind of food NEC E63.8
  intoxication – *see* Poisoning, food
  lack of T73.0
  poisoning – *see* Poisoning, food
  rejection NEC – *see* Disorder, eating
  strangulation or suffocation - *see* As-
      phyxia, food
  toxemia – *see* Poisoning, food
Foot - *see* condition
Foramen ovale (nonclosure) (patent)
    (persistent) Q21.1
Forbes' glycogen storage disease E74.03
Fordyce-Fox disease L75.2
Fordyce's disease (mouth) Q38.6
Forearm - *see* condition
Foreign body
  with
    laceration - *see* Laceration, by site,
        with foreign body
    puncture wound - *see* Puncture, by
        site, with foreign body
  accidentally left following a procedure
      T81.509
    aspiration T81.506
      resulting in
        adhesions T81.516
        obstruction T81.526
        perforation T81.536
        specified complication NEC
            T81.596
    cardiac catheterization T81.505
      resulting in
        acute reaction T81.60
          aseptic peritonitis T81.61
          specified NEC T81.69
        adhesions T81.515
        obstruction T81.525

Foreign body *(Continued)*
    accidentally left following a procedure
        (Continued)
        cardiac catheterization *(Continued)*
            resulting in *(Continued)*
                perforation T81.535
                specified complication NEC T81.595
        endoscopy T81.504
            resulting in
                adhesions T81.514
                obstruction T81.524
                perforation T81.534
                specified complication NEC T81.594
        immunization T81.503
            resulting in
                adhesions T81.513
                obstruction T81.523
                perforation T81.533
                specified complication NEC T81.593
        infusion T81.501
            resulting in
                adhesions T81.511
                obstruction T81.521
                perforation T81.531
                specified complication NEC T81.591
        injection T81.503
            resulting in
                adhesions T81.513
                obstruction T81.523
                perforation T81.533
                specified complication NEC T81.593
        kidney dialysis T81.502
            resulting in
                adhesions T81.512
                obstruction T81.522
                perforation T81.532
                specified complication NEC T81.592
        packing removal T81.507
            resulting in
                acute reaction T81.60
                    aseptic peritonitis T81.61
                    specified NEC T81.69
                adhesions T81.517
                obstruction T81.527
                perforation T81.537
                specified complication NEC
                    T81.597
        puncture T81.506
            resulting in
                adhesions T81.516
                obstruction T81.526
                perforation T81.536
                specified complication NEC
                    T81.596
        specified procedure NEC T81.508
            resulting in
                acute reaction T81.60
                    aseptic peritonitis T81.61
                    specified NEC T81.69
                adhesions T81.518
                obstruction T81.528
                perforation T81.538
                specified complication NEC
                    T81.598
        surgical operation T81.500
            resulting in
                acute reaction T81.60
                    aseptic peritonitis T81.61
                    specified NEC T81.69
                adhesions T81.510
                obstruction T81.520
                perforation T81.530
                specified complication NEC
                    T81.590

Foreign body *(Continued)*
    accidentally left following a procedure
        (Continued)
        transfusion T81.501
            resulting in
                adhesions T81.511
                obstruction T81.521
                perforation T81.531
                specified complication NEC
                    T81.591
            causing
                acute reaction T81.60
                    aseptic peritonitis T81.61
                    specified complication NEC
                        T81.69
                adhesions T81.519
                aseptic peritonitis T81.61
                obstruction T81.529
                perforation T81.539
                specified complication NEC
                    T81.599
    alimentary tract T18.9
        anus T18.5
        colon T18.4
        esophagus - *see* Foreign body,
            esophagus
        mouth T18.0
        multiple sites T18.8
        rectosigmoid (junction) T18.5
        rectum T18.5
        small intestine T18.3
        specified site NEC T18.8
        stomach T18.2
    anterior chamber (eye) S05.5-
    auditory canal – *see* Foreign body, enter-
        ing through orifice, ear
    bronchus T17.508
        causing
            asphyxiation T17.500
                food (bone) (seed) T17.520
                gastric contents (vomitus)
                    T17.510
                specified type NEC T17.590
            injury NEC T17.508
                food (bone) (seed) T17.528
                gastric contents (vomitus)
                    T17.518
                specified type NEC T17.598
    canthus – *see* Foreign body, conjunctival
        sac
    ciliary body (eye) S05.5-
    conjunctival sac T15.1-
    cornea T15.0-
    entering through orifice
        accessory sinus T17.0
        alimentary canal T18.9
            multiple parts T18.8
            specified part NEC T18.8
        alveolar process T18.0
        antrum (Highmore's) T17.0
        anus T18.5
        appendix T18.4
        auditory canal – *see* Foreign body,
            entering through orifice, ear
        auricle – *see* Foreign body, entering
            through orifice, ear
        bladder T19.1
        bronchioles - *see* Foreign body, respi-
            ratory tract, specified site NEC
        bronchus (main) - *see* Foreign body,
            bronchus
        buccal cavity T18.0
        canthus (inner) – *see* Foreign body,
            conjunctival sac

Foreign body *(Continued)*
    entering through orifice *(Continued)*
        cecum T18.4
        cervix (canal) (uteri) T19.3
        colon T18.4
        conjunctival sac – *see* Foreign body,
            conjunctival sac
        cornea – *see* Foreign body, cornea
        digestive organ or tract NOS T18.9
            multiple parts T18.8
            specified part NEC T18.8
        duodenum T18.3
        ear (external) T16.-
        esophagus - *see* Foreign body,
            esophagus
        eye (external) NOS T15.90
            conjunctival sac – *see* Foreign body,
                conjunctival sac
            cornea – *see* Foreign body, cornea
            specified part NEC T15.8-
        eyeball – *see also* Foreign body,
            entering through orifice, eye,
            specified part NEC
            with penetrating wound – *see*
                Puncture, eyeball
        eyelid – *see also* Foreign body,
            conjunctival sac
            with
                laceration – *see* Laceration,
                    eyelid, with foreign body
                puncture – *see* Puncture, eyelid,
                    with foreign body
                superficial injury – *see* Foreign
                    body, superficial, eyelid
        gastrointestinal tract T18.9
            multiple parts T18.8
            specified part NEC T18.8
        genitourinary tract T19.9
            multiple parts T19.8
            specified part NEC T19.8
        globe – *see* Foreign body, entering
            through orifice, eyeball
        gum T18.0
        Highmore's antrum T17.0
        hypopharynx - *see* Foreign body,
            pharynx
        ileum T18.3
        intestine (small) T18.3
            large T18.4
        lacrimal apparatus (punctum) –
            see Foreign body, entering
            through orifice, eye, specified
            part NEC
        large intestine T18.4
        larynx - *see* Foreign body, larynx
        lung - *see* Foreign body, respiratory
            tract, specified site NEC
        maxillary sinus T17.0
        mouth T18.0
        nasal sinus T17.0
        nasopharynx - *see* Foreign body,
            pharynx
        nose (passage) T17.1
        nostril T17.1
        oral cavity T18.0
        palate T18.0
        penis T19.8
        pharynx - *see* Foreign body, pharynx
        piriform sinus - *see* Foreign body,
            pharynx
        rectosigmoid (junction) T18.5
        rectum T18.5
        respiratory tract - *see* Foreign body,
            respiratory tract

243

Foreign body *(Continued)*
  entering through orifice *(Continued)*
    sinus (accessory) (frontal) (maxillary) (nasal) T17.0
      piriform - *see* Foreign body, pharynx
    small intestine T18.3
    stomach T18.2
    suffocation by - *see* Asphyxia, food
    tear ducts or glands – *see* Foreign body, entering through orifice, eye, specified part NEC
    throat - *see* Foreign body, pharynx
    tongue T18.0
    tonsil, tonsillar (fossa) - *see* Foreign body, pharynx
    trachea - *see* Foreign body, trachea
    ureter T19.8
    urethra T19.0
    uterus (any part) T19.3
    vagina T19.2
    vulva T19.2
  esophagus T18.108
    causing
      injury NEC T18.108
        food (bone) (seed) T18.128
        gastric contents (vomitus) T18.118
        specified type NEC T18.198
      tracheal compression T18.100
        food (bone) (seed) T18.120
        gastric contents (vomitus) T18.110
        specified type NEC T18.190
  felling of, in throat R09.89
  genitourinary tract T19.9
    bladder T19.1
    multiple parts T19.8
    penis T19.4
    specified site NEC T19.8
    urethra T19.0
    uterus T19.3
      IUD Z97.5
    vagina T19.2
      contraceptive device Z97.5
    vulva T19.2
  granuloma (old) (soft tissue) - *see also* Granuloma, foreign body
    skin L92.3
  in
    laceration - *see* Laceration, by site, with foreign body
    puncture wound - *see* Puncture, by site, with foreign body
    soft tissue (residual) M79.5
  inadvertently left in operation wound – *see* Foreign body, accidentally left during a procedure
  ingestion, ingested NOS T18.9
  inhalation or inspiration - *see* Asphyxia, food
  internal organ, not entering through a natural orifice - code as specific injury with foreign body
  intraocular S05.5-
    old, retained (nonmagnetic) H44.70-
      anterior chamber H44.71-
      ciliary body H44.72-
      iris H44.72-
      lens H44.73-
      magnetic H44.60-
        anterior chamber H44.61-
        ciliary body H44.62-
        iris H44.62-

Foreign body *(Continued)*
  intraocular *(Continued)*
    old, retained *(Continued)*
      magnetic *(Continued)*
        lens H44.63-
        posterior wall H44.64-
        specified site NEC H44.69-
        vitreous body H44.65-
      posterior wall H44.74-
      specified site NEC H44.79-
      vitreous body H44.75-
    iris – *see* Foreign body, intraocular
    lacrimal punctum – *see* Foreign body, entering through orifice, eye, specified part NEC
  larynx T17.308
    causing
      asphyxiation T17.300
        food (bone) (seed) T17.320
        gastric contents (vomitus) T17.310
        specified type NEC T17.390
      injury NEC T17.308
        food (bone) (seed) T17.328
        gastric contents (vomitus) T17.318
        specified type NEC T17.398
    lens – *see* Foreign body, intraocular
  ocular muscle S05.4-
    old, retained - *see* Foreign body, orbit, old
  old or residual
    soft tissue (residual) M79.5
  operation wound, left accidentally – *see* Foreign body, accidentally left during a procedure
  orbit S05.4-
    old, retained H05.5-
  pharynx T17.208
    causing
      asphyxiation T17.200
        food (bone) (seed) T17.220
        gastric contents (vomitus) T17.210
        specified type NEC T17.290
      injury NEC T17.208
        food (bone) (seed) T17.228
        gastric contents (vomitus) T17.218
        specified type NEC T17.298
  respiratory tract T17.908
    bronchioles - *see* Foreign body, respiratory tract, specified site NEC
    bronchus - *see* Foreign body, bronchus
    causing
      asphyxiation T17.900
        food (bone) (seed) T17.920
        gastric contents (vomitus) T17.910
        specified type NEC T17.990
      injury NEC T17.908
        food (bone) (seed) T17.928
        gastric contents (vomitus) T17.918
        specified type NEC T17.998
    larynx - *see* Foreign body, larynx
    lung - *see* Foreign body, respiratory tract, specified site NEC
    multiple parts - *see* Foreign body, respiratory tract, specified site NEC
    nasal sinus T17.0
    nasopharynx - *see* Foreign body, pharynx
    nose T17.1

Foreign body *(Continued)*
  respiratory tract *(Continued)*
    nostril T17.1
    pharynx - *see* Foreign body, pharynx
    specified site NEC T17.808
      causing
        asphyxiation T17.800
          food (bone) (seed) T17.820
          gastric contents (vomitus) T17.810
          specified type NEC T17.890
        injury NEC T17.808
          food (bone) (seed) T17.828
          gastric contents (vomitus) T17.818
          specified type NEC T17.898
    throat - *see* Foreign body, pharynx
    trachea - *see* Foreign body, trachea
  retained (old) (nonmagnetic) (in)
    anterior chamber (eye) - *see* Foreign body, intraocular, old, retained, anterior chamber
      magnetic - *see* Foreign body, intraocular, old, retained, magnetic, anterior chamber
    ciliary body - *see* Foreign body, intraocular, old, retained, ciliary body
      magnetic - *see* Foreign body, intraocular, old, retained, magnetic, ciliary body
    eyelid H02.819
      left H02.816
        lower H02.815
        upper H02.814
      right H02.813
        lower H02.812
        upper H02.811
    globe - *see* Foreign body, intraocular, old, retained
      magnetic - *see* Foreign body, intraocular, old, retained, magnetic
    intraocular - *see* Foreign body, intraocular, old, retained
      magnetic - *see* Foreign body, intraocular, old, retained, magnetic
    iris - *see* Foreign body, intraocular, old, retained, iris
      magnetic - *see* Foreign body, intraocular, old, retained, magnetic, iris
    lens - *see* Foreign body, intraocular, old, retained, lens
      magnetic - *see* Foreign body, intraocular, old, retained, magnetic, lens
    muscle - *see* Foreign body, retained, soft tissue
    orbit - *see* Foreign body, orbit, old
    posterior wall of globe - *see* Foreign body, intraocular, old, retained, posterior wall
      magnetic - *see* Foreign body, intraocular, old, retained, magnetic, posterior wall
    retrobulbar - *see* Foreign body, orbit, old, retrobulbar
    soft tissue M79.5
    vitreous - *see* Foreign body, intraocular, old, retained, vitreous body
      magnetic - *see* Foreign body, intraocular, old, retained, magnetic, vitreous body
  retina S05.5-

Foreign body *(Continued)*
  superficial, without open wound
    abdomen, abdominal (wall) S30.851
    alveolar process S00.552
    ankle S90.55-
    antecubital space – *see* Foreign body,
      superficial, forearm
    anus S30.857
    arm (upper) S40.85-
    auditory canal – *see* Foreign body,
      superficial, ear
    auricle – *see* Foreign body, superficial,
      ear
    axilla – *see* Foreign body, superficial,
      arm
    back, lower S30.850
    breast S20.15-
    brow S00.85
    buttock S30.850
    calf – *see* Foreign body, superficial, leg
    canthus – *see* Foreign body, superfi-
      cial, eyelid
    cheek S00.85
      internal S00.552
    chest wall – *see* Foreign body, superfi-
      cial, thorax
    chin S00.85
    clitoris S30.854
    costal region - *see* Foreign body,
      superficial, thorax
    digit(s)
      hand – *see* Foreign body, superfi-
        cial, finger
      foot - *see* Foreign body, superficial,
        toe
    ear S00.45-
    elbow S50.35-
    epididymis S30.853
    epigastric region S30.851
    epiglottis S10.15
    esophagus, cervical S10.15
    eyebrow – *see* Foreign body, superfi-
      cial, eyelid
    eyelid S00.25-
    face S00.85
    finger(s) S60.459
      index S60.45-
      little S60.45-
      middle S60.45-
      ring S60.45-
    flank S30.851
    foot (except toe(s) alone) S90.85-
      toe - *see* Foreign body, superficial,
        toe
    forearm S50.85-
      elbow only – *see* Foreign body,
        superficial, elbow
    forehead S00.85
    genital organs, external
      female S30.856
      male S30.855
    groin S30.851
    gum S00.552
    hand S60.55-
    head S00.95
      ear - *see* Foreign body, superficial,
        ear
      eyelid - *see* Foreign body, superfi-
        cial, eyelid
      lip S00.551
      nose S00.35
      oral cavity S00.552
      scalp S00.05
      specified site NEC S00.85

Foreign body *(Continued)*
  superficial, without open wound
    (Continued)
    heel – *see* Foreign body, superficial,
      foot
    hip S70.25-
    inguinal region S30.851
    interscapular region S20.459
    jaw S00.85
    knee S80.25-
    labium (majus) (minus) S30.854
    larynx S10.15
    leg (lower) S80.85-
      knee – *see* Foreign body, superficial,
        knee
      upper - *see* Foreign body, superfi-
        cial, thigh
    lip S00.551
    lower back S30.850
    lumbar region S30.850
    malar region S00.85
    mammary – *see* Foreign body, superfi-
      cial, breast
    mastoid region S00.85
    mouth S00.552
    nail
      finger – *see* Foreign body, superfi-
        cial, finger
      toe – *see* Foreign body, superficial,
        toe
    nape S10.85
    nasal S00.35
    neck S10.95
      specified site NEC S10.85
      throat S10.15
    nose S00.35
    occipital region S00.05
    oral cavity S00.552
    orbital region – *see* Foreign body,
      superficial, eyelid
    palate S00.552
    palm – *see* Foreign body, superficial,
      hand
    parietal region S00.05
    pelvis S30.850
    penis S30.852
    perineum
      female S30.854
      male S30.850
    periocular area – *see* Foreign body,
      superficial, eyelid
    phalanges
      finger – *see* Foreign body, superfi-
        cial, finger
      toe – *see* Foreign body, superficial,
        toe
    pharynx S10.15
    pinna – *see* Foreign body, superficial,
      ear
    popliteal space – *see* Foreign body,
      superficial, knee
    prepuce S30.852
    pubic region S30.850
    pudendum
      female S30.856
      male S30.855
    sacral region S30.850
    scalp S00.05
    scapular region – *see* Foreign body,
      superficial, shoulder
    scrotum S30.853
    shin – *see* Foreign body, superficial,
      leg
    shoulder S40.25-

Foreign body *(Continued)*
  superficial, without open wound
    (Continued)
    sternal region S20.359
    submaxillary region S00.85
    submental region S00.85
    subungual
      finger(s) – *see* Foreign body, super-
        ficial, finger
      toe(s) – *see* Foreign body, superfi-
        cial, toe
    supraclavicular fossa S10.85
    supraorbital S00.85
    temple S00.85
    temporal region S00.85
    testis S30.853
    thigh S70.35-
    thorax, thoracic (wall) S20.95
      back S20.45-
      front S20.35-
    throat S10.15
    thumb S60.35-
    toe(s) (lesser) S90.456
      great S90.45-
    tongue S00.552
    trachea S10.15
    tunica vaginalis S30.853
    tympanum, tympanic membrane
      – *see* Foreign body, superficial,
      ear
    uvula S00.552
    vagina S30.854
    vocal cords S10.15
    vulva S30.854
    wrist S60.85-
  swallowed T18.9
  trachea T17.408
    causing
      asphyxiation T17.400
        food (bone) (seed) T17.420
        gastric contents (vomitus)
          T17.410
        specified type NEC T17.490
      injury NEC T17.408
        food (bone) (seed) T17.428
        gastric contents (vomitus)
          T17.418
        specified type NEC T17.498
  vitreous (humor) S05.5-
Forestier's disease (rhizomelic pseudopolyarthritis) M35.3 - meaning
  ankylosing hyperostosis - *see*
  Hyperostosis, ankylosing
Formation
  hyalin in cornea - *see* Degeneration,
    cornea
  sequestrum in bone (due to infection) -
    see Osteomyelitis, chronic
  valve
    colon, congenital Q43.8
    ureter (congenital) Q62.39
Formication R20.2
Fort Bragg fever A27.89
Fossa - *see also* condition
  pyriform - *see* condition
Fothergill's
  disease (trigeminal neuralgia) - *see also*
    Neuralgia, trigeminal
  scarlatina anginosa A38.9
Foul breath R19.6
Foundling Z76.1
Fournier's disease or gangrene
  N49.3
  female N76.89

Fourth
  cranial nerve - *see* condition
  molar K00.1
Foville's (peduncular) disease or syndrome G46.3
Fox(-Fordyce) disease (apocrine miliaria) L75.2
Fracture, burst - *see* Fracture, traumatic, by site
Fracture, chronic - *see* Fracture, pathological
Fracture, insufficiency - *see* Fracture, pathologic, by site
Fracture, pathological (pathologic) M84.40
  - *see also* Fracture, traumatic
  ankle M84.47-
  carpus M84.44-
  clavicle M84.41-
  dental implant M27.63
  dental restorative material K08.539
    with loss of material K08.531
    without loss of material K08.530
  due to
    neoplastic disease NEC (*see also* Neoplasm) M84.50
      ankle M84.57-
      carpus M84.54-
      clavicle M84.51-
      femur M84.55-
      fibula M84.56-
      finger M84.54-
      hip M84.559
      humerus M84.52-
      ilium M84.550
      ischium M84.550
      metacarpus M84.54-
      metatarsus M84.57-
      neck M84.58
      pelvis M84.550
      radius M84.53-
      rib M84.58
      scapula M84.51-
      skull M84.58
      tarsus M84.57-
      tibia M84.56-
      toe M84.57-
      ulna M84.53-
      vertebra M84.58
    osteoporosis M80.80
      disuse - *see* Osteoporosis, specified type NEC, with pathological fracture
      drug-induced - *see* Osteoporosis, drug induced, with pathological fracture
      idiopathic - *see* Osteoporosis, specified type NEC, with pathological fracture
      postmenopausal - *see* Osteoporosis, postmenopausal, with pathological fracture
      postoophorectomy - *see* Osteoporosis, postoophorectomy, with pathological fracture
      postsurgical malabsorption - *see* Osteoporosis, specified type NEC, with pathological fracture
      specified cause NEC - *see* Osteoporosis, specified type NEC, with pathological fracture
    specified disease NEC M84.60
      ankle M84.67-
      carpus M84.64-
      clavicle M84.61-

Fracture, pathologic (*Continued*)
  due to (*Continued*)
    specified disease NEC (*Continued*)
      femur M84.65-
      fibula M84.66-
      finger M84.64-
      hip M84.65-
      humerus M84.62-
      ilium M84.650
      ischium M84.650
      metacarpus M84.64-
      metatarsus M84.67-
      neck M84.68
      radius M84.63-
      rib M84.68
      scapula M84.61-
      skull M84.68
      tarsus M84.67-
      tibia M84.66-
      toe M84.67-
      ulna M84.63-
      vertebra M84.68
  femur M84.45-
  fibula M84.46-
  finger M84.44-
  hip M84.459
  humerus M84.42-
  ilium M84.454
  ischium M84.454
  joint prosthesis - *see* Complications, joint prosthesis, mechanical, breakdown, by site
    periprosthetic - *see* Complications, joint prosthesis, mechanical, periprosthesis, fracture, by site
  metacarpus M84.44-
  metatarsus M84.47-
  neck M84.48
  pelvis M84.454
  radius M84.43-
  restorative material (dental) K08.539
    with loss of material K08.531
    without loss of material K08.530
  rib M84.48
  scapula M84.41-
  skull M84.48
  tarsus M84.47-
  tibia M84.46-
  toe M84.47-
  ulna M84.43-
  vertebra M84.48
Fracture, traumatic (abduction) (adduction) (separation) (*see also* Fracture, pathological) T14.8
  acetabulum S32.409
    column
      anterior (displaced) (iliopubic) S32.43-
        nondisplaced S32.436
      posterior (displaced) (ilioischial) S32.443
        nondisplaced S32.44-
    dome (displaced) S32.48-
      nondisplaced S32.48
    specified NEC S32.49-
    transverse (displaced) S32.45-
      with associated posterior wall fracture (displaced) S32.46-
        nondisplaced S32.46-
      nondisplaced S32.45-
    wall
      anterior (displaced) S32.41-
        nondisplaced S32.41-
      medial (displaced) S32.47-
        nondisplaced S32.47-

Fracture, traumatic (*Continued*)
  acetabulum (*Continued*)
    wall (*Continued*)
      posterior (displaced) S32.42-
        with associated transverse fracture (displaced) S32.46-
          nondisplaced S32.46-
        nondisplaced S32.42-
  acromion – *see* Fracture, scapula, acromial process
  alveolus S02.83
    mandible S02.82
    maxilla S02.81
  ankle S82.899
    bimalleolar (displaced) S82.84-
      nondisplaced S82.84-
    lateral malleolus only (displaced) S82.6-
      nondisplaced S82.6-
    medial malleolus (displaced) S82.5-
      associated with Maisonneuve's fracture - *see* Fracture, Maisonneuve's
      nondisplaced S82.5-
    talus - *see* Fracture, tarsal, talus
    trimalleolar (displaced) S82.85-
      nondisplaced S82.85-
  arm (upper) – *see also* Fracture, humerus, shaft
    humerus – *see* Fracture, humerus
    radius – *see* Fracture, radius
    ulna – *see* Fracture, ulna
  astragalus – *see* Fracture, tarsal, talus
  atlas - *see* Fracture, neck, cervical vertebra, first
  axis - *see* Fracture, neck, cervical vertebra, second
  back - *see* Fracture, vertebra
  Barton's – *see* Barton's fracture
  base of skull - *see* Fracture, skull, base
  Bennett's - *see* Bennett's fracture
  bimalleolar - *see* Fracture, ankle, bimalleolar
  blow-out S02.3
  bone NEC T14.8
    birth injury P13.9
    following insertion of orthopedic implant, joint prosthesis or bone plate - *see* Fracture, following insertion of orthopedic implant, joint prosthesis or bone plate
    in (due to) neoplastic disease NEC - *see* Fracture, pathological, due to, neoplastic disease
    pathological (cause unknown) -*see* Fracture, pathological
  breast bone - *see* Fracture, sternum
  bucket handle (semilunar cartilage) - *see* Tear, meniscus
  burst - *see* Fracture, traumatic, by site
  calcaneus - *see* Fracture, tarsal, calcaneus
  carpal bone(s) S62.109
    capitate (displaced) S62.13-
      nondisplaced S62.13-
    cuneiform - *see* Fracture, carpal bone, triquetrum
    hamate (body) (displaced) S62.143
      hook process (displaced) S62.15-
        nondisplaced S62.15-
      nondisplaced S62.14-
    larger multangular - *see* Fracture, carpal bones, trapezium

Fracture, traumatic *(Continued)*
  carpal bone(s) *(Continued)*
    lunate (displaced) S62.12-
      nondisplaced S62.12-
    navicular S62.00-
      distal pole (displaced) S62.01-
        nondisplaced S62.01-
      middle third (displaced) S62.02-
        nondisplaced S62.02-
      proximal third (displaced) S62.03-
        nondisplaced S62.03-
      volar tuberosity - *see* Fracture,
        carpal bones, navicular, distal
        pole
    os magnum - *see* Fracture, carpal
      bones, capitate
    pisiform (displaced) S62.16-
      nondisplaced S62.16-
    semilunar - *see* Fracture, carpal bones,
      lunate
    smaller multangular - *see* Fracture,
      carpal bones, trapezoid
    trapezium (displaced) S62.17-
      nondisplaced S62.17-
    trapezoid (displaced) S62.18-
      nondisplaced S62.18-
    triquetrum (displaced) S62.11-
      nondisplaced S62.11-
    unciform - *see* Fracture, carpal bones,
      hamate
  cervical - *see* Fracture, vertebra, cervical
  clavicle S42.00-
    acromial end (displaced) S42.03-
      nondisplaced S42.03-
    birth injury P13.4
    lateral end - *see* Fracture, clavicle,
      acromial end
    shaft (displaced) S42.02-
      nondisplaced S42.02-
    sternal end (anterior) (displaced)
      S42.01-
      nondisplaced S42.01-
      posterior S42.01-
  coccyx S32.2
  collapsed – *see* Collapse, vertebra
  collar bone - *see* Fracture, clavicle
  Colles' - *see* Colles' fracture
  compression, not due to trauma – *see*
    Collapse, vertebra
  coronoid process – *see* Fracture, ulna,
    upper end, coronoid process
  corpus cavernosum penis S39.840
  costochondral cartilage S23.41
  costochondral, costosternal junction -
    see Fracture, rib
  cranium - *see* Fracture, skull
  cricoid cartilage S12.8
  cuboid (ankle) – *see* Fracture, tarsal,
    cuboid
  cuneiform
    foot – *see* Fracture, tarsal, cuneiform
    wrist - *see* Fracture, carpal, triquetrum
  delayed union - *see* Delay, union,
    fracture
  dental restorative material K08.539
    with loss of material K08.531
    without loss of material K08.530
  due to
    birth injury - *see* Birth, injury, fracture
    osteoporosis – *see* Osteoporosis, with
      fracture
  Dupuytren's – *see* Fracture, ankle,
    lateral malleolus
  elbow S42.40-

Fracture, traumatic *(Continued)*
  ethmoid (bone) (sinus) – *see* Fracture,
    skull, base
  face bone S02.92
  fatigue - *see also* Fracture, stress
    vertebra M48.40
      cervical region M48.42
      cervicothoracic region M48.43
      lumbar region M48.46
      lumbosacral region M48.47
      occipito-atlanto-axial region
        M48.41
      sacrococcygeal region M48.48
      thoracic region M48.44
      thoracolumbar region M48.45
  femur, femoral S72.9-
    birth injury P13.2
    capital epiphyseal S79.01-
    condyles, epicondyles - *see* Fracture,
      femur, lower end
    distal end - *see* Fracture, femur,
      lower end
    epiphysis
      head - *see* Fracture, femur, upper
        end, epiphysis
      lower - *see* Fracture, femur, lower
        end, epiphysis
      upper - *see* Fracture, femur, upper
        end, epiphysis
    following insertion of implant, pros-
      thesis or plate M96.66-
    head - *see* Fracture, femur, upper end,
      head
    intertrochanteric - *see* Fracture, femur,
      trochanteric
    intratrochanteric - *see* Fracture, femur,
      trochanteric
    lower end S72.40-
      condyle (displaced) S72.41-
        lateral (displaced) S72.42-
          nondisplaced S72.42-
        medial (displaced) S72.43-
          nondisplaced S72.43-
        nondisplaced S72.41-
      epiphysis (displaced) S72.44-
        nondisplaced S72.44-
      physeal S79.10-
        Salter-Harris
          Type I S79.11-
          Type II S79.12-
          Type III S79.13-
          Type IV S79.14-
        specified NEC S79.19-
      specified NEC S72.49-
      supracondylar (displaced)
        S72.45-
        with intracondylar extension
          (displaced) S72.46-
          nondisplaced S72.46-
        nondisplaced S72.45-
      torus S72.47-
    neck - *see* Fracture, femur, upper end,
      neck
    pertrochanteric - *see* Fracture, femur,
      trochanteric
    shaft (lower third) (middle third)
      (upper third) S72.30-
      comminuted (displaced) S72.35-
        nondisplaced S72.35-
      oblique (displaced) S72.33-
        nondisplaced S72.33-
      segmental (displaced) S72.36-
        nondisplaced S72.36-
      specified NEC S72.39-

Fracture, traumatic *(Continued)*
  femur, femoral *(Continued)*
    shaft *(Continued)*
      spiral (displaced) S72.34-
        nondisplaced S72.34-
      transverse (displaced) S72.32-
        nondisplaced S72.32-
    specified site NEC - *see* subcategory
      S72.8
    subcapital (displaced) S72.01-
    subtrochanteric (region) (section)
      (displaced) S72.2-
      nondisplaced S72.2-
    transcervical - *see* Fracture, femur,
      upper end, neck
    transtrochanteric - *see* Fracture,
      femur, trochanteric
    trochanteric S72.10-
      apophyseal (displaced) S72.14-
        nondisplaced S72.14-
      greater trochanter (displaced)
        S72.11-
        nondisplaced S72.11-
      intertrochanteric (displaced) S72.13-
        nondisplaced S72.13-
      lesser trochanter (displaced)
        S72.12-
        nondisplaced S72.12-
    upper end S72.00-
      apophyseal (displaced) S72.13-
        nondisplaced S72.13-
      cervicotrochanteric - *see* Fracture,
        femur, upper end, neck, base
      epiphysis (displaced) S72.02-
        nondisplaced S72.02-
      head S72.05-
        articular (displaced) S72.06-
          nondisplaced S72.06-
        specified NEC S72.09-
      intertrochanteric (displaced)
        S72.14-
        nondisplaced S72.14-
      intracapsular S72.01-
      midcervical (displaced) S72.03-
        nondisplaced S72.03-
      neck S72.00-
        base (displaced) S72.04-
          nondisplaced S72.04-
        specified NEC S72.09-
      pertrochanteric - *see* Fracture,
        femur, upper end, trochanteric
      physeal S79.00-
        Salter-Harris type I S79.01-
        specified NEC S79.09-
      subcapital (displaced) S72.01-
      subtrochanteric (displaced) S72.2-
        nondisplaced S72.2-
      transcervical - *see* Fracture, femur,
        upper end, midcervical
      trochanteric S72.10-
        greater (displaced) S72.11-
          nondisplaced S72.11-
        lesser (displaced) S72.12-
          nondisplaced S72.12-
  fibula (shaft) (styloid) S82.40-
    comminuted (displaced) S82.45-
      nondisplaced S82.45-
    following insertion of implant, pros-
      thesis or plate M96.67-
    involving ankle or malleolus –
      see Fracture, fibula, lateral
      malleolus
    lateral malleolus (displaced) S82.6-
      nondisplaced S82.6-

Fracture, traumatic (Continued)
  fibula (Continued)
    lower end
      physeal S89.30-
        Salter-Harris
          Type I S89.31-
          Type II S89.32-
        specified NEC S89.39-
      specified NEC S82.83-
      torus S82.82-
    oblique (displaced) S82.43-
      nondisplaced S82.43-
    segmental (displaced) S82.46-
      nondisplaced S82.46-
    specified NEC S82.49-
    spiral (displaced) S82.44-
      nondisplaced S82.44-
    transverse (displaced) S82.42-
      nondisplaced S82.42-
    upper end
      physeal S89.20-
        Salter-Harris
          Type I S89.21-
          Type II S89.22-
        specified NEC S89.29-
      specified NEC S82.83-
      torus S82.81-
  finger (except thumb) S62.60-
    distal phalanx (displaced) S62.63-
      nondisplaced S62.66-
    index S62.60-
      distal phalanx (displaced) S62.63-
        nondisplaced S62.66-
      medial phalanx (displaced) S62.62-
        nondisplaced S62.65-
      proximal phalanx (displaced)
        S62.61-
        nondisplaced S62.64-
    little S62.60-
      distal phalanx (displaced) S62.63-
        nondisplaced S62.66-
      medial phalanx (displaced) S62.62-
        nondisplaced S62.65-
      proximal phalanx (displaced)
        S62.61-
        nondisplaced S62.64-
    medial phalanx (displaced) S62.62-
      nondisplaced S62.65-
    middle S62.60-
      distal phalanx (displaced) S62.63-
        nondisplaced S62.66-
      medial phalanx (displaced) S62.62-
        nondisplaced S62.65-
      proximal phalanx (displaced)
        S62.61-
        nondisplaced S62.64-
    proximal phalanx (displaced) S62.61-
      nondisplaced S62.64-
    ring S62.60-
      distal phalanx (displaced) S62.63-
        nondisplaced S62.66-
      medial phalanx (displaced) S62.62-
        nondisplaced S62.65-
      proximal phalanx (displaced)
        S62.61-
        nondisplaced S62.64-
    thumb – see Fracture, thumb
  following insertion (intraoperative)
    (postoperative) of orthopedic
    implant, joint prosthesis or bone
    plate M96.69
    femur M96.66-
    fibula M96.67-
    humerus M96.62-

Fracture, traumatic (Continued)
  following insertion (intraoperative)
    (postoperative) of orthopedic
    implant, joint prosthesis or bone
    plate (Continued)
    pelvis M96.65
    radius M96.63-
    specified bone NEC M96.69
    tibia M96.67-
    ulna M96.63-
  foot S92.90-
    astragalus - see Fracture, tarsal, talus
    calcaneus – see Fracture, tarsal,
      calcaneus
    cuboid – see Fracture, tarsal, cuboid
    cuneiform - see Fracture, tarsal,
      cuneiform
    metatarsal – see Fracture, metatarsal
    navicular – see Fracture, tarsal,
      navicular
    talus – see Fracture, tarsal, talus
    tarsal – see Fracture, tarsal
    toe – see Fracture, toe
  forearm S52.9-
    radius – see Fracture, radius
    ulna – see Fracture, ulna
  fossa (anterior) (middle) (posterior)
    S02.19
  frontal (bone) (skull) S02.0
    sinus S02.19
  glenoid (cavity) (scapula) – see Fracture,
    scapula, glenoid cavity
  greenstick - see Fracture, by site
  hallux – see Fracture, toe, great
  hand S62.9-
    carpal – see Fracture, carpal bone
    finger (except thumb) – see Fracture,
      finger
    metacarpal – see Fracture, metacarpal
    navicular (scaphoid) (hand) – see
      Fracture, carpal bone, navicular
    thumb - see Fracture, thumb
  healed or old
    with complications - code by Nature
      of the complication
  heel bone - see Fracture, tarsal, calcaneus
  Hill-Sachs S42.29-
  hip - see Fracture, femur, neck
  humerus S42.30-
    anatomical neck– see Fracture,
      humerus, upper end
    articular process – see Fracture,
      humerus, lower end
    capitellum - see Fracture, humerus,
      lower end, condyle, lateral
    distal end – see Fracture, humerus,
      lower end
    epiphysis
      lower – see Fracture, humerus,
        lower end, physeal
      upper – see Fracture, humerus,
        upper end, physeal
    external condyle – see Fracture, hu-
      merus, lower end, condyle, lateral
    following insertion of implant,
      prosthesis or plate M96.62-
    great tuberosity – see Fracture,
      humerus, upper end, greater
      tuberosity
    intercondylar – see Fracture, humerus,
      lower end
    internal epicondyle – see Fracture,
      humerus, lower end, epicon-
      dyle, medial

Fracture, traumatic (Continued)
  humerus (Continued)
    lesser tuberosity – see Fracture,
      humerus, upper end, specified
      NEC
    lower end S42.40-
      condyle
        lateral (displaced) S42.45-
          nondisplaced S42.45-
        medial (displaced) S42.46-
          nondisplaced S42.46-
      epicondyle
        lateral (displaced) S42.43-
          nondisplaced S42.43-
        medial (displaced) S42.44-
          incarcerated S42.44-
          nondisplaced S42.44-
      physeal S49.10-
        Salter-Harris
          Type I S49.11-
          Type II S49.12-
          Type III S49.13-
          Type IV S49.14-
        specified NEC S49.19-
      specified NEC (displaced)
        S42.49-
        nondisplaced S42.49-
      supracondylar (simple) (displaced)
        S42.41-
        comminuted (displaced)
          S42.42-
          nondisplaced S42.42-
        nondisplaced S42.41-
      torus S42.48-
      transcondylar (displaced) S42.47-
        nondisplaced S42.47-
    proximal end – see Fracture, humerus,
      upper end
    shaft S42.30-
      comminuted (displaced) S42.35-
        nondisplaced S42.35-
      greenstick S42.31-
      oblique (displaced) S42.33-
        nondisplaced S42.33-
      segmental (displaced) S42.36-
        nondisplaced S42.36-
      specified NEC S42.39-
      spiral (displaced) S42.34-
        nondisplaced S42.34-
      transverse (displaced) S42.32-
        nondisplaced S42.32-
    supracondylar – see Fracture, hu-
      merus, lower end
    surgical neck – see Fracture, humerus,
      upper end, surgical neck
    trochlea – see Fracture, humerus,
      lower end, condyle, medial
    tuberosity – see Fracture, humerus,
      upper end
    upper end S42.20-
      anatomical neck - see Fracture,
        humerus, upper end, specified
        NEC
      articular head - see Fracture, hu-
        merus, upper end, specified
        NEC
      epiphysis - see Fracture, humerus,
        upper end, physeal
      greater tuberosity (displaced)
        S42.25-
        nondisplaced S42.25-
      lesser tuberosity (displaced)
        S42.26-
        nondisplaced S42.26-

Fracture, traumatic *(Continued)*
  newborn – *see* Birth, injury, fracture
  nontraumatic – *see* Fracture,
    pathological
  nonunion - *see* Nonunion, fracture
  nose, nasal (bone) (septum) S02.2
  occiput - *see* Fracture, skull, base, occiput
  odontoid process – *see* Fracture, neck,
    cervical vertebra, second
  olecranon (process) (ulna) – *see* Frac-
    ture, ulna, upper end, olecranon
    process
  orbit, orbital (bone) (region) S02.89
    floor (blow-out) S02.3
    roof S02.19
  os
    calcis - *see* Fracture, tarsal, calcaneus
    magnum - *see* Fracture, carpal, capitate
    pubis - *see* Fracture, pubis
  palate S02.89
  parietal bone (skull) S02.0
  patella S82.00-
    comminuted (displaced) S82.04-
      nondisplaced S82.04-
    longitudinal (displaced) S82.02-
      nondisplaced S82.02-
    osteochondral (displaced) S82.01-
      nondisplaced S82.01-
    specified NEC S82.09-
    transverse (displaced) S82.03-
      nondisplaced S82.03-
  pedicle (of vertebral arch) - *see* Fracture,
    vertebra
  pelvis, pelvic (bone) S32.9
    acetabulum - *see* Fracture, acetabulum
    following insertion of implant, pros-
      thesis or plate M96.65
    ilium - *see* Fracture, ilium
    ischium - *see* Fracture, ischium
    multiple with disruption of pelvic
      circle - *see* Disruption, pelvic
      circle
    pubis - *see* Fracture, pubis
    specified site NEC S32.89
    sacrum - *see* Fracture, sacrum
  phalanx
    foot - *see* Fracture, toe
    hand - *see* Fracture, finger
  pisiform - *see* Fracture, carpal, pisiform
  pond - *see* Fracture, skull
  prosthetic device, internal - *see* Compli-
    cations, prosthetic device, by site,
    mechanical
  pubis S32.5-
    with disruption of pelvic circle - *see*
      Disruption, pelvic circle
    specified site NEC S32.5-
    superior rim S32.51-
  radius S52.9-
    distal end – *see* Fracture, radius,
      lower end
    following insertion of implant, pros-
      thesis or plate M96.63-
    head – *see* Fracture, radius, upper
      end, head
    lower end S52.50-
      Barton's - *see* Barton's fracture
      Colles' - *see* Colles' fracture
      extraarticular NEC S52.55-
      intraarticular NEC S52.57-
      physeal S59.20-
        Salter-Harris
          Type I S59.21-
          Type II S59.22-

Fracture, traumatic *(Continued)*
  radius *(Continued)*
    lower end *(Continued)*
      physeal *(Continued)*
        Salter-Harris *(Continued)*
          Type III S59.23-
          Type IV S59.24-
        specified NEC S59.29-
      Smith's - *see* Smith's fracture
      specified NEC S52.59-
      styloid process (displaced)
        S52.51-
        nondisplaced S52.51-
      torus S52.52-
    neck – *see* Fracture, radius, upper end
    proximal end – *see* Fracture, radius,
      upper end
    shaft S52.30-
      bent bone S52.38-
      comminuted (displaced) S52.35-
        nondisplaced S52.35-
      Galeazzi's - *see* Galeazzi's fracture
      greenstick S52.31-
      oblique (displaced) S52.33-
        nondisplaced S52.33-
      segmental (displaced) S52.36-
        nondisplaced S52.36-
      specified NEC S52.39-
      spiral (displaced) S52.34-
        nondisplaced S52.34-
      transverse (displaced) S52.32-
        nondisplaced S52.32-
    upper end S52.10-
      head (displaced) S52.12-
        nondisplaced S52.12-
      neck (displaced) S52.13-
        nondisplaced S52.13-
      specified NEC S52.18-
      physeal S59.10-
        Salter-Harris
          Type I S59.11-
          Type II S59.12-
          Type III S59.13-
          Type IV S59.14-
        specified NEC S59.19-
      torus S52.11-
  ramus
    inferior or superior, pubis - *see* Frac-
      ture, pubis
    mandible - *see* Fracture, mandible
  restorative material (dental) K08.539
    with loss of material K08.531
    without loss of material K08.530
  rib S22.3-
    with flail chest - *see* Flail, chest
    multiple S22.4-
      with flail chest - *see* Flail, chest
  root, tooth - *see* Fracture, tooth
  sacrum S32.10
    specified NEC S32.19
    Type
      1 S32.14
      2 S32.15
      3 S32.16
      4 S32.17
    Zone
      I S32.119
        displaced (minimally) S32.111
          severely S32.112
        nondisplaced S32.110
      II S32.129
        displaced (minimally) S32.121
          severely S32.122
        nondisplaced S32.120

Fracture, traumatic *(Continued)*
  sacrum *(Continued)*
    Zone *(Continued)*
      III S32.139
        displaced (minimally) S32.131
          severely S32.132
        nondisplaced S32.130
  scaphoid (hand) – *see also* Fracture,
    carpal, navicular
    foot – *see* Fracture, tarsal, navicular
  scapula S42.10-
    acromial process (displaced) S42.12-
      nondisplaced S42.12-
    body (displaced) S42.11-
      nondisplaced S42.11-
    coracoid process (displaced) S42.13-
      nondisplaced S42.13-
    glenoid cavity (displaced) S42.14-
      nondisplaced S42.14-
    neck (displaced) S42.15-
      nondisplaced S42.15-
    specified NEC S42.19-
  semilunar bone, wrist - *see* Fracture,
    carpal, lunate
  sequelae - *see* Sequelae, fracture
  sesamoid bone
    hand - *see* Fracture, carpal
    other - code by site under Fracture
  shepherd's – *see* Fracture, tarsal, talus
  shoulder (girdle) S42.9-
    blade - *see* Fracture, scapula
  sinus (ethmoid) (frontal) S02.19
  skull S02.91
    base S02.10
      occiput S02.119
        condyle S02.113
          type I S02.110
          type II S02.111
          type III S02.112
        specified NEC S02.118
      specified NEC S02.19
    birth injury P13.0
    frontal bone S02.0
    parietal bone S02.0
    specified site NEC S02.89
    temporal bone S02.19
    vault S02.0
  Smith's - *see* Smith's fracture
  sphenoid (bone) (sinus) S02.19
  spine - *see* Fracture, vertebra
  spinous process - *see* Fracture, vertebra
  spontaneous (cause unknown) - *see*
    Fracture, pathological
  stave (of thumb) – *see* Fracture, metacar-
    pal, first
  sternum S22.20
    with flail chest - *see* Flail, chest
    body S22.22
    manubrium S22.21
    xiphoid (process) S22.24
  stress M84.30
    ankle M84.37-
    carpus M84.34-
    clavicle M84.31-
    femoral neck M84.359
    femur M84.35-
    fibula M84.36-
    finger M84.34-
    hip M84.359
    humerus M84.32-
    ilium M84.350
    ischium M84.350
    metacarpus M84.34-
    metatarsus M84.37-

Fracture, traumatic *(Continued)*
  stress *(Continued)*
    neck - *see* Fracture, fatigue, vertebra
    pelvis M84.350
    radius M84.33-
    rib M84.38
    scapula M84.31-
    skull M84.38
    tarsus M84.37-
    tibia M84.36-
    toe M84.37-
    ulna M84.33-
    vertebra - *see* Fracture, fatigue, vertebra
  supracondylar, elbow - *see* Fracture, humerus, lower end, supracondylar
  symphysis pubis - *see* Fracture, pubis
  talus (ankle bone) – *see* Fracture, tarsal, talus
  tarsal bone(s) S92.20-
    astragalus – *see* Fracture, tarsal, talus
    calcaneus S92.00-
      anterior process (displaced) S92.02-
        nondisplaced S92.02-
      body (displaced) S92.01-
        nondisplaced S92.01-
      extraarticular NEC (displaced) S92.05-
        nondisplaced S92.05-
      intraarticular (displaced) S92.06-
        nondisplaced S92.06-
      tuberosity (displaced) S92.04-
        avulsion (displaced) S92.03-
          nondisplaced S92.03-
        nondisplaced S92.04-
    cuboid (displaced) S92.21-
      nondisplaced S92.21-
    cuneiform
      intermediate (displaced) S92.23-
        nondisplaced S92.23-
      lateral (displaced) S92.22-
        nondisplaced S92.22-
      medial (displaced) S92.24-
        nondisplaced S92.24-
    navicular (displaced) S92.25-
      nondisplaced S92.25-
    scaphoid - *see* Fracture, tarsal, navicular
    talus S92.10-
      avulsion (displaced) S92.15-
        nondisplaced S92.15-
      body (displaced) S92.12-
        nondisplaced S92.12-
      dome (displaced) S92.14-
        nondisplaced S92.14-
      head (displaced) S92.12-
        nondisplaced S92.12-
      lateral process (displaced) S92.14-
        nondisplaced S92.14-
      neck (displaced) S92.11-
        nondisplaced S92.11-
      posterior process (displaced) S92.13-
        nondisplaced S92.13-
      specified NEC S92.19-
  temporal bone (styloid) S02.19
  thorax (bony) S22.9
    with flail chest - *see* Flail, chest
    rib S22.3-
      multiple S22.4-
        with flail chest - *see* Flail, chest
    sternum S22.20
      body S22.22
      manubrium S22.21
      xiphoid process S22.24

Fracture, traumatic *(Continued)*
  thorax *(Continued)*
    vertebra (displaced) S22.009
      burst (stable) S22.001
        unstable S22.002
      eighth S22.069
        burst (stable) S22.061
          unstable S22.062
        specified type NEC S22.068
        wedge compression S22.060
      eleventh S22.089
        burst (stable) S22.081
          unstable S22.082
        specified type NEC S22.088
        wedge compression S22.080
      fifth S22.059
        burst (stable) S22.051
          unstable S22.052
        specified type NEC S22.058
        wedge compression S22.050
      first S22.019
        burst (stable) S22.011
          unstable S22.012
        specified type NEC S22.018
        wedge compression S22.010
      fourth S22.049
        burst (stable) S22.041
          unstable S22.042
        specified type NEC S22.048
        wedge compression S22.040
      ninth S22.079
        burst (stable) S22.071
          unstable S22.072
        specified type NEC S22.078
        wedge compression S22.070
      nondisplaced S22.001
      second S22.029
        burst (stable) S22.021
          unstable S22.022
        specified type NEC S22.028
        wedge compression S22.020
      seventh S22.069
        burst (stable) S22.061
          unstable S22.062
        specified type NEC S22.068
        wedge compression S22.060
      sixth S22.059
        burst (stable) S22.051
          unstable S22.052
        specified type NEC S22.058
        wedge compression S22.050
      specified type NEC S22.008
      tenth S22.079
        burst (stable) S22.071
          unstable S22.072
        specified type NEC S22.078
        wedge compression S22.070
      third S22.039
        burst (stable) S22.031
          unstable S22.032
        specified type NEC S22.038
        wedge compression S22.030
      twelfth S22.089
        burst (stable) S22.081
          unstable S22.082
        specified type NEC S22.088
        wedge compression S22.080
      wedge compression S22.000
    thumb S62.50-
      distal phalanx (displaced) S62.52-
        nondisplaced S62.52-
      proximal phalanx (displaced) S62.51-
        nondisplaced S62.51-
    thyroid cartilage S12.8

Fracture, traumatic *(Continued)*
  tibia (shaft) S82.20-
    comminuted (displaced) S82.25-
      nondisplaced S82.25-
    condyles – *see* Fracture, tibia, upper end
    distal end – *see* Fracture, tibia, lower end
    epiphysis
      lower - *see* Fracture, tibia, lower end
      upper – *see* Fracture, tibia, upper end
    following insertion of implant, prosthesis or plate M96.67-
    head (involving knee joint) – *see* Fracture, tibia, upper end
    intercondyloid eminence– *see* Fracture, tibia, upper end
    involving ankle or malleolus - *see* Fracture, ankle, medial malleolus
    lower end S82.30-
      physeal S89.10-
        Salter-Harris
          Type I S89.11-
          Type II S89.12-
          Type III S89.13-
          Type IV S89.14-
        specified NEC S89.19-
      pilon (displaced) S82.87-
        nondisplaced S82.87-
      specified NEC S82.39-
      torus S82.31-
    malleolus – *see* Fracture, ankle, medial malleolus
    oblique (displaced) S82.23-
      nondisplaced S82.23-
    pilon - *see* Fracture, tibia, lower end, pilon
    proximal end – *see* Fracture, tibia, upper end
    segmental (displaced) S82.26-
      nondisplaced S82.26-
    specified NEC S82.29-
    spine - *see* Fracture, upper end, spine
    spiral (displaced) S82.24-
      nondisplaced S82.24-
    transverse (displaced) S82.22-
      nondisplaced S82.22-
    tuberosity – *see* Fracture, tibia, upper end, tuberosity
    upper end S82.10-
      bicondylar (displaced) S82.14-
        nondisplaced S82.14-
      lateral condyle (displaced) S82.12-
        nondisplaced S82.12-
      medial condyle (displaced) S82.13-
        nondisplaced S82.13-
      physeal S89.00-
        Salter-Harris
          Type I S89.01-
          Type II S89.02-
          Type III S89.03-
          Type IV S89.04-
        specified NEC S89.09-
      plateau - *see* Fracture, tibia, upper end, bicondylar
      spine (displaced) S82.11-
        nondisplaced S82.11-
      torus S82.16-
      specified NEC S82.19-
      tuberosity (displaced) S82.15-
        nondisplaced S82.15-

Fracture, traumatic *(Continued)*
  toe S92.91-
    great (displaced) S92.40-
      distal phalanx (displaced) S92.42-
        nondisplaced S92.42-
      nondisplaced S92.40-
      proximal phalanx (displaced) S92.41-
        nondisplaced S92.41-
      specified NEC S92.49-
    lesser (displaced) S92.50-
      distal phalanx (displaced) S92.53-
        nondisplaced S92.53-
      medial phalanx (displaced) S92.52-
        nondisplaced S92.52-
      nondisplaced S92.50-
      proximal phalanx (displaced) S92.51-
        nondisplaced S92.51-
      specified NEC S92.59-
  tooth (root) S02.5
  trachea (cartilage) S12.8
  transverse process - *see* Fracture, vertebra
  trapezium or trapezoid bone - *see* Fracture, carpal
  trimalleolar - *see* Fracture, ankle, trimalleolar
  triquetrum (cuneiform of carpus) - *see* Fracture, carpal, triquetrum
  trochanter – *see* Fracture, femur, trochanteric
  tuberosity (external) - code by site under Fracture
  ulna (shaft) S52.20-
    bent bone S52.28-
    coronoid process – *see* Fracture, ulna, upper end, coronoid process
    distal end – *see* Fracture, ulna, lower end
    following insertion of implant, prosthesis or plate M96.63-
    head S52.00-
    lower end S52.60-
      physeal S59.00-
        Salter-Harris
          Type I S59.01-
          Type II S59.02-
          Type III S59.03-
          Type IV S59.04-
        specified NEC S59.09-
      specified NEC S52.69-
      styloid process (displaced) S52.61-
        nondisplaced S52.61-
      torus S52.62-
    proximal end – *see* Fracture, ulna, upper end
    shaft S52.20-
      comminuted (displaced) S52.25-
        nondisplaced S52.25-
      greenstick S52.21-
      Monteggia's - *see* Monteggia's fracture
      oblique (displaced) S52.23-
        nondisplaced S52.23-
      segmental (displaced) S52.26-
        nondisplaced S52.26-
      specified NEC S52.29-
      spiral (displaced) S52.24-
        nondisplaced S52.24-
      transverse (displaced) S52.22-
        nondisplaced S52.22-

Fracture, traumatic *(Continued)*
  ulna *(Continued)*
    upper end S52.00-
      coronoid process (displaced) S52.04-
        nondisplaced S52.04-
      olecranon process (displaced) S52.02-
        with intraarticular extension S52.03-
          with intraarticular extension S52.03-
        nondisplaced S52.02-
          with intraarticular extension S52.03-
            with intraarticular extension S52.03-
            with intraarticular extension S52.03-
              with intraarticular extension S52.03-
      specified NEC S52.09-
      torus S52.01-
  unciform - *see* Fracture, carpal, hamate
  vault of skull S02.0
  vertebra, vertebral (arch) (body) (column) (neural arch) (pedicle) (spinous process) (transverse process)
    atlas – *see* Fracture, neck, cervical vertebra, first
    axis - *see* Fracture, neck, cervical vertebra, second
    cervical (teardrop) S12.9
      axis - *see* Fracture, neck, cervical vertebra, second
      first (atlas) - *see* Fracture, neck, cervical vertebra, first
      second (axis) - *see* Fracture, neck, cervical vertebra, second
    chronic M84.48
    coccyx S32.2
    dorsal – *see* Fracture, thorax, vertebra
    lumbar S32.009
      burst (stable) S32.001
        unstable S32.002
      fifth S32.059
        burst (stable) S32.051
          unstable S32.052
        specified type NEC S32.058
        wedge compression S32.050
      first S32.019
        burst (stable) S32.011
          unstable S32.012
        specified type NEC S32.018
        wedge compression S32.010
      fourth S32.049
        burst (stable) S32.041
          unstable S32.042
        specified type NEC S32.048
        wedge compression S32.040
      second S32.029
        burst (stable) S32.021
          unstable S32.022
        specified type NEC S32.028
        wedge compression S32.020
      specified type NEC S32.008
      third S32.039
        burst (stable) S32.031
          unstable S32.032
        specified type NEC S32.038
        wedge compression S32.030
      wedge compression S32.000

Fracture, traumatic *(Continued)*
  vertebra, vertebral *(Continued)*
    metastatic (*see also* Neoplasm) - *see* Collapse, vertebra, in, specified disease NEC
    newborn (birth injury) P11.5
    sacrum S32.10
      specified NEC S32.19
      Type
        1 S32.14
        2 S32.15
        3 S32.16
        4 S32.17
      Zone
        I S32.119
          displaced (minimally) S32.111
            severely S32.112
          nondisplaced S32.110
        II S32.129
          displaced (minimally) S32.121
            severely S32.122
          nondisplaced S32.120
        III S32.139
          displaced (minimally) S32.131
            severely S32.132
          nondisplaced S32.130
    thoracic – *see* Fracture, thorax, vertebra
  vertex S02.0
  vomer (bone) S02.2
  wrist S62.10-
    carpal – *see* Fracture, carpal bone
    navicular (scaphoid) (hand) – *see* Fracture, carpal, navicular
  xiphisternum, xiphoid (process) S22.24
  zygoma S02.44
Fragile, fragility
  autosomal site Q95.5
  bone, congenital (with blue sclera) Q78.0
  capillary (hereditary) D69.8
  hair L67.8
  nails L60.3
  non-sex chromosome site Q95.5
  X chromosome Q99.2
Fragilitas
  crinium L67.8
  ossium (with blue sclerae) (hereditary) Q78.0
  unguium L60.3
    congenital Q84.6
Fragments, cataract (lens), following cataract surgery H59.02-
Frailty (frail) R54
  mental R41.81
Frambesia, frambesial (tropica) - *see also* Yaws
  initial lesion or ulcer A66.0
  primary A66.0
Frambeside
  gummatous A66.4
  of early yaws A66.2
Frambesioma A66.1
Franceschetti-Klein(-Wildervanck) **disease or syndrome** Q75.4
Francis' disease - *see* Tularemia
Franklin disease C88.2
Frank's essential thrombocytopenia D69.3
Fraser's syndrome Q87.0
Freckle(s) L81.2
  malignant melanoma in - *see* Melanoma
  melanotic (Hutchinson's) - *see* Melanoma, in situ
  retinal D49.81

Frederickson's hyperlipoproteinemia,
   type
   I and V E78.3
   IIA E78.0
   IIB and III E78.2
   IV E78.1
Freeman Sheldon syndrome Q87.0
Freezing - *see also* Effect, adverse, cold
   T69.9
Freiberg's disease (infraction of metatar-
   sal head or osteochondrosis) - *see* Os-
   teochondrosis, juvenile, metatarsus
Frei's disease A55
Fremitus, friction, cardiac R01.2
Frenum, frenulum
   external os Q51.8
   tongue (shortening) (congenital) Q38.1
Frequency micturition (nocturnal)
   R35.0
   psychogenic F45.8
Frey's syndrome
   auriculotemporal G50.8
   hyperhidrosis L74.52
Friction
   burn - *see* Burn, by site
   fremitus, cardiac R01.2
   precordial R01.2
   sounds, chest R09.89
Friderichsen-Waterhouse syndrome or
   disease A39.1
Friedländer's B (bacillus) NEC (*see also*
   condition) A49.8
Friedreich's
   ataxia G11.1
   combined systemic disease G11.1
   facial hemihypertrophy Q67.4
   sclerosis (cerebellum) (spinal cord)
      G11.1
Frigidity F52.22
Fröhlich's syndrome E23.6
Frontal - *see also* condition
   lobe syndrome F07.0
Frostbite (superficial) T33.90
   with
      partial thickness skin loss - *see* Frost-
         bite (superficial), by site
      tissue necrosis T34.90
   abdominal wall T33.3
      with tissue necrosis T34.3
   ankle T33.81-
      with tissue necrosis T34.81-
   arm T33.4-
   with tissue necrosis T34.4-
      finger(s) - *see* Frostbite, finger
      hand - *see* Frostbite, hand
      wrist - *see* Frostbite, wrist
   ear T33.01-
      with tissue necrosis T34.01-
   face T33.09
      with tissue necrosis T34.09
   finger T33.53-
      with tissue necrosis T34.53-
   foot T33.82-
      with tissue necrosis T34.82-
   hand T33.52-
      with tissue necrosis T34.52-
   head T33.09
      with tissue necrosis T34.09
      ear - *see* Frostbite, ear
      nose - *see* Frostbite, nose
   hip (and thigh) T33.6-
      with tissue necrosis T34.6-
   knee T33.7-
      with tissue necrosis T34.7-

Frostbite *(Continued)*
   leg T33.9-
      with tissue necrosis T34.9-
      ankle – *see* Frostbite, ankle
      foot – *see* Frostbite, foot
      knee - *see* Frostbite, knee
      lower T33.7-
         with tissue necrosis T34.7-
      thigh – *see* Frostbite, hip
      toe - *see* Frostbite, toe
   limb
      lower T33.99
         with tissue necrosis T34.99
      upper - *see* Frostbite, arm
   neck T33.1
      with tissue necrosis T34.1
   nose T33.02
      with tissue necrosis T34.02
   pelvis T33.3
      with tissue necrosis T34.3
   specified site NEC T33.99
      with tissue necrosis T34.99
   thigh – *see* Frostbite, hip
   thorax T33.2
      with tissue necrosis T34.2
   toes T33.83-
      with tissue necrosis T34.83-
   trunk T33.99
      with tissue necrosis T34.99
   wrist T33.51-
      with tissue necrosis T34.51-
Frotteurism F65.81
Frozen - *see also* Effect, adverse, cold T69.9
   pelvis (female) N94.89
      male K66.8
   shoulder - *see* Capsulitis, adhesive
Fructokinase deficiency E74.11
Fructose 1,6 diphosphatase deficiency
   E74.19
Fructosemia (benign) (essential) E74.19
Fructosuria (benign) (essential) E74.11
Fuchs'
   black spot (myopic) - *see* Disorder,
      globe, degenerative, myopia
   dystrophy (corneal endothelium)
      H18.52
   heterochromic cyclitis - *see* Cyclitis,
      Fuchs' heterochromic
Fucosidosis E77.1
Fugue R68.89
   dissociative F44.1
   hysterical (dissociative) F44.1
   postictal in epilepsy – *see* Epilepsy
   reaction to exceptional stress (transient)
      F43.0
Fulminant, fulminating - *see* condition
Functional - *see also* condition
   bleeding (uterus) N93.89
Functioning, intellectual, borderline
   R41.83
Fundus - *see* condition
Fungemia NOS B49
Fungus, fungous
   cerebral G93.89
   disease NOS B49
   infection - *see* Infection, fungus
Funiculitis (acute) (chronic) (endemic)
   N49.1
   gonococcal (acute) (chronic) A54.23
   tuberculous A18.15
Funnel
   breast (acquired) M95.4
      congenital Q67.6
      sequelae (late effect) of rickets E64.3

Funnel *(Continued)*
   chest (acquired) M95.4
      congenital Q67.6
      sequelae (late effect) of rickets E64.3
   pelvis (acquired) M95.5
      with disproportion (fetopelvic) O33.3
         causing obstructed labor O65.3
      congenital Q74.2
FUO (fever of unknown origin) R50.9
Furfur L21.0
   microsporon B36.0
Furrier's lung J67.8
Furrowed K14.5
   nail(s) (transverse) L60.4
      congenital Q84.6
   tongue K14.5
      congenital Q38.3
Furuncle L02.92
   abdominal wall L02.221
   ankle - *see* Furuncle, lower limb
   anus K61.0
   antecubital space - *see* Furuncle, upper
      limb
   arm - *see* Furuncle, upper limb
   auditory canal, external - *see* Abscess,
      ear, external
   auricle (ear) - *see* Abscess, ear, external
   axilla (region) L02.42-
   back (any part) L02.222
   breast N61
   buttock L02.32
   cheek (external) L02.02
   chest wall L02.223
   chin L02.02
   corpus cavernosum N48.21
   ear, external - *see* Abscess, ear, external
   external auditory canal - *see* Abscess,
      ear, external
   eyelid - *see* Abscess, eyelid
   face L02.02
   femoral (region) - *see* Furuncle, lower
      limb
   finger - *see* Furuncle, hand
   flank L02.221
   foot L02.62-
   forehead L02.02
   gluteal (region) L02.32
   groin L02.224
   hand L02.52-
   head L02.821
      face L02.02
   hip - *see* Furuncle, lower limb
   kidney – *see* Abscess, kidney
   knee - *see* Furuncle, lower limb
   labium (majus) (minus) N76.4
   lacrimal
      gland - *see* Dacryoadenitis
      passages (duct) (sac) - *see* Inflamma-
         tion, lacrimal, passages, acute
   leg (any part) - *see* Furuncle, lower limb
   lower limb L02.42-
   malignant A22.0
   mouth K12.2
   navel L02.226
   neck L02.12
   nose J34.0
   orbit, orbital - *see* Abscess, orbit
   palmar (space) - *see* Furuncle, hand
   partes posteriores L02.32
   pectoral region L02.223
   penis N48.21
   perineum L02.225
   pinna - *see* Abscess, ear, external
   popliteal - *see* Furuncle, lower limb

Furuncle (*Continued*)
  prepatellar - *see* Furuncle, lower limb
  scalp L02.821
  seminal vesicle N49.0
  shoulder - *see* Furuncle, upper limb
  specified site NEC L02.828
  submandibular K12.2
  temple (region) L02.02
  thumb - *see* Furuncle, hand
  toe - *see* Furuncle, foot
  trunk L02.229
    abdominal wall L02.221
    back L02.222
    chest wall L02.223
    groin L02.224
    perineum L02.225
    umbilicus L02.226
  umbilicus L02.226
  upper limb L02.42-
  vulva N76.4
Furunculosis — *see* Abscess, by site
Fusion, fused (congenital)
  astragaloscaphoid Q74.2
  atria Q21.1
  auditory canal Q16.1
  auricles, heart Q21.1
  binocular with defective stereopsis
      H53.32
  bone Q79.8
  cervical spine M43.22
  choanal Q30.0

Fusion, fused (*Continued*)
  commissure, mitral valve Q23.2
  cusps, heart valve NEC Q24.8
    mitral Q23.2
    pulmonary Q22.1
    tricuspid Q22.4
  ear ossicles Q16.3
  fingers – *see* Syndactyly, complex, fingers
  hymen Q52.3
  joint (acquired) - *see also* Ankylosis
    congenital Q74.8
  kidneys (incomplete) Q63.1
  labium (majus) (minus) Q52.5
  larynx and trachea Q34.8
  limb, congenital Q74.8
    lower Q74.2
    upper Q74.0
  lobes, lung Q33.8
  lumbosacral (acquired) M43.27
    arthrodesis status Z98.1
    congenital Q76.49
    postprocedural status Z98.1
  nares, nose, nasal, nostril(s) Q30.0
  organ or site not listed - *see* Anomaly,
      by site
  ossicles Q79.9
    auditory Q16.3
  pulmonic cusps Q22.1
  ribs Q76.6
  sacroiliac (joint) (acquired) M43.25
    arthrodesis status Z98.1

Fusion, fused (*Continued*)
  sacroiliac (*Continued*)
    congenital Q74.2
    postprocedural status Z98.1
  spine (acquired) NEC M43.20
    arthrodesis status Z98.1
    cervical region M43.22
    cervicothoracic region M43.23
    congenital Q76.49
    lumbar M43.26
    lumbosacral region M43.27
    occipito-atlanto-axial region M43.21
    postoperative status Z98.1
    sacrococcygeal region M43.28
    thoracic region M43.24
    thoracolumbar region M43.25
  sublingual duct with submaxillary
      duct at opening in mouth
      Q38.4
  testes Q55.1
  toes Q70.2
  tooth, teeth K00.2
  trachea and esophagus Q39.8
  twins Q89.4
  vagina Q52.4
  ventricles, heart Q21.0
  vertebra (arch) - *see* Fusion, spine
  vulva Q52.5
Fusospirillosis (mouth) (tongue)
    (tonsil) A69.1
Fussy baby R68.12

G

Gain in weight (abnormal) (excessive) - *see also* Weight, gain
Gaisböck's disease (polycythemia hypertonica) D75.1
Gait abnormality R26.9
  ataxic R26.0
  falling R29.6
  hysterical (ataxic) (staggering) F44.4
  paralytic R26.1
  spastic R26.1
  specified type NEC R26.89
  staggering R26.0
  unsteadiness R26.81
  walking difficulty NEC R26.2
Galactocele (breast) N64.89
  puerperal, postpartum O92.79
Galactokinase deficiency E74.29
Galactophoritis N61
  gestational, puerperal, postpartum – *see* Mastitis, obstetric, purulent
Galactorrhea O92.6
  not associated with childbirth N64.3
Galactosemia (classic) (congenital) E74.21
Galactosuria E74.29
Galacturia R82.0
  schistosomiasis (bilharziasis) B65.0
Galeazzi's fracture S52.37-
Galen's vein - *see* condition
Galeophobia F40.218
Gall duct - *see* condition
Gallbladder - *see also* condition
  acute K81.0
Gallop rhythm R00.8
Gallstone (colic) (cystic duct) (gallbladder) (impacted) (multiple) - *see also* Calculus, gallbladder
  with
    cholecystitis – *see* Calculus, gallbladder, with cholecystitis
    bile duct (common) (hepatic) - *see* Calculus, bile duct
  causing intestinal obstruction K56.3
  specified NEC K80.80
    with obstruction K80.81
Gambling Z72.6
  pathological (compulsive) F63.0
Gammopathy (of undetermined significance [MGUS]) D47.2
  associated with lymphoplasmacytic dyscrasia D47.2
  monoclonal D47.2
    of undetermined significance D47.2
  polyclonal D89.0
Gamna's disease (siderotic splenomegaly) D73.1
Gamophobia F40.298
Gampsodactylia (congenital) Q66.7
Gamstorp's disease (adynamia episodica hereditaria) G72.3
Gandy-Nanta disease (siderotic splenomegaly) D73.1
Gang
  membership offenses Z72.810
Gangliocytoma D36.10
Ganglioglioma - *see* Neoplasm, uncertain behavior
Ganglion (compound) (diffuse) (joint) (tendon (sheath)) M67.40
  ankle M67.47-
  foot M67.47-
  forearm M67.43-
  hand M67.44-

Ganglion (*Continued*)
  lower leg M67.46-
  multiple sites M67.49
  of yaws (early) (late) A66.6
  pelvic region M67.45-
  periosteal – *see* Periostitis
  shoulder region M67.41-
  specified site NEC M67.48
  thigh region M67.45-
  tuberculous A18.09
  upper arm M67.42-
  wrist M67.43-
Ganglioneuroblastoma - *see* Neoplasm, nerve, malignant
Ganglioneuroma D36.10
  malignant - *see* Neoplasm, nerve, malignant
Ganglioneuromatosis D36.10
Ganglionitis
  fifth nerve - *see* Neuralgia, trigeminal
  gasserian (postherpetic) (postzoster) B02.21
  geniculate G51.1
    newborn (birth injury) P11.3
    postherpetic, postzoster B02.21
  herpes zoster B02.21
  postherpetic geniculate B02.21
Gangliosidosis E75.10
  GM1 E75.19
  GM2 E75.00
    other specified E75.09
    Sandhoff disease E75.01
    Tay-Sachs disease E75.02
  GM3 E75.19
  mucolipidosis IV E75.11
Gangosa A66.5
Gangrene, gangrenous (connective tissue) (dropsical) (dry) (moist) (skin) (ulcer) (*see also* Necrosis) I96
  with diabetes (mellitus) – *see* Diabetes, gangrene
  abdomen (wall) I96
  alveolar M27.3
  appendix K35.9
    with
      perforation or rupture K35.0
      peritoneal abscess K35.1
      peritonitis, localized K35.9
        with perforation or rupture K35.0
        generalized K35.0
  arteriosclerotic (general) (senile) - *see* Arteriosclerosis, extremities, with, gangrene
  auricle I96
  Bacillus welchii A48.0
  bladder (infectious) – *see* Cystitis, specified type NEC
  bowel, cecum, or colon - *see* Gangrene, intestine
  Clostridium perfringens or welchii A48.0
  cornea H18.89-
  corpora cavernosa N48.29
    noninfective N48.89
  cutaneous, spreading I96
  decubital - *see* Ulcer, pressure, by site
  diabetic (any site) - *see* Diabetes, gangrene
  epidemic - *see* Poisoning, food, noxious, plant
  epididymis (infectional) N45.1
  erysipelas – *see* Erysipelas
  emphysematous – *see* Gangrene, gas
  extremity (lower) (upper) I96

Gangrene, gangrenous (*Continued*)
  Fournier's N49.3
    female N76.89
  fusospirochetal A69.0
  gallbladder - *see* Cholecystitis, acute
  gas (bacillus) A48.0
    following
      abortion - *see* Abortion by type complicated by infection
      ectopic or molar pregnancy O08.0
  glossitis K14.0
  hernia - *see* Hernia, by site, with gangrene
  intestine, intestinal (hemorrhagic) (massive) K55.0
    with
      mesenteric embolism K55.0
      obstruction - *see* Obstruction, intestine
  laryngitis J04.0
  limb (lower) (upper) I96
  lung J85.0
    spirochetal A69.8
  lymphangitis I89.1
  Meleney's (synergistic) - *see* Ulcer, skin
  mesentery K55.0
    with
      embolism K55.0
      intestinal obstruction - *see* Obstruction, intestine
  mouth A69.0
  ovary - *see* Oophoritis
  pancreas K85.9
  penis N48.29
    noninfective N48.89
  perineum I96
  pharynx - *see also* Pharyngitis
    Vincent's A69.1
  presenile I73.1
  progressive synergistic – *see* Ulcer, skin
  pulmonary J85.0
  pulpal (dental) K04.1
  quinsy J36
  Raynaud's (symmetric gangrene) I73.01
  retropharyngeal J39.2
  scrotum N49.3
    noninfective N50.8
  senile (atherosclerotic) - *see* Arteriosclerosis, extremities, with, gangrene
  spermatic cord N49.1
    noninfective N50.8
  spine I96
  spirochetal NEC A69.8
  spreading cutaneous I96
  stomatitis A69.0
  symmetrical I73.01
  testis (infectional) N45.2
    noninfective N44.8
  throat - *see also* Pharyngitis
    diphtheritic A36.0
    Vincent's A69.1
  thyroid (gland) E07.89
  tooth (pulp) K04.1
  tuberculous NEC - *see* Tuberculosis
  tunica vaginalis N49.1
    noninfective N50.8
  umbilicus I96
  uterus - *see* Endometritis
  uvulitis K12.2
  vas deferens N49.1
    noninfective N50.8
  vulva N76.89
Ganister disease J62.8
Ganser's syndrome (hysterical) F44.89

Gardner-Diamond syndrome (autoeryth-
    rocyte sensitization) D69.2
Gargoylism E76.01
Garré's disease, osteitis (sclerosing),
    osteomyelitis - see Osteomyelitis,
    specified type NEC
Garrod's pad, knuckle M72.1
Gartner's duct
    cyst Q52.4
    persistent Q50.6
Gas R14.3
    asphyxiation, inhalation, poisoning,
        suffocation NEC - see Table of
        drugs and chemicals
    excessive R14.8
    gangrene A48.0
        following
            abortion - see Abortion by type
                complicated by infection
            ectopic or molar pregnancy O08.0
    on stomach R14.8
    pains R14.1
Gastralgia - see also Pain, abdominal
Gastrectasis K31.0
    psychogenic F45.8
Gastric - see condition
Gastrinoma
    malignant
        pancreas C25.4
        specified site NEC - see Neoplasm,
            malignant
        unspecified site C25.4
    specified site - see Neoplasm, uncertain
        behavior
    unspecified site D37.7
Gastritis (simple) K29.70
    with bleeding K29.71
    acute (erosive) K29.00
        with bleeding K29.01
    alcoholic K29.20
        with bleeding K29.21
    allergic K29.60
        with bleeding K29.61
    atrophic (chronic) K29.40
        with bleeding K29.41
    chronic (antral) (fundal) K29.50
        with bleeding K29.51
        atrophic K29.40
            with bleeding K29.41
        superficial K29.30
            with bleeding K29.31
    dietary counseling and surveillance
        Z71.3
    due to diet deficiency E63.9
    eosinophilic K52.81
    giant hypertrophic K29.60
        with bleeding K29.61
    granulomatous K29.60
        with bleeding K29.61
    hypertrophic (mucosa) K29.60
        with bleeding K29.61
    nervous F54
    spastic K29.60
        with bleeding K29.61
    specified NEC K29.60
        with bleeding K29.61
    superficial chronic K29.30
        with bleeding K29.31
    tuberculous A18.83
    viral NEC A08.4
Gastrocarcinoma - see Neoplasm,
    malignant, stomach
Gastrocolic - see condition
Gastrodisciasis, gastrodiscoidiasis B66.8

Gastroduodenitis K29.90
    with bleeding K29.91
    virus, viral A08.4
        specified type NEC A08.3
Gastrodynia - see Pain, abdominal
Gastroenteritis (acute) (chronic) (nonin-
    fectious) (see also Enteritis) K52.9
    allergic K52.2
    dietetic K52.2
    due to
        Cryptosporidium A07.2
        food poisoning - see Intoxication,
            foodborne
        radiation K52.0
    eosinophilic K52.81
    epidemic (infectious) A09
    food hypersensitivity K52.2
    infectious - see Enteritis, infectious
    noninfectious K52.9
        specified NEC K52.89
    rotaviral A08.0
    Salmonella A02.0
    toxic K52.1
    viral NEC A08.4
        acute infectious A08.3
            type Norwalk A08.11
        infantile (acute) A08.3
        Norwalk agent A08.11
        rotaviral A08.0
        severe of infants A08.3
        specified type NEC A08.3
Gastroenteropathy (see also Gastroenteri-
    tis) K52.9
    acute, due to Norovirus A08.11
    acute, due to Norwalk agent A08.11
    infectious A09
Gastroenteroptosis K63.4
    Gastroesophageal lacerationhemor-
        rhage syndrome K22.6
Gastrointestinal - see condition
Gastrojejunal - see condition
Gastrojejunitis (see also Enteritis) K52.9
Gastrojejunocolic - see condition
Gastroliths K31.89
Gastromalacia K31.89
Gastroparalysis K31.89
    diabetic – see Diabetes, gastroparalysis
Gastroparesis K31.89
    diabetic – see Diabetes, by type, with
        gastroparesis
Gastropathy K31.9
    congestive portal K31.89
    erythematous K29.70
    exudative K90.89
    portal hypertensive K31.89
Gastroptosis K31.89
Gastrorrhagia K92.2
    psychogenic F45.8
Gastroschisis (congenital) Q79.3
Gastrospasm (neurogenic) (reflex) K31.89
    neurotic F45.8
    psychogenic F45.8
Gastrostaxis – see Gastritis, with bleeding
Gastrostenosis K31.89
Gastrostomy
    attention to Z43.1
    status Z93.1
Gastrosuccorrhea (continuous) (intermit-
    tent) K31.89
    neurotic F45.8
    psychogenic F45.8
Gatophobia F40.218
Gaucher's disease or splenomegaly
    (adult) (infantile) E75.22

Gee(-Herter)(-Thaysen) disease (non-
    tropical sprue) K90.0
Gélineau's syndrome G47.419
    with cataplexy G47.411
Gemination, tooth, teeth K00.2
Gemistocytoma
    specified site - see Neoplasm, malignant
    unspecified site C71.9
General, generalized - see condition
Genetic
    carrier (status)
        cystic fibrosis Z14.1
        hemophilia A (asymptomatic) Z14.01
            symptomatic Z14.02
        specified NEC Z14.8
    susceptibility to disease NEC Z15.89
        malignant neoplasm Z15.00
            breast Z15.01
            endometrium Z15.04
            ovary Z15.02
            prostate Z15.03
            specified NEC Z15.09
        multiple endocrine neoplasia Z15.81
Genital - see condition
Genito-anorectal syndrome A55
Genitourinary system - see condition
Genu
    congenital Q74.1
    extrorsum (acquired) - see also Defor-
        mity, varus, knee
        congenital Q74.1
        sequelae (late effect) of rickets E64.3
    introrsum (acquired) - see also Defor-
        mity, valgus, knee
        congenital Q74.1
        sequelae (late effect) of rickets E64.3
    rachitic (old) E64.3
    recurvatum (acquired) - see also Defor-
        mity, limb, specified type NEC,
        lower leg
        congenital Q68.2
        sequelae (late effect) of rickets E64.3
    valgum (acquired) (knock-knee)
        M21.06-
        congenital Q74.1
        sequelae (late effect) of rickets E64.3
    varum (acquired) (bowleg) M21.16-
        congenital Q74.1
        sequelae (late effect) of rickets
            E64.3
Geographic tongue K14.1
Geophagia – see Pica
Geotrichosis B48.3
    stomatitis B48.3
Gephyrophobia F40.242
Gerbode defect Q21.0
GERD (gastroesophageal reflux disease)
    K21.9
Gerhardt's
    disease (erythromelalgia) I73.81
    syndrome (vocal cord paralysis) J38.00
        bilateral J38.02
        unilateral J38.01
German measles - see also Rubella
    exposure to Z20.4
Germinoblastoma (diffuse) C85.9-
    follicular C82.9-
Germinoma - see Neoplasm, malignant
Gerontoxon - see Degeneration, cornea,
    senile
Gerstmann-Sträussler-Scheinker
    syndrome (GSS) A81.82
Gerstmann's syndrome (developmental)
    F81.2

Gestation (period) - *see also* Pregnancy
  ectopic - *see* Pregnancy, by site
  multiple O30.9-
    specified NEC - *see* subcategory
      O30.8-
Gestational
  mammary abscess O91.11-
  purulent mastitis O91.11-
  subareolar abscess O91.11-
Ghon tubercle, primary infection
  A15.7
Ghost
  teeth K00.4
  vessels (cornea) H16.41-
Ghoul hand A66.3
Gianotti-Crosti disease L44.4
Giant
  cell
    epulis K06.8
    peripheral granuloma K06.8
  esophagus, congenital Q39.5
  kidney, congenital Q63.3
  oesophagus, congenital Q39.5
  urticaria T78.3
    hereditary D84.1
Giardiasis A07.1
Gibert's disease or pityriasis L42
Giddiness R42
  hysterical F44.89
  psychogenic F45.8
Gierke's disease (glycogenosis I)
  E74.01
Gigantism (cerebral) (hypophyseal)
  (pituitary) E22.0
  constitutional E34.4
Gilbert's disease or syndrome E80.4
Gilchrist's disease B40.9
Gilford-Hutchinson disease E34.8
Gilles de la Tourette's disease
  or syndrome (motor-verbal tic)
  F95.2
Gingivitis K05.10
  acute (catarrhal) K05.00
    necrotizing A69.1
    plaque induced K05.00
    nonplaque induced K05.01
  chronic (desquamative) (hyperplastic)
    (simple marginal) (ulcerative)
    K05.10
    plaque induced K05.10
    nonplaque induced K05.11
  expulsiva - *see* Periodontitis
  necrotizing ulcerative (acute) A69.1
  pellagrous E52
    acute necrotizing A69.1
  Vincent's A69.1
Gingivoglossitis K14.0
Gingivopericementitis - *see*
  Periodontitis
Gingivosis - *see* Gingivitis, chronic
Gingivostomatitis B00.2
  herpesviral B00.2
  necrotizing ulcerative (acute) A69.1
Gland, glandular - *see* condition
Glanders A24.0
Glanzmann (-Naegeli) disease or throm-
  basthenia D69.1
Glass-blower's disease (cataract) - *see*
  Cataract, specified NEC
Glaucoma H40.9
  with
    increased episcleral venous pressure
      H40.81-

Glaucoma *(Continued)*
  with *(Continued)*
    pseudoexfoliation of lens - *see*
      Glaucoma, open angle, primary,
      capsular
  absolute H44.51-
  angle-closure (primary) H40.20
    acute H40.21-
    chronic H40.22-
    intermittent H40.23-
    residual stage H40.24-
  borderline H40.0
  capsular (with pseudoexfoliation of
    lens) - *see* Glaucoma, open angle,
    primary, capsular
  childhood Q15.0
  closed angle - *see* Glaucoma,
    angle-closure
  congenital Q15.0
  corticosteroid-induced - *see* Glaucoma,
    secondary, drugs
  hypersecretion H40.82-
  in (due to)
    amyloidosis E85.4 *[H42]*
    aniridia Q13.1 *[H42]*
    concussion of globe - *see* Glaucoma,
      secondary, trauma
    dislocation of lens - *see* Glaucoma,
      secondary
    disorder of lens NEC - *see* Glaucoma,
      secondary
    drugs - *see* Glaucoma, secondary,
      drugs
    endocrine disease NOS E34.9 *[H42]*
    eye
      inflammation - *see* Glaucoma, sec-
        ondary, inflammation
      trauma - *see* Glaucoma, secondary,
        trauma
    hypermature cataract - *see* Glaucoma,
      secondary
    iridocyclitis - *see* Glaucoma, second-
      ary, inflammation
    lens disorder - *see* Glaucoma, second-
      ary, Lowe's syndrome E72.03
      [H42]
    metabolic disease NOS E88.9 *[H42]*
    ocular disorders NEC - *see* Glaucoma,
      secondary
    onchocerciasis B73.02
    pupillary block - *see* Glaucoma,
      secondary
    retinal vein occlusion - *see* Glaucoma,
      secondary
    Rieger's anomaly Q13.81 *[H42]*
    rubeosis of iris - *see* Glaucoma,
      secondary
    tumor of globe - *see* Glaucoma,
      secondary
  infantile Q15.0
  low tension - *see* Glaucoma, open angle,
    low-tension
  malignant H40.83-
  narrow angle - *see* Glaucoma,
    angle-closure
  newborn Q15.0
  noncongestive (chronic) - *see* Glaucoma,
    open angle
  nonobstructive - *see* Glaucoma, open
    angle
  obstructive - *see also* Glaucoma,
    angle-closure
    due to lens changes - *see* Glaucoma,
      secondary

Glaucoma *(Continued)*
  open angle H40.10
    primary H40.11
      capsular (with pseudoexfoliation of
        lens) H40.14-
      low-tension H40.12-
      pigmentary H40.13-
      residual stage H40.15-
    phacolytic - *see* Glaucoma, secondary
    pigmentary - *see* Glaucoma, open angle,
      pigmentary
    postinfectious - *see* Glaucoma, secondary,
      inflammation
  secondary (to) H40.5-
    drugs H40.6-
    inflammation H40.4-
    trauma H40.3-
  simple (chronic) - *see* Glaucoma, open
    angle
  simplex - *see* Glaucoma, open angle
  specified type NEC H40.89
  suspect H40.0
  syphilitic A52.71
  traumatic - *see also* Glaucoma, second-
    ary, trauma
    newborn (birth injury) P15.3
  tuberculous A18.59
Glaucomatous flecks (subcapsular) - *see*
  Cataract, complicated
Glazed tongue K14.4
Gleet (gonococcal) A54.01
Glénard's disease K63.4
Glioblastoma (multiforme)
  with sarcomatous component
    specified site - *see* Neoplasm,
      malignant
    unspecified site C71.9
  giant cell
    specified site - *see* Neoplasm,
      malignant
    unspecified site C71.9
  specified site - *see* Neoplasm,
    malignant
  unspecified site C71.9
Glioma (malignant)
  astrocytic
    specified site - *see* Neoplasm,
      malignant
    unspecified site C71.9
  mixed
    specified site - *see* Neoplasm,
      malignant
    unspecified site C71.9
  nose Q30.8
  specified site NEC - *see* Neoplasm,
    malignant
  subependymal D43.2
    specified site - *see* Neoplasm,
      uncertain behavior
    unspecified site D43.2
  unspecified site C71.9
Gliomatosis cerebri C71.0
Glioneuroma - *see* Neoplasm, uncertain
  behavior
Gliosarcoma
  specified site - *see* Neoplasm,
    malignant
  unspecified site C71.9
Gliosis (cerebral) G93.89
  spinal G95.89
Glisson's disease – *see* Rickets
Globinuria R82.3
Globus (hystericus) F45.8

Glomangioma D18.00
  intra-abdominal D18.03
  intracranial D18.02
  skin D18.01
  specified site NEC D18.09
Glomangiomyoma D18.00
  intra-abdominal D18.03
  intracranial D18.02
  skin D18.01
  specified site NEC D18.09
Glomangiosarcoma - *see* Neoplasm,
  connective tissue, malignant
Glomerular
  disease in syphilis A52.75
  nephritis - *see* Glomerulonephritis
Glomerulitis - *see* Glomerulonephritis
Glomerulonephritis (*see also* Nephritis)
  N05.9
  with
    edema - *see* Nephrosis
    minimal change N05.0
    minor glomerular abnormality N05.0
  acute N00.9
  chronic N03.9
  crescentic (diffuse) NEC (*see also* N00-
    N07 with fourth character .7)
    N05.7
  dense deposit (*see also* N00-N07 with
    fourth character .6) N05.6
  diffuse
    crescentic (*see also* N00-N07 with
      fourth character .7) N05.7
    endocapillary proliferative (*see also*
      N00N07 with fourth character .4)
      N05.4
    membranous (*see also* N00-N07 with
      fourth character .2) N05.2
    mesangial proliferative (*see also*
      N00N07 with fourth character .3)
      N05.3
    mesangiocapillary (*see also* N00-N07
      with fourth character .5) N05.5
    sclerosing N05.8
  endocapillary proliferative (diffuse)
    NEC (*see also* N00-N07 with fourth
    character .4) N05.4
  extracapillary NEC (*see also* N00-N07
    with fourth character .7) N05.7
  focal (and segmental) (*see also* N00-N07
    with fourth character .1) N05.1
  hypocomplementemic - *see* Glomerulo-
    nephritis, membranoproliferative
  IgA - *see* Nephropathy, IgA
  immune complex (circulating) NEC N05.8
  in (due to)
    amyloidosis E85.4 [N08]
    bilharziasis B65.9 [N08]
    cryoglobulinemia D89.1 [N08]
    defibrination syndrome D65 [N08]
    diabetes mellitus - *see* Diabetes,
      glomerulosclerosis
    disseminated intravascular coagula-
      tion D65 [N08]
    Fabry(-Anderson) disease E75.21
      [N08]
    Goodpasture's syndrome M31.0
    hemolytic-uremic syndrome D59.3
    Henoch(-Schönlein) purpura D69.0
      [N08]
    lecithin cholesterol acyltransferase
      deficiency E78.6 [N08]
    microscopic polyangiitis M31.7
      [N08]
    multiple myeloma C90.00 [N08]

Glomerulonephritis (*Continued*)
  in (due to) (*Continued*)
    Plasmodium malariae B52.0
    schistosomiasis B65.9 [N08]
    sepsis A41.9- [N08]
      streptococcal A40.- [N08]
    sickle-cell disorders D57.[N08]
    strongyloidiasis B78.9 [N08]
    subacute bacterial endocarditis I33.0
      [N08]
    syphilis (late) congenital A50.59
      [N08]
    systemic lupus erythematosus
      M32.14
    thrombotic thrombocytopenic pur-
      pura M31.1 [N08]
    typhoid fever A01.09
    Waldenström macroglobulinemia
      C88.0 [N08]
    Wegener's granulomatosis M31.31
  latent or quiescent N03.9
  lobular, lobulonodular - *see* Glomerulo-
    nephritis, membranoproliferative
  membranoproliferative (diffuse)(type 1
    or 3)(*see also* N00-N07 with fourth
    character .5) N05.5
    dense deposit (type 2) NEC (*see also*
      N00-N07 with fourth character
      .6) N05.6
  membranous (diffuse) NEC (*see also*
    N00-N07 with fourth character .2)
    N05.2
  mesangial
    IgA/IgG - *see* Nephropathy, IgA
    proliferative (diffuse) NEC (*see also*
      N00-N07 with fourth character
      .3) N05.3
  mesangiocapillary (diffuse) NEC (*see
    also* N00-N07 with fourth character
    .5) N05.5
  necrotic, necrotizing NEC (*see also* N00-
    N07 with fourth character .8) N05.8
  nodular - *see* Glomerulonephritis,
    membranoproliferative
  poststreptococcal NEC N05.9
    acute N00.9
    chronic N03.9
    rapidly progressive N01.9
  proliferative NEC (*see also* N00-N07
    with fourth character .8) N05.8
    diffuse (lupus) M32.14
  rapidly progressive N01.9
  sclerosing, diffuse N05.8
  specified pathology NEC (*see also*
    N00N07 with fourth character .8)
    N05.8
  subacute N01.9
Glomerulopathy - *see* Glomerulonephritis
Glomerulosclerosis - *see also* Sclerosis,
  renal
  intercapillary (nodular) (with diabetes)
    – *see* Diabetes, glomerulosclerosis
  intracapillary – *see* Diabetes,
    glomerulosclerosis
Glossagra K14.6
Glossalgia K14.6
Glossitis (chronic superficial) (gangrenous) (Moeller's) K14.0
  areata exfoliativa K14.1
  atrophic K14.4
  benign migratory K14.1
  cortical superficial, sclerotic K14.0
  Hunter's D51.0
  interstitial, sclerous K14.0

Glossitis (*Continued*)
  median rhomboid K14.2
  pellagrous E52
  superficial, chronic K14.0
Glossocele K14.8
Glossodynia K14.6
  exfoliativa K14.0
Glossoncus K14.8
Glossopathy K14.9
Glossophytia K14.3
Glossoplegia K14.8
Glossoptosis K14.8
Glossopyrosis K14.6
Glossotrichia K14.3
Glossy skin L90.8
Glottis - *see* condition
Glottitis (*see also* Laryngitis) J04.0
Glucagonoma
  pancreas
    benign D13.7
    malignant C25.4
    uncertain behavior D37.7
  specified site NEC
    benign - *see* Neoplasm, benign
    malignant - *see* Neoplasm,
      malignant
    uncertain behavior - *see* Neoplasm,
      uncertain behavior
  unspecified site
    benign D13.7
    malignant C25.4
    uncertain behavior D37.7
Glucoglycinuria E72.51
Glucose-galactose malabsorption E74.39
Glue
  ear - *see* Otitis, media, nonsuppurative,
    chronic, mucoid
  sniffing (airplane) – *see* Abuse, drug,
    inhalant
    dependence - *see* Dependence, drug,
      inhalant
Glutaric aciduria E72.3
Glycinemia E72.51
Glycinuria (renal) (with ketosis) E72.09
Glycogen
  infiltration - *see* Disease, glycogen
    storage
  storage disease - *see* Disease, glycogen
    storage
Glycogenosis (diffuse) (generalized) - *see
  also* Disease, glycogen storage
  cardiac E74.02 [I43]
  diabetic, secondary – *see* Diabetes,
    glycogenosis, secondary
Glycopenia E16.2
Glycosuria R81
  renal E74.8
Gnathostoma spinigerum (infection)
  (infestation), **gnathostomiasis** (wandering swelling) B83.1
Goiter (plunging) (substernal) E04.9
  with
    hyperthyroidism (recurrent) – *see*
      Hyperthyroidism, with,
      goiter
    thyrotoxicosis – *see* Hyperthyroidism,
      with, goiter
  adenomatous - *see* Goiter, nodular
  cancerous C73
  congenital (nontoxic) E03.0
    diffuse E03.0
    parenchymatous E03.0
    transitory, with normal functioning
      P72.0

Gout, gouty *(Continued)*
  secondary NEC *(Continued)*
    hand joint M10.44-
    hip M10.45-
    knee M10.46-
    multiple site M10.49
    shoulder M10.41-
    specified joint NEC M10.48
    wrist M10.43-
   syphilitic *(see also* subcategory M14.8-)
    A52.77
  tophi NEC - *see* Gout by type
Gout, chronic M1a.9 - *see also* Gout (acute)
  drug-induced M1a.20
    ankle M1a.27-
    elbow M1a.22-
    foot joint M1a.27-
    hand joint M1a.24-
    hip M1a.25-
    knee M1a.26-
    multiple site M1a.29-
    shoulder M1a.21-
    specified joint NEC M1a.28
    wrist M1a.23-
  idiopathic M1a.00
    ankle M1a.07-
    elbow M1a.02-
    foot joint M1a.07-
    hand joint M1a.04-
    hip M1a.05-
    knee M1a.06-
    multiple site M1a.09
    shoulder M1a.01-
    specified joint NEC M1a.08
    wrist M1a.03-
  in (due to) renal impairment M1a.30
    ankle M1a.37-
    elbow M1a.32-
    foot joint M1a.37-
    hand joint M1a.34-
    hip M1a.35-
    knee M1a.36-
    multiple site M1a.39
    shoulder M1a.31-
    specified joint NEC M1a.38
    wrist M1a.33-
  lead-induced M1a.10
    ankle M1a.17-
    elbow M1a.12-
    foot joint M1a.17-
    hand joint M1a.14-
    hip M1a.15-
    knee M1a.16-
    multiple site M1a.19
    shoulder M1a.11-
    specified joint NEC M1a.18
    wrist M1a.13-
  primary - *see* Gout, chronic, idiopathic
  saturnine - *see* Gout, chronic,
    lead-induced
  secondary NEC M1a.40
    ankle M1a.47-
    elbow M1a.42-
    foot joint M1a.47-
    hand joint M1a.44-
    hip M1a.45-
    knee M1a.46-
    multiple site M1a.49
    shoulder M1a.41-
    specified joint NEC M1a.48
    wrist M1a.43-
  syphilitic *(see also* subcategory M1a.8-)
    A52.77
  tophi - *see* Gout by type

Gower's
  muscular dystrophy G71.0
  syndrome (vasovagal attack) R55
Gradenigo's syndrome – *see* Otitis, media,
  suppurative, acute
Graefe's disease - *see* Strabismus, paralytic, ophthalmoplegia, progressive
Graft-versus-host disease D89.813
  acute D89.810
  acute on chronic D89.812
  chronic D89.811
Grainhandler's disease or lung J67.8
Grain mite (itch) B88.0
Grand mal – *see* Epilepsy, generalized,
  idiopathic
Grand multipara status only (not pregnant) Z64.1
  pregnant - *see* Pregnancy, complicated
    by, grand multiparity
Granite worker's lung J62.8
Granular - *see also* condition
  inflammation, pharynx J31.2
  kidney (contracting) - *see* Sclerosis,
    renal
  liver K74.69
Granulation tissue (abnormal) (excessive)
  L92.9
  postmastoidectomy cavity - *see* Com-
    plications, postmastoidectomy,
    granulation
Granulocytopenia (primary) (malignant) -
  see Agranulocytosis
Granuloma L92.9
  abdomen K66.8
    from residual foreign body L92.3
    pyogenicum L98.0
  actinic L57.5
  annulare (perforating) L92.0
  apical K04.5
  aural - *see* Otitis, externa, specified NEC
  beryllium (skin) L92.3
  bone
    eosinophilic C96.6
    from residual foreign body - *see*
      Osteomyelitis, specified type
      NEC
    lung C96.6
  brain (any site) G06.0
    schistosomiasis B65.9 *[G07]*
  canaliculus lacrimalis - *see* Granuloma,
    lacrimal
  candidal (cutaneous) B37.2
  cerebral (any site) G06.0
  coccidioidal (primary) (progressive)
    B38.7
    lung B38.1
    meninges B38.4
  colon K63.89
  conjunctiva H11.22-
  dental K04.5
  ear, middle – *see* Cholesteatoma
  eosinophilic C96.6
    bone C96.6
    lung C96.6
    oral mucosa K13.4
    skin L92.2
  eyelid H01.8
  facial(e) L92.2
  foreign body (in soft tissue) NEC
    M60.20
    ankle M60.27-
    foot M60.27-
    forearm M60.23-
    hand M60.24-

Granuloma *(Continued)*
  foreign body *(Continued)*
    in operation wound – *see* Foreign
      body, accidentally left during a
      procedure
    lower leg M60.26-
    pelvic region M60.25-
    shoulder region M60.21-
    skin L92.3
    specified site NEC M60.28
    subcutaneous tissue L92.3
    thigh M60.25-
    upper arm M60.22-
  gangraenescens M31.2
  genito-inguinale A58
  giant cell (central) (reparative) (jaw)
    M27.1
    gingiva (peripheral) K06.8
  gland (lymph) I88.8
  hepatic NEC K75.3
    in (due to)
      berylliosis J63.2 *[K77]*
      sarcoidosis D86.89
  Hodgkin C81.9
  ileum K63.89
  infectious B99.9
    specified NEC B99.8
  inguinale (Donovan) (venereal) A58
  intestine NEC K63.89
  intracranial (any site) G06.0
  intraspinal (any part) G06.1
  iridocyclitis - *see* Iridocyclitis, chronic
  jaw (bone) (central) M27.1
    reparative giant cell M27.1
  kidney *(see also* Infection, kidney)
    N15.8
  lacrimal H04.81-
  larynx J38.7
  lethal midline (faciale(e)) M31.2
  liver NEC - *see* Granuloma, hepatic
  lung (infectious) - *see also* Fibrosis, lung
    coccidioidal B38.1 *[J99]*
    eosinophilic C96.6
  Majocchi's B35.8
  malignant (facial(e)) M31.2
  mandible (central) M27.1
  midline (lethal) M31.2
  monilial (cutaneous) B37.2
  nasal sinus – *see* Sinusitis
  operation wound T81.89
    foreign body – *see* Foreign body,
      accidentally left during a
      procedure
    stitch T81.89
    talc – *see* Foreign body, accidentally
      left during a procedure
  oral mucosa K13.4
  orbit, orbital H05.11-
  paracoccidioidal B41.8
  penis, venereal A58
  periapical K04.5
  peritoneum K66.8
    due to ova of helminths NOS *(see also*
      Helminthiasis) B83.9 *[K67]*
  postmastoidectomy cavity - *see* Com-
    plications, postmastoidectomy,
    recurrent cholesteatoma
  prostate N42.89
  pudendi (ulcerating) A58
  pulp, internal (tooth) K03.3
  pyogenic, pyogenicum (of) (skin) L98.0
    gingiva K06.8
    maxillary alveolar ridge K04.5
    oral mucosa K13.4

Granuloma *(Continued)*
rectum K62.8
reticulohistiocytic D76.3
rubrum nasi L74.8
Schistosoma - *see* Schistosomiasis
septic (skin) L98.0
silica (skin) L92.3
sinus (accessory) (infective) (nasal) - *see*
Sinusitis
skin L92.9
from residual foreign body L92.3
pyogenicum L98.0
spine
syphilitic (epidural) A52.19
tuberculous A18.01
stitch (postoperative) T81.89
suppurative (skin) L98.0
swimming pool A31.1
talc - *see also* Granuloma, foreign body
in operation wound – *see* Foreign
body, accidentally left during a
procedure
telangiectaticum (skin) L98.0
tracheostomy J95.09
trichophyticum B35.8
tropicum A66.4
umbilicus L92.9
urethra N36.8
uveitis - *see* Iridocyclitis, chronic
vagina A58
venereum A58
vocal cord J38.3
Granulomatosis L92.9
lymphoid C83.8-
miliary (listerial) A32.89
necrotizing, respiratory M31.30
progressive septic D71
specified NEC L92.8
Wegener's M31.30
with renal involvement M31.31
Granulomatous tissue (abnormal) (excessive) L92.9
Granulosis rubra nasi L74.8
Graphite fibrosis (of lung) J63.3
Graphospasm F48.8
organic G25.89
Grating scapula M89.8x1
Gravel (urinary) - *see* Calculus, urinary
Graves' disease – *see* Hyperthyroidism,
with, goiter
Gravis - *see* condition
Grawitz tumor C64.-
Gray syndrome (newborn) P93.0
Grayness, hair (premature) L67.1
congenital Q84.2
Green sickness D50.8

Greenfield's disease
meaning
concentric sclerosis (encephalitis peri-
axialis concentrica) G37.5
metachromatic leukodystrophy
E75.25
Greenstick fracture - code as Fracture,
by site
Grey syndrome (newborn) P93.0
Grief F43.21
prolonged F43.29
reaction (*see also* Disorder, adjustment)
F43.20
Griesinger's disease B76.9
Grinder's lung or pneumoconiosis J62.8
Grinding, teeth
psychogenic F45.8
sleep related G47.63
Grip
Dabney's B33.0
devil's B33.0
Grippe, grippal - *see also* Influenza
Balkan A78
summer, of Italy A93.1
Grisel's disease M43.6
Groin - *see* condition
Grooved tongue K14.5
Ground itch B76.9
Grover's disease or syndrome L11.1
Growing pains, children R29.898
Growth (fungoid) (neoplastic) (new) - *see*
also Neoplasm
adenoid (vegetative) J35.8
benign - *see* Neoplasm, benign
malignant - *see* Neoplasm, malignant
rapid, childhood Z00.2
secondary - *see* Neoplasm, secondary
Gruby's disease B35.0
Gubler-Millard paralysis or syndrome
G46.3
Guerin-Stern syndrome Q74.3
Guidance, insufficient anterior (occlusal)
M26.54
Guillain-Barré disease or syndrome G61.0
sequelae G65.0
Guinea worms (infection) (infestation) B72
Guinon's disease (motor-verbal tic) F95.2
Gull's disease E03.4
Gum - *see* condition
Gumboil K04.7
with sinus K04.6
Gumma (syphilitic) A52.79
artery A52.09
cerebral A52.04
bone A52.77
of yaws (late) A66.6

Gumma *(Continued)*
brain A52.19
cauda equina A52.19
central nervous system A52.3
ciliary body A52.71
congenital A50.59
eyelid A52.71
heart A52.06
intracranial A52.19
iris A52.71
kidney A52.75
larynx A52.73
leptomeninges A52.19
liver A52.74
meninges A52.19
myocardium A52.06
nasopharynx A52.73
neurosyphilitic A52.3
nose A52.73
orbit A52.71
palate (soft) A52.79
penis A52.76
pericardium A52.06
pharynx A52.73
pituitary A52.79
scrofulous (tuberculous) A18.4
skin A52.79
specified site NEC A52.79
spinal cord A52.19
tongue A52.79
tonsil A52.73
trachea A52.73
tuberculous A18.4
ulcerative due to yaws A66.4
ureter A52.75
yaws A66.4
bone A66.6
Gunn's syndrome Q07.8
Gunshot wound - *see also* Wound, open
fracture - code as Fracture, by site
internal organs - *see* Injury, by site
Gynandrism Q56.0
Gynandroblastoma
specified site - *see* Neoplasm, uncertain
behavior
unspecified site
female D39.10
male D40.10
Gynecological examination (periodic)
(routine) Z01.419
with abnormal findings Z01.411
Gynecomastia N62
Gynephobia F40.291
Gyrate scalp Q82.8

H

H (Hartnup's) disease E72.02
Haas' disease or osteochondrosis (juvenile) (head of humerus) - *see* Osteochondrosis, juvenile, humerus
Habit, habituation
  bad sleep Z72.821
  chorea F95.8
  disturbance, child F98.9
  drug - *see* Dependence, drug
  irregular Z72.821
  laxative F55.2
  spasm - *see* Tic
  tic - *see* Tic
Haemophilus (H.) influenzae, as cause of disease classified elsewhere B96.3
Haff disease – *see* Poisoning, mercury
Hageman's factor defect, deficiency or disease D68.2
Haglund's disease or osteochondrosis (juvenile) (os tibiale externum) - *see* Osteochondrosis, juvenile, tarsus
Hailey-Hailey disease Q82.8
Hair - *see also* condition
  plucking F63.3
    in stereotyped movement disorder F98.4
  tourniquet syndrome - *see also* Constriction, external, by site
    finger S60.44-
    penis S30.842
    thumb S60.34-
    toe S90.44-
Hairball in stomach T18.2
Hair-pulling, pathological (compulsive) F63.3
Hairy black tongue K14.3
Half vertebra Q76.49
Halitosis R19.6
Hallerman-Streiff syndrome Q87.0
Hallervorden-Spatz disease G23.0
Hallopeau's acrodermatitis or disease L40.2
Hallucination R44.3
  auditory R44.0
  gustatory R44.2
  olfactory R44.2
  specified NEC R44.2
  tactile R44.2
  visual R44.1
Hallucinosis (chronic) F28
  alcoholic (acute) F10.951
    in
      abuse F10.151
      dependence F10.251
  drug-induced F19.951
    cannabis F12.951
    cocaine F14.951
    hallucinogen F16.151
    in
      abuse F19.151
        cannabis F12.151
        cocaine F14.151
        hallucinogen F16.151
        inhalant F18.151
        opioid F11.151
        sedative, anxiolytic or hypnotic F13.151
        stimulant NEC F15.151
      dependence F19.251
        cannabis F12.251
        cocaine F14.251
        hallucinogen F16.251

Hallucinosis (*Continued*)
  drug-induced (*Continued*)
    in (*Continued*)
      dependence (*Continued*)
        inhalant F18.251
        opioid F11.251
        sedative, anxiolytic or hypnotic F13.251
        stimulant NEC F15.251
      inhalant F18.951
      opioid F11.951
      sedative, anxiolytic or hypnotic F13.951
      stimulant NEC F15.951
    organic F06.0
Hallux
  deformity (acquired) NEC M20.5x-
  limitus M20.5x-
  malleus (acquired) NEC M20.3-
  rigidus (acquired) M20.2-
    congenital Q74.2
    sequelae (late effect) of rickets E64.3
  valgus (acquired) M20.1-
    congenital Q66.6
  varus (acquired) M20.3-
    congenital Q66.3
Halo, visual H53.19
Hamartoma, hamartoblastoma Q85.9
  epithelial (gingival), odontogenic, central or peripheral - *see* Cyst, calcifying odontogenic
Hamartosis Q85.9
Hamman-Rich syndrome J84.1
Hammer toe (acquired) NEC - *see also* Deformity, toe, hammer toe
  congenital Q66.8
  sequelae (late effect) of rickets E64.3
Hand - *see* condition
Hand-foot syndrome L27.1
Handicap, handicapped
  educational Z55.9
    specified NEC Z55.8
Hand-Schüller-Christian disease or syndrome C96.5
Hanging (asphyxia) (strangulation) (suffocation) - *see* Asphyxia, traumatic, due to mechanical threat
Hangnail - *see also* Cellulitis, digit
  with lymphangitis - *see* Lymphangitis, acute, digit
Hangover (alcohol) F10.129
Hanhart's syndrome Q87.0
Hanot-Chauffard(-Troisier) syndrome E83.19
Hanot's cirrhosis or disease K74.3
Hansen's disease - *see* Leprosy
Hantaan virus disease (Korean hemorrhagic fever) A98.5
Hantavirus disease (with renal manifestations) (Dobrava) (Puumala) (Seoul) A98.5
  with pulmonary manifestations (Andes) (Bayou) (Bermejo) (Black Creek Canal) (Choclo) (Juquitiba) (Laguna negra) (Lechiguanas) (New York) (Oran) (Sin nombre) B33.4
Happy puppet syndrome Q93.5
Harada's disease or syndrome H30.81-
Hardening
  artery - *see* Arteriosclerosis
  brain G93.89
Harelip (complete) (incomplete) - *see* Cleft, lip
Harlequin (newborn) Q80.4
Harley's disease D59.6

Harmful use (of)
  alcohol F10.10
  anxiolytics - *see* Abuse, drug, sedative
  cannabinoids – *see* Abuse, drug, cannabis
  cocaine – *see* Abuse, drug, cocaine
  drug - *see* Abuse, drug
  hallucinogens – *see* Abuse, drug, hallucinogen
  hypnotics - *see* Abuse, drug, sedative
    - opioids – *see* Abuse, drug, opioid
  PCP (phencyclidine) – *see* Abuse, drug NEC
  sedatives - *see* Abuse, drug, sedative
  stimulants NEC – *see* Abuse, drug, stimulant
Harris' lines - *see* Arrest, epiphyseal
Hartnup's disease E72.02
Harvester's lung J67.0
Harvesting ovum for in vitro fertilization Z31.83
Hashimoto's disease or thyroiditis E06.3
Hashitoxicosis (transient) E06.3
Hassal-Henle bodies or warts (cornea) H18.49
Haut mal – *see* Epilepsy, generalized, idiopathic
Haverhill fever A25.1
Hay fever J30.1
Hayem-Widal syndrome D59.8
Haygarth's nodes M15.8
Haymaker's lung J67.0
Hb (abnormal)
  Bart's disease D56.8
  disease - *see* Disease, hemoglobin
  trait - *see* Trait
Head - *see* condition
Headache R51
  allergic NEC G44.89
  associated with sexual activity G44.82
  chronic daily R51
  cluster G44.009
    chronic G44.029
      intractable G44.021
      not intractable G44.029
    episodic G44.019
      intractable G44.011
      not intractable G44.019
    intractable G44.001
    not intractable G44.009
  cough (primary) G44.83
  daily chronic R51
  drug-induced NEC G44.40
    intractable G44.41
    not intractable G44.40
  exertional (primary) G44.84
  histamine G44.009
    intractable G44.001
    not intractable G44.009
  hypnic G44.81
  lumbar puncture G97.1
  medication overuse G44.40
    intractable G44.41
    not intractable G44.40
  menstrual - *see* Migraine, menstrual
  migraine (type) (*see also* Migraine) G43.909
  nasal septum R51
  neuralgiform, short lasting unilateral, with conjunctival injection and tearing (SUNCT) G44.059
    intractable G44.051
    not intractable G44.059
  new daily persistent (NDPH) G44.52
  orgasmic G44.82

Headache (Continued)
  periodic
    periodic syndromes in adults and children G43.c09
      intractable G43.c19
        with status migrainosus G43.c11
        without status migrainosus G43.c19
      not intractable G43.c09
        with status migrainosus G43.c01
        without status migrainosus G43.c09
  postspinal puncture G97.1
  post-traumatic G44.309
    acute G44.319
      intractable G44.311
      not intractable G44.319
    chronic G44.329
      intractable G44.321
      not intractable G44.329
    intractable G44.301
    not intractable G44.309
  pre-menstrual - see Migraine, menstrual
  preorgasmic G44.82
  primary
    cough G44.83
    exertional G44.84
    stabbing G44.85
    thunderclap G44.53
  rebound G44.40
    intractable G44.41
    not intractable G44.40
  short lasting unilateral neuralgiform, with conjunctival injection and tearing (SUNCT) G44.059
    intractable G44.051
    not intractable G44.059
  specified syndrome NEC G44.89
  spinal and epidural anesthesia - induced T88.59
    in labor and delivery O74.5
    in pregnancy O29.4-
    postpartum, puerperal O89.4
  spinal fluid loss (from puncture) G97.1
  stabbing (primary) G44.85
  tension(-type) G44.209
    chronic G44.229
      intractable G44.221
      not intractable G44.229
    episodic G44.219
      intractable G44.211
      not intractable G44.219
    intractable G44.201
    not intractable G44.209
  thunderclap (primary) G44.53
  vascular NEC G44.10
    intractable G44.11
    not intractable G44.10
Healthy
  infant
    accompanying sick mother Z76.3
    receiving care Z76.2
  person accompanying sick person Z76.3
Hearing examination Z01.10
  with abnormal findings NEC Z01.118
  following failed hearing screening Z01.110
  for hearing conservation and treatment Z01.12
Heart - see condition
Heart beat
  abnormality R00.9
    specified NEC R00.8
  awareness R00.2
  rapid R00.0
  slow R00.1

Heartburn R12
  psychogenic F45.8
Heat (effects) T67.9
  apoplexy T67.0
  burn - see also Burn L55.9
  collapse T67.1
  cramps T67.2
  dermatitis or eczema L59.0
  edema T67.7
  erythema - code by site under Burn, first degree
  excessive T67.9
    specified effect NEC T67.8
  exhaustion T67.5
    anhydrotic T67.3
    due to
      salt (and water) depletion T67.4
      water depletion T67.3
        with salt depletion T67.4
  fatigue (transient) T67.6
  fever T67.0
  hyperpyrexia T67.0
  prickly L74.0
  prostration - see Heat, exhaustion
  pyrexia T67.0
  rash L74.0
  specified effect NEC T67.8
  stroke T67.0
  sunburn - see Sunburn
  syncope T67.1
Heavy-for-dates NEC (infant) (4000g to 4499g) P08.1
  exceptionally (4500g or more) P08.0
Hebephrenia, hebephrenic (schizophrenia) F20.1
Heberden's disease or nodes (with arthropathy) M15.1
Hebra's
  pityriasis L26
  prurigo L28.2
Heel - see condition
Heerfordt's disease D86.89
Hegglin's anomaly or syndrome D72.0
Heilmeyer-Schoner disease D45
Heine-Medin disease A80.9
Heinz body anemia, congenital D58.2
Heliophobia F40.228
Heller's disease or syndrome F84.3
Hellp syndrome O14.1-
Helminthiasis - see also Infestation, helminth
  Ancylostoma B76.0
  intestinal B82.0
    mixed types (types classifiable to more than one of the titles B65.0-B81.3 and B81.8) B81.4
    specified type NEC B81.8
  mixed types (intestinal) (types classifiable to more than one of the titles B65.0-B81.3 and B81.8) B81.4
  Necator (americanus) B76.1
  specified type NEC B83.8
Heloma L84
Hemangioblastoma - see Neoplasm, connective tissue, uncertain behavior
  malignant - see Neoplasm, connective tissue, malignant
Hemangioendothelioma – see also Neoplasm, uncertain behavior
  benign D18.00
    intra-abdominal D18.03
    intracranial D18.02
    skin D18.01
    specified site NEC D18.09

Hemangioendothelioma (Continued)
  bone (diffuse) - see Neoplasm, bone, malignant
  epithelioid - see also Neoplasm, uncertain behavior
    malignant - see Neoplasm, malignant
  malignant - see Neoplasm, connective tissue, malignant
Hemangiofibroma - see Neoplasm, benign
Hemangiolipoma - see Lipoma
Hemangioma D18.00
  arteriovenous D18.00
    intra-abdominal D18.03
    intracranial D18.02
    skin D18.01
    specified site NEC D18.09
  capillary D18.00
    intra-abdominal D18.03
    intracranial D18.02
    skin D18.01
    specified site NEC D18.09
  cavernous D18.00
    intra-abdominal D18.03
    intracranial D18.02
    skin D18.01
    specified site NEC D18.09
  epithelioid D18.00
    intra-abdominal D18.03
    intracranial D18.02
    skin D18.01
    specified site NEC D18.09
  histiocytoid D18.00
    intra-abdominal D18.03
    intracranial D18.02
    skin D18.01
    specified site NEC D18.09
  infantile D18.00
    intra-abdominal D18.03
    intracranial D18.02
    skin D18.01
    specified site NEC D18.09
  intra-abdominal D18.03
  intracranial D18.02
  intramuscular D18.00
    intra-abdominal D18.03
    intracranial D18.02
    skin D18.01
    specified site NEC D18.09
  juvenile D18.00
  malignant - see Neoplasm, connective tissue, malignant
  plexiform D18.00
    intra-abdominal D18.03
    intracranial D18.02
    skin D18.01
    specified site NEC D18.09
  racemose D18.00
    intra-abdominal D18.03
    intracranial D18.02
    skin D18.01
    specified site NEC D18.09
  sclerosing - see Neoplasm, skin, benign
  simplex D18.00
    intra-abdominal D18.03
    intracranial D18.02
    skin D18.01
    specified site NEC D18.09
  skin D18.01
  specified site NEC D18.09
  venous D18.00
    intra-abdominal D18.03
    intracranial D18.02
    skin D18.01
    specified site NEC D18.09

Hemangioma (Continued)
  verrucous keratotic D18.00
    intra-abdominal D18.03
    intracranial D18.02
    skin D18.01
    specified site NEC D18.09
Hemangiomatosis (systemic) I78.8
  involving single site - see
    Hemangioma
Hemangiopericytoma - see also
    Neoplasm, connective tissue,
    uncertain behavior
  benign - see Neoplasm, connective
    tissue, benign
  malignant - see Neoplasm, connective
    tissue, malignant
Hemangiosarcoma - see Neoplasm,
    connective tissue, malignant
Hemarthrosis (nontraumatic)
    M25.00
  ankle M25.07-
  elbow M25.02-
  foot joint M25.07-
  hand joint M25.04-
  hip M25.05-
  in hemophilic arthropathy - see
    Arthropathy, hemophilic
  knee M25.06-
  shoulder M25.01-
  specified joint NEC M25.08
  traumatic - see Sprain, by site
  wrist M25.03-
Hematemesis K92.0
  with ulcer - code by site under Ulcer,
    with hemorrhage K27.4
  newborn, neonatal P54.0
    due to swallowed maternal blood
    P78.2
Hematidrosis L74.8
Hematinuria - see also Hemoglobinuria
  malarial B50.8
Hematobilia K83.8
Hematocele
  female NEC N94.89
    with ectopic pregnancy O00.9
    ovary N83.8
  male N50.1
Hematochezia (see also Melena) K92.1
Hematochyluria - see also Infestation,
    filarial
  schistosomiasis (bilharziasis) B65.0
Hematocolpos (with hematometra or
    hematosalpinx) N89.7
Hematocornea - see Pigmentation, cornea,
    stromal
Hematogenous - see condition
Hematoma (traumatic) (skin surface
    intact) - see also Contusion
  with
    injury of internal organs - see Injury,
      by site
    open wound - see Wound, open
  amputation stump (surgical) (late)
    T87.8
  aorta, dissecting I71.00
    abdominal I71.02
    thoracic I71.01
    thoracoabdominal I71.03
  arterial (complicating trauma) - see
    Injury, blood vessel, by site
  auricle - see Contusion, ear
    nontraumatic - see Disorder, pinna,
      hematoma
  birth injury NEC P15.8

Hematoma (Continued)
  brain (traumatic)
    with
      cerebral laceration or contusion
        (diffuse) - see Injury, intracra-
        nial, diffuse
        focal - see Injury, intracranial,
          focal
    cerebellar, traumatic S06.37-
    newborn NEC P52.4
      birth injury P10.1
    intracerebral, traumatic - see Injury,
      intracranial, intracerebral
      hemorrhage
    nontraumatic - see Hemorrhage,
      intracranial
    subarachnoid, arachnoid, traumatic -
      see Injury, intracranial, subarach-
      noid hemorrhage
    subdural, traumatic - see Injury, intra-
      cranial, subdural hemorrhage
  breast (nontraumatic) N64.89
  broad ligament (nontraumatic) N83.7
    traumatic S37.892
  cerebellar, traumatic S06.37-
  cerebral - see Hematoma, brain
  cerebrum S06.36-
    left S06.35-
    right S06.34-
  cesarean delivery wound O90.2
  complicating delivery (perineal) (pel-
    vic) (vagina) (vulva) O71.7
  corpus cavernosum (nontraumatic)
    N48.89
  epididymis (nontraumatic) N50.1
  epidural (traumatic) - see Injury, intra-
    cranial, epidural hemorrhage
    spinal - see Injury, spinal cord, by
      region
  episiotomy O90.2
  face, birth injury P15.4
  genital organ NEC (nontraumatic)
    female (nonobstetric) N94.89
      traumatic S30.202
    male N50.1
      traumatic S30.201
  internal organs - see Injury, by site
  intracerebral, traumatic - see In-
    jury, intracranial, intracerebral
    hemorrhage
  intraoperative - see Complications,
    intraoperative, hemorrhage
  labia (nontraumatic) (nonobstetric)
    N90.8
  liver (subcapsular) (nontraumatic)
    K76.8
    birth injury P15.0
  mediastinum - see Injury, intrathoracic
  mesosalpinx (nontraumatic) N83.7
    traumatic S37.529
      bilateral S37.522
      unilateral S37.521
  muscle - code by site under Contusion
  nontraumatic
    muscle M79.81
    soft tissue M79.81
  obstetrical surgical wound O90.2
  orbit, orbital (nontraumatic) - see also
    Hemorrhage, orbit
    traumatic - see Contusion, orbit
  pelvis (female) (nontraumatic) (nonob-
    stetric) N94.89
    obstetric O71.7
    traumatic - see Injury, by site

Hematoma (Continued)
  penis (nontraumatic) N48.89
    birth injury P15.5
  perineal S30.23
    complicating delivery O71.7
  perirenal - see Injury, kidney
  pinna - see Contusion, ear
    nontraumatic - see Disorder, pinna,
      hematoma
  placenta O43.89-
  postoperative (postprocedural) - see
    Complication, postprocedural,
    hemorrhage
  retroperitoneal (nontraumatic) K66.1
    traumatic S36.892
  scrotum, superficial S30.22
    birth injury P15.5
  seminal vesicle (nontraumatic) N50.1
    traumatic S37.892
  spermatic cord (traumatic) S37.892
    nontraumatic N50.1
  spinal (cord) (meninges) - see also Injury,
    spinal cord, by region
    newborn (birth injury) P11.5
  spleen D73.5
    intraoperative see Complications,
      intraoperative, hemorrhage,
      spleen
    postprocedural (postoperative) see
      Complications, postprocedural,
      hemorrhage, spleen
  sternocleidomastoid, birth injury P15.2
  sternomastoid, birth injury P15.2
  subarachnoid (traumatic) - see Injury,
    intracranial, subarachnoid
    hemorrhage
    newborn (nontraumatic) P52.5
      due to birth injury P10.3
    nontraumatic - see Hemorrhage,
      intracranial, subarachnoid
  subdural (traumatic) - see Injury, intra-
    cranial, subdural hemorrhage
    newborn (localized) P52.8
      birth injury P10.0
    nontraumatic - see Hemorrhage,
      intracranial, subdural
  superficial, newborn P54.5
  testis (nontraumatic) N50.1
    birth injury P15.5
  tunica vaginalis (nontraumatic) N50.1
  umbilical cord, complicating delivery
    O69.5
  uterine ligament (broad) (nontraumatic)
    N83.7
    traumatic S37.62
  vagina (ruptured) (nontraumatic)
    N89.8
    complicating delivery O71.7
  vas deferens (nontraumatic) N50.1
    traumatic S37.892
  vitreous - see Hemorrhage, vitreous
  vulva (nontraumatic) (nonobstetric)
    N90.8
    complicating delivery O71.7
    newborn (birth injury) P15.5
Hematometra N85.7
  with hematocolpos N89.7
Hematomyelia (central) G95.19
  newborn (birth injury) P11.5
  traumatic T14.8
Hematomyelitis G04.90
Hematoperitoneum - see
    Hemoperitoneum
Hematophobia F40.230

Hematopneumothorax (see Hemothorax)
Hematopoiesis, cyclic D70.4
Hematoporphyria - see Porphyria
Hematorachis, hematorrhachis G95.19
  newborn (birth injury) P11.5
Hematosalpinx N83.6
  with
    hematocolpos N89.7
    hematometra N85.7
      with hematocolpos N89.7
  infectional - see Salpingitis
Hematospermia R36.1
Hematothorax (see Hemothorax)
Hematuria R31.9
  due to sulphonamide, sulfonamide - see
    Table of drugs and chemicals, by
    drug
  benign (familial) (of childhood) - see also
    Hematuria, idiopathic
    essential microscopic R31.1
  endemic (see also Schistosomiasis)
    B65.0
  gross R31.0
  idiopathic N02.9
    with glomerular lesion
      crescentic (diffuse) glomerulone-
        phritis N02.7
      dense deposit disease N02.6
      endocapillary proliferative glo-
        merulonephritis N02.4
      focal and segmental hyalinosis or
        sclerosis N02.1
      membranoproliferative (diffuse)
        N02.5
      membranous (diffuse) N02.2
      mesangial proliferative (diffuse)
        N02.3
      mesangiocapillary (diffuse) N02.5
      minor abnormality N02.0
      proliferative NEC N02.8
      specified pathology NEC N02.8
  intermittent - see Hematuria, idiopathic
  malarial B50.8
  microscopic NEC R31.2
    benign essential R31.1
  paroxysmal - see also Hematuria,
    idiopathic
    nocturnal D59.5
  persistent - see Hematuria, idiopathic
  recurrent - see Hematuria, idiopathic
  tropical (see also Schistosomiasis)
    B65.0
  tuberculous A18.13
Hemeralopia (day blindness) H53.11
  vitamin A deficiency E50.5
Hemi-akinesia R41.4
Hemianalgesia R20.0
Hemianencephaly Q00.0
Hemianesthesia R20.0
Hemianopia, hemianopsia (heterony-
    mous) H53.47
  homonymous H53.46-
  syphilitic A52.71
Hemiathetosis R25.8
Hemiatrophy R68.89
  cerebellar G31.9
  face, facial, progressive (Romberg)
    G51.8
  tongue K14.8
Hemiballism(us) G25.5
Hemicardia Q24.8
Hemicephalus, hemicephaly Q00.0
Hemichorea G25.5
Hemicolitis, left - see Colitis, left sided

Hemicrania
  congenital malformation Q00.0
  continua G44.51
  meaning migraine (see also Migraine)
    G43.909
  paroxysmal G44.039
    chronic G44.049
      intractable G44.041
      not intractable G44.049
    episodic G44.039
      intractable G44.031
      not intractable G44.039
    intractable G44.031
    not intractable G44.039
Hemidystrophy - see Hemiatrophy
Hemiectromelia Q73.8
Hemihypalgesia R20.8
Hemihypesthesia R20.1
Hemi-inattention R41.4
Hemimelia Q73.8
  lower limb – see Defect, reduction,
    lower limb, specified type NEC
  upper limb - see Defect, reduction,
    upper limb, specified type NEC
Hemiparalysis - see Hemiplegia
Hemiparesis - see Hemiplegia
Hemiparesthesia R20.2
Hemiparkinsonism G20
Hemiplegia G81.9-
  alternans facialis G83.89
  ascending NEC G81.90
    spinal G95.89
  congenital (cerebral) G80.8
    spastic G80.2
  embolic (current episode) I63.4-
  flaccid G81.0-
    following
      cerebrovascular disease I69.959
        cerebral infarction I69.35-
        intracerebral hemorrhage I69.15-
        nontraumatic intracranial hem-
          orrhage NEC I69.25-
        specified disease NEC I69.85-
        stroke NOS I69.35-
        subarachnoid hemorrhage I69.05-
  hysterical F44.4
  newborn NEC P91.8
    birth injury P11.9
  spastic G81.1-
    congenital G80.2
  thrombotic (current episode) I63.3
Hemisection, spinal cord - see Injury,
    spinal cord, by region
Hemispasm (facial) R25.2
Hemisporosis B48.8
Hemitremor R25.1
Hemivertebra Q76.49
  failure of segmentation with scoliosis
    Q76.3
  fusion with scoliosis Q76.3
Hemochromatosis (diabetic) (hereditary)
    (liver) (myocardium) (primary
    idiopathic) (secondary) E83.11
  with refractory anemia D46.1
Hemoglobin - see also condition
  abnormal (disease) - see Disease,
    hemoglobin
  AS genotype D57.3
  fetal, hereditary persistence (HPFH)
    D56.4
  low NOS D64.9
  S (Hb S), heterozygous D57.3
Hemoglobinemia D59.9
  due to blood transfusion T80.89

Hemoglobinemia (Continued)
  paroxysmal D59.6
    nocturnal D59.5
Hemoglobinopathy (mixed) D58.2
  with thalassemia D56.9
  sickle-cell D57.1
    with thalassemia D57.40
      with crisis (vasoocclusive pain)
        D57.419
      with
        acute chest syndrome
          D57.411
        splenic sequestration
          D57.412
      without crisis D57.40
Hemoglobinuria R82.3
  with anemia, hemolytic, acquired
    (chronic) NEC D59.6
  cold (agglutinin) (paroxysmal) (with
    Raynaud's syndrome) D59.6
  due to exertion or hemolysis NEC
    D59.6
  intermittent D59.6
  malarial B50.8
  march D59.6
  nocturnal (paroxysmal) D59.5
  paroxysmal (cold) D59.6
    nocturnal D59.5
Hemolymphangioma D18.1
Hemolysis
  intravascular
    with
      abortion - see Abortion, by type,
        complicated by, hemorrhage
      ectopic or molar pregnancy O08.1
      hemorrhage
        antepartum - see Hemorrhage,
          antepartum
        intrapartum - see also Hemor-
          rhage, complicating, deliv-
          ery O67.0
      postpartum O72.3
  neonatal (excessive) P58.8
Hemolytic - see condition
Hemopericardium I31.2
  following acute myocardial infarction
    (current complication) I23.0
  newborn P54.8
  traumatic – see Injury, heart, with
    hemopericardium
Hemoperitoneum K66.1
  infectional K65.9
  traumatic S36.899
    with open wound - see Wound, open,
      with penetration into peritoneal
      cavity
Hemophilia (classical) (familial) (heredi-
    tary) D66
  A D66
  B D67
  C D68.1
  calcipriva (see also Defect, coagulation)
    D68.4
  nonfamilial (see also Defect, coagulation)
    D68.4
  secondary D68.31
  vascular D68.0
Hemophthalmos H44.81-
Hemopneumothorax - see also
    Hemothorax
  traumatic S27.2
Hemoptysis R04.2
  newborn P26.9

Hemoptysis *(Continued)*
  tuberculous - *see* Tuberculosis,
    pulmonary
Hemorrhage, hemorrhagic (concealed)
    R58
  abdomen R58
  accidental antepartum – *see* Hemor-
    rhage, antepartum
  adenoid J35.8
  adrenal (capsule) (gland) E27.49
    medulla E27.8
    newborn P54.4
  after delivery - *see* Hemorrhage,
    postpartum
  alveolar
    lung, newborn P26.8
    process K08.8
  alveolus K08.8
  amputation stump (surgical) T87.8
  anemia (chronic) D50.0
    acute D62
  antepartum (with) O46.90
    with coagulation defect O46.00-
      afibrinogenemia O46.01-
      disseminated intravascular coagu-
        lation O46.02-
      hypofibrinogenemia – *see* Hem-
        orrhage, antepartum,
        with coagulation defect,
        afibrinogenemia
      specified defect NEC O46.09-
    before 20 weeks gestation O20.9
      specified type NEC O20.8
      threatened abortion O20.0
    due to
      abruptio placenta O45.— *See also*
        Abruptio placentae
      leiomyoma, uterus – *see* Hemor-
        rhage, antepartum, specified
        cause NEC
      placenta previa O44.1-
      specified cause NEC - *see* subcategory
        O46.8x-
  anus (sphincter) K62.5
  apoplexy (stroke) - *see* Hemorrhage,
    intracranial, intracerebral
  arachnoid - *see* Hemorrhage, intracra-
    nial, subarachnoid
  artery R58
    brain - *see* Hemorrhage, intracranial,
      intracerebral
    basilar (ganglion) I61.0
  bladder N32.89
  bowel K92.2
    newborn P54.3
  brain (miliary) (nontraumatic) –
    see Hemorrhage, intracranial,
      intracerebral
    due to
      birth injury P10.1
      syphilis A52.05
    epidural or extradural (traumatic)
      – *see* Injury, intracranial, epidu-
        ral hemorrhage
    newborn P52.4
      birth injury P10.1
    subarachnoid - *see* Hemorrhage,
      intracranial, subarachnoid
    subdural - *see* Hemorrhage, intracra-
      nial, subdural
  brainstem (nontraumatic) I61.3
    traumatic S06.38-
  breast N64.59

Hemorrhage, hemorrhagic *(Continued)*
  bronchial tube - *see* Hemorrhage,
    lung
  bronchopulmonary - *see* Hemorrhage,
    lung
  bronchus - *see* Hemorrhage, lung
  bulbar I61.5
  capillary I78.8
    primary D69.8
  cecum K92.2
  cerebellar, cerebellum (nontraumatic)
    I61.4
    newborn P52.6
    traumatic S06.37-
  cerebral, cerebrum - *see also* Hemor-
    rhage, intracranial, intracerebral
    newborn (anoxic) P52.4
      birth injury P10.1
    lobe I61.1
  cerebromeningeal I61.8
  cerebrospinal - *see* Hemorrhage, intra-
    cranial, intracerebral
  cervix (uteri) (stump) NEC N88.8
  chamber, anterior (eye) - *see*
    Hyphema
  childbirth - *see* Hemorrhage, compli-
    cating, delivery
  choroid H31.30-
    expulsive H31.31-
  ciliary body - *see* Hyphema
  cochlea - *see* subcategory H83.8
  colon K92.2
  complicating
    abortion – *see* Abortion, by type, com-
      plicated by, hemorrhage
    delivery O67.9
      associated with coagulation defect
        (afibrinogenemia) (DIC) (hy-
        perfibrinolysis) O67.0
      specified cause NEC O67.8
    surgical procedure – *see* Hemorrhage,
      intraoperative
  conjunctiva H11.3-
    newborn P54.8
  cord, newborn (stump) P51.9
  corpus luteum (ruptured) cyst N83.1
  cortical (brain) I61.1
  cranial - *see* Hemorrhage, intracranial
  cutaneous R23.3
    due to autosensitivity, erythrocyte
      D69.2
    newborn P54.5
  delayed
    following ectopic or molar pregnancy
      O08.1
    postpartum O72.2
  diathesis (familial) D69.9
  disease D69.9
    newborn P53
    specified type NEC D69.8
  due to or associated with
    afibrinogenemia or other coagulation
      defect (conditions in categories
      D65D69)
      antepartum – *see* Hemorrhage,
        antepartum, with coagulation
        defect
      intrapartum O67.0
    dental implant M27.61
    device, implant or graft (*see also*
      Complications, by site and type,
      specified NEC) T85.83
      arterial graft NEC T82.838
      breast T85.83

Hemorrhage, hemorrhagic *(Continued)*
  due to or associated with *(Continued)*
    device, implant or graft *(Continued)*
      catheter NEC T85.83
        dialysis (renal) T82.838
          intraperitoneal T85.83
        infusion NEC T82.838
          spinal (epidural) (subdural)
            T85.83
        urinary (indwelling) T83.83
      electronic (electrode) (pulse genera-
        tor) (stimulator)
        bone T84.83
        cardiac T82.837
        nervous system (brain) (peri-
          pheral nerve) (spinal)
          T85.83
        urinary T83.83
      fixation, internal (orthopedic) NEC
        T84.83
      gastrointestinal (bile duct) (esopha-
        gus) T85.83
      genital NEC T83.83
      heart NEC T82.837
      joint prosthesis T84.83
      ocular (corneal graft) (orbital im-
        plant) NEC T85.83
      orthopedic NEC T84.83
        bone graft T86.838
      specified NEC T85.83
      urinary NEC T83.83
      vascular NEC T82.838
      ventricular intracranial shunt
        T85.83
    duodenum, duodenal K92.2
      ulcer - *see* Ulcer, duodenum, with
        hemorrhage
    dura mater - *see* Hemorrhage, intracra-
      nial, subdural
    endotracheal - *see* Hemorrhage, lung
    epicranial subaponeurotic (massive),
      birth injury P12.2
    epidural (traumatic) – *see also* Injury,
      intracranial, epidural hemorrhage
      nontraumatic I62.1
    esophagus K22.8
      varix I85.01
        secondary I85.11
    excessive, following ectopic gestation
      (subsequent episode) O08.1
    extradural (traumatic) – *see* Injury, intra-
      cranial, epidural hemorrhage
      birth injury P10.8
      newborn (anoxic) (nontraumatic)
        P52.8
      nontraumatic I62.1
    eye NEC H57.8
      fundus - *see* Hemorrhage, retina
      lid - *see* Disorder, eyelid, specified
        type NEC
    fallopian tube N83.6
    fibrinogenolysis - *see* Fibrinolysis
    fibrinolytic (acquired) - *see* Fibrinolysis
    from
      ear (nontraumatic) - *see* Otorrhagia
      tracheostomy stoma J95.01
    fundus, eye - *see* Hemorrhage, retina
    funis - *see* Hemorrhage, umbilicus, cord
    gastric - *see* Hemorrhage, stomach
    gastroenteric K92.2
      newborn P54.3
    gastrointestinal (tract) K92.2
      newborn P54.3
    genital organ, male N50.1

Hemorrhage, hemorrhagic *(Continued)*
genitourinary (tract) NOS R31.9
gingiva K06.8
globe (eye) - *see* Hemophthalmos
graafian follicle cyst (ruptured) N83.0
gum K06.8
heart I51.89
hypopharyngeal (throat) R58
intermenstrual (regular) N92.3
  irregular N92.1
internal (organs) NEC R58
  capsule I61.0
  ear - *see* subcategory H83.8
  newborn P54.8
intestine K92.2
  newborn P54.3
intra-abdominal R58
intra-alveolar (lung), newborn P26.8
intracerebral (nontraumatic) - *see* Hemorrhage, intracranial, intracerebral
intracranial (nontraumatic) I62.9
  birth injury P10.9
  epidural, nontraumatic I62.1
  extradural, nontraumatic I62.1
  newborn P52.9
    specified NEC P52.8
  intracerebral (nontraumatic) (in) I61.9
    brain stem I61.3
    cerebellum I61.4
    newborn P52.4
      birth injury P10.1
    hemisphere I61.2
      cortical (superficial) I61.1
      subcortical (deep) I61.0
    intraoperative
      during a nervous system procedure G97.31
      during other procedure G97.32
    intraventricular I61.5
    multiple localized I61.6
    postprocedural
      during a nervous system procedure G97.51
      during other procedure G97.52
    specified NEC I61.8
    superficial I61.1
    traumatic (diffuse) – *see* Injury, intracranial, diffuse
      focal – *see* Injury, intracranial, focal
  subarachnoid (nontraumatic) (from) I60.9
    newborn P52.5
      birth injury P10.3
    intracranial (cerebral) artery I60.7
      anterior communicating I60.2-
      basilar I60.4
      carotid siphon and bifurcation I60.0-
      communicating I60.7
        anterior I60.2-
        posterior I60.3-
      middle cerebral I60.1-
      posterior communicating I60.3-
      specified artery NEC I60.6
      vertebral I60.5-
    specified NEC I60.8
    traumatic S06.6x-
  subdural (nontraumatic) I62.00
    acute I62.01
    birth injury P10.0
    chronic I62.03

Hemorrhage, hemorrhagic *(Continued)*
intracranial *(Continued)*
  subdural *(Continued)*
    newborn (anoxic) (hypoxic) P52.8
      birth injury P10.0
    spinal G95.19
    subacute I62.02
    traumatic – *see* Injury, intracranial, subdural hemorrhage
    traumatic – *see* Injury, intracranial, focal brain injury
intramedullary NEC G95.19
intraocular - *see* Hemophthalmos
intraoperative, intraprocedural - *see* Complication, hemorrhage (hematoma), intraoperative (intraprocedural), by site
intrapartum - *see* Hemorrhage, complicating, delivery
intrapelvic
  female N94.89
  male K66.1
intraperitoneal K66.1
intrapontine I61.3
intraprocedural - *see* Complication, hemorrhage (hematoma), intraoperative (intraprocedural), by site
intrauterine N85.7
  complicating delivery - *see also* Hemorrhage, complicating, delivery O67.9
  postpartum - *see* Hemorrhage, postpartum
intraventricular I61.5
  newborn (nontraumatic) (*see also* Newborn, affected by, hemorrhage) P52.3
  due to birth injury P10.2
  grade
    1 P52.0
    2 P52.1
    3 P52.21
    4 P52.22
intravesical N32.89
iris (postinfectional) (postinflammatory) (toxic) - *see* Hyphema
joint (nontraumatic) - *see* Hemarthrosis
kidney N28.89
knee (joint) (nontraumatic) - *see* Hemarthrosis, knee
labyrinth - *see* subcategory H83.8
lenticular striate artery I61.0
ligature, vessel – *see* Hemorrhage, postoperative
liver K76.8
lung R04.8
  newborn P26.9
    massive P26.1
    specified NEC P26.8
  tuberculous - *see* Tuberculosis, pulmonary
massive umbilical, newborn P51.0
mediastinum - *see* Hemorrhage, lung
medulla I61.3
membrane (brain) I60.8
  spinal cord - *see* Hemorrhage, spinal cord
meninges, meningeal (brain) (middle) I60.8
  spinal cord - *see* Hemorrhage, spinal cord
mesentery K66.1

Hemorrhage, hemorrhagic *(Continued)*
metritis - *see* Endometritis
mouth K13.79
mucous membrane NEC R58
  newborn P54.8
muscle M62.89
nail (subungual) L60.8
nasal turbinate R04.0
  newborn P54.8
navel, newborn P51.9
newborn P54.9
  specified NEC P54.8
nipple N64.59
nose R04.0
  newborn P54.8
omentum K66.1
optic nerve (sheath) H47.02-
orbit, orbital H05.23-
ovary NEC N83.8
oviduct N83.6
pancreas K86.8
parathyroid (gland) (spontaneous) E21.4
parturition - *see* Hemorrhage, complicating, delivery
penis N48.89
pericardium, pericarditis I31.2
peritoneum, peritoneal K66.1
peritonsillar tissue J35.8
  due to infection J36
petechial R23.3
  due to autosensitivity, erythrocyte D69.2
pituitary (gland) E23.6
pleura - *see* Hemorrhage, lung
polioencephalitis, superior E51.2
polymyositis - *see* Polymyositis
pons, pontine I61.3
posterior fossa (nontraumatic) I61.8
  newborn P52.6
postmenopausal N95.0
postnasal R04.0
postoperative - *see* Complications, postprocedural, hemorrhage, by site
postpartum NEC (following delivery of placenta) O72.1
  delayed or secondary O72.2
  retained placenta O72.0
  third stage O72.0
pregnancy - *see* Hemorrhage, antepartum
preretinal - *see* Hemorrhage, retina
prostate N42.1
puerperal - *see* Hemorrhage, postpartum
  delayed or secondary O72.2
pulmonary R04.8
  newborn P26.9
    massive P26.1
    specified NEC P26.8
  tuberculous - *see* Tuberculosis, pulmonary
purpura (primary) D69.3
rectum (sphincter) K62.5
  newborn P54.2
recurring, following initial hemorrhage at time of injury T79.2
renal N28.89
respiratory passage or tract R04.9
  specified NEC R04.8
retina, retinal (vessels) H35.6-
  diabetic – *see* Diabetes, retinal, hemorrhage

Hemorrhage, hemorrhagic *(Continued)*
retroperitoneal R58
scalp R58
scrotum N50.1
secondary (nontraumatic) R58
  following initial hemorrhage at time
    of injury T79.2
seminal vesicle N50.1
skin R23.3
  newborn P54.5
slipped umbilical ligature P51.8
spermatic cord N50.1
spinal (cord) G95.19
  newborn (birth injury) P11.5
spleen D73.5
  intraoperative *see* Complications,
    intraoperative, hemorrhage,
    spleen
  postprocedural *see* Complications,
    postprocedural, hemorrhage,
    spleen
stomach K92.2
  newborn P54.3
  ulcer - *see* Ulcer, stomach, with
    hemorrhage
subarachnoid (nontraumatic) - *see*
    Hemorrhage, intracranial,
    subarachnoid
subconjunctival - *see also* Hemorrhage,
    conjunctiva
  birth injury P15.3
subcortical (brain) I61.0
subcutaneous R23.3
subdiaphragmatic R58
subdural (acute) (nontraumatic)
    - *see* Hemorrhage, intracranial,
    subarachnoid
subependymal
  newborn P52.0
    with intraventricular extension
      P52.1
    and intracerebral extension
      P52.22
subhyaloid - *see* Hemorrhage, retina
subperiosteal - *see* Disorder, bone,
    specified type NEC
subretinal - *see* Hemorrhage, retina
subtentorial - *see* Hemorrhage, intracra-
    nial, subarachnoid
subungual L60.8
suprarenal (capsule) (gland) E27.49
  newborn P54.4
tentorium (traumatic) NEC – *see* Hem-
    orrhage, brain
  newborn (birth injury) P10.4
testis N50.1
third stage (postpartum) O72.0
thorax - *see* Hemorrhage, lung
throat R04.1
thymus (gland) E32.8
thyroid (cyst) (gland) E07.89
tongue K14.8
tonsil J35.8
trachea - *see* Hemorrhage, lung
tracheobronchial R04.8
  newborn P26.0
traumatic - code to specific injury
  cerebellar – *see* Hemorrhage, brain
  intracranial – *see* Hemorrhage,
    brain
  recurring or secondary (following
    initial hemorrhage at time of
    injury) T79.2

Hemorrhage, hemorrhagic *(Continued)*
tuberculous NEC - *see also* Tuberculosis,
    pulmonary A15.0
tunica vaginalis N50.1
ulcer - code by site under Ulcer, with
    hemorrhage K27.4
umbilicus, umbilical
  cord
    after birth, newborn P51.9
    complicating delivery O69.5
  newborn P51.9
    massive P51.0
    slipped ligature P51.8
  stump P51.9
urethra (idiopathic) N36.8
uterus, uterine (abnormal) N93.9
  climacteric N92.4
  complicating delivery - *see*
    Hemorrhage, complicating,
    delivery
  dysfunctional or functional
    N93.8
  intermenstrual (regular)
    N92.3
    irregular N92.1
  postmenopausal N95.0
  postpartum - *see* Hemorrhage,
    postpartum
  preclimacteric or premenopausal
    N92.4
  prepubertal N93.8
  pubertal N92.2
vagina (abnormal) N93.9
  newborn P54.6
vas deferens N50.1
vasa previa O69.4
ventricular I61.5
vesical N32.89
viscera NEC R58
  newborn P54.8
vitreous (humor) (intraocular)
    H43.1-
vulva N90.8
Hemorrhoids I84.20
  bleeding I84.101
  external I84.22
    with internal I84.23
      bleeding I84.131
      prolapsed I84.132
      strangulated I84.133
      thrombosed I84.03
      ulcerated I84.134-
    bleeding I84.121
    prolapsed I84.122
    strangulated I84.123
    thrombosed I84.02
    ulcerated I84.124
  internal I84.21
    with external I84.23
      bleeding I84.131
      prolapsed I84.132
      strangulated I84.133
      thrombosed I84.03
      ulcerated I84.134-
    bleeding I84.111
    prolapsed I84.112
    strangulated I84.113
    thrombosed I84.01
    ulcerated I84.114
  prolapsed I84.102
  skin tags, residual I84.6
  strangulated I84.103
  thrombosed I84.00
  ulcerated I84.104

Hemosalpinx N83.6
  with
    hematocolpos N89.7
    hematometra N85.7
      with hematocolpos N89.7
Hemosiderosis (dietary) E83.19
  pulmonary, idiopathic E83.19 *[J99]*
  transfusion T80.89
Hemothorax (bacterial) (nontuberculous)
    J94.2
  newborn P54.8
  traumatic S27.1
    with pneumothorax S27.2
  tuberculous NEC A15.6
Henoch(-Schönlein) disease or syndrome
    (purpura) D69.0
Henpue, henpuye A66.6
Hepar lobatum (syphilitic) A52.74
Hepatalgia K76.8
Hepatitis K75.9
  acute B17.9
    with coma K72.01
    with hepatic failure - *see* Failure,
      hepatic
    alcoholic – *see* Hepatitis, alcoholic
    infectious B15.9
      with hepatic coma B15.0
    viral B17.9
  alcoholic (acute) (chronic) K70.10
    with ascites K70.11
  amebic - *see* Abscess, liver, amebic
  anicteric, acute (viral) - *see* Hepatitis,
    viral
  antigen-associated (HAA) - *see*
    Hepatitis, B
  Australia-antigen (positive) - *see*
    Hepatitis, B
  autoimmune K75.4
  B B19.10
    with hepatic coma B19.11
    acute B16.9
      with
        delta-agent (coinfection) (with-
          out hepatic coma) B16.1
        with hepatic coma B16.0
        hepatic coma (without delta-
          agent coinfection) B16.2
    chronic B18.1
      with delta-agent B18.0
  bacterial NEC K75.89
  C (viral) B19.20
    with hepatic coma B19.21
    acute B17.10
      with hepatic coma B17.11
    chronic B18.2
  catarrhal (acute) B15.9
    with hepatic coma B15.0
  cholangiolitic K75.89
  cholestatic K75.89
  chronic K73.9
    active NEC K73.2
    lobular NEC K73.1
    persistent NEC K73.0
    specified NEC K73.8
  cytomegaloviral B25.1
  due to ethanol (acute) (chronic) – *see*
    Hepatitis, alcoholic
  epidemic B15.9
    with hepatic coma B15.0
  fulminant NEC (viral) - *see* Hepatitis,
    viral
  giant cell P59.29
  granulomatous NEC K75.3
  herpesviral B00.81

Hepatitis *(Continued)*
history of
B Z86.19
C Z86.19
homologous serum - *see* Hepatitis, viral,
type B
in (due to)
mumps B26.81
toxoplasmosis (acquired) B58.1
congenital (active) P37.1 *[K77]*
infectious, infective (acute) (chronic)
(subacute) B15.9
with hepatic coma B15.0
inoculation - *see* Hepatitis, viral, type B
interstitial (chronic) K74.69
lupoid NEC K73.2
malignant NEC (with hepatic failure)
K72.90
with coma K72.91
neonatal (idiopathic) (toxic) P59.29
newborn P59.29
postimmunization - *see* Hepatitis, viral,
type B
post-transfusion - *see* Hepatitis, viral,
type B
reactive, nonspecific K75.2
serum - *see* Hepatitis, viral, type B
specified type NEC
with hepatic failure – *see* Failure,
hepatic
syphilitic (late) A52.74
congenital (early) A50.08 *[K77]*
late A50.59 *[K77]*
secondary A51.45
toxic (*see also* Disease, liver, toxic) K71.6
tuberculous A18.83
viral, virus B19.9
with hepatic coma B19.0
acute B17.9
chronic B18.9
specified NEC B18.8
type
B B18.1
with delta-agent B18.0
C B18.2
congenital P35.3
coxsackie B33.8 *[K77]*
cytomegalic inclusion B25.1
in remission, any type - code to
Hepatitis, chronic, by type
non-A, non-B B17.8
specified type NEC (with or without
coma) B17.8
type
A B15.9
with hepatic coma B15.0
B B19.10
with hepatic coma B19.11
acute B16.9
with
delta-agent (coinfection)
(without hepatic coma)
B16.1
with hepatic coma B16.0
hepatic coma (without
delta-agent coinfection)
B16.2
chronic B18.1
with delta-agent B18.0
C B19.20
with hepatic coma B19.21
acute B17.10
with hepatic coma B17.11
chronic B18.2

Hepatitis *(Continued)*
viral, virus *(Continued)*
type *(Continued)*
E B17.2
non-A, non-B B17.8
Hepatization lung (acute) - *see* Pneumo-
nia, lobar
Hepatoblastoma C22.2
Hepatocarcinoma C22.0
Hepatocholangiocarcinoma C22.0
Hepatocholangioma, benign D13.4
Hepatocholangitis K75.89
Hepatolenticular degeneration E83.01
Hepatoma (malignant) C22.0
benign D13.4
embryonal C22.0
Hepatomegaly - *see also* Hypertrophy,
liver
with splenomegaly R16.2
congenital Q44.7
in infectious mononucleosis (gamma-
herpesviral) B27.09
Hepatoptosis K76.8
Hepatorenal syndrome following labor
and delivery O90.4
Hepatosis K76.8
Hepatosplenomegaly R16.2
hyperlipemic (Bürger-Grütz type) E78.3
[K77]
Hereditary - *see* condition
Heredodegeneration, macular - *see* Dystrophy, retina
Heredopathia atactica polyneuritiformis
G60.1
Heredosyphilis - *see* Syphilis, congenital
Herlitz' syndrome Q81.1
Hermansky-Pudlak syndrome E70.331
Hermaphrodite, hermaphroditism (true)
Q56.0
46,XX with streak gonads Q99.1
46,XX/46,XY Q99.0
46,XY with streak gonads Q99.1
chimera 46,XX/46,XY Q99.0
Hernia, hernial (acquired) (recurrent)
K46.9
with
gangrene - *see* Hernia, by site, with,
gangrene
incarceration - *see* Hernia, by site,
with, obstruction
irreducible - *see* Hernia, by site, with,
obstruction
obstruction - *see* Hernia, by site, with,
obstruction
strangulation - *see* Hernia, by site,
with, obstruction
abdomen, abdominal K46.9
with
gangrene (and obstruction) K46.1
obstruction K46.0
femoral – *see* Hernia, femoral
incisional – *see* Hernia, incisional
inguinal – *see* Hernia, inguinal
specified site NEC K45.8
with
gangrene (and obstruction) K45.1
obstruction K45.0
umbilical – *see* Hernia, umbilical
wall - *see* Hernia, ventral
appendix - *see* Hernia, abdomen
bladder (mucosa) (sphincter)
congenital (female) (male) Q79.51
female - *see* Cystocele
male N32.89

Hernia, hernial *(Continued)*
brain, congenital - *see* Encephalocele
cartilage, vertebra - *see* Displacement,
intervertebral disc
cerebral, congenital - *see also*
Encephalocele
endaural Q01.8
ciliary body (traumatic) S05.2-
colon - *see* Hernia, abdomen
Cooper's - *see* Hernia, abdomen, specified site NEC
crural - *see* Hernia, femoral
diaphragm, diaphragmatic K44.9
with
gangrene (and obstruction) K44.1
obstruction K44.0
congenital Q79.0
direct (inguinal) - *see* Hernia, inguinal
diverticulum, intestine - *see* Hernia,
abdomen
double (inguinal) - *see* Hernia, inguinal,
bilateral
due to adhesions (with obstruction)
K56.5
epigastric - *see* Hernia, ventral
esophageal hiatus - *see* Hernia, hiatal
external (inguinal) - *see* Hernia, inguinal
fallopian tube N83.4
fascia M62.89
femoral K41.90
with
gangrene (and obstruction) K41.40
not specified as recurrent K41.40
recurrent K41.41
obstruction K41.30
not specified as recurrent K41.30
recurrent K41.31
bilateral K41.20
with
gangrene (and obstruction)
K41.10
not specified as recurrent
K41.10
recurrent K41.11
obstruction K41.00
not specified as recurrent
K41.00
recurrent K41.01
not specified as recurrent K41.20
recurrent K41.21
unilateral K41.90
with
gangrene (and obstruction)
K41.40
not specified as recurrent
K41.40
recurrent K41.41
obstruction K41.30
not specified as recurrent
K41.30
recurrent K41.31
not specified as recurrent K41.90
recurrent K41.91
not specified as recurrent K41.90
recurrent K41.91
foramen magnum G93.5
congenital Q01.8
funicular (umbilical) - *see also* Hernia,
umbilicus
spermatic (cord) - *see* Hernia,
inguinal
gastrointestinal tract - *see* Hernia,
abdomen

Hernia, hernial *(Continued)*
  Hesselbach's - *see* Hernia, femoral,
      specified site NEC
  hiatal (esophageal) (sliding) K44.9
    with
      gangrene (and obstruction) K44.1
      obstruction K44.0
    congenital Q40.1
  incarcerated - *see also* Hernia, by site,
      with obstruction
    with gangrene - *see* Hernia, by site,
      with gangrene
  incisional K43.91
    with
      gangrene (and obstruction) K43.11
      obstruction K43.01
  indirect (inguinal) - *see* Hernia,
      inguinal
  inguinal (direct) (external) (funicular)
      (indirect) (internal) (oblique) (scro-
      tal) (sliding) K40.90
    with
      gangrene (and obstruction) K40.40
        not specified as recurrent K40.40
        recurrent K40.41
      obstruction K40.30
        not specified as recurrent K40.30
        recurrent K40.31
    not specified as recurrent K40.90
    recurrent K40.91
    bilateral K40.20
      with
        gangrene (and obstruction)
            K40.10
          not specified as recurrent
              K40.10
          recurrent K40.11
        obstruction K40.00
          not specified as recurrent
              K40.00
          recurrent K40.01
      not specified as recurrent K40.20
      recurrent K40.21
    unilateral K40.90
      with
        gangrene (and obstruction)
            K40.40
          not specified as recurrent
              K40.40
          recurrent K40.41
        obstruction K40.30
          not specified as recurrent
              K40.30
          recurrent K40.31
      not specified as recurrent K40.90
      recurrent K40.91
  internal - *see also* Hernia, abdomen
    inguinal - *see* Hernia, inguinal
  interstitial - *see* Hernia, abdomen
  intervertebral cartilage or disc - *see*
      Displacement, intervertebral disc
  intestine, intestinal - *see* Hernia, by site
  intra-abdominal - *see* Hernia, abdomen
  iris (traumatic) S05.2-
  irreducible - *see also* Hernia, by site,
      with obstruction
    with gangrene - *see* Hernia, by site,
      with gangrene
  ischiatic - *see* Hernia, abdomen, speci-
      fied site NEC
  ischiorectal - *see* Hernia, abdomen,
      specified site NEC
  lens (traumatic) S05.2-

Hernia, hernial *(Continued)*
  linea (alba) (semilunaris) - *see* Hernia,
      ventral
  Littre's - *see* Hernia, abdomen
  lumbar - *see* Hernia, abdomen, specified
      site NEC
  lung (subcutaneous) J98.4
  mediastinum J98.5
  mesenteric (internal) - *see* Hernia,
      abdomen
  muscle (sheath) M62.89
  nucleus pulposus - *see* Displacement,
      intervertebral disc
  oblique (inguinal) - *see* Hernia, inguinal
  obstructive - *see also* Hernia, by site,
      with obstruction
    with gangrene - *see* Hernia, by site,
      with gangrene
  obturator - *see* Hernia, abdomen, speci-
      fied site NEC
  omental - *see* Hernia, abdomen
  ovary N83.4
  oviduct N83.4
  paraesophageal - *see also* Hernia,
      diaphragm
    congenital Q40.1
  paraumbilical - *see* Hernia, umbilicus
  perineal - *see* Hernia, abdomen, speci-
      fied site NEC
  Petit's - *see* Hernia, abdomen, specified
      site NEC
  postoperative - *see* Hernia, incisional
  pregnant uterus – *see* Abnormal, uterus
      in pregnancy or childbirth
  prevesical N32.89
  properitoneal - *see* Hernia, abdomen,
      specified site NEC
  pudendal - *see* Hernia, abdomen, speci-
      fied site NEC
  rectovaginal N81.6
  retroperitoneal - *see* Hernia, abdomen,
      specified site NEC
  Richter's - *see* Hernia, abdomen, with
      obstruction
  Rieux's, Riex's - *see* Hernia, abdomen,
      specified site NEC
  sac condition (adhesion) (dropsy) (in-
      flammation) (laceration) (suppura-
      tion) - code by site under Hernia
  sciatic - *see* Hernia, abdomen, specified
      site NEC
  scrotum, scrotal - *see* Hernia, inguinal
  sliding (inguinal) - *see also* Hernia,
      inguinal
    hiatus - *see* Hernia, hiatal
  spigelian - *see* Hernia, ventral
  spinal - *see* Spina bifida
  strangulated - *see also* Hernia, by site,
      with obstruction
    with gangrene - *see* Hernia, by site,
      with gangrene
  supra-umbilicus - *see* Hernia, ventral
  tendon – *see* Disorder, tendon, specified
      type NEC
  Treitz's (fossa) - *see* Hernia, abdomen,
      specified site NEC
  tunica vaginalis Q55.29
  umbilicus, umbilical K42.9
    with
      gangrene (and obstruction) K42.1
      obstruction K42.0
  ureter N28.89
  urethra, congenital Q64.79
  urinary meatus, congenital Q64.79

Hernia, hernial *(Continued)*
  uterus N81.4
    pregnant – *see* Abnormal, uterus in
        pregnancy or childbirth
  vaginal (anterior) (wall) - *see*
      Cystocele
  Velpeau's - *see* Hernia, femoral
  ventral K43.90
    with
      gangrene (and obstruction)
          K43.10
      obstruction K43.00
    recurrent - *see* Hernia, incisional
    incisional K43.91
      with
        gangrene (and obstruction)
            K43.11
        obstruction K43.01
    specified NEC K43.99
      with
        gangrene (and obstruction)
            K43.19
        obstruction K43.09
  vesical
    congenital (female) (male)
        Q79.51
    female - *see* Cystocele
    male N32.89
  vitreous (into wound) S05.2-
    into anterior chamber - *see* Prolapse,
        vitreous
Herniation - *see also* Hernia
  brain (stem) G93.5
  cerebral G93.5
  mediastinum J98.5
  nucleus pulposus - *see* Displacement,
      intervertebral disc
Herpangina B08.5
Herpes, herpesvirus, herpetic B00.9
  anogenital A60.9
    perianal skin A60.1
    rectum A60.1
    urogenital tract A60.00
      cervix A60.03
      male genital organ NEC
          A60.02
      penis A60.01
      specified site NEC A60.09
      vagina A60.04
      vulva A60.04
  blepharitis (zoster) B02.39
    simplex B00.59
  circinatus B35.4
    bullosus L12.0
  conjunctivitis (simplex) B00.53
    zoster B02.31
  cornea B02.33
  encephalitis B00.4
    due to herpesvirus 6 B10.01
    due to herpesvirus 7 B10.09
    specified NEC B10.09
  eye (zoster) B02.30
    simplex B00.50
  eyelid (zoster) B02.39
    simplex B00.59
  facialis B00.1
  febrilis B00.1
  geniculate ganglionitis B02.21
  genital, genitalis A60.00
    female A60.09
    male A60.01
  gestational, gestationis
      O26.4-
  gingivostomatitis B00.2

Herpes, herpesvirus, herpetic *(Continued)*
  human B00.9
    1 - *see* Herpes, simplex
    2 - *see* Herpes, simplex
    3 - *see* Varicella
    4 - *see* Mononucleosis, Epstein-Barr
      (virus)
    5 - *see* Disease, cytomegalic inclusion
      (generalized)
    6
      encephalitis B10.01
      specified NEC B10.81
    7
      encephalitis B10.09
      specified NEC B10.82
    8 B10.89
  infection NEC B10.89
    Kaposi's sarcoma associated B10.89
  iridocyclitis (simplex) B00.51
    zoster B02.32
  iris (vesicular erythema multiforme)
    L51.9
  iritis (simplex) B00.51
  Kaposi's sarcoma associated B10.89
  keratitis (simplex) (dendritic) (disci-
    form) (interstitial) B00.52
    zoster (interstitial) B02.33
  keratoconjunctivitis (simplex) B00.52
    zoster B02.33
  labialis B00.1
  lip B00.1
  meningitis (simplex) B00.3
    zoster B02.1
  ophthalmicus (zoster) NEC B02.30
    simplex B00.50
  penis A60.01
  perianal skin A60.1
  pharyngitis, pharyngotonsillitis B00.2
  rectum A60.1
  scrotum A60.02
  sepsis B00.7
  simplex B00.9
    complicated NEC B00.89
    congenital P35.2
    conjunctivitis B00.53
    external ear B00.1
    eyelid B00.59
    hepatitis B00.81
    keratitis (interstitial) B00.52
    myelitis B00.82
    specified complication NEC B00.89
    visceral B00.89
  stomatitis B00.2
  tonsurans B35.0
  visceral B00.89
  vulva A60.04
  whitlow B00.89
  zoster *(see also* condition) B02.9
    auricularis B02.21
    complicated NEC B02.8
    conjunctivitis B02.31
    disseminated B02.7
    encephalitis B02.0
    eye(lid) B02.39
    geniculate ganglionitis B02.21
    keratitis (interstitial) B02.33
    meningitis B02.1
    myelitis B02.24
    neuritis, neuralgia B02.29
    ophthalmicus NEC B02.30
    oticus B02.21
    polyneuropathy B02.23
    specified complication NEC B02.8
    trigeminal neuralgia B02.22

Herpesvirus (human) - *see* Herpes
Herpetophobia F40.218
Herrick's anemia - *see* Disease,
  sickle-cell
Hers' disease E74.09
Herter-Gee syndrome K90.0
Herxheimer's reaction T88.6
Hesitancy
  of micturition R39.11
  urinary R39.11
Hesselbach's hernia - *see* Hernia, femoral,
  specified site NEC
Heterochromia (congenital) Q13.2
  cataract - *see* Cataract, complicated
  cyclitis (Fuchs) - *see* Cyclitis, Fuchs'
    heterochromic
  hair L67.1
  iritis - *see* Cyclitis, Fuchs' heterochromic
  retained metallic foreign body (non-
    magnetic) - *see* Foreign body,
    intraocular, old, retained
    magnetic - *see* Foreign body, intra-
      ocular, old, retained, magnetic
  uveitis - *see* Cyclitis, Fuchs'
    heterochromic
Heterophoria - *see* Strabismus,
  heterophoria
Heterophyes, heterophyiasis (small
  intestine) B66.8
Heterotopia, heterotopic - *see also* Malposition, congenital
  cerebralis Q04.8
Heterotropia - *see* Strabismus
Heubner-Herter disease K90.0
Hexadactylism Q69.9
HGSIL (cytology finding) (high grade
  squamous intraepithelial lesion
  on cytologic smear) (Pap smear
  finding)
  anus R85.613
  cervix R87.613
    biopsy (histology) finding - code to
      CIN II or CIN III
  vagina R87.623
    biopsy (histology) finding - code to
      VAIN II or VAIN III
Hibernoma (M8880/0) - *see* Lipoma
Hiccup, hiccough R06.6
  epidemic B33.0
  psychogenic F45.8
Hidradenitis (axillaris) (suppurative)
  L73.2
Hidradenoma (nodular) - *see also*
  Neoplasm, skin, benign
  clear cell - *see* Neoplasm, skin, benign
  papillary - *see* Neoplasm, skin, benign
Hidrocystoma - *see* Neoplasm, skin,
  benign
High
  altitude effects T70.20
    anoxia T70.20
    on
      ears T70.0
      sinuses T70.1
    polycythemia D75.1
  arch
    foot Q66.7
    palate, congenital Q38.5
  arterial tension - *see* Hypertension
  basal metabolic rate R94.8
  blood pressure - *see also* Hypertension
    reading (incidental) (isolated) (non-
      specific), without diagnosis of
      hypertension R03.0

High *(Continued)*
  cholesterol E78.0
    with high triglycerides E78.2
  diaphragm (congenital) Q79.1
  expressed emotional level within family
    Z63.8
  head at term O32.4
  palate, congenital Q38.5
    infant NEC Z76.2
    sexual behavior (heterosexual) Z72.51
      bisexual Z72.53
      homosexual Z72.52
    temperature (of unknown origin) R50.9
  thoracic rib Q76.6
  triglycerides E78.1
    with high cholesterol E78.2
Hildenbrand's disease A75.0
Hilum - *see* condition Hip - *see* condition
Hippel's disease Q85.8
Hippophobia F40.218
Hippus H57.09
Hirschsprung's disease or megacolon
  Q43.1
Hirsutism, hirsuties L68.0
Hirudiniasis
  external B88.3
  internal B83.4
Hiss-Russell dysentery A03.1
Histidinemia, histidinuria E70.41
Histiocytoma - *see also* Neoplasm, skin,
  benign
  fibrous - *see also* Neoplasm, skin,
    benign
    atypical - *see* Neoplasm, connective
      tissue, uncertain behavior
    malignant - *see* Neoplasm, connective
      tissue, malignant
Histiocytosis D76.3
  acute differentiated progressive C96.0
  Langerhans' cell NEC C96.6
    multifocal X
      multisystemic (disseminated)
        C96.0
      unisystemic C96.5
    unifocal (X) C96.6
  lipid, lipoid (essential) D76.3
  malignant C96.a
  mononuclear phagocytes NEC D76.1
    Langerhans' cells C96.6
  non-Langerhans cell D76.3
  polyostotic sclerosing D76.3
  sinus, with massive lymphadenopathy
    D76.3
  syndrome NEC D76.3
  X NEC C96.6
    acute (progressive) C96.0
    chronic C96.6
    multifocal C96.5
    multisystemic C96.0
    unifocal C96.6
Histoplasmosis B39.9
  with pneumonia NEC B39.2 *[J17]*
  African B39.5
  American - *see* Histoplasmosis,
    capsulati
  capsulati B39.4
    disseminated B39.3
    generalized B39.3
    pulmonary B39.2
      acute B39.0
      chronic B39.1
  Darling's B39.4
  duboisii B39.5
  lung NEC B39.2

History
    family (of) - *see also* History, personal
        (of)
        alcohol abuse Z81.1
        allergy NEC Z84.89
        anemia Z83.2
        arthritis Z82.61
        asthma Z82.5
        blindness Z82.1
        cardiac death (sudden) Z82.41
        carrier of genetic disease Z84.81
        chromosomal anomaly Z82.79
        chronic
           disabling disease NEC Z82.8
           lower respiratory disease Z82.5
        colonic polyps Z83.71
        congenital malformations and defor-
           mations Z82.79
           polycystic kidney Z82.71
        consanguinity Z84.3
        deafness Z82.2
        diabetes mellitus Z83.3
        disability NEC Z82.8
        disease or disorder (of)
           allergic NEC Z84.89
           behavioral NEC Z81.8
           blood and blood-forming organs
             Z83.2
           cardiovascular NEC Z82.49
           chronic disabling NEC Z82.8
           digestive Z83.79
           ear NEC Z83.5
           endocrine NEC Z83.49
           eye NEC Z83.5
           genitourinary NEC Z84.2
           hematological Z83.2
           immune mechanism Z83.2
           infectious NEC Z83.1
           ischemic heart Z82.49
           kidney Z84.1
           mental NEC Z81.8
           metabolic Z83.49
           musculoskeletal NEC Z82.69
           neurological NEC Z82.0
           nutritional Z83.49
           parasitic NEC Z83.1
           psychiatric NEC Z81.8
           respiratory NEC Z83.6
           skin and subcutaneous tissue NEC
             Z84.0
           specified NEC Z84.89
        drug abuse NEC Z81.3
        epilepsy Z82.0
        genetic disease carrier Z84.81
        hearing loss Z82.2
        human immunodeficiency virus
           (HIV) infection Z83.0
        Huntington's chorea Z82.0
        leukemia Z80.6
        malignant neoplasm (of) NOS
           Z80.9
           bladder Z80.52
           breast Z80.3
           bronchus Z80.1
           digestive organ Z80.0
           gastrointestinal tract Z80.0
           genital organ Z80.49
             ovary Z80.41
             prostate Z80.42
             specified organ NEC Z80.49
             testis Z80.43
           hematopoietic NEC Z80.7
           intrathoracic organ NEC Z80.2
           kidney Z80.51

History *(Continued)*
    family *(Continued)*
        malignant neoplasm *(Continued)*
           lung Z80.1
           lymphatic NEC Z80.7
           ovary Z80.41
           prostate Z80.42
           respiratory organ NEC Z80.2
           specified site NEC Z80.8
           testis Z80.43
           trachea Z80.1
           urinary organ or tract Z80.59
             bladder Z80.52
             kidney Z80.51
        mental
           disorder NEC Z81.8
           retardation Z81.0
        multiple endocrine neoplasia [MEN]
           syndrome Z83.41
        osteoporosis Z82.62
        polycystic kidney Z82.71
        polyps (colon) Z83.71
        psychiatric disorder Z81.8
        psychoactive substance abuse NEC
           Z81.3
        respiratory condition NEC Z83.6
           asthma and other lower respiratory
             conditions Z82.5
        self-harmful behavior Z81.8
        skin condition Z84.0
        specified condition NEC Z84.89
        stroke (cerebrovascular) Z82.3
        substance abuse NEC Z81.4
           alcohol Z81.1
           drug NEC Z81.3
           psychoactive NEC Z81.3
           tobacco Z81.2
        sudden cardiac death Z82.41
        tobacco abuse Z81.2
        violence, violent behavior Z81.8
        visual loss Z82.1
    personal (of) - *see also* History, family
        (of)
        abuse
           childhood Z62.819
             physical Z62.810
             psychological Z62.811
             sexual Z62.810
           adult Z91.419
             physical and sexual Z91.410
             psychological Z91.411
        alcohol dependence F10.21
        allergy to
           analgesic agent NEC Z88.6
           anesthetic Z88.4
           antibiotic agent NEC Z88.1
           anti-infective agent NEC Z88.3
           contrast media Z91.041
           drugs, medicaments and biological
             substances Z88.9
             specified NEC Z88.8
           food Z91.018
             additives Z91.02
             eggs Z91.012
             milk products Z91.011
             peanuts Z91.010
             seafood Z91.013
             specified food NEC Z91.018
           insect Z91.038
             bee Z91.030
           latex Z91.040
           medicinal agents Z88.9
             specified NEC Z88.8
           narcotic agent NEC Z88.5

History *(Continued)*
    personal *(Continued)*
        allergy to *(Continued)*
           nonmedicinal agents Z91.048
           penicillin Z88.0
           serum Z88.7
           specified NEC Z91.09
           sulfonamides Z88.2
           vaccine Z88.7
        benign carcinoid tumor Z86.012
        benign neoplasm Z86.018
           brain Z86.011
           carcinoid Z86.012
           colonic polyps Z86.010
        brain injury (traumatic) Z87.820
        breast implant removal Z98.86
        calculi, renal Z87.43
        cancer - *see* History, personal (of),
           malignant neoplasm (of)
        cardiac arrest (death), successfully
           resuscitated Z86.74
        cerebral infarction without residual
           deficit Z86.73
        cervical dysplasia Z87.44
        chemotherapy for neoplastic condi-
           tion Z92.21
        childhood abuse - *see* History, per-
           sonal (of), abuse
           collapsed vertebra (healed) Z87.311
           due to osteoporosis Z87.310
        congenital malformation (surgically
           corrected) Z87.79
           hypospadias (surgically corrected)
             Z87.71
        contraception Z92.0
        deployment (military) Z91.82
        disease or disorder (of) Z87.898
           blood and blood-forming organs
             Z86.2
           circulatory system Z86.79
             specified condition NEC Z86.79
           connective tissue NEC Z87.39
           digestive system Z87.19
             colonic polyp Z86.010
             peptic ulcer disease Z87.11
             specified condition NEC
               Z87.19
           ear Z86.69
           endocrine Z86.39
             diabetic foot ulcer Z86.31
             specified type NEC Z86.39
           eye Z86.69
           genital system Z87.49
           hematological Z86.2
           Hodgkin Z85.71
           immune mechanism Z86.2
           infectious Z86.19
             malaria Z86.13
             poliomyelitis Z86.12
             specified NEC Z86.19
             tuberculosis Z86.11
           mental NEC Z87.898
           metabolic Z86.39
             diabetic foot ulcer Z86.31
             specified type NEC Z86.39
           musculoskeletal NEC Z87.39
           nervous system Z86.69
           nutritional Z86.39
           parasitic Z86.19
           respiratory system NEC Z87.09
           sense organs Z86.69
           skin Z87.2
           specified site or type NEC Z87.898
           subcutaneous tissue Z87.2

History *(Continued)*
  personal *(Continued)*
    disease or disorder *(Continued)*
      trophoblastic Z87.59
      urinary system Z87.49
    drug dependence - *see* Dependence,
      drug, by type, in remission
    drug therapy
      antineoplastic chemotherapy
        Z92.21
      estrogen Z92.23
      immunosupression Z92.25
      inhaled steroids Z92.240
      monoclonal drug Z92.22
      specified NEC Z92.29
      steroid Z92.241
      systemic steroids Z92.241
    embolism (venous) Z86.71
    encephalitis Z86.61
    estrogen therapy Z92.23
    extracorporeal membrane oxygen-
      ation (ECMO) Z92.81
    failed moderate sedation Z92.83
    failed conscious sedation Z92.83
    fall, falling Z91.81
    fracture (healed)
      fatigue Z87.312
      fragility Z87.310
      osteoporosis Z87.310
      pathological NEC Z87.311
      stress Z87.312
      traumatic Z87.81
    hepatitis
      B Z86.19
      C Z86.19
    Hodgkin disease Z85.71
    hyperthermia, malignant Z88.4
    hypospadias Z87.71
    hysterectomy Z90.710
    immunosupression therapy Z92.25
    in situ neoplasm
      breast Z86.000
      cervix uteri Z86.001
      specified NEC Z86.008
    infection NEC Z86.61
      central nervous system Z86.61
      urinary (tract) Z87.41
    injury NEC Z87.828
    in utero procedure during pregnancy
      Z98.870
    in utero procedure while a fetus
      Z98.871
    irradiation Z92.3
    kidney stones Z87.43
    leukemia Z85.6
    lymphoma (non-Hodgkin) Z85.72
    malignant melanoma (skin) Z85.820
    malignant neoplasm (of) Z85.9
      anus NEC Z85.048
        carcinoid Z85.040
      bladder Z85.51
      bone Z85.830
      brain Z85.841
      breast Z85.3
      bronchus NEC Z85.118
        carcinoid Z85.110
      carcinoid - *see* History, personal
        (of), malignant neoplasm, by
        site, carcinoid
      cervix Z85.41
      colon NEC Z85.038
        carcinoid Z85.030
      digestive organ Z85.00
      endocrine gland NEC Z85.858

History *(Continued)*
  personal *(Continued)*
    malignant neoplasm *(Continued)*
      epididymis Z85.48
      eye Z85.840
      gastrointestinal tract - *see* History,
        malignant neoplasm, diges-
        tive organ
      genital organ
        female Z85.40
          specified NEC Z85.44
        male Z85.45
          specified NEC Z85.49
      hematopoietic NEC Z85.79
      intrathoracic organ Z85.20-
      kidney NEC Z85.528
        carcinoid Z85.520
      large intestine NEC Z85.030
        carcinoid Z85.030
      liver Z85.05
      lung NEC Z85.118
        carcinoid Z85.110
      mediastinum Z85.29
      Merkel cell Z85.821
      nervous system NEC Z85.848
      oral cavity Z85.819
        specified site NEC Z85.818
      ovary Z85.43
      pancreas Z85.07
      pharynx Z85.819
        specified site NEC Z85.818
      pelvis Z85.53
      pleura Z85.29
      prostate Z85.46
      rectosigmoid junction NEC Z85.048
        carcinoid Z85.040
      rectum NEC Z85.048
        carcinoid Z85.040
      respiratory organ Z85.20
      skin NEC Z85.828
        melanoma Z85.820
        Merkel cell Z85.821
      small intestine NEC Z85.068
        carcinoid Z85.060
      soft tissue Z85.831
      specified site NEC Z85.89
      stomach NEC Z85.028
        carcinoid Z85.020
      testis Z85.47
      thymus NEC Z85.238
        carcinoid Z85.230
      thyroid Z85.850
      tongue Z85.810
      trachea Z85.12
      urinary organ or tract Z85.50
        specified NEC Z85.59
      uterus Z85.42
    maltreatment Z91.89
    medical treatment NEC Z92.89
    melanoma (malignant) (skin) Z85.820
    meningitis Z86.61
    Merkel cell carcinoma (skin) Z85.821
    military deployment Z91.82
    military war, peacekeeping and hu-
      manitarian deployment (current
      or past conflict) Z91.82
    myocardial infarction (old) I25.2
    neglect (in)
      adult Z91.412
      childhood Z62.812
    neoplasm
      benign Z86.018
        brain Z86.011
        colon polyp Z86.010

History *(Continued)*
  personal *(Continued)*
    neoplasm *(Continued)*
      in situ
        breast Z86.000
        cervix uteri Z86.001
        specified NEC Z86.008
      malignant – *see* History of, malig-
        nant neoplasm
      uncertain behavior Z86.03
    nephrotic syndrome Z87.42
    nicotine dependence Z87.891
    noncompliance with medical
      treatment or regimen – *see*
      Noncompliance
    nutritional deficiency Z86.39
    obstetric complications Z87.59
      childbirth Z87.59
      pregnancy Z87.59
      pre-term labor Z87.51
      puerperium Z87.59
    osteoporosis fractures Z87.31
    parasuicide (attempt) Z91.5
    perinatal problems Z87.89
    physical trauma NEC Z87.828
      self-harm or suicide attempt Z91.5
    poisoning NEC Z91.89
      self-harm or suicide attempt Z91.5
    poor personal hygiene Z91.89
    pneumonia (recurrent) Z87.01
    preterm labor Z87.51
    prolonged reversible ischemic neuro-
      logic deficit (PRINO) Z86.73
    procedure during pregnancy Z98.870
    procedure while a fetus Z98.871
    psychiatric disorder NEC Z87.89
    psychological abuse
      adult Z91.411
      child Z62.811
    radiation therapy Z92.3
    removal
      implant
        breast Z98.86
    renal calculi Z87.43
    respiratory condition NEC Z87.09
    risk factors NEC Z91.89
    self-harm Z91.5
    self-poisoning attempt Z91.5
    sex reassignment Z87.890
    sleep-wake cycle problem Z72.821
    specified NEC Z87.898
    steroid therapy (systemic) Z92.241
      inhaled Z92.240
    stroke without residual deficits
      Z86.73
    substance abuse NEC F10
F19 with fifth character 1
    sudden cardiac arrest Z86.74
    sudden cardiac death successfully
      resuscitated Z86.74
    suicide attempt Z91.5
    surgery NEC Z98.89
      sex reassignment Z87.890
      transplant - *see* Transplant
    thrombophlebitis Z86.72
    thrombosis (venous) Z86.71
    tobacco dependence Z87.82
    transient ischemic attack (TIA)
      without residual deficits Z86.73
    trauma (physical) NEC Z87.828
      self-harm Z91.5
    traumatic brain injury Z87.820
    unhealthy sleep-wake cycle Z72.821
    urinary calculi Z87.43

History *(Continued)*
  F19 with fifth character 1 *(Continued)*
    urinary (tract) infection(s) Z87.41
    venous thrombosis or embolism
      Z86.71
His-Werner disease A79.0
HIV B20
  laboratory evidence (nonconclusive)
    R75
  positive, seropositive Z21
  nonconclusive test in infants R75
Hives (bold) - *see* Urticaria
Hoarseness R49.0
Hobo Z59.0
Hodgkin disease - *see* Lymphoma,
  Hodgkin
Hodgson's disease I71.2
  ruptured I71.1
Hoffa-Kastert disease E88.89
Hoffa's disease E88.89
Hoffmann-Bouveret syndrome I47.9
Hoffmann's syndrome E03.9 *[G73.7]*
Hole (round)
  macula H35.34-
  retina (without detachment) - *see* Break,
    retina, round hole
    with detachment - *see* Detachment,
      retina, with retinal, break
Holiday relief care Z75.5
Hollenhorst's plaque - *see* Occlusion,
  artery, retina
Hollow foot (congenital) Q66.7
  acquired - *see* Deformity, limb, foot,
    specified NEC
Holoprosencephaly Q04.2
Holt-Oram syndrome Q87.2
Homelessness Z59.0
Homesickness – *see* Disorder,
  adjustment
Homocystinemia, homocystinuria
  E72.11
Homogentisate 1,2-dioxygenase defi-
  ciency E70.29
Homologous serum hepatitis (prophy-
  lactic) (therapeutic) - *see* Hepatitis,
  viral, type B
Honeycomb lung J98.4
  congenital Q33.0
Hooded
  clitoris Q52.6
  penis Q55.69
Hookworm (anemia) (disease) (infection)
  (infestation) B76.9
  specified NEC B76.8
Hordeolum (eyelid) (externum) (recurrent) H00.019
  internum H00.029
    left H00.026
      lower H00.025
      upper H00.024
    right H00.023
      lower H00.022
      upper H00.021
    left H00.016
      lower H00.015
      upper H00.014
    right H00.013
      lower H00.012
      upper H00.011
Horn
  cutaneous L85.8
  nail L60.2
    congenital Q84.6

Horner(-Claude Bernard) **syndrome**
  G90.2
  traumatic – *see* Injury, nerve, cervical
    sympathetic
Horseshoe kidney (congenital) Q63.1
Horton's headache or neuralgia G44.099
  intractable G44.091
  not intractable G44.099
Hospital hopper syndrome – *see* Disorder,
  factitious
Hospitalism in children – *see* Disorder,
  adjustment
Hostility R45.5
  towards child Z62.3
Hot flashes
  menopausal N95.11
Hourglass (contracture) - *see also*
  Contraction, hourglass
  stomach K31.89
    congenital Q40.2
    stricture K31.2
Household, housing circumstance affect-
  ing care Z59.9
  specified NEC Z59.8
Housemaid's knee - *see* Bursitis,
  prepatellar
Hudson(-Stähli) **line** (cornea) - *see* Pigmentation, cornea, anterior
Human
  bite (open wound) - *see also* Bite
    intact skin surface - *see* Bite,
      superficial
  herpesvirus - *see* Herpes
  immunodeficiency virus (HIV) disease
    (infection) B20
    asymptomatic status Z21
    contact Z20.6
    counseling Z71.7
    dementia B20 *[F02.80]*
      with behavioral disturbance B20
        [F02.81]
    exposure to Z20.6
    laboratory evidence R75
    type-2 (HIV 2) as cause of disease
      classified elsewhere B97.35
  papillomavirus (HPV)
    DNA test positive
      high risk
        cervix R87.810
        vagina R87.811
      low risk
        cervix R87.820
        vagina R87.821
    screening for Z11.51
  T-cell lymphotropic virus
    type-1 (HTLV-I) infection B33.3
      as cause of disease classified else-
        where B97.33
      carrier Z22.6
    type-2 (HTLV-II) as cause of disease
      classified elsewhere B97.34
Humidifier lung or pneumonitis J67.7
Humiliation (experience) **in childhood**
  Z62.898
Humpback (acquired) - *see* Kyphosis
Hunchback (acquired) - *see* Kyphosis
Hunger T73.0
  air, psychogenic F45.8
Hungry bone syndrome E83.81
Hunner's ulcer – *see* Cystitis, chronic,
  interstitial
Hunter's
  glossitis D51.0
  syndrome E76.1

Huntington's disease or chorea G10
  with dementia G10 *[F02.80]*
    with behavioral disturbance G10
      [F02.81]
Hunt's
  disease or syndrome (herpetic genicu-
    late ganglionitis) B02.21
  dyssynergia cerebellaris myoclonica
    G11.1
  neuralgia B02.21
Hurler(-Scheie) **disease or syndrome**
  E76.02
Hurst's disease G36.1
Hurthle cell
  adenocarcinoma C73
  adenoma D34
  carcinoma C73
  tumor D34
Hutchinson-Boeck disease or syndrome
  - *see* Sarcoidosis
Hutchinson-Gilford disease or syndrome
  E34.8
Hutchinson's
  disease meaning
    angioma serpiginosum L81.7
    pompholyx L30.1
    prurigo estivalis L56.4
    summer eruption or summer prurigo
      L56.4
  melanotic freckle - *see* Melanoma, in
    situ
    malignant melanoma in - *see*
      Melanoma
  teeth or incisors (congenital syphilis)
    A50.52
  triad (congenital syphilis) A50.53
Hyalin plaque, sclera, senile H15.89
Hyaline membrane (disease) (lung) (pulmonary) (newborn) P22.0
Hyalinosis
  cutis (et mucosae) E78.89
  focal and segmental (glomerular) (*see*
    also N00-N07 with fourth character
    .1) N05.1
Hyalitis, hyalosis, asteroid - *see also*
  Deposit, crystalline
  syphilitic (late) A52.71
Hydatid
  cyst or tumor - *see* Echinococcus
  mole - *see* Hydatidiform mole
  Morgagni
    female Q50.5
    male (epididymal) Q55.4
    testicular Q55.29
Hydatidiform mole (benign) (complicating pregnancy) (delivered) (undelivered) O01.9
  classical O01.0
  complete O01.0
  incomplete O01.1
  invasive D39.2
  malignant D39.2
  partial O01.1
Hydatidosis - *see* Echinococcus
Hydradenitis (axillaris) (suppurative)
  L73.2
Hydradenoma - *see* Hidradenoma
Hydramnios O40.-
Hydrancephaly, hydranencephaly
  Q04.3
  with spina bifida - *see* Spina bifida, with
    hydrocephalus
Hydrargyrism NEC – *see* Poisoning,
  mercury

Hydrarthrosis - *see also* Effusion, joint
  gonococcal A54.42
  intermittent M12.40
    ankle M12.47-
    elbow M12.42-
    foot joint M12.47-
    hand joint M12.44-
    hip M12.45-
    knee M12.46-
    multiple site M12.49
    shoulder M12.41-
    specified joint NEC M12.48
    wrist M12.43-
  of yaws (early) (late) (*see also* subcategory M14.8-) A66.6
  syphilitic (late) A52.77
    congenital A50.55 [M12.80]
Hydremia D64.89
Hydrencephalocele (congenital) - *see* Encephalocele
Hydrencephalomeningocele (congenital) - *see* Encephalocele
Hydroa R23.8
  aestivale L56.4
  vacciniforme L56.4
Hydroadenitis (axillaris) (suppurative) L73.2
Hydrocalycosis - *see* Hydronephrosis
Hydrocele (spermatic cord) (testis) (tunica vaginalis) N43.3
  canal of Nuck N94.89
  congenital P83.5
  encysted N43.0
  female NEC N94.89
  infected N43.1
  newborn P83.5
  round ligament N94.89
  specified NEC N43.2
  spinalis - *see* Spina bifida
  vulva N90.8
Hydrocephalus (acquired) (external) (internal) (malignant) (recurrent) G91.9
  aqueduct Sylvius stricture Q03.0
  causing disproportion O33.6
    with obstructed labor O66.3
  communicating G91.0
  congenital (external) (internal) Q03.9
    with spina bifida Q05.4
      cervical Q05.0
      dorsal Q05.1
      lumbar Q05.2
      lumbosacral Q05.2
      sacral Q05.3
      thoracic Q05.1
      thoracolumbar Q05.1
    specified NEC Q03.8
  due to toxoplasmosis (congenital) P37.1
  foramen Magendie block (acquired) G91.1
    congenital (*see also* Hydrocephalus, congenital) Q03.1
  in (due to)
    infectious disease NEC G91.4
    neoplastic disease NEC (*see also* Neoplasm) G91.4
    parasitic disease G91.4
  newborn Q03.9
    with spina bifida - *see* Spina bifida, with hydrocephalus
  noncommunicating G91.1
  normal pressure G91.2
    secondary G91.0

Hydrocephalus (*Continued*)
  obstructive G91.1
  otitic G93.2
  post-traumatic NEC G91.3
  secondary G91.4
    post-traumatic G91.3
  specified NEC G91.8
  syphilitic, congenital A50.49
Hydrocolpos (congenital) N89.8
Hydrocystoma - *see* Neoplasm, skin, benign
Hydroencephalocele (congenital) - *see* Encephalocele
Hydroencephalomeningocele (congenital) - *see* Encephalocele
Hydrohematopneumothorax - *see* Hemothorax
Hydromeningitis - *see* Meningitis
Hydromeningocele (spinal) - *see also* Spina bifida
  cranial - *see* Encephalocele
Hydrometra N85.8
Hydrometrocolpos N89.8
Hydromicrocephaly Q02
Hydromphalos (since birth) Q45.8
Hydromyelia Q06.4
Hydromyelocele - *see* Spina bifida
Hydronephrosis (atrophic) (early) (functionless) (intermittent) (primary) (secondary) NEC N13.30
  with
    infection N13.6
    obstruction (by) (of)
      renal calculus N13.2
        with infection N13.6
      ureteral NEC N13.1
        with infection N13.6
        calculus N13.2
          with infection N13.6
      ureteropelvic junction (congenital) Q62.0
        with infection N13.6
    ureteral stricture NEC N13.1
      with infection N13.6
  congenital Q62.0
  specified type NEC N13.39
  tuberculous A18.11
Hydropericarditis - *see* Pericarditis
Hydropericardium - *see* Pericarditis
Hydroperitoneum R18.8
Hydrophobia - *see* Rabies
Hydrophthalmos Q15.0
Hydropneumohemothorax - *see* Hemothorax
Hydropneumopericarditis - *see* Pericarditis
Hydropneumopericardium - *see* Pericarditis
Hydropneumothorax J94.8
  traumatic – *see* Injury, intrathoracic, lung
  tuberculous NEC A15.6
Hydrops R60.9
  abdominis R18.8
  articulorum intermittens - *see* Hydrarthrosis, intermittent
  cardiac - *see* Failure, heart, congestive
  causing obstructed labor (mother) O66.3
  endolymphatic H81.0
  gallbladder K82.1
  joint - *see* Effusion, joint
  labyrinth H81.0

Hydrops (*Continued*)
  newborn (idiopathic) P83.2
    due to
      ABO isoimmunization P56.0
      hemolytic disease P56.90
        specified NEC P56.99
      isoimmunization (ABO) (Rh) P56.0
      Rh incompatibility P56.0
  nutritional - *see* Malnutrition, severe
  pericardium - *see* Pericarditis
  pleura - *see* Hydrothorax
  spermatic cord - *see* Hydrocele
Hydropyonephrosis N13.6
Hydrorachis Q06.4
Hydrorrhea (nasal) J34.89
  pregnancy - *see* Rupture, membranes, premature
Hydrosadenitis (axillaris) (suppurative) L73.2
Hydrosalpinx (fallopian tube) (follicularis) N70.11
Hydrothorax (double) (pleura) J94.8
  chylous (nonfilarial) I89.8
  filarial (*see also* Infestation, filarial) B74.9 [J91.8]
  traumatic – *see* Injury, intrathoracic
  tuberculous NEC (non primary) A15.6
Hydroureter (*see also* Hydronephrosis) N13.4
  with infection N13.6
  congenital Q62.39
Hydroureteronephrosis - *see* Hydronephrosis
Hydrourethra N36.8
Hydroxykynureninuria E70.8
Hydroxylysinemia E72.3
Hydroxyprolinemia E72.59
Hygiene, sleep
  abuse Z72.821
  inadequate Z72.821
  poor Z72.821
Hygroma (congenital) (cystic) D18.1
  praepatellare, prepatellar - *see* Bursitis, prepatellar
Hymen - *see* condition
Hymenolepis, hymenolepiasis (diminuta) (infection) (infestation) (nana) B71.0
Hypalgesia R20.8
Hyperacidity (gastric) K31.89
  psychogenic F45.8
Hyperactive, hyperactivity F90.9
  basal cell, uterine cervix - *see* Dysplasia, cervix
  bowel sounds R19.12
  cervix epithelial (basal) - *see* Dysplasia, cervix
  child F90.9
    attention deficit – *see* Disorder, attention-deficit hyperactivity
  destrusor muscle N32.81
  gastrointestinal K31.89
    psychogenic F45.8
  nasal mucous membrane J34.3
  stomach K31.89
  thyroid (gland) - *see* Hyperthyroidism
Hyperacusis H93.23-
Hyperadrenalism E27.5
Hyperadrenocorticism E24.9
  congenital E25.0
  iatrogenic E24.2

Hyperadrenocorticism *(Continued)*
  correct substance properly admin-
    istered - *see* Table of drugs and
    chemicals, by drug, adverse
    effect
    overdose or wrong substance given
      or taken - *see* Table of drugs
      and chemicals, by drug,
      poisoning
  not associated with Cushing's syn-
    drome E27.0
  pituitary-dependent E24.0
Hyperaldosteronism E26.9
  familial (type I) E26.02
  glucocorticoid-remediable E26.02
  primary (due to (bilateral) adrenal
    hyperplasia) E26.09
  primary NEC E26.09
  secondary E26.1
  specified NEC E26.89
Hyperalgesia R20.8
Hyperalimentation R63.2
  carotene, carotin E67.1
  specified NEC E67.8
  vitamin
    A E67.0
    D E67.3
Hyperaminoaciduria
  arginine E72.21
  cystine E72.01
  lysine E72.3
  ornithine E72.4
Hyperammonemia (congenital) E72.20
Hyperazotemia - *see* Uremia
Hyperbetalipoproteinemia (familial)
    E78.0
  with prebetalipoproteinemia E78.2
Hyperbilirubinemia
  constitutional E80.6
  familial conjugated E80.6
  neonatal (transient) - *see* Jaundice,
    newborn
Hypercalcemia, hypocalciuric, familial
    E83.52
Hypercalciuria, idiopathic E83.52
Hypercapnia R06.89
  newborn P84
Hypercarotenemia, hypercarotinemia
    (dietary) E67.1
Hypercementosis K03.4
Hyperchloremia E87.8
Hyperchlorhydria K31.89
  neurotic F45.8
  psychogenic F45.8
Hypercholesterinemia - *see*
  Hypercholesterolemia
Hypercholesterolemia (essential) (famil-
    ial) (hereditary) (primary) (pure)
    E78.0
  with hyperglyceridemia, endogenous
    E78.2
  dietary counseling and surveillance
    Z71.3
Hyperchylia gastrica, psychogenic F45.8
Hyperchylomicronemia (familial) (pri-
    mary) E78.3
  with hyperbetalipoproteinemia E78.3
Hypercoagulable (state) D68.59
  activated protein C resistance D68.51
  antithrombin (III) deficiency D68.59
  factor V Leiden mutation D68.51
  primary NEC D68.59
  protein C deficiency D68.59
  protein S deficiency D68.59

Hypercoagulable *(Continued)*
  prothrombin gene mutation D68.52
  secondary D68.69
  specified NEC D68.69
Hypercoagulation (state) D68.59
Hypercorticalism, pituitary-dependent
    E24.0
Hypercorticosolism - *see* Cushing's
  syndrome
Hypercorticosteronism E24.2
  correct substance properly administered-
    see Table of drugs and chemicals, by
    drug, adverse effect
  overdose or wrong substance given
    or taken - *see* Table of drugs and
    chemicals, by drug, poisoning
Hypercortisonism E24.2
  correct substance properly administered-
    see Table of drugs and chemicals, by
    drug, adverse effect
  overdose or wrong substance given
    or taken - *see* Table of drugs and
    chemicals, by drug, poisoning
Hyperekplexia Q89.8
Hyperelectrolytemia E87.8
Hyperemesis R11.10
  with nausea R11.2
  gravidarum (mild) O21.0
    with
      carbohydrate depletion O21.1
      dehydration O21.1
      electrolyte imbalance O21.1
      metabolic disturbance O21.1
    severe (with metabolic disturbance)
      O21.1
  projectile R11.12
  psychogenic F45.8
Hyperemia (acute) (passive) R68.89
  anal mucosa K62.8
  bladder N32.89
  cerebral I67.8
  conjunctiva H11.43-
  ear internal, acute - *see* subcategory H83.0
  enteric K59.8
  eye - *see* Hyperemia, conjunctiva
  eyelid (active) (passive) - *see* Disorder,
    eyelid, specified type NEC
  intestine K59.8
  iris - *see* Disorder, iris, vascular
  kidney N28.89
  labyrinth - *see* subcategory H83.0
  liver (active) K76.8
  lung (passive) - *see* Edema, lung
  pulmonary (passive) - *see* Edema, lung
  renal N28.89
  retina H35.89
  stomach K31.89
Hyperesthesia (body surface) R20.3
  larynx (reflex) J38.7
    hysterical F44.89
  pharynx (reflex) J39.2
    hysterical F44.89
Hyperestrogenism (drug-induced)
    (iatrogenic) E28.0
Hyperexplexia Q89.8
Hyperfibrinolysis - *see* Fibrinolysis
Hyperfructosemia E74.19
Hyperfunction
  adrenal cortex, not associated with
    Cushing's syndrome E27.0
  medulla E27.5
    adrenomedullary E27.5
  virilism E25.9
    congenital E25.0

Hyperfunction *(Continued)*
  ovarian E28.8
  pancreas K86.8
  parathyroid (gland) E21.3
  pituitary (gland) (anterior) E22.9
    specified NEC E22.8
  polyglandular E31.1
  testicular E29.0
Hypergammaglobulinemia D89.2
  polyclonal D89.0
  Waldenström's D89.0
Hypergastrinemia E16.4
Hyperglobulinemia R77.1
Hyperglycemia, hyperglycemic (tran-
    sient) R73.9
  coma - *see* Diabetes, by type, with
    coma
  postpancreatectomy E89.1
Hyperglyceridemia (endogenous)
    (essential) (familial) (hereditary)
    (pure) E78.1
  mixed E78.3
Hyperglycinemia (non-ketotic)
    E72.51
Hypergonadism
  ovarian E28.8
  testicular (primary) (infantile)
    E29.0
Hyperheparinemia - *see* Circulating
  anticoagulants
Hyperhidrosis, hyperidrosis R61
  focal
    primary L74.519
      axilla L74.510
      face L74.511
      palms L74.512
      soles L74.513
    secondary L74.52
  generalized R61
  localized
    primary L74.519
      axilla L74.510
      face L74.511
      palms L74.512
      soles L74.513
    secondary L74.52
  psychogenic F45.8
  secondary R61
    focal L74.52
Hyperhistidinemia E70.41
Hyperhomocysteinemia E72.11
Hyperhydroxyprolinemia E72.59
Hyperinsulinism (functional) E16.1
  with
    coma (hypoglycemic) E15
    encephalopathy E16.1 *[G94]*
  ectopic E16.1
  therapeutic misadventure (from
    administration of insulin) - *see*
    subcategory T38.3
Hyperkalemia E87.5
Hyperkeratosis *(see also* Keratosis)
    L85.9
  cervix N88.0
  due to yaws (early) (late) (palmar or
    plantar) A66.3
  follicularis Q82.8
    penetrans (in cutem) L87.0
  palmoplantaris climacterica L85.1
  pinta A67.1
  senile (with pruritus) L57.0
  universalis congenita Q80.8
  vocal cord J38.3
  vulva N90.4

Hyperkinesia, hyperkinetic (disease) (reaction) (syndrome) (childhood) (adolescence) – see also Disorder, attention-deficit hyperactivity
heart I51.89
Hyperleucine-isoleucinemia E71.19
Hyperlipemia, hyperlipidemia E78.5
combined E78.2
familial E78.4
group
A E78.0
B E78.1
C E78.2
D E78.3
mixed E78.2
specified NEC E78.4
Hyperlipidosis E75.6
hereditary NEC E75.5
Hyperlipoproteinemia E78.5
Fredrickson's type
I E78.3
IIa E78.0
IIb E78.2
III E78.2
IV E78.1
V E78.3
low-density-lipoprotein-type (LDL) E78.0
very-low-density-lipoprotein-type (VLDL) E78.1
Hyperlucent lung, unilateral J43.0
Hyperlysinemia E72.3
Hypermagnesemia E83.41
neonatal P71.8
Hypermenorrhea N92.0
Hypermethioninemia E72.19
Hypermetropia (congenital) H52.0-
Hypermobility, hypermotility
cecum - see Syndrome, irritable bowel
coccyx - see subcategory M53.2
colon - see Syndrome, irritable bowel
psychogenic F45.8
ileum K58.9
intestine - see also Syndrome, irritable bowel K58.9
psychogenic F45.8
meniscus (knee) - see Derangement, knee, meniscus
scapula - see Instability, joint, shoulder
stomach K31.89
psychogenic F45.8
syndrome M35.7
urethra N36.41
with intrinsic sphincter deficiency N36.43
Hypernasality R49.21
Hypernatremia E87.0
Hypernephroma C64.-
Hyperopia - see Hypermetropia
Hyperorexia nervosa F50.2
Hyperornithinemia E72.4
Hyperosmia R43.1
Hyperosmolality E87.0
Hyperostosis (monomelic) - see also Disorder, bone, density and structure, specified NEC
ankylosing (spine) M48.10
cervical region M48.12
cervicothoracic region M48.13
lumbar region M48.16
lumbosacral region M48.17
multiple sites M48.19
occipito-atlanto-axial region M48.11

Hyperostosis (Continued)
ankylosing (Continued)
sacrococcygeal region M48.18
thoracic region M48.14
thoracolumbar region M48.15
cortical (skull) M85.2
infantile M89.8x-
frontal, internal of skull M85.2
interna frontalis M85.2
skeletal, diffuse idiopathic - see Hyperostosis, ankylosing
skull M85.2
congenital Q75.8
vertebral, ankylosing - see Hyperostosis, ankylosing
Hyperovarism E28.8
Hyperoxaluria (primary) E72.53
Hyperparathyroidism E21.3
primary E21.0
secondary (renal) N25.81
non-renal E21.1
specified NEC E21.2
tertiary E21.2
Hyperpathia R20.8
Hyperperistalsis R19.2
psychogenic F45.8
Hyperpermeability, capillary I78.8
Hyperphagia R63.2
Hyperphenylalaninemia NEC E70.1
Hyperphoria (alternating) H50.53
Hyperphosphatemia E83.39
Hyperpiesis, hyperpiesia - see Hypertension
Hyperpigmentation - see also Pigmentation
melanin NEC L81.4
postinflammatory L81.0
Hyperpinealism E34.8
Hyperpituitarism E22.9
Hyperplasia, hyperplastic
adenoids J35.2
adrenal (capsule) (cortex) (gland) E27.8
with
sexual precocity (male) E25.9
congenital E25.0
virilism, adrenal E25.9
congenital E25.0
virilization (female) E25.9
congenital E25.0
congenital E25.0
salt-losing E25.0
adrenomedullary E27.5
appendix (lymphoid) K38.0
artery, fibromuscular I77.3
bone - see also Hypertrophy, bone
marrow D75.89
breast - see also Hypertrophy, breast
ductal (atypical) N60.9-
C-cell, thyroid E07.0
cementation (tooth) (teeth) K03.4
cervical gland R59.0
cervix (uteri) (basal cell) (endometrium) (polypoid) - see also Dysplasia, cervix
congenital Q51.8
clitoris, congenital Q52.6
denture K06.2
endocervicitis N72
endometrium, endometrial (adenomatous) (benign) (cystic) (glandular) (glandular-cystic) (polypoid) N85.00
with atypia N85.02

Hyperplasia, hyperplastic (Continued)
endometrium (Continued)
cervix - see Dysplasia, cervix
complex (without atypia) N85.01
simple (without atypia) N85.01
epithelial L85.9
focal, oral, including tongue K13.29
nipple N62
skin L85.9
tongue K13.29
vaginal wall N89.3
erythroid D75.89
fibromuscular of artery (carotid) (renal) I77.3
genital
female NEC N94.89
male N50.8
gingiva K06.1
glandularis cystica uteri (interstitialis) N85.00 - see also Hyperplasia, endometrial
gum K06.1
hymen, congenital Q52.4
irritative, edentulous (alveolar) K06.2
jaw M26.09
alveolar M26.79
lower M26.03
alveolar M26.72
upper M26.01
alveolar M26.71
kidney (congenital) Q63.3
labia N90.6
epithelial N90.3
liver (congenital) Q44.7
nodular, focal K76.8
lymph gland or node R59.9
mandible, mandibular M26.03
alveolar M26.72
unilateral condylar M27.8
maxilla, maxillary M26.01
alveolar M26.71
myometrium, myometrial N85.2
nose
lymphoid J34.89
polypoid J33.9
oral mucosa (irritative) K13.6
organ or site, congenital NEC - see Anomaly, by site
ovary N83.8
palate, papillary (irritative) K13.6
pancreatic islet cells E16.9
alpha E16.8
with excess
gastrin E16.4
glucagon E16.3
beta E16.1
parathyroid (gland) E21.0
pharynx (lymphoid) J39.2
prostate (adenofibromatous) (nodular) - see Enlargement, enlarged, prostate
renal artery I77.8
reticulo-endothelial (cell) D75.89
salivary gland (any) K11.1
Schimmelbusch's – see Mastopathy, cystic
suprarenal capsule (gland) E27.8
thymus (gland) (persistent) E32.0
thyroid (gland) - see Goiter
tonsils (faucial) (infective) (lingual) (lymphoid) J35.1
with adenoids J35.3
unilateral condylar M27.8

Hyperplasia, hyperplastic *(Continued)*
 uterus, uterine N85.2
  endometrium (glandular) N85.00 -
   see also Hyperplasia, endometrial
 vulva N90.6
  epithelial N90.3
Hyperpnea - *see* Hyperventilation
Hyperpotassemia E87.5
Hyperprebetalipoproteinemia (familial)
   E78.1
Hyperprolactinemia E22.1
Hyperprolinemia (type I) (type II)
   E72.59
Hyperproteinemia E88.09
Hyperprothrombinemia, causing
   coagulation factor deficiency
   D68.4
Hyperpyrexia R50.9
 heat (effects) T67.0
 malignant, due to anesthetic T88.3
 rheumatic - *see* Fever, rheumatic
 unknown origin R50.9
Hyper-reflexia R29.2
Hypersalivation K11.7
Hypersecretion
 ACTH (not associated with Cushing's
   syndrome) E27.0
  pituitary E24.0
 adrenaline E27.5
 adrenomedullary E27.5
 androgen (testicular) E29.0
  ovarian (drug-induced) (iatrogenic)
   E28.1
 calcitonin E07.0
 catecholamine E27.5
 corticoadrenal E24.9
 cortisol E24.9
 epinephrine E27.5
 estrogen E28.0
 gastric K31.89
  psychogenic F45.8
 gastrin E16.4
 glucagon E16.3
 hormone(s)
  ACTH (not associated with Cushing's
   syndrome) E27.0
  pituitary E24.0
  antidiuretic E22.2
  growth E22.0
  intestinal NEC E34.1
  ovarian androgen E28.1
  pituitary E22.9
  testicular E29.0
  thyroid stimulating E05.80
   with thyroid storm E05.81
 insulin - *see* Hyperinsulinism
 lacrimal glands - *see* Epiphora
 medulloadrenal E27.5
 milk O92.6
 ovarian androgens E28.1
 salivary gland (any) K11.7
 thyrocalcitonin E07.0
 upper respiratory J39.8
Hypersegmentation, leukocytic, heredi-
   tary D72.0
Hypersensitive, hypersensitiveness,
   hypersensitivity - *see also* Allergy
 carotid sinus G90.01
 colon - *see* Irritable, colon
 drug T88.7 This code not for use in the
   inpatient setting
 gastrointestinal K52.2
  psychogenic F45.8
 labyrinth - *see* subcategory H83.2

Hypersensitive, hypersensitiveness,
   hypersensitivity *(Continued)*
 pain R20.8
 pneumonitis - *see* Pneumonitis,
   allergic
 reaction T78.40
  upper respiratory tract NEC
   J39.3
Hypersomnia (organic) G47.10
 due to
  alcohol
   abuse F10.182
   dependence F10.282
   use F10.982
  amphetamines
   abuse F15.182
   dependence F15.282
   use F15.982
  caffeine
   abuse F15.182
   dependence F15.282
   use F15.982
  cocaine
   abuse F14.182
   dependence F14.282
   use F14.982
  drug NEC
   abuse F19.182
   dependence F19.282
   use F19.982
  medical condition G47.14
  mental disorder F51.13
  opioid
   abuse F11.182
   dependence F11.282
   use F11.982
  psychoactive substance NEC
   abuse F19.182
   dependence F19.282
   use F19.982
  sedative, hypnotic, or anxiolytic
   abuse F13.182
   dependence F13.282
   use F13.982
  stimulant NEC
   abuse F15.182
   dependence F15.282
   use F15.982
 idiopathic G47.11
  with long sleep time G47.11
  without long sleep time G47.12
 menstrual related G47.13
 nonorganic origin F51.11
  specified NEC F51.19
 not due to a substance or known
   physiological condition F51.11
  specified NEC F51.19
 primary F51.11
 recurrent G47.13
 specified NEC G47.19
Hypersplenia, hypersplenism D73.1
Hyperstimulation, ovaries (associated
   with induced ovulation) N98.1
Hypersusceptibility - *see* Allergy
Hypertelorism (ocular) (orbital)
   Q75.2
Hypertension, hypertensive (accelerated) (benign) (essential) (idiopathic)
   (malignant) (systemic) I10
 with
  heart involvement (conditions in
   I51.4-I51.9 due to hypertension) -
   see Hypertension, heart

Hypertension, hypertensive *(Continued)*
 with *(Continued)*
  kidney involvement - *see* Hypertension, kidney
  renal sclerosis (conditions in N26) -
   see Hypertension, kidney
 benign, intracranial G93.2
 cardiorenal (disease) I13.10
  with heart failure I13.0
   with stage I through stage IV
    chronic kidney disease
    I13.0
   with stage V or end stage renal
    disease I13.2
  without heart failure I13.10
   with stage I through stage IV
    chronic kidney disease
    I13.10
   with stage V or end stage renal
    disease I13.11
 cardiovascular
  disease (arteriosclerotic) (sclerotic) -
   see Hypertension, heart
  renal (disease) (sclerosis) - *see*
   Hypertension, cardiorenal
 chronic venous - *see* Hypertension,
   venous (chronic)
 complicating
  childbirth (labor) O10.92
   with
    heart disease O10.12
     with renal disease
      O10.32
    renal disease O10.22
     with heart disease
      O10.32
   essential O10.02
   secondary O10.42
  pregnancy O16.-
   with edema (*see also* Pre-eclampsia)
    O14.9-
   gestational (pregnancy induced)
    (transient) (without protein-
    uria) O13.-
    with proteinuria O14.9-
     mild pre-eclampsia O14.0-
     severe pre-eclampsia O14.1-
   pre-existing O10.91-
    with
     heart disease O10.11-
      with renal disease O10.31-
     proteinuria O11.-
     renal disease O10.21-
      with heart disease
       O10.31-
    essential O10.01-
    secondary O10.41-
  puerperium O10.93
   with
    heart disease O10.13
     with renal disease O10.33
    renal disease O10.23
     with heart disease O10.33
   essential O10.03
   secondary O10.43
 due to
  endocrine disorders I15.2
  pheochromocytoma I15.2
  renal disorders NEC I15.1
   arterial I15.0
  renovascular disorders I15.0
  specified disease NEC I15.8
 encephalopathy I67.4

Hypertension, hypertensive *(Continued)*
  gestational (without significant pro-
    teinuria) (pregnancy-induced)
    (transient) O13.-
    with significant proteinuria – *see*
      Pre-eclampsia
  Goldblatt's I70.1
  heart (disease) (conditions in I51.4-I51.9
    due to hypertension) I11.9
    with
      heart failure (congestive) I11.0
      kidney disease (chronic) - *see* Hy-
        pertension, cardiorenal
  intracranial (benign) G93.2
  kidney I12.9
    with
      heart disease - *see* Hypertension,
        cardiorenal
      stage V chronic kidney disease
        (CKD) or end stage renal
        disease (ESRD) I12.0
      stage I through stage IV chronic
        kidney disease I12.9
  lesser circulation I27.0
  newborn P29.2
    pulmonary (persistent) P29.3
  ocular H40.0
  pancreatic duct - code to underlying
    condition
    with chronic pancreatitis K86.1
  portal (due to chronic liver disease)
    (idiopathic) K76.6
    gastropathy K31.89
    in (due to) schistosomiasis (bilharzia-
      sis) B65.9 *[K77]*
  postoperative I97.3
  psychogenic F45.8
  pulmonary (artery) (secondary) NEC
    I27.2
    of newborn (persistent) P29.3
    primary (idiopathic) I27.0
  renal - *see* Hypertension, kidney
  renovascular I15.0
  secondary NEC I15.9
    due to
      endocrine disorders I15.2
      pheochromocytoma I15.2
      renal disorders NEC I15.1
        arterial I15.0
      renovascular disorders I15.0
    specified NEC I15.8
  venous (chronic)
    due to
      deep vein thrombosis - *see* Syn-
        drome, postthrombotic
    idiopathic I87.309
      with
        inflammation I87.32-
          with ulcer I87.33-
        specified complication NEC
          I87.39-
        ulcer I87.31-
          with inflammation
            I87.33-
      asymptomatic I87.30-
Hyperthecosis ovary E28.8
Hyperthermia (of unknown origin) - *see
  also* Hyperpyrexia
  malignant, due to anesthesia T88.3
  newborn P81.9
    environmental P81.0
Hyperthyroid (recurrent) - *see*
  Hyperthyroidism

Hyperthyroidism (latent) (pre-adult)
  (recurrent) E05.90
  with
    goiter (diffuse) E05.00
      with thyroid storm E05.01
      nodular (multinodular) E05.20
        with thyroid storm E05.21
        uninodular E05.10
          with thyroid storm E05.11
    storm E05.91
  due to ectopic thyroid tissue E05.30
    with thyroid storm E05.31
  neonatal, transitory P72.1
  specified NEC E05.80
    with thyroid storm E05.81
Hypertony, hypertonia, hypertonicity
  bladder N31.8
  congenital P94.1
  stomach K31.89
    psychogenic F45.8
  uterus, uterine (contractions) (compli-
    cating delivery) O62.4
Hypertrichosis L68.9
  congenital Q84.2
  eyelid H02.869
    left H02.866
      lower H02.865
      upper H02.864
    right H02.863
      lower H02.862
      upper H02.861
  lanuginosa Q84.2
    acquired L68.1
  localized L68.2
  specified NEC L68.8
Hypertriglyceridemia, essential E78.1
Hypertrophy, hypertrophic
  adenofibromatous, prostate - *see* En-
    largement, enlarged, prostate
  adenoids (infective) J35.2
    with tonsils J35.3
  adrenal cortex E27.8
  alveolar process or ridge – *see* Anomaly,
    alveolar
  anal papillae K62.8
  artery I77.8
    congenital NEC Q27.8
      digestive system Q27.8
      lower limb Q27.8
      specified site NEC Q27.8
      upper limb Q27.8
  auricular - *see* Hypertrophy, cardiac
  Bartholin's gland N75.8
  bile duct (common) (hepatic) K83.8
  bladder (sphincter) (trigone) N32.89
  bone M89.30
    carpus M89.34-
    clavicle M89.31-
    femur M89.35-
    fibula M89.36-
    finger M89.34-
    humerus M89.32-
    ilium M89.359
    ischium M89.359
    metacarpus M89.34-
    metatarsus M89.37-
    multiple sites M89.39
    neck M89.38
    radius M89.33-
    rib M89.38
    scapula M89.31-
    skull M89.38
    tarsus M89.37-
    tibia M89.36-

Hypertrophy, hypertrophic *(Continued)*
  bone *(Continued)*
    toe M89.37-
    ulna M89.33-
    vertebra M89.38
  brain G93.89
  breast N62
    cystic – *see* Mastopathy, cystic
    newborn P83.4
    pubertal, massive N62
    puerperal, postpartum – *see* Disorder,
      breast, specified type NEC
    senile (parenchymatous) N62
  cardiac (chronic) (idiopathic) I51.7
    with rheumatic fever (conditions in I00)
      active I01.8
      inactive or quiescent (with chorea)
        I09.89
    congenital NEC Q24.8
    fatty - *see* Degeneration, myocardial
    hypertensive - *see* Hypertension,
      heart
    rheumatic (with chorea) I09.89
      active or acute I01.8
        with chorea I02.0
    valve - *see* Endocarditis
  cartilage - *see* Disorder, cartilage, speci-
    fied type NEC
  cecum - *see* Megacolon
  cervix (uteri) N88.8
    congenital Q51.8
    elongation N88.4
  clitoris (cirrhotic) N90.8
    congenital Q52.6
  colon - *see also* Megacolon
    congenital Q43.2
  conjunctiva, lymphoid H11.89
  corpora cavernosa N48.89
  cystic duct K82.8
  duodenum K31.89
  endometrium (glandular) N85.00 -
    see also Hyperplasia, endometrial
    cervix N88.8
  epididymis N50.8
  esophageal hiatus (congenital) Q79.1
    with hernia - *see* Hernia, hiatal
  eyelid - *see* Disorder, eyelid, specified
    type NEC
  fat pad E65
    knee (infrapatellar) (popliteal) (pre-
      patellar) (retropatellar) M79.4
  foot (congenital) Q74.2
  frenulum, frenum (tongue) K14.8
    lip K13.0
  gallbladder K82.8
  gastric mucosa K29.60
    with bleeding K29.61
  gland, glandular R59.9
    generalized R59.1
    localized R59.0
  gum (mucous membrane) K06.1
  heart (idiopathic) – *see also* Hypertro-
    phy, cardiac
    valve - *see also* Endocarditis I38
  hemifacial Q67.4
  hepatic - *see* Hypertrophy, liver
  hiatus (esophageal) Q79.1
  hilus gland R59.0
  hymen, congenital Q52.4
  ileum K63.89
  intestine NEC K63.89
  jejunum K63.89
  kidney (compensatory) N28.81
    congenital Q63.3

Hypertrophy, hypertrophic (*Continued*)
labium (majus) (minus) N90.6
ligament - *see* Disorder, ligament
lingual tonsil (infective) J35.1
  with adenoids J35.3
lip K13.0
  congenital Q18.6
liver R16.0
  acute K76.8
  congenital Q44.7
  cirrhotic - *see* Cirrhosis, liver
  fatty - *see* Fatty, liver
lymph, lymphatic gland R59.9
  generalized R59.1
  localized R59.0
  tuberculous - *see* Tuberculosis, lymph
    gland
mammary gland - *see* Hypertrophy,
  breast
Meckel's diverticulum (congenital)
  Q43.0
median bar – *see* Hyperplasia,
  prostate
meibomian gland - *see* Chalazion
meniscus, knee, congenital Q74.1
metatarsal head - *see* Hypertrophy,
  bone, metatarsus
metatarsus - *see* Hypertrophy, bone,
  metatarsus
mucous membrane
  alveolar ridge K06.2
  gum K06.1
  nose (turbinate) J34.3
muscle M62.89
muscular coat, artery I77.8
myocardium - *see also* Hypertrophy,
  cardiac
  idiopathic I42.2
myometrium N85.2
nail L60.2
  congenital Q84.5
nasal J34.89
  alae J34.89
  bone J34.89
  cartilage J34.89
  mucous membrane (septum) J34.3
  sinus J34.89
  turbinate J34.3
nasopharynx, lymphoid (infectional)
  (tissue) (wall) J35.2
nipple N62
organ or site, congenital NEC - *see*
  Anomaly, by site - ovary N83.8
palate (hard) M27.8
  soft K13.79
pancreas, congenital Q45.3
parathyroid (gland) E21.0
parotid gland K11.1
penis N48.89
pharyngeal tonsil J35.2
pharynx J39.2
  lymphoid (infectional) (tissue) (wall)
    J35.2
pituitary (anterior) (fossa) (gland)
  E23.6
prepuce (congenital) N47.8
  female N90.8
prostate - *see* Enlargement, enlarged,
  prostate
  congenital Q55.4
pseudomuscular G71.0

Hypertrophy, hypertrophic (*Continued*)
pylorus (adult) (muscle) (sphincter)
  K31.1
  congenital or infantile Q40.0
rectal, rectum (sphincter) K62.8
rhinitis (turbinate) J31.0
salivary gland (any) K11.1
  congenital Q38.4
scaphoid (tarsal) - *see* Hypertrophy,
  bone, tarsus
scar L91.0
scrotum N50.8
seminal vesicle N50.8
sigmoid - *see* Megacolon
skin L91.9
  specified NEC L91.8
spermatic cord N50.8
spleen - *see* Splenomegaly
spondylitis - *see* Spondylosis
stomach K31.89
sublingual gland K11.1
submandibular gland K11.1
suprarenal cortex (gland) E27.8
synovial NEC M67.20
  acromioclavicular M67.21-
  ankle M67.27-
  elbow M67.22-
  foot M67.27-
  hand M67.24-
  hip M67.25-
  knee M67.26-
  multiple sites M67.29
  specified site NEC M67.28
  wrist M67.23-
tendon – *see* Disorder, tendon, specified
  type NEC
testis N44.8
  congenital Q55.29
thymic, thymus (gland) (congenital)
  E32.0
thyroid (gland) - *see* Goiter
toe (congenital) Q74.2
  acquired - *see also* Deformity, toe,
    specified NEC
tongue K14.8
  congenital Q38.2
  papillae (foliate) K14.3
tonsils (faucial) (infective) (lingual)
  (lymphoid) J35.1
  with adenoids J35.3
tunica vaginalis N50.8
ureter N28.89
urethra N36.8
uterus N85.2
  neck (with elongation) N88.4
  puerperal O90.89
uvula K13.79
vagina N89.8
vas deferens N50.8
vein I87.8
ventricle, ventricular (heart) - *see also*
  Hypertrophy, cardiac
  congenital Q24.8
  in tetralogy of Fallot Q21.3
verumontanum N36.8
vocal cord J38.3
vulva N90.6
  stasis (nonfilarial) N90.6
Hypertropia H50.2-
Hypertyrosinemia E70.21
Hyperuricemia (asymptomatic) E79.0
Hypervalinemia E71.19

Hyperventilation (tetany) R06.4
hysterical F45.8
psychogenic F45.8
syndrome F45.8
Hypervitaminosis (dietary) NEC E67.8
A E67.0
  administered as drug (prolonged
    intake) - *see* Table of drugs and
    chemicals, vitamins, adverse
    effect
  overdose or wrong substance given
    or taken - *see* Table of drugs and
    chemicals, vitamins,
    poisoning
B6 E67.2
D E67.3
  administered as drug (prolonged
    intake) - *see* Table of drugs and
    chemicals, vitamins, adverse
    effect
  overdose or wrong substance given
    or taken - *see* Table of drugs and
    chemicals, vitamins,
    poisoning
K E67.8
  administered as drug (prolonged
    intake) - *see* Table of drugs and
    chemicals, vitamins, adverse
    effect
  overdose or wrong substance given
    or taken - *see* Table of drugs and
    chemicals, vitamins, poisoning
Hypervolemia E87.7
Hypesthesia R20.1
cornea - *see* Anesthesia, cornea
Hyphema H21.0-
traumatic S05.1-
Hypoacidity, gastric K31.89
psychogenic F45.8
Hypoadrenalism, hypoadrenia E27.40
primary E27.1
tuberculous A18.7
Hypoadrenocorticism E27.40
pituitary E23.0
primary E27.1
Hypoalbuminemia E88.09
Hypoaldosteronism E27.40
Hypoalphalipoproteinemia E78.6
Hypobarism T70.29
Hypobaropathy T70.29
Hypobetalipoproteinemia (familial) E78.6
Hypocalcemia E83.51
dietary E58
neonatal P71.1
  due to cow's milk P71.0
phosphate-loading (newborn) P71.1
Hypochloremia E87.8
Hypochlorhydria K31.89
neurotic F45.8
psychogenic F45.8
Hypochondria, hypochondriac,
  hypochondriasis (reaction) F45.21
sleep F51.03
Hypochondrogenesis Q77.0
Hypochondroplasia Q77.4
Hypochromasia, blood cells D50.8
Hypodontia - *see* Anodontia
Hypoeosinophilia D72.89
Hypoesthesia R20.1
Hypofibrinogenemia D68.8
acquired D65
congenital (hereditary) D68.2

Hypofunction
  adrenocortical E27.40
    drug-induced E27.3
    postprocedural E89.6
    primary E27.1
  adrenomedullary, postprocedural E89.6
  cerebral R29.81
  corticoadrenal NEC E27.49
  intestinal K59.8
  labyrinth - *see* subcategory H83.2
  ovary E28.39
  pituitary (gland) (anterior) E23.0
  testicular E29.1
    postprocedural (postsurgical) (postir-
      radiation) (iatrogenic) E89.5
Hypogalactia O92.4
Hypogammaglobulinemia (*see also*
    Agammaglobulinemia) D80.1
  hereditary D80.0
  nonfamilial D80.1
  transient, of infancy D80.7
Hypogenitalism (congenital) - *see*
    Hypogonadism
Hypoglossia Q38.3
Hypoglycemia (spontaneous) E16.2
  coma E15
    diabetic – *see* Diabetes, coma
  diabetic - *see* Diabetes, hypoglycemia
  dietary counseling and surveillance
    Z71.3
  drug-induced E16.0
    with coma (nondiabetic) E15
  due to insulin E16.0
    with coma (nondiabetic) E15
      therapeutic misadventure - *see* sub-
        category T38.3
  functional, nonhyperinsulinemic E16.1
  iatrogenic E16.0
    with coma (nondiabetic) E15
  in infant of diabetic mother P70.1
    gestational diabetes P70.0
  infantile E16.1
  leucine-induced E71.19
  neonatal (transitory) P70.4
  reactive (not drug-induced) E16.1
  transitory neonatal P70.4
Hypogonadism
  female E28.39
  hypogonadotropic E23.0
  male E29.1
  ovarian (primary) E28.39
  pituitary E23.0
  testicular (primary) E29.1
Hypohidrosis, hypoidrosis L74.4
Hypoinsulinemia, postprocedural E89.1
Hypokalemia E87.6
Hypoleukocytosis - *see* Agranulocytosis
Hypolipoproteinemia (alpha) (beta) E78.6
Hypomagnesemia E83.42
  neonatal P71.2
Hypomania, hypomanic reaction F30.8
Hypomenorrhea - *see* Oligomenorrhea
Hypometabolism R63.8
Hypomotility
  gastrointestinal (tract) K31.89
    psychogenic F45.8
  intestine K59.8
    psychogenic F45.8
  stomach K31.89
    psychogenic F45.8
Hyponasality R49.22
Hyponatremia E87.1

Hypo-osmolality E87.1
Hypo-ovarianism, hypo-ovarism E28.39
Hypoparathyroidism E20.9
  familial E20.8
  idiopathic E20.0
  neonatal, transitory P71.4
  postprocedural E89.2
  specified NEC E20.8
Hypopharyngitis - *see*
    Laryngopharyngitis
Hypophoria H50.53
Hypophosphatemia, hypophosphatasia
    (acquired) (congenital) (renal)
    E83.39
  familial E83.31
Hypophyseal, hypophysis - *see also*
    condition
  dwarfism E23.0
  gigantism E22.0
Hypopiesis - *see* Hypotension
Hypopinealism E34.8
Hypopituitarism (juvenile) E23.0
  drug-induced E23.1
  due to
    hypophysectomy E89.3
    radiotherapy E89.3
  iatrogenic NEC E23.1
  postirradiation E89.3
  postpartum E23.0
  postprocedural E89.3
Hypoplasia, hypoplastic
  adrenal (gland), congenital Q89.1
  alimentary tract, congenital Q45.8
    upper Q40.8
  anus, anal (canal) Q42.3
    with fistula Q42.2
  aorta, aortic Q25.4
    ascending, in hypoplastic left heart
      syndrome Q23.4
    valve Q23.1
      in hypoplastic left heart syndrome
        Q23.4
  areola, congenital Q83.8
  arm (congenital) - *see* Defect, reduction,
    upper limb
  artery (peripheral) Q27.8
    brain (congenital) Q28.3
    coronary Q24.5
    digestive system Q27.8
    lower limb Q27.8
    pulmonary Q25.7
      functional, unilateral J43.0
    retinal (congenital) Q14.1
    specified site NEC Q27.8
    umbilical Q27.0
    upper limb Q27.8
  auditory canal Q17.8
    causing impairment of hearing
      Q16.9
  biliary duct or passage Q44.5
  bone NOS Q79.9
    face Q75.8
    marrow D61.9
      megakaryocytic D69.49
    skull - *see* Hypoplasia, skull
  brain Q02
    gyri Q04.3
    part of Q04.3
  breast (areola) N64.82
  bronchus Q32.4
  cardiac Q24.8

Hypoplasia, hypoplastic (*Continued*)
  carpus - *see* Defect, reduction, upper
    limb, specified type NEC
  cartilage hair Q78.5
  cecum Q42.8
  cementum K00.4
  cephalic Q02
  cerebellum Q04.3
  cervix (uteri), congenital Q51.8
  clavicle (congenital) Q74.0
  coccyx Q76.49
  colon Q42.9
    specified NEC Q42.8
  corpus callosum Q04.0
  cricoid cartilage Q31.2
  digestive organ(s) or tract NEC
    Q45.8
    upper (congenital) Q40.8
  ear (auricle) (lobe) Q17.2
    middle Q16.4
  enamel of teeth (neonatal) (postnatal)
    (prenatal) K00.4
  endocrine (gland) NEC Q89.2
  endometrium N85.8
  epididymis (congenital) Q55.4
  epiglottis Q31.2
  erythroid, congenital D61.09
  esophagus (congenital) Q39.8
  eustachian tube Q17.8
  eye Q11.2
  eyelid (congenital) Q10.3
  face Q18.8
    bone(s) Q75.8
  femur (congenital) – *see* Defect, reduc-
    tion, lower limb, specified type
    NEC
  fibula (congenital) – *see* Defect, reduc-
    tion, lower limb, specified type
    NEC
  finger (congenital) - *see* Defect, reduc-
    tion, upper limb, specified type
    NEC
  focal dermal Q82.8
  foot – *see* Defect, reduction, lower limb,
    specified type NEC
  gallbladder Q44.0
  genitalia, genital organ(s)
    female, congenital Q52.8
      external Q52.79
      internal NEC Q52.8
    in adiposogenital dystrophy E23.6
  glottis Q31.2
  hair Q84.2
  hand (congenital) - *see* Defect, reduc-
    tion, upper limb, specified type
    NEC
  heart Q24.8
  humerus (congenital) - *see* Defect,
    reduction, upper limb, specified
    type NEC
  intestine (small) Q41.9
    large Q42.9
      specified NEC Q42.8
  jaw M26.09
    alveolar M26.79
      lower M26.04
        alveolar M26.74
      upper M26.02
        alveolar M26.73
  kidney(s) Q60.5
    bilateral Q60.4
    unilateral Q60.3

Hypoplasia, hypoplastic *(Continued)*
  labium (majus) (minus), congenital
    Q52.79
  larynx Q31.2
  left heart syndrome Q23.4
  leg (congenital) – *see* Defect, reduction,
    lower limb
  limb Q73.8
    lower (congenital) – *see* Defect, reduc-
      tion, lower limb
    upper (congenital) - *see* Defect, reduc-
      tion, upper limb
  liver Q44.7
  lung (lobe) (not associated with short
    gestation) Q33.6
    associated with immaturity, low birth
      weight, prematurity, or short
      gestation P28.0
  mammary (areola), congenital
    Q83.8
  mandible, mandibular M26.04
    alveolar M26.74
    unilateral condylar M27.8
  maxillary M26.02
    alveolar M26.73
  medullary D61.9
  megakaryocytic D69.49
  metacarpus - *see* Defect, reduction, up-
    per limb, specified type NEC
  metatarsus – *see* Defect, reduction,
    lower limb, specified type NEC
  muscle Q79.8
  nail(s) Q84.6
  nose, nasal Q30.1
  optic nerve H47.03-
  osseous meatus (ear) Q17.8
  ovary, congenital Q50.39
  pancreas Q45.0
  parathyroid (gland) Q89.2
  parotid gland Q38.4
  patella Q74.1
  pelvis, pelvic girdle Q74.2
  penis (congenital) Q55.62
  peripheral vascular system Q27.8
    digestive system Q27.8
    lower limb Q27.8
    specified site NEC Q27.8
    upper limb Q27.8
  pituitary (gland) (congenital) Q89.2
  pulmonary (not associated with short
    gestation) Q33.6
    artery, functional J43.0
    associated with short gestation
      P28.0
  radioulnar - *see* Defect, reduction, upper
    limb, specified type NEC
  radius - *see* Defect, reduction, upper
    limb
  rectum Q42.1
    with fistula Q42.0
  respiratory system NEC Q34.8
  rib Q76.6
  right heart syndrome Q22.6
  sacrum Q76.49
  scapula Q74.0
  scrotum Q55.1
  shoulder girdle Q74.0
  skin Q82.8
  skull (bone) Q75.8
    with
      anencephaly Q00.0
      encephalocele - *see* Encephalocele

Hypoplasia, hypoplastic *(Continued)*
  skull *(Continued)*
    with *(Continued)*
      hydrocephalus Q03.9
        with spina bifida - *see* Spina
          bifida, by site, with
          hydrocephalus
      microcephaly Q02
  spinal (cord) (ventral horn cell) Q06.1
  spine Q76.49
  sternum Q76.7
  tarsus – *see* Defect, reduction, lower
    limb, specified type NEC
  testis Q55.1
  thymic, with immunodeficiency D82.1
  thymus (gland) Q89.2
    with immunodeficiency D82.1
  thyroid (gland) E03.1
    cartilage Q31.2
  tibiofibular (congenital) – *see* Defect,
    reduction, lower limb, specified
    type NEC
  toe – *see* Defect, reduction, lower limb,
    specified type NEC
  tongue Q38.3
  Turner's K00.4
  ulna (congenital) - *see* Defect, reduction,
    upper limb
  umbilical artery Q27.0
  unilateral condylar M27.8
  ureter Q62.8
  uterus, congenital Q51.8
  vagina Q52.4
  vascular NEC peripheral Q27.8
    brain Q28.3
    digestive system Q27.8
    lower limb Q27.8
    specified site NEC Q27.8
    upper limb Q27.8
  vein(s) (peripheral) Q27.8
    brain Q28.3
    digestive system Q27.8
    great Q26.8
    lower limb Q27.8
    specified site NEC Q27.8
    upper limb Q27.8
  vena cava (inferior) (superior) Q26.8
  vertebra Q76.49
  vulva, congenital Q52.79
  zonule (ciliary) Q12.8
Hypopotassemia E87.6
Hypoproconvertinemia, congenital (hereditary) D68.2
Hypoproteinemia E77.8
Hypoprothrombinemia (congenital)
  (hereditary) (idiopathic) D68.2
  acquired D68.4
  newborn, transient P61.6
Hypoptyalism K11.7
Hypopyon (eye) (anterior chamber) - *see*
  Iridocyclitis, acute, hypopyon
Hypopyrexia R68.0
Hyporeflexia R29.2
Hyposecretion
  ACTH E23.0
  antidiuretic hormone E23.2
  ovary E28.39
  salivary gland (any) K11.7
  vasopressin E23.2
**Hyposegmentation, leukocytic, heredi-
  tary** D72.0
Hyposiderinemia D50.9

Hypospadias Q54.9
  balanic Q54.0
  coronal Q54.0
  glandular Q54.0
  penile Q54.1
  penoscrotal Q54.2
  perineal Q54.3
  specified NEC Q54.8
Hypospermatogenesis - *see* Oligospermia
Hyposplenism D73.0
Hypostasis pulmonary, passive - *see*
  Edema, lung
Hypostatic - *see* condition
Hyposthenuria N28.89
Hypotension (arterial) (constitutional)
  I95.9
  chronic I95.89
  due to (of) hemodialysis I95.3
  drug-induced I95.2
  iatrogenic I95.89
  idiopathic (permanent) I95.0
  intracranial, following ventricular
    shunting (ventriculostomy)
    G97.2
  intra-dialytic I95.3
  maternal, syndrome (following labor
    and delivery) O26.5-
  neurogenic, orthostatic G90.3
  orthostatic (chronic) I95.1
    due to drugs I95.2
    neurogenic G90.3
  postoperative I95.81
  postural I95.1
  specified NEC I95.89
Hypothermia (accidental) T68
  due to anesthesia, anesthetic T88.51
  low environmental temperature T68
  neonatal P80.9
    environmental (mild) NEC P80.8
    mild P80.8
    severe (chronic) (cold injury syn-
      drome) P80.0
    specified NEC P80.8
  not associated with low environmental
    temperature R68.0
Hypothyroidism (acquired) E03.9
  congenital (without goiter) E03.1
    with goiter (diffuse) E03.0
  due to
    exogenous substance NEC E03.2
    iodine-deficiency, acquired E01.8
      subclinical E02
    irradiation therapy E89.0
    medicament NEC E03.2
    P-aminosalicylic acid (PAS) E03.2
    phenylbutazone E03.2
    resorcinol E03.2
    sulfonamide E03.2
    surgery E89.0
    thiourea group drugs E03.2
  iatrogenic NEC E03.2
  iodine-deficiency (acquired) E01.8
  congenital - *see* Syndrome, iodinedefi-
    ciency, congenital
    subclinical E02
  neonatal, transitory P72.2
  postinfectious E03.3
  postirradiation E89.0
  postprocedural E89.0
  postsurgical E89.0
  specified NEC E03.8
  subclinical, iodine-deficiency related E02

Hypotonia, hypotonicity, hypotony
    bladder N31.2
    congenital (benign) P94.2
    eye - *see* Disorder, globe, hypotony
Hypotrichosis - *see* Alopecia
Hypotropia H50.2-
Hypoventilation R06.89
    congenital central alveolar G47.35
    sleep related
        idiopathic nonobstructive alveolar
            G47.34
        in conditions classified elsewhere
            G47.36

Hypovitaminosis - *see* Deficiency, vitamin
Hypovolemia E86.1
    surgical shock T81.1
    traumatic (shock) T79.4
Hypoxemia R09.02
    newborn P84
    sleep related, in conditions classified
        elsewhere G47.36
Hypoxia (*see also* Anoxia) R09.01
    cerebral, during a procedure NEC
        G97.81
        postprocedural NEC G97.82
    intrauterine P84

Hypoxia (*Continued*)
    myocardial - *see* Insufficiency, coronary
    newborn P84
    sleep-related G47.34
Hypsarhythmia – *see* Epilepsy, general-
    ized, specified NEC
Hysteralgia, pregnant uterus O26.89-
Hysteria, hysterical (conversion) (dis-
    sociative state) F44.9
    anxiety F41.8
    convulsions F44.5
    psychosis, acute F44.9
Hysteroepilepsy F44.5

I

Ichthyoparasitism due to Vandellia cirrhosa B88.8
Ichthyosis (congenital) Q80.9
  acquired L85.0
  fetalis Q80.4
  hystrix Q80.8
  lamellar Q80.2
  lingual K13.29
  palmaris and plantaris Q82.8
  simplex Q80.0
  vera Q80.8
  vulgaris Q80.0
  X-linked Q80.1
Ichthyotoxism - *see* Poisoning, fish
  bacterial - *see* Intoxication, foodborne
Icteroanemia, hemolytic (acquired) D59.9
  congenital - *see* Spherocytosis
Icterus - *see also* Jaundice
  conjunctiva R17
  newborn P59.9
  gravis, newborn P55.0
  hematogenous (acquired) D59.9
  hemolytic (acquired) D59.9
    congenital - *see* Spherocytosis
  hemorrhagic (acute) (leptospiral) (spirochetal) A27.0
    newborn P53
  infectious B15.9
    with hepatic coma B15.0
    leptospiral A27.0
    spirochetal A27.0
  neonatorum - *see* Jaundice, newborn
  spirochetal A27.0
Ictus solaris, solis T67.0
Ideation
  suicidal R45.85
    associated with a specific mental disorder - code to the disorder
Identity disorder (child) F64.9
  gender role F64.2
  psychosexual F64.2
Id reaction (due to bacteria) L30.2
Idioglossia F80.0
Idiopathic - *see* condition
Idiot, idiocy (congenital) F73
  amaurotic (Bielschowsky(-Jansky)) (family) (infantile (late)) (juvenile (late)) (Vogt-Spielmeyer) E75.4
  microcephalic Q02
IgE asthma J45.909
Ileitis (chronic) (noninfectious) - *see also* Enteritis K52.9
  backwash – *see* Pancolitis, ulcerative (chronic)
  infectious A09
  regional (ulcerative) – *see* Enteritis, regional, small intestine
  segmental – *see* Enteritis, regional
  terminal (ulcerative) – *see* Enteritis, regional, small intestine
Ileocolitis (*see also* Enteritis) K52.9
  regional – *see* Enteritis, regional
  infectious A09
Ileostomy
  attention to Z43.2
  malfunctioning K94.13
  status Z93.2
    with complication - *see* Complications, enterostomy
Ileotyphus - *see* Typhoid
Ileum - *see* condition

Ileus (bowel) (colon) (inhibitory) (intestine) K56.7
  adynamic K56.0
  due to gallstone (in intestine) K56.3
  duodenal (chronic) K31.5
  gallstone K56.3
  mechanical NEC K56.69
  meconium P76.0
    in cystic fibrosis E84.11
    meaning meconium plug (without cystic fibrosis) P76.0
  myxedema K59.8
  neurogenic K56.0
    Hirschsprung's disease or megacolon Q43.1
  newborn
    due to meconium P76.0
      in cystic fibrosis E84.11
      meaning meconium plug (without cystic fibrosis) P76.0
    transitory P76.1
  obstructive K56.69
  paralytic K56.0
Iliac - *see* condition
Iliotibial band syndrome M76.3-
Illiteracy Z55.0
Illness - *see also* Disease R69
  manic-depressive - *see* Disorder, bipolar
Imbalance R26.89
  autonomic G90.8
  constituents of food intake E63.1
  electrolyte E87.8
    with molar pregnancy O08.5
    due to hyperemesis gravidarum O21.1
    following ectopic or molar pregnancy O08.5
    neonatal, transitory NEC P74.4
      potassium P74.3
      sodium P74.2
  endocrine E34.9
  eye muscle NOS H50.9
  hormone E34.9
  hysterical F44.4
  labyrinth - *see* subcategory H83.2
  posture R29.3
  protein-energy - *see* Malnutrition
  sympathetic G90.8
Imbecile, imbecility (I.Q. 35-49) F71
Imbedding, intrauterine device T83.39
Imbibition, cholesterol (gallbladder) K82.4
Imbrication, teeth,, fully erupted M26.30
Imerslund(-Gräsbeck) syndrome D51.1
Immature - *see also* Immaturity
  birth (less than 37 completed weeks) *see* Preterm infant, newborn
    extremely (less than 28 completed weeks) - *see* Immaturity, extreme
  personality F60.89
Immaturity (less than 37 completed weeks) - *see* Preterm infant, newborn
  extreme P07.20
    with gestation of:
      less than 24 weeks P07.21
      24-26 weeks P07.22
      27 weeks P07.23
  fetus or infant light-for-dates - *see* Light-for-dates
  lung, newborn P28.0
  organ or site NEC - *see* Hypoplasia
  pulmonary, newborn P28.0
  reaction F60.89
  sexual (female) (male), after puberty E30.0

Immersion T75.1
  hand T69.01-
  foot T69.02-
Immobile, immobility
  complete, due to severe physical disability or frailty R53.2
  intestine K59.8
  syndrome (paraplegic) M62.3
Immune reconstitution syndrome D89.3
Immunization - *see also* Vaccination
  ABO - *see* Incompatibility, ABO
    in newborn P55.1
  complication - *see* Complications, vaccination
  not done (not carried out) Z28.9
    because (of)
      contraindication NEC Z28.09
      encounter for Z23
        acute illness of patient Z28.01
        allergy to vaccine (or component) Z28.04
        caregiver refusal Z28.82
        chronic illness of patient Z28.02
        group pressure Z28.1
        guardian refusal Z28.82
        immune compromised state of patient Z28.03
        parent refusal Z28.82
        patient's belief Z28.1
        patient had disease being vaccinated against Z28.81
        patient refusal Z28.21
        religious beliefs of patient Z28.1
        specified reason NEC Z28.89
          of patient Z28.29
        unspecified patient reason Z28.20
  Rh factor - *see* Incompatibility, Rh
    affecting management of pregnancy NEC O36.09-
      anti-D antibody O36.01-
    from transfusion T80.4
Immunocytoma – *see* Lymphoma, non-Hodgkin's, diffuse, small cell
Immunodeficiency D84.9
  with
    adenosine-deaminase deficiency D81.3
    antibody defects D80.9
      specified type NEC D80.8
    hyperimmunoglobulinemia D80.6
    increased immunoglobulin M (IgM) D80.5
    major defect D82.9
      specified type NEC D82.8
    partial albinism D82.8
    short-limbed stature D82.2
    thrombocytopenia and eczema D82.0
  antibody with
    hyperimmunoglobulinemia D80.6
    near-normal immunoglobulins D80.6
  autosomal recessive, Swiss type D80.0
  combined D81.9
    biotin-dependent carboxylase D81.819
      biotinidase D81.810
      holocarboxylase synthetase D81.818
      specified type NEC D81.818
    severe (SCID) D81.9
      with
        low or normal B-cell numbers D81.2
        low T- and B-cell numbers D81.1
        reticular dysgenesis D81.0
    specified type NEC D81.89

Immunodeficiency *(Continued)*
common variable D83.9
with
abnormalities of B-cell numbers and function D83.0
autoantibodies to B- or T-cells D83.2
immunoregulatory T-cell disorders D83.1
specified type NEC D83.8
following hereditary defective response to Epstein-Barr virus (EBV) D82.3
selective, immunoglobulin
A (IgA) D80.2
G (IgG) (subclasses) D80.3
M (IgM) D80.4
severe combined (SCID) D81.9
specified type NEC D84.8
X-linked, with increased IgM D80.5
Immunotherapy (encounter for)
antineoplastic Z51.12
Impaction, impacted
bowel, colon, rectum (fecal) K56.4
by gallstone K56.3
calculus - *see* Calculus
cerumen (ear) (external) H61.2-
cuspid - *see* Impaction, tooth
dental (same or adjacent tooth) K01.1
fecal, feces K56.4
fracture - *see* Fracture, by site
gallbladder - *see* Calculus, gallbladder
gallstone(s) - *see* Calculus, gallbladder
bile duct (common) (hepatic) – *see* Calculus, bile duct
cystic duct - *see* Calculus, gallbladder
in intestine, with obstruction (any part) K56.3
intestine (calculous) (fecal) NEC K56.4
gallstone, with ileus K56.3
intrauterine device (IUD) T83.39
molar - *see* Impaction, tooth
shoulder, causing obstructed labor O66.0
tooth, teeth K01.1
turbinate J34.89
Impaired, impairment (function)
auditory discrimination - *see* Abnormal, auditory perception
cognitive, mild, so stated G31.84
dual sensory Z73.82
fasting glucose R73.01
glucose tolerance (oral) R73.02
hearing - *see* Deafness
heart - *see* Disease, heart
kidney N28.9
disorder resulting from N25.9
specified NEC N25.89
liver K72.90
with coma K72.91
mastication K08.8
mild cognitive, so stated G31.84
mobility
ear ossicles - *see* Ankylosis, ear ossicles
requiring care provider Z74.09
myocardium, myocardial - *see* Insufficiency, myocardial
rectal sphincter R19.8
renal (acute) (chronic) N28.9
disorder resulting from N25.9
specified NEC N25.89
vision NEC H54.7
both eyes H54.3
Impediment, speech R47.9
psychogenic (childhood) F98.8
slurring R47.81
specified NEC R47.89

Impending
coronary syndrome I20.0
delirium tremens F10.239
myocardial infarction I20.0
Imperception auditory (acquired) - *see also* Deafness
congenital H93.25
Imperfect
aeration, lung (newborn) NEC - *see* Atelectasis
closure (congenital)
alimentary tract NEC Q45.8
lower Q43.8
upper Q40.8
atrioventricular ostium Q21.2
atrium (secundum) Q21.1
branchial cleft or sinus Q18.0
choroid Q14.3
cricoid cartilage Q31.8
cusps, heart valve NEC Q24.8
pulmonary Q22.3
ductus
arteriosus Q25.0
Botalli Q25.0
ear drum (causing impairment of hearing) Q16.4
esophagus with communication to bronchus or trachea Q39.1
eyelid Q10.3
foramen
botalli Q21.1
ovale Q21.1
genitalia, genital organ(s) or system
female Q52.8
external Q52.79
internal NEC Q52.8
male Q55.8
glottis Q31.8
interatrial ostium or septum Q21.1
interauricular ostium or septum Q21.1
interventricular ostium or septum Q21.0
larynx Q31.8
lip - *see* Cleft, lip
nasal septum Q30.3
nose Q30.2
omphalomesenteric duct Q43.0
optic nerve entry Q14.2
organ or site not listed - *see* Anomaly, by site
ostium
interatrial Q21.1
interauricular Q21.1
interventricular Q21.0
palate - *see* Cleft, palate
preauricular sinus Q18.1
retina Q14.1
roof of orbit Q75.8
sclera Q13.5
septum
aorticopulmonary Q21.4
atrial (secundum) Q21.1
between aorta and pulmonary artery Q21.4
heart Q21.9
interatrial (secundum) Q21.1
interauricular (secundum) Q21.1
interventricular Q21.0
in tetralogy of Fallot Q21.3
nasal Q30.3

Imperfect *(Continued)*
closure *(Continued)*
septum *(Continued)*
ventricular Q21.0
with pulmonary stenosis or atresia, dextraposition of aorta, and hypertrophy of right ventricle Q21.3
in tetralogy of Fallot Q21.3
skull Q75.0
with
anencephaly Q00.0
encephalocele - *see* Encephalocele
hydrocephalus Q03.9
with spina bifida - *see* Spina bifida, by site, with hydrocephalus
microcephaly Q02
spine (with meningocele) - *see* Spina bifida
trachea Q32.1
tympanic membrane (causing impairment of hearing) Q16.4
uterus Q51.8
vitelline duct Q43.0
erection – *see* Dysfunction, sexual, male, erectile
fusion - *see* Imperfect, closure
inflation, lung (newborn) - *see* Atelectasis
posture R29.3
rotation, intestine Q43.3
septum, ventricular Q21.0
Imperfectly descended testis – *see* Cryptorchid
Imperforate (congenital) - *see also* Atresia
anus Q42.3
with fistula Q42.2
cervix (uteri) Q51.8
esophagus Q39.0
with tracheoesophageal fistula Q39.1
hymen Q52.3
jejunum Q41.1
pharynx Q38.8
rectum Q42.1
with fistula Q42.0
urethra Q64.39
vagina Q52.4
Impervious (congenital) - *see also* Atresia
anus Q42.3
with fistula Q42.2
bile duct Q44.2
esophagus Q39.0
with tracheoesophageal fistula Q39.1
intestine (small) Q41.9
large Q42.9
specified NEC Q42.8
rectum Q42.1
with fistula Q42.0
ureter – *see* Atresia, ureter
urethra Q64.39
Impetiginization of dermatoses L01.1
Impetigo (any organism) (any site) (circinate) (contagiosa) (simplex) (vulgaris) L01.00
Bockhart's L01.02
bullous, bullosa L01.03
external ear L01.00 *[H62.40]*
follicularis L01.02
furfuracea L30.5
herpetiformis L40.1
nonobstetrical L40.1
neonatorum L01.03
nonbullous L01.01

Impetigo *(Continued)*
  specified type NEC L01.09
  ulcerative L01.09
Impingement (on teeth)
  soft tissue
    anterior M26.81
    posterior M26.82
Implant, endometrial N80.9
Implantation
  anomalous - *see* Anomaly, by site
    ureter Q62.63
  cyst
    external area or site (skin) NEC L72.0
    iris - *see* Cyst, iris, implantation
    vagina N89.8
    vulva N90.7
  dermoid (cyst) - *see* Implantation, cyst
Impotence (sexual) N52.9
  counseling Z70.1
  organic origin N52.9 – *see also* Dysfunction, sexual, male, erectile
  psychogenic F52.21
Impression, basilar Q75.8
Imprisonment, anxiety concerning Z65.1
Improper care (child) (newborn) – *see* Neglect
Improperly tied umbilical cord (causing hemorrhage) P51.8
Impulsiveness (impulsive) R45.87
Inability to swallow – *see* Aphagia
Inaccessible, inaccessibility
  health care NEC Z75.3
    due to
      waiting period Z75.2
        for admission to facility elsewhere Z75.1
    other helping agencies Z75.4
Inactive - *see* condition
Inadequate, inadequacy
  aesthetics of dental restoration K08.56
  biologic, constitutional, functional, or social F60.7
  development
    child R62.50
    genitalia
      after puberty NEC E30.0
      congenital
        female Q52.8
          external Q52.79
          internal Q52.8
        male Q55.8
    lungs Q33.6
      associated with short gestation P28.0
    organ or site not listed - *see* Anomaly, by site
  diet (causing nutritional deficiency) E63.9
  eating habits Z72.4
  environment, household Z59.1
  family support Z63.8
  food (supply) NEC Z59.4
    hunger effects T73.0
  functional F60.7
  household care, due to
    family member
      handicapped or ill Z74.2
      on vacation Z75.5
      temporarily away from home Z74.2
    technical defects in home Z59.1
    temporary absence from home of person rendering care Z74.2
  housing (heating) (space) Z59.1
  income (financial) Z59.6

Inadequate, inadequacy *(Continued)*
  intrafamilial communication Z63.8
  material resources Z59.9
  mental - *see* Retardation, mental
  parental supervision or control of child Z62.0
  personality F60.7
  pulmonary
    function R06.89
      newborn P28.5
    ventilation, newborn P28.5
  sample of cytologic smear
    anus R85.615
    cervix R87.615
    vagina R87.625
  social F60.7
    insurance Z59.7
    skills NEC Z73.4
  supervision of child by parent Z62.0
  teaching affecting education Z55.8
  welfare support Z59.7
Inanition R64
  with edema - *see* Malnutrition, severe
  due to
    deprivation of food T73.0
    malnutrition - *see* Malnutrition
  fever R50.9
Inappropriate
  diet or eating habits Z72.4
  secretion
    antidiuretic hormone (ADH) (excessive) E22.2
    deficiency E23.2
    pituitary (posterior) E22.2
Inattention at or after birth – *see* Neglect
Incarceration, incarcerated
  enterocele K46.0
    gangrenous K46.1
  epiplocele K46.0
    gangrenous K46.1
  exophthalmos K42.0
    gangrenous K42.1
  hernia - *see also* Hernia, by site, with obstruction
    with gangrene - *see* Hernia, by site, with gangrene
  iris, in wound – *see* Injury, eye, laceration, with prolapse
  lens, in wound – *see* Injury, eye, laceration, with prolapse
  omphalocele K42.0
  prison, anxiety concerning Z65.1
  rupture - *see* Hernia, by site
  sarcoepiplocele K46.0
    gangrenous K46.1
  sarcoepiplomphalocele K42.0
    with gangrene K42.1
  uterus N85.8
    gravid O34.51-
      causing obstructed labor O65.5
Incised wound
  external - *see* Laceration
  internal organs - *see* Injury, by site
Incision, incisional
  hernia - *see* Hernia, ventral
  surgical, complication - *see* Complications, surgical procedure
  traumatic
    external - *see* Laceration
    internal organs - *see* Injury, by site

Inclusion
  azurophilic leukocytic D72.0
  blennorrhea (neonatal) (newborn) P39.1
  gallbladder in liver (congenital) Q44.1
Incompatibility
  ABO
    affecting management of pregnancy O36.11-
      anti-A sensitization O36.11-
      anti-B sensitization O36.19-
      specified NEC O36.19-
    infusion or transfusion reaction T80.89
    newborn P55.1
  blood (group) (Duffy) (K(ell)) (Kidd) (Lewis) (M) (S) NEC
    affecting management of pregnancy O36.11-
      anti-A sensitization O36.11-
      anti-B sensitization O36.19-
    infusion or transfusion reaction T80.89
    newborn P55.8
  divorce or estrangement Z63.5
  Rh (blood group) (factor) Z31.82
    affecting management of pregnancy NEC O36.09-
      anti-D antibody O36.01-
    infusion or transfusion reaction T80.4
    newborn P55.0
  rhesus - *see* Incompatibility, Rh
Incompetency, incompetent, incompetence
  annular
    aortic (valve) - *see* Insufficiency, aortic
    mitral (valve) I34.0
    pulmonary valve (heart) I37.1
  aortic (valve) - *see* Insufficiency, aortic
  cardiac valve - *see* Endocarditis
  cervix, cervical (os) N88.3
    in pregnancy O34.3-
  chronotropic I45.89
    with
      autonomic dysfunction G90.8
      ischemic heart disease I25.89
      left ventricular dysfunction I51.89
      sinus node dysfunction I49.8
  esophagogastric (junction) (sphincter) K22.0
  mitral (valve) - *see* Insufficiency, mitral
  pelvic fundus N81.89
  pubocervical tissue N81.82
  pulmonary valve (heart) I37.1
    congenital Q22.3
  rectovaginal tissue N81.83
  tricuspid (annular) (valve) - *see* Insufficiency, tricuspid
  valvular - *see* Endocarditis
    congenital Q24.8
  vein, venous (saphenous) (varicose) - *see* Varix, leg
Incomplete - *see also* condition
  bladder, emptying R33.9
  expansion lungs (newborn) NEC - *see* Atelectasis
  rotation, intestine Q43.3
Inconclusive
  diagnostic imaging due to excess body fat of patient R93.9
  findings on diagnostic imaging of breast NEC R92.8
  mammogram (due to dense breasts) R92.2

Incontinence R32
  anal sphincter R15
  feces R15
    nonorganic origin F98.1
  overflow N39.490
  psychogenic F45.8
  rectal R15
  reflex N39.498
  stress (female) (male) N39.3
    and urge N39.46
  urethral sphincter R32
  urge N39.41
    and stress (female) (male) N39.46
  urine (urinary) R32
    continuous N39.45
    due to cognitive impairment, or
        severe physical disability or
        immobility R39.81
    functional R39.81
    mixed (stress and urge) N39.46
    nocturnal N39.44
    nonorganic origin F98.0
    overflow N39.490
    post dribbling N39.43
    reflex N39.498
    specified NEC N39.498
    stress (female) (male) N39.3
      and urge N39.46
    total N39.498
    unaware N39.42
    urge N39.41
      and stress (female) (male)
          N39.46
Incontinentia pigmenti Q82.3
Incoordinate, incoordination
  esophageal-pharyngeal (newborn) – see
      Dysphagia
  muscular R27.8
  uterus (action) (contractions) (compli-
      cating delivery) O62.4
Increase, increased
  abnormal, in development R63.8
  androgens (ovarian) E28.1
  anticoagulants (antithrombin)
      (anti-VIIIa) (anti-IXa) (anti-
      Xa) (anti-XIa) - see Circulating
      anticoagulants)
  cold sense R20.8
  estrogen E28.0
  function
    adrenal
      cortex - see Cushing's syndrome
      medulla E27.5
    pituitary (gland) (anterior) (lobe)
        E22.9
      posterior E22.2
  heat sense R20.8
  intracranial pressure (benign) G93.2
  permeability, capillaries I78.8
  pressure, intracranial G93.2
  secretion
    gastrin E16.4
    glucagon E16.3
    pancreas, endocrine E16.9
      growth hormone-releasing hor-
          mone E16.8
      pancreatic polypeptide E16.8
      somatostatin E16.8
      vasoactive-intestinal polypeptide
          E16.8
  sphericity, lens Q12.4
  splenic activity D73.1
  venous pressure I87.8
    portal K76.6

Increta placenta O43.22-
Incrustation, cornea, foreign body
      (lead)(zinc)—see Foreign body,
      cornea
Incyclophoria H50.54
Incyclotropia - see Cyclotropia
Indeterminate sex Q56.4
India rubber skin Q82.8
Indigestion (acid) (bilious) (functional)
      K30
  catarrhal K31.89
  due to decomposed food NOS A05.9
  nervous F45.8
  psychogenic F45.8
Indirect - see condition
Induratio penis plastica N48.6
Induration, indurated
  brain G93.89
  breast (fibrous) N64.51
    puerperal, postpartum O92.29
  broad ligament N83.8
  chancre
    anus A51.1
    congenital A50.07
    extragenital NEC A51.2
  corpora cavernosa (penis) (plastic)
      N48.6
  liver (chronic) K76.8
  lung (black) (brown) (chronic) (fibroid) -
      see Fibrosis, lung
  penile (plastic) N48.6
  phlebitic - see Phlebitis
  skin R23.4
Inebriety (without dependence) - see
      Alcohol, intoxication
Inefficiency, kidney N28.9
Inelasticity, skin R23.4
Inequality, leg (length) (acquired) - see
      also Deformity, limb, unequal length
  congenital – see Defect, reduction, lower
      limb
  lower leg - see Deformity, limb, unequal
      length
Inertia
  bladder (neurogenic) N31.2
  stomach K31.89
    psychogenic F45.8
  uterus, uterine during labor O62.2
    during latent phase of labor O62.0
    primary O62.0
    secondary O62.1
  vesical (neurogenic) N31.2
Infancy, infantile, infantilism - see also
      condition
  celiac K90.0
  genitalia, genitals (after puberty) E30.0
  Herter's (nontropical sprue) K90.0
  intestinal K90.0
  Lorain E23.0
  pancreatic K86.8
  pelvis M95.5
    with disproportion (fetopelvic) O33.1
      causing obstructed labor O65.1
  pituitary E23.0
  renal N25.0
  uterus - see Infantile, genitalia
Infant(s) - see also Infancy
  excessive crying R68.11
  irritable child R68.12
  lack of care – see Neglect
  liveborn (singleton) Z38.2
    born in hospital Z38.00
      by cesarean Z38.01
    born outside hospital Z38.1

Infant(s) (Continued)
  liveborn (Continued)
    multiple NEC Z38.8
      born in hospital Z38.68
        by cesarean Z38.69
      born outside hospital Z38.7
    quadruplet Z38.8
      born in hospital Z38.63
        by cesarean Z38.64
      born outside hospital Z38.7
    quintuplet Z38.8
      born in hospital Z38.65
        by cesarean Z38.66
      born outside hospital Z38.7
    triplet Z38.8
      born in hospital Z38.61
        by cesarean Z38.62
      born outside hospital Z38.7
    twin Z38.5
      born in hospital Z38.30
        by cesarean Z38.31
      born outside hospital Z38.4
  of diabetic mother (syndrome of) P70.1
    gestational diabetes P70.0
Infantile - see also condition
  genitalia, genitals E30.0
  os, uterine E30.0
  penis E30.0
  testis E29.1
  uterus E30.0
Infantilism - see Infancy
Infarct, infarction
  adrenal (capsule) (gland) E27.49
  appendices epiploicae K55.0
  bowel K55.0
  brain (stem) - see Infarct, cerebral
  breast N64.89
  brewer's (kidney) N28.0
  cardiac - see Infarct, myocardium
  cerebellar - see Infarct, cerebral
  cerebral I63.9 - see also Occlusion, artery
      cerebral or precerebral, with
      infarction
    aborted I63.9
    cortical I63.9
    due to
      cerebral venous thrombosis, non-
          pyogenic I63.6
      embolism
        cerebral arteries I63.4-
        precerebral arteries I63.1-
      occlusion NEC
        cerebral arteries I63.5-
        precerebral arteries I63.2-
      stenosis NEC
        cerebral arteries I63.5-
        precerebral arteries I63.2-
      thrombosis
        cerebral artery I63.3-
        precerebral artery I63.0-
    intraoperative
      during cardiac surgery I97.810
      during other surgery I97.811
    postprocedural
      following cardiac surgery
          I97.820
      following other surgery I97.821
    specified NEC I63.8
  colon (acute) (agnogenic) (embolic)
      (hemorrhagic) (nonocclusive)
      (nonthrombotic) (occlusive)
      (segmental) (thrombotic) (with
      gangrene) K55.0

Infarct, infarction (Continued)
  coronary artery - see Infarct,
    myocardium
  embolic - see Embolism
  fallopian tube N83.8
  gallbladder K82.8
  heart - see Infarct, myocardium
  hepatic K76.3
  hypophysis (anterior lobe) E23.6
  impending (myocardium) I20.0
  intestine (acute) (agnogenic) (embolic)
    (hemorrhagic) (nonocclusive)
    (nonthrombotic) (occlusive)
    (thrombotic) (with gangrene)
    K55.0
  kidney N28.0
  liver K76.3
  lung (embolic) (thrombotic) - see Embo-
    lism, pulmonary
  lymph node I89.8
  mesentery, mesenteric (embolic)
    (thrombotic) (with gangrene)
    K55.0
  muscle (ischemic) M62.20
    ankle M62.27-
    foot M62.27-
    forearm M62.23-
    hand M62.24-
    lower leg M62.26-
    pelvic region M62.25-
    shoulder region M62.21-
    specified site NEC M62.28
    thigh M62.25-
    upper arm M62.22-
  myocardium, myocardial (acute) (with
    stated duration of 4 weeks or less)
    I21.3
    diagnosed on ECG, but presenting no
      symptoms I25.2
    healed or old I25.2
    intraoperative
      during cardiac surgery I97.790
      during other surgery I97.791
    non-Q wave I21.4
    non-ST elevation (NSTEMI) I21.4
      subsequent I22.2
    nontransmural I21.4
    past (diagnosed on ECG or other
      investigation, but currently pre-
      senting no symptoms) I25.2
    postprocedural
      following cardiac surgery I97.190
      following other surgery I97.191
    Q wave (see also, Infarct, myocar-
      dium, by site) I21.3
    ST elevation (STEMI) I21.3
      anterior (anteroapical) (anterolat-
        eral) (anteroseptal) (Q wave)
        (wall) I21.09
        subsequent I22.0
      inferior (diaphragmatic) (inferolat-
        eral) (inferoposterior) (wall)
        NEC I21.19
        subsequent I22.1
      inferoposterior transmural (Q
        wave) I21.11
      involving
        coronary artery of anterior wall
          NEC I21.09
        coronary artery of inferior wall
          NEC I21.19
        diagonal coronary artery I21.02
        left anterior descending coronary
          artery I21.02

Infarct, infarction (Continued)
  myocardium, myocardial (Continued)
    ST elevation (Continued)
      involving (Continued)
        left circumflex coronary artery
          I21.21
        left main coronary artery
          I21.01
        oblique marginal coronary artery
          I21.21
        right coronary artery I21.11
      lateral (apical-lateral) (basal-lateral)
        (high) I21.29
        subsequent I22.8
      posterior (posterobasal) (postero-
        lateral) (posteroseptal) (true)
        I21.29
        subsequent I22.8
      septal I21.29
        subsequent I22.8
      specified NEC I21.29
        subsequent I22.8
      subsequent I22.9
    subsequent (recurrent) (reinfarction)
      I22.9
      anterior (anteroapical) (anterolat-
        eral) (anteroseptal) (wall)
        I22.0
      diaphragmatic (wall) I22.1
      inferior (diaphragmatic) (inferolat-
        eral) (inferoposterior) (wall)
        I22.1
      lateral (apical-lateral) (basal-lateral)
        (high) I22.8
      non-ST elevation (NSTEMI) I22.2
      posterior (posterobasal) (postero-
        lateral) (posteroseptal) (true)
        I22.8
      septal I22.8
      specified NEC I22.8
      ST elevation I22.9
        anterior (anteroapical) (antero-
          lateral) (anteroseptal) (wall)
          I22.0
        inferior (diaphragmatic) (in-
          ferolateral) (inferoposterior)
          (wall) I22.1
        specified NEC I22.8
      subendocardial I22.2
      transmural I22.9
        anterior (anteroapical) (antero-
          lateral) (anteroseptal) (wall)
          I22.0
        diaphragmatic (wall) I22.1
        inferior (diaphragmatic) (in-
          ferolateral) (inferoposterior)
          (wall) I22.1
        lateral (apical-lateral) (basal-
          lateral) (high) I22.8
        posterior (posterobasal) (pos-
          terolateral) (posteroseptal)
          (true) I22.8
        specified NEC I22.8
    syphilitic A52.06
    transmural I21.3
      anterior (anteroapical) (anterolat-
        eral) (anteroseptal) (Q wave)
        (wall) NEC I21.09
      inferior (diaphragmatic) (inferolat-
        eral) (inferoposterior)
        (Q wave) (wall) NEC
        I21.19
      inferoposterior (Q wave) I21.11

Infarct, infarction (Continued)
  myocardium, myocardial (Continued)
    transmural (Continued)
      lateral (apical-lateral) (basal-lateral)
        (high) NEC I21.29
      posterior (posterobasal) (postero-
        lateral) (posteroseptal) (true)
        NEC I21.29
      septal NEC I21.29
      specified NEC I21.29
    nontransmural I21.4
    omentum K55.0
    ovary N83.8
    pancreas
    papillary muscle - see Infarct,
      myocardium
    parathyroid gland E21.4
    pituitary (gland) E23.6
    placenta O43.81-
    prostate N42.89
    pulmonary (artery) (vein) (hemor-
      rhagic) - see Embolism, pulmonary
    renal (embolic) (thrombotic) N28.0
    retina, retinal (artery) - see Occlusion,
      artery, retina
    spinal (cord) (acute) (embolic) (nonem-
      bolic) G95.11
    spleen D73.5
      embolic or thrombotic I74.8
    subendocardial (acute) (nontransmural)
      I21.4
    suprarenal (capsule) (gland) E27.49
    testis N50.1
    thrombotic - see also Thrombosis
      artery, arterial - see Embolism
    thyroid (gland) E07.89
    ventricle (heart) - see Infarct,
      myocardium
Infecting - see condition
Infection, infected, infective (opportunistic) B99.9
  with
    drug resistant organism (see also
      specific organism) Z16
    lymphangitis - see Lymphangitis
    organ dysfunction (acute) R65.20
      with septic shock R65.21
  abscess (skin) - code by site under
    Abscess
  Absidia - see Mucormycosis
  Acanthocheilonema (perstans) (strepto-
    cerca) B74.4
  accessory sinus (chronic) - see Sinusitis
  achorion - see Dermatophytosis
  Acremonium falciforme B47.0
  acromioclavicular M00.9
  Actinobacillus (actinomycetem-
    comitans) A28.8
    mallei A24.0
    muris A25.1
  Actinomadura B47.1
  Actinomyces (israelii) - see also Actino-
    mycosis A42.9
  Actinomycetales - see Actinomycosis
  actinomycotic NOS - see Actinomycosis
  adenoid (and tonsil) J03.90
    chronic J35.02
  adenovirus NEC
    as cause of disease classified else-
      where B97.0
    unspecified nature or site B34.0
  aerogenes capsulatus A48.0
  aertrycke - see Infection, salmonella

Infection, infected, infective *(Continued)*
   alimentary canal NOS - *see* Enteritis,
      infectious
   Allescheria boydii B48.2
   Alternaria B48.8
   alveolus, alveolar (process) K04.7
   Ameba, amebic (histolytica) - *see*
      Amebiasis
   amniotic fluid, sac or cavity O41.10-
      chorioamnionitis O41.12-
      placentitis O41.14-
   amputation stump (surgical) – *see*
         Complication, amputation stump,
         infection
   Ancylostoma (duodenalis) B76.0
   Anisakiasis, Anisakis larvae B81.0
   anthrax - *see* Anthrax
   antrum (chronic) - *see* Sinusitis,
      maxillary
   anus, anal (papillae) (sphincter) K62.8
   arbovirus (arbor virus) A94
      specified type NEC A93.8
   artificial insemination N98.0
   Ascaris lumbricoides - *see* Ascariasis
   Ascomycetes B47.0
   Aspergillus (flavus) (fumigatus) (ter-
      reus) - *see* Aspergillosis
   atypical
      acid-fast (bacilli) - *see* Mycobacte-
         rium, atypical
      mycobacteria - *see* Mycobacterium,
         atypical
      virus A81.9
         specified type NEC A81.89
   auditory meatus (external) - *see* Otitis,
      externa, infective
   auricle (ear) - *see* Otitis, externa,
      infective
   axillary gland (lymph) L04.2
   Bacillus A49.9
      abortus A23.1
      anthracis - *see* Anthrax
      Ducrey's (any location) A57
      Flexner's A03.1
      Friedländer's NEC A49.8
      gas (gangrene) A48.0
      mallei A24.0
      melitensis A23.0
      paratyphoid, paratyphosus A01.4
         A A01.1
         B A01.2
         C A01.3
      Shiga(-Kruse) A03.0
      suipestifer - *see* Infection, salmonella
      swimming pool A31.1
      typhosa A01.00
      welchii - *see* Gangrene, gas
   bacterial NOS A49.9
      as cause of disease classified else-
         where B96.89
         Clostridium perfringens
            [C. perfringens] B96.7
         Bacteroides fragilis [B. fragilis]
            B96.6
         Enterobacter sakazakii B96.89
         Enterococcus B95.2
         Escherichia coli [E. coli] B96.2
         Helicobacter pylori [H.pylori]
            B96.81
         Hemophilus influenzae
            [H. influenzae] B96.3
         Klebsiella pneumoniae
            [K. pneumoniae] B96.1

Infection, infected, infective *(Continued)*
   bacterial NOS *(Continued)*
      as cause of disease classified else-
         where *(Continued)*
         Mycoplasma pneumoniae
            [M. pneumoniae] B96.0
         Proteus (mirabilis) (morganii)
            B96.4
         Pseudomonas (aeruginosa)
            (mallei) (pseudomallei)
            B96.5
         Staphylococcus B95.8
            aureus B95.6
            specified NEC B95.7
         Streptococcus B95.5
            group A B95.0
            group B B95.1
            pneumoniae B95.3
            specified NEC B95.4
         Vibrio vulnificus B96.82
      specified NEC A48.8
   Bacterium
      paratyphosum A01.4
         A A01.1
         B A01.2
         C A01.3
      typhosum A01.00
   Bacteroides NEC A49.8
      fragilis, as cause of disease classified
         elsewhere B96.6
   Balantidium coli A07.0
   Bartholin's gland N75.8
   Basidiobolus B46.8
   bile duct (common) (hepatic) - *see*
      Cholangitis
   bladder - *see* Cystitis
   Blastomyces, blastomycotic - *see also*
      Blastomycosis
      brasiliensis - *see*
         Paracoccidioidomycosis
      dermatitidis - *see* Blastomycosis
      European - *see* Cryptococcosis
      Loboi B48.0
      North American B40.9
      South American - *see*
         Paracoccidioidomycosis
   bleb, postprocedure - *see* Blebitis
   bone - *see* Osteomyelitis
   Bordetella - *see* Whooping cough
   Borrelia bergdorfi A69.20
   brain *(see also* Encephalitis) G04.90
      membranes - *see* Meningitis
      septic G06.0
         meninges - *see* Meningitis,
            bacterial
   branchial cyst Q18.0
   breast - *see* Mastitis
   bronchus - *see* Bronchitis
   Brucella A23.9
      abortus A23.1
      canis A23.3
      melitensis A23.0
      mixed A23.8
      specified NEC A23.8
      suis A23.2
   Brugia (malayi) B74.1
      timori B74.2
   bursa - *see* Bursitis, infective
   buttocks (skin) L08.9
   Campylobacter, intestinal A04.5
      as cause of disease classified else-
         where B96.81
   Candida (albicans) (tropicalis) - *see*
      Candidiasis

Infection, infected, infective *(Continued)*
   candiru B88.8
   Capillaria (intestinal) B81.1
      hepatica B83.8
      philippinensis B81.1
   cartilage - *see* Disorder, cartilage,
      specified type NEC
   catheter-related bloodstream (CRBSI)
      T80.21
   cat liver fluke B66.0
   cellulitis - code by site under Cellulitis
   Cephalosporium falciforme B47.0
   cerebrospinal - *see* Meningitis
   cervical gland (lymph) L04.0
   cervix - *see* Cervicitis
   cesarean delivery wound (puerperal)
      O86.0
   cestodes - *see* Infestation, cestodes
   chest J22
   Chilomastix (intestinal) A07.8
   Chlamydia, chlamydial A74.9
      anus A56.3
      genitourinary tract A56.2
         lower A56.00
         specified NEC A56.19
      lymphogranuloma A55
      pharynx A56.4
      psittaci A70
      rectum A56.3
      sexually transmitted NEC A56.8
   cholera - *see* Cholera
   Cladosporium
      bantianum (brain abscess) B43.1
      carrionii B43.0
      castellanii B36.1
      trichoides (brain abscess) B43.1
      werneckii B36.1
   Clonorchis (sinensis) (liver) B66.1
   Clostridium NEC
      bifermentans A48.0
      botulinum (food poisoning) A05.1
         infant A48.51
         wound A48.52
      difficile
         as cause of disease classified else-
            where B96.89
         foodborne (disease) A05.8
         gas gangrene A48.0
         necrotizing enterocolitis A05.8
         sepsis A41.4
      gas-forming NEC A48.0
      histolyticum A48.0
      novyi, causing gas gangrene A48.0
      oedematiens A48.0
      perfringens
         as cause of disease classified else-
            where B96.7
         due to food A05.2
         foodborne (disease) A05.2
         gas gangrene A48.0
         sepsis A41.4
      septicum, causing gas gangrene A48.0
      sordellii, causing gas gangrene A48.0
      welchii
         as cause of disease classified else-
            where B96.7
         foodborne (disease) A05.2
         gas gangrene A48.0
         necrotizing enteritis A05.2
         sepsis A41.4
   Coccidioides (immitis) - *see*
      Coccidioidomycosis
   colon - *see* Enteritis, infectious
   colostomy K94.02

Infection, infected, infective *(Continued)*
  common duct - *see* Cholangitis
  congenital NOS P39.9
    Candida (albicans) P37.5
    cytomegalovirus P35.1
    hepatitis, viral P35.3
    herpes simplex P35.2
    infectious or parasitic disease P37.9
      specified NEC P37.8
    listeriosis (disseminated) P37.2
    malaria NEC P37.4
      falciparum P37.3
    Plasmodium falciparum P37.3
    poliomyelitis P35.8
    rubella P35.0
    skin P39.4
    toxoplasmosis (acute) (subacute) (chronic) P37.1
    tuberculosis P37.0
    urinary (tract) P39.3
    vaccinia P35.8
    virus P35.9
      specified type NEC P35.8
  Conidiobolus B46.8
  coronavirus NEC B34.2
    as cause of disease classified elsewhere B97.29
    severe acute respiratory syndrome (SARS associated) B97.21
  corpus luteum – *see* Salpingo-oophoritis
  Corynebacterium diphtheriae - *see* Diphtheria
  cotia virus B08.8
  Coxiella burnetii A78
  coxsackie - *see* Coxsackie
  Cryptococcus neoformans - *see* Cryptococcosis
  Cryptosporidium A07.2
  Cunninghamella - *see* Mucormycosis
  cyst - *see* Cyst
  cystic duct (*see also* Cholecystitis) K81.9
  Cysticercus cellulosae - *see* Cysticercosis
  cytomegalovirus, cytomegaloviral B25.9
    congenital P35.1
    maternal, maternal care for (suspected) damage to fetus O35.3
    mononucleosis B27.10
      with
        complication NEC B27.19
        meningitis B27.12
        polyneuropathy B27.11
  delta-agent (acute), in hepatitis B carrier B17.0
  dental (pulpal origin) K04.7
  Deuteromycetes B47.0
  Dicrocoelium dendriticum B66.2
  Dipetalonema (perstans) (streptocerca) B74.4
  diphtherial - *see* Diphtheria
  Diphyllobothrium (adult) (latum) (pacificum) B70.0
    larval B70.1
  Diplogonoporus (grandis) B71.8
  Dipylidium caninum B67.4
  Dirofilaria B74.8
  Dracunculus medinensis B72
  Drechslera (hawaiiensis) B43.8
  Ducrey Haemophilus (any location) A57
  due to or resulting from
    artificial insemination N98.0
    central venous catheter T80.21

Infection, infected, infective *(Continued)*
  due to or resulting from *(Continued)*
    device, implant or graft (*see also* Complications, by site and type, infection or inflammation) T85.79
      arterial graft NEC T82.7
      breast (implant) T85.79
      catheter NEC T85.79
        dialysis (renal) T82.7
          intraperitoneal T85.71
        infusion NEC T82.7
          spinal (epidural) (subdural) T85.79
        urinary (indwelling) T83.51
      electronic (electrode) (pulse generator) (stimulator)
        bone T84.7
        cardiac T82.7
        nervous system (brain) (peripheral nerve) (spinal) T85.79
        urinary T83.59
      fixation, internal (orthopedic) NEC - *see* Complication, fixation device, infection
      gastrointestinal (bile duct) (esophagus) T85.79
      genital NEC T83.6
      heart NEC T82.7
        valve (prosthesis) T82.6
          graft T82.7
      joint prosthesis - *see* Complication, joint prosthesis, infection
      ocular (corneal graft) (orbital implant) NEC T85.79
      orthopedic NEC T84.7
      specified NEC T85.79
      urinary NEC T83.59
      vascular NEC T82.7
      ventricular intracranial shunt T85.79
    immunization or vaccination T88.0
    infusion, injection or transfusion NEC T80.29
    injury NEC - code by site under Wound, open
    portacath (port-a-cath) T80.21
    surgery T81.4
    umbilical venous catheter T80.21
  during labor NEC O75.3
  ear (middle) - *see also* Otitis media
    external - *see* Otitis, externa, infective
    inner - *see* subcategory H83.0
  Eberthella typhosa A01.00
  Echinococcus - *see* Echinococcus
  echovirus
    as cause of disease classified elsewhere B97.12
    unspecified nature or site B34.1
  endocardium I33.0
  endocervix - *see* Cervicitis
  Entamoeba - *see* Amebiasis
  enteric - *see* Enteritis, infectious
  Enterobacter sakazakii B96.89
  Enterobius vermicularis B80
  enterostomy K94.12
  enterovirus B34.1
    as cause of disease classified elsewhere B97.10
      coxsackievirus B97.11
      echovirus B97.12
      specified NEC B97.19
  Entomophthora B46.8

Infection, infected, infective *(Continued)*
  Epidermophyton - *see* Dermatophytosis
  epididymis - *see* Epididymitis
  episiotomy (puerperal) O86.0
  Erysipelothrix (insidiosa) (rhusiopathiae) - *see* Erysipeloid
  erythema infectiosum B08.3
  Escherichia (E.) coli NEC A49.8
    as cause of disease classified elsewhere B96.2
    congenital B39.8
      sepsis P36.4
    generalized A41.51
    intestinal - *see* Enteritis, infectious, due to, Escherichia coli
  ethmoidal (chronic) (sinus) - *see* Sinusitis, ethmoidal
  eustachian tube (ear) – *see* Salpingitis, eustachian
  external auditory canal (meatus) NEC - *see* Otitis, externa, infective
  eye (purulent) - *see* Endophthalmitis, purulent
  eyelid - *see* Inflammation, eyelid
  fallopian tube - *see* Salpingo-oophoritis
  Fasciola (gigantica) (hepatica) (indica) B66.3
  Fasciolopsis (buski) B66.5
  filarial - *see* Infestation, filarial
  finger (skin) L08.9
    nail L03.01-
      fungus B35.1
  fish tapeworm B70.0
    larval B70.1
  flagellate, intestinal A07.9
  fluke - *see* Infestation, fluke
  focal
    teeth (pulpal origin) K04.7
    tonsils J35.01
  Fonsecaea (compactum) (pedrosoi) B43.0
  food - *see* Intoxication, foodborne
  foot (skin) L08.9
    dermatophytic fungus B35.3
  Francisella tularensis - *see* Tularemia
  frontal (sinus) (chronic) - *see* Sinusitis, frontal
  fungus NOS B49
    beard B35.0
    dermatophytic - *see* Dermatophytosis
    foot B35.3
    groin B35.6
    hand B35.2
    nail B35.1
    pathogenic to compromised host only B48.8
    perianal (area) B35.6
    scalp B35.0
    skin B36.9
      foot B35.3
      hand B35.2
      toenails B35.1
  Fusarium B48.8
  gallbladder - *see* Cholecystitis
  gas bacillus - *see* Gangrene, gas
  gastrointestinal - *see* Enteritis, infectious
  generalized NEC - *see* Sepsis
  genital organ or tract
    female - *see* Disease, pelvis, inflammatory
    male N49.9
      multiple sites N49.8
      specified NEC N49.8

Infection, infected, infective *(Continued)*
Ghon tubercle, primary A15.7
Giardia lamblia A07.1
gingiva (chronic) K05.10
   acute K05.00
      plaque induced K05.00
      nonplaque induced K05.01
   plaque induced K05.10
   nonplaque induced K05.11
glanders A24.0
glenosporopsis B48.0
Gnathostoma (spinigerum) B83.1
Gongylonema B83.8
gonococcal - *see* Gonococcus
gram-negative bacilli NOS A49.9
guinea worm B72
gum (chronic) K05.10
   acute K05.00
      plaque induced K05.00
      nonplaque induced K05.01
   plaque induced K05.10
   nonplaque induced K05.11
Haemophilus - *see* Infection,
   Hemophilus
heart - *see* Carditis
Helicobacter pylori A04.5
   as cause of disease classified else-
      where B96.81
helminths B83.9
   intestinal B82.0
      mixed (types classifiable to more
         than one of the titles B65.0-
         B81.3 and B81.8) B81.4
      specified type NEC B81.8
   specified type NEC B83.8
Hemophilus
   aegyptius, systemic A48.4
   ducrey (any location) A57
   influenzae NEC A49.2
      as cause of disease classified else-
         where B96.3
      generalized A41.3
herpes (simplex) - *see also* Herpes
   congenital P35.2
   disseminated B00.7
   zoster B02.9
herpesvirus, herpesviral - *see* Herpes
Heterophyes (heterophyes) B66.8
Histoplasma - *see* Histoplasmosis
   American B39.4
   capsulatum B39.4
hookworm B76.9
human
   papilloma virus A63.0
   T-cell lymphotropic virus type-1
      (HTLV-1) B33.3
hydrocele N43.0
Hymenolepis B71.0
hypopharynx - *see* Pharyngitis
inguinal (lymph) glands L04.1
   due to soft chancre A57
intervertebral disc, pyogenic M46.30
   cervical region M46.32
   cervicothoracic region M46.33
   lumbar region M46.36
   lumbosacral region M46.37
   multiple sites M46.39
   occipito-atlanto-axial region M46.31
   sacrococcygeal region M46.38
   thoracic region M46.34
   thoracolumbar region M46.35
intestine, intestinal - *see* Enteritis,
   infectious
   specified NEC A08.8

Infection, infected, infective *(Continued)*
Isospora belli or hominis A07.3
Japanese B encephalitis A83.0
jaw (bone) (lower) (upper) M27.2
joint - *see* Arthritis, pyogenic or
   pyemic
kidney (cortex) (hematogenous) N15.9
   with calculus N20.0
      with hydronephrosis N13.6
   following ectopic gestation O08.89
   pelvis and ureter (cystic) N28.85
   puerperal (postpartum) O86.21
   specified NEC N15.8
Klebsiella (K.) pneumoniae NEC
   A49.8
   as cause of disease classified else-
      where B96.1
knee (skin) NEC L08.9
   joint M00.9
Koch's - *see* Tuberculosis
labia (majora) (minora) (acute) - *see*
   Vulvitis
lacrimal
   gland - *see* Dacryoadenitis
   passages (duct) (sac) - *see* Inflamma-
      tion, lacrimal, passages
lancet fluke B66.2
larynx NEC J38.7
leg (skin) NOS L08.9
Legionella pneumophila A48.1
   nonpneumonic A48.2
Leishmania – *see also* Leishmaniasis
   aethiopica B55.1
   braziliensis B55.2
   chagasi B55.0
   donovani B55.0
   infantum B55.0
   major B55.1
   mexicana B55.1
   tropica B55.1
lentivirus, as cause of disease classified
   elsewhere B97.31
Leptosphaeria senegalensis B47.0
Leptospira interrogans A27.9
   autumnalis A27.89
   canicola A27.89
   hebdomadis A27.89
   icterohaemorrhagiae A27.0
   pomona A27.89
   specified type NEC A27.89
leptospirochetal NEC – *see*
   Leptospirosis
Listeria monocytogenes – *see also*
   Listeriosis
   congenital P37.2
Loa loa B74.3
   with conjunctival infestation B74.3
   eyelid B74.3
Loboa loboi B48.0
local, skin (staphylococcal) (streptococcal) L08.9
   abscess - code by site under Abscess
   cellulitis - code by site under
      Cellulitis
   specified NEC L08.89
   ulcer - *see* Ulcer, skin
Loefflerella mallei A24.0
lung (*see also* Pneumonia) J18.9
   atypical Mycobacterium A31.0
   spirochetal A69.8
   tuberculous - *see* Tuberculosis,
      pulmonary
   virus - *see* Pneumonia, viral

Infection, infected, infective *(Continued)*
lymph gland - *see also* Lymphadenitis,
   acute
   mesenteric I88.0
lymphoid tissue, base of tongue or
   posterior pharynx, NEC (chronic)
   J35.03
Madurella (grisea) (mycetomii)
   B47.0
major
   following ectopic or molar pregnancy
      O08.0
   puerperal, postpartum, childbirth
      O85
Malassezia furfur B36.0
Malleomyces
   mallei A24.0
   pseudomallei (whitmori) - *see*
      Melioidosis
mammary gland N61
Mansonella (ozzardi) (perstans)
   (streptocerca) B74.4
mastoid - *see* Mastoiditis
maxilla, maxillary M27.2
   sinus (chronic) - *see* Sinusitis,
      maxillary
mediastinum J98.5
Medina (worm) B72
meibomian cyst or gland - *see*
   Hordeolum
meninges - *see* Meningitis, bacterial
meningococcal (*see also* condition)
   A39.9
   adrenals A39.1
   brain A39.81
   cerebrospinal A39.0
   conjunctiva A39.89
   endocardium A39.51
   heart A39.50
      endocardium A39.51
      myocardium A39.52
      pericardium A39.53
   joint A39.83
   meninges A39.0
   meningococcemia A39.4
      acute A39.2
      chronic A39.3
   myocardium A39.52
   pericardium A39.53
   retrobulbar neuritis A39.82
   specified site NEC A39.89
mesenteric lymph nodes or glands NEC
   I88.0
Metagonimus B66.8
metatarsophalangeal M00.9
Microsporum, microsporic - *see*
   Dermatophytosis
mixed flora (bacterial) NEC A49.8
Monilia - *see* Candidiasis
Monosporium apiospermum
   B48.2
mouth, parasitic B37.0
Mucor - *see* Mucormycosis
muscle NEC - *see* Myositis,
   infective
mycelium NOS B49
mycetoma
   actinomycotic NEC B47.1
   mycotic NEC B47.0
Mycobacterium, mycobacterial - *see*
   Mycobacterium
Mycoplasma NEC A49.3
   pneumoniae, as cause of disease
      classified elsewhere B96.0

Infection, infected, infective *(Continued)*
  mycotic NOS B49
    pathogenic to compromised host only
      B48.8
    skin NOS B36.9
  myocardium NEC I40.0
  nail (chronic)
    with lymphangitis - *see* Lymphangitis, acute, digit
    finger L03.01-
      fungus B35.1
    ingrowing L60.0
    toe L03.03-
      fungus B35.1
  nasal sinus (chronic) - *see* Sinusitis
  nasopharynx - *see* Nasopharyngitis
  navel L08.82
  Necator americanus B76.1
  Neisseria - *see* Gonococcus
  Neotestudina rosatii B47.0
  newborn P39.9
    skin P39.4
    specified type NEC P39.8
  nipple N61
    associated with
      lactation O91.03
      pregnancy O91.01-
      puerperium O91.02
  Nocardia - *see* Nocardiosis
  obstetrical surgical wound (puerperal)
    O86.0
  Oesophagostomum (apiostomum)
    B81.8
  Oestrus ovis - *see* Myiasis
  Oidium albicans B37.9
  Onchocerca (volvulus) - *see* Onchocerciasis - oncovirus, as cause of disease classified elsewhere B97.32
  operation wound T81.4
  Opisthorchis (felineus) (viverrini)
    B66.0
  orbit, orbital - *see* Inflammation, orbit
  orthopoxvirus NEC B08.09
  ovary - *see* Salpingo-oophoritis
  Oxyuris vermicularis B80
  pancreas (acute) K85.9
    abscess - *see* Pancreatitis, acute
    specified NEC K85.8
  papillomavirus, as cause of disease classified elsewhere B97.7
  papovavirus NEC B34.4
  Paracoccidioides brasiliensis - *see* Paracoccidioidomycosis
  Paragonimus (westermani)
    B66.4
  parainfluenza virus B34.8
  parameningococcus NOS A39.9
  parapoxvirus B08.60
    specified NEC B08.69
  parasitic B89
  Parastrongylus
    cantonensis B83.2
    costaricensis B81.3
    paratyphoid A01.4
      Type A A01.1
      Type B A01.2
      Type C A01.3
  paraurethral ducts N34.2
  parotid gland – *see* Sialoadenitis
  parvovirus NEC B34.3
    as cause of disease classified elsewhere B97.6

Infection, infected, infective *(Continued)*
  Pasteurella NEC A28.0
    multocida A28.0
    pestis - *see* Plague
    pseudotuberculosis A28.0
    septica (cat bite) (dog bite) A28.0
    tularensis - *see* Tularemia
  pelvic, female - *see* Disease, pelvis, inflammatory
  Penicillium (marneffei) B48.4
  penis (glans) (retention) NEC N48.29
  periapical K04.5
  peridental, periodontal K05.20
    generalized K05.22
    localized K05.21
  perinatal period P39.9
    specified type NEC P39.8
  perineal repair (puerperal) O86.0
  periorbital - *see* Inflammation, orbit
  perirectal K62.8
  perirenal - *see* Infection, kidney
  peritoneal - *see* Peritonitis
  periureteral N28.89
  Petriellidium boydii B48.2
  pharynx - *see also* Pharyngitis
    coxsackievirus B08.5
    posterior, lymphoid (chronic)
      J35.03
  Phialophora
    gougerotii (subcutaneous abscess or cyst) B43.2
    jeanselmei (subcutaneous abscess or cyst) B43.2
    verrucosa (skin) B43.0
  Piedraia hortae B36.3
  pinta A67.9
    intermediate A67.1
    late A67.2
    mixed A67.3
    primary A67.0
  pinworm B80
  pityrosporum furfur B36.0
  pleuro-pneumonia-like organism (PPLO) NEC A49.3
    as cause of disease classified elsewhere B96.0
  pneumococcus, pneumococcal NEC A49.1
    as cause of disease classified elsewhere B95.3
    generalized (purulent) A40.3
      with pneumonia J13
  Pneumocystis carinii (pneumonia)
    B59
  Pneumocystis jiroveci (pneumonia)
    B59
  postoperative T81.4
  postoperative wound T81.4
  postprocedural T81.4
  postvaccinal T88.0
  prepuce NEC N47.7
    with penile inflammation N47.6
  prion - *see* Disease, prion, central nervous system
  prostate (capsule) - *see* Prostatitis
  Proteus (mirabilis) (morganii) (vulgaris) NEC A49.8
    as cause of disease classified elsewhere B96.4
  protozoal NEC B64
    intestinal A07.9
      specified NEC A07.8
    specified NEC B60.8
  Pseudoallescheria boydii B48.2

Infection, infected, infective *(Continued)*
  Pseudomonas NEC A49.8
    as cause of disease classified elsewhere B96.5
    mallei A24.0
    pneumonia J15.1
    pseudomallei - *see* Melioidosis
  puerperal O86.4
    genitourinary tract NEC O86.89
    major or generalized O85
    minor O86.4
    specified NEC O86.89
  pulmonary - *see* Infection, lung
  purulent - *see* Abscess
  Pyrenochaeta romeroi B47.0
  Q fever A78
  rectum (sphincter) K62.8
  renal - *see also* Infection, kidney
    pelvis and ureter (cystic) N28.85
  reovirus, as cause of disease classified elsewhere B97.5
  respiratory (tract) NEC J98.8
    acute J22
    chronic J98.8
    influenzal (upper) (acute) - *see* Influenza, with, respiratory manifestations
    lower (acute) J22
      chronic - *see* Bronchitis, chronic
    rhinovirus J00
    syncytial virus, as cause of disease classified elsewhere B97.4
    upper (acute) NOS J06.9
      chronic J39.8
      streptococcal J06.9
      viral NOS J06.9
  resulting from
    presence of internal prosthesis, implant, graft - *see* Complications, by site and type, infection
  retortamoniasis A07.8
  retroperitoneal NEC K68.9
  retrovirus B33.3
    as cause of disease classified elsewhere B97.30
    human
      immunodeficiency, type 2 [HIV 2] B97.35
      T-cell lymphotropic
        type I [HTLV-I] B97.33
        type II [HTLV-II] B97.34
    lentivirus B97.31
    oncovirus B97.32
    specified NEC B97.39
  Rhinosporidium (seeberi) B48.1
  rhinovirus
    as cause of disease classified elsewhere B97.8
    unspecified nature or site B34.8
  Rhizopus - *see* Mucormycosis
  rickettsial NOS A79.9
  roundworm (large) NEC B82.0
    Ascariasis (*see also* Ascariasis) B77.9
  rubella - *see* Rubella
  Saccharomyces - *see* Candidiasis
  salivary duct or gland (any) – *see* Sialoadenitis
  Salmonella (aertrycke) (arizonae) (callinarum) (cholerae-suis) (enteritidis) (suipestifer) (typhimurium) A02.9
    with
      (gastro)enteritis A02.0
      sepsis A02.1

Infection, infected, infective *(Continued)*
  Salmonella *(Continued)*
    with *(Continued)*
      specified manifestation NEC
        A02.8
      due to food (poisoning) A02.9
      hirschfeldii A01.3
      localized A02.20
        arthritis A02.23
        meningitis A02.21
        osteomyelitis A02.24
        pneumonia A02.22
        pyelonephritis A02.25
        specified NEC A02.29
    paratyphi A01.4
      A A01.1
      B A01.2
      C A01.3
    schottmuelleri A01.2
    typhi, typhosa - *see* Typhoid
  Sarcocystis A07.8
  scabies B86
  Schistosoma - *see* Infestation,
    Schistosoma
  scrotum (acute) NEC N49.2
  seminal vesicle - *see* Vesiculitis
  septic
    localized, skin - *see* Abscess
  sheep liver fluke B66.3
  Shigella A03.9
    boydii A03.2
    dysenteriae A03.0
    flexneri A03.1
    group
      A A03.0
      B A03.1
      C A03.2
      D A03.3
    Schmitz (-Stutzer) A03.0
    schmitzii A03.0
    shigae A03.0
    sonnei A03.3
    specified NEC A03.8
  sinus (accessory) (chronic) (nasal) - *see
    also* Sinusitis
    pilonidal - *see* Sinus, pilonidal
    skin NEC L08.89
  Skene's duct or gland - *see* Urethritis
  skin (local) (staphylococcal) (streptococ-
    cal) L08.9
    abscess - code by site under Abscess
    cellulitis - code by site under
      Cellulitis
    due to fungus B36.9
      specified type NEC B36.8
    mycotic B36.9
      specified type NEC B36.8
    newborn P39.4
    ulcer - *see* Ulcer, skin
  slow virus A81.89
    specified NEC A81.8
  Sparganum (mansoni) (proliferum)
    (baxteri) B70.1
  specific - *see also* Syphilis
    to perinatal period – *see* Infection,
      congenital
  specified NEC B99.8
  spermatic cord NEC N49.1
  sphenoidal (sinus) - *see* Sinusitis,
    sphenoidal
  spinal cord NOS (*see also* Myelitis) G04.91
    abscess G06.1
    meninges - *see* Meningitis
    streptococcal G04.89

Infection, infected, infective *(Continued)*
  Spirillum A25.0
  spirochetal NOS A69.9
    lung A69.8
    specified NEC A69.8
  Spirometra larvae B70.1
  spleen D73.89
  Sporotrichum, Sporothrix (schenckii)
    - *see* Sporotrichosis
  staphylococcal NEC A49.0
    as cause of disease classified else-
      where B95.8
      aureus B95.6
      specified NEC B95.7
    food poisoning A05.0
    generalized (purulent) A41.2
    pneumonia - *see* Pneumonia,
      staphylococcal
  Stellantchasmus falcatus B66.8
  streptobacillus moniliformis A25.1
  streptococcal NEC A49.1
    as cause of disease classified else-
      where B95.5
    B genitourinary complicating
      childbirth O98.82
      pregnancy O98.81-
      puerperium O98.83
    congenital
      sepsis P36.10
        group B P36.0
        specified NEC P36.19
    generalized (purulent) A40.9
  Streptomyces B47.1
  Strongyloides (stercoralis) - *see*
    Strongyloidiasis
  stump (amputation) (surgical) – *see*
    Complication, amputation stump,
    infection
  subcutaneous tissue, local L08.9
  suipestifer - *see* Infection, salmonella
  swimming pool bacillus A31.1
  Taenia - *see* Infestation, Taenia
  Taeniarhynchus saginatus B68.1
  tapeworm - *see* Infestation, tapeworm
  tendon (sheath) - *see* Tenosynovitis,
    infective NEC
  Ternidens diminutus B81.8
  testis - *see* Orchitis
  threadworm B80
  throat - *see* Pharyngitis
  thyroglossal duct K14.8
  toe (skin) L08.9
    cellulitis L03.03-
    fungus B35.1
    nail L03.03-
    fungus B35.1
  tongue NEC K14.0
    parasitic B37.0
  tonsil (and adenoid) (faucial) (lingual)
    (pharyngeal) – *see* Tonsillitis
  tooth, teeth K04.7
    periapical K04.7
    peridental, periodontal K05.20
      generalized K05.22
      localized K05.21
    pulp K04.0
    socket M27.3
  TORCH - *see* Infection, congenital
    without active infection P00.2
  Torula histolytica - *see* Cryptococcosis
  Toxocara (canis) (cati) (felis) B83.0
  Toxoplasma gondii - *see* Toxoplasma
  trachea, chronic J42
  trematode NEC - *see* Infestation, fluke

Infection, infected, infective *(Continued)*
  trench fever A79.0
  Treponema pallidum - *see* Syphilis
  Trichinella (spiralis) B75
  Trichomonas A59.9
    cervix A59.09
    intestine A07.8
    prostate A59.02
    specified site NEC A59.8
    urethra A59.03
    urogenitalis A59.00
    vagina A59.01
    vulva A59.01
  Trichophyton, trichophytic - *see*
    Dermatophytosis
  Trichosporon (beigelii) cutaneum
    B36.2
  Trichostrongylus B81.2
  Trichuris (trichiura) B79
  Trombicula (irritans) B88.0
  Trypanosoma
    brucei
      gambiense B56.0
      rhodesiense B56.1
    cruzi - *see* Chagas' disease
  tubal - *see* Salpingo-oophoritis
  tuberculous NEC - *see* Tuberculosis
  tubo-ovarian - *see* Salpingo-oophoritis
  tunica vaginalis N49.1
  tympanic membrane NEC - *see*
    Myringitis
  typhoid (abortive) (ambulant) (bacillus) -
    see Typhoid
  typhus A75.9
    flea-borne A75.2
    mite-borne A75.3
    recrudescent A75.1
    tick-borne A77.9
      African A77.1
      North Asian A77.2
  umbilicus L08.82
  ureter N28.86
  urethra - *see* Urethritis
  urinary (tract) N39.0
    bladder – *see* Cystitis
    complicating
      pregnancy O23.4-
        specified type NEC O23.3-
    kidney – *see* Infection, kidney
    newborn P39.3
    puerperal (postpartum) O86.20
    tuberculous A18.13
    urethra – *see* Urethritis
  uterus, uterine - *see* Endometritis
  vaccination T88.0
  vaccinia not from vaccination
    B08.011
  vagina (acute) - *see* Vaginitis
  varicella B01.9
  varicose veins -*see* Varix
  vas deferens NEC N49.1
  vesical - *see* Cystitis
  Vibrio
    cholerae A00.0
      El Tor A00.1
    parahaemolyticus (food poisoning)
      A05.3
    vulnificus
      as cause of disease classified
        elsewhere B96.82
      foodborne intoxication A05.5
  Vincent's (gum) (mouth) (tonsil)
    A69.1

Infection, infected, infective (Continued)
  virus, viral NOS B34.9
    adenovirus
      as cause of disease classified else-
        where B97.0
      unspecified nature or site
        B34.0
    arborvirus, arbovirus arthropod-
      borne A94
    as cause of disease classified else-
      where B97.8
      adenovirus B97.0
      coronavirus B97.29
        SARS-associated B97.21
      coxsackievirus B97.11
      echovirus B97.12
      enterovirus B97.10
        coxsackievirus B97.11
        echovirus B97.12
        specified NEC B97.19
      human
        immunodeficiency, type 2
          [HIV 2] B97.35
        T-cell lymphotropic,
          type I [HTLV-I] B97.33
          type II [HTLV-II] B97.34
      metapneumovirus B97.8
      papillomavirus B97.7
      parvovirus B97.6
      reovirus B97.5
      respiratory syncytial B97.4
      retrovirus B97.30
        human
          immunodeficiency, type 2
            [HIV 2] B97.35
          T-cell lymphotropic,
            type I [HTLV-I] B97.33
            type II [HTLV-II]
              B97.34
        lentivirus B97.31
        oncovirus B97.32
        specified NEC B97.39
      specified NEC B97.8
    central nervous system A89
      atypical A81.9
        specified NEC A81.89
      enterovirus NEC A88.8
        meningitis A87.0
      slow virus A81.9
        specified NEC A81.89
      specified NEC A88.8
    chest J98.8
    cotia B08.8
    coxsackie - see also Infection, cox-
      sackie B34.1
      as cause of disease classified else-
        where B97.11
    ECHO
      as cause of disease classified else-
        where B97.12
      unspecified nature or site B34.1
    encephalitis, tick-borne A84.9
    enterovirus, as cause of disease classi-
      fied elsewhere B97.10
      coxsackievirus B97.11
      echovirus B97.12
      specified NEC B97.19
    exanthem NOS B09
    human papilloma as cause of disease
      classified elsewhere B97.7
    human metapneumovirus as cause
      of disease classified elsewhere
      B97.8
    intestine - see Enteritis, viral

Infection, infected, infective (Continued)
  virus, viral NOS (Continued)
    respiratory syncytial
      as cause of disease classified else-
        where B97.4
      bronchopneumonia J12.1
      common cold syndrome J00
      nasopharyngitis (acute) J00
    rhinovirus
      as cause of disease classified else-
        where B97.8
      unspecified nature or site B34.8
    slow A81.9
      specified NEC A81.89
    specified type NEC B33.8
      as cause of disease classified else-
        where B97.8
      unspecified nature or site B34.8
    unspecified nature or site B34.9
    West Nile - see Virus, West Nile
    vulva (acute) - see Vulvitis
    West Nile - see Virus, West Nile
    whipworm B79
    worms B83.9
      specified type NEC B83.8
    Wuchereria (bancrofti) B74.0
      malayi B74.1
      yatapoxvirus B08.70
        specified NEC B08.79
    yeast (see also Candidiasis) B37.9
    yellow fever - see Fever, yellow
    Yersinia
      enterocolitica (intestinal) A04.6
      pestis - see Plague
      pseudotuberculosis A28.2
    Zeis' gland - see Hordeolum
    zoonotic bacterial NOS A28.9
    Zopfia senegalensis B47.0
Infective, infectious - see condition
Infertility
  female N97.9
    age-related N97.8
    associated with
      anovulation N97.0
      cervical (mucus) disease or
        anomaly N88.3
      congenital anomaly
        cervix N88.3
        fallopian tube N97.1
        uterus N97.2
        vagina N97.8
      dysmucorrhea N88.3
      fallopian tube disease or anomaly
        N97.1
      pituitary-hypothalamic origin
        E23.0
      specified origin NEC N97.8
      Stein-Leventhal syndrome E28.2
      uterine disease or anomaly N97.2
      vaginal disease or anomaly N97.8
    due to
      cervical anomaly N88.3
      fallopian tube anomaly N97.1
      ovarian failure E28.39
      Stein-Leventhal syndrome E28.2
      uterine anomaly N97.2
      vaginal anomaly N97.8
    nonimplantation N97.2
    origin
      cervical N88.3
      tubal (block) (occlusion) (stenosis)
        N97.1
      uterine N97.2
      vaginal N97.8

Infertility (Continued)
  male N46.9
    azoospermia N46.01
      extratesticular cause N46.029
        drug therapy N46.021
        efferent duct obstruction N46.023
        infection N46.022
        radiation N46.024
        specified cause NEC N46.029
        systemic disease N46.025
    oligospermia N46.11
      extratesticular cause N46.129
        drug therapy N46.121
        efferent duct obstruction N46.123
        infection N46.122
        radiation N46.124
        specified cause NEC N46.129
        systemic disease N46.125
    specified type NEC N46.8
Infestation B88.9
  Acanthocheilonema (perstans) (strepto-
    cerca) B74.4
  Acariasis B88.0
    demodex folliculorum B88.0
    sarcoptes scabiei B86
    trombiculae B88.0
  Agamofilaria streptocerca B74.4
  Ancylostoma, ankylostoma (brazil-
    iense) (caninum) (ceylanicum)
    (duodenale) B76.0
    americanum B76.1
    new world B76.1
  Anisakis larvae, anisakiasis B81.0
  arthropod NEC B88.2
  Ascaris lumbricoides - see Ascariasis
  Balantidium coli A07.0
  beef tapeworm B68.1
  Bothriocephalus (latus) B70.0
    larval B70.1
  broad tapeworm B70.0
    larval B70.1
  Brugia (malayi) B74.1
    timori B74.2
  candiru B88.8
  Capillaria
    hepatica B83.8
    philippinensis B81.1
  cat liver fluke B66.0
  cestodes B71.9
    diphyllobothrium – see Infestation,
      diphyllobothrium
    dipylidiasis B71.1
    hymenolepiasis B71.0
    specified type NEC B71.8
  chigger B88.0
  chigo, chigoe B88.1
  Clonorchis (sinensis) (liver) B66.1
  coccidial A07.3
  crab-lice B85.3
  Cysticercus cellulosae - see Cysticercosis
  Demodex (folliculorum) B88.0
  Dermanyssus gallinae B88.0
  Dermatobia (hominis) - see Myiasis
  Dibothriocephalus (latus) B70.0
    larval B70.1
  Dicrocoelium dendriticum B66.2
  Diphyllobothrium (adult) (latum) (in-
    testinal) (pacificum) B70.0
    larval B70.1
  Diplogonoporus (grandis) B71.8
  Dipylidium caninum B67.4
  Distoma hepaticum B66.3
  dog tapeworm B67.4
  Dracunculus medinensis B72

Infestation *(Continued)*
  dragon worm B72
  dwarf tapeworm B71.0
  Echinococcus - *see* Echinococcus
  Echinostomum ilocanum B66.8
  Entamoeba (histolytica) - *see* Infection,
    Ameba
  Enterobius vermicularis B80
  eyelid
    in (due to)
      leishmaniasis B55.1
      loiasis B74.3
      onchocerciasis B73.00
      phthiriasis B85.3
      parasitic NOS B89
  eyeworm B74.3
  Fasciola (gigantica) (hepatica) (indica)
    B66.3
  Fasciolopsis (buski) (intestine) B66.5
  filarial B74.9
    bancroftian B74.0
    conjunctiva B74.3
    due to
      Acanthocheilonema (perstans)
        (streptocerca) B74.4
      Brugia (malayi) B74.1
        timori B74.2
      Dracunculus medinensis B72
      guinea worm B72
      loa loa B74.3
      Mansonella (ozzardi) (perstans)
        (streptocerca) B74.4
      Onchocerca volvulus B73.00
        eye B73.00
        eyelid B73.09
      Wuchereria (bancrofti) B74.0
    Malayan B74.1
    ozzardi B74.4
    specified type NEC B74.8
  fish tapeworm B70.0
    larval B70.1
  fluke B66.9
    blood NOS - *see* Schistosomiasis
    cat liver B66.0
    intestinal B66.5
    liver (sheep) B66.3
      cat B66.0
      Chinese B66.1
      due to clonorchiasis B66.1
      oriental B66.1
    lancet B66.2
    lung (oriental) B66.4
    sheep liver B66.3
    specified type NEC B66.8
  fly larvae - *see* Myiasis
  Gasterophilus (intestinalis) - *see* Myiasis
  Gastrodiscoides hominis B66.8
  Giardia lamblia A07.1
  Gnathostoma (spinigerum) B83.1
  Gongylonema B83.8
  guinea worm B72
  helminth B83.9
    angiostrongyliasis B83.2
      intestinal B81.3
    gnathostomiasis B83.1
    hirudiniasis, internal B83.4
    intestinal B82.0
      angiostrongyliasis B81.3
      anisakiasis B81.0
      ascariasis – *see* Ascariasis
      capillariasis B81.1
      cysticercosis – *see* Cysticercosis
      diphyllobothriasis – *see* Infestation,
        diphyllobothriasis

Infestation *(Continued)*
  helminth *(Continued)*
    intestinal *(Continued)*
      dracunculiasis B72
      echinococcus – *see* Echinococcosis
      enterobiasis B80
      filariasis - *see* Infestation, filarial
      fluke – *see* Infestation, fluke
      hookworm – *see* Infestation,
        hookworm
      mixed (types classifiable to more
        than one of the titles B65.0-
        B81.3 and B81.8) B81.4
      onchocerciasis – *see* Onchocerciasis
      schistosomiasis – *see* Infestation,
        schistosoma
      specified
        cestode NEC – *see* Infestation,
          cestode
        type NEC B81.8
      strongyloidiasis – *see*
        Strongyloidiasis
      taenia – *see* Infestation, taenia
      trichinellosis B75
      trichostrongyliasis B81.2
      trichuriasis B79
    specified type NEC B83.8
    syngamiasis B83.3
    visceral larva migrans B83.0
  Heterophyes (heterophyes) B66.8
  hookworm B76.9
    ancylostomiasis B76.0
    necatoriasis B76.1
    specified type NEC B76.8
  Hymenolepis (diminuta) (nana)
    B71.0
  intestinal NEC B82.9
  leeches (aquatic) (land) - *see*
    Hirudiniasis
  Leishmania - *see* Leishmaniasis
  lice, louse - *see* Infestation, Pediculus
  Linguatula B88.8
  Liponyssoides sanguineus B88.0
  Loa loa B74.3
    conjunctival B74.3
    eyelid B74.3
  louse - *see* Infestation, Pediculus
  maggots - *see* Myiasis
  Mansonella (ozzardi) (perstans)
    (streptocerca) B74.4
  Medina (worm) B72
  Metagonimus (yokogawai) B66.8
  microfilaria streptocerca B74.4
    eye B73.00
    eyelid B73.09
  mites B88.9
    scabic B86
  Monilia (albicans) - *see* Candidiasis
  mouth B37.0
  Necator americanus B76.1
  nematode NEC (intestinal) B82.0
    Ancylostoma B76.0
    conjunctiva NEC B83.9
    Enterobius vermicularis B80
    Gnathostoma spinigerum B83.1
    intestinal NEC B81.8
    physaloptera B80
    trichostrongylus B81.2
    trichuris (trichuria) B79
  Oesophagostomum (apiostomum)
    B81.8
  Oestrus ovis (*see also* Myiasis) B87.9
  Onchocerca (volvulus) - *see*
    Onchocerciasis

Infestation *(Continued)*
  Opisthorchis (felineus) (viverrini) B66.0
  orbit, parasitic NOS B89
  Oxyuris vermicularis B80
  Paragonimus (westermani) B66.4
  parasite, parasitic B89
    eyelid B89
    intestinal NOS B82.9
    mouth B37.0
    skin B88.9
    tongue B37.0
  Parastrongylus
    cantonensis B83.2
    costaricensis B81.3
  Pediculus B85.2
    body B85.1
    capitis (humanus) (any site) B85.0
    corporis (humanus) (any site) B85.1
    head B85.0
    mixed (classifiable to more than one
      of the titles B85.0-B85.3) B85.4
    pubis (any site) B85.3
  Pentastoma B88.8
  Phthirus (pubis) (any site) B85.3
    with any infestation classifiable to
      B85.0-B85.2 B85.4
  pinworm B80
  pork tapeworm (adult) B68.0
  protozoal NEC B64
    intestinal A07.9
      specified NEC A07.8
    specified NEC B60.8
  pubic, louse B85.3
  rat tapeworm B71.0
  red bug B88.0
  roundworm (large) NEC B82.0
    Ascariasis (*see also* Ascariasis) B77.9
  sandflea B88.1
  Sarcoptes scabiei B86
  scabies B86
  Schistosoma B65.9
    bovis B65.8
    cercariae B65.3
    haematobium B65.0
    intercalatum B65.8
    japonicum B65.2
    mansoni B65.1
    mattheei B65.8
    mekongi B65.8
    specified type NEC B65.8
    spindale B65.8
  screw worms - *see* Myiasis
  skin NOS B88.9
  Sparganum (mansoni) (proliferum)
    (baxteri) B70.1
    larval B70.1
  specified type NEC B88.8
  Spirometra larvae B70.1
  Stellantchasmus falcatus B66.8
  Strongyloides stercoralis - *see*
    Strongyloidiasis
  Taenia B68.9
    diminuta B71.0
    echinococcus - *see* Echinococcus
    mediocanellata B68.1
    nana B71.0
    saginata B68.1
    solium (intestinal form) B68.0
      larval form - *see* Cysticercosis
  Taeniarhynchus saginatus B68.1
  tapeworm B71.9
    beef B68.1
    broad B70.0
      larval B70.1

Infestation (Continued)

tapeworm (Continued)

dog

dwarf B71.0

fish B70.0

larval B70.1

pork B68.0

rat B71.0

Ternidens diminutus B81.8

Tetranychus molestissimus B88.0

threadworm B80

tongue B37.0

Toxocara (canis) (cati) (felis) B83.0

trematode(s) NEC - see Infestation, fluke

Trichinella (spiralis) B75

Trichocephalus B79

Trichomonas - see Trichomoniasis

Trichostrongylus B81.2

Trichuris (trichiura) B79

Trombicula (irritans) B88.0

Tunga penetrans B88.1

Uncinaria americana B76.1

Vandellia cirrhosa B88.8

whipworm B79

worms B83.9

intestinal B82.0

Wuchereria (bancrofti) B74.0

Infiltrate, infiltration

amyloid (generalized) (localized) - see Amyloidosis

calcareous NEC R89.7

localized - see Degeneration, by site

calcium salt R89.7

cardiac

fatty - see Degeneration, myocardial

glycogenic E74.02

corneal - see Edema, cornea

eyelid - see Inflammation, eyelid

glycogen, glycogenic - see Disease, glycogen storage

heart, cardiac

fatty - see Degeneration, myocardial

glycogenic E74.02 [I43]

inflammatory in vitreous H43.89

kidney N28.89

leukemic - see Leukemia

liver K76.8

fatty - see Fatty, liver NEC

glycogen (see also Disease, glycogen storage) E74.03 [K77]

lung (eosinophilic) J82

lymphatic (see also Leukemia, lymphatic) C91.90

gland I88.9

muscle, fatty M62.89

myocardium, myocardial

fatty - see Degeneration, myocardial

glycogenic E74.02 [I43]

on chest x-ray R91

pulmonary J82

with eosinophilia J82

skin (lymphocytic) L98.6

thymus (gland) (fatty) E32.8

urine R39.0

vesicant agent

antineoplastic chemotherapy T80.810

other agent T80.818

vitreous body H43.89

Infirmity R68.89

senile R54

Inflammation, inflamed, inflammatory

(with exudation)

Inflammation, inflamed, inflammatory (Continued)

abducent (nerve) - see Strabismus, paralytic, sixth nerve

accessory sinus (chronic) - see Sinusitis

adrenal (gland) E27.8

alveoli, teeth M27.3

scorbutic E54

anal canal, anus K62.8

antrum (chronic) - see Sinusitis, maxillary

appendix - see Appendicitis

arachnoid - see Meningitis

areola N61

puerperal, postpartum or gestational – see Infection, nipple

areolar tissue NOS L08.9

artery - see Arteritis

auditory meatus (external) - see Otitis, externa

Bartholin's gland N75.8

bile duct (common) (hepatic) or passage - see Cholangitis

bladder - see Cystitis

bone - see Osteomyelitis

brain - see also Encephalitis

membrane - see Meningitis

breast N61

puerperal, postpartum, gestational – see Mastitis, obstetric

broad ligament - see Disease, pelvis, inflammatory

bronchi - see Bronchitis

catarrhal J00

cecum - see Appendicitis

cerebral - see also Encephalitis

membrane - see Meningitis

cerebrospinal

meningococcal A39.0

cervix (uteri) - see Cervicitis

chest J98.8

chorioretinal H30.9-

cyclitis - see Cyclitis

disseminated H30.10-

generalized H30.13-

peripheral H30.12-

posterior pole H30.11-

epitheliopathy - see Epitheliopathy

focal H30.00-

juxtapapillary H30.01-

macular H30.04-

paramacular - see Inflammation, chorioretinal, focal, macular

peripheral H30.03-

posterior pole H30.02-

specified type NEC H30.89-

choroid - see Inflammation, chorioretinal

chronic, postmastoidectomy cavity - see Complications, postmastoidectomy, inflammation

colon - see Enteritis

connective tissue (diffuse) NEC – see Disorder, soft tissue, specified type NEC

cornea - see Keratitis

corpora cavernosa N48.29

cranial nerve - see Disorder, nerve, cranial

Douglas' cul-de-sac or pouch (chronic) N73.0

Inflammation, inflamed, inflammatory (Continued)

due to device, implant or graft - see also Complications, by site and type, infection or inflammation

arterial graft T82.7

breast (implant) T85.79

catheter T85.79

dialysis (renal) T82.7

intraperitoneal T85.71

infusion T82.7

spinal (epidural) (subdural) T85.79

urinary (indwelling) T83.51

electronic (electrode) (pulse generator) (stimulator)

bone T84.7

cardiac T82.7

nervous system (brain) (peripheral nerve) (spinal) T85.79

urinary T83.59

fixation, internal (orthopedic) NEC - see Complication, fixation device, infection

gastrointestinal (bile duct) (esophagus) T85.79

genital NEC T83.6

heart NEC T82.7

valve (prosthesis) T82.6

graft T82.7

joint prosthesis - see Complication, joint prosthesis, infection

ocular (corneal graft) (orbital implant) NEC T85.79

orthopedic NEC T84.7

specified NEC T85.79

urinary NEC T83.59

vascular NEC T82.7

ventricular intracranial shunt T85.79

duodenum K29.80

with bleeding K29.81

dura mater - see Meningitis

ear (middle) - see also Otitis, media

external - see Otitis, externa

inner - see subcategory H83.0

epididymis - see Epididymitis

esophagus K20.9

ethmoidal (sinus) (chronic) - see Sinusitis, ethmoidal

eustachian tube (catarrhal) – see Salpingitis, eustachian

eyelid H01.9

abscess - see Abscess, eyelid

blepharitis - see Blepharitis

chalazion - see Chalazion

dermatosis (noninfectious) - see Dermatosis, eyelid

hordeolum - see Hordeolum

specified NEC H01.8

fallopian tube - see Salpingo-oophoritis

fascia - see Myositis

follicular, pharynx J31.2

frontal (sinus) (chronic) - see Sinusitis, frontal

gallbladder - see Cholecystitis

gastric - see Gastritis

gastrointestinal - see Enteritis

genital organ (internal) (diffuse)

female - see Disease, pelvis, inflammatory

male N49.9

multiple sites N49.8

specified NEC N49.8

gland (lymph) - see Lymphadenitis

Inflammation, inflamed, inflammatory
(*Continued*)
glottis - *see* Laryngitis
granular, pharynx J31.2
gum K05.10
    plaque induced K05.10
    nonplaque induced K05.11
heart - *see* Carditis
hepatic duct - *see* Cholangitis
ileoanal (internal) pouch K91.850
ileum - *see also* Enteritis
    regional or terminal – *see* Enteritis,
        regional
intestinal pouch K91.850
intestine (any part) - *see* Enteritis
jaw (acute) (bone) (chronic) (lower)
        (suppurative) (upper) M27.2
joint NEC - *see* Arthritis
    sacroiliac M46.1
kidney - *see* Nephritis
knee (joint) M13.169
    tuberculous A18.02
labium (majus) (minus) - *see* Vulvitis
lacrimal
    gland - *see* Dacryoadenitis
    passages (duct) (sac) - *see also*
        Dacryocystitis
        canaliculitis - *see* Canaliculitis,
            lacrimal
larynx - *see* Laryngitis
leg NOS L08.9
lip K13.0
liver (capsule) - *see also* Hepatitis
    chronic K73.9
    suppurative K75.0
lung (acute) - *see also* Pneumonia
    chronic J98.4
lymph gland or node - *see* Lymphadenitis
lymphatic vessel - *see* Lymphangitis
maxilla, maxillary M27.2
    sinus (chronic) - *see* Sinusitis,
        maxillary
membranes of brain or spinal cord - *see*
        Meningitis
meninges - *see* Meningitis
mouth K12.1
muscle - *see* Myositis
myocardium - *see* Myocarditis
nasal sinus (chronic) - *see* Sinusitis
nasopharynx - *see* Nasopharyngitis
navel L08.82
nerve NEC - *see* Neuralgia
nipple N61
    puerperal, postpartum or gestational –
        see Infection, nipple
nose - *see* Rhinitis
oculomotor (nerve) - *see* Strabismus,
        paralytic, third nerve
optic nerve - *see* Neuritis, optic
orbit (chronic) H05.10
    acute H05.00
        abscess - *see* Abscess, orbit
        cellulitis - *see* Cellulitis, orbit
        osteomyelitis - *see* Osteomyelitis,
            orbit
        periostitis - *see* Periostitis, orbital
        tenonitis - *see* Tenonitis, eye
    granuloma - *see* Granuloma, orbit
    myositis - *see* Myositis, orbital
ovary - *see* Salpingo-oophoritis
oviduct - *see* Salpingo-oophoritis
pancreas (acute) - *see* Pancreatitis
parametrium N73.0
parotid region L08.9

Inflammation, inflamed, inflammatory
(*Continued*)
pelvis, female - *see* Disease, pelvis,
        inflammatory
penis (corpora cavernosa) N48.29
perianal K62.8
pericardium - *see* Pericarditis
perineum (female) (male) L08.9
perirectal K62.8
peritoneum - *see* Peritonitis
periuterine - *see* Disease, pelvis,
        inflammatory
perivesical - *see* Cystitis
petrous bone (acute) (chronic) – *see*
        Petrositis
pharynx (acute) - *see* Pharyngitis
pia mater - *see* Meningitis
pleura - *see* Pleurisy
polyp, colon (*see also* Polyp, colon,
        inflammatory) K51.40
prostate - *see also* Prostatitis
    specified type NEC N41.8
rectosigmoid - *see* Rectosigmoiditis
rectum (*see also* Proctitis) K62.8
respiratory, upper (*see also* Infection,
        respiratory, upper) J06.9
    acute, due to radiation J70.0
    chronic, due to external agent - *see*
        condition, respiratory, chronic,
        due to
    due to
        chemicals, gases, fumes or vapors
            (inhalation) J68.2
        radiation J70.1
retina - *see* Chorioretinitis
retrocecal - *see* Appendicitis
retroperitoneal - *see* Peritonitis
salivary duct or gland (any) (suppura-
        tive) - *see* Sialoadenitis
scorbutic, alveoli, teeth E54
scrotum N49.2
seminal vesicle - *see* Vesiculitis
sigmoid - *see* Enteritis
sinus - *see* Sinusitis
Skene's duct or gland - *see* Urethritis
skin L08.9
spermatic cord N49.1
sphenoidal (sinus) - *see* Sinusitis,
        sphenoidal
spinal
    cord - *see* Encephalitis
    membrane - *see* Meningitis
    nerve - *see* Disorder, nerve
spine - *see* Spondylopathy,
        inflammatory
spleen (capsule) D73.89
stomach - *see* Gastritis
subcutaneous tissue L08.9
suprarenal (gland) E27.8
synovial - *see* Tenosynovitis
tendon (sheath) NEC - *see* Tenosynovitis
testis - *see* Orchitis
throat (acute) - *see* Pharyngitis
thymus (gland) E32.8
thyroid (gland) - *see* Thyroiditis
tongue K14.0
tonsil - *see* Tonsillitis
trachea - *see* Tracheitis
trochlear (nerve) - *see* Strabismus, para-
        lytic, fourth nerve
tubal - *see* Salpingo-oophoritis
tuberculous NEC - *see* Tuberculosis
tubo-ovarian - *see* Salpingo-oophoritis
tunica vaginalis N49.1

Inflammation, inflamed, inflammatory
(*Continued*)
tympanic membrane - *see* Tympanitis
umbilicus, umbilical L08.82
uterine ligament - *see* Disease, pelvis,
        inflammatory
uterus (catarrhal) - *see* Endometritis
uveal tract (anterior) NOS - *see also*
        Iridocyclitis
    posterior - *see* Chorioretinitis
vagina - *see* Vaginitis
vas deferens N49.1
vein - *see also* Phlebitis
    intracranial or intraspinal (septic)
        G08
    thrombotic I80.9
        leg - *see* Phlebitis, leg
        lower extremity - *see* Phlebitis, leg
vocal cord J38.3
vulva - *see* Vulvitis
Wharton's duct (suppurative) – *see*
        Sialoadenitis
Inflation, lung, imperfect (newborn) - *see*
        Atelectasis
Influenza, influenzal (bronchial) (epi-
        demic) (respiratory (upper)) J10.1
    with
        digestive manifestations J10.81
        enteritis J10.81
        gastroenteritis J10.81
        involvement of
            gastrointestinal tract J10.81
            nervous system NEC J10.89
        laryngitis J10.1
        manifestations NEC J10.89
        meningismus J10.89
        myocarditis J10.89
        pharyngitis J10.1
        pleural effusion NEC J10.1
        respiratory manifestations NEC J10.1
        upper respiratory infection (acute)
            NEC J10.1
    due to identified avian influenza virus
        J09.01
        with
            digestive manifestations J09.090
            enteritis J09.090
            gastroenteritis J09.090
            involvement of
                gastrointestinal tract J09.090
                nervous system NEC J09.098
            laryngitis J09.01
            manifestations NEC J09.098
            meningismus J09.098
            myocarditis J09.098
            pharyngitis J09.01
            pleural effusion NEC J09.01
            respiratory manifestations NEC
                J09.01
            upper respiratory infection (acute)
                NEC J09.01
    due to identified novel H1N1 influenza
        virus J09.11
        with
            digestive manifestations J09.190
            enteritis J09.190
            gastroenteritis J09.190
            involvement of
                gastrointestinal tract J09.190
                nervous system NEC J09.198
            laryngitis J09.11
            manifestations NEC J09.198
            meningismus J09.198
            myocarditis J09.198

Influenza, influenzal *(Continued)*
  due to identified novel H1N1 influenza virus *(Continued)*
    with *(Continued)*
      pharyngitis J09.11
      pleural effusion NEC J09.11
      respiratory manifestations NEC J09.11
      upper respiratory infection (acute) NEC J09.11
    summer, of Italy A93.1
Influenza-like disease - *see* Influenza
Infraction, Freiberg's (metatarsal head) - *see* Osteochondrosis, juvenile, metatarsus
Infraeruption of tooth (teeth) M26.34
Infusion complication, misadventure, or reaction - *see* Complications, infusion
Ingestion
  chemical - *see* Table of drugs and chemicals, by substance, poisoning
  drug or medicament
    correct substance properly administered- *see* Table of drugs and chemicals, by drug, adverse effect
    overdose or wrong substance given or taken - *see* Table of drugs and chemicals, by drug, poisoning
  foreign body - *see* Foreign body, alimentary tract
  tularemia A21.3
Ingrowing
  hair (beard) L73.1
  nail (finger) (toe) L60.0
Inguinal - *see also* condition
  testicle Q53.9
    bilateral Q53.21
    unilateral Q53.11
Inhalation
  anthrax A22.1
  carbon monoxide – *see* Table of drugs and chemicals
  flame T27.3
  food or foreign body - *see* Asphyxia, food
  gases, fumes, or vapors NEC - *see* Table of drugs and chemicals, by substance
  liquid or vomitus - *see* Asphyxia
  meconium (newborn) P24.00
    with
      pneumonia (pneumonitis) P24.01
      with respiratory symptoms P24.01
  mucus - *see* Asphyxia, mucus
  oil or gasoline (causing suffocation) - *see* Asphyxia, food
  smoke – *see* Toxicity, vapors
  steam – *see* Toxicity, vapors
  stomach contents or secretions - *see also* Asphyxia, food
    due to anesthesia (general) (local) or other sedation T88.59
    in labor and delivery O74.0
    in pregnancy O29.01-
    postpartum, puerperal O89.01
Inhibition, orgasm
  female F52.32
  male F52.31
Inhibitor, systemic lupus erythematosus (presence of) D68.62
Iniencephalus, iniencephaly Q00.2

Injection, traumatic jet (air) (industrial) (water) (paint or dye) T70.4
Injury (*see also* specified injury type) T14.90
  abdomen, abdominal S39.91
    blood vessel – *see* Injury, blood vessel, abdomen
    cavity – *see* Injury, intra-abdominal
    contusion S30.1
    internal – *see* Injury, intra-abdominal
    intra-abdominal organ – *see* Injury, intra-abdominal
    nerve – *see* Injury, nerve, abdomen
    open – *see* Wound, open, abdomen
    specified NEC S39.81
    superficial – *see* Injury, superficial, abdomen
  Achilles tendon S86.00-
    laceration S86.02-
    specified type NEC S86.09-
    strain S86.01-
  acoustic, resulting in deafness – *see* Injury, nerve, acoustic
  adrenal (gland) S37.819
    contusion S37.812
    laceration S37.813
    specified type NEC S37.818
  alveolar (process) S09.93
  ankle S99.91-
    contusion – *see* Contusion, ankle
    dislocation – *see* Dislocation, ankle
    fracture – *see* Fracture, ankle
    nerve – *see* Injury, nerve, ankle
    open – *see* Wound, open, ankle
    specified type NEC S99.81-
    sprain – *see* Sprain, ankle
    superficial – *see* Injury, superficial, ankle
  anterior chamber, eye – *see* Injury, eye, specified site NEC
  anus – *see* Injury, abdomen
  aorta (thoracic) S25.00
    abdominal S35.00
      laceration (minor) (superficial) S35.01
      major S35.02
      specified type NEC S35.09
    laceration (minor) (superficial) S25.01
      major S25.02
    specified type NEC S25.09
  arm (upper) S49.9-
    blood vessel – *see* Injury, blood vessel, arm
    contusion – *see* Contusion, arm, upper
    fracture – *see* Fracture, humerus
    lower - *see* Injury, forearm
    muscle – *see* Injury, muscle, shoulder
    nerve – *see* Injury, nerve, arm
    open – *see* Wound, open, arm
    specified type NEC S49.8-
    superficial – *see* Injury, superficial, arm
  artery (complicating trauma) - *see also* Injury, blood vessel, by site
  cerebral or meningeal – *see* Injury, intracranial
  auditory canal (external) (meatus) S09.91
  auricle, auris, ear S09.91
  axilla – *see* Injury, shoulder

Injury *(Continued)*
  back – *see* Injury, back, lower
  bile duct - *see* Injury, gallbladder
  birth - *see also* Birth, injury P15.9
  bladder (sphincter) S37.20
    at delivery O71.5
    contusion S37.22
    laceration S37.23
    obstetrical trauma O71.5
    specified type NEC S37.28
  blast (air) (hydraulic) (immersion) (underwater) NEC T14.8
    acoustic nerve trauma – *see* Injury, nerve, acoustic
    bladder – *see* Injury, bladder, blast injury
    brain – *see* Concussion
    colon - *see* Injury, intestine, large, blast injury
    ear (primary) S09.31-
      secondary S09.39-
    generalized T70.8
    lung - *see* Injury, intrathoracic, lung, blast injury
    multiple body organs T70.8
    peritoneum S36.81
    rectum S36.61
    retroperitoneum S36.898
    small intestine S36.419
      duodenum S36.410
      specified site NEC S36.418
    specified
      intra-abdominal organ NEC S36.898
      pelvic organ NEC S37.899
  blood vessel NEC T14.8
    abdomen S35.90
      aorta - *see* Injury, aorta, abdominal
      celiac artery - *see* Injury, blood vessel, celiac artery
      iliac vessel - *see* Injury, blood vessel, iliac
      laceration S35.91
      mesenteric vessel - *see* Injury, mesenteric
      portal vein - *see* Injury, blood vessel, portal vein
      renal vessel - *see* Injury, blood vessel, renal
      specified T14.8
      site NEC - *see* subcategory S35.8
      type NEC S35.99
      splenic vessel - *see* Injury, blood vessel, splenic
      vena cava - *see* Injury, vena cava, inferior
    ankle – *see* Injury, blood vessel, foot
    aorta (abdominal) (thoracic) - *see* Injury, aorta
    arm (upper) NEC S45.90-
      forearm – *see* Injury, blood vessel, forearm
      laceration S45.91-
      specified
        site NEC S45.80-
        laceration S45.81-
        specified type NEC S45.89-
      type NEC S45.99-
      superficial vein S45.30-
        laceration S45.31-
        specified type NEC S45.39-

Injury *(Continued)*
  blood vessel NEC *(Continued)*
    axillary
      artery S45.00-
        laceration S45.01-
          specified type NEC S45.09-
      vein S45.20-
        laceration S45.21-
          specified type NEC S45.29-
    azygos vein – *see* Injury, blood vessel,
        thoracic, specified site NEC
    brachial
      artery S45.10-
        laceration S45.11-
          specified type NEC S45.19-
      vein S45.20-
        laceration S45.219
          specified type NEC S45.29-
    carotid artery (common) (external)
        (internal, extracranial) S15.00-
      internal, intracranial S06.8-
      laceration (minor) (superficial)
          S15.01-
        major S15.02-
      specified type NEC S15.09-
    celiac artery S35.219
      branch S35.299
        laceration (minor) (superficial)
            S35.291
          major S35.292
        specified NEC S35.298
      laceration (minor) (superficial)
          S35.211
        major S35.212
      specified type NEC S35.218
    cerebral - *see* Injury, intracranial
    deep plantar - *see* Injury, nerve, me-
        dial plantar
    digital (hand) – *see* Injury, blood ves-
        sel, finger
    dorsal
      artery (foot) S95.00-
        laceration S95.01-
          specified type NEC S95.09-
      vein (foot) S95.20-
        laceration S95.21-
          specified type NEC S95.29-
    due to accidental laceration during
        procedure – *see* Laceration,
        accidental complicating
        surgery
    extremity - *see* Injury, blood vessel,
        limb
    femoral
      artery (common) (superficial)
          S75.00-
        laceration (minor) (superficial)
            S75.01-
          major S75.02-
        specified type NEC S75.09-
      vein (hip level) (thigh level)
          S75.10-
        laceration (minor) (superficial)
            S75.11-
          major S75.12-
        specified type NEC S75.19-
    finger S65.50-
      index S65.50-
        laceration S65.51-
          specified type NEC S65.59-
      laceration S65.51-
      little S65.50-
        laceration S65.51-
          specified type NEC S65.59-

Injury *(Continued)*
  blood vessel NEC *(Continued)*
    finger *(Continued)*
      middle S65.50-
        laceration S65.51-
          specified type NEC S65.59-
        laceration S65.51-
          specified type NEC S65.59-
      specified type NEC S65.59-
      thumb – *see* Injury, blood vessel,
          thumb
    foot S95.90-
      dorsal
        artery – *see* Injury, blood vessel,
            dorsal, artery
        vein – *see* Injury, blood vessel,
            dorsal, vein
      laceration S95.91-
      plantar artery – *see* Injury, blood
          vessel, plantar artery
      specified
        site NEC S95.80-
          laceration S95.81-
            specified type NEC S95.89-
        specified type NEC S95.99-
    forearm S55.90-
      laceration S55.91-
      radial artery – *see* Injury, blood
          vessel, radial artery
      specified
        site NEC S55.80-
          laceration S55.81-
            specified type NEC S55.89-
        type NEC S55.99-
      ulnar artery – *see* Injury, blood
          vessel, ulnar artery
      vein S55.20-
        laceration S55.21-
          specified type NEC S55.29-
    gastric
      artery – *see* Injury, mesenteric,
          artery, branch
      vein – *see* Injury, blood vessel,
          abdomen
    gastroduodenal artery – *see* Injury,
        mesenteric, artery, branch
    greater saphenous vein (lower leg
        level) S85.309
      hip (and thigh) level S75.20-
        laceration (minor) (superficial)
            S75.21-
          major S75.22-
        specified type NEC S75.29-
      laceration S85.31-
      specified type NEC S85.39-
    hand (level) S65.90-
      finger – *see* Injury, blood vessel,
          finger
      laceration S65.91-
      palmar arch – *see* Injury, blood
          vessel, palmar arch
      radial artery – *see* Injury, blood
          vessel, radial artery, hand
      specified
        site NEC S65.80-
          laceration S65.81-
            specified type NEC
                S65.89-
        type NEC S65.99-
      thumb – *see* Injury, blood vessel,
          thumb
      ulnar artery – *see* Injury, blood
          vessel, ulnar artery,
          hand

Injury *(Continued)*
  blood vessel NEC *(Continued)*
    head S09.0
      intracranial – *see* Injury,
          intracranial
      multiple S09.0
    hepatic
      artery – *see* Injury, mesenteric,
          artery
      vein – *see* Injury, vena cava,
          inferior
    hip S75.909
      femoral artery – *see* Injury, blood
          vessel, femoral, artery
      femoral vein – *see* Injury, blood
          vessel, femoral, vein
      greater saphenous vein – *see* Injury,
          blood vessel, greater saphe-
          nous, hip level
      laceration S75.91-
      specified
        site NEC S75.80-
          laceration S75.81-
            specified type NEC S75.89-
        type NEC S75.99-
    hypogastric (artery) (vein) – *see*
        Injury, blood vessel, iliac
    iliac S35.5-
      artery S35.51-
        specified vessel NEC S35.5-
      uterine vessel - *see* Injury, blood
          vessel, uterine
      vein S35.51-
    innominate – *see* Injury, blood vessel,
        thoracic, innominate
    intercostal (artery) (vein) – *see*
        Injury, blood vessel, thoracic,
        intercostal
    jugular vein (external) S15.20-
      internal S15.30-
        laceration (minor) (superficial)
            S15.31-
          major S15.32-
        specified type NEC S15.39-
      laceration (minor) (superficial)
          S15.21-
        major S15.22-
      specified type NEC S15.29-
    leg (level) (lower) S85.90-
      greater saphenous – *see* In-
          jury, blood vessel, greater
          saphenous
      laceration S85.91-
      lesser saphenous – *see* Injury, blood
          vessel, lesser saphenous
      peroneal artery – *see* Injury, blood
          vessel, peroneal artery
      popliteal
        artery – *see* Injury, blood vessel,
            popliteal, artery
        vein – *see* Injury, blood vessel,
            popliteal, vein
      specified
        site NEC S85.80-
          laceration S85.81-
            specified type NEC S85.89-
        type NEC S85.99-
      thigh – *see* Injury, blood vessel, hip
      tibial artery – *see* Injury, blood
          vessel, tibial artery
    lesser saphenous vein (lower leg
        level) S85.40-
      laceration S85.41-
        specified type NEC S85.49-

299

Injury *(Continued)*
  blood vessel NEC *(Continued)*
    limb
      lower – *see* Injury, blood vessel, leg
      upper – *see* Injury, blood vessel, arm
    lower back – *see* Injury, blood vessel, abdomen
      specified NEC – *see* Injury, blood vessel, abdomen, specified, site NEC
    mammary (artery) (vein) – *see* Injury, blood vessel, thoracic, specified site NEC
    mesenteric (inferior) (superior)
      artery – *see* Injury, mesenteric, artery
      vein – *see* Injury, blood vessel, portal vein
    neck S15.9
      specified site NEC S15.8
    ovarian (artery) (vein) - *see* subcategory S35.8
    palmar arch (superficial) S65.20-
      deep S65.30-
        laceration S65.31-
        specified type NEC S65.39-
      laceration S65.21-
      specified type NEC S65.29-
    pelvis – *see* Injury, blood vessel, abdomen
      specified NEC – *see* Injury, blood vessel, abdomen, specified, site NEC
    peroneal artery S85.20-
      laceration S85.21-
      specified type NEC S85.29-
    plantar artery (deep) (foot) S95.10-
      laceration S95.11-
      specified type NEC S95.19-
    popliteal
      artery S85.00-
        laceration S85.01-
        specified type NEC S85.09-
      vein S85.50-
        laceration S85.51-
        specified type NEC S85.59-
    portal vein S35.319
      laceration S35.311
      specified type NEC S35.318
    precerebral – *see* Injury, blood vessel, neck
    pulmonary (artery) (vein) – *see* Injury, blood vessel, thoracic, pulmonary
    radial artery (forearm level) S55.10-
      hand and wrist (level) S65.10-
        laceration S65.11-
        specified type NEC S65.19-
      laceration S55.11-
      specified type NEC S55.19-
    renal
      artery S35.40-
        laceration S35.41-
        specified NEC S35.49-
      vein S35.40-
        laceration S35.41-
        specified NEC S35.49-
    saphenous vein (greater) (lower leg level) – *see* Injury, blood vessel, greater saphenous

Injury *(Continued)*
  blood vessel NEC *(Continued)*
    saphenous vein *(Continued)*
      hip and thigh level – *see* Injury, blood vessel, greater saphenous, hip level
      lesser – *see* Injury, blood vessel, lesser saphenous
    shoulder
      specified NEC – *see* Injury, blood vessel, arm, specified site NEC
      superficial vein – *see* Injury, blood vessel, arm, superficial vein
    specified NEC
    splenic
      artery – *see* Injury, blood vessel, celiac artery, branch
      vein S35.329
        laceration S35.321
        specified NEC S35.328
    subclavian – *see* Injury, blood vessel, thoracic, innominate
    thigh – *see* Injury, blood vessel, hip
    thoracic S25.90
      aorta S25.00
        laceration (minor) (superficial) S25.01
        major S25.02
        specified type NEC S25.09
      azygos vein - *see* Injury, blood vessel, thoracic, specified, site NEC
      innominate
        artery S25.10-
          laceration (minor) (superficial) S25.11-
          major S25.12-
          specified type NEC S25.19-
        vein S25.30-
          laceration (minor) (superficial) S25.31-
          major S25.32-
          specified type NEC S25.39-
      intercostal S25.50-
        laceration S25.51-
        specified type NEC S25.59-
      laceration S25.91
      mammary vessel - *see* Injury, blood vessel, thoracic, specified, site NEC
      pulmonary S25.40-
        laceration (minor) (superficial) S25.41-
        major S25.42-
        specified type NEC S25.49-
      specified
        site NEC S25.80-
          laceration S25.81-
          specified type NEC S25.89-
        type NEC S25.99
      subclavian – *see* Injury, blood vessel, thoracic, innominate
      vena cava (superior) S25.20
        laceration (minor) (superficial) S25.21
        major S25.22
        specified type NEC S25.29
    thumb S65.40-
      laceration S65.41-
      specified type NEC S65.49-
    tibial artery S85.10-
      anterior S85.13-
        laceration S85.14-
        specified injury NEC S85.15-

Injury *(Continued)*
  blood vessel NEC *(Continued)*
    tibial artery *(Continued)*
      laceration S85.11-
      posterior S85.16-
        laceration S85.17-
        specified injury NEC S85.18-
      specified injury NEC S85.12-
    ulnar artery (forearm level) S55.00-
      hand and wrist (level) S65.00-
        laceration S65.01-
        specified type NEC S65.09-
      laceration S55.01-
      specified type NEC S55.09-
      upper arm (level) – *see* Injury, blood vessel, arm
      superficial vein – *see* Injury, blood vessel, arm, superficial vein
    uterine S35.5-
      artery S35.53-
      vein S35.53-
    vena cava – *see* Injury, vena cava
    vertebral artery S15.10-
      laceration (minor) (superficial) S15.11-
      major S15.12-
      specified type NEC S15.19-
    wrist (level) – *see* Injury, blood vessel, hand
  brachial plexus S14.3
    newborn P14.3
  brain (traumatic) S06.9-
    diffuse (axonal) S06.2x-
    focal S06.30-
    traumatic - *see* category S06
  brainstem S06.38-
  breast NOS S29.9
  broad ligament – *see* Injury, pelvic organ, specified site NEC
  bronchus, bronchi – *see* Injury, intrathoracic, bronchus
  brow S09.90
  buttock S39.92
  canthus, eye S05.90
  cardiac plexus – *see* Injury, nerve, thorax, sympathetic
  cauda equina S34.3
  cavernous sinus – *see* Injury, intracranial
  cecum – *see* Injury, colon
  celiac ganglion or plexus – *see* Injury, nerve, lumbosacral, sympathetic
  cerebellum – *see* Injury, intracranial
  cerebral – *see* Injury, intracranial
  cervix (uteri) – *see* Injury, uterus
  cheek (wall) S09.93
  chest – *see* Injury, thorax
  childbirth (newborn) - *see also* Birth, injury
    maternal NEC O71.9
  chin S09.93
  choroid (eye) – *see* Injury, eye, specified site NEC
  clitoris S39.94
  coccyx – *see also* Injury, back, lower
    complicating delivery O71.6
  colon - *see* Injury, intestine, large
  common bile duct – *see* Injury, liver
  conjunctiva (superficial) – *see* Injury, eye, conjunctiva
  conus medullaris - *see* Injury, spinal, sacral

Injury *(Continued)*
  cord
    spermatic (pelvic region) S37.898
      scrotal region S39.848
    spinal - *see* Injury, spinal cord, by
      region
  cornea – *see* Injury, eye, specified site
    NEC
    abrasion – *see* Injury, eye, cornea,
      abrasion
  cortex (cerebral) – *see also* Injury,
    intracranial
    visual – *see* Injury, nerve, optic
  costal region NEC S29.9
  costochondral NEC S29.9
  cranial
    cavity - *see* Injury, intracranial
    nerve - *see* Injury, nerve, cranial
  crushing - *see* Crush
  cutaneous sensory nerve
  cystic duct – *see* Injury, liver
  deep tissue - *see* Contusion, by site
    meaning pressure ulcer - *see* Ulcer,
      pressure, unstageable, by site
  delivery (newborn) P15.9
    maternal NEC O71.9
  Descemet's membrane - *see* Injury,
    eyeball, penetrating
  diaphragm – *see* Injury, intrathoracic,
    diaphragm
  duodenum – *see* Injury, intestine, small,
    duodenum
  ear (auricle) (external) (canal) S09.91
    abrasion - *see* Abrasion, ear
    bite - *see* Bite, ear
    blister - *see* Blister, ear
    bruise - *see* Contusion, ear
    contusion - *see* Contusion, ear
    external constriction - *see* Constric-
      tion, external, ear
    hematoma - *see* Hematoma, ear
    inner - *see* Injury, ear, middle
    laceration - *see* Laceration, ear
    middle S09.30-
      blast - *see* Injury, blast, ear
      specified NEC S09.39-
    puncture - *see* Puncture, ear
    superficial - *see* Injury, superficial, ear
  eighth cranial nerve (acoustic or audi-
    tory) – *see* Injury, nerve, acoustic
  elbow S59.90-
    contusion – *see* Contusion, elbow
    dislocation – *see* Dislocation, elbow
    fracture – *see* Fracture, ulna, upper
      end
    open – *see* Wound, open, elbow
    specified NEC S59.80-
    sprain – *see* Sprain, elbow
    superficial – *see* Injury, superficial,
      elbow
  eleventh cranial nerve (accessory) – *see*
    Injury, nerve, accessory
  epididymis S39.94
  epigastric region S39.91
  epiglottis NEC S19.89
  esophageal plexus – *see* Injury, nerve,
    thorax, sympathetic
  esophagus (thoracic part) – *see also*
    Injury, intrathoracic, esophagus
    cervical NEC S19.85
  eustachian tube S09.91
  eye S05.9-
    avulsion S05.7-
    ball – *see* Injury, eyeball

Injury *(Continued)*
  eye *(Continued)*
    conjunctiva S05.0-
    cornea
      abrasion S05.0-
    laceration S05.3-
      with prolapse S05.2-
    lacrimal apparatus S05.8x-
    orbit penetration S05.4-
    specified site NEC S05.8x-
  eyeball S05.8x-
    contusion S05.1-
    penetrating S05.6-
      with
        foreign body S05.5-
        prolapse or loss of intraocular
          tissue S05.2-
      without prolapse or loss of intra-
        ocular tissue S05.3-
    specified type NEC S05.80
  eyebrow S09.93
  eyelid S09.93
    abrasion – *see* Abrasion, eyelid
    contusion – *see* Contusion, eyelid
    open – *see* Wound, open, eyelid
  face S09.93
  fallopian tube S37.509
    bilateral S37.502
      blast injury S37.512
      contusion S37.522
      laceration S37.532
      specified type NEC S37.592
    blast injury (primary) S37.519
      bilateral S37.512
      secondary - *see* Injury, fallopian
        tube, specified type NEC
      unilateral S37.511
    contusion S37.529
      bilateral S37.522
      unilateral S37.521
    laceration S37.539
      bilateral S37.532
      unilateral S37.531
    specified type NEC S37.599
      bilateral S37.592
      unilateral S37.591
    unilateral S37.501
      blast injury S37.511
      contusion S37.521
      laceration S37.531
      specified type NEC S37.591
  fascia - *see* Injury, muscle
  fifth cranial nerve (trigeminal) – *see*
    Injury, nerve, trigeminal
  finger (nail) S69.9-
    blood vessel – *see* Injury, blood vessel,
      finger
    contusion – *see* Contusion, finger
    dislocation – *see* Dislocation, finger
    fracture – *see* Fracture, finger
    muscle – *see* Injury, muscle, finger
    nerve – *see* Injury, nerve, digital,
      finger
    open – *see* Wound, open, finger
    specified NEC S69.8-
    sprain – *see* Sprain, finger
    superficial – *see* Injury, superficial,
      finger
  first cranial nerve (olfactory) – *see*
    Injury, nerve, olfactory
  flank – *see* Injury, abdomen
  foot S99.92-
    blood vessel – *see* Injury, blood vessel,
      foot

Injury *(Continued)*
  foot *(Continued)*
    contusion – *see* Contusion, foot
    dislocation – *see* Dislocation, foot
    fracture – *see* Fracture, foot
    muscle – *see* Injury, muscle, foot
    open – *see* Wound, open, foot
    specified type NEC S99.82-
    sprain – *see* Sprain, foot
    superficial – *see* Injury, superficial, foot
  forceps NOS P15.9
  forearm S59.91-
    blood vessel – *see* Injury, blood vessel,
      forearm
    contusion – *see* Contusion, forearm
    fracture – *see* Fracture, forearm
    muscle – *see* Injury, muscle, forearm
    nerve – *see* Injury, nerve, forearm
    open – *see* Wound, open, forearm
    specified NEC S59.81-
    superficial – *see* Injury, superficial,
      forearm
  forehead S09.90
  fourth cranial nerve (trochlear) – *see*
    Injury, nerve, trochlear
  gallbladder S36.129
    contusion S36.122
    laceration S36.123
    specified NEC S36.128
  ganglion
    celiac, coeliac – *see* Injury, nerve,
      lumbosacral, sympathetic
    gasserian – *see* Injury, nerve,
      trigeminal
    stellate – *see* Injury, nerve, thorax,
      sympathetic
    thoracic sympathetic – *see* Injury,
      nerve, thorax, sympathetic
  gasserian ganglion – *see* Injury, nerve,
    trigeminal
  gastric artery – *see* Injury, blood vessel,
    celiac artery, branch
  gastroduodenal artery – *see* Injury,
    blood vessel, celiac artery, branch
  gastrointestinal tract - *see* Injury,
    intra-abdominal
    with open wound into abdominal
      cavity - *see* Wound, open, with
      penetration into peritoneal
      cavity
    colon - *see* Injury, intestine, large
    rectum - *see* Injury, intestine, large,
      rectum
      with open wound into abdominal
        cavity S36.61
    specified site NEC - *see* Injury, intra-
      abdominal, specified, site NEC
    stomach – *see* Injury, stomach
    small intestine - *see* Injury, intestine,
      small
  genital organ(s)
    external S39.94
      specified NEC S39.848
    internal S37.90
      fallopian tube - *see* Injury, fallopian
        tube
      ovary - *see* Injury, ovary
      prostate – *see* Injury, prostate
      seminal vesicle - *see* Injury, pelvis,
        organ, specified site NEC
      uterus - *see* Injury, uterus
      vas deferens - *see* Injury, pelvis,
        organ, specified site NEC
  obstetrical trauma O71.9

Injury *(Continued)*
  gland
    lacrimal laceration – *see* Injury, eye,
      specified site NEC
    salivary S09.90
    thyroid NEC S19.84
  globe (eye) S05.90
    specified NEC S05.8x-
  groin – *see* Injury, abdomen
  gum S09.90
  hand S69.9-
    blood vessel – *see* Injury, blood vessel,
      hand
    contusion – *see* Contusion, hand
    fracture – *see* Fracture, hand
    muscle – *see* Injury, muscle, hand
    nerve – *see* Injury, nerve, hand
    open – *see* Wound, open, hand
    specified NEC S69.8-
    sprain – *see* Sprain, hand
    superficial – *see* Injury, superficial,
      hand
  head S09.90
    with loss of consciousness S06.9-
    specified NEC S09.89-
  heart S26.90
    with hemopericardium S26.00
      contusion S26.01
      laceration (mild) S26.020
        moderate S26.021
        major S26.022
      specified type NEC S26.09
    contusion S26.91
    laceration S26.92
    specified type NEC S26.99
    without hemopericardium S26.10
      contusion S26.11
      laceration S26.12
      specified type NEC S26.19
  heel – *see* Injury, foot
  hepatic
    artery – *see* Injury, blood vessel, celiac
      artery, branch
    duct – *see* Injury, liver
    vein – *see* Injury, vena cava,
      inferior
  hip S79.91-
    blood vessel – *see* Injury, blood
      vessel, hip
    contusion – *see* Contusion, hip
    dislocation – *see* Dislocation, hip
    fracture – *see* Fracture, femur, neck
    muscle – *see* Injury, muscle, hip
    nerve – *see* Injury, nerve, hip
    open – *see* Wound, open, hip
    sprain – *see* Sprain, hip
    superficial – *see* Injury, superficial,
      hip
    specified NEC S79.81-
  hymen S39.94
  hypogastric
    blood vessel – *see* Injury, blood vessel,
      iliac
    plexus – *see* Injury, nerve, lumbosa-
      cral, sympathetic
  ileum – *see* Injury, intestine, small
  iliac region S39.91
  instrumental (during surgery) – *see*
    Laceration, accidental complicat-
    ing surgery
    birth injury - *see* Birth, injury
    nonsurgical - *see* Injury, by site
    obstetrical O71.9
      bladder O71.5

Injury *(Continued)*
  instrumental *(Continued)*
    obstetrical *(Continued)*
      cervix O71.3
      high vaginal O71.4
      perineal NOS O70.9
      urethra O71.5
      uterus O71.5
        with rupture or perforation
          O71.1
  internal T14.8
    aorta - *see* Injury, aorta
    bladder (sphincter) – *see* Injury,
      bladder
    with
      ectopic or molar pregnancy
        O08.6
      following ectopic or molar preg-
        nancy O08.6
      obstetrical trauma O71.5
    bronchus, bronchi – *see* Injury, intra-
      thoracic, bronchus
    cecum - *see* Injury, intestine, large
    cervix (uteri) - *see also* Injury, uterus
      with ectopic or molar pregnancy
        O08.6
      following ectopic or molar preg-
        nancy O08.6
      obstetrical trauma O71.3
    chest - *see* Injury, intrathoracic
    gastrointestinal tract - *see* Injury,
      intra-abdominal
    heart - *see* Injury, heart
    intestine NEC - *see* Injury, intestine
    intrauterine - *see* Injury, uterus
    mesentery - *see* Injury, intra-
      abdominal, specified, site NEC
    pelvis, pelvic (organ) S37.90
      following ectopic or molar preg-
        nancy (subsequent episode)
        O08.6
      obstetrical trauma NEC O71.5
      rupture or perforation O71.1
      specified NEC S39.83
    rectum - *see* Injury, intestine, large,
      rectum
    stomach - *see* Injury, stomach
    ureter - *see* Injury, ureter
    urethra (sphincter) following ectopic
      or molar pregnancy O08.6
    uterus - *see* Injury, uterus
  interscapular area – *see* Injury, thorax
  intestine
    large S36.509
      ascending (right) S36.500
        blast injury (primary) S36.510
          secondary S36.590
        contusion S36.520
        laceration S36.530
        specified type NEC S36.590
      blast injury (primary) S36.519
        ascending (right) S36.510
        descending (left) S36.512
        rectum S36.61
        sigmoid S36.513
        specified site NEC S36.518
        transverse S36.511
      contusion S36.529
        ascending (right) S36.520
        descending (left) S36.522
        rectum S36.62
        sigmoid S36.523
        specified site NEC S36.528
        transverse S36.521

Injury *(Continued)*
  intestine *(Continued)*
    large *(Continued)*
      descending (left) S36.502
        blast injury (primary) S36.512
          secondary S36.592
        contusion S36.522
        laceration S36.532
        specified type NEC S36.592
      laceration S36.539
        ascending (right) S36.530
        descending (left) S36.532
        rectum S36.63
        sigmoid S36.533
        specified site NEC S36.538
        transverse S36.531
      rectum S36.60
        blast injury (primary) S36.61
          secondary S36.69
        contusion S36.62
        laceration S36.63
        specified type NEC S36.69
      sigmoid S36.503
        blast injury (primary) S36.513
          secondary S36.593
        contusion S36.523
        laceration S36.533
        specified type NEC S36.593
      specified
        site NEC S36.508
          blast injury (primary)
            S36.518
            secondary S36.598
          contusion S36.528
          laceration S36.538
          specified type NEC S36.598
        type NEC S36.599
          ascending (right) S36.590
          descending (left) S36.592
          rectum S36.69
          sigmoid S36.593
          specified site NEC S36.598
          transverse S36.591
      transverse S36.501
        blast injury (primary) S36.511
          secondary S36.591
        contusion S36.521
        laceration S36.531
        specified type NEC S36.591
    small S36.409
      blast injury (primary) S36.419
        duodenum S36.410
          secondary S36.499
            duodenum S36.490
            specified site NEC S36.498
        specified site NEC S36.418
      contusion S36.429
        duodenum S36.420
        specified site NEC S36.428
      duodenum S36.400
        blast injury (primary)
          S36.410
          secondary S36.490
        contusion S36.420
        laceration S36.430
        specified NEC S36.490
      laceration S36.439
        duodenum S36.430
        specified site NEC S36.438
      specified
        type NEC S36.499
          duodenum S36.490
          specified site NEC S36.498
        site NEC S36.408

Injury *(Continued)*
  intra-abdominal S36.90
    adrenal gland - *see* Injury, adrenal
      gland
    bladder – *see* Injury, bladder
    colon - *see* Injury, intestine,
      large
    contusion S36.92
    fallopian tube - *see* Injury, fallopian
      tube
    gallbladder - *see* Injury, gallbladder
    intestine – *see* Injury, intestine
    laceration S36.93
    liver - *see* Injury, liver
    kidney - *see* Injury, kidney
    ovary - *see* Injury, ovary
    pancreas - *see* Injury, pancreas
    pelvic NOS S37.90
    peritoneum - *see* Injury, intra-
      abdominal, specified,
      site NEC
    prostate – *see* Injury, prostate
    rectum - *see* Injury, intestine, large,
      rectum
    retroperitoneum - *see* Injury, intra-
      abdominal, specified,
      site NEC
    seminal vesicle - *see* Injury, pelvis,
      organ, specified
      site NEC
    small intestine - *see* Injury, intestine,
      small
    specified
      site NEC S36.899
        contusion S36.892
        laceration S36.893
        specified type NEC S36.898
      type NEC S36.99
    pelvic S37.90
      specified
        site NEC S37.899
          specified type NEC
            S37.898
        type NEC S37.99
    spleen – *see* Injury, spleen
    stomach - *see* Injury, stomach
    ureter - *see* Injury, ureter
    urethra - *see* Injury, urethra
    uterus - *see* Injury, uterus
    vas deferens - *see* Injury, pelvis,
      organ, specified site NEC
  intracranial S06.9-
    cerebellar hemorrhage, traumatic –
      see Injury, intracranial, focal
    cerebral edema, traumatic S06.1x-
      diffuse S06.1x-
      focal S06.1x-
    diffuse (axonal) S06.2x-
    epidural hemorrhage (traumatic)
      S06.4x-
    focal brain injury S06.30-
      contusion - *see* Contusion,
        cerebral
      laceration - *see* Laceration, cerebral
    intracerebral hemorrhage, traumatic
      S06.36-
      left side S06.35-
      right side S06.34-
    subarachnoid hemorrhage, traumatic
      S06.6x-
    subdural hemorrhage, traumatic
      S06.5x-
  intraocular – *see* Injury, eyeball,
    penetrating

Injury *(Continued)*
  intrathoracic S27.9
    bronchus S27.409
      bilateral S27.402
      blast injury (primary) S27.419
        bilateral S27.412
        secondary - *see* Injury, intratho-
          racic, bronchus, specified
          type NEC
        unilateral S27.411
      contusion S27.429
        bilateral S27.422
        unilateral S27.421
      laceration S27.439
        bilateral S27.432
        unilateral S27.431
      specified type NEC S27.499
        bilateral S27.492
        unilateral S27.491
      unilateral S27.401
    diaphragm S27.809
      contusion S27.802
      laceration S27.803
      specified type NEC S27.808
    esophagus (thoracic) S27.819
      contusion S27.812
      laceration S27.813
      specified type NEC S27.818
    heart – *see* Injury, heart
    hemopneumothorax S27.2
    hemothorax S27.1
    lung S27.309
      bilateral S27.302
      blast injury (primary) S27.319
        bilateral S27.312
        secondary - *see* Injury, intratho-
          racic, lung, specified type
          NEC
        unilateral S27.311
      contusion S27.329
        bilateral S27.322
        unilateral S27.321
      laceration S27.339
        bilateral S27.332
        unilateral S27.331
      specified type NEC S27.399
        bilateral S27.392
        unilateral S27.391
      unilateral S27.301
    pleura S27.60
      laceration S27.63
      specified type NEC S27.69
    pneumothorax S27.0
    specified organ NEC S27.899
      contusion S27.892
      laceration S27.893
      specified type NEC S27.898
    thoracic duct – *see* Injury, intratho-
      racic, specified organ NEC
    thymus gland – *see* Injury, intratho-
      racic, specified organ NEC
    trachea, thoracic S27.50
      blast (primary) S27.51
      contusion S27.52
      laceration S27.53
      specified type NEC S27.59
  iris – *see* Injury, eye, specified site NEC
    penetrating – *see* Injury, eyeball,
      penetrating
  jaw S09.93
  jejunum - *see* Injury, intestine, small
  joint NOS T14.8
    old or residual - *see* Disorder, joint,
      specified type NEC

Injury *(Continued)*
  kidney S37.00-
    acute (nontraumatic) N17.9
    contusion (minor) S37.019
      major S37.029
    laceration S37.039
      major (massive) (stellate) S37.069
      minor S37.049
      moderate S37.059
    contusion (minor) S37.012
      major S37.022
    laceration S37.032
      major (massive) (stellate) S37.062
      minor S37.042
      moderate S37.052
    specified type NEC S37.092
    contusion (minor) S37.011
      major S37.021
    laceration S37.031
      major (massive) (stellate) S37.061
      minor S37.041
      moderate S37.051
    specified type NEC S37.091
    specified type NEC S37.099
  knee S89.9-
    contusion – *see* Contusion, knee
    dislocation – *see* Dislocation, knee
    meniscus (lateral) (medial) – *see*
      Sprain, knee, specified site NEC
    old injury or tear - *see* Derange-
      ment, knee, meniscus, due to
      old injury
    open – *see* Wound, open, knee
    specified NEC S89.8-
    sprain – *see* Sprain, knee
    superficial – *see* Injury, superficial,
      knee
  labium (majus) (minus) S39.94
  labyrinth, ear S09.91
  lacrimal apparatus, duct, gland, or sac -
    see Injury, eye, specified site NEC
  larynx NEC S19.81
    with
  leg (lower) S89.9-
    blood vessel – *see* Injury, blood vessel,
      leg
    contusion – *see* Contusion, leg
    fracture – *see* Fracture, leg
    muscle – *see* Injury, muscle, leg
    nerve – *see* Injury, nerve, leg
    open – *see* Wound, open, leg
    specified NEC S89.8-
    superficial – *see* Injury, superficial, leg
  lens, eye – *see* Injury, eye, specified site
    NEC
    penetrating – *see* Injury, eyeball,
      penetrating
  limb NEC T14.8
  lip S09.93
  liver S36.119
    contusion S36.112
    laceration S36.113
      major (stellate) S36.116
      minor S36.114
      moderate S36.115
    specified NEC S36.118
  lower back S39.92
    specified NEC S39.82
  lumbar, lumbosacral (region) S39.92
    plexus - *see* Injury, lumbosacral
      plexus
  lumbosacral plexus S34.4
  lung – *see also* Injury, intrathoracic, lung
    transfusion-related (TRALI) J95.84

Injury *(Continued)*
  lymphatic thoracic duct – *see* Injury,
    intrathoracic, specified organ NEC
  malar region S09.93
  mastoid region S09.90
  maxilla S09.93
  mediastinum – *see* Injury, intrathoracic,
    specified organ NEC
  membrane, brain – *see* Injury,
    intracranial
  meningeal artery – *see* Injury, intracra-
    nial, subdural hemorrhage
  meninges (cerebral) – *see* Injury,
    intracranial
  mesenteric
    artery
      branch S35.299
        laceration (minor) (superficial)
          S35.291
          major S35.292
          specified NEC S35.298
      inferior S35.239
        laceration (minor) (superficial)
          S35.231
          major S35.232
          specified NEC S35.238
      superior S35.229
        laceration (minor) (superficial)
          S35.221
          major S35.222
          specified NEC S35.228
    plexus (inferior) (superior) – *see*
      Injury, nerve, lumbosacral,
      sympathetic
    vein
      inferior S35.349
        laceration S35.341
        specified NEC S35.348
      superior S35.339
        laceration S35.331
        specified NEC S35.338
  mesentery – *see* Injury, intra-abdominal,
    specified site NEC
  mesosalpinx – *see* Injury, pelvic organ,
    specified site NEC
  middle ear S09.91
  midthoracic region NOS S29.9
  mouth S09.93
  multiple NOS T07
  muscle (and fascia) (and tendon)
    abdomen S39.001
      laceration S39.021
      specified type NEC S39.091
      strain S39.011
    abductor
      thumb, forearm level – *see* Injury,
        muscle, thumb, abductor
    adductor
      thigh S76.20-
        laceration S76.22-
        specified type NEC S76.29-
        strain S76.21-
    ankle – *see* Injury, muscle, foot
    anterior muscle group, at leg level
      (lower) S86.20-
      laceration S86.22-
      specified type NEC S86.29-
      strain S86.21-
    arm (upper) – *see* Injury, muscle,
      shoulder
    biceps (parts NEC) S46.20-
      laceration S46.22-
      long head S46.10-
        laceration S46.12-

Injury *(Continued)*
  muscle *(Continued)*
    biceps *(Continued)*
      long head *(Continued)*
        strain S46.11-
        specified type NEC S46.19-
      specified type NEC S46.29-
      strain S46.21-
    extensor
      finger(s) (other than thumb)– *see*
        Injury, muscle, finger by site,
        extensor
      forearm level, specified NEC –
        see Injury, muscle, forearm,
        extensor
      thumb – *see* Injury, muscle, thumb,
        extensor
      toe (large) (ankle level) (foot level) –
        see Injury, muscle, toe,
        extensor
    finger
      extensor (forearm level) S56.409
        hand level S66.309
          laceration S66.329
          specified type NEC S66.399
          strain S66.319
        laceration S56.429
        specified type NEC S56.499
        strain S56.419
      flexor (forearm level) S56.109
        hand level S66.109
          laceration S66.129
          specified type NEC S66.199
          strain S66.119
        laceration S56.129
        specified type NEC S56.199
        strain S56.119
      intrinsic S66.509
        laceration S66.529
        specified type NEC S66.599
        strain S66.519
      index
        extensor (forearm level)
          hand level S66.308
            laceration S66.32-
            specified type NEC S66.39-
            strain S66.31-
          specified type NEC S56.492-
        flexor (forearm level)
          hand level S66.108
            laceration S66.12-
            specified type NEC S66.19-
            strain S66.11-
          specified type NEC S56.19-
          strain S56.11-
        intrinsic S66.50-
          laceration S66.52-
          specified type NEC S66.59-
          strain S66.51-
      little
        extensor (forearm level)
          hand level S66.30-
            laceration S66.32-
            specified type NEC S66.39-
            strain S66.31-
          laceration S56.42-
          specified type NEC S56.49-
          strain S56.41-
        flexor (forearm level)
          hand level S66.10-
            laceration S66.12-
            specified type NEC S66.19-
            strain S66.11-
          laceration S56.12-

Injury *(Continued)*
  muscle *(Continued)*
    finger *(Continued)*
      little *(Continued)*
        flexor *(Continued)*
          specified type NEC S56.19-
          strain S56.11-
        intrinsic S66.50-
          laceration S66.52-
          specified type NEC S66.59-
          strain S66.51-
      middle
        extensor (forearm level)
          hand level S66.30-
            laceration S66.32-
            specified type NEC S66.39-
            strain S66.31-
          laceration S56.42-
          specified type NEC S56.49-
          strain S56.41-
        flexor (forearm level)
          hand level S66.10-
            laceration S66.12-
            specified type NEC S66.19-
            strain S66.11-
          laceration S56.12-
          specified type NEC S56.19-
          strain S56.11-
        intrinsic S66.50-
          laceration S66.52-
          specified type NEC S66.59-
          strain S66.51-
      ring
        extensor (forearm level)
          hand level S66.30-
            laceration S66.32-
            specified type NEC S66.39-
            strain S66.31-
          laceration S56.42-
          specified type NEC S56.49-
          strain S56.41-
        flexor (forearm level)
          hand level S66.10-
            laceration S66.12-
            specified type NEC S66.19-
            strain S66.11-
          laceration S56.12-
          specified type NEC S56.19-
          strain S56.11-
        intrinsic S66.50-
          laceration S66.52-
          specified type NEC S66.59-
          strain S66.51-
    flexor
      finger(s) (other than thumb) – *see*
        Injury, muscle, finger
      forearm level, specified NEC –
        see Injury, muscle, forearm,
        flexor
      thumb – *see* Injury, muscle, thumb,
        flexor
      toe (long) (ankle level) (foot level) –
        see Injury, muscle, toe,
        flexor
    foot S96.90-
      intrinsic S96.20-
        laceration S96.22-
        specified type NEC S96.29-
        strain S96.21-
      laceration S96.92-
      long extensor, toe - *see* Injury,
        muscle, toe, extensor
      long flexor, toe - *see* Injury, muscle,
        toe, flexor

Injury *(Continued)*
  nerve NEC *(Continued)*
    acoustic *(Continued)*
      laceration S04.6-
      specified type NEC S04.6-
    ankle S94.9-
      cutaneous sensory S94.3-
      specified site NEC - *see* subcategory
        S94.8
    anterior crural, femoral – *see* Injury,
      nerve, femoral
    arm (upper) S44.9-
      axillary – *see* Injury, nerve,
        axillary
      cutaneous - *see* Injury, nerve, cuta-
        neous, arm
      median - *see* Injury, nerve, median,
        upper arm
      musculocutaneous - *see* Injury,
        nerve, musculocutaneous
      radial - *see* Injury, nerve, radial,
        upper arm
      specified site NEC - *see* subcategory
        S44.8
      ulnar - *see* Injury, nerve, ulnar, arm
    auditory – *see* Injury, nerve, acoustic
    axillary S44.3-
    brachial plexus – *see* Injury, brachial
      plexus
    cervical sympathetic S14.5
    cranial S04.9
      contusion S04.9
      eighth (acoustic or auditory) – *see*
        Injury, nerve, acoustic
      eleventh (accessory) – *see* Injury,
        nerve, accessory
      fifth (trigeminal) – *see* Injury, nerve,
        trigeminal
      first (olfactory) – *see* Injury, nerve,
        olfactory
      fourth (trochlear) – *see* Injury,
        nerve, trochlear
      laceration S04.9
      ninth (glossopharyngeal) – *see*
        Injury, nerve, glossopharyngeal
      second (optic) – *see* Injury, nerve,
        optic
      seventh (facial) – *see* Injury, nerve,
        facial
      sixth (abducent) – *see* Injury, nerve,
        abducens
      specified
        nerve NEC S04.89-
          contusion S04.89-
          laceration S04.89-
          specified type NEC S04.89-
        type NEC S04.9
      tenth (pneumogastric or vagus) –
        see Injury, nerve, vagus
      third (oculomotor) – *see* Injury,
        nerve, oculomotor
      twelfth (hypoglossal) – *see* Injury,
        nerve, hypoglossal
    cutaneous sensory
      ankle (level) S94.3-
      arm (upper) (level) S44.5-
      foot (level) – *see* Injury, nerve, cuta-
        neous sensory, ankle
      forearm (level) S54.3-
      hip (level) S74.2-
      leg (lower level) S84.2-
      shoulder (level) - *see* Injury, nerve,
        cutaneous sensory, arm

Injury *(Continued)*
  nerve NEC *(Continued)*
    cutaneous sensory *(Continued)*
      thigh (level) - *see* Injury, nerve,
        cutaneous sensory, hip
      deep peroneal – *see* Injury, nerve,
        peroneal, foot
    digital
      finger S64.4-
        index S64.49-
        little S64.49-
        middle S64.49-
        ring S64.49-
        thumb S64.3-
      toe – *see* Injury, nerve, ankle, speci-
        fied site NEC
    eighth cranial (acoustic or auditory) –
      see Injury, nerve, acoustic
    eleventh cranial (accessory) – *see*
      Injury, nerve, accessory
    facial S04.5-
      contusion S04.5-
      laceration S04.5-
      newborn P11.3
      specified type NEC S04.5-
    femoral (hip level) (thigh level)
      S74.1-
    fifth cranial (trigeminal) – *see* Injury,
      nerve, trigeminal
    finger (digital) – *see* Injury, nerve,
      digital, finger
    first cranial (olfactory) – *see* Injury,
      nerve, olfactory
    foot S94.9-
      cutaneous sensory S94.3-
      deep peroneal S94.2-
      lateral plantar S94.0-
      medial plantar S94.1-
      specified site NEC - *see* subcategory
        S94.8
    forearm (level) S54.9-
      cutaneous sensory - *see* Injury,
        nerve, cutaneous sensory,
        forearm
      median - *see* Injury, nerve, median
      radial - *see* Injury, nerve, radial
      specified site NEC - *see* subcategory
        S54.8
      ulnar - *see* Injury, nerve, ulnar
    fourth cranial (trochlear) – *see* Injury,
      nerve, trochlear
    glossopharyngeal S04.89-
      specified type NEC S04.89-
    hand S64.9-
      median – *see* Injury, nerve, median,
        hand
      radial – *see* Injury, nerve, radial,
        hand
      specified NEC - *see* subcategory
        S64.8
      ulnar – *see* Injury, nerve, ulnar,
        hand
    hip (level) S74.9-
      cutaneous sensory - *see* Injury,
        nerve, cutaneous sensory,
        hip
      femoral - *see* Injury, nerve,
        femoral
      sciatic - *see* Injury, nerve, sciatic
      specified site NEC - *see* subcategory
        S74.8
    hypoglossal S04.89-
      specified type NEC S04.89-
    lateral plantar S94.0-

Injury *(Continued)*
  nerve NEC *(Continued)*
    leg (lower) S84.9-
      cutaneous sensory – *see* Injury,
        nerve, cutaneous sensory, leg
      peroneal – *see* Injury, nerve,
        peroneal
      specified site NEC - *see* subcategory
        S84.8
      tibial – *see* Injury, nerve, tibial
      upper - *see* Injury, nerve, thigh
    lower
      back – *see* Injury, nerve, abdomen,
        specified site NEC
      peripheral – *see* Injury, nerve,
        abdomen, peripheral
      limb - *see* Injury, nerve, leg
    lumbar plexus - *see* Injury, lumbosa-
      cral plexus
    lumbosacral
      plexus - *see* Injury, lumbosacral
        plexus
      sympathetic S34.5
    medial plantar S94.1-
    median (forearm level) S54.1-
      hand (level) S64.1-
      upper arm (level) S44.1-
      wrist (level) – *see* Injury, nerve,
        median, hand
    musculocutaneous S44.4-
    musculospiral (upper arm level) –
      see Injury, nerve, radial, upper
      arm
    neck S14.9
      peripheral S14.4
      specified site NEC S14.8
      sympathetic S14.5
    ninth cranial (glossopharyngeal) –
      see Injury, nerve,
      glossopharyngeal
    oculomotor S04.1-
      contusion S04.1-
      laceration S04.1-
      specified type NEC S04.1-
    olfactory S04.81-
      specified type NEC S04.81-
    optic S04.01-
      contusion S04.01-
      laceration S04.01-
      specified type NEC S04.01-
    pelvic girdle – *see* Injury, nerve,
      hip
    pelvis – *see* Injury, nerve, abdomen,
      specified site NEC
    peripheral – *see* Injury, nerve, abdo-
      men, peripheral
    peripheral NEC T14.8
      abdomen – *see* Injury, nerve, abdo-
        men, peripheral
      lower back – *see* Injury, nerve,
        abdomen, peripheral
      neck – *see* Injury, nerve, neck,
        peripheral
      pelvis – *see* Injury, nerve, abdomen,
        peripheral
      specified NEC T14.8
    peroneal (lower leg level) S84.1-
      foot S94.2-
    plexus
      brachial – *see* Injury, brachial
        plexus
      celiac, coeliac – *see* Injury, nerve,
        lumbosacral, sympathetic

306

Injury *(Continued)*
  nerve NEC *(Continued)*
    plexus *(Continued)*
      mesenteric, inferior – *see* Injury, nerve, lumbosacral, sympathetic
      sacral - *see* Injury, lumbosacral plexus
      spinal
        brachial – *see* Injury, brachial plexus
        lumbosacral - *see* Injury, lumbosacral plexus
    pneumogastric – *see* Injury, nerve, vagus
    radial (forearm level) S54.2-
      hand (level) S64.2-
      upper arm (level) S44.2-
      wrist (level) – *see* Injury, nerve, radial, hand
    sacral plexus - *see* Injury, lumbosacral plexus
    sciatic (hip level) (thigh level) S74.0-
    second cranial (optic) – *see* Injury, nerve, optic
    seventh cranial (facial) – *see* Injury, nerve, facial
    shoulder - *see* Injury, nerve, arm
    sixth cranial (abducent) – *see* Injury, nerve, abducens
    spinal
      plexus - *see* Injury, nerve, plexus, spinal
      root
        cervical S14.2
        dorsal S24.2
        lumbar S34.21
        sacral S34.22
        thoracic – *see* Injury, nerve, spinal, root, dorsal
    splanchnic – *see* Injury, nerve, lumbosacral, sympathetic
    sympathetic NEC – *see* Injury, nerve, lumbosacral, sympathetic
      cervical – *see* Injury, nerve, cervical sympathetic
    tenth cranial (pneumogastric or vagus) – *see* Injury, nerve, vagus
    thigh (level) – *see* Injury, nerve, hip
      cutaneous sensory – *see* Injury, nerve, cutaneous sensory, hip
      femoral – *see* Injury, nerve, femoral
      sciatic – *see* Injury, nerve, sciatic
      specified NEC – *see* Injury, nerve, hip
    third cranial (oculomotor) – *see* Injury, nerve, oculomotor
    thorax S24.9
      peripheral S24.3
      specified site NEC S24.8
      sympathetic S24.4
    thumb, digital – *see* Injury, nerve, digital, thumb
    tibial (lower leg level) (posterior) S84.0-
    toe – *see* Injury, nerve, ankle
    trigeminal S04.3-
      contusion S04.3-
      laceration S04.3-
      specified type NEC S04.3-
    trochlear S04.2-
      contusion S04.2-
      laceration S04.2-
      specified type NEC S04.2-

Injury *(Continued)*
  nerve NEC *(Continued)*
    twelfth cranial (hypoglossal) – *see* Injury, nerve, hypoglossal
    ulnar (forearm level) S54.0-
      arm (upper) (level) S44.0-
      hand (level) S64.0-
      wrist (level) – *see* Injury, nerve, ulnar, hand
    vagus S04.89-
      specified type NEC S04.89-
    wrist (level) – *see* Injury, nerve, hand
    ninth cranial nerve (glossopharyngeal) – *see* Injury, nerve, glossopharyngeal
  nose (septum) S09.92
  obstetrical O71.9
    specified NEC O71.89
  occipital (region) (scalp) S09.90
    lobe - *see* Injury, intracranial
  optic chiasm S04.02
  optic radiation S04.03-
  optic tract and pathways S04.03-
  orbit, orbital (region) – *see* Injury, eye
    penetrating (with foreign body) – *see* Injury, eye, orbit, penetrating
    specified NEC – *see* Injury, eye, specified site NEC
  ovary, ovarian S37.409
    bilateral S37.402
      contusion S37.422
      laceration S37.432
      specified type NEC S37.492
    blood vessel – *see* Injury, blood vessel, ovarian
    contusion S37.429
      bilateral S37.422
      unilateral S37.421
    laceration S37.439
      bilateral S37.432
      unilateral S37.431
    specified type NEC S37.499
      bilateral S37.492
      unilateral S37.491
    unilateral S37.401
      contusion S37.421
      laceration S37.431
      specified type NEC S37.491
  palate (hard) (soft) S09.93
  pancreas S36.209
    body S36.201
      contusion S36.221
      laceration S36.231
        major S36.261
        minor S36.241
        moderate S36.251
      specified type NEC S36.291
    contusion S36.229
    head S36.200
      contusion S36.220
      laceration S36.230
        major S36.260
        minor S36.240
        moderate S36.250
      specified type NEC S36.290
    laceration S36.239
      major S36.269
      minor S36.249
      moderate S36.259
    specified type NEC S36.299
    tail S36.202
      contusion S36.222
      laceration S36.232
        major S36.262

Injury *(Continued)*
  pancreas *(Continued)*
    tail *(Continued)*
      laceration *(Continued)*
        minor S36.242
        moderate S36.252
      specified type NEC S36.292
  parietal (region) (scalp) S09.90
    lobe - *see* Injury, intracranial
  patellar ligament (tendon) S76.10-
    laceration S76.12-
    specified NEC S76.19-
    strain S76.11-
  pelvis, pelvic (floor) S39.93
    complicating delivery O70.1
    joint or ligament, complicating delivery O71.6
    organ S37.90
      with ectopic or molar pregnancy O08.6
      complication of abortion - *see* Abortion
      contusion S37.92
      following ectopic or molar pregnancy O08.6
      laceration S37.93
      obstetrical trauma NEC O71.5
      specified
        site NEC S37.899
          contusion S37.892
          laceration S37.893
          specified type NEC S37.898
        type NEC S37.99
    specified NEC S39.83
  penis S39.94
  perineum S39.94
  peritoneum – *see* Injury, intra-abdominal, specified site NEC
  periurethral tissue – *see* Injury, urethra
  phalanges
    foot – *see* Injury, foot
    hand – *see* Injury, hand
  pharynx S09.93
  pleura – *see* Injury, intrathoracic, pleura
  plexus
    brachial – *see* Injury, brachial plexus
    cardiac – *see* Injury, nerve, thorax, sympathetic
    celiac, coeliac – *see* Injury, nerve, lumbosacral, sympathetic
    esophageal – *see* Injury, nerve, thorax, sympathetic
    hypogastric – *see* Injury, nerve, lumbosacral, sympathetic
    lumbar, lumbosacral - *see* Injury, lumbosacral plexus
    mesenteric – *see* Injury, nerve, lumbosacral, sympathetic
    pulmonary – *see* Injury, nerve, thorax, sympathetic
  postcardiac surgery (syndrome) I97.0
  prepuce S39.94
  prostate S37.829
    contusion S37.822
    laceration S37.823
    specified type NEC S37.828
  pubic region S39.94
  pudendum S39.94
  pulmonary plexus – *see* Injury, nerve, thorax, sympathetic
  rectovaginal septum NEC S39.83
  rectum - *see* Injury, intestine, large, rectum

Injury (Continued)
  retina – see Injury, eye, specified site
    NEC
    penetrating – see Injury, eyeball,
      penetrating
  retroperitoneal – see Injury, intra-
    abdominal, specified site NEC
  rotator cuff (muscles(s)) (tendon(s))
    S46.00-
    laceration S46.02-
    specified type NEC S46.09-
    strain S46.01-
  round ligament – see Injury, pelvic
    organ, specified site NEC
  sacral plexus - see Injury, lumbosacral
    plexus
  salivary duct or gland S09.93
  scalp S09.90
    newborn (birth injury) P12.9
      due to monitoring (electrode)
        (sampling incision) P12.4
      specified NEC P12.89
        caput succedaneum P12.81
  scapular region – see Injury, shoulder
  sclera – see Injury, eye, specified site
    NEC
    penetrating – see Injury, eyeball,
      penetrating
  scrotum S39.94
  second cranial nerve (optic) – see Injury,
    nerve, optic
  seminal vesicle – see Injury, pelvic
    organ, specified site NEC
  seventh cranial nerve (facial) – see
    Injury, nerve, facial
  shoulder S49.9-
    blood vessel – see Injury, blood vessel,
      arm
    contusion – see Contusion, shoulder
    dislocation – see Dislocation,
      shoulder
    fracture – see Fracture, shoulder
    muscle – see Injury, muscle,
      shoulder
    nerve – see Injury, nerve, shoulder
    open – see Wound, open, shoulder
    specified type NEC S49.8-
    sprain – see Sprain, shoulder
      girdle
    superficial – see Injury, superficial,
      shoulder
  sinus
    cavernous – see Injury, intracranial
    nasal S09.92
  sixth cranial nerve (abducent) – see
    Injury, nerve, abducens
  skeleton, birth injury P13.9
    specified part NEC P13.8
  skin NEC T14.8
    surface intact - see Injury, superficial
  skull NEC S09.90
  specified NEC T14.8
  spermatic cord (pelvic region) S37.898
    spinal (cord) S39.848
  spinal (cord)
    cervical (neck) S14.109
      anterior cord syndrome S14.139
        C1 level S14.131
        C2 level S14.132
        C3 level S14.133
        C4 level S14.134
        C5 level S14.135
        C6 level S14.136
        C7 level S14.137

Injury (Continued)
  spinal (Continued)
    cervical (Continued)
      Brown-Séquard syndrome S14.149
        C1 level S14.141
        C2 level S14.142
        C3 level S14.143
        C4 level S14.144
        C5 level S14.145
        C6 level S14.146
        C7 level S14.147
      C1 level S14.101
      C2 level S14.102
      C3 level S14.103
      C4 level S14.104
      C5 level S14.105
      C6 level S14.106
      C7 level S14.107
      central cord syndrome S14.129
        C1 level S14.121
        C2 level S14.122
        C3 level S14.123
        C4 level S14.124
        C5 level S14.125
        C6 level S14.126
        C7 level S14.127
      complete lesion S14.119
        C1 level S14.111
        C2 level S14.112
        C3 level S14.113
        C4 level S14.114
        C5 level S14.115
        C6 level S14.116
        C7 level S14.117
      concussion S14.0
      edema S14.0
      incomplete lesion specified NEC
        S14.159
        C1 level S14.151
        C2 level S14.152
        C3 level S14.153
        C4 level S14.154
        C5 level S14.155
        C6 level S14.156
        C7 level S14.157
      posterior cord syndrome S14.159
        C1 level S14.151
        C2 level S14.152
        C3 level S14.153
        C4 level S14.154
        C5 level S14.155
        C6 level S14.156
        C7 level S14.157
    dorsal - see Injury, spinal, thoracic
    lumbar S34.109
      complete lesion S34.119
        C1 level S34.111
        C2 level S34.112
        C3 level S34.113
        C4 level S34.114
        C5 level S34.115
      concussion S34.01
      edema S34.01
      incomplete lesion S34.129
        C1 level S34.121
        C2 level S34.122
        C3 level S34.123
        C4 level S34.124
        C5 level S34.125
      L1 level S34.101
      L2 level S34.102
      L3 level S34.103
      L4 level S34.104
      L5 level S34.105

Injury (Continued)
  spinal (Continued)
    nerve root NEC
      cervical – see Injury, nerve, spinal,
        root, cervical
      dorsal – see Injury, nerve, spinal,
        root, dorsal
      lumbar S34.21
      sacral S34.22
      thoracic – see Injury, nerve, spinal,
        root, dorsal
    plexus
      brachial – see Injury, brachial
        plexus
      lumbosacral - see Injury, lumbosa-
        cral plexus
    sacral S34.139
      complete lesion S34.131
      incomplete lesion S34.132
    thoracic S24.109
      anterior cord syndrome S24.139
        T1 level S24.131
        T2-T6 level S24.132
        T7-T10 level S24.133
        T11-T12 level S24.134
      Brown-Séquard syndrome S24.149
        T1 level S24.141
        T2-T6 level S24.142
        T7-T10 level S24.143
        T11-T12 level S24.144
      complete lesion S24.119
        T1 level S24.111
        T2-T6 level S24.112
        T7-T10 level S24.113
        T11-T12 level S24.114
      concussion S24.0
      edema S24.0
      incomplete lesion specified NEC
        S24.159
        T1 level S24.151
        T2-T6 level S24.152
        T7-T10 level S24.153
        T11-T12 level S24.154
      posterior cord syndrome S24.159
        T1 level S24.151
        T2-T6 level S24.152
        T7-T10 level S24.153
        T11-T12 level S24.154
      T1 level S24.101
      T2-T6 level S24.102
      T7-T10 level S24.103
      T11-T12 level S24.104
    splanchnic nerve – see Injury, nerve,
      lumbosacral, sympathetic
    spleen S36.00
      contusion S36.029
        major S36.021
        minor S36.020
      laceration S36.039
        major (massive) (stellate) S36.032
        moderate S36.031
        superficial (capsular) (minor)
          S36.030
      specified type NEC S36.09
    splenic artery – see Injury, blood vessel,
      celiac artery, branch
    stellate ganglion – see Injury, nerve,
      thorax, sympathetic
    sternal region S29.9
    stomach S36.30
      contusion S36.32
      laceration S36.33
      specified type NEC S36.39

Injury *(Continued)*
   subconjunctival – *see* Injury, eye,
      conjunctiva
   subcutaneous NEC T14.8
   submaxillary region S09.93
   submental region S09.93
   subungual
      fingers – *see* Injury, hand
      toes – *see* Injury, foot
   superficial NEC T14.8
      abdomen, abdominal (wall) S30.92
         abrasion S30.811
         bite S30.871
            insect S30.861
         contusion S30.1
         external constriction S30.841
         foreign body S30.851
      abrasion – *see* Abrasion, by site
      adnexa, eye NEC – *see* Injury, eye,
         specified site NEC
      alveolar process – *see* Injury, superfi-
         cial, oral cavity
      ankle S90.91-
         abrasion - *see* Abrasion, ankle
         blister - *see* Blister, ankle
         bite - *see* Bite, ankle
         contusion - *see* Contusion, ankle
         external constriction - *see*
            Constriction, external,
            ankle
         foreign body - *see* Foreign body,
            superficial, ankle
      anus S30.98
      arm (upper) S40.92-
         abrasion – *see* Abrasion, arm
         bite – *see* Bite, superficial, arm
         blister - *see* Blister, arm (upper)
         contusion – *see* Contusion, arm
         external constriction – *see*
            Constriction, external, arm
         foreign body – *see* Foreign body,
            superficial, arm
      auditory canal (external) (meatus) –
         see Injury, superficial, ear
      auricle – *see* Injury, superficial, ear
      axilla – *see* Injury, superficial, arm
      back - *see also* Injury, superficial,
         thorax, back
         lower S30.91
            abrasion S30.810
            contusion S30.0
            external constriction S30.840
            superficial
               bite NEC S30.870
                  insect S30.860
               foreign body S30.850
      bite NEC – *see* Bite, superficial NEC,
         by site
      blister – *see* Blister, by site
      breast S20.10-
         abrasion – *see* Abrasion, breast
         bite – *see* Bite, superficial, breast
         contusion – *see* Contusion, breast
         external constriction – *see*
            Constriction, external,
            breast
         foreign body – *see* Foreign body,
            superficial, breast
      brow – *see* Injury, superficial, head,
         specified NEC
      buttock S30.91
      calf – *see* Injury, superficial, leg
      canthus, eye – *see* Injury, superficial,
         periocular area

Injury *(Continued)*
   superficial NEC *(Continued)*
      cheek (external) – *see* Injury, superfi-
         cial, head, specified NEC
         internal – *see* Injury, superficial,
            oral cavity
      chest wall – *see* Injury, superficial,
         thorax
      chin - *see* Injury, superficial, head
         NEC
      clitoris S30.95
      conjunctiva – *see* Injury, eye,
         conjunctiva
         with foreign body (in conjunctival
            sac) – *see* Foreign body, con-
            junctival sac
      contusion – *see* Contusion, by site
      costal region - *see* Injury, superficial,
         thorax
      digit(s)
         hand – *see* Injury, superficial, finger
      ear (auricle) (canal) (external) S00.40-
         abrasion – *see* Abrasion, ear
         bite – *see* Bite, superficial, ear
         contusion – *see* Contusion, ear
         external constriction – *see* Constric-
            tion, external, ear
         foreign body – *see* Foreign body,
            superficial, ear
      elbow S50.90-
         abrasion – *see* Abrasion, elbow
         bite – *see* Bite, superficial, elbow
         blister - *see* Blister, elbow
         contusion – *see* Contusion, elbow
         external constriction – *see* Constric-
            tion, external, elbow
         foreign body – *see* Foreign body,
            superficial, elbow
      epididymis S30.94
      epigastric region S30.92
      epiglottis – *see* Injury, superficial,
         throat
      esophagus
         cervical – *see* Injury, superficial,
            throat
      external constriction – *see* Constric-
         tion, external, by site
      extremity NEC T14.8
      eyeball NEC – *see* Injury, eye, speci-
         fied site NEC
      eyebrow – *see* Injury, superficial,
         periocular area
      eyelid S00.20-
         abrasion – *see* Abrasion, eyelid
         bite – *see* Bite, superficial, eyelid
         contusion – *see* Contusion, eyelid
         external constriction – *see* Constric-
            tion, external, eyelid
         foreign body – *see* Foreign body,
            superficial, eyelid
      face NEC – *see* Injury, superficial,
         head, specified NEC
      finger(s) S60.949
         abrasion – *see* Abrasion, finger
         bite – *see* Bite, superficial, finger
         blister - *see* Blister, finger
         contusion – *see* Contusion, finger
         external constriction – *see* Constric-
            tion, external, finger
         foreign body – *see* Foreign body,
            superficial, finger
         insect bite - *see* Bite, insect, finger
         index S60.94-
         little S60.94-

Injury *(Continued)*
   superficial NEC *(Continued)*
      finger(s) *(Continued)*
         middle S60.94-
         ring S60.94-
      flank S30.92
      foot S90.92-
         abrasion – *see* Abrasion, foot
         bite – *see* Bite, foot
         blister - *see* Blister, foot
         contusion – *see* Contusion, foot
         external constriction – *see* Constric-
            tion, external, foot
         foreign body – *see* Foreign body,
            superficial, foot
      forearm S50.91-
         abrasion - *see* Abrasion, forearm
         bite - *see* Bite, forearm, superficial
         blister - *see* Blister, forearm
         contusion - *see* Contusion, forearm
         elbow only – *see* Injury, superficial,
            elbow
         external constriction - *see*
            Constriction, external,
            forearm
         foreign body - *see* Foreign body,
            superficial, forearm
      forehead – *see* Injury, superficial, head
         NEC
      foreign body – *see* Foreign body,
         superficial
      genital organs, external
         female S30.97
         male S30.96
      globe (eye) – *see* Injury, eye, specified
         site NEC
      groin S30.92
      gum – *see* Injury, superficial, oral
         cavity
      hand S60.92-
         abrasion – *see* Abrasion, hand
         bite – *see* Bite, superficial, hand
         contusion – *see* Contusion, hand
         external constriction – *see*
            Constriction, external, hand
         foreign body – *see* Foreign body,
            superficial, hand
      head S00.90
         ear – *see* Injury, superficial, ear
         eyelid – *see* Injury, superficial,
            eyelid
         nose S00.30
         oral cavity S00.502
         scalp S00.00
         specified site NEC S00.80
      heel – *see* Injury, superficial, foot
      hip S70.91-
         abrasion – *see* Abrasion, hip
         bite – *see* Bite, superficial, hip
         blister - *see* Blister, hip
         contusion – *see* Contusion, hip
         external constriction – *see*
            Constriction, external, hip
         foreign body – *see* Foreign body,
            superficial, hip
      iliac region – *see* Injury, superficial,
         abdomen
      inguinal region – *see* Injury, superfi-
         cial, abdomen
      insect bite – *see* Bite, insect, by site
      interscapular region – *see* Injury,
         superficial, thorax, back
      jaw – *see* Injury, superficial, head,
         specified NEC

Injury *(Continued)*
  superficial NEC *(Continued)*
    knee S80.91-
      abrasion – *see* Abrasion, knee
      bite – *see* Bite, superficial, knee
      blister - *see* Blister, knee
      contusion – *see* Contusion, knee
      external constriction – *see*
        Constriction, external,
        knee
      foreign body – *see* Foreign body,
        superficial, knee
    labium (majus) (minus) S30.95
    lacrimal (apparatus) (gland) (sac) –
      see Injury, eye, specified site
      NEC
    larynx – *see* Injury, superficial, throat
    leg (lower) S80.92-
      abrasion – *see* Abrasion, leg
      bite – *see* Bite, superficial, leg
      contusion – *see* Contusion, leg
      external constriction – *see*
        Constriction, external, leg
      foreign body – *see* Foreign body,
        superficial, leg
      knee – *see* Injury, superficial,
        knee
    limb NEC T14.8
    lip S00.501
    lower back S30.91
    lumbar region S30.91
    malar region – *see* Injury, superficial,
      head, specified NEC
    mammary – *see* Injury, superficial,
      breast
    mastoid region – *see* Injury, superfi-
      cial, head, specified NEC
    mouth – *see* Injury, superficial, oral
      cavity
    muscle NEC T14.8
    nail NEC T14.8
      finger – *see* Injury, superficial,
        finger
      toe – *see* Injury, superficial, toe
    nasal (septum) – *see* Injury, superfi-
      cial, nose
    neck S10.90
      specified site NEC S10.80
    nose (septum) S00.30
    occipital region – *see* Injury, superfi-
      cial, scalp
    oral cavity S00.502
    orbital region – *see* Injury, superficial,
      periocular area
    palate – *see* Injury, superficial, oral
      cavity
    palm – *see* Injury, superficial, hand
    parietal region – *see* Injury, superfi-
      cial, scalp
    pelvis S30.91
      girdle – *see* Injury, superficial, hip
    penis S30.93
    perineum
      female S30.95
      male S30.91
    periocular area S00.20-
      abrasion – *see* Abrasion, eyelid
      bite – *see* Bite, superficial, eyelid
      contusion – *see* Contusion, eyelid
      external constriction – *see*
        Constriction, external,
        eyelid
      foreign body – *see* Foreign body,
        superficial, eyelid

Injury *(Continued)*
  superficial NEC *(Continued)*
    phalanges
      finger – *see* Injury, superficial,
        finger
      toe – *see* Injury, superficial, toe
    pharynx – *see* Injury, superficial,
      throat
    pinna – *see* Injury, superficial, ear
    popliteal space – *see* Injury, superfi-
      cial, knee
    prepuce S30.93
    pubic region S30.91
    pudendum
      female S30.97
      male S30.96
    sacral region S30.91
    scalp S00.00
    scapular region – *see* Injury, superfi-
      cial, shoulder
    sclera – *see* Injury, eye, specified site
      NEC
    scrotum S30.94
    shin – *see* Injury, superficial, leg
    shoulder S40.91-
      abrasion – *see* Abrasion, shoulder
      bite – *see* Bite, superficial, shoulder
      blister - *see* Blister, shoulder
      contusion – *see* Contusion,
        shoulder
      external constriction – *see* Constric-
        tion, external, shoulder
      foreign body – *see* Foreign body,
        superficial, shoulder
    skin NEC T14.8
    sternal region – *see* Injury, superficial,
      thorax, front
    subconjunctival – *see* Injury, eye,
      specified site NEC
    subcutaneous NEC T14.8
    submaxillary region – *see* Injury, su-
      perficial, head, specified NEC
    submental region – *see* Injury, superfi-
      cial, head, specified NEC
    subungual
      finger(s) – *see* Injury, superficial,
        finger
      toe(s) – *see* Injury, superficial, toe
    supraclavicular fossa – *see* Injury,
      superficial, neck
    supraorbital – *see* Injury, superficial,
      head, specified NEC
    temple – *see* Injury, superficial, head,
      specified NEC
    temporal region – *see* Injury, superfi-
      cial, head, specified NEC
    testis S30.94
    thigh S70.92-
      abrasion – *see* Abrasion, thigh
      bite – *see* Bite, superficial, thigh
      blister - *see* Blister, thigh
      contusion – *see* Contusion, thigh
      external constriction – *see* Constric-
        tion, external, thigh
      foreign body – *see* Foreign body,
        superficial, thigh
    thorax, thoracic (wall) S20.90
      abrasion – *see* Abrasion, thorax
      back S20.40-
      bite – *see* Bite, thorax, superficial
      blister - *see* Blister, thorax
      contusion – *see* Contusion, thorax
      external constriction – *see* Constric-
        tion, external, thorax

Injury *(Continued)*
  superficial NEC *(Continued)*
    thorax, thoracic *(Continued)*
      foreign body – *see* Foreign body,
        superficial, thorax
      front S20.30-
    throat S10.10
      abrasion S10.11
      bite S10.17
        insect S10.16
      blister S10.12
      contusion S10.0
      external constriction S10.14
      foreign body S10.15
    thumb S60.93-
      abrasion - *see* Abrasion, thumb
      bite - *see* Bite, superficial, thumb
      blister - *see* Blister, thumb
      contusion - *see* Contusion, thumb
      external constriction - *see* Constric-
        tion, external, thumb
      foreign body - *see* Foreign body,
        superficial, thumb
      insect bite - *see* Bite, insect, thumb
        specified type NEC S60.392
        specified type NEC S60.391
        specified type NEC S60.399
    toe(s) S90.93-
      abrasion – *see* Abrasion, toe
      bite – *see* Bite, toe
      blister - *see* Blister, toe
      contusion – *see* Contusion, toe
      external constriction – *see* Constric-
        tion, external, toe
      foreign body – *see* Foreign body,
        superficial, toe
      great S90.93-
    tongue – *see* Injury, superficial, oral
      cavity
    tooth, teeth – *see* Injury, superficial,
      oral cavity
    trachea S10.10
    tunica vaginalis S30.94
    tympanum, tympanic membrane –
      see Injury, superficial, ear
    uvula – *see* Injury, superficial, oral
      cavity
    vagina S30.95
    vocal cords – *see* Injury, superficial,
      throat
    vulva S30.95
    wrist S60.91-
  supraclavicular region – *see* Injury,
    neck
  supraorbital S09.93
  suprarenal gland (multiple) – *see* Injury,
    adrenal
  surgical complication (external or
    internal site) – *see* Laceration,
    accidental complicating
    surgery
  temple S09.90
  temporal region S09.90
  tendon - *see also* Injury, muscle, by site
    abdomen – *see* Injury, muscle,
      abdomen
    Achilles – *see* Injury, Achilles tendon
    lower back – *see* Injury, muscle,
      lower back
    pelvic organs – *see* Injury, muscle,
      pelvis
  tenth cranial nerve (pneumogastric
    or vagus) – *see* Injury, nerve,
    vagus

Injury *(Continued)*
  testis S39.94
  thigh S79.92-
    blood vessel – *see* Injury, blood
        vessel, hip
    contusion – *see* Contusion, thigh
    fracture – *see* Fracture, femur
    muscle – *see* Injury, muscle, thigh
    nerve – *see* Injury, nerve, thigh
    open – *see* Wound, open, thigh
    specified NEC S79.82-
    superficial – *see* Injury, superficial,
        thigh
  third cranial nerve (oculomotor) –
      see Injury, nerve, oculomotor
  thorax, thoracic S29.9
    blood vessel – *see* Injury, blood
        vessel, thorax
    cavity - *see* Injury, intrathoracic
    dislocation - *see* Dislocation, thorax
    external (wall) S29.9
      contusion – *see* Contusion,
          thorax
      nerve – *see* Injury, nerve, thorax
      open – *see* Wound, open, thorax
      specified NEC S29.8
      sprain – *see* Sprain, thorax
      superficial – *see* Injury, superficial,
          thorax
    fracture – *see* Fracture, thorax
    internal - *see* Injury, intrathoracic
    intrathoracic organ - *see* Injury,
        intrathoracic
    sympathetic ganglion – *see* Injury,
        nerve, thorax, sympathetic
  throat – *see* Injury, neck
  thumb S69.9-
    blood vessel – *see* Injury, blood
        vessel, thumb
    contusion – *see* Contusion, thumb
    dislocation – *see* Dislocation, thumb
    fracture – *see* Fracture, thumb
    muscle – *see* Injury, muscle, thumb
    nerve – *see* Injury, nerve, digital,
        thumb
    open – *see* Wound, open, thumb
    specified NEC S69.8-
    sprain – *see* Sprain, thumb
    superficial – *see* Injury, superficial,
        thumb
  thymus (gland) – *see* Injury, intra-
      thoracic, specified organ NEC
  thyroid (gland) NEC S19.84
  toe S99.92-
    contusion – *see* Contusion, toe
    dislocation – *see* Dislocation, toe
    fracture – *see* Fracture, toe
    muscle – *see* Injury, muscle, toe
    open – *see* Wound, open, toe
    specified type NEC S99.82-
    sprain – *see* Sprain, toe
    superficial – *see* Injury, superficial,
        toe
  tongue S09.93
  tonsil S09.93
  tooth S09.93
  trachea (cervical) NEC S19.82
    thoracic – *see* Injury, intrathoracic,
        trachea, thoracic
  transfusion-related acute lung (TRALI)
      J95.84
  tunica vaginalis S39.94
  twelfth cranial nerve (hypoglossal) –
      see Injury, nerve, hypoglossal

Injury *(Continued)*
  ureter S37.10
    contusion S37.12
    laceration S37.13
    specified type NEC S37.19
  urethra (sphincter) S37.30
    at delivery O71.5
    contusion S37.32
    laceration S37.33
    specified type NEC S37.38
  urinary organ S37.899
    specified NEC S37.898
  uterus, uterine S37.60
    with ectopic or molar pregnancy
        O08.6
    blood vessel – *see* Injury, blood vessel,
        iliac
    contusion S37.62
    laceration S37.63
      cervix at delivery O71.3
    rupture associated with obstetrics -
        see Rupture, uterus
    specified type NEC S37.69
  uvula S09.93
  vagina S39.93
    abrasion S30.814
    bite S31.45
      insect S30.864
      superficial NEC S30.874
    contusion S30.23
    crush S38.03
    during delivery – *see* Laceration,
        vagina, during delivery
    external constriction S30.844
    insect bite S30.864
    laceration S31.41
      with foreign body S31.42
    open wound S31.40
    puncture S31.43
      with foreign body S31.44
    superficial S30.95
      foreign body S30.854
  vas deferens – *see* Injury, pelvic organ,
      specified site NEC
  vascular NEC T14.8
  vein - *see* Injury, blood vessel
  vena cava (superior) S25.20
    inferior S35.10
      laceration (minor) (superficial)
          S35.11
        major S35.12
      specified type NEC S35.19
    laceration (minor) (superficial) S25.21
      major S25.22
    specified type NEC S25.29
  vesical (sphincter) – *see* Injury, bladder
  visual cortex S04.04-
  vitreous (humor) S05.90
    specified NEC S05.8x-
  vocal cord S19.83
  vulva S39.94
    abrasion S30.814
    bite S31.45
      insect S30.864
      superficial NEC S30.874
    contusion S30.23
    crush S38.03
    during delivery – *see* Laceration,
        perineum, female, during
        delivery
    external constriction S30.844
    insect bite S30.864
    laceration S31.41
      with foreign body S31.42

Injury *(Continued)*
  vulva *(Continued)*
    open wound S31.40
    puncture S31.43
      with foreign body S31.44
    superficial S30.95
      foreign body S30.854
  whiplash (cervical spine) S13.4
  wrist S69.9-
    blood vessel – *see* Injury, blood vessel,
        hand
    contusion – *see* Contusion, wrist
    dislocation – *see* Dislocation, wrist
    fracture – *see* Fracture, wrist
    muscle – *see* Injury, muscle, hand
    nerve – *see* Injury, nerve, hand
    open – *see* Wound, open, wrist
    specified NEC S69.8-
    sprain – *see* Sprain, wrist
    superficial – *see* Injury, superficial,
        wrist
Inoculation - *see also* Vaccination
  complication or reaction - *see*
      Complications, vaccination
Insanity, insane - *see also* Psychosis
  adolescent - *see* Schizophrenia
  confusional F28
    acute or subacute F05
  delusional F22
  senile F03
Insect
  bite - *see* Bite, insect, by site
  venomous, poisoning NEC (by) –
      see Venom, arthropod
Insensitivity
  adrenocorticotropin hormone (ACTH)
      E27.49
  androgen E34.50
    complete E35.51
    partial E34.52
Insertion
  cord (umbilical) lateral or velamentous
      O43.12-
Insolation (sunstroke) T67.0
Insomnia (organic) G47.00
  adjustment F51.02
  adjustment disorder F51.02
  behavioral, of childhood Z73.819
    combined type Z73.812
    limit setting type Z73.811
    sleep-onset association type
        Z73.810
  childhood Z73.819
  chronic F51.04
    somatized tension F51.04
  conditioned F51.04
  due to
    alcohol
      abuse F10.182
      dependence F10.282
      use F10.982
    amphetamines
      abuse F15.182
      dependence F15.282
      use F15.982
    anxiety disorder F51.05
    caffeine
      abuse F15.182
      dependence F15.282
      use F15.982
    cocaine
      abuse F14.182
      dependence F14.282
      use F14.982

311

Insomnia *(Continued)*
  due to *(Continued)*
    depression F51.05
    drug NEC
      abuse F19.182
      dependence F19.282
      use F19.982
    medical condition G47.01
    mental disorder NEC F51.05
    opioid
      abuse F11.182
      dependence F11.282
      use F11.982
    psychoactive substance NEC
      abuse F19.182
      dependence F19.282
      use F19.982
    sedative, hypnotic, or anxiolytic
      abuse F13.182
      dependence F13.282
      use F13.982
    stimulant NEC
      abuse F15.182
      dependence F15.282
      use F15.982
  fatal familial (FFI) A81.83
  idiopathic F51.01
  learned F51.3
  nonorganic origin F51.01
  not due to a substance or known physiological condition F51.01
    specified NEC F51.09
  organic G47.00
    specified NEC G47.09
  paradoxical F51.03
  primary F51.01
  psychiatric F51.05
  psychophysiologic F51.04
  related to psychopathology F51.05
  short-term F51.02
  specified NEC G47.09
  stress-related F51.02
  transient F51.02
  without objective findings F51.02
Inspiration
  food or foreign body - *see* Asphyxia, food
  mucus - *see* Asphyxia, mucus
Inspissated bile syndrome (newborn) P59.1
Instability
  emotional (excessive) F60.3
  joint (post-traumatic) M25.30
    ankle M25.37-
    due to old ligament injury - *see* Disorder, ligament
    elbow M25.32-
    flail - *see* Flail, joint
    foot M25.37-
    hand M25.34-
    hip M25.35-
    knee M25.36-
    lumbosacral - *see* subcategory M53.2
    prosthesis - *see* Complications, joint prosthesis, mechanical, displacement, by site
    sacroiliac - *see* subcategory M53.2
    secondary to
      old ligament injury – *see* Disorder, ligament
      removal of joint prosthesis M96.89
    shoulder (region) M25.31-
    spine - *see* subcategory M53.2
    wrist M25.33-

Instability *(Continued)*
  knee (chronic) M23.5-
  lumbosacral - *see* subcategory M53.2
  nervous F48.8
  personality (emotional) F60.3
  spine - *see* Instability, joint, spine
  vasomotor R55
Institutional syndrome (childhood) F94.2
Institutionalization, affecting child Z62.22
  disinhibited attachment F94.2
Insufficiency, insufficient
  accommodation, old age H52.4
  adrenal (gland) E27.40
    primary E27.1
  adrenocortical E27.40
    drug-induced E27.3
    iatrogenic E27.3
    primary E27.1
  anterior (occlusal) guidance M26.54
  anus K62.8
  aortic (valve) I35.1
    with
      mitral (valve) disease I08.0
        with tricuspid (valve) disease I08.3
      stenosis I35.2
      tricuspid (valve) disease I08.2
        with mitral (valve) disease I08.3
    congenital Q23.1
    rheumatic I06.1
      with
        mitral (valve) disease I08.0
          with tricuspid (valve) disease I08.3
        stenosis I06.2
          with mitral (valve) disease I08.0
            with tricuspid (valve) disease I08.3
        tricuspid (valve) disease I08.2
          with mitral (valve) disease I08.3
    specified cause NEC I35.1
    syphilitic A52.03
  arterial I77.1
    basilar G45.0
    carotid (hemispheric) G45.1
    cerebral I67.8
    coronary (acute or subacute) I24.9
    mesenteric K55.1
    peripheral I73.9
    precerebral (multiple) (bilateral) G45.2
    vertebral G45.0
  arteriovenous I99.8
  biliary K83.8
  cardiac - *see also* Insufficiency, myocardial
    due to presence of (cardiac) prosthesis I97.11-
    postprocedural I97.11-
  cardiorenal, hypertensive I13.2
  cardiovascular - *see* Disease, cardiovascular
  cerebrovascular (acute) I67.8
    with transient focal neurological signs and symptoms G45.8
  circulatory NEC I99.8
    newborn P29.89
  convergence H51.11
  coronary (acute or subacute) I24.8
    chronic or with a stated duration of over 4 weeks I25.89
  corticoadrenal E27.40
    primary E27.1

Insufficiency, insufficient *(Continued)*
  dietary E63.9
  divergence H51.8
  food T73.0
  gastroesophageal K22.8
  gonadal
    ovary E28.39
    testis E29.1
  heart - *see also* Insufficiency, myocardial
    newborn P29.0
    valve - *see* Endocarditis
  hepatic - *see* Failure, hepatic
  idiopathic autonomic G90.09
  interocclusal distance of fully erupted teeth (ridge) M26.36
  kidney N28.9
    acute N28.9
    chronic N18.9
  lacrimal (secretion) H04.12-
    passages - *see* Stenosis, lacrimal
  liver - *see* Failure, hepatic
  lung - *see* Insufficiency, pulmonary
  mental (congenital) - *see* Retardation, mental
  mesenteric K55.1
  mitral (valve) I34.0
    with
      aortic valve disease I08.0
        with tricuspid (valve) disease I08.3
      obstruction or stenosis I05.2
        with aortic valve disease I08.0
      tricuspid (valve) disease I08.1
        with aortic (valve) disease I08.3
    congenital Q23.3
    rheumatic I05.1
      with
        aortic valve disease I08.0
          with tricuspid (valve) disease I08.3
        obstruction or stenosis I05.2
          with aortic valve disease I08.0
            with tricuspid (valve) disease I08.3
        tricuspid (valve) disease I08.1
        tricuspid (valve) disease I08.1
          with aortic (valve) disease I08.3
    active or acute I01.1
      with chorea, rheumatic (Sydenham's) I02.0
    specified cause, except rheumatic I34.0
  muscle - *see also* Disease, muscle
    heart - *see* Insufficiency, myocardial
  ocular NEC H50.9
  myocardial, myocardium (with arteriosclerosis) I50.9
    with
      rheumatic fever (conditions in I00) I09.0
        active, acute or subacute I01.2
          with chorea I02.0
        inactive or quiescent (with chorea) I09.0
    congenital Q24.8
    hypertensive - *see* Hypertension, heart
    newborn P29.0

Insufficiency, insufficient *(Continued)*
 myocardial, myocardium *(Continued)*
  rheumatic I09.0
   active, acute, or subacute I01.2
  syphilitic A52.06
 nourishment T73.0
 pancreatic K86.8
 parathyroid (gland) E20.9
 peripheral vascular (arterial) I73.9
 pituitary E23.0
 placental (mother) O36.51-
 platelets D69.6
 prenatal care affecting management of
  pregnancy O09.3-
 progressive pluriglandular E31.0
 pulmonary J98.4
  acute, following surgery (nonthoracic) J95.2
   thoracic J95.1
  chronic, following surgery J95.3
  following
   shock J80
   trauma J80
  newborn P28.5
 valve I37.1
  with stenosis I37.2
  congenital Q22.2
  rheumatic I09.89
   with aortic, mitral or tricuspid
    (valve) disease I08.8
 pyloric K31.89
 renal (acute) N28.9
  chronic N18.9
 respiratory R06.89
  newborn P28.5
 rotation - *see* Malrotation
 sleep syndrome F51.12
 social insurance Z59.7
 suprarenal E27.40
  primary E27.1
 tarso-orbital fascia, congenital Q10.3
 testis E29.1
 thyroid (gland) (acquired) E03.9
  congenital E03.1
 tricuspid (valve) (rheumatic) I07.1
  with
   aortic (valve) disease I08.2
    with mitral (valve) disease
     I08.3
   mitral (valve) disease I08.1
    with aortic (valve) disease
     I08.3
   obstruction or stenosis I07.2
    with aortic (valve) disease
     I08.2
     with mitral (valve) disease
      I08.3
  congenital Q22.8
  nonrheumatic I36.1
   with stenosis I36.2
 urethral sphincter R32
 valve, valvular (heart) - *see* Endocarditis
  congenital Q24.8
 vascular I99.8
  intestine K55.9
   acute K55.0
  mesenteric K55.1
  peripheral I73.9
  renal - *see* Hypertension, kidney
 velopharyngeal
  acquired K13.79
  congenital Q38.8
 venous (chronic) (peripheral) I87.2

Insufficiency, insufficient *(Continued)*
 ventricular - *see* Insufficiency,
  myocardial
 welfare support Z59.7
Insufflation, fallopian Z31.41
Insular - *see* condition
Insulinoma
 pancreas
  benign D13.7
  malignant C25.4
  uncertain behavior D37.7
 specified site
  benign - *see* Neoplasm, by site,
   benign
  malignant - *see* Neoplasm, by site,
   malignant
  uncertain behavior - *see* Neoplasm,
   by site, uncertain behavior
 unspecified site
  benign D13.7
  malignant C25.4
  uncertain behavior D37.7
Insulinoma
 specified site NEC - *see* Neoplasm,
  malignant
 unspecified site C25.4
 pancreas D13.7
 specified site NEC - *see* Neoplasm,
  benign
 unspecified site D13.7
Insuloma - *see* Insulinoma
Interference
 balancing side M26.56
 non-working side M26.56
Intermenstrual - *see* condition
Intermittent - *see* condition
Internal - *see* condition
Interruption
 bundle of His I44.30
 phase-shift, sleep cycle
 sleep phase-shift, or 24 hour sleep-wake
  cycle
Interstitial - *see* condition
Intertrigo L30.4
 labialis K13.0
Intervertebral disc - *see* condition
Intestine, intestinal - *see* condition
Intolerance
 carbohydrate K90.4
 disaccharide, hereditary E73.0
 fat NEC K90.4
  pancreatic K90.3
 food K90.4
  dietary counseling and surveillance
   Z71.3
 fructose E74.10
  hereditary E74.12
 glucose(-galactose) E74.39
 gluten K90.0
 lactose E73.9
  specified NEC E73.8
 lysine E72.3
 milk NEC K90.4
  lactose E73.9
 protein K90.4
 starch NEC K90.4
 sucrose(-isomaltose) E74.31
Intoxicated NEC (without dependence) –
 see Alcohol, intoxication
Intoxication
 acid E87.2
 alcoholic (acute) (without dependence) –
  see Alcohol, intoxication
 alimentary canal K52.1

Intoxication *(Continued)*
 amphetamine (without dependence) -
  see Abuse, drug, stimulant,
  with intoxication
  with dependence - *see* Dependence,
   drug, stimulant,
   with intoxication
 anxiolytic (acute) (without dependence) -
  see Abuse, drug, sedative, with
  intoxication
  with dependence - *see* Dependence,
   drug, sedative, with intoxication
 caffeine (acute) (without dependence) -
  see Abuse, drug, stimulant, with
  intoxication
  with dependence - *see* Dependence,
   drug, stimulant, with intoxication
 cannabinoids (acute) (without dependence) - *see* Abuse, drug, cannabis,
  with intoxication
  with dependence - *see* Dependence,
   drug, cannabis, with intoxication
 chemical - *see* Table of drugs and
  chemicals
  via placenta or breast milk - *see* -
   Absorption, chemical, through
   placenta
 cocaine (acute) (without dependence) -
  see Abuse, drug, cocaine, with
  intoxication
  with dependence - *see* Dependence,
   drug, cocaine, with intoxication
 drug
  acute (without dependence) -
   see Abuse, drug, by type with
   intoxication
   with dependence – *see* Dependence,
    drug, by type with intoxication
  addictive
   via placenta or breast milk - *see*
    Absorption, drug, addictive,
    through placenta
  newborn P93.8
   gray baby syndrome P93.0
  overdose or wrong substance given
   or taken - *see* Table of drugs and
   chemicals, by drug, poisoning
 enteric - *see* Intoxication, intestinal
 foodborne A05.9
  bacterial A05.9
  classical (Clostridium botulinum)
   A05.1
  due to
   Bacillus cereus A05.4
   bacterium A05.9
    specified NEC A05.8
   Clostridium
    botulinum A05.1
    perfringens A05.2
    welchii A05.2
   Salmonella A02.9
    with
     (gastro)enteritis A02.0
     localized infection(s) A02.20
      arthritis A02.23
      meningitis A02.21
      osteomyelitis A02.24
      pneumonia A02.22
      pyelonephritis A02.25
      specified NEC A02.29
     sepsis A02.1
     specified manifestation NEC
      A02.8
   Staphylococcus A05.0

313

Intoxication (Continued)
  foodborne (Continued)
    due to (Continued)
      Vibrio
        parahaemolyticus A05.3
        vulnificus A05.5
      enterotoxin, staphylococcal A05.0
    noxious - see Poisoning, food,
      noxious
  gastrointestinal K52.1
  hallucinogenic (without dependence) -
    see Abuse, drug, hallucinogen,
    with intoxication
    with dependence - see Dependence,
      drug, hallucinogen, with
      intoxication
  hypnotic (acute) (without dependence) -
    see Abuse, drug, sedative, with
    intoxication
    with dependence - see Dependence,
      drug, sedative, with intoxication
  inhalant (acute) (without dependence) -
    see Abuse, drug, inhalant, with
    intoxication
    with dependence - see Dependence,
      drug, inhalant, with intoxication
  meaning
    inebriation - see category F10
    poisoning - see Table of drugs and
      chemicals
  methyl alcohol (acute) (without depen-
    dence) – see Alcohol, intoxication
  opioid (acute) (without dependence) –
    see Abuse, drug, opioid, with
    intoxication
    with dependence – see Dependence,
      drug, opioid, with
      intoxication
  pathologic NEC (without dependence) -
    see Alcohol, intoxication
  phencyclidine (without dependence) -
    see Abuse, drug, psychoactive
    NEC, with intoxication
    with dependence - see Dependence,
      drug, psychoactive NEC, with
      intoxication
  potassium (K) E87.5
  psychoactive substance NEC (with-
    out dependence) - see Abuse,
    drug, psychoactive NEC, with
    intoxication
    with dependence - see Dependence,
      drug, psychoactive NEC, with
      intoxication
  sedative (acute) (without dependence) -
    see Abuse, drug, sedative, with
    intoxication
    with dependence - see Dependence,
      drug, sedative, with
      intoxication
  serum (prophylactic) (therapeutic)
    T80.6
  uremic - see Uremia
  volatile solvents (acute) (without
    dependence) - see Abuse, drug,
    inhalant, with intoxication
    with dependence - see Dependence,
      drug, inhalant, with intoxication
  water E87.7
Intracranial - see condition
Intrahepatic gallbladder Q44.1
Intraligamentous - see condition
Intrathoracic - see also condition
  kidney Q63.2

Intrauterine contraceptive device
  checking, reinsertion, removal Z30.43
  in situ Z97.5
  management Z30.43
  retention in pregnancy O26.3-
Intraventricular - see condition
Intrinsic deformity - see Deformity
Intubation, difficult or failed T88.4
Intumescence, lens (eye) (cataract) - see
  Cataract
Intussusception (bowel) (colon) (enteric)
  (ileocecal) (ileocolic) (intestine)
  (rectum) K56.1
  appendix K38.8
  congenital Q43.8
  ureter (with obstruction) N13.5
Invagination (bowel, colon, intestine or
  rectum) K56.1
Inversion
  albumin-globulin (A-G) ratio E88.09
  bladder N32.89
  cecum - see Intussusception
  cervix N88.8
  chromosome in normal individual Q95.1
  circadian rhythm – see Disorder, sleep,
    circadian rhythm
  nipple N64.59
    congenital Q83.8
    gestational – see Retraction, nipple
    puerperal, postpartum – see Retrac-
      tion, nipple
  nyctohemeral rhythm – see Disorder,
    sleep, circadian rhythm
  optic papilla Q14.2
  organ or site, congenital NEC - see
    Anomaly, by site
  sleep rhythm – see Disorder, sleep,
    circadian rhythm
  testis (congenital) Q55.29
  uterus (chronic) (postinfectional)
    (postpartal, old) N85.5
    postpartum O71.2
  vagina (posthysterectomy) N99.3
  ventricular Q20.5
Investigation - see also Examination Z04.9
  clinical research subject (control) Z00.6
Involuntary movement, abnormal R25.9
Involution, involutional - see also
    condition
  breast, cystic – see Dysplasia, mammary,
    specified type NEC
  depression (single episode) F32.8
    recurrent episode F33.9
  melancholia (recurrent episode) (single
    episode) F32.8
  ovary, senile – see Atrophy, ovary
  thymus failure E32.8
I.Q.
  under 20 F73
  20-34 F72
  35-49 F71
  50-69 F70
IRDS (type I) P22.0
  type II P22.1
Irideremia Q13.1
Iridis rubeosis - see Disorder, iris, vascular
Iridochoroiditis (panuveitis) - see Panuveitis
Iridocyclitis H20.9-
  acute H20.0-
    hypopyon H20.05-
    primary H20.01-
    recurrent H20.02-
    secondary (noninfectious) H20.04-
      infectious H20.03-

Iridocyclitis (Continued)
  chronic H20.1-
  due to allergy - see Iridocyclitis, acute,
    secondary
  endogenous - see Iridocyclitis, acute,
    primary
  Fuchs' - see Cyclitis, Fuchs' heterochromic
  gonococcal A54.32
  granulomatous - see Iridocyclitis,
    chronic
  herpes, herpetic (simplex) B00.51
    zoster B02.32
  hypopyon - see Iridocyclitis, acute,
    hypopyon
  in (due to)
    ankylosing spondylitis M45.9
    gonococcal infection A54.32
    herpes (simplex) virus B00.51
      zoster B02.32
    infectious disease NOS B99
    parasitic disease NOS B89
    sarcoidosis D86.83
    syphilis A51.43
    tuberculosis A18.54
    zoster B02.32
  lens-induced H20.2-
  nongranulomatous - see Iridocyclitis,
    acute
  recurrent - see Iridocyclitis, acute, recurrent
  rheumatic - see Iridocyclitis, chronic
  subacute - see Iridocyclitis, acute
  sympathetic - see Uveitis, sympathetic
  syphilitic (secondary) A51.43
  tuberculous (chronic) A18.54
  Vogt-Koyanagi H20.82-
Iridocyclochoroiditis (panuveitis) - see
  Panuveitis
Iridodialysis H21.53-
Iridodonesis H21.89
Iridoplegia (complete) (partial) (reflex)
  H57.09
Iridoschisis H21.25-
Iris - see also condition
  bombé - see Membrane, pupillary
Iritis - see also Iridocyclitis
  chronic - see Iridocyclitis, chronic
  diabetic – see E09-E13 with .39
  due to
    herpes simplex B00.51
    leprosy A30.9
  gonococcal A54.32
  gouty M10.9
  granulomatous - see Iridocyclitis, chronic
  lens induced - see Iridocyclitis,
    lens-induced
  papulosa (syphilitic) A52.71
  rheumatic - see Iridocyclitis, chronic
  syphilitic (secondary) A51.43
    congenital (early) A50.01
    late A52.71
  tuberculous A18.54
Iron - see condition
Iron-miner's lung J63.4
Irradiated enamel (tooth, teeth) K03.89
Irradiation effects, adverse T66
Irreducible, irreducibility - see condition
Irregular, irregularity
  action, heart I49.9
  alveolar process K08.8
  bleeding N92.6
  breathing R06.89
  contour of cornea (acquired) - see Defor-
    mity, cornea
    congenital Q13.4

Irregular, irregularity *(Continued)*
  contour, reconstructed breast N65.0
  dentin (in pulp) K04.3
  eye movements H55.89
    nystagmus - *see* Nystagmus
    saccadic H55.81
  labor O62.2
  menstruation (cause unknown) N92.6
  periods N92.6
  prostate N42.9
  pupil - *see* Abnormality, pupillary
  reconstructed breast N65.0
  respiratory R06.89
  septum (nasal) J34.2
  shape, organ or site, congenital NEC -
    see Distortion
  sleep-wake pattern (rhythm) G47.23
Irritable, irritability R45.4
  bladder N32.89
  bowel (syndrome) K58.9
    with diarrhea K58.0
    psychogenic F45.8
  bronchial - *see* Bronchitis
  cerebral, in newborn P91.3
  colon K58.9
    with diarrhea K58.0
    psychogenic F45.8
  duodenum K59.8
  heart (psychogenic) F45.8
  hip - *see* Derangement, joint, specified
    type NEC, hip
  ileum K59.8
  infant R68.12
  jejunum K59.8
  rectum K59.8
  stomach K31.89
    psychogenic F45.8
  sympathetic G90.8
  urethra N36.8
Irritation
  anus K62.8
  axillary nerve G54.0
  bladder N32.89
  brachial plexus G54.0
  bronchial - *see* Bronchitis
  cervical plexus G54.2
  cervix - *see* Cervicitis
  choroid, sympathetic - *see* Endophthalmitis
  cranial nerve - *see* Disorder, nerve, cranial
  gastric K31.89
    psychogenic F45.8
  globe, sympathetic - *see* Uveitis,
    sympathetic
  labyrinth - *see* subcategory H83.2
  lumbosacral plexus G54.1
  meninges (traumatic) - *see* Injury,
    intracranial
    nontraumatic - *see* Meningismus
  nerve - *see* Disorder, nerve
  nervous R45.0
  penis N48.89
  perineum NEC L29.3
  peripheral autonomic nervous system
    G90.8
  peritoneum - *see* Peritonitis
  pharynx J39.2
  plantar nerve – *see* Lesion, nerve, plantar
  spinal (cord) (traumatic) - *see also* Injury,
    spinal cord, by region
    nerve G58.9
      root NEC – *see* Radiculopathy
    nontraumatic - *see* Myelopathy
  stomach K31.89
    psychogenic F45.8

Irritation *(Continued)*
  sympathetic nerve NEC G90.8
  ulnar nerve –*see* Lesion, nerve, ulnar
  vagina N89.8
Ischemia, ischemic I99.8
  brain - *see* Ischemia, cerebral
  bowel (transient)
    acute K55.0
    chronic K55.1
    due to mesenteric artery insufficiency
      K55.1
  cardiac (*see* Disease, heart, ischemic)
  cardiomyopathy I25.5
  cerebral (chronic) (generalized) I67.8
    arteriosclerotic I67.2
    intermittent G45.9
    newborn P91.0
    recurrent focal G45.8
    transient G45.9
  colon chronic(due to mesenteric artery
    insufficiency K55.1
  coronary - *see* Disease, heart, ischemic
  heart (chronic or with a stated
    duration of over 4 weeks)
    I25.9
    acute or with a stated duration of
      4 weeks or less I24.9
    subacute I24.9
  infarction, muscle - *see* Infarct,
    muscle
  intestine (large) (small) (transient)
    K55.9
    acute K55.0
    chronic K55.1
    due to mesenteric artery
      insufficiency K55.1
  kidney N28.0
  mesenteric, acute K55.0
  muscle, traumatic T79.6
  myocardium, myocardial (chronic or
    with a stated duration of over
    4 weeks) I25.9
    acute, without myocardial infarction
      I24.0
    silent (asymptomatic) I25.6
    transient of newborn P29.4
  renal N28.0
  retina, retinal - *see* Occlusion, artery,
    retina
  small bowel
    acute K55.0
    chronic K55.1
    due to mesenteric artery
      insufficiency
  spinal cord G95.11
  subendocardial - *see* Insufficiency,
    coronary
Ischial spine - *see* condition
Ischialgia - *see* Sciatica
Ischiopagus Q89.4
Ischium, ischial - *see* condition
Ischuria R34
Iselin's disease or osteochondrosis -
    see Osteochondrosis, juvenile,
    metatarsus
Islands of
  parotid tissue in
    lymph nodes Q38.6
    neck structures Q38.6
  submaxillary glands in
    fascia Q38.6
    lymph nodes Q38.6
    neck muscles Q38.6
Islet cell tumor, pancreas D13.7

Isoimmunization NEC - *see also*
    Incompatibility
  affecting management of pregnancy
    (ABO) (with hydrops fetalis)
    O36.11-
    anti-A sensitization O36.11-
    anti-B sensitization O36.19-
    anti-E sensitization O36.19-
    Rh NEC O36.09-
      anti-D antibody O36.01-
    specified NEC O36.19-
  newborn P55.9
    with
      hydrops fetalis P56.0
      kernicterus P57.0
    ABO (blood groups) P55.1
    Rhesus (Rh) factor P55.0
    specified type NEC P55.8
Isolation, isolated
  dwelling Z59.8
  family Z63.79
  social Z60.4
Isoleucinosis E71.19
Isomerism atrial appendages (with
    asplenia or polysplenia) Q20.6
Isosporiasis, isosporosis A07.3
Isovaleric acidemia E71.110
Issue of
  medical certificate Z02.79
    for disability determination Z02.71
  repeat prescription (appliance)
    (glasses) (medicinal substance,
    medicament, medicine) Z76.0
    contraceptive pill Z30.41
      device (intrauterine) Z30.43
Itch, itching - *see also* Pruritus
  baker's L23.6
  barber's B35.0
  bricklayer's L24.5
  cheese B88.0
  clam digger's B65.3
  coolie B76.9
  copra B88.0
  dew B76.9
  dhobi B35.6
  filarial - *see* Infestation, filarial
  grain B88.0
  grocer's B88.0
  ground B76.9
  harvest B88.0
  jock B35.6
  Malabar B35.5
    beard B35.0
    foot B35.3
    scalp B35.0
  meaning scabies B86
  Norwegian B86
  perianal L29.0
  poultrymen's B88.0
  sarcoptic B86
  scabies B86
  scrub B88.0
  straw B88.0
  swimmer's B65.3
  water B76.9
  winter L29.8
Ivemark's syndrome (asplenia with
    congenital heart disease)
    Q89.01
Ivory bones Q78.2
Ixodiasis NEC B88.8

J

Jaccoud's syndrome - *see* Arthropathy, postrheumatic, chronic
Jackson's
  membrane Q43.3
  paralysis or syndrome G83.89
  veil Q43.3
Jacquet's dermatitis (diaper dermatitis) L22
Jadassohn-Pellizari's disease or aneto-derma L90.2
Jadassohn's
  blue nevus - *see* Nevus
  intraepidermal epithelioma - *see* Neoplasm, skin, benign
Jaffe-Lichtenstein (-Uehlinger) syn-drome - *see* Dysplasia, fibrous, bone NEC
Jakob-Creutzfeldt disease or syndrome - *see* Creutzfeldt-Jakob disease or syndrome
Jaksch-Luzet disease D64.89
Jamaican
  neuropathy G92
  paraplegic tropical ataxic-spastic syn-drome G92
Janet's disease F48.8
Janiceps Q89.4
Jansky-Bielschowsky amaurotic idiocy E75.4
Japanese
  B-type encephalitis A83.0
  river fever R17
Jaundice (yellow) R17
  acholuric (familial) (splenomegalic) - *see also* Spherocytosis
    acquired D59.8
  breast-milk (inhibitor) P59.3
  catarrhal (acute) B15.9
    with hepatic coma B15.0
  cholestatic (benign) R17
  due to or associated with
    delayed conjugation P59.8
      associated with (due to) preterm delivery P59.0
    preterm delivery P59.0
  epidemic (catarrhal)
    with hepatic coma B15.0
    leptospiral A27.0
    spirochetal A27.0
  familial nonhemolytic E80.4
    congenital E80.5
  febrile (acute) B15.9
    with hepatic coma B15.0
    leptospiral A27.0
    spirochetal A27.0
    due to or associated with
      ABO
        antibodies P55.1
        incompatibility, maternal/fetal P55.1
        isoimmunization P55.1

Jaundice *(Continued)*
  febrile *(Continued)*
    due to or associated with *(Continued)*
      absence or deficiency of en-zyme system for bilirubin conjugation (congenital) P59.8
      bleeding P58.1
      breast milk inhibitors to conjuga-tion P59.3
        associated with preterm delivery P59.0
      bruising P58.0
      Crigler-Najjar syndrome E80.5
      delayed conjugation P59.8
        associated with preterm delivery P59.0
      drugs or toxins
        given to newborn P58.42
        transmitted from mother P58.41
      excessive hemolysis P58.9
        due to
          bleeding P58.1
          bruising P58.0
          drugs or toxins
            given to newborn P58.42
            transmitted from mother P58.41
          infection P58.2
          polycythemia P58.3
          swallowed maternal blood P58.5
        specified type NEC P58.8
      galactosemia E74.21
      Gilbert's syndrome E80.4
      hemolytic disease P55.9
        ABO isoimmunization P55.1
        Rh isoimmunization P55.0
        specified NEC P55.8
      hepatocellular damage P59.20
        specified NEC P59.29
      hereditary hemolytic anemia P58.8
      hypothyroidism, congenital E03.1
      incompatibility, maternal/fetal NOS P55.9
      infection P58.2
      inspissated bile syndrome P59.1
      isoimmunization NOS P55.9
      mucoviscidosis E84.9
      polycythemia P58.3
      preterm delivery P59.0
      Rh
        antibodies P55.0
        incompatibility, maternal/fetal P55.0
        isoimmunization P55.0
      specified cause NEC P59.8
      swallowed maternal blood P58.5
      spherocytosis (congenital) D58.0
  hematogenous D59.9

Jaundice *(Continued)*
  hemolytic (acquired) D59.9
    congenital - *see* Spherocytosis
  hemorrhagic (acute) (leptospiral) (spirochetal) A27.0
    newborn P53
  infectious (acute) (subacute) B15.9
    with hepatic coma B15.0
    leptospiral A27.0
    spirochetal A27.0
  leptospiral (hemorrhagic) A27.0
  malignant (without coma) K72.90
    with coma K72.91
  newborn P59.9
  neonatal - *see* Jaundice, newborn
  nonhemolytic congenital familial (Gilbert) E80.4
  nuclear, newborn (see also Kernicterus of newborn) K57.9
  obstructive (see also Obstruction, bile duct) K83.1
  post-immunization - *see* Hepatitis, viral, type, B
  post-transfusion - *see* Hepatitis, viral, type, B
  regurgitation (see also Obstruction, bile duct) K83.1
  serum (homologous) (prophylactic) (therapeutic) - *see* Hepatitis, viral, type, B
  spirochetal (hemorrhagic) A27.0
  symptomatic R17
    newborn P59.9
Jaw - *see* condition
Jaw-winking phenomenon or syndrome Q07.8
Jealousy
  alcoholic F10.988
  childhood F93.8
  sibling F93.8
Jejunitis - *see* Enteritis
Jejunostomy status Z93.4
Jejunum, jejunal - *see* condition
Jensen's disease - *see* Inflammation, chorioretinal, focal, juxtapapillary
Jerks, myoclonic G25.3
Jervell-Lange-Nielson syndrome I45.81
Jeune's disease Q77.2
Jigger disease B88.1
Job's syndrome (chronic granulomatous disease) D71
Joint - *see also* condition
  mice - *see* Loose, body, joint
    knee M23.4-
Jordan's anomaly or syndrome D72.0
Joseph-Diamond-Blackfan anemia (congenital hypoplastic) D61.09
Jungle yellow fever A95.0
Jüngling's disease - *see* Sarcoidosis
Juvenile - *see* condition

K

Kahler's disease C90.0-
Kakke E51.11
Kala-azar B55.0
Kallmann's syndrome E23.0
Kanner's syndrome (autism) - *see*
    Psychosis, childhood
Kaposi's
  dermatosis (xeroderma pigmentosum)
    Q82.1
  lichen ruber L44.0
    acuminatus L44.0
  sarcoma
    colon C46.4
    connective tissue C46.1
    gastrointestinal organ C46.4
    lung C46.5-
    lymph node (multiple) C46.3
    palate (hard) (soft) C46.2
    rectum C46.4
    skin (multiple sites) C46.0
    specified site NEC C46.7
    stomach C46.4
    unspecified site C46.9
  varicelliform eruption B00.0
    vaccinia T88.1
Kartagener's syndrome or triad
    (sinusitis, bronchiectasis, situs
    inversus) Q89.3
Karyotype
  with abnormality except iso (Xq)
    Q96.2
  45,X Q96.0
  46,X
    iso (Xq) Q96.1
  46,XX Q98.3
    with streak gonads Q50.32
    hermaphrodite (true) Q99.1
    male Q98.3
  46,XY
    with streak gonads Q56.1
    female Q97.3
    hermaphrodite (true) Q99.1
  47,XXX Q97.0
  47,XXY Q98.0
  47,XYY Q98.5
Kaschin-Beck disease - *see* Disease,
    Kaschin-Beck
Katayama's disease or fever B65.2
Kawasaki's syndrome M30.3
Kayser-Fleischer ring (cornea) (pseudo-
    sclerosis) H18.04-
Kaznelson's syndrome (congenital hypo-
    plastic anemia) D61.01
Kearns-Sayre syndrome H49.81-
Kedani fever A75.3
Kelis L91.0
Kelly (-Patterson) syndrome (sideropenic
    dysphagia) D50.1
Keloid, cheloid L91.0
  acne L73.0
  Addison's L94.0
  cornea - *see* Opacity, cornea
  Hawkin's L91.0
  scar L91.0
Keloma L91.0
Kenya fever A77.1
Keratectasia - *see also* Ectasia, cornea
  congenital Q13.4
Keratinization of alveolar ridge
    mucosa
  excessive K13.23
  minimal K13.22

Keratinized residual ridge mucosa
  excessive K13.23
  minimal K13.22
Keratitis (nodular) (nonulcerative)
    (simple) (zonular) H16.9
  with ulceration (central) (marginal) (per-
    forated) (ring) - *see* Ulcer, cornea
  actinic - *see* Photokeratitis
  arborescens (herpes simplex) B00.52
  areolar - *see* Keratitis, macular
  bullosa H16.8
  deep H16.309
    specified type NEC H16.399
  dendritic(a) (herpes simplex) B00.52
  disciform(is) (herpes simplex) B00.52
    varicella B01.81
  filamentary H16.12-
  gonococcal (congenital or prenatal)
    A54.33
  herpes, herpetic (simplex) B00.52
    zoster B02.33
  in (due to)
    acanthamebiasis B60.13
    adenovirus B30.0
    exanthema (see also Exanthem) B09
    herpes (simplex) virus B00.52
    measles B05.81
    syphilis A50.31
    tuberculosis A18.52
    zoster B02.33
  interstitial (nonsyphilitic) H16.30-
    diffuse H16.32-
    herpes, herpetic (simplex) B00.5-
      zoster B02.3-
    sclerosing H16.33-
    specified type NEC H16.39-
    syphilitic (congenital) (late) A50.31
    tuberculous A18.52
  macular H16.11-
  nummular - *see* Keratitis, macular
  oyster shuckers' H16.8
  parenchymatous - *see* Keratitis,
    interstitial
  petrificans H16.8
  postmeasles B05.81
  punctata
    leprosa A30.9
    syphilitic (profunda) A50.31
  punctate H16.14-
  purulent H16.8
  rosacea L71.8
  sclerosing - *see* Keratitis, interstitial,
    sclerosing
  specified type NEC H16.8
  superficial (stellate) (striate) H16.10-
    with conjunctivitis - *see*
      Keratoconjunctivitis
    due to light - *see* Photokeratitis
    filamentary - *see* Keratitis, filamentary
    macular - *see* Keratitis, macular
    punctate - *see* Keratitis, punctate
  suppurative H16.8
  syphilitic (congenital) (prenatal) A50.31
  trachomatous A71.1
    sequelae B94.0
  tuberculous A18.52
  vesicular H16.8
  xerotic (see also Keratomalacia) H16.8
    vitamin A deficiency E50.4
Keratoacanthoma L85.8
Keratocele - *see* Descemetocele
Keratoconjunctivitis H16.20-
  Acanthamoeba B60.13
  adenoviral B30.0

Keratoconjunctivitis *(Continued)*
  epidemic B30.0
  exposure H16.21-
  herpes, herpetic (simplex) B00.52
    zoster B02.33
  in exanthema (see also Exanthem) B09
  infectious B30.0
  lagophthalmic - *see* Keratoconjunctivitis,
    specified type NEC
  neurotrophic H16.23-
  phlyctenular H16.25-
  postmeasles B05.81
  shipyard B30.0
  sicca (Sjogren's) M35.0-
    not Sjogren's H16.22-
  specified type NEC H16.29-
  tuberculous (phlyctenular) A18.52
  vernal H16.26-
Keratoconus H18.60-
  congenital Q13.4
  stable H18.61-
  unstable H18.62-
Keratocyst (dental) (odontogenic) - *see*
    Cyst, calcifying odontogenic
Keratoderma, keratodermia (congenital)
    (palmaris et plantaris) (symmetrical)
    Q82.8
  acquired L85.1
  climactericum L85.1
  gonococcal A54.89
  gonorrheal A54.89
  punctata L85.2
  Reiter's - *see* Reiter's disease
Keratodermatocele - *see* Descemetocele
Keratoglobus (congenital) H18.79
  congenital Q15.8
    with glaucoma Q15.0
Keratohemia - *see* Pigmentation, cornea,
    stromal
Keratoiritis - *see also* Iridocyclitis
  syphilitic A50.39
  tuberculous A18.54
Keratoma L57.0
  palmaris and plantaris hereditarium
    Q82.8
  senile L57.0
Keratomalacia H18.44-
  vitamin A deficiency E50.4
Keratomegaly Q13.4
Keratomycosis B49
  nigrans, nigricans (palmaris) B36.1
Keratopathy H18.9
  band H18.42-
  bullous H18.1-
  bullous (aphakic), following cataract
    surgery H59.01-
Keratoscleritis, tuberculous A18.52
Keratosis L57.0
  actinic L57.0
  arsenical L85.8
  congenital, specified NEC Q80.8
  female genital NEC N94.89
  follicularis Q82.8
    acquired L11.0
    congenita Q82.8
    et parafollicularis in cutem penetrans
      L87.0
    spinulosa (decalvans) Q82.8
    vitamin A deficiency E50.8
  gonococcal A54.89
  male genital (external) N50.8
  nigricans L83
  obturans, external ear (canal) - *see*
    Cholesteatoma, external ear

317

Keratosis *(Continued)*
  palmaris et plantaris (inherited) (symmetrical) Q82.8
    acquired L85.1
  penile N48.89
  pharynx J39.2
  pilaris, acquired L85.8
  punctata (palmaris et plantaris) L85.2
  scrotal N50.8
  seborrheic L82.1
    inflamed L82.0
  senile L57.0
  solar L57.0
  tonsillaris J35.8
  vagina N89.4
  vegetans Q82.8
  vitamin A deficiency E50.8
  vocal cord J38.3
Kerato-uveitis - *see* Iridocyclitis
Kerunoparalysis T75.09
Kerion (celsi) B35.0
Kernicterus of newborn (not due to isoimmunization) P57.9
  due to isoimmunization (conditions in P55.0-P55.9) P57.0
  specified type NEC P57.8
Keshan disease E59
Ketoacidosis E87.2
  diabetic - *see* Diabetes, by type, with complication, ketosis
Ketonuria R82.4
Ketosis NEC E88.89
  diabetic - *see* Diabetes, by type, with complication, ketosis
Kew Garden fever A79.1
Kidney - *see* condition
Kienböck's disease - *see also* Osteochondrosis, juvenile, hand, carpal lunate
  adult M93.1
Kimmelstiel (-Wilson) disease - *see* Diabetes, Kimmelstiel (-Wilson) disease
Kink, kinking
  artery I77.1
  hair (acquired) L67.8
  ileum or intestine - *see* Obstruction, intestine
  Lane's - *see* Obstruction, intestine
  organ or site, congenital NEC - *see* Anomaly, by site
  ureter (pelvic junction) N13.5
    with
      hydronephrosis N13.1
        with infection N13.6
      pyelonephritis (chronic) N11.1
    congenital Q62.39
  vein(s) I87.8
    caval I87.1
    peripheral I87.1
Kinnier Wilson's disease (hepatolenticular degeneration) E83.01
Kissing spine M48.20
  cervical region M48.22
  cervicothoracic region M48.23
  lumbar region M48.26
  lumbosacral region M48.27
  occipito-atlanto-axial region M48.21
  thoracic region M48.24
  thoracolumbar region M48.25
Klatskin's tumor C22.1
Klauder's disease A26.8
Klebs' disease (*see also* Glomerulonephritis) N05.-
Klebsiella (K.) pneumoniae, as cause of disease classified elsewhere B96.1

Klein(e)-Levin syndrome G47.13
Kleptomania F63.2
Klinefelter's syndrome Q98.4
  karyotype 47,XXY Q98.0
  male with more than two X chromosomes Q98.1
Klippel-Feil deficiency, disease, or syndrome (brevicollis) Q76.1
Klippel's disease I67.2
Klippel-Trenaunay (-Weber) syndrome Q87.2
Klumpke(-Déjerine) palsy, paralysis (birth) (newborn) P14.1
Knee - *see* condition
Knock knee (acquired) M21.06-
  congenital Q74.1
Knot(s)
  intestinal, syndrome (volvulus) K56.2
  surfer S89.8-
  umbilical cord (true) O69.2
Knotting (of)
  hair L67.8
  intestine K56.2
Knuckle pad (Garrod's) M72.1
Koch's
  infection - *see* Tuberculosis
  relapsing fever A68.9
Koch-Weeks' conjunctivitis - *see* Conjunctivitis, acute, mucopurulent
Köebner's syndrome Q81.8
Köenig's disease (osteochondritis dissecans) - *see* Osteochondritis, dissecans
Köhler-Pellegrini-Steida disease or syndrome (calcification, knee joint) - *see* Bursitis, tibial collateral
Köhler's
  disease
    patellar - *see* Osteochondrosis, juvenile, patella
    tarsal navicular - *see* Osteochondrosis, juvenile, tarsus
Koilonychia L60.3
  congenital Q84.6
Kojevnikov's, Kozhevnikof's epilepsy G40.509
  intractable G40.519
    with status epilepticus G40.511
    without status epilepticus G40.519
  not intractable G50.509
    with status epilepticus G40.501
    without status epilepticus G40.509
Koplik's spots B05.9
Kopp's asthma E32.8
Korsakoff's (Wernicke) disease, psychosis or syndrome (alcoholic) F10.96
  with dependence F10.26
  drug-induced
    due to drug abuse - *see* Abuse, drug, by type, with amnestic disorder
    due to drug dependence - *see* Dependence, drug, by type, with amnestic disorder
  nonalcoholic F04
Korsakov's disease, psychosis or syndrome - *see* Korsakoff's disease
Korsakow's disease, psychosis or syndrome - *see* Korsakoff's disease
Kostmann's disease or syndrome (infantile genetic agranulocytosis) - *see* Agranulocytosis
Krabbe's
  disease E75.23
  syndrome, congenital muscle hypoplasia Q79.8

Kraepelin-Morel disease - *see* Schizophrenia
Kraft-Weber-Dimitri disease Q85.8
Kraurosis
  ani K62.8
  penis N48.0
  vagina N89.8
  vulva N90.4
Kreotoxism A05.9
Krukenberg's
  spindle - *see* Pigmentation, cornea, posterior
  tumor C79.6-
Kufs' disease E75.4
Kugelberg-Welander disease G12.1
Kuhnt-Junius degeneration - *see* Degeneration, macula
Kümmell's disease or spondylitis - *see* Spondylopathy, traumatic
Kupffer cell sarcoma C22.3
Kuru A81.81
Kussmaul's
  disease M30.0
  respiration E87.2
    in diabetic acidosis - *see* Diabetes, by type, with ketoacidosis
Kwashiorkor E40
  marasmic, marasmus type E42
Kyasanur Forest disease A98.2
Kyphoscoliosis, kyphoscoliotic (acquired) (*see also* Scoliosis) M41.9
  congenital Q67.5
  heart (disease) I27.1
  sequelae of rickets E64.3
  tuberculous A18.01
Kyphosis, kyphotic (acquired) M40.209
  cervical region M40.202
  cervicothoracic region M40.203
  congenital Q76.419
    cervical region Q76.412
    cervicothoracic region Q76.413
    occipito-atlanto-axial region Q76.411
    thoracic region Q76.414
    thoracolumbar region Q76.415
  Morquio-Brailsford type (spinal) (*see also* subcategory M49.8) E76.219
  postlaminectomy M96.3
  postradiation therapy M96.2
  postural (adolescent) M40.00
    cervical region M40.02
    cervicothoracic region M40.03
    thoracic region M40.04
    thoracolumbar region M40.05
  secondary NEC M40.10
    cervical region M40.12
    cervicothoracic region M40.13
    thoracic region M40.14
    thoracolumbar region M40.15
  sequelae of rickets E64.3
  specified type NEC M40.299
    cervical region M40.292
    cervicothoracic region M40.293
    thoracic region M40.294
    thoracolumbar region M40.295
  syphilitic, congenital A50.56
  thoracic region M40.204
  thoracolumbar region M40.205
  tuberculous A18.01
Kyrle's disease L87.0

L

Labia, labium - *see* condition
Labile
blood pressure R09.89
vasomotor system I73.9
Labioglossal paralysis G12.29
Labium leporinum - *see* Cleft, lip
Labor - *see* Delivery
Labored breathing - *see* Hyperventilation
Labyrinthitis (circumscribed) (destructive) (diffuse) (inner ear) (latent) (purulent) (suppurative) - *see also* subcategory H83.0
syphilitic A52.79
Laceration
with abortion – *see* Abortion, by type, complicated by laceration of pelvic organs
abdomen, abdominal
wall S31.119
with
foreign body S31.129
penetration into peritoneal cavity S31.619
with foreign body S31.629
epigastric region S31.112
with
foreign body S31.122
penetration into peritoneal cavity S31.612
with foreign body S31.622
left
lower quadrant S31.114
with
foreign body S31.124
penetration into peritoneal cavity S31.614
with foreign body S31.624
upper quadrant S31.111
with
foreign body S31.121
penetration into peritoneal cavity S31.611
with foreign body S31.621
periumbilic region S31.115
with
foreign body S31.125
penetration into peritoneal cavity S31.615
with foreign body S31.625
right
lower quadrant S31.113
with
foreign body S31.123
penetration into peritoneal cavity S31.613
with foreign body S31.623
upper quadrant S31.110
with
foreign body S31.120
penetration into peritoneal cavity S31.610
with foreign body S31.620
accidental, complicating surgery - *see* Complications, surgical, accidental puncture or laceration
Achilles tendon S86.02-

Laceration *(Continued)*
adrenal gland S37.813
alveolar (process) – *see* Laceration, oral cavity
ankle S91.01-
with
foreign body S91.02-
antecubital space – *see* Laceration, elbow
anus (sphincter) S31.831
with
ectopic or molar pregnancy O08.6
foreign body S31.832
complicating delivery - *see* Delivery, complicated, by, laceration, anus (sphincter)
following ectopic or molar pregnancy O08.6
nontraumatic, nonpuerperal - *see* Fissure, anus
arm (upper) S41.11-
with foreign body S41.12-
lower – *see* Laceration, forearm
auditory canal (external) (meatus) – *see* Laceration, ear
auricle, ear – *see* Laceration, ear
axilla – *see* Laceration, arm
back - *see also* Laceration, thorax, back
lower S31.010
with
foreign body S31.020
with penetration into retroperitoneal space S31.021
penetration into retroperitoneal space S31.011
bile duct S36.13
bladder S37.23
with ectopic or molar pregnancy O08.6
following ectopic or molar pregnancy O08.6
obstetrical trauma O71.5
blood vessel - *see* Injury, blood vessel
bowel - *see also* Laceration, intestine
with ectopic or molar pregnancy O08.6
complicating abortion - *see* Abortion, by type, complicated by, specified condition NEC
following ectopic or molar pregnancy O08.6
obstetrical trauma O71.5
brain (any part) (cortex) (diffuse) (membrane) – *see also* Injury, intracranial, diffuse
during birth P10.8
with hemorrhage P10.1
focal – *see* Injury, intracranial, focal brain injury
brainstem S06.38-
breast S21.01-
with foreign body S21.02-
broad ligament S37.893
with ectopic or molar pregnancy O08.6
following ectopic or molar pregnancy O08.6
laceration syndrome N83.8
obstetrical trauma O71.6
syndrome (laceration) N83.8
buttock S31.80-
with foreign body S31.80-

Laceration *(Continued)*
calf – *see* Laceration, leg
canaliculus lacrimalis – *see* Laceration, eyelid
canthus, eye – *see* Laceration, eyelid
capsule, joint - *see* Sprain
causing eversion of cervix uteri (old) N86
central (perineal), complicating delivery O70.9
cerebellum, traumatic S06.37-
cerebral S06.33-
left side S06.32-
during birth P10.8
with hemorrhage P10.1
right side S06.31-
cervix (uteri)
with ectopic or molar pregnancy O08.6
following ectopic or molar pregnancy O08.6
nonpuerperal, nontraumatic N88.1
obstetrical trauma (current) O71.3
old (postpartal) N88.1
traumatic S37.63
cheek (external) S01.41-
with foreign body S01.42-
internal – *see* Laceration, oral cavity
chest wall – *see* Laceration, thorax
chin – *see* Laceration, head, specified site NEC
chordae tendinae NEC I51.1
concurrent with acute myocardial infarction - *see* Infarct, myocardium
following acute myocardial infarction (current complication) I23.4
clitoris – *see* Laceration, vulva
colon - *see* Laceration, intestine, large, colon
common bile duct S36.13
cortex (cerebral) – *see* Injury, intracranial, diffuse
costal region - *see* Laceration, thorax
cystic duct S36.13
diaphragm S27.803
digit(s)
hand – *see* Laceration, finger
foot - *see* Laceration, toe
duodenum S36.430
ear (canal) (external) S01.31-
with foreign body S01.32-
drum S09.2-
elbow S51.01-
with
foreign body S51.02-
epididymis – *see* Laceration, testis
epigastric region - *see* Laceration, abdomen, wall, epigastric region
esophagus K22.8
traumatic
cervical S11.21
with foreign body S11.22
thoracic S27.813
eye(ball) S05.3-
with prolapse or loss of intraocular tissue S05.2-
penetrating S05.6-
eyebrow – *see* Laceration, eyelid

Laceration *(Continued)*
  thigh S71.11-
    with foreign body S71.12-
  thorax, thoracic (wall) S21.91
    with foreign body S21.92
      back S21.229
      front S21.129
    back S21.21-
      with foreign body S21.22-
    breast – *see* Laceration, breast
    front S21.11-
      with foreign body S21.12-
  thumb S61.019
    with
      damage to nail S61.119
        with
          foreign body S61.129
      foreign body S61.029
    left S61.012
      with
        damage to nail S61.112
          with
            foreign body S61.122
        foreign body S61.022
    right S61.011
      with
        damage to nail S61.111
          with
            foreign body S61.121
        foreign body S61.021
  thyroid gland S11.11
    with foreign body S11.12
  toe(s) S91.119
    with
      damage to nail S91.219
        with
          foreign body S91.229
      foreign body S91.129
    great S91.113
      with
        damage to nail S91.213
          with
            foreign body S91.223
        foreign body S91.123
      left S91.112
        with
          damage to nail S91.212
            with
              foreign body S91.222
          foreign body S91.122
      right S91.111
        with
          damage to nail S91.211
            with
              foreign body S91.221
          foreign body S91.121
    lesser S91.116
      with
        damage to nail S91.216
          with
            foreign body S91.226
        foreign body S91.126
      left S91.115
        with
          damage to nail S91.215
            with
              foreign body S91.225
          foreign body S91.125
      right S91.114
        with
          damage to nail S91.214
            with
              foreign body S91.224
          foreign body S91.124

Laceration *(Continued)*
  tongue – *see* Laceration, oral cavity
  trachea S11.021
    with foreign body S11.022
  tunica vaginalis – *see* Laceration, testis
  tympanum, tympanic membrane – *see*
    Laceration, ear, drum
  umbilical region S31.115
    with foreign body S31.125
  ureter S37.13
  urethra S37.33
    with or following ectopic or molar
      pregnancy O08.6
    obstetrical trauma O71.5
  urinary organ NEC S37.893
  uterus S37.63
    with ectopic or molar pregnancy O08.6
    following ectopic or molar pregnancy
      O08.6
    nonpuerperal, nontraumatic N85.8
    obstetrical trauma NEC O71.81
    old (postpartal) N85.8
  uvula – *see* Laceration, oral cavity
  vagina S31.41
    with
      ectopic or molar pregnancy O08.6
      foreign body S31.42
    during delivery O71.4
      with perineal laceration – *see* Laceration,
        perineum, female, during delivery
    following ectopic or molar pregnancy
      O08.6
    nonpuerperal, nontraumatic N89.8
    old (postpartal) N89.8
  vas deferens S37.893
  vesical – *see* Laceration, bladder
  vulva S31.41
    with
      ectopic or molar pregnancy O08.6
      foreign body S31.42
    complicating delivery O70.0
    following ectopic or molar pregnancy
      O08.6
    nonpuerperal, nontraumatic N90.8
    old (postpartal) N90.8
  wrist S61.519
    with
      foreign body S61.529
    left S61.512
      with
        foreign body S61.522
    right S61.511
      with
        foreign body S61.521

Lack of
  achievement in school Z55.3
  adequate
    food Z59.4
    intermaxillary vertical dimension of
      fully erupted teeth M26.36
    sleep Z72.820
  appetite - *see* Anorexia
  care
    in home Z74.2
    of infant (at or after birth) T76.02
      confirmed T74.02
  coordination R27.9
    ataxia R27.0
    specified type NEC R27.8
  development (physiological) R62.50
    failure to thrive (child over 28 days
      old) R62.51
    adult R62.7
    newborn P92.6

Lack of *(Continued)*
  development *(Continued)*
    short stature R62.52
    specified type NEC R62.59
  energy R53.83
  financial resources Z59.6
  food T73.0
  growth R62.52
  heating Z59.1
  housing (permanent) (temporary) Z59.0
    adequate Z59.1
  learning experiences in childhood
    Z62.8
  leisure time (affecting life-style) Z73.2
  material resources Z59.9
  memory - *see also* Amnesia
    mild, following organic brain damage
      F06.8
  ovulation N97.0
  parental supervision or control of child
    Z62.0
  person able to render necessary care
    Z74.2
  physical exercise Z72.3
  play experience in childhood Z62.8
  posterior occlusal support M26.57
  relaxation (affecting life-style) Z73.2
  sexual
    desire F52.0
    enjoyment F52.1
  shelter Z59.0
  sleep (adequate) Z72.820
  supervision of child by parent Z62.0
  support, posterior occlusal M26.57
  water T73.1
Lacrimal - *see* condition
Lacrimation, abnormal - *see* Epiphora
Lacrimonasal duct - *see* condition
Lactation, lactating (breast) (puerperal,
  postpartum)
  associated
    cracked nipple O92.13
    retracted nipple O92.03
  defective O92.4
  disorder NEC O92.79
  excessive O92.6
  failed (complete) O92.3
    partial O92.4
  mastitis NEC – *see* Mastitis, obstetric
  mother (care and/or examination)
    Z39.1
  nonpuerperal N64.3
Lacticemia, excessive E87.2
Lacunar skull Q75.8
Laennec's cirrhosis K74.69
  alcoholic K70.30
    with ascites K70.31
Lafora's disease - *see* Epilepsy, generalized, idiopathic
Lag, lid (nervous) - *see* Retraction, lid
Lagophthalmos (eyelid) (nervous)
  H02.209
  cicatricial H02.219
    left H02.216
      lower H02.215
      upper H02.214
    right H02.213
      lower H02.212
      upper H02.211
  keratoconjunctivitis - *see*
    Keratoconjunctivitis
  left H02.206
    lower H02.205
    upper H02.204

Lagophthalmos *(Continued)*
  mechanical H02.229
    left H02.226
      lower H02.225
      upper H02.224
    right H02.223
      lower H02.222
      upper H02.221
  paralytic H02.239
    left H02.236
      lower H02.235
      upper H02.234
    right H02.233
      lower H02.232
      upper H02.231
    right H02.203
      lower H02.202
      upper H02.201
Laki-Lorand factor deficiency - *see* Defect,
    coagulation, specified type NEC
Lalling F80.0
Lambert-Eaton syndrome G73.1
  not associated with neoplasm G70.8
Lambliasis, lambliosis A07.1
Landau-Kleffner syndrome F80.3
Landouzy-Déjérine dystrophy or fa-
    cioscapulohumeral atrophy G71.0
Landouzy's disease (icterohemorrhagic
    leptospirosis) A27.0
Landry-Guillain-Barré, syndrome or
    paralysis G61.0
Landry's disease or paralysis G61.0
Lane's
  band Q43.3
  kink - *see* Obstruction, intestine
  syndrome K90.2
Langdon Down's syndrome - *see* Trisomy, 21
Lapsed immunization schedule status Z28.3
Large
  baby (regardless of gestational age)
      (4000g to 4499g) P08.1
  ear, congenital Q17.1
  physiological cup Q14.2
  stature R68.89
Large-for-dates NEC (infant) (4000g to
    4499g) P08.1
  affecting management of pregnancy
      O36.6-
  exceptionally (4500g or more) P08.0
Larsen-Johansson disease orosteo-
    chondrosis - *see* Osteochondrosis,
    juvenile, patella
Larsen's syndrome (flattened facies and
    multiple congenital dislocations) Q74.8
Larva migrans
  cutaneous B76.9
    Ancylostoma B76.0
  visceral B83.0
Laryngeal - *see* condition
Laryngismus (stridulus) J38.5
  congenital P28.89
  diphtheritic A36.2
Laryngitis (acute) (edematous) (fibrinous)
    (infective) (infiltrative) (malignant)
    (membranous) (phlegmonous)
    (pneumococcal) (pseudomembra-
    nous) (septic) (subglottic) (suppura-
    tive) (ulcerative) J04.0
  with
    influenza, flu, or grippe - *see*
        Influenza, with, respiratory
        manifestations
    tracheitis (acute) - *see*
        Laryngotracheitis

Laryngitis *(Continued)*
  atrophic J37.0
  catarrhal J37.0
  chronic J37.0
    with tracheitis (chronic) J37.1
  diphtheritic A36.2
  due to external agent – *see* Inflamma-
      tion, respiratory, upper, due to
  Hemophilus influenzae J04.0
  H. influenzae J04.0
  hypertrophic J37.0
  influenzal - *see* Influenza, with, respira-
      tory manifestations
  obstructive J05.0
  sicca J37.0
  spasmodic J05.0
    acute J04.0
  streptococcal J04.0
  stridulous J05.0
  syphilitic (late) A52.73
    congenital A50.59 *[J99]*
    early A50.03 *[J99]*
  tuberculous A15.5
  Vincent's A69.1
Laryngocele (congenital) (ventricular) Q31.3
Laryngofissure J38.7
  congenital Q31.8
Laryngomalacia (congenital) Q31.5
Laryngopharyngitis (acute) J06.0
  chronic J37.0
  due to external agent - *see* Inflamma-
      tion, respiratory, upper, due to
Laryngoplegia J38.00
  bilateral J38.02
  unilateral J38.01
Laryngoptosis J38.7
Laryngospasm J38.5
Laryngostenosis J38.6
Laryngotracheitis (acute) (Infectional)
      (infective) (viral) J04.2
  atrophic J37.1
  catarrhal J37.1
  chronic J37.1
  diphtheritic A36.2
  due to external agent - *see* Inflamma-
      tion, respiratory, upper, due to
  Hemophilus influenzae J04.2
  hypertrophic J37.1
  influenzal - *see* Influenza, with, respira-
      tory manifestations
  pachydermic J38.7
  sicca J37.1
  spasmodic J38.5
    acute J05.0
  streptococcal J04.2
  stridulous J38.5
  syphilitic (late) A52.73
    congenital A50.59 *[J99]*
    early A50.03 *[J99]*
  tuberculous A15.5
  Vincent's A69.1
Laryngotracheobronchitis - *see* Bronchitis
Larynx, laryngeal - *see* condition
Lassa fever A96.2
Lassitude - *see* Weakness
Late
  talker R62.0
  walker R62.0
Late effect(s) - *see* Sequelae
Latent - *see* condition
Laterocession - *see* Lateroversion
Lateroflexion - *see* Lateroversion
Lateroversion
  cervix - *see* Lateroversion, uterus

Lateroversion *(Continued)*
  uterus, uterine (cervix) (postinfectional)
      (postpartal, old) N85.4
    congenital Q51.8
    in pregnancy or childbirth - *see* sub-
        category O34.5
Lathyrism - *see* Poisoning, food, noxious,
    plant
Launois' syndrome (pituitary gigantism)
    E22.0
Launois-Bensaude adenolipomatosis
    E88.89
Laurence-Moon(-Bardet)-Biedl syn-
    drome Q87.89
Lax, laxity - *see also* Relaxation
  ligament(ous) - *see also* Disorder, ligament
    familial M35.7
    knee - *see* Derangement, knee
  skin (acquired) L57.4
    congenital Q82.8
Laxative habit F55.2
Lazy leukocyte syndrome D70.8
Lead miner's lung J63.6
Leak, leakage
  amniotic fluid - *see* Rupture, mem-
      branes, premature
  blood (microscopic), fetal, into maternal
      circulation affecting management
      of pregnancy – *see* Pregnancy,
      complicated by
  cerebrospinal fluid G96.0
    from spinal (lumbar) puncture G97.0
  device, implant or graft - *see also*
      Complications, by site and type,
      mechanical
    arterial graft NEC - *see* Complication,
        cardiovascular device, mechani-
        cal, vascular
    breast (implant) T85.43
    catheter NEC T85.638
      cystostomy T83.030
      dialysis (renal) T82.43
        intraperitoneal T85.631
      infusion NEC T82.534
        spinal (epidural) (subdural) T85.630
    gastrointestinal - *see* Complications,
        prosthetic device, mechanical,
        gastrointestinal device
    genital NEC T83.498
      penile prosthesis T83.490
    heart NEC - *see* Complication, cardio-
        vascular device, mechanical
    joint prosthesis - *see* Complications,
        joint prosthesis, mechanical,
        specified NEC, by site
    ocular NEC - *see* Complications,
        prosthetic device, mechanical,
        ocular device
    orthopedic NEC - *see* Complication,
        orthopedic, device, mechanical
    specified NEC T85.638
    urinary NEC - *see also* Complication,
        genitourinary, device, urinary,
        mechanical
      graft T83.23
    vascular NEC - *see* Complication, car-
        diovascular device, mechanical
    ventricular intracranial shunt T85.03
  joint prosthesis - *see* Complications,
      joint prosthesis, mechanical,
      specified NEC, by site
  urine - *see* Incontinence
Leaky heart - *see* Endocarditis
Learning defect (specific) F81.9

Leather bottle stomach C16.9
Leber's
  congenital amaurosis H35.50
  optic atrophy (hereditary) H47.22
Lederer's anemia D59.1
Leeches (external) - see Hirudiniasis
Leg - see condition
Legg(-Calvé)-Perthes disease, syndrome
  or osteochondrosis M91.1-
Legionellosis A48.1
  nonpneumonic A48.2
Legionnaire's
  disease A48.1
    nonpneumonic A48.2
    pneumonia A48.1
Leigh's disease G31.82
Leiner's disease L21.1
Leiofibromyoma - see Leiomyoma
Leiomyoblastoma - see Neoplasm,
  connective tissue, benign
Leiomyofibroma - see also Neoplasm,
  connective tissue, benign
  uterus (cervix) (corpus) D25.9
Leiomyoma - see also Neoplasm,
  connective tissue, benign
  bizarre - see Neoplasm, connective
    tissue, benign
  cellular - see Neoplasm, connective
    tissue, benign
  epithelioid - see Neoplasm, connective
    tissue, benign
  uterus (cervix) (corpus) D25.9
    intramural D25.1
    submucous D25.0
    subserosal D25.2
  vascular -see Neoplasm,
    connective tissue, benign
Leiomyoma, leiomyomatosis (intravascular) - see Neoplasm, connective
  tissue, uncertain behavior
Leiomyosarcoma - see also Neoplasm,
  connective tissue, malignant
  epithelioid - see Neoplasm, connective
    tissue, malignant
  myxoid - see Neoplasm, connective
    tissue, malignant
Leishmaniasis B55.9
  American (mucocutaneous) B55.2
    cutaneous B55.1
  Asian Desert B55.1
  Brazilian B55.2
  cutaneous (any type) B55.1
  dermal - see also Leishmaniasis,
    cutaneous
    post-kala-azar B55.0
  eyelid B55.1
  infantile B55.0
  Mediterranean B55.0
  mucocutaneous (American) (New
    World) B55.2
  naso-oral B55.2
  nasopharyngeal B55.2
  old world B55.1
  tegumentaria diffusa B55.1
  visceral B55.0
Leishmanoid, dermal - see also Leishmaniasis, cutaneous
  post-kala-azar B55.0
Lenegre's disease I44.2
Lengthening, leg - see Deformity, limb,
  unequal length
Lennert's lymphoma – see Lymphoma,
  Lennert's

Lennox-Gastaut syndrome - see Epilepsy,
  generalized, specified NEC
Lens - see condition
Lenticonus (anterior) (posterior) (con-
  genital) Q12.8
Lenticular degeneration, progressive
  E83.01
Lentiglobus (posterior) (congenital)
  Q12.8
Lentigo (congenital) L81.4
  maligna - see also Melanoma, in situ
    melanoma - see Melanoma
Lentivirus, as cause of disease classified
  elsewhere B97.31
Leontiasis
  ossium M85.2
  syphilitic (late) A52.78
    congenital A50.59
Lepothrix A48.8
Lepra - see Leprosy
Leprechaunism E34.8
Leprosy A30.-
  with muscle disorder A30.9 [M63.80]
    ankle A30.9 [M63.87-]
    foot A30.9 [M63.87-]
    forearm A30.9 [M63.83-]
    hand A30.9 [M63.84-]
    lower leg A30.9 [M63.86-]
    multiple sites A30.9 [M63.89]
    pelvic region A30.9 [M63.85-]
    shoulder region A30.9 [M63.81-]
    specified site NEC A30.9 [M63.88]
    thigh A30.9 [M63.85-]
    upper arm A30.9 [M63.82-]
  anesthetic A30.9
  BB A30.3
  BL A30.4
  borderline (infiltrated) (neuritic) A30.3
    lepromatous A30.4
    tuberculoid A30.2
  BT A30.2
  dimorphous (infiltrated) (neuritic) A30.3
  I A30.0
  indeterminate (macular) (neuritic)
    A30.0
  lepromatous (diffuse) (infiltrated)
    (macular) (neuritic) (nodular)
    A30.5
  LL A30.5
  macular (early) (neuritic) (simple)
    A30.9
  maculoanesthetic A30.9
  mixed A30.3
  neural A30.9
  nodular A30.5
  primary neuritic A30.3
  specified type NEC A30.8
  TT A30.1
  tuberculoid (major) (minor) A30.1
Leptocytosis, hereditary D56.9
Leptomeningitis (chronic) (circumscribed) (hemorrhagic) (nonsuppurative) - see Meningitis
Leptomeningopathy G96.19
Leptospiral - see condition
Leptospirochetal - see condition
Leptospirosis A27.9
  canicola A27.89
  due to Leptospira interrogans serovar
    icterohaemorrhagiae A27.0
  icterohemorrhagica A27.0
  pomona A27.89
  Weil's disease A27.0
Leptus dermatitis B88.0

Leriche's syndrome (aortic bifurcation
  occlusion) I74.0
Leri's pleonosteosis Q78.8
Leri-Weill syndrome Q77.8
Lermoyez' syndrome - see Vertigo, peripheral NEC
Lesch-Nyhan syndrome E79.1
Leser-Trélat disease L82.1
  inflamed L82.0
Lesion(s) (nontraumatic)
  abducens nerve - see Strabismus, para-
    lytic, sixth nerve
  alveolar process K08.9
  angiocentric immunoproliferative
    D47.z9
  anorectal K62.9
  aortic (valve) I35.9
  auditory nerve - see subcategory
    H93.3
  basal ganglion G25.9
  bile duct - see Disease, bile duct
  biomechanical M99.9
    specified type NEC M99.89
      abdomen M99.89
      acromioclavicular M99.87
      cervical region M99.81
      cervicothoracic M99.81
      costochondral M99.88
      costovertebral M99.88
      head region M99.80
      hip M99.85
      lower extremity M99.86
      lumbar region M99.83
      lumbosacral M99.83
      occipitocervical M99.80
      pelvic region M99.85
      pubic M99.85
      rib cage M99.88
      sacral region M99.84
      sacrococcygeal M99.84
      sacroiliac M99.84
      specified NEC M99.89
      sternochondral M99.88
      sternoclavicular M99.87
      thoracic region M99.82
      thoracolumbar M99.82
      upper extremity M99.87
  bladder N32.9
  bone - see Disorder, bone
  brachial plexus G54.0
  brain G93.9
    congenital Q04.9
    vascular I67.9
      degenerative I67.9
      hypertensive I67.4
  buccal cavity K13.79
  calcified - see Calcification
  canthus - see Disorder, eyelid
  carate - see Pinta, lesions
  cardia K22.9
  cardiac - see also Disease, heart I51.9
    congenital Q24.9
    valvular - see Endocarditis
  cauda equina G83.4
  cecum K63.9
  cerebral - see Lesion, brain
  cerebrovascular I67.9
    degenerative I67.9
    hypertensive I67.4
  cervical (nerve) root NEC G54.2
  chiasmal - see Disorder, optic, chiasm
  chorda tympani G51.8
  coin, lung R91
  colon K63.9

Lesion *(Continued)*
 congenital - *see* Anomaly, by site
 conjunctiva H11.9
 coronary artery - *see* Ischemia, heart
 cranial nerve G52.9
  eighth - *see* Disorder, ear
  eleventh G52.9
  fifth G50.9
  first G52.0
  fourth - *see* Strabismus, paralytic,
   fourth nerve
  seventh G51.9
  sixth - *see* Strabismus, paralytic, sixth
   nerve
  tenth G52.2
  twelfth G52.3
 cystic - *see* Cyst
 degenerative - *see* Degeneration
 duodenum K31.9
 edentulous (alveolar) ridge, associated
  with trauma, due to traumatic occlusion K06.2
 en coup de sabre L94.1
 eyelid - *see* Disorder, eyelid
 gasserian ganglion G50.8
 gastric K31.9
 gastroduodenal K31.9
 gastrointestinal K63.9
 gingiva, associated with trauma K06.2
 glomerular
  focal and segmental (see also N00-N07
   with fourth character .1) N05.1
  minimal change (see also N00-N07
   with fourth character .0) N05.0
 heart (organic) - *see* Disease, heart
 hyperchromic, due to pinta (carate) A67.1
 hyperkeratotic - *see* Hyperkeratosis
 hypothalamic E23.7
 ileocecal K63.9
 ileum K63.9
 iliohypogastric nerve G57.8-
 inflammatory - *see* Inflammation
 intestine K63.9
 intracerebral - *see* Lesion, brain
 intrachiasmal (optic) - *see* Disorder,
  optic, chiasm
 intracranial, space-occupying R90.0
 joint - *see* Disorder, joint
  sacroiliac (old) M53.3
 keratotic - *see* Keratosis
 kidney - *see* Disease, renal
 laryngeal nerve (recurrent) G52.2
 lip K13.0
 liver K76.9
 lumbosacral
  plexus G54.1
  root (nerve) NEC G54.4
 lung (coin) R91
 maxillary sinus J32.0
 mitral I05.9
 Morel-Lavallée - *see* Hematoma, by site
 motor cortex NEC G93.89
 mouth K13.79
 nerve G58.9
  femoral G57.2-
  median G56.1-
   carpal tunnel syndrome – *see* Syn-
    drome, carpal tunnel
  plantar G57.6-
  popliteal (lateral) G57.3-
  medial G57.4-
  radial G56.3-
  sciatic G57.0-
  ulnar G56.2-

Lesion *(Continued)*
 nervous system, congenital Q07.9
 nonallopathic - *see* Lesion, biomechanical
 nose (internal) J34.89
 obstructive - *see* Obstruction
 obturator nerve G57.8-
 oral mucosa K13.70
 organ or site NEC - *see* Disease, by site
 osteolytic - *see* Osteolysis
 peptic K27.9
 periodontal, due to traumatic occlusion
  K05.5
 pharynx J39.2
 pigment, pigmented (skin) L81.9
 pinta - *see* Pinta, lesions
 polypoid - *see* Polyp
 prechiasmal (optic) - *see* Disorder, optic,
  chiasm
 primary - *see also* Syphilis, primary A51.0
  carate A67.0
  pinta A67.0
  yaws A66.0
 pulmonary J98.4
  valve I37.9
 pylorus K31.9
 rectosigmoid K63.9
 retina, retinal H35.9
 sacroiliac (joint) (old) M53.3
 salivary gland K11.9
  benign lymphoepithelial K11.8
 saphenous nerve G57.8-
 sciatic nerve G57.0-
 secondary - *see* Syphilis, secondary
 shoulder (region) M75.9-
  specified NEC M75.8-
 sigmoid K63.9
 sinus (accessory) (nasal) J34.89
 skin L98.9
  suppurative L08.0
 SLAP S43.43
 spinal cord G95.9
  congenital Q06.9
 spleen D73.89
 stomach K31.9
 superior glenoid labrum S43.43
 syphilitic - *see* Syphilis
 tertiary - *see* Syphilis, tertiary
 thoracic root (nerve) NEC G54.3
 tonsillar fossa J35.9
 tooth, teeth K08.9
  white spot
   chewing surface K02.51
   pit and fissure surface K02.51
   smooth surface K02.61
 traumatic – *see* specific type of injury
  by site
 tricuspid (valve) I07.9
  nonrheumatic I36.9
 trigeminal nerve G50.9
 ulcerated or ulcerative - *see* Ulcer, skin
 uterus N85.9
 vagus nerve G52.2
 valvular - *see* Endocarditis
 vascular I99.9
  affecting central nervous system I67.9
  following trauma NEC T14.8
  umbilical cord, complicating delivery
   O69.5
 warty - *see* Verruca
 white spot (tooth)
  chewing surface K02.51
  pit and fissure surface K02.51
  smooth surface K02.61
Lethargic - *see* condition

Lethargy R53.83
Leukemia, leukemic C95.9-
 acute basophilic C94.8-
 acute bilineal C95.0-
 acute erythoid C94.0-
 acute lymphoblastic C91.0-
 acute megakaryoblastic C94.2-
 acute megakaryocytic C94.2-
 acute mixed lineage C95.0-
 acute monoblastic (monoblastic/mono-
  cytic) C93.0-
 acute monocytic (monoblastic/mono-
  cytic) C93.0-
 acute myeloblastic (minimal differentiation) (with maturation) C92.0-
 acute myeloid
  with
   11q23-abnormality C92.6-
   dysplasia of remaining hematopoe-
    sis and/or myelodysplastic
    disease in its history) C92.a-
   multilineage dysplasia 92.a-
   variation of MLL-gene C92.6-
   M6(a)(b) C94.0-
   M7 C94.2-
 acute myelomonocytic C92.5-
 acute promyelocytic C92.4-
 adult T-cell (HTLV-1-associated) (acute
  variant) (chronic variant) (lymphomatoid variant) (smouldering
  variant) C91.5-
 aggressive NK-cell C94.8-
 AML (1/ETO) (M0) (M1) (M2) (without
  a FAB classification) C92.0-
 AML M3 C92.4-
 AML M4 (Eo with inv(16) or t(16;16))
  C92.5-
 AML M5 C93.0-
 AML M5a C93.0-
 AML M5b C93.0-
 AML Me with t(15;17) and variants C92.4-
 atypical chronic myeloid, BCR/ABL-
  negative C92.2-
 biphenotypic acute C95.0-
 blast cell C95.0-
 Burkitt-type, mature B-cell C91.a-
 chronic lymphocytic, of B-cell type
  C91.1-
 chronic monocytic C93.1-
 chronic myelogenous (Philadelphia
  chromosome (Ph1) positive)
  (t(9:22) (q34;q11) (with crisis of
  blast cells) C92.1-
 chronic myeloid, BCR/ABL-positive
  C92.1-
  atypical, BCR/ABL-negative C92.2-
 chronic myelomonocytic C93.1-
 chronic neutrophilic D47.1
 CMML (-1) (-2) (with eosinophilia)
  C93.1-
 granulocytic C92.9- - *see also* Category
  C92
 hairy-cell C91.4-
 juvenile myelomonocytic C93.3-
 lymphoid C91.9-
  specified NEC C91.z-
 mast cell C94.3-
 mature B-cell, Burkitt-type C91.a-
 monocytic (subacute) C93.9-
  specified NEC C93.z-
 myelogenous C92.9- - *see also* Category
  C92
 myeloid C92.9-
  specified NEC C92.z-

Leukemia, leukemic *(Continued)*
plasma cell C90.10-
plasmacytic C90.10-
prolymphocytic
of B-cell type C91.3-
of T-cell type C91.6-
specified NEC C94.8-
stem cell, of unclear lineage C95.0-
subacute lymphocytic C91.9-
T-cell large granular lymphocytic C91.z-
unspecified cell type C95.9-
acute C95.0-
chronic C95.1-
Leukemoid reaction D72.823 - *see also*
Reaction, leukemoid
Leukoaraiosis (hypertensive) I67.8
Leukoariosis - *see* Leukoaraiosis
Leukocoria - *see* Disorder, globe, degenerated condition, leucocoria
Leukocytopenia D72.819
Leukocytosis D72.829
eosinophilic D72.1
Leukoderma, leukodermia NEC L81.5
syphilitic A51.39
late A52.79
Leukodystrophy E75.29
Leukoedema, oral epithelium K13.29
Leukoencephalitis G04.81
acute (subacute) hemorrhagic G36.1
postimmunization or postvaccinal
G04.01
postinfectious G04.00
subacute sclerosing A81.1
van Bogaert's (sclerosing) A81.1
Leukoencephalopathy (*see also* Encephalopathy) G93.49
Binswanger's F03
heroin vapor G92
metachromatic E75.25
multifocal (progressive) A81.2
postimmunization and postvaccinal
G04.01
progressive multifocal A81.2
reversible, posterior G93.6
van Bogaert's (sclerosing) A81.1
vascular, progressive I67.3
Leukoerythroblastosis D75.9
Leukokeratosis - *see also* Leukoplakia
mouth K13.21
nicotina palati K13.24
oral mucosa K31.21
tongue K13.21
vocal cord J38.3
Leukokraurosis vulva(e) N90.4
Leukoma (cornea) - *see also* Opacity, cornea
adherent H17.0-
interfering with central vision - *see*
Opacity, cornea, central
Leukomalacia, cerebral, newborn P91.2
periventricular P91.2
Leukomelanopathy, hereditary D72.0
Leukonychia (punctata) (striata) L60.8
congenital Q84.4
Leukopathia unguium L60.8
congenital Q84.4
Leukopenia D72.819
basophilic D72.818
chemotherapy (cancer) induced
D70.1
congenital D70.0
cyclic D70.0
drug induced NEC D70.2
due to cytoreductive cancer chemotherapy D70.1

Leukopenia *(Continued)*
eosinophilic D72.818
familial D70.0
infantile genetic D70.0
malignant D70.9
periodic D70.0
transitory neonatal P61.5
Leukopenic - *see* condition
Leukoplakia
anus K62.8
bladder (postinfectional) N32.89
buccal K13.21
cervix (uteri) N88.0
esophagus K22.8
gingiva K13.21
hairy (oral mucosa) (tongue) K13.3
kidney (pelvis) N28.89
larynx J38.7
lip K13.21
mouth K13.21
oral epithelium, including tongue (mucosa) K13.21
palate K13.21
pelvis (kidney) N28.89
penis (infectional) N48.0
rectum K62.8
syphilitic (late) A52.79
tongue K13.21
ureter (postinfectional) N28.89
urethra (postinfectional) N36.8
uterus N85.8
vagina N89.4
vocal cord J38.3
vulva N90.4
Leukorrhea N89.8
due to Trichomonas (vaginalis)
A59.00
trichomonal A59.00
Leukosarcoma C85.9
Levocardia (isolated) Q24.1
with situs inversus Q89.3
Levotransposition Q20.5
Lev's disease or syndrome (acquired
complete heart block) I44.2
Levulosuria - *see* Fructosuria
Levurid L30.2
Lewy body(ies) (dementia) (disease)
G31.83
Leyden-Moebius dystrophy G71.0
Leydig cell
carcinoma
specified site - *see* Neoplasm,
malignant
unspecified site
female C56.9-
male C62.9-
tumor
benign
specified site - *see* Neoplasm,
benign
unspecified site
female D27.-
male D29.2-
malignant
specified site - *see* Neoplasm,
malignant
unspecified site
female C56.-
male C62.9-
specified site - *see* Neoplasm, uncertain behavior
unspecified site
female D39.1-
male D40.1-

Leydig-Sertoli cell tumor
specified site - *see* Neoplasm, benign
unspecified site
female D27.-
male D29.2-
LGSIL (Low grade squamous intraepithelial lesion on cytologic smear of)
anus R85.612
cervix R87.612
vagina R87.622
Liar, pathologic F60.2
Libido
decreased R68.82
Libman-Sacks disease M32.11
Lice (infestation) B85.2
body (Pediculus corporis) B85.1
crab B85.3
head (Pediculus capitis) B85.0
mixed (classifiable to more than one of
the titles B85.0-B85.3) B85.4
pubic (Phthirus pubis) B85.3
Lichen L28.0
albus L90.0
penis N48.0
vulva N90.4
amyloidosis E85.4 *[L99]*
atrophicus L90.0
penis N48.0
vulva N90.4
congenital Q82.8
myxedematosus L98.5
nitidus L44.1
pilaris Q82.8
acquired L85.8
planopilaris L66.1
planus (chronicus) L43.9
annularis L43.8
bullous L43.1
follicular L66.1
hypertrophic L43.0
moniliformis L44.3
of Wilson L43.9
specified NEC L43.8
subacute (active) L43.3
tropicus L43.3
ruber
acuminatus L44.0
moniliformis L44.3
planus L43.9
sclerosus (et atrophicus) L90.0
penis N48.0
vulva N90.4
scrofulosus (primary) (tuberculous)
A18.4
simplex (chronicus) (circumscriptus)
L28.0
striatus L44.2
urticatus L28.2
Lichenification L28.0
Lichenoides tuberculosis (primary) A18.4
Lichtheim's disease or syndrome - *see*
Degeneration, combined
Lien migrans D73.89
Ligament - *see* condition
Light
for gestational age - *see* Light for dates
headedness R42
Light-for-dates (infant) P05.00
with weight of
499 grams or less P05.01
500-749 grams P05.02
750-999 grams P05.03
1000-1249 grams P05.04
1250-1499 grams P05.05

Light-for-dates *(Continued)*
  with weight of *(Continued)*
    1500-1749 grams P05.06
    1750-1999 grams P05.07
    2000-2499 grams P05.08
    and small-for-dates - *see* Small for dates
  affecting management of pregnancy O36.59-
Lightning (effects) (stroke) (struck by) T75.00
  burn - *see* Burn
  foot E53.8
  shock T75.01
  specified effect NEC T75.09
Lightwood-Albright syndrome N25.89
Lightwood's disease or syndrome (renal tubular acidosis) N25.89
Lignac(-de Toni) (-Fanconi) (-Debré) disease or syndrome E72.09
  with cystinosis E72.04
Ligneous thyroiditis E06.5
Likoff's syndrome I20.8
Limb - *see* condition
Limbic epilepsy personality syndrome F07.0
Limitation, limited
  activities due to disability Z73.6
  cardiac reserve - *see* Disease, heart
  eye muscle duction, traumatic - *see* Strabismus, mechanical
  mandibular range of motion M26.52
Lindau(-von Hippel) disease Q85.8
Line(s)
  Beau's L60.4
  Harris' - *see* Arrest, epiphyseal
  Hudson's (cornea) - *see* Pigmentation, cornea, anterior
  Stähli's (cornea) - *see* Pigmentation, cornea, anterior
Linea corneae senilis - *see* Change, cornea, senile
Lingua
  geographica K14.1
  nigra (villosa) K14.3
  plicata K14.5
  tylosis K13.29
Lingual - *see* condition
Linguatulosis B88.8
Linitis (gastric) plastica C16.9
Lip - *see* condition
Lipedema - *see* Edema
Lipemia - *see also* Hyperlipidemia
  retina, retinalis E78.3
Lipidosis E75.6
  cerebral (infantile) (juvenile) (late) E75.4
  cerebroretinal E75.4
  cerebroside E75.22
  cholesterol (cerebral) E75.5
  glycolipid E75.21
  hepatosplenomegalic E78.3
  sphingomyelin - *see* Niemann-Pick disease or syndrome
  sulfatide E75.29
Lipoadenoma - *see* Neoplasm, benign
Lipoblastoma - *see* Lipoma
Lipoblastomatosis - *see* Lipoma
Lipochondrodystrophy E76.01
Lipodermatosclerosis - *see* Varix, leg, with, inflammation
  ulcerated - *see* Varix, leg, with, ulcer, with inflammation by site
Lipochrome histiocytosis (familial) D71
Lipodystrophia progressiva E88.1
Lipodystrophy (progressive) E88.1
  insulin E88.1
  intestinal K90.81
  mesenteric K65.4

Lipofibroma - *see* Lipoma
Lipofuscinosis, neuronal (with ceroidosis) E75.4
Lipogranuloma, sclerosing L92.8
Lipogranulomatosis E78.89
Lipoid - *see also* condition
  histiocytosis D76.0
    essential E75.29
  nephrosis N04.9
  proteinosis of Urbach E78.89
Lipoidemia - *see* Hyperlipidemia
Lipoidosis - *see* Lipidosis
Lipoma D17.9
  fetal D17.9
    fat cell D17.9
  infiltrating D17.9
  intramuscular D17.9
  pleomorphic D17.9
  site classification
    arms (skin) (subcutaneous) D17.2-
    connective tissue D17.30
      intra-abdominal D17.5
      intrathoracic D17.4
      peritoneum D17.7
      retroperitoneum D17.7
      specified site NEC D17.39
      spermatic cord D17.6
    face (skin) (subcutaneous) D17.0
    head (skin) (subcutaneous) D17.0
    intra-abdominal D17.5
    intrathoracic D17.4
    legs (skin) (subcutaneous) D17.2-
    neck (skin) (subcutaneous) D17.0
    peritoneum D17.7
    retroperitoneum D17.7
    skin D17.30
      specified site NEC D17.39
    specified site NEC D17.7
    spermatic cord D17.6
    subcutaneous D17.30
      specified site NEC D17.39
    trunk (skin) (subcutaneous) D17.1
    unspecified D17.9
  spindle cell D17.9
Lipomatosis E88.2
  dolorosa (Dercum) E88.2
  fetal - *see* Lipoma
  Launois-Bensaude E88.89
Lipomyoma - *see* Lipoma
Lipomyxoma - *see* Lipoma
Lipomyxosarcoma - *see* Neoplasm, connective tissue, malignant
Lipoprotein metabolism disorder E78.9
Lipoproteinemia E78.5
  broad-beta E78.2
  floating-beta E78.2
  hyper-pre-beta E78.1
Liposarcoma - *see also* Neoplasm, connective tissue, malignant
  dedifferentiated - *see* Neoplasm, connective tissue, malignant
  differentiated type - *see* Neoplasm, connective tissue, malignant
  embryonal - *see* Neoplasm, connective tissue, malignant
  mixed type - *see* Neoplasm, connective tissue, malignant
  myxoid - *see* Neoplasm, connective tissue, malignant
  pleomorphic - *see* Neoplasm, connective tissue, malignant
  round cell - *see* Neoplasm, connective tissue, malignant
  well differentiated type - *see* Neoplasm, connective tissue, malignant

Liposynovitis prepatellaris E88.89
Lipping, cervix N86
Lipschütz disease or ulcer N76.6
Lipuria R82.0
  schistosomiasis (bilharziasis) B65.0
Lisping F80.0
Lissauer's paralysis A52.17
Lissencephalia, lissencephaly Q04.3
Listeriosis, listerellosis A32.9
  congenital (disseminated) P37.2
  cutaneous A32.0
  neonatal, newborn (disseminated) P37.2
  oculoglandular A32.81
  specified NEC A32.89
Lithemia E79.0
Lithiasis - *see* Calculus
Lithosis J62.8
Lithuria R82.99
Litigation, anxiety concerning Z65.3
Little leaguer's elbow - *see* Epicondylitis, medial
Little's disease G80.9
Littre's
  gland - *see* condition
  hernia - *see* Hernia, abdomen
Littritis - *see* Urethritis
Livedo (annularis) (racemosa) (reticularis) R23.1
Liver - *see* condition
Living alone (problems with) Z60.2
  with handicapped person Z74.2
Lloyd's syndrome - *see* Adenomatosis, endocrine
Loa loa, loaiasis, loasis B74.3
Lobar - *see* condition
Lobomycosis B48.0
Lobo's disease B48.0
Lobotomy syndrome F07.0
Lobstein(-Ekman) disease or syndrome Q78.0
Lobster-claw hand Q71.6-
Lobulation (congenital) - *see also* Anomaly, by site
  kidney, Q63.1
  liver, abnormal Q44.7
  spleen Q89.09
Lobule, lobular - *see* condition
Local, localized - *see* condition
Locked-in state G83.5
Locked twins causing obstructed labor O66.1
Locking
  joint - *see* Derangement, joint, specified type NEC
  knee - *see* Derangement, knee
Lockjaw - *see* Tetanus
Löffler's
  endocarditis I42.3
  eosinophilia J82
  pneumonia J82
  syndrome (eosinophilic pneumonitis) J82
Loiasis (with conjunctival infestation) (eyelid) B74.3
Lone Star fever A77.0
Long
  labor O63.9
    first stage O63.0
    second stage O63.1
  QT syndrome I45.81
Long-term (current) drug therapy (use of)
  agents affecting estrogen receptors and estrogen levels NEC Z79.818
  anastrozole (Arimidex) Z79.811

Long-term *(Continued)*
    antibiotics Z79.2
    anticoagulants Z79.01
    anti-inflammatory, non-steroidal
        (NSAID) Z79.1
    antiplatelet Z79.02
    antithrombotics Z79.02
    aromatase inhibitors Z79.811
    aspirin Z79.82
    birth control pill or patch Z79.3
    contraceptive, oral Z79.3
    drug, specified NEC Z79.899
    estrogen receptor downregulators
        Z79.818
    Evista Z79.810
    exemestane (Aromasin) Z79.811
    Fareston Z79.810
    fulvestrant (Faslodex) Z79.818
    gonadotropin-releasing hormone
        (GnRH) agonist Z79.818
    goserelin acetate (Zoladex)
        Z79.818
    hormone replacement (postmeno-
        pausal) Z79.890
    insulin Z79.4
    letrozole (Femara) Z79.811
    leuprolide acetate (leuprorelin)
        (Lupron) Z79.818
    megestrol acetate (Megace) Z79.818
    methadone for pain management
        Z79.891
    Nolvadex Z79.810
    non-steroidal anti-inflammatories
        (NSAID) Z79.1
    opiate analgesic Z79.891
    oral contraceptive Z79.3
    raloxifene (Evista) Z79.810
    selective estrogen receptor modulators
        (SERMs) Z79.810
    steroids
        inhaled Z79.51
        systemic Z79.52
    tamoxifen (Nolvadex) Z79.810
    toremifene (Fareston) Z79.810
Longitudinal stripes or grooves, nails
    L60.8
    congenital Q84.6
Loop
    intestine - *see* Volvulus
    vascular on papilla (optic) Q14.2
Loose - *see also* condition
    body
        joint M24.00
            ankle M24.07-
            elbow M24.02-
            hand M24.04-
            hip M24.05-
            knee M23.4-
            shoulder (region) M24.01-
            specified site NEC M24.08
            vertebra M24.08
            toe M24.07-
            wrist M24.03-
        knee M23.4-
        sheath, tendon - *see* Disorder, tendon,
            specified type NEC
    cartilage - *see* Loose, body, joint
    tooth, teeth K08.8
Loosening
    aseptic
        joint prosthesis - *see* Complications,
            joint prosthesis, mechanical,
            loosening, by site
    epiphysis - *see* Osteochondropathy

Loosening *(Continued)*
    mechanical
        joint prosthesis - *see* Complications,
            joint prosthesis, mechanical,
            loosening, by site
Looser-Milkman(-Debray) syndrome
    M83.8
Lop ear (deformity) Q17.3
Lorain(-Levi) short stature syndrome
    E23.0
Lordosis M40.50
    acquired - *see* Lordosis, specified type
        NEC
    congenital Q76.429
        lumbar region Q76.426
        lumbosacral region Q76.427
        sacral region Q76.428
        sacrococcygeal region Q76.428
        thoracolumbar region Q76.425
    lumbar region M40.56
    lumbosacral region M40.57
    postsurgical M96.4
    postural - *see* Lordosis, specified type
        NEC
    rachitic (late effect) (sequelae) E64.3
    sequelae of rickets E64.3
    specified type NEC M40.40
        lumbar region M40.46
        lumbosacral region M40.47
        thoracolumbar region M40.45
    thoracolumbar region M40.55
    tuberculous A18.01
Loss (of)
    appetite R63.0
        hysterical F50.8
        nonorganic origin F50.8
        psychogenic F50.8
    blood - *see* Hemorrhage
    control, sphincter, rectum R15
        nonorganic origin F98.1
    consciousness, transient R55
        traumatic - *see* Injury, intracranial
    elasticity, skin R23.4
    family (member) in childhood
        Z62.898
    fluid (acute) E86.9
        with
            hypernatremia E87.0
            hyponatremia E87.1
    function of labyrinth - *see* subcategory
        H83.2
    hair, nonscarring - *see* Alopecia
    hearing - *see also* Deafness
        central NOS H90.5
        neural NOS H90.5
        perceptive NOS H90.5
        sensorineural NOS H90.5
        sensory NOS H90.5
    height R29.890
    limb or member, traumatic, current - *see*
        Amputation, traumatic
    love relationship in childhood
        Z62.898
    memory - *see also* Amnesia
        mild, following organic brain damage
            F06.8
    mind - *see* Psychosis
    occlusal vertical dimension of fully
        erupted teeth M26.37
    organ or part - *see* Absence, by site,
        acquired
    ossicles, ear (partial) H74.32-
    parent in childhood Z63.4
    self-esteem, in childhood Z62.898

Loss (of) *(Continued)*
    sense of
        smell - *see* Disturbance, sensation,
            smell
        taste - *see* Disturbance, sensation,
            taste
        touch R20.8
    sensory R44.9
        dissociative F44.6
    sexual desire F52.0
    sight (acquired) (complete) (congenital)
        - *see* Blindness
    substance of
        bone - *see* Disorder, bone, density and
            structure, specified NEC
        cartilage - *see* Disorder, cartilage,
            specified type NEC
        auricle (ear) - *see* Disorder, pinna,
            specified type NEC
        vitreous (humor) H15.89
    tooth, teeth *see* Absence, teeth, acquired
    vision, visual H54.7
        both eyes H54.3
        one eye H54.60
            left (normal vision on right) H54.62
            right (normal vision on left) H54.61
            specified as blindness – *see* Blindness
        subjective
            sudden H53.13-
            transient H53.12-
    vitreous - *see* Prolapse, vitreous
    voice - *see* Aphonia
    weight (abnormal) (cause unknown)
        R63.4
Louis-Bar syndrome (ataxia-
    telangiectasia) G11.3
Louping ill (encephalitis) A84.8
Louse, lousiness - *see* Lice
Low
    achiever, school Z55.3
    back syndrome M54.5
    basal metabolic rate R94.8
    birthweight (2499 grams or less) P07.10
        with weight of
            1000-1249 grams P07.14
            1250-1499 grams P07.15
            1500-1749 grams P07.16
            1750-1999 grams P07.17
            2000-2499 grams P07.18
        extreme (999 grams or less) P07.00
            with weight of
                499 grams or less P07.01
                500-749 grams P07.02
                750-999 grams P07.03
        for gestational age - *see* Light for
            dates
    blood pressure - *see also* Hypotension
        reading (incidental) (isolated) (non-
            specific) R03.1
    cardiac reserve - *see* Disease, heart
    function - *see also* Hypofunction
        kidney N28.9
    hematocrit D64.9
    hemoglobin D64.9
    income Z59.6
    level of literacy Z55.0
    lying
        kidney N28.89
        organ or site, congenital - *see* Malpo-
            sition, congenital
    output syndrome (cardiac) - *see* Failure,
        heart
    platelets (blood) - *see*
        Thrombocytopenia

Low *(Continued)*
  reserve, kidney N28.89
  salt syndrome E87.1
  self esteem R45.81
  set ears Q17.4
  vision H54.2
    one eye (other eye normal) H54.50
      left (normal vision on right) H54.52
      other eye blind - *see* Blindness
      right (normal vision on left) H54.51
Low-density-lipoprotein-type (LDL)
  hyperlipoproteinemia E78.0
Lowe's syndrome E72.03
Lown-Ganong-Levine syndrome I45.6
LSD reaction (acute) (without depen-
  dence) F16.90
  with dependence F16.20
L-shaped kidney Q63.8
Ludwig's angina or disease K12.2
Lues (venerea), luetic - *see* Syphilis
Luetscher's syndrome (dehydration)E86.0
Lumbago, lumbalgia M54.5
  with sciatica M54.4-
    due to intervertebral disc disorder
      M51.17
  due to displacement, intervertebral disc
    M51.27
    with sciatica M51.17
Lumbar - *see* condition
Lumbarization, vertebra, congenital
  Q76.49
Lumbermen's itch B88.0
Lump - *see* Mass
Lunacy - *see* Psychosis
Lung - *see* condition
Lupoid (miliary) of Boeck D86.3
Lupus
  anticoagulant D68.62
  discoid (local) L93.0
  erythematosus (discoid) (local) L93.0
    disseminated - *see* Lupus, erythema-
      tosus, systemic
    eyelid H01.129
      left H01.126
        lower H01.125
        upper H01.124
      right H01.123
        lower H01.122
        upper H01.121
    profundus L93.2
    specified NEC L93.2
    subacute cutaneous L93.1
    systemic M32.9
      with
        with organ or system involvement
          M32.10
        endocarditis M32.11
        lung M32.13
        pericarditis M32.12
        renal (glomerular) M32.14
          tubulo-interstitial M32.15
        specified organ or system NEC
          M32.19
      drug-induced M32.0
      inhibitor (presence of) D68.62
      specified NEC M32.8
  exedens A18.4
  hydralazine M32.0
    correct substance properly admin-
      istered- *see* Table of drugs and
      chemicals, by drug, adverse effect
    overdose or wrong substance given
      or taken - *see* Table of drugs and
      chemicals, by drug, poisoning

Lupus *(Continued)*
  nephritis (chronic) M32.14
  nontuberculous, not disseminated L93.0
  panniculitis L93.2
  pernio (Besnier) D86.3
  systemic - *see* Lupus, erythematosus,
    systemic
  tuberculous A18.4
    eyelid A18.4
  vulgaris A18.4
    eyelid A18.4
Luteinoma D27.-
Lutembacher's disease or syndrome
  (atrial septal defect with mitral
  stenosis) Q21.1
Luteoma D27.-
Lutz(-Splendore-de Almeida) disease
  - *see* Paracoccidioidomycosis
Luxation - *see also* Dislocation
  eyeball (nontraumatic) - *see* Luxation,
    globe
    birth injury P15.3
  globe, nontraumatic H44.82-
  lacrimal gland - *see* Dislocation, lacrimal
    gland
  lens (old) (partial) (spontaneous)
    congenital
      syphilitic A50.39
Lycanthropy F22
Lyell's syndrome L51.2
  due to drug L51.2
    correct substance properly admin-
      istered- *see* Table of drugs and
      chemicals, by drug, adverse effect
    overdose or wrong substance given
      or taken - *see* Table of drugs and
      chemicals, by drug, poisoning
Lyme disease A69.20
Lymph
  gland or node - *see* condition
  scrotum - *see* Infestation, filarial
Lymphadenitis I88.9
  with ectopic or molar pregnancy O08.0
  acute L04.9
    axilla L04.2
    face L04.0
    head L04.0
    hip L04.3
    limb
      lower L04.3
      upper L04.2
    neck L04.0
    shoulder L04.2
    specified site NEC L04.8
    trunk L04.1
  anthracosis (occupational) J60
  any site, except mesenteric I88.9
    chronic I88.1
    subacute I88.1
  breast
    gestational – *see* Mastitis, obstetric
    puerperal, postpartum (nonpurulent)
      O91.22
  chancroidal (congenital) A57
  chronic I88.1
    mesenteric I88.0
  due to
    Brugia (malayi) B74.1
      timori B74.2
    chlamydial lymphogranuloma A55
    diphtheria (toxin) A36.89
    lymphogranuloma venereum A55
    Wuchereria bancrofti B74.0

Lymphadenitis *(Continued)*
  following ectopic or molar pregnancy
    O08.0
  gonorrheal A54.89
  infective - *see* Lymphadenitis, acute
  mesenteric (acute) (chronic) (nonspe-
    cific) (subacute) I88.0
    due to Salmonella typhi A01.09
    tuberculous A18.39
  mycobacterial A31.8
  purulent - *see* Lymphadenitis, acute
  pyogenic - *see* Lymphadenitis, acute
  regional, nonbacterial I88.8
  septic - *see* Lymphadenitis, acute
  subacute, unspecified site I88.1
  suppurative - *see* Lymphadenitis,
    acute
  syphilitic (early) (secondary) A51.49
    late A52.79
  tuberculous - *see* Tuberculosis, lymph
    gland
  venereal (chlamydial) A55
Lymphadenoid goiter E06.3
Lymphadenopathy (generalized) R59.1
  angioimmunoblastic, with dysprotein-
    emia (AILD) C86.5
  due to toxoplasmosis (acquired)
    B58.89
    congenital (acute) (subacute)
      (chronic) P37.1
  localized R59.0
  syphilitic (early) (secondary) A51.49
Lymphadenosis R59.1
Lymphangiectasis I89.0
  conjunctiva H11.89
  postinfectional I89.0
  scrotum I89.0
Lymphangiectatic elephantiasis, nonfilarial I89.0
Lymphangioendothelioma D18.1
  malignant - *see* Neoplasm, connective
    tissue, malignant
Lymphangioma D18.1
  capillary D18.1
  cavernous D18.1
  cystic D18.1
  malignant - *see* Neoplasm, connective
    tissue, malignant
Lymphangiomyoma D18.1
Lymphangiomyomatosis - *see* Neoplasm,
  connective tissue, uncertain
  behavior
Lymphangiosarcoma - *see* Neoplasm,
  connective tissue, malignant
Lymphangitis I89.1
  with
    abscess - code by site under Abscess
    cellulitis - code by site under
      Cellulitis
    ectopic or molar pregnancy O08.0
  acute L03.91
    abdominal wall L03.321
    ankle - *see* Lymphangitis, acute, lower
      limb
    arm - *see* Lymphangitis, acute, upper
      limb
    auricle (ear) - *see* Lymphangitis,
      acute, ear
    axilla L03.12-
    back (any part) L03.322
    buttock L03.327
    cervical (meaning neck) L03.222
    cheek (external) L03.212
    chest wall L03.323

Lymphangitis (Continued)
  acute (Continued)
    digit
      finger - see Lymphangitis, acute, finger
      toe - see Lymphangitis, acute, toe
    ear (external) H60.1-
    external auditory canal - see Lymphangitis, acute, ear
    eyelid - see Abscess, eyelid
    face NEC L03.212
    finger (intrathecal) (periosteal) (subcutaneous) (subcuticular) L03.02-
    foot - see Lymphangitis, acute, lower limb
    gluteal (region) L03.327
    groin L03.324
    hand - see Lymphangitis, acute, upper limb
    head NEC L03.891
      face (any part, except ear, eye and nose) L03.212
    heel - see Lymphangitis, acute, lower limb
    hip - see Lymphangitis, acute, lower limb
    jaw (region) L03.212
    knee - see Lymphangitis, acute, lower limb
    leg - see Lymphangitis, acute, lower limb
    lower limb L03.12-
      toe - see Lymphangitis, acute, toe
    navel L03.326
    neck (region) L03.222
    orbit, orbital - see Cellulitis, orbit
    pectoral (region) L03.323
    perineal, perineum L03.325
    scalp (any part) L03.891
    shoulder - see Lymphangitis, acute, upper limb
    specified site NEC L03.898
    thigh - see Lymphangitis, acute, lower limb
    thumb (intrathecal) (periosteal) (subcutaneous) (subcuticular) - see Lymphangitis, acute, finger
    toe (intrathecal) (periosteal) (subcutaneous) (subcuticular) L03.04-
    trunk L03.329
      abdominal wall L03.321
      back (any part) L03.322
      buttock L03.327
      chest wall L03.323
      groin L03.324
      perineal, perineum L03.325
      umbilicus L03.326
    umbilicus L03.326
    upper limb L03.12-
      axilla - see Lymphangitis, acute, axilla
      finger - see Lymphangitis, acute, finger
      thumb - see Lymphangitis, acute, finger
      wrist - see Lymphangitis, acute, upper limb
  breast
    gestational – see Mastitis, obstetric
  chancroidal A57
  chronic (any site) I89.1

Lymphangitis (Continued)
  due to
    Brugia (malayi) B74.1
      timori B74.2
    Wuchereria bancrofti B74.0
  following ectopic or molar pregnancy O08.89
  penis
    acute N48.29
    gonococcal (acute) (chronic) A54.09
  puerperal, postpartum, childbirth O86.89
  strumous, tuberculous A18.2
  subacute (any site) I89.1
  tuberculous - see Tuberculosis, lymph gland
Lymphatic (vessel) - see condition
Lymphatism E32.8
Lymphectasia I89.0
Lymphedema (acquired) - see also Elephantiasis
  congenital Q82.0
  hereditary (chronic) (idiopathic) Q82.0
  postmastectomy I97.2
  praecox I89.0
  secondary I89.0
  surgical NEC I97.89
    postmastectomy (syndrome) I97.2
Lymphoblastic - see condition
Lymphoblastoma (diffuse) – see Lymphoma, lymphoblastic (diffuse)
  giant follicular – see Lymphoma, lymphoblastic (diffuse)
  macrofollicular – see Lymphoma, lymphoblastic (diffuse)
Lymphocele I89.8
Lymphocytic
  chorioencephalitis (acute) (serous) A87.2
  choriomeningitis (acute) (serous) A87.2
  meningoencephalitis A87.2
Lymphocytoma, benign cutis L98.8
Lymphocytopenia D72.810
Lymphocytosis (symptomatic) D72.820
  infectious (acute) B33.8
Lymphoepithelioma (M8082/3) - see Neoplasm, malignant
Lymphogranuloma (malignant) (M9650/3) –see also Hodgkin's, disease
  chlamydial A55
  inguinale A55
  venereum (any site) (chlamydial) (with stricture of rectum) A55
Lymphogranulomatosis (malignant) (M9650/3) – see also Hodgkin's, disease
  benign (Boeck's sarcoid) (Schaumann's) D86.1
Lymphohistiocytosis, hemophagocytic (familial) D76.1
Lymphoid - see condition
Lymphoma (of) (malignant) C85.90
  adult T-cell (HTLV-1-associated) (acute variant) (chronic variant) (lymphomatoid variant) (smouldering variant) C91.5-
  anaplastic large cell
    ALK-negative C84.7-
    ALK-positive C84.6-
    CD30-positive C84.6-
    primary cutaneous C86.6
  angioimmunoblastic T-cell C86.5
  BALT C88.4
  B-cell C85.1-

Lymphoma (Continued)
  B-precursor C83.5-
  blastic NK-cell C86.4
  bronchial-associated lymphoid tissue [BALT-lymphoma] C88.4
  Burkitt (atypical) C83.7-
  Burkitt-like C83.7-
  centrocytic C83.1-
  cutaneous follicle center C82.6-
  cutaneous T-cell C84.a-
  diffuse follicle center C82.5-
  diffuse large cell C83.3-
    anaplastic C83.3-
    B-cell C83.3-
    CD30-positive C83.3-
    centroblastic C83.3-
    immunoblastic C83.3-
    plasmablastic C83.3-
    subtype not specified C83.3-
    T-cell rich C83.3-
  enteropathy-type (associated) (intestinal) T-cell C86.2
  extranodal NK/T-cell, nasal type C86.0
  extranodal marginal zone B-cell lymphoma of mucosa-associated lymphoid tissue [MALT-lymphoma] C88.4
  follicular C82.9-
    grade
      I C82.0
      II C82.1-
      III C82.2-
      IIIa C82.3-
      IIIb C82.4-
    specified NEC C82.8-
  hepatosplenic T-cell (alpha-beta) (gamma-delta) C86.1
  histiocytic C85.9-
    true C96.a
  Hodgkin C81.9
    classical C81.7-
      lymphocyte-rich C81.4-
      lymphocytic depletion C81.3-
      mixed cellularity C81.2-
      nodular sclerosis C81.1-
      specified NEC C81.7-
    lymphocyte-rich classical C81.4-
    lymphocytic depletion classical C81.3-
    mixed cellularity classical C81.2-
    nodular
      lymphocyte predominant C81.0-
      sclerosis classical C81.1-
  intravascular large B-cell C83.8-
  Lennert's C84.4-
  lymphoblastic B-cell C83.5-
  lymphoblastic (diffuse) C83.5-
  lymphoblastic T-cell C83.5-
  lymphoepithelioid C84.4-
  lymphoplasmacytic C83.0-
    with IgM-production C88.0
  MALT C88.4
  mantle cell C83.1-
  mature T-cell NEC C84.4-
  mature T/NK-cell C84.9-
    specified NEC C84.z-
  mediastinal (thymic) large B-cell C85.2-
  Mediterranean C88.3
  mucosa-associated lymphoid tissue [MALT-lymphoma] C88.4
  NK/T cell C84.9-
  nodal marginal zone C83.0-
  non-follicular C83.9-
    specified NEC C83.8-

Lymphoma *(Continued)*
   non-Hodgkin C85.9-
   see also Lymphoma, by type
      specified NEC C85.8-
   non-leukemic variant of B-CLL C83.0-
   peripheral T-cell, not classified C84.4-
   primary cutaneous
      anaplastic large cell C86.6
      CD30-positive T-cell C86.6
   primary effusion B-cell C83.8-
   SALT C88.4
   skin-associated lymphoid tissue [SALT-
      lymphoma] C88.4
   small cell B-cell C83.0-

Lymphoma *(Continued)*
   splenic marginal zone C83.0
   subcutaneous panniculitis-like T-cell
      C86.3
   T-precursor C83.5-
   true histiocytic C96.a
Lymphomatosis - *see* Lymphoma
Lymphopathia venereum, veneris A55
Lymphopenia D72.810
Lymphoplasmacyticleukemia - *see* Leuke-
   mia, chronic lymphocytic, B-cell type
Lymphoproliferation, X-linked disease
   D82.3

Lymphoreticulosis, benign (of inocula-
   tion) A28.1
Lymphorrhea I89.8
Lymphosarcoma (diffuse) C85.9- - *see also*
   Lymphoma
Lymphostasis I89.8
Lypemania -*see* Melancholia
Lysine and hydroxylysine metabolism
   disorder E72.3
Lyssa - *see* Rabies

M

Macacus ear Q17.3
Maceration, wet feet, tropical (syndrome) T69.02-
MacLeod's syndrome J43.0
Macrocephalia, macrocephaly Q75.3
Macrocheilia, macrochilia (congenital)Q18.6
Macrocolon (*see also* Megacolon) Q43.1
Macrocornea Q15.8
  with glaucoma Q15.0
Macrocytic - *see* condition
Macrocytosis D75.89
Macrodactylia, macrodactylism (fingers) (thumbs) Q74.0
  toes Q74.2
Macrodontia K00.2
Macrogenia M26.05
Macrogenitosomia (adrenal) (male) (praecox) E25.9
  congenital E25.0
Macroglobulinemia (idiopathic) (primary) C88.0
  Waldenström C88.0
Macroglossia (congenital) Q38.2
  acquired K14.8
Macrognathia, macrognathism (congenital) (mandibular) (maxillary) M26.09
Macrogyria (congenital) Q04.8
Macrohydrocephalus - *see* Hydrocephalus
Macromastia - *see* Hypertrophy, breast
Macrophthalmos Q11.3
  in congenital glaucoma Q15.0
Macropsia H53.18
Macrosigmoid K59.3
  congenital Q43.2
Macrospondylitis , acromegalic E22.0
Macrostomia (congenital) Q18.4
Macrotia (external ear) (congenital) Q17.1
Macula
  cornea, corneal - *see* Opacity, cornea
  degeneration (atrophic) (exudative) (senile) - *see also* Degeneration, macula
    hereditary - *see* Dystrophy, retina
Maculae ceruleae — B85.1
Maculopathy, toxic - *see* Degeneration, macula, toxic
Madarosis (eyelid) H02.729
  left H02.726
    lower H02.725
    upper H02.724
  right H02.723
    lower H02.722
    upper H02.721
Madelung's
  deformity (radius) Q74.0
  disease
    radial deformity Q74.0
    symmetrical lipomas, neck E88.89
Madness - *see* Psychosis
Madura
  foot B47.9
    actinomycotic B47.1
    mycotic B47.0
Maduromycosis B47.0
Maffucci's syndrome Q78.4
Magnesium metabolism disorder - *see* Disorder, metabolism, magnesium
Main en griffe (acquired) - *see also* Deformity, limb, clawhand
  congenital Q74.0

Maintenance (encounter for)
  antineoplastic chemotherapy Z51.11
  antineoplastic radiation therapy Z51.0
Majocchi's
  disease L81.7
  granuloma B35.8
Major - *see* condition
Malabar itch (any site) B35.5
Malabsorption K90.9
  calcium K90.89
  carbohydrate K90.4
  disaccharide E73.9
  fat K90.4
  galactose E74.20
  glucose(-galactose) E74.39
  intestinal K90.9
    specified NEC K90.89
  isomaltose E74.31
  lactose E73.9
  methionine E72.19
  monosaccharide E74.39
  postgastrectomy K91.2
  postsurgical K91.2
  protein K90.4
  starch K90.4
  sucrose E74.39
  syndrome K90.9
    postsurgical K91.2
Malacia, bone (adult) M83.9
  juvenile - *see* Rickets
Malacoplakia
  bladder N32.89
  pelvis (kidney) N28.89
  ureter N28.89
  urethra N36.8
Malacosteon, juvenile - *see* Rickets
Maladaptation - *see* Maladjustment
Maladie de Roger Q21.0
Maladjustment
  conjugal Z63.0
    involving divorce or estrangement Z63.5
  educational Z55.4
  family Z63.9
  marital Z63.0
    involving divorce or estrangement Z63.5
  occupational NEC Z56.89
  simple, adult – *see* Disorder, adjustment
  situational – *see* Disorder, adjustment
  social Z60.9
    due to
      acculturation difficulty Z60.3
      discrimination and persecution (perceived) Z60.5
      exclusion and isolation Z60.4
      life-cycle (phase of life) transition Z60.0
      rejection Z60.4
      specified reason NEC Z60.8
Malaise R53.81
Malakoplakia - *see* Malacoplakia
Malaria, malarial (fever) B54
  with
    blackwater fever B50.8
      hemoglobinuric (bilious) B50.8
    hemoglobinuria B50.8
  accidentally induced (therapeutically) - code by type under Malaria
  algid B50.9
  cerebral B50.0 *[G94]*
  clinically diagnosed (without parasitological confirmation) B54

Malaria, malarial (*Continued*)
  congenital NEC P37.4
    falciparum P37.3
  congestion, congestive B54
  continued (fever) B50.9
  estivo-autumnal B50.9
  falciparum B50.9
    with complications NEC B50.8
      cerebral B50.0 *[G94]*
    severe B50.8
  hemorrhagic B54
  malariae B52.9
    with
      complications NEC B52.8
      glomerular disorder B52.0
  malignant (tertian) - *see* Malaria, falciparum
  mixed infections - code to first listed type in B50-B53
  ovale B53.0
  parasitologically confirmed NEC B53.8
  pernicious, acute - *see* Malaria, falciparum
  Plasmodium (P.)
    falciparum NEC - *see* Malaria, falciparum
    malariae NEC B52.9
      with Plasmodium
        falciparum (and or vivax) - *see* Malaria, falciparum
        vivax - *see also* Malaria, vivax
        and falciparum - *see* Malaria, falciparum
    ovale B53.0
      with Plasmodium malariae - *see also* Malaria, malariae
      and vivax - *see also* Malaria, vivax
      and falciparum - *see* Malaria, falciparum
    simian B53.1
      with Plasmodium malariae – *see also* Malaria, malariae
      and vivax - *see also* Malaria, vivax
      and falciparum - *see* Malaria, falciparum
    vivax NEC B51.9
      with Plasmodium falciparum - *see* Malaria, falciparum
  quartan - *see* Malaria, malariae
  quotidian - *see* Malaria, falciparum
  recurrent B54
  remittent B54
  specified type NEC (parasitologically confirmed) B53.8
  spleen B54
  subtertian (fever) - *see* Malaria, falciparum
  tertian (benign) - *see also* Malaria, vivax
    malignant B50.9
  tropical B50.9
  typhoid B54
  vivax B51.9
    with
      complications NEC B51.8
      ruptured spleen B51.0
Malassimilation K90.9
Malassez's disease (cystic) N50.8
Mal de los pintos - *see* Pinta
Mal de mer T75.3
Maldescent, testis Q53.9
  bilateral Q53.20
    abdominal Q53.21
    perineal Q53.22

Maldescent, testis *(Continued)*
unilateral Q53.10
  abdominal Q53.11
  perineal Q53.12
Maldevelopment - *see also* Anomaly
brain Q07.9
colon Q43.9
hip Q74.2
  congenital dislocation Q65.2
    bilateral Q65.1
    unilateral Q65.0-
mastoid process Q75.8
middle ear Q16.4
  except ossicles Q16.4
  ossicles Q16.3
ossicles Q16.3
spine Q76.49
toe Q74.2
Male type pelvis Q74.2
with disproportion (fetopelvic)
    O33.3
  causing obstructed labor O65.3
Malformation (congenital) - *see also*
    Anomaly
adrenal gland Q89.1
affecting multiple systems with
    skeletal changes NEC Q87.5
alimentary tract Q45.9
  specified type NEC Q45.8
  upper Q40.9
    specified type NEC Q40.8
aorta Q25.9
  atresia Q25.2
  coarctation (preductal) (postductal)
    Q25.1
  patent ductus arteriosus Q25.0
  specified type NEC Q25.4
  stenosis (supravalvular) Q25.3
aortic valve Q23.9
  specified NEC Q23.8
arteriovenous, aneurysmatic (congeni-
    tal) Q27.30
  brain Q28.2
  cerebral Q28.2
  peripheral Q27.30
    digestive system Q27.33
    lower limb Q27.32
    other specified site Q27.39
    renal vessel Q27.34
    upper limb Q27.31
  precerebral vessels (nonruptured)
    Q28.0
auricle
  ear (congenital) Q17.3
    acquired H61.119
      left H61.112
        with right H61.113
      right H61.111
        with left H61.113
bile duct Q44.5
bladder Q64.79
  aplasia Q64.5
  diverticulum Q64.6
  exstrophy – *see* Exstrophy, bladder
  neck obstruction Q64.31
bone Q79.9
  face Q75.9
    specified type NEC Q75.8
  skull Q75.9
    specified type NEC Q75.8
brain (multiple) Q04.9
  arteriovenous Q28.2
  specified type NEC Q04.8
branchial cleft Q18.2

Malformation *(Continued)*
breast Q83.9
  specified type NEC Q83.8
broad ligament Q50.6
bronchus Q32.4
bursa Q79.9
cardiac
  chambers Q20.9
    specified type NEC Q20.8
  septum Q21.9
    specified type NEC Q21.8
cerebral Q04.9
  vessels Q28.3
cervix uteri Q51.9
  specified type NEC Q51.8
Chiari
  Type I G93.5
  Type II Q07.01
choroid (congenital) Q14.3
  plexus Q07.8
circulatory system Q28.9
cochlea Q16.5
cornea Q13.4
coronary vessels Q24.5
corpus callosum (congenital) Q04.0
diaphragm Q79.1
digestive system NEC, specified type
    NEC Q45.8
dura Q07.9
  brain Q04.9
  spinal Q06.9
ear Q17.9
  causing impairment of hearing Q16.9
  external Q17.9
    accessory auricle Q17.0
    causing impairment of hearing
        Q16.9
      absence of
        auditory canal Q16.1
        auricle Q16.0
    macrotia Q17.1
    microtia Q17.2
    misplacement Q17.4
    misshapen NEC Q17.3
    prominence Q17.5
    specified type NEC Q17.8
  inner Q16.5
  middle Q16.4
    absence of eustachian tube Q16.2
    ossicles (fusion) Q16.3
  ossicles Q16.3
  specified type NEC Q17.8
epididymis Q55.4
esophagus Q39.9
  specified type NEC Q39.8
eye Q15.9
  lid Q10.3
  specified NEC Q15.8
fallopian tube Q50.6
genital organ
  male Q55.9
    epididymis – *see* Malformation,
        epididymis
    penis – *see* Malformation, penis
    prostate – *see* Malformation, prostate
    scrotum – *see* Malformation,
        scrotum
    seminal vesicle – *see* Malformation,
        seminal vesicle
    specified type NEC Q55.8
    testis – *see* Malformation, testis
    vas deferens – *see* Malformation,
        vas deferens
    vasocutaneous fistula Q55.7

Malformation *(Continued)*
great
  artery Q25.9
    aorta – *see* Malformation, aorta
    pulmonary artery – *see* Malforma-
        tion, pulmonary, artery
    specified type NEC Q25.8
  vein Q26.9
    anomalous
      portal venous connection Q26.5
      pulmonary venous connection
          Q26.4
        partial Q26.3
        total Q26.2
    persistent left superior vena cava
        Q26.1
    portal vein-hepatic artery fistula
        Q26.6
    specified type NEC Q26.8
    vena cava stenosis, congenital
        Q26.0
gum Q38.6
hair Q84.2
heart Q24.9
  specified type NEC Q24.8
integument Q84.9
  specified type NEC Q84.8
internal ear Q16.5
intestine Q43.9
  specified type NEC Q43.8
iris Q13.2
joint Q74.9
  ankle Q74.2
  lumbosacral Q76.49
  sacroiliac Q74.2
  specified type NEC Q74.8
kidney Q63.9
  accessory Q63.0
  giant Q63.3
  horseshoe Q63.1
  hydronephrosis Q62.0
  malposition Q63.2
  specified type NEC Q63.8
lacrimal apparatus Q10.6
lip Q38.0
lingual Q38.3
liver Q44.7
lung Q33.9
meninges or membrane (congenital)
    Q07.9
  cerebral Q04.8
  spinal (cord) Q06.9
middle ear Q16.4
  ossicles Q16.3
mitral valve Q23.9
  specified NEC Q23.8
Mondini's (congenital) (malformation,
    cochlea) Q16.5
mouth (congenital) Q38.6
multiple types NEC Q89.7
musculoskeletal system Q79.9
myocardium Q24.8
nail Q84.6
nervous system (central) Q07.9
nose Q30.9
  specified type NEC Q30.8
optic disc Q14.2
orbit Q10.7
ovary Q50.39
palate Q38.5
parathyroid gland Q89.2
pelvic organs or tissues NEC
  in pregnancy or childbirth O34.8-
    causing obstructed labor O65.5

333

Malformation *(Continued)*
penis Q55.69
  aplasia Q55.5
  curvature (lateral) Q55.61
  hypoplasia Q55.62
pericardium Q24.8
peripheral vascular system
  Q27.9
  specified type NEC Q27.8
pharynx Q38.8
precerebral vessels Q28.1
prostate Q55.4
pulmonary
  artery Q25.9
    atresia Q25.5
    specified type NEC Q25.7
    stenosis Q25.6
  valve Q22.3
renal artery Q27.2
respiratory system Q34.9
retina Q14.1
scrotum - *see* Malformation, testis
  and scrotum
seminal vesicles Q55.4
sense organs NEC Q07.9
skin Q82.9
specified NEC Q89.8
spinal
  cord Q06.9
  nerve root Q07.8
spine Q76.49
  kyphosis - *see* Kyphosis,
    congenital
  lordosis - *see* Lordosis,
    congenital
spleen Q89.09
stomach Q40.3
  specified type NEC Q40.2
teeth, tooth K00.9
tendon Q79.9
testis and scrotum Q55.20
  aplasia Q55.0
  hypoplasia Q55.1
  polyorchism Q55.21
  retractile testis Q55.22
  scrotal transposition Q55.23
  specified NEC Q55.29
throat Q38.8
thorax, bony Q76.9
thyroid gland Q89.2
tongue (congenital) Q38.3
  hypertrophy Q38.2
  tie Q38.1
trachea Q32.1
tricuspid valve Q22.9
  specified type NEC Q22.8
umbilical cord NEC (complicating
  delivery) O69.89
umbilicus Q89.9
ureter Q62.8
  agenesis Q62.4
  duplication Q62.5
  malposition – *see* Malposition,
    congenital, ureter
  obstructive defect – *see* Defect,
    obstructive, ureter
  vesico-uretero-renal reflux
    Q62.7
urethra Q64.79
  aplasia Q64.5
  duplication Q64.74
  posterior valves Q64.2
  prolapse Q64.71
  stricture Q64.32

Malformation *(Continued)*
urinary system Q64.9
uterus Q51.9
  specified type NEC Q51.8
vagina Q52.4
vascular system, peripheral Q27.9
vas deferens Q55.4
  atresia Q55.3
venous - *see* Anomaly, vein(s)
vulva Q52.70
Malfunction - *see also* Dysfunction
cardiac electronic device T82.119
  electrode T82.110
  pulse generator T82.111
  specified type NEC T82.118
catheter device NEC T85.618
  cystostomy T83.010
  dialysis (renal) (vascular) T82.41
    intraperitoneal T85.611
  infusion NEC T82.514
    spinal (epidural) (subdural) T85.610
  urinary, indwelling T83.018
colostomy K94.03
  valve K94.03
cystostomy (stoma) N99.512
  catheter T83.010
enteric stoma K94.13
enterostomy K94.13
esophagostomy K94.33
gastroenteric K31.89
gastrostomy K94.23
ileostomy K94.13
  valve K94.13
jejunostomy K94.13
pacemaker - *see* Malfunction, cardiac
  electronic device
prosthetic device, internal - *see*
  Complications, prosthetic device,
  by site, mechanical
tracheostomy J95.03
urinary device NEC - *see* Complication,
  genitourinary, device, urinary,
  mechanical
valve
  colostomy K94.03
  heart T82.09
  ileostomy K94.13
vascular graft or shunt NEC - *see*
  Complication, cardiovascular
  device, mechanical, vascular
ventricular (communicating shunt)
  T85.01
Malherbe's tumor - *see* Neoplasm, skin,
  benign
Malibu disease L98.8-
Malignancy - *see also* Neoplasm,
  malignant
  unspecified site (primary) (secondary)
    C80.1
Malignant - *see* condition
Malingerer, malingering Z76.5
Mallet finger (acquired) - *see* Deformity,
  finger, mallet finger
  congenital Q74.0
  sequelae of rickets E64.3
Malleus A24.0
Mallory's bodies R89.7
Mallory-Weiss syndrome K22.6
Malnutrition E46
degree
  first E44.1
  mild E44.1
  moderate E44.0
  second E44.0

Malnutrition *(Continued)*
degree *(Continued)*
  severe (protein-energy) E43
    intermediate form E42
      with
        kwashiorkor (and marasmus)
        E42
        marasmus E41
  third E43
following gastrointestinal surgery K91.2
intrauterine
  light-for-dates - *see* Light for dates
  small-for-dates - *see* Small for dates
lack of care, or neglect (child) (infant)
  T76.02
  confirmed T74.02
malignant E40
protein E46
  calorie
    mild E44.1
    moderate E44.0
    severe E43
      intermediate form E42
        with
          kwashiorkor (and maras-
          mus) E42
          marasmus E41
  energy E46
    mild E44.1
    moderate E44.0
    severe E43
      intermediate form E42
        with
          kwashiorkor (and maras-
          mus) E42
          marasmus E41
  severe (protein-energy) E43
    with
      kwashiorkor (and marasmus) E42
      marasmus E41
Malocclusion (teeth) M26.4
Angle's M26.219
  class I M26.211
  class II M26.212
  class III M26.213
due to
  abnormal swallowing M26.59
  mouth breathing M26.59
  tongue, lip or finger habits M26.59
temporomandibular (joint) M26.69
Malposition
cervix - *see* Malposition, uterus
congenital
  adrenal (gland) Q89.1
  alimentary tract Q45.8
    lower Q43.8
    upper Q40.8
  aorta Q25.4
  appendix Q43.8
  arterial trunk Q20.0
  artery (peripheral) Q27.8
    coronary Q24.5
    digestive system Q27.8
    lower limb Q27.8
    pulmonary Q25.7
    specified site NEC Q27.8
    upper limb Q27.8
  auditory canal Q17.8
    causing impairment of hearing
      Q16.9
  auricle (ear) Q17.4
    causing impairment of hearing
      Q16.9
  cervical Q18.2

Malposition *(Continued)*
  congenital *(Continued)*
    biliary duct or passage Q44.5
    bladder (mucosa) – *see* Exstrophy,
        bladder
    brachial plexus Q07.8
    brain tissue Q04.8
    breast Q83.8
    bronchus Q32.4
    cecum Q43.8
    clavicle Q74.0
    colon Q43.8
    digestive organ or tract NEC Q45.8
      lower Q43.8
      upper Q40.8
    ear (auricle) (external) Q17.4
      ossicles Q16.3
    endocrine (gland) NEC Q89.2
    epiglottis Q31.8
    eustachian tube Q17.8
    eye Q15.8
    facial features Q18.8
    fallopian tube Q50.6
    finger(s) Q68.1
      supernumerary Q69.0
    foot Q66.9
    gallbladder Q44.1
    gastrointestinal tract Q45.8
    genitalia, genital organ(s) or tract
      female Q52.8
        external Q52.79
        internal NEC Q52.8
      male Q55.8
    glottis Q31.8
    hand Q68.1
    heart Q24.8
      dextrocardia Q24.0
        with complete transposition of
            viscera Q89.3
    hepatic duct Q44.5
    hip (joint) Q65.8
    intestine (large) (small) Q43.8
      with anomalous adhesions, fixation
          or malrotation Q43.3
    joint NEC Q68.8
    kidney Q63.2
    larynx Q31.8
    limb Q68.8
      lower Q68.8
      upper Q68.8
    liver Q44.7
    lung (lobe) Q33.8
    nail(s) Q84.6
    nerve Q07.8
    nervous system NEC Q07.8
    nose, nasal (septum) Q30.8
    organ or site not listed - *see* Anomaly,
        by site
    ovary Q50.39
    pancreas Q45.3
    parathyroid (gland) Q89.2
    patella Q74.1
    peripheral vascular system Q27.8
    pituitary (gland) Q89.2
    respiratory organ or system NEC
        Q34.8
    rib (cage) Q76.6
      supernumerary in cervical region
          Q76.5
    scapula Q74.0
    shoulder Q74.0
    spinal cord Q06.8
    spleen Q89.09
    sternum NEC Q76.7

Malposition *(Continued)*
  congenital *(Continued)*
    stomach Q40.2
    symphysis pubis Q74.2
    thymus (gland) Q89.2
    thyroid (gland) (tissue) Q89.2
      cartilage Q31.8
    toe(s) Q66.9
      supernumerary Q69.2
    tongue Q38.3
    trachea Q32.1
    ureter Q62.60
      deviation Q62.61
      displacement Q62.62
      ectopia Q62.63
      specified type NEC Q62.69
    uterus Q51.8
    vein(s) (peripheral) Q27.8
      great Q26.8
    vena cava (inferior) (superior)
        Q26.8
  device, implant or graft (*see also*
      Complications, by site and type,
      mechanical) T85.628
    arterial graft NEC - *see* Complication,
        cardiovascular device, mechani-
        cal, vascular
    breast (implant) T85.42
    catheter NEC T85.628
      cystostomy T83.020
      dialysis (renal) T82.42
        intraperitoneal T85.621
      infusion NEC T82.524
        spinal (epidural) (subdural)
            T85.620
    electronic (electrode) (pulse genera-
        tor) (stimulator)
      bone T84.320
      cardiac T82.129
        electrode T82.120
        pulse generator T82.121
        specified type NEC T82.128
      nervous system - *see* Complication,
          prosthetic device, mechani-
          cal, electronic nervous system
          stimulator
      urinary - *see* Complication,
          genitourinary, device, urinary,
          mechanical
    fixation, internal (orthopedic) NEC
        - *see* Complication, fixation
        device, mechanical
    gastrointestinal - *see* Complications,
        prosthetic device, mechanical,
        gastrointestinal device
    genital NEC T83.428
      intrauterine contraceptive device
          T83.32
      penile prosthesis T83.420
    heart NEC - *see* Complication,
        cardiovascular device,
        mechanical
    joint prosthesis – *see* Complication,
        joint prosthesis, mechanical
    ocular NEC - *see* Complications,
        prosthetic device, mechanical,
        ocular device
    orthopedic NEC - *see* Complication,
        orthopedic, device, mechanical
    specified NEC T85.628
    urinary NEC - *see also* Complication,
        genitourinary, device, urinary,
        mechanical
      graft T83.22

Malposition *(Continued)*
  device, implant or graft *(Continued)*
    vascular NEC - *see* Complication,
        cardiovascular device,
        mechanical
    ventricular intracranial shunt T85.02
  fetus - *see* Pregnancy, complicated by
      (management affected by), presen-
      tation, fetal
  gallbladder K82.8
  gastrointestinal tract, congenital Q45.8
  heart, congenital NEC Q24.8
  joint prosthesis - *see* Complications,
      joint prosthesis, mechanical, dis-
      placement, by site
  stomach K31.89
    congenital Q40.2
  tooth, teeth, fully erupted M26.30
  uterus (acute) (acquired) (adherent)
      (asymptomatic) (postinfectional)
      (postpartal, old) N85.4
    anteflexion or anteversion N85.4
      congenital Q51.8
    flexion N85.4
      lateral - *see* Lateroversion, uterus
    inversion N85.5
    lateral (flexion) (version) - *see* Latero-
        version, uterus
    retroflexion or retroversion - *see* Ret-
        roversion, uterus
Malposture R29.3
Malrotation
  cecum Q43.3
  colon Q43.3
  intestine Q43.3
  kidney Q63.2
Maltreatment
  adult
    abandonment
      confirmed T74.01
      suspected T76.01
    confirmed T74.91
    history of Z91.419
    neglect
      confirmed T74.01
      suspected T76.01
    physical abuse
      confirmed T74.11
      suspected T76.11
    psychological abuse
      confirmed T74.31
      suspected T76.31
      history of Z91.411
    sexual abuse
      confirmed T74.21
      suspected T76.21
    suspected T76.91
  child
    abandonment
      confirmed T74.02
      suspected T76.02
    confirmed T74.92
    history of - *see* History, personal (of),
        abuse
    neglect
      confirmed T74.02
      history of - *see* History, personal
          (of), abuse
      suspected T76.02
    physical abuse
      confirmed T74.12
      history of - *see* History, personal
          (of), abuse
      suspected T76.12

Maltreatment *(Continued)*
  child *(Continued)*
    psychological abuse
      confirmed T74.32
      history of - *see* History, personal
        (of), abuse
      suspected T76.32
    sexual abuse
      confirmed T74.22
      history of - *see* History, personal
        (of), abuse
      suspected T76.22
    suspected T76.92
  personal history of Z91.89
Malta fever - *see* Brucellosis
Maltworker's lung J67.4
Malunion, fracture - *see* Fracture, by site
Mammillitis N61
  puerperal, postpartum O91.02
Mammitis - *see* Mastitis
Mammogram (examination) Z12.39
  routine Z12.31
Mammoplasia N62
Management (of)
  bone conduction hearing device (implanted) Z45.320
  cardiac pacemaker NEC Z45.018
  cerebrospinal fluid drainage device Z45.41
  cochlear device (implanted) Z45.321
  contraceptive Z30.9
    specified NEC Z30.8
  implanted device Z45.9
    specified NEC Z45.89
  infusion pump Z45.1
  procreative Z31.9
    male factor infertility in female Z31.81
    specified NEC Z31.89
  prosthesis (external) (see also Fitting) Z44.9
    implanted Z45.9
      specified NEC Z45.89
  renal dialysis catheter Z49.01
  vascular access device Z45.2
Mangled – *see* specified injury by site
Mania (monopolar) - *see also* Disorder, mood, manic episode
  with psychotic symptoms F30.2
  without psychotic symptoms F30.10
    mild F30.11
    moderate F30.12
    severe F30.13
  Bell's F30.8
  chronic (recurrent) F31.89
  hysterical F44.89
  puerperal F30.8
  recurrent F31.89
Manic-depressive insanity, psychosis, or syndrome - *see* Disorder, bipolar
Mannosidosis E77.1
Mansonelliasis, mansonellosis B74.4
Manson's
  disease B65.1
  schistosomiasis B65.1
Manual - *see* condition
Maple-bark-stripper's lung (disease) J67.6
Maple-syrup-urine disease E71.0
Marable's syndrome (celiac artery compression) I77.4
Marasmus E41
  due to malnutrition E41
  intestinal E41
  nutritional E41
  senile R54
  tuberculous NEC - *see* Tuberculosis

Marble
  bones Q78.2
  skin R23.8
Marburg virus disease A98.3
March
  fracture - *see* Fracture, traumatic, stress, by site
  hemoglobinuria D59.6
Marchesani(-Weill) syndrome Q87.0
Marchiafava(-Bignami) syndrome or disease G37.1
Marchiafava-Micheli syndrome D59.5
Marcus Gunn's syndrome Q07.8
Marfan's syndrome - *see* Syndrome, Marfan's
Marie-Bamberger disease - *see* Osteoarthropathy, hypertrophic, specified NEC
Marie-Charcot-Tooth neuropathic muscular atrophy G60.0
Marie's
  cerebellar ataxia (late-onset) G11.2
  disease or syndrome (acromegaly) E22.0
Marie-Strümpell arthritis, disease or spondylitis - *see* Spondylitis, ankylosing
Marion's disease (bladder neck obstruction) N32.0
Marital conflict Z63.0
Mark
  port wine Q82.5
  raspberry Q82.5
  strawberry Q82.5
  stretch L90.6
  tattoo L81.8
Marker heterochromatin - *see* Extra, marker chromosomes
Maroteaux-Lamy syndrome (mild) (severe) E76.29
Marrow (bone)
  arrest D61.9
  poor function D75.89
Marseilles fever A77.1
Marsh fever - *see* Malaria
Marshall's (hidrotic) ectodermal dysplasia Q82.4
Marsh's disease (exophthalmic goiter) E05.00
  with storm E05.01
Masculinization (female) with adrenal hyperplasia E25.9
  congenital E25.0
Masculinovoblastoma D27.-
Masochism (sexual) F65.51
Mason's lung J62.8
Mass
  abdominal R19.00
    epigastric R19.06
    generalized R19.07
    left lower quadrant R19.04
    left upper quadrant R19.02
    periumbilic R19.05
    right lower quadrant R19.03
    right upper quadrant R19.01
    specified site NEC R19.09
  breast N63
  chest R22.2
  cystic - *see* Cyst
  ear - *see* subcategory H93.8
  head R22.0
  intra-abdominal (diffuse) (generalized) – *see* Mass, abdominal
  kidney N28.89
  liver R16.0

Mass *(Continued)*
  localized (skin) R22.9
    chest R22.2
    head R22.0
    limb
      lower R22.4-
      upper R22.3-
    neck R22.1
    trunk R22.2
  lung R91
  malignant - *see* Neoplasm, malignant
  neck R22.1
  pelvic (diffuse) (generalized) – *see* Mass, abdominal
  specified organ NEC - *see* Disease, by site
  splenic R16.1
  substernal thyroid - *see* Goiter
  superficial (localized) R22.9
  umbilical (diffuse) (generalized) R19.09
Massive - *see* condition
Mast cell
  disease, systemic tissue D47.0
  leukemia C94.3-
  sarcoma C96.2
  tumor D47.0
    malignant C96.2
Mastalgia N64.4
Masters-Allen syndrome N83.8
Mastitis (acute) (diffuse) (nonpuerperal) (subacute) N61
  chronic (cystic) – *see* Mastopathy, cystic
  cystic (Schimmelbusch's type) – *see* Mastopathy, cystic
  fibrocystic – *see* Mastopathy, cystic
  infective N61
    newborn P39.0
  interstitial, gestational or puerperal – *see* Mastitis, obstetric
  neonatal (noninfective) P83.4
    infective P39.0
  obstetric (interstitial) (nonpurulent)
    associated with
      lactation O91.23
      pregnancy O91.21-
      puerperium O91.22
    purulent
      associated with
        lactation O91.13
        pregnancy O91.11-
        puerperium O91.12
  periductal – *see* Ectasia, mammary duct
  phlegmonous – *see* Mastopathy, cystic
  plasma cell - *see* Ectasia, mammary duct
Mastocytoma D47.0
  malignant C96.2
Mastocytosis Q82.2
  aggressive systemic C96.2
  indolent systemic D47.0
  malignant C96.2
  systemic, associated with clonal hematopoetic non-mast-cell disease (SM-AHNMD) D47.0
Mastodynia N64.4
Mastoid - *see* condition
Mastoidalgia - *see* subcategory H92.0
Mastoiditis (coalescent) (hemorrhagic) (suppurative) H70.9-
  acute, subacute H70.00-
    complicated NEC H70.09-
    subperiosteal H70.01-
  chronic (necrotic) (recurrent) H70.1-

Mastoiditis (Continued)
  in (due to)
    infectious disease NEC B99 [H75.0-]
    parasitic disease NEC B89 [H75.0-]
    tuberculosis A18.03
  petrositis – see Petrositis
  postauricular fistula – see Fistula,
    postauricular
  specified NEC H70.89-
  tuberculous A18.03
Mastopathy, mastopathia N64.9
  chronica cystica – see Mastopathy, cystic
  cystic (chronic) (diffuse) N60.1
    with epithelial proliferation N60.3-
  diffuse cystic—see Mastopathy, cystic
  estrogenic, oestrogenica N64.89
  ovarian origin N64.89
Mastoplasia, mastoplastia N62
Masturbation (excessive) F98.8
Maternal care (for) - see Pregnancy (com-
    plicated by) (management affected
    by)
Matheiu's disease (leptospiral jaundice)
    A27.0
Mauclaire's disease or osteochondrosis
    - see Osteochondrosis, juvenile, hand,
    metacarpal
Maxcy's disease A75.2
Maxilla, maxillary - see condition
May(-Hegglin) anomaly or syndrome
    D72.0
McArdle(-Schmid)(-Pearson) disease
    (glycogen storage) E74.04
McCune-Albright syndrome Q78.1
McQuarrie's syndrome (idiopathic famil-
    ial hypoglycemia) E16.2
Meadow's syndrome Q86.1
Measles (black) (hemorrhagic) (sup-
    pressed) B05.9
  with
    complications NEC B05.89
    encephalitis B05.0
    intestinal complications B05.4
    keratitis (keratoconjunctivitis)
      B05.81
    meningitis B05.1
    otitis media B05.3
    pneumonia B05.2
  French - see Rubella
  German - see Rubella
  Liberty - see Rubella
Meatitis, urethral - see Urethritis
Meatus, meatal - see condition
Meat-wrappers' asthma J68.9
Meckel-Gruber syndrome Q61.9
Meckel's diverticulitis, diverticulum
    (displaced) (hypertrophic) Q43.0
Meconium
  ileus, newborn P76.0
    in cystic fibrosis E84.11
  obstruction, newborn P76.0
    in mucoviscidosis E84.11
  peritonitis P78.0
  plug syndrome (newborn) NEC P76.0
Median - see also condition
  arcuate ligament syndrome I77.4
  bar (prostate) (vesical orifice) - see Hy-
    perplasia, prostate
  rhomboid glossitis K14.2
Mediastinal shift R93.1
Mediastinitis (acute) (chronic) J98.5
  syphilitic A52.73
  tuberculous A15.8

Mediastinopericarditis - see also
    Pericarditis
  acute I30.9
  adhesive I31.0
  chronic I31.8
  rheumatic I09.2
Mediastinum, mediastinal - see condition
Medical services provided for - see Health,
    services provided because (of)
Medicine poisoning - see Table of drugs
    and chemicals, by drug, poisoning
Mediterranean
  fever - see Brucellosis
    familial E85.0
    tick A77.1
  kala-azar B55.0
  leishmaniasis B55.0
  tick fever A77.1
Medulla - see condition
Medullary cystic kidney Q61.5
Medullated fibers
  optic (nerve) Q14.8
  retina Q14.1
Medulloblastoma
  desmoplastic C71.6
  specified site - see Neoplasm, malignant
  unspecified site C71.6
Medulloepithelioma - see also Neoplasm,
    malignant
  teratoid - see Neoplasm, malignant
Medullomyoblastoma
  specified site - see Neoplasm, malignant
  unspecified site C71.6
Meekeren-Ehlers-Danlos syndrome Q79.6
Megacolon (acquired) (functional) (not
    Hirschsprung's disease) (in) K59.3
  Chagas' disease B57.32
  congenital, congenitum (aganglionic) Q43.1
  Hirschsprung's (disease) Q43.1
  toxic K59.3
Megaesophagus (functional) K22.0
  congenital Q39.5
  in (due to) Chagas' disease B57.31
Megalencephaly Q04.5
Megalerythema (epidemic) B08.3
Megaloappendix Q43.8
Megalocephalus, megalocephaly NEC Q75.3
Megalocornea Q15.8
  with glaucoma Q15.0
Megalocytic anemia D53.9
Megalodactylia (fingers) (thumbs) (con-
    genital) Q74.0
  toes Q74.2
Megaloduodenum Q43.8
Megaloesophagus (functional) K22.0
  congenital Q39.5
Megalogastria (acquired) K31.89
  congenital Q40.2
Megalophthalmos Q11.3
Megalopsia H53.18
Megalosplenia - see Splenomegaly
Megaloureter N28.82
  congenital Q62.2
Megarectum K62.8
Megasigmoid K59.3
  congenital Q43.2
Megaureter N28.82
  congenital Q62.2
Megavitamin-B6 syndrome E67.2
Megrim - see Migraine
Meibomian
  cyst, infected - see Hordeolum
  gland - see condition
  sty, stye - see Hordeolum

Meibomitis - see Hordeolum
Meige-Milroy disease (chronic hereditary
    edema) Q82.0
Meige's syndrome Q82.0
Melalgia, nutritional E53.8
Melancholia F32.9
  climacteric (single episode) F32.8
    recurrent episode F33.9
  hypochondriac F45.29
  intermittent (single episode) F32.8
    recurrent episode F33.9
  involutional (single episode) E32.8
    recurrent episode F33.9
  menopausal (single episode) F32.8
    recurrent episode F33.9
  puerperal F32.8
  reactive (emotional stress or trauma)
    F32.3
  recurrent F33.9
  senile F03
  stuporous (single episode) F32.8
    recurrent episode F33.9
Melanemia R79.89
Melanoameloblastoma - see Neoplasm,
    bone, benign
Melanoblastoma - see Melanoma
Melanocarcinoma - see Melanoma
Melanocytoma, eyeball D31.4-
Melanoderma, melanodermia L81.4
Melanodontia, infantile K03.89
Melanodontoclasia K03.89
Melanoepithelioma - see Melanoma
Melanoma (malignant) C43.9
  acral lentiginous, malignant
  amelanotic
  balloon cell
  benign - see Nevus
  desmoplastic, malignant
  epithelioid cell
    with spindle cell, mixed
  in
    giant pigmented nevus
    Hutchinson's melanotic freckle
    junctional nevus
    precancerous melanosis
  in situ D03.9
    abdominal wall D03.59
    ala nasi D03.39
    ankle D03.7-
    anus, anal (margin) (skin) D03.51
    arm D03.6-
    auditory canal D03.2-
    auricle (ear) D03.2-
    auricular canal (external) D03.2-
    axilla, axillary fold D03.59
    back D03.59
    breast D03.52
    brow D03.39
    buttock D03.59
    canthus (eye) D03.1-
    cheek (external) D03.39
    chest wall D03.59
    chin D03.39
    choroid D03.8
    conjunctiva D03.8
    ear (external) D03.2-
    external meatus (ear) D03.2-
    eye D03.8
    eyebrow D03.39
    eyelid (lower) (upper) D03.1-
    face D03.30
      specified NEC D03.39
    female genital organ (external) NEC
      D03.8

Membrane(s), membranous *(Continued)*
Jackson's Q43.3
over face of newborn P28.9
premature rupture - *see* Rupture, membranes, premature
pupillary H21.4-
persistent Q13.89
retained (with hemorrhage) (complicating delivery) O72.2
without hemorrhage O73.1
secondary cataract - *see* Cataract, secondary
unruptured (causing asphyxia) - *see* Asphyxia, newborn
vitreous - *see* Opacity, vitreous, membranes and strands
Membranitis – *see* Chorioamnionitis
Memory disturbance, lack or loss - *see also* Amnesia
mild, following organic brain damage F06.8
Menadione deficiency E56.1
Menarche
delayed E30.0
precocious E30.1
Mendacity, pathologic F60.2
Mendelson's syndrome (due to anesthesia) J95.4
in labor and delivery O74.0
in pregnancy O29.01-
obstetric O74.0
postpartum, puerperal O89.01
Ménétrier's disease or syndrome K29.60
with bleeding K29.61
Méniére's disease, syndrome or vertigo H81.0
Meninges, meningeal - *see* condition
Meningioma - *see also* Neoplasm, meninges, benign
angioblastic - *see* Neoplasm, meninges, benign
angiomatous - *see* Neoplasm, meninges, benign
endotheliomatous - *see* Neoplasm, meninges, benign
fibroblastic - *see* Neoplasm, meninges, benign
fibrous - *see* Neoplasm, meninges, benign
hemangioblastic - *see* Neoplasm, meninges, benign
hemangiopericytic - *see* Neoplasm, meninges, benign
malignant - *see* Neoplasm, meninges, malignant
meningiothelial - *see* Neoplasm, meninges, benign
meningotheliomatous - *see* Neoplasm, meninges, benign
mixed - *see* Neoplasm, meninges, benign
multiple - *see* Neoplasm, meninges, uncertain behavior
papillary - *see* Neoplasm, meninges, uncertain behavior
psammomatous - *see* Neoplasm, meninges, benign
syncytial - *see* Neoplasm, meninges, benign
transitional - *see* Neoplasm, meninges, benign
Meningiomatosis (diffuse) - *see* Neoplasm, meninges, uncertain behavior

Meningism - *see* Meningismus
Meningismus (infectional) (pneumococcal) R29.1
due to serum or vaccine R29.1
influenzal - *see* Influenza, with, manifestations NEC
Meningitis (basal) (basic) (brain) (cerebral) (cervical) (congestive) (diffuse) (hemorrhagic) infantile) (membranous) (metastatic) (nonspecific) (pontine) (progressive) (simple) (spinal) (subacute) (sympathetic) (toxic) G03.9
abacterial G03.0
actinomycotic A42.81
adenoviral A87.1
arbovirus A87.8
aseptic (acute) G03.0
bacterial G00.9
Escherichia coli (E. coli) G00.8
Friedländer (bacillus) G00.8
gram-negative G00.9
H. influenzae G00.0
Klebsiella G00.8
pneumococcal G00.1
specified organism NEC G00.8
staphylococcal G00.3
streptococcal (acute) G00.2
benign recurrent (Mollaret) G03.2
candidal B37.5
caseous (tuberculous) A17.0
cerebrospinal A39.0
chronic NEC G03.1
clear cerebrospinal fluid NEC G03.0
coxsackievirus A87.0
cryptococcal B45.1
diplococcal (gram positive) A39.0
echovirus A87.0
enteroviral A87.0
eosinophilic B83.2
epidemic NEC A39.0
Escherichia coli (E. coli) G00.8
fibrinopurulent G00.9
specified organism NEC G00.8
Friedländer (bacillus) G00.8
gonococcal A54.81
gram-negative cocci G00.9
gram-positive cocci G00.9
Haemophilus (influenzae) G00.0
H. influenzae G00.0
in (due to)
adenovirus A87.1
African trypanosomiasis B56.9
anthrax A22.8
bacterial disease NEC A48.8 [G01]
Chagas' disease (chronic) B57.41
chickenpox B01.0
coccidioidomycosis B38.4
Diplococcus pneumoniae G00.1
enterovirus A87.0
herpes (simplex) virus B00.3
zoster B02.1
infectious mononucleosis B27.92
leptospirosis A27.81
Listeria monocytogenes A32.11
Lyme disease A69.21
measles B05.1
mumps (virus) B26.1
neurosyphilis (late) A52.13
parasitic disease NEC B89 [G02]
poliovirus A80.9 [G02]
preventive immunization, inoculation or vaccination G03.8
rubella B06.02

Meningitis *(Continued)*
in *(Continued)*
Salmonella infection A02.21
specified cause NEC G03.8
typhoid fever A01.01
varicella B01.0
viral disease NEC A87.8
whooping cough A37.90
zoster B02.1
infectious G00.9
influenzal (H. influenzae) G00.0
Klebsiella G00.8
leptospiral (aseptic) A27.81
lymphocytic (acute) (benign) (serous) A87.2
meningococcal A39.0
Mima polymorpha G00.8
Mollaret (benign recurrent) G03.2
monilial B37.5
mycotic NEC B49 [G02]
Neisseria A39.0
nonbacterial G03.0
nonpyogenic NEC G03.0
ossificans G96.19
pneumococcal G00.1
poliovirus A80.9 [G02]
postmeasles B05.1
purulent G00.9
specified organism NEC G00.8
pyogenic G00.9
specified organism NEC G00.8
Salmonella (arizonae) (Cholerae-Suis) (enteritidis) (typhimurium) A02.21
septic G00.9
specified organism NEC G00.8
serosa circumscripta NEC G03.0
serous NEC G93.2
specified organism NEC G00.8
sporotrichosis B42.81
staphylococcal G00.3
sterile G03.0
streptococcal (acute) G00.2
suppurative G00.9
specified organism NEC G00.8
syphilitic (late) (tertiary) A52.13
acute A51.41
congenital A50.41
secondary A51.41
Torula histolytica (cryptococcal) B45.1
traumatic (complication of injury) T79.8
tuberculous A17.0
typhoid A01.01
viral NEC A87.9
Yersinia pestis A20.3
Meningocele (spinal) - *see also* Spina bifida
with hydrocephalus - *see* Spina bifida, by site, with hydrocephalus
acquired (traumatic) G96.19
cerebral - *see* Encephalocele
Meningocerebritis - *see* Meningoencephalitis
Meningococcemia A39.4
acute A39.2
chronic A39.3
Meningococcus, meningococcal *(see also* condition) A39.9
adrenalitis, hemorrhagic A39.1
carrier (suspected) of Z22.31
meningitis (cerebrospinal) A39.0
Meningoencephalitis *(see also* Encephalitis) G04.90
acute NEC (see also Encephalitis, viral) A86
bacterial NEC G04.2

Meningoencephalitis (Continued)
  California A83.5
  diphasic A84.1
  eosinophilic B83.2
  epidemic A39.81
  herpesviral, herpetic B00.4
    due to herpesvirus 6 B10.01
    due to herpesvirus 7 B10.09
    specified NEC B10.09
  in (due to)
    blastomycosis NEC B40.81
    diseases classified elsewhere G05.3
    free-living amebae B60.2
    Hemophilus influenzae (H .influenzae) G04.2
    herpes B00.4
      due to herpesvirus 6 B10.01
      due to herpesvirus 7 B10.09
      specified NEC B10.09
    H. influenzae G00.0
    Lyme disease A69.22
    mercury - see subcategory T56.1
    mumps B26.2
    Naegleria (amebae) (organisms) (fowleri) B60.2
    Parastrongylus cantonensis B83.2
    toxoplasmosis (acquired) B58.2
      congenital P37.1
  infectious (acute) (viral) A86
  influenzal (H. influenzae) G04.2
  Listeria monocytogenes A32.12
  lymphocytic (serous) A87.2
  mumps B26.2
  parasitic NEC B89 [G05.3]
  pneumococcal G00.1
  primary amebic B60.2
  specific (syphilitic) A52.14
  specified organism NEC G04.81
  staphylococcal G04.2
  streptococcal G04.2
  syphilitic A52.14
  toxic NEC G92
    due to mercury - see subcategory T56.1
  tuberculous A17.82
  virus NEC A86
Meningoencephalocele - see also Encephalocele
  syphilitic A52.19
    congenital A50.49
Meningoencephalomyelitis - see also Meningoencephalitis
  acute NEC (viral) A86
    disseminated G04.00
      postimmunization or postvaccination G04.01
      postinfectious G04.00
  due to
    actinomycosis A42.82
    Torula B45.1
    Toxoplasma or toxoplasmosis (acquired) B58.2
      congenital P37.1
  postimmunization or postvaccination G04.01
Meningoencephalomyelopathy G96.9
Meningoencephalopathy G96.9
Meningomyelitis - see also Meningoencephalitis
  bacterial NEC G04.2
  blastomycotic NEC B40.81
  cryptococcal B45.1
  in diseases classified elsewhere G05.4
  meningococcal A39.81

Meningomyelitis (Continued)
  syphilitic A52.14
  tuberculous A17.82
Meningomyelocele - see also Spina bifida
  syphilitic A52.19
Meningomyeloneuritis - see Meningoencephalitis
Meningoradiculitis - see Meningitis
Meningovascular - see condition
Menkes' disease or syndrome E83.09
  meaning maple-syrup-urine disease E71.0
Menometrorrhagia N92.1
Menopause, menopausal (state) N95.10
  arthritis (any site) NEC - see Arthritis, specified form NEC
  bleeding N92.4
  depression (single episode) F32.8
    agitated (single episode) F32.2
      recurrent episode F33.9
    psychotic (single episode) F32.8
      recurrent episode F33.9
    recurrent episode F33.9
  melancholia (single episode) F32.8
    recurrent episode F33.9
  paranoid state F22
  premature E28.319
    asymptomatic E28.319
      postirradiation E89.40
      postsurgical E89.40
    symptomatic E28.310
      postirradiation E89.41
      postsurgical E89.41
  psychosis NEC F28
  toxic polyarthritis NEC - see Arthritis, specified form NEC
Menorrhagia (primary) N92.0
  climacteric N92.4
    menopausal N92.4
  menopausal N92.4
  postclimacteric N95.0
  postmenopausal N95.0
  preclimacteric or premenopausal N92.4
  pubertal (menses retained) N92.2
Menostaxis N92.0
Menses, retention N94.89
Menstrual - see Menstruation
Menstruation
  absent - see Amenorrhea
  anovulatory N97.0
  cycle, irregular N92.6
  delayed N91.0
  disorder N93.9
    psychogenic F45.8
  during pregnancy O20.8
  excessive (with regular cycle) N92.0
    with irregular cycle N92.1
    at puberty N92.2
  frequent N92.0
  infrequent - see Oligomenorrhea
  irregular N92.6
    specified NEC N92.5
  latent N92.5
  membranous N92.5
  painful (see also Dysmenorrhea) N94.6
    primary N94.4
    psychogenic F45.8
    secondary N94.5
  passage of clots N92.0
  precocious E30.1
  protracted N92.5
  rare - see Oligomenorrhea
  retained N94.89
  retrograde N92.5

Menstruation (Continued)
  scanty - see Oligomenorrhea
  suppression N94.89
  vicarious (nasal) N94.89
Mental - see also condition
  deficiency - see Retardation, mental
  deterioration - see Psychosis
  disorder - see Disorder, mental
  exhaustion F48.8
  insufficiency (congenital) - see Retardation, mental
  observation without need for further medical care Z03.89
  retardation - see Retardation, mental
  subnormality - see Retardation, mental
  upset - see Disorder, mental
Meralgia paresthetica G57.1-
Mercurial - see condition
Mercurialism - see subcategory T56.1
MERFF syndrome E88.42
Merkel cell tumor - see Carcinoma, Merkel cell
Merocele - see Hernia, femoral
Meromelia
  lower limb - see Defect, reduction, lower limb
    intercalary
      femur - see Defect, reduction, lower limb, specified type NEC
      tibiofibular (complete) (incomplete) - see Defect, reduction, lower limb
  upper limb – see Defect, reduction, upper limb
    intercalary, humeral, radioulnar – see Agenesis, arm, with hand present
Merzbacher-Pelizaeus disease E75.29
Mesaortitis - see Aortitis
Mesarteritis - see Arteritis
Mesencephalitis - see Encephalitis
Mesenchymoma - see also Neoplasm, connective tissue, uncertain behavior
  benign - see Neoplasm, connective tissue, benign
  malignant - see Neoplasm, connective tissue, malignant
Mesenteritis
  retractile K65.4
  sclerosing K65.4
Mesentery, mesenteric - see condition
Mesiodens, mesiodentes K00.1
Mesio-occlusion M26.213
Mesocolon - see condition
Mesonephroma (malignant) - see Neoplasm, malignant
  benign - see Neoplasm, benign
Mesophlebitis - see Phlebitis
Mesostromal dysgenesia Q13.89
Mesothelioma (malignant) C45.9
  benign
    mesentery D19.1
    mesocolon D19.1
    omentum D19.1
    peritoneum D19.1
    pleura D19.0
    specified site NEC D19.7
    unspecified site D19.9
  biphasic C45.9
    benign
      mesentery D19.1
      mesocolon D19.1
      omentum D19.1
      peritoneum D19.1
      pleura D19.0

Mesothelioma *(Continued)*
  biphasic *(Continued)*
    benign *(Continued)*
      specified site NEC D19.7
      unspecified site D19.9
  cystic D48.4
  epithelioid C45.9
    benign
      mesentery D19.1
      mesocolon D19.1
      omentum D19.1
      peritoneum D19.1
      pleura D19.0
      specified site NEC D19.7
      unspecified site D19.9
  fibrous C45.9
    benign
      mesentery D19.1
      mesocolon D19.1
      omentum D19.1
      peritoneum D19.1
      pleura D19.0
      specified site NEC D19.7
      unspecified site D19.9
  site classification
    liver C45.7
    lung C45.7
    mediastinum C45.7
    mesentery C45.1
    mesocolon C45.1
    omentum C45.1
    pericardium C45.2
    peritoneum C45.1
    pleura C45.0
      parietal C45.0
    retroperitoneum C45.7
    specified site NEC C45.7
    unspecified C45.9
Metabolic syndrome E88.81
Metagonimiasis B66.8
Metagonimus infestation (intestine) B66.8
Metal
  pigmentation L81.8
  polisher's disease J62.8
Metamorphopsia H53.15
Metaplasia
  apocrine (breast) – *see* Dysplasia,
    mammary, specified type NEC
  cervix (squamous) - *see* Dysplasia, cervix
  endometrium (squamous) (uterus) N85.8
  esophagus
  kidney (pelvis) (squamous) N28.89
  myelogenous D73.1
  myeloid (agnogenic) (megakaryocytic)
    D73.1
  spleen D73.1
  squamous cell, bladder N32.89
Metastasis, metastatic
  abscess - *see* Abscess
  calcification E83.59
  cancer
    from specified site - *see* Neoplasm,
      malignant, by site
    to specified site - *see* Neoplasm,
      secondary, by site
  deposits (in) - *see* Neoplasm, secondary,
    by site
  disease C79.9
  spread (to) - *see* Neoplasm, secondary,
    by site
Metastrongyliasis B83.8
Metatarsalgia M77.4-
  anterior G57.6-
  Morton's G57.6-

Metatarsus, metatarsal - *see also* condition
  valgus (abductus), congenital Q66.6
  varus (adductus) (congenital) Q66.2
Methadone use F11.20
Methemoglobinemia D74.9
  acquired (with sulfhemoglobinemia)
    D74.8
  congenital D74.0
  enzymatic (congenital) D74.0
  Hb M disease D74.0
  hereditary D74.0
  toxic D74.8
Methemoglobinuria — *see*
  Hemoglobinuria
Methioninemia E72.19
Methylmalonic acidemia E71.120
Metritis (catarrhal) (hemorrhagic) (septic)
  (suppurative) - *see also* Endometritis
  cervical - *see* Cervicitis
Metropathia hemorrhagica N93.8
Metroperitonitis - *see* Peritonitis, pelvic,
  female
Metrorrhagia N92.1
  climacteric N92.4
  menopausal N92.4
  postpartum NEC (atonic) (following
    delivery of placenta) O72.1
    delayed or secondary O72.2
  preclimacteric or premenopausal N92.4
  psychogenic F45.8
Metrorrhexis - *see* Rupture, uterus
Metrosalpingitis N70.91
Metrostaxis N93.8
Metrovaginitis - *see* Endometritis
Meyer-Schwickerath and Weyers syn-
  drome Q87.0
Meynert's amentia (nonalcoholic) F04
  alcoholic F10.96
    with dependence F10.26
Mibelli's disease (porokeratosis) Q82.8
Mice, joint - *see* Loose, body, joint
  knee M23.4
Micrencephalon, micrencephaly Q02
Microalbuminuria R80.9
Microaneurysm, retinal - *see also* Disor-
  der, retina, microaneurysms
  diabetic - *see* E09-E13 with .31
Microangiopathy (peripheral) I73.9
  thrombotic M31.1
Microcalcifications, breast R92.0
Microcephalus, microcephalic, micro-
  cephaly Q02
  due to toxoplasmosis (congenital) P37.1
Microcheilia Q18.7
Microcolon (congenital) Q43.8
Microcornea (congenital) Q13.4
Microcytic - *see* condition
Microdeletions NEC Q93.88
Microdontia K00.2
Microdrepanocytosis D56.8
Microembolism
  atherothrombotic - *see* Atheroembolism
  retinal - *see* Occlusion, artery, retina
Microencephalon Q02
Microfilaria streptocerca infestation
  B73.1
Microgastria (congenital) Q40.2
Microgenia M26.06
Microgenitalia, congenital
  female Q52.8
  male Q55.8
Microglioma – *see* Lymphoma, non-
  Hodgkin, specified type NEC
Microglossia (congenital) Q38.3

Micrognathia, micrognathism (congeni-
  tal) (mandibular) (maxillary) M26.09
Microgyria (congenital) Q04.3
Microinfarct of heart - *see* Insufficiency,
  coronary
Microlentia (congenital) Q12.8
Microlithiasis, alveolar, pulmonary J84.0
Micromastia N64.82
Micromyelia (congenital) Q06.8
Micropenis Q55.62
Microphakia (congenital) Q12.8
Microphthalmos, microphthalmia (con-
  genital) Q11.2
  due to toxoplasmosis P37.1
Micropsia H53.18
Microscopic polyangiitis (polyarteritis)
  M31.7
Microsporidiosis B60.8
  intestinal A07.8
Microsporon furfur infestation B36.0
Microsporosis - *see also* Dermatophytosis
  nigra B36.1
Microstomia (congenital) Q18.5
Microtia (congenital) (external ear) Q17.2
Microtropia H50.40
Micturition
  disorder NEC R39.19
    psychogenic F45.8
  frequency R35.0
    psychogenic F45.8
  hesitancy R39.11
  incomplete emptying R39.14
  nocturnal R35.1
  painful R30.9
    dysuria R30.0
    psychogenic F45.8
    tenesmus R30.1
  poor stream R39.12
  split stream R39.13
  straining R39.16
  urgency R39.15
Mid plane - *see* condition
Middle
  ear - *see* condition
  lobe (right) syndrome J98.19
Miescher's elastoma L87.2
Mietens' syndrome Q87.2
Migraine (idiopathic) G43.909
  basilar - *see* Migraine, with aura
  classical - *see* Migraine, with aura
  common - *see* Migraine, without aura
  equivalents - *see* Migraine, with aura
  familiar - *see* Migraine, hemiplegic
  hemiplegic G43.409
    intractable G43.419
      with status migrainosus G43.411
      without status migrainosus
        G43.419
    not intractable G43.409
      with status migrainosus G43.401
      without status migrainosus
        G43.409
  intractable G43.919
    with status migrainosus G43.911
    without status migrainosus G43.919
  menstrual G43.d09
    intractable G43.d19
      with status migrainosus G43.d11
      without status migrainosus
        G43.d19
    not intractable G43.d09
      with status migrainosus G43.d01
      without status migrainosus
        G43.d09

Migraine *(Continued)*
  menstrually related - *see* Migraine,
      menstrual
  not intractable G43.909
      with status migrainosus G43.901
      without status migrainosus G43.919
  ophthalmoplegic G43.b09
      intractable G43.b19
          with status migrainosus G43.b11
          without status migrainosus
              G43.b19
      not intractable G43.b09
          with status migrainosus G43.b01
          without status migrainosus
              G43.b09
  persistent aura (with, without) cerebral
      infarction - *see* Migraine, with
      aura, persistent
  preceded or accompanied by transient
      focal neurological phenomena - *see*
      Migraine, with aura
  pre-menstrual - *see* Migraine,
      menstrual
  pure menstrual - *see* Migraine,
      menstrual
  retinal - *see* Migraine, with aura
  specified NEC G43.809
      intractable G43.819
          with status migrainosus G43.811
          without status migrainosus
              G43.819
      not intractable G43.809
          with status migrainosus G43.801
          without status migrainosus
              G43.809
  sporadic - *see* Migraine, hemiplegic
  transformed - *see* Migraine, without
      aura, chronic
  triggered seizures - *see* Migraine, with
      aura
  with aura (acute-onset) (prolonged)
      (typical) (without headache)
      G43.109
      intractable G43.119
          with status migrainosus G43.111
          without status migrainosus
              G43.119
      not intractable G43.109
          with status migrainosus G43.101
          without status migrainosus
              G43.109
      persistent G43.509
          with cerebral infarction G43.609
              intractable G43.619
                  with status migrainosus
                      G43.611
                  without status migrainosus
                      G43.619
              not intractable G43.609
                  with status migrainosus
                      G43.601
                  without status migrainosus
                      G43.609
          without cerebral infarction G43.509
              intractable G43.519
                  with status migrainosus
                      G43.511
                  without status migrainosus
                      G43.519
              not intractable G43.509
                  with status migrainosus
                      G43.501
                  without status migrainosus
                      G43.509

Migraine *(Continued)*
  without aura G43.009
      chronic G43.709
          intractable
              with status migrainosus G43.711
              without status migrainosus
                  G43.719
          not intractable
              with status migrainosus G43.701
              without status migrainosus
                  G43.709
      intractable
          with status migrainosus G43.011
          without status migrainosus
              G43.019
      not intractable
          with status migrainosus G43.001
          without status migrainosus
              G43.009
Migrant, social Z59.0
Migration, anxiety concerning Z60.3
Migratory, migrating - *see also* condition
  person Z59.0
  testis Q55.29
Mikity-Wilson disease or syndrome
    P27.0
Mikulicz' disease or syndrome K11.8
Miliaria L74.3
  alba L74.1
  apocrine L75.2
  crystallina L74.1
  profunda L74.2
  rubra L74.0
  tropicalis L74.2
Miliary - *see* condition
Milium L72.0
  colloid L57.8
Milk
  crust L21.0
  excessive secretion O92.6
  poisoning - *see* Poisoning, food, noxious
  retention O92.79
  sickness - *see* Poisoning, food, noxious
  spots I31.0
Milk-alkali disease or syndrome E83.59
Milk-leg (deep vessels) (nonpuerperal)
    - *see* Embolism, vein, lower extremity
  complicating pregnancy O22.3-
  puerperal, postpartum, childbirth
      O87.1
Milkman's disease or syndrome M83.8
Milky urine - *see* Chyluria
Millard-Gubler(-Foville) paralysis or
    syndrome G46.3
Millar's asthma J38.5
Miller-Fisher syndrome G61.0
Mills' disease - *see* Hemiplegia
Millstone maker's pneumoconiosis J62.8
Milroy's disease (chronic hereditary
    edema) Q82.0
Minamata disease T26.1
Minkowski-Chauffard syndrome - *see*
    Spherocytosis
Miners' asthma or lung J60
Minkowski-Chauffard syndrome - *see*
    Spherocytosis
Minor - *see* condition
Minor's disease (hematomyelia) G95.19
Minot's disease (hemorrhagic disease),
    newborn P53
Minot-von Willebrand-Jurgens disease
    or syndrome (angiohemophilia)
    D68.0

Minus (and plus) hand (intrinsic) - *see*
    Deformity, limb, specified type NEC,
    forearm
Miosis (pupil) H57.03
Mirizzi's syndrome (hepatic duct steno-
    sis) K83.1
Mirror writing F81.0
Misadventure (of) (prophylactic)
    (therapeutic) - *see also* Complications
    T88.9
  administration of insulin (by accident)
      - *see* subcategory T38.3
  infusion - *see* Complications, infusion
  local applications (of fomentations,
      plasters, etc.) T88.9
      burn or scald - *see* Burn
      specified NEC T88.8
  medical care (early) (late) T88.9
      adverse effect of drugs or chemicals -
          see Table of drugs and chemicals
  medical care (early) (late)
      burn or scald - *see* Burn
      specified NEC T88.8
  specified NEC T88.8
  surgical procedure (early) (late) - *see*
      Complications, surgical procedure
  transfusion - *see* Complications,
      transfusion
  vaccination or other immunological
      procedure - *see* Complications,
      vaccination
Miscarriage O03.9
Misdirection, aqueous H40.83-
Misperception, sleep state R51.02
Misplaced, misplacement
  ear Q17.4
  kidney (acquired) N28.89
      congenital Q63.2
  organ or site, congenital NEC - *see*
      Malposition, congenital
Missed
  abortion O02.1
  delivery O36.4
Missing - *see* Absence
Misuse of drugs F19.99
Mitchell's disease (erythromelalgia) I73.81
Mite(s) (infestation) B88.9
  diarrhea B88.0
  grain (itch) B88.0
  hair follicle (itch) B88.0
  in sputum B88.0
Mitral - *see* condition
Mittelschmerz N94.0
Mixed - *see* condition
MNGIE (Mitochondrial Neurogastroin-
    testinal Encephalopathy) syndrome
    E88.49
Mobile, mobility
  cecum Q43.3
  excessive - *see* Hypermobility
  gallbladder, congenital Q44.1
  kidney N28.89
  organ or site, congenital NEC - *see*
      Malposition, congenital
Mobitz heart block (atrioventricular)
    I44.30
Moebius, Möbius
  disease (ophthalmoplegic migraine)
      - *see* Migraine, ophthalmoplegic
  syndrome Q87.0
      congenital oculofacial paralysis (with
          other anomalies) Q87.0
      ophthalmoplegic migraine - *see*
          Migraine, ophthalmoplegic

Moeller's glossitis K14.0
Mohr's syndrome (Types I and II) Q87.0
Mola destruens D39.2
Molar pregnancy O02.0
Molarization of premolars K00.2
Molding, head (during birth) - omit code
Mole (pigmented) - *see also* Nevus
  blood O02.0
  Breus' O02.0
  cancerous - *see* Melanoma
  carneous O02.0
  destructive D39.2
  fleshy O02.0
  hydatid, hydatidiform (benign) (complicating pregnancy) (delivered) (undelivered) O01.9
    classical O01.0
    complete O01.0
    incomplete O01.1
    invasive D39.2
    malignant D39.2
    partial O01.1
  intrauterine O02.0
  invasive (hydatidiform) D39.2
  malignant
    meaning
      malignant hydatidiform mole D39.2
    melanoma - *see* Melanoma
  nonhydatidiform O02.0
  nonpigmented - *see* Nevus
  pregnancy NEC O02.0
  skin - *see* Nevus
  tubal O00.1
  vesicular - *see* Mole, hydatidiform
Molimen, molimina (menstrual) N94.3
Molluscum contagiosum (epitheliale) B08.1
Mönckeberg's arteriosclerosis, disease, or sclerosis – *see* Arteriosclerosis, extremities
Mondini's malformation (cochlea) Q16.5
Mondor's disease I80.8
Monge's disease T70.29
Monilethrix (congenital) Q84.1
Moniliasis - *see also* Candidiasis B37.9
  neonatal P37.5
Monitoring (encounter for)
  therapeutic drug level Z51.81
Monkey malaria B53.1
Monkeypox B04
Monoarthritis M13.10
  ankle M13.17-
  elbow M13.12-
  foot joint M13.17-
  hand joint M13.14-
  hip M13.15-
  knee M13.16-
  shoulder M13.11-
  wrist M13.13-
Monoblastic - *see* condition
Monochromat(ism), monochromatopsia (acquired) (congenital) H53.51
Monocytic - *see* condition
Monocytopenia D72.818
Monocytosis (symptomatic) D72.821
Monomania - *see* Psychosis
Mononeuritis G58.9
  cranial nerve - *see* Disorder, nerve, cranial
  femoral nerve G57.2-
  lateral
    cutaneous nerve of thigh G57.1-
    popliteal nerve G57.3-

Mononeuritis *(Continued)*
  lower limb G57.9-
    specified nerve NEC G57.8-
  medial popliteal nerve G57.4-
  median nerve G56.1-
  multiplex G58.7
  plantar nerve G57.6-
  posterior tibial nerve G57.5-
  radial nerve G56.3-
  sciatic nerve G57.0-
  specified NEC G58.8
  tibial nerve G57.4-
  ulnar nerve G56.2-
  upper limb G56.9-
    specified nerve NEC G56.8-
  vestibular - *see* subcategory H93.3
Mononeuropathy G58.9
  carpal tunnel syndrome – *see* Syndrome, carpal tunnel
  diabetic NEC - *see* E09-E13 with .41
  femoral nerve – *see* Lesion, nerve, femoral
  ilioinguinal nerve G57.8-
  intercostal G58.0
  lower limb G57.9-
    causalgia – *see* Causalgia, lower limb
    femoral nerve – *see* Lesion, nerve, femoral
    meralgia paresthetica G57.1-
    plantar nerve – *see* Lesion, nerve, plantar
    popliteal nerve – *see* Lesion, nerve, popliteal
    sciatic nerve – *see* Lesion, nerve, sciatic
    specified NEC G57.8-
    tarsal tunnel syndrome – *see* Syndrome, tarsal tunnel
  median nerve – *see* Lesion, nerve, median
  multiplex G58.7
  obturator nerve G57.80
  popliteal nerve – *see* Lesion, nerve, popliteal
  radial nerve – *see* Lesion, nerve, radial
  saphenous nerve G57.8-
  specified NEC G58.8
  tarsal tunnel syndrome – *see* Syndrome, tarsal tunnel
  tuberculous A17.83
  ulnar nerve – *see* Lesion, nerve, ulnar
  upper limb G56.9-
    carpal tunnel syndrome – *see* Syndrome, carpal tunnel
    causalgia – *see* Causalgia
    median nerve – *see* Lesion, nerve, median
    radial nerve – *see* Lesion, nerve, radial
    specified site NEC G56.8-
    ulnar nerve – *see* Lesion, nerve, ulnar
Mononucleosis, infectious B27.90
  with
    complication NEC B27.99
    meningitis B27.92
    polyneuropathy B27.91
  cytomegaloviral B27.10
    with
      complication NEC B27.19
      meningitis B27.12
      polyneuropathy B27.11

Mononucleosis, infectious *(Continued)*
  Epstein-Barr (virus) B27.00
    with
      complication NEC B27.09
      meningitis B27.02
      polyneuropathy B27.01
  gammaherpesviral B27.00
    with
      complication NEC B27.09
      meningitis B27.02
      polyneuropathy B27.01
  specified NEC B27.80
    with
      complication NEC B27.89
      meningitis B27.82
      polyneuropathy B27.81
Monoplegia G83.3-
  congenital (cerebral) G80.8
    spastic G80.1
  embolic (current episode) I63.4
  following
    cerebrovascular disease
      cerebral infarction
        lower limb I69.34-
        upper limb I69.33-
      intracerebral hemorrhage
        lower limb I69.14-
        upper limb I69.13-
      lower limb I69.94-
      nontraumatic intracranial hemorrhage NEC
        lower limb I69.24-
        upper limb I69.23-
      specified disease NEC
        lower limb I69.84-
        upper limb I69.83-
      stroke NOS
        lower limb I69.34-
        upper limb I69.33-
      subarachnoid hemorrhage
        lower limb I69.04-
        upper limb I69.03-
      upper limb I69.93-
  hysterical (transient) F44.4
  lower limb G83.1-
  psychogenic (conversion reaction) F44.4
  thrombotic (current episode) I63.3
  transient R29.81
  upper limb G83.2-
Monorchism, monorchidism Q55.0
Monosomy - *see also* Deletion, chromosome Q93.9
  specified NEC Q93.89
  whole chromosome
    meiotic nondisjunction Q93.0
    mitotic nondisjunction Q93.1
    mosaicism Q93.1
  X Q96.9
Monster, monstrosity (single) Q89.7
  acephalic Q00.0
  twin Q89.4
Monteggia's fracture(-dislocation) S52.27-
Mooren's ulcer (cornea) - *see* Ulcer, cornea, Mooren's
Moore's syndrome - *see* Epilepsy, specified NEC
Mooser-Neill reaction A75.2
Mooser's bodies A75.2
Morbidity not stated or unknown R69
Morbilli - *see* Measles
Morbus (*see also* Disease)
  angelicus, anglorum E55.0
  Beigel B36.2

Morbus *(Continued)*
  caducus - *see* Epilepsy
  celiacus K90.0
  comitialis - *see* Epilepsy
  cordis - *see also* Disease, heart I51.9
    valvulorum - *see* Endocarditis
  coxae senilis M16.9
    tuberculous A18.02
  hemorrhagicus neonatorum P53
  maculosus neonatorum P54.5
Morel(-Stewart)(-Morgagni) syndrome
    M85.2
Morel-Kraepelin disease - *see*
    Schizophrenia
Morel-Moore syndrome M85.2
Morgagni's
  cyst, organ, hydatid, or appendage
    female Q50.5
    male (epididymal) Q55.4
      testicular Q55.29
  syndrome M85.2
Morgagni-Stokes-Adams syndrome I45.9
Morgagni-Stewart-Morel syndrome M85.2
Morgagni-Turner(-Albright) syndrome
    Q96.9
Moria F07.0
Moron (I.Q. 50-69) F70
Morphea L94.0
Morphinism (without remission) F11.20
  with remission F11.21
Morphinomania (without remission)
    F11.20
  with remission F11.21
Morquio(-Ullrich)(-Brailsford)
    disease or syndrome - *see*
    Mucopolysaccharidosis
Mortification (dry) (moist) - *see* Gangrene
Morton's metatarsalgia
    (neuralgia)(neuroma) (syndrome)
    G57.6
Morvan's disease or syndrome G60.8
Mosaicism, mosaic (autosomal)
    (chromosomal)
  45,X/other cell lines NEC with abnor-
    mal sex chromosome Q96.4
  45,X/46,XX Q96.3
  sex chromosome
    female Q97.8
    lines with various numbers of X
      chromosomes Q97.2
    male Q98.7
    XY Q96.3
Moschowitz' disease M31.1
Mother yaw A66.0
Motion sickness (from travel, any vehicle)
    (from roundabouts or swings) T75.3
Mottled, mottling, teeth (enamel) (en-
    demic) (nonendemic) K00.3
Mounier-Kuhn syndrome Q32.4
  with bronchiectasis J47.9
    exacerbation (acute) J47.1
    lower respiratory infection J47.0
  acquired J98.09
    with bronchiectasis J47.9
      with
        exacerbation (acute) J47.1
        lower respiratory infection J47.0
Mountain
  sickness T70.29
    with polycythemia , acquired (acute)
      D75.1
  tick fever A93.2
Mouse, joint - *see* Loose, body, joint
  knee M23.4-

Mouth - *see* condition
Movable
  coccyx - *see* subcategory M53.2
  kidney N28.89
    congenital Q63.8
  spleen D73.89
Movements, dystonic R25.8
Moyamoya disease I67.5
MRSA (Methacillin Resistant Staphylo-
    coccus Aureus) Z16
Mucha-Habermann disease L41.0
Mucinosis (cutaneous) (focal) (papular)
    (skin) L98.5
  oral K13.79
Mucocele
  appendix K38.8
  buccal cavity K13.79
  gallbladder K82.1
  lacrimal sac, chronic H04.43-
  nasal sinus J34.1
  nose J34.1
  salivary gland (any) K11.6
  sinus (accessory) (nasal) J34.1
  turbinate (bone) (middle) (nasal) J34.1
  uterus N85.8
Mucolipidosis
  I E77.1
  II, III E77.0
  IV E75.11
Mucopolysaccharidosis E76.3
  beta-gluduronidase deficiency E76.29
  cardiopathy E76.3 [152]
  Hunter's syndrome E76.1
  Hurler's syndrome E76.01
  Hurler-Scheie syndrome E76.02
  Maroteaux-Lamy syndrome E76.29
  Morquio syndrome E76.219
    A E76.210
    B E76.211
    classic E76.210
  Sanfilippo syndrome E76.22
  Scheie's syndrome E76.03
  specified NEC E76.29
  type
    I
      Hurler's syndrome E76.01
      Hurler-Scheie syndrome E76.02
      Scheie's syndrome E76.03
    II E76.1
    III E76.22
    IV E76.219
    IVA E76.210
    IVB E76.211
    VI E76.29
    VII E76.29
Mucormycosis B46.5
  cutaneous B46.3
  disseminated B46.4
  gastrointestinal B46.2
  generalized B46.4
  pulmonary B46.0
  rhinocerebral B46.1
  skin B46.3
  subcutaneous B46.3
Mucositis (ulcerative) K12.30
  due to drugs NEC K12.32
  gastrointestinal K92.81
  mouth (oral) (oropharyngeal) K12.30
    due to antineoplastic therapy K12.31
    due to drugs NEC K12.32
    due to radiation K12.33
    specified NEC K12.39
    viral K12.39
  nasal J34.81

Mucositis *(Continued)*
  oral cavity - *see* Mucositis, mouth
  oral soft tissues - *see* Mucositis, mouth
  vagina and vulva N76.81
Mucositis necroticans agranulocytica
    - *see* Agranulocytosis
Mucous - *see also* condition
  patches (syphilitic) A51.39
    congenital A50.07
Mucoviscidosis E84.9
  with meconium obstruction E84.11
Mucus
  asphyxia or suffocation - *see* Asphyxia,
    mucus
  in stool R19.5
  plug - *see* Asphyxia, mucus
Muguet B37.0
Mulberry molars (congenital syphilis)
    A50.52
Müllerian mixed tumor
  specified site - *see* Neoplasm,
    malignant
  unspecified site C54.9
Multicystic kidney (development) Q61.4
Multiparity (grand) Z64.1
  affecting management of pregnancy,
    labor and delivery (supervision
    only) O09.4-
  requiring contraceptive management
    - *see* Contraception
Multipartita placenta O43.19-
Multiple, multiplex - *see also* condition
  digits (congenital) Q69.9
  endocrine neoplasia - *see* Neoplasia,
    endocrine, multiple [MEN}
  personality F44.81
Mumps B26.9
  arthritis B26.85
  complication NEC B26.89
  encephalitis B26.2
  hepatitis B26.81
  meningitis (aseptic) B26.1
  meningoencephalitis B26.2
  myocarditis B26.82
  oophoritis B26.89
  orchitis B26.0
  pancreatitis B26.3
  polyneuropathy B26.84
Mumu (*see also* Infestation, filarial) B74.9
    [N51]
Münchhausen's syndrome – *see* Disorder,
    factitious
Münchmeyer's syndrome - *see* Myositis,
    ossificans, progressiva
Mural - *see* condition
Murmur (cardiac) (heart) (organic) R01.1
  abdominal R19.15
  aortic (valve) - *see* Endocarditis, aortic
  benign R01.0
  diastolic - *see* Endocarditis
  Flint I35.1
  functional R01.0
  Graham Steell I37.1
  innocent R01.0
  mitral (valve) - *see* Insufficiency, mitral
  nonorganic R01.0
  presystolic, mitral - *see* Insufficiency,
    mitral
  pulmonic (valve) I37.8
  systolic (valvular) - *see* Endocarditis
  tricuspid (valve) I07.9
  valvular - *see* Endocarditis
Murri's disease (intermittent hemoglobin-
    uria) D59.6

Muscle, muscular - *see also* condition
  carnitine (palmityltransferase) deficiency E71.314
Musculoneuralgia - *see* Neuralgia
Mushroom-workers' (pickers') disease or lung J67.5
Mushrooming hip - *see* Derangement, joint, specified NEC, hip
Mutation
  factor V Leiden D68.51
  prothrombin gene D68.52
Mutism - *see also* Aphasia
  deaf (acquired) (congenital) NEC H91.3
  elective (adjustment reaction) (childhood) F94.0
  hysterical F44.4
  selective (childhood) F94.0
Myalgia M79.1
  epidemic (cervical) B33.0
  traumatic NEC T14.8
Myasthenia G70.9
  congenital G70.2
  cordis - *see* Failure, heart
  developmental G70.2
  gravis G70.00
    with exacerbation (acute) G70.01
    in crisis G70.01
    neonatal, transient P94.0
    pseudoparalytica G70.00
      with exacerbation (acute) G70.01
      in crisis G70.01
  stomach, psychogenic F45.8
  syndrome
    in
      diabetes mellitus - *see* E09-E13 with .44
      neoplastic disease (*see also* Neoplasm) D49.9 *[G73.3]*
      pernicious anemia D51.0 *[G73.3]*
      thyrotoxicosis E05.90 *[G73.3]*
        with thyroid storm E05.91 *[G73.3]*
Myasthenic M62.81
Mycelium infection B49
Mycetismus - *see* Poisoning, food, noxious, mushroom
Mycetoma B47.9
  actinomycotic B47.1
  bone (mycotic) B47.9 *[M90.80]*
  eumycotic B47.0
  foot B47.9
    actinomycotic B47.1
    mycotic B47.0
  madurae NEC B47.9
    mycotic B47.0
  maduromycotic B47.0
  mycotic B47.0
  nocardial B47.1
Mycobacteriosis - *see* Mycobacterium
Mycobacterium, mycobacterial (infection) A31.9
  anonymous A31.9
  atypical A31.9
    cutaneous A31.1
    pulmonary A31.0
      tuberculous - *see* Tuberculosis, pulmonary
    specified site NEC A31.8
  avium (intracellulare complex) A31.0
  balnei A31.1
  Battey A31.0
  chelonei A31.8
  cutaneous A31.1

Mycobacterium, mycobacterial
  (*Continued*)
  extrapulmonary systemic A31.8
  fortuitum A31.8
  intracellulare (Battey bacillus) A31.0
  kansasii (yellow bacillus) A31.0
  kakaferifu A31.8
  kasongo A31.8
  leprae (see also Leprosy) A30.9
  luciflavum A31.1
  marinum (M. balnei) A31.1
  nonspecific - *see* Mycobacterium, atypical
  pulmonary (atypical) A31.0
    tuberculous - *see* Tuberculosis, pulmonary
  scrofulaceum A31.8
  simiae A31.8
  systemic, extrapulmonary A31.8
  szulgai A31.8
  terrae A31.8
  triviale A31.8
  tuberculosis (human, bovine) - *see* Tuberculosis
  ulcerans A31.1
  xenopi A31.8
Mycoplasma (M.) pneumoniae, as cause of disease classified elsewhere B96.0
Mycosis, mycotic B49
  cutaneous NEC B36.9
  ear B36.8
  fungoides (extranodal) (solid organ) C84.0-
  mouth B37.0
  nails B35.1
  opportunistic B48.8
  skin NEC B36.9
  specified NEC B48.8
  stomatitis B37.0
  vagina, vaginitis (candidal) B37.3
Mydriasis (pupil) H57.04
Myelatelia Q06.1
Myelinolysis, pontine, central G37.2
Myelitis (acute) (ascending) (childhood) (chronic) (descending) (diffuse) (disseminated) (idiopathic) (pressure) (progressive) (spinal cord) (subacute) (*see also* Encephalitis) G04.91
  herpes simplex B00.82
  herpes zoster B02.24
  in diseases classified elsewhere G05.4
  necrotizing, subacute G37.4
  optic neuritis in G36.0
  postchickenpox B01.12
  postherpetic B02.24
  postimmunization G04.89
  postinfectious NEC G04.89
  postvaccinal G04.89
  specified NEC G04.89
  syphilitic (transverse) A52.14
  toxic G92
  transverse (in demyelinating diseases of central nervous system) G37.3
  tuberculous A17.82
  varicella B01.12
Myeloblastic - *see* condition
Myeloblastoma
  granular cell - *see also* Neoplasm, connective tissue
    malignant - *see* Neoplasm, connective tissue, malignant
    tongue D10.1

Myelocele - *see* Spina bifida
Myelocystocele - *see* Spina bifida
Myelocytic - *see* condition
Myelodysplasia D46.9
  specified NEC D46.Z
  spinal cord (congenital) Q06.1
Myelodysplastic syndrome D46.9
  with
    5q deletion D46.c
    isolated del(5q) chromosomal abnormality C46.c
    specified NEC D46.z
Myeloencephalitis - *see* Encephalitis
Myelofibrosis D75.81
  with myeloid metaplasia D47.4
  acute C94.4
  idiopathic (chronic) D47.4
  primary D75.81
  secondary D75.81
    in myeloproliferative disease D47.4
Myelogenous - *see* condition
Myeloid - *see* condition
Myelokathexis D70.9
Myeloleukodystrophy E75.29
Myelolipoma - *see* Lipoma
Myeloma (multiple) C90.0-
  plasma cell C90.0-
  solitary C90.3- - *see also* Plasmacytoma, solitary
Myelomalacia G95.89
Myelomatosis C90.0-
Myelomeningitis - *see* Meningoencephalitis
Myelomeningocele (spinal cord) - *see* Spina bifida
Myelo-osteo-musculodysplasia hereditaria Q79.8
Myelopathic
  anemia D64.89
  muscle atrophy - *see* Atrophy, muscle, spinal
  pain syndrome G89.0
Myelopathy (spinal cord) G95.9
  drug-induced G95.89
  in (due to)
    degeneration or displacement, intervertebral disc NEC - *see* Disorder, disc, with, myelopathy
    infection - *see* Encephalitis
    intervertebral disc disorder - *see also* Disorder, disc, with, myelopathy
    mercury - *see* subcategory T56.1
    neoplastic disease (see also Neoplasm) D49.9 *[G99.2]*
    pernicious anemia D51.0 *[G99.2]*
    spondylosis - *see* Spondylosis, with myelopathy NEC
  necrotic (subacute) (vascular) G95.19
  radiation-induced G95.89
  spondylogenic NEC - *see* Spondylosis, with myelopathy NEC
  toxic G95.89
  transverse, acute G37.3
  vascular G95.19
  vitamin B$_{12}$ E53.8 *[G32.0]*
Myelophthisis D61.82
Myeloradiculitis G04.91
Myeloradiculodysplasia (spinal) Q06.1
Myelosarcoma C92.3-
Myelosclerosis D75.89
  with myeloid metaplasia D47.4
  disseminated, of nervous system G35
  megakaryocytic D47.4
    with myeloid metaplasia D47.4

Myelosis
  acute C92.0-
  aleukemic C92.9-
  chronic D47.1
  erythremic (acute) C94.0-
  megakaryocytic C94.2-
  nonleukemic D72.828
  subacute C92.9-
Myiasis (cavernous) B87.9
  aural B87.4
  creeping B87.0
  cutaneous B87.0
  dermal B87.0
  ear (external) (middle) B87.4
  eye B87.2
  genitourinary B87.81
  intestinal B87.82
  laryngeal B87.3
  nasopharyngeal B87.3
  ocular B87.2
  orbit B87.2
  skin B87.0
  specified site NEC B87.89
  traumatic B87.1
  wound B87.1
Myoadenoma, prostate - *see* Hyperplasia,
    prostate
Myoblastoma
  granular cell - *see also* Neoplasm,
    connective tissue, benign
    malignant - *see* Neoplasm, connective
      tissue, malignant
  tongue D10.1
Myocardial - *see* condition
Myocardiopathy (congestive) (constric-
    tive) (familial) (hypertrophic nonob-
    structive) (idiopathic) (infiltrative)
    (obstructive) (primary) (restrictive)
    (sporadic) (*see also* Cardiomyopathy)
    I42.9
  alcoholic I42.6
  cobalt-beer I42.6
  glycogen storage E74.02 *[I43]*
  hypertrophic obstructive I42.1
  in (due to)
    beriberi E51.12 *[I43]*
    cardiac glycogenosis E74.02 *[I43]*
    Friedreich's ataxia G11.1 *[I43]*
    myotonia atrophica G71.19 *[I43]*
    progressive muscular dystrophy
      G71.0 *[I43]*
  obscure (African) I42.8
  secondary I42.7
  thyrotoxic E05.90 *[I43]*
    with storm E05.91 *[I43]*
  toxic NEC I42.7
Myocarditis (with arteriosclerosis)
    (chronic)(fibroid) (interstitial) (old)
    (progressive) (senile) I51.4
  with
    rheumatic fever (conditions in I00)
      I09.0
      active - *see* Myocarditis, acute,
        rheumatic
      inactive or quiescent (with chorea)
        I09.0
  active I40.9
    rheumatic I01.2
      with chorea (acute) (rheumatic)
        (Sydenham's) I02.0
  acute or subacute (interstitial) I40.9
    due to
      streptococcus (beta-hemolytic)
        I01.2

Myocarditis *(Continued)*
  acute or subacute *(Continued)*
    idiopathic I40.1
    rheumatic I01.2
      with chorea (acute) (rheumatic)
        (Sydenham's) I02.0
    specified NEC I40.8
  aseptic of newborn B33.22
  bacterial (acute) I40.0
  Coxsackie (virus) B33.22
  diphtheritic A36.81
  eosinophilic I40.1
  epidemic of newborn (Coxsackie)
    B33.22
  Fiedler's (acute) (isolated) I40.1
  giant cell (acute) (subacute) I40.1
  gonococcal A54.83
  granulomatous (idiopathic) (isolated)
    (nonspecific) I40.1
  hypertensive - *see* Hypertension, heart
  idiopathic (granulomatous) I40.1
  in (due to)
    diphtheria A36.81
    epidemic louse-borne typhus A75.0
      [I41]
    Lyme disease A69.29
    sarcoidosis D86.85
    scarlet fever A38.1
    toxoplasmosis (acquired) B58.81
    typhoid A01.02
    typhus NEC A75.9 *[I41]*
  infective I40.0
  influenzal - *see* Influenza, with,
    manifestations NEC
  isolated (acute) I40.1
  meningococcal A39.52
  mumps B26.82
  nonrheumatic, active I40.9
  parenchymatous I40.9
  pneumococcal I40.0
  rheumatic (chronic) (inactive) (with
    chorea) I09.0
    active or acute I01.2
      with chorea (acute) (rheumatic)
        (Sydenham's) I02.0
  rheumatoid - *see* Rheumatoid, carditis
  septic I40.0
  staphylococcal I40.0
  suppurative I40.0
  syphilitic (chronic) A52.06
  toxic I40.8
    rheumatic - *see* Myocarditis, acute,
      rheumatic
  tuberculous A18.84
  typhoid A01.02
  valvular - *see* Endocarditis
  virus, viral I40.0
    of newborn (Coxsackie) B33.22
Myocardium, myocardial - *see* condition
Myocardosis - *see* Cardiomyopathy
Myoclonus, myoclonic, myoclonia
    (familial) (essential) (multifocal)
    (simplex) G25.3
  drug-induced G25.3
  epilepsy, familial (progressive) G25.3
  epileptica G40.309
    with status epilepticus G40.301
  facial G51.3
  familial progressive G25.3
  Friedreich's G25.3
  jerks G25.3
  massive G25.3
  palatal G25.3
  pharyngeal G25.3

Myocytolysis I51.5
Myodiastasis - *see* Diastasis, muscle
Myoendocarditis - *see* Endocarditis
Myoepithelioma - *see* Neoplasm, benign
Myofasciitis (acute) - *see* Myositis
Myofibroma - *see also* Neoplasm,
    connective tissue, benign
  uterus (cervix) (corpus) - *see*
    Leiomyoma
Myofibromatosis D48.1
  infantile Q89.8
Myofibrosis M62.89
  heart - *see* Myocarditis
  scapulohumeral - *see* Lesion, shoulder,
    specified NEC
Myofibrositis M79.7
  scapulohumeral - *see* Lesion, shoulder,
    specified NEC
Myoglobulinuria, myoglobinuria (pri-
    mary) R82.1
Myokymia, facial G51.4
Myolipoma - *see* Lipoma
Myoma - *see also* Neoplasm, connective
    tissue, benign
  malignant - *see* Neoplasm, connective
    tissue, malignant
  prostate D29.1
  uterus (cervix) (corpus) - *see*
    Leiomyoma
Myomalacia M62.89
Myometritis - *see* Endometritis
Myometrium - *see* condition
Myonecrosis, clostridial A48.0
Myopathy G72.9
  alcoholic G72.1
  benign congenital G70.9
  central core G70.9
  centronuclear G71.2
  congenital (benign) G71.2
  distal G71.0
  drug-induced G72.0
  endocrine NEC E34.9 *[G73.7]*
  extraocular muscles H05.82-
  facioscapulohumeral G71.0
  hereditary G71.9
    specified NEC G71.8
  immune NEC G72.49
  in (due to)
    Addison's disease E27.1 *[G73.7]*
    alcohol G72.1
    amyloidosis E85.0 *[G73.7]*
    cretinism E00.9 *[G73.7]*
    Cushing's syndrome E24.9 *[G73.7]*
    drugs G72.0
    endocrine disease NEC E34.9 *[G73.7]*
    giant cell arteritis M31.6 *[G73.7]*
    glycogen storage disease E74.00
      [G73.7]
    hyperadrenocorticism E24.9 *[G73.7]*
    hyperparathyroidism NEC E21.3
      [G73.7]
    hypoparathyroidism E20.9 *[G73.7]*
    hypopituitarism E23.0 *[G73.7]*
    hypothyroidism E03.9 *[G73.7]*
    infectious disease NEC B99 *[G73.7]*
    lipid storage disease E75.6 *[G73.7]*
    metabolic disease NEC E88.9 *[G73.7]*
    myxedema E03.9 *[G73.7]*
    parasitic disease NEC B89 *[G73.7]*
    polyarteritis nodosa M30.0 *[G73.7]*
    rheumatoid arthritis - *see* Rheuma-
      toid, myopathy
    sarcoidosis D86.87
    scleroderma M34.82

Myopathy (Continued)
  in (Continued)
    sicca syndrome M35.03
    Sjögren's syndrome M35.03
    systemic lupus erythematosus
      M32.19
    thyrotoxicosis (hyperthyroidism)
      E05.90 [G73.7]
      with thyroid storm E05.91 [G73.7]
    toxic agent NEC G72.2
  inflammatory NEC G72.49
  limb-girdle G71.0
  mitochondrial NEC G71.3
  mytonic, proximal (PROMM) G71.11
  myotubular G71.2
  nemaline G71.2
  ocular G71.0
  oculopharyngeal G71.0
  primary G71.9
    specified NEC G71.8
  progressive NEC G72.8
  proximal myotonic (PROMM) G71.11
  rod G71.2
  scapulohumeral G71.0
  specified NEC G72.8
  toxic G72.2
Myopericarditis - see also Pericarditis
  chronic rheumatic I09.2
Myopia (axial) (congenital) (progressive)
  H52.1-
  degenerative (malignant) - see Disorder,
    globe, degenerative, myopia
  malignant - see Disorder, globe, degen-
    erative, myopia
  pernicious - see Disorder, globe, degen-
    erative, myopia
  progressive high (degenerative) - see
    Disorder, globe, degenerative,
    myopia
Myosarcoma - see Neoplasm, connective
  tissue, malignant
Myosis (pupil) H57.03
  stromal (endolymphatic) D39.0
Myositis M60.9
  clostridial A48.0
  due to posture - see Myositis, specified
    type NEC
  epidemic B33.0
  fibrosa or fibrous (chronic), Volkmann's
    T79.6
  foreign body granuloma - see Granu-
    loma, foreign body
  in (due to)
    bilharziasis B65.9 [M63]
    cysticercosis B69.81
    leprosy A30.9 [M63]
    mycosis B49 [M63]
    sarcoidosis D86.87
    schistosomiasis B65.9 [M63]
    syphilis
      late A52.78
      secondary A51.49
    toxoplasmosis (acquired) B58.82
    trichinellosis B75 [M63]
    tuberculosis A18.09
  inclusion body [IBM] G72.41
  infective M60.009
    lower limb M60.005
      ankle M60.07-
      foot M60.07-
      lower leg M60.06-
      thigh M60.05-
      toe M60.07-
    multiple sites M60.09

Myositis (Continued)
  infective (Continued)
    specified site NEC M60.08
    upper limb M60.002
      finger M60.04-
      forearm M60.03-
      hand M60.04-
      shoulder region M60.01-
      upper arm M60.02-
  interstitial M60.10
    ankle M60.17-
    foot M60.17-
    forearm M60.13-
    hand M60.14-
    lower leg M60.16-
    multiple sites M60.19
    shoulder region M60.11-
    specified site NEC M60.18
    thigh M60.15-
    upper arm M60.12-
  mycotic B49 [M63] - orbital, chronic
    H05.12-
  ossificans or ossifying (circumscripta) -
    see also Ossification, muscle,
    specified NEC
    in (due to)
      burns M61.30
        ankle M61.37-
        foot M61.37-
        forearm M61.33-
        hand M61.34-
        lower leg M61.36-
        multiple sites M61.39
        pelvic region M61.35-
        shoulder region M61.21-
        specified site NEC M61.28
        thigh M61.25-
        upper arm M61.22-
      quadriplegia or paraplegia M61.20
        ankle M61.27-
        foot M61.27-
        forearm M61.23-
        hand M61.24-
        lower leg M61.26-
        multiple sites M61.29
        pelvic region M61.25-
        shoulder region M61.21-
        specified site NEC M61.28
        thigh M61.25-
        upper arm M61.22-
  progressiva M61.10
    ankle M61.17-
    finger M61.14-
    foot M61.17-
    forearm M61.13-
    hand M61.14-
    lower leg M61.16-
    multiple sites M61.19
    pelvic region M61.15-
    shoulder region M61.11-
    specified site NEC M61.18
    thigh M61.15-
    toe M61.17-
    upper arm M61.12-
  traumatica M61.00
    ankle M61.07-
    foot M61.07-
    forearm M61.03-
    hand M61.04-
    lower leg M61.06-
    multiple sites M61.09
    pelvic region M61.05-
    shoulder region M61.01-
    specified site NEC M61.08

Myositis (Continued)
  ossificans or ossifying (Continued)
    traumatica (Continued)
      thigh M61.05-
      upper arm M61.02-
    purulent - see Myositis, infective
    specified type NEC M60.80
      ankle M60.87-
      foot M60.87-
      forearm M60.83-
      hand M60.84-
      lower leg M60.86-
      multiple sites M60.89
      pelvic region M60.85-
      shoulder region M60.81-
      specified site NEC M60.88
      thigh M60.85-
      upper arm M60.82-
    suppurative - see Myositis, infective
    traumatic (old) - see Myositis, specified
      type NEC
Myospasia impulsiva F95.2
Myotonia (acquisita) (intermittens) M62.89
  atrophica G71.11
  chondrodystrophic G71.13
  congenita (acetazolamide responsive)
    (dominant) (recessive) G71.12
  drug-induced G71.14
  dystrophica G71.11
  fluctuans G71.19
  levior G71.12
  permanens G71.19
  symptomatic G71.19
Myotonic pupil - see Anomaly, pupil,
  function, tonic pupil
Myriapodiasis B88.2
Myringitis H73.2-
  with otitis media - see Otitis, media
  acute H73.00
    bullous H73.01-
    specified NEC H73.09-
  bullous - see Myringitis, acute, bullous
  chronic H73.1-
Mysophobia F40.228
Mytilotoxism - see Poisoning, fish
Myxadenitis labialis K13.0
Myxedema (adult) (idiocy) (infantile) (juvenile) (see also Hypothyroidism) E03.9
  circumscribed E05.90
    with storm E05.91
  coma E03.5
  congenital E00.1
  cutis L98.5
  localized (pretibial) E05.90
    with storm E05.91
  papular L98.5
Myxochondrosarcoma - see Neoplasm,
  cartilage, malignant
Myxofibroma - see Neoplasm, connective
  tissue, benign
  odontogenic - see Cyst, calcifying
    odontogenic
Myxofibrosarcoma - see Neoplasm,
  connective tissue, malignant
Myxolipoma D17.9
Myxoliposarcoma - see Neoplasm,
  connective tissue, malignant
Myxoma - see also Neoplasm, connective
  tissue, benign
  nerve sheath - see Neoplasm, nerve, benign
  odontogenic - see Cyst, calcifying
    odontogenic
Myxosarcoma - see Neoplasm, connective
  tissue, malignant

N

Naegeli's
  disease Q82.8
  leukemia, monocytic C93.1-
Naegleriasis (with meningoencephalitis)
  B60.2
Naffziger's syndrome G54.0
Naga sore - see Ulcer, skin
Nägele's pelvis M95.5
  with disproportion (fetopelvic) O33.0
    causing obstructed labor O65.0
Nail - see also condition
  biting F98.8
  patella syndrome Q87.2
Nanism, nanosomia - see Dwarfism
Nanophyetiasis B66.8
Nanukayami A27.89
Napkin rash L22
Narcolepsy G47.419
  with cataplexy G47.411
  in conditions classified elsewhere
    G47.429
    with cataplexy G47.421
Narcosis R06.89
Narcotism - see Dependence
NARP (Neuropathy, Ataxia and Retinitis
  pigmentosa) syndrome E88.49
Narrow
  anterior chamber angle H40.0
  pelvis - see Contraction, pelvis
Narrowing - see also Stenosis
  artery I77.1
    auditory, internal I65.8
    basilar - see Occlusion, artery, basilar
    carotid - see Occlusion, artery, carotid
    cerebellar – see Occlusion, artery,
      cerebellar
    cerebral – see Occlusion artery,
      cerebral
    choroidal – see Occlusion, artery,
      cerebral, specified NEC
    communicating posterior – see Occlu-
      sion, artery, cerebral, specified
      NEC
    coronary – see also Disease, heart,
      ischemic, atherosclerotic
      congenital Q24.5
      syphilitic A50.54 [I52]
      due to syphilis NEC A52.06
    hypophyseal – see Occlusion, artery,
      cerebral, specified NEC
    pontine – see Occlusion, artery, cere-
      bral, specified NEC
    precerebral - see Occlusion, artery,
      precerebral
    vertebral - see Occlusion, artery,
      vertebral
  auditory canal (external) - see Stenosis,
    external ear canal
  eustachian tube – see Obstruction,
    eustachian tube
  eyelid - see Disorder, eyelid function
  larynx J38.6
  mesenteric artery K55.0
  palate M26.89
  palpebral fissure - see Disorder, eyelid
    function
  ureter N13.5
    with infection N13.6
  urethra - see Stricture, urethra
Narrowness, abnormal, eyelid Q10.3
Nasal - see condition

Nasolachrymal, nasolacrimal - see
  condition
Nasopharyngeal - see also condition
  pituitary gland Q89.2
  torticollis M43.6
Nasopharyngitis (acute) (infective) (strep-
  tococcal) (subacute) J00
  chronic (suppurative) (ulcerative) J31.1
Nasopharynx, nasopharyngeal - see
  condition
Natal tooth, teeth K00.6
Nausea (without vomiting) R11.0
  with vomiting R11.2
  gravidarum - see Hyperemesis,
    gravidarum
  marina T75.3
  navalis T75.3
Navel - see condition
Neapolitan fever - see Brucellosis
Near drowning T75.1
Nearsightedness - see Myopia
Near-syncope R55
Nebula, cornea - see Opacity, cornea
Necator americanus infestation B76.1
Necatoriasis B76.1
Neck - see condition
Necrobiosis R68.89
  lipoidica NEC L92.1
    with diabetes - see E09-E13 with .63
Necrolysis, toxic epidermal L51.2
  due to drug
    correct substance properly admin-
      istered- see Table of drugs and
      chemicals, by drug, adverse
      effect
    overdose or wrong substance given
      or taken - see Table of drugs and
      chemicals, by drug, poisoning
Necrophilia F65.89
Necrosis, necrotic (ischemic) - see also
  Gangrene
  adrenal (capsule) (gland) E27.49
  amputation stump (surgical) (late)
    T87.50
    arm T87.5-
    leg T87.5-
  antrum J32.0
  aorta (hyaline) - see also Aneurysm, aorta
    cystic medial - see Dissection, aorta
  artery I77.5
  bladder (aseptic) (sphincter) N32.89
  bone (see also Osteonecrosis) M87.9
    aseptic or avascular - see
      Osteonecrosis
      idiopathic M87.00
    ethmoid J32.2
    jaw M27.2
    tuberculous - see Tuberculosis, bone
  brain I67.8
  breast (aseptic) (fat) (segmental) N64.1
  bronchus J98.09
  central nervous system NEC I67.8
  cerebellar I67.8
  cerebral I67.8
  colon K55.0
  cornea H18.40
  cortical (acute) (renal) N17.1
  cystic medial (aorta) - see Dissection,
    aorta
  dental pulp K04.1
  esophagus K22.8
  ethmoid (bone) J32.2
  eyelid - see Disorder, eyelid,
    degenerative

Necrosis, necrotic (Continued)
  fat, fatty (generalized) - see also Disor-
    der, soft tissue, specified type NEC
    abdominal wall K65.4
    breast (aseptic) (segmental) N64.1
    localized - see Degeneration, by site,
      fatty
    mesentery K65.4
    omentum K65.4
    pancreas K86.8
    peritoneum K65.4
    skin (subcutaneous), newborn P83.0
    subcutaneous, due to birth injury
      P15.6
  gallbladder - see Cholecystitis, acute
  heart - see Infarct, myocardium
  hip, aseptic or avascular - see Osteone-
    crosis, by type, femur
  intestine (acute) (hemorrhagic) (mas-
    sive) K55.0
  jaw M27.2
  kidney (bilateral) N28.0
    acute N17.9
    cortical (acute) (bilateral) N17.1
      with ectopic or molar pregnancy
        O08.4
    medullary (bilateral) (in acute renal
      failure) (papillary) - see Pyelitis
    papillary (bilateral) (in acute renal
      failure) - see Pyelitis
    tubular N17.0
      with ectopic or molar pregnancy
        O08.4
      complicating
        abortion – see Abortion, by type,
          complicated by, tubular
          necrosis
        ectopic or molar pregnancy
          O08.4
        pregnancy – see Pregnancy,
          complicated by, diseases
          of, specified type or system
          NEC
      following ectopic or molar preg-
        nancy O08.4
      traumatic T79.5
  larynx J38.7
  liver (with hepatic failure) (cell) see
    Failure, hepatic
    hemorrhagic, central K76.2
  lung J85.0
  lymphatic gland - see Lymphadenitis,
    acute
  mammary gland (fat) (segmental) N64.1
  mastoid (chronic) – see Mastoiditis,
    chronic
  medullary (acute) (renal) N17.2
  mesentery K55.0
    fat K65.4
  mitral valve - see Insufficiency, mitral
  myocardium, myocardial - see Infarct,
    myocardium
  nose J34.0
  omentum (with mesenteric infarction)
    K55.0
    fat K65.4
  orbit, orbital - see Osteomyelitis, orbit
  ossicles, ear - see Abnormal, ear ossicles
  ovary N70.92
  pancreas (aseptic) (duct) (fat) K86.8
    acute (infective) - see Pancreatitis,
      acute
    infective - see Pancreatitis, acute
  papillary (acute) (renal) N17.2

Necrosis, necrotic (Continued)
perineum N90.89
peritoneum (with mesenteric infarction) K55.0
fat K65.4
pharynx J02.9
in granulocytopenia – see Neutropenia
Vincent's A69.1
phosphorus - see subcategory T54.2
pituitary (gland) (postpartum) (Sheehan) E23.0
pressure - see Ulcer, pressure, by site
pulmonary J85.0
pulp (dental) K04.1
radiation - see Necrosis, by site
radium - see Necrosis, by site
renal – see Necrosis, kidney
sclera H15.89
scrotum N50.8
skin or subcutaneous tissue NEC I96
spine, spinal (column) - see also Osteonecrosis, by type, vertebra
cord G95.19
spleen D73.5
stomach K31.89
stomatitis (ulcerative) A69.0
subcutaneous fat, newborn P83.8
subendocardial (acute) I21.4
chronic I25.89
suprarenal (capsule) (gland) E27.49
testis N50.8
thymus (gland) E32.8
tonsil J35.8
trachea J39.8
tuberculous NEC - see Tuberculosis
tubular (acute) (anoxic) (renal) (toxic) N17.0
postprocedural N99.0
vagina N89.8
vertebra - see also Osteonecrosis, by type, vertebra
tuberculous A18.01
vulva N90.89
X-ray - see Necrosis, by site
Necrospermia - see Infertility, male
Need (for)
care provider because of)
assistance with personal care Z74.1
continuous supervision required Z74.3
impaired mobility Z74.09
no other household member able to render care Z74.2
specified reason NEC Z74.8
immunization - see Vaccination
vaccination - see Vaccination
Neglect
adult
confirmed T74.01
history of Z91.412
suspected T76.01
child (childhood)
confirmed T74.02
history of Z62.812
suspected T76.02
emotional, in childhood Z62.8
hemispatial R41.4
left-sided R41.4
sensory R41.4
visuospatial R41.4
Neisserian infection NEC - see Gonococcus

Nelaton's syndrome G60.8
Nelson's syndrome E24.1
Nematodiasis (intestinal) B82.0
Ancylostoma B76.0
Neonatal - see also Newborn
acne L70.4
bradycardia P29.12
tachycardia P29.11
screening, abnormal findings on P09
tooth, teeth K00.6
Neonatorum - see condition
Neoplasia
endocrine, multiple (MEN) E31.20
type I E31.21
type IIA E31.22
type IIB E31.23
intraepithelial (histologically confirmed)
anal (AIN) (histologically confirmed) K62.82
grade I K62.82
grade II K62.82
severe D01.3
cervical glandular (histologically confirmed) D06.9
cervix (uteri) (CIN) (histologically confirmed) N87.9
glandular D06.9
grade I N87.0
grade II N87.1
grade III (severe dysplasia) D06.9
see also Carcinoma, cervix uteri, in situ
prostate (histologically confirmed) (PIN I) (PIN II) N42.3
grade I N42.3
grade II N42.3
vagina (histologically confirmed) (VAIN) N89.3
grade I N89.0
grade II N89.1
grade III (severe dysplasia) D07.2
vulva (histologically confirmed) (VIN) N90.3
grade I N90.0
grade II N90.1
grade III (severe dysplasia) D07.1
Neoplasm, neoplastic - see also Neoplasm table
malignant, associated with transplant organ C80.2
Neovascularization
ciliary body - see Disorder, iris, vascular
cornea H16.40-
deep H16.44-
ghost vessels -see Ghost, vessels
localized H16.43-
pannus - see Pannus
iris - see Disorder, iris, vascular
retina H35.05-
Nephralgia N23
Nephritis, nephritic (albuminuric) (azotemic) (congenital) (disseminated) (epithelial) (familial) (focal) (granulomatous) (hemorrhagic) (infantile) (nonsuppurative, excretory) (uremic) N05.9
with
dense deposit disease N05.6
diffuse
crescentic glomerulonephritis N05.7
endocapillary proliferative glomerulonephritis N05.4
membranous glomerulonephritis N05.2

Nephritis, nephritic (Continued)
with (Continued)
diffuse (Continued)
mesangial proliferative glomerulonephritis N05.3
mesangiocapillary glomerulonephritis N05.5
edema - see Nephrosis
focal and segmental glomerular lesions N05.1
foot process disease N04.9
glomerular lesion
diffuse sclerosing N05.8
hypocomplementemic - see Nephritis, membranoproliferative
IgA - see Nephropathy, IgA
lobular, lobulonodular - see Nephritis, membranoproliferative
nodular - see Nephritis, membranoproliferative
lesion of
glomerulonephritis, proliferative N05.8
renal necrosis N05.9
minor glomerular abnormality N05.0
specified morphological changes NEC N05.8
acute N00.9
with
dense deposit disease N00.6
diffuse
crescentic glomerulonephritis N00.7
endocapillary proliferative glomerulonephritis N00.4
membranous glomerulonephritis N00.2
mesangial proliferative glomerulonephritis N00.3
mesangiocapillary glomerulonephritis N00.5
focal and segmental glomerular lesions N00.1
minor glomerular abnormality N00.0
specified morphological changes NEC N00.8
amyloid E85.4 [N08]
antiglomerular basement membrane (anti-GBM) antibody NEC
in Goodpasture's syndrome M31.0
antitubular basement membrane (tubulo-interstitial) NEC N12
toxic - see Nephropathy, toxic
arteriolar - see Hypertension, kidney
arteriosclerotic - see Hypertension, kidney
ascending - see Nephritis, tubulo-interstitial
atrophic N03.9
Balkan (endemic) N15.0
calculous, calculus - see Calculus, kidney
cardiac - see Hypertension, kidney
cardiovascular - see Hypertension, kidney
chronic N03.9
with
dense deposit disease N03.6
diffuse
crescentic glomerulonephritis N03.7
endocapillary proliferative glomerulonephritis N03.4
membranous glomerulonephritis N03.2
mesangial proliferative glomerulonephritis N03.3
mesangiocapillary glomerulonephritis N03.5

Nephritis, nephritic *(Continued)*
  chronic *(Continued)*
    with *(Continued)*
      focal and segmental glomerular
        lesions N03.1
      minor glomerular abnormality
        N03.0
      specified morphological changes
        NEC N03.8
    arteriosclerotic - *see* Hypertension,
      kidney
  cirrhotic N26.9
  croupous N00.9
  degenerative - *see* Nephrosis
  diffuse sclerosing N05.8
  due to
    diabetes mellitus - *see* E09-E13 with .21
    subacute bacterial endocarditis I33.0
    systemic lupus erythematosus
      (chronic) M32.14
    typhoid fever A01.09
  gonococcal (acute) (chronic) A54.21
  hypocomplementemic - *see* Nephritis,
    membranoproliferative
  IgA - *see* Nephropathy, IgA
  immune complex (circulating) NEC
    N05.8
  infective - *see* Nephritis,
    tubulo-interstitial
  interstitial - *see* Nephritis,
    tubulo-interstitial
  lead N14.3
  membranoproliferative (diffuse) (type 1
    or 3) (*see also* N00-N07 with fourth
    character .5) N05.5
    type 2 (*see also* N00-N07 with fourth
      character .6) N05.6
  minimal change N05.0
  necrotic, necrotizing NEC (*see also* N00-
    N07 with fourth character .8) N05.8
  nephrotic - *see* Nephrosis
  nodular - *see* Nephritis,
    membranoproliferative
  polycystic Q61.3
    adult type Q61.2
    autosomal
      dominant Q61.2
      recessive NEC Q61.19
    childhood type NEC Q61.19
    infantile type NEC Q61.19
  poststreptococcal N05.9
    acute N00.9
    chronic N03.9
    rapidly progressive N01.9
  proliferative NEC (*see also* N00-N07
    with fourth character .8) N05.8
  purulent - *see* Nephritis,
    tubulo-interstitial
  rapidly progressive N01.9
    with
      dense deposit disease N01.6
      diffuse
        crescentic glomerulonephritis
          N01.7
        endocapillary proliferative glo-
          merulonephritis N01.4
        membranous glomerulonephritis
          N01.2
        mesangial proliferative glomeru-
          lonephritis N01.3
        mesangiocapillary glomerulone-
          phritis N01.5
      focal and segmental glomerular
        lesions N01.1

Nephritis, nephritic *(Continued)*
  rapidly progressive *(Continued)*
    with *(Continued)*
      minor glomerular abnormality
        N01.0
      specified morphological changes
        NEC N01.8
  salt losing or wasting NEC N28.89
  saturnine N14.3
  sclerosing, diffuse N05.8
  septic - *see* Nephritis, tubulo-
    interstitial
  specified pathology NEC (*see also*
    N00-N07 with fourth character .8)
    N05.8
  subacute N01.9
  suppurative - *see* Nephritis,
    tubulo-interstitial
  syphilitic (late) A52.75
    congenital A50.59 *[N08]*
    early (secondary) A51.44
  toxic - *see* Nephropathy, toxic
  tubal, tubular - *see* Nephritis,
    tubulo-interstitial
  tuberculous A18.11
  tubulo-interstitial (in) N12
    acute (infectious) N10
    chronic (infectious) N11.9
      nonobstructive N11.8
        reflux-associated N11.0
      obstructive N11.1
      specified NEC N11.8
    due to
      brucellosis A23.9 *[N16]*
      cryoglobulinemia D89.1 *[N16]*
      glycogen storage disease E74.00
        [N16]
      Sjögren's syndrome M35.04
  vascular - *see* Hypertension, kidney
  war N00.9
Nephroblastoma (epithelial) (mesenchymal) C64.-
Nephrocalcinosis E83.59 *[N29]*
Nephrocystitis, pustular - *see* Nephritis,
  tubulo-interstitial
Nephrolithiasis (congenital) (pelvis)
  (recurrent) - *see also* Calculus,
  kidney
Nephroma C64.-
  mesoblastic D41.0-
Nephronephritis - *see* Nephrosis
Nephronophthisis Q61.5
Nephropathia epidemica A98.5
Nephropathy (*see also* Nephritis)
  N28.9
  with
    edema - *see* Nephrosis
    glomerular lesion - *see*
      Glomerulonephritis
  amyloid, hereditary E85.0
  analgesic N14.0
    with medullary necrosis, acute
      N17.2
  Balkan (endemic) N15.0
  chemical - *see* Nephropathy, toxic
  diabetic - *see* E09-E13 with .21
  drug-induced N14.2
    specified NEC N14.1
  focal and segmental hyalinosis or scle-
    rosis N02.1
  heavy metal-induced N14.3
  hereditary NEC N07.9
    with
      dense deposit disease N07.6

Nephropathy *(Continued)*
  hereditary *(Continued)*
    with *(Continued)*
      diffuse
        crescentic glomerulonephritis
          N07.7
        endocapillary proliferative glo-
          merulonephritis N07.4
        membranous glomerulonephritis
          N07.2
        mesangial proliferative glomeru-
          lonephritis N07.3
        mesangiocapillary glomerulone-
          phritis N07.5
      focal and segmental glomerular
        lesions N07.1
      minor glomerular abnormality N07.0
      specified morphological changes
        NEC N07.8
  hypercalcemic N25.89
  hypertensive - *see* Hypertension, kidney
  hypokalemic (vacuolar) N25.89
  IgA N02.8
    with glomerular lesion N02.9
      focal and segmental hyalinosis or
        sclerosis N02.1
      membranoproliferative (diffuse)
        N02.5
      membranous (diffuse) N02.2
      mesangial proliferative (diffuse)
        N02.3
      mesangiocapillary (diffuse) N02.5
      proliferative NEC N02.8
      specified pathology NEC N02.8
  lead N14.3
  membranoproliferative (diffuse) N02.5
  membranous (diffuse) N02.2
  mesangial (IgA/IgG) - *see* Nephropathy,
    IgA
    proliferative (diffuse) N02.3
  mesangiocapillary (diffuse) N02.5
  obstructive N13.8
  phenacetin N17.2
  phosphate-losing N25.0
  potassium depletion N25.89
  pregnancy-related O26.83-
  proliferative NEC (*see also* N00-N07
    with fourth character .8) N05.8
  protein-losing N25.89
  saturnine N14.3
  sickle-cell D57.*[N08]*
  toxic NEC N14.4
    due to
      drugs N14.2
        analgesic N14.0
        specified NEC N14.1
      heavy metals N14.3
  vasomotor N17.0
  water-losing N25.89
Nephroptosis N28.83
Nephropyosis - *see* Abscess, kidney
Nephrorrhagia N28.89
Nephrosclerosis (arteriolar)(arteriosclerotic) (chronic) (hyaline) - *see also*
  Hypertension, kidney
  hyperplastic - *see* Hypertension, kidney
  senile N26.9
Nephrosis, nephrotic (Epstein's) (syndrome) (congenital) N04.9
  with glomerular lesion N04.1
    foot process disease N04.9
    hypocomplementemic N04.5
  acute N04.9
  anoxic - *see* Nephrosis, tubular

Nephrosis, nephrotic *(Continued)*
  chemical - *see* Nephrosis, tubular
  cholemic K76.7
  diabetic - *see* E09-E13 with .21
  Finnish type (congenital) Q89.8
  hemoglobin N10
  hemoglobinuric - *see* Nephrosis, tubular
  in
    amyloidosis E85.4 *[N08]*
    diabetes mellitus - *see* E09-E13 with .21
    epidemic hemorrhagic fever A98.5
    malaria (malariae) B52.0
  ischemic - *see* Nephrosis, tubular
  lipoid N04.9
  lower nephron - *see* Nephrosis, tubular
  malarial (malariae) B52.0
  minimal change N04.0
  myoglobin N10
  necrotizing - *see* Nephrosis, tubular
  osmotic (sucrose) N25.89
  radiation N04.9
  syphilitic (late) A52.75
  toxic - *see* Nephrosis, tubular
  tubular (acute) N17.0
    postprocedural N99.0
    radiation N04.9
Nephrosonephritis, hemorrhagic (en-
  demic) A98.5
Nephrostomy
  attention to Z43.6
  status Z93.6
Nerve - *see also* condition
  injury - *see* Injury, nerve, by body site
Nerves R45.0
Nervous (*see also* condition) R45.0
  heart F45.8
  stomach F45.8
  tension R45.0
Nervousness R45.0
Nesidioblastoma
  pancreas D13.7
  specified site NEC - *see* Neoplasm, benign
  unspecified site D13.7
Nettleship's syndrome Q82.2
Neumann's disease or syndrome L10.1
Neuralgia, neuralgic (acute) M79.2
  accessory (nerve) G52.8
  acoustic (nerve) - *see* subcategory H93.3
  auditory (nerve) - *see* subcategory H93.3
  ciliary G44.009
    intractable G44.001
    not intractable G44.009
  cranial
    nerve - *see also* Disorder, nerve, cranial
      fifth or trigeminal - *see* Neuralgia,
        trigeminal
      postherpetic, postzoster B02.29
  ear - *see* subcategory H92.0
  facialis vera G51.1
  Fothergill's - *see* Neuralgia, trigeminal
  glossopharyngeal (nerve) G52.1
  Horton's G43.809
  Hunt's B02.21
  hypoglossal (nerve) G52.3
  infraorbital - *see* Neuralgia, trigeminal
  malarial - *see* Malaria
  migrainous G44.009
    intractable G44.001
    not intractable G44.009
  Morton's G57.6-
  nerve, cranial - *see* Disorder, nerve,
    cranial
  nose G52.0
  occipital M54.81

Neuralgia, neuralgic *(Continued)*
  olfactory G52.0
  penis N48.9
  perineum R10.2
  postherpetic NEC B02.29
    trigeminal B02.22
  pubic region R10.2
  scrotum R10.2
  Sluder's G90.09
  specified nerve NEC G58.8
  spermatic cord R10.2
  sphenopalatine (ganglion) G44.89
  trifacial - *see* Neuralgia, trigeminal
  trigeminal G50.0
    postherpetic, postzoster B02.22
  vagus (nerve) G52.2
  writer's F48.8
    organic G25.89
Neurapraxia - *see* Injury, nerve
Neurasthenia F48.8
  cardiac F45.8
  gastric F45.8
  heart F45.8
Neurilemmoma - *see also* Neoplasm,
  nerve, benign
  acoustic (nerve) D33.3
  malignant - *see also* Neoplasm, nerve,
    malignant
    acoustic (nerve) C72.4
Neurilemmosarcoma - *see* Neoplasm,
  nerve, malignant
Neurinoma - *see* Neoplasm, nerve, benign
Neurinomatosis - *see* Neoplasm, nerve,
  uncertain behavior
Neuritis (rheumatoid) M79.2
  abducens (nerve) - *see* Strabismus, para-
    lytic, sixth nerve
  accessory (nerve) G52.8
  acoustic (nerve) - *see also* subcategory
    H93.3
    in (due to)
      infectious disease NEC B99
        [H94.0-]
      parasitic disease NEC B89 *[H94.0-]*
    syphilitic A52.15
  alcoholic G62.1
    with psychosis - *see* Psychosis,
      alcoholic
  amyloid, any site E85.4 *[G63]*
  auditory (nerve) - *see* subcategory
    H93.3
  brachial - *see* Radiculopathy
    due to displacement, intervertebral
      disc - *see* Disorder, disc, cervical,
      with neuritis
  cranial nerve
    due to Lyme disease A69.22
    eighth or acoustic or auditory - *see*
      subcategory H93.3
    eleventh or accessory G52.8
    fifth or trigeminal G51.0
    first or olfactory G52.0
    fourth or trochlear - *see* Strabismus,
      paralytic, fourth nerve
    second or optic - *see* Neuritis, optic
    seventh or facial G51.8
      newborn (birth injury) P11.3
    sixth or abducent - *see* Strabismus,
      paralytic, sixth nerve
    tenth or vagus G52.2
    third or oculomotor - *see* Strabismus,
      paralytic, third nerve
    twelfth or hypoglossal G52.3
  Déjérine-Sottas G60.0

Neuritis *(Continued)*
  diabetic (mononeuropathy) - *see* E09-
    E13 with .41
    polyneuropathy - *see* E09-E13 with .42
  due to
    beriberi E51.11 *[G63]*
    displacement, prolapse or rupture,
      intervertebral disc - *see* Disorder,
      disc, with, radiculopathy
    herniation, nucleus pulposus M51.9
      [G55]
  endemic E51.11 *[G63]*
  facial G51.8
    newborn (birth injury) P11.3
  general - *see* Polyneuropathy
  geniculate ganglion G51.1
    due to herpes (zoster) B02.21
  gouty M10.00 *[G63]*
  hypoglossal (nerve) G52.3
  ilioinguinal (nerve) G57.9-
  infectious (multiple) NEC G61.0
  interstitial hypertrophic progressive
    G60.0
  lumbar M54.16
  lumbosacral M54.17
  multiple - *see also* Polyneuropathy
    endemic E51.11
    infective, acute G61.0
  multiplex endemica E51.11
  nerve root - *see* Radiculopathy
  oculomotor (nerve) - *see* Strabismus,
    paralytic, third nerve
  olfactory nerve G52.0
  optic (nerve) (hereditary) (sympathetic)
    H46.9
    with demyelination G36.0
    in myelitis G36.0
    nutritional H46.2
    papillitis - *see* Papillitis, optic
    retrobulbar H46.1-
    specified type NEC H46.8
    toxic H46.3
  peripheral (nerve) G62.9
    multiple - *see* Polyneuropathy
    single - *see* Mononeuritis
  pneumogastric (nerve) G52.2
  postherpetic, postzoster B02.29
  progressive hypertrophic interstitial
    G60.0
  retrobulbar - *see also* Neuritis, optic,
    retrobulbar
    in (due to)
      late syphilis A52.15
      meningococcal infection A39.82
    meningococcal A39.82
    syphilitic A52.15
  sciatic (nerve) - *see also* Sciatica
    due to displacement of intervertebral
      disc - *see* Disorder, disc, with,
      radiculopathy
  serum T80.6
  shoulder-girdle G54.5
  specified nerve NEC G58.8
  spinal (nerve) root - *see* Radiculopathy
  syphilitic A52.15
  thenar (median) G56.1-
  thoracic M54.14
  toxic NEC G62.2
  trochlear (nerve) - *see* Strabismus, para-
    lytic, fourth nerve
  vagus (nerve) G52.2
Neuroastrocytoma - *see* Neoplasm, uncertain behavior
Neuroavitaminosis E56.9 *[G99.8]*

Neuroblastoma
olfactory C30.0
specified site - *see* Neoplasm, malignant
unspecified site C74.90
Neurochorioretinitis - *see* Chorioretinitis
Neurocirculatory asthenia F45.8
Neurocysticercosis B69.0
Neurocytoma - *see* Neoplasm, benign
Neurodermatitis (circumscribed) (circumscripta) (local) L28.0
atopic L20.81
diffuse (Brocq) L20.81
disseminated L20.81
Neuroencephalomyelopathy, optic G36.0
Neuroepithelioma - *see also* Neoplasm, malignant
olfactory C30.0
Neurofibroma - *see also* Neoplasm, nerve, benign
melanotic - *see* Neoplasm, nerve, benign
multiple - *see* Neurofibromatosis
plexiform - *see* Neoplasm, nerve, benign
Neurofibromatosis (multiple) (nonmalignant) Q85.0
malignant - *see* Neoplasm, nerve, malignant
Neurofibrosarcoma - *see* Neoplasm, nerve, malignant
Neurogenic - *see also* condition
bladder - *see also* Dysfunction, bladder, neuromuscular N31.9
cauda equina syndrome G83.4
bowel NEC K59.2
heart F45.8
Neuroglioma - *see* Neoplasm, uncertain behavior
Neurolabyrinthitis (of Dix and Hallpike) - *see* Neuronitis, vestibular
Neurolathyrism - *see* Poisoning, food, noxious, plant
Neuroleprosy A30.9
Neuroma - *see also* Neoplasm, nerve, benign
acoustic (nerve) D33.3
amputation (stump) (traumatic) (surgical complication) (late) T87.3-
arm T87.3-
leg T87.3-
digital (toe) G57.6-
interdigital (toe) G58.8
lower limb G57.8-
upper limb G56.8-
intermetatarsal G57.8-
Morton's G57.6-
nonneoplastic
arm G56.9-
leg G57.9-
lower extremity G57.9-
upper extremity G56.9-
optic (nerve) D33.3
plantar G57.6-
plexiform - *see* Neoplasm, nerve, benign
surgical (nonneoplastic)
arm G56.9-
leg G57.9-
lower extremity G57.9-
upper extremity G56.9-
Neuromyalgia - *see* Neuralgia
Neuromyasthenia (epidemic) (postinfectious) G93.3

Neuromyelitis G36.9
ascending G61.0
optica G36.0
Neuromyopathy G70.9
paraneoplastic D49.9 *[G13.0]*
Neuromyotonia (Isaacs) G71.19
Neuronevus - *see* Nevus
Neuronitis G58.9
ascending (acute) G57.2-
vestibular H81.23
left H81.21
with right H81.22
right H81.20
with left H81.22
Neuroparalytic - *see* condition
Neuropathy, neuropathic G62.9
acute motor G62.81
alcoholic G62.1
with psychosis - *see* Psychosis, alcoholic
arm G56.9-
autonomic, peripheral - *see* Neuropathy, peripheral, autonomic
axillary G56.9-
bladder N31.9
atonic (motor) (sensory) N31.2
autonomous N31.2
flaccid N31.2
nonreflex N31.2
reflex N31.1
uninhibited N31.0
brachial plexus G54.0
cervical plexus G54.2
chronic
progressive segmentally demyelinating G62.89
relapsing demyelinating G62.89
Déjérine-Sottas G60.0
diabetic - *see* E09-E13 with .40
mononeuropathy - *see* E09-E13 with .41
polyneuropathy - *see* E09-E13 with .42
entrapment G58.9
iliohypogastric nerve G57.8-
ilioinguinal nerve G57.8-
lateral cutaneous nerve of thigh G57.1-
median nerve G56.0-
obturator nerve G57.8-
peroneal nerve G57.3-
posterior tibial nerve G57.5-
saphenous nerve G57.8-
ulnar nerve G56.2-
facial nerve G51.9
hereditary G60.9
motor and sensory (types I-IV) G60.0
sensory G60.8
specified NEC G60.8
hypertrophic G60.0
Charcot-Marie-Tooth G60.0
Déjérine-Sottas G60.0
interstitial progressive G60.0
of infancy G60.0
Refsum G60.1
idiopathic G60.9
progressive G60.3
specified NEC G60.8
in association with hereditary ataxia G60.2
intercostal G58.0
ischemic - *see* Disorder, nerve
Jamaica (ginger) G62.2
leg NEC G57.9-
lower extremity G57.9-

Neuropathy, neuropathic *(Continued)*
lumbar plexus G54.1
median nerve G56.1-
motor and sensory - *see also* Polyneuropathy
hereditary (types I-IV) G60.0
multiple (acute) (chronic) - *see* Polyneuropathy
optic (nerve) - *see also* Neuritis, optic
ischemic - *see* Disorder, nerve, optic, ischemic
paraneoplastic (sensorial) (Denny Brown) D49.9 *[G13.0]*
peripheral (nerve) (*see also* Polyneuropathy) G62.9
autonomic G90.9
idiopathic G90.09
in (due to)
amyloidosis E85.4 *[G99.0]*
diabetes mellitus - *see* E09-E13 with .43
endocrine disease NEC E34.9 *[G99.0]*
gout M10.00 *[G99.0]*
hyperthyroidism E05.90 *[G99.0]*
with thyroid storm E05.91 *[G99.0]*
metabolic disease NEC E88.9 *[G99.0]*
idiopathic G60.9
progressive G60.3
in (due to)
antitetanus serum G62.0
arsenic G62.2
drugs NEC G62.0
lead G62.2
organophosphate compounds G62.2
toxic agent NEC G62.2
plantar nerves G57.6-
progressive
hypertrophic interstitial G60.9
inflammatory G62.81
radicular NEC - *see* Radiculopathy
sacral plexus G54.1
sciatic G57.0-
serum G61.1
toxic NEC G62.2
trigeminal sensory G50.8
ulnar nerve G56.2-
uremic N18.9 *[G63]*
vitamin B_{12} E53.8 *[G63]*
with anemia (pernicious) D51.0 *[G63]*
due to dietary deficiency D51.3 *[G63]*
Neurophthisis - *see also* Disorder, nerve
peripheral, diabetic - *see* E09-E13 with .42
Neuroretinitis - *see* Chorioretinitis
Neuroretinopathy, hereditary optic H47.22
Neurosarcoma - *see* Neoplasm, nerve, malignant
Neurosclerosis - *see* Disorder, nerve
Neurosis, neurotic F48.9
anankastic F42
anxiety (state) F41.1
panic type F41.0
asthenic F48.8
bladder F45.8
cardiac (reflex) F45.8
cardiovascular F45.8
character F60.9
colon F45.8
compensation F68.8

Neurosis, neurotic (*Continued*)
  compulsive, compulsion F42
  conversion F44.9
  craft F48.8
  cutaneous F45.8
  depersonalization F48.1
  depressive (reaction) (type) F34.1
  environmental F48.8
  excoriation L98.1
  fatigue F48.8
  functional - *see* Disorder, somatoform
  gastric F45.8
  gastrointestinal F45.8
  heart F45.8
  hypochondriacal F45.21
  hysterical F44.9
  incoordination F45.8
    larynx F45.8
    vocal cord F45.8
  intestine F45.8
  larynx (sensory) F45.8
    hysterical F44.4
  mixed NEC F48.8
  musculoskeletal F45.8
  obsessional F42
  obsessive-compulsive F42
  occupational F48.8
  ocular NEC F45.8
  organ - *see* Disorder, somatoform
  pharynx F45.8
  phobic F40.9
  posttraumatic (acute) (situational) F43.9
  psychasthenic (type) F48.8
  railroad F48.8
  rectum F45.8
  respiratory F45.8
  rumination F45.8
  sexual F65.9
  situational F48.8
  social F40.10
    generalized F40.11
  specified type NEC F48.8
  state F48.9
    with depersonalization episode
      F48.1
  stomach F45.8
  traumatic F43.10
    acute F43.11
    chronic F43.12
  vasomotor F45.8
  visceral F45.8
  war F48.8
Neurospongioblastosis diffusa Q85.1
Neurosyphilis (arrested) (early) (gumma)
    (late) (latent) (recurrent) (relapse)
    A52.3
  with ataxia (cerebellar) (locomotor)
    (spastic) (spinal) A52.19
  aneurysm (cerebral) A52.05
  arachnoid (adhesive) A52.13
  arteritis (any artery) (cerebral) A52.04
  asymptomatic A52.2
  congenital A50.40
  dura (mater) A52.13
  general paresis A52.17
  hemorrhagic A52.05
  juvenile (asymptomatic) (meningeal)
    A50.40
  leptomeninges (aseptic) A52.13
  meningeal, meninges (adhesive) A52.13
  meningitis A52.12
  meningovascular (diffuse) A52.13
  optic atrophy A52.15
  parenchymatous (degenerative) A52.19

Neurosyphilis (*Continued*)
  paresis, paretic A52.17
    juvenile A50.45
  remission in (sustained) A52.3
  serological (without symptoms) A52.2
  specified nature or site NEC A52.19
  tabes, tabetic (dorsalis) A52.11
    juvenile A50.45
  taboparesis A52.17
    juvenile A50.45
  thrombosis (cerebral) A52.05
  vascular (cerebral) NEC A52.05
Neurothekeoma - *see* Neoplasm, nerve,
    benign
Neurotic - *see* Neurosis
Neurotoxemia - *see* Toxemia
Neutroclusion M26.211
Neutropenia, neutropenic (chronic)
    (genetic) (idiopathic) (immune)
    (infantile) (malignant) (pernicious)
    (splenic) D70.9
  congenital (primary) D70.0
  cyclic D70.4
  cytoreductive cancer chemotherapy
    sequela D70.1
  drug-induced D70.2
    due to cytoreductive cancer chemo-
      therapy D70.1
  due to infection D70.3
  fever D70.9
  neonatal, transitory (isoimmune) (ma-
    ternal transfer) P61.5
  periodic D70.4
  secondary (cyclic) (periodic) (splenic)
    D70.4
    drug-induced D70.2
      due to cytoreductive cancer chemo-
        therapy D70.1
  toxic D70.8
Neutrophilia, hereditary giant D72.0
Nevocarcinoma - *see* Melanoma
Nevus D22.9
  achromic
  amelanotic
  angiomatous D18.00
    intra-abdominal D18.03
    intracranial D18.02
    skin D18.01
    specified site NEC D18.09
  araneus I78.1
  balloon cell
  bathing trunk D48.5
  blue
    cellular
    giant
    Jadassohn's
    malignant - *see* Melanoma
  capillary D18.00
    intra-abdominal D18.03
    intracranial D18.02
    skin D18.01
    specified site NEC D18.09
  cavernous D18.00
    intra-abdominal D18.03
    intracranial D18.02
    skin D18.01
    specified site NEC D18.09
  cellular
    blue
  choroid D31.3-
  comedonicus Q82.5
  conjunctiva D31.0-
  dermal
    with epidermal nevus

Nevus (*Continued*)
  dysplastic
  eye D31.9-
  flammeus Q82.5
  hemangiomatous D18.00
    intra-abdominal D18.03
    intracranial D18.02
    skin D18.01
    specified site NEC D18.09
  iris D31.4-
  lacrimal gland D31.5-
  lymphatic D18.1
    specified site - *see* Neoplasm, benign
    unspecified site D31.40
  malignant (M8720/3) - *see* Melanoma
  meaning hemangioma D18.00
    intra-abdominal D18.03
    intracranial D18.02
    skin D18.01
    specified site NEC D18.09
  mouth (mucosa) D10.30
    specified site NEC D10.39
    white sponge Q38.6
  multiplex Q85.1
  non-neoplastic I78.1
  oral mucosa D10.30
    specified site NEC D10.39
    white sponge Q38.6
  orbit D31.6-
    giant - *see also* Neoplasm, skin, uncer-
      tain behavior D48.5
    malignant melanoma in - *see*
      Melanoma
  portwine Q82.5
  retina D31.2-
  retrobulbar D31.6-
  sanguineous Q82.5
  senile I78.1
  skin D22.9
    abdominal wall D22.5
    ala nasi D22.39
    ankle D22.7-
    anus, anal D22.5
    arm D22.6-
    auditory canal (external) D22.2-
    auricle (ear) D22.2-
    auricular canal (external) D22.2-
    axilla, axillary fold D22.5
    back D22.5
    breast D22.5
    brow D22.39
    buttock D22.5
    canthus (eye) D22.1-
    cheek (external) D22.39
    chest wall D22.5
    chin D22.39
    ear (external) D22.2-
    external meatus (ear) D22.2-
    eyebrow D22.39
    eyelid (lower) (upper) D22.1-
    face D22.30
      specified NEC D22.39
    female genital organ (external) NEC
      D28.0
    finger D22.6-
    flank D22.5
    foot D22.7-
    forearm D22.6-
    forehead D22.39
    foreskin D29.0
    genital organ (external) NEC
      female D28.0
      male D29.9
    gluteal region D22.5

Nevus *(Continued)*
  skin *(Continued)*
    groin D22.5
    hand D22.6-
    heel D22.7-
    helix D22.2-
    hip D22.7-
    interscapular region D22.5
    jaw D22.39
    knee D22.7-
    labium (majus) (minus) D28.0
    leg D22.7-
    lip (lower) (upper) D22.0
    lower limb D22.7-
    male genital organ (external) D29.9
    nail D22.9
      finger D22.6-
      toe D22.7-
    nasolabial groove D22.39
    nates D22.5
    neck D22.4
    nose (external) D22.39
    palpebra D22.1-
    penis D29.0
    perianal skin D22.5
    perineum D22.5
    pinna D22.2-
    popliteal fossa or space D22.7-
    prepuce D29.0
    pudendum D28.0
    scalp D22.4
    scrotum D29.4
    shoulder D22.6-
    skin D22.9
    specified site NEC - *see* Neoplasm,
      benign
    submammary fold D22.5
    temple D22.39
    thigh D22.7-
    toe D22.7-
    trunk NEC D22.5
    umbilicus D22.5
    upper limb D22.6-
    vulva D28.0
  spider I78.1
  stellar I78.1
  strawberry Q82.5
  Sutton's
  unius lateris Q82.5
  Unna's Q82.5
  vascular Q82.5
  verrucous Q82.5
Newborn (infant) (liveborn) (singleton)
  Z38.2
  acne L70.4
  abstinence syndrome P96.1
  affected by (suspected to be)
    abnormalities of membranes P02.9
      specified NEC P02.8
    abruptio placenta P02.1
    amino-acid metabolic disorder, tran-
      sitory P74.8
    amniocentesis (while in utero) P00.6
    amnionitis P02.7
    apparent life threatening event ALTE
      R68.13
    bleeding (into)
      cerebral cortex P52.22
      germinal matrix P52.0
      ventricles P52.1
    breech delivery P03.0
    cardiac arrest P29.81
    cardiomyopathy I42.8
    congenital I42.4

Newborn *(Continued)*
  affected by *(Continued)*
    cerebral ischemia P91.0
    Cesarean delivery P03.4
    chemotherapy agents P04.1
    chorioamnionitis P02.7
    cocaine (crack) P04.41
    complications of labor and delivery
      P03.9
      specified NEC P03.89
    compression of umbilical cord NEC
      P02.5
    contracted pelvis P03.1
    delivery P03.9
      Cesarean P03.4
      forceps P03.2
      vacuum extractor P03.3
    environmental chemicals P04.6
    entanglement (knot) in umbilical cord
      P02.5
    forceps delivery P03.2
    heart rate abnormalities P29.1
      bradycardia P29.12
      intrauterine P03.819
        before onset of labor P03.810
        during labor P03.811
      tachycardia P29.11
    hemorrhage (antepartum) P02.1
      cerebellar (nontraumatic) P52.6
      intracerebral (nontraumatic) P52.4
      intracranial (nontraumatic) P52.9
        specified NEC P52.8
      intraventricular (nontraumatic)
        P52.3
        grade 1 P52.0
        grade 2 P52.1
        grade 3 P52.21
        grade 4 P52.22
      posterior fossa (nontraumatic)
        P52.6
      subarachnoid (nontraumatic)
        P52.5
      subependymal P52.0
        with intracerebral extension
          P52.22
        with intraventricular extension
          P52.1
          with enlargment of ventricles
            P52.21
        without intraventricular exten-
          sion P52.0
    hypoxic ischemic encephalopathy
      [HIE] P91.60
      mild P91.61
      moderate P91.62
      severe P91.63
    induction of labor P03.89
    intestinal perforation P78.0
    intrauterine (fetal) blood loss P50.9
      due to (from)
        cut end of co-twin cord P50.5
        hemorrhage into
          co-twin P50.3
          maternal circulation P50.4
        placenta P50.2
        ruptured cord blood P50.1
        vasa previa P50.0
      specified NEC P50.8
    intrauterine (fetal) hemorrhage
      P50.9
    intrauterine (in utereo) procedure
      P96.5
    malpresentation (malposition) NEC
      P03.1

Newborn *(Continued)*
  affected by *(Continued)*
    maternal (complication of) (use of)
      alcohol P04.3
      analgesia (maternal) P04.0
      anesthesia (maternal) P04.0
      blood loss P02.1
      circulatory disease P00.3
      condition P00.9
        specified NEC P00.89
      delivery P03.9
        Cesarean P03.4
        forceps P03.2
        vacuum extractor P03.3
      diabetes mellitus (pre-existing)
        P70.1
      disorder P00.9
        specified NEC P00.89
      drugs (addictive) (illegal) NEC
        P04.49
      ectopic pregnancy P01.4
      gestational diabetes P70.0
      hemorrhage P02.1
      hypertensive disorder P00.0
      incompetent cervix P01.0
      infectious disease P00.2
      injury P00.5
      labor and delivery P03.9
      malpresentation before labor P01.7
      maternal death P01.6
      medical procedure P00.7
      medication P04.1
      multiple pregnancy P01.5
      nutritional disorder P00.4
      oligohydramnios P01.2
      parasitic disease P00.2
      periodontal disease P00.81
      placenta previa P02.0
      polyhydramnios P01.3
      precipitate delivery P03.5
      pregnancy P01.9
        specified P01.8
      premature rupture of membranes
        P01.1
      renal disease P00.1
      respiratory disease P00.3
      surgical procedure P00.6
      urinary tract disease P00.1
      uterine contraction (abnormal)
        P03.6
    meconium peritonitis P78.0
    medication (legal) (maternal use)
      (prescribed) P04.1
    membrane abnormalities P02.9
      specified NEC P02.8
    membranitis P02.7
    methamphetamine(s) P04.49
    mixed metabolic and respiratory
      acidosis P84
    neonatal abstinence syndrome P96.1
    noxious substances transmitted via
      placenta or breast milk P04.9
      specified NEC P04.8
    nutritional supplements P04.5
    placenta previa P02.0
    placental
      abnormality (functional) (morpho-
        logical) P02.20
        specified NEC P02.29
      dysfunction P02.29
      infarction P02.29
      insufficiency P02.29
      separation NEC P02.1
      transfusion syndromes P02.3

Newborn *(Continued)*
  affected by *(Continued)*
    placentitis P02.7
    precipitate delivery P03.5
    prolapsed cord P02.4
    respiratory arrest P28.81
    tobacco P04.2
    twin to twin transplacental transfu-
      sion P02.3
    umbilical cord (tightly) around neck
      P02.5
    umbilical cord condition P02.60
      short cord P02.69
      specified NEC P02.69
    uterine contractions (abnormal)
      P03.6
    vasa previa P02.69
      from intrauterine blood loss P50.0
  apnea P28.3
    primary P28.3
    obstructive P28.4
    specified P28.4
  born in hospital Z38.00
    by cesarean Z38.01
  born outside hospital Z38.1
  breast buds P96.89
  breast engorgement P83.4
  check-up - *see* Newborn, examination
  convulsion P90
  dehydration P74.1
  examination
    8 to 28 days old Z00.111
    under 8 days old Z00.110
  fever P81.9
    environmentally-induced P81.0
  hyperbilirubinemia P59.9
    of prematurity P59.0
  hypernatremia P74.2
  hyponatremia P74.2
  infection P39.9
    candidal P37.5
    specified NEC P39.8
    urinary tract P39.3
  jaundice P59.8
    due to
      breast milk inhibitor P593.
      hepatocellular damage P59.20
        specified NEC P59.29
      preterm delivery P59.0
    of prematurity P59.0
    specified NEC P59.8
  late metabolic acidosis P74.0
  mastitis P39.0
    infective P39.0
    noninfective P83.4
  multiple born NEC Z38.8
    born in hospital Z38.68
      by cesarean Z38.69
    born outside hospital Z38.7
  omphalitis P38.9
    with mild hemorrhage P38.1
    without hemorrhage P38.9
  post-term P08.21
  prolonged gestation (over 42 completed
    weeks) P08.22
  quadruplet Z38.8
    born in hospital Z38.63
      by cesarean Z38.64
    born outside hospital Z38.7
  quintuplet Z38.8
    born in hospital Z38.65
      by cesarean Z38.66
    born outside hospital Z38.7
  seizure P90

Newborn *(Continued)*
  sepsis (congenital) P36.9
    due to
      anaerobes NEC P36.5
      Escherichia coli P36.4
      Staphylococcus P36.30
        aureus P36.2
        specified NEC P36.39
      Streptococcus P36.10
        group B P36.0
        specified NEC P36.19
      specified NEC P36.8
  triplet Z38.8
    born in hospital Z38.61
      by cesarean Z38.62
    born outside hospital Z38.7
  twin Z38.5
    born in hospital Z38.30
      by cesarean Z38.31
    born outside hospital Z38.4
  vomiting P92.09
    bilious P92.01
  weight check Z00.111
Newcastle conjunctivitis or disease B30.8
Nezelof's syndrome (pure alymphocyto-
  sis) D81.4
Niacin(amide) deficiency E52
Nicolas(-Durand)-Favre disease A55
Nicotine - *see* Tobacco
Nicotinic acid deficiency E52
Niemann-Pick disease or syndrome
  E75.249
  specified NEC E75.248
  type
    A E75.240
    B E75.241
    C E75.242
    D E75.243
Night
  blindness - *see* Blindness, night
  sweats R61
  terrors (child) F51.4
Nightmares (REM sleep type) F51.5
Nipple - *see* condition
Nisbet's chancre A57
Nishimoto (-Takeuchi) disease I67.5
Nitritoid crisis or reaction - *see* Crisis,
  nitritoid
Nitrosohemoglobinemia D74.8
Njovera A65
Nocardiosis, nocardiasis A43.9
  cutaneous A43.1
  lung A43.0
  pneumonia A43.0
  pulmonary A43.0
  specified site NEC A43.8
Nocturia R35.1
  psychogenic F45.8
Nocturnal - *see* condition
Nodal rhythm I49.8
Node(s) - *see also* Nodule
  Bouchard's (with arthropathy) M15.2
  Haygarth's M15.8
  Heberden's (with arthropathy) M15.1
  larynx J38.7
  lymph - *see* condition
  milker's B08.03
  Osler's I33.0
  Schmorl's - *see* Schmorl's disease
  singer's J38.2
  teacher's J38.2
  tuberculous - *see* Tuberculosis, lymph
    gland
  vocal cord J38.2

Nodule(s), nodular
  actinomycotic - *see* Actinomycosis
  breast NEC N63
  colloid (cystic), thyroid E04.1
  cutaneous - *see* Swelling, localized
  endometrial (stromal) D26.1
  Haygarth's M15.8
  inflammatory - *see* Inflammation
  juxta-articular
    syphilitic A52.77
    yaws A66.7
  larynx J38.7
  milker's B08.03
  prostate - *see* Enlargement, enlarged,
    prostate
  retrocardiac R09.89
  rheumatoid M06.30
    ankle M06.37-
    elbow M06.32-
    foot joint M06.37-
    hand joint M06.34-
    hip M06.35-
    knee M06.36-
    multiple site M06.39
    shoulder M06.31-
    vertebra M06.38
    wrist M06.33-
  scrotum (inflammatory) N49.2
  singer's J38.2
  solitary, lung J98.4
  subcutaneous - *see* Swelling, localized
  teacher's J38.2
  thyroid (cold) (gland) (nontoxic) E04.1
    with thyrotoxicosis E05.20
      with thyroid storm E05.21
    toxic or with hyperthyroidism
      E05.20
      with thyroid storm E05.21
  vocal cord J38.2
Noma (gangrenous) (hospital) (infective)
  A69.0
  auricle I96
  mouth A69.0
  pudendi N76.89
  vulvae N76.89
Nomad, nomadism Z59.0
Nonautoimmune hemolytic anemia D59.4
  drug-induced D59.2
Nonclosure - *see also* Imperfect, closure
  ductus arteriosus (Botallo's) Q25.0
  foramen
    botalli Q21.1
    ovale Q21.1
Noncompliance Z91.19
  with
    dietary regimen Z91.11
    dialysis Z91.15
    medical treatment Z91.19
    medication regimen NEC Z91.14
      underdosing Z91.14 - *see also*
        Table of drugs and chemicals,
        categories T36-T50, with final
        character 6
      intentional NEC Z91.128
        due to financial hardship of
          patient Z91.120
      unintentional NEC Z91.138
        due to patient's age related
          debility Z91.130
      renal dialysis Z91.15
Nondescent (congenital) - *see also* Malposition, congenital
  cecum Q43.3
  colon Q43.3

Nondescent *(Continued)*
  testicle Q53.9
    bilateral Q53.20
      abdominal Q53.21
      perineal Q53.22
    unilateral Q53.10
      abdominal Q53.11
      perineal Q53.12
Nondevelopment
  brain Q02
    part of Q04.3
  heart Q24.8
  organ or site, congenital NEC - *see*
    Hypoplasia
Nonengagement
  head NEC O32.4
    in labor, causing obstructed labor
      O64.8
Nonexanthematous tick fever A93.2
Nonexpansion, lung (newborn) P28.0
Nonfunctioning
  cystic duct (*see also* Disease, gall-
    bladder) K82.8
  gallbladder (*see also* Disease, gall-
    bladder) K82.8
  kidney N28.9
  labyrinth - *see* subcategory H83.2
Non-Hodgkin lymphoma NEC – *see*
    Lymphoma, non-Hodgkin type
Non-working side interference M26.56
Nonimplantation, ovum N97.2
Noninsufflation, fallopian tube
    N97.1
Non-ketotic hyperglycinemia E72.51
Nonne-Milroy syndrome Q82.0
Nonovulation N97.0
Nonpatent fallopian tube N97.1

Nonpneumatization, lung NEC P28.0
Nonrotation - *see* Malrotation
Nonsecretion, urine - *see* Anuria
Nonunion
  fracture - *see* Fracture, by site
  organ or site, congenital NEC - *see*
    Imperfect, closure
  symphysis pubis, congenital Q74.2
Nonvisualization, gallbladder R93.2
Nonvital, nonvitalized tooth K04.99
Noonan's syndrome Q87.1
Normocytic anemia (infectional) due to
    blood loss (chronic) D50.0
  acute D62
Norrie's disease (congenital) Q15.8
North American blastomycosis B40.9
Norwegian itch B86
Nose, nasal - *see* condition
Nosebleed R04.0
Nose-picking F98.8
Nosomania F45.21
Nosophobia F45.22
Nostalgia F43.20
Notch of iris Q13.2
Notching nose, congenital (tip) Q30.2
Nothnagel's
  syndrome - *see* Strabismus, paralytic,
    third nerve
  vasomotor acroparesthesia I73.89
Novy's relapsing fever A68.9
  louse-borne A68.0
  tick-borne A68.1
Noxious
  foodstuffs, poisoning by - *see* Poisoning,
    food, noxious, plant
  substances transmitted through pla-
    centa or breast milk P04.9

Nucleus pulposus - *see* condition
Numbness R20.0
Nuns' knee - *see* Bursitis, prepatellar
Nursemaid's elbow S53.03-
Nutcracker esophagus K22.4
Nutmeg liver K76.1
Nutrient element deficiency E61.9
  specified NEC E61.8
Nutrition deficient or insufficient - *see*
    also Malnutrition E46
  due to
    insufficient food T73.0
    lack of
      care (child) T76.02
        adult T76.01
      food T73.0
Nutritional stunting E45
Nyctalopia (night blindness) - *see* Blind-
    ness, night
Nycturia R35.1
  psychogenic F45.8
Nymphomania F52.8
Nystagmus H55.00
  benign paroxysmal - *see* Vertigo, benign
    paroxysmal
  central positional - *see* subcategory
    H81.4
  congenital H55.01
  dissociated H55.04
  latent H55.02
  miners' H55
  positional
    benign paroxysmal - *see* subcategory
      H81.4
    central - *see* subcategory H81.4
  specified form NEC H55.09
  visual deprivation H55.03

O

Obermeyer's relapsing fever (European)
A68.0
Obesity E66.9
  with alveolar hyperventilation
    E66.2
  adrenal E27.8
  complicating
    childbirth O99.214
    pregnancy O99.21-
    puerperium O99.215
  constitutional E66.8
  dietary counseling and surveillance
    Z71.3
  drug-induced E66.1
  due to
    drug E66.1
    excess calories E66.09
      morbid E66.01
      severe E66.01
  endocrine E66.8
  endogenous E66.8
  familial E66.8
  glandular E66.8
  hypothyroid - see Hypothyroidism
  morbid E66.01
    with alveolar hypoventilation
      E66.2
    due to excess calories E66.01
  nutritional E66.09
  pituitary E23.6
  severe E66.01
  specified type NEC E66.8
Oblique - see condition
Obliteration
  appendix (lumen) K38.8
  artery I77.1
  bile duct (noncalculous) K83.1
  common duct (noncalculous)
    K83.1
  cystic duct - see Obstruction,
    gallbladder
  disease, arteriolar I77.1
  endometrium N85.8
  eye, anterior chamber - see Disorder,
    globe, hypotony
  fallopian tube N97.1
  lymphatic vessel I89.0
    due to mastectomy I97.2
  organ or site, congenital NEC - see
    Atresia, by site
  ureter N13.5
    with infection N13.6
  urethra - see Stricture, urethra
  vein I87.8
  vestibule (oral) K08.8
Observation (following) (for) (without
    need for further medical care)
    Z04.9
  accident NEC Z04.3
    at work Z04.2
    transport Z04.1
  adverse effect of drug Z03.6
  alleged rape or sexual assault (victim),
    ruled out
    adult Z04.41
    child Z04.42
  criminal assault Z04.8
  development state
    adolescent Z00.3
    period of rapid growth in childhood
      Z00.2
    puberty Z00.3

Observation (Continued)
  disease, specified NEC Z03.89
  following work accident Z04.2
  growth and development state - see
    Observation, development state
  injuries (accidental) NEC - see also Ob-
    servation, accident
  newborn (for suspected condition,
    ruled out) see - Newborn, affected
    by (suspected to be), maternal
    (complication of) (use of)
  postpartum
    immediately after delivery Z39.0
    routine follow-up Z39.2
  pregnancy (normal) (without complica-
    tion) Z34.9-
    high risk O09.9-
  suicide attempt, alleged NEC Z03.89
    self-poisoning Z03.6
  suspected, ruled out - see also Suspected
    condition, ruled out
    abuse, physical
      adult Z04.71
      child Z04.72
    accident at work Z04.2
    adult battering victim Z04.71
    child battering victim Z04.72
    condition NEC Z03.89
      newborn see - Newborn, affected
        by (suspected to be),
        maternal (complication of)
        (use of)
    drug poisoning or adverse effect
      Z03.6
    exposure (to)
      anthrax Z03.810
      biological agent NEC Z03.818
    inflicted injury NEC Z04.8
    suicide attempt, alleged Z03.89
      self-poisoning Z03.6
    toxic effects from ingested substance
      (drug) (poison) Z03.6
  toxic effects from ingested substance
    (drug) (poison) Z03.6
Obsession, obsessional state F42
Obsessive-compulsive neurosis or reac-
    tion F42
Obstetric embolism, septic – see Embo-
    lism, obstetric, septic
Obstetrical trauma (complicating deliv-
    ery) O71.9
  with or following ectopic or molar
    pregnancy O08.6
  specified type NEC O71.89
Obstipation - see Constipation
Obstruction, obstructed, obstructive
  airway J98.8
    with
      allergic alveolitis J67.9
      asthma J45.909
        with
          exacerbation (acute) J45.901
          status asthmaticus J45.902
      bronchiectasis J47.9
        with
          exacerbation (acute) J47.1
          lower respiratory infection
            J47.0
      bronchitis (chronic) J44.9
      emphysema J43.9
    chronic J44.9
      with
        allergic alveolitis – see Pneumo-
          nitis, hypersensitivity

Obstruction, obstructed, obstructive
    (Continued)
  airway (Continued)
    chronic (Continued)
      with (Continued)
        bronchiectasis J47.9
          with
            exacerbation (acute) J47.1
            lower respiratory infection
              J47.0
      due to
        foreign body - see Foreign body,
          by site, causing asphyxia
        inhalation of fumes or vapors
          J68.9
        laryngospasm J38.5
  ampulla of Vater K83.1
  aortic (heart) (valve) - see Stenosis,
    aortic
  aortoiliac I74.0
  aqueduct of Sylvius G91.1
    congenital Q03.0
      with spina bifida - see Spina
        bifida, by site, with
        hydrocephalus
  Arnold-Chiari - see Arnold-Chiari
    disease
  artery (see also Embolism, artery)
    I74.9
    basilar (complete) (partial) - see
      Occlusion, artery, basilar
    carotid (complete) (partial) - see
      Occlusion, artery, carotid
    cerebellar – see Occlusion, artery,
      cerebellar
    cerebral (anterior) (middle) (pos-
      terior) – see Occlusion, artery,
      cerebral
    precerebral - see Occlusion, artery,
      precerebral
    renal N28.0
    retinal NEC - see Occlusion, artery,
      retina
    vertebral (complete) (partial) - see
      Occlusion, artery, vertebral
  band (intestinal) K56.69
  bile duct or passage (common) (hepatic)
    (noncalculous) K83.1
    with calculus K80.51
    congenital (causing jaundice)
      Q44.3
  biliary (duct) (tract) K83.1
    gallbladder K82.0
  bladder-neck (acquired) N32.0
    congenital Q64.31
    due to hyperplasia (hypertrophy)
      of prostate - see Hyperplasia,
      prostate, specified type, with
      obstruction
  bowel - see Obstruction, intestine
  bronchus J98.09
  canal, ear - see Stenosis, external ear
    canal
  cardia K22.2
  caval veins (inferior) (superior) I87.1
  cecum - see Obstruction, intestine
  circulatory I99.8
  colon - see Obstruction, intestine
  common duct (noncalculous) K83.1
  coronary (artery) – see Occlusion,
    coronary
  cystic duct - see also Obstruction,
    gallbladder
    with calculus K80.21

Obstruction, obstructed, obstructive
(Continued)
device, implant or graft (*see also*
    Complications, by site and type,
    mechanical) T85.628
  arterial graft NEC - *see* Complication,
    cardiovascular device, mechani-
    cal, vascular
  catheter NEC T85.628
    cystostomy T83.090
    dialysis (renal) T82.49
      intraperitoneal T85.691
    infusion NEC T82.594
      spinal (epidural) (subdural)
        T85.690
    due to infection T85.79
  gastrointestinal - *see* Complications,
    prosthetic device, mechanical,
    gastrointestinal device
  genital NEC T83.498
    intrauterine contraceptive device
      T83.39
    penile prosthesis T83.490
  heart NEC - *see* Complication,
    cardiovascular device,
    mechanical
  joint prosthesis – *see* Complications,
    joint prosthesis, mechanical,
    specified NEC, by site
  orthopedic NEC - *see* Complication,
    orthopedic, device, mechanical
  specified NEC T85.628
  urinary NEC - *see also* Complication,
    genitourinary, device, urinary,
    mechanical
    graft T83.29
  vascular NEC - *see* Complica-
    tion, cardiovascular device,
    mechanical
  ventricular intracranial shunt
    T85.09
due to foreign body accidentally left in
    operative wound T81.529
duodenum K31.5
ejaculatory duct N50.8
esophagus K22.2
eustachian tube (complete) (partial)
    H68.10-
  cartilagenous (extrinsic) H68.13-
    intrinsic H68.12-
  osseous H68.11-
fallopian tube (bilateral) N97.1
fecal K56.4
  with hernia - *see* Hernia, by site, with
    obstruction
foramen of Monro (congenital) Q03.8
  with spina bifida - *see* Spina bifida,
    by site, with hydrocephalus
foreign body - *see* Foreign body
gallbladder K82.0
  with calculus, stones K80.21
  congenital Q44.1
gastric outlet K31.1
gastrointestinal - *see* Obstruction,
    intestine
hepatic K76.8
  duct (noncalculous) K83.1
ileum - *see* Obstruction, intestine
iliofemoral (artery) I74.5
intestine K56.60
  with
    adhesions (intestinal) (peritoneal)
      K56.5
    adynamic K56.0

Obstruction, obstructed, obstructive
(Continued)
intestine *(Continued)*
  by gallstone K56.3
  congenital (small) Q41.9
    large Q42.9
      specified part NEC Q42.8
  neurogenic K56.0
    Hirschsprung's disease or megaco-
      lon Q43.1
  newborn P76.9
    due to
      fecaliths P76.8
      inspissated milk P76.2
      meconium (plug) P76.0
        in mucoviscidosis E84.11
      specified NEC P76.8
  postoperative K91.3
  reflex K56.0
  specified NEC K56.69
  volvulus K56.2
intracardiac ball valve prosthesis
    T82.09
jejunum - *see* Obstruction, intestine
joint prosthesis - *see* Complications,
    joint prosthesis, mechanical, speci-
    fied NEC, by site
kidney (calices) N28.89
labor - *see* Delivery
lacrimal (passages) (duct)
  by
    dacryolith - *see* Dacryolith
    stenosis - *see* Stenosis, lacrimal
  congenital Q10.5
  neonatal H04.53-
lacrimonasal duct - *see* Obstruction,
    lacrimal
lacteal, with steatorrhea K90.2
laryngitis - *see* Laryngitis
larynx NEC J38.6
  congenital Q31.8
lung J98.4
  disease, chronic J44.9
lymphatic I89.0
meconium (plug)
  newborn P76.0
    due to fecaliths P76.0
    in mucoviscidosis E84.11
mitral - *see* Stenosis, mitral
nasal J34.89
nasolacrimal duct - *see also* Obstruction,
    lacrimal
  congenital Q10.5
nasopharynx J39.2
nose J34.89
organ or site, congenital NEC - *see*
    Atresia, by site
pancreatic duct K86.8
parotid duct or gland K11.8
pelviureteral junction N13.5
  congenital Q62.39
pharynx J39.2
portal (circulation) (vein) I81
prostate - *see also* Hyperplasia, prostate,
    with obstruction
  valve (urinary) N32.0
pulmonary valve (heart) I37.0
pyelonephritis (chronic) N11.1
pylorus
  adult K31.1
  congenital or infantile Q40.0
rectosigmoid - *see* Obstruction,
    intestine
rectum K62.4

Obstruction, obstructed, obstructive
(Continued)
renal N28.89
  outflow N13.8
  pelvis, congenital Q62.39
respiratory J98.8
  chronic J44.9
retinal (vessels) H34.9
salivary duct (any) K11.8
  with calculus K11.5
sigmoid - *see* Obstruction,
    intestine
sinus (accessory) (nasal) J34.89
Stensen's duct K11.8
stomach NEC K31.89
  acute K31.0
  congenital Q40.2
  due to pylorospasm K31.3
submandibular duct K11.8
submaxillary gland K11.8
  with calculus K11.5
thoracic duct I89.0
thrombotic - *see* Thrombosis
trachea J39.8
tracheostomy airway J95.03
tricuspid (valve) - *see* Stenosis,
    tricuspid
upper respiratory, congenital
    Q34.8
ureter (functional) (pelvic junction)
    NEC N13.5
  with
    hydronephrosis N13.1
      with infection N13.6
    pyelonephritis (chronic) N11.1
  congenital Q62.39
  due to calculus - *see* Calculus,
    ureter
urethra NEC N36.8
  congenital Q64.39
urinary (moderate) N13.9
  due to hyperplasia (hypertrophy)
    of prostate - *see* Hyperplasia,
    prostate, specified type, with
    obstruction
  organ or tract (lower) N13.9
  prostatic valve N32.0
  specified NEC N13.8
uropathy N13.9
uterus N85.8
vagina N89.5
valvular - *see* Endocarditis
vein, venous I87.1
  caval (inferior) (superior) I87.1
  thrombotic - *see* Thrombosis
vena cava (inferior) (superior) I87.1
vesical NEC N32.0
vesicourethral orifice N32.0
  congenital Q64.31
vessel NEC I99.8
Obturator - *see* condition
Occlusal wear, teeth K03.0
Occlusio pupillae - *see* Membrane,
    pupillary
Occlusion, occluded
  anus K62.4
    congenital Q42.3
      with fistula Q42.2
  aortoiliac (chronic) I74.0
  aqueduct of Sylvius G91.1
    congenital Q03.0
      with spina bifida - *see* Spina
        bifida, by site, with
        hydrocephalus

Occlusion, occluded (Continued)
artery (*see also* Embolism, artery) I74.9
  auditory, internal I65.8
  basilar I65.1
    with
      infarction I63.22
        due to
          embolism I63.12
          thrombosis I63.02
  brain or cerebral I66.9
    with infarction (due to) I63.5
      embolism I63.4
      thrombosis I63.3
  carotid I65.2-
    with
      infarction I63.23-
        due to
          embolism I63.13-
          thrombosis I63.03-
  cerebellar (anterior inferior) (posterior inferior) (superior) I66.3
    with infarction I63.54-
      due to
        embolism I63.44-
        thrombosis I63.34-
  cerebral I66.9
    with infarction I63.50
      due to
        embolism I63.40
          specified NEC I63.49
        thrombosis I63.30
          specified NEC I63.39
    anterior I66.1-
      with infarction I63.52-
        due to
          embolism I63.42-
          thrombosis I63.32-
    middle I66.0-
      with infarction I63.51-
        due to
          embolism I63.41-
          thrombosis I63.31-
    posterior I66.2-
      with infarction I63.53-
        due to
          embolism I63.43-
          thrombosis I63.33-
    specified NEC I66.8
      with infarction I63.59
        due to
          embolism I63.4
          thrombosis I63.3
  choroidal (anterior) – *see* Occlusion, artery, cerebral, specified NEC
  communicating posterior – *see* Occlusion, artery, cerebral, specified NEC
  complete
    coronary I25.82
    extremities I70.92
  coronary (acute) (thrombotic) (without myocardial infarction) I24.0
    with myocardial infarction – *see* Infarction, myocardium
    chronic total I25.82
    complete I25.82
    healed or old I25.2
    total (chronic) I25.82
  hypophyseal – *see* Occlusion, artery, precerebral, specified NEC
  iliac I74.5
  lower extremities due to stenosis or stricture I77.1

Occlusion, occluded (Continued)
artery (Continued)
  mesenteric (embolic) (thrombotic) K55.0
  perforating – *see* Occlusion, artery, cerebral, specified NEC
  peripheral I77.9
    thrombotic or embolic I74.4
  pontine – *see* Occlusion, artery, cerebral, specified NEC
  precerebral I65.9
    specified NEC I65.8
    with infarction I63.20
      specified NEC I63.29
      due to
        embolism I63.10
          specified NEC I63.19
        thrombosis I63.00
          specified NEC I63.09
    basilar – *see* Occlusion, artery, basilar
    carotid – *see* Occlusion, artery, carotid
      with infarction I63.2
      due to
        embolism I63.13-
        thrombosis I63.03-
    puerperal O88.23
    specified NEC I65.8
      with infarction I63.2
      due to
        embolism I63.1
        thrombosis I63.00
    vertebral – *see* Occlusion, artery, vertebral
  renal N28.0
  retinal
    central H34.1-
    partial H34.21-
    branch H34.23-
    transient H34.0-
  spinal – *see* Occlusion, artery, precerebral, vertebral
  total (chronic)
    coronary I25.82
    extremities I70.92
  vertebral I65.0-
    with
      infarction I63.21-
        due to
          embolism I63.11-
          thrombosis I63.01-
basilar artery - *see* Occlusion, artery, basilar
bile duct (common) (hepatic) (noncalculous) K83.1
bowel - *see* Obstruction, intestine
carotid (artery) (common) (internal) - *see* Occlusion, artery, carotid
centric (of teeth) M26.59
  maximum intercuspation discrepancy M26.55
cerebellar (artery) - *see* Occlusion, artery, cerebellar
cerebral (artery) - *see* Occlusion, artery, cerebral
cerebrovascular - *see also* Occlusion, artery, cerebral
  with infarction I63.5
cervical canal - *see* Stricture, cervix
cervix (uteri) - *see* Stricture, cervix
choanal Q30.0
choroidal (artery) I65.8
colon - *see* Obstruction, intestine

Occlusion, occluded (Continued)
communicating posterior artery – *see* Occlusion, artery, precerebral, specified NEC
coronary (artery) (vein) (thrombotic) - *see also* Infarct, myocardium
  chronic total I25.82
  healed or old I25.2
  not resulting in infarction I24.0
  total (chronic) I25.82
cystic duct - *see* Obstruction, gallbladder
embolic - *see* Embolism
fallopian tube N97.1
  congenital Q50.6
gallbladder - *see also* Obstruction, gallbladder
  congenital (causing jaundice) Q44.1
gingiva, traumatic K06.2
hymen N89.6
  congenital Q52.3
hypophyseal (artery) – *see* Occlusion, artery, precerebral, specified NEC
iliac artery I74.5
intestine - *see* Obstruction, intestine
lacrimal passages - *see* Obstruction, lacrimal
lung J98.4
lymph or lymphatic channel I89.0
mammary duct N64.89
mesenteric artery (embolic) (thrombotic) K55.0
nose J34.89
congenital Q30.0
organ or site, congenital NEC - *see* Atresia, by site
oviduct N97.1
  congenital Q50.6
peripheral arteries
  due to stricture or stenosis I77.1
  upper extremity I74.3
pontine (artery) – *see* Occlusion, artery, precerebral, specified NEC
posterior lingual, of mandibular teeth M26.29
precerebral artery - *see* Occlusion, artery, precerebral
punctum lacrimale - *see* Obstruction, lacrimal
pupil - *see* Membrane, pupillary
pylorus, adult (*see also* Stricture, pylorus) K31.1
renal artery N28.0
retina, retinal
  artery - *see* Occlusion, artery, retinal
  vein (central) H34.81-
    engorgement H34.82-
    tributary H34.83-
  vessels H34.9
spinal artery – *see* Occlusion, artery, precerebral, vertebral
teeth (mandibular) (posterior lingual) M26.29
thoracic duct I89.0
thrombotic – *see* Thrombosis, artery
traumatic
  edentulous (alveolar) ridge K06.2
  gingiva K06.2
  periodontal K05.5
tubal N97.1
ureter (complete) (partial) N13.5
  congenital Q62.10
ureteropelvic junction N13.5
  congenital Q62.11

Occlusion, occluded *(Continued)*
  ureterovesical orifice N13.5
    congenital Q62.12
  urethra - *see* Stricture, urethra
  uterus N85.8
  vagina N89.5
  vascular NEC I99.8
  vein - *see* Thrombosis
    retinal - *see* Occlusion, retinal, vein
  vena cava (inferior) (superior) - *see*
      Embolism, vena cava
  ventricle (brain) NEC G91.1
  vertebral (artery) - *see* Occlusion, artery,
      vertebral
  vessel (blood) I99.8
  vulva N90.5
Occult
  blood in feces (stools) R19.5
Occupational
  problems NEC Z56.89
Ochlophobia – *see* Agoraphobia
Ochronosis (endogenous) E70.29
Ocular muscle - *see* condition
Oculogyric crisis or disturbance
      H51.8
  psychogenic F45.8
Oculomotor syndrome H51.9
Oculopathy
  syphilitic NEC A52.71
    congenital
      early A50.01
      late A50.30
    early (secondary) A51.43
    late A52.71
Oddi's sphincter spasm K83.4
Odontalgia K08.8
Odontoameloblastoma - *see* Cyst, calcify-
      ing odontogenic
Odontoclasia K03.89
Odontodysplasia, regional K00.4
Odontogenesis imperfecta K00.5
Odontoma (ameloblastic) (complex)
      (compound) (fibroameloblastic) - *see*
      Cyst, calcifying odontogenic
Odontomyelitis (closed) (open)
      K04.0
Odontorrhagia K08.8
Odontosarcoma, ameloblastic C41.1
  upper jaw (bone) C41.0
Oedema, oedematous - *see* Edema
Oesophag(o) - *see* Esophag(o)-
Oestriasis - *see* Myiasis
Oguchi's disease H53.63
Ohara's disease - *see* Tularemia
Oidiomycosis - *see* Candidiasis
Oidium albicans infection - *see*
      Candidiasis
Old age (without mention of debility) R54-
  dementia F03
Old (previous) myocardial infarction
      I25.2
Olfactory - *see* condition
Oligemia - *see* Anemia
  specified site - *see* Neoplasm, malignant
  unspecified site C71.9
Oligocythemia D64.9
  specified site - *see* Neoplasm, malignant
  unspecified site C71.9
    specified site - *see* Neoplasm,
        malignant
    unspecified site C71.9
Oligodontia - *see* Anodontia
Oligoencephalon Q02
Oligohidrosis L74.4

Oligohydramnios O41.0-
Oligohydrosis L74.4
Oligomenorrhea N91.5
  primary N91.3
  secondary N91.4
Oligophrenia — *see also* Retardation,
      mental
  phenylpyruvic E70.0
Oligospermia N46.11
  due to
    drug therapy N46.121
    efferent duct obstruction N46.123
    infection N46.122
    radiation N46.124
    specified cause NEC N46.129
    systemic disease N46.125
Oligotrichia - *see* Alopecia
Oliguria R34
  with, complicating or following ectopic
      or molar pregnancy O08.4
  postprocedural N99.0
Ollier's disease Q78.4
Omentitis - *see* Peritonitis
Omenotocele - *see* Hernia, abdomen,
      specified site NEC
Omentum, omental - *see* condition
Omphalitis (congenital) (newborn)
      P38.9
  with mild hemorrhage P38.1
  without hemorrhage P38.9
  not of newborn L08.82
  tetanus A33
Omphalocele Q79.2
Omphalomesenteric duct, persistent
      Q43.0
Omphalorrhagia, newborn P51.9
Omsk hemorrhagic fever A98.1
Onanism (excessive) F98.8
Onchocerciasis, onchocercosis B73.1
  with
    eye disease B73.00
      endophthalmitis B73.01
      eyelid B73.09
      glaucoma B73.02
      specified NEC B73.09
    eye NEC B73.00
    eyelid B73.09
Oncocytoma - *see* Neoplasm, benign
Oncovirus, as cause of disease classified
      elsewhere B97.32
Ondine's curse - *see* Apnea, sleep
Oneirophrenia F23
Onychauxis L60.2
  congenital Q84.5
Onychia - *see also* Cellulitis, digit
  with lymphangitis - *see* Lymphangitis,
      acute, digit
  candidal B37.2
  dermatophytic B35.1
Onychitis - *see also* Cellulitis, digit
  with lymphangitis - *see* Lymphangitis,
      acute, digit
Onychocryptosis L60.0
Onychodystrophy L60.3
  congenital Q84.6
Onychogryphosis, onychogryposis L60.2
Onycholysis L60.1
Onychomadesis L60.8
Onychomalacia L60.3
Onychomycosis (finger) (toe) B35.1
Onycho-osteodysplasia Q79.8
Onychophagia F98.8
Onychophosis L60.8
Onychoptosis L60.8

Onychorrhexis L60.3
  congenital Q84.6
Onychoschizia L60.3
Onyxis (finger) (toe) L60.0
Onyxitis - *see also* Cellulitis, digit
  with lymphangitis - *see* Lymphangitis,
      acute, digit
Oophoritis (cystic) (infectional) (intersti-
      tial) N70.92
  with salpingitis N70.93
  acute N70.02
    with salpingitis N70.03
  chronic N70.12
    with salpingitis N70.13
  complicating abortion – *see* Abortion,
      by type, complicated by, oophoritis
Oophorocele N83.4
Opacity, opacities
  cornea H17.
    central H17.1-
    congenital Q13.3
    degenerative - *see* Degeneration,
        cornea
    hereditary - *see* Dystrophy, cornea
    inflammatory - *see* Keratitis
    minor H17.81-
    peripheral H17.82-
    sequelae of trachoma (healed) B94.0
    specified NEC H17.89
  enamel (teeth) (fluoride) (nonfluoride)
      K00.3
  lens - *see* Cataract
  snowball - *see* Deposit, crystalline
  vitreous (humor) NEC H43.39-
    congenital Q14.0
    membranes and strands H43.31-
Opalescent dentin (hereditary) K00.5
Open, opening
  abnormal, organ or site, congenital - *see*
      Imperfect, closure
  angle with
    borderline intraocular pressure H40.0
    cupping of discs H40.0
    glaucoma (primary) - *see* Glaucoma,
        open angle
  bite
    anterior M26.220
    posterior M26.221
  false - *see* Imperfect, closure
  margin on tooth restoration K08.51
  restoration margins of tooth K08.51
  wound - *see* Wound, open
Operation R69
Operational fatigue F48.8
Operative - *see* condition
Operculitis - *see* Periodontitis
Operculum - *see* Break, retina
Ophiasis L63.2
Ophthalmia (*see also* Conjunctivitis)
      H10.9
  actinic rays - *see* Photokeratitis
  allergic (acute) - *see* Conjunctivitis,
      acute, atopic
  blennorrhagic (gonococcal) (neonato-
      rum) A54.31
  diphtheritic A36.86
  Egyptian A71.1
  electrica - *see* Photokeratitis
  gonococcal (neonatorum) A54.31
  metastatic - *see* Endophthalmitis,
      purulent
  migraine - *see* Migraine, ophthalmoplegic
  neonatorum, newborn P39.1
    gonococcal A54.31

Osteitis *(Continued)*
  Garr's (sclerosing) - *see* Osteomyelitis,
      specified type NEC
  jaw (acute) (chronic) (lower) (suppura-
      tive) (upper) M27.2
  parathyroid E21.0
  petrous bone (acute) (chronic) – *see*
      Petrositis
  sclerotic, nonsuppurative - *see* Osteo-
      myelitis, specified type NEC
  tuberculosa A18.09
      cystica D86.89
      multiplex cystoides D86.89
Osteoarthritis M19.90
  ankle M19.07-
  elbow M19.02-
  foot joint M19.07-
  generalized M15.9
      erosive M15.4
      primary M15.0
      specified NEC M15.8
  hand joint M19.04-
      first carpometacarpal joint M18.1-
          bilateral M18.0
  hip M16.1-
      bilateral M16.0
      due to hip dysplasia (unilateral)
          M16.3-
          bilateral M16.2
  interphalangeal
      distal (Heberden) M15.1
      proximal (Bouchard) M15.2
  knee M17.1-
      bilateral M17.0
  shoulder M19.01-
  spine - *see* Spondylosis
  wrist M19.03-
  post-traumatic NEC M19.92
      ankle M19.17-
      elbow M19.12-
      foot joint M19.17-
      hand joint M19.14-
          first carpometacarpal joint M18.3-
              bilateral M18.2
      hip M16.5-
          bilateral M16.4
      knee M17.3-
          bilateral M17.2
      shoulder M19.11-
      wrist M19.13-
  primary M19.91
      ankle M19.07-
      elbow M19.02-
      foot joint M19.07-
      hand joint M19.04-
          first carpometacarpal joint M18.1-
              bilateral M18.0
      hip M16.1-
          bilateral M16.0
      knee M17.1-
          bilateral M17.0
      shoulder M19.01-
      spine - *see* Spondylosis
      wrist M19.03-
  secondary M19.93
      ankle M19.27-
      elbow M19.22-
      foot joint M19.27-
      hand joint M19.24-
          first carpometacarpal joint
              M18.5-
              bilateral M18.4
      hip M16.7
          bilateral M16.6

Osteoarthritis *(Continued)*
  secondary *(Continued)*
      knee M17.5
          bilateral M17.4
      multiple M15.3
      shoulder M19.21-
      spine - *see* Spondylosis
      wrist M19.23-
Osteoarthropathy (hypertrophic) M19.90
  ankle - *see* Osteoarthritis, primary,
      ankle
  elbow - *see* Osteoarthritis, primary,
      elbow
  foot joint - *see* Osteoarthritis, primary,
      foot
  hand joint - *see* Osteoarthritis, primary,
      hand joint
  knee joint - *see* Osteoarthritis, primary,
      knee
  multiple site - *see* Osteoarthritis, pri-
      mary, multiple joint
  pulmonary - *see also* Osteoarthropathy,
      specified type NEC
      hypertrophic - *see* Osteoarthropathy,
          hypertrophic, specified type
          NEC
  secondary hypertrophic - *see* Osteoar-
      thropathy, specified type NEC
  shoulder - *see* Osteoarthritis, primary,
      shoulder
  specified joint NEC - *see* Osteoarthritis,
      primary, specified joint NEC
  specified type NEC M89.40
      carpus M89.44-
      clavicle M89.41-
      femur M89.45-
      fibula M89.46-
      finger M89.44-
      humerus M89.42-
      ilium M89.459
      ischium M89.459
      metacarpus M89.44-
      metatarsus M89.47-
      multiple sites M89.49
      neck M89.48
      radius M89.43-
      rib M89.48
      scapula M89.41-
      skull M89.48
      tarsus M89.47-
      tibia M89.46-
      toe M89.47-
      ulna M89.43-
      vertebra M89.48
  secondary - *see* Osteoarthropathy, speci-
      fied type NEC
  spine - *see* Spondylosis
  wrist - *see* Osteoarthritis, primary, wrist
Osteoarthrosis (degenerative) (hypertro-
      phic) (joint) - *see also* Osteoarthritis
  deformans alkaptonurica E70.29
      [M36.8]
  erosive M15.4
  generalized M15.9
      primary M15.0
  polyarticular M15.9
  spine - *see* Spondylosis
Osteoblastoma - *see* Neoplasm, bone,
      benign
  aggressive - *see* Neoplasm, bone, uncer-
      tain behavior
Osteochondroarthrosis deformans
      endemica – *see* Disease, Kaschin-
      Beck

Osteochondritis - *see also* Osteochondrop-
      athy, by site
  Brailsford's - *see* Osteochondrosis,
      juvenile, radius
  dissecans M93.20
      ankle M93.27-
      elbow M93.22-
      foot M93.27-
      hand M93.24-
      hip M93.25-
      knee M93.26-
      multiple sites M93.29
      shoulder joint M93.21-
      specified site NEC M93.28
      wrist M93.23-
  juvenile M92.9
      patellar - *see* Osteochondrosis, juve-
          nile, patella
  syphilitic (congenital) (early) A50.02
      [M90.80]
      ankle A50.02 [M90.87-]
      elbow A50.02 [M90.82-]
      foot A50.02 [M90.87-]
      forearm A50.02 [M90.83-]
      hand A50.02 [M90.84-]
      hip A50.02 [M90.85-]
      knee A50.02 [M90.86-]
      multiple sites A50.02 [M90.89]
      shoulder joint A50.02 [M90.81-]
      specified site NEC A50.02
          [M90.88]
Osteochondrodysplasia Q78.9
  with defects of growth of tubular bones
      and spine Q77.9
      specified NEC Q77.8
  specified NEC Q78.8
Osteochondrodystrophy E78.9
Osteochondrolysis – *see* Osteochondritis,
      dissecans
Osteochondroma - *see* Neoplasm, bone,
      benign
Osteochondromatosis D48.0
  syndrome Q78.4
Osteochondromyxosarcoma - *see* Neo-
      plasm, bone, malignant
Osteochondropathy M93.90
  ankle M93.97-
  elbow M93.92-
  foot M93.97-
  hand M93.94-
  hip M93.95-
  Kienböck's disease of adults
      M93.1
  knee M93.96-
  multiple joints M93.99
  osteochondritis dissecans – *see* Osteo-
      chondritis, dissecans
  osteochondrosis – *see* Osteochondrosis
  shoulder region M93.91-
  slipped upper femoral epiphysis - *see*
      Slipped, epiphysis, upper
      femoral
  specified joint NEC M93.98
  specified type NEC M93.80
      ankle M93.87
      elbow M93.82
      foot M93.87-
      hand M93.84
      hip M93.85
      knee M93.86
      multiple joints M93.89
      shoulder region M93.81
      specified joint NEC M93.88
      wrist M93.83-

Osteochondropathy *(Continued)*
 syphilitic, congenital
  early A50.02 *[M90.80]*
  late A50.56 *[M90.80]*
 wrist M93.93-
Osteochondrosarcoma - *see* Neoplasm,
  bone, malignant
Osteochondrosis - *see also* Osteochondropathy, by site
 acetabulum (juvenile) M91.0
 adult – *see* Osteochondropathy,
  specified type NEC, by site
 astragalus (juvenile) - *see* Osteochondrosis, juvenile, tarsus
 Blount's - *see* Osteochondrosis, juvenile,
  tibia
 Buchanan's M91.0
 Burns' - *see* Osteochondrosis, juvenile,
  ulna
 calcaneus (juvenile) - *see* Osteochondrosis, juvenile, tarsus
 capitular epiphysis (femur) (juvenile) -
  see Legg-Calve-Perthes disease
 carpal (juvenile) (lunate) (scaphoid) -
  see Osteochondrosis, juvenile,
  hand, carpal lunate
  adult M93.1
 coxae juvenilis - *see* Legg-Calve-Perthes
  disease
 deformans juvenilis, coxae - *see* Legg-
  Calve-Perthes disease
 Diaz's - *see* Osteochondrosis, juvenile,
  tarsus
 dissecans (knee) (shoulder) – *see* Osteochondritis, dissecans
 femoral capital epiphysis (juvenile) -
  see Legg-Calve-Perthes disease
 femur (head), juvenile - *see* Legg-Calve-
  Perthes disease
 fibula (juvenile) - *see* Osteochondrosis,
  juvenile, fibula
 foot NEC (juvenile) M92.8
 Freiberg's - *see* Osteochondrosis,
  juvenile, metatarsus
 Haas' (juvenile) - *see* Osteochondrosis,
  juvenile, humerus
 Haglund's - *see* Osteochondrosis,
  juvenile, tarsus
 hip (juvenile) - *see* Legg-Calve-Perthes
  disease
 humerus (capitulum) (head) (juvenile) -
  see Osteochondrosis, juvenile,
  humerus
 ilium, iliac crest (juvenile) M91.0
 ischiopubic synchondrosis M91.0
 Iselin's - *see* Osteochondrosis, juvenile,
  metatarsus
 juvenile, juvenilis M92.9
  after congenital dislocation of
   hip reduction - *see* Osteochondrosis, juvenile, hip, specified
   NEC
  arm - *see* Osteochondrosis, juvenile,
   upper limb NEC
  capitular epiphysis (femur) - *see*
   Legg-Calve-Perthes disease
  clavicle, sternal epiphysis - *see* Osteochondrosis, juvenile, upper limb
   NEC
  coxae - *see* Legg-Calve-Perthes
   disease
  deformans M92.9
  fibula M92.5-
  foot NEC M92.8

Osteochondrosis *(Continued)*
 juvenile, juvenilis *(Continued)*
  hand M92.20-
   carpal lunate M92.21-
   metacarpal head M92.22-
   specified site NEC M92.29-
  head of femur - *see* Legg-Calve-
   Perthes disease
  hip and pelvis M91.9-
   coxa plana - *see* Coxa, plana
   femoral head - *see* Legg-Calve-
    Perthes disease
   pelvis M91.0
   pseudocoxalgia - *see* Pseudocoxalgia
   specified NEC M91.8-
  humerus M92.0-
  limb
   lower NEC M92.8
   upper NEC - *see* Osteochondrosis,
    juvenile, upper limb NEC
  medial cuneiform bone - *see* Osteochondrosis, juvenile, tarsus
  metatarsus M92.7-
  patella M92.4-
  radius M92.1-
  specified site NEC M92.8
  spine M42.00
   cervical region M42.02
   cervicothoracic region M42.03
   lumbar region M42.06
   lumbosacral region M42.07
   multiple sites M42.09
   occipito-atlanto-axial region
    M42.01
   sacrococcygeal region M42.08
   thoracic region M42.04
   thoracolumbar region M42.05
  tarsus M92.6-
  tibia M92.5-
  ulna M92.1-
  upper limb NEC M92.3-
  vertebra (body) (epiphyseal plates)
   (Calvés) (Scheuermann's) - *see*
   Osteochondrosis, juvenile,
   spine
 Kienböck's - *see* Osteochondrosis, juvenile, hand, carpal lunate
  adult M93.1
 Köhler's
  patellar - *see* Osteochondrosis, juvenile, patella
  tarsal navicular - *see* Osteochondrosis,
   juvenile, tarsus
 Legg-Perthes(-Calvés)(-Waldenström) -
  see Legg-Calve-Perthes disease
 limb
  lower NEC (juvenile) M92.8
  upper NEC (juvenile) - *see* Osteochondrosis, juvenile, upper limb
   NEC
 lunate bone (carpal) (juvenile) - *see also*
  Osteochondrosis, juvenile, hand,
  carpal lunate
  adult M93.1
 Mauclaire's - *see* Osteochondrosis, juvenile, hand, metacarpal
 metacarpal (head) (juvenile) - *see*
  Osteochondrosis, juvenile, hand,
  metacarpal
 metatarsus (fifth) (head) (juvenile)
  (second) - *see* Osteochondrosis,
  juvenile, metatarsus
 navicular (juvenile) - *see* Osteochondrosis, juvenile, tarsus

Osteochondrosis *(Continued)*
 os
  calcis (juvenile) - *see* Osteochondrosis,
   juvenile, tarsus
  tibiale externum (juvenile) - *see* Osteochondrosis, juvenile, tarsus
 Osgood-Schlatter - *see* Osteochondrosis,
  juvenile, tibia
 Panner's - *see* Osteochondrosis, juvenile, humerus
 patellar center (juvenile) (primary)
  (secondary) - *see* Osteochondrosis,
  juvenile, patella
 pelvis (juvenile) M91.0
 Pierson's M91.0
 radius (head) (juvenile) - *see* Osteochondrosis, juvenile, radius
 Scheuermann's - *see* Osteochondrosis,
  juvenile, spine
 Sever's - *see* Osteochondrosis, juvenile,
  tarsus
 Sinding-Larsen - *see* Osteochondrosis,
  juvenile, patella
 spine M42.9
  adult M42.10
   cervical region M42.12
   cervicothoracic region M42.13
   lumbar region M42.16
   lumbosacral region M42.17
   multiple sites M42.19
   occipito-atlanto-axial region
    M42.11
   sacrococcygeal region M42.18
   thoracic region M42.14
   thoracolumbar region M42.15
  juvenile - *see* Osteochondrosis, juvenile, spine
 symphysis pubis (juvenile) M91.0
 syphilitic (congenital) A50.02
 talus (juvenile) - *see* Osteochondrosis,
  juvenile, tarsus
 tarsus (navicular) (juvenile) - *see* Osteochondrosis, juvenile, tarsus
 tibia (proximal) (tubercle) (juvenile) -
  see Osteochondrosis, juvenile, tibia
 tuberculous - *see* Tuberculosis, bone
 ulna (lower) (juvenile) - *see* Osteochondrosis, juvenile, ulna
 van Neck's M91.0
 vertebral - *see* Osteochondrosis, spine
Osteoclastoma D48.0
 malignant - *see* Neoplasm, bone,
  malignant
Osteodynia - *see* Disorder, bone, specified
  type NEC
Osteodystrophy Q78.9
 azotemic N25.0
 congenital Q78.9
 parathyroid, secondary E21.1
 renal N25.0
Osteofibroma - *see* Neoplasm, bone,
  benign
Osteofibrosarcoma - *see* Neoplasm, bone,
  malignant
Osteogenesis imperfecta Q78.0
Osteogenic - *see* condition
Osteolysis M89.50
 carpus M89.54-
 clavicle M89.51-
 femur M89.55-
 fibula M89.56-
 finger M89.54-
 humerus M89.52-
 ilium M89.559

Osteolysis *(Continued)*
  ischium M89.559
  joint prosthesis (periprosthetic) - *see*
    Complications, joint prosthe-
    sis, mechanical, periprosthetic,
    osteolysis, by site
  metacarpus M89.54-
  metatarsus M89.57-
  multiple sites M89.59
  neck M89.58
  periprosthetic - *see* Complications, joint
    prosthesis, mechanical, peripros-
    thetic, osteolysis, by site
  radius M89.53-
  rib M89.58
  scapula M89.51-
  skull M89.58
  tarsus M89.57-
  tibia M89.56-
  toe M89.57-
  ulna M89.53-
  vertebra M89.58
Osteoma - *see also* Neoplasm, bone,
  benign
  osteoid - *see also* Neoplasm, bone,
    benign
  giant - *see* Neoplasm, bone, benign
Osteomalacia M83.9
  adult M83.9
    drug-induced NEC M83.5
    due to
      malabsorption (postsurgical)
        M83.2
      malnutrition M83.3
    specified NEC M83.8
  aluminium-induced M83.4
  infantile - *see* Rickets
  juvenile - *see* Rickets
  pelvis M83.8
  puerperal M83.0
  senile M83.1
  vitamin-D-resistant in adults E83.31
    [M90.8-]
    carpus E83.31 [M90.84-]
    clavicle E83.31 [M90.81-]
    femur E83.31 [M90.85-]
    fibula E83.31 [M90.86-]
    finger E83.31 [M90.84-]
    humerus E83.31 [M90.82-]
    ilium E83.31 [M90.859]
    ischium E83.31 [M90.859]
    metacarpus E83.31 [M90.84-]
    metatarsus E83.31 [M90.87-]
    multiple sites E83.31 [M90.89]
    neck E83.31 [M90.88]
    radius E83.31 [M90.83-]
    rib E83.31 [M90.88]
    scapula E83.31 [M90.819]
    skull E83.31 [M90.88]
    tarsus E83.31 [M90.879]
    tibia E83.31 [M90.869]
    toe E83.31 [M90.879]
    ulna E83.31 [M90.839]
    vertebra E83.31 [M90.88]
Osteomyelitis (general) (infective) (localized) (neonatal) (purulent) (septic)
  (staphylococcal) (streptococcal) (suppurative) (with periostitis) M86.9
  acute M86.10
    carpus M86.14
    clavicle M86.11
    femur M86.15
    fibula M86.16
    finger M86.14-

Osteomyelitis *(Continued)*
  acute *(Continued)*
    hematogenous M86.00
      carpus M86.04
      clavicle M86.01
      femur M86.05-
      fibula M86.06
      finger M86.04-
      humerus M86.02-
      ilium M86.059
      ischium M86.059
      mandible M27.2
      metacarpus M86.04
      metatarsus M86.07
      multiple sites M86.09
      neck M86.08
      orbit H05.02-
      petrous bone - *see* Petrositis
      radius M86.03-
      rib M86.08
      scapula M86.01-
      skull M86.08
      tarsus M86.07-
      tibia M86.06-
      toe M86.07-
      ulna M86.03-
      vertebra - *see* Osteomyelitis,
        vertebra
    humerus M86.12-
    ilium M86.159
    ischium M86.159
    mandible M27.2
    metacarpus M86.14-
    metatarsus M86.17-
    multiple sites M86.19
    neck M86.18
    orbit H05.02-
    petrous bone - *see* Petrositis
    radius M86.13-
    rib M86.18
    scapula M86.11-
    skull M86.18
    tarsus M86.17-
    tibia M86.16-
    toe M86.17-
    ulna M86.13-
    vertebra - *see* Osteomyelitis,
      vertebra
  chronic (or old) M86.60
    with draining sinus M86.40
      carpus M86.44-
      clavicle M86.41-
      femur M86.45-
      fibula M86.46-
      finger M86.44-
      humerus M86.42-
      ilium M86.459
      ischium M86.459
      mandible M27.2
      metacarpus M86.44-
      metatarsus M86.47-
      multiple sites M86.49
      neck M86.48
      orbit H05.02-
      petrous bone - *see* Petrositis
      radius M86.43-
      rib M86.48
      scapula M86.41-
      skull M86.48
      tarsus M86.47-
      tibia M86.46-
      toe M86.47-
      ulna M86.43-
      vertebra - *see* Osteomyelitis, vertebra

Osteomyelitis *(Continued)*
  chronic *(Continued)*
    carpus M86.64-
    clavicle M86.61-
    femur M86.65-
    fibula M86.66-
    finger M86.64-
    hematogenous NEC M86.50
      carpus M86.54-
      clavicle M86.51-
      femur M86.55-
      fibula M86.56-
      finger M86.54-
      humerus M86.52-
      ilium M86.559
      ischium M86.559
      mandible M27.2
      metacarpus M86.54-
      metatarsus M86.57-
      multifocal M86.30
        carpus M86.34-
        clavicle M86.31-
        femur M86.35-
        fibula M86.36-
        finger M86.34-
        humerus M86.32-
        ilium M86.359
        ischium M86.359
        metacarpus M86.34-
        metatarsus M86.37-
        multiple sites M86.39
        neck M86.38
        radius M86.33-
        rib M86.38
        scapula M86.31-
        skull M86.38
        tarsus M86.37-
        tibia M86.36-
        toe M86.37-
        ulna M86.33-
        vertebra - *see* Osteomyelitis,
          vertebra
      multiple sites M86.59
      neck M86.58
      orbit H05.02-
      petrous bone - *see* Petrositis
      radius M86.53-
      rib M86.58
      scapula M86.51-
      skull M86.58
      tarsus M86.57-
      tibia M86.56-
      toe M86.57-
      ulna M86.53-
      vertebra - *see* Osteomyelitis,
        vertebra
    humerus M86.62-
    ilium M86.659
    ischium M86.659
    mandible M27.2
    metacarpus M86.64-
    metatarsus M86.67-
    multifocal - *see* Osteomyelitis,
      chronic, hematogenous,
      multifocal
    multiple sites M86.69
    neck M86.68
    orbit H05.02-
    petrous bone - *see* Petrositis
    radius M86.63-
    rib M86.68
    scapula M86.61-
    skull M86.68
    tarsus M86.67-

Osteomyelitis *(Continued)*
  chronic *(Continued)*
    tibia M86.66-
    toe M86.67-
    ulna M86.63-
    vertebra - *see* Osteomyelitis,
      vertebra
  echinococcal B67.2
  Garr's - *see* Osteomyelitis, specified
    type NEC
  jaw (acute) (chronic) (lower) (neonatal)
    (suppurative) (upper) M27.2
  nonsuppurating - *see* Osteomyelitis,
    specified type NEC
  orbit H05.02-
  petrous bone – *see* Petrositis
  Salmonella (arizonae) (cholerae-suis)
    (enteritidis) (typhimurium)
    A02.24
  sclerosing, nonsuppurative - *see*
    Osteomyelitis, specified type
    NEC
  specified type NEC - *see also* subcat-
    egory M86.8x
    mandible M27.2
    orbit H05.02
    petrous bone - *see* Petrositis
    vertebra - *see* Osteomyelitis,
      vertebra
  subacute M86.20
    carpus M86.24
    clavicle M86.21
    femur M86.25
    fibula M86.26
    finger M86.24-
    humerus M86.22
    mandible M27.2
    metacarpus M86.24
    metatarsus M86.27-
    multiple sites M86.29
    neck M86.28
    orbit H05.02
    petrous bone - *see* Petrositis
    radius M86.23
    rib M86.28
    scapula M86.21
    skull M86.28
    tarsus M86.27-
    tibia M86.26
    toe M86.27
    ulna M86.23
    vertebra - *see* Osteomyelitis, vertebra
  syphilitic A52.77
    congenital (early) A50.02 [M90.80]
  tuberculous - *see* Tuberculosis, bone
  typhoid A01.05
  vertebra M46.20
    cervical region M46.22
    cervicothoracic region M46.23
    lumbar region M46.26
    lumbosacral region M46.27
    occipito-atlanto-axial region
      M46.21
    sacrococcygeal region M46.28
    thoracic region M46.24
    thoracolumbar region M46.25
Osteomyelofibrosis D75.89
Osteomyelosclerosis D75.89
Osteonecrosis M87.9
  due to
    drugs - *see* Osteonecrosis, secondary,
      due to, drugs
    trauma - *see* Osteonecrosis, secondary,
      due to, trauma

Osteonecrosis *(Continued)*
  idiopathic aseptic M87.00
    ankle M87.07-
    carpus M87.03-
    clavicle M87.01-
    femur M87.05-
    fibula M87.06-
    finger M87.04-
    humerus M87.02-
    ilium M87.050
    ischium M87.050
    metacarpus M87.04-
    metatarsus M87.07-
    neck M87.08
    pelvis M87.050
    radius M87.03-
    rib M87.08
    scapula M87.01-
    skull M87.08
    tarsus M87.07-
    tibia M87.06-
    toe M87.07-
    ulna M87.03-
    vertebra M87.08
  secondary NEC M87.30
    carpus M87.34-
    clavicle M87.31-
    due to
      drugs M87.10
        carpus M87.14-
        clavicle M87.11-
        femur M87.15-
        fibula M87.16-
        finger M87.14-
        humerus M87.12-
        ilium M87.159
        ischium M87.159
        jaw M87.180
        metacarpus M87.14-
        metatarsus M87.17-
        multiple sites M87.19
        neck M87.18
        radius M87.13-
        rib M87.18
        scapula M87.11-
        skull M87.18
        tarsus M87.17-
        tibia M87.16-
        toe M87.17-
        ulna M87.13-
        vertebra M87.18
      hemoglobinopathy NEC D58.2
        [M90.50]
        carpus D58.2 [M90.54-]
        clavicle D58.2 [M90.51-]
        femur D58.2 [M90.55-]
        fibula D58.2 [M90.56-]
        finger D58.2 [M90.54-]
        humerus D58.2 [M90.52-]
        ilium D58.2 [M90.55-]
        ischium D58.2 [M90.55-]
        metacarpus D58.2 [M90.54-]
        metatarsus D58.2 [M90.57-]
        multiple sites D58.2 [M90.58]
        neck D58.2 [M90.58]
        radius D58.2 [M90.539]
        rib D58.2 [M90.58]
        scapula D58.2 [M90.51-]
        skull D58.2 [M90.58]
        tarsus D58.2 [M90.57-]
        tibia D58.2 [M90.56-]
        toe D58.2 [M90.57-]
        ulna D58.2 [M90.53-]
        vertebra D58.2 [M90.58]

Osteonecrosis *(Continued)*
  secondary NEC *(Continued)*
    due to *(Continued)*
      trauma (previous) M87.20
        carpus M87.24-
        clavicle M87.21-
        femur M87.25-
        fibula M87.26-
        finger M87.24-
        humerus M87.22-
        ilium M87.25-
        ischium M87.25-
        metacarpus M87.24-
        metatarsus M87.27-
        multiple sites M87.29
        neck M87.28
        radius M87.23-
        rib M87.28
        scapula M87.21-
        skull M87.28
        tarsus M87.27-
        tibia M87.26-
        toe M87.27-
        ulna M87.23-
        vertebra M87.28
      femur M87.35-
      fibula M87.36-
      finger M87.34-
      humerus M87.32
      ilium M87.359
      in
        caisson disease T70.3 [M90.50]
          carpus T70.3 [M90.54-]
          clavicle T70.3 [M90.51-]
          femur T70.3 [M90.55-]
          fibula T70.3 [M90.56-]
          finger T70.3 [M90.54-]
          humerus T70.3 [M90.52-]
          ilium T70.3 [M90.55-]
          ischium T70.3 [M90.55-]
          metacarpus T70.3 [M90.54-]
          metatarsus T70.3 [M90.57-]
          multiple sites T70.3 [M90.59]
          neck T70.3 [M90.58]
          radius T70.3 [M90.53-]
          rib T70.3 [M90.58]
          scapula T70.3 [M90.51-]
          skull T70.3 [M90.58]
          tarsus T70.3 [M90.57-]
          tibia T70.3 [M90.56-]
          toe T70.3 [M90.57-]
          ulna T70.3 [M90.53-]
          vertebra T70.3 [M90.58]
      ischium M87.359
      metacarpus M87.34
      metatarsus M87.37-
      multiple site M87.39
      neck M87.38
      radius M87.339
      rib M87.38
      scapula M87.319
      skull M87.38
      tarsus M87.379
      tibia M87.366
      toe M87.379
      ulna M87.339
      vertebra M87.38
    specified type NEC M87.80
      carpus M87.84-
      clavicle M87.81-
      femur M87.85-
      fibula M87.86-
      finger M87.84-
      humerus M87.82-

Osteonecrosis *(Continued)*
  specified type NEC *(Continued)*
    ilium M87.85-
    ischium M87.85-
    metacarpus M87.84-
    metatarsus M87.87-
    multiple sites M87.89
    neck M87.88
    radius M87.83-
    rib M87.88-
    scapula M87.81-
    skull M87.88
    tarsus M87.87-
    tibia M87.86-
    toe M87.87-
    ulna M87.83-
    vertebra M87.88
Osteo-onycho-arthro-dysplasia Q79.8
Osteo-onychodysplasia, hereditary Q79.8
Osteopathia condensans disseminata
    Q78.8
Osteopathy – *see also* Osteomyelitis,
    Osteonecrosis, Osteoporosis
  after poliomyelitis M89.60
    carpus M89.64-
    clavicle M89.61-
    femur M89.65-
    fibula M89.66-
    finger M89.64-
    humerus M89.62-
    ilium M89.659
    ischium M89.659
    metacarpus M89.64-
    metatarsus M89.67-
    multiple sites M89.69
    neck M89.68
    radius M89.63-
    rib M89.68
    scapula M89.61-
    skull M89.68
    tarsus M89.67-
    tibia M89.66-
    toe M89.67-
    ulna M89.63-
    vertebra M89.68
  in (due to)
    renal osteodystrophy N25.0
    specified diseases classified else-
        where – *see* subcategory M90.8
Osteopenia M85.8-
  borderline M85.8-
Osteoperiostitis - *see* Osteomyelitis, speci-
    fied type NEC
Osteopetrosis (familial) Q78.2
Osteophyte M25.70
  ankle M25.77-
  elbow M25.72-
  foot joint M25.77-
  hand joint M25.74-
  hip M25.75-
  knee M25.76-
  shoulder M25.71-
  spine M25.78
  vertebrae M25.78
  wrist M25.73-
Osteopoikilosis Q78.8
Osteoporosis (female) (male) M81.0
  with current pathological fracture
      M80.00
  age-related M81.0
    with current pathologic fracture
        M80.00
      carpus M80.04-
      clavicle M80.01-

Osteoporosis *(Continued)*
  age-related *(Continued)*
    with current pathologic fracture
        (Continued)
      fibula M80.06-
      finger M80.04-
      humerus M80.02-
      ilium M80.05-
      ischium M80.05-
      metacarpus M80.04-
      metatarsus M80.07-
      pelvis M80.05-
      radius M80.03-
      scapula M80.01-
      tarsus M80.07-
      tibia M80.06-
      toe M80.07-
      ulna M80.03-
      vertebra M80.08
  disuse M81.8
    with current pathological fracture
        M80.80
      carpus M80.84-
      clavicle M80.81-
      fibula M80.86-
      finger M80.84-
      humerus M80.82-
      ilium M80.85-
      ischium M80.85-
      metacarpus M80.84-
      metatarsus M80.87-
      pelvis M80.85-
      radius M80.83-
      scapula M80.81-
      tarsus M80.87-
      tibia M80.86-
      toe M80.87-
      ulna M80.83-
      vertebra M80.88
  drug-induced - *see* Osteoporosis, speci-
      fied type NEC
  idiopathic - *see* Osteoporosis, specified
      type NEC
  involutional - *see* Osteoporosis,
      age-related
  Lequesne M81.6
  localized M81.6
  postmenopausal M81.0
    with pathological fracture
        M80.00
      carpus M80.04-
      clavicle M80.01-
      fibula M80.06-
      finger M80.04-
      humerus M80.02-
      ilium M80.05-
      ischium M80.05-
      metacarpus M80.04-
      metatarsus M80.07-
      pelvis M80.05-
      radius M80.03-
      scapula M80.01-
      tarsus M80.07-
      tibia M80.06-
      toe M80.07-
      ulna M80.03-
      vertebra M80.08
  postoophorectomy - *see* Osteoporosis,
      specified type NEC
  postsurgical malabsorption - *see* Osteo-
      porosis, specified type NEC
  post-traumatic - *see* Osteoporosis, speci-
      fied type NEC
  senile - *see* Osteoporosis, age-related

Osteoporosis *(Continued)*
  specified type NEC M81.8
    with pathological fracture M80.80
      carpus M80.84-
      clavicle M80.81-
      fibula M80.86-
      finger M80.84-
      humerus M80.82-
      ilium M80.85-
      ischium M80.85-
      metacarpus M80.84-
      metatarsus M80.87-
      pelvis M80.85-
      radius M80.83-
      scapula M80.81-
      tarsus M80.87-
      tibia M80.86-
      toe M80.87-
      ulna M80.83-
      vertebra M80.88
Osteopsathyrosis (idiopathica) Q78.0
Osteoradionecrosis, jaw (acute)
    (chronic) (lower) (suppurative)
    (upper) M27.2
Osteosarcoma (any form) - *see* Neoplasm,
    bone, malignant
Osteosclerosis Q78.2
  acquired M85.8-
  congenita Q77.4
  fragilitas (generalisata) Q78.2
  myelofibrosis D75.81
Osteosclerotic anemia D64.89
Osteosis
  cutis L94.2
  renal fibrocystic N25.0
Österreicher-Turner syndrome Q87.2
Ostium
  atrioventriculare commune Q21.2
  primum (arteriosum) (defect) (persis-
      tent) Q21.2
  secundum (arteriosum) (defect) (patent)
      (persistent) Q21.1
Ostrum-Furst syndrome Q75.8
Otalgia - *see* subcategory H92.0
Otitis (acute) H66.90
  with effusion - *see also* Otitis, media,
      nonsuppurative
    purulent - *see* Otitis, media,
        suppurative
  adhesive - *see* subcategory H74.1
  chronic - *see also* Otitis, media, chronic
    with effusion - *see also* Otitis, media,
        nonsuppurative, chronic
  externa H60.90
    abscess - *see* Abscess, ear, external
    acute (noninfective) H60.50-
      actinic H60.51-
      chemical H60.52-
      contact H60.53-
      eczematoid H60.54-
      infective - *see* Otitis, externa,
          infective
      reactive H60.55-
      specified NEC H60.59-
    cellulitis - *see* Cellulitis, ear
    chronic H60.6-
    diffuse - *see* Otitis, externa, infective,
        diffuse
    hemorrhagic - *see* Otitis, externa,
        infective, hemorrhagic
    in (due to)
      aspergillosis B44.89
      candidiasis B37.84
      erysipelas A46 *[H62.40]*

Otitis *(Continued)*
  externa *(Continued)*
    in (due to) *(Continued)*
      herpes (simplex) virus infection
        B00.1
        zoster B02.8
      impetigo L01.00 *[H62.40]*
      infectious disease NEC B99
        [H62.4-]
      mycosis NEC B36.9 *[H62.40]*
      parasitic disease NEC B89 *[H62.40]*
      viral disease NEC B34.9 *[H62.40]*
      zoster B02.8
    infective NEC H60.39-
      abscess - *see* Abscess, ear, external
      cellulitis - *see* Cellulitis, ear
      diffuse H60.31-
      hemorrhagic H60.32-
      swimmer's ear - *see* Swimmer's,
        ear
    malignant H60.2-
    mycotic B36.9 *[H62.40]*
    necrotizing - *see* Otitis, externa,
      malignant
    Pseudomonas aeruginosa - *see* Otitis,
      externa, malignant
    reactive - *see* Otitis, externa, acute,
      reactive
    specified NEC - *see* subcategory
      H60.8
    tropical B36.8
  insidiosa - *see* Otosclerosis
  interna - *see* subcategory H83.0
  media (hemorrhagic) (staphylococcal)
    (streptococcal) H66.9-
    with effusion (nonpurulent) - *see* Oti-
      tis, media, nonsuppurative
    acute, subacute H66.90
      allergic – *see* Otitis, media, nonsup-
        purative, acute, allergic
      exudative – *see* Otitis, media, non-
        suppurative, acute
      mucoid – *see* Otitis, media, nonsup-
        purative, acute
      necrotizing – *see also* Otitis, media,
        suppurative, acute
      in
        measles B05.3
        scarlet fever A38.0
      nonsuppurative NEC – *see* Otitis,
        media, nonsuppurative,
        acute
      purulent – *see* Otitis, media, sup-
        purative, acute
      sanguinous – *see* Otitis, media,
        nonsuppurative, acute
      secretory – *see* Otitis, media, non-
        suppurative, acute, serous
      seromucinous – *see* Otitis, media,
        nonsuppurative, acute
      serous – *see* Otitis, media, nonsup-
        purative, acute, serous
      suppurative – *see* Otitis, media,
        suppurative, acute
      allergic – *see* Otitis, media,
        nonsuppurative
      catarrhal – *see* Otitis, media,
        nonsuppurative
    chronic H66.90
      with effusion (nonpurulent) - *see*
        Otitis, media, nonsuppura-
        tive, chronic
      allergic - *see* Otitis, media, nonsup-
        purative, chronic, allergic

Otitis *(Continued)*
  media *(Continued)*
    chronic H66.90 *(Continued)*
      benign suppurative - *see* Otitis,
        media, suppurative, chronic,
        tubotympanic
      catarrhal - *see* Otitis, media, non-
        suppurative, chronic, serous
      exudative - *see* Otitis, media, non-
        suppurative, chronic
      mucinous - *see* Otitis, media, non-
        suppurative, chronic, mucoid
      mucoid - *see* Otitis, media, nonsup-
        purative, chronic, mucoid
      nonsuppurative NEC - *see* Otitis, me-
        dia, nonsuppurative, chronic
      purulent - *see* Otitis, media, sup-
        purative, chronic
      secretory - *see* Otitis, media, non-
        suppurative, chronic, mucoid
      seromucinous - *see* Otitis, media,
        nonsuppurative, chronic
      serous - *see* Otitis, media, nonsup-
        purative, chronic, serous
      suppurative - *see* Otitis, media,
        suppurative, chronic
      transudative - *see* Otitis, media, non-
        suppurative, chronic, mucoid
    exudative – *see* Otitis, media,
      nonsuppurative
    in (due to)
      influenza - *see* Influenza, with,
        manifestations NEC
      measles B05.3
      scarlet fever A38.0
      tuberculosis A18.6
      viral disease NEC B34.*[H67.9]*
    mucoid – *see* Otitis, media,
      nonsuppurative
    nonsuppurative H65.9-
      acute or subacute NEC H65.19-
        allergic H65.11-
          recurrent H65.11-
        recurrent H65.19-
        secretory - *see* Otitis, media,
          nonsuppurative, serous
        serous H65.0-
          recurrent H65.0-
      chronic H65.49-
        allergic H65.41-
        mucoid H65.3-
        serous H65.2-
      postmeasles B05.3
    purulent – *see* Otitis, media,
      suppurative
    secretory – *see* Otitis, media,
      nonsuppurative
    seromucinous – *see* Otitis, media,
      nonsuppurative
    serous – *see* Otitis, media,
      nonsuppurative
    suppurative H66.4-
      acute H66.00-
        with rupture of ear drum
          H66.01-
        recurrent H66.00-
          with rupture of ear drum
          H66.01-
      chronic - *see also* subcategory H66.3
        atticoantral H66.2-
        benign - *see* Otitis, media,
          suppurative, chronic,
          tubotympanic
        tubotympanic H66.1-

Otitis *(Continued)*
  media *(Continued)*
    transudative – *see* Otitis, media,
      nonsuppurative
    tuberculous A18.6
Otocephaly Q18.2
Otolith syndrome - *see* subcategory
  H81.8
Otomycosis (diffuse) NEC B36.9
  [H62.40]
  in
    aspergillosis B44.89
    candidiasis B37.84
    moniliasis B37.84
Otoporosis - *see* Otosclerosis
Otorrhagia (nontraumatic) H92.2-
  traumatic - code by Type of injury
Otorrhea H92.1-
  cerebrospinal G96.0
Otosclerosis (general) H80.9-
  cochlear (endosteal) H80.2-
  involving
    otic capsule - *see* Otosclerosis,
      cochlear
    oval window
      nonobliterative H80.0-
      obliterative H80.1-
    round window - *see* Otosclerosis,
      cochlear
  nonobliterative - *see* Otosclero-
    sis, involving, oval window,
    nonobliterative
  obliterative - *see* Otosclerosis, involving,
    oval window, obliterative
  specified NEC H80.8-
Otospongiosis - *see* Otosclerosis
Otto's disease or pelvis M24.7
Outcome of delivery Z37.9
  multiple births Z37.9
    all liveborn Z37.50
      quadruplets Z37.52
      quintuplets Z37.53
      sextuplets Z37.54
      specified number NEC Z37.59
      triplets Z37.51
    all stillborn Z37.7
    some liveborn Z37.60
      quadruplets Z37.62
      quintuplets Z37.63
      sextuplets Z37.64
      specified number NEC
        Z37.69
      triplets Z37.61
  single NEC Z37.9
    liveborn Z37.0
    stillborn Z37.1
  twins NEC Z37.9
    both liveborn Z37.2
    both stillborn Z37.4
    one liveborn, one stillborn Z37.3
Outlet - *see* condition
Ovalocytosis (congenital) (hereditary) -
  see Elliptocytosis
Ovarian - *see* Condition
Ovariocele N83.4
Ovaritis (cystic) - *see* Oophoritis
Ovary, ovarian - *see also* condition
  resistant syndrome E28.39
  vein syndrome N13.8
Overactive - *see also* Hyperfunction
  adrenal cortex NEC E27.0
  bladder N32.81
  hypothalamus E23.3
  thyroid - *see* Hyperthyroidism

Overactivity R46.3
   child – *see* Disorder, attention-deficit
      hyperactivity
Overbite (deep) (excessive) (horizontal)
   (vertical) M26.29
Overbreathing - *see* Hyperventilation
Overconscientious personality F60.5
Overdevelopment - *see* Hypertrophy
Overdistension - *see* Distension
Overdose, overdosage (drug) - *see* Table
   of drugs and chemicals, by drug,
   poisoning
Overeating R63.2
   nonorganic origin F50.8
   psychogenic F50.8
Overexertion (effects) (exhaustion) T73.3
Overexposure (effects) T73.9
   exhaustion T73.2
Overfeeding - *see* Overeating
   newborn P92.4
Overfill, endodontic M27.52
Overgrowth, bone - *see* Hypertrophy,
   bone
Overhanging of dental restorative mate-
   rial (unrepairable) K08.52

Overheated (places) (effects) - *see* Heat
Overjet (excessive horizontal) M26.23
Overlaid, overlying (suffocation) - *see*
   Asphyxia, traumatic, due to me-
   chanical threat
Overlap, excessive horizontal (teeth)
   M26.23
Overlapping toe (acquired) - *see also*
   Deformity, toe, specified NEC
   congenital (fifth toe) Q66.8
Overload
   fluid E87.7
   potassium (K) E87.5
   sodium (Na) E87.0
Overnutrition - *see* Hyperalimentation
Overproduction - *see also* Hypersecretion
   ACTH E27.0
   catecholamine E27.5
   growth hormone E22.0
Overprotection, child by parent Z62.1
Overriding
   aorta Q25.4
   finger (acquired) - *see* Deformity,
      finger
      congenital Q68.1

Overriding *(Continued)*
   toe (acquired) - *see also* Deformity, toe,
      specified NEC
      congenital Q66.8
Overstrained R53.83
   heart - *see* Hypertrophy, cardiac
Overuse, muscle NEC M70.8-
Overweight E66.3
Overworked R53.83
Oviduct - *see* condition
Ovotestis Q56.0
Ovulation (cycle)
   failure or lack of N97.0
   pain N94.0
Ovum - *see* condition
Owren's disease or syndrome (parahe-
   mophilia) D68.2
Ox heart - *see* Hypertrophy, cardiac
Oxalosis E72.53
Oxaluria E72.53
Oxycephaly, oxycephalic Q75.0
   syphilitic, congenital A50.02
Oxyuriasis B80
Oxyuris vermicularis (infestation) B80
Ozena J31.0

P

Pachyderma, pachydermia L85.9
 larynx (verrucosa) J38.7
Pachydermatocele (congenital) Q82.8
Pachydermoperiostosis - see also Osteoarthropathy, hypertrophic, specified
  type NEC
 clubbed nail M89.40 [L62]
Pachygyria Q04.3
Pachymeningitis (adhesive)
  (basal) (brain) (cervical)
  (chronic)(circumscribed) (external)
  (fibrous) (hemorrhagic) (hypertrophic) (internal) (purulent) (spinal)
  (suppurative) - see Meningitis
Pachyonychia (congenital) Q84.5
Pacinian tumor -see Neoplasm, skin,
  benign
Pad, knuckle or Garrod's M72.1
Paget-Schroetter syndrome I82.890
Paget's disease
 with infiltrating duct carcinoma - see
    Neoplasm, breast, malignant
 bone M88.9
  carpus M88.84-
  clavicle M88.81-
  femur M88.85-
  fibula M88.86-
  finger M88.84-
  humerus M88.82-
  ilium M88.85-
  in neoplastic disease - see Osteitis,
       deformans, in neoplastic disease
  ischium M88.85-
  metacarpus M88.84-
  metatarsus M88.87-
  multiple sites M88.89
  neck M88.88
  radius M88.83-
  rib M88.88
  scapula M88.81-
  skull M88.0
  tarsus M88.87-
  tibia M88.86-
  toe M88.87-
  ulna M88.83-
  vertebra M88.88
 breast (female) C50.01-
  male C50.02-
 extramammary - see also Neoplasm,
    skin, malignant
  anus C21.0
   margin C44.51
   skin C44.51
 intraductal carcinoma - see Neoplasm,
    breast, malignant
 malignant - see Neoplasm, skin,
    malignant
  breast (female) C50.01-
   male C50.02-
  specified site NEC - see Neoplasm,
     skin, malignant
  unspecified site (female) C50.01-
   male C50.02-
 mammary – see Paget's disease, breast
 nipple – see Paget's disease, breast
 osteitis deformans - see Paget's disease,
    bone
Pain(s) (see also Painful) R52
 abdominal R10.9
  colic R10.83
  generalized R10.84
   with acute abdomen R10.0

Pain(s) (Continued)
 abdominal (Continued)
  lower R10.30
   left quadrant R10.32
   pelvic or perineal R10.2
   periumbilical R10.33
   right quadrant R10.31
  rebound - see Tenderness, abdominal,
     rebound
  severe with abdominal rigidity
     R10.0
  tenderness - see Tenderness,
     abdominal
  upper R10.10
   epigastric R10.13
   left quadrant R10.12
   right quadrant R10.11
 acute R52
  due to trauma G89.11
  neoplasm related G89.3
  postprocedural NEC G89.18
  post-thoracotomy G89.12
  specified by site - code to Pain,
     by site
 adnexa (uteri) R10.2
 anginoid - see Pain, precordial
 anus K62.8
 arm – see Pain, limb, upper
 axillary (axilla) M79.62-
 back (postural) M54.9
 bladder R39.89
  associated with micturition – see
     Micturition, painful
 bone - see Disorder, bone, specified type
     NEC
 breast N64.4
 broad ligament R10.2
 cancer associated (acute) (chronic)
     G89.3
 cecum - see Pain, abdominal
 cervicobrachial M53.1
 chest (central) R07.9
  anterior wall R07.89
  atypical R07.89
  ischemic I20.9
  musculoskeletal R07.89
  non-cardiac R07.89
  on breathing R07.1
  pleurodynia R07.81
  precordial R07.2
  wall (anterior) R07.89
 chronic R52
  associated with significant psychoso-
     cial dysfunction G89.4
  due to trauma G89.21
  neoplasm related G89.3
  postoperative NEC G89.28
  postprocedural NEC G89.28
  post-thoracotomy G89.22
  specified by site - code to Pain, by site
 coccyx M53.3
 colon – see Pain, abdominal
 coronary - see Angina
 costochondral R07.1
 diaphragm R07.1
 due to cancer G89.3
 due to device, implant or graft (see also
     Complications, by site and type,
     specified NEC) T85.84
  arterial graft NEC T82.848
  breast (implant) T85.84
  catheter NEC T85.84
   dialysis (renal) T82.848
    intraperitoneal T85.84

Pain(s) (Continued)
 due to device, implant or graft
     (Continued)
  catheter NEC (Continued)
   infusion NEC T82.848
    spinal (epidural) (subdural)
       T85.84
   urinary (indwelling) T83.84
  electronic (electrode) (pulse genera-
     tor) (stimulator)
   bone T84.84
   cardiac T82.847
   nervous system (brain) (peripheral
      nerve) (spinal) T85.84
   urinary T83.84
  fixation, internal (orthopedic) NEC
     T84.84
  gastrointestinal (bile duct) (esopha-
     gus) T85.84
  genital NEC T83.84
  heart NEC T82.847
  infusion NEC T85.84
  joint prosthesis T84.84
  ocular (corneal graft) (orbital im-
     plant) NEC T85.84
  orthopedic NEC T84.84
  specified NEC T85.84
  urinary NEC T83.84
  vascular NEC T82.848
  ventricular intracranial shunt
     T85.84
 due to malignancy (primary) (second-
     ary) G89.3
 ear - see subcategory H92.0
 epigastric, epigastrium R10.13
 eye - see Pain, ocular
 face, facial R51
  atypical G50.1
 female genital organs NEC N94.89
 finger – see Pain, limb, upper
 flank – see Pain, abdominal
 foot – see Pain, limb, lower
 gallbladder K82.9
 gas (intestinal) R14.1
 gastric - see Pain, abdominal
 generalized NOS R52
 genital organ
  female N94.89
  male N50.8
 groin – see Pain, abdominal, lower
 hand – see Pain, limb, upper
 head - see Headache
 heart - see Pain, precordial
 infra-orbital - see Neuralgia, trigeminal
 intercostal R07.82
 intermenstrual N94.0
 jaw M27.8
 joint M25.50
  ankle M25.57-
  elbow M25.52-
  finger M79.64-
  foot M79.67-
  hand M79.64-
  hip M25.55-
  knee M25.56-
  shoulder M25.51-
  toe M79.67-
  wrist M25.53-
 kidney N23
 laryngeal R07.0
 leg – see Pain, limb, lower
 limb M79.609
  lower M79.60-
   lower leg M79.66-

Pain(s) *(Continued)*
  limb *(Continued)*
    lower *(Continued)*
      thigh M79.65-
      toe M79.67-
    upper M79.60-
      axilla M79.62-
      finger M79.64-
      forearm M79.63-
      hand M79.64-
      upper arm M79.62-
  loin M54.5
  low back M54.5
  lumbar region M54.5
  mastoid - *see* subcategory H92.0
  maxilla M27.8
  menstrual (*see also* Dysmenorrhea)
    N94.6
  metacarpophalangeal (joint) - *see* Pain,
    joint, hand
  metatarsophalangeal (joint) - *see* Pain,
    joint, foot
  mouth K13.79
  muscle - *see* Myalgia
  musculoskeletal (*see also* Pain, by site)
    M79.1
  myofascial M79.1
  nasal J34.89
  nasopharynx J39.2
  neck NEC M54.2
  nerve NEC - *see* Neuralgia
  neuromuscular - *see* Neuralgia
  nose J34.89
  ocular H57.1-
  ophthalmic - *see* Pain, ocular
  orbital region - *see* Pain, ocular
  ovary N94.89
  over heart - *see* Pain, precordial
  ovulation N94.0
  pelvic (female) R10.2
  penis N48.89
  pericardial - *see* Pain, precordial
  perineal, perineum R10.2
  pharynx J39.2
  pleura, pleural, pleuritic R07.89
  postoperative NOS G89.18
  postprocedural NOS G89.18
  post-thoracotomy G89.12
  precordial (region) R07.2
  premenstrual N94.3
  psychogenic (persistent) (any site)
    F45.41
  radicular (spinal) - *see* Radiculopathy
  rectum K62.8
  respiration R07.1
  retrosternal R07.2
  rheumatoid, muscular - *see* Myalgia
  rib R07.81
  root (spinal) - *see* Radiculopathy
  round ligament (stretch) R10.2
  sacroiliac M53.3
  sciatic - *see* Sciatica
  scrotum N50.8
  seminal vesicle N50.8
  shoulder M25.51-
  spermatic cord N50.8
  spinal root - *see* Radiculopathy
  spine M54.9
    cervical M54.2
    low back M54.5
      with sciatica M54.4-
    thoracic M54.6
  stomach - *see* Pain, abdominal
  substernal R07.2

Pain(s) *(Continued)*
  temporomandibular (joint) M26.62
  testis N50.8
  thoracic spine M54.6
    with radicular and visceral pain
      M54.14
  throat R07.0
  tibia – *see* Pain, limb, lower
  toe – *see* Pain, limb, lower
  tongue K14.6
  tooth K08.8
  trigeminal - *see* Neuralgia, trigeminal
  tumor associated G89.3
  ureter N23
  urinary (organ) (system) N23
  uterus NEC N94.89
  vagina R10.2
  vertebrogenic (syndrome) M54.89
  vesical R39.89
    associated with micturition – *see*
      Micturition, painful
  vulva R10.2
Painful - *see also* Pain
  coitus
    female N94.1
    male N53.12
    psychogenic F52.6
  ejaculation (semen) N53.12
    psychogenic F52.6
  erection - *see* Priapism
  feet syndrome E53.8
  joint replacement (hip) (knee)
    T84.84
  menstruation - *see* Dysmenorrhea
    psychogenic F45.8
  micturition – *see* Micturition, painful
  respiration R07.1
  scar NEC L90.5
  wire sutures T81.89
Painter's colic - *see* subcategory T56.0
Palate - *see* condition
Palatoplegia K13.79
Palatoschisis - *see* Cleft, palate
Palilalia R48.8
Palliative care Z51.5
Pallor R23.1
  optic disc, temporal - *see* Atrophy,
    optic
Palmar - *see also* condition
  fascia - *see* condition
Palpable
  cecum K63.89
  kidney N28.89
  ovary N83.8
  prostate N42.9
  spleen - *see* Splenomegaly
Palpitations (heart) R00.2
  psychogenic F45.8
Palsy - *see also* Paralysis G83.9
  atrophic diffuse (progressive) G12.22
  Bell's - *see also* Palsy, facial
    newborn P11.3
  brachial plexus NEC G54.0
    newborn (birth injury) P14.3
  brain - *see* Palsy, cerebral
  bulbar (progressive) (chronic)
    G12.22
    of childhood (Fazio-Londe) G12.1
    pseudo NEC G12.29
    supranuclear NEC G12.22
  cerebral (congenital) G80.9
    ataxic G80.4
    athetoid G80.3
    choreathetoid G80.3

Palsy *(Continued)*
  cerebral *(Continued)*
    diplegic G80.8
      spastic G80.1
    dyskinetic G80.3
      athetoid G80.3
      choreathetoid G80.3
      distonic G80.3
    dystonic G80.3
    hemiplegic G80.8
      spastic G80.2
    mixed G80.8
    monoplegic G80.8
      spastic G80.1
    paraplegic G80.8
      spastic G80.1
    quadriplegic G80.8
      spastic G80.0
    spastic G80.1
      diplegic G80.1
      hemiplegic G80.2
      monoplegic G80.1
      quadriplegic G80.0
      specified NEC G80.1
      tetrapelgic G80.0
    specified NEC G80.8
    syphilitic A52.12
      congenital A50.49
    tetraplegic G80.8
      spastic G80.0
  cranial nerve - *see also* Disorder, nerve,
    cranial
    multiple G52.7
      in
        infectious disease B99 *[G53]*
        neoplastic disease (*see also*
          Neoplasm) D49.9 *[G53]*
        parasitic disease B89 *[G53]*
        sarcoidosis D86.82
  creeping G12.22
  diver's T70.3
  Erb's P14.0
  facial G51.0
    newborn (birth injury) P11.3
  glossopharyngeal G52.1
  Klumpke(-Déjérine) P14.1
  lead - *see* subcategory T56.0
  median nerve (tardy) G56.1-
  nerve G58.9
    specified NEC G58.8
  peroneal nerve (acute) (tardy) G57.3-
  pseudobulbar NEC G12.29
  radial nerve (acute) G56.3-
  seventh nerve - *see also* Palsy, facial
    newborn P11.3
  shaking - *see* Parkinsonism
  spastic (cerebral) (spinal) G80.9
  ulnar nerve (tardy) G56.2-
  wasting G12.29
Paludism - *see* Malaria
Panangiitis M30.0
Panaris, panaritium - *see also* Cellulitis,
  digit
  with lymphangitis - *see* Lymphangitis,
    acute, digit
Panarteritis nodosa M30.0
  brain or cerebral I67.7
Pancake heart R93.1
  with cor pulmonale (chronic)
    I27.81
Pancarditis (acute) (chronic) I51.89
  rheumatic I09.89
    active or acute I01.8
Pancoast's syndrome or tumor C34.1-

Pancolitis, ulcerative (chronic) K51.00
  with
    complication K51.019
    abscess K51.014
    fistula K51.013
    obstruction K51.012
    rectal bleeding K51.011
    specified complication NEC K51.018
Pancreas, pancreatic - *see* condition
Pancreatitis (annular) (apoplectic) (cal-
    careous) (edematous) (hemorrhagic)
    (malignant) (recurrent) (subacute)
    (suppurative) K85.9
  acute K85.9
    alcohol induced K85.2
    biliary K85.1
    drug induced K85.3
    gallstone K85.1
    idiopathic K85.0
    specified NEC K85.8
  chronic (infectious) K86.1
    alcohol-induced K86.0
    recurrent K86.1
    relapsing K86.1
  cystic (chronic) K86.1
  cytomegaloviral B25.2
  fibrous (chronic) K86.1
  gangrenous K85.8
  gallstone K85.1
  interstitial (chronic) K86.1
    acute K85.8
  mumps B26.3
  recurrent (chronic) K86.1
  relapsing, chronic K86.1
  syphilitic A52.74
Pancreatoblastoma - *see* Neoplasm,
    pancreas, malignant
Pancreolithiasis K86.8
Pancytolysis D75.89
Pancytopenia (acquired) D61.81
  with malformations D61.09
  congenital D61.09
Panencephalitis, subacute, sclerosing
    A81.1
Panhematopenia D61.9
  congenital D61.09
  constitutional D61.09
  splenic, primary D73.1
Panhemocytopenia D61.9
  congenital D61.09
  constitutional D61.09
Panhypogonadism E29.1
Panhypopituitarism E23.0
  prepubertal E23.0
Panic (attack) (state) F41.0
  reaction to exceptional stress (transient)
    F43.0
Panmyelopathy, familial, constitutional
    D61.09
Panmyelophthisis D61.82
  congenital D61.09
Panmyelosis (acute) (with myelofibrosis)
    C94.4-
Panner's disease - *see* Osteochondrosis,
    juvenile, humerus
Panneuritis endemica E51.11
Panniculitis (nodular) (nonsuppurative)
    M79.3
  back M54.00
    cervical region M54.02
    cervicothoracic region M54.03
    lumbar region M54.06
    lumbosacral region M54.07
    multiple sites M54.09

Panniculitis *(Continued)*
  back *(Continued)*
    occipito-atlanto-axial region
      M54.01
    sacrococcygeal region M54.08
    thoracic region M54.04
    thoracolumbar region M54.05
  lupus L93.2
  mesenteric K65.4
  neck M54.02
    cervicothoracic region M54.03
    occipito-atlanto-axial region
      M54.01
  relapsing M35.6
Panniculus adiposus (abdominal) E65
Pannus (allergic) (cornea) (degenerativus)
    (keratic) H16.42-
  abdominal (symptomatic) E65
  trachomatosus, trachomatous (active)
    A71.1
Panophthalmitis H44.01-
Pansinusitis (chronic) (hyperplastic)
    (nonpurulent) (purulent) J32.4
  acute J01.40
    recurrent J01.41
  tuberculous A15.8
Panuveitis (sympathetic) H44.11-
Panvalvular disease I08.9
  specified NEC I08.8
Papanicolaou smear, cervix Z12.4
  as part of routine gynecological exami-
    nation Z01.419
    with abnormal findings Z01.411
  for suspected neoplasm Z12.4
  nonspecific abnormal finding R87.619
  routine Z01.419
    with abnormal findings Z01.411
Papilledema (choked disc) H47.10
  associated with
    decreased ocular pressure H47.12
    increased intracranial pressure
      H47.11
    retinal disorder H47.13
  Foster Kennedy syndrome H47.14-
Papillitis H46.00
  anus K62.8
  chronic lingual K14.4
  necrotizing, kidney N17.2
  optic H46.0-
  rectum K62.8
  renal, necrotizing N17.2
  tongue K14.0
Papilloma - *see also* Neoplasm, benign
  acuminatum (female) (male) (anogeni-
    tal) A63.0
  benign pinta (primary) A67.0
  bladder (urinary) (transitional cell)
    D41.4
  choroid plexus (lateral ventricle) (third
    ventricle) D33.0
    anaplastic C71.5
    fourth ventricle D33.1
    malignant C71.5
  renal pelvis (transitional cell) D41.1-
    benign D30.1-
    specified site - *see* Neoplasm,
      benign
    unspecified site D14.0
      specified site - *see* Neoplasm,
        uncertain behavior
      unspecified site D39.10
    specified site - *see* Neoplasm,
      benign
    unspecified site D27.9

Papilloma *(Continued)*
  transitional (cell)
    bladder (urinary) D41.4
    inverted type - *see* Neoplasm, uncer-
      tain behavior
    renal pelvis D41.1-
    ureter D41.2-
  ureter (transitional cell) D41.2-
    benign D30.2-
  urothelial - *see* Neoplasm, uncertain
    behavior
  villous - *see* Neoplasm, uncertain
    behavior
    adenocarcinoma in - *see* Neoplasm,
      malignant
    in situ - *see* Neoplasm, in situ
  yaws, plantar or palmar A66.1
Papillomata, multiple, of yaws A66.1
Papillomatosis - *see also* Neoplasm,
    benign
  confluent and reticulated L83
  cystic, breast – *see* Mastopathy, cystic
  ductal, breast – *see* Mastopathy, cystic
  intraductal (diffuse) - *see* Neoplasm,
    benign
  subareolar duct (female) D24.0-
Papillomavirus, as cause of disease clas-
    sified elsewhere B97.7
Papillon-Léage and Psaume syndrome
    Q87.0
Papule(s) R23.8
  carate (primary) A67.0
  fibrous, of nose (M8724/0) D22.39
  Gottron's L94.4
  pinta (primary) A67.0
Papulosis
  lymphomatoid C86.6
  malignant I77.8
Papyraceous fetus O31.0-
Para-albuminemia E88.09
Paracephalus Q89.7
Parachute mitral valve Q23.2
Paracoccidioidomycosis B41.9
  disseminated B41.7
  generalized B41.7
  mucocutaneous-lymphangitic
    B41.8
  pulmonary B41.0
  specified NEC B41.8
  visceral B41.8
Paradentosis K05.4
Paraffinoma T88.8
Paraganglioma
  adrenal D35.0-
    malignant C74.1-
  aortic body D44.7
    malignant C75.5
  carotid body D44.6
    malignant C75.4
  chromaffin - *see also* Neoplasm,
    benign
    malignant - *see* Neoplasm,
      malignant
    specified site - *see* Neoplasm,
      malignant
    unspecified site C75.5
  specified site - *see* Neoplasm, uncer-
    tain behavior
  unspecified site D44.7
  specified site - *see* Neoplasm,
    benign
  unspecified site D13.2
  glomus jugulare D44.7
    malignant C75.5

Paraganglioma *(Continued)*
　jugular D44.7
　　specified site - *see* Neoplasm,
　　　malignant
　　unspecified site C75.5
　　　specified site - *see* Neoplasm,
　　　　malignant
　　　unspecified site C75.5
　　specified site - *see* Neoplasm, uncer-
　　　tain behavior
　　unspecified site D44.7
　　specified site - *see* Neoplasm, uncer-
　　　tain behavior
　　unspecified site D44.7
　　specified site - *see* Neoplasm, uncertain
　　　behavior
　　specified site - *see* Neoplasm, uncer-
　　　tain behavior
　　unspecified site D44.7
　　unspecified site D44.7
Parageusia R43.2
　psychogenic F45.8
Paragonimiasis B66.4
Paragranuloma, Hodgkin – *see* Hodgkin,
　disease, specified type NEC
Parahemophilia (*see also* Defect, coagula-
　tion) D68.2
Parakeratosis R23.4
　variegata L41.0
Paralysis, paralytic (complete) (incom-
　plete) G83.9
　with
　　syphilis A52.17
　abducens, abducent (nerve) - *see* Stra-
　　bismus, paralytic, sixth nerve
　abductor, lower extremity G57.9-
　accessory nerve G52.8
　accommodation - *see also* Paresis, of
　　accommodation
　　hysterical F44.89
　acoustic nerve (except Deafness) - *see*
　　subcategory H93.3
　agitans (*see also* Parkinsonism) G20
　　arteriosclerotic G21.4
　alternating (oculomotor) G83.89
　amyotrophic G12.21
　ankle G57.9-
　anus (sphincter) K62.8
　arm – *see* Monoplegia, upper limb
　ascending (spinal), acute G61.0
　association G12.29
　asthenic bulbar G70.00
　　with exacerbation (acute) G70.01
　　in crisis G70.01
　ataxic (hereditary) G11.9
　　general (syphilitic) A52.17
　atrophic G58.9
　　infantile, acute - *see* Poliomyelitis,
　　　paralytic
　　progressive G12.22
　　spinal (acute) - *see* Poliomyelitis,
　　　paralytic
　axillary G54.0
　Babinski-Nageotte's G83.89
　Bell's G51.0
　　newborn P11.3
　Benedikt's G46.3
　birth injury P14.9
　　spinal cord P11.5
　bladder (neurogenic) (sphincter) N31.2
　bowel, colon or intestine K56.0
　brachial plexus G54.0
　　birth injury P14.3
　　newborn (birth injury) P14.3

Paralysis, paralytic *(Continued)*
　brain G83.9
　　diplegia G83.0
　　triplegia G83.89
　bronchial J98.09
　Brown-Séquard G83.81
　bulbar (chronic) (progressive) G12.22
　　infantile - *see* Poliomyelitis, paralytic
　　poliomyelitic - *see* Poliomyelitis,
　　　paralytic
　　pseudo G12.29
　　supranuclear G12.22
　bulbospinal G70.00
　　with exacerbation (acute) G70.01
　　in crisis G70.01
　cardiac - *see also* Failure, heart I50.9
　cerebrocerebellar, diplegic G80.1
　cervical
　　plexus G54.2
　　sympathetic G90.09
　Cestan-Chenais G46.3
　Charcot-Marie-Tooth type G60.0
　Clark's G80.9
　colon K56.0
　compressed air T70.3
　compression
　　arm G56.9-
　　leg G57.9-
　　lower extremity G57.9-
　　upper extremity G56.9-
　congenital (cerebral) - *see* Palsy, cerebral
　conjugate movement (gaze) (of eye) H51.0
　　cortical (nuclear) (supranuclear) H51.0
　cordis - *see* Failure, heart
　cranial or cerebral nerve G52.9
　creeping G12.22
　crossed leg G83.89
　crutch - *see* Injury, brachial plexus
　deglutition R13.0
　　hysterical F44.4
　dementia A52.17
　descending (spinal) NEC G12.29
　diaphragm (flaccid) J98.6
　　due to accidental dissection of
　　　phrenic nerve during procedure –
　　　see Puncture, accidental compli-
　　　cating surgery
　digestive organs NEC K59.8
　diplegic - *see* Diplegia
　divergence (nuclear) H51.8
　diver's T70.3
　Duchenne's
　　birth injury P14.0
　　due to or associated with
　　　motor neuron disease G12.22
　　　muscular dystrophy G71.0
　　due to intracranial or spinal birth
　　　injury - *see* Palsy, cerebral
　　embolic (current episode) I63.4
　Erb(-Duchenne) (birth) (newborn) P14.0
　Erb's syphilitic spastic spinal A52.17
　esophagus K22.8
　eye muscle (extrinsic) H49.9
　　intrinsic - *see also* Paresis, of
　　　accommodation
　facial (nerve) G51.0
　　birth injury P11.3
　　congenital P11.3
　　following operation NEC – *see* Punc-
　　　ture, accidental complicating
　　　surgery
　　newborn (birth injury) P11.3
　familial (recurrent) (periodic) G72.3
　　spastic G11.4

Paralysis, paralytic *(Continued)*
　fauces J39.2
　finger G56.9-
　gait R26.1
　gastric nerve (nondiabetic) G52.2
　gaze, conjugate H51.0
　general (progressive) (syphilitic)
　　A52.17
　　juvenile A50.45
　glottis J38.00
　　bilateral J38.02
　　unilateral J38.01
　gluteal G54.1
　Gubler(-Millard) G46.3
　hand – *see* Monoplegia, upper limb
　heart – *see* Arrest, cardiac
　hemiplegic - *see* Hemiplegia
　hyperkalemic periodic (familial)
　　G72.3
　hypoglossal (nerve) G52.3
　hypokalemic periodic G72.3
　hysterical F44.4
　ileus K56.0
　infantile (*see also* Poliomyelitis, para-
　　lytic) A80.30
　　bulbar - *see* Poliomyelitis, paralytic
　　cerebral - *see* Palsy, cerebral
　　spastic - *see* Palsy, cerebral, spastic
　　infective - *see* Poliomyelitis, paralytic
　inferior nuclear G83.9
　internuclear - *see* Ophthalmoplegia,
　　internuclear
　intestine K56.0
　iris H57.09
　　due to diphtheria (toxin) A36.89
　ischemic, Volkmann's (complicating
　　trauma) T79.6
　Jackson's G83.89
　jake - *see* Poisoning, food, noxious,
　　plant
　Jamaica ginger (jake) G62.2
　juvenile general A50.45
　Klumpke(-Déjérine) (birth) (newborn)
　　P14.1
　labioglossal (laryngeal) (pharyngeal)
　　G12.29
　Landry's G61.0
　laryngeal nerve (recurrent) (superior)
　　(unilateral) J38.00
　　bilateral J38.02
　　unilateral J38.01
　larynx J38.00
　　bilateral J38.02
　　due to diphtheria (toxin) A36.2
　　unilateral J38.01
　lateral G12.21
　lead - *see* subcategory T56.0
　left side - *see* Hemiplegia
　leg G83.1-
　　both - *see* Paraplegia
　　crossed G83.89
　　hysterical F44.4
　　psychogenic F44.4
　　transient or transitory R29.81
　　　traumatic NEC – *see* Injury, nerve,
　　　　leg
　levator palpebrae superioris - *see*
　　Blepharoptosis, paralytic
　limb – *see* Monoplegia
　lip K13.0
　Lissauer's A52.17
　lower limb – *see* Monoplegia, lower
　　limb
　　both - *see* Paraplegia

Paralysis, paralytic *(Continued)*
lung J98.4
median nerve G56.1-
medullary (tegmental) G83.89
mesencephalic NEC G83.89
tegmental G83.89
middle alternating G83.89
Millard-Gubler-Foville G46.3
monoplegic - *see* Monoplegia
motor G83.9
muscle, muscular NEC G72.8
due to nerve lesion G58.9
eye (extrinsic) H49.9
intrinsic - *see* Paresis, of
accommodation
oblique - *see* Strabismus, paralytic,
fourth nerve
iris sphincter H21.9
ischemic (Volkmann's) (complicating
trauma) T79.6
progressive G12.21
pseudohypertrophic G71.0
musculocutaneous nerve G56.9-
musculospiral G56.9-
nerve - *see also* Disorder, nerve
abducent - *see* Strabismus, paralytic,
sixth nerve
accessory G52.8
auditory (except Deafness) - *see* subcategory H93.3
birth injury P14.9
cranial or cerebral G52.9
facial G51.0
birth injury P11.3
newborn (birth injury) P11.3
fourth or trochlear - *see* Strabismus,
paralytic, fourth nerve
newborn (birth injury) P14.9
oculomotor - *see* Strabismus, paralytic, third nerve
phrenic (birth injury) P14.2
radial G56.3-
seventh or facial G51.0
newborn (birth injury) P11.3
sixth or abducent - *see* Strabismus,
paralytic, sixth nerve
syphilitic A52.15
third or oculomotor - *see* Strabismus,
paralytic, third nerve
trigeminal G50.9
trochlear - *see* Strabismus, paralytic,
fourth nerve
ulnar G56.2-
normokalemic periodic G72.3
ocular H49.9
alternating G83.89
oculofacial, congenital (Moebius) Q87.0
oculomotor (external bilateral) (nerve) -
see Strabismus, paralytic, third
nerve
palate (soft) K13.79
paratrigeminal G50.9
periodic (familial) (hyperkalemic)
(hypokalemic) (myotonic) (normokalemic) (potassium sensitive)
(secondary) G72.3
peripheral autonomic nervous system -
see Neuropathy, peripheral,
autonomic
peroneal (nerve) G57.3-
pharynx J39.2
phrenic nerve G56.8-
plantar nerve(s) G57.6-
pneumogastric nerve G52.2

Paralysis, paralytic *(Continued)*
poliomyelitis (current) - *see* Poliomyelitis, paralytic
popliteal nerve G57.3-
postepileptic transitory G83.84
progressive (atrophic) (bulbar) (spinal)
G12.22
general A52.17
infantile acute - *see* Poliomyelitis,
paralytic
pseudobulbar G12.29
pseudohypertrophic (muscle) G71.0
psychogenic F44.4
quadriceps G57.9-
quadriplegic - *see* Tetraplegia
radial nerve G56.3-
rectus muscle (eye) H49.9
recurrent isolated sleep G47.53
respiratory (muscle) (system) (tract)
R06.81
center NEC G93.89
congenital P28.89
newborn P28.89
right side - *see* Hemiplegia
saturnine - *see* subcategory T56.0
sciatic nerve G57.0-
senile G83.9
shaking - *see* Parkinsonism
shoulder G56.9-
sleep, recurrent isolated G47.53
spastic G83.9
cerebral - *see* Palsy, cerebral, spastic
congenital (cerebral) - *see* Palsy, cerebral, spastic
familial G11.4
hereditary G11.4
quadriplegic G80.0
syphilitic (spinal) A52.17
sphincter, bladder - *see* Paralysis,
bladder
spinal (cord) G83.9
accessory nerve G52.8
acute - *see* Poliomyelitis, paralytic
ascending acute G61.0
atrophic (acute) - *see also* Poliomyelitis, paralytic
spastic, syphilitic A52.17
congenital NEC - *see* Palsy, cerebral
infantile - *see* Poliomyelitis,
paralytic
hereditary G95.89
progressive G12.21
sequelae NEC G83.89
sternomastoid G52.8
stomach K31.89
diabetic - *see* Diabetes, by type, with
gastroparesis
nerve G52.2
diabetic - *see* Diabetes, by type,
with gastroparesis
stroke - *see* Infarct, brain
subcapsularis G56.8-
supranuclear G12.29
sympathetic G90.8
cervical G90.09
nervous system - *see* Neuropathy,
peripheral, autonomic
syndrome G83.9
specified NEC G83.89
syphilitic spastic spinal (Erb's) A52.17
thigh G57.9-
throat J39.2
diphtheritic A36.0
muscle J39.2

Paralysis, paralytic *(Continued)*
thrombotic (current episode) I63.3
thumb G56.9-
tick - *see* Toxicity, venom, arthropod,
specified NEC
Todd's (postepileptic transitory
paralysis) G83.84
toe G57.6-
tongue K14.8
transient R29.5
arm or leg NEC R29.81
traumatic NEC - *see* Injury, nerve
trapezius G52.8
traumatic, transient NEC - *see* Injury,
nerve
trembling - *see* Parkinsonism
triceps brachii G56.9-
trigeminal nerve G50.9
trochlear (nerve) - *see* Strabismus,
paralytic, fourth nerve
ulnar nerve G56.2-
upper limb – *see* Monoplegia, upper
limb
uremic N18.9 *[G99.8]*
uveoparotitic D86.89
uvula K13.79
postdiphtheritic A36.0
vagus nerve G52.2
vasomotor NEC G90.8
velum palati K13.79
vesical - *see* Paralysis, bladder
vestibular nerve (except Vertigo) - *see*
subcategory H93.3
vocal cords J38.00
bilateral J38.02
unilateral J38.01
Volkmann's (complicating trauma)
T79.6
wasting G12.29
Weber's G46.3
wrist G56.9-
Paramedial urethrovesical orifice
Q64.79
Paramenia N92.6
Parametritis (*see also* Disease, pelvis,
inflammatory) N73.2
acute N73.0
complicating abortion – *see* Abortion,
by type, complicated by,
parametritis
Parametrium, parametric - *see* condition
Paramnesia - *see* Amnesia
Paramolar K00.1
Paramyloidosis E85.8
Paramyoclonus multiplex G25.3
Paramyotonia (congenita) G71.19
Parangi - *see* Yaws
Paranoia (querulans) F22
senile F03
Paranoid
dementia (senile) F03
praecox - *see* Schizophrenia
personality F60.0
psychosis (climacteric) (involutional)
(menopausal) F22
psychogenic (acute) F23
senile F03
reaction (acute) F23
chronic F22
schizophrenia F20.0
state (climacteric) (involutional) (menopausal) (simple) F22
senile F03
tendencies F60.0

Paranoid (*Continued*)
traits F60.0
trends F60.0
type, psychopathic personality F60.0
Paraparesis - *see* Paraplegia
Paraphasia R47.02
Paraphilia F65.9
Paraphimosis (congenital) N47.2
chancroidal A57
Paraphrenia, paraphrenic (late) F22
schizophrenia F20.0
Paraplegia (lower) G82.20
ataxic - *see* Degeneration, combined, spinal cord
complete G82.21
congenital (cerebral) G80.8
spastic G80.1
familial spastic G11.4
functional (hysterical) F44.4
hereditary, spastic G11.4
hysterical F44.4
incomplete G82.22
Pott's A18.01
psychogenic F44.4
spastic
Erb's spinal, syphilitic A52.17
hereditary G11.4
tropical G04.1
syphilitic (spastic) A52.17
tropical spastic G04.1
Parapoxvirus B08.60
specified NEC B08.69
Paraproteinemia D89.2
benign (familial) D89.2
monoclonal D47.2
secondary to malignant disease D47.2
Parapsoriasis L41.9
en plaques L41.4
guttata L41.1
large plaque L41.4
retiform, retiformis L41.5
small plaque L41.3
specified NEC L41.8
varioliformis (acuta) L41.0
Parasitic - *see also* condition
disease NEC B89
stomatitis B37.0
sycosis (beard) (scalp) B35.0
twin Q89.4
Parasitism B89
intestinal B82.9
skin B88.9
specified - *see* Infestation
Parasitophobia F40.218
Parasomnia G47.50
due to
alcohol
abuse F10.182
dependence F10.282
use F10.982
amphetamines
abuse F15.182
dependence F15.282
use F15.982
caffeine
abuse F15.182
dependence F15.282
use F15.982
cocaine
abuse F14.182
dependence F14.282
use F14.982

Parasomnia (*Continued*)
due to (*Continued*)
drug NEC
abuse F19.182
dependence F19.282
use F19.982
opioid
abuse F11.182
dependence F11.282
use F11.982
psychoactive substance NEC
abuse F19.182
dependence F19.282
use F19.982
sedative, hypnotic, or anxiolytic
abuse F13.182
dependence F13.282
use F13.982
stimulant NEC
abuse F15.182
dependence F15.282
use F15.982
in conditions classified elsewhere G47.54
nonorganic origin F51.8
organic G47.50
specified NEC G47.59
Paraspadias Q54.9
Paraspasmus facialis G51.8
Parasuicide (attempt)
history of (personal) Z91.5
in family Z81.8
Parathyroid gland - *see* condition
Parathyroid tetany E20.9
Paratrachoma A74.0
Paratyphilitis - *see* Appendicitis
Paratyphoid (fever) - *see* Fever, paratyphoid
Paratyphus - *see* Fever, paratyphoid
Paraurethral duct Q64.79
nonorganic origin F51.5
Paraurethritis - *see also* Urethritis
gonococcal (acute) (chronic) (with abscess) A54.1
Paravaccinia NEC B08.04
Paravaginitis - *see* Vaginitis
Parencephalitis - *see also* Encephalitis
sequelae G09
Parent-child conflict - *see* Conflict, parent-child
estrangement NEC Z62.890
Paresis - *see also* Paralysis
accommodation - *see* Paresis, of accommodation
Bernhardt's G57.1-
bladder (sphincter) - *see also* Paralysis, bladder
tabetic A52.17
bowel, colon or intestine K56.0
extrinsic muscle, eye H49.9
general (progressive) (syphilitic) A52.17
juvenile A50.45
heart - *see* Failure, heart
insane (syphilitic) A52.17
juvenile (general) A50.45
of accommodation H52.52-
peripheral progressive (idiopathic) G60.3
pseudohypertrophic G71.0
senile G83.9
syphilitic (general) A52.17
congenital A50.45
vesical NEC N31.2

Paresthesia - *see also* Disturbance, sensation
Bernhardt G57.1-
Paretic - *see* condition
Parinaud's
conjunctivitis H10.89
oculoglandular syndrome H10.89
ophthalmoplegia H49.88
Parkinsonism (primary) G20
with neurogenic orthostatic hypotension (idiopathic) (symptomatic) G90.3
arteriosclerotic G21.4
dementia G31.83 [*F02.80*]
with behavioral disturbance G31.83 [*F02.81*]
due to
drugs NEC G21.19
neuroleptic G21.11
neuroleptic induced G21.11
postencephalitic G21.3
secondary G21.9
due to
arteriosclerosis G21.4
drugs NEC G21.19
neuroleptic G21.11
encephalitis G21.3
external agents NEC G21.2
syphilis A52.19
specified NEC G21.8
syphilitic A52.19
treatment-induced NEC G21.19
vascular G21.4
Parkinson's disease, syndrome or tremor - *see* Parkinsonism
Parodontitis - *see* Periodontitis
Parodontosis K05.4
Paronychia - *see also* Cellulitis, digit
with lymphangitis - *see* Lymphangitis, acute, digit
candidal (chronic) B37.2
tuberculous (primary) A18.4
Parorexia (psychogenic) F50.8
Parosmia R43.1
psychogenic F45.8
Parotid gland - *see* condition
Parotitis, parotiditis (allergic) (nonspecific toxic) (purulent) (septic) (suppurative) *see also* Sialoadenitis
epidemic - *see* Mumps
infectious - *see* Mumps
postoperative K91.89
surgical K91.89
Parrot fever A70
Parrot's disease (early congenital syphilitic pseudoparalysis) A50.02
Parry-Romberg syndrome G51.8
Parry's disease or syndrome E05.00
with thyroid storm E05.01
Pars planitis - *see* Cyclitis
Parsonage(-Aldren)-Turner syndrome G54.5
Parson's disease (exophthalmic goiter) E05.00
with thyroid storm E05.01
Particolored infant Q82.8
Parturition - *see* Delivery
Parulis K04.7
with sinus K04.6
Parvovirus, as cause of disease classified elsewhere B97.6
Pasini and Pierini's atrophoderma L90.3

Passage
  false, urethra N36.0
  meconium (newborn) during delivery P03.82
  of sounds or bougies - *see* Attention to, artificial, opening
Passive - *see* condition
  smoking Z77.22
Pasteurella septica A28.0
Pasteurellosis - *see* Infection, Pasteurella
PAT (paroxysmal atrial tachycardia) I47.1
Patau's syndrome - *see* Trisomy, 13
Patches
  mucous (syphilitic) A51.39
    congenital A50.07
  smokers' (mouth) K13.24
Patellar - *see* condition
Patent - *see also* Imperfect, closure
  canal of Nuck Q52.4
  cervix N88.3
  ductus arteriosus or Botallo's Q25.0
  foramen
    botalli Q21.1
    ovale Q21.1
  interauricular septum Q21.1
  interventricular septum Q21.0
  omphalomesenteric duct Q43.0
  os (uteri) - *see* Patent, cervix
  ostium secundum Q21.1
  urachus Q64.4
  vitelline duct Q43.0
Paterson(-Brown)(-Kelly) syndrome or web D50.1
Pathologic, pathological - *see also* condition
  asphyxia R09.01
  fire-setting F63.1
  gambling F63.0
  ovum O02.0
  resorption, tooth K03.3
  stealing F63.2
Pathology (of) - *see* Disease
  periradicular, associated with previous endodontic treatment NEC M27.59
Pattern, sleep-wake, irregular G47.2
Patulous - *see also* Imperfect, closure (congenital)
  alimentary tract Q45.8
    lower Q43.8
    upper Q40.8
  eustachian tube H69.0-
Pause, sinoatrial I49.5
Paxton's disease B36.8
Pearl(s)
  enamel K00.2
  Epstein's K09.8
Pearl-worker's disease - *see* Osteomyelitis, specified type NEC
Pectenosis K62.4
Pectoral - *see* condition
Pectus
  carinatum (congenital) Q67.7
    acquired M95.4
    rachitic sequelae (late effect) E64.3
  excavatum (congenital) Q67.6
    acquired M95.4
    rachitic sequelae (late effect) E64.3
  recurvatum (congenital) Q67.6
Pedatrophia E41
Pederosis F65.4
Pediculosis (infestation) B85.2
  capitis (head-louse) (any site) B85.0
  corporis (body-louse) (any site) B85.1
  eyelid B85.0

Pediculosis (Continued)
  mixed (classifiable to more than one of the titles B85.0-B85.3) B85.4
  pubis (pubic louse) (any site) B85.3
  vestimenti B85.1
  vulvae B85.3
Pediculus (infestation) - *see* Pediculosis
Pedophilia F65.4
Peg-shaped teeth K00.2
Pelade - *see* Alopecia, areata
Pelger-Huët anomaly or syndrome D72.0
Peliosis (rheumatica) D69.0
  hepatis K76.4
  with toxic liver disease K71.8
Pelizaeus-Merzbacher disease E75.29
Pellagra (alcoholic) (with polyneuropathy) E52
Pellagra-cerebellar-ataxia-renal aminoaciduria syndrome E72.02
Pellegrini (-Stieda) disease or syndrome - *see* Bursitis, tibial collateral
Pellizzi's syndrome E34.8
Pel's crisis A52.17
Pelvic - *see also* condition
  examination (periodic) (routine) Z01.419
    with abnormal findings Z01.411
  kidney, congenital Q63.2
Pelviolithiasis - *see* Calculus, kidney
Pelviperitonitis - *see also* Peritonitis, pelvic
  gonococcal A54.24
  puerperal O85
Pelvis - *see* condition or type
Pemphigoid L12.9
  benign, mucous membrane L12.1
  bullous L12.0
  cicatricial L12.1
  juvenile L12.2
  ocular L12.1
  specified NEC L12.8
Pemphigus L10.9
  benign familial (chronic) Q82.8
  Brazilian L10.3
  circinatus L13.0
  conjunctiva L12.1
  drug-induced L10.5
  erythematosus L10.4
  foliaceous L10.2
  gangrenous - *see* Gangrene
  neonatorum L01.03
  ocular L12.1
  paraneoplastic L10.81
  specified NEC L10.89
  syphilitic (congenital) A50.06
  vegetans L10.1
  vulgaris L10.0
  wildfire L10.3
Pendred's syndrome E07.1
Pendulous
  abdomen, in pregnancy – *see* Pregnancy, complicated by, abnormal, pelvic organs or tissues NEC
  breast N64.89
Penetrating wound - *see also* Puncture
  with internal injury - *see* Injury, by site
  eyeball – *see* Puncture, eyeball
  orbit (with or without foreign body) – *see* Puncture, orbit
  uterus by instrument with or following ectopic or molar pregnancy O08.6
Penicillosis B48.4
Penis - *see* condition
Penitis N48.29

Pentalogy of Fallot Q21.8
Pentasomy X syndrome Q97.1
Pentosuria (essential) E74.8
Percreta placenta O43.23-
Peregrinating patient - *see* Disorder, factitious
Perforation, perforated (nontraumatic) (of)
  accidental during procedure (blood vessel) (nerve) (organ) – *see* Complication, accidental puncture or laceration
  antrum - *see* Sinusitis, maxillary
  appendix K35.2
  atrial septum, multiple Q21.1
  attic, ear - *see* Perforation, tympanum, attic
  bile duct (common) (hepatic) K83.2
    cystic K82.2
  bladder (urinary)
    with or following ectopic or molar pregnancy O08.6
    obstetrical trauma O71.5
    traumatic S37.28
      at delivery O71.5
  bowel K63.1
    with or following ectopic or molar pregnancy O08.6
    newborn P78.0
    obstetrical trauma O71.5
    traumatic - *see* Laceration, intestine
  broad ligament N83.8
    with or following ectopic or molar pregnancy O08.6
    obstetrical trauma O71.6
  by
    device, implant or graft (*see also* Complications, by site and type, mechanical) T85.628
      arterial graft NEC - *see* Complication, cardiovascular device, mechanical, vascular
      breast (implant) T85.49
      catheter NEC T85.628
        cystostomy T83.090
        dialysis (renal) T82.49
          intraperitoneal T85.691
        infusion NEC T82.594
          spinal (epidural) (subdural) T85.690
      electronic (electrode) (pulse generator) (stimulator)
        bone T84.390
        cardiac T82.199
          electrode T82.190
          pulse generator T82.191
          specified type NEC T82.198
        nervous system - *see* Complication, prosthetic device, mechanical, electronic nervous system stimulator
        urinary - *see* Complication, genitourinary, device, urinary, mechanical
      fixation, internal (orthopedic) NEC - *see* Complication, fixation device, mechanical
      gastrointestinal - *see* Complications, prosthetic device, mechanical, gastrointestinal device
      genital NEC T83.498
        intrauterine contraceptive device T83.39
        penile prosthesis T83.490

Perforation, perforated *(Continued)*
  by *(Continued)*
    device, implant or graft *(Continued)*
      heart NEC - *see* Complication,
        cardiovascular device,
        mechanical
      joint prosthesis – *see* Complications, joint prosthesis, mechanical, specified NEC, by site
      ocular NEC - *see* Complications, prosthetic device, mechanical, ocular device
      orthopedic NEC - *see* Complication, orthopedic, device, mechanical
      specified NEC T85.628
      urinary NEC - *see also* Complication, genitourinary, device, urinary, mechanical
        graft T83.29
      vascular NEC - *see* Complication, cardiovascular device, mechanical
      ventricular intracranial shunt T85.09
    foreign body left accidentally in operative wound T81.539
    instrument (any) during a procedure, accidental – *see* Puncture, accidental complicating surgery
  cecum K35.0
  cervix (uteri) N88.8
    with or following ectopic or molar pregnancy O08.6
    obstetrical trauma O71.3
  colon K63.1
    newborn P78.0
    obstetrical trauma O71.5
    traumatic - *see* Laceration, intestine, large
  common duct (bile) K83.2
  cornea (due to ulceration) - *see* Ulcer, cornea, perforated
  cystic duct K82.2
  diverticulum (intestine) K57.80
    with bleeding K57.81
    large intestine K57.20
      with
        bleeding K57.21
        small intestine K57.40
          with bleeding K57.41
    small intestine K57.00
      with
        bleeding K57.01
        large intestine K57.40
          with bleeding K57.41
  ear drum - *see* Perforation, tympanum
  esophagus K22.3
  ethmoidal sinus - *see* Sinusitis, ethmoidal
  frontal sinus - *see* Sinusitis, frontal
  gallbladder K82.2
  heart valve - *see* Endocarditis
  ileum K63.1
    newborn P78.0
    obstetrical trauma O71.5
    traumatic - *see* Laceration, intestine, small
  instrumental, surgical (accidental) (blood vessel) (nerve) (organ) – *see* Puncture, accidental complicating surgery

Perforation, perforated *(Continued)*
  intestine NEC K63.1
    with ectopic or molar pregnancy O08.6
    newborn P78.0
    obstetrical trauma O71.5
    traumatic - *see* Laceration, intestine
    ulcerative NEC K63.1
      newborn P78.0
  jejunum, jejunal K63.1
    obstetrical trauma O71.5
    traumatic - *see* Laceration, intestine, small
    ulcer - *see* Ulcer, gastrojejunal, with perforation
  joint prosthesis - *see* Complications, joint prosthesis, mechanical, specified NEC, by site
  mastoid (antrum) (cell) – *see* Disorder, mastoid, specified NEC
  maxillary sinus - *see* Sinusitis, maxillary
  membrana tympani - *see* Perforation, tympanum
  nasal
    septum J34.89
      congenital Q30.3
      syphilitic A52.73
    sinus J34.89
      congenital Q30.8
      due to sinusitis - *see* Sinusitis
  palate (*see also* Cleft, palate) Q35.9
    syphilitic A52.79
  palatine vault (*see also* Cleft, palate, hard) Q35.1
    syphilitic A52.79
    congenital A50.59
  pars flaccida (ear drum) - *see* Perforation, tympanum, attic
  pelvic
    floor S31.030
      with
        ectopic or molar pregnancy O08.6
        penetration into retroperitoneal space S31.031
        retained foreign body S31.040
          with penetration into retroperitoneal space S31.041
      following ectopic or molar pregnancy O08.6
      obstetrical trauma O70.1
    organ S37.99
      adrenal gland S37.818
      bladder – *see* Perforation, bladder
      fallopian tube S37.599
        bilateral S37.592
        unilateral S37.591
      kidney S37.09-
      obstetrical trauma O71.5
      ovary S37.499
        bilateral S37.492
        unilateral S37.491
      prostate S37.828
      specified organ NEC S37.898
      ureter – *see* Perforation, ureter
      urethra – *see* Perforation, urethra
      uterus – *see* Perforation, uterus
  perineum - *see* Laceration, perineum
  pharynx J39.2
  rectum K63.1
    newborn P78.0
    obstetrical trauma O71.5
    traumatic S36.63

Perforation, perforated *(Continued)*
  root canal space due to endodontic treatment M27.51
  sigmoid K63.1
    newborn P78.0
    obstetrical trauma O71.5
    traumatic S36.533
  sinus (accessory) (chronic) (nasal) J34.89
  sphenoidal sinus - *see* Sinusitis, sphenoidal
  surgical (accidental) (by instrument) (blood vessel) (nerve) (organ) – *see* Puncture, accidental complicating surgery
  traumatic
    external - *see* Puncture
    eye – *see* Puncture, eyeball
    internal organ - *see* Injury, by site
  tympanum, tympanic (membrane) (persistent post-traumatic) (postinflammatory) H72.9-
    attic H72.1-
      multiple - *see* Perforation, tympanum, multiple
      total - *see* Perforation, tympanum, total
    central H72.0-
      multiple - *see* Perforation, tympanum, multiple
      total - *see* Perforation, tympanum, total
    marginal NEC - *see* subcategory H72.2
    multiple H72.81-
    pars flaccida - *see* Perforation, tympanum, attic
    total H72.82-
    traumatic, current episode S09.2-
  typhoid, gastrointestinal - *see* Typhoid
  ulcer - *see* Ulcer, by site, with perforation
  ureter N28.89
    traumatic S37.19
  urethra N36.8
    with ectopic or molar pregnancy O08.6
    following ectopic or molar pregnancy O08.6
    obstetrical trauma O71.5
    traumatic S37.38
      at delivery O71.5
  uterus
    with ectopic or molar pregnancy O08.6
    by intrauterine contraceptive device T83.39
    following ectopic or molar pregnancy O08.6
    obstetrical trauma O71.1
    traumatic S37.69
      obstetric O71.1
  uvula K13.79
    syphilitic A52.79
  vagina - *see also* Puncture, vagina O71.4
Periadenitis mucosa necrotica recurrens K12.0
Periappendicitis (acute) - *see* Appendicitis
Periarteritis nodosa (disseminated) (infectious) (necrotizing) M30.0

Periarthritis (joint) - *see also* Enthesopathy
Duplay's M75.0-
gonococcal A54.42
humeroscapularis - *see* Capsulitis, adhesive
scapulohumeral - *see* Capsulitis, adhesive
shoulder - *see* Capsulitis, adhesive
wrist M77.2-
Periarthrosis (angioneural) - *see* Enthesopathy
Pericapsulitis, adhesive (shoulder) - *see* Capsulitis, adhesive
Pericarditis (with decompensation) (with effusion) I31.9
with rheumatic fever (conditions in I00)
active - *see* Pericarditis, rheumatic
inactive or quiescent I09.2
acute (hemorrhagic) (infective) (non-rheumatic) (Sicca) I30.9
with chorea (acute) (rheumatic) (Sydenham's) I02.0
benign I30.8
nonspecific I30.0
rheumatic I01.0
with chorea (acute) (Sydenham's) I02.0
adhesive or adherent (chronic) (external) (internal) I31.0
acute - *see* Pericarditis, acute
rheumatic I09.2
bacterial (acute) (subacute) (with serous or seropurulent effusion) I30.1
calcareous I31.1
cholesterol (chronic) I31.8
acute I30.9
chronic (nonrheumatic) I31.9
rheumatic I09.2
constrictive (chronic) I31.1
coxsackie B33.23
fibrinocaseous (tuberculous) A18.84
fibrinopurulent I30.1
fibrinous I30.8
fibrous I31.0
gonococcal A54.83
idiopathic I30.0
in systemic lupus erythematosus M32.12
infective I30.1
meningococcal A39.53
neoplastic (chronic) I31.8
acute I30.9
obliterans, obliterating I31.0
plastic I31.0
pneumococcal I30.1
postinfarction I24.1
purulent I30.1
rheumatic (active) (acute) (with effusion) (with pneumonia) I01.0
with chorea (acute) (rheumatic) (Sydenham's) I02.0
chronic or inactive (with chorea) I09.2
rheumatoid - *see* Rheumatoid, carditis
septic I30.1
serofibrinous I30.8
staphylococcal I30.1
streptococcal I30.1
suppurative I30.1
syphilitic A52.06
tuberculous A18.84
uremic N18.9 *[I32]*
viral I30.1
Pericardium, pericardial - *see* condition
Pericellulitis - *see* Cellulitis

Pericementitis (chronic) (suppurative) - *see also* Periodontitis
acute K05.20
generalized K05.22
localized K05.21
Perichondritis
auricle - *see* Perichondritis, ear
bronchus J98.09
ear (external) H61.00-
acute H61.01-
chronic H61.02-
external auditory canal - *see* Perichondritis, ear
larynx J38.7
syphilitic A52.73
typhoid A01.09
nose J34.89
pinna - *see* Perichondritis, ear
trachea J39.8
Periclasia K05.4
Pericoronitis - *see* Periodontitis
Pericystitis N30.90
with hematuria N30.91
Peridiverticulitis (intestine) K57.92
cecum - *see* Diverticulitis, intestine, large
colon - *see* Diverticulitis, intestine, large
duodenum - *see* Diverticulitis, intestine, small
intestine - *see* Diverticulitis, intestine
jejunum - *see* Diverticulitis, intestine, small
rectosigmoid - *see* Diverticulitis, intestine, large
rectum - *see* Diverticulitis, intestine, large
sigmoid - *see* Diverticulitis, intestine, large
Periendocarditis - *see* Endocarditis
Periepididymitis N45.1
Perifolliculitis L01.02
abscedens, caput, scalp L66.3
capitis, abscedens (et suffodiens) L66.3
superficial pustular L01.02
Perihepatitis K65.8
Perilabyrinthitis (acute) - *see* subcategory H83.0
Perimeningitis - *see* Meningitis
Perimetritis - *see* Endometritis
Perimetrosalpingitis - *see* Salpingo-oophoritis
Perineocele N81.81
Perinephric, perinephritic - *see* condition
Perinephritis - *see also* Infection, kidney
purulent - *see* Abscess, kidney
Perineum, perineal - *see* condition
Perineuritis NEC - *see* Neuralgia
Periodic - *see* condition
Periodontitis (chronic) (complex) (compound) (local) (simplex) K05.30
acute K05.20
generalized K05.22
localized K05.21
apical K04.5
acute (pulpal origin) K04.4
generalized K05.32
localized K05.31
Periodontoclasia K05.4
Periodontosis (juvenile) K05.4
Periods - *see also* Menstruation
heavy N92.0
irregular N92.6
shortened intervals (irregular) N92.1

Perionychia - *see also* Cellulitis, digit
with lymphangitis - *see* Lymphangitis, acute, digit
Perioophoritis - *see* Salpingo-oophoritis
Periorchitis N45.2
Periosteum, periosteal - *see* condition
Periostitis (albuminosa) (circumscribed) (diffuse) (infective) (monomelic) - *see also* Osteomyelitis
alveolar M27.3
alveolodental M27.3
dental M27.3
gonorrheal A54.43
jaw (lower) (upper) M27.2
orbit H05.03-
syphilitic A52.77
congenital (early) A50.02 *[M90.80]*
secondary A51.46
tuberculous - *see* Tuberculosis, bone
yaws (hypertrophic) (early) (late) A66.6 *[M90.80]*
Periostosis (hyperplastic) - *see also* Disorder, bone, specified type NEC
with osteomyelitis - *see* Osteomyelitis, specified type NEC
Peripartum
cardiomyopathy O90.3
Periphlebitis - *see* Phlebitis
Periproctitis K62.8
Periprostatitis - *see* Prostatitis
Perirectal - *see* condition
Perirenal - *see* condition
Perisalpingitis - *see* Salpingo-oophoritis
Perisplenitis (infectional) D73.89
Peristalsis, visible or reversed R19.2
Peritendinitis - *see* Enthesopathy
Peritoneum, peritoneal - *see* condition
Peritonitis (adhesive) (bacterial) (fibrinous) (hemorrhagic) (idiopathic) (localized) (perforative) (primary) (with adhesions) (with effusion) K65.9
with or following
abscess K65.1
appendicitis K35.9
with perforation or rupture K35.0
localized K35.9
generalized K35.0
diverticular disease (intestine) K57.80
with bleeding K57.81
large intestine K57.20
with
bleeding K57.21
small intestine K57.40
with bleeding K57.41
small intestine K57.00
with
bleeding K57.01
large intestine K57.40
with bleeding K57.41
ectopic or molar pregnancy O08.0
acute (generalized) K65.0
aseptic T81.61
bile, biliary K65.3
chemical T81.61
chlamydial A74.81
complicating abortion – *see* Abortion, by type, complicated by, pelvic peritonitis
congenital P78.1
chronic proliferative K65.8
diaphragmatic K65.0
diffuse K65.0

377

Peritonitis *(Continued)*
  diphtheritic A36.89
  disseminated K65.0
  due to
    bile K65.3
    foreign
      body or object accidentally left dur-
        ing a procedure (instrument)
        (sponge) (swab) T81.599
      substance accidentally left during
        a procedure (chemical) (pow-
        der) (talc) T81.61
    talc T81.61
    urine K65.8
  fibrocaseous (tuberculous) A18.31
  fibropurulent K65.0
  following ectopic or molar pregnancy
    O08.0
  general(ized) K65.0
  gonococcal A54.85
  meconium (newborn) P78.0
  neonatal P78.1
    meconium P78.0
  pancreatic K65.0
  paroxysmal, familial E85.0
    benign E85.0
  pelvic
    female N73.5
      acute N73.3
      chronic N73.4
        with adhesions N73.6
    male K65.0
  periodic, familial E85.0
  proliferative, chronic K65.8
  puerperal, postpartum, childbirth O85
  purulent K65.0
  septic K65.0
  specified NEC K65.8
  spontaneous bacterial K65.2
  subdiaphragmatic K65.0
  subphrenic K65.0
  suppurative K65.0
  syphilitic A52.74
    congenital (early) A50.08 *[K67]*
  talc T81.61
  tuberculous A18.31
  urine K65.8
Peritonsillar - *see* condition
Peritonsillitis J36
Perityphlitis K37
Periureteritis N28.89
Periurethral - *see* condition
Periurethritis (gangrenous) - *see* Urethritis
Periuterine - *see* condition
Perivaginitis - *see* Vaginitis
Perivasculitis, retinal - *see* Vasculitis,
  retina
Perivasitis (chronic) N49.1
Perivesiculitis (seminal) - *see* Vesiculitis
Perlèche NEC K13.0
  due to
    candidiasis B37.83
    moniliasis B37.83
    riboflavin deficiency E53.0
    vitamin B$_2$ (riboflavin) deficiency
      E53.0
Pernicious - *see* condition
Pernio, perniosis T69.1
Perpetrator (of abuse) - *see* Index to
  External Cause of Injury,
  Perpetrator
Persecution
  delusion F22
  social Z60.5

Perseveration (tonic) R48.8
Persistence, persistent (congenital)
  anal membrane Q42.3
    with fistula Q42.2
  arteria stapedia Q16.3
  atrioventricular canal Q21.2
  branchial cleft Q18.0
  bulbus cordis in left ventricle Q21.8
  canal of Cloquet Q14.0
  capsule (opaque) Q12.8
  cilioretinal artery or vein Q14.8
  cloaca Q43.7
  communication - *see* Fistula, congenital
  convolutions
    aortic arch Q25.4
    fallopian tube Q50.6
    oviduct Q50.6
    uterine tube Q50.6
  double aortic arch Q25.4
  ductus arteriosus (Botalli) Q25.0
  fetal
    circulation P29.3
    form of cervix (uteri) Q51.8
    hemoglobin, hereditary (HPFH)
      D56.4
  foramen
    Botalli Q21.1
    ovale Q21.1
  Gartner's duct Q52.4
  hemoglobin, fetal (hereditary) (HPFH)
    D56.4
  hyaloid
    artery (generally incomplete) Q14.0
    system Q14.8
  hymen, in pregnancy or childbirth –
    see Pregnancy, complicated by,
    abnormal, vulva
  lanugo Q84.2
  left
    posterior cardinal vein Q26.8
    root with right arch of aorta Q25.4
    superior vena cava Q26.1
  Meckel's diverticulum Q43.0
  mucosal disease (middle ear) - *see* Oti-
    tis, media, suppurative, chronic,
    tubotympanic
  nail(s), anomalous Q84.6
  omphalomesenteric duct Q43.0
  organ or site not listed - *see* Anomaly,
    by site - ostium
    atrioventriculare commune Q21.2
    primum Q21.2
    secundum Q21.1
  ovarian rests in fallopian tube Q50.6
  pancreatic tissue in intestinal tract
    Q43.8
  primary (deciduous)
    teeth K00.6
    vitreous hyperplasia Q14.0
  pupillary membrane Q13.89
  right aortic arch Q25.4
  rhesus (Rh) titer T80.4
  sinus
    urogenitalis
      female Q52.8
      male Q55.8
    venosus with imperfect incorporation
      in right auricle Q26.8
  thymus (gland) (hyperplasia) E32.0
  thyroglossal duct Q89.2
  thyrolingual duct Q89.2
  truncus arteriosus or communis
    Q20.0
  tunica vasculosa lentis Q12.2

Persistence, persistent *(Continued)*
  umbilical sinus Q64.4
  urachus Q64.4
  vitelline duct Q43.0
Person (with)
  admitted for clinical research, as a con-
    trol subject Z00.6
  awaiting admission to adequate facility
    elsewhere Z75.1
  concern (normal) about sick person in
    family Z63.6
  consulting on behalf of another Z71.0
  feigning illness Z76.5
  living (in)
    alone Z60.2
    boarding school Z59.3
    residential institution Z59.3
    without
      adequate housing (heating) (space)
        Z59.1
      housing (permanent) (temporary)
        Z59.0
      person able to render necessary
        care Z74.2
      shelter Z59.0
  on waiting list Z75.1
  sick or handicapped in family Z63.6
Personality (disorder) F60.9
  accentuation of traits (type A pattern)
    Z73.1
  affective F34.0
  aggressive F60.3
  amoral F60.2
  anacastic, anankastic F60.5
  antisocial F60.2
  anxious F60.6
  asocial F60.2
  asthenic F60.7
  avoidant F60.6
  borderline F60.3
  change due to organic condition (en-
    during) F07.0
  compulsive F60.5
  cycloid F34.0
  cyclothymic F34.0
  dependent F60.7
  depressive F34.1
  dissocial F60.2
  dual F44.81
  eccentric F60.89
  emotionally unstable F60.3
  expansive paranoid F60.0
  explosive F60.3
  fanatic F60.0
  haltose type F60.89
  histrionic F60.4
  hyperthymic F34.0
  hypothymic F34.1
  hysterical F60.4
  immature F60.89
  inadequate F60.7
  labile (emotional) F60.3
  mixed (nonspecific) F60.81
  morally defective F60.2
  multiple F44.81
  narcissistic F60.81
  obsessional F60.5
  obsessive(-compulsive) F60.5
  organic F07.0
  overconscientious F60.5
  paranoid F60.0
  passive(-dependent) F60.7
  passive-aggressive F60.89
  pathologic F60.9

Personality *(Continued)*
  pattern defect or disturbance F60.9
  pseudopsychopathic (organic) F07.0
  pseudoretarded (organic) F07.0
  psychoinfantile F60.4
  psychoneurotic NEC F60.89
  psychopathic F60.2
  querulant F60.0
  sadistic F60.89
  schizoid F60.1
  self-defeating F60.7
  sensitive paranoid F60.0
  sociopathic (amoral) (antisocial) (aso-
    cial) (dissocial) F60.2
  specified NEC F60.89
  type A Z73.1
  unstable (emotional) F60.3
Perthes' disease - *see* Legg-Calve-Perthes
    disease
Pertussis - *see also* Whooping cough
    A37.90
Perversion, perverted
  appetite F50.8
    psychogenic F50.8
  function
    pituitary gland E23.2
      posterior lobe E22.2
  sense of smell and taste R43.8
    psychogenic F45.8
  sexual - *see* Deviation, sexual
Pervious, congenital - *see also* Imperfect,
    closure
  ductus arteriosus Q25.0
Pes (congenital) - *see also* Talipes
  acquired - *see also* Deformity, limb, foot,
    specified NEC
    planus - *see* Deformity, limb, flat foot
  adductus Q66.8
  cavus Q66.7
  deformity NEC, acquired - *see* Defor-
    mity, limb, foot, specified NEC
  planus (acquired) (any degree) - *see also*
    Deformity, limb, flat foot
    rachitic sequelae (late effect) E64.3
  valgus Q66.6
Pest, pestis - *see* Plague
Petechia, petechiae R23.3
  newborn P54.5
Petechial typhus A75.9
Peter's anomaly Q13.4
Petit mal seizure - *see* Epilepsy, general-
    ized, idiopathic
Petit's hernia - *see* Hernia, abdomen,
    specified site NEC
Petrellidosis B48.2
Petrositis H70.20-
  acute H70.21-
  chronic H70.22-
Peutz-Jeghers disease or syndrome Q85.8
Peyronie's disease N48.6
Pfeiffer's disease - *see* Mononucleosis,
    infectious
Phagedena (dry) (moist) (sloughing) - *see*
    also Gangrene
  geometric L88
  penis N48.29
  tropical - *see* Ulcer, skin
  vulva N76.6
Phagedenic - *see* condition
Phakoma H35.89
Phakomatosis *(see also* specific eponymous
    syndromes) Q85.9
  Bourneville's Q85.1
  specified NEC Q85.8

Phantom limb syndrome (without pain)
    G54.7
  with pain G54.6
Pharyngeal pouch syndrome D82.1
**Pharyngitis (acute)(catarrhal) (gan-
    grenous) (infective) (malignant)
    (membranous) (phlegmonous)
    (pseudomembranous) (simple)
    (subacute) (suppurative) (ulcerative)
    (viral)** J02.9
  with influenza, flu, or grippe - *see*
    Influenza, with, respiratory
    manifestations
  aphthous B08.5
  atrophic J31.2
  chlamydial A56.4
  chronic (atrophic) (granular) (hypertro-
    phic) J31.2
  coxsackievirus B08.5
  diphtheritic A36.0
  enteroviral vesicular B08.5
  follicular (chronic) J31.2
  fusospirochetal A69.1
  gonococcal A54.5
  granular (chronic) J31.2
  herpesviral B00.2
  hypertrophic J31.2
  infectional, chronic J31.2
  influenzal - *see* Influenza, with, respira-
    tory manifestations
  lymphonodular, acute (enteroviral)
    B08.8
  pneumococcal J02.8
  purulent J02.9
  putrid J02.9
  septic J02.0
  sicca J31.2
  specified organism NEC J02.8
  staphylococcal J02.8
  streptococcal J02.0
  syphilitic, congenital (early) A50.03
  tuberculous A15.8
  vesicular, enteroviral B08.5
  viral NEC J02.8
Pharyngoconjunctivitis, viral B30.2
Pharyngolaryngitis (acute) J06.0
  chronic J37.0
Pharyngoplegia J39.2
Pharyngotonsillitis, herpesviral B00.2
Pharyngotracheitis, chronic J42
Pharynx, pharyngeal - *see* condition
Phenomenon
  Arthus' - *see* Arthus' phenomenon
  jaw-winking Q07.8
  lupus erythematosus (LE) cell M32.9
  Raynaud's (secondary) I73.00
    with gangrene I73.01
  vasomotor R55
  vasospastic I73.9
  vasovagal R55
  Wenckebach's I44.1
Phenylketonuria E70.1
  classical E70.0
  maternal E70.1
  specified site - *see* Neoplasm, malignant
  unspecified site C74.10
Pheochromocytoma
    specified site - *see* Neoplasm,
      malignant
    unspecified site C74.10
  specified site - *see* Neoplasm, benign
  unspecified site D35.00
Pheohyphomycosis - *see* Chromomycosis
Pheomycosis - *see* Chromomycosis

Phimosis (congenital) (due to infection)
    N47.1
  chancroidal A57
Phlebectasia - *see also* Varix
  congenital Q27.4
**Phlebitis (infective) (pyemic) (septic)
    (suppurative)** I80.9
  antepartum - *see* Thrombophlebitis,
    antepartum
  blue - *see* Phlebitis, leg, deep
  breast, superficial I80.8
  cavernous (venous) sinus - *see* Phlebitis,
    intracranial (venous) sinus
  cerebral (venous) sinus - *see* Phlebitis,
    intracranial (venous) sinus
  chest wall, superficial I80.8
  cranial (venous) sinus - *see* Phlebitis,
    intracranial (venous) sinus
  deep (vessels) - *see* Phlebitis, leg, deep
  due to implanted device - *see* Complica-
    tions, by site and type, specified
    NEC
  during or resulting from a procedure
    T81.72
  femoral vein (superficial) I80.1-
  femoropopliteal vein I80.0-
  following infusion, therapeutic injection
    or transfusion T80.1
  gestational - *see* Phlebopathy,
    gestational
  hepatic veins I80.8
  iliofemoral - *see* Phlebitis, femoral
    vein
  intracranial (venous) sinus (any) G08
    nonpyogenic I67.6
  intraspinal venous sinuses and veins
    G08
    nonpyogenic G95.19
  lateral (venous) sinus - *see* Phlebitis,
    intracranial (venous) sinus
  leg I80.3
    antepartum – *see* Thrombophlebitis,
      antepartum
    deep (vessels) NEC I80.20-
      iliac I80.21-
      popliteal vein I80.22-
      specified vessel NEC I80.29-
      tibial vein I80.23-
    femoral vein (superficial) I80.1-
    superficial (vessels) I80.0-
  longitudinal sinus - *see* Phlebitis, intra-
    cranial (venous) sinus
  lower limb - *see* Phlebitis, leg
  migrans, migrating (superficial) I82.1
  pelvic
    with ectopic or molar pregnancy
      O08.0
    following ectopic or molar pregnancy
      O08.0
    puerperal, postpartum O87.1
  popliteal vein - *see* Phlebitis, leg, deep,
    popliteal
  portal (vein) K75.1
  postoperative T81.72
  pregnancy – *see* Thrombophlebitis,
    antepartum
  puerperal, postpartum, childbirth O87.0
    deep O87.1
    pelvic O87.1
    superficial O87.0
  retina - *see* Vasculitis, retina
  saphenous (accessory) (great) (long)
    (small) - *see* Phlebitis, leg,
    superficial

Phlebitis *(Continued)*
  sinus (meninges) - *see* Phlebitis, intra-
    cranial (venous) sinus
  specified site NEC I80.8
  syphilitic A52.09
  tibial vein - *see* Phlebitis, leg, deep, tibial
  ulcerative I80.9
    leg - *see* Phlebitis, leg
  umbilicus I80.8
  uterus (septic) - *see* Endometritis
  varicose (leg) (lower limb) - *see* Varix,
    leg, with, inflammation
Phlebofibrosis I87.8
Phleboliths I87.8
Phlebopathy,
  gestational O22.9-
  puerperal O87.9
Phlebosclerosis I87.8
Phlebothrombosis - *see also* Thrombosis
  antepartum – *see* Thrombophlebitis,
    antepartum
  pregnancy – *see* Thrombophlebitis,
    antepartum
  puerperal – *see* Thrombophlebitis,
    puerperal
Phlebotomus fever A93.1
Phlegmasia
  alba dolens O87.1
    nonpuerperal - *see* Phlebitis, femoral
      vein
  cerulea dolens - *see* Phlebitis, leg, deep
Phlegmon - *see* Abscess
Phlegmonous - *see* condition
Phlyctenulosis (allergic) (keratoconjunc-
    tivitis) (nontuberculous) - *see also*
    Keratoconjunctivitis
  cornea - *see* Keratoconjunctivitis
  tuberculous A18.52
Phobia, phobic F40.9
  animal F40.218
    spiders F40.210
  examination F40.298
  reaction F40.9
  simple F40.298
  social F40.10
    generalized F40.11
  specific (isolated) F40.298
    animal F40.218
      spiders F40.210
    blood F40.230
    injection F40.231
    injury F40.233
    men F40.290
    natural environment F40.228
      thunderstorms F40.220
    situational F40.248
      bridges F40.242
      closed in spaces F40.240
      flying F40.243
      heights F40.241
    specified focus NEC F40.298
    transfusion F40.231
    women F40.291
  specified NEC F40.8
    medical care NEC F40.232
  state F40.9
Phocas' disease – *see* Mastopathy, cystic
Phocomelia Q73.1
  lower limb – *see* Agenesis, leg, with foot
    present
  upper limb – *see* Agenesis, arm, with
    hand present
Phoria H50.50
Phosphate-losing tubular disorder N25.0

Phosphatemia E83.39
Phosphaturia E83.39
Photodermatitis (sun) L56.8
  chronic L57.8
  due to drug L56.8
  light other than sun L59.8
Photokeratitis H16.13-
Photophobia H53.19
Photophthalmia - *see* Photokeratitis
Photopsia H53.19
Photoretinitis - *see* Retinopathy, solar
Photosensitivity, photosensitization
    (sun) skin L56.8
  light other than sun L59.8
Phrenitis - *see* Encephalitis
Phrynoderma (vitamin A deficiency) E50.8
Phthiriasis (pubis) B85.3
  with any infestation classifiable to
    B85.0-B85.2 B85.4
Phthirus infestation - *see* Phthiriasis
Phthisis - *see also* Tuberculosis
  bulbi (infectional) - *see* Disorder, globe,
    degenerated condition, atrophy
  eyeball (due to infection) - *see* Disorder,
    globe, degenerated condition,
    atrophy
Phycomycosis - *see* Zygomycosis
Physalopteriasis B81.8
Phytobezoar T18.9
  intestine T18.3
  stomach T18.2
Pian - *see* Yaws
Pianoma A66.1
Pica F50.8
  in adults F50.8
  infant or child F98.3
Picking, nose F98.8
Pick-Niemann disease - *see* Niemann-
    Pick disease or syndrome
Pick's
  cerebral atrophy G31.01 *[F02.80]*
    with behavioral disturbance G31.01
      [F02.81]
  disease or syndrome (brain) G31.01
    [F02.80]
    with behavioral disturbance G31.01
      [F02.81]
Pickwickian syndrome E66.2
Piebaldism E70.39
Piedra (beard) (scalp) B36.8
  black B36.3
  white B36.2
Pierre Robin deformity or syndrome Q87.0
Pierson's disease or osteochondrosis M91.0
Pig-bel A05.2
Pigeon
  breast or chest (acquired) M95.4
    congenital Q67.7
    rachitic sequelae (late effect) E64.3
  breeder's disease or lung J67.2
  fancier's disease or lung J67.2
  toe - *see* Deformity, toe, specified NEC
Pigmentation (abnormal) (anomaly) L81.9
  conjunctiva H11.13-
  cornea (anterior) H18.01-
    posterior H18.05-
    stromal H18.06-
  diminished melanin formation NEC L81.6
  iron L81.8
  lids, congenital Q82.8
  limbus corneae - *see* Pigmentation,
    cornea
  metals L81.8
  optic papilla, congenital Q14.2

Pigmentation *(Continued)*
  retina, congenital (grouped) (nevoid)
    Q14.1
  scrotum, congenital Q82.8
  tattoo L81.8
Piles - *see* Hemorrhoids
Pili
  annulati or torti (congenital) Q84.1
  incarnati L73.1
Pill roller hand (intrinsic) - *see*
    Parkinsonism
Pilomatrixoma - *see* Neoplasm, skin, benign
  malignant - *see* Neoplasm, skin, malignant
Pilonidal - *see* condition
Pimple R23.8
Pinched nerve - *see* Neuropathy, entrapment
Pindborg tumor - *see* Cyst, calcifying
    odontogenic
Pineal body or gland - *see* condition
Pinealoblastoma C75.3
Pinealoma D44.5
  malignant C75.3
Pineoblastoma C75.3
Pineocytoma D44.5
Pinguecula H11.15-
Pingueculitis H10.81-
Pinhole meatus (*see also* Stricture, urethra)
    N35.9
Pink
  disease - *see* subcategory T56.1
  eye - *see* Conjunctivitis, acute,
    mucopurulent
Pinkus' disease (lichen nitidus) L44.1
Pinpoint
  meatus - *see* Stricture, urethra
  os (uteri) - *see* Stricture, cervix
Pins and needles R20.2
Pinta A67.9
  cardiovascular lesions A67.2
  chancre (primary) A67.0
  erythematous plaques A67.1
  hyperchromic lesions A67.1
  hyperkeratosis A67.1
  lesions A67.9
    cardiovascular A67.2
    hyperchromic A67.1
    intermediate A67.1
    late A67.2
    mixed A67.3
    primary A67.0
    skin (achromic) (cicatricial) (dyschro-
      mic) A67.2
      hyperchromic A67.1
      mixed (achromic and hyperchro-
        mic) A67.3
  papule (primary) A67.0
  skin lesions (achromic) (cicatricial) (dys-
    chromic) A67.2
    hyperchromic A67.1
    mixed (achromic and hyperchromic)
      A67.3
  vitiligo A67.2
Pintids A67.1
Pinworm (disease) (infection) (infesta-
    tion) B80
Piroplasmosis B60.0
Pistol wound - *see* Gunshot wound
Pitchers' elbow - *see* Derangement, joint,
    specified type NEC, elbow
Pithecoid pelvis Q74.2
  with disproportion (fetopelvic) O33.0
    causing obstructed labor O65.0
Pithiatism F48.8
Pitted - *see* Pitting

Pitting - *see also* Edema R60.9
  lip R60.0
  nail L60.8
  teeth K00.4
Pituitary gland - *see* condition
Pituitary-snuff-taker's disease J67.8
Pityriasis (capitis) L21.0
  alba L30.5
  circinata (et maculata) L42
  furfuracea L21.0
  Hebra's L26
  lichenoides L41.0
    chronica L41.1
    et varioliformis (acuta) L41.0
  maculata (et circinata) L30.5
  nigra B36.1
  pilaris, Hebra's L44.0
  rosea L42
  rotunda L44.8
  rubra (Hebra) pilaris L44.0
  simplex L30.5
  specified type NEC L30.5
  streptogenes L30.5
  versicolor (scrotal) B36.0
Placenta, placental - *see* Pregnancy, complicated by (care of) (management affected by), specified condition
Placentitis O41.14-
Plagiocephaly Q67.3
Plague A20.9
  abortive A20.8
  ambulatory A20.8
  asymptomatic A20.8
  bubonic A20.0
  cellulocutaneous A20.1
  cutaneobubonic A20.1
  lymphatic gland A20.0
  meningitis A20.3
  pharyngeal A20.8
  pneumonic (primary) (secondary) A20.2
  pulmonary, pulmonic A20.2
  septicemic A20.7
  tonsillar A20.8
    septicemic A20.7
Planning, family
  contraception Z30.9
  procreation Z31.69
Plaque(s)
  artery, arterial - *see* Arteriosclerosis
  calcareous - *see* Calcification
  coronary, lipid rich I25.83
  epicardial I31.8
  erythematous, of pinta A67.1
  Hollenhorst's - *see* Occlusion, artery, retina
  lipid rich, coronary I25.83
  pleural (without asbestos) J92.9
    with asbestos J92.0
  tongue K13.29
Plasmacytoma C90.3-
  extramedullary C90.2-
  medullary C90.0-
  solitary C90.3-
Plasmacytopenia D72.818
Plasmacytosis D72.822
Plaster ulcer - *see* Ulcer, pressure, by site
Plateau iris syndrome (post-iridectomy) (postprocedural) H21.82
Platybasia Q75.8
Platyonychia (congenital) Q84.6
  acquired L60.8
Platypelloid pelvis M95.5
  with disproportion (fetopelvic) O33.0
    causing obstructed labor O65.0
  congenital Q74.2

Platyspondylisis Q76.49
Plaut(-Vincent) disease - *see also* Vincent's A69.1
Plethora R23.2
  newborn P61.1
Pleura, pleural - *see* condition
Pleuralgia R07.89
Pleurisy (acute) (adhesive) (chronic) (costal) (diaphragmatic) (double) (dry) (fibrinous) (fibrous) (interlobar) (latent) (plastic) (primary) (residual) (sicca) (sterile) (subacute) (unresolved) R09.1
  with
    adherent pleura J86.0
    effusion J90
      chylous, chyliform J94.0
      influenzal - *see* Influenza, with, respiratory manifestations
      tuberculous (non primary) A15.6
        primary (progressive) A15.7
    influenza, flu, or grippe - *see* Influenza, with, respiratory manifestations
    tuberculosis - *see* Pleurisy, tuberculous (non primary)
  encysted - *see* Pleurisy, with effusion
  exudative - *see* Pleurisy, with effusion
  fibrinopurulent, fibropurulent - *see* Pyothorax
  hemorrhagic - *see* Hemothorax
  influenzal - *see* Influenza, with, respiratory manifestations
  pneumococcal J90
  purulent - *see* Pyothorax
  septic – *see* Pyothorax
  serofibrinous - *see* Pleurisy, with effusion
  seropurulent - *see* Pyothorax
  serous - *see* Pleurisy, with effusion
  staphylococcal J86.9
  streptococcal J90
  suppurative - *see* Pyothorax
  traumatic (post) (current) – *see* Injury, intrathoracic, pleura
  tuberculous (with effusion) (non primary) A15.6
    primary (progressive) A15.7
Pleuritis sicca - *see* Pleurisy
Pleurobronchopneumonia - *see* Pneumonia, broncho
Pleurodynia R07.81
  epidemic B33.0
  viral B33.0
Pleuropericarditis - *see also* Pericarditis
  acute I30.9
Pleuropneumonia (acute) (bilateral) (double) (septic) (*see also* Pneumonia) J18.8
  chronic - *see* Fibrosis, lung
Pleuro-pneumonia-like-organism (PPLO), as cause of disease classified elsewhere B96.0
Pleurorrhea - *see* Pleurisy, with effusion
Plexitis, brachial G54.0
Plica
  polonica B85.0
  syndrome, knee M67.5
  tonsil J35.8
Plicated tongue K14.5
Plug
  bronchus NEC J98.09
  meconium (newborn) NEC syndrome P76.0
  mucus - *see* Asphyxia, mucus

Plumbism - *see* subcategory T56.0
Plummer's disease E05.20
  with thyroid storm E05.21
Plummer-Vinson syndrome D50.1
Pluricarential syndrome of infancy E40
Plus (and minus) hand (intrinsic) - *see* Deformity, limb, specified type NEC, forearm
Pneumathemia - *see* Air, embolism
Pneumatic hammer (drill) syndrome T75.21
Pneumatocele (lung) J98.4
  intracranial G93.89
  tension J44.9
Pneumatosis
  cystoides intestinalis K63.89
  intestinalis K63.89
  peritonei K66.8
Pneumaturia R39.89
Pneumoblastoma - *see* Neoplasm, lung, malignant
Pneumocephalus G93.89
Pneumococcemia A40.3
Pneumococcus, pneumococcal - *see* condition
Pneumoconiosis (due to) (inhalation of) J64
  with tuberculosis (any type in A15) J65
  aluminum J63.0
  asbestos J61
  bagasse, bagassosis J67.1
  bauxite J63.1
  beryllium J63.2
  coal miners' (simple) J60
  coalworkers' (simple) J60
  collier's J60
  cotton dust J66.0
  diatomite (diatomaceous earth) J62.8
  dust
    inorganic NEC J63.6
    lime J62.8
    marble J62.8
    organic NEC J66.8
  fumes or vapors (from silo) J68.9
  graphite J63.3
  grinder's J62.8
  kaolin J62.8
  mica J62.8
  millstone maker's J62.8
  mineral fibers NEC J61
  miner's J60
  moldy hay J67.0
  potter's J62.8
  rheumatoid - *see* Rheumatoid, lung
  sandblaster's J62.8
  silica, silicate NEC J62.8
    with carbon J60
  stonemason's J62.8
  talc (dust) J62.0
Pneumocystis carinii pneumonia B59
Pneumocystis jiroveci (pneumonia) B59
Pneumocystosis (with pneumonia) B59
Pneumohemopericardium I31.2
Pneumohemothorax J94.2
  traumatic S27.2
Pneumohydropericardium - *see* Pericarditis
Pneumohydrothorax - *see* Hydrothorax
Pneumomediastinum J98.2
  congenital or perinatal P25.2
Pneumomycosis B49 *[J99]*

Pneumonia (acute) (Alpenstich) (benign) (bilateral) (brain) (cerebral) (circum-scribed) (congestive) (creeping) (de-layed resolution) (double) (epidemic) (fever) (flash) (fulminant) (fungoid) (granulomatous) (hemorrhagic) (incipient) (infantile) (infectious) (infiltration) (insular) (intermittent) (latent) (migratory) (organized) (overwhelming) (primary (atypical)) (progressive) (pseudolobar) (puru-lent) (resolved) (secondary) (senile) (septic) (suppurative) (terminal) (true) (unresolved) (vesicular) J18.9
  with
    lung abscess J85.1
      due to specified organism - *see* Pneumonia, in (due to)
  adenoviral J12.0
  adynamic J18.2
  alba A50.04
  allergic (eosinophilic) J82
  alveolar - *see* Pneumonia, lobar
  anaerobes J15.8
  anthrax A22.1
  apex, apical - *see* Pneumonia, lobar
  Ascaris B77.81
  aspiration J69.0
    due to
      aspiration of microorganisms
        bacterial J15.9
        viral J12.9
      food (regurgitated) J69.0
      gastric secretions J69.0
      milk (regurgitated) J69.0
      oils, essences J69.1
      solids, liquids NEC J69.8
      vomitus J69.0
    newborn P24.81
      amniotic fluid (clear) P24.11
      blood P24.21
      liquor (amnii) P24.11
      meconium P24.01
      milk P24.31
      mucus P24.11
      food (regurgitated) P24.31
      specified NEC P24.81
      stomach contents P24.31
  atypical NEC J18.9
  bacillus J15.9
    specified NEC J15.8
  bacterial J15.9
    specified NEC J15.8
  Bacteroides (fragilis) (oralis) (melanino-genicus) J15.8
  basal, basic, basilar - *see* Pneumonia, lobar
  bronchiolitis obliterans organized (BOOP) J84.8
  broncho-, bronchial (confluent) (croup-ous) (diffuse) (disseminated) (hemorrhagic) (involving lobes) (lobar) (terminal) J18.0
    allergic (eosinophilic) J82
    aspiration - *see* Pneumonia, aspiration
    bacterial J15.9
      specified NEC J15.8
    chronic - *see* Fibrosis, lung
    diplococcal J13
    Eaton's agent J15.7
    Escherichia coli (E. coli) J15.5
    Friedländer's bacillus J15.0

Pneumonia *(Continued)*
  broncho-, bronchial *(Continued)*
    Hemophilus influenzae J14
    hypostatic J18.2
    inhalation (*see also* Pneumonia, aspiration
      due to fumes or vapors (chemical) J68.0
      of oils or essences J69.1
    Klebsiella (pneumoniae) J15.0
    lipid, lipoid J69.1
      endogenous J84.8
    Mycoplasma (pneumoniae) J15.7
    pleuro-pneumonia-like-organisms (PPLO) J15.7
    pneumococcal J13
    Proteus J15.6
    Pseudomonas J15.1
    Serratia marcescens J15.6
    specified organism NEC J16.8
    staphylococcal - *see* Pneumonia, staphylococcal
    streptococcal NEC J15.4
      group B J15.3
      pneumoniae J13
    viral, virus - *see* Pneumonia, viral
  Butyrivibrio (fibriosolvens) J15.8
  Candida B37.1
  caseous - *see* Tuberculosis, pulmonary
  catarrhal - *see* Pneumonia, broncho
  chlamydial J16.0
    congenital P23.1
  cholesterol J84.8
  cirrhotic (chronic) - *see* Fibrosis, lung
  Clostridium (haemolyticum) (novyi) J15.8
  confluent - *see* Pneumonia, broncho
  congenital (infective) P23.9
    due to
      bacterium NEC P23.6
      Chlamydia P23.1
      Escherichia coli P23.4
      Haemophilus influenzae P23.6
      infective organism NEC P23.8
      Klebsiella pneumoniae P23.6
      Mycoplasma P23.6
      Pseudomonas P23.5
      Staphylococcus P23.2
      Streptococcus (except group B) P23.6
        group B P23.3
      viral agent P23.0
      specified NEC P23.8
  croupous - *see* Pneumonia, lobar
  cytomegalic inclusion B25.0
  cytomegaloviral B25.0
  deglutition - *see* Pneumonia, aspiration
  desquamative interstitial J84.8
  diffuse - *see* Pneumonia, broncho
  diplococcal, diplococcus (broncho-) (lobar) J13
  disseminated (focal) - *see* Pneumonia, broncho
  Eaton's agent J15.7
  embolic, embolism - *see* Embolism, pulmonary
  Enterobacter J15.6
  eosinophilic J82
  Escherichia coli (E. coli) J15.5
  Eubacterium J15.8
  fibrinous - *see* Pneumonia, lobar
  fibroid, fibrous (chronic) - *see* Fibrosis, lung
  Friedländer's bacillus J15.0

Pneumonia *(Continued)*
  Fusobacterium (nucleatum) J15.8
  gangrenous J85.0
  giant cell (measles) B05.2
  gonococcal A54.84
  gram-negative bacteria NEC J15.6
    anaerobic J15.8
  Hemophilus influenzae ((broncho) (lobar) J14
  human metapneumovirus J12.3
  hypostatic (broncho) (lobar) J18.2
  in (due to)
    actinomycosis A42.0
    adenovirus J12.0
    anthrax A22.1
    ascariasis B77.81
    aspergillosis B44.9
    Bacillus anthracis A22.1
    Bacterium anitratum J15.6
    candidiasis B37.1
    chickenpox B01.2
    Chlamydia J16.0
      neonatal P23.1
    coccidioidomycosis B38.2
      acute B38.0
      chronic B38.1
    cytomegalovirus disease B25.0
    Diplococcus (pneumoniae) J13
    Eaton's agent J15.7
    Enterobacter J15.6
    Escherichia coli (E. coli) J15.5
    Friedländer's bacillus J15.0
    fumes and vapors (chemical) (inhalation) J68.0
    gonorrhea A54.84
    Hemophilus influenzae (H. influenzae) J14
    Herellea J15.6
    histoplasmosis B39.2
      acute B39.0
      chronic B39.1
    human metapneumovirus J12.3
    Klebsiella (pneumoniae) J15.0
    measles B05.2
    Mycoplasma (pneumoniae) J15.7
    nocardiosis, nocardiasis A43.0
    ornithosis A70
    parainfluenza virus J12.2
    pleuro-pneumonia-like-organism (PPLO) J15.7
    pneumococcus J13
    pneumocystosis (Pneumocystis carinii) (Pneumocystis jiroveci) B59
    Proteus J15.6
    Pseudomonas NEC J15.1
      pseudomallei A24.1
    psittacosis A70
    Q fever A78
    respiratory syncytial virus J12.1
    rheumatic fever I00 *[J17]*
    rubella B06.81
    Salmonella (infection) A02.22
      typhi A01.03
    schistosomiasis B65.9 *[J17]*
    Serratia marcescens J15.6
    specified
      bacterium NEC J15.8
      organism NEC J16.8
    spirochetal NEC A69.8
    Staphylococcus J15.20
      aureus J15.21
      specified NEC J15.29

Pneumonia *(Continued)*
  in (due to) *(Continued)*
    Streptococcus J15.4
      group B J15.3
      pneumoniae J13
      specified NEC J15.4
    toxoplasmosis B58.3
    tularemia A21.2
    typhoid (fever) A01.03
    varicella B01.2
    virus - *see* Pneumonia, viral
    whooping cough A37.91
      due to
        Bordetella parapertussis A37.11
        Bordetella pertussis A37.01
        specified NEC A37.81
    Yersinia pestis A20.2
  inhalation of food or vomit - *see* Pneumonia, aspiration
  interstitial J84.9
    chronic J84.1
    lymphoid J84.2
    plasma cell B59
    pseudomonas J15.1
    usual J84.1
  Klebsiella (pneumoniae) J15.0
  lipid, lipoid (exogenous) J69.1
    endogenous J84.2
  lobar (disseminated) (double) (interstitial) J18.1
    bacterial J15.9
      specified NEC J15.8
    chronic - *see* Fibrosis, lung
    Escherichia coli (E. coli) J15.5
    Friedländer's bacillus J15.0
    Hemophilus influenzae J14
    hypostatic J18.2
    Klebsiella (pneumoniae) J15.0
    pneumococcal J13
    Proteus J15.6
    Pseudomonas J15.1
    specified organism NEC J16.8
    staphylococcal - *see* Pneumonia, staphylococcal
    streptococcal NEC J15.4
    Streptococcus pneumoniae J13
    viral, virus - *see* Pneumonia, viral
  lobular - *see* Pneumonia, broncho
  Löffler's J82
  lymphoid interstitial J84.2
  massive - *see* Pneumonia, lobar
  meconium P24.01
  Mycoplasma (pneumoniae) J15.7
  necrotic J85.0
  neonatal P23.9
    aspiration - *see* Aspiration, by substance, with pneumonia
  nitrogen dioxide J68.9
  orthostatic J18.2
  parainfluenza virus J12.2
  parenchymatous - *see* Fibrosis, lung
  passive J18.2
  patchy - *see* Pneumonia, broncho
  Peptococcus J15.8
  Peptostreptococcus J15.8
  plasma cell (of infants) B59
  pleurolobar - *see* Pneumonia, lobar
  pleuro-pneumonia-like organism (PPLO) J15.7
  pneumococcal (broncho) (lobar) J13
  Pneumocystis (carinii) (jiroveci) B59
  postinfectional NEC B99 *[J17]*
  postmeasles B05.2
  Proteus J15.6

Pneumonia *(Continued)*
  Pseudomonas J15.1
  psittacosis A70
  radiation J70.0
  respiratory syncytial virus J12.1
  resulting from a procedure J95.89
  rheumatic I00 *[J17]*
  Salmonella (arizonae) (cholerae-suis) (enteritidis) (typhimurium) A02.22
    typhi A01.03
    typhoid fever A01.03
  SARS-associated coronavirus J12.81
  segmented, segmental - *see* Pneumonia, broncho-
  Serratia marcescens J15.6
  specified NEC J18.8
    bacterium NEC J15.8
    organism NEC J16.8
    virus NEC J12.89
  spirochetal NEC A69.8
  staphylococcal (broncho) (lobar) J15.20
    aureus J15.21
    specified NEC J15.29
  static, stasis J18.2
  streptococcal NEC (broncho) (lobar) J15.4
    group
      A J15.4
      B J15.3
      specified NEC J15.4
  Streptococcus pneumoniae J13
  syphilitic, congenital (early) A50.04
  traumatic (complication) (early) (secondary) T79.8
  tuberculous (any) - *see* Tuberculosis, pulmonary
  tularemic A21.2
  varicella B01.2
  Veillonella J15.8
  ventilator associated J95.851
  viral, virus (broncho) (interstitial) (lobar) J12.9
    adenoviral J12.0
    congenital P23.0
    human metapneumovirus J12.3
    parainfluenza J12.2
    respiratory syncytial J12.1
    SARS-associated coronavirus J12.81
    specified NEC J12.89
  white (congenital) A50.04
Pneumonic - *see* condition
Pneumonitis (acute) (primary) - *see also* Pneumonia
  air-conditioner J67.7
  allergic (due to) J67.9
    organic dust NEC J67.8
    red cedar dust J67.8
    sequoiosis J67.8
    wood dust J67.8
  aspiration J69.0
    due to
      anesthesia J95.4
        during
          labor and delivery O74.0
          pregnancy O29.01-
          puerperium O89.01
      fumes or gases J68.0
    obstetric O74.0
  chemical (due to gases, fumes or vapors) (inhalation) J68.0
  cholesterol J84.8
  crack (cocaine) J68.0
  chronic - *see* Fibrosis, lung

Pneumonitis *(Continued)*
  congenital rubella P35.0
  due to
    beryllium J68.0
    cadmium J68.0
    crack (cocaine) J68.0
    detergent J69.8
    fluorocarbon-polymer J68.0
    food, vomit (aspiration) J69.0
    fumes or vapors J68.0
    gases, fumes or vapors (inhalation) J68.0
    inhalation
      blood J69.8
      essences J69.1
      food (regurgitated), milk, vomit J69.0
      oils, essences J69.1
      saliva J69.0
      solids, liquids NEC J69.8
    manganese J68.0
    nitrogen dioxide J68.0
    oils, essences J69.1
    solids, liquids NEC J69.8
    toxoplasmosis (acquired) B58.3
      congenital P37.1
    vanadium J68.0
    ventilator J95.851
  eosinophilic J82
  hypersensitivity J67.9
    air conditioner lung J67.7
    bagassosis J67.1
    bird fancier's lung J67.2
    farmer's lung J67.0
    maltworker's lung J67.4
    maple bark-stripper's lung J67.6
    mushroom worker's lung J67.5
    specified organic dust NEC J67.8
    suberosis J67.3
  interstitial (chronic) J84.1
    lymphoid J84.2
  lymphoid, interstitial J84.2
  meconium P24.01
  postanesthetic J95.4
    correct substance properly administered - *see* Table of drugs and chemcials, by drug, adverse effect
    in labor and delivery O74.0
    in pregnancy O29.01-
    obstetric O74.0
    overdose or wrong substance given or taken (by accident) - *see* Table of drugs and chemicals, by drug, poisoning
    postpartum, puerperal O89.01
  postoperative J95.4
    obstetric O74.0
  radiation J70.0
  rubella, congenital P35.0
  ventilation (air-conditioning) J67.7
  ventilator associated J95.851
  wood-dust J67.8
Pneumonoconiosis - *see* Pneumoconiosis
Pneumoparotid K11.8
Pneumopathy NEC J98.4
  alveolar J84.0
  due to organic dust NEC J66.8
  parietoalveolar J84.0
Pneumopericarditis - *see also* Pericarditis
  acute I30.9
Pneumopericardium - *see also* Pericarditis
  congenital P25.3
  newborn P25.3
  traumatic (post) – *see* Injury, heart

Pneumophagia (psychogenic) F45.8
Pneumopleurisy, pneumopleuritis (*see also* Pneumonia) J18.8
Pneumopyopericardium I30.1
Pneumopyothorax - *see* Pyopneumothorax
with fistula J86.0
Pneumorrhagia - *see also* Hemorrhage, lung
tuberculous - *see* Tuberculosis, pulmonary
Pneumothorax J93.9
acute J93.8
chronic J93.8
congenital P25.1
perinatal period P25.1
postprocedural J95.81
specified NEC J93.8
spontaneous NEC J93.1
newborn P25.1
tension J93.0
tense valvular, infectional J93.0
tension (spontaneous) J93.0
traumatic S27.0
with hemothorax S27.2
tuberculous - *see* Tuberculosis, pulmonary
Podagra M10.9 - *see also* Gout
Podencephalus Q01.9
Poikilocytosis R71.8
Poikiloderma L81.6
Civatte's L57.3
congenital Q82.8
vasculare atrophicans L94.5
Poikilodermatomyositis M33.10
with
myopathy M33.12
respiratory involvement M33.11
specified organ involvement NEC M33.19
Pointed ear (congenital) Q17.3
Poison ivy, oak, sumac or other plant dermatitis (allergic) (contact) L23.7
Poisoning (acute) - *see also* Table of drugs and chemicals
algae and toxins T65.82-
Bacillus B (aertrycke) (cholerae (suis)) (paratyphosus) (suipestifer) A02.9
botulinus A05.1
bacterial toxins A05.9
berries, noxious - *see* Poisoning, food, noxious, berries
botulism A05.1
ciguatera fish T61.0-
Clostridium botulinum A05.1
death-cap (Amanita phalloides) (Amanita verna) - *see* Poisoning, food, noxious, mushrooms
drug - *see* Table of drugs and chemicals, by drug, poisoning
epidemic, fish (noxious) - *see* Poisoning, seafood
bacterial A05.9
fava bean D55.0
fish (noxious) T61.9-
bacterial - *see* Intoxication, foodborne, by agent
ciguatera fish - *see* Poisoning, ciguatera fish
scombroid fish - *see* Poisoning, scombroid fish
specified type NEC T61.77-

Poisoning (*Continued*)
food (acute) (diseased) (infected) (noxious) NEC T62.9-
bacterial - *see* Intoxication, foodborne, by agent
due to
Bacillus (aertrycke) (choleraesuis) (paratyphosus) (suipestifer) A02.9
botulinus A05.1
Clostridium (perfringens) Welchii A05.2
salmonella (aertrycke) (callinarum) (choleraesuis) (enteritidis) (paratyphi) (suipestifer) A02.9
with
gastroenteritis A02.0
sepsis A02.1
staphylococcus A05.0
Vibrio
parahaemolyticus A05.3
vulnificus A05.5
noxious or naturally toxic T62.9-
berries - *see* subcategory T62.1-
fish - *see* Poisoning, seafood
mushrooms - *see* subcategory T62.0x-
plants NEC - *see* subcategory T62.2x
seafood - *see* Poisoning, seafood
specified NEC - *see* subcategory T62.8x-
ichthyotoxism - *see* Poisoning, seafood
kreotoxism, food A05.9
latex T65.81-
lead T56.0-
mushroom - *see* Poisoning, food, noxious, mushroom
mussels - *see also* Poisoning, shellfish
bacterial - *see* Intoxication, foodborne, by agent
nicotine (tobacco) T65.2-
noxious foodstuffs - *see* Poisoning, food, noxious
plants, noxious - *see* Poisoning, food, noxious, plants NEC
ptomaine - *see* Poisoning, food
radiation J70.0
Salmonella (arizonae) (cholerae-suis) (enteritidis) (typhimurium) A02.9
scombroid fish T61.1-
seafood (noxious) T61.9-
bacterial - *see* Intoxication, foodborne, by agent
fish - *see* Poisoning, fish
shellfish - *see* Poisoning, shellfish
specified NEC - *see* subcategory T61.8x-
shellfish (amnesic) (azaspiracid) (diarrheic) (neurotoxic) (noxious) (paralytic) T61.78-
bacterial - *see* Intoxication, foodborne, by agent
ciguatera mollusk - *see* Poisoning, ciguatera fish
specified substance NEC T65.891
Staphylococcus, food A05.0
tobacco (nicotine) T65.2-
water E87.7
Poker spine - *see* Spondylitis, ankylosing
Poland's syndrome Q79.8

Polioencephalitis (acute) (bulbar) A80.9
inferior G12.22
influenzal - *see* Influenza, with, manifestations NEC
superior hemorrhagic (acute) (Wernicke's) E51.2
Wernicke's E51.2
Polioencephalomyelitis (acute) (anterior) A80.9
with beriberi E51.2
Polioencephalopathy, superior hemorrhagic E51.8
with
beriberi E51.11
pellagra E52
Poliomeningoencephalitis - *see* Meningoencephalitis
Poliomyelitis (acute) (anterior) (epidemic) A80.9
with paralysis (bulbar) - *see* Poliomyelitis, paralytic
abortive A80.4
ascending (progressive) - *see* Poliomyelitis, paralytic
bulbar (paralytic) - *see* Poliomyelitis, paralytic
congenital P35.8
nonepidemic A80.9
nonparalytic A80.4
paralytic A80.30
specified NEC A80.39
vaccine-associated A80.0
wild virus
imported A80.1
indigenous A80.2
spinal, acute A80.9
Poliosis (eyebrow) (eyelashes) L67.1
circumscripta, acquired L67.1
Pollakiuria R35.0
psychogenic F45.8
Pollinosis J30.1
Pollitzer's disease L73.2
Polyadenitis - *see also* Lymphadenitis
malignant A20.0
Polyalgia M79.89
Polyangiitis M30.0
microscopic M31.7
overlap syndrome M30.8
Polyarteritis
microscopic M31.7
nodosa M30.0
with lung involvement M30.1
juvenile M30.2
related condition NEC M30.8
Polyarthralgia - *see* Pain, joint
Polyarthritis, polyarthropathy (*see also* Arthritis) M13.0
due to or associated with other specified conditions - *see* Arthritis
epidemic (Australian) (with exanthema) B33.1
infective - *see* Arthritis, pyogenic or pyemic
inflammatory M06.4
juvenile (chronic) (seronegative) M08.3
migratory - *see* Fever, rheumatic
rheumatic, acute - *see* Fever, rheumatic
Polyarthrosis M15.9
post-traumatic M15.3
primary M15.0
specified NEC M15.8

Polycarential syndrome of infancy E40
Polychondritis (atrophic) (chronic) - *see also* Disorder, cartilage, specified type NEC
  relapsing M94.1
Polycoria Q13.2
Polycystic (disease)
  degeneration, kidney Q61.3
    autosomal dominant (adult type) Q61.2
    autosomal recessive (infantile type) NEC Q61.19
  kidney Q61.3
    autosomal
      dominant Q61.2
      recessive NEC Q61.19
    autosomal dominant (adult type) Q61.2
    autosomal recessive (childhood type) NEC Q61.19
    infantile type NEC Q61.19
  liver Q44.6
  lung J98.4
    congenital Q33.0
  ovary, ovaries E28.2
  spleen Q89.09
Polycythemia (secondary) D75.1
  acquired D75.1
  benign (familial) D75.0
  due to
    donor twin P61.1
    erythropoietin D75.1
    fall in plasma volume D75.1
    high altitude D75.1
    maternal-fetal transfusion P61.1
    stress D75.1
  emotional D75.1
  erythropoietin D75.1
  familial (benign) D75.0
  Gaisböck's (hypertonica) D75.1
  high altitude D75.1
  hypertonica D75.1
  hypoxemic D75.1
  neonatorum P61.1
  nephrogenous D75.1
  relative D75.1
  secondary D75.1
  spurious D75.1
  stress D75.1
  vera D45
Polycytosis cryptogenica D75.1
Polydactylism, polydactyly Q69.9
  toes Q69.2
Polydipsia R63.1
Polydystrophy, pseudo-Hurler E77.0
Polyembryoma - *see* Neoplasm, malignant
Polyglandular
  deficiency E31.0
  dyscrasia E31.9
  dysfunction E31.9
  syndrome E31.8
Polyhydramnios O40.-
Polymastia Q83.1
Polymenorrhea N92.0
Polymyalgia M35.3
  arteritica, giant cell M31.5
  rheumatica M35.3
    with giant cell arteritis M31.5
Polymyositis (acute) (chronic) (hemorrhagic) M33.20
  with
    myopathy M33.22
    respiratory involvement M33.21

Polymyositis *(Continued)*
  with
    skin involvement - *see* Dermatopolymyositis
    specified organ involvement NEC M33.29
  ossificans (generalisata) (progressiva) - *see* Myositis, ossificans, progressiva
Polyneuritis, polyneuritic - *see also* Polyneuropathy
  acute (post-)infective G61.0
  alcoholic G62.1
  cranialis G52.7
  demyelinating, chronic inflammatory (CIDP) G61.81
  diabetic – *see* Diabetes, polyneuropathy
  diphtheritic A36.83
  due to lack of vitamin NEC E56.9 *[G63]*
  endemic E51.11
  erythredema - *see* subcategory T56.1
  febrile, acute G61.0
  hereditary ataxic G60.1
  idiopathic, acute G61.0
  infective (acute) G61.0
  inflammatory, chronic demyelinating (CIDP) G61.81
  nutritional E63.9 *[G63]*
  postinfective (acute) G61.0
  specified NEC G62.89
Polyneuropathy (peripheral) G62.9
  alcoholic G62.1
  amyloid (Portuguese) E85.1 *[G63]*
  arsenical G62.2
  critical illness G62.81
  demyelinating, chronic inflammatory (CIDP) G61.81
  diabetic – *see* Diabetes, polyneuropathy
  drug-induced G62.0
  hereditary G60.9
    specified NEC G60.8
  idiopathic G60.9
    progressive G60.3
  in (due to)
    alcohol G62.1
      sequelae G65.2
    amyloidosis, familial (Portuguese) E85.1 *[G63]*
    antitetanus serum G61.1
    arsenic G62.2
      sequelae G65.2
    avitaminosis NEC E56.9 *[G63]*
    beriberi E51.11
    collagen vascular disease NEC M35.9 *[G63]*
    deficiency (of)
      B(-complex) vitamins E53.9 *[G63]*
      vitamin B_6 E53.1 *[G63]*
    diabetes – *see* Diabetes, polyneuropathy
    diphtheria A36.83
    drug or medicament G62.0
      correct substance properly administered - *see* Table of drugs and chemicals, by drug, adverse effect
      overdose or wrong substance given or taken - *see* Table of drugs and chemicals, by drug, poisoning
    endocrine disease NEC E34.9 *[G63]*
    herpes zoster B02.23

Polyneuropathy *(Continued)*
  in (due to) *(Continued)*
    hypoglycemia E16.2 *[G63]*
    infectious
      disease NEC B99 *[G63]*
      mononucleosis B27.91
    lack of vitamin NEC E56.9 *[G63]*
    lead G62.2
      sequelae G65.2
    leprosy A30.9
    Lyme disease A69.22
    metabolic disease NEC E88.9 *[G63]*
    microscopic polyangiitis M31.7 *[G63]*
    mumps B26.84
    neoplastic disease (*see also* Neoplasm) D49.9 *[G63]*
    nutritional deficiency NEC E63.9 *[G63]*
    organophosphate compounds G62.2
      sequelae G65.2
    parasitic disease NEC B89 *[G63]*
    pellagra E52 *[G63]*
    polyarteritis nodosa M30.0
    porphyria E80.20 *[G63]*
    radiation G62.82
    rheumatoid arthritis - *see* Rheumatoid, polyneuropathy
    sarcoidosis D86.9
    serum G61.1
    syphilis (late) A52.15
      congenital A50.43
    systemic
      connective tissue disorder M35.9 *[G63]*
      lupus erythematosus M32.19
    toxic agent NEC G62.2
      sequelae G65.2
    triorthocresyl phosphate G62.2
      sequelae G65.2
    tuberculosis A17.89
    uremia N18.9 *[G63]*
    vitamin B12 deficiency E53.8 *[G63]*
      with anemia (pernicious) D51.0 *[G63]*
        due to dietary deficiency D51.3 *[G63]*
    zoster B02.23
  inflammatory G61.9
    chronic demyelinating (CIDP) G61.81
    sequelae G65.1
    specified NEC G61.89
  lead G62.2
    sequelae G65.2
  nutritional NEC E63.9 *[G63]*
  postherpetic (zoster) B02.23
  progressive G60.3
  radiation-induced G62.82
  sensory (hereditary) (idiopathic) G60.8
  specified NEC G62.89
  syphilitic (late) A52.15
    congenital A50.43
Polyopia H53.8
Polyorchism, polyorchidism Q55.21
Polyosteoarthritis M15.9 - *see also* Osteoarthritis, generalized
  post-traumatic M15.3
  specified NEC M15.8
Polyostotic fibrous dysplasia Q78.1
Polyotia Q17.0

Polyp, polypus
- accessory sinus J33.8
- adenocarcinoma in - *see* Neoplasm, malignant
- adenocarcinoma in situ in - *see* Neoplasm, in situ
- adenoid tissue J33.0
- adenomatous - *see also* Neoplasm, benign
  - adenocarcinoma in - *see* Neoplasm, malignant
  - adenocarcinoma in situ in - *see* Neoplasm, in situ
  - carcinoma in - *see* Neoplasm, malignant
  - carcinoma in situ in - *see* Neoplasm, in situ
  - multiple - *see* Neoplasm, benign
    - adenocarcinoma in - *see* Neoplasm, malignant
    - adenocarcinoma in situ in - *see* Neoplasm, in situ
- antrum J33.8
- anus, anal (canal) K62.0
- Bartholin's gland N84.3
- bladder D41.4
- carcinoma in - *see* Neoplasm, malignant
- carcinoma in situ in - *see* Neoplasm, in situ
- cecum D12.0
- cervix (uteri) N84.1
  - in pregnancy or childbirth – *see* Pregnancy, complicated by, abnormal, cervix
  - mucous N84.1
  - nonneoplastic N84.1
- choanal J33.0
- cholesterol K82.4
- clitoris N84.3
- colon K63.5
  - adenomatous D12.6
  - ascending D12.2
  - cecum D12.0
  - descending D12.4
  - inflammatory K51.40
    - with
      - abscess K51.414
      - complication K51.419
        - specified NEC K51.418
      - fistula K51.413
      - intestinal obstruction K51.412
      - rectal bleeding K51.411
  - sigmoid D12.5
  - transverse D12.3
- corpus uteri N84.0
- dental K04.0
- duodenum K31.7
- ear (middle) H74.4-
- endometrium N84.0
- ethmoidal (sinus) J33.8
- fallopian tube N84.8
- female genital tract N84.9
  - specified NEC N84.8
- frontal (sinus) J33.8
- gallbladder K82.4
- gingiva, gum K06.8
- labia, labium (majus) (minus) N84.3
- larynx (mucous) J38.1
  - adenomatous D14.1
- malignant (M8000/3) - *see* Neoplasm, malignant
- maxillary (sinus) J33.8
- middle ear - *see* Polyp, ear (middle)
- myometrium N84.0

Polyp, polypus *(Continued)*
- nares
  - anterior J33.9
  - posterior J33.0
- nasal (mucous) J33.9
  - cavity J33.0
  - septum J33.9
- nasopharyngeal J33.0
- nose (mucous) J33.9
- oviduct N84.8
- pharynx J39.2
- placenta O90.89
- prostate - *see* Enlargement, enlarged, prostate
- pudenda, pudendum N84.3
- pulpal (dental) K04.0
- rectum (nonadenomatous) K62.1
  - adenomatous - *see* Polyp, adenomatous
- septum (nasal) J33.0
- sinus (accessory) (ethmoidal) (frontal) (maxillary) (sphenoidal) J33.8
- sphenoidal (sinus) J33.8
- stomach K31.7
  - adenomatous D13.1
- tube, fallopian N84.8
- turbinate, mucous membrane J33.8
- umbilical, newborn P83.6
- ureter N28.89
- urethra N36.2
- uterus (body) (corpus) (mucous) N84.0
  - cervix N84.1
  - in pregnancy or childbirth – *see* Pregnancy, complicated by, tumor, uterus
- vagina N84.2
- vocal cord (mucous) J38.1
- vulva N84.3

Polyphagia R63.2
Polyploidy Q92.7
Polypoid - *see* condition
Polyposis - *see also* Polyp
- coli (adenomatous) D12.6
  - adenocarcinoma in C18.9
  - adenocarcinoma in situ in - *see* Neoplasm, in situ
  - carcinoma in C18.9
- colon (adenomatous) D12.6
- familial D12.6
  - adenocarcinoma in situ in - *see* Neoplasm, in situ
- intestinal (adenomatous) D12.6
  - malignant lymphomatous C83.1
- multiple, adenomatous - *see also* Neoplasm, benign D36.9

Polyradiculitis - *see* Polyneuropathy
Polyradiculoneuropathy (acute) (postinfective) (segmentally demyelinating) G61.0
Polyserositis
- due to pericarditis I31.1
- pericardial I31.1
- periodic, familial E85.0
- tuberculous A19.9
  - acute A19.1
  - chronic A19.8

Polysplenia syndrome Q89.09
Polysyndactyly Q70.4
Polytrichia L68.3
Polyunguia Q84.6
Polyuria R35.8
- nocturnal R35.1
- psychogenic F45.8

Pompe's disease (glycogen storage) E74.02
Pompholyx L30.1
Poncet's disease (tuberculous rheumatism) A18.09
Pond fracture - *see* Fracture, skull
Ponos B55.0
Pons, pontine - *see* condition
Poor
- aesthetic of existing restoration of tooth K08.56
- contractions, labor O62.2
- gingival margin to tooth restoration K08.51
- personal hygiene R46.0
- prenatal care, affecting management of pregnancy – *see* Pregnancy, complicated by, insufficient, prenatal care
- sucking reflex (newborn) R29.2
- urinary stream R39.12
- vision NEC H54.7

Poradenitis, nostras inguinalis or venerea A55
Porencephaly (congenital) (developmental) (true) Q04.6
- acquired G93.0
- nondevelopmental G93.0
- traumatic (post) F07.89
Porocephaliasis B88.8
Porokeratosis Q82.8
Poroma, eccrine - *see* Neoplasm, skin, benign
Porphyria (South African) E80.20
- acquired E80.20
- acute intermittent (hepatic) (Swedish) E80.21
- cutanea tarda (hereditary) (symptomatic) E80.1
- due to drugs E80.20
  - correct substance properly administered - *see* Table of drugs and chemicals, by drug, adverse effect
  - overdose or wrong substance given or taken - *see* Table of drugs and chemicals, by drug, poisoning
- erythropoietic (congenital) (hereditary) E80.0
- hepatocutaneous type E80.1
- secondary E80.20
- toxic NEC E80.20
- variegata E80.20
Porphyrinuria - *see* Porphyria
Porphyruria - *see* Porphyria
Portal -*see* condition
Port wine nevus, mark, or stain Q82.5
Posada-Wernicke disease B38.7
Positive
- culture (nonspecific)
  - blood R78.81
  - bronchial washings R84.5
  - cerebrospinal fluid R83.5
  - cervix uteri R87.5
  - nasal secretions R84.5
  - nipple discharge R89.5
  - nose R84.5
    - staphylococcus Z22.32
  - peritoneal fluid R85.5
  - pleural fluid R84.5
  - prostatic secretions R86.5
  - saliva R85.5

Positive *(Continued)*
culture *(Continued)*
seminal fluid R86.5
sputum R84.5
synovial fluid R89.5
throat scrapings R84.5
urine R82.7
vagina R87.5
vulva R87.5
wound secretions R89.5
PPD (skin test) R76.1
serology for syphilis A53.0
false R76.8
with signs or symptoms - code as
Syphilis, by site and stage
skin test, tuberculin (without active
tuberculosis) R76.1
test, human immunodeficiency virus
(HIV) R75
VDRL A53.0
with signs or symptoms - code
by site and stage under Syphilis
A53.9
Wassermann reaction A53.0
Postcardiotomy syndrome I97.0
Postcaval ureter Q62.62
Postcholecystectomy syndrome
K91.5
Postclimacteric bleeding N95.0
Postcommissurotomy syndrome
I97.0
Postconcussional syndrome F07.81
Postcontusional syndrome F07.81
Postcricoid region - *see* condition
Post-dates (40-42 weeks) (pregnancy)
(mother) O48.0
more than 42 weeks gestation O48.1
Postencephalitic syndrome F07.89
Posterior - *see* condition
Posterolateral sclerosis (spinal cord) - *see*
Degeneration, combined
Postexanthematous - *see* condition
Postfebrile - *see* condition
Postgastrectomy dumping syndrome
K91.1
Posthemiplegic chorea – *see*
Monoplegia
Posthemorrhagic anemia (chronic)
D50.0
acute (D62
newborn P61.3
Postherpetic neuralgia (zoster) B02.29
trigeminal B02.22
Posthitis N47.7
Postimmunization complication or
reaction - *see* Complications,
vaccination
Postinfectious - *see* condition
Postlaminectomy syndrome NEC M96.1
Postleukotomy syndrome F07.0
Postmastectomy lymphedema (syn-
drome) I97.2
Postmaturity, postmature (over 42 weeks)
maternal (over 42 weeks gestation)
O48.1
newborn P08.22
Postmeasles complication NEC *(see also*
condition) B05.89
Postmenopausal
endometrium (atrophic) N95.8
suppurative *(see also* Endometritis)
N71.9
osteoporosis - *see* Osteoporosis,
postmenopausal

Postnasal drip R09.82
due to
allergic rhinitis - *see* Rhinitis, allergic
common cold J00
gastroesophageal reflux - *see* Reflux,
gastroesophageal
nasopharyngitis - *see* Nasopharyngitis
other know condition - code to
condition
sinusitis - *see* Sinusitis
Postnatal - *see* condition
Postoperative (postprocedural) - *see* Complication, postoperative
pneumothorax, therapeutic Z98.3
state NEC Z98.89
Postpancreatectomy hyperglycemia E89.1
Postpartum - *see* Puerperal
Postphlebitic syndrome - *see* Syndrome,
postthrombotic
Postpoliomyelitic - *see also* condition
osteopathy - *see* Osteopathy, after
poliomyelitis
Postpolio (myelitic) syndrome G14
Postprocedural - *see also* Postoperative
hypoinsulinemia E89.1
Postschizophrenic depression F32.8
Postsurgery status - *see also* Status
(post)
pneumothorax, therapeutic Z98.3
Post-term (40-42 weeks) (pregnancy)
(mother) O48.0
infant P08.21
more than 42 weeks gestation (mother)
O48.1
Post-traumatic brain syndrome, nonpsychotic F07.81
Post-typhoid abscess A01.09
Postures, hysterical F44.2
Postvaccinal reaction or complication -
see Complications, vaccination
Postvalvulotomy syndrome I97.0
Potain's
disease (pulmonary edema) - *see*
Edema, lung
syndrome (gastrectasis with dyspepsia)
K31.0
Potter's
asthma J62.8
facies Q60.6
lung J62.8
syndrome (with renal agenesis) Q60.6
Pott's
curvature (spinal) A18.01
disease or paraplegia A18.01
spinal curvature A18.01
tumor, puffy - *see* Osteomyelitis, speci-
fied type NEC
Pouch
bronchus Q32.4
Douglas' - *see* condition
esophagus, esophageal, congenital
Q39.6
acquired K22.5
gastric K31.4
Hartmann's K82.8
pharynx, pharyngeal (congenital)
Q38.7
Pouchitis K91.850
Poultrymen's itch B88.0
Poverty NEC Z59.6
extreme Z59.5
Poxvirus NEC B08.8
Prader-Willi syndrome Q87.1
Preauricular appendage or tag Q17.0

Prebetalipoproteinemia (acquired)
(essential) (familial) (hereditary)
(primary) (secondary) E78.1
with chylomicronemia E78.3
Precipitate labor or delivery O62.3
Preclimacteric bleeding (menorrhagia)
N92.4
Precocious
adrenarche E30.1
menarche E30.1
menstruation E30.1
pubarche E30.1
puberty E30.1
central E22.8
sexual development NEC E30.1
thelarche E30.8
Precocity, sexual (constitutional) (cryptogenic) (female) (idiopathic) (male)
E30.1
with adrenal hyperplasia E25.9
congenital E25.0
Precordial pain R07.2
Predeciduous teeth K00.2
Prediabetes, prediabetic R73.09
complicating
pregnancy – *see* Pregnancy, complicated by, diseases of, specified
type or system NEC
puerperium O99.89
Predislocation status of hip at birth Q65.6
Pre-eclampsia O14.9-
with pre-existing hypertension –*see* Hypertension, complicating pregnancy,
pre-existing, with, proteinuria
mild O14.0-
severe (H.E.L.L.P.) O14.1-
Pre-eruptive color change, teeth, tooth
K00.8
Pre-excitation atrioventricular conduction I45.6
Pregnancy (childbirth) (labor) (puerperium) - *see also* Delivery and Puerperal

---
Note: the tabular must be reviewed for
assignment of the final character for
trimester

Note: the tabular must be reviewed
for assignment of the correct extension
for multiple gestations for all chapter
15 codes
---

abdominal (ectopic) O00.0
with viable fetus O36.7-
ampullar O00.1
broad ligament O00.8
cervical O00.8
complicated NOS O26.9-
complicated by (care of) (management
affected by)
abnormal, abnormality
cervix O34.4-
causing obstructed labor O65.5
cord (umbilical) O69.9
findings on antenatal screening of
mother O28.9
biochemical O28.1
cytological O28.2
chromosomal O28.5
genetic O28.5
hematological O28.0
radiological O28.4
specified NEC O28.8
ultrasonic O28.3

Pregnancy *(Continued)*
  complicated by *(Continued)*
    abnormal, abnormality *(Continued)*
      glucose (tolerance) NEC O99.810
      pelvic organs O34.9-
        specified NEC O34.8-
          causing obstructed labor O65.5
      pelvis (bony) (major) NEC O33.0
      perineum O34.7-
      position
        placenta O44.1-
          without hemorrhage O44.0-
        uterus O34.59-
      uterus O34.59-
        causing obstructed labor O65.5
        congenital O34.0-
      vagina O34.6-
        causing obstructed labor O65.5
      vulva O34.7-
        causing obstructed labor O65.5
    abruptio placentae - *see* Abruptio
      placentae
    abscess or cellulitis
      bladder O23.1-
      breast O91.11-
      genital organ or tract O23.9-
    abuse
      physical O9A.31-
      psychological O9A.51-
      sexual O9A.41-
    adverse effect anesthesia O29.9-
      aspiration pneumonitis O29.01-
      cardiac arrest O29.11-
      cardiac complication NEC O29.19-
      cardiac failure O29.12-
      central nervous system complica-
        tion NEC O29.29-
      cerebral anoxia O29.21-
      failed or difficult intubation O29.6-
      inhalation of stomach contents or
        secretions NOS O29.01-
      local, toxic reaction O29.3x
      Mendelson's syndrome O29.01-
      pressure collapse of lung O29.02-
      pulmonary complications NEC
        O29.09-
      specified NEC O29.8x
      spinal and epidural type NEC O29.5x
        induced headache O29.4-
    albuminuria O12.1-
    alcohol use O99.31-
    amnionitis O41.12-
    anaphylactoid syndrome of pregnancy
      O88.01-
    anemia (conditions in D50-D64) (pre-
      exisiting) O99.01-
      postpartum O90.81
    antepartum hemorrhage O46.9-
      with coagulation defect - *see* Hem-
        orrhage, antepartum, with
        coagulation defect
      specified NEC O46.8x
    appendicitis O99.61-
    atrophy (yellow) (acute) liver (sub-
      acute) O26.61-
    bariatric surgery status O99.84-
    bicornis or bicornuate uterus O34.59-
    biliary problems O99.61-
    breech presentation O32.1
    cardiovascular diseases (conditions in
      I00-I09, I20-I52, I70-I99) O99.41-
    cerebrovascular disorders (conditions
      in I60-I69) O99.41-
    cervical shortening O26.87-

Pregnancy *(Continued)*
  complicated by *(Continued)*
    cervicitis O23.51-
    chloasma (gravidarum) O26.89-
    cholestasis (intrahepatic) O26.61-
    cholecystitis O99.61-
    chorioamnionitis O41.12-
    circulatory system disorder (condi-
      tions in I00-I09, I20-I99) O99.41-
    compound presentation O32.6
    connective system disorders (condi-
      tions in M00-M99) O99.89
    contracted pelvis (general) O33.1
      inlet O33.2
      outlet O33.3
    convulsions (eclamptic) (uremic)
      O15.9 – *see also* Eclampsia
    cracked nipple O92.11-
    cystitis O23.1-
    cystocele O34.8-
    death of fetus (near term) O36.4
      early pregnancy O02.1
      of one fetus or more in multiple
        gestation O31.2-
    deciduitis O41.14-
    decreased fetal movement O36.81-
    dental problems O99.61-
    diabetes (mellitus) O24.91-
      gestational (pregnancy induced)
        see - Diabetes, gestational
      pre-exisiting O24.31-
        specified NEC O24.81-
        type 1 O24.01-
        type 2 O24.11-
    digestive system disorders (condi-
      tions in K00-K93) O99.61-
    diseases of - *see* Pregnancy, compli-
      cated by, specified body system
      disease
      blood NEC (conditions in D65-D77)
        O99.11-
      liver O26.61-
      specified NEC O99.89
    disorders of - *see* Pregnancy, compli-
      cated by, specified body system
      disorder
      amniotic fluid and membranes
        O41.9-
        specified NEC O41.8x-
      ear and mastoid process (condi-
        tions in H60-H95) O99.89
      eye and adnexa (conditions in
        H00-H59) O99.89
      liver O26.61-
      skin (conditions in L00-L99) O99.7-
      specified NEC O99.89
    displacement, uterus NEC O34.59-
      causing obstructed labor O65.5
    disproportion (due to) O33.9
      fetal deformities NEC O33.7
      generally contracted pelvis O33.1
      hydrocephalic fetus O33.6
      inlet contraction of pelvis O33.2
      mixed maternal and fetal origin
        O33.4
      specified NEC O33.8
    double uterus O34.59-
      causing obstructed labor O65.5
    drug use (conditions in F11-F19)
      O99.32-
    eclampsia, eclamptic (coma) (con-
      vulsions) (delirium) (nephri-
      tis) (uremia) O15.– *see also*
      Eclampsia

Pregnancy *(Continued)*
  complicated by *(Continued)*
    ectopic pregnancy - *see* Pregnancy,
      ectopic
    edema O12.0-
      with proteinuria O12.2-
    effusion, amniotic fluid - *see* Preg-
      nancy, complicated by, prema-
      ture rupture of membranes
    elderly
      multigravida O09.52-
      primigravida O09.51-
    embolism O88. – *see also* Embolism,
      obstetric, pregnancy
    endocrine diseases NEC O99.28-
    endometritis O86.12
    excessive weight gain O26.0-
    exhaustion O26.81-
      during labor and delivery O75.81
    face presentation O32.3
    failed induction of labor O61.9
      instrumental O61.1
      mechanical O61.1
      medical O61.0
      specified NEC O61.8
      surgical O61.1
    failed or difficult intubation for
      anesthesia O29.6-
    false labor (pains) O47.9
      at or after 37 completed weeks of
        pregnancy O47.1
      before 37 completed weeks of
        pregnancy O47.0-
    fatigue O26.81-
      during labor and delivery O75.81
    fatty metamorphosis of liver O26.61-
    female genital mutilation
      O34.8*[N90.81-]*
    fetal (maternal care for)
      abnormality or damage O35.9
        acid-base balance O68
        specified type NEC O35.8
      acidemia O68
      acidosis O68
      alkalosis O68
      anemia and thrombocytopenia
        O36.82-
      anencephaly O35.0
      chromosomal abnormality (condi-
        tions in Q90-Q99) O35.1
      conjoined twins O30.02-
      damage from
        amniocentesis O35.7
        biopsy procedures O35.7
        drug addiction O35.5
        hematological investigation O35.7
        intrauterine contraceptive device
          O35.7
        maternal
          alcohol addiction O35.4
          cytomegalovirus infection O35.3
          disease NEC O35.8
          drug addiction O35.5
          listeriosis O35.8
          rubella O35.3
          toxoplasmosis O35.8
          viral infection O35.3
        medical procedure NEC O35.7
        radiation O35.6
      death (near term) O36.4
        early pregnancy O02.1
      decreased movement O36.81-
      disproportion due to deformity
        (fetal) O33.7

Pregnancy (Continued)
   complicated by (Continued)
      fetal (Continued)
         excessive growth (large for dates)
            O36.6-
         growth retardation O36.59-
            light for dates O36.59-
            small for dates O36.59-
         heart rate irregularity (bradycardia)
            (decelerations) (tachycardia)
            O76
         hereditary disease O35.2
         hydrocephalus O35.0
         intrauterine death O36.4
         poor growth O36.59-
            light for dates O36.59-
            small for dates O36.59-
         problem O36.9-
            specified NEC O36.89-
         reduction (elective) O31.3-
         selective termination O31.3-
         spina bifida O35.0
         thrombocytopenia O36.82-
      fibroid (tumor) (uterus) O34.1-
      fissure of nipple O92.11-
      gallstones O99.61-
      gastric banding status O99.84-
      gastric bypass status O99.84-
      genital tract infection O23.9-
      glomerular diseases (conditions in
            N00-N07) O26.83-
         with hypertension, pre-existing
            – see Hypertension,
            complicating, pregnancy, pre-
            existing, with, renal disease
      gonorrhea O98.21-
      grand multiparity O09.4
      habitual aborter O26.2-
      HELLP syndrome O14.2
      hemorrhage
         antepartum – see Hemorrhage,
            antepartum
         before 20 completed weeks
            gestation O20.9
            specified NEC O20.8
         due to premature separation,
            placenta O45. - see also
            Abruptio placentae
         early O20.9
            specified NEC O20.8
         threatened abortion O20.0
      hemorrhoids O22.4-
      hepatitis (viral) O98.41-
      herniation of uterus O34.59-
      high
         head at term O32.4
         risk - see Supervision (of) (for),
            high-risk
      history of in utereo procedure during
            previous pregnancy O09.82-
      HIV O98.71-
      human immunodeficiency [HIV]
            disease O98.71-
      hydatidiform mole O01.9 - see also
            Mole, hydatidiform
      hydramnios O40.-
      hydrocephalic fetus (disproportion)
            O33.6
      hydrops
         amnii O40.
         fetalis O36.2-
            associated with isoimmunization
               O36.11-
      hydrorrhea O42.90

Pregnancy (Continued)
   complicated by (Continued)
      hyperemesis (gravidarum) (mild)
            O21.0 - see also Hyperemesis,
            gravidarum
      hypertension - see Hypertension, com-
            plicating pregnancy
      hypertensive
         heart and renal disease, pre-
            existing – see Hypertension,
            complicating, pregnancy, pre-
            existing, with, heart disease,
            with renal disease
         heart disease, pre-existing – see
            Hypertension, complicating,
            pregnancy, pre-existing, with,
            heart disease
         renal disease, pre-existing – see
            Hypertension, complicating,
            pregnancy, pre-existing, with,
            renal disease
      hypotension O26.5-
      immune disorders NEC (conditions in
            D80-D89) O99.11-
      incarceration, uterus O34.51-
      incompetent cervix O34.3-
      infection(s) O98.91-
         amniotic fluid or sac O41.10-
         bladder O23.1-
         carrier state NEC O99.830
            streptococcus B O99.820
         genital organ or tract O23.9-
            specified NEC O23.59-
         genitourinary tract O23.9-
         gonorrhea O98.21-
         hepatitis (viral) O98.41-
         HIV O98.71-
         human immunodeficiency [HIV]
            O98.71-
         kidney O23.0-
         nipple O91.01-
         parasitic disease O98.91-
            specified NEC O98.81-
         protozoal disease O98.61-
         sexually transmitted NEC O98.31-
         specified type NEC O98.81-
         syphilis O98.11-
         tuberculosis O98.01-
         urethra O23.2-
         urinary (tract) O23.4-
            specified NEC O23.3-
         viral disease O98.51
      injury or poisoning (conditions in S00-
            T88) O9A.21-
         due to abuse
            physical O9A.31
            psychological O9A.51-
            sexual O9A.41-
      insufficient
         prenatal care O09.3-
         weight gain O26.1-
      intrauterine fetal death (near term) O36.4
         early pregnancy O02.1
         multiple gestation (one fetus or
            more) O31.2-
      isoimmunization, Rh O36.09-
         anti-D antibody O36.01-
      laceration of uterus NEC O71.81
      malformation
         placenta, placental (vessel) O43.10-
            specified NEC O43.19-
         uterus (congenital) O34.0-
      malnutrition (conditions in E40-E46)
            O25.1-

Pregnancy (Continued)
   complicated by (Continued)
      maternal hypotension syndrome O26.5-
      mental disorders (conditions in F01-
            F09, F20-F99) O99.34-
         alcohol use O99.31-
         drug use O99.32-
         smoking O99.33-
      mentum presentation O32.3
      metabolic disorders O99.28-
      missed
         abortion O02.1
         delivery O36.4
      multiple gestations O30.9 - see Tabu-
            lar for required extensions
         conjoined twins O30.02-
         specified number of multiples NEC
            O30.8-
         quadruplet O30.2-
         specified complication NEC
            O31.8x-
         triplet O30.1-
         twin O30.00-
            conjoined O30.02-
            monoamniotic/monochorionic
               O30.01-
            specified NEC O30.09-
      musculoskeletal condition (condi-
            tions is M00-M99) O99.89
      necrosis, liver (conditions in K72)
            O26.61-
      neoplasm
         benign
            cervix O34.4-
            corpus uteri O34.1-
            uterus O34.1-
         malignant O9A.11-
      nephropathy NEC O26.83-
      nervous system condition (conditions
            in G00-G99) O99.35-
      nutritional diseases NEC O99.28-
      obesity (pre-existing) O99.21-
      obesity surgery status O99.84-
      oblique lie or presentation O32.2
      older mother
         multigravida O09.52-
         primigravida O09.51-
      oligohydramnios O41.0-
         with premature rupture of mem-
            branes O42. - see also Preg-
            nancy, complicated by, prema-
            ture rupture of membranes
      oophoritis O23.52-
      overdose, drug O9A.21– see also Table
            of drugs and chemicals, by drug,
            poisoning
      oversize fetus O33.5
      papyraceous fetus O31.0-
      pelvic inflammatory disease O99.89
      periodontal disease O99.61-
      peripheral neuritis O26.82-
      peritoneal (pelvic) adhesions O99.89
      phlebitis O22.9-
      phlebopathy O22.9-
      phlebothrombosis (superficial) O22.2-
         deep O22.3-
      placenta accreta O43.21-
      placenta increta O43.22-
      placenta percreta O43.23-
      placenta previa O44.1-
         without hemorrhage O44.0-
      placental disorder O43.9-
         specified NEC O43.89-
      placental dysfunction O43.89-

Pregnancy *(Continued)*
  complicated by *(Continued)*
    placental infarction O43.81-
    placental insufficiency O36.51-
    placental transfusion syndromes
      fetomaternal O43.01-
      fetus to fetus O43.02-
      maternofetal O43.01-
    placentitis O41.14-
    poisoning O9A.21 - *see also* Table of
        drugs and chemicals
    polyhydramnios O40.
    polymorphic eruption of pregnancy
        O26.86
    poor obstetric history NEC O09.29-
    postmaturity (post-term) (40 to 42
        weeks) O48.0
      more than 42 completed weeks
          gestation (prolonged) O48.1
    pre-eclampsia O14.9-
      mild O14.0-
      severe O14.1
        with HELLP O14.2
    premature labor - *see* Pregnancy,
        complicated by, preterm labor
    premature rupture of membranes
        O42.90
      full-term O42.92
      with onset of labor
        within 24 hours O42.00
          after 37 weeks gestation O42.02
          pre-term (before 37 completed
              weeks of gestation) O42.01-
        after 24 hours O42.10
          after 37 weeks gestation O42.12
          pre-term (before 37 completed
              weeks of gestation) O42.11-
      after 37 weeks gestation O42.92
      pre-term (before 37 completed
          weeks of gestation) O42.91-
    premature separation of placenta O45.
        - *see also* Abruptio placentae
    presentation, fetal -*see* Delivery (child-
        birth) (labor) (complicated by)
    preterm delivery O60.10
    preterm labor
      with delivery O60.10
        preterm O60.10
        term O60.20
      second trimester
        with term delivery O60.22
        without delivery O60.02
        with preterm delivery
          second trimester O60.12
          third trimester O60.13
      third trimester
        with term delivery O60.23
        without delivery O60.03
        with third trimester preterm
            delivery O60.14
      without delivery O60.00
        second trimester O60.02
        third trimester O60.03
    previous history of - *see* Pregnancy,
        supervision of, high-risk
    prolapse, uterus O34.52-
    proteinuria (gestational) O12.1-
      with edema O12.2-
    pruritic urticarial papules and plaques
        of pregnancy (PUPPP) O26.86
    pruritus (neurogenic) O26.89-
    psychosis or psychoneurosis
        (puerperal) F53
    ptyalism O26.89-

Pregnancy *(Continued)*
  complicated by *(Continued)*
    PUPPP (pruritic urticarial papules and
        plaques of pregnancy) O26.86
    pyelitis O23.0-
    renal disease or failure NEC O26.83-
      with secondary hypertension,
          pre-existing – *see* Hyperten-
          sion, complicating, pregnancy,
          pre-existing, secondary
      hypertensive, pre-existing – *see*
          Hypertension, complicating,
          pregnancy, pre-existing, with,
          renal disease
    respiratory condition (conditions in
        J00-J99) O99.51-
    retained, retention
      dead ovum O02.0
      intrauterine contraceptive device
          O26.3-
    retroversion, uterus O34.53-
    Rh immunization, incompatibility or
        sensitization NEC O36.09-
      anti-D antibody O36.01-
    rupture
      amnion (premature) O42. - *see
          also* Pregnancy, complicated
          by, premature rupture of
          membranes
      membranes (premature) O42. - *see
          also* Pregnancy, complicated
          by, premature rupture of
          membranes
      uterus (during labor) O71.1
        before onset of labor O71.0-
    salivation (excessive) O26.89-
    salpingitis O23.52-
    salpingo-oophoritis O23.52-
    sepsis (conditions in A40, A41)
        O98.81-
    size date discrepancy (uterine)
        O26.84-
    skin condition (conditions in L00-
        L99) O99.7-
    smoking (tobacco) O99.33-
    social problem O09.7-
    specified condition NEC O26.89-
    spotting O26.85-
    streptococcus B carrier state O99.820
    subluxation of symphysis (pubis)
        O26.71-
    syphilis (conditions in A50-A53)
        O98.11-
    threatened
      abortion O20.0
      labor O47.9
        at or after 37 completed weeks of
            gestation O47.1
        before 37 completed weeks of
            gestation O47.0-
    thrombophlebitis (superficial) O22.2-
    thrombosis O22.9-
      cerebral venous O22.5-
      cerebrovenous sinus O22.5-
      deep O22.3-
    torsion of uterus O34.59-
    toxemia O14.9-
    transverse lie or presentation O32.2
    tuberculosis (conditions in A15-A19)
        O98.01-
    tumor (benign)
      cervix O34.4-
      malignant O9A.11-
      uterus O34.1-

Pregnancy *(Continued)*
  complicated by *(Continued)*
    unstable lie O32.0
    upper respiratory infection O99.51-
    urethritis O23.2-
    uterine size date discrepancy O26.84-
    vaginitis or vulvitis O23.59-
    varicose veins (lower extremities)
        O22.0-
      genitals O22.1-
      legs O22.0-
      perineal O22.1-
      vaginal or vulval O22.1-
    venereal disease NEC (conditions in
        A63.8) O98.31-
    venous disorders O22.9-
      specified NEC O22.8x
    viral diseases (conditions in A80-B09,
        B25-B34) O98.51-
    very young
      multigravida O09.62-
      primigravida O09.61-
    vomiting O21.9
      due to diseases classified elsewhere
          O21.8
      hyperemesis gravidarum (mild)
          O21.0 – *see also* Hyperemesis,
          gravidarum
      late (occurring after 20 weeks of
          gestation) O21.2
  concealed O09.3-
  continuing following
    elective fetal reduction of one or more
        fetus O31.3-
    intrauterine death of one or more
        fetus O31.2-
    spontaneous abortion of one or more
        fetus O31.1-
  cornual O00.8
  ectopic (ruptured) O00.9
    abdominal O00.0
      with viable fetus O36.7-
    cervical O00.8
    complicated (by) O07.30
      afibrinogenemia O07.1
      cardiac arrest O07.39
      chemical damage of pelvic organ(s)
          O07.39
      circulatory collapse O07.39
      defibrination syndrome O07.1
      electrolyte imbalance O07.39
      embolism (amniotic fluid) (blood
          clot) (pulmonary) (septic)
          O07.2
      endometritis O07.0
      genital tract and pelvic infection
          O07.0
      hemorrhage (delayed) (excessive)
          O07.1
      infection
        genital tract or pelvic O07.0
        urinary tract O07.39
      intravascular coagulation O07.1
      laceration of pelvic organ(s) O07.39
      metabolic disorder O07.39
      oliguria O07.39
      oophoritis O07.0
      parametritis O07.0
      pelvic peritonitis O07.0
      perforation of pelvic organ(s)
          O07.39
      renal failure or shutdown O07.39
      salpingitis or salpingo-oophoritis
          O07.0

Pregnancy *(Continued)*
 ectopic *(Continued)*
  complicated (by) *(Continued)*
   sepsis O07.0
   shock O07.39
    septic O07.0
   specified condition NEC O07.39
   tubular necrosis (renal) O07.39
   uremia O07.39
   urinary infection O07.39
   venous complication NEC O07.39
    embolism O07.2
  cornual O00.8
  intraligamentous O00.8
  mural O00.8
  ovarian O00.2
  specified site NEC O00.8
  tubal (ruptured) O00.1
 examination (normal) Z34.9-
  high-risk - *see* Pregnancy, supervision of, high-risk
  first Z34.0-
  specified Z34.8-
 extrauterine – *see* Pregnancy, ectopic
 fallopian O00.1
 false F45.8
 hidden O09.3-
 high-risk - *see* Pregnancy, supervision of, high-risk
 incidental finding Z33.1
 interstitial O00.8
 intraligamentous O00.8
 intramural O00.8
 intraperitoneal O00.0
 isthmian O00.1
 mesometric (mural) O00.8
 molar NEC O02.0
  complicated (by) O07.30
   afibrinogenemia O07.1
   cardiac arrest O07.39
   chemical damage of pelvic organ(s) O07.39
   circulatory collapse O07.39
   defibrination syndrome O07.1
   electrolyte imbalance O07.39
   embolism (amniotic fluid) (blood clot) (pulmonary) (septic) O07.2
   endometritis O07.0
   genital tract and pelvic infection O07.0
   hemorrhage (delayed) (excessive) O07.1
   infection
    genital tract or pelvic O07.0
    urinary tract O07.39
   intravascular coagulation O07.1
   laceration of pelvic organ(s) O07.39
   metabolic disorder O07.39
   oliguria O07.39
   oophoritis O07.0
   parametritis O07.0
   pelvic peritonitis O07.0
   perforation of pelvic organ(s) O07.39
   renal failure or shutdown O07.39
   salpingitis or salpingo-oophoritis O07.0
   sepsis O07.0
   shock O07.39
    septic O07.0
   specified condition NEC O07.39

Pregnancy *(Continued)*
 molar NEC *(Continued)*
  complicated (by) *(Continued)*
   tubular necrosis (renal) O07.39
   uremia O07.39
   urinary infection O07.39
   venous complication NEC O07.39
    embolism O07.2
  hydatidiform O01.9 - *see also* Mole, hydatidiform
 mural O00.8
 normal (supervision of) Z34.9-
  high-risk - *see* Pregnancy, supervision of, high-risk
  first Z34.0-
  specified Z34.8-
 ovarian O00.2
 postmature (40 to 42 weeks) O48.0
  more than 42 weeks gestation O48.1
 post-term (40 to 42 weeks) O48.0
 prenatal care only Z34.9-
  high-risk - *see* Pregnancy, supervision of, high-risk
  first Z34.0-
  specified Z34.8-
 prolonged (more than 42 weeks gestation) O48.1
 quadruplet O30.2 - *see* Tabular for required extensions
 quintuplet O30.8 - *see* Tabular for required extensions
 sextuplet O30.8 - *see* Tabular for required extensions
 supervision of
  high-risk O09.9-
   due to (history of)
    ectopic pregnancy O09.1-
    grand multiparity O09.4
    infertility O09.0-
    insufficient prenatal care O09.3-
    in utereo procedure during previous pregnancy O09.82-
    in vitro fertilization O09.81-
    molar pregnancy O09.1-
    multiple previous pregnancies O09.4-
    older mother
     multigravida O09.52-
     primigravida O09.51-
    poor reproductive or obstetric history NEC O09.29-
    pre-term labor O09.21-
    previous
     neonatal death O09.29-
    social problems O09.7-
    specified NEC O09.89-
    very young mother
     multigravida O09.62-
     primigravida O09.61-
    resulting from in vitro fertilization O09.81-
  normal Z34.9-
   first Z34.0-
   specified NEC Z34.8-
  older mother
   multigravida O09.52-
   primigravida O09.51-
  very young mother
   multigravida O09.62-
   primigravida O09.61-
 triplet O30.1 - *see* Tabular for required extensions
 tubal (with abortion) (with rupture) O00.1

Pregnancy *(Continued)*
 twin O30.00 - *see* Tabular for required extensions
  monoamniotic/monochorionic O30.01-
  specified NEC O30.09-
 unwanted Z64.0
Preiser's disease - *see* Osteonecrosis, secondary, due to, trauma, metacarpus
Pre-kwashiorkor - *see* Malnutrition, severe
Preleukemia (syndrome) D46.9
Preluxation, hip, congenital Q65.6
Premature - *see also* condition
 adrenarche E27.0
 aging E34.8
 beats I49.40
  atrial I49.1
  auricular I49.1
  supraventricular I49.1
 birth NEC - *see* Preterm infant, newborn
 closure, foramen ovale Q21.8
 contraction
  atrial I49.1
  atrioventricular I49.2
  auricular I49.1
  auriculoventricular I49.2
  heart (extrasystole) I49.49
  junctional I49.2
  ventricular I49.3
 delivery (*see also* Pregnancy, complicated by, preterm labor) O60.10
 ejaculation F52.4
 infant NEC - *see* Preterm infant, newborn
 light-for-dates - *see* Light for dates
 labor - *see* Pregnancy, complicated by, preterm labor
 lungs P28.0
 menopause E28.319
  asymptomatic E28.319
  symptomatic E28.310
 newborn
  extreme (less than 28 completed weeks) - *see* Immaturity, extreme
  less than 37 completed weeks - *see* Preterm infant, newborn
 puberty E30.1
 rupture membranes or amnion - *see* Pregnancy, complicated by, premature rupture of membranes
 senility E34.8
 thelarche E30.8
 ventricular systole I49.3
Prematurity NEC (less than 37 completed weeks) - *see* Preterm infant, newborn
 extreme (less than 28 completed weeks) - *see* Immaturity, extreme
Premenstrual
 dysphoric disorder (PMDD) N94.3
 tension (syndrome) N94.3
Premolarization, cuspids K00.2
Prenatal
 care, normal pregnancy – *see* Pregnancy, normal
 screening of mother Z36
 teeth K00.6
Preparatory care for subsequent treatment NEC
 for dialysis Z49.01
  peritoneal Z49.02
Prepartum - *see* condition

Preponderance, left or right ventricular
I51.7
Prepuce - *see* condition
PRES (Posterior Reversible Encephalopathy Syndrome) G93.49
Presbycardia R54
Presbycusis, presbyacusia H91.1-
Presbyesophagus K22.8
Presbyophrenia F03
Presbyopia H52.4
Prescription of contraceptives (initial)
Z30.019
  emergency (postcoital) Z30.012
  implantable subdermal Z30.019
  injectable Z30.013
  intrauterine contraceptive device
    Z30.014
  pills Z30.011
  postcoital (emergency) Z30.012
  repeat Z30.40
    implantable subdermal Z30.49
    injectable Z30.42
    intrauterine contraceptive device
      Z30.43
    pills Z30.41
    specified type NEC Z30.49
  specified type NEC Z30.018
Presence (of)
  ankle-joint implant (functional) (prosthesis) Z96.66-
  aortocoronary (bypass) graft Z95.1
  arterial-venous shunt (dialysis) Z99.2
  artificial
    eye (globe) Z97.0
    heart (fully implantable) (mechanical)
      Z95.812
      valve Z95.2
    larynx Z96.3
    lens (intraocular) Z96.1
    limb (complete) (partial) Z97.1-
      arm Z97.1-
        bilateral Z97.15
      leg Z97.1-
        bilateral Z97.16
  audiological implant (functional) Z96.29
  bladder implant (functional) Z96.0
  bone
    conduction hearing device Z96.29
    implant (functional) NEC Z96.7
    joint (prosthesis) – *see* Presence, joint
      implant
  cardiac
    defibrillator (functional) Z95.810
    implant or graft Z95.9
      specified type NEC Z95.818
    pacemaker Z95.0
  cerebrospinal fluid drainage device
    Z98.2
  cochlear implant (functional) Z96.21
  contact lens(es) Z97.3
  coronary artery graft or prosthesis Z95.5
  CSF shunt Z98.2
  dental prosthesis device Z97.2
  dentures Z97.2
  device (external) NEC Z97.8
    cardiac NEC Z95.818
    heart assist Z95.811
    implanted (functional) Z96.9
      specified NEC Z96.89
    prosthetic Z97.8
  ear implant Z96.20
    cochlear implant Z96.21
    myringotomy tube Z96.22
    specified type NEC Z96.29

Presence (of) *(Continued)*
  elbow-joint implant (functional)
    (prosthesis) Z96.62-
  endocrine implant (functional) NEC
    Z96.49
  eustachian tube stent or device (functional) Z96.29
  external hearing-aid or device Z97.4
  finger-joint implant (functional) (prosthetic) Z96.69-
  functional implant Z96.9
    specified NEC Z96.89
  graft
    cardiac NEC Z95.818
    vascular NEC Z95.828
  hearing-aid or device (external)
    Z97.4
    implant (bone) (cochlear) (functional)
      Z96.21
  heart assist device Z95.811
  heart valve implant (functional)
    Z95.2
    prosthetic Z95.2
    specified type NEC Z95.4
    xenogenic Z95.3
  hip-joint implant (functional) (prosthesis) Z96.64-
  implanted device (artificial) (functional)
    (prosthetic) Z96.9
    automatic cardiac defibrillator
      Z95.810
    cardiac pacemaker Z95.0
    cochlear Z96.21
    dental Z96.5
    heart Z95.812
    heart valve Z95.2
      prosthetic Z95.2
      specified NEC Z95.4
      xenogenic Z95.3
    insulin pump Z96.41
    intraocular lens Z96.1
    joint Z96.60
      ankle Z96.66-
      elbow Z96.62-
      finger Z96.69-
      hip Z96.64-
      knee Z96.65-
      shoulder Z96.61-
      specified NEC Z96.698
      wrist Z96.63-
    larynx Z96.3
    myringotomy tube Z96.22
    otological Z96.20
      cochlear Z96.21
      eustachian stent Z96.29
      myringotomy Z96.22
      specified NEC Z96.29
      stapes Z96.29
    skin Z96.81
    skull plate Z96.7
    specified NEC Z96.89
    urogenital Z96.0
  insulin pump (functional) Z96.41
  intestinal bypass or anastomosis
    Z98.0
  intraocular lens (functional) Z96.1
  intrauterine contraceptive device (IUD)
    Z97.5
  intravascular implant (functional)
    (prosthetic) NEC Z95.9
    coronary artery Z95.5
    defibrillator Z95.810
    peripheral vessel (with angioplasty)
      Z95.820

Presence (of) *(Continued)*
  joint implant (prosthetic) (any) Z96.60
    ankle - *see* Presence, ankle joint
      implant
    elbow - *see* Presence, elbow joint
      implant
    finger - *see* Presence, finger joint
      implant
    hip - *see* Presence, hip joint implant
    knee - *see* Presence, knee joint
      implant
    shoulder - *see* Presence, shoulder
      joint implant
    specified joint NEC Z96.698
    wrist - *see* Presence, wrist joint
      implant
  knee-joint implant (functional) (prosthesis) Z96.65-
  laryngeal implant (functional) Z96.3
  mandibular implant (dental) Z96.5
  myringotomy tube(s) Z96.22
  orthopedic-joint implant (prosthetic)
    (any) – *see* Presence, joint implant
  otological implant (functional) Z96.29
  shoulder-joint implant (functional)
    (prosthesis) Z96.61-
  skull-plate implant Z96.7
  spectacles Z97.3
  stapes implant (functional) Z96.29
  systemic lupus erythematosus [SLE]
    inhibitor D68.62
  tendon implant (functional) (graft)
    Z96.7
  tooth root(s) implant Z96.5
  ureteral stent Z96.0
  urethral stent Z96.0
  urogenital implant (functional) Z96.0
  vascular implant or device Z95.9
    access port device Z95.828
    specified type NEC Z95.828
  wrist-joint implant (functional) (prosthesis) Z96.63-
Presenile - *see also* condition
  dementia F03
  premature aging E34.8
Presentation, fetal - *see* Delivery (childbirth) (labor) (complicated by),
  malposition, malpresentation
Prespondylolisthesis (congenital) Q76.2
Pressure
  area, skin - *see* Ulcer, pressure, by site
  brachial plexus G54.0
  brain G93.5
    injury at birth NEC P11.1
  cerebral - *see* Pressure, brain
  chest R07.89
  cone, tentorial G93.5
  hyposystolic - *see also* Hypotension
    incidental reading, without diagnosis
      of hypotension R03.1
  increased
    intracranial (benign) G93.2
      injury at birth P11.0
    intraocular H40.0
  lumbosacral plexus G54.1
  mediastinum J98.5
  necrosis (chronic) - *see* Ulcer, pressure,
    by site
  sore (chronic) - *see* Ulcer, pressure, by
    site
  spinal cord G95.20
  ulcer (chronic) - *see* Ulcer, pressure, by
    site
  venous, increased I87.8

Pre-syncope R55
Preterm
  delivery (*see also* Pregnancy, complicated
    by, preterm labor) O60.10
  infant, newborn P07.30
    with gestation of: -
      28-31 weeks P07.31
      32-36 weeks P07.32
  labor - *see* Pregnancy, complicated by,
    preterm labor
Previa
  placenta (low) (marginal) (partial)
    (total) (with hemorrhage) O44.1-
    without hemorrhage O44.0-
  vasa O69.4
Priapism N48.30
  due to
    disease classified elsewhere
      N48.32
    drug N48.33
    specified cause NEC N48.39
    trauma N48.31
Prickling sensation (skin) R20.2
Prickly heat L74.0
Primary - *see* condition
Primigravida
  elderly, affecting management of
    pregnancy, labor and delivery
    (supervision only) – *see* Preg-
    nancy, complicated by, elderly,
    primigravida
  very young, affecting management of
    pregnancy, labor and delivery
    (supervision only) – *see* Pregnancy,
    complicated by, very young,
    primigravida
Primipara
  elderly, affecting management of
    pregnancy, labor and delivery
    (supervision only) – *see* Preg-
    nancy, complicated by, elderly,
    primigravida
  very young, affecting management of
    pregnancy, labor and delivery
    (supervision only) – *see* Pregnancy,
    complicated by, very young,
    primigravida
Primus varus (bilateral) Q66.3
PRIND (Prolonged reversible ischemic
  neurologic deficit) I63.9
Pringle's disease (tuberous
  sclerosis)Q85.1
Prinzmetal angina I20.1
Prizefighter ear - *see* Cauliflower ear
Problem (with) (related to)
  academic Z55.8
  acculturation Z60.3
  adjustment (to)
    change of job Z56.1
    life-cycle transition Z60.0
    pension Z60.0
    retirement Z60.0
  adopted child Z62.821
  alcoholism in family Z63.72
  atypical parenting situation Z62.6
  bankruptcy Z59.8
  behavioral (adult) F69
    drug seeking Z72.89
  birth of sibling affecting child Z62.898
  care (of)
    provider dependency Z74.9
      specified NEC Z74.8
    sick or handicapped person in family
      or household Z63.6

Problem (*Continued*)
  child
    abuse (affecting the child) - *see* Mal-
      treatment, child
    custody or support proceedings Z65.3
    in welfare custody Z62.21
    in care of non-parental family mem-
      ber Z62.21
    in foster care Z62.21
    living in orphanage or group home
      Z62.22
  child-rearing Z62.9
    specified NEC Z62.8
  communication (developmental) F80.9
  conflict or discord (with)
    boss Z56.4
    classmates Z55.4
    counselor Z64.4
    employer Z56.4
    family Z63.9
      specified NEC Z63.8
    probation officer Z64.4
    social worker Z64.4
    teachers Z55.4
    workmates Z56.4
  conviction in legal proceedings Z65.0
    with imprisonment Z65.1
  counselor Z64.4
  creditors Z59.8
  digestive K92.9
  drug addict in family Z63.72
  ear - *see* Disorder, ear
  economic Z59.9
    affecting care Z59.9
    specified NEC Z59.8
  education Z55.9
    specified NEC Z55.8
  employment Z56.9
    change of job Z56.1
    discord Z56.4
    environment Z56.5
    sexual harassment Z56.81
    specified NEC Z56.89
    stress NEC Z56.6
    stressful schedule Z56.3
    threat of job loss Z56.2
    unemployment Z56.0
  enuresis, child F98.0
  eye H57.9
  failed examinations (school) Z55.2
  falling Z91.81
  family Z63.9 - *see also* Disruption, family
    specified NEC Z63.8
  feeding (elderly) (infant) R63.3
    newborn P92.9
      breast P92.5
      overfeeding P92.4
      slow P92.2
      specified NEC P92.8
      underfeeding P92.3
    nonorganic F50.8
  finance Z59.9
    specified NEC Z59.8
  foreclosure on loan Z59.8
  foster child Z63.822
  frightening experience(s) in childhood
    Z62.898
  genital NEC
    female N94.9
    male N50.9
  health care Z75.9
    specified NEC Z75.8
  hearing - *see* Deafness
  homelessness Z59.0

Problem (*Continued*)
  housing Z59.9
    inadequate Z59.1
    isolated Z59.8
    specified NEC Z59.8
  identity (of childhood) F93.8
  illegitimate pregnancy (unwanted) Z64.0
  illiteracy Z55.0
  impaired mobility Z74.09
  imprisonment or incarceration Z65.1
  inadequate teaching affecting education
    Z55.8
  inappropriate (excessive) parental pres-
    sure Z62.6
  influencing health status NEC Z91.89
  in-law Z63.1
  institutionalization, affecting child Z62.22
  intrafamilial communication Z63.8
  jealousy, child F93.8
  landlord Z59.2
  language (developmental) F80.9
  learning (developmental) F81.9
  legal Z65.3
    conviction without imprisonment Z65.0
    imprisonment Z65.1
    release from prison Z65.2
  life-management Z73.9
    specified NEC Z73.89
  life-style Z72.9
    gambling Z72.6
    high-risk sexual behavior (hetero-
      sexual) Z72.51
      bisexual Z72.53
      homosexual Z72.52
    inappropriate eating habits Z72.4
    self-damaging behavior NEC Z72.89
    specified NEC Z72.89
    tobacco use Z72.0
  literacy Z55.9
    low level Z55.0
    specified NEC Z55.8
  living alone Z60.2
  lodgers Z59.2
  loss of love relationship in childhood
    Z62.898
  marital Z63.0
    involving
      divorce Z63.5
      estrangement Z63.5
      gender identity F66
  mastication K08.8
  medical
    care, within family Z63.6
    facilities Z75.9
      specified NEC Z75.8
  mental F48.9
  multiparity Z64.1
  negative life events in childhood Z62.9
    altered pattern of family relationships
      Z62.898
    frightening experience Z62.898
    loss of
      love relationship Z62.898
      self-esteem Z62.898
    physical abuse (alleged) - *see* Mal-
      treatment, child
    removal from home Z62.9
    specified event NEC Z61.88
  neighbor Z59.2
  neurological NEC R29.81
  new step-parent affecting child Z62.898
  none (feared complaint unfounded) Z71.1
  occupational NEC Z56.89
  parent-child - *see* Conflict, parent-child

Problem *(Continued)*
  personal hygiene Z91.89
  personality F69
  phase-of-life transition, adjustment Z60.0
  presence of sick or disabled person in
      family or household Z63.79
    needing care Z63.6
  primary support group (family) Z63.9
    specified NEC Z63.8
  probation officer Z64.4
  psychiatric F99
  psychosexual (development) F66
  psychosocial Z65.9
    specified NEC Z65.8
  relationship Z63.9
    childhood F93.8
  release from prison Z65.2
  removal from home affecting child Z62.29
  seeking and accepting known hazard-
      ous and harmful
    behavioral or psychological inter-
        ventions Z65.8
    chemical, nutritional or physical
        interventions Z65.8
  sexual function (nonorganic) F52.9
  sight H54.7
  sleep disorder, child F51.9
  smell - *see* Disturbance, sensation, smell
  social
    environment Z60.9
      specified NEC Z60.8
    exclusion and rejection Z60.4
    worker Z64.4
  speech R47.9
    developmental F80.9
    specified NEC R47.89
  swallowing – *see* Dysphagia
  taste - *see* Disturbance, sensation, taste
  tic, child F95.0
  underachievement in school Z55.3
  unemployment Z56.0
    threatened Z56.2
  unwanted pregnancy Z64.0
  upbringing Z62.9
    specified NEC Z62.898
  urinary N39.9
  voice production R47.89
  work schedule (stressful) Z56.3
Procedure (surgical)
  ear piercing Z41.3
    specified NEC Z41.8
  for purpose other than remedying
      health state Z41.9
    specified NEC Z41.8
  not done Z53.9
    because of
      administrative reasons Z53.8
      contraindication Z53.09
        smoking Z53.01
      patient's decision Z53.20
        for reasons of belief or group
            pressure Z53.1
        left against medical advice
            (AMA) Z53.21
        specified reason NEC Z53.29
      specified reason NEC Z53.8
Procidentia (uteri) N81.3
Proctalgia K62.8
  fugax K59.4
  spasmodic K59.4
Proctitis K62.8
  amebic (acute) A06.0
  chlamydial A56.3
  gonococcal A54.6

Proctitis *(Continued)*
  granulomatous - *see* Enteritis, regional,
      large intestine
  herpetic A60.1
  radiation K62.7
  tuberculous A18.32
  ulcerative (chronic) K51.20
    with
      complication K51.219
        abscess K51.214
        fistula K51.213
        obstruction K51.212
        rectal bleeding K51.211
        specified NEC K51.218
Proctocele
  female (without uterine prolapse) N81.6
    with uterine prolapse N81.2
      complete N81.3
  male K62.3
Proctocolitis, mucosal - *see* Rectosigmoid-
    itis, ulcerative
Proctoptosis K62.3
Proctorrhagia K62.5
Proctosigmoiditis K63.89
  ulcerative (chronic) – *see* Rectosigmoid-
      itis, ulcerative
Proctospasm K59.4
  psychogenic F45.8
Profichet's disease - *see* Disorder, soft tis-
    sue, specified type NEC
Progeria E34.8
Prognathism (mandibular) (maxillary)
    M26.19
Progonoma (melanotic) - *see* Neoplasm,
    benign
Progressive - *see* condition
Prolactinoma
  specified site - *see* Neoplasm, benign
  unspecified site D35.2
Prolapse, prolapsed
  anus, anal (canal) (sphincter) K62.2
  arm or hand O32.2
    causing obstructed labor O64.4
  bladder (mucosa) (sphincter) (acquired)
    congenital Q79.4
    female - *see* Cystocele
    male N32.89
  breast implant (prosthetic) T85.49
  cecostomy K94.19
  cecum K63.4
  cervix, cervical (hypertrophied) N81.2
    anterior lip, obstructing labor O65.5
    congenital Q51.8
    postpartal, old N81.2
    stump N81.85
  ciliary body (traumatic) – *see* Lacera-
      tion, eye(ball), with prolapse or
      loss of interocular tissue
  colon (pedunculated) K63.4
  colostomy K94.09
  disc (intervertebral) - *see* Displacement,
      intervertebral disc
  eye implant (orbital) T85.398
    lens (ocular) - *see* Complications,
        intraocular lens
  fallopian tube N83.4
  gastric (mucosa) K31.89
  genital, female N81.9
    specified NEC N81.89
  globe, nontraumatic - *see* Luxation, globe
  ileostomy bud K94.19
  intervertebral disc - *see* Displacement,
      intervertebral disc
  intestine (small) K63.4

Prolapse, prolapsed *(Continued)*
  iris (traumatic) – *see* Laceration,
      eye(ball), with prolapse or loss of
      interocular tissue
    nontraumatic H21.89
  kidney N28.83
    congenital Q63.2
  laryngeal muscles or ventricle J38.7
  liver K76.8
  meatus urinarius N36.8
  mitral (valve) I34.1
  ocular lens implant - *see* Complications,
      intraocular lens
  organ or site, congenital NEC - *see* Mal-
      position, congenital
  ovary N83.4
  pelvic floor, female N81.89
  perineum, female N81.89
  rectum (mucosa) (sphincter) K62.3
    due to trichuris trichuria B79
  spleen D73.89
  stomach K31.89
  umbilical cord
    complicating delivery O69.0
  urachus, congenital Q64.4
  ureter N28.89
    with obstruction N13.5
      with infection N13.6
  ureterovesical orifice N28.89
  urethra (acquired) (infected) (mucosa)
      N36.8
    congenital Q64.71
  urinary meatus N36.8
    congenital Q64.72
  uterovaginal N81.4
    complete N81.3
    incomplete N81.2
  uterus (with prolapse of vagina) N81.4
    complete N81.3
    congenital Q51.8
    first degree N81.2
    in pregnancy or childbirth - *see* Preg-
        nancy, complicated by, abnor-
        mal, uterus
    incomplete N81.2
    postpartal (old) N81.4
    second degree N81.2
    third degree N81.3
  uveal (traumatic) - *see* Laceration,
      eye(ball), with prolapse or loss of
      interocular tissue
  vagina (anterior) (wall) - *see* Cystocele
    with prolapse of uterus N81.4
      complete N81.3
      incomplete N81.2
    posterior wall N81.6
    posthysterectomy N99.3
  vitreous (humor) H43.0-
    in wound – *see* Laceration, eye(ball),
        with prolapse or loss of in-
        terocular tissue
  womb - *see* Prolapse, uterus
Prolapsus, female N81.9
  specified NEC N81.89
Proliferation(s)
  primary cutaneous CD30-positive T-cell
      C86.6
Proliferative - *see* condition
Prolonged, prolongation (of)
  bleeding (time) (idiopathic) R79.1
  coagulation (time) R79.1
  gestation (over 42 completed weeks)
    mother O48.1
    newborn P08.22

Prolonged, prolongation (Continued)
interval I44.0
labor O63.9
first stage O63.0
second stage O63.1
partial thromboplastin time (PTT)
R79.1
pregnancy (more than 42 weeks gestation) O48.1
prothrombin time R79.1
QT interval I45.81
uterine contractions in labor O62.4
Prominence, prominent
auricle (congenital) (ear) Q17.5
ischial spine or sacral promontory
with disproportion (fetopelvic) O33.0
causing obstructed labor O65.0
nose (congenital) acquired M95.0
Promiscuity – see High, risk, sexual
behavior
Pronation
ankle - see Deformity, limb, foot, specified NEC
foot - see also Deformity, limb, foot,
specified NEC
congenital Q74.2
Prophylactic
administration of
drug Z79.899 - see also Long-term
(current) drug therapy
(use of)
medication Z79.899
organ removal (for neoplasia management) Z40.00
breast Z40.01
ovary Z40.02
specified site NEC Z40.09
surgery Z40.9
for risk factors related to malignant
neoplasm – see Prophylactic,
organ removal
specified NEC Z40.8
vaccination Z23
Propionic acidemia E71.121
Proptosis (ocular) - see also Exophthalmos
thyroid - see Hyperthyroidism, with
goiter
Prosecution, anxiety concerning Z65.3
Prosopagnosia H53.16
Prostadynia N42.81
Prostate, prostatic - see condition
Prostatism – see Hyperplasia, prostate
Prostatitis (congestive) (suppurative)
(with cystitis) N41.9
acute N41.00
with hematuria N41.01
cavitary N41.8
chronic N41.10
with hematuria N41.11
diverticular N41.8
due to Trichomonas (vaginalis) A59.02
fibrous N41.10
with hematuria N41.11
gonococcal (acute) (chronic) A54.22
granulomatous N41.4
hypertrophic N41.10
with hematuria N41.11
subacute N41.10
with hematuria N41.11
trichomonal A59.02
tuberculous A18.14
Prostatocystitis N41.3
Prostatorrhea N42.89
Prostatosis N42.82

Prostration R53.83
heat - see also Heat, exhaustion
anhydrotic T67.3
due to
salt (and water) depletion T67.4
water depletion T67.3
nervous F48.8
senile R54
Protanomaly (anomalous trichromat)
H53.54
Protanopia (complete) (incomplete)
H53.54
Protection (against) (from) - see
Prophylactic
Protein
deficiency NEC - see Malnutrition
malnutrition - see Malnutrition
sickness (prophylactic) (therapeutic)
T80.6
Proteinemia R77.9
Proteinosis
alveolar (pulmonary) J84.0
lipid or lipoid (of Urbach) E78.89
Proteinuria R80.9
Bence Jones R80.3
complicating pregnancy – see Proteinuria, gestational
superimposed on pre-existing
hypertensive disorder – see
Hypertension, complicating,
pregnancy, pre-existing, with,
proteinuria
gestational O12.1-
with edema O12.2-
idiopathic R80.0
isolated R80.0
with glomerular lesion N06.9
dense deposit disease N06.6
diffuse
crescentic glomerulonephritis
N06.7
endocapillary proliferative glomerulonephritis N06.4
mesangiocapillary glomerulonephritis N06.5
focal and segmental hyalinosis or
sclerosis N06.1
membranous (diffuse) N06.2
mesangial proliferative (diffuse)
N06.3
minimal change N06.0
specified pathology NEC N06.8
orthostatic R80.2
with glomerular lesion - see Proteinuria, isolated, with glomerular
lesion
persistent R80.1
with glomerular lesion - see Proteinuria, isolated, with glomerular
lesion
postural R80.2
with glomerular lesion - see Proteinuria, isolated, with glomerular
lesion
pre-eclamptic - see Pre-eclampsia
specified type NEC R80.8
Proteolysis, pathologic D65
Proteus (mirabilis) (morganii), as cause of
disease classified elsewhere B96.4
Prothrombin gene mutation D68.52
Protoporphyria, erythropoietic E80.0
Protozoal - see also condition
disease B64
specified NEC B60.8

Protrusion, protrusio
acetabuli M24.7
acetabulum (into pelvis) M24.7
device, implant or graft (see also
Complications, by site and type,
mechanical) T85.628
arterial graft NEC - see Complication,
cardiovascular device, mechanical, vascular
breast (implant) T85.49
catheter NEC T85.628
cystostomy T83.090
dialysis (renal) T82.49
intraperitoneal T85.691
infusion NEC T82.594
spinal (epidural) (subdural)
T85.690
electronic (electrode) (pulse generator) (stimulator)
bone T84.390
nervous system - see Complication,
prosthetic device, mechanical, electronic nervous system
stimulator
fixation, internal (orthopedic) NEC -
see Complication, fixation device, mechanical
gastrointestinal - see Complications,
prosthetic device, mechanical,
gastrointestinal device
genital NEC T83.498
intrauterine contraceptive device
T83.39
penile prosthesis T83.490
heart NEC - see Complication,
cardiovascular device,
mechanical
joint prosthesis – see Complications,
joint prosthesis, mechanical,
specified NEC, by site
ocular NEC - see Complications,
prosthetic device, mechanical,
ocular device
orthopedic NEC - see Complication,
orthopedic, device, mechanical
specified NEC T85.628
urinary NEC - see also Complication,
genitourinary, device, urinary,
mechanical
graft T83.29
vascular NEC - see Complication, cardiovascular device,
mechanical
ventricular intracranial shunt T85.09
intervertebral disc - see Displacement,
intervertebral disc
joint prosthesis - see Complications,
joint prosthesis, mechanical, specified NEC, by site
nucleus pulposus - see Displacement,
intervertebral disc
Prune belly (syndrome) Q79.4
Prurigo (ferox) (gravis) (Hebrae) (Hebra's)
(mitis) (simplex) L28.2
Besnier's L20.0
estivalis L56.4
nodularis L28.1
psychogenic F45.8
Pruritus, pruritic (essential) L29.9
ani, anus L29.0
psychogenic F45.8
anogenital L29.3
psychogenic F45.8
due to onchocerca volvulus B73.1

Pruritus, pruritic (Continued)
  gravidarum – see Pregnancy, compli-
    cated by, specified pregnancy-
    related condition NEC
  hiemalis L29.8
  neurogenic (any site) F45.8
  perianal L29.0
  psychogenic (any site) F45.8
  scroti, scrotum L29.1
    psychogenic F45.8
  senile, senilis L29.8
  specified NEC L29.8
    psychogenic F45.8
  Trichomonas A59.9
  vulva, vulvae L29.2
    psychogenic F45.8
Pseudarthrosis, pseudoarthrosis (bone) -
    see Nonunion, fracture
  clavicle, congenital Q74.0
  joint, following fusion or arthrodesis
    M96.0
Pseudoaneurysm - see Aneurysm
Pseudoangioma I81
Pseudoangina (pectoris) - see Angina
Pseudoarteriosus Q28.8
Pseudoarthrosis - see Pseudarthrosis
Pseudobulbar affect (PBA) F48.8
Pseudochromhidrosis L67.8
Pseudocirrhosis, liver, pericardial I31.1
Pseudocowpox B08.03
Pseudocoxalgia M91.3-
Pseudocroup J38.5
Pseudo-Cushing's syndrome, alcohol-
    induced E24.4
Pseudocyesis F45.8
Pseudocyst
  lung J98.4
  pancreas K86.3
  retina - see Cyst, retina
Pseudoelephantiasis neuroarthritica
    Q82.0
Pseudoexfoliation, capsule (lens) – see
    Cataract, specified NEC
Pseudofolliculitis barbae L73.1
Pseudoglioma H44.89
Pseudohemophilia (Bernuth's) (heredi-
    tary) (type B) D68.0
  Type A D69.8
  vascular D69.8
Pseudohermaphroditism Q56.3
  adrenal E25.8
  female Q56.2
    with adrenocortical disorder E25.8
    without adrenocortical disorder
      Q56.2
    adrenal, congenital E25.0
  male Q56.1
    with
      adrenocortical disorder E25.8
      androgen resistance E34.51
      cleft scrotum Q56.1
      feminizing testis E34.51
      5-alpha-reductase deficiency
        E29.1
    without gonadal disorder Q56.1
    adrenal E25.8
Pseudo-Hurler's polydystrophy
    E77.0
Pseudohydrocephalus G93.2
Pseudohypertrophic muscular dystrophy
    (Erb's) G71.0
Pseudohypertrophy, muscle G71.0
Pseudohypoparathyroidism E20.1
Pseudoinsomnia F51.03

Pseudoleukemia, infantile D64.89
Pseudomembranous - see condition
Pseudomenses (newborn) P54.6
Pseudomenstruation (newborn) P54.6
Pseudomeningocele (cerebral) (infective)
    (post-traumatic) G96.19
  postprocedural (spinal) G97.82
Pseudomonas
  aeruginosa, as cause of disease classi-
    fied elsewhere B96.5
  mallei infection A24.0
    as cause of disease classified else-
      where B96.5
  pseudomallei, as cause of disease
    classified elsewhere B96.5
Pseudomyotonia G71.19
Pseudomyxoma peritonei (M8480/6) C78.6
Pseudoneuritis, optic (nerve) (disc)
    (papilla), congenital Q14.2
Pseudo-obstruction intestine (acute)
    (chronic) (idiopathic) (intermittent
    secondary) (primary) K59.8
Pseudopapilledema H47.33-
  congenital Q14.2
Pseudoparalysis
  arm or leg R29.81
  atonic, congenital P94.2
Pseudopelade L66.0
Pseudophakia Z96.1
Pseudopolyarthritis, rhizomelic M35.3
Pseudopolycythemia D75.1
Pseudopseudohypoparathyroidism
    E20.1
Pseudopterygium H11.81-
Pseudoptosis (eyelid) - see
    Blepharochalasis
Pseudopuberty, precocious
  female heterosexual E25.8
  male isosexual E25.8
Pseudorickets (renal) N25.0
Pseudorubella B08.20
Pseudosclerema, newborn P83.8
Pseudosclerosis (brain)
  of Westphal (Strüümpell) E83.01
  Jakob's - see Creutzfeldt-Jakob disease
    or syndrome
  spastic - see Creutzfeldt-Jakob disease
    or syndrome
Pseudotetanus - see Convulsions
Pseudotetany R29.0
  hysterical F44.5
Pseudotruncus arteriosus Q25.4
Pseudotuberculosis A28.2
  enterocolitis A04.8
  pasteurella (infection) A28.0
Pseudotumor
  cerebri G93.2
  orbital - see Inflammation, orbit
Pseudoxanthoma elasticum Q82.8
Psilosis (sprue) (tropical) K90.1
  nontropical K90.0
Psittacosis A70
Psoitis M60.88
Psoriasis L40.9
  arthropathic L40.50
    arthritis mutilans L40.52
    distal interphalangeal L40.51
    juvenile L40.54
    other specified L40.59
    spondylitis L40.53
  buccal K13.29
  flexural L40.8
  guttate L40.4
  mouth K13.29

Psoriasis (Continued)
  nummular L40.0
  plaque L40.0
  psychogenic F54
  pustular (generalized) L40.1
    palmaris et plantaris L40.3
  specified NEC L40.8
  vulgaris L40.0
Psychasthenia F48.8
Psychiatric disorder or problem F99
Psychogenic - see also condition
  factors associated with physical
    conditions F54
Psychological and behavioral factors
    affecting medical condition F59
Psychoneurosis, psychoneurotic -
    see also Neurosis
  anxiety (state) F41.1
  depersonalization F48.1
  hypochondriacal F45.21
  hysteria F44.9
  neurasthenic F48.8
  personality NEC F60.89
Psychopathy, psychopathic
  affectionless F94.2
  autistic F84.5
  constitution, post-traumatic F07.81
  personality - see Disorder, personality
  sexual - see Deviation, sexual
  state F60.2
Psychosexual identity disorder of
    childhood F64.2
Psychosis, psychotic F29
  acute (transient) F23
    hysterical F44.9
  affective – see Disorder, mood
  alcoholic F10.959
    with
      abuse F10.159
      anxiety disorder F10.980
        with
          abuse F10.180
          dependence F10.280
      delirium tremens F10.231
      delusions F10.950
        with
          abuse F10.150
          dependence F10.250
      dementia F10.97
        with dependence F10.27
      dependence F10.259
      hallucinosis F10.951
        with
          abuse F10.151
          dependence F10.251
      mood disorder F10.94
        with
          abuse F10.14
          dependence F10.24
      paranoia F10.950
        with
          abuse F10.150
          dependence F10.250
      persisting amnesia F10.96
        with dependence F10.26
    amnestic confabulatory F10.96
      with dependence F10.26
    delirium tremens F10.231
    Korsakoff's, Korsakov's, Korsakow's
      F10.26
    paranoid type F10.950
      with
        abuse F10.150
        dependence F10.250

Psychosis, psychotic *(Continued)*
  anergastic - *see* Psychosis, organic
  arteriosclerotic (simple type) (uncomplicated) F01.50
    with behavioral disturbance F01.51
  childhood F84.0
    atypical F84.8
  climacteric - *see* Psychosis, involutional
  confusional F29
    acute or subacute F05
    reactive F23
  cycloid F23
  depressive – *see* Disorder, depressive
  disintegrative (childhood) F84.3
  drug-induced - *see* F11-F19 with .x59
    paranoid and hallucinatory states - *see* F11-F19 with .x50 or .x51
  due to or associated with
    addiction, drug - *see* F11 - F19 with .x59
    dependence
      alcohol F10.259
      drug - *see* F11-F19 with .x59
    epilepsy F06.8
    Huntington's chorea F06.8
    ischemia, cerebrovascular (generalized) F06.8
    multiple sclerosis F06.8
    physical disease F06.8
    presenile dementia F03
    senile dementia F03
    vascular disease (arteriosclerotic) (cerebral) F01.50
      with behavioral disturbance F01.51
  epileptic F06.8
  episode F23
    due to or associated with physical condition F06.8
  exhaustive F43.0
  hallucinatory, chronic F28
  hypomanic F30.8
  hysterical (acute) F44.9
  induced F24
  infantile F84.0
    atypical F84.8
  infective (acute) (subacute) F05
  involutional F28
    depressive – *see* Disorder, depressive
    melancholic – *see* Disorder, depressive
    paranoid (state) F22
  Korsakoff's, Korsakov's, Korsakow's (nonalcoholic) F04
    alcoholic F10.96
      in dependence F10.26
    induced by other psychoactive substance - *see* categories F11-F19 with .x5x
  mania, manic (single episode) F30.2
    recurrent type F31.89
  manic-depressive – *see* Disorder, mood
  menopausal - *see* Psychosis, involutional
  mixed schizophrenic and affective F25.8
  multi-infarct (cerebrovascular) F01.50
    with behavioral disturbance F01.51
  nonorganic F29
    specified NEC F28

Psychosis, psychotic *(Continued)*
  organic F09
    due to or associated with
      arteriosclerosis (cerebral) - *see* Psychosis, arteriosclerotic
      cerebrovascular disease, arteriosclerotic - *see* Psychosis, arteriosclerotic
      childbirth - *see* Psychosis, puerperal
      Creutzfeldt-Jakob disease or syndrome - *see* Creutzfeldt-Jakob disease or syndrome
      dependence, alcohol F10.259
      disease
        alcoholic liver F10.259
        brain, arteriosclerotic - *see* Psychosis, arteriosclerotic
        cerebrovascular F01.50
          with behavioral disturbance F01.51
        Creutzfeldt-Jakob - *see* Creutzfeldt-Jakob disease or syndrome
        endocrine or metabolic F06.8
          acute or subacute F05
        liver, alcoholic F10.259
      epilepsy transient (acute) F05
      infection
        brain (intracranial) F06.8
          acute or subacute F05
      intoxication
        alcoholic (acute) F10.259
        drug F11 - F19 with .x59
      ischemia, cerebrovascular (generalized) - *see* Psychosis, arteriosclerotic
      puerperium - *see* Psychosis, puerperal
      trauma, brain (birth) (from electric current) (surgical) F06.8
        acute or subacute F05
    infective F06.8
      acute or subacute F05
    post-traumatic F06.8
      acute or subacute F05
  paranoiac F22
  paranoid (climacteric) (involutional) (menopausal) F22
    psychogenic (acute) F23
    schizophrenic F20.0
    senile F03
  postpartum F53
  presbyophrenic (type) F03
  presenile F03
  psychogenic (paranoid) F23
    depressive F32.3
  puerperal F53
    specified type - *see* Psychosis, by type
  reactive (brief) (transient) (emotional stress) (psychological trauma) F23
    depressive F32.3
      recurrent F33.3
    excitative type F30.8
  schizoaffective F25.9
    depressive type F25.1
    manic type F25.0
  schizophrenia, schizophrenic - *see* Schizophrenia
  schizophrenia-like, in epilepsy F06.2
  schizophreniform F20.81
    affective type F25.9
    brief F23
    confusional type F23

Psychosis, psychotic *(Continued)*
  schizophreniform *(Continued)*
    depressive type F25.1
    manic type F25.0
    mixed type F25.8
    senile NEC F03
      depressed or paranoid type F03
      simple deterioration F03
      specified type - code to condition
    shared F24
    situational (reactive) F23
    symbiotic (childhood) F84.3
    symptomatic F09
Psychosomatic - *see* Disorder, psychosomatic
Psychosyndrome, organic F07.9
Psychotic episode due to or associated with physical condition F06.8
Pterygium (eye) H11.00-
  amyloid H11.01-
  central H11.02-
  colli Q18.3
  double H11.03-
  peripheral
    progressive H11.05-
    stationary H11.04-
  recurrent H11.06-
Ptilosis (eyelid) - *see* Madarosis
Ptomaine (poisoning) - *see* Poisoning, food
Ptosis - *see also* Blepharoptosis
  adiposa (false) - *see* Blepharoptosis
  breast N64.81
  cecum K63.4
  colon K63.4
  congenital (eyelid) Q10.0
    specified site NEC - *see* Anomaly, by site
  eyelid - *see* Blepharoptosis
    congenital Q10.0
  gastric K31.89
  intestine K63.4
  kidney N28.83
  liver K76.8
  renal N28.83
  splanchnic K63.4
  spleen D73.89
  stomach K31.89
  viscera K63.4
Ptyalism (periodic) K11.7
  hysterical F45.8
  pregnancy – *see* Pregnancy, complicated by, specified pregnancy-related condition NEC
  psychogenic F45.8
Ptyalolithiasis K11.5
Pubarche, precocious E30.1
Pubertas praecox E30.1
Puberty (development state) Z00.3
  bleeding (excessive) N92.2
  delayed E30.0
  precocious (constitutional) (cryptogenic) (idiopathic) E30.1
    central E22.8
    due to
      ovarian hyperfunction E28.1
        estrogen E28.0
      testicular hyperfunction E29.0
  premature E30.1
    due to
      adrenal cortical hyperfunction E25.8
      pineal tumor E34.8
      pituitary (anterior) hyperfunction E22.8

Puckering, macula - *see* Degeneration, macula, puckering
Pudenda, pudendum - *see* condition
Puente's disease (simple glandular cheilitis) K13.0
Puerperal, puerperium (complicated by, complications)
　abnormal glucose (tolerance test) O99.815
　abscess
　　areola O91.02
　　　associated with lactation O91.03
　　Bartholin's gland O86.19
　　breast O91.12
　　　associated with lactation O91.13
　　cervix (uteri) O86.11
　　genital organ O86.19
　　kidney O86.21
　　mammary O91.12
　　　associated with lactation O91.13
　　nipple O91.02
　　　associated with lactation O91.03
　　peritoneum O85
　　subareolar O91.12
　　　associated with lactation O91.13
　　urinary tract – *see* Puerperal, infection, urinary
　　uterus O86.19
　　vagina (wall) O86.13
　　vaginorectal O86.13
　　vulvovaginal gland O86.13
　adnexitis O86.19
　afibrinogenemia, or other coagulation defect O72.3
　albuminuria (acute) (subacute) – *see* Proteinuria, gestational
　alcohol use O99.315
　anemia (pre-exisitng) O99.03
　anesthetic death O89.8
　apoplexy O99.43
　bariatric surgery status O99.845
　blood disorder NEC O99.13
　blood dyscrasia O72.3
　cardiomyopathy O90.3
　cerebrovascular disorder (conditions in I60-I69) O99.43
　cervicitis O86.11
　circulatory system disorder O99.43
　coagulopathy (any) O72.3
　complications O90.9
　　specified NEC O90.89
　convulsions – *see* Eclampsia
　cystitis O86.22
　cystopyelitis O86.29
　delirium NEC F05
　diabetes O24.93
　　gestational - *see* Puerperal, gestational diabetes
　　pre-existing O24.33
　　　specified NEC O24.83
　　　type 1 O24.03
　　　type 2 O24.13
　digestive system disorder O99.63
　disease O90.9
　　breast NEC O92.29
　　cerebrovascular (acute) O99.43
　　nonobstetric NEC O99.89
　　tubo-ovarian O86.19
　　Valsuani's O99.03
　disorder O90.9
　　lactation O92.79
　　nonobstetric NEC O99.89

Puerperal, puerperium (Continued)
　disruption
　　cesarean wound O90.0
　　episiotomy wound O90.1
　　perineal laceration wound O90.1
　drug use O99.325
　eclampsia (with pre-existing hypertension) O15.2
　embolism (pulmonary) (blood clot) – *see* Embolism, obstetric, puerperal
　endocrine, nutritional or metabolic disease NEC O99.285
　endophlebitis - *see* Puerperal, phlebitis
　endotrachelitis O86.19
　failure
　　lactation (complete) O92.3
　　　partial O92.4
　　renal, acute O90.4
　fever (sepsis) O85
　　pyrexia (of unknown origin) O86.4
　fissure, nipple O92.12
　　associated with lactation O92.13
　fistula
　　breast (due to mastitis) O91.12
　　　associated with lactation O91.13
　　nipple O91.02
　　　associated with lactation O91.03
　galactophoritis O91.22
　　associated with lactation O91.23
　galactorrhea O92.6
　gastric banding status O99.845
　gastric bypass status O99.845
　gastrointestinal disease NEC O99.63
　gestational diabetes O24.439
　　diet controlled O24.430
　　insulin (and diet) controlled O24.431
　gonorrhea O98.23
　hematoma, subdural O99.43
　hemiplegia, cerebral O99.35-
　　due to cerebrovascular disorder O99.43
　hemorrhage O72.1
　　brain O99.43
　　bulbar O99.43
　　cerebellar O99.43
　　cerebral O99.43
　　cortical O99.43
　　delayed or secondary O72.2
　　extradural O99.43
　　internal capsule O99.43
　　intracranial O99.43
　　intrapontine O99.43
　　meningeal O99.43
　　pontine O99.43
　　retained placenta O72.0
　　subarachnoid O99.43
　　subcortical O99.43
　　subdural O99.43
　　third stage O72.0
　　uterine, delayed O72.2
　　ventricular O99.43
　hemorrhoids O87.2
　hepatorenal syndrome O90.4
　hypertension - *see* Hypertension, complicating, puerperium
　hypertrophy, breast O92.29
　induration breast (fibrous) O92.29
　infection O86.4
　　cervix O86.11
　　generalized O85
　　genital tract NEC O86.19
　　　obstetric surgical wound O86.0
　　kidney (bacillus coli) O86.21

Puerperal, puerperium (Continued)
　infection (Continued)
　　maternal O98.93
　　　carrier state NEC O99.835
　　　gonorrhea O98.23
　　　human immunodeficiency [HIV] O98.73
　　　protozoal O98.63
　　　sexually transmitted NEC O98.33
　　　specified NEC O98.83
　　　streptococcus B carrier state O99.825
　　　syphilis O98.13
　　　tuberculosis O98.03
　　　viral hepatitis O98.43
　　　viral NEC O98.53
　　nipple O91.02
　　　associated with lactation O91.03
　　peritoneum O85
　　renal O86.21
　　specified NEC O86.89
　　urinary (asymptomatic) (tract) NEC O86.20
　　　bladder O86.22
　　　kidney O86.21
　　　specified site NEC O86.29
　　　urethra O86.22
　　vagina O86.13
　　vein - *see* Puerperal, phlebitis
　ischemia, cerebral O99.43
　lymphangitis O86.89
　　breast O91.22
　　　associated with lactation O91.23
　malignancy O9A.13
　malnutrition O25.3
　mammillitis O91.02
　　associated with lactation O91.03
　mammitis O91.22
　　associated with lactation O91.23
　mania F30.8
　mastitis O91.22
　　associated with lactation O91.23
　　purulent O91.12
　　　associated with lactation O91.13
　melancholia – *see* Disorder, depressive
　mental disorder NEC O99.345
　metroperitonitis O85
　metrorrhagia - *see* Hemorrhage, postpartum
　metrosalpingitis O86.19
　metrovaginitis O86.13
　milk leg O87.1
　monoplegia, cerebral O99.43
　mood disturbance O90.6
　necrosis, liver (acute) (subacute) (conditions in subcategory K72.0) O26.63
　　with renal failure O90.4
　nervous system disorder O99.355
　obesity (pre-exisiting prior to pregnancy) O99.215
　obesity surgery status O99.845
　occlusion, precerebral artery O99.43
　paralysis
　　bladder (sphincter) O90.89
　　cerebral O99.43
　paralytic stroke O99.43
　parametritis O85
　paravaginitis O86.13
　pelviperitonitis O85
　perimetritis O86.19
　perimetrosalpingitis O86.19
　perinephritis O86.21
　periphlebitis - *see* Puerperal phlebitis
　peritoneal infection O85

P

Puerperal, puerperium *(Continued)*
  peritonitis (pelvic) O85
  perivaginitis O86.13
  phlebitis O87.0
    deep O87.1
    pelvic O87.1
    superficial O87.0
  phlebothrombosis, deep O87.1
  phlegmasia alba dolens O87.1
  placental polyp O90.89
  pneumonia, embolic - *see* Embolism,
      obstetric, puerperal
  pre-eclampsia - *see* Pre-eclampsia
  psychosis F53
  pyelitis O86.21
  pyelocystitis O86.29
  pyelonephritis O86.21
  pyelonephrosis O86.21
  pyemia O85
  pyocystitis O86.29
  pyohemia O85
  pyometra O86.19
  pyonephritis O86.21
  pyosalpingitis O86.19
  pyrexia (of unknown origin)
      O86.4
  renal
    disease NEC O90.89
    failure O90.4
  respiratory disease NEC O99.53
  retention
    decidua - *see* Retention, decidua
    placenta O72.0
    secundines - *see* Retention,
        secundines
  retrated nipple O92.02
  salpingo-ovaritis O86.19
  salpingoperitonitis O85
  secondary perineal tear O90.1
  sepsis (pelvic) O85
  sepsis O85
  septic thrombophlebitis O86.81
  skin disorder NEC O99.73
  specified condition NEC O99.89
  stroke O99.43
  subinvolution (uterus) O90.89
  subluxation of symphysis (pubis)
      O26.73
  suppuration - *see* Puerperal, abscess
  tetanus A34
  thelitis O91.02
    associated with lactation O91.03
  thrombocytopenia O72.3
  thrombophlebitis (superficial)
      O87.0
    deep O87.1
    pelvic O87.1
    septic O86.81
  thrombosis (venous) - *see* Thrombosis,
      puerperal
  thyroiditis O90.5
  toxemia (eclamptic) (pre-eclamptic)
      (with convulsions) O15.2
  trauma, non-obstetric O9A.23
    caused by abuse (physical) (sus-
        pected) O9A.33
      confirmed O9A.33
      psychological (suspected)
          O9A.53
        confirmed O9A.53
      sexual (suspected) O9A.43
        confirmed O9A.43
  uremia (due to renal failure)
      O90.4

Puerperal, puerperium *(Continued)*
  urethritis O86.22
  vaginitis O86.13
  varicose veins (legs) O87.4
    vulva or perineum O87.8
  venous O87.9
  vulvitis O86.19
  vulvovaginitis O86.13
  white leg O87.1
Puerperium - *see* Puerperal
Pulmolithiasis J98.4
Pulmonary - *see* condition
Pulpitis (acute) (anachoretic) (chronic)
    (hyperplastic) (putrescent)
    (suppurative) (ulcerative) K04.0
Pulpless tooth K04.99
Pulse
  alternating R00.8
  bigeminal R00.8
  fast R00.0
  feeble, rapid due to shock following
      injury T79.4
  rapid R00.0
  weak R09.89
Pulsus alternans or trigeminus
    R00.8
Punch drunk F07.81
Punctum lacrimale occlusion - *see*
    Obstruction, lacrimal
Puncture
  abdomen, abdominal
    wall S31.139
      with
        foreign body S31.149
        penetration into peritoneal
            cavity S31.639
          with foreign body S31.649
      epigastric region S31.132
        with
          foreign body S31.142
          penetration into peritoneal
              cavity S31.632
            with foreign body
                S31.642
      left
        lower quadrant S31.134
          with
            foreign body S31.144
            penetration into peritoneal
                cavity S31.634
              with foreign body
                  S31.644
        upper quadrant S31.131
          with
            foreign body S31.141
            penetration into peritoneal
                cavity S31.631
              with foreign body
                  S31.641
      periumbilic region S31.135
        with
          foreign body S31.145
          penetration into peritoneal
              cavity S31.635
            with foreign body
                S31.645
      right
        lower quadrant S31.133
          with
            foreign body S31.143
            penetration into peritoneal
                cavity S31.633
              with foreign body
                  S31.643

Puncture *(Continued)*
  abdomen, abdominal *(Continued)*
    wall *(Continued)*
      right *(Continued)*
        upper quadrant S31.130
          with
            foreign body S31.140
            penetration into peritoneal
                cavity S31.630
              with foreign body
                  S31.640
  accidental, complicating surgery - *see*
      Complication, accidental puncture
      or laceration
  alveolar (process) – *see* Puncture, oral
      cavity
  ankle S91.039
    with
      foreign body S91.049
    left S91.032
      with
        foreign body S91.042
    right S91.031
      with
        foreign body S91.041
  anus S31.833
    with foreign body S31.834
  arm (upper) S41.139
    with foreign body S41.149
    left S41.132
      with foreign body S41.142
    lower – *see* Puncture, forearm
    right S41.131
      with foreign body S41.141
  auditory canal (external) (meatus) –
      see Puncture, ear
  auricle, ear – *see* Puncture, ear
  axilla – *see* Puncture, arm
  back - *see also* Puncture, thorax, back
    lower S31.030
      with
        foreign body S31.040
          with penetration into
              retroperitoneal space
              S31.041
        penetration into retroperitoneal
            space S31.031
  bladder (traumatic) S37.28
    nontraumatic N32.89
  breast S21.039
    with foreign body S21.049
    left S21.032
      with foreign body S21.042
    right S21.031
      with foreign body S21.041
  buttock S31.803
    with foreign body S31.804
    left S31.823
      with foreign body S31.824
    right S31.813
      with foreign body S31.814
  by
    device, implant or graft - *see* Com-
        plications, by site and type,
        mechanical
    foreign body left accidentally in
        operative wound T81.539
    instrument (any) during a procedure,
        accidental – *see* Puncture, ac-
        cidental complicating surgery
  calf – *see* Puncture, leg
  canaliculus lacrimalis – *see* Puncture,
      eyelid
  canthus, eye – *see* Puncture, eyelid

Puncture *(Continued)*
  cervical esophagus S11.23
    with foreign body S11.24
  cheek (external) S01.439
    with foreign body S01.449
    left S01.432
      with foreign body S01.442
    right S01.431
      with foreign body S01.441
    internal – *see* Puncture, oral
      cavity
  chest wall – *see* Puncture, thorax
  chin – *see* Puncture, head, specified
    site NEC
  clitoris – *see* Puncture, vulva
  costal region - *see* Puncture,
    thorax
  digit(s)
    hand – *see* Puncture, finger
    foot - *see* Puncture, toe
  ear (canal) (external) S01.339
    with foreign body S01.349
    left S01.332
      with foreign body S01.342
    right S01.331
      with foreign body S01.341
    drum S09.2-
  elbow S51.039
    with
      foreign body S51.049
    left S51.032
      with
        foreign body S51.042
    right S51.031
      with
        foreign body S51.041
  epididymis – *see* Puncture, testis
  epigastric region - *see* Puncture,
    abdomen, wall, epigastric
  epiglottis S11.83
    with foreign body S11.84
  esophagus
    cervical S11.23
      with foreign body S11.24
    thoracic S27.818
  eyeball S05.6-
    with foreign body S05.5-
  eyebrow – *see* Puncture, eyelid
  eyelid S01.13-
    with foreign body S01.14-
    left S01.132
      with foreign body S01.142
    right S01.131
      with foreign body S01.141
  face NEC – *see* Puncture, head,
    specified site NEC
  finger(s) S61.239
    with
      damage to nail S61.339
        with
          foreign body S61.349
      foreign body S61.249
    index S61.238
      with
        damage to nail S61.338
          with
            foreign body S61.348
        foreign body S61.248
      left S61.231
        with
          damage to nail S61.331
            with
              foreign body S61.341
        foreign body S61.241

Puncture *(Continued)*
  finger(s) *(Continued)*
    index *(Continued)*
      right S61.230
        with
          damage to nail S61.330
            with
              foreign body S61.340
          foreign body S61.240
    little S61.238
      with
        damage to nail S61.338
          with
            foreign body S61.348
        foreign body S61.248
      left S61.237
        with
          damage to nail S61.337
            with
              foreign body S61.347
          foreign body S61.247
      right S61.236
        with
          damage to nail S61.336
            with
              foreign body S61.346
          foreign body S61.246
    middle S61.238
      with
        damage to nail S61.338
          with
            foreign body S61.348
        foreign body S61.248
      left S61.233
        with
          damage to nail S61.333
            with
              foreign body S61.343
          foreign body S61.243
      right S61.232
        with
          damage to nail S61.332
            with
              foreign body S61.342
          foreign body S61.242
    ring S61.238
      with
        damage to nail S61.338
          with
            foreign body S61.348
        foreign body S61.248
      left S61.235
        with
          damage to nail S61.335
            with
              foreign body
                S61.345
          foreign body S61.245
      right S61.234
        with
          damage to nail S61.334
            with
              foreign body S61.344
          foreign body S61.244
  flank S31.139
    with foreign body S31.149
  foot (except toe(s) alone)
    S91.339
    with foreign body S91.349
    left S91.332
      with foreign body S91.342
    right S91.331
      with foreign body S91.341
  toe – *see* Puncture, toe

Puncture *(Continued)*
  forearm S51.839
    with
      foreign body S51.849
    elbow only – *see* Puncture, elbow
    left S51.832
      with
        foreign body S51.842
    right S51.831
      with
        foreign body S51.841
  forehead – *see* Puncture, head, specified
    site NEC
  genital organs, external
    female S31.532
      with foreign body S31.542
      vagina – *see* Puncture, vagina
      vulva – *see* Puncture, vulva
    male S31.531
      with foreign body S31.541
      penis – *see* Puncture, penis
      scrotum – *see* Puncture, scrotum
      testis – *see* Puncture, testis
  groin - *see* Puncture, abdomen,
    wall
  gum – *see* Puncture, oral cavity
  hand S61.439
    with
      foreign body S61.449
    finger - *see* Puncture, finger
    left S61.432
      with
        foreign body S61.442
    right S61.431
      with
        foreign body S61.441
    thumb - *see* Puncture, thumb
  head S01.93
    with foreign body S01.94
    cheek – *see* Puncture, cheek
    ear – *see* Puncture, ear
    eyelid – *see* Puncture, eyelid
    lip – *see* Puncture, oral cavity
    nose – *see* Puncture, nose
    oral cavity – *see* Puncture, oral
      cavity
    scalp S01.03
      with foreign body S01.04
    specified site NEC S01.83
      with foreign body S01.84
    temporomandibular area – *see* Punc-
      ture, cheek
  heart S26.99
    with hemopericardium S26.09
    without hemopericardium
      S26.19
  heel – *see* Puncture, foot
  hip S71.039
    with foreign body S71.049
    left S71.032
      with foreign body S71.042
    right S71.031
      with foreign body S71.041
  hymen – *see* Puncture, vagina
  hypochondrium - *see* Puncture, abdo-
    men, wall
  hypogastric region - *see* Puncture, abdo-
    men, wall
  inguinal region - *see* Puncture, abdo-
    men, wall
  instep – *see* Puncture, foot
  internal organs - *see* Injury, by site
  interscapular region - *see* Puncture,
    thorax, back

Puncture *(Continued)*
  intestine
    large
      colon S36.599
        ascending S36.590
        descending S36.592
        sigmoid S36.593
        specified site NEC S36.598
        transverse S36.591
      rectum S36.69
    small S36.499
      duodenum S36.490
      specified site NEC S36.498
  intra-abdominal organ S36.99
    gallbladder S36.128
    intestine - *see* Puncture, intestine
    liver S36.118
    pancreas - *see* Puncture,
      pancreas
    peritoneum S36.81
    specified site NEC S36.898
    spleen S36.09
    stomach S36.39
  jaw – *see* Puncture, head, specified site
    NEC
  knee S81.039
    with foreign body S81.049
    left S81.032
      with foreign body S81.042
    right S81.031
      with foreign body S81.041
  labium (majus) (minus) – *see* Puncture,
    vulva
  lacrimal duct – *see* Puncture,
    eyelid
  larynx S11.013
    with foreign body S11.014
  leg (lower) S81.839
    with foreign body S81.849
    foot – *see* Puncture, foot
    knee – *see* Puncture, knee
    left S81.832
      with foreign body S81.842
    right S81.831
      with foreign body S81.841
    upper – *see* Puncture, thigh
  lip S01.531
    with foreign body S01.541
  loin - *see* Puncture, abdomen, wall
  lower back - *see* Puncture, back,
    lower
  lumbar region – *see* Puncture, back,
    lower
  malar region – *see* Puncture, head,
    specified site NEC
  mammary – *see* Puncture, breast
  mastoid region – *see* Puncture, head,
    specified site NEC
  mouth – *see* Puncture, oral cavity
  nail
    finger – *see* Puncture, finger, with
      damage to nail
    toe – *see* Puncture, toe, with damage
      to nail
  nasal (septum) (sinus) – *see* Puncture,
    nose
  nasopharynx – *see* Puncture, head,
    specified site NEC
  neck S11.93
    with foreign body S11.94
    involving
      cervical esophagus – *see* Puncture,
        cervical esophagus
      larynx – *see* Puncture, larynx

Puncture *(Continued)*
  neck *(Continued)*
    involving *(Continued)*
      pharynx – *see* Puncture, pharynx
      thyroid gland – *see* Puncture,
        thyroid gland
      trachea – *see* Puncture, trachea
    specified site NEC S11.83
      with foreign body S11.84
  nose (septum) (sinus) S01.23
    with foreign body S01.24
  ocular – *see* Puncture, eyeball - oral
    cavity S01.532
    with foreign body S01.542
  orbit S05.4-
  palate – *see* Puncture, oral cavity
  palm – *see* Puncture, hand
  pancreas S36.299
    body S36.291
    head S36.290
    tail S36.292
  pelvis - *see* Puncture, back, lower
  penis S31.23
    with foreign body S31.24
  perineum
    female S31.43
      with foreign body S31.44
    male S31.139
      with foreign body S31.149
  periocular area (with or without
    lacrimal passages) - *see* Puncture,
    eyelid
  phalanges
    finger – *see* Puncture, finger
    toe – *see* Puncture, toe
  pharynx S11.23
    with foreign body S11.24
  pinna – *see* Puncture, ear
  popliteal space – *see* Puncture, knee
  prepuce – *see* Puncture, penis
  pubic region S31.139
    with foreign body S31.149
  pudendum – *see* Puncture, genital
    organs, external
  rectovaginal septum - *see* Puncture,
    vagina
  sacral region – *see* Puncture, back,
    lower
  sacroiliac region - *see* Puncture, back,
    lower
  salivary gland – *see* Puncture, oral
    cavity
  scalp S01.03
    with foreign body S01.04
  scapular region – *see* Puncture, shoulder
  scrotum S31.33
    with foreign body S31.34
  shin – *see* Puncture, leg
  shoulder S41.039
    with foreign body S41.049
    left S41.032
      with foreign body S41.042
    right S41.031
      with foreign body S41.041
  spermatic cord - *see* Puncture, testis
  sternal region - *see* Puncture, thorax,
    front
  submaxillary region – *see* Puncture,
    head, specified site NEC
  submental region – *see* Puncture, head,
    specified site NEC
  subungual
    finger(s) – *see* Puncture, finger, with
      damage to nail

Puncture *(Continued)*
  subungual *(Continued)*
    toe – *see* Puncture, toe, with damage
      to nail
  supraclavicular fossa - *see*
    Puncture, neck, specified
    site NEC
  temple, temporal region – *see*
    Puncture, head, specified
    site NEC
  temporomandibular area – *see*
    Puncture, cheek
  testis S31.33
    with foreign body S31.34
  thigh S71.139
    with foreign body S71.149
    left S71.132
      with foreign body S71.142
    right S71.131
      with foreign body S71.141
  thorax, thoracic (wall) S21.93
    with foreign body S21.94
    back S21.239
      with foreign body S21.249
      left S21.232
        with foreign body S21.242
      right S21.231
        with foreign body S21.241
    breast – *see* Puncture, breast
    front S21.139
      with foreign body S21.149
      left S21.132
        with foreign body S21.142
      right S21.131
        with foreign body S21.141
  throat – *see* Puncture, neck
  thumb S61.039
    with
      damage to nail S61.139
        with
          foreign body S61.149
      foreign body S61.049
    left S61.032
      with
        damage to nail S61.132
          with
            foreign body S61.142
        foreign body S61.042
    right S61.031
      with
        damage to nail S61.131
          with
            foreign body S61.141
        foreign body S61.041
  thyroid gland S11.13
    with foreign body S11.14
  toe(s) S91.139
    with
      damage to nail S91.239
        with
          foreign body S91.249
      foreign body S91.149
    great S91.133
      with
        damage to nail S91.233
          with
            foreign body S91.243
        foreign body S91.143
      left S91.132
        with
          damage to nail S91.232
            with
              foreign body S91.242
          foreign body S91.142

401

Puncture (Continued)
  toe(s) (Continued)
    great (Continued)
      right S91.131
        with
          damage to nail S91.231
            with
              foreign body S91.241
          foreign body S91.141
      lesser S91.136
        with
          damage to nail S91.236
            with
              foreign body S91.246
          foreign body S91.146
      left S91.135
        with
          damage to nail S91.235
            with
              foreign body S91.245
          foreign body S91.145
      right S91.134
        with
          damage to nail S91.234
            with
              foreign body S91.244
          foreign body S91.144
  tongue – see Puncture, oral cavity
  trachea S11.023
    with foreign body S11.024
  tunica vaginalis – see Puncture, testis
  tympanum, tympanic membrane S09.2-
  umbilical region S31.135
    with foreign body S31.145
  uvula – see Puncture, oral cavity
  vagina S31.43
    with foreign body S31.44
  vocal cords S11.83
    with foreign body S11.84
  vulva S31.43
    with foreign body S31.44
  wrist S61.539
    with
      foreign body S61.549
    left S61.532
      with
        foreign body S61.542
    right S61.531
      with
        foreign body S61.541
PUO (pyrexia of unknown origin) R50.9
Pupillary membrane (persistent) Q13.89
Pupillotonia - see Anomaly, pupil, function, tonic pupil
Purpura D69.2
  abdominal D69.0
  allergic D69.0
  anaphylactoid D69.0
  annularis telangiectodes L81.7
  arthritic D69.0
  autoerythrocyte sensitization D69.2
  autoimmune D69.0
  bacterial D69.0
  Bateman's (senile) D69.2
  capillary fragility (hereditary)
    (idiopathic)D69.8
  cryoglobulinemic D89.1
  Devil's pinches D69.2
  fibrinolytic - see Fibrinolysis
  fulminans, fulminous D65
  gangrenous D65
  hemorrhagic, hemorrhagica D69.3
    not due to thrombocytopenia D69.0
  Henoch(-Schönlein) (allergic) D69.0

Purpura (Continued)
  hypergammaglobulinemic (benign)
    (Waldenström's) D89.0
  idiopathic (thrombocytopenic) D69.3
    nonthrombocytopenic D69.0
  immune thrombocytopenic D69.3
  infectious D69.0
  malignant D69.0
  neonatorum P54.5
  nervosa D69.0
  newborn P54.5
  nonthrombocytopenic D69.2
    hemorrhagic D69.0
    idiopathic D69.0
  nonthrombopenic D69.2
  peliosis rheumatica D69.0
  post-transfusion D69.5
  primary D69.49
  red cell membrane sensitivity D69.2
  rheumatica D69.0
  Schönlein(-Henoch) (allergic) D69.0
  scorbutic E54 [D77]
  senile D69.2
  simplex D69.2
  symptomatica D69.0
  telangiectasia annularis L81.7
  thrombocytopenic D69.49
    congenital D69.42
    hemorrhagic D69.3
    hereditary D69.42
    idiopathic D69.3
    immune D69.3
    neonatal, transitory P61.0
    thrombotic M31.1
  thrombohemolytic - see Fibrinolysis
  thrombolytic - see Fibrinolysis
  thrombopenic D69.49
  thrombotic, thrombocytopenic
    M31.1
  toxic D69.0
  vascular D69.0
  visceral symptoms D69.0
Purpuric spots R23.3
Purulent - see condition
Pus
  in
    stool R19.5
    urine N39.0
  tube (rupture) - see Salpingo-oophoritis
Pustular rash L08.0
Pustule (nonmalignant) L08.9
  malignant A22.0
Pustulosis palmaris et plantaris L40.3
Putnam(-Dana) disease or syndrome -
  see Degeneration, combined
Putrescent pulp (dental) K04.1
Pyarthritis, pyarthrosis - see Arthritis,
  pyogenic or pyemic
  tuberculous - see Tuberculosis, joint
Pyelectasis - see Hydronephrosis
Pyelitis (congenital) (uremic) - see also
  Pyelonephritis)
  with
    calculus - see category N20
      with hydronephrosis N13.2
    contracted kidney N11.9
  acute N10
  chronic N11.9
    with calculus - see category N20
      with hydronephrosis N13.2
  cystica N28.84
  puerperal (postpartum) O86.21
  tuberculous A18.11
Pyelocystitis - see Pyelonephritis

Pyelonephritis - see also Nephritis,
  tubulo-interstitial
  with
    calculus - see category N20
      with hydronephrosis N13.2
    contracted kidney N11.9
  acute N10
  calculous - see category N20
    with hydronephrosis N13.2
  chronic N11.9
    with calculus - see category N20
      with hydronephrosis N13.2
    associated with ureteral obstruction
      or stricture N11.1
    nonobstructive N11.8
      with reflux (vesicoureteral) N11.0
    obstructive N11.1
    specified NEC N11.8
  in (due to)
    brucellosis A23.9 [N16]
    cryoglobulinemia (mixed) D89.1
      [N16]
    cystinosis E72.04
    diphtheria A36.84
    glycogen storage disease E74.09
      [N16]
    leukemia NEC C95.90 [N16]
    lymphoma NEC C85.90 [N16]
    multiple myeloma C90.00 [N16]
    obstruction N11.1
    Salmonella infection A02.25
    sarcoidosis D86.84
    sepsis A41.9 [N16]
    Sjögren's disease M35.04
    toxoplasmosis B58.83
    transplant rejection T86.91 [N16]
    Wilson's disease E83.01 [N16]
  nonobstructive N12
    with reflux (vesicoureteral) N11.0
    chronic N11.8
  syphilitic A52.75
Pyelonephrosis (obstructive) N11.1
  chronic N11.9
Pyelophlebitis I80.8
Pyeloureteritis cystica N28.85
Pyemia, pyemic (fever) (infection)
  (purulent) - see also Sepsis
  joint - see Arthritis, pyogenic or
    pyemic
  liver K75.1
  pneumococcal A40.3
  portal K75.1
  postvaccinal T88.0
  puerperal, postpartum, childbirth
    O85
  specified organism NEC A41.89
  tuberculous - see Tuberculosis, miliary
Pygopagus Q89.4
Pyknoepilepsy, pyknolepsy (idiopathic) -
  see Epilepsy, generalized, idiopathic
Pyknolepsy - see Epilepsy, generalized,
  idiopathic
Pylephlebitis K75.1
Pyle's syndrome Q78.5
Pylethrombophlebitis K75.1
Pylethrombosis K75.1
Pyloritis K29.90
  with bleeding K29.91
Pylorospasm (reflex) NEC K31.3
  congenital or infantile Q40.0
  newborn Q40.0
  neurotic F45.8
  psychogenic F45.8
Pylorus, pyloric - see condition

Pyoarthrosis - *see* Arthritis, pyogenic or
    pyemic
Pyocele
    mastoid – *see* Mastoiditis, acute
    sinus (accessory) - *see* Sinusitis
    turbinate (bone) J32.9
    urethra (*see also* Urethritis) N34.0
Pyocolpos – *see* Vaginitis
Pyocystitis N30.80
    with hematuria N30.81
Pyoderma, pyodermia L08.0
    gangrenosum L88
    newborn P39.4
    phagedenic L88
    vegetans L08.81
Pyodermatitis L08.0
    vegetans L08.81
Pyogenic - *see* condition
Pyohydronephrosis N13.6

Pyometra, pyometrium, pyometritis -
    see Endometritis
Pyomyositis (tropical) - *see* Myositis,
    infective
Pyonephritis N12
Pyonephrosis N13.6
    tuberculous A18.11
Pyo-oophoritis - *see* Salpingo-
    oophoritis
Pyo-ovarium - *see* Salpingo-oophoritis
Pyopericarditis, pyopericardium
    I30.1
Pyophlebitis - *see* Phlebitis
Pyopneumopericardium I30.1
Pyopneumothorax (infective) J86.9
    with fistula J86.0
    tuberculous NEC A15.6
Pyosalpinx, pyosalpingitis - *see also*
    Salpingo-oophoritis

Pyothorax J86.9
    with fistula J86.0
    tuberculous NEC A15.6
Pyoureter N28.89
    tuberculous A18.11
Pyramidopallidonigral syndrome
    G20
Pyrexia (of unknown origin) R50.9
    atmospheric T67.0
    during labor NEC O75.2
    heat T67.0
    newborn P81.9
        environmentally-induced P81.0
    persistent R50.9
    puerperal O86.4
Pyroglobulinemia NEC E88.09
Pyromania F63.1
Pyrosis R12
Pyuria (bacterial) N39.0

Q

Q fever A78
  with pneumonia A78
Quadricuspid aortic valve Q23.8
Quadrilateral fever A78
Quadriparesis - *see* Quadriplegia
  meaning muscle weakness M62.81
Quadriplegia G82.50-
  complete
    C1-C4 level G82.51
    C5-C7 level G82.53
  congenital (cerebral) (spinal) G80.8
    spastic G80.0

Quadriplegia *(Continued)*
  embolic (current episode) I63.4
  incomplete
    C1-C4 level G82.52
    C5-C7 level G82.54
  functional R53.2
  thrombotic (current episode) I63.3
  traumatic — code to injury with extension s
    current episode – *see* Injury, spinal
      (cord), cervical
  functional R53.2
Quadruplet, pregnancy - *see* Pregnancy,
  quadruplet

Quarrelsomeness F60.3
Queensland fever A77.3
Quervain's disease M65.4
  thyroid E06.1
Queyrat's erythroplasia D07.4
  penis D07.4
  specified site - *see* Neoplasm, skin, in situ
  unspecified site D07.4
Quincke's disease or edema T78.3
  hereditary D84.1
Quinsy (gangrenous) J36
Quintan fever A79.0
Quintuplet, pregnancy - *see* Pregnancy,
  quintuplet

R

Rabbit fever - *see* Tularemia
Rabies A82.9
  contact Z20.3
  exposure to Z20.3
  inoculation reaction - *see* Complications, vaccination
  sylvatic A82.0
  urban A82.1
Rachischisis - *see* Spina bifida
Rachitic - *see also* condition
  deformities of spine (late effect) (sequelae) E64.3
  pelvis (late effect) (sequelae) E64.3
    with disproportion (fetopelvic) O33.0
      causing obstructed labor O65.0
Rachitis, rachitism (acute) (tarda) - *see also* Rickets
  renalis N25.0
  sequelae E64.3
Radial nerve - *see* condition
Radiation
  burn – *see* Burn
  effects NOS T66
  sickness NOS T66
  therapy, encounter for Z51.0
Radiculitis (pressure) (vertebrogenic) - *see* Radiculopathy
Radiculomyelitis - *see also* Encephalitis
  toxic, due to
    Clostridium tetani A35
    Corynebacterium diphtheriae A36.82
Radiculopathy M54.10
  cervical region M54.12
  cervicothoracic region M54.13
  due to displacement of intervertebral disc *see* Disorder, disc, with, radiculopathy
  leg M54.1-
  lumbar region M54.16
  lumbosacral region M54.17
  occipito-atlanto-axial region M54.11
  postherpetic B02.29
  sacrococcygeal region M54.18
  syphilitic A52.11
  thoracic region (with visceral pain) M54.14
  thoracolumbar region M54.15
Radiodermal burns (acute, chronic, or occupational) - *see* Burn
Radiodermatitis L58.9
  acute L58.0
  chronic L58.1
Radiotherapy session Z51.0
Rage, meaning rabies - *see* Rabies
Ragpicker's disease A22.1
Ragsorter's disease A22.1
Raillietiniasis B71.8
Railroad neurosis F48.8
Railway spine F48.8
Raised - *see also* Elevated
  antibody titer R76.0
Rake teeth, tooth M26.39
Rales R09.89
Ramifying renal pelvis Q63.8
Ramsay-Hunt disease or syndrome - *see also* Hunt's disease B02.21
  meaning dyssynergia cerebellaris myoclonica G11.1
Ranula K11.6
  congenital Q38.4

Rape
  adult
    confirmed T74.21
    suspected T76.21
  alleged, observation or examination, ruled out
    adult Z04.41
    child Z04.42
  child
    confirmed T74.22
    suspected T76.22
Rapid
  feeble pulse, due to shock, following injury T79.4
  heart (beat) R00.0
    psychogenic F45.8
  second stage (delivery) O62.3
  time-zone change syndrome - *see* Disorder, sleep, circadian rhythm, psychogenic
Rarefaction, bone - *see* Disorder, bone, density and structure, specified NEC
Rash (toxic) R21
  canker A38.9
  diaper L22
  drug (internal use) L27.0
    contact - *see also* Dermatitis, due to, drugs, external L25.1
  following immunization T88.1
  food - *see* Dermatitis, due to, food
  heat L74.0
  napkin (psoriasiform) L22
  nettle - *see* Urticaria
  pustular L08.0
  rose R21
    epidemic B06.9
  scarlet A38.9
  serum (prophylactic) (therapeutic) T80.6
  wandering tongue K14.1
Rasmussen aneurysm - *see* Tuberculosis, pulmonary
Rat-bite fever A25.9
  due to Streptobacillus moniliformis A25.1
  spirochetal (morsus muris) A25.0
Rathke's pouch tumor D44.3
Raymond (-Cestan) syndrome I65.8
Raynaud's disease, phenomenon or syndrome (secondary) I73.00
  with gangrene (symmetric) I73.01
RDS (newborn) (type I) P22.0
  type II P22.1
Reaction - *see also* Disorder
  adaptation – *see* Disorder, adjustment
  adjustment (anxiety) (conduct disorder) (depressiveness) (distress) – *see* Disorder, adjustment
    with
      mutism, elective (child) (adolescent) F94.0
  affective - *see* Disorder, mood
  allergic - *see* Allergy
  anaphylactic - *see* Shock, anaphylactic
  anesthesia - *see* Anesthesia, complication
  antitoxin (prophylactic) (therapeutic) - *see* Complications, vaccination
  anxiety F41.1
  Arthus - *see* Arthus' phenomenon
  asthenic F48.8
  compulsive F42
  conversion F44.9
  crisis, acute F43.0

Reaction (*Continued*)
  deoxyribonuclease (DNA) (DNase) hypersensitivity D69.2
  depressive (single episode) F32.9
    affective (single episode) F31.4
      recurrent episode F33.9
    neurotic F34.1
    psychoneurotic F34.1
    psychotic F32.3
    recurrent - *see* Disorder, depressive, recurrent
  dissociative F44.9
  drug NEC T88.7 This code not for use in the inpatient setting
    addictive - *see* Dependence, drug transmitted via placenta or breast milk - *see* Absorption, drug, addictive, through placenta
    allergic - *see* Allergy, drug
    lichenoid L43.2
    newborn P93.8
      gray baby syndrome P93.0
    overdose or poisoning (by accident) - *see* Table of drugs and chemicals, by drug, poisoning
    photoallergic L56.1
    phototoxic L56.0
    withdrawal – *see* Dependence, by drug, with, withdrawal
      infant of dependent mother P96.1
      newborn P96.1
    wrong substance given or taken (by accident) - *see* Table of drugs and chemicals, by drug, poisoning
  fear F40.9
    child (abnormal) F93.8
  fluid loss, cerebrospinal G97.1
  foreign
    body NEC - *see* Granuloma, foreign body
      in operative wound (inadvertently left) – *see* Foreign body, accidentally left during a procedure
    substance accidentally left during a procedure (chemical) (powder) (talc) T81.60
      aseptic peritonitis T81.61
      body or object (instrument) (sponge) (swab) – *see* Foreign body, accidentally left during a procedure
      specified reaction NEC T81.69
  grief – *see* Disorder, adjustment
  Herxheimer's T88.6
  hyperkinetic - *see* Hyperkinesia
  hypochondriacal F45.20
  hypoglycemic, due to insulin E16.0
    with coma (diabetic) - *see* Diabetes, coma
    nondiabetic E15
    therapeutic misadventure - *see* subcategory T38.3
  hypomanic F30.8
  hysterical F44.9
  immunization - *see* Complications, vaccination
  incompatibility
    ABO blood group (infusion) (transfusion) T80.3
    minor blood group (Duffy) (E) (K(ell)) (Kidd) (Lewis) (M) (N) (P) (S) T80.89
    Rh (factor) (infusion) (transfusion) T80.4

Reaction *(Continued)*
  inflammatory - *see* Infection
  infusion - *see* Complications, infusion
  inoculation (immune serum) - *see* Complications, vaccination
  insulin T38.3-
  involutional psychotic - *see* Disorder, depressive
  leukemoid D72.823
    basophilic D72.823
    lymphocytic D72.823
    monocytic D72.823
    myelocytic D72.823
    neutrophilic D72.823
  LSD (acute)
    due to drug abuse - *see* Abuse, drug, hallucinogen
    due to drug dependence - *see* Dependence, drug, hallucinogen
  lumbar puncture G97.1
  manic-depressive - *see* Disorder, bipolar
  neurasthenic F48.8
  neurogenic - *see* Neurosis
  neurotic F48.9
  neurotic-depressive F34.1
  nitritoid - *see* Crisis, nitritoid -
    obsessive-compulsive F42
  organic, acute or subacute - *see* Delirium
  paranoid (acute) F23
    chronic F22
    senile F03
  passive dependency F60.7
  phobic F40.9
  post-traumatic stress, uncomplicated Z73.3
  psychogenic F99
  psychoneurotic - *see also* Neurosis
    compulsive F42
    depersonalization F48.1
    depressive F34.1
    hypochondriacal F45.20
    neurasthenic F48.8
    obsessive F42
  psychophysiologic - *see* Disorder, somatoform
  psychosomatic - *see* Disorder, somatoform
  psychotic - *see* Psychosis
  scarlet fever toxin - *see* Complications, vaccination
  schizophrenic F23
    acute (brief) (undifferentiated) F23
    latent F21
    undifferentiated (acute) (brief) F23
  serological for syphilis - *see* Serology for syphilis
  serum (prophylactic) (therapeutic) T80.6
    anaphylactic (immediate) T80.5
  situational – *see* Disorder, adjustment
  somatization - *see* Disorder, somatoform
  spinal puncture G97.1
  stress (severe) F43.9
    acute (agitation) ("daze") (disorientation) (disturbance of consciousness) (flight reaction) (fugue) F43.0
    specified NEC F43.8
  surgical procedure - *see* Complications, surgical procedure
  tetanus antitoxin - *see* Complications, vaccination
  toxic, to local anesthesia T81.89
    in labor and delivery O74.4
    in pregnancy O29.3x
    postpartum, puerperal O89.3

Reaction *(Continued)*
  toxin-antitoxin - *see* Complications, vaccination
  transfusion (blood) (bone marrow) (lymphocytes) (allergic) - *see* Complications, transfusion
  tuberculin skin test, abnormal R76.1
  vaccination (any) - *see* Complications, vaccination
  withdrawing, child or adolescent F93.8
Reactive airway disease - *see* Asthma
Reactive depression - *see* Reaction, depressive
Rearrangement
  chromosomal
    balanced (in) Q95.9
      abnormal individual (autosomal) Q95.2
        non-sex (autosomal) chromosomes Q95.2
        sex/non-sex chromosomes Q95.3
      specified NEC Q95.8
Recalcitrant patient - *see* Noncompliance
Recanalization, thrombus - *see* Thrombosis
Recession, receding
  chamber angle (eye) H21.55-
  chin M26.09
  gingival (generalized) (localized) (postinfective) (postoperative) K06.0
Recklinghausen's disease Q85.0
  bones E21.0
Reclus' disease (cystic) - *see* Mastopathy, cystic
Recrudescent typhus (fever) A75.1
Recruitment, auditory H93.21-
Rectalgia K62.8
Rectitis K62.8
Rectocele
  female (without uterine prolapse) N81.6
    with uterine prolapse N81.4
      incomplete N81.2
  in pregnancy – *see* Pregnancy, complicated by, abnormal, pelvic organs or tissues NEC
  male K62.3
Rectosigmoid junction - *see* condition
Rectosigmoiditis K63.89
  ulcerative (chronic) K51.30
    with
      complication K51.319
        abscess K51.314
        fistula K51.313
        obstruction K51.312
        rectal bleeding K51.311
        specified NEC K51.318
Rectourethral - *see* condition
Rectovaginal - *see* condition
Rectovesical - *see* condition
Rectum, rectal - *see* condition
Recurrent - *see* condition
Red bugs B88.0
Red-cedar lung or pneumonitis J67.8
Red tide T65.82-
  see also Table of Drugs and Chemicals
Reduced
  mobility Z74.09
  ventilatory or vital capacity R94.2
Redundant, redundancy
  anus (congenital) Q43.8
  clitoris N90.8
  colon (congenital) Q43.8
  foreskin (congenital) N47.8

Redundant, redundancy *(Continued)*
  intestine (congenital) Q43.8
  labia N90.6
  organ or site, congenital NEC - *see* Accessory
  panniculus (abdominal) E65
  prepuce (congenital) N47.8
  pylorus K31.89
  rectum (congenital) Q43.8
  scrotum N50.8
  sigmoid (congenital) Q43.8
  skin (of face) L57.4
    eyelids - *see* Blepharochalasis
  stomach K31.89
Reduplication - *see* Duplication
Reflex R29.2
  hyperactive gag J39.2
  pupillary, abnormal - *see* Anomaly, pupil, function
  vasoconstriction I73.9
  vasovagal R55
Reflux K21.9
  acid K21.9
  esophageal K21.9
    with esophagitis K21.0
    newborn P78.83
  gastroesophageal K21.9
    with esophagitis K21.0
  mitral - *see* Insufficiency, mitral
  ureteral - *see* Reflux, vesicoureteral
  vesicoureteral (with scarring) N13.70
    with
      nephropathy N13.729
        with hydroureter N13.739
          bilateral N13.732
          unilateral N13.731
        bilateral N13.722
        unilateral N13.721
        without hydroureter N13.729
          bilateral N13.722
          unilateral N13.721
      pyelonephritis (chronic) N11.1
    congenital Q62.7
    without nephropathy N13.71
Reforming, artificial openings - *see* Attention to, artificial, opening
Refractive error - *see* Disorder, refraction
Refsum's disease or syndrome G60.1
Refusal of
  food, psychogenic F50.8
  treatment (because of) Z53.20
    left against medical advice (AMA) Z53.21
    patient's decision NEC Z53.29
    reasons of belief or group pressure Z53.1
Regional - *see* condition
Regurgitation R11.10
  aortic (valve) - *see* Insufficiency, aortic
  food - *see also* Vomiting
    with reswallowing - *see* Rumination
    newborn P92.1
  gastric contents - *see* Vomiting
  heart - *see* Endocarditis
  mitral (valve) - *see* Insufficiency, mitral
    congenital Q23.3
  myocardial - *see* Endocarditis
  pulmonary (valve) (heart) I37.1
    congenital Q22.2
    syphilitic A52.03
  tricuspid - *see* Insufficiency, tricuspid
  valve, valvular - *see* Endocarditis
    congenital Q24.8

Regurgitation *(Continued)*
  vesicoureteral - *see* Reflux,
      vesicoureteral
Reifenstein syndrome E34.52
Reinsertion, contraceptive device Z30.43
Reiter's disease, syndrome, or urethritis
      M02.30
  ankle M02.37-
  elbow M02.32-
  foot joint M02.37-
  hand joint M02.34-
  hip M02.35-
  knee M02.36-
  multiple site M02.39
  shoulder M02.31-
  vertebra M02.38
  wrist M02.33-
Reichmann's disease or syndrome
      K31.89
Rejection
  food, psychogenic F50.8
  transplant T86.91
    bone T86.830
      marrow T86.09
    cornea T86.840
    heart T86.21
      with lung(s) T86.31
    intestine T86.890
    kidney T86.11
    liver T86.41
    lung(s) T86.810
      with heart T86.31
    organ (immune or nonimmune cause)
        T86.91
    pancreas T86.890
    skin (allograft) (autograft) T86.820
    specified NEC T86.890
Relapsing fever A68.9
  Carter's (Asiatic) A68.0
  Dutton's (West African) A68.1
  Koch's A68.9
  louse-borne (epidemic) A68.0
  Novy's (American) A68.1
  Obermeyers's (European) A68.0
  Spirillum A68.9
  tick-borne (endemic) A68.1
Relationship
  occlusal
    open anterior M26.220
    open posterior M26.221
Relaxation
  anus (sphincter) K62.8
    psychogenic F45.8
  arch (foot) - *see also* Deformity, limb,
      flat foot
  back ligaments - *see* Instability, joint,
      spine
  bladder (sphincter) N31.2
  cardioesophageal K21.9
  cervix - *see* Incompetency, cervix
  diaphragm J98.6
  joint (capsule) (ligament) (paralytic) -
      see Flail, joint
    congenital NEC Q74.8
  lumbosacral (joint) - *see* subcategory
      M53.2
  pelvic floor N81.89
  perineum N81.89
  posture R29.3
  rectum (sphincter) K62.8
  sacroiliac (joint) - *see* subcategory M53.2
  scrotum N50.8
  urethra (sphincter) N36.44
  vesical N31.2

Release from prison, anxiety concerning
      Z65.2
Remains
  canal of Cloquet Q14.0
  capsule (opaque) Q14.8
Remittent fever (malarial) B54
Remnant
  canal of Cloquet Q14.0
  capsule (opaque) Q14.8
  cervix, cervical stump (acquired)
      (postoperative) N88.8
  cystic duct, postcholecystectomy
      K91.5
  fingernail L60.8
    congenital Q84.6
  meniscus, knee - *see* Derangement,
      knee, meniscus, specified NEC
  thyroglossal duct Q89.2
  tonsil J35.8
    infected (chronic) J35.01
  urachus Q64.4
Removal (from) (of)
  artificial
    arm Z44.00-
      complete Z44.01-
      partial Z44.02-
    eye Z44.2-
    leg Z44.10-
      complete Z44.11-
      partial Z44.12-
  breast implant Z45.81
  cardiac pulse generator (battery)
      (end-of-life) Z45.010
  catheter (urinary) (indwelling)
      Z46.6
    from artificial opening - *see* Attention
        to, artificial, opening
    non-vascular Z46.82
    vascular NEC Z45.2
  drains Z48.03
  device Z46.9
    contraceptive Z30.43
    implanted NEC Z45.89
    specified NEC Z46.89
  dressing (nonsurgical) Z48.00
    surgical Z48.01
  external
    fixation device - code to fracture with
        extension d
    prosthesis, prosthetic device Z44.9
      breast Z44.3-
      specified NEC Z44.8
  home in childhood (to foster home or
      institution) Z62.29
  ileostomy Z43.2
  insulin pump Z46.81
  myringotomy device (stent) (tube)
      Z45.82
  nervous system device NEC Z46.2
    brain neuropacemaker Z46.2
    visual substitution device Z46.2
      implanted Z45.31
  non-vascular catheter Z46.82
  orthodontic device Z46.4
  organ, prophylactic (for neoplasia
      management) – *see* Prophylactic,
      organ removal
  staples Z48.02
  stent
    ureteral Z46.6
  suture Z48.02
  urinary device Z46.6
  vascular access device or catheter
      Z45.2

Ren
  arcuatus Q63.1
  mobile, mobilis N28.89
    congenital Q63.8
  unguliformis Q63.1
Renal - *see* condition
Rendu-Osler-Weber disease or syndrome
      I78.0
Reninoma D41.0-
Renon-Delille syndrome E23.3
Reovirus, as cause of disease classified
      elsewhere B97.5
Repeated falls NEC R29.6
Replaced chromosome by dicentric ring
      Q93.2
Replacement by artificial or mechanical
      device or prosthesis of
  bladder Z96.0
  blood vessel NEC Z95.828
  bone NEC Z96.7
  cochlea Z96.21
  coronary artery Z95.5
  eustachian tube Z96.29
  eye globe Z97.0
  heart Z95.812
    valve Z95.2
      prosthetic Z95.2
      specified NEC Z95.4
      xenogenic Z95.3
  intestine Z96.89
  joint Z96.60
    hip - *see* Presence, hip joint implant
    knee - *see* Presence, knee joint implant
    specified site NEC Z96.698
  larynx Z96.3
  lens Z96.1
  limb(s) – *see* Presence, artificial, limb
  mandible NEC (for tooth root
      implant(s) Z96.5
  organ NEC Z96.89
  peripheral vessel NEC Z95.828
  stapes Z96.29
  teeth Z97.2
  tendon Z96.7
  tissue NEC Z96.89
  tooth root(s) Z96.5
  vessel NEC Z95.828
    coronary (artery) Z95.5
Request for expert evidence Z04.8
Reserve, decreased or low
  cardiac - *see* Disease, heart
  kidney N28.89
Residual - *see also* condition - ovary syn-
      drome N99.83
  state, schizophrenic F20.5
  urine R39.19
Resistance, resistant
  activated protein C D68.51
  insulin E88.81
  organism, to multiple drugs (MDRO)
      Z16
  thyroid hormone E07.89
Resorption
  dental (roots) K03.3
    alveoli M26.79
  teeth (external) (internal) (pathological)
      (roots) K03.3
Respiration
  Cheyne-Stokes R06.3
  decreased due to shock, following
      injury T79.4
  disorder of, psychogenic F45.8
  insufficient, or poor R06.89
    newborn P28.5

Respiration *(Continued)*
  painful R07.1
  sighing, psychogenic F45.8
Respiratory - *see also* condition
  distress syndrome (newborn) (type I) P22.0
    type II P22.1
  syncytial virus, as cause of disease classified elsewhere B97.4
Respite care Z75.5
Response (drug)
  photoallergic L56.1
  phototoxic L56.0
Restless legs (syndrome) G25.81
Restlessness R45.1
Restriction of housing space Z59.1
Restoration (of)
  dental
    aesthetically inadequate or displeasing K08.87
    defective K08.50
      specified NEC K08.59
    failure of marginal integrity K08.51
    failure of periodontal anatomical intergrity K08.54
    organ continuity from previous sterilization (tuboplasty) (vasoplasty) Z31.0
      aftercare Z31.42
    tooth (existing)
      contours biologically incompatible with oral health K08.54
      open margins K08.51
      overhanging K08.52
      poor aesthetic K08.56
      poor gingival margins K08.51
    unsatisfactory, of tooth K08.50
      specified NEC K08.59
Restorative material (dental)
  allergy to K08.55
  fractured K08.539
    with loss of material K08.531
    without loss of material K08.530
  unrepairable overhanging of K08.52
Rests, ovarian, in fallopian tube Q50.6
Restzustand (schizophrenic) F20.5
Retained - *see* Retention
Retardation
  development, developmental, specific - *see* Disorder, developmental
  endochondral bone growth - *see* Disorder, bone, development or growth
  growth R62.50
    due to malnutrition E45
  mental F79
    with
      autistic features F84.9
      mild (I.Q. 50-69) F70
      moderate (I.Q. 35-49) F71
      profound (I.Q. under 20) F73
      severe (I.Q. 20-34) F72
      specified level NEC F78
  motor function, specific F82
  physical (child) R62.50
    due to malnutrition E45
  reading (specific) F81.0
  spelling (specific) (without reading disorder) F81.81
Retching - *see* Vomiting
Retention, retained
  bladder – *see* Retention, urine
  carbon dioxide E87.2
  cholelithiasis K91.89
  cyst - *see* Cyst

Retention, retained *(Continued)*
  dead
    fetus (at or near term) (mother) O36.4
      early fetal death O02.1
    ovum O02.0
  decidua (fragments) (following delivery) (with hemorrhage) O72.2
    without hemorrhage O73.1
  deciduous tooth K00.6
  dental root K08.3
  fecal - *see* Constipation
  fetus
    dead O36.4
    early O02.1
  fluid R60.9
  foreign body - *see also* Foreign body, retained
    current trauma - code as Foreign body, by site or type
  gallstones K91.89
  gastric K31.89
  intrauterine contraceptive device, in pregnancy – *see* Pregnancy, complicated by, retention, intrauterine device
  membranes (complicating delivery) (with hemorrhage) O72.2
    with abortion - *see* Abortion, by type
    without hemorrhage O73.1
  meniscus - *see* Derangement, meniscus
  menses N94.89
  milk (puerperal, postpartum) O92.79
  nitrogen, extrarenal R39.2
  ovary syndrome N99.83
  placenta (total) (with hemorrhage) O72.0
    without hemorrhage O73.0
    portions or fragments (with hemorrhage) O72.2
      without hemorrhage O73.1
  products of conception
    early pregnancy (dead fetus) O02.1
    following
      delivery (with hemorrhage) O72.2
        without hemorrhage O73.1
  secundines (following delivery) (with hemorrhage) O72.0
    without hemorrhage O73.0
    complicating puerperium (delayed hemorrhage) O72.2
    partial O72.2
      without hemorrhage O73.1
  smegma, clitoris N90.8
  urine R33.9
    due to hyperplasia (hypertrophy) of prostate - *see* Hyperplasia, prostate, specified type, with obstruction
    drug-induced R33.0
    organic R33.8
      drug-induced R33.0
    psychogenic F45.8
    specified NEC R33.8
  water (in tissues) - *see* Edema
Reticulation, dust - *see* Pneumoconiosis
Reticulocytosis R70.1
Reticuloendotheliosis
  acute infantile C96.0
  leukemic C91.4-
  malignant C96.9
  nonlipid C96.0
Reticulohistiocytoma (giant-cell) D76.3

Reticuloid, actinic L57.1
Reticulolymphosarcoma (diffuse) (M9675/3) – *see* Lymphoma, non-Hodgkin's, diffuse, mixed small and large cell
  follicular (M9691/3) – *see* Lymphoma, non-Hodgkin's, follicular, mixed small cleaved cell and large cell
  nodular (M9691/3) – *see* Lymphoma, non-Hodgkin's, follicular, mixed small cleaved cell and large cell
Reticulosarcoma (diffuse) (M9593/3) C83.3-
  nodular (M9593/3) – *see* Lymphoma, non-Hodgkin's, follicular, large cell
Reticulosis (skin)
  acute of infancy C96.0
  hemophagocytic, familial D76.1
  histiocytic medullary C96.9
  lipomelanotic I89.8
  malignant (midline) C86.0
  nonlipid C96.0
  polymorphic C83.8-
  Sézary - *see* Sézary disease
Retina, retinal - *see also* condition
  dark area D49.81
Retinitis - *see also* Inflammation, chorioretinal
  albuminurica N18.9 *[H32]*
  diabetic – *see* Diabetes, retinitis
  disciformis - *see* Degeneration, macula
  focal - *see* Inflammation, chorioretinal, focal
  gravidarum – *see* Pregnancy, complicated by, specified pregnancy-related condition NEC
  juxtapapillaris - *see* Inflammation, chorioretinal, focal, juxtapapillary
  luetic - *see* Retinitis, syphilitic
  pigmentosa H35.52
  proliferans - *see* Disorder, globe, degenerative, specified type NEC
  proliferating - *see* Disorder, globe, degenerative, specified type NEC
  renal N18.9 *[H32]*
  syphilitic (early) (secondary) A51.43
    central, recurrent A52.71
    congenital (early) A50.01 *[H32]*
    late A52.71
  tuberculous A18.53
Retinoblastoma C69.2-
  differentiated C69.2-
  undifferentiated C69.2-
Retinochoroiditis - *see also* Inflammation, chorioretinal
  disseminated - *see* Inflammation, chorioretinal, disseminated
    syphilitic A52.71
  focal - *see* Inflammation, chorioretinal
  juxtapapillaris - *see* Inflammation, chorioretinal, focal, juxtapapillary
Retinopathy (background) (Coats) H35.9
  arteriosclerotic I70.90 *[H36]*
  atherosclerotic I70.90 *[H36]*
  central serous - *see* Chorioretinopathy, central serous
  diabetic – *see* Diabetes, retinopathy
  exudative H35.02-
  hypertensive H35.03-
  in (due to)
    diabetes – *see* Diabetes, retinopathy

Retinopathy *(Continued)*
  sickle-cell disorders D57.*[H36]*
  of prematurity H35.10-
    stage 0 H35.11-
    stage 1 H35.12-
    stage 2 H35.13-
    stage 3 H35.14-
    stage 4 H35.15-
    stage 5 H35.16-
  pigmentary, congenital - *see* Dystrophy, retina
  proliferative NEC H35.2-
    diabetic – *see* Diabetes, retinopathy, proliferative
  sickle-cell D57.-*[H36]*
  solar H31.02-
Retinoschisis H33.10-
  congenital Q14.1
  specified type NEC H33.19-
Retortamoniasis A07.8
Retractile testis Q55.22
Retraction
  cervix - *see* Retroversion, uterus
  drum (membrane) - *see* Disorder, tympanic membrane, specified NEC
  finger - *see* Deformity, finger
  lid H02.539
    left H02.536
      lower H02.535
      upper H02.534
    right H02.533
      lower H02.532
      upper H02.531
  lung J98.4
  mediastinum J98.5
  nipple N64.53
    associated with
      lactation O92.03
      pregnancy O92.01-
      puerperium O92.02
    congenital Q83.8
  palmar fascia M72.0
  pleura - *see* Pleurisy
  ring, uterus (Bandl's) (pathological) O62.4
  sternum (congenital) Q76.7
    acquired M95.4
  uterus - *see* Retroversion, uterus
  valve (heart) - *see* Endocarditis
Retrobulbar - *see* condition
Retrocecal - *see* condition
Retrocession - *see* Retroversion
Retrodisplacement - *see* Retroversion
Retroflection, retroflexion - *see* Retroversion
Retrognathia, retrognathism (mandibular) (maxillary) M26.19
Retrograde menstruation N92.5
Retroperineal - *see* condition
Retroperitoneal - *see* condition
Retroperitonitis K68.9
Retropharyngeal - *see* condition
Retroplacental - *see* condition
Retroposition - *see* Retroversion
Retrosternal thyroid (congenital) Q89.2
Retroversion, retroverted
  cervix - *see* Retroversion, uterus
  female NEC - *see* Retroversion, uterus
  iris H21.89
  testis (congenital) Q55.29
  uterus (acquired) (acute) (any degree) (asymptomatic) (cervix) (postinfectional) (postpartal, old) N85.4
    congenital Q51.8

Retroversion, retroverted *(Continued)*
  uterus *(Continued)*
    in pregnancy – *see* Pregnancy, complicated by, abnormal, uterus
Retrovirus, as cause of disease classified elsewhere B97.30
  human
    immunodeficiency, type 2 [HIV 2] B97.35
    T-cell lymphotropic
      type I [HTLV-I] B97.33
      type II [HTLV-II] B97.34
  lentivirus B97.31
  oncovirus B97.32
  specified NEC B97.39
Retrusion, premaxilla (developmental) M26.09
Rett's disease or syndrome F84.2
Reverse peristalsis R19.2
Reye's syndrome G93.7
Rh (factor)
  hemolytic disease (newborn) P55.0
  incompatibility, immunization or sensitization
    affecting management of pregnancy NEC O36.09-
      anti-D antibody O36.01-
    newborn P55.0
    transfusion reaction T80.4
  negative mother affecting newborn P55.0
  titer elevated T80.4
  transfusion reaction T80.4
Rhabdomyolysis (idiopathic) NEC M62.82
  traumatic T79.6
Rhabdomyoma - *see also* Neoplasm, connective tissue, benign
  adult - *see* Neoplasm, connective tissue, benign
  fetal - *see* Neoplasm, connective tissue, benign
  glycogenic - *see* Neoplasm, connective tissue, benign
Rhabdomyosarcoma (any type) - *see also* Neoplasm, connective tissue, malignant
Rhabdosarcoma - *see* Rhabdomyosarcoma
Rhesus (factor) incompatibility - *see* Rh, incompatibility
Rheumatic (acute) (subacute) (chronic)
  adherent pericardium I09.2
  coronary arteritis I01.9
  degeneration, myocardium I09.0
  fever (acute) - *see* Fever, rheumatic
  heart - *see* Disease, heart, rheumatic
  myocardial degeneration - *see* Degeneration, myocardium
  myocarditis (chronic) (inactive) (with chorea) I09.0
    active or acute I01.2
      with chorea (acute) (rheumatic) (Sydenham's) I02.0
  pancarditis, acute I01.8
    with chorea (acute (rheumatic) Sydenham's) I02.0
  pericarditis (active) (acute) (with effusion) (with pneumonia) I01.0
    with chorea (acute) (rheumatic) (Sydenham's) I02.0
  chronic or inactive I09.2
  pneumonia I00 *[J17]*
  torticollis M43.6
  typhoid fever A01.09

Rheumatism (articular) (neuralgic) (non-articular) M79.0
  intercostal, meaning Tietze's disease M94.0
  palindromic (any site) M12.30
    ankle M12.37-
    elbow M12.32-
    foot joint M12.37-
    hand joint M12.34-
    hip M12.35-
    knee M12.36-
    multiple site M12.39
    shoulder M12.31-
    specified joint NEC M12.38
    wrist M12.33-
  sciatic M54.4-
Rheumatoid - *see also* condition
  arthritis - *see also* Arthritis, rheumatoid
    with involvement of organs NEC M05.60
      ankle M05.67-
      elbow M05.62-
      foot joint M05.67-
      hand joint M05.64-
      hip M05.65-
      knee M05.66-
      multiple site M05.69
      shoulder M05.61-
      vertebra - *see* Spondylitis, ankylosing
      wrist M05.63-
    seronegative - *see* Arthritis, rheumatoid, seronegative
    seropositive - *see* Arthritis, rheumatoid, seropositive
  carditis M05.30
    ankle M05.37-
    elbow M05.32-
    foot joint M05.37-
    hand joint M05.34-
    hip M05.35-
    knee M05.36-
    multiple site M05.39
    shoulder M05.31-
    vertebra - *see* Spondylitis, ankylosing
    wrist M05.33-
  endocarditis - *see* Rheumatoid, carditis
  lung (disease) M05.10
    ankle M05.17-
    elbow M05.12-
    foot joint M05.17-
    hand joint M05.14-
    hip M05.15-
    knee M05.16-
    multiple site M05.19
    shoulder M05.11-
    vertebra - *see* Spondylitis, ankylosing
    wrist M05.13-
  myocarditis - *see* Rheumatoid, carditis
  myopathy M05.40
    ankle M05.47-
    elbow M05.42-
    foot joint M05.47-
    hand joint M05.44-
    hip M05.45-
    knee M05.46-
    multiple site M05.49
    shoulder M05.41-
    vertebra - *see* Spondylitis, ankylosing
    wrist M05.43-
  pericarditis - *see* Rheumatoid, carditis

Rheumatoid *(Continued)*
  polyarthritis - *see* Arthritis, rheumatoid
  polyneuropathy M05.50
    ankle M05.57-
    elbow M05.52-
    foot joint M05.57-
    hand joint M05.54-
    hip M05.55-
    knee M05.56-
    multiple site M05.59
    shoulder M05.51-
    vertebra - *see* Spondylitis,
      ankylosing
    wrist M05.53-
  vasculitis M05.20
    ankle M05.27-
    elbow M05.22-
    foot joint M05.27-
    hand joint M05.24-
    hip M05.25-
    knee M05.26-
    multiple site M05.29
    shoulder M05.21-
    vertebra - *see* Spondylitis, ankylosing
    wrist M05.23-
Rhinitis (atrophic) (catarrhal) (chronic)
  (croupous) (fibrinous) (granulomatous) (hyperplastic) (hypertrophic)
  (membranous) (obstructive)
  (purulent) (suppurative)
  (ulcerative) J31.0
  with
    sore throat - *see* Nasopharyngitis
  acute J00
  allergic J30.9
    with asthma J45.909
      with
        exacerbation (acute) J45.901
        status asthmaticus J45.902
    due to
      food J30.5
      pollen J30.1
    nonseasonal J30.89
    perennial J30.89
    seasonal NEC J30.2
    specified NEC J30.89
  infective J00
  pneumococcal J00
  syphilitic A52.73
    congenital A50.05 *[J99]*
  tuberculous A15.8
  vasomotor J30.0
Rhinoantritis (chronic) - *see* Sinusitis,
  maxillary
Rhinodacryolith - *see* Dacryolith
Rhinolith (nasal sinus) J34.89
Rhinomegaly J34.89
Rhinopharyngitis (acute) (subacute) - *see
  also* Nasopharyngitis
  chronic J31.1
  destructive ulcerating A66.5
  mutilans A66.5
Rhinophyma L71.1
Rhinorrhea J34.89
  cerebrospinal (fluid) G96.0
  paroxysmal - *see* Rhinitis, allergic
  spasmodic - *see* Rhinitis, allergic
Rhinosalpingitis – *see* Salpingitis,
  eustachian
Rhinoscleroma A48.8
Rhinosporidiosis B48.1
Rhinovirus infection NEC B34.8
Rhizomelic chondrodysplasia punctata
  E71.540

Rhythm
  atrioventricular nodal I49.8
  disorder I49.9
    coronary sinus I49.8
    ectopic I49.8
    nodal I49.8
  escape I49.9
  heart, abnormal I49.9
  idioventricular I44.2
  nodal I49.8
  sleep, inversion G47.2
    nonorganic origin - *see* Disorder,
      sleep, circadian rhythm,
      psychogenic
Rhytidosis facialis L98.8
Rib - *see also* condition
  cervical Q76.5
Riboflavin deficiency E53.0
Rice bodies - *see also* Loose, body, joint
  knee M23.4-
Richter syndrome - *see* Leukemia, chronic
  lymphocytic, B-cell type
Richter's hernia - *see* Hernia, abdomen,
  with obstruction
Ricinism - *see* Poisoning, food, noxious,
  plant
Rickets (active) (acute) (adolescent) (chest
  wall) (congenital) (current) (infantile)
  (intestinal) E55.0
  adult - *see* Osteomalacia
  celiac K90.0
  hypophosphatemic with nephrotic-
    glycosuric dwarfism E72.09
  inactive E64.3
  kidney N25.0
  renal N25.0
  sequelae, any E64.3
  vitamin-D-resistant E83.31 *[M90.80]*
Rickettsial disease A79.9
  specified type NEC A79.89
Rickettsialpox (Rickettsia akari) A79.1
Rickettsiosis A79.9
  due to
    Ehrlichia sennetsu A79.81
    Rickettsia akari (rickettsialpox) A79.1
  specified type NEC A79.89
  tick-borne A77.9
  vesicular A79.1
Rider's bone - *see* Ossification, muscle,
  specified NEC
Ridge, alveolus - *see also* condition
  flabby K06.8
Ridged ear, congenital Q17.3
Riedel's
  lobe, liver Q44.7
  struma, thyroiditis or disease E06.5
Rieger's anomaly or syndrome Q13.81
Riehl's melanosis L81.4
Rietti-Greppi-Micheli anemia D56.9
Rieux's hernia - *see* Hernia, abdomen,
  specified site NEC
Riga (-Fede) disease K14.0
Riggs' disease - *see* Periodontitis
Right middle lobe syndrome J98.11
Rigid, rigidity - *see also* condition
  abdominal R19.30
    with severe abdominal pain R10.0
    epigastric R19.36
    generalized R19.37
    left lower quadrant R19.34
    left upper quadrant R19.32
    periumbilic R19.35
    right lower quadrant R19.33
    right upper quadrant R19.31

Rigid, rigidity *(Continued)*
  articular, multiple, congenital Q68.8
  cervix (uteri) in pregnancy – *see* Preg-
    nancy, complicated by, abnormal,
    cervix
  hymen (acquired) (congenital) N89.6
  nuchal R29.1
  pelvic floor in pregnancy – *see*
    Pregnancy, complicated by,
    abnormal, pelvic organs or
    tissues NEC
  perineum or vulva in pregnancy – *see*
    Pregnancy, complicated by, abnor-
    mal, vulva
  spine - *see* Dorsopathy, specified NEC
  vagina in pregnancy – *see* Pregnancy,
    complicated by, abnormal, vagina
Rigors R68.89
  with fever R50.9
Riley-Day syndrome G90.1
RIND (reversible ischemic neurologic
  deficit) I63.9
Ring(s)
  aorta (vascular) Q25.4
  Bandl's O62.4
  contraction, complicating delivery
    O62.4
  esophageal, lower (muscular) K22.2
  Fleischer's (cornea) H18.04-
  hymenal, tight (acquired) (congenital)
    N89.6
  Kayser-Fleischer (cornea) H18.04-
  retraction, uterus, pathological O62.4
  Schatzki's (esophagus) (lower) K22.4
    congenital Q39.8
  Soemmerring's - *see* Cataract, secondary
  vascular (congenital) Q25.8
    aorta Q25.4
Ringed hair (congenital) Q84.1
Ringworm B35.9
  beard B35.0
  black dot B35.0
  body B35.4
  Burmese B35.5
  corporeal B35.4
  foot B35.3
  groin B35.6
  hand B35.2
  honeycomb B35.0
  nails B35.1
  perianal (area) B35.6
  scalp B35.0
  specified NEC B35.8
  Tokelau B35.5
Rise, venous pressure I87.8
Risk, suicidal
  meaning personal history of attempted
    suicide Z91.5
  meaning suicidal ideation R45.85
Ritter's disease L00
Rivalry, sibling Z62.891
Rivalta's disease A42.2
River blindness B73.01
Robert's pelvis Q74.2
  with disproportion (fetopelvic) O33.0
    causing obstructed labor O65.0
Robin(-Pierre) syndrome Q87.0
Robinow-Silvermann-Smith syndrome
  Q87.1
Robinson's (hidrotic) ectodermal dyspla-
  sia or syndrome Q82.4
Robles' disease - *see* Onchocerciasis
Rocky Mountain (spotted) fever A77.0
Roetheln - *see* Rubella

Roger's disease Q21.0
Rokitansky-Aschoff sinuses (gallbladder) K82.8
Rolando's fracture (displaced) S62.22-
  nondisplaced S62.22-
Romano-Ward (prolonged QT interval) syndrome I45.81
Romberg's disease or syndrome G51.8
Roof, mouth - *see* condition
Rosacea L71.9
  acne L71.9
  keratitis L71.8
  specified NEC L71.8
Rosary, rachitic E55.0
Rose
  cold J30.1
  fever J30.1
  rash R21
    epidemic B06.9
Rosenbach's erysipeloid A26.0
Rosenthal's disease or syndrome D68.1
Roseola B09
  infantum B08.20
    due to human herpesvirus 6 B08.21
    due to human herpesvirus 7 B08.22
Rossbach's disease K31.89
  psychogenic F45.8
Ross River disease or fever B33.1
Rostan's asthma (cardiac) - *see* Failure, ventricular, left
Rotation
  anomalous, incomplete or insufficient, intestine Q43.3
  cecum (congenital) Q43.3
  colon (congenital) Q43.3
  spine, incomplete or insufficient - *see* Dorsopathy, deforming, specified NEC
  tooth, teeth, fully erupted M26.35
  vertebra, incomplete or insufficient - *see* Dorsopathy, deforming, specified NEC
Rotes Quérol disease or syndrome - *see* Hyperstosis, ankylosing
Roth(-Bernhardt) disease or syndrome - *see* Meralgia paraesthetica
Rothmund(-Thomson) syndrome Q82.8
Rotor's disease or syndrome E80.6
Round
  back (with wedging of vertebrae) - *see* Kyphosis
  sequelae (late effect) of rickets E64.3
  worms (large) (infestation) NEC B82.0
    Ascariasis (*see also* Ascariasis) B77.9
Roussy-Lévy syndrome G60.0
Rubella (German measles) B06.9
  complication NEC B06.09
    neurological B06.00
  congenital P35.0
  contact Z20.4
  exposure to Z20.4
  maternal
    manifest rubella in infant P35.0
    care for (suspected) damage to fetus O35.3
    suspected damage to fetus affecting management of pregnancy O35.3
  specified complications NEC B06.89
Rubeola (meaning measles) - *see* Measles
  meaning rubella - *see* Rubella
Rubeosis, iris - *see* Disorder, iris, vascular
Rubinstein-Taybi syndrome Q87.2

Rudimentary (congenital) - *see also* Agenesis
  arm – *see* Defect, reduction, upper limb
  bone Q79.9
  cervix uteri Q51.8
  eye Q11.2
  lobule of ear Q17.3
  patella Q74.1
  respiratory organs in thoracopagus Q89.4
  tracheal bronchus Q32.4
  uterus Q51.8
    in male Q56.1
  vagina Q52.0
Ruled out condition - *see* Observation, suspected
Rumination R11.10
  with nausea R11.2
  disorder of infancy F98.21
  neurotic F42
  newborn P92.1
  obsessional F42
  psychogenic F42
Runeberg's disease D51.0
Runny nose R09.89
Rupia (syphilitic) A51.39
  congenital A50.06
  tertiary A52.79
Rupture, ruptured
  abscess (spontaneous) - code by site under Abscess
  aneurysm - *see* Aneurysm
  anus (sphincter) - *see* Laceration, anus
  aorta, aortic I71.8
    abdominal I71.3
    arch I71.1
    ascending I71.1
    descending I71.8
      abdominal I71.3
      thoracic I71.1
    syphilitic A52.01
    thoracoabdominal I71.5
    thorax, thoracic I71.1
    transverse I71.1
    traumatic – *see* Injury, aorta, laceration, major
    valve or cusp (*see also* Endocarditis, aortic) I35.8
  appendix (with peritonitis) K35.0
  arteriovenous fistula, brain I60.8
  artery I77.2
    brain - *see* Hemorrhage, intracranial, intracerebral
    coronary - *see* Infarct, myocardium
    heart - *see* Infarct, myocardium
    pulmonary I28.8
    traumatic (complication) - *see* Injury, blood vessel
  bile duct (common) (hepatic) K83.2
    cystic K82.2
  bladder (sphincter) (nontraumatic) (spontaneous) N32.89
    following ectopic or molar pregnancy O08.6
    obstetrical trauma O71.5
    traumatic S37.28
  blood vessel - *see also* Hemorrhage
    brain - *see* Hemorrhage, intracranial, intracerebral
    heart - *see* Infarct, myocardium
    traumatic (complication) - *see* Injury, blood vessel, laceration, major, by site
  bone - *see* Fracture

Rupture, ruptured (*Continued*)
  bowel (nontraumatic) K63.1
  brain
    aneurysm (congenital) - *see also* Hemorrhage, intracranial, subarachnoid
      syphilitic A52.05
    hemorrhagic - *see* Hemorrhage, intracranial, intracerebral
  capillaries I78.8
  cardiac (auricle) (ventricle) (wall) I23.3
    with hemopericardium I23.0
    infectional I40.9
    traumatic – *see* Injury, heart
  cartilage (articular) (current) - *see also* Sprain
    knee S83.3-
    semilunar - *see* Tear, meniscus
  cecum (with peritonitis) K65.0
    with peritoneal abscess K35.1
    traumatic S36.598
  celiac artery, traumatic - *see* Injury, blood vessel, celiac artery, laceration, major
  cerebral aneurysm (congenital) (*see* Hemorrhage, intracranial, subarachnoid)
  cervix (uteri)
    with ectopic or molar pregnancy O08.6
    following ectopic or molar pregnancy O08.6
    obstetrical trauma O71.3
    traumatic S37.69
  chordae tendineae NEC I51.1
    concurrent with acute myocardial infarction - *see* Infarct, myocardium
    following acute myocardial infarction (current complication) I23.4
  choroid (direct) (indirect) (traumatic) H31.32-
  circle of Willis I60.6
  colon (nontraumatic) K63.1
    traumatic – *see* Injury, intestine, large
  cornea (traumatic) - *see* Injury, eye, laceration
  coronary (artery) (thrombotic) - *see* Infarct, myocardium
  corpus luteum (infected) (ovary) N83.1
  cyst - *see* Cyst
  cystic duct K82.2
  Descemet's membrane - *see* Change, corneal membrane, Descemet's, rupture
    traumatic - *see* Injury, eye, laceration
  diaphragm, traumatic – *see* Injury, intrathoracic, diaphragm
  disc - *see* Rupture, intervertebral disc
  diverticulum (intestine) K57.80
    with bleeding K57.81
    bladder N32.3
    large intestine K57.20
      with
        bleeding K57.21
        small intestine K57.40
          with bleeding K57.41
    small intestine K57.00
      with
        bleeding K57.01
        large intestine K57.40
          with bleeding K57.41
  duodenal stump K31.89

Rupture, ruptured *(Continued)*
  ear drum (nontraumatic) - *see also* Perfo-
      ration, tympanum
    traumatic S09.2-
      due to blast injury - *see* Injury,
          blast, ear
  esophagus K22.3
  eye (without prolapse or loss of intra-
      ocular tissue) – *see* Injury, eye,
      laceration
  fallopian tube NEC (nonobstetric) (non-
      traumatic) N83.8
    due to pregnancy O00.1
  fontanel P13.1
  gallbladder K82.2
    traumatic S36.128
  gastric - *see also* Rupture, stomach
      vessel K92.2
  globe (eye) (traumatic) - *see* Injury, eye,
      laceration
  graafian follicle (hematoma) N83.0
  heart - *see* Rupture, cardiac
  hymen (nontraumatic) (nonintentional)
      N89.8
  internal organ, traumatic - *see* Injury,
      by site
  intervertebral disc - *see* Displacement,
      intervertebral disc
    traumatic - *see* Rupture, traumatic,
        intervertebral disc
  intestine NEC (nontraumatic) K63.1
    traumatic – *see* Injury, intestine
  iris - *see also* Abnormality, pupillary
    traumatic - *see* Injury, eye, laceration
  joint capsule, traumatic - *see* Sprain
  kidney (traumatic) S37.06-
    birth injury P15.8
    nontraumatic N28.89
  lacrimal duct (traumatic) – *see* Injury,
      eye, specified site NEC
  lens (cataract) (traumatic) - *see* Cataract,
      traumatic
  ligament, traumatic - *see* Rupture, trau-
      matic, ligament, by site
  liver S36.116
    birth injury P15.0
  lymphatic vessel I89.8
  marginal sinus (placental) (with hemor-
      rhage) – *see* Hemorrhage, antepar-
      tum, specified cause NEC
  membrana tympani (nontraumatic) - *see*
      Perforation, tympanum
  membranes (spontaneous)
    artificial
      delayed delivery following O75.5
    delayed delivery following – *see* Preg-
        nancy, complicated by, prema-
        ture rupture of membranes
  meningeal artery I60.8
  meniscus (knee) - *see also* Tear, meniscus
    old - *see* Derangement, meniscus
    site other than knee - code as Sprain
  mesenteric artery, traumatic - *see* Injury,
      mesenteric, artery, laceration,
      major
  mesentery (nontraumatic) K66.8
    traumatic - *see* Injury, intra-
        abdominal, specified, site NEC
  mitral (valve) I34.8
  muscle (traumatic) - *see also* Strain
    diastasis - *see* Diastasis, muscle
    nontraumatic M62.10
      ankle M62.17-
      foot M62.17-

Rupture, ruptured *(Continued)*
  muscle *(Continued)*
    nontraumatic *(Continued)*
      forearm M62.13-
      hand M62.14-
      lower leg M62.16-
      pelvic region M62.15-
      shoulder region M62.11-
      specified site NEC M62.18
      thigh M62.15-
      upper arm M62.12-
    traumatic - *see* Strain, by site
  musculotendinous junction NEC, non-
      traumatic - *see* Rupture, tendon,
      spontaneous
  mycotic aneurysm causing cerebral
      hemorrhage - *see* Hemorrhage,
      intracranial, subarachnoid
  myocardium, myocardial - *see* Rupture,
      cardiac
    traumatic – *see* Injury, heart
  nontraumatic, meaning hernia - *see*
      Hernia
  obstructed - *see* Hernia, by site,
      obstructed
  operation wound - *see* Disruption,
      wound, operation
  ovary, ovarian N83.8
    corpus luteum cyst N83.1
    follicle (graafian) N83.0
  oviduct (nonobstetric) (nontraumatic)
      N83.8
    due to pregnancy O00.1
  pancreas (nontraumatic) K86.8
    traumatic S36.299
  papillary muscle NEC I51.2
    following acute myocardial
        infarction (current complication)
        I23.5
  pelvic
    floor, complicating delivery O70.1
    organ NEC, obstetrical trauma
        O71.5
  perineum (nonobstetric) (nontraumatic)
      N90.8
    complicating delivery - *see* Delivery,
        complicated, by, laceration, anus
        (sphincter)
  postoperative wound - *see* Disruption,
      wound, operation
  prostate (traumatic) S37.828
  pulmonary
    artery I28.8
    valve (heart) I37.8
    vein I28.8
    vessel I28.8
  pus tube - *see* Salpingitis
  pyosalpinx - *see* Salpingitis
  rectum (nontraumatic) K63.1
    traumatic S36.69
  retina, retinal (traumatic) (without
      detachment) - *see also* Break,
      retina
    with detachment - *see* Detachment,
        retina, with retinal, break
  rotator cuff (complete) (incomplete)
      (nontraumatic) M75.1-
  sclera – *see* Injury, eye, laceration
  sigmoid (nontraumatic) K63.1
    traumatic S36.593
  spinal cord - *see also* Injury, spinal cord,
      by region
    due to injury at birth P11.5
    newborn (birth injury) P11.5

Rupture, ruptured *(Continued)*
  spleen (traumatic) S36.09
    birth injury P15.1
    congenital (birth injury) P15.1
    due to P. vivax malaria B51.0
    nontraumatic D73.5
    spontaneous D73.5
  splenic vein R58
    traumatic – *see* Injury, blood vessel,
        portal vein
  stomach (nontraumatic) (spontaneous)
      K31.89
    traumatic S36.39
  supraspinatus (complete)
      (incomplete) (nontraumatic)
      M75.1-
  symphysis pubis
    obstetric O71.6
    traumatic S33.4
  synovium (cyst) M66.10
    ankle M66.17
    elbow M66.12
    finger M66.14-
    foot M66.17-
    forearm M66.13
    hand M66.14
    pelvic region M66.15
    shoulder region M66.11
      specified site NEC M66.18
    thigh M66.15
    toe M66.17
    upper arm M66.12-
    wrist M66.13-
  tendon (traumatic) - *see* Strain
    nontraumatic (spontaneous)
        M66.9
      ankle M66.87-
      extensor M66.20
        ankle M66.27-
        foot M66.27-
        forearm M66.23-
        hand M66.24-
        lower leg M66.26-
        multiple sites M66.29
        pelvic region M66.25-
        shoulder region M66.21-
        specified site NEC M66.28
        thigh M66.25-
        upper arm M66.22-
      flexor M66.30
        ankle M66.37-
        foot M66.37-
        forearm M66.33-
        hand M66.34-
        lower leg M66.36-
        multiple sites M66.39
        pelvic region M66.35-
        shoulder region M66.31-
        specified site NEC M66.38
        thigh M66.35-
        upper arm M66.32-
      foot M66.87-
      forearm M66.83-
      hand M66.84-
      lower leg M66.86-
      multiple sites M66.89
      pelvic region M66.85-
      shoulder region M66.81-
      specified
          site NEC M66.88
          tendon M66.80
      thigh M66.85-
      upper arm M66.82-
    thoracic duct I89.8

Rupture, ruptured *(Continued)*
tonsil J35.8
traumatic
aorta — *see* Injury, aorta, laceration, major
diaphragm – *see* Injury, intrathoracic, diaphragm
external site - *see* Wound, open, by site
eye – *see* Injury, eye, laceration
internal organ - *see* Injury, by site
intervertebral disc
cervical S13.0
lumbar S33.0
thoracic S23.0
kidney S37.06-
ligament - *see also* Sprain
ankle - *see* Sprain, ankle
carpus - *see* Rupture, traumatic, ligament, wrist
collateral (hand) - *see* Rupture, traumatic, ligament, finger, collateral
finger (metacarpophalangeal) (interphalangeal) S63.40-
collateral S63.41-
index S63.41-
little S63.41-
middle S63.41-
ring S63.41-
index S63.40-
little S63.40-
middle S63.40-
palmar S63.42-
index S63.42-
little S63.42-
middle S63.42-
ring S63.42-
ring S63.40-
specified site NEC S63.499
index S63.49-
little S63.49-
middle S63.49-
ring S63.49-

Rupture, ruptured *(Continued)*
traumatic *(Continued)*
ligament *(Continued)*
finger *(Continued)*
volar plate S63.43-
index S63.43-
little S63.43-
middle S63.43-
ring S63.43-
foot - *see* Sprain, foot
radial collateral S53.2-
radiocarpal - *see* Rupture, traumatic, ligament, wrist, radiocarpal
ulnar collateral S53.3-
ulnocarpal - *see* Rupture, traumatic, ligament, wrist, ulnocarpal
wrist S63.30-
collateral S63.31-
radiocarpal S63.32-
specified site NEC S63.39-
ulnocarpal (palmar) S63.33-
liver S36.116
membrana tympani – *see* Rupture, ear drum, traumatic
muscle or tendon - *see* Strain
myocardium - *see* Injury, heart
pancreas S36.299
rectum S36.69
sigmoid S36.593
spleen S36.09
stomach S36.39
symphysis pubis S33.4
tympanum, tympanic (membrane) – *see* Rupture, ear drum, traumatic
ureter S37.19
uterus S37.69
vagina – *see* Injury, vagina
vena cava – *see* Injury, vena cava, laceration, major
tricuspid (heart) (valve) I07.8
tube, tubal (nonobstetric) (nontraumatic) N83.8
abscess - *see* Salpingitis
due to pregnancy O00.1

Rupture, ruptured *(Continued)*
tympanum, tympanic (membrane) (nontraumatic) (*see also* Perforation, tympanic membrane) H72.9-
traumatic – *see* Rupture, ear drum, traumatic
umbilical cord, complicating delivery O69.89
ureter (traumatic) S37.19
nontraumatic N28.89
urethra (nontraumatic) N36.8
with ectopic or molar pregnancy O08.6
following ectopic or molar pregnancy O08.6
obstetrical trauma O71.5
traumatic S37.38
uterosacral ligament (nonobstetric) (nontraumatic) N83.8
uterus (traumatic) S37.69
before labor O71.0-
during or after labor O71.1
nonpuerperal, nontraumatic N85.8
pregnant (during labor) O71.1
before labor O71.0-
vagina – *see* Injury, vagina
valve, valvular (heart) - *see* Endocarditis
varicose vein - *see* Varix
varix - *see* Varix
vena cava R58
traumatic - *see* Injury, vena cava, laceration, major
vesical (urinary) N32.89
vessel (blood) R58
pulmonary I28.8
traumatic – *see* Injury, blood vessel
viscus R19.8
vulva complicating delivery O70.0
Russell-Silver syndrome Q87.1
Russian spring-summer type encephalitis A84.0
Rust's disease (tuberculous cervical spondylitis) A18.01
Ruvalcaba-Myhre-Smith syndrome E71.440
Rytand-Lipsitch syndrome I44.2

S

Saber, sabre shin or tibia (syphilitic) A50.56 [M90.80]
Sac lacrimal - see condition
Saccharomyces infection B37.9
Saccharopinuria E72.3
Saccular - see condition
Sacculation
  aorta (nonsyphilitic) - see Aneurysm, aorta
  bladder N32.3
  intralaryngeal (congenital) (ventricular) Q31.3
  larynx (congenital) (ventricular) Q31.3
  organ or site, congenital - see Distortion
  pregnant uterus - see Pregnancy, complicated by, abnormal, uterus
  ureter N28.89
  urethra N36.1
  vesical N32.3
Sachs' amaurotic familial idiocy or disease E75.02
Sachs-Tay disease E75.02
Sacks-Libman disease M32.11
Sacralgia M53.3
Sacralization Q76.49
Sacrodynia M53.3
Sacroiliac joint - see condition
Sacroiliitis NEC M46.1
Sacrum - see condition
Saddle
  back - see Lordosis
  embolus, aorta I74.0
  nose M95.0
    due to syphilis A50.57
Sadism (sexual) F65.52
Sadness, postpartal O90.6
Sadomasochism F65.50
Saemisch's ulcer (cornea) - see Ulcer, cornea, central
Sahib disease B55.0
Sailors' skin L57.8
Saint
  Anthony's fire - see Erysipelas
  triad - see Hernia, diaphragm
  Vitus' dance - see Chorea, Sydenham's
Salaam
  attack(s) - see Epilepsy, generalized, specified NEC
  tic R25.8
Salicylism
  abuse F55.8
  overdose or wrong substance given - see Table of drugs and chemicals, by drug, poisoning
Salivary duct or gland - see condition
Salivation, excessive K11.7
Salmonella - see Infection, Salmonella
Salmonellosis A02.0
Salpingitis (catarrhal) (fallopian tube) (nodular) (pseudofollicular) (purulent) (septic) N70.91
  with oophoritis N70.93
  acute N70.01
    with oophoritis N70.03
  chlamydial A56.11
  chronic N70.11
    with oophoritis N70.13
  complicating abortion – see Abortion, by type, complicated by, salpingitis

Salpingitis (Continued)
  ear – see Salpingitis, eustachian
  eustachian (tube) H68.00-
    acute H68.01-
    chronic H68.02-
  follicularis N70.11
    with oophoritis N70.13
  gonococcal (acute) (chronic) A54.24
  interstitial, chronic N70.11
    with oophoritis N70.13
  isthmica nodosa N70.11
    with oophoritis N70.13
  specific (gonococcal) (acute) (chronic) A54.24
  tuberculous (acute) (chronic) A18.17
  venereal (gonococcal) (acute) (chronic) A54.24
Salpingocele N83.4
Salpingo-oophoritis (catarrhal) (purulent) (ruptured) (septic) (suppurative) N70.93
  acute N70.03
    with ectopic or molar pregnancy O08.0
    following ectopic or molar pregnancy O08.0
    gonococcal A54.24
  chronic N70.13
  following ectopic or molar pregnancy O08.0
  gonococcal (acute) (chronic) A54.24
  puerperal O86.19
  specific (gonococcal) (acute) (chronic) A54.24
  subacute N70.03
  tuberculous (acute) (chronic) A18.17
  venereal (gonococcal) (acute) (chronic) A54.24
Salpingo-ovaritis - see Salpingo-oophoritis
Salpingoperitonitis - see Salpingo-oophoritis
Salzmann's nodular dystrophy - see Degeneration, cornea, nodular
Sampson's cyst or tumor N80.1
San Joaquin (Valley) fever B38.0
Sandblaster's asthma, lung or pneumoconiosis J62.8
Sander's disease (paranoia) F22
Sandfly fever A93.1
Sandhoff's disease E75.01
Sanfilippo (Type B) (Type C) (Type D) syndrome E76.22
Sanger-Brown ataxia G11.2
Sao Paulo fever or typhus A77.0
Saponification, mesenteric K65.8
Sarcocele (benign)
  syphilitic A52.76
    congenital A50.59
Sarcocystosis A07.8
Sarcoepiplocele - see Hernia
Sarcoepiplomphalocele Q79.2
Sarcoid - see also Sarcoidosis
  arthropathy D86.86
  Boeck's D86.9
  Darier-Roussy D86.3
  iridocyclitis D86.83
  meningitis D86.81
  myocarditis D86.85
  myositis D86.87
  pyelonephritis D86.84
  Spiegler-Fendt L08.89

Sarcoidosis D86.9
  with
    cranial nerve palsies D86.82
    hepatic granuloma D86.89
    polyarthritis D86.86
    tubulo-interstitial nephropathy D86.84
  combined sites NEC D86.89
  lung D86.0
    and lymph nodes D86.2
  lymph nodes D86.1
    and lung D86.2
  meninges D86.81
  skin D86.3
  specified type NEC D86.89
Sarcoma (of) - see also Neoplasm, connective tissue, malignant
  alveolar soft part - see Neoplasm, connective tissue, malignant
  ameloblastic C41.1
    upper jaw (bone) C41.0
  botryoid - see Neoplasm, connective tissue, malignant
  botryoides - see Neoplasm, connective tissue, malignant
  cerebellar C71.6
    circumscribed (arachnoidal) C71.6
  circumscribed (arachnoidal) cerebellar C71.6
  clear cell - see also Neoplasm, connective tissue, malignant
    kidney C64.-
  dendritic cells (accessory cells) C96.4
  embryonal - see Neoplasm, connective tissue, malignant
  endometrial (stromal) C54.1
    isthmus C54.0
  epithelioid (cell) - see Neoplasm, connective tissue, malignant
  Ewing's - see Neoplasm, bone, malignant
  follicular dendritic cell C96.4
  germinoblastic (diffuse) – see Lymphoma, non-Hodgkin type, diffuse, large cell
    follicular – see Lymphoma, non-Hodgkin type, follicular, specified type NEC
  giant cell (except of bone) - see also Neoplasm, connective tissue, malignant
    bone - see Neoplasm, bone, malignant
  glomoid - see Neoplasm, connective tissue, malignant
  granulocytic C92.3-
    in remission C92.31
  hemangioendothelial - see Neoplasm, connective tissue, malignant
  hemorrhagic, multiple - see Sarcoma, Kaposi's
  histiocytic C96.a
  Hodgkin - see Lymphoma, Hodgkin
  immunoblastic (diffuse) - see Lymphoma, diffuse large cell
  interdigitating dendritic cell C96.4
  Kaposi's
    colon C46.4
    connective tissue C46.1
    gastrointestinal organ C46.4
    lung C46.5-
    lymph node(s) C46.3
    palate (hard) (soft) C46.2
    rectum C46.4
    skin C46.0
    specified site NEC C46.7

Sarcoma *(Continued)*
  Kaposi's *(Continued)*
    stomach C46.4
    unspecified site C46.9
  Kupffer cell C22.3
  Langerhans cell C96.4
  leptomeningeal - *see* Neoplasm, meninges, malignant
  liver NEC C22.4
  lymphangioendothelial - *see* Neoplasm, connective tissue, malignant
  lymphoblastic - *see* Lymphoma, lymphoblastic (diffuse)
  lymphocytic - *see* Lymphoma, small cell B-cell
  mast cell C96.2
  melanotic - *see* Melanoma
  meningeal - *see* Neoplasm, meninges, malignant
  meningothelial - *see* Neoplasm, meninges, malignant
  mesenchymal - *see also* Neoplasm, connective tissue, malignant
    mixed - *see* Neoplasm, connective tissue, malignant
  mesothelial - *see* Mesothelioma
  monstrocellular
    specified site - *see* Neoplasm, malignant
    unspecified site C71.9
  myeloid C92.3-
  neurogenic - *see* Neoplasm, nerve, malignant
  odontogenic C41.1
    upper jaw (bone) C41.0
  osteoblastic - *see* Neoplasm, bone, malignant
  osteogenic - *see also* Neoplasm, bone, malignant
    juxtacortical - *see* Neoplasm, bone, malignant
    periosteal - *see* Neoplasm, bone, malignant
  periosteal - *see also* Neoplasm, bone, malignant
    osteogenic - *see* Neoplasm, bone, malignant
  pleomorphic cell - *see* Neoplasm, connective tissue, malignant
  reticulum cell (diffuse) - *see* Lymphoma, diffuse large cell
  nodular - *see* Lymphoma, follicular
  pleomorphic cell type - *see* Lymphoma, diffuse large cell
  rhabdoid - *see* Neoplasm, malignant
  round cell - *see* Neoplasm, connective tissue, malignant
  small cell - *see* Neoplasm, connective tissue, malignant
  soft tissue - *see* Neoplasm, connective tissue, malignant
  spindle cell - *see* Neoplasm, connective tissue, malignant
  stromal (endometrial) C54.1
    isthmus C54.0
  synovial - *see also* Neoplasm, connective tissue, malignant
    biphasic - *see* Neoplasm, connective tissue, malignant
    epithelioid cell - *see* Neoplasm, connective tissue, malignant
    spindle cell - *see* Neoplasm, connective tissue, malignant

Sarcomatosis
  meningeal - *see* Neoplasm, meninges, malignant
  specified site NEC - *see* Neoplasm, connective tissue, malignant
  unspecified site C80.1
Sarcosinemia E72.59
Sarcosporidiosis (intestinal) A07.8
Satiety, early R68.81
Saturnine - *see* condition
Saturnism
  overdose or wrong substance given or taken - *see* Table of drugs and chemicals, by drug, poisoning
Satyriasis F52.8
Sauriasis - *see* Ichthyosis
SBE (subacute bacterial endocarditis) I28.8
Scabs R23.4
Scabies (any site) B86
Scaglietti-Dagnini syndrome E22.0
Scald - *see* Burn
Scalenus anticus (anterior) syndrome G54.0
Scales R23.4
Scaling, skin R23.4
Scalp - *see* condition
Scapegoating affecting child Z62.3
Scaphocephaly Q75.0
Scapulalgia M89.8x1
Scapulohumeral myopathy G71.0
Scar, scarring (*see also* Cicatrix) L90.5
  adherent L90.5
  atrophic L90.5
  cervix
    in pregnancy or childbirth - *see* Pregnancy, complicated by, abnormal cervix
  cheloid L91.0
  chorioretinal H31.00-
    posterior pole macula H31.01-
    postsurgical H59.81-
    solar retinopathy H31.02-
    specified type NEC H31.09-
  choroid - *see* Scar, chorioretinal
  conjunctiva H11.24-
  cornea H17.9
    xerophthalmic - *see also* Opacity, cornea
      vitamin A deficiency E50.6
  duodenum, obstructive K31.5
  hypertrophic L91.0
  keloid L91.0
  labia N90.8
  lung (base) J98.4
  macula - *see* Scar, chorioretinal, posterior pole
  muscle M62.89
  myocardium, myocardial I25.2
  painful L90.5
  posterior pole (eye) - *see* Scar, chorioretinal, posterior pole
  retina - *see* Scar, chorioretinal
  trachea J39.8
  uterus N85.8
    in pregnancy O34.29
  vagina N89.8
    postoperative N99.2
  vulva N90.8
Scarabiasis B88.2
Scarlatina (anginosa) (maligna) (ulcerosa) A38.9
  myocarditis (acute) A38.1
    old - *see* Myocarditis
    otitis media A38.0

Scarlet fever (albuminuria) (angina) A38.9
Schamberg's disease (progressive pigmentary dermatosis) L81.7
Schatzki's ring (acquired) (esophagus) (lower) K22.2
  congenital Q39.8
Schaufenster krankheit I20.8
Schaumann's
  benign lymphogranulomatosis D86.1
  disease or syndrome - *see* Sarcoidosis
Scheie's syndrome E76.03
Schenck's disease B42.1
Scheuermann's disease or osteochondrosis - *see* Osteochondrosis, juvenile, spine
Schilder(-Flatau) disease G37.0
Schilling-type monocytic leukemia C93.0-
Schimmelbusch's disease, cystic mastitis, or hyperplasia - *see* Mastopathy, cystic
Schistosoma infestation - *see* Infestation, Schistosoma
Schistosomiasis B65.9
  with muscle disorder B65.9 *[M63.80]*
    ankle B65.9 *[M63.87-]*
    foot B65.9 *[M63.87-]*
    forearm B65.9 *[M63.83-]*
    hand B65.9 *[M63.849]*
    lower leg B65.9 *[M63.86-]*
    multiple sites B65.9 *[M63.89]*
    pelvic region B65.9 *[M63.85-]*
    shoulder region B65.9 *[M63.81-]*
    specified site NEC B65.9 *[M63.88]*
    thigh B65.9 *[M63.85-]*
    upper arm B65.9 *[M63.82-]*
  Asiatic B65.2
  bladder B65.0
  chestermani B65.8
  colon B65.1
  cutaneous B65.3
  due to
    S. haematobium B65.0
    S. japonicum B65.2
    S. mansoni B65.1
    S. mattheii B65.8
  Eastern B65.2
  genitourinary tract B65.0
  intestinal B65.1
  lung NEC B65.9 *[J99]*
    pneumonia B65.9 *[J17]*
  Manson's (intestinal) B65.1
  oriental B65.2
  pulmonary NEC B65.9 *[J99]*
    pneumonia B65.9
  Schistosoma
    haematobium B65.0
    japonicum B65.2
    mansoni B65.1
  specified type NEC B65.8
  urinary B65.0
  vesical B65.0
Schizencephaly Q04.6
Schizoaffective psychosis F25.9
Schizodontia K00.2
Schizoid personality F60.1
Schizophrenia, schizophrenic F20.9
  acute (brief) (undifferentiated) F23
  atypical (form) F20.3
  borderline F21
  catalepsy F20.2
  catatonic (type) (excited) (withdrawn) F20.2

Schizophrenia, schizophrenic (Continued)
  cenesthopathic, cenesthesiopathic
    F20.89
  childhood type F84.5
  chronic undifferentiated F20.5
  cyclic F25.0
  disorganized (type) F20.1
  flexibilitas cerea F20.2
  hebephrenic (type) F20.1
  incipient F21
  latent F21
  negative type F20.5
  paranoid (type) F20.0
  paraphrenic F20.0
  post-psychotic depression F32.8
  prepsychotic F21
  prodromal F21
  pseudoneurotic F21
  pseudopsychopathic F21
  reaction F23
  residual (state) (type) F20.5
  restzustand F20.5
  schizoaffective (type) - see Psychosis,
    schizoaffective
  simple (type) F20.89
  simplex F20.89
  specified type NEC F20.89
  stupor F20.2
  syndrome of childhood F84.5
  undifferentiated (type) F20.3
    chronic F20.5
Schizothymia (persistent) F60.1
Schlatter-Osgood disease or osteo-
    chondrosis - see Osteochondrosis,
    juvenile, tibia
Schlatter's tibia - see Osteochondrosis,
    juvenile, tibia
Schmidt's syndrome (polyglandular,
    autoimmune) E31.0
Schmincke's carcinoma or tumor -
    see Neoplasm, nasopharynx,
    malignant
Schmitz(-Stutzer) dysentery A03.0
Schmorl's disease or nodes
  lumbar region M51.46
  lumbosacral region M51.47
  sacrococcygeal region M53.3
  thoracic region M51.44
  thoracolumbar region M51.45
Schneiderian
    specified site - see Neoplasm, malignant
    unspecified site C30.0
    papilloma - see Neoplasm, nasopharynx
      benign
    specified site - see Neoplasm, benign
    unspecified site D14.0
Scholte's syndrome (malignant carcinoid)
    E34.0
Scholz(-Bielchowsky-Henneberg) dis-
    ease or syndrome E75.25
Schönlein(-Henoch) disease or
    purpura (primary) (rheumatic)
    D69.0
Schottmuller's disease A01.4
Schroeder's syndrome (endocrine hyper-
    tensive) E27.0
Schüller-Christian disease or syndrome
    C96.5
Schultze's type acroparesthesia, simple
    I73.89
Schultz's disease or syndrome - see
    Agranulocytosis
Schwalbe-Ziehen-Oppenheim disease
    G24.1

Schwannoma - see also Neoplasm, nerve,
    benign
  malignant - see also Neoplasm, nerve,
    malignant
    with rhabdomyoblastic differen-
      tiation - see Neoplasm, nerve,
      malignant
    melanocytic - see Neoplasm, nerve,
      benign
    pigmented - see Neoplasm, nerve, benign
Schwartz(-Jampel) syndrome G71.13
Schwartz-Bartter syndrome E22.2
Schweniger-Buzzi anetoderma L90.1
Sciatic - see condition
Sciatica (infective)
  with lumbago M54.4-
    due to intervertebral disc disor-
      der - see Disorder, disc, with,
      radiculopathy
    due to displacement of intervertebral
      disc (with lumbago) - see Disorder,
      disc, with, radiculopathy
    wallet M54.3-
Scimitar syndrome Q26.8
Sclera - see condition
Sclerectasia H15.84-
Scleredema
  adultorum - see Sclerosis, systemic
  Buschke's - see Sclerosis, systemic
  newborn P83.0
Sclerema (adiposum) (edematosum)
    (neonatorum) (newborn) P83.0
  adultorum see Sclerosis, systemic
Scleriasis - see Scleroderma
Scleritis H15.00-
  with corneal involvement H15.04-
  anterior H15.01-
  brawny H15.02-
  in (due to) zoster B02.34
  posterior H15.03-
  specified type NEC H15.09-
  syphilitic A52.71
  tuberculous (nodular) A18.51
Sclerochoroiditis H31.8
Scleroconjunctivitis - see Scleritis
Sclerocystic ovary syndrome E28.2
Sclerodactyly, sclerodactylia L94.3
Scleroderma, sclerodermia (acrosclerotic)
    (diffuse) (generalized) (progressive)
    (pulmonary) M34.9 - see also
    Sclerosis, systemic
  circumscribed L94.0
  linear L94.1
  localized L94.0
  newborn P83.8
  systemic M34.9
Sclerokeratitis H16.8
  tuberculous A18.52
Scleroma nasi A48.8
Scleromalacia (perforans) H15.05-
Scleromyxedema L98.5
Sclérose en plaques G35
Sclerosis, sclerotic
  adrenal (gland) E27.8
  Alzheimer's – see Disease, Alzheimer's
  amyotrophic (lateral) G12.21
  aorta, aortic I70.0
    valve - see Endocarditis, aortic
  artery, arterial, arteriolar, arteriovascu-
    lar - see Arteriosclerosis
  ascending multiple G35
  brain (generalized) (lobular) G37.9
    artery, arterial I67.2
    diffuse G37.0

Sclerosis, sclerotic (Continued)
  brain (Continued)
    disseminated G35
    insular G35
    Krabbe's E75.23
    miliary G35
    multiple G35
    presenile (Alzheimer's) – see Disease,
      Alzheimer's, early onset
    senile (arteriosclerotic) I67.2
    stem, multiple G35
    tuberous Q85.1
  bulbar, multiple G35
  bundle of His I44.39
  cardiac - see Disease, heart, ischemic,
    atherosclerotic
  cardiorenal - see Hypertension,
    cardiorenal
  cardiovascular - see also Disease,
    cardiovascular
    renal - see Hypertension, cardiorenal
  cerebellar - see Sclerosis, brain
  cerebral - see Sclerosis, brain
  cerebrospinal (disseminated) (multiple)
    G35
  cerebrovascular I67.2
  choroid - see Degeneration, choroid
  combined (spinal cord) - see also Degen-
    eration, combined
    multiple G35
  concentric (Balo) G37.5
  cornea - see Opacity, cornea
  coronary (artery) I25.10
    with angina pectoris - see Arterioscle-
      rosis, coronary (artery),
  corpus cavernosum
    female N90.8
    male N48.6
  diffuse (brain) (spinal cord) G37.0
  disseminated G35
  dorsal G35
  dorsolateral (spinal cord) - see Degen-
    eration, combined
  endometrium N85.5
  extrapyramidal G25.9
  eye, nuclear (senile) – see Cataract,
    senile, nuclear
  focal and segmental (glomerular) (see
    also N00-N07 with fourth character
    .1) N05.1
  Friedreich's (spinal cord) G11.1
  funicular (spermatic cord) N50.8
  general (vascular) - see Arteriosclerosis
  gland (lymphatic) I89.8
  hepatic K74.1
    alcoholic K70.2
  hereditary
    cerebellar G11.9
    spinal (Friedreich's ataxia) G11.1
  hippocampal G93.81
  insular G35
  kidney - see Sclerosis, renal
  larynx J38.7
  lateral (amyotrophic) (descending)
    (primary) (spinal) G12.21
  lens, senile nuclear - see Cataract, senile,
    nuclear
  liver K74.1
    with fibrosis K74.2
      alcoholic K70.2
    alcoholic K70.2
    cardiac K76.1
  lung - see Fibrosis, lung
  mastoid – see Mastoiditis, chronic

Sclerosis, sclerotic *(Continued)*
  mesial temporal G93.81
  mitral I05.8
  Mönckeberg's (medial) - *see* Arteriosclerosis, extremities
  multiple (brain stem) (cerebral) (generalized) (spinal cord) G35
  myocardium, myocardial – *see* Disease, heart, ischemic, atherosclerotic
  nuclear (senile), eye – *see* Cataract, senile, nuclear
  ovary N83.8
  pancreas K86.8
  penis N48.6
  peripheral arteries - *see* Arteriosclerosis, extremities
  plaques G35
  pluriglandular E31.8
  polyglandular E31.8
  posterolateral (spinal cord) - *see* Degeneration, combined
  presenile (Alzheimer's) – *see* Disease, Alzheimer's, early onset
  primary, lateral G12.29
  progressive, systemic M34.0
  pulmonary - *see* Fibrosis, lung
    artery I27.0
    valve (heart) - *see* Endocarditis, pulmonary
  renal N26.9
    with
      cystine storage disease E72.09
      hypertension - *see* Hypertension, kidney
      hypertensive heart disease (conditions in I11) - *see* Hypertension, cardiorenal
    arteriolar (hyaline) (hyperplastic) - *see* Hypertension, kidney
  retina (senile) (vascular) H35.00
  senile (vascular) - *see* Arteriosclerosis
  spinal (cord) (progressive) G95.89
    ascending G61.0
    combined - *see also* Degeneration, combined
      multiple G35
      syphilitic A52.11
    disseminated G35
    dorsolateral - *see* Degeneration, combined
    hereditary (Friedreich's) (mixed form) G11.1
    lateral (amyotrophic) G12.21
    multiple G35
    posterior (syphilitic) A52.11
  stomach K31.89
  subendocardial, congenital I42.4
  systemic M34.9
    with
      lung involvement M34.81
      myopathy M34.82
      polyneuropathy M34.83
    drug-induced M34.2
    due to chemicals NEC M34.2
    progressive M34.0
    specified NEC M34.89
  temporal (mesial) G93.81
  tricuspid (heart) (valve) I07.8
  tuberous (brain) Q85.1
  tympanic membrane - *see* Disorder, tympanic membrane, specified NEC
  valve, valvular (heart) - *see* Endocarditis
  vascular - *see* Arteriosclerosis
  vein I87.8

Scoliosis (acquired) (postural) M41.9
  adolescent (idiopathic) - *see* Scoliosis, idiopathic, juvenile
  congenital Q67.5
    due to bony malformation Q76.3
    failure of segmentation (hemivertebra) Q76.3
    hemivertebra fusion Q76.3
    postural Q67.5
  idiopathic M41.20
    adolescent M41.129
      cervical region M41.122
      cervicothoracic region M41.123
      lumbar region M41.126
      lumbosacral region M41.127
      multiple sites M41.129
      thoracic region M41.124
      thoracolumbar region M41.125
    cervical region M41.22
    cervicothoracic region M41.23
    infantile M41.00
      cervical region M41.02
      cervicothoracic region M41.03
      lumbar region M41.06
      lumbosacral region M41.07
      sacrococcygeal region M41.08
      thoracic region M41.04
      thoracolumbar region M41.05
    juvenile M41.119
      cervical region M41.112
      cervicothoracic region M41.113
      lumbar region M41.116
      lumbosacral region M41.117
      multiple sites M41.119
      thoracic region M41.114
      thoracolumbar region M41.115
    lumbar region M41.26
    lumbosacral region M41.27
    thoracic region M41.24
    thoracolumbar region M41.25
  neuromuscular M41.40
    cervical region M41.42
    cervicothoracic region M41.43
    lumbar region M41.46
    lumbosacral region M41.47
    occipito-atlanto-axial region M41.41
    thoracic region M41.44
    thoracolumbar region M41.45
  paralytic - *see* Scoliosis, neuromuscular
  postradiation therapy M96.5
  rachitic (late effect or sequelae) E64.3 *[M49.80]*
    cervical region E64.3 *[M49.82]*
    cervicothoracic region E64.3 *[M49.83]*
    lumbar region E64.3 *[M49.86]*
    lumbosacral region E64.3 *[M49.87]*
    multiple sites E64.3 *[M49.89]*
    occipito-atlanto-axial region E64.3 *[M49.81]*
    sacrococcygeal region E64.3 *[M49.88]*
    thoracic region E64.3 *[M49.84]*
    thoracolumbar region E64.3 *[M49.85]*
  sciatic M54.4-
  secondary (to) NEC M41.50
    cerebral palsy, Friedreich's ataxia, poliomyelitis, neuromuscular disorders - *see* Scoliosis, neuromuscular
    cervical region M41.52
    cervicothoracic region M41.53
    lumbar region M41.56
    lumbosacral region M41.57
    thoracic region M41.54
    thoracolumbar region M41.55

Scoliosis *(Continued)*
  specified form NEC M41.80
    cervical region M41.82
    cervicothoracic region M41.83
    lumbar region M41.86
    lumbosacral region M41.87
    thoracic region M41.84
    thoracolumbar region M41.85
  thoracogenic M41.30
    thoracic region M41.34
    thoracolumbar region M41.35
  tuberculous A18.01
Scoliotic pelvis
  with disproportion (fetopelvic) O33.0
    causing obstructed labor O65.0
Scorbutus, scorbutic - *see also* Scurvy
  anemia D53.2
Scotoma (arcuate) (Bjerrum) (central) (ring) - *see also* Defect, visual field, localized, scotoma
  scintillating H53.19
Scratch - *see* Abrasion
Scratchy throat R09.89
Screening (for) Z13.9
  alcoholism Z13.89
  anemia Z13.0
  anomaly, congenital Z13.89
  antenatal, of mother Z36
  arterial hypertension Z13.6
  arthropod-borne viral disease NEC Z11.59
  bacteriuria, asymptomatic Z13.89
  behavioral disorder Z13.89
  brain injury, traumatic Z13.850
  bronchitis, chronic Z13.83
  brucellosis Z11.2
  cardiovascular disorder Z13.6
  cataract Z13.5
  chlamydial diseases Z11.8
  cholera Z11.0
  chromosomal abnormalities (nonprocreative) NEC Z13.79
  congenital
    dislocation of hip Z13.89
    eye disorder Z13.5
    malformation or deformation Z13.89
  contamination NEC Z13.88
  cystic fibrosis Z13.228
  dengue fever Z11.59
  dental disorder Z13.84
  depression Z13.89
  developmental handicap Z13.4
    in early childhood Z13.4
  diabetes mellitus Z13.1
  diphtheria Z11.2
  disease or disorder Z13.9
    bacterial NEC Z11.2
      intestinal infectious Z11.0
      respiratory tuberculosis Z11.1
    blood or blood-forming organ Z13.0
    cardiovascular Z13.6
    Chagas' Z11.6
    chlamydial Z11.8
    dental Z13.89
    developmental Z13.4
    digestive tract NEC Z13.818
      lower GI Z13.811
      upper GI Z13.810
    ear Z13.5
    endocrine Z13.29
    eye Z13.5
    genitourinary Z13.89
    heart Z13.6

Screening *(Continued)*
  disease or disorder *(Continued)*
    human immunodeficiency virus
        (HIV) infection Z11.4
    immunity Z13.0
    infection
        intestinal Z11.0
            specified NEC Z11.6
    infectious Z11.9
    mental Z13.89
    metabolic Z13.228
    neurological Z13.89
    nutritional Z13.21
        metabolic Z13.228
            lipoid disorders Z13.220
    protozoal Z11.6
        intestinal Z11.0
    respiratory Z13.83
    rheumatic Z13.828
    rickettsial Z11.8
    sexually-transmitted NEC Z11.3
        human immunodeficiency
            virus (HIV) Z11.4
    sickle-cell (trait) Z13.0
    skin Z13.89
    specified NEC Z13.89
    spirochetal Z11.8
    thyroid Z13.29
    vascular Z13.6
    venereal Z11.3
    viral NEC Z11.59
        human immunodeficiency virus
            (HIV) Z11.4
        intestinal Z11.0
  elevated titer Z13.89
  emphysema Z13.83
  encephalitis, viral (mosquitoor tick-
        borne) Z11.59
  exposure to contaminants (toxic) Z13.88
  fever
    dengue Z11.59
    hemorrhagic Z11.59
    yellow Z11.59
  filariasis Z11.6
  galactosemia Z13.228
  gastrointestinal condition Z13.818
  genetic (nonprocreative) - for procre-
        ative management *see* Testing, ge-
        netic, for procreative management
    disease carrier status (nonprocre-
        ative) Z13.71
    specified NEC (nonprocreative) Z13.79
  genitourinary condition Z13.89
  glaucoma Z13.5
  gonorrhea Z11.3
  gout Z13.89
  helminthiasis (intestinal) Z11.6
  hematopoietic malignancy Z12.89
  hemoglobinopathies NEC Z13.0
  hemorrhagic fever Z11.59
  Hodgkin disease Z12.89
  human immunodeficiency virus (HIV)
        Z11.4
  human papillomavirus Z11.51
  hypertension Z13.6
  immunity disorders Z13.0
  infection
    mycotic Z11.8
    parasitic Z11.8
  ingestion of radioactive substance
        Z13.88
  intestinal
    helminthiasis Z11.6
    infectious disease Z11.0

Screening *(Continued)*
  leishmaniasis Z11.6
  leprosy Z11.2
  leptospirosis Z11.8
  leukemia Z12.89
  lymphoma Z12.89
  malaria Z11.6
  malnutrition Z13.29
    metabolic Z13.228
    nutritional Z13.21
  measles Z11.59
  mental
    disorder Z13.89
    retardation Z13.4
  metabolic errors, inborn Z13.228
  multiphasic Z13.89
  musculoskeletal disorder Z13.828
    osteoporosis Z13.820
  mycoses Z11.8
  myocardial infarction (acute) Z13.6
  neoplasm (malignant) (of) Z12.9
    bladder Z12.6
    blood Z12.89
    breast Z12.39
        routine mammogram Z12.31
    cervix Z12.4
    colon Z12.11
    genitourinary organs NEC
        Z12.79
        bladder Z12.6
        cervix Z12.4
        ovary Z12.73
        prostate Z12.5
        testis Z12.71
        vagina Z12.72
    hematopoietic system Z12.89
    intestinal tract Z12.10
        colon Z12.11
        rectum Z12.12
        small intestine Z12.13
    lung Z12.2
    lymph (glands) Z12.89
    nervous system Z12.82
    oral cavity Z12.81
    prostate Z12.5
    rectum Z12.12
    respiratory organs Z12.2
    skin Z12.83
    small intestine Z12.13
    specified site NEC Z12.89
    stomach Z12.0
  nephropathy Z13.89
  nervous system disorders NEC Z13.858
  neurological condition Z13.89
  osteoporosis Z13.820
  parasitic infestation Z11.9
    specified NEC Z11.8
  phenylketonuria Z13.228
  plague Z11.2
  poisoning (chemical) (heavy metal)
        Z13.88
  poliomyelitis Z11.59
  postnatal, chromosomal abnormalities
        Z13.89
  prenatal, of mother Z36
  protozoal disease Z11.6
    intestinal Z11.0
  pulmonary tuberculosis Z11.1
  radiation exposure Z13.88
  respiratory condition Z13.83
  respiratory tuberculosis Z11.1
  rheumatoid arthritis Z13.828
  rubella Z11.59
  schistosomiasis Z11.6

Screening *(Continued)*
  sexually-transmitted disease NEC Z11.3
    human immunodeficiency virus
        (HIV) Z11.4
  sickle-cell disease or trait Z13.0
  skin condition Z13.89
  sleeping sickness Z11.6
  special Z13.9
    specified NEC Z13.89
  syphilis Z11.3
  tetanus Z11.2
  trachoma Z11.8
  traumatic brain injury Z13.850
  trypanosomiasis Z11.6
  tuberculosis, respiratory Z11.1
  venereal disease Z11.3
  viral encephalitis (mosquito- or tick-
        borne) Z11.59
  whooping cough Z11.2
  worms, intestinal Z11.6
  yaws Z11.8
  yellow fever Z11.59
Scrofula, scrofulosis (tuberculosis of
      cervical lymph glands) A18.2
Scrofulide (primary) (tuberculous) A18.4
Scrofuloderma, scrofulodermia (any site)
      (primary) A18.4
Scrofulosus lichen (primary) (tubercu-
      lous) A18.4
Scrofulous - *see* condition
Scrotal tongue K14.5
Scrotum - *see* condition
Scurvy, scorbutic E54
  anemia D53.2
  gum E54
  infantile E54
  rickets E55.9 *[M90.80]*
Sealpox B08.62
Seasickness T75.3
Seatworm (infection) (infestation) B80
Sebaceous - *see also* condition
  cyst - *see* Cyst, sebaceous
Seborrhea, seborrheic L21.9
  capillitii R23.8
  capitis L21.0
  dermatitis L21.9
    infantile L21.1
  eczema L21.9
    infantile L21.1
  sicca L21.0
Seckel's syndrome Q87.1
Seclusion, pupil - *see* Membrane,
      pupillary
Second hand tobacco smoke exposure
      (acute) (chronic) Z77.22
Secondary
  dentin (in pulp) K04.3
  neoplasm, secondaries - *see* Table of
      Neoplasms, secondary
Secretion
  antidiuretic hormone, inappropriate
        E22.2
  catecholamine, by pheochromocytoma
        E27.5
  hormone
    antidiuretic, inappropriate (syn-
        drome) E22.2
    by
        carcinoid tumor E34.0
        pheochromocytoma E27.5
    ectopic NEC E34.2
  urinary
    excessive R35.8
    suppression R34

Section
  nerve, traumatic - *see* Injury, nerve
Segmentation, incomplete (congenital) -
      see also Fusion
  bone NEC Q78.8
  lumbosacral (joint) (vertebra) Q76.49
Seitelberger's syndrome (infantile neur-
      axonal dystrophy) G31.89
Seizure(s) (*see also* Convulsions) R56.9
  akinetic - *see* Epilepsy, generalized,
      idiopathic
  atonic - *see* Epilepsy, generalized,
      idiopathic
  autonomic (hysterical) F44.5
  convulsive - *see* Convulsions
  cortical (focal) (motor) - *see* Epilepsy,
      localization-related, symptomatic,
      with simple partial seizures
  disorder (*see also* Epilepsy) G40.909
  due to stroke - *see* Sequelae (of), disease,
      cerebrovascular, by type, specified
      NEC
  epileptic - *see* Epilepsy
  febrile (simple) R56.00
    with status epilepticus G40.901
    complex (atypical) (complicated) R56.01
      with status epilepticus G40.901
  grand mal G40.309
    intractable G40.319
      with status epilepticus G40.311
      without status epilepticus G40.319
    not intractable G40.309
      with status epilepticus G40.301
      without status epilepticus G40.309
  heart - *see* Disease, heart
  hysterical F44.5
  intractable G40.919
    with status epilepticus G40.911
  Jacksonian (focal) (motor type) (sensory
      type) - *see* Epilepsy, localization-
      related, symptomatic, with simple
      partial seizures
  newborn P90
  nonspecific epileptic
    atonic - *see* Epilepsy, generalized,
        idiopathic
    clonic - *see* Epilepsy, generalized,
        idiopathic
    myoclonic - *see* Epilepsy, generalized,
        idiopathic
    tonic - *see* Epilepsy, generalized,
        idiopathic
    tonic-clonic - *see* Epilepsy, general-
        ized, idiopathic
  partial, developing into secondarily
      generalized seizures
    complex - *see* Epilepsy, localization-
        related, symptomatic, with
        complex partial seizures
    simple - *see* Epilepsy, localization-
        related, symptomatic, with
        simple partial seizures
  petit mal G40.309
    intractable G40.319
      with status epilepticus G40.311
      without status epilepticus G40.319
    not intractable G40.309
      with status epilepticus G40.301
      without status epilepticus G40.309
  recurrent G40.909
  specified NEC G40.89
  uncinate - *see* Epilepsy, localization-
      related, symptomatic, with com-
      plex partial seizures

Selenium deficiency, dietary E59
Self-damaging behavior (life-style) Z72.89
Self-harm (attempted)
  history (personal) Z91.5
    in family Z81.8
Self-mutilation (attempted)
  history (personal) Z91.5
    in family Z81.8
Self-poisoning
  history (personal) Z91.5
    in family Z81.8
Semicoma R40.1
Seminal vesiculitis N49.0
Seminoma C62.9-
  anaplastic
    specified site - *see* Neoplasm,
        malignant
    unspecified site C62.9-
  specified site - *see* Neoplasm, malignant
  spermatocytic
    specified site - *see* Neoplasm,
        malignant
    unspecified site C62.9-
Senear-Usher disease or syndrome
      L10.4
Senectus R54
Senescence (without mention of psycho-
      sis) R54
Senile, senility (*see also* condition) R54
  with
    acute confusional state F05
    mental changes NOS F03
    psychosis NEC - *see* Psychosis, senile
  asthenia R54
  cervix (atrophic) N88.8
  debility R54
  endometrium (atrophic) N85.8
  fallopian tube (atrophic) – *see* Atrophy,
      fallopian tube
  heart (failure) R54
  ovary (atrophic) – *see* Atrophy, ovary
  premature E34.8
  vagina, vaginitis (atrophic) N95.2
  wart L82.1
Sensation
  burning (skin) R20.8
    tongue K14.6
  loss of R20.8
  prickling (skin) R20.2
  tingling (skin) R20.2
Sense loss
  smell - *see* Disturbance, sensation, smell
  taste - *see* Disturbance, sensation, taste
  touch R20.8
Sensibility disturbance (cortical) (deep)
      (vibratory) R20.9
Sensitive, sensitivity - *see also* Allergy
  carotid sinus G90.01
  child (excessive) F93.8
  cold, autoimmune D59.1
  dentin K03.89
  latex Z91.040
  methemoglobin D74.8
  tuberculin, without clinical or radiologi-
      cal symptoms R76.1
  visual
    glare H53.71
    impaired contrast H53.72
Sensitiver Beziehungswahn F22
Sensitization, auto-erythrocytic D69.2
Separation
  anxiety, abnormal (of childhood) F93.0
  apophysis, traumatic - code as Fracture,
      by site

Separation (*Continued*)
  choroid - *see* Detachment, choroid
  epiphysis, epiphyseal
    nontraumatic – *see also* Osteochon-
        dropathy, specified type NEC
      upper femoral - *see* Slipped,
          epiphysis, upper femoral
    traumatic - code as Fracture, by site
  fracture - *see* Fracture
  infundibulum cardiac from right ven-
      tricle by a partition Q24.3
  joint (traumatic) (current) - code by site
      under Dislocation
  pubic bone, obstetrical trauma O71.6
  retina, retinal - *see* Detachment, retina
  symphysis pubis, obstetrical trauma
      O71.6
  tracheal ring, incomplete, congenital
      Q32.1
Sepsis (generalized) A41.9
  with
    acute organ dysfunction R65.2
    multiple organ dysfunction R65.2
  actinomycotic A42.7
  adrenal hemorrhage syndrome (menin-
      gococcal) A39.1
  anaerobic A41.4
  Bacillus anthracis A22.7
  Brucella (*see also* Brucellosis) A23.9
  candidal B37.7
  cryptogenic A41.9
  due to device, implant or graft T85.79
    arterial graft NEC T82.7
    breast (implant) T85.79
    catheter NEC T85.79
      dialysis (renal) T82.7
        intraperitoneal T85.71
      infusion NEC T82.7
        spinal (epidural) (subdural)
            T85.79
      urinary (indwelling) T83.51
    ectopic or molar pregnancy O08.82
    electronic (electrode) (pulse genera-
        tor) (stimulator)
      bone T84.7
      cardiac T82.7
      nervous system (brain) (peripheral
          nerve) (spinal) T85.79
      urinary T83.59
    fixation, internal (orthopedic) - *see*
        Complication, fixation device,
        infection
    gastrointestinal (bile duct) (esopha-
        gus) T85.79
    genital T83.6
    heart NEC T82.7
      valve (prosthesis) T82.6
        graft T82.7
    joint prosthesis - *see* Complication,
        joint prosthesis, infection
    ocular (corneal graft) (orbital im-
        plant) T85.79
    orthopedic NEC T84.7
      fixation device, internal - *see*
          Complication, fixation device,
          infection
    specified NEC T85.79
    vascular T82.7
    ventricular intracranial shunt T85.79
  during labor O75.3
  Enterococcus A41.81
  Erysipelothrix (rhusiopathiae) (erysip-
      eloid) A26.7
  Escherichia coli (E. coli) A41.5

Sepsis *(Continued)*
  extraintestinal yersiniosis A28.2
  following
    abortion (subsequent episode) O08.0
      current episode - *see* Abortion
    ectopic or molar pregnancy O08.82
    immunization T88.0
    infusion, therapeutic injection or
      transfusion NEC T80.29
  gangrenous A41.9
  gonococcal A54.8
  Gram-negative (organism) A41.5
    anaerobic A41.4
  Haemophilus influenzae A41.3
  herpesviral B00.7
  intraocular - *see* Endophthalmitis,
    purulent
  Listeria monocytogenes A32.7
  localized
    in operation wound T81.4
    skin - *see* Abscess
  malleus A24.0
  melioidosis A24.1
  meningeal - *see* Meningitis
  meningococcal A39.4
    acute A39.2
    chronic A39.3
  newborn P36.9
    due to
      anaerobes NEC P36.5
      Escherichia coli P36.4
      Staphylococcus P36.30
        aureus P36.2
        specified NEC P36.39
      Streptococcus P36.10
        group B P36.0
        specified NEC P36.19
      specified NEC P36.8
  Pasteurella multocida A28.0
  pelvic, puerperal, postpartum, child-
    birth O85
  postprocedural T81.4
  pneumococcal A40.3
  puerperal, postpartum, childbirth
    (pelvic) O85
  Salmonella (arizonae) (cholerae-suis)
    (enteritidis) (typhimurium) A02.1
  severe R65.20
    with septic shock R65.21
  skin, localized - *see* Abscess
  Shigella (*see also* Dysentery, bacillary)
    A03.9
  specified organism NEC A41.89
  Staphylococcus, staphylococcal A41.2
    aureus A41.0
    coagulase-negative A41.1
    specified NEC A41.1
  Streptococcus, streptococcal A40.9
    agalactiae A40.1
    group
      A A40.0
      B A40.1
      D A41.81
    neonatal P36.10
      group B P36.0
      specified NEC P36.19
    pneumoniae A40.3
    pyogenes A40.0
    specified NEC A40.8
  tracheostomy stoma J95.02
  tularemic A21.7
  umbilical, umbilical cord (newborn) -
    see Sepsis, newborn
  Yersinia pestis A20.7

Septate - *see* Septum
Septic - *see* condition
  arm - *see* Cellulitis, upper limb
    with lymphangitis - *see* Lymphangi-
      tis, acute, upper limb
  embolus - *see* Embolism
  finger - *see* Cellulitis, digit
    with lymphangitis - *see* Lymphangi-
      tis, acute, digit
  foot - *see* Cellulitis, lower limb
    with lymphangitis - *see* Lymphangi-
      tis, acute, lower limb
  gallbladder (acute) K81.0
  hand - *see* Cellulitis, upper limb
    with lymphangitis - *see* Lymphangi-
      tis, acute, upper limb
  joint - *see* Arthritis, pyogenic or pyemic
  leg - *see* Cellulitis, lower limb
    with lymphangitis - *see* Lymphangi-
      tis, acute, lower limb
  nail - *see also* Cellulitis, digit
    with lymphangitis - *see* Lymphangi-
      tis, acute, digit
  sore - *see also* Abscess
    throat J02.0
      streptococcal J02.0
  spleen (acute) D73.89
  teeth, tooth (pulpal origin) K04.4
  throat - *see* Pharyngitis
  thrombus - *see* Thrombosis
  toe - *see* Cellulitis, digit
    with lymphangitis - *see* Lymphangi-
      tis, acute, digit
  tonsils, chronic J35.01
    with adenoiditis J35.03
  uterus - *see* Endometritis
Septicemia A41.9
  meaning sepsis - *see* Sepsis
Septum, septate (congenital) - *see also*
    Anomaly, by site
  anal Q42.3
    with fistula Q42.2
  aqueduct of Sylvius Q03.0
    with spina bifida - *see* Spina bifida, by
      site, with hydrocephalus
  uterus - *see* Double, uterus
  vagina Q52.1
    in pregnancy - *see* Pregnancy, compli-
      cated by, abnormal vagina
    causing obstructed labor O65.5
Sequelae (of) - *see also* condition
  abscess, intracranial or intraspinal (con-
    ditions in G06) G09
  amputation — code to injury with
    extension s
  burn and corrosion — code to injury
    with extension s
  calcium deficiency E64.8
  cerebrovascular disease – *see* Sequelae,
    disease, cerebrovascular
  childbirth O94
  contusion — code to injury with exten-
    sion s
  corrosion - *see* Sequelae, burn and
    corrosion
  crushing injury — code to injury with
    extension s
  disease
    cerebrovascular I69.90
      alteration of sensation I69.998
      aphasia I69.920
      apraxia I69.990
      ataxia I69.993
      cognitive defects I69.91

Sequelae (of) *(Continued)*
  disease *(Continued)*
    cerebrovascular *(Continued)*
      disturbance of vision I69.998
      dysarthria I69.922
      dysphagia I69.991
      dysphasia I69.921
      facial droop I69.992
      facial weakness I69.992
      fluency disorder I69.923
      hemiplegia I69.95-
      hemorrhage
        intracerebral - *see* Sequelae, hem-
          orrhage, intracerebral
        intracranial, nontraumatic NEC
          - *see* Sequelae, hemorrhage,
          intracranial, nontraumatic
        subarachnoid - *see* Sequelae,
          hemorrhage, subarachnoid
      language deficit I69.928
      monoplegia
        lower limb I69.84-
        upper limb I69.93-
      paralytic syndrome I69.96-
      specified effect NEC I69.998
      specified type NEC I69.80
        alteration of sensation I69.898
        aphasia I69.820
        apraxia I69.890
        ataxia I69.893
        cognitive defects I69.81
        disturbance of vision I69.898
        dysarthria I69.822
        dysphagia I69.891
        dysphasia I69.821
        facial droop I69.892
        facial weakness I69.892
        fluency disorder I69.823
        hemiplegia I69.85-
        language deficit I69.828
        monoplegia
          lower limb I69.84-
          upper limb I69.83-
        paralytic syndrome I69.86-
        specified effect NEC I69.898
      speech deficit I69.928
        speech deficit I69.828
      stroke NOS - *see* Sequelae, stroke
        NOS
    dislocation - code to injury with
      extensions
    encephalitis or encephalomyelitis (con-
      ditions in G04) G09
      in infectious disease NEC B94.8
      viral B94.1
    external cause
      code to injury with extensions
    foreign body entering natural orifice
      code to injury with extension s
    fracture
      code to injury with extensions
    frostbite
      code to injury with extensions
    Hansen's disease B92
    hemorrhage
      intracerebral I69.10
        alteration of sensation I69.198
        aphasia I69.120
        apraxia I69.190
        ataxia I69.193
        cognitive defects I69.11
        disturbance of vision I69.198
        dysarthria I69.122
        dysphagia I69.191

Sequelae (of) (Continued)
  hemorrhage (Continued)
    intracerebral (Continued)
      dysphasia I69.121
      facial droop I69.192
      facial weakness I69.192
      fluency disorder I69.123
      hemiplegia I69.15-
      language deficit NEC I69.128
      monoplegia
        lower limb I69.14-
        upper limb I69.13-
      paralytic syndrome I69.16-
      specified effect NEC I69.198
      speech deficit NEC I69.128
    intracranial, nontraumatic NEC
        I69.20
      alteration of sensation I69.298
      aphasia I69.220
      apraxia I69.290
      ataxia I69.293
      cognitive defects I69.21
      disturbance of vision I69.298
      dysarthria I69.222
      dysphagia I69.291
      dysphasia I69.221
      facial droop I69.292
      facial weakness I69.292
      fluency disorder I69.223
      hemiplegia I69.25-
      language deficit NEC I69.228
      monoplegia
        lower limb I69.24-
        upper limb I69.23-
      paralytic syndrome I69.26-
      specified effect NEC I69.298
      speech deficit NEC I69.228
    subarachnoid I69.00
      alteration of sensation I69.098
      aphasia I69.020
      apraxia I69.090
      ataxia I69.093
      cognitive defects I69.01
      disturbance of vision I69.098
      dysarthria I69.022
      dysphagia I69.091
      dysphasia I69.021
      facial droop I69.092
      facial weakness I69.092
      fluency disorder I69.023
      hemiplegia I69.05-
      language deficit NEC I69.028
      monoplegia
        lower limb I69.04-
        upper limb I69.03-
      paralytic syndrome I69.06-
      specified effect NEC I69.098
      speech deficit NEC I69.028
  hepatitis, viral B94.2
  hyperalimentation E68
  infarction
    cerebral I69.30
      alteration of sensation I69.398
      aphasia I69.320
      apraxia I69.390
      ataxia I69.393
      cognitive defects I69.31
      disturbance of vision I69.398
      dysarthria I69.322
      dysphagia I69.391
      dysphasia I69.321
      facial droop I69.392
      facial weakness I69.392
      fluency disorder I69.323

Sequelae (of) (Continued)
  infarction (Continued)
    cerebral (Continued)
      hemiplegia I69.35-
      language deficit NEC I69.328
      monoplegia
        lower limb I69.34-
        upper limb I69.33-
      paralytic syndrome I69.36-
      specified effect NEC I69.398
      speech deficit NEC I69.328
  infection, pyogenic, intracranial or
      intraspinal G09
  infectious disease B94.9
    specified NEC B94.8
  injury
    code to injury with extensions
  leprosy B92
  meningitis
    bacterial (conditions in G00) G09
    other or unspecified cause (condi-
      tions in G03) G09
  muscle (and tendon) injury
    code to injury with extension s
  myelitis - see Sequelae, encephalitis
  niacin deficiency E64.8
  nutritional deficiency E64.9
    specified NEC E64.8
  obstetrical condition O94
  parasitic disease B94.9
  phlebitis or thrombophlebitis of
      intracranial or intraspinal venous
      sinuses and veins (conditions in
      G08) G09
  poisoning
    code to poisoning with extensions
    nonmedicinal substance - see
        Sequelae, toxic effect, nonmed-
        icinal substance
  poliomyelitis (acute) B91
  pregnancy O94
  protein-energy malnutrition E64.0
  puerperium O94
  rickets E64.3
  selenium deficiency E64.8
  sprain and strain
    code to injury with extensions
  stroke NOS I69.30
    alteration in sensation I69.398
    aphasia I69.320
    apraxia I69.390
    ataxia I69.393
    cognitive defects I69.31
    disturbance of vision I69.398
    dysarthria I69.322
    dysphagia I69.391
    dysphasia I69.321
    facial droop I69.392
    facial weakness I69.392
    hemiplegia I69.35-
    language deficit NEC I69.328
    monoplegia
      lower limb I69.34-
      upper limb I69.33-
    paralytic syndrome I69.36-
    specified effect NEC I69.398
    speech deficit NEC I69.328
  tendon and muscle injury — code to
      injury with extension s
  thiamine deficiency E64.8
  trachoma B94.0
  tuberculosis B90.9
    bones and joints B90.2
    central nervous system B90.0

Sequelae (of) (Continued)
  tuberculosis (Continued)
    genitourinary B90.1
    pulmonary (respiratory) B90.9
    specified organs NEC B90.8
  viral
    encephalitis B94.1
    hepatitis B94.2
  vitamin deficiency NEC E64.8
    A E64.1
    B E64.8
    C E64.2
  wound, open — code to injury with
      extension s
Sequestration - see also Sequestrum
  lung, congenital Q33.2
Sequestrum
  bone - see Osteomyelitis, chronic
  dental M27.2
  jaw bone M27.2
  orbit - see Osteomyelitis, orbit
  sinus (accessory) (nasal) - see Sinusitis
Sequoiosis lung or pneumonitis J67.8
Serology for syphilis
  doubtful
    with signs or symptoms - code
        by site and stage under
        Syphilis
    follow-up of latent syphilis - see
        Syphilis, latent
  negative, with signs or symptoms -
      code by site and stage under
      Syphilis
  positive A53.0
    with signs or symptoms - code
        by site and stage under
        Syphilis
  reactivated A53.0
Seroma - see also Hematoma
  traumatic, secondary and recurrent
      T79.2
Seropurulent - see condition
Serositis, multiple K65.8
  pericardial I31.1
  peritoneal K65.8
Serous - see condition
Sertoli cell
    specified site - see Neoplasm, benign
    unspecified site
      female D27.9
      male D29.20
    specified site - see Neoplasm, malignant
    unspecified site (male) C62.9-
      female C56.9
        specified site - see Neoplasm,
            benign
        unspecified site
          female D27.9
          male D29.20
    specified site - see Neoplasm, benign
    unspecified site
      female D27.9
      male D29.20
Sertoli-Leydig cell tumor - see Neoplasm,
    benign
  specified site - see Neoplasm, benign
  unspecified site
    female D27.9
    male D29.20
Serum
  allergy, allergic reaction T80.6
    shock T80.5
  arthritis T80.6
  complication or reaction NEC T80.6

421

Serum (*Continued*)
  disease NEC T80.6
  hepatitis - *see also* Hepatitis, viral,
     type B
    carrier (suspected) of Z22.51
  intoxication T80.6
  neuritis T80.6
  neuropathy G61.1
  poisoning NEC T80.6
  rash NEC T80.6
  reaction NEC T80.6
  sickness NEC T80.6
  urticaria T80.6
Sesamoiditis - *see* Osteomyelitis, specified
  type NEC
Sever's disease or osteochondrosis - *see*
  Osteochondrosis, juvenile, tarsus
Severe sepsis R65.20
  with septic shock R65.21
Sex
  chromosome mosaics Q97.8
    lines with various numbers of X
     chromosomes Q97.2
  education Z70.8
  reassignment surgery status Z87.890
Sextuplet pregnancy – *see* Pregnancy,
  sextuplet
Sexual
  function, disorder of (psychogenic)
    F52.9
  immaturity (female) (male) E30.0
  impotence (psychogenic) organic origin
    NEC - *see* Dysfunction, sexual,
    male
  precocity (constitutional)
    (cryptogenic)(female) (idiopathic)
    (male) E30.1
Sexuality, pathologic - *see* Deviation,
  sexual
Sézary's disease C84.1-
Shadow, lung R91
Shaking palsy or paralysis - *see*
  Parkinsonism
Shallowness, acetabulum - *see* Derange-
  ment, joint, specified type NEC, hip
Shaver's disease J63.1
Sheath (tendon) - *see* condition
Sheathing, retinal vessels H35.00
Shedding
  nail L60.8
  premature, primary (deciduous) teeth
    K00.6
Sheehan's disease or syndrome E23.0
Shelf, rectal K62.8
Shell teeth K00.5
Shellshock (current) F43.0
  lasting state – *see* Disorder, post-
    traumatic stress
Shield kidney Q63.1
Shift
  auditory threshold (temporary)
    H93.24-
  mediastinal R93.8
Shifting sleep-work schedule (affecting
  sleep) G47.26
Shiga(-Kruse) dysentery A03.0
Shiga's bacillus A03.0
Shigella (dysentery) - *see* Dysentery,
  bacillary
Shigellosis A03.9
  Group A A03.0
  Group B A03.1
  Group C A03.2
  Group D A03.3

Shin splints T79.6
Shingles - *see* Herpes, zoster
Shipyard disease or eye B30.0
Shirodkar suture, in pregnancy - *see*
  Pregnancy, complicated by, incompetent cervix
Shock R57.9
  with ectopic or molar pregnancy
    O08.3
  adrenal (cortical) (Addisonian) E27.2
  adverse food reaction (anaphylactic) –
    see Shock, anaphylactic, food
  allergic - *see* Shock, anaphylactic
  anaphylactic T78.2
    chemical - *see* Table of drugs and
     chemicals
    due to drug or medicinal substance
     correct substance properly admin-
      istered T88.6
     overdose or wrong substance given
      or taken (by accident) - *see*
      Table of drugs and chemicals,
      by drug, poisoning
    due to food T78.00
     additives T78.06
     dairy products T78.07
     eggs T78.08
     fish T78.03
      shellfish T78.02
     fruit T78.04
     milk T78.07
     nuts T78.05
      peanuts T78.01
     peanuts T78.01
     seeds T78.05
     specified type NEC T78.09
     vegetable T78.04
    following sting(s) – *see* Venom
    immunization T80.5
    serum T80.5
  anaphylactoid - *see* Shock, anaphylactic
  anesthetic
    correct substance properly adminis-
     tered T88.2
    overdose or wrong substance given
     or taken - *see* Table of drugs and
     chemicals, by drug, poisoning
    specified anesthetic - *see* Table of
     drugs and chemicals, by drug,
     poisoning
  cardiogenic R57.0
  chemical substance - *see* Table of drugs
    and chemicals
  complicating ectopic or molar preg-
    nancy O08.3
  culture - *see* Disorder, adjustment
  drug
    due to correct substance properly
     administered T88.6
    overdose or wrong substance given
     or taken (by accident) - *see* Table
     of drugs and chemicals, by drug,
     poisoning
  during or after labor and delivery
    O75.1
  electric T75.4
    (taser) T75.4
  endotoxic R65.21
  following
    ectopic or molar pregnancy O08.3
    injury (immediate) (delayed) T79.4
    labor and delivery O75.1
  food (anaphylactic) – *see* Shock, ana-
    phylactic, food

Shock (*Continued*)
  from electroshock gun (taser) T75.4
  gram-negative R65.21
  hematologic R57.8
  hemorrhagic
    surgery (intraoperative) (postopera-
     tive) T81.1
    trauma T79.4
  hypovolemic R57.1
    surgical T81.1
    traumatic T79.4
  insulin E15
    therapeutic misadventure - *see* sub-
     category T38.3
  kidney N17.0
    traumatic (following crushing)
     T79.5
  lightning T75.01
  lung J80
  obstetric O75.1
    with ectopic or molar pregnancy
     O08.3
    following ectopic or molar pregnancy
     O08.3
  pleural (surgical) T81.1
    due to trauma T79.4
  postoperative T81.1
    with ectopic or molar pregnancy
     O08.3
    following ectopic or molar pregnancy
     O08.3
  psychic F43.0
  septic (due to severe sepsis) R65.21
  specified NEC R57.8
  surgical T81.1
  taser gun (taser) T75.4
  therapeutic misadventure NEC T81.1
  thyroxin
    overdose or wrong substance given
     or taken - *see* Table of drugs
     and chemicals, by drug,
     poisoning
  toxic, syndrome A48.3
  transfusion - *see* Complications,
    transfusion
  traumatic (immediate) (delayed) T79.4
Shoemaker's chest M95.4
Short, shortening, shortness
  arm (acquired) - *see also* Deformity,
    limb, unequal length
    congenital – *see* Defect, reduction,
     upper limb, specified type NEC
    forearm - *see* Deformity, limb, un-
     equal length
  bowel syndrome K91.2
  breath R06.02
  cervical (complicating pregnancy) O26.87-
    non-gravid uterus N88.3
  common bile duct, congenital Q44.5
  cord (umbilical), complicating delivery
    O69.3
  cystic duct, congenital Q44.5
  esophagus (congenital) Q39.8
  femur (acquired) - *see* Deformity, limb,
    unequal length, femur
    congenital – *see* Defect, reduction,
     lower limb, longitudinal, femur
  frenum, frenulum, linguae (congenital)
    Q38.1
  hip (acquired) - *see also* Deformity, limb,
    unequal length
    congenital Q65.8
  leg (acquired) - *see also* Deformity, limb,
    unequal length

Short, shortening, shortness *(Continued)*
  leg (acquired) *(Continued)*
    congenital – *see* Defect, reduction, lower limb, specified type NEC
    lower leg - *see also* Deformity, limb, unequal length
    limbed stature, with immunodeficiency D82.2
    lower limb (acquired) - *see also* Deformity, limb, unequal length
      congenital – *see* Defect, reduction, lower limb, specified type NEC
    organ or site, congenital NEC - *see* Distortion
    palate, congenital Q38.5
    radius (acquired) - *see also* Deformity, limb, unequal length
      congenital – *see* Defect, reduction, upper limb, longitudinal, radius
    rib syndrome Q77.2
    stature (child) (hereditary) (idiopathic) NEC R62.52
      constitutional E34.3
      due to endocrine disorder E34.3
      Laron-type E34.3
    tendon – *see also* Contraction, tendon
      with contracture of joint - *see* Contraction, joint
      Achilles (acquired) M67.0-
        congenital Q66.8
      congenital Q79.8
    thigh (acquired) - *see also* Deformity, limb, unequal length, femur
      congenital – *see* Defect, reduction, lower limb, longitudinal, femur
    tibialis anterior (tendon) – *see* Contraction, tendon
    umbilical cord
      complicating delivery O69.3
    upper limb, congenital – *see* Defect, reduction, upper limb, specified type NEC
    urethra N36.8
    uvula, congenital Q38.5
    vagina (congenital) Q52.4
Shortsightedness - *see* Myopia
Shoshin (acute fulminating beriberi) E51.11
Shoulder - *see* condition
Shovel-shaped incisors K00.2
Shower, thromboembolic - *see* Embolism
Shunt
  arterial-venous (dialysis) Z99.2
  arteriovenous, pulmonary (acquired) I28.0
    congenital Q25.7
  cerebral ventricle (communicating) in situ Z98.2
  surgical, prosthetic, with complications - *see* Complications, cardiovascular, device or implant Shutdown, renal N28.9
Shy-Drager syndrome G90.3
Sialadenitis, sialadenosis (any gland) (chronic) (periodic) (suppurative) - *see* Sialoadenitis
Sialectasia K11.8
Sialidosis E77.1
Sialitis, silitis (any gland) (chronic) (suppurative) - *see* Sialoadenitis
Sialoadenitis (any gland) (periodic) (suppurative) K11.20
  acute K11.21
    recurrent K11.22
  chronic K11.23

Sialoadenopathy K11.9
Sialoangitis - *see* Sialoadenitis
Sialodochitis (fibrinosa) - *see* Sialoadenitis
Sialodocholithiasis K11.5
Sialolithiasis K11.5
Sialometaplasia, necrotizing K11.8
Sialorrhea - *see also* Ptyalism
  periodic - *see* Sialoadenitis
Sialosis K11.7
Siamese twin Q89.4
Sibling rivalry Z62.891
Sicard's syndrome G52.7
Sicca syndrome M35.00
  with
    keratoconjunctivitis M35.01
    lung involvement M35.02
    myopathy M35.03
    renal tubulo-interstitial disorders M35.04
  specified organ involvement NEC M35.09
Sick R69
  or handicapped person in family Z63.79
    needing care at home Z63.6
  sinus (syndrome) I49.5
Sick-euthyroid syndrome E07.81
Sickle-cell
  anemia - *see* Disease, sickle-cell
  trait D57.3
Sicklemia - *see also* Disease, sickle-cell
  trait D57.3
Sickness
  air (travel) T75.3
  airplane T75.3
  alpine T70.29
  altitude T70.20
  Andes T70.29
  aviator's T70.29
  balloon T70.29
  car T75.3
  compressed air T70.3
  decompression T70.3
  green D50.9
  milk - *see* Poisoning, food, noxious
  motion T75.3
  mountain T70.20
    acute D75.1
  protein T80.6
  radiation T66
  roundabout (motion) T75.3
  sea T75.3
  serum NEC T80.6
  sleeping (African) B56.9
    by Trypanosoma B56.9
      brucei
        gambiense B56.0
        rhodesiense B56.1
      East African B56.1
      Gambian B56.0
      Rhodesian B56.1
      West African B56.0
  swing (motion) T75.3
  train (railway) (travel) T75.3
  travel (any vehicle) T75.3
Sideropenia - *see* Anemia, iron deficiency
Siderosilicosis J62.8
Siderosis (lung) J63.4
  eye (globe) - *see* Disorder, globe, degenerative, siderosis
Siemens' syndrome (ectodermal dysplasia) Q82.8
Sighing R06.89
  psychogenic F45.8

Sigmoid - *see also* condition
  flexure - *see* condition
  kidney Q63.1
Sigmoiditis (*see also* Enteritis) K52.9
  infectious A09
  noninfectious K52.9
Silfversköld's syndrome Q78.9
Silicosiderosis J62.8
Silicosis, silicotic (simple) (complicated) J62.8
  with tuberculosis J65
Silicotuberculosis J65
Silo-fillers' disease J68.8
Silver's syndrome Q87.1
Simian malaria B53.1
Simmonds' cachexia or disease E23.0
Simons' disease or syndrome (progressive lipodystrophy) E88.1
Simple, simplex - *see* condition
Simulation, conscious (of illness) Z76.5
Sin Nombre virus disease (Hantavirus (cardio)-pulmonary syndrome) B33.4
Sinding-Larsen disease or osteochondrosis - *see* Osteochondrosis, juvenile, patella
Singapore hemorrhagic fever A91
Singer's node or nodule J38.2
Single
  atrium Q21.2
  coronary artery Q24.5
  umbilical artery Q27.0
  ventricle Q20.4
Singultus R06.6
  epidemicus B33.0
Sinus - *see also* Fistula
  abdominal K63.89
  arrest I45.5
  arrhythmia I49.8
  bradycardia R00.1
  branchial cleft (internal) (external) Q18.0
  coccygeal - *see* Sinus, pilonidal
  dental K04.6
  dermal (congenital) Q06.8
    with abscess Q06.8
    coccygeal, pilonidal - *see* Sinus, coccygeal
  infected, skin NEC L08.89
  marginal, ruptured or bleeding – *see* Hemorrhage, antepartum, specified cause NEC
  medial, face and neck Q18.8
  pause I45.5
  pericranii Q01.9
  pilonidal (infected) (rectum) L05.92
    with abscess L05.02
  preauricular Q18.1
  rectovaginal N82.3
  Rokitansky-Aschoff (gallbladder) K82.8
  sacrococcygeal (dermoid) (infected) - *see* Sinus, pilonidal
  tachycardia R00.0
    paroxysmal I47.1
  tarsi syndrome - *see* Syndrome, tarsal tunnel
  testis N50.8
  tract (postinfective) - *see* Fistula
  urachus Q64.4
Sinusitis (accessory) (chronic) (hyperplastic) (nasal) (nonpurulent) (purulent) J32.9
  acute J01.90
    ethmoidal J01.20
      recurrent J01.21

423

Sinusitis (Continued)
  acute (Continued)
    frontal J01.10
      recurrent J01.11
    involving more than one sinus, other
        than pansinusitis J01.80
      recurrent J01.81
    maxillary J01.00
      recurrent J01.01
    pansinusitis J01.40
      recurrent J01.41
    recurrent J01.91
    specified NEC J01.80
      recurrent J01.81
    sphenoidal J01.30
      recurrent J01.31
  allergic - see Rhinitis, allergic
  due to high altitude T70.1
  ethmoidal J32.2
    acute J01.20
      recurrent J01.21
  frontal J32.1
    acute J01.10
      recurrent J01.11
  influenzal - see Influenza, with, respira-
      tory manifestations
  involving more than one sinus but not
        pansinusitis J32.8
    acute J01.80
      recurrent J01.81
  maxillary J32.0
    acute J01.00
      recurrent J01.01
  sphenoidal J32.3
    acute J01.30
      recurrent J01.31
  tuberculous, any sinus A15.8
Sinusitis-bronchiectasis-situs inversus
    (syndrome) (triad) Q89.3
Sipple's syndrome E31.22
Sirenomelia (syndrome) Q87.2
Siriasis T67.0
Sirkari's disease B55.0
Siti A65
Situation, psychiatric F99
Situational
  disturbance (transient) – see Disorder,
      adjustment
    acute F43.0
  maladjustment – see Disorder,
      adjustment
  reaction – see Disorder, adjustment
    acute F43.0
Situs inversus or transversus (abdomina-
    lis) (thoracis) Q89.3
Sixth disease B08.20
  due to human herpesvirus 6 B08.21
  due to human herpesvirus 7 B08.22
Sjögren-Larsson syndrome Q87.1
Sjögren's syndrome or disease - see Sicca
    syndrome
Skeletal - see condition
Skene's gland - see condition
Skenitis - see Urethritis
Skerljevo A65
Skevas-Zerfus disease - see Toxicity,
    venom, marine animal, sea
    anemone
Skin - see also condition
  clammy R23.1
  donor - see Donor, skin
  hidebound M35.9
Slate-dressers' or slate-miners' lung
    J62.8

Sleep
  apnea - see Apnea, sleep
  deprivation Z72.820
  disorder or disturbance G47.9
    child F51.9
      nonorganic origin F51.9
      specified NEC G47.8
    disturbance G47.9
      nonorganic origin F51.9
    drunkenness F51.5
    rhythm inversion G47.2
    terrors F51.4
    walking F51.3
      hysterical F44.89
Sleep hygiene
  abuse Z72.821
  inadequate Z72.821
  poor Z72.821
Sleeping sickness — see Sickness, sleeping
Sleeplessness - see Insomnia
  menopausal N95.11
Sleep-wake schedule disorder G47.2
Slim disease (in HIV infection) B20
Slipped, slipping
  epiphysis (traumatic) – see also Osteo-
        chondropathy, specified type NEC
    capital femoral (traumatic)
      acute (on chronic) S79.01-
    current traumatic - code as Fracture,
        by site
    upper femoral (nontraumatic)
        M93.00-
      acute M93.01-
        on chronic M93.03-
      chronic M93.02-
  intervertebral disc - see Displacement,
      intervertebral disc
  ligature, umbilical P51.8
  patella - see Disorder, patella, derange-
      ment NEC
  rib M89.8x8
  sacroiliac joint - see subcategory M53.2
  tendon - see Disorder, tendon
  ulnar nerve, nontraumatic – see Lesion,
      nerve, ulnar
  vertebra NEC - see Spondylolisthesis
Slocumb's syndrome E27.0
Sloughing (multiple) (phagedena) (skin) -
      see also Gangrene
  abscess - see Abscess
  appendix K38.8
  fascia - see Disorder, soft tissue, speci-
      fied type NEC
  scrotum N50.8
  tendon - see Disorder, tendon
  transplanted organ – see Rejection,
      transplant
  ulcer - see Ulcer, skin
Slow
  feeding, newborn P92.2
  heart(beat) R00.1
Slowing, urinary stream R39.19
Sluder's neuralgia (syndrome) G44.89
Slurred, slurring speech R47.81
Small(ness)
  for gestational age – see Small for dates
  introitus, vagina N89.6
  kidney (unknown cause) N27.9
    bilateral N27.1
    unilateral N27.0
  ovary (congenital) Q50.39
  pelvis
    with disproportion (fetopelvic) O33.1
      causing obstructed labor O65.1

Small(ness) (Continued)
  uterus N85.8
  white kidney N03.9
Small-and-light-for-dates - see Small for
    dates
Small-for-dates (infant) P05.10
  with weight of
    499 grams or less P05.11
    500-749 grams P05.12
    750-999 grams P05.13
    1000-1249 grams P05.14
    1250-1499 grams P05.15
    1500-1749 grams P05.16
    1750-1999 grams P05.17
    2000-2499 grams P05.18
Smallpox B03
Smith-Lemli-Opitz syndrome Q87.1
Smith's fracture S52.54-
Smoker - see Dependence, drug, nicotine
Smoker's
  bronchitis J41.0
  cough J41.0
  palate K13.24
  throat J31.2
  tongue K13.24
Smoking
  passive Z77.22
Smothering spells R06.81
Snaggle teeth, tooth M26.39
Snapping
  finger - see Trigger finger
  hip - see Derangement, joint, specified
      type NEC, hip
    involving the iliotiblial band M76.3-
  knee - see Derangement, knee
    involving the iliotiblial band M76.3-
Sneddon-Wilkinson disease or syn-
    drome L13.1
Sneddon-Wilkinson disease or syn-
    drome (sub-corneal pustular derma-
    tosis) L13.1
Sneezing (intractable) R06.7
Sniffing
  cocaine
    abuse - see Abuse, drug, cocaine
    dependence - see Dependence, drug,
        cocaine
  gasoline
    abuse - see Abuse, drug, inhalant
    dependence - see Dependence, drug,
        inhalant
  glue (airplane)
    abuse - see Abuse, drug, inhalant
    drug dependence - see Dependence,
        drug, inhalant
Sniffles
  newborn P28.89
Snoring R06.83
Snow blindness - see Photokeratitis
Snuffles (non-syphilitic) R06.5
  newborn P28.89
  syphilitic (infant) A50.05 [J99]
Social
  exclusion Z60.4
    due to discrimination or persecution
        (perceived) Z60.5
  migrant Z59.0
    acculturation difficulty Z60.3
  rejection Z60.4
    due to discrimination or persecution
        Z60.5
  role conflict NEC Z73.5
  skills inadequacy NEC Z73.4
  transplantation Z60.3

Sperm counts *(Continued)*
  postvasectomy Z30.8
    reversal Z31.42
Spermatic cord - *see* condition
Spermatocele N43.40
  congenital Q55.4
  multiple N43.42
  single N43.41
Spermatocystitis N49.0
Spermatocytoma C62.9-
  specified site - *see* Neoplasm, malignant
Spermatorrhea N50.8
Sphacelus - *see* Gangrene
Sphenoidal - *see* condition
Sphenoiditis (chronic) - *see* Sinusitis,
    sphenoidal
Sphenopalatine ganglion neuralgia G90.09
Sphericity, increased, lens (congenital)
    Q12.4
Spherocytosis (congenital) (familial)
    (hereditary) D58.0
  hemoglobin disease D58.0
  sickle-cell (disease) D57.8-
Spherophakia Q12.4
Sphincter - *see* condition
Sphincteritis, sphincter of Oddi - *see*
    Cholangitis
Sphingolipidosis E75.3
  specified NEC E75.29
Sphingomyelinosis E75.3
Spicule tooth K00.2
Spider
  bite - *see* Toxicity, venom, spider
  fingers - *see* Syndrome, Marfan's
  nevus I78.1
  toes - *see* Syndrome, Marfan's
  vascular I78.1
Spiegler-Fendt
  benign lymphocytoma L98.8
  sarcoid L08.0
Spielmeyer-Vogt disease E75.4
Spina bifida (aperta) Q05.9
  with hydrocephalus NEC Q05.4
  cervical Q05.5
    with hydrocephalus Q05.0
  dorsal Q05.6
    with hydrocephalus Q05.1
  lumbar Q05.7
    with hydrocephalus Q05.2
  lumbosacral Q05.7
    with hydrocephalus Q05.2
  occulta Q76.0
  sacral Q05.8
    with hydrocephalus Q05.3
  thoracic Q05.6
    with hydrocephalus Q05.1
  thoracolumbar Q05.6
    with hydrocephalus Q05.1
Spindle, Krukenberg's - *see* Pigmenta-
    tion, cornea, posterior
Spine, spinal - *see* condition
Spiradenoma (eccrine) - *see* Neoplasm,
    skin, benign
Spirillosis A25.0
Spirillum
  minus A25.0
  obermeieri infection A68.0
Spirochetal - *see* condition
Spirochetosis A69.9
  arthritic, arthritica A69.9
  bronchopulmonary A69.8
  icterohemorrhagic A27.0
  lung A69.8
Spirometrosis B70.1

Spitting blood - *see* Hemoptysis
Splanchnoptosis K63.4
Spleen, splenic - *see* condition
Splenectasis - *see* Splenomegaly
Splenitis (interstitial) (malignant) (non-
    specific) D73.89
  malarial B54
  tuberculous A18.85
Splenocele D73.89
Splenomegaly, splenomegalia (Bengal)
    (cryptogenic) (idiopathic) (tropical)
    R16.1
  with hepatomegaly R16.2
  cirrhotic D73.2
  congenital Q89.09
  congestive, chronic D73.2
  Egyptian B65.1
  Gaucher's E75.22
  malarial (*see also* Malaria) B54 *[D77]*
  neutropenic D73.81
  Niemann-Pick - *see* Niemann-Pick
    disease or syndrome
  siderotic D73.2
  syphilitic A52.79
    congenital (early) A50.08 *[D77]*
Splenopathy D73.9
Splenoptosis D73.89
Splenosis D73.89
Splinter - *see* Foreign body, superficial,
    by site
Split, splitting
  foot Q72.7-
  heart sounds R01.2
  lip, congenital - *see* Cleft, lip
  nails L60.3
  urinary stream R39.13
Spondylarthrosis - *see* Spondylosis
Spondylitis (chronic) - *see also* Spondy-
    lopathy, inflammatory
  ankylopoietica - *see* Spondylitis,
    ankylosing
  ankylosing (chronic) M45.9
    with lung involvement M45.9 *[J99]*
    cervical region M45.2
    cervicothoracic region M45.3
    juvenile M08.1
    lumbar region M45.6
    lumbosacral region M45.7
    multiple sites M45.0
    occipito-atlanto-axial region M45.1
    sacrococcygeal region M45.8
    thoracic region M45.4
    thoracolumbar region M45.5
  atrophic (ligamentous) - *see* Spondylitis,
    ankylosing
  deformans (chronic) - *see* Spondylosis
  gonococcal A54.41
  gouty M10.08
  in (due to)
    brucellosis A23.9 *[M49.80]*
      cervical region A23.9 *[M49.82]*
      cervicothoracic region A23.9
        [M49.83]
      lumbar region A23.9 *[M49.86]*
      lumbosacral region A23.9
        [M49.87]
      multiple sites A23.9 *[M49.89]*
      occipito-atlanto-axial region A23.9
        [M49.81]
      sacrococcygeal region A23.9
        [M49.88]
      thoracic region A23.9 *[M49.84]*
      thoracolumbar region A23.9
        [M49.85]

Spondylitis *(Continued)*
  in (due to) *(Continued)*
    enterobacteria (*see also* subcategory
      M49.8) A04.9
    tuberculosis A18.01
  infectious NEC - *see* Spondylopathy,
    infective
  juvenile ankylosing (chronic) M08.1
  Kümmell's - *see* Spondylopathy,
    traumatic
  Marie-Strümpell - *see* Spondylitis,
    ankylosing
  muscularis - *see* Spondylopathy, speci-
    fied NEC
  psoriatic L40.53
  rheumatoid - *see* Spondylitis,
    ankylosing
  rhizomelica - *see* Spondylitis,
    ankylosing
  sacroiliac NEC M46.1
  senescent, senile - *see* Spondylosis
  traumatic (chronic) or post-traumatic -
    see Spondylopathy, traumatic
  tuberculous A18.01
  typhosa A01.05
Spondylarthrosis - *see* Spondylosis
Spondylolisthesis (acquired) (degenera-
    tive) M43.10
  with disproportion (fetopelvic) O33.0
    causing obstructed labor O65.0
  cervical region M43.12
  cervicothoracic region M43.13
  congenital Q76.2
  lumbar region M43.16
  lumbosacral region M43.17
  multiple sites M43.19
  occipito-atlanto-axial region M43.11
  sacrococcygeal region M43.18
  thoracic region M43.14
  thoracolumbar region M43.15
  traumatic (old) M43.10
    acute
      fifth cervical (displaced) S12.430
        nondisplaced S12.431
        specified type NEC (displaced)
          S12.450
          nondisplaced S12.451
        type III S12.44
      fourth cervical (displaced)
        S12.330
        nondisplaced S12.331
        specified type NEC (displaced)
          S12.350
          nondisplaced S12.351
        type III S12.34
      second cervical (displaced)
        S12.130
        nondisplaced S12.131
        specified type NEC (displaced)
          S12.150
          nondisplaced S12.151
        type III S12.14
      seventh cervical (displaced) S12.630
        nondisplaced S12.631
        specified type NEC (displaced)
          S12.650
          nondisplaced S12.651
        type III S12.64
      sixth cervical (displaced) S12.530
        nondisplaced S12.531
        specified type NEC (displaced)
          S12.550
          nondisplaced S12.551
        type III S12.54

Spondylolisthesis *(Continued)*
  traumatic *(Continued)*
    acute *(Continued)*
      third cervical (displaced)
        S12.230
        nondisplaced S12.231
        specified type NEC (displaced)
          S12.250
          nondisplaced S12.251
        type III S12.24
Spondylolysis (acquired) M43.00
  cervical region M43.02
  cervicothoracic region M43.03
  congenital Q76.2
  lumbar region M43.06
  lumbosacral region M43.07
    with disproportion (fetopelvic)
      O33.0
      causing obstructed labor O65.8
  multiple sites M43.09
  occipito-atlanto-axial region M43.01
  sacrococcygeal region M43.08
  thoracic region M43.04
  thoracolumbar region M43.05
Spondylopathy M48.9
  infective NEC M46.50
    cervical region M46.52
    cervicothoracic region M46.53
    lumbar region M46.56
    lumbosacral region M46.57
    multiple sites M46.59
    occipito-atlanto-axial region
      M46.51
    sacrococcygeal region M46.58
    thoracic region M46.54
    thoracolumbar region M46.55
  inflammatory M46.90
    cervical region M46.92
    cervicothoracic region M46.93
    lumbar region M46.96
    lumbosacral region M46.97
    multiple sites M46.99
    occipito-atlanto-axial region
      M46.91
    sacrococcygeal region M46.98
  specified type NEC M46.80
    cervical region M46.82
    cervicothoracic region
      M46.83
    lumbar region M46.86
    lumbosacral region M46.87
    multiple sites M46.89
    occipito-atlanto-axial region
      M46.81
    sacrococcygeal region M46.88
    thoracic region M46.84
    thoracolumbar region M46.85
    thoracic region M46.94
    thoracolumbar region M46.95
  neuropathic, in
    syringomyelia and syringobulbia
      G95.0
    tabes dorsalis A52.11
  specified NEC - *see* subcategory M48.8
  traumatic M48.30
    cervical region M48.32
    cervicothoracic region M48.33
    lumbar region M48.36
    lumbosacral region M48.37
    occipito-atlanto-axial region
      M48.31
    sacrococcygeal region M48.38
    thoracic region M48.34
    thoracolumbar region M48.35

Spondylosis M47.9
  with
    disproportion (fetopelvic)
      O33.0
      causing obstructed labor
        O65.0
    myelopathy NEC M47.10
      cervical region M47.12
      cervicothoracic region M47.13
      lumbar region M47.16
      lumbosacral region M47.17
      occipito-atlanto-axial region
        M47.11
      sacrococcygeal region
        M47.18
      thoracic region M47.14
      thoracolumbar region
        M47.15
    radiculopathy M47.20
      cervical region M47.22
      cervicothoracic region M47.23
      lumbar region M47.26
      lumbosacral region M47.27
      occipito-atlanto-axial region
        M47.21
      sacrococcygeal region M47.28
      thoracic region M47.24
      thoracolumbar region M47.25
  traumatic - *see* Spondylopathy, traumatic
  without myelopathy or radiculopathy
    M47.819
    cervical region M47.812
    cervicothoracic region M47.813
    lumbar region M47.816
    lumbosacral region M47.817
    occipito-atlanto-axial region
      M47.811
    sacrococcygeal region
      M47.818
    thoracic region M47.814
    thoracolumbar region M47.815
Sponge
  inadvertently left in operation wound –
    see Foreign body, accidentally left
    during a procedure
  kidney (medullary) Q61.5
Sponge-diver's disease - *see* Toxicity,
  venom, marine animal, sea anemone
Spongioblastoma (any type) - *see*
  Neoplasm, malignant
  specified site - *see* Neoplasm,
    malignant
    unspecified site C71.9
  specified site - *see* Neoplasm,
    malignant
  unspecified site C71.9
Spongioneuroblastoma - *see* Neoplasm,
  malignant
Spontaneous - *see also* condition
  fracture (cause unknown) - *see* Fracture,
    pathological
Spoon nail L60.3
  congenital Q84.6
Sporadic - *see* condition
Sporothrix schenckii infection - *see*
  Sporotrichosis
Sporotrichosis B42.9
  arthritis B42.82
  disseminated B42.7
  generalized B42.7
  lymphocutaneous (fixed) (progressive)
    B42.1
  pulmonary B42.0
  specified NEC B42.89

Spots, spotting (in) (of)
  Bitot's - *see also* Pigmentation,
    conjunctiva
    in the young child E50.1
    vitamin A deficiency E50.1
  café, au lait L81.3
  Cayenne pepper I78.1
  cotton wool, retina - *see* Occlusion,
    artery, retina
  de Morgan's (senile angiomas) I78.1
  Fuchs' black (myopic) - *see* Disorder,
    globe, degenerative, myopia
  intermenstrual (regular) N92.0
    irregular N92.1
  Koplik's B05.9
  liver L81.4
  pregnancy O26.85-
  purpuric R23.3
  ruby I78.1
Spotted fever - *see* Fever, spotted N92.3
Sprain (joint) (ligament)
  acromioclavicular joint or ligament
    S43.50-
  ankle S93.409
    calcaneofibular ligament S93.41-
    deltoid ligament S93.42-
    internal collateral ligament - *see*
      Sprain, ankle, specified ligament
      NEC
    specified ligament NEC S93.49-
    talofibular ligament - *see* Sprain,
      ankle, specified ligament NEC
    tibiofibular ligament S93.43-
  anterior longitudinal, cervical S13.4
  atlas, atlanto-axial, atlanto-occipital
    S13.4
  breast bone - *see* Sprain, sternum
  calcaneofibular – *see* Sprain, ankle
  carpal – *see* Sprain, wrist
  carpometacarpal – *see* Sprain, hand,
    specified site NEC
  cartilage
    costal S23.41
    semilunar (knee) – *see* Sprain, knee,
      specified site NEC
      with current tear – *see* Tear,
        meniscus
    thyroid region S13.5
    xiphoid - *see* Sprain, sternum
  cervical, cervicodorsal, cervicothoracic
    S13.4
  chondrosternal S23.421
  coracoclavicular S43.8-
  coracohumeral S43.41-
  coronary, knee – *see* Sprain, knee, speci-
    fied site NEC
  costal cartilage S23.41
  cricoarytenoid articulation or ligament
    S13.5
  cricothyroid articulation S13.5
  cruciate, knee – *see* Sprain, knee,
    cruciate
  deltoid, ankle – *see* Sprain, ankle
  dorsal (spine) S23.3
  elbow S53.40-
    radial collateral ligament S53.43-
    radiohumeral S53.41-
    rupture
      radial collateral ligament - *see*
        Rupture, traumatic, ligament,
        radial collateral
      ulnar collateral ligament - *see*
        Rupture, traumatic, ligament,
        ulnar collateral

Sprain *(Continued)*
  elbow *(Continued)*
    specified type NEC S53.49-
    ulnar collateral ligament S53.44-
    ulnohumeral S53.42-
  femur, head – *see* Sprain, hip
  fibular collateral, knee – *see* Sprain,
      knee, collateral
  fibulocalcaneal – *see* Sprain, ankle
  finger(s) S63.61-
    index S63.61-
    interphalangeal (joint) S63.63-
      index S63.63-
      little S63.63-
      middle S63.63-
      ring S63.63-
    little S63.61-
    middle S63.61-
    ring S63.61-
    specified site NEC S63.69-
      index S63.69-
      little S63.69-
      middle S63.69-
      ring S63.69-
  foot S93.60-
    specified ligament NEC S93.69-
    tarsal ligament S93.61-
    tarsometatarsal ligament S93.62-
    toe - *see* Sprain, toe
  hand S63.9-
    finger – *see* Sprain, finger
    specified site NEC - *see* subcategory
        S63.8
    thumb – *see* Sprain, thumb
  head S03.9
  hip S73.109
    iliofemoral ligament S73.11-
    ischiocapsular (ligament)
        S73.12-
    specified NEC S73.19-
  iliofemoral – *see* Sprain, hip
  innominate
    acetabulum – *see* Sprain, hip
    sacral junction S33.6
  internal
    collateral, ankle – *see* Sprain,
        ankle
    semilunar cartilage – *see* Sprain,
        knee, specified site NEC
  interphalangeal
    finger – *see* Sprain, finger, interpha-
        langeal (joint)
    toe – *see* Sprain, toe, interphalangeal
        joint
  ischiocapsular – *see* Sprain, hip
  ischiofemoral – *see* Sprain, hip
  jaw (articular disc) (cartilage) (menis-
      cus) S03.4
    old M26.69
  knee S83.9-
    collateral ligament S83.40-
      lateral (fibular) S83.42-
      medial (tibial) S83.41-
    cruciate ligament S83.50-
      anterior S83.51-
      posterior S83.52-
    lateral (fibular) collateral ligament
        S83.42-
    medial (tibial) collateral ligament
        S83.41-
    patellar ligament S76.11-
    specified site NEC S83.8x-
    superior tibiofibular joint (ligament)
        S83.6-

Sprain *(Continued)*
  lateral collateral, knee – *see* Sprain,
      knee, collateral
  lumbar (spine) S33.5
  lumbosacral S33.9
  mandible (articular disc) S03.4
    old M26.69
  medial collateral, knee – *see* Sprain,
      knee, collateral
  meniscus
    jaw S03.4
      old M26.69
    knee – *see* Sprain, knee, specified site
        NEC
      with current tear – *see* Tear,
          meniscus
        old - *see* Derangement, knee,
            meniscus, due to old tear
    mandible S03.4
      old M26.69
  metacarpal (distal) (proximal) – *see*
      Sprain, hand, specified site NEC
  metacarpophalangeal – *see* Sprain, fin-
      ger, metacarpophalangeal (joint)
  metatarsophalangeal – *see* Sprain, toe,
      metatarsophalangeal joint
  midcarpal – *see* Sprain, hand, specified
      site NEC
  midtarsal – *see* Sprain, foot, specified
      site NEC
  neck S13.9
    anterior longitudinal cervical liga-
        ment S13.4
    atlanto-axial joint S13.4
    atlanto-occipital joint S13.4
    cervical spine S13.4
    cricoarytenoid ligament S13.5
    cricothyroid ligament S13.5
    specified site NEC S13.8
    thyroid region (cartilage) S13.5
  nose S03.8
  orbicular, hip – *see* Sprain, hip
  patella – *see* Sprain, knee, specified site
      NEC
  patellar ligament S76.11-
  pelvis NEC S33.8
  phalanx
    finger – *see* Sprain, finger
    toe – *see* Sprain, toe
  pubofemoral – *see* Sprain, hip
  radiocarpal – *see* Sprain, wrist
  radiohumeral – *see* Sprain, elbow
  radius, collateral – *see* Rupture, trau-
      matic, ligament, radial collateral
  rib (cage) S23.41
  rotator cuff (capsule) S43.42-
  sacroiliac (region)
    chronic or old - *see* subcategory M53.2
    joint S33.6
  scaphoid (hand) – *see* Sprain, hand,
      specified site NEC
  scapula(r) – *see* Sprain, shoulder girdle,
      specified site NEC
  semilunar cartilage (knee) – *see* Sprain,
      knee, specified site NEC
    with current tear – *see* Tear, meniscus
      old - *see* Derangement, knee, me-
          niscus, due to old tear
  shoulder joint S43.409
    acromioclavicular joint (ligament) –
        see Sprain, acromioclavicular
        joint
    blade – *see* Sprain, shoulder, girdle,
        specified site NEC

Sprain *(Continued)*
  shoulder joint *(Continued)*
    coracoclavicular joint (ligament) – *see*
        Sprain, coracoclavicular joint
    coracohumeral ligament – *see* Sprain,
        coracohumeral joint
    girdle S43.9-
      specified site NEC S43.8-
    rotator cuff – *see* Sprain, rotator cuff
    specified site NEC S43.49-
    sternoclavicular joint (ligament)
        – *see* Sprain, sternoclavicular
        joint
  spine
    cervical S13.4
    lumbar S33.5
    thoracic S23.3
  sternoclavicular joint S43.6-
  sternum S23.429
    chondrosternal joint S23.421
    specified site NEC S23.428
    sternoclavicular (joint) (ligament)
        S23.420
  symphysis
    jaw S03.4
      old M26.69
    mandibular S03.4
      old M26.69
  talofibular – *see* Sprain, ankle
  tarsal – *see* Sprain, foot, specified site
      NEC
  tarsometatarsal – *see* Sprain, foot, speci-
      fied site NEC
  temporomandibular S03.4
    old M26.69
  thorax S23.9
    specified site NEC S23.8
    spine S23.3
  thorax S23.9
    ribs S23.41
    specified site NEC S23.8
    spine S23.3
    sternum - *see* Sprain, sternum
  thumb S63.60-
    interphalangeal (joint) S63.62-
    metacarpophalangeal (joint)
        S63.64-
    specified site NEC S63.68-
  thyroid cartilage or region S13.5
  tibia (proximal end) – *see* Sprain, knee,
      specified site NEC
  tibial collateral, knee – *see* Sprain, knee,
      collateral
  tibiofibular
    distal – *see* Sprain, ankle
    superior – *see* Sprain, knee, specified
        site NEC
  toe(s) S93.50-
    great S93.50-
      interphalangeal joint S93.51-
        great S93.51-
        lesser S93.51-
      lesser S93.50-
      metatarsophalangeal joint S93.52-
        great S93.52-
        lesser S93.52-
  ulna, collateral – *see* Rupture, traumatic,
      ligament, ulnar collateral
  ulnohumeral – *see* Sprain, elbow
  wrist S63.50-
    carpal S63.51-
    radiocarpal S63.52-
    specified site NEC S63.59-
  xiphoid cartilage - *see* Sprain, sternum

Sprengel's deformity (congenital)
Q74.0
Sprue (tropical) K90.1
celiac K90.0
idiopathic K90.0
meaning thrush B37.0
nontropical K90.0
Spur, bone - see also Enthesopathy
calcaneal M77.3-
iliac crest M76.2-
nose (septum) J34.89
Spurway's syndrome Q78.0
Sputum
abnormal (amount) (color) (odor) (purulent) R09.3
blood-stained R04.2
excessive (cause unknown) R09.3
Squamous - see also condition
epithelium in
cervical canal (congenital) Q51.8
uterine mucosa (congenital) Q51.8
Squashed nose M95.0
congenital Q67.4
Squeeze, divers' T70.3
Squint - see also Strabismus
accommodative - see Strabismus, convergent concomitant
St. Hubert's disease A82.9
Stab - see also Laceration
internal organs - see Injury, by site
Stafne's cyst or cavity M27.0
Staggering gait R26.0
hysterical F44.4
Staghorn calculus - see Calculus, kidney
Stähli's line (cornea) (pigment) - see Pigmentation, cornea, anterior
Stain, staining
meconium (newborn) P96.83
port wine Q82.5
tooth, teeth (hard tissues) (extrinsic) K03.6
due to
accretions K03.6
deposits (betel) (black) (green) (materia alba) (orange) (soft) (tobacco) K03.6
metals (copper) (silver) K03.7
nicotine K03.6
pulpal bleeding K03.7
tobacco K03.6
intrinsic K00.8
Stammering F98.5
Standstill
auricular I45.5
cardiac - see Arrest, cardiac
sinoatrial I45.5
ventricular - see Arrest, cardiac
Stannosis J63.5
Stanton's disease - see Melioidosis
Staphylitis (acute) (catarrhal) (chronic) (gangrenous) (membranous) (suppurative) (ulcerative) K12.2
Staphylococcal scalded skin syndrome L00
Staphylococcemia A41.2
Staphylococcus, staphylococcal - see also condition
as cause of disease classified elsewhere B95.8
aureus, as cause of disease classified elsewhere B95.6
specified NEC, as cause of disease classified elsewhere B95.7

Staphyloma (sclera)
cornea H18.72-
equatorial H15.81-
localized (anterior) H15.82-
posticum H15.83-
ring H15.85-
Stargardt's disease - see Dystrophy, retina
Starvation (inanition) (due to lack of food) T73.0
edema - see Malnutrition, severe
Stasis
bile (noncalculous) K83.1
bronchus J98.09
with infection - see Bronchitis
cardiac - see Failure, heart, congestive
cecum K59.8
colon K59.8
dermatitis - see Varix, leg, with, inflammation
duodenal K31.5
eczema - see Varix, leg, with, inflammation
edema - see Hypertension, venous (chronic), idiopathic
foot T69.0-
ileocecal coil K59.8
ileum K59.8
intestinal K59.8
jejunum K59.8
kidney N19
liver (cirrhotic) K76.1
lymphatic I89.8
pneumonia J18.2
pulmonary - see Edema, lung
rectal K59.8
renal N19
tubular N17.0
ulcer - see Varix, leg, with, ulcer
without varicose veins I87.2
urine – see Retention, urine
venous I87.8
State (of)
affective and paranoid, mixed, organic psychotic F06.8
agitated R45.1
acute reaction to stress F43.0
anxiety (neurotic) F41.1
apprehension F41.1
burn-out Z73.0
climacteric, female N95.10
symptomatic N95.11
compulsive F42
mixed with obsessional thoughts F42
confusional (psychogenic) F44.89
acute - see also Delirium
with
arteriosclerotic dementia F01.50
with behavioral disturbance F01.51
senility or dementia F05
alcoholic F10.231
epileptic F05
reactive (from emotional stress, psychological trauma) F44.89
subacute - see Delirium
convulsive - see Convulsions
crisis F43.0
depressive F32.9
neurotic F34.1
dissociative F44.9
emotional shock (stress) R45.7
hypercoagulation - see Hypercoagulable
locked-in G83.5

State (of) (Continued)
menopausal N95.10
symptomatic N95.11
neurotic F48.9
with depersonalization F48.1
obsessional F42
oneiroid (schizophrenia-like) F23
organic
hallucinatory (nonalcoholic) F06.0
paranoid(-hallucinatory) F06.2
panic F41.0
paranoid F22
climacteric F22
involutional F22
menopausal F22
organic F06.2
senile F03
simple F22
persistent vegetative R40.3
phobic F40.9
postleukotomy F07.0
pregnant, incidental Z33.1
psychogenic, twilight F44.89
psychopathic (constitutional) F60.2
psychotic, organic - see also Psychosis, organic
mixed paranoid and affective F06.8
senile or presenile F03
transient NEC F06.8
with
hallucinations F06.0
depression F06.31
residual schizophrenic F20.5
restlessness R45.1
stress (emotional) R45.7
tension (mental) F48.9
specified NEC F48.8
transient organic psychotic NEC F06.8
depressive type F06.31
hallucinatory type F06.30
twilight
epileptic F05
psychogenic F44.89
vegetative, persistent R40.3
vital exhaustion Z73.0
withdrawal, see Withdrawal, state
Status (post) - see also Presence (of)
absence, epileptic – see Epilepsy, by type, with status epilepticus
administration of tPA (rtPA) in a different facility within the last 24 hours prior to admission to the current facility Z92.82
adrenalectomy (unilateral) (bilateral) E89.6
anastomosis Z98.0
angioplasty (peripheral) Z98.62
with implant Z95.820
coronary artery Z98.61
with implant Z95.5
anginosus I20.9
aortocoronary bypass Z95.1
arthrodesis Z98.1
artificial opening (of) Z93.9
gastrointestinal tract Z93.4
specified NEC Z93.8
urinary tract Z93.6
vagina Z93.8
asthmaticus - see Asthma, by type, with status asthmaticus
awaiting organ transplant Z76.82
bariatric surgery Z98.84
bed confinement Z74.01

Status (*Continued*)
bleb, filtering (vitreous), after glaucoma surgery Z98.83
breast implant Z98.82
  removal Z98.86
cataract extraction Z98.4-
cholecystectomy Z90.4
clitorectomy N90.811
  with excision of labia minora N90.812
colectomy (complete) (partial) Z90.4
colonization - *see* Carrier (suspected) of
colostomy Z93.3
convulsivus idiopathicus – *see* Epilepsy, by type, with status epilepticus
coronary artery angioplasty – *see* Status, angioplasty, coronary artery
cystectomy (urinary bladder) Z90.6
cystostomy Z93.50
  appendico-vesicostomy Z93.52
  cutaneous Z93.51
  specified NEC Z93.59
delinquent immunization Z28.3
dental Z98.818
  crown Z98.811
  fillings Z98.811
  restoration Z98.811
  sealant Z98.810
  specified NEC Z98.818
deployment (current) (military) Z56.82
dialysis (hemodialysis) (peritoneal) Z99.2
do not resuscitate (DNR) Z66
donor - *see* Donor
enterostomy Z93.4
epileptic, epilepticus G40.901 – *see also* Epilepsy, by type, with status epilepticus
estrogen receptor
  negative Z17.0
  positive Z17.1
female genital cutting - *see* Female genital mutilation status
female genital mutilation - *see* Female genital mutilation status
filtering (vitreous) bleb after glaucoma surgery Z98.83
gastrectomy (complete) (partial) Z90.3
gastric banding Z98.84
gastric bypass for obesity Z98.84
gastrostomy Z93.1
human immunodeficiency virus (HIV) infection, asymptomatic Z21
hysterectomy (complete) (total) Z90.710
  partial (with remaining cervial stump) Z90.711
ileostomy Z93.2
implant
  breast Z98.82
infibulation N90.813
intestinal bypass Z98.0
jejunostomy Z93.4
lapsed immunization schedule Z28.3
laryngectomy Z90.02
lymphaticus E32.8
marmoratus G80.3
mastectomy (unilateral) (bilateral) Z90.1-
military deployment status (current) Z56.82
  in theater or in support of military war, peacekeeping and humanitarian operations Z56.82
nephrectomy (unilateral) (bilateral) Z90.5
nephrostomy Z93.6

Status (*Continued*)
obesity surgery Z98.84
oophorectomy
  bilateral Z90.722
  unilateral Z90.721
organ replacement
  by artificial or mechanical device or prosthesis of
   artery Z95.828
   bladder Z96.0
   blood vessel Z95.829
   breast Z97.8
   eye globe Z97.0
   heart Z95.812
    valve Z95.2
   intestine Z97.8
   joint Z96.60
    hip - *see* Presence, hip joint implant
    knee - *see* Presence, knee joint implant
    specified site NEC Z96.698
   kidney Z97.8
   larynx Z96.3
   lens Z96.1
   limbs – *see* Presence, artificial, limb
   liver Z97.8
   lung Z97.8
   pancreas Z97.8
  by organ transplant (heterologous)(homologous) - *see* Transplant
pacemaker
  brain Z96.89
  cardiac Z95.0
  specified NEC Z96.89
pancreatectomy Z90.4
pneumonectomy (complete) (partial) Z90.2
pneumothorax, therapeutic Z98.3
postcommotio cerebri F07.81
postoperative (postprocedural) NEC Z98.89
  breast implant Z98.82
  dental Z98.818
   crown Z98.811
   fillings Z98.811
   restoration Z98.811
   sealant Z98.810
   specified NEC Z98.818
  pneumothorax, therapeutic Z98.3
postpartum (routine follow-up) Z39.2
  care immediately after delivery Z39.0
postsurgical (postprocedural) NEC Z98.89
  pneumothorax, therapeutic Z98.3
pregnancy, incidental Z33.1
prosthesis coronary angioplasty Z95.5
pseudophakia Z96.1
renal dialysis (hemodialysis) (peritoneal) Z99.2
reversed jejunal transposition (for bypass) Z98.0
salpingo-oophorectomy
  bilateral Z90.722
  unilateral Z90.721
sex reassignment surgery status Z87.890
shunt
  arteriovenous (for dialysis) Z99.2
  cerebrospinal fluid Z98.2
  ventricular (communicating) (for drainage) Z98.2
splenectomy D73.0
thymicolymphaticus E32.8
thymicus E32.8

Status (*Continued*)
thymolymphaticus E32.8
thyroidectomy (hypothyroidism) E89.0
tooth (teeth) extraction K08.409 *See also* Absence, teeth, acquired
tPA (rtPA) administration in a different facility within the last 24 hours prior to admission to current facility Z92.82
tracheostomy Z93.0
transplant - *see* Transplant
  organ removed Z98.85
tubal ligation Z98.51
underimmunization Z28.3
ureterostomy Z93.6
urethrostomy Z93.6
vagina, artificial Z93.8
vasectomy Z98.52
wheelchair confinement Z99.3
Stealing
child problem F91.8
  in company with others Z72.810
pathological (compulsive) F63.2
Steam burn - *see* Burn
Steatocystoma multiplex L72.2
Steatohepatitis (nonalcoholic) (NASH) K75.81
Steatoma L72.1
eyelid (cystic) - *see* Dermatosis, eyelid
infected - *see* Hordeolum
Steatorrhea (chronic) K90.4
with lacteal obstruction K90.2
idiopathic (adult) (infantile) K90.0
pancreatic K90.3
primary K90.0
tropical K90.1
Steatosis E88.89
heart - *see* Degeneration, myocardial
kidney N28.89
liver NEC K76.0
Steele-Richardson-Olszewski disease or syndrome G23.1
Steinbrocker's syndrome G90.8
Steinert's disease G71.11
Stein-Leventhal syndrome E28.2
Stein's syndrome E28.2
STEMI I21.3 (*see also* - Infarct, myocardium, ST elevation)
Stenocardia I20.8
Stenocephaly Q75.8
Stenosis, stenotic (cicatricial) - *see also* Stricture
ampulla of Vater K83.1
anus, anal (canal) (sphincter) K62.4
  and rectum K62.4
  congenital Q42.3
   with fistula Q42.2
aorta (ascending) (supraventricular) (congenital) Q25.3
  arteriosclerotic I70.0
  calcified I70.0
aortic (valve) I35.0
  with insufficiency I35.2
  congenital Q23.0
  rheumatic I06.0
   with
    incompetency, insufficiency or regurgitation I06.2
     with mitral (valve) disease I08.0
      with tricuspid (valve) disease I08.3
    mitral (valve) disease I08.0
     with tricuspid (valve) disease I08.3

Stenosis, stenotic *(Continued)*
  aortic *(Continued)*
    rheumatic *(Continued)*
      with *(Continued)*
        tricuspid (valve) disease I08.2
          with mitral (valve) disease I08.3
    specified cause NEC I35.0
    syphilitic A52.03
  aqueduct of Sylvius (congenital) Q03.0
    with spina bifida - *see* Spina bifida, by site, with hydrocephalus
    acquired G91.1
  artery NEC (*see also* Arteriosclerosis) I77.1
    celiac I77.4
    cerebral - *see* Occlusion, artery, cerebral
    extremities - *see* Arteriosclerosis, extremities
    precerebral - *see* Occlusion, artery, precerebral
    pulmonary (congenital) Q25.6
      acquired I28.8
    renal I70.1
  bile duct (common) (hepatic) K83.1
    congenital Q44.3
  bladder-neck (acquired) N32.0
    congenital Q64.31
  brain G93.89
  bronchus J98.09
    congenital Q32.3
    syphilitic A52.72
  cardia (stomach) K22.2
    congenital Q40.2
  cardiovascular - *see* Disease, cardiovascular
  caudal M48.08
  cervix, cervical (canal) N88.2
    congenital Q51.8
    in pregnancy or childbirth - *see* Pregnancy, complicated by, abnormal cervix
  colon - *see also* Obstruction, intestine
    congenital Q42.9
      specified NEC Q42.8
  colostomy K94.03
  common (bile) duct K83.1
    congenital Q44.3
  coronary (artery) – *see* Disease, heart, ischemic, atherosclerotic
  cystic duct - *see* Obstruction, gallbladder
  due to presence of device, implant or graft (*see also* Complications, by site and type, specified NEC) T85.85
    arterial graft NEC T82.858
    breast (implant) T85.85
    catheter T83.85
      dialysis (renal) T82.858
        intraperitoneal T85.85
      infusion NEC T82.858
        spinal (epidural) (subdural) T85.85
      urinary (indwelling) T83.85
    fixation, internal (orthopedic) NEC T84.85
    gastrointestinal (bile duct) (esophagus) T85.85
    genital NEC T83.85
    heart NEC T82.857
    joint prosthesis T84.85
    ocular (corneal graft) (orbital implant) NEC T85.85

Stenosis, stenotic *(Continued)*
  due to presence of device, implant or graft *(Continued)*
    orthopedic NEC T84.85
    specified NEC T85.85
    urinary NEC T83.85
    vascular NEC T82.858
    ventricular intracranial shunt T85.85
  duodenum K31.5
    congenital Q41.0
  ejaculatory duct NEC N50.8
  endocervical os - *see* Stenosis, cervix
  enterostomy K94.13
  esophagus K22.2
    congenital Q39.3
    syphilitic A52.79
      congenital A50.59 *[K23]*
  eustachian tube – *see* Obstruction, eustachian tube
  external ear canal (acquired) H61.30-
    congenital Q16.1
    due to
      inflammation H61.32-
      trauma H61.31-
    postprocedural H95.81-
    specified cause NEC H61.39-
  gallbladder - *see* Obstruction, gallbladder
  glottis J38.6
  heart valve (congenital) Q24.8
    aortic Q23.0
    mitral Q23.2
    pulmonary Q22.1
    tricuspid Q22.4
  hepatic duct K83.1
  hymen N89.6
  hypertrophic subaortic (idiopathic) I42.1
  ileum K56.69
    congenital Q41.2
  infundibulum cardia Q24.3
  intervertebral foramina - *see also* Lesion, biomechanical, specified NEC
    connective tissue M99.79
      abdomen M99.79
      cervical region M99.71
      cervicothoracic M99.71
      head region M99.70
      lumbar region M99.73
      lumbosacral M99.73
      occipitocervical M99.70
      sacral region M99.74
      sacrococcygeal M99.74
      sacroiliac M99.74
      specified NEC M99.79
      thoracic region M99.72
      thoracolumbar M99.72
    disc M99.79
      abdomen M99.79
      cervical region M99.71
      cervicothoracic M99.71
      head region M99.70
      lower extremity M99.76
      lumbar region M99.73
      lumbosacral M99.73
      occipitocervical M99.70
      pelvic M99.75
      rib cage M99.78
      sacral region M99.74
      sacrococcygeal M99.74
      sacroiliac M99.74
      specified NEC M99.79

Stenosis, stenotic *(Continued)*
  intervertebral foramina *(Continued)*
    disc *(Continued)*
      thoracic region M99.72
      thoracolumbar M99.72
      upper extremity M99.77
    osseous M99.69
      abdomen M99.69
      cervical region M99.61
      cervicothoracic M99.61
      head region M99.60
      lower extremity M99.66
      lumbar region M99.63
      lumbosacral M99.63
      occipitocervical M99.60
      pelvic M99.65
      rib cage M99.68
      sacral region M99.64
      sacrococcygeal M99.64
      sacroiliac M99.64
      specified NEC M99.69
      thoracic region M99.62
      thoracolumbar M99.62
      upper extremity M99.67
    subluxation - *see* Stenosis, intervertebral foramina, osseous
  intestine - *see also* Obstruction, intestine
    congenital (small) Q41.9
      large Q42.9
        specified NEC Q42.8
      specified NEC Q41.8
  jejunum K56.69
    congenital Q41.1
  lacrimal (passage)
    canaliculi H04.54-
    congenital Q10.5
    duct H04.55-
    punctum H04.56-
    sac H04.57-
  lacrimonasal duct - *see* Stenosis, lacrimal, duct
    congenital Q10.5
  larynx J38.6
    congenital NEC Q31.8
      subglottic Q31.1
    syphilitic A52.73
      congenital A50.59 *[J99]*
  mitral (chronic) (inactive) (valve) I05.0
    with
      aortic valve disease I08.0
      incompetency, insufficiency or regurgitation I05.2
    active or acute I01.1
      with rheumatic or Sydenham's chorea I02.0
    congenital Q23.2
    specified cause, except rheumatic I34.2
    syphilitic A52.03
  myocardium, myocardial - *see also* Degeneration, myocardial
    hypertrophic subaortic (idiopathic) I42.1
  nares (anterior) (posterior) J34.89
    congenital Q30.0
  nasal duct - *see also* Stenosis, lacrimal, duct
    congenital Q10.5
  nasolacrimal duct - *see also* Stenosis, lacrimal, duct
    congenital Q10.5
  neural canal - *see also* Lesion, biomechanical, specified NEC

Stenosis, stenotic *(Continued)*
  neural canal *(Continued)*
    connective tissue M99.49
      abdomen M99.49
      cervical region M99.41
      cervicothoracic M99.41
      head region M99.40
      lower extremity M99.46
      lumbar region M99.43
      lumbosacral M99.43
      occipitocervical M99.40
      pelvic M99.45
      rib cage M99.48
      sacral region M99.44
      sacrococcygeal M99.44
      sacroiliac M99.44
      specified NEC M99.49
      thoracic region M99.42
      thoracolumbar M99.42
      upper extremity M99.47
    intervertebral disc M99.59
      abdomen M99.59
      cervical region M99.51
      cervicothoracic M99.51
      head region M99.50
      lower extremity M99.56
      lumbar region M99.53
      lumbosacral M99.53
      occipitocervical M99.50
      pelvic M99.55
      rib cage M99.58
      sacral region M99.54
      sacrococcygeal M99.54
      sacroiliac M99.54
      specified NEC M99.59
      thoracic region M99.52
      thoracolumbar M99.52
      upper extremity M99.57
    osseous M99.39
      abdomen M99.39
      cervical region M99.31
      cervicothoracic M99.31
      head region M99.30
      lower extremity M99.36
      lumbar region M99.33
      lumbosacral M99.33
      pelvic M99.35
      rib cage M99.38
      occipitocervical M99.30
      sacral region M99.34
      sacrococcygeal M99.34
      sacroiliac M99.34
      specified NEC M99.39
      thoracic region M99.32
      thoracolumbar M99.32
      upper extremity M99.37
    subluxation M99.29
      cervical region M99.21
      cervicothoracic M99.21
      head region M99.20
      lower extremity M99.26
      lumbar region M99.23
      lumbosacral M99.23
      occipitocervical M99.20
      pelvic M99.25
      rib cage M99.28
      sacral region M99.24
      sacrococcygeal M99.24
      sacroiliac M99.24
      specified NEC M99.29
      thoracic region M99.22
      thoracolumbar M99.22
      upper extremity M99.27
  oesophagus - *see* Stenosis, esophagus

Stenosis, stenotic *(Continued)*
  organ or site, congenital NEC - *see* Atresia, by site
  papilla of Vater K83.1
  pulmonary (artery) (congenital) Q25.6
    with ventricular septal defect, transposition of aorta, and hypertrophy of right ventricle Q21.3
    acquired I28.8
    in tetralogy of Fallot Q21.3
    infundibular Q24.3
    valve I37.0
      with insufficiency I37.2
      congenital Q22.1
      rheumatic I09.89
        with aortic, mitral or tricuspid (valve) disease I08.8
    subvalvular Q24.3
    supravalvular Q25.6
    vein, acquired I28.8
    vessel NEC I28.8
  pulmonic (congenital) Q22.1
    infundibular Q24.3
    subvalvular Q24.3
  pylorus (hypertrophic) (acquired) K31.1
    adult K31.1
    congenital Q40.0
    infantile Q40.0
  rectum (sphincter) - *see* Stricture, rectum
  renal artery I70.1
    congenital Q27.1
  salivary duct (any) K11.8
  sphincter of Oddi K83.1
  spinal M48.00
    cervical region M48.02
    cervicothoracic region M48.03
    lumbar region M48.06
    lumbosacral region M48.07
    occipito-atlanto-axial region M48.01
    sacrococcygeal region M48.08
    thoracic region M48.04
    thoracolumbar region M48.05
  stomach, hourglass K31.2
  subaortic (congenital) Q24.4
    hypertrophic (idiopathic) I42.1
  subglottic
    congenital Q31.1
    postprocedural J95.5
  trachea J39.8
    congenital Q32.1
    syphilitic A52.73
    tuberculous NEC A15.5
  tracheostomy J95.03
  tricuspid (valve) I07.0
    with
      aortic (valve) disease I08.2
      incompetency, insufficiency or regurgitation I07.2
        with aortic (valve) disease I08.2
          with mitral (valve) disease I08.3
      mitral (valve) disease I08.1
        with aortic (valve) disease I08.3
    congenital Q22.4
    nonrheumatic I36.0
      with insufficiency I36.2
  tubal N97.1
  ureter – *see* Atresia, ureter
  ureteropelvic junction, congenital Q62.11

Stenosis, stenotic *(Continued)*
  ureterovesical orifice, congenital Q62.12
  urethra (valve) - *see also* Stricture, urethra
    congenital Q64.32
  urinary meatus, congenital Q64.33
  vagina N89.5
    congenital Q52.4
    in pregnancy - *see* Pregnancy, complicated by, abnormal vagina
      causing obstructed labor O65.5
  valve (cardiac) (heart) (*see also* Endocarditis) I38
    congenital Q24.8
      aortic Q23.0
      mitral Q23.2
      pulmonary Q22.1
      tricuspid Q22.4
  vena cava (inferior) (superior) I87.1
    congenital Q26.0
  vesicourethral orifice Q64.31
  vulva N90.5
Stercolith (impaction) K56.4
  appendix K38.1
Stercoraceous, stercoral ulcer K63.3
  anus or rectum K62.6
Stereotypies NEC F98.4
Sterility – *see* Infertility
Sterilization - *see* Encounter (for), sterilization
Sternalgia - *see* Angina
Sternopagus Q89.4
Sternum bifidum Q76.7
Steroid
  effects (adverse) (adrenocortical) (iatrogenic)
    cushingoid E24.2
      correct substance properly administered - *see* Table of drugs and chemicals, by drug, adverse effect
      overdose or wrong substance given or taken - *see* Table of drugs and chemicals, by drug, poisoning
    diabetes - *see* category E09
      correct substance properly administered – Table of drugs and chemicals, by drug, adverse effect
      overdose or wrong substance given or taken - *see* Table of drugs and chemicals, by drug, poisoning
    fever R50.2
    insufficiency E27.3
      correct substance properly administered - *see* Table of drugs and chemicals, by drug, adverse effect
      overdose or wrong substance given or taken - *see* Table of drugs and chemicals, by drug, poisoning
Stevens-Johnson disease or syndrome L51.1
  toxic epidermal necrolysis overlap L51.3
Stewart-Morel syndrome M85.2
Sticker's disease B08.3
Sticky eye - *see* Conjunctivitis, acute, mucopurulent

Stieda's disease - *see* Bursitis, tibial
    collateral
Stiff neck —*see* Torticollis
Stiff-man syndrome G25.82
Stiffness, joint NEC M25.60
    ankle M25.67-
    ankylosis - *see* Ankylosis, joint
    contracture - *see* Contraction, joint
    elbow M25.6-
    foot M25.6-
    hand M25.6-
    hip M25.6-
    knee M25.6-
    shoulder M25.1-
    wrist M25.3-
Stigmata congenital syphilis A50.59
Stillbirth P95
Still-Felty syndrome - *see* Felty's
    syndrome
Still's disease or syndrome (juvenile)
    M08.20
    adult-onset M06.1
    ankle M08.27-
    elbow M08.22-
    foot joint M08.27-
    hand joint M08.24-
    hip M08.25-
    knee M08.26-
    multiple site M08.29
    shoulder M08.21-
    vertebra M08.28
    wrist M08.23-
Stimulation, ovary E28.1
Sting (venomous) (with allergic or
    anaphylactic shock) - *see* Toxicity,
    venom
Stippled epiphyses Q78.8
Stitch
    abscess T81.4
    burst (in operation wound) - *see*
        Disruption, wound, operation
Stokes-Adams disease or syndrome
    I45.9
Stokes' disease E05.00
    with thyroid storm E05.01
Stokvis(-Talma) disease D74.8BD
Stoma malfunction
    colostomy K94.03
    enterostomy K94.13
    gastrostomy K94.23
    ileostomy K94.13
    tracheostomy J95.03
Stomach - *see* condition
Stomatitis (denture) (ulcerative) K12.1
    angular K13.0
        due to dietary or vitamin deficiency
        E53.0
    aphthous K12.0
    bovine B08.61
    candidal B37.0
    catarrhal K12.1
    diphtheritic A36.89
    due to
        dietary deficiency E53.0
        thrush B37.0
        vitamin deficiency
            B group NEC E53.9
            B$_2$ (riboflavin) E53.0
    epidemic B08.8
    epizootic B08.8
    follicular K12.1
    gangrenous A69.0
    Geotrichum B48.3
    herpesviral, herpetic B00.2

Stomatitis (Continued)
    herpetiformis K12.0
    malignant K12.1
    membranous acute K12.1
    monilial B37.0
    mycotic B37.0
    necrotizing ulcerative A69.0
    parasitic B37.0
    septic K12.1
    spirochetal A69.1
    suppurative (acute) K12.2
    ulceromembranous A69.1
    vesicular K12.1
        with exanthem (enteroviral) B08.4
        virus disease A93.8
    Vincent's A69.1
Stomatocytosis D58.8
Stomatomycosis B37.0
Stomatorrhagia K13.79
Stone(s) - *see also* Calculus
    bladder (diverticulum) N21.0
    cystine E72.09
    heart syndrome I50.1
    kidney N20.0
    prostate N42.0
    pulpal (dental) K04.2
    renal N20.0
    salivary gland or duct (any) K11.5
    urethra (impacted) N21.1
    urinary (duct) (impacted) (passage)
        N20.9
        bladder (diverticulum) N21.0
        lower tract N21.9
        specified NEC N21.8
    xanthine E79.8 *[N22]*
Stonecutter's lung J62.8
Stonemason's asthma, disease, lung or
    pneumoconiosis J62.8
Stoppage
    heart - *see* Arrest, cardiac
    urine - *see* Retention, urine
Storm, thyroid - *see* Thyrotoxicosis
Strabismus (congenital) (nonparalytic)
    H50.9
    concomitant H50.40
        convergent - *see* Strabismus, conver-
            gent concomitant
        divergent - *see* Strabismus, divergent
            concomitant
    convergent concomitant H50.00
        accommodative component
            H50.43
        alternating H50.05
            with
                A pattern H50.06
                specified nonconcomitances
                    NEC H50.08
                V pattern H50.07
        monocular
            with
                A pattern H50.02-
                specified nonconcomitances
                    NEC H50.04-
                V pattern H50.03-
        intermittent H50.01-
            alternating H50.32
    cyclotropia H50.1-
    divergent concomitant H50.10
        alternating H50.15
            with
                A pattern H50.16
                specified noncomitances NEC
                    H50.18
                V pattern H50.17

Strabismus (Continued)
    divergent concomitant (Continued)
        monocular
            with
                A pattern H50.12-
                specified noncomitances NEC
                    H50.14-
                V pattern H50.13-
        intermittent H50.11-
            alternating H50.34
    Duane's syndrome H50.81-
    due to adhesions, scars H50.60
    heterophoria H50.50
        alternating H50.55
        cyclophoria H50.54
        esophoria H50.51
        exophoria H50.52
        vertical H50.53
    heterotropia H50.40
        intermittent H50.30
    hypertropia H50.2-
    hypotropia - *see* Hypertropia
    latent H50.50
    mechanical H50.60
        Brown's sheath syndrome H50.61-
        specified type NEC H50.69
    monofixation syndrome H50.42
    paralytic H49.9
        abducens nerve H49.2-
        fourth nerve H49.1-
        Kearns-Sayre syndrome H49.81-
        ophthalmoplegia (external)
            progressive H49.4-
                with pigmentary retinopathy
                    H49.81-
            total H49.3-
        sixth nerve H49.2-
        specified type NEC H49.88-
        third nerve H49.0-
        trochlear nerve H49.1-
    specified type NEC H50.89
    vertical H50.2-
Strain
    back S39.012
    cervical S16.1
    eye NEC - *see* Disturbance, vision,
        subjective
    heart - *see* Disease, heart
    low back S39.012
    mental NOS Z73.3
        work-related Z56.6
    muscle (tendon) - *see* Injury, muscle,
        by site, strain
    neck S16.1
    postural - *see also* Disorder, soft tissue,
        due to use
    physical NOS Z73.3
        work-related Z56.6
    psychological NEC Z73.3
    tendon - *see* Injury, muscle, by site,
        strain
Straining, on urination R39.16
Strand, vitreous - *see* Opacity, vitreous,
    membranes and strands
Strangulation, strangulated - *see also*
    Asphyxia, traumatic
    appendix K38.8
    bladder-neck N32.0
    bowel or colon K56.2
    food or foreign body - *see* Asphyxia, food
    hemorrhoids - *see* Hemorrhoids, with
        complication
    hernia - *see also* Hernia, by site, with
        obstruction

Strangulation, strangulated *(Continued)*
hernia *(Continued)*
with gangrene - *see* Hernia, by site, with gangrene
intestine (large) (small) K56.2
with hernia - *see also* Hernia, by site, with obstruction
with gangrene - *see* Hernia, by site, with gangrene
mesentery K56.2
mucus - *see* Asphyxia, mucus
omentum K56.2
organ or site, congenital NEC - *see* Atresia, by site
ovary – *see* Torsion, ovary
penis N48.89
foreign body T19.8
rupture - *see* Hernia, by site, with obstruction
stomach due to hernia - *see also* Hernia, by site, with obstruction
with gangrene - *see* Hernia, by site, with gangrene
vesicourethral orifice N32.0
Strangury R30.0
Straw itch B88.0
Strawberry
gallbladder K82.4
mark Q82.5
tongue (red) (white) K14.3
Streak(s)
macula, angioid H35.33
ovarian Q50.32
Strephosymbolia F81.0
secondary to organic lesion R48.8
Streptobacillary fever A25.1
Streptobacillosis A25.1
Streptobacillus moniliformis A25.1
Streptococcus, streptococcal - *see also* condition
as cause of disease classified elsewhere B95.5
group
A, as cause of disease classified elsewhere B95.0
B, as cause of disease classified elsewhere B95.1
D, as cause of disease classified elsewhere B95.2
pneumoniae, as cause of disease classified elsewhere B95.3
specified NEC, as cause of disease classified elsewhere B95.4
Streptomycosis B47.1
Streptotrichosis A48.8
Stress F43.9
family - *see* Disruption, family
fetal P84
complicating pregnancy O77.9
due to drug administration O77.1
mental NEC Z73.3
work-related Z56.6
physical NEC Z73.3
work-related Z56.6
polycythemia D75.1
reaction (*see also* Reaction, stress) F43.9
work schedule Z56.3
Stretching, nerve - *see* Injury, nerve
Striae albicantes, atrophicae or distensae (cutis) L90.6
Stricture - *see also* Stenosis
ampulla of Vater K83.1
anus (sphincter) K62.4

Stricture *(Continued)*
anus *(Continued)*
congenital Q42.3
with fistula Q42.2
infantile Q42.3
with fistula Q42.2
aorta (ascending) (congenital) Q25.3
arteriosclerotic I70.0
calcified I70.0
supravalvular, congenital Q25.3
aortic (valve) - *see* Stenosis, aortic
aqueduct of Sylvius (congenital) Q03.0
with spina bifida - *see* Spina bifida, by site, with hydrocephalus
acquired G91.1
artery I77.1
basilar - *see* Occlusion, artery, basilar
carotid - *see* Occlusion, artery, carotid
celiac I77.4
congenital (peripheral) Q27.8
cerebral Q28.3
coronary Q24.5
digestive system Q27.8
lower limb Q27.8
retinal Q14.1
specified site NEC Q27.8
umbilical Q27.0
upper limb Q27.8
coronary – *see* Disease, heart, ischemic, atherosclerotic
congenital Q24.5
precerebral - *see* Occlusion, artery, precerebral
pulmonary (congenital) Q25.6
acquired I28.8
renal I70.1
vertebral - *see* Occlusion, artery, vertebral
auditory canal (external) (congenital)
acquired - *see* Stenosis, external ear canal
bile duct (common) (hepatic) K83.1
congenital Q44.3
postoperative K91.89
bladder N32.89
neck N32.0
bowel - *see* Obstruction, intestine
brain G93.89
bronchus J98.09
congenital Q32.3
syphilitic A52.72
cardia (stomach) K22.2
congenital Q40.2
cardiac - *see also* Disease, heart
orifice (stomach) K22.2
cecum - *see* Obstruction, intestine
cervix, cervical (canal) N88.2
congenital Q51.8
in pregnancy - *see* Pregnancy, complicated by, abnormal cervix
causing obstructed labor O65.5
colon - *see also* Obstruction, intestine
congenital Q42.9
specified NEC Q42.8
colostomy K94.03
common (bile) duct K83.1
coronary (artery) – *see* Disease, heart, ischemic, atherosclerotic
cystic duct - *see* Obstruction, gallbladder
digestive organs NEC, congenital Q45.8
duodenum K31.5
congenital Q41.0

Stricture *(Continued)*
ear canal (external) (congenital) Q16.1
acquired - *see* Stricture, auditory canal, acquired
ejaculatory duct N50.8
enterostomy K94.13
esophagus K22.2
congenital Q39.3
syphilitic A52.79
congenital A50.59 *[K23]*
eustachian tube – *see also* Obstruction, eustachian tube
congenital Q17.8
fallopian tube N97.1
gonococcal A54.24
tuberculous A18.17
gallbladder - *see* Obstruction, gallbladder
glottis J38.6
heart - *see also* Disease, heart
valve (*see also* Endocarditis) I38
aortic Q23.0
mitral Q23.4
pulmonary Q22.1
tricuspid Q22.4
hepatic duct K83.1
hourglass, of stomach K31.2
hymen N89.6
hypopharynx J39.2
ileum K56.69
congenital Q41.2
intestine - *see also* Obstruction, intestine
congenital (small) Q41.9
large Q42.9
specified NEC Q42.8
specified NEC Q41.8
ischemic K55.1
jejunum K56.69
congenital Q41.1
lacrimal passages - *see also* Stenosis, lacrimal
congenital Q10.5
larynx J38.6
congenital NEC Q31.8
subglottic Q31.1
syphilitic A52.73
congenital A50.59 *[J99]*
meatus
ear (congenital) Q16.1
acquired - *see* Stricture, auditory canal, acquired
osseous (ear) (congenital) Q16.1
acquired - *see* Stricture, auditory canal, acquired
urinarius - *see also* Stricture, urethra
congenital Q64.33
mitral (valve) - *see* Stenosis, mitral
myocardium, myocardial I51.5
hypertrophic subaortic (idiopathic) I42.1
nares (anterior) (posterior) J34.89
congenital Q30.0
nasal duct - *see also* Stenosis, lacrimal, duct
congenital Q10.5
nasolacrimal duct - *see also* Stenosis, lacrimal, duct
congenital Q10.5
nasopharynx J39.2
syphilitic A52.73
nose J34.89
congenital Q30.0
nostril (anterior) (posterior) J34.89
congenital Q30.0

Stricture *(Continued)*
  nostril *(Continued)*
    syphilitic A52.73
      congenital A50.59 *[J99]*
  oesophagus - *see* Stricture, esophagus
  organ or site, congenital NEC - *see*
      Atresia, by site
  os uteri - *see* Stricture, cervix
  osseous meatus (ear) (congenital) Q16.1
    acquired - *see* Stricture, auditory
        canal, acquired
  oviduct - *see* Stricture, fallopian tube
  pelviureteric junction (congenital)
      Q62.0
  penis, by foreign body T19.8
  pharynx J39.2
  prostate N42.89
  pulmonary, pulmonic
    artery (congenital) Q25.6
      acquired I28.8
      noncongenital I28.8
    infundibulum (congenital) Q24.3
    valve I37.0
      congenital Q22.1
    vein, acquired I28.8
    vessel NEC I28.8
  punctum lacrimale - *see also* Stenosis,
      lacrimal, punctum
    congenital Q10.5
  pylorus (hypertrophic) K31.1
    adult K31.1
    congenital Q40.0
    infantile Q40.0
  rectosigmoid K56.69
  rectum (sphincter) K62.4
    congenital Q42.1
      with fistula Q42.0
    due to
      chlamydial lymphogranuloma
          A55
      irradiation K91.89
      lymphogranuloma venereum A55
    gonococcal A54.6
    inflammatory (chlamydial) A55
    syphilitic A52.74
    tuberculous A18.32
  renal artery I70.1
    congenital Q27.1
  salivary duct or gland (any) K11.8
  sigmoid (flexure) - *see* Obstruction,
      intestine
  spermatic cord N50.8
  stoma (following) (of)
    colostomy K94.03
    enterostomy K94.13
    gastrostomy K94.23
    ileostomy K94.13
    tracheostomy J95.03
  stomach K31.89
    congenital Q40.2
    hourglass K31.2
  subaortic Q24.4
    hypertrophic (acquired) (idiopathic)
        I42.1
  subglottic J38.6
  syphilitic NEC A52.79
  trachea J39.8
    congenital Q32.1
    syphilitic A52.73
    tuberculous NEC A15.5
  tracheostomy J95.03
  tricuspid (valve) - *see* Stenosis,
      tricuspid
  tunica vaginalis N50.8

Stricture *(Continued)*
  ureter (postoperative) N13.5
    with
      hydronephrosis N13.1
        with infection N13.6
      pyelonephritis (chronic) N11.1
    congenital – *see* Atresia, ureter
    tuberculous A18.11
  ureteropelvic junction (congenital) Q62.0
  ureterovesical orifice N13.5
    with infection N13.6
  urethra (organic) (spasmodic) N35.9
    associated with schistosomiasis
        B65.0 *[N29]*
    congenital Q64.39
      valvular (posterior) Q64.2
    due to
      infection – *see* Stricture, urethra,
          postinfective
      trauma – *see* Stricture, urethra,
          post-traumatic
    gonococcal, gonorrheal A54.01
    infective NEC – *see* Stricture, urethra,
        postinfective
    late effect (sequelae) of injury – *see*
        Stricture, urethra, post-traumatic
    postcatheterization – *see* Stricture,
        urethra, postprocedural
    postinfective NEC
      female N35.12
      male N35.119
        anterior urethra N35.114
        bulbous urethra N35.112
        meatal N35.111
        membranous urethra N35.113
    postobstetric N35.021
    postoperative– *see* Stricture, urethra,
        postprocedural
    postprocedural
      female N99.12
      male N99.114
        anterior urethra N99.113
        bulbous urethra N99.111
        meatal N99.110
        membranous urethra N99.112
    post-traumatic
      female N35.028
        due to childbirth N35.021
      male N35.014
        anterior urethra N35.013
        bulbous urethra N35.011
        meatal N35.010
        membranous urethra N35.012
    sequela (late effect) of
      childbirth N35.021
      injury – *see* Stricture, urethra,
          post-traumatic
    specified cause NEC N35.8
    syphilitic A52.76
    traumatic – *see* Stricture, urethra,
        post-traumatic
    valvular (posterior), congenital Q64.2
  urinary meatus - *see* Stricture, urethra
  uterus, uterine (synechiae) N85.6
    os (external) (internal) - *see* Stricture,
        cervix
  vagina (outlet) - *see* Stenosis, vagina
  valve (cardiac) (heart) - *see also*
      Endocarditis
    congenital
      aortic Q23.0
      mitral Q23.2
      pulmonary Q22.1
      tricuspid Q22.4

Stricture *(Continued)*
  vas deferens N50.8
    congenital Q55.4
  vein I87.1
  vena cava (inferior) (superior) NEC
      I87.1
    congenital Q26.0
  vesicourethral orifice N32.0
    congenital Q64.31
  vulva (acquired) N90.5
Stridor R06.1
  congenital (larynx) P28.89
Stridulous - *see* condition
Stroke (apoplectic) (brain) (embolic)
    (ischemic) (paralytic) (thrombotic)
    I63.9
  epileptic - *see* Epilepsy
  heat T67.0
  in evolution I63.9
  intraoperative
    during cardiac surgery I97.810
    during other surgery I97.811
  lightning - *see* Lightning
  meaning
    cerebral hemorrhage - code to Hem-
        orrhage, intracranial
    cerebral infarction - code to Infarc-
        tion, cerebral
  postprocedural
    following cardiac surgery I97.820
    following other surgery I97.821
  unspecified (NOS) I63.9
Stromatosis, endometrial D39.0
Strongyloidiasis, strongyloidosis B78.9
  cutaneous B78.1
  disseminated B78.7
  intestinal B78.0
Strophulus pruriginosus L28.2
Struck by lightning - *see* Lightning
Struma - *see also* Goiter
  Hashimoto E06.3
  lymphomatosa E06.3
  nodosa (simplex) E04.9
    endemic E01.2
      multinodular E01.1
    multinodular E04.2
      iodine-deficiency related E01.1
    toxic or with hyperthyroidism E05.20
      with thyroid storm E05.21
      multinodular E05.20
        with thyroid storm E05.21
      uninodular E05.10
        with thyroid storm E05.11
    toxicosa E05.20
      with thyroid storm E05.21
      multinodular E05.20
        with thyroid storm E05.21
      uninodular E05.10
        with thyroid storm E05.11
    uninodular E04.1
  ovarii D27.-
  Riedel's E06.5
Strumipriva cachexia E03.4
Strümpell-Marie spine - *see* Spondylitis,
    ankylosing
Strümpell-Westphal pseudosclerosis
    E83.01
Stuart deficiency disease (factor X) D68.2
Stuart-Prower factor deficiency (factor
    X) D68.2
Student's elbow - *see* Bursitis, elbow,
    olecranon
Stump - *see* Amputation
Stunting, nutritional E45

Stupor (catatonic) R40.1
  depressive F32.8
  dissociative F44.2
  manic F30.2
  manic-depressive F31.89
  psychogenic (anergic) F44.2
  reaction to exceptional stress (transient)
    F43.0
Sturge (-Weber) (-Dimitri) (-Kalischer)
  disease or syndrome Q85.8
Stuttering F98.5
  following cerebrovascular disease - *see*
    Disorder, fluency, following cere-
    brovascular disease
Sty, stye (external) (internal) (meibomian)
  (zeisian) - *see* Hordeolum
Subacidity, gastric K31.89
  psychogenic F45.8
Subacute - *see* condition
Subarachnoid - *see* condition
Subcortical - *see* condition
Subcostal syndrome, nerve compression -
  see Mononeuropathy, upper limb,
  specified site NEC
Subcutaneous, subcuticular - *see*
  condition
Subdural - *see* condition
Subendocardium - *see* condition
Subependymoma
  specified site - *see* Neoplasm, uncertain
    behavior
  unspecified site D43.2
Suberosis J67.3
Subglossitis - *see* Glossitis
Subhemophilia D66
Subinvolution
  breast (postlactational) (postpuerperal)
    N64.89
  puerperal O90.89
  uterus (chronic) (nonpuerperal) N85.3
    puerperal O90.89
Sublingual - *see* condition
Sublinguitis - *see* Sialoadenitis
Subluxatable hip Q65.6
Subluxation - *see also* Dislocation
  acromioclavicular S43.11-
  ankle S93.0-
  atlantoaxial, recurrent M43.4
    with myelopathy M43.3
  carpometacarpal (joint) NEC S63.05-
    thumb S63.04-
  complex, vertebral - *see* Complex,
    subluxation
  congenital - *see also* Malposition,
    congenital
    hip – *see* Dislocation, hip, congenital,
      partial
    joint (excluding hip)
      lower limb Q68.8
      shoulder Q68.8
      upper limb Q68.8
  elbow (traumatic) S53.10-
    anterior S53.11-
    lateral S53.14-
    medial S53.13-
    posterior S53.12-
    specified type NEC S53.19-
  finger S63.20-
    index S63.20-
    interphalangeal S63.22-
      distal S63.24-
        index S63.24-
        little S63.24-
        middle S63.24-

Subluxation *(Continued)*
  finger *(Continued)*
    interphalangeal *(Continued)*
      distal *(Continued)*
        ring S63.24-
      index S63.22-
      little S63.22-
      middle S63.22-
      proximal S63.23-
        index S63.23-
        little S63.23-
        middle S63.23-
        ring S63.23-
      ring S63.22-
    little S63.20-
    metacarpophalangeal S63.21-
      index S63.21-
      little S63.21-
      middle S63.21-
      ring S63.21-
    middle S63.20-
    ring S63.20-
  foot S93.30-
    specified site NEC S93.33-
    tarsal joint S93.31-
    tarsometatarsal joint S93.32-
    toe – *see* Subluxation, toe
  hip S73.00-
    anterior S73.03-
      obturator S73.02-
    central S73.04-
    posterior S73.01-
  interphalangeal (joint)
    finger S63.22-
      distal joint S63.24-
        index S63.24-
        little S63.24-
        middle S63.24-
        ring S63.24-
      index S63.22-
      little S63.22-
      middle S63.22-
      proximal joint S63.23-
        index S63.23-
        little S63.23-
        middle S63.23-
        ring S63.23-
      ring S63.22-
    thumb S63.12-
      distal joint S63.14-
      proximal joint S63.13-
    toe S93.13-
      great S93.13-
      lesser S93.13-
  joint prosthesis - *see* Complications,
    joint prosthesis, mechanical,
    displacement, by site
  knee S83.10-
    cap – *see* Subluxation, patella
    patella - *see* Subluxation, patella
    proximal tibia
      anteriorly S83.11-
      laterally S83.14-
      medially S83.13-
      posteriorly S83.12-
    specified type NEC S83.19-
  lens - *see* Dislocation, lens, partial
  ligament, traumatic – *see* Sprain,
    by site
  metacarpal (bone)
    proximal end S63.06-
  metacarpophalangeal (joint)
    finger S63.21-
      index S63.21-

Subluxation *(Continued)*
  metacarpophalangeal *(Continued)*
    finger *(Continued)*
      little S63.21-
      middle S63.21-
      ring S63.21-
      thumb S63.11-
  metatarsophalangeal joint S93.14-
    great toe S93.14-
    lesser toe S93.14-
  midcarpal (joint) S63.03-
  patella S83.00-
    lateral S83.01-
    recurrent (nontraumatic) - *see*
      Dislocation, patella, recurrent,
      incomplete
    specified type NEC S83.09-
  pathological - *see* Dislocation,
    pathological
  nursemaid's elbow S53.03-
  radial head S53.00-
    anterior S53.01-
    posterior S53.02-
    specified type NEC S53.09-
  radiocarpal (joint) S63.02-
  radioulnar (joint)
    distal S63.01-
    proximal - *see* Subluxation,
      elbow
  shoulder
    congenital Q68.8
    girdle S43.30-
      scapula S43.31-
      specified site NEC S43.39-
    traumatic S43.00-
      anterior S43.01-
      inferior S43.03-
      posterior S43.02-
      specified type NEC S43.08-
  sternoclavicular (joint) S43.20-
    anterior S43.21-
    posterior S43.22-
  symphysis (pubis)
  thumb S63.103
    interphalangeal joint - *see* Sublux-
      ation, interphalangeal (joint),
      thumb
    metacarpophalangeal joint -
      see Subluxation, metacarpo-
      phalangeal (joint), thumb
  toe(s) S93.10-
    great S93.10-
      interphalangeal joint S93.13-
      metatarsophalangeal joint S93.14-
    interphalangeal joint S93.13-
    lesser S93.10-
      interphalangeal joint S93.13-
      metatarsophalangeal joint S93.14-
    metatarsophalangeal joint S93.149
  ulnohumeral joint - *see* Subluxation,
    elbow
  vertebral
    recurrent NEC - *see* subcategory
      M43.5
    traumatic
      cervical S13.100
        atlantoaxial joint S13.120
        atlantooccipital joint S13.110
        atloidooccipital joint S13.110
        joint between
          C0 and C1 S13.110
          C1 and C2 S13.120
          C2 and C3 S13.130
          C3 and C4 S13.140

Subluxation (Continued)
  vertebral (Continued)
    traumatic (Continued)
      cervical (Continued)
        joint between (Continued)
          C4 and C5 S13.150
          C5 and C6 S13.160
          C6 and C7 S13.170
          C7 and T1 S13.180
          occipitoatloid joint S13.110
      lumbar S33.100
        joint between
          L1and L2 S33.110
          L2and L3 S33.120
          L3 and L4 S33.130
          L4 and L5 S33.140
      thoracic S23.100
        joint between
          T1 and T2 S23.110
          T2 and T3 S23.120
          T3 and T4 S23.122
          T4 and T5 S23.130
          T5 and T6 S23.132
          T6 and T7 S23.140
          T7 and T8 S23.142
          T8 and T9 S23.150
          T9 and T10 S23.152
          T10 and T11 S23.160
          T11 and T12 S23.162
          T12 and L1
  ulna
    distal end S63.07-
    proximal end - see Subluxation, elbow
  wrist (carpal bone) S63.00-
    carpometacarpal joint - see Subluxation, carpometacarpal (joint)
    distal radioulnar joint - see Subluxation, radioulnar (joint), distal
    metacarpal bone, proximal - see Subluxation, metacarpal (bone), proximal end
    midcarpal - see Subluxation, midcarpal (joint)
    radiocarpal joint - see Subluxation, radiocarpal (joint)
    recurrent - see Dislocation, recurrent, wrist
    specified site NEC S63.09-
    ulna - see Subluxation, ulna, distal end
Submaxillary - see condition
Submersion (fatal) (nonfatal) T75.1
Submucous - see condition
Subnormal, subnormality
  accommodation (old age) H52.4
  mental F79
    mild F70
    moderate F71
    profound F73
    severe F72
  temperature (accidental) T68
Subphrenic - see condition
Subscapular nerve - see condition
Subseptus uterus Q51.8
Subsiding appendicitis K36
Substernal thyroid E04.9
  congenital Q89.2
Substitution disorder F44.9
Subtentorial - see condition
Subthyroidism (acquired) - see also Hypothyroidism
  congenital E03.1
Succenturiate placenta O43.19-
Sucking thumb, child (excessive) F98.8

Sudamen, sudamina L74.1
Sudanese kala-azar B55.0
Sudden
  heart failure - see Failure, heart
  hearing loss - see Deafness, sudden
Sudeck's atrophy, disease, or syndrome - see Algoneurodystrophy
Suffocation - see Asphyxia, traumatic
Sugar
  blood
    high (transient) R73.9
    low (transient) E16.2
  in urine R81
Suicide, suicidal (attempted) T14.91
  by poisoning - see Table of drugs and chemicals
  history of (personal) Z91.5
    in family Z81.8
  ideation R45.85
  risk
    meaning personal history of attempted suicide Z91.5
    meaning suicidal ideation R45.85
  tendencies
    meaning personal history of attempted suicide Z91.5
    meaning suicidal ideation R45.85
  trauma - see nature of injury by site
Suipestifer infection - see Infection, salmonella
Sulfhemoglobinemia, sulphemoglobinemia (acquired) (with methemoglobinemia) D74.8
Sumatran mite fever A75.3
Summer - see condition
Sunburn L55.9
  first degree L55.0
  second degree L55.1
  third degree L55.2
SUNCT (short lasting unilateral neural-giform headache with conjunctival injection and tearing) G44.059
  intractable G44.051
  not intractable G44.059
Sunken acetabulum - see Derangement, joint, specified type NEC, hip
Sunstroke T67.0
Superfecundation - see Pregnancy, multiple
Superfetation - see Pregnancy, multiple
Superinvolution (uterus) N85.8
Supernumerary (congenital)
  aortic cusps Q23.8
  auditory ossicles Q16.3
  bone Q79.8
  breast Q83.1
  carpal bones Q74.0
  cusps, heart valve NEC Q24.8
    aortic Q23.8
    mitral Q23.2
    pulmonary Q22.3
  digit(s) Q69.9
  ear (lobule) Q17.0
  fallopian tube Q50.6
  finger Q69.0
  hymen Q52.4
  kidney Q63.0
  lacrimonasal duct Q10.6
  lobule (ear) Q17.0
  mitral cusps Q23.2
  muscle Q79.8
  nipple(s) Q83.3
  organ or site not listed - see Accessory
  ossicles, auditory Q16.3

Supernumerary (Continued)
  ovary Q50.31
  oviduct Q50.6
  pulmonary, pulmonic cusps Q22.3
  rib Q76.6
    cervical or first (syndrome) Q76.5
  roots (of teeth) K00.2
  spleen Q89.09
  tarsal bones Q74.2
  teeth K00.1
  testis Q55.29
  thumb Q69.1
  toe Q69.2
  uterus Q51.2
  vagina Q52.1
  vertebra Q76.49
Supervision (of)
  contraceptive – see Prescription, contraceptives
  dietary (for) Z71.3
    allergy (food) Z71.3
    colitis Z71.3
    diabetes mellitus Z71.3
    food allergy or intolerance Z71.3
    gastritis Z71.3
    hypercholesterolemia Z71.3
    hypoglycemia Z71.3
    intolerance (food) Z71.3
    obesity Z71.3
    specified NEC Z71.3
  healthy infant or child Z76.2
    foundling Z76.1
  high-risk pregnancy – see Pregnancy, complicated by, high, risk
  lactation Z39.1
  pregnancy - see Pregnancy, supervision of
Supplemental teeth K00.1
Suppression
  binocular vision H53.34
  lactation O92.5
  menstruation N94.89
  ovarian secretion E28.39
  renal N28.9
  urine, urinary secretion R34
Suppuration, suppurative - see also condition
  accessory sinus (chronic) - see Sinusitis
  adrenal gland
  antrum (chronic) - see Sinusitis, maxillary
  bladder - see Cystitis
  brain G06.0
    sequelae G09
  breast N61
    puerperal, postpartum or gestational – see Mastitis, obstetric, purulent
  dental periosteum M27.3
  ear (middle) - see also Otitis, media
    external NEC - see Otitis, externa, infective
    internal - see subcategory H83.0
  ethmoidal (chronic) (sinus) - see Sinusitis, ethmoidal
  fallopian tube - see Salpingo-oophoritis
  frontal (chronic) (sinus) - see Sinusitis, frontal
  gallbladder (acute) K81.0
  gum K05.20
    generalized K05.22
    localized K05.21
  intracranial G06.0

Suppuration, suppurative *(Continued)*
  joint - *see* Arthritis, pyogenic or
      pyemic
  labyrinthine - *see* subcategory H83.0
  lung - *see* Abscess, lung
  mammary gland N61
      puerperal, postpartum O91.12
          associated with lactation O91.13
  maxilla, maxillary M27.2
      sinus (chronic) - *see* Sinusitis,
          maxillary
  muscle - *see* Myositis, infective
  nasal sinus (chronic) - *see* Sinusitis
  pancreas, acute K85.8
  parotid gland - *see* Sialoadenitis
  pelvis, pelvic
      female - *see* Disease, pelvis,
          inflammatory
      male K65.0
  pericranial - *see* Osteomyelitis
  salivary duct or gland (any) - *see*
      Sialoadenitis
  sinus (accessory) (chronic) (nasal) -
      see Sinusitis
  sphenoidal sinus (chronic) - *see* Sinus-
      itis, sphenoidal
  thymus (gland) E32.1
  thyroid (gland) E06.0
  tonsil - *see* Tonsillitis
  uterus - *see* Endometritis
Supraeruption of tooth (teeth) M26.34
Supraglottitis J04.30
  with obstruction J04.31
Suprarenal (gland) - *see* condition
Suprascapular nerve - *see* condition
Suprasellar - *see* condition
Surfer's knots or nodules S89.8-
Surgical
  emphysema T81.82
  operation R69
  procedures, complication or misadven-
      ture - *see* Complications, surgical
      procedures
  shock T81.1
Surveillance (of) (for) - *see also*
      Observation
  alcohol abuse Z71.41
  contraceptive – *see* Prescription,
      contraceptives
  dietary Z71.3
  drug abuse Z71.51
Susceptibility to disease, genetic Z15.89
  malignant neoplasm Z15.00
      breast Z15.01
      endometrium Z15.04
      ovary Z15.02
      prostate Z15.03
      specified NEC Z15.09
  multiple endocrine neoplasia Z15.81
Suspected condition, ruled out - *see also*
      Observation, suspected
  amniotic cavity and membrane Z03.71
  cervical shortening Z03.75
  fetal anomaly Z03.73
  fetal growth Z03.74
  maternal and fetal conditions NEC
      Z03.70
  oligohydramnios Z03.71
  placental problem Z03.72
  polyhydramnios Z03.71
Suspended uterus
  in pregnancy or childbirth - *see* Preg-
      nancy, complicated by, abnormal
      uterus

Sutton's nevus D22.9
Suture
  burst (in operation wound) T81.31
      external operation wound T81.31
      internal operation wound T81.32
  inadvertently left in operation wound –
      see Foreign body, accidentally left
      during a procedure
  removal Z48.02
Swab inadvertently left in operation
      wound – *see* Foreign body, acciden-
      tally left during a procedure
Swallowed, swallowing
  difficulty - *see* Dysphagia
  foreign body - *see* Foreign body, alimen-
      tary tract
Swan-neck deformity (finger) - *see* Defor-
      mity, finger, swan-neck
Swearing, compulsive F42
  in Gilles de la Tourette's syndrome F95.2
Sweat, sweats
  fetid L75.0
  night R61
Sweating, excessive R61
Sweet's disease or dermatosis L98.2
Swelling (of) R60.9
  abdomen, abdominal (not referable to
      any particular organ) – *see* Mass,
      abdominal
  ankle - *see* Effusion, joint, ankle
  arm M79.89
      forearm M79.89
  breast N63
  Calabar B74.3
  cervical gland R59.0
  chest, localized R22.2
  ear - *see* subcategory H93.8
  extremity (lower) (upper) - *see* Disorder,
      soft tissue, specified type NEC
  finger M79.89
  foot M79.89
  glands R59.9
      generalized R59.1
      localized R59.0
  hand M79.89
  head (localized) R22.0
  inflammatory - *see* Inflammation
  intra-abdominal – *see* Mass,
      abdominal
  joint - *see* Effusion, joint
  leg M79.89
      lower M79.89
  limb - *see* Disorder, soft tissue, specified
      type NEC
  localized (skin) R22.9
      chest R22.2
      head R22.0
      limb
          lower – *see* Mass, localized, limb,
              lower
          upper – *see* Mass, localized, limb,
              upper
      neck R22.1
      trunk R22.2
  neck (localized) R22.1
  pelvic – *see* Mass, abdominal
  scrotum N50.8
  splenic - *see* Splenomegaly
  testis N50.8
  toe M79.89
  umbilical R19.09
  wandering, due to Gnathostoma (spini-
      gerum) B83.1
  white - *see* Tuberculosis, arthritis

Swift(-Feer) disease
  overdose or wrong substance given
      or taken - *see* Table of drugs and
      chemicals, by drug, poisoning
Swimmer's
  cramp T75.1
  ear H60.33-
  itch B65.3
Swimming in the head R42
Swollen - *see* Swelling
Swyer syndrome Q99.1
Sycosis L73.8
  barbae (not parasitic) L73.8
  contagiosa (mycotic) B35.0
  lupoides L73.8
  mycotic B35.0
  parasitic B35.0
  vulgaris L73.8
Sydenham's chorea - *see* Chorea,
      Sydenham's
Sylvatic yellow fever A95.0
Sylvest's disease B33.0
Symblepharon H11.23-
  congenital Q10.3
Symond's syndrome G93.2
Sympathetic - *see* condition
Sympatheticotonia G90.8
Sympathicoblastoma
  specified site - *see* Neoplasm, malignant
  unspecified site C74.90
Symphalangy (fingers) (toes) Q70.9
Symptoms NEC R68.89
  breast NEC N64.59
  development NEC R63.8
  factitious, self-induced – *see* Disorder,
      factitious
  genital organs, female R10.2
  involving
      abdomen NEC R19.8
      appearance NEC R46.89
      awareness R41.9
          altered mental status R41.82
          amnesia - *see* Amnesia
          borderline intellectual functioning
              R41.83
          coma - *see* Coma
          disorientation R41.0
          neurologic neglect syndrome R41.4
          senile cognitive decline R41.81
          specified symptom NEC R41.89
      behavior NEC R46.89
      cardiovascular system NEC R09.89
      chest NEC R09.89
      circulatory system NEC R09.89
      cognitive functions R41.9
          altered mental status R41.82
          amnesia - *see* Amnesia
          borderline intellectual functioning
              R41.83
          coma - *see* Coma
          disorientation R41.0
          neurologic neglect syndrome R41.4
          senile cognitive decline R41.81
          specified symptom NEC R41.89
      development NEC R62.50
      digestive system NEC R19.8
      emotional state NEC R45.89
          emotional lability R45.86
      food and fluid intake R63.8
      general perceptions and sensations
          R44.9
          specified NEC R44.8
      musculoskeletal system R29.91
          specified NEC R29.898

Symptoms NEC *(Continued)*
  involving *(Continued)*
    nervous system R29.90
      specified NEC R29.818
    pelvis NEC R19.8
    respiratory system NEC R09.89
    skin and integument R23.9
    urinary system R39.9
  menopausal N95.11
  metabolism NEC R63.8
  neurotic F48.8
  of infancy R68.19
  pelvis NEC, female R10.2
  skin and integument NEC R23.8
  subcutaneous tissue NEC R23.8
Sympus Q74.2
Syncephalus Q89.4
Synchondrosis
  abnormal (congenital) Q78.8
  ischiopubic M91.0
Synchysis (scintillans) (senile) (vitreous
    body) H43.89
Syncope (near) (pre-) R55
  anginosa I20.8
  bradycardia R00.1
  cardiac R55
  carotid sinus G90.01
  due to spinal (lumbar) puncture
    G97.1
  heart R55
  heat T67.1
  laryngeal R05
  psychogenic F48.8
  tussive R05
  vasoconstriction R55
  vasodepressor R55
  vasomotor R55
  vasovagal R55
Syndactylism, syndactyly Q70.9
  complex (with synostosis) Q70.9
    fingers Q70.0-
    toes Q70.2
  fingers Q70.1-
  simple (without synostosis) Q70.9
    fingers Q70.1-
    toes Q70.3
  toes Q70.3
Syndrome - *see also* Disease
  5q minus NOS D46.C
  48,XXXX Q97.1
  49,XXXXX Q97.1
  abdominal
    acute R10.0
    muscle deficiency Q79.4
  abnormal innervation H02.519
    left H02.516
      lower H02.515
      upper H02.514
    right H02.513
      lower H02.512
      upper H02.511
  abstinence, neonatal P96.1
  acid pulmonary aspiration, obstetric
    O74.0
  acquired immunodeficiency - *see* Hu-
    man, immunodeficiency virus
    (HIV) disease
  acute abdominal R10.0
  acute respiratory distress (adult) (child)
    J80
  Adair-Dighton Q78.0
  Adams-Stokes(-Morgagni) I45.9
  adiposogenital E23.6
  adrenal

Syndrome *(Continued)*
  adrenal *(Continued)*
    hemorrhage (meningococcal) A39.1
    meningococcic A39.1
  adrenocortical - *see* Cushing's syndrome
  adrenogenital E25.9
    congenital, associated with enzyme
      deficiency E25.0
  afferent loop NEC K91.89
  Alagille's Q44.7
  alcohol withdrawal (without convul-
    sions) – *see* Dependence, alcohol,
    with, withdrawal
  Alder's D72.0
  Aldrich(-Wiskott) D82.0
  alien hand R41.4
  Alport Q87.81
  alveolar hypoventilation E66.2
  alveolocapillary block J84.1
  amnesic, amnestic (confabulatory) (due
    to) – *see* Disorder, amnesic
  amyostatic (Wilson's disease) E83.01
  androgen insensitivity E34.50
    complete E34.51
    partial E34.52
  androgen resistance E34.50 - *see also*
    Syndrome, androgen insensitivity
  Angelman Q93.5
  anginal - *see* Angina
  ankyloglossia superior Q38.1
  anterior
    chest wall R07.89
    cord G83.82
    spinal artery G95.19
      compression M47.019
        cervical region M47.012
        cervicothoracic region M47.013
        lumbar region M47.016
        occipito-atlanto-axial region
          M47.011
        thoracic region M47.014
        thoracolumbar region M47.015
  antibody deficiency D80.9
    agammaglobulinemic D80.1
      hereditary D80.0
    congenital D80.0
    hypogammaglobulinemic D80.1
      hereditary D80.0
  anticardiolipin (-antibody) D68.61
  antiphospholipid (-antibody) D68.61
  aortic
    arch M31.4
    bifurcation I74.0
  aortomesenteric duodenum occlusion
    K31.5
  apical ballooning (transient left ven-
    tricular) I51.81
  arcuate ligament I77.4
  argentaffin, argintaffinoma E34.0
  Arnold-Chiari - *see* Arnold-Chiari
    disease
  Arrillaga-Ayerza I27.0
  Asherman's N85.6
  aspiration, of newborn - *see* Aspiration,
    by substance, with pneumonia
    meconium P24.01
  ataxia-telangiectasia G11.3
  auriculotemporal G50.8
  autoerythrocyte sensitization (Gardner-
    Diamond) D69.2
  autoimmune lymphoproliferative
    [ALPS] D89.82
  autoimmune polyglandular E31.0
  autosomal - *see* Abnormal, autosomes

Syndrome *(Continued)*
  Avellis' G83.89
  Ayerza(-Arrillaga) I27.0
  Babinski-Nageotte G83.89
  Bakwin-Krida Q79.8
  bare lymphocyte D81.6
  Barré-Guillain G61.0
  Barré-Liéou M53.0
  Barrett's - *see* Barrett's, esophagus
  Barsony-Polgar K22.4
  Barsony-Teschendorf K22.4
  Barth E78.71
  Bartter's E26.81
  basal cell nevus Q87.89
  Basedow's E05.00
    with thyroid storm E05.01
  basilar artery G45.0
  Batten-Steinert G71.11
  battered
    baby or child – *see* Maltreatment,
      child, physical abuse
    spouse – *see* Maltreatment, adult,
      physical abuse
  Beals Q87.40
  Beau's I51.5
  Beck's I65.8
  Benedikt's G83.89
  Béquez César (-Steinbrinck-Chédiak-
    Higashi) D72.0
  Bernhardt-Roth – *see* Meralgia
    paresthetica
  Bernheim's I50.9
  big spleen D73.1
  bilateral polycystic ovarian E28.2
  Bing-Horton's G43.809
  Birt-Hogg-Dube syndrome Q87.89
  Björck(-Thorsen) E34.0
  black
    lung J60
    widow spider bite - *see* Toxicity,
      venom, spider, black widow
  Blackfan-Diamond D61.01
  blind loop K90.2
    congenital Q43.8
    postsurgical K91.2
  blue sclera Q78.0
  blue toe I75.02-
  Boder-Sedgewick G11.3
  Boerhaave's K22.3
  Borjeson Forssman Lehmann Q89.8
  Bouillaud's I01.9
  Bourneville(-Pringle) Q85.1
  Bouveret(-Hoffman) I47.9
  brachial plexus G54.0
  bradycardia-tachycardia I49.5
  brain (nonpsychotic) F06.9
    with psychosis, psychotic reaction
      F09
    acute or subacute - *see* Delirium
    congenital - *see* Retardation, mental
    organic F09
      post-traumatic (nonpsychotic)
        F07.81
        psychotic F09
    personality change F07.0
    postcontusional F07.81
    post-traumatic, nonpsychotic F07.81
    psycho-organic F06.9
    psychotic F06.8
  brain stem stroke G46.3
  Brandt's L08.0
  broad ligament laceration N83.8
  Brock's J98.11
  bronze baby P83.8

Syndrome *(Continued)*
  Brown-Sequard G83.81
  bubbly lung P27.0
  Buchem's M85.2
  Budd-Chiari I82.0
  bulbar (progressive) G12.22
  Bürger-Grütz E78.3
  Burke's K86.8
  Burnett's (milk-alkali) E83.52
  burning feet E53.9
  Bywaters' T79.5
  carbohydrate-deficient glycoprotein
      (CDGS) E77.8
  carcinogenic thrombophlebitis I82.1
  carcinoid E34.0
  cardiac asthma I50.1
  cardiacos negros I27.0
  cardiofasciocutaneous Q87.89
  cardiopulmonary-obesity E66.2
  cardiorenal - *see* Hypertension,
      cardiorenal
  cardiorespiratory distress (idiopathic),
      newborn P22.0
  cardiovascular renal - *see* Hypertension,
      cardiorenal
  carotid
      artery (hemispheric) (internal) G45.1
      body G90.01
      sinus G90.01
  carpal tunnel G56.0-
  Cassidy(-Scholte) M34.0
  cat-cry Q93.4
  cauda equina G83.4
  causalgia – *see* Causalgia
  celiac K90.0
      artery compression I77.4
      axis I77.4
  central pain G89.0
  cerebellar
      hereditary G11.9
      stroke G46.4
  cerebellomedullary malformation - *see*
      Spina bifida
  cerebral
      artery
          anterior G46.1
          middle G46.0
          posterior G46.2
      gigantism E22.0
  cervical (root) M53.1
      disc - *see* Disorder, disc, cervical, with
          neuritis
      fusion Q76.1
      posterior, sympathicus M53.0
      rib Q76.5
      sympathetic paralysis G90.2
  cervicobrachial (diffuse) M53.1
  cervicocranial M53.0
  cervicodorsal outlet G54.2
  cervicothoracic outlet G54.0
  Céstan(-Raymond) I65.8
  Charcot's (angina cruris) (intermittent
      claudication) I73.9
  Charcot-Weiss-Baker G90.09
  CHARGE Q89.8
  Chédiak-Higashi(-Steinbrinck) D72.0
  chest wall R07.1
  Chiari's (hepatic vein thrombosis) I82.0
  Chilaiditi's Q43.3
  child maltreatment – *see* Maltreatment,
      child
  chondrocostal junction M94.0
  chondroectodermal dysplasia Q77.6
  chromosome 4 short arm deletion Q93.3

Syndrome *(Continued)*
  chromosome 5 short arm deletion Q93.4
  chronic
      pain G89.4
          personality F68.8
  Clarke-Hadfield K86.8
  Clerambault's automatism G93.89
  Clouston's (hidrotic ectodermal dyspla-
      sia) Q82.4
  clumsiness, clumsy child F82
  cluster headache G44.009
      intractable G44.001
      not intractable G44.009
  Coffin-Lowry Q89.8
  cold injury (newborn) P80.0
  combined immunity deficiency D81.9
  compartment (deep) (posterior) (trau-
      matic) T79.A0
      abdomen T79.A3
      lower extremity (hip, buttock, thigh,
          leg, foot, toes) T79.A2
      nontraumatic
          abdomen M79.A3
          lower extremity (hip, buttock,
              thigh, leg, foot, toes) M79.A2-
          specified site NEC M79.A9
          upper extremity (shoulder, arm,
              forearm, wrist, hand, fingers)
              M79.A1-
      postprocedural - *see* Syndrome com-
          partment, nontraumatic
      specified site NEC T79.A9
      upper extremity (shoulder, arm,
          forearm, wrist, hand, fingers)
          T79.A1
  complex regional pain - *see* Syndrome,
      pain, complex regional
  compression T79.5
      anterior spinal - *see* Syndrome, ante-
          rior, spinal artery, compression
      cauda equina G83.4
      celiac artery I77.4
      vertebral artery M47.029
          occipito-atlanto-axial region
              M47.021
          cervical region M47.022
  concussion F07.81
  congenital
      affecting multiple systems NEC
          Q87.89
      central alveolar hypoventilation
          G47.35
      facial diplegia Q87.0
      muscular hypertrophy-cerebral Q87.89
      oculo-auriculovertebral Q87.0
      oculofacial diplegia (Moebius) Q87.0
      rubella (manifest) P35.0
  congestion-fibrosis (pelvic), female
      N94.89
  congestive dysmenorrhea N94.6
  Conn's E26.01
  connective tissue M35.9
      overlap NEC M35.1
  conus medullaris G95.81
  cord
      anterior G83.82
      posterior G83.83
  coronary
      acute NEC I24.9
      insufficiency or intermediate I20.0
  Costen's (complex) M26.69
  costochondral junction M94.0
  costoclavicular G54.0
  costovertebral E22.0

Syndrome *(Continued)*
  Cowden Q85.8
  craniovertebral M53.0
  Creutzfeldt-Jakob - *see* Creutzfeldt-
      Jakob disease or syndrome
  cri-du-chat Q93.4
  crib death R99
  cricopharyngeal – *see* Dysphagia
  croup J05.0
  CRPS I - *see* Syndrome, pain, complex
      regional I
  crush T79.5
  cubital tunnel – *see* Lesion, nerve, ulnar
  Curschmann (-Batten) (-Steinert) G71.11
  Cushing's E24.9
      alcohol-induced E24.4
      due to
          alcohol
              drugs E24.2
              ectopic ACTH E24.3
              overproduction of pituitary ACTH
                  E24.0
      drug-induced E24.2
      overdose or wrong substance given
          or taken - *see* Table of drugs and
          chemicals, by drug, poisoning
      pituitary-dependent E24.0
      specified type NEC E24.8
  cryptophthalmos Q87.0
  cystic duct stump K91.5
  Dana-Putnam D51.0
  Danbolt (-Closs) L08.0
  Dandy-Walker Q03.0
      with spina bifida Q07.01
  Danlos' Q79.8
  defibrination - *see also* Fibrinolysis
      with
          antepartum hemorrhage – *see* Hem-
              orrhage, antepartum
          intrapartum hemorrhage – *see*
              Hemorrhage, complicating,
              delivery
      newborn P60
      postpartum O72.3
  Degos' I77.8
  Déjérine-Roussy G89.0
  delayed sleep phase G47.21
  demyelinating G37.9
  dependence - *see* F10-F19 with fourth
      character .2
  depersonalization(-derealization) F48.1
  De Quervain E34.51
  de Toni-Fanconi (-Debré) E72.09
      with cystinosis E72.04
  diabetes mellitus-hypertension-
      nephrosis – *see* Diabetes, nephrosis
  diabetes mellitus in newborn infant
      P70.2
  diabetes-nephrosis – *see* Diabetes,
      nephrosis
  diabetic amyotrophy – *see* Diabetes,
      amyotrophy
  Diamond-Blackfan D61.01
  Diamond-Gardener D69.2
  DIC (diffuse or disseminated intravas-
      cular coagulopathy) D65
  di George's D82.1
  Dighton's Q78.0
  disequilibrium E87.8
  Döhle body-panmyelopathic D72.0
  dorsolateral medullary G46.4
  double athetosis G80.3
  Down (*see also* Down syndrome) Q90.9
  Dresbach's (elliptocytosis) D58.1

Syndrome *(Continued)*
  Dressler's (postmyocardial infarction) I24.1
    postcardiotomy I97.0
  drug withdrawal, infant of dependent mother P96.1
  dry eye H04.12-
  due to abnormality
    chromosomal Q99.9
      sex
        female phenotype Q97.9
        male phenotype Q98.9
      specified NEC Q99.8
  dumping (postgastrectomy) K91.1
    nonsurgical K31.89
  Dupré's (meningism) R29.1
  dysmetabolic X E88.81
  dyspraxia, developmental F82
  Eagle-Barrett Q79.4
  Eaton-Lambert G73.1
    not associated with neoplasm G70.8
  Ebstein's Q22.5
  ectopic ACTH E24.3
  eczema-thrombocytopenia D82.0
  Eddowes' Q78.0
  effort (psychogenic) F45.8
  Eisenmenger's I27.89
  Ehlers-Danlos Q79.6
  Ekman's Q78.0
  electric feet E53.8
  Ellis-van Creveld Q77.6
  empty nest Z60.0
  endocrine-hypertensive E27.0
  entrapment - *see* Neuropathy, entrapment
  eosinophilia-myalgia M35.8
  epileptic - *see* Epilepsy
  Erdheim-Chester (ECD) E88.89
  Erdheim's E22.0
  erythrocyte fragmentation D59.4
  Evans D69.41
  exhaustion F48.8
  extrapyramidal G25.9
    specified NEC G25.89
  eye retraction - *see* Strabismus
  eyelid-malar-mandible Q87.0
  Faber's D50.9
  facial pain, paroxysmal G50.0
  Fallot's Q21.3
  familial eczema-thrombocytopenia (Wiskott-Aldrich) D82.0
  Fanconi (-de Toni) (-Debré) E72.09
    with cystinosis E72.04
  Fanconi's (anemia) (congenital pancyto-penia) D61.09
  fatigue
    chronic R53.82
    psychogenic F48.8
  faulty bowel habit K59.3
  Feil-Klippel (brevicollis) Q76.1
  Felty's - *see* Felty's syndrome
  fertile eunuch E23.0
  fetal
    alcohol (dysmorphic) Q86.0
    hydantoin Q86.1
  Fiedler's I40.1
  first arch Q87.0
  fish odor E72.8
  Fisher's G61.0
  Fitzhugh-Curtis
    due to
      Chlamydia trachomatis A74.81
      Neisseria gonorrhorea (gonococcal peritonitis) A54.85

Syndrome *(Continued)*
  Fitz's K85.8
  Flajani (-Basedow) E05.00
    with thyroid storm E05.01
  flatback - *see* Flatback syndrome
  floppy
    baby P94.2
    iris (intraoperative) (IFIS) H21.81
    mitral valve I34.1
  flush E34.0
  Foix-Alajouanine G95.19
  Fong's Q79.8
  foramen magnum G93.5
  Foville's (peduncular) G83.89
  fragile X Q99.2
  Franceschetti Q75.4
  Frey's
    auriculotemporal G50.8
    hyperhidrosis L74.52
  Friderichsen-Waterhouse A39.1
  Froin's G95.89
  frontal lobe F07.0
  Fukuhara E88.49
  functional
    bowel K59.9
    prepubertal castrate E29.1
  Gaisböck's D75.1
  ganglion (basal ganglia brain) G25.9
    geniculi G51.1
  Gardner-Diamond D69.2
  gastroesophageal
    junction K22.0
    laceration-hemorrhage K22.6
  gastrojejunal loop obstruction K91.89
  Gee-Herter-Heubner K90.0
  Gelineau's G47.419
    with cataplexy G47.411
  genito-anorectal A55
  Gerstmann-Sträussler-Scheinker (GSS) A81.82
  Gianotti-Crosti L44.4
  giant platelet (Bernard-Soulier) D69.1
  Gilles de la Tourette's F95.2
  goiter-deafness E07.1
  Goldberg Q89.8
  Goldberg-Maxwell E34.51
  Good's D83.8
  Gopalan' (burning feet) E53.8
  Gorlin's Q87.89
  Gougerot-Blum L81.7
  Gouley's I31.1
  Gower's R55
  gray or grey (newborn) P93.0
    platelet D69.1
  Gubler-Millard G83.89
  Guillain-Barré (-Strohl) G61.0
  gustatory sweating G50.8
  Hadfield-Clarke K86.8
  hair tourniquet - *see* Constriction, external, by site
  Hamman's J98.19
  hand-foot L27.1
  hand-shoulder G90.8
  hantavirus (cardio)-pulmonary (HPS) (HCPS) B33.4
  happy puppet Q93.5
  Harada's H30.81-
  Hayem-Faber D50.9
  headache NEC G44.89
    complicated NEC G44.59
  Heberden's I20.8
  Hedinger's E34.0
  Hegglin's D72.0
  HELLP O14.1-

Syndrome *(Continued)*
  hemolytic-uremic D59.3
  hemophagocytic, infection-associated D76.2
  Henoch-Schönlein D69.0
  hepatic flexure K59.8
  hepatorenal K76.7
    following delivery O90.4
    postoperative or postprocedural K91.83
    postpartum, puerperal O90.4
  hepatourologic K76.7
  Herter (-Gee) (nontropical sprue) K90.0
  Heubner-Herter K90.0
  Heyd's K76.7
  Hilger's G90.09
  histamine-like (fish poisoning) - *see* Poisoning, fish
  histiocytic D76.9
  histiocytosis NEC D76.3
  HIV infection, acute B20
  Hoffmann-Werdnig G12.0
  Hollander-Simons E88.1
  Hoppe-Goldflam G70.00
    with exacerbation (acute) G70.01
    in crisis G70.01
  Horner's G90.2
  hungry bone E83.81
  hunterian glossitis K14.4
  Hutchinson's triad A50.53
  hyperabduction G54.0
  hyperammonemia-hyperornithinemia-homocitrullinemia E72.4
  hypereosinophilic (idiopathic) D72.1
  hyperimmunoglobulin E (IgE) D82.4
  hyperkalemic E87.5
  hyperkinetic - *see* Hyperkinesia
  hypermobility M35.7
  hypernatremia E87.0
  hyperosmolarity E87.0
  hyperperfusion G97.82
  hypersplenic D73.1
  hypertransfusion, newborn P61.1
  hyperventilation F45.8
  hyperviscosity (of serum)
    polycythemic D75.1
    sclerothymic D58.8
  hypoglycemic (familial) (neonatal) E16.2
  hypokalemic E87.6
  hyponatremic E87.1
  hypopituitarism E23.0
  hypoplastic left-heart Q23.4
  hypopotassemia E87.6
  hyposmolality E87.1
  hypotension, maternal O26.5-
  hypothenar hammer I73.89
  ICF (intravascular coagulation-fibrinolysis) D65
  idiopathic
    cardiorespiratory distress, newborn P22.0
    nephrotic (infantile) N04.9
  iliotibial band M76.3-
  immobility, immobilization (paraplegic) M62.3
  immune reconstitution D89.3
  immunity deficiency, combined D81.9
  immunodeficiency
    acquired - *see* Human, immuno-deficiency virus (HIV) disease
    combined D81.9

Syndrome *(Continued)*
 impending coronary I20.0
 impingement, shoulder M75.4-
 inappropriate secretion of antidiuretic
  hormone E22.2
 infant
  of diabetic mother P70.1
   gestational diabetes P70.0
 infantilism (pituitary) E23.0
 inferior vena cava I87.1
 inspissated bile (newborn) P59.1
 institutional (childhood) F94.2
 insufficient sleep F51.12
 intermediate coronary (artery) I20.0
 interspinous ligament - *see* Spondylopathy, specified NEC
 intestinal
  carcinoid E34.0
  knot K56.2
 intravascular coagulation-fibrinolysis
  (ICF) D65
 iodine-deficiency, congenital E00.9
  type
   mixed E00.2
   myxedematous E00.1
   neurological E00.0
 IRDS (idiopathic respiratory distress,
  newborn) P22.0
 irritable
  bowel K58.9
   with diarrhea K58.0
   psychogenic F45.8
  heart (psychogenic) F45.8
  weakness F48.8
 ischemic bowel (transient) K55.9
  chronic K55.1
  due to mesenteric artery insufficiency
   K55.1
 IVC (intravascular coagulopathy) D65
 Ivemark's Q89.01
 Jaccoud's - *see* Arthropathy, postrheu-
  matic, chronic
 Jackson's G83.89
 Jakob-Creutzfeldt - *see* Creutzfeldt-
  Jakob disease or syndrome
 jaw-winking Q07.8
 Jervell-Lange-Nielsen I45.81
 jet lag G47.25
 Job's D71
 Joseph-Diamond-Blackfan D61.01
 jugular foramen G52.7
 Kabuki Q89.8
 Kanner's (autism) F84.0
 Kartagener's Q89.3
 Kelly's D50.1
 Kimmelstiel-Wilson – *see* Diabetes,
  specified type, with Kimmelstiel-
  Wilson disease
 Klein(e)-Levine G47.13
 Klippel-Feil (brevicollis) Q76.1
 Köhler-Pellegrini-Steida - *see* Bursitis,
  tibial collateral
 König's K59.8
 Korsakoff (-Wernicke) (nonalcoholic)
  F04
  alcoholic F10.26
 Kostmann's D70.0
 Krabbe's congenital muscle hypoplasia
  Q79.8
 labyrinthine - *see* subcategory H83.2
 lacunar NEC G46.7
 Lambert-Eaton G73.1
  not associated with neoplasm G70.8
 Landau-Kleffner F80.3

Syndrome *(Continued)*
 Larsen's Q74.8
 lateral
  cutaneous nerve of thigh D57.1-
   medullary G46.4
 Launois' E22.0
 lazy
  leukocyte D70.8
  posture M62.3
 Lemiere I80.8
 Lennox-Gastaut - *see* Epilepsy, generalized, specified NEC
 lenticular, progressive E83.01
 Leopold-Levi's E05.90
 Lev's I44.2
 Li-Fraumeni Z15.01
 Lichtheim's D51.0
 Lightwood's N25.89
 Lignac (de Toni) (-Fanconi) (-Debré)
  E72.09
  with cystinosis E72.04
 Likoff's I20.8
 limbic epilepsy personality F07.0
 liver-kidney K76.7
 lobotomy F07.0
 Loffler's J82
 long arm 18 or 21 deletion Q93.89
 long QT I45.81
 Louis-Barré G11.3
 low
  atmospheric pressure T70.20
  back M54.5
  output (cardiac) I50.9
 lower radicular, newborn (birth injury)
  P14.8
 Luetscher's (dehydration) E86.0
 Lupus anticoagulant D68.62
 Lutembacher's Q21.1
 macrophage activation D76.1
  due to infection D76.2
 Mal de Debarquement R42
 malabsorption K90.9
  postsurgical K91.2
 magnesium-deficiency R29.0
 malabsorption K90.9
  postsurgical K91.2
 malformation, congenital, due to
  alcohol Q86.0
  exogenous cause NEC Q86.8
  hydantoin Q86.1
   warfarin Q86.2
 malignant
  carcinoid E34.0
  neuroleptic G21.0
 Mallory-Weiss K22.6
 mandibulofacial dysostosis Q75.4
 manic-depressive - *see* Disorder, bipolar,
  affective
 maple-syrup-urine E71.0
 Marable's I77.4
 Marfan's Q87.40
  with
   cardiovascular manifestations
    Q87.418
    aortic dilation Q87.410
   ocular manifestations Q87.42
   skeletal manifestations Q87.43
 Marie's (acromegaly) E22.0
 maternal hypotension – *see* Syndrome,
  hypotension, maternal
 May (-Hegglin) D72.0
 McArdle (-Schmidt) (-Pearson) E74.04
 McQuarrie's E16.2
 meconium plug (newborn) P76.0

Syndrome *(Continued)*
 median arcuate ligament I77.4
 Meekeren-Ehlers-Danlos Q79.6
 megavitamin-B6 E67.2
 Meige G24.4
 MELAS E88.41
 Mendelson's O74.0
 MERFF E88.42
 mesenteric
  artery (superior) K55.1
  vascular insufficiency K55.1
 metabolic E88.81
 metastatic carcinoid E34.0
 micrognathia-glossoptosis Q87.0
 midbrain NEC G93.89
 middle lobe (lung) J98.19
 middle radicular G54.0
 migraine G43.909 - *see also* Migraine
 Mikulicz' K11.8
 milk-alkali E83.52
 Millard-Gubler G83.89
 Miller-Dieker Q93.88
 Miller-Fisher G61.0
 Minkowski-Chauffard D58.0
 Mirizzi's K83.1
 MNGIE (Mitochondrial Neurogastroin-
  testinal Encephalopathy) E88.49
 Möbius, ophthalmoplegic migraine - *see*
  Migraine, ophthalmoplegic
 monofixation H50.42
 Morel-Moore M85.2
 Morel-Morgagni M85.2
 Morgagni (-Morel) (-Stewart) M85.2
 Morgagni-Adams-Stokes I45.9
 mucocutaneous lymph node (acute
  febrile) (MCLS) M30.3
 multiple endocrine neoplasia [MEN] -
  see Neoplasia, endocrine, multiple
  [MEN]
 multiple operations – *see* Disorder,
  factitious
 Mounier-Kuhn Q32.4
  with bronchiectasis J47.9
   with
    exacerbation (acute) J47.1
    lower respiratory infection
     J47.0
  acquired J98.09
   with bronchiectasis J47.9
    with
     exacerbation (acute) J47.1
     lower respiratory infection
      J47.0
 myasthenic G70.9
  in
   diabetes mellitus – *see* Diabetes,
    amyotrophy
   endocrine disease NEC E34.9
    [G73.3]
   neoplastic disease (*see also* Neo-
    plasm) D49.9 [G73.3]
   thyrotoxicosis (hyperthyroidism)
    E05.90 [G73.3]
    with thyroid storm E05.91
     [G73.3]
 myelodysplastic D46.9
  with 5q deletion D46.c
  with isolated del(5q) chromosomal
   abnormality C46.c
  specified NEC D46.z
 myelopathic pain G89.0
 myeloproliferative (chronic) D47.1
 myofascial pain M79.1
 Naffziger's G54.0

Syndrome *(Continued)*
  nail patella Q87.2
  NARP (Neuropathy, Ataxia and Retinitis pigmentosa) E88.49
  neonatal abstinence P96.1
  nephritic - *see also* Nephritis
    with edema - *see* Nephrosis
    acute N00.9
    chronic N03.9
    rapidly progressive N01.9
  nephrotic (congenital) *(see also* Nephrosis) N04.9
    with
      dense deposit disease N04.6
      diffuse
        crescentic glomerulonephritis N04.7
        endocapillary proliferative glomerulonephritis N04.4
        membranous glomerulonephritis N04.2
        mesangial proliferative glomerulonephritis N04.3
        mesangiocapillary glomerulonephritis N04.5
      focal and segmental glomerular lesions N04.1
      minor glomerular abnormality N04.0
      specified morphological changes NEC N04.8
    diabetic – *see* Diabetes, nephrosis
  neurologic neglect R41.4
  Nezelof's D81.4
  Nonne-Milroy-Meige Q82.0
  Nothnagel's vasomotor acroparesthesia I73.89
  oculomotor H51.9
  ophthalmoplegia-cerebellar ataxia - *see* Strabismus, paralytic, third nerve
  oral-facial-digital Q87.0
  organic
    affective F06.30
    amnesic (not alcohol- or drug-induced) F04
    brain F09
    depressive F06.31
    hallucinosis F06.0
    personality F07.0
  Ormond's N13.5
  oro-facial-digital Q87.0
  os trigonum Q68.8
  Osler-Weber-Rendu I78.0
  osteoporosis-osteomalacia M83.8
  Osterreicher-Turner Q79.8
  otolith - *see* subcategory H81.8
  oto-palatal-digital Q87.0
  outlet (thoracic) G54.0
  ovary
    polycystic E28.2
    resistant E28.39
    sclerocystic E28.2
  Owren's D68.2
  Paget-Schroetter I82.890
  pain - *see also* Pain
    complex regional I G90.50
      lower limb G90.52-
        specified site NEC G90.59
      upper limb G90.51-
    complex regional II - *see* Causalgia
  painful
    bruising D69.2
    feet E53.8
    prostate N42.81

Syndrome *(Continued)*
  paralysis agitans - *see* Parkinsonism
  paralytic G83.9
    specified NEC G83.89
  Parinaud's H51.0
  parkinsonian - *see* Parkinsonism
  Parkinson's - *see* Parkinsonism
  paroxysmal facial pain G50.0
  Parry's E05.00
    with thyroid storm E05.01
  Parsonage(-Aldren)-Turner G54.5
  patella clunk M25.86-
  Paterson(-Brown) (-Kelly) D50.1
  pectoral girdle I77.8
  pectoralis minor I77.8
  Pelger-Huet D72.0
  pellagra-cerebellar ataxia-renal aminoaciduria E72.02
  pellagroid E52
  Pellegrini-Stieda - *see* Bursitis, tibial collateral
  pelvic congestion-fibrosis, female N94.89
  penta X Q97.1
  peptic ulcer - *see* Ulcer, peptic
  perabduction I77.8
  periodic headache, in adults and children G43.c09
    intractable G43.c19
      with status migrainosus G43.c11
      without status migrainosus G43.c19
    not intractable G43.c09
      with status migrainosus G43.c01
      without status migrainosus G43.c09
  periurethral fibrosis N13.5
  phantom limb (without pain) G54.7
    with pain G54.6
  pharyngeal pouch D82.1
  Pick's (heart) (liver) I31.1
  Pickwickian E66.2
  PIE (pulmonary infiltration with eosinophilia) J82
  pigmentary pallidal degeneration progressive) G23.0
  pineal E34.8
  pituitary E22.0
  plantar fascia M72.2
  placental transfusion - *see* Pregnancy, complicated by, placental transfusion syndromes
  plateau iris (post-iridectomy) (postprocedural) H21.82
  Plummer-Vinson D50.1
  pluricarential of infancy E40
  plurideficiency E40
  pluriglandular (compensatory) E31.20
    autoimmune E31.0
  pneumatic hammer T75.21
  polyangiitis overlap M30.8
  polycarential of infancy E40
  polyglandular E31.20
    autoimmune E31.0
  polysplenia Q89.09
  pontine NEC G93.89
  popliteal
    artery entrapment I77.8
    web Q87.89
  postcardiac injury
    postcardiotomy I97.0
    postmyocardial infarction I24.1
  postcardiotomy I97.0
  postcholecystectomy K91.5

Syndrome *(Continued)*
  postcommissurotomy I97.0
  postconcussional F07.81
  postcontusional F07.81
  postencephalitic F07.89
  posterior
    cervical sympathetic M53.0
    cord G83.83
    fossa compression G93.5
    reversible encephalopathy (PRES) G93.49
  postgastrectomy (dumping) K91.1
  postgastric surgery K91.1
  postinfarction I24.1
  postlaminectomy NEC M96.1
  postleukotomy F07.0
  postmastectomy lymphedema I97.2
  postmyocardial infarction I24.1
  postoperative NEC T81.9
    blind loop K90.2
  postpartum panhypopituitary (Sheehan) E23.0
  postpolio (myelitic) G14
  postthrombotic I87.009
    with
      inflammation I87.02-
        with ulcer I87.03-
        specified complication NEC I87.09-
      ulcer I87.01-
        with inflammation I87.03-
    asymptomatic I87.00-
  postvagotomy K91.1
  postvalvulotomy I97.0
  postviral NEC G93.3
    fatigue G93.3
  Potain's K31.0
  potassium intoxication E87.5
  precerebral artery (multiple) (bilateral) G45.2
  preinfarction I20.0
  preleukemic D46.9
  premature senility E34.8
  premenstrual dysphoric N94.3
  premenstrual tension N94.3
  Prinzmetal-Massumi R07.1
  prune belly Q79.4
  pseudocarpal tunnel (sublimis) - *see* Syndrome, carpal tunnel
  pseudoparalytica G70.00
    with exacerbation (acute) G70.01
    in crisis G70.01
  pseudo -Turner's Q87.1
  psycho-organic (nonpsychotic severity) F07.9
    acute or subacute F05
    depressive type F06.31
    hallucinatory type F06.0
    nonpsychotic severity F07.0
    specified NEC F07.89
  pulmonary
    arteriosclerosis I27.0
    dysmaturity (Wilson-Mikity) P27.0
    hypoperfusion (idiopathic) P22.0
    renal (hemorrhagic) (Goodpasture's) M31.0
  pure
    motor lacunar G46.5
    sensory lacunar G46.6
  Putnam-Dana D51.0
  pyramidopallidonigral G20
  pyriformis - *see* Lesion, nerve, sciatic

Syndrome *(Continued)*
 QT interval prolongation I45.81
 radicular NEC - *see* Radiculopathy
  upper limbs, newborn (birth injury)
   P14.3
 rapid time-zone change G47.25
 Raymond (-Céstan) I65.8
 Raynaud's I73.00
  with gangrene I73.01
 RDS (respiratory distress syndrome,
   newborn) P22.0
 reactive airways dysfunction J68.3
 Refsum's G60.1
 Reifenstein E34.52
 renal glomerulohyalinosis-diabetic –
   see Diabetes, nephrosis
 Rendu-Osler-Weber I78.0
 residual ovary N99.83
 resistant ovary E28.39
 respiratory
  distress
   acute J80
    adult J80
    child J80
    newborn (idiopathic) (type I)
     P22.0
    type II P22.1
 restless legs G25.81
 retinoblastoma (familial) C69.2
 retroperitoneal fibrosis N13.8
 retroviral seroconversion (acute) Z21
 Reye's G93.7
 Richter - *see* Leukemia, chronic lymphocytic, B-cell type
 Ridley's I50.1
 right
  heart, hypoplastic Q22.6
  ventricular obstruction - *see* Failure,
    heart, congestive
 Romano-Ward (prolonged QT interval)
   I45.81
 rotator cuff, shoulder M75.1-
 Rotes Quérol - *see* Hyperostosis,
   ankylosing
 Roth - *see* Meralgia paresthetica
 rubella (congenital) P35.0
 Ruvalcaba-Myhre-Smith E71.440
 Rytand-Lipsitch I44.2
 salt
  depletion E87.1
   due to heat NEC T67.8
    causing heat exhaustion or pros-
     tration T67.4
  low E87.1
 salt-losing N28.89
 Scaglietti-Dagnini E22.0
 scalenus anticus (anterior) G54.0
 scapulocostal - *see* Mononeuropathy,
   upper limb, specified site NEC
 scapuloperoneal G71.0
 schizophrenic, of childhood NEC F84.5
 Schnitzler D47.2
 Scholte's E34.0
 Schroeder's E27.0
 Schwachman's - *see* Syndrome,
   Shwachman's
 Schwartz (-Jampel) G71.13
 Schwartz-Bartter E22.2
 scimitar Q26.8
 sclerocystic ovary E28.2
 Seitelberger's G31.89
 septicemic adrenal hemorrhage A39.1
 seroconversion, retroviral (acute) Z21
 serous meningitis G93.2

Syndrome *(Continued)*
 severe acute respiratory (SARS) J12.81
 shaken infant T74.4
 shock (traumatic) T79.4
  kidney N17.0
   following crush injury T79.5
  toxic A48.3
 shock-lung J80
 Shone's - code to specific anomalies
 short
  bowel K91.2
  rib Q77.2
 shoulder-hand - *see*
    Algoneurodystrophy
 Shwachman's D70.4
 sicca - *see* Sicca syndrome
 sick
  cell E87.1
  sinus I49.5
 sick-euthyroid E07.81
 sideropenic D50.1
 Siemens' ectodermal dysplasia Q82.4
 Silfversköld's Q78.9
 Simon's E88.1
 sinus tarsi - *see* Syndrome, tarsal tunnel
 sinusitis-bronchiectasis-situs inversus
   Q89.3
 Sipple's E31.22
 sirenomelia Q87.2
 Slocumb's E27.0
 Sluder's
 Smith-Magenis Q93.88
 Sneddon-Wilkinson L13.1
 Sotos' E22.0
 South African cardiomyopathy I42.8
 spasmodic
  upward movement, eyes H51.8
  winking F95.8
 Spen's I45.9
 splenic
  agenesis Q89.01
  flexure K59.8
  neutropenia D73.81
 Spurway's Q78.0
 staphylococcal scalded skin L00
 Stein-Leventhal E28.2
 Stein's E28.2
 Stevens-Johnson syndrome L51.1
  toxic epidermal necrolysis overlap
   L51.3
 Stewart-Morel M85.2
 Stickler Q89.8
 stiff baby Q89.8
 stiff man G25.82
 Still-Felty - *see* Felty's syndrome
 Stokes (-Adams) I45.9
 stone heart I50.1
 straight back, congenital Q76.49
 subclavian steal G45.8
 subcoracoid-pectoralis minor G54.0
 subcostal nerve compression I77.8
 subphrenic interposition Q43.3
 superior
  cerebellar artery I63.8
  mesenteric artery K55.1
  vena cava I87.1
 supine hypotensive (maternal) – *see*
   Syndrome, hypotension, maternal
 suprarenal cortical E27.0
 supraspinatus M75.1-
 Susac G93.49
 swallowed blood P78.2
 sweat retention L74.0
 Swyer Q99.1

Syndrome *(Continued)*
 Symond's G93.2
 sympathetic
  cervical paralysis G90.2
  pelvic, female N94.89
 systemic inflammatory response (SIRS),
   of non-infectious origin (without
   organ dysfunction) R65.10
  with acute organ dysfunction
   R65.11
 tachycardia-bradycardia I49.5
 takotsubo I51.81
 TAR (thrombocytopenia with absent
   radius) Q87.2
 tarsal tunnel G57.5-
 teething K00.7
 tegmental G93.89
 telangiectasic-pigmentation-cataract
   Q82.8
 temporal pyramidal apex - *see* Otitis,
   media, suppurative, acute
 temporomandibular joint-pain-
   dysfunction M26.62
 Terry's - *see* Disorder, globe, degenerative, myopia
 testicular feminization E34.51
   - *see also* Syndrome, androgen
   insensitivity
 thalamic pain (hyperesthetic) G89.0
 thoracic outlet (compression) G54.0
 Thorson-Björck E34.0
 thrombocytopenia with absent radius
   (TAR) Q87.2
 thyroid-adrenocortical insufficiency
   E31.0
 tibial (anterior) (posterior) - *see* Enthesopathy, lower limb, lower leg,
   specified type NEC
 Tietze's M94.0
 time-zone (rapid) G47.25
 Toni-Fanconi E72.09
  with cystinosis E72.04
 Touraine's Q79.8
 tourniquet - *see* Constriction, external,
   by site
 toxic shock A48.3
 transient left ventricular apical ballooning I51.81
 traumatic vasospastic T75.22
 Treacher Collins Q75.4
 triple X, female Q97.0
 trisomy Q92.9
  13 Q91.7
   meiotic nondisjunction Q91.4
   mitotic nondisjunction Q91.5
   mosaicism Q91.5
   translocation Q91.6
  18 Q91.3
   meiotic nondisjunction Q91.0
   mitotic nondisjunction Q91.1
   mosaicism Q91.1
   translocation Q91.2
  20(q)(p) Q92.8
  21 Q90.9
   meiotic nondisjunction Q90.0
   mitotic nondisjunction Q90.1
   mosaicism Q90.1
   translocation Q90.2
  22 Q92.8
 tropical wet feet T69.0-
 Trousseau's I82.1
 tumor lysis (following antineoplastic
   chemotherapy) (spontaneous)
   NEC E88.3

Syphilis, syphilitic *(Continued)*
  central nervous system *(Continued)*
    serology doubtful, negative, or
      positive A52.3
    specified nature or site NEC
      A52.19
    vascular A52.05
  cerebral A52.17
    meningovascular A52.13
    nerves (multiple palsies) A52.15
    sclerosis A52.17
    thrombosis A52.05
  cerebrospinal (tabetic type) A52.12
  cerebrovascular A52.05
  cervix (late) A52.76
  chancre (multiple) A51.0
    extragenital A51.2
    Rollet's A51.0
  Charcot's joint A52.16
  chorioretinitis A51.43
    congenital A50.01
    late A52.71
    prenatal A50.01
  choroiditis - *see* Syphilitic
    chorioretinitis
  choroidoretinitis - *see* Syphilitic
    chorioretinitis
  ciliary body (secondary) A51.43
    late A52.71
  colon (late) A52.74
  combined spinal sclerosis A52.11
  condyloma (latum) A51.31
  congenital A50.9
    with
      paresis (general) A50.45
      tabes (dorsalis) A50.45
      taboparesis A50.45
    chorioretinitis, choroiditis A50.01 *[H32]*
    early, or less than 2 years after birth
      NEC A50.2
      with manifestations - *see* Syphilis,
        congenital, early, symptomatic
      latent (without manifestations) A50.1
        negative spinal fluid test A50.1
        serology positive A50.1
      symptomatic A50.09
        cutaneous A50.06
        mucocutaneous A50.07
        oculopathy A50.01
        osteochondropathy A50.02
        pharyngitis A50.03
        pneumonia A50.04
        rhinitis A50.05
        visceral A50.08
    interstitial keratitis A50.31
    juvenile neurosyphilis A50.45
    late, or 2 years or more after birth
      NEC A50.7
      chorioretinitis, choroiditis A50.32
      interstitial keratitis A50.31
      juvenile neurosyphilis A50.45
      latent (without manifestations)
        A50.6
        negative spinal fluid test A50.6
        serology positive A50.6
      symptomatic or with manifesta-
        tions NEC A50.59
        arthropathy A50.55
        cardiovascular A50.54
        Clutton's joints A50.51
        Hutchinson's teeth A50.52
        Hutchinson's triad A50.53
        osteochondropathy A50.56
        saddle nose A50.57

Syphilis, syphilitic *(Continued)*
  conjugal A53.9
    tabes A52.11
  conjunctiva (late) A52.71
  contact Z20.2
  cord bladder A52.19
  cornea, late A52.71
  coronary (artery) (sclerosis) A52.06
  coryza, congenital A50.05
  cranial nerve A52.15
    multiple palsies A52.15
  cutaneous - *see* Syphilis, skin
  dacryocystitis (late) A52.71
  degeneration, spinal cord A52.12
  dementia paralytica A52.17
    juvenilis A50.45
  destruction of bone A52.77
  dilatation, aorta A52.01
  due to blood transfusion A53.9
  dura mater A52.13
  ear A52.79
    inner A52.79
      nerve (eighth) A52.15
      neurorecurrence A52.15
  early A51.9
    cardiovascular A52.00
    central nervous system A52.3
    latent (without manifestations) (less
      than 2 years after infection) A51.5
      negative spinal fluid test A51.5
      serological relapse after treatment
        A51.5
      serology positive A51.5
    relapse (treated, untreated) A51.9
    skin A51.39
    symptomatic A51.9
      extragenital chancre A51.2
      primary, except extragenital chan-
        cre A51.0
      secondary (*see also* Syphilis, sec-
        ondary) A51.39
        relapse (treated, untreated) A51.49
    ulcer A51.39
  eighth nerve (neuritis) A52.15
  endemic A65
  endocarditis A52.03
    aortic A52.03
    pulmonary A52.03
  epididymis (late) A52.76
  epiglottis (late) A52.73
  epiphysitis (congenital) (early) A50.02
    [M90.80]
  episcleritis (late) A52.71
  esophagus A52.79
  eustachian tube A52.73
  exposure to Z20.2
  eye A52.71
  eyelid (late) (with gumma) A52.71
  fallopian tube (late) A52.76
  fracture A52.77
  gallbladder (late) A52.74
  gastric (polyposis) (late) A52.74
  general A53.9
    paralysis A52.17
      juvenile A50.45
  genital (primary) A51.0
  glaucoma A52.71
  gumma NEC A52.79
    cardiovascular system A52.00
    central nervous system A52.3
    congenital A50.59
  heart (block) (decompensation) (dis-
    ease) (failure) A52.06 *[I52]*
    valve NEC A52.03

Syphilis, syphilitic *(Continued)*
  hemianesthesia A52.19
  hemianopsia A52.71
  hemiparesis A52.17
  hemiplegia A52.17
  hepatic artery A52.09
  hepatis A52.74
  hepatomegaly, congenital A50.08
  hereditaria tarda - *see* Syphilis, congeni-
    tal, late
  hereditary - *see* Syphilis, congenital
  Hutchinson's teeth A50.52
  hyalitis A52.71
  inactive - *see* Syphilis, latent
  infantum - *see* Syphilis, congenital
  inherited - *see* Syphilis, congenital
  internal ear A52.79
  intestine (late) A52.74
  iris, iritis (secondary) A51.43
    late A52.71
  joint (late) A52.77
  keratitis (congenital) (interstitial) (late)
    A50.31
  kidney (late) A52.75
  lacrimal passages (late) A52.71
  larynx (late) A52.73
  late A52.9
    cardiovascular A52.00
    central nervous system A52.3
    kidney A52.75
    latent or 2 years or more after infec-
      tion (without manifestations)
      A52.8
      negative spinal fluid test A52.8
      serology positive A52.8
    paresis A52.17
    specified site NEC A52.79
    symptomatic or with manifestations
      A52.79
    tabes A52.11
  latent A53.0
    with signs or symptoms - code by site
      and stage under Syphilis
    central nervous system A52.2
    date of infection unspecified A53.0
    early, or less than 2 years after infec-
      tion A51.5
    follow-up of latent syphilis A53.0
      date of infection unspecified
        A53.0
      late, or 2 years or more after infec-
        tion A52.8
    late, or 2 years or more after infection
      A52.8
    positive serology (only finding) A53.0
      date of infection unspecified A53.0
      early, or less than 2 years after
        infection A51.5
      late, or 2 years or more after infec-
        tion A52.8
  lens (late) A52.71
  leukoderma A51.39
    late A52.79
  lienitis A52.79
  lip A51.39
    chancre (primary) A51.2
    late A52.79
  Lissauer's paralysis A52.17
  liver A52.74
  locomotor ataxia A52.11
  lung A52.72
  lymph gland (early) (secondary) A51.49
    late A52.79
  lymphadenitis (secondary) A51.49

Syphilis, syphilitic *(Continued)*
  macular atrophy of skin A51.39
    striated A52.79
  mediastinum (late) A52.73
  meninges (adhesive) (brain) (spinal
    cord) A52.13
  meningitis A52.13
    acute (secondary) A51.41
    congenital A50.41
  meningoencephalitis A52.14
  meningovascular A52.13
    congenital A50.41
  mesarteritis A52.09
    brain A52.04
  middle ear A52.77
  mitral stenosis A52.03
  monoplegia A52.17
  mouth (secondary) A51.39
    late A52.79
  mucocutaneous (secondary) A51.39
    late A52.79
  mucous
    membrane (secondary) A51.39
      late A52.79
    patches A51.39
      congenital A50.07
  mulberry molars A50.52
  muscle A52.78
  myocardium A52.06
  nasal sinus (late) A52.73
  neonatorum - *see* Syphilis, congenital
  nephrotic syndrome (secondary)
    A51.44
  nerve palsy (any cranial nerve) A52.15
    multiple A52.15
  nervous system, central A52.3
  neuritis A52.15
    acoustic A52.15
  neurorecidive of retina A52.19
  neuroretinitis A52.19
  newborn - *see* Syphilis, congenital
  nodular superficial (late) A52.79
  nonvenereal A65
  nose (late) A52.73
    saddle back deformity A50.57
  occlusive arterial disease A52.09
  oculopathy A52.71
  oesophagus (late) A52.79
  ophthalmic (late) A52.71
  optic nerve (atrophy) (neuritis) (papilla)
    A52.15
  orbit (late) A52.71
  organic A53.9
  osseous (late) A52.77
  osteochondritis (congenital) (early)
    A50.02 *[M90.80]*
  osteoporosis A52.77
  ovary (late) A52.76
  oviduct (late) A52.76
  palate (late) A52.79
  pancreas (late) A52.74
  paralysis A52.17
    general A52.17
      juvenile A50.45
  paresis (general) A52.17
    juvenile A50.45
  paresthesia A52.19
  Parkinson's disease or syndrome A52.19
  paroxysmal tachycardia A52.06
  pemphigus (congenital) A50.06
  penis (chancre) A51.0
    late A52.76
  pericardium A52.06
  perichondritis, larynx (late) A52.73

Syphilis, syphilitic *(Continued)*
  periosteum (late) A52.77
    congenital (early) A50.02 *[M90.80]*
    early (secondary) A51.46
  peripheral nerve A52.79
  petrous bone (late) A52.77
  pharynx (late) A52.73
    secondary A51.39
  pituitary (gland) A52.79
  pleura (late) A52.73
  pneumonia, white A50.04
  pontine lesion A52.17
  portal vein A52.09
  primary A51.0
    anal A51.1
    and secondary - *see* Syphilis, secondary
    central nervous system A52.3
    extragenital chancre NEC A51.2
    fingers A51.2
    genital A51.0
    lip A51.2
    specified site NEC A51.2
    tonsils A51.2
  prostate (late) A52.76
  ptosis (eyelid) A52.71
  pulmonary (late) A52.72
    artery A52.09
  pyelonephritis (late) A52.75
  recently acquired, symptomatic A51.9
  rectum (late) A52.74
  respiratory tract (late) A52.73
  retina, late A52.71
  retrobulbar neuritis A52.15
  salpingitis A52.76
  sclera (late) A52.71
  sclerosis
    cerebral A52.17
    coronary A52.06
    multiple A52.11
  scotoma (central) A52.71
  scrotum (late) A52.76
  secondary (and primary) A51.49
    adenopathy A51.49
    anus A51.39
    bone A51.46
    chorioretinitis, choroiditis A51.43
    hepatitis A51.45
    liver A51.45
    lymphadenitis A51.49
    meningitis (acute) A51.41
    mouth A51.39
    mucous membranes A51.39
    periosteum, periostitis A51.46
    pharynx A51.39
    relapse (treated, untreated) A51.49
    skin A51.39
    specified form NEC A51.49
    tonsil A51.39
    ulcer A51.39
    viscera NEC A51.49
    vulva A51.39
  seminal vesicle (late) A52.76
  seronegative with signs or symptoms -
    code by site and stage under
    Syphilis
  seropositive
    with signs or symptoms - code by site
      and stage under Syphilis
    follow-up of latent syphilis - *see*
      Syphilis, latent
    only finding - *see* Syphilis, latent
  seventh nerve (paralysis) A52.15
  sinus, sinusitis (late) A52.73
  skeletal system A52.77

Syphilis, syphilitic *(Continued)*
  skin (with ulceration) (early) (second-
    ary) A51.39
    late or tertiary A52.79
  small intestine A52.74
  spastic spinal paralysis A52.17
  spermatic cord (late) A52.76
  spinal (cord) A52.12
  spleen A52.79
  splenomegaly A52.79
  spondylitis A52.77
  staphyloma A52.71
  stigmata (congenital) A50.59
  stomach A52.74
  synovium A52.78
  tabes dorsalis (late) A52.11
    juvenile A50.45
  tabetic type A52.11
    juvenile A50.45
  taboparesis A52.11
    juvenile A50.45
  tachycardia A52.06
  tendon (late) A52.78
  tertiary A52.9
    with symptoms NEC A52.79
    cardiovascular A52.00
    central nervous system A52.3
    multiple NEC A52.79
    specified site NEC A52.79
  testis A52.76
  thorax A52.73
  throat A52.73
  thymus (gland) (late) A52.79
  thyroid (late) A52.79
  tongue (late) A52.79
  tonsil (lingual) (late) A52.73
    primary A51.2
    secondary A51.39
  trachea (late) A52.73
  tunica vaginalis (late) A52.76
  ulcer (any site) (early) (secondary)
    A51.39
    late A52.79
    perforating A52.79
      foot A52.11
  urethra (late) A52.76
  urogenital (late) A52.76
  uterus (late) A52.76
  uveal tract (secondary) A51.43
    late A52.71
  uveitis (secondary) A51.43
    late A52.71
  uvula (late) (perforated) A52.79
  vagina A51.0
    late A52.76
  valvulitis NEC A52.03
  vascular A52.00
    brain (cerebral) A52.05
  ventriculi A52.74
  vesicae urinariae (late) A52.76
  viscera (abdominal) (late) A52.74
    secondary A51.49
  vitreous (opacities) (late) A52.71
    hemorrhage A52.71
  vulva A51.0
    late A52.76
    secondary A51.39
Syphiloma A52.79
  cardiovascular system A52.00
  central nervous system A52.3
  circulatory system A52.00
  congenital A50.59
Syphilophobia F45.29

Syringadenoma - *see also* Neoplasm, skin, benign
  papillary - *see* Neoplasm, skin, benign
Syringobulbia G95.0
Syringocystadenoma - *see* Neoplasm, skin, benign
  papillary - *see* Neoplasm, skin, benign
Syringoma - *see also* Neoplasm, skin, benign
  chondroid - *see* Neoplasm, skin, benign

Syringomyelia G95.0
Syringomyelitis - *see* Encephalitis
Syringomyelocele - *see* Spina bifida
Syringopontia G95.0
System, systemic - *see also* condition
  disease, combined - *see* Degeneration, combined

System, systemic *(Continued)*
  inflammatory response syndrome (SIRS) of non-infectious origin (without organ dysfunction) R65.10
  with acute organ dysfunction R65.11
  lupus erythematosus M32.9
    inhibitor present D68.62

T

Tabacism, tabacosis, tabagism - *see also*
 Poisioning, tobacco
 meaning dependence (without remission) F17.200
  with
   disorder F17.299
    remission F17.211
    specified disorder NEC F17.298
    withdrawal F17.203
Tabardillo A75.9
 flea-borne A75.2
 louse-borne A75.0
Tabes, tabetic A52.10
 with
  central nervous system syphilis A52.10
  Charcot's joint A52.16
  cord bladder A52.19
  crisis, viscera (any) A52.19
  paralysis, general A52.17
  paresis (general) A52.17
  perforating ulcer (foot) A52.19
 arthropathy (Charcot) A52.16
 bladder A52.19
 bone A52.11
 cerebrospinal A52.12
 congenital A50.45
 conjugal A52.10
 dorsalis A52.11
  juvenile A50.49
 juvenile A50.49
 latent A52.19
 mesenterica A18.39
 paralysis, insane, general A52.17
 spasmodic A52.17
 syphilis (cerebrospinal) A52.12
Taboparalysis A52.17
Taboparesis (remission) A52.17
 juvenile A50.45
TAC (trigeminal autonomic cephalgia)
  NEC G44.099
 intractable G44.091
 not intractable G44.099
Tache noir S60.22-
Tachyalimentation K91.2
Tachyarrhythmia, tachyrhythmia - *see*
  Tachycardia
Tachycardia R00.0
 atrial I47.1
 auricular I47.1
 AV nodal re-entry (re-entrant) I49.8
 newborn P29.11
 nodal I47.1
 non-paroxysmal AV nodal I45.89
 paroxysmal (sustained) (nonsustained)
  I47.9
  with sinus bradycardia I49.5
  atrial (PAT) I47.1
  atrioventricular (AV) I47.1
   psychogenic F54
  junctional I47.1
   ectopic I47.1
  nodal I47.1
  psychogenic (atrial) (supraventricular) (ventricular) F54
  supraventricular (sustained) I47.1
   psychogenic F54
  ventricular I47.2
   psychogenic F54
 psychogenic F45.8
 sick sinus I49.5
 sinoauricular NOS R00.0
  paroxysmal I47.1

Tachycardia (*Continued*)
 sinus [sinusal] NOS R00.0
  paroxysmal I47.1
 supraventricular I47.1
 ventricular (paroxysmal) (sustained) I47.2
  psychogenic F54
Tachygastria K31.89
Tachypnea R06.82
 hysterical F45.8
 newborn (idiopathic) (transitory) P22.1
 psychogenic F45.8
 transitory, of newborn P22.1
Taenia (infection) (infestation) B68.9
 diminuta B71.0
 echinococcal infestation B67.90
 mediocanellata B68.1
 nana B71.0
 saginata B68.1
 solium (intestinal form) B68.0
  larval form - *see* Cysticercosis
Taeniasis (intestine) - *see* Taenia
Tag (hypertrophied skin) (infected) L91.8
 adenoid J35.8
 anus I84.6
 hemorrhoidal I84.6
 hymen N89.8
 perineal N90.8
 preauricular Q17.0
 rectum I84.6
 sentinel I84.6
 skin L91.8
  accessory (congenital) Q82.8
  anus I84.6
  congenital Q82.8
  preauricular Q17.0
  rectum I84.6
 tonsil J35.8
 urethra, urethral N36.8
 vulva N90.8
Tahyna fever B33.8
Takahara's disease E80.3
Takayasu's disease or syndrome M31.4
Talcosis (pulmonary) J62.0
Talipes (congenital) Q66.8
 acquired, planus - *see* Deformity, limb,
  flat foot
 asymmetric Q66.8
 calcaneovalgus Q66.4
 calcaneovarus Q66.1
 calcaneus Q66.8
 cavus Q66.7
 equinovalgus Q66.6
 equinovarus Q66.0
 equinus Q66.8
 percavus Q66.7
 planovalgus Q66.6
 planus (acquired) (any degree) - *see also*
  Deformity, limb, flat foot
  due to rickets (sequelae) E64.3
 valgus Q66.6
 varus Q66.3
Tall stature, constitutional E34.4
Talma's disease M62.89
Talon noir S90.3-
 hand S60.22-
 heel S90.3-
 toe S90.1-
Tamponade, heart I31.4
Tanapox (virus disease) B08.71
Tangier disease E78.6
Tantrum, child problem F91.8
Tapeworm (infection) (infestation) - *see*
  Infestation, tapeworm
Tapia's syndrome G52.7

TAR (thrombocytopenia with absent
  radius) **syndrome** Q87.2
Tarral-Besnier disease L44.0
Tarsal tunnel syndrome - *see* Syndrome,
  tarsal tunnel
Tarsalgia - *see* Pain, limb, lower
Tarsitis (eyelid) H01.8
 syphilitic A52.71
 tuberculous A18.4
Tartar (teeth) (dental calculus) K03.6
Tattoo (mark) L81.8
Tauri's disease E74.09
Taurodontism K00.2
Taussig-Bing syndrome Q20.1
Taybi's syndrome Q87.2
**Tay-Sachs amaurotic familial idiocy or
 disease** E75.02
TBI (traumatic brain injury) - *see* category
  S06
Teacher's node or nodule J38.2
Tear, torn (traumatic) - *see also* Laceration
 with abortion – *see* Abortion
 anus, anal (sphincter) S31.831
  complicating delivery
   with third degree perineal lacera-
    tion O70.2
    with mucosa O70.3
   without third degree perineal
    laceration O70.4
  nontraumatic (healed) (old) K62.81
 articular cartilage, old - *see* Derangement, joint, articular cartilage, by
  site
 bladder
  with ectopic or molar pregnancy
   O08.6
  following ectopic or molar pregnancy
   O08.6
  obstetrical O71.5
  traumatic – *see* Injury, bladder
 bowel
  with ectopic or molar pregnancy
   O08.6
  following ectopic or molar pregnancy
   O08.6
  obstetrical trauma O71.5
 broad ligament
  with ectopic or molar pregnancy
   O08.6
  following ectopic or molar pregnancy
   O08.6
  obstetrical trauma O71.6
 bucket handle (knee) (meniscus) – *see*
  Tear, meniscus
 capsule, joint - *see* Sprain
 cartilage - *see also* Sprain
  articular, old - *see* Derangement, joint,
   articular cartilage, by site
 cervix
  with ectopic or molar pregnancy
   O08.6
  following ectopic or molar pregnancy
   O08.6
  obstetrical trauma (current) O71.3
  old N88.1
  traumatic *see* Injury, uterus
 dural
  nontraumatic G96.11
 internal organ - *see* Injury, by site
 knee cartilage
  articular (current) S83.3-
  old - *see* Derangement, knee, meniscus, due to old tear
 ligament - *see* Sprain

Tear, torn *(Continued)*
  meniscus (knee) (current injury)
    S83.209
    bucket-handle S83.20-
    lateral
      bucket-handle S83.25-
      complex S83.27-
      peripheral S83.26-
      specified type NEC S83.28-
    medial
      bucket-handle S83.21-
      complex S83.23-
      peripheral S83.22-
      specified type NEC S83.24-
    old - *see* Derangement, knee, meniscus, due to old tear
    site other than knee - code as Sprain
    specified type NEC S83.20-
  muscle - *see* Strain
  pelvic
    floor, complicating delivery O70.1
    organ NEC, obstetrical trauma O71.5
      with ectopic or molar pregnancy O08.6
      following ectopic or molar pregnancy O08.6
  perineal, secondary O90.1
  periurethral tissue, obstetrical trauma O71.5
    with ectopic or molar pregnancy O08.6
    following ectopic or molar pregnancy O08.6
  rectovaginal septum - *see* Laceration, vagina
  retina, retinal (without detachment) (horseshoe) - *see also* Break, retina, horseshoe
    with detachment - *see* Detachment, retina, with retinal, break
  rotator cuff (complete) (incomplete) (nontraumatic) M75.1-
    traumatic S46.01-
      capsule S43.42-
  semilunar cartilage, knee - *see* Tear, meniscus
  supraspinatus (complete) (incomplete) (nontraumatic) M75.1
  tendon - *see* Strain
  tentorial, at birth P10.4
  umbilical cord
    complicating delivery O69.89
  urethra
    with ectopic or molar pregnancy O08.6
    following ectopic or molar pregnancy O08.6
    obstetrical trauma O71.5
  uterus - *see* Injury, uterus
  vagina - *see* Laceration, vagina
  vessel, from catheter - *see* Puncture, accidental complicating surgery
  vulva, complicating delivery O70.0
Tear-stone - *see* Dacryolith
Teeth - *see also* condition
  grinding
    psychogenic F45.8
    sleep related G47.63
Teething (syndrome) K00.7
Telangiectasia, telangiectasis (verrucous) I78.1
  ataxic (cerebellar) (Louis-Bar) G11.3
  familial I78.0

Telangiectasia, telangiectasis *(Continued)*
  hemorrhagic, hereditary (congenital) (senile) I78.0
  hereditary, hemorrhagic (congenital) (senile) I78.0
  retina H35.07-
  spider I78.1
Telephone scatologia F65.89
Telescoped bowel or intestine K56.1
  congenital Q43.8
Temperature
  body, high (of unknown origin) R50.9
  cold, trauma from T69.9
    newborn P80.0
    specified effect NEC T69.8
Temple - *see* condition
Temporal - *see* condition
Temporomandibular joint pain-dysfunction syndrome M26.62
Temporosphenoidal - *see* condition
Tendency
  bleeding - *see* Defect, coagulation
  suicide
    meaning personal history of attempted suicide Z91.5
    meaning suicidal ideation R45.85
  to fall R29.6
Tenderness, abdominal R10.819
  epigastric R10.816
  generalized R10.817
  left lower quadrant R10.814
  left upper quadrant R10.812
  periumbilic R10.815
  right lower quadrant R10.813
  right upper quadrant R10.811
  rebound R10.829
    epigastric R10.826
    generalized R10.827
    left lower quadrant R10.824
    left upper quadrant R10.822
    periumbilic R10.825
    right lower quadrant R10.823
    right upper quadrant R10.821
Tendinitis, tendonitis - *see also* Enthesopathy
  Achilles M76.6-
  adhesive - *see* Tenosynovitis, specified type NEC
    shoulder - *see* Capsulitis, adhesive
  bicipital M75.2-
  calcific M65.2-
    ankle M65.27-
    foot M65.27-
    forearm M65.23-
    hand M65.24-
    lower leg M65.26-
    multiple sites M65.29
    pelvic region M65.25-
    shoulder M75.3-
    specified site NEC M65.28
    thigh M65.25-
    upper arm M65.22-
  due to use, overuse, pressure - *see also* Disorder, soft tissue, due to use
    specified NEC - *see* Disorder, soft tissue, due to use, specified NEC
  gluteal M76.0-
  patellar M76.5-
  peroneal M76.7-
  psoas M76.1-
  tibialis (anterior) (posterior) - *see* Enthesopathy, lower limb, lower leg, specified type NEC

Tendinitis, tendonitis *(Continued)*
  trochanteric - *see* Bursitis, hip, trochanteric
Tendon - *see* condition
Tendosynovitis - *see* Tenosynovitis
Tenesmus (rectal) R19.8
  vesical R30.1
Tennis elbow - *see* Epicondylitis, lateral
Tenonitis - *see also* Tenosynovitis
  eye (capsule) H05.04-
Tenontosynovitis - *see* Tenosynovitis
Tenontothecitis - *see* Tenosynovitis
Tenophyte - *see* Disorder, synovium, specified type NEC
Tenosynovitis (*see also* Synovitis) M65.9
  adhesive - *see* Tenosynovitis, specified type NEC
    shoulder - *see* Capsulitis, adhesive
  bicipital (calcifying) - *see* Tendinitis, bicipital
  gonococcal A54.49
  in (due to)
    crystals M65.8-
    gonorrhea A54.49
    syphilis (late) A52.78
    use, overuse, pressure - *see also* Disorder, soft tissue, due to use
      specified NEC - *see* Disorder, soft tissue, due to use, specified NEC
  infective NEC M65.1-
    ankle M65.17-
    foot M65.17-
    forearm M65.13-
    hand M65.14-
    lower leg M65.16-
    multiple sites M65.19
    pelvic region M65.15-
    shoulder region M65.11-
    specified site NEC M65.18
    thigh M65.15-
    upper arm M65.12-
  radial styloid M65.4
  shoulder region M65.81-
    adhesive - *see* Capsulitis, adhesive
  specified type NEC M65.88
    ankle M65.87-
    foot M65.87-
    forearm M65.83-
    hand M65.84-
    lower leg M65.86-
    multiple sites M65.89
    pelvic region M65.85-
    shoulder region M65.81-
    specified site NEC M65.88
    thigh M65.85-
    upper arm M65.82-
  tuberculous - *see* Tuberculosis, tenosynovitis
Tenovaginitis - *see* Tenosynovitis
Tension
  arterial, high - *see also* Hypertension
    without diagnosis of hypertension R03.0
  headache G44.209
    intractable G44.201
    not intractable G44.209
  nervous R45.0
  pneumothorax J93.0
  premenstrual N94.3
  state (mental) F48.9
Tentorium - *see* condition
Teratencephalus Q89.8
Teratism Q89.7

Teratoblastoma (malignant) - *see* Neoplasm,
  malignant
Teratocarcinoma - *see also* Neoplasm,
  malignant
  liver C22.7
Teratoma (solid) - *see also* Neoplasm,
  uncertain behavior
  with embryonal carcinoma, mixed - *see*
    Neoplasm, malignant
  with malignant transformation - *see*
    Neoplasm, malignant
  adult (cystic) - *see* Neoplasm, benign
  benign - *see* Neoplasm, benign
  combined with choriocarcinoma - *see*
    Neoplasm, malignant
  cystic (adult) - *see* Neoplasm, benign
  differentiated - *see* Neoplasm, benign
  embryonal - *see also* Neoplasm,
    malignant
    liver C22.7
  immature - *see* Neoplasm, malignant
  liver C22.7
    adult, benign, cystic, differentiated
      type or mature D13.4
  malignant - *see also* Neoplasm,
    malignant
    anaplastic - *see* Neoplasm, malignant
    intermediate - *see* Neoplasm,
      malignant
      specified site - *see* Neoplasm,
        malignant
      unspecified site C62.90
    undifferentiated - *see* Neoplasm,
      malignant
  mature - *see* Neoplasm, uncertain
    behavior
    malignant - *see* Neoplasm, by site,
      malignant
  ovary D27.-
    embryonal, immature or malignant
      C56.-
  solid - *see* Neoplasm, uncertain
    behavior
  testis C62.9-
    adult, benign, cystic, differentiated
      type or mature D29.2-
    scrotal C62.1-
    undescended C62.0-
Termination
  anomalous - *see also* Malposition,
    congenital
    right pulmonary vein Q26.3
  pregnancy, elective Z33.2
Ternidens diminutus infestation B81.8
Ternidensiasis B81.8
Terror(s) night (child) F51.4
Terrorism, victim of Z65.4
Terry's syndrome - *see* Disorder, globe,
  degenerative, myopia
Tertiary - *see* condition
Test, tests, testing (for)
  adequacy (for dialysis)
    hemodialysis Z49.31
    peritoneal Z49.32
  blood pressure Z01.30
    abnormal reading - *see* Blood, pressure
  blood-alcohol Z04.8
    positive - *see* Findings, abnormal, in
      blood
  blood-drug Z04.8
    positive - *see* Findings, abnormal, in
      blood
  blood typing Z01.83
    Rh typing Z01.83

Test, tests, testing (for) *(Continued)*
  cardiac pulse generator (battery)
    Z45.010
  fertility Z31.41
  genetic
    disease carrier status for procreative
      management
      female Z31.430
      male Z31.440
      male partner of habitual aborter
        Z31.441
    procreative management NEC
      female Z31.438
      male Z31.448
  hearing Z01.10
    with abnormal findings NEC Z01.118
  HIV (human immunodeficiency virus)
    nonconclusive in infants R75
    positive Z21
    seropositive Z21
  immunity status Z01.84
  intelligence NEC Z01.89
  laboratory (as part of a general medical
    examination) Z00.00
    with abnormal finding Z00.01
    for medicolegal reason NEC Z04.8
  male partner of habitual aborter
    Z31.441
  Mantoux (for tuberculosis) Z11.1
    abnormal result R76.1
  pregnancy, positive first pregnancy - *see*
    Pregnancy, normal, first
  procreative Z31.49
    fertility Z31.41
  skin, diagnostic
    allergy Z01.82
    special screening examination -
      see Screening, by name of
      disease
    Mantoux Z11.1
    tuberculin Z11.1
  specified NEC Z01.89
  tuberculin Z11.1
    abnormal result R76.1
  vision Z01.00
    with abnormal findings Z01.01
  Wassermann Z11.3
    positive - *see* Serology for syphilis,
      positive
Testicle, testicular, testis - *see also*
  condition
  feminization syndrome E34.50 - *see also*
    Syndrome, androgen insensitivity
  migrans Q55.29
Tetanus, tetanic (cephalic) (convulsions)
  A35
  with
    abortion A34
    ectopic or molar pregnancy O08.0
  following ectopic or molar pregnancy
    O08.0
  inoculation reaction (due to serum) - *see*
    Complications, vaccination
  neonatorum A33
  obstetrical A34
  puerperal, postpartum, childbirth A34
Tetany (due to) R29.0
  alkalosis E87.3
  associated with rickets E55.0
  convulsions R29.0
    hysterical F44.5
  functional (hysterical) F44.5
  hyperkinetic R29.0
    hysterical F44.5

Tetany *(Continued)*
  hyperpnea R06.4
    hysterical F44.5
    psychogenic F45.8
  hyperventilation (*see also* Hyperventila-
    tion) R06.4
    hysterical F44.5
  neonatal (without calcium or magne-
    sium deficiency) P71.3
  parathyroid (gland) E20.9
  parathyroprival E89.2
  post-(para)thyroidectomy E89.2
  postoperative E89.2
  pseudotetany R29.0
  psychogenic (conversion reaction) F44.5
Tetralogy of Fallot Q21.3
Tetraplegia (chronic) (*see also* Quadriplegia) G82.50-
Thailand hemorrhagic fever A91
Thalassanemia - *see* Thalassemia
Thalassemia (anemia) (disease) D56.9
  with other hemoglobinopathy NEC
    D56.9
  alpha (major) (severe) (triple gene
    defect) D56.0
    minor D56.3
  beta (severe) D56.1
    minor D56.3
  delta-beta (homozygous) D56.2
    minor D56.3
  intermedia D56.1
  major D56.1
  minor D56.3
  mixed (with other hemoglobinopathy)
    D56.9
  sickle cell - *see* Disease, sickle cell,
    thalassemia
  specified type NEC D56.8
  trait D56.3
  variants D56.8
Thanatophoric dwarfism or short stature
  Q77.1
Thaysen-Gee disease (nontropical sprue)
  K90.0
Thaysen's disease K90.0
Thecoma D27.-
  luteinized D27.-
  malignant C56.-
Thelarche, premature E30.8
Thelaziasis B83.8
Thelitis N61
  puerperal, postpartum or gestational –
    see Infection, nipple
Therapeutic - *see* condition
Therapy
  drug, long-term (current)
    agents affecting estrogen recep-
      tors and estrogen levels NEC
      Z79.818
    anastrozole (Arimidex) Z79.811
    antibiotics Z79.2
    anticoagulants Z79.01
    anti-inflammatory Z79.1
    antiplatelet Z79.02
    antithrombotics Z79.02
    aromatase inhibitors Z79.811
    aspirin Z79.82
    birth control pill or patch Z79.3
    contraceptive, oral Z79.3
    drug, specified NEC Z79.899
    estrogen receptor downregulators
      Z79.818
    Evista Z79.810
    exemestane (Aromasin) Z79.811

Therapy *(Continued)*
  drug, long-term *(Continued)*
    Fareston Z79.810
    fulvestrant (Faslodex) Z79.818
    gonadotropin-releasing hormone
      (GnRH) agonist Z79.818
    goserelin acetate (Zoladex) Z79.818
    hormone replacement (postmeno-
      pausal) Z79.890
    insulin Z79.4
    letrozole (Femara) Z79.811
    leuprolide acetate (leuprorelin)
      (Lupron) Z79.818
    megestrol acetate (Megace) Z79.818
    methadone for pain management
      Z79.891
    Nolvadex Z79.810
    opiate analgesic Z79.891
    oral contraceptive Z79.3
    raloxifene (Evista) Z79.810
    selective estrogen receptor modula-
      tors (SERMs) Z79.810
    steroids
      inhaled Z79.51
      systemic Z79.52
    tamoxifen (Nolvadex) Z79.810
    toremifene (Fareston) Z79.810
Thermic - *see* condition
Thermography (abnormal) R93.8
  breast R92.8
Thermoplegia T67.0
Thesaurismosis, glycogen - *see* Disease,
  glycogen storage
Thiamin deficiency E51.9
  specified NEC E51.8
Thiaminic deficiency with beriberi E51.11
Thibierge-Weissenbach syndrome - *see*
  Sclerosis, systemic
Thickening
  bone - *see* Hypertrophy, bone
  breast N64.59
  epidermal L85.9
    specified NEC L85.8
  hymen N89.6
  larynx J38.7
  nail L60.2
    congenital Q84.5
  periosteal - *see* Hypertrophy, bone
  pleura J92.9
    with asbestos J92.0
  skin R23.4
  subepiglottic J38.7
  tongue K14.8
  valve, heart - *see* Endocarditis
Thigh - *see* condition
Thinning vertebra - *see* Spondylopathy,
  specified NEC
Thirst, excessive R63.1
  due to deprivation of water T73.1
Thomsen disease G71.12
Thoracic - *see also* condition
  kidney Q63.2
  outlet syndrome G54.0
Thoracogastroschisis (congenital)
  Q79.8
Thoracopagus Q89.4
Thorax - *see* condition
Thorn's syndrome N28.89
Thorson-Björck syndrome E34.0
Threadworm (infection) (infestation) B80
Threatened
  abortion O20.0
    with subsequent abortion O03.9
  job loss, anxiety concerning Z56.2

Threatened *(Continued)*
  labor (without delivery) O47.9
    after 37 completed weeks of gestation
      O47.1
    before 37 completed weeks of gesta-
      tion O47.0-
  loss of job, anxiety concerning Z56.2
  miscarriage O20.0
  unemployment, anxiety concerning
    Z56.2
Three-day fever A93.1
ThresHers' lung J67.0
Thrix annulata (congenital) Q84.1
Throat - *see* condition
Thrombasthenia (Glanzmann) (hemor-
  rhagic) (hereditary) D69.1
Thromboangiitis I73.1
  obliterans (general) I73.1
    cerebral I67.8
    vessels
      brain I67.8
      spinal cord I67.8
Thromboarteritis - *see* Arteritis
Thromboasthenia (Glanzmann) (hemorrhagic) (hereditary) D69.1
Thrombocytasthenia (Glanzmann) D69.1
Thrombocythemia (essential) (hemorrhagic) (idiopathic) (primary) D47.3
Thrombocytopathy (dystrophic) (granu-
  lopenic) D69.1
Thrombocytopenia, thrombocytopenic
  D69.6
  with absent radius (TAR) Q87.2
  congenital D69.42
  dilutional D69.5
  due to
    drugs D69.5
    extracorporeal circulation of blood
      D69.5
    massive blood transfusion D69.5
    platelet alloimmunization D69.5
  essential D69.3
  heparin induced (HIT) D75.82
  hereditary D69.42
  idiopathic D69.3
  neonatal, transitory P61.0
    due to
      exchange transfusion P61.0
      idiopathic maternal thrombocyto-
        penia P61.0
      isoimmunization P61.0
  primary NEC D69.49
    idiopathic D69.3
  puerperal, postpartum O72.3
  secondary D69.5
  transient neonatal P61.0
Thrombocytosis, essential D47.3
  primary D47.3
Thromboembolism - *see* Embolism
Thrombopathy (Bernard-Soulier) D69.1
  constitutional D68.0
  Willebrand-Jurgens D68.0
Thrombopenia - *see* Thrombocytopenia
Thrombophilia D68.59
  primary NEC D68.59
  secondary NEC D68.69
  specified NEC D68.69
Thrombophlebitis I80.9
  antepartum O22.2-
    deep O22.3-
    superficial O22.2-
  cavernous (venous) sinus G08
    complicating pregnancy O22.5-
    nonpyogenic I67.6

Thrombophlebitis *(Continued)*
  cerebral (sinus) (vein) G08
    nonpyogenic I67.6
    sequelae G09
  due to implanted device - *see* Complica-
    tions, by site and type, specified
    NEC
  during or resulting from a procedure
    NEC T81.72
  femoral vein (superficial) I80.1-
  femoropopliteal vein I80.0-
  following infusion, perfusion, therapeu-
    tic injection or transfusion T80.1
  hepatic (vein) I80.8
  idiopathic, recurrent I82.1
  iliofemoral I80.1-
  intracranial venous sinus (any) G08
    nonpyogenic I67.6
    sequelae G09
  intraspinal venous sinuses and veins
    G08
    nonpyogenic G95.19
  lateral (venous) sinus G08
    nonpyogenic I67.6
  leg I80.299
    superficial I80.0-
  longitudinal (venous) sinus G08
    nonpyogenic I67.6
  lower extremity I80.299
  migrans, migrating I82.1
  pelvic
    with ectopic or molar pregnancy
      O08.0
    following ectopic or molar pregnancy
      O08.0
    puerperal O87.1
  popliteal vein - *see* Phlebitis, leg, deep,
    popliteal
  portal (vein) K75.1
  postoperative T81.72
  pregnancy – *see* Thrombophlebitis,
    antepartum
  puerperal, postpartum, childbirth
    O87.0
    deep O87.1
    pelvic O87.1
    septic O86.81
    superficial O87.0
  saphenous (greater) (lesser) I80.0-
  sinus (intracranial) G08
    nonpyogenic I67.6
  specified site NEC I80.8
  tibial vein I80.23-
Thrombosis, thrombotic (bland) (multiple) (progressive) (silent) (vessel)
  I82.90
  antepartum – *see* Thrombophlebitis,
    antepartum
  aorta, aortic I74.10
    abdominal I74.0
    bifurcation I74.0
    saddle I74.0
    specified site NEC I74.19
    terminal I74.0
    thoracic I74.11
    valve - *see* Endocarditis, aortic
  apoplexy I63.3
  appendix, septic K35.9
  artery, arteries (postinfectional) I74.9
    auditory, internal – *see* Occlusion, ar-
      tery, precerebral, specified NEC
    basilar - *see* Occlusion, artery, basilar
    carotid (common) (internal) - *see* Oc-
      clusion, artery, carotid

Thrombosis, thrombotic *(Continued)*
  artery, arteries *(Continued)*
    cerebellar (anterior inferior) (posterior inferior) (superior) - *see* Occlusion, artery, cerebellar
    cerebral - *see* Occlusion, artery, cerebral
    choroidal (anterior) – *see* Occlusion, artery, cerebral, specified NEC
    communicating, posterior – *see* Occlusion, artery, cerebral, specified NEC
    coronary - *see also* Infarct, myocardium
      not resulting in infarction I24.0
    hepatic I74.8
    hypophyseal – *see* Occlusion, artery, cerebral, specified NEC
    iliac I74.5
    limb I74.4
      lower I74.3
      upper I74.2
    meningeal, anterior or posterior – *see* Occlusion, artery, cerebral, specified NEC
    mesenteric (with gangrene) K55.0
    ophthalmic - *see* Occlusion, artery, retina
    pontine – *see* Occlusion, artery, cerebral, specified NEC
    precerebral - *see* Occlusion, artery, precerebral
    pulmonary (iatrogenic) - *see* Embolism, pulmonary
    renal N28.0
    retinal - *see* Occlusion, artery, retina
    spinal, anterior or posterior G95.11
    traumatic NEC T14.8
    vertebral - *see* Occlusion, artery, vertebral
  atrium, auricular - *see also* Infarct, myocardium
    following acute myocardial infarction (current complication) I23.6
    not resulting in infarction I24.0
  basilar (artery) - *see* Occlusion, artery, basilar
  brain (artery) (stem) - *see also* Occlusion, artery, cerebral
    due to syphilis A52.05
    puerperal O99.43
    sinus - *see* Thrombosis, intracranial venous sinus
  capillary I78.8
  cardiac - *see also* Infarct, myocardium
    not resulting in infarction I24.0
    valve - *see* Endocarditis
  carotid (artery) (common) (internal) - *see* Occlusion, artery, carotid
  cavernous (venous) sinus - *see* Thrombosis, intracranial venous sinus
  cerebellar artery (anterior inferior) (posterior inferior) (superior) I65.8
  cerebral (artery) - *see* Occlusion, artery, cerebral
  cerebrovenous sinus - *see also* Thrombosis, intracranial venous sinus
    puerperium O87.3
  chronic I82.91
  coronary (artery) (vein) - *see also* Infarct, myocardium
    not resulting in infarction I24.0
  corpus cavernosum N48.89
  cortical I66.9

Thrombosis, thrombotic *(Continued)*
  deep - *see* Embolism, vein, lower extremity
  due to device, implant or graft *(see also* Complications, by site and type, specified NEC) T85.86
    arterial graft NEC T82.868
    breast (implant) T85.86
    catheter NEC T85.86
      dialysis (renal) T82.868
        intraperitoneal T85.86
      infusion NEC T82.868
        spinal (epidural) (subdural) T85.86
      urinary (indwelling) T83.86
    electronic (electrode) (pulse generator) (stimulator)
      bone T84.86
      cardiac T82.867
      nervous system (brain) (peripheral nerve) (spinal) T85.86
      urinary T83.86
    fixation, internal (orthopedic) NEC T84.86
    gastrointestinal (bile duct) (esophagus) T85.86
    genital NEC T83.86
    heart T82.867
    joint prosthesis T84.86
    ocular (corneal graft) (orbital implant) NEC T85.86
    orthopedic NEC T84.86
    specified NEC T85.86
    urinary NEC T83.86
    vascular NEC T82.868
    ventricular intracranial shunt T85.86
  during the puerperium - *see* Thrombosis, puerperal
  endocardial - *see also* Infarct, myocardium
    not resulting in infarction I24.0
  eye - *see* Occlusion, retina
  genital organ
    female NEC N94.89
      pregnancy – *see* Thrombophlebitis, antepartum
    male N50.1
  gestational – *see* Phlebopathy, gestational
  heart (chamber) - *see also* Infarct, myocardium
    not resulting in infarction I24.0
  hepatic (vein) I82.0
    artery I74.8
  history (of) Z86.71
  intestine (with gangrene) K55.0
  intracardiac NEC (apical) (atrial) (auricular) (ventricular) (old) I51.3
  intracranial (arterial) I66.9
    venous sinus (any) G08
      nonpyogenic origin I67.6
      puerperium O87.3
  intramural - *see also* Infarct, myocardium
    not resulting in infarction I24.0
  intraspinal venous sinuses and veins G08
    nonpyogenic G95.19
  kidney (artery) N28.0
  lateral (venous) sinus - *see* Thrombosis, intracranial venous sinus
  leg - *see* Embolism, vein, lower extremity
    arterial I74.3

Thrombosis, thrombotic *(Continued)*
  liver (venous) I82.0
    artery I74.8
    portal vein I81
  longitudinal (venous) sinus - *see* Thrombosis, intracranial venous sinus
  lower limb - *see* Embolism, vein, lower extremity
  lung (iatrogenic) (postoperative) - *see* Embolism, pulmonary
  meninges (brain) (arterial) I66.8
  mesenteric (artery) (with gangrene) K55.0
    vein (inferior) (superior) I81
  mitral I34.8
  mural - *see also* Infarct, myocardium
    due to syphilis A52.06
    not resulting in infarction I24.0
  omentum (with gangrene) K55.0
  ophthalmic - *see* Occlusion, retina
  pampiniform plexus (male) N50.1
  parietal - *see also* Infarct, myocardium
    not resulting in infarction I24.0
  penis, superficial vein N48.81
  peripheral arteries I74.4
    upper I74.3
  personal history (of) Z86.71
  portal I81
    due to syphilis A52.09
  precerebral artery - *see* Occlusion, artery, precerebral
  puerperal, postpartum O87.0
    brain (artery) O99.43
      venous (sinus) O87.3
    cardiac O99.43
    cerebral (artery) O99.43
      venous (sinus) O87.3
    superficial O87.0
  pulmonary (artery) (iatrogenic) (postoperative) (vein) - *see* Embolism, pulmonary
  renal (artery) N28.0
    vein I82.3
  resulting from presence of device, implant or graft - *see* Complications, by site and type, specified NEC
  retina, retinal - *see* Occlusion, retina
  scrotum N50.1
  seminal vesicle N50.1
  sigmoid (venous) sinus - *see* Thrombosis, intracranial venous sinus
  sinus, intracranial (any) - *see* Thrombosis, intracranial venous sinus
  specified site NEC I82.890
    chronic I82.891
  spermatic cord N50.1
  spinal cord (arterial) G95.11
    due to syphilis A52.09
    pyogenic origin G06.1
  spleen, splenic D73.5
    artery I74.8
  testis N50.1
  tumor - *see* Neoplasm, by site
  traumatic NEC T14.8
  tricuspid I07.8
  tunica vaginalis N50.1
  umbilical cord (vessels), complicating delivery O69.5
  vas deferens N50.1
  vein (acute) I82.90
    antecubital I82.61-
    axillary I82.a1-
    basilic I82.61-

Tinea *(Continued)*
  barbae B35.0
  beard B35.0
  black dot B35.0
  blanca B36.2
  capitis B35.0
  corporis B35.4
  cruris B35.6
  flava B36.0
  foot B35.3
  furfuracea B36.0
  imbricata (Tokelau) B35.5
  kerion B35.0
  manuum B35.2
  microsporic - *see* Dermatophytosis
  nigra B36.1
  nodosa - *see* Piedra
  pedis B35.3
  scalp B35.0
  specified site NEC B35.8
  sycosis B35.0
  tonsurans B35.0
  trichophytic - *see* Dermatophytosis
  unguium B35.1
  versicolor B36.0
Tingling sensation (skin) R20.2
Tinnitus (audible) (aurium) (subjective) -
  see subcategory H93.1
Tipped tooth (teeth) M26.33
Tipping
  pelvis M95.5
    with disproportion (fetopelvic) O33.0
      causing obstructed labor O65.0
  tooth (teeth), fully erupted M26.33
Tiredness R53.83
Tissue - *see* condition
Tobacco (nicotine)
  dependence - *see* Dependence, drug,
    nicotine
  harmful use Z72.0
  heart - *see* Tobacco, toxic effect
  maternal use, affecting newborn P04.2
  toxic effect - *see* Table of drugs and
    chemicals, by substance, poisoning
  chewing tobacco - *see* Table of drugs
    and chemicals, by substance,
    poisoning
  cigarettes - *see* Table of drugs and
    chemicals, by substance,
    poisoning
  use Z72.0
    complicating
      childbirth O99.334
      pregnancy O99.33-
      puerperium O99.335
    counseling and surveillance Z71.6
  withdrawal state - *see* Dependence,
    drug, nicotine
Tocopherol deficiency E56.0
Todd's
  cirrhosis K74.3
  paralysis (postepileptic) (transitory)
    G83.84
Toe - *see* condition
Toilet, artificial opening - *see* Attention
  to, artificial, opening
Tokelau (ringworm) B35.5
Tollwut - *see* Rabies
Tommaselli's disease R31.9
  correct substance properly admin-
    istered - *see* Table of drugs and
    chemicals, by drug, adverse
    effect

Tommaselli's disease *(Continued)*
  overdose or wrong substance given
    or taken - *see* Table of drugs and
    chemicals, by drug, poisoning
Tongue - *see also* condition
  tie Q38.1
Tonic pupil - *see* Anomaly, pupil, function, tonic pupil
Toni-Fanconi syndrome (cystinosis) E72.09
  with cystinosis E72.04
Tonsil - *see* condition
Tonsillitis (acute) (catarrhal) (croupous)
    (follicular) (gangrenous) (infec-
    tive) (lacunar) (lingual) (malignant)
    (membranous) (parenchymatous)
    (phlegmonous) (pseudomembra-
    nous) (purulent) (septic) (subacute)
    (suppurative) (toxic) (ulcerative)
    (vesicular) (viral) J03.90
  chronic J35.01
    with adenoiditis J35.03
  diphtheritic A36.0
  hypertrophic J35.01
    with adenoiditis J35.03
  recurrent J03.91
  specified organism NEC J03.80
    recurrent J03.81
  staphylococcal J03.80
    recurrent J03.81
  streptococcal J03.00
    recurrent J03.01
  tuberculous A15.8
  Vincent's A69.1
Tooth, teeth - *see* condition
Toothache K08.8
Topagnosis R20.8
Tophi - *see* Gout
TORCH infection - *see* Infection, congenital
  without active infection P00.2
Torn - *see* Tear
Tornwaldt's cyst or disease J39.2
Torsion
  accessory tube - *see* Torsion, fallopian
    tube
  adnexa (female) - *see* Torsion, fallopian
    tube
  aorta, acquired I77.1
  appendix epididymis N44.04
  appendix testis N44.03
  bile duct (common) (hepatic) K83.8
    congenital Q44.5
  bowel, colon or intestine K56.2
  cervix - *see* Malposition, uterus
  cystic duct K82.8
  dystonia - *see* Dystonia, torsion
  epididymis (appendix) N44.04
  fallopian tube N83.52
    with ovary N83.53
  gallbladder K82.8
    congenital Q44.1
  hydatid of Morgagni
    female N83.52
    male N44.03
  kidney (pedicle) (leading to infarction)
    N28.0
  Meckel's diverticulum (congenital)
    Q43.0
  mesentery K56.2
  omentum K56.2
  organ or site, congenital NEC - *see*
    Anomaly, by site
  ovary (pedicle) N83.51
    with fallopian tube N83.53
    congenital Q50.2

Torsion *(Continued)*
  oviduct - *see* Torsion, fallopian tube
  penis N48.89
    congenital Q55.69
  spasm - *see* Dystonia, torsion
  spermatic cord N44.02
    extravaginal N44.01
    intravaginal N44.02
  spleen D73.5
  testis, testicle N44.00
    appendix N44.03
  tibia - *see* Deformity, limb, specified
    type NEC, lower leg
  uterus - *see* Malposition, uterus
Torticollis (intermittent) (spastic)
    M43.6
  congenital (sternomastoid)
    Q68.0
  due to birth injury P15.2
  hysterical F44.4
  ocular R29.891
  psychogenic F45.8
    conversion reaction F44.4
  rheumatoid M06.88
  spasmodic G24.3
  traumatic, current S13.4
Tortipelvis G24.1
Tortuous
  artery I77.1
  organ or site, congenital NEC -
    see Distortion
  retinal vessel, congenital Q14.1
  ureter N13.8
  urethra N36.8
  vein - *see* Varix
Torture, victim of Z65.4
Torula, torular (histolytica) (infection) -
  see Cryptococcosis
Torulosis - *see* Cryptococcosis
Torus (mandibularis) (palatinus)
    M27.0
  fracture - *see* Fracture, by site,
    torus
Touraine's syndrome Q79.8
Tourette's syndrome F95.2
Tourniquet syndrome - *see* Constriction,
  external, by site
Tower skull Q75.0
  with exophthalmos Q87.0
Toxemia R68.89
  bacterial - *see* Sepsis
  burn - *see* Burn
  eclamptic (with pre-existing hyperten-
    sion) - *see* Eclampsia
  erysipelatous - *see* Erysipelas
  fatigue R68.89
  food - *see* Poisoning, food
  gastrointestinal K52.1
  intestinal K52.1
  kidney - *see* Uremia
  malarial - *see* Malaria
  myocardial - *see* Myocarditis, toxic
  of pregnancy - *see* Pre-eclampsia
  pre-eclamptic - *see* Pre-eclampsia
  small intestine K52.1
  staphylococcal, due to food A05.0
  stasis R68.89
  uremic - *see* Uremia
  urinary - *see* Uremia
Toxemica cerebropathia psychica
    (nonalcoholic) F04
  alcoholic - *see* Alcohol, amnestic
    disorder

Toxic (poisoning) - *see also* condition
T65.91
    effect - *see* Table of drugs and chemicals,
      by substance, poisoning
    shock syndrome A48.3
    thyroid (gland) - *see* Thyrotoxicosis
Toxicemia - *see* Toxemia
Toxicity - *see* Table of drugs and chemi-
    cals, by substance, poisoning
    fava bean D55.0
    food, noxious - *see* Poisoning, food
    from drug or nonmedicinal substance -
      see Table of drugs and chemicals,
      by drug
Toxicosis - *see also* Toxemia
    capillary, hemorrhagic D69.0
Toxinfection, gastrointestinal K52.1
Toxocariasis B83.0
Toxoplasma, toxoplasmosis (acquired)
    B58.9
    with
      hepatitis B58.1
      meningoencephalitis B58.2
      ocular involvement B58.00
      other organ involvement B58.89
      pneumonia, pneumonitis B58.3
    congenital (acute) (subacute) (chronic)
      P37.1
    maternal, manifest toxoplasmosis in
      infant (acute) (subacute) (chronic)
      P37.1
tPA (rtPA) administation in a different fa-
    cility within the last 24 hours prior to
    admission to current facility Z92.82
Trabeculation, bladder N32.89
Trachea - *see* condition
Tracheitis (catarrhal) (infantile) (membra-
    nous) (plastic) (septal) (suppurative)
    (viral) J04.10
    with
      bronchitis (15 years of age and above)
        J40
        acute or subacute - *see* Bronchitis,
          acute
        chronic J42
        tuberculous NEC A15.5
        under 15 years of age J20.9
      laryngitis (acute) J04.2
        chronic J37.1
        tuberculous NEC A15.5
    acute J04.10
      with obstruction J04.11
    chronic J42
      with
        bronchitis (chronic) J42
        laryngitis (chronic) J37.1
    diphtheritic (membranous) A36.89
    due to external agent - *see* Inflamma-
      tion, respiratory, upper, due to
    syphilitic A52.73
    tuberculous A15.5
Trachelitis (nonvenereal) - *see* Cervicitis
Tracheobronchial - *see* condition
Tracheobronchitis (15 years of age and
    above) - *see also* Bronchitis
    due to
      Bordetella bronchiseptica A37.80
        with pneumonia A37.81
      Francisella tularensis A21.8
Tracheobronchomegaly Q32.4
    with bronchiectasis J47.9
      with
        exacerbation (acute) J47.1
        lower respiratory infection J47.0

Tracheobronchomegaly *(Continued)*
    acquired J98.09
      with bronchiectasis J47.9
        with
          exacerbation (acute) J47.1
          lower respiratory infection J47.0
Tracheobronchopneumonitis - *see* Pneu-
    monia, broncho-
Tracheocele (external) (internal) J39.8
    congenital Q32.1
Tracheomalacia J39.8
    congenital Q32.0
Tracheopharyngitis
    chronic J42
    due to external agent - *see* Inflamma-
      tion, respiratory, upper, due to
Tracheostenosis J39.8
Tracheostomy
    complication – *see* Complication,
      tracheostomy
    status Z93.0
      attention to Z43.0
      malfunctioning J95.03
Trachoma, trachomatous A71.9
    active (stage) A71.1
    contraction of conjunctiva A71.1
    dubium A71.0
    initial (stage) A71.0
    healed or sequelae B94.0
    pannus A71.1
    Türck's J37.0
Train sickness T75.3
Trait(s)
    Hb-S D57.3
    hemoglobin
      abnormal NEC D58.2
        with thalassemia D56.3
      C - *see* Disease, hemoglobin C
      S (Hb-S) D57.3
    Lepore D56.3
    personality, accentuated Z73.1
    sickle-cell D57.3
      with elliptocytosis or spherocytosis
        D57.3
    type A personality Z73.1
Tramp Z59.0
Trance R41.89
    hysterical F44.89
Transection
    abdomen (partial) S38.3
    aorta (incomplete) - *see also* Injury, aorta
      complete - *see* Injury, aorta, lacera-
        tion, major
    carotid artery (incomplete) - *see also* In-
      jury, blood vessel, carotid, laceration
      complete - *see* Injury, blood vessel,
        carotid, laceration, major
    celiac artery (incomplete) S35.211
      branch (incomplete) S35.291
        complete S35.292
      complete S35.212
    innominate
      artery (incomplete) - *see also* Injury,
        blood vessel, thoracic, innomi-
        nate, artery, laceration
        complete - *see* Injury, blood vessel,
          thoracic, innominate, artery,
          laceration, major
      vein (incomplete) - *see also* Injury,
        blood vessel, thoracic, innomi-
        nate, vein, laceration
        complete - *see* Injury, blood vessel,
          thoracic, innominate, vein,
          laceration, major

Transection *(Continued)*
    jugular vein (external) (incomplete) - *see*
      also Injury, blood vessel, jugular
      vein, laceration
      complete - *see* Injury, blood vessel,
        jugular vein, laceration,
        major
      internal (incomplete) - *see also* Injury,
        blood vessel, jugular vein, inter-
        nal, laceration
        complete - *see* Injury, blood vessel,
          jugular vein, internal, lacera-
          tion, major
    mesenteric artery (incomplete) - *see*
      also Injury, mesenteric, artery,
      laceration
      complete - *see* Injury, mesenteric
        artery, laceration, major
    pulmonary vessel (incomplete) - *see*
      also Injury, blood vessel, thoracic,
      pulmonary, laceration
      complete - *see* Injury, blood vessel,
        thoracic, pulmonary, laceration,
        major
    subclavian - *see* Transection, innominate
    vena cava (incomplete) - *see also* Injury,
      vena cava
      complete - *see* Injury, vena cava,
        laceration, major
    vertebral artery (incomplete) - *see also*
      Injury, blood vessel, vertebral,
      laceration
      complete - *see* Injury, blood vessel,
        vertebral, laceration, major
Transaminasemia R74.0
Transfusion
    blood
      ABO incompatible T80.3
      minor blood group (Duffy) (E)
        (K(ell)) (Kidd) (Lewis) (M) (N)
        (P) (S) T80.89
      reaction or complication - *see*
        Complications, transfusion
    fetomaternal (mother) – *see* Pregnancy,
      complicated by, placenta, transfu-
      sion syndrome
    maternofetal (mother) – *see* Pregnancy,
      complicated by, placenta, transfu-
      sion syndrome
    placental (syndrome) (mother) – *see*
      Pregnancy, complicated by, pla-
      centa, transfusion syndrome
    reaction (adverse) - *see* Complications,
      transfusion
    related acute lung injury (TRALI)
      J95.84
    twin-to-twin – *see* Pregnancy, compli-
      cated by, placenta, transfusion
      syndrome, fetus to fetus
Transient (meaning homeless) (*see also*
    condition) Z59.0
Translocation
    balanced autosomal Q95.9
      in normal individual Q95.0
    chromosomes NEC Q99.8
      balanced and insertion in normal
        individual Q95.0
    Down's syndrome Q90.2
    trisomy
      13 Q91.6
      18 Q91.2
      21 Q90.2
Translucency, iris - *see* Degeneration,
    iris

Transmission of chemical substances through the placenta - see Absorption, chemical, through placenta
Transparency, lung, unilateral J43.0
Transplant(ed) (status) Z94.9
  awaiting organ Z76.82
  bone Z94.6
    marrow Z94.81
  candidate Z76.82
  complication – see Complication, transplant
  cornea Z94.7
  heart Z94.1
    and lung(s) Z94.3
    valve Z95.2
      prosthetic Z95.2
      specified NEC Z95.4
      xenogenic Z95.3
  intestine Z94.82
  kidney Z94.0
  liver Z94.4
  lung(s) Z94.2
    and heart Z94.3
  organ (failure) (infection) (rejection)Z94.9
    removal status Z98.85
  pancreas Z94.83
  skin Z94.5
  social Z60.3
  specified organ or tissue NEC Z94.89
  stem cells Z94.84
  tissue Z94.9
Transplants, ovarian, endometrial N80.1
Transposed - see Transposition
Transposition (congenital) - see also Malposition, congenital
  abdominal viscera Q89.3
  aorta (dextra) Q20.3
  appendix Q43.8
  colon Q43.8
  corrected Q20.5
  great vessels (complete) (partial) Q20.3
  heart Q24.0
    with complete transposition of viscera Q89.3
  intestine (large) (small) Q43.8
  reversed jejunal (for bypass) (status) Z98.0
  scrotum Q55.23
  stomach Q40.2
    with general transposition of viscera Q89.3
  tooth, teeth, fully erupted M26.30
  vessels, great (complete) (partial) Q20.3
  viscera (abdominal) (thoracic) Q89.3
Transsexualism F64.1
Transverse - see also condition
  arrest (deep), in labor O64.0
  lie (mother) O32.2
    causing obstructed labor O64.8
Transvestism, transvestitism (dual-role) F64.1
  fetishistic F65.1
Trapped placenta (with hemorrhage) O72.0
  without hemorrhage O73.0
Trauma, traumatism - see also Injury
  acoustic - see subcategory H83.3
  birth - see Birth, injury
  complicating ectopic or molar pregnancy O08.6
  during delivery O71.9

Trauma, traumatism (Continued)
  following ectopic or molar pregnancy O08.6
  obstetric O71.9
    specified NEC O71.89
Traumatic - see also condition
  brain injury - see category S06
Treacher Collins syndrome Q75.4
Treitz's hernia - see Hernia, abdomen, specified site NEC
Trematode infestation - see Infestation, fluke
Trematodiasis - see Infestation, fluke
Trembling paralysis - see Parkinsonism
Tremor(s) R25.1
  drug induced G25.1
  essential (benign) G25.0
  familial G25.0
  hereditary G25.0
  hysterical F44.4
  intention G25.2
  medication induced postural G25.1
  mercurial - see subcategory T56.1
  Parkinson's - see Parkinsonism
  psychogenic (conversion reaction) F44.4
  senilis R54
  specified type NEC G25.2
Trench
  fever A79.0
  foot – see Immersion, foot
  mouth A69.1
Treponema pallidum infection - see Syphilis
Treponematosis
  due to
    T. pallidum - see Syphilis
    T. pertenue - see Yaws
Triad
  Hutchinson's (congenital syphilis) A50.53
  Kartagener's Q89.3
  Saint's - see Hernia, diaphragm
Trichiasis (eyelid) H02.059
  with entropion - see Entropion
  left H02.056
    lower H02.055
    upper H02.054
  right H02.053
    lower H02.052
    upper H02.051
Trichinella spiralis (infection) (infestation) B75
Trichinellosis, trichiniasis, trichinelliasis, trichinosis B75
  with muscle disorder B75 [M63.80]
    ankle B75 [M63.87-]
    foot B75 [M63.87-]
    forearm B75 [M63.83-]
    hand B75 [M63.849]
    lower leg B75 [M63.86-]
    multiple sites B75 [M63.89]
    pelvic region B75 [M63.85-]
    shoulder region B75 [M63.81-]
    specified site NEC B75 [M63.88]
    thigh B75 [M63.85-]
    upper arm B75 [M63.82-]
Trichobezoar T18.9
  intestine T18.3
  stomach T18.2
Trichocephaliasis, trichocephalosis B79
Trichocephalus infestation B79
Trichoclasis L67.8

Trichoepithelioma - see also Neoplasm, skin, benign
  malignant - see Neoplasm, skin, malignant
Trichofolliculoma - see Neoplasm, skin, benign
Tricholemmoma 4 - see Neoplasm, skin, benign
Trichomoniasis A59.9
  bladder A59.03
  cervix A59.09
  intestinal A07.8
  prostate A59.02
  seminal vesicles A59.09
  specified site NEC A59.8
  urethra A59.03
  urogenitalis A59.00
  vagina A59.01
  vulva A59.01
Trichomycosis
  axillaris A48.8
  nodosa, nodularis B36.8
Trichonodosis L67.8
Trichophytid, trichophyton infection - see Dermatophytosis
Trichophytobezoar T18.9
  intestine T18.3
  stomach T18.2
Trichophytosis - see Dermatophytosis
Trichoptilosis L67.8
Trichorrhexis (nodosa) (invaginata) L67.0
Trichosis axillaris A48.8
Trichosporosis nodosa B36.2
Trichostasis spinulosa (congenital) Q84.1
Trichostrongyliasis, trichostrongylosis (small intestine) B81.2
Trichostrongylus infection B81.2
Trichotillomania F63.3
Trichromat, trichromatopsia, anomalous (congenital) H53.55
Trichuriasis B79
Trichuris trichiura (infection) (infestation) (any site) B79
Tricuspid (valve) - see condition
Trifid - see also Accessory
  kidney (pelvis) Q63.8
  tongue Q38.3
Trigeminal neuralgia - see Neuralgia, trigeminal
Trigeminy R00.8
Trigger finger (acquired) M65.30
  congenital Q74.0
  index finger M65.32-
  little finger M65.35-
  middle finger M65.33-
  ring finger M65.34-
  thumb M65.31-
Trigonitis (bladder) (chronic) (pseudomembranous) N30.30
  with hematuria N30.31
Trigonocephaly Q75.0
Trilocular heart - see Cor triloculare
Trimethylaminuria E72.52
Tripartite placenta O43.19-
Triphalangeal thumb Q74.0
Triple - see also Accessory
  kidneys Q63.0
  uteri Q51.8
  X, female Q97.0
Triplegia G83.89
  congenital G80.8

Triplet (newborn) – *see also* Newborn, triplet
  complicating pregnancy – *see* Pregnancy, triplet
Triplication - *see* Accessory
Triploidy Q92.7
Trismus R25.2
  neonatorum A33
  newborn A33
Trisomy (syndrome) Q92.9
  autosomes Q92.9
  chromosome specified NEC Q92.8
    partial Q92.2
      due to unbalanced translocation Q92.5
    whole (nonsex chromosome)
      meiotic nondisjunction Q92.0
      mitotic nondisjunction Q92.1
      mosaicism Q92.1
    specified NEC Q92.8
  due to
    dicentrics - *see* Extra, marker chromosomes
    extra rings - *see* Extra, marker chromosomes
    isochromosomes -*see* Extra, marker chromosomes
  specified NEC Q92.8
  whole chromosome Q92.9
    meiotic nondisjunction Q92.0
    mitotic nondisjunction Q92.1
    mosaicism Q92.1
    partial Q92.9
    specified NEC Q92.8
  13 (partial) Q91.7
    meiotic nondisjunction Q91.4
    mitotic nondisjunction Q91.5
    mosaicism Q91.5
    translocation Q91.6
  18 (partial) Q91.3
    meiotic nondisjunction Q91.0
    mitotic nondisjunction Q91.1
    mosaicism Q91.1
    translocation Q91.2
  20 Q92.8
  21 (partial) Q90.9
    meiotic nondisjunction Q90.0
    mitotic nondisjunction Q90.1
    mosaicism Q90.1
    translocation Q90.2
  22 Q92.8
Tritanomaly, tritanopia H53.55
Trombiculosis, trombiculiasis, trombidiosis B88.0
Trophedema (congenital) (hereditary) Q82.0
Trophoblastic disease (*see also* Mole, hydatidiform) O01.9
Tropholymphedema Q82.0
Trophoneurosis NEC G96.8
  disseminated M34.9
Tropical - *see* condition
Trouble - *see also* Disease
  heart - *see* Disease, heart
  kidney - *see* Disease, renal
  nervous R45.0
  sinus - *see* Sinusitis
Trousseau's syndrome (thrombophlebitis migrans) I82.1
Truancy, childhood
  from school Z72.810
Truncus
  arteriosus (persistent) Q20.0
  communis Q20.0

Trunk - *see* condition
Trypanosomiasis
  African B56.9
    by Trypanosoma brucei
      gambiense B56.0
      rhodesiense B56.1
  American - *see* Chagas' disease
  Brazilian - *see* Chagas' disease
  by Trypanosoma
    brucei gambiense B56.0
    brucei rhodesiense B56.1
    cruzi - *see* Chagas' disease
  gambiensis, Gambian B56.0
  rhodesiensis, Rhodesian B56.1
  South American - *see* Chagas' disease
  where
    African trypanosomiasis is prevalent B56.9
    Chagas' disease is prevalent B57.2
T-shaped incisors K00.2
Tsutsugamushi (disease) (fever) A75.3
Tube, tubal, tubular - *see* condition
Tubercle - *see also* Tuberculosis
  brain, solitary A17.81
  Darwin's Q17.8
  Ghon, primary infection A15.7
Tuberculid, tuberculide (indurating, subcutaneous) (lichenoid) (miliary) (papulonecrotic) (primary) (skin) A18.4
Tuberculoma - *see also* Tuberculosis
  brain A17.81
  meninges (cerebral) (spinal) A17.1
  spinal cord A17.81
Tuberculosis, tubercular, tuberculous (calcification) (calcified) (caseous) (chromogenic acid-fast bacilli) (degeneration) (fibrocaseous) (fistula) (interstitial) (isolated circumscribed lesions) (necrosis) (parenchymatous) (ulcerative) A15.9
  with pneumoconiosis (any condition in J60-J64) J65
  abdomen (lymph gland) A18.39
  abscess (respiratory) A15.9
    bone A18.03
      hip A18.02
      knee A18.02
      sacrum A18.01
      specified site NEC A18.03
      spinal A18.01
      vertebra A18.01
    brain A17.81
    breast A18.89
    Cowper's gland A18.15
    dura (mater) (cerebral) (spinal) A17.81
    epidural (cerebral) (spinal) A17.81
    female pelvis A18.17
    frontal sinus A15.8
    genital organs NEC A18.10
    genitourinary A18.10
    gland (lymphatic) - *see* Tuberculosis, lymph gland
    hip A18.02
    intestine A18.32
    ischiorectal A18.32
    joint NEC A18.02
      hip A18.02
      knee A18.02
      specified NEC A18.02
      vertebral A18.01
    kidney A18.11
    knee A18.02

Tuberculosis, tubercular, tuberculous (Continued)
  abscess (Continued)
    lumbar (spine) A18.01
    lung - *see* Tuberculosis, pulmonary
    meninges (cerebral) (spinal) A17.0
    muscle A18.09
    perianal (fistula) A18.32
    perinephritic A18.11
    perirectal A18.32
    rectum A18.32
    retropharyngeal A15.8
    sacrum A18.01
    scrofulous A18.2
    scrotum A18.15
    skin (primary) A18.4
    spinal cord A17.81
    spine or vertebra (column) A18.01
    subdiaphragmatic A18.31
    testis A18.15
    urinary A18.13
    uterus A18.17
  accessory sinus - *see* Tuberculosis, sinus
  Addison's disease A18.7
  adenitis - *see* Tuberculosis, lymph gland
  adenoids A15.8
  adenopathy - *see* Tuberculosis, lymph gland
  adherent pericardium A18.84
  adnexa (uteri) A18.17
  adrenal (capsule) (gland) A18.7
  alimentary canal A18.32
  anemia A18.89
  ankle (joint) (bone) A18.02
  anus A18.32
  apex, apical - *see* Tuberculosis, pulmonary
  appendicitis, appendix A18.32
  arachnoid A17.0
  artery, arteritis A18.89
    cerebral A18.89
  arthritis (chronic) (synovial) A18.02
    spine or vertebra (column) A18.01
  articular - *see* Tuberculosis, joint
  ascites A18.31
  asthma - *see* Tuberculosis, pulmonary
  axilla, axillary (gland) A18.2
  bladder A18.12
  bone A18.03
    hip A18.02
    knee A18.02
    limb NEC A18.03
    sacrum A18.01
    spine or vertebral column A18.01
  bowel (miliary) A18.32
  brain A17.81
  breast A18.89
  broad ligament A18.17
  bronchi, bronchial, bronchus A15.5
    ectasia, ectasis (bronchiectasis) - *see* Tuberculosis, pulmonary
    fistula A15.5
      primary (progressive) A15.7
    gland or node A15.4
      primary (progressive) A15.7
    lymph gland or node A15.4
      primary (progressive) A15.7
  bronchiectasis - *see* Tuberculosis, pulmonary
  bronchitis A15.5
  bronchopleural A15.6
  bronchopneumonia, bronchopneumonic - *see* Tuberculosis, pulmonary

Tuberculosis, tubercular, tuberculous
(Continued)
bronchorrhagia A15.5
bronchotracheal A15.5
bronze disease A18.7
buccal cavity A18.83
bulbourethral gland A18.15
bursa A18.09
cachexia A15.9
cardiomyopathy A18.84
caries - *see* Tuberculosis, bone
cartilage A18.02
 intervertebral A18.01
catarrhal - *see* Tuberculosis, respiratory
cecum A18.32
cellulitis (primary) A18.4
cerebellum A17.81
cerebral, cerebrum A17.81
cerebrospinal A17.81
 meninges A17.0
cervical (lymph gland or node) A18.2
cervicitis, cervix (uteri) A18.16
chest - *see* Tuberculosis, respiratory
chorioretinitis A18.53
choroid, choroiditis A18.53
ciliary body A18.54
colitis A18.32
collier's J65
colliquativa (primary) A18.4
colon A18.32
complex, primary A15.7
congenital P37.0
conjunctiva A18.59
connective tissue (systemic) A18.89
contact Z20.1
cornea (ulcer) A18.52
Cowper's gland A18.15
coxae A18.02
coxalgia A18.02
cul-de-sac of Douglas A18.17
curvature, spine A18.01
cutis (colliquativa) (primary) A18.4
cyst, ovary A18.18
cystitis A18.12
dactylitis A18.03
diarrhea A18.32
diffuse - *see* Tuberculosis, miliary
digestive tract A18.32
disseminated - *see* Tuberculosis, miliary
duodenum A18.32
dura (mater) (cerebral) (spinal) A17.0
 abscess (cerebral) (spinal) A17.81
dysentery A18.32
ear (inner) (middle) A18.6
 bone A18.03
 external (primary) A18.4
 skin (primary) A18.4
elbow A18.02
emphysema - *see* Tuberculosis,
 pulmonary
empyema A15.6
encephalitis A17.82
endarteritis A18.89
endocarditis A18.84
 aortic A18.84
 mitral A18.84
 pulmonary A18.84
 tricuspid A18.84
endocrine glands NEC A18.82
endometrium A18.17
enteric, enterica, enteritis A18.32
enterocolitis A18.32
epididymis, epididymitis A18.15

Tuberculosis, tubercular, tuberculous
(Continued)
epidural abscess (cerebral) (spinal)
 A17.81
epiglottis A15.5
episcleritis A18.51
erythema (induratum) (nodosum)
 (primary) A18.4
esophagus A18.83
eustachian tube A18.6
exposure (to) Z20.1
exudative - *see* Tuberculosis, pulmonary
eye A18.50
eyelid (primary) (lupus) A18.4
fallopian tube (acute) (chronic) A18.17
fascia A18.09
fauces A15.8
female pelvic inflammatory disease
 A18.17
finger A18.03
first infection A15.7
gallbladder A18.83
ganglion A18.09
gastritis A18.83
gastrocolic fistula A18.32
gastroenteritis A18.32
gastrointestinal tract A18.32
general, generalized - *see* Tuberculosis,
 miliary
genital organs A18.10
genitourinary A18.10
genu A18.02
glandula suprarenalis A18.7
glandular, general A18.2
glottis A15.5
grinder's J65
gum A18.83
hand A18.03
heart A18.84
hematogenous - *see* Tuberculosis,
 miliary
hemoptysis - *see* Tuberculosis,
 pulmonary
hemorrhage NEC - *see* Tuberculosis,
 pulmonary
hemothorax A15.6
hepatitis A18.83
hilar lymph nodes A15.4
 primary (progressive) A15.7
hip (joint) (disease) (bone) A18.02
hydropneumothorax A15.6
hydrothorax A15.6
hypoadrenalism A18.7
hypopharynx A15.8
ileocecal (hyperplastic) A18.32
ileocolitis A18.32
ileum A18.32
iliac spine (superior) A18.03
immunological findings only A15.7
indurativa (primary) A18.4
infantile A15.7
infection A15.9
 without clinical manifestations A15.7
infraclavicular gland A18.2
inguinal gland A18.2
inguinalis A18.2
intestine (any part) A18.32
iridocyclitis A18.54
iris, iritis A18.54
ischiorectal A18.32
jaw A18.03
jejunum A18.32
joint A18.02
 vertebral A18.01

Tuberculosis, tubercular, tuberculous
(Continued)
keratitis (interstitial) A18.52
keratoconjunctivitis A18.52
kidney A18.11
knee (joint) A18.02
kyphosis, kyphoscoliosis A18.01
laryngitis A15.5
larynx A15.5
leptomeninges, leptomeningitis (cerebral) (spinal) A17.0
lichenoides (primary) A18.4
linguae A18.83
lip A18.83
liver A18.83
lordosis A18.01
lung - *see* Tuberculosis, pulmonary
lupus vulgaris A18.4
lymph gland or node (peripheral) A18.2
 abdomen A18.39
 bronchial A15.4
 primary (progressive) A15.7
 cervical A18.2
 hilar A15.4
 primary (progressive) A15.7
 intrathoracic A15.4
 primary (progressive) A15.7
 mediastinal A15.4
 primary (progressive) A15.7
 mesenteric A18.39
 retroperitoneal A18.39
 tracheobronchial A15.4
 primary (progressive) A15.7
lymphadenitis - *see* Tuberculosis, lymph
 gland
lymphangitis - *see* Tuberculosis, lymph
 gland
lymphatic (gland) (vessel) - *see* Tuberculosis, lymph gland
mammary gland A18.89
marasmus A15.9
mastoiditis A18.03
mediastinal lymph gland or node A15.4
 primary (progressive) A15.7
mediastinitis A15.8
 primary (progressive) A15.7
mediastinum A15.8
 primary (progressive) A15.7
medulla A17.81
melanosis, Addisonian A18.7
meninges, meningitis (basilar) (cerebral)
 (cerebrospinal) (spinal) A17.0
meningoencephalitis A17.82
mesentery, mesenteric (gland or node)
 A18.39
miliary A19.9
 acute A19.2
 multiple sites A19.1
 single specified site A19.0
 chronic A19.8
 specified NEC A19.8
millstone makers' J65
miner's J65
molder's J65
mouth A18.83
multiple A19.9
 acute A19.1
 chronic A19.8
muscle A18.09
myelitis A17.82
myocardium, myocarditis A18.84
nasal (passage) (sinus) A15.8
nasopharynx A15.8
neck gland A18.2

459

Tuberculosis, tubercular, tuberculous
(Continued)
nephritis A18.11
nerve (mononeuropathy) A17.83
nervous system A17.9
nose (septum) A15.8
ocular A18.50
omentum A18.31
oophoritis (acute) (chronic) A18.17
optic (nerve trunk) (papilla) A18.59
orbit A18.59
orchitis A18.15
organ, specified NEC A18.89
osseous - *see* Tuberculosis, bone
osteitis - *see* Tuberculosis, bone
osteomyelitis - *see* Tuberculosis, bone
otitis media A18.6
ovary, ovaritis (acute) (chronic) A18.17
oviduct (acute) (chronic) A18.17
pachymeningitis A17.0
palate (soft) A18.83
pancreas A18.83
papulonecrotic(a) (primary) A18.4
parathyroid glands A18.82
paronychia (primary) A18.4
parotid gland or region A18.83
pelvis (bony) A18.03
penis A18.15
peribronchitis A15.5
pericardium, pericarditis A18.84
perichondritis, larynx A15.5
periostitis - *see* Tuberculosis, bone
perirectal fistula A18.32
peritoneum NEC A18.31
peritonitis A18.31
pharynx, pharyngitis A15.8
phlyctenulosis (keratoconjunctivitis) A18.52
phthisis NEC - *see* Tuberculosis, pulmonary
pituitary gland A18.82
pleura, pleural, pleurisy, pleuritis (fibrinous) (obliterative) (purulent) (simple plastic) (with effusion) A15.6
primary (progressive) A15.7
pneumonia, pneumonic - *see* Tuberculosis, pulmonary
pneumothorax (spontaneous) (tense valvular) - *see* Tuberculosis, pulmonary
polyneuropathy A17.89
polyserositis A19.9
acute A19.1
chronic A19.8
potter's J65
prepuce A18.15
primary (complex) A15.7
proctitis A18.32
prostate, prostatitis A18.14
pulmonalis - *see* Tuberculosis, pulmonary
pulmonary (cavitated) (fibrotic) (infiltrative) (nodular) A15.0
childhood type or first infection A15.7
primary (complex) A15.7
pyelitis A18.11
pyelonephritis A18.11
pyemia - *see* Tuberculosis, miliary
pyonephrosis A18.11
pyopneumothorax A15.6
pyothorax A15.6
rectum (fistula) (with abscess) A18.32

Tuberculosis, tubercular, tuberculous
(Continued)
reinfection stage - *see* Tuberculosis, pulmonary
renal A18.11
renis A18.11
respiratory A15.9
primary A15.7
specified site NEC A15.8
retina, retinitis A18.53
retroperitoneal (lymph gland or node) A18.39
rheumatism NEC A18.09
rhinitis A15.8
sacroiliac (joint) A18.01
sacrum A18.01
salivary gland A18.83
salpingitis (acute) (chronic) A18.17
sandblaster's J65
sclera A18.51
scoliosis A18.01
scrofulous A18.2
scrotum A18.15
seminal tract or vesicle A18.15
senile A15.9
septic - *see* Tuberculosis, miliary
shoulder (joint) A18.02
blade A18.03
sigmoid A18.32
sinus (any nasal) A15.8
bone A18.03
epididymis A18.15
skeletal NEC A18.03
skin (any site) (primary) A18.4
small intestine A18.32
soft palate A18.83
spermatic cord A18.15
spine, spinal (column) A18.01
cord A17.81
medulla A17.81
membrane A17.0
meninges A17.0
spleen, splenitis A18.85
spondylitis A18.01
sternoclavicular joint A18.02
stomach A18.83
stonemason's J65
subcutaneous tissue (cellular) (primary) A18.4
subcutis (primary) A18.4
subdeltoid bursa A18.83
submaxillary (region) A18.83
supraclavicular gland A18.2
suprarenal (capsule) (gland) A18.7
swelling, joint (*see also* Tuberculosis, joint) A18.02 (*see also* category M01)
symphysis pubis A18.02
synovitis A18.09
articular A18.02
spine or vertebra A18.01
systemic - *see* Tuberculosis, miliary
tarsitis A18.4
tendon (sheath) - *see* Tuberculosis, tenosynovitis
tenosynovitis A18.09
spine or vertebra A18.01
testis A18.15
throat A15.8
thymus gland A18.82
thyroid gland A18.81
tongue A18.83
tonsil, tonsillitis A15.8

Tuberculosis, tubercular, tuberculous
(Continued)
trachea, tracheal A15.5
lymph gland or node A15.4
primary (progressive) A15.7
tracheobronchial A15.5
lymph gland or node A15.4
primary (progressive) A15.7
tubal (acute) (chronic) A18.17
tunica vaginalis A18.15
ulcer (skin) (primary) A18.4
bowel or intestine A18.32
specified NEC - code under Tuberculosis, by site
unspecified site A15.9
ureter A18.11
urethra, urethral (gland) A18.13
urinary organ or tract A18.13
uterus A18.17
uveal tract A18.54
uvula A18.83
vagina A18.18
vas deferens A18.15
verruca, verrucosa (cutis) (primary) A18.4
vertebra (column) A18.01
vesiculitis A18.15
vulva A18.18
wrist (joint) A18.02
Tuberculum
Carabelli - *see* Note at K00.2
occlusal - *see* Note at K00.2
paramolare K00.2
Tuberosity, enitre maxillary M26.07
Tuberous sclerosis (brain) Q85.1
Tubo-ovarian - *see* condition
Tuboplasty, after previous sterilization Z31.0
aftercare Z31.42
Tubotympanitis, catarrhal (chronic) - *see* Otitis, media, nonsuppurative, chronic, serous
Tularemia A21.9
with
conjunctivitis A21.1
pneumonia A21.2
abdominal A21.3
bronchopneumonic A21.2
conjunctivitis A21.1
cryptogenic A21.3
enteric A21.3
gastrointestinal A21.3
generalized A21.7
ingestion A21.3
intestinal A21.3
oculoglandular A21.1
ophthalmic A21.1
pneumonia (any), pneumonic A21.2
pulmonary A21.2
sepsis A21.7
specified NEC A21.8
typhoidal A21.7
ulceroglandular A21.0
Tularensis conjunctivitis A21.1
Tumefaction - *see also* Swelling
liver - *see* Hypertrophy, liver
Tumor - *see also* Neoplasm, unspecified behavior
acinar cell - *see* Neoplasm, uncertain behavior
acinic cell - *see* Neoplasm, uncertain behavior
adenocarcinoid - *see* Neoplasm, malignant

Tumor *(Continued)*
  adenomatoid - *see also* Neoplasm,
    benign
    odontogenic - *see* Cyst, calcifying
      odontogenic
  adnexal (skin) - *see* Neoplasm, skin,
    benign
  adrenal
    cortical (benign) D35.0-
      malignant C74.0-
    rest - *see* Neoplasm, benign
      pancreas C25.4
      specified site NEC - *see* Neoplasm,
        malignant
      unspecified site C25.4
    pancreas D13.7
    specified site NEC - *see* Neoplasm,
      benign
    unspecified site D13.7
  aneurysmal - *see* Aneurysm
  aortic body D44.7
    malignant C75.5
  Askin's - *see* Neoplasm, connective
    tissue, malignant
  basal cell - *see also* Neoplasm, skin,
    uncertain behavior D48.5
  Bednar - *see* Neoplasm, skin,
    malignant
  benign (unclassified) - *see* Neoplasm,
    benign
    pancreas C25.4
      specified site NEC - *see* Neoplasm,
        malignant
      unspecified site C25.4
      pancreas D13.7
    specified site NEC - *see* Neoplasm,
      benign
    unspecified site D13.7
  Brenner D27.9
    borderline malignancy D39.1-
    malignant C56.-
    proliferating D39.1
  bronchial alveolar, intravascular
    D38.1
  Brooke's - *see* Neoplasm, skin, benign
  brown fat - *see* Lipoma
  Burkitt- *see* Lymphoma, Burkitt
  calcifying epithelial odontogenic - *see*
    Cyst, calcifying odontogenic
  carcinoid
    benign D3a.00
      appendix D3a.020
      ascending colon D3a.022
      bronchus (lung) D3a.090
      cecum D3a.021
      colon D3a.029
      descending colon D3a.024
      duodenum D3a.010
      foregut NOS D3a.094
      hindgut NOS D3a.096
      ileum D3a.012
      jejunum D3a.011
      kidney D3a.093
      large intestine D3a.029
      lung (bronchus) D3a.090
      midgut NOS D3a.095
      rectum D3a.026
      sigmoid colon D3a.025
      small intestine D3a.019
      specified NEC D3a.098
      stomach D3a.092
      thymus D3a.091
      transverse colon
        D3a.023

Tumor *(Continued)*
  carcinoid *(Continued)*
    malignant C7a.00
      appendix C7a.020
      ascending colon C7a.022
      bronchus (lung) C7a.090
      cecum C7a.021
      colon C7a.029
      descending colon C7a.024
      duodenum C7a.010
      foregut NOS C7a.094
      hindgut NOS C7a.096
      ileum C7a.012
      jejunum C7a.011
      kidney C7a.093
      large intestine C7a.029
      lung (bronchus) C7a.090
      midgut NOS C7a.095
      rectum C7a.026
      sigmoid colon C7a.025
      small intestine C7a.019
      specified NEC C7a.098
      stomach C7a.092
      thymus C7a.091
      transverse colon C7a.023
    mesentary metastasis C7b.01
    secondary C7b.00
      bone C7b.03
      distant lymph nodes C7b.01
      liver C7b.02
      peritoneum C7b.04
      specified NEC C7b.09
  carotid body D44.6
    malignant C75.4
  cells - *see also* Neoplasm, unspecified
    behavior
    benign - *see* Neoplasm, benign
    malignant - *see* Neoplasm, malignant
    uncertain whether benign or
      malignant - *see* Neoplasm,
      uncertain behavior
  cervix, in pregnancy or childbirth - *see*
    Pregnancy, complicated by, tumor,
    cervix
  chondromatous giant cell - *see* Neo-
    plasm, bone, benign
  chromaffin - *see also* Neoplasm, benign
    malignant - *see* Neoplasm, malignant
  Cock's peculiar L72.1
  Codman's - *see* Neoplasm, bone, benign
  dentigerous, mixed - *see* Cyst, calcifying
    odontogenic
  dermoid - *see* Neoplasm, benign
    with malignant transformation C56.-
  desmoid (extra-abdominal) - *see also*
    Neoplasm, connective tissue,
    uncertain behavior
    abdominal - *see* Neoplasm, connec-
      tive tissue, uncertain behavior
  embolus - *see* Neoplasm, secondary
  embryonal (mixed) - *see also* Neoplasm,
    uncertain behavior
    liver C22.7
    specified site - *see* Neoplasm,
      malignant
    unspecified site
      female C56.-
      male C62.90
  epithelial
    benign - *see* Neoplasm, benign
    malignant - *see* Neoplasm, malignant
  Ewing's - *see* Neoplasm, bone,
    malignant
  fatty - *see* Lipoma

Tumor *(Continued)*
  fibroid - *see* Leiomyoma
    pancreas C25.4
    specified site NEC - *see* Neoplasm,
      malignant
    unspecified site C25.4
    specified site - *see* Neoplasm, uncer-
      tain behavior
    unspecified site D37.7
  germ cell - *see also* Neoplasm,
    malignant
    mixed - *see* Neoplasm, malignant
  ghost cell, odontogenic - *see* Cyst,
    calcifying odontogenic
  giant cell - *see also* Neoplasm, uncertain
    behavior
    bone D48.0
      malignant - *see* Neoplasm, bone,
        malignant
      chondromatous - *see* Neoplasm, bone,
        benign
      malignant - *see* Neoplasm,
        malignant
      soft parts - *see* Neoplasm, connective
        tissue, uncertain behavior
        malignant - *see* Neoplasm, connec-
          tive tissue, malignant
  glomus D18.00
    intra-abdominal D18.03
    intracranial D18.02
    jugulare D44.7
      malignant C75.5
    skin D18.01
    specified site NEC D18.09
  gonadal stromal - *see* Neoplasm, uncer-
    tain behavior
  granular cell - *see also* Neoplasm, con-
    nective tissue, benign
    malignant - *see* Neoplasm, connective
      tissue, malignant
  granulosa cell D39.1-
    juvenile D39.1-
    malignant C56.-
  granulosa cell-theca cell D39.1-
    malignant C56.-
  Grawitz's C64.-
  hemorrhoidal - *see* Hemorrhoids
  hilar cell D27.-
  hilus cell D27.-
  Hurthle cell (benign) D34
    malignant C73
  hydatid - *see* Echinococcus
  hypernephroid - *see also* Neoplasm,
    uncertain behavior
  interstitial cell - *see also* Neoplasm,
    uncertain behavior
    benign - *see* Neoplasm, benign
    malignant - *see* Neoplasm,
      malignant
  intravascular bronchial alveolar D38.1
  islet cell - *see* Neoplasm, benign
    malignant - *see* Neoplasm,
      malignant
      pancreas C25.4
      specified site NEC - *see* Neoplasm,
        malignant
      unspecified site C25.4
    pancreas D13.7
    specified site NEC - *see* Neoplasm,
      benign
    unspecified site D13.7
  juxtaglomerular D41.0-
  Klatskin's C22.1
  Krukenberg's C79.6-

Tumor *(Continued)*

Leydig cell - *see* Neoplasm, uncertain behavior
  benign - *see* Neoplasm, benign
    specified site - *see* Neoplasm, benign
    unspecified site
      female D27.9
      male D29.20
  malignant - *see* Neoplasm, malignant
    specified site - *see* Neoplasm, malignant
    unspecified site
      female C56.9
      male C62.90
  specified site - *see* Neoplasm, uncertain behavior
  unspecified site
    female D39.10
    male D40.10
lipid cell, ovary D27.-
lipoid cell, ovary D27.-
malignant (*see also* Neoplasm, malignant) C80.1
  fusiform cell (type) C80.1
  giant cell (type) C80.1
  localized, plasma cell - *see* Plasmacytoma, solitary
  mixed NEC C80.1
  small cell (type) C80.1
  spindle cell (type) C80.1
  unclassified C80.1
mast cell D47.0
  malignant C96.2
melanotic, neuroectodermal - *see* Neoplasm, benign
Merkel cell - *see* Carcinoma, Merkel cell
mesenchymal- - malignant - *see* Neoplasm, connective tissue, malignant
  mixed - *see* Neoplasm, connective tissue, uncertain behavior
mesodermal, mixed - *see also* Neoplasm, malignant
  liver C22.4
mesonephric - *see also* Neoplasm, uncertain behavior
  malignant - *see* Neoplasm, malignant
metastatic
  from specified site - *see* Neoplasm, malignant, by site
  of specified site - *see* Neoplasm, malignant, by site
  to specified site - *see* Neoplasm, secondary, by site
mixed NEC - *see also* Neoplasm, benign
  malignant - *see* Neoplasm, malignant
    specified site - *see* Neoplasm, malignant
    unspecified site C56.9
  specified site - *see* Neoplasm, malignant
  unspecified site C18.1
mucoepidermoid - *see* Neoplasm, uncertain behavior
Müllerian, mixed
  specified site - *see* Neoplasm, malignant
  unspecified site C54.9
myoepithelial - *see* Neoplasm, benign
neuroectodermal (peripheral) (primative) - *see* Neoplasm, malignant
  specified site - *see* Neoplasm, malignant
  unspecified site C71.9

Tumor *(Continued)*

neuroendocrine
  malignant poorly differentiated C7a.1
  secondary NEC C7b.8
  specified NEC C7a.8
neurogenic olfactory C30.0
nonencapsulated sclerosing C73
odontogenic (adenomatoid) (benign) (calcifying epithelial) (keratocystic) (squamous) - *see* Cyst, calcifying odontogenic
  malignant C41.1
    upper jaw (bone) C41.0
ovarian stromal D39.1-
ovary, in pregnancy - *see* Pregnancy, complicated by
pacinian - *see* Neoplasm, skin, benign
Pancoast's - *see* Pancoast's syndrome
papillary - *see also* Papilloma
  cystic D37.7
  mucinous of low malignant potential C56.-
    specified site - *see* Neoplasm, malignant
    unspecified site C56.9
  specified site - *see* Neoplasm, malignant
  unspecified site C56.9
pelvic, in pregnancy or childbirth - *see* Pregnancy, complicated by
phantom F45.8
phyllodes
  female D48.61-
  male D48.62-
  benign D24.0-
  malignant - *see* Neoplasm, breast, malignant
Pindborg - *see* Cyst, calcifying odontogenic
placental site trophoblastic D39.2
plasma cell (malignant) (localized) - *see* Plasmacytoma, solitary
  specified site - *see* Neoplasm, malignant
  unspecified site
    female C56.9
    male C62.90
Pott's puffy - *see* Osteomyelitis, specified NEC
Rathke's pouch D44.3
retinal anlage - *see* Neoplasm, benign
salivary gland type, mixed - *see* Neoplasm, salivary gland, benign
  malignant - *see* Neoplasm, salivary gland, malignant
Sampson's N80.1
Schmincke's - *see* Neoplasm, nasopharynx, malignant
sclerosing stromal D27.-
sebaceous - *see* Cyst, sebaceous
secondary - *see* Neoplasm, secondary
  carcinoid C7b.00
    bone C7b.03
    distant lymph nodes C7b.01
    liver C7b.02
    peritoneum C7b.04
    specified NEC C7b.09
  neuroendocrine NEC C7b.8
  specified site - *see* Neoplasm, malignant
  unspecified site C56.9

Tumor *(Continued)*

Sertoli cell - *see* Neoplasm, benign
  specified site - *see* Neoplasm, benign
  unspecified site
    female D27.9
    male D29.20
  specified site - *see* Neoplasm, benign
  unspecified site
    female D27.9
    male D29.20
Sertoli-Leydig cell - *see* Neoplasm, benign
  specified site - *see* Neoplasm, benign
  unspecified site
    female D27.9
    male D29.20
sex cord(-stromal) - *see* Neoplasm, uncertain behavior
  with annular tubules D39.1-
skin appendage - *see* Neoplasm, skin, benign
smooth muscle - *see* Neoplasm, connective tissue, uncertain behavior
soft tissue
  benign - *see* Neoplasm, connective tissue, benign
  malignant - *see* Neoplasm, connective tissue, malignant
sternomastoid (congenital) Q68.0
stromal
  gastric D48.1
    benign D21.4
    malignant C16.9
    uncertain behavior D48.1
  gastrointestinal
    benign D21.4
    malignant C49.4
    uncertain behavior D48.1
  intestine
    benign D21.4
    malignant C49.4
    uncertain behavior D48.1
  ovarian D39.1-
  stomach
    benign D21.4
    malignant C16.9
    uncertain behavior D48.1
testicular D40.10
sweat gland - *see also* Neoplasm, skin, uncertain behavior
  benign - *see* Neoplasm, skin, benign
  malignant - *see* Neoplasm, skin, malignant
syphilitic, brain A52.17
testicular stromal D40.1-
theca cell D27.-
theca cell-granulosa cell D39.1-
Triton, malignant - *see* Neoplasm, nerve, malignant
trophoblastic, placental site D39.2
turban D23.4
uterus (body), in pregnancy or childbirth - *see* Pregnancy, complicated by, tumor, uterus
vagina, in pregnancy or childbirth - *see* Pregnancy, complicated by
varicose - *see* Varix
von Recklinghausen's - *see* Neurofibromatosis
vulva or perineum, in pregnancy or childbirth - *see* Pregnancy, complicated by
  causing obstructed labor O65.5

Tumor *(Continued)*
  Warthin's - *see* Neoplasm, salivary
      gland, benign
  Wilms' C64.-
    yolk sac - *see* Neoplasm, malignant
      specified site - *see* Neoplasm,
        malignant
      unspecified site
        female C56.9
        male C62.90
Tumor lysis syndrome (following
      antineoplastic chemotherapy)
      (spontaneous) NEC E88.3
Tumorlet - *see* Neoplasm, uncertain
      behavior
Tungiasis B88.1
Tunica vasculosa lentis Q12.2
Turban tumor D23.4
Türck's trachoma J37.0
Turner-Kieser syndrome Q79.8
Turner-like syndrome Q87.1
Turner's
  hypoplasia (tooth) K00.4
  syndrome Q96.9
    specified NEC Q96.8
  tooth K00.4
Turner-Ullrich syndrome Q96.9
Tussis convulsiva - *see* Whooping cough
Twiddler's syndrome (due to)
  automatic implantable defibrillator
      T82.198
  cardiac pacemaker T82.198
Twilight state
  epileptic F05
  psychogenic F44.89
Twin (newborn) – *see also* Newborn, twin
  complicating pregnancy – *see* Preg-
      nancy, complicated by, multiple
      gestations, conjoined twin
  conjoined Q89.4
Twinning, teeth K00.2
Twist, twisted
  bowel, colon or intestine K56.2
  hair (congenital) Q84.1
  mesentery K56.2

Twist, twisted *(Continued)*
  omentum K56.2
  organ or site, congenital NEC - *see*
      Anomaly, by site
  ovarian pedicle – *see* Torsion, ovary
Twitching R25.3
Tylosis (acquired) L84
  buccalis K13.29
  linguae K13.29
  palmaris et plantaris (congenital) (in-
      herited) Q82.8
    acquired L85.1
Tympanism R14.0
Tympanites (abdominal) (intestinal) R14.0
Tympanitis - *see* Myringitis
Tympanosclerosis - *see* subcategory H74.0
Tympanum - *see* condition
Tympany
  abdomen R14.0
  chest R09.89
Type A behavior pattern Z73.1
Typhlitis - *see* Appendicitis
Typhoenteritis - *see* Typhoid
Typhoid (abortive) (ambulant) (any
      site) (clinical) (fever) (hemorrhagic)
      (infection) (intermittent) (malignant)
      (rheumatic) (Widal negative) A01.00
  with pneumonia A01.03
  abdominal A01.09
  arthritis A01.04
  carrier (suspected) of Z22.0
  cholecystitis (current) A01.09
  endocarditis A01.02
  heart involvement A01.02
  inoculation reaction - *see* Complications,
      vaccination
  meningitis A01.01
  mesenteric lymph nodes A01.09
  myocarditis A01.02
  osteomyelitis A01.05
  perichondritis, larynx A01.09
  pneumonia A01.03
  spine A01.05
  specified NEC A01.09
  ulcer (perforating) A01.09

Typhomalaria (fever) - *see* Malaria
Typhomania A01.00
Typhoperitonitis A01.09
Typhus (fever) A75.9
  abdominal, abdominalis - *see* Typhoid
  African tick A77.1
  amarillic A95.9
  brain A75.9 [G94]
  cerebral A75.9 [G94]
  classical A75.0
  due to Rickettsia
    prowazekii A75.0
      recrudescent A75.1
    tsutsugamushi A75.3
    typhi A75.2
  endemic (flea-borne) A75.2
  epidemic (louse-borne) A75.0
  exanthematic NEC A75.0
  exanthematicus SAI A75.0
    brillii SAI A75.1
    mexicanus SAI A75.2
    typhus murinus A75.2
  flea-borne A75.2
  India tick A77.1
  Kenya (tick) A77.1
  louse-borne A75.0
  Mexican A75.2
  mite-borne A75.3
  murine A75.2
  North Asian tick-borne A77.2
  petechial A75.9
  Queensland tick A77.3
  rat A75.2
  recrudescent A75.1
  recurrens - *see* Fever, relapsing
  Sao Paulo A77.0
  scrub (China) (India) (Malaysia) (New
      Guinea) A75.3
  shop (of Malaysia) A75.2
  Siberian tick A77.2
  tick-borne A77.9
  tropical (mite-borne) A75.3
Tyrosinemia E70.21
  newborn, transitory P74.5
Tyrosinosis E70.21
Tyrosinuria E70.29

U

Uhl's anomaly or disease Q24.8

Ulcer, ulcerated, ulcerating, ulceration, ulcerative
- alveolar process M27.3
- amebic (intestine) A06.1
  - skin A06.7
- anastomotic - *see* Ulcer, gastrojejunal
- anorectal K62.6
- antral - *see* Ulcer, stomach
- anus (sphincter) (solitary) K62.6
  - varicose - *see* Varicose, ulcer, anus
- aorta - *see* Aneurysm
- aphthous (oral) (recurrent) K12.0
  - genital organ(s)
    - female N76.6
    - male N50.8
- artery I77.2
- atrophic - *see* Ulcer, skin
  - decubitus - *see* Ulcer, pressure, by site
- Barrett's (esophagus) K22.10
  - with bleeding K22.11
- bile duct (common) (hepatic) K83.8
- bladder (solitary) (sphincter) NEC N32.89
  - bilharzial B65.9 *[N33]*
  - in schistosomiasis (bilharzial) B65.9 *[N33]*
  - submucosal - *see* Cystitis, interstitial
  - tuberculous A18.12
- bleeding K27.4
- bone - *see* Osteomyelitis, specified type NEC
- bowel - *see* Ulcer, intestine
- breast N61
- bronchus J98.09
- buccal (cavity) (traumatic) K12.1
- Buruli A31.1
- cancerous - *see* Neoplasm, malignant
- cardia K22.10
  - with bleeding K22.11
- cardioesophageal (peptic) K22.10
  - with bleeding K22.11
- cecum - *see* Ulcer, intestine
- cervix (uteri) (decubitus) (trophic) N86
  - with cervicitis N72
- chancroidal A57
- chiclero B55.1
- chronic (cause unknown) - *see* Ulcer, skin
- Cochin-China B55.1
- colon - *see* Ulcer, intestine
- conjunctiva H10.89
- cornea H16.00-
  - with hypopyon H16.03-
  - central H16.01-
  - dendritic (herpes simplex) B00.52
  - marginal H16.04-
  - Mooren's H16.05-
  - mycotic H16.06-
  - perforated H16.07-
  - ring H16.02-
  - tuberculous (phlyctenular) A18.52
- corpus cavernosum (chronic) N48.5
- crural - *see* Ulcer, lower limb
- Curling's - *see* Ulcer, peptic, acute
- Cushing's - *see* Ulcer, peptic, acute
- cystic duct K82.8
- cystitis (interstitial) - *see* Cystitis, interstitial
- decubitus - *see* Ulcer, pressure, by site
- dendritic, cornea (herpes simplex) B00.52

Ulcer, ulcerated, ulcerating, ulceration, ulcerative *(Continued)*
- diabetes, diabetic - *see* Diabetes, ulcer
- Dieulafoy's K25.0
- due to
  - infection NEC - *see* Ulcer, skin
  - radiation NEC L59.8
  - trophic disturbance (any region) - *see* Ulcer, skin
  - X-ray L58.1
- duodenum, duodenal (eroded) (peptic) K26.9
  - with
    - hemorrhage K26.4
      - and perforation K26.6
    - perforation K26.5
  - acute K26.3
    - with
      - hemorrhage K26.0
        - and perforation K26.2
      - perforation K26.1
  - chronic K26.7
    - with
      - hemorrhage K26.4
        - and perforation K26.6
      - perforation K26.5
- dysenteric A09
- elusive - *see* Cystitis, interstitial
- endocarditis (acute) (chronic) (subacute) I28.8
- epiglottis J38.7
- esophagus (peptic) K22.10
  - with bleeding K22.11
  - due to
    - aspirin K22.10
      - with bleeding K22.11
    - gastrointestinal reflux disease K21.0
    - ingestion of chemical or medicament K22.10
      - with bleeding K22.11
    - fungal K22.10
      - with bleeding K22.11
    - infective K22.10
      - with bleeding K22.11
  - varicose - *see* Varix, esophagus
- eyelid (region) H01.8
- fauces J39.2
- Fenwick (-Hunner) (solitary) - *see* Cystitis, interstitial
- fistulous - *see* Ulcer, skin
- foot (indolent) (trophic) - *see* Ulcer, lower limb
- frambesial, initial A66.0
- frenum (tongue) K14.0
- gallbladder or duct K82.8
- gangrenous - *see* Gangrene
- gastric - *see* Ulcer, stomach
- gastrocolic - *see* Ulcer, gastrojejunal
- gastroduodenal - *see* Ulcer, peptic
- gastroesophageal - *see* Ulcer, stomach
- gastrointestinal - *see* Ulcer, gastrojejunal
- gastrojejunal (peptic) K28.9
  - with
    - hemorrhage K28.4
      - and perforation K28.6
    - perforation K28.5
  - acute K28.3
    - with
      - hemorrhage K28.0
        - and perforation K28.2
      - perforation K28.1

Ulcer, ulcerated, ulcerating, ulceration, ulcerative *(Continued)*
- gastrojejunal *(Continued)*
  - chronic K28.7
    - with
      - hemorrhage K28.4
        - and perforation K28.6
      - perforation K28.5
- gastrojejunocolic - *see* Ulcer, gastrojejunal
- gingiva K06.8
- gingivitis K05.10
  - plaque induced K05.10
  - nonplaque induced K05.11
- glottis J38.7
- granuloma of pudenda A58
- gum K06.8
- gumma, due to yaws A66.4
- heel - *see* Ulcer, lower limb
- hemorrhoids - *see* Hemorrhoids
- Hunner's - *see* Cystitis, interstitial
- hypopharynx J39.2
- hypopyon (chronic) (subacute) - *see* Ulcer, cornea, with hypopyon
- hypostaticum - *see* Ulcer, varicose
- ileum - *see* Ulcer, intestine
- intestine, intestinal K63.3
  - with perforation K63.1
  - amebic A06.1
  - duodenal - *see* Ulcer, duodenum
  - granulocytopenic (with hemorrhage) - *see* Neutropenia
  - marginal - *see* Ulcer, gastrojejunal
  - perforating K63.1
    - newborn P78.0
  - primary, small intestine K63.3
  - rectum K62.6
  - stercoraceous, stercoral K63.3
  - tuberculous A18.32
  - typhoid (fever) - *see* Typhoid
  - varicose I86.8
- jejunum, jejunal - *see* Ulcer, gastrojejunal
- keratitis - *see* Ulcer, cornea
- knee - *see* Ulcer, lower limb
- labium (majus) (minus) N76.6
- laryngitis - *see* Laryngitis
- larynx (aphthous) (contact) J38.7
  - diphtheritic A36.2
- leg - *see* Ulcer, lower limb
- lip K13.0
- Lipschütz's N76.6
- lower limb (atrophic) (chronic) (neurogenic) (perforating) (pyogenic) (trophic) (tropical) L97.909
  - with
    - bone necrosis L97.904
    - exposed fat layer L97.902
    - muscle necrosis L97.903
    - skin breakdown only L97.901
  - ankle L97.309
    - with
      - bone necrosis L97.304
      - exposed fat layer L97.302
      - muscle necrosis L97.303
      - skin breakdown only L97.301
    - left L97.329
      - with
        - bone necrosis L97.324
        - exposed fat layer L97.322
        - muscle necrosis L97.323
        - skin breakdown only L97.321

Ulcer, ulcerated, ulcerating, ulceration,
ulcerative (Continued)
 lower limb (Continued)
  ankle (Continued)
   right L97.319
    with
     bone necrosis L97.314
     exposed fat layer L97.312
     muscle necrosis L97.313
     skin breakdown only
      L97.311
  calf L97.209
   with
    bone necrosis L97.204
    exposed fat layer L97.202
    muscle necrosis L97.203
    skin breakdown only L97.201
   left L97.229
    with
     bone necrosis L97.224
     exposed fat layer L97.222
     muscle necrosis L97.223
     skin breakdown only L97.221
   right L97.219
    with
     bone necrosis L97.214
     exposed fat layer L97.212
     muscle necrosis L97.213
     skin breakdown only L97.211
  decubitus - see Ulcer, pressure,
   by site
  foot specified NEC L97.509
   with
    bone necrosis L97.504
    exposed fat layer L97.502
    muscle necrosis L97.503
    skin breakdown only L97.501
   left L97.529
    with
     bone necrosis L97.524
     exposed fat layer L97.522
     muscle necrosis L97.523
     skin breakdown only
      L97.521
   right L97.519
    with
     bone necrosis L97.514
     exposed fat layer L97.512
     muscle necrosis L97.513
     skin breakdown only L97.511
  heel L97.409
   with
    bone necrosis L97.404
    exposed fat layer L97.402
    muscle necrosis L97.403
    skin breakdown only L97.401
   left L97.429
    with
     bone necrosis L97.424
     exposed fat layer L97.422
     muscle necrosis L97.423
     skin breakdown only L97.421
   right L97.419
    with
     bone necrosis L97.414
     exposed fat layer L97.412
     muscle necrosis L97.413
     skin breakdown only L97.411
  left L97.929
   with
    bone necrosis L97.924
    exposed fat layer L97.922
    muscle necrosis L97.923
    skin breakdown only L97.921

Ulcer, ulcerated, ulcerating, ulceration,
ulcerative (Continued)
 lower limb (Continued)
  lower leg NOS L97.909
   with
    bone necrosis L97.904
    exposed fat layer L97.902
    muscle necrosis L97.903
    skin breakdown only L97.901
   left L97.929
    with
     bone necrosis L97.924
     exposed fat layer L97.922
     muscle necrosis L97.923
     skin breakdown only
      L97.921
   right L97.919
    with
     bone necrosis L97.914
     exposed fat layer L97.912
     muscle necrosis L97.913
     skin breakdown only L97.911
  specified site NEC L97.809
   with
    bone necrosis L97.804
    exposed fat layer L97.802
    muscle necrosis L97.803
    skin breakdown only
     L97.801
   left L97.829
    with
     bone necrosis L97.824
     exposed fat layer L97.822
     muscle necrosis L97.823
     skin breakdown only
      L97.821
   right L97.819
    with
     bone necrosis L97.814
     exposed fat layer L97.812
     muscle necrosis L97.813
     skin breakdown only
      L97.811
  midfoot L97.409
   with
    bone necrosis L97.404
    exposed fat layer L97.402
    muscle necrosis L97.403
    skin breakdown only L97.401
   left L97.429
    with
     bone necrosis L97.424
     exposed fat layer L97.422
     muscle necrosis L97.423
     skin breakdown only
      L97.421
   right L97.419
    with
     bone necrosis L97.414
     exposed fat layer L97.412
     muscle necrosis L97.413
     skin breakdown only L97.411
  right L97.919
   with
    bone necrosis L97.914
    exposed fat layer L97.912
    muscle necrosis L97.913
    skin breakdown only L97.911
  thigh L97.109
   with
    bone necrosis L97.104
    exposed fat layer L97.102
    muscle necrosis L97.103
    skin breakdown only L97.101

Ulcer, ulcerated, ulcerating, ulceration,
ulcerative (Continued)
 lower limb (Continued)
  thigh (Continued)
   left L97.129
    with
     bone necrosis L97.124
     exposed fat layer L97.122
     muscle necrosis L97.123
     skin breakdown only L97.121
   right L97.119
    with
     bone necrosis L97.114
     exposed fat layer L97.112
     muscle necrosis L97.113
     skin breakdown only L97.111
  toe L97.509
   with
    bone necrosis L97.504
    exposed fat layer L97.502
    muscle necrosis L97.503
    skin breakdown only L97.501
   left L97.529
    with
     bone necrosis L97.524
     exposed fat layer L97.522
     muscle necrosis L97.523
     skin breakdown only L97.521
   right L97.519
    with
     bone necrosis L97.514
     exposed fat layer L97.512
     muscle necrosis L97.513
     skin breakdown only
      L97.511
  leprous A30.1
  syphilitic A52.19
  varicose - see Varix, leg, with, ulcer
 luetic - see Ulcer, syphilitic
 lung J98.4
  tuberculous - see Tuberculosis,
   pulmonary
 malignant - see Neoplasm, malignant
 marginal NEC - see Ulcer,
  gastrojejunal
 meatus (urinarius) N34.2
 Meckel's diverticulum Q43.0
 Meleney's (chronic undermining) –
  see Ulcer, skin
 Mooren's (cornea) - see Ulcer, cornea,
  Mooren's
 mycobacterial (skin) A31.1
 nasopharynx J39.2
 neck, uterus N86
 neurogenic NEC - see Ulcer, skin
 nose, nasal (passage) (infective)
  (septum) J34.0
  skin - see Ulcer, skin
  spirochetal A69.8
  varicose (bleeding) I86.8
 oral mucosa (traumatic) K12.1
 palate (soft) K12.1
 penis (chronic) N48.5
 peptic (site unspecified) K27.9
  with
   hemorrhage K27.4
    and perforation K27.6
   perforation K27.5
  acute K27.3
   with
    hemorrhage K27.0
     and perforation K27.2
    perforation K27.1

Ulcer, ulcerated, ulcerating, ulceration, ulcerative (Continued)
tunica vaginalis N50.8
turbinate J34.89
typhoid (perforating) - see Typhoid
unspecified site - see Ulcer, skin
urethra (meatus) - see Urethritis
uterus N85.8
cervix N86
with cervicitis N72
neck N86
with cervicitis N72
vagina N76.5
in Behçet's disease M35.2 [N77.0]
pessary N89.8
valve, heart I33.0
varicose (lower limb, any part) - see also
Varix, leg, with, ulcer
anus - see Varicose, ulcer, anus
broad ligament I86.2
esophagus - see Varix, esophagus
inflamed or infected - see Varix, leg,
with ulcer, with inflammation
nasal septum I86.8
perineum I86.3
rectum - see Varicose, ulcer, anus
scrotum I86.1
specified site NEC I86.8
sublingual I86.0
vulva I86.3
vas deferens N50.8
vulva (acute) (infectional) N76.6
in (due to)
Behçet's disease M35.2 [N77.0]
herpesviral (herpes simplex)
infection A60.04
tuberculosis A18.18
vulvobuccal, recurring N76.6
X-ray L58.1
yaws A66.4
Ulcerosa scarlatina A38.8
Ulcus - see also Ulcer
cutis tuberculosum A18.4
duodeni - see Ulcer, duodenum
durum (syphilitic) A51.0
extragenital A51.2
gastrojejunale - see Ulcer, gastrojejunal
hypostaticum - see Ulcer, varicose
molle (cutis) (skin) A57
serpens corneae - see Ulcer, cornea,
central
ventriculi - see Ulcer, stomach
Ulegyria Q04.8
Ulerythema
ophryogenes, congenital Q84.2
sycosiforme L73.8
Ullrich(-Bonnevie)(-Turner) syndrome
Q87.1
Ullrich-Feichtiger syndrome Q87.0
Ulnar - see condition
Ulorrhagia, ulorrhea K06.8
Umbilicus, umbilical - see condition
Unacceptable
contours of tooth K08.54
morphology of tooth K08.54
Unavailability (of)
bed at medical facility Z75.1
health service-related agencies
Z75.4
medical facilities (at) Z75.3
due to
investigation by social service
agency Z75.2
lack of services at home Z75.0

Unavailability (Continued)
medical facilities (Continued)
due to (Continued)
remoteness from facility Z75.3
waiting list Z75.1
home Z75.0
outpatient clinic Z75.3
schooling Z55.1
social service agencies Z75.4
Uncinaria americana infestation
B76.9
Uncinariasis B76.9
Uncongenial work Z56.5
Unconscious(ness) - see Coma
Under observation - see Observation
Underachievement in school Z55.3
Underdevelopment - see also
Undeveloped
nose Q30.1
sexual E30.0
Underdosing Z91.14 - see also Table of
drugs and chemicals, categories
T36-T50, with final character 6
intentional NEC Z91.128
due to financial hardship of patient
Z91.120
unintentional NEC Z91.138
due to patient's age related debility
Z91.130
Underfeeding, newborn P92.3
Underfill, endodontic M27.53
Underimmunization status Z28.3
Undernourishment - see Malnutrition
Undernutrition - see Malnutrition
Underweight R63.6
for gestational age - see Light for dates
Underwood's disease P83.0
Undescended - see also Malposition,
congenital
cecum Q43.3
colon Q43.3
testicle – see Cryptorchid
Undetermined cause R69
Undeveloped, undevelopment - see also
Hypoplasia
brain (congenital) Q02
cerebral (congenital) Q02
heart Q24.8
lung Q33.6
testis E29.1
uterus E30.0
Undiagnosed (disease) R69
Undulant fever - see Brucellosis
Unemployment, anxiety concerning Z56.0
threatened Z56.2
Unequal length (acquired) (limb) - see also
Deformity, limb, unequal length
leg - see also Deformity, limb, unequal
length
congenital Q72.9-
Unextracted dental root K08.3
Unguis incarnatus L60.0
Unhappiness R45.2
Unicornate uterus Q51.4
Unilateral - see also condition
development, breast N64.89
organ or site, congenital NEC - see
Agenesis, by site
Unilocular heart Q20.8
Union, abnormal - see also Fusion
larynx and trachea Q34.8
Universal mesentery Q43.3
Unknown cause, morbidity R69

Unrepairable overhanging of dental
restorative materials K08.52
Unsatisfactory
restoration of tooth K08.50
specified NEC K08.59
sample of cytologic smear
anus R85.615
cervix R87.615
vagina R87.625
surroundings Z59.1
work Z56.5
Unsoundness of mind - see Psychosis
Unspecified cause, morbidity R69
Unstable
back NEC - see Instability, joint, spine
hip (congenital) Q65.6
acquired - see Derangement, joint,
specified type NEC, hip
joint - see Instability, joint
secondary to removal of joint prosthesis M96.89
lie (mother) O32.0
lumbosacral joint (congenital)
acquired - see subcategory M53.2
sacroiliac - see subcategory M53.2
spine NEC - see Instability, joint, spine
Unsteadiness on feet R26.81
Untruthfulness, child problem F91.8
Unverricht(-Lundborg) disease or
epilepsy - see Epilepsy, generalized,
idiopathic
Unwanted pregnancy Z64.0
Upbringing, institutional Z62.22
away from parents NEC Z62.29
in care of non-parental family member
Z62.21
in foster care Z62.21
in orphanage or group home Z62.22
in welfare custody Z62.21
Upper respiratory - see condition
Upset
gastric K30
gastrointestinal K30
psychogenic F45.8
intestinal (large) (small) K59.9
psychogenic F45.8
menstruation N93.9
mental F48.9
stomach K30
psychogenic F45.8
Urachus - see also condition
patent or persistent Q64.4
Urbach-Oppenheim disease E88.89
Urbach's lipoid proteinosis E78.89
Urbach-Wiethe disease E78.89
Urban yellow fever A95.1
Urea
blood, high - see Uremia
cycle metabolism disorder – see
Disorder, urea cycle metabolism
Uremia, uremic N19
with
ectopic or molar pregnancy O08.4
polyneuropathy N19 [G63]
chronic (see also Disease, kidney,
chronic) N18.9
due to hypertension - see
Hypertensive
complicating
ectopic or molar pregnancy O08.4
congenital P96.0
extrarenal R39.2
following ectopic or molar pregnancy
O08.4

Uremia, uremic (Continued)
  newborn P96.0
  prerenal R39.2
Ureter, ureteral - see condition
Ureteralgia N23
Ureterectasis - see Hydroureter
Ureteritis N28.89
  cystica N28.86
  due to calculus N20.1
    with calculus, kidney N20.2
      with hydronephrosis N13.2
  gonococcal (acute) (chronic)
    A54.21
  nonspecific N28.89
Ureterocele N28.89
  congenital (orthotopic) Q62.31
    ectopic Q62.32
Ureterolith, ureterolithiasis - see
    Calculus, ureter
Ureterostomy
  attention to Z43.6
  status Z93.6
Urethra, urethral - see condition
Urethralgia R39.89
Urethritis (anterior) (posterior) N34.2
  calculous N21.1
  candidal B37.41
  chlamydial A56.01
  diplococcal (gonococcal) A54.01
    with abscess (accessory gland)
      (periurethral) A54.1
  gonococcal A54.01
    with abscess (accessory gland)
      (periurethral) A54.1
  nongonococcal N34.1
    Reiter's - see Reiter's disease
  nonspecific N34.1
  nonvenereal N34.1
  postmenopausal N34.2
  puerperal O86.29
  Reiter's - see Reiter's disease
  specified NEC N34.2
  trichomonal or due to Trichomonas
    (vaginalis) A59.03
Urethrocele N81.0
  with
    cystocele - see Cystocele
    prolapse of uterus - see Prolapse,
      uterus
Urethrolithiasis (with colic or infection)
    N21.1
Urethrorectal - see condition
Urethrorrhagia N36.8
Urethrorrhea R36.9
Urethrostomy
  attention to Z43.6
  status Z93.6
Urethrotrigonitis - see Trigonitis
Urethrovaginal - see condition
Urhidrosis, uridrosis L74.8
Uric acid in blood (increased)
    E79.0
Uricacidemia (asymptomatic) E79.0
Uricemia (asymptomatic) E79.0
Uricosuria R82.99
Urinary - see condition
Urination
  frequent R35.0
  painful R30.9
Urine
  blood in - see Hematuria
  discharge, excessive R35.8
  enuresis, nonorganic origin F98.0
  extravasation R39.0

Urine (Continued)
  frequency R35.0
  incontinence R32
    nonorganic origin F98.0
  intermittent stream R39.19
  pus in N39.0
  retention or stasis R33.9
    organic R33.8
      drug-induced R33.0
    psychogenic F45.8
  secretion
    deficient R34
    excessive R35.8
    frequency R35.0
  stream
    intermittent R39.19
    slowing R39.19
    splitting R39.13
    weak R39.12
Urinemia - see Uremia
Urinoma, urethra N36.8
Uroarthritis, infectious (Reiter's) -
    see Reiter's disease
Urodialysis R34
Urolithiasis - see Calculus, urinary
Uronephrosis - see Hydronephrosis
Uropathy N39.9
  obstructive N13.9
    specified NEC N13.8
  reflux N13.9
    specified NEC N13.8
  vesicoureteral reflux-associated -
    see Reflux, vesicoureteral
Urosepsis - code to condition
Urticaria L50.9
  with angioneurotic edema T78.3
    hereditary D84.1
  allergic L50.0
  cholinergic L50.5
  chronic L50.8
  cold, familial L50.2
  contact L50.6
  dermatographic L50.3
  due to
    cold or heat L50.2
    drugs L50.0
    food L50.0
    inhalants L50.0
    plants L50.6
    serum T80.6
  factitial L50.3
  giant T78.3
    hereditary D84.1
  gigantea T78.3
  idiopathic L50.1
  larynx T78.3
    hereditary D84.1
  neonatorum P83.8
  nonallergic L50.1
  papulosa (Hebra) L28.2
  pigmentosa Q82.2
  recurrent periodic L50.8
  serum T80.6
  solar L56.3
  specified type NEC L50.8
  thermal (cold) (heat) L50.2
  vibratory L50.4
  xanthelasmoidea Q82.2
Use (of)
  alcohol F10.99
    with sleep disorder F10.982
    harmful – see Abuse, alcohol
  amphetamines - see Use, stimulant
    NEC

Use (Continued)
  caffeine - see Use, stimulant NEC
  cocaine F14.90
    with sleep disorder F14.982
    harmful - see Abuse, drug, cocaine
  drug(s) NEC F19.90
    with sleep disorder F19.982
    harmful - see Abuse, drug, by type
  inhalants F18.90
    harmful – see Abuse, drug, inhalant
  methadone F11.20
  nonprescribed drugs F19.90
    harmful – see Abuse, non-
      psychoactive substance
  opioid F11.90
    with sleep disorder F11.982
    harmful - see Abuse, drug, opioid
  patent medicines F19.90
    harmful – see Abuse, non-
      psychoactive substance
  psychoactive drug NEC F19.90
    with sleep disorder F19.982
    harmful - see Abuse, drug NEC,
      psychoactive NEC
  sedative, hypnotic, or anxiolytic
    F13.90
    with sleep disorder F13.982
    harmful - see Abuse, drug,
      sedative, hypnotic, or
      anxiolytic
  stimulant NEC F15.90
    with sleep disorder F15.982
    harmful - see Abuse, drug, stimulant
      NEC
  volatile solvents F18.90
    harmful – see Abuse, drug, inhalant
  tobacco Z72.0
    with dependence - see Dependence,
      drug, nicotine
Usher-Senear disease or syndrome
    L10.4
Uta B55.1
Uteromegaly N85.2
Uterovaginal - see condition
Uterovesical - see condition
Uveal - see condition
Uveitis (anterior) - see also
    Iridocyclitis
  acute - see Iridocyclitis, acute
  chronic - see Iridocyclitis, chronic
  due to toxoplasmosis (acquired)
    B58.09
    congenital P37.1
  granulomatous - see Iridocyclitis,
    chronic
  heterochromic - see Cyclitis, Fuchs'
    heterochromic
  lens-induced - see Iridocyclitis,
    lens-induced
  posterior - see Chorioretinitis
  sympathetic H44.13-
  syphilitic (secondary) A51.43
    congenital (early) A50.01
    late A52.71
  tuberculous A18.54
Uveoencephalitis - see Inflammation,
    chorioretinal
Uveokeratitis - see Iridocyclitis
Uveoparotitis D86.89
Uvula - see condition
Uvulitis (acute) (catarrhal) (chronic)
    (membranous) (suppurative)
    (ulcerative) K12.2

V

Vaccination (prophylactic)
   complication or reaction - *see* Complications, vaccination
   delayed Z28.9
   encounter for Z23
   not done - *see* Immunization, not done, because (of)
Vaccinia (generalized) (localized) T88.1
   congenital P35.8
   without vaccination B08.011
Vacuum, in sinus (accessory) (nasal) J34.89
Vagabond, vagabondage Z59.0
Vagabond's disease B85.1
Vagina, vaginal - *see* condition
Vaginalitis (tunica) (testis) N49.1
Vaginismus (reflex) N94.2
   functional F52.5
   nonorganic F52.5
   psychogenic F52.5
   secondary N94.2
Vaginitis (acute) (circumscribed) (diffuse) (emphysematous) (nonvenereal) (ulcerative) N76.0
   with ectopic or molar pregnancy O08.0
   amebic A06.82
   atrophic, postmenopausal N95.2
   bacterial N76.0
   blennorrhagic (gonococcal) A54.02
   candidal B37.3
   chlamydial A56.02
   chronic N76.1
   due to Trichomonas (vaginalis) A59.01
   following ectopic or molar pregnancy O08.0
   gonococcal A54.02
      with abscess (accessory gland) (periurethral) A54.1
   granuloma A58
   in (due to)
      candidiasis B37.3
      herpesviral (herpes simplex) infection A60.04
      pinworm infection B80 *[N77.1]*
   monilial B37.3
   mycotic (candidal) B37.3
   postmenopausal atrophic N95.2
   puerperal (postpartum) O86.13
   senile (atrophic) N95.2
   subacute or chronic N76.1
   syphilitic (early) A51.0
      late A52.76
   trichomonal A59.01
   tuberculous A18.18
Vaginosis - *see* Vaginitis
Vagotonia G52.2
Vagrancy Z59.0
VAIN - *see* Neoplasia, intraepithelial, vagina
Vallecula - *see* condition
Valley fever B38.0
Valsuani's disease - *see* Anemia, obstetric
Valve, valvular (formation) - *see also* condition
   cerebral ventricle (communicating) in situ Z98.2
   cervix, internal os Q51.8
   congenital NEC - *see* Atresia, by site
   ureter (pelvic junction) (vesical orifice) Q62.39
   urethra (congenital) (posterior) Q64.2
Valvulitis (chronic) - *see* Endocarditis

Valvulopathy - *see* Endocarditis
Van Bogaert's leukoencephalopathy (sclerosing) (subacute) A81.1
Van Bogaert-Scherer-Epstein disease or syndrome E75.5
Van Buchem's syndrome M85.2
Van Creveld-von Gierke disease E74.01
Van der Hoeve(-de Kleyn) syndrome Q78.0
Van der Woude's syndrome Q38.0
Van Neck's disease or osteochondrosis M91.0
Vanishing lung J44.9
Vapor asphyxia or suffocation T59.9
   specified agent - *see* Table of drugs and chemicals
Variance, lethal ball, prosthetic heart valve T82.09
Variants, thalassemic D56.8
Variations in hair color L67.1
Varicella B01.9
   with
      complications NEC B01.89
      encephalitis B01.11
      encephalomyelitis B01.11
      meningitis B01.0
      myelitis B01.12
      pneumonia B01.2
   congenital P35.8
Varices - *see* Varix
Varicocele (scrotum) (thrombosed) I86.1
   ovary I86.2
   perineum I86.3
   spermatic cord (ulcerated) I86.1
Varicose
   aneurysm (ruptured) I77.0
   dermatitis - *see* Varix, leg, with, inflammation
   eczema - *see* Varix, leg, with, inflammation
   phlebitis - *see* Varix, with, inflammation
   tumor - *see* Varix
   ulcer (lower limb, any part) - *see also* Varix, leg, with, ulcer
      anus - *see* Hemorrhoids, with complication
      esophagus - *see* Varix, esophagus
      inflamed or infected - *see* Varix, leg, with ulcer, with inflammation
      nasal septum I86.8
      perineum I86.3
      rectum - *see* Varicose, ulcer, anus
      scrotum I86.1
      specified site NEC I86.8
   vein – *see* Varix
   vessel - *see* Varix, leg
Varicosis, varicosities, varicosity - *see* Varix
Variola (major) (minor) B03
Varioloid B03
Varix (lower limb) (ruptured) I83.90
   with
      edema I83.899
      inflammation I83.10
         with ulcer (venous) I83.209
      pain I83.819
      specified complication NEC I83.899
      stasis dermatitis I83.10
         with ulcer (venous) I83.209
      swelling I83.899
      ulcer I83.009
         with inflammation I83.209
   aneurysmal I77.0
   anus - *see* Hemorrhoids
   asymptomatic I83.9-

Varix *(Continued)*
   bladder I86.2
   broad ligament I86.2
   complicating
      childbirth (lower extremity) O87.4
         anus or rectum O87.2
         genital (vagina, vulva or perineum) O87.8
      pregnancy (lower extremity) O22.0-
         anus or rectum O22.4-
         genital (vagina, vulva or perineum) O22.1-
      puerperium (lower extremity) O87.4
         anus or rectum O87.2
         genital (vagina, vulva, perineum) O87.8
   congenital (any site) Q27.8
   esophagus (idiopathic) (primary) (ulcerated) I85.00
      bleeding I85.01
      congenital Q27.8
      in (due to)
         alcoholic liver disease I85.10
            bleeding I85.11
         cirrhosis of liver I85.10
            bleeding I85.11
         portal hypertension I85.10
            bleeding I85.11
         schistosomiasis I85.10
            bleeding I85.11
         toxic liver disease I85.10
            bleeding I85.11
      secondary I85.10
         bleeding I85.11
   gastric I86.4
   inflamed or infected I83.10
      ulcerated I83.209
   labia (majora) I86.3
   leg (asymptomatic) I83.90
      with
         edema I83.899
         inflammation I83.10
            with ulcer - *see* Varix, leg, with, ulcer, with inflammation by site
         pain I83.819
         specified complication NEC I83.899
         swelling I83.899
         ulcer I83.009
            with inflammation I83.209
            ankle I83.003
               with inflammation I83.203
            calf I83.002
               with inflammation I83.202
            foot NEC I83.005
               with inflammation I83.205
            heel I83.004
               with inflammation I83.204
            lower leg NEC I83.008
               with inflammation I83.208
            midfoot I83.004
               with inflammation I83.204
            thigh I83.001
               with inflammation I83.201
      bilateral (asymptomatic) I83.93
         with
            edema I83.893
            pain I83.813
            specified complication NEC I83.893
            swelling I83.893
            ulcer I83.009
               with inflammation I83.209

Varix *(Continued)*
  leg *(Continued)*
    left (asymptomatic) I83.92
      with
        edema I83.892
        pain I83.812
        specified complication NEC
          I83.892
        swelling I83.892
        inflammation I83.12
          with ulcer - *see* Varix, leg,
            with, ulcer, with
            inflammation by site
        ulcer I83.029
          with inflammation I83.229
          ankle I83.023
            with inflammation
              I83.223
          calf I83.022
            with inflammation
              I83.222
          foot NEC I83.025
            with inflammation
              I83.225
          heel I83.024
            with inflammation
              I83.224
          lower leg NEC I83.028
            with inflammation
              I83.228
          midfoot I83.024
            with inflammation
              I83.224
          thigh I83.021
            with inflammation
              I83.221
    right (asymptomatic) I83.91
      with
        edema I83.891
        pain I83.811
        specified complication NEC
          I83.891
        swelling I83.891
        inflammation I83.11
          with ulcer - *see* Varix, leg,
            with, ulcer, with
            inflammation by site
        ulcer I83.019
          with inflammation I83.219
          ankle I83.013
            with inflammation
              I83.213
          calf I83.012
            with inflammation
              I83.212
          foot NEC I83.015
            with inflammation
              I83.215
          heel I83.014
            with inflammation
              I83.214
          lower leg NEC I83.018
            with inflammation
              I83.218
          midfoot I83.014
            with inflammation
              I83.214
          thigh I83.011
            with inflammation
              I83.211
  nasal septum I86.8
  orbit I86.8
    congenital Q27.8
  ovary I86.2

Varix *(Continued)*
  papillary I78.1
  pelvis I86.2
  perineum I86.3
  pharynx I86.8
  placenta O43.89-
  rectum - *see* Hemorrhoids, internal
  renal papilla I86.8
  retina H35.09
  scrotum (ulcerated) I86.1
  sigmoid colon I86.8
  specified site NEC I86.8
  spinal (cord) (vessels) I86.8
  spleen, splenic (vein) (with phlebolith)
    I86.8
  stomach I86.4
  sublingual I86.0
  ulcerated I83.009
    inflamed or infected I83.209
  uterine ligament I86.2
  vagina I86.8
  vocal cord I86.8
  vulva I86.3
Vas deferens - *see* condition
Vas deferentitis N49.1
Vasa previa O69.4
  hemorrhage from, affecting newborn
    P50.0
Vascular - *see also* condition
  loop on optic papilla Q14.2
  spasm I73.9
  spider I78.1
Vascularization, cornea - *see* Neovascular-
    ization, cornea
Vasculitis I77.6
  allergic D69.0
  cryoglobulinemic D89.1
  disseminated I77.6
  hypocomplementemic M31.8
  kidney I77.8
  livedoid L95.0
  nodular L95.8
  retina H35.06-
  rheumatic - *see* Fever, rheumatic
  rheumatoid - *see* Rheumatoid,
    vasculitis
  skin (limited to) L95.9
    specified NEC L95.8
Vasculopathy, necrotizing M31.9
  cardiac allograft T86.290
  specified NEC M31.8
Vasitis (nodosa) N49.1
  tuberculous A18.15
Vasodilation I73.9
Vasomotor - *see* condition
Vasoplasty, after previous sterilization
    Z31.0
  aftercare Z31.42
Vasospasm I73.9
  cerebral (artery) G45.9
  coronary I20.9
  nerve
    arm – *see* Mononeuropathy, upper
      limb
    brachial plexus G54.0
    cervical plexus G54.2
    leg – *see* Mononeuropathy, lower
      limb
  peripheral NOS I73.9
  retina (artery) - *see* Occlusion, artery,
    retina
Vasospastic - *see* condition
Vasovagal attack (paroxysmal) R55
  psychogenic F45.8

VATER syndrome Q87.2
Vater's ampulla - *see* condition
Vegetation, vegetative
  adenoid (nasal fossa) J35.8
  endocarditis (acute) (any valve)
    (subacute) I33.0
  heart (mycotic) (valve) I33.0
Veil
  Jackson's Q43.3
Vein, venous - *see* condition
Veldt sore - *see* Ulcer, skin
Velpeau's hernia - *see* Hernia, femoral
Venereal
  bubo A55
  disease A64
  granuloma inguinale A58
  lymphogranuloma (Durand-Nicolas-
    Favre) A55
Venofibrosis I87.8
Venom, venomous - *see* Table of drugs
    and chemicals, by animal or sub-
    stance, poisoning
Venous - *see* condition
Ventilator lung, newborn P27.8
Ventral - *see* condition
Ventricle, ventricular - *see also* condition
  escape I49.3
  inversion Q20.5
Ventriculitis (cerebral) (*see also* Encepha-
    litis) G04.90
Ventriculostomy status Z98.2
Vernet's syndrome G52.7
Verneuil's disease (syphilitic bursitis)
    A52.78
Verruca (due to HPV) (filiformis)
    (simplex) (viral) (vulgaris) B07
  acuminata A63.0
  necrogenica (primary) (tuberculosa)
    A18.4
  plana B07.8
  plantaris B07.0
  seborrheica L82.1
    inflamed L82.0
  senile (seborrheic) L82.1
    inflamed L82.0
  tuberculosa (primary) A18.4
  venereal A63.0
Verrucosities - *see* Verruca
Verruga peruana, peruviana A44.1
Version
  with extraction
  cervix - *see* Malposition, uterus
  uterus (postinfectional) (postpartal,
    old) - *see* Malposition, uterus
Vertebra, vertebral - *see* condition
Vertical talus Q66.8
Vertigo R42
  auditory - *see* Vertigo, aural
  aural H81.31-
  benign paroxysmal (positional)
    H81.1-
  central (origin) - *see* subcategory
    H81.4
  cerebral - *see* subcategory H81.4
  Dix and Hallpike (epidemic) - *see*
    Neuronitis, vestibular
  due to infrasound T75.23
  epidemic A88.1
    Dix and Hallpike - *see* Neuronitis,
      vestibular
    Pedersen's - *see* Neuronitis,
      vestibular
    vestibular neuronitis - *see* Neuronitis,
      vestibular

470

Vertigo *(Continued)*
  hysterical F44.89
  infrasound T75.23
  labyrinthine - *see* subcategory H81.0
  laryngeal R05
  malignant positional - *see* subcategory H81.4
  Ménière's - *see* subcategory H81.0
  menopausal N95.11
  otogenic - *see* Vertigo, aural
  paroxysmal positional, benign - *see* Vertigo, benign paroxysmal
  Pedersen's (epidemic) - *see* Neuronitis, vestibular
  peripheral NEC H81.39-
  positional
    benign paroxysmal - *see* Vertigo, benign paroxysmal
    malignant - *see* subcategory H81.4
Very-low-density-lipoprotein-type (VLDL) hyperlipoproteinemia E78.1
Vesania - *see* Psychosis
Vesical - *see* condition
Vesicle
  cutaneous R23.8
  seminal - *see* condition
  skin R23.8
Vesicocolic - *see* condition
Vesicoperineal - *see* condition
Vesicorectal - *see* condition
Vesicourethrorectal - *see* condition
Vesicovaginal - *see* condition
Vesicular - *see* condition
Vesiculitis (seminal) N49.0
  amebic A06.82
  gonorrheal (acute) (chronic) A54.23
  trichomonal A59.09
  tuberculous A18.15
Vestibulitis (ear) - *see also* subcategory H83.0
  nose (external) J34.89
  vulvar N94.810
Vestibulopathy , acute peripheral (recurrent) - *see* Neuronitis, vestibular
Vestige, vestigial - *see also* Persistence
  branchial Q18.0
  structures in vitreous Q14.0
Vibration
  adverse effects T75.20
    pneumatic hammer syndrome T75.21
    specified effect NEC T75.29
    vasospastic syndrome T75.22
    vertigo from infrasound T75.23
  exposure (occupational) Z57.7
  vertigo T75.23
Vibriosis A28.9
Victim (of)
  crime Z65.4
  disaster Z65.5
  terrorism Z65.4
  torture Z65.4
  war Z65.5
Vidal's disease L28.0
Villaret's syndrome G52.7
Villous - *see* condition
VIN - *see* Neoplasia, intraepithelial, vulva
Vincent's infection (angina) (gingivitis) A69.1
  stomatitis A69.0
Vinson-Plummer syndrome D50.1

Violence, physical R45.6
Viosterol deficiency - *see* Deficiency, calciferol
Vipoma - *see* Neoplasm, malignant
Viremia B34.9
Virilism (adrenal) E25.9
  congenital E25.0
Virilization (female) (suprarenal) E25.9
  congenital E25.0
  isosexual E28.2
Virulent bubo A57
Virus, viral - *see also* condition
  as cause of disease classified elsewhere B97.8
  cytomegalovirus B25.9
  human immunodeficiency (HIV) - *see* Human, immunodeficiency virus (HIV) disease
  infection - *see* Infection, virus
  specified NEC B34.8
  West Nile (fever) A92.30
    with
      complications NEC A92.39
      cranial nerve disorders A92.32
      encephalitis A92.31
      encephalomyelitis A92.31
      neurologic manifestation NEC A92.32
      optic neuritis A92.32
      polyradiculitis A92.32
Viscera, visceral - *see* condition
Visceroptosis K63.4
Visible peristalsis R19.2
Vision, visual
  binocular, suppression H53.34
  blurred, blurring H53.8
    hysterical F44.6
  defect, defective NEC H54.7
  disorientation (syndrome) H53.8
  disturbance H53.9
    hysterical F44.6
  double H53.2
  examination Z01.00
    with abnormal findings Z01.01
  field, limitation (defect) - *see* Defect, visual field
  hallucinations R44.1
  halos H53.19
  loss - *see* Loss, vision
    sudden - *see* Disturbance, vision, subjective, loss, sudden
  low (both eyes) - *see* Low, vision
  perception, simultaneous without fusion H53.33
Vitality, lack or want of R53.83
  newborn P96.89
Vitamin deficiency - *see* Deficiency, vitamin
Vitelline duct, persistent Q43.0
Vitiligo L80
  eyelid H02.739
    left H02.736
      lower H02.735
      upper H02.734
    right H02.733
      lower H02.732
      upper H02.731
  pinta A67.2
  vulva N90.8
Vitreal corneal syndrome H59.01-
Vitreoretinopathy, proliferative - *see also* Retinopathy, proliferative
  with retinal detachment - *see* Detachment, retina, traction

Vitreous - *see also* condition
  touch syndrome - *see* Complication, postprocedural, following cataract surgery
Vocal cord - *see* condition
Vogt-Koyanagi syndrome H20.82-
Vogt's disease or syndrome G80.3
Vogt-Spielmeyer amaurotic idiocy or disease E75.4
Voice
  change R49.9
    specified NEC R49.8
  loss - *see* Aphonia
Volhynian fever A79.0
Volkmann's ischemic contracture or paralysis (complicating trauma) T79.6
Volvulus (bowel) (colon) (duodenum) (intestine) K56.2
  with perforation K56.2
  congenital Q43.8
  fallopian tube – *see* Torsion, fallopian tube
  oviduct – *see* Torsion, fallopian tube
  stomach (due to absence of gastrocolic ligament) K31.89
Vomiting R11.10
  with nausea R11.2
  asphyxia - *see* Foreign body, by site, causing asphyxia, gastric contents
  bilious (cause unknown) R11.14
    in newborn P92.01
    following gastro-intestinal surgery K91.0
  blood - *see* Hematemesis
  causing asphyxia, choking, or suffocation - *see* Asphyxia, food
  cyclical G43.a09
    intractable G43.a19
      with status migrainosus G43.a11
      without status migrainosus G43.a19
    not intractable G43.a09
      with status migrainosus G43.a01
      without status migrainosus G43.a09
    psychogenic F50.8
  fecal mater R11.13
  following gastrointestinal surgery K91.0
    psychogenic F50.8
  functional K31.89
  hysterical F50.8
  nervous F50.8
  neurotic F50.8
  newborn NEC P92.09
    bilious P92.01
  periodic R11.10
    psychogenic F50.8
  projectile R11.12
  psychogenic F50.8
  uremic - *see* Uremia
  without nausea R11.11
Vomito negro - *see* Fever, yellow
Von Bezold's abscess - *see* Mastoiditis, acute
Von Economo-Cruchet disease A85.8
Von Eulenburg's disease G71.19
Von Gierke's disease E74.01
Von Hippel(-Lindau) disease or syndrome Q85.8
Von Jaksch's anemia or disease D64.89
Von Recklinghausen's
  disease (neurofibromatosis) (M9540/1) Q85.0
    bones E21.0

Von Schroetter's syndrome I82.890
Von Willebrand(-Jurgens)(-Minot) disease or syndrome D68.0
Von Zumbusch's disease L40.1
Voyeurism F65.3
Vrolik's disease Q78.0
Vulva - *see* condition
Vulvismus N94.2
Vulvitis (acute) (allergic) (atrophic) (hypertrophic) (intertriginous) (senile) N76.2
  with ectopic or molar pregnancy O08.0
  adhesive, congenital Q52.79

Vulvitis *(Continued)*
  blennorrhagic (gonococcal) A54.02
  candidal B37.3
Vulvitis (acute) (allergic) (atrophic) (hypertrophic) (intertriginous) (senile) N76.2
  chlamydial A56.02
  due to Haemophilus ducreyi A57
  following ectopic or molar pregnancy O08.0
  gonococcal A54.02
    with abscess (accessory gland) (periurethral) A54.1
  herpesviral A60.04

Vulvitis *(Continued)*
  leukoplakic N90.4
  monilial B37.3
  puerperal (postpartum) O86.19
  subacute or chronic N76.3
  syphilitic (early) A51.0
    late A52.76
  trichomonal A59.01
  tuberculous A18.18
Vulvodynia N94.819
  specified NEC N94.818
Vulvorectal - *see* condition
Vulvovaginitis (acute) - *see* Vaginitis

W

Waiting list, person on Z75.1
  for organ transplant Z76.82
  undergoing social agency investigation Z75.2
Waldenström-Kjellberg syndrome D50.1
Waldenström
  hypergammaglobulinemia D89.0
  syndrome or macroglobulinemia C88.0
Walking
  difficulty R26.2
    psychogenic F44.4
  sleep F51.3
    hysterical F44.89
Wall, abdominal - see condition
Wallenberg's disease or syndrome G46.3
Wallgren's disease I87.8
Wandering
  gallbladder, congenital Q44.1
  kidney, congenital Q63.8
  organ or site, congenital NEC - see Malposition, congenital, by site
  pacemaker (heart) I49.8
  spleen D73.89
War neurosis F48.8
Wart (due to HPV) (filiform) (infectious) (viral) B07.9
  anogenital region (venereal) A63.0
  common B07.8
  external genital organs (venereal) A63.0
  flat B07.8
  Hassal-Henle's (of cornea) H18.49
  Peruvian A44.1
  plantar B07.0
  prosector (tuberculous) A18.4
  seborrheic L82.1
    inflamed L82.0
  senile (seborrheic) L82.1
    inflamed L82.0
  tuberculous A18.4
  venereal A63.0
Warthin's tumor - see Neoplasm, salivary gland, benign
Wassilieff's disease A27.0
Wasting
  disease R64
    due to malnutrition E41
  extreme (due to malnutrition) E41
  muscle NEC - see Atrophy, muscle
Water
  clefts (senile cataract) - see Cataract, senile, incipient
  deprivation of T73.1
  intoxication E87.7
  itch B76.9
  lack of T73.1
  loading E87.7
  on
    brain - see Hydrocephalus
    chest J94.8
  poisoning E87.7
Waterbrash R12
Waterhouse(-Friderichsen) syndrome or disease (meningococcal) A39.1
Water-losing nephritis N25.89
Watermelon stomach K31.819
  with hemorrhage K31.811
  without hemorrhage K31.819
Watsoniasis B66.8
Wax in ear - see Impaction, cerumen

Weak, weakening, weakness (generalized) R53.1
  arches (acquired) - see also Deformity, limb, flat foot
  bladder (sphincter) R32
  facial R29.810
    following
      cerebrovascular disease I69.992
        specified NEC I69.892
        cerebral infarction I69.392
        intracerebral hemorrhage I69.192
        nontraumatic intracranial hemorrhage NEC I69.292
        specified disease NEC I69.892
        stroke I69.392
        subarachnoid hemorrhage I69.092
  foot (double) - see Weak, arches
  heart, cardiac - see Failure, heart
  mind F70
  muscle M62.81
  myocardium - see Failure, heart
  newborn P96.89
  pelvic fundus N81.89
  pubocervical tissue N81.82
  senile R54
  rectovaginal tissue N81.83
  urinary stream R39.12
  valvular - see Endocarditis
Wear, worn (with normal or routine use)
  articular bearing surface of internal joint prosthesis - see Complications, joint prosthesis, mechanical, wear of articular bearing surfaces, by site
  device, implant or graft - see Complications, by site, mechanical complication
  tooth, teeth (approximal) (hard tissues) (interproximal) (occlusal) K03.0
Weather, weathered
  effects of
    cold T69.9
      specified effect NEC T69.8
    hot - see Heat
    skin L57.8
Weaver's syndrome Q87.3
Web, webbed (congenital)
  duodenal Q43.8
  esophagus Q39.4
  fingers - see Syndactylism, simple
  larynx (glottic) (subglottic) Q31.0
  neck (pterygium colli) Q18.3
  Paterson-Kelly D50.1
  popliteal syndrome Q87.89
  toes Q70.3
Weber-Christian disease M35.6
Weber-Cockayne syndrome (epidermolysis bullosa) Q81.8
Weber-Gubler syndrome G46.3
Weber-Leyden syndrome G46.3
Weber-Osler syndrome I78.0
Weber's paralysis or syndrome G46.3
Wedge-shaped or wedging vertebra - see Collapse, vertebra NEC
Wegener's granulomatosis or syndrome M31.30
  with
    kidney involvement M31.31
    lung involvement M31.30
      with kidney involvement M31.31
Wegner's disease A50.02
Weight
  1000-2499 grams at birth (low) - see Low, birthweight

Weight (Continued)
  999 grams or less at birth (extremely low) - see Low, birthweight, extreme
  gain (abnormal) (excessive) R63.5
    in pregnancy - see Pregnancy, complicated by, excessive weight gain
    low - see Pregnancy, complicated by, insufficient, weight gain
  loss (abnormal) (cause unknown) R63.4
Weightlessness (effect of) T75.82
Weil(l)-Marchesani syndrome Q87.1
Weil's disease A27.0
Weingarten's syndrome J82
Weir Mitchell's disease I73.81
Weiss-Baker syndrome G90.09
Wells' disease L98.3
Wen - see Cyst, sebaceous
Wenckebach's block or phenomenon I44.1
Werdnig-Hoffmann syndrome (muscular atrophy) G12.0
Werlhof's disease D69.3
Wermer's disease or syndrome E31.21
Werner-His disease A79.0
Werner's disease or syndrome E34.8
Wernicke-Korsakoff's syndrome or psychosis (alcoholic) F10.96
  with dependence F10.26
  drug-induced
    due to drug abuse - see Abuse, drug, by type, with amnestic disorder
    due to drug dependence - see Dependence, drug, by type, with amnestic disorder
  nonalcoholic F04
Wernicke-Posada disease B38.7
Wernicke's
  developmental aphasia F80.2
  disease or syndrome E51.2
  encephalopathy E51.2
  polioencephalitis, superior E51.2
West African fever B50.8
Westphal-Strümpell syndrome E83.01
West's syndrome - see Epilepsy, generalized, specified NEC
Wet
  feet, tropical (maceration) (syndrome) - see Immersion, foot
  lung (syndrome), newborn P22.1
Wharton's duct - see condition
Wheal - see Urticaria
Wheezing R06.2
Whiplash injury S13.4
Whipple's disease (see also subcategory M14.8-) K90.81
Whipworm (disease) (infection) (infestation) B79
Whistling face Q87.0
White - see also condition
  kidney, small N03.9
  leg, puerperal, postpartum, childbirth O87.1
  mouth B37.0
  patches of mouth K13.29
  spot lesions, teeth
    chewing surface K02.51
    pit and fissure surface K02.51
    smooth surface K02.61
Whitehead L70.0
Whitlow - see also Cellulitis, digit
  with lymphangitis - see Lymphangitis, acute, digit
  herpesviral B00.89

Whitmore's disease or fever - *see* Melioidosis
Whooping cough A37.90
  with pneumonia A37.91
    due to Bordetella
      bronchiseptica A37.81
      parapertussis A37.11
      pertussis A37.01
    specified organism NEC A37.81
  due to
    Bordetella
      bronchiseptica A37.80
        with pneumonia A37.81
      parapertussis A37.10
        with pneumonia A37.11
      pertussis A37.00
        with pneumonia A37.01
      specified NEC A37.80
        with pneumonia A37.81
Wichman's asthma J38.5
Wide cranial sutures, newborn P96.3
Widening aorta - *see* Aneurysm, aorta
Wilkie's disease or syndrome K55.1
Wilkinson-Sneddon disease or syndrome L13.1
Willebrand (-Jurgens) thrombopathy D68.0
Willige-Hunt disease or syndrome G23.1
Wilms' tumor C64.-
Wilson-Mikity syndrome P27.0
Wilson's
  disease or syndrome E83.01
  hepatolenticular degeneration E83.01
  lichen ruber L43.9
Window - *see also* Imperfect, closure
  aorticopulmonary Q21.4
Winter - *see* condition
Wiskott-Aldrich syndrome D82.0
Withdrawal state– *see also* Dependence, drug by type, with withdrawal
  newborn
    correct therapeutic substance properly administered P96.2
    infant of dependent mother P96.1
    therapeutic substance, neonatal P96.2
Witts' anemia D50.8
Witzelsucht F07.0
Woakes' ethmoiditis or syndrome J33.1
Wolff-Hirschorn syndrome Q93.3
Wolff-Parkinson-White syndrome I45.6
Wolhynian fever A79.0
Wolman's disease E75.5
Wood lung or pneumonitis J67.8
Woolly, wooly hair (congenital) (nevus) Q84.1
Woolsorter's disease A22.1
Word
  blindness (congenital) (developmental) F81.0
  deafness (congenital) (developmental) H93.25
Worm(s) (infection) (infestation) - *see also* Infestation, helminth
  guinea B72
  in intestine NEC B82.0
Worm-eaten soles A66.3
Worn out - *see* Exhaustion
  cardiac defibrillator Z45.02
  cardiace pacemaker
    battery Z45.010
    lead Z45.018
  device, implant or graft - *see* Complications, by site, mechanical
Worried well Z71.1
Worries R45.82

Wound, open
  abdomen, abdominal
    wall S31.109
      with penetration into peritoneal cavity S31.609
      bite – *see* Bite, abdomen, wall
      epigastric region S31.102
        with penetration into peritoneal cavity S31.602
        bite - *see* Bite, abdomen, wall, epigastric region
        laceration - *see* Laceration, abdomen, wall, epigastric region
        puncture - *see* Puncture, abdomen, wall, epigastric region
      laceration – *see* Laceration, abdomen, wall
      left
        lower quadrant S31.104
          with penetration into peritoneal cavity S31.604
          bite - *see* Bite, abdomen, wall, left, lower quadrant
          laceration - *see* Laceration, abdomen, wall, left, lower quadrant
          puncture - *see* Puncture, abdomen, wall, left, lower quadrant
        upper quadrant S31.101
          with penetration into peritoneal cavity S31.601
          bite - *see* Bite, abdomen, wall, left, upper quadrant
          laceration - *see* Laceration, abdomen, wall, left, upper quadrant
          puncture - *see* Puncture, abdomen, wall, left, upper quadrant
      periumbilic region S31.105
        with penetration into peritoneal cavity S31.605
        bite - *see* Bite, abdomen, wall, periumbilic region
        laceration - *see* Laceration, abdomen, wall, periumbilic region
        puncture - *see* Puncture, abdomen, wall, periumbilic region
      puncture – *see* Puncture, abdomen, wall
      right
        lower quadrant S31.103
          with penetration into peritoneal cavity S31.603
          bite - *see* Bite, abdomen, wall, right, lower quadrant
          laceration - *see* Laceration, abdomen, wall, right, lower quadrant
          puncture - *see* Puncture, abdomen, wall, right, lower quadrant
        upper quadrant S31.100
          with penetration into peritoneal cavity S31.600
          bite - *see* Bite, abdomen, wall, right, upper quadrant
          laceration - *see* Laceration, abdomen, wall, right, upper quadrant
          puncture - *see* Puncture, abdomen, wall, right, upper quadrant

Wound, open *(Continued)*
  alveolar (process) – *see* Wound, open, oral cavity
  ankle S91.00-
    bite – *see* Bite, ankle
    laceration – *see* Laceration, ankle
    puncture – *see* Puncture, ankle
  antecubital space – *see* Wound, open, elbow
  anterior chamber, eye - *see* Wound, open, ocular
  anus S31.839
    bite S31.835
    laceration – *see* Laceration, anus
    puncture – *see* Puncture, anus
  arm (upper) S41.10-
    with amputation - *see* Amputation, traumatic, arm
    bite – *see* Bite, arm
    forearm – *see* Wound, open, forearm
    laceration – *see* Laceration, arm
    puncture – *see* Puncture, arm
  auditory canal (external) (meatus) – *see* Wound, open, ear
  auricle, ear – *see* Wound, open, ear
  axilla – *see* Wound, open, arm
  back - *see also* Wound, open, thorax, back
    lower S31.000
      with penetration into retroperitoneal space S31.001
      bite - *see* Bite, back, lower
      laceration – *see* Laceration, back, lower
      puncture – *see* Puncture, back, lower
  bite – *see* Bite
  blood vessel - *see* Injury, blood vessel
  breast S21.00-
    with amputation - *see* Amputation, traumatic, breast
    bite – *see* Bite, breast
    laceration – *see* Laceration, breast
    puncture – *see* Puncture, breast
  buttock S31.80-
    bite - *see* Bite, buttock
    laceration - *see* Laceration, buttock
    puncture - *see* Puncture, buttock
  calf - *see* Wound, open, leg
  canaliculus lacrimalis - *see* Wound, open, eyelid
  canthus, eye - *see* Wound, open, eyelid
  cervical esophagus S11.20
    bite S11.25
    laceration - *see* Laceration, esophagus, traumatic, cervical
    puncture - *see* Puncture, cervical esophagus
  cheek (external) S01.40-
    bite - *see* Bite, cheek
    laceration - *see* Laceration, cheek
    puncture - *see* Puncture, cheek
    internal - *see* Wound, open, oral cavity
  chest wall - *see* Wound, open, thorax
  chin - *see* Wound, open, head, specified site NEC
  choroid - *see* Wound, open, ocular
  ciliary body (eye) - *see* Wound, open, ocular
  clitoris S31.40
    with amputation - *see* Amputation, traumatic, clitoris
    bite S31.45

Wound, open *(Continued)*
  clitoris *(Continued)*
    laceration - *see* Laceration, vulva
    puncture - *see* Puncture, vulva
  conjunctiva - *see* Wound, open, ocular
  cornea - *see* Wound, open, ocular
  costal region - *see* Wound, open, thorax
  Descemet's membrane - *see* Wound, open, ocular
  digit(s)
    foot - *see* Wound, open, toe
    hand - *see* Wound, open, finger
  ear (canal) (external) S01.30-
    with amputation - *see* Amputation, traumatic, ear
    bite - *see* Bite, ear
    laceration - *see* Laceration, ear
    puncture - *see* Puncture, ear
    drum S09.2-
  elbow S51.00-
    bite - *see* Bite, elbow
    laceration - *see* Laceration, elbow
    puncture - *see* Puncture, elbow
  epididymis - *see* Wound, open, testis
  epigastric region S31.102
    with penetration into peritoneal cavity S31.602
    bite - *see* Bite, abdomen, wall, epigastric region
    laceration - *see* Laceration, abdomen, wall, epigastric region
    puncture - *see* Puncture, abdomen, wall, epigastric region
  epiglottis - *see* Wound, open, neck, specified site NEC
  esophagus (thoracic) S27.819
    cervical - *see* Wound, open, cervical esophagus
    laceration S27.813
    specified type NEC S27.818
  eye - *see* Wound, open, ocular
  eyeball - *see* Wound, open, ocular
  eyebrow - *see* Wound, open, eyelid
  eyelid S01.10-
    bite - *see* Bite, eyelid
    laceration - *see* Laceration, eyelid
    puncture - *see* Puncture, eyelid
  face NEC – *see* Wound, open, head, specified site NEC
  finger(s) S61.209
    with
      amputation - *see* Amputation, traumatic, finger
      damage to nail S61.309
    bite – *see* Bite, finger
    index S61.208
      with
        damage to nail S61.308
      left S61.201
        with
          damage to nail S61.301
      right S61.200
        with
          damage to nail S61.300
    laceration – *see* Laceration, finger
    little S61.208
      with
        damage to nail S61.308
      left S61.207
        with damage to nail S61.307
      right S61.206
        with damage to nail S61.306

Wound, open *(Continued)*
  finger(s) *(Continued)*
    middle S61.208
      with
        damage to nail S61.308
      left S61.203
        with damage to nail S61.303
      right S61.202
        with damage to nail S61.302
    puncture – *see* Puncture, finger
    ring S61.208
      with
        damage to nail S61.308
      left S61.205
        with damage to nail S61.305
      right S61.204
        with damage to nail S61.304
  flank – *see* Wound, open, abdomen, wall
  foot (except toe(s) alone) S91.30-
    with amputation - *see* Amputation, traumatic, foot
    bite – *see* Bite, foot
    laceration – *see* Laceration, foot
    puncture – *see* Puncture, foot
    toe – *see* Wound, open, toe
  forearm S51.80-
    with
      amputation - *see* Amputation, traumatic, forearm
    bite – *see* Bite, forearm
    elbow only – *see* Wound, open, elbow
    laceration – *see* Laceration, forearm
    puncture – *see* Puncture, forearm
  forehead – *see* Wound, open, head, specified site NEC
  genital organs, external
    with amputation - *see* Amputation, traumatic, genital organs
    bite – *see* Bite, genital organ
    female S31.502
      vagina S31.40
      vulva S31.40
    laceration – *see* Laceration, genital organ
    male S31.501
      penis S31.20
      scrotum S31.30
      testes S31.30
    puncture – *see* Puncture, genital organ
  globe (eye) - *see* Wound, open, ocular
  groin – *see* Wound, open, abdomen, wall
  gum – *see* Wound, open, oral cavity
  hand S61.40-
    with
      amputation - *see* Amputation, traumatic, hand
    bite – *see* Bite, hand
    finger(s) - *see* Wound, open, finger
    laceration – *see* Laceration, hand
    puncture – *see* Puncture, hand
    thumb - *see* Wound, open, thumb
  head S01.90
    bite – *see* Bite, head
    cheek - *see* Wound, open, cheek
    ear - *see* Wound, open, ear
    eyelid - *see* Wound, open, eyelid
    laceration – *see* Laceration, head
    lip - *see* Wound, open, lip
    nose S01.20
    oral cavity - *see* Wound, open, oral cavity
    puncture – *see* Puncture, head

Wound, open *(Continued)*
  head *(Continued)*
    scalp - *see* Wound, open, scalp
    specified site NEC S01.80
    temporomandibular area - *see* Wound, open, cheek
  heel – *see* Wound, open, foot
  hip S71.00-
    with amputation - *see* Amputation, traumatic, hip
    bite – *see* Bite, hip
    laceration – *see* Laceration, hip
    puncture – *see* Puncture, hip
  hymen S31.40
    bite - *see* Bite, vulva
    laceration – *see* Laceration, vagina
    puncture – *see* Puncture, vagina
  hypochondrium S31.109
    bite - *see* Bite, hypochondrium
    laceration – *see* Laceration, hypochondrium
    puncture – *see* Puncture, hypochondrium
  hypogastric region S31.109
    bite - *see* Bite, hypogastric region
    laceration – *see* Laceration, hypogastric region
    puncture – *see* Puncture, hypogastric region
  iliac (region) – *see* Wound, open, inguinal region
  inguinal region S31.109
    bite - *see* Bite, abdomen, wall, lower quadrant
    laceration – *see* Laceration, inguinal region
    puncture – *see* Puncture, inguinal region
  instep – *see* Wound, open, foot
  interscapular region - *see* Wound, open, thorax, back
  intraocular - *see* Wound, open, ocular
  iris - *see* Wound, open, ocular
  jaw – *see* Wound, open, head, specified site NEC
  knee S81.00-
    bite - *see* Bite, knee
    laceration – *see* Laceration, knee
    puncture – *see* Puncture, knee
  labium (majus) (minus) – *see* Wound, open, vulva
  laceration – *see* Laceration, by site
  lacrimal duct – *see* Wound, open, eyelid
  larynx S11.019
    bite - *see* Bite, larynx
    laceration – *see* Laceration, larynx
    puncture – *see* Puncture, larynx
  left
    lower quadrant S31.104
      with penetration into peritoneal cavity S31.604
      bite - *see* Bite, abdomen, wall, left, lower quadrant
      laceration - *see* Laceration, abdomen, wall, left, lower quadrant
      puncture - *see* Puncture, abdomen, wall, left, lower quadrant
    upper quadrant S31.101
      with penetration into peritoneal cavity S31.601
      bite - *see* Bite, abdomen, wall, left, upper quadrant

Wound, open *(Continued)*
  left *(Continued)*
    upper quadrant *(Continued)*
      laceration - *see* Laceration, abdo-
        men, wall, left, upper quadrant
      puncture - *see* Puncture, abdomen,
        wall, left, upper quadrant
    leg (lower) S81.80-
      with amputation - *see* Amputation,
        traumatic, leg
      ankle – *see* Wound, open, ankle
      bite – *see* Bite, leg
      foot – *see* Wound, open, foot
      knee – *see* Wound, open, knee
      laceration – *see* Laceration, leg
      puncture – *see* Puncture, leg
      toe – *see* Wound, open, toe
      upper – *see* Wound, open, thigh
    lip S01.501
      bite - *see* Bite, lip
      laceration - *see* Laceration, lip
      puncture – *see* Puncture, lip
    loin S31.109
      bite - *see* Bite, abdomen, wall
      laceration – *see* Laceration, loin
      puncture – *see* Puncture, loin
    lower back - *see* Wound, open, back,
      lower
    lumbar region – *see* Wound, open, back,
      lower
    malar region – *see* Wound, open, head,
      specified site NEC
    mammary – *see* Wound, open, breast
    mastoid region – *see* Wound, open,
      head, specified site NEC
    mouth – *see* Wound, open, oral cavity
    nail
      finger – *see* Wound, open, finger,
        with damage to nail
      toe – *see* Wound, open, toe, with
        damage to nail
    nape (neck) – *see* Wound, open, neck
    nasal (septum) (sinus) – *see* Wound,
      open, nose
    nasopharynx - *see* Wound, open, head,
      specified site NEC
    neck S11.90
      bite – *see* Bite, neck
      involving
        cervical esophagus S11.20
        larynx - *see* Wound, open, larynx
        pharynx S11.20
        thyroid S11.10
        trachea (cervical) S11.029
          bite - *see* Bite, trachea
          laceration S11.021
            with foreign body S11.022
          puncture S11.023
            with foreign body S11.024
      laceration – *see* Laceration, neck
      puncture – *see* Puncture, neck
      specified site NEC S11.80
        specified type NEC S11.89
    nose (septum) (sinus) S01.20
      with amputation - *see* Amputation,
        traumatic, nose
      bite - *see* Bite, nose
      laceration – *see* Laceration, nose
      puncture – *see* Puncture, nose - ocular
        S05.90
      avulsion (traumatic enucleation) S05.7-
      eyeball S05.6-
        with foreign body S05.5-
      eyelid – *see* Wound, open, eyelid

Wound, open *(Continued)*
  nose *(Continued)*
    laceration and rupture S05.3-
      with prolapse or loss of intraocular
        tissue S05.2-
      orbit (penetrating) (with or without
        foreign body) S05.4-
      periocular area – *see* Wound, open,
        eyelid
      specified NEC S05.8x
    oral cavity S01.502
      bite S01.552
      laceration – *see* Laceration, oral
        cavity
      puncture – *see* Puncture, oral cavity
    orbit – *see* Wound, open, ocular, orbit
    palate – *see* Wound, open, oral cavity
    palm – *see* Wound, open, hand
    pelvis, pelvic - *see also* Wound, open,
      back, lower
      girdle – *see* Wound, open, hip
    penetrating – *see* Puncture, by site
    penis S31.20
      with amputation - *see* Amputation,
        traumatic, penis
      bite S31.25
      laceration – *see* Laceration, penis
      puncture – *see* Puncture, penis
    perineum
      bite – *see* Bite, perineum
      female S31.502
        laceration – *see* Laceration,
          perineum
      male S31.501
        puncture – *see* Puncture,
          perineum
    periocular area (with or without
      lacrimal passages) - *see* Wound,
      open, eyelid
    periumbilic region S31.105
      with penetration into peritoneal
        cavity S31.605
      bite - *see* Bite, abdomen, wall,
        periumbilic region
      laceration - *see* Laceration, abdomen,
        wall, periumbilic region
      puncture - *see* Puncture, abdomen,
        wall, periumbilic region
    phalanges
      finger – *see* Wound, open, finger
      toe – *see* Wound, open, toe
    pharynx S11.20
    pinna – *see* Wound, open, ear
    popliteal space – *see* Wound, open,
      knee
    prepuce – *see* Wound, open, penis
    pubic region - *see* Wound, open, back,
      lower
    pudendum – *see* Wound, open, genital
      organs, external
    puncture wound – *see* Puncture
    rectovaginal septum – *see* Wound, open,
      vagina
    right
      lower quadrant S31.103
        with penetration into peritoneal
          cavity S31.603
        bite - *see* Bite, abdomen, wall, right,
          lower quadrant
        laceration - *see* Laceration, abdo-
          men, wall, right, lower
          quadrant
        puncture - *see* Puncture, abdomen,
          wall, right, lower quadrant

Wound, open *(Continued)*
  right *(Continued)*
    upper quadrant S31.100
      with penetration into peritoneal
        cavity S31.600
      bite - *see* Bite, abdomen, wall, right,
        upper quadrant
      laceration - *see* Laceration, abdomen,
        wall, right, upper quadrant
      puncture - *see* Puncture, abdomen,
        wall, right, upper quadrant
    sacral region – *see* Wound, open, back,
      lower
    sacroiliac region – *see* Wound, open,
      back, lower
    salivary gland – *see* Wound, open, oral
      cavity
    scalp S01.00
      bite S01.05
      laceration – *see* Laceration, scalp
      puncture – *see* Puncture, scalp
    scalpel, newborn (birth injury) P15.8
    scapular region – *see* Wound, open,
      shoulder
    sclera - *see* Wound, open, ocular
    scrotum S31.30
      with amputation - *see* Amputation,
        traumatic, scrotum
      bite S31.35
      laceration – *see* Laceration, scrotum
      puncture – *see* Puncture, scrotum
    shin – *see* Wound, open, leg
    shoulder S41.00-
      with amputation - *see* Amputation,
        traumatic, arm
      bite – *see* Bite, shoulder
      laceration – *see* Laceration, shoulder
      puncture – *see* Puncture, shoulder
    skin NOS T14.8
    spermatic cord – *see* Wound, open, testis
    sternal region - *see* Wound, open, tho-
      rax, front wall
    submaxillary region – *see* Wound, open,
      head, specified site NEC
    submental region – *see* Wound, open,
      head, specified site NEC
    subungual
      finger(s) – *see* Wound, open, finger
      toe(s) – *see* Wound, open, toe
    supraclavicular region – *see* Wound,
      open, neck, specified site NEC
    temple, temporal region – *see* Wound,
      open, head, specified site NEC
    temporomandibular area – *see* Wound,
      open, cheek
    testis S31.30
      with amputation - *see* Amputation,
        traumatic, testes
      bite S31.35
      laceration – *see* Laceration, testis
      puncture – *see* Puncture, testis
    thigh S71.10-
      with amputation - *see* Amputation,
        traumatic, hip
      bite – *see* Bite, thigh
      laceration – *see* Laceration, thigh
      puncture – *see* Puncture, thigh
    thorax, thoracic (wall) S21.90
      back S21.20-
      bite – *see* Bite, thorax
      breast – *see* Wound, open, breast
      front S21.10-
      laceration – *see* Laceration, thorax
      puncture – *see* Puncture, thorax

Wound, open *(Continued)*
  throat - *see* Wound, open, neck
  thumb S61.009
    with
      amputation - *see* Amputation,
        traumatic, thumb
      damage to nail S61.109
    bite – *see* Bite, thumb
    laceration – *see* Laceration, thumb
    left S61.002
      with
        damage to nail S61.102
    puncture – *see* Puncture, thumb
    right S61.001
      with
        damage to nail S61.101
  thyroid (gland) – *see* Wound, open,
    neck, thyroid
  toe(s) S91.109
    with
      amputation - *see* Amputation,
        traumatic, toe
      damage to nail S91.209
    bite – *see* Bite, toe
    great S91.103
      with
      left S91.102
        with
          damage to nail S91.202
      right S91.101
        with
          damage to nail S91.201

Wound, open *(Continued)*
  toe(s) *(Continued)*
    laceration – *see* Laceration, toe
    lesser S91.106
      with
        damage to nail S91.206
      left S91.105
        with
          damage to nail S91.205
      right S91.104
        with
          damage to nail S91.204
    puncture – *see* Puncture, toe
  tongue – *see* Wound, open, oral
    cavity
  trachea (cervical region) – *see* Wound,
    open, neck, trachea
  tunica vaginalis – *see* Wound, open,
    testis
  tympanum, tympanic membrane
    S09.2-
    laceration – *see* Laceration, ear,
      drum
    puncture – *see* Puncture, tympanum
  umbilical region – *see* Wound, open,
    abdomen, wall, periumbilic
    region
  uvula – *see* Wound, open, oral cavity
  vagina S31.40
    bite S31.45
    laceration – *see* Laceration, vagina
    puncture – *see* Puncture, vagina

Wound, open *(Continued)*
  vocal cord S11.039
    bite - *see* Bite, vocal cord
    laceration S11.031
      with foreign body S11.032
    puncture S11.033
      with foreign body S11.034
  vitreous (humor) - *see* Wound, open,
    ocular
  vulva S31.40
    with amputation - *see* Amputation,
      traumatic, vulva
    bite S31.45
    laceration – *see* Laceration, vulva
    puncture – *see* Puncture, vulva
  wrist S61.50-
    bite – *see* Bite, wrist
    laceration – *see* Laceration, wrist
    puncture – *see* Puncture, wrist
Wound, superficial (*see also* specified
  injury type) - *see* Injury
Wright's syndrome G54.0
Wrist - *see* condition
Wrong drug (by accident) (given in error) -
  see Table of drugs and chemicals, by
  drug, poisoning
Wry neck - *see* Torticollis
Wuchereria (bancrofti) infestation B74.0
Wuchereriasis B74.0
Wuchernde Struma Langhans (M8332/3)
  C73

X

Xanthelasma (eyelid) (palpebrarum)
    H02.60
  left H02.66
    lower H02.65
    upper H02.64
  right H02.63
    lower H02.62
    upper H02.61
Xanthelasmatosis (essential) E78.2
Xanthinuria, hereditary E79.8
  specified site - *see* Neoplasm,
    malignant
  unspecified site C71.9
Xanthofibroma - *see* Neoplasm, connective tissue, benign
Xanthogranuloma D76.3
Xanthoma(s), xanthomatosis (primary)
    (familial) (hereditary) E75.5
  with
    hyperlipoproteinemia
      Type I E78.3
      Type III E78.2
      Type IV E78.1
      Type V E78.3
  cerebrotendinous E75.5
  cutaneotendinous E75.5
  disseminatum (skin) E78.2
  eruptive E78.2

Xanthoma(s), xanthomatosis
    (Continued)
  hypercholesterinemic E78.0
  hypercholesterolemic E78.0
  hyperlipidemic E78.5
  joint E75.5
  multiple (skin) E78.2
  tendon (sheath) E75.5
  tubo-eruptive E78.2
  tuberosum E78.2
  tuberous E78.2
  verrucous, oral mucosa K13.4
Xanthosis R23.8
Xenophobia F40.10
Xeroderma - *see also* Ichthyosis
  acquired L85.0
  eyelid H01.149
    left H01.146
      lower H01.145
      upper H01.144
    right H01.143
      lower H01.142
      upper H01.141
  pigmentosum Q82.1
  vitamin A deficiency E50.8
Xerophthalmia (vitamin A deficiency)
    E50.7
  unrelated to vitamin A deficiency - *see*
    Keratoconjunctivitis

Xerosis
  conjunctiva H11.14-
    with Bitot's spots - *see also* Pigmenta-
      tion, conjunctiva
      vitamin A deficiency E50.1
    vitamin A deficiency E50.0
  cornea H18.89-
    with ulceration - *see* Ulcer, cornea
      vitamin A deficiency E50.3
    vitamin A deficiency E50.2
  cutis L85.3
  skin L85.3
Xerostomia K11.7
Xiphopagus Q89.4
XO syndrome Q96.9
X-ray (of)
  abnormal findings - *see* Abnormal,
    diagnostic imaging
  breast (mammogram) (routine)
    Z12.31
  chest
    routine (as part of a general medical
      examination) Z00.00
      with abnormal findings Z00.01
  routine (as part of a general medical
    examination) Z00.00
    with abnormal findings Z00.01
XXXXY syndrome Q98.1
XXY syndrome Q98.0

Y

Yaba pox virus disease B08.72
Yatapoxvirus B08.70
    specified NEC B08.79
Yawning R06.89
    psychogenic F45.8
Yaws A66.9
    bone lesions A66.6
    butter A66.1
    chancre A66.0
    cutaneous, less than five years after
            infection A66.2
    early (cutaneous) (macular) (maculo-
            papular) (micropapular) (papular)
            A66.2
        frambeside A66.2
        skin lesions NEC A66.2
    eyelid A66.2
    ganglion A66.6
    gangosis, gangosa A66.5
    gumma, gummata A66.4
        bone A66.6
    gummatous
        frambeside A66.4
        osteitis A66.6
        periostitis A66.6
    hydrarthrosis (see also subcategory
            M14.8-) A66.6

Yaws (Continued)
    hyperkeratosis (early) (late) A66.3
    initial lesions A66.0
    joint lesions (see also subcategory
            M14.8-) A66.6
    juxta-articular nodules A66.7
    late nodular (ulcerated) A66.4
    latent (without clinical manifestations)
            (with positive serology) A66.8
    mother A66.0
    mucosal A66.7
    multiple papillomata A66.1
    nodular, late (ulcerated) A66.4
    osteitis A66.6
    papilloma, plantar or palmar A66.1
    periostitis (hypertrophic) A66.6
    specified NEC A66.7
    ulcers A66.4
    wet crab A66.1
Yeast infection (see also Candidiasis) B37.9
Yellow
    atrophy (liver) - see Failure, hepatic
    fever - see Fever, yellow
    jack - see Fever, yellow
    jaundice - see Jaundice
    nail syndrome L60.5
Yersiniosis - see also Infection, Yersinia
    extraintestinal A28.2
    intestinal A04.6

Z

Zahorsky's syndrome (herpangina)
        B08.5
Zellweger's syndrome Q87.89
Zenker's diverticulum (esophagus)
        K22.5
Ziehen-Oppenheim disease G24.1
Zieve's syndrome K70.0
Zinc
    deficiency, dietary E60
    metabolism disorder E83.2
Zollinger-Ellison syndrome E16.4
Zona - see Herpes, zoster
Zoophobia F40.218
Zoster (herpes) - see Herpes, zoster
Zygomycosis B46.9
    specified NEC B46.8
Zymotic - see condition

ICD-10-CM
Table of
Neoplasms

2010

	Malignant Primary	Malignant Secondary	Ca in situ	Benign	Uncertain	Unspecified Behavior
Neoplasm, neoplastic	C80	C80	D09.9	D36.9	D48.9	D49.9

Notes - 1. The list below gives the code numbers for neoplasms by anatomical site. For each site there are six possible code numbers according to whether the neoplasm in question is malignant, benign, in situ, of uncertain behavior, or of unspecified nature. The description of the neoplasm will often indicate which of the six columns is appropriate; e.g., malignant melanoma of skin, benign fibroadenoma of breast, carcinoma in situ of cervix uteri.

Where such descriptors are not present, the remainder of the Index should be consulted where guidance is given to the appropriate column for each morphological (histological) variety listed; e.g., Mesonephroma-see Neoplasm, malignant; Embryoma-see also Neoplasm, uncertain behavior; Disease, Bowen's-see Neoplasm, skin, in situ. However, the guidance in the Index can be overridden if one of the descriptors mentioned above is present; e.g., malignant adenoma of colon is coded to C18.9 and not to D12.6 as the adjective "malignant" overrides the Index entry "Adenoma-see also Neoplasm, benign."

2. Sites marked with the sign * (e.g., face NEC*) should be classified to malignant neoplasm of skin of these sites if the variety of neoplasm is a squamous cell carcinoma or an epidermoid carcinoma and to benign neoplasm of skin of these sites if the variety of neoplasm is a papilloma (any type).

	Malignant Primary	Malignant Secondary	Ca in situ	Benign	Uncertain	Unspecified Behavior
abdomen, abdominal	C76.2	C79.89	D09.7	D36.7	D48.7	D49.89
cavity	C76.2	C79.89	D09.7	D36.7	D48.7	D49.89
organ	C76.2	C79.89	D09.7	D36.7	D48.7	D49.89
viscera	C76.2	C79.89	D09.7	D36.7	D48.7	D49.89
wall	C44.59	C79.2	D04.5	D23.5	D48.5	D49.2
connective tissue	C49.4	C79.89	—	D21.4	D48.1	D49.2
abdominopelvic	C76.7	C79.89	D09.7	D36.7	D48.7	D49.89
accessory sinus-see Neoplasm, sinus						
acoustic nerve (unspecified side)	C72.4-	C79.49	—	D33.3	D43.3	D49.7
left side	C72.42	C79.49	—	D33.3	D43.3	D49.7
right side	C72.41	C79.49	—	D33.3	D43.3	D49.7
acromion (process)						
left side	C40.02	C79.51	—	D16.02	D48.0	D49.2
marrow NEC	C96.9	C79.52	—	—	—	D47.9
right side	C40.01	C79.51	—	D16.01	D48.0	D49.2
marrow NEC	C96.9	C79.52	—	—	—	D47.9
unspecified side	C40.00	C79.51	—	D16.00	D48.0	D49.2
marrow NEC	C96.9	C79.52	—	—	—	D47.9
adenoid (pharynx) (tissue)	C11.1	C79.89	D00.08	D10.6	D37.05	D49.0
adipose tissue (see also Neoplasm, connective tissue)	C49.9	C79.89	—	D21.9	D48.1	D49.2
adnexa (uterine)	C57.4	C79.89	D07.39	D28.7	D39.7	D49.5
adrenal						
capsule	C74.9-	C79.7-	D09.3	D35.0-	D44.1-	D49.7
cortex	C74.0-	C79.70	D09.3	D35.00	D44.10	D49.7
gland	C74.0-	C79.70	D09.3	D35.00	D44.10	D49.7
medulla	C74.1-	C79.70	D09.3	D35.00	D44.10	D49.7
unspecified site	C74.9-	C79.70	D09.3	D35.00	D44.10	D49.7

	Malignant Primary	Malignant Secondary	Ca in situ	Benign	Uncertain	Unspecified Behavior
ala nasi (external)	C44.31	C79.2	D04.39	D23.39	D48.5	D49.2
alimentary canal or tract NEC	C26.9	C78.80	D01.9	D13.9	D37.9	D49.0
alveolar	C03.9	C79.89	D00.03	D10.39	D37.09	D49.0
mucosa	C03.9	C79.89	D00.03	D10.39	D37.09	D49.0
lower	C03.1	C79.89	D00.03	D10.39	D37.09	D49.0
upper	C03.0	C79.89	D00.03	D10.39	D37.09	D49.0
ridge or process	C41.1	C79.51	—	D16.5	D48.0	D49.2
carcinoma	C03.9	—	—	—	—	—
lower	C03.1	—	—	—	—	—
upper	C03.0	—	—	—	—	—
lower	C41.1	C79.51	—	D16.5	D48.0	D49.2
marrow NEC	C96.9	C79.52	—	—	—	D47.9
marrow NEC	C96.9	C79.52	—	—	—	D47.9
mucosa	C03.9	C79.89	D00.03	D10.39	D37.09	D49.0
lower	C03.1	C79.89	D00.03	D10.39	D37.09	D49.0
upper	C03.0	C79.89	D00.03	D10.39	D37.09	D49.0
upper	C41.0	C79.51	—	D16.4	D48.0	D49.2
marrow NEC	C96.9	C79.52	—	—	—	D47.9
sulcus	C06.1	C79.89	D00.02	D10.39	D37.09	D49.0
alveolus	C03.9	C79.89	D00.03	D10.39	D37.09	D49.0
lower	C03.1	C79.89	D00.03	D10.39	D37.09	D49.0
upper	C03.0	C79.89	D00.03	D10.39	D37.09	D49.0
ampulla of Vater	C24.1	C78.89	D01.5	D13.5	D37.6	D49.0
ankle NEC*	C76.5-	C79.89	D04.7-	D36.7	D48.7	D49.89
anorectum, anorectal (junction)	C21.8	C78.5	D01.3	D12.9	D37.7	D49.0
antecubital fossa or space*	C76.4-	C79.89	D04.6-	D36.7	D48.7	D49.89
antrum (Highmore) (maxillary)	C31.0	C78.39	D02.3	D14.0	D38.5	D49.1
pyloric	C16.3	C78.89	D00.2	D13.1	D37.1	D49.0
tympanicum	C30.1	C78.39	D02.3	D14.0	D38.5	D49.1
anus, anal	C21.0	C78.5	D01.3	D12.9	D37.7	D49.0
canal	C21.1	C78.5	D01.3	D12.9	D37.7	D49.0
cloacogenic zone	C21.2	C78.5	D01.3	D12.9	D37.7	D49.0
margin	C44.51	C79.2	D04.5	D23.5	D48.5	D49.2
overlapping lesion with rectosigmoid junction or rectum	C21.8	—	—	—	—	—
skin	C44.51	C79.2	D04.5	D23.5	D48.5	D49.2
sphincter	C21.1	C78.5	D01.3	D12.9	D37.7	D49.0
aorta (thoracic)	C49.3	C79.89	—	D21.3	D48.1	D49.2
abdominal	C49.4	C79.89	—	D21.4	D48.1	D49.2
aortic body	C75.5	C79.89	—	D35.6	D44.7	D49.7
aponeurosis	C49.9	C79.89	—	D21.9	D48.1	D49.2
palmar	C49.1-	C79.89	—	D21.1-	D48.1	D49.2
plantar	C49.2-	C79.89	—	D21.2-	D48.1	D49.2
appendix	C18.1	C78.5	D01.0	D12.1	D37.3	D49.0
arachnoid	C70.9	C79.49		D32.9	D42.9	D49.7

	Malignant Primary	Malignant Secondary	Ca in situ	Benign	Uncertain	Unspecified Behavior
arachnoid *(Continued)*						
cerebral	C70.0	C79.32	—	D32.0	D42.0	D49.7
spinal	C70.1	C79.49	—	D32.1	D42.1	D49.7
areola						
female	D50.01-	C79.81	D05.9-	D24.00	D48.6-	D49.3
male	D50.02-	C79.81	D05.9-	D24.10	D48.6-	D49.3
arm NEC*	C76.4-	C79.89	D04.6-	D36.7	D48.7	D49.89
artery-*see* Neoplasm, connective tissue						
aryepiglottic fold	C13.1	C79.89	D00.08	D10.7	D37.05	D49.0
hypopharyngeal aspect	C13.1	C79.89	D00.08	D10.7	D37.05	D49.0
laryngeal aspect	C32.1	C78.39	D02.0	D14.1	D38.0	D49.1
marginal zone	C13.1	C79.89	D00.08	D10.7	D37.05	D49.0
arytenoid (cartilage)	C32.3	C78.39	D02.0	D14.1	D38.0	D49.1
fold-*see* Neoplasm, aryepiglottic						
atlas	C41.2	C79.51	—	D16.6	D48.0	D49.2
marrow NEC	C96.9	C79.52	—	—	—	D47.9
atrium, cardiac	C38.0	C79.89	—	D15.1	D48.7	D49.89
auditory						
canal (external) (skin)	C44.2-	C79.2	D04.2-	D23.2-	D48.5	D49.2
internal	C30.1	C78.39	D02.3	D14.0	D38.5	D49.1
nerve	C72.4-	C79.49	—	D33.3	D43.3	D49.7
tube	C30.1	C78.39	D02.3	D14.0	D38.5	D49.1
opening	C11.2	C79.89	D00.08	D10.6	D37.05	D49.0
auricle, ear						
left side	C44.22	C79.2	D04.22	D23.22	D48.5	D49.2
cartilage	C49.0	C79.89	—	D21.0	D48.1	D49.2
right side	C44.21	C79.2	D04.21	D23.21	D48.5	D49.2
cartilage	C49.0	C79.89	—	D21.0	D48.1	D49.2
unspecified side	C44.20	C79.2	D04.20	D23.20	D48.5	D49.2
cartilage	C49.0	C79.89	—	D21.0	D48.1	D49.2
auricular canal (external)						
left side	C44.22	C79.2	D04.22	D23.22	D48.5	D49.2
internal	C30.1	C78.39	D02.3	D14.0	D38.5	D49.2
right side	C44.21	C79.2	D04.21	D23.21	D48.5	D49.2
internal	C30.1	C78.39	D02.3	D14.0	D38.5	D49.2
unspecified side	C44.20	C79.2	D04.20	D23.20	D48.5	D49.2
internal	C30.1	C78.39	D02.3	D14.0	D38.5	D49.2
autonomic nerve or nervous system NEC (*see also* Neoplasm, nerve, peripheral)	C47.9	C79.89	—	D36.10	D48.2	D49.2
axilla, axillary	C76.1	C79.89	D09.7	D36.7	D48.7	D49.89
fold	C44.59	C79.2	D04.5	D23.5	D48.5	D49.2
back NEC*	C76.7	C79.89	D04.5	D36.7	D48.7	D49.89
Bartholin's gland	C51.0	C79.82	D07.1	D28.0	D39.7	D49.5
basal ganglia	C71.0	C79.31	—	D33.0	D43.0	D49.6
basis pedunculi	C71.7	C79.31	—	D33.1	D43.1	D49.6

	Malignant Primary	Malignant Secondary	Ca in situ	Benign	Uncertain	Unspecified Behavior
bile or biliary (tract)	C24.9	C78.89	D01.5	D13.5	D37.6	D49.0
canaliculi (biliferi) (intrahepatic)	C22.1	C78.7	D01.5	D13.4	D37.6	D49.0
canals, interlobular	C22.1	C78.89	D01.5	D13.4	D37.6	D49.0
overlapping lesion	C24.8	—	—	—	—	—
duct or passage (common) (cystic) (extrahepatic)	C24.0	C78.89	D01.5	D13.5	D37.6	D49.0
interlobular	C22.1	C78.89	D01.5	D13.4	D37.6	D49.0
intrahepatic	C22.1	C78.7	D01.5	D13.4	D37.6	D49.0
and extrahepatic	C24.8	C78.89	D01.5	D13.5	D37.6	D49.0
overlapping lesion with gallbladder	C24.8	—	—	—	—	—
bladder (urinary)	C67.9	C79.11	D09.0	D30.3	D41.4	D49.4
dome	C67.1	C79.11	D09.0	D30.3	D41.4	D49.4
neck	C67.5	C79.11	D09.0	D30.3	D41.4	D49.4
orifice	C67.9	C79.11	D09.0	D30.3	D41.4	D49.4
ureteric	C67.6	C79.11	D09.0	D30.3	D41.4	D49.4
urethral	C67.5	C79.11	D09.0	D30.3	D41.4	D49.4
overlapping lesion	C67.8	—	—	—	—	—
sphincter	C67.8	C79.11	D09.0	D30.3	D41.4	D49.4
trigone	C67.0	C79.11	D09.0	D30.3	D41.4	D49.4
urachus	C67.7	—	D09.0	D30.3	D41.4	D49.4
wall	C67.9	C79.11	D09.0	D30.3	D41.4	D49.4
anterior	C67.3	C79.11	D09.0	D30.3	D41.4	D49.4
lateral	C67.2	C79.11	D09.0	D30.3	D41.4	D49.4
posterior	C67.4	C79.11	D09.0	D30.3	D41.4	D49.4
blood vessel-*see* Neoplasm, connective tissue						
bone (periosteum)	C41.9	C79.51	—	D16.9	D48.0	D49.2

Note-Carcinomas and adenocarcinomas, of any type other than intraosseous or odontogenic, of the sites listed under "Neoplasm, bone" should be considered as constituting metastatic spread from an unspecified primary site and coded to C79.51 for morbidity coding and to C80.1 for underlying cause of death coding.

	Malignant Primary	Malignant Secondary	Ca in situ	Benign	Uncertain	Unspecified Behavior
acetabulum	C41.4	C79.51	—	D16.8	D48.0	D49.2
marrow NEC	C96.9	C79.52	—	—	—	D47.9
acromion (process)						
left side	C40.02	C79.51	—	D16.02	D48.0	D49.2
marrow NEC	C96.9	C79.52	—	—	—	D47.9
right side	C40.01	C79.51	—	D16.01	D48.0	D49.2
marrow NEC	C96.9	C79.52	—	—	—	D47.9
unspecified side	C40.00	C79.51	—	D16.00	D48.0	D49.2
marrow NEC	C96.9	C79.52	—	—	—	D47.9
ankle						
left side	C40.32	C79.51	—	D16.32	D48.0	D49.2
marrow NEC	C96.9	C79.52	—	—	—	D47.9
right side	C40.31	C79.51	—	D16.31	D48.0	D49.2
marrow NEC	C96.9	C79.52	—	—	—	D47.9

	Malignant Primary	Malignant Secondary	Ca in situ	Benign	Uncertain	Unspecified Behavior
bone *(Continued)*						
ankle *(Continued)*						
unspecified side	C40.30	C79.51	—	D16.30	D48.0	D49.2
marrow NEC	C96.9	C79.52	—	—	—	D47.9
arm NEC						
left side	C40.02	C79.51	—	D16.02	D48.0	D49.2
marrow NEC	C96.9	C79.52	—	—	—	D47.9
right side	C40.01	C79.51	—	D16.01	D48.0	D49.2
marrow NEC	C96.9	C79.52	—	—	—	D47.9
unspecified side	C40.00	C79.51	—	D16.00	D48.0	D49.2
marrow NEC	C96.9	C79.52	—	—	—	D47.9
astragalus						
left side	C40.32	C79.51	—	D16.32	D48.0	D49.2
marrow NEC	C96.9	C79.52	—	—	—	D47.9
right side	C40.31	C79.51	—	D16.31	D48.0	D49.2
marrow NEC	C96.9	C79.52	—	—	—	D47.9
unspecified side	C40.30	C79.51	—	D16.30	D48.0	D49.2
marrow NEC	C96.9	C79.52	—	—	—	D47.9
atlas	C41.2	C79.51	—	D16.6	D48.0	D49.2
marrow NEC	C96.9	C79.52	—	—	—	D47.9
axis	C41.2	C79.51	—	D16.6	D48.0	D49.2
marrow NEC	C96.9	C79.52	—	—	—	D47.9
back NEC	C41.2	C79.51	—	D16.6	D48.0	D49.2
marrow NEC	C96.9	C79.52	—	—	—	D47.9
calcaneus						
left side	C40.32	C79.51	—	D16.32	D48.0	D49.2
marrow NEC	C96.9	C79.52	—	—	—	D47.9
right side	C40.31	C79.51	—	D16.31	D48.0	D49.2
marrow NEC	C96.9	C79.52	—	—	—	D47.9
unspecified side	C40.30	C79.51	—	D16.30	D48.0	D49.2
marrow NEC	C96.9	C79.52	—	—	—	D47.9
calvarium	C41.0	C79.51	—	D16.4	D48.0	D49.2
marrow NEC	C96.9	C79.52	—	—	—	D47.9
carpus (any)						
left side	C40.12	C79.51	—	D16.12	D48.0	D49.2
marrow NEC	C96.9	C79.52	—	—	—	D47.9
right side	C40.11	C79.51	—	D16.11	D48.0	D49.2
marrow NEC	C96.9	C79.52	—	—	—	D47.9
unspecified side	C40.10	C79.51	—	D16.10	D48.0	D49.2
marrow NEC	C96.9	C79.52	—	—	—	D47.9
cartilage NEC	C41.9	C79.51	—	D16.9	D48.0	D49.2
clavicle	C41.3	C79.51	—	D16.7	D48.0	D49.2
marrow NEC	C96.9	C79.52	—	—	—	D47.9
clivus	C41.0	C79.51	—	D16.4	D48.0	D49.2

	Malignant Primary	Malignant Secondary	Ca in situ	Benign	Uncertain	Unspecified Behavior
bone (Continued)						
clivus (Continued)						
marrow NEC	C96.9	C79.52	—	—	—	D47.9
coccygeal vertebra	C41.4	C79.51	—	D16.8	D48.0	D49.2
marrow NEC	C96.9	C79.52	—	—	—	D47.9
coccyx	C41.4	C79.51	—	D16.8	D48.0	D49.2
marrow NEC	C96.9	C79.52	—	—	—	D47.9
costal cartilage	C41.3	C79.51	—	D16.7	D48.0	D49.2
costovertebral joint	C41.3	C79.51	—	D16.7	D48.0	D49.2
marrow NEC	C96.9	C79.52	—	—	—	D47.9
cranial	C41.0	C79.51	—	D16.4	D48.0	D49.2
marrow NEC	C96.9	C79.52	—	—	—	D47.9
cuboid						
left side	C40.32	C79.51	—	D16.32	D48.0	D49.2
marrow NEC	C96.9	C79.52	—	—	—	D47.9
right side	C40.31	C79.51	—	D16.31	D48.0	D49.2
marrow NEC	C96.9	C79.52	—	—	—	D47.9
unspecified side	C40.30	C79.51	—	D16.30	D48.0	D49.2
marrow NEC	C96.9	C79.52	—	—	—	D47.9
cuneiform	C41.9	C79.51	—	D16.9	D48.0	D49.2
ankle						
left side	C40.32	C79.51	—	D16.32	D48.0	D49.2
marrow NEC	C96.9	C79.52	—	—	—	D47.9
right side	C40.31	C79.51	—	D16.31	D48.0	D49.2
marrow NEC	C96.9	C79.52	—	—	—	D47.9
unspecified side	C40.30	C79.51	—	D16.30	D48.0	D49.2
marrow NEC	C96.9	C79.52	—	—	—	D47.9
wrist						
left side	C40.12	C79.51	—	D16.12	D48.0	D49.2
marrow NEC	C96.9	C79.52	—	—	—	D47.9
right side	C40.11	C79.51	—	D16.11	D48.0	D49.2
marrow NEC	C96.9	C79.52	—	—	—	D47.9
unspecified side	C40.10	C79.51	—	D16.10	D48.0	D49.2
marrow NEC	C96.9	C79.52	—	—	—	D47.9
digital						
finger						
left side	C40.12	C79.51	—	D16.12	D48.0	D49.2
marrow NEC	C96.9	C79.52	—	—	—	D47.9
right side	C40.11	C79.51	—	D16.11	D48.0	D49.2
marrow NEC	C96.9	C79.52	—	—	—	D47.9
unspecified side	C40.10	C79.51	—	D16.10	D48.0	D49.2
marrow NEC	C96.9	C79.52	—	—	—	D47.9
toe						
left side	C40.32	C79.51	—	D16.32	D48.0	D49.2
marrow NEC	C96.9	C79.52	—	—	—	D47.9

	Malignant Primary	Malignant Secondary	Ca in situ	Benign	Uncertain	Unspecified Behavior
bone *(Continued)*						
digital *(Continued)*						
toe *(Continued)*						
right side	C40.31	C79.51	—	D16.31	D48.0	D49.2
marrow NEC	C96.9	C79.52	—	—	—	D47.9
unspecified side	C40.30	C79.51	—	D16.30	D48.0	D49.2
marrow NEC	C96.9	C79.52	—	—	—	D47.9
unspecified site						
left side	C40.92	C79.51	—	D16.9	D48.0	D49.2
marrow NEC	C96.9	C79.52	—	—	—	D47.9
right side	C40.91	C79.51	—	D16.9	D48.0	D49.2
marrow NEC	C96.9	C79.52	—	—	—	D47.9
unspecified side	C40.90	C79.51	—	D16.9	D48.0	D49.2
marrow NEC	C96.9	C79.52	—	—	—	D47.9
elbow						
left side	C40.02	C79.51	—	D16.02	D48.0	D49.2
marrow NEC	C96.9	C79.52	—	—	—	D47.9
right side	C40.01	C79.51	—	D16.01	D48.0	D49.2
marrow NEC	C96.9	C79.52	—	—	—	D47.9
unspecified side	C40.00	C79.51	—	D16.00	D48.0	D49.2
marrow NEC	C96.9	C79.52	—	—	—	D47.9
ethmoid (labyrinth)	C41.0	C79.51	—	D16.4	D48.0	D49.2
marrow NEC	C96.9	C79.52	—	—	—	D47.9
face	C41.0	C79.51	—	D16.4	D48.0	D49.2
lower jaw	C41.1	C79.51	—	D16.5	D48.0	D49.2
marrow NEC	C96.9	C79.52	—	—	—	D47.9
marrow NEC	C96.9	C79.52	—	—	—	D47.9
femur (any part)						
left side	C40.22	C79.51	—	D16.22	D48.0	D49.2
marrow NEC	C96.9	C79.52	—	—	—	D47.9
right side	C40.21	C79.51	—	D16.21	D48.0	D49.2
marrow NEC	C96.9	C79.52	—	—	—	D47.9
unspecified side	C40.20	C79.51	—	D16.20	D48.0	D49.2
marrow NEC	C96.9	C79.52	—	—	—	D47.9
fibula (any part)						
left side	C40.22	C79.51	—	D16.22	D48.0	D49.2
marrow NEC	C96.9	C79.52	—	—	—	D47.9
right side	C40.21	C79.51	—	D16.21	D48.0	D49.2
marrow NEC	C96.9	C79.52	—	—	—	D47.9
unspecified side	C40.20	C79.51	—	D16.20	D48.0	D49.2
marrow NEC	C96.9	C79.52	—	—	—	D47.9
finger (any)						
left side	C40.12	C79.51	—	D16.12	D48.0	D49.2
marrow NEC	C96.9	C79.52	—	—	—	D47.9

	Malignant Primary	Malignant Secondary	Ca in situ	Benign	Uncertain	Unspecified Behavior
bone *(Continued)*						
finger *(Continued)*						
right side	C40.11	C79.51	—	D16.11	D48.0	D49.2
marrow NEC	C96.9	C79.52	—	—	—	D47.9
unspecified side	C40.10	C79.51	—	D16.10	D48.0	D49.2
marrow NEC	C96.9	C79.52	—	—	—	D47.9
foot						
left side	C40.32	C79.51	—	D16.32	D48.0	D49.2
marrow NEC	C96.9	C79.52	—	—	—	D47.9
right side	C40.31	C79.51	—	D16.31	D48.0	D49.2
marrow NEC	C96.9	C79.52	—	—	—	D47.9
unspecified side	C40.30	C79.51	—	D16.30	D48.0	D49.2
marrow NEC	C96.9	C79.52	—	—	—	D47.9
forearm						
left side	C40.02	C79.51	—	D16.02	D48.0	D49.2
marrow NEC	C96.9	C79.52	—	—	—	D47.9
right side	C40.01	C79.51	—	D16.01	D48.0	D49.2
marrow NEC	C96.9	C79.52	—	—	—	D47.9
unspecified side	C40.00	C79.51	—	D16.00	D48.0	D49.2
marrow NEC	C96.9	C79.52	—	—	—	D47.9
frontal	C41.0	C79.51	—	D16.4	D48.0	D49.2
marrow NEC	C96.9	C79.52	—	—	—	D47.9
hand						
left side	C40.12	C79.51	—	D16.12	D48.0	D49.2
marrow NEC	C96.9	C79.52	—	—	—	D47.9
right side	C40.11	C79.51	—	D16.11	D48.0	D49.2
marrow NEC	C96.9	C79.52	—	—	—	D47.9
unspecified side	C40.10	C79.51	—	D16.10	D48.0	D49.2
marrow NEC	C96.9	C79.52	—	—	—	D47.9
heel						
left side	C40.32	C79.51	—	D16.32	D48.0	D49.2
marrow NEC	C96.9	C79.52	—	—	—	D47.9
right side	C40.31	C79.51	—	D16.31	D48.0	D49.2
marrow NEC	C96.9	C79.52	—	—	—	D47.9
unspecified side	C40.30	C79.51	—	D16.30	D48.0	D49.2
marrow NEC	C96.9	C79.52	—	—	—	D47.9
hip	C41.4	C79.51	—	D16.8	D48.0	D49.2
marrow NEC	C96.9	C79.52	—	—	—	D47.9
humerus (any part)						
left side	C40.02	C79.51	—	D16.02	D48.0	D49.2
marrow NEC	C96.9	C79.52	—	—	—	D47.9
right side	C40.01	C79.51	—	D16.01	D48.0	D49.2
marrow NEC	C96.9	C79.52	—	—	—	D47.9

	Malignant Primary	Malignant Secondary	Ca in situ	Benign	Uncertain	Unspecified Behavior
bone *(Continued)*						
humerus *(Continued)*						
unspecified side	C40.00	C79.51	—	D16.00	D48.0	D49.2
marrow NEC	C96.9	C79.52	—	—	—	D47.9
hyoid	C41.0	C79.51	—	D16.4	D48.0	D49.2
marrow NEC	C96.9	C79.52	—	—	—	D47.9
ilium	C41.4	C79.51	—	D16.8	D48.0	D49.2
marrow NEC	C96.9	C79.52	—	—	—	D47.9
innominate	C41.4	C79.51	—	D16.8	D48.0	D49.2
marrow NEC	C96.9	C79.52	—	—	—	D47.9
intervertebral cartilage or disc	C41.2	C79.51	—	D16.6	D48.0	D49.2
marrow NEC	C96.9	C79.52	—	—	—	D47.9
ischium	C41.4	C79.51	—	D16.8	D48.0	D49.2
marrow NEC	C96.9	C79.52	—	—	—	D47.9
jaw (lower)	C41.1	C79.51	—	D16.5	D48.0	D49.2
marrow NEC	C96.9	C79.52	—	—	—	D47.9
upper	C41.0	C79.51	—	D16.4	D48.0	D49.2
marrow NEC	C96.9	C79.52	—	—	—	D47.9
knee						
left side	C40.22	C79.51	—	D16.22	D48.0	D49.2
marrow NEC	C96.9	C79.52	—	—	—	D47.9
right side	C40.21	C79.51	—	D16.21	D48.0	D49.2
marrow NEC	C96.9	C79.52	—	—	—	D47.9
unspecified side	C40.20	C79.51	—	D16.20	D48.0	D49.2
marrow NEC	C96.9	C79.52	—	—	—	D47.9
leg NEC						
left side	C40.22	C79.51	—	D16.22	D48.0	D49.2
marrow NEC	C96.9	C79.52	—	—	—	D47.9
right side	C40.21	C79.51	—	D16.21	D48.0	D49.2
marrow NEC	C96.9	C79.52	—	—	—	D47.9
unspecified side	C40.20	C79.51	—	D16.20	D48.0	D49.2
marrow NEC	C96.9	C79.52	—	—	—	D47.9
limb NEC						
lower						
long bones						
left side	C40.20	C79.51	—	D16.21	D48.0	D49.2
marrow NEC	C96.9	C79.52	—	—	—	D47.9
right side	C40.22	C79.51	—	D16.22	D48.0	D49.2
marrow NEC	C96.9	C79.52	—	—	—	D47.9
unspecified side	C40.21	C79.51	—	D16.20	D48.0	D49.2
marrow NEC	C96.9	C79.52	—	—	—	D47.9
short bones						
left side	C40.32	C79.51	—	D16.32	D48.0	D49.2
marrow NEC	C96.9	C79.52	—	—	—	D47.9

	Malignant Primary	Malignant Secondary	Ca in situ	Benign	Uncertain	Unspecified Behavior
bone *(Continued)*						
limb NEC *(Continued)*						
lower *(Continued)*						
short bones *(Continued)*						
right side	C40.31	C79.51	—	D16.31	D48.0	D49.2
marrow NEC	C96.9	C79.52	—	—	—	D47.9
unspecified side	C40.30	C79.51	—	D16.30	D48.0	D49.2
marrow NEC	C96.9	C79.52	—	—	—	D47.9
unspecified site						
left side	C40.22	C79.51	—	D16.22	D48.0	D49.2
marrow NEC	C96.9	C79.52	—	—	—	D47.9
right side	C40.21	C79.51	—	D16.21	D48.0	D49.2
marrow NEC	C96.9	C79.52	—	—	—	D47.9
unspecified side	C40.20	C79.51	—	D16.20	D48.0	D49.2
marrow NEC	C96.9	C79.52	—	—	—	D47.9
unspecified site						
left side	C40.92	C79.51	—	D16.9	D48.0	D49.2
marrow NEC	C96.9	C79.52	—	—	—	D47.9
right side	C40.91	C79.51	—	D16.9	D48.0	D49.2
marrow NEC	C96.9	C79.52	—	—	—	D47.9
unspecified side	C40.90	C79.51	—	D16.9	D48.0	D49.2
marrow NEC	C96.9	C79.52	—	—	—	D47.9
upper						
long bones						
left side	C40.02	C79.51	—	D16.02	D48.0	D49.2
marrow NEC	C96.9	C79.52	—	—	—	D47.9
right side	C40.01	C79.51	—	D16.01	D48.0	D49.2
marrow NEC	C96.9	C79.52	—	—	—	D47.9
unspecified side	C40.00	C79.51	—	D16.00	D48.0	D49.2
marrow NEC	C96.9	C79.52	—	—	—	D47.9
short bones						
left side	C40.12	C79.51	—	D16.12	D48.0	D49.2
marrow NEC	C96.9	C79.52	—	—	—	D47.9
right side	C40.11	C79.51	—	D16.11	D48.0	D49.2
marrow NEC	C96.9	C79.52	—	—	—	D47.9
unspecified side	C40.10	C79.51	—	D16.10	D48.0	D49.2
marrow NEC	C96.9	C79.52	—	—	—	D47.9
unspecified site						
left side	C40.02	C79.51	—	D16.02	D48.0	D49.2
marrow NEC	C96.9	C79.52	—	—	—	D47.9
right side	C40.01	C79.51	—	D16.01	D48.0	D49.2
marrow NEC	C96.9	C79.52	—	—	—	D47.9
unspecified side	C40.00	C79.51	—	D16.00	D48.0	D49.2
marrow NEC	C96.9	C79.52	—	—	—	D47.9

	Malignant Primary	Malignant Secondary	Ca in situ	Benign	Uncertain	Unspecified Behavior
bone *(Continued)*						
long						
lower limbs NEC						
left side	C40.22	C79.51	—	D16.22	D48.0	D49.2
marrow NEC	C96.9	C79.52	—	—	—	D47.9
right side	C40.21	C79.51	—	D16.21	D48.0	D49.2
marrow NEC	C96.9	C79.52	—	—	—	D47.9
unspecified side	C40.20	C79.51	—	D16.20	D48.0	D49.2
marrow NEC	C96.9	C79.52	—	—	—	D47.9
unspecified site						
left side	C40.92	C79.51	—	D16.9	D48.0	D49.2
marrow NEC	C96.9	C79.52	—	—	—	D47.9
right side	C40.91	C79.51	—	D16.9	D48.0	D49.2
marrow NEC	C96.9	C79.52	—	—	—	D47.9
unspecified side	C40.90	C79.51	—	D16.9	D48.0	D49.2
marrow NEC	C96.9	C79.52	—	—	—	D47.9
upper limbs NEC						
left side	C40.02	C79.51	—	D16.02	D48.0	D49.2
marrow NEC	C96.9	C79.52	—	—	—	D47.9
right side	C40.01	C79.51	—	D16.01	D48.0	D49.2
marrow NEC	C96.9	C79.52	—	—	—	D47.9
unspecified side	C40.00	C79.51	—	D16.00	D48.0	D49.2
marrow NEC	C96.9	C79.52	—	—	—	D47.9
malar	C41.0	C79.51	—	D16.4	D48.0	D49.2
marrow NEC	C96.9	C79.52	—	—	—	D47.9
mandible	C41.1	C79.51	—	D16.5	D48.0	D49.2
marrow NEC	C96.9	C79.52	—	—	—	D47.9
marrow NEC	C96.9	C79.52	—	—	—	D47.9
mastoid	C41.0	C79.51	—	D16.4	D48.0	D49.2
marrow NEC	C96.9	C79.52	—	—	—	D47.9
maxilla, maxillary (superior)	C41.0	C79.51	—	D16.4	D48.0	D49.2
marrow NEC	C96.9	C79.52	—	—	—	D47.9
inferior	C41.1	C79.51	—	D16.5	D48.0	D49.2
marrow NEC	C96.9	C79.52	—	—	—	D47.9
metacarpus (any)						
left side	C40.12	C79.51	—	D16.12	D48.0	D49.2
marrow NEC	C96.9	C79.52	—	—	—	D47.9
right side	C40.11	C79.51	—	D16.11	D48.0	D49.2
marrow NEC	C96.9	C79.52	—	—	—	D47.9
unspecified side	C40.10	C79.51	—	D16.10	D48.0	D49.2
marrow NEC	C96.9	C79.52	—	—	—	D47.9
metatarsus (any)						
left side	C40.32	C79.51	—	D16.32	D48.0	D49.2
marrow NEC	C96.9	C79.52	—	—	—	D47.9

	Malignant Primary	Malignant Secondary	Ca in situ	Benign	Uncertain	Unspecified Behavior
bone *(Continued)*						
metatarsus *(Continued)*						
right side	C40.31	C79.51	—	D16.31	D48.0	D49.2
marrow NEC	C96.9	C79.52	—	—	—	D47.9
unspecified side	C40.30	C79.51	—	D16.30	D48.0	D49.2
marrow NEC	C96.9	C79.52	—	—	—	D47.9
navicular						
ankle						
left side	C40.32	C79.51	—	D16.32	D48.0	D49.2
marrow NEC	C96.9	C79.52	—	—	—	D47.9
right side	C40.31	C79.51	—	D16.31	D48.0	D49.2
marrow NEC	C96.9	C79.52	—	—	—	D47.9
unspecified side	C40.30	C79.51	—	D16.30	D48.0	D49.2
marrow NEC	C96.9	C79.52	—	—	—	D47.9
hand						
left side	C40.12	C79.51	—	D16.12	D48.0	D49.2
marrow NEC	C96.9	C79.52	—	—	—	D47.9
right side	C40.11	C79.51	—	D16.11	D48.0	D49.2
marrow NEC	C96.9	C79.52	—	—	—	D47.9
unspecified side	C40.10	C79.51	—	D16.10	D48.0	D49.2
marrow NEC	C96.9	C79.52	—	—	—	D47.9
unspecified site						
left side	C40.32	C79.51	—	D16.32	D48.0	D49.2
marrow NEC	C96.9	C79.52	—	—	—	D47.9
right side	C40.31	C79.51	—	D16.31	D48.0	D49.2
marrow NEC	C96.9	C79.52	—	—	—	D47.9
unspecified side	C40.30	C79.51	—	D16.30	D48.0	D49.2
marrow NEC	C96.9	C79.52	—	—	—	D47.9
nose, nasal	C41.0	C79.51	—	D16.4	D48.0	D49.2
marrow NEC	C96.9	C79.52	—	—	—	D47.9
occipital	C41.0	C79.51	—	D16.4	D48.0	D49.2
marrow NEC	C96.9	C79.52	—	—	—	D47.9
orbit	C41.0	C79.51	—	D16.4	D48.0	D49.2
marrow NEC	C96.9	C79.52	—	—	—	D47.9
parietal	C41.0	C79.51	—	D16.4	D48.0	D49.2
marrow NEC	C96.9	C79.52	—	—	—	D47.9
patella						
left side	C40.32	C79.51	—	D16.32	D48.0	D49.2
marrow NEC	C96.9	C79.52	—	—	—	D47.9
right side	C40.31	C79.51	—	D16.31	D48.0	D49.2
marrow NEC	C96.9	C79.52	—	—	—	D47.9
unspecified side	C40.30	C79.51	—	D16.30	D48.0	D49.2
marrow NEC	C96.9	C79.52	—	—	—	D47.9

	Malignant Primary	Malignant Secondary	Ca in situ	Benign	Uncertain	Unspecified Behavior
bone *(Continued)*						
pelvic	C41.4	C79.51	—	D16.8	D48.0	D49.2
marrow NEC	C96.9	C79.52	—	—	—	D47.9
phalanges						
foot						
left side	C40.32	C79.51	—	D16.32	D48.0	D49.2
marrow NEC	C96.9	C79.52	—	—	—	D47.9
right side	C40.31	C79.51	—	D16.31	D48.0	D49.2
marrow NEC	C96.9	C79.52	—	—	—	D47.9
unspecified side	C40.30	C79.51	—	D16.30	D48.0	D49.2
marrow NEC	C96.9	C79.52	—	—	—	D47.9
hand						
left side	C40.12	C79.51	—	D16.12	D48.0	D49.2
marrow NEC	C96.9	C79.52	—	—	—	D47.9
right side	C40.11	C79.51	—	D16.11	D48.0	D49.2
marrow NEC	C96.9	C79.52	—	—	—	D47.9
unspecified side	C40.10	C79.51	—	D16.10	D48.0	D49.2
marrow NEC	C96.9	C79.52	—	—	—	D47.9
unspecified site						
left side	C40.92	C79.51	—	D16.9	D48.0	D49.2
marrow NEC	C96.9	C79.52	—	—	—	D47.9
right side	C40.91	C79.51	—	D16.9	D48.0	D49.2
marrow NEC	C96.9	C79.52	—	—	—	D47.9
unspecified side	C40.90	C79.51	—	D16.9	D48.0	D49.2
marrow NEC	C96.9	C79.52	—	—	—	D47.9
pubic	C41.4	C79.51	—	D16.8	D48.0	D49.2
marrow NEC	C96.9	C79.52	—	—	—	D47.9
radius (any part)						
left side	C40.02	C79.51	—	D16.02	D48.0	D49.2
marrow NEC	C96.9	C79.52	—	—	—	D47.9
right side	C40.01	C79.51	—	D16.01	D48.0	D49.2
marrow NEC	C96.9	C79.52	—	—	—	D47.9
unspecified side	C40.00	C79.51	—	D16.00	D48.0	D49.2
marrow NEC	C96.9	C79.52	—	—	—	D47.9
rib	C41.3	C79.51	—	D16.7	D48.0	D49.2
marrow NEC	C96.9	C79.52	—	—	—	D47.9
sacral vertebra	C41.4	C79.51	—	D16.8	D48.0	D49.2
marrow NEC	C96.9	C79.52	—	—	—	D47.9
sacrum	C41.4	C79.51	—	D16.8	D48.0	D49.2
marrow NEC	C96.9	C79.52	—	—	—	D47.9
scaphoid						
of ankle						
left side	C40.32	C79.51	—	D16.32	D48.0	D49.2
marrow NEC	C96.9	C79.52	—	—	—	D47.9

	Malignant Primary	Malignant Secondary	Ca in situ	Benign	Uncertain	Unspecified Behavior
bone *(Continued)*						
scaphoid *(Continued)*						
of ankle *(Continued)*						
right side	C40.31	C79.51	—	D16.31	D48.0	D49.2
marrow NEC	C96.9	C79.52	—	—	—	D47.9
unspecified side	C40.30	C79.51	—	D16.30	D48.0	D49.2
marrow NEC	C96.9	C79.52	—	—	—	D47.9
of hand						
left side	C40.12	C79.51	—	D16.12	D48.0	D49.2
marrow NEC	C96.9	C79.52	—	—	—	D47.9
right side	C40.11	C79.51	—	D16.11	D48.0	D49.2
marrow NEC	C96.9	C79.52	—	—	—	D47.9
unspecified side	C40.10	C79.51	—	D16.10	D48.0	D49.2
marrow NEC	C96.9	C79.52	—	—	—	D47.9
unspecified site						
left side	C40.12	C79.51	—	D16.12	D48.0	D49.2
marrow NEC	C96.9	C79.52	—	—	—	D47.9
right side	C40.11	C79.51	—	D16.11	D48.0	D49.2
marrow NEC	C96.9	C79.52	—	—	—	D47.9
unspecified side	C40.10	C79.51	—	D16.10	D48.0	D49.2
marrow NEC	C96.9	C79.52	—	—	—	D47.9
scapula (any part)						
left side	C40.02	C79.51	—	D16.02	D48.0	D49.2
marrow NEC	C96.9	C79.52	—	—	—	D47.9
right side	C40.01	C79.51	—	D16.01	D48.0	D49.2
marrow NEC	C96.9	C79.52	—	—	—	D47.9
unspecified side	C40.00	C79.51	—	D16.00	D48.0	D49.2
marrow NEC	C96.9	C79.52	—	—	—	D47.9
sella turcica	C41.0	C79.51	—	D16.4	D48.0	D49.2
marrow NEC	C96.9	C79.52	—	—	—	D47.9
short						
lower limb						
left side	C40.32	C79.51	—	D16.32	D48.0	D49.2
marrow NEC	C96.9	C79.52	—	—	—	D47.9
right side	C40.31	C79.51	—	D16.31	D48.0	D49.2
marrow NEC	C96.9	C79.52	—	—	—	D47.9
unspecified side	C40.30	C79.51	—	D16.30	D48.0	D49.2
marrow NEC	C96.9	C79.52	—	—	—	D47.9
unspecified site						
left side	C40.92	C79.51	—	D16.9	D48.0	D49.2
marrow NEC	C96.9	C79.52	—	—	—	D47.9
right side	C40.91	C79.51	—	D16.9	D48.0	D49.2
marrow NEC	C96.9	C79.52	—	—	—	D47.9
unspecified side	C40.90	C79.51	—	D16.9	D48.0	D49.2
marrow NEC	C96.9	C79.52	—	—	—	D47.9

	Malignant Primary	Malignant Secondary	Ca in situ	Benign	Uncertain	Unspecified Behavior
bone *(Continued)*						
short *(Continued)*						
upper limb						
left side	C40.12	C79.51	—	D16.12	D48.0	D49.2
marrow NEC	C96.9	C79.52	—	—	—	D47.9
right side	C40.11	C79.51	—	D16.11	D48.0	D49.2
marrow NEC	C96.9	C79.52	—	—	—	D47.9
unspecified side	C40.10	C79.51	—	D16.10	D48.0	D49.2
marrow NEC	C96.9	C79.52	—	—	—	D47.9
shoulder						
left side	C40.02	C79.51	—	D16.02	D48.0	D49.2
marrow NEC	C96.9	C79.52	—	—	—	D47.9
right side	C40.01	C79.51	—	D16.01	D48.0	D49.2
marrow NEC	C96.9	C79.52	—	—	—	D47.9
unspecified side	C40.00	C79.51	—	D16.00	D48.0	D49.2
marrow NEC	C96.9	C79.52	—	—	—	D47.9
skeleton, skeletal NEC	C41.9	C79.51	—	D16.9	D48.0	D49.2
marrow NEC	C96.9	C79.52	—	—	—	D47.9
skull	C41.0	C79.51	—	D16.4	D48.0	D49.2
marrow NEC	C96.9	C79.52	—	—	—	D47.9
sphenoid	C41.0	C79.51	—	D16.4	D48.0	D49.2
marrow NEC	C96.9	C79.52	—	—	—	D47.9
spine, spinal (column)	C41.2	C79.51	—	D16.6	D48.0	D49.2
coccyx	C41.4	C79.51	—	D16.8	D48.0	D49.2
marrow NEC	C96.9	C79.52	—	—	—	D47.9
marrow NEC	C96.9	C79.52	—	—	—	D47.9
sacrum	C41.4	C79.51	—	D16.8	D48.0	D49.2
marrow NEC	C96.9	C79.52	—	—	—	D47.9
sternum	C41.3	C79.51	—	D16.7	D48.0	D49.2
marrow NEC	C96.9	C79.52	—	—	—	D47.9
tarsus (any)						
left side	C40.32	C79.51	—	D16.32	D48.0	D49.2
marrow NEC	C96.9	C79.52	—	—	—	D47.9
right side	C40.31	C79.51	—	D16.31	D48.0	D49.2
marrow NEC	C96.9	C79.52	—	—	—	D47.9
unspecified side	C40.30	C79.51	—	D16.30	D48.0	D49.2
marrow NEC	C96.9	C79.52	—	—	—	D47.9
temporal	C41.0	C79.51	—	D16.4	D48.0	D49.2
marrow NEC	C96.9	C79.52	—	—	—	D47.9
thumb						
left side	C40.12	C79.51	—	D16.12	D48.0	D49.2
marrow NEC	C96.9	C79.52	—	—	—	D47.9
right side	C40.11	C79.51	—	D16.11	D48.0	D49.2
marrow NEC	C96.9	C79.52	—	—	—	D47.9

	Malignant Primary	Malignant Secondary	Ca in situ	Benign	Uncertain	Unspecified Behavior
bone *(Continued)*						
thumb *(Continued)*						
unspecified side	C40.10	C79.51	—	D16.10	D48.0	D49.2
marrow NEC	C96.9	C79.52	—	—	—	D47.9
tibia (any part)						
left side	C40.22	C79.51	—	D16.22	D48.0	D49.2
marrow NEC	C96.9	C79.52	—	—	—	D47.9
right side	C40.21	C79.51	—	D16.21	D48.0	D49.2
marrow NEC	C96.9	C79.52	—	—	—	D47.9
unspecified side	C40.20	C79.51	—	D16.20	D48.0	D49.2
marrow NEC	C96.9	C79.52	—	—	—	D47.9
toe (any)						
left side	C40.32	C79.51	—	D16.32	D48.0	D49.2
marrow NEC	C96.9	C79.52	—	—	—	D47.9
right side	C40.31	C79.51	—	D16.31	D48.0	D49.2
marrow NEC	C96.9	C79.52	—	—	—	D47.9
unspecified side	C40.30	C79.51	—	D16.30	D48.0	D49.2
marrow NEC	C96.9	C79.52	—	—	—	D47.9
trapezium						
left side	C40.12	C79.51	—	D16.12	D48.0	D49.2
marrow NEC	C96.9	C79.52	—	—	—	D47.9
right side	C40.11	C79.51	—	D16.11	D48.0	D49.2
marrow NEC	C96.9	C79.52	—	—	—	D47.9
unspecified side	C40.10	C79.51	—	D16.10	D48.0	D49.2
marrow NEC	C96.9	C79.52	—	—	—	D47.9
trapezoid						
left side	C40.12	C79.51	—	D16.12	D48.0	D49.2
marrow NEC	C96.9	C79.52	—	—	—	D47.9
right side	C40.11	C79.51	—	D16.11	D48.0	D49.2
marrow NEC	C96.9	C79.52	—	—	—	D47.9
unspecified side	C40.10	C79.51	—	D16.10	D48.0	D49.2
marrow NEC	C96.9	C79.52	—	—	—	D47.9
turbinate	C41.0	C79.51	—	D16.4	D48.0	D49.2
marrow NEC	C96.9	C79.52	—	—	—	D47.9
ulna (any part)						
left side	C40.02	C79.51	—	D16.02	D48.0	D49.2
marrow NEC	C96.9	C79.52	—	—	—	D47.9
right side	C40.01	C79.51	—	D16.01	D48.0	D49.2
marrow NEC	C96.9	C79.52	—	—	—	D47.9
unspecified side	C40.00	C79.51	—	D16.00	D48.0	D49.2
marrow NEC	C96.9	C79.52	—	—	—	D47.9
unciform						
left side	C40.12	C79.51	—	D16.12	D48.0	D49.2
marrow NEC	C96.9	C79.52	—	—	—	D47.9

TABLE OF NEOPLASMS

	Malignant Primary	Malignant Secondary	Ca in situ	Benign	Uncertain	Unspecified Behavior
bone *(Continued)*						
unciform *(Continued)*						
right side	C40.11	C79.51	—	D16.11	D48.0	D49.2
marrow NEC	C96.9	C79.52	—	—	—	D47.9
unspecified side	C40.10	C79.51	—	D16.10	D48.0	D49.2
marrow NEC	C96.9	C79.52	—	—	—	D47.9
vertebra (column)	C41.2	C79.51	—	D16.6	D48.0	D49.2
coccyx	C41.4	C79.51	—	D16.8	D48.0	D49.2
marrow NEC	C96.9	C79.52	—	—	—	D47.9
marrow NEC	C96.9	C79.52	—	—	—	D47.9
sacrum	C41.4	C79.51	—	D16.8	D48.0	D49.2
marrow NEC	C96.9	C79.52	—	—	—	D47.9
vomer	C41.0	C79.51	—	D16.4	D48.0	D49.2
marrow NEC	C96.9	C79.52	—	—	—	D47.9
wrist						
left side	C40.12	C79.51	—	D16.12	D48.0	D49.2
marrow NEC	C96.9	C79.52	—	—	—	D47.9
right side	C40.11	C79.51	—	D16.11	D48.0	D49.2
marrow NEC	C96.9	C79.52	—	—	—	D47.9
unspecified side	C40.10	C79.51	—	D16.10	D48.0	D49.2
marrow NEC	C96.9	C79.52	—	—	—	D47.9
xiphoid process	C41.3	C79.51	—	D16.7	D48.0	D49.2
marrow NEC	C96.9	C79.52	—	—	—	D47.9
zygomatic	C41.0	C79.51	—	D16.4	D48.0	D49.2
marrow NEC	C96.9	C79.52	—	—	—	D47.9
book-leaf (mouth) [ventral surface of tongue and floor of mouth]	C06.89	C79.89	D00.00	D10.39	D37.09	D49.0
bowel -*see* Neoplasm, intestine						
brachial plexus	C47.1-	C79.89	—	D36.12	D48.2	D49.2
brain NEC	C71.9	C79.31	—	D33.2	D43.2	D49.6
basal ganglia	C71.0	C79.31	—	D33.0	D43.0	D49.6
cerebellopontine angle	C71.6	C79.31	—	D33.1	D43.1	D49.6
cerebellum NOS	C71.6	C79.31	—	D33.1	D43.1	D49.6
cerebrum	C71.0	C79.31	—	D33.0	D43.0	D49.6
choroid plexus	C71.7	C79.31	—	D33.1	D43.1	D49.6
corpus callosum	C71.8	C79.31	—	D33.2	D43.2	D49.6
corpus striatum	C71.0	C79.31	—	D33.0	D43.0	D49.6
cortex (cerebral)	C71.0	C79.31	—	D33.0	D43.0	D49.6
frontal lobe	C71.1	C79.31	—	D33.0	D43.0	D49.6
globus pallidus	C71.0	C79.31	—	D33.0	D43.0	D49.6
hippocampus	C71.2	C79.31	—	D33.0	D43.0	D49.6
hypothalamus	C71.0	C79.31	—	D33.0	D43.0	D49.6
internal capsule	C71.0	C79.31	—	D33.0	D43.0	D49.6
medulla oblongata	C71.7	C79.31	—	D33.1	D43.1	D49.6
meninges	C70.0	C79.32	—	D32.0	D42.0	D49.7

	Malignant Primary	Malignant Secondary	Ca in situ	Benign	Uncertain	Unspecified Behavior
brain NEC *(Continued)*						
midbrain	C71.7	C79.31	—	D33.1	D43.1	D49.6
occipital lobe	C71.4	C79.31	—	D33.0	D43.0	D49.6
overlapping lesion	C71.8	C79.31	—	—	—	—
parietal lobe	C71.3	C79.31	—	D33.0	D43.0	D49.6
peduncle	C71.7	C79.31	—	D33.1	D43.1	D49.6
pons	C71.7	C79.31	—	D33.1	D43.1	D49.6
stem	C71.7	C79.31	—	D33.1	D43.1	D49.6
tapetum	C71.8	C79.31	—	D33.2	D43.2	D49.6
temporal lobe	C71.2	C79.31	—	D33.0	D43.0	D49.6
thalamus	C71.0	C79.31	—	D33.0	D43.0	D49.6
uncus	C71.2	C79.31	—	D33.0	D43.0	D49.6
ventricle (floor)	C71.5	C79.31	—	D33.0	D43.0	D49.6
fourth	C71.7	C79.31	—	D33.1	D43.1	D49.6
branchial (cleft) (cyst) (vestiges)	C10.4	C79.89	D00.08	D10.5	D37.05	D49.0
breast (connective tissue) (glandular tissue) (soft parts)						
female						
areola	C50.01-	C79.81	D05.9-	D24.0-	D48.6-	D49.3
axillary tail	C50.61-	C79.81	D05.9-	D24.0-	D48.6-	D49.3
central portion	C50.11-	C79.81	D05.9-	D24.0-	D48.6-	D49.3
inner	C50.81-	C79.81	D05.9-	D24.0-	D48.6-	D49.3
lower	C50.81-	C79.81	D05.9-	D24.0-	D48.6-	D49.3
lower-inner quadrant	C50.31-	C79.81	D05.9-	D24.0-	D48.6-	D49.3
lower-outer quadrant	C50.51-	C79.81	D05.9-	D24.0-	D48.6-	D49.3
mastectomy site (skin)	C44.52	C79.2	—	—	—	—
specified as breast tissue	C50.81-	C79.81	—	—	—	—
midline	C50.81-	C79.81	D05.9-	D24.0-	D48.6-	D49.3
nipple	C50.01-	C79.81	D05.9-	D24.0-	D48.6-	D49.3
outer	C50.81-	C79.81	D05.9-	D24.0-	D48.6-	D49.3
overlapping lesion	C50.81-	—	—	—	—	—
skin	C44.52	C79.2	D04.5	D23.5	D48.5	D49.2
tail (axillary)	C50.61-	C79.81	D05.9-	D24.0-	D48.6-	D49.3
unspecified site	C50.91-	C79.81	D05.9-	D24.0-	D48.6-	D49.3
upper	C50.81-	C79.81	D05.9-	D24.0-	D48.6-	D49.3
upper-inner quadrant	C50.21-	C79.81	D05.9-	D24.0-	D48.6-	D49.3
upper-outer quadrant	C50.41-	C79.81	D05.9-	D24.0-	D48.6-	D49.3
male						
areola	C50.02-	C79.81	D05.9-	D24.1-	D48.6-	D49.3
axillary tail	C50.62-	C79.81	D05.9-	D24.1-	D48.6-	D49.3
central portion	C50.12-	C79.81	D05.9-	D24.1-	D48.6-	D49.3
inner	C50.82-	C79.81	D05.9-	D24.1-	D48.6-	D49.3
lower	C50.82-	C79.81	D05.9-	D24.1-	D48.6-	D49.3
lower-inner quadrant	C50.32-	C79.81	D05.9-	D24.1-	D48.6-	D49.3
lower-outer quadrant	C50.52-	C79.81	D05.9-	D24.1-	D48.6-	D49.3

	Malignant Primary	Malignant Secondary	Ca in situ	Benign	Uncertain	Unspecified Behavior
breast *(Continued)*						
male *(Continued)*						
mastectomy site (skin)	C44.52	C79.2	—	—	—	—
specified as breast tissue	C50.82-	C79.81	—	—	—	—
midline	C50.82-	C79.81	D05.9-	D24.1-	D48.6-	D49.3
nipple	C50.02-	C79.81	D05.9-	D24.1-	D48.6-	D49.3
outer	C50.82-	C79.81	D05.9-	D24.1-	D48.6-	D49.3
overlapping lesion	C50.82-	—	—	—	—	—
skin	C44.52	C79.2	D04.5	D23.5	D48.5	D49.2
tail (axillary)	C50.62-	C79.81	D05.9-	D24.1-	D48.6-	D49.3
unspecified site	C50.92-	C79.81	D05.9-	D24.1-	D48.6-	D49.3
upper	C50.82-	C79.81	D05.9-	D24.1-	D48.6-	D49.3
upper-inner quadrant	C50.22-	C79.81	D05.9-	D24.1-	D48.6-	D49.3
upper-outer quadrant	C50.42-	C79.81	D05.9-	D24.1-	D48.6-	D49.3
skin	C44.52	C79.2	D04.5	D23.5	D48.5	D49.2
broad ligament	C57.1	C79.82	D07.39	D28.2	D39.7	D49.5
bronchiogenic, bronchogenic (lung)	C34.9-	C78.0-	D02.2-	D14.3-	D38.1	D49.1
bronchiole	C34.9-	C78.0-	D02.2-	D14.3-	D38.1	D49.1
bronchus						
carina	C34.0-.	C78.0-	D02.2-	D14.3-	D38.1	D49.1
lower lobe of lung	C34.3-	C78.0-	D02.2-	D14.3-	D38.1	D49.1
main	C34.0-	C78.0-	D02.2-	D14.3-	D38.1	D49.1
middle lobe of lung	C34.2	C78.01	D02.21	D14.31	D38.1	D49.1
overlapping lesion	C34.8-	—	—	—	—	—
unspecified site	C34.9-	C78.0-	D02.2-	D14.3-	D38.1	D49.1
upper lobe of lung	C34.1-	C78.0-	D02.2-	D14.3-	D38.1	D49.1
brow	C44.39	C79.2	D04.39	D23.39	D48.5	D49.2
buccal (cavity)	C06.9	C79.89	D00.00	D10.39	D37.09	D49.0
commissure	C06.0	C79.89	D00.02	D10.39	D37.09	D49.0
groove (lower) (upper)	C06.1	C79.89	D00.02	D10.39	D37.09	D49.0
mucosa	C06.0	C79.89	D00.02	D10.39	D37.09	D49.0
sulcus (lower) (upper)	C06.1	C79.89	D00.02	D10.39	D37.09	D49.0
bulbourethral gland	C68.0	C79.19	D09.19	D30.4	D41.3	D49.5
bursa-*see* Neoplasm, connective tissue						
buttock NEC*	C76.3	C79.89	D04.5	D36.7	D48.7	D49.89
caecum - *see* Neoplasm, cecum						
calf*	C76.5-	C79.89	D04.7-	D36.7	D48.7	D49.89
calvarium	C41.0	C79.51	—	D16.4	D48.0	D49.2
marrow NEC	C96.9	C79.52	—	—	—	D47.9
calyx, renal	C65.-	C79.0-	D09.19	D30.1-	D41.1-	D49.5
canal						
anal	C21.1	C78.5	D01.3	D12.9	D37.7	D49.0
auditory (external)	C44.2-	C79.2	D04.2-	D23.2-	D48.5	D49.2
auricular (external)	C44.2-	C79.2	D04.2-	D23.2-	D48.5	D49.2

	Malignant Primary	Malignant Secondary	Ca in situ	Benign	Uncertain	Unspecified Behavior
canaliculi, biliary (biliferi) (intrahepatic)	C22.1	C78.7	D01.5	D13.4	D37.6	D49.0
canthus (eye) (inner) (outer)	C44.1-	C79.2	D04.1-	D23.1-	D48.5	D49.2
capillary-see Neoplasm, connective tissue						
caput coli	C18.0	C78.5	D01.0	D12.0	D37.4	D49.0
cardia (gastric)	C16.0	C78.89	D00.2	D13.1	D37.1	D49.0
cardiac orifice (stomach)	C16.0	C78.89	D00.2	D13.1	D37.1	D49.0
cardio-esophageal junction	C16.0	C78.89	D00.2	D13.1	D37.1	D49.0
cardio-esophagus	C16.0	C78.89	D00.2	D13.1	D37.1	D49.0
carina (bronchus)	C34.0-	C78.0-	D02.2-	D14.3-	D38.1	D49.1
carotid (artery)	C49.0	C79.89	—	D21.0	D48.1	D49.2
body	C75.4	C79.89	—	D35.5	D44.6	D49.7
carpus (any bone)						
left side	C40.12	C79.51	—	D16.12	D48.0	D49.2
marrow NEC	C96.9	C79.52	—	—	—	D47.9
right side	C40.11	C79.51	—	D16.11	D48.0	D49.2
marrow NEC	C96.9	C79.52	—	—	—	D47.9
unspecified side	C40.10	C79.51	—	D16.10	D48.0	D49.2
marrow NEC	C96.9	C79.52	—	—	—	D47.9
cartilage (articular) (joint) NEC (see also Neoplasm, bone)	C41.9	C79.51	—	D16.9	D48.0	D49.2
arytenoid	C32.3	C78.39	D02.0	D14.1	D38.0	D49.1
auricular	C49.0	C79.89	—	D21.0	D48.1	D49.2
bronchi	C34.0-	C78.39	—	D14.3-	D38.1	D49.1
connective tissue-see Neoplasm, connective tissue						
costal	C41.3	C79.51	—	D16.7	D48.0	D49.2
cricoid	C32.3	C78.39	D02.0	D14.1	D38.0	D49.1
cuneiform	C32.3	C78.39	D02.0	D14.1	D38.0	D49.1
ear (external)	C49.0	C79.89	—	D21.0	D48.1	D49.2
ensiform	C41.3	C79.51	—	D16.7	D48.0	D49.2
epiglottis	C32.1	C78.39	D02.0	D14.1	D38.0	D49.1
anterior surface	C10.1	C79.89	D00.08	D10.5	D37.05	D49.0
eyelid	C49.0	C79.89	—	D21.0	D48.1	D49.2
intervertebral	C41.2	C79.51	—	D16.6	D48.0	D49.2
larynx, laryngeal	C32.3	C78.39	D02.0	D14.1	D38.0	D49.1
nose, nasal	C30.0	C78.39	D02.3	D14.0	D38.5	D49.1
pinna	C49.0	C79.89	—	D21.0	D48.1	D49.2
rib	C41.3	C79.51	—	D16.7	D48.0	D49.2
semilunar (knee)	C40.2-	C79.51	—	D16.2-	D48.0	D49.2
thyroid	C32.3	C78.39	D02.0	D14.1	D38.0	D49.1
trachea	C33	C78.39	D02.1	D14.2	D38.1	D49.1
cauda equina	C72.1	C79.49	—	D33.4	D43.4	D49.7
cavity						
buccal	C06.9	C79.89	D00.00	D10.30	D37.09	D49.0
nasal	C30.0	C78.39	D02.3	D14.0	D38.5	D49.1

	Malignant Primary	Malignant Secondary	Ca in situ	Benign	Uncertain	Unspecified Behavior
cavity *(Continued)*						
oral	C06.9	C79.89	D00.00	D10.30	D37.09	D49.0
peritoneal	C48.2	C78.6	—	D20.1	D48.4	D49.0
tympanic	C30.1	C78.39	D02.3	D14.0	D38.5	D49.1
cecum	C18.0	C78.5	D01.0	D12.0	D37.4	D49.0
central nervous system-*see also* Neoplasm, nervous system						
white matter	C71.0	C79.31	—	D33.0	D43.0	D49.6
cerebellopontine (angle)	C71.6	C79.31	—	D33.1	D43.1	D49.6
cerebellum, cerebellar	C71.6	C79.31	—	D33.1	D43.1	D49.6
cerebrum, cerebral (cortex) (hemisphere) (white matter)	C71.0	C79.31	—	D33.0	D43.0	D49.6
meninges	C70.0	C79.32	—	D32.0	D42.0	D49.7
peduncle	C71.7	C79.31	—	D33.1	D43.1	D49.6
ventricle	C71.5	C79.31	—	D33.0	D43.0	D49.6
fourth	C71.7	C79.31	—	D33.1	D43.1	D49.6
cervical region	C76.0	C79.89	D09.7	D36.7	D48.7	D49.89
cervix (cervical) (uteri) (uterus)	C53.9	C79.82	D06.9	D26.0	D39.0	D49.5
canal	C53.0	C79.82	D06.0	D26.0	D39.0	D49.5
endocervix (canal) (gland)	C53.0	C79.82	D06.0	D26.0	D39.0	D49.5
exocervix	C53.1	C79.82	D06.1	D26.0	D39.0	D49.5
external os	C53.1	C79.82	D06.1	D26.0	D39.0	D49.5
internal os	C53.0	C79.82	D06.0	D26.0	D39.0	D49.5
nabothian gland	C53.0	C79.82	D06.0	D26.0	D39.0	D49.5
overlapping lesion	C53.8	—	—	—	—	—
squamocolumnar junction	C53.8	C79.82	D06.7	D26.0	D39.0	D49.5
stump	C53.8	C79.82	D06.7	D26.0	D39.0	D49.5
cheek	C76.0	C79.89	D09.7	D36.7	D48.7	D49.89
external	C44.39	C79.2	D04.39	D23.39	D48.5	D49.2
inner aspect	C06.0	C79.89	D00.02	D10.39	D37.09	D49.0
internal	C06.0	C79.89	D00.02	D10.39	D37.09	D49.0
mucosa	C06.0	C79.89	D00.02	D10.39	D37.09	D49.0
chest (wall) NEC	C76.1	C79.89	D09.7	D36.7	D48.7	D49.89
chiasma opticum	C72.3-	C79.49	—	D33.3	D43.3	D49.7
chin	C44.39	C79.2	D04.39	D23.39	D48.5	D49.2
choana	C11.3	C79.89	D00.08	D10.6	D37.05	D49.0
cholangiole	C22.1	C78.89	D01.5	D13.4	D37.6	D49.0
choledochal duct	C24.0	C78.89	D01.5	D13.5	D37.6	D49.0
choroid	C69.3-	C79.49	D09.2-	D31.3-	D48.7	D49.81
plexus	C71.5	C79.31	—	D33.0	D43.0	D49.6
ciliary body	C69.4-	C79.49	D09.2-	D31.40	D48.7	D49.89
clavicle	C41.3	C79.51	—	D16.7	D48.0	D49.2
marrow NEC	C96.9	C79.52	—	—	—	D47.9
clitoris	C51.2	C79.82	D07.1	D28.0	D39.7	D49.5
clivus	C41.0	C79.51	—	D16.4	D48.0	D49.2
marrow NEC	C96.9	C79.52	—	—	—	D47.9

	Malignant Primary	Malignant Secondary	Ca in situ	Benign	Uncertain	Unspecified Behavior
cloacogenic zone	C21.2	C78.5	D01.3	D12.9	D37.7	D49.0
coccygeal						
body or glomus	C75.5	C79.89	—	D35.6	D44.7	D49.7
vertebra	C41.4	C79.51	—	D16.8	D48.0	D49.2
marrow NEC	C96.9	C79.52	—	—	—	D47.9
coccyx	C41.4	C79.51	—	D16.8	D48.0	D49.2
marrow NEC	C96.9	C79.52	—	—	—	D47.9
colon-see also Neoplasm, intestine, large						
and rectum	C19	C78.5	D01.1	D12.7	D37.5	D49.0
column, spinal-see Neoplasm, spine						
columnella	C44.39	C79.2	D04.39	D23.39	D48.5	D49.2
commissure						
labial, lip	C00.6	C79.89	D00.01	D10.39	D37.01	D49.0
laryngeal	C32.0	C78.39	D02.0	D14.1	D38.0	D49.1
common (bile) duct	C24.0	C78.89	D01.5	D13.5	D37.6	D49.0
concha						
left side	C44.22	C79.2	D04.22	D23.22	D48.5	D49.2
nose	C30.0	C78.39	D02.3	D14.0	D38.5	D49.1
right side	C44.21	C79.2	D04.21	D23.21	D48.5	D49.2
nose	C30.0	C78.39	D02.3	D14.0	D38.5	D49.1
unspecified side	C44.20	C79.2	D04.20	D23.20	D48.5	D49.2
nose	C30.0	C78.39	D02.3	D14.0	D38.5	D49.1
conjunctiva	C69.0-	C79.49	D09.2-	D31.0-	D48.7	D49.8
connective tissue NEC	C49.9	C79.89	—	D21.9	D48.1	D49.2

Note-For neoplasms of connective tissue (blood vessel, bursa, fascia, ligament, muscle, synovia, tendon, etc.) or of morphological types that indicate connective tissue, code according to the list under "Neoplasm, connective tissue;" for sites that do not appear in this list, code to neoplasm of that site; e.g.,

liposarcoma, shoulder	C49.10					
leiomyosarcoma, stomach	C16.9					

Morphological types that indicate connective tissue appear in their proper place in the alphabetic index with the instruction "*see* Neoplasm, connective tissue ...."

abdomen	C49.4	C79.89	—	D21.4	D48.1	D49.2
abdominal wall	C49.4	C79.89	—	D21.4	D48.1	D49.2
ankle	C49.2-	C79.89	—	D21.2-	D48.1	D49.2
antecubital fossa or space	C49.1-	C79.89	—	D21.2-	D48.1	D49.2
arm	C49.1-	C79.89	—	D21.1-	D48.1	D49.2
auricle (ear)	C49.0	C79.89	—	D21.0	D48.1	D49.2
axilla	C49.3	C79.89	—	D21.3	D48.1	D49.2
back	C49.6	C79.89	—	D21.6	D48.1	D49.2
breast-see Neoplasm, breast						

	Malignant Primary	Malignant Secondary	Ca in situ	Benign	Uncertain	Unspecified Behavior
connective tissue NEC *(Continued)*						
leiomyosarcoma, stomach *(Continued)*						
buttock	C49.5	C79.89	—	D21.5	D48.1	D49.2
calf	C49.2-	C79.89	—	D21.2-	D48.1	D49.2
cervical region	C49.0	C79.89	—	D21.0	D48.1	D49.2
cheek	C49.0	C79.89	—	D21.0	D48.1	D49.2
chest (wall)	C49.3	C79.89	—	D21.3	D48.1	D49.2
chin	C49.0	C79.89	—	D21.0	D48.1	D49.2
diaphragm	C49.3	C79.89	—	D21.3	D48.1	D49.2
ear (external)	C49.0	C79.89	—	D21.0	D48.1	D49.2
elbow	C49.1-	C79.89	—	D21.1-	D48.1	D49.2
extrarectal	C49.5	C79.89	—	D21.5	D48.1	D49.2
extremity	C49.9	C79.89	—	D21.9	D48.1	D49.2
lower	C49.2-	C79.89	—	D21.2-	D48.1	D49.2
upper	C49.1-	C79.89	—	D21.1-	D48.1	D49.2
eyelid	C49.0	C79.89	—	D21.0	D48.1	D49.2
face	C49.0	C79.89	—	D21.0	D48.1	D49.2
finger	C49.1-	C79.89	—	D21.1-	D48.1	D49.2
flank	C49.6	C79.89	—	D21.6	D48.1	D49.2
foot	C49.2-	C79.89	—	D21.2-	D48.1	D49.2
forearm	C49.1-	C79.89	—	D21.1-	D48.1	D49.2
forehead	C49.0	C79.89	—	D21.0	D48.1	D49.2
gastric	C49.4	C79.89		D21.4	D48.1	D49.2
gastrointestinal	C49.4	C79.89		D21.4	D48.1	D49.2
gluteal region	C49.5	C79.89	—	D21.5	D48.1	D49.2
great vessels NEC	C49.3	C79.89	—	D21.3	D48.1	D49.2
groin	C49.5	C79.89	—	D21.5	D48.1	D49.2
hand	C49.1-	C79.89	—	D21.1-	D48.1	D49.2
head	C49.0	C79.89	—	D21.0	D48.1	D49.2
heel	C49.2-	C79.89	—	D21.2-	D48.1	D49.2
hip	C49.2-	C79.89	—	D21.2-	D48.1	D49.2
hypochondrium	C49.4	C79.89	—	D21.4	D48.1	D49.2
iliopsoas muscle	C49.5	C79.89	—	D21.5	D48.1	D49.2
infraclavicular region	C49.3	C79.89	—	D21.3	D48.1	D49.2
inguinal (canal) (region)	C49.5	C79.89	—	D21.5	D48.1	D49.2
intestinal	C49.4	C79.89		D21.4	D48.1	D49.2
intrathoracic	C49.3	C79.89	—	D21.3	D48.1	D49.2
ischiorectal fossa	C49.5	C79.89	—	D21.5	D48.1	D49.2
jaw	C03.9	C79.89	D00.03	D10.39	D48.1	D49.0
knee	C49.2-	C79.89	—	D21.2-	D48.1	D49.2
leg	C49.2-	C79.89	—	D21.2-	D48.1	D49.2
limb NEC	C49.9	C79.89	—	D21.9	D48.1	D49.2
lower	C49.2-	C79.89	—	D21.2-	D48.1	D49.2
upper	C49.1-	C79.89	—	D21.1-	D48.1	D49.2

	Malignant Primary	Malignant Secondary	Ca in situ	Benign	Uncertain	Unspecified Behavior
connective tissue NEC *(Continued)*						
nates	C49.5	C79.89	—	D21.5	D48.1	D49.2
neck	C49.0	C79.89	—	D21.0	D48.1	D49.2
orbit	C69.6-	C79.49	D09.2-	D31.6-	D48.7	D49.89
overlapping lesion	C49.8	—	—	—	—	—
pararectal	C49.5	C79.89	—	D21.5	D48.1	D49.2
para-urethral	C49.5	C79.89	—	D21.5	D48.1	D49.2
paravaginal	C49.5	C79.89	—	D21.5	D48.1	D49.2
pelvis (floor)	C49.5	C79.89	—	D21.5	D48.1	D49.2
pelvo-abdominal	C49.8	C79.89	—	D21.6	D48.1	D49.2
perineum	C49.5	C79.89	—	D21.5	D48.1	D49.2
perirectal (tissue)	C49.5	C79.89	—	D21.5	D48.1	D49.2
periurethral (tissue)	C49.5	C79.89	—	D21.5	D48.1	D49.2
popliteal fossa or space	C49.2-	C79.89	—	D21.2-	D48.1	D49.2
presacral	C49.5	C79.89	—	D21.5	D48.1	D49.2
psoas muscle	C49.4	C79.89	—	D21.4	D48.1	D49.2
pterygoid fossa	C49.0	C79.89	—	D21.0	D48.1	D49.2
rectovaginal septum or wall	C49.5	C79.89	—	D21.5	D48.1	D49.2
rectovesical	C49.5	C79.89	—	D21.5	D48.1	D49.2
retroperitoneum	C48.0	C78.6	—	D20.0	D48.3	D49.0
sacrococcygeal region	C49.5	C79.89	—	D21.5	D48.1	D49.2
scalp	C49.0	C79.89	—	D21.0	D48.1	D49.2
scapular region	C49.3	C79.89	—	D21.3	D48.1	D49.2
shoulder	C49.1-	C79.89	—	D21.1-	D48.1	D49.2
skin (dermis) NEC	C44.9	C79.2	D04.9	D23.9	D48.5	D49.2
stomach	C49.4	C79.89		D21.4	D48.1	D49.2
submental	C49.0	C79.89	—	D21.0	D48.1	D49.2
supraclavicular region	C49.0	C79.89	—	D21.0	D48.1	D49.2
temple	C49.0	C79.89	—	D21.0	D48.1	D49.2
temporal region	C49.0	C79.89	—	D21.0	D48.1	D49.2
thigh	C49.2-	C79.89	—	D21.2-	D48.1	D49.2
thoracic (duct) (wall)	C49.3	C79.89	—	D21.3	D48.1	D49.2
thorax	C49.3	C79.89	—	D21.3	D48.1	D49.2
thumb	C49.1-	C79.89	—	D21.1-	D48.1	D49.2
toe	C49.2-	C79.89	—	D21.2-	D48.1	D49.2
trunk	C49.6	C79.89		D21.6	D48.1	D49.2
umbilicus	C49.4	C79.89	—	D21.4	D48.1	D49.2
vesicorectal	C49.5	C79.89	—	D21.5	D48.1	D49.2
wrist	C49.1-	C79.89	—	D21.1-	D48.1	D49.2
conus medullaris	C72.0	C79.49	—	D33.4	D43.4	D49.7
cord (true) (vocal)	C32.0	C78.39	D02.0	D14.1	D38.0	D49.1
false	C32.1	C78.39	D02.0	D14.1	D38.0	D49.1
spermatic	C63.1-	C79.82	D07.69	D29.7	D40.7	D49.5
spinal (cervical) (lumbar) (thoracic)	C72.0	C79.49	—	D33.4	D43.4	D49.7

	Malignant Primary	Malignant Secondary	Ca in situ	Benign	Uncertain	Unspecified Behavior
cornea (limbus)	C69.1-	C79.49	D09.2-	D31.1-	D48.7	D49.89
corpus						
albicans	C56.-	C79.6-	D07.39	D27.9	D39.1-	D49.5
callosum, brain	C71.0	C79.31	—	D33.2	D43.2	D49.6
cavernosum	C60.2	C79.82	D07.4	D29.0	D40.7	D49.5
gastric	C16.2	C78.89	D00.2	D13.1	D37.1	D49.0
penis	C60.2	C79.82	D07.4	D29.0	D40.7	D49.5
striatum, cerebrum	C71.0	C79.31	—	D33.0	D43.0	D49.6
uteri	C54.9	C79.82	D07.0	D26.1	D39.0	D49.5
isthmus	C54.0	C79.82	D07.0	D26.1	D39.0	D49.5
cortex						
adrenal	C74.0-	C79.7-	D09.3	D35.0-	D44.1-	D49.7
cerebral	C71.0	C79.31	—	D33.0	D43.0	D49.6
costal cartilage	C41.3	C79.51	—	D16.7	D48.0	D49.2
costovertebral joint	C41.3	C79.51	—	D16.7	D48.0	D49.2
marrow NEC	C96.9	C79.52	—	—	—	D47.9
Cowper's gland	C68.0	C79.19	D09.19	D30.4	D41.3	D49.5
cranial (fossa, any)	C71.9	C79.31	—	D33.2	D43.2	D49.6
meninges	C70.0	C79.32	—	D32.0	D42.0	D49.7
nerve	C72.50	C79.49	—	D33.3	D43.3	D49.7
specified NEC	C72.59	C79.49	—	D33.3	D43.3	D49.7
craniobuccal pouch	C75.2	C79.89	D09.3	D35.2	D44.3	D49.7
craniopharyngeal (duct) (pouch)	C75.2	C79.89	D09.3	D35.3	D44.4	D49.7
cricoid	C13.0	C79.89	D00.08	D10.7	D37.05	D49.0
cartilage	C32.3	C79.39	D02.0	D14.1	D38.0	D49.1
cricopharynx	C13.0	C79.89	D00.08	D10.7	D37.05	D49.0
crypt of Morgagni	C21.8	C78.5	D01.3	D12.9	D37.7	D49.0
crystalline lens	C69.4-	C79.49	D09.2-	D31.4-	D48.7	D49.89
cul-de-sac (Douglas')	C48.1	C78.6	—	D20.1	D48.4	D49.0
cuneiform cartilage	C32.3	C78.39	D02.0	D14.1	D38.0	D49.1
cutaneous-see Neoplasm, skin						
cutis-see Neoplasm, skin						
cystic (bile) duct (common)	C24.0	C78.89	D01.5	D13.5	D37.6	D49.0
dermis-see Neoplasm, skin						
diaphragm	C49.3	C79.89	—	D21.3	D48.1	D49.2
digestive organs, system, tube, or tract NEC	C26.9	C78.89	D01.9	D13.9	D37.9	D49.0
disc, intervertebral	C41.2	C79.51	—	D16.6	D48.0	D49.2
marrow NEC	C96.9	C79.52	—	—	—	D47.9
disease, generalized	C80.0	C80.0	D09.9	D36.9	D48.9	C80.0
disseminated	C80.0	C80.0	D09.9	D36.9	D48.9	C80.0
Douglas' cul-de-sac or pouch	C48.1	C78.6	—	D20.1	D48.4	D49.0
duodenojejunal junction	C17.8	C78.4	D01.49	D13.39	D37.2	D49.0
duodenum	C17.0	C78.4	D01.41	D13.2	D37.2	D49.0

	Malignant Primary	Malignant Secondary	Ca in situ	Benign	Uncertain	Unspecified Behavior
dura (cranial) (mater)	C70.9	C79.49	—	D32.9	D42.9	D49.7
cerebral	C70.0	C79.32	—	D32.0	D42.0	D49.7
spinal	C70.1	C79.49	—	D32.1	D42.1	D49.7
ear (external)						
left side	C44.22	C79.2	D04.22	D23.22	D48.5	D49.2
auricle or auris	C44.22	C79.2	D04.22	D23.22	D48.5	D49.2
canal, external	C44.22	C79.2	D04.22	D23.22	D48.5	D49.2
cartilage	C49.0	C79.89	—	D21.0	D48.1	D49.2
external meatus	C44.22	C79.2	D04.22	D23.22	D48.5	D49.2
inner	C30.1	C78.39	D02.3	D14.0	D38.5	D49.1
lobule	C44.20	C79.2	D04.20	D23.20	D48.5	D49.2
middle	C30.1	C78.39	D02.3	D14.0	D38.5	D49.1
overlapping lesion with accessory sinuses	C31.8	—	—	—	—	—
skin	C44.22	C79.2	D04.22	D23.22	D48.5	D49.2
right side	C44.21	C79.2	D04.21	D23.21	D48.5	D49.2
auricle or auris	C44.21	C79.2	D04.21	D23.21	D48.5	D49.2
canal, external	C44.21	C79.2	D04.21	D23.21	D48.5	D49.2
cartilage	C49.0	C79.89	—	D21.0	D48.1	D49.2
external meatus	C44.21	C79.2	D04.21	D23.21	D48.5	D49.2
inner	C30.1	C78.39	D02.3	D14.0	D38.5	D49.1
lobule	C44.21	C79.2	D04.21	D23.21	D48.5	D49.2
middle	C30.1	C78.39	D02.3	D14.0	D38.5	D49.1
overlapping lesion with accessory sinuses	C31.8	—	—	—	—	—
skin	C44.21	C79.2	D04.21	D23.21	D48.5	D49.2
unspecified side	C44.20	C79.2	D04.20	D23.20	D48.5	D49.2
auricle or auris	C44.20	C79.2	D04.20	D23.20	D48.5	D49.2
canal, external	C44.20	C79.2	D04.20	D23.20	D48.5	D49.2
cartilage	C49.0	C79.89	—	D21.0	D48.1	D49.2
external meatus	C44.20	C79.2	D04.20	D23.20	D48.5	D49.2
inner	C30.1	C78.39	D02.3	D14.0	D38.5	D49.1
lobule	C44.20	C79.2	D04.20	D23.20	D48.5	D49.2
middle	C30.1	C78.39	D02.3	D14.0	D38.5	D49.1
overlapping lesion with accessory sinuses	C31.8	—	—	—	—	—
skin	C44.20	C79.2	D04.20	D23.20	D48.5	D49.2
earlobe	C44.2-	C79.2	D04.2-	D23.2-	D48.5	D49.2
ejaculatory duct	C63.7	C79.82	D07.69	D29.7	D40.7	D49.5
elbow NEC*	C76.4-	C79.89	D04.6-	D36.7	D48.7	D49.89
endocardium	C38.0	C79.89	—	D15.1	D48.7	D49.89
endocervix (canal) (gland)	C53.0	C79.82	D06.0	D26.0	D39.0	D49.5
endocrine gland NEC	C75.9	C79.89	D09.3	D35.9	D44.9	D49.7
pluriglandular NEC	C75.8	C79.89	D09.3	D35.8	D44.8	D49.7
endometrium (gland) (stroma)	C54.1	C79.82	D07.0	D26.1	D39.0	D49.5
ensiform cartilage	C41.3	C79.51	—	D16.7	D48.0	D49.2
enteric-see Neoplasm, intestine						

	Malignant Primary	Malignant Secondary	Ca in situ	Benign	Uncertain	Unspecified Behavior
ependyma (brain)	C71.5	C79.31	—	D33.0	D43.0	D49.6
fourth ventricle	C71.7	C79.31	—	D33.1	D43.1	D49.6
epicardium	C38.0	C79.89	—	D15.1	D48.7	D49.89
epididymis	C63.0-	C79.82	D07.69	D29.3-	D40.7	D49.5
epidural	C72.9	C79.49	—	D33.9	D43.9	D49.7
epiglottis	C32.1	C78.39	D02.0	D14.1	D38.0	D49.1
anterior aspect or surface	C10.1	C79.89	D00.08	D10.5	D37.05	D49.0
cartilage	C32.3	C78.39	D02.0	D14.1	D38.0	D49.1
free border (margin)	C10.1	C79.89	D00.08	D10.5	D37.05	D49.0
junctional region	C10.8	C79.89	D00.08	D10.5	D37.05	D49.0
posterior (laryngeal) surface	C32.1	C78.39	D02.0	D14.1	D38.0	D49.1
suprahyoid portion	C32.1	C78.39	D02.0	D14.1	D38.0	D49.1
esophagogastric junction	C16.0	C78.89	D00.2	D13.1	D37.1	D49.0
esophagus	C15.9	C78.89	D00.1	D13.0	D37.7	D49.0
abdominal	C15.5	C78.89	D00.1	D13.0	D37.7	D49.0
cervical	C15.3	C78.89	D00.1	D13.0	D37.7	D49.0
distal (third)	C15.5	C78.89	D00.1	D13.0	D37.7	D49.0
lower (third)	C15.5	C78.89	D00.1	D13.0	D37.7	D49.0
middle (third)	C15.4	C78.89	D00.1	D13.0	D37.7	D49.0
overlapping lesion	C15.8	—	—	—	—	—
proximal (third)	C15.3	C78.89	D00.1	D13.0	D37.7	D49.0
thoracic	C15.4	C78.89	D00.1	D13.0	D37.7	D49.0
upper (third)	C15.3	C78.89	D00.1	D13.0	D37.7	D49.0
ethmoid (sinus)	C31.1	C78.39	D02.3	D14.0	D38.5	D49.1
bone or labyrinth	C41.0	C79.51	—	D16.4	D48.0	D49.2
marrow NEC	C96.9	C79.52	—	—	—	D47.9
Eustachian tube	C30.1	C78.39	D02.3	D14.0	D38.5	D49.1
exocervix	C53.1	C79.82	D06.1	D26.0	D39.0	D49.5
external						
meatus (ear)	C44.2-	C79.2	D04.2-	D23.2-	D48.5	D49.2
os, cervix uteri	C53.1	C79.82	D06.1	D26.0	D39.0	D49.5
extradural	C72.9	C79.49	—	D33.9	D43.9	D49.7
extrahepatic (bile) duct	C24.0	C78.89	D01.5	D13.5	D37.6	D49.0
overlapping lesion with gallbladder	C24.8	—	—	—	—	—
extraocular muscle	C69.6-	C79.49	D09.2-	D31.6-	D48.7	D49.89
extrarectal	C76.3	C79.89	D09.7	D36.7	D48.7	D49.89
extremity*	C76.7	C79.89	D04.8	D36.7	D48.7	D49.89
lower*	C76.5-	C79.89	D04.7-	D36.7	D48.7	D49.89
upper*	C76.4-	C79.89	D04.6-	D36.7	D48.7	D49.89
eye NEC						
left side	C69.92	C79.49	D09.22	D31.92	D48.7	D49.89
overlapping lesion	C69.82	—	—	—	—	—
right side	C69.91	C79.49	D09.21	D31.91	D48.7	D49.89
overlapping lesion	C69.81	—	—	—	—	—

	Malignant Primary	Malignant Secondary	Ca in situ	Benign	Uncertain	Unspecified Behavior
eye NEC *(Continued)*						
unspecified side	C69.90	C79.49	D09.20	D31.90	D48.7	D49.89
overlapping lesion	C69.80	—	—	—	—	—
eyeball	C69.4-	C79.49	D09.2-	D31.4-	D48.7	D49.89
eyebrow	C44.31	C79.2	D04.39	D23.39	D48.5	D49.2
eyelid (lower) (skin) (upper)						
left side	C44.12	C79.2	D04.12	D23.12	D48.5	D49.2
cartilage	C49.0	C79.89	—	D21.0	D48.1	D49.2
right side	C44.11	C79.2	D04.11	D23.11	D48.5	D49.2
cartilage	C49.0	C79.89	—	D21.0	D48.1	D49.2
unspecified side	C44.10	C79.2	D04.10	D23.10	D48.5	D49.2
cartilage	C49.0	C79.89	—	D21.0	D48.1	D49.2
face NEC*	C76.0	C79.89	D04.39	D36.7	D48.7	D49.89
fallopian tube (accessory)	C57.0-	C79.82	D07.39	D28.2	D39.7	D49.5
falx (cerebella) (cerebri)	C70.0	C79.32	—	D32.0	D42.0	D49.7
fascia-*see also* Neoplasm, connective tissue						
palmar	C49.1-	C79.89	—	D21.1-	D48.1	D49.2
plantar	C49.2-	C79.89	—	D21.2-	D48.1	D49.2
fatty tissue-*see* Neoplasm, connective tissue						
fauces, faucial NEC	C10.9	C79.89	D00.00	D10.5	D37.05	D49.0
pillars	C09.1	C79.89	D00.08	D10.5	D37.05	D49.0
tonsil	C09.9	C79.89	D00.08	D10.4	D37.05	D49.0
femur (any part)						
left side	C40.22	C79.51	—	D16.22	D48.0	D49.2
marrow NEC	C96.9	C79.52	—	—	—	D47.9
right side	C40.21	C79.51	—	D16.21	D48.0	D49.2
marrow NEC	C96.9	C79.52	—	—	—	D47.9
unspecified side	C40.20	C79.51	—	D16.20	D48.0	D49.2
marrow NEC	C96.9	C79.52	—	—	—	D47.9
fetal membrane	C58	C79.82	D07.0	D26.7	D39.2	D49.5
fibrous tissue-*see* Neoplasm, connective tissue						
fibula (any part)						
left side	C40.22	C79.51	—	D16.22	D48.0	D49.2
marrow NEC	C96.9	C79.52	—	—	—	D47.9
right side	C40.21	C79.51	—	D16.21	D48.0	D49.2
marrow NEC	C96.9	C79.52	—	—	—	D47.9
unspecified side	C40.20	C79.51	—	D16.20	D48.0	D49.2
marrow NEC	C96.9	C79.52	—	—	—	D47.9
filum terminale	C72.0	C79.49	—	D33.4	D43.4	D49.7
finger NEC*	C76.4-	C79.89	D04.6-	D36.7	D48.7	D49.89
flank NEC*	C76.7	C79.89	D04.5	D36.7	D48.7	D49.89
follicle, nabothian	C53.0	C79.82	D06.0	D26.0	D39.0	D49.5
foot NEC*	C76.5-	C79.89	D04.7-	D36.7	D48.7	D49.89
forearm NEC*	C76.4-	C79.89	D04.6-	D36.7	D48.7	D49.89

	Malignant Primary	Malignant Secondary	Ca in situ	Benign	Uncertain	Unspecified Behavior
forehead (skin)	C44.39	C79.2	D04.39	D23.39	D48.5	D49.2
foreskin	C60.0	C79.82	D07.4	D29.0	D40.7	D49.5
fornix						
pharyngeal	C11.3	C79.89	D00.08	D10.6	D37.05	D49.0
vagina	C52	C79.82	D07.2	D28.1	D39.7	D49.5
fossa (of)						
anterior (cranial)	C71.9	C79.31	—	D33.2	D43.2	D49.6
cranial	C71.9	C79.31	—	D33.2	D43.2	D49.6
ischiorectal	C76.3	C79.89	D09.7	D36.7	D48.7	D49.89
middle (cranial)	C71.9	C79.31	—	D33.2	D43.2	D49.6
piriform	C12	C79.89	D00.08	D10.7	D37.05	D49.0
pituitary	C75.1	C79.89	D09.3	D35.2	D44.3	D49.7
posterior (cranial)	C71.9	C79.31	—	D33.2	D43.2	D49.6
pterygoid	C49.0	C79.89	—	D21.0	D48.1	D49.2
pyriform	C12	C79.89	D00.08	D10.7	D37.05	D49.0
Rosenmüller	C11.2	C79.89	D00.08	D10.6	D37.05	D49.0
tonsillar	C09.0	C79.89	D00.08	D10.5	D37.05	D49.0
fourchette	C51.9	C79.82	D07.1	D28.0	D39.7	D49.5
frenulum						
labii-see Neoplasm, lip, internal						
linguae	C02.2	C79.89	D00.07	D10.1	D37.02	D49.0
frontal						
bone	C41.0	C79.51	—	D16.4	D48.0	D49.2
marrow NEC	C96.9	C79.52	—	—	—	D47.9
lobe, brain	C71.1	C79.31	—	D33.0	D43.0	D49.6
meninges	C70.0	C79.32	—	D32.0	D42.0	D49.7
pole	C71.1	C79.31	—	D33.0	D43.0	D49.6
sinus	C31.2	C78.39	D02.3	D14.0	D38.5	D49.1
fundus						
stomach	C16.1	C78.89	D00.2	D13.1	D37.1	D49.0
uterus	C54.3	C79.82	D07.0	D26.1	D39.0	D49.5
gall duct (extrahepatic)	C24.0	C78.89	D01.5	D13.5	D37.6	D49.0
intrahepatic	C22.1	C78.89	D01.5	D13.4	D37.6	D49.0
gallbladder	C23	C78.89	D01.5	D13.5	D37.6	D49.0
overlapping lesion with extrahepatic bile ducts	C24.8	—	—	—	—	—
ganglia (see also Neoplasm, nerve, peripheral)	C47.9	C79.89	—	D36.10	D48.2	D49.2
basal	C71.0	C79.31	—	D33.0	D43.0	D49.6
cranial nerve	C72.50	C79.49	—	D33.3	D43.3	D49.7
Gartner's duct	C52	C79.82	D07.2	D28.1	D39.7	D49.5
gastric-see Neoplasm, stomach						
gastrocolic	C26.9	C78.89	D01.9	D13.9	D37.9	D49.0
gastroesophageal junction	C16.0	C78.89	D00.2	D13.1	D37.1	D49.0
gastrointestinal (tract) NEC	C26.9	C78.89	D01.9	D13.9	D37.9	D49.0
generalized	C80.0	C80.0	D09.9	D36.9	D48.9	C80.0

	Malignant Primary	Malignant Secondary	Ca in situ	Benign	Uncertain	Unspecified Behavior
genital organ or tract						
female NEC	C57.9	C79.82	D07.30	D28.9	D39.9	D49.5
overlapping lesion	C57.8	—	—	—	—	—
specified site NEC	C57.7	C79.82	D07.39	D28.7	D39.7	D49.5
male NEC	C63.9	C79.82	D07.60	D29.9	D40.9	D49.5
overlapping lesion	C63.8	—	—	—	—	—
specified site NEC	C63.7	C79.82	D07.69	D29.7	D40.7	D49.5
genitourinary tract						
female	C57.9	C79.82	D07.30	D28.9	D39.9	D49.5
male	C63.9	C79.82	D07.60	D29.9	D40.9	D49.5
gingiva (alveolar) (marginal)	C03.9	C79.89	D00.03	D10.39	D37.09	D49.0
lower	C03.1	C79.89	D00.03	D10.39	D37.09	D49.0
mandibular	C03.1	C79.89	D00.03	D10.39	D37.09	D49.0
maxillary	C03.0	C79.89	D00.03	D10.39	D37.09	D49.0
upper	C03.0	C79.89	D00.03	D10.39	D37.09	D49.0
gland, glandular (lymphatic) (system)-see also Neoplasm, lymph gland						
endocrine NEC	C75.9	C79.89	D09.3	D35.9	D44.9	D49.7
salivary-see Neoplasm, salivary gland						
glans penis	C60.1	C79.82	D07.4	D29.0	D40.7	D49.5
globus pallidus	C71.0	C79.31	—	D33.0	D43.0	D49.6
glomus						
coccygeal	C75.5	C79.89	—	D35.6	D44.7	D49.7
jugularis	C75.5	C79.89	—	D35.6	D44.7	D49.7
glosso-epiglottic fold(s)	C10.1	C79.89	D00.08	D10.5	D37.05	D49.0
glossopalatine fold	C09.1	C79.89	D00.08	D10.5	D37.05	D49.0
glossopharyngeal sulcus	C09.0	C79.89	D00.08	D10.5	D37.05	D49.0
glottis	C32.0	C78.39	D02.0	D14.1	D38.0	D49.1
gluteal region*	C76.3	C79.89	D04.5	D36.7	D48.7	D49.89
great vessels NEC	C49.3	C79.89	—	D21.3	D48.1	D49.2
groin NEC	C76.3	C79.89	D04.5	D36.7	D48.7	D49.89
gum	C03.9	C79.89	D00.03	D10.39	D37.09	D49.0
lower	C03.1	C79.89	D00.03	D10.39	D37.09	D49.0
upper	C03.0	C79.89	D00.03	D10.39	D37.09	D49.0
hand NEC*	C76.4-	C79.89	D04.6-	D36.7	D48.7	D49.89
head NEC*	C76.0	C79.89	D04.4	D36.7	D48.7	D49.89
heart	C38.0	C79.89	—	D15.1	D48.7	D49.89
overlapping lesion with mediastinum or pleura	C38.8	—	—	—	—	—
heel NEC*	C76.5-	C79.89	D04.7-	D36.7	D48.7	D49.89
helix	C44.2-	C79.2	D04.2-	D23.2-	D48.5	D49.2
hematopoietic, hemopoietic tissue NEC	C96.9	C79.89	—	—	—	D47.9
hemisphere, cerebral	C71.0	C79.31	—	D33.0	D43.0	D49.6
hemorrhoidal zone	C21.1	C78.5	D01.3	D12.9	D37.7	D49.0
hepatic	C22.9	C78.7	D01.5	D13.4	D37.6	D49.0
duct (bile)	C24.0	C78.89	D01.5	D13.5	D37.6	D49.0

	Malignant Primary	Malignant Secondary	Ca in situ	Benign	Uncertain	Unspecified Behavior
hepatic *(Continued)*						
flexure (colon)	C18.3	C78.5	D01.0	D12.3	D37.4	D49.0
primary	C22.8	—	—	—	—	—
hilus of lung	C34.0-	C78.0-	D02.2-	D14.3-	D38.1	D49.1
hip NEC*	C76.5-	C79.89	D04.7-	D36.7	D48.7	D49.89
hippocampus, brain	C71.2	C79.31	—	D33.0	D43.0	D49.6
humerus (any part)						
left side	C40.02	C79.51	—	D16.02	D48.0	D49.2
marrow NEC	C96.9	C79.52	—	—	—	D47.9
right side	C40.01	C79.51	—	D16.01	D48.0	D49.2
marrow NEC	C96.9	C79.52	—	—	—	D47.9
unspecified side	C40.00	C79.51	—	D16.00	D48.0	D49.2
marrow NEC	C96.9	C79.52	—	—	—	D47.9
hymen	C52	C79.82	D07.2	D28.1	D39.7	D49.5
hypopharynx, hypopharyngeal NEC	C13.9	C79.89	D00.08	D10.7	D37.05	D49.0
overlapping lesion	C13.8	—	—	—	—	—
postcricoid region	C13.0	C79.89	D00.08	D10.7	D37.05	D49.0
posterior wall	C13.2	C79.89	D00.08	D10.7	D37.05	D49.0
pyriform fossa (sinus)	C12	C79.89	D00.08	D10.7	D37.05	D49.0
wall	C13.9	C79.89	D00.08	D10.7	D37.05	D49.0
posterior	C13.2	C79.89	D00.08	D10.7	D37.05	D49.0
hypophysis	C75.1	C79.89	D09.3	D35.2	D44.3	D49.7
hypothalamus	C71.0	C79.31	—	D33.0	D43.0	D49.6
ileocecum, ileocecal (coil) (junction) (valve)	C18.0	C78.5	D01.0	D12.0	D37.4	D49.0
ileum	C17.2	C78.4	D01.49	D13.39	D37.2	D49.0
ilium	C41.4	C79.51	—	D16.8	D48.0	D49.2
marrow NEC	C96.9	C79.52	—	—	—	D47.9
immunoproliferative NEC	C88.9	—	—	—	—	—
infraclavicular (region)*	C76.1	C79.89	D04.5	D36.7	D48.7	D49.89
inguinal (region)*	C76.3	C79.89	D04.5	D36.7	D48.7	D49.89
insula	C71.0	C79.31	—	D33.0	D43.0	D49.6
insular tissue (pancreas)	C25.4	C78.89	D01.7	D13.7	D37.7	D49.0
brain	C71.0	C79.31	—	D33.0	D43.0	D49.6
interarytenoid fold	C13.1	C79.89	D00.08	D10.7	D37.05	D49.0
hypopharyngeal aspect	C13.1	C79.89	D00.08	D10.7	D37.05	D49.0
laryngeal aspect	C32.1	C79.39	D02.0	D14.1	D38.0	D49.1
marginal zone	C13.1	C79.89	D00.08	D10.7	D37.05	D49.0
interdental papillae	C03.9	C79.89	D00.03	D10.39	D37.09	D49.0
lower	C03.1	C79.89	D00.03	D10.39	D37.09	D49.0
upper	C03.0	C79.89	D00.03	D10.39	D37.09	D49.0
internal						
capsule	C71.0	C79.31	—	D33.0	D43.0	D49.6
os (cervix)	C53.0	C79.82	D06.0	D26.0	D39.0	D49.5
intervertebral cartilage or disc	C41.2	C79.51	—	D16.6	D48.0	D49.2
marrow NEC	C96.9	C79.52	—	—	—	D47.9

	Malignant Primary	Malignant Secondary	Ca in situ	Benign	Uncertain	Unspecified Behavior
intestine, intestinal	C26.0	C78.80	D01.40	D13.9	D37.7	D49.0
large	C18.9	C78.5	D01.0	D12.6	D37.4	D49.0
appendix	C18.1	C78.5	D01.0	D12.1	D37.3	D49.0
caput coli	C18.0	C78.5	D01.0	D12.0	D37.4	D49.0
cecum	C18.0	C78.5	D01.0	D12.0	D37.4	D49.0
colon	C18.9	C78.5	D01.0	D12.6	D37.4	D49.0
and rectum	C19	C78.5	D01.1	D12.7	D37.5	D49.0
ascending	C18.2	C78.5	D01.0	D12.2	D37.4	D49.0
caput	C18.0	C78.5	D01.0	D12.0	D37.4	D49.0
descending	C18.6	C78.5	D01.0	D12.4	D37.4	D49.0
distal	C18.6	C78.5	D01.0	D12.4	D37.4	D49.0
left	C18.6	C78.5	D01.0	D12.4	D37.4	D49.0
overlapping lesion	C18.8	—	—	—	—	—
pelvic	C18.7	C78.5	D01.0	D12.5	D37.4	D49.0
right	C18.2	C78.5	D01.0	D12.2	D37.4	D49.0
sigmoid (flexure)	C18.7	C78.5	D01.0	D12.5	D37.4	D49.0
transverse	C18.4	C78.5	D01.0	D12.3	D37.4	D49.0
hepatic flexure	C18.3	C78.5	D01.0	D12.3	D37.4	D49.0
ileocecum, ileocecal (coil) (valve)	C18.0	C78.5	D01.0	D12.0	D37.4	D49.0
overlapping lesion	C18.8	—	—	—	—	—
sigmoid flexure (lower) (upper)	C18.7	C78.5	D01.0	D12.5	D37.4	D49.0
splenic flexure	C18.5	C78.5	D01.0	D12.3	D37.4	D49.0
small	C17.9	C78.4	D01.40	D13.30	D37.2	D49.0
duodenum	C17.0	C78.4	D01.49	D13.2	D37.2	D49.0
ileum	C17.2	C78.4	D01.49	D13.39	D37.2	D49.0
jejunum	C17.1	C78.4	D01.49	D13.39	D37.2	D49.0
overlapping lesion	C17.8	—	—	—	—	—
tract NEC	C26.0	C78.89	D01.40	D13.9	D37.7	D49.0
intra-abdominal	C76.2	C79.89	D09.7	D36.7	D48.7	D49.89
intracranial NEC	C71.9	C79.31	—	D33.2	D43.2	D49.6
intrahepatic (bile) duct	C22.1	C78.7	D01.5	D13.4	D37.6	D49.0
intraocular	C69.4-	C79.49	D09.2-	D31.4-	D48.7	D49.89
intraorbital	C69.6-	C79.49	D09.2-	D31.6-	D48.7	D49.89
intrasellar	C75.1	C79.89	D09.3	D35.2	D44.3	D49.7
intrathoracic (cavity) (organs NEC)	C76.1	C79.89	D09.7	D36.7	D48.7	D49.89
overlapping lesion with respiratory organs	C39.8	—	—	—	—	—
iris	C69.4-	C79.49	D09.2-	D31.4-	D48.7	D49.89
ischiorectal (fossa)	C76.3	C79.89	D09.7	D36.7	D48.7	D49.89
ischium	C41.4	C79.51	—	D16.8	D48.0	D49.2
marrow NEC	C96.9	C79.52	—	—	—	D47.9
island of Reil	C71.0	C79.31	—	D33.0	D43.0	D49.6
islands or islets of Langerhans	C25.4	C78.89	D01.7	D13.7	D37.7	D49.0
isthmus uteri	C54.0	C79.82	D07.0	D26.1	D39.0	D49.5

	Malignant Primary	Malignant Secondary	Ca in situ	Benign	Uncertain	Unspecified Behavior
jaw	C76.0	C79.89	D09.7	D36.7	D48.7	D49.89
bone	C41.1	C79.51	—	D16.5	D48.0	D49.2
carcinoma	C03.9	—	—	—	—	—
lower	C03.1	—	—	—	—	—
upper	C03.0	—	—	—	—	—
lower	C41.1	C79.51	—	D16.5	D48.0	D49.2
marrow NEC	C96.9	C79.52	—	—	—	D47.9
marrow NEC	C96.9	C79.52	—	—	—	D47.9
upper	C41.0	C79.51	—	D16.4	D48.0	D49.2
marrow NEC	C96.9	C79.52	—	—	—	D47.9
carcinoma (any type) (lower) (upper)	C76.0	—	—	—	—	—
skin	C44.39	C79.2	D04.39	D23.39	D48.5	D49.2
soft tissues	C03.9	C79.89	D00.03	D10.39	D37.09	D49.0
lower	C03.1	C79.89	D00.03	D10.39	D37.09	D49.0
upper	C03.0	C79.89	D00.03	D10.39	D37.09	D49.0
jejunum	C17.1	C79.4	D01.49	D13.39	D37.2	D49.0
joint NEC (*see also* Neoplasm, bone)	C41.9	C79.51	—	D16.9	D48.0	D49.2
acromioclavicular	C40.0-	C79.51	—	D16.0-	D48.0	D49.2
bursa or synovial membrane-*see* Neoplasm, connective tissue						
costovertebral	C41.3	C79.51	—	D16.7	D48.0	D49.2
sternocostal	C41.3	C79.51	—	D16.7	D48.0	D49.2
temporomandibular	C41.1	C79.51	—	D16.5	D48.0	D49.2
junction						
anorectal	C21.8	C78.5	D01.3	D12.9	D37.7	D49.0
cardioesophageal	C16.0	C78.89	D00.2	D13.1	D37.1	D49.0
esophagogastric	C16.0	C78.89	D00.2	D13.1	D37.1	D49.0
gastroesophageal	C16.0	C78.89	D00.2	D13.1	D37.1	D49.0
hard and soft palate	C05.9	C79.89	D00.00	D10.39	D37.09	D49.0
ileocecal	C18.0	C78.5	D01.0	D12.0	D37.4	D49.0
pelvirectal	C19	C78.5	D01.1	D12.7	D37.5	D49.0
pelviureteric	C65.-	C79.0-	D09.19	D30.1-	D41.1-	D49.5
rectosigmoid	C19	C78.5	D01.1	D12.7	D37.5	D49.0
squamocolumnar, of cervix	C53.8	C79.82	D06.7	D26.0	D39.0	D49.5
kidney (parenchymal)						
calyx	C65.-	C79.0-	D09.19	D30.1-	D41.1-	D49.5
hilus	C65.-	C79.0-	D09.19	D30.1-	D41.1-	D49.5
pelvis	C65.-	C79.0-	D09.19	D30.1-	D41.1-	D49.5
unspecified site	C64.-	C79.0-	D09.19	D30.0-	D41.0-	D49.5
knee NEC*	C76.5-	C79.89	D04.7-	D36.7	D48.7	D49.89
labia (skin)	C51.9	C79.82	D07.0	D28.0	D39.7	D49.5
majora	C51.0	C79.82	D07.0	D28.0	D39.7	D49.5
minora	C51.1	C79.82	D07.0	D28.0	D39.7	D49.5
labial-*see also* Neoplasm, lip						
sulcus (lower) (upper)	C06.1	C79.89	D00.02	D10.39	D37.09	D49.0

	Malignant Primary	Malignant Secondary	Ca in situ	Benign	Uncertain	Unspecified Behavior
labium (skin)	C51.9	C79.82	D07.1	D28.0	D39.7	D49.5
majus	C51.0	C79.82	D07.1	D28.0	D39.7	D49.5
minus	C51.1	C79.82	D07.1	D28.0	D39.7	D49.5
lacrimal						
canaliculi	C69.5-	C79.49	D09.2-	D31.5-	D48.7	D49.89
duct (nasal)	C69.5-	C79.49	D09.2-	D31.5-	D48.7	D49.89
gland	C69.5-	C79.49	D09.2-	D31.5-	D48.7	D49.89
punctum	C69.5-	C79.49	D09.2-	D31.5-	D48.7	D49.89
sac	C69.5-	C79.49	D09.2-	D31.5-	D48.7	D49.89
Langerhans, islands or islets	C25.4	C78.89	D01.7	D13.7	D37.7	D49.0
laryngopharynx	C14.1	C79.89	D00.08	D10.7	D37.05	D49.0
larynx, laryngeal NEC	C32.9	C78.39	D02.0	D14.1	D38.0	D49.1
aryepiglottic fold	C32.1	C78.39	D02.0	D14.1	D38.0	D49.1
cartilage (arytenoid) (cricoid) (cuneiform) (thyroid)	C32.3	C78.39	D02.0	D14.1	D38.0	D49.1
commissure (anterior) (posterior)	C32.0	C78.39	D02.0	D14.1	D38.0	D49.1
extrinsic NEC	C32.1	C78.39	D02.0	D14.1	D38.0	D49.1
meaning hypopharynx	C13.9	C79.89	D00.08	D10.7	D37.05	D49.0
interarytenoid fold	C32.1	C78.39	D02.0	D14.1	D38.0	D49.1
intrinsic	C32.0	C78.39	D02.0	D14.1	D38.0	D49.1
overlapping lesion	C32.8	—	—	—	—	—
ventricular band	C32.1	C78.39	D02.0	D14.1	D38.0	D49.1
leg NEC*	C76.5-	C79.89	D04.7-	D36.7	D48.7	D49.89
lens, crystalline	C69.4-	C79.49	D09.2-	D31.4-	D48.7	D49.89
lid (lower) (upper)	C44.1-	C79.2	D04.1-	D23.1-	D48.5	D49.2
ligament-see also Neoplasm, connective tissue						
broad	C57.1	C79.82	D07.39	D28.2	D39.7	D49.5
Mackenrodt's	C57.7	C79.82	D07.39	D28.7	D39.7	D49.5
non-uterine-see Neoplasm, connective tissue						
round	C57.2	C79.82	—	D28.2	D39.7	D49.5
sacro-uterine	C57.3	C79.82	—	D28.2	D39.7	D49.5
uterine	C57.3	C79.82	—	D28.2	D39.7	D49.5
utero-ovarian	C57.7	C79.82	D07.39	D28.2	D39.7	D49.5
uterosacral	C57.3	C79.82	—	D28.2	D39.7	D49.5
limb*	C76.7	C79.89	D04.8	D36.7	D48.7	D49.89
lower*	C76.5-	C79.89	D04.7-	D36.7	D48.7	D49.89
upper*	C76.4-	C79.89	D04.6-	D36.7	D48.7	D49.89
limbus of cornea	C69.1-	C79.49	D09.2-	D31.1-	D48.7	D49.89
lingual NEC (see also Neoplasm, tongue)	C02.9	C79.89	D00.07	D10.1	D37.02	D49.0
lingula, lung	C34.1-	C78.00	D02.2-	D14.3-	D38.1	D49.1
lip	C00.9	C79.89	D00.01	D10.0	D37.01	D49.0
buccal aspect-see Neoplasm, lip, internal						
commissure	C00.6	C79.89	D00.01	D10.0	D37.01	D49.0
external	C00.2	C79.89	D00.01	D10.0	D37.01	D49.0
lower	C00.1	C79.89	D00.01	D10.0	D37.01	D49.0
upper	C00.0	C79.89	D00.01	D10.0	D37.01	D49.0

	Malignant Primary	Malignant Secondary	Ca in situ	Benign	Uncertain	Unspecified Behavior
lip *(Continued)*						
frenulum-*see* Neoplasm, lip, internal						
inner aspect-*see* Neoplasm, lip, internal						
internal	C00.5	C79.89	D00.01	D10.0	D37.01	D49.0
lower	C00.4	C79.89	D00.01	D10.0	D37.01	D49.0
upper	C00.3	C79.89	D00.01	D10.0	D37.01	D49.0
lipstick area	C00.2	C79.89	D00.01	D10.0	D37.01	D49.0
lower	C00.1	C79.89	D00.01	D10.0	D37.01	D49.0
upper	C00.0	C79.89	D00.01	D10.0	D37.01	D49.0
lower	C00.1	C79.89	D00.01	D10.0	D37.01	D49.0
internal	C00.4	C79.89	D00.01	D10.0	D37.01	D49.0
mucosa-*see* Neoplasm, lip, internal						
oral aspect-*see* Neoplasm, lip, internal						
overlaping lesion	C00.8	—	—	—	—	—
with oral cavity or pharynx	C14.8	—	—	—	—	—
skin (commissure) (lower) (upper)	C44.0	C79.2	D04.0	D23.0	D48.5	D49.2
upper	C00.0	C79.89	D00.01	D10.0	D37.01	D49.0
internal	C00.3	C79.89	D00.01	D10.0	D37.01	D49.0
vermilion border	C00.2	C79.89	D00.01	D10.0	D37.01	D49.0
lower	C00.1	C79.89	D00.01	D10.0	D37.01	D49.0
upper	C00.0	C79.89	D00.01	D10.0	D37.01	D49.0
liver	C22.9	C78.7	D01.5	D13.4	D37.6	D49.0
primary	C22.8	—	—	—	—	—
lobe						
azygos	C34.1-	C78.0-	D02.2-	D14.3-	D38.1	D49.1
frontal	C71.1	C79.31	—	D33.0	D43.0	D49.6
lower	C34.3-	C78.0-	D02.2-	D14.3-	D38.1	D49.1
middle	C34.2	C78.01	D02.21	D14.31	D38.1	D49.1
occipital	C71.4	C79.31	—	D33.0	D43.0	D49.6
parietal	C71.3	C79.31	—	D33.0	D43.0	D49.6
temporal	C71.2	C79.31	—	D33.0	D43.0	D49.6
upper	C34.1-	C78.0-	D02.2-	D14.3-	D38.1	D49.1
lumbosacral plexus	C47.5	C79.49	—	D36.16	D48.2	D49.2
lung						
azygos lobe	C34.1-	C78.0-	D02.2-	D14.3-	D38.1	D49.1
carina	C34.0-	C78.0-	D02.2-	D14.3-	D38.1	D49.1
hilus	C34.0-	C78.0-	D02.2-	D14.3-	D38.1	D49.1
lingula	C34.1-	C78.0-	D02.2-	D14.3-	D38.1	D49.1
lobe NEC	C34.9-	C78.0-	D02.2-	D14.3-	D38.1	D49.1
lower lobe	C34.3-	C78.0-	D02.2-	D14.3-	D38.1	D49.1
main bronchus	C34.0-	C78.0-	D02.2-	D14.3-	D38.1	D49.1
middle lobe	C34.2	C78.01	D02.21	D14.31	D38.1	D49.1
overlapping lesion	C34.8-	—	—	—	—	—
unspecified site	C34.9-	C78.0-	D02.2-	D14.3-	D38.1	D49.1
upper lobe	C34.1-	C78.0-	D02.2-	D14.3-	D38.1	D49.1

	Malignant Primary	Malignant Secondary	Ca in situ	Benign	Uncertain	Unspecified Behavior
lymph, lymphatic channel NEC (*see also* Neoplasm, connective tissue)	C49.9	C79.89	—	D21.9	D48.1	D49.2
gland (secondary)	—	C77.9	—	D36.0	D48.7	D49.89
abdominal	—	C77.2	—	D36.0	D48.7	D49.89
aortic	—	C77.2	—	D36.0	D48.7	D49.89
arm	—	C77.3	—	D36.0	D48.7	D49.89
auricular (anterior) (posterior)	—	C77.0	—	D36.0	D48.7	D49.89
axilla, axillary	—	C77.3	—	D36.0	D48.7	D49.89
brachial	—	C77.3	—	D36.0	D48.7	D49.89
bronchial	—	C77.1	—	D36.0	D48.7	D49.89
bronchopulmonary	—	C77.1	—	D36.0	D48.7	D49.89
celiac	—	C77.2	—	D36.0	D48.7	D49.89
cervical	—	C77.0	—	D36.0	D48.7	D49.89
cervicofacial	—	C77.0	—	D36.0	D48.7	D49.89
Cloquet	—	C77.4	—	D36.0	D48.7	D49.89
colic	—	C77.2	—	D36.0	D48.7	D49.89
common duct	—	C77.2	—	D36.0	D48.7	D49.89
cubital	—	C77.3	—	D36.0	D48.7	D49.89
diaphragmatic	—	C77.1	—	D36.0	D48.7	D49.89
epigastric, inferior	—	C77.1	—	D36.0	D48.7	D49.89
epitrochlear	—	C77.3	—	D36.0	D48.7	D49.89
esophageal	—	C77.1	—	D36.0	D48.7	D49.89
face	—	C77.0	—	D36.0	D48.7	D49.89
femoral	—	C77.4	—	D36.0	D48.7	D49.89
gastric	—	C77.2	—	D36.0	D48.7	D49.89
groin	—	C77.4	—	D36.0	D48.7	D49.89
head	—	C77.0	—	D36.0	D48.7	D49.89
hepatic	—	C77.2	—	D36.0	D48.7	D49.89
hilar (pulmonary)	—	C77.1	—	D36.0	D48.7	D49.89
splenic	—	C77.2	—	D36.0	D48.7	D49.89
hypogastric	—	C77.5	—	D36.0	D48.7	D49.89
ileocolic	—	C77.2	—	D36.0	D48.7	D49.89
iliac	—	C77.5	—	D36.0	D48.7	D49.89
infraclavicular	—	C77.3	—	D36.0	D48.7	D49.89
inguina, inguinal	—	C77.4	—	D36.0	D48.7	D49.89
innominate	—	C77.1	—	D36.0	D48.7	D49.89
intercostal	—	C77.1	—	D36.0	D48.7	D49.89
intestinal	—	C77.2	—	D36.0	D48.7	D49.89
intrabdominal	—	C77.2	—	D36.0	D48.7	D49.89
intrapelvic	—	C77.5	—	D36.0	D48.7	D49.89
intrathoracic	—	C77.1	—	D36.0	D48.7	D49.89
jugular	—	C77.0	—	D36.0	D48.7	D49.89
leg	—	C77.4	—	D36.0	D48.7	D49.89
limb	—					
lower	—	C77.4	—	D36.0	D48.7	D49.89
upper	—	C77.3	—	D36.0	D48.7	D49.89

	Malignant Primary	Malignant Secondary	Ca in situ	Benign	Uncertain	Unspecified Behavior
lymph, lymphatic channel NEC *(Continued)*						
gland *(Continued)*						
lower limb	—	C77.4	—	D36.0	D48.7	D49.89
lumbar	—	C77.2	—	D36.0	D48.7	D49.89
mandibular	—	C77.0	—	D36.0	D48.7	D49.89
mediastinal	—	C77.1	—	D36.0	D48.7	D49.89
mesenteric (inferior) (superior)	—	C77.2	—	D36.0	D48.7	D49.89
midcolic	—	C77.2	—	D36.0	D48.7	D49.89
multiple sites in categories C77.0 - C77.5	—	C77.8	—	D36.0	D48.7	D49.89
neck	—	C77.0	—	D36.0	D48.7	D49.89
obturator	—	C77.5	—	D36.0	D48.7	D49.89
occipital	—	C77.0	—	D36.0	D48.7	D49.89
pancreatic	—	C77.2	—	D36.0	D48.7	D49.89
para-aortic	—	C77.2	—	D36.0	D48.7	D49.89
paracervical	—	C77.5	—	D36.0	D48.7	D49.89
parametrial	—	C77.5	—	D36.0	D48.7	D49.89
parasternal	—	C77.1	—	D36.0	D48.7	D49.89
parotid	—	C77.0	—	D36.0	D48.7	D49.89
pectoral	—	C77.3	—	D36.0	D48.7	D49.89
pelvic	—	C77.5	—	D36.0	D48.7	D49.89
peri-aortic	—	C77.2	—	D36.0	D48.7	D49.89
peripancreatic	—	C77.2	—	D36.0	D48.7	D49.89
popliteal	—	C77.4	—	D36.0	D48.7	D49.89
porta hepatis	—	C77.2	—	D36.0	D48.7	D49.89
portal	—	C77.2	—	D36.0	D48.7	D49.89
preauricular	—	C77.0	—	D36.0	D48.7	D49.89
prelaryngeal	—	C77.0	—	D36.0	D48.7	D49.89
presymphysial	—	C77.5	—	D36.0	D48.7	D49.89
pretracheal	—	C77.0	—	D36.0	D48.7	D49.89
primary (any site) NEC	C96.9	—	—	—	—	—
pulmonary (hiler)	—	C77.1	—	D36.0	D48.7	D49.89
pyloric	—	C77.2	—	D36.0	D48.7	D49.89
retroperitoneal	—	C77.2	—	D36.0	D48.7	D49.89
retropharyngeal	—	C77.0	—	D36.0	D48.7	D49.89
Rosenmüller's	—	C77.4	—	D36.0	D48.7	D49.89
sacral	—	C77.5	—	D36.0	D48.7	D49.89
scalene	—	C77.0	—	D36.0	D48.7	D49.89
site NEC	—	C77.9	—	D36.0	D48.7	D49.89
splenic (hilar)	—	C77.2	—	D36.0	D48.7	D49.89
subclavicular	—	C77.3	—	D36.0	D48.7	D49.89
subinguinal	—	C77.4	—	D36.0	D48.7	D49.89
sublingual	—	C77.0	—	D36.0	D48.7	D49.89
submandibular	—	C77.0	—	D36.0	D48.7	D49.89
submaxillary	—	C77.0	—	D36.0	D48.7	D49.89

	Malignant Primary	Malignant Secondary	Ca in situ	Benign	Uncertain	Unspecified Behavior
lymph, lymphatic channel NEC *(Continued)*						
gland *(Continued)*						
submental	—	C77.0	—	D36.0	D48.7	D49.89
subscapular	—	C77.3	—	D36.0	D48.7	D49.89
supraclavicular	—	C77.0	—	D36.0	D48.7	D49.89
thoracic	—	C77.1	—	D36.0	D48.7	D49.89
tibial	—	C77.4	—	D36.0	D48.7	D49.89
tracheal	—	C77.1	—	D36.0	D48.7	D49.89
tracheobronchial	—	C77.1	—	D36.0	D48.7	D49.89
upper limb	—	C77.3	—	D36.0	D48.7	D49.89
Virchow's	—	C77.0	—	D36.0	D48.7	D49.89
node-*see also* Neoplasm, lymph gland						
primary NEC	C96.9	—	—	—	—	—
vessel (*see also* Neoplasm, connective tissue)	C49.9	C79.89	—	D21.9	D48.1	D49.2
Mackenrodt's ligament	C57.7	C79.82	D07.39	D28.7	D39.7	D49.5
malar	C41.0	C79.51	—	D16.4	D48.0	D49.2
marrow NEC	C96.9	C79.52	—	—	—	D47.9
region-*see* Neoplasm, cheek						
mammary gland-*see* Neoplasm, breast						
mandible	C41.1	C79.51	—	D16.5	D48.0	D49.2
alveolar						
mucosa	C03.1	C79.89	D00.03	D10.39	D37.09	D49.0
ridge or process	C41.1	C79.51	—	D16.5	D48.0	D49.2
carcinoma	C03.1	—	—	—	—	—
marrow NEC	C96.9	C79.52	—	—	—	D47.9
carcinoma	C03.1	—	—	—	—	—
marrow NEC	C96.9	C79.52	—	—	—	D47.9
marrow (bone) NEC	C96.9	C79.52	—	—	—	D47.9
mastectomy site (skin)	C44.5	C79.2	—	—	—	—
specified as breast tissue						
female	C50.81-	C79.81	—	—	—	—
male	C50.82-	C79.81	—	—	—	—
mastoid (air cells) (antrum) (cavity)	C30.1	C78.39	D02.3	D14.0	D38.5	D49.1
bone or process	C41.0	C79.51	—	D16.4	D48.0	D49.2
marrow NEC	C96.9	C79.52	—	—	—	D47.9
maxilla, maxillary (superior)	C41.0	C79.51	—	D16.4	D48.0	D49.2
alveolar						
mucosa	C03.0	C79.89	D00.03	D10.39	D37.09	D49.0
ridge or process	C41.0	C79.51	—	D16.4	D48.0	D49.2
carcinoma	C03.0	—	—	—	—	—
marrow NEC	C96.9	C79.52	—	—	—	D47.9
antrum	C31.0	C78.39	D02.3	D14.0	D38.5	D49.1
carcinoma	C03.0	—	—	—	—	—
inferior-*see* Neoplasm, mandible						

	Malignant Primary	Malignant Secondary	Ca in situ	Benign	Uncertain	Unspecified Behavior
maxilla, maxillary *(Continued)*						
marrow NEC	C96.9	C79.52	—	—	—	D47.9
sinus	C31.0	C78.39	D02.3	D14.0	D38.5	D49.1
meatus						
external (ear)	C44.2-	C79.2	D04.2-	D23.2-	D48.5	D49.2
Meckel's diverticulum	C17.3	C78.4	D01.49	D13.39	D37.2	D49.0
mediastinum, mediastinal	C38.3	C78.1	—	D15.2	D38.3	D49.89
anterior	C38.1	C78.1	—	D15.2	D38.3	D49.89
overlapping lesion with heart or pleura	C38.8	—	—	—	—	—
posterior	C38.2	C78.1	—	D15.2	D38.3	D49.89
medulla						
adrenal	C74.1-	C79.7-	D09.3	D35.0-	D44.1-	D49.7
oblongata	C71.7	C79.31	—	D33.1	D43.1	D49.6
meibomian gland	C44.1-	C79.2	D04.1-	D23.1-	D48.5	D49.2
melanoma-*see* Melanoma						
meninges	C70.9	C79.49	—	D32.9	D42.9	D49.7
brain	C70.0	C79.32	—	D32.0	D42.0	D49.7
cerebral	C70.0	C79.32	—	D32.0	D42.0	D49.7
crainial	C70.0	C79.32	—	D32.0	D42.0	D49.7
intracranial	C70.0	C79.32	—	D32.0	D42.0	D49.7
spinal (cord)	C70.1	C79.49	—	D32.1	D42.1	D49.7
meniscus, knee joint (lateral) (medial)	C40.2-	C79.51	—	D16.2-	D48.0	D49.2
mesentery, mesenteric	C48.1	C78.6	—	D20.1	D48.4	D49.0
mesoappendix	C48.1	C78.6	—	D20.1	D48.4	D49.0
mesocolon	C48.1	C78.6	—	D20.1	D48.4	D49.0
mesopharynx-*see* Neoplasm, oropharynx						
mesosalpinx	C57.1	C79.82	D07.39	D28.2	D39.7	D49.5
mesovarium	C57.1	C79.82	D07.39	D28.2	D39.7	D49.5
metacarpus (any bone)						
left side	C40.12	C79.51	—	D16.12	D48.0	D49.2
marrow NEC	C96.9	C79.52	—	—	—	D47.9
right side	C40.11	C79.51	—	D16.11	D48.0	D49.2
marrow NEC	C96.9	C79.52	—	—	—	D47.9
unspecified side	C40.10	C79.51	—	D16.10	D48.0	D49.2
marrow NEC	C96.9	C79.52	—	—	—	D47.9
metastatic NEC-*see also* Neoplasm, by site, secondary	—	C80	—	—	—	—
metatarsus (any bone)						
left side	C40.32	C79.51	—	D16.32	D48.0	D49.2
marrow NEC	C96.9	C79.52	—	—	—	D47.9
right side	C40.31	C79.51	—	D16.31	D48.0	D49.2
marrow NEC	C96.9	C79.52	—	—	—	D47.9
unspecified side	C40.30	C79.51	—	D16.30	D48.0	D49.2
marrow NEC	C96.9	C79.52	—	—	—	D47.9
midbrain	C71.7	C79.31	—	D33.1	D43.1	D49.6

	Malignant Primary	Malignant Secondary	Ca in situ	Benign	Uncertain	Unspecified Behavior
milk duct-*see* Neoplasm, breast						
mons						
pubis	C51.9	C79.82	D07.1	D28.0	D39.7	D49.5
veneris	C51.9	C79.82	D07.1	D28.0	D39.7	D49.5
motor tract	C72.9	C79.49	—	D33.9	D43.9	D49.7
brain	C71.9	C79.31	—	D33.2	D43.2	D49.6
cauda equina	C72.1	C79.49	—	D33.4	D43.4	D49.7
spinal	C72.0	C79.49	—	D33.4	D43.4	D49.7
mouth	C06.9	C79.89	D00.00	D10.30	D37.09	D49.0
floor	C04.9	C79.89	D00.06	D10.2	D37.09	D49.0
anterior portion	C04.0	C79.89	D00.06	D10.2	D37.09	D49.0
lateral portion	C04.1	C79.89	D00.06	D10.2	D37.09	D49.0
overlapping lesion	C04.8	—	—	—	—	—
overlapping lesion of						
other parts of mouth	C06.89	—	—	—	—	—
unspecified parts of mouth	C06.80	—	—	—	—	—
roof	C05.9	C79.89	D00.00	D10.39	D37.09	D49.0
specified part NEC	C06.89	C79.89	D00.00	D10.39	D37.09	D49.0
vestibule	C06.1	C79.89	D00.00	D10.39	D37.09	D49.0
mucosa						
alveolar (ridge or process)	C03.9	C79.89	D00.03	D10.39	D37.09	D49.0
lower	C03.1	C79.89	D00.03	D10.39	D37.09	D49.0
upper	C03.0	C79.89	D00.03	D10.39	D37.09	D49.0
buccal	C06.0	C79.89	D00.02	D10.39	D37.09	D49.0
cheek	C06.0	C79.89	D00.02	D10.39	D37.09	D49.0
lip-*see* Neoplasm, lip, internal						
nasal	C30.0	C78.39	D02.3	D14.0	D38.5	D49.1
oral	C06.0	C79.89	D00.02	D10.39	D37.09	D49.0
Müllerian duct						
female	C57.7	C79.82	D07.39	D28.7	D39.7	D49.5
male	C63.7	C79.82	D07.69	D29.7	D40.7	D49.5
multiple sites NEC	C80.0	C80.0	D09.9	D36.9	D48.9	C80.0
muscle-*see also* Neoplasm, connective tissue						
extraocular	C69.6-	C79.49	D09.2-	D31.6-	D48.7	D49.89
myocardium	C38.0	C79.89	—	D15.1	D48.7	D49.89
myometrium	C54.2	C79.82	D07.0	D26.1	D39.0	D49.5
myopericardium	C38.0	C79.89	—	D15.1	D48.7	D49.89
nabothian gland (follicle)	C53.0	C79.82	D06.0	D26.0	D39.0	D49.5
nail	C44.9	C79.2	D04.9	D23.9	D48.5	D49.2
finger	C44.6-	C79.2	D04.6-	D23.6-	D48.5	D49.2
toe	C44.7-	C79.2	D04.6-	D23.7-	D48.5	D49.2
nares, naris (anterior) (posterior)	C30.0	C78.39	D02.3	D14.0	D38.5	D49.1
nasal-*see* Neoplasm, nose						
nasolabial groove	C44.39	C79.2	D04.39	D23.39	D48.5	D49.2

	Malignant Primary	Malignant Secondary	Ca in situ	Benign	Uncertain	Unspecified Behavior
nasolacrimal duct	C69.5-	C79.49	D09.2-	D31.5-	D48.7	D49.89
nasopharynx, nasopharyngeal	C11.9	C79.89	D00.08	D10.6	D37.05	D49.0
floor	C11.3	C79.89	D00.08	D10.6	D37.05	D49.0
overlapping lesion	C11.8	—	—	—	—	—
roof	C11.0	C79.89	D00.08	D10.6	D37.05	D49.0
wall	C11.9	C79.89	D00.08	D10.6	D37.05	D49.0
anterior	C11.3	C79.89	D00.08	D10.6	D37.05	D49.0
lateral	C11.2	C79.89	D00.08	D10.6	D37.05	D49.0
posterior	C11.1	C79.89	D00.08	D10.6	D37.05	D49.0
superior	C11.0	C79.89	D00.08	D10.6	D37.05	D49.0
nates	C44.59	C79.2	D04.5	D23.5	D48.5	D49.2
neck NEC*	C76.0	C79.89	D09.7	D36.7	D48.7	D49.89
nerve (ganglion)	C47.9	C79.89	—	D36.10	D48.2	D49.2
abducens	C72.59	C79.49	—	D33.3	D43.3	D49.7
accessory (spinal)	C72.59	C79.49	—	D33.3	D43.3	D49.7
acoustic	C72.4-	C79.49	—	D33.3	D43.3	D49.7
auditory	C72.4-	C79.49	—	D33.3	D43.3	D49.7
autonomic NEC (see also Neoplasm, nerve, peripheral)	C47.9	C79.89	—	D36.10	D48.2	D49.2
brachial	C47.1-	C79.89	—	D36.12	D48.2	D49.2
cranial	C72.50	C79.49	—	D33.3	D43.3	D49.7
specified NEC	C72.59	C79.49	—	D33.3	D43.3	D49.7
facial	C72.59	C79.49	—	D33.3	D43.3	D49.7
femoral	C47.2-	C79.89	—	D36.13	D48.2	D49.2
ganglion NEC (see also Neoplasm, nerve, peripheral)	C47.9	C79.89	—	D36.10	D48.2	D49.2
glossopharyngeal	C72.59	C79.49	—	D33.3	D43.3	D49.7
hypoglossal	C72.59	C79.49	—	D33.3	D43.3	D49.7
intercostal	C47.3	C79.89	—	D36.14	D48.2	D49.2
lumbar	C47.6	C79.89	—	D36.17	D48.2	D49.2
median	C47.1-	C79.89	—	D36.12	D48.2	D49.2
obturator	C47.2-	C79.89	—	D36.13	D48.2	D49.2
oculomotor	C72.59	C79.49	—	D33.3	D43.3	D49.7
olfactory	C47.2-	C79.49	—	D33.3	D43.3	D49.7
optic	C72.3-	C79.49	—	D33.3	D43.3	D49.7
parasympathetic NEC - (see also Neoplasm, nerve, peripheral)	C47.9	C79.89	—	D36.10	D48.2	D49.2
peripheral NEC	C47.9	C79.89	—	D36.10	D48.2	D49.2
abdomen	C47.4	C79.89	—	D36.15	D48.2	D49.2
abdominal wall	C47.4	C79.89	—	D36.15	D48.2	D49.2
ankle	C47.2-	C79.89	—	D36.13	D48.2	D49.2
antecubital fossa or space	C47.1-	C79.89	—	D36.12	D48.2	D49.2
arm	C47.1-	C79.89	—	D36.12	D48.2	D49.2
auricle (ear)	C47.0	C79.89	—	D36.11	D48.2	D49.2
axilla	C47.3	C79.89	—	D36.12	D48.2	D49.2
back	C47.6	C79.89	—	D36.17	D48.2	D49.2
buttock	C47.5	C79.89	—	D36.16	D48.2	D49.2

	Malignant Primary	Malignant Secondary	Ca in situ	Benign	Uncertain	Unspecified Behavior
nerve *(Continued)*						
peripheral NEC *(Continued)*						
calf	C47.2-	C79.89	—	D36.13	D48.2	D49.2
cervical region	C47.0	C79.89	—	D36.11	D48.2	D49.2
cheek	C47.0	C79.89	—	D36.11	D48.2	D49.2
chest (wall)	C47.3	C79.89	—	D36.14	D48.2	D49.2
chin	C47.0	C79.89	—	D36.11	D48.2	D49.2
ear (external)	C47.0	C79.89	—	D36.11	D48.2	D49.2
elbow	C47.1-	C79.89	—	D36.12	D48.2	D49.2
extrarectal	C47.5	C79.89	—	D36.16	D48.2	D49.2
extremity	C47.9	C79.89	—	D36.10	D48.2	D49.2
lower	C47.2-	C79.89	—	D36.13	D48.2	D49.2
upper	C47.1-	C79.89	—	D36.12	D48.2	D49.2
eyelid	C47.0	C79.89	—	D36.11	D48.2	D49.2
face	C47.0	C79.89	—	D36.11	D48.2	D49.2
finger	C47.1-	C79.89	—	D36.12	D48.2	D49.2
flank	C47.6	C79.89	—	D36.17	D48.2	D49.2
foot	C47.2-	C79.89	—	D36.13	D48.2	D49.2
forearm	C47.1-	C79.89	—	D36.12	D48.2	D49.2
forehead	C47.0	C79.89	—	D36.11	D48.2	D49.2
gluteal region	C47.5	C79.89	—	D36.16	D48.2	D49.2
groin	C47.5	C79.89	—	D36.16	D48.2	D49.2
hand	C47.1-	C79.89	—	D36.12	D48.2	D49.2
head	C47.0	C79.89	—	D36.11	D48.2	D49.2
heel	C47.2-	C79.89	—	D36.13	D48.2	D49.2
hip	C47.2-	C79.89	—	D36.13	D48.2	D49.2
infraclavicular region	C47.3	C79.89	—	D36.14	D48.2	D49.2
inguinal (canal) (region)	C47.5	C79.89	—	D36.16	D48.2	D49.2
intrathoracic	C47.3	C79.89	—	D36.14	D48.2	D49.2
ischiorectal fossa	C47.5	C79.89	—	D36.16	D48.2	D49.2
knee	C47.2-	C79.89	—	D36.13	D48.2	D49.2
leg	C47.2-	C79.89	—	D36.13	D48.2	D49.2
limb NEC	C47.9	C79.89	—	D36.10	D48.2	D49.2
lower	C47.2-	C79.89	—	D36.13	D48.2	D49.2
upper	C47.1-	C79.89	—	D36.12	D48.2	D49.2
nates	C47.5	C79.89	—	D36.16	D48.2	D49.2
neck	C47.0	C79.89	—	D36.11	D48.2	D49.2
orbit	C69.6-	C79.49	—	D31.60	D48.7	D49.2
pararectal	C47.5	C79.89	—	D36.16	D48.2	D49.2
paraurethral	C47.5	C79.89	—	D36.16	D48.2	D49.2
paravaginal	C47.5	C79.89	—	D36.16	D48.2	D49.2
pelvis (floor)	C47.5	C79.89	—	D36.16	D48.2	D49.2
pelvoabdominal	C47.8	C79.89	—	D36.17	D48.2	D49.2
perineum	C47.5	C79.89	—	D36.16	D48.2	D49.2

	Malignant Primary	Malignant Secondary	Ca in situ	Benign	Uncertain	Unspecified Behavior
nerve *(Continued)*						
peripheral NEC *(Continued)*						
perirectal (tissue)	C47.5	C79.89	—	D36.16	D48.2	D49.2
periurethral (tissue)	C47.5	C79.89	—	D36.16	D48.2	D49.2
popliteal fossa or space	C47.2-	C79.89	—	D36.13	D48.2	D49.2
presacral	C47.5	C79.89	—	D36.16	D48.2	D49.2
pterygoid fossa	C47.0	C79.89	—	D36.11	D48.2	D49.2
rectovaginal septum or wall	C47.5	C79.89	—	D36.16	D48.2	D49.2
rectovesical	C47.5	C79.89	—	D36.16	D48.2	D49.2
sacrococcygeal region	C47.5	C79.89	—	D36.16	D48.2	D49.2
scalp	C47.0	C79.89	—	D36.11	D48.2	D49.2
scapular region	C47.3	C79.89	—	D36.14	D48.2	D49.2
shoulder	C47.1-	C79.89	—	D36.12	D48.2	D49.2
submental	C47.0	C79.89	—	D36.11	D48.2	D49.2
supraclavicular region	C47.0	C79.89	—	D36.11	D48.2	D49.2
temple	C47.0	C79.89	—	D36.11	D48.2	D49.2
temporal region	C47.0	C79.89	—	D36.11	D48.2	D49.2
thigh	C47.2-	C79.89	—	D36.13	D48.2	D49.2
thoracic (duct) (wall)	C47.3	C79.89	—	D36.14	D48.2	D49.2
thorax	C47.3	C79.89	—	D36.14	D48.2	D49.2
thumb	C47.1-	C79.89	—	D36.12	D48.2	D49.2
toe	C47.2-	C79.89	—	D36.13	D48.2	D49.2
trunk	C47.6	C79.89	—	D36.17	D48.2	D49.2
umbilicus	C47.4	C79.89	—	D36.15	D48.2	D49.2
vesicorectal	C47.5	C79.89	—	D36.16	D48.2	D49.2
wrist	C47.1-	C79.89	—	D36.12	D48.2	D49.2
radial	C47.1-	C79.89	—	D36.12	D48.2	D49.2
sacral	C47.5	C79.89	—	D36.16	D48.2	D49.2
sciatic	C47.2-	C79.89	—	D36.13	D48.2	D49.2
spinal NEC	C47.9	C79.89	—	D36.10	D48.2	D49.2
accessory	C72.59	C79.49	—	D33.3	D43.3	D49.7
sympathetic NEC *(see also* Neoplasm, nerve, peripheral)	C47.9	C79.89	—	D36.10	D48.2	D49.2
trigeminal	C72.59	C79.49	—	D33.3	D43.3	D49.7
trochlear	C72.59	C79.49	—	D33.3	D43.3	D49.7
ulnar	C47.1-	C79.89	—	D36.12	D48.2	D49.2
vagus	C72.59	C79.49	—	D33.3	D43.3	D49.7
nervous system (central) NEC	C72.9	C79.40	—	D33.9	D43.9	D49.7
autonomic NEC *(see also* Neoplasm, nerve, peripheral)	C47.9	C79.89	—	D36.10	D48.2	D49.2
brain-*see also* Neoplasm, brain						
membrane or meninges	C70.0	C79.32	—	D32.0	D42.0	D49.7
overlapping lesion	C72.9	—	—	—	—	—
parasympathetic NEC *(see also* Neoplasm, nerve, peripheral)	C47.9	C79.89	—	D36.10	D48.2	D49.2
sympathetic NEC *(see also* Neoplasm, nerve, peripheral)	C47.9	C79.89	—	D36.10	D48.2	D49.2

	Malignant Primary	Malignant Secondary	Ca in situ	Benign	Uncertain	Unspecified Behavior
nipple						
female	C50.01-	C79.81	D05.9-	D24.0-	D48.6-	D49.3
male	C50.02-	C79.81	D05.9-	D24.1-	D48.6-	D49.3
nose, nasal	C76.0	C79.89	D09.7	D36.7	D48.7	D49.89
ala (external) (nasi)	C44.31	C79.2	D04.39	D23.39	D48.5	D49.2
bone	C41.0	C79.51	—	D16.4	D48.0	D49.2
marrow NEC	C96.9	C79.52	—	—	—	D47.9
cartilage	C30.0	C78.39	D02.3	D14.0	D38.5	D49.1
cavity	C30.0	C78.39	D02.3	D14.0	D38.5	D49.1
overlapping lesion with accessory sinuses	C31.8	—	—	—	—	—
choana	C11.3	C79.89	D00.08	D10.6	D37.05	D49.0
external (skin)	C44.31	C79.2	D04.39	D23.39	D48.5	D49.2
fossa	C30.0	C78.39	D02.3	D14.0	D38.5	D49.1
internal	C30.0	C78.39	D02.3	D14.0	D38.5	D49.1
mucosa	C30.0	C78.39	D02.3	D14.0	D38.5	D49.1
septum	C30.0	C78.39	D02.3	D14.0	D38.5	D49.1
posterior margin	C11.3	C79.89	D00.08	D10.6	D37.05	D49.0
sinus-*see* Neoplasm, sinus						
skin	C44.31	C79.2	D04.39	D23.39	D48.5	D49.2
turbinate (mucosa)	C30.0	C78.39	D02.3	D14.0	D38.5	D49.1
bone	C41.0	C79.51	—	D16.4	D48.0	D49.2
marrow NEC	C96.9	C79.52	—	—	—	D47.9
vestibule	C30.0	C78.39	D02.3	D14.0	D38.5	D49.1
nostril	C30.0	C78.39	D02.3	D14.0	D38.5	D49.1
nucleus pulposus	C41.2	C79.51	—	D16.6	D48.0	D49.2
marrow NEC	C96.9	C79.52	—	—	—	D47.9
occipital						
bone	C41.0	C79.51	—	D16.4	D48.0	D49.2
marrow NEC	C96.9	C79.52	—	—	—	D47.9
lobe or pole, brain	C71.4	C79.31	—	D33.0	D43.0	D49.6
odontogenic-*see* Neoplasm, jaw bone						
oesophagus-*see* Neoplasm, esophagus						
olfactory nerve or bulb	C72.2-	C79.49	—	D33.3	D43.3	D49.7
olive (brain)	C71.7	C79.31	—	D33.1	D43.1	D49.6
omentum	C48.1	C78.6	—	D20.1	D48.4	D49.0
overlaping lesion with retroperitoneum	C48.8	—	—	—	—	—
operculum (brain)	C71.0	C79.31	—	D33.0	D43.0	D49.6
optic nerve, chiasm, or tract	C72.3-	C79.49	—	D33.3	D43.3	D49.7
oral (cavity)	C06.9	C79.89	D00.00	D10.30	D37.09	D49.0
ill-defined	C14.8	C79.89	D00.00	D10.30	D37.09	D49.0
mucosa	C06.0	C79.89	D00.02	D10.39	D37.09	D49.0
overlapping lesion with lip or pharynx	C14.8	—	—	—	—	—
orbit						
autonomic nerve	C69.6-	C79.49	—	D31.6-	D48.7	D49.2

	Malignant Primary	Malignant Secondary	Ca in situ	Benign	Uncertain	Unspecified Behavior
orbit *(Continued)*						
bone	C41.0	C79.51	—	D16.4	D48.0	D49.2
marrow NEC	C96.9	C79.52	—	—	—	D47.9
eye	C69.6-	C79.49	D09.2-	D31.6-	D48.7	D49.89
peripheral nerves	C69.6-	C79.49	—	D31.6-	D48.7	D49.2
soft parts	C69.6-	C79.49	D09.2-	D31.6-	D48.7	D49.89
unspecified site	C69.6-	C79.49	D09.2-	D31.6-	D48.7	D49.89
organ of Zuckerkandl	C75.5	C79.89	—	D35.6	D44.7	D49.7
oropharynx	C10.9	C79.89	D00.08	D10.5	D37.05	D49.0
branchial cleft (vestige)	C10.4	C79.89	D00.08	D10.5	D37.05	D49.0
junctional region	C10.8	C79.89	D00.08	D10.5	D37.05	D49.0
lateral wall	C10.2	C79.89	D00.08	D10.5	D37.05	D49.0
overlapping lesion	C10.8	—	—	—	—	—
pillars or fauces	C09.1	C79.89	D00.08	D10.5	D37.05	D49.0
posterior wall	C10.3	C79.89	D00.08	D10.5	D37.05	D49.0
vallecula	C10.0	C79.89	D00.08	D10.5	D37.05	D49.0
os						
external	C53.1	C79.82	D06.1	D26.0	D39.0	D49.5
internal	C53.0	C79.82	D06.0	D26.0	D39.0	D49.5
ovary	C56.-	C79.6-	D07.39	D27.-	D39.1-	D49.5
oviduct	C57.0-	C79.82	D07.39	D28.2	D39.7	D49.5
palate	C05.9	C79.89	D00.00	D10.39	D37.09	D49.0
hard	C05.0	C79.89	D00.05	D10.39	D37.09	D49.0
junction of hard and soft palate	C05.9	C79.89	D00.00	D10.39	D37.09	D49.0
overlapping lesions	C05.8	—	—	—	—	—
soft	C05.1	C79.89	D00.04	D10.39	D37.09	D49.0
nasopharyngeal surface	C11.3	C79.89	D00.08	D10.6	D37.05	D49.0
posterior surface	C11.3	C79.89	D00.08	D10.6	D37.05	D49.0
superior surface	C11.3	C79.89	D00.08	D10.6	D37.05	D49.0
palatoglossal arch	C09.1	C79.89	D00.00	D10.5	D37.09	D49.0
palatopharyngeal arch	C09.1	C79.89	D00.00	D10.5	D37.09	D49.0
pallium	C71.0	C79.31	—	D33.0	D43.0	D49.6
palpebra	C44.1-	C79.2	D04.1-	D23.1-	D48.5	D49.2
pancreas	C25.9	C78.89	D01.7	D13.6	D37.7	D49.0
body	C25.1	C78.89	D01.7	D13.6	D37.7	D49.0
duct (of Santorini) (of Wirsung)	C25.3	C78.89	D01.7	D13.6	D37.7	D49.0
ectopic tissue	C25.7	C78.89	—	D13.6	D37.7	D49.0
head	C25.0	C78.89	D01.7	D13.6	D37.7	D49.0
islet cells	C25.4	C78.89	D01.7	D13.7	D37.7	D49.0
neck	C25.7	C78.89	D01.7	D13.6	D37.7	D49.0
overlapping lesion	C25.8	—	—	—	—	—
tail	C25.2	C78.89	D01.7	D13.6	D37.7	D49.0
para-aortic body	C75.5	C79.89	—	D35.6	D44.7	D49.7
paraganglion NEC	C75.5	C79.89	—	D35.6	D44.7	D49.7

	Malignant Primary	Malignant Secondary	Ca in situ	Benign	Uncertain	Unspecified Behavior
parametrium	C57.3	C79.82	—	D28.2	D39.7	D49.5
paranephric	C48.0	C78.6	—	D20.0	D48.3	D49.0
pararectal	C76.3	C79.89	—	D36.7	D48.7	D49.89
parasagittal (region)	C76.0	C79.89	D09.7	D36.7	D48.7	D49.89
parasellar	C72.9	C79.49	—	D33.9	D43.7	D49.7
parathyroid (gland)	C75.0	C79.89	D09.3	D35.1	D44.2	D49.7
paraurethral	C76.3	C79.89	—	D36.7	D48.7	D49.89
gland	C68.1	C79.19	D09.19	D30.7	D41.7	D49.5
paravaginal	C76.3	C79.89	—	D36.7	D48.7	D49.89
parenchyma, kidney	C64.-	D79.0-	D09.19	D30.0-	D41.0-	D49.5
parietal						
bone	C41.0	C79.51	—	D16.4	D48.0	D49.2
marrow NEC	C96.9	C79.52	—	—	—	D47.9
lobe, brain	C71.3	C79.31	—	D33.0	D43.0	D49.6
paroophoron	C57.1	C79.82	D07.39	D28.2	D39.7	D49.5
parotid (duct) (gland)	C07	C79.89	D00.00	D11.0	D37.030	D49.0
parovarium	C57.1	C79.82	D07.39	D28.2	D39.7	D49.5
patella						
left side	C40.32	C79.51	—	D16.32	D48.0	D49.2
marrow NEC	C96.9	C79.52	—	—	—	D47.9
right side	C40.31	C79.51	—	D16.31	D48.0	D49.2
marrow NEC	C96.9	C79.52	—	—	—	D47.9
unspecified side	C40.30	C79.51	—	D16.30	D48.0	D49.2
marrow NEC	C96.9	C79.52	—	—	—	D47.9
peduncle, cerebral	C71.7	C79.31	—	D33.1	D43.1	D49.6
pelvirectal junction	C19	C78.5	D01.1	D12.7	D37.5	D49.0
pelvis, pelvic	C76.3	C79.89	D09.7	D36.7	D48.7	D49.89
bone	C41.4	C79.51	—	D16.8	D48.0	D49.2
marrow NEC	C96.9	C79.52	—	—	—	D47.9
floor	C76.3	C79.89	D09.7	D36.7	D48.7	D49.89
renal	C69.-	D79.0-	D09.19	D30.1-	D41.1-	D49.5
viscera	C76.3	C79.89	D09.7	D36.7	D48.7	D49.89
wall	C76.3	C79.89	D09.7	D36.7	D48.7	D49.89
pelvo-abdominal	C76.7	C79.89	D09.7	D36.7	D48.7	D49.89
penis	C60.9	C79.82	D07.4	D29.0	D40.7	D49.5
body	C60.2	C79.82	D07.4	D29.0	D40.7	D49.5
corpus (cavernosum)	C60.2	C79.82	D07.4	D29.0	D40.7	D49.5
glans	C60.1	C79.82	D07.4	D29.0	D40.7	D49.5
skin NEC	C60.9	C79.82	D07.4	D29.0	D40.7	D49.5
periadrenal (tissue)	C48.0	C78.6	—	D20.0	D48.3	D49.0
perianal (skin)	C44.51	C79.2	D04.5	D23.5	D48.5	D49.2
pericardium	C38.0	C79.89	—	D15.1	D48.7	D49.89
perinephric	C48.0	C78.6	—	D20.0	D48.3	D49.0
perineum	C76.3	C79.89	D09.7	D36.7	D48.7	D49.89

	Malignant Primary	Malignant Secondary	Ca in situ	Benign	Uncertain	Unspecified Behavior
periodontal tissue NEC	C03.9	C79.89	D00.03	D10.39	D37.09	D49.0
periosteum-*see* Neoplasm, bone						
peripancreatic	C48.0	C78.6	—	D20.0	D48.3	D49.0
peripheral nerve NEC	C47.9	C79.89	—	D36.10	D48.2	D49.2
perirectal (tissue)	C76.3	C79.89	—	D36.7	D48.7	D49.89
perirenal (tissue)	C48.0	C78.6	—	D20.0	D48.3	D49.0
peritoneum, peritoneal (cavity)	C48.2	C78.6	—	D20.1	D48.4	D49.0
overlapping lesion	C48.9	—	—	—	—	—
with digestive organs	C26.9	—	—	—	—	—
parietal	C48.1	C78.6	—	D20.1	D48.4	D49.0
pelvic	C48.1	C78.6	—	D20.1	D48.4	D49.0
specified part NEC	C48.1	C78.6	—	D20.1	D48.4	D49.0
peritonsillar (tissue)	C76.0	C79.89	D09.7	D36.7	D48.7	D49.89
periurethral tissue	C76.3	C79.89	—	D36.7	D48.7	D49.89
phalanges						
foot						
left side	C40.32	C79.51	—	D16.32	D48.0	D49.2
marrow NEC	C96.9	C79.52	—	—	—	D47.9
right side	C40.31	C79.51	—	D16.31	D48.0	D49.2
marrow NEC	C96.9	C79.52	—	—	—	D47.9
unspecified side	C40.30	C79.51	—	D16.30	D48.0	D49.2
marrow NEC	C96.9	C79.52	—	—	—	D47.9
hand						
left side	C40.12	C79.51	—	D16.12	D48.0	D49.2
marrow NEC	C96.9	C79.52	—	—	—	D47.9
right side	C40.11	C79.51	—	D16.11	D48.0	D49.2
marrow NEC	C96.9	C79.52	—	—	—	D47.9
unspecified side	C40.10	C79.51	—	D16.10	D48.0	D49.2
marrow NEC	C96.9	C79.52	—	—	—	D47.9
unspecified site						
left side	C40.92	C79.51	—	D16.9	D48.0	D49.2
marrow NEC	C96.9	C79.52	—	—	—	D47.9
right side	C40.91	C79.51	—	D16.9	D48.0	D49.2
marrow NEC	C96.9	C79.52	—	—	—	D47.9
unspecified side	C40.90	C79.51	—	D16.9	D48.0	D49.2
marrow NEC	C96.9	C79.52	—	—	—	D47.9
pharynx, pharyngeal	C14.0	C79.89	D00.08	D10.9	D37.05	D49.0
bursa	C11.1	C79.89	D00.08	D10.6	D37.05	D49.0
fornix	C11.3	C79.89	D00.08	D10.6	D37.05	D49.0
recess	C11.2	C79.89	D00.08	D10.6	D37.05	D49.0
region	C14.0	C79.89	D00.08	D10.9	D37.05	D49.0
tonsil	C11.1	C79.89	D00.08	D10.6	D37.05	D49.0
wall (lateral) (posterior)	C14.0	C79.89	D00.08	D10.9	D37.05	D49.0

	Malignant Primary	Malignant Secondary	Ca in situ	Benign	Uncertain	Unspecified Behavior
pia mater	C70.9	C79.40	—	D32.9	D42.9	D49.7
cerebral	C70.0	C79.32	—	D32.0	D42.0	D49.7
cranial	C70.0	C79.32	—	D32.0	D42.0	D49.7
spinal	C70.1	C79.49	—	D32.1	D42.1	D49.7
pillars of fauces	C09.1	C79.89	D00.08	D10.5	D37.05	D49.0
pineal (body) (gland)	C75.3	C79.89	D09.3	D35.4	D44.5	D49.7
pinna (ear) NEC						
left side	C44.22	C79.2	D04.22	D23.22	D48.5	D49.2
cartilage	C49.0	C79.89	—	D21.0	D48.1	D49.2
right side	C44.21	C79.2	D04.21	D23.21	D48.5	D49.2
cartilage	C49.0	C79.89	—	D21.0	D48.1	D49.2
unspecified side	C44.20	C79.2	D04.20	D23.20	D48.5	D49.2
cartilage	C49.0	C79.89	—	D21.0	D48.1	D49.2
piriform fossa or sinus	C12	C79.89	D00.08	D10.7	D37.05	D49.0
pituitary (body) (fossa) (gland) (lobe)	C75.1	C79.89	D09.3	D35.2	D44.3	D49.7
placenta	C58	C79.82	D07.0	D26.7	D39.2	D49.5
pleura, pleural (cavity)	C38.4	C78.2	—	D19.0	D38.2	D49.1
overlapping lesion with heart or mediastinum	C38.8	—	—	—	—	—
parietal	C38.4	C78.2	—	D19.0	D38.2	D49.1
visceral	C38.4	C78.2	—	D19.0	D38.2	D49.1
plexus						
brachial	C47.10	C79.89	—	D36.12	D48.2	D49.2
left side	C47.12	C79.89	—	D36.12	D48.2	D49.2
right side	C47.11	C79.89	—	D36.12	D48.2	D49.2
cervical	C47.0	C79.89	—	D36.11	D48.2	D49.2
choroid	C71.5	C79.31	—	D33.0	D43.0	D49.6
lumbosacral	C47.5	C79.89	—	D36.16	D48.2	D49.2
sacral	C47.5	C79.89	—	D36.16	D48.2	D49.2
pluri-endocrine	C75.8	C79.89	D09.3	D35.8	D44.8	D49.7
pole						
frontal	C71.1	C79.31	—	D33.0	D43.0	D49.6
occipital	C71.4	C79.31	—	D33.0	D43.0	D49.6
pons (varolii)	C71.7	C79.31	—	D33.1	D43.1	D49.6
popliteal fossa or space*	C76.5-	C79.89	D04.7-	D36.7	D48.7	D49.89
postcricoid (region)	C13.0	C79.89	D00.08	D10.7	D37.05	D49.0
posterior fossa (cranial)	C71.9	C79.31	—	D33.2	D43.2	D49.6
postnasal space	C11.9	C79.89	D00.08	D10.6	D37.05	D49.0
prepuce	C60.0	C79.82	D07.4	D29.0	D40.7	D49.5
prepylorus	C16.4	C78.89	D00.2	D13.1	D37.1	D49.0
presacral (region)	C76.3	C79.89	—	D36.7	D48.7	D49.89
prostate (gland)	C61	C79.82	D07.5	D29.1	D40.0	D49.5
utricle	C68.0	C79.19	D09.19	D30.4	D41.3	D49.5
pterygoid fossa	C49.0	C79.89	—	D21.0	D48.1	D49.2

	Malignant Primary	Malignant Secondary	Ca in situ	Benign	Uncertain	Unspecified Behavior
pubic bone	C41.4	C79.51	—	D16.8	D48.0	D49.2
marrow NEC	C96.9	C79.52	—	—	—	D47.9
pudenda, pudendum (female)	C51.9	C79.82	D07.1	D28.0	D39.7	D49.5
pulmonary (*see also* Neoplasm, lung)	C34.9-	C78.0-	D02.2-	D14.30	D38.1	D49.1
putamen	C71.0	C79.31	—	D33.0	D43.0	D49.6
pyloric						
antrum	C16.3	C78.89	D00.2	D13.1	D37.1	D49.0
canal	C16.4	C78.89	D00.2	D13.1	D37.1	D49.0
pylorus	C16.4	C78.89	D00.2	D13.1	D37.1	D49.0
pyramid (brain)	C71.7	C79.31	—	D33.1	D43.1	D49.6
pyriform fossa or sinus	C12	C79.89	D00.08	D10.7	D37.05	D49.0
radius (any part)						
left side	C40.02	C79.51	—	D16.02	D48.0	D49.2
marrow NEC	C96.9	C79.52	—	—	—	D47.9
right side	C40.01	C79.51	—	D16.01	D48.0	D49.2
marrow NEC	C96.9	C79.52	—	—	—	D47.9
unspecified side	C40.00	C79.51	—	D16.00	D48.0	D49.2
marrow NEC	C96.9	C79.52	—	—	—	D47.9
Rathke's pouch	C75.1	C79.89	D09.3	D35.2	D44.3	D49.7
rectosigmoid (junction)	C19	C78.5	D01.1	D12.7	D37.5	D49.0
overlapping lesion with anus or rectum	C21.8	—	—	—	—	—
rectouterine pouch	C48.1	C78.6	—	D20.1	D48.4	D49.0
rectovaginal septum or wall	C76.3	C79.89	D09.7	D36.7	D48.7	D49.89
rectovesical septum	C76.3	C79.89	D09.7	D36.7	D48.7	D49.89
rectum (ampulla)	C20	C78.5	D01.2	D12.8	D37.5	D49.0
and colon	C19	C78.5	D01.1	D12.7	D37.5	D49.0
overlapping lesion with anus or rectosigmoid junction	C21.8	—	—	—	—	—
renal						
calyx	C65.-	C79.0-	D09.19	D30.1-	D41.1-	D49.5
hilus	C65.-	C79.0-	D09.19	D30.1-	D41.1-	D49.5
parenchyma	C64.-	C79.0-	D09.19	D30.1-	D41.1-	D49.5
pelvis	C65.-	C79.0-	D09.19	D30.1-	D41.1-	D49.5
unspecified site	C64.-	C79.0-	D09.19	D30.1-	D41.1-	D49.5
respiratory						
organs or system NEC	C39.9	C78.30	D02.4	D14.4	D38.6	D49.1
tract NEC	C39.9	C78.30	D02.4	D14.4	D38.5	D49.1
upper	C39.0	C78.30	D02.4	D14.4	D38.5	D49.1
retina	C69.2-	C79.49	D09.20	D31.2-	D48.7	D49.81
retrobulbar	C69.6-	C79.49	—	D31.6-	D48.7	D49.89
retrocecal	C48.0	C78.6	—	D20.0	D48.3	D49.0
retromolar (area) (triangle) (trigone)	C06.2	C79.89	D00.00	D10.39	D37.09	D49.0
retro-orbital	C76.0	C79.89	D09.7	D36.7	D48.7	D49.89
retroperitoneal (space) (tissue)	C48.0	C78.6	—	D20.0	D48.3	D49.0
overlapping lesion	C48.8	—	—	—	—	—

	Malignant Primary	Malignant Secondary	Ca in situ	Benign	Uncertain	Unspecified Behavior
retroperitoneum	C48.0	C78.6	—	D20.0	D48.3	D49.0
overlapping lesion	C48.8	—	—	—	—	—
retropharyngeal	C14.0	C79.89	D00.08	D10.9	D37.05	D49.0
retrovesical (septum)	C76.3	C79.89	D09.7	D36.7	D48.7	D49.89
rhinencephalon	C71.0	C79.31	—	D33.0	D43.0	D49.6
rib	C41.3	C79.51	—	D16.7	D48.0	D49.2
marrow NEC	C96.9	C79.52	—	—	—	D47.9
Rosenmüller's fossa	C11.2	C79.89	D00.08	D10.6	D37.05	D49.0
round ligament	C57.2	C79.82	—	D28.2	D39.7	D49.5
sacrococcyx, sacrococcygeal	C41.4	C79.51	—	D16.8	D48.0	D49.2
marrow NEC	C96.9	C79.52	—	—	—	D47.9
region	C76.3	C79.89	D09.7	D36.7	D48.7	D49.89
sacrouterine ligament	C57.3	C79.82	—	D28.2	D39.7	D49.5
sacrum, sacral (vertebra)	C41.4	C79.51	—	D16.8	D48.0	D49.2
marrow NEC	C96.9	C79.52	—	—	—	D47.9
salivary gland or duct (major)	C08.9	C79.89	D00.00	D11.9	D37.039	D49.0
minor NEC	C06.9	C79.89	D00.00	D10.39	D37.04	D49.0
overlapping lesion	C08.9	—	—	—	—	—
parotid	C07	C79.89	D00.00	D11.0	D37.030	D49.0
pluriglandular	C08.8	C79.89	D00.00	D11.9	D37.039	D49.0
sublingual	C08.1	C79.89	D00.00	D11.7	D37.031	D49.0
submandibular	C08.0	C79.89	D00.00	D11.7	D37.032	D49.0
submaxillary	C08.0	C79.89	D00.00	D11.7	D37.032	D49.0
salpinx (uterine)	C57.0-	C79.82	D07.39	D28.2	D39.7	D49.5
Santorini's duct	C25.3	C78.89	D01.7	D13.6	D37.7	D49.0
scalp	C44.4	C79.2	D04.4	D23.4	D48.5	D49.2
scapula (any part)						
left side	C40.02	C79.51	—	D16.02	D48.0	D49.2
marrow NEC	C96.9	C79.52	—	—	—	D47.9
right side	C40.01	C79.51	—	D16.01	D48.0	D49.2
marrow NEC	C96.9	C79.52	—	—	—	D47.9
unspecified side	C40.00	C79.51	—	D16.00	D48.0	D49.2
marrow NEC	C96.9	C79.52	—	—	—	D47.9
scapular region	C76.1	C79.89	D09.7	D36.7	D48.7	D49.89
scar NEC (*see also* Neoplasm, skin)	C44.9	C79.2	D04.9	D23.9	D48.5	D49.2
sciatic nerve	C47.2-	C79.89	—	D36.13	D48.2	D49.2
sclera	C69.4-	C79.49	D09.2-	D31.4-	D48.7	D49.89
scrotum (skin)	C63.2	C79.82	D07.61	D29.4	D40.7	D49.5
sebaceous gland-*see* Neoplasm, skin						
sella turcica	C75.1	C79.89	D09.3	D35.2	D44.3	D49.7
bone	C41.0	C79.51	—	D16.4	D48.0	D49.2
marrow NEC	C96.9	C79.52	—	—	—	D47.9
semilunar cartilage (knee)	C40.2-	C79.51	—	D16.2-	D48.0	D49.2
seminal vesicle	C63.7	C79.82	D07.69	D29.7	D40.7	D49.5

	Malignant Primary	Malignant Secondary	Ca in situ	Benign	Uncertain	Unspecified Behavior
septum						
nasal	C30.0	C78.39	D02.3	D14.0	D38.5	D49.1
posterior margin	C11.3	C79.89	D00.08	D10.6	D37.05	D49.0
rectovaginal	C76.3	C79.89	D09.7	D36.7	D48.7	D49.89
rectovesical	C76.3	C79.89	D09.7	D36.7	D48.7	D49.89
urethrovaginal	C57.9	C79.82	D07.30	D28.9	D39.9	D49.5
vesicovaginal	C57.9	C79.82	D07.30	D28.9	D39.9	D49.5
shoulder NEC*	C76.4-	C79.89	D04.6-	D36.7	D48.7	D49.89
sigmoid flexure (lower) (upper)	C18.7	C78.5	D01.0	D12.5	D37.4	D49.0
sinus (accessory)	C31.9	C78.39	D02.3	D14.0	D38.5	D49.1
bone (any)	C41.0	C79.51	—	D16.4	D48.0	D49.2
marrow NEC	C96.9	C79.52	—	—	—	D47.9
ethmoidal	C31.1	C78.39	D02.3	D14.0	D38.5	D49.1
frontal	C31.2	C78.39	D02.3	D14.0	D38.5	D49.1
maxillary	C31.0	C78.39	D02.3	D14.0	D38.5	D49.1
nasal, paranasal NEC	C31.9	C78.39	D02.3	D14.0	D38.5	D49.1
overlapping lesion	C31.8	—	—	—	—	—
pyriform	C12	C79.89	D00.08	D10.7	D37.05	D49.0
sphenoid	C31.3	C78.39	D02.3	D14.0	D38.5	D49.1
skeleton, skeletal NEC	C41.9	C79.51	—	D16.9	D48.0	D49.2
marrow NEC	C96.9	C79.52	—	—	—	D47.9
Skene's gland	C68.1	C79.19	D09.19	D30.7	D41.7	D49.5
skin NEC	C44.9	C79.2	D04.9	D23.9	D48.5	D49.2
abdominal wall	C44.59	C79.2	D04.5	D23.5	D48.5	D49.2
ala nasi	C44.31	C79.2	D04.39	D23.39	D48.5	D49.2
ankle	C44.7-	C79.2	D04.7-	D23.7-	D48.5	D49.2
antecubital space	C44.6-	C79.2	D04.6-	D23.6-	D48.5	D49.2
anus	C44.51	C79.2	D04.5	D23.5	D48.5	D49.2
arm	C44.6-	C79.2	D04.6-	D23.6-	D48.5	D49.2
auditory canal (external)	C44.2-	C79.2	D04.2-	D23.2-	D48.5	D49.2
auricle (ear)	C44.2-	C79.2	D04.2-	D23.2-	D48.5	D49.2
auricular canal (external)	C44.2-	C79.2	D04.2-	D23.2-	D48.5	D49.2
axilla, axillary fold	C44.59	C79.2	D04.5	D23.5	D48.5	D49.2
back	C44.59	C79.2	D04.5	D23.5	D48.5	D49.2
breast	C44.52	C79.2	D04.5	D23.5	D48.5	D49.2
brow	C44.39	C79.2	D04.39	D23.39	D48.5	D49.2
buttock	C44.59	C79.2	D04.5	D23.5	D48.5	D49.2
calf	C44.7-	C79.2	D04.7-	D23.7-	D48.5	D49.2
canthus (eye) (inner) (outer)	C44.1-	C79.2	D04.1-	D23.1-	D48.5	D49.2
cervical region	C44.4	C79.2	D04.4	D23.4	D48.5	D49.2
cheek (external)	C44.39	C79.2	D04.39	D23.39	D48.5	D49.2
chest (wall)	C44.59	C79.2	D04.5	D23.5	D48.5	D49.2
chin	C44.39	C79.2	D04.39	D23.39	D48.5	D49.2
clavicular area	C44.59	C79.2	D04.5	D23.5	D48.5	D49.2

	Malignant Primary	Malignant Secondary	Ca in situ	Benign	Uncertain	Unspecified Behavior
skin NEC *(Continued)*						
clitoris	C51.2	C79.82	D07.1	D28.0	D39.7	D49.5
columnella	C44.39	C79.2	D04.39	D23.39	D48.5	D49.2
concha	C44.2-	C79.2	D04.2-	D23.2-	D48.5	D49.2
ear (external)	C44.2-	C79.2	D04.2-	D23.2-	D48.5	D49.2
elbow	C44.6-	C79.2	D04.6-	D23.6-	D48.5	D49.2
eyebrow	C44.39	C79.2	D04.39	D23.39	D48.5	D49.2
eyelid	C44.1-	C79.2	D04.1-	D23.1-	D48.5	D49.2
face NEC	C44.30	C79.2	D04.30	D23.30	D48.5	D49.2
female genital organs (external)	C51.9	C79.82	D07.1	D28.0	D39.7	D49.5
clitoris	C51.2	C79.82	D07.1	D28.0	D39.7	D49.5
labium NEC	C51.9	C79.82	D07.1	D28.0	D39.7	D49.5
majus	C51.0	C79.82	D07.1	D28.0	D39.7	D49.5
minus	C51.1	C79.82	D07.1	D28.0	D39.7	D49.5
pudendum	C51.9	C79.82	D07.1	D28.0	D39.7	D49.5
vulva	C51.9	C79.82	D07.1	D28.0	D39.7	D49.5
finger	C44.6-	C79.2	D04.6-	D23.6-	D48.5	D49.2
flank	C44.59	C79.2	D04.5	D23.5	D48.5	D49.2
foot	C44.7-	C79.2	D04.7-	D23.7-	D48.5	D49.2
forearm	C44.6-	C79.2	D04.6-	D23.6-	D48.5	D49.2
forehead	C44.39	C79.2	D04.39	D23.39	D48.5	D49.2
glabella	C44.39	C79.2	D04.39	D23.39	D48.5	D49.2
gluteal region	C44.59	C79.2	D04.5	D23.5	D48.5	D49.2
groin	C44.59	C79.2	D04.5	D23.5	D48.5	D49.2
hand	C44.6-	C79.2	D04.6-	D23.6-	D48.5	D49.2
head NEC	C44.4	C79.2	D04.4	D23.4	D48.5	D49.2
heel	C44.7-	C79.2	D04.7-	D23.7-	D48.5	D49.2
helix	C44.2-	C79.2	D04.2-	D23.2-	D48.5	D49.2
hip	C44.7-	C79.2	D04.7-	D23.7-	D48.5	D49.2
infraclavicular region	C44.59	C79.2	D04.5	D23.5	D48.5	D49.2
inguinal region	C44.59	C79.2	D04.5	D23.5	D48.5	D49.2
jaw	C44.39	C79.2	D04.39	D23.39	D48.5	D49.2
knee	C44.7-	C79.2	D04.7-	D23.7-	D48.5	D49.2
labia						
majora	C51.0	C79.82	D07.1	D28.0	D39.7	D49.5
minora	C51.1	C79.82	D07.1	D28.0	D39.7	D49.5
leg	C44.7-	C79.2	D04.7-	D23.7-	D48.5	D49.2
lid (lower) (upper)	C44.1-	C79.2	D04.1-	D23.1-	D48.5	D49.2
limb NEC	C44.9	C79.2	D04.9	D23.9	D48.5	D49.2
lower	C44.7-	C79.2	D04.7-	D23.7-	D48.5	D49.2
upper	C44.6-	C79.2	D04.6-	D23.6-	D48.5	D49.2
lip (lower) (upper)	C44.0	C79.2	D04.0	D23.0	D48.5	D49.2
male genital organs	C63.9	C79.82	D07.60	D29.9	D40.7	D49.5
penis	C60.9	C79.82	D07.4	D29.0	D40.7	D49.5

	Malignant Primary	Malignant Secondary	Ca in situ	Benign	Uncertain	Unspecified Behavior
skin NEC *(Continued)*						
male genital organs *(Continued)*						
prepuce	C60.0	C79.82	D07.4	D29.0	D40.7	D49.5
scrotum	C63.2	C79.82	D07.61	D29.4	D40.7	D49.5
mastectomy site (skin)	C44.52	C79.2	—	—	—	—
specified as breast tissue						
female	C50.81-	C79.81	—	—	—	—
male	C50.82-	C79.81	—	—	—	—
meatus, acoustic (external)	C44.2-	C79.2	D04.2-	D23.2-	D48.5	D49.2
melanotic - *see* Melanoma						
nates	C44.59	C79.2	D04.5	D23.5	D48.5	D49.2
neck	C44.4	C79.2	D04.4	D23.4	D48.5	D49.2
nose (external)	C44.31	C79.2	D04.39	D23.39	D48.5	D49.2
overlapping lesion	C44.8	—	—	—	—	—
palm	C44.6-	C79.2	D04.6-	D23.6-	D48.5	D49.2
palpebra	C44.1-	C79.2	D04.1-	D23.1-	D48.5	D49.2
penis NEC	C60.9	C79.82	D07.4	D29.0	D40.7	D49.5
perianal	C44.51	C79.2	D04.5	D23.5	D48.5	D49.2
perineum	C44.59	C79.2	D04.5	D23.5	D48.5	D49.2
pinna	C44.2-	C79.2	D04.2-	D23.2-	D48.5	D49.2
plantar	C44.7-	C79.2	D04.7-	D23.7-	D48.5	D49.2
popliteal fossa or space	C44.7-	C79.2	D04.7-	D23.7-	D48.5	D49.2
prepuce	C60.0	C79.82	D07.4	D29.0	D40.7	D49.5
pubes	C44.59	C79.2	D04.5	D23.5	D48.5	D49.2
sacrococcygeal region	C44.59	C79.2	D04.5	D23.5	D48.5	D49.2
scalp	C44.4	C79.2	D04.4	D23.4	D48.5	D49.2
scapular region	C44.59	C79.2	D04.5	D23.5	D48.5	D49.2
scrotum	C63.2	C79.82	D07.61	D29.4	D40.7	D49.5
shoulder	C44.6-	C79.2	D04.6-	D23.6-	D48.5	D49.2
sole (foot)	C44.7-	C79.2	D04.7-	D23.7-	D48.5	D49.2
specified sites NEC	C44.8	C79.2	D04.8	D23.9	D48.5	D49.2
submammary fold	C44.59	C79.2	D04.5	D23.5	D48.5	D49.2
supraclavicular region	C44.4	C79.2	D04.4	D23.4	D48.5	D49.2
temple	C44.39	C79.2	D04.39	D23.39	D48.5	D49.2
thigh	C44.7-	C79.2	D04.7-	D23.7-	D48.5	D49.2
thoracic wall	C44.59	C79.2	D04.5	D23.5	D48.5	D49.2
thumb	C44.6-	C79.2	D04.6-	D23.6-	D48.5	D49.2
toe	C44.7-	C79.2	D04.7-	D23.7-	D48.5	D49.2
tragus	C44.2-	C79.2	D04.2-	D23.2-	D48.5	D49.2
trunk	C44.59	C79.2	D04.5	D23.5	D48.5	D49.2
umbilicus	C44.59	C79.2	D04.5	D23.5	D48.5	D49.2
vulva	C51.9	C79.82	D07.1	D28.0	D39.7	D49.5
wrist	C44.6-	C79.2	D04.6-	D23.6-	D48.5	D49.2

	Malignant Primary	Malignant Secondary	Ca in situ	Benign	Uncertain	Unspecified Behavior
skull	C41.0	C79.51	—	D16.4	D48.0	D49.2
marrow NEC	C96.9	C79.52	—	—	—	D47.9
soft parts or tissues-*see* Neoplasm, connective tissue						
specified site NEC	C76.7	C79.89	D09.7	D36.7	D48.7	D49.89
spermatic cord	C63.1-	C79.82	D07.69	D29.7	D40.7	D49.5
sphenoid	C31.3	C78.39	D02.3	D14.0	D38.5	D49.1
bone	C41.0	C79.51	—	D16.4	D48.0	D49.2
marrow NEC	C96.9	C79.52	—	—	—	D47.9
sinus	C31.3	C78.39	D02.3	D14.0	D38.5	D49.1
sphincter						
anal	C21.1	C78.5	D01.3	D12.9	D37.7	D49.0
of Oddi	C24.0	C78.89	D01.5	D13.5	D37.6	D49.0
spine, spinal (column)	C41.2	C79.51	—	D16.6	D48.0	D49.2
bulb	C71.7	C79.31	—	D33.1	D43.1	D49.6
coccyx	C41.4	C79.51	—	D16.8	D48.0	D49.2
marrow NEC	C96.9	C79.52	—	—	—	D47.9
cord (cervical) (lumbar) (sacral) (thoracic)	C72.0	C79.49	—	D33.4	D43.4	D49.7
dura mater	C70.1	C79.49	—	D32.1	D42.1	D49.7
lumbosacral	C41.2	C79.51	—	D16.6	D48.0	D49.2
marrow NEC	C96.9	C79.52	—	—	—	D47.9
marrow NEC	C96.9	C79.52	—	—	—	D47.9
membrane	C70.1	C79.49	—	D32.1	D42.1	D49.7
meninges	C70.1	C79.49	—	D32.1	D42.1	D49.7
nerve (root)	C47.9	C79.89	—	D36.10	D48.2	D49.2
pia mater	C70.1	C79.49	—	D32.1	D42.1	D49.7
root	C47.9	C79.89	—	D36.10	D48.2	D49.2
sacrum	C41.4	C79.51	—	D16.8	D48.0	D49.2
marrow NEC	C96.9	C79.52	—	—	—	D47.9
spleen, splenic NEC	C26.1	C78.89	D01.7	D13.9	D37.7	D49.0
flexure (colon)	C18.5	C78.5	D01.0	D12.3	D37.4	D49.0
stem, brain	C71.7	C79.31	—	D33.1	D43.1	D49.6
Stensen's duct	C07	C79.89	D00.00	D11.0	D37.030	D49.0
sternum	C41.3	C79.51	—	D16.7	D48.0	D49.2
marrow NEC	C96.9	C79.52	—	—	—	D47.9
stomach	C16.9	C78.89	D00.2	D13.1	D37.1	D49.0
antrum (pyloric)	C16.3	C78.89	D00.2	D13.1	D37.1	D49.0
body	C16.2	C78.89	D00.2	D13.1	D37.1	D49.0
cardia	C16.0	C78.89	D00.2	D13.1	D37.1	D49.0
cardiac orifice	C16.0	C78.89	D00.2	D13.1	D37.1	D49.0
corpus	C16.2	C78.89	D00.2	D13.1	D37.1	D49.0
fundus	C16.1	C78.89	D00.2	D13.1	D37.1	D49.0
greater curvature NEC	C16.6	C78.89	D00.2	D13.1	D37.1	D49.0
lesser curvature NEC	C16.5	C78.89	D00.2	D13.1	D37.1	D49.0
overlapping lesion	C16.8	—	—	—	—	—

	Malignant Primary	Malignant Secondary	Ca in situ	Benign	Uncertain	Unspecified Behavior
stomach *(Continued)*						
prepylorus	C16.4	C78.89	D00.2	D13.1	D37.1	D49.0
pylorus	C16.4	C78.89	D00.2	D13.1	D37.1	D49.0
wall NEC	C16.9	C78.89	D00.2	D13.1	D37.1	D49.0
anterior NEC	C16.8	C78.89	D00.2	D13.1	D37.1	D49.0
posterior NEC	C16.8	C78.89	D00.2	D13.1	D37.1	D49.0
stroma, endometrial	C54.1	C79.82	D07.0	D26.1	D39.0	D49.5
stump, cervical	C53.8	C79.82	D06.7	D26.0	D39.0	D49.5
subcutaneous (nodule) (tissue) NEC-*see* Neoplasm, connective tissue						
subdural	C70.9	C79.32	—	D32.9	D42.9	D49.7
subglottis, subglottic	C32.2	C78.39	D02.0	D14.1	D38.0	D49.1
sublingual	C04.9	C79.89	D00.06	D10.2	D37.09	D49.0
gland or duct	C08.1	C79.89	D00.00	D11.7	D37.031	D49.0
submandibular gland	C08.0	C79.89	D00.00	D11.7	D37.032	D49.0
submaxillary gland or duct	C08.0	C79.89	D00.00	D11.7	D37.032	D49.0
submental	C76.0	C79.89	D09.7	D36.7	D48.7	D49.89
subpleural	C34.9-	C78.00	—	D14.3-	D38.1	D49.1
substernal	C38.1	C78.1	—	D15.2	D38.3	D49.89
sudoriferous, sudoriparous gland, site unspecified	C44.9	C79.2	D04.9	D23.9	D48.5	D49.2
specified site-*see* Neoplasm, skin						
supraclavicular region	C76.0	C79.89	D09.7	D36.7	D48.7	D49.89
supraglottis	C32.1	C78.39	D02.0	D14.1	D38.0	D49.1
suprarenal						
capsule	C74.9-	C79.7-	D09.3	D35.0-	D44.1-	D49.7
cortex	C74.0-	C79.7-	D09.3	D35.0-	D44.1-	D49.7
gland	C74.9-	C79.7-	D09.3	D35.0-	D44.1-	D49.7
medulla	C74.1-	C79.7-	D09.3	D35.0-	D44.1-	D49.7
unspecified site	C74.9-	C79.7-	D09.3	D35.0-	D44.1-	D49.7
suprasellar (region)	C71.9	C79.31	—	D33.2	D43.2	D49.6
supratentorial (brain) NEC	C71.0	C79.31	—	D33.0	D43.0	D49.6
sweat gland (apocrine) (eccrine), site unspecified	C44.9	C79.2	D04.9	D23.9	D48.5	D49.2
specified site-*see* Neoplasm, skin						
sympathetic nerve or nervous system NEC	C47.9	C79.89	—	D36.10	D48.2	D49.2
symphysis pubis	C41.4	C79.51	—	D16.8	D48.0	D49.2
marrow NEC	C96.9	C79.52	—	—	—	D47.9
synovial membrane-*see* Neoplasm, connective tissue						
tapetum, brain	C71.8	C79.31	—	D33.2	D43.2	D49.6
tarsus (any bone)						
left side	C40.32	C79.51	—	D16.32	D48.0	D49.2
marrow NEC	C96.9	C79.52	—	—	—	D47.9
right side	C40.31	C79.51	—	D16.31	D48.0	D49.2
marrow NEC	C96.9	C79.52	—	—	—	D47.9
unspecified side	C40.30	C79.51	—	D16.30	D48.0	D49.2
marrow NEC	C96.9	C79.52	—	—	—	D47.9

	Malignant Primary	Malignant Secondary	Ca in situ	Benign	Uncertain	Unspecified Behavior
temple (skin)	C44.39	C79.2	D04.39	D23.39	D48.5	D49.2
temporal						
bone	C41.0	C79.51	—	D16.4	D48.0	D49.2
marrow NEC	C96.9	C79.52	—	—	—	D47.9
lobe or pole	C71.2	C79.31	—	D33.0	D43.0	D49.6
region	C76.0	C79.89	D09.7	D36.7	D48.7	D49.89
skin	C44.39	C79.2	D04.39	D23.39	D48.5	D49.2
tendon (sheath)-see Neoplasm, connective tissue						
tentorium (cerebelli)	C70.0	C79.32	—	D32.0	D42.0	D49.7
testis, testes						
descended	C62.1-	C79.82	D07.69	D29.2-	D40.1-	D49.5
ectopic	C62.0-	C79.82	D07.69	D29.2-	D40.1-	D49.5
retained	C62.0-	C79.82	D07.69	D29.2-	D40.1-	D49.5
scrotal	C62.1-	C79.82	D07.69	D29.2-	D40.1-	D49.5
undescended	C62.0-	C79.82	D07.69	D29.2-	D40.1-	D49.5
unspecified site	C62.9-	C79.82	D07.69	D29.2-	D40.1-	D49.5
thalamus	C71.0	C79.31	—	D33.0	D43.0	D49.6
thigh NEC*	C76.5-	C79.89	D04.7-	D36.7	D48.7	D49.89
thorax, thoracic (cavity) (organs NEC)	C76.1	C79.89	D09.7	D36.7	D48.7	D49.89
duct	C49.3	C79.89	—	D21.3	D48.1	D49.2
wall NEC	C76.1	C79.89	D09.7	D36.7	D48.7	D49.89
throat	C14.0	C79.89	D00.08	D10.9	D37.05	D49.0
thumb NEC*	C76.4-	C79.89	D04.6-	D36.7	D48.7	D49.89
thymus (gland)	C37	C79.89	—	D15.0	D38.4	D49.89
overlapping lesion with heart or mediastinum	C38.8	—	—	—	—	—
thyroglossal duct	C73	C79.89	D09.3	D34	D44.0	D49.7
thyroid (gland)	C73	C79.89	D09.3	D34	D44.0	D49.7
cartilage	C32.3	C78.39	D02.0	D14.1	D38.0	D49.1
tibia (any part)						
left side	C40.22	C79.51	—	D16.22	D48.0	D49.2
marrow NEC	C96.9	C79.52	—	—	—	D47.9
right side	C40.21	C79.51	—	D16.21	D48.0	D49.2
marrow NEC	C96.9	C79.52	—	—	—	D47.9
unspecified side	C40.20	C79.51	—	D16.20	D48.0	D49.2
marrow NEC	C96.9	C79.52	—	—	—	D47.9
toe NEC*	C76.5-	C79.89	D04.7-	D36.7	D47.7	D49.89
tongue	C02.9	C79.89	D00.07	D10.1	D37.02	D49.0
anterior (two-thirds) NEC	C02.3	C79.89	D00.07	D10.1	D37.02	D49.0
dorsal surface	C02.0	C79.89	D00.07	D10.1	D37.02	D49.0
ventral surface	C02.2	C79.89	D00.07	D10.1	D37.02	D49.0
base (dorsal surface)	C01	C79.89	D00.07	D10.1	D37.02	D49.0
border (lateral)	C02.1	C79.89	D00.07	D10.1	D37.02	D49.0
dorsal surface NEC	C02.0	C79.89	D00.07	D10.1	D37.02	D49.0
fixed part NEC	C01	C79.89	D00.07	D10.1	D37.02	D49.0

	Malignant Primary	Malignant Secondary	Ca in situ	Benign	Uncertain	Unspecified Behavior
tongue *(Continued)*						
foreamen cecum	C02.0	C79.89	D00.07	D10.1	D37.02	D49.0
frenulum linguae	C02.2	C79.89	D00.07	D10.1	D37.02	D49.0
junctional zone	C02.8	C79.89	D00.07	D10.1	D37.02	D49.0
margin (lateral)	C02.1	C79.89	D00.07	D10.1	D37.02	D49.0
midline NEC	C02.0	C79.89	D00.07	D10.1	D37.02	D49.0
mobile part NEC	C02.3	C79.89	D00.07	D10.1	D37.02	D49.0
overlapping lesion	C02.8	—	—	—	—	—
posterior (third)	C01	C79.89	D00.07	D10.1	D37.02	D49.0
root	C01	C79.89	D00.07	D10.1	D37.02	D49.0
surface (dorsal)	C02.0	C79.89	D00.07	D10.1	D37.02	D49.0
base	C01	C79.89	D00.07	D10.1	D37.02	D49.0
ventral	C02.2	C79.89	D00.07	D10.1	D37.02	D49.0
with floor of mouth [book-leaf]	C06.89					
tip	C02.1	C79.89	D00.07	D10.1	D37.02	D49.0
tonsil	C02.4	C79.89	D00.07	D10.1	D37.02	D49.0
tonsil	C09.9	C79.89	D00.08	D10.4	D37.05	D49.0
fauces, faucial	C09.9	C79.89	D00.08	D10.4	D37.05	D49.0
lingual	C02.4	C79.89	D00.07	D10.1	D37.02	D49.0
palatine	C09.9	C79.89	D00.08	D10.4	D37.05	D49.0
pharyngeal	C11.1	C79.89	D00.08	D10.6	D37.05	D49.0
pillar (anterior) (posterior)	C09.1	C79.89	D00.08	D10.5	D37.05	D49.0
tonsillar fossa	C09.0	C79.89	D00.08	D10.5	D37.05	D49.0
tooth socket NEC	C03.9	C79.89	D00.03	D10.39	D37.09	D49.0
trachea (cartilage) (mucosa)	C33	C78.39	D02.1	D14.2	D38.1	D49.1
overlapping lesion with bronchus or lung	C34.8-	—	—	—	—	—
tracheobronchial						
overlapping lesion with lung	C34.8-	—	—	—	—	—
unspecified site	C34.8-	C78.39	D02.1	D14.2	D38.1	D49.1
tragus	C44.2-	C79.2	D04.2-	D23.2-	D48.5	D49.2
trunk NEC*	C76.7	C79.89	D04.5	D36.7	D48.7	D49.89
tubo-ovarian	C57.8	C79.82	D07.39	D28.7	D39.7	D49.5
tunica vaginalis	C63.7	C79.82	D07.69	D29.7	D40.7	D49.5
turbinate (bone)	C41.0	C79.51	—	D16.4	D48.0	D49.2
marrow NEC	C96.9	C79.52	—	—	—	D47.9
nasal	C30.0	C78.39	D02.3	D14.0	D38.5	D49.1
tympanic cavity	C30.1	C78.39	D02.3	D14.0	D38.5	D49.1
ulna (any part)						
left side	C40.02	C79.51	—	D16.01	D48.0	D49.2
marrow NEC	C96.9	C79.52	—	—	—	D47.9
right side	C40.01	C79.51	—	D16.02	D48.0	D49.2
marrow NEC	C96.9	C79.52	—	—	—	D47.9
unspecified side	C40.00	C79.51	—	D16.00	D48.0	D49.2
marrow NEC	C96.9	C79.52	—	—	—	D47.9

	Malignant Primary	Malignant Secondary	Ca in situ	Benign	Uncertain	Unspecified Behavior
umbilicus, umbilical	C44.59	C79.2	D04.5	D23.5	D48.5	D49.2
uncus, brain	C71.2	C79.31	—	D33.0	D43.0	D49.6
unknown site or unspecified	C80	C80	D09.9	D36.9	D48.9	D49.9
urachus	C67.7	C79.11	D09.0	D30.3	D41.4	D49.4
ureter, ureteral						
orifice (bladder)	C67.6	C79.11	D09.0	D30.3	D41.4	D49.4
unspecified site	C66.-	C79.19	D09.19	D30.2-	D41.2-	D49.5
ureter-bladder (junction)	C67.6	C79.11	D09.0	D30.3	D41.4	D49.4
urethra, urethral (gland)	C68.0	C79.19	D09.19	D30.4	D41.3	D49.5
orifice, internal	C67.5	C79.11	D09.0	D30.3	D41.4	D49.4
urethrovaginal (septum)	C57.9	C79.82	D07.39	D28.9	D39.7	D49.5
urinary organ or system NEC	C68.9	C79.10	D09.10	D30.9	D41.9	D49.5
bladder-*see* Neoplasm, bladder						
overlapping lesion	C68.8	—	—	—	—	—
specified sites NEC	C68.8	C79.19	D09.19	D30.7	D41.7	D49.5
utero-ovarian	C57.8	C79.82	D07.39	D28.7	D39.7	D49.5
ligament	C57.1	C79.82	D07.39	D28.2	D39.7	D49.5
uterosacral ligament	C57.3	C79.82	—	D28.2	D39.7	D49.5
uterus, uteri, uterine	C55	C79.82	D07.0	D26.9	D39.0	D49.5
adnexa NEC	C57.4	C79.82	D07.39	D28.7	D39.7	D49.5
overlapping lesion	C57.8	—	—	—	—	—
body	C54.9	C79.82	D07.0	D26.1	D39.0	D49.5
overlapping lesion	C54.8	—	—	—	—	—
cervix	C53.9	C79.82	D06.9	D26.0	D39.0	D49.5
cornu	C54.9	C79.82	D07.0	D26.1	D39.0	D49.5
corpus	C54.9	C79.82	D07.0	D26.1	D39.0	D49.5
endocervix (canal) (gland)	C53.0	C79.82	D06.0	D26.0	D39.0	D49.5
endometrium	C54.1	C79.82	D07.0	D26.1	D39.0	D49.5
exocervix	C53.1	C79.82	D06.1	D26.0	D39.0	D49.5
external os	C53.1	C79.82	D06.1	D26.0	D39.0	D49.5
fundus	C54.3	C79.82	D07.0	D26.1	D39.0	D49.5
internal os	C53.0	C79.82	D06.0	D26.0	D39.0	D49.5
isthmus	C54.0	C79.82	D07.0	D26.1	D39.0	D49.5
ligament	C57.3	C79.82	—	D28.2	D39.7	D49.5
broad	C57.1	C79.82	D07.39	D28.2	D39.7	D49.5
round	C57.2	C79.82	—	D28.2	D39.7	D49.5
lower segment	C54.0	C79.82	D07.0	D26.1	D39.0	D49.5
myometrium	C54.2	C79.82	D07.0	D26.1	D39.0	D49.5
squamocolumnar junction	C53.8	C79.82	D06.7	D26.0	D39.0	D49.5
tube	C57.0-	C79.82	D07.39	D28.2	D39.7	D49.5
utricle, prostatic	C68.0	C79.19	D09.19	D30.4	D41.3	D49.5
uveal tract	C69.4-	C79.49	D09.2-	D31.4-	D48.7	D49.89
uvula	C05.2	C79.89	D00.04	D10.39	D37.09	D49.0

	Malignant Primary	Malignant Secondary	Ca in situ	Benign	Uncertain	Unspecified Behavior
vagina, vaginal (fornix) (vault) (wall)	C52	C79.82	D07.2	D28.1	D39.7	D49.5
vaginovesical	C57.9	C79.82	D07.30	D28.9	D39.9	D49.5
septum	C57.9	C79.82	D07.30	D28.9	D39.9	D49.5
vallecula (epigiottis)	C10.0	C79.89	D00.08	D10.5	D37.05	D49.0
vascular-see Neoplasm, connective tissue						
vas deferens	C63.1-	C79.82	D07.69	D29.7	D40.7	D49.5
Vater's ampulla	C24.1	C78.89	D01.5	D13.5	D37.6	D49.0
vein, venous-see Neoplasm, connective tissue						
vena cava (abdominal) (inferior)	C49.4	C79.89	—	D21.4	D48.1	D49.2
superior	C49.3	C79.89	—	D21.3	D48.1	D49.2
ventricle (cerebral) (floor) (lateral) (third)	C71.5	C79.31	—	D33.0	D43.0	D49.6
cardiac (left) (right)	C38.0	C79.89	—	D15.1	D48.7	D49.89
fourth	C71.7	C79.31	—	D33.1	D43.1	D49.6
ventricular band of larynx	C32.1	C78.39	D02.0	D14.1	D38.0	D49.1
ventriculus-see Neoplasm, stomach						
vermillion border-see Neoplasm, lip						
vermis, cerebellum	C71.6	C79.31	—	D33.1	D43.1	D49.6
vertebra (column)	C41.2	C79.51	—	D16.6	D48.0	D49.2
coccyx	C41.4	C79.51	—	D16.8	D48.0	D49.2
marrow NEC	C96.9	C79.52	—	—	—	D47.9
marrow NEC	C96.9	C79.52	—	—	—	D47.9
sacrum	C41.4	C79.51	—	D16.8	D48.0	D49.2
marrow NEC	C96.9	C79.52	—	—	—	D47.9
vesical-see Neoplasm, bladder						
vesicle, seminal	C63.7	C79.82	D07.69	D29.7	D40.7	D49.5
vesicocervical tissue	C57.9	C79.82	D07.30	D28.9	D39.9	D49.5
vesicorectal	C76.3	C79.82	D09.7	D36.7	D48.7	D49.89
vesicovaginal	C57.9	C79.82	D07.30	D28.9	D39.9	D49.5
septum	C57.9	C79.82	D07.39	D28.9	D39.7	D49.5
vessel (blood)-see Neoplasm, connective tissue						
vestibular gland, greater	C51.0	C79.82	D07.1	D28.0	D39.7	D49.5
vestibule						
mouth	C06.1	C79.89	D00.00	D10.30	D37.09	D49.0
nose	C30.0	C78.39	D02.3	D14.0	D38.5	D49.1
Virchow's gland	—	C77.0	—	D36.0	D48.7	D49.89
viscera NEC	C76.7	C79.89	D09.7	D36.7	D48.7	D49.89
vocal cords (true)	C32.0	C78.39	D02.0	D14.1	D38.0	D49.1
false	C32.1	C78.39	D02.0	D14.1	D38.0	D49.1
vomer	C41.0	C79.51	—	D16.4	D48.0	D49.2
marrow NEC	C96.9	C79.52	—	—	—	D47.9
vulva	C51.9	C79.82	D07.1	D28.0	D39.7	D49.5
vulvovaginal gland	C51.9	C79.82	D07.1	D28.0	D39.7	D49.5
Waldeyer's ring	C14.2	C79.89	D00.08	D10.9	D37.05	D49.0

TABLE OF NEOPLASMS

541

	Malignant Primary	Malignant Secondary	Ca in situ	Benign	Uncertain	Unspecified Behavior
Wharton's duct	C08.0	C79.89	D00.00	D11.7	D37.032	D49.0
white matter (central) (cerebral)	C71.0	C79.31	—	D33.0	D43.0	D49.6
windpipe	C33	C78.39	D02.1	D14.2	D38.1	D49.1
Wirsung's duct	C25.3	C78.89	D01.7	D13.6	D37.7	D49.0
wolffian (body) (duct)						
female	C57.7	C79.82	D07.39	D28.7	D39.7	D49.5
male	C63.7	C79.82	D07.69	D29.7	D40.7	D49.5
womb-*see* Neoplasm, uterus						
wrist NEC*	C76.4-	C79.89	D04.6-	D36.7	D48.7	D49.89
xiphoid process	C41.3	C79.51	—	D16.7	D48.0	D49.2
Zuckerkandl's organ	C75.5	C79.89	—	D35.6	D44.7	D49.7

ICD-10-CM
Table of Drugs
and Chemicals

Substance	External Cause (T-Code)					
	Poisoning, Accidental (Unintentional)	Poisoning, Intentional Self-Harm	Poisoning, Assault	Poisoning, Undetermined	Adverse Effect	Underdosing
1-propanol	T51.3x1	T51.3x2	T51.3x3	T51.3x4	—	—
2-propanol	T51.2x1	T51.2x2	T51.2x3	T51.2x4	—	—
2,4-D (dichlorophen-oxyacetic acid)	T60.3x1	T60.3x2	T60.3x3	T60.3x4	—	—
2,4-toluene diisocyanate	T65.0x1	T65.0x2	T65.0x3	T65.0x4	—	—
2,4,5-T (trichloro-phenoxyacetic acid)	T60.1x1	T60.1x2	T60.1x3	T60.1x4	—	—
14-hydroxydihydro-morphinone	T40.2x1	T40.2x2	T40.2x3	T40.2x4	T40.2x5	T40.2x6
ABOB	T37.5x1	T37.5x2	T37.5x3	T37.5x4	T37.5x5	T37.5x6
Abrine	T62.2x1	T62.2x2	T62.2x3	T62.2x4	—	—
Abrus (seed)	T62.2x1	T62.2x2	T62.2x3	T62.2x4	—	—
Absinthe	T51.0x1	T51.0x2	T51.0x3	T51.0x4	—	—
beverage	T51.0x1	T51.0x2	T51.0x3	T51.0x4	—	—
Acaricide	T60.8x1	T60.8x2	T60.8x3	T60.8x4	—	—
Acebutolol	T44.7x1	T44.7x2	T44.7x3	T44.7x4	T44.7x5	T44.7x6
Acecarbromal	T42.6x1	T42.6x2	T42.6x3	T42.6x4	T42.6x5	T42.6x6
Aceclidine	T44.1x1	T44.1x2	T44.1x3	T44.1x4	T44.1x5	T44.1x6
Acedapsone	T37.0x1	T37.0x2	T37.0x3	T37.0x4	T37.0x5	T37.0x6
Acefylline piperazine	T48.6x1	T48.6x2	T48.6x3	T48.6x4	T48.6x5	T48.6x6
Acemorphan	T40.2x1	T40.2x2	T40.2x3	T40.2x4	T40.2x5	T40.2x6
Acenocoumarin	T45.511	T45.512	T45.513	T45.514	T45.515	T45.516
Acenocoumarol	T45.511	T45.512	T45.513	T45.514	T45.515	T45.516
Acepifylline	T48.6x1	T48.6x2	T48.6x3	T48.6x4	T48.6x5	T48.6x6
Acepromazine	T43.3x1	T43.3x2	T43.3x3	T43.3x4	T43.3x5	T43.3x6
Acesulfamethoxypyridazine	T37.0x1	T37.0x2	T37.0x3	T37.0x4	T37.0x5	T37.0x6
Acetal	T52.8x1	T52.8x2	T52.8x3	T52.8x4	—	—
Acetaldehyde (vapor)	T52.8x1	T52.8x2	T52.8x3	T52.8x4	—	—
liquid	T65.891	T65.892	T65.893	T65.894	—	—
P-Acetamidophenol	T39.1x1	T39.1x2	T39.1x3	T39.1x4	T39.1x5	T39.1x6
Acetaminophen	T39.1x1	T39.1x2	T39.1x3	T39.1x4	T39.1x5	T39.1x6
Acetaminosalol	T39.1x1	T39.1x2	T39.1x3	T39.1x4	T39.1x5	T39.1x6
Acetanilide	T39.1x1	T39.1x2	T39.1x3	T39.1x4	T39.1x5	T39.1x6
Acetarsol	T37.3x1	T37.3x2	T37.3x3	T37.3x4	T37.3x5	T37.3x6
Acetazolamide	T50.2x1	T50.2x2	T50.2x3	T50.2x4	T50.2x5	T50.2x6
Acetiamine	T45.2x1	T45.2x2	T45.2x3	T45.2x4	T45.2x5	T45.2x6
Acetic						
acid	T54.2x1	T54.2x2	T54.2x3	T54.2x4	—	—
with sodium acetate (ointment)	T49.3x1	T49.3x2	T49.3x3	T49.3x4	T49.3x5	T49.3x6
ester (solvent) (vapor)	T52.8x1	T52.8x2	T52.8x3	T52.8x4	—	—
irrigating solution	T50.3x1	T50.3x2	T50.3x3	T50.3x4	T50.3x5	T50.3x6
medicinal (lotion)	T49.2x1	T49.2x2	T49.2x3	T49.2x4	T49.2x5	T49.2x6

Substance	External Cause (T-Code)					
	Poisoning, Accidental (Unintentional)	Poisoning, Intentional Self-Harm	Poisoning, Assault	Poisoning, Undetermined	Adverse Effect	Underdosing
Acetic *(Continued)*						
anhydride	T65.891	T65.892	T65.893	T65.894	—	—
ether (vapor)	T52.8x1	T52.8x2	T52.8x3	T52.8x4	—	—
Acetohexamide	T38.3x1	T38.3x2	T38.3x3	T38.3x4	T38.3x5	T38.3x6
Acetohydroxamic acid	T50.991	T50.992	T50.993	T50.994	T50.995	T50.996
Acetomenaphihone	T45.7x1	T45.7x2	T45.7x3	T45.7x4	T45.7x5	T45.7x6
Acetomorphine	T40.1x1	T40.1x2	T40.1x3	T40.1x4	T40.1x5	T40.1x6
Acetone (oils)	T52.4x1	T52.4x2	T52.4x3	T52.4x4	—	—
chlorinated	T52.4x1	T52.4x2	T52.4x3	T52.4x4	—	—
vapor	T52.4x1	T52.4x2	T52.4x3	T52.4x4	—	—
Acetonitrile	T52.8x1	T52.8x2	T52.8x3	T52.8x4	—	—
Acetophenazine	T43.3x1	T43.3x2	T43.3x3	T43.3x4	T43.3x5	T43.3x6
Acetophenetedin	T39.1x1	T39.1x2	T39.1x3	T39.1x4	T39.1x5	T39.1x6
Acetophenone	T52.4x1	T52.4x2	T52.4x3	T52.4x4	—	—
Acetorphine	T40.2x1	T40.2x2	T40.2x3	T40.2x4	T40.2x5	T40.2x6
Acetosulfone (sodium)	T37.1x1	T37.1x2	T37.1x3	T37.1x4	T37.1x5	T37.1x6
Acetrizoate (sodium)	T50.8x1	T50.8x2	T50.8x3	T50.8x4	T50.8x5	T50.8x6
Acetylcarbromal	T42.6x1	T42.6x2	T42.6x3	T42.6x4	T42.6x5	T42.6x6
Acetrizoic acid	T50.8x1	T50.8x2	T50.8x3	T50.8x4	T50.8x5	T50.8x6
Acetyl						
bromide	T53.6x1	T53.6x2	T53.6x3	T53.6x4	—	—
chloride	T53.6x1	T53.6x2	T53.6x3	T53.6x4	—	—
Acetylcholine						
chloride	T44.1x1	T44.1x2	T44.1x3	T44.1x4	T44.1x5	T44.1x6
derivative	T44.1x1	T44.1x2	T44.1x3	T44.1x4	T44.1x5	T44.1x6
Acetylcysteine	T48.4x1	T48.4x2	T48.4x3	T48.4x4	T48.4x5	T48.4x6
Acetyldigitoxin	T46.0x1	T46.0x2	T46.0x3	T46.0x4	T46.0x5	T46.0x6
Acetyldigoxin	T46.0x1	T46.0x2	T46.0x3	T46.0x4	T46.0x5	T46.0x6
Acetyldihydrocodeine	T40.2x1	T40.2x2	T40.2x3	T40.2x4	T40.2x5	T40.2x6
Acetyldihydrocodeinone	T40.2x1	T40.2x2	T40.2x3	T40.2x4	T40.2x5	T40.2x6
Acetylene (gas)	T59.891	T59.892	T59.893	T59.894	—	—
dichloride	T53.6x1	T53.6x2	T53.6x3	T53.6x4	—	—
incomplete combustion of - *see* Carbon, monoxide, industrial fuels or gases						
industrial	T59.891	T59.892	T59.893	T59.894	—	—
tetrachloride	T53.6x1	T53.6x2	T53.6x3	T53.6x4	—	—
vapor	T53.6x1	T53.6x2	T53.6x3	T53.6x4	—	—
Acetylphenylhydrazine	T39.8x1	T39.8x2	T39.8x3	T39.8x4	T39.8x5	T39.8x6
Acetylpheneturide	T42.6x1	T42.6x2	T42.6x3	T42.6x4	T42.6x5	T42.6x6
Acetylsalicylic acid (salts)	T39.011	T39.012	T39.013	T39.014	T39.015	T39.016
enteric coated	T39.011	T39.012	T39.013	T39.014	T39.015	T39.016

Substance	External Cause (T-Code)					
	Poisoning, Accidental (Unintentional)	Poisoning, Intentional Self-Harm	Poisoning, Assault	Poisoning, Undetermined	Adverse Effect	Underdosing
Acetylsulfamethoxypyridazine	T37.0x1	T37.0x2	T37.0x3	T37.0x4	T37.0x5	T37.0x6
Achromycin	T36.4x1	T36.4x2	T36.4x3	T36.4x4	T36.4x5	T36.4x6
ophthalmic preparation	T49.5x1	T49.5x2	T49.5x3	T49.5x4	T49.5x5	T49.5x6
topical NEC	T49.0x1	T49.0x2	T49.0x3	T49.0x4	T49.0x5	T49.0x6
Aciclovir	T37.5x1	T37.5x2	T37.5x3	T37.5x4	T37.5x5	T37.5x6
Acid (corrosive) NEC	T54.2x1	T54.2x2	T54.2x3	T54.2x4	—	—
Acidifying agent NEC	T50.901	T50.902	T50.903	T50.904	T50.905	T50.906
Acipimox	T46.6x1	T46.6x2	T46.6x3	T46.6x4	T46.6x5	T46.6x6
Acitretin	T50.991	T50.992	T50.993	T50.994	T50.995	T50.996
Aclarubicin	T45.1x1	T45.1x2	T45.1x3	T45.1x4	T45.1x5	T45.1x6
Aclatonium napadisilate	T48.1x1	T48.1x2	T48.1x3	T48.1x4	T48.1x5	T48.1x6
Aconite (wild)	T46.991	T46.992	T46.993	T46.994	T46.995	T46.996
Aconitine	T46.991	T46.992	T46.993	T46.994	T46.995	T46.996
Aconitum ferox	T46.991	T46.992	T46.993	T46.994	T46.995	T46.996
Acridine	T65.6x1	T65.6x2	T65.6x3	T65.6x4	—	—
vapor	T59.891	T59.892	T59.893	T59.894	—	—
Acriflavine	T37.91	T37.92	T37.93	T37.94	T37.95	T37.96
Acriflavinium chloride	T49.0x1	T49.0x2	T49.0x3	T49.0x4	T49.0x5	T49.0x6
Acrinol	T49.0x1	T49.0x2	T49.0x3	T49.0x4	T49.0x5	T49.0x6
Acrisorcin	T49.0x1	T49.0x2	T49.0x3	T49.0x4	T49.0x5	T49.0x6
Acrivastine	T45.0x1	T45.0x2	T45.0x3	T45.0x4	T45.0x5	T45.0x6
Acrolein (gas)	T59.891	T59.892	T59.893	T59.894	—	—
liquid	T54.1x1	T54.1x2	T54.1x3	T54.1x4	—	—
Acrylamide	T65.891	T65.892	T65.893	T65.894	—	—
Acrylic resin	T49.3x1	T49.3x2	T49.3x3	T49.3x4	T49.3x5	T49.3x6
Acrylonitrile	T65.891	T65.892	T65.893	T65.894	—	—
Actaea spicata	T62.2x1	T62.2x2	T62.2x3	T62.2x4	—	—
berry	T62.1x1	T62.1x2	T62.1x3	T62.1x4	—	—
Acterol	T37.3x1	T37.3x2	T37.3x3	T37.3x4	T37.3x5	T37.3x6
ACTH	T38.811	T38.812	T38.813	T38.814	T38.815	T38.816
Actinomycin C	T45.1x1	T45.1x2	T45.1x3	T45.1x4	T45.1x5	T45.1x6
Actinomycin D	T45.1x1	T45.1x2	T45.1x3	T45.1x4	T45.1x5	T45.1x6
Activated charcoal	T47.6x1	T47.6x2	T47.6x3	T47.6x4	T47.6x5	T47.6x6
Acyclovir	T37.5x1	T37.5x2	T37.5x3	T37.5x4	T37.5x5	T37.5x6
Adenine	T45.2x1	T45.2x2	T45.2x3	T45.2x4	T45.2x5	T45.2x6
arabinoside	T37.5x1	T37.5x2	T37.5x3	T37.5x4	T37.5x5	T37.5x6
Adenosine (phosphate)	T46.2x1	T46.2x2	T46.2x3	T46.2x4	T46.2x5	T46.2x6
ADH	T38.891	T38.892	T38.893	T38.894	T38.895	T38.896
Adhesive NEC	T65.891	T65.892	T65.893	T65.894	—	—
Adicillin	T36.0x1	T36.0x2	T36.0x3	T36.0x4	T36.0x5	T36.0x6

	External Cause (T-Code)					
Substance	Poisoning, Accidental (Unintentional)	Poisoning, Intentional Self-Harm	Poisoning, Assault	Poisoning, Undetermined	Adverse Effect	Underdosing
Adiphenine	T44.3x1	T44.3x2	T44.3x3	T44.3x4	T44.3x5	T44.3x6
Adipiodone	T50.8x1	T50.8x2	T50.8x3	T50.8x4	T50.8x5	T50.8x6
Adjunct, pharmaceutical	T50.901	T50.902	T50.903	T50.904	T50.905	T50.906
Adrenal (extract, cortex or medulla) (glucocorticoids) (hormones) (mineralocorticoids)	T38.0x1	T38.0x2	T38.0x3	T38.0x4	T38.0x5	T38.0x6
ENT agent	T49.6x1	T49.6x2	T49.6x3	T49.6x4	T49.6x5	T49.6x6
ophthalmic preparation	T49.5x1	T49.5x2	T49.5x3	T49.5x4	T49.5x5	T49.5x6
topical NEC	T49.0x1	T49.0x2	T49.0x3	T49.0x4	T49.0x5	T49.0x6
Adrenaline	T44.5x1	T44.5x2	T44.5x3	T44.5x4	T44.5x5	T44.5x6
Adrenalin - see Adrenaline						
Adrenergic NEC	T44.901	T44.902	T44.903	T44.904	T44.905	T44.906
blocking agent NEC	T44.8x1	T44.8x2	T44.8x3	T44.8x4	T44.8x5	T44.8x6
beta, heart	T44.7x1	T44.7x2	T44.7x3	T44.7x4	T44.7x5	T44.7x6
specified NEC	T44.991	T44.992	T44.993	T44.994	T44.995	T44.996
Adrenochrome						
(mono) semicarbazone	T46.991	T46.992	T46.993	T46.994	T46.995	T46.996
derivative	T46.991	T46.992	T46.993	T46.994	T46.995	T46.996
Adrenocorticotrophic hormone	T38.811	T38.812	T38.813	T38.814	T38.815	T38.816
Adrenocorticotrophin	T38.811	T38.812	T38.813	T38.814	T38.815	T38.816
Adriamycin	T45.1x1	T45.1x2	T45.1x3	T45.1x4	T45.1x5	T45.1x6
Aerosol spray NEC	T65.91	T65.92	T65.93	T65.94	—	—
Aerosporin	T36.8x1	T36.8x2	T36.8x3	T36.8x4	T36.8x5	T36.8x6
ENT agent	T49.6x1	T49.6x2	T49.6x3	T49.6x4	T49.6x5	T49.6x6
ophthalmic preparation	T49.5x1	T49.5x2	T49.5x3	T49.5x4	T49.5x5	T49.5x6
topical NEC	T49.0x1	T49.0x2	T49.0x3	T49.0x4	T49.0x5	T49.0x6
Aethusa cynapium	T62.2x1	T62.2x2	T62.2x3	T62.2x4	—	—
Afghanistan black	T40.7x1	T40.7x2	T40.7x3	T40.7x4	T40.7x5	T40.7x6
Aflatoxin	T64.01	T64.02	T64.03	T64.04	—	—
Afloqualone	T42.8x1	T42.8x2	T42.8x3	T42.8x4	T42.8x5	T42.8x6
African boxwood	T62.2x1	T62.2x2	T62.2x3	T62.2x4	—	—
Agar	T47.4x1	T47.4x2	T47.4x3	T47.4x4	T47.4x5	T47.4x6
Agricultural agent NEC	T65.91	T65.92	T65.93	T65.94	—	—
Agrypnal	T42.3x1	T42.3x2	T42.3x3	T42.3x4	T42.3x5	T42.3x6
AHLG	T50.Z11	T50.Z12	T50.Z13	T50.Z14	T50.Z15	T50.Z16
Air contaminant(s), source/type NOS	T65.91	T65.92	T65.93	T65.94	—	—
Ajmaline	T46.2x1	T46.2x2	T46.2x3	T46.2x4	T46.2x5	T46.2x6
Akritoin	T37.8x1	T37.8x2	T37.8x3	T37.8x4	T37.8x5	T37.8x6
Akee	T62.1x1	T62.1x2	T62.1x3	T62.1x4	—	—
Akrinol	T49.0x1	T49.0x2	T49.0x3	T49.0x4	T49.0x5	T49.0x6
Alacepril	T46.4x1	T46.4x2	T46.4x3	T46.4x4	T46.4x5	T46.4x6

Substance	External Cause (T-Code)					
	Poisoning, Accidental (Unintentional)	Poisoning, Intentional Self-Harm	Poisoning, Assault	Poisoning, Undetermined	Adverse Effect	Underdosing
Alantolactone	T37.4x1	T37.4x2	T37.4x3	T37.4x4	T37.4x5	T37.4x6
Albamycin	T36.8x1	T36.8x2	T36.8x3	T36.8x4	T36.8x5	T36.8x6
Albendazole	T37.4x1	T37.4x2	T37.4x3	T37.4x4	T37.4x5	T37.4x6
Albumin						
bovine	T45.8x1	T45.8x2	T45.8x3	T45.8x4	T45.8x5	T45.8x6
human serum	T45.8x1	T45.8x2	T45.8x3	T45.8x4	T45.8x5	T45.8x6
salt-poor	T45.8x1	T45.8x2	T45.8x3	T45.8x4	T45.8x5	T45.8x6
normal human serum	T45.8x1	T45.8x2	T45.8x3	T45.8x4	T45.8x5	T45.8x6
Albuterol	T48.6x1	T48.6x2	T48.6x3	T48.6x4	T48.6x5	T48.6x6
Albutoin	T42.0x1	T42.0x2	T42.0x3	T42.0x4	T42.0x5	T42.0x6
Alclometasone	T49.0x1	T49.0x2	T49.0x3	T49.0x4	T49.0x5	T49.0x6
Alcohol	T51.91	T51.92	T51.93	T51.94	—	—
absolute	T51.0x1	T51.0x2	T51.0x3	T51.0x4	—	—
beverage	T51.0x1	T51.0x2	T51.0x3	T51.0x4	—	—
allyl	T51.8x1	T51.8x2	T51.8x3	T51.8x4	—	—
antifreeze	T51.1x1	T51.1x2	T51.1x3	T51.1x4	—	—
amyl	T51.3x1	T51.3x2	T51.3x3	T51.3x4	—	—
beverage	T51.0x1	T51.0x2	T51.0x3	T51.0x4	—	—
butyl	T51.3x1	T51.3x2	T51.3x3	T51.3x4	—	—
dehydrated	T51.0x1	T51.0x2	T51.0x3	T51.0x4	—	—
beverage	T51.0x1	T51.0x2	T51.0x3	T51.0x4	—	—
denatured	T51.0x1	T51.0x2	T51.0x3	T51.0x4	—	—
deterrent NEC	T50.6x1	T50.6x2	T50.6x3	T50.6x4	T50.6x5	T50.6x6
diagnostic (gastric function)	T50.8x1	T50.8x2	T50.8x3	T50.8x4	T50.8x5	T50.8x6
ethyl	T51.0x1	T51.0x2	T51.0x3	T51.0x4	—	—
beverage	T51.0x1	T51.0x2	T51.0x3	T51.0x4	—	—
grain	T51.0x1	T51.0x2	T51.0x3	T51.0x4	—	—
beverage	T51.0x1	T51.0x2	T51.0x3	T51.0x4	—	—
industrial	T51.0x1	T51.0x2	T51.0x3	T51.0x4	—	—
isopropyl	T51.2x1	T51.2x2	T51.2x3	T51.2x4	—	—
methyl	T51.1x1	T51.1x2	T51.1x3	T51.1x4	—	—
preparation for consumption	T51.0x1	T51.0x2	T51.0x3	T51.0x4	—	—
propyl	T51.3x1	T51.3x2	T51.3x3	T51.3x4	—	—
secondary	T51.2x1	T51.2x2	T51.2x3	T51.2x4	—	—
radiator	T51.1x1	T51.1x2	T51.1x3	T51.1x4	—	—
rubbing	T51.2x1	T51.2x2	T51.2x3	T51.2x4	—	—
specified type NEC	T51.8x1	T51.8x2	T51.8x3	T51.8x4	—	—
surgical	T51.0x1	T51.0x2	T51.0x3	T51.0x4	—	—
vapor (from any type of Alcohol)	T59.891	T59.892	T59.893	T59.894	—	—
wood	T51.1x1	T51.1x2	T51.1x3	T51.1x4	—	—

Substance	Poisoning, Accidental (Unintentional)	Poisoning, Intentional Self-Harm	Poisoning, Assault	Poisoning, Undetermined	Adverse Effect	Underdosing
	External Cause (T-Code)					
Alcuronium (chloride)	T48.1x1	T48.1x2	T48.1x3	T48.1x4	T48.1x5	T48.1x6
Aldactone	T50.0x1	T50.0x2	T50.0x3	T50.0x4	T50.0x5	T50.0x6
Aldesulfone sodium	T37.1x1	T37.1x2	T37.1x3	T37.1x4	T37.1x5	T37.1x6
Aldicarb	T60.0x1	T60.0x2	T60.0x3	T60.0x4	—	—
Aldomet	T46.5x1	T46.5x2	T46.5x3	T46.5x4	T46.5x5	T46.5x6
Aldosterone	T50.0x1	T50.0x2	T50.0x3	T50.0x4	T50.0x5	T50.0x6
Aldrin (dust)	T60.1x1	T60.1x2	T60.1x3	T60.1x4	—	—
Aleve - *see* Naproxen						
Alexitol sodium	T47.1x1	T47.1x2	T47.1x3	T47.1x4	T47.1x5	T47.1x6
Alfacalcidol	T45.2x1	T45.2x2	T45.2x3	T45.2x4	T45.2x5	T45.2x6
Alfadolone	T41.1x1	T41.1x2	T41.1x3	T41.1x4	T41.1x5	T41.1x6
Alfaxalone	T41.1x1	T41.1x2	T41.1x3	T41.1x4	T41.1x5	T41.1x6
Alfentanil	T40.4x1	T40.4x2	T40.4x3	T40.4x4	T40.4x5	T40.4x6
Alfuzosin (hydrochloride)	T44.8x1	T44.8x2	T44.8x3	T44.8x4	T44.8x5	T44.8x6
Algae (harmful) (toxin)	T65.821	T65.822	T65.823	T65.824	—	—
Algeldrate	T47.1x1	T47.1x2	T47.1x3	T47.1x4	T47.1x5	T47.1x6
Algin	T47.8x1	T47.8x2	T47.8x3	T47.8x4	T47.8x5	T47.8x6
Alglucerase	T45.3x1	T45.3x2	T45.3x3	T45.3x4	T45.3x5	T45.3x6
Alidase	T45.3x1	T45.3x2	T45.3x3	T45.3x4	T45.3x5	T45.3x6
Alimemazine	T43.3x1	T43.3x2	T43.3x3	T43.3x4	T43.3x5	T43.3x6
Aliphatic thiocyanates	T65.0x1	T65.0x2	T65.0x3	T65.0x4	—	—
Alizapride	T45.0x1	T45.0x2	T45.0x3	T45.0x4	T45.0x5	T45.0x6
Alkali (caustic)	T54.3x1	T54.3x2	T54.3x3	T54.3x4	—	—
Alkalizing agent NEC	T50.901	T50.902	T50.903	T50.904	T50.905	T50.906
Alkaline antiseptic solution (aromatic)	T49.6x1	T49.6x2	T49.6x3	T49.6x4	T49.6x5	T49.6x6
Alkalinizing agents (medicinal)	T50.901	T50.902	T50.903	T50.904	T50.905	T50.906
Alka-seltzer	T39.011	T39.012	T39.013	T39.014	T39.015	T39.016
Alkavervir	T46.5x1	T46.5x2	T46.5x3	T46.5x4	T46.5x5	T46.5x6
Alkonium (bromide)	T49.0x1	T49.0x2	T49.0x3	T49.0x4	T49.0x5	T49.0x6
Alkylating drug NEC	T45.1x1	T45.1x2	T45.1x3	T45.1x4	T45.1x5	T45.1x6
antimyeloproliferative	T45.1x1	T45.1x2	T45.1x3	T45.1x4	T45.1x5	T45.1x6
lymphatic	T45.1x1	T45.1x2	T45.1x3	T45.1x4	T45.1x5	T45.1x6
Alkylisocyanate	T65.0x1	T65.0x2	T65.0x3	T65.0x4	—	—
Allantoin	T49.411	T49.412	T49.413	T49.414	T49.415	T49.416
Allegron	T43.0x1	T43.0x2	T43.0x3	T43.0x4	T43.0x5	T43.0x6
Allethrin	T49.0x1	T49.0x2	T49.0x3	T49.0x4	T49.0x5	T49.0x6
Allobarbital	T42.3x1	T42.3x2	T42.3x3	T42.3x4	T42.3x5	T42.3x6
Allopurinol	T50.4x1	T50.4x2	T50.4x3	T50.4x4	T50.4x5	T50.4x6
Allyl						
alcohol	T51.8x1	T51.8x2	T51.8x3	T51.8x4	—	—
disulfide	T46.6x1	T46.6x2	T46.6x3	T46.6x4	T46.6x5	T46.6x6

Substance	External Cause (T-Code)					
	Poisoning, Accidental (Unintentional)	Poisoning, Intentional Self-Harm	Poisoning, Assault	Poisoning, Undetermined	Adverse Effect	Underdosing
Allylestrenol	T38.5x1	T38.5x2	T38.5x3	T38.5x4	T38.5x5	T38.5x6
Allylisopropylacetylurea	T42.6x1	T42.6x2	T42.6x3	T42.6x4	T42.6x5	T42.6x6
Allylisopropylmalonylurea	T42.3x1	T42.3x2	T42.3x3	T42.3x4	T42.3x5	T42.3x6
Allylthiourea	T49.3x1	T49.3x2	T49.3x3	T49.3x4	T49.3x5	T49.3x6
Allyltribromide	T42.6x1	T42.6x2	T42.6x3	T42.6x4	T42.6x5	T42.6x6
Allypropymal	T42.3x1	T42.3x2	T42.3x3	T42.3x4	T42.3x5	T42.3x6
Almagate	T47.1x1	T47.1x2	T47.1x3	T47.1x4	T47.1x5	T47.1x6
Almasilate	T47.1x1	T47.1x2	T47.1x3	T47.1x4	T47.1x5	T47.1x6
Almitrine	T50.7x1	T50.7x2	T50.7x3	T50.7x4	T50.7x5	T50.7x6
Aloes	T47.2x1	T47.2x2	T47.2x3	T47.2x4	T47.2x5	T47.2x6
Aloglutamol	T47.1x1	T47.1x2	T47.1x3	T47.1x4	T47.1x5	T47.1x6
Aloin	T47.2x1	T47.2x2	T47.2x3	T47.2x4	T47.2x5	T47.2x6
Aloxidone	T42.2x1	T42.2x2	T42.2x3	T42.2x4	T42.2x5	T42.2x6
Alpha						
Acetyldigoxin	T46.0x1	T46.0x2	T46.0x3	T46.0x4	T46.0x5	T46.0x6
amylase	T45.3x1	T45.3x2	T45.3x3	T45.3x4	T45.3x5	T45.3x6
tocoferol (acetate)	T45.2x1	T45.2x2	T45.2x3	T45.2x4	T45.2x5	T45.2x6
Alpha-adrenergic blocking drug	T44.6x1	T44.6x2	T44.6x3	T44.6x4	T44.6x5	T44.6x6
Alpha tocopherol	T45.2x1	T45.2x2	T45.2x3	T45.2x4	T45.2x5	T45.2x6
Alphadolone	T41.1x1	T41.1x2	T41.1x3	T41.1x4	T41.1x5	T41.1x6
Alphaprodine	T40.4x1	T40.4x2	T40.4x3	T40.4x4	T40.4x5	T40.4x6
Alphaxalone	T41.1x1	T41.1x2	T41.1x3	T41.1x4	T41.1x5	T41.1x6
Alprazolam	T42.4x1	T42.4x2	T42.4x3	T42.4x4	T42.4x5	T42.4x6
Alprenolol	T44.7x1	T44.7x2	T44.7x3	T44.7x4	T44.7x5	T44.7x6
Alprostadil	T46.7x1	T46.7x2	T46.7x3	T46.7x4	T46.7x5	T46.7x6
Alsactide	T38.811	T38.812	T38.813	T38.814	T38.815	T38.816
Alseroxylon	T46.5x1	T46.5x2	T46.5x3	T46.5x4	T46.5x5	T46.5x6
Alteplase	T45.611	T45.612	T45.613	T45.614	T45.615	T45.616
Altizide	T50.2x1	T50.2x2	T50.2x3	T50.2x4	T50.2x5	T50.2x6
Altretamine	T45.1x1	T45.1x2	T45.1x3	T45.1x4	T45.1x5	T45.1x6
Alum (medicinal)	T49.4x1	T49.4x2	T49.4x3	T49.4x4	T49.4x5	T49.4x6
nonmedicinal (ammonium) (potassium)	T56.891	T56.892	T56.893	T56.894	—	—
Aluminium, aluminum						
acetate	T49.2x1	T49.2x2	T49.2x3	T49.2x4	T49.2x5	T49.2x6
solution	T49.0x1	T49.0x2	T49.0x3	T49.0x4	T49.0x5	T49.0x6
aspirin	T39.011	T39.012	T39.013	T39.014	T39.015	T39.016
bis (acetylsalicylate)	T39.011	T39.012	T39.013	T39.014	T39.015	T39.016
carbonate (gel, basic)	T47.1x1	T47.1x2	T47.1x3	T47.1x4	T47.1x5	T47.1x6
chlorhydroxide-complex	T47.1x1	T47.1x2	T47.1x3	T47.1x4	T47.1x5	T47.1x6
chloride	T49.2x1	T49.2x2	T49.2x3	T49.2x4	T49.2x5	T49.2x6

Substance	External Cause (T-Code)					
	Poisoning, Accidental (Unintentional)	Poisoning, Intentional Self-Harm	Poisoning, Assault	Poisoning, Undetermined	Adverse Effect	Underdosing
Aluminium, aluminum *(Continued)*						
clofibrate	T46.6x1	T46.6x2	T46.6x3	T46.6x4	T46.6x5	T46.6x6
diacetate	T49.2x1	T49.2x2	T49.2x3	T49.2x4	T49.2x5	T49.2x6
glycinate	T47.1x1	T47.1x2	T47.1x3	T47.1x4	T47.1x5	T47.1x6
hydroxide (gel)	T47.1x1	T47.1x2	T47.1x3	T47.1x4	T47.1x5	T47.1x6
hydroxide-magnesium carb. gel	T47.1x1	T47.1x2	T47.1x3	T47.1x4	T47.1x5	T47.1x6
magnesium silicate	T47.1x1	T47.1x2	T47.1x3	T47.1x4	T47.1x5	T47.1x6
nicotinate	T46.7x1	T46.7x2	T46.7x3	T46.7x4	T46.7x5	T46.7x6
ointment (surgical) (topical)	T49.3x1	T49.3x2	T49.3x3	T49.3x4	T49.3x5	T49.3x6
phosphate	T47.1x1	T47.1x2	T47.1x3	T47.1x4	T47.1x5	T47.1x6
salicylate	T39.091	T39.092	T39.093	T39.094	T39.095	T39.096
silicate	T47.1x1	T47.1x2	T47.1x3	T47.1x4	T47.1x5	T47.1x6
sodium silicate	T47.1x1	T47.1x2	T47.1x3	T47.1x4	T47.1x5	T47.1x6
subacetate	T49.2x1	T49.2x2	T49.2x3	T49.2x4	T49.2x5	T49.2x6
sulfate	T49.0x1	T49.0x2	T49.0x3	T49.0x4	T49.0x5	T49.0x6
tannate	T47.6x1	T47.6x2	T47.6x3	T47.6x4	T47.6x5	T47.6x6
topical NEC	T49.3x1	T49.3x2	T49.3x3	T49.3x4	T49.3x5	T49.3x6
Alurate	T42.3x1	T42.3x2	T42.3x3	T42.3x4	T42.3x5	T42.3x6
Alverine	T44.3x1	T44.3x2	T44.3x3	T44.3x4	T44.3x5	T44.3x6
Alvodine	T40.2x1	T40.2x2	T40.2x3	T40.2x4	T40.2x5	T40.2x6
Amanita phalloides	T62.0x1	T62.0x2	T62.0x3	T62.0x4	—	—
Amanitine	T62.0x1	T62.0x2	T62.0x3	T62.0x4	—	—
Amantadine	T42.8x1	T42.8x2	T42.8x3	T42.8x4	T42.8x5	T42.8x6
Ambazone	T49.6x1	T49.6x2	T49.6x3	T49.6x4	T49.6x5	T49.6x6
Ambenonium (chloride)	T44.0x1	T44.0x2	T44.0x3	T44.0x4	T44.0x5	T44.0x6
Ambroxol	T48.4x1	T48.4x2	T48.4x3	T48.4x4	T48.4x5	T48.4x6
Ambuphylline	T48.6x1	T48.6x2	T48.6x3	T48.6x4	T48.6x5	T48.6x6
Ambutonium bromide	T44.3x1	T44.3x2	T44.3x3	T44.3x4	T44.3x5	T44.3x6
Amcinonide	T49.0x1	T49.0x2	T49.0x3	T49.0x4	T49.0x5	T49.0x6
Amdinocilline	T36.0x1	T36.0x2	T36.0x3	T36.0x4	T36.0x5	T36.0x6
Ametazole	T50.8x1	T50.8x2	T50.8x3	T50.8x4	T50.8x5	T50.8x6
Amethocaine	T41.3x1	T41.3x2	T41.3x3	T41.3x4	T41.3x5	T41.3x6
regional	T41.3x1	T41.3x2	T41.3x3	T41.3x4	T41.3x5	T41.3x6
spinal	T41.3x1	T41.3x2	T41.3x3	T41.3x4	T41.3x5	T41.3x6
Amethopterin	T45.1x1	T45.1x2	T45.1x3	T45.1x4	T45.1x5	T45.1x6
Amezinium metilsulfate	T44.991	T44.992	T44.993	T44.994	T44.995	T44.996
Amfebutamone	T43.291	T43.292	T43.293	T43.294	T43.295	T43.296
Amfepramone	T50.5x1	T50.5x2	T50.5x3	T50.5x4	T50.5x5	T50.5x6
Amfetamine	T43.621	T43.622	T43.623	T43.624	T43.625	T43.626
Amfetaminil	T43.621	T43.622	T43.623	T43.624	T43.625	T43.626

Substance	Poisoning, Accidental (Unintentional)	Poisoning, Intentional Self-Harm	Poisoning, Assault	Poisoning, Undetermined	Adverse Effect	Underdosing
			External Cause (T-Code)			
Amfomycin	T36.8x1	T36.8x2	T36.8x3	T36.8x4	T36.8x5	T36.8x6
Amidefrine mesilate	T48.5x1	T48.5x2	T48.5x3	T48.5x4	T48.5x5	T48.5x6
Amidone	T40.3x1	T40.3x2	T40.3x3	T40.3x4	T40.3x5	T40.3x6
Amidopyrine	T39.2x1	T39.2x2	T39.2x3	T39.2x4	T39.2x5	T39.2x6
Amidotrizoate	T50.8x1	T50.8x2	T50.8x3	T50.8x4	T50.8x5	T50.8x6
Amiflamine	T43.1x1	T43.1x2	T43.1x3	T43.1x4	T43.1x5	T43.1x6
Amikacin	T36.5x1	T36.5x2	T36.5x3	T36.5x4	T36.5x5	T36.5x6
Amikhelline	T46.3x1	T46.3x2	T46.3x3	T46.3x4	T46.3x5	T46.3x6
Amiloride	T50.2x1	T50.2x2	T50.2x3	T50.2x4	T50.2x5	T50.2x6
Aminacrine	T49.0x1	T49.0x2	T49.0x3	T49.0x4	T49.0x5	T49.0x6
Amineptine	T43.011	T43.012	T43.013	T43.014	T43.015	T43.016
Aminitrozole	T37.3x1	T37.3x2	T37.3x3	T37.3x4	T37.3x5	T37.3x6
Aminoacetic acid (derivatives)	T50.3x1	T50.3x2	T50.3x3	T50.3x4	T50.3x5	T50.3x6
Amino acids	T50.3x1	T50.3x2	T50.3x3	T50.3x4	T50.3x5	T50.3x6
Aminoacridine	T49.0x1	T49.0x2	T49.0x3	T49.0x4	T49.0x5	T49.0x6
Aminobenzoic acid (-p)	T49.3x1	T49.3x2	T49.3x3	T49.3x4	T49.3x5	T49.3x6
4-Aminobutyric acid	T43.8x1	T43.8x2	T43.8x3	T43.8x4	T43.8x5	T43.8x6
Aminocaproic acid	T45.621	T45.622	T45.623	T45.624	T45.625	T45.626
Aminofenazone	T39.2x1	T39.2x2	T39.2x3	T39.2x4	T39.2x5	T39.2x6
Aminoethylisothiourium	T45.8x1	T45.8x2	T45.8x3	T45.8x4	T45.8x5	T45.8x6
Aminoglutethimide	T45.1x1	T45.1x2	T45.1x3	T45.1x4	T45.1x5	T45.1x6
Aminohippuric acid	T50.8x1	T50.8x2	T50.8x3	T50.8x4	T50.8x5	T50.8x6
Aminomethylbenzoic acid	T45.691	T45.692	T45.693	T45.694	T45.695	T45.696
Aminometradine	T50.2x1	T50.2x2	T50.2x3	T50.2x4	T50.2x5	T50.2x6
Aminopentamide	T44.3x1	T44.3x2	T44.3x3	T44.3x4	T44.3x5	T44.3x6
Aminophenazone	T39.2x1	T39.2x2	T39.2x3	T39.2x4	T39.2x5	T39.2x6
Aminophenol	T54.0x1	T54.0x2	T54.0x3	T54.0x4	—	—
4-Aminophenol derivatives	T39.1x1	T39.1x2	T39.1x3	T39.1x4	T39.1x5	T39.1x6
Aminophenylpyridone	T43.591	T43.592	T43.593	T43.594	T43.595	T43.596
Aminophylline	T48.6x1	T48.6x2	T48.6x3	T48.6x4	T48.6x5	T48.6x6
Aminopterin sodium	T45.1x1	T45.1x2	T45.1x3	T45.1x4	T45.1x5	T45.1x6
Aminopyrine	T39.2x1	T39.2x2	T39.2x3	T39.2x4	T39.2x5	T39.2x6
8-Aminoquinoline drugs	T37.2x1	T37.2x2	T37.2x3	T37.2x4	T37.2x5	T37.2x6
Aminorex	T50.5x1	T50.5x2	T50.5x3	T50.5x4	T50.5x5	T50.5x6
Aminosalicylic acid	T37.1x1	T37.1x2	T37.1x3	T37.1x4	T37.1x5	T37.1x6
Aminosalylum	T37.1x1	T37.1x2	T37.1x3	T37.1x4	T37.1x5	T37.1x6
Amiodarone	T46.2x1	T46.2x2	T46.2x3	T46.2x4	T46.2x5	T46.2x6
Amiphenazole	T50.7x1	T50.7x2	T50.7x3	T50.7x4	T50.7x5	T50.7x6
Amiquinsin	T46.5x1	T46.5x2	T46.5x3	T46.5x4	T46.5x5	T46.5x6
Amisometradine	T50.2x1	T50.2x2	T50.2x3	T50.2x4	T50.2x5	T50.2x6

Substance	Poisoning, Accidental (Unintentional)	Poisoning, Intentional Self-Harm	Poisoning, Assault	Poisoning, Undetermined	Adverse Effect	Underdosing
			External Cause (T-Code)			
Amisulpride	T43.591	T43.592	T43.593	T43.594	T43.595	T43.596
Amitriptyline	T43.021	T43.022	T43.023	T43.024	T43.025	T43.026
Amitriptylinoxide	T43.021	T43.022	T43.023	T43.024	T43.025	T43.026
Amlexanox	T48.6x1	T48.6x2	T48.6x3	T48.6x4	T48.6x5	T48.6x6
Ammonia (fumes) (gas) (vapor)	T59.891	T59.892	T59.893	T59.894	—	—
aromatic spirit	T48.991	T48.992	T48.993	T48.994	T48.995	T48.996
liquid (household)	T54.3x1	T54.3x2	T54.3x3	T54.3x4	—	—
Ammoniated mercury	T49.0x1	T49.0x2	T49.0x3	T49.0x4	T49.0x5	T49.0x6
Ammonium						
acid tartrate	T49.5x1	T49.5x2	T49.5x3	T49.5x4	T49.5x5	T49.5x6
bromide	T42.6x1	T42.6x2	T42.6x3	T42.6x4	T42.6x5	T42.6x6
carbonate	T54.3x1	T54.3x2	T54.3x3	T54.3x4	—	—
chloride	T50.991	T50.992	T50.993	T50.994	T50.995	T50.996
expectorant	T48.4x1	T48.4x2	T48.4x3	T48.4x4	T48.4x5	T48.4x6
compounds (household) NEC	T54.3x1	T54.3x2	T54.3x3	T54.3x4	—	—
fumes (any usage)	T59.891	T59.892	T59.893	T59.894	—	—
industrial	T54.3x1	T54.3x2	T54.3x3	T54.3x4	—	—
ichthyosulronate	T49.4x1	T49.4x2	T49.4x3	T49.4x4	T49.4x5	T49.4x6
mandelate	T37.91	T37.92	T37.93	T37.94	T37.95	T37.96
sulfamate	T60.3x1	T60.3x2	T60.3x3	T60.3x4	—	—
sulfonate resin	T47.8x1	T47.8x2	T47.8x3	T47.8x4	T47.8x5	T47.8x6
Amobarbital (sodium)	T42.3x1	T42.3x2	T42.3x3	T42.3x4	T42.3x5	T42.3x6
Amodiaquine	T37.2x1	T37.2x2	T37.2x3	T37.2x4	T37.2x5	T37.2x6
Amopyroquin(e)	T37.2x1	T37.2x2	T37.2x3	T37.2x4	T37.2x5	T37.2x6
Amoxapine	T43.011	T43.012	T43.013	T43.014	T43.015	T43.016
Amoxicillin	T36.0x1	T36.0x2	T36.0x3	T36.0x4	T36.0x5	T36.0x6
Amperozide	T43.591	T43.592	T43.593	T43.594	T43.595	T43.596
Amphenidone	T43.591	T43.592	T43.593	T43.594	T43.595	T43.596
Amphetamine NEC	T43.621	T43.622	T43.623	T43.624	T43.625	T43.626
Amphomycin	T36.8x1	T36.8x2	T36.8x3	T36.8x4	T36.8x5	T36.8x6
Amphotalide	T37.4x1	T37.4x2	T37.4x3	T37.4x4	T37.4x5	T37.4x6
Amphotericin B	T36.7x1	T36.7x2	T36.7x3	T36.7x4	T36.7x5	T36.7x6
topical	T49.0x1	T49.0x2	T49.0x3	T49.0x4	T49.0x5	T49.0x6
Ampicillin	T36.0x1	T36.0x2	T36.0x3	T36.0x4	T36.0x5	T36.0x6
Amprotropine	T44.3x1	T44.3x2	T44.3x3	T44.3x4	T44.3x5	T44.3x6
Amsacrine	T45.1x1	T45.1x2	T45.1x3	T45.1x4	T45.1x5	T45.1x6
Amygdaline	T62.2x1	T62.2x2	T62.2x3	T62.2x4	—	—
Amyl						
acetate	T52.8x1	T52.8x2	T52.8x3	T52.8x4	—	—
vapor	T59.891	T59.892	T59.893	T59.894	—	—

Substance	External Cause (T-Code)					
	Poisoning, Accidental (Unintentional)	Poisoning, Intentional Self-Harm	Poisoning, Assault	Poisoning, Undetermined	Adverse Effect	Underdosing
Amyl *(Continued)*						
alcohol	T51.3x1	T51.3x2	T51.3x3	T51.3x4	—	—
chloride	T53.6x1	T53.6x2	T53.6x3	T53.6x4	—	—
formate	T52.8x1	T52.8x2	T52.8x3	T52.8x4	—	—
nitrite	T46.3x1	T46.3x2	T46.3x3	T46.3x4	T46.3x5	T46.3x6
propionate	T65.891	T65.892	T65.893	T65.894	—	—
Amylase	T47.5x1	T47.5x2	T47.5x3	T47.5x4	T47.5x5	T47.5x6
Amyleine, regional	T41.3x1	T41.3x2	T41.3x3	T41.3x4	T41.3x5	T41.3x6
Amylene						
dichloride	T53.6x1	T53.6x2	T53.6x3	T53.6x4	—	—
hydrate	T51.3x1	T51.3x2	T51.3x3	T51.3x4	—	—
Amylmetacresol	T49.6x1	T49.6x2	T49.6x3	T49.6x4	T49.6x5	T49.6x6
Amylobarbitone	T42.3x1	T42.3x2	T42.3x3	T42.3x4	T42.3x5	T42.3x6
Amylocaine, regional	T41.3x1	T41.3x2	T41.3x3	T41.3x4	T41.3x5	T41.3x6
infiltration (subcutaneous)	T41.3x1	T41.3x2	T41.3x3	T41.3x4	T41.3x5	T41.3x6
nerve block (peripheral) (plexus)	T41.3x1	T41.3x2	T41.3x3	T41.3x4	T41.3x5	T41.3x6
spinal	T41.3x1	T41.3x2	T41.3x3	T41.3x4	T41.3x5	T41.3x6
topical (surface)	T41.3x1	T41.3x2	T41.3x3	T41.3x4	T41.3x5	T41.3x6
Amylopectin	T47.6x1	T47.6x2	T47.6x3	T47.6x4	T47.6x5	T47.6x6
Amytal (sodium)	T42.3x1	T42.3x2	T42.3x3	T42.3x4	T42.3x5	T42.3x6
Anabolic steroid	T38.7x1	T38.7x2	T38.7x3	T38.7x4	T38.7x5	T38.7x6
Analeptic NEC	T50.7x1	T50.7x2	T50.7x3	T50.7x4	T50.7x5	T50.7x6
Analgesic NEC	T39.8x1	T39.8x2	T39.8x3	T39.8x4	T39.8x5	T39.8x6
anti-inflammatory NEC	T39.91	T39.92	T39.93	T39.94	T39.95	T39.96
propionic acid derivative	T39.311	T39.312	T39.313	T39.314	T39.315	T39.316
antirheumatic NEC	T39.91	T39.92	T39.93	T39.94	T39.95	T39.96
aromatic NEC	T39.1x1	T39.1x2	T39.1x3	T39.1x4	T39.1x5	T39.1x6
narcotic NEC	T40.601	T40.602	T40.603	T40.604	T40.605	T40.606
combination	T40.601	T40.602	T40.603	T40.604	T40.605	T40.606
obstetric	T40.601	T40.602	T40.603	T40.604	T40.605	T40.606
non-narcotic NEC	T39.91	T39.92	T39.93	T39.94	T39.95	T39.96
combination	T39.91	T39.92	T39.93	T39.94	T39.95	T39.96
pyrazole	T39.2x1	T39.2x2	T39.2x3	T39.2x4	T39.2x5	T39.2x6
specified NEC	T39.8x1	T39.8x2	T39.8x3	T39.8x4	T39.8x5	T39.8x6
Analgin	T39.2x1	T39.2x2	T39.2x3	T39.2x4	T39.2x5	T39.2x6
Anamirta cocculus	T62.1x1	T62.1x2	T62.1x3	T62.1x4	—	—
Ancillin	T36.0x1	T36.0x2	T36.0x3	T36.0x4	T36.0x5	T36.0x6
Ancrod	T45.691	T45.692	T45.693	T45.694	T45.695	T45.696
Androgen	T38.7x1	T38.7x2	T38.7x3	T38.7x4	T38.7x5	T38.7x6
Androgen-estrogen mixture	T38.7x1	T38.7x2	T38.7x3	T38.7x4	T38.7x5	T38.7x6
Androstalone	T38.7x1	T38.7x2	T38.7x3	T38.7x4	T38.7x5	T38.7x6

Substance	External Cause (T-Code)					
	Poisoning, Accidental (Unintentional)	Poisoning, Intentional Self-Harm	Poisoning, Assault	Poisoning, Undetermined	Adverse Effect	Underdosing
Androstanolone	T38.7x1	T38.7x2	T38.7x3	T38.7x4	T38.7x5	T38.7x6
Androsterone	T38.7x1	T38.7x2	T38.7x3	T38.7x4	T38.7x5	T38.7x6
Anemone pulsatilla	T62.2x1	T62.2x2	T62.2x3	T62.2x4	—	—
Anesthesia						
caudal	T41.3x1	T41.3x2	T41.3x3	T41.3x4	T41.3x5	T41.3x6
endotracheal	T41.0x1	T41.0x2	T41.0x3	T41.0x4	T41.0x5	T41.0x6
epidural	T41.3x1	T41.3x2	T41.3x3	T41.3x4	T41.3x5	T41.3x6
inhalation	T41.0x1	T41.0x2	T41.0x3	T41.0x4	T41.0x5	T41.0x6
local	T41.3x1	T41.3x2	T41.3x3	T41.3x4	T41.3x5	T41.3x6
mucosal	T41.3x1	T41.3x2	T41.3x3	T41.3x4	T41.3x5	T41.3x6
muscle relaxation	T48.1x1	T48.1x2	T48.1x3	T48.1x4	T48.1x5	T48.1x6
nerve blocking	T41.3x1	T41.3x2	T41.3x3	T41.3x4	T41.3x5	T41.3x6
plexus blocking	T41.3x1	T41.3x2	T41.3x3	T41.3x4	T41.3x5	T41.3x6
potentiated	T41.201	T41.202	T41.203	T41.204	T41.205	T41.206
rectal	T41.201	T41.202	T41.203	T41.204	T41.205	T41.206
general	T41.201	T41.202	T41.203	T41.204	T41.205	T41.206
local	T41.3x1	T41.3x2	T41.3x3	T41.3x4	T41.3x5	T41.3x6
regional	T41.3x1	T41.3x2	T41.3x3	T41.3x4	T41.3x5	T41.3x6
surface	T41.3x1	T41.3x2	T41.3x3	T41.3x4	T41.3x5	T41.3x6
Anesthetic NEC (see also Anesthesia)	T41.41	T41.42	T41.43	T41.44	T41.45	T41.46
with muscle relaxant	T41.201	T41.202	T41.203	T41.204	T41.205	T41.206
general	T41.201	T41.202	T41.203	T41.204	T41.205	T41.206
local	T41.3x1	T41.3x2	T41.3x3	T41.3x4	T41.3x5	T41.3x6
gaseous NEC	T40.0x1	T40.0x2	T40.0x3	T40.0x4	T40.0x5	T40.0x6
general NEC	T41.201	T41.202	T41.203	T41.204	T41.205	T41.206
halogenated hydrocarbon derivatives NEC	T40.0x1	T40.0x2	T40.0x3	T40.0x4	T40.0x5	T40.0x6
infiltration NEC	T41.3x1	T41.3x2	T41.3x3	T41.3x4	T41.3x5	T41.3x6
intravenous NEC	T41.1x1	T41.1x2	T41.1x3	T41.1x4	T41.1x5	T41.1x6
local NEC	T41.3x1	T41.3x2	T41.3x3	T41.3x4	T41.3x5	T41.3x6
rectal	T41.201	T41.202	T41.203	T41.204	T41.205	T41.206
general	T41.201	T41.202	T41.203	T41.204	T41.205	T41.206
local	T41.3x1	T41.3x2	T41.3x3	T41.3x4	T41.3x5	T41.3x6
regional NEC	T41.3x1	T41.3x2	T41.3x3	T41.3x4	T41.3x5	T41.3x6
spinal NEC	T41.3x1	T41.3x2	T41.3x3	T41.3x4	T41.3x5	T41.3x6
thiobarbiturate	T41.1x1	T41.1x2	T41.1x3	T41.1x4	T41.1x5	T41.1x6
topical	T41.3x1	T41.3x2	T41.3x3	T41.3x4	T41.3x5	T41.3x6
Aneurine	T45.2x1	T45.2x2	T45.2x3	T45.2x4	T45.2x5	T45.2x6
Angio-Conray	T50.8x1	T50.8x2	T50.8x3	T50.8x4	T50.8x5	T50.8x6
Angiotensin	T44.5x1	T44.5x2	T44.5x3	T44.5x4	T44.5x5	T44.5x6
Angiotensinamide	T44.991	T44.992	T44.993	T44.994	T44.995	T44.996

Substance	External Cause (T-Code)					
	Poisoning, Accidental (Unintentional)	Poisoning, Intentional Self-Harm	Poisoning, Assault	Poisoning, Undetermined	Adverse Effect	Underdosing
Anhydrohydroxy-progesterone	T38.5x1	T38.5x2	T38.5x3	T38.5x4	T38.5x5	T38.5x6
Anhydron	T50.2x1	T50.2x2	T50.2x3	T50.2x4	T50.2x5	T50.2x6
Anileridine	T40.4x1	T40.4x2	T40.4x3	T40.4x4	T40.4x5	T40.4x6
Aniline (dye) (liquid)	T65.3x1	T65.3x2	T65.3x3	T65.3x4	—	—
analgesic	T39.1x1	T39.1x2	T39.1x3	T39.1x4	T39.1x5	T39.1x6
derivatives, therapeutic NEC	T39.1x1	T39.1x2	T39.1x3	T39.1x4	T39.1x5	T39.1x6
vapor	T65.3x1	T65.3x2	T65.3x3	T65.3x4	—	—
Anise oil	T47.5x1	T47.5x2	T47.5x3	T47.5x4	T47.5x5	T47.5x6
Aniscoropine	T44.3x1	T44.3x2	T44.3x3	T44.3x4	T44.3x5	T44.3x6
Anisidine	T65.3x1	T65.3x2	T65.3x3	T65.3x4	—	—
Anisindione	T45.511	T45.512	T45.513	T45.514	T45.515	T45.516
Anisotropine methyl-bromide	T44.3x1	T44.3x2	T44.3x3	T44.3x4	T44.3x5	T44.3x6
Anistreplase	T45.611	T45.612	T45.613	T45.614	T45.615	T45.616
Anorexiant (central)	T50.5x1	T50.5x2	T50.5x3	T50.5x4	T50.5x5	T50.5x6
Anorexic agents	T50.5x1	T50.5x2	T50.5x3	T50.5x4	T50.5x5	T50.5x6
Ansamycin	T36.6x1	T36.6x2	T36.6x3	T36.6x4	T36.6x5	T36.6x6
Ant (bite) (sting)	T63.421	T63.422	T63.423	T63.424	—	—
Antabuse	T50.6x1	T50.6x2	T50.6x3	T50.6x4	T50.6x5	T50.6x6
Ant poison - *see* Insecticide						
Antacid NEC	T47.1x1	T47.1x2	T47.1x3	T47.1x4	T47.1x5	T47.1x6
Antagonist						
Aldosterone	T50.0x1	T50.0x2	T50.0x3	T50.0x4	T50.0x5	T50.0x6
anticoagulant	T45.7x1	T45.7x2	T45.7x3	T45.7x4	T45.7x5	T45.7x6
extrapyramidal NEC	T44.3x1	T44.3x2	T44.3x3	T44.3x4	T44.3x5	T44.3x6
folic acid	T45.1x1	T45.1x2	T45.1x3	T45.1x4	T45.1x5	T45.1x6
heavy metal	T45.8x1	T45.8x2	T45.8x3	T45.8x4	T45.8x5	T45.8x6
H2 receptor	T47.1x1	T47.1x2	T47.1x3	T47.1x4	T47.1x5	T47.1x6
narcotic analgesic	T50.7x1	T50.7x2	T50.7x3	T50.7x4	T50.7x5	T50.7x6
opiate	T50.7x1	T50.7x2	T50.7x3	T50.7x4	T50.7x5	T50.7x6
pyrimidine	T45.1x1	T45.1x2	T45.1x3	T45.1x4	T45.1x5	T45.1x6
serotonin	T46.5x1	T46.5x2	T46.5x3	T46.5x4	T46.5x5	T46.5x6
Antazolin(e)	T45.0x1	T45.0x2	T45.0x3	T45.0x4	T45.0x5	T45.0x6
Anterior pituitary hormone NEC	T38.811	T38.812	T38.813	T38.814	T38.815	T38.816
Anthelmintic NEC	T37.4x1	T37.4x2	T37.4x3	T37.4x4	T37.4x5	T37.4x6
Anthiolimine	T37.4x1	T37.4x2	T37.4x3	T37.4x4	T37.4x5	T37.4x6
Anthralin	T49.4x1	T49.4x2	T49.4x3	T49.4x4	T49.4x5	T49.4x6
Anthramycin	T45.1x1	T45.1x2	T45.1x3	T45.1x4	T45.1x5	T45.1x6
Antiadrenergic NEC	T44.8x1	T44.8x2	T44.8x3	T44.8x4	T44.8x5	T44.8x6
Antiallergic NEC	T45.0x1	T45.0x2	T45.0x3	T45.0x4	T45.0x5	T45.0x6
Anti-anemic (drug) (preparation)	T45.8x1	T45.8x2	T45.8x3	T45.8x4	T45.8x5	T45.8x6

Substance	Poisoning, Accidental (Unintentional)	Poisoning, Intentional Self-Harm	Poisoning, Assault	Poisoning, Undetermined	Adverse Effect	Underdosing
Antianxiety drug NEC	T43.501	T43.502	T43.503	T43.504	T43.505	T43.506
Antiaris toxicaria	T65.891	T65.892	T65.893	T65.894	—	—
Antiarteriosclerotic drug	T46.6x1	T46.6x2	T46.6x3	T46.6x4	T46.6x5	T46.6x6
Antiasthmatic drug NEC	T48.6x1	T48.6x2	T48.6x3	T48.6x4	T48.6x5	T48.6x6
Antibiotic NEC	T36.91	T36.92	T36.93	T36.94	T36.95	T36.96
aminoglycoside	T36.5x1	T36.5x2	T36.5x3	T36.5x4	T36.5x5	T36.5x6
anticancer	T45.1x1	T45.1x2	T45.1x3	T45.1x4	T45.1x5	T45.1x6
antifungal	T36.7x1	T36.7x2	T36.7x3	T36.7x4	T36.7x5	T36.7x6
antimycobacterial	T36.5x1	T36.5x2	T36.5x3	T36.5x4	T36.5x5	T36.5x6
antineoplastic	T45.1x1	T45.1x2	T45.1x3	T45.1x4	T45.1x5	T45.1x6
cephalosporin (group)	T36.1x1	T36.1x2	T36.1x3	T36.1x4	T36.1x5	T36.1x6
chloramphenicol (group)	T36.2x1	T36.2x2	T36.2x3	T36.2x4	T36.2x5	T36.2x6
ENT	T49.6x1	T49.6x2	T49.6x3	T49.6x4	T49.6x5	T49.6x6
eye	T49.5x1	T49.5x2	T49.5x3	T49.5x4	T49.5x5	T49.5x6
fungicidal (local)	T49.0x1	T49.0x2	T49.0x3	T49.0x4	T49.0x5	T49.0x6
intestinal	T36.8x1	T36.8x2	T36.8x3	T36.8x4	T36.8x5	T36.8x6
b-lactam NEC	T36.1x1	T36.1x2	T36.1x3	T36.1x4	T36.1x5	T36.1x6
local	T49.0x1	T49.0x2	T49.0x3	T49.0x4	T49.0x5	T49.0x6
macrolides	T36.3x1	T36.3x2	T36.3x3	T36.3x4	T36.3x5	T36.3x6
polypeptide	T36.8x1	T36.8x2	T36.8x3	T36.8x4	T36.8x5	T36.8x6
specified NEC	T36.8x1	T36.8x2	T36.8x3	T36.8x4	T36.8x5	T36.8x6
tetracycline (group)	T36.4x1	T36.4x2	T36.4x3	T36.4x4	T36.4x5	T36.4x6
throat	T49.6x1	T49.6x2	T49.6x3	T49.6x4	T49.6x5	T49.6x6
Anticancer agents NEC	T45.1x1	T45.1x2	T45.1x3	T45.1x4	T45.1x5	T45.1x6
Anticholesterolemic drug NEC	T46.6x1	T46.6x2	T46.6x3	T46.6x4	T46.6x5	T46.6x6
Anticholinergic NEC	T44.3x1	T44.3x2	T44.3x3	T44.3x4	T44.3x5	T44.3x6
Anticholinesterase	T44.0x1	T44.0x2	T44.0x3	T44.0x4	T44.0x5	T44.0x6
organophosphorus	T44.0x1	T44.0x2	T44.0x3	T44.0x4	T44.0x5	T44.0x6
insecticide	T60.0x1	T60.0x2	T60.0x3	T60.0x4	—	—
nerve gas	T59.891	T59.892	T59.893	T59.894	—	—
reversible	T44.0x1	T44.0x2	T44.0x3	T44.0x4	T44.0x5	T44.0x6
ophthalmological	T49.5x1	T49.5x2	T49.5x3	T49.5x4	T49.5x5	T49.5x6
Anticoagulant NEC	T45.511	T45.512	T45.513	T45.514	T45.515	T45.516
Antagonist	T45.7x1	T45.7x2	T45.7x3	T45.7x4	T45.7x5	T45.7x6
Anti-common-cold drug NEC	T48.5x1	T48.5x2	T48.5x3	T48.5x4	T48.5x5	T48.5x6
Anticonvulsant NEC	T42.6x1	T42.6x2	T42.6x3	T42.6x4	T42.6x5	T42.6x6
barbiturate	T42.3x1	T42.3x2	T42.3x3	T42.3x4	T42.3x5	T42.3x6
combination (with barbiturate)	T42.3x1	T42.3x2	T42.3x3	T42.3x4	T42.3x5	T42.3x6
hydantoin	T42.0x1	T42.0x2	T42.0x3	T42.0x4	T42.0x5	T42.0x6
hypnotic NEC	T42.6x1	T42.6x2	T42.6x3	T42.6x4	T42.6x5	T42.6x6
oxazolidinedione	T42.2x1	T42.2x2	T42.2x3	T42.2x4	T42.2x5	T42.2x6

Substance	External Cause (T-Code)					
	Poisoning, Accidental (Unintentional)	Poisoning, Intentional Self-Harm	Poisoning, Assault	Poisoning, Undetermined	Adverse Effect	Underdosing
Anticonvulsant NEC *(Continued)*						
pyrimidinedione	T42.6x1	T42.6x2	T42.6x3	T42.6x4	T42.6x5	T42.6x6
succinimide	T42.2x1	T42.2x2	T42.2x3	T42.2x4	T42.2x5	T42.2x6
Anti-D immunoglobulin (human)	T50.Z11	T50.Z12	T50.Z13	T50.Z14	T50.Z15	T50.Z16
Antidepressant NEC	T43.201	T43.202	T43.203	T43.204	T43.205	T43.206
selective serotonin norepinephrine reuptake inhibitor	T43.211	T43.212	T43.213	T43.214	T43.215	T43.216
selective serotonin reuptake inhibitor	T43.221	T43.222	T43.223	T43.224	T43.225	T43.226
specified NEC	T43.291	T43.292	T43.293	T43.294	T43.295	T43.296
tetracyclic	T43.021	T43.022	T43.023	T43.024	T43.025	T43.026
triazolopyridine	T43.221	T43.222	T43.223	T43.224	T43.225	T43.226
tricyclic	T43.011	T43.012	T43.013	T43.014	T43.015	T43.016
Antidiabetic NEC	T38.3x1	T38.3x2	T38.3x3	T38.3x4	T38.3x5	T38.3x6
biguanide	T38.3x1	T38.3x2	T38.3x3	T38.3x4	T38.3x5	T38.3x6
and sulfonyl combined	T38.3x1	T38.3x2	T38.3x3	T38.3x4	T38.3x5	T38.3x6
combined	T38.3x1	T38.3x2	T38.3x3	T38.3x4	T38.3x5	T38.3x6
sulfonylurea	T38.3x1	T38.3x2	T38.3x3	T38.3x4	T38.3x5	T38.3x6
Antidiarrheal drug NEC	T47.6x1	T47.6x2	T47.6x3	T47.6x4	T47.6x5	T47.6x6
absorbent	T47.6x1	T47.6x2	T47.6x3	T47.6x4	T47.6x5	T47.6x6
Antidiphtheria serum	T50.Z11	T50.Z12	T50.Z13	T50.Z14	T50.Z15	T50.Z16
Antidiuretic hormone	T38.891	T38.892	T38.893	T38.894	T38.895	T38.896
Antidote NEC	T50.6x1	T50.6x2	T50.6x3	T50.6x4	T50.6x5	T50.6x6
heavy metal	T45.8x1	T45.8x2	T45.8x3	T45.8x4	T45.8x5	T45.8x6
Antiemetic drug	T45.0x1	T45.0x2	T45.0x3	T45.0x4	T45.0x5	T45.0x6
Antiepilepsy agent	T42.71	T42.72	T42.73	T42.74	T42.75	T42.76
combination	T42.5x1	T42.5x2	T42.5x3	T42.5x4	T42.5x5	T42.5x6
mixed	T42.5x1	T42.5x2	T42.5x3	T42.5x4	T42.5x5	T42.5x6
specified, NEC	T42.6x1	T42.6x2	T42.6x3	T42.6x4	T42.6x5	T42.6x6
Antifertility pill	T38.4x1	T38.4x2	T38.4x3	T38.4x4	T38.4x5	T38.4x6
Antifibrinolytic drug	T45.621	T45.622	T45.623	T45.624	T45.625	T45.626
Antifilarial drug	T37.4x1	T37.4x2	T37.4x3	T37.4x4	T37.4x5	T37.4x6
Antiflatulent	T47.5x1	T47.5x2	T47.5x3	T47.5x4	T47.5x5	T47.5x6
Antifreeze	T65.91	T65.92	T65.93	T65.94	—	—
alcohol	T51.1x1	T51.1x2	T51.1x3	T51.1x4	—	—
ethylene glycol	T51.8x1	T51.8x2	T51.8x3	T51.8x4	—	—
Antifungal						
antibiotic (systemic)	T36.7x1	T36.7x2	T36.7x3	T36.7x4	T36.7x5	T36.7x6
anti-infective NEC	T37.91	T37.92	T37.93	T37.94	T37.95	T37.96
disinfectant, local	T49.0x1	T49.0x2	T49.0x3	T49.0x4	T49.0x5	T49.0x6
nonmedicinal (spray)	T60.3x1	T60.3x2	T60.3x3	T60.3x4	—	—
topical	T49.0x1	T49.0x2	T49.0x3	T49.0x4	T49.0x5	T49.0x6
Anti-gastric-secretion drug NEC	T47.1x1	T47.1x2	T47.1x3	T47.1x4	T47.1x5	T47.1x6

Substance	External Cause (T-Code)					
	Poisoning, Accidental (Unintentional)	Poisoning, Intentional Self-Harm	Poisoning, Assault	Poisoning, Undetermined	Adverse Effect	Underdosing
Antihallucinogen	T43.501	T43.502	T43.503	T43.504	T43.505	T43.506
Antihelmintics	T37.4x1	T37.4x2	T37.4x3	T37.4x4	T37.4x5	T37.4x6
Antihemophilic						
factor	T45.8x1	T45.8x2	T45.8x3	T45.8x4	T45.8x5	T45.8x6
fraction	T45.8x1	T45.8x2	T45.8x3	T45.8x4	T45.8x5	T45.8x6
globulin concentrate	T45.7x1	T45.7x2	T45.7x3	T45.7x4	T45.7x5	T45.7x6
human plasma	T45.8x1	T45.8x2	T45.8x3	T45.8x4	T45.8x5	T45.8x6
plasma, dried	T45.7x1	T45.7x2	T45.7x3	T45.7x4	T45.7x5	T45.7x6
Antihemorrhoidal preparation	T49.2x1	T49.2x2	T49.2x3	T49.2x4	T49.2x5	T49.2x6
Antiheparin drug	T45.7x1	T45.7x2	T45.7x3	T45.7x4	T45.7x5	T45.7x6
Antihistamine	T45.0x1	T45.0x2	T45.0x3	T45.0x4	T45.0x5	T45.0x6
Antihookworm drug	T37.4x1	T37.4x2	T37.4x3	T37.4x4	T37.4x5	T37.4x6
Anti-human lymphocytic globulin	T50.Z11	T50.Z12	T50.Z13	T50.Z14	T50.Z15	T50.Z16
Antihypertensive drug NEC	T46.5x1	T46.5x2	T46.5x3	T46.5x4	T46.5x5	T46.5x6
Anti-infective NEC	T37.91	T37.92	T37.93	T37.94	T37.95	T37.96
antibiotics	T36.91	T36.92	T36.93	T36.94	T36.95	T36.96
specified NEC	T36.8x1	T36.8x2	T36.8x3	T36.8x4	T36.8x5	T36.8x6
anthelmintic	T37.4x1	T37.4x2	T37.4x3	T37.4x4	T37.4x5	T37.4x6
antimalarial	T37.2x1	T37.2x2	T37.2x3	T37.2x4	T37.2x5	T37.2x6
antimycobacterial NEC	T37.1x1	T37.1x2	T37.1x3	T37.1x4	T37.1x5	T37.1x6
antibiotics	T36.5x1	T36.5x2	T36.5x3	T36.5x4	T36.5x5	T36.5x6
antiprotozoal NEC	T37.3x1	T37.3x2	T37.3x3	T37.3x4	T37.3x5	T37.3x6
blood	T37.2x1	T37.2x2	T37.2x3	T37.2x4	T37.2x5	T37.2x6
antiviral	T37.5x1	T37.5x2	T37.5x3	T37.5x4	T37.5x5	T37.5x6
arsenical	T37.8x1	T37.8x2	T37.8x3	T37.8x4	T37.8x5	T37.8x6
bismuth, local	T49.0x1	T49.0x2	T49.0x3	T49.0x4	T49.0x5	T49.0x6
ENT	T49.6x1	T49.6x2	T49.6x3	T49.6x4	T49.6x5	T49.6x6
eye NEC	T49.5x1	T49.5x2	T49.5x3	T49.5x4	T49.5x5	T49.5x6
heavy metals NEC	T37.8x1	T37.8x2	T37.8x3	T37.8x4	T37.8x5	T37.8x6
local NEC	T49.0x1	T49.0x2	T49.0x3	T49.0x4	T49.0x5	T49.0x6
specified NEC	T49.0x1	T49.0x2	T49.0x3	T49.0x4	T49.0x5	T49.0x6
mixed	T37.91	T37.92	T37.93	T37.94	T37.95	T37.96
ophthalmic preparation	T49.5x1	T49.5x2	T49.5x3	T49.5x4	T49.5x5	T49.5x6
topical NEC	T49.0x1	T49.0x2	T49.0x3	T49.0x4	T49.0x5	T49.0x6
Anti-inflammatory drug, local, NEC	T49.0x1	T49.0x2	T49.0x3	T49.0x4	T49.0x5	T49.0x6
Antikaluretic	T50.3x1	T50.3x2	T50.3x3	T50.3x4	T50.3x5	T50.3x6
Antiknock (tetraethyl lead)	T56.0x1	T56.0x2	T56.0x3	T56.0x4	—	—
Antilipemic drug NEC	T46.6x1	T46.6x2	T46.6x3	T46.6x4	T46.6x5	T46.6x6
Antimalarial	T37.2x1	T37.2x2	T37.2x3	T37.2x4	T37.2x5	T37.2x6
prophylactic NEC	T37.2x1	T37.2x2	T37.2x3	T37.2x4	T37.2x5	T37.2x6
pyrimidine derivative	T37.2x1	T37.2x2	T37.2x3	T37.2x4	T37.2x5	T37.2x6

Substance	External Cause (T-Code)					
	Poisoning, Accidental (Unintentional)	Poisoning, Intentional Self-Harm	Poisoning, Assault	Poisoning, Undetermined	Adverse Effect	Underdosing
Antimetabolite	T45.1x1	T45.1x2	T45.1x3	T45.1x4	T45.1x5	T45.1x6
Antimitotic agent	T45.1x1	T45.1x2	T45.1x3	T45.1x4	T45.1x5	T45.1x6
Antimony (compounds) (vapor) NEC	T56.891	T56.892	T56.893	T56.894	—	—
anti-infectives	T37.8x1	T37.8x2	T37.8x3	T37.8x4	T37.8x5	T37.8x6
dimercaptosuccinate	T37.3x1	T37.3x2	T37.3x3	T37.3x4	T37.3x5	T37.3x6
hydride	T56.891	T56.892	T56.893	T56.894	—	—
pesticide (vapor)	T60.8x1	T60.8x2	T60.8x3	T60.8x4	—	—
potassium (sodium) Tartrate	T37.8x1	T37.8x2	T37.8x3	T37.8x4	T37.8x5	T37.8x6
tartrated	T37.8x1	T37.8x2	T37.8x3	T37.8x4	T37.8x5	T37.8x6
sodium dimercaptosuccinate	T37.3x1	T37.3x2	T37.3x3	T37.3x4	T37.3x5	T37.3x6
Antimuscarinic NEC	T44.3x1	T44.3x2	T44.3x3	T44.3x4	T44.3x5	T44.3x6
Antimycobacterial drug NEC	T37.1x1	T37.1x2	T37.1x3	T37.1x4	T37.1x5	T37.1x6
antibiotics	T36.5x1	T36.5x2	T36.5x3	T36.5x4	T36.5x5	T36.5x6
combination	T37.1x1	T37.1x2	T37.1x3	T37.1x4	T37.1x5	T37.1x6
Antinausea drug	T45.0x1	T45.0x2	T45.0x3	T45.0x4	T45.0x5	T45.0x6
Antinematode drug	T37.4x1	T37.4x2	T37.4x3	T37.4x4	T37.4x5	T37.4x6
Antineoplastic NEC	T45.1x1	T45.1x2	T45.1x3	T45.1x4	T45.1x5	T45.1x6
antibiotics	T45.1x1	T45.1x2	T45.1x3	T45.1x4	T45.1x5	T45.1x6
alkaloidal	T45.1x1	T45.1x2	T45.1x3	T45.1x4	T45.1x5	T45.1x6
combination	T45.1x1	T45.1x2	T45.1x3	T45.1x4	T45.1x5	T45.1x6
estrogen	T38.5x1	T38.5x2	T38.5x3	T38.5x4	T38.5x5	T38.5x6
steroid	T38.7x1	T38.7x2	T38.7x3	T38.7x4	T38.7x5	T38.7x6
Antiparasitic drug, local	T49.0x1	T49.0x2	T49.0x3	T49.0x4	T49.0x5	T49.0x6
Antiparkinsonism drug NEC	T42.8x1	T42.8x2	T42.8x3	T42.8x4	T42.8x5	T42.8x6
Antiperspirant NEC	T49.2x1	T49.2x2	T49.2x3	T49.2x4	T49.2x5	T49.2x6
Antiphlogistic NEC	T39.4x1	T39.4x2	T39.4x3	T39.4x4	T39.4x5	T39.4x6
Antiplatyhelmintic drug	T37.4x1	T37.4x2	T37.4x3	T37.4x4	T37.4x5	T37.4x6
Antiprotozoal drug NEC	T37.3x1	T37.3x2	T37.3x3	T37.3x4	T37.3x5	T37.3x6
blood	T37.2x1	T37.2x2	T37.2x3	T37.2x4	T37.2x5	T37.2x6
local	T49.0x1	T49.0x2	T49.0x3	T49.0x4	T49.0x5	T49.0x6
Antipruritic drug NEC	T49.1x1	T49.1x2	T49.1x3	T49.1x4	T49.1x5	T49.1x6
Antipsychotic drug NEC	T43.501	T43.502	T43.503	T43.504	T43.505	T43.506
Antipyretic NEC	T39.8x1	T39.8x2	T39.8x3	T39.8x4	T39.8x5	T39.8x6
Antipyrine	T39.2x1	T39.2x2	T39.2x3	T39.2x4	T39.2x5	T39.2x6
Antirabies hyperimmune serum	T50.Z11	T50.Z12	T50.Z13	T50.Z14	T50.Z15	T50.Z16
Antirheumatic NEC	T39.4x1	T39.4x2	T39.4x3	T39.4x4	T39.4x5	T39.4x6
Antirigidity drug NEC	T42.8x1	T42.8x2	T42.8x3	T42.8x4	T42.8x5	T42.8x6
Antischistosomal drug	T37.4x1	T37.4x2	T37.4x3	T37.4x4	T37.4x5	T37.4x6
Antiscorpion sera	T50.Z11	T50.Z12	T50.Z13	T50.Z14	T50.Z15	T50.Z16
Antiseborrheics	T49.4x1	T49.4x2	T49.4x3	T49.4x4	T49.4x5	T49.4x6
Antiseptics (external) (medicinal)	T49.0x1	T49.0x2	T49.0x3	T49.0x4	T49.0x5	T49.0x6

	External Cause (T-Code)					
Substance	Poisoning, Accidental (Unintentional)	Poisoning, Intentional Self-Harm	Poisoning, Assault	Poisoning, Undetermined	Adverse Effect	Underdosing
Antistine	T45.0x1	T45.0x2	T45.0x3	T45.0x4	T45.0x5	T45.0x6
Antitapeworm drug	T37.4x1	T37.4x2	T37.4x3	T37.4x4	T37.4x5	T37.4x6
Antitetanus immunoglobulin	T50.Z11	T50.Z12	T50.Z13	T50.Z14	T50.Z15	T50.Z16
Antithyroid drug NEC	T38.2x1	T38.2x2	T38.2x3	T38.2x4	T38.2x5	T38.2x6
Antitoxin	T50.Z11	T50.Z12	T50.Z13	T50.Z14	T50.Z15	T50.Z16
diphtheria	T50.Z11	T50.Z12	T50.Z13	T50.Z14	T50.Z15	T50.Z16
gas gangrene	T50.Z11	T50.Z12	T50.Z13	T50.Z14	T50.Z15	T50.Z16
tetanus	T50.Z11	T50.Z12	T50.Z13	T50.Z14	T50.Z15	T50.Z16
Antitoxin, any	T50.901	T50.902	T50.903	T50.904	T50.905	T50.906
Antitrichomonal drug	T37.3x1	T37.3x2	T37.3x3	T37.3x4	T37.3x5	T37.3x6
Antituberculars	T37.1x1	T37.1x2	T37.1x3	T37.1x4	T37.1x5	T37.1x6
antibiotics	T36.5x1	T36.5x2	T36.5x3	T36.5x4	T36.5x5	T36.5x6
Antitussive NEC	T48.3x1	T48.3x2	T48.3x3	T48.3x4	T48.3x5	T48.3x6
codeine mixture	T40.2x1	T40.2x2	T40.2x3	T40.2x4	T40.2x5	T40.2x6
opiate	T40.2x1	T40.2x2	T40.2x3	T40.2x4	T40.2x5	T40.2x6
Antivaricose drug	T46.8x1	T46.8x2	T46.8x3	T46.8x4	T46.8x5	T46.8x6
Antivenin, antivenom (sera)	T50.Z11	T50.Z12	T50.Z13	T50.Z14	T50.Z15	T50.Z16
crotaline	T50.Z11	T50.Z12	T50.Z13	T50.Z14	T50.Z15	T50.Z16
spider bite	T50.Z11	T50.Z12	T50.Z13	T50.Z14	T50.Z15	T50.Z16
Antivertigo drug	T45.0x1	T45.0x2	T45.0x3	T45.0x4	T45.0x5	T45.0x6
Antiviral drug NEC	T37.5x1	T37.5x2	T37.5x3	T37.5x4	T37.5x5	T37.5x6
eye	T49.5x1	T49.5x2	T49.5x3	T49.5x4	T49.5x5	T49.5x6
Antiwhipworm drug	T37.4x1	T37.4x2	T37.4x3	T37.4x4	T37.4x5	T37.4x6
Ant poisons - *see* Pesticides						
Antrol (*see also* by specific chemical substance)	T60.91	T60.92	T60.93	T60.94	—	—
fungicide	T60.91	T60.92	T60.93	T60.94	—	—
ANTU (alpha naphthylthiourea)	T60.4x1	T60.4x2	T60.4x3	T60.4x4	—	—
Apalcillin	T36.0x1	T36.0x2	T36.0x3	T36.0x4	T36.0x5	T36.0x6
APC	T48.5x1	T48.5x2	T48.5x3	T48.5x4	T48.5x5	T48.5x6
Aplonidine	T44.4x1	T44.4x2	T44.4x3	T44.4x4	T44.4x5	T44.4x6
Apomorphine	T47.7x1	T47.7x2	T47.7x3	T47.7x4	T47.7x5	T47.7x6
Appetite depressants, central	T50.5x1	T50.5x2	T50.5x3	T50.5x4	T50.5x5	T50.5x6
Apraclonidine (hydrochloride)	T44.4x1	T44.4x2	T44.4x3	T44.4x4	T44.4x5	T44.4x6
Apresoline	T46.5x1	T46.5x2	T46.5x3	T46.5x4	T46.5x5	T46.5x6
Aprindine	T46.2x1	T46.2x2	T46.2x3	T46.2x4	T46.2x5	T46.2x6
Aprobarbital	T42.3x1	T42.3x2	T42.3x3	T42.3x4	T42.3x5	T42.3x6
Apronalide	T42.6x1	T42.6x2	T42.6x3	T42.6x4	T42.6x5	T42.6x6
Aprotinin	T45.621	T45.622	T45.623	T45.624	T45.625	T45.626
Aptocaine	T41.3x1	T41.3x2	T41.3x3	T41.3x4	T41.3x5	T41.3x6
Aqua fortis	T54.2x1	T54.2x2	T54.2x3	T54.2x4	—	—

Substance	Poisoning, Accidental (Unintentional)	Poisoning, Intentional Self-Harm	Poisoning, Assault	Poisoning, Undetermined	Adverse Effect	Underdosing
	External Cause (T-Code)					
Ara-A	T37.5x1	T37.5x2	T37.5x3	T37.5x4	T37.5x5	T37.5x6
Ara-C	T45.1x1	T45.1x2	T45.1x3	T45.1x4	T45.1x5	T45.1x6
Arachis oil	T49.3x1	T49.3x2	T49.3x3	T49.3x4	T49.3x5	T49.3x6
cathartic	T47.4x1	T47.4x2	T47.4x3	T47.4x4	T47.4x5	T47.4x6
Aralen	T37.2x1	T37.2x2	T37.2x3	T37.2x4	T37.2x5	T37.2x6
Arecoline	T44.1x1	T44.1x2	T44.1x3	T44.1x4	T44.1x5	T44.1x6
Arginine	T50.991	T50.992	T50.993	T50.994	T50.995	T50.996
glutamate	T50.991	T50.992	T50.993	T50.994	T50.995	T50.996
Argyrol	T49.0x1	T49.0x2	T49.0x3	T49.0x4	T49.0x5	T49.0x6
ENT agent	T49.6x1	T49.6x2	T49.6x3	T49.6x4	T49.6x5	T49.6x6
ophthalmic preparation	T49.5x1	T49.5x2	T49.5x3	T49.5x4	T49.5x5	T49.5x6
Aristocort	T38.0x1	T38.0x2	T38.0x3	T38.0x4	T38.0x5	T38.0x6
ENT agent	T49.6x1	T49.6x2	T49.6x3	T49.6x4	T49.6x5	T49.6x6
ophthalmic preparation	T49.5x1	T49.5x2	T49.5x3	T49.5x4	T49.5x5	T49.5x6
topical NEC	T49.0x1	T49.0x2	T49.0x3	T49.0x4	T49.0x5	T49.0x6
Aromatics, corrosive	T54.1x1	T54.1x2	T54.1x3	T54.1x4	—	—
disinfectants	T54.1x1	T54.1x2	T54.1x3	T54.1x4	—	—
Arsenate of lead	T57.0x1	T57.0x2	T57.0x3	T57.0x4	—	—
herbicide	T57.0x1	T57.0x2	T57.0x3	T57.0x4	—	—
Arsenic, arsenicals (compounds) (dust) (vapor) NEC	T57.0x1	T57.0x2	T57.0x3	T57.0x4	—	—
anti-infectives	T37.8x1	T37.8x2	T37.8x3	T37.8x4	T37.8x5	T37.8x6
pesticide (dust) (fumes)	T57.0x1	T57.0x2	T57.0x3	T57.0x4	—	—
Arsine (gas)	T57.0x1	T57.0x2	T57.0x3	T57.0x4	—	—
Arsphenamine (silver)	T37.8x1	T37.8x2	T37.8x3	T37.8x4	T37.8x5	T37.8x6
Arsthinol	T37.3x1	T37.3x2	T37.3x3	T37.3x4	T37.3x5	T37.3x6
Artane	T44.3x1	T44.3x2	T44.3x3	T44.3x4	T44.3x5	T44.3x6
Arthropod (venomous) NEC	T63.481	T63.482	T63.483	T63.484	—	—
Articaine	T41.3x1	T41.3x2	T41.3x3	T41.3x4	T41.3x5	T41.3x6
Asbestos	T57.8x1	T57.8x2	T57.8x3	T57.8x4	—	—
Ascaridole	T37.4x1	T37.4x2	T37.4x3	T37.4x4	T37.4x5	T37.4x6
Ascorbic acid	T45.2x1	T45.2x2	T45.2x3	T45.2x4	T45.2x5	T45.2x6
Asiaticoside	T49.0x1	T49.0x2	T49.0x3	T49.0x4	T49.0x5	T49.0x6
Asparaginase	T45.1x1	T45.1x2	T45.1x3	T45.1x4	T45.1x5	T45.1x6
Aspidium (oleoresin)	T37.4x1	T37.4x2	T37.4x3	T37.4x4	T37.4x5	T37.4x6
Aspirin (aluminum) (soluble)	T39.011	T39.012	T39.013	T39.014	T39.015	T39.016
Aspoxicillin	T36.0x1	T36.0x2	T36.0x3	T36.0x4	T36.0x5	T36.0x6
Astemizole	T45.0x1	T45.0x2	T45.0x3	T45.0x4	T45.0x5	T45.0x6
Astringent (local)	T49.2x1	T49.2x2	T49.2x3	T49.2x4	T49.2x5	T49.2x6
specified NEC	T49.2x1	T49.2x2	T49.2x3	T49.2x4	T49.2x5	T49.2x6
Astromicin	T36.5x1	T36.5x2	T36.5x3	T36.5x4	T36.5x5	T36.5x6

Substance	Poisoning, Accidental (Unintentional)	Poisoning, Intentional Self-Harm	Poisoning, Assault	Poisoning, Undetermined	Adverse Effect	Underdosing
Atabrine	T37.8x1	T37.8x2	T37.8x3	T37.8x4	T37.8x5	T37.8x6
Ataractic drug NEC	T43.501	T43.502	T43.503	T43.504	T43.505	T43.506
Atenolol	T44.7x1	T44.7x2	T44.7x3	T44.7x4	T44.7x5	T44.7x6
Atonia drug, intestinal	T47.4x1	T47.4x2	T47.4x3	T47.4x4	T47.4x5	T47.4x6
Atophan	T50.4x1	T50.4x2	T50.4x3	T50.4x4	T50.4x5	T50.4x6
Atracurium besilate	T48.1x1	T48.1x2	T48.1x3	T48.1x4	T48.1x5	T48.1x6
Atropine	T44.3x1	T44.3x2	T44.3x3	T44.3x4	T44.3x5	T44.3x6
derivative	T44.3x1	T44.3x2	T44.3x3	T44.3x4	T44.3x5	T44.3x6
methonitrate	T44.3x1	T44.3x2	T44.3x3	T44.3x4	T44.3x5	T44.3x6
Attapulgite	T47.6x1	T47.6x2	T47.6x3	T47.6x4	T47.6x5	T47.6x6
Attenuvax	T50.991	T50.992	T50.993	T50.994	T50.995	T50.996
Auramine	T65.891	T65.892	T65.893	T65.894	—	—
dye	T65.6x1	T65.6x2	T65.6x3	T65.6x4	—	—
fungicide	T60.3x1	T60.3x2	T60.3x3	T60.3x4	—	—
Auranofin	T39.4x1	T39.4x2	T39.4x3	T39.4x4	T39.4x5	T39.4x6
Aurantiin	T46.991	T46.992	T46.993	T46.994	T46.995	T46.996
Aureomycin	T36.4x1	T36.4x2	T36.4x3	T36.4x4	T36.4x5	T36.4x6
ophthalmic preparation	T49.5x1	T49.5x2	T49.5x3	T49.5x4	T49.5x5	T49.5x6
topical NEC	T49.0x1	T49.0x2	T49.0x3	T49.0x4	T49.0x5	T49.0x6
Aurothioglucose	T39.4x1	T39.4x2	T39.4x3	T39.4x4	T39.4x5	T39.4x6
Aurothioglycanide	T39.4x1	T39.4x2	T39.4x3	T39.4x4	T39.4x5	T39.4x6
Aurothiomalate sodium	T39.4x1	T39.4x2	T39.4x3	T39.4x4	T39.4x5	T39.4x6
Aurotioprol	T39.4x1	T39.4x2	T39.4x3	T39.4x4	T39.4x5	T39.4x6
Automobile fuel	T52.0x1	T52.0x2	T52.0x3	T52.0x4	—	—
Autonomic nervous system agent NEC	T44.901	T44.902	T44.903	T44.904	T44.905	T44.906
Avlosulfon	T37.1x1	T37.1x2	T37.1x3	T37.1x4	T37.1x5	T37.1x6
Avomine	T42.6x1	T42.6x2	T42.6x3	T42.6x4	T42.6x5	T42.6x6
Axerophthol	T45.2x1	T45.2x2	T45.2x3	T45.2x4	T45.2x5	T45.2x6
Azacitidine	T45.1x1	T45.1x2	T45.1x3	T45.1x4	T45.1x5	T45.1x6
Azacyclonol	T43.591	T43.592	T43.593	T43.594	T43.595	T43.596
Azadirachta	T60.2x1	T60.2x2	T60.2x3	T60.2x4	—	—
Azanidazole	T37.3x1	T37.3x2	T37.3x3	T37.3x4	T37.3x5	T37.3x6
Azapetine	T46.7x1	T46.7x2	T46.7x3	T46.7x4	T46.7x5	T46.7x6
Azapropazone	T39.2x1	T39.2x2	T39.2x3	T39.2x4	T39.2x5	T39.2x6
Azaribine	T45.1x1	T45.1x2	T45.1x3	T45.1x4	T45.1x5	T45.1x6
Azaserine	T45.1x1	T45.1x2	T45.1x3	T45.1x4	T45.1x5	T45.1x6
Azatadine	T45.0x1	T45.0x2	T45.0x3	T45.0x4	T45.0x5	T45.0x6
Azatepa	T45.1x1	T45.1x2	T45.1x3	T45.1x4	T45.1x5	T45.1x6
Azathioprine	T45.1x1	T45.1x2	T45.1x3	T45.1x4	T45.1x5	T45.1x6
Azelaic acid	T49.0x1	T49.0x2	T49.0x3	T49.0x4	T49.0x5	T49.0x6

Substance	Poisoning, Accidental (Unintentional)	Poisoning, Intentional Self-Harm	Poisoning, Assault	Poisoning, Undetermined	Adverse Effect	Underdosing
			External Cause (T-Code)			
Azelastine	T45.0x1	T45.0x2	T45.0x3	T45.0x4	T45.0x5	T45.0x6
Azidocillin	T36.0x1	T36.0x2	T36.0x3	T36.0x4	T36.0x5	T36.0x6
Azidothymidine	T37.5x1	T37.5x2	T37.5x3	T37.5x4	T37.5x5	T37.5x6
Azinphos (ethyl) (methyl)	T60.0x1	T60.0x2	T60.0x3	T60.0x4	—	—
Aziridine (chelating)	T54.1x1	T54.1x2	T54.1x3	T54.1x4	—	—
Azithromycin	T36.3x1	T36.3x2	T36.3x3	T36.3x4	T36.3x5	T36.3x6
Azlocillin	T36.01	T36.02	T36.03	T36.04	T36.05	T36.06
Azobenzene smoke	T65.3x1	T65.3x2	T65.3x3	T65.3x4	—	—
acaricide	T60.8x1	T60.8x2	T60.8x3	T60.8x4	—	—
Azosulfamide	T37.0x1	T37.0x2	T37.0x3	T37.0x4	T37.0x5	T37.0x6
AZT	T37.5x1	T37.5x2	T37.5x3	T37.5x4	T37.5x5	T37.5x6
Aztreonam	T36.1x1	T36.1x2	T36.1x3	T36.1x4	T36.1x5	T36.1x6
Azulfidine	T37.0x1	T37.0x2	T37.0x3	T37.0x4	T37.0x5	T37.0x6
Azuresin	T50.8x1	T50.8x2	T50.8x3	T50.8x4	T50.8x5	T50.8x6
Bacampicillin	T36.0x1	T36.0x2	T36.0x3	T36.0x4	T36.0x5	T36.0x6
Bacillus						
lactobacillus	T47.8x1	T47.8x2	T47.8x3	T47.8x4	T47.8x5	T47.8x6
subtilis	T47.6x1	T47.6x2	T47.6x3	T47.6x4	T47.6x5	T47.6x6
Bacimycin	T49.0x1	T49.0x2	T49.0x3	T49.0x4	T49.0x5	T49.0x6
ophthalmic preparation	T49.5x1	T49.5x2	T49.5x3	T49.5x4	T49.5x5	T49.5x6
Bacitracin zinc	T49.0x1	T49.0x2	T49.0x3	T49.0x4	T49.0x5	T49.0x6
with neomycin	T49.0x1	T49.0x2	T49.0x3	T49.0x4	T49.0x5	T49.0x6
ENT agent	T49.6x1	T49.6x2	T49.6x3	T49.6x4	T49.6x5	T49.6x6
ophthalmic preparation	T49.5x1	T49.5x2	T49.5x3	T49.5x4	T49.5x5	T49.5x6
topical NEC	T49.0x1	T49.0x2	T49.0x3	T49.0x4	T49.0x5	T49.0x6
Baclofen	T42.8x1	T42.8x2	T42.8x3	T42.8x4	T42.8x5	T42.8x6
Baking soda	T50.991	T50.992	T50.993	T50.994	T50.995	T50.996
BAL	T45.8x1	T45.8x2	T45.8x3	T45.8x4	T45.8x5	T45.8x6
Bambuterol	T48.6x1	T48.6x2	T48.6x3	T48.6x4	T48.6x5	T48.6x6
Bamethan (sulfate)	T46.7x1	T46.7x2	T46.7x3	T46.7x4	T46.7x5	T46.7x6
Bamifylline	T48.6x1	T48.6x2	T48.6x3	T48.6x4	T48.6x5	T48.6x6
Bamipine	T45.0x1	T45.0x2	T45.0x3	T45.0x4	T45.0x5	T45.0x6
Baneberry - *see* Actaea spicata						
Banewort - *see* Belladonna						
Barbenyl	T42.3x1	T42.3x2	T42.3x3	T42.3x4	T42.3x5	T42.3x6
Barbexaclone	T42.6x1	T42.6x2	T42.6x3	T42.6x4	T42.6x5	T42.6x6
Barbital	T42.3x1	T42.3x2	T42.3x3	T42.3x4	T42.3x5	T42.3x6
sodium	T42.3x1	T42.3x2	T42.3x3	T42.3x4	T42.3x5	T42.3x6
Barbitone	T42.3x1	T42.3x2	T42.3x3	T42.3x4	T42.3x5	T42.3x6

Substance	Poisoning, Accidental (Unintentional)	Poisoning, Intentional Self-Harm	Poisoning, Assault	Poisoning, Undetermined	Adverse Effect	Underdosing
Barbiturate NEC	T42.3x1	T42.3x2	T42.3x3	T42.3x4	T42.3x5	T42.3x6
with tranquilizer	T42.3x1	T42.3x2	T42.3x3	T42.3x4	T42.3x5	T42.3x6
anesthetic (intravenous)	T41.1x1	T41.1x2	T41.1x3	T41.1x4	T41.1x5	T41.1x6
Barium (carbonate) (chloride) (sulfite)	T57.8x1	T57.8x2	T57.8x3	T57.8x4	—	—
diagnostic agent	T50.8x1	T50.8x2	T50.8x3	T50.8x4	T50.8x5	T50.8x6
pesticide	T60.4x1	T60.4x2	T60.4x3	T60.4x4	—	—
rodenticide	T60.4x1	T60.4x2	T60.4x3	T60.4x4	—	—
sulfate (medicinal)	T50.8x1	T50.8x2	T50.8x3	T50.8x4	T50.8x5	T50.8x6
Barrier cream	T49.3x1	T49.3x2	T49.3x3	T49.3x4	T49.3x5	T49.3x6
Basic fuchsin	T49.0x1	T49.0x2	T49.0x3	T49.0x4	T49.0x5	T49.0x6
Battery acid or fluid	T54.2x1	T54.2x2	T54.2x3	T54.2x4	—	—
Bay rum	T51.8x1	T51.8x2	T51.8x3	T51.8x4	—	—
BCG (vaccine)	T50.A91	T50.A92	T50.A93	T50.A94	T50.A95	T50.A96
BCNU	T45.1x1	T45.1x2	T45.1x3	T45.1x4	T45.1x5	T45.1x6
Bearsfoot	T62.2x1	T62.2x2	T62.2x3	T62.2x4	—	—
Beclamide	T42.6x1	T42.6x2	T42.6x3	T42.6x4	T42.6x5	T42.6x6
Beclomethasone	T44.5x1	T44.5x2	T44.5x3	T44.5x4	T44.5x5	T44.5x6
Bee (sting) (venom)	T63.441	T63.442	T63.443	T63.444	—	—
Befunolol	T49.5x1	T49.5x2	T49.5x3	T49.5x4	T49.5x5	T49.5x6
Bekanamycin	T36.5x1	T36.5x2	T36.5x3	T36.5x4	T36.5x5	T36.5x6
Belladonna (see also Nightshade)						
alkaloids	T44.3x1	T44.3x2	T44.3x3	T44.3x4	T44.3x5	T44.3x6
extract	T44.3x1	T44.3x2	T44.3x3	T44.3x4	T44.3x5	T44.3x6
herb	T44.3x1	T44.3x2	T44.3x3	T44.3x4	T44.3x5	T44.3x6
Bemegride	T50.7x1	T50.7x2	T50.7x3	T50.7x4	T50.7x5	T50.7x6
Benactyzine	T44.3x1	T44.3x2	T44.3x3	T44.3x4	T44.3x5	T44.3x6
Benadryl	T45.0x1	T45.0x2	T45.0x3	T45.0x4	T45.0x5	T45.0x6
Benaprizine	T44.3x1	T44.3x2	T44.3x3	T44.3x4	T44.3x5	T44.3x6
Benazepril	T46.4x1	T46.4x2	T46.4x3	T46.4x4	T46.4x5	T46.4x6
Bencyclane	T46.7x1	T46.7x2	T46.7x3	T46.7x4	T46.7x5	T46.7x6
Bendazol	T46.3x1	T46.3x2	T46.3x3	T46.3x4	T46.3x5	T46.3x6
Bendrofluazide	T50.2x1	T50.2x2	T50.2x3	T50.2x4	T50.2x5	T50.2x6
Bendroflumethiazide	T50.2x1	T50.2x2	T50.2x3	T50.2x4	T50.2x5	T50.2x6
Benemid	T50.4x1	T50.4x2	T50.4x3	T50.4x4	T50.4x5	T50.4x6
Benethamine penicillin	T36.0x1	T36.0x2	T36.0x3	T36.0x4	T36.0x5	T36.0x6
Benisone	T49.0x1	T49.0x2	T49.0x3	T49.0x4	T49.0x5	T49.0x6
Benexate	T47.1x1	T47.1x2	T47.1x3	T47.1x4	T47.1x5	T47.1x6
Benfluorex	T46.6x1	T46.6x2	T46.6x3	T46.6x4	T46.6x5	T46.6x6
Benfotiamine	T45.2x1	T45.2x2	T45.2x3	T45.2x4	T45.2x5	T45.2x6

Substance	External Cause (T-Code)					
	Poisoning, Accidental (Unintentional)	Poisoning, Intentional Self-Harm	Poisoning, Assault	Poisoning, Undetermined	Adverse Effect	Underdosing
Benomyl	T60.0x1	T60.0x2	T60.0x3	T60.0x4	—	—
Benoquin	T49.8x1	T49.8x2	T49.8x3	T49.8x4	T49.8x5	T49.8x6
Benoxinate	T41.3x1	T41.3x2	T41.3x3	T41.3x4	T41.3x5	T41.3x6
Benperidol	T43.4x1	T43.4x2	T43.4x3	T43.4x4	T43.4x5	T43.4x6
Benproperine	T48.3x1	T48.3x2	T48.3x3	T48.3x4	T48.3x5	T48.3x6
Benserazide	T42.8x1	T42.8x2	T42.8x3	T42.8x4	T42.8x5	T42.8x6
Bentazepam	T42.4x1	T42.4x2	T42.4x3	T42.4x4	T42.4x5	T42.4x6
Bentiromide	T50.8x1	T50.8x2	T50.8x3	T50.8x4	T50.8x5	T50.8x6
Bentonite	T49.3x1	T49.3x2	T49.3x3	T49.3x4	T49.3x5	T49.3x6
Benzalbutyramide	T46.6x1	T46.6x2	T46.6x3	T46.6x4	T46.6x5	T46.6x6
Benzalkonium (chloride)	T49.0x1	T49.0x2	T49.0x3	T49.0x4	T49.0x5	T49.0x6
ophthalmic preparation	T49.5x1	T49.5x2	T49.5x3	T49.5x4	T49.5x5	T49.5x6
Benzamine	T41.3x1	T41.3x2	T41.3x3	T41.3x4	T41.3x5	T41.3x6
lactate	T49.1x1	T49.1x2	T49.1x3	T49.1x4	T49.1x5	T49.1x6
Benzamidosalicylate (calcium)	T37.1x1	T37.1x2	T37.1x3	T37.1x4	T37.1x5	T37.1x6
Benzamphetamine	T50.5x1	T50.5x2	T50.5x3	T50.5x4	T50.5x5	T50.5x6
Benzapril hydrochloride	T46.5x1	T46.5x2	T46.5x3	T46.5x4	T46.5x5	T46.5x6
Benzathine benzylpenicillin	T36.0x1	T36.0x2	T36.0x3	T36.0x4	T36.0x5	T36.0x6
Benzathine penicillin	T36.0x1	T36.0x2	T36.0x3	T36.0x4	T36.0x5	T36.0x6
Benzatropine	T42.8x1	T42.8x2	T42.8x3	T42.8x4	T42.8x5	T42.8x6
Benzbromarone	T50.4x1	T50.4x2	T50.4x3	T50.4x4	T50.4x5	T50.4x6
Benzcarbimine	T45.1x1	T45.1x2	T45.1x3	T45.1x4	T45.1x5	T45.1x6
Benzedrex	T44.991	T44.992	T44.993	T44.994	T44.995	T44.996
Benzedrine (amphetamine)	T43.621	T43.622	T43.623	T43.624	T43.625	T43.626
Benzenamine	T65.3x1	T65.3x2	T65.3x3	T65.3x4	—	—
Benzene	T52.1x1	T52.1x2	T52.1x3	T52.1x4	—	—
homologues (acetyl) (dimethyl) (methyl) (solvent)	T52.2x1	T52.2x2	T52.2x3	T52.2x4	—	—
Benzethonium (chloride)	T49.0x1	T49.0x2	T49.0x3	T49.0x4	T49.0x5	T49.0x6
Benzfetamine	T50.5x1	T50.5x2	T50.5x3	T50.5x4	T50.5x5	T50.5x6
Benzhexol	T44.3x1	T44.3x2	T44.3x3	T44.3x4	T44.3x5	T44.3x6
Benzhydramine (chloride)	T45.0x1	T45.0x2	T45.0x3	T45.0x4	T45.0x5	T45.0x6
Benzidine	T65.891	T65.892	T65.893	T65.894	—	—
Benzilonium bromide	T44.3x1	T44.3x2	T44.3x3	T44.3x4	T44.3x5	T44.3x6
Benzimidazole	T60.3x1	T60.3x2	T60.3x3	T60.3x4	—	—
Benzin(e) - *see* Ligroin						
Benziodarone	T46.3x1	T46.3x2	T46.3x3	T46.3x4	T46.3x5	T46.3x6
Benznidazole	T37.3x1	T37.3x2	T37.3x3	T37.3x4	T37.3x5	T37.3x6
Benzocaine	T41.3x1	T41.3x2	T41.3x3	T41.3x4	T41.3x5	T41.3x6
Benzoctamine	T43.0x1	T43.0x2	T43.0x3	T43.0x4	T43.0x5	T43.0x6

Substance	External Cause (T-Code)					
	Poisoning, Accidental (Unintentional)	Poisoning, Intentional Self-Harm	Poisoning, Assault	Poisoning, Undetermined	Adverse Effect	Underdosing
Benzodiapin	T42.4x1	T42.4x2	T42.4x3	T42.4x4	T42.4x5	T42.4x6
Benzodiazepine NEC	T42.4x1	T42.4x2	T42.4x3	T42.4x4	T42.4x5	T42.4x6
Benzoic acid	T49.0x1	T49.0x2	T49.0x3	T49.0x4	T49.0x5	T49.0x6
with salicylic acid	T49.0x1	T49.0x2	T49.0x3	T49.0x4	T49.0x5	T49.0x6
Benzoin (tincture)	T48.5x1	T48.5x2	T48.5x3	T48.5x4	T48.5x5	T48.5x6
Benzol (benzene)	T52.1x1	T52.1x2	T52.1x3	T52.1x4	—	—
vapor	T52.0x1	T52.0x2	T52.0x3	T52.0x4	—	—
Benzomorphan	T40.2x1	T40.2x2	T40.2x3	T40.2x4	T40.2x5	T40.2x6
Benzonatate	T48.3x1	T48.3x2	T48.3x3	T48.3x4	T48.3x5	T48.3x6
Benzophenones	T49.3x1	T49.3x2	T49.3x3	T49.3x4	T49.3x5	T49.3x6
Benzopyrone	T46.991	T46.992	T46.993	T46.994	T46.995	T46.996
Benzothiadiazides	T50.2x1	T50.2x2	T50.2x3	T50.2x4	T50.2x5	T50.2x6
Benzoxonium chloride	T49.0x1	T49.0x2	T49.0x3	T49.0x4	T49.0x5	T49.0x6
Benzoyl peroxide	T49.0x1	T49.0x2	T49.0x3	T49.0x4	T49.0x5	T49.0x6
Benzoylpas calcium	T37.1x1	T37.1x2	T37.1x3	T37.1x4	T37.1x5	T37.1x6
Benzperidin	T43.591	T43.592	T43.593	T43.594	T43.595	T43.596
Benzperidol	T43.591	T43.592	T43.593	T43.594	T43.595	T43.596
Benzphetamine	T43.621	T43.622	T43.623	T43.624	T43.625	T43.626
Benzpyrinium bromide	T44.1x1	T44.1x2	T44.1x3	T44.1x4	T44.1x5	T44.1x6
Benzquinamide	T45.0x1	T45.0x2	T45.0x3	T45.0x4	T45.0x5	T45.0x6
Benzthiazide	T50.2x1	T50.2x2	T50.2x3	T50.2x4	T50.2x5	T50.2x6
Benztropine						
anticholinergic	T44.3x1	T44.3x2	T44.3x3	T44.3x4	T44.3x5	T44.3x6
antiparkinson	T42.8x1	T42.8x2	T42.8x3	T42.8x4	T42.8x5	T42.8x6
Benzydamine	T49.0x1	T49.0x2	T49.0x3	T49.0x4	T49.0x5	T49.0x6
Benzyl						
acetate	T52.8x1	T52.8x2	T52.8x3	T52.8x4	—	—
alcohol	T49.0x1	T49.0x2	T49.0x3	T49.0x4	T49.0x5	T49.0x6
benzoate	T49.0x1	T49.0x2	T49.0x3	T49.0x4	T49.0x5	T49.0x6
Benzoic acid	T49.0x1	T49.0x2	T49.0x3	T49.0x4	T49.0x5	T49.0x6
morphine	T40.2x1	T40.2x2	T40.2x3	T40.2x4	T40.2x5	T40.2x6
nicotinate	T46.6x1	T46.6x2	T46.6x3	T46.6x4	T46.6x5	T46.6x6
penicillin	T36.0x1	T36.0x2	T36.0x3	T36.0x4	T36.0x5	T36.0x6
Benzylhydrochlorthia-zide	T50.2x1	T50.2x2	T50.2x3	T50.2x4	T50.2x5	T50.2x6
Benzylpenicillin	T36.0x1	T36.0x2	T36.0x3	T36.0x4	T36.0x5	T36.0x6
Benzylthiouracil	T38.2x1	T38.2x2	T38.2x3	T38.2x4	T38.2x5	T38.2x6
Bephenium hydroxy-naphthoate	T37.4x1	T37.4x2	T37.4x3	T37.4x4	T37.4x5	T37.4x6
Bepridil	T46.1x1	T46.1x2	T46.1x3	T46.1x4	T46.1x5	T46.1x6
Bergamot oil	T65.891	T65.892	T65.893	T65.894	—	—
Bergapten	T50.991	T50.992	T50.993	T50.994	T50.995	T50.996

Substance	Poisoning, Accidental (Unintentional)	Poisoning, Intentional Self-Harm	Poisoning, Assault	Poisoning, Undetermined	Adverse Effect	Underdosing
	External Cause (T-Code)					
Berries, poisonous	T62.1x1	T62.1x2	T62.1x3	T62.1x4	—	—
Beryllium (compounds)	T56.7x1	T56.7x2	T56.7x3	T56.7x4	—	—
b-acetyldigoxin	T46.0x1	T46.0x2	T46.0x3	T46.0x4	T46.0x5	T46.0x6
b-adrenergic blocking agent, heart	T44.7x1	T44.7x2	T44.7x3	T44.7x4	T44.7x5	T44.7x6
b-benzalbutyramide	T46.6x1	T46.6x2	T46.6x3	T46.6x4	T46.6x5	T46.6x6
Betacarotene	T45.2x1	T45.2x2	T45.2x3	T45.2x4	T45.2x5	T45.2x6
b-eucaine	T49.1x1	T49.1x2	T49.1x3	T49.1x4	T49.1x5	T49.1x6
Beta-Chlor	T42.6x1	T42.6x2	T42.6x3	T42.6x4	T42.6x5	T42.6x6
b-galactosidase	T47.5x1	T47.5x2	T47.5x3	T47.5x4	T47.5x5	T47.5x6
Betahistine	T46.7x1	T46.7x2	T46.7x3	T46.7x4	T46.7x5	T46.7x6
Betaine	T47.5x1	T47.5x2	T47.5x3	T47.5x4	T47.5x5	T47.5x6
Betamethasone	T49.0x1	T49.0x2	T49.0x3	T49.0x4	T49.0x5	T49.0x6
topical	T49.0x1	T49.0x2	T49.0x3	T49.0x4	T49.0x5	T49.0x6
Betamicin	T36.8x1	T36.8x2	T36.8x3	T36.8x4	T36.8x5	T36.8x6
Betanidine	T46.5x1	T46.5x2	T46.5x3	T46.5x4	T46.5x5	T46.5x6
b-sitosterol(s)	T46.6x1	T46.6x2	T46.6x3	T46.6x4	T46.6x5	T46.6x6
Betaxolol	T44.7x1	T44.7x2	T44.7x3	T44.7x4	T44.7x5	T44.7x6
Betazole	T50.8x1	T50.8x2	T50.8x3	T50.8x4	T50.8x5	T50.8x6
Bethanechol	T44.1x1	T44.1x2	T44.1x3	T44.1x4	T44.1x5	T44.1x6
chloride	T44.1x1	T44.1x2	T44.1x3	T44.1x4	T44.1x5	T44.1x6
Bethanidine	T46.5x1	T46.5x2	T46.5x3	T46.5x4	T46.5x5	T46.5x6
Betoxycaine	T41.3x1	T41.3x2	T41.3x3	T41.3x4	T41.3x5	T41.3x6
Betula oil	T49.3x1	T49.3x2	T49.3x3	T49.3x4	T49.3x5	T49.3x6
Bevantolol	T44.7x1	T44.7x2	T44.7x3	T44.7x4	T44.7x5	T44.7x6
Bevonium metilsulfate	T44.3x1	T44.3x2	T44.3x3	T44.3x4	T44.3x5	T44.3x6
Bezafibrate	T46.6x1	T46.6x2	T46.6x3	T46.6x4	T46.6x5	T46.6x6
Bezitramide	T40.4x1	T40.4x2	T40.4x3	T40.4x4	T40.4x5	T40.4x6
BHA	T50.991	T50.992	T50.993	T50.994	T50.995	T50.996
Bhang	T40.7x1	T40.7x2	T40.7x3	T40.7x4	T40.7x5	T40.7x6
BHC (medicinal)	T49.0x1	T49.0x2	T49.0x3	T49.0x4	T49.0x5	T49.0x6
nonmedicinal (vapor)	T53.6x1	T53.6x2	T53.6x3	T53.6x4	—	—
Bialamicol	T37.3x1	T37.3x2	T37.3x3	T37.3x4	T37.3x5	T37.3x6
Bibenzonium bromide	T48.3x1	T48.3x2	T48.3x3	T48.3x4	T48.3x5	T48.3x6
Bibrocathol	T49.5x1	T49.5x2	T49.5x3	T49.5x4	T49.5x5	T49.5x6
Bichloride of mercury - *see* Mercury, chloride						
Bichromates (calcium) (potassium) (sodium) (crystals)	T57.8x1	T57.8x2	T57.8x3	T57.8x4	—	—
fumes	T56.2x1	T56.2x2	T56.2x3	T56.2x4	—	—
Biclotymol	T49.6x1	T49.6x2	T49.6x3	T49.6x4	T49.6x5	T49.6x6
Bicucculine	T50.7x1	T50.7x2	T50.7x3	T50.7x4	T50.7x5	T50.7x6
Bifemelane	T43.291	T43.292	T43.293	T43.294	T43.295	T43.296

Substance	External Cause (T-Code)					
	Poisoning, Accidental (Unintentional)	Poisoning, Intentional Self-Harm	Poisoning, Assault	Poisoning, Undetermined	Adverse Effect	Underdosing
Biguanide derivatives, oral	T38.3x1	T38.3x2	T38.3x3	T38.3x4	T38.3x5	T38.3x6
Biligrafin	T50.8x1	T50.8x2	T50.8x3	T50.8x4	T50.8x5	T50.8x6
Bile salts	T47.5x1	T47.5x2	T47.5x3	T47.5x4	T47.5x5	T47.5x6
Bilopaque	T50.8x1	T50.8x2	T50.8x3	T50.8x4	T50.8x5	T50.8x6
Binifibrate	T46.6x1	T46.6x2	T46.6x3	T46.6x4	T46.6x5	T46.6x6
Binitrobenzol	T65.3x1	T65.3x2	T65.3x3	T65.3x4	—	—
Bioflavonoid(s)	T46.991	T46.992	T46.993	T46.994	T46.995	T46.996
Biological substance NEC	T50.901	T50.902	T50.903	T50.904	T50.905	T50.906
Biotin	T45.2x1	T45.2x2	T45.2x3	T45.2x4	T45.2x5	T45.2x6
Biperiden	T44.3x1	T44.3x2	T44.3x3	T44.3x4	T44.3x5	T44.3x6
Bisacodyl	T47.2x1	T47.2x2	T47.2x3	T47.2x4	T47.2x5	T47.2x6
Bisbentiamine	T45.2x1	T45.2x2	T45.2x3	T45.2x4	T45.2x5	T45.2x6
Bisbutiamine	T45.2x1	T45.2x2	T45.2x3	T45.2x4	T45.2x5	T45.2x6
Bisdequalinium (salts) (diacetate)	T49.6x1	T49.6x2	T49.6x3	T49.6x4	T49.6x5	T49.6x6
Bishydroxycoumarin	T45.511	T45.512	T45.513	T45.514	T45.515	T45.516
Bismarsen	T37.8x1	T37.8x2	T37.8x3	T37.8x4	T37.8x5	T37.8x6
Bismuth salts	T47.6x1	T47.6x2	T47.6x3	T47.6x4	T47.6x5	T47.6x6
aluminate	T47.1x1	T47.1x2	T47.1x3	T47.1x4	T47.1x5	T47.1x6
anti-infectives	T37.8x1	T37.8x2	T37.8x3	T37.8x4	T37.8x5	T37.8x6
formic iodide	T49.0x1	T49.0x2	T49.0x3	T49.0x4	T49.0x5	T49.0x6
glycolylarsenate	T49.0x1	T49.0x2	T49.0x3	T49.0x4	T49.0x5	T49.0x6
nonmedicinal (compounds) NEC	T65.91	T65.92	T65.93	T65.94	—	—
subcarbonate	T47.6x1	T47.6x2	T47.6x3	T47.6x4	T47.6x5	T47.6x6
subsalicylate	T37.8x1	T37.8x2	T37.8x3	T37.8x4	T37.8x5	T37.8x6
sulfarsphenamine	T37.8x1	T37.8x2	T37.8x3	T37.8x4	T37.8x5	T37.8x6
Bisoprolol	T44.7x1	T44.7x2	T44.7x3	T44.7x4	T44.7x5	T44.7x6
Bisoxatin	T47.2x1	T47.2x2	T47.2x3	T47.2x4	T47.2x5	T47.2x6
Bisulepin (hydrochloride)	T45.0x1	T45.0x2	T45.0x3	T45.0x4	T45.0x5	T45.0x6
Bithionol	T37.8x1	T37.8x2	T37.8x3	T37.8x4	T37.8x5	T37.8x6
Bitolterol	T48.6x1	T48.6x2	T48.6x3	T48.6x4	T48.6x5	T48.6x6
Bitoscanate	T37.4x1	T37.4x2	T37.4x3	T37.4x4	T37.4x5	T37.4x6
Bitter almond oil	T62.8x1	T62.8x2	T62.8x3	T62.8x4	—	—
Bittersweet	T62.2x1	T62.2x2	T62.2x3	T62.2x4	—	—
Black						
flag	T60.91	T60.92	T60.93	T60.94	—	—
henbane	T62.2x1	T62.2x2	T62.2x3	T62.2x4	—	—
leaf (40)	T60.91	T60.92	T60.93	T60.94	—	—
widow spider (bite)	T63.311	T63.312	T63.313	T63.314	—	—
antivenin	T50.Z11	T50.Z12	T50.Z13	T50.Z14	T50.Z15	T50.Z16
Blast furnace gas (carbon monoxide from)	T58.8x1	T58.8x2	T58.8x3	T58.8x4	—	—

Substance	External Cause (T-Code)					
	Poisoning, Accidental (Unintentional)	Poisoning, Intentional Self-Harm	Poisoning, Assault	Poisoning, Undetermined	Adverse Effect	Underdosing
Bleach	T54.91	T54.92	T54.93	T54.94	—	—
Bleaching agent (medicinal)	T49.4x1	T49.4x2	T49.4x3	T49.4x4	T49.4x5	T49.4x6
Bleomycin	T45.1x1	T45.1x2	T45.1x3	T45.1x4	T45.1x5	T45.1x6
Blockain	T41.3x1	T41.3x2	T41.3x3	T41.3x4	T41.3x5	T41.3x6
infiltration (subcutaneous)	T41.3x1	T41.3x2	T41.3x3	T41.3x4	T41.3x5	T41.3x6
nerve block (peripheral) (plexus)	T41.3x1	T41.3x2	T41.3x3	T41.3x4	T41.3x5	T41.3x6
topical (surface)	T41.3x1	T41.3x2	T41.3x3	T41.3x4	T41.3x5	T41.3x6
Blood (derivatives) (natural) (plasma) (whole)	T45.8x1	T45.8x2	T45.8x3	T45.8x4	T45.8x5	T45.8x6
dried	T45.8x1	T45.8x2	T45.8x3	T45.8x4	T45.8x5	T45.8x6
drug affecting NEC	T45.91	T45.92	T45.93	T45.94	T45.95	T45.96
expander NEC	T45.8x1	T45.8x2	T45.8x3	T45.8x4	T45.8x5	T45.8x6
fraction NEC	T45.8x1	T45.8x2	T45.8x3	T45.8x4	T45.8x5	T45.8x6
substitute (macromolecular)	T45.8x1	T45.8x2	T45.8x3	T45.8x4	T45.8x5	T45.8x6
Blue velvet	T40.2x1	T40.2x2	T40.2x3	T40.2x4	T40.2x5	T40.2x6
Bone meal	T62.8x1	T62.8x2	T62.8x3	T62.8x4	—	—
Bonine	T45.0x1	T45.0x2	T45.0x3	T45.0x4	T45.0x5	T45.0x6
Bopindolol	T44.7x1	T44.7x2	T44.7x3	T44.7x4	T44.7x5	T44.7x6
Boracic acid	T49.0x1	T49.0x2	T49.0x3	T49.0x4	T49.0x5	T49.0x6
ENT agent	T49.6x1	T49.6x2	T49.6x3	T49.6x4	T49.6x5	T49.6x6
ophthalmic preparation	T49.5x1	T49.5x2	T49.5x3	T49.5x4	T49.5x5	T49.5x6
Borane complex	T57.8x1	T57.8x2	T57.8x3	T57.8x4	—	—
Borate(s)	T57.8x1	T57.8x2	T57.8x3	T57.8x4	—	—
buffer	T50.991	T50.992	T50.993	T50.994	T50.995	T50.996
cleanser	T54.91	T54.92	T54.93	T54.94	—	—
sodium	T57.8x1	T57.8x2	T57.8x3	T57.8x4	—	—
Borax (cleanser)	T54.91	T54.92	T54.93	T54.94	—	—
Bordeaux mixture	T60.3x1	T60.3x2	T60.3x3	T60.3x4	—	—
Boric acid	T49.0x1	T49.0x2	T49.0x3	T49.0x4	T49.0x5	T49.0x6
ENT agent	T49.6x1	T49.6x2	T49.6x3	T49.6x4	T49.6x5	T49.6x6
ophthalmic preparation	T49.5x1	T49.5x2	T49.5x3	T49.5x4	T49.5x5	T49.5x6
Bornaprine	T44.3x1	T44.3x2	T44.3x3	T44.3x4	T44.3x5	T44.3x6
Boron	T57.8x1	T57.8x2	T57.8x3	T57.8x4	—	—
hydride NEC	T57.8x1	T57.8x2	T57.8x3	T57.8x4	—	—
fumes or gas	T57.8x1	T57.8x2	T57.8x3	T57.8x4	—	—
trifluoride	T59.891	T59.892	T59.893	T59.894	—	—
Botox	T48.291	T48.292	T48.293	T48.294	T48.295	T48.296
Botulinus anti-toxin (type A, B)	T50.Z11	T50.Z12	T50.Z13	T50.Z14	T50.Z15	T50.Z16
Brake fluid vapor	T59.891	T59.892	T59.893	T59.894	—	—
Brallobarbital	T42.3x1	T42.3x2	T42.3x3	T42.3x4	T42.3x5	T42.3x6
Bran (wheat)	T47.4x1	T47.4x2	T47.4x3	T47.4x4	T47.4x5	T47.4x6

Substance	External Cause (T-Code)					
	Poisoning, Accidental (Unintentional)	Poisoning, Intentional Self-Harm	Poisoning, Assault	Poisoning, Undetermined	Adverse Effect	Underdosing
Brass (fumes)	T56.4x1	T56.4x2	T56.4x3	T56.4x4	—	—
Brasso	T52.0x1	T52.0x2	T52.0x3	T52.0x4	—	—
Bretylium tosilate	T46.2x1	T46.2x2	T46.2x3	T46.2x4	T46.2x5	T46.2x6
Brevital (sodium)	T41.1x1	T41.1x2	T41.1x3	T41.1x4	T41.1x5	T41.1x6
Brinase	T45.3x1	T45.3x2	T45.3x3	T45.3x4	T45.3x5	T45.3x6
British antilewisite	T45.8x1	T45.8x2	T45.8x3	T45.8x4	T45.8x5	T45.8x6
Brodifacoum	T60.4x1	T60.4x2	T60.4x3	T60.4x4	—	—
Bromal (hydrate)	T42.6x1	T42.6x2	T42.6x3	T42.6x4	T42.6x5	T42.6x6
Bromazepam	T42.4x1	T42.4x2	T42.4x3	T42.4x4	T42.4x5	T42.4x6
Bromazine	T45.0x1	T45.0x2	T45.0x3	T45.0x4	T45.0x5	T45.0x6
Brombenzylcyanide	T59.3x1	T59.3x2	T59.3x3	T59.3x4	—	—
Bromelains	T45.3x1	T45.3x2	T45.3x3	T45.3x4	T45.3x5	T45.3x6
Bromethalin	T60.4x1	T60.4x2	T60.4x3	T60.4x4	—	—
Bromhexine	T48.4x1	T48.4x2	T48.4x3	T48.4x4	T48.4x5	T48.4x6
Bromide salts	T42.6x1	T42.6x2	T42.6x3	T42.6x4	T42.6x5	T42.6x6
Bromindione	T45.511	T45.512	T45.513	T45.514	T45.515	T45.516
Bromine						
compounds (medicinal)	T42.6x1	T42.6x2	T42.6x3	T42.6x4	T42.6x5	T42.6x6
sedative	T42.6x1	T42.6x2	T42.6x3	T42.6x4	T42.6x5	T42.6x6
vapor	T59.891	T59.892	T59.893	T59.894	—	—
Bromisovalum	T42.6x1	T42.6x2	T42.6x3	T42.6x4	T42.6x5	T42.6x6
Bromisoval	T42.6x1	T42.6x2	T42.6x3	T42.6x4	T42.6x5	T42.6x6
Bromobenzylcyanide	T59.3x1	T59.3x2	T59.3x3	T59.3x4	—	—
Bromochlorosalicylani-lide	T49.0x1	T49.0x2	T49.0x3	T49.0x4	T49.0x5	T49.0x6
Bromocriptine	T42.8x1	T42.8x2	T42.8x3	T42.8x4	T42.8x5	T42.8x6
Bromodiphenhydramine	T45.0x1	T45.0x2	T45.0x3	T45.0x4	T45.0x5	T45.0x6
Bromoform	T42.6x1	T42.6x2	T42.6x3	T42.6x4	T42.6x5	T42.6x6
Bromophenol blue reagent	T50.991	T50.992	T50.993	T50.994	T50.995	T50.996
Bromopride	T47.8x1	T47.8x2	T47.8x3	T47.8x4	T47.8x5	T47.8x6
Bromosalicylchloranitide	T49.0x1	T49.0x2	T49.0x3	T49.0x4	T49.0x5	T49.0x6
Bromosalicylhydroxamic acid	T37.1x1	T37.1x2	T37.1x3	T37.1x4	T37.1x5	T37.1x6
Bromo-seltzer	T39.1x1	T39.1x2	T39.1x3	T39.1x4	T39.1x5	T39.1x6
Bromoxynil	T60.3x1	T60.3x2	T60.3x3	T60.3x4	—	—
Bromperidol	T43.4x1	T43.4x2	T43.4x3	T43.4x4	T43.4x5	T43.4x6
Brompheniramine	T45.0x1	T45.0x2	T45.0x3	T45.0x4	T45.0x5	T45.0x6
Bromsulfophthalein	T50.8x1	T50.8x2	T50.8x3	T50.8x4	T50.8x5	T50.8x6
Bromural	T42.6x1	T42.6x2	T42.6x3	T42.6x4	T42.6x5	T42.6x6
Bromvaletone	T42.6x1	T42.6x2	T42.6x3	T42.6x4	T42.6x5	T42.6x6
Bronchodilator NEC	T48.6x1	T48.6x2	T48.6x3	T48.6x4	T48.6x5	T48.6x6
Brotizolam	T42.4x1	T42.4x2	T42.4x3	T42.4x4	T42.4x5	T42.4x6

Substance	External Cause (T-Code)					
	Poisoning, Accidental (Unintentional)	Poisoning, Intentional Self-Harm	Poisoning, Assault	Poisoning, Undetermined	Adverse Effect	Underdosing
Brovincamine	T46.7x1	T46.7x2	T46.7x3	T46.7x4	T46.7x5	T46.7x6
Brown spider (bite) (venom)	T63.391	T63.392	T63.393	T63.394	—	—
Brown recluse spider (bite) (venom)	T63.331	T63.332	T63.333	T63.334	—	—
Broxaterol	T48.6x1	T48.6x2	T48.6x3	T48.6x4	T48.6x5	T48.6x6
Broxuridine	T45.1x1	T45.1x2	T45.1x3	T45.1x4	T45.1x5	T45.1x6
Broxyquinoline	T37.8x1	T37.8x2	T37.8x3	T37.8x4	T37.8x5	T37.8x6
Bruceine	T48.291	T48.292	T48.293	T48.294	T48.295	T48.296
Brucia	T62.2x1	T62.2x2	T62.2x3	T62.2x4	—	—
Brucine	T65.1x1	T65.1x2	T65.1x3	T65.1x4	—	—
Brunswick green - see Copper						
Bruten - see Ibuprofen						
Bryonia	T47.2x1	T47.2x2	T47.2x3	T47.2x4	T47.2x5	T47.2x6
Buclizine	T45.0x1	T45.0x2	T45.0x3	T45.0x4	T45.0x5	T45.0x6
Buclosamide	T49.0x1	T49.0x2	T49.0x3	T49.0x4	T49.0x5	T49.0x6
Budesonide	T44.5x1	T44.5x2	T44.5x3	T44.5x4	T44.5x5	T44.5x6
Budralazine	T46.5x1	T46.5x2	T46.5x3	T46.5x4	T46.5x5	T46.5x6
Bufferin	T39.011	T39.012	T39.013	T39.014	T39.015	T39.016
Buflomedil	T46.7x1	T46.7x2	T46.7x3	T46.7x4	T46.7x5	T46.7x6
Buformin	T38.3x1	T38.3x2	T38.3x3	T38.3x4	T38.3x5	T38.3x6
Bufotenine	T40.991	T40.992	T40.993	T40.994	T40.995	T40.996
Bufrolin	T48.6x1	T48.6x2	T48.6x3	T48.6x4	T48.6x5	T48.6x6
Bufylline	T48.6x1	T48.6x2	T48.6x3	T48.6x4	T48.6x5	T48.6x6
Bulk filler	T50.5x1	T50.5x2	T50.5x3	T50.5x4	T50.5x5	T50.5x6
cathartic	T47.4x1	T47.4x2	T47.4x3	T47.4x4	T47.4x5	T47.4x6
Bumetanide	T50.1x1	T50.1x2	T50.1x3	T50.1x4	T50.1x5	T50.1x6
Bunaftine	T46.2x1	T46.2x2	T46.2x3	T46.2x4	T46.2x5	T46.2x6
Bunamiodyl	T50.8x1	T50.8x2	T50.8x3	T50.8x4	T50.8x5	T50.8x6
Bunazosin	T44.6x1	T44.6x2	T44.6x3	T44.6x4	T44.6x5	T44.6x6
Bunitrolol	T44.7x1	T44.7x2	T44.7x3	T44.7x4	T44.7x5	T44.7x6
Buphenine	T46.7x1	T46.7x2	T46.7x3	T46.7x4	T46.7x5	T46.7x6
Bupivacaine	T41.3x1	T41.3x2	T41.3x3	T41.3x4	T41.3x5	T41.3x6
infiltration (subcutaneous)	T41.3x1	T41.3x2	T41.3x3	T41.3x4	T41.3x5	T41.3x6
nerve block (peripheral) (plexus)	T41.3x1	T41.3x2	T41.3x3	T41.3x4	T41.3x5	T41.3x6
spinal	T41.3x1	T41.3x2	T41.3x3	T41.3x4	T41.3x5	T41.3x6
Bupranolol	T44.7x1	T44.7x2	T44.7x3	T44.7x4	T44.7x5	T44.7x6
Buprenorphine	T40.4x1	T40.4x2	T40.4x3	T40.4x4	T40.4x5	T40.4x6
Bupropion	T43.291	T43.292	T43.293	T43.294	T43.295	T43.296
Burimamide	T47.1x1	T47.1x2	T47.1x3	T47.1x4	T47.1x5	T47.1x6
Buserelin	T38.891	T38.892	T38.893	T38.894	T38.895	T38.896
Buspirone	T43.591	T43.592	T43.593	T43.594	T43.595	T43.596

Substance	Poisoning, Accidental (Unintentional)	Poisoning, Intentional Self-Harm	Poisoning, Assault	Poisoning, Undetermined	Adverse Effect	Underdosing
			External Cause (T-Code)			
Busulfan, busulphan	T45.1x1	T45.1x2	T45.1x3	T45.1x4	T45.1x5	T45.1x6
Butabarbital (sodium)	T42.3x1	T42.3x2	T42.3x3	T42.3x4	T42.3x5	T42.3x6
Butabarbitone	T42.3x1	T42.3x2	T42.3x3	T42.3x4	T42.3x5	T42.3x6
Butabarpal	T42.3x1	T42.3x2	T42.3x3	T42.3x4	T42.3x5	T42.3x6
Butacaine	T41.3x1	T41.3x2	T41.3x3	T41.3x4	T41.3x5	T41.3x6
Butalamine	T46.7x1	T46.7x2	T46.7x3	T46.7x4	T46.7x5	T46.7x6
Butalbital	T42.3x1	T42.3x2	T42.3x3	T42.3x4	T42.3x5	T42.3x6
Butallylonal	T42.3x1	T42.3x2	T42.3x3	T42.3x4	T42.3x5	T42.3x6
Butamben	T41.3x1	T41.3x2	T41.3x3	T41.3x4	T41.3x5	T41.3x6
Butamirate	T48.3x1	T48.3x2	T48.3x3	T48.3x4	T48.3x5	T48.3x6
Butane (distributed in mobile container)	T59.891	T59.892	T59.893	T59.894	—	—
distributed through pipes	T59.891	T59.892	T59.893	T59.894	—	—
incomplete combustion	T58.11	T58.12	T58.13	T58.14	—	—
Butanilicaine	T41.3x1	T41.3x2	T41.3x3	T41.3x4	T41.3x5	T41.3x6
Butanol	T51.3x1	T51.3x2	T51.3x3	T51.3x4	—	—
Butanone, 2-butanone	T52.4x1	T52.4x2	T52.4x3	T52.4x4	—	—
Butantrone	T49.4x1	T49.4x2	T49.4x3	T49.4x4	T49.4x5	T49.4x6
Butaperazine	T43.3x1	T43.3x2	T43.3x3	T43.3x4	T43.3x5	T43.3x6
Butazolidin	T39.2x1	T39.2x2	T39.2x3	T39.2x4	T39.2x5	T39.2x6
Butetamate	T48.6x1	T48.6x2	T48.6x3	T48.6x4	T48.6x5	T48.6x6
Butethal	T42.3x1	T42.3x2	T42.3x3	T42.3x4	T42.3x5	T42.3x6
Butethamate	T44.3x1	T44.3x2	T44.3x3	T44.3x4	T44.3x5	T44.3x6
Buthalitone (sodium)	T41.1x1	T41.1x2	T41.1x3	T41.1x4	T41.1x5	T41.1x6
Butisol (sodium)	T42.3x1	T42.3x2	T42.3x3	T42.3x4	T42.3x5	T42.3x6
Butizide	T50.2x1	T50.2x2	T50.2x3	T50.2x4	T50.2x5	T50.2x6
Butobarbital	T42.3x1	T42.3x2	T42.3x3	T42.3x4	T42.3x5	T42.3x6
sodium	T42.3x1	T42.3x2	T42.3x3	T42.3x4	T42.3x5	T42.3x6
Butobarbitone	T42.3x1	T42.3x2	T42.3x3	T42.3x4	T42.3x5	T42.3x6
Butoconazole (nitrate)	T49.0x1	T49.0x2	T49.0x3	T49.0x4	T49.0x5	T49.0x6
Butorphanol	T40.4x1	T40.4x2	T40.4x3	T40.4x4	T40.4x5	T40.4x6
Butriptyline	T43.011	T43.012	T43.013	T43.014	T43.015	T43.016
Butropium bromide	T44.3x1	T44.3x2	T44.3x3	T44.3x4	T44.3x5	T44.3x6
Buttercups	T62.2x1	T62.2x2	T62.2x3	T62.2x4	—	—
Butter of antimony - see Antimony						
Butyl						
acetate (secondary)	T52.8x1	T52.8x2	T52.8x3	T52.8x4	—	—
alcohol	T51.3x1	T51.3x2	T51.3x3	T51.3x4	—	—
aminobenzoate	T41.3x1	T41.3x2	T41.3x3	T41.3x4	T41.3x5	T41.3x6
butyrate	T52.8x1	T52.8x2	T52.8x3	T52.8x4	—	—
carbinol	T51.3x1	T51.3x2	T51.3x3	T51.3x4	—	—

Substance	External Cause (T-Code)					
	Poisoning, Accidental (Unintentional)	Poisoning, Intentional Self-Harm	Poisoning, Assault	Poisoning, Undetermined	Adverse Effect	Underdosing
Butyl *(Continued)*						
carbitol	T52.3x1	T52.3x2	T52.3x3	T52.3x4	—	—
cellosolve	T52.3x1	T52.3x2	T52.3x3	T52.3x4	—	—
chloral (hydrate)	T42.6x1	T42.6x2	T42.6x3	T42.6x4	T42.6x5	T42.6x6
formate	T52.8x1	T52.8x2	T52.8x3	T52.8x4	—	—
lactate	T52.8x1	T52.8x2	T52.8x3	T52.8x4	—	—
propionate	T52.8x1	T52.8x2	T52.8x3	T52.8x4	—	—
scopolamine bromide	T44.3x1	T44.3x2	T44.3x3	T44.3x4	T44.3x5	T44.3x6
thiobarbital sodium	T41.1x1	T41.1x2	T41.1x3	T41.1x4	T41.1x5	T41.1x6
Butylated hydroxy-anisole	T50.991	T50.992	T50.993	T50.994	T50.995	T50.996
Butylchloral hydrate	T42.6x1	T42.6x2	T42.6x3	T42.6x4	T42.6x5	T42.6x6
Butyltoluene	T52.2x1	T52.2x2	T52.2x3	T52.2x4	—	—
Butyn	T41.3x1	T41.3x2	T41.3x3	T41.3x4	T41.3x5	T41.3x6
Butyrophenone (-based tranquilizers)	T43.4x1	T43.4x2	T43.4x3	T43.4x4	T43.4x5	T43.4x6
Cabergoline	T42.8x1	T42.8x2	T42.8x3	T42.8x4	T42.8x5	T42.8x6
Cacodyl, cacodylic acid	T57.0x1	T57.0x2	T57.0x3	T57.0x4	—	—
Cactinomycin	T45.1x1	T45.1x2	T45.1x3	T45.1x4	T45.1x5	T45.1x6
Cade oil	T49.4x1	T49.4x2	T49.4x3	T49.4x4	T49.4x5	T49.4x6
Cadexomer iodine	T49.0x1	T49.0x2	T49.0x3	T49.0x4	T49.0x5	T49.0x6
Cadmium (chloride) (fumes) (oxide)	T56.3x1	T56.3x2	T56.3x3	T56.3x4	—	—
sulfide (medicinal) NEC	T49.4x1	T49.4x2	T49.4x3	T49.4x4	T49.4x5	T49.4x6
Cadralazine	T46.5x1	T46.5x2	T46.5x3	T46.5x4	T46.5x5	T46.5x6
Caffeine	T43.611	T43.612	T43.613	T43.614	T43.615	T43.616
Calabar bean	T62.2x1	T62.2x2	T62.2x3	T62.2x4	—	—
Caladium seguinum	T62.2x1	T62.2x2	T62.2x3	T62.2x4	—	—
Calamine (lotion)	T49.3x1	T49.3x2	T49.3x3	T49.3x4	T49.3x5	T49.3x6
Calcifediol	T45.2x1	T45.2x2	T45.2x3	T45.2x4	T45.2x5	T45.2x6
Calciferol	T45.2x1	T45.2x2	T45.2x3	T45.2x4	T45.2x5	T45.2x6
Calcitonin	T50.991	T50.992	T50.993	T50.994	T50.995	T50.996
Calcitriol	T45.2x1	T45.2x2	T45.2x3	T45.2x4	T45.2x5	T45.2x6
Calcium	T50.3x1	T50.3x2	T50.3x3	T50.3x4	T50.3x5	T50.3x6
actylsalicylate	T39.011	T39.012	T39.013	T39.014	T39.015	T39.016
benzamidosalicylate	T37.1x1	T37.1x2	T37.1x3	T37.1x4	T37.1x5	T37.1x6
bromide	T42.6x1	T42.6x2	T42.6x3	T42.6x4	T42.6x5	T42.6x6
bromolactobionate	T42.6x1	T42.6x2	T42.6x3	T42.6x4	T42.6x5	T42.6x6
carbaspirin	T39.011	T39.012	T39.013	T39.014	T39.015	T39.016
carbimide	T50.6x1	T50.6x2	T50.6x3	T50.6x4	T50.6x5	T50.6x6
carbonate	T47.1x1	T47.1x2	T47.1x3	T47.1x4	T47.1x5	T47.1x6
chloride	T50.991	T50.992	T50.993	T50.994	T50.995	T50.996
anhydrous	T50.991	T50.992	T50.993	T50.994	T50.995	T50.996

Substance	Poisoning, Accidental (Unintentional)	Poisoning, Intentional Self-Harm	Poisoning, Assault	Poisoning, Undetermined	Adverse Effect	Underdosing
Calcium *(Continued)*						
cyanide	T57.8x1	T57.8x2	T57.8x3	T57.8x4	—	—
dioctyl sulfosuccinate	T47.4x1	T47.4x2	T47.4x3	T47.4x4	T47.4x5	T47.4x6
disodium edathamil	T45.8x1	T45.8x2	T45.8x3	T45.8x4	T45.8x5	T45.8x6
disodium edetate	T45.8x1	T45.8x2	T45.8x3	T45.8x4	T45.8x5	T45.8x6
dobesilate	T46.991	T46.992	T46.993	T46.994	T46.995	T46.996
EDTA	T45.8x1	T45.8x2	T45.8x3	T45.8x4	T45.8x5	T45.8x6
ferrous citrate	T45.4x1	T45.4x2	T45.4x3	T45.4x4	T45.4x5	T45.4x6
folinate	T45.8x1	T45.8x2	T45.8x3	T45.8x4	T45.8x5	T45.8x6
glubionate	T50.3x1	T50.3x2	T50.3x3	T50.3x4	T50.3x5	T50.3x6
gluconate	T50.3x1	T50.3x2	T50.3x3	T50.3x4	T50.3x5	T50.3x6
gluconogalactogluconate	T50.3x1	T50.3x2	T50.3x3	T50.3x4	T50.3x5	T50.3x6
hydrate, hydroxide	T54.3x1	T54.3x2	T54.3x3	T54.3x4	—	—
hypochlorite	T37.91	T37.92	T37.93	T37.94	T37.95	T37.96
iodide	T48.4x1	T48.4x2	T48.4x3	T48.4x4	T48.4x5	T48.4x6
ipodate	T50.8x1	T50.8x2	T50.8x3	T50.8x4	T50.8x5	T50.8x6
lactate	T50.3x1	T50.3x2	T50.3x3	T50.3x4	T50.3x5	T50.3x6
leucovorin	T45.8x1	T45.8x2	T45.8x3	T45.8x4	T45.8x5	T45.8x6
mandelate	T37.91	T37.92	T37.93	T37.94	T37.95	T37.96
oxide	T54.3x1	T54.3x2	T54.3x3	T54.3x4	—	—
pantothenate	T45.2x1	T45.2x2	T45.2x3	T45.2x4	T45.2x5	T45.2x6
phosphate	T50.3x1	T50.3x2	T50.3x3	T50.3x4	T50.3x5	T50.3x6
salicylate	T39.091	T39.092	T39.093	T39.094	T39.095	T39.096
salts	T50.3x1	T50.3x2	T50.3x3	T50.3x4	T50.3x5	T50.3x6
Calculus-dissolving drug	T50.991	T50.992	T50.993	T50.994	T50.995	T50.996
Calomel	T49.0x1	T49.0x2	T49.0x3	T49.0x4	T49.0x5	T49.0x6
Caloric agent	T50.3x1	T50.3x2	T50.3x3	T50.3x4	T50.3x5	T50.3x6
Calusterone	T38.7x1	T38.7x2	T38.7x3	T38.7x4	T38.7x5	T38.7x6
Camazepam	T42.4x1	T42.4x2	T42.4x3	T42.4x4	T42.4x5	T42.4x6
Camomile	T49.0x1	T49.0x2	T49.0x3	T49.0x4	T49.0x5	T49.0x6
Camoquin	T37.2x1	T37.2x2	T37.2x3	T37.2x4	T37.2x5	T37.2x6
Camphor						
insecticide	T60.2x1	T60.2x2	T60.2x3	T60.2x4	—	—
medicinal	T49.8x1	T49.8x2	T49.8x3	T49.8x4	T49.8x5	T49.8x6
Camylofin	T44.3x1	T44.3x2	T44.3x3	T44.3x4	T44.3x5	T44.3x6
Cancer chemotherapy drug regimen	T45.1x1	T45.1x2	T45.1x3	T45.1x4	T45.1x5	T45.1x6
Candeptin	T49.0x1	T49.0x2	T49.0x3	T49.0x4	T49.0x5	T49.0x6
Candicidin	T49.0x1	T49.0x2	T49.0x3	T49.0x4	T49.0x5	T49.0x6
Cannabinol	T40.7x1	T40.7x2	T40.7x3	T40.7x4	T40.7x5	T40.7x6
Cannabis (derivatives)	T40.7x1	T40.7x2	T40.7x3	T40.7x4	T40.7x5	T40.7x6

Substance	External Cause (T-Code)					
	Poisoning, Accidental (Unintentional)	Poisoning, Intentional Self-Harm	Poisoning, Assault	Poisoning, Undetermined	Adverse Effect	Underdosing
Canned heat	T51.1x1	T51.1x2	T51.1x3	T51.1x4	—	—
Canrenoic acid	T50.0x1	T50.0x2	T50.0x3	T50.0x4	T50.0x5	T50.0x6
Canrenone	T50.0x1	T50.0x2	T50.0x3	T50.0x4	T50.0x5	T50.0x6
Cantharides, cantharidin, cantharis	T49.8x1	T49.8x2	T49.8x3	T49.8x4	T49.8x5	T49.8x6
Canthaxanthin	T50.991	T50.992	T50.993	T50.994	T50.995	T50.996
Capillary-active drug NEC	T46.901	T46.902	T46.903	T46.904	T46.905	T46.906
Capreomycin	T36.8x1	T36.8x2	T36.8x3	T36.8x4	T36.8x5	T36.8x6
Capsicum	T49.4x1	T49.4x2	T49.4x3	T49.4x4	T49.4x5	T49.4x6
Captafol	T60.3x1	T60.3x2	T60.3x3	T60.3x4	—	—
Captan	T60.3x1	T60.3x2	T60.3x3	T60.3x4	—	—
Captodiame, captodiamine	T43.591	T43.592	T43.593	T43.594	T43.595	T43.596
Captopril	T46.4x1	T46.4x2	T46.4x3	T46.4x4	T46.4x5	T46.4x6
Caramiphen	T44.3x1	T44.3x2	T44.3x3	T44.3x4	T44.3x5	T44.3x6
Carazolol	T44.7x1	T44.7x2	T44.7x3	T44.7x4	T44.7x5	T44.7x6
Carbachol	T44.1x1	T44.1x2	T44.1x3	T44.1x4	T44.1x5	T44.1x6
Carbacrylamine (resin)	T50.3x1	T50.3x2	T50.3x3	T50.3x4	T50.3x5	T50.3x6
Carbamate (insecticide)	T60.0x1	T60.0x2	T60.0x3	T60.0x4	—	—
Carbamate (sedative)	T42.6x1	T42.6x2	T42.6x3	T42.6x4	T42.6x5	T42.6x6
herbicide	T60.0x1	T60.0x2	T60.0x3	T60.0x4	—	—
insecticide	T60.0x1	T60.0x2	T60.0x3	T60.0x4	—	—
Carbamazepine	T42.1x1	T42.1x2	T42.1x3	T42.1x4	T42.1x5	T42.1x6
Carbamide	T47.3x1	T47.3x2	T47.3x3	T47.3x4	T47.3x5	T47.3x6
peroxide	T49.0x1	T49.0x2	T49.0x3	T49.0x4	T49.0x5	T49.0x6
topical	T49.8x1	T49.8x2	T49.8x3	T49.8x4	T49.8x5	T49.8x6
Carbamylcholine chloride	T44.1x1	T44.1x2	T44.1x3	T44.1x4	T44.1x5	T44.1x6
Carbaril	T49.0x1	T49.0x2	T49.0x3	T49.0x4	T49.0x5	T49.0x6
Carbarsone	T37.3x1	T37.3x2	T37.3x3	T37.3x4	T37.3x5	T37.3x6
Carbaryl	T60.0x1	T60.0x2	T60.0x3	T60.0x4	—	—
Carbaspirin	T39.011	T39.012	T39.013	T39.014	T39.015	T39.016
Carbazochrome (salicylate) (sodium sulfonate)	T49.4x1	T49.4x2	T49.4x3	T49.4x4	T49.4x5	T49.4x6
Carbenicillin	T36.0x1	T36.0x2	T36.0x3	T36.0x4	T36.0x5	T36.0x6
Carbenoxolone	T47.1x1	T47.1x2	T47.1x3	T47.1x4	T47.1x5	T47.1x6
Carbetapentane	T48.3x1	T48.3x2	T48.3x3	T48.3x4	T48.3x5	T48.3x6
Carbethyl salicylate	T39.091	T39.092	T39.093	T39.094	T39.095	T39.096
Carbidopa (with levodopa)	T42.8x1	T42.8x2	T42.8x3	T42.8x4	T42.8x5	T42.8x6
Carbimazole	T38.2x1	T38.2x2	T38.2x3	T38.2x4	T38.2x5	T38.2x6
Carbinol	T51.1x1	T51.1x2	T51.1x3	T51.1x4	—	—
Carbinoxamine	T45.0x1	T45.0x2	T45.0x3	T45.0x4	T45.0x5	T45.0x6
Carbiphene	T39.8x1	T39.8x2	T39.8x3	T39.8x4	T39.8x5	T39.8x6
Carbitol	T52.3x1	T52.3x2	T52.3x3	T52.3x4	—	—

Substance	Poisoning, Accidental (Unintentional)	Poisoning, Intentional Self-Harm	Poisoning, Assault	Poisoning, Undetermined	Adverse Effect	Underdosing
Carbocaine	T41.3x1	T41.3x2	T41.3x3	T41.3x4	T41.3x5	T41.3x6
infiltration (subcutaneous)	T41.3x1	T41.3x2	T41.3x3	T41.3x4	T41.3x5	T41.3x6
nerve block (peripheral) (plexus)	T41.3x1	T41.3x2	T41.3x3	T41.3x4	T41.3x5	T41.3x6
topical (surface)	T41.3x1	T41.3x2	T41.3x3	T41.3x4	T41.3x5	T41.3x6
Carbo medicinalis	T47.6x1	T47.6x2	T47.6x3	T47.6x4	T47.6x5	T47.6x6
Carbomycin	T36.8x1	T36.8x2	T36.8x3	T36.8x4	T36.8x5	T36.8x6
Carbocisteine	T48.4x1	T48.4x2	T48.4x3	T48.4x4	T48.4x5	T48.4x6
Carbocromen	T46.3x1	T46.3x2	T46.3x3	T46.3x4	T46.3x5	T46.3x6
Carbol fuchsin	T49.0x1	T49.0x2	T49.0x3	T49.0x4	T49.0x5	T49.0x6
Carbolic acid (*see also* Phenol)	T54.0x1	T54.0x2	T54.0x3	T54.0x4	—	—
Carbolonium (bromide)	T48.1x1	T48.1x2	T48.1x3	T48.1x4	T48.1x5	T48.1x6
Carbon						
bisulfide (liquid)	T65.4x1	T65.4x2	T65.4x3	T65.4x4	—	—
vapor	T65.4x1	T65.4x2	T65.4x3	T65.4x4	—	—
dioxide (gas)	T59.7x1	T59.7x2	T59.7x3	T59.7x4	—	—
medicinal	T41.5x1	T41.5x2	T41.5x3	T41.5x4	T41.5x5	T41.5x6
nonmedicinal	T59.7x1	T59.7x2	T59.7x3	T59.7x4	—	—
snow	T49.4x1	T49.4x2	T49.4x3	T49.4x4	T49.4x5	T49.4x6
disulfide (liquid)	T65.4x1	T65.4x2	T65.4x3	T65.4x4	—	—
vapor	T65.4x1	T65.4x2	T65.4x3	T65.4x4	—	—
monoxide (from incomplete combustion)	T58.91	T58.92	T58.93	T58.94	—	—
blast furnace gas	T58.8x1	T58.8x2	T58.8x3	T58.8x4	—	—
butane (distributed in mobile container)	T58.11	T58.12	T58.13	T58.14	—	—
distributed through pipes	T58.11	T58.12	T58.13	T58.14	—	—
charcoal fumes	T58.2x1	T58.2x2	T58.2x3	T58.2x4	—	—
coal	T58.2x1	T58.2x2	T58.2x3	T58.2x4		
gas (piped)	T58.11	T58.12	T58.13	T58.14	—	—
solid (in domestic stoves, fireplaces)	T58.2x1	T58.2x2	T58.2x3	T58.2x4	—	—
coke (in domestic stoves, fireplaces)	T58.2x1	T58.2x2	T58.2x3	T58.2x4	—	—
exhaust gas (motor)	T58.01	T58.02	T58.03	T58.04	—	—
not in transit	T58.01	T58.02	T58.03	T58.04	—	—
combustion engine, any not in watercraft	T58.01	T58.02	T58.03	T58.04	—	—
farm tractor, not in transit	T58.01	T58.02	T58.03	T58.04	—	—
gas engine	T58.01	T58.02	T58.03	T58.04	—	—
motor pump	T58.01	T58.02	T58.03	T58.04	—	—
motor vehicle, not in transit	T58.01	T58.02	T58.03	T58.04	—	—
fuel (in domestic use)	T58.2x1	T58.2x2	T58.2x3	T58.2x4	—	—
gas (piped)	T58.11	T58.12	T58.13	T58.14	—	—
in mobile container	T58.11	T58.12	T58.13	T58.14	—	—

Substance	External Cause (T-Code)					
	Poisoning, Accidental (Unintentional)	Poisoning, Intentional Self-Harm	Poisoning, Assault	Poisoning, Undetermined	Adverse Effect	Underdosing
Carbon *(Continued)*						
monoxide *(Continued)*						
fuel *(Continued)*						
utility	T58.11	T58.12	T58.13	T58.14	—	—
in mobile container	T58.11	T58.12	T58.13	T58.14	—	—
piped (natural)	T58.11	T58.12	T58.13	T58.14	—	—
illuminating gas	T58.11	T58.12	T58.13	T58.14	—	—
industrial fuels or gases, any	T58.8x1	T58.8x2	T58.8x3	T58.8x4	—	—
kerosene (in domestic stoves, fireplaces)	T58.2x1	T58.2x2	T58.2x3	T58.2x4	—	—
kiln gas or vapor	T58.8x1	T58.8x2	T58.8x3	T58.8x4	—	—
motor exhaust gas, not in transit	T58.01	T58.02	T58.03	T58.04	—	—
piped gas (manufactured) (natural)	T58.11	T58.12	T58.13	T58.14	—	—
producer gas	T58.8x1	T58.8x2	T58.8x3	T58.8x4	—	—
propane (distributed in mobile container)	T58.11	T58.12	T58.13	T58.14	—	—
distributed through pipes	T58.11	T58.12	T58.13	T58.14	—	—
specified source NEC	T58.8x1	T58.8x2	T58.8x3	T58.8x4	—	—
stove gas	T58.11	T58.12	T58.13	T58.14	—	—
piped	T58.11	T58.12	T58.13	T58.14	—	—
utility gas	T58.11	T58.12	T58.13	T58.14	—	—
piped	T58.11	T58.12	T58.13	T58.14	—	—
water gas	T58.8x1	T58.8x2	T58.8x3	T58.8x4	—	—
wood (in domestic stoves, fireplaces)	T58.2x1	T58.2x2	T58.2x3	T58.2x4	—	—
tetrachloride (vapor) NEC	T53.0x1	T53.0x2	T53.0x3	T53.0x4	—	—
liquid (cleansing agent) NEC	T53.0x1	T53.0x2	T53.0x3	T53.0x4	—	—
solvent	T53.0x1	T53.0x2	T53.0x3	T53.0x4	—	—
Carbonic acid gas	T59.7x1	T59.7x2	T59.7x3	T59.7x4	—	—
anhydrase inhibitor NEC	T50.2x1	T50.2x2	T50.2x3	T50.2x4	T50.2x5	T50.2x6
Carbophenothion	T60.0x1	T60.0x2	T60.0x3	T60.0x4	—	—
Carboplatin	T45.1x1	T45.1x2	T45.1x3	T45.1x4	T45.1x5	T45.1x6
Carboprost	T48.0x1	T48.0x2	T48.0x3	T48.0x4	T48.0x5	T48.0x6
Carboquone	T45.1x1	T45.1x2	T45.1x3	T45.1x4	T45.1x5	T45.1x6
Carbowax	T49.3x1	T49.3x2	T49.3x3	T49.3x4	T49.3x5	T49.3x6
Carboxymethyl-cellulose	T47.4x1	T47.4x2	T47.4x3	T47.4x4	T47.4x5	T47.4x6
S-Carboxymethyl-cysteine	T48.4x1	T48.4x2	T48.4x3	T48.4x4	T48.4x5	T48.4x6
Carbrital	T42.3x1	T42.3x2	T42.3x3	T42.3x4	T42.3x5	T42.3x6
Carbromal	T42.6x1	T42.6x2	T42.6x3	T42.6x4	T42.6x5	T42.6x6
Carbutamide	T38.3x1	T38.3x2	T38.3x3	T38.3x4	T38.3x5	T38.3x6
Carbuterol	T48.6x1	T48.6x2	T48.6x3	T48.6x4	T48.6x5	T48.6x6
Cardiac rhythm regulator NEC	T46.2x1	T46.2x2	T46.2x3	T46.2x4	T46.2x5	T46.2x6
specified NEC	T46.2x1	T46.2x2	T46.2x3	T46.2x4	T46.2x5	T46.2x6

Substance	Poisoning, Accidental (Unintentional)	Poisoning, Intentional Self-Harm	Poisoning, Assault	Poisoning, Undetermined	Adverse Effect	Underdosing
Cardiac						
depressants	T46.2x1	T46.2x2	T46.2x3	T46.2x4	T46.2x5	T46.2x6
rhythm regulators	T46.2x1	T46.2x2	T46.2x3	T46.2x4	T46.2x5	T46.2x6
Cardiografin	T50.8x1	T50.8x2	T50.8x3	T50.8x4	T50.8x5	T50.8x6
Cardio-green	T50.8x1	T50.8x2	T50.8x3	T50.8x4	T50.8x5	T50.8x6
Cardiotonic (glycoside) NEC	T46.0x1	T46.0x2	T46.0x3	T46.0x4	T46.0x5	T46.0x6
Cardiovascular drug NEC	T46.901	T46.902	T46.903	T46.904	T46.905	T46.906
Cardrase	T50.2x1	T50.2x2	T50.2x3	T50.2x4	T50.2x5	T50.2x6
Carfusin	T49.0x1	T49.0x2	T49.0x3	T49.0x4	T49.0x5	T49.0x6
Carfecillin	T36.0x1	T36.0x2	T36.0x3	T36.0x4	T36.0x5	T36.0x6
Carfenazine	T43.3x1	T43.3x2	T43.3x3	T43.3x4	T43.3x5	T43.3x6
Carindacillin	T36.0x1	T36.0x2	T36.0x3	T36.0x4	T36.0x5	T36.0x6
Carisoprodol	T42.8x1	T42.8x2	T42.8x3	T42.8x4	T42.8x5	T42.8x6
Carmellose	T47.4x1	T47.4x2	T47.4x3	T47.4x4	T47.4x5	T47.4x6
Carminative	T47.5x1	T47.5x2	T47.5x3	T47.5x4	T47.5x5	T47.5x6
Carmofur	T45.1x1	T45.1x2	T45.1x3	T45.1x4	T45.1x5	T45.1x6
Carmustine	T45.1x1	T45.1x2	T45.1x3	T45.1x4	T45.1x5	T45.1x6
Carotene	T45.2x1	T45.2x2	T45.2x3	T45.2x4	T45.2x5	T45.2x6
Carphenazine	T43.3x1	T43.3x2	T43.3x3	T43.3x4	T43.3x5	T43.3x6
Carpipramine	T42.4x1	T42.4x2	T42.4x3	T42.4x4	T42.4x5	T42.4x6
Carprofen	T39.311	T39.312	T39.313	T39.314	T39.315	T39.316
Carpronium chloride	T44.3x1	T44.3x2	T44.3x3	T44.3x4	T44.3x5	T44.3x6
Carrageenan	T47.8x1	T47.8x2	T47.8x3	T47.8x4	T47.8x5	T47.8x6
Carteolol	T44.7x1	T44.7x2	T44.7x3	T44.7x4	T44.7x5	T44.7x6
Carter's Little Pills	T47.2x1	T47.2x2	T47.2x3	T47.2x4	T47.2x5	T47.2x6
Cascara (sagrada)	T47.2x1	T47.2x2	T47.2x3	T47.2x4	T47.2x5	T47.2x6
Cassava	T62.2x1	T62.2x2	T62.2x3	T62.2x4	—	—
Castellani's paint	T49.0x1	T49.0x2	T49.0x3	T49.0x4	T49.0x5	T49.0x6
Castor						
bean	T62.2x1	T62.2x2	T62.2x3	T62.2x4	—	—
oil	T47.2x1	T47.2x2	T47.2x3	T47.2x4	T47.2x5	T47.2x6
Catalase	T45.3x1	T45.3x2	T45.3x3	T45.3x4	T45.3x5	T45.3x6
Caterpillar (sting)	T63.431	T63.432	T63.433	T63.434	—	—
Catha (tea)	T43.691	T43.692	T43.693	T43.694	—	—
Cathartic NEC	T47.4x1	T47.4x2	T47.4x3	T47.4x4	T47.4x5	T47.4x6
anthacene derivative	T47.2x1	T47.2x2	T47.2x3	T47.2x4	T47.2x5	T47.2x6
bulk	T47.4x1	T47.4x2	T47.4x3	T47.4x4	T47.4x5	T47.4x6
contact	T47.2x1	T47.2x2	T47.2x3	T47.2x4	T47.2x5	T47.2x6
emollient NEC	T47.4x1	T47.4x2	T47.4x3	T47.4x4	T47.4x5	T47.4x6
irritant NEC	T47.2x1	T47.2x2	T47.2x3	T47.2x4	T47.2x5	T47.2x6

Substance	Poisoning, Accidental (Unintentional)	Poisoning, Intentional Self-Harm	Poisoning, Assault	Poisoning, Undetermined	Adverse Effect	Underdosing
			External Cause (T-Code)			
Cathartic NEC *(Continued)*						
mucilage	T47.4x1	T47.4x2	T47.4x3	T47.4x4	T47.4x5	T47.4x6
saline	T47.3x1	T47.3x2	T47.3x3	T47.3x4	T47.3x5	T47.3x6
vegetable	T47.2x1	T47.2x2	T47.2x3	T47.2x4	T47.2x5	T47.2x6
Cathine	T50.5x1	T50.5x2	T50.5x3	T50.5x4	T50.5x5	T50.5x6
Cathomycin	T36.8x1	T36.8x2	T36.8x3	T36.8x4	T36.8x5	T36.8x6
Cation exchange resin	T50.3x1	T50.3x2	T50.3x3	T50.3x4	T50.3x5	T50.3x6
Caustic(s) NEC	T54.91	T54.92	T54.93	T54.94	—	—
alkali	T54.3x1	T54.3x2	T54.3x3	T54.3x4	—	—
hydroxide	T54.3x1	T54.3x2	T54.3x3	T54.3x4	—	—
potash	T54.3x1	T54.3x2	T54.3x3	T54.3x4	—	—
specified NEC	T54.91	T54.92	T54.93	T54.94	—	—
soda	T54.3x1	T54.3x2	T54.3x3	T54.3x4	—	—
Ceepryn	T49.0x1	T49.0x2	T49.0x3	T49.0x4	T49.0x5	T49.0x6
ENT agent	T49.6x1	T49.6x2	T49.6x3	T49.6x4	T49.6x5	T49.6x6
lozenges	T49.6x1	T49.6x2	T49.6x3	T49.6x4	T49.6x5	T49.6x6
Cefacetrile	T36.1x1	T36.1x2	T36.1x3	T36.1x4	T36.1x5	T36.1x6
Cefaclor	T36.1x1	T36.1x2	T36.1x3	T36.1x4	T36.1x5	T36.1x6
Cefadroxil	T36.1x1	T36.1x2	T36.1x3	T36.1x4	T36.1x5	T36.1x6
Cefalexin	T36.1x1	T36.1x2	T36.1x3	T36.1x4	T36.1x5	T36.1x6
Cefaloglycin	T36.1x1	T36.1x2	T36.1x3	T36.1x4	T36.1x5	T36.1x6
Cefaloridine	T36.1x1	T36.1x2	T36.1x3	T36.1x4	T36.1x5	T36.1x6
Cefalosporins	T36.1x1	T36.1x2	T36.1x3	T36.1x4	T36.1x5	T36.1x6
Cefalotin	T36.1x1	T36.1x2	T36.1x3	T36.1x4	T36.1x5	T36.1x6
Cefamandole	T36.1x1	T36.1x2	T36.1x3	T36.1x4	T36.1x5	T36.1x6
Cefamycin antibiotic	T36.1x1	T36.1x2	T36.1x3	T36.1x4	T36.1x5	T36.1x6
Cefapirin	T36.1x1	T36.1x2	T36.1x3	T36.1x4	T36.1x5	T36.1x6
Cefatrizine	T36.1x1	T36.1x2	T36.1x3	T36.1x4	T36.1x5	T36.1x6
Cefazedone	T36.1x1	T36.1x2	T36.1x3	T36.1x4	T36.1x5	T36.1x6
Cefazolin	T36.1x1	T36.1x2	T36.1x3	T36.1x4	T36.1x5	T36.1x6
Cefbuperazone	T36.1x1	T36.1x2	T36.1x3	T36.1x4	T36.1x5	T36.1x6
Cefetamet	T36.1x1	T36.1x2	T36.1x3	T36.1x4	T36.1x5	T36.1x6
Cefixime	T36.1x1	T36.1x2	T36.1x3	T36.1x4	T36.1x5	T36.1x6
Cefmenoxime	T36.1x1	T36.1x2	T36.1x3	T36.1x4	T36.1x5	T36.1x6
Cefmetazole	T36.1x1	T36.1x2	T36.1x3	T36.1x4	T36.1x5	T36.1x6
Cefminox	T36.1x1	T36.1x2	T36.1x3	T36.1x4	T36.1x5	T36.1x6
Cefonicid	T36.1x1	T36.1x2	T36.1x3	T36.1x4	T36.1x5	T36.1x6
Cefoperazone	T36.1x1	T36.1x2	T36.1x3	T36.1x4	T36.1x5	T36.1x6
Ceforanide	T36.1x1	T36.1x2	T36.1x3	T36.1x4	T36.1x5	T36.1x6
Cefotaxime	T36.1x1	T36.1x2	T36.1x3	T36.1x4	T36.1x5	T36.1x6

Substance	External Cause (T-Code)					
	Poisoning, Accidental (Unintentional)	Poisoning, Intentional Self-Harm	Poisoning, Assault	Poisoning, Undetermined	Adverse Effect	Underdosing
Cefotetan	T36.1x1	T36.1x2	T36.1x3	T36.1x4	T36.1x5	T36.1x6
Cefotiam	T36.1x1	T36.1x2	T36.1x3	T36.1x4	T36.1x5	T36.1x6
Cefoxitin	T36.1x1	T36.1x2	T36.1x3	T36.1x4	T36.1x5	T36.1x6
Cefpimizole	T36.1x1	T36.1x2	T36.1x3	T36.1x4	T36.1x5	T36.1x6
Cefpiramide	T36.1x1	T36.1x2	T36.1x3	T36.1x4	T36.1x5	T36.1x6
Cefradine	T36.1x1	T36.1x2	T36.1x3	T36.1x4	T36.1x5	T36.1x6
Cefroxadine	T36.1x1	T36.1x2	T36.1x3	T36.1x4	T36.1x5	T36.1x6
Cefsulodin	T36.1x1	T36.1x2	T36.1x3	T36.1x4	T36.1x5	T36.1x6
Ceftazidime	T36.1x1	T36.1x2	T36.1x3	T36.1x4	T36.1x5	T36.1x6
Cefteram	T36.1x1	T36.1x2	T36.1x3	T36.1x4	T36.1x5	T36.1x6
Ceftezole	T36.1x1	T36.1x2	T36.1x3	T36.1x4	T36.1x5	T36.1x6
Ceftizoxime	T36.1x1	T36.1x2	T36.1x3	T36.1x4	T36.1x5	T36.1x6
Ceftriaxone	T36.1x1	T36.1x2	T36.1x3	T36.1x4	T36.1x5	T36.1x6
Cefuroxime	T36.1x1	T36.1x2	T36.1x3	T36.1x4	T36.1x5	T36.1x6
Cefuzonam	T36.1x1	T36.1x2	T36.1x3	T36.1x4	T36.1x5	T36.1x6
Celestone	T38.0x1	T38.0x2	T38.0x3	T38.0x4	T38.0x5	T38.0x6
topical	T49.0x1	T49.0x2	T49.0x3	T49.0x4	T49.0x5	T49.0x6
Celiprolol	T44.7x1	T44.7x2	T44.7x3	T44.7x4	T44.7x5	T44.7x6
Cellosolve	T52.91	T52.92	T52.93	T52.94	—	—
Cell stimulants and proliferants	T49.8x1	T49.8x2	T49.8x3	T49.8x4	T49.8x5	T49.8x6
Cellulose						
cathartic	T47.4x1	T47.4x2	T47.4x3	T47.4x4	T47.4x5	T47.4x6
hydroxyethyl	T47.4x1	T47.4x2	T47.4x3	T47.4x4	T47.4x5	T47.4x6
nitrates (topical)	T49.3x1	T49.3x2	T49.3x3	T49.3x4	T49.3x5	T49.3x6
oxidized	T49.4x1	T49.4x2	T49.4x3	T49.4x4	T49.4x5	T49.4x6
Centipede (bite)	T63.411	T63.412	T63.413	T63.414	—	—
Central nervous system						
depressants	T41.201	T41.202	T41.203	T41.204	T41.205	T41.206
anesthetic (general) NEC	T41.201	T41.202	T41.203	T41.204	T41.205	T41.206
gases NEC	T41.0x1	T41.0x2	T41.0x3	T41.0x4	T41.0x5	T41.0x6
intravenous	T41.1x1	T41.1x2	T41.1x3	T41.1x4	T41.1x5	T41.1x6
barbiturates	T42.3x1	T42.3x2	T42.3x3	T42.3x4	T42.3x5	T42.3x6
benzodiazepines	T42.4x1	T42.4x2	T42.4x3	T42.4x4	T42.4x5	T42.4x6
bromides	T42.6x1	T42.6x2	T42.6x3	T42.6x4	T42.6x5	T42.6x6
cannabis sativa	T40.7x1	T40.7x2	T40.7x3	T40.7x4	T40.7x5	T40.7x6
chloral hydrate	T42.6x1	T42.6x2	T42.6x3	T42.6x4	T42.6x5	T42.6x6
ethanol	T51.0x1	T51.0x2	T51.0x3	T51.0x4	—	—
hallucinogenics	T40.901	T40.902	T40.903	T40.904	T40.905	T40.906
hypnotics	T42.71	T42.72	T42.73	T42.74	T42.75	T42.76
specified NEC	T42.6x1	T42.6x2	T42.6x3	T42.6x4	T42.6x5	T42.6x6

Substance	External Cause (T-Code)					
	Poisoning, Accidental (Unintentional)	Poisoning, Intentional Self-Harm	Poisoning, Assault	Poisoning, Undetermined	Adverse Effect	Underdosing
Central nervous system *(Continued)*						
depressants *(Continued)*						
muscle relaxants	T42.8x1	T42.8x2	T42.8x3	T42.8x4	T42.8x5	T42.8x6
paraldehyde	T42.6x1	T42.6x2	T42.6x3	T42.6x4	T42.6x5	T42.6x6
sedatives; sedative-hypnotics	T42.71	T42.72	T42.73	T42.74	T42.75	T42.76
mixed NEC	T42.71	T42.72	T42.73	T42.74	T42.75	T42.76
specified NEC	T42.6x1	T42.6x2	T42.6x3	T42.6x4	T42.6x5	T42.6x6
muscle-tone depressants	T42.8x1	T42.8x2	T42.8x3	T42.8x4	T42.8x5	T42.8x6
stimulants	T43.601	T43.602	T43.603	T43.604	T43.605	T43.606
amphetamines	T43.621	T43.622	T43.623	T43.624	T43.625	T43.626
analeptics	T50.7x1	T50.7x2	T50.7x3	T50.7x4	T50.7x5	T50.7x6
antidepressants	T43.201	T43.202	T43.203	T43.204	T43.205	T43.206
opiate antagonists	T50.7x1	T50.7x2	T50.7x3	T50.7x4	T50.7x5	T50.7x6
specified NEC	T43.691	T43.692	T43.693	T43.694	T43.695	T43.696
Cephalexin	T36.1x1	T36.1x2	T36.1x3	T36.1x4	T36.1x5	T36.1x6
Cephaloglycin	T36.1x1	T36.1x2	T36.1x3	T36.1x4	T36.1x5	T36.1x6
Cephaloridine	T36.1x1	T36.1x2	T36.1x3	T36.1x4	T36.1x5	T36.1x6
Cephalosporins	T36.1x1	T36.1x2	T36.1x3	T36.1x4	T36.1x5	T36.1x6
N (adicillin)	T36.0x1	T36.0x2	T36.0x3	T36.0x4	T36.0x5	T36.0x6
Cephalothin	T36.1x1	T36.1x2	T36.1x3	T36.1x4	T36.1x5	T36.1x6
Cephalotin	T36.1x1	T36.1x2	T36.1x3	T36.1x4	T36.1x5	T36.1x6
Cephradine	T36.1x1	T36.1x2	T36.1x3	T36.1x4	T36.1x5	T36.1x6
Cerbera (odallam)	T62.2x1	T62.2x2	T62.2x3	T62.2x4	—	—
Cerberin	T46.0x1	T46.0x2	T46.0x3	T46.0x4	T46.0x5	T46.0x6
Cerebral stimulants	T43.601	T43.602	T43.603	T43.604	T43.605	T43.606
psychotherapeutic	T43.601	T43.602	T43.603	T43.604	T43.605	T43.606
specified NEC	T43.691	T43.692	T43.693	T43.694	T43.695	T43.696
Cerium oxalate	T45.0x1	T45.0x2	T45.0x3	T45.0x4	T45.0x5	T45.0x6
Cerous oxalate	T45.0x1	T45.0x2	T45.0x3	T45.0x4	T45.0x5	T45.0x6
Ceruletide	T50.8x1	T50.8x2	T50.8x3	T50.8x4	T50.8x5	T50.8x6
Cetalkonium (chloride)	T49.0x1	T49.0x2	T49.0x3	T49.0x4	T49.0x5	T49.0x6
Cethexonium chloride	T49.0x1	T49.0x2	T49.0x3	T49.0x4	T49.0x5	T49.0x6
Cetiedil	T46.7x1	T46.7x2	T46.7x3	T46.7x4	T46.7x5	T46.7x6
Cetirizine	T45.0x1	T45.0x2	T45.0x3	T45.0x4	T45.0x5	T45.0x6
Cetomacrogol	T50.991	T50.992	T50.993	T50.994	T50.995	T50.996
Cetotiamine	T45.2x1	T45.2x2	T45.2x3	T45.2x4	T45.2x5	T45.2x6
Cetoxime	T45.0x1	T45.0x2	T45.0x3	T45.0x4	T45.0x5	T45.0x6
Cetraxate	T47.1x1	T47.1x2	T47.1x3	T47.1x4	T47.1x5	T47.1x6
Cetrimide	T49.0x1	T49.0x2	T49.0x3	T49.0x4	T49.0x5	T49.0x6
Cetrimonium (bromide)	T49.0x1	T49.0x2	T49.0x3	T49.0x4	T49.0x5	T49.0x6

Substance	External Cause (T-Code)					
	Poisoning, Accidental (Unintentional)	Poisoning, Intentional Self-Harm	Poisoning, Assault	Poisoning, Undetermined	Adverse Effect	Underdosing
Cetylpyridinium chloride	T49.0x1	T49.0x2	T49.0x3	T49.0x4	T49.0x5	T49.0x6
ENT agent	T49.6x1	T49.6x2	T49.6x3	T49.6x4	T49.6x5	T49.6x6
lozenges	T49.6x1	T49.6x2	T49.6x3	T49.6x4	T49.6x5	T49.6x6
Cevadillasee Sabadilla						
Cevitamic acid	T45.2x1	T45.2x2	T45.2x3	T45.2x4	T45.2x5	T45.2x6
Chalk, precipitated	T47.1x1	T47.1x2	T47.1x3	T47.1x4	T47.1x5	T47.1x6
Chamomile	T49.0x1	T49.0x2	T49.0x3	T49.0x4	T49.0x5	T49.0x6
Ch'an su	T46.0x1	T46.0x2	T46.0x3	T46.0x4	T46.0x5	T46.0x6
Charcoal	T47.6x1	T47.6x2	T47.6x3	T47.6x4	T47.6x5	T47.6x6
activated	T47.6x1	T47.6x2	T47.6x3	T47.6x4	T47.6x5	T47.6x6
fumes (Carbon monoxide)	T58.2x1	T58.2x2	T58.2x3	T58.2x4	—	—
industrial	T58.8x1	T58.8x2	T58.8x3	T58.8x4	—	—
medicinal (activated)	T47.8x1	T47.8x2	T47.8x3	T47.8x4	T47.8x5	T47.8x6
Chaulmosulfone	T37.1x1	T37.1x2	T37.1x3	T37.1x4	T37.1x5	T37.1x6
Chelating agent NEC	T50.6x1	T50.6x2	T50.6x3	T50.6x4	T50.6x5	T50.6x6
Chelidonium majus	T62.2x1	T62.2x2	T62.2x3	T62.2x4	—	—
Chemical substance NEC	T65.91	T65.92	T65.93	T65.94	—	—
Chenodeoxycholic acid	T47.5x1	T47.5x2	T47.5x3	T47.5x4	T47.5x5	T47.5x6
Chenodiol	T47.5x1	T47.5x2	T47.5x3	T47.5x4	T47.5x5	T47.5x6
Chenopodium	T37.4x1	T37.4x2	T37.4x3	T37.4x4	T37.4x5	T37.4x6
Cherry laurel	T62.2x1	T62.2x2	T62.2x3	T62.2x4	—	—
Chinidin(e)	T46.2x1	T46.2x2	T46.2x3	T46.2x4	T46.2x5	T46.2x6
Chiniofon	T37.8x1	T37.8x2	T37.8x3	T37.8x4	T37.8x5	T37.8x6
Chlophedianol	T48.3x1	T48.3x2	T48.3x3	T48.3x4	T48.3x5	T48.3x6
Chloral (betaine) (formamide) (hydrate)	T42.6x1	T42.6x2	T42.6x3	T42.6x4	T42.6x5	T42.6x6
Chloral	T42.6x1	T42.6x2	T42.6x3	T42.6x4	T42.6x5	T42.6x6
derivative	T42.6x1	T42.6x2	T42.6x3	T42.6x4	T42.6x5	T42.6x6
hydrate	T42.6x1	T42.6x2	T42.6x3	T42.6x4	T42.6x5	T42.6x6
Chloralamide	T42.6x1	T42.6x2	T42.6x3	T42.6x4	T42.6x5	T42.6x6
Chloralodol	T42.6x1	T42.6x2	T42.6x3	T42.6x4	T42.6x5	T42.6x6
Chloralose	T60.4x1	T60.4x2	T60.4x3	T60.4x4	—	—
Chlorambucil	T45.1x1	T45.1x2	T45.1x3	T45.1x4	T45.1x5	T45.1x6
Chloramine (-T)	T49.0x1	T49.0x2	T49.0x3	T49.0x4	T49.0x5	T49.0x6
Chloramphenicol	T36.2x1	T36.2x2	T36.2x3	T36.2x4	T36.2x5	T36.2x6
ENT agent	T49.6x1	T49.6x2	T49.6x3	T49.6x4	T49.6x5	T49.6x6
ophthalmic preparation	T49.5x1	T49.5x2	T49.5x3	T49.5x4	T49.5x5	T49.5x6
topical NEC	T49.0x1	T49.0x2	T49.0x3	T49.0x4	T49.0x5	T49.0x6
Chloramphencolum	T36.2x1	T36.2x2	T36.2x3	T36.2x4	T36.2x5	T36.2x6
Chlorate (potassium) (sodium) NEC	T60.3x1	T60.3x2	T60.3x3	T60.3x4	—	—
herbicide	T60.3x1	T60.3x2	T60.3x3	T60.3x4	—	—

Substance	Poisoning, Accidental (Unintentional)	Poisoning, Intentional Self-Harm	Poisoning, Assault	Poisoning, Undetermined	Adverse Effect	Underdosing
	External Cause (T-Code)					
Chlorazanil	T50.2x1	T50.2x2	T50.2x3	T50.2x4	T50.2x5	T50.2x6
Chlorbenzene, chlorbenzol	T53.7x1	T53.7x2	T53.7x3	T53.7x4	—	—
Chlorbenzoxamine	T44.3x1	T44.3x2	T44.3x3	T44.3x4	T44.3x5	T44.3x6
Chlorbutol	T42.6x1	T42.6x2	T42.6x3	T42.6x4	T42.6x5	T42.6x6
Chlorcyclizine	T45.0x1	T45.0x2	T45.0x3	T45.0x4	T45.0x5	T45.0x6
Chlordan(e) (dust)	T60.1x1	T60.1x2	T60.1x3	T60.1x4	—	—
Chlordantoin	T49.0x1	T49.0x2	T49.0x3	T49.0x4	T49.0x5	T49.0x6
Chlordiazepoxide	T42.4x1	T42.4x2	T42.4x3	T42.4x4	T42.4x5	T42.4x6
Chlordiethyl benzamide	T49.3x1	T49.3x2	T49.3x3	T49.3x4	T49.3x5	T49.3x6
Chloresium	T49.8x1	T49.8x2	T49.8x3	T49.8x4	T49.8x5	T49.8x6
Chlorethiazol	T42.6x1	T42.6x2	T42.6x3	T42.6x4	T42.6x5	T42.6x6
Chlorethyl - see Ethyl chloride						
Chloretone	T42.6x1	T42.6x2	T42.6x3	T42.6x4	T42.6x5	T42.6x6
Chlorex	T53.6x1	T53.6x2	T53.6x3	T53.6x4	—	—
insecticide	T60.1x1	T60.1x2	T60.1x3	T60.1x4	—	—
Chlorfenvinphos	T60.0x1	T60.0x2	T60.0x3	T60.0x4	—	—
Chlorhexadol	T42.6x1	T42.6x2	T42.6x3	T42.6x4	T42.6x5	T42.6x6
Chlorhexamide	T45.1x1	T45.1x2	T45.1x3	T45.1x4	T45.1x5	T45.1x6
Chlorhexidine	T49.0x1	T49.0x2	T49.0x3	T49.0x4	T49.0x5	T49.0x6
Chlorhydroxyquinolin	T49.0x1	T49.0x2	T49.0x3	T49.0x4	T49.0x5	T49.0x6
Chloride of lime (bleach)	T54.3x1	T54.3x2	T54.3x3	T54.3x4	—	—
Chlorimipramine	T43.011	T43.012	T43.013	T43.014	T43.015	T43.016
Chlorinated						
camphene	T53.6x1	T53.6x2	T53.6x3	T53.6x4	—	—
diphenyl	T53.7x1	T53.7x2	T53.7x3	T53.7x4	—	—
hydrocarbons NEC	T53.91	T53.92	T53.93	T53.94	—	—
solvents	T53.91	T53.92	T53.93	T53.94	—	—
lime (bleach)	T54.3x1	T54.3x2	T54.3x3	T54.3x4	—	—
and boric acid solution	T49.0x1	T49.0x2	T49.0x3	T49.0x4	T49.0x5	T49.0x6
naphthalene (insecticide)	T60.1x1	T60.1x2	T60.1x3	T60.1x4	—	—
industrial (non-pesticide)	T53.7x1	T53.7x2	T53.7x3	T53.7x4	—	—
pesticide NEC	T60.8x1	T60.8x2	T60.8x3	T60.8x4	—	—
soda - see also sodium hypochlorite						
solution	T49.0x1	T49.0x2	T49.0x3	T49.0x4	T49.0x5	T49.0x6
Chlorine (fumes) (gas)	T59.4x1	T59.4x2	T59.4x3	T59.4x4	—	—
bleach	T54.3x1	T54.3x2	T54.3x3	T54.3x4	—	—
compound gas NEC	T59.4x1	T59.4x2	T59.4x3	T59.4x4	—	—
disinfectant	T59.4x1	T59.4x2	T59.4x3	T59.4x4	—	—
releasing agents NEC	T59.4x1	T59.4x2	T59.4x3	T59.4x4	—	—
Chlorisondamine chloride	T46.991	T46.992	T46.993	T46.994	T46.995	T46.996

Substance	External Cause (T-Code)					
	Poisoning, Accidental (Unintentional)	Poisoning, Intentional Self-Harm	Poisoning, Assault	Poisoning, Undetermined	Adverse Effect	Underdosing
Chlormadinone	T38.5x1	T38.5x2	T38.5x3	T38.5x4	T38.5x5	T38.5x6
Chlormephos	T60.0x1	T60.0x2	T60.0x3	T60.0x4	—	—
Chlormerodrin	T50.2x1	T50.2x2	T50.2x3	T50.2x4	T50.2x5	T50.2x6
Chlormethiazole	T42.6x1	T42.6x2	T42.6x3	T42.6x4	T42.6x5	T42.6x6
Chlormethine	T45.1x1	T45.1x2	T45.1x3	T45.1x4	T45.1x5	T45.1x6
Chlormethylenecycline	T36.4x1	T36.4x2	T36.4x3	T36.4x4	T36.4x5	T36.4x6
Chlormezanone	T42.6x1	T42.6x2	T42.6x3	T42.6x4	T42.6x5	T42.6x6
Chloroacetic acid	T60.3x1	T60.3x2	T60.3x3	T60.3x4	—	—
Chloroacetone	T59.3x1	T59.3x2	T59.3x3	T59.3x4	—	—
Chloroacetophenone	T59.3x1	T59.3x2	T59.3x3	T59.3x4	—	—
Chloroaniline	T53.7x1	T53.7x2	T53.7x3	T53.7x4	—	—
Chlorobenzene, chlorobenzol	T53.7x1	T53.7x2	T53.7x3	T53.7x4	—	—
Chlorobromomethane (fire extinguisher)	T53.6x1	T53.6x2	T53.6x3	T53.6x4	—	—
Chlorobutanol	T49.0x1	T49.0x2	T49.0x3	T49.0x4	T49.0x5	T49.0x6
Chlorocresol	T49.0x1	T49.0x2	T49.0x3	T49.0x4	T49.0x5	T49.0x6
Chlorodehydro-methyltestosterone	T38.7x1	T38.7x2	T38.7x3	T38.7x4	T38.7x5	T38.7x6
Chlorodinitrobenzene	T53.7x1	T53.7x2	T53.7x3	T53.7x4	—	—
dust or vapor	T53.7x1	T53.7x2	T53.7x3	T53.7x4	—	—
Chlorodiphenyl	T53.7x1	T53.7x2	T53.7x3	T53.7x4	—	—
Chloroethane - *see* Ethyl chloride						
Chloroethylene	T53.6x1	T53.6x2	T53.6x3	T53.6x4	—	—
Chlorofluorocarbons	T53.5x1	T53.5x2	T53.5x3	T53.5x4	—	—
Chloroform (fumes) (vapor)	T53.1x1	T53.1x2	T53.1x3	T53.1x4	—	—
anesthetic	T41.0x1	T41.0x2	T41.0x3	T41.0x4	T41.0x5	T41.0x6
solvent	T53.1x1	T53.1x2	T53.1x3	T53.1x4	—	—
water, concentrated	T41.0x1	T41.0x2	T41.0x3	T41.0x4	T41.0x5	T41.0x6
Chloroguanide	T37.2x1	T37.2x2	T37.2x3	T37.2x4	T37.2x5	T37.2x6
Chloromycetin	T36.2x1	T36.2x2	T36.2x3	T36.2x4	T36.2x5	T36.2x6
ENT agent	T49.6x1	T49.6x2	T49.6x3	T49.6x4	T49.6x5	T49.6x6
ophthalmic preparation	T49.5x1	T49.5x2	T49.5x3	T49.5x4	T49.5x5	T49.5x6
otic solution	T49.6x1	T49.6x2	T49.6x3	T49.6x4	T49.6x5	T49.6x6
topical NEC	T49.0x1	T49.0x2	T49.0x3	T49.0x4	T49.0x5	T49.0x6
Chloronitrobenzene	T53.7x1	T53.7x2	T53.7x3	T53.7x4	—	—
dust or vapor	T53.7x1	T53.7x2	T53.7x3	T53.7x4	—	—
Chlorophacinone	T60.4x1	T60.4x2	T60.4x3	T60.4x4	—	—
Chlorophenol	T53.7x1	T53.7x2	T53.7x3	T53.7x4	—	—
Chlorophenothane	T60.1x1	T60.1x2	T60.1x3	T60.1x4	—	—
Chlorophyll	T50.991	T50.992	T50.993	T50.994	T50.995	T50.996
Chloropicrin (fumes)	T53.6x1	T53.6x2	T53.6x3	T53.6x4	—	—
fumigant	T60.8x1	T60.8x2	T60.8x3	T60.8x4	—	—

Substance	External Cause (T-Code)					
	Poisoning, Accidental (Unintentional)	Poisoning, Intentional Self-Harm	Poisoning, Assault	Poisoning, Undetermined	Adverse Effect	Underdosing
Chloropicrin *(Continued)*						
fungicide	T60.3x1	T60.3x2	T60.3x3	T60.3x4	—	—
pesticide	T60.8x1	T60.8x2	T60.8x3	T60.8x4	—	—
Chloroprocaine	T41.3x1	T41.3x2	T41.3x3	T41.3x4	T41.3x5	T41.3x6
infiltration (subcutaneous)	T41.3x1	T41.3x2	T41.3x3	T41.3x4	T41.3x5	T41.3x6
nerve block (peripheral) (plexus)	T41.3x1	T41.3x2	T41.3x3	T41.3x4	T41.3x5	T41.3x6
spinal	T41.3x1	T41.3x2	T41.3x3	T41.3x4	T41.3x5	T41.3x6
Chloroptic	T49.5x1	T49.5x2	T49.5x3	T49.5x4	T49.5x5	T49.5x6
Chloropurine	T45.1x1	T45.1x2	T45.1x3	T45.1x4	T45.1x5	T45.1x6
Chloropyramine	T45.0x1	T45.0x2	T45.0x3	T45.0x4	T45.0x5	T45.0x6
Chloropyrifos	T60.0x1	T60.0x2	T60.0x3	T60.0x4	—	—
Chloropyrilene	T45.0x1	T45.0x2	T45.0x3	T45.0x4	T45.0x5	T45.0x6
Chloroquine	T37.2x1	T37.2x2	T37.2x3	T37.2x4	T37.2x5	T37.2x6
Chlorothalonil	T60.3x1	T60.3x2	T60.3x3	T60.3x4	—	—
Chlorothen	T45.0x1	T45.0x2	T45.0x3	T45.0x4	T45.0x5	T45.0x6
Chlorothiazide	T50.2x1	T50.2x2	T50.2x3	T50.2x4	T50.2x5	T50.2x6
Chlorothymol	T49.4x1	T49.4x2	T49.4x3	T49.4x4	T49.4x5	T49.4x6
Chlorotrianisene	T38.5x1	T38.5x2	T38.5x3	T38.5x4	T38.5x5	T38.5x6
Chlorovinyldichloro-arsine, not in war	T57.0x1	T57.0x2	T57.0x3	T57.0x4	—	—
Chloroxine	T49.4x1	T49.4x2	T49.4x3	T49.4x4	T49.4x5	T49.4x6
Chloroxylenol	T49.0x1	T49.0x2	T49.0x3	T49.0x4	T49.0x5	T49.0x6
Chlorphenamine	T45.0x1	T45.0x2	T45.0x3	T45.0x4	T45.0x5	T45.0x6
Chlorphenesin	T42.8x1	T42.8x2	T42.8x3	T42.8x4	T42.8x5	T42.8x6
topical (antifungal)	T49.0x1	T49.0x2	T49.0x3	T49.0x4	T49.0x5	T49.0x6
Chlorpheniramine	T45.0x1	T45.0x2	T45.0x3	T45.0x4	T45.0x5	T45.0x6
Chlorphenoxamine	T45.0x1	T45.0x2	T45.0x3	T45.0x4	T45.0x5	T45.0x6
Chlorphentermine	T50.5x1	T50.5x2	T50.5x3	T50.5x4	T50.5x5	T50.5x6
Chlorprocaine - *see* Chloroprocaine						
Chlorproguanil	T37.2x1	T37.2x2	T37.2x3	T37.2x4	T37.2x5	T37.2x6
Chlorpromazine	T43.3x1	T43.3x2	T43.3x3	T43.3x4	T43.3x5	T43.3x6
Chlorpropamide	T38.3x1	T38.3x2	T38.3x3	T38.3x4	T38.3x5	T38.3x6
Chlorprothixene	T43.4x1	T43.4x2	T43.4x3	T43.4x4	T43.4x5	T43.4x6
Chlorquinaldol	T49.0x1	T49.0x2	T49.0x3	T49.0x4	T49.0x5	T49.0x6
Chlorquinol	T49.0x1	T49.0x2	T49.0x3	T49.0x4	T49.0x5	T49.0x6
Chlortalidone	T50.2x1	T50.2x2	T50.2x3	T50.2x4	T50.2x5	T50.2x6
Chlortetracycline	T36.4x1	T36.4x2	T36.4x3	T36.4x4	T36.4x5	T36.4x6
Chlorthalidone	T50.2x1	T50.2x2	T50.2x3	T50.2x4	T50.2x5	T50.2x6
Chlorthiophos	T60.0x1	T60.0x2	T60.0x3	T60.0x4	—	—
Chlorotrianisene	T38.5x1	T38.5x2	T38.5x3	T38.5x4	T38.5x5	T38.5x6
Chlor-Trimeton	T45.0x1	T45.0x2	T45.0x3	T45.0x4	T45.0x5	T45.0x6

Substance	External Cause (T-Code)					
	Poisoning, Accidental (Unintentional)	Poisoning, Intentional Self-Harm	Poisoning, Assault	Poisoning, Undetermined	Adverse Effect	Underdosing
Chlorthion	T60.0x1	T60.0x2	T60.0x3	T60.0x4	—	—
Chlorzoxazone	T42.8x1	T42.8x2	T42.8x3	T42.8x4	T42.8x5	T42.8x6
Choke damp	T59.7x1	T59.7x2	T59.7x3	T59.7x4	—	—
Cholagogues	T47.5x1	T47.5x2	T47.5x3	T47.5x4	T47.5x5	T47.5x6
Cholebrine	T50.8x1	T50.8x2	T50.8x3	T50.8x4	T50.8x5	T50.8x6
Cholecalciferol	T45.2x1	T45.2x2	T45.2x3	T45.2x4	T45.2x5	T45.2x6
Cholecystokinin	T50.8x1	T50.8x2	T50.8x3	T50.8x4	T50.8x5	T50.8x6
Cholera vaccine	T50.A91	T50.A92	T50.A93	T50.A94	T50.A95	T50.A96
Choleretic	T47.5x1	T47.5x2	T47.5x3	T47.5x4	T47.5x5	T47.5x6
Cholesterol-lowering agents	T46.6x1	T46.6x2	T46.6x3	T46.6x4	T46.6x5	T46.6x6
Cholestyramine (resin)	T46.6x1	T46.6x2	T46.6x3	T46.6x4	T46.6x5	T46.6x6
Cholic acid	T47.5x1	T47.5x2	T47.5x3	T47.5x4	T47.5x5	T47.5x6
Choline	T48.6x1	T48.6x2	T48.6x3	T48.6x4	T48.6x5	T48.6x6
chloride	T50.991	T50.992	T50.993	T50.994	T50.995	T50.996
dihydrogen citrate	T50.991	T50.992	T50.993	T50.994	T50.995	T50.996
salicylate	T39.091	T39.092	T39.093	T39.094	T39.095	T39.096
theophyllinate	T48.6x1	T48.6x2	T48.6x3	T48.6x4	T48.6x5	T48.6x6
Cholinergic (drug) NEC	T44.1x1	T44.1x2	T44.1x3	T44.1x4	T44.1x5	T44.1x6
muscle tone enhancer	T44.1x1	T44.1x2	T44.1x3	T44.1x4	T44.1x5	T44.1x6
organophosphorus	T44.0x1	T44.0x2	T44.0x3	T44.0x4	T44.0x5	T44.0x6
insecticide	T60.0x1	T60.0x2	T60.0x3	T60.0x4	—	—
nerve gas	T59.891	T59.892	T59.893	T59.894	—	—
trimethyl ammonium propanediol	T44.1x1	T44.1x2	T44.1x3	T44.1x4	T44.1x5	T44.1x6
Cholinesterase reactivator	T50.6x1	T50.6x2	T50.6x3	T50.6x4	T50.6x5	T50.6x6
Cholografin	T50.8x1	T50.8x2	T50.8x3	T50.8x4	T50.8x5	T50.8x6
Chorionic gonadotropin	T38.891	T38.892	T38.893	T38.894	T38.895	T38.896
Chromate	T56.2x1	T56.2x2	T56.2x3	T56.2x4	—	—
dust or mist	T56.2x1	T56.2x2	T56.2x3	T56.2x4	—	—
lead (see also lead)	T56.0x1	T56.0x2	T56.0x3	T56.0x4	—	—
paint	T56.0x1	T56.0x2	T56.0x3	T56.0x4	—	—
Chromic						
acid	T56.2x1	T56.2x2	T56.2x3	T56.2x4	—	—
dust or mist	T56.2x1	T56.2x2	T56.2x3	T56.2x4	—	—
phosphate 32P	T45.1x1	T45.1x2	T45.1x3	T45.1x4	T45.1x5	T45.1x6
Chromium	T56.2x1	T56.2x2	T56.2x3	T56.2x4	—	—
compounds - see Chromate						
sesquioxide	T50.8x1	T50.8x2	T50.8x3	T50.8x4	T50.8x5	T50.8x6
Chromomycin A3	T45.1x1	T45.1x2	T45.1x3	T45.1x4	T45.1x5	T45.1x6
Chromonar	T46.3x1	T46.3x2	T46.3x3	T46.3x4	T46.3x5	T46.3x6
Chromyl chloride	T56.2x1	T56.2x2	T56.2x3	T56.2x4	—	—

Substance	Poisoning, Accidental (Unintentional)	Poisoning, Intentional Self-Harm	Poisoning, Assault	Poisoning, Undetermined	Adverse Effect	Underdosing
			External Cause (T-Code)			
Chrysarobin	T49.4x1	T49.4x2	T49.4x3	T49.4x4	T49.4x5	T49.4x6
Chrysazin	T47.2x1	T47.2x2	T47.2x3	T47.2x4	T47.2x5	T47.2x6
Chymar	T45.3x1	T45.3x2	T45.3x3	T45.3x4	T45.3x5	T45.3x6
ophthalmic preparation	T49.5x1	T49.5x2	T49.5x3	T49.5x4	T49.5x5	T49.5x6
Chymopapain	T45.3x1	T45.3x2	T45.3x3	T45.3x4	T45.3x5	T45.3x6
Chymotrypsin	T45.3x1	T45.3x2	T45.3x3	T45.3x4	T45.3x5	T45.3x6
ophthalmic preparation	T49.5x1	T49.5x2	T49.5x3	T49.5x4	T49.5x5	T49.5x6
Cianidanol	T50.991	T50.992	T50.993	T50.994	T50.995	T50.996
Cianopramine	T43.011	T43.012	T43.013	T43.014	T43.015	T43.016
Cibenzoline	T46.2x1	T46.2x2	T46.2x3	T46.2x4	T46.2x5	T46.2x6
Ciclacillin	T36.0x1	T36.0x2	T36.0x3	T36.0x4	T36.0x5	T36.0x6
Ciclobarbital - see Hexobarbital						
Ciclonicate	T46.7x1	T46.7x2	T46.7x3	T46.7x4	T46.7x5	T46.7x6
Ciclopirox (olamine)	T49.0x1	T49.0x2	T49.0x3	T49.0x4	T49.0x5	T49.0x6
Ciclosporin	T45.1x1	T45.1x2	T45.1x3	T45.1x4	T45.1x5	T45.1x6
Cicuta maculata or virosa	T62.2x1	T62.2x2	T62.2x3	T62.2x4	—	—
Cicutoxin	T62.2x1	T62.2x2	T62.2x3	T62.2x4	—	—
Cigarette lighter fluid	T52.0x1	T52.0x2	T52.0x3	T52.0x4	—	—
Cigarettes (tobacco)	T65.221	T65.222	T65.223	T65.224	—	—
Ciguatoxin	T61.01	T61.02	T61.03	T61.04	—	—
Cilazapril	T46.4x1	T46.4x2	T46.4x3	T46.4x4	T46.4x5	T46.4x6
Cimetidine	T47.0x1	T47.0x2	T47.0x3	T47.0x4	T47.0x5	T47.0x6
Cimetropium bromide	T44.3x1	T44.3x2	T44.3x3	T44.3x4	T44.3x5	T44.3x6
Cinchocaine	T41.3x1	T41.3x2	T41.3x3	T41.3x4	T41.3x5	T41.3x6
topical (surface)	T41.3x1	T41.3x2	T41.3x3	T41.3x4	T41.3x5	T41.3x6
Cinchona	T37.2x1	T37.2x2	T37.2x3	T37.2x4	T37.2x5	T37.2x6
Cinchonine alkaloids	T37.2x1	T37.2x2	T37.2x3	T37.2x4	T37.2x5	T37.2x6
Cinchophen	T50.4x1	T50.4x2	T50.4x3	T50.4x4	T50.4x5	T50.4x6
Cinepazide	T46.7x1	T46.7x2	T46.7x3	T46.7x4	T46.7x5	T46.7x6
Cinnamedrine	T48.5x1	T48.5x2	T48.5x3	T48.5x4	T48.5x5	T48.5x6
Cinnarizine	T45.0x1	T45.0x2	T45.0x3	T45.0x4	T45.0x5	T45.0x6
Cinoxacin	T37.8x1	T37.8x2	T37.8x3	T37.8x4	T37.8x5	T37.8x6
Ciprofibrate	T46.6x1	T46.6x2	T46.6x3	T46.6x4	T46.6x5	T46.6x6
Ciprofloxacin	T36.8x1	T36.8x2	T36.8x3	T36.8x4	T36.8x5	T36.8x6
Cisapride	T47.8x1	T47.8x2	T47.8x3	T47.8x4	T47.8x5	T47.8x6
Cisplatin	T45.1x1	T45.1x2	T45.1x3	T45.1x4	T45.1x5	T45.1x6
Citalopram	T43.221	T43.222	T43.223	T43.224	T43.225	T43.226
Citanest	T41.3x1	T41.3x2	T41.3x3	T41.3x4	T41.3x5	T41.3x6
infiltration (subcutaneous)	T41.3x1	T41.3x2	T41.3x3	T41.3x4	T41.3x5	T41.3x6
nerve block (peripheral) (plexus)	T41.3x1	T41.3x2	T41.3x3	T41.3x4	T41.3x5	T41.3x6
Citric acid	T47.5x1	T47.5x2	T47.5x3	T47.5x4	T47.5x5	T47.5x6

Substance	Poisoning, Accidental (Unintentional)	Poisoning, Intentional Self-Harm	Poisoning, Assault	Poisoning, Undetermined	Adverse Effect	Underdosing
Citrovorum (factor)	T45.8x1	T45.8x2	T45.8x3	T45.8x4	T45.8x5	T45.8x6
Claviceps purpurea	T62.2x1	T62.2x2	T62.2x3	T62.2x4	—	—
Clavulanic acid	T36.1x1	T36.1x2	T36.1x3	T36.1x4	T36.1x5	T36.1x6
Cleaner, cleansing agent NEC	T52.91	T52.92	T52.93	T52.94	—	—
of paint or varnish	T52.91	T52.92	T52.93	T52.94	—	—
Clebopride	T47.8x1	T47.8x2	T47.8x3	T47.8x4	T47.8x5	T47.8x6
Clefamide	T37.3x1	T37.3x2	T37.3x3	T37.3x4	T37.3x5	T37.3x6
Clemastine	T45.0x1	T45.0x2	T45.0x3	T45.0x4	T45.0x5	T45.0x6
Clematis vitalba	T62.2x1	T62.2x2	T62.2x3	T62.2x4	—	—
Clemizole	T45.0x1	T45.0x2	T45.0x3	T45.0x4	T45.0x5	T45.0x6
penicillin	T36.0x1	T36.0x2	T36.0x3	T36.0x4	T36.0x5	T36.0x6
Clenbuterol	T48.6x1	T48.6x2	T48.6x3	T48.6x4	T48.6x5	T48.6x6
Clidinium bromide	T44.3x1	T44.3x2	T44.3x3	T44.3x4	T44.3x5	T44.3x6
Clindamycin	T36.8x1	T36.8x2	T36.8x3	T36.8x4	T36.8x5	T36.8x6
Clinofibrate	T46.6x1	T46.6x2	T46.6x3	T46.6x4	T46.6x5	T46.6x6
Clioquinol	T37.8x1	T37.8x2	T37.8x3	T37.8x4	T37.8x5	T37.8x6
Cliradon	T40.2x1	T40.2x2	T40.2x3	T40.2x4	T40.2x5	T40.2x6
Clobazam	T42.4x1	T42.4x2	T42.4x3	T42.4x4	T42.4x5	T42.4x6
Clobenzorex	T50.5x1	T50.5x2	T50.5x3	T50.5x4	T50.5x5	T50.5x6
Clobetasol	T49.0x1	T49.0x2	T49.0x3	T49.0x4	T49.0x5	T49.0x6
Clobetasone	T49.0x1	T49.0x2	T49.0x3	T49.0x4	T49.0x5	T49.0x6
Clobutinol	T48.3x1	T48.3x2	T48.3x3	T48.3x4	T48.3x5	T48.3x6
Clocapramine	T43.0x1	T43.0x2	T43.0x3	T43.0x4	T43.0x5	T43.0x6
Clocortolone	T38.0x1	T38.0x2	T38.0x3	T38.0x4	T38.0x5	T38.0x6
Clodantoin	T49.0x1	T49.0x2	T49.0x3	T49.0x4	T49.0x5	T49.0x6
Clodronic acid	T50.991	T50.992	T50.993	T50.994	T50.995	T50.996
Clofazimine	T37.1x1	T37.1x2	T37.1x3	T37.1x4	T37.1x5	T37.1x6
Clofedanol	T48.3x1	T48.3x2	T48.3x3	T48.3x4	T48.3x5	T48.3x6
Clofenamide	T50.2x1	T50.2x2	T50.2x3	T50.2x4	T50.2x5	T50.2x6
Clofenotane	T49.0x1	T49.0x2	T49.0x3	T49.0x4	T49.0x5	T49.0x6
Clofezone	T39.2x1	T39.2x2	T39.2x3	T39.2x4	T39.2x5	T39.2x6
Clofibrate	T46.6x1	T46.6x2	T46.6x3	T46.6x4	T46.6x5	T46.6x6
Clofibride	T46.6x1	T46.6x2	T46.6x3	T46.6x4	T46.6x5	T46.6x6
Cloforex	T50.5x1	T50.5x2	T50.5x3	T50.5x4	T50.5x5	T50.5x6
Clomacran	T43.0x1	T43.0x2	T43.0x3	T43.0x4	T43.0x5	T43.0x6
Clomethiazole	T42.6x1	T42.6x2	T42.6x3	T42.6x4	T42.6x5	T42.6x6
Clometocillin	T36.0x1	T36.0x2	T36.0x3	T36.0x4	T36.0x5	T36.0x6
Clomifene	T38.5x1	T38.5x2	T38.5x3	T38.5x4	T38.5x5	T38.5x6
Clomiphene	T38.5x1	T38.5x2	T38.5x3	T38.5x4	T38.5x5	T38.5x6
Clomipramine	T43.011	T43.012	T43.013	T43.014	T43.015	T43.016

	External Cause (T-Code)					
Substance	Poisoning, Accidental (Unintentional)	Poisoning, Intentional Self-Harm	Poisoning, Assault	Poisoning, Undetermined	Adverse Effect	Underdosing
Clomocycline	T36.4x1	T36.4x2	T36.4x3	T36.4x4	T36.4x5	T36.4x6
Clonazepam	T42.4x1	T42.4x2	T42.4x3	T42.4x4	T42.4x5	T42.4x6
Clonidine	T46.5x1	T46.5x2	T46.5x3	T46.5x4	T46.5x5	T46.5x6
Clonixin	T39.8x1	T39.8x2	T39.8x3	T39.8x4	T39.8x5	T39.8x6
Clopamide	T50.2x1	T50.2x2	T50.2x3	T50.2x4	T50.2x5	T50.2x6
Clopenthixol	T43.4x1	T43.4x2	T43.4x3	T43.4x4	T43.4x5	T43.4x6
Cloperastine	T48.3x1	T48.3x2	T48.3x3	T48.3x4	T48.3x5	T48.3x6
Clophedianol	T48.3x1	T48.3x2	T48.3x3	T48.3x4	T48.3x5	T48.3x6
Cloponone	T36.2x1	T36.2x2	T36.2x3	T36.2x4	T36.2x5	T36.2x6
Cloprednol	T38.0x1	T38.0x2	T38.0x3	T38.0x4	T38.0x5	T38.0x6
Cloral betaine	T42.6x1	T42.6x2	T42.6x3	T42.6x4	T42.6x5	T42.6x6
Cloramfenicol	T36.2x1	T36.2x2	T36.2x3	T36.2x4	T36.2x5	T36.2x6
Clorazepate (dipotassium)	T42.4x1	T42.4x2	T42.4x3	T42.4x4	T42.4x5	T42.4x6
Clorexolone	T50.2x1	T50.2x2	T50.2x3	T50.2x4	T50.2x5	T50.2x6
Clorox (bleach)	T54.91	T54.92	T54.93	T54.94	—	—
Clorfenamine	T45.0x1	T45.0x2	T45.0x3	T45.0x4	T45.0x5	T45.0x6
Clorgiline	T43.1x1	T43.1x2	T43.1x3	T43.1x4	T43.1x5	T43.1x6
Clorotepine	T44.3x1	T44.3x2	T44.3x3	T44.3x4	T44.3x5	T44.3x6
Clorprenaline	T48.6x1	T48.6x2	T48.6x3	T48.6x4	T48.6x5	T48.6x6
Clortermine	T50.5x1	T50.5x2	T50.5x3	T50.5x4	T50.5x5	T50.5x6
Clotiapine	T43.591	T43.592	T43.593	T43.594	T43.595	T43.596
Clotiazepam	T42.4x1	T42.4x2	T42.4x3	T42.4x4	T42.4x5	T42.4x6
Clotibric acid	T46.6x1	T46.6x2	T46.6x3	T46.6x4	T46.6x5	T46.6x6
Clotrimazole	T49.0x1	T49.0x2	T49.0x3	T49.0x4	T49.0x5	T49.0x6
Cloxacillin	T36.0x1	T36.0x2	T36.0x3	T36.0x4	T36.0x5	T36.0x6
Cloxazolam	T42.4x1	T42.4x2	T42.4x3	T42.4x4	T42.4x5	T42.4x6
Cloxiquine	T49.0x1	T49.0x2	T49.0x3	T49.0x4	T49.0x5	T49.0x6
Clozapine	T42.4x1	T42.4x2	T42.4x3	T42.4x4	T42.4x5	T42.4x6
Coagulant NEC	T45.7x1	T45.7x2	T45.7x3	T45.7x4	T45.7x5	T45.7x6
Coal (carbon monoxide from) - *see also* Carbon, monoxide, coal	T58.2x1	T58.2x2	T58.2x3	T58.2x4	—	—
oil - *see* Kerosene						
tar	T49.1x1	T49.1x2	T49.1x3	T49.1x4	T49.1x5	T49.1x6
fumes	T59.891	T59.892	T59.893	T59.894	—	—
medicinal (ointment)	T49.4x1	T49.4x2	T49.4x3	T49.4x4	T49.4x5	T49.4x6
analgesics NEC	T39.2x1	T39.2x2	T39.2x3	T39.2x4	T39.2x5	T39.2x6
naphtha (solvent)	T52.0x1	T52.0x2	T52.0x3	T52.0x4		
Cobalamine	T45.2x1	T45.2x2	T45.2x3	T45.2x4	T45.2x5	T45.2x6
Cobalt (nonmedicinal) (fumes) (industrial)	T56.891	T56.892	T56.893	T56.894		
medicinal (trace) (chloride)	T45.8x1	T45.8x2	T45.8x3	T45.8x4	T45.8x5	T45.8x6
Cobra (venom)	T63.041	T63.042	T63.043	T63.044		

TABLE OF DRUGS AND CHEMICALS

Substance	Poisoning, Accidental (Unintentional)	Poisoning, Intentional Self-Harm	Poisoning, Assault	Poisoning, Undetermined	Adverse Effect	Underdosing
Coca (leaf)	T43.621	T43.622	T43.623	T43.624	T43.625	T43.626
Cocaine	T40.5x1	T40.5x2	T40.5x3	T40.5x4	T40.5x5	T40.5x6
topical anesthetic	T41.3x1	T41.3x2	T41.3x3	T41.3x4	T41.3x5	T41.3x6
Cocarboxylase	T45.3x1	T45.3x2	T45.3x3	T45.3x4	T45.3x5	T45.3x6
Coccidioidin	T50.8x1	T50.8x2	T50.8x3	T50.8x4	T50.8x5	T50.8x6
Cocculus indicus	T62.1x1	T62.1x2	T62.1x3	T62.1x4		
Cochineal	T65.6x1	T65.6x2	T65.6x3	T65.6x4		
medicinal products	T50.991	T50.992	T50.993	T50.994	T50.995	T50.996
Codeine	T40.2x1	T40.2x2	T40.2x3	T40.2x4	T40.2x5	T40.2x6
Cod-liver oil	T45.2x1	T45.2x2	T45.2x3	T45.2x4	T45.2x5	T45.2x6
Coenzyme A	T50.991	T50.992	T50.993	T50.994	T50.995	T50.996
Coffee	T62.8x1	T62.8x2	T62.8x3	T62.8x4	—	—
Cogalactoisomerase	T50.991	T50.992	T50.993	T50.994	T50.995	T50.996
Cogentin	T44.3x1	T44.3x2	T44.3x3	T44.3x4	T44.3x5	T44.3x6
Coke fumes or gas (carbon monoxide)	T58.2x1	T58.2x2	T58.2x3	T58.2x4	—	—
industrial use	T58.8x1	T58.8x2	T58.8x3	T58.8x4	—	—
Colace	T47.4x1	T47.4x2	T47.4x3	T47.4x4	T47.4x5	T47.4x6
Colaspase	T45.1x1	T45.1x2	T45.1x3	T45.1x4	T45.1x5	T45.1x6
Colchicine	T50.4x1	T50.4x2	T50.4x3	T50.4x4	T50.4x5	T50.4x6
Colchicum	T62.2x1	T62.2x2	T62.2x3	T62.2x4	—	—
Cold cream	T49.3x1	T49.3x2	T49.3x3	T49.3x4	T49.3x5	T49.3x6
Colecalciferol	T45.2x1	T45.2x2	T45.2x3	T45.2x4	T45.2x5	T45.2x6
Colestipol	T46.6x1	T46.6x2	T46.6x3	T46.6x4	T46.6x5	T46.6x6
Colestyramine	T46.6x1	T46.6x2	T46.6x3	T46.6x4	T46.6x5	T46.6x6
Colimycin	T36.8x1	T36.8x2	T36.8x3	T36.8x4	T36.8x5	T36.8x6
Colistimethate	T36.8x1	T36.8x2	T36.8x3	T36.8x4	T36.8x5	T36.8x6
Colistin	T36.8x1	T36.8x2	T36.8x3	T36.8x4	T36.8x5	T36.8x6
sulfate (eye preparation)	T49.5x1	T49.5x2	T49.5x3	T49.5x4	T49.5x5	T49.5x6
Collagen	T50.991	T50.992	T50.993	T50.994	T50.995	T50.996
Collagenase	T49.4x1	T49.4x2	T49.4x3	T49.4x4	T49.4x5	T49.4x6
Collodion	T49.3x1	T49.3x2	T49.3x3	T49.3x4	T49.3x5	T49.3x6
Colocynth	T47.2x1	T47.2x2	T47.2x3	T47.2x4	T47.2x5	T47.2x6
Colophony adhesive	T49.3x1	T49.3x2	T49.3x3	T49.3x4	T49.3x5	T49.3x6
Colorant (see also Dye)	T50.991	T50.992	T50.993	T50.994	T50.995	T50.996
Coloring matter - see Dye(s)						
Combustion gas (after combustion) - see Carbon, monoxide						
prior to combustion	T59.891	T59.892	T59.893	T59.894	—	—
Compazine	T43.3x1	T43.3x2	T43.3x3	T43.3x4	T43.3x5	T43.3x6
Compound						
42 (warfarin)	T60.4x1	T60.4x2	T60.4x3	T60.4x4	—	—
269 (endrin)	T60.1x1	T60.1x2	T60.1x3	T60.1x4	—	—

Substance	External Cause (T-Code)					
	Poisoning, Accidental (Unintentional)	Poisoning, Intentional Self-Harm	Poisoning, Assault	Poisoning, Undetermined	Adverse Effect	Underdosing
Compound *(Continued)*						
497 (dieldrin)	T60.1x1	T60.1x2	T60.1x3	T60.1x4	—	—
L80 (sodium fluoroacetate)	T60.4x1	T60.4x2	T60.4x3	T60.4x4	—	—
3422 (parathion)	T60.0x1	T60.0x2	T60.0x3	T60.0x4	—	—
3911 (phorate)	T60.0x1	T60.0x2	T60.0x3	T60.0x4	—	—
3956 (toxaphene)	T60.1x1	T60.1x2	T60.1x3	T60.1x4	—	—
4049 (malathion)	T60.0x1	T60.0x2	T60.0x3	T60.0x4	—	—
4069 (malathion)	T60.0x1	T60.0x2	T60.0x3	T60.0x4	—	—
4124 (dicapthon)	T60.0x1	T60.0x2	T60.0x3	T60.0x4	—	—
E (cortisone)	T38.0x1	T38.0x2	T38.0x3	T38.0x4	T38.0x5	T38.0x6
F (hydrocortisone)	T38.0x1	T38.0x2	T38.0x3	T38.0x4	T38.0x5	T38.0x6
Congo red	T50.8x1	T50.8x2	T50.8x3	T50.8x4	T50.8x5	T50.8x6
Coniine, conine	T62.2x1	T62.2x2	T62.2x3	T62.2x4	—	—
Conium (maculatum)	T62.2x1	T62.2x2	T62.2x3	T62.2x4	—	—
Conjugated estrogenic substances	T38.5x1	T38.5x2	T38.5x3	T38.5x4	T38.5x5	T38.5x6
Contac	T48.5x1	T48.5x2	T48.5x3	T48.5x4	T48.5x5	T48.5x6
Contact lens solution	T49.5x1	T49.5x2	T49.5x3	T49.5x4	T49.5x5	T49.5x6
Contraceptive (oral)	T38.4x1	T38.4x2	T38.4x3	T38.4x4	T38.4x5	T38.4x6
vaginal	T49.8x1	T49.8x2	T49.8x3	T49.8x4	T49.8x5	T49.8x6
Contrast medium, radiography	T50.8x1	T50.8x2	T50.8x3	T50.8x4	T50.8x5	T50.8x6
Convallaria glycosides	T46.0x1	T46.0x2	T46.0x3	T46.0x4	T46.0x5	T46.0x6
Convallaria majalis	T62.2x1	T62.2x2	T62.2x3	T62.2x4	—	—
berry	T62.1x1	T62.1x2	T62.1x3	T62.1x4	—	—
Copper (dust) (fumes) (nonmedicinal) NEC	T56.4x1	T56.4x2	T56.4x3	T56.4x4	—	—
arsenate, arsenite	T57.0x1	T57.0x2	T57.0x3	T57.0x4	—	—
insecticide	T60.2x1	T60.2x2	T60.2x3	T60.2x4	—	—
emetic	T47.7x1	T47.7x2	T47.7x3	T47.7x4	T47.7x5	T47.7x6
fungicide	T60.3x1	T60.3x2	T60.3x3	T60.3x4	—	—
gluconate	T49.0x1	T49.0x2	T49.0x3	T49.0x4	T49.0x5	T49.0x6
insecticide	T60.2x1	T60.2x2	T60.2x3	T60.2x4	—	—
medicinal (trace)	T45.8x1	T45.8x2	T45.8x3	T45.8x4	T45.8x5	T45.8x6
oleate	T49.0x1	T49.0x2	T49.0x3	T49.0x4	T49.0x5	T49.0x6
sulfate	T56.4x1	T56.4x2	T56.4x3	T56.4x4	—	—
cupric	T56.4x1	T56.4x2	T56.4x3	T56.4x4	—	—
fungicide	T60.3x1	T60.3x2	T60.3x3	T60.3x4	—	—
medicinal						
ear	T49.6x1	T49.6x2	T49.6x3	T49.6x4	T49.6x5	T49.6x6
emetic	T47.7x1	T47.7x2	T47.7x3	T47.7x4	T47.7x5	T47.7x6
eye	T49.5x1	T49.5x2	T49.5x3	T49.5x4	T49.5x5	T49.5x6
cuprous	T56.4x1	T56.4x2	T56.4x3	T56.4x4	—	—

Substance	External Cause (T-Code)					
	Poisoning, Accidental (Unintentional)	Poisoning, Intentional Self-Harm	Poisoning, Assault	Poisoning, Undetermined	Adverse Effect	Underdosing
Copper NEC *(Continued)*						
sulfate *(Continued)*						
fungicide	T60.3x1	T60.3x2	T60.3x3	T60.3x4	—	—
medicinal						
ear	T49.6x1	T49.6x2	T49.6x3	T49.6x4	T49.6x5	T49.6x6
emetic	T47.7x1	T47.7x2	T47.7x3	T47.7x4	T47.7x5	T47.7x6
eye	T49.5x1	T49.5x2	T49.5x3	T49.5x4	T49.5x5	T49.5x6
Copperhead snake (bite) (venom)	T63.061	T63.062	T63.063	T63.064	—	—
Coral (sting)	T63.691	T63.692	T63.693	T63.694	—	—
snake (bite) (venom)	T63.021	T63.022	T63.023	T63.024	—	—
Corbadrine	T49.6x1	T49.6x2	T49.6x3	T49.6x4	T49.6x5	T49.6x6
Cordran	T49.0x1	T49.0x2	T49.0x3	T49.0x4	T49.0x5	T49.0x6
Cordite	T65.891	T65.892	T65.893	T65.894	—	—
vapor	T59.891	T59.892	T59.893	T59.894	—	—
Corn cures	T49.4x1	T49.4x2	T49.4x3	T49.4x4	T49.4x5	T49.4x6
Cornhusker's lotion	T49.3x1	T49.3x2	T49.3x3	T49.3x4	T49.3x5	T49.3x6
Corn starch	T49.3x1	T49.3x2	T49.3x3	T49.3x4	T49.3x5	T49.3x6
Coronary vasodilator NEC	T46.3x1	T46.3x2	T46.3x3	T46.3x4	T46.3x5	T46.3x6
Corrosive NEC	T54.91	T54.92	T54.93	T54.94	—	—
acid NEC	T54.2x1	T54.2x2	T54.2x3	T54.2x4	—	—
aromatics	T54.1x1	T54.1x2	T54.1x3	T54.1x4	—	—
disinfectant	T54.1x1	T54.1x2	T54.1x3	T54.1x4	—	—
fumes NEC	T54.91	T54.92	T54.93	T54.94	—	—
specified NEC	T54.91	T54.92	T54.93	T54.94	—	—
sublimate	T56.1x1	T56.1x2	T56.1x3	T56.1x4	—	—
Cortate	T38.0x1	T38.0x2	T38.0x3	T38.0x4	T38.0x5	T38.0x6
Cort-Dome	T38.0x1	T38.0x2	T38.0x3	T38.0x4	T38.0x5	T38.0x6
ENT agent	T49.6x1	T49.6x2	T49.6x3	T49.6x4	T49.6x5	T49.6x6
ophthalmic preparation	T49.5x1	T49.5x2	T49.5x3	T49.5x4	T49.5x5	T49.5x6
topical NEC	T49.0x1	T49.0x2	T49.0x3	T49.0x4	T49.0x5	T49.0x6
Cortef	T38.0x1	T38.0x2	T38.0x3	T38.0x4	T38.0x5	T38.0x6
ENT agent	T49.6x1	T49.6x2	T49.6x3	T49.6x4	T49.6x5	T49.6x6
ophthalmic preparation	T49.5x1	T49.5x2	T49.5x3	T49.5x4	T49.5x5	T49.5x6
topical NEC	T49.0x1	T49.0x2	T49.0x3	T49.0x4	T49.0x5	T49.0x6
Corticosteroid	T38.0x1	T38.0x2	T38.0x3	T38.0x4	T38.0x5	T38.0x6
ENT agent	T49.6x1	T49.6x2	T49.6x3	T49.6x4	T49.6x5	T49.6x6
mineral	T50.0x1	T50.0x2	T50.0x3	T50.0x4	T50.0x5	T50.0x6
ophthalmic	T49.5x1	T49.5x2	T49.5x3	T49.5x4	T49.5x5	T49.5x6
topical NEC	T49.0x1	T49.0x2	T49.0x3	T49.0x4	T49.0x5	T49.0x6
Corticotropin	T38.811	T38.812	T38.813	T38.814	T38.815	T38.816

	External Cause (T-Code)					
Substance	Poisoning, Accidental (Unintentional)	Poisoning, Intentional Self-Harm	Poisoning, Assault	Poisoning, Undetermined	Adverse Effect	Underdosing
Cortisol	T49.0x1	T49.0x2	T49.0x3	T49.0x4	T49.0x5	T49.0x6
ENT agent	T49.6x1	T49.6x2	T49.6x3	T49.6x4	T49.6x5	T49.6x6
ophthalmic preparation	T49.5x1	T49.5x2	T49.5x3	T49.5x4	T49.5x5	T49.5x6
topical NEC	T49.0x1	T49.0x2	T49.0x3	T49.0x4	T49.0x5	T49.0x6
Cortisone (acetate)	T38.0x1	T38.0x2	T38.0x3	T38.0x4	T38.0x5	T38.0x6
ENT agent	T49.6x1	T49.6x2	T49.6x3	T49.6x4	T49.6x5	T49.6x6
ophthalmic preparation	T49.5x1	T49.5x2	T49.5x3	T49.5x4	T49.5x5	T49.5x6
topical NEC	T49.0x1	T49.0x2	T49.0x3	T49.0x4	T49.0x5	T49.0x6
Cortivazol	T38.0x1	T38.0x2	T38.0x3	T38.0x4	T38.0x5	T38.0x6
Cortogen	T38.0x1	T38.0x2	T38.0x3	T38.0x4	T38.0x5	T38.0x6
ENT agent	T49.6x1	T49.6x2	T49.6x3	T49.6x4	T49.6x5	T49.6x6
ophthalmic preparation	T49.5x1	T49.5x2	T49.5x3	T49.5x4	T49.5x5	T49.5x6
Cortone	T38.0x1	T38.0x2	T38.0x3	T38.0x4	T38.0x5	T38.0x6
ENT agent	T49.6x1	T49.6x2	T49.6x3	T49.6x4	T49.6x5	T49.6x6
ophthalmic preparation	T49.5x1	T49.5x2	T49.5x3	T49.5x4	T49.5x5	T49.5x6
Cortril	T38.0x1	T38.0x2	T38.0x3	T38.0x4	T38.0x5	T38.0x6
ENT agent	T49.6x1	T49.6x2	T49.6x3	T49.6x4	T49.6x5	T49.6x6
ophthalmic preparation	T49.5x1	T49.5x2	T49.5x3	T49.5x4	T49.5x5	T49.5x6
topical NEC	T49.0x1	T49.0x2	T49.0x3	T49.0x4	T49.0x5	T49.0x6
Corynebacterium parvum	T45.1x1	T45.1x2	T45.1x3	T45.1x4	T45.1x5	T45.1x6
Cosmetic preparation	T49.8x1	T49.8x2	T49.8x3	T49.8x4	T49.8x5	T49.8x6
Cosmetics	T49.8x1	T49.8x2	T49.8x3	T49.8x4	T49.8x5	T49.8x6
Cosyntropin	T38.811	T38.812	T38.813	T38.814	T38.815	T38.816
Cotarnine	T45.7x1	T45.7x2	T45.7x3	T45.7x4	T45.7x5	T45.7x6
Co-trimoxazole	T36.8x1	T36.8x2	T36.8x3	T36.8x4	T36.8x5	T36.8x6
Cottonseed oil	T49.3x1	T49.3x2	T49.3x3	T49.3x4	T49.3x5	T49.3x6
Cough mixture (syrup)	T48.4x1	T48.4x2	T48.4x3	T48.4x4	T48.4x5	T48.4x6
containing opiates	T40.2x1	T40.2x2	T40.2x3	T40.2x4	T40.2x5	T40.2x6
expectorants	T48.4x1	T48.4x2	T48.4x3	T48.4x4	T48.4x5	T48.4x6
Coumadin	T45.511	T45.512	T45.513	T45.514	T45.515	T45.516
rodenticide	T60.4x1	T60.4x2	T60.4x3	T60.4x4	—	—
Coumaphos	T60.0x1	T60.0x2	T60.0x3	T60.0x4	—	—
Coumarin	T45.511	T45.512	T45.513	T45.514	T45.515	T45.516
Coumetarol	T45.511	T45.512	T45.513	T45.514	T45.515	T45.516
Cowbane	T62.2x1	T62.2x2	T62.2x3	T62.2x4	—	—
Cozyme	T45.2x1	T45.2x2	T45.2x3	T45.2x4	T45.2x5	T45.2x6
Crack	T40.5x1	T40.5x2	T40.5x3	T40.5x4	T40.5x5	T40.5x6
Crataegus extract	T46.0x1	T46.0x2	T46.0x3	T46.0x4	T46.0x5	T46.0x6
Creolin	T54.1x1	T54.1x2	T54.1x3	T54.1x4	—	—
disinfectant	T54.1x1	T54.1x2	T54.1x3	T54.1x4	—	—

Substance	Poisoning, Accidental (Unintentional)	Poisoning, Intentional Self-Harm	Poisoning, Assault	Poisoning, Undetermined	Adverse Effect	Underdosing
Creosol (compound)	T49.0x1	T49.0x2	T49.0x3	T49.0x4	T49.0x5	T49.0x6
Creosote (coal tar) (beechwood)	T49.0x1	T49.0x2	T49.0x3	T49.0x4	T49.0x5	T49.0x6
medicinal (expectorant)	T48.4x1	T48.4x2	T48.4x3	T48.4x4	T48.4x5	T48.4x6
syrup	T48.4x1	T48.4x2	T48.4x3	T48.4x4	T48.4x5	T48.4x6
Cresol(s)	T49.0x1	T49.0x2	T49.0x3	T49.0x4	T49.0x5	T49.0x6
and soap solution	T49.0x1	T49.0x2	T49.0x3	T49.0x4	T49.0x5	T49.0x6
Cresyl acetate	T49.0x1	T49.0x2	T49.0x3	T49.0x4	T49.0x5	T49.0x6
Cresylic acid	T49.0x1	T49.0x2	T49.0x3	T49.0x4	T49.0x5	T49.0x6
Crimidine	T60.4x1	T60.4x2	T60.4x3	T60.4x4	—	—
Croconazole	T37.8x1	T37.8x2	T37.8x3	T37.8x4	T37.8x5	T37.8x6
Cromoglicic acid	T48.6x1	T48.6x2	T48.6x3	T48.6x4	T48.6x5	T48.6x6
Cromolyn	T48.6x1	T48.6x2	T48.6x3	T48.6x4	T48.6x5	T48.6x6
Cromonar	T46.3x1	T46.3x2	T46.3x3	T46.3x4	T46.3x5	T46.3x6
Cropropamide	T39.8x1	T39.8x2	T39.8x3	T39.8x4	T39.8x5	T39.8x6
with crotethamide	T50.7x1	T50.7x2	T50.7x3	T50.7x4	T50.7x5	T50.7x6
Crotamiton	T49.0x1	T49.0x2	T49.0x3	T49.0x4	T49.0x5	T49.0x6
Crotethamide	T39.8x1	T39.8x2	T39.8x3	T39.8x4	T39.8x5	T39.8x6
with cropropamide	T50.7x1	T50.7x2	T50.7x3	T50.7x4	T50.7x5	T50.7x6
Croton (oil)	T47.2x1	T47.2x2	T47.2x3	T47.2x4	T47.2x5	T47.2x6
chloral	T42.6x1	T42.6x2	T42.6x3	T42.6x4	T42.6x5	T42.6x6
Crude oil	T52.0x1	T52.0x2	T52.0x3	T52.0x4	—	—
Cryogenine	T39.8x1	T39.8x2	T39.8x3	T39.8x4	T39.8x5	T39.8x6
Cryolite (vapor)	T60.1x1	T60.1x2	T60.1x3	T60.1x4	—	—
insecticide	T60.1x1	T60.1x2	T60.1x3	T60.1x4	—	—
Cryptenamine (tannates)	T46.5x1	T46.5x2	T46.5x3	T46.5x4	T46.5x5	T46.5x6
Crystal violet	T49.0x1	T49.0x2	T49.0x3	T49.0x4	T49.0x5	T49.0x6
Cuckoopint	T62.2x1	T62.2x2	T62.2x3	T62.2x4	—	—
Cumetharol	T45.511	T45.512	T45.513	T45.514	T45.515	T45.516
Cupric						
acetate	T60.3x1	T60.3x2	T60.3x3	T60.3x4	—	—
acetoarsenite	T57.0x1	T57.0x2	T57.0x3	T57.0x4	—	—
arsenate	T57.0x1	T57.0x2	T57.0x3	T57.0x4	—	—
gluconate	T49.0x1	T49.0x2	T49.0x3	T49.0x4	T49.0x5	T49.0x6
oleate	T49.0x1	T49.0x2	T49.0x3	T49.0x4	T49.0x5	T49.0x6
sulfate	T56.4x1	T56.4x2	T56.4x3	T56.4x4	—	—
Cuprous sulfate (see also Copper sulfate)	T56.4x1	T56.4x2	T56.4x3	T56.4x4	—	—
Curare, curarine	T48.1x1	T48.1x2	T48.1x3	T48.1x4	T48.1x5	T48.1x6
Cyamemazine	T43.3x1	T43.3x2	T43.3x3	T43.3x4	T43.3x5	T43.3x6
Cyamopsis tetragono-loba	T46.6x1	T46.6x2	T46.6x3	T46.6x4	T46.6x5	T46.6x6
Cyanacetyl hydrazide	T37.1x1	T37.1x2	T37.1x3	T37.1x4	T37.1x5	T37.1x6

Substance	External Cause (T-Code)					
	Poisoning, Accidental (Unintentional)	Poisoning, Intentional Self-Harm	Poisoning, Assault	Poisoning, Undetermined	Adverse Effect	Underdosing
Cyanic acid (gas)	T59.891	T59.892	T59.893	T59.894	—	—
Cyanide(s) (compounds) (potassium) (sodium) NEC	T65.0x1	T65.0x2	T65.0x3	T65.0x4	—	—
dust or gas (inhalation) NEC	T57.3x1	T57.3x2	T57.3x3	T57.3x4	—	—
fumigant	T65.0x1	T65.0x2	T65.0x3	T65.0x4	—	—
hydrogen	T57.3x1	T57.3x2	T57.3x3	T57.3x4	—	—
mercuric - *see* Mercury						
pesticide (dust) (fumes)	T65.0x1	T65.0x2	T65.0x3	T65.0x4	—	—
Cyanoacrylate adhesive	T49.3x1	T49.3x2	T49.3x3	T49.3x4	T49.3x5	T49.3x6
Cyanocobalamin	T45.8x1	T45.8x2	T45.8x3	T45.8x4	T45.8x5	T45.8x6
Cyanogen (chloride) (gas) NEC	T59.891	T59.892	T59.893	T59.894	—	—
Cyclacillin	T36.0x1	T36.0x2	T36.0x3	T36.0x4	T36.0x5	T36.0x6
Cyclaine	T41.3x1	T41.3x2	T41.3x3	T41.3x4	T41.3x5	T41.3x6
Cyclamate	T50.991	T50.992	T50.993	T50.994	T50.995	T50.996
Cyclamen europaeum	T62.2x1	T62.2x2	T62.2x3	T62.2x4	—	—
Cyclandelate	T46.7x1	T46.7x2	T46.7x3	T46.7x4	T46.7x5	T46.7x6
Cyclazocine	T50.7x1	T50.7x2	T50.7x3	T50.7x4	T50.7x5	T50.7x6
Cyclizine	T45.0x1	T45.0x2	T45.0x3	T45.0x4	T45.0x5	T45.0x6
Cyclobarbital	T42.3x1	T42.3x2	T42.3x3	T42.3x4	T42.3x5	T42.3x6
Cyclobarbitone	T42.3x1	T42.3x2	T42.3x3	T42.3x4	T42.3x5	T42.3x6
Cyclobenzaprine	T48.1x1	T48.1x2	T48.1x3	T48.1x4	T48.1x5	T48.1x6
Cyclodrine	T44.3x1	T44.3x2	T44.3x3	T44.3x4	T44.3x5	T44.3x6
Cycloguanil embonate	T37.2x1	T37.2x2	T37.2x3	T37.2x4	T37.2x5	T37.2x6
Cycloheptadiene	T43.291	T43.292	T43.293	T43.294	T43.295	T43.296
Cyclohexane	T52.8x1	T52.8x2	T52.8x3	T52.8x4	—	—
Cyclohexanol	T51.8x1	T51.8x2	T51.8x3	T51.8x4	—	—
Cyclohexanone	T52.4x1	T52.4x2	T52.4x3	T52.4x4	—	—
Cycloheximide	T60.3x1	T60.3x2	T60.3x3	T60.3x4	—	—
Cyclohexyl acetate	T52.8x1	T52.8x2	T52.8x3	T52.8x4	—	—
Cycloleucin	T45.1x1	T45.1x2	T45.1x3	T45.1x4	T45.1x5	T45.1x6
Cyclomethycaine	T41.3x1	T41.3x2	T41.3x3	T41.3x4	T41.3x5	T41.3x6
Cyclopentamine	T44.4x1	T44.4x2	T44.4x3	T44.4x4	T44.4x5	T44.4x6
Cyclopenthiazide	T50.2x1	T50.2x2	T50.2x3	T50.2x4	T50.2x5	T50.2x6
Cyclopentolate	T44.3x1	T44.3x2	T44.3x3	T44.3x4	T44.3x5	T44.3x6
Cyclophosphamide	T45.1x1	T45.1x2	T45.1x3	T45.1x4	T45.1x5	T45.1x6
Cycloplegic drug	T49.5x1	T49.5x2	T49.5x3	T49.5x4	T49.5x5	T49.5x6
Cyclopropane	T41.291	T41.292	T41.293	T41.294	T41.295	T41.296
Cyclopyrabital	T39.8x1	T39.8x2	T39.8x3	T39.8x4	T39.8x5	T39.8x6
Cycloserine	T37.1x1	T37.1x2	T37.1x3	T37.1x4	T37.1x5	T37.1x6
Cyclosporin	T45.1x1	T45.1x2	T45.1x3	T45.1x4	T45.1x5	T45.1x6
Cyclothiazide	T50.2x1	T50.2x2	T50.2x3	T50.2x4	T50.2x5	T50.2x6

Substance	External Cause (T-Code)					
	Poisoning, Accidental (Unintentional)	Poisoning, Intentional Self-Harm	Poisoning, Assault	Poisoning, Undetermined	Adverse Effect	Underdosing
Cycrimine	T44.3x1	T44.3x2	T44.3x3	T44.3x4	T44.3x5	T44.3x6
Cyhalothrin	T60.1x1	T60.1x2	T60.1x3	T60.1x4	—	—
Cymarin	T46.0x1	T46.0x2	T46.0x3	T46.0x4	T46.0x5	T46.0x6
Cypermethrin	T60.1x1	T60.1x2	T60.1x3	T60.1x4	—	—
Cyphenothrin	T60.2x1	T60.2x2	T60.2x3	T60.2x4	—	—
Cyproheptadine	T45.0x1	T45.0x2	T45.0x3	T45.0x4	T45.0x5	T45.0x6
Cyprolidol	T43.291	T43.292	T43.293	T43.294	T43.295	T43.296
Cyproterone	T38.6x1	T38.6x2	T38.6x3	T38.6x4	T38.6x5	T38.6x6
Cysteamine	T50.6x1	T50.6x2	T50.6x3	T50.6x4	T50.6x5	T50.6x6
Cytarabine	T45.1x1	T45.1x2	T45.1x3	T45.1x4	T45.1x5	T45.1x6
Cytisus						
laburnum	T62.2x1	T62.2x2	T62.2x3	T62.2x4	—	—
scoparius	T62.2x1	T62.2x2	T62.2x3	T62.2x4	—	—
Cytochrome C	T47.5x1	T47.5x2	T47.5x3	T47.5x4	T47.5x5	T47.5x6
Cytomel	T38.1x1	T38.1x2	T38.1x3	T38.1x4	T38.1x5	T38.1x6
Cytosine arabinoside	T45.1x1	T45.1x2	T45.1x3	T45.1x4	T45.1x5	T45.1x6
Cytosine (antineoplastic)	T45.1x1	T45.1x2	T45.1x3	T45.1x4	T45.1x5	T45.1x6
Cytoxan	T45.1x1	T45.1x2	T45.1x3	T45.1x4	T45.1x5	T45.1x6
Cytozyme	T45.7x1	T45.7x2	T45.7x3	T45.7x4	T45.7x5	T45.7x6
2,4-D	T60.3x1	T60.3x2	T60.3x3	T60.3x4	—	—
Dacarbazine	T45.1x1	T45.1x2	T45.1x3	T45.1x4	T45.1x5	T45.1x6
Dactinomycin	T45.1x1	T45.1x2	T45.1x3	T45.1x4	T45.1x5	T45.1x6
DADPS	T37.1x1	T37.1x2	T37.1x3	T37.1x4	T37.1x5	T37.1x6
Dakin's solution	T49.0x1	T49.0x2	T49.0x3	T49.0x4	T49.0x5	T49.0x6
Dalapon (sodium)	T60.3x1	T60.3x2	T60.3x3	T60.3x4	—	—
Dalmane	T42.4x1	T42.4x2	T42.4x3	T42.4x4	T42.4x5	T42.4x6
Danazol	T38.6x1	T38.6x2	T38.6x3	T38.6x4	T38.6x5	T38.6x6
Danilone	T45.511	T45.512	T45.513	T45.514	T45.515	T45.516
Danthron	T47.2x1	T47.2x2	T47.2x3	T47.2x4	T47.2x5	T47.2x6
Dantrolene	T42.8x1	T42.8x2	T42.8x3	T42.8x4	T42.8x5	T42.8x6
Dantron	T47.2x1	T47.2x2	T47.2x3	T47.2x4	T47.2x5	T47.2x6
Daphne (gnidium) (mezereum)	T62.2x1	T62.2x2	T62.2x3	T62.2x4	—	—
berry	T62.1x1	T62.1x2	T62.1x3	T62.1x4	—	—
Dapsone	T37.1x1	T37.1x2	T37.1x3	T37.1x4	T37.1x5	T37.1x6
Daraprim	T37.2x1	T37.2x2	T37.2x3	T37.2x4	T37.2x5	T37.2x6
Darnel	T62.2x1	T62.2x2	T62.2x3	T62.2x4	—	—
Darvon	T39.8x1	T39.8x2	T39.8x3	T39.8x4	T39.8x5	T39.8x6
Daunomycin	T45.1x1	T45.1x2	T45.1x3	T45.1x4	T45.1x5	T45.1x6
Daunorubicin	T45.1x1	T45.1x2	T45.1x3	T45.1x4	T45.1x5	T45.1x6
DBI	T38.3x1	T38.3x2	T38.3x3	T38.3x4	T38.3x5	T38.3x6

Substance	External Cause (T-Code)					
	Poisoning, Accidental (Unintentional)	Poisoning, Intentional Self-Harm	Poisoning, Assault	Poisoning, Undetermined	Adverse Effect	Underdosing
D-Con	T60.91	T60.92	T60.93	T60.94	—	—
insecticide	T60.2x1	T60.2x2	T60.2x3	T60.2x4	—	—
rodenticide	T60.4x1	T60.4x2	T60.4x3	T60.4x4	—	—
DDAVP	T38.891	T38.892	T38.893	T38.894	T38.895	T38.896
DDE (bis(chlorophenyl)-dichloroethylene)	T60.2x1	T60.2x2	T60.2x3	T60.2x4	—	—
DDS	T37.1x1	T37.1x2	T37.1x3	T37.1x4	T37.1x5	T37.1x6
DDT (dust)	T60.1x1	T60.1x2	T60.1x3	T60.1x4	—	—
Deadly nightshade (*see also* Belladonna)	T62.2x1	T62.2x2	T62.2x3	T62.2x4	—	—
berry	T62.1x1	T62.1x2	T62.1x3	T62.1x4	—	—
Deamino-D-arginine vasopressin	T38.891	T38.892	T38.893	T38.894	T38.895	T38.896
Deanol (aceglumate)	T50.991	T50.992	T50.993	T50.994	T50.995	T50.996
Debrisoquine	T46.5x1	T46.5x2	T46.5x3	T46.5x4	T46.5x5	T46.5x6
Decaborane	T57.8x1	T57.8x2	T57.8x3	T57.8x4	—	—
fumes	T59.891	T59.892	T59.893	T59.894	—	—
Decadron	T38.0x1	T38.0x2	T38.0x3	T38.0x4	T38.0x5	T38.0x6
ENT agent	T49.6x1	T49.6x2	T49.6x3	T49.6x4	T49.6x5	T49.6x6
ophthalmic preparation	T49.5x1	T49.5x2	T49.5x3	T49.5x4	T49.5x5	T49.5x6
topical NEC	T49.0x1	T49.0x2	T49.0x3	T49.0x4	T49.0x5	T49.0x6
Decahydronaphthalene	T52.8x1	T52.8x2	T52.8x3	T52.8x4	—	—
Decalin	T52.8x1	T52.8x2	T52.8x3	T52.8x4	—	—
Decamethonium (bromide)	T48.1x1	T48.1x2	T48.1x3	T48.1x4	T48.1x5	T48.1x6
Decholin	T47.5x1	T47.5x2	T47.5x3	T47.5x4	T47.5x5	T47.5x6
Declomycin	T36.4x1	T36.4x2	T36.4x3	T36.4x4	T36.4x5	T36.4x6
Decongestant, nasal (mucosa)	T48.5x1	T48.5x2	T48.5x3	T48.5x4	T48.5x5	T48.5x6
combination	T48.5x1	T48.5x2	T48.5x3	T48.5x4	T48.5x5	T48.5x6
Deet	T60.8x1	T60.8x2	T60.8x3	T60.8x4	—	—
Deferoxamine	T45.8x1	T45.8x2	T45.8x3	T45.8x4	T45.8x5	T45.8x6
Deflazacort	T38.0x1	T38.0x2	T38.0x3	T38.0x4	T38.0x5	T38.0x6
Deglycyrrhizinized extract of licorice	T48.4x1	T48.4x2	T48.4x3	T48.4x4	T48.4x5	T48.4x6
Dehydrocholic acid	T47.5x1	T47.5x2	T47.5x3	T47.5x4	T47.5x5	T47.5x6
Dehydroemetine	T37.3x1	T37.3x2	T37.3x3	T37.3x4	T37.3x5	T37.3x6
Dekalin	T52.8x1	T52.8x2	T52.8x3	T52.8x4	—	—
Delalutin	T38.5x1	T38.5x2	T38.5x3	T38.5x4	T38.5x5	T38.5x6
Delphinium	T62.2x1	T62.2x2	T62.2x3	T62.2x4	—	—
Deltasone	T38.0x1	T38.0x2	T38.0x3	T38.0x4	T38.0x5	T38.0x6
Deltra	T38.0x1	T38.0x2	T38.0x3	T38.0x4	T38.0x5	T38.0x6
Delvinal	T42.3x1	T42.3x2	T42.3x3	T42.3x4	T42.3x5	T42.3x6
Delorazepam	T42.4x1	T42.4x2	T42.4x3	T42.4x4	T42.4x5	T42.4x6
Deltamethrin	T60.1x1	T60.1x2	T60.1x3	T60.1x4	—	—
Demecarium (bromide)	T49.5x1	T49.5x2	T49.5x3	T49.5x4	T49.5x5	T49.5x6

TABLE OF DRUGS AND CHEMICALS DRAFT / Demeclocycline

Substance	Poisoning, Accidental (Unintentional)	Poisoning, Intentional Self-Harm	Poisoning, Assault	Poisoning, Undetermined	Adverse Effect	Underdosing
Demeclocycline	T36.4x1	T36.4x2	T36.4x3	T36.4x4	T36.4x5	T36.4x6
Demecolcine	T45.1x1	T45.1x2	T45.1x3	T45.1x4	T45.1x5	T45.1x6
Demegestone	T38.5x1	T38.5x2	T38.5x3	T38.5x4	T38.5x5	T38.5x6
Demelanizing agents	T49.8x1	T49.8x2	T49.8x3	T49.8x4	T49.8x5	T49.8x6
Demephion -O and -S	T60.0x1	T60.0x2	T60.0x3	T60.0x4	—	—
Demerol	T40.2x1	T40.2x2	T40.2x3	T40.2x4	T40.2x5	T40.2x6
Demethylchlortetracycline	T36.4x1	T36.4x2	T36.4x3	T36.4x4	T36.4x5	T36.4x6
Demethyltetracycline	T36.4x1	T36.4x2	T36.4x3	T36.4x4	T36.4x5	T36.4x6
Demeton -O and -S	T60.0x1	T60.0x2	T60.0x3	T60.0x4	—	—
Demulcent (external)	T49.3x1	T49.3x2	T49.3x3	T49.3x4	T49.3x5	T49.3x6
specified NEC	T49.3x1	T49.3x2	T49.3x3	T49.3x4	T49.3x5	T49.3x6
Demulen	T38.4x1	T38.4x2	T38.4x3	T38.4x4	T38.4x5	T38.4x6
Denatured alcohol	T51.0x1	T51.0x2	T51.0x3	T51.0x4	—	—
Dendrid	T49.5x1	T49.5x2	T49.5x3	T49.5x4	T49.5x5	T49.5x6
Dental drug, topical application NEC	T49.7x1	T49.7x2	T49.7x3	T49.7x4	T49.7x5	T49.7x6
Dentifrice	T49.7x1	T49.7x2	T49.7x3	T49.7x4	T49.7x5	T49.7x6
Deodorant spray (feminine hygiene)	T49.8x1	T49.8x2	T49.8x3	T49.8x4	T49.8x5	T49.8x6
Deoxycortone	T50.0x1	T50.0x2	T50.0x3	T50.0x4	T50.0x5	T50.0x6
2-Deoxy-5-fluorouridine	T45.1x1	T45.1x2	T45.1x3	T45.1x4	T45.1x5	T45.1x6
5-Deoxy-5-fluorouridine	T45.1x1	T45.1x2	T45.1x3	T45.1x4	T45.1x5	T45.1x6
Deoxyribonuclease (pancreatic)	T45.3x1	T45.3x2	T45.3x3	T45.3x4	T45.3x5	T45.3x6
Depilatory	T49.4x1	T49.4x2	T49.4x3	T49.4x4	T49.4x5	T49.4x6
Deprenalin	T42.8x1	T42.8x2	T42.8x3	T42.8x4	T42.8x5	T42.8x6
Deprenyl	T42.8x1	T42.8x2	T42.8x3	T42.8x4	T42.8x5	T42.8x6
Depressant, appetite	T50.5x1	T50.5x2	T50.5x3	T50.5x4	T50.5x5	T50.5x6
Depressants						
appetite, central	T50.5x1	T50.5x2	T50.5x3	T50.5x4	T50.5x5	T50.5x6
cardiac	T46.2x1	T46.2x2	T46.2x3	T46.2x4	T46.2x5	T46.2x6
Central nervous system (anesthetic) (see also Central nervous system, depressants)	T41.41	T41.42	T41.43	T41.44	T41.45	T41.46
general anesthetic	T41.201	T41.202	T41.203	T41.204	T41.205	T41.206
psychotherapeutic	T43.501	T43.502	T43.503	T43.504	T43.505	T43.506
Deptropine	T45.0x1	T45.0x2	T45.0x3	T45.0x4	T45.0x5	T45.0x6
Dequalinium (chloride)	T49.0x1	T49.0x2	T49.0x3	T49.0x4	T49.0x5	T49.0x6
Derris root	T60.2x1	T60.2x2	T60.2x3	T60.2x4	—	—
Deserpidine	T43.011	T43.012	T43.013	T43.014	T43.015	T43.016
Desferrioxamine	T45.8x1	T45.8x2	T45.8x3	T45.8x4	T45.8x5	T45.8x6
Desipramine	T43.0x1	T43.0x2	T43.0x3	T43.0x4	T43.0x5	T43.0x6
Desianoside	T46.0x1	T46.0x2	T46.0x3	T46.0x4	T46.0x5	T46.0x6
Deslanoside	T46.0x1	T46.0x2	T46.0x3	T46.0x4	T46.0x5	T46.0x6

TABLE OF DRUGS AND CHEMICALS

600

Substance	External Cause (T-Code)					
	Poisoning, Accidental (Unintentional)	Poisoning, Intentional Self-Harm	Poisoning, Assault	Poisoning, Undetermined	Adverse Effect	Underdosing
Desloughing agent	T49.4x1	T49.4x2	T49.4x3	T49.4x4	T49.4x5	T49.4x6
Desmethylimipramine	T43.011	T43.012	T43.013	T43.014	T43.015	T43.016
Desmopressin	T38.891	T38.892	T38.893	T38.894	T38.895	T38.896
Desocodeine	T40.2x1	T40.2x2	T40.2x3	T40.2x4	T40.2x5	T40.2x6
Desogestrel	T38.5x1	T38.5x2	T38.5x3	T38.5x4	T38.5x5	T38.5x6
Desomorphine	T40.2x1	T40.2x2	T40.2x3	T40.2x4	T40.2x5	T40.2x6
Desonide	T49.0x1	T49.0x2	T49.0x3	T49.0x4	T49.0x5	T49.0x6
Desoximetasone	T49.0x1	T49.0x2	T49.0x3	T49.0x4	T49.0x5	T49.0x6
Desoxycorticosteroid	T50.0x1	T50.0x2	T50.0x3	T50.0x4	T50.0x5	T50.0x6
Desoxycortone	T50.0x1	T50.0x2	T50.0x3	T50.0x4	T50.0x5	T50.0x6
Desoxyephedrine	T43.621	T43.622	T43.623	T43.624	T43.625	T43.626
Detaxtran	T46.6x1	T46.6x2	T46.6x3	T46.6x4	T46.6x5	T46.6x6
Detergent (local) (medicinal) NEC	T55.1x1	T55.1x2	T55.1x3	T55.1x4	T55.1x5	T55.1x6
external medication	T49.2x1	T49.2x2	T49.2x3	T49.2x4	T49.2x5	T49.2x6
nonmedicinal	T55.1x1	T55.1x2	T55.1x3	T55.1x4	—	—
specified NEC	T55.1x1	T55.1x2	T55.1x3	T55.1x4	T55.1x5	T55.1x6
Deterrent, alcohol	T50.6x1	T50.6x2	T50.6x3	T50.6x4	T50.6x5	T50.6x6
Detoxifying agent	T50.6x1	T50.6x2	T50.6x3	T50.6x4	T50.6x5	T50.6x6
Detrothyronine	T38.1x1	T38.1x2	T38.1x3	T38.1x4	T38.1x5	T38.1x6
Dettol (external medication)	T49.0x1	T49.0x2	T49.0x3	T49.0x4	T49.0x5	T49.0x6
Dexamethasone	T38.0x1	T38.0x2	T38.0x3	T38.0x4	T38.0x5	T38.0x6
ENT agent	T49.6x1	T49.6x2	T49.6x3	T49.6x4	T49.6x5	T49.6x6
ophthalmic preparation	T49.5x1	T49.5x2	T49.5x3	T49.5x4	T49.5x5	T49.5x6
topical NEC	T49.0x1	T49.0x2	T49.0x3	T49.0x4	T49.0x5	T49.0x6
Dexamfetamine	T43.621	T43.622	T43.623	T43.624	T43.625	T43.626
Dexamphetamine	T43.621	T43.622	T43.623	T43.624	T43.625	T43.626
Dexbrompheniramine	T45.0x1	T45.0x2	T45.0x3	T45.0x4	T45.0x5	T45.0x6
Dexchlorpheniramine	T45.0x1	T45.0x2	T45.0x3	T45.0x4	T45.0x5	T45.0x6
Dexedrine	T43.621	T43.622	T43.623	T43.624	T43.625	T43.626
Dexetimide	T44.3x1	T44.3x2	T44.3x3	T44.3x4	T44.3x5	T44.3x6
Dexfenfluramine	T50.5x1	T50.5x2	T50.5x3	T50.5x4	T50.5x5	T50.5x6
Dexpanthenol	T45.2x1	T45.2x2	T45.2x3	T45.2x4	T45.2x5	T45.2x6
Dextran (40) (70) (150)	T45.8x1	T45.8x2	T45.8x3	T45.8x4	T45.8x5	T45.8x6
Dextriferron	T45.4x1	T45.4x2	T45.4x3	T45.4x4	T45.4x5	T45.4x6
Dextroamphetamine	T43.621	T43.622	T43.623	T43.624	T43.625	T43.626
Dextro calcium pantothenate	T45.2x1	T45.2x2	T45.2x3	T45.2x4	T45.2x5	T45.2x6
Dextromethorphan	T48.3x1	T48.3x2	T48.3x3	T48.3x4	T48.3x5	T48.3x6
Dextromoramide	T40.4x1	T40.4x2	T40.4x3	T40.4x4	T40.4x5	T40.4x6
Dextro pantothenyl alcohol	T45.2x1	T45.2x2	T45.2x3	T45.2x4	T45.2x5	T45.2x6
topical	T49.8x1	T49.8x2	T49.8x3	T49.8x4	T49.8x5	T49.8x6

Substance	External Cause (T-Code)					
	Poisoning, Accidental (Unintentional)	Poisoning, Intentional Self-Harm	Poisoning, Assault	Poisoning, Undetermined	Adverse Effect	Underdosing
Dextropropoxyphene	T40.4x1	T40.4x2	T40.4x3	T40.4x4	T40.4x5	T40.4x6
Dextrorphan	T40.2x1	T40.2x2	T40.2x3	T40.2x4	T40.2x5	T40.2x6
Dextrose	T50.3x1	T50.3x2	T50.3x3	T50.3x4	T50.3x5	T50.3x6
concentrated solution, intravenous	T46.8x1	T46.8x2	T46.8x3	T46.8x4	T46.8x5	T46.8x6
Dextrothyroxin	T38.1x1	T38.1x2	T38.1x3	T38.1x4	T38.1x5	T38.1x6
Dextrothyroxine sodium	T38.1x1	T38.1x2	T38.1x3	T38.1x4	T38.1x5	T38.1x6
DFP	T44.0x1	T44.0x2	T44.0x3	T44.0x4	T44.0x5	T44.0x6
DHE	T37.3x1	T37.3x2	T37.3x3	T37.3x4	T37.3x5	T37.3x6
45	T46.5x1	T46.5x2	T46.5x3	T46.5x4	T46.5x5	T46.5x6
Diabinese	T38.3x1	T38.3x2	T38.3x3	T38.3x4	T38.3x5	T38.3x6
Diacetone alcohol	T52.4x1	T52.4x2	T52.4x3	T52.4x4	—	—
Diacetyl monoxime	T50.991	T50.992	T50.993	T50.994	—	—
Diacetylmorphine	T40.1x1	T40.1x2	T40.1x3	T40.1x4	T40.1x5	T40.1x6
Diachylon plaster	T49.4x1	T49.4x2	T49.4x3	T49.4x4	T49.4x5	T49.4x6
Diaethylstilboestrolum	T38.5x1	T38.5x2	T38.5x3	T38.5x4	T38.5x5	T38.5x6
Diagnostic agent NEC	T50.8x1	T50.8x2	T50.8x3	T50.8x4	T50.8x5	T50.8x6
Dial (soap)	T49.2x1	T49.2x2	T49.2x3	T49.2x4	T49.2x5	T49.2x6
sedative	T42.3x1	T42.3x2	T42.3x3	T42.3x4	T42.3x5	T42.3x6
Dialkyl carbonate	T52.91	T52.92	T52.93	T52.94	—	—
Diallylbarbituric acid	T42.3x1	T42.3x2	T42.3x3	T42.3x4	T42.3x5	T42.3x6
Diallymal	T42.3x1	T42.3x2	T42.3x3	T42.3x4	T42.3x5	T42.3x6
Dialysis solution (intraperitoneal)	T50.3x1	T50.3x2	T50.3x3	T50.3x4	T50.3x5	T50.3x6
Diaminodiphenylsulfone	T37.1x1	T37.1x2	T37.1x3	T37.1x4	T37.1x5	T37.1x6
Diamorphine	T40.1x1	T40.1x2	T40.1x3	T40.1x4	T40.1x5	T40.1x6
Diamox	T50.2x1	T50.2x2	T50.2x3	T50.2x4	T50.2x5	T50.2x6
Diamthazole	T49.0x1	T49.0x2	T49.0x3	T49.0x4	T49.0x5	T49.0x6
Dianthone	T47.2x1	T47.2x2	T47.2x3	T47.2x4	T47.2x5	T47.2x6
Diaphenylsulfone	T37.0x1	T37.0x2	T37.0x3	T37.0x4	T37.0x5	T37.0x6
Diasone (sodium)	T37.1x1	T37.1x2	T37.1x3	T37.1x4	T37.1x5	T37.1x6
Diastase	T47.5x1	T47.5x2	T47.5x3	T47.5x4	T47.5x5	T47.5x6
Diatrizoate	T50.8x1	T50.8x2	T50.8x3	T50.8x4	T50.8x5	T50.8x6
Diazepam	T42.4x1	T42.4x2	T42.4x3	T42.4x4	T42.4x5	T42.4x6
Diazinon	T60.0x1	T60.0x2	T60.0x3	T60.0x4	—	—
Diazomethane (gas)	T59.891	T59.892	T59.893	T59.894	—	—
Diazoxide	T46.5x1	T46.5x2	T46.5x3	T46.5x4	T46.5x5	T46.5x6
Dibekacin	T36.5x1	T36.5x2	T36.5x3	T36.5x4	T36.5x5	T36.5x6
Dibenamine	T44.6x1	T44.6x2	T44.6x3	T44.6x4	T44.6x5	T44.6x6
Dibenzepin	T43.011	T43.012	T43.013	T43.014	T43.015	T43.016
Dibenzheptropine	T45.0x1	T45.0x2	T45.0x3	T45.0x4	T45.0x5	T45.0x6
Dibenzyline	T44.6x1	T44.6x2	T44.6x3	T44.6x4	T44.6x5	T44.6x6

Substance	External Cause (T-Code)					
	Poisoning, Accidental (Unintentional)	Poisoning, Intentional Self-Harm	Poisoning, Assault	Poisoning, Undetermined	Adverse Effect	Underdosing
Diborane (gas)	T59.891	T59.892	T59.893	T59.894	—	—
Dibromochloropropane	T60.8x1	T60.8x2	T60.8x3	T60.8x4	—	—
Dibromodulcitol	T45.1x1	T45.1x2	T45.1x3	T45.1x4	T45.1x5	T45.1x6
Dibromoethane	T53.6x1	T53.6x2	T53.6x3	T53.6x4	—	—
Dibromomannitol	T45.1x1	T45.1x2	T45.1x3	T45.1x4	T45.1x5	T45.1x6
Dibromopropamidine isethionate	T49.0x1	T49.0x2	T49.0x3	T49.0x4	T49.0x5	T49.0x6
Dibrompropamidine	T49.0x1	T49.0x2	T49.0x3	T49.0x4	T49.0x5	T49.0x6
Dibucaine	T41.3x1	T41.3x2	T41.3x3	T41.3x4	T41.3x5	T41.3x6
topical (surface)	T41.3x1	T41.3x2	T41.3x3	T41.3x4	T41.3x5	T41.3x6
Dibunate sodium	T48.3x1	T48.3x2	T48.3x3	T48.3x4	T48.3x5	T48.3x6
Dibutoline sulfate	T44.3x1	T44.3x2	T44.3x3	T44.3x4	T44.3x5	T44.3x6
Dicamba	T60.3x1	T60.3x2	T60.3x3	T60.3x4	—	—
Dicapthon	T60.0x1	T60.0x2	T60.0x3	T60.0x4	—	—
Dichlobenil	T60.3x1	T60.3x2	T60.3x3	T60.3x4	—	—
Dichlone	T60.3x1	T60.3x2	T60.3x3	T60.3x4	—	—
Dichloralphenozone	T42.6x1	T42.6x2	T42.6x3	T42.6x4	T42.6x5	T42.6x6
Dichlorbenzidine	T65.3x1	T65.3x2	T65.3x3	T65.3x4	—	—
Dichlorhydrin	T52.8x1	T52.8x2	T52.8x3	T52.8x4	—	—
Dichlorhydroxyquinoline	T37.8x1	T37.8x2	T37.8x3	T37.8x4	T37.8x5	T37.8x6
Dichlorobenzene	T53.7x1	T53.7x2	T53.7x3	T53.7x4	—	—
Dichlorobenzyl alcohol	T49.6x1	T49.6x2	T49.6x3	T49.6x4	T49.6x5	T49.6x6
Dichlorodifluoromethane	T53.5x1	T53.5x2	T53.5x3	T53.5x4	—	—
Dichloroethane	T52.8x1	T52.8x2	T52.8x3	T52.8x4	—	—
Sym-Dichloroethyl ether	T53.6x1	T53.6x2	T53.6x3	T53.6x4	—	—
Dichloroethyl sulfide, not in war	T59.891	T59.892	T59.893	T59.894	—	—
Dichloroethylene	T53.6x1	T53.6x2	T53.6x3	T53.6x4	—	—
Dichloroformoxine, not in war	T59.891	T59.892	T59.893	T59.894		
Dichlorohydrin, alpha-dichlorohydrin	T52.8x1	T52.8x2	T52.8x3	T52.8x4		
Dichloromethane (solvent)	T53.4x1	T53.4x2	T53.4x3	T53.4x4	—	—
vapor	T53.4x1	T53.4x2	T53.4x3	T53.4x4	—	—
Dichloronaphthoquinone	T60.3x1	T60.3x2	T60.3x3	T60.3x4	—	—
Dichlorophen	T37.4x1	T37.4x2	T37.4x3	T37.4x4	T37.4x5	T37.4x6
2,4-Dichlorophenoxy-acetic acid	T60.3x1	T60.3x2	T60.3x3	T60.3x4	—	—
Dichloropropene	T60.3x1	T60.3x2	T60.3x3	T60.3x4	—	—
Dichloropropionic acid	T60.3x1	T60.3x2	T60.3x3	T60.3x4	—	—
Dichlorphenamide	T50.2x1	T50.2x2	T50.2x3	T50.2x4	T50.2x5	T50.2x6
Dichlorvos	T60.0x1	T60.0x2	T60.0x3	T60.0x4	—	—
Diclofenac	T39.391	T39.392	T39.393	T39.394	T39.395	T39.396
Diclofenamide	T50.2x1	T50.2x2	T50.2x3	T50.2x4	T50.2x5	T50.2x6
Diclofensine	T43.291	T43.292	T43.293	T43.294	T43.295	T43.296

Substance	External Cause (T-Code)					
	Poisoning, Accidental (Unintentional)	Poisoning, Intentional Self-Harm	Poisoning, Assault	Poisoning, Undetermined	Adverse Effect	Underdosing
Diclonixine	T39.8x1	T39.8x2	T39.8x3	T39.8x4	T39.8x5	T39.8x6
Dicloxacillin	T36.0x1	T36.0x2	T36.0x3	T36.0x4	T36.0x5	T36.0x6
Dicophane	T49.0x1	T49.0x2	T49.0x3	T49.0x4	T49.0x5	T49.0x6
Dicoumarol, dicoumarin, dicumarol	T45.511	T45.512	T45.513	T45.514	T45.515	T45.516
Dicrotophos	T60.0x1	T60.0x2	T60.0x3	T60.0x4	—	—
Dicyanogen (gas)	T65.0x1	T65.0x2	T65.0x3	T65.0x4	—	—
Dicyclomine	T44.3x1	T44.3x2	T44.3x3	T44.3x4	T44.3x5	T44.3x6
Dicycloverine	T44.3x1	T44.3x2	T44.3x3	T44.3x4	T44.3x5	T44.3x6
Dideoxycytidine	T37.5x1	T37.5x2	T37.5x3	T37.5x4	T37.5x5	T37.5x6
Dideoxyinosine	T37.5x1	T37.5x2	T37.5x3	T37.5x4	T37.5x5	T37.5x6
Dieldrin (vapor)	T60.1x1	T60.1x2	T60.1x3	T60.1x4	—	—
Diemal	T42.3x1	T42.3x2	T42.3x3	T42.3x4	T42.3x5	T42.3x6
Dienestrol	T38.5x1	T38.5x2	T38.5x3	T38.5x4	T38.5x5	T38.5x6
Dienoestrol	T38.5x1	T38.5x2	T38.5x3	T38.5x4	T38.5x5	T38.5x6
Dietetic drug NEC	T50.901	T50.902	T50.903	T50.904	T50.905	T50.906
Diethazine	T42.8x1	T42.8x2	T42.8x3	T42.8x4	T42.8x5	T42.8x6
Diethyl						
barbituric acid	T42.3x1	T42.3x2	T42.3x3	T42.3x4	T42.3x5	T42.3x6
carbamazine	T37.4x1	T37.4x2	T37.4x3	T37.4x4	T37.4x5	T37.4x6
carbinol	T51.3x1	T51.3x2	T51.3x3	T51.3x4	—	—
carbonate	T52.8x1	T52.8x2	T52.8x3	T52.8x4	—	—
ether (vapor) (see also ether)	T41.0x1	T41.0x2	T41.0x3	T41.0x4	T41.0x5	T41.0x6
oxide	T52.8x1	T52.8x2	T52.8x3	T52.8x4	—	—
propion	T50.5x1	T50.5x2	T50.5x3	T50.5x4	T50.5x5	T50.5x6
stilbestrol	T38.5x1	T38.5x2	T38.5x3	T38.5x4	T38.5x5	T38.5x6
toluamide (nonmedicinal)	T60.8x1	T60.8x2	T60.8x3	T60.8x4	—	—
medicinal	T49.3x1	T49.3x2	T49.3x3	T49.3x4	T49.3x5	T49.3x6
Diethylcarbamazine	T37.4x1	T37.4x2	T37.4x3	T37.4x4	T37.4x5	T37.4x6
Diethylene						
dioxide	T52.8x1	T52.8x2	T52.8x3	T52.8x4	—	—
glycol (monoacetate) (monobutyl ether) (monoethyl ether)	T52.3x1	T52.3x2	T52.3x3	T52.3x4	—	—
Diethylhexylphthalate	T65.891	T65.892	T65.893	T65.894	—	—
Diethylpropion	T50.5x1	T50.5x2	T50.5x3	T50.5x4	T50.5x5	T50.5x6
Diethylstilbestrol	T38.5x1	T38.5x2	T38.5x3	T38.5x4	T38.5x5	T38.5x6
Diethylstilboestrol	T38.5x1	T38.5x2	T38.5x3	T38.5x4	T38.5x5	T38.5x6
Diethylsulfone-diethylmethane	T42.6x1	T42.6x2	T42.6x3	T42.6x4	T42.6x5	T42.6x6
Diethyltoluamide	T49.0x1	T49.0x2	T49.0x3	T49.0x4	T49.0x5	T49.0x6
Diethyltryptamine (DET)	T40.991	T40.992	T40.993	T40.994	T40.995	T40.996
Difebarbamate	T42.3x1	T42.3x2	T42.3x3	T42.3x4	T42.3x5	T42.3x6
Difencloxazine	T40.2x1	T40.2x2	T40.2x3	T40.2x4	T40.2x5	T40.2x6

Substance	External Cause (T-Code)					
	Poisoning, Accidental (Unintentional)	Poisoning, Intentional Self-Harm	Poisoning, Assault	Poisoning, Undetermined	Adverse Effect	Underdosing
Difenidol	T45.0x1	T45.0x2	T45.0x3	T45.0x4	T45.0x5	T45.0x6
Difenoxin	T47.6x1	T47.6x2	T47.6x3	T47.6x4	T47.6x5	T47.6x6
Difetarsone	T37.3x1	T37.3x2	T37.3x3	T37.3x4	T37.3x5	T37.3x6
Diffusin	T45.3x1	T45.3x2	T45.3x3	T45.3x4	T45.3x5	T45.3x6
Diflorasone	T49.0x1	T49.0x2	T49.0x3	T49.0x4	T49.0x5	T49.0x6
Diflubenzuron	T60.1x1	T60.1x2	T60.1x3	T60.1x4	—	—
Diflos	T44.0x1	T44.0x2	T44.0x3	T44.0x4	T44.0x5	T44.0x6
Diflucortolone	T49.0x1	T49.0x2	T49.0x3	T49.0x4	T49.0x5	T49.0x6
Diflunisal	T39.091	T39.092	T39.093	T39.094	T39.095	T39.096
Difluoromethyldopa	T42.8x1	T42.8x2	T42.8x3	T42.8x4	T42.8x5	T42.8x6
Difluorophate	T44.0x1	T44.0x2	T44.0x3	T44.0x4	T44.0x5	T44.0x6
Digestant NEC	T47.5x1	T47.5x2	T47.5x3	T47.5x4	T47.5x5	T47.5x6
Digitalin(e)	T46.0x1	T46.0x2	T46.0x3	T46.0x4	T46.0x5	T46.0x6
Digitalis (leaf) (glycoside)	T46.0x1	T46.0x2	T46.0x3	T46.0x4	T46.0x5	T46.0x6
lanata	T46.0x1	T46.0x2	T46.0x3	T46.0x4	T46.0x5	T46.0x6
purpurea	T46.0x1	T46.0x2	T46.0x3	T46.0x4	T46.0x5	T46.0x6
Digitoxin	T46.0x1	T46.0x2	T46.0x3	T46.0x4	T46.0x5	T46.0x6
Digitoxose	T46.0x1	T46.0x2	T46.0x3	T46.0x4	T46.0x5	T46.0x6
Digoxin	T46.0x1	T46.0x2	T46.0x3	T46.0x4	T46.0x5	T46.0x6
Digoxine	T46.0x1	T46.0x2	T46.0x3	T46.0x4	T46.0x5	T46.0x6
Dihydralazine	T46.5x1	T46.5x2	T46.5x3	T46.5x4	T46.5x5	T46.5x6
Dihydrazine	T46.5x1	T46.5x2	T46.5x3	T46.5x4	T46.5x5	T46.5x6
Dihydrocodein	T40.2x1	T40.2x2	T40.2x3	T40.2x4	T40.2x5	T40.2x6
Dihydrocodeinone	T40.2x1	T40.2x2	T40.2x3	T40.2x4	T40.2x5	T40.2x6
Dihydroergocornine	T46.7x1	T46.7x2	T46.7x3	T46.7x4	T46.7x5	T46.7x6
Dihydroergocristine (mesilate)	T46.7x1	T46.7x2	T46.7x3	T46.7x4	T46.7x5	T46.7x6
Dihydroergokryptine	T46.7x1	T46.7x2	T46.7x3	T46.7x4	T46.7x5	T46.7x6
Dihydroergotamine	T46.5x1	T46.5x2	T46.5x3	T46.5x4	T46.5x5	T46.5x6
Dihydroergotoxine	T46.7x1	T46.7x2	T46.7x3	T46.7x4	T46.7x5	T46.7x6
mesilate	T46.7x1	T46.7x2	T46.7x3	T46.7x4	T46.7x5	T46.7x6
Dihydrohydroxycodein-one	T40.2x1	T40.2x2	T40.2x3	T40.2x4	T40.2x5	T40.2x6
Dihydrohydroxymorphinone	T40.2x1	T40.2x2	T40.2x3	T40.2x4	T40.2x5	T40.2x6
Dihydroisocodeine	T40.2x1	T40.2x2	T40.2x3	T40.2x4	T40.2x5	T40.2x6
Dihydromorphine	T40.2x1	T40.2x2	T40.2x3	T40.2x4	T40.2x5	T40.2x6
Dihydromorphinone	T40.2x1	T40.2x2	T40.2x3	T40.2x4	T40.2x5	T40.2x6
Dihydrostreptomycin	T36.5x1	T36.5x2	T36.5x3	T36.5x4	T36.5x5	T36.5x6
Dihydrotachysterol	T45.2x1	T45.2x2	T45.2x3	T45.2x4	T45.2x5	T45.2x6
Dihydroxyaluminum aminoacetate	T47.1x1	T47.1x2	T47.1x3	T47.1x4	T47.1x5	T47.1x6
Dihydroxyaluminum sodium carbonate	T47.1x1	T47.1x2	T47.1x3	T47.1x4	T47.1x5	T47.1x6
Dihydroxyanthraquinone	T47.2x1	T47.2x2	T47.2x3	T47.2x4	T47.2x5	T47.2x6

Substance	External Cause (T-Code)					
	Poisoning, Accidental (Unintentional)	Poisoning, Intentional Self-Harm	Poisoning, Assault	Poisoning, Undetermined	Adverse Effect	Underdosing
Dihydroxycodeinone	T40.2x1	T40.2x2	T40.2x3	T40.2x4	T40.2x5	T40.2x6
Dihydroxypropyl theophylline	T50.2x1	T50.2x2	T50.2x3	T50.2x4	T50.2x5	T50.2x6
Diiodohydroxyquin	T37.8x1	T37.8x2	T37.8x3	T37.8x4	T37.8x5	T37.8x6
topical	T49.0x1	T49.0x2	T49.0x3	T49.0x4	T49.0x5	T49.0x6
Diiodohydroxyquinoline	T37.8x1	T37.8x2	T37.8x3	T37.8x4	T37.8x5	T37.8x6
Diiodotyrosine	T38.2x1	T38.2x2	T38.2x3	T38.2x4	T38.2x5	T38.2x6
Diisopromine	T44.3x1	T44.3x2	T44.3x3	T44.3x4	T44.3x5	T44.3x6
Diisopropylamine	T46.3x1	T46.3x2	T46.3x3	T46.3x4	T46.3x5	T46.3x6
Diisopropylfluorophosphonate	T44.0x1	T44.0x2	T44.0x3	T44.0x4	T44.0x5	T44.0x6
Dilantin	T42.0x1	T42.0x2	T42.0x3	T42.0x4	T42.0x5	T42.0x6
Dilaudid	T40.2x1	T40.2x2	T40.2x3	T40.2x4	T40.2x5	T40.2x6
Dilazep	T46.3x1	T46.3x2	T46.3x3	T46.3x4	T46.3x5	T46.3x6
Dill	T47.5x1	T47.5x2	T47.5x3	T47.5x4	T47.5x5	T47.5x6
Diloxanide	T37.3x1	T37.3x2	T37.3x3	T37.3x4	T37.3x5	T37.3x6
Diltiazem	T46.1x1	T46.1x2	T46.1x3	T46.1x4	T46.1x5	T46.1x6
Dimazole	T49.0x1	T49.0x2	T49.0x3	T49.0x4	T49.0x5	T49.0x6
Dimefline	T50.7x1	T50.7x2	T50.7x3	T50.7x4	T50.7x5	T50.7x6
Dimefox	T60.0x1	T60.0x2	T60.0x3	T60.0x4	—	—
Dimemorfan	T48.3x1	T48.3x2	T48.3x3	T48.3x4	T48.3x5	T48.3x6
Dimenhydrinate	T45.0x1	T45.0x2	T45.0x3	T45.0x4	T45.0x5	T45.0x6
Dimercaprol (British anti-lewisite)	T45.8x1	T45.8x2	T45.8x3	T45.8x4	T45.8x5	T45.8x6
Dimercaptopropanol	T45.8x1	T45.8x2	T45.8x3	T45.8x4	T45.8x5	T45.8x6
Dimestrol	T38.5x1	T38.5x2	T38.5x3	T38.5x4	T38.5x5	T38.5x6
Dimetane	T45.0x1	T45.0x2	T45.0x3	T45.0x4	T45.0x5	T45.0x6
Dimethicone	T47.1x1	T47.1x2	T47.1x3	T47.1x4	T47.1x5	T47.1x6
Dimethindene	T45.0x1	T45.0x2	T45.0x3	T45.0x4	T45.0x5	T45.0x6
Dimethisoquin	T49.1x1	T49.1x2	T49.1x3	T49.1x4	T49.1x5	T49.1x6
Dimethisterone	T38.5x1	T38.5x2	T38.5x3	T38.5x4	T38.5x5	T38.5x6
Dimethoate	T60.0x1	T60.0x2	T60.0x3	T60.0x4	—	—
Dimethocaine	T41.3x1	T41.3x2	T41.3x3	T41.3x4	T41.3x5	T41.3x6
Dimethoxanate	T48.3x1	T48.3x2	T48.3x3	T48.3x4	T48.3x5	T48.3x6
Dimethyl						
arsine, arsinic acid	T57.0x1	T57.0x2	T57.0x3	T57.0x4	—	—
carbinol	T51.2x1	T51.2x2	T51.2x3	T51.2x4	—	—
carbonate	T52.8x1	T52.8x2	T52.8x3	T52.8x4	—	—
diguanide	T38.3x1	T38.3x2	T38.3x3	T38.3x4	T38.3x5	T38.3x6
ketone	T52.4x1	T52.4x2	T52.4x3	T52.4x4	—	—
vapor	T52.4x1	T52.4x2	T52.4x3	T52.4x4	—	—
meperidine	T40.2x1	T40.2x2	T40.2x3	T40.2x4	T40.2x5	T40.2x6
parathion	T60.0x1	T60.0x2	T60.0x3	T60.0x4	—	—

Substance	External Cause (T-Code)					
	Poisoning, Accidental (Unintentional)	Poisoning, Intentional Self-Harm	Poisoning, Assault	Poisoning, Undetermined	Adverse Effect	Underdosing
Dimethyl *(Continued)*						
phthlate	T49.3x1	T49.3x2	T49.3x3	T49.3x4	T49.3x5	T49.3x6
polysiloxane	T47.8x1	T47.8x2	T47.8x3	T47.8x4	T47.8x5	T47.8x6
sulfate (fumes)	T59.891	T59.892	T59.893	T59.894	—	—
liquid	T65.891	T65.892	T65.893	T65.894	—	—
sulfoxide (nonmedicinal)	T52.8x1	T52.8x2	T52.8x3	T52.8x4	—	—
medicinal	T49.4x1	T49.4x2	T49.4x3	T49.4x4	T49.4x5	T49.4x6
tryptamine	T40.991	T40.992	T40.993	T40.994	T40.995	T40.996
tubocurarine	T48.1x1	T48.1x2	T48.1x3	T48.1x4	T48.1x5	T48.1x6
Dimethylamine sulfate	T49.4x1	T49.4x2	T49.4x3	T49.4x4	T49.4x5	T49.4x6
Dimethylformamide	T52.8x1	T52.8x2	T52.8x3	T52.8x4	—	—
Dimethyltubocurarinium chloride	T48.1x1	T48.1x2	T48.1x3	T48.1x4	T48.1x5	T48.1x6
Dimeticone	T47.1x1	T47.1x2	T47.1x3	T47.1x4	T47.1x5	T47.1x6
Dimetilan	T60.0x1	T60.0x2	T60.0x3	T60.0x4	—	—
Dimetindene	T45.0x1	T45.0x2	T45.0x3	T45.0x4	T45.0x5	T45.0x6
Dimetotiazine	T43.3x1	T43.3x2	T43.3x3	T43.3x4	T43.3x5	T43.3x6
Dimorpholamine	T50.7x1	T50.7x2	T50.7x3	T50.7x4	T50.7x5	T50.7x6
Dimoxyline	T46.3x1	T46.3x2	T46.3x3	T46.3x4	T46.3x5	T46.3x6
Dinitrobenzene	T65.3x1	T65.3x2	T65.3x3	T65.3x4	—	—
vapor	T59.891	T59.892	T59.893	T59.894	—	—
Dinitrobenzol	T65.3x1	T65.3x2	T65.3x3	T65.3x4	—	—
vapor	T59.891	T59.892	T59.893	T59.894	—	—
Dinitrobutylphenol	T65.3x1	T65.3x2	T65.3x3	T65.3x4	—	—
Dinitro(-ortho-)cresol (pesticide) (spray)	T65.3x1	T65.3x2	T65.3x3	T65.3x4	—	—
Dinitrocyclohexylphenol	T65.3x1	T65.3x2	T65.3x3	T65.3x4	—	—
Dinitrophenol	T65.3x1	T65.3x2	T65.3x3	T65.3x4	—	—
Dinoprost	T48.0x1	T48.0x2	T48.0x3	T48.0x4	T48.0x5	T48.0x6
Dinoprostone	T48.0x1	T48.0x2	T48.0x3	T48.0x4	T48.0x5	T48.0x6
Dinoseb	T60.3x1	T60.3x2	T60.3x3	T60.3x4	—	—
Dioctyl sulfosuccinate (calcium) (sodium)	T47.4x1	T47.4x2	T47.4x3	T47.4x4	T47.4x5	T47.4x6
Diodone	T50.8x1	T50.8x2	T50.8x3	T50.8x4	T50.8x5	T50.8x6
Diodoquin	T37.8x1	T37.8x2	T37.8x3	T37.8x4	T37.8x5	T37.8x6
Dionin	T40.2x1	T40.2x2	T40.2x3	T40.2x4	T40.2x5	T40.2x6
Diosmin	T46.991	T46.992	T46.993	T46.994	T46.995	T46.996
Dioxane	T52.8x1	T52.8x2	T52.8x3	T52.8x4	—	—
Dioxathion	T60.0x1	T60.0x2	T60.0x3	T60.0x4	—	—
Dioxin	T53.7x1	T53.7x2	T53.7x3	T53.7x4	—	—
Dioxopromethazine	T43.3x1	T43.3x2	T43.3x3	T43.3x4	T43.3x5	T43.3x6
Dioxyline	T46.3x1	T46.3x2	T46.3x3	T46.3x4	T46.3x5	T46.3x6
Dipentene	T52.8x1	T52.8x2	T52.8x3	T52.8x4	—	—

Substance	External Cause (T-Code)					
	Poisoning, Accidental (Unintentional)	Poisoning, Intentional Self-Harm	Poisoning, Assault	Poisoning, Undetermined	Adverse Effect	Underdosing
Diperodon	T41.3x1	T41.3x2	T41.3x3	T41.3x4	T41.3x5	T41.3x6
Diphacinone	T60.4x1	T60.4x2	T60.4x3	T60.4x4	—	—
Diphemanil	T44.3x1	T44.3x2	T44.3x3	T44.3x4	T44.3x5	T44.3x6
metilsulfate	T44.3x1	T44.3x2	T44.3x3	T44.3x4	T44.3x5	T44.3x6
Diphenadione	T45.511	T45.512	T45.513	T45.514	T45.515	T45.516
rodenticide	T60.4x1	T60.4x2	T60.4x3	T60.4x4	—	—
Diphenhydramine	T45.0x1	T45.0x2	T45.0x3	T45.0x4	T45.0x5	T45.0x6
Diphenidol	T45.0x1	T45.0x2	T45.0x3	T45.0x4	T45.0x5	T45.0x6
Diphenoxylate	T47.6x1	T47.6x2	T47.6x3	T47.6x4	T47.6x5	T47.6x6
Diphenylamine	T65.3x1	T65.3x2	T65.3x3	T65.3x4	—	—
Diphenylbutazone	T39.2x1	T39.2x2	T39.2x3	T39.2x4	T39.2x5	T39.2x6
Diphenylchloroarsine, not in war	T57.0x1	T57.0x2	T57.0x3	T57.0x4	—	—
Diphenylhydantoin	T42.0x1	T42.0x2	T42.0x3	T42.0x4	T42.0x5	T42.0x6
Diphenylmethane dye	T52.1x1	T52.1x2	T52.1x3	T52.1x4	—	—
Diphenylpyraline	T45.0x1	T45.0x2	T45.0x3	T45.0x4	T45.0x5	T45.0x6
Diphtheria						
antitoxin	T50.Z11	T50.Z12	T50.Z13	T50.Z14	T50.Z15	T50.Z16
toxoid	T50.A91	T50.A92	T50.A93	T50.A94	T50.A95	T50.A96
with tetanus toxoid	T50.A21	T50.A22	T50.A23	T50.A24	T50.A25	T50.A26
with pertussis component	T50.A11	T50.A12	T50.A13	T50.A14	T50.A15	T50.A16
vaccine (combination)	T50.A91	T50.A92	T50.A93	T50.A94	T50.A95	T50.A96
combination						
including pertussis	T50.A11	T50.A12	T50.A13	T50.A14	T50.A15	T50.A16
without pertussis	T50.A21	T50.A22	T50.A23	T50.A24	T50.A25	T50.A26
Diphylline	T50.2x1	T50.2x2	T50.2x3	T50.2x4	T50.2x5	T50.2x6
Dipipanone	T40.4x1	T40.4x2	T40.4x3	T40.4x4	T40.4x5	T40.4x6
Dipivefrine	T49.5x1	T49.5x2	T49.5x3	T49.5x4	T49.5x5	T49.5x6
Diplovax	T50.B91	T50.B92	T50.B93	T50.B94	T50.B95	T50.B96
Diprophylline	T50.2x1	T50.2x2	T50.2x3	T50.2x4	T50.2x5	T50.2x6
Dipropyline	T48.291	T48.292	T48.293	T48.294	T48.295	T48.296
Dipyridamole	T46.3x1	T46.3x2	T46.3x3	T46.3x4	T46.3x5	T46.3x6
Dipyrone	T39.2x1	T39.2x2	T39.2x3	T39.2x4	T39.2x5	T39.2x6
Diquat (dibromide)	T60.3x1	T60.3x2	T60.3x3	T60.3x4	—	—
Disinfectant	T65.891	T65.892	T65.893	T65.894	—	—
alkaline	T54.3x1	T54.3x2	T54.3x3	T54.3x4	—	—
aromatic	T54.1x1	T54.1x2	T54.1x3	T54.1x4	—	—
intestinal	T37.8x1	T37.8x2	T37.8x3	T37.8x4	T37.8x5	T37.8x6
Disipal	T42.8x1	T42.8x2	T42.8x3	T42.8x4	T42.8x5	T42.8x6
Disodium edetate	T50.6x1	T50.6x2	T50.6x3	T50.6x4	T50.6x5	T50.6x6
Disoprofol	T41.291	T41.292	T41.293	T41.294	T41.295	T41.296

	External Cause (T-Code)					
Substance	Poisoning, Accidental (Unintentional)	Poisoning, Intentional Self-Harm	Poisoning, Assault	Poisoning, Undetermined	Adverse Effect	Underdosing
Disopyramide	T46.2x1	T46.2x2	T46.2x3	T46.2x4	T46.2x5	T46.2x6
Distigmine (bromide)	T44.0x1	T44.0x2	T44.0x3	T44.0x4	T44.0x5	T44.0x6
Disulfamide	T50.2x1	T50.2x2	T50.2x3	T50.2x4	T50.2x5	T50.2x6
Disulfanilamide	T37.0x1	T37.0x2	T37.0x3	T37.0x4	T37.0x5	T37.0x6
Disulfiram	T50.6x1	T50.6x2	T50.6x3	T50.6x4	T50.6x5	T50.6x6
Disulfoton	T60.0x1	T60.0x2	T60.0x3	T60.0x4	—	—
Dithiazanine iodide	T37.4x1	T37.4x2	T37.4x3	T37.4x4	T37.4x5	T37.4x6
Dithiocarbamate	T60.0x1	T60.0x2	T60.0x3	T60.0x4	—	—
Dithranol	T49.4x1	T49.4x2	T49.4x3	T49.4x4	T49.4x5	T49.4x6
Diucardin	T50.2x1	T50.2x2	T50.2x3	T50.2x4	T50.2x5	T50.2x6
Diupres	T50.2x1	T50.2x2	T50.2x3	T50.2x4	T50.2x5	T50.2x6
Diuretic NEC	T50.2x1	T50.2x2	T50.2x3	T50.2x4	T50.2x5	T50.2x6
carbonic acid anhydrase inhibitors	T50.2x1	T50.2x2	T50.2x3	T50.2x4	T50.2x5	T50.2x6
benzothiadiazine	T50.2x1	T50.2x2	T50.2x3	T50.2x4	T50.2x5	T50.2x6
furfuryl NEC	T50.2x1	T50.2x2	T50.2x3	T50.2x4	T50.2x5	T50.2x6
mercurial NEC	T50.2x1	T50.2x2	T50.2x3	T50.2x4	T50.2x5	T50.2x6
osmotic	T50.2x1	T50.2x2	T50.2x3	T50.2x4	T50.2x5	T50.2x6
purine NEC	T50.2x1	T50.2x2	T50.2x3	T50.2x4	T50.2x5	T50.2x6
saluretic NEC	T50.2x1	T50.2x2	T50.2x3	T50.2x4	T50.2x5	T50.2x6
sulfonamide	T50.2x1	T50.2x2	T50.2x3	T50.2x4	T50.2x5	T50.2x6
thiazide NEC	T50.2x1	T50.2x2	T50.2x3	T50.2x4	T50.2x5	T50.2x6
xanthine	T50.2x1	T50.2x2	T50.2x3	T50.2x4	T50.2x5	T50.2x6
Diurgin	T50.2x1	T50.2x2	T50.2x3	T50.2x4	T50.2x5	T50.2x6
Diuril	T50.2x1	T50.2x2	T50.2x3	T50.2x4	T50.2x5	T50.2x6
Diuron	T60.3x1	T60.3x2	T60.3x3	T60.3x4	—	—
Divalproex	T42.6x1	T42.6x2	T42.6x3	T42.6x4	T42.6x5	T42.6x6
Divinyl ether	T41.0x1	T41.0x2	T41.0x3	T41.0x4	T41.0x5	T41.0x6
Dixanthogen	T49.0x1	T49.0x2	T49.0x3	T49.0x4	T49.0x5	T49.0x6
Dixyrazine	T43.3x1	T43.3x2	T43.3x3	T43.3x4	T43.3x5	T43.3x6
D-lysergic acid diethylamide	T40.8x1	T40.8x2	T40.8x3	T40.8x4	T40.8x5	T40.8x6
DMCT	T36.4x1	T36.4x2	T36.4x3	T36.4x4	T36.4x5	T36.4x6
DMSO - see Dimethyl sulfoxide						
DNBP	T60.3x1	T60.3x2	T60.3x3	T60.3x4	—	—
DNOC	T65.3x1	T65.3x2	T65.3x3	T65.3x4	—	—
DOCA	T38.0x1	T38.0x2	T38.0x3	T38.0x4	T38.0x5	T38.0x6
Dobutamine	T44.5x1	T44.5x2	T44.5x3	T44.5x4	T44.5x5	T44.5x6
Docusate sodium	T47.4x1	T47.4x2	T47.4x3	T47.4x4	T47.4x5	T47.4x6
Dodicin	T49.0x1	T49.0x2	T49.0x3	T49.0x4	T49.0x5	T49.0x6
Dofamium chloride	T49.0x1	T49.0x2	T49.0x3	T49.0x4	T49.0x5	T49.0x6
Dolophine	T40.3x1	T40.3x2	T40.3x3	T40.3x4	T40.3x5	T40.3x6

Substance	Poisoning, Accidental (Unintentional)	Poisoning, Intentional Self-Harm	Poisoning, Assault	Poisoning, Undetermined	Adverse Effect	Underdosing
	External Cause (T-Code)					
Doloxene	T39.8x1	T39.8x2	T39.8x3	T39.8x4	T39.8x5	T39.8x6
Domestic gas (after combustion) - *see* Gas, utility						
prior to combustion	T59.891	T59.892	T59.893	T59.894	—	—
Domiodol	T48.4x1	T48.4x2	T48.4x3	T48.4x4	T48.4x5	T48.4x6
Domiphen (bromide)	T49.0x1	T49.0x2	T49.0x3	T49.0x4	T49.0x5	T49.0x6
Domperidone	T45.0x1	T45.0x2	T45.0x3	T45.0x4	T45.0x5	T45.0x6
Dopa	T42.8x1	T42.8x2	T42.8x3	T42.8x4	T42.8x5	T42.8x6
Dopamine	T44.991	T44.992	T44.993	T44.994	T44.995	T44.996
Doriden	T42.6x1	T42.6x2	T42.6x3	T42.6x4	T42.6x5	T42.6x6
Dormiral	T42.3x1	T42.3x2	T42.3x3	T42.3x4	T42.3x5	T42.3x6
Dormison	T42.6x1	T42.6x2	T42.6x3	T42.6x4	T42.6x5	T42.6x6
Dornase	T48.4x1	T48.4x2	T48.4x3	T48.4x4	T48.4x5	T48.4x6
Dorsacaine	T41.3x1	T41.3x2	T41.3x3	T41.3x4	T41.3x5	T41.3x6
Dosulepin	T43.011	T43.012	T43.013	T43.014	T43.015	T43.016
Dothiepin	T43.011	T43.012	T43.013	T43.014	T43.015	T43.016
Doxantrazole	T48.6x1	T48.6x2	T48.6x3	T48.6x4	T48.6x5	T48.6x6
Doxapram	T50.7x1	T50.7x2	T50.7x3	T50.7x4	T50.7x5	T50.7x6
Doxazosin	T44.6x1	T44.6x2	T44.6x3	T44.6x4	T44.6x5	T44.6x6
Doxepin	T43.011	T43.012	T43.013	T43.014	T43.015	T43.016
Doxifluridine	T45.1x1	T45.1x2	T45.1x3	T45.1x4	T45.1x5	T45.1x6
Doxorubicin	T45.1x1	T45.1x2	T45.1x3	T45.1x4	T45.1x5	T45.1x6
Doxycycline	T36.4x1	T36.4x2	T36.4x3	T36.4x4	T36.4x5	T36.4x6
Doxylamine	T45.0x1	T45.0x2	T45.0x3	T45.0x4	T45.0x5	T45.0x6
Dramamine	T45.0x1	T45.0x2	T45.0x3	T45.0x4	T45.0x5	T45.0x6
Drano (drain cleaner)	T54.3x1	T54.3x2	T54.3x3	T54.3x4	—	—
Dressing, live pulp	T49.7x1	T49.7x2	T49.7x3	T49.7x4	T49.7x5	T49.7x6
Drocode	T40.2x1	T40.2x2	T40.2x3	T40.2x4	T40.2x5	T40.2x6
Dromoran	T40.2x1	T40.2x2	T40.2x3	T40.2x4	T40.2x5	T40.2x6
Dromostanolone	T38.7x1	T38.7x2	T38.7x3	T38.7x4	T38.7x5	T38.7x6
Dronabinol	T40.7x1	T40.7x2	T40.7x3	T40.7x4	T40.7x5	T40.7x6
Droperidol	T43.591	T43.592	T43.593	T43.594	T43.595	T43.596
Dropropizine	T48.3x1	T48.3x2	T48.3x3	T48.3x4	T48.3x5	T48.3x6
Drostanolone	T38.7x1	T38.7x2	T38.7x3	T38.7x4	T38.7x5	T38.7x6
Drotaverine	T44.3x1	T44.3x2	T44.3x3	T44.3x4	T44.3x5	T44.3x6
Drotrecogin alfa	T45.511	T45.512	T45.513	T45.514	T45.515	T45.516
Drug NEC	T50.901	T50.902	T50.903	T50.904	T50.905	T50.906
specified NEC	T50.991	T50.992	T50.993	T50.994	T50.995	T50.996
DTIC	T45.1x1	T45.1x2	T45.1x3	T45.1x4	T45.1x5	T45.1x6
Duboisine	T44.3x1	T44.3x2	T44.3x3	T44.3x4	T44.3x5	T44.3x6

Substance	Poisoning, Accidental (Unintentional)	Poisoning, Intentional Self-Harm	Poisoning, Assault	Poisoning, Undetermined	Adverse Effect	Underdosing
	External Cause (T-Code)					
Dulcolax	T47.2x1	T47.2x2	T47.2x3	T47.2x4	T47.2x5	T47.2x6
Duponol (C) (EP)	T49.2x1	T49.2x2	T49.2x3	T49.2x4	T49.2x5	T49.2x6
Durabolin	T38.7x1	T38.7x2	T38.7x3	T38.7x4	T38.7x5	T38.7x6
Dyclone	T41.3x1	T41.3x2	T41.3x3	T41.3x4	T41.3x5	T41.3x6
Dyclonine	T41.3x1	T41.3x2	T41.3x3	T41.3x4	T41.3x5	T41.3x6
Dydrogesterone	T38.5x1	T38.5x2	T38.5x3	T38.5x4	T38.5x5	T38.5x6
Dye NEC	T65.6x1	T65.6x2	T65.6x3	T65.6x4	—	—
antiseptic	T49.0x1	T49.0x2	T49.0x3	T49.0x4	T49.0x5	T49.0x6
diagnostic agents	T50.8x1	T50.8x2	T50.8x3	T50.8x4	T50.8x5	T50.8x6
pharmaceutical NEC	T50.901	T50.902	T50.903	T50.904	T50.905	T50.906
Dyflos	T44.0x1	T44.0x2	T44.0x3	T44.0x4	T44.0x5	T44.0x6
Dymelor	T38.3x1	T38.3x2	T38.3x3	T38.3x4	T38.3x5	T38.3x6
Dynamite	T65.3x1	T65.3x2	T65.3x3	T65.3x4	—	—
fumes	T59.891	T59.892	T59.893	T59.894	—	—
Dyphylline	T44.3x1	T44.3x2	T44.3x3	T44.3x4	T44.3x5	T44.3x6
Ear drug NEC	T49.6x1	T49.6x2	T49.6x3	T49.6x4	T49.6x5	T49.6x6
Ear preparations	T49.6x1	T49.6x2	T49.6x3	T49.6x4	T49.6x5	T49.6x6
Econazole	T49.0x1	T49.0x2	T49.0x3	T49.0x4	T49.0x5	T49.0x6
Ecothiopate iodide	T49.5x1	T49.5x2	T49.5x3	T49.5x4	T49.5x5	T49.5x6
Echothiophate, echothiopate, ecothiopate	T49.5x1	T49.5x2	T49.5x3	T49.5x4	T49.5x5	T49.5x6
Ecstasy	T43.621	T43.622	T43.623	T43.624	T43.625	T43.626
Ectylurea	T42.6x1	T42.6x2	T42.6x3	T42.6x4	T42.6x5	T42.6x6
Edathamil disodium	T45.8x1	T45.8x2	T45.8x3	T45.8x4	T45.8x5	T45.8x6
Edecrin	T50.1x1	T50.1x2	T50.1x3	T50.1x4	T50.1x5	T50.1x6
Edetate, disodium (calcium)	T45.8x1	T45.8x2	T45.8x3	T45.8x4	T45.8x5	T45.8x6
Edoxudine	T49.5x1	T49.5x2	T49.5x3	T49.5x4	T49.5x5	T49.5x6
Edrophonium	T44.0x1	T44.0x2	T44.0x3	T44.0x4	T44.0x5	T44.0x6
chloride	T44.0x1	T44.0x2	T44.0x3	T44.0x4	T44.0x5	T44.0x6
EDTA	T50.6x1	T50.6x2	T50.6x3	T50.6x4	T50.6x5	T50.6x6
Eflornithine	T37.2x1	T37.2x2	T37.2x3	T37.2x4	T37.2x5	T37.2x6
Efloxate	T46.3x1	T46.3x2	T46.3x3	T46.3x4	T46.3x5	T46.3x6
Elase	T49.8x1	T49.8x2	T49.8x3	T49.8x4	T49.8x5	T49.8x6
Elastase	T47.5x1	T47.5x2	T47.5x3	T47.5x4	T47.5x5	T47.5x6
Elaterium	T47.2x1	T47.2x2	T47.2x3	T47.2x4	T47.2x5	T47.2x6
Elcatonin	T50.991	T50.992	T50.993	T50.994	T50.995	T50.996
Elder	T62.2x1	T62.2x2	T62.2x3	T62.2x4	—	—
berry (unripe)	T62.1x1	T62.1x2	T62.1x3	T62.1x4	—	—
Electrolyte balance drug	T50.3x1	T50.3x2	T50.3x3	T50.3x4	T50.3x5	T50.3x6
Electrolytes NEC	T50.3x1	T50.3x2	T50.3x3	T50.3x4	T50.3x5	T50.3x6
Electrolytic agent NEC	T50.3x1	T50.3x2	T50.3x3	T50.3x4	T50.3x5	T50.3x6

Substance	Poisoning, Accidental (Unintentional)	Poisoning, Intentional Self-Harm	Poisoning, Assault	Poisoning, Undetermined	Adverse Effect	Underdosing
	External Cause (T-Code)					
Elemental diet	T50.901	T50.902	T50.903	T50.904	T50.905	T50.906
Elliptinium acetate	T45.1x1	T45.1x2	T45.1x3	T45.1x4	T45.1x5	T45.1x6
Embramine	T45.0x1	T45.0x2	T45.0x3	T45.0x4	T45.0x5	T45.0x6
Emepronium (salts)	T44.3x1	T44.3x2	T44.3x3	T44.3x4	T44.3x5	T44.3x6
bromide	T44.3x1	T44.3x2	T44.3x3	T44.3x4	T44.3x5	T44.3x6
Emetic NEC	T47.7x1	T47.7x2	T47.7x3	T47.7x4	T47.7x5	T47.7x6
Emetine	T37.3x1	T37.3x2	T37.3x3	T37.3x4	T37.3x5	T37.3x6
Emollient NEC	T49.3x1	T49.3x2	T49.3x3	T49.3x4	T49.3x5	T49.3x6
Emorfazone	T39.8x1	T39.8x2	T39.8x3	T39.8x4	T39.8x5	T39.8x6
Emylcamate	T43.591	T43.592	T43.593	T43.594	T43.595	T43.596
Enalapril	T46.4x1	T46.4x2	T46.4x3	T46.4x4	T46.4x5	T46.4x6
Enalaprilat	T46.4x1	T46.4x2	T46.4x3	T46.4x4	T46.4x5	T46.4x6
Encainide	T46.2x1	T46.2x2	T46.2x3	T46.2x4	T46.2x5	T46.2x6
Endocaine	T41.3x1	T41.3x2	T41.3x3	T41.3x4	T41.3x5	T41.3x6
Endosulfan	T60.2x1	T60.2x2	T60.2x3	T60.2x4	—	—
Endothall	T60.3x1	T60.3x2	T60.3x3	T60.3x4	—	—
Endralazine	T46.5x1	T46.5x2	T46.5x3	T46.5x4	T46.5x5	T46.5x6
Endrin	T60.1x1	T60.1x2	T60.1x3	T60.1x4	—	—
Enflurane	T41.0x1	T41.0x2	T41.0x3	T41.0x4	T41.0x5	T41.0x6
Enhexymal	T42.3x1	T42.3x2	T42.3x3	T42.3x4	T42.3x5	T42.3x6
Enocitabine	T45.1x1	T45.1x2	T45.1x3	T45.1x4	T45.1x5	T45.1x6
Enovid	T38.4x1	T38.4x2	T38.4x3	T38.4x4	T38.4x5	T38.4x6
Enoxacin	T36.8x1	T36.8x2	T36.8x3	T36.8x4	T36.8x5	T36.8x6
Enoxaparin (sodium)	T45.511	T45.512	T45.513	T45.514	T45.515	T45.516
Enpiprazole	T43.591	T43.592	T43.593	T43.594	T43.595	T43.596
Enprofylline	T48.6x1	T48.6x2	T48.6x3	T48.6x4	T48.6x5	T48.6x6
Enprostil	T47.1x1	T47.1x2	T47.1x3	T47.1x4	T47.1x5	T47.1x6
Enterogastrone	T38.891	T38.892	T38.893	T38.894	T38.895	T38.896
ENT preparations (anti-infectives)	T49.6x1	T49.6x2	T49.6x3	T49.6x4	T49.6x5	T49.6x6
Enviomycin	T36.8x1	T36.8x2	T36.8x3	T36.8x4	T36.8x5	T36.8x6
Enzodase	T45.3x1	T45.3x2	T45.3x3	T45.3x4	T45.3x5	T45.3x6
Enzyme NEC	T45.3x1	T45.3x2	T45.3x3	T45.3x4	T45.3x5	T45.3x6
depolymerizing	T49.8x1	T49.8x2	T49.8x3	T49.8x4	T49.8x5	T49.8x6
fibrolytic	T45.3x1	T45.3x2	T45.3x3	T45.3x4	T45.3x5	T45.3x6
gastric	T45.3x1	T45.3x2	T45.3x3	T45.3x4	T45.3x5	T45.3x6
intestinal	T47.5x1	T47.5x2	T47.5x3	T47.5x4	T47.5x5	T47.5x6
local action	T49.4x1	T49.4x2	T49.4x3	T49.4x4	T49.4x5	T49.4x6
proteolytic	T49.4x1	T49.4x2	T49.4x3	T49.4x4	T49.4x5	T49.4x6
thrombolytic	T45.3x1	T45.3x2	T45.3x3	T45.3x4	T45.3x5	T45.3x6
EPAB	T41.3x1	T41.3x2	T41.3x3	T41.3x4	T41.3x5	T41.3x6

Substance	External Cause (T-Code)					
	Poisoning, Accidental (Unintentional)	Poisoning, Intentional Self-Harm	Poisoning, Assault	Poisoning, Undetermined	Adverse Effect	Underdosing
Epanutin	T42.0x1	T42.0x2	T42.0x3	T42.0x4	T42.0x5	T42.0x6
Ephedra	T44.991	T44.992	T44.993	T44.994	T44.995	T44.996
Ephedrine	T44.991	T44.992	T44.993	T44.994	T44.995	T44.996
Epichlorhydrin, epichlorohydrin	T52.8x1	T52.8x2	T52.8x3	T52.8x4	—	—
Epicillin	T36.0x1	T36.0x2	T36.0x3	T36.0x4	T36.0x5	T36.0x6
Epiestriol	T38.5x1	T38.5x2	T38.5x3	T38.5x4	T38.5x5	T38.5x6
Epilim - *see* Sodium valproate						
Epimestrol	T38.5x1	T38.5x2	T38.5x3	T38.5x4	T38.5x5	T38.5x6
Epinephrine	T44.5x1	T44.5x2	T44.5x3	T44.5x4	T44.5x5	T44.5x6
Epirubicin	T45.1x1	T45.1x2	T45.1x3	T45.1x4	T45.1x5	T45.1x6
Epitiostanol	T38.7x1	T38.7x2	T38.7x3	T38.7x4	T38.7x5	T38.7x6
Epitizide	T50.2x1	T50.2x2	T50.2x3	T50.2x4	T50.2x5	T50.2x6
EPN	T60.0x1	T60.0x2	T60.0x3	T60.0x4	—	—
EPO	T45.8x1	T45.8x2	T45.8x3	T45.8x4	T45.8x5	T45.8x6
Epoetin alpha	T45.8x1	T45.8x2	T45.8x3	T45.8x4	T45.8x5	T45.8x6
Epomediol	T50.991	T50.992	T50.993	T50.994	T50.995	T50.996
Epoprostenol	T45.521	T45.522	T45.523	T45.524	T45.525	T45.526
Epoxy resin	T65.891	T65.892	T65.893	T65.894	—	—
Eprazinone	T48.4x1	T48.4x2	T48.4x3	T48.4x4	T48.4x5	T48.4x6
Epsilon amino-caproic acid	T45.621	T45.622	T45.623	T45.624	T45.625	T45.626
Epsom salt	T47.3x1	T47.3x2	T47.3x3	T47.3x4	T47.3x5	T47.3x6
Eptazocine	T40.4x1	T40.4x2	T40.4x3	T40.4x4	T40.4x5	T40.4x6
Equanil	T43.591	T43.592	T43.593	T43.594	T43.595	T43.596
Equisetum	T62.2x1	T62.2x2	T62.2x3	T62.2x4	—	—
diuretic	T50.2x1	T50.2x2	T50.2x3	T50.2x4	T50.2x5	T50.2x6
Ergobasine	T48.0x1	T48.0x2	T48.0x3	T48.0x4	T48.0x5	T48.0x6
Ergocalciferol	T45.2x1	T45.2x2	T45.2x3	T45.2x4	T45.2x5	T45.2x6
Ergoloid mesylates	T46.7x1	T46.7x2	T46.7x3	T46.7x4	T46.7x5	T46.7x6
Ergometrine	T48.0x1	T48.0x2	T48.0x3	T48.0x4	T48.0x5	T48.0x6
Ergonovine	T48.0x1	T48.0x2	T48.0x3	T48.0x4	T48.0x5	T48.0x6
Ergot NEC	T64.81	T64.82	T64.83	T64.84	—	—
derivative	T48.0x1	T48.0x2	T48.0x3	T48.0x4	T48.0x5	T48.0x6
medicinal (alkaloids)	T48.0x1	T48.0x2	T48.0x3	T48.0x4	T48.0x5	T48.0x6
prepared	T48.0x1	T48.0x2	T48.0x3	T48.0x4	T48.0x5	T48.0x6
Ergotamine	T46.5x1	T46.5x2	T46.5x3	T46.5x4	T46.5x5	T46.5x6
Ergotocine	T48.0x1	T48.0x2	T48.0x3	T48.0x4	T48.0x5	T48.0x6
Ergotrate	T48.0x1	T48.0x2	T48.0x3	T48.0x4	T48.0x5	T48.0x6
Eritrityl tetranitrate	T46.3x1	T46.3x2	T46.3x3	T46.3x4	T46.3x5	T46.3x6
Erythrityl tetranitrate	T46.3x1	T46.3x2	T46.3x3	T46.3x4	T46.3x5	T46.3x6
Erythrol tetranitrate	T46.3x1	T46.3x2	T46.3x3	T46.3x4	T46.3x5	T46.3x6

Substance	External Cause (T-Code)					
	Poisoning, Accidental (Unintentional)	Poisoning, Intentional Self-Harm	Poisoning, Assault	Poisoning, Undetermined	Adverse Effect	Underdosing
Erythromycin (salts)	T36.3x1	T36.3x2	T36.3x3	T36.3x4	T36.3x5	T36.3x6
ophthalmic preparation	T49.5x1	T49.5x2	T49.5x3	T49.5x4	T49.5x5	T49.5x6
topical NEC	T49.0x1	T49.0x2	T49.0x3	T49.0x4	T49.0x5	T49.0x6
Erythropoietin	T45.8x1	T45.8x2	T45.8x3	T45.8x4	T45.8x5	T45.8x6
human	T45.8x1	T45.8x2	T45.8x3	T45.8x4	T45.8x5	T45.8x6
Escin	T46.991	T46.992	T46.993	T46.994	T46.995	T46.996
Esculin	T45.2x1	T45.2x2	T45.2x3	T45.2x4	T45.2x5	T45.2x6
Esculoside	T45.2x1	T45.2x2	T45.2x3	T45.2x4	T45.2x5	T45.2x6
ESDT (ether-soluble tar distillate)	T49.1x1	T49.1x2	T49.1x3	T49.1x4	T49.1x5	T49.1x6
Eserine	T49.5x1	T49.5x2	T49.5x3	T49.5x4	T49.5x5	T49.5x6
Esflurbiprofen	T39.311	T39.312	T39.313	T39.314	T39.315	T39.316
Eskabarb	T42.3x1	T42.3x2	T42.3x3	T42.3x4	T42.3x5	T42.3x6
Eskalith	T43.8x1	T43.8x2	T43.8x3	T43.8x4	T43.8x5	T43.8x6
Esmolol	T44.7x1	T44.7x2	T44.7x3	T44.7x4	T44.7x5	T44.7x6
Estanozolol	T38.7x1	T38.7x2	T38.7x3	T38.7x4	T38.7x5	T38.7x6
Estazolam	T42.4x1	T42.4x2	T42.4x3	T42.4x4	T42.4x5	T42.4x6
Estradiol	T38.5x1	T38.5x2	T38.5x3	T38.5x4	T38.5x5	T38.5x6
with testosterone	T38.7x1	T38.7x2	T38.7x3	T38.7x4	T38.7x5	T38.7x6
benzoate	T38.5x1	T38.5x2	T38.5x3	T38.5x4	T38.5x5	T38.5x6
Estramustine	T45.1x1	T45.1x2	T45.1x3	T45.1x4	T45.1x5	T45.1x6
Estriol	T38.5x1	T38.5x2	T38.5x3	T38.5x4	T38.5x5	T38.5x6
Estrogen	T38.5x1	T38.5x2	T38.5x3	T38.5x4	T38.5x5	T38.5x6
with progesterone	T38.5x1	T38.5x2	T38.5x3	T38.5x4	T38.5x5	T38.5x6
conjugated	T38.5x1	T38.5x2	T38.5x3	T38.5x4	T38.5x5	T38.5x6
Estrone	T38.5x1	T38.5x2	T38.5x3	T38.5x4	T38.5x5	T38.5x6
Estropipate	T38.5x1	T38.5x2	T38.5x3	T38.5x4	T38.5x5	T38.5x6
Etacrynate sodium	T50.1x1	T50.1x2	T50.1x3	T50.1x4	T50.1x5	T50.1x6
Etacrynic acid	T50.1x1	T50.1x2	T50.1x3	T50.1x4	T50.1x5	T50.1x6
Etafedrine	T48.6x1	T48.6x2	T48.6x3	T48.6x4	T48.6x5	T48.6x6
Etafenone	T46.3x1	T46.3x2	T46.3x3	T46.3x4	T46.3x5	T46.3x6
Etambutol	T37.1x1	T37.1x2	T37.1x3	T37.1x4	T37.1x5	T37.1x6
Etamiphyllin	T48.6x1	T48.6x2	T48.6x3	T48.6x4	T48.6x5	T48.6x6
Etamivan	T50.7x1	T50.7x2	T50.7x3	T50.7x4	T50.7x5	T50.7x6
Etamsylate	T45.7x1	T45.7x2	T45.7x3	T45.7x4	T45.7x5	T45.7x6
Etebenecid	T50.4x1	T50.4x2	T50.4x3	T50.4x4	T50.4x5	T50.4x6
Ethacridine	T49.0x1	T49.0x2	T49.0x3	T49.0x4	T49.0x5	T49.0x6
Ethacrynic acid	T50.1x1	T50.1x2	T50.1x3	T50.1x4	T50.1x5	T50.1x6
Ethadione	T42.2x1	T42.2x2	T42.2x3	T42.2x4	T42.2x5	T42.2x6
Ethambutol	T37.1x1	T37.1x2	T37.1x3	T37.1x4	T37.1x5	T37.1x6
Ethamide	T50.2x1	T50.2x2	T50.2x3	T50.2x4	T50.2x5	T50.2x6

Substance	External Cause (T-Code)					
	Poisoning, Accidental (Unintentional)	Poisoning, Intentional Self-Harm	Poisoning, Assault	Poisoning, Undetermined	Adverse Effect	Underdosing
Ethamivan	T50.7x1	T50.7x2	T50.7x3	T50.7x4	T50.7x5	T50.7x6
Ethamsylate	T45.7x1	T45.7x2	T45.7x3	T45.7x4	T45.7x5	T45.7x6
Ethanol	T51.0x1	T51.0x2	T51.0x3	T51.0x4	—	—
beverage	T51.0x1	T51.0x2	T51.0x3	T51.0x4	—	—
Ethanolamine oleate	T46.8x1	T46.8x2	T46.8x3	T46.8x4	T46.8x5	T46.8x6
Ethaverine	T44.3x1	T44.3x2	T44.3x3	T44.3x4	T44.3x5	T44.3x6
Ethchlorvynol	T42.6x1	T42.6x2	T42.6x3	T42.6x4	T42.6x5	T42.6x6
Ethebenecid	T50.4x1	T50.4x2	T50.4x3	T50.4x4	T50.4x5	T50.4x6
Ether (vapor)	T41.0x1	T41.0x2	T41.0x3	T41.0x4	T41.0x5	T41.0x6
anesthetic	T41.0x1	T41.0x2	T41.0x3	T41.0x4	T41.0x5	T41.0x6
divinyl	T41.0x1	T41.0x2	T41.0x3	T41.0x4	T41.0x5	T41.0x6
ethyl (medicinal)	T41.0x1	T41.0x2	T41.0x3	T41.0x4	T41.0x5	T41.0x6
nonmedicinal	T52.8x1	T52.8x2	T52.8x3	T52.8x4	—	—
petroleum - *see* Ligroin						
solvent	T52.8x1	T52.8x2	T52.8x3	T52.8x4	—	—
Ethiazide	T50.2x1	T50.2x2	T50.2x3	T50.2x4	T50.2x5	T50.2x6
Ethidium chloride (vapor)	T59.891	T59.892	T59.893	T59.894	—	—
Ethinamate	T42.6x1	T42.6x2	T42.6x3	T42.6x4	T42.6x5	T42.6x6
Ethinylestradiol, ethinyloestradiol	T38.5x1	T38.5x2	T38.5x3	T38.5x4	T38.5x5	T38.5x6
with						
levonorgestrel	T38.4x1	T38.4x2	T38.4x3	T38.4x4	T38.4x5	T38.4x6
norethisterone	T38.4x1	T38.4x2	T38.4x3	T38.4x4	T38.4x5	T38.4x6
Ethiodized oil (131 I)	T50.8x1	T50.8x2	T50.8x3	T50.8x4	T50.8x5	T50.8x6
Ethion	T60.0x1	T60.0x2	T60.0x3	T60.0x4	—	—
Ethionamide	T37.1x1	T37.1x2	T37.1x3	T37.1x4	T37.1x5	T37.1x6
Ethioniamide	T37.1x1	T37.1x2	T37.1x3	T37.1x4	T37.1x5	T37.1x6
Ethisterone	T38.5x1	T38.5x2	T38.5x3	T38.5x4	T38.5x5	T38.5x6
Ethobral	T42.3x1	T42.3x2	T42.3x3	T42.3x4	T42.3x5	T42.3x6
Ethocaine (infiltration) (topical)	T41.3x1	T41.3x2	T41.3x3	T41.3x4	T41.3x5	T41.3x6
nerve block (peripheral) (plexus)	T41.3x1	T41.3x2	T41.3x3	T41.3x4	T41.3x5	T41.3x6
spinal	T41.3x1	T41.3x2	T41.3x3	T41.3x4	T41.3x5	T41.3x6
Ethoheptazine	T40.4x1	T40.4x2	T40.4x3	T40.4x4	T40.4x5	T40.4x6
Ethopropazine	T44.3x1	T44.3x2	T44.3x3	T44.3x4	T44.3x5	T44.3x6
Ethosuximide	T42.2x1	T42.2x2	T42.2x3	T42.2x4	T42.2x5	T42.2x6
Ethotoin	T42.0x1	T42.0x2	T42.0x3	T42.0x4	T42.0x5	T42.0x6
Ethoxazene	T37.91	T37.92	T37.93	T37.94	T37.95	T37.96
Ethoxazorutoside	T46.991	T46.992	T46.993	T46.994	T46.995	T46.996
2-Ethoxyethanol	T52.3x1	T52.3x2	T52.3x3	T52.3x4	—	—
Ethoxzolamide	T50.2x1	T50.2x2	T50.2x3	T50.2x4	T50.2x5	T50.2x6

Substance	External Cause (T-Code)					
	Poisoning, Accidental (Unintentional)	Poisoning, Intentional Self-Harm	Poisoning, Assault	Poisoning, Undetermined	Adverse Effect	Underdosing
Ethyl						
acetate	T52.8x1	T52.8x2	T52.8x3	T52.8x4	—	—
alcohol	T51.0x1	T51.0x2	T51.0x3	T51.0x4	—	—
beverage	T51.0x1	T51.0x2	T51.0x3	T51.0x4	—	—
aldehyde (vapor)	T59.891	T59.892	T59.893	T59.894	—	—
liquid	T52.8x1	T52.8x2	T52.8x3	T52.8x4	—	—
aminobenzoate	T41.3x1	T41.3x2	T41.3x3	T41.3x4	T41.3x5	T41.3x6
aminophenothiazine	T43.3x1	T43.3x2	T43.3x3	T43.3x4	T43.3x5	T43.3x6
benzoate	T52.8x1	T52.8x2	T52.8x3	T52.8x4	—	—
biscoumacetate	T45.511	T45.512	T45.513	T45.514	T45.515	T45.516
bromide (anesthetic)	T41.0x1	T41.0x2	T41.0x3	T41.0x4	T41.0x5	T41.0x6
carbamate	T45.1x1	T45.1x2	T45.1x3	T45.1x4	T45.1x5	T45.1x6
carbinol	T51.2x1	T51.2x2	T51.2x3	T51.2x4	—	—
carbonate	T52.8x1	T52.8x2	T52.8x3	T52.8x4	—	—
chaulmoograte	T37.1x1	T37.1x2	T37.1x3	T37.1x4	T37.1x5	T37.1x6
chloride (anesthetic)	T41.0x1	T41.0x2	T41.0x3	T41.0x4	T41.0x5	T41.0x6
anesthetic (local)	T41.3x1	T41.3x2	T41.3x3	T41.3x4	T41.3x5	T41.3x6
inhaled	T41.0x1	T41.0x2	T41.0x3	T41.0x4	T41.0x5	T41.0x6
local	T49.4x1	T49.4x2	T49.4x3	T49.4x4	T49.4x5	T49.4x6
solvent	T53.6x1	T53.6x2	T53.6x3	T53.6x4	—	—
dibunate	T48.3x1	T48.3x2	T48.3x3	T48.3x4	T48.3x5	T48.3x6
dichloroarsine (vapor)	T57.0x1	T57.0x2	T57.0x3	T57.0x4	—	—
estranol	T38.7x1	T38.7x2	T38.7x3	T38.7x4	T38.7x5	T38.7x6
ether (see also ether)	T52.8x1	T52.8x2	T52.8x3	T52.8x4	—	—
formate NEC (solvent)	T52.0x1	T52.0x2	T52.0x3	T52.0x4	—	—
fumarate	T49.4x1	T49.4x2	T49.4x3	T49.4x4	T49.4x5	T49.4x6
hydroxyisobutyrate NEC (solvent)	T52.8x1	T52.8x2	T52.8x3	T52.8x4	—	—
iodoacetate	T59.3x1	T59.3x2	T59.3x3	T59.3x4	—	—
lactate NEC (solvent)	T52.8x1	T52.8x2	T52.8x3	T52.8x4	—	—
loflazepate	T42.4x1	T42.4x2	T42.4x3	T42.4x4	T42.4x5	T42.4x6
mercuric chloride	T56.1x1	T56.1x2	T56.1x3	T56.1x4	—	—
methylcarbinol	T51.8x1	T51.8x2	T51.8x3	T51.8x4	—	—
morphine	T40.2x1	T40.2x2	T40.2x3	T40.2x4	T40.2x5	T40.2x6
noradrenaline	T48.6x1	T48.6x2	T48.6x3	T48.6x4	T48.6x5	T48.6x6
oxybutyrate NEC (solvent)	T52.8x1	T52.8x2	T52.8x3	T52.8x4	—	—
Ethylene (gas)	T59.891	T59.892	T59.893	T59.894	—	—
anesthetic (general)	T41.0x1	T41.0x2	T41.0x3	T41.0x4	T41.0x5	T41.0x6
chlorohydrin	T52.8x1	T52.8x2	T52.8x3	T52.8x4	—	—
vapor	T53.6x1	T53.6x2	T53.6x3	T53.6x4	—	—
dichloride	T52.8x1	T52.8x2	T52.8x3	T52.8x4	—	—
vapor	T53.6x1	T53.6x2	T53.6x3	T53.6x4	—	—

Substance	External Cause (T-Code)					
	Poisoning, Accidental (Unintentional)	Poisoning, Intentional Self-Harm	Poisoning, Assault	Poisoning, Undetermined	Adverse Effect	Underdosing
Ethylene *(Continued)*						
dinitrate	T52.3x1	T52.3x2	T52.3x3	T52.3x4	—	—
glycol(s)	T52.8x1	T52.8x2	T52.8x3	T52.8x4	—	—
dinitrate	T52.3x1	T52.3x2	T52.3x3	T52.3x4	—	—
monobutyl ether	T52.3x1	T52.3x2	T52.3x3	T52.3x4	—	—
imine	T54.1x1	T54.1x2	T54.1x3	T54.1x4	—	—
oxide (fumigant) (nonmedicinal)	T59.891	T59.892	T59.893	T59.894	—	—
medicinal	T49.0x1	T49.0x2	T49.0x3	T49.0x4	T49.0x5	T49.0x6
Ethylenediamine theophylline	T48.6x1	T48.6x2	T48.6x3	T48.6x4	T48.6x5	T48.6x6
Ethylenediaminetetra-acetic acid	T50.6x1	T50.6x2	T50.6x3	T50.6x4	T50.6x5	T50.6x6
Ethylenedinitrilotetra-acetate	T50.6x1	T50.6x2	T50.6x3	T50.6x4	T50.6x5	T50.6x6
Ethylestrenol	T38.7x1	T38.7x2	T38.7x3	T38.7x4	T38.7x5	T38.7x6
Ethylhydroxycellulose	T47.4x1	T47.4x2	T47.4x3	T47.4x4	T47.4x5	T47.4x6
Ethylidene						
chloride NEC	T53.6x1	T53.6x2	T53.6x3	T53.6x4	—	—
diacetate	T60.3x1	T60.3x2	T60.3x3	T60.3x4	—	—
dicoumarin	T45.511	T45.512	T45.513	T45.514	T45.515	T45.516
dicoumarol	T45.511	T45.512	T45.513	T45.514	T45.515	T45.516
diethyl ether	T52.0x1	T52.0x2	T52.0x3	T52.0x4	—	—
Ethylmorphine	T40.2x1	T40.2x2	T40.2x3	T40.2x4	T40.2x5	T40.2x6
Ethylnorepinephrine	T48.6x1	T48.6x2	T48.6x3	T48.6x4	T48.6x5	T48.6x6
Ethylparachlorophen-oxyisobutyrate	T46.6x1	T46.6x2	T46.6x3	T46.6x4	T46.6x5	T46.6x6
Ethynodiol	T38.4x1	T38.4x2	T38.4x3	T38.4x4	T38.4x5	T38.4x6
with mestranol diacetate	T38.4x1	T38.4x2	T38.4x3	T38.4x4	T38.4x5	T38.4x6
Etidocaine	T41.3x1	T41.3x2	T41.3x3	T41.3x4	T41.3x5	T41.3x6
infiltration (subcutaneous)	T41.3x1	T41.3x2	T41.3x3	T41.3x4	T41.3x5	T41.3x6
nerve (peripheral) (plexus)	T41.3x1	T41.3x2	T41.3x3	T41.3x4	T41.3x5	T41.3x6
Etidronate	T50.991	T50.992	T50.993	T50.994	T50.995	T50.996
Etidronic acid (disodium salt)	T50.991	T50.992	T50.993	T50.994	T50.995	T50.996
Etifoxine	T42.6x1	T42.6x2	T42.6x3	T42.6x4	T42.6x5	T42.6x6
Etilefrine	T44.4x1	T44.4x2	T44.4x3	T44.4x4	T44.4x5	T44.4x6
Etilfen	T42.3x1	T42.3x2	T42.3x3	T42.3x4	T42.3x5	T42.3x6
Etinodiol	T38.4x1	T38.4x2	T38.4x3	T38.4x4	T38.4x5	T38.4x6
Etiroxate	T46.6x1	T46.6x2	T46.6x3	T46.6x4	T46.6x5	T46.6x6
Etizolam	T42.4x1	T42.4x2	T42.4x3	T42.4x4	T42.4x5	T42.4x6
Etodolac	T39.391	T39.392	T39.393	T39.394	T39.395	T39.396
Etofamide	T37.3x1	T37.3x2	T37.3x3	T37.3x4	T37.3x5	T37.3x6
Etofibrate	T46.6x1	T46.6x2	T46.6x3	T46.6x4	T46.6x5	T46.6x6
Etofylline	T46.7x1	T46.7x2	T46.7x3	T46.7x4	T46.7x5	T46.7x6
clofibrate	T46.6x1	T46.6x2	T46.6x3	T46.6x4	T46.6x5	T46.6x6
Etoglucid	T45.1x1	T45.1x2	T45.1x3	T45.1x4	T45.1x5	T45.1x6

Substance	External Cause (T-Code)					
	Poisoning, Accidental (Unintentional)	Poisoning, Intentional Self-Harm	Poisoning, Assault	Poisoning, Undetermined	Adverse Effect	Underdosing
Etomidate	T41.1x1	T41.1x2	T41.1x3	T41.1x4	T41.1x5	T41.1x6
Etomide	T39.8x1	T39.8x2	T39.8x3	T39.8x4	T39.8x5	T39.8x6
Etomidoline	T44.3x1	T44.3x2	T44.3x3	T44.3x4	T44.3x5	T44.3x6
Etoposide	T45.1x1	T45.1x2	T45.1x3	T45.1x4	T45.1x5	T45.1x6
Etorphine	T40.2x1	T40.2x2	T40.2x3	T40.2x4	T40.2x5	T40.2x6
Etoval	T42.3x1	T42.3x2	T42.3x3	T42.3x4	T42.3x5	T42.3x6
Etoval	T42.3x1	T42.3x2	T42.3x3	T42.3x4	T42.3x5	T42.3x6
Etozolin	T50.1x1	T50.1x2	T50.1x3	T50.1x4	T50.1x5	T50.1x6
Etretinate	T50.991	T50.992	T50.993	T50.994	T50.995	T50.996
Etryptamine	T43.691	T43.692	T43.693	T43.694	T43.695	T43.696
Etybenzatropine	T44.3x1	T44.3x2	T44.3x3	T44.3x4	T44.3x5	T44.3x6
Etynodiol	T38.4x1	T38.4x2	T38.4x3	T38.4x4	T38.4x5	T38.4x6
Eucaine	T41.3x1	T41.3x2	T41.3x3	T41.3x4	T41.3x5	T41.3x6
Eucalyptus oil	T49.7x1	T49.7x2	T49.7x3	T49.7x4	T49.7x5	T49.7x6
Eucatropine	T49.5x1	T49.5x2	T49.5x3	T49.5x4	T49.5x5	T49.5x6
Eucodal	T40.2x1	T40.2x2	T40.2x3	T40.2x4	T40.2x5	T40.2x6
Euneryl	T42.3x1	T42.3x2	T42.3x3	T42.3x4	T42.3x5	T42.3x6
Euphthalmine	T44.3x1	T44.3x2	T44.3x3	T44.3x4	T44.3x5	T44.3x6
Eurax	T49.0x1	T49.0x2	T49.0x3	T49.0x4	T49.0x5	T49.0x6
Euresol	T49.4x1	T49.4x2	T49.4x3	T49.4x4	T49.4x5	T49.4x6
Euthroid	T38.1x1	T38.1x2	T38.1x3	T38.1x4	T38.1x5	T38.1x6
Evans blue	T50.8x1	T50.8x2	T50.8x3	T50.8x4	T50.8x5	T50.8x6
Evipal	T42.3x1	T42.3x2	T42.3x3	T42.3x4	T42.3x5	T42.3x6
sodium	T41.1x1	T41.1x2	T41.1x3	T41.1x4	T41.1x5	T41.1x6
Evipan	T42.3x1	T42.3x2	T42.3x3	T42.3x4	T42.3x5	T42.3x6
sodium	T41.1x1	T41.1x2	T41.1x3	T41.1x4	T41.1x5	T41.1x6
Exalamide	T49.0x1	T49.0x2	T49.0x3	T49.0x4	T49.0x5	T49.0x6
Exalgin	T39.1x1	T39.1x2	T39.1x3	T39.1x4	T39.1x5	T39.1x6
Excipients, pharmaceutical	T50.901	T50.902	T50.903	T50.904	T50.905	T50.906
Exhaust gas (engine) (motor vehicle)	T58.01	T58.02	T58.03	T58.04	—	—
Ex-Lax (phenolphthalein)	T47.2x1	T47.2x2	T47.2x3	T47.2x4	T47.2x5	T47.2x6
Expectorant NEC	T48.4x1	T48.4x2	T48.4x3	T48.4x4	T48.4x5	T48.4x6
Extended insulin zinc suspension	T38.3x1	T38.3x2	T38.3x3	T38.3x4	T38.3x5	T38.3x6
External medications (skin) (mucous membrane)	T49.91	T49.92	T49.93	T49.94	T49.95	T49.96
dental agent	T49.7x1	T49.7x2	T49.7x3	T49.7x4	T49.7x5	T49.7x6
ENT agent	T49.6x1	T49.6x2	T49.6x3	T49.6x4	T49.6x5	T49.6x6
ophthalmic preparation	T49.5x1	T49.5x2	T49.5x3	T49.5x4	T49.5x5	T49.5x6
specified NEC	T49.8x1	T49.8x2	T49.8x3	T49.8x4	T49.8x5	T49.8x6
Extrapyramidal antagonist NEC	T44.3x1	T44.3x2	T44.3x3	T44.3x4	T44.3x5	T44.3x6
Eye agents (anti-infective)	T49.5x1	T49.5x2	T49.5x3	T49.5x4	T49.5x5	T49.5x6

Substance	Poisoning, Accidental (Unintentional)	Poisoning, Intentional Self-Harm	Poisoning, Assault	Poisoning, Undetermined	Adverse Effect	Underdosing
			External Cause (T-Code)			
Eye drug NEC	T49.5x1	T49.5x2	T49.5x3	T49.5x4	T49.5x5	T49.5x6
FAC (fluorouracil + doxorubicin + cyclophosphamide)	T45.1x1	T45.1x2	T45.1x3	T45.1x4	T45.1x5	T45.1x6
Factor						
I (fibrinogen)	T45.8x1	T45.8x2	T45.8x3	T45.8x4	T45.8x5	T45.8x6
III (thromboplastin)	T45.8x1	T45.8x2	T45.8x3	T45.8x4	T45.8x5	T45.8x6
VIII (antihemophilic Factor) (Concentrate)	T45.8x1	T45.8x2	T45.8x3	T45.8x4	T45.8x5	T45.8x6
IX complex	T45.7x1	T45.7x2	T45.7x3	T45.7x4	T45.7x5	T45.7x6
human	T45.8x1	T45.8x2	T45.8x3	T45.8x4	T45.8x5	T45.8x6
Famotidine	T47.0x1	T47.0x2	T47.0x3	T47.0x4	T47.0x5	T47.0x6
Fat suspension, intravenous	T50.991	T50.992	T50.993	T50.994	T50.995	T50.996
Fazadinium bromide	T48.1x1	T48.1x2	T48.1x3	T48.1x4	T48.1x5	T48.1x6
Febarbamate	T42.3x1	T42.3x2	T42.3x3	T42.3x4	T42.3x5	T42.3x6
Fecal softener	T47.4x1	T47.4x2	T47.4x3	T47.4x4	T47.4x5	T47.4x6
Fedrilate	T48.3x1	T48.3x2	T48.3x3	T48.3x4	T48.3x5	T48.3x6
Felodipine	T46.1x1	T46.1x2	T46.1x3	T46.1x4	T46.1x5	T46.1x6
Felypressin	T38.891	T38.892	T38.893	T38.894	T38.895	T38.896
Femoxetine	T43.221	T43.222	T43.223	T43.224	T43.225	T43.226
Fenalcomine	T46.3x1	T46.3x2	T46.3x3	T46.3x4	T46.3x5	T46.3x6
Fenamisal	T37.1x1	T37.1x2	T37.1x3	T37.1x4	T37.1x5	T37.1x6
Fenazone	T39.2x1	T39.2x2	T39.2x3	T39.2x4	T39.2x5	T39.2x6
Fenbendazole	T37.4x1	T37.4x2	T37.4x3	T37.4x4	T37.4x5	T37.4x6
Fenbutrazate	T50.5x1	T50.5x2	T50.5x3	T50.5x4	T50.5x5	T50.5x6
Fencamfamine	T43.691	T43.692	T43.693	T43.694	T43.695	T43.696
Fendiline	T46.1x1	T46.1x2	T46.1x3	T46.1x4	T46.1x5	T46.1x6
Fenetylline	T43.691	T43.692	T43.693	T43.694	T43.695	T43.696
Fenflumizole	T39.391	T39.392	T39.393	T39.394	T39.395	T39.396
Fenfluramine	T50.5x1	T50.5x2	T50.5x3	T50.5x4	T50.5x5	T50.5x6
Fenobarbital	T42.3x1	T42.3x2	T42.3x3	T42.3x4	T42.3x5	T42.3x6
Fenofibrate	T46.6x1	T46.6x2	T46.6x3	T46.6x4	T46.6x5	T46.6x6
Fenoprofen	T39.311	T39.312	T39.313	T39.314	T39.315	T39.316
Fenoterol	T48.6x1	T48.6x2	T48.6x3	T48.6x4	T48.6x5	T48.6x6
Fenoverine	T44.3x1	T44.3x2	T44.3x3	T44.3x4	T44.3x5	T44.3x6
Fenoxazoline	T48.5x1	T48.5x2	T48.5x3	T48.5x4	T48.5x5	T48.5x6
Fenproporex	T50.5x1	T50.5x2	T50.5x3	T50.5x4	T50.5x5	T50.5x6
Fenquizone	T50.2x1	T50.2x2	T50.2x3	T50.2x4	T50.2x5	T50.2x6
Fentanyl	T40.4x1	T40.4x2	T40.4x3	T40.4x4	T40.4x5	T40.4x6
Fentazin	T43.3x1	T43.3x2	T43.3x3	T43.3x4	T43.3x5	T43.3x6
Fenthion	T60.0x1	T60.0x2	T60.0x3	T60.0x4	—	—
Fenticlor	T49.0x1	T49.0x2	T49.0x3	T49.0x4	T49.0x5	T49.0x6
Fenylbutazone	T39.2x1	T39.2x2	T39.2x3	T39.2x4	T39.2x5	T39.2x6

Substance	External Cause (T-Code)					
	Poisoning, Accidental (Unintentional)	Poisoning, Intentional Self-Harm	Poisoning, Assault	Poisoning, Undetermined	Adverse Effect	Underdosing
Feprazone	T39.2x1	T39.2x2	T39.2x3	T39.2x4	T39.2x5	T39.2x6
Fer de lance (bite) (venom)	T63.061	T63.062	T63.063	T63.064	—	—
Ferric - *see also* Iron						
chloride	T45.4x1	T45.4x2	T45.4x3	T45.4x4	T45.4x5	T45.4x6
citrate	T45.4x1	T45.4x2	T45.4x3	T45.4x4	T45.4x5	T45.4x6
hydroxide						
colloidal	T45.4x1	T45.4x2	T45.4x3	T45.4x4	T45.4x5	T45.4x6
polymaltose	T45.4x1	T45.4x2	T45.4x3	T45.4x4	T45.4x5	T45.4x6
pyrophosphate	T45.4x1	T45.4x2	T45.4x3	T45.4x4	T45.4x5	T45.4x6
Ferritin	T45.4x1	T45.4x2	T45.4x3	T45.4x4	T45.4x5	T45.4x6
Ferrocholinate	T45.4x1	T45.4x2	T45.4x3	T45.4x4	T45.4x5	T45.4x6
Ferrodextrane	T45.4x1	T45.4x2	T45.4x3	T45.4x4	T45.4x5	T45.4x6
Ferropolimaler	T45.4x1	T45.4x2	T45.4x3	T45.4x4	T45.4x5	T45.4x6
Ferrous - *see also* Iron						
phosphate	T45.4x1	T45.4x2	T45.4x3	T45.4x4	T45.4x5	T45.4x6
salt	T45.4x1	T45.4x2	T45.4x3	T45.4x4	T45.4x5	T45.4x6
with folic acid	T45.4x1	T45.4x2	T45.4x3	T45.4x4	T45.4x5	T45.4x6
Ferrous fumerate, gluconate, lactate, salt NEC, sulfate (medicinal)	T45.4x1	T45.4x2	T45.4x3	T45.4x4	T45.4x5	T45.4x6
Ferrovanadium (fumes)	T59.891	T59.892	T59.893	T59.894	—	—
Ferrum - *see* Iron						
Fertilizers NEC	T65.891	T65.892	T65.893	T65.894	—	—
with herbicide mixture	T60.3x1	T60.3x2	T60.3x3	T60.3x4	—	—
Fetoxilate	T47.6x1	T47.6x2	T47.6x3	T47.6x4	T47.6x5	T47.6x6
Fiber, dietary	T47.4x1	T47.4x2	T47.4x3	T47.4x4	T47.4x5	T47.4x6
Fibrinogen (human)	T45.8x1	T45.8x2	T45.8x3	T45.8x4	T45.8x5	T45.8x6
Fibrinolysin (human)	T45.691	T45.692	T45.693	T45.694	T45.695	T45.696
Fibrinolysis-affecting drug	T45.601	T45.602	T45.603	T45.604	T45.605	T45.606
Fibrinolysis inhibitor NEC	T45.621	T45.622	T45.623	T45.624	T45.625	T45.626
Fibrinolytic drug	T45.611	T45.612	T45.613	T45.614	T45.615	T45.616
Filix mas	T37.4x1	T37.4x2	T37.4x3	T37.4x4	T37.4x5	T37.4x6
Filtering cream	T49.3x1	T49.3x2	T49.3x3	T49.3x4	T49.3x5	T49.3x6
Fiorinal	T39.011	T39.012	T39.013	T39.014	T39.015	T39.016
Firedamp	T59.891	T59.892	T59.893	T59.894	—	—
Fish, noxious, nonbacterial	T61.771	T61.772	T61.773	T61.774	—	—
ciguatera	T61.01	T61.02	T61.03	T61.04	—	—
scombroid	T61.11	T61.12	T61.13	T61.14	—	—
shell	T61.781	T61.782	T61.783	T61.784	—	—
Flagyl	T37.3x1	T37.3x2	T37.3x3	T37.3x4	T37.3x5	T37.3x6
Flavine adenine dinucleotide	T45.2x1	T45.2x2	T45.2x3	T45.2x4	T45.2x5	T45.2x6
Flavodic acid	T46.991	T46.992	T46.993	T46.994	T46.995	T46.996

Substance	External Cause (T-Code)					
	Poisoning, Accidental (Unintentional)	Poisoning, Intentional Self-Harm	Poisoning, Assault	Poisoning, Undetermined	Adverse Effect	Underdosing
Flavoxate	T44.3x1	T44.3x2	T44.3x3	T44.3x4	T44.3x5	T44.3x6
Flaxedil	T48.1x1	T48.1x2	T48.1x3	T48.1x4	T48.1x5	T48.1x6
Flaxseed (medicinal)	T49.3x1	T49.3x2	T49.3x3	T49.3x4	T49.3x5	T49.3x6
Flecainide	T46.2x1	T46.2x2	T46.2x3	T46.2x4	T46.2x5	T46.2x6
Fleroxacin	T36.8x1	T36.8x2	T36.8x3	T36.8x4	T36.8x5	T36.8x6
Floctafenine	T39.8x1	T39.8x2	T39.8x3	T39.8x4	T39.8x5	T39.8x6
Flomax	T44.6x1	T44.6x2	T44.6x3	T44.6x4	T44.6x5	T44.6x6
Flomoxef	T36.1x1	T36.1x2	T36.1x3	T36.1x4	T36.1x5	T36.1x6
Flopropione	T44.3x1	T44.3x2	T44.3x3	T44.3x4	T44.3x5	T44.3x6
Florantyrone	T47.5x1	T47.5x2	T47.5x3	T47.5x4	T47.5x5	T47.5x6
Floraquin	T37.8x1	T37.8x2	T37.8x3	T37.8x4	T37.8x5	T37.8x6
Florinef	T38.0x1	T38.0x2	T38.0x3	T38.0x4	T38.0x5	T38.0x6
ENT agent	T49.6x1	T49.6x2	T49.6x3	T49.6x4	T49.6x5	T49.6x6
ophthalmic preparation	T49.5x1	T49.5x2	T49.5x3	T49.5x4	T49.5x5	T49.5x6
topical NEC	T49.0x1	T49.0x2	T49.0x3	T49.0x4	T49.0x5	T49.0x6
Flowers of sulfur	T49.4x1	T49.4x2	T49.4x3	T49.4x4	T49.4x5	T49.4x6
Floxuridine	T45.1x1	T45.1x2	T45.1x3	T45.1x4	T45.1x5	T45.1x6
Fluanisone	T43.4x1	T43.4x2	T43.4x3	T43.4x4	T43.4x5	T43.4x6
Flubendazole	T37.4x1	T37.4x2	T37.4x3	T37.4x4	T37.4x5	T37.4x6
Fluclorolone acetonide	T49.0x1	T49.0x2	T49.0x3	T49.0x4	T49.0x5	T49.0x6
Flucloxacillin	T36.0x1	T36.0x2	T36.0x3	T36.0x4	T36.0x5	T36.0x6
Fluconazole	T37.8x1	T37.8x2	T37.8x3	T37.8x4	T37.8x5	T37.8x6
Flucytosine	T37.8x1	T37.8x2	T37.8x3	T37.8x4	T37.8x5	T37.8x6
Fludeoxyglucose (18F)	T50.8x1	T50.8x2	T50.8x3	T50.8x4	T50.8x5	T50.8x6
Fludiazepam	T42.4x1	T42.4x2	T42.4x3	T42.4x4	T42.4x5	T42.4x6
Fludrocortisone	T50.0x1	T50.0x2	T50.0x3	T50.0x4	T50.0x5	T50.0x6
ENT agent	T49.6x1	T49.6x2	T49.6x3	T49.6x4	T49.6x5	T49.6x6
ophthalmic preparation	T49.5x1	T49.5x2	T49.5x3	T49.5x4	T49.5x5	T49.5x6
topical NEC	T49.0x1	T49.0x2	T49.0x3	T49.0x4	T49.0x5	T49.0x6
Fludroxycortide	T49.0x1	T49.0x2	T49.0x3	T49.0x4	T49.0x5	T49.0x6
Flufenamic acid	T39.391	T39.392	T39.393	T39.394	T39.395	T39.396
Fluindione	T45.511	T45.512	T45.513	T45.514	T45.515	T45.516
Flumequine	T37.8x1	T37.8x2	T37.8x3	T37.8x4	T37.8x5	T37.8x6
Flumethasone	T49.0x1	T49.0x2	T49.0x3	T49.0x4	T49.0x5	T49.0x6
Flumethiazide	T50.2x1	T50.2x2	T50.2x3	T50.2x4	T50.2x5	T50.2x6
Flumidin	T37.5x1	T37.5x2	T37.5x3	T37.5x4	T37.5x5	T37.5x6
Flunarizine	T46.7x1	T46.7x2	T46.7x3	T46.7x4	T46.7x5	T46.7x6
Flunidazole	T37.8x1	T37.8x2	T37.8x3	T37.8x4	T37.8x5	T37.8x6
Flunisolide	T48.6x1	T48.6x2	T48.6x3	T48.6x4	T48.6x5	T48.6x6
Flunitrazepam	T42.4x1	T42.4x2	T42.4x3	T42.4x4	T42.4x5	T42.4x6

Substance	External Cause (T-Code)					
	Poisoning, Accidental (Unintentional)	Poisoning, Intentional Self-Harm	Poisoning, Assault	Poisoning, Undetermined	Adverse Effect	Underdosing
Fluocinolone (acetonide)	T49.0x1	T49.0x2	T49.0x3	T49.0x4	T49.0x5	T49.0x6
Fluocinolone	T49.0x1	T49.0x2	T49.0x3	T49.0x4	T49.0x5	T49.0x6
Fluocinonide	T49.0x1	T49.0x2	T49.0x3	T49.0x4	T49.0x5	T49.0x6
Fluocortin (butyl)	T49.0x1	T49.0x2	T49.0x3	T49.0x4	T49.0x5	T49.0x6
Fluocortolone	T49.0x1	T49.0x2	T49.0x3	T49.0x4	T49.0x5	T49.0x6
Fluohydrocortisone	T38.0x1	T38.0x2	T38.0x3	T38.0x4	T38.0x5	T38.0x6
ENT agent	T49.6x1	T49.6x2	T49.6x3	T49.6x4	T49.6x5	T49.6x6
ophthalmic preparation	T49.5x1	T49.5x2	T49.5x3	T49.5x4	T49.5x5	T49.5x6
topical NEC	T49.0x1	T49.0x2	T49.0x3	T49.0x4	T49.0x5	T49.0x6
Fluonid	T49.0x1	T49.0x2	T49.0x3	T49.0x4	T49.0x5	T49.0x6
Fluopromazine	T43.3x1	T43.3x2	T43.3x3	T43.3x4	T43.3x5	T43.3x6
Fluoroacetate, fluoracetate	T60.8x1	T60.8x2	T60.8x3	T60.8x4	—	—
Fluorescein	T50.8x1	T50.8x2	T50.8x3	T50.8x4	T50.8x5	T50.8x6
Fluorhydrocortisone	T50.0x1	T50.0x2	T50.0x3	T50.0x4	T50.0x5	T50.0x6
Fluoride (nonmedicinal) (pesticide) (sodium) NEC	T60.8x1	T60.8x2	T60.8x3	T60.8x4	—	—
hydrogen - see Hydrofluoric acid						
medicinal NEC	T50.991	T50.992	T50.993	T50.994	T50.995	T50.996
dental use	T49.7x1	T49.7x2	T49.7x3	T49.7x4	T49.7x5	T49.7x6
not pesticide NEC	T54.91	T54.92	T54.93	T54.94	—	—
stannous	T49.7x1	T49.7x2	T49.7x3	T49.7x4	T49.7x5	T49.7x6
Fluorinated corticosteroids	T38.0x1	T38.0x2	T38.0x3	T38.0x4	T38.0x5	T38.0x6
Fluorine (gas)	T59.5x1	T59.5x2	T59.5x3	T59.5x4	—	—
salt - see Fluoride(s)						
Fluoristan	T49.7x1	T49.7x2	T49.7x3	T49.7x4	T49.7x5	T49.7x6
Fluormetholone	T49.0x1	T49.0x2	T49.0x3	T49.0x4	T49.0x5	T49.0x6
Fluoroacetate	T60.4x1	T60.4x2	T60.4x3	T60.4x4	—	—
Fluorocarbon monomer	T53.6x1	T53.6x2	T53.6x3	T53.6x4	—	—
Fluorocytosine	T37.8x1	T37.8x2	T37.8x3	T37.8x4	T37.8x5	T37.8x6
Fluorodeoxyuridine	T45.1x1	T45.1x2	T45.1x3	T45.1x4	T45.1x5	T45.1x6
Fluorometholone	T49.0x1	T49.0x2	T49.0x3	T49.0x4	T49.0x5	T49.0x6
ophthalmic preparation	T49.5x1	T49.5x2	T49.5x3	T49.5x4	T49.5x5	T49.5x6
Fluorophosphate insecticide	T60.0x1	T60.0x2	T60.0x3	T60.0x4	—	—
Fluorosol	T46.3x1	T46.3x2	T46.3x3	T46.3x4	T46.3x5	T46.3x6
Fluorouracil	T45.1x1	T45.1x2	T45.1x3	T45.1x4	T45.1x5	T45.1x6
Fluorphenylalanine	T49.5x1	T49.5x2	T49.5x3	T49.5x4	T49.5x5	T49.5x6
Fluothane	T41.0x1	T41.0x2	T41.0x3	T41.0x4	T41.0x5	T41.0x6
Fluoxetine	T43.221	T43.222	T43.223	T43.224	T43.225	T43.226
Fluoxymesterone	T38.7x1	T38.7x2	T38.7x3	T38.7x4	T38.7x5	T38.7x6
Flupenthixol	T43.4x1	T43.4x2	T43.4x3	T43.4x4	T43.4x5	T43.4x6
Flupentixol	T43.4x1	T43.4x2	T43.4x3	T43.4x4	T43.4x5	T43.4x6
Fluphenazine	T43.3x1	T43.3x2	T43.3x3	T43.3x4	T43.3x5	T43.3x6

Substance	External Cause (T-Code)					
	Poisoning, Accidental (Unintentional)	Poisoning, Intentional Self-Harm	Poisoning, Assault	Poisoning, Undetermined	Adverse Effect	Underdosing
Fluprednidene	T49.0x1	T49.0x2	T49.0x3	T49.0x4	T49.0x5	T49.0x6
Fluprednisolone	T38.0x1	T38.0x2	T38.0x3	T38.0x4	T38.0x5	T38.0x6
Fluradoline	T39.8x1	T39.8x2	T39.8x3	T39.8x4	T39.8x5	T39.8x6
Flurandrenolide	T49.0x1	T49.0x2	T49.0x3	T49.0x4	T49.0x5	T49.0x6
Flurandrenolone	T49.0x1	T49.0x2	T49.0x3	T49.0x4	T49.0x5	T49.0x6
Flurazepam	T42.4x1	T42.4x2	T42.4x3	T42.4x4	T42.4x5	T42.4x6
Flurbiprofen	T39.311	T39.312	T39.313	T39.314	T39.315	T39.316
Flurobate	T49.0x1	T49.0x2	T49.0x3	T49.0x4	T49.0x5	T49.0x6
Flurotyl	T43.291	T43.292	T43.293	T43.294	T43.295	T43.296
Fluroxene	T41.0x1	T41.0x2	T41.0x3	T41.0x4	T41.0x5	T41.0x6
Fluspirilene	T43.591	T43.592	T43.593	T43.594	T43.595	T43.596
Flutamide	T38.6x1	T38.6x2	T38.6x3	T38.6x4	T38.6x5	T38.6x6
Flutazolam	T42.4x1	T42.4x2	T42.4x3	T42.4x4	T42.4x5	T42.4x6
Fluticasone propionate	T49.1x1	T49.1x2	T49.1x3	T49.1x4	T49.1x5	T49.1x6
Flutoprazepam	T42.4x1	T42.4x2	T42.4x3	T42.4x4	T42.4x5	T42.4x6
Flutropium bromide	T48.6x1	T48.6x2	T48.6x3	T48.6x4	T48.6x5	T48.6x6
Fluvoxamine	T43.221	T43.222	T43.223	T43.224	T43.225	T43.226
Folacin	T45.8x1	T45.8x2	T45.8x3	T45.8x4	T45.8x5	T45.8x6
Folic acid	T45.8x1	T45.8x2	T45.8x3	T45.8x4	T45.8x5	T45.8x6
with ferrous salt	T45.2x1	T45.2x2	T45.2x3	T45.2x4	T45.2x5	T45.2x6
antagonist	T45.1x1	T45.1x2	T45.1x3	T45.1x4	T45.1x5	T45.1x6
Folinic acid	T45.8x1	T45.8x2	T45.8x3	T45.8x4	T45.8x5	T45.8x6
Folium stramoniae	T48.6x1	T48.6x2	T48.6x3	T48.6x4	T48.6x5	T48.6x6
Follicle-stimulating hormone, human	T38.811	T38.812	T38.813	T38.814	T38.815	T38.816
Folpet	T60.3x1	T60.3x2	T60.3x3	T60.3x4	—	—
Fominoben	T48.3x1	T48.3x2	T48.3x3	T48.3x4	T48.3x5	T48.3x6
Food, foodstuffs, noxious, nonbacterial, NEC	T62.91	T62.92	T62.93	T62.94	—	—
berries	T62.1x1	T62.1x2	T62.1x3	T62.1x4	—	—
fish	T61.771	T61.772	T61.773	T61.774	—	—
mushrooms	T62.0x1	T62.0x2	T62.0x3	T62.0x4	—	—
plants	T62.2x1	T62.2x2	T62.2x3	T62.2x4	—	—
seafood	T61.91	T61.92	T61.93	T61.94	—	—
specified NEC	T61.8x1	T61.8x2	T61.8x3	T61.8x4	—	—
seeds	T62.2x1	T62.2x2	T62.2x3	T62.2x4	—	—
specified type NEC	T62.8x1	T62.8x2	T62.8x3	T62.8x4	—	—
shellfish	T61.781	T61.782	T61.783	T61.784	—	—
specified NEC	T62.8x1	T62.8x2	T62.8x3	T62.8x4	—	—
Fool's parsley	T62.2x1	T62.2x2	T62.2x3	T62.2x4	—	—
Formaldehyde (solution), gas or vapor	T59.2x1	T59.2x2	T59.2x3	T59.2x4	—	—
fungicide	T60.3x1	T60.3x2	T60.3x3	T60.3x4	—	—

Substance	External Cause (T-Code)					
	Poisoning, Accidental (Unintentional)	Poisoning, Intentional Self-Harm	Poisoning, Assault	Poisoning, Undetermined	Adverse Effect	Underdosing
Formalin	T59.2x1	T59.2x2	T59.2x3	T59.2x4	—	—
fungicide	T60.3x1	T60.3x2	T60.3x3	T60.3x4	—	—
vapor	T59.2x1	T59.2x2	T59.2x3	T59.2x4	—	—
Formic acid	T54.2x1	T54.2x2	T54.2x3	T54.2x4		
vapor	T59.891	T59.892	T59.893	T59.894	—	—
Foscarnet sodium	T37.5x1	T37.5x2	T37.5x3	T37.5x4	T37.5x5	T37.5x6
Fosfestrol	T38.5x1	T38.5x2	T38.5x3	T38.5x4	T38.5x5	T38.5x6
Fosfomycin	T36.8x1	T36.8x2	T36.8x3	T36.8x4	T36.8x5	T36.8x6
Fosfonet sodium	T37.5x1	T37.5x2	T37.5x3	T37.5x4	T37.5x5	T37.5x6
Fosinopril	T46.4x1	T46.4x2	T46.4x3	T46.4x4	T46.4x5	T46.4x6
sodium	T46.4x1	T46.4x2	T46.4x3	T46.4x4	T46.4x5	T46.4x6
Fowler's solution	T57.0x1	T57.0x2	T57.0x3	T57.0x4	—	—
Foxglove	T62.2x1	T62.2x2	T62.2x3	T62.2x4	—	—
Framycetin	T36.5x1	T36.5x2	T36.5x3	T36.5x4	T36.5x5	T36.5x6
Frangula	T47.2x1	T47.2x2	T47.2x3	T47.2x4	T47.2x5	T47.2x6
extract	T47.2x1	T47.2x2	T47.2x3	T47.2x4	T47.2x5	T47.2x6
Frei antigen	T50.8x1	T50.8x2	T50.8x3	T50.8x4	T50.8x5	T50.8x6
Freon	T53.5x1	T53.5x2	T53.5x3	T53.5x4	—	—
Fructose	T50.3x1	T50.3x2	T50.3x3	T50.3x4	T50.3x5	T50.3x6
Frusemide	T50.1x1	T50.1x2	T50.1x3	T50.1x4	T50.1x5	T50.1x6
FSH	T38.811	T38.812	T38.813	T38.814	T38.815	T38.816
Ftorafur	T45.1x1	T45.1x2	T45.1x3	T45.1x4	T45.1x5	T45.1x6
Fuel						
automobile	T52.0x1	T52.0x2	T52.0x3	T52.0x4	—	—
exhaust gas, not in transit	T58.01	T58.02	T58.03	T58.04	—	—
vapor NEC	T52.0x1	T52.0x2	T52.0x3	T52.0x4	—	—
gas (domestic use) *see also* Carbon, monoxide, fuel, utility	T59.891	T59.892	T59.893	T59.894	—	—
utility	T59.891	T59.892	T59.893	T59.894	—	—
incomplete combustion of - *see* Carbon, monoxide, fuel, utility						
in mobile container	T59.891	T59.892	T59.893	T59.894	—	—
piped (natural)	T59.891	T59.892	T59.893	T59.894	—	—
industrial, incomplete combustion	T58.8x1	T58.8x2	T58.8x3	T58.8x4	—	
Fugillin	T36.8x1	T36.8x2	T36.8x3	T36.8x4	T36.8x5	T36.8x6
Fulminate of mercury	T56.1x1	T56.1x2	T56.1x3	T56.1x4		
Fulvicin	T36.7x1	T36.7x2	T36.7x3	T36.7x4	T36.7x5	T36.7x6
Fumadil	T36.8x1	T36.8x2	T36.8x3	T36.8x4	T36.8x5	T36.8x6
Fumagillin	T36.8x1	T36.8x2	T36.8x3	T36.8x4	T36.8x5	T36.8x6
Fumaric acid	T49.4x1	T49.4x2	T49.4x3	T49.4x4	T49.4x5	T49.4x6
Fumes (from)	T59.91	T59.92	T59.93	T59.94	—	—
carbon monoxide - *see* Carbon, monoxide						
charcoal (domestic use) - *see* Charcoal, fumes						

Substance	External Cause (T-Code)					
	Poisoning, Accidental (Unintentional)	Poisoning, Intentional Self-Harm	Poisoning, Assault	Poisoning, Undetermined	Adverse Effect	Underdosing
Fumes *(Continued)*						
chloroform - *see* Chloroform						
coke (in domestic stoves, fireplaces) - *see* Coke, fumes						
corrosive NEC	T59.891	T59.892	T59.893	T59.894	—	—
ether - *see* ether						
freons	T53.5x1	T53.5x2	T53.5x3	T53.5x4	—	—
hydrocarbons	T59.891	T59.892	T59.893	T59.894	—	—
petroleum (liquefied)	T59.891	T59.892	T59.893	T59.894	—	—
distributed through pipes (pure or mixed with air)	T59.891	T59.892	T59.893	T59.894	—	—
lead - *see* lead						
metal - *see* Metals, or the specified metal						
nitrogen dioxide	T59.0x1	T59.0x2	T59.0x3	T59.0x4	—	—
pesticides - *see* Pesticides						
petroleum (liquefied)	T59.891	T59.892	T59.893	T59.894	—	—
distributed through pipes (pure or mixed with air)	T59.891	T59.892	T59.893	T59.894	—	—
polyester	T59.891	T59.892	T59.893	T59.894	—	—
specified source NEC	T59.91	T59.92	T59.93	T59.94	—	—
sulfur dioxide	T59.1x1	T59.1x2	T59.1x3	T59.1x4	—	—
Fumigant NEC	T60.91	T60.92	T60.93	T60.94		
Fungi, noxious, used as food	T62.0x1	T62.0x2	T62.0x3	T62.0x4	—	—
Fungicide NEC (nonmedicinal)	T60.3x1	T60.3x2	T60.3x3	T60.3x4	—	—
Fungizone	T36.7x1	T36.7x2	T36.7x3	T36.7x4	T36.7x5	T36.7x6
topical	T49.0x1	T49.0x2	T49.0x3	T49.0x4	T49.0x5	T49.0x6
Furacin	T49.0x1	T49.0x2	T49.0x3	T49.0x4	T49.0x5	T49.0x6
Furadantin	T37.91	T37.92	T37.93	T37.94	T37.95	T37.96
Furazolidone	T37.8x1	T37.8x2	T37.8x3	T37.8x4	T37.8x5	T37.8x6
Furazolium chloride	T49.0x1	T49.0x2	T49.0x3	T49.0x4	T49.0x5	T49.0x6
Furfural	T52.8x1	T52.8x2	T52.8x3	T52.8x4	—	—
Furnace (coal burning) (domestic), gas from industrial	T58.2x1	T58.2x2	T58.2x3	T58.2x4	—	—
industrial	T58.8x1	T58.8x2	T58.8x3	T58.8x4	—	—
Furniture polish	T65.891	T65.892	T65.893	T65.894	—	—
Furosemide	T50.1x1	T50.1x2	T50.1x3	T50.1x4	T50.1x5	T50.1x6
Furoxone	T37.91	T37.92	T37.93	T37.94	T37.95	T37.96
Fursultiamine	T45.2x1	T45.2x2	T45.2x3	T45.2x4	T45.2x5	T45.2x6
Fusafungine	T36.8x1	T36.8x2	T36.8x3	T36.8x4	T36.8x5	T36.8x6
Fusel oil (any) (amyl) (butyl) (propyl), vapor	T51.3x1	T51.3x2	T51.3x3	T51.3x4	—	—
Fusidate (ethanolamine) (sodium)	T36.8x1	T36.8x2	T36.8x3	T36.8x4	T36.8x5	T36.8x6
Fusidic acid	T36.8x1	T36.8x2	T36.8x3	T36.8x4	T36.8x5	T36.8x6
Fytic acid, nonasodium	T50.6x1	T50.6x2	T50.6x3	T50.6x4	T50.6x5	T50.6x6
GABA	T43.8x1	T43.8x2	T43.8x3	T43.8x4	T43.8x5	T43.8x6

Substance	External Cause (T-Code)					
	Poisoning, Accidental (Unintentional)	Poisoning, Intentional Self-Harm	Poisoning, Assault	Poisoning, Undetermined	Adverse Effect	Underdosing
Gadopentetic acid	T50.8x1	T50.8x2	T50.8x3	T50.8x4	T50.8x5	T50.8x6
Galactose	T50.3x1	T50.3x2	T50.3x3	T50.3x4	T50.3x5	T50.3x6
b-Galactosidase	T47.5x1	T47.5x2	T47.5x3	T47.5x4	T47.5x5	T47.5x6
Galantamine	T44.0x1	T44.0x2	T44.0x3	T44.0x4	T44.0x5	T44.0x6
Gallamine (triethiodide)	T48.1x1	T48.1x2	T48.1x3	T48.1x4	T48.1x5	T48.1x6
Gallium citrate	T50.991	T50.992	T50.993	T50.994	T50.995	T50.996
Gallopamil	T46.1x1	T46.1x2	T46.1x3	T46.1x4	T46.1x5	T46.1x6
Gamboge	T47.2x1	T47.2x2	T47.2x3	T47.2x4	T47.2x5	T47.2x6
Gamimune	T50.Z11	T50.Z12	T50.Z13	T50.Z14	T50.Z15	T50.Z16
Gamma-aminobutyric acid	T43.8x1	T43.8x2	T43.8x3	T43.8x4	T43.8x5	T43.8x6
Gamma-benzene hexachloride (medicinal)	T49.0x1	T49.0x2	T49.0x3	T49.0x4	T49.0x5	T49.0x6
nonmedicinal, vapor	T53.6x1	T53.6x2	T53.6x3	T53.6x4	—	—
Gamma-BHC (medicinal)	T49.0x1	T49.0x2	T49.0x3	T49.0x4	T49.0x5	T49.0x6
Gamma globulin	T50.Z11	T50.Z12	T50.Z13	T50.Z14	T50.Z15	T50.Z16
Gamulin	T50.Z11	T50.Z12	T50.Z13	T50.Z14	T50.Z15	T50.Z16
Ganciclovir (sodium)	T37.5x1	T37.5x2	T37.5x3	T37.5x4	T37.5x5	T37.5x6
Ganglionic blocking drug NEC	T44.2x1	T44.2x2	T44.2x3	T44.2x4	T44.2x5	T44.2x6
specified NEC	T44.2x1	T44.2x2	T44.2x3	T44.2x4	T44.2x5	T44.2x6
Ganja	T40.7x1	T40.7x2	T40.7x3	T40.7x4	T40.7x5	T40.7x6
Garamycin	T36.8x1	T36.8x2	T36.8x3	T36.8x4	T36.8x5	T36.8x6
ophthalmic preparation	T49.5x1	T49.5x2	T49.5x3	T49.5x4	T49.5x5	T49.5x6
topical NEC	T49.0x1	T49.0x2	T49.0x3	T49.0x4	T49.0x5	T49.0x6
Gardenal	T42.3x1	T42.3x2	T42.3x3	T42.3x4	T42.3x5	T42.3x6
Gardepanyl	T42.3x1	T42.3x2	T42.3x3	T42.3x4	T42.3x5	T42.3x6
Gas	T59.91	T59.92	T59.93	T59.94	—	—
acetylene	T59.891	T59.892	T59.893	T59.894	—	—
incomplete combustion of - *see* Carbon, monoxide, industrial fuels or gases						
air contaminants, source or type not specified	T59.91	T59.92	T59.93	T59.94	—	—
anesthetic	T41.0x1	T41.0x2	T41.0x3	T41.0x4	T41.0x5	T41.0x6
blast furnace	T58.8x1	T58.8x2	T58.8x3	T58.8x4	—	—
butane - *see* butane						
carbon monoxide - *see* Carbon, monoxide						
chlorine	T59.4x1	T59.4x2	T59.4x3	T59.4x4	—	—
coal	T58.2x1	T58.2x2	T58.2x3	T58.2x4	—	—
cyanide	T57.3x1	T57.3x2	T57.3x3	T57.3x4	—	—
dicyanogen	T65.0x1	T65.0x2	T65.0x3	T65.0x4	—	—
domestic - *see* Domestic gas	T57.91	T57.92	T57.93	T57.94	—	—
exhaust	T57.91	T57.92	T57.93	T57.94	—	—
from utility (for cooking, heating, or lighting) (after combustion) - *see* Carbon, monoxide, fuel, utility						
prior to combustion	T59.891	T59.892	T59.893	T59.894	—	—

| | External Cause (T-Code) | | | | | |
Substance	Poisoning, Accidental (Unintentional)	Poisoning, Intentional Self-Harm	Poisoning, Assault	Poisoning, Undetermined	Adverse Effect	Underdosing
Gas *(Continued)*						
from wood or coal-burning stove or fireplace	T57.91	T57.92	T57.93	T57.94	—	—
fuel (domestic use) (after combustion) - *see also* Carbon, monoxide, fuel	T57.91	T57.92	T57.93	T57.94	—	—
industrial use	T58.8x1	T58.8x2	T58.8x3	T58.8x4	—	—
prior to combustion	T59.891	T59.892	T59.893	T59.894	—	—
utility	T59.891	T59.892	T59.893	T59.894	—	—
in mobile container	T59.891	T59.892	T59.893	T59.894	—	—
incomplete combustion of - *see* Carbon, monoxide, fuel, utility						
piped (natural)	T59.891	T59.892	T59.893	T59.894	—	—
garage	T58.01	T58.02	T58.03	T58.04	—	—
hydrocarbon NEC	T59.891	T59.892	T59.893	T59.894	—	—
incomplete combustion of - *see* Carbon, monoxide, fuel, utility						
liquefied - *see* butane						
piped	T59.891	T59.892	T59.893	T59.894	—	—
hydrocyanic acid	T57.3x1	T57.3x2	T57.3x3	T57.3x4	—	—
illuminating (after combustion)	T58.11	T58.12	T58.13	T58.14	—	—
prior to combustion	T59.891	T59.892	T59.893	T59.894	—	—
incomplete combustion, any - *see* Carbon, monoxide						
kiln	T58.8x1	T58.8x2	T58.8x3	T58.8x4	—	—
lacrimogenic	T59.3x1	T59.3x2	T59.3x3	T59.3x4	—	—
liquefied petroleum - *see* butane						
marsh	T59.891	T59.892	T59.893	T59.894	—	—
motor exhaust, not in transit	T58.01	T58.02	T58.03	T58.04	—	—
mustard, not in war	T59.891	T59.892	T59.893	T59.894	—	—
natural	T59.891	T59.892	T59.893	T59.894	—	—
nerve, not in war	T59.91	T59.92	T59.93	T59.94	—	—
oil	T52.0x1	T52.0x2	T52.0x3	T52.0x4	—	—
petroleum (liquefied) (distributed in mobile containers)	T59.891	T59.892	T59.893	T59.894	—	—
piped (pure or mixed with air)	T59.891	T59.892	T59.893	T59.894	—	—
piped (manufactured) (natural) NEC	T59.891	T59.892	T59.893	T59.894	—	—
producer	T58.8x1	T58.8x2	T58.8x3	T58.8x4	—	—
propane - *see* propane						
refrigerant (chlorofluoro-carbon)	T53.5x1	T53.5x2	T53.5x3	T53.5x4	—	—
not chlorofluoro-carbon	T59.891	T59.892	T59.893	T59.894	—	—
sewer	T59.91	T59.92	T59.93	T59.94	—	—
specified source NEC	T59.91	T59.92	T59.93	T59.94	—	—
stove (after combustion)	T58.11	T58.12	T58.13	T58.14	—	—
tear	T59.3x1	T59.3x2	T59.3x3	T59.3x4	—	—
utility (for cooking, heating, or lighting) (piped) NEC	T59.891	T59.892	T59.893	T59.894	—	—
in mobile container	T59.891	T59.892	T59.893	T59.894	—	—
incomplete combustion of - *see* Carbon, monoxide, fuel, utilty						

Substance	Poisoning, Accidental (Unintentional)	Poisoning, Intentional Self-Harm	Poisoning, Assault	Poisoning, Undetermined	Adverse Effect	Underdosing
Gas *(Continued)*						
utility *(Continued)*						
piped (natural)	T59.891	T59.892	T59.893	T59.894	—	—
water	T58.8x1	T58.8x2	T58.8x3	T58.8x4	—	—
incomplete combustion of - *see* Carbon, monoxide, fuel, utility						
Gaseous substance - *see* Gas						
Gasoline, gasoline	T52.0x1	T52.0x2	T52.0x3	T52.0x4	—	—
vapor	T52.0x1	T52.0x2	T52.0x3	T52.0x4	—	—
Gastric enzymes	T47.5x1	T47.5x2	T47.5x3	T47.5x4	T47.5x5	T47.5x6
Gastrografin	T50.8x1	T50.8x2	T50.8x3	T50.8x4	T50.8x5	T50.8x6
Gastrointestinal drug	T47.91	T47.92	T47.93	T47.94	T47.95	T47.96
biological	T47.8x1	T47.8x2	T47.8x3	T47.8x4	T47.8x5	T47.8x6
specified NEC	T47.8x1	T47.8x2	T47.8x3	T47.8x4	T47.8x5	T47.8x6
Gaultheria procumbens	T62.2x1	T62.2x2	T62.2x3	T62.2x4	—	—
Gelatin (intravenous)	T45.8x1	T45.8x2	T45.8x3	T45.8x4	T45.8x5	T45.8x6
absorbable (sponge)	T45.7x1	T45.7x2	T45.7x3	T45.7x4	T45.7x5	T45.7x6
Gefarnate	T44.3x1	T44.3x2	T44.3x3	T44.3x4	T44.3x5	T44.3x6
Gelfilm	T49.8x1	T49.8x2	T49.8x3	T49.8x4	T49.8x5	T49.8x6
Gelfoam	T45.7x1	T45.7x2	T45.7x3	T45.7x4	T45.7x5	T45.7x6
Gelsemine	T50.991	T50.992	T50.993	T50.994	T50.995	T50.996
Gelsemium (sempervirens)	T62.2x1	T62.2x2	T62.2x3	T62.2x4	—	—
Gemeprost	T48.0x1	T48.0x2	T48.0x3	T48.0x4	T48.0x5	T48.0x6
Gemfibrozil	T46.6x1	T46.6x2	T46.6x3	T46.6x4	T46.6x5	T46.6x6
Gemonil	T42.3x1	T42.3x2	T42.3x3	T42.3x4	T42.3x5	T42.3x6
Gentamicin	T36.5x1	T36.5x2	T36.5x3	T36.5x4	T36.5x5	T36.5x6
ophthalmic preparation	T49.5x1	T49.5x2	T49.5x3	T49.5x4	T49.5x5	T49.5x6
topical NEC	T49.0x1	T49.0x2	T49.0x3	T49.0x4	T49.0x5	T49.0x6
Gentian	T47.5x1	T47.5x2	T47.5x3	T47.5x4	T47.5x5	T47.5x6
violet	T49.0x1	T49.0x2	T49.0x3	T49.0x4	T49.0x5	T49.0x6
Gepefrine	T44.4x1	T44.4x2	T44.4x3	T44.4x4	T44.4x5	T44.4x6
Gestonorone caproate	T38.5x1	T38.5x2	T38.5x3	T38.5x4	T38.5x5	T38.5x6
Gexane	T49.0x1	T49.0x2	T49.0x3	T49.0x4	T49.0x5	T49.0x6
Gila monster (venom)	T63.111	T63.112	T63.113	T63.114	—	—
Ginger	T47.5x1	T47.5x2	T47.5x3	T47.5x4	T47.5x5	T47.5x6
jamaica	T62.2x1	T62.2x2	T62.2x3	T62.2x4	—	—
Gitalin	T46.0x1	T46.0x2	T46.0x3	T46.0x4	T46.0x5	T46.0x6
amorphous	T46.0x1	T46.0x2	T46.0x3	T46.0x4	T46.0x5	T46.0x6
Gitaloxin	T46.0x1	T46.0x2	T46.0x3	T46.0x4	T46.0x5	T46.0x6
Gitoxin	T46.0x1	T46.0x2	T46.0x3	T46.0x4	T46.0x5	T46.0x6
Glafenine	T39.8x1	T39.8x2	T39.8x3	T39.8x4	T39.8x5	T39.8x6

Substance	External Cause (T-Code)					
	Poisoning, Accidental (Unintentional)	Poisoning, Intentional Self-Harm	Poisoning, Assault	Poisoning, Undetermined	Adverse Effect	Underdosing
Glandular extract (medicinal) NEC	T50.Z91	T50.Z92	T50.Z93	T50.Z94	T50.Z95	T50.Z96
Glaucarubin	T37.3x1	T37.3x2	T37.3x3	T37.3x4	T37.3x5	T37.3x6
Glibenclamide	T38.3x1	T38.3x2	T38.3x3	T38.3x4	T38.3x5	T38.3x6
Glibornuride	T38.3x1	T38.3x2	T38.3x3	T38.3x4	T38.3x5	T38.3x6
Gliclazide	T38.3x1	T38.3x2	T38.3x3	T38.3x4	T38.3x5	T38.3x6
Glimidine	T38.3x1	T38.3x2	T38.3x3	T38.3x4	T38.3x5	T38.3x6
Glipizide	T38.3x1	T38.3x2	T38.3x3	T38.3x4	T38.3x5	T38.3x6
Gliquidone	T38.3x1	T38.3x2	T38.3x3	T38.3x4	T38.3x5	T38.3x6
Glisolamide	T38.3x1	T38.3x2	T38.3x3	T38.3x4	T38.3x5	T38.3x6
Glisoxepide	T38.3x1	T38.3x2	T38.3x3	T38.3x4	T38.3x5	T38.3x6
Globin zinc insulin	T38.3x1	T38.3x2	T38.3x3	T38.3x4	T38.3x5	T38.3x6
Globulin						
antilymphocytic	T50.Z11	T50.Z12	T50.Z13	T50.Z14	T50.Z15	T50.Z16
antirhesus	T50.Z11	T50.Z12	T50.Z13	T50.Z14	T50.Z15	T50.Z16
antivenin	T50.Z11	T50.Z12	T50.Z13	T50.Z14	T50.Z15	T50.Z16
antiviral	T50.Z11	T50.Z12	T50.Z13	T50.Z14	T50.Z15	T50.Z16
Glucagon	T38.3x1	T38.3x2	T38.3x3	T38.3x4	T38.3x5	T38.3x6
Glucocorticoids	T38.0x1	T38.0x2	T38.0x3	T38.0x4	T38.0x5	T38.0x6
Glucocorticosteroid	T38.0x1	T38.0x2	T38.0x3	T38.0x4	T38.0x5	T38.0x6
Gluconic acid	T50.991	T50.992	T50.993	T50.994	T50.995	T50.996
Glucosamine sulfate	T39.4x1	T39.4x2	T39.4x3	T39.4x4	T39.4x5	T39.4x6
Glucose	T50.3x1	T50.3x2	T50.3x3	T50.3x4	T50.3x5	T50.3x6
with sodium chloride	T50.3x1	T50.3x2	T50.3x3	T50.3x4	T50.3x5	T50.3x6
Glucosulfone sodium	T37.1x1	T37.1x2	T37.1x3	T37.1x4	T37.1x5	T37.1x6
Glucurolactone	T47.8x1	T47.8x2	T47.8x3	T47.8x4	T47.8x5	T47.8x6
Glue NEC	T52.8x1	T52.8x2	T52.8x3	T52.8x4	—	—
Glutamic acid	T47.5x1	T47.5x2	T47.5x3	T47.5x4	T47.5x5	T47.5x6
Glutaral (medicinal)	T49.0x1	T49.0x2	T49.0x3	T49.0x4	T49.0x5	T49.0x6
nonmedicinal	T65.891	T65.892	T65.893	T65.894	—	—
Glutaraldehyde (nonmedicinal)	T65.891	T65.892	T65.893	T65.894	—	—
medicinal	T49.0x1	T49.0x2	T49.0x3	T49.0x4	T49.0x5	T49.0x6
Glutathione	T50.6x1	T50.6x2	T50.6x3	T50.6x4	T50.6x5	T50.6x6
Glutethimide	T42.6x1	T42.6x2	T42.6x3	T42.6x4	T42.6x5	T42.6x6
Glyburide	T38.3x1	T38.3x2	T38.3x3	T38.3x4	T38.3x5	T38.3x6
Glycerin	T47.4x1	T47.4x2	T47.4x3	T47.4x4	T47.4x5	T47.4x6
Glycerol	T47.4x1	T47.4x2	T47.4x3	T47.4x4	T47.4x5	T47.4x6
borax	T49.6x1	T49.6x2	T49.6x3	T49.6x4	T49.6x5	T49.6x6
intravenous	T50.3x1	T50.3x2	T50.3x3	T50.3x4	T50.3x5	T50.3x6
iodinated	T48.4x1	T48.4x2	T48.4x3	T48.4x4	T48.4x5	T48.4x6
Glycerophosphate	T50.991	T50.992	T50.993	T50.994	T50.995	T50.996

Substance	Poisoning, Accidental (Unintentional)	Poisoning, Intentional Self-Harm	Poisoning, Assault	Poisoning, Undetermined	Adverse Effect	Underdosing
Glyceryl						
gualacolate	T48.4x1	T48.4x2	T48.4x3	T48.4x4	T48.4x5	T48.4x6
nitrate	T46.3x1	T46.3x2	T46.3x3	T46.3x4	T46.3x5	T46.3x6
triacetate (topical)	T49.0x1	T49.0x2	T49.0x3	T49.0x4	T49.0x5	T49.0x6
trinitrate	T46.3x1	T46.3x2	T46.3x3	T46.3x4	T46.3x5	T46.3x6
Glycine	T50.3x1	T50.3x2	T50.3x3	T50.3x4	T50.3x5	T50.3x6
Glyclopyramide	T38.3x1	T38.3x2	T38.3x3	T38.3x4	T38.3x5	T38.3x6
Glycobiarsol	T37.3x1	T37.3x2	T37.3x3	T37.3x4	T37.3x5	T37.3x6
Glycols (ether)	T52.3x1	T52.3x2	T52.3x3	T52.3x4	—	—
Glyconiazide	T37.1x1	T37.1x2	T37.1x3	T37.1x4	T37.1x5	T37.1x6
Glycopyrrolate	T44.3x1	T44.3x2	T44.3x3	T44.3x4	T44.3x5	T44.3x6
Glycopyrronium	T44.3x1	T44.3x2	T44.3x3	T44.3x4	T44.3x5	T44.3x6
bromide	T44.3x1	T44.3x2	T44.3x3	T44.3x4	T44.3x5	T44.3x6
Glycyclamide	T38.3x1	T38.3x2	T38.3x3	T38.3x4	T38.3x5	T38.3x6
Glycyrrhiza extract	T48.4x1	T48.4x2	T48.4x3	T48.4x4	T48.4x5	T48.4x6
Glycyrrhizic acid	T48.4x1	T48.4x2	T48.4x3	T48.4x4	T48.4x5	T48.4x6
Glycyrrhizinate potassium	T48.4x1	T48.4x2	T48.4x3	T48.4x4	T48.4x5	T48.4x6
Glymidine sodium	T38.3x1	T38.3x2	T38.3x3	T38.3x4	T38.3x5	T38.3x6
Glyphosate	T60.3x1	T60.3x2	T60.3x3	T60.3x4	—	—
Glyphylline	T48.6x1	T48.6x2	T48.6x3	T48.6x4	T48.6x5	T48.6x6
Gold						
colloidal (l98Au)	T45.1x1	T45.1x2	T45.1x3	T45.1x4	T45.1x5	T45.1x6
salts	T39.4x1	T39.4x2	T39.4x3	T39.4x4	T39.4x5	T39.4x6
Golden sulfide of antimony	T56.891	T56.892	T56.893	T56.894	—	—
Goldylocks	T62.2x1	T62.2x2	T62.2x3	T62.2x4	—	—
Gonadal tissue extract	T38.901	T38.902	T38.903	T38.904	T38.905	T38.906
female	T38.5x1	T38.5x2	T38.5x3	T38.5x4	T38.5x5	T38.5x6
male	T38.7x1	T38.7x2	T38.7x3	T38.7x4	T38.7x5	T38.7x6
Gonadorelin	T38.891	T38.892	T38.893	T38.894	T38.895	T38.896
Gonadotropin	T38.891	T38.892	T38.893	T38.894	T38.895	T38.896
chorionic	T38.891	T38.892	T38.893	T38.894	T38.895	T38.896
pituitary	T38.811	T38.812	T38.813	T38.814	T38.815	T38.816
Goserelin	T45.1x1	T45.1x2	T45.1x3	T45.1x4	T45.1x5	T45.1x6
Grain alcohol	T51.0x1	T51.0x2	T51.0x3	T51.0x4	—	—
Gramicidin	T49.0x1	T49.0x2	T49.0x3	T49.0x4	T49.0x5	T49.0x6
Granisetron	T45.0x1	T45.0x2	T45.0x3	T45.0x4	T45.0x5	T45.0x6
Gratiola officinalis	T62.2x1	T62.2x2	T62.2x3	T62.2x4	—	—
Grease	T65.891	T65.892	T65.893	T65.894	—	—
Green hellebore	T62.2x1	T62.2x2	T62.2x3	T62.2x4	—	—
Green soap	T49.2x1	T49.2x2	T49.2x3	T49.2x4	T49.2x5	T49.2x6

Substance	Poisoning, Accidental (Unintentional)	Poisoning, Intentional Self-Harm	Poisoning, Assault	Poisoning, Undetermined	Adverse Effect	Underdosing
	External Cause (T-Code)					
Grifulvin	T36.7x1	T36.7x2	T36.7x3	T36.7x4	T36.7x5	T36.7x6
Griseofulvin	T36.7x1	T36.7x2	T36.7x3	T36.7x4	T36.7x5	T36.7x6
Growth hormone	T38.811	T38.812	T38.813	T38.814	T38.815	T38.816
Guaiacol derivatives	T48.4x1	T48.4x2	T48.4x3	T48.4x4	T48.4x5	T48.4x6
Guaiac reagent	T50.991	T50.992	T50.993	T50.994	T50.995	T50.996
Guaifenesin	T48.4x1	T48.4x2	T48.4x3	T48.4x4	T48.4x5	T48.4x6
Guaimesal	T48.4x1	T48.4x2	T48.4x3	T48.4x4	T48.4x5	T48.4x6
Guaiphenesin	T48.4x1	T48.4x2	T48.4x3	T48.4x4	T48.4x5	T48.4x6
Guamecycline	T36.4x1	T36.4x2	T36.4x3	T36.4x4	T36.4x5	T36.4x6
Guanabenz	T46.5x1	T46.5x2	T46.5x3	T46.5x4	T46.5x5	T46.5x6
Guanacline	T46.5x1	T46.5x2	T46.5x3	T46.5x4	T46.5x5	T46.5x6
Guanadrel	T46.5x1	T46.5x2	T46.5x3	T46.5x4	T46.5x5	T46.5x6
Guanatol	T37.2x1	T37.2x2	T37.2x3	T37.2x4	T37.2x5	T37.2x6
Guanethidine	T46.5x1	T46.5x2	T46.5x3	T46.5x4	T46.5x5	T46.5x6
Guanfacine	T46.5x1	T46.5x2	T46.5x3	T46.5x4	T46.5x5	T46.5x6
Guano	T65.891	T65.892	T65.893	T65.894	—	—
Guanochlor	T46.5x1	T46.5x2	T46.5x3	T46.5x4	T46.5x5	T46.5x6
Guanoclor	T46.5x1	T46.5x2	T46.5x3	T46.5x4	T46.5x5	T46.5x6
Guanoctine	T46.5x1	T46.5x2	T46.5x3	T46.5x4	T46.5x5	T46.5x6
Guanoxabenz	T46.5x1	T46.5x2	T46.5x3	T46.5x4	T46.5x5	T46.5x6
Guanoxan	T46.5x1	T46.5x2	T46.5x3	T46.5x4	T46.5x5	T46.5x6
Guar gum (medicinal)	T46.6x1	T46.6x2	T46.6x3	T46.6x4	T46.6x5	T46.6x6
Hachimycin	T36.7x1	T36.7x2	T36.7x3	T36.7x4	T36.7x5	T36.7x6
Hair						
dye	T49.4x1	T49.4x2	T49.4x3	T49.4x4	T49.4x5	T49.4x6
preparation NEC	T49.4x1	T49.4x2	T49.4x3	T49.4x4	T49.4x5	T49.4x6
Halazepam	T42.4x1	T42.4x2	T42.4x3	T42.4x4	T42.4x5	T42.4x6
Halcinolone	T49.0x1	T49.0x2	T49.0x3	T49.0x4	T49.0x5	T49.0x6
Halcinonide	T49.0x1	T49.0x2	T49.0x3	T49.0x4	T49.0x5	T49.0x6
Halethazole	T49.0x1	T49.0x2	T49.0x3	T49.0x4	T49.0x5	T49.0x6
Hallucinogen NEC	T40.901	T40.902	T40.903	T40.904	T40.905	T40.906
Halofantrine	T37.2x1	T37.2x2	T37.2x3	T37.2x4	T37.2x5	T37.2x6
Halofenate	T46.6x1	T46.6x2	T46.6x3	T46.6x4	T46.6x5	T46.6x6
Halometasone	T49.0x1	T49.0x2	T49.0x3	T49.0x4	T49.0x5	T49.0x6
Haloperidol	T43.4x1	T43.4x2	T43.4x3	T43.4x4	T43.4x5	T43.4x6
Haloprogin	T49.0x1	T49.0x2	T49.0x3	T49.0x4	T49.0x5	T49.0x6
Halotex	T49.0x1	T49.0x2	T49.0x3	T49.0x4	T49.0x5	T49.0x6
Halothane	T41.0x1	T41.0x2	T41.0x3	T41.0x4	T41.0x5	T41.0x6
Haloxazolam	T42.4x1	T42.4x2	T42.4x3	T42.4x4	T42.4x5	T42.4x6
Halquinols	T49.0x1	T49.0x2	T49.0x3	T49.0x4	T49.0x5	T49.0x6

Substance	External Cause (T-Code)					
	Poisoning, Accidental (Unintentional)	Poisoning, Intentional Self-Harm	Poisoning, Assault	Poisoning, Undetermined	Adverse Effect	Underdosing
Hamamelis	T49.2x1	T49.2x2	T49.2x3	T49.2x4	T49.2x5	T49.2x6
Haptendextran	T45.8x1	T45.8x2	T45.8x3	T45.8x4	T45.8x5	T45.8x6
Harmonyl	T46.5x1	T46.5x2	T46.5x3	T46.5x4	T46.5x5	T46.5x6
Hartmann's solution	T50.3x1	T50.3x2	T50.3x3	T50.3x4	T50.3x5	T50.3x6
Hashish	T40.7x1	T40.7x2	T40.7x3	T40.7x4	T40.7x5	T40.7x6
Hawaiian wood rose seeds	T40.991	T40.992	T40.993	T40.994	T40.995	T40.996
HCB	T60.3x1	T60.3x2	T60.3x3	T60.3x4	—	—
HCH	T53.6x1	T53.6x2	T53.6x3	T53.6x4	—	—
medicinal	T49.0x1	T49.0x2	T49.0x3	T49.0x4	T49.0x5	T49.0x6
HCN	T57.3x1	T57.3x2	T57.3x3	T57.3x4	—	—
Headache cures, drugs, powders NEC	T50.901	T50.902	T50.903	T50.904	T50.905	T50.906
Heavenly Blue (morning glory)	T40.991	T40.992	T40.993	T40.994	T40.995	T40.996
Heavy metal antidote	T45.8x1	T45.8x2	T45.8x3	T45.8x4	T45.8x5	T45.8x6
Hedaquinium	T49.0x1	T49.0x2	T49.0x3	T49.0x4	T49.0x5	T49.0x6
Hedge hyssop	T62.2x1	T62.2x2	T62.2x3	T62.2x4	—	—
Heet	T49.8x1	T49.8x2	T49.8x3	T49.8x4	T49.8x5	T49.8x6
Helium	T48.991	T48.992	T48.993	T48.994	T48.995	T48.996
Helenin	T37.4x1	T37.4x2	T37.4x3	T37.4x4	T37.4x5	T37.4x6
Hellebore (black) (green) (white)	T62.2x1	T62.2x2	T62.2x3	T62.2x4	—	—
Hematin	T45.8x1	T45.8x2	T45.8x3	T45.8x4	T45.8x5	T45.8x6
Hematinic preparation	T45.8x1	T45.8x2	T45.8x3	T45.8x4	T45.8x5	T45.8x6
Hemlock	T62.2x1	T62.2x2	T62.2x3	T62.2x4	—	—
Hemostatic	T49.4x1	T49.4x2	T49.4x3	T49.4x4	T49.4x5	T49.4x6
drug, systemic	T45.7x1	T45.7x2	T45.7x3	T45.7x4	T45.7x5	T45.7x6
Hemostyptic	T49.4x1	T49.4x2	T49.4x3	T49.4x4	T49.4x5	T49.4x6
Henbane	T62.2x1	T62.2x2	T62.2x3	T62.2x4	—	—
Heparin (sodium)	T45.511	T45.512	T45.513	T45.514	T45.515	T45.516
action reverser	T45.7x1	T45.7x2	T45.7x3	T45.7x4	T45.7x5	T45.7x6
Heparin-fraction	T45.511	T45.512	T45.513	T45.514	T45.515	T45.516
Heparinoid (systemic)	T45.511	T45.512	T45.513	T45.514	T45.515	T45.516
Hepatic secretion stimulant	T47.8x1	T47.8x2	T47.8x3	T47.8x4	T47.8x5	T47.8x6
Hepatitis B						
immune globulin	T50.Z11	T50.Z12	T50.Z13	T50.Z14	T50.Z15	T50.Z16
vaccine	T50.B91	T50.B92	T50.B93	T50.B94	T50.B95	T50.B96
Hepronicate	T46.7x1	T46.7x2	T46.7x3	T46.7x4	T46.7x5	T46.7x6
Heptabarb	T42.3x1	T42.3x2	T42.3x3	T42.3x4	T42.3x5	T42.3x6
Heptabarbitone	T42.3x1	T42.3x2	T42.3x3	T42.3x4	T42.3x5	T42.3x6
Heptabarbital, heptabarbitone	T42.3x1	T42.3x2	T42.3x3	T42.3x4	T42.3x5	T42.3x6
Heptachlor	T60.1x1	T60.1x2	T60.1x3	T60.1x4	—	—
Heptalgin	T40.2x1	T40.2x2	T40.2x3	T40.2x4	T40.2x5	T40.2x6

TABLE OF DRUGS AND CHEMICALS

Substance	External Cause (T-Code)					
	Poisoning, Accidental (Unintentional)	Poisoning, Intentional Self-Harm	Poisoning, Assault	Poisoning, Undetermined	Adverse Effect	Underdosing
Heptaminol	T46.3x1	T46.3x2	T46.3x3	T46.3x4	T46.3x5	T46.3x6
Herbicide NEC	T60.3x1	T60.3x2	T60.3x3	T60.3x4	—	—
Heroin	T40.1x1	T40.1x2	T40.1x3	T40.1x4	T40.1x5	T40.1x6
Herplex	T49.5x1	T49.5x2	T49.5x3	T49.5x4	T49.5x5	T49.5x6
HES	T45.8x1	T45.8x2	T45.8x3	T45.8x4	T45.8x5	T45.8x6
Hesperidin	T46.991	T46.992	T46.993	T46.994	T46.995	T46.996
Hetacillin	T36.0x1	T36.0x2	T36.0x3	T36.0x4	T36.0x5	T36.0x6
Hetastarch	T45.8x1	T45.8x2	T45.8x3	T45.8x4	T45.8x5	T45.8x6
HETP	T60.0x1	T60.0x2	T60.0x3	T60.0x4	—	—
Hexachlorobenzene (vapor)	T60.3x1	T60.3x2	T60.3x3	T60.3x4	—	—
Hexachlorocyclohexane	T53.6x1	T53.6x2	T53.6x3	T53.6x4	—	—
Hexachlorophene	T49.0x1	T49.0x2	T49.0x3	T49.0x4	T49.0x5	T49.0x6
Hexadiline	T46.3x1	T46.3x2	T46.3x3	T46.3x4	T46.3x5	T46.3x6
Hexadimethrine (bromide)	T45.7x1	T45.7x2	T45.7x3	T45.7x4	T45.7x5	T45.7x6
Hexadylamine	T46.3x1	T46.3x2	T46.3x3	T46.3x4	T46.3x5	T46.3x6
Hexaethyl tetraphosphate	T60.0x1	T60.0x2	T60.0x3	T60.0x4	—	—
Hexafluorenium bromide	T48.1x1	T48.1x2	T48.1x3	T48.1x4	T48.1x5	T48.1x6
Hexafluorodiethyl ether	T43.291	T43.292	T43.293	T43.294	T43.295	T43.296
Hexafluronium (bromide)	T48.1x1	T48.1x2	T48.1x3	T48.1x4	T48.1x5	T48.1x6
Hexahydrobenzol	T52.8x1	T52.8x2	T52.8x3	T52.8x4	—	—
Hexahydrocresol (s)	T51.8x1	T51.8x2	T51.8x3	T51.8x4	—	—
arsenide	T57.0x1	T57.0x2	T57.0x3	T57.0x4	—	—
arseniurated	T57.0x1	T57.0x2	T57.0x3	T57.0x4	—	—
cyanide	T57.3x1	T57.3x2	T57.3x3	T57.3x4	—	—
gas	T59.891	T59.892	T59.893	T59.894	—	—
Fluoride (liquid)	T57.8x1	T57.8x2	T57.8x3	T57.8x4	—	—
vapor	T59.891	T59.892	T59.893	T59.894	—	—
phophorated	T60.0x1	T60.0x2	T60.0x3	T60.0x4	—	—
sulfate	T57.8x1	T57.8x2	T57.8x3	T57.8x4	—	—
sulfide (gas)	T59.6x1	T59.6x2	T59.6x3	T59.6x4	—	—
arseniurated	T57.0x1	T57.0x2	T57.0x3	T57.0x4	—	—
sulfurated	T57.8x1	T57.8x2	T57.8x3	T57.8x4	—	—
Hexahydrophenol	T51.8x1	T51.8x2	T51.8x3	T51.8x4	—	—
Hexa-germ	T49.2x1	T49.2x2	T49.2x3	T49.2x4	T49.2x5	T49.2x6
Hexalen	T51.8x1	T51.8x2	T51.8x3	T51.8x4	—	—
Hexamethonium bromide	T44.2x1	T44.2x2	T44.2x3	T44.2x4	T44.2x5	T44.2x6
Hexamethylene	T52.8x1	T52.8x2	T52.8x3	T52.8x4	—	—
Hexamethylmelamine	T45.1x1	T45.1x2	T45.1x3	T45.1x4	T45.1x5	T45.1x6
Hexamidine	T49.0x1	T49.0x2	T49.0x3	T49.0x4	T49.0x5	T49.0x6
Hexamine (mandelate)	T37.8x1	T37.8x2	T37.8x3	T37.8x4	T37.8x5	T37.8x6

Substance	Poisoning, Accidental (Unintentional)	Poisoning, Intentional Self-Harm	Poisoning, Assault	Poisoning, Undetermined	Adverse Effect	Underdosing
Hexanone, 2-hexanone	T52.4x1	T52.4x2	T52.4x3	T52.4x4	—	—
Hexanuorenium	T48.1x1	T48.1x2	T48.1x3	T48.1x4	T48.1x5	T48.1x6
Hexapropymate	T42.6x1	T42.6x2	T42.6x3	T42.6x4	T42.6x5	T42.6x6
Hexasonium iodide	T44.3x1	T44.3x2	T44.3x3	T44.3x4	T44.3x5	T44.3x6
Hexcarbacholine bromide	T48.1x1	T48.1x2	T48.1x3	T48.1x4	T48.1x5	T48.1x6
Hexemal	T42.3x1	T42.3x2	T42.3x3	T42.3x4	T42.3x5	T42.3x6
Hexestrol	T38.5x1	T38.5x2	T38.5x3	T38.5x4	T38.5x5	T38.5x6
Hexethal (sodium)	T42.3x1	T42.3x2	T42.3x3	T42.3x4	T42.3x5	T42.3x6
Hexetidine	T37.8x1	T37.8x2	T37.8x3	T37.8x4	T37.8x5	T37.8x6
Hexobarbital	T42.3x1	T42.3x2	T42.3x3	T42.3x4	T42.3x5	T42.3x6
rectal	T41.291	T41.292	T41.293	T41.294	T41.295	T41.296
sodium	T41.1x1	T41.1x2	T41.1x3	T41.1x4	T41.1x5	T41.1x6
Hexobendine	T46.3x1	T46.3x2	T46.3x3	T46.3x4	T46.3x5	T46.3x6
Hexocyclium	T44.3x1	T44.3x2	T44.3x3	T44.3x4	T44.3x5	T44.3x6
metilsulfate	T44.3x1	T44.3x2	T44.3x3	T44.3x4	T44.3x5	T44.3x6
Hexoestrol	T38.5x1	T38.5x2	T38.5x3	T38.5x4	T38.5x5	T38.5x6
Hexone	T52.4x1	T52.4x2	T52.4x3	T52.4x4	—	—
Hexoprenaline	T48.6x1	T48.6x2	T48.6x3	T48.6x4	T48.6x5	T48.6x6
Hexylcaine	T41.3x1	T41.3x2	T41.3x3	T41.3x4	T41.3x5	T41.3x6
Hexylresorcinol	T52.2x1	T52.2x2	T52.2x3	T52.2x4	—	—
HGH (human growth hormone)	T38.811	T38.812	T38.813	T38.814	T38.815	T38.816
Hinkle's pills	T47.2x1	T47.2x2	T47.2x3	T47.2x4	T47.2x5	T47.2x6
Histalog	T50.8x1	T50.8x2	T50.8x3	T50.8x4	T50.8x5	T50.8x6
Histamine (phosphate)	T50.8x1	T50.8x2	T50.8x3	T50.8x4	T50.8x5	T50.8x6
Histoplasmin	T50.8x1	T50.8x2	T50.8x3	T50.8x4	T50.8x5	T50.8x6
Holly berries	T62.2x1	T62.2x2	T62.2x3	T62.2x4	—	—
Homatropine	T44.3x1	T44.3x2	T44.3x3	T44.3x4	T44.3x5	T44.3x6
methylbromide	T44.3x1	T44.3x2	T44.3x3	T44.3x4	T44.3x5	T44.3x6
Homochlorcyclizine	T45.0x1	T45.0x2	T45.0x3	T45.0x4	T45.0x5	T45.0x6
Homosalate	T49.3x1	T49.3x2	T49.3x3	T49.3x4	T49.3x5	T49.3x6
Homo-tet	T50.Z11	T50.Z12	T50.Z13	T50.Z14	T50.Z15	T50.Z16
Hormone	T38.801	T38.802	T38.803	T38.804	T38.805	T38.806
adrenal cortical steroids	T38.0x1	T38.0x2	T38.0x3	T38.0x4	T38.0x5	T38.0x6
androgenic	T38.7x1	T38.7x2	T38.7x3	T38.7x4	T38.7x5	T38.7x6
anterior pituitary NEC	T38.811	T38.812	T38.813	T38.814	T38.815	T38.816
antidiabetic agents	T38.3x1	T38.3x2	T38.3x3	T38.3x4	T38.3x5	T38.3x6
antidiuretic	T38.891	T38.892	T38.893	T38.894	T38.895	T38.896
cancer therapy	T45.1x1	T45.1x2	T45.1x3	T45.1x4	T45.1x5	T45.1x6
follicle stimulating	T38.811	T38.812	T38.813	T38.814	T38.815	T38.816
gonadotropic	T38.891	T38.892	T38.893	T38.894	T38.895	T38.896
pituitary	T38.811	T38.812	T38.813	T38.814	T38.815	T38.816

Substance	External Cause (T-Code)					
	Poisoning, Accidental (Unintentional)	Poisoning, Intentional Self-Harm	Poisoning, Assault	Poisoning, Undetermined	Adverse Effect	Underdosing
Hormone *(Continued)*						
growth	T38.811	T38.812	T38.813	T38.814	T38.815	T38.816
luteinizing	T38.811	T38.812	T38.813	T38.814	T38.815	T38.816
ovarian	T38.5x1	T38.5x2	T38.5x3	T38.5x4	T38.5x5	T38.5x6
oxytocic	T48.0x1	T48.0x2	T48.0x3	T48.0x4	T48.0x5	T48.0x6
parathyroid (derivatives)	T50.991	T50.992	T50.993	T50.994	T50.995	T50.996
pituitary (posterior) NEC	T38.891	T38.892	T38.893	T38.894	T38.895	T38.896
anterior	T38.811	T38.812	T38.813	T38.814	T38.815	T38.816
specified, NEC	T38.891	T38.892	T38.893	T38.894	T38.895	T38.896
thyroid	T38.1x1	T38.1x2	T38.1x3	T38.1x4	T38.1x5	T38.1x6
Hornet (sting)	T63.451	T63.452	T63.453	T63.454	—	—
Horse anti-human lymphocytic serum	T50.Z11	T50.Z12	T50.Z13	T50.Z14	T50.Z15	T50.Z16
Horticulture agent NEC	T65.91	T65.92	T65.93	T65.94	—	—
with pesticide	T60.91	T60.92	T60.93	T60.94	—	—
Human						
albumin	T45.8x1	T45.8x2	T45.8x3	T45.8x4	T45.8x5	T45.8x6
growth hormone (HGH)	T38.811	T38.812	T38.813	T38.814	T38.815	T38.816
immune serum	T50.Z11	T50.Z12	T50.Z13	T50.Z14	T50.Z15	T50.Z16
Hyaluronidase	T45.3x1	T45.3x2	T45.3x3	T45.3x4	T45.3x5	T45.3x6
Hyazyme	T45.3x1	T45.3x2	T45.3x3	T45.3x4	T45.3x5	T45.3x6
Hycodan	T40.2x1	T40.2x2	T40.2x3	T40.2x4	T40.2x5	T40.2x6
Hydantoin derivative NEC	T42.0x1	T42.0x2	T42.0x3	T42.0x4	T42.0x5	T42.0x6
Hydeltra	T38.0x1	T38.0x2	T38.0x3	T38.0x4	T38.0x5	T38.0x6
Hydergine	T44.6x1	T44.6x2	T44.6x3	T44.6x4	T44.6x5	T44.6x6
Hydrabamine penicillin	T36.0x1	T36.0x2	T36.0x3	T36.0x4	T36.0x5	T36.0x6
Hydralazine	T46.5x1	T46.5x2	T46.5x3	T46.5x4	T46.5x5	T46.5x6
Hydrargaphen	T49.0x1	T49.0x2	T49.0x3	T49.0x4	T49.0x5	T49.0x6
Hydrargyri amino-chloridum	T49.0x1	T49.0x2	T49.0x3	T49.0x4	T49.0x5	T49.0x6
Hydrastine	T48.291	T48.292	T48.293	T48.294	T48.295	T48.296
Hydrazine	T54.1x1	T54.1x2	T54.1x3	T54.1x4	—	—
monoamine oxidase inhibitors	T43.1x1	T43.1x2	T43.1x3	T43.1x4	T43.1x5	T43.1x6
Hydrazoic acid, azides	T54.2x1	T54.2x2	T54.2x3	T54.2x4	—	—
Hydriodic acid	T48.4x1	T48.4x2	T48.4x3	T48.4x4	T48.4x5	T48.4x6
Hydrocarbon gas	T59.891	T59.892	T59.893	T59.894	—	—
incomplete combustion of - *see* Carbon, monoxide, fuel, utility						
liquefied (mobile container)	T59.891	T59.892	T59.893	T59.894	—	—
piped (natural)	T59.891	T59.892	T59.893	T59.894	—	—
Hydrochloric acid (liquid)	T54.2x1	T54.2x2	T54.2x3	T54.2x4	—	—
medicinal (digestant)	T47.5x1	T47.5x2	T47.5x3	T47.5x4	T47.5x5	T47.5x6
vapor	T59.891	T59.892	T59.893	T59.894	—	—

Substance	External Cause (T-Code)					
	Poisoning, Accidental (Unintentional)	Poisoning, Intentional Self-Harm	Poisoning, Assault	Poisoning, Undetermined	Adverse Effect	Underdosing
Hydrochlorothiazide	T50.2x1	T50.2x2	T50.2x3	T50.2x4	T50.2x5	T50.2x6
Hydrocodone	T40.2x1	T40.2x2	T40.2x3	T40.2x4	T40.2x5	T40.2x6
Hydrocortisone (derivatives)	T49.0x1	T49.0x2	T49.0x3	T49.0x4	T49.0x5	T49.0x6
aceponate	T49.0x1	T49.0x2	T49.0x3	T49.0x4	T49.0x5	T49.0x6
ENT agent	T49.6x1	T49.6x2	T49.6x3	T49.6x4	T49.6x5	T49.6x6
ophthalmic preparation	T49.5x1	T49.5x2	T49.5x3	T49.5x4	T49.5x5	T49.5x6
topical NEC	T49.0x1	T49.0x2	T49.0x3	T49.0x4	T49.0x5	T49.0x6
Hydrocortone	T38.0x1	T38.0x2	T38.0x3	T38.0x4	T38.0x5	T38.0x6
ENT agent	T49.6x1	T49.6x2	T49.6x3	T49.6x4	T49.6x5	T49.6x6
ophthalmic preparation	T49.5x1	T49.5x2	T49.5x3	T49.5x4	T49.5x5	T49.5x6
topical NEC	T49.0x1	T49.0x2	T49.0x3	T49.0x4	T49.0x5	T49.0x6
Hydrocyanic acid (liquid)	T57.3x1	T57.3x2	T57.3x3	T57.3x4	—	—
gas	T65.0x1	T65.0x2	T65.0x3	T65.0x4	—	—
Hydroflumethiazide	T50.2x1	T50.2x2	T50.2x3	T50.2x4	T50.2x5	T50.2x6
Hydrofluoric acid (liquid)	T54.2x1	T54.2x2	T54.2x3	T54.2x4	—	—
vapor	T59.891	T59.892	T59.893	T59.894	—	—
Hydrogen	T59.891	T59.892	T59.893	T59.894	—	—
arsenide	T57.0x1	T57.0x2	T57.0x3	T57.0x4	—	—
arseniureted	T57.0x1	T57.0x2	T57.0x3	T57.0x4	—	—
cyanide (salts)	T57.3x1	T57.3x2	T57.3x3	T57.3x4	—	—
gas	T57.3x1	T57.3x2	T57.3x3	T57.3x4	—	—
chloride	T57.8x1	T57.8x2	T57.8x3	T57.8x4	—	—
cyanide (gas)	T57.3x1	T57.3x2	T57.3x3	T57.3x4	—	—
Fluoride	T59.5x1	T59.5x2	T59.5x3	T59.5x4	—	—
vapor	T59.5x1	T59.5x2	T59.5x3	T59.5x4	—	—
peroxide	T49.0x1	T49.0x2	T49.0x3	T49.0x4	T49.0x5	T49.0x6
phosphureted	T57.1x1	T57.1x2	T57.1x3	T57.1x4	—	—
sulfide	T59.6x1	T59.6x2	T59.6x3	T59.6x4	—	—
arseniureted	T57.0x1	T57.0x2	T57.0x3	T57.0x4	—	—
sulfureted	T59.6x1	T59.6x2	T59.6x3	T59.6x4	—	—
Hydromethylpyridine	T46.7x1	T46.7x2	T46.7x3	T46.7x4	T46.7x5	T46.7x6
Hydromorphinol	T40.2x1	T40.2x2	T40.2x3	T40.2x4	T40.2x5	T40.2x6
Hydromorphinone	T40.2x1	T40.2x2	T40.2x3	T40.2x4	T40.2x5	T40.2x6
Hydromorphone	T40.2x1	T40.2x2	T40.2x3	T40.2x4	T40.2x5	T40.2x6
Hydromox	T50.2x1	T50.2x2	T50.2x3	T50.2x4	T50.2x5	T50.2x6
Hydrophilic lotion	T49.3x1	T49.3x2	T49.3x3	T49.3x4	T49.3x5	T49.3x6
Hydroquinidine	T46.2x1	T46.2x2	T46.2x3	T46.2x4	T46.2x5	T46.2x6
Hydroquinone	T52.2x1	T52.2x2	T52.2x3	T52.2x4	—	—
vapor	T59.891	T59.892	T59.893	T59.894	—	—

Substance	External Cause (T-Code)					
	Poisoning, Accidental (Unintentional)	Poisoning, Intentional Self-Harm	Poisoning, Assault	Poisoning, Undetermined	Adverse Effect	Underdosing
Hydrosulfuric acid (gas)	T59.6x1	T59.6x2	T59.6x3	T59.6x4	—	—
Hydrotalcite	T47.1x1	T47.1x2	T47.1x3	T47.1x4	T47.1x5	T47.1x6
Hydrous wool fat	T49.3x1	T49.3x2	T49.3x3	T49.3x4	T49.3x5	T49.3x6
Hydroxide, caustic	T54.3x1	T54.3x2	T54.3x3	T54.3x4	—	—
Hydroxocobalamin	T45.8x1	T45.8x2	T45.8x3	T45.8x4	T45.8x5	T45.8x6
Hydroxyamphetamine	T49.5x1	T49.5x2	T49.5x3	T49.5x4	T49.5x5	T49.5x6
Hydroxycarbamide	T45.1x1	T45.1x2	T45.1x3	T45.1x4	T45.1x5	T45.1x6
Hydroxychloroquine	T37.8x1	T37.8x2	T37.8x3	T37.8x4	T37.8x5	T37.8x6
Hydroxydihydrocodeinone	T40.2x1	T40.2x2	T40.2x3	T40.2x4	T40.2x5	T40.2x6
Hydroxyestrone	T38.5x1	T38.5x2	T38.5x3	T38.5x4	T38.5x5	T38.5x6
Hydroxyethyl starch	T45.8x1	T45.8x2	T45.8x3	T45.8x4	T45.8x5	T45.8x6
Hydroxymethylpentanone	T52.4x1	T52.4x2	T52.4x3	T52.4x4	—	—
Hydroxyphenamate	T43.591	T43.592	T43.593	T43.594	T43.595	T43.596
Hydroxyphenylbutazone	T39.2x1	T39.2x2	T39.2x3	T39.2x4	T39.2x5	T39.2x6
Hydroxyprogesterone	T38.5x1	T38.5x2	T38.5x3	T38.5x4	T38.5x5	T38.5x6
caproate	T38.5x1	T38.5x2	T38.5x3	T38.5x4	T38.5x5	T38.5x6
Hydroxyquinoline (derivatives) NEC	T37.8x1	T37.8x2	T37.8x3	T37.8x4	T37.8x5	T37.8x6
Hydroxystilbamidine	T37.3x1	T37.3x2	T37.3x3	T37.3x4	T37.3x5	T37.3x6
Hydroxytoluene (nonmedicinal)	T54.0x1	T54.0x2	T54.0x3	T54.0x4	—	—
medicinal	T49.0x1	T49.0x2	T49.0x3	T49.0x4	T49.0x5	T49.0x6
Hydroxyurea	T45.1x1	T45.1x2	T45.1x3	T45.1x4	T45.1x5	T45.1x6
Hydroxyzine	T43.591	T43.592	T43.593	T43.594	T43.595	T43.596
Hyoscine	T44.3x1	T44.3x2	T44.3x3	T44.3x4	T44.3x5	T44.3x6
Hyoscyamine	T44.3x1	T44.3x2	T44.3x3	T44.3x4	T44.3x5	T44.3x6
Hyoscyamus	T44.3x1	T44.3x2	T44.3x3	T44.3x4	T44.3x5	T44.3x6
dry extract	T44.3x1	T44.3x2	T44.3x3	T44.3x4	T44.3x5	T44.3x6
Hypaque	T50.8x1	T50.8x2	T50.8x3	T50.8x4	T50.8x5	T50.8x6
Hypertussis	T50.Z11	T50.Z12	T50.Z13	T50.Z14	T50.Z15	T50.Z16
Hypnotic	T42.71	T42.72	T42.73	T42.74	T42.75	T42.76
anticonvulsant	T42.71	T42.72	T42.73	T42.74	T42.75	T42.76
specified NEC	T42.6x1	T42.6x2	T42.6x3	T42.6x4	T42.6x5	T42.6x6
Hypochlorite	T49.0x1	T49.0x2	T49.0x3	T49.0x4	T49.0x5	T49.0x6
Hypophysis, posterior	T38.891	T38.892	T38.893	T38.894	T38.895	T38.896
Hypotensive NEC	T46.5x1	T46.5x2	T46.5x3	T46.5x4	T46.5x5	T46.5x6
Hypromellose	T49.5x1	T49.5x2	T49.5x3	T49.5x4	T49.5x5	T49.5x6
Ibacitabine	T37.5x1	T37.5x2	T37.5x3	T37.5x4	T37.5x5	T37.5x6
Ibopamine	T44.991	T44.992	T44.993	T44.994	T44.995	T44.996
Ibufenac	T39.311	T39.312	T39.313	T39.314	T39.315	T39.316
Ibuprofen	T39.311	T39.312	T39.313	T39.314	T39.315	T39.316
Ibuproxam	T39.311	T39.312	T39.313	T39.314	T39.315	T39.316

Substance	Poisoning, Accidental (Unintentional)	Poisoning, Intentional Self-Harm	Poisoning, Assault	Poisoning, Undetermined	Adverse Effect	Underdosing
	External Cause (T-Code)					
Ibuterol	T48.6x1	T48.6x2	T48.6x3	T48.6x4	T48.6x5	T48.6x6
Ichthammol	T49.0x1	T49.0x2	T49.0x3	T49.0x4	T49.0x5	T49.0x6
Ichthyol	T49.4x1	T49.4x2	T49.4x3	T49.4x4	T49.4x5	T49.4x6
Idarubicin	T45.1x1	T45.1x2	T45.1x3	T45.1x4	T45.1x5	T45.1x6
Idoxuridine	T37.5x1	T37.5x2	T37.5x3	T37.5x4	T37.5x5	T37.5x6
IDU	T49.5x1	T49.5x2	T49.5x3	T49.5x4	T49.5x5	T49.5x6
Idrocilamide	T42.8x1	T42.8x2	T42.8x3	T42.8x4	T42.8x5	T42.8x6
Ifenprodil	T46.7x1	T46.7x2	T46.7x3	T46.7x4	T46.7x5	T46.7x6
Ifosfamide	T45.1x1	T45.1x2	T45.1x3	T45.1x4	T45.1x5	T45.1x6
Iletin	T38.3x1	T38.3x2	T38.3x3	T38.3x4	T38.3x5	T38.3x6
Ilex	T62.2x1	T62.2x2	T62.2x3	T62.2x4	—	—
Illuminating gas (after combustion)	T58.11	T58.12	T58.13	T58.14	—	—
prior to combustion	T59.891	T59.892	T59.893	T59.894	—	—
Ilopan	T45.2x1	T45.2x2	T45.2x3	T45.2x4	T45.2x5	T45.2x6
Iloprost	T46.7x1	T46.7x2	T46.7x3	T46.7x4	T46.7x5	T46.7x6
Ilotycin	T36.3x1	T36.3x2	T36.3x3	T36.3x4	T36.3x5	T36.3x6
ophthalmic preparation	T49.5x1	T49.5x2	T49.5x3	T49.5x4	T49.5x5	T49.5x6
topical NEC	T49.0x1	T49.0x2	T49.0x3	T49.0x4	T49.0x5	T49.0x6
Imidazole-4-carboxamide	T45.1x1	T45.1x2	T45.1x3	T45.1x4	T45.1x5	T45.1x6
Imipenem	T36.0x1	T36.0x2	T36.0x3	T36.0x4	T36.0x5	T36.0x6
Imipramine	T43.011	T43.012	T43.013	T43.014	T43.015	T43.016
Immu-G	T50.Z11	T50.Z12	T50.Z13	T50.Z14	T50.Z15	T50.Z16
Immune						
globulin	T50.Z11	T50.Z12	T50.Z13	T50.Z14	T50.Z15	T50.Z16
serum globulin	T50.Z11	T50.Z12	T50.Z13	T50.Z14	T50.Z15	T50.Z16
Immunoglobin human (intravenous) (normal)	T50.Z11	T50.Z12	T50.Z13	T50.Z14	T50.Z15	T50.Z16
unmodified	T50.Z11	T50.Z12	T50.Z13	T50.Z14	T50.Z15	T50.Z16
Immunosuppressive drug	T45.1x1	T45.1x2	T45.1x3	T45.1x4	T45.1x5	T45.1x6
Immu-tetanus	T50.Z11	T50.Z12	T50.Z13	T50.Z14	T50.Z15	T50.Z16
Indalpine	T43.221	T43.222	T43.223	T43.224	T43.225	T43.226
Indanazoline	T48.5x1	T48.5x2	T48.5x3	T48.5x4	T48.5x5	T48.5x6
Indandione (derivatives)	T45.511	T45.512	T45.513	T45.514	T45.515	T45.516
Indapamide	T46.5x1	T46.5x2	T46.5x3	T46.5x4	T46.5x5	T46.5x6
Indendione (derivatives)	T45.511	T45.512	T45.513	T45.514	T45.515	T45.516
Indenolol	T44.7x1	T44.7x2	T44.7x3	T44.7x4	T44.7x5	T44.7x6
Inderal	T44.7x1	T44.7x2	T44.7x3	T44.7x4	T44.7x5	T44.7x6
Indian hemp	T40.7x1	T40.7x2	T40.7x3	T40.7x4	T40.7x5	T40.7x6
Indian						
hemp	T40.991	T40.992	T40.993	T40.994	T40.995	T40.996
tobacco	T62.2x1	T62.2x2	T62.2x3	T62.2x4	—	—

Substance	External Cause (T-Code)					
	Poisoning, Accidental (Unintentional)	Poisoning, Intentional Self-Harm	Poisoning, Assault	Poisoning, Undetermined	Adverse Effect	Underdosing
Indigo carmine	T50.8x1	T50.8x2	T50.8x3	T50.8x4	T50.8x5	T50.8x6
Indobufen	T45.521	T45.522	T45.523	T45.524	T45.525	T45.526
Indocin	T39.2x1	T39.2x2	T39.2x3	T39.2x4	T39.2x5	T39.2x6
Indocyanine green	T50.8x1	T50.8x2	T50.8x3	T50.8x4	T50.8x5	T50.8x6
Indometacin	T39.391	T39.392	T39.393	T39.394	T39.395	T39.396
Indomethacin	T39.391	T39.392	T39.393	T39.394	T39.395	T39.396
farnesil	T39.4x1	T39.4x2	T39.4x3	T39.4x4	T39.4x5	T39.4x6
Indoramin	T44.6x1	T44.6x2	T44.6x3	T44.6x4	T44.6x5	T44.6x6
Industrial						
alcohol	T51.91	T51.92	T51.93	T51.94	—	—
fumes	T59.891	T59.892	T59.893	T59.894	—	—
solvents (fumes) (vapors)	T52.91	T52.92	T52.93	T52.94	—	—
Influenza vaccine	T50.B91	T50.B92	T50.B93	T50.B94	T50.B95	T50.B96
Ingested substance NEC	T65.91	T65.92	T65.93	T65.94	—	—
INH	T37.1x1	T37.1x2	T37.1x3	T37.1x4	T37.1x5	T37.1x6
Inhalation, gas (noxious) - *see* Gas						
Inhibitor						
fibrinolysis	T45.621	T45.622	T45.623	T45.624	T45.625	T45.626
monoamine oxidase NEC	T43.1x1	T43.1x2	T43.1x3	T43.1x4	T43.1x5	T43.1x6
hydrazine	T43.1x1	T43.1x2	T43.1x3	T43.1x4	T43.1x5	T43.1x6
postsynaptic	T43.8x1	T43.8x2	T43.8x3	T43.8x4	T43.8x5	T43.8x6
prothrombin synthesis	T45.511	T45.512	T45.513	T45.514	T45.515	T45.516
Ink	T65.891	T65.892	T65.893	T65.894	—	—
Innovar	T42.71	T42.72	T42.73	T42.74	T42.75	T42.76
Inosine pranobex	T37.5x1	T37.5x2	T37.5x3	T37.5x4	T37.5x5	T37.5x6
Inositol	T50.991	T50.992	T50.993	T50.994	T50.995	T50.996
nicotinate	T46.7x1	T46.7x2	T46.7x3	T46.7x4	T46.7x5	T46.7x6
Inproquone	T45.1x1	T45.1x2	T45.1x3	T45.1x4	T45.1x5	T45.1x6
Insect (sting), venomous	T63.481	T63.482	T63.483	T63.484	—	—
ant	T63.421	T63.422	T63.423	T63.424	—	—
bee	T63.441	T63.442	T63.443	T63.444	—	—
caterpillar	T63.431	T63.432	T63.433	T63.434	—	—
hornet	T63.451	T63.452	T63.453	T63.454	—	—
wasp	T63.461	T63.462	T63.463	T63.464	—	—
Insecticide NEC	T60.91	T60.92	T60.93	T60.94	—	—
carbamate	T60.0x1	T60.0x2	T60.0x3	T60.0x4	—	—
chlorinated	T60.1x1	T60.1x2	T60.1x3	T60.1x4	—	—
mixed	T60.91	T60.92	T60.93	T60.94	—	—
organochlorine	T60.1x1	T60.1x2	T60.1x3	T60.1x4	—	—
organophosphorus	T60.0x1	T60.0x2	T60.0x3	T60.0x4	—	—

Substance	External Cause (T-Code)					
	Poisoning, Accidental (Unintentional)	Poisoning, Intentional Self-Harm	Poisoning, Assault	Poisoning, Undetermined	Adverse Effect	Underdosing
Insular tissue extract	T38.3x1	T38.3x2	T38.3x3	T38.3x4	T38.3x5	T38.3x6
Insulin NEC	T38.3x1	T38.3x2	T38.3x3	T38.3x4	T38.3x5	T38.3x6
defalan	T38.3x1	T38.3x2	T38.3x3	T38.3x4	T38.3x5	T38.3x6
human	T38.3x1	T38.3x2	T38.3x3	T38.3x4	T38.3x5	T38.3x6
injection, soluble	T38.3x1	T38.3x2	T38.3x3	T38.3x4	T38.3x5	T38.3x6
biphasic	T38.3x1	T38.3x2	T38.3x3	T38.3x4	T38.3x5	T38.3x6
intermediate acting	T38.3x1	T38.3x2	T38.3x3	T38.3x4	T38.3x5	T38.3x6
protamine zinc	T38.3x1	T38.3x2	T38.3x3	T38.3x4	T38.3x5	T38.3x6
slow acting	T38.3x1	T38.3x2	T38.3x3	T38.3x4	T38.3x5	T38.3x6
zinc						
protamine injection	T38.3x1	T38.3x2	T38.3x3	T38.3x4	T38.3x5	T38.3x6
suspension (amorphous) (crystalline)	T38.3x1	T38.3x2	T38.3x3	T38.3x4	T38.3x5	T38.3x6
Insulin (amorphous) (globin) (isophane) (Lente) (NPH) (prolamine) (Semilente) (Ultralente) (zinc)	T38.3x1	T38.3x2	T38.3x3	T38.3x4	T38.3x5	T38.3x6
Interferon (alpha) (beta) (gamma)	T37.5x1	T37.5x2	T37.5x3	T37.5x4	T37.5x5	T37.5x6
Intestinal motility control drug	T47.6x1	T47.6x2	T47.6x3	T47.6x4	T47.6x5	T47.6x6
biological	T47.8x1	T47.8x2	T47.8x3	T47.8x4	T47.8x5	T47.8x6
Intranarcon	T41.1x1	T41.1x2	T41.1x3	T41.1x4	T41.1x5	T41.1x6
Intravenous						
amino acids	T50.991	T50.992	T50.993	T50.994	T50.995	T50.996
fat suspension	T50.991	T50.992	T50.993	T50.994	T50.995	T50.996
Inulin	T50.8x1	T50.8x2	T50.8x3	T50.8x4	T50.8x5	T50.8x6
Invert sugar	T50.3x1	T50.3x2	T50.3x3	T50.3x4	T50.3x5	T50.3x6
Inza - see Naproxen						
Iobenzamic acid	T50.8x1	T50.8x2	T50.8x3	T50.8x4	T50.8x5	T50.8x6
Iocarmic acid	T50.8x1	T50.8x2	T50.8x3	T50.8x4	T50.8x5	T50.8x6
Iocetamic acid	T50.8x1	T50.8x2	T50.8x3	T50.8x4	T50.8x5	T50.8x6
Iodamide	T50.8x1	T50.8x2	T50.8x3	T50.8x4	T50.8x5	T50.8x6
Iodide NEC (see also Iodine)	T49.0x1	T49.0x2	T49.0x3	T49.0x4	T49.0x5	T49.0x6
mercury (ointment)	T49.0x1	T49.0x2	T49.0x3	T49.0x4	T49.0x5	T49.0x6
methylate	T49.0x1	T49.0x2	T49.0x3	T49.0x4	T49.0x5	T49.0x6
potassium (expectorant) NEC	T48.4x1	T48.4x2	T48.4x3	T48.4x4	T48.4x5	T48.4x6
Iodinated						
contrast medium	T50.8x1	T50.8x2	T50.8x3	T50.8x4	T50.8x5	T50.8x6
glycerol	T48.4x1	T48.4x2	T48.4x3	T48.4x4	T48.4x5	T48.4x6
human serum albumin (131I)	T50.8x1	T50.8x2	T50.8x3	T50.8x4	T50.8x5	T50.8x6
Iodine (antiseptic, external) (tincture) NEC	T49.0x1	T49.0x2	T49.0x3	T49.0x4	T49.0x5	T49.0x6
solution	T49.0x1	T49.0x2	T49.0x3	T49.0x4	T49.0x5	T49.0x6
125 (see also Radiation sickness, and Exposure to radioactivce isotopes)	T50.8x1	T50.8x2	T50.8x3	T50.8x4	T50.8x5	T50.8x6
therapeutic	T50.991	T50.992	T50.993	T50.994	T50.995	T50.996

Substance	External Cause (T-Code)					
	Poisoning, Accidental (Unintentional)	Poisoning, Intentional Self-Harm	Poisoning, Assault	Poisoning, Undetermined	Adverse Effect	Underdosing
Iodine *(Continued)*						
131 (*see also* Radiation sickness, and Exposure to radioactivce isotopes)	T50.8x1	T50.8x2	T50.8x3	T50.8x4	T50.8x5	T50.8x6
therapeutic	T38.2x1	T38.2x2	T38.2x3	T38.2x4	T38.2x5	T38.2x6
diagnostic	T50.8x1	T50.8x2	T50.8x3	T50.8x4	T50.8x5	T50.8x6
for thyroid conditions (antithyroid)	T38.2x1	T38.2x2	T38.2x3	T38.2x4	T38.2x5	T38.2x6
vapor	T59.891	T59.892	T59.893	T59.894	—	—
Iodinated glycerol	T48.4x1	T48.4x2	T48.4x3	T48.4x4	T48.4x5	T48.4x6
Iodipamide	T50.8x1	T50.8x2	T50.8x3	T50.8x4	T50.8x5	T50.8x6
Iodized (poppy seed) oil	T50.8x1	T50.8x2	T50.8x3	T50.8x4	T50.8x5	T50.8x6
Iodobismitol	T37.8x1	T37.8x2	T37.8x3	T37.8x4	T37.8x5	T37.8x6
Iodochlorhydroxyquin	T37.8x1	T37.8x2	T37.8x3	T37.8x4	T37.8x5	T37.8x6
topical	T49.0x1	T49.0x2	T49.0x3	T49.0x4	T49.0x5	T49.0x6
Iodochlorhydroxyquinoline	T37.8x1	T37.8x2	T37.8x3	T37.8x4	T37.8x5	T37.8x6
Iodocholesterol (131I)	T50.8x1	T50.8x2	T50.8x3	T50.8x4	T50.8x5	T50.8x6
Iodoform	T49.0x1	T49.0x2	T49.0x3	T49.0x4	T49.0x5	T49.0x6
Iodohippuric acid	T50.8x1	T50.8x2	T50.8x3	T50.8x4	T50.8x5	T50.8x6
Iodopanoic acid	T50.8x1	T50.8x2	T50.8x3	T50.8x4	T50.8x5	T50.8x6
Iodophthalein (sodium)	T50.8x1	T50.8x2	T50.8x3	T50.8x4	T50.8x5	T50.8x6
Iodopyracet	T50.8x1	T50.8x2	T50.8x3	T50.8x4	T50.8x5	T50.8x6
Iodoquinol	T37.8x1	T37.8x2	T37.8x3	T37.8x4	T37.8x5	T37.8x6
Iodoxamic acid	T50.8x1	T50.8x2	T50.8x3	T50.8x4	T50.8x5	T50.8x6
Iofendylate	T50.8x1	T50.8x2	T50.8x3	T50.8x4	T50.8x5	T50.8x6
Ioglycamic acid	T50.8x1	T50.8x2	T50.8x3	T50.8x4	T50.8x5	T50.8x6
Iohexol	T50.8x1	T50.8x2	T50.8x3	T50.8x4	T50.8x5	T50.8x6
Ion exchange resin						
anion	T47.8x1	T47.8x2	T47.8x3	T47.8x4	T47.8x5	T47.8x6
cation	T50.3x1	T50.3x2	T50.3x3	T50.3x4	T50.3x5	T50.3x6
cholestyramine	T46.6x1	T46.6x2	T46.6x3	T46.6x4	T46.6x5	T46.6x6
intestinal	T47.8x1	T47.8x2	T47.8x3	T47.8x4	T47.8x5	T47.8x6
Iopamidol	T50.8x1	T50.8x2	T50.8x3	T50.8x4	T50.8x5	T50.8x6
Iopanoic acid	T50.8x1	T50.8x2	T50.8x3	T50.8x4	T50.8x5	T50.8x6
Iophenoic acid	T50.8x1	T50.8x2	T50.8x3	T50.8x4	T50.8x5	T50.8x6
Iopodate, sodium	T50.8x1	T50.8x2	T50.8x3	T50.8x4	T50.8x5	T50.8x6
Iopodic acid	T50.8x1	T50.8x2	T50.8x3	T50.8x4	T50.8x5	T50.8x6
Iopromide	T50.8x1	T50.8x2	T50.8x3	T50.8x4	T50.8x5	T50.8x6
Iopydol	T50.8x1	T50.8x2	T50.8x3	T50.8x4	T50.8x5	T50.8x6
Iotalamic acid	T50.8x1	T50.8x2	T50.8x3	T50.8x4	T50.8x5	T50.8x6
Iothalamate	T50.8x1	T50.8x2	T50.8x3	T50.8x4	T50.8x5	T50.8x6
Iothiouracil	T38.2x1	T38.2x2	T38.2x3	T38.2x4	T38.2x5	T38.2x6
Iotrol	T50.8x1	T50.8x2	T50.8x3	T50.8x4	T50.8x5	T50.8x6

	External Cause (T-Code)					
Substance	Poisoning, Accidental (Unintentional)	Poisoning, Intentional Self-Harm	Poisoning, Assault	Poisoning, Undetermined	Adverse Effect	Underdosing
Iotrolan	T50.8x1	T50.8x2	T50.8x3	T50.8x4	T50.8x5	T50.8x6
Iotroxate	T50.8x1	T50.8x2	T50.8x3	T50.8x4	T50.8x5	T50.8x6
Iotroxic acid	T50.8x1	T50.8x2	T50.8x3	T50.8x4	T50.8x5	T50.8x6
Ioversol	T50.8x1	T50.8x2	T50.8x3	T50.8x4	T50.8x5	T50.8x6
Ioxaglate	T50.8x1	T50.8x2	T50.8x3	T50.8x4	T50.8x5	T50.8x6
Ioxaglic acid	T50.8x1	T50.8x2	T50.8x3	T50.8x4	T50.8x5	T50.8x6
Ioxitalamic acid	T50.8x1	T50.8x2	T50.8x3	T50.8x4	T50.8x5	T50.8x6
Ipecac	T47.7x1	T47.7x2	T47.7x3	T47.7x4	T47.7x5	T47.7x6
Ipecacuanha	T48.4x1	T48.4x2	T48.4x3	T48.4x4	T48.4x5	T48.4x6
Ipodate, calcium	T50.8x1	T50.8x2	T50.8x3	T50.8x4	T50.8x5	T50.8x6
Ipral	T42.3x1	T42.3x2	T42.3x3	T42.3x4	T42.3x5	T42.3x6
Ipratropium (bromide)	T48.6x1	T48.6x2	T48.6x3	T48.6x4	T48.6x5	T48.6x6
Ipriflavone	T46.3x1	T46.3x2	T46.3x3	T46.3x4	T46.3x5	T46.3x6
Iprindole	T43.011	T43.012	T43.013	T43.014	T43.015	T43.016
Iproclozide	T43.1x1	T43.1x2	T43.1x3	T43.1x4	T43.1x5	T43.1x6
Iprofenin	T50.8x1	T50.8x2	T50.8x3	T50.8x4	T50.8x5	T50.8x6
Iproheptine	T49.2x1	T49.2x2	T49.2x3	T49.2x4	T49.2x5	T49.2x6
Iproniazid	T43.1x1	T43.1x2	T43.1x3	T43.1x4	T43.1x5	T43.1x6
Iproplatin	T45.1x1	T45.1x2	T45.1x3	T45.1x4	T45.1x5	T45.1x6
Iproveratril	T46.1x1	T46.1x2	T46.1x3	T46.1x4	T46.1x5	T46.1x6
Iron (compounds) (medicinal) NEC	T45.4x1	T45.4x2	T45.4x3	T45.4x4	T45.4x5	T45.4x6
ammonium	T45.4x1	T45.4x2	T45.4x3	T45.4x4	T45.4x5	T45.4x6
dextran injection	T45.4x1	T45.4x2	T45.4x3	T45.4x4	T45.4x5	T45.4x6
nonmedicinal	T56.891	T56.892	T56.893	T56.894	—	—
salts	T45.4x1	T45.4x2	T45.4x3	T45.4x4	T45.4x5	T45.4x6
sorbitex	T45.4x1	T45.4x2	T45.4x3	T45.4x4	T45.4x5	T45.4x6
sorbitol citric acid complex	T45.4x1	T45.4x2	T45.4x3	T45.4x4	T45.4x5	T45.4x6
Irrigating fluid (vaginal)	T49.8x1	T49.8x2	T49.8x3	T49.8x4	T49.8x5	T49.8x6
eye	T49.5x1	T49.5x2	T49.5x3	T49.5x4	T49.5x5	T49.5x6
Isepamicin	T36.5x1	T36.5x2	T36.5x3	T36.5x4	T36.5x5	T36.5x6
Isoaminile (citrate)	T48.3x1	T48.3x2	T48.3x3	T48.3x4	T48.3x5	T48.3x6
Isoamyl nitrite	T46.3x1	T46.3x2	T46.3x3	T46.3x4	T46.3x5	T46.3x6
Isobenzan	T60.1x1	T60.1x2	T60.1x3	T60.1x4	—	—
Isobutyl acetate	T52.8x1	T52.8x2	T52.8x3	T52.8x4	—	—
Isocarboxazid	T43.1x1	T43.1x2	T43.1x3	T43.1x4	T43.1x5	T43.1x6
Isoconazole	T49.0x1	T49.0x2	T49.0x3	T49.0x4	T49.0x5	T49.0x6
Isocyanate	T65.0x1	T65.0x2	T65.0x3	T65.0x4	—	—
Isoephedrine	T44.991	T44.992	T44.993	T44.994	T44.995	T44.996
Isoetarine	T48.6x1	T48.6x2	T48.6x3	T48.6x4	T48.6x5	T48.6x6
Isoethadione	T42.2x1	T42.2x2	T42.2x3	T42.2x4	T42.2x5	T42.2x6

Substance	Poisoning, Accidental (Unintentional)	Poisoning, Intentional Self-Harm	Poisoning, Assault	Poisoning, Undetermined	Adverse Effect	Underdosing
	External Cause (T-Code)					
Isoetharine	T44.5x1	T44.5x2	T44.5x3	T44.5x4	T44.5x5	T44.5x6
Isoflurane	T41.0x1	T41.0x2	T41.0x3	T41.0x4	T41.0x5	T41.0x6
Isoflurophate	T44.0x1	T44.0x2	T44.0x3	T44.0x4	T44.0x5	T44.0x6
Isomaltose, ferric complex	T45.4x1	T45.4x2	T45.4x3	T45.4x4	T45.4x5	T45.4x6
Isometheptene	T44.3x1	T44.3x2	T44.3x3	T44.3x4	T44.3x5	T44.3x6
Isoniazid	T37.1x1	T37.1x2	T37.1x3	T37.1x4	T37.1x5	T37.1x6
with						
rifampicin	T36.6x1	T36.6x2	T36.6x3	T36.6x4	T36.6x5	T36.6x6
thioacetazone	T37.1x1	T37.1x2	T37.1x3	T37.1x4	T37.1x5	T37.1x6
Isonicotinic acid hydrazide	T37.1x1	T37.1x2	T37.1x3	T37.1x4	T37.1x5	T37.1x6
Isonipecaine	T40.4x1	T40.4x2	T40.4x3	T40.4x4	T40.4x5	T40.4x6
Isopentaquine	T37.2x1	T37.2x2	T37.2x3	T37.2x4	T37.2x5	T37.2x6
Isophane insulin	T38.3x1	T38.3x2	T38.3x3	T38.3x4	T38.3x5	T38.3x6
Isophorone	T65.891	T65.892	T65.893	T65.894	—	—
Isophosphamide	T45.1x1	T45.1x2	T45.1x3	T45.1x4	T45.1x5	T45.1x6
Isopregnenone	T38.5x1	T38.5x2	T38.5x3	T38.5x4	T38.5x5	T38.5x6
Isoprenaline	T48.6x1	T48.6x2	T48.6x3	T48.6x4	T48.6x5	T48.6x6
Isopromethazine	T43.3x1	T43.3x2	T43.3x3	T43.3x4	T43.3x5	T43.3x6
Isopropamide	T44.3x1	T44.3x2	T44.3x3	T44.3x4	T44.3x5	T44.3x6
iodide	T44.3x1	T44.3x2	T44.3x3	T44.3x4	T44.3x5	T44.3x6
Isopropanol	T51.2x1	T51.2x2	T51.2x3	T51.2x4	—	—
Isopropyl						
acetate	T52.8x1	T52.8x2	T52.8x3	T52.8x4	—	—
alcohol	T51.2x1	T51.2x2	T51.2x3	T51.2x4	—	—
medicinal	T49.4x1	T49.4x2	T49.4x3	T49.4x4	T49.4x5	T49.4x6
ether	T52.8x1	T52.8x2	T52.8x3	T52.8x4	—	—
Isopropylaminophenazone	T39.2x1	T39.2x2	T39.2x3	T39.2x4	T39.2x5	T39.2x6
Isoproterenol	T48.6x1	T48.6x2	T48.6x3	T48.6x4	T48.6x5	T48.6x6
Isosorbide dinitrate	T46.3x1	T46.3x2	T46.3x3	T46.3x4	T46.3x5	I46.3x6
Isothipendyl	T45.0x1	T45.0x2	T45.0x3	T45.0x4	T45.0x5	T45.0x6
Isotretinoin	T50.991	T50.992	T50.993	T50.994	T50.995	T50.996
Isoxazolyl penicillin	T36.0x1	T36.0x2	T36.0x3	T36.0x4	T36.0x5	T36.0x6
Isoxicam	T39.391	T39.392	T39.393	T39.394	T39.395	T39.396
Isoxsuprine	T46.7x1	T46.7x2	T46.7x3	T46.7x4	T46.7x5	T46.7x6
Ispagula	T47.4x1	T47.4x2	T47.4x3	T47.4x4	T47.4x5	T47.4x6
husk	T47.4x1	T47.4x2	T47.4x3	T47.4x4	T47.4x5	T47.4x6
Isradipine	T46.1x1	T46.1x2	T46.1x3	T46.1x4	T46.1x5	T46.1x6
l-thyroxine sodium	T38.1x1	T38.1x2	T38.1x3	T38.1x4	T38.1x5	T38.1x6
Itraconazole	T37.8x1	T37.8x2	T37.8x3	T37.8x4	T37.8x5	T37.8x6
Itramin tosilate	T46.3x1	T46.3x2	T46.3x3	T46.3x4	T46.3x5	T46.3x6
Ivermectin	T37.4x1	T37.4x2	T37.4x3	T37.4x4	T37.4x5	T37.4x6

Substance	Poisoning, Accidental (Unintentional)	Poisoning, Intentional Self-Harm	Poisoning, Assault	Poisoning, Undetermined	Adverse Effect	Underdosing
	External Cause (T-Code)					
Izoniazid	T37.1x1	T37.1x2	T37.1x3	T37.1x4	T37.1x5	T37.1x6
with thioacetazone	T37.1x1	T37.1x2	T37.1x3	T37.1x4	T37.1x5	T37.1x6
Jalap	T47.2x1	T47.2x2	T47.2x3	T47.2x4	T47.2x5	T47.2x6
Jamaica ginger	T62.2x1	T62.2x2	T62.2x3	T62.2x4	—	—
Jamaica						
dogwood (bark)	T39.8x1	T39.8x2	T39.8x3	T39.8x4	T39.8x5	T39.8x6
ginger	T65.891	T65.892	T65.893	T65.894	—	—
Jatropha	T62.2x1	T62.2x2	T62.2x3	T62.2x4	—	—
curcas	T62.2x1	T62.2x2	T62.2x3	T62.2x4	—	—
Jectofer	T45.4x1	T45.4x2	T45.4x3	T45.4x4	T45.4x5	T45.4x6
Jellyfish (sting)	T63.621	T63.622	T63.623	T63.624	—	—
Jequirity (bean)	T62.2x1	T62.2x2	T62.2x3	T62.2x4	—	—
Jimson weed (stramonium)	T62.2x1	T62.2x2	T62.2x3	T62.2x4	—	—
seeds	T62.2x1	T62.2x2	T62.2x3	T62.2x4	—	—
Josamycin	T36.3x1	T36.3x2	T36.3x3	T36.3x4	T36.3x5	T36.3x6
Juniper tar	T49.1x1	T49.1x2	T49.1x3	T49.1x4	T49.1x5	T49.1x6
Kallidinogenase	T46.7x1	T46.7x2	T46.7x3	T46.7x4	T46.7x5	T46.7x6
Kallikrein	T46.7x1	T46.7x2	T46.7x3	T46.7x4	T46.7x5	T46.7x6
Kanamycin	T36.5x1	T36.5x2	T36.5x3	T36.5x4	T36.5x5	T36.5x6
Kantrex	T36.5x1	T36.5x2	T36.5x3	T36.5x4	T36.5x5	T36.5x6
Kaolin	T47.6x1	T47.6x2	T47.6x3	T47.6x4	T47.6x5	T47.6x6
light	T47.6x1	T47.6x2	T47.6x3	T47.6x4	T47.6x5	T47.6x6
Karaya (gum)	T47.4x1	T47.4x2	T47.4x3	T47.4x4	T47.4x5	T47.4x6
Kebuzone	T39.2x1	T39.2x2	T39.2x3	T39.2x4	T39.2x5	T39.2x6
Kelevan	T60.1x1	T60.1x2	T60.1x3	T60.1x4	—	—
Kemithal	T41.1x1	T41.1x2	T41.1x3	T41.1x4	T41.1x5	T41.1x6
Kenacort	T38.0x1	T38.0x2	T38.0x3	T38.0x4	T38.0x5	T38.0x6
Keratolytic drug NEC	T49.4x1	T49.4x2	T49.4x3	T49.4x4	T49.4x5	T49.4x6
anthracene	T49.4x1	T49.4x2	T49.4x3	T49.4x4	T49.4x5	T49.4x6
Keratoplastic NEC	T49.4x1	T49.4x2	T49.4x3	T49.4x4	T49.4x5	T49.4x6
Kerosene, kerosine (fuel) (solvent) NEC	T52.0x1	T52.0x2	T52.0x3	T52.0x4	—	—
insecticide	T52.0x1	T52.0x2	T52.0x3	T52.0x4	—	—
vapor	T52.0x1	T52.0x2	T52.0x3	T52.0x4	—	—
Ketamine	T41.291	T41.292	T41.293	T41.294	T41.295	T41.296
Ketazolam	T42.4x1	T42.4x2	T42.4x3	T42.4x4	T42.4x5	T42.4x6
Ketazon	T39.2x1	T39.2x2	T39.2x3	T39.2x4	T39.2x5	T39.2x6
Ketobemidone	T40.4x1	T40.4x2	T40.4x3	T40.4x4	T40.4x5	T40.4x6
Ketoconazole	T49.0x1	T49.0x2	T49.0x3	T49.0x4	T49.0x5	T49.0x6
Ketols	T52.4x1	T52.4x2	T52.4x3	T52.4x4	—	—
Ketone oils	T52.4x1	T52.4x2	T52.4x3	T52.4x4	—	—

Substance	External Cause (T-Code)					
	Poisoning, Accidental (Unintentional)	Poisoning, Intentional Self-Harm	Poisoning, Assault	Poisoning, Undetermined	Adverse Effect	Underdosing
Ketoprofen	T39.311	T39.312	T39.313	T39.314	T39.315	T39.316
Ketorolac	T39.8x1	T39.8x2	T39.8x3	T39.8x4	T39.8x5	T39.8x6
Ketotifen	T45.0x1	T45.0x2	T45.0x3	T45.0x4	T45.0x5	T45.0x6
Khat	T43.691	T43.692	T43.693	T43.694	—	—
Khellin	T46.3x1	T46.3x2	T46.3x3	T46.3x4	T46.3x5	T46.3x6
Khelloside	T46.3x1	T46.3x2	T46.3x3	T46.3x4	T46.3x5	T46.3x6
Kiln gas or vapor (carbon monoxide)	T58.8x1	T58.8x2	T58.8x3	T58.8x4	—	—
Kitasamycin	T36.3x1	T36.3x2	T36.3x3	T36.3x4	T36.3x5	T36.3x6
Konsyl	T47.4x1	T47.4x2	T47.4x3	T47.4x4	T47.4x5	T47.4x6
Kosam seed	T62.2x1	T62.2x2	T62.2x3	T62.2x4	—	—
Krait (venom)	T63.091	T63.092	T63.093	T63.094	—	—
Kwell (insecticide)	T60.1x1	T60.1x2	T60.1x3	T60.1x4	—	—
anti-infective (topical)	T49.0x1	T49.0x2	T49.0x3	T49.0x4	T49.0x5	T49.0x6
Labetalol	T44.8x1	T44.8x2	T44.8x3	T44.8x4	T44.8x5	T44.8x6
Laburnum (seeds)	T62.2x1	T62.2x2	T62.2x3	T62.2x4		
leaves	T62.2x1	T62.2x2	T62.2x3	T62.2x4	—	—
Lachesine	T49.5x1	T49.5x2	T49.5x3	T49.5x4	T49.5x5	T49.5x6
Lacidipine	T46.5x1	T46.5x2	T46.5x3	T46.5x4	T46.5x5	T46.5x6
Lacquer	T65.6x1	T65.6x2	T65.6x3	T65.6x4	—	—
Lacrimogenic gas	T59.3x1	T59.3x2	T59.3x3	T59.3x4	—	—
Lactated potassic saline	T50.3x1	T50.3x2	T50.3x3	T50.3x4	T50.3x5	T50.3x6
Lactic acid	T49.8x1	T49.8x2	T49.8x3	T49.8x4	T49.8x5	T49.8x6
Lactobacillus						
acidophilus	T47.6x1	T47.6x2	T47.6x3	T47.6x4	T47.6x5	T47.6x6
compound	T47.6x1	T47.6x2	T47.6x3	T47.6x4	T47.6x5	T47.6x6
bifidus, lyophilized	T47.6x1	T47.6x2	T47.6x3	T47.6x4	T47.6x5	T47.6x6
bulgaricus	T47.6x1	T47.6x2	T47.6x3	T47.6x4	T47.6x5	T47.6x6
sporogenes	T47.6x1	T47.6x2	T47.6x3	T47.6x4	T47.6x5	T47.6x6
Lactoflavin	T45.2x1	T45.2x2	T45.2x3	T45.2x4	T45.2x5	T45.2x6
Lactose (as excipient)	T50.901	T50.902	T50.903	T50.904	T50.905	T50.906
Lactuca (virosa) (extract)	T42.6x1	T42.6x2	T42.6x3	T42.6x4	T42.6x5	T42.6x6
Lactucarium	T42.6x1	T42.6x2	T42.6x3	T42.6x4	T42.6x5	T42.6x6
Lactulose	T47.3x1	T47.3x2	T47.3x3	T47.3x4	T47.3x5	T47.3x6
Laevo - see Levo-						
Lanatosides	T46.0x1	T46.0x2	T46.0x3	T46.0x4	T46.0x5	T46.0x6
Lanolin	T49.3x1	T49.3x2	T49.3x3	T49.3x4	T49.3x5	T49.3x6
Largactil	T43.3x1	T43.3x2	T43.3x3	T43.3x4	T43.3x5	T43.3x6
Larkspur	T62.2x1	T62.2x2	T62.2x3	T62.2x4	—	—
Laroxyl	T43.011	T43.012	T43.013	T43.014	T43.015	T43.016
Lassar's paste	T49.4x1	T49.4x2	T49.4x3	T49.4x4	T49.4x5	T49.4x6

Substance	External Cause (T-Code)					
	Poisoning, Accidental (Unintentional)	Poisoning, Intentional Self-Harm	Poisoning, Assault	Poisoning, Undetermined	Adverse Effect	Underdosing
Lasix	T50.1x1	T50.1x2	T50.1x3	T50.1x4	T50.1x5	T50.1x6
Latamoxef	T36.1x1	T36.1x2	T36.1x3	T36.1x4	T36.1x5	T36.1x6
Latex	T65.811	T65.812	T65.813	T65.814	—	—
Lathyrus (seed)	T62.2x1	T62.2x2	T62.2x3	T62.2x4	—	—
Laudanum	T40.0x1	T40.0x2	T40.0x3	T40.0x4	T40.0x5	T40.0x6
Laudexium	T48.1x1	T48.1x2	T48.1x3	T48.1x4	T48.1x5	T48.1x6
Laughing gas	T41.0x1	T41.0x2	T41.0x3	T41.0x4	T41.0x5	T41.0x6
Laurel, black or cherry	T62.2x1	T62.2x2	T62.2x3	T62.2x4	—	—
Laurolinium	T49.0x1	T49.0x2	T49.0x3	T49.0x4	T49.0x5	T49.0x6
Lauryl sulfoacetate	T49.2x1	T49.2x2	T49.2x3	T49.2x4	T49.2x5	T49.2x6
Laxative NEC	T47.4x1	T47.4x2	T47.4x3	T47.4x4	T47.4x5	T47.4x6
L-dopa	T42.8x1	T42.8x2	T42.8x3	T42.8x4	T42.8x5	T42.8x6
Lead (dust) (fumes) (vapor) NEC	T56.0x1	T56.0x2	T56.0x3	T56.0x4	—	—
acetate	T49.2x1	T49.2x2	T49.2x3	T49.2x4	T49.2x5	T49.2x6
alkyl (fuel additive)	T56.0x1	T56.0x2	T56.0x3	T56.0x4	—	—
anti-infectives	T37.8x1	T37.8x2	T37.8x3	T37.8x4	T37.8x5	T37.8x6
antiknock compound (tetraethyl)	T56.0x1	T56.0x2	T56.0x3	T56.0x4	—	—
arsenate, arsenite (dust) (herbicide) (insecticide) (vapor)	T57.0x1	T57.0x2	T57.0x3	T57.0x4	—	—
carbonate	T56.0x1	T56.0x2	T56.0x3	T56.0x4	—	—
paint	T56.0x1	T56.0x2	T56.0x3	T56.0x4	—	—
chromate	T56.0x1	T56.0x2	T56.0x3	T56.0x4	—	—
paint	T56.0x1	T56.0x2	T56.0x3	T56.0x4	—	—
dioxide	T56.0x1	T56.0x2	T56.0x3	T56.0x4	—	—
inorganic	T56.0x1	T56.0x2	T56.0x3	T56.0x4	—	—
iodide	T56.0x1	T56.0x2	T56.0x3	T56.0x4	—	—
pigment (paint)	T56.0x1	T56.0x2	T56.0x3	T56.0x4	—	—
monoxide (dust)	T56.0x1	T56.0x2	T56.0x3	T56.0x4	—	—
paint	T56.0x1	T56.0x2	T56.0x3	T56.0x4	—	—
organic	T56.0x1	T56.0x2	T56.0x3	T56.0x4	—	—
oxide	T56.0x1	T56.0x2	T56.0x3	T56.0x4	—	—
paint	T56.0x1	T56.0x2	T56.0x3	T56.0x4	—	—
paint	T56.0x1	T56.0x2	T56.0x3	T56.0x4	—	—
salts	T56.0x1	T56.0x2	T56.0x3	T56.0x4	—	—
specified compound NEC	T56.0x1	T56.0x2	T56.0x3	T56.0x4	—	—
tetra-ethyl	T56.0x1	T56.0x2	T56.0x3	T56.0x4	—	—
Lebanese red	T40.991	T40.992	T40.993	T40.994	T40.995	T40.996
Lefetamine	T39.8x1	T39.8x2	T39.8x3	T39.8x4	T39.8x5	T39.8x6
Lenperone	T43.4x1	T43.4x2	T43.4x3	T43.4x4	T43.4x5	T43.4x6
Lente lietin (insulin)	T38.3x1	T38.3x2	T38.3x3	T38.3x4	T38.3x5	T38.3x6
Leptazol	T50.7x1	T50.7x2	T50.7x3	T50.7x4	T50.7x5	T50.7x6

Substance	External Cause (T-Code)					
	Poisoning, Accidental (Unintentional)	Poisoning, Intentional Self-Harm	Poisoning, Assault	Poisoning, Undetermined	Adverse Effect	Underdosing
Leptophos	T60.0x1	T60.0x2	T60.0x3	T60.0x4	—	—
Leritine	T40.2x1	T40.2x2	T40.2x3	T40.2x4	T40.2x5	T40.2x6
Letosteine	T48.4x1	T48.4x2	T48.4x3	T48.4x4	T48.4x5	T48.4x6
Letter	T38.1x1	T38.1x2	T38.1x3	T38.1x4	T38.1x5	T38.1x6
Lettuce opium	T42.6x1	T42.6x2	T42.6x3	T42.6x4	T42.6x5	T42.6x6
Leucinocaine	T41.3x1	T41.3x2	T41.3x3	T41.3x4	T41.3x5	T41.3x6
Leucocianidol	T46.991	T46.992	T46.993	T46.994	T46.995	T46.996
Leucovorin (factor)	T45.8x1	T45.8x2	T45.8x3	T45.8x4	T45.8x5	T45.8x6
Leukeran	T45.1x1	T45.1x2	T45.1x3	T45.1x4	T45.1x5	T45.1x6
Leuprolide	T38.891	T38.892	T38.893	T38.894	T38.895	T38.896
Levalbuterol	T48.6x1	T48.6x2	T48.6x3	T48.6x4	T48.6x5	T48.6x6
Levallorphan	T50.7x1	T50.7x2	T50.7x3	T50.7x4	T50.7x5	T50.7x6
Levamisole	T37.4x1	T37.4x2	T37.4x3	T37.4x4	T37.4x5	T37.4x6
Levanil	T42.6x1	T42.6x2	T42.6x3	T42.6x4	T42.6x5	T42.6x6
Levarterenol	T44.4x1	T44.4x2	T44.4x3	T44.4x4	T44.4x5	T44.4x6
Levdropropizine	T48.3x1	T48.3x2	T48.3x3	T48.3x4	T48.3x5	T48.3x6
Levobunolol	T49.5x1	T49.5x2	T49.5x3	T49.5x4	T49.5x5	T49.5x6
Levocabastine (hydrochloride)	T45.0x1	T45.0x2	T45.0x3	T45.0x4	T45.0x5	T45.0x6
Levocarnitine	T50.991	T50.992	T50.993	T50.994	T50.995	T50.996
Levodopa	T42.8x1	T42.8x2	T42.8x3	T42.8x4	T42.8x5	T42.8x6
with carbidopa	T42.8x1	T42.8x2	T42.8x3	T42.8x4	T42.8x5	T42.8x6
Levo-dromoran	T40.2x1	T40.2x2	T40.2x3	T40.2x4	T40.2x5	T40.2x6
Levoglutamide	T50.991	T50.992	T50.993	T50.994	T50.995	T50.996
Levoid	T38.1x1	T38.1x2	T38.1x3	T38.1x4	T38.1x5	T38.1x6
Levo-iso-methadone	T40.3x1	T40.3x2	T40.3x3	T40.3x4	T40.3x5	T40.3x6
Levomepromazine	T43.3x1	T43.3x2	T43.3x3	T43.3x4	T43.3x5	T43.3x6
Levonordefrin	T49.6x1	T49.6x2	T49.6x3	T49.6x4	T49.6x5	T49.6x6
Levonorgestrel	T38.4x1	T38.4x2	T38.4x3	T38.4x4	T38.4x5	T38.4x6
with ethinylestradiol	T38.5x1	T38.5x2	T38.5x3	T38.5x4	T38.5x5	T38.5x6
Levopromazine	T43.3x1	T43.3x2	T43.3x3	T43.3x4	T43.3x5	T43.3x6
Levoprome	T42.6x1	T42.6x2	T42.6x3	T42.6x4	T42.6x5	T42.6x6
Levopropoxyphene	T40.4x1	T40.4x2	T40.4x3	T40.4x4	T40.4x5	T40.4x6
Levopropylhexedrine	T50.5x1	T50.5x2	T50.5x3	T50.5x4	T50.5x5	T50.5x6
Levoproxyphylline	T48.6x1	T48.6x2	T48.6x3	T48.6x4	T48.6x5	T48.6x6
Levorphanol	T40.4x1	T40.4x2	T40.4x3	T40.4x4	T40.4x5	T40.4x6
Levothyroxine	T38.1x1	T38.1x2	T38.1x3	T38.1x4	T38.1x5	T38.1x6
sodium	T38.1x1	T38.1x2	T38.1x3	T38.1x4	T38.1x5	T38.1x6
Levsin	T44.3x1	T44.3x2	T44.3x3	T44.3x4	T44.3x5	T44.3x6
Levulose	T50.3x1	T50.3x2	T50.3x3	T50.3x4	T50.3x5	T50.3x6
Lewisite (gas), not in war	T57.0x1	T57.0x2	T57.0x3	T57.0x4	—	—

Substance	External Cause (T-Code)					
	Poisoning, Accidental (Unintentional)	Poisoning, Intentional Self-Harm	Poisoning, Assault	Poisoning, Undetermined	Adverse Effect	Underdosing
Librium	T42.4x1	T42.4x2	T42.4x3	T42.4x4	T42.4x5	T42.4x6
Lidex	T49.0x1	T49.0x2	T49.0x3	T49.0x4	T49.0x5	T49.0x6
Lidocaine	T41.3x1	T41.3x2	T41.3x3	T41.3x4	T41.3x5	T41.3x6
regional	T41.3x1	T41.3x2	T41.3x3	T41.3x4	T41.3x5	T41.3x6
spinal	T41.3x1	T41.3x2	T41.3x3	T41.3x4	T41.3x5	T41.3x6
Lidofenin	T50.8x1	T50.8x2	T50.8x3	T50.8x4	T50.8x5	T50.8x6
Lidoflazine	T46.1x1	T46.1x2	T46.1x3	T46.1x4	T46.1x5	T46.1x6
Lighter fluid	T52.0x1	T52.0x2	T52.0x3	T52.0x4	—	—
Lignin hemicellulose	T47.6x1	T47.6x2	T47.6x3	T47.6x4	T47.6x5	T47.6x6
Lignocaine	T41.3x1	T41.3x2	T41.3x3	T41.3x4	T41.3x5	T41.3x6
regional	T41.3x1	T41.3x2	T41.3x3	T41.3x4	T41.3x5	T41.3x6
spinal	T41.3x1	T41.3x2	T41.3x3	T41.3x4	T41.3x5	T41.3x6
Ligroin(e) (solvent)	T52.0x1	T52.0x2	T52.0x3	T52.0x4	—	—
vapor	T59.891	T59.892	T59.893	T59.894	—	—
Ligustrum vulgare	T62.2x1	T62.2x2	T62.2x3	T62.2x4	—	—
Lily of the valley	T62.2x1	T62.2x2	T62.2x3	T62.2x4	—	—
Lime (chloride)	T54.3x1	T54.3x2	T54.3x3	T54.3x4	—	—
Limonene	T52.8x1	T52.8x2	T52.8x3	T52.8x4	—	—
Lincomycin	T36.8x1	T36.8x2	T36.8x3	T36.8x4	T36.8x5	T36.8x6
Lindane (insecticide) (nonmedicinal) (vapor)	T53.6x1	T53.6x2	T53.6x3	T53.6x4	—	—
medicinal	T49.0x1	T49.0x2	T49.0x3	T49.0x4	T49.0x5	T49.0x6
Liniments NEC	T49.91	T49.92	T49.93	T49.94	T49.95	T49.96
Linoleic acid	T46.6x1	T46.6x2	T46.6x3	T46.6x4	T46.6x5	T46.6x6
Linolenic acid	T46.6x1	T46.6x2	T46.6x3	T46.6x4	T46.6x5	T46.6x6
Linseed	T47.4x1	T47.4x2	T47.4x3	T47.4x4	T47.4x5	T47.4x6
Liothyronine	T38.1x1	T38.1x2	T38.1x3	T38.1x4	T38.1x5	T38.1x6
Liotrix	T38.1x1	T38.1x2	T38.1x3	T38.1x4	T38.1x5	T38.1x6
Lipancreatin	T47.5x1	T47.5x2	T47.5x3	T47.5x4	T47.5x5	T47.5x6
Lipo-alprostadil	T46.7x1	T46.7x2	T46.7x3	T46.7x4	T46.7x5	T46.7x6
Lipo-Lutin	T38.5x1	T38.5x2	T38.5x3	T38.5x4	T38.5x5	T38.5x6
Lipotropic drug NEC	T50.901	T50.902	T50.903	T50.904	T50.905	T50.906
Liquefied petroleum gases	T59.891	T59.892	T59.893	T59.894	—	—
piped (pure or mixed with air)	T59.891	T59.892	T59.893	T59.894	—	—
Liquid						
paraffin	T47.4x1	T47.4x2	T47.4x3	T47.4x4	T47.4x5	T47.4x6
substance NEC	T65.91	T65.92	T65.93	T65.94	—	—
Liquid petrolatum	T47.4x1	T47.4x2	T47.4x3	T47.4x4	T47.4x5	T47.4x6
substance	T65.91	T65.92	T65.93	T65.94	—	—
specified NEC	T65.891	T65.892	T65.893	T65.894	—	—
Liquor creosolis compositus	T65.891	T65.892	T65.893	T65.894	—	—

Substance	External Cause (T-Code)					
	Poisoning, Accidental (Unintentional)	Poisoning, Intentional Self-Harm	Poisoning, Assault	Poisoning, Undetermined	Adverse Effect	Underdosing
Liquorice	T48.4x1	T48.4x2	T48.4x3	T48.4x4	T48.4x5	T48.4x6
extract	T47.8x1	T47.8x2	T47.8x3	T47.8x4	T47.8x5	T47.8x6
Lirugen	T50.991	T50.992	T50.993	T50.994	T50.995	T50.996
Lisinopril	T46.4x1	T46.4x2	T46.4x3	T46.4x4	T46.4x5	T46.4x6
Lisuride	T42.8x1	T42.8x2	T42.8x3	T42.8x4	T42.8x5	T42.8x6
Lithane	T43.8x1	T43.8x2	T43.8x3	T43.8x4	T43.8x5	T43.8x6
Lithium	T56.891	T56.892	T56.893	T56.894	—	—
gluconate	T43.591	T43.592	T43.593	T43.594	T43.595	T43.596
salts (carbonate)	T43.591	T43.592	T43.593	T43.594	T43.595	T43.596
Lithonate	T43.8x1	T43.8x2	T43.8x3	T43.8x4	T43.8x5	T43.8x6
Liver						
extract	T45.8x1	T45.8x2	T45.8x3	T45.8x4	T45.8x5	T45.8x6
for parenteral use	T45.8x1	T45.8x2	T45.8x3	T45.8x4	T45.8x5	T45.8x6
fraction 1	T45.8x1	T45.8x2	T45.8x3	T45.8x4	T45.8x5	T45.8x6
hydrolysate	T45.8x1	T45.8x2	T45.8x3	T45.8x4	T45.8x5	T45.8x6
Lizard (bite) (venom)	T63.121	T63.122	T63.123	T63.124	—	—
LMD	T45.8x1	T45.8x2	T45.8x3	T45.8x4	T45.8x5	T45.8x6
Lobelia	T62.2x1	T62.2x2	T62.2x3	T62.2x4	—	—
Lobeline	T50.7x1	T50.7x2	T50.7x3	T50.7x4	T50.7x5	T50.7x6
Local action drug NEC	T49.8x1	T49.8x2	T49.8x3	T49.8x4	T49.8x5	T49.8x6
Locorten	T49.0x1	T49.0x2	T49.0x3	T49.0x4	T49.0x5	T49.0x6
Lofepramine	T43.011	T43.012	T43.013	T43.014	T43.015	T43.016
Lolium temulentum	T62.2x1	T62.2x2	T62.2x3	T62.2x4	—	—
Lomotil	T47.6x1	T47.6x2	T47.6x3	T47.6x4	T47.6x5	T47.6x6
Lomustine	T45.1x1	T45.1x2	T45.1x3	T45.1x4	T45.1x5	T45.1x6
Lonidamine	T45.1x1	T45.1x2	T45.1x3	T45.1x4	T45.1x5	T45.1x6
Loperamide	T47.6x1	T47.6x2	T47.6x3	T47.6x4	T47.6x5	T47.6x6
Loprazolam	T42.4x1	T42.4x2	T42.4x3	T42.4x4	T42.4x5	T42.4x6
Lorajmine	T46.2x1	T46.2x2	T46.2x3	T46.2x4	T46.2x5	T46.2x6
Loratidine	T45.0x1	T45.0x2	T45.0x3	T45.0x4	T45.0x5	T45.0x6
Lorazepam	T42.4x1	T42.4x2	T42.4x3	T42.4x4	T42.4x5	T42.4x6
Lorcainide	T46.2x1	T46.2x2	T46.2x3	T46.2x4	T46.2x5	T46.2x6
Lormetazepam	T42.4x1	T42.4x2	T42.4x3	T42.4x4	T42.4x5	T42.4x6
Lotions NEC	T49.91	T49.92	T49.93	T49.94	T49.95	T49.96
Lotusate	T42.3x1	T42.3x2	T42.3x3	T42.3x4	T42.3x5	T42.3x6
Lovastatin	T46.6x1	T46.6x2	T46.6x3	T46.6x4	T46.6x5	T46.6x6
Loxapine	T43.591	T43.592	T43.593	T43.594	T43.595	T43.596
Lowila	T49.2x1	T49.2x2	T49.2x3	T49.2x4	T49.2x5	T49.2x6
Lozenges (throat)	T49.6x1	T49.6x2	T49.6x3	T49.6x4	T49.6x5	T49.6x6
LSD	T40.8x1	T40.8x2	T40.8x3	T40.8x4	T40.8x5	T40.8x6

	External Cause (T-Code)					
Substance	Poisoning, Accidental (Unintentional)	Poisoning, Intentional Self-Harm	Poisoning, Assault	Poisoning, Undetermined	Adverse Effect	Underdosing
L-Tryptophan - *see* amino acid						
Lubricant, eye	T49.5x1	T49.5x2	T49.5x3	T49.5x4	T49.5x5	T49.5x6
Lubricating oil NEC	T52.0x1	T52.0x2	T52.0x3	T52.0x4	—	—
Lucanthone	T37.4x1	T37.4x2	T37.4x3	T37.4x4	T37.4x5	T37.4x6
Luminal	T42.3x1	T42.3x2	T42.3x3	T42.3x4	T42.3x5	T42.3x6
Lung irritant (gas) NEC	T59.91	T59.92	T59.93	T59.94	—	—
Luteinizing hormone	T38.811	T38.812	T38.813	T38.814	T38.815	T38.816
Lutocylol	T38.5x1	T38.5x2	T38.5x3	T38.5x4	T38.5x5	T38.5x6
Lutromone	T38.5x1	T38.5x2	T38.5x3	T38.5x4	T38.5x5	T38.5x6
Lututrin	T48.291	T48.292	T48.293	T48.294	T48.295	T48.296
Lye (Concentrated)	T54.3x1	T54.3x2	T54.3x3	T54.3x4	—	—
Lygranum (skin test)	T50.8x1	T50.8x2	T50.8x3	T50.8x4	T50.8x5	T50.8x6
Lymecycline	T36.4x1	T36.4x2	T36.4x3	T36.4x4	T36.4x5	T36.4x6
Lymphogranuloma venereum antigen	T50.8x1	T50.8x2	T50.8x3	T50.8x4	T50.8x5	T50.8x6
Lynestrenol	T38.4x1	T38.4x2	T38.4x3	T38.4x4	T38.4x5	T38.4x6
Lypressin	T38.891	T38.892	T38.893	T38.894	T38.895	T38.896
Lyovac Sodium Edecrin	T50.1x1	T50.1x2	T50.1x3	T50.1x4	T50.1x5	T50.1x6
Lysergic acid diethylamide	T40.8x1	T40.8x2	T40.8x3	T40.8x4	T40.8x5	T40.8x6
Lysergide	T40.8x1	T40.8x2	T40.8x3	T40.8x4	T40.8x5	T40.8x6
Lysine vasopressin	T38.891	T38.892	T38.893	T38.894	T38.895	T38.896
Lysol	T54.1x1	T54.1x2	T54.1x3	T54.1x4	—	—
Lysozyme	T49.0x1	T49.0x2	T49.0x3	T49.0x4	T49.0x5	T49.0x6
Lytta (vitatta)	T49.8x1	T49.8x2	T49.8x3	T49.8x4	T49.8x5	T49.8x6
Mace	T59.3x1	T59.3x2	T59.3x3	T59.3x4	—	—
Macrogol	T50.991	T50.992	T50.993	T50.994	T50.995	T50.996
Macrolide						
anabolic drug	T38.7x1	T38.7x2	T38.7x3	T38.7x4	T38.7x5	T38.7x6
antibiotic	T36.3x1	T36.3x2	T36.3x3	T36.3x4	T36.3x5	T36.3x6
Mafenide	T49.0x1	T49.0x2	T49.0x3	T49.0x4	T49.0x5	T49.0x6
Magaldrate	T47.1x1	T47.1x2	T47.1x3	T47.1x4	T47.1x5	T47.1x6
Magic mushroom	T40.991	T40.992	T40.993	T40.994	T40.995	T40.996
Magnamycin	T36.8x1	T36.8x2	T36.8x3	T36.8x4	T36.8x5	T36.8x6
Magnesia magma	T47.1x1	T47.1x2	T47.1x3	T47.1x4	T47.1x5	T47.1x6
Magnesium NEC	T56.891	T56.892	T56.893	T56.894	—	—
carbonate	T47.1x1	T47.1x2	T47.1x3	T47.1x4	T47.1x5	T47.1x6
citrate	T47.4x1	T47.4x2	T47.4x3	T47.4x4	T47.4x5	T47.4x6
hydroxide	T47.1x1	T47.1x2	T47.1x3	T47.1x4	T47.1x5	T47.1x6
oxide	T47.1x1	T47.1x2	T47.1x3	T47.1x4	T47.1x5	T47.1x6
peroxide	T49.0x1	T49.0x2	T49.0x3	T49.0x4	T49.0x5	T49.0x6
salicylate	T39.091	T39.092	T39.093	T39.094	T39.095	T39.096

Substance	External Cause (T-Code)					
	Poisoning, Accidental (Unintentional)	Poisoning, Intentional Self-Harm	Poisoning, Assault	Poisoning, Undetermined	Adverse Effect	Underdosing
Magnesium NEC *(Continued)*						
silicofluoride	T50.3x1	T50.3x2	T50.3x3	T50.3x4	T50.3x5	T50.3x6
sulfate	T47.4x1	T47.4x2	T47.4x3	T47.4x4	T47.4x5	T47.4x6
thiosulfate	T45.0x1	T45.0x2	T45.0x3	T45.0x4	T45.0x5	T45.0x6
trisilicate	T47.1x1	T47.1x2	T47.1x3	T47.1x4	T47.1x5	T47.1x6
Malathion (medicinal)	T49.0x1	T49.0x2	T49.0x3	T49.0x4	T49.0x5	T49.0x6
insecticide	T60.0x1	T60.0x2	T60.0x3	T60.0x4	—	—
Male fern extract	T37.4x1	T37.4x2	T37.4x3	T37.4x4	T37.4x5	T37.4x6
M-AMSA	T45.1x1	T45.1x2	T45.1x3	T45.1x4	T45.1x5	T45.1x6
Mandelic acid	T37.8x1	T37.8x2	T37.8x3	T37.8x4	T37.8x5	T37.8x6
Manganese (dioxide) (salts)	T57.2x1	T57.2x2	T57.2x3	T57.2x4	—	—
medicinal	T50.991	T50.992	T50.993	T50.994	T50.995	T50.996
Mannitol	T47.3x1	T47.3x2	T47.3x3	T47.3x4	T47.3x5	T47.3x6
hexanitrate	T46.3x1	T46.3x2	T46.3x3	T46.3x4	T46.3x5	T46.3x6
Mannomustine	T45.1x1	T45.1x2	T45.1x3	T45.1x4	T45.1x5	T45.1x6
MAO inhibitors	T43.1x1	T43.1x2	T43.1x3	T43.1x4	T43.1x5	T43.1x6
Mapharsen	T37.8x1	T37.8x2	T37.8x3	T37.8x4	T37.8x5	T37.8x6
Maphenide	T49.0x1	T49.0x2	T49.0x3	T49.0x4	T49.0x5	T49.0x6
Maprotiline	T43.021	T43.022	T43.023	T43.024	T43.025	T43.026
Marcaine	T41.3x1	T41.3x2	T41.3x3	T41.3x4	T41.3x5	T41.3x6
infiltration (subcutaneous)	T41.3x1	T41.3x2	T41.3x3	T41.3x4	T41.3x5	T41.3x6
nerve block (peripheral) (plexus)	T41.3x1	T41.3x2	T41.3x3	T41.3x4	T41.3x5	T41.3x6
Marezine	T45.0x1	T45.0x2	T45.0x3	T45.0x4	T45.0x5	T45.0x6
Marihuana	T40.7x1	T40.7x2	T40.7x3	T40.7x4	T40.7x5	T40.7x6
Marijuana	T40.7x1	T40.7x2	T40.7x3	T40.7x4	T40.7x5	T40.7x6
Marine (sting)	T63.691	T63.692	T63.693	T63.694	—	—
animals (sting)	T63.691	T63.692	T63.693	T63.694	—	—
plants (sting)	T63.711	T63.712	T63.713	T63.714	—	—
Marplan	T43.1x1	T43.1x2	T43.1x3	T43.1x4	T43.1x5	T43.1x6
Marsh gas	T59.891	T59.892	T59.893	T59.894	—	—
Marsilid	T43.1x1	T43.1x2	T43.1x3	T43.1x4	T43.1x5	T43.1x6
Matulane	T45.1x1	T45.1x2	T45.1x3	T45.1x4	T45.1x5	T45.1x6
Mazindol	T50.5x1	T50.5x2	T50.5x3	T50.5x4	T50.5x5	T50.5x6
MCPA	T60.3x1	T60.3x2	T60.3x3	T60.3x4	—	—
MDMA	T43.621	T43.622	T43.623	T43.624	T43.625	T43.626
Meadow saffron	T62.2x1	T62.2x2	T62.2x3	T62.2x4	—	—
Measles virus vaccine (attenuated)	T50.B91	T50.B92	T50.B93	T50.B94	T50.B95	T50.B96
Meat, noxious	T62.8x1	T62.8x2	T62.8x3	T62.8x4	—	—
Meballymal	T42.3x1	T42.3x2	T42.3x3	T42.3x4	T42.3x5	T42.3x6
Mebanazine	T43.1x1	T43.1x2	T43.1x3	T43.1x4	T43.1x5	T43.1x6

Substance	External Cause (T-Code)					
	Poisoning, Accidental (Unintentional)	Poisoning, Intentional Self-Harm	Poisoning, Assault	Poisoning, Undetermined	Adverse Effect	Underdosing
Mebaral	T42.3x1	T42.3x2	T42.3x3	T42.3x4	T42.3x5	T42.3x6
Mebendazole	T37.4x1	T37.4x2	T37.4x3	T37.4x4	T37.4x5	T37.4x6
Mebeverine	T44.3x1	T44.3x2	T44.3x3	T44.3x4	T44.3x5	T44.3x6
Mebhydrolin	T45.0x1	T45.0x2	T45.0x3	T45.0x4	T45.0x5	T45.0x6
Mebumal	T42.3x1	T42.3x2	T42.3x3	T42.3x4	T42.3x5	T42.3x6
Mebutamate	T43.591	T43.592	T43.593	T43.594	T43.595	T43.596
Mecamylamine	T44.2x1	T44.2x2	T44.2x3	T44.2x4	T44.2x5	T44.2x6
Mechlorethamine	T45.1x1	T45.1x2	T45.1x3	T45.1x4	T45.1x5	T45.1x6
Mecillinam	T36.0x1	T36.0x2	T36.0x3	T36.0x4	T36.0x5	T36.0x6
Meclizine (hydrochloride)	T45.0x1	T45.0x2	T45.0x3	T45.0x4	T45.0x5	T45.0x6
Meclocycline	T36.4x1	T36.4x2	T36.4x3	T36.4x4	T36.4x5	T36.4x6
Meclofenamate	T39.391	T39.392	T39.393	T39.394	T39.395	T39.396
Meclofenamic acid	T39.391	T39.392	T39.393	T39.394	T39.395	T39.396
Meclofenoxate	T43.691	T43.692	T43.693	T43.694	T43.695	T43.696
Meclozine	T45.0x1	T45.0x2	T45.0x3	T45.0x4	T45.0x5	T45.0x6
Mecobalamin	T45.8x1	T45.8x2	T45.8x3	T45.8x4	T45.8x5	T45.8x6
Mecoprop	T60.3x1	T60.3x2	T60.3x3	T60.3x4	—	—
Mecrilate	T49.3x1	T49.3x2	T49.3x3	T49.3x4	T49.3x5	T49.3x6
Mecysteine	T48.4x1	T48.4x2	T48.4x3	T48.4x4	T48.4x5	T48.4x6
Medazepam	T42.4x1	T42.4x2	T42.4x3	T42.4x4	T42.4x5	T42.4x6
Medicament NEC	T50.901	T50.902	T50.903	T50.904	T50.905	T50.906
Medinal	T42.3x1	T42.3x2	T42.3x3	T42.3x4	T42.3x5	T42.3x6
Medomin	T42.3x1	T42.3x2	T42.3x3	T42.3x4	T42.3x5	T42.3x6
Medrogestone	T38.5x1	T38.5x2	T38.5x3	T38.5x4	T38.5x5	T38.5x6
Medroxalol	T44.8x1	T44.8x2	T44.8x3	T44.8x4	T44.8x5	T44.8x6
Medroxyprogesterone acetate (depot)	T38.5x1	T38.5x2	T38.5x3	T38.5x4	T38.5x5	T38.5x6
Medrysone	T49.0x1	T49.0x2	T49.0x3	T49.0x4	T49.0x5	T49.0x6
Mefenamic acid	T39.391	T39.392	T39.393	T39.394	T39.395	T39.396
Mefenorex	T50.5x1	T50.5x2	T50.5x3	T50.5x4	T50.5x5	T50.5x6
Mefloquine	T37.2x1	T37.2x2	T37.2x3	T37.2x4	T37.2x5	T37.2x6
Mefruside	T50.2x1	T50.2x2	T50.2x3	T50.2x4	T50.2x5	T50.2x6
Megahallucinogen	T40.901	T40.902	T40.903	T40.904	T40.905	T40.906
Megestrol	T38.5x1	T38.5x2	T38.5x3	T38.5x4	T38.5x5	T38.5x6
Meglumine						
antimoniate	T37.8x1	T37.8x2	T37.8x3	T37.8x4	T37.8x5	T37.8x6
diatrizoate	T50.8x1	T50.8x2	T50.8x3	T50.8x4	T50.8x5	T50.8x6
iodipamide	T50.8x1	T50.8x2	T50.8x3	T50.8x4	T50.8x5	T50.8x6
iotroxate	T50.8x1	T50.8x2	T50.8x3	T50.8x4	T50.8x5	T50.8x6
MEK (methyl ethyl ketone)	T52.4x1	T52.4x2	T52.4x3	T52.4x4	—	—
Meladrazine	T44.3x1	T44.3x2	T44.3x3	T44.3x4	T44.3x5	T44.3x6
Meladinin	T49.3x1	T49.3x2	T49.3x3	T49.3x4	T49.3x5	T49.3x6

Substance	External Cause (T-Code)					
	Poisoning, Accidental (Unintentional)	Poisoning, Intentional Self-Harm	Poisoning, Assault	Poisoning, Undetermined	Adverse Effect	Underdosing
Melaleuca alternifolia oil	T49.0x1	T49.0x2	T49.0x3	T49.0x4	T49.0x5	T49.0x6
Melanizing agents	T49.3x1	T49.3x2	T49.3x3	T49.3x4	T49.3x5	T49.3x6
Melanocyte-stimulating hormone	T38.891	T38.892	T38.893	T38.894	T38.895	T38.896
Melarsonyl potassium	T37.3x1	T37.3x2	T37.3x3	T37.3x4	T37.3x5	T37.3x6
Melarsoprol	T37.3x1	T37.3x2	T37.3x3	T37.3x4	T37.3x5	T37.3x6
Melia azedarach	T62.2x1	T62.2x2	T62.2x3	T62.2x4	—	—
Melitracen	T43.011	T43.012	T43.013	T43.014	T43.015	T43.016
Mellaril	T43.3x1	T43.3x2	T43.3x3	T43.3x4	T43.3x5	T43.3x6
Meloxine	T49.3x1	T49.3x2	T49.3x3	T49.3x4	T49.3x5	T49.3x6
Melperone	T43.4x1	T43.4x2	T43.4x3	T43.4x4	T43.4x5	T43.4x6
Melphalan	T45.1x1	T45.1x2	T45.1x3	T45.1x4	T45.1x5	T45.1x6
Memantine	T43.8x1	T43.8x2	T43.8x3	T43.8x4	T43.8x5	T43.8x6
Menadiol	T45.7x1	T45.7x2	T45.7x3	T45.7x4	T45.7x5	T45.7x6
sodium sulfate	T45.7x1	T45.7x2	T45.7x3	T45.7x4	T45.7x5	T45.7x6
Menadione	T45.7x1	T45.7x2	T45.7x3	T45.7x4	T45.7x5	T45.7x6
sodium bisulfite	T45.7x1	T45.7x2	T45.7x3	T45.7x4	T45.7x5	T45.7x6
Menaphthone	T45.7x1	T45.7x2	T45.7x3	T45.7x4	T45.7x5	T45.7x6
Menaquinone	T45.7x1	T45.7x2	T45.7x3	T45.7x4	T45.7x5	T45.7x6
Menatetrenone	T45.7x1	T45.7x2	T45.7x3	T45.7x4	T45.7x5	T45.7x6
Meningococcal vaccine	T50.A91	T50.A92	T50.A93	T50.A94	T50.A95	T50.A96
Menningovax (-AC) (-C)	T50.A91	T50.A92	T50.A93	T50.A94	T50.A95	T50.A96
Menotropins	T38.811	T38.812	T38.813	T38.814	T38.815	T38.816
Menthol	T48.5x1	T48.5x2	T48.5x3	T48.5x4	T48.5x5	T48.5x6
Mepacrine	T37.2x1	T37.2x2	T37.2x3	T37.2x4	T37.2x5	T37.2x6
Meparfynol	T42.6x1	T42.6x2	T42.6x3	T42.6x4	T42.6x5	T42.6x6
Mepartricin	T36.7x1	T36.7x2	T36.7x3	T36.7x4	T36.7x5	T36.7x6
Mepazine	T43.3x1	T43.3x2	T43.3x3	T43.3x4	T43.3x5	T43.3x6
Mepenzolate	T44.3x1	T44.3x2	T44.3x3	T44.3x4	T44.3x5	T44.3x6
bromide	T44.3x1	T44.3x2	T44.3x3	T44.3x4	T44.3x5	T44.3x6
Meperidine	T40.4x1	T40.4x2	T40.4x3	T40.4x4	T40.4x5	T40.4x6
Mephebarbital	T42.3x1	T42.3x2	T42.3x3	T42.3x4	T42.3x5	T42.3x6
Mephenamin(e)	T42.8x1	T42.8x2	T42.8x3	T42.8x4	T42.8x5	T42.8x6
Mephenesin	T42.8x1	T42.8x2	T42.8x3	T42.8x4	T42.8x5	T42.8x6
Mephenhydramine	T45.0x1	T45.0x2	T45.0x3	T45.0x4	T45.0x5	T45.0x6
Mephenoxalone	T42.8x1	T42.8x2	T42.8x3	T42.8x4	T42.8x5	T42.8x6
Mephentermine	T44.991	T44.992	T44.993	T44.994	T44.995	T44.996
Mephenytoin	T42.0x1	T42.0x2	T42.0x3	T42.0x4	T42.0x5	T42.0x6
with phenobarbital	T42.3x1	T42.3x2	T42.3x3	T42.3x4	T42.3x5	T42.3x6
Mephobarbital	T42.3x1	T42.3x2	T42.3x3	T42.3x4	T42.3x5	T42.3x6
Mephosfolan	T60.0x1	T60.0x2	T60.0x3	T60.0x4	—	—
Mepindolol	T44.7x1	T44.7x2	T44.7x3	T44.7x4	T44.7x5	T44.7x6

Substance	Poisoning, Accidental (Unintentional)	Poisoning, Intentional Self-Harm	Poisoning, Assault	Poisoning, Undetermined	Adverse Effect	Underdosing
Mepiperphenidol	T44.3x1	T44.3x2	T44.3x3	T44.3x4	T44.3x5	T44.3x6
Mepitiostane	T38.7x1	T38.7x2	T38.7x3	T38.7x4	T38.7x5	T38.7x6
Mepivacaine	T41.3x1	T41.3x2	T41.3x3	T41.3x4	T41.3x5	T41.3x6
epidural	T41.3x1	T41.3x2	T41.3x3	T41.3x4	T41.3x5	T41.3x6
Meprednisone	T38.0x1	T38.0x2	T38.0x3	T38.0x4	T38.0x5	T38.0x6
Meprobam	T43.591	T43.592	T43.593	T43.594	T43.595	T43.596
Meprobamate	T43.591	T43.592	T43.593	T43.594	T43.595	T43.596
Meproscillarin	T46.0x1	T46.0x2	T46.0x3	T46.0x4	T46.0x5	T46.0x6
Meprylcaine	T41.3x1	T41.3x2	T41.3x3	T41.3x4	T41.3x5	T41.3x6
Meptazinol	T39.8x1	T39.8x2	T39.8x3	T39.8x4	T39.8x5	T39.8x6
Mepyramine	T45.0x1	T45.0x2	T45.0x3	T45.0x4	T45.0x5	T45.0x6
Mequitazine	T43.3x1	T43.3x2	T43.3x3	T43.3x4	T43.3x5	T43.3x6
Meralluride	T50.2x1	T50.2x2	T50.2x3	T50.2x4	T50.2x5	T50.2x6
Merbaphen	T50.2x1	T50.2x2	T50.2x3	T50.2x4	T50.2x5	T50.2x6
Merbromin	T49.0x1	T49.0x2	T49.0x3	T49.0x4	T49.0x5	T49.0x6
Mercaptobenzothiazole salts	T49.0x1	T49.0x2	T49.0x3	T49.0x4	T49.0x5	T49.0x6
Mercaptomerin	T50.2x1	T50.2x2	T50.2x3	T50.2x4	T50.2x5	T50.2x6
Mercaptopurine	T45.1x1	T45.1x2	T45.1x3	T45.1x4	T45.1x5	T45.1x6
Mercumatilin	T50.2x1	T50.2x2	T50.2x3	T50.2x4	T50.2x5	T50.2x6
Mercuramide	T50.2x1	T50.2x2	T50.2x3	T50.2x4	T50.2x5	T50.2x6
Mercurochrome	T49.0x1	T49.0x2	T49.0x3	T49.0x4	T49.0x5	T49.0x6
Mercurophylline	T50.2x1	T50.2x2	T50.2x3	T50.2x4	T50.2x5	T50.2x6
Mercury, mercurial, mercuric, mercurous (compounds) (cyanide) (fumes) (nonmedicinal) (vapor) NEC	T56.1x1	T56.1x2	T56.1x3	T56.1x4	—	—
ammoniated	T49.0x1	T49.0x2	T49.0x3	T49.0x4	T49.0x5	T49.0x6
anti-infective						
local	T49.0x1	T49.0x2	T49.0x3	T49.0x4	T49.0x5	T49.0x6
systemic	T37.8x1	T37.8x2	T37.8x3	T37.8x4	T37.8x5	T37.8x6
topical	T49.0x1	T49.0x2	T49.0x3	T49.0x4	T49.0x5	T49.0x6
chloride (ammoniated)	T49.0x1	T49.0x2	T49.0x3	T49.0x4	T49.0x5	T49.0x6
fungicide	T56.1x1	T56.1x2	T56.1x3	T56.1x4	—	—
diuretic NEC	T50.2x1	T50.2x2	T50.2x3	T50.2x4	T50.2x5	T50.2x6
fungicide	T56.1x1	T56.1x2	T56.1x3	T56.1x4	—	—
organic (fungicide)	T56.1x1	T56.1x2	T56.1x3	T56.1x4	—	—
oxide, yellow	T49.0x1	T49.0x2	T49.0x3	T49.0x4	T49.0x5	T49.0x6
Mersalyl	T50.2x1	T50.2x2	T50.2x3	T50.2x4	T50.2x5	T50.2x6
Merthiolate	T49.0x1	T49.0x2	T49.0x3	T49.0x4	T49.0x5	T49.0x6
ophthalmic preparation	T49.5x1	T49.5x2	T49.5x3	T49.5x4	T49.5x5	T49.5x6
Meruvax	T50.B91	T50.B92	T50.B93	T50.B94	T50.B95	T50.B96
Mesalazine	T47.8x1	T47.8x2	T47.8x3	T47.8x4	T47.8x5	T47.8x6

Substance	External Cause (T-Code)					
	Poisoning, Accidental (Unintentional)	Poisoning, Intentional Self-Harm	Poisoning, Assault	Poisoning, Undetermined	Adverse Effect	Underdosing
Mescal buttons	T40.991	T40.992	T40.993	T40.994	T40.995	T40.996
Mescaline	T40.991	T40.992	T40.993	T40.994	T40.995	T40.996
Mesna	T48.4x1	T48.4x2	T48.4x3	T48.4x4	T48.4x5	T48.4x6
Mesoglycan	T46.6x1	T46.6x2	T46.6x3	T46.6x4	T46.6x5	T46.6x6
Mesoridazine	T43.3x1	T43.3x2	T43.3x3	T43.3x4	T43.3x5	T43.3x6
Mestanolone	T38.7x1	T38.7x2	T38.7x3	T38.7x4	T38.7x5	T38.7x6
Mesterolone	T38.7x1	T38.7x2	T38.7x3	T38.7x4	T38.7x5	T38.7x6
Mestranol	T38.5x1	T38.5x2	T38.5x3	T38.5x4	T38.5x5	T38.5x6
Mesulergine	T42.8x1	T42.8x2	T42.8x3	T42.8x4	T42.8x5	T42.8x6
Mesulfen	T49.0x1	T49.0x2	T49.0x3	T49.0x4	T49.0x5	T49.0x6
Mesuximide	T42.2x1	T42.2x2	T42.2x3	T42.2x4	T42.2x5	T42.2x6
Metabutethamine	T41.3x1	T41.3x2	T41.3x3	T41.3x4	T41.3x5	T41.3x6
Metactesylacetate	T49.0x1	T49.0x2	T49.0x3	T49.0x4	T49.0x5	T49.0x6
Metacycline	T36.4x1	T36.4x2	T36.4x3	T36.4x4	T36.4x5	T36.4x6
Metaldehyde (snail killer) NEC	T60.8x1	T60.8x2	T60.8x3	T60.8x4	—	—
Metals (heavy) (nonmedicinal)	T56.91	T56.92	T56.93	T56.94	—	—
dust, fumes, or vapor NEC	T56.91	T56.92	T56.93	T56.94	—	—
light NEC	T56.91	T56.92	T56.93	T56.94	—	—
dust, fumes, or vapor NEC	T56.91	T56.92	T56.93	T56.94	—	—
specified NEC	T56.891	T56.892	T56.893	T56.894	—	—
thallium	T56.811	T56.812	T56.813	T56.814	—	—
Metamfetamine	T43.621	T43.622	T43.623	T43.624	T43.625	T43.626
Metamizole sodium	T39.2x1	T39.2x2	T39.2x3	T39.2x4	T39.2x5	T39.2x6
Metampicillin	T36.0x1	T36.0x2	T36.0x3	T36.0x4	T36.0x5	T36.0x6
Metamucil	T47.4x1	T47.4x2	T47.4x3	T47.4x4	T47.4x5	T47.4x6
Metaphen	T49.0x1	T49.0x2	T49.0x3	T49.0x4	T49.0x5	T49.0x6
Metandienone	T38.7x1	T38.7x2	T38.7x3	T38.7x4	T38.7x5	T38.7x6
Metandrostenolone	T38.7x1	T38.7x2	T38.7x3	T38.7x4	T38.7x5	T38.7x6
Metaphos	T60.0x1	T60.0x2	T60.0x3	T60.0x4	—	—
Metapramine	T43.011	T43.012	T43.013	T43.014	T43.015	T43.016
Metaproterenol	T48.291	T48.292	T48.293	T48.294	T48.295	T48.296
Metaraminol	T44.4x1	T44.4x2	T44.4x3	T44.4x4	T44.4x5	T44.4x6
Metaxalone	T42.8x1	T42.8x2	T42.8x3	T42.8x4	T42.8x5	T42.8x6
Metenolone	T38.7x1	T38.7x2	T38.7x3	T38.7x4	T38.7x5	T38.7x6
Metergoline	T42.8x1	T42.8x2	T42.8x3	T42.8x4	T42.8x5	T42.8x6
Metescufylline	T46.991	T46.992	T46.993	T46.994	T46.995	T46.996
Metetoin	T42.0x1	T42.0x2	T42.0x3	T42.0x4	T42.0x5	T42.0x6
Metformin	T38.3x1	T38.3x2	T38.3x3	T38.3x4	T38.3x5	T38.3x6
Methacholine	T44.1x1	T44.1x2	T44.1x3	T44.1x4	T44.1x5	T44.1x6
Methacycline	T36.4x1	T36.4x2	T36.4x3	T36.4x4	T36.4x5	T36.4x6

Substance	External Cause (T-Code)					
	Poisoning, Accidental (Unintentional)	Poisoning, Intentional Self-Harm	Poisoning, Assault	Poisoning, Undetermined	Adverse Effect	Underdosing
Methadone	T40.3x1	T40.3x2	T40.3x3	T40.3x4	T40.3x5	T40.3x6
Methallenestril	T38.5x1	T38.5x2	T38.5x3	T38.5x4	T38.5x5	T38.5x6
Methallenoestril	T38.5x1	T38.5x2	T38.5x3	T38.5x4	T38.5x5	T38.5x6
Methamphetamine	T43.621	T43.622	T43.623	T43.624	T43.625	T43.626
Methampyrone	T39.2x1	T39.2x2	T39.2x3	T39.2x4	T39.2x5	T39.2x6
Methandienone	T38.7x1	T38.7x2	T38.7x3	T38.7x4	T38.7x5	T38.7x6
Methandriol	T38.7x1	T38.7x2	T38.7x3	T38.7x4	T38.7x5	T38.7x6
Methandrostenolone	T38.7x1	T38.7x2	T38.7x3	T38.7x4	T38.7x5	T38.7x6
Methane	T59.891	T59.892	T59.893	T59.894	—	—
Methanethiol	T59.891	T59.892	T59.893	T59.894	—	—
Methaniazide	T37.1x1	T37.1x2	T37.1x3	T37.1x4	T37.1x5	T37.1x6
Methanol (vapor)	T51.1x1	T51.1x2	T51.1x3	T51.1x4	—	—
Methantheline	T44.3x1	T44.3x2	T44.3x3	T44.3x4	T44.3x5	T44.3x6
Methanthelinium bromide	T44.3x1	T44.3x2	T44.3x3	T44.3x4	T44.3x5	T44.3x6
Methaphenilene	T45.0x1	T45.0x2	T45.0x3	T45.0x4	T45.0x5	T45.0x6
Methapyrilene	T45.0x1	T45.0x2	T45.0x3	T45.0x4	T45.0x5	T45.0x6
Methaqualone (compound)	T42.6x1	T42.6x2	T42.6x3	T42.6x4	T42.6x5	T42.6x6
Metharbital	T42.3x1	T42.3x2	T42.3x3	T42.3x4	T42.3x5	T42.3x6
Methazolamide	T50.2x1	T50.2x2	T50.2x3	T50.2x4	T50.2x5	T50.2x6
Methdilazine	T43.3x1	T43.3x2	T43.3x3	T43.3x4	T43.3x5	T43.3x6
Methedrine	T43.621	T43.622	T43.623	T43.624	T43.625	T43.626
Methenamine (mandelate)	T37.8x1	T37.8x2	T37.8x3	T37.8x4	T37.8x5	T37.8x6
Methenolone	T38.7x1	T38.7x2	T38.7x3	T38.7x4	T38.7x5	T38.7x6
Methergine	T48.0x1	T48.0x2	T48.0x3	T48.0x4	T48.0x5	T48.0x6
Methetoin	T42.0x1	T42.0x2	T42.0x3	T42.0x4	T42.0x5	T42.0x6
Methiacil	T38.2x1	T38.2x2	T38.2x3	T38.2x4	T38.2x5	T38.2x6
Methicillin	T36.0x1	T36.0x2	T36.0x3	T36.0x4	T36.0x5	T36.0x6
Methimazole	T38.2x1	T38.2x2	T38.2x3	T38.2x4	T38.2x5	T38.2x6
Methiodal sodium	T50.8x1	T50.8x2	T50.8x3	T50.8x4	T50.8x5	T50.8x6
Methionine	T50.991	T50.992	T50.993	T50.994	T50.995	T50.996
Methisazone	T37.5x1	T37.5x2	T37.5x3	T37.5x4	T37.5x5	T37.5x6
Methisoprinol	T37.5x1	T37.5x2	T37.5x3	T37.5x4	T37.5x5	T37.5x6
Methitural	T42.3x1	T42.3x2	T42.3x3	T42.3x4	T42.3x5	T42.3x6
Methixene	T44.3x1	T44.3x2	T44.3x3	T44.3x4	T44.3x5	T44.3x6
Methobarbital, methobarbitone	T42.3x1	T42.3x2	T42.3x3	T42.3x4	T42.3x5	T42.3x6
Methocarbamol	T42.8x1	T42.8x2	T42.8x3	T42.8x4	T42.8x5	T42.8x6
skeletal muscle relaxant	T48.1x1	T48.1x2	T48.1x3	T48.1x4	T48.1x5	T48.1x6
Methohexital	T41.1x1	T41.1x2	T41.1x3	T41.1x4	T41.1x5	T41.1x6
Methohexitone	T41.1x1	T41.1x2	T41.1x3	T41.1x4	T41.1x5	T41.1x6
Methoin	T42.0x1	T42.0x2	T42.0x3	T42.0x4	T42.0x5	T42.0x6
Methopholine	T39.8x1	T39.8x2	T39.8x3	T39.8x4	T39.8x5	T39.8x6

Substance	External Cause (T-Code)					
	Poisoning, Accidental (Unintentional)	Poisoning, Intentional Self-Harm	Poisoning, Assault	Poisoning, Undetermined	Adverse Effect	Underdosing
Methopromazine	T43.3x1	T43.3x2	T43.3x3	T43.3x4	T43.3x5	T43.3x6
Methorate	T48.3x1	T48.3x2	T48.3x3	T48.3x4	T48.3x5	T48.3x6
Methoserpidine	T46.5x1	T46.5x2	T46.5x3	T46.5x4	T46.5x5	T46.5x6
Methotrexate	T45.1x1	T45.1x2	T45.1x3	T45.1x4	T45.1x5	T45.1x6
Methotrimeprazine	T43.3x1	T43.3x2	T43.3x3	T43.3x4	T43.3x5	T43.3x6
Methoxa-Dome	T49.3x1	T49.3x2	T49.3x3	T49.3x4	T49.3x5	T49.3x6
Methoxamine	T44.4x1	T44.4x2	T44.4x3	T44.4x4	T44.4x5	T44.4x6
Methoxsalen	T50.991	T50.992	T50.993	T50.994	T50.995	T50.996
Methoxyaniline	T65.3x1	T65.3x2	T65.3x3	T65.3x4	—	—
Methoxybenzyl penicillin	T36.0x1	T36.0x2	T36.0x3	T36.0x4	T36.0x5	T36.0x6
Methoxychlor	T53.7x1	T53.7x2	T53.7x3	T53.7x4	—	—
Methoxy-DDT	T53.7x1	T53.7x2	T53.7x3	T53.7x4	—	—
2-Methoxyethanol	T52.3x1	T52.3x2	T52.3x3	T52.3x4	—	—
Methoxyflurane	T41.0x1	T41.0x2	T41.0x3	T41.0x4	T41.0x5	T41.0x6
Methoxyphenamine	T48.6x1	T48.6x2	T48.6x3	T48.6x4	T48.6x5	T48.6x6
Methoxypromazine	T43.3x1	T43.3x2	T43.3x3	T43.3x4	T43.3x5	T43.3x6
5-Methoxypsoralen (5-MOP)	T50.991	T50.992	T50.993	T50.994	T50.995	T50.996
8-Methoxypsoralen (8-MOP)	T50.991	T50.992	T50.993	T50.994	T50.995	T50.996
Methscopolamine bromide	T44.3x1	T44.3x2	T44.3x3	T44.3x4	T44.3x5	T44.3x6
Methsuximide	T42.2x1	T42.2x2	T42.2x3	T42.2x4	T42.2x5	T42.2x6
Methyclothiazide	T50.2x1	T50.2x2	T50.2x3	T50.2x4	T50.2x5	T50.2x6
Methyl						
acetate	T52.4x1	T52.4x2	T52.4x3	T52.4x4	—	—
acetone	T52.4x1	T52.4x2	T52.4x3	T52.4x4	—	—
acrylate	T65.891	T65.892	T65.893	T65.894	—	—
alcohol	T51.1x1	T51.1x2	T51.1x3	T51.1x4	—	—
aminophenol	T65.3x1	T65.3x2	T65.3x3	T65.3x4	—	—
amphetamine	T43.621	T43.622	T43.623	T43.624	T43.625	T43.626
androstanolone	T38.7x1	T38.7x2	T38.7x3	T38.7x4	T38.7x5	T38.7x6
atropine	T44.3x1	T44.3x2	T44.3x3	T44.3x4	T44.3x5	T44.3x6
benzene	T52.2x1	T52.2x2	T52.2x3	T52.2x4	—	—
benzoate	T52.8x1	T52.8x2	T52.8x3	T52.8x4	—	—
benzol	T52.2x1	T52.2x2	T52.2x3	T52.2x4	—	—
bromide (gas)	T59.891	T59.892	T59.893	T59.894	—	—
fumigant	T60.8x1	T60.8x2	T60.8x3	T60.8x4	—	—
butanol	T51.3x1	T51.3x2	T51.3x3	T51.3x4	—	—
carbonate	T52.8x1	T52.8x2	T52.8x3	T52.8x4	—	—
carbinol	T51.1x1	T51.1x2	T51.1x3	T51.1x4	—	—
CCNU	T45.1x1	T45.1x2	T45.1x3	T45.1x4	T45.1x5	T45.1x6
cellosolve	T52.91	T52.92	T52.93	T52.94	—	—

Substance	Poisoning, Accidental (Unintentional)	Poisoning, Intentional Self-Harm	Poisoning, Assault	Poisoning, Undetermined	Adverse Effect	Underdosing
Methyl *(Continued)*						
cellulose	T47.4x1	T47.4x2	T47.4x3	T47.4x4	T47.4x5	T47.4x6
chloride (gas)	T59.891	T59.892	T59.893	T59.894	—	—
chloroformate	T59.3x1	T59.3x2	T59.3x3	T59.3x4	—	—
cyclohexane	T52.8x1	T52.8x2	T52.8x3	T52.8x4	—	—
cyclohexanol	T51.8x1	T51.8x2	T51.8x3	T51.8x4	—	—
cyclohexanone	T52.8x1	T52.8x2	T52.8x3	T52.8x4	—	—
cyclohexyl acetate	T52.8x1	T52.8x2	T52.8x3	T52.8x4	—	—
demeton	T60.0x1	T60.0x2	T60.0x3	T60.0x4	—	—
dihydromorphinone	T40.2x1	T40.2x2	T40.2x3	T40.2x4	T40.2x5	T40.2x6
ergometrine	T48.0x1	T48.0x2	T48.0x3	T48.0x4	T48.0x5	T48.0x6
ergonovine	T48.0x1	T48.0x2	T48.0x3	T48.0x4	T48.0x5	T48.0x6
ethyl ketone	T52.4x1	T52.4x2	T52.4x3	T52.4x4	—	—
glucamine antimonate	T37.8x1	T37.8x2	T37.8x3	T37.8x4	T37.8x5	T37.8x6
hydrazine	T65.891	T65.892	T65.893	T65.894	—	—
iodide	T65.891	T65.892	T65.893	T65.894	—	—
isobutyl ketone	T52.4x1	T52.4x2	T52.4x3	T52.4x4	—	—
isothiocyanate	T60.3x1	T60.3x2	T60.3x3	T60.3x4	—	—
mercaptan	T59.891	T59.892	T59.893	T59.894	—	—
morphine NEC	T40.2x1	T40.2x2	T40.2x3	T40.2x4	T40.2x5	T40.2x6
nicotinate	T49.4x1	T49.4x2	T49.4x3	T49.4x4	T49.4x5	T49.4x6
paraben	T49.0x1	T49.0x2	T49.0x3	T49.0x4	T49.0x5	T49.0x6
parafynol	T42.6x1	T42.6x2	T42.6x3	T42.6x4	T42.6x5	T42.6x6
parathion	T60.0x1	T60.0x2	T60.0x3	T60.0x4	—	—
propylcarbinol	T51.3x1	T51.3x2	T51.3x3	T51.3x4	—	—
peridol	T43.4x1	T43.4x2	T43.4x3	T43.4x4	T43.4x5	T43.4x6
phenidate	T43.631	T43.632	T43.633	T43.634	T43.635	T43.636
prednisolone	T38.0x1	T38.0x2	T38.0x3	T38.0x4	T38.0x5	T38.0x6
ENT agent	T49.6x1	T49.6x2	T49.6x3	T49.6x4	T49.6x5	T49.6x6
ophthalmic preparation	T49.5x1	T49.5x2	T49.5x3	T49.5x4	T49.5x5	T49.5x6
topical NEC	T49.0x1	T49.0x2	T49.0x3	T49.0x4	T49.0x5	T49.0x6
propylcarbinol	T51.8x1	T51.8x2	T51.8x3	T51.8x4	—	—
rosaniline NEC	T49.0x1	T49.0x2	T49.0x3	T49.0x4	T49.0x5	T49.0x6
salicylate	T49.2x1	T49.2x2	T49.2x3	T49.2x4	T49.2x5	T49.2x6
sulfate (fumes)	T59.891	T59.892	T59.893	T59.894	—	—
liquid	T52.8x1	T52.8x2	T52.8x3	T52.8x4	—	—
sulfonal	T42.6x1	T42.6x2	T42.6x3	T42.6x4	T42.6x5	T42.6x6
testosterone	T38.7x1	T38.7x2	T38.7x3	T38.7x4	T38.7x5	T38.7x6
thiouracil	T38.2x1	T38.2x2	T38.2x3	T38.2x4	T38.2x5	T38.2x6
Methylamphetamine	T43.621	T43.622	T43.623	T43.624	T43.625	T43.626

Substance	Poisoning, Accidental (Unintentional)	Poisoning, Intentional Self-Harm	Poisoning, Assault	Poisoning, Undetermined	Adverse Effect	Underdosing
Methylated spirit	T51.1x1	T51.1x2	T51.1x3	T51.1x4	—	—
Methylatropine nitrate	T44.3x1	T44.3x2	T44.3x3	T44.3x4	T44.3x5	T44.3x6
Methylbenactyzium bromide	T44.3x1	T44.3x2	T44.3x3	T44.3x4	T44.3x5	T44.3x6
Methylbenzethonium chloride	T49.0x1	T49.0x2	T49.0x3	T49.0x4	T49.0x5	T49.0x6
Methylcellulose	T47.4x1	T47.4x2	T47.4x3	T47.4x4	T47.4x5	T47.4x6
laxative	T47.4x1	T47.4x2	T47.4x3	T47.4x4	T47.4x5	T47.4x6
Methylchlorophenoxy-acetic acid	T60.3x1	T60.3x2	T60.3x3	T60.3x4	—	—
Methyldopa	T46.5x1	T46.5x2	T46.5x3	T46.5x4	T46.5x5	T46.5x6
Methyldopate	T46.5x1	T46.5x2	T46.5x3	T46.5x4	T46.5x5	T46.5x6
Methylene						
blue	T50.6x1	T50.6x2	T50.6x3	T50.6x4	T50.6x5	T50.6x6
chloride or dichloride (solvent) NEC	T53.4x1	T53.4x2	T53.4x3	T53.4x4	—	—
Methylenedioxyamphet-amine	T43.621	T43.622	T43.623	T43.624	T43.625	T43.626
Methylenedioxymethamphetamine	T43.621	T43.622	T43.623	T43.624	T43.625	T43.626
Methylergometrine	T48.0x1	T48.0x2	T48.0x3	T48.0x4	T48.0x5	T48.0x6
Methylergonovine	T48.0x1	T48.0x2	T48.0x3	T48.0x4	T48.0x5	T48.0x6
Methylestrenolone	T38.5x1	T38.5x2	T38.5x3	T38.5x4	T38.5x5	T38.5x6
Methylethyl cellulose	T50.991	T50.992	T50.993	T50.994	T50.995	T50.996
Methylhexabital	T42.3x1	T42.3x2	T42.3x3	T42.3x4	T42.3x5	T42.3x6
Methylmorphine	T40.2x1	T40.2x2	T40.2x3	T40.2x4	T40.2x5	T40.2x6
Methylparaben (ophthalmic)	T49.5x1	T49.5x2	T49.5x3	T49.5x4	T49.5x5	T49.5x6
Methylparafynol	T42.6x1	T42.6x2	T42.6x3	T42.6x4	T42.6x5	T42.6x6
Methylpentynol, methylpenthynol	T42.6x1	T42.6x2	T42.6x3	T42.6x4	T42.6x5	T42.6x6
Methylphenidate	T43.631	T43.632	T43.633	T43.634	T43.635	T43.636
Methylphenobarbital	T42.3x1	T42.3x2	T42.3x3	T42.3x4	T42.3x5	T42.3x6
Methylpolysiloxane	T47.1x1	T47.1x2	T47.1x3	T47.1x4	T47.1x5	T47.1x6
Methylprednisolone	T49.0x1	T49.0x2	T49.0x3	T49.0x4	T49.0x5	T49.0x6
Methylrosaniline	T49.0x1	T49.0x2	T49.0x3	T49.0x4	T49.0x5	T49.0x6
Methylrosanilinium chloride	T49.0x1	T49.0x2	T49.0x3	T49.0x4	T49.0x5	T49.0x6
Methyltestosterone	T38.7x1	T38.7x2	T38.7x3	T38.7x4	T38.7x5	T38.7x6
Methylthionine chloride	T50.6x1	T50.6x2	T50.6x3	T50.6x4	T50.6x5	T50.6x6
Methylthioninium chloride	T50.6x1	T50.6x2	T50.6x3	T50.6x4	T50.6x5	T50.6x6
Methylthiouracil	T38.2x1	T38.2x2	T38.2x3	T38.2x4	T38.2x5	T38.2x6
Methyprylon	T42.6x1	T42.6x2	T42.6x3	T42.6x4	T42.6x5	T42.6x6
Methysergide	T46.5x1	T46.5x2	T46.5x3	T46.5x4	T46.5x5	T46.5x6
Metiamide	T47.1x1	T47.1x2	T47.1x3	T47.1x4	T47.1x5	T47.1x6
Meticillin	T36.0x1	T36.0x2	T36.0x3	T36.0x4	T36.0x5	T36.0x6
Meticrane	T50.2x1	T50.2x2	T50.2x3	T50.2x4	T50.2x5	T50.2x6
Metildigoxin	T46.0x1	T46.0x2	T46.0x3	T46.0x4	T46.0x5	T46.0x6
Metipranolol	T49.5x1	T49.5x2	T49.5x3	T49.5x4	T49.5x5	T49.5x6

Substance	External Cause (T-Code)					
	Poisoning, Accidental (Unintentional)	Poisoning, Intentional Self-Harm	Poisoning, Assault	Poisoning, Undetermined	Adverse Effect	Underdosing
Metirosine	T46.5x1	T46.5x2	T46.5x3	T46.5x4	T46.5x5	T46.5x6
Metisazone	T37.5x1	T37.5x2	T37.5x3	T37.5x4	T37.5x5	T37.5x6
Metixene	T44.3x1	T44.3x2	T44.3x3	T44.3x4	T44.3x5	T44.3x6
Metizoline	T48.5x1	T48.5x2	T48.5x3	T48.5x4	T48.5x5	T48.5x6
Metoclopramide	T45.0x1	T45.0x2	T45.0x3	T45.0x4	T45.0x5	T45.0x6
Metofenazate	T43.3x1	T43.3x2	T43.3x3	T43.3x4	T43.3x5	T43.3x6
Metofoline	T39.8x1	T39.8x2	T39.8x3	T39.8x4	T39.8x5	T39.8x6
Metolazone	T50.2x1	T50.2x2	T50.2x3	T50.2x4	T50.2x5	T50.2x6
Metopon	T40.2x1	T40.2x2	T40.2x3	T40.2x4	T40.2x5	T40.2x6
Metoprine	T45.1x1	T45.1x2	T45.1x3	T45.1x4	T45.1x5	T45.1x6
Metoprolol	T44.7x1	T44.7x2	T44.7x3	T44.7x4	T44.7x5	T44.7x6
Metrifonate	T60.0x1	T60.0x2	T60.0x3	T60.0x4	—	—
Metrizamide	T50.8x1	T50.8x2	T50.8x3	T50.8x4	T50.8x5	T50.8x6
Metrizoic acid	T50.8x1	T50.8x2	T50.8x3	T50.8x4	T50.8x5	T50.8x6
Metronidazole	T37.8x1	T37.8x2	T37.8x3	T37.8x4	T37.8x5	T37.8x6
Metycaine	T41.3x1	T41.3x2	T41.3x3	T41.3x4	T41.3x5	T41.3x6
infiltration (subcutaneous)	T41.3x1	T41.3x2	T41.3x3	T41.3x4	T41.3x5	T41.3x6
nerve block (peripheral) (plexus)	T41.3x1	T41.3x2	T41.3x3	T41.3x4	T41.3x5	T41.3x6
topical (surface)	T41.3x1	T41.3x2	T41.3x3	T41.3x4	T41.3x5	T41.3x6
Metyrapone	T50.8x1	T50.8x2	T50.8x3	T50.8x4	T50.8x5	T50.8x6
Mevinphos	T60.0x1	T60.0x2	T60.0x3	T60.0x4	—	—
Mexazolam	T42.4x1	T42.4x2	T42.4x3	T42.4x4	T42.4x5	T42.4x6
Mexenone	T49.3x1	T49.3x2	T49.3x3	T49.3x4	T49.3x5	T49.3x6
Mexiletine	T46.2x1	T46.2x2	T46.2x3	T46.2x4	T46.2x5	T46.2x6
Mezereon	T62.2x1	T62.2x2	T62.2x3	T62.2x4	—	—
berries	T62.1x1	T62.1x2	T62.1x3	T62.1x4	—	—
Mezlocillin	T36.0x1	T36.0x2	T36.0x3	T36.0x4	T36.0x5	T36.0x6
Mianserin	T43.021	T43.022	T43.023	T43.024	T43.025	T43.026
Micatin	T49.0x1	T49.0x2	T49.0x3	T49.0x4	T49.0x5	T49.0x6
Miconazole	T49.0x1	T49.0x2	T49.0x3	T49.0x4	T49.0x5	T49.0x6
Micronomicin	T36.5x1	T36.5x2	T36.5x3	T36.5x4	T36.5x5	T36.5x6
Midazolam	T42.4x1	T42.4x2	T42.4x3	T42.4x4	T42.4x5	T42.4x6
Midecamycin	T36.3x1	T36.3x2	T36.3x3	T36.3x4	T36.3x5	T36.3x6
Mifepristone	T38.6x1	T38.6x2	T38.6x3	T38.6x4	T38.6x5	T38.6x6
Milk of magnesia	T47.1x1	T47.1x2	T47.1x3	T47.1x4	T47.1x5	T47.1x6
Millipede (tropical) (venomous)	T63.411	T63.412	T63.413	T63.414	—	—
Miltown	T43.591	T43.592	T43.593	T43.594	T43.595	T43.596
Milverine	T44.3x1	T44.3x2	T44.3x3	T44.3x4	T44.3x5	T44.3x6
Minaprine	T43.291	T43.292	T43.293	T43.294	T43.295	T43.296
Minaxolone	T41.291	T41.292	T41.293	T41.294	T41.295	T41.296

Substance	External Cause (T-Code)					
	Poisoning, Accidental (Unintentional)	Poisoning, Intentional Self-Harm	Poisoning, Assault	Poisoning, Undetermined	Adverse Effect	Underdosing
Mineral						
acids	T54.2x1	T54.2x2	T54.2x3	T54.2x4	—	—
oil (laxative) (medicinal)	T47.4x1	T47.4x2	T47.4x3	T47.4x4	T47.4x5	T47.4x6
emulsion	T47.2x1	T47.2x2	T47.2x3	T47.2x4	T47.2x5	T47.2x6
nonmedicinal	T52.0x1	T52.0x2	T52.0x3	T52.0x4	—	—
topical	T49.3x1	T49.3x2	T49.3x3	T49.3x4	T49.3x5	T49.3x6
salt NEC	T50.3x1	T50.3x2	T50.3x3	T50.3x4	T50.3x5	T50.3x6
spirits	T52.0x1	T52.0x2	T52.0x3	T52.0x4	—	—
Mineralocorticosteroid	T50.0x1	T50.0x2	T50.0x3	T50.0x4	T50.0x5	T50.0x6
Minocycline	T36.4x1	T36.4x2	T36.4x3	T36.4x4	T36.4x5	T36.4x6
Minoxidil	T46.7x1	T46.7x2	T46.7x3	T46.7x4	T46.7x5	T46.7x6
Miokamycin	T36.3x1	T36.3x2	T36.3x3	T36.3x4	T36.3x5	T36.3x6
Miotic drug	T49.5x1	T49.5x2	T49.5x3	T49.5x4	T49.5x5	T49.5x6
Mipafox	T60.0x1	T60.0x2	T60.0x3	T60.0x4	—	—
Mirex	T60.1x1	T60.1x2	T60.1x3	T60.1x4	—	—
Mirtazapine	T43.021	T43.022	T43.023	T43.024	T43.025	T43.026
Misonidazole	T37.3x1	T37.3x2	T37.3x3	T37.3x4	T37.3x5	T37.3x6
Misoprostol	T47.1x1	T47.1x2	T47.1x3	T47.1x4	T47.1x5	T47.1x6
Mithramycin	T45.1x1	T45.1x2	T45.1x3	T45.1x4	T45.1x5	T45.1x6
Mitobronitol	T45.1x1	T45.1x2	T45.1x3	T45.1x4	T45.1x5	T45.1x6
Mitoguazone	T45.1x1	T45.1x2	T45.1x3	T45.1x4	T45.1x5	T45.1x6
Mitolactol	T45.1x1	T45.1x2	T45.1x3	T45.1x4	T45.1x5	T45.1x6
Mitomycin	T45.1x1	T45.1x2	T45.1x3	T45.1x4	T45.1x5	T45.1x6
Mitopodozide	T45.1x1	T45.1x2	T45.1x3	T45.1x4	T45.1x5	T45.1x6
Mitotane	T45.1x1	T45.1x2	T45.1x3	T45.1x4	T45.1x5	T45.1x6
Mitoxantrone	T45.1x1	T45.1x2	T45.1x3	T45.1x4	T45.1x5	T45.1x6
Mivacurium chloride	T48.1x1	T48.1x2	T48.1x3	T48.1x4	T48.1x5	T48.1x6
Miyari bacteria	T47.6x1	T47.6x2	T47.6x3	T47.6x4	T47.6x5	T47.6x6
Moclobemide	T43.1x1	T43.1x2	T43.1x3	T43.1x4	T43.1x5	T43.1x6
Moderil	T46.5x1	T46.5x2	T46.5x3	T46.5x4	T46.5x5	T46.5x6
Mofebutazone	T39.2x1	T39.2x2	T39.2x3	T39.2x4	T39.2x5	T39.2x6
Mogadon - *see* Nitrazepam						
Molindone	T43.591	T43.592	T43.593	T43.594	T43.595	T43.596
Molsidomine	T46.3x1	T46.3x2	T46.3x3	T46.3x4	T46.3x5	T46.3x6
Mometasone	T49.0x1	T49.0x2	T49.0x3	T49.0x4	T49.0x5	T49.0x6
Monistat	T49.0x1	T49.0x2	T49.0x3	T49.0x4	T49.0x5	T49.0x6
Monkshood	T62.2x1	T62.2x2	T62.2x3	T62.2x4	—	—
Monoamine oxidase inhibitor NEC	T43.1x1	T43.1x2	T43.1x3	T43.1x4	T43.1x5	T43.1x6
hydrazine	T43.1x1	T43.1x2	T43.1x3	T43.1x4	T43.1x5	T43.1x6
Monobenzone	T49.4x1	T49.4x2	T49.4x3	T49.4x4	T49.4x5	T49.4x6

Substance	Poisoning, Accidental (Unintentional)	Poisoning, Intentional Self-Harm	Poisoning, Assault	Poisoning, Undetermined	Adverse Effect	Underdosing
Monochloroacetic acid	T60.3x1	T60.3x2	T60.3x3	T60.3x4	—	—
Monochlorobenzene	T53.7x1	T53.7x2	T53.7x3	T53.7x4	—	—
Monoethanolamine	T46.8x1	T46.8x2	T46.8x3	T46.8x4	T46.8x5	T46.8x6
oleate	T46.8x1	T46.8x2	T46.8x3	T46.8x4	T46.8x5	T46.8x6
Monooctanoin	T50.991	T50.992	T50.993	T50.994	T50.995	T50.996
Monophenylbutazone	T39.2x1	T39.2x2	T39.2x3	T39.2x4	T39.2x5	T39.2x6
Monosodium glutamate	T65.891	T65.892	T65.893	T65.894	—	—
Monosulfiram	T49.0x1	T49.0x2	T49.0x3	T49.0x4	T49.0x5	T49.0x6
Monoxide, carbon - *see* Carbon, monoxide	T57.91	T57.92	T57.93	T57.94	—	—
Monoxidine hydrochloride	T46.1x1	T46.1x2	T46.1x3	T46.1x4	T46.1x5	T46.1x6
Monuron	T60.3x1	T60.3x2	T60.3x3	T60.3x4	—	—
Moperone	T43.4x1	T43.4x2	T43.4x3	T43.4x4	T43.4x5	T43.4x6
Mopidamol	T45.1x1	T45.1x2	T45.1x3	T45.1x4	T45.1x5	T45.1x6
MOPP (mechlorethamine + vincristine + prednisone + procarbazine)	T45.1x1	T45.1x2	T45.1x3	T45.1x4	T45.1x5	T45.1x6
Morfin	T40.2x1	T40.2x2	T40.2x3	T40.2x4	T40.2x5	T40.2x6
Morinamide	T37.1x1	T37.1x2	T37.1x3	T37.1x4	T37.1x5	T37.1x6
Morning glory seeds	T40.991	T40.992	T40.993	T40.994	T40.995	T40.996
Moroxydine	T37.5x1	T37.5x2	T37.5x3	T37.5x4	T37.5x5	T37.5x6
Morphazinamide	T37.1x1	T37.1x2	T37.1x3	T37.1x4	T37.1x5	T37.1x6
Morphine	T40.2x1	T40.2x2	T40.2x3	T40.2x4	T40.2x5	T40.2x6
antagonist	T50.7x1	T50.7x2	T50.7x3	T50.7x4	T50.7x5	T50.7x6
Morpholinylethylmorphine	T40.2x1	T40.2x2	T40.2x3	T40.2x4	T40.2x5	T40.2x6
Morsuximide	T42.2x1	T42.2x2	T42.2x3	T42.2x4	T42.2x5	T42.2x6
Mosapramine	T43.591	T43.592	T43.593	T43.594	T43.595	T43.596
Moth balls (*see also* Pesticides)	T60.2x1	T60.2x2	T60.2x3	T60.2x4	—	—
naphthalene	T60.2x1	T60.2x2	T60.2x3	T60.2x4	—	—
paradichlorobenzene	T60.1x1	T60.1x2	T60.1x3	T60.1x4	—	—
Motor exhaust gas	T58.01	T58.02	T58.03	T58.04	—	—
Mouthwash (antiseptic) (zinc chloride)	T49.6x1	T49.6x2	T49.6x3	T49.6x4	T49.6x5	T49.6x6
Moxastine	T45.0x1	T45.0x2	T45.0x3	T45.0x4	T45.0x5	T45.0x6
Moxaverine	T44.3x1	T44.3x2	T44.3x3	T44.3x4	T44.3x5	T44.3x6
Moxifensine	T43.291	T43.292	T43.293	T43.294	T43.295	T43.296
Moxisylyte	T46.7x1	T46.7x2	T46.7x3	T46.7x4	T46.7x5	T46.7x6
Mucilage, plant	T47.4x1	T47.4x2	T47.4x3	T47.4x4	T47.4x5	T47.4x6
Mucolytic drug	T48.4x1	T48.4x2	T48.4x3	T48.4x4	T48.4x5	T48.4x6
Mucomyst	T48.4x1	T48.4x2	T48.4x3	T48.4x4	T48.4x5	T48.4x6
Mucous membrane agents (external)	T49.91	T49.92	T49.93	T49.94	T49.95	T49.96
specified NEC	T49.8x1	T49.8x2	T49.8x3	T49.8x4	T49.8x5	T49.8x6
Mumps						
immune globulin (human)	T50.Z11	T50.Z12	T50.Z13	T50.Z14	T50.Z15	T50.Z16

Substance	Poisoning, Accidental (Unintentional)	Poisoning, Intentional Self-Harm	Poisoning, Assault	Poisoning, Undetermined	Adverse Effect	Underdosing
Mumps *(Continued)*						
skin test antigen	T50.8x1	T50.8x2	T50.8x3	T50.8x4	T50.8x5	T50.8x6
vaccine	T50.B91	T50.B92	T50.B93	T50.B94	T50.B95	T50.B96
Mumpsvax	T50.B91	T50.B92	T50.B93	T50.B94	T50.B95	T50.B96
Mupirocin	T49.0x1	T49.0x2	T49.0x3	T49.0x4	T49.0x5	T49.0x6
Muriatic acid - *see* Hydrochloric acid						
Muromonab-CD3	T45.1x1	T45.1x2	T45.1x3	T45.1x4	T45.1x5	T45.1x6
Muscle relaxant - *see* Relaxant, muscle						
Muscle-action drug NEC	T48.201	T48.202	T48.203	T48.204	T48.205	T48.206
Muscle affecting agents NEC	T48.201	T48.202	T48.203	T48.204	T48.205	T48.206
oxytocic	T48.0x1	T48.0x2	T48.0x3	T48.0x4	T48.0x5	T48.0x6
relaxants	T48.201	T48.202	T48.203	T48.204	T48.205	T48.206
central nervous system	T42.8x1	T42.8x2	T42.8x3	T42.8x4	T42.8x5	T42.8x6
skeletal	T48.1x1	T48.1x2	T48.1x3	T48.1x4	T48.1x5	T48.1x6
smooth	T44.3x1	T44.3x2	T44.3x3	T44.3x4	T44.3x5	T44.3x6
Muscle-tone depressant, central NEC	T42.8x1	T42.8x2	T42.8x3	T42.8x4	T42.8x5	T42.8x6
specified NEC	T42.8x1	T42.8x2	T42.8x3	T42.8x4	T42.8x5	T42.8x6
Mushroom, noxious	T62.0x1	T62.0x2	T62.0x3	T62.0x4	—	—
Mussel, noxious	T61.781	T61.782	T61.783	T61.784	—	—
Mustard (emetic)	T47.7x1	T47.7x2	T47.7x3	T47.7x4	T47.7x5	T47.7x6
black	T47.7x1	T47.7x2	T47.7x3	T47.7x4	T47.7x5	T47.7x6
gas, not in war	T59.91	T59.92	T59.93	T59.94	—	—
nitrogen	T45.1x1	T45.1x2	T45.1x3	T45.1x4	T45.1x5	T45.1x6
Mustine	T45.1x1	T45.1x2	T45.1x3	T45.1x4	T45.1x5	T45.1x6
M-vac	T45.1x1	T45.1x2	T45.1x3	T45.1x4	T45.1x5	T45.1x6
Mycifradin	T36.8x1	T36.8x2	T36.8x3	T36.8x4	T36.8x5	T36.8x6
topical	T49.0x1	T49.0x2	T49.0x3	T49.0x4	T49.0x5	T49.0x6
Mycitracin	T36.8x1	T36.8x2	T36.8x3	T36.8x4	T36.8x5	T36.8x6
ophthalmic preparation	T49.5x1	T49.5x2	T49.5x3	T49.5x4	T49.5x5	T49.5x6
Mycostatin	T36.7x1	T36.7x2	T36.7x3	T36.7x4	T36.7x5	T36.7x6
topical	T49.0x1	T49.0x2	T49.0x3	T49.0x4	T49.0x5	T49.0x6
Mycotoxins	T64.81	T64.82	T64.83	T64.84	—	—
aflatoxin	T64.01	T64.02	T64.03	T64.04	—	—
specified NEC	T64.81	T64.82	T64.83	T64.84	—	—
Mydriacyl	T44.3x1	T44.3x2	T44.3x3	T44.3x4	T44.3x5	T44.3x6
Mydriatic drug	T49.5x1	T49.5x2	T49.5x3	T49.5x4	T49.5x5	T49.5x6
Myelobromal	T45.1x1	T45.1x2	T45.1x3	T45.1x4	T45.1x5	T45.1x6
Myleran	T45.1x1	T45.1x2	T45.1x3	T45.1x4	T45.1x5	T45.1x6
Myochrysin(e)	T39.2x1	T39.2x2	T39.2x3	T39.2x4	T39.2x5	T39.2x6
Myoneural blocking agents	T48.1x1	T48.1x2	T48.1x3	T48.1x4	T48.1x5	T48.1x6
Myralact	T49.0x1	T49.0x2	T49.0x3	T49.0x4	T49.0x5	T49.0x6

Substance	Poisoning, Accidental (Unintentional)	Poisoning, Intentional Self-Harm	Poisoning, Assault	Poisoning, Undetermined	Adverse Effect	Underdosing
Myristica fragrans	T62.2x1	T62.2x2	T62.2x3	T62.2x4	—	—
Myristicin	T65.891	T65.892	T65.893	T65.894	—	—
Mysoline	T42.3x1	T42.3x2	T42.3x3	T42.3x4	T42.3x5	T42.3x6
Nabilone	T40.7x1	T40.7x2	T40.7x3	T40.7x4	T40.7x5	T40.7x6
Nabumetone	T39.391	T39.392	T39.393	T39.394	T39.395	T39.396
Nadolol	T44.7x1	T44.7x2	T44.7x3	T44.7x4	T44.7x5	T44.7x6
Nafcillin	T36.0x1	T36.0x2	T36.0x3	T36.0x4	T36.0x5	T36.0x6
Nafoxidine	T38.6x1	T38.6x2	T38.6x3	T38.6x4	T38.6x5	T38.6x6
Naftazone	T46.991	T46.992	T46.993	T46.994	T46.995	T46.996
Naftidrofuryl (oxalate)	T46.7x1	T46.7x2	T46.7x3	T46.7x4	T46.7x5	T46.7x6
Naftifine	T49.0x1	T49.0x2	T49.0x3	T49.0x4	T49.0x5	T49.0x6
Nail polish remover	T52.91	T52.92	T52.93	T52.94	—	—
Nalbuphine	T40.4x1	T40.4x2	T40.4x3	T40.4x4	T40.4x5	T40.4x6
Naled	T60.0x1	T60.0x2	T60.0x3	T60.0x4	—	—
Nalidixic acid	T37.8x1	T37.8x2	T37.8x3	T37.8x4	T37.8x5	T37.8x6
Nalorphine	T50.7x1	T50.7x2	T50.7x3	T50.7x4	T50.7x5	T50.7x6
Naloxone	T50.7x1	T50.7x2	T50.7x3	T50.7x4	T50.7x5	T50.7x6
Naltrexone	T50.7x1	T50.7x2	T50.7x3	T50.7x4	T50.7x5	T50.7x6
Namenda	T43.8x1	T43.8x2	T43.8x3	T43.8x4	T43.8x5	T43.8x6
Nandrolone	T38.7x1	T38.7x2	T38.7x3	T38.7x4	T38.7x5	T38.7x6
Naphazoline	T48.5x1	T48.5x2	T48.5x3	T48.5x4	T48.5x5	T48.5x6
Naphtha (painters') (petroleum)	T52.0x1	T52.0x2	T52.0x3	T52.0x4	—	—
solvent	T52.0x1	T52.0x2	T52.0x3	T52.0x4	—	—
vapor	T52.0x1	T52.0x2	T52.0x3	T52.0x4	—	—
Naphthalene (non-chlorinated)	T60.2x1	T60.2x2	T60.2x3	T60.2x4	—	—
chlorinated	T60.1x1	T60.1x2	T60.1x3	T60.1x4	—	—
vapor	T60.1x1	T60.1x2	T60.1x3	T60.1x4	—	—
insecticide or moth repellent	T60.2x1	T60.2x2	T60.2x3	T60.2x4	—	—
chlorinated	T60.1x1	T60.1x2	T60.1x3	T60.1x4	—	—
vapor	T60.2x1	T60.2x2	T60.2x3	T60.2x4	—	—
chlorinated	T60.1x1	T60.1x2	T60.1x3	T60.1x4	—	—
Naphthol	T65.891	T65.892	T65.893	T65.894	—	—
Naphthylamine	T65.891	T65.892	T65.893	T65.894	—	—
Naphthylthiourea (ANTU)	T60.4x1	T60.4x2	T60.4x3	T60.4x4	—	—
Naprosyn - see Naproxen						
Naproxen	T39.311	T39.312	T39.313	T39.314	T39.315	T39.316
Narcotic (drug)	T40.601	T40.602	T40.603	T40.604	T40.605	T40.606
analgesic NEC	T39.8x1	T39.8x2	T39.8x3	T39.8x4	T39.8x5	T39.8x6
antagonist	T50.7x1	T50.7x2	T50.7x3	T50.7x4	T50.7x5	T50.7x6
specified NEC	T40.691	T40.692	T40.693	T40.694	T40.695	T40.696

Substance	Poisoning, Accidental (Unintentional)	Poisoning, Intentional Self-Harm	Poisoning, Assault	Poisoning, Undetermined	Adverse Effect	Underdosing
			External Cause (T-Code)			
Narcotine	T48.3x1	T48.3x2	T48.3x3	T48.3x4	T48.3x5	T48.3x6
Nardil	T43.1x1	T43.1x2	T43.1x3	T43.1x4	T43.1x5	T43.1x6
Nasal drug NEC	T49.6x1	T49.6x2	T49.6x3	T49.6x4	T49.6x5	T49.6x6
Natamycin	T49.0x1	T49.0x2	T49.0x3	T49.0x4	T49.0x5	T49.0x6
Natrium cyanide - *see* Cyanide(s)						
Natural gas	T59.891	T59.892	T59.893	T59.894	—	—
incomplete combustion	T57.91	T57.92	T57.93	T57.94	—	—
Natural						
blood (product)	T45.8x1	T45.8x2	T45.8x3	T45.8x4	T45.8x5	T45.8x6
gas (piped)	T59.891	T59.892	T59.893	T59.894	—	—
incomplete combustion	T58.11	T58.12	T58.13	T58.14	—	—
Nealbarbital	T42.3x1	T42.3x2	T42.3x3	T42.3x4	T42.3x5	T42.3x6
Nectadon	T48.3x1	T48.3x2	T48.3x3	T48.3x4	T48.3x5	T48.3x6
Nedocromil	T48.6x1	T48.6x2	T48.6x3	T48.6x4	T48.6x5	T48.6x6
Nefopam	T39.8x1	T39.8x2	T39.8x3	T39.8x4	T39.8x5	T39.8x6
Nematocyst (sting)	T63.691	T63.692	T63.693	T63.694	—	—
Nembutal	T42.3x1	T42.3x2	T42.3x3	T42.3x4	T42.3x5	T42.3x6
Nemonapride	T43.591	T43.592	T43.593	T43.594	T43.595	T43.596
Neoarsphenamine	T37.8x1	T37.8x2	T37.8x3	T37.8x4	T37.8x5	T37.8x6
Neocinchophen	T50.4x1	T50.4x2	T50.4x3	T50.4x4	T50.4x5	T50.4x6
Neomycin (derivatives)	T36.5x1	T36.5x2	T36.5x3	T36.5x4	T36.5x5	T36.5x6
with						
bacitracin	T49.0x1	T49.0x2	T49.0x3	T49.0x4	T49.0x5	T49.0x6
neostigmine	T44.0x1	T44.0x2	T44.0x3	T44.0x4	T44.0x5	T44.0x6
ENT agent	T49.6x1	T49.6x2	T49.6x3	T49.6x4	T49.6x5	T49.6x6
ophthalmic preparation	T49.5x1	T49.5x2	T49.5x3	T49.5x4	T49.5x5	T49.5x6
topical NEC	T49.0x1	T49.0x2	T49.0x3	T49.0x4	T49.0x5	T49.0x6
Neonal	T42.3x1	T42.3x2	T42.3x3	T42.3x4	T42.3x5	T42.3x6
Neoprontosil	T37.0x1	T37.0x2	T37.0x3	T37.0x4	T37.0x5	T37.0x6
Neosalvarsan	T37.8x1	T37.8x2	T37.8x3	T37.8x4	T37.8x5	T37.8x6
Neosilversalvarsan	T37.8x1	T37.8x2	T37.8x3	T37.8x4	T37.8x5	T37.8x6
Neosporin	T36.8x1	T36.8x2	T36.8x3	T36.8x4	T36.8x5	T36.8x6
ENT agent	T49.6x1	T49.6x2	T49.6x3	T49.6x4	T49.6x5	T49.6x6
opthalmic preparation	T49.5x1	T49.5x2	T49.5x3	T49.5x4	T49.5x5	T49.5x6
topical NEC	T49.0x1	T49.0x2	T49.0x3	T49.0x4	T49.0x5	T49.0x6
Neostigmine bromide	T44.0x1	T44.0x2	T44.0x3	T44.0x4	T44.0x5	T44.0x6
Neraval	T42.3x1	T42.3x2	T42.3x3	T42.3x4	T42.3x5	T42.3x6
Neravan	T42.3x1	T42.3x2	T42.3x3	T42.3x4	T42.3x5	T42.3x6
Nerium oleander	T62.2x1	T62.2x2	T62.2x3	T62.2x4	—	—
Nerve gas, not in war	T59.891	T59.892	T59.893	T59.894	—	—

Substance	Poisoning, Accidental (Unintentional)	Poisoning, Intentional Self-Harm	Poisoning, Assault	Poisoning, Undetermined	Adverse Effect	Underdosing
Nesacaine	T41.3x1	T41.3x2	T41.3x3	T41.3x4	T41.3x5	T41.3x6
infiltration (subcutaneous)	T41.3x1	T41.3x2	T41.3x3	T41.3x4	T41.3x5	T41.3x6
nerve block (peripheral) (plexus)	T41.3x1	T41.3x2	T41.3x3	T41.3x4	T41.3x5	T41.3x6
Netilmicin	T36.5x1	T36.5x2	T36.5x3	T36.5x4	T36.5x5	T36.5x6
Neurobarb	T42.3x1	T42.3x2	T42.3x3	T42.3x4	T42.3x5	T42.3x6
Neuroleptic drug NEC	T43.501	T43.502	T43.503	T43.504	T43.505	T43.506
Neuromuscular blocking drug	T48.1x1	T48.1x2	T48.1x3	T48.1x4	T48.1x5	T48.1x6
Neutral insulin injection	T38.3x1	T38.3x2	T38.3x3	T38.3x4	T38.3x5	T38.3x6
Neutral spirits	T51.0x1	T51.0x2	T51.0x3	T51.0x4	—	—
beverage	T51.0x1	T51.0x2	T51.0x3	T51.0x4	—	—
Niacin	T46.7x1	T46.7x2	T46.7x3	T46.7x4	T46.7x5	T46.7x6
Niacinamide	T45.2x1	T45.2x2	T45.2x3	T45.2x4	T45.2x5	T45.2x6
Nialamide	T43.1x1	T43.1x2	T43.1x3	T43.1x4	T43.1x5	T43.1x6
Niaprazine	T42.6x1	T42.6x2	T42.6x3	T42.6x4	T42.6x5	T42.6x6
Nicametate	T46.7x1	T46.7x2	T46.7x3	T46.7x4	T46.7x5	T46.7x6
Nicardipine	T46.1x1	T46.1x2	T46.1x3	T46.1x4	T46.1x5	T46.1x6
Nicergoline	T46.7x1	T46.7x2	T46.7x3	T46.7x4	T46.7x5	T46.7x6
Nickel (carbonyl) (tetra-carbonyl) (fumes) (vapor)	T56.891	T56.892	T56.893	T56.894	—	—
Nickelocene	T56.891	T56.892	T56.893	T56.894	—	—
Niclosamide	T37.4x1	T37.4x2	T37.4x3	T37.4x4	T37.4x5	T37.4x6
Nicofuranose	T46.7x1	T46.7x2	T46.7x3	T46.7x4	T46.7x5	T46.7x6
Nicomorphine	T40.2x1	T40.2x2	T40.2x4	T40.2x4	T40.2x5	T40.2x6
Nicorandil	T46.3x1	T46.3x2	T46.3x3	T46.3x4	T46.3x5	T46.3x6
Nicotiana (plant)	T62.2x1	T62.2x2	T62.2x3	T62.2x4	—	—
Nicotinamide	T45.2x1	T45.2x2	T45.2x3	T45.2x4	T45.2x5	T45.2x6
Nicotine (insecticide) (spray) (sulfate) NEC	T60.2x1	T60.2x2	T60.2x3	T60.2x4	—	—
from tobacco	T65.291	T65.292	T65.293	T65.294	—	—
cigarettes	T65.221	T65.222	T65.223	T65.224	—	—
not insecticide	T65.291	T65.292	T65.293	T65.294	—	—
Nicotinic acid	T46.7x1	T46.7x2	T46.7x3	T46.7x4	T46.7x5	T46.7x6
Nicotinyl alcohol	T46.7x1	T46.7x2	T46.7x3	T46.7x4	T46.7x5	T46.7x6
Nicoumalone	T45.511	T45.512	T45.513	T45.514	T45.515	T45.516
Nifedipine	T46.1x1	T46.1x2	T46.1x3	T46.1x4	T46.1x5	T46.1x6
Nifenazone	T39.2x1	T39.2x2	T39.2x3	T39.2x4	T39.2x5	T39.2x6
Nifuraldezone	T37.91	T37.92	T37.93	T37.94	T37.95	T37.96
Nifuratel	T37.8x1	T37.8x2	T37.8x3	T37.8x4	T37.8x5	T37.8x6
Nifurtimox	T37.3x1	T37.3x2	T37.3x3	T37.3x4	T37.3x5	T37.3x6
Nifurtoinol	T37.8x1	T37.8x2	T37.8x3	T37.8x4	T37.8x5	T37.8x6
Nightshade, deadly (solanum) (see also Belladonna)	T62.2x1	T62.2x2	T62.2x3	T62.2x4	—	—
berry	T62.1x1	T62.1x2	T62.1x3	T62.1x4	—	—

Substance	External Cause (T-Code)					
	Poisoning, Accidental (Unintentional)	Poisoning, Intentional Self-Harm	Poisoning, Assault	Poisoning, Undetermined	Adverse Effect	Underdosing
Nikethamide	T50.7x1	T50.7x2	T50.7x3	T50.7x4	T50.7x5	T50.7x6
Nilstat	T36.7x1	T36.7x2	T36.7x3	T36.7x4	T36.7x5	T36.7x6
topical	T49.0x1	T49.0x2	T49.0x3	T49.0x4	T49.0x5	T49.0x6
Nilutamide	T38.6x1	T38.6x2	T38.6x3	T38.6x4	T38.6x5	T38.6x6
Nimesulide	T39.391	T39.392	T39.393	T39.394	T39.395	T39.396
Nimetazepam	T42.4x1	T42.4x2	T42.4x3	T42.4x4	T42.4x5	T42.4x6
Nimodipine	T46.1x1	T46.1x2	T46.1x3	T46.1x4	T46.1x5	T46.1x6
Nimorazole	T37.3x1	T37.3x2	T37.3x3	T37.3x4	T37.3x5	T37.3x6
Nimustine	T45.1x1	T45.1x2	T45.1x3	T45.1x4	T45.1x5	T45.1x6
Niridazole	T37.4x1	T37.4x2	T37.4x3	T37.4x4	T37.4x5	T37.4x6
Nisentil	T40.2x1	T40.2x2	T40.2x3	T40.2x4	T40.2x5	T40.2x6
Nisoldipine	T46.1x1	T46.1x2	T46.1x3	T46.1x4	T46.1x5	T46.1x6
Nitramine	T65.3x1	T65.3x2	T65.3x3	T65.3x4	—	—
Nitrate, organic	T46.3x1	T46.3x2	T46.3x3	T46.3x4	T46.3x5	T46.3x6
Nitrazepam	T42.4x1	T42.4x2	T42.4x3	T42.4x4	T42.4x5	T42.4x6
Nitrefazole	T50.6x1	T50.6x2	T50.6x3	T50.6x4	T50.6x5	T50.6x6
Nitrendipine	T46.1x1	T46.1x2	T46.1x3	T46.1x4	T46.1x5	T46.1x6
Nitric						
acid (liquid)	T54.2x1	T54.2x2	T54.2x3	T54.2x4	—	—
vapor	T59.891	T59.892	T59.893	T59.894	—	—
oxide (gas)	T59.0x1	T59.0x2	T59.0x3	T59.0x4	—	—
Nitrimidazine	T37.3x1	T37.3x2	T37.3x3	T37.3x4	T37.3x5	T37.3x6
Nitrite, amyl (medicinal) (vapor)	T46.3x1	T46.3x2	T46.3x3	T46.3x4	T46.3x5	T46.3x6
Nitroaniline	T65.3x1	T65.3x2	T65.3x3	T65.3x4	—	—
vapor	T59.891	T59.892	T59.893	T59.894	—	—
Nitrobenzene, nitrobenzol	T65.3x1	T65.3x2	T65.3x3	T65.3x4	—	—
vapor	T65.3x1	T65.3x2	T65.3x3	T65.3x4	—	—
Nitrocellulose	T65.891	T65.892	T65.893	T65.894	—	—
lacquer	T65.891	T65.892	T65.893	T65.894	—	—
Nitrodiphenyl	T65.3x1	T65.3x2	T65.3x3	T65.3x4	—	—
Nitrofural	T49.0x1	T49.0x2	T49.0x3	T49.0x4	T49.0x5	T49.0x6
Nitrofurantoin	T37.8x1	T37.8x2	T37.8x3	T37.8x4	T37.8x5	T37.8x6
Nitrofurazone	T49.0x1	T49.0x2	T49.0x3	T49.0x4	T49.0x5	T49.0x6
Nitrogen	T59.0x1	T59.0x2	T59.0x3	T59.0x4	—	—
mustard	T45.1x1	T45.1x2	T45.1x3	T45.1x4	T45.1x5	T45.1x6
Nitroglycerin, nitro-glycerol (medicinal)	T46.3x1	T46.3x2	T46.3x3	T46.3x4	T46.3x5	T46.3x6
nonmedicinal	T65.5x1	T65.5x2	T65.5x3	T65.5x4	—	—
fumes	T65.5x1	T65.5x2	T65.5x3	T65.5x4	—	—
Nitroglycol	T52.3x1	T52.3x2	T52.3x3	T52.3x4	—	—
Nitrohydrochloric acid	T54.2x1	T54.2x2	T54.2x3	T54.2x4	—	—

Substance	External Cause (T-Code)					
	Poisoning, Accidental (Unintentional)	Poisoning, Intentional Self-Harm	Poisoning, Assault	Poisoning, Undetermined	Adverse Effect	Underdosing
Nitromersol	T49.0x1	T49.0x2	T49.0x3	T49.0x4	T49.0x5	T49.0x6
Nitronaphthalene	T65.891	T65.892	T65.893	T65.894	—	—
Nitrophenol	T54.0x1	T54.0x2	T54.0x3	T54.0x4	—	—
Nitropropane	T52.8x1	T52.8x2	T52.8x3	T52.8x4	—	—
Nitroprusside	T46.5x1	T46.5x2	T46.5x3	T46.5x4	T46.5x5	T46.5x6
Nitrosodimethylamine	T65.3x1	T65.3x2	T65.3x3	T65.3x4	—	—
Nitrothiazol	T37.4x1	T37.4x2	T37.4x3	T37.4x4	T37.4x5	T37.4x6
Nitrotoluene, nitrotoluol	T65.3x1	T65.3x2	T65.3x3	T65.3x4	—	—
vapor	T65.3x1	T65.3x2	T65.3x3	T65.3x4	—	—
Nitrous						
acid (liquid)	T54.2x1	T54.2x2	T54.2x3	T54.2x4	—	—
fumes	T59.891	T59.892	T59.893	T59.894	—	—
ether spirit	T46.3x1	T46.3x2	T46.3x3	T46.3x4	T46.3x5	T46.3x6
oxide	T41.0x1	T41.0x2	T41.0x3	T41.0x4	T41.0x5	T41.0x6
Nitroxoline	T37.8x1	T37.8x2	T37.8x3	T37.8x4	T37.8x5	T37.8x6
Nitrozone	T49.0x1	T49.0x2	T49.0x3	T49.0x4	T49.0x5	T49.0x6
Nizatidine	T47.0x1	T47.0x2	T47.0x3	T47.0x4	T47.0x5	T47.0x6
Nizofenone	T43.8x1	T43.8x2	T43.8x3	T43.8x4	T43.8x5	T43.8x6
Noctec	T42.6x1	T42.6x2	T42.6x3	T42.6x4	T42.6x5	T42.6x6
Noludar	T42.6x1	T42.6x2	T42.6x3	T42.6x4	T42.6x5	T42.6x6
Noptil	T42.3x1	T42.3x2	T42.3x3	T42.3x4	T42.3x5	T42.3x6
Nomegestrol	T38.5x1	T38.5x2	T38.5x3	T38.5x4	T38.5x5	T38.5x6
Nomifensine	T43.291	T43.292	T43.293	T43.294	T43.295	T43.296
Nonoxinol	T49.8x1	T49.8x2	T49.8x3	T49.8x4	T49.8x5	T49.8x6
Nonylphenoxy (polyethoxy-ethanol)	T49.8x1	T49.8x2	T49.8x3	T49.8x4	T49.8x5	T49.8x6
Noptil	T42.3x1	T42.3x2	T42.3x3	T42.3x4	T42.3x5	T42.3x6
Noradrenaline	T44.4x1	T44.4x2	T44.4x3	T44.4x4	T44.4x5	T44.4x6
Noramidopyrine	T39.2x1	T39.2x2	T39.2x3	T39.2x4	T39.2x5	T39.2x6
methanesulfonate sodium	T39.2x1	T39.2x2	T39.2x3	T39.2x4	T39.2x5	T39.2x6
Norbormide	T60.4x1	T60.4x2	T60.4x3	T60.4x4	—	—
Nordazepam	T42.4x1	T42.4x2	T42.4x3	T42.4x4	T42.4x5	T42.4x6
Norepinephrine	T44.4x1	T44.4x2	T44.4x3	T44.4x4	T44.4x5	T44.4x6
Norethandrolone	T38.7x1	T38.7x2	T38.7x3	T38.7x4	T38.7x5	T38.7x6
Norethindrone	T38.4x1	T38.4x2	T38.4x3	T38.4x4	T38.4x5	T38.4x6
Norethisterone (acetate) (enantate)	T38.4x1	T38.4x2	T38.4x3	T38.4x4	T38.4x5	T38.4x6
with ethinylestradiol	T38.5x1	T38.5x2	T38.5x3	T38.5x4	T38.5x5	T38.5x6
Noretynodrel	T38.5x1	T38.5x2	T38.5x3	T38.5x4	T38.5x5	T38.5x6
Norfenefrine	T44.4x1	T44.4x2	T44.4x3	T44.4x4	T44.4x5	T44.4x6
Norfloxacin	T36.8x1	T36.8x2	T36.8x3	T36.8x4	T36.8x5	T36.8x6
Norgestrel	T38.4x1	T38.4x2	T38.4x3	T38.4x4	T38.4x5	T38.4x6
Norgestrienone	T38.4x1	T38.4x2	T38.4x3	T38.4x4	T38.4x5	T38.4x6

Substance	External Cause (T-Code)					
	Poisoning, Accidental (Unintentional)	Poisoning, Intentional Self-Harm	Poisoning, Assault	Poisoning, Undetermined	Adverse Effect	Underdosing
Norlestrin	T38.4x1	T38.4x2	T38.4x3	T38.4x4	T38.4x5	T38.4x6
Norlutin	T38.4x1	T38.4x2	T38.4x3	T38.4x4	T38.4x5	T38.4x6
Normal serum albumin (human), salt-poor	T45.8x1	T45.8x2	T45.8x3	T45.8x4	T45.8x5	T45.8x6
Normethandrone	T38.5x1	T38.5x2	T38.5x3	T38.5x4	T38.5x5	T38.5x6
Normison - see Benzodiazepines						
Normorphine	T40.2x1	T40.2x2	T40.2x3	T40.2x4	T40.2x5	T40.2x6
Norpseudoephedrine	T50.5x1	T50.5x2	T50.5x3	T50.5x4	T50.5x5	T50.5x6
Nortestosterone (furanpropionate)	T38.7x1	T38.7x2	T38.7x3	T38.7x4	T38.7x5	T38.7x6
Nortriptyline	T43.011	T43.012	T43.013	T43.014	T43.015	T43.016
Noscapine	T48.3x1	T48.3x2	T48.3x3	T48.3x4	T48.3x5	T48.3x6
Nose preparations	T49.6x1	T49.6x2	T49.6x3	T49.6x4	T49.6x5	T49.6x6
Novobiocin	T36.5x1	T36.5x2	T36.5x3	T36.5x4	T36.5x5	T36.5x6
Novocain (infiltration) (topical)	T41.3x1	T41.3x2	T41.3x3	T41.3x4	T41.3x5	T41.3x6
nerve block (peripheral) (plexus)	T41.3x1	T41.3x2	T41.3x3	T41.3x4	T41.3x5	T41.3x6
spinal	T41.3x1	T41.3x2	T41.3x3	T41.3x4	T41.3x5	T41.3x6
Noxious foodstuff	T62.91	T62.92	T62.93	T62.94	—	—
specified NEC	T62.8x1	T62.8x2	T62.8x3	T62.8x4	—	—
Noxiptiline	T43.011	T43.012	T43.013	T43.014	T43.015	T43.016
Noxytiolin	T49.0x1	T49.0x2	T49.0x3	T49.0x4	T49.0x5	T49.0x6
NPH Iletin (insulin)	T38.3x1	T38.3x2	T38.3x3	T38.3x4	T38.3x5	T38.3x6
Numorphan	T40.2x1	T40.2x2	T40.2x3	T40.2x4	T40.2x5	T40.2x6
Nunol	T42.3x1	T42.3x2	T42.3x3	T42.3x4	T42.3x5	T42.3x6
Nupercaine (spinal anesthetic)	T41.3x1	T41.3x2	T41.3x3	T41.3x4	T41.3x5	T41.3x6
topical (surface)	T41.3x1	T41.3x2	T41.3x3	T41.3x4	T41.3x5	T41.3x6
Nutmeg oil (liniment)	T49.3x1	T49.3x2	T49.3x3	T49.3x4	T49.3x5	T49.3x6
Nutritional supplement	T50.901	T50.902	T50.903	T50.904	T50.905	T50.906
Nux vomica	T65.1x1	T65.1x2	T65.1x3	T65.1x4	—	—
Nydrazid	T37.1x1	T37.1x2	T37.1x3	T37.1x4	T37.1x5	T37.1x6
Nylidrin	T46.7x1	T46.7x2	T46.7x3	T46.7x4	T46.7x5	T46.7x6
Nystatin	T36.7x1	T36.7x2	T36.7x3	T36.7x4	T36.7x5	T36.7x6
topical	T49.0x1	T49.0x2	T49.0x3	T49.0x4	T49.0x5	T49.0x6
Nytol	T45.0x1	T45.0x2	T45.0x3	T45.0x4	T45.0x5	T45.0x6
Oblivion	T42.6x1	T42.6x2	T42.6x3	T42.6x4	T42.6x5	T42.6x6
Obidoxime chloride	T50.6x1	T50.6x2	T50.6x3	T50.6x4	T50.6x5	T50.6x6
Octafonium (chloride)	T49.3x1	T49.3x2	T49.3x3	T49.3x4	T49.3x5	T49.3x6
Octamethyl pyrophos-phoramide	T60.0x1	T60.0x2	T60.0x3	T60.0x4	—	—
Octanoin	T50.991	T50.992	T50.993	T50.994	T50.995	T50.996
Octatropine methyl-bromide	T44.3x1	T44.3x2	T44.3x3	T44.3x4	T44.3x5	T44.3x6
Octotiamine	T45.2x1	T45.2x2	T45.2x3	T45.2x4	T45.2x5	T45.2x6
Octoxinol (9)	T49.8x1	T49.8x2	T49.8x3	T49.8x4	T49.8x5	T49.8x6
Octreotide	T38.991	T38.992	T38.993	T38.994	T38.995	T38.996

Substance	Poisoning, Accidental (Unintentional)	Poisoning, Intentional Self-Harm	Poisoning, Assault	Poisoning, Undetermined	Adverse Effect	Underdosing
			External Cause (T-Code)			
Octyl nitrite	T46.3x1	T46.3x2	T46.3x3	T46.3x4	T46.3x5	T46.3x6
Oestradiol	T38.5x1	T38.5x2	T38.5x3	T38.5x4	T38.5x5	T38.5x6
Oestriol	T38.5x1	T38.5x2	T38.5x3	T38.5x4	T38.5x5	T38.5x6
Oestrogen	T38.5x1	T38.5x2	T38.5x3	T38.5x4	T38.5x5	T38.5x6
Oestrone	T38.5x1	T38.5x2	T38.5x3	T38.5x4	T38.5x5	T38.5x6
Ofloxacin	T36.8x1	T36.8x2	T36.8x3	T36.8x4	T36.8x5	T36.8x6
Oil (of)	T65.891	T65.892	T65.893	T65.894	—	—
bitter almond	T62.8x1	T62.8x2	T62.8x3	T62.8x4	—	—
cloves	T49.7x1	T49.7x2	T49.7x3	T49.7x4	T49.7x5	T49.7x6
colors	T65.6x1	T65.6x2	T65.6x3	T65.6x4	—	—
fumes	T59.891	T59.892	T59.893	T59.894	—	—
lubricating	T52.0x1	T52.0x2	T52.0x3	T52.0x4	—	—
Niobe	T52.8x1	T52.8x2	T52.8x3	T52.8x4	—	—
vitriol (liquid)	T54.2x1	T54.2x2	T54.2x3	T54.2x4	—	—
fumes	T54.2x1	T54.2x2	T54.2x3	T54.2x4	—	—
wintergreen (bitter) NEC	T49.3x1	T49.3x2	T49.3x3	T49.3x4	T49.3x5	T49.3x6
Oily preparation (for skin)	T49.3x1	T49.3x2	T49.3x3	T49.3x4	T49.3x5	T49.3x6
Ointment NEC	T49.3x1	T49.3x2	T49.3x3	T49.3x4	T49.3x5	T49.3x6
Oleander	T62.2x1	T62.2x2	T62.2x3	T62.2x4	—	—
Oleandomycin	T36.3x1	T36.3x2	T36.3x3	T36.3x4	T36.3x5	T36.3x6
Oleandrin	T46.0x1	T46.0x2	T46.0x3	T46.0x4	T46.0x5	T46.0x6
Oleic acid	T46.6x1	T46.6x2	T46.6x3	T46.6x4	T46.6x5	T46.6x6
Oleovitamin A	T45.2x1	T45.2x2	T45.2x3	T45.2x4	T45.2x5	T45.2x6
Oleum ricini	T47.2x1	T47.2x2	T47.2x3	T47.2x4	T47.2x5	T47.2x6
Olive oil (medicinal) NEC	T47.4x1	T47.4x2	T47.4x3	T47.4x4	T47.4x5	T47.4x6
Olivomycin	T45.1x1	T45.1x2	T45.1x3	T45.1x4	T45.1x5	T45.1x6
Olsalazine	T47.8x1	T47.8x2	T47.8x3	T47.8x4	T47.8x5	T47.8x6
Omeprazole	T47.1x1	T47.1x2	T47.1x3	T47.1x4	T47.1x5	T47.1x6
OMPA	T60.0x1	T60.0x2	T60.0x3	T60.0x4	—	—
Ondansetron	T45.0x1	T45.0x2	T45.0x3	T45.0x4	T45.0x5	T45.0x6
Oncovin	T45.1x1	T45.1x2	T45.1x3	T45.1x4	T45.1x5	T45.1x6
Ophthaine	T41.3x1	T41.3x2	T41.3x3	T41.3x4	T41.3x5	T41.3x6
Ophthetic	T41.3x1	T41.3x2	T41.3x3	T41.3x4	T41.3x5	T41.3x6
Opiate NEC	T40.601	T40.602	T40.603	T40.604	T40.605	T40.606
antagonists	T50.7x1	T50.7x2	T50.7x3	T50.7x4	T50.7x5	T50.7x6
Opipramol	T43.011	T43.012	T43.013	T43.014	T43.015	T43.016
Opium alkaloids (total)	T40.0x1	T40.0x2	T40.0x3	T40.0x4	T40.0x5	T40.0x6
standardized powdered	T40.0x1	T40.0x2	T40.0x3	T40.0x4	T40.0x5	T40.0x6
tincture (camphorated)	T40.0x1	T40.0x2	T40.0x3	T40.0x4	T40.0x5	T40.0x6
Oracon	T38.4x1	T38.4x2	T38.4x3	T38.4x4	T38.4x5	T38.4x6

Substance	External Cause (T-Code)					
	Poisoning, Accidental (Unintentional)	Poisoning, Intentional Self-Harm	Poisoning, Assault	Poisoning, Undetermined	Adverse Effect	Underdosing
Oragrafin	T50.8x1	T50.8x2	T50.8x3	T50.8x4	T50.8x5	T50.8x6
Oral contraceptives	T38.4x1	T38.4x2	T38.4x3	T38.4x4	T38.4x5	T38.4x6
Oral rehydration salts	T50.3x1	T50.3x2	T50.3x3	T50.3x4	T50.3x5	T50.3x6
Orazamide	T50.991	T50.992	T50.993	T50.994	T50.995	T50.996
Orciprenaline	T48.291	T48.292	T48.293	T48.294	T48.295	T48.296
Organidin	T48.4x1	T48.4x2	T48.4x3	T48.4x4	T48.4x5	T48.4x6
Organonitrate NEC	T46.3x1	T46.3x2	T46.3x3	T46.3x4	T46.3x5	T46.3x6
Organophosphates	T60.0x1	T60.0x2	T60.0x3	T60.0x4	—	—
Orimune	T50.B91	T50.B92	T50.B93	T50.B94	T50.B95	T50.B96
Orinase	T38.3x1	T38.3x2	T38.3x3	T38.3x4	T38.3x5	T38.3x6
Ormeloxifene	T38.6x1	T38.6x2	T38.6x3	T38.6x4	T38.6x5	T38.6x6
Ornidazole	T37.3x1	T37.3x2	T37.3x3	T37.3x4	T37.3x5	T37.3x6
Ornithine aspartate	T50.991	T50.992	T50.993	T50.994	T50.995	T50.996
Ornoprostil	T47.1x1	T47.1x2	T47.1x3	T47.1x4	T47.1x5	T47.1x6
Orphenadrine (hydrochloride)	T42.8x1	T42.8x2	T42.8x3	T42.8x4	T42.8x5	T42.8x6
Ortal (sodium)	T42.3x1	T42.3x2	T42.3x3	T42.3x4	T42.3x5	T42.3x6
Orthoboric acid	T49.0x1	T49.0x2	T49.0x3	T49.0x4	T49.0x5	T49.0x6
ENT agent	T49.6x1	T49.6x2	T49.6x3	T49.6x4	T49.6x5	T49.6x6
ophthalmic preparation	T49.5x1	T49.5x2	T49.5x3	T49.5x4	T49.5x5	T49.5x6
Orthocaine	T41.3x1	T41.3x2	T41.3x3	T41.3x4	T41.3x5	T41.3x6
Orthodichlorobenzene	T53.7x1	T53.7x2	T53.7x3	T53.7x4	—	—
Ortho-Novum	T38.4x1	T38.4x2	T38.4x3	T38.4x4	T38.4x5	T38.4x6
Orthotolidine (reagent)	T54.2x1	T54.2x2	T54.2x3	T54.2x4	—	—
Osmic acid (liquid)	T54.2x1	T54.2x2	T54.2x3	T54.2x4	—	—
fumes	T54.2x1	T54.2x2	T54.2x3	T54.2x4	—	—
Osmotic diuretics	T50.2x1	T50.2x2	T50.2x3	T50.2x4	T50.2x5	T50.2x6
Otilonium bromide	T44.3x1	T44.3x2	T44.3x3	T44.3x4	T44.3x5	T44.3x6
Ouabain(e)	T46.0x1	T46.0x2	T46.0x3	T46.0x4	T46.0x5	T46.0x6
Ovarian						
hormone	T38.5x1	T38.5x2	T38.5x3	T38.5x4	T38.5x5	T38.5x6
stimulant	T38.5x1	T38.5x2	T38.5x3	T38.5x4	T38.5x5	T38.5x6
Ovral	T38.4x1	T38.4x2	T38.4x3	T38.4x4	T38.4x5	T38.4x6
Ovulen	T38.4x1	T38.4x2	T38.4x3	T38.4x4	T38.4x5	T38.4x6
Oxacillin	T36.0x1	T36.0x2	T36.0x3	T36.0x4	T36.0x5	T36.0x6
Oxalic acid	T54.2x1	T54.2x2	T54.2x3	T54.2x4	—	—
ammonium salt	T50.991	T50.992	T50.993	T50.994	T50.995	T50.996
Oxamniquine	T37.4x1	T37.4x2	T37.4x3	T37.4x4	T37.4x5	T37.4x6
Oxanamide	T43.591	T43.592	T43.593	T43.594	T43.595	T43.596
Oxandrolone	T38.7x1	T38.7x2	T38.7x3	T38.7x4	T38.7x5	T38.7x6
Oxantel	T37.4x1	T37.4x2	T37.4x3	T37.4x4	T37.4x5	T37.4x6

Substance	External Cause (T-Code)					
	Poisoning, Accidental (Unintentional)	Poisoning, Intentional Self-Harm	Poisoning, Assault	Poisoning, Undetermined	Adverse Effect	Underdosing
Oxapium iodide	T44.3x1	T44.3x2	T44.3x3	T44.3x4	T44.3x5	T44.3x6
Oxaprotiline	T43.021	T43.022	T43.023	T43.024	T43.025	T43.026
Oxaprozin	T39.311	T39.312	T39.313	T39.314	T39.315	T39.316
Oxatomide	T45.0x1	T45.0x2	T45.0x3	T45.0x4	T45.0x5	T45.0x6
Oxazepam	T42.4x1	T42.4x2	T42.4x3	T42.4x4	T42.4x5	T42.4x6
Oxazimedrine	T50.5x1	T50.5x2	T50.5x3	T50.5x4	T50.5x5	T50.5x6
Oxazolam	T42.4x1	T42.4x2	T42.4x3	T42.4x4	T42.4x5	T42.4x6
Oxazolidine derivatives	T42.2x1	T42.2x2	T42.2x3	T42.2x4	T42.2x5	T42.2x6
Ox bile extract	T47.5x1	T47.5x2	T47.5x3	T47.5x4	T47.5x5	T47.5x6
Oxcarbazepine	T42.1x1	T42.1x2	T42.1x3	T42.1x4	T42.1x5	T42.1x6
Oxedrine	T44.4x1	T44.4x2	T44.4x3	T44.4x4	T44.4x5	T44.4x6
Oxeladin (citrate)	T48.3x1	T48.3x2	T48.3x3	T48.3x4	T48.3x5	T48.3x6
Oxendolone	T38.5x1	T38.5x2	T38.5x3	T38.5x4	T38.5x5	T38.5x6
Oxetacaine	T41.3x1	T41.3x2	T41.3x3	T41.3x4	T41.3x5	T41.3x6
Oxethazine	T41.3x1	T41.3x2	T41.3x3	T41.3x4	T41.3x5	T41.3x6
Oxetorone	T39.8x1	T39.8x2	T39.8x3	T39.8x4	T39.8x5	T39.8x6
Oxiconazole	T49.0x1	T49.0x2	T49.0x3	T49.0x4	T49.0x5	T49.0x6
Oxidizing agent NEC	T54.91	T54.92	T54.93	T54.94	—	—
Oxipurinol	T50.4x1	T50.4x2	T50.4x3	T50.4x4	T50.4x5	T50.4x6
Oxitriptan	T43.291	T43.292	T43.293	T43.294	T43.295	T43.296
Oxitropium bromide	T48.6x1	T48.6x2	T48.6x3	T48.6x4	T48.6x5	T48.6x6
Oxodipine	T46.1x1	T46.1x2	T46.1x3	T46.1x4	T46.1x5	T46.1x6
Oxolamine	T48.3x1	T48.3x2	T48.3x3	T48.3x4	T48.3x5	T48.3x6
Oxolinic acid	T37.8x1	T37.8x2	T37.8x3	T37.8x4	T37.8x5	T37.8x6
Oxomemazine	T43.3x1	T43.3x2	T43.3x3	T43.3x4	T43.3x5	T43.3x6
Oxophenarsine	T37.3x1	T37.3x2	T37.3x3	T37.3x4	T37.3x5	T37.3x6
Oxprenolol	T44.7x1	T44.7x2	T44.7x3	T44.7x4	T44.7x5	T44.7x6
Oxsoralen	T49.3x1	T49.3x2	T49.3x3	T49.3x4	T49.3x5	T49.3x6
Oxtriphylline	T48.6x1	T48.6x2	T48.6x3	T48.6x4	T48.6x5	T48.6x6
Oxybate sodium	T41.291	T41.292	T41.293	T41.294	T41.295	T41.296
Oxybuprocaine	T41.3x1	T41.3x2	T41.3x3	T41.3x4	T41.3x5	T41.3x6
Oxybutynin	T44.3x1	T44.3x2	T44.3x3	T44.3x4	T44.3x5	T44.3x6
Oxychlorosene	T49.0x1	T49.0x2	T49.0x3	T49.0x4	T49.0x5	T49.0x6
Oxycodone	T40.2x1	T40.2x2	T40.2x3	T40.2x4	T40.2x5	T40.2x6
Oxyfedrine	T46.3x1	T46.3x2	T46.3x3	T46.3x4	T46.3x5	T46.3x6
Oxygen	T41.5x1	T41.5x2	T41.5x3	T41.5x4	T41.5x5	T41.5x6
Oxylone	T49.0x1	T49.0x2	T49.0x3	T49.0x4	T49.0x5	T49.0x6
ophthalmic preparation	T49.5x1	T49.5x2	T49.5x3	T49.5x4	T49.5x5	T49.5x6
Oxymesterone	T38.7x1	T38.7x2	T38.7x3	T38.7x4	T38.7x5	T38.7x6
Oxymetazoline	T48.5x1	T48.5x2	T48.5x3	T48.5x4	T48.5x5	T48.5x6

Substance	External Cause (T-Code)					
	Poisoning, Accidental (Unintentional)	Poisoning, Intentional Self-Harm	Poisoning, Assault	Poisoning, Undetermined	Adverse Effect	Underdosing
Oxymetholone	T38.7x1	T38.7x2	T38.7x3	T38.7x4	T38.7x5	T38.7x6
Oxymorphone	T40.2x1	T40.2x2	T40.2x3	T40.2x4	T40.2x5	T40.2x6
Oxypertine	T43.591	T43.592	T43.593	T43.594	T43.595	T43.596
Oxyphenbutazone	T39.2x1	T39.2x2	T39.2x3	T39.2x4	T39.2x5	T39.2x6
Oxyphencyclimine	T44.3x1	T44.3x2	T44.3x3	T44.3x4	T44.3x5	T44.3x6
Oxyphenisatine	T47.2x1	T47.2x2	T47.2x3	T47.2x4	T47.2x5	T47.2x6
Oxyphenonium bromide	T44.3x1	T44.3x2	T44.3x3	T44.3x4	T44.3x5	T44.3x6
Oxypolygelatin	T45.8x1	T45.8x2	T45.8x3	T45.8x4	T45.8x5	T45.8x6
Oxyquinoline (derivatives)	T37.8x1	T37.8x2	T37.8x3	T37.8x4	T37.8x5	T37.8x6
Oxytetracycline	T36.4x1	T36.4x2	T36.4x3	T36.4x4	T36.4x5	T36.4x6
Oxytocic drug NEC	T48.0x1	T48.0x2	T48.0x3	T48.0x4	T48.0x5	T48.0x6
Oxytocin (synthetic)	T48.0x1	T48.0x2	T48.0x3	T48.0x4	T48.0x5	T48.0x6
Ozone	T59.891	T59.892	T59.893	T59.894	—	—
PABA	T49.3x1	T49.3x2	T49.3x3	T49.3x4	T49.3x5	T49.3x6
Packed red cells	T45.8x1	T45.8x2	T45.8x3	T45.8x4	T45.8x5	T45.8x6
Padimate	T49.3x1	T49.3x2	T49.3x3	T49.3x4	T49.3x5	T49.3x6
Paint NEC	T65.6x1	T65.6x2	T65.6x3	T65.6x4	—	—
cleaner	T52.91	T52.92	T52.93	T52.94	—	—
fumes NEC	T59.891	T59.892	T59.893	T59.894	—	—
lead (fumes)	T56.0x1	T56.0x2	T56.0x3	T56.0x4	—	—
solvent NEC	T52.8x1	T52.8x2	T52.8x3	T52.8x4	—	—
stripper	T52.8x1	T52.8x2	T52.8x3	T52.8x4	—	—
Palfium	T40.2x1	T40.2x2	T40.2x3	T40.2x4	T40.2x5	T40.2x6
Palm kernel oil	T50.991	T50.992	T50.993	T50.994	T50.995	T50.996
Paludrine	T37.2x1	T37.2x2	T37.2x3	T37.2x4	T37.2x5	T37.2x6
PAM (pralidoxime)	T50.6x1	T50.6x2	T50.6x3	T50.6x4	T50.6x5	T50.6x6
Pamaquine (naphthoute)	T37.2x1	T37.2x2	T37.2x3	T37.2x4	T37.2x5	T37.2x6
Panadol	T39.1x1	T39.1x2	T39.1x3	T39.1x4	T39.1x5	T39.1x6
Pancreatic						
digestive secretion stimulant	T47.8x1	T47.8x2	T47.8x3	T47.8x4	T47.8x5	T47.8x6
dornase	T45.3x1	T45.3x2	T45.3x3	T45.3x4	T45.3x5	T45.3x6
Pancreatin	T47.5x1	T47.5x2	T47.5x3	T47.5x4	T47.5x5	T47.5x6
Pancrelipase	T47.5x1	T47.5x2	T47.5x3	T47.5x4	T47.5x5	T47.5x6
Pancuronium (bromide)	T48.1x1	T48.1x2	T48.1x3	T48.1x4	T48.1x5	T48.1x6
Pangamic acid	T45.2x1	T45.2x2	T45.2x3	T45.2x4	T45.2x5	T45.2x6
Panthenol	T45.2x1	T45.2x2	T45.2x3	T45.2x4	T45.2x5	T45.2x6
topical	T49.8x1	T49.8x2	T49.8x3	T49.8x4	T49.8x5	T49.8x6
Pantopon	T40.0x1	T40.0x2	T40.0x3	T40.0x4	T40.0x5	T40.0x6
Pantothenic acid	T45.2x1	T45.2x2	T45.2x3	T45.2x4	T45.2x5	T45.2x6
Panwarfin	T45.511	T45.512	T45.513	T45.514	T45.515	T45.516

Substance	Poisoning, Accidental (Unintentional)	Poisoning, Intentional Self-Harm	Poisoning, Assault	Poisoning, Undetermined	Adverse Effect	Underdosing
			External Cause (T-Code)			
Papain	T47.5x1	T47.5x2	T47.5x3	T47.5x4	T47.5x5	T47.5x6
digestant	T47.5x1	T47.5x2	T47.5x3	T47.5x4	T47.5x5	T47.5x6
Papaveretum	T40.0x1	T40.0x2	T40.0x3	T40.0x4	T40.0x5	T40.0x6
Papaverine	T44.3x1	T44.3x2	T44.3x3	T44.3x4	T44.3x5	T44.3x6
Para-acetamidophenol	T39.1x1	T39.1x2	T39.1x3	T39.1x4	T39.1x5	T39.1x6
Para-aminobenzoic acid	T49.3x1	T49.3x2	T49.3x3	T49.3x4	T49.3x5	T49.3x6
Para-aminophenol derivatives	T39.1x1	T39.1x2	T39.1x3	T39.1x4	T39.1x5	T39.1x6
Para-aminosalicylic acid	T37.1x1	T37.1x2	T37.1x3	T37.1x4	T37.1x5	T37.1x6
Paracetaldehyde	T42.6x1	T42.6x2	T42.6x3	T42.6x4	T42.6x5	T42.6x6
Paracetamol	T39.1x1	T39.1x2	T39.1x3	T39.1x4	T39.1x5	T39.1x6
Parachlorophenol (camphorated)	T49.0x1	T49.0x2	T49.0x3	T49.0x4	T49.0x5	T49.0x6
Paracodin	T40.2x1	T40.2x2	T40.2x3	T40.2x4	T40.2x5	T40.2x6
Paradione	T42.2x1	T42.2x2	T42.2x3	T42.2x4	T42.2x5	T42.2x6
Paraffin(s) (wax)	T52.0x1	T52.0x2	T52.0x3	T52.0x4	—	—
liquid (medicinal)	T47.4x1	T47.4x2	T47.4x3	T47.4x4	T47.4x5	T47.4x6
nonmedicinal	T52.0x1	T52.0x2	T52.0x3	T52.0x4	—	—
Paraformaldehyde	T60.3x1	T60.3x2	T60.3x3	T60.3x4	—	—
Paraldehyde	T42.6x1	T42.6x2	T42.6x3	T42.6x4	T42.6x5	T42.6x6
Paramethadione	T42.2x1	T42.2x2	T42.2x3	T42.2x4	T42.2x5	T42.2x6
Paramethasone	T38.0x1	T38.0x2	T38.0x3	T38.0x4	T38.0x5	T38.0x6
acetate	T49.0x1	T49.0x2	T49.0x3	T49.0x4	T49.0x5	T49.0x6
Paraoxon	T60.0x1	T60.0x2	T60.0x3	T60.0x4	—	—
Paraquat	T60.3x1	T60.3x2	T60.3x3	T60.3x4	—	—
Parasympatholytic NEC	T44.3x1	T44.3x2	T44.3x3	T44.3x4	T44.3x5	T44.3x6
Parasympathomimetic drug NEC	T44.1x1	T44.1x2	T44.1x3	T44.1x4	T44.1x5	T44.1x6
Parathion	T60.0x1	T60.0x2	T60.0x3	T60.0x4	—	—
Parathormone	T50.991	T50.992	T50.993	T50.994	T50.995	T50.996
Parathyroid extract	T50.991	T50.992	T50.993	T50.994	T50.995	T50.996
Paratyphoid vaccine	T50.A91	T50.A92	T50.A93	T50.A94	T50.A95	T50.A96
Paredrine	T44.4x1	T44.4x2	T44.4x3	T44.4x4	T44.4x5	T44.4x6
Paregoric	T40.0x1	T40.0x2	T40.0x3	T40.0x4	T40.0x5	T40.0x6
Pargyline	T46.5x1	T46.5x2	T46.5x3	T46.5x4	T46.5x5	T46.5x6
Paris green	T57.0x1	T57.0x2	T57.0x3	T57.0x4	—	—
insecticide	T57.0x1	T57.0x2	T57.0x3	T57.0x4	—	—
Parnate	T43.1x1	T43.1x2	T43.1x3	T43.1x4	T43.1x5	T43.1x6
Paromomycin	T36.5x1	T36.5x2	T36.5x3	T36.5x4	T36.5x5	T36.5x6
Paroxypropione	T45.1x1	T45.1x2	T45.1x3	T45.1x4	T45.1x5	T45.1x6
Parzone	T40.2x1	T40.2x2	T40.2x3	T40.2x4	T40.2x5	T40.2x6
PAS	T37.1x1	T37.1x2	T37.1x3	T37.1x4	T37.1x5	T37.1x6
Pasiniazid	T37.1x1	T37.1x2	T37.1x3	T37.1x4	T37.1x5	T37.1x6

Substance	External Cause (T-Code)					
	Poisoning, Accidental (Unintentional)	Poisoning, Intentional Self-Harm	Poisoning, Assault	Poisoning, Undetermined	Adverse Effect	Underdosing
PBB (polybrominated biphenyls)	T65.891	T65.892	T65.893	T65.894	—	—
PCB	T65.891	T65.892	T65.893	T65.894	—	—
PCP (pentachlorophenol)	T60.1x1	T60.1x2	T60.1x3	T60.1x4	—	—
fungicide	T60.3x1	T60.3x2	T60.3x3	T60.3x4	—	—
herbicide	T60.3x1	T60.3x2	T60.3x3	T60.3x4	—	—
insecticide	T60.1x1	T60.1x2	T60.1x3	T60.1x4	—	—
phencyclidine	T40.991	T40.992	T40.993	T40.994	T40.995	T40.996
Peach kernel oil (emulsion)	T47.4x1	T47.4x2	T47.4x3	T47.4x4	T47.4x5	T47.4x6
Peanut oil (emulsion) NEC	T47.4x1	T47.4x2	T47.4x3	T47.4x4	T47.4x5	T47.4x6
topical	T49.3x1	T49.3x2	T49.3x3	T49.3x4	T49.3x5	T49.3x6
Pearly Gates (morning glory seeds)	T40.991	T40.992	T40.993	T40.994	T40.995	T40.996
Pecazine	T43.3x1	T43.3x2	T43.3x3	T43.3x4	T43.3x5	T43.3x6
Pectin	T47.6x1	T47.6x2	T47.6x3	T47.6x4	T47.6x5	T47.6x6
Pefloxacin	T37.8x1	T37.8x2	T37.8x3	T37.8x4	T37.8x5	T37.8x6
Pegademase, bovine	T50.Z91	T50.Z92	T50.Z93	T50.Z94	T50.Z95	T50.Z96
Pelletierine tannate	T37.4x1	T37.4x2	T37.4x3	T37.4x4	T37.4x5	T37.4x6
Pemirolast (potassium)	T48.6x1	T48.6x2	T48.6x3	T48.6x4	T48.6x5	T48.6x6
Pemoline	T50.7x1	T50.7x2	T50.7x3	T50.7x4	T50.7x5	T50.7x6
Pempidine	T44.2x1	T44.2x2	T44.2x3	T44.2x4	T44.2x5	T44.2x6
Penamecillin	T36.0x1	T36.0x2	T36.0x3	T36.0x4	T36.0x5	T36.0x6
Penbutolol	T44.7x1	T44.7x2	T44.7x3	T44.7x4	T44.7x5	T44.7x6
Penethamate	T36.0x1	T36.0x2	T36.0x3	T36.0x4	T36.0x5	T36.0x6
Penfluridol	T43.591	T43.592	T43.593	T43.594	T43.595	T43.596
Penflutizide	T50.2x1	T50.2x2	T50.2x3	T50.2x4	T50.2x5	T50.2x6
Pengitoxin	T46.0x1	T46.0x2	T46.0x3	T46.0x4	T46.0x5	T46.0x6
Penicillamine	T50.6x1	T50.6x2	T50.6x3	T50.6x4	T50.6x5	T50.6x6
Penicillin (any)	T36.0x1	T36.0x2	T36.0x3	T36.0x4	T36.0x5	T36.0x6
Penicillinase	T45.3x1	T45.3x2	T45.3x3	T45.3x4	T45.3x5	T45.3x6
Penicilloyl polylysine	T50.8x1	T50.8x2	T50.8x3	T50.8x4	T50.8x5	T50.8x6
Penimepicycline	T36.4x1	T36.4x2	T36.4x3	T36.4x4	T36.4x5	T36.4x6
Pentachloroethane	T53.6x1	T53.6x2	T53.6x3	T53.6x4	—	—
Pentachloronaphthalene	T53.7x1	T53.7x2	T53.7x3	T53.7x4	—	—
Pentachlorophenol (pesticide)	T60.3x1	T60.3x2	T60.3x3	T60.3x4	—	—
herbicide	T60.3x1	T60.3x2	T60.3x3	T60.3x4	—	—
insecticide	T60.1x1	T60.1x2	T60.1x3	T60.1x4	—	—
Pentaerythritol tetranitrate	T46.3x1	T46.3x2	T46.3x3	T46.3x4	T46.3x5	T46.3x6
Pentaerythritol	T46.3x1	T46.3x2	T46.3x3	T46.3x4	T46.3x5	T46.3x6
chloral	T42.6x1	T42.6x2	T42.6x3	T42.6x4	T42.6x5	T42.6x6
tetranitrate NEC	T46.3x1	T46.3x2	T46.3x3	T46.3x4	T46.3x5	T46.3x6

Substance	External Cause (T-Code)					
	Poisoning, Accidental (Unintentional)	Poisoning, Intentional Self-Harm	Poisoning, Assault	Poisoning, Undetermined	Adverse Effect	Underdosing
Pentaerythrityl tetranitrate	T46.3x1	T46.3x2	T46.3x3	T46.3x4	T46.3x5	T46.3x6
Pentagastrin	T50.8x1	T50.8x2	T50.8x3	T50.8x4	T50.8x5	T50.8x6
Pentalin	T53.6x1	T53.6x2	T53.6x3	T53.6x4	—	—
Pentamethonium bromide	T44.2x1	T44.2x2	T44.2x3	T44.2x4	T44.2x5	T44.2x6
Pentamidine	T37.3x1	T37.3x2	T37.3x3	T37.3x4	T37.3x5	T37.3x6
Pentanol	T51.3x1	T51.3x2	T51.3x3	T51.3x4	—	—
Pentapyrrolinium (bitartrate)	T44.2x1	T44.2x2	T44.2x3	T44.2x4	T44.2x5	T44.2x6
Pentaquine	T37.2x1	T37.2x2	T37.2x3	T37.2x4	T37.2x5	T37.2x6
Pentazocine	T40.4x1	T40.4x2	T40.4x3	T40.4x4	T40.4x5	T40.4x6
Pentetrazole	T50.7x1	T50.7x2	T50.7x3	T50.7x4	T50.7x5	T50.7x6
Penthienate bromide	T44.3x1	T44.3x2	T44.3x3	T44.3x4	T44.3x5	T44.3x6
Pentifylline	T46.7x1	T46.7x2	T46.7x3	T46.7x4	T46.7x5	T46.7x6
Pentobarbital	T42.3x1	T42.3x2	T42.3x3	T42.3x4	T42.3x5	T42.3x6
sodium	T42.3x1	T42.3x2	T42.3x3	T42.3x4	T42.3x5	T42.3x6
Pentobarbitone	T42.3x1	T42.3x2	T42.3x3	T42.3x4	T42.3x5	T42.3x6
Pentolonium tartrate	T44.2x1	T44.2x2	T44.2x3	T44.2x4	T44.2x5	T44.2x6
Pentosan polysulfate (sodium)	T45.511	T45.512	T45.513	T45.514	T45.515	T45.516
Pentostatin	T45.1x1	T45.1x2	T45.1x3	T45.1x4	T45.1x5	T45.1x6
Pentothal	T41.1x1	T41.1x2	T41.1x3	T41.1x4	T41.1x5	T41.1x6
Pentoxifylline	T46.7x1	T46.7x2	T46.7x3	T46.7x4	T46.7x5	T46.7x6
Pentoxyverine	T48.3x1	T48.3x2	T48.3x3	T48.3x4	T48.3x5	T48.3x6
Pentrinat	T46.3x1	T46.3x2	T46.3x3	T46.3x4	T46.3x5	T46.3x6
Pentylenetetrazole	T50.7x1	T50.7x2	T50.7x3	T50.7x4	T50.7x5	T50.7x6
Pentylsalicylamide	T37.1x1	T37.1x2	T37.1x3	T37.1x4	T37.1x5	T37.1x6
Pentymal	T42.3x1	T42.3x2	T42.3x3	T42.3x4	T42.3x5	T42.3x6
Peplomycin	T45.1x1	T45.1x2	T45.1x3	T45.1x4	T45.1x5	T45.1x6
Peppermint (oil)	T47.5x1	T47.5x2	T47.5x3	T47.5x4	T47.5x5	T47.5x6
Pepsin	T47.5x1	T47.5x2	T47.5x3	T47.5x4	T47.5x5	T47.5x6
digestant	T47.5x1	T47.5x2	T47.5x3	T47.5x4	T47.5x5	T47.5x6
Pepstatin	T47.1x1	T47.1x2	T47.1x3	T47.1x4	T47.1x5	T47.1x6
Peptavlon	T50.8x1	T50.8x2	T50.8x3	T50.8x4	T50.8x5	T50.8x6
Perazine	T43.3x1	T43.3x2	T43.3x3	T43.3x4	T43.3x5	T43.3x6
Percaine (spinal)	T41.3x1	T41.3x2	T41.3x3	T41.3x4	T41.3x5	T41.3x6
topical (surface)	T41.3x1	T41.3x2	T41.3x3	T41.3x4	T41.3x5	T41.3x6
Perchloroethylene	T53.3x1	T53.3x2	T53.3x3	T53.3x4	—	—
vapor	T53.3x1	T53.3x2	T53.3x3	T53.3x4	—	—
medicinal	T37.4x1	T37.4x2	T37.4x3	T37.4x4	T37.4x5	T37.4x6
Percodan	T40.2x1	T40.2x2	T40.2x3	T40.2x4	T40.2x5	T40.2x6
Percogesic	T40.2x1	T40.2x2	T40.2x3	T40.2x4	T40.2x5	T40.2x6
Percorten	T38.0x1	T38.0x2	T38.0x3	T38.0x4	T38.0x5	T38.0x6
Pergolide	T42.8x1	T42.8x2	T42.8x3	T42.8x4	T42.8x5	T42.8x6

Substance	External Cause (T-Code)					
	Poisoning, Accidental (Unintentional)	Poisoning, Intentional Self-Harm	Poisoning, Assault	Poisoning, Undetermined	Adverse Effect	Underdosing
Pergonal	T38.811	T38.812	T38.813	T38.814	T38.815	T38.816
Perhexilene	T46.3x1	T46.3x2	T46.3x3	T46.3x4	T46.3x5	T46.3x6
Perhexiline (maleate)	T46.3x1	T46.3x2	T46.3x3	T46.3x4	T46.3x5	T46.3x6
Periactin	T45.0x1	T45.0x2	T45.0x3	T45.0x4	T45.0x5	T45.0x6
Periciazine	T43.3x1	T43.3x2	T43.3x3	T43.3x4	T43.3x5	T43.3x6
Periclor	T42.6x1	T42.6x2	T42.6x3	T42.6x4	T42.6x5	T42.6x6
Perindopril	T46.4x1	T46.4x2	T46.4x3	T46.4x4	T46.4x5	T46.4x6
Perisoxal	T39.8x1	T39.8x2	T39.8x3	T39.8x4	T39.8x5	T39.8x6
Peritrate	T46.3x1	T46.3x2	T46.3x3	T46.3x4	T46.3x5	T46.3x6
Peritoneal dialysis solution	T50.3x1	T50.3x2	T50.3x3	T50.3x4	T50.3x5	T50.3x6
Perlapine	T42.4x1	T42.4x2	T42.4x3	T42.4x4	T42.4x5	T42.4x6
Permanganate	T65.891	T65.892	T65.893	T65.894	—	—
Permethrin	T60.1x1	T60.1x2	T60.1x3	T60.1x4	—	—
Pernocton	T42.3x1	T42.3x2	T42.3x3	T42.3x4	T42.3x5	T42.3x6
Pernoston	T42.3x1	T42.3x2	T42.3x3	T42.3x4	T42.3x5	T42.3x6
Peronin(e)	T40.2x1	T40.2x2	T40.2x3	T40.2x4	T40.2x5	T40.2x6
Perphenazine	T43.3x1	T43.3x2	T43.3x3	T43.3x4	T43.3x5	T43.3x6
Pertofrane	T43.011	T43.012	T43.013	T43.014	T43.015	T43.016
Pertussis vaccine	T50.A11	T50.A12	T50.A13	T50.A14	T50.A15	T50.A16
Pertussis						
immune serum (human)	T50.Z11	T50.Z12	T50.Z13	T50.Z14	T50.Z15	T50.Z16
vaccine (with diphtheria toxoid) (with tetanus toxoid)	T50.A11	T50.A12	T50.A13	T50.A14	T50.A15	T50.A16
Peruvian balsam	T49.0x1	T49.0x2	T49.0x3	T49.0x4	T49.0x5	T49.0x6
Peruvoside	T46.0x1	T46.0x2	T46.0x3	T46.0x4	T46.0x5	T46.0x6
Pesticide (dust) (fumes) (vapor) NEC	T60.91	T60.92	T60.93	T60.94	—	—
arsenic	T57.0x1	T57.0x2	T57.0x3	T57.0x4	—	—
chlorinated	T60.1x1	T60.1x2	T60.1x3	T60.1x4	—	—
cyanide	T65.0x1	T65.0x2	T65.0x3	T65.0x4	—	—
kerosene	T52.0x1	T52.0x2	T52.0x3	T52.0x4	—	—
mixture (of compounds)	T60.91	T60.92	T60.93	T60.94	—	—
naphthalene	T60.2x1	T60.2x2	T60.2x3	T60.2x4	—	—
organochlorine (compounds)	T60.1x1	T60.1x2	T60.1x3	T60.1x4	—	—
petroleum (distillate) (products) NEC	T52.0x1	T52.0x2	T52.0x3	T52.0x4	—	—
specified ingredient NEC	T60.8x1	T60.8x2	T60.8x3	T60.8x4	—	—
strychnine	T65.1x1	T65.1x2	T65.1x3	T65.1x4	—	—
thallium	T60.4x1	T60.4x2	T60.4x3	T60.4x4	—	—
Pethidine	T40.4x1	T40.4x2	T40.4x3	T40.4x4	T40.4x5	T40.4x6
Petrichloral	T42.6x1	T42.6x2	T42.6x3	T42.6x4	T42.6x5	T42.6x6
Petrol	T52.0x1	T52.0x2	T52.0x3	T52.0x4	—	—
vapor	T52.0x1	T52.0x2	T52.0x3	T52.0x4	—	—

Substance	Poisoning, Accidental (Unintentional)	Poisoning, Intentional Self-Harm	Poisoning, Assault	Poisoning, Undetermined	Adverse Effect	Underdosing
Petrolatum	T49.3x1	T49.3x2	T49.3x3	T49.3x4	T49.3x5	T49.3x6
hydrophilic	T49.3x1	T49.3x2	T49.3x3	T49.3x4	T49.3x5	T49.3x6
liquid	T47.4x1	T47.4x2	T47.4x3	T47.4x4	T47.4x5	T47.4x6
topical	T49.3x1	T49.3x2	T49.3x3	T49.3x4	T49.3x5	T49.3x6
nonmedicinal	T52.0x1	T52.0x2	T52.0x3	T52.0x4	—	—
red veterinary	T49.3x1	T49.3x2	T49.3x3	T49.3x4	T49.3x5	T49.3x6
white	T49.3x1	T49.3x2	T49.3x3	T49.3x4	T49.3x5	T49.3x6
Petroleum (products) NEC	T52.0x1	T52.0x2	T52.0x3	T52.0x4	—	—
benzine(s) - *see* Ligroin						
ether - *see* Ligroin						
jelly - *see* Petrolatum						
naphtha - *see* Ligroin						
pesticide	T60.8x1	T60.8x2	T60.8x3	T60.8x4	—	—
solids	T52.0x1	T52.0x2	T52.0x3	T52.0x4	—	—
solvents	T52.0x1	T52.0x2	T52.0x3	T52.0x4	—	—
vapor	T52.0x1	T52.0x2	T52.0x3	T52.0x4	—	—
Peyote	T40.991	T40.992	T40.993	T40.994	T40.995	T40.996
Phanodorm, phanodorn	T42.3x1	T42.3x2	T42.3x3	T42.3x4	T42.3x5	T42.3x6
Phanquinone	T37.3x1	T37.3x2	T37.3x3	T37.3x4	T37.3x5	T37.3x6
Phanquone	T37.3x1	T37.3x2	T37.3x3	T37.3x4	T37.3x5	T37.3x6
Pharmaceutical						
adjunct NEC	T50.901	T50.902	T50.903	T50.904	T50.905	T50.906
excipient NEC	T50.901	T50.902	T50.903	T50.904	T50.905	T50.906
sweetener	T50.901	T50.902	T50.903	T50.904	T50.905	T50.906
viscous agent	T50.901	T50.902	T50.903	T50.904	T50.905	T50.906
Phemitone	T42.3x1	T42.3x2	T42.3x3	T42.3x4	T42.3x5	T42.3x6
Phenacaine	T41.3x1	T41.3x2	T41.3x3	T41.3x4	T41.3x5	T41.3x6
Phenacemide	T42.6x1	T42.6x2	T42.6x3	T42.6x4	T42.6x5	T42.6x6
Phenacetin	T39.1x1	T39.1x2	T39.1x3	T39.1x4	T39.1x5	T39.1x6
Phenadoxone	T40.2x1	T40.2x2	T40.2x3	T40.2x4	T40.2x5	T40.2x6
Phenaglycodol	T43.591	T43.592	T43.593	T43.594	T43.595	T43.596
Phenantoin	T42.0x1	T42.0x2	T42.0x3	T42.0x4	T42.0x5	T42.0x6
Phenaphthazine reagent	T50.991	T50.992	T50.993	T50.994	T50.995	T50.996
Phenazocine	T40.4x1	T40.4x2	T40.4x3	T40.4x4	T40.4x5	T40.4x6
Phenazone	T39.2x1	T39.2x2	T39.2x3	T39.2x4	T39.2x5	T39.2x6
Phenazopyridine	T37.8x1	T37.8x2	T37.8x3	T37.8x4	T37.8x5	T37.8x6
Phenbenicillin	T36.0x1	T36.0x2	T36.0x3	T36.0x4	T36.0x5	T36.0x6
Phenbutrazate	T50.5x1	T50.5x2	T50.5x3	T50.5x4	T50.5x5	T50.5x6
Phencyclidine	T41.1x1	T41.1x2	T41.1x3	T41.1x4	T41.1x5	T41.1x6
Phendimetrazine	T50.5x1	T50.5x2	T50.5x3	T50.5x4	T50.5x5	T50.5x6

Substance	External Cause (T-Code)					
	Poisoning, Accidental (Unintentional)	Poisoning, Intentional Self-Harm	Poisoning, Assault	Poisoning, Undetermined	Adverse Effect	Underdosing
Phenelzine	T43.1x1	T43.1x2	T43.1x3	T43.1x4	T43.1x5	T43.1x6
Phenemal	T42.3x1	T42.3x2	T42.3x3	T42.3x4	T42.3x5	T42.3x6
Phenergan	T42.6x1	T42.6x2	T42.6x3	T42.6x4	T42.6x5	T42.6x6
Pheneticillin	T36.0x1	T36.0x2	T36.0x3	T36.0x4	T36.0x5	T36.0x6
Pheneturide	T42.6x1	T42.6x2	T42.6x3	T42.6x4	T42.6x5	T42.6x6
Phenformin	T38.3x1	T38.3x2	T38.3x3	T38.3x4	T38.3x5	T38.3x6
Phenglutarimide	T44.3x1	T44.3x2	T44.3x3	T44.3x4	T44.3x5	T44.3x6
Phenicarbazide	T39.8x1	T39.8x2	T39.8x3	T39.8x4	T39.8x5	T39.8x6
Phenindamine	T45.0x1	T45.0x2	T45.0x3	T45.0x4	T45.0x5	T45.0x6
Phenindione	T45.511	T45.512	T45.513	T45.514	T45.515	T45.516
Pheniprazine	T43.1x1	T43.1x2	T43.1x3	T43.1x4	T43.1x5	T43.1x6
Pheniramine	T45.0x1	T45.0x2	T45.0x3	T45.0x4	T45.0x5	T45.0x6
Phenisatin	T47.2x1	T47.2x2	T47.2x3	T47.2x4	T47.2x5	T47.2x6
Phenmetrazine	T50.5x1	T50.5x2	T50.5x3	T50.5x4	T50.5x5	T50.5x6
Phenobal	T42.3x1	T42.3x2	T42.3x3	T42.3x4	T42.3x5	T42.3x6
Phenobarbital	T42.3x1	T42.3x2	T42.3x3	T42.3x4	T42.3x5	T42.3x6
with						
mephenytoin	T42.3x1	T42.3x2	T42.3x3	T42.3x4	T42.3x5	T42.3x6
phenytoin	T42.3x1	T42.3x2	T42.3x3	T42.3x4	T42.3x5	T42.3x6
sodium	T42.3x1	T42.3x2	T42.3x3	T42.3x4	T42.3x5	T42.3x6
Phenobarbitone	T42.3x1	T42.3x2	T42.3x3	T42.3x4	T42.3x5	T42.3x6
Phenobutiodil	T50.8x1	T50.8x2	T50.8x3	T50.8x4	T50.8x5	T50.8x6
Phenoctide	T49.0x1	T49.0x2	T49.0x3	T49.0x4	T49.0x5	T49.0x6
Phenol	T49.0x1	T49.0x2	T49.0x3	T49.0x4	T49.0x5	T49.0x6
disinfectant	T54.0x1	T54.0x2	T54.0x3	T54.0x4	—	—
in oil injection	T46.8x1	T46.8x2	T46.8x3	T46.8x4	T46.8x5	T46.8x6
medicinal	T49.1x1	T49.1x2	T49.1x3	T49.1x4	T49.1x5	T49.1x6
nonmedicinal NEC	T54.0x1	T54.0x2	T54.0x3	T54.0x4	—	—
pesticide	T60.8x1	T60.8x2	T60.8x3	T60.8x4	—	—
red	T50.8x1	T50.8x2	T50.8x3	T50.8x4	T50.8x5	T50.8x6
Phenolic preparation	T49.1x1	T49.1x2	T49.1x3	T49.1x4	T49.1x5	T49.1x6
Phenolphthalein	T47.2x1	T47.2x2	T47.2x3	T47.2x4	T47.2x5	T47.2x6
Phenolsulfonphthalein	T50.8x1	T50.8x2	T50.8x3	T50.8x4	T50.8x5	T50.8x6
Phenomorphan	T40.2x1	T40.2x2	T40.2x3	T40.2x4	T40.2x5	T40.2x6
Phenonyl	T42.3x1	T42.3x2	T42.3x3	T42.3x4	T42.3x5	T42.3x6
Phenoperidine	T40.4x1	T40.4x2	T40.4x3	T40.4x4	T40.4x5	T40.4x6
Phenopyrazone	T46.991	T46.992	T46.993	T46.994	T46.995	T46.996
Phenoquin	T50.4x1	T50.4x2	T50.4x3	T50.4x4	T50.4x5	T50.4x6
Phenothiazine (psychotropic) NEC	T43.3x1	T43.3x2	T43.3x3	T43.3x4	T43.3x5	T43.3x6
insecticide	T60.2x1	T60.2x2	T60.2x3	T60.2x4	—	—

Substance	External Cause (T-Code)					
	Poisoning, Accidental (Unintentional)	Poisoning, Intentional Self-Harm	Poisoning, Assault	Poisoning, Undetermined	Adverse Effect	Underdosing
Phenothrin	T49.0x1	T49.0x2	T49.0x3	T49.0x4	T49.0x5	T49.0x6
Phenoxybenzamine	T46.7x1	T46.7x2	T46.7x3	T46.7x4	T46.7x5	T46.7x6
Phenoxyethanol	T49.0x1	T49.0x2	T49.0x3	T49.0x4	T49.0x5	T49.0x6
Phenoxymethyl penicillin	T36.0x1	T36.0x2	T36.0x3	T36.0x4	T36.0x5	T36.0x6
Phenprobamate	T42.8x1	T42.8x2	T42.8x3	T42.8x4	T42.8x5	T42.8x6
Phenprocoumon	T45.511	T45.512	T45.513	T45.514	T45.515	T45.516
Phensuximide	T42.2x1	T42.2x2	T42.2x3	T42.2x4	T42.2x5	T42.2x6
Phentermine	T50.5x1	T50.5x2	T50.5x3	T50.5x4	T50.5x5	T50.5x6
Phenthicillin	T36.0x1	T36.0x2	T36.0x3	T36.0x4	T36.0x5	T36.0x6
Phentolamine	T46.7x1	T46.7x2	T46.7x3	T46.7x4	T46.7x5	T46.7x6
Phenyl						
butazone	T39.2x1	T39.2x2	T39.2x3	T39.2x4	T39.2x5	T39.2x6
enediamine	T65.3x1	T65.3x2	T65.3x3	T65.3x4	—	—
hydrazine	T65.3x1	T65.3x2	T65.3x3	T65.3x4	—	—
antineoplastic	T45.1x1	T45.1x2	T45.1x3	T45.1x4	T45.1x5	T45.1x6
mercuric compounds - *see* Mercury						
salicylate	T49.3x1	T49.3x2	T49.3x3	T49.3x4	T49.3x5	T49.3x6
Phenylalanine mustard	T45.1x1	T45.1x2	T45.1x3	T45.1x4	T45.1x5	T45.1x6
Phenylbutazone	T39.2x1	T39.2x2	T39.2x3	T39.2x4	T39.2x5	T39.2x6
Phenylenediamine	T65.3x1	T65.3x2	T65.3x3	T65.3x4	—	—
Phenylephrine	T44.4x1	T44.4x2	T44.4x3	T44.4x4	T44.4x5	T44.4x6
Phenylethylbiguanide	T38.3x1	T38.3x2	T38.3x3	T38.3x4	T38.3x5	T38.3x6
Phenylmercuric						
acetate	T49.0x1	T49.0x2	T49.0x3	T49.0x4	T49.0x5	T49.0x6
borate	T49.0x1	T49.0x2	T49.0x3	T49.0x4	T49.0x5	T49.0x6
nitrate	T49.0x1	T49.0x2	T49.0x3	T49.0x4	T49.0x5	T49.0x6
Phenylmethylbarbitone	T42.3x1	T42.3x2	T42.3x3	T42.3x4	T42.3x5	T42.3x6
Phenylpropanol	T47.5x1	T47.5x2	T47.5x3	T47.5x4	T47.5x5	T47.5x6
Phenylpropanolamine	T44.991	T44.992	T44.993	T44.994	T44.995	T44.996
Phenylsulfthion	T60.0x1	T60.0x2	T60.0x3	T60.0x4	—	—
Phenyltoloxamine	T45.0x1	T45.0x2	T45.0x3	T45.0x4	T45.0x5	T45.0x6
Phenyramidol, phenyramidon	T39.8x1	T39.8x2	T39.8x3	T39.8x4	T39.8x5	T39.8x6
Phenytoin	T42.0x1	T42.0x2	T42.0x3	T42.0x4	T42.0x5	T42.0x6
with Phenobarbital	T42.3x1	T42.3x2	T42.3x3	T42.3x4	T42.3x5	T42.3x6
pHisoHex	T49.2x1	T49.2x2	T49.2x3	T49.2x4	T49.2x5	T49.2x6
Pholcodine	T48.3x1	T48.3x2	T48.3x3	T48.3x4	T48.3x5	T48.3x6
Pholedrine	T46.991	T46.992	T46.993	T46.994	T46.995	T46.996
Phorate	T60.0x1	T60.0x2	T60.0x3	T60.0x4	—	—
Phosdrin	T60.0x1	T60.0x2	T60.0x3	T60.0x4	—	—
Phosfolan	T60.0x1	T60.0x2	T60.0x3	T60.0x4	—	—

Substance	External Cause (T-Code)					
	Poisoning, Accidental (Unintentional)	Poisoning, Intentional Self-Harm	Poisoning, Assault	Poisoning, Undetermined	Adverse Effect	Underdosing
Phosgene (gas)	T59.891	T59.892	T59.893	T59.894	—	—
Phosphamidon	T60.0x1	T60.0x2	T60.0x3	T60.0x4	—	—
Phosphate	T65.891	T65.892	T65.893	T65.894	—	—
laxative	T47.4x1	T47.4x2	T47.4x3	T47.4x4	T47.4x5	T47.4x6
organic	T60.0x1	T60.0x2	T60.0x3	T60.0x4	—	—
solvent	T52.91	T52.92	T52.93	T52.94	—	—
tricresyl	T65.891	T65.892	T65.893	T65.894	—	—
Phosphine	T57.1x1	T57.1x2	T57.1x3	T57.1x4	—	—
fumigant	T57.1x1	T57.1x2	T57.1x3	T57.1x4	—	—
Phospholine	T49.5x1	T49.5x2	T49.5x3	T49.5x4	T49.5x5	T49.5x6
Phosphoric acid	T54.2x1	T54.2x2	T54.2x3	T54.2x4	—	—
Phosphorus (compound) NEC	T57.1x1	T57.1x2	T57.1x3	T57.1x4	—	—
pesticide	T60.0x1	T60.0x2	T60.0x3	T60.0x4	—	—
Phthalates	T65.891	T65.892	T65.893	T65.894	—	—
Phthalic anhydride	T65.891	T65.892	T65.893	T65.894	—	—
Phthalimidoglutarimide	T42.6x1	T42.6x2	T42.6x3	T42.6x4	T42.6x5	T42.6x6
Phthalylsulfathiazole	T37.0x1	T37.0x2	T37.0x3	T37.0x4	T37.0x5	T37.0x6
Phylloquinone	T45.7x1	T45.7x2	T45.7x3	T45.7x4	T45.7x5	T45.7x6
Physeptone	T40.3x1	T40.3x2	T40.3x3	T40.3x4	T40.3x5	T40.3x6
Physostigma venenosum	T62.2x1	T62.2x2	T62.2x3	T62.2x4	—	—
Physostigmine	T49.5x1	T49.5x2	T49.5x3	T49.5x4	T49.5x5	T49.5x6
Phytolacca decandra	T62.2x1	T62.2x2	T62.2x3	T62.2x4	—	—
berries	T62.1x1	T62.1x2	T62.1x3	T62.1x4	—	—
Phytomenadione	T45.7x1	T45.7x2	T45.7x3	T45.7x4	T45.7x5	T45.7x6
Phytonadione	T45.7x1	T45.7x2	T45.7x3	T45.7x4	T45.7x5	T45.7x6
Picoperine	T48.3x1	T48.3x2	T48.3x3	T48.3x4	T48.3x5	T48.3x6
Picosulfate (sodium)	T47.2x1	T47.2x2	T47.2x3	T47.2x4	T47.2x5	T47.2x6
Picric (acid)	T54.2x1	T54.2x2	T54.2x3	T54.2x4	—	—
Picrotoxin	T50.7x1	T50.7x2	T50.7x3	T50.7x4	T50.7x5	T50.7x6
Piketoprofen	T49.0x1	T49.0x2	T49.0x3	T49.0x4	T49.0x5	T49.0x6
Pilocarpine	T44.1x1	T44.1x2	T44.1x3	T44.1x4	T44.1x5	T44.1x6
Pilocarpus (jaborandi) extract	T44.1x1	T44.1x2	T44.1x3	T44.1x4	T44.1x5	T44.1x6
Pilsicainide (hydrochloride)	T46.2x1	T46.2x2	T46.2x3	T46.2x4	T46.2x5	T46.2x6
Pimaricin	T36.7x1	T36.7x2	T36.7x3	T36.7x4	T36.7x5	T36.7x6
Pimeclone	T50.7x1	T50.7x2	T50.7x3	T50.7x4	T50.7x5	T50.7x6
Pimelic ketone	T52.8x1	T52.8x2	T52.8x3	T52.8x4	—	—
Pimethixene	T45.0x1	T45.0x2	T45.0x3	T45.0x4	T45.0x5	T45.0x6
Piminodine	T40.2x1	T40.2x2	T40.2x3	T40.2x4	T40.2x5	T40.2x6
Pimozide	T43.591	T43.592	T43.593	T43.594	T43.595	T43.596
Pinacidil	T46.5x1	T46.5x2	T46.5x3	T46.5x4	T46.5x5	T46.5x6

	External Cause (T-Code)					
Substance	Poisoning, Accidental (Unintentional)	Poisoning, Intentional Self-Harm	Poisoning, Assault	Poisoning, Undetermined	Adverse Effect	Underdosing
Pinaverium bromide	T44.3x1	T44.3x2	T44.3x3	T44.3x4	T44.3x5	T44.3x6
Pinazepam	T42.4x1	T42.4x2	T42.4x3	T42.4x4	T42.4x5	T42.4x6
Pindolol	T44.7x1	T44.7x2	T44.7x3	T44.7x4	T44.7x5	T44.7x6
Pindone	T60.4x1	T60.4x2	T60.4x3	T60.4x4	—	—
Pine oil (disinfectant)	T65.891	T65.892	T65.893	T65.894	—	—
Pinkroot	T37.4x1	T37.4x2	T37.4x3	T37.4x4	T37.4x5	T37.4x6
Pipadone	T40.2x1	T40.2x2	T40.2x3	T40.2x4	T40.2x5	T40.2x6
Pipamazine	T45.0x1	T45.0x2	T45.0x3	T45.0x4	T45.0x5	T45.0x6
Pipamperone	T43.4x1	T43.4x2	T43.4x3	T43.4x4	T43.4x5	T43.4x6
Pipazetate	T48.3x1	T48.3x2	T48.3x3	T48.3x4	T48.3x5	T48.3x6
Pipemidic acid	T37.8x1	T37.8x2	T37.8x3	T37.8x4	T37.8x5	T37.8x6
Pipenzolate bromide	T44.3x1	T44.3x2	T44.3x3	T44.3x4	T44.3x5	T44.3x6
Piperacetazine	T43.3x1	T43.3x2	T43.3x3	T43.3x4	T43.3x5	T43.3x6
Piperacillin	T36.0x1	T36.0x2	T36.0x3	T36.0x4	T36.0x5	T36.0x6
Piperazine	T37.4x1	T37.4x2	T37.4x3	T37.4x4	T37.4x5	T37.4x6
estrone sulfate	T38.5x1	T38.5x2	T38.5x3	T38.5x4	T38.5x5	T38.5x6
Piper cubeba	T62.2x1	T62.2x2	T62.2x3	T62.2x4	—	—
Piperidione	T48.3x1	T48.3x2	T48.3x3	T48.3x4	T48.3x5	T48.3x6
Piperidolate	T44.3x1	T44.3x2	T44.3x3	T44.3x4	T44.3x5	T44.3x6
Piperocaine	T41.3x1	T41.3x2	T41.3x3	T41.3x4	T41.3x5	T41.3x6
infiltration (subcutaneous)	T41.3x1	T41.3x2	T41.3x3	T41.3x4	T41.3x5	T41.3x6
nerve block (peripheral) (plexus)	T41.3x1	T41.3x2	T41.3x3	T41.3x4	T41.3x5	T41.3x6
topical (surface)	T41.3x1	T41.3x2	T41.3x3	T41.3x4	T41.3x5	T41.3x6
Piperonyl butoxide	T60.8x1	T60.8x2	T60.8x3	T60.8x4	—	—
Pipethanate	T44.3x1	T44.3x2	T44.3x3	T44.3x4	T44.3x5	T44.3x6
Pipobroman	T45.1x1	T45.1x2	T45.1x3	T45.1x4	T45.1x5	T45.1x6
Pipofezine	T43.0x1	T43.0x2	T43.0x3	T43.0x4	T43.0x5	T43.0x6
Pipotiazine	T43.3x1	T43.3x2	T43.3x3	T43.3x4	T43.3x5	T43.3x6
Pipoxizine	T45.0x1	T45.0x2	T45.0x3	T45.0x4	T45.0x5	T45.0x6
Pipradrol	T43.691	T43.692	T43.693	T43.694	T43.695	T43.696
Piprinhydrinate	T45.0x1	T45.0x2	T45.0x3	T45.0x4	T45.0x5	T45.0x6
Pirarubicin	T45.1x1	T45.1x2	T45.1x3	T45.1x4	T45.1x5	T45.1x6
Pirazinamide	T37.1x1	T37.1x2	T37.1x3	T37.1x4	T37.1x5	T37.1x6
Pirbuterol	T48.6x1	T48.6x2	T48.6x3	T48.6x4	T48.6x5	T48.6x6
Pirenzepine	T47.1x1	T47.1x2	T47.1x3	T47.1x4	T47.1x5	T47.1x6
Piretanide	T50.1x1	T50.1x2	T50.1x3	T50.1x4	T50.1x5	T50.1x6
Piribedil	T42.8x1	T42.8x2	T42.8x3	T42.8x4	T42.8x5	T42.8x6
Piridoxilate	T46.3x1	T46.3x2	T46.3x3	T46.3x4	T46.3x5	T46.3x6
Piritramide	T40.4x1	T40.4x2	T40.4x3	T40.4x4	T40.4x5	T40.4x6
Pirlindole	T43.0x1	T43.0x2	T43.0x3	T43.0x4	T43.0x5	T43.0x6

Substance	External Cause (T-Code)					
	Poisoning, Accidental (Unintentional)	Poisoning, Intentional Self-Harm	Poisoning, Assault	Poisoning, Undetermined	Adverse Effect	Underdosing
Piromidic acid	T37.8x1	T37.8x2	T37.8x3	T37.8x4	T37.8x5	T37.8x6
Piroxicam	T39.391	T39.392	T39.393	T39.394	T39.395	T39.396
beta-cyclodextrin complex	T39.8x1	T39.8x2	T39.8x3	T39.8x4	T39.8x5	T39.8x6
Pirozadil	T46.6x1	T46.6x2	T46.6x3	T46.6x4	T46.6x5	T46.6x6
Piscidia (bark) (erythrina)	T39.8x1	T39.8x2	T39.8x3	T39.8x4	T39.8x5	T39.8x6
Pitch	T65.891	T65.892	T65.893	T65.894	—	—
Pitkin's solution	T41.3x1	T41.3x2	T41.3x3	T41.3x4	T41.3x5	T41.3x6
Pitocin	T48.0x1	T48.0x2	T48.0x3	T48.0x4	T48.0x5	T48.0x6
Pitressin (tannate)	T38.891	T38.892	T38.893	T38.894	T38.895	T38.896
Pituitary extracts (posterior)	T38.891	T38.892	T38.893	T38.894	T38.895	T38.896
anterior	T38.811	T38.812	T38.813	T38.814	T38.815	T38.816
Pituitrin	T38.891	T38.892	T38.893	T38.894	T38.895	T38.896
Pivampicillin	T36.0x1	T36.0x2	T36.0x3	T36.0x4	T36.0x5	T36.0x6
Pivmecillinam	T36.0x1	T36.0x2	T36.0x3	T36.0x4	T36.0x5	T36.0x6
Placental hormone	T38.891	T38.892	T38.893	T38.894	T38.895	T38.896
Placidyl	T42.6x1	T42.6x2	T42.6x3	T42.6x4	T42.6x5	T42.6x6
Plague vaccine	T50.A91	T50.A92	T50.A93	T50.A94	T50.A95	T50.A96
Plant						
food or fertilizer NEC	T65.891	T65.892	T65.893	T65.894	—	—
containing herbicide	T60.3x1	T60.3x2	T60.3x3	T60.3x4	—	—
noxious, used as food	T62.2x1	T62.2x2	T62.2x3	T62.2x4	—	—
berries	T62.1x1	T62.1x2	T62.1x3	T62.1x4	—	—
seeds	T62.2x1	T62.2x2	T62.2x3	T62.2x4	—	—
specified type NEC	T62.2x1	T62.2x2	T62.2x3	T62.2x4	—	—
Plasma	T45.8x1	T45.8x2	T45.8x3	T45.8x4	T45.8x5	T45.8x6
expander NEC	T45.8x1	T45.8x2	T45.8x3	T45.8x4	T45.8x5	T45.8x6
protein fraction (human)	T45.8x1	T45.8x2	T45.8x3	T45.8x4	T45.8x5	T45.8x6
Plasmanate	T45.8x1	T45.8x2	T45.8x3	T45.8x4	T45.8x5	T45.8x6
Plasminogen (tissue) activator	T45.611	T45.612	T45.613	T45.614	T45.615	T45.616
Plaster dressing	T49.3x1	T49.3x2	T49.3x3	T49.3x4	T49.3x5	T49.3x6
Plastic dressing	T49.3x1	T49.3x2	T49.3x3	T49.3x4	T49.3x5	T49.3x6
Plegicil	T43.3x1	T43.3x2	T43.3x3	T43.3x4	T43.3x5	T43.3x6
Plicamycin	T45.1x1	T45.1x2	T45.1x3	T45.1x4	T45.1x5	T45.1x6
Podophyllotoxin	T49.8x1	T49.8x2	T49.8x3	T49.8x4	T49.8x5	T49.8x6
Podophyllum (resin)	T49.4x1	T49.4x2	T49.4x3	T49.4x4	T49.4x5	T49.4x6
Poison NEC	T65.91	T65.92	T65.93	T65.94	—	—
Poisonous berries	T62.1x1	T62.1x2	T62.1x3	T62.1x4	—	—
Pokeweed (any part)	T62.2x1	T62.2x2	T62.2x3	T62.2x4	—	—
Poldine metilsulfate	T44.3x1	T44.3x2	T44.3x3	T44.3x4	T44.3x5	T44.3x6
Polidexide (sulfate)	T46.6x1	T46.6x2	T46.6x3	T46.6x4	T46.6x5	T46.6x6

Substance	Poisoning, Accidental (Unintentional)	Poisoning, Intentional Self-Harm	Poisoning, Assault	Poisoning, Undetermined	Adverse Effect	Underdosing
Polidocanol	T46.8x1	T46.8x2	T46.8x3	T46.8x4	T46.8x5	T46.8x6
Poliomyelitis vaccine	T50.B91	T50.B92	T50.B93	T50.B94	T50.B95	T50.B96
Polish (car) (floor) (furniture) (metal) (porcelain) (silver)	T65.891	T65.892	T65.893	T65.894	—	—
abrasive	T65.891	T65.892	T65.893	T65.894	—	—
porcelain	T65.891	T65.892	T65.893	T65.894	—	—
Poloxalkol	T47.4x1	T47.4x2	T47.4x3	T47.4x4	T47.4x5	T47.4x6
Poloxamer	T47.4x1	T47.4x2	T47.4x3	T47.4x4	T47.4x5	T47.4x6
Polyaminostyrene resins	T50.3x1	T50.3x2	T50.3x3	T50.3x4	T50.3x5	T50.3x6
Polycarbophil	T47.4x1	T47.4x2	T47.4x3	T47.4x4	T47.4x5	T47.4x6
Polychlorinated biphenyl	T65.891	T65.892	T65.893	T65.894	—	—
Polycycline	T36.4x1	T36.4x2	T36.4x3	T36.4x4	T36.4x5	T36.4x6
Polyester fumes	T59.891	T59.892	T59.893	T59.894	—	—
Polyester resin hardener	T52.91	T52.92	T52.93	T52.94	—	—
fumes	T59.891	T59.892	T59.893	T59.894	—	—
Polyestradiol phosphate	T38.5x1	T38.5x2	T38.5x3	T38.5x4	T38.5x5	T38.5x6
Polyethanolamine alkyl sulfate	T49.2x1	T49.2x2	T49.2x3	T49.2x4	T49.2x5	T49.2x6
Polyethylene adhesive	T49.3x1	T49.3x2	T49.3x3	T49.3x4	T49.3x5	T49.3x6
Polyferose	T45.4x1	T45.4x2	T45.4x3	T45.4x4	T45.4x5	T45.4x6
Polygeline	T45.8x1	T45.8x2	T45.8x3	T45.8x4	T45.8x5	T45.8x6
Polymyxin	T36.8x1	T36.8x2	T36.8x3	T36.8x4	T36.8x5	T36.8x6
B	T36.8x1	T36.8x2	T36.8x3	T36.8x4	T36.8x5	T36.8x6
ENT agent	T49.6x1	T49.6x2	T49.6x3	T49.6x4	T49.6x5	T49.6x6
ophthalmic preparation	T49.5x1	T49.5x2	T49.5x3	T49.5x4	T49.5x5	T49.5x6
topical NEC	T49.0x1	T49.0x2	T49.0x3	T49.0x4	T49.0x5	T49.0x6
E sulfate (eye preparation)	T49.5x1	T49.5x2	T49.5x3	T49.5x4	T49.5x5	T49.5x6
Polynoxylin	T49.0x1	T49.0x2	T49.0x3	T49.0x4	T49.0x5	T49.0x6
Polyoestradiol phosphate	T38.5x1	T38.5x2	T38.5x3	T38.5x4	T38.5x5	T38.5x6
Polyoxymethyleneurea	T49.0x1	T49.0x2	T49.0x3	T49.0x4	T49.0x5	T49.0x6
Polysilane	T47.8x1	T47.8x2	T47.8x3	T47.8x4	T47.8x5	T47.8x6
Polytetrafluoroethylene (inhaled)	T59.891	T59.892	T59.893	T59.894	—	—
Polythiazide	T50.2x1	T50.2x2	T50.2x3	T50.2x4	T50.2x5	T50.2x6
Polyvidone	T45.8x1	T45.8x2	T45.8x3	T45.8x4	T45.8x5	T45.8x6
Polyvinylpyrrolidone	T45.8x1	T45.8x2	T45.8x3	T45.8x4	T45.8x5	T45.8x6
Pontocaine (hydrochloride) (infiltration) (topical)	T41.3x1	T41.3x2	T41.3x3	T41.3x4	T41.3x5	T41.3x6
nerve block (peripheral) (plexus)	T41.3x1	T41.3x2	T41.3x3	T41.3x4	T41.3x5	T41.3x6
spinal	T41.3x1	T41.3x2	T41.3x3	T41.3x4	T41.3x5	T41.3x6
Porfiromycin	T45.1x1	T45.1x2	T45.1x3	T45.1x4	T45.1x5	T45.1x6
Posterior pituitary hormone NEC	T38.891	T38.892	T38.893	T38.894	T38.895	T38.896
Pot	T40.7x1	T40.7x2	T40.7x3	T40.7x4	T40.7x5	T40.7x6
Potash (caustic)	T54.3x1	T54.3x2	T54.3x3	T54.3x4	—	—

Substance	External Cause (T-Code)					
	Poisoning, Accidental (Unintentional)	Poisoning, Intentional Self-Harm	Poisoning, Assault	Poisoning, Undetermined	Adverse Effect	Underdosing
Potassic saline injection (lactated)	T50.3x1	T50.3x2	T50.3x3	T50.3x4	T50.3x5	T50.3x6
Potassium (salts) NEC	T50.3x1	T50.3x2	T50.3x3	T50.3x4	T50.3x5	T50.3x6
aminobenzoate	T45.8x1	T45.8x2	T45.8x3	T45.8x4	T45.8x5	T45.8x6
aminosalicylate	T37.1x1	T37.1x2	T37.1x3	T37.1x4	T37.1x5	T37.1x6
antimony 'tartrate'	T37.8x1	T37.8x2	T37.8x3	T37.8x4	T37.8x5	T37.8x6
arsenite (solution)	T57.0x1	T57.0x2	T57.0x3	T57.0x4	—	—
bichromate	T56.2x1	T56.2x2	T56.2x3	T56.2x4	—	—
bisulfate	T47.3x1	T47.3x2	T47.3x3	T47.3x4	T47.3x5	T47.3x6
bromide	T42.6x1	T42.6x2	T42.6x3	T42.6x4	T42.6x5	T42.6x6
canrenoate	T50.0x1	T50.0x2	T50.0x3	T50.0x4	T50.0x5	T50.0x6
carbonate	T54.3x1	T54.3x2	T54.3x3	T54.3x4	—	—
chlorate NEC	T65.891	T65.892	T65.893	T65.894	—	—
chloride	T50.3x1	T50.3x2	T50.3x3	T50.3x4	T50.3x5	T50.3x6
citrate	T50.991	T50.992	T50.993	T50.994	T50.995	T50.996
cyanide	T65.0x1	T65.0x2	T65.0x3	T65.0x4	—	—
ferric hexacyanoferrate (medicinal)	T50.6x1	T50.6x2	T50.6x3	T50.6x4	T50.6x5	T50.6x6
nonmedicinal	T65.891	T65.892	T65.893	T65.894	—	—
Fluoride	T57.8x1	T57.8x2	T57.8x3	T57.8x4	—	—
glucaldrate	T47.1x1	T47.1x2	T47.1x3	T47.1x4	T47.1x5	T47.1x6
hydroxide	T54.3x1	T54.3x2	T54.3x3	T54.3x4	—	—
iodate	T49.0x1	T49.0x2	T49.0x3	T49.0x4	T49.0x5	T49.0x6
iodide	T48.4x1	T48.4x2	T48.4x3	T48.4x4	T48.4x5	T48.4x6
nitrate	T57.8x1	T57.8x2	T57.8x3	T57.8x4	—	—
oxalate	T65.891	T65.892	T65.893	T65.894	—	—
perchlorate (nonmedicinal) NEC	T65.891	T65.892	T65.893	T65.894	—	—
antithyroid	T38.2x1	T38.2x2	T38.2x3	T38.2x4	T38.2x5	T38.2x6
medicinal	T38.2x1	T38.2x2	T38.2x3	T38.2x4	T38.2x5	T38.2x6
Permanganate (nonmedicinal)	T65.891	T65.892	T65.893	T65.894	—	—
medicinal	T49.0x1	T49.0x2	T49.0x3	T49.0x4	T49.0x5	T49.0x6
sulfate	T47.2x1	T47.2x2	T47.2x3	T47.2x4	T47.2x5	T47.2x6
Potassium-removing resin	T50.3x1	T50.3x2	T50.3x3	T50.3x4	T50.3x5	T50.3x6
Potassium-retaining drug	T50.3x1	T50.3x2	T50.3x3	T50.3x4	T50.3x5	T50.3x6
Povidone	T45.8x1	T45.8x2	T45.8x3	T45.8x4	T45.8x5	T45.8x6
iodine	T49.0x1	T49.0x2	T49.0x3	T49.0x4	T49.0x5	T49.0x6
Practolol	T44.7x1	T44.7x2	T44.7x3	T44.7x4	T44.7x5	T44.7x6
Prajmalium bitartrate	T46.2x1	T46.2x2	T46.2x3	T46.2x4	T46.2x5	T46.2x6
Pralidoxime (iodide)	T50.6x1	T50.6x2	T50.6x3	T50.6x4	T50.6x5	T50.6x6
chloride	T50.6x1	T50.6x2	T50.6x3	T50.6x4	T50.6x5	T50.6x6
Pramiverine	T44.3x1	T44.3x2	T44.3x3	T44.3x4	T44.3x5	T44.3x6
Pramocaine	T49.1x1	T49.1x2	T49.1x3	T49.1x4	T49.1x5	T49.1x6

Substance	External Cause (T-Code)					
	Poisoning, Accidental (Unintentional)	Poisoning, Intentional Self-Harm	Poisoning, Assault	Poisoning, Undetermined	Adverse Effect	Underdosing
Pramoxine	T49.1x1	T49.1x2	T49.1x3	T49.1x4	T49.1x5	T49.1x6
Prasterone	T38.7x1	T38.7x2	T38.7x3	T38.7x4	T38.7x5	T38.7x6
Pravastatin	T46.6x1	T46.6x2	T46.6x3	T46.6x4	T46.6x5	T46.6x6
Prazepam	T42.4x1	T42.4x2	T42.4x3	T42.4x4	T42.4x5	T42.4x6
Praziquantel	T37.4x1	T37.4x2	T37.4x3	T37.4x4	T37.4x5	T37.4x6
Prazitone	T43.291	T43.292	T43.293	T43.294	T43.295	T43.296
Prazosin	T44.6x1	T44.6x2	T44.6x3	T44.6x4	T44.6x5	T44.6x6
Prednicarbate	T49.0x1	T49.0x2	T49.0x3	T49.0x4	T49.0x5	T49.0x6
Prednimustine	T45.1x1	T45.1x2	T45.1x3	T45.1x4	T45.1x5	T45.1x6
Prednisolone	T49.0x1	T49.0x2	T49.0x3	T49.0x4	T49.0x5	T49.0x6
ENT agent	T49.6x1	T49.6x2	T49.6x3	T49.6x4	T49.6x5	T49.6x6
ophthalmic preparation	T49.5x1	T49.5x2	T49.5x3	T49.5x4	T49.5x5	T49.5x6
steaglate	T49.0x1	T49.0x2	T49.0x3	T49.0x4	T49.0x5	T49.0x6
topical NEC	T49.0x1	T49.0x2	T49.0x3	T49.0x4	T49.0x5	T49.0x6
Prednisone	T38.0x1	T38.0x2	T38.0x3	T38.0x4	T38.0x5	T38.0x6
Prednylidene	T38.0x1	T38.0x2	T38.0x3	T38.0x4	T38.0x5	T38.0x6
Pregnandiol	T38.5x1	T38.5x2	T38.5x3	T38.5x4	T38.5x5	T38.5x6
Pregneninolone	T38.5x1	T38.5x2	T38.5x3	T38.5x4	T38.5x5	T38.5x6
Preludin	T43.691	T43.692	T43.693	T43.694	T43.695	T43.696
Premarin	T38.5x1	T38.5x2	T38.5x3	T38.5x4	T38.5x5	T38.5x6
Premedication anesthetic	T41.201	T41.202	T41.203	T41.204	T41.205	T41.206
Prenalterol	T44.5x1	T44.5x2	T44.5x3	T44.5x4	T44.5x5	T44.5x6
Prenoxdiazine	T48.3x1	T48.3x2	T48.3x3	T48.3x4	T48.3x5	T48.3x6
Prenylamine	T46.3x1	T46.3x2	T46.3x3	T46.3x4	T46.3x5	T46.3x6
Preparation, local	T49.4x1	T49.4x2	T49.4x3	T49.4x4	T49.4x5	T49.4x6
Preparation H	T49.8x1	T49.8x2	T49.8x3	T49.8x4	T49.8x5	T49.8x6
Preservative (nonmedicinal)	T65.891	T65.892	T65.893	T65.894	—	—
medicinal	T50.901	T50.902	T50.903	T50.904	T50.905	T50.906
Prethcamide	T50.7x1	T50.7x2	T50.7x3	T50.7x4	T50.7x5	T50.7x6
Pride of China	T62.2x1	T62.2x2	T62.2x3	T62.2x4	—	—
Pridinol	T44.3x1	T44.3x2	T44.3x3	T44.3x4	T44.3x5	T44.3x6
Prifinium bromide	T44.3x1	T44.3x2	T44.3x3	T44.3x4	T44.3x5	T44.3x6
Prilocaine	T41.3x1	T41.3x2	T41.3x3	T41.3x4	T41.3x5	T41.3x6
infiltration (subcutaneous)	T41.3x1	T41.3x2	T41.3x3	T41.3x4	T41.3x5	T41.3x6
nerve block (peripheral) (plexus)	T41.3x1	T41.3x2	T41.3x3	T41.3x4	T41.3x5	T41.3x6
regional	T41.3x1	T41.3x2	T41.3x3	T41.3x4	T41.3x5	T41.3x6
Primaquine	T37.2x1	T37.2x2	T37.2x3	T37.2x4	T37.2x5	T37.2x6
Primidone	T42.6x1	T42.6x2	T42.6x3	T42.6x4	T42.6x5	T42.6x6
Primula (veris)	T62.2x1	T62.2x2	T62.2x3	T62.2x4	—	—
Prinadol	T40.2x1	T40.2x2	T40.2x3	T40.2x4	T40.2x5	T40.2x6

	External Cause (T-Code)					
Substance	Poisoning, Accidental (Unintentional)	Poisoning, Intentional Self-Harm	Poisoning, Assault	Poisoning, Undetermined	Adverse Effect	Underdosing
Priscol, Priscoline	T44.6x1	T44.6x2	T44.6x3	T44.6x4	T44.6x5	T44.6x6
Pristinamycin	T36.3x1	T36.3x2	T36.3x3	T36.3x4	T36.3x5	T36.3x6
Privet	T62.2x1	T62.2x2	T62.2x3	T62.2x4	—	—
berries	T62.1x1	T62.1x2	T62.1x3	T62.1x4	—	—
Privine	T44.4x1	T44.4x2	T44.4x3	T44.4x4	T44.4x5	T44.4x6
Pro-Banthine	T44.3x1	T44.3x2	T44.3x3	T44.3x4	T44.3x5	T44.3x6
Probarbital	T42.3x1	T42.3x2	T42.3x3	T42.3x4	T42.3x5	T42.3x6
Probenecid	T50.4x1	T50.4x2	T50.4x3	T50.4x4	T50.4x5	T50.4x6
Probucol	T46.6x1	T46.6x2	T46.6x3	T46.6x4	T46.6x5	T46.6x6
Procainamide	T46.2x1	T46.2x2	T46.2x3	T46.2x4	T46.2x5	T46.2x6
Procaine	T41.3x1	T41.3x2	T41.3x3	T41.3x4	T41.3x5	T41.3x6
benzylpenicillin	T36.0x1	T36.0x2	T36.0x3	T36.0x4	T36.0x5	T36.0x6
nerve block (periphreal) (plexus)	T41.3x1	T41.3x2	T41.3x3	T41.3x4	T41.3x5	T41.3x6
penicillin G	T36.0x1	T36.0x2	T36.0x3	T36.0x4	T36.0x5	T36.0x6
regional	T41.3x1	T41.3x2	T41.3x3	T41.3x4	T41.3x5	T41.3x6
spinal	T41.3x1	T41.3x2	T41.3x3	T41.3x4	T41.3x5	T41.3x6
Procalmidol	T43.591	T43.592	T43.593	T43.594	T43.595	T43.596
Procarbazine	T45.1x1	T45.1x2	T45.1x3	T45.1x4	T45.1x5	T45.1x6
Procaterol	T44.5x1	T44.5x2	T44.5x3	T44.5x4	T44.5x5	T44.5x6
Prochlorperazine	T43.3x1	T43.3x2	T43.3x3	T43.3x4	T43.3x5	T43.3x6
Procyclidine	T44.3x1	T44.3x2	T44.3x3	T44.3x4	T44.3x5	T44.3x6
Producer gas	T58.8x1	T58.8x2	T58.8x3	T58.8x4	—	—
Profadol	T40.4x1	T40.4x2	T40.4x3	T40.4x4	T40.4x5	T40.4x6
Profenamine	T44.3x1	T44.3x2	T44.3x3	T44.3x4	T44.3x5	T44.3x6
Profenil	T44.3x1	T44.3x2	T44.3x3	T44.3x4	T44.3x5	T44.3x6
Proflavine	T49.0x1	T49.0x2	T49.0x3	T49.0x4	T49.0x5	T49.0x6
Progabide	T42.6x1	T42.6x2	T42.6x3	T42.6x4	T42.6x5	T42.6x6
Progestin	T38.5x1	T38.5x2	T38.5x3	T38.5x4	T38.5x5	T38.5x6
oral contraceptive	T38.4x1	T38.4x2	T38.4x3	T38.4x4	T38.4x5	T38.4x6
Progesterone	T38.5x1	T38.5x2	T38.5x3	T38.5x4	T38.5x5	T38.5x6
Progestogen NEC	T38.5x1	T38.5x2	T38.5x3	T38.5x4	T38.5x5	T38.5x6
Progestone	T38.5x1	T38.5x2	T38.5x3	T38.5x4	T38.5x5	T38.5x6
Proglumide	T47.1x1	T47.1x2	T47.1x3	T47.1x4	T47.1x5	T47.1x6
Proguanil	T37.2x1	T37.2x2	T37.2x3	T37.2x4	T37.2x5	T37.2x6
Prolactin	T38.811	T38.812	T38.813	T38.814	T38.815	T38.816
Prolintane	T43.691	T43.692	T43.693	T43.694	T43.695	T43.696
Proloid	T38.1x1	T38.1x2	T38.1x3	T38.1x4	T38.1x5	T38.1x6
Proluton	T38.5x1	T38.5x2	T38.5x3	T38.5x4	T38.5x5	T38.5x6
Promacetin	T37.1x1	T37.1x2	T37.1x3	T37.1x4	T37.1x5	T37.1x6
Promazine	T43.3x1	T43.3x2	T43.3x3	T43.3x4	T43.3x5	T43.3x6

Substance	Poisoning, Accidental (Unintentional)	Poisoning, Intentional Self-Harm	Poisoning, Assault	Poisoning, Undetermined	Adverse Effect	Underdosing
			External Cause (T-Code)			
Promedol	T40.2x1	T40.2x2	T40.2x3	T40.2x4	T40.2x5	T40.2x6
Promegestone	T38.5x1	T38.5x2	T38.5x3	T38.5x4	T38.5x5	T38.5x6
Promethazine (teoclate)	T43.3x1	T43.3x2	T43.3x3	T43.3x4	T43.3x5	T43.3x6
Promin	T37.1x1	T37.1x2	T37.1x3	T37.1x4	T37.1x5	T37.1x6
Pronase	T45.3x1	T45.3x2	T45.3x3	T45.3x4	T45.3x5	T45.3x6
Pronestyl (hydrochloride)	T46.2x1	T46.2x2	T46.2x3	T46.2x4	T46.2x5	T46.2x6
Pronetalol	T44.7x1	T44.7x2	T44.7x3	T44.7x4	T44.7x5	T44.7x6
Prontosil	T37.0x1	T37.0x2	T37.0x3	T37.0x4	T37.0x5	T37.0x6
Propachlor	T60.3x1	T60.3x2	T60.3x3	T60.3x4	—	—
Propafenone	T46.2x1	T46.2x2	T46.2x3	T46.2x4	T46.2x5	T46.2x6
Propallylonal	T42.3x1	T42.3x2	T42.3x3	T42.3x4	T42.3x5	T42.3x6
Propamidine	T49.0x1	T49.0x2	T49.0x3	T49.0x4	T49.0x5	T49.0x6
Propane (distributed in mobile container)	T59.891	T59.892	T59.893	T59.894	—	—
distributed through pipes	T59.891	T59.892	T59.893	T59.894	—	—
incomplete combustion	T57.11	T57.12	T57.13	T57.14	—	—
Propanidid	T41.291	T41.292	T41.293	T41.294	T41.295	T41.296
Propanil	T60.3x1	T60.3x2	T60.3x3	T60.3x4	—	—
1-Propanol	T51.3x1	T51.3x2	T51.3x3	T51.3x4	—	—
2-Propanol	T51.2x1	T51.2x2	T51.2x3	T51.2x4	—	—
Propantheline	T44.3x1	T44.3x2	T44.3x3	T44.3x4	T44.3x5	T44.3x6
bromide	T44.3x1	T44.3x2	T44.3x3	T44.3x4	T44.3x5	T44.3x6
Proparacaine	T41.3x1	T41.3x2	T41.3x3	T41.3x4	T41.3x5	T41.3x6
Propatylnitrate	T46.3x1	T46.3x2	T46.3x3	T46.3x4	T46.3x5	T46.3x6
Propicillin	T36.0x1	T36.0x2	T36.0x3	T36.0x4	T36.0x5	T36.0x6
Propiolactone	T49.0x1	T49.0x2	T49.0x3	T49.0x4	T49.0x5	T49.0x6
Propiomazine	T45.0x1	T45.0x2	T45.0x3	T45.0x4	T45.0x5	T45.0x6
Propionaldehyde (medicinal)	T42.6x1	T42.6x2	T42.6x3	T42.6x4	T42.6x5	T42.6x6
Propionate (calcium) (sodium)	T49.0x1	T49.0x2	T49.0x3	T49.0x4	T49.0x5	T49.0x6
Propion gel	T49.0x1	T49.0x2	T49.0x3	T49.0x4	T49.0x5	T49.0x6
Propitocaine	T41.3x1	T41.3x2	T41.3x3	T41.3x4	T41.3x5	T41.3x6
infiltration (subcutaneous)	T41.3x1	T41.3x2	T41.3x3	T41.3x4	T41.3x5	T41.3x6
nerve block (peripheral) (plexus)	T41.3x1	T41.3x2	T41.3x3	T41.3x4	T41.3x5	T41.3x6
Propofol	T41.291	T41.292	T41.293	T41.294	T41.295	T41.296
Propoxur	T60.0x1	T60.0x2	T60.0x3	T60.0x4	—	—
Propoxycaine	T41.3x1	T41.3x2	T41.3x3	T41.3x4	T41.3x5	T41.3x6
infiltration (subcutaneous)	T41.3x1	T41.3x2	T41.3x3	T41.3x4	T41.3x5	T41.3x6
nerve block (peripheral) (plexus)	T41.3x1	T41.3x2	T41.3x3	T41.3x4	T41.3x5	T41.3x6
topical (surface)	T41.3x1	T41.3x2	T41.3x3	T41.3x4	T41.3x5	T41.3x6
Propoxyphene	T40.4x1	T40.4x2	T40.4x3	T40.4x4	T40.4x5	T40.4x6
Propranolol	T44.7x1	T44.7x2	T44.7x3	T44.7x4	T44.7x5	T44.7x6

Substance	External Cause (T-Code)					
	Poisoning, Accidental (Unintentional)	Poisoning, Intentional Self-Harm	Poisoning, Assault	Poisoning, Undetermined	Adverse Effect	Underdosing
Propyl						
alcohol	T51.3x1	T51.3x2	T51.3x3	T51.3x4	—	—
carbinol	T51.3x1	T51.3x2	T51.3x3	T51.3x4	—	—
hexadrine	T44.4x1	T44.4x2	T44.4x3	T44.4x4	T44.4x5	T44.4x6
iodone	T50.8x1	T50.8x2	T50.8x3	T50.8x4	T50.8x5	T50.8x6
thiouracil	T38.2x1	T38.2x2	T38.2x3	T38.2x4	T38.2x5	T38.2x6
Propylaminophenothiazine	T43.3x1	T43.3x2	T43.3x3	T43.3x4	T43.3x5	T43.3x6
Propylene	T59.891	T59.892	T59.893	T59.894	—	—
Propylhexedrine	T48.5x1	T48.5x2	T48.5x3	T48.5x4	T48.5x5	T48.5x6
Propyliodone	T50.8x1	T50.8x2	T50.8x3	T50.8x4	T50.8x5	T50.8x6
Propylthiouracil	T38.2x1	T38.2x2	T38.2x3	T38.2x4	T38.2x5	T38.2x6
Propylparaben (ophthalmic)	T49.5x1	T49.5x2	T49.5x3	T49.5x4	T49.5x5	T49.5x6
Propyphenazone	T39.2x1	T39.2x2	T39.2x3	T39.2x4	T39.2x5	T39.2x6
Proquazone	T39.391	T39.392	T39.393	T39.394	T39.395	T39.396
Proscillaridin	T46.0x1	T46.0x2	T46.0x3	T46.0x4	T46.0x5	T46.0x6
Prostacyclin	T45.521	T45.522	T45.523	T45.524	T45.525	T45.526
Prostaglandin (I2)	T45.521	T45.522	T45.523	T45.524	T45.525	T45.526
E1	T46.7x1	T46.7x2	T46.7x3	T46.7x4	T46.7x5	T46.7x6
E2	T48.0x1	T48.0x2	T48.0x3	T48.0x4	T48.0x5	T48.0x6
F2 alpha	T48.0x1	T48.0x2	T48.0x3	T48.0x4	T48.0x5	T48.0x6
Prostigmin	T44.0x1	T44.0x2	T44.0x3	T44.0x4	T44.0x5	T44.0x6
Prosultiamine	T45.2x1	T45.2x2	T45.2x3	T45.2x4	T45.2x5	T45.2x6
Protamine sulfate	T45.7x1	T45.7x2	T45.7x3	T45.7x4	T45.7x5	T45.7x6
zinc insulin	T38.3x1	T38.3x2	T38.3x3	T38.3x4	T38.3x5	T38.3x6
Protease	T47.5x1	T47.5x2	T47.5x3	T47.5x4	T47.5x5	T47.5x6
Protectant, skin NEC	T49.3x1	T49.3x2	T49.3x3	T49.3x4	T49.3x5	T49.3x6
Protein hydrolysate	T50.991	T50.992	T50.993	T50.994	T50.995	T50.996
Prothiaden - see Dothiepin hydrochloride						
Prothionamide	T37.1x1	T37.1x2	T37.1x3	T37.1x4	T37.1x5	T37.1x6
Prothipendyl	T43.591	T43.592	T43.593	T43.594	T43.595	T43.596
Prothoate	T60.0x1	T60.0x2	T60.0x3	T60.0x4	—	—
Prothrombin						
activator	T45.7x1	T45.7x2	T45.7x3	T45.7x4	T45.7x5	T45.7x6
synthesis inhibitor	T45.511	T45.512	T45.513	T45.514	T45.515	T45.516
Protionamide	T37.1x1	T37.1x2	T37.1x3	T37.1x4	T37.1x5	T37.1x6
Protirelin	T38.891	T38.892	T38.893	T38.894	T38.895	T38.896
Protokylol	T48.6x1	T48.6x2	T48.6x3	T48.6x4	T48.6x5	T48.6x6
Protopam	T50.6x1	T50.6x2	T50.6x3	T50.6x4	T50.6x5	T50.6x6
Protoveratrine(s) (A) (B)	T46.5x1	T46.5x2	T46.5x3	T46.5x4	T46.5x5	T46.5x6
Protriptyline	T43.011	T43.012	T43.013	T43.014	T43.015	T43.016

Substance	Poisoning, Accidental (Unintentional)	Poisoning, Intentional Self-Harm	Poisoning, Assault	Poisoning, Undetermined	Adverse Effect	Underdosing
	External Cause (T-Code)					
Provera	T38.5x1	T38.5x2	T38.5x3	T38.5x4	T38.5x5	T38.5x6
Provitamin A	T45.2x1	T45.2x2	T45.2x3	T45.2x4	T45.2x5	T45.2x6
Proxibarbal	T42.3x1	T42.3x2	T42.3x3	T42.3x4	T42.3x5	T42.3x6
Proxymetacaine	T41.3x1	T41.3x2	T41.3x3	T41.3x4	T41.3x5	T41.3x6
Proxyphylline	T48.6x1	T48.6x2	T48.6x3	T48.6x4	T48.6x5	T48.6x6
Prozac - *see* Fluoxetine hydrochloride						
Prunus						
laurocerasus	T62.2x1	T62.2x2	T62.2x3	T62.2x4	—	—
virginiana	T62.2x1	T62.2x2	T62.2x3	T62.2x4	—	—
Prussian blue						
commercial	T65.891	T65.892	T65.893	T65.894	—	—
therapeutic	T50.6x1	T50.6x2	T50.6x3	T50.6x4	T50.6x5	T50.6x6
Prussic acid	T65.0x1	T65.0x2	T65.0x3	T65.0x4	—	—
vapor	T57.3x1	T57.3x2	T57.3x3	T57.3x4	—	—
Pseudoephedrine	T44.991	T44.992	T44.993	T44.994	T44.995	T44.996
Psilocin	T40.991	T40.992	T40.993	T40.994	T40.995	T40.996
Psilocybin	T40.991	T40.992	T40.993	T40.994	T40.995	T40.996
Psilocybine	T40.991	T40.992	T40.993	T40.994	T40.995	T40.996
Psoralene (nonmedicinal)	T65.891	T65.892	T65.893	T65.894	—	—
Psoralens (medicinal)	T50.991	T50.992	T50.993	T50.994	T50.995	T50.996
PSP (phenolsulfonphthalein)	T50.8x1	T50.8x2	T50.8x3	T50.8x4	T50.8x5	T50.8x6
Psychodysleptic drug NEC	T40.901	T40.902	T40.903	T40.904	T40.905	T40.906
Psychostimulant	T43.601	T43.602	T43.603	T43.604	T43.605	T43.606
amphetamine	T43.621	T43.622	T43.623	T43.624	T43.625	T43.626
caffeine	T43.611	T43.612	T43.613	T43.614	T43.615	T43.616
methylphenidate	T43.631	T43.632	T43.633	T43.634	T43.635	T43.636
specified NEC	T43.691	T43.692	T43.693	T43.694	T43.695	T43.696
Psychotherapeutic drug NEC	T43.91	T43.92	T43.93	T43.94	T43.95	T43.96
antidepressants (*see also* Antidepressant)	T43.201	T43.202	T43.203	T43.204	T43.205	T43.206
specified NEC	T43.8x1	T43.8x2	T43.8x3	T43.8x4	T43.8x5	T43.8x6
tranquilizers NEC	T43.501	T43.502	T43.503	T43.504	T43.505	T43.506
Psychotomimetic agents	T40.901	T40.902	T40.903	T40.904	T40.905	T40.906
Psychotropic drug NEC	T43.91	T43.92	T43.93	T43.94	T43.95	T43.96
specified NEC	T43.8x1	T43.8x2	T43.8x3	T43.8x4	T43.8x5	T43.8x6
Psyllium hydrophilic mucilloid	T47.4x1	T47.4x2	T47.4x3	T47.4x4	T47.4x5	T47.4x6
Pteroylglutamic acid	T45.8x1	T45.8x2	T45.8x3	T45.8x4	T45.8x5	T45.8x6
Pteroyltriglutamate	T45.1x1	T45.1x2	T45.1x3	T45.1x4	T45.1x5	T45.1x6
PTFE - *see* Polytetrafluoroethylene						
Pulp						
devitalizing paste	T49.7x1	T49.7x2	T49.7x3	T49.7x4	T49.7x5	T49.7x6
dressing	T49.7x1	T49.7x2	T49.7x3	T49.7x4	T49.7x5	T49.7x6

Substance	External Cause (T-Code)					
	Poisoning, Accidental (Unintentional)	Poisoning, Intentional Self-Harm	Poisoning, Assault	Poisoning, Undetermined	Adverse Effect	Underdosing
Pulsatilla	T62.2x1	T62.2x2	T62.2x3	T62.2x4	—	—
Pumpkin seed extract	T37.4x1	T37.4x2	T37.4x3	T37.4x4	T37.4x5	T37.4x6
Purex (bleach)	T54.91	T54.92	T54.93	T54.94	—	—
Purgative NEC (*see also* Cathartic)	T47.4x1	T47.4x2	T47.4x3	T47.4x4	T47.4x5	T47.4x6
Purine analogue (antineoplastic)	T45.1x1	T45.1x2	T45.1x3	T45.1x4	T45.1x5	T45.1x6
Purine diuretics	T50.2x1	T50.2x2	T50.2x3	T50.2x4	T50.2x5	T50.2x6
Purinethol	T45.1x1	T45.1x2	T45.1x3	T45.1x4	T45.1x5	T45.1x6
PVP	T45.8x1	T45.8x2	T45.8x3	T45.8x4	T45.8x5	T45.8x6
Pyrabital	T39.8x1	T39.8x2	T39.8x3	T39.8x4	T39.8x5	T39.8x6
Pyramidon	T39.2x1	T39.2x2	T39.2x3	T39.2x4	T39.2x5	T39.2x6
Pyrantel	T37.4x1	T37.4x2	T37.4x3	T37.4x4	T37.4x5	T37.4x6
Pyrathiazine	T45.0x1	T45.0x2	T45.0x3	T45.0x4	T45.0x5	T45.0x6
Pyrazinamide	T37.1x1	T37.1x2	T37.1x3	T37.1x4	T37.1x5	T37.1x6
Pyrazinoic acid (amide)	T37.1x1	T37.1x2	T37.1x3	T37.1x4	T37.1x5	T37.1x6
Pyrazole (derivatives)	T39.2x1	T39.2x2	T39.2x3	T39.2x4	T39.2x5	T39.2x6
Pyrazolone analgesic NEC	T39.2x1	T39.2x2	T39.2x3	T39.2x4	T39.2x5	T39.2x6
Pyrethrin, pyrethrum (nonmedicinal)	T60.2x1	T60.2x2	T60.2x3	T60.2x4	—	—
Pyrethrum extract	T49.0x1	T49.0x2	T49.0x3	T49.0x4	T49.0x5	T49.0x6
Pyribenzamine	T45.0x1	T45.0x2	T45.0x3	T45.0x4	T45.0x5	T45.0x6
Pyridine	T52.8x1	T52.8x2	T52.8x3	T52.8x4	—	—
aldoxime methiodide	T50.6x1	T50.6x2	T50.6x3	T50.6x4	T50.6x5	T50.6x6
aldoxime methyl chloride	T50.6x1	T50.6x2	T50.6x3	T50.6x4	T50.6x5	T50.6x6
vapor	T59.891	T59.892	T59.893	T59.894	—	—
Pyridium	T49.1x1	T49.1x2	T49.1x3	T49.1x4	T49.1x5	T49.1x6
Pyridostigmine bromide	T44.0x1	T44.0x2	T44.0x3	T44.0x4	T44.0x5	T44.0x6
Pyridoxal phosphate	T45.2x1	T45.2x2	T45.2x3	T45.2x4	T45.2x5	T45.2x6
Pyridoxine	T45.2x1	T45.2x2	T45.2x3	T45.2x4	T45.2x5	T45.2x6
Pyrilamine	T45.0x1	T45.0x2	T45.0x3	T45.0x4	T45.0x5	T45.0x6
Pyrimethamine	T37.2x1	T37.2x2	T37.2x3	T37.2x4	T37.2x5	T37.2x6
with sulfadoxine	T37.2x1	T37.2x2	T37.2x3	T37.2x4	T37.2x5	T37.2x6
Pyrimidine antagonist	T45.1x1	T45.1x2	T45.1x3	T45.1x4	T45.1x5	T45.1x6
Pyriminil	T60.4x1	T60.4x2	T60.4x3	T60.4x4	—	—
Pyrithione zinc	T49.4x1	T49.4x2	T49.4x3	T49.4x4	T49.4x5	T49.4x6
Pyrithyldione	T42.6x1	T42.6x2	T42.6x3	T42.6x4	T42.6x5	T42.6x6
Pyrogallic acid	T49.0x1	T49.0x2	T49.0x3	T49.0x4	T49.0x5	T49.0x6
Pyrogallol	T49.0x1	T49.0x2	T49.0x3	T49.0x4	T49.0x5	T49.0x6
Pyroxylin	T49.3x1	T49.3x2	T49.3x3	T49.3x4	T49.3x5	T49.3x6
Pyrrobutamine	T45.0x1	T45.0x2	T45.0x3	T45.0x4	T45.0x5	T45.0x6
Pyrrolizidine alkaloids	T62.8x1	T62.8x2	T62.8x3	T62.8x4	—	—
Pyrvinium chloride	T37.4x1	T37.4x2	T37.4x3	T37.4x4	T37.4x5	T37.4x6
PZI	T38.3x1	T38.3x2	T38.3x3	T38.3x4	T38.3x5	T38.3x6

Substance	Poisoning, Accidental (Unintentional)	Poisoning, Intentional Self-Harm	Poisoning, Assault	Poisoning, Undetermined	Adverse Effect	Underdosing
Quaalude	T42.6x1	T42.6x2	T42.6x3	T42.6x4	T42.6x5	T42.6x6
Quarternary ammonium						
anti-infective	T49.0x1	T49.0x2	T49.0x3	T49.0x4	T49.0x5	T49.0x6
ganglion blocking	T44.2x1	T44.2x2	T44.2x3	T44.2x4	T44.2x5	T44.2x6
parasympatholytic	T44.3x1	T44.3x2	T44.3x3	T44.3x4	T44.3x5	T44.3x6
Quazepam	T42.4x1	T42.4x2	T42.4x3	T42.4x4	T42.4x5	T42.4x6
Quicklime	T54.3x1	T54.3x2	T54.3x3	T54.3x4	—	—
Quillaja extract	T48.4x1	T48.4x2	T48.4x3	T48.4x4	T48.4x5	T48.4x6
Quinacrine	T37.2x1	T37.2x2	T37.2x3	T37.2x4	T37.2x5	T37.2x6
Quinaglute	T46.2x1	T46.2x2	T46.2x3	T46.2x4	T46.2x5	T46.2x6
Quinalbarbital	T42.3x1	T42.3x2	T42.3x3	T42.3x4	T42.3x5	T42.3x6
Quinalbarbitone sodium	T42.3x1	T42.3x2	T42.3x3	T42.3x4	T42.3x5	T42.3x6
Quinalphos	T60.0x1	T60.0x2	T60.0x3	T60.0x4	—	—
Quinapril	T46.4x1	T46.4x2	T46.4x3	T46.4x4	T46.4x5	T46.4x6
Quinestradiol	T38.5x1	T38.5x2	T38.5x3	T38.5x4	T38.5x5	T38.5x6
Quinestradol	T38.5x1	T38.5x2	T38.5x3	T38.5x4	T38.5x5	T38.5x6
Quinestrol	T38.5x1	T38.5x2	T38.5x3	T38.5x4	T38.5x5	T38.5x6
Quinethazone	T50.2x1	T50.2x2	T50.2x3	T50.2x4	T50.2x5	T50.2x6
Quingestanol	T38.4x1	T38.4x2	T38.4x3	T38.4x4	T38.4x5	T38.4x6
Quinidine	T46.2x1	T46.2x2	T46.2x3	T46.2x4	T46.2x5	T46.2x6
Quinine	T37.2x1	T37.2x2	T37.2x3	T37.2x4	T37.2x5	T37.2x6
Quiniobine	T37.8x1	T37.8x2	T37.8x3	T37.8x4	T37.8x5	T37.8x6
Quinisocaine	T49.1x1	T49.1x2	T49.1x3	T49.1x4	T49.1x5	T49.1x6
Quinocide	T37.2x1	T37.2x2	T37.2x3	T37.2x4	T37.2x5	T37.2x6
Quinoline (derivatives) NEC	T37.8x1	T37.8x2	T37.8x3	T37.8x4	T37.8x5	T37.8x6
Quinupramine	T43.011	T43.012	T43.013	T43.014	T43.015	T43.016
Quotane	T41.3x1	T41.3x2	T41.3x3	T41.3x4	T41.3x5	T41.3x6
Rabies						
immune globulin (human)	T50.Z11	T50.Z12	T50.Z13	T50.Z14	T50.Z15	T50.Z16
vaccine	T50.B91	T50.B92	T50.B93	T50.B94	T50.B95	T50.B96
Racemoramide	T40.2x1	T40.2x2	T40.2x3	T40.2x4	T40.2x5	T40.2x6
Racemorphan	T40.2x1	T40.2x2	T40.2x3	T40.2x4	T40.2x5	T40.2x6
Racepinefrin	T44.5x1	T44.5x2	T44.5x3	T44.5x4	T44.5x5	T44.5x6
Raclopride	T43.591	T43.592	T43.593	T43.594	T43.595	T43.596
Radiator alcohol	T51.1x1	T51.1x2	T51.1x3	T51.1x4	—	—
Radioactive drug NEC	T50.8x1	T50.8x2	T50.8x3	T50.8x4	T50.8x5	T50.8x6
Radio-opaque (drugs) (materials)	T50.8x1	T50.8x2	T50.8x3	T50.8x4	T50.8x5	T50.8x6
Ramifenazone	T39.2x1	T39.2x2	T39.2x3	T39.2x4	T39.2x5	T39.2x6
Ramipril	T46.4x1	T46.4x2	T46.4x3	T46.4x4	T46.4x5	T46.4x6
Ranitidine	T47.0x1	T47.0x2	T47.0x3	T47.0x4	T47.0x5	T47.0x6

Substance	External Cause (T-Code)					
	Poisoning, Accidental (Unintentional)	Poisoning, Intentional Self-Harm	Poisoning, Assault	Poisoning, Undetermined	Adverse Effect	Underdosing
Ranunculus	T62.2x1	T62.2x2	T62.2x3	T62.2x4	—	—
Rat poison NEC	T60.4x1	T60.4x2	T60.4x3	T60.4x4	—	—
Rattlesnake (venom)	T63.011	T63.012	T63.013	T63.014	—	—
Raubasine	T46.7x1	T46.7x2	T46.7x3	T46.7x4	T46.7x5	T46.7x6
Raudixin	T46.5x1	T46.5x2	T46.5x3	T46.5x4	T46.5x5	T46.5x6
Rautensin	T46.5x1	T46.5x2	T46.5x3	T46.5x4	T46.5x5	T46.5x6
Rautina	T46.5x1	T46.5x2	T46.5x3	T46.5x4	T46.5x5	T46.5x6
Rautotal	T46.5x1	T46.5x2	T46.5x3	T46.5x4	T46.5x5	T46.5x6
Rauwiloid	T46.5x1	T46.5x2	T46.5x3	T46.5x4	T46.5x5	T46.5x6
Rauwoldin	T46.5x1	T46.5x2	T46.5x3	T46.5x4	T46.5x5	T46.5x6
Rauwolfia (alkaloids)	T46.5x1	T46.5x2	T46.5x3	T46.5x4	T46.5x5	T46.5x6
Razoxane	T45.1x1	T45.1x2	T45.1x3	T45.1x4	T45.1x5	T45.1x6
Realgar	T57.0x1	T57.0x2	T57.0x3	T57.0x4	—	—
Recombinant (R) - *see* specific protein						
Red blood cells, packed	T45.8x1	T45.8x2	T45.8x3	T45.8x4	T45.8x5	T45.8x6
Red squill (scilliroside)	T60.4x1	T60.4x2	T60.4x3	T60.4x4	—	—
Reducing agent, industrial NEC	T65.891	T65.892	T65.893	T65.894	—	—
Refrigerant gas (chlorofluoro-carbon)	T53.5x1	T53.5x2	T53.5x3	T53.5x4	—	—
not chlorofluoro-carbon	T59.891	T59.892	T59.893	T59.894	—	—
Regroton	T50.2x1	T50.2x2	T50.2x3	T50.2x4	T50.2x5	T50.2x6
Rehydration salts (oral)	T50.3x1	T50.3x2	T50.3x3	T50.3x4	T50.3x5	T50.3x6
Rela	T42.8x1	T42.8x2	T42.8x3	T42.8x4	T42.8x5	T42.8x6
Relaxant, muscle						
anesthetic	T48.1x1	T48.1x2	T48.1x3	T48.1x4	T48.1x5	T48.1x6
central nervous system	T42.8x1	T42.8x2	T42.8x3	T42.8x4	T42.8x5	T42.8x6
skeletal NEC	T48.1x1	T48.1x2	T48.1x3	T48.1x4	T48.1x5	T48.1x6
smooth NEC	T44.3x1	T44.3x2	T44.3x3	T44.3x4	T44.3x5	T44.3x6
Remoxipride	T43.591	T43.592	T43.593	T43.594	T43.595	T43.596
Renese	T50.2x1	T50.2x2	T50.2x3	T50.2x4	T50.2x5	T50.2x6
Renografin	T50.8x1	T50.8x2	T50.8x3	T50.8x4	T50.8x5	T50.8x6
Replacement solution	T50.3x1	T50.3x2	T50.3x3	T50.3x4	T50.3x5	T50.3x6
Reproterol	T48.6x1	T48.6x2	T48.6x3	T48.6x4	T48.6x5	T48.6x6
Rescinnamine	T46.5x1	T46.5x2	T46.5x3	T46.5x4	T46.5x5	T46.5x6
Reserpin(e)	T46.5x1	T46.5x2	T46.5x3	T46.5x4	T46.5x5	T46.5x6
Resorcin, resorcinol (nonmedicinal)	T65.891	T65.892	T65.893	T65.894	—	—
medicinal	T49.4x1	T49.4x2	T49.4x3	T49.4x4	T49.4x5	T49.4x6
Respaire	T48.4x1	T48.4x2	T48.4x3	T48.4x4	T48.4x5	T48.4x6
Respiratory drug NEC	T48.901	T48.902	T48.903	T48.904	T48.905	T48.906
antiasthmatic NEC	T48.6x1	T48.6x2	T48.6x3	T48.6x4	T48.6x5	T48.6x6
anti-common-cold NEC	T48.5x1	T48.5x2	T48.5x3	T48.5x4	T48.5x5	T48.5x6

Substance	External Cause (T-Code)					
	Poisoning, Accidental (Unintentional)	Poisoning, Intentional Self-Harm	Poisoning, Assault	Poisoning, Undetermined	Adverse Effect	Underdosing
Respiratory drug NEC *(Continued)*						
expectorant NEC	T48.4x1	T48.4x2	T48.4x3	T48.4x4	T48.4x5	T48.4x6
stimulant	T48.901	T48.902	T48.903	T48.904	T48.905	T48.906
Retinoic acid	T49.0x1	T49.0x2	T49.0x3	T49.0x4	T49.0x5	T49.0x6
Retinol	T45.2x1	T45.2x2	T45.2x3	T45.2x4	T45.2x5	T45.2x6
Rh (D) immune globulin (human)	T50.Z11	T50.Z12	T50.Z13	T50.Z14	T50.Z15	T50.Z16
Rhodine	T39.011	T39.012	T39.013	T39.014	T39.015	T39.016
RhoGAM	T50.Z11	T50.Z12	T50.Z13	T50.Z14	T50.Z15	T50.Z16
Rhubarb						
dry extract	T47.2x1	T47.2x2	T47.2x3	T47.2x4	T47.2x5	T47.2x6
tincture, compound	T47.2x1	T47.2x2	T47.2x3	T47.2x4	T47.2x5	T47.2x6
Ribavirin	T37.5x1	T37.5x2	T37.5x3	T37.5x4	T37.5x5	T37.5x6
Riboflavin	T45.2x1	T45.2x2	T45.2x3	T45.2x4	T45.2x5	T45.2x6
Ribostamycin	T36.5x1	T36.5x2	T36.5x3	T36.5x4	T36.5x5	T36.5x6
Ricin	T62.2x1	T62.2x2	T62.2x3	T62.2x4	—	—
Ricinus communis	T62.2x1	T62.2x2	T62.2x3	T62.2x4	—	—
Rickettsial vaccine NEC	T50.A91	T50.A92	T50.A93	T50.A94	T50.A95	T50.A96
Rifabutin	T36.6x1	T36.6x2	T36.6x3	T36.6x4	T36.6x5	T36.6x6
Rifamide	T36.6x1	T36.6x2	T36.6x3	T36.6x4	T36.6x5	T36.6x6
Rifampicin	T36.6x1	T36.6x2	T36.6x3	T36.6x4	T36.6x5	T36.6x6
with isoniazid	T37.1x1	T37.1x2	T37.1x3	T37.1x4	T37.1x5	T37.1x6
Rifampin	T36.6x1	T36.6x2	T36.6x3	T36.6x4	T36.6x5	T36.6x6
Rifamycin	T36.6x1	T36.6x2	T36.6x3	T36.6x4	T36.6x5	T36.6x6
Rifaximin	T36.6x1	T36.6x2	T36.6x3	T36.6x4	T36.6x5	T36.6x6
Rimantadine	T37.5x1	T37.5x2	T37.5x3	T37.5x4	T37.5x5	T37.5x6
Rimazolium metilsulfate	T39.8x1	T39.8x2	T39.8x3	T39.8x4	T39.8x5	T39.8x6
Rimifon	T37.1x1	T37.1x2	T37.1x3	T37.1x4	T37.1x5	T37.1x6
Rimiterol	T48.6x1	T48.6x2	T48.6x3	T48.6x4	T48.6x5	T48.6x6
Ringer (lactate) solution	T50.3x1	T50.3x2	T50.3x3	T50.3x4	T50.3x5	T50.3x6
Ristocetin	T36.8x1	T36.8x2	T36.8x3	T36.8x4	T36.8x5	T36.8x6
Ritalin	T43.631	T43.632	T43.633	T43.634	T43.635	T43.636
Ritodrine	T44.5x1	T44.5x2	T44.5x3	T44.5x4	T44.5x5	T44.5x6
Roach killer - *see* Insecticide						
Rociverine	T44.3x1	T44.3x2	T44.3x3	T44.3x4	T44.3x5	T44.3x6
Rocky Mountain spotted fever vaccine	T50.A91	T50.A92	T50.A93	T50.A94	T50.A95	T50.A96
Rodenticide NEC	T60.4x1	T60.4x2	T60.4x3	T60.4x4	—	—
Rohypnol	T42.4x1	T42.4x2	T42.4x3	T42.4x4	T42.4x5	T42.4x6
Rokitamycin	T36.3x1	T36.3x2	T36.3x3	T36.3x4	T36.3x5	T36.3x6
Rolaids	T47.1x1	T47.1x2	T47.1x3	T47.1x4	T47.1x5	T47.1x6
Rolitetracycline	T36.4x1	T36.4x2	T36.4x3	T36.4x4	T36.4x5	T36.4x6

Substance	Poisoning, Accidental (Unintentional)	Poisoning, Intentional Self-Harm	Poisoning, Assault	Poisoning, Undetermined	Adverse Effect	Underdosing
	External Cause (T-Code)					
Romilar	T48.3x1	T48.3x2	T48.3x3	T48.3x4	T48.3x5	T48.3x6
Ronifibrate	T46.6x1	T46.6x2	T46.6x3	T46.6x4	T46.6x5	T46.6x6
Rosaprostol	T47.1x1	T47.1x2	T47.1x3	T47.1x4	T47.1x5	T47.1x6
Rose bengal sodium (131I)	T50.8x1	T50.8x2	T50.8x3	T50.8x4	T50.8x5	T50.8x6
Rose water ointment	T49.3x1	T49.3x2	T49.3x3	T49.3x4	T49.3x5	T49.3x6
Rosoxacin	T37.8x1	T37.8x2	T37.8x3	T37.8x4	T37.8x5	T37.8x6
Rotenone	T60.2x1	T60.2x2	T60.2x3	T60.2x4	—	—
Rotoxamine	T45.0x1	T45.0x2	T45.0x3	T45.0x4	T45.0x5	T45.0x6
Rough-on-rats	T60.4x1	T60.4x2	T60.4x3	T60.4x4	—	—
Roxatidine	T47.0x1	T47.0x2	T47.0x3	T47.0x4	T47.0x5	T47.0x6
Roxithromycin	T36.3x1	T36.3x2	T36.3x3	T36.3x4	T36.3x5	T36.3x6
Rt-PA	T45.611	T45.612	T45.613	T45.614	T45.615	T45.616
Rubbing alcohol	T51.2x1	T51.2x2	T51.2x3	T51.2x4	—	—
Rubefacient	T49.4x1	T49.4x2	T49.4x3	T49.4x4	T49.4x5	T49.4x6
Rubella vaccine	T50.B91	T50.B92	T50.B93	T50.B94	T50.B95	T50.B96
Rubelogen	T50.B91	T50.B92	T50.B93	T50.B94	T50.B95	T50.B96
Rubeovax	T50.991	T50.992	T50.993	T50.994	T50.995	T50.996
Rubidium chloride Rb82	T50.8x1	T50.8x2	T50.8x3	T50.8x4	T50.8x5	T50.8x6
Rubidomycin	T45.1x1	T45.1x2	T45.1x3	T45.1x4	T45.1x5	T45.1x6
Rue	T62.2x1	T62.2x2	T62.2x3	T62.2x4	—	—
Rufocromomycin	T45.1x1	T45.1x2	T45.1x3	T45.1x4	T45.1x5	T45.1x6
Russel's viper venin	T45.7x1	T45.7x2	T45.7x3	T45.7x4	T45.7x5	T45.7x6
Ruta (graveolens)	T62.2x1	T62.2x2	T62.2x3	T62.2x4	—	—
Rutinum	T46.991	T46.992	T46.993	T46.994	T46.995	T46.996
Rutoside	T46.991	T46.992	T46.993	T46.994	T46.995	T46.996
Sabadilla (plant)	T62.2x1	T62.2x2	T62.2x3	T62.2x4	—	—
pesticide	T60.2x1	T60.2x2	T60.2x3	T60.2x4	—	—
Saccharated iron oxide	T45.8x1	T45.8x2	T45.8x3	T45.8x4	T45.8x5	T45.8x6
Saccharin	T50.901	T50.902	T50.903	T50.904	T50.905	T50.906
Saccharomyces boulardii	T47.6x1	T47.6x2	T47.6x3	T47.6x4	T47.6x5	T47.6x6
Safflower oil	T46.6x1	T46.6x2	T46.6x3	T46.6x4	T46.6x5	T46.6x6
Safrazine	T43.1x1	T43.1x2	T43.1x3	T43.1x4	T43.1x5	T43.1x6
Salazosulfapyridine	T37.0x1	T37.0x2	T37.0x3	T37.0x4	T37.0x5	T37.0x6
Salbutamol	T48.6x1	T48.6x2	T48.6x3	T48.6x4	T48.6x5	T48.6x6
Salicylamide	T39.091	T39.092	T39.093	T39.094	T39.095	T39.096
Salicylate NEC	T39.091	T39.092	T39.093	T39.094	T39.095	T39.096
methyl	T49.3x1	T49.3x2	T49.3x3	T49.3x4	T49.3x5	T49.3x6
theobromine calcium	T50.2x1	T50.2x2	T50.2x3	T50.2x4	T50.2x5	T50.2x6
Salicylazosulfapyridine	T37.0x1	T37.0x2	T37.0x3	T37.0x4	T37.0x5	T37.0x6
Salicylhydroxamic acid	T49.0x1	T49.0x2	T49.0x3	T49.0x4	T49.0x5	T49.0x6

Substance	Poisoning, Accidental (Unintentional)	Poisoning, Intentional Self-Harm	Poisoning, Assault	Poisoning, Undetermined	Adverse Effect	Underdosing
			External Cause (T-Code)			
Salicylic acid	T49.4x1	T49.4x2	T49.4x3	T49.4x4	T49.4x5	T49.4x6
with benzoic acid	T49.4x1	T49.4x2	T49.4x3	T49.4x4	T49.4x5	T49.4x6
congeners	T39.091	T39.092	T39.093	T39.094	T39.095	T39.096
derivative	T39.091	T39.092	T39.093	T39.094	T39.095	T39.096
salts	T39.091	T39.092	T39.093	T39.094	T39.095	T39.096
Salinazid	T37.1x1	T37.1x2	T37.1x3	T37.1x4	T37.1x5	T37.1x6
Salmeterol	T48.6x1	T48.6x2	T48.6x3	T48.6x4	T48.6x5	T48.6x6
Salol	T49.3x1	T49.3x2	T49.3x3	T49.3x4	T49.3x5	T49.3x6
Salsalate	T39.091	T39.092	T39.093	T39.094	T39.095	T39.096
Salt substitute	T50.901	T50.902	T50.903	T50.904	T50.905	T50.906
Salt-replacing drug	T50.901	T50.902	T50.903	T50.904	T50.905	T50.906
Salt-retaining mineralocorticoid	T50.0x1	T50.0x2	T50.0x3	T50.0x4	T50.0x5	T50.0x6
Saluretic NEC	T50.2x1	T50.2x2	T50.2x3	T50.2x4	T50.2x5	T50.2x6
Saluron	T50.2x1	T50.2x2	T50.2x3	T50.2x4	T50.2x5	T50.2x6
Salvarsan 606 (neosilver) (silver)	T37.8x1	T37.8x2	T37.8x3	T37.8x4	T37.8x5	T37.8x6
Sambucus canadensis	T62.2x1	T62.2x2	T62.2x3	T62.2x4	—	—
berry	T62.1x1	T62.1x2	T62.1x3	T62.1x4	—	—
Sandril	T46.5x1	T46.5x2	T46.5x3	T46.5x4	T46.5x5	T46.5x6
Sanguinaria canadensis	T62.2x1	T62.2x2	T62.2x3	T62.2x4	—	—
Saniflush (cleaner)	T54.2x1	T54.2x2	T54.2x3	T54.2x4	—	—
Santonin	T37.4x1	T37.4x2	T37.4x3	T37.4x4	T37.4x5	T37.4x6
Santyl	T49.8x1	T49.8x2	T49.8x3	T49.8x4	T49.8x5	T49.8x6
Saralasin	T46.5x1	T46.5x2	T46.5x3	T46.5x4	T46.5x5	T46.5x6
Sarcolysin	T45.1x1	T45.1x2	T45.1x3	T45.1x4	T45.1x5	T45.1x6
Sarkomycin	T45.1x1	T45.1x2	T45.1x3	T45.1x4	T45.1x5	T45.1x6
Saroten	T43.011	T43.012	T43.013	T43.014	T43.015	T43.016
Saturnine - *see* Lead						
Savin (oil)	T49.4x1	T49.4x2	T49.4x3	T49.4x4	T49.4x5	T49.4x6
Scammony	T47.2x1	T47.2x2	T47.2x3	T47.2x4	T47.2x5	T47.2x6
Scarlet red	T49.8x1	T49.8x2	T49.8x3	T49.8x4	T49.8x5	T49.8x6
Scheele's green	T57.0x1	T57.0x2	T57.0x3	T57.0x4	—	—
insecticide	T57.0x1	T57.0x2	T57.0x3	T57.0x4	—	—
Schizontozide (blood) (tissue)	T37.2x1	T37.2x2	T37.2x3	T37.2x4	T37.2x5	T37.2x6
Schradan	T60.0x1	T60.0x2	T60.0x3	T60.0x4	—	—
Schweinfurth green	T57.0x1	T57.0x2	T57.0x3	T57.0x4	—	—
insecticide	T57.0x1	T57.0x2	T57.0x3	T57.0x4	—	—
Scilla, rat poison	T60.4x1	T60.4x2	T60.4x3	T60.4x4	—	—
Scillaren	T60.4x1	T60.4x2	T60.4x3	T60.4x4	—	—
Sclerosing agent	T46.8x1	T46.8x2	T46.8x3	T46.8x4	T46.8x5	T46.8x6
Scombrotoxin	T61.11	T61.12	T61.13	T61.14	—	—

Substance	External Cause (T-Code)					
	Poisoning, Accidental (Unintentional)	Poisoning, Intentional Self-Harm	Poisoning, Assault	Poisoning, Undetermined	Adverse Effect	Underdosing
Scopolamine	T44.3x1	T44.3x2	T44.3x3	T44.3x4	T44.3x5	T44.3x6
Scopolia extract	T44.3x1	T44.3x2	T44.3x3	T44.3x4	T44.3x5	T44.3x6
Scouring powder	T65.891	T65.892	T65.893	T65.894	—	—
Sea						
anemone (sting)	T63.631	T63.632	T63.633	T63.634	—	—
cucumber (sting)	T63.691	T63.692	T63.693	T63.694	—	—
snake (bite) (venom)	T63.091	T63.092	T63.093	T63.094	—	—
urchin spine (puncture)	T63.691	T63.692	T63.693	T63.694	—	—
Seafood	T61.91	T61.92	T61.93	T61.94	—	—
specified NEC	T61.8x1	T61.8x2	T61.8x3	T61.8x4	—	—
Secbutabarbital	T42.3x1	T42.3x2	T42.3x3	T42.3x4	T42.3x5	T42.3x6
Secbutabarbitone	T42.3x1	T42.3x2	T42.3x3	T42.3x4	T42.3x5	T42.3x6
Secnidazole	T37.3x1	T37.3x2	T37.3x3	T37.3x4	T37.3x5	T37.3x6
Secobarbital	T42.3x1	T42.3x2	T42.3x3	T42.3x4	T42.3x5	T42.3x6
Seconal	T42.3x1	T42.3x2	T42.3x3	T42.3x4	T42.3x5	T42.3x6
Secretin	T50.8x1	T50.8x2	T50.8x3	T50.8x4	T50.8x5	T50.8x6
Sedative NEC	T42.71	T42.72	T42.73	T42.74	T42.75	T42.76
mixed NEC	T42.6x1	T42.6x2	T42.6x3	T42.6x4	T42.6x5	T42.6x6
Sedormid	T42.6x1	T42.6x2	T42.6x3	T42.6x4	T42.6x5	T42.6x6
Seed disinfectant or dressing	T60.8x1	T60.8x2	T60.8x3	T60.8x4	—	—
Seeds (poisonous)	T62.2x1	T62.2x2	T62.2x3	T62.2x4	—	—
disinfectant or dressing	T65.891	T65.892	T65.893	T65.894	—	—
Selegiline	T42.8x1	T42.8x2	T42.8x3	T42.8x4	T42.8x5	T42.8x6
Selenium NEC	T56.891	T56.892	T56.893	T56.894	—	—
disulfide or sulfide	T49.4x1	T49.4x2	T49.4x3	T49.4x4	T49.4x5	T49.4x6
fumes	T59.891	T59.892	T59.893	T59.894	—	—
sulfide	T49.4x1	T49.4x2	T49.4x3	T49.4x4	T49.4x5	T49.4x6
Selenomethionine (75Se)	T50.8x1	T50.8x2	T50.8x3	T50.8x4	T50.8x5	T50.8x6
Selsun	T49.4x1	T49.4x2	T49.4x3	T49.4x4	T49.4x5	T49.4x6
Semustine	T45.1x1	T45.1x2	T45.1x3	T45.1x4	T45.1x5	T45.1x6
Senega syrup	T48.4x1	T48.4x2	T48.4x3	T48.4x4	T48.4x5	T48.4x6
Senna	T47.2x1	T47.2x2	T47.2x3	T47.2x4	T47.2x5	T47.2x6
Sennoside A+B	T47.2x1	T47.2x2	T47.2x3	T47.2x4	T47.2x5	T47.2x6
Septisol	T49.2x1	T49.2x2	T49.2x3	T49.2x4	T49.2x5	T49.2x6
Seractide	T38.811	T38.812	T38.813	T38.814	T38.815	T38.816
Serax	T42.4x1	T42.4x2	T42.4x3	T42.4x4	T42.4x5	T42.4x6
Serenesil	T42.6x1	T42.6x2	T42.6x3	T42.6x4	T42.6x5	T42.6x6
Serenium (hydrochloride)	T37.91	T37.92	T37.93	T37.94	T37.95	T37.96
Serepax - see Oxazepam						
Sermorelin	T38.891	T38.892	T38.893	T38.894	T38.895	T38.896

Substance	Poisoning, Accidental (Unintentional)	Poisoning, Intentional Self-Harm	Poisoning, Assault	Poisoning, Undetermined	Adverse Effect	Underdosing
			External Cause (T-Code)			
Sernyl	T41.1x1	T41.1x2	T41.1x3	T41.1x4	T41.1x5	T41.1x6
Serotonin	T50.991	T50.992	T50.993	T50.994	T50.995	T50.996
Serpasil	T46.5x1	T46.5x2	T46.5x3	T46.5x4	T46.5x5	T46.5x6
Serrapeptase	T45.3x1	T45.3x2	T45.3x3	T45.3x4	T45.3x5	T45.3x6
Serum						
antibotulinus	T50.Z11	T50.Z12	T50.Z13	T50.Z14	T50.Z15	T50.Z16
anticytotoxic	T50.Z11	T50.Z12	T50.Z13	T50.Z14	T50.Z15	T50.Z16
antidiphtheria	T50.Z11	T50.Z12	T50.Z13	T50.Z14	T50.Z15	T50.Z16
antimeningococcus	T50.Z11	T50.Z12	T50.Z13	T50.Z14	T50.Z15	T50.Z16
anti-Rh	T50.Z11	T50.Z12	T50.Z13	T50.Z14	T50.Z15	T50.Z16
anti-snake-bite	T50.Z11	T50.Z12	T50.Z13	T50.Z14	T50.Z15	T50.Z16
antitetanic	T50.Z11	T50.Z12	T50.Z13	T50.Z14	T50.Z15	T50.Z16
antitoxic	T50.Z11	T50.Z12	T50.Z13	T50.Z14	T50.Z15	T50.Z16
complement (inhibitor)	T45.8x1	T45.8x2	T45.8x3	T45.8x4	T45.8x5	T45.8x6
convalescent	T50.Z11	T50.Z12	T50.Z13	T50.Z14	T50.Z15	T50.Z16
hemolytic complement	T45.8x1	T45.8x2	T45.8x3	T45.8x4	T45.8x5	T45.8x6
immune (human)	T50.Z11	T50.Z12	T50.Z13	T50.Z14	T50.Z15	T50.Z16
protective NEC	T50.Z11	T50.Z12	T50.Z13	T50.Z14	T50.Z15	T50.Z16
Setastine	T45.0x1	T45.0x2	T45.0x3	T45.0x4	T45.0x5	T45.0x6
Setoperone	T43.591	T43.592	T43.593	T43.594	T43.595	T43.596
Sewer gas	T59.891	T59.892	T59.893	T59.894	—	—
Shampoo	T54.91	T54.92	T54.93	T54.94	—	—
Shellfish, noxious, nonbacterial	T61.781	T61.782	T61.783	T61.784	—	—
Silibinin	T50.991	T50.992	T50.993	T50.994	T50.995	T50.996
Silicone NEC	T65.891	T65.892	T65.893	T65.894	—	—
medicinal	T49.3x1	T49.3x2	T49.3x3	T49.3x4	T49.3x5	T49.3x6
Silvadene	T49.0x1	T49.0x2	T49.0x3	T49.0x4	T49.0x5	T49.0x6
Silver	T49.0x1	T49.0x2	T49.0x3	T49.0x4	T49.0x5	T49.0x6
anti-infectives	T49.0x1	T49.0x2	T49.0x3	T49.0x4	T49.0x5	T49.0x6
arsphenamine	T37.8x1	T37.8x2	T37.8x3	T37.8x4	T37.8x5	T37.8x6
colloidal	T49.0x1	T49.0x2	T49.0x3	T49.0x4	T49.0x5	T49.0x6
nitrate	T49.0x1	T49.0x2	T49.0x3	T49.0x4	T49.0x5	T49.0x6
ophthalmic preparation	T49.5x1	T49.5x2	T49.5x3	T49.5x4	T49.5x5	T49.5x6
toughened (keratolytic)	T49.4x1	T49.4x2	T49.4x3	T49.4x4	T49.4x5	T49.4x6
nonmedicinal (dust)	T56.891	T56.892	T56.893	T56.894	—	—
protein	T49.5x1	T49.5x2	T49.5x3	T49.5x4	T49.5x5	T49.5x6
salvarsan	T37.8x1	T37.8x2	T37.8x3	T37.8x4	T37.8x5	T37.8x6
sulfadiazine	T49.4x1	T49.4x2	T49.4x3	T49.4x4	T49.4x5	T49.4x6
Silymarin	T50.991	T50.992	T50.993	T50.994	T50.995	T50.996
Simaldrate	T47.1x1	T47.1x2	T47.1x3	T47.1x4	T47.1x5	T47.1x6
Simazine	T60.3x1	T60.3x2	T60.3x3	T60.3x4	—	—

Substance	Poisoning, Accidental (Unintentional)	Poisoning, Intentional Self-Harm	Poisoning, Assault	Poisoning, Undetermined	Adverse Effect	Underdosing
	External Cause (T-Code)					
Simethicone	T47.1x1	T47.1x2	T47.1x3	T47.1x4	T47.1x5	T47.1x6
Simfibrate	T46.6x1	T46.6x2	T46.6x3	T46.6x4	T46.6x5	T46.6x6
Simvastatin	T46.6x1	T46.6x2	T46.6x3	T46.6x4	T46.6x5	T46.6x6
Sincalide	T50.8x1	T50.8x2	T50.8x3	T50.8x4	T50.8x5	T50.8x6
Sinequan	T43.011	T43.012	T43.013	T43.014	T43.015	T43.016
Singoserp	T46.5x1	T46.5x2	T46.5x3	T46.5x4	T46.5x5	T46.5x6
Sintrom	T45.511	T45.512	T45.513	T45.514	T45.515	T45.516
Sisomicin	T36.5x1	T36.5x2	T36.5x3	T36.5x4	T36.5x5	T36.5x6
Sitosterols	T46.6x1	T46.6x2	T46.6x3	T46.6x4	T46.6x5	T46.6x6
Skeletal muscle relaxants	T48.1x1	T48.1x2	T48.1x3	T48.1x4	T48.1x5	T48.1x6
Skin						
agents (external)	T49.91	T49.92	T49.93	T49.94	T49.95	T49.96
specified NEC	T49.8x1	T49.8x2	T49.8x3	T49.8x4	T49.8x5	T49.8x6
test antigen	T50.8x1	T50.8x2	T50.8x3	T50.8x4	T50.8x5	T50.8x6
Sleep-eze	T45.0x1	T45.0x2	T45.0x3	T45.0x4	T45.0x5	T45.0x6
Sleeping draught, pill	T42.71	T42.72	T42.73	T42.74	T42.75	T42.76
Smallpox vaccine	T50.B11	T50.B12	T50.B13	T50.B14	T50.B15	T50.B16
Smelter fumes NEC	T56.91	T56.92	T56.93	T56.94	—	—
Smog	T59.1x1	T59.1x2	T59.1x3	T59.1x4	—	—
Smoke NEC	T59.811	T59.812	T59.813	T59.814	—	—
Smooth muscle relaxant	T44.3x1	T44.3x2	T44.3x3	T44.3x4	T44.3x5	T44.3x6
Snail killer NEC	T60.8x1	T60.8x2	T60.8x3	T60.8x4	—	—
Snake venom or bite	T63.001	T63.002	T63.003	T63.004	—	—
hemocoagulase	T45.7x1	T45.7x2	T45.7x3	T45.7x4	T45.7x5	T45.7x6
Snuff	T65.211	T65.212	T65.213	T65.214	—	—
Soap (powder) (product)	T54.91	T54.92	T54.93	T54.94	—	—
enema	T47.4x1	T47.4x2	T47.4x3	T47.4x4	T47.4x5	T47.4x6
medicinal, soft	T49.2x1	T49.2x2	T49.2x3	T49.2x4	T49.2x5	T49.2x6
superfatted	T49.2x1	T49.2x2	T49.2x3	T49.2x4	T49.2x5	T49.2x6
Sobrerol	T48.4x1	T48.4x2	T48.4x3	T48.4x4	T48.4x5	T48.4x6
Soda (caustic)	T54.3x1	T54.3x2	T54.3x3	T54.3x4	—	—
bicarb	T47.1x1	T47.1x2	T47.1x3	T47.1x4	T47.1x5	T47.1x6
chlorinated - *see* Sodium, hypochlorite						
Sodium						
acetosulfone	T37.1x1	T37.1x2	T37.1x3	T37.1x4	T37.1x5	T37.1x6
acetrizoate	T50.8x1	T50.8x2	T50.8x3	T50.8x4	T50.8x5	T50.8x6
acid phosphate	T50.3x1	T50.3x2	T50.3x3	T50.3x4	T50.3x5	T50.3x6
alginate	T47.8x1	T47.8x2	T47.8x3	T47.8x4	T47.8x5	T47.8x6
amidotrizoate	T50.8x1	T50.8x2	T50.8x3	T50.8x4	T50.8x5	T50.8x6
aminopterin	T45.1x1	T45.1x2	T45.1x3	T45.1x4	T45.1x5	T45.1x6
amylosulfate	T47.8x1	T47.8x2	T47.8x3	T47.8x4	T47.8x5	T47.8x6

	External Cause (T-Code)					
Substance	Poisoning, Accidental (Unintentional)	Poisoning, Intentional Self-Harm	Poisoning, Assault	Poisoning, Undetermined	Adverse Effect	Underdosing
Sodium *(Continued)*						
amytal	T42.3x1	T42.3x2	T42.3x3	T42.3x4	T42.3x5	T42.3x6
antimony gluconate	T37.3x1	T37.3x2	T37.3x3	T37.3x4	T37.3x5	T37.3x6
arsenate	T57.0x1	T57.0x2	T57.0x3	T57.0x4	—	—
aurothiomalate	T39.4x1	T39.4x2	T39.4x3	T39.4x4	T39.4x5	T39.4x6
aurothiosulfate	T39.4x1	T39.4x2	T39.4x3	T39.4x4	T39.4x5	T39.4x6
barbiturate	T42.3x1	T42.3x2	T42.3x3	T42.3x4	T42.3x5	T42.3x6
basic phosphate	T47.4x1	T47.4x2	T47.4x3	T47.4x4	T47.4x5	T47.4x6
bicarbonate	T47.1x1	T47.1x2	T47.1x3	T47.1x4	T47.1x5	T47.1x6
bichromate	T57.8x1	T57.8x2	T57.8x3	T57.8x4	—	—
biphosphate	T50.3x1	T50.3x2	T50.3x3	T50.3x4	T50.3x5	T50.3x6
bisulfate	T65.891	T65.892	T65.893	T65.894	—	—
borate						
cleanser	T57.8x1	T57.8x2	T57.8x3	T57.8x4	—	—
eye	T49.5x1	T49.5x2	T49.5x3	T49.5x4	T49.5x5	T49.5x6
therapeutic	T49.8x1	T49.8x2	T49.8x3	T49.8x4	T49.8x5	T49.8x6
bromide	T42.6x1	T42.6x2	T42.6x3	T42.6x4	T42.6x5	T42.6x6
cacodylate (nonmedicinal) NEC	T50.8x1	T50.8x2	T50.8x3	T50.8x4	T50.8x5	T50.8x6
anti-infective	T37.8x1	T37.8x2	T37.8x3	T37.8x4	T37.8x5	T37.8x6
herbicide	T60.3x1	T60.3x2	T60.3x3	T60.3x4	—	—
calcium edetate	T45.8x1	T45.8x2	T45.8x3	T45.8x4	T45.8x5	T45.8x6
carbonate NEC	T54.3x1	T54.3x2	T54.3x3	T54.3x4	—	—
chlorate NEC	T65.891	T65.892	T65.893	T65.894	—	—
herbicide	T54.91	T54.92	T54.93	T54.94	—	—
chloride	T50.3x1	T50.3x2	T50.3x3	T50.3x4	T50.3x5	T50.3x6
with glucose	T50.3x1	T50.3x2	T50.3x3	T50.3x4	T50.3x5	T50.3x6
chromate	T65.891	T65.892	T65.893	T65.894	—	—
citrate	T50.991	T50.992	T50.993	T50.994	T50.995	T50.996
cromoglicate	T48.6x1	T48.6x2	T48.6x3	T48.6x4	T48.6x5	T48.6x6
cyanide	T57.8x1	T57.8x2	T57.8x3	T57.8x4	—	—
cyclamate	T50.3x1	T50.3x2	T50.3x3	T50.3x4	T50.3x5	T50.3x6
dehydrocholate	T45.8x1	T45.8x2	T45.8x3	T45.8x4	T45.8x5	T45.8x6
diatrizoate	T50.8x1	T50.8x2	T50.8x3	T50.8x4	T50.8x5	T50.8x6
dibunate	T48.4x1	T48.4x2	T48.4x3	T48.4x4	T48.4x5	T48.4x6
dioctyl sulfosuccinate	T47.4x1	T47.4x2	T47.4x3	T47.4x4	T47.4x5	T47.4x6
dipantoyl ferrate	T45.8x1	T45.8x2	T45.8x3	T45.8x4	T45.8x5	T45.8x6
edetate	T45.8x1	T45.8x2	T45.8x3	T45.8x4	T45.8x5	T45.8x6
ethacrynate	T50.1x1	T50.1x2	T50.1x3	T50.1x4	T50.1x5	T50.1x6
feredetate	T45.8x1	T45.8x2	T45.8x3	T45.8x4	T45.8x5	T45.8x6
Fluoride - *see* Fluoride						

	External Cause (T-Code)					
Substance	Poisoning, Accidental (Unintentional)	Poisoning, Intentional Self-Harm	Poisoning, Assault	Poisoning, Undetermined	Adverse Effect	Underdosing
Sodium *(Continued)*						
fluoroacetate (dust) (pesticide)	T60.4x1	T60.4x2	T60.4x3	T60.4x4	—	—
free salt	T50.3x1	T50.3x2	T50.3x3	T50.3x4	T50.3x5	T50.3x6
fusidate	T36.8x1	T36.8x2	T36.8x3	T36.8x4	T36.8x5	T36.8x6
glucaldrate	T47.1x1	T47.1x2	T47.1x3	T47.1x4	T47.1x5	T47.1x6
glucosulfone	T37.1x1	T37.1x2	T37.1x3	T37.1x4	T37.1x5	T37.1x6
glutamate	T45.8x1	T45.8x2	T45.8x3	T45.8x4	T45.8x5	T45.8x6
hydrogen carbonate	T50.3x1	T50.3x2	T50.3x3	T50.3x4	T50.3x5	T50.3x6
hydroxide	T54.3x1	T54.3x2	T54.3x3	T54.3x4	—	—
hypochlorite (bleach) NEC	T54.3x1	T54.3x2	T54.3x3	T54.3x4	—	—
disinfectant	T54.3x1	T54.3x2	T54.3x3	T54.3x4	—	—
medicinal (anti-infective) (external)	T49.0x1	T49.0x2	T49.0x3	T49.0x4	T49.0x5	T49.0x6
vapor	T54.3x1	T54.3x2	T54.3x3	T54.3x4	—	—
hyposulfite	T49.0x1	T49.0x2	T49.0x3	T49.0x4	T49.0x5	T49.0x6
indigotin disulfonate	T50.8x1	T50.8x2	T50.8x3	T50.8x4	T50.8x5	T50.8x6
iodide	T50.991	T50.992	T50.993	T50.994	T50.995	T50.996
I-131	T50.8x1	T50.8x2	T50.8x3	T50.8x4	T50.8x5	T50.8x6
therapeutic	T38.2x1	T38.2x2	T38.2x3	T38.2x4	T38.2x5	T38.2x6
iodohippurate (131I)	T50.8x1	T50.8x2	T50.8x3	T50.8x4	T50.8x5	T50.8x6
iopodate	T50.8x1	T50.8x2	T50.8x3	T50.8x4	T50.8x5	T50.8x6
iothalamate	T50.8x1	T50.8x2	T50.8x3	T50.8x4	T50.8x5	T50.8x6
iron edetate	T45.4x1	T45.4x2	T45.4x3	T45.4x4	T45.4x5	T45.4x6
lactate (compound solution)	T45.8x1	T45.8x2	T45.8x3	T45.8x4	T45.8x5	T45.8x6
lauryl (sulfate)	T49.2x1	T49.2x2	T49.2x3	T49.2x4	T49.2x5	T49.2x6
L-triiodothyronine	T38.1x1	T38.1x2	T38.1x3	T38.1x4	T38.1x5	T38.1x6
magnesium citrate	T50.991	T50.992	T50.993	T50.994	T50.995	T50.996
mersalate	T50.2x1	T50.2x2	T50.2x3	T50.2x4	T50.2x5	T50.2x6
metasilicate	T65.891	T65.892	T65.893	T65.894	—	—
metrizoate	T50.8x1	T50.8x2	T50.8x3	T50.8x4	T50.8x5	T50.8x6
monofluoroacetate (pesticide)	T60.1x1	T60.1x2	T60.1x3	T60.1x4	—	—
morrhuate	T46.8x1	T46.8x2	T46.8x3	T46.8x4	T46.8x5	T46.8x6
nafcillin	T36.0x1	T36.0x2	T36.0x3	T36.0x4	T36.0x5	T36.0x6
nitrate (oxidizing agent)	T65.891	T65.892	T65.893	T65.894	—	—
nitrite	T50.6x1	T50.6x2	T50.6x3	T50.6x4	T50.6x5	T50.6x6
nitroferricyanide	T46.5x1	T46.5x2	T46.5x3	T46.5x4	T46.5x5	T46.5x6
nitroprusside	T46.5x1	T46.5x2	T46.5x3	T46.5x4	T46.5x5	T46.5x6
oxalate	T65.891	T65.892	T65.893	T65.894	—	—
oxide/peroxide	T65.891	T65.892	T65.893	T65.894	—	—
oxybate	T41.291	T41.292	T41.293	T41.294	T41.295	T41.296
para-aminohippurate	T50.8x1	T50.8x2	T50.8x3	T50.8x4	T50.8x5	T50.8x6

	External Cause (T-Code)					
Substance	Poisoning, Accidental (Unintentional)	Poisoning, Intentional Self-Harm	Poisoning, Assault	Poisoning, Undetermined	Adverse Effect	Underdosing
Sodium *(Continued)*						
perborate (nonmedicinal) NEC	T65.891	T65.892	T65.893	T65.894	—	—
medicinal	T49.0x1	T49.0x2	T49.0x3	T49.0x4	T49.0x5	T49.0x6
soap	T55.0x1	T55.0x2	T55.0x3	T55.0x4	—	—
percarbonate - *see* Sodium, perborate						
pertechnetate Tc99m	T50.8x1	T50.8x2	T50.8x3	T50.8x4	T50.8x5	T50.8x6
phosphate						
cellulose	T45.8x1	T45.8x2	T45.8x3	T45.8x4	T45.8x5	T45.8x6
dibasic	T47.2x1	T47.2x2	T47.2x3	T47.2x4	T47.2x5	T47.2x6
monobasic	T47.2x1	T47.2x2	T47.2x3	T47.2x4	T47.2x5	T47.2x6
phytate	T50.6x1	T50.6x2	T50.6x3	T50.6x4	T50.6x5	T50.6x6
picosulfate	T47.2x1	T47.2x2	T47.2x3	T47.2x4	T47.2x5	T47.2x6
polyhydroxyaluminium monocarbonate	T47.1x1	T47.1x2	T47.1x3	T47.1x4	T47.1x5	T47.1x6
polystyrene sulfonate	T50.3x1	T50.3x2	T50.3x3	T50.3x4	T50.3x5	T50.3x6
propionate	T49.0x1	T49.0x2	T49.0x3	T49.0x4	T49.0x5	T49.0x6
propyl hydroxybenzoate	T50.991	T50.992	T50.993	T50.994	T50.995	T50.996
psylliate	T46.8x1	T46.8x2	T46.8x3	T46.8x4	T46.8x5	T46.8x6
removing resins	T50.3x1	T50.3x2	T50.3x3	T50.3x4	T50.3x5	T50.3x6
salicylate	T39.091	T39.092	T39.093	T39.094	T39.095	T39.096
salt NEC	T50.3x1	T50.3x2	T50.3x3	T50.3x4	T50.3x5	T50.3x6
selenate	T60.2x1	T60.2x2	T60.2x3	T60.2x4	—	—
stibogluconate	T37.3x1	T37.3x2	T37.3x3	T37.3x4	T37.3x5	T37.3x6
sulfate	T47.4x1	T47.4x2	T47.4x3	T47.4x4	T47.4x5	T47.4x6
sulfoxone	T37.1x1	T37.1x2	T37.1x3	T37.1x4	T37.1x5	T37.1x6
tetradecyl sulfate	T46.8x1	T46.8x2	T46.8x3	T46.8x4	T46.8x5	T46.8x6
thiopental	T41.1x1	T41.1x2	T41.1x3	T41.1x4	T41.1x5	T41.1x6
thiosalicylate	T39.091	T39.092	T39.093	T39.094	T39.095	T39.096
thiosulfate	T50.6x1	T50.6x2	T50.6x3	T50.6x4	T50.6x5	T50.6x6
tolbutamide	T38.3x1	T38.3x2	T38.3x3	T38.3x4	T38.3x5	T38.3x6
l-triiodothyronine	T38.1x1	T38.1x2	T38.1x3	T38.1x4	T38.1x5	T38.1x6
tyropanoate	T50.8x1	T50.8x2	T50.8x3	T50.8x4	T50.8x5	T50.8x6
valproate	T42.6x1	T42.6x2	T42.6x3	T42.6x4	T42.6x5	T42.6x6
versenate	T50.6x1	T50.6x2	T50.6x3	T50.6x4	T50.6x5	T50.6x6
Sodium-free salt	T50.901	T50.902	T50.903	T50.904	T50.905	T50.906
Sodium-removing resin	T50.3x1	T50.3x2	T50.3x3	T50.3x4	T50.3x5	T50.3x6
Soft soap	T54.91	T54.92	T54.93	T54.94	—	—
Solanine	T62.2x1	T62.2x2	T62.2x3	T62.2x4	—	—
berries	T62.1x1	T62.1x2	T62.1x3	T62.1x4	—	—
Solanum dulcamara	T62.2x1	T62.2x2	T62.2x3	T62.2x4	—	—
berries	T62.1x1	T62.1x2	T62.1x3	T62.1x4	—	—

Substance	Poisoning, Accidental (Unintentional)	Poisoning, Intentional Self-Harm	Poisoning, Assault	Poisoning, Undetermined	Adverse Effect	Underdosing
			External Cause (T-Code)			
Solapsone	T37.1x1	T37.1x2	T37.1x3	T37.1x4	T37.1x5	T37.1x6
Solar lotion	T49.3x1	T49.3x2	T49.3x3	T49.3x4	T49.3x5	T49.3x6
Solasulfone	T37.1x1	T37.1x2	T37.1x3	T37.1x4	T37.1x5	T37.1x6
Soldering fluid	T65.891	T65.892	T65.893	T65.894	—	—
Solid substance	T65.91	T65.92	T65.93	T65.94	—	—
specified NEC	T65.891	T65.892	T65.893	T65.894	—	—
Solvent, industrial NEC	T52.91	T52.92	T52.93	T52.94	—	—
naphtha	T52.0x1	T52.0x2	T52.0x3	T52.0x4	—	—
petroleum	T52.0x1	T52.0x2	T52.0x3	T52.0x4	—	—
specified NEC	T52.91	T52.92	T52.93	T52.94	—	—
Soma	T42.8x1	T42.8x2	T42.8x3	T42.8x4	T42.8x5	T42.8x6
Somatorelin	T38.891	T38.892	T38.893	T38.894	T38.895	T38.896
Somatostatin	T38.991	T38.992	T38.993	T38.994	T38.995	T38.996
Somatotropin	T38.811	T38.812	T38.813	T38.814	T38.815	T38.816
Somatrem	T38.811	T38.812	T38.813	T38.814	T38.815	T38.816
Somatropin	T38.811	T38.812	T38.813	T38.814	T38.815	T38.816
Sominex	T45.0x1	T45.0x2	T45.0x3	T45.0x4	T45.0x5	T45.0x6
Somnos	T42.6x1	T42.6x2	T42.6x3	T42.6x4	T42.6x5	T42.6x6
Somonal	T42.3x1	T42.3x2	T42.3x3	T42.3x4	T42.3x5	T42.3x6
Soneryl	T42.3x1	T42.3x2	T42.3x3	T42.3x4	T42.3x5	T42.3x6
Soothing syrup	T50.901	T50.902	T50.903	T50.904	T50.905	T50.906
Sopor	T42.6x1	T42.6x2	T42.6x3	T42.6x4	T42.6x5	T42.6x6
Soporific	T42.71	T42.72	T42.73	T42.74	T42.75	T42.76
Soporific drug	T42.71	T42.72	T42.73	T42.74	T42.75	T42.76
specified type NEC	T42.6x1	T42.6x2	T42.6x3	T42.6x4	T42.6x5	T42.6x6
Sorbide nitrate	T46.3x1	T46.3x2	T46.3x3	T46.3x4	T46.3x5	T46.3x6
Sorbitol	T47.4x1	T47.4x2	T47.4x3	T47.4x4	T47.4x5	T47.4x6
Sotalol	T44.7x1	T44.7x2	T44.7x3	T44.7x4	T44.7x5	T44.7x6
Sotradecol	T46.8x1	T46.8x2	T46.8x3	T46.8x4	T46.8x5	T46.8x6
Soysterol	T46.6x1	T46.6x2	T46.6x3	T46.6x4	T46.6x5	T46.6x6
Spacoline	T44.3x1	T44.3x2	T44.3x3	T44.3x4	T44.3x5	T44.3x6
Spanish fly	T49.8x1	T49.8x2	T49.8x3	T49.8x4	T49.8x5	T49.8x6
Sparine	T43.3x1	T43.3x2	T43.3x3	T43.3x4	T43.3x5	T43.3x6
Sparteine	T48.0x1	T48.0x2	T48.0x3	T48.0x4	T48.0x5	T48.0x6
Spasmolytic						
anticholinergics	T44.3x1	T44.3x2	T44.3x3	T44.3x4	T44.3x5	T44.3x6
autonomic	T44.3x1	T44.3x2	T44.3x3	T44.3x4	T44.3x5	T44.3x6
bronchial NEC	T48.6x1	T48.6x2	T48.6x3	T48.6x4	T48.6x5	T48.6x6
quaternary ammonium	T44.3x1	T44.3x2	T44.3x3	T44.3x4	T44.3x5	T44.3x6
skeletal muscle NEC	T48.1x1	T48.1x2	T48.1x3	T48.1x4	T48.1x5	T48.1x6

TABLE OF DRUGS AND CHEMICALS

Substance	External Cause (T-Code)					
	Poisoning, Accidental (Unintentional)	Poisoning, Intentional Self-Harm	Poisoning, Assault	Poisoning, Undetermined	Adverse Effect	Underdosing
Spectinomycin	T36.5x1	T36.5x2	T36.5x3	T36.5x4	T36.5x5	T36.5x6
Speed	T43.621	T43.622	T43.623	T43.624	T43.625	T43.626
Spermicide	T49.8x1	T49.8x2	T49.8x3	T49.8x4	T49.8x5	T49.8x6
Spider (bite) (venom)	T63.391	T63.392	T63.393	T63.394	—	—
antivenin	T50.Z11	T50.Z12	T50.Z13	T50.Z14	T50.Z15	T50.Z16
Spigelia (root)	T37.4x1	T37.4x2	T37.4x3	T37.4x4	T37.4x5	T37.4x6
Spindle inactivator	T50.4x1	T50.4x2	T50.4x3	T50.4x4	T50.4x5	T50.4x6
Spiperone	T43.4x1	T43.4x2	T43.4x3	T43.4x4	T43.4x5	T43.4x6
Spiramycin	T36.3x1	T36.3x2	T36.3x3	T36.3x4	T36.3x5	T36.3x6
Spirapril	T46.4x1	T46.4x2	T46.4x3	T46.4x4	T46.4x5	T46.4x6
Spirilene	T43.591	T43.592	T43.593	T43.594	T43.595	T43.596
Spirit(s) (neutral) NEC	T51.0x1	T51.0x2	T51.0x3	T51.0x4	—	—
beverage	T51.0x1	T51.0x2	T51.0x3	T51.0x4	—	—
industrial	T51.0x1	T51.0x2	T51.0x3	T51.0x4	—	—
mineral	T52.0x1	T52.0x2	T52.0x3	T52.0x4	—	—
of salt - see Hydrochloric acid						
surgical	T51.0x1	T51.0x2	T51.0x3	T51.0x4	—	—
Spironolactone	T50.0x1	T50.0x2	T50.0x3	T50.0x4	T50.0x5	T50.0x6
Spiroperidol	T43.4x1	T43.4x2	T43.4x3	T43.4x4	T43.4x5	T43.4x6
Sponge, absorbable (gelatin)	T45.7x1	T45.7x2	T45.7x3	T45.7x4	T45.7x5	T45.7x6
Sporostacin	T49.0x1	T49.0x2	T49.0x3	T49.0x4	T49.0x5	T49.0x6
Spray (aerosol)	T65.91	T65.92	T65.93	T65.94	—	—
cosmetic	T65.891	T65.892	T65.893	T65.894	—	—
medicinal NEC	T50.901	T50.902	T50.903	T50.904	T50.905	T50.906
pesticides - see Pesticides						
specified content - see specific substance						
Spurge flax	T62.2x1	T62.2x2	T62.2x3	T62.2x4	—	—
Spurges	T62.2x1	T62.2x2	T62.2x3	T62.2x4	—	—
Sputum viscosity-lowering drug	T48.4x1	T48.4x2	T48.4x3	T48.4x4	T48.4x5	T48.4x6
Squill	T46.0x1	T46.0x2	T46.0x3	T46.0x4	T46.0x5	T46.0x6
rat poison	T60.4x1	T60.4x2	T60.4x3	T60.4x4	—	—
Squirting cucumber (cathartic)	T47.2x1	T47.2x2	T47.2x3	T47.2x4	T47.2x5	T47.2x6
Stains	T65.6x1	T65.6x2	T65.6x3	T65.6x4	—	—
Stannous fluoride	T49.7x1	T49.7x2	T49.7x3	T49.7x4	T49.7x5	T49.7x6
Stanolone	T38.7x1	T38.7x2	T38.7x3	T38.7x4	T38.7x5	T38.7x6
Stanozolol	T38.7x1	T38.7x2	T38.7x3	T38.7x4	T38.7x5	T38.7x6
Staphisagria or stavesacre (pediculicide)	T49.0x1	T49.0x2	T49.0x3	T49.0x4	T49.0x5	T49.0x6
Starch	T50.901	T50.902	T50.903	T50.904	T50.905	T50.906
Stelazine	T43.3x1	T43.3x2	T43.3x3	T43.3x4	T43.3x5	T43.3x6
Stemetil	T43.3x1	T43.3x2	T43.3x3	T43.3x4	T43.3x5	T43.3x6

Substance	External Cause (T-Code)					
	Poisoning, Accidental (Unintentional)	Poisoning, Intentional Self-Harm	Poisoning, Assault	Poisoning, Undetermined	Adverse Effect	Underdosing
Stepronin	T48.4x1	T48.4x2	T48.4x3	T48.4x4	T48.4x5	T48.4x6
Sterculia	T47.4x1	T47.4x2	T47.4x3	T47.4x4	T47.4x5	T47.4x6
Sternutator gas	T59.891	T59.892	T59.893	T59.894	—	—
Steroid	T38.0x1	T38.0x2	T38.0x3	T38.0x4	T38.0x5	T38.0x6
anabolic	T38.7x1	T38.7x2	T38.7x3	T38.7x4	T38.7x5	T38.7x6
androgenic	T38.7x1	T38.7x2	T38.7x3	T38.7x4	T38.7x5	T38.7x6
antineoplastic, hormone	T38.7x1	T38.7x2	T38.7x3	T38.7x4	T38.7x5	T38.7x6
estrogen	T38.5x1	T38.5x2	T38.5x3	T38.5x4	T38.5x5	T38.5x6
ENT agent	T49.6x1	T49.6x2	T49.6x3	T49.6x4	T49.6x5	T49.6x6
ophthalmic preparation	T49.5x1	T49.5x2	T49.5x3	T49.5x4	T49.5x5	T49.5x6
topical NEC	T49.0x1	T49.0x2	T49.0x3	T49.0x4	T49.0x5	T49.0x6
Stibine	T56.891	T56.892	T56.893	T56.894	—	—
Stibogluconate	T37.3x1	T37.3x2	T37.3x3	T37.3x4	T37.3x5	T37.3x6
Stibophen	T37.4x1	T37.4x2	T37.4x3	T37.4x4	T37.4x5	T37.4x6
Stilbamidine (isetionate)	T37.3x1	T37.3x2	T37.3x3	T37.3x4	T37.3x5	T37.3x6
Stilbestrol	T38.5x1	T38.5x2	T38.5x3	T38.5x4	T38.5x5	T38.5x6
Stilboestrol	T38.5x1	T38.5x2	T38.5x3	T38.5x4	T38.5x5	T38.5x6
Stimulant						
central nervous system (*see also* Psychostimulant)	T43.601	T43.602	T43.603	T43.604	T43.605	T43.606
analeptics	T50.7x1	T50.7x2	T50.7x3	T50.7x4	T50.7x5	T50.7x6
opiate antagonist	T50.7x1	T50.7x2	T50.7x3	T50.7x4	T50.7x5	T50.7x6
psychotherapeutic NEC (*see also* Psychotherapeutic drug)	T43.601	T43.602	T43.603	T43.604	T43.605	T43.606
specified NEC	T43.691	T43.692	T43.693	T43.694	T43.695	T43.696
respiratory	T48.901	T48.902	T48.903	T48.904	T48.905	T48.906
Stone-dissolving drug	T50.901	T50.902	T50.903	T50.904	T50.905	T50.906
Storage battery (cells) (acid)	T54.2x1	T54.2x2	T54.2x3	T54.2x4	—	—
Stovaine	T41.3x1	T41.3x2	T41.3x3	T41.3x4	T41.3x5	T41.3x6
infiltration (subcutaneous)	T41.3x1	T41.3x2	T41.3x3	T41.3x4	T41.3x5	T41.3x6
nerve block (peripheral) (plexus)	T41.3x1	T41.3x2	T41.3x3	T41.3x4	T41.3x5	T41.3x6
spinal	T41.3x1	T41.3x2	T41.3x3	T41.3x4	T41.3x5	T41.3x6
topical (surface)	T41.3x1	T41.3x2	T41.3x3	T41.3x4	T41.3x5	T41.3x6
Stovarsal	T37.8x1	T37.8x2	T37.8x3	T37.8x4	T37.8x5	T37.8x6
Stove gas - *see* Gas, stove	T57.91	T57.92	T57.93	T57.94	—	—
Stoxil	T49.5x1	T49.5x2	T49.5x3	T49.5x4	T49.5x5	T49.5x6
Stramonium	T48.6x1	T48.6x2	T48.6x3	T48.6x4	T48.6x5	T48.6x6
natural state	T62.2x1	T62.2x2	T62.2x3	T62.2x4	—	—
Streptodornase	T45.3x1	T45.3x2	T45.3x3	T45.3x4	T45.3x5	T45.3x6
Streptoduocin	T36.5x1	T36.5x2	T36.5x3	T36.5x4	T36.5x5	T36.5x6
Streptokinase	T45.611	T45.612	T45.613	T45.614	T45.615	T45.616
Streptomycin (derivative)	T36.5x1	T36.5x2	T36.5x3	T36.5x4	T36.5x5	T36.5x6

Substance	External Cause (T-Code)					
	Poisoning, Accidental (Unintentional)	Poisoning, Intentional Self-Harm	Poisoning, Assault	Poisoning, Undetermined	Adverse Effect	Underdosing
Streptonivicin	T36.5x1	T36.5x2	T36.5x3	T36.5x4	T36.5x5	T36.5x6
Streptovarycin	T36.5x1	T36.5x2	T36.5x3	T36.5x4	T36.5x5	T36.5x6
Streptozocin	T45.1x1	T45.1x2	T45.1x3	T45.1x4	T45.1x5	T45.1x6
Streptozotocin	T45.1x1	T45.1x2	T45.1x3	T45.1x4	T45.1x5	T45.1x6
Stripper (paint) (solvent)	T52.8x1	T52.8x2	T52.8x3	T52.8x4	—	—
Strobane	T60.1x1	T60.1x2	T60.1x3	T60.1x4	—	—
Strofantina	T46.0x1	T46.0x2	T46.0x3	T46.0x4	T46.0x5	T46.0x6
Strophanthin (g) (k)	T46.0x1	T46.0x2	T46.0x3	T46.0x4	T46.0x5	T46.0x6
Strophanthus	T46.0x1	T46.0x2	T46.0x3	T46.0x4	T46.0x5	T46.0x6
Strophantin	T46.0x1	T46.0x2	T46.0x3	T46.0x4	T46.0x5	T46.0x6
Strophantin-g	T46.0x1	T46.0x2	T46.0x3	T46.0x4	T46.0x5	T46.0x6
Strychnine (nonmedicinal) (pesticide) (salts)	T65.1x1	T65.1x2	T65.1x3	T65.1x4	—	—
medicinal	T48.291	T48.292	T48.293	T48.294	T48.295	T48.296
Strychnos (ignatii) - see Strychnine						
Styramate	T42.8x1	T42.8x2	T42.8x3	T42.8x4	T42.8x5	T42.8x6
Styrene	T65.891	T65.892	T65.893	T65.894	—	—
Succinimide, antiepileptic or anticonvulsant	T42.2x1	T42.2x2	T42.2x3	T42.2x4	T42.2x5	T42.2x6
mercuric - see Mercury						
Succinylcholine	T48.1x1	T48.1x2	T48.1x3	T48.1x4	T48.1x5	T48.1x6
Succinylsulfathiazole	T37.0x1	T37.0x2	T37.0x3	T37.0x4	T37.0x5	T37.0x6
Sucralfate	T47.1x1	T47.1x2	T47.1x3	T47.1x4	T47.1x5	T47.1x6
Sucrose	T50.3x1	T50.3x2	T50.3x3	T50.3x4	T50.3x5	T50.3x6
Sufentanil	T40.4x1	T40.4x2	T40.4x3	T40.4x4	T40.4x5	T40.4x6
Sulbactam	T36.0x1	T36.0x2	T36.0x3	T36.0x4	T36.0x5	T36.0x6
Sulbenicillin	T36.0x1	T36.0x2	T36.0x3	T36.0x4	T36.0x5	T36.0x6
Sulbentine	T49.0x1	T49.0x2	T49.0x3	T49.0x4	T49.0x5	T49.0x6
Sulfacetamide	T49.5x1	T49.5x2	T49.5x3	T49.5x4	T49.5x5	T49.5x6
ophthalmic preparation	T49.5x1	T49.5x2	T49.5x3	T49.5x4	T49.5x5	T49.5x6
Sulfachlorpyridazine	T37.0x1	T37.0x2	T37.0x3	T37.0x4	T37.0x5	T37.0x6
Sulfacitine	T37.0x1	T37.0x2	T37.0x3	T37.0x4	T37.0x5	T37.0x6
Sulfadiasulfone sodium	T37.0x1	T37.0x2	T37.0x3	T37.0x4	T37.0x5	T37.0x6
Sulfadiazine	T37.0x1	T37.0x2	T37.0x3	T37.0x4	T37.0x5	T37.0x6
silver (topical)	T49.0x1	T49.0x2	T49.0x3	T49.0x4	T49.0x5	T49.0x6
Sulfadimethoxine	T37.0x1	T37.0x2	T37.0x3	T37.0x4	T37.0x5	T37.0x6
Sulfadimidine	T37.0x1	T37.0x2	T37.0x3	T37.0x4	T37.0x5	T37.0x6
Sulfadoxine	T37.0x1	T37.0x2	T37.0x3	T37.0x4	T37.0x5	T37.0x6
with pyrimethamine	T37.2x1	T37.2x2	T37.2x3	T37.2x4	T37.2x5	T37.2x6
Sulfaethidole	T37.0x1	T37.0x2	T37.0x3	T37.0x4	T37.0x5	T37.0x6
Sulfafurazole	T37.0x1	T37.0x2	T37.0x3	T37.0x4	T37.0x5	T37.0x6
Sulfaguanidine	T37.0x1	T37.0x2	T37.0x3	T37.0x4	T37.0x5	T37.0x6

Substance	External Cause (T-Code)					
	Poisoning, Accidental (Unintentional)	Poisoning, Intentional Self-Harm	Poisoning, Assault	Poisoning, Undetermined	Adverse Effect	Underdosing
Sulfalene	T37.0x1	T37.0x2	T37.0x3	T37.0x4	T37.0x5	T37.0x6
Sulfaloxate	T37.0x1	T37.0x2	T37.0x3	T37.0x4	T37.0x5	T37.0x6
Sulfaloxic acid	T37.0x1	T37.0x2	T37.0x3	T37.0x4	T37.0x5	T37.0x6
Sulfamazone	T39.2x1	T39.2x2	T39.2x3	T39.2x4	T39.2x5	T39.2x6
Sulfamerazine	T37.0x1	T37.0x2	T37.0x3	T37.0x4	T37.0x5	T37.0x6
Sulfameter	T37.0x1	T37.0x2	T37.0x3	T37.0x4	T37.0x5	T37.0x6
Sulfamethazine	T37.0x1	T37.0x2	T37.0x3	T37.0x4	T37.0x5	T37.0x6
Sulfamethizole	T37.0x1	T37.0x2	T37.0x3	T37.0x4	T37.0x5	T37.0x6
Sulfamethoxazole	T37.0x1	T37.0x2	T37.0x3	T37.0x4	T37.0x5	T37.0x6
with trimethoprim	T36.8x1	T36.8x2	T36.8x3	T36.8x4	T36.8x5	T36.8x6
Sulfamethoxydiazine	T37.0x1	T37.0x2	T37.0x3	T37.0x4	T37.0x5	T37.0x6
Sulfamethoxypyridazine	T37.0x1	T37.0x2	T37.0x3	T37.0x4	T37.0x5	T37.0x6
Sulfamethylthiazole	T37.0x1	T37.0x2	T37.0x3	T37.0x4	T37.0x5	T37.0x6
Sulfametoxydiazine	T37.0x1	T37.0x2	T37.0x3	T37.0x4	T37.0x5	T37.0x6
Sulfamidopyrine	T39.2x1	T39.2x2	T39.2x3	T39.2x4	T39.2x5	T39.2x6
Sulfamonomethoxine	T37.0x1	T37.0x2	T37.0x3	T37.0x4	T37.0x5	T37.0x6
Sulfamoxole	T37.0x1	T37.0x2	T37.0x3	T37.0x4	T37.0x5	T37.0x6
Sulfamylon	T49.0x1	T49.0x2	T49.0x3	T49.0x4	T49.0x5	T49.0x6
Sulfan blue (diagnostic dye)	T50.8x1	T50.8x2	T50.8x3	T50.8x4	T50.8x5	T50.8x6
Sulfanilamide	T37.0x1	T37.0x2	T37.0x3	T37.0x4	T37.0x5	T37.0x6
Sulfanilylguanidine	T37.0x1	T37.0x2	T37.0x3	T37.0x4	T37.0x5	T37.0x6
Sulfaperin	T37.0x1	T37.0x2	T37.0x3	T37.0x4	T37.0x5	T37.0x6
Sulfaphenazole	T37.0x1	T37.0x2	T37.0x3	T37.0x4	T37.0x5	T37.0x6
Sulfaphenylthiazole	T37.0x1	T37.0x2	T37.0x3	T37.0x4	T37.0x5	T37.0x6
Sulfaproxyline	T37.0x1	T37.0x2	T37.0x3	T37.0x4	T37.0x5	T37.0x6
Sulfapyridine	T37.0x1	T37.0x2	T37.0x3	T37.0x4	T37.0x5	T37.0x6
Sulfapyrimidine	T37.0x1	T37.0x2	T37.0x3	T37.0x4	T37.0x5	T37.0x6
Sulfarsphenamine	T37.8x1	T37.8x2	T37.8x3	T37.8x4	T37.8x5	T37.8x6
Sulfasalazine	T37.0x1	T37.0x2	T37.0x3	T37.0x4	T37.0x5	T37.0x6
Sulfasuxidine	T37.0x1	T37.0x2	T37.0x3	T37.0x4	T37.0x5	T37.0x6
Sulfasymazine	T37.0x1	T37.0x2	T37.0x3	T37.0x4	T37.0x5	T37.0x6
Sulfated amylopectin	T47.8x1	T47.8x2	T47.8x3	T47.8x4	T47.8x5	T47.8x6
Sulfathiazole	T37.0x1	T37.0x2	T37.0x3	T37.0x4	T37.0x5	T37.0x6
Sulfatostearate	T49.2x1	T49.2x2	T49.2x3	T49.2x4	T49.2x5	T49.2x6
Sulfinpyrazone	T50.4x1	T50.4x2	T50.4x3	T50.4x4	T50.4x5	T50.4x6
Sulfiram	T49.0x1	T49.0x2	T49.0x3	T49.0x4	T49.0x5	T49.0x6
Sulfisomidine	T37.0x1	T37.0x2	T37.0x3	T37.0x4	T37.0x5	T37.0x6
Sulfisoxazole	T37.0x1	T37.0x2	T37.0x3	T37.0x4	T37.0x5	T37.0x6
ophthalmic preparation	T49.5x1	T49.5x2	T49.5x3	T49.5x4	T49.5x5	T49.5x6
Sulfobromophthalein (sodium)	T50.8x1	T50.8x2	T50.8x3	T50.8x4	T50.8x5	T50.8x6

Substance	External Cause (T-Code)					
	Poisoning, Accidental (Unintentional)	Poisoning, Intentional Self-Harm	Poisoning, Assault	Poisoning, Undetermined	Adverse Effect	Underdosing
Sulfobromphthalein	T50.8x1	T50.8x2	T50.8x3	T50.8x4	T50.8x5	T50.8x6
Sulfogaiacol	T48.4x1	T48.4x2	T48.4x3	T48.4x4	T48.4x5	T48.4x6
Sulfomyxin	T36.8x1	T36.8x2	T36.8x3	T36.8x4	T36.8x5	T36.8x6
Sulfonal	T42.6x1	T42.6x2	T42.6x3	T42.6x4	T42.6x5	T42.6x6
Sulfonamide NEC	T37.0x1	T37.0x2	T37.0x3	T37.0x4	T37.0x5	T37.0x6
eye	T49.5x1	T49.5x2	T49.5x3	T49.5x4	T49.5x5	T49.5x6
Sulfonazide	T37.1x1	T37.1x2	T37.1x3	T37.1x4	T37.1x5	T37.1x6
Sulfones	T37.1x1	T37.1x2	T37.1x3	T37.1x4	T37.1x5	T37.1x6
Sulfonethylmethane	T42.6x1	T42.6x2	T42.6x3	T42.6x4	T42.6x5	T42.6x6
Sulfonmethane	T42.6x1	T42.6x2	T42.6x3	T42.6x4	T42.6x5	T42.6x6
Sulfonphthal, sulfonphthol	T50.8x1	T50.8x2	T50.8x3	T50.8x4	T50.8x5	T50.8x6
Sulfonylurea derivatives, oral	T38.3x1	T38.3x2	T38.3x3	T38.3x4	T38.3x5	T38.3x6
Sulforidazine	T43.3x1	T43.3x2	T43.3x3	T43.3x4	T43.3x5	T43.3x6
Sulfoxone	T37.1x1	T37.1x2	T37.1x3	T37.1x4	T37.1x5	T37.1x6
Sulfur, sulfurated, sulfuric, sulfurous, sulfuryl (compounds NEC) (medicinal)	T49.4x1	T49.4x2	T49.4x3	T49.4x4	T49.4x5	T49.4x6
acid	T54.2x1	T54.2x2	T54.2x3	T54.2x4	—	—
dioxide (gas)	T59.1x1	T59.1x2	T59.1x3	T59.1x4	—	—
ether - *see* Ether(s)						
hydrogen	T59.6x1	T59.6x2	T59.6x3	T59.6x4	—	—
medicinal (keratolytic) (ointment) NEC	T49.4x1	T49.4x2	T49.4x3	T49.4x4	T49.4x5	T49.4x6
ointment	T49.0x1	T49.0x2	T49.0x3	T49.0x4	T49.0x5	T49.0x6
pesticide (vapor)	T60.91	T60.92	T60.93	T60.94	—	—
vapor NEC	T59.891	T59.892	T59.893	T59.894	—	—
Sulfuric acid	T54.2x1	T54.2x2	T54.2x3	T54.2x4	—	—
Sulglicotide	T47.1x1	T47.1x2	T47.1x3	T47.1x4	T47.1x5	T47.1x6
Sulindac	T39.391	T39.392	T39.393	T39.394	T39.395	T39.396
Sulisatin	T47.2x1	T47.2x2	T47.2x3	T47.2x4	T47.2x5	T47.2x6
Sulisobenzone	T49.3x1	T49.3x2	T49.3x3	T49.3x4	T49.3x5	T49.3x6
Sulkowitch's reagent	T50.8x1	T50.8x2	T50.8x3	T50.8x4	T50.8x5	T50.8x6
Sulmetozine	T44.3x1	T44.3x2	T44.3x3	T44.3x4	T44.3x5	T44.3x6
Suloctidil	T46.7x1	T46.7x2	T46.7x3	T46.7x4	T46.7x5	T46.7x6
Sulph - *see also* Sulf-						
Sulphadiazine	T37.0x1	T37.0x2	T37.0x3	T37.0x4	T37.0x5	T37.0x6
Sulphadimethoxine	T37.0x1	T37.0x2	T37.0x3	T37.0x4	T37.0x5	T37.0x6
Sulphadimidine	T37.0x1	T37.0x2	T37.0x3	T37.0x4	T37.0x5	T37.0x6
Sulphadione	T37.1x1	T37.1x2	T37.1x3	T37.1x4	T37.1x5	T37.1x6
Sulphafurazole	T37.0x1	T37.0x2	T37.0x3	T37.0x4	T37.0x5	T37.0x6
Sulphamethizole	T37.0x1	T37.0x2	T37.0x3	T37.0x4	T37.0x5	T37.0x6
Sulphamethoxazole	T37.0x1	T37.0x2	T37.0x3	T37.0x4	T37.0x5	T37.0x6
Sulphan blue	T50.8x1	T50.8x2	T50.8x3	T50.8x4	T50.8x5	T50.8x6

TABLE OF DRUGS AND CHEMICALS

Substance	External Cause (T-Code)					
	Poisoning, Accidental (Unintentional)	Poisoning, Intentional Self-Harm	Poisoning, Assault	Poisoning, Undetermined	Adverse Effect	Underdosing
Sulphaphenazole	T37.0x1	T37.0x2	T37.0x3	T37.0x4	T37.0x5	T37.0x6
Sulphapyridine	T37.0x1	T37.0x2	T37.0x3	T37.0x4	T37.0x5	T37.0x6
Sulphasalazine	T37.0x1	T37.0x2	T37.0x3	T37.0x4	T37.0x5	T37.0x6
Sulphinpyrazone	T50.4x1	T50.4x2	T50.4x3	T50.4x4	T50.4x5	T50.4x6
Sulpiride	T43.591	T43.592	T43.593	T43.594	T43.595	T43.596
Sulprostone	T48.0x1	T48.0x2	T48.0x3	T48.0x4	T48.0x5	T48.0x6
Sulpyrine	T39.2x1	T39.2x2	T39.2x3	T39.2x4	T39.2x5	T39.2x6
Sultamicillin	T36.0x1	T36.0x2	T36.0x3	T36.0x4	T36.0x5	T36.0x6
Sulthiame	T42.6x1	T42.6x2	T42.6x3	T42.6x4	T42.6x5	T42.6x6
Sultiame	T42.6x1	T42.6x2	T42.6x3	T42.6x4	T42.6x5	T42.6x6
Sultopride	T43.591	T43.592	T43.593	T43.594	T43.595	T43.596
Sumatriptan	T39.8x1	T39.8x2	T39.8x3	T39.8x4	T39.8x5	T39.8x6
Sunflower seed oil	T46.6x1	T46.6x2	T46.6x3	T46.6x4	T46.6x5	T46.6x6
Superinone	T48.4x1	T48.4x2	T48.4x3	T48.4x4	T48.4x5	T48.4x6
Suprofen	T39.311	T39.312	T39.313	T39.314	T39.315	T39.316
Suramin (sodium)	T37.4x1	T37.4x2	T37.4x3	T37.4x4	T37.4x5	T37.4x6
Surfacaine	T41.3x1	T41.3x2	T41.3x3	T41.3x4	T41.3x5	T41.3x6
Surital	T41.1x1	T41.1x2	T41.1x3	T41.1x4	T41.1x5	T41.1x6
Sutilains	T45.3x1	T45.3x2	T45.3x3	T45.3x4	T45.3x5	T45.3x6
Suxamethonium (chloride)	T48.1x1	T48.1x2	T48.1x3	T48.1x4	T48.1x5	T48.1x6
Suxethonium (chloride)	T48.1x1	T48.1x2	T48.1x3	T48.1x4	T48.1x5	T48.1x6
Suxibuzone	T39.2x1	T39.2x2	T39.2x3	T39.2x4	T39.2x5	T39.2x6
Sweet oil (birch)	T49.3x1	T49.3x2	T49.3x3	T49.3x4	T49.3x5	T49.3x6
Sweet niter spirit	T46.3x1	T46.3x2	T46.3x3	T46.3x4	T46.3x5	T46.3x6
Sweetener	T50.901	T50.902	T50.903	T50.904	T50.905	T50.906
Sym-dichloroethyl ether	T53.6x1	T53.6x2	T53.6x3	T53.6x4	—	—
Sympatholytic NEC	T44.8x1	T44.8x2	T44.8x3	T44.8x4	T44.8x5	T44.8x6
haloalkylamine	T44.8x1	T44.8x2	T44.8x3	T44.8x4	T44.8x5	T44.8x6
Sympathomimetic NEC	T44.901	T44.902	T44.903	T44.904	T44.905	T44.906
anti-common-cold	T48.5x1	T48.5x2	T48.5x3	T48.5x4	T48.5x5	T48.5x6
bronchodilator	T48.6x1	T48.6x2	T48.6x3	T48.6x4	T48.6x5	T48.6x6
specified NEC	T44.991	T44.992	T44.993	T44.994	T44.995	T44.996
Synagis	T50.B91	T50.B92	T50.B93	T50.B94	T50.B95	T50.B96
Synalar	T49.0x1	T49.0x2	T49.0x3	T49.0x4	T49.0x5	T49.0x6
Synthroid	T38.1x1	T38.1x2	T38.1x3	T38.1x4	T38.1x5	T38.1x6
Syntocinon	T48.0x1	T48.0x2	T48.0x3	T48.0x4	T48.0x5	T48.0x6
Syrosingopine	T46.5x1	T46.5x2	T46.5x3	T46.5x4	T46.5x5	T46.5x6
Systemic drug	T45.91	T45.92	T45.93	T45.94	T45.95	T45.96
specified NEC	T45.8x1	T45.8x2	T45.8x3	T45.8x4	T45.8x5	T45.8x6
2,4,5-T	T60.3x1	T60.3x2	T60.3x3	T60.3x4	—	—

Substance	External Cause (T-Code)					
	Poisoning, Accidental (Unintentional)	Poisoning, Intentional Self-Harm	Poisoning, Assault	Poisoning, Undetermined	Adverse Effect	Underdosing
Tablets (see also specified substance)	T50.901	T50.902	T50.903	T50.904	T50.905	T50.906
Tace	T38.5x1	T38.5x2	T38.5x3	T38.5x4	T38.5x5	T38.5x6
Tacrine	T44.0x1	T44.0x2	T44.0x3	T44.0x4	T44.0x5	T44.0x6
Talampicillin	T36.0x1	T36.0x2	T36.0x3	T36.0x4	T36.0x5	T36.0x6
Talbutal	T42.3x1	T42.3x2	T42.3x3	T42.3x4	T42.3x5	T42.3x6
Talc powder	T49.3x1	T49.3x2	T49.3x3	T49.3x4	T49.3x5	T49.3x6
Talcum	T49.3x1	T49.3x2	T49.3x3	T49.3x4	T49.3x5	T49.3x6
Taleranol	T38.6x1	T38.6x2	T38.6x3	T38.6x4	T38.6x5	T38.6x6
Tamoxifen	T38.6x1	T38.6x2	T38.6x3	T38.6x4	T38.6x5	T38.6x6
Tamsulosin	T44.6x1	T44.6x2	T44.6x3	T44.6x4	T44.6x5	T44.6x6
Tandearil, tanderil	T39.2x1	T39.2x2	T39.2x3	T39.2x4	T39.2x5	T39.2x6
Tannic acid	T49.2x1	T49.2x2	T49.2x3	T49.2x4	T49.2x5	T49.2x6
medicinal (astringent)	T49.2x1	T49.2x2	T49.2x3	T49.2x4	T49.2x5	T49.2x6
Tannin - see Tannic acid						
Tansy	T62.2x1	T62.2x2	T62.2x3	T62.2x4	—	—
TAO	T36.3x1	T36.3x2	T36.3x3	T36.3x4	T36.3x5	T36.3x6
Tapazole	T38.2x1	T38.2x2	T38.2x3	T38.2x4	T38.2x5	T38.2x6
Tar NEC	T52.0x1	T52.0x2	T52.0x3	T52.0x4	—	—
camphor	T60.1x1	T60.1x2	T60.1x3	T60.1x4	—	—
distillate	T49.1x1	T49.1x2	T49.1x3	T49.1x4	T49.1x5	T49.1x6
fumes	T59.891	T59.892	T59.893	T59.894	—	—
medicinal	T49.1x1	T49.1x2	T49.1x3	T49.1x4	T49.1x5	T49.1x6
ointment	T49.1x1	T49.1x2	T49.1x3	T49.1x4	T49.1x5	T49.1x6
Taractan	T43.591	T43.592	T43.593	T43.594	T43.595	T43.596
Tarantula (venomous)	T63.321	T63.322	T63.323	T63.324	—	—
Tartar emetic	T37.8x1	T37.8x2	T37.8x3	T37.8x4	T37.8x5	T37.8x6
Tartaric acid	T65.891	T65.892	T65.893	T65.894	—	—
Tartrated antimony (anti-infective)	T37.8x1	T37.8x2	T37.8x3	T37.8x4	T37.8x5	T37.8x6
Tartrate, laxative	T47.4x1	T47.4x2	T47.4x3	T47.4x4	T47.4x5	T47.4x6
Tauromustine	T45.1x1	T45.1x2	T45.1x3	T45.1x4	T45.1x5	T45.1x6
TCA - see Trichloroacetic acid						
TCDD	T65.891	T65.892	T65.893	T65.894	—	—
TDI (vapor)	T65.0x1	T65.0x2	T65.0x3	T65.0x4	—	—
Tear						
gas	T59.3x1	T59.3x2	T59.3x3	T59.3x4	—	—
solution	T49.5x1	T49.5x2	T49.5x3	T49.5x4	T49.5x5	T49.5x6
Teclothiazide	T50.2x1	T50.2x2	T50.2x3	T50.2x4	T50.2x5	T50.2x6
Teclozan	T37.3x1	T37.3x2	T37.3x3	T37.3x4	T37.3x5	T37.3x6
Tegafur	T45.1x1	T45.1x2	T45.1x3	T45.1x4	T45.1x5	T45.1x6
Tegretol	T42.1x1	T42.1x2	T42.1x3	T42.1x4	T42.1x5	T42.1x6

Substance	External Cause (T-Code)					
	Poisoning, Accidental (Unintentional)	Poisoning, Intentional Self-Harm	Poisoning, Assault	Poisoning, Undetermined	Adverse Effect	Underdosing
Teicoplanin	T36.8x1	T36.8x2	T36.8x3	T36.8x4	T36.8x5	T36.8x6
Telepaque	T50.8x1	T50.8x2	T50.8x3	T50.8x4	T50.8x5	T50.8x6
Tellurium	T56.891	T56.892	T56.893	T56.894	—	—
fumes	T56.891	T56.892	T56.893	T56.894	—	—
TEM	T45.1x1	T45.1x2	T45.1x3	T45.1x4	T45.1x5	T45.1x6
Temazepam	T42.4x1	T42.4x2	T42.4x3	T42.4x4	T42.4x5	T42.4x6
Temocillin	T36.0x1	T36.0x2	T36.0x3	T36.0x4	T36.0x5	T36.0x6
Tenamfetamine	T43.621	T43.622	T43.623	T43.624	T43.625	T43.626
Teniposide	T45.1x1	T45.1x2	T45.1x3	T45.1x4	T45.1x5	T45.1x6
Tenitramine	T46.3x1	T46.3x2	T46.3x3	T46.3x4	T46.3x5	T46.3x6
Tenoglicin	T48.4x1	T48.4x2	T48.4x3	T48.4x4	T48.4x5	T48.4x6
Tenonitrozole	T37.3x1	T37.3x2	T37.3x3	T37.3x4	T37.3x5	T37.3x6
Tenoxicam	T39.391	T39.392	T39.393	T39.394	T39.395	T39.396
TEPA	T45.1x1	T45.1x2	T45.1x3	T45.1x4	T45.1x5	T45.1x6
TEPP	T60.0x1	T60.0x2	T60.0x3	T60.0x4	—	—
Teprotide	T46.5x1	T46.5x2	T46.5x3	T46.5x4	T46.5x5	T46.5x6
Terazosin	T44.6x1	T44.6x2	T44.6x3	T44.6x4	T44.6x5	T44.6x6
Terbufos	T60.0x1	T60.0x2	T60.0x3	T60.0x4	—	—
Terbutaline	T48.6x1	T48.6x2	T48.6x3	T48.6x4	T48.6x5	T48.6x6
Terconazole	T49.0x1	T49.0x2	T49.0x3	T49.0x4	T49.0x5	T49.0x6
Terfenadine	T45.0x1	T45.0x2	T45.0x3	T45.0x4	T45.0x5	T45.0x6
Teriparatide (acetate)	T50.991	T50.992	T50.993	T50.994	T50.995	T50.996
Terizidone	T37.1x1	T37.1x2	T37.1x3	T37.1x4	T37.1x5	T37.1x6
Terlipressin	T38.891	T38.892	T38.893	T38.894	T38.895	T38.896
Terodiline	T46.3x1	T46.3x2	T46.3x3	T46.3x4	T46.3x5	T46.3x6
Teroxalene	T37.4x1	T37.4x2	T37.4x3	T37.4x4	T37.4x5	T37.4x6
Terpin(cis) hydrate	T48.4x1	T48.4x2	T48.4x3	T48.4x4	T48.4x5	T48.4x6
Terramycin	T36.4x1	T36.4x2	T36.4x3	T36.4x4	T36.4x5	T36.4x6
Tertatolol	T44.7x1	T44.7x2	T44.7x3	T44.7x4	T44.7x5	T44.7x6
Tessalon	T48.3x1	T48.3x2	T48.3x3	T48.3x4	T48.3x5	T48.3x6
Testolactone	T38.7x1	T38.7x2	T38.7x3	T38.7x4	T38.7x5	T38.7x6
Testosterone	T38.7x1	T38.7x2	T38.7x3	T38.7x4	T38.7x5	T38.7x6
Tetanus toxoid or vaccine	T50.A91	T50.A92	T50.A93	T50.A94	T50.A95	T50.A96
antitoxin	T50.Z11	T50.Z12	T50.Z13	T50.Z14	T50.Z15	T50.Z16
immune globulin (human)	T50.Z11	T50.Z12	T50.Z13	T50.Z14	T50.Z15	T50.Z16
toxoid	T50.A91	T50.A92	T50.A93	T50.A94	T50.A95	T50.A96
with diphtheria toxoid	T50.A21	T50.A22	T50.A23	T50.A24	T50.A25	T50.A26
with pertussis	T50.A11	T50.A12	T50.A13	T50.A14	T50.A15	T50.A16
Tetrabenazine	T43.591	T43.592	T43.593	T43.594	T43.595	T43.596

Substance	External Cause (T-Code)					
	Poisoning, Accidental (Unintentional)	Poisoning, Intentional Self-Harm	Poisoning, Assault	Poisoning, Undetermined	Adverse Effect	Underdosing
Tetracaine	T41.3x1	T41.3x2	T41.3x3	T41.3x4	T41.3x5	T41.3x6
nerve block (peripheral) (plexus)	T41.3x1	T41.3x2	T41.3x3	T41.3x4	T41.3x5	T41.3x6
regional	T41.3x1	T41.3x2	T41.3x3	T41.3x4	T41.3x5	T41.3x6
spinal	T41.3x1	T41.3x2	T41.3x3	T41.3x4	T41.3x5	T41.3x6
Tetrachlorethylene - *see* Tetrachloroethylene						
Tetrachlormethiazide	T50.2x1	T50.2x2	T50.2x3	T50.2x4	T50.2x5	T50.2x6
2,3,7,8-Tetrachlorodi-benzo-p-dioxin	T53.7x1	T53.7x2	T53.7x3	T53.7x4	—	—
Tetrachloroethane	T53.6x1	T53.6x2	T53.6x3	T53.6x4	—	—
vapor	T53.6x1	T53.6x2	T53.6x3	T53.6x4	—	—
paint or varnish	T53.6x1	T53.6x2	T53.6x3	T53.6x4	—	—
Tetrachloroethylene (liquid)	T53.3x1	T53.3x2	T53.3x3	T53.3x4	—	—
medicinal	T37.4x1	T37.4x2	T37.4x3	T37.4x4	T37.4x5	T37.4x6
vapor	T53.3x1	T53.3x2	T53.3x3	T53.3x4		
Tetrachloromethane - *see* Carbon tetrachloride						
Tetracosactide	T38.811	T38.812	T38.813	T38.814	T38.815	T38.816
Tetracosactrin	T38.811	T38.812	T38.813	T38.814	T38.815	T38.816
Tetracycline	T36.4x1	T36.4x2	T36.4x3	T36.4x4	T36.4x5	T36.4x6
ophthalmic preparation	T49.5x1	T49.5x2	T49.5x3	T49.5x4	T49.5x5	T49.5x6
topical NEC	T49.0x1	T49.0x2	T49.0x3	T49.0x4	T49.0x5	T49.0x6
Tetradifon	T60.8x1	T60.8x2	T60.8x3	T60.8x4	—	—
Tetradotoxin	T61.771	T61.772	T61.773	T61.774	—	—
Tetraethyl						
lead	T56.0x1	T56.0x2	T56.0x3	T56.0x4	—	—
pyrophosphate	T60.0x1	T60.0x2	T60.0x3	T60.0x4	—	—
Tetraethylammonium chloride	T44.2x1	T44.2x2	T44.2x3	T44.2x4	T44.2x5	T44.2x6
Tetraethylthiuram disulfide	T50.6x1	T50.6x2	T50.6x3	T50.6x4	T50.6x5	T50.6x6
Tetrahydroaminoacridine	T44.0x1	T44.0x2	T44.0x3	T44.0x4	T44.0x5	T44.0x6
Tetrahydrocannabinol	T40.7x1	T40.7x2	T40.7x3	T40.7x4	T40.7x5	T40.7x6
Tetrahydrofuran	T52.8x1	T52.8x2	T52.8x3	T52.8x4	—	—
Tetrahydronaphthalene	T52.8x1	T52.8x2	T52.8x3	T52.8x4	—	—
Tetrahydrozoline	T49.5x1	T49.5x2	T49.5x3	T49.5x4	T49.5x5	T49.5x6
Tetralin	T52.8x1	T52.8x2	T52.8x3	T52.8x4	—	—
Tetramethrin	T60.2x1	T60.2x2	T60.2x3	T60.2x4	—	—
Tetramethylthiuram (disulfide) NEC	T60.3x1	T60.3x2	T60.3x3	T60.3x4	—	—
medicinal	T49.0x1	T49.0x2	T49.0x3	T49.0x4	T49.0x5	T49.0x6
Tetramisole	T37.4x1	T37.4x2	T37.4x3	T37.4x4	T37.4x5	T37.4x6
Tetranicotinoyl fructose	T46.7x1	T46.7x2	T46.7x3	T46.7x4	T46.7x5	T46.7x6
Tetronal	T42.6x1	T42.6x2	T42.6x3	T42.6x4	T42.6x5	T42.6x6
Tetrazepam	T42.4x1	T42.4x2	T42.4x3	T42.4x4	T42.4x5	T42.4x6
Tetryl	T65.3x1	T65.3x2	T65.3x3	T65.3x4	—	—

Substance	External Cause (T-Code)					
	Poisoning, Accidental (Unintentional)	Poisoning, Intentional Self-Harm	Poisoning, Assault	Poisoning, Undetermined	Adverse Effect	Underdosing
Tetrylammonium chloride	T44.2x1	T44.2x2	T44.2x3	T44.2x4	T44.2x5	T44.2x6
Tetryzoline	T49.5x1	T49.5x2	T49.5x3	T49.5x4	T49.5x5	T49.5x6
Thalidomide	T45.1x1	T45.1x2	T45.1x3	T45.1x4	T45.1x5	T45.1x6
Thallium (compounds) (dust) NEC	T56.811	T56.812	T56.813	T56.814	—	—
pesticide	T60.4x1	T60.4x2	T60.4x3	T60.4x4	—	—
THC	T40.7x1	T40.7x2	T40.7x3	T40.7x4	T40.7x5	T40.7x6
Thebacon	T48.3x1	T48.3x2	T48.3x3	T48.3x4	T48.3x5	T48.3x6
Thebaine	T40.2x1	T40.2x2	T40.2x3	T40.2x4	T40.2x5	T40.2x6
Thenoic acid	T49.6x1	T49.6x2	T49.6x3	T49.6x4	T49.6x5	T49.6x6
Thenyldiamine	T45.0x1	T45.0x2	T45.0x3	T45.0x4	T45.0x5	T45.0x6
Theobromine (calcium salicylate)	T48.6x1	T48.6x2	T48.6x3	T48.6x4	T48.6x5	T48.6x6
sodium salicylate	T48.6x1	T48.6x2	T48.6x3	T48.6x4	T48.6x5	T48.6x6
Theophyllamine	T48.6x1	T48.6x2	T48.6x3	T48.6x4	T48.6x5	T48.6x6
Theophylline	T48.6x1	T48.6x2	T48.6x3	T48.6x4	T48.6x5	T48.6x6
aminobenzoic acid	T48.6x1	T48.6x2	T48.6x3	T48.6x4	T48.6x5	T48.6x6
ethylenediamine	T48.6x1	T48.6x2	T48.6x3	T48.6x4	T48.6x5	T48.6x6
piperazine p-amino-benzoate	T48.6x1	T48.6x2	T48.6x3	T48.6x4	T48.6x5	T48.6x6
Thiabendazole	T37.4x1	T37.4x2	T37.4x3	T37.4x4	T37.4x5	T37.4x6
Thialbarbital	T41.1x1	T41.1x2	T41.1x3	T41.1x4	T41.1x5	T41.1x6
Thiamazole	T38.2x1	T38.2x2	T38.2x3	T38.2x4	T38.2x5	T38.2x6
Thiambutosine	T37.1x1	T37.1x2	T37.1x3	T37.1x4	T37.1x5	T37.1x6
Thiamine	T45.2x1	T45.2x2	T45.2x3	T45.2x4	T45.2x5	T45.2x6
Thiamphenicol	T36.2x1	T36.2x2	T36.2x3	T36.2x4	T36.2x5	T36.2x6
Thiamylal	T41.1x1	T41.1x2	T41.1x3	T41.1x4	T41.1x5	T41.1x6
sodium	T41.1x1	T41.1x2	T41.1x3	T41.1x4	T41.1x5	T41.1x6
Thiazesim	T43.291	T43.292	T43.293	T43.294	T43.295	T43.296
Thiazides (diuretics)	T50.2x1	T50.2x2	T50.2x3	T50.2x4	T50.2x5	T50.2x6
Thiazinamium metilsulfate	T43.3x1	T43.3x2	T43.3x3	T43.3x4	T43.3x5	T43.3x6
Thiethylperazine	T43.3x1	T43.3x2	T43.3x3	T43.3x4	T43.3x5	T43.3x6
Thimerosal	T49.0x1	T49.0x2	T49.0x3	T49.0x4	T49.0x5	T49.0x6
ophthalmic preparation	T49.5x1	T49.5x2	T49.5x3	T49.5x4	T49.5x5	T49.5x6
Thioacetazone	T37.1x1	T37.1x2	T37.1x3	T37.1x4	T37.1x5	T37.1x6
with isoniazid	T37.1x1	T37.1x2	T37.1x3	T37.1x4	T37.1x5	T37.1x6
Thiobarbital sodium	T41.1x1	T41.1x2	T41.1x3	T41.1x4	T41.1x5	T41.1x6
Thiobarbiturate anesthetic	T41.1x1	T41.1x2	T41.1x3	T41.1x4	T41.1x5	T41.1x6
Thiobismol	T37.8x1	T37.8x2	T37.8x3	T37.8x4	T37.8x5	T37.8x6
Thiobutabarbital sodium	T41.1x1	T41.1x2	T41.1x3	T41.1x4	T41.1x5	T41.1x6
Thiocarbamate (insecticide)	T60.0x1	T60.0x2	T60.0x3	T60.0x4	—	—
Thiocarbamide	T38.2x1	T38.2x2	T38.2x3	T38.2x4	T38.2x5	T38.2x6

Substance	External Cause (T-Code)					
	Poisoning, Accidental (Unintentional)	Poisoning, Intentional Self-Harm	Poisoning, Assault	Poisoning, Undetermined	Adverse Effect	Underdosing
Thiocarbarsone	T37.8x1	T37.8x2	T37.8x3	T37.8x4	T37.8x5	T37.8x6
Thiocarlide	T37.1x1	T37.1x2	T37.1x3	T37.1x4	T37.1x5	T37.1x6
Thioctamide	T50.991	T50.992	T50.993	T50.994	T50.995	T50.996
Thioctic acid	T50.991	T50.992	T50.993	T50.994	T50.995	T50.996
Thiofos	T60.0x1	T60.0x2	T60.0x3	T60.0x4	—	—
Thioglycolate	T49.4x1	T49.4x2	T49.4x3	T49.4x4	T49.4x5	T49.4x6
Thioglycolic acid	T65.891	T65.892	T65.893	T65.894	—	—
Thioguanine	T45.1x1	T45.1x2	T45.1x3	T45.1x4	T45.1x5	T45.1x6
Thiomercaptomerin	T50.2x1	T50.2x2	T50.2x3	T50.2x4	T50.2x5	T50.2x6
Thiomerin	T50.2x1	T50.2x2	T50.2x3	T50.2x4	T50.2x5	T50.2x6
Thiomersal	T49.0x1	T49.0x2	T49.0x3	T49.0x4	T49.0x5	T49.0x6
Thionazin	T60.0x1	T60.0x2	T60.0x3	T60.0x4	—	—
Thiopental (sodium)	T41.1x1	T41.1x2	T41.1x3	T41.1x4	T41.1x5	T41.1x6
Thiopentone (sodium)	T41.1x1	T41.1x2	T41.1x3	T41.1x4	T41.1x5	T41.1x6
Thiopropazate	T43.3x1	T43.3x2	T43.3x3	T43.3x4	T43.3x5	T43.3x6
Thioproperazine	T43.3x1	T43.3x2	T43.3x3	T43.3x4	T43.3x5	T43.3x6
Thioridazine	T43.3x1	T43.3x2	T43.3x3	T43.3x4	T43.3x5	T43.3x6
Thiosinamine	T49.3x1	T49.3x2	T49.3x3	T49.3x4	T49.3x5	T49.3x6
Thiotepa	T45.1x1	T45.1x2a	T45.1x3	T45.1x4	T45.1x5	T45.1x6
Thiothixene	T43.4x1	T43.4x2	T43.4x3	T43.4x4	T43.4x5	T43.4x6
Thiouracil (benzyl) (methyl) (propyl)	T38.2x1	T38.2x2	T38.2x3	T38.2x4	T38.2x5	T38.2x6
Thiourea	T38.2x1	T38.2x2	T38.2x3	T38.2x4	T38.2x5	T38.2x6
Thiphenamil	T44.3x1	T44.3x2	T44.3x3	T44.3x4	T44.3x5	T44.3x6
Thiram	T60.3x1	T60.3x2	T60.3x3	T60.3x4	—	—
medicinal	T49.2x1	T49.2x2	T49.2x3	T49.2x4	T49.2x5	T49.2x6
Thonzylamine (systemic)	T45.0x1	T45.0x2	T45.0x3	T45.0x4	T45.0x5	T45.0x6
mucosal decongestant	T48.5x1	T48.5x2	T48.5x3	T48.5x4	T48.5x5	T48.5x6
Thorazine	T43.3x1	T43.3x2	T43.3x3	T43.3x4	T43.3x5	T43.3x6
Thorium dioxide suspension	T50.8x1	T50.8x2	T50.8x3	T50.8x4	T50.8x5	T50.8x6
Thornapple	T62.2x1	T62.2x2	T62.2x3	T62.2x4	—	—
Throat drug NEC	T49.6x1	T49.6x2	T49.6x3	T49.6x4	T49.6x5	T49.6x6
Thrombin	T45.7x1	T45.7x2	T45.7x3	T45.7x4	T45.7x5	T45.7x6
Thrombolysin	T45.611	T45.612	T45.613	T45.614	T45.615	T45.616
Thromboplastin	T45.7x1	T45.7x2	T45.7x3	T45.7x4	T45.7x5	T45.7x6
Thurfyl nicotinate	T46.7x1	T46.7x2	T46.7x3	T46.7x4	T46.7x5	T46.7x6
Thymol	T49.0x1	T49.0x2	T49.0x3	T49.0x4	T49.0x5	T49.0x6
Thymopentin	T37.5x1	T37.5x2	T37.5x3	T37.5x4	T37.5x5	T37.5x6
Thymoxamine	T46.7x1	T46.7x2	T46.7x3	T46.7x4	T46.7x5	T46.7x6
Thymus extract	T38.891	T38.892	T38.893	T38.894	T38.895	T38.896
Thyreotrophic hormone	T38.811	T38.812	T38.813	T38.814	T38.815	T38.816

	External Cause (T-Code)					
Substance	Poisoning, Accidental (Unintentional)	Poisoning, Intentional Self-Harm	Poisoning, Assault	Poisoning, Undetermined	Adverse Effect	Underdosing
Thyroglobulin	T38.1x1	T38.1x2	T38.1x3	T38.1x4	T38.1x5	T38.1x6
Thyroid (hormone)	T38.1x1	T38.1x2	T38.1x3	T38.1x4	T38.1x5	T38.1x6
Thyrolar	T38.1x1	T38.1x2	T38.1x3	T38.1x4	T38.1x5	T38.1x6
Thyrotrophin	T38.811	T38.812	T38.813	T38.814	T38.815	T38.816
Thyrotropic hormone	T38.811	T38.812	T38.813	T38.814	T38.815	T38.816
Thyroxine	T38.1x1	T38.1x2	T38.1x3	T38.1x4	T38.1x5	T38.1x6
Tiabendazole	T37.4x1	T37.4x2	T37.4x3	T37.4x4	T37.4x5	T37.4x6
Tiamizide	T50.2x1	T50.2x2	T50.2x3	T50.2x4	T50.2x5	T50.2x6
Tianeptine	T43.291	T43.292	T43.293	T43.294	T43.295	T43.296
Tiapamil	T46.1x1	T46.1x2	T46.1x3	T46.1x4	T46.1x5	T46.1x6
Tiapride	T43.591	T43.592	T43.593	T43.594	T43.595	T43.596
Tiaprofenic acid	T39.311	T39.312	T39.313	T39.314	T39.315	T39.316
Tiaramide	T39.8x1	T39.8x2	T39.8x3	T39.8x4	T39.8x5	T39.8x6
Ticarcillin	T36.0x1	T36.0x2	T36.0x3	T36.0x4	T36.0x5	T36.0x6
Ticlatone	T49.0x1	T49.0x2	T49.0x3	T49.0x4	T49.0x5	T49.0x6
Ticlopidine	T45.521	T45.522	T45.523	T45.524	T45.525	T45.526
Ticrynafen	T50.1x1	T50.1x2	T50.1x3	T50.1x4	T50.1x5	T50.1x6
Tidiacic	T50.991	T50.992	T50.993	T50.994	T50.995	T50.996
Tiemonium	T44.3x1	T44.3x2	T44.3x3	T44.3x4	T44.3x5	T44.3x6
iodide	T44.3x1	T44.3x2	T44.3x3	T44.3x4	T44.3x5	T44.3x6
Tienilic acid	T50.1x1	T50.1x2	T50.1x3	T50.1x4	T50.1x5	T50.1x6
Tifenamil	T44.3x1	T44.3x2	T44.3x3	T44.3x4	T44.3x5	T44.3x6
Tigan	T45.0x1	T45.0x2	T45.0x3	T45.0x4	T45.0x5	T45.0x6
Tigloidine	T44.3x1	T44.3x2	T44.3x3	T44.3x4	T44.3x5	T44.3x6
Tilactase	T47.5x1	T47.5x2	T47.5x3	T47.5x4	T47.5x5	T47.5x6
Tiletamine	T41.291	T41.292	T41.293	T41.294	T41.295	T41.296
Tilidine	T40.4x1	T40.4x2	T40.4x3	T40.4x4	T40.4x5	T40.4x6
Timepidium bromide	T44.3x1	T44.3x2	T44.3x3	T44.3x4	T44.3x5	T44.3x6
Timiperone	T43.4x1	T43.4x2	T43.4x3	T43.4x4	T43.4x5	T43.4x6
Timolol	T44.7x1	T44.7x2	T44.7x3	T44.7x4	T44.7x5	T44.7x6
Tin (chloride) (dust) (oxide) NEC	T56.6x1	T56.6x2	T56.6x3	T56.6x4	—	—
anti-infectives	T37.8x1	T37.8x2	T37.8x3	T37.8x4	T37.8x5	T37.8x6
Tincture, iodine - *see* Iodine						
Tindal	T43.3x1	T43.3x2	T43.3x3	T43.3x4	T43.3x5	T43.3x6
Tinidazole	T37.3x1	T37.3x2	T37.3x3	T37.3x4	T37.3x5	T37.3x6
Tinoridine	T39.8x1	T39.8x2	T39.8x3	T39.8x4	T39.8x5	T39.8x6
Tiocarlide	T37.1x1	T37.1x2	T37.1x3	T37.1x4	T37.1x5	T37.1x6
Tioclomarol	T45.511	T45.512	T45.513	T45.514	T45.515	T45.516
Tioconazole	T49.0x1	T49.0x2	T49.0x3	T49.0x4	T49.0x5	T49.0x6
Tioguanine	T45.1x1	T45.1x2	T45.1x3	T45.1x4	T45.1x5	T45.1x6

TABLE OF DRUGS AND CHEMICALS

Substance	Poisoning, Accidental (Unintentional)	Poisoning, Intentional Self-Harm	Poisoning, Assault	Poisoning, Undetermined	Adverse Effect	Underdosing
Tiopronin	T50.991	T50.992	T50.993	T50.994	T50.995	T50.996
Tiotixene	T43.4x1	T43.4x2	T43.4x3	T43.4x4	T43.4x5	T43.4x6
Tioxolone	T49.4x1	T49.4x2	T49.4x3	T49.4x4	T49.4x5	T49.4x6
Tipepidine	T48.3x1	T48.3x2	T48.3x3	T48.3x4	T48.3x5	T48.3x6
Tiquizium bromide	T44.3x1	T44.3x2	T44.3x3	T44.3x4	T44.3x5	T44.3x6
Tiratricol	T38.1x1	T38.1x2	T38.1x3	T38.1x4	T38.1x5	T38.1x6
Tisopurine	T50.4x1	T50.4x2	T50.4x3	T50.4x4	T50.4x5	T50.4x6
Titanium (compounds) (vapor)	T56.891	T56.892	T56.893	T56.894	—	—
dioxide	T49.3x1	T49.3x2	T49.3x3	T49.3x4	T49.3x5	T49.3x6
ointment	T49.3x1	T49.3x2	T49.3x3	T49.3x4	T49.3x5	T49.3x6
oxide	T49.3x1	T49.3x2	T49.3x3	T49.3x4	T49.3x5	T49.3x6
tetrachloride	T56.891	T56.892	T56.893	T56.894	—	—
Titanocene	T56.891	T56.892	T56.893	T56.894	—	—
Titroid	T38.1x1	T38.1x2	T38.1x3	T38.1x4	T38.1x5	T38.1x6
Tizanidine	T42.8x1	T42.8x2	T42.8x3	T42.8x4	T42.8x5	T42.8x6
TMTD	T60.3x1	T60.3x2	T60.3x3	T60.3x4	—	—
TNT (fumes)	T65.3x1	T65.3x2	T65.3x3	T65.3x4	—	—
TNT	T65.891	T65.892	T65.893	T65.894	—	—
fumes	T59.891	T59.892	T59.893	T59.894	—	—
Toadstool	T62.0x1	T62.0x2	T62.0x3	T62.0x4	—	—
Tobacco NEC	T65.291	T65.292	T65.293	T65.294	—	—
cigarettes	T65.221	T65.222	T65.223	T65.224	—	—
Indian	T62.2x1	T62.2x2	T62.2x3	T62.2x4	—	—
smoke, second-hand	T59.811	T59.812	T59.813	T59.814	—	—
Tobramycin	T36.5x1	T36.5x2	T36.5x3	T36.5x4	T36.5x5	T36.5x6
Tocainide	T46.2x1	T46.2x2	T46.2x3	T46.2x4	T46.2x5	T46.2x6
Tocoferol	T45.2x1	T45.2x2	T45.2x3	T45.2x4	T45.2x5	T45.2x6
Tocopherol	T45.2x1	T45.2x2	T45.2x3	T45.2x4	T45.2x5	T45.2x6
acetate	T45.2x1	T45.2x2	T45.2x3	T45.2x4	T45.2x5	T45.2x6
Tocosamine	T48.0x1	T48.0x2	T48.0x3	T48.0x4	T48.0x5	T48.0x6
Todralazine	T46.5x1	T46.5x2	T46.5x3	T46.5x4	T46.5x5	T46.5x6
Tofisopam	T42.4x1	T42.4x2	T42.4x3	T42.4x4	T42.4x5	T42.4x6
Tofranil	T43.011	T43.012	T43.013	T43.014	T43.015	T43.016
Toilet deodorizer	T65.891	T65.892	T65.893	T65.894	—	—
Tolamolol	T44.7x1	T44.7x2	T44.7x3	T44.7x4	T44.7x5	T44.7x6
Tolazamide	T38.3x1	T38.3x2	T38.3x3	T38.3x4	T38.3x5	T38.3x6
Tolazoline	T46.7x1	T46.7x2	T46.7x3	T46.7x4	T46.7x5	T46.7x6
Tolbutamide (sodium)	T38.3x1	T38.3x2	T38.3x3	T38.3x4	T38.3x5	T38.3x6
Tolciclate	T49.0x1	T49.0x2	T49.0x3	T49.0x4	T49.0x5	T49.0x6
Tolmetin	T39.391	T39.392	T39.393	T39.394	T39.395	T39.396

Substance	External Cause (T-Code)					
	Poisoning, Accidental (Unintentional)	Poisoning, Intentional Self-Harm	Poisoning, Assault	Poisoning, Undetermined	Adverse Effect	Underdosing
Tolnaftate	T49.0x1	T49.0x2	T49.0x3	T49.0x4	T49.0x5	T49.0x6
Tolonidine	T46.5x1	T46.5x2	T46.5x3	T46.5x4	T46.5x5	T46.5x6
Toloxatone	T42.6x1	T42.6x2	T42.6x3	T42.6x4	T42.6x5	T42.6x6
Tolperisone	T44.3x1	T44.3x2	T44.3x3	T44.3x4	T44.3x5	T44.3x6
Tolserol	T42.8x1	T42.8x2	T42.8x3	T42.8x4	T42.8x5	T42.8x6
Toluene (liquid)	T52.2x1	T52.2x2	T52.2x3	T52.2x4	—	—
diisocyanate	T65.0x1	T65.0x2	T65.0x3	T65.0x4	—	—
Toluidine	T65.891	T65.892	T65.893	T65.894	—	—
vapor	T59.891	T59.892	T59.893	T59.894	—	—
Toluol (liquid)	T52.2x1	T52.2x2	T52.2x3	T52.2x4	—	—
vapor	T52.2x1	T52.2x2	T52.2x3	T52.2x4	—	—
Toluylenediamine	T65.3x1	T65.3x2	T65.3x3	T65.3x4	—	—
Tolylene-2,4-diisocyanate	T65.0x1	T65.0x2	T65.0x3	T65.0x4	—	—
Tonic NEC	T50.901	T50.902	T50.903	T50.904	T50.905	T50.906
Topical action drug NEC	T49.91	T49.92	T49.93	T49.94	T49.95	T49.96
ear, nose or throat	T49.6x1	T49.6x2	T49.6x3	T49.6x4	T49.6x5	T49.6x6
eye	T49.5x1	T49.5x2	T49.5x3	T49.5x4	T49.5x5	T49.5x6
skin	T49.4x1	T49.4x2	T49.4x3	T49.4x4	T49.4x5	T49.4x6
specified NEC	T49.8x1	T49.8x2	T49.8x3	T49.8x4	T49.8x5	T49.8x6
Toquizine	T44.3x1	T44.3x2	T44.3x3	T44.3x4	T44.3x5	T44.3x6
Toremifene	T38.6x1	T38.6x2	T38.6x3	T38.6x4	T38.6x5	T38.6x6
Tosylchloramide sodium	T49.8x1	T49.8x2	T49.8x3	T49.8x4	T49.8x5	T49.8x6
Toxaphene (dust) (spray)	T60.1x1	T60.1x2	T60.1x3	T60.1x4	—	—
Toxin, diphtheria (Schick Test)	T50.8x1	T50.8x2	T50.8x3	T50.8x4	T50.8x5	T50.8x6
Toxoid						
combined	T50.A21	T50.A22	T50.A23	T50.A24	T50.A25	T50.A26
diphtheria	T50.A91	T50.A92	T50.A93	T50.A94	T50.A95	T50.A96
tetanus	T50.A91	T50.A92	T50.A93	T50.A94	T50.A95	T50.A96
Trace element NEC	T45.8x1	T45.8x2	T45.8x3	T45.8x4	T45.8x5	T45.8x6
Tractor fuel NEC	T52.0x1	T52.0x2	T52.0x3	T52.0x4	—	—
Tragacanth	T50.991	T50.992	T50.993	T50.994	T50.995	T50.996
Tramadol	T40.4x1	T40.4x2	T40.4x3	T40.4x4	T40.4x5	T40.4x6
Tramazoline	T48.5x1	T48.5x2	T48.5x3	T48.5x4	T48.5x5	T48.5x6
Tranexamic acid	T45.621	T45.622	T45.623	T45.624	T45.625	T45.626
Tranilast	T45.0x1	T45.0x2	T45.0x3	T45.0x4	T45.0x5	T45.0x6
Tranquilizer NEC	T43.501	T43.502	T43.503	T43.504	T43.505	T43.506
with hypnotic or sedative	T42.6x1	T42.6x2	T42.6x3	T42.6x4	T42.6x5	T42.6x6
benzodiazepine NEC	T42.4x1	T42.4x2	T42.4x3	T42.4x4	T42.4x5	T42.4x6
butyrophenone NEC	T43.4x1	T43.4x2	T43.4x3	T43.4x4	T43.4x5	T43.4x6
carbamate	T43.591	T43.592	T43.593	T43.594	T43.595	T43.596
dimethylamine	T43.3x1	T43.3x2	T43.3x3	T43.3x4	T43.3x5	T43.3x6

Substance	Poisoning, Accidental (Unintentional)	Poisoning, Intentional Self-Harm	Poisoning, Assault	Poisoning, Undetermined	Adverse Effect	Underdosing
Tranquilizer NEC *(Continued)*						
ethylamine	T43.3x1	T43.3x2	T43.3x3	T43.3x4	T43.3x5	T43.3x6
hydroxyzine	T43.591	T43.592	T43.593	T43.594	T43.595	T43.596
major NEC	T43.501	T43.502	T43.503	T43.504	T43.505	T43.506
penothiazine NEC	T43.3x1	T43.3x2	T43.3x4	T43.3x4	T43.3x5	T43.3x6
phenothiazine-based	T43.3x1	T43.3x2	T43.3x3	T43.3x4	T43.3x5	T43.3x6
piperazine NEC	T43.3x1	T43.3x2	T43.3x3	T43.3x4	T43.3x5	T43.3x6
piperidine	T43.3x1	T43.3x2	T43.3x3	T43.3x4	T43.3x5	T43.3x6
propylamine	T43.3x1	T43.3x2	T43.3x3	T43.3x4	T43.3x5	T43.3x6
specified NEC	T43.591	T43.592	T43.593	T43.594	T43.595	T43.596
thioxanthene NEC	T43.591	T43.592	T43.593	T43.594	T43.595	T43.596
Trantoin	T37.91	T37.92	T37.93	T37.94	T37.95	T37.96
Tranxene	T42.4x1	T42.4x2	T42.4x3	T42.4x4	T42.4x5	T42.4x6
Tranylcypromine	T43.1x1	T43.1x2	T43.1x3	T43.1x4	T43.1x5	T43.1x6
Trapidil	T46.3x1	T46.3x2	T46.3x3	T46.3x4	T46.3x5	T46.3x6
Trasentine	T44.3x1	T44.3x2	T44.3x3	T44.3x4	T44.3x5	T44.3x6
Travert	T50.3x1	T50.3x2	T50.3x3	T50.3x4	T50.3x5	T50.3x6
Trazodone	T43.211	T43.212	T43.213	T43.214	T43.215	T43.216
Trecator	T37.1x1	T37.1x2	T37.1x3	T37.1x4	T37.1x5	T37.1x6
Treosulfan	T45.1x1	T45.1x2	T45.1x3	T45.1x4	T45.1x5	T45.1x6
Tretamine	T45.1x1	T45.1x2	T45.1x3	T45.1x4	T45.1x5	T45.1x6
Tretinoin	T49.0x1	T49.0x2	T49.0x3	T49.0x4	T49.0x5	T49.0x6
Tretoquinol	T48.6x1	T48.6x2	T48.6x3	T48.6x4	T48.6x5	T48.6x6
Triacetin	T49.0x1	T49.0x2	T49.0x3	T49.0x4	T49.0x5	T49.0x6
Triacetoxyanthracene	T49.4x1	T49.4x2	T49.4x3	T49.4x4	T49.4x5	T49.4x6
Triacetyloleandomycin	T36.3x1	T36.3x2	T36.3x3	T36.3x4	T36.3x5	T36.3x6
Triamcinolone	T49.0x1	T49.0x2	T49.0x3	T49.0x4	T49.0x5	T49.0x6
ENT agent	T49.6x1	T49.6x2	T49.6x3	T49.6x4	T49.6x5	T49.6x6
hexacetonide	T49.0x1	T49.0x2	T49.0x3	T49.0x4	T49.0x5	T49.0x6
ophthalmic preparation	T49.5x1	T49.5x2	T49.5x3	T49.5x4	T49.5x5	T49.5x6
topical NEC	T49.0x1	T49.0x2	T49.0x3	T49.0x4	T49.0x5	T49.0x6
Triampyzine	T44.3x1	T44.3x2	T44.3x3	T44.3x4	T44.3x5	T44.3x6
Triamterene	T50.2x1	T50.2x2	T50.2x3	T50.2x4	T50.2x5	T50.2x6
Triazine (herbicide)	T60.3x1	T60.3x2	T60.3x3	T60.3x4	—	—
Triaziquone	T45.1x1	T45.1x2	T45.1x3	T45.1x4	T45.1x5	T45.1x6
Triazolam	T42.4x1	T42.4x2	T42.4x3	T42.4x4	T42.4x5	T42.4x6
Triazole (herbicide)	T60.3x1	T60.3x2	T60.3x3	T60.3x4	—	—
Tribenoside	T46.991	T46.992	T46.993	T46.994	T46.995	T46.996
Tribromacetaldehyde	T42.6x1	T42.6x2	T42.6x3	T42.6x4	T42.6x5	T42.6x6
Tribromoethanol, rectal	T41.291	T41.292	T41.293	T41.294	T41.295	T41.296

Substance	External Cause (T-Code)					
	Poisoning, Accidental (Unintentional)	Poisoning, Intentional Self-Harm	Poisoning, Assault	Poisoning, Undetermined	Adverse Effect	Underdosing
Tribromomethane	T42.6x1	T42.6x2	T42.6x3	T42.6x4	T42.6x5	T42.6x6
Trichlorethane	T53.2x1	T53.2x2	T53.2x3	T53.2x4	—	—
Trichlorethylene	T53.2x1	T53.2x2	T53.2x3	T53.2x4	—	—
Trichlorfon	T60.0x1	T60.0x2	T60.0x3	T60.0x4	—	—
Trichlormethiazide	T50.2x1	T50.2x2	T50.2x3	T50.2x4	T50.2x5	T50.2x6
Trichlormethine	T45.1x1	T45.1x2	T45.1x3	T45.1x4	T45.1x5	T45.1x6
Trichloroacetic acid, Trichloracetic acid	T54.2x1	T54.2x2	T54.2x3	T54.2x4	—	—
medicinal	T49.4x1	T49.4x2	T49.4x3	T49.4x4	T49.4x5	T49.4x6
Trichloroethane	T53.2x1	T53.2x2	T53.2x3	T53.2x4	—	—
Trichloroethanol	T42.6x1	T42.6x2	T42.6x3	T42.6x4	T42.6x5	T42.6x6
Trichloroethylene (liquid) (vapor)	T53.2x1	T53.2x2	T53.2x3	T53.2x4	—	—
anesthetic (gas)	T41.0x1	T41.0x2	T41.0x3	T41.0x4	T41.0x5	T41.0x6
vapor NEC	T53.2x1	T53.2x2	T53.2x3	T53.2x4	—	—
Trichloroethyl phosphate	T42.6x1	T42.6x2	T42.6x3	T42.6x4	T42.6x5	T42.6x6
Trichlorofluoromethane NEC	T53.5x1	T53.5x2	T53.5x3	T53.5x4	—	—
Trichloronat(e)	T60.0x1	T60.0x2	T60.0x3	T60.0x4	—	—
2,4,5-Trichlorophen-oxyacetic acid	T60.3x1	T60.3x2	T60.3x3	T60.3x4	—	—
Trichloropropane	T53.6x1	T53.6x2	T53.6x3	T53.6x4	—	—
Trichlorotriethylamine	T45.1x1	T45.1x2	T45.1x3	T45.1x4	T45.1x5	T45.1x6
Trichomonacides NEC	T37.3x1	T37.3x2	T37.3x3	T37.3x4	T37.3x5	T37.3x6
Trichomycin	T36.7x1	T36.7x2	T36.7x3	T36.7x4	T36.7x5	T36.7x6
Triclobisonium chloride	T49.0x1	T49.0x2	T49.0x3	T49.0x4	T49.0x5	T49.0x6
Triclocarban	T49.0x1	T49.0x2	T49.0x3	T49.0x4	T49.0x5	T49.0x6
Triclofos	T42.6x1	T42.6x2	T42.6x3	T42.6x4	T42.6x5	T42.6x6
Triclosan	T49.0x1	T49.0x2	T49.0x3	T49.0x4	T49.0x5	T49.0x6
Tricresyl phosphate	T65.891	T65.892	T65.893	T65.894	—	—
solvent	T52.91	T52.92	T52.93	T52.94	—	—
Tricyclamol chloride	T44.3x1	T44.3x2	T44.3x3	T44.3x4	T44.3x5	T44.3x6
Tridesilon	T49.0x1	T49.0x2	T49.0x3	T49.0x4	T49.0x5	T49.0x6
Tridihexethyl iodide	T44.3x1	T44.3x2	T44.3x3	T44.3x4	T44.3x5	T44.3x6
Tridione	T42.2x1	T42.2x2	T42.2x3	T42.2x4	T42.2x5	T42.2x6
Trientine	T45.8x1	T45.8x2	T45.8x3	T45.8x4	T45.8x5	T45.8x6
Triethanolamine NEC	T54.3x1	T54.3x2	T54.3x3	T54.3x4	—	—
detergent	T54.3x1	T54.3x2	T54.3x3	T54.3x4	—	—
trinitrate (biphosphate)	T46.3x1	T46.3x2	T46.3x3	T46.3x4	T46.3x5	T46.3x6
Triethanomelamine	T45.1x1	T45.1x2	T45.1x3	T45.1x4	T45.1x5	T45.1x6
Triethylenemelamine	T45.1x1	T45.1x2	T45.1x3	T45.1x4	T45.1x5	T45.1x6
Triethylenephosphoramide	T45.1x1	T45.1x2	T45.1x3	T45.1x4	T45.1x5	T45.1x6
Triethylenethiophosphoramide	T45.1x1	T45.1x2	T45.1x3	T45.1x4	T45.1x5	T45.1x6
Trifluoperazine	T43.3x1	T43.3x2	T43.3x3	T43.3x4	T43.3x5	T43.3x6

Substance	Poisoning, Accidental (Unintentional)	Poisoning, Intentional Self-Harm	Poisoning, Assault	Poisoning, Undetermined	Adverse Effect	Underdosing
	External Cause (T-Code)					
Trifluoroethyl vinyl ether	T41.0x1	T41.0x2	T41.0x3	T41.0x4	T41.0x5	T41.0x6
Trifluperidol	T43.4x1	T43.4x2	T43.4x3	T43.4x4	T43.4x5	T43.4x6
Triflupromazine	T43.3x1	T43.3x2	T43.3x3	T43.3x4	T43.3x5	T43.3x6
Trifluridine	T37.5x1	T37.5x2	T37.5x3	T37.5x4	T37.5x5	T37.5x6
Triflusal	T45.521	T45.522	T45.523	T45.524	T45.525	T45.526
Trihexyphenidyl	T44.3x1	T44.3x2	T44.3x3	T44.3x4	T44.3x5	T44.3x6
Triiodothyronine	T38.1x1	T38.1x2	T38.1x3	T38.1x4	T38.1x5	T38.1x6
Trilene	T41.0x1	T41.0x2	T41.0x3	T41.0x4	T41.0x5	T41.0x6
Trilostane	T38.991	T38.992	T38.993	T38.994	T38.995	T38.996
Trimebutine	T44.3x1	T44.3x2	T44.3x3	T44.3x4	T44.3x5	T44.3x6
Trimecaine	T41.3x1	T41.3x2	T41.3x3	T41.3x4	T41.3x5	T41.3x6
Trimeprazine (tartrate)	T44.3x1	T44.3x2	T44.3x3	T44.3x4	T44.3x5	T44.3x6
Trimetaphan camsilate	T44.2x1	T44.2x2	T44.2x3	T44.2x4	T44.2x5	T44.2x6
Trimetazidine	T46.7x1	T46.7x2	T46.7x3	T46.7x4	T46.7x5	T46.7x6
Trimethadione	T42.2x1	T42.2x2	T42.2x3	T42.2x4	T42.2x5	T42.2x6
Trimethaphan	T44.2x1	T44.2x2	T44.2x3	T44.2x4	T44.2x5	T44.2x6
Trimethidinium	T44.2x1	T44.2x2	T44.2x3	T44.2x4	T44.2x5	T44.2x6
Trimethobenzamide	T45.0x1	T45.0x2	T45.0x3	T45.0x4	T45.0x5	T45.0x6
Trimethoprim	T37.8x1	T37.8x2	T37.8x3	T37.8x4	T37.8x5	T37.8x6
with sulfamethoxazole	T36.8x1	T36.8x2	T36.8x3	T36.8x4	T36.8x5	T36.8x6
Trimethylcarbinol	T51.3x1	T51.3x2	T51.3x3	T51.3x4	—	—
Trimethylpsoralen	T49.3x1	T49.3x2	T49.3x3	T49.3x4	T49.3x5	T49.3x6
Trimeton	T45.0x1	T45.0x2	T45.0x3	T45.0x4	T45.0x5	T45.0x6
Trimetrexate	T45.1x1	T45.1x2	T45.1x3	T45.1x4	T45.1x5	T45.1x6
Trimipramine	T43.011	T43.012	T43.013	T43.014	T43.015	T43.016
Trimustine	T45.1x1	T45.1x2	T45.1x3	T45.1x4	T45.1x5	T45.1x6
Trinitrine	T46.3x1	T46.3x2	T46.3x3	T46.3x4	T46.3x5	T46.3x6
Trinitrobenzol	T65.3x1	T65.3x2	T65.3x3	T65.3x4	—	—
Trinitrophenol	T65.3x1	T65.3x2	T65.3x3	T65.3x4	—	—
Trinitrotoluene (fumes)	T65.3x1	T65.3x2	T65.3x3	T65.3x4	—	—
Trinitrotoluene	T65.891	T65.892	T65.893	T65.894		
fumes	T59.891	T59.892	T59.893	T59.894	—	—
Trional	T42.6x1	T42.6x2	T42.6x3	T42.6x4	T42.6x5	T42.6x6
Triorthocresyl phosphate	T65.891	T65.892	T65.893	T65.894	—	—
Trioxide of arsenic	T57.0x1	T57.0x2	T57.0x3	T57.0x4	—	—
Trioxysalen	T49.4x1	T49.4x2	T49.4x3	T49.4x4	T49.4x5	T49.4x6
Tripamide	T50.2x1	T50.2x2	T50.2x3	T50.2x4	T50.2x5	T50.2x6
Triparanol	T46.6x1	T46.6x2	T46.6x3	T46.6x4	T46.6x5	T46.6x6
Tripelennamine	T45.0x1	T45.0x2	T45.0x3	T45.0x4	T45.0x5	T45.0x6
Triperiden	T44.3x1	T44.3x2	T44.3x3	T44.3x4	T44.3x5	T44.3x6

Substance	External Cause (T-Code)					
	Poisoning, Accidental (Unintentional)	Poisoning, Intentional Self-Harm	Poisoning, Assault	Poisoning, Undetermined	Adverse Effect	Underdosing
Triperidol	T43.4x1	T43.4x2	T43.4x3	T43.4x4	T43.4x5	T43.4x6
Triphenylphosphate	T65.891	T65.892	T65.893	T65.894	—	—
Triple						
bromides	T42.6x1	T42.6x2	T42.6x3	T42.6x4	T42.6x5	T42.6x6
carbonate	T47.1x1	T47.1x2	T47.1x3	T47.1x4	T47.1x5	T47.1x6
vaccine						
DPT	T50.A11	T50.A12	T50.A13	T50.A14	T50.A15	T50.A16
including pertussis	T50.A11	T50.A12	T50.A13	T50.A14	T50.A15	T50.A16
MMR	T50.B91	T50.B92	—	—	—	—
Triprolidine	T45.0x1	T45.0x2	T45.0x3	T45.0x4	T45.0x5	T45.0x6
Trisodium hydrogen edetate	T50.6x1	T50.6x2	T50.6x3	T50.6x4	T50.6x5	T50.6x6
Trisoralen	T49.3x1	T49.3x2	T49.3x3	T49.3x4	T49.3x5	T49.3x6
Trisulfapyrimidines	T37.0x1	T37.0x2	T37.0x3	T37.0x4	T37.0x5	T37.0x6
Trithiozine	T44.3x1	T44.3x2	T44.3x3	T44.3x4	T44.3x5	T44.3x6
Tritiozine	T44.3x1	T44.3x2	T44.3x3	T44.3x4	T44.3x5	T44.3x6
Tritoqualine	T45.0x1	T45.0x2	T45.0x3	T45.0x4	T45.0x5	T45.0x6
Trofosfamide	T45.1x1	T45.1x2	T45.1x3	T45.1x4	T45.1x5	T45.1x6
Troleandomycin	T36.3x1	T36.3x2	T36.3x3	T36.3x4	T36.3x5	T36.3x6
Trolnitrate (phosphate)	T46.3x1	T46.3x2	T46.3x3	T46.3x4	T46.3x5	T46.3x6
Tromantadine	T37.5x1	T37.5x2	T37.5x3	T37.5x4	T37.5x5	T37.5x6
Trometamol	T50.2x1	T50.2x2	T50.2x3	T50.2x4	T50.2x5	T50.2x6
Tromethamine	T50.2x1	T50.2x2	T50.2x3	T50.2x4	T50.2x5	T50.2x6
Tronothane	T41.3x1	T41.3x2	T41.3x3	T41.3x4	T41.3x5	T41.3x6
Tropacine	T44.3x1	T44.3x2	T44.3x3	T44.3x4	T44.3x5	T44.3x6
Tropatepine	T44.3x1	T44.3x2	T44.3x3	T44.3x4	T44.3x5	T44.3x6
Tropicamide	T44.3x1	T44.3x2	T44.3x3	T44.3x4	T44.3x5	T44.3x6
Trospium chloride	T44.3x1	T44.3x2	T44.3x3	T44.3x4	T44.3x5	T44.3x6
Troxerutin	T46.991	T46.992	T46.993	T46.994	T46.995	T46.996
Troxidone	T42.2x1	T42.2x2	T42.2x3	T42.2x4	T42.2x5	T42.2x6
Tryparsamide	T37.3x1	T37.3x2	T37.3x3	T37.3x4	T37.3x5	T37.3x6
Trypsin	T45.3x1	T45.3x2	T45.3x3	T45.3x4	T45.3x5	T45.3x6
Tryptizol	T43.011	T43.012	T43.013	T43.014	T43.015	T43.016
TSH	T38.811	T38.812	T38.813	T38.814	T38.815	T38.816
Tuaminoheptane	T48.5x1	T48.5x2	T48.5x3	T48.5x4	T48.5x5	T48.5x6
Tuberculin, purified protein derivative (PPD)	T50.8x1	T50.8x2	T50.8x3	T50.8x4	T50.8x5	T50.8x6
Tubocurare	T48.1x1	T48.1x2	T48.1x3	T48.1x4	T48.1x5	T48.1x6
Tubocurarine (chloride)	T48.1x1	T48.1x2	T48.1x3	T48.1x4	T48.1x5	T48.1x6
Tulobuterol	T48.6x1	T48.6x2	T48.6x3	T48.6x4	T48.6x5	T48.6x6
Turpentine (spirits of)	T52.8x1	T52.8x2	T52.8x3	T52.8x4	—	—
vapor	T52.8x1	T52.8x2	T52.8x3	T52.8x4	—	—

Substance	External Cause (T-Code)					
	Poisoning, Accidental (Unintentional)	Poisoning, Intentional Self-Harm	Poisoning, Assault	Poisoning, Undetermined	Adverse Effect	Underdosing
Tybamate	T43.591	T43.592	T43.593	T43.594	T43.595	T43.596
Tyloxapol	T48.4x1	T48.4x2	T48.4x3	T48.4x4	T48.4x5	T48.4x6
Tymazoline	T48.5x1	T48.5x2	T48.5x3	T48.5x4	T48.5x5	T48.5x6
Typhoid-paratyphoid vaccine	T50.A91	T50.A92	T50.A93	T50.A94	T50.A95	T50.A96
Typhus vaccine	T50.A91	T50.A92	T50.A93	T50.A94	T50.A95	T50.A96
Tyropanoate	T50.8x1	T50.8x2	T50.8x3	T50.8x4	T50.8x5	T50.8x6
Tyrothricin	T49.6x1	T49.6x2	T49.6x3	T49.6x4	T49.6x5	T49.6x6
ENT agent	T49.6x1	T49.6x2	T49.6x3	T49.6x4	T49.6x5	T49.6x6
ophthalmic preparation	T49.5x1	T49.5x2	T49.5x3	T49.5x4	T49.5x5	T49.5x6
Ufenamate	T39.391	T39.392	T39.393	T39.394	T39.395	T39.396
Ultraviolet light protectant	T49.3x1	T49.3x2	T49.3x3	T49.3x4	T49.3x5	T49.3x6
Undecenoic acid	T49.0x1	T49.0x2	T49.0x3	T49.0x4	T49.0x5	T49.0x6
Undecoylium	T49.0x1	T49.0x2	T49.0x3	T49.0x4	T49.0x5	T49.0x6
Undecylenic acid (derivatives)	T49.0x1	T49.0x2	T49.0x3	T49.0x4	T49.0x5	T49.0x6
Unna's boot	T49.3x1	T49.3x2	T49.3x3	T49.3x4	T49.3x5	T49.3x6
Unsaturated fatty acid	T46.6x1	T46.6x2	T46.6x3	T46.6x4	T46.6x5	T46.6x6
Uracil mustard	T45.1x1	T45.1x2	T45.1x3	T45.1x4	T45.1x5	T45.1x6
Uramustine	T45.1x1	T45.1x2	T45.1x3	T45.1x4	T45.1x5	T45.1x6
Urapidil	T46.5x1	T46.5x2	T46.5x3	T46.5x4	T46.5x5	T46.5x6
Urari	T48.1x1	T48.1x2	T48.1x3	T48.1x4	T48.1x5	T48.1x6
Urate oxidase	T50.4x1	T50.4x2	T50.4x3	T50.4x4	T50.4x5	T50.4x6
Urea	T47.3x1	T47.3x2	T47.3x3	T47.3x4	T47.3x5	T47.3x6
peroxide	T49.0x1	T49.0x2	T49.0x3	T49.0x4	T49.0x5	T49.0x6
stibamine	T37.4x1	T37.4x2	T37.4x3	T37.4x4	T37.4x5	T37.4x6
topical	T49.8x1	T49.8x2	T49.8x3	T49.8x4	T49.8x5	T49.8x6
Urethane	T45.1x1	T45.1x2	T45.1x3	T45.1x4	T45.1x5	T45.1x6
Urginea (maritima) (scilla) *see* Squill						
Uric acid metabolism drug NEC	T50.4x1	T50.4x2	T50.4x3	T50.4x4	T50.4x5	T50.4x6
Uricosuric agent	T50.4x1	T50.4x2	T50.4x3	T50.4x4	T50.4x5	T50.4x6
Urinary anti-infective	T37.8x1	T37.8x2	T37.8x3	T37.8x4	T37.8x5	T37.8x6
Urofollitropin	T38.811	T38.812	T38.813	T38.814	T38.815	T38.816
Urokinase	T45.611	T45.612	T45.613	T45.614	T45.615	T45.616
Urokon	T50.8x1	T50.8x2	T50.8x3	T50.8x4	T50.8x5	T50.8x6
Urotropin	T37.91	T37.92	T37.93	T37.94	T37.95	T37.96
Ursodeoxycholic acid	T50.991	T50.992	T50.993	T50.994	T50.995	T50.996
Ursodiol	T50.991	T50.992	T50.993	T50.994	T50.995	T50.996
Uterine relaxing factor	T44.5x1	T44.5x2	T44.5x3	T44.5x4	T44.5x5	T44.5x6
Urtica	T62.2x1	T62.2x2	T62.2x3	T62.2x4	—	—
Utility gas - *see* Gas, utility						
Vaccine NEC	T50.Z91	T50.Z92	T50.Z93	T50.Z94	T50.Z95	T50.Z96
antineoplastic	T50.Z91	T50.Z92	T50.Z93	T50.Z94	T50.Z95	T50.Z96

TABLE OF DRUGS AND CHEMICALS

Substance	External Cause (T-Code)					
	Poisoning, Accidental (Unintentional)	Poisoning, Intentional Self-Harm	Poisoning, Assault	Poisoning, Undetermined	Adverse Effect	Underdosing
Vaccine NEC (Continued)						
bacterial NEC	T50.A91	T50.A92	T50.A93	T50.A94	T50.A95	T50.A96
with						
other bacterial component	T50.A91	T50.A92	T50.A93	T50.A94	T50.A95	T50.A96
pertussis component	T50.A91	T50.A92	T50.A93	T50.A94	T50.A95	T50.A96
viral-rickettsial component	T50.A91	T50.A92	T50.A93	T50.A94	T50.A95	T50.A96
mixed NEC	T50.A91	T50.A92	T50.A93	T50.A94	T50.A95	T50.A96
BCG	T50.A91	T50.A92	T50.A93	T50.A94	T50.A95	T50.A96
cholera	T50.A91	T50.A92	T50.A93	T50.A94	T50.A95	T50.A96
diphtheria	T50.A91	T50.A92	T50.A93	T50.A94	T50.A95	T50.A96
with tetanus	T50.A21	T50.A22	T50.A23	T50.A24	T50.A25	T50.A26
and pertussis	T50.A11	T50.A12	T50.A13	T50.A14	T50.A15	T50.A16
influenza	T50.B91	T50.B92	T50.B93	T50.B94	T50.B95	T50.B96
measles	T50.B91	T50.B92	T50.B93	T50.B94	T50.B95	T50.B96
with mumps and rubella	T50.B91	T50.B92	T50.B93	T50.B94	T50.B95	T50.B96
meningococcal	T50.A91	T50.A92	T50.A93	T50.A94	T50.A95	T50.A96
mumps	T50.B91	T50.B92	T50.B93	T50.B94	T50.B95	T50.B96
paratyphoid	T50.A91	T50.A92	T50.A93	T50.A94	T50.A95	T50.A96
pertussis	T50.A11	T50.A12	T50.A13	T50.A14	T50.A15	T50.A16
with diphtheria	T50.A11	T50.A12	T50.A13	T50.A14	T50.A15	T50.A16
and tetanus	T50.A11	T50.A12	T50.A13	T50.A14	T50.A15	T50.A16
plague	T50.A91	T50.A92	T50.A93	T50.A94	T50.A95	T50.A96
poliomyelitis	T50.B91	T50.B92	T50.B93	T50.B94	T50.B95	T50.B96
poliovirus	T50.B91	T50.B92	T50.B93	T50.B94	T50.B95	T50.B96
rabies	T50.B91	T50.B92	T50.B93	T50.B94	T50.B95	T50.B96
respiratory syncytial virus	T50.B91	T50.B92	T50.B93	T50.B94	T50.B95	T50.B96
rickettsial NEC	T50.A91	T50.A92	T50.A93	T50.A94	T50.A95	T50.A96
with						
bacterial component	T50.A21	T50.A22	T50.A23	T50.A24	T50.A25	T50.A26
Rocky Mountain spotted fever	T50.A91	T50.A92	T50.A93	T50.A94	T50.A95	T50.A96
rubella	T50.B91	T50.B92	T50.B93	T50.B94	T50.B95	T50.B96
sabin oral	T50.B91	T50.B92	T50.B93	T50.B94	T50.B95	T50.B96
smallpox	T50.B11	T50.B12	T50.B13	T50.B14	T50.B15	T50.B16
TAB	T50.A91	T50.A92	T50.A93	T50.A94	T50.A95	T50.A96
tetanus	T50.A91	T50.A92	T50.A93	T50.A94	T50.A95	T50.A96
typhoid	T50.A91	T50.A92	T50.A93	T50.A94	T50.A95	T50.A96
typhus	T50.A91	T50.A92	T50.A93	T50.A94	T50.A95	T50.A96
viral NEC	T50.B91	T50.B92	T50.B93	T50.B94	T50.B95	T50.B96
yellow fever	T50.B91	T50.B92	T50.B93	T50.B94	T50.B95	T50.B96
Vaccinia immune globulin	T50.Z11	T50.Z12	T50.Z13	T50.Z14	T50.Z15	T50.Z16

Substance	Poisoning, Accidental (Unintentional)	Poisoning, Intentional Self-Harm	Poisoning, Assault	Poisoning, Undetermined	Adverse Effect	Underdosing
			External Cause (T-Code)			
Vaginal contraceptives	T49.8x1	T49.8x2	T49.8x3	T49.8x4	T49.8x5	T49.8x6
Valerian						
root	T42.6x1	T42.6x2	T42.6x3	T42.6x4	T42.6x5	T42.6x6
tincture	T42.6x1	T42.6x2	T42.6x3	T42.6x4	T42.6x5	T42.6x6
Valethamate bromide	T44.3x1	T44.3x2	T44.3x3	T44.3x4	T44.3x5	T44.3x6
Valisone	T49.0x1	T49.0x2	T49.0x3	T49.0x4	T49.0x5	T49.0x6
Valium	T42.4x1	T42.4x2	T42.4x3	T42.4x4	T42.4x5	T42.4x6
Valmid	T42.6x1	T42.6x2	T42.6x3	T42.6x4	T42.6x5	T42.6x6
Valnoctamide	T42.6x1	T42.6x2	T42.6x3	T42.6x4	T42.6x5	T42.6x6
Valproate (sodium)	T42.6x1	T42.6x2	T42.6x3	T42.6x4	T42.6x5	T42.6x6
Valproic acid	T42.6x1	T42.6x2	T42.6x3	T42.6x4	T42.6x5	T42.6x6
Valpromide	T42.6x1	T42.6x2	T42.6x3	T42.6x4	T42.6x5	T42.6x6
Vanadium	T56.891	T56.892	T56.893	T56.894	—	—
Vancomycin	T36.8x1	T36.8x2	T36.8x3	T36.8x4	T36.8x5	T36.8x6
Vapor (see also Gas)	T59.91	T59.92	T59.93	T59.94	—	—
kiln (carbon monoxide)	T58.8x1	T58.8x2	T58.8x3	T58.8x4	—	—
lead - see lead						
specified source NEC	T59.91	T59.92	T59.93	T59.94	—	—
Varicose reduction drug	T46.8x1	T46.8x2	T46.8x3	T46.8x4	T46.8x5	T46.8x6
Varnish	T65.4x1	T65.4x2	T65.4x3	T65.4x4	—	—
cleaner	T52.91	T52.92	T52.93	T52.94	—	—
Vaseline	T49.3x1	T49.3x2	T49.3x3	T49.3x4	T49.3x5	T49.3x6
Vasodilan	T46.7x1	T46.7x2	T46.7x3	T46.7x4	T46.7x5	T46.7x6
Vasodilator						
coronary NEC	T46.3x1	T46.3x2	T46.3x3	T46.3x4	T46.3x5	T46.3x6
peripheral NEC	T46.7x1	T46.7x2	T46.7x3	T46.7x4	T46.7x5	T46.7x6
Vasopressin	T38.891	T38.892	T38.893	T38.894	T38.895	T38.896
Vasopressor drugs	T38.891	T38.892	T38.893	T38.894	T38.895	T38.896
Vecuronium bromide	T48.1x1	T48.1x2	T48.1x3	T48.1x4	T48.1x5	T48.1x6
Vegetable extract, astringent	T49.2x1	T49.2x2	T49.2x3	T49.2x4	T49.2x5	T49.2x6
Venlafaxine	T43.211	T43.212	T43.213	T43.214	T43.215	T43.216
Venom, venomous (bite) (sting)	T63.91	T63.92	T63.93	T63.94	—	—
ant	T63.421	T63.422	T63.423	T63.424	—	—
amphibian NEC	T63.831	T63.832	T63.833	T63.834	—	—
animal NEC	T63.891	T63.892	T63.893	T63.894	—	—
arthropod NEC	T63.481	T63.482	T63.483	T63.484	—	—
bee	T63.441	T63.442	T63.443	T63.444	—	—
centipede	T63.411	T63.412	T63.413	T63.414	—	—
fish	T63.591	T63.592	T63.593	T63.594	—	—
frog	T63.811	T63.812	T63.813	T63.814	—	—

Substance	External Cause (T-Code)					
	Poisoning, Accidental (Unintentional)	Poisoning, Intentional Self-Harm	Poisoning, Assault	Poisoning, Undetermined	Adverse Effect	Underdosing
Venom, venomous *(Continued)*						
hornet	T63.451	T63.452	T63.453	T63.454	—	—
insect NEC	T63.481	T63.482	T63.483	T63.484	—	—
lizard	T63.121	T63.122	T63.123	T63.124	—	—
marine						
animals	T63.691	T63.692	T63.693	T63.694	—	—
bluebottle	T63.611	T63.612	T63.613	T63.614	—	—
jellyfish NEC	T63.621	T63.622	T63.623	T63.624	—	—
Portugese Man-o-war	T63.611	T63.612	T63.613	T63.614	—	—
sea anemone	T63.631	T63.632	T63.633	T63.634	—	—
specified NEC	T63.691	T63.692	T63.693	T63.694	—	—
fish	T63.591	T63.592	T63.593	T63.594	—	—
sting ray	T63.511	T63.512	T63.513	T63.514	—	—
plants	T63.711	T63.712	T63.713	T63.714	—	—
millipede (tropical)	T63.411	T63.412	T63.413	T63.414	—	—
plant NEC	T63.791	T63.792	T63.793	T63.794	—	—
marine	T63.711	T63.712	T63.713	T63.714	—	—
reptile	T63.191	T63.192	T63.193	T63.194	—	—
gila monster	T63.111	T63.112	T63.113	T63.114	—	—
lizard NEC	T63.121	T63.122	T63.123	T63.124	—	—
scorpion	T63.2x1	T63.2x2	T63.2x3	T63.2x4	—	—
snake	T63.001	T63.002	T63.003	T63.004	—	—
African NEC	T63.081	T63.082	T63.083	T63.084	—	—
American (North) (South) NEC	T63.061	T63.062	T63.063	T63.064	—	—
Asian	T63.081	T63.082	T63.083	T63.084	—	—
Australian	T63.071	T63.072	T63.073	T63.074	—	—
cobra	T63.041	T63.042	T63.043	T63.044	—	—
coral snake	T63.021	T63.022	T63.023	T63.024	—	—
rattlesnake	T63.011	T63.012	T63.013	T63.014	—	—
specified NEC	T63.091	T63.092	T63.093	T63.094	—	—
taipan	T63.031	T63.032	T63.033	T63.034	—	—
specified NEC	T63.891	T63.892	T63.893	T63.894	—	—
spider	T63.301	T63.302	T63.303	T63.304	—	—
black widow	T63.311	T63.312	T63.313	T63.314	—	—
brown recluse	T63.331	T63.332	T63.333	T63.334	—	—
specified NEC	T63.391	T63.392	T63.393	T63.394	—	—
tarantula	T63.321	T63.322	T63.323	T63.324	—	—
sting ray	T63.511	T63.512	T63.513	T63.514	—	—
toad	T63.821	T63.822	T63.823	T63.824	—	—
wasp	T63.461	T63.462	T63.463	T63.464	—	—

Substance	External Cause (T-Code)					
	Poisoning, Accidental (Unintentional)	Poisoning, Intentional Self-Harm	Poisoning, Assault	Poisoning, Undetermined	Adverse Effect	Underdosing
Venous sclerosing drug NEC	T46.8x1	T46.8x2	T46.8x3	T46.8x4	T46.8x5	T46.8x6
Ventolin - *see* Albuterol						
Verapamil	T46.1x1	T46.1x2	T46.1x3	T46.1x4	T46.1x5	T46.1x6
Veramon	T42.3x1	T42.3x2	T42.3x3	T42.3x4	T42.3x5	T42.3x6
Veratrine	T46.5x1	T46.5x2	T46.5x3	T46.5x4	T46.5x5	T46.5x6
Veratrum						
album	T62.2x1	T62.2x2	T62.2x3	T62.2x4	—	—
alkaloids	T46.5x1	T46.5x2	T46.5x3	T46.5x4	T46.5x5	T46.5x6
viride	T62.2x1	T62.2x2	T62.2x3	T62.2x4	—	—
Verdigris	T60.3x1	T60.3x2	T60.3x3	T60.3x4	—	—
Veronal	T42.3x1	T42.3x2	T42.3x3	T42.3x4	T42.3x5	T42.3x6
Veroxil	T37.4x1	T37.4x2	T37.4x3	T37.4x4	T37.4x5	T37.4x6
Versenate	T50.6x1	T50.6x2	T50.6x3	T50.6x4	T50.6x5	T50.6x6
Versidyne	T39.8x1	T39.8x2	T39.8x3	T39.8x4	T39.8x5	T39.8x6
Vetrabutine	T48.0x1	T48.0x2	T48.0x3	T48.0x4	T48.0x5	T48.0x6
Vidarabine	T37.5x1	T37.5x2	T37.5x3	T37.5x4	T37.5x5	T37.5x6
Vienna						
green	T57.0x1	T57.0x2	T57.0x3	T57.0x4	—	—
insecticide	T60.2x1	T60.2x2	T60.2x3	T60.2x4	—	—
red	T57.0x1	T57.0x2	T57.0x3	T57.0x4	—	—
pharmaceutical dye	T50.991	T50.992	T50.993	T50.994	T50.995	T50.996
Vigabatrin	T42.6x1	T42.6x2	T42.6x3	T42.6x4	T42.6x5	T42.6x6
Viloxazine	T43.291	T43.292	T43.293	T43.294	T43.295	T43.296
Viminol	T39.8x1	T39.8x2	T39.8x3	T39.8x4	T39.8x5	T39.8x6
Vinbarbital, vinbarbitone	T42.3x1	T42.3x2	T42.3x3	T42.3x4	T42.3x5	T42.3x6
Vinblastine	T45.1x1	T45.1x2	T45.1x3	T45.1x4	T45.1x5	T45.1x6
Vinburnine	T46.7x1	T46.7x2	T46.7x3	T46.7x4	T46.7x5	T46.7x6
Vincamine	T45.1x1	T45.1x2	T45.1x3	T45.1x4	T45.1x5	T45.1x6
Vincristine	T45.1x1	T45.1x2	T45.1x3	T45.1x4	T45.1x5	T45.1x6
Vindesine	T45.1x1	T45.1x2	T45.1x3	T45.1x4	T45.1x5	T45.1x6
Vinesthene, vinethene	T41.0x1	T41.0x2	T41.0x3	T41.0x4	T41.0x5	T41.0x6
Vinorelbine tartrate	T45.1x1	T45.1x2	T45.1x3	T45.1x4	T45.1x5	T45.1x6
Vinpocetine	T46.7x1	T46.7x2	T46.7x3	T46.7x4	T46.7x5	T46.7x6
Vinyl						
acetate	T65.891	T65.892	T65.893	T65.894	—	—
bital	T42.3x1	T42.3x2	T42.3x3	T42.3x4	T42.3x5	T42.3x6
bromide	T65.891	T65.892	T65.893	T65.894	—	—
chloride	T59.891	T59.892	T59.893	T59.894	—	—
ether	T41.0x1	T41.0x2	T41.0x3	T41.0x4	T41.0x5	T41.0x6
Vinylbital	T42.3x1	T42.3x2	T42.3x3	T42.3x4	T42.3x5	T42.3x6

Substance	External Cause (T-Code)					
	Poisoning, Accidental (Unintentional)	Poisoning, Intentional Self-Harm	Poisoning, Assault	Poisoning, Undetermined	Adverse Effect	Underdosing
Vinylidene chloride	T65.891	T65.892	T65.893	T65.894	—	—
Vioform	T37.8x1	T37.8x2	T37.8x3	T37.8x4	T37.8x5	T37.8x6
topical	T49.0x1	T49.0x2	T49.0x3	T49.0x4	T49.0x5	T49.0x6
Viomycin	T36.8x1	T36.8x2	T36.8x3	T36.8x4	T36.8x5	T36.8x6
Viosterol	T45.2x1	T45.2x2	T45.2x3	T45.2x4	T45.2x5	T45.2x6
Viper (venom)	T63.091	T63.092	T63.093	T63.094	—	—
Viprynium	T37.4x1	T37.4x2	T37.4x3	T37.4x4	T37.4x5	T37.4x6
Viquidil	T46.7x1	T46.7x2	T46.7x3	T46.7x4	T46.7x5	T46.7x6
Viral vaccine NEC	T50.B91	T50.B92	T50.B93	T50.B94	T50.B95	T50.B96
Virginiamycin	T36.8x1	T36.8x2	T36.8x3	T36.8x4	T36.8x5	T36.8x6
Virugon	T37.5x1	T37.5x2	T37.5x3	T37.5x4	T37.5x5	T37.5x6
Viscous agent	T50.901	T50.902	T50.903	T50.904	T50.905	T50.906
Visine	T49.5x1	T49.5x2	T49.5x3	T49.5x4	T49.5x5	T49.5x6
Visnadine	T46.3x1	T46.3x2	T46.3x3	T46.3x4	T46.3x5	T46.3x6
Vitamin NEC	T45.2x1	T45.2x2	T45.2x3	T45.2x4	T45.2x5	T45.2x6
A	T45.2x1	T45.2x2	T45.2x3	T45.2x4	T45.2x5	T45.2x6
B NEC	T45.2x1	T45.2x2	T45.2x3	T45.2x4	T45.2x5	T45.2x6
nicotinic acid	T46.7x1	T46.7x2	T46.7x3	T46.7x4	T46.7x5	T46.7x6
B1	T45.2x1	T45.2x2	T45.2x3	T45.2x4	T45.2x5	T45.2x6
B2	T45.2x1	T45.2x2	T45.2x3	T45.2x4	T45.2x5	T45.2x6
B6	T45.2x1	T45.2x2	T45.2x3	T45.2x4	T45.2x5	T45.2x6
B12	T45.2x1	T45.2x2	T45.2x3	T45.2x4	T45.2x5	T45.2x6
B15	T45.2x1	T45.2x2	T45.2x3	T45.2x4	T45.2x5	T45.2x6
C	T45.2x1	T45.2x2	T45.2x3	T45.2x4	T45.2x5	T45.2x6
D	T45.2x1	T45.2x2	T45.2x3	T45.2x4	T45.2x5	T45.2x6
D2	T45.2x1	T45.2x2	T45.2x3	T45.2x4	T45.2x5	T45.2x6
D3	T45.2x1	T45.2x2	T45.2x3	T45.2x4	T45.2x5	T45.2x6
E	T45.2x1	T45.2x2	T45.2x3	T45.2x4	T45.2x5	T45.2x6
E acetate	T45.2x1	T45.2x2	T45.2x3	T45.2x4	T45.2x5	T45.2x6
hematopoietic	T45.8x1	T45.8x2	T45.8x3	T45.8x4	T45.8x5	T45.8x6
K NEC	T45.7x1	T45.7x2	T45.7x3	T45.7x4	T45.7x5	T45.7x6
K1	T45.7x1	T45.7x2	T45.7x3	T45.7x4	T45.7x5	T45.7x6
K2	T45.7x1	T45.7x2	T45.7x3	T45.7x4	T45.7x5	T45.7x6
PP	T45.2x1	T45.2x2	T45.2x3	T45.2x4	T45.2x5	T45.2x6
ulceroprotectant	T47.1x1	T47.1x2	T47.1x3	T47.1x4	T47.1x5	T47.1x6
Vleminckx's solution	T49.4x1	T49.4x2	T49.4x3	T49.4x4	T49.4x5	T49.4x6
Voltaren - see Diclofenac sodium						
Warfarin	T45.511	T45.512	T45.513	T45.514	T45.515	T45.516
rodenticide	T60.4x1	T60.4x2	T60.4x3	T60.4x4	—	—
sodium	T60.4x1	T60.4x2	T60.4x3	T60.4x4	—	—

Substance	External Cause (T-Code)					
	Poisoning, Accidental (Unintentional)	Poisoning, Intentional Self-Harm	Poisoning, Assault	Poisoning, Undetermined	Adverse Effect	Underdosing
Wasp (sting)	T63.461	T63.462	T63.463	T63.464	—	—
Water						
balance drug	T50.3x1	T50.3x2	T50.3x3	T50.3x4	T50.3x5	T50.3x6
distilled	T50.3x1	T50.3x2	T50.3x3	T50.3x4	T50.3x5	T50.3x6
gas - see Gas, water						
incomplete combustion of - see Carbon, monoxide, fuel, utility						
hemlock	T62.2x1	T62.2x2	T62.2x3	T62.2x4	—	—
moccasin (venom)	T63.061	T63.062	T63.063	T63.064	—	—
purified	T50.3x1	T50.3x2	T50.3x3	T50.3x4	T50.3x5	T50.3x6
Wax (paraffin) (petroleum)	T52.0x1	T52.0x2	T52.0x3	T52.0x4	—	—
automobile	T65.891	T65.892	T65.893	T65.894	—	—
floor	T52.0x1	T52.0x2	T52.0x3	T52.0x4	—	—
Weed killers NEC	T60.3x1	T60.3x2	T60.3x3	T60.3x4	—	—
Welldorm	T42.6x1	T42.6x2	T42.6x3	T42.6x4	T42.6x5	T42.6x6
White						
arsenic	T57.0x1	T57.0x2	T57.0x3	T57.0x4	—	—
hellebore	T62.2x1	T62.2x2	T62.2x3	T62.2x4	—	—
lotion (keratolytic)	T49.4x1	T49.4x2	T49.4x3	T49.4x4	T49.4x5	T49.4x6
spirit	T52.0x1	T52.0x2	T52.0x3	T52.0x4	—	—
Whitewash	T65.891	T65.892	T65.893	T65.894	—	—
Whole blood (human)	T45.8x1	T45.8x2	T45.8x3	T45.8x4	T45.8x5	T45.8x6
Wild						
black cherry	T62.2x1	T62.2x2	T62.2x3	T62.2x4	—	—
poisonous plants NEC	T62.2x1	T62.2x2	T62.2x3	T62.2x4	—	—
Window cleaning fluid	T65.891	T65.892	T65.893	T65.894	—	—
Wintergreen (oil)	T49.3x1	T49.3x2	T49.3x3	T49.3x4	T49.3x5	T49.3x6
Witch hazel	T49.2x1	T49.2x2	T49.2x3	T49.2x4	T49.2x5	T49.2x6
Wisterine	T62.2x1	T62.2x2	T62.2x3	T62.2x4	—	—
Witch hazel	T49.2x1	T49.2x2	T49.2x3	T49.2x4	T49.2x5	T49.2x6
Wood alcohol or spirit	T51.1x1	T51.1x2	T51.1x3	T51.1x4	—	—
Wool fat (hydrous)	T49.3x1	T49.3x2	T49.3x3	T49.3x4	T49.3x5	T49.3x6
Woorali	T48.1x1	T48.1x2	T48.1x3	T48.1x4	T48.1x5	T48.1x6
Wormseed, American	T37.4x1	T37.4x2	T37.4x3	T37.4x4	T37.4x5	T37.4x6
Xamoterol	T44.5x1	T44.5x2	T44.5x3	T44.5x4	T44.5x5	T44.5x6
Xanthine diuretics	T50.2x1	T50.2x2	T50.2x3	T50.2x4	T50.2x5	T50.2x6
Xanthinol nicotinate	T46.7x1	T46.7x2	T46.7x3	T46.7x4	T46.7x5	T46.7x6
Xanthotoxin	T49.3x1	T49.3x2	T49.3x3	T49.3x4	T49.3x5	T49.3x6
Xantinol nicotinate	T46.7x1	T46.7x2	T46.7x3	T46.7x4	T46.7x5	T46.7x6
Xantocillin	T36.0x1	T36.0x2	T36.0x3	T36.0x4	T36.0x5	T36.0x6
Xenon (127Xe) (133Xe)	T50.8x1	T50.8x2	T50.8x3	T50.8x4	T50.8x5	T50.8x6

Substance	External Cause (T-Code)					
	Poisoning, Accidental (Unintentional)	Poisoning, Intentional Self-Harm	Poisoning, Assault	Poisoning, Undetermined	Adverse Effect	Underdosing
Xenysalate	T49.4x1	T49.4x2	T49.4x3	T49.4x4	T49.4x5	T49.4x6
Xibornol	T37.8x1	T37.8x2	T37.8x3	T37.8x4	T37.8x5	T37.8x6
Xigris	T45.511	T45.512	T45.513	T45.514	T45.515	T45.516
Xipamide	T50.2x1	T50.2x2	T50.2x3	T50.2x4	T50.2x5	T50.2x6
Xylene (vapor)	T52.2x1	T52.2x2	T52.2x3	T52.2x4	—	—
Xylocaine (infiltration) (topical)	T41.3x1	T41.3x2	T41.3x3	T41.3x4	T41.3x5	T41.3x6
nerve block (peripheral) (plexus)	T41.3x1	T41.3x2	T41.3x3	T41.3x4	T41.3x5	T41.3x6
spinal	T41.3x1	T41.3x2	T41.3x3	T41.3x4	T41.3x5	T41.3x6
Xylol (vapor)	T52.2x1	T52.2x2	T52.2x3	T52.2x4	—	—
Xylometazoline	T48.5x1	T48.5x2	T48.5x3	T48.5x4	T48.5x5	T48.5x6
Yeast	T45.2x1	T45.2x2	T45.2x3	T45.2x4	T45.2x5	T45.2x6
dried	T45.2x1	T45.2x2	T45.2x3	T45.2x4	T45.2x5	T45.2x6
Yellow						
fever vaccine	T50.B91	T50.B92	T50.B93	T50.B94	T50.B95	T50.B96
jasmine	T62.2x1	T62.2x2	T62.2x3	T62.2x4	—	—
phenolphthalein	T47.2x1	T47.2x2	T47.2x3	T47.2x4	T47.2x5	T47.2x6
Yew	T62.2x1	T62.2x2	T62.2x3	T62.2x4	—	—
Yohimbic acid	T40.991	T40.992	T40.993	T40.994	T40.995	T40.996
Zactane	T39.8x1	T39.8x2	T39.8x3	T39.8x4	T39.8x5	T39.8x6
Zalcitabine	T37.5x1	T37.5x2	T37.5x3	T37.5x4	T37.5x5	T37.5x6
Zaroxolyn	T50.2x1	T50.2x2	T50.2x3	T50.2x4	T50.2x5	T50.2x6
Zephiran (topical)	T49.0x1	T49.0x2	T49.0x3	T49.0x4	T49.0x5	T49.0x6
ophthalmic preparation	T49.5x1	T49.5x2	T49.5x3	T49.5x4	T49.5x5	T49.5x6
Zeranol	T38.7x1	T38.7x2	T38.7x3	T38.7x4	T38.7x5	T38.7x6
Zerone	T51.1x1	T51.1x2	T51.1x3	T51.1x4	—	—
Zidovudine	T37.5x1	T37.5x2	T37.5x3	T37.5x4	T37.5x5	T37.5x6
Zimeldine	T43.221	T43.222	T43.223	T43.224	T43.225	T43.226
Zinc (compounds) (fumes) (vapor) NEC	T56.5x1	T56.5x2	T56.5x3	T56.5x4	—	—
anti-infectives	T49.0x1	T49.0x2	T49.0x3	T49.0x4	T49.0x5	T49.0x6
antivaricose	T46.8x1	T46.8x2	T46.8x3	T46.8x4	T46.8x5	T46.8x6
bacitracin	T49.0x1	T49.0x2	T49.0x3	T49.0x4	T49.0x5	T49.0x6
chloride (mouthwash)	T49.6x1	T49.6x2	T49.6x3	T49.6x4	T49.6x5	T49.6x6
chromate	T56.5x1	T56.5x2	T56.5x3	T56.5x4	—	—
gelatin	T49.3x1	T49.3x2	T49.3x3	T49.3x4	T49.3x5	T49.3x6
oxide	T49.3x1	T49.3x2	T49.3x3	T49.3x4	T49.3x5	T49.3x6
plaster	T49.3x1	T49.3x2	T49.3x3	T49.3x4	T49.3x5	T49.3x6
peroxide	T49.0x1	T49.0x2	T49.0x3	T49.0x4	T49.0x5	T49.0x6
pesticides	T56.5x1	T56.5x2	T56.5x3	T56.5x4	—	—
phosphide	T60.4x1	T60.4x2	T60.4x3	T60.4x4	—	—
pyrithionate	T49.4x1	T49.4x2	T49.4x3	T49.4x4	T49.4x5	T49.4x6

Substance	External Cause (T-Code)					
	Poisoning, Accidental (Unintentional)	Poisoning, Intentional Self-Harm	Poisoning, Assault	Poisoning, Undetermined	Adverse Effect	Underdosing
Zinc NEC *(Continued)*						
stearate	T49.3x1	T49.3x2	T49.3x3	T49.3x4	T49.3x5	T49.3x6
sulfate	T49.5x1	T49.5x2	T49.5x3	T49.5x4	T49.5x5	T49.5x6
ENT agent	T49.6x1	T49.6x2	T49.6x3	T49.6x4	T49.6x5	T49.6x6
ophthalmic solution	T49.5x1	T49.5x2	T49.5x3	T49.5x4	T49.5x5	T49.5x6
topical NEC	T49.0x1	T49.0x2	T49.0x3	T49.0x4	T49.0x5	T49.0x6
undecylenate	T49.0x1	T49.0x2	T49.0x3	T49.0x4	T49.0x5	T49.0x6
Zineb	T60.0x1	T60.0x2	T60.0x3	T60.0x4	—	—
Zinostatin	T45.1x1	T45.1x2	T45.1x3	T45.1x4	T45.1x5	T45.1x6
Zipeprol	T48.3x1	T48.3x2	T48.3x3	T48.3x4	T48.3x5	T48.3x6
Zofenopril	T46.4x1	T46.4x2	T46.4x3	T46.4x4	T46.4x5	T46.4x6
Zolpidem	T42.6x1	T42.6x2	T42.6x3	T42.6x4	T42.6x5	T42.6x6
Zomepirac	T39.391	T39.392	T39.393	T39.394	T39.395	T39.396
Zopiclone	T42.6x1	T42.6x2	T42.6x3	T42.6x4	T42.6x5	T42.6x6
Zorubicin	T45.1x1	T45.1x2	T45.1x3	T45.1x4	T45.1x5	T45.1x6
Zotepine	T43.591	T43.592	T43.593	T43.594	T43.595	T43.596
Zovant	T45.511	T45.512	T45.513	T45.514	T45.515	T45.516
Zoxazolamine	T42.8x1	T42.8x2	T42.8x3	T42.8x4	T42.8x5	T42.8x6
Zuclopenthixol	T43.4x1	T43.4x2	T43.4x3	T43.4x4	T43.4x5	T43.4x6
Zygadenus (venenosus)	T62.2x1	T62.2x2	T62.2x3	T62.2x4	—	—

External Cause Index

ICD-10-CM EXTERNAL CAUSE INDEX DRAFT

A

Abandonment (causing exposure to weather conditions) (with intent to injure or kill) NEC X58

Abuse (adult) (child) (mental) (physical) (sexual) X58

Accident (to) X58

  aircraft (in transit) (powered) - *see also* Accident, transport, aircraft

    due to, caused by cataclysm - *see* Forces of nature, by type

  animal-rider - *see* Accident, transport, animal-rider

  animal-drawn vehicle - *see* Accident, transport, animal-drawn vehicle occupant

  automobile - *see* Accident, transport, car occupant

  bare foot water skiier V94.4

  boat, boating - *see also* Accident, watercraft

    striking swimmer

      powered V94.11

      unpowered V94.12

  bus - *see* Accident, transport, bus occupant

  cable car, not on rails V98.0

    on rails - *see* Accident, transport, streetcar occupant

  car - *see* Accident, transport, car occupant

  caused by, due to

    animal NEC W64

    chain hoist W24.0

    cold (excessive) - *see* Exposure, cold

    corrosive liquid, substance - *see* Table of drugs and chemicals

    cutting or piercing instrument - *see* Contact, with, by type of instrument

    drive belt W24.0

    electric

      current - *see* Exposure, electric current

      motor (*see also* Contact, with, by type of machine) W31.3

        current (of) W86.8

    environmental factor NEC X58

    explosive material - *see* Explosion

    fire, flames - *see* Exposure, fire

    firearm missile - *see* Discharge, firearm by type

    heat (excessive) - *see* Heat

    hot - *see* Contact, with, hot

    ignition - *see* Ignition

    lifting device W24.0

    lightning X33

      causing fire - *see* Exposure, fire

    machine, machinery - *see* Contact, with, by type of machine

    natural factor NEC X58

    pulley (block) W24.0

    radiation - *see* Radiation

    steam X13.1

      inhalation X13.0

      pipe X16

    thunderbolt X33

      causing fire - *see* Exposure, fire

    transmission device W24.1

  coach - *see* Accident, transport, bus occupant

Accident (*Continued*)

  coal car - *see* Accident, transport, industrial vehicle occupant

  diving - *see also* Fall, into, water

    with

      drowning or submersion - *see* Drowning

  forklift - *see* Accident, transport, industrial vehicle occupant

  heavy transport vehicle NOS - *see* Accident, transport, truck occupant

  ice yacht V98.2

  in

    medical, surgical procedure

      as, or due to misadventure - *see* Misadventure

      causing an abnormal reaction or later complication without mention of misadventure (*see also* Complication of or following, by type of procedure) Y84.9

  land yacht V98.1

  late effect of - *see* W00-X58 with q as terminal character

  logging car - *see* Accident, transport, industrial vehicle occupant

  machine, machinery - *see also* Contact, with, by type of machine

    on board watercraft V93.69

      explosion - *see* Explosion, in, watercraft

      fire - *see* Burn, on board watercraft

      powered craft V93.63

        ferry boat V93.61

        fishing boat V93.62

        jetskis V93.63

        liner V93.61

        merchant ship V93.60

        passenger ship V93.61

        sailboat V93.64

  mine tram - *see* Accident, transport, industrial vehicle occupant

  mobility scooter (motorized) - *see* Accident, transport, pedestrian, conveyance, specified type NEC

  motor scooter - *see* Accident, transport, motorcyclist

  motor vehicle NOS (traffic) (*see also* Accident, transport) V89.2

    nontraffic V89.0

    three-wheeled NOS - *see* Accident, transport, three-wheeled motor vehicle occupant

  motorcycle NOS - *see* Accident, transport, motorcyclist

  nonmotor vehicle NOS (nontraffic) (*see also* Accident, transport) V89.1

    traffic NOS V89.3

  nontraffic (victim's mode of transport NOS) V88.9

    collision (between) V88.7

      bus and truck V88.5

      car and:

        bus V88.3

        pickup V88.2

        three-wheeled motor vehicle V88.0

        train V88.6

        truck V88.4

        two-wheeled motor vehicle V88.0

        van V88.2

      specified vehicle NEC and:

        three-wheeled motor vehicle V88.1

        two-wheeled motor vehicle V88.1

Accident (*Continued*)

  nontraffic (*Continued*)

    known mode of transport - *see* Accident, transport, by type of vehicle

    noncollision V88.8

  on board watercraft V93.89

    powered craft V93.83

      ferry boat V93.81

      fishing boat V93.82

      jetskis V93.83

      liner V93.81

      merchant ship V93.80

      passenger ship V93.81

    unpowered craft V93.88

      canoe V93.85

      inflatable V93.86

        in tow

          recreational V94.31

          specified NEC V94.32

      kayak V93.85

      sailboat V93.84

      surf-board V93.88

      water skis V93.87

      windsurfer V93.88

  parachutist V97.29

    entangled in object V97.21

    injured on landing V97.22

  pedal cycle - *see* Accident, transport, pedal cyclist

  pedestrian (on foot)

    with

      another pedestrian W51

        with fall W03

          due to ice or snow W00.0

        on pedestrian conveyance NEC V00.09

      roller skater (in-line) V00.01

      skate boarder V00.02

      transport vehicle - *see* Accident, transport

    on pedestrian conveyance - *see* Accident, transport, pedestrian, conveyance

  pick-up truck or van - *see* Accident, transport, pickup truck occupant

  quarry truck - *see* Accident, transport, industrial vehicle occupant

  railway vehicle (any) (in motion) - *see* Accident, transport, railway vehicle occupant

    due to cataclysm - *see* Forces of nature, by type

  scooter (non-motorized) - *see* Accident, transport, pedestrian, conveyance, scooter

  sequelae of - *see* W00-X58 with q as terminal character

  skateboard - *see* Accident, transport, pedestrian, conveyance, skateboard

  ski(ing) - *see* Accident, transport, pedestrian, conveyance

    lift V98.3

  specified cause NEC X58

  streetcar - *see* Accident, transport, streetcar occupant

  traffic (victim's mode of transport NOS) V87.9

    collision (between) V87.7

      bus and truck V87.5

      car and:

        bus V87.3

Accident *(Continued)*
  traffic *(Continued)*
    collision *(Continued)*
      car and: *(Continued)*
        pickup V87.2
        three-wheeled motor vehicle
          V87.0
        train V87.6
        truck V87.4
        two-wheeled motor vehicle V87.0
        van V87.2
      specified vehicle NEC and:
        three-wheeled motor vehicle V87.1
        two-wheeled motor vehicle V87.1
    known mode of transport - *see* Accident,
      transport, by type of vehicle
    noncollision V87.8
  transport (involving injury to) V99
    18 wheeler - *see* Accident, transport,
      truck occupant
    agricultural vehicle occupant
      (nontraffic) V84.9
      driver V84.5
      hanger-on V84.7
      passenger V84.6
      traffic V84.3
        driver V84.0
        hanger-on V84.2
        passenger V84.1
      while boarding or alighting V84.4
    aircraft
      aircraft NEC Y97.89
        military NEC V97.818
          with civilian aircraft V97.810
          civilian injured by V97.811
      occupant injured (in)
        nonpowered craft accident V96.9
          balloon V96.00
            collision V96.03
            crash V96.01
            explosion V96.05
            fire V96.04
            forced landing V96.02
            specified type NEC V96.09
          glider V96.20
            collision V96.23
            crash V96.21
            explosion V96.25
            fire V96.24
            forced landing V96.22
            specified type NEC V96.29
          hang glider V96.10
            collision V96.13
            crash V96.11
            explosion V96.15
            fire V96.14
            forced landing V96.12
            specified type NEC V96.19
          specified craft NEC V96.8
        powered craft accident V95.9
          fixed wing NEC
            commercial V95.30
              collision V95.33
              crash V95.31
              explosion V95.35
              fire V95.34
              forced landing V95.32
              specified type NEC V95.39
            private V95.20
              collision V95.23
              crash V95.21
              explosion V95.25
              fire V95.24
              forced landing V95.22
              specified type NEC V95.29

Accident *(Continued)*
  transport *(Continued)*
    aircraft *(Continued)*
      occupant injured *(Continued)*
        powered craft accident
          (Continued)
          glider V95.10
            collision V95.13
            crash V95.11
            explosion V95.15
            fire V95.14
            forced landing V95.12
            specified type NEC V95.19
          helicopter V95.00
            collision V95.03
            crash V95.01
            explosion V95.05
            fire V95.04
            forced landing V95.02
            specified type NEC V95.09
          spacecraft V95.40
            collision V95.43
            crash V95.41
            explosion V95.45
            fire V95.44
            forced landing V95.42
            specified type NEC V95.49
          specified craft NEC V95.8
          ultralight V95.10
            collision V95.13
            crash V95.11
            explosion V95.15
            fire V95.14
            forced landing V95.12
            specified type NEC V95.19
        specified accident NEC V97.0
        while boarding or alighting
          V97.1
      person (injured by)
        falling from, in or on aircraft
          V97.0
        machinery on aircraft V97.89
        on ground with aircraft
          involvement V97.39
        rotating propeller V97.32
        struck by object falling from
          aircraft V97.31
        sucked into aircraft jet V97.33
        while boarding or alighting
          aircraft V97.1
    airport (battery-powered) passenger
      vehicle - *see* Accident, transport,
      industrial vehicle occupant
    all-terrain vehicle occupant
      (nontraffic) V86.99
      driver V86.59
      dune buggy - *see* Accident,
        transport, dune buggy
        occupant
      hanger-on V86.79
      passenger V86.69
      snowmobile - *see* Accident,
        transport, snowmobile
        occupant
      traffic V86.39
        driver V86.09
        hanger-on V86.29
        passenger V86.19
      while boarding or alighting V86.49
    ambulance occupant (traffic) V86.31
      driver V86.01
      hanger-on V86.21
      nontraffic V86.91
        driver V86.51

Accident *(Continued)*
  transport *(Continued)*
    ambulance occupant *(Continued)*
      nontraffic *(Continued)*
        hanger-on V86.71
        passenger V86.61
      passenger V86.11
      while boarding or alighting V86.41
    animal-drawn vehicle occupant (in)
      V80.929
      collision (with)
        animal V80.12
          being ridden V80.711
        animal-drawn vehicle V80.721
        bus V80.42
        car V80.42
        fixed or stationary object V80.82
        military vehicle V80.920
        nonmotor vehicle V80.791
        pedal cycle V80.22
        pedestrian V80.12
        pickup V80.42
        railway train or vehicle V80.62
        specified motor vehicle NEC
          V80.52
        streetcar V80.731
        truck V80.42
        two-or three-wheeled motor
          vehicle V80.32
        van V80.42
      noncollision V80.02
      specified circumstance NEC V80.928
    animal-rider V80.919
      collision (with)
        animal V80.11
          being ridden V80.710
        animal-drawn vehicle V80.720
        bus V80.41
        car V80.41
        fixed or stationary object V80.81
        military vehicle V80.910
        nonmotor vehicle V80.790
        pedal cycle V80.21
        pedestrian V80.11
        pickup V80.41
        railway train or vehicle V80.61
        specified motor vehicle NEC
          V80.51
        streetcar V80.730
        truck V80.41
        two- or three-wheeled motor
          vehicle V80.31
        van V80.41
      noncollision V80.018
        specified as horse rider V80.010
      specified circumstance NEC V80.918
    armored car - *see* Accident, transport,
      truck occupant
    battery-powered truck (baggage)
      (mail) - *see* Accident, transport,
      industrial vehicle occupant
    bus occupant V79.9
      collision (with)
        animal (traffic) V70.9
          being ridden (traffic) V76.9
            nontraffic V76.3
              while boarding or alighting
                V76.4
          nontraffic V70.3
            while boarding or alighting
              V70.4
        animal-drawn vehicle (traffic)
          V76.9
          nontraffic V76.3
            while boarding or alighting V76.4

733

Accident *(Continued)*
  transport *(Continued)*
    bus occupant *(Continued)*
      collision *(Continued)*
        bus (traffic) V74.9
          nontraffic V74.3
          while boarding or alighting
            V74.4
        car (traffic) V73.9
          nontraffic V73.3
          while boarding or alighting
            V73.4
        motor vehicle NOS (traffic)
          V79.60
          nontraffic V79.20
          specified type NEC (traffic)
          V79.69
          nontraffic V79.29
        pedal cycle (traffic) V71.9
          nontraffic V71.3
          while boarding or alighting
            V71.4
        pickup truck (traffic) V73.9
          nontraffic V73.3
          while boarding or alighting
            V73.4
        railway vehicle (traffic) V75.9
          nontraffic V75.3
          while boarding or alighting
            V75.4
        specified vehicle NEC (traffic)
          V76.9
          nontraffic V76.3
          while boarding or alighting
            V76.4
        stationary object (traffic) V77.9
          nontraffic V77.3
          while boarding or alighting
            V77.4
        streetcar (traffic) V76.9
          nontraffic V76.3
          while boarding or alighting
            V76.4
        three wheeled motor vehicle
          (traffic) V72.9
          nontraffic V72.3
          while boarding or alighting
            V72.4
        truck (traffic) V74.9
          nontraffic V74.3
          while boarding or alighting
            V74.4
        two wheeled motor vehicle
          (traffic) V72.9
          nontraffic V72.3
          while boarding or alighting
            V72.4
        van (traffic) V73.9
          nontraffic V73.3
          while boarding or alighting V73.4
      driver
        collision (with)
          animal (traffic) V70.5
            being ridden (traffic) V76.5
              nontraffic V76.0
            nontraffic V70.0
          animal-drawn vehicle (traffic)
            V76.5
            nontraffic V76.0
          bus (traffic) V74.5
            nontraffic V74.0
          car (traffic) V73.5
            nontraffic V73.0

Accident *(Continued)*
  transport *(Continued)*
    bus occupant *(Continued)*
      driver *(Continued)*
        collision *(Continued)*
          motor vehicle NOS (traffic)
          V79.40
          nontraffic V79.00
          specified type NEC (traffic)
          V79.49
          nontraffic V79.09
        pedal cycle (traffic) V71.5
          nontraffic V71.0
        pickup truck (traffic) V73.5
          nontraffic V73.0
        railway vehicle (traffic) V75.5
          nontraffic V75.0
        specified vehicle NEC (traffic)
          V76.5
          nontraffic V76.0
        stationary object (traffic) V77.5
          nontraffic V77.0
        streetcar (traffic) V76.5
          nontraffic V76.0
        three wheeled motor vehicle
          (traffic) V72.5
          nontraffic V72.0
        truck (traffic) V74.5
          nontraffic V74.0
        two wheeled motor vehicle
          (traffic) V72.5
          nontraffic V72.0
        van (traffic) V73.5
          nontraffic V73.0
        noncollision accident (traffic)
          V78.5
          nontraffic V78.0
      noncollision accident (traffic) V78.9
        nontraffic V78.3
        while boarding or alighting V78.4
      nontraffic V79.3
      hanger-on
        collision (with)
          animal (traffic) V70.7
            being ridden (traffic) V76.7
              nontraffic V76.2
            nontraffic V70.2
          animal-drawn vehicle (traffic)
            V76.7
            nontraffic V76.2
          bus (traffic) V74.7
            nontraffic V74.2
          car (traffic) V73.7
            nontraffic V73.2
          pedal cycle (traffic) V71.7
            nontraffic V71.2
          pickup truck (traffic) V73.7
            nontraffic V73.2
          railway vehicle (traffic) V75.7
            nontraffic V75.2
          specified vehicle NEC (traffic)
            V76.7
            nontraffic V76.2
          stationary object (traffic) V77.7
            nontraffic V77.2
          streetcar (traffic) V76.7
            nontraffic V76.2
          three wheeled motor vehicle
          (traffic) V72.7
            nontraffic V72.2
          truck (traffic) V74.7
            nontraffic V74.2

Accident *(Continued)*
  transport *(Continued)*
    bus occupant *(Continued)*
      hanger-on *(Continued)*
        collision *(Continued)*
          two wheeled motor vehicle
          (traffic) V72.7
          nontraffic V72.2
          van (traffic) V73.7
          nontraffic V73.2
        noncollision accident (traffic)
          V78.7
          nontraffic V78.2
      passenger
        collision (with)
          animal (traffic) V70.6
            being ridden (traffic) V76.6
              nontraffic V76.1
            nontraffic V70.1
          animal-drawn vehicle (traffic)
            V76.6
            nontraffic V76.1
          bus (traffic) V74.6
            nontraffic V74.1
          car (traffic) V73.6
            nontraffic V73.1
          motor vehicle NOS (traffic)
          V79.50
          nontraffic V79.10
          specified type NEC (traffic)
          V79.59
          nontraffic V79.19
        pedal cycle (traffic) V71.6
          nontraffic V71.1
        pickup truck (traffic) V73.6
          nontraffic V73.1
        railway vehicle (traffic) V75.6
          nontraffic V75.1
        specified vehicle NEC (traffic)
          V76.6
          nontraffic V76.1
        stationary object (traffic) V77.6
          nontraffic V77.1
        streetcar (traffic) V76.6
          nontraffic V76.1
        three wheeled motor vehicle
          (traffic) V72.6
          nontraffic V72.1
        truck (traffic) V74.6
          nontraffic V74.1
        two wheeled motor vehicle
          (traffic) V72.6
          nontraffic V72.1
        van (traffic) V73.6
          nontraffic V73.1
        noncollision accident (traffic)
          V78.6
          nontraffic V78.1
      specified type NEC V79.88
      military vehicle V79.81
    cable car, not on rails V98.0
    on rails - *see* Accident, transport,
      streetcar occupant
    car occupant V49.9
      ambulance occupant - *see* Accident,
        transport, ambulance occupant
      collision (with)
        animal (traffic) V40.9
          being ridden (traffic) V46.9
            nontraffic V46.3
            while boarding or alighting
              V46.4

Accident *(Continued)*
 transport *(Continued)*
  car occupant *(Continued)*
   collision *(Continued)*
    animal *(Continued)*
     nontraffic V40.3
     while boarding or alighting
      V40.4
    animal-drawn vehicle (traffic)
     V46.9
     nontraffic V46.3
     while boarding or alighting
      V46.4
    bus (traffic) V44.9
     nontraffic V44.3
     while boarding or alighting
      V44.4
    car (traffic) V43.92
     nontraffic V43.32
     while boarding or alighting
      V43.42
    motor vehicle NOS (traffic)
     V49.60
     nontraffic V49.20
     specified type NEC (traffic)
      V49.69
      nontraffic V49.29
    pedal cycle (traffic) V41.9
     nontraffic V41.3
     while boarding or alighting
      V41.4
    pickup truck (traffic) V43.93
     nontraffic V43.33
     while boarding or alighting
      V43.43
    railway vehicle (traffic) V45.9
     nontraffic V45.3
     while boarding or alighting
      V45.4
    specified vehicle NEC (traffic)
     V46.9
     nontraffic V46.3
     while boarding or alighting
      V46.4
    sport utility vehicle (traffic)
     V43.91
     nontraffic V43.31
     while boarding or alighting
      V43.41
    stationary object (traffic) V47.92
     nontraffic V47.32
     while boarding or alighting
      V47.4
    streetcar (traffic) V46.9
     nontraffic V46.3
     while boarding or alighting
      V46.4
    three wheeled motor vehicle
     (traffic) V42.9
     nontraffic V42.3
     while boarding or alighting
      V42.4
    truck (traffic) V44.9
     nontraffic V44.3
     while boarding or alighting
      V44.4
    two wheeled motor vehicle
     (traffic) V42.9
     nontraffic V42.3
     while boarding or alighting
      V42.4
    van (traffic) V43.94
     nontraffic V43.34
     while boarding or alighting
      V43.44

Accident *(Continued)*
 transport *(Continued)*
  car occupant *(Continued)*
   driver
    collision (with)
     animal (traffic) V40.5
      being ridden (traffic) V46.5
       nontraffic V46.0
      nontraffic V40.0
     animal-drawn vehicle (traffic)
      V46.5
      nontraffic V46.0
     bus (traffic) V44.5
      nontraffic V44.0
     car (traffic) V43.52
      nontraffic V43.02
     motor vehicle NOS (traffic)
      V49.40
      nontraffic V49.00
      specified type NEC (traffic)
       V49.49
       nontraffic V49.09
     pedal cycle (traffic) V41.5
      nontraffic V41.0
     pickup truck (traffic) V43.53
      nontraffic V43.03
     railway vehicle (traffic) V45.5
      nontraffic V45.0
     specified vehicle NEC (traffic)
      V46.5
      nontraffic V46.0
     sport utility vehicle (traffic)
      V43.51
      nontraffic V43.01
     stationary object (traffic)
      V47.52
      nontraffic V47.02
     streetcar (traffic) V46.5
      nontraffic V46.0
     three wheeled motor vehicle
      (traffic) V42.5
      nontraffic V42.0
     truck (traffic) V44.5
      nontraffic V44.0
     two wheeled motor vehicle
      (traffic) V42.5
      nontraffic V42.0
     van (traffic) V43.54
      nontraffic V43.04
    noncollision accident (traffic)
     V48.5
     nontraffic V48.0
    noncollision accident (traffic) V48.9
     nontraffic V48.3
     while boarding or alighting V48.4
   nontraffic V49.3
   hanger-on
    collision (with)
     animal (traffic) V40.7
      being ridden (traffic) V46.7
       nontraffic V46.2
      nontraffic V40.2
     animal-drawn vehicle (traffic)
      V46.7
      nontraffic V46.2
     bus (traffic) V44.7
      nontraffic V44.2
     car (traffic) V43.72
      nontraffic V43.22
     pedal cycle (traffic) V41.7
      nontraffic V41.2
     pickup truck (traffic) V43.73
      nontraffic V43.23
     railway vehicle (traffic) V45.7
      nontraffic V45.2

Accident *(Continued)*
 transport *(Continued)*
  car occupant *(Continued)*
   hanger-on *(Continued)*
    collision *(Continued)*
     specified vehicle NEC (traffic)
      V46.7
      nontraffic V46.2
     sport utility vehicle (traffic)
      V43.71
      nontraffic V43.21
     stationary object (traffic) V47.7
      nontraffic V47.2
     streetcar (traffic) V46.7
      nontraffic V46.2
     three wheeled motor vehicle
      (traffic) V42.7
      nontraffic V42.2
     truck (traffic) V44.7
      nontraffic V44.2
     two wheeled motor vehicle
      (traffic) V42.7
      nontraffic V42.2
     van (traffic) V43.74
      nontraffic V43.24
    noncollision accident (traffic)
     V48.7
     nontraffic V48.2
   passenger
    collision (with)
     animal (traffic) V40.6
      being ridden (traffic) V46.6
       nontraffic V46.1
      nontraffic V40.1
     animal-drawn vehicle (traffic)
      V46.6
      nontraffic V46.1
     bus (traffic) V44.6
      nontraffic V44.1
     car (traffic) V43.62
      nontraffic V43.12
     motor vehicle NOS (traffic)
      V49.50
      nontraffic V49.10
      specified type NEC (traffic)
       V49.59
       nontraffic V49.19
     pedal cycle (traffic) V41.6
      nontraffic V41.1
     pickup truck (traffic) V43.63
      nontraffic V43.13
     railway vehicle (traffic) V45.6
      nontraffic V45.1
     specified vehicle NEC (traffic)
      V46.6
      nontraffic V46.1
     sport utility vehicle (traffic)
      V43.61
      nontraffic V43.11
     stationary object (traffic) V47.62
      nontraffic V47.12
     streetcar (traffic) V46.6
      nontraffic V46.1
     three wheeled motor vehicle
      (traffic) V42.6
      nontraffic V42.1
     truck (traffic) V44.6
      nontraffic V44.1
     two wheeled motor vehicle
      (traffic) V42.6
      nontraffic V42.1
     van (traffic) V43.64
      nontraffic V43.14

Accident *(Continued)*
  transport *(Continued)*
    car occupant *(Continued)*
      passenger *(Continued)*
        noncollision accident (traffic)
          V48.6
          nontraffic V48.1
        specified type NEC V49.88
          military vehicle V49.81
      coal car - *see* Accident, transport,
        industrial vehicle occupant
      construction vehicle occupant
        (nontraffic) V85.9
        driver V85.5
        hanger-on V85.7
        passenger V85.6
        traffic V85.3
          driver V85.0
          hanger-on V85.2
          passenger V85.1
        while boarding or alighting V85.4
      dirt bike rider - *see* Accident,
        transport, all-terrain vehicle
        occupant
      due to cataclysm - *see* Forces of
        nature, by type
      dune buggy occupant (nontraffic)
        V86.93
        driver V86.53
        hanger-on V86.73
        passenger V86.63
        traffic V86.33
          driver V86.03
          hanger-on V86.23
          passenger V86.13
        while boarding or alighting
          V86.43
      forklift - *see* Accident, transport,
        industrial vehicle occupant
      go cart - *see* Accident, transport,
        all-terrain vehicle occupant
      golf cart - *see* Accident, transport,
        all-terrain vehicle occupant
      heavy transport vehicle occupant
        - *see* Accident, transport, truck
        occupant
      ice yacht V98.2
      industrial vehicle occupant
        (nontraffic) V83.9
        driver V83.5
        hanger-on V83.7
        passenger V83.6
        traffic V83.3
          driver V83.0
          hanger-on V83.2
          passenger V83.1
        while boarding or alighting V83.4
      interurban electric car - *see* Accident,
        transport, streetcar
      land yacht V98.1
      logging car - *see* Accident, transport,
        industrial vehicle occupant
      military vehicle occupant (traffic)
        V86.34
        driver V86.04
        hanger-on V86.24
        nontraffic V86.94
          driver V86.54
          hanger-on V86.74
          passenger V86.64
        passenger V86.14
        while boarding or alighting
          V86.44

Accident *(Continued)*
  transport *(Continued)*
    mine tram - *see* Accident, transport,
      industrial vehicle occupant
    motorcoach - *see* Accident, transport,
      bus occupant
    motorcyclist V29.9
      collision (with)
        animal (traffic) V20.9
          being ridden (traffic) V26.9
            nontraffic V26.2
            while boarding or alighting
              V26.3
          nontraffic V20.2
          while boarding or alighting
            V20.3
        animal-drawn vehicle (traffic)
          V26.9
          nontraffic V26.2
          while boarding or alighting
            V26.3
        bus (traffic) V24.9
          nontraffic V24.2
          while boarding or alighting
            V24.3
        car (traffic) V23.9
          nontraffic V23.2
          while boarding or alighting
            V23.3
        motor vehicle NOS (traffic)
          V29.60
          nontraffic V29.20
          specified type NEC (traffic)
            V29.69
            nontraffic V29.29
        pedal cycle (traffic) V21.9
          nontraffic V21.2
          while boarding or alighting
            V21.3
        pickup truck (traffic) V23.9
          nontraffic V23.2
          while boarding or alighting
            V23.3
        railway vehicle (traffic) V25.9
          nontraffic V25.2
          while boarding or alighting
            V25.3
        specified vehicle NEC (traffic)
          V26.9
          nontraffic V26.2
          while boarding or alighting
            V26.3
        stationary object (traffic) V27.9
          nontraffic V27.2
          while boarding or alighting
            V27.3
        streetcar (traffic) V26.9
          nontraffic V26.2
          while boarding or alighting
            V26.3
        three wheeled motor vehicle
          (traffic) V22.9
          nontraffic V22.2
          while boarding or alighting
            V22.3
        truck (traffic) V24.9
          nontraffic V24.2
          while boarding or alighting V24.3
        two wheeled motor vehicle
          (traffic) V22.9
          nontraffic V22.2
          while boarding or alighting
            V22.3

Accident *(Continued)*
  transport *(Continued)*
    motorcyclist *(Continued)*
      collision *(Continued)*
        van (traffic) V23.9
          nontraffic V23.2
          while boarding or alighting V23.3
      driver
        collision (with)
          animal (traffic) V20.4
            being ridden (traffic) V26.4
              nontraffic V26.0
            nontraffic V20.0
          animal-drawn vehicle (traffic)
            V26.4
            nontraffic V26.0
          bus (traffic) V24.4
            nontraffic V24.0
          car (traffic) V23.4
            nontraffic V23.0
          motor vehicle NOS (traffic)
            V29.40
            nontraffic V29.00
            specified type NEC (traffic)
              V29.49
              nontraffic V29.09
          pedal cycle (traffic) V21.4
            nontraffic V21.0
          pickup truck (traffic) V23.4
            nontraffic V23.0
          railway vehicle (traffic) V25.4
            nontraffic V25.0
          specified vehicle NEC (traffic)
            V26.4
            nontraffic V26.0
          stationary object (traffic) V27.4
            nontraffic V27.0
          streetcar (traffic) V26.4
            nontraffic V26.0
          three wheeled motor vehicle
            (traffic) V22.4
            nontraffic V22.0
          truck (traffic) V24.4
            nontraffic V24.0
          two wheeled motor vehicle
            (traffic) V22.4
            nontraffic V22.0
          van (traffic) V23.4
            nontraffic V23.0
        noncollision accident (traffic)
          V28.4
          nontraffic V28.0
      noncollision accident (traffic) V28.9
        nontraffic V28.2
        while boarding or alighting V28.3
      nontraffic V29.3
      passenger
        collision (with)
          animal (traffic) V20.5
            being ridden (traffic) V26.5
              nontraffic V26.1
            nontraffic V20.1
          animal-drawn vehicle (traffic)
            V26.5
            nontraffic V26.1
          bus (traffic) V24.5
            nontraffic V24.1
          car (traffic) V23.5
            nontraffic V23.1
          motor vehicle NOS (traffic)
            V29.50
            nontraffic V29.10

Accident *(Continued)*
  transport *(Continued)*
    motorcyclist *(Continued)*
      passenger *(Continued)*
        collision *(Continued)*
          motor vehicle NOS *(Continued)*
            specified type NEC (traffic) V29.59
              nontraffic V29.19
            pedal cycle (traffic) V21.5
              nontraffic V21.1
            pickup truck (traffic) V23.5
              nontraffic V23.1
            railway vehicle (traffic) V25.5
              nontraffic V25.1
            specified vehicle NEC (traffic) V26.5
              nontraffic V26.1
            stationary object (traffic) V27.5
              nontraffic V27.1
            streetcar (traffic) V26.5
              nontraffic V26.1
            three wheeled motor vehicle (traffic) V22.5
              nontraffic V22.1
            truck (traffic) V24.5
              nontraffic V24.1
            two wheeled motor vehicle (traffic) V22.5
              nontraffic V22.1
            van (traffic) V23.5
              nontraffic V23.1
          noncollision accident (traffic) V28.5
            nontraffic V28.1
        specified type NEC V29.88
        military vehicle V29.81
      motor vehicle NEC occupant (traffic) V86.39
        driver V86.09
        hanger-on V86.29
        nontraffic V86.99
          driver V86.59
          hanger-on V86.79
          passenger V86.69
        passenger V86.19
        while boarding or alighting V86.49
    occupant (of)
      aircraft (powered) V95.9
        fixed wing
          commercial - *see* Accident, transport, aircraft, occupant, powered, fixed wing, commercial
          private - *see* Accident, transport, aircraft, occupant, powered, fixed wing, private
        nonpowered V96.9
        specified NEC V95.8
      airport battery-powered vehicle - *see* Accident, transport, industrial vehicle occupant
      all-terrain vehicle (ATV) - *see* Accident, transport, all-terrain vehicle occupant
      animal-drawn vehicle - *see* Accident, transport, animal-drawn vehicle occupant
      automobile - *see* Accident, transport, car occupant
      balloon V96.00

Accident *(Continued)*
  transport *(Continued)*
    occupant *(Continued)*
      battery-powered vehicle - *see* Accident, transport, industrial vehicle occupant
      bicycle - *see* Accident, transport, pedal cyclist
        motorized - *see* Accident, transport, motorcycle rider
      boat NEC - *see* Accident, watercraft
      bulldozer - *see* Accident, transport, construction vehicle occupant
      bus - *see* Accident, transport, bus occupant
      cable car (on rails) - *see also* Accident, transport, streetcar occupant
        not on rails V98.0
      car - *see also* Accident, transport, car occupant
        cable (on rails) - *see also* Accident, transport, streetcar occupant
          not on rails V98.0
      coach - *see* Accident, transport, bus occupant
      coal-car - *see* Accident, transport, industrial vehicle occupant
      digger - *see* Accident, transport, construction vehicle occupant
      dump truck - *see* Accident, transport, construction vehicle occupant
      earth-leveler - *see* Accident, transport, construction vehicle occupant
      farm machinery (self-propelled) - *see* Accident, transport, agricultural vehicle occupant
      forklift - *see* Accident, transport, industrial vehicle occupant
      glider (unpowered) V96.20
        hang V96.10
        powered (microlight) (ultralight) - *see* Accident, transport, aircraft, occupant, powered, glider
      glider (unpowered) NEC V96.20
      hang-glider V96.10
      harvester - *see* Accident, transport, agricultural vehicle occupant
      heavy (transport) vehicle - *see* Accident, transport, truck occupant
      helicopter - *see* Accident, transport, aircraft, occupant, helicopter
      ice-yacht V98.2
      kite (carrying person) V96.8
      land-yacht V98.1
      logging car - *see* Accident, transport, industrial vehicle occupant
      mechanical shovel - *see* Accident, transport, construction vehicle occupant
      microlight - *see* Accident, transport, aircraft, occupant, powered, glider
      minibus - *see* Accident, transport, car occupant
      minivan - *see* Accident, transport, car occupant

Accident *(Continued)*
  transport *(Continued)*
    occupant *(Continued)*
      moped - *see* Accident, transport, motorcycle
      motor scooter - *see* Accident, transport, motorcycle
      motorcycle (with sidecar) - *see* Accident, transport, motorcycle
      pedal cycle - *see also* Accident, transport, pedal cyclist
      pick-up (truck) - *see* Accident, transport, pickup truck occupant
      railway (train) (vehicle) (subterranean) (elevated) - *see* Accident, transport, railway vehicle occupant
      rickshaw - *see* Accident, transport, pedal cycle
        motorized - *see* Accident, transport, three-wheeled motor vehicle)
        pedal driven - *see* Accident, transport, pedal cyclist
      road-roller - *see* Accident, transport, construction vehicle occupant
      ship NOS V94.9
      ski-lift (chair) (gondola) V98.3
      snowmobile - *see* Accident, transport, snowmobile occupant
      spacecraft, spaceship - *see* Accident, transport, aircraft, occupant, spacecraft
      sport utility vehicle - *see* Accident, transport, car occupant
      streetcar (interurban) (operating on public street or highway) - *see* Accident, transport, streetcar occupant
      SUV - *see* Accident, transport, car occupant
      téléférique V98.0
      three-wheeled vehicle (motorized) - *see also* Accident, transport, three-wheeled motor vehicle occupant
        nonmotorized - *see* Accident, transport, pedal cycle
      tractor (farm) (and trailer) - *see* Accident, transport, agricultural vehicle occupant
      train - *see* Accident, transport, railway vehicle occupant
      tram - *see* Accident, transport, streetcar occupant
        in mine or quarry - *see* Accident, transport, industrial vehicle occupant
      tricycle - *see* Accident, transport, pedal cycle
        motorized - *see* Accident, transport, three-wheeled motor vehicle
      trolley - *see* Accident, transport, streetcar occupant
        in mine or quarry - *see* Accident, transport, industrial vehicle occupant
      tub, in mine or quarry - *see* Accident, transport, industrial vehicle occupant

Accident *(Continued)*
  transport *(Continued)*
    occupant *(Continued)*
      ultralight - *see* Accident, transport,
        aircraft, occupant, powered,
        glider
      van - *see* Accident, transport, van
        occupant
      vehicle NEC V89.9
        heavy transport - *see* Accident,
          transport, truck occupant
        motor (traffic) NEC V89.2
        nontraffic NEC V89.0
      watercraft NOS V94.9
        causing drowning - *see*
          Drowning, resulting from
          accident to boat
    parachutist V97.29
      after accident to aircraft *see* Accident,
        transport, aircraft
      entangled in object V97.21
      injured on landing V97.22
    pedal cyclist V19.9
      collision (with)
        animal (traffic) V10.9
          being ridden (traffic) V16.9
            nontraffic V16.2
              while boarding or alighting
                V16.3
          nontraffic V10.2
            while boarding or alighting
              V10.3
        animal-drawn vehicle (traffic) V16.9
          nontraffic V16.2
            while boarding or alighting
              V16.3
        bus (traffic) V14.9
          nontraffic V14.2
            while boarding or alighting
              V14.3
        car (traffic) V13.9
          nontraffic V13.2
            while boarding or alighting
              V13.3
        motor vehicle NOS (traffic)
          V19.60
          nontraffic V19.20
          specified type NEC (traffic)
            V19.69
            nontraffic V19.29
        pedal cycle (traffic) V11.9
          nontraffic V11.2
            while boarding or alighting
              V11.3
        pickup truck (traffic) V13.9
          nontraffic V13.2
            while boarding or alighting
              V13.3
        railway vehicle (traffic) V15.9
          nontraffic V15.2
            while boarding or alighting
              V15.3
        specified vehicle NEC (traffic)
          V16.9
          nontraffic V16.2
            while boarding or alighting
              V16.3
        stationary object (traffic) V17.9
          nontraffic V17.2
            while boarding or alighting
              V17.3
        streetcar (traffic) V16.9
          nontraffic V16.2
            while boarding or alighting
              V16.3

Accident *(Continued)*
  transport *(Continued)*
    pedal cyclist *(Continued)*
      collision *(Continued)*
        three wheeled motor vehicle
          (traffic) V12.9
          nontraffic V12.2
          while boarding or alighting V12.3
        truck (traffic) V14.9
          nontraffic V14.2
            while boarding or alighting
              V14.3
        two wheeled motor vehicle
          (traffic) V12.9
          nontraffic V12.2
            while boarding or alighting
              V12.3
        van (traffic) V13.9
          nontraffic V13.2
            while boarding or alighting
              V13.3
      driver
        collision (with)
          animal (traffic) V10.4
            being ridden (traffic) V16.4
              nontraffic V16.0
            nontraffic V10.0
          animal-drawn vehicle (traffic)
            V16.4
            nontraffic V16.0
          bus (traffic) V14.4
            nontraffic V14.0
          car (traffic) V13.4
            nontraffic V13.0
          motor vehicle NOS (traffic)
            V19.40
            nontraffic V19.00
            specified type NEC (traffic)
              V19.49
              nontraffic V19.09
          pedal cycle (traffic) V11.4
            nontraffic V11.0
          pickup truck (traffic) V13.4
            nontraffic V13.0
          railway vehicle (traffic) V15.4
            nontraffic V15.0
          specified vehicle NEC (traffic)
            V16.4
            nontraffic V16.0
          stationary object (traffic) V17.4
            nontraffic V17.0
          streetcar (traffic) V16.4
            nontraffic V16.0
          three wheeled motor vehicle
            (traffic) V12.4
            nontraffic V12.0
          truck (traffic) V14.4
            nontraffic V14.0
          two wheeled motor vehicle
            (traffic) V12.4
            nontraffic V12.0
          van (traffic) V13.4
            nontraffic V13.0
          noncollision accident (traffic)
            V18.4
            nontraffic V18.0
        noncollision accident (traffic) V18.9
          nontraffic V18.2
            while boarding or alighting
              V18.3
        nontraffic V19.3
      passenger
        collision (with)
          animal (traffic) V10.5

Accident *(Continued)*
  transport *(Continued)*
    pedal cyclist *(Continued)*
      passenger *(Continued)*
        collision *(Continued)*
          animal (traffic) *(Continued)*
            being ridden (traffic)
              V16.5
              nontraffic V16.1
            nontraffic V10.1
          animal-drawn vehicle (traffic)
            V16.5
            nontraffic V16.1
          bus (traffic) V14.5
            nontraffic V14.1
          car (traffic) V13.5
            nontraffic V13.1
          motor vehicle NOS (traffic)
            V19.50
            nontraffic V19.10
            specified type NEC (traffic)
              V19.59
              nontraffic V19.19
          pedal cycle (traffic) V11.5
            nontraffic V11.1
          pickup truck (traffic) V13.5
            nontraffic V13.1
          railway vehicle (traffic) V15.5
            nontraffic V15.1
          specified vehicle NEC (traffic)
            V16.5
            nontraffic V16.1
          stationary object (traffic)
            V17.5
            nontraffic V17.1
          streetcar (traffic) V16.5
            nontraffic V16.1
          three wheeled motor vehicle
            (traffic) V12.5
            nontraffic V12.1
          truck (traffic) V14.5
            nontraffic V14.1
          two wheeled motor vehicle
            (traffic) V12.5
            nontraffic V12.1
          van (traffic) V13.5
            nontraffic V13.1
        noncollision accident (traffic)
          V18.5
          nontraffic V18.1
      specified type NEC V19.88
        military vehicle V19.81
    pedestrian
      conveyance occupant V09.9
        babystroller V00.828
        collision (with) V09.9
          animal being ridden or animal
            drawn vehicle V06.99
            nontraffic V06.09
            traffic V06.19
          bus or heavy transport
            V04.99
            nontraffic V04.09
            traffic V04.19
          car V03.99
            nontraffic V03.09
            traffic V03.19
          pedal cycle V01.99
            nontraffic V01.09
            traffic V01.19
          pick-up truck or van V03.99
            nontraffic V03.09
            traffic V03.19

Accident *(Continued)*
 transport *(Continued)*
  pedestrian *(Continued)*
   conveyance occupant *(Continued)*
    babystroller *(Continued)*
     collision *(Continued)*
      railway (train) (vehicle)
       V05.99
       nontraffic V05.09
       traffic V05.19
      streetcar V06.99
       nontraffic V06.09
       traffic V06.19
      stationary object V00.822
      two- or three-wheeled motor
       vehicle V02.99
       nontraffic V02.09
       traffic V02.19
      vehicle V09.9
       animal-drawn V06.99
        nontraffic V06.09
        traffic V06.19
       motor
        nontraffic V09.00
        traffic V09.20
     fall V00.821
     nontraffic V09.1
      involving motor vehicle
       NEC V09.00
     traffic V09.3
      involving motor vehicle
       NEC V09.20
    flat-bottomed NEC V00.388
     collision (with) V09.9
      animal being ridden or
       animal drawn vehicle
       V06.99
       nontraffic V06.09
       traffic V06.19
      bus or heavy transport
       V04.99
       nontraffic V04.09
       traffic V04.19
      car V03.99
       nontraffic V03.09
       traffic V03.19
      pedal cycle V01.99
       nontraffic V01.09
       traffic V01.19
      pick-up truck or van V03.99
       nontraffic V03.09
       traffic V03.19
      railway (train) (vehicle)
       V05.99
       nontraffic V05.09
       traffic V05.19
      stationary object V00.382
      streetcar V06.99
       nontraffic V06.09
       traffic V06.19
      two-or three-wheeled motor
       vehicle V02.99
       nontraffic V02.09
       traffic V02.19
      vehicle V09.9
       animal-drawn V06.99
        nontraffic V06.09
        traffic V06.19
       motor
        nontraffic V09.00
        traffic V09.20
     fall V00.381
     nontraffic V09.1
      involving motor vehicle
       NEC V09.00

Accident *(Continued)*
 transport *(Continued)*
  pedestrian *(Continued)*
   conveyance occupant *(Continued)*
    flat-bottomed NEC *(Continued)*
     snow
      board - *see* Accident,
       transport, pedestrian,
       conveyance, snow board
      ski - *see* Accident, transport,
       pedestrian, conveyance,
       skis (snow)
     traffic V09.3
      involving motor vehicle
       NEC V09.20
    gliding type NEC V00.288
     collision (with) V09.9
      animal being ridden or animal
       drawn vehicle V06.99
       nontraffic V06.09
       traffic V06.19
      bus or heavy transport V04.99
       nontraffic V04.09
       traffic V04.19
      car V03.99
       nontraffic V03.09
       traffic V03.19
      pedal cycle V01.99
       nontraffic V01.09
       traffic V01.19
      pick-up truck or van V03.99
       nontraffic V03.09
       traffic V03.19
      railway (train) (vehicle)
       V05.99
       nontraffic V05.09
       traffic V05.19
      stationary object V00.282
      streetcar V06.99
       nontraffic V06.09
       traffic V06.19
      two- or three-wheeled motor
       vehicle V02.99
       nontraffic V02.09
       traffic V02.19
      vehicle V09.9
       animal-drawn V06.99
        nontraffic V06.09
        traffic V06.19
       motor
        nontraffic V09.00
        traffic V09.20
     fall V00.281
     heelies - *see* Accident, transport,
      pedestrian, conveyance,
      heelies
     ice skate - *see* Accident,
      transport, pedestrian,
      conveyance, ice skate
     nontraffic V09.1
      involving motor vehicle
       NEC V09.00
     sled - *see* Accident, transport,
      pedestrian, conveyance,
      sled
     traffic V09.3
      involving motor vehicle
       NEC V09.20
     wheelies - *see* Accident,
      transport, pedestrian,
      conveyance, heelies
    heelies V00.158
     colliding with stationary object
      V00.152
     fall V00.151

Accident *(Continued)*
 transport *(Continued)*
  pedestrian *(Continued)*
   conveyance occupant *(Continued)*
    ice skates V00.218
     collision (with) V09.9
      animal being ridden or
       animal drawn vehicle
       V06.99
       nontraffic V06.09
       traffic V06.19
      bus or heavy transport
       V04.99
       nontraffic V04.09
       traffic V04.19
      car V03.99
       nontraffic V03.09
       traffic V03.19
      pedal cycle V01.99
       nontraffic V01.09
       traffic V01.19
      pick-up truck or van
       V03.99
       nontraffic V03.09
       traffic V03.19
      railway (train) (vehicle)
       V05.99
       nontraffic V05.09
       traffic V05.19
      streetcar V06.99
       nontraffic V06.09
       traffic V06.19
      stationary object V00.212
      two- or three-wheeled motor
       vehicle V02.99
       nontraffic V02.09
       traffic V02.19
      vehicle V09.9
       animal-drawn V06.99
        nontraffic V06.09
        traffic V06.19
       motor
        nontraffic V09.00
        traffic V09.20
     fall V00.211
     nontraffic V09.1
      involving motor vehicle
       NEC V09.00
     traffic V09.3
      involving motor vehicle
       NEC V09.20
    nontraffic V09.1
     involving motor vehicle
      V09.00
      military V09.01
      specified type NEC
       V09.09
    roller skates (non in-line)
     V00.128
     collision (with) V09.9
      animal being ridden or
       animal drawn vehicle
       V06.91
       nontraffic V06.01
       traffic V06.11
      bus or heavy transport
       V04.91
       nontraffic V04.01
       traffic V04.11
      car V03.91
       nontraffic V03.01
       traffic V03.11
      pedal cycle V01.91
       nontraffic V01.01
       traffic V01.11

Accident *(Continued)*
  transport *(Continued)*
    pedestrian *(Continued)*
      conveyance occupant *(Continued)*
        roller skates *(Continued)*
          collision *(Continued)*
            pick-up truck or van V03.91
              nontraffic V03.01
              traffic V03.11
            railway (train) (vehicle)
                V05.91
              nontraffic V05.01
              traffic V05.11
            streetcar V06.91
              nontraffic V06.01
              traffic V06.11
            stationary object V00.122
            two- or three-wheeled motor
                vehicle V02.91
              nontraffic V02.01
              traffic V02.11
            vehicle V09.9
              animal-drawn V06.91
                nontraffic V06.01
                traffic V06.11
              motor
                nontraffic V09.00
                traffic V09.20
          fall V00.121
          in-line V00.118
            collision - *see* also Accident,
                transport, pedestrian,
                conveyance occupant,
                roller skates, collision
                with stationary object
                V00.112
            fall V00.111
            nontraffic V09.1
              involving motor vehicle
                  NEC V09.00
            traffic V09.3
              involving motor vehicle NEC
                  V09.20
        rolling type NEC V00.188
          collision (with) V09.9
            animal being ridden or
                animal drawn vehicle
                V06.99
              nontraffic V06.09
              traffic V06.19
            bus or heavy transport
                V04.99
              nontraffic V04.09
              traffic V04.19
            car V03.99
              nontraffic V03.09
              traffic V03.19
            pedal cycle V01.99
              nontraffic V01.09
              traffic V01.19
            pick-up truck or van V03.99
              nontraffic V03.09
              traffic V03.19
            railway (train) (vehicle)
                V05.99
              nontraffic V05.09
              traffic V05.19
            stationary object V00.182
            streetcar V06.99
              nontraffic V06.09
              traffic V06.19
            two- or three-wheeled motor
                vehicle V02.99
              nontraffic V02.09
              traffic V02.19

Accident *(Continued)*
  transport *(Continued)*
    pedestrian *(Continued)*
      conveyance occupant *(Continued)*
        rolling type NEC *(Continued)*
          collision *(Continued)*
            vehicle V09.9
              animal-drawn V06.99
                nontraffic V06.09
                traffic V06.19
              motor
                nontraffic V09.00
                traffic V09.20
          fall V00.181
        in-line roller skate - *see*
            Accident, transport,
            pedestrian, conveyance,
            roller skate, in-line
          nontraffic V09.1
            involving motor vehicle
                NEC V09.00
        roller skate - *see* Accident,
            transport, pedestrian,
            conveyance, roller skate
        scooter (non-motorized)
            - *see* Accident, transport,
            pedestrian, conveyance,
            scooter
        skateboard - *see* Accident,
            transport, pedestrian,
            conveyance, skateboard
          traffic V09.3
            involving motor vehicle
                NEC V09.20
        scooter (non-motorized) V00.148
          collision (with) V09.9
            animal being ridden or
                animal drawn vehicle
                V06.99
              nontraffic V06.09
              traffic V06.19
            bus or heavy transport
                V04.99
              nontraffic V04.09
              traffic V04.19
            car V03.99
              nontraffic V03.09
              traffic V03.19
            pedal cycle V01.99
              nontraffic V01.09
              traffic V01.19
            pick-up truck or van
                V03.99
              nontraffic V03.09
              traffic V03.19
            railway (train) (vehicle)
                V05.99
              nontraffic V05.09
              traffic V05.19
            streetcar V06.99
              nontraffic V06.09
              traffic V06.19
            stationary object V00.142
            two- or three-wheeled motor
                vehicle V02.99
              nontraffic V02.09
              traffic V02.19
            vehicle V09.9
              animal-drawn V06.99
                nontraffic V06.09
                traffic V06.19
              motor
                nontraffic V09.00
                traffic V09.20
          fall V00.141

Accident *(Continued)*
  transport *(Continued)*
    pedestrian *(Continued)*
      conveyance occupant *(Continued)*
        scooter *(Continued)*
          nontraffic V09.1
            involving motor vehicle
                NEC V09.00
          traffic V09.3
            involving motor vehicle
                NEC V09.20
        skate board V00.138
          collision (with) V09.9
            animal being ridden or
                animal drawn vehicle
                V06.92
              nontraffic V06.02
              traffic V06.12
            bus or heavy transport
                V04.92
              nontraffic V04.02
              traffic V04.12
            car V03.92
              nontraffic V03.02
              traffic V03.12
            pedal cycle V01.92
              nontraffic V01.02
              traffic V01.12
            pick-up truck or van
                V03.92
              nontraffic V03.02
              traffic V03.12
            railway (train) (vehicle)
                V05.92
              nontraffic V05.02
              traffic V05.12
            streetcar V06.92
              nontraffic V06.02
              traffic V06.12
            stationary object V00.132
            two- or three-wheeled motor
                vehicle V02.92
              nontraffic V02.02
              traffic V02.12
            vehicle V09.9
              animal-drawn V06.92
                nontraffic V06.02
                traffic V06.12
              motor
                nontraffic V09.00
                traffic V09.20
          fall V00.131
          nontraffic V09.1
            involving motor vehicle
                NEC V09.00
          traffic V09.3
            involving motor vehicle
                NEC V09.20
        sled V00.228
          collision (with) V09.9
            animal being ridden or
                animal drawn vehicle
                V06.99
              nontraffic V06.09
              traffic V06.19
            bus or heavy transport
                V04.99
              nontraffic V04.09
              traffic V04.19
            car V03.99
              nontraffic V03.09
              traffic V03.19
            pedal cycle V01.99
              nontraffic V01.09
              traffic V01.19

Accident *(Continued)*
  transport *(Continued)*
    pedestrian *(Continued)*
      conveyance occupant *(Continued)*
        sled *(Continued)*
          collision *(Continued)*
            pick-up truck or van V03.99
              nontraffic V03.09
              traffic V03.19
            railway (train) (vehicle)
              V05.99
              nontraffic V05.09
              traffic V05.19
            streetcar V06.99
              nontraffic V06.09
              traffic V06.19
            stationary object V00.222
            two- or three-wheeled motor
              vehicle V02.99
              nontraffic V02.09
              traffic V02.19
            vehicle V09.9
              animal-drawn V06.99
                nontraffic V06.09
                traffic V06.19
              motor
                nontraffic V09.00
                traffic V09.20
          fall V00.221
            nontraffic V09.1
              involving motor vehicle
                NEC V09.00
            traffic V09.3
              involving motor vehicle
                NEC V09.20
        skis (snow) V00.328
          collision (with) V09.9
            animal being ridden or
              animal drawn vehicle
              V06.99
              nontraffic V06.09
              traffic V06.19
            bus or heavy transport
              V04.99
              nontraffic V04.09
              traffic V04.19
            car V03.99
              nontraffic V03.09
              traffic V03.19
            pedal cycle V01.99
              nontraffic V01.09
              traffic V01.19
            pick-up truck or van
              V03.99
              nontraffic V03.09
              traffic V03.19
            railway (train) (vehicle)
              V05.99
              nontraffic V05.09
              traffic V05.19
            streetcar V06.99
              nontraffic V06.09
              traffic V06.19
            stationary object V00.322
            two-or three-wheeled
              motor vehicle V02.99
              nontraffic V02.09
              traffic V02.19
            vehicle V09.9
              animal-drawn V06.99
                nontraffic V06.09
                traffic V06.19
              motor
                nontraffic V09.00
                traffic V09.20

Accident *(Continued)*
  transport *(Continued)*
    pedestrian *(Continued)*
      conveyance occupant *(Continued)*
        skis *(Continued)*
          fall V00.321
            nontraffic V09.1
              involving motor vehicle
                NEC V09.00
            traffic V09.3
              involving motor vehicle
                NEC V09.20
        snow board V00.318
          collision (with) V09.9
            animal being ridden or
              animal drawn vehicle
              V06.99
              nontraffic V06.09
              traffic V06.19
            bus or heavy transport
              V04.99
              nontraffic V04.09
              traffic V04.19
            car V03.99
              nontraffic V03.09
              traffic V03.19
            pedal cycle V01.99
              nontraffic V01.09
              traffic V01.19
            pick-up truck or van V03.99
              nontraffic V03.09
              traffic V03.19
            railway (train) (vehicle)
              V05.99
              nontraffic V05.09
              traffic V05.19
            streetcar V06.99
              nontraffic V06.09
              traffic V06.19
            stationary object V00.312
            two- or three-wheeled motor
              vehicle V02.99
              nontraffic V02.09
              traffic V02.19
            vehicle V09.9
              animal-drawn V06.99
                nontraffic V06.09
                traffic V06.19
              motor
                nontraffic V09.00
                traffic V09.20
          fall V00.311
            nontraffic V09.1
              involving motor vehicle
                NEC V09.00
            traffic V09.3
              involving motor vehicle
                NEC V09.20
        specified type NEC V00.989
          collision (with) V09.9
            animal being ridden or
              animal drawn vehicle
              V06.99
              nontraffic V06.09
              traffic V06.19
            bus or heavy transport
              V04.99
              nontraffic V04.09
              traffic V04.19
            car V03.99
              nontraffic V03.09
              traffic V03.19
            pedal cycle V01.99
              nontraffic V01.09
              traffic V01.19

Accident *(Continued)*
  transport *(Continued)*
    pedestrian *(Continued)*
      conveyance occupant *(Continued)*
        specified type NEC *(Continued)*
          collision *(Continued)*
            pick-up truck or van
              V03.99
              nontraffic V03.09
              traffic V03.19
            railway (train) (vehicle)
              V05.99
              nontraffic V05.09
              traffic V05.19
            streetcar V06.99
              nontraffic V06.09
              traffic V06.19
            stationary object V00.89
            two- or three-wheeled motor
              vehicle V02.99
              nontraffic V02.09
              traffic V02.19
            vehicle V09.9
              animal-drawn V06.99
                nontraffic V06.09
                traffic V06.19
              motor
                nontraffic V09.00
                traffic V09.20
          fall V00.891
            nontraffic V09.1
              involving motor vehicle
                NEC V09.00
            traffic V09.3
              involving motor vehicle
                NEC V09.20
        traffic V09.3
          involving motor vehicle NEC
           V09.20
          military V09.21
          specified type NEC
           V09.29
        wheelchair (powered) V00.818
          collision (with) V09.9
            animal being ridden or
              animal drawn vehicle
              V06.99
              nontraffic V06.09
              traffic V06.19
            bus or heavy transport
              V04.99
              nontraffic V04.09
              traffic V04.19
            car V03.99
              nontraffic V03.09
              traffic V03.19
            pedal cycle V01.99
              nontraffic V01.09
              traffic V01.19
            pick-up truck or van
              V03.99
              nontraffic V03.09
              traffic V03.19
            railway (train) (vehicle)
              V05.99
              nontraffic V05.09
              traffic V05.19
            streetcar V06.99
              nontraffic V06.09
              traffic V06.19
            stationary object V00.812
            two- or three-wheeled motor
              vehicle V02.99
              nontraffic V02.09
              traffic V02.19

Accident *(Continued)*
  transport *(Continued)*
    pedestrian *(Continued)*
      conveyance occupant *(Continued)*
        wheelchair *(Continued)*
          collision *(Continued)*
            vehicle V09.9
              animal-drawn V06.99
                nontraffic V06.09
                traffic V06.19
              motor
                nontraffic V09.00
                traffic V09.20
            fall V00.811
            nontraffic V09.1
              involving motor vehicle
                NEC V09.00
            traffic V09.3
              involving motor vehicle
                NEC V09.20
      on foot - *see* also Accident,
        pedestrian
      collision (with)
        animal being ridden or animal
            drawn vehicle V06.90
          nontraffic V06.00
          traffic V06.10
        bus or heavy transport
            V04.90
          nontraffic V04.00
          traffic V04.10
        car V03.90
          nontraffic V03.00
          traffic V03.10
        pedal cycle V01.90
          nontraffic V01.00
          traffic V01.10
        pick-up truck or van V03.90
          nontraffic V03.00
          traffic V03.10
        railway (train) (vehicle) V05.90
          nontraffic V05.00
          traffic V05.10
        streetcar V06.90
          nontraffic V06.00
          traffic V06.10
        two- or three-wheeled motor
            vehicle V02.90
          nontraffic V02.00
          traffic V02.10
        vehicle V09.9
          animal-drawn V06.90
            nontraffic V06.00
            traffic V06.10
          motor
            nontraffic V09.00
            traffic V09.20
          nontraffic V09.1
            involving motor vehicle
              V09.00
            military V09.01
            specified type NEC V09.09
          traffic V09.3
            involving motor vehicle
              V09.20
            military V09.21
            specified type NEC
              V09.29
    person NEC (unknown way or
        transportation) V99
      collision (between)
        bus (with)
          heavy transport vehicle
            (traffic) V87.5
          nontraffic V88.5

Accident *(Continued)*
  transport *(Continued)*
    person NEC *(Continued)*
      collision *(Continued)*
        car (with)
          nontraffic V88.5
          bus (traffic) V87.3
            nontraffic V88.3
          heavy transport vehicle
            (traffic) V87.4
            nontraffic V88.4
          pick-up truck or van (traffic)
            V87.2
            nontraffic V88.2
          train or railway vehicle
            (traffic) V87.6
            nontraffic V88.6
          two- or three-wheeled motor
            vehicle (traffic) V87.0
            nontraffic V88.0
          motor vehicle (traffic) NEC
            V87.7
            nontraffic V88.7
          two- or three-wheeled vehicle
            (with) (traffic)
          motor vehicle NEC V87.1
            nontraffic V88.1
        nonmotor vehicle (collision)
          (noncollision) (traffic) V87.9
          nontraffic V88.9
    pickup truck occupant V59.9
      collision (with)
        animal (traffic) V50.9
          being ridden (traffic) V56.9
            nontraffic V56.3
            while boarding or alighting
              V56.4
          nontraffic V50.3
          while boarding or alighting
            V50.4
        animal-drawn vehicle (traffic)
            V56.9
          nontraffic V56.3
          while boarding or alighting
            V56.4
        bus (traffic) V54.9
          nontraffic V54.3
          while boarding or alighting
            V54.4
        car (traffic) V53.9
          nontraffic V53.3
          while boarding or alighting
            V53.4
        motor vehicle NOS (traffic)
            V59.60
          nontraffic V59.20
          specified type NEC (traffic)
            V59.69
          nontraffic V59.29
        pedal cycle (traffic) V51.9
          nontraffic V51.3
          while boarding or alighting V51.4
        pickup truck (traffic) V53.9
          nontraffic V53.3
          while boarding or alighting
            V53.4
        railway vehicle (traffic) V55.9
          nontraffic V55.3
          while boarding or alighting
            V55.4
        specified vehicle NEC (traffic)
            V56.9
          nontraffic V56.3
          while boarding or alighting
            V56.4

Accident *(Continued)*
  transport *(Continued)*
    pickup truck occupant *(Continued)*
      collision *(Continued)*
        stationary object (traffic) V57.9
          nontraffic V57.3
          while boarding or alighting
            V57.4
        streetcar (traffic) V56.9
          nontraffic V56.3
          while boarding or alighting V56.4
        three wheeled motor vehicle
            (traffic) V52.9
          nontraffic V52.3
          while boarding or alighting
            V52.4
        truck (traffic) V54.9
          nontraffic V54.3
          while boarding or alighting
            V54.4
        two wheeled motor vehicle
            (traffic) V52.9
          nontraffic V52.3
          while boarding or alighting
            V52.4
        van (traffic) V53.9
          nontraffic V53.3
          while boarding or alighting
            V53.4
      driver
        collision (with)
          animal (traffic) V50.5
            being ridden (traffic) V56.5
              nontraffic V56.0
            nontraffic V50.0
          animal-drawn vehicle (traffic)
              V56.5
            nontraffic V56.0
          bus (traffic) V54.5
            nontraffic V54.0
          car (traffic) V53.5
            nontraffic V53.0
          motor vehicle NOS (traffic)
              V59.40
            nontraffic V59.00
            specified type NEC (traffic)
              V59.49
            nontraffic V59.09
          pedal cycle (traffic) V51.5
            nontraffic V51.0
          pickup truck (traffic) V53.5
            nontraffic V53.0
          railway vehicle (traffic) V55.5
            nontraffic V55.0
          specified vehicle NEC (traffic)
              V56.5
            nontraffic V56.0
          stationary object (traffic) V57.5
            nontraffic V57.0
          streetcar (traffic) V56.5
            nontraffic V56.0
          three wheeled motor vehicle
              (traffic) V52.5
            nontraffic V52.0
          truck (traffic) V54.5
            nontraffic V54.0
          two wheeled motor vehicle
              (traffic) V52.5
            nontraffic V52.0
          van (traffic) V53.5
            nontraffic V53.0
          noncollision accident (traffic)
              V58.5
            nontraffic V58.0

Accident *(Continued)*
  transport *(Continued)*
    pickup truck occupant *(Continued)*
      noncollision accident (traffic) V58.9
        nontraffic V58.3
          while boarding or alighting
            V58.4
        nontraffic V59.3
      hanger-on
        collision (with)
          animal (traffic) V50.7
            being ridden (traffic) V56.7
              nontraffic V56.2
            nontraffic V50.2
          animal-drawn vehicle (traffic)
            V56.7
            nontraffic V56.2
          bus (traffic) V54.7
            nontraffic V54.2
          car (traffic) V53.7
            nontraffic V53.2
          pedal cycle (traffic) V51.7
            nontraffic V51.2
          pickup truck (traffic) V53.7
            nontraffic V53.2
          railway vehicle (traffic) V55.7
            nontraffic V55.2
          specified vehicle NEC (traffic)
            V56.7
            nontraffic V56.2
          stationary object (traffic) V57.7
            nontraffic V57.2
          streetcar (traffic) V56.7
            nontraffic V56.2
          three wheeled motor vehicle
            (traffic) V52.7
            nontraffic V52.2
          truck (traffic) V54.7
            nontraffic V54.2
          two wheeled motor vehicle
            (traffic) V52.7
            nontraffic V52.2
          van (traffic) V53.7
            nontraffic V53.2
        noncollision accident (traffic)
          V58.7
          nontraffic V58.2
      passenger
        collision (with)
          animal (traffic) V50.6
            being ridden (traffic) V56.6
              nontraffic V56.1
            nontraffic V50.1
          animal-drawn vehicle (traffic)
            V56.6
            nontraffic V56.1
          bus (traffic) V54.6
            nontraffic V54.1
          car (traffic) V53.6
            nontraffic V53.1
          motor vehicle NOS (traffic)
            V59.50
            nontraffic V59.10
              specified type NEC (traffic)
                V59.59
                nontraffic V59.19
          pedal cycle (traffic) V51.6
            nontraffic V51.1
          pickup truck (traffic) V53.6
            nontraffic V53.1
          railway vehicle (traffic) V55.6
            nontraffic V55.1
          specified vehicle NEC (traffic)
            V56.6
            nontraffic V56.1

Accident *(Continued)*
  transport *(Continued)*
    pickup truck occupant *(Continued)*
      passenger *(Continued)*
        collision *(Continued)*
          stationary object (traffic) V57.6
            nontraffic V57.1
          streetcar (traffic) V56.6
            nontraffic V56.1
          three wheeled motor vehicle
            (traffic) V52.6
            nontraffic V52.1
          truck (traffic) V54.6
            nontraffic V54.1
          two wheeled motor vehicle
            (traffic) V52.6
            nontraffic V52.1
          van (traffic) V53.6
            nontraffic V53.1
        noncollision accident (traffic)
          V58.6
          nontraffic V58.1
      specified type NEC V59.88
      military vehicle V59.81
    quarry truck - *see* Accident, transport,
      industrial vehicle occupant
    race car - *see* Accident, transport,
      motor vehicle NEC occupant
    railway vehicle occupant V81.9
      collision (with) V81.3
        motor vehicle (non-military)
          (traffic) V81.1
        military V81.83
          nontraffic V81.0
        rolling stock V81.2
        specified object NEC V81.3
      during derailment V81.7
        with antecedent collision - *see*
          Accident, transport, railway
          vehicle occupant, collision
      explosion V81.81
      fall (in railway vehicle) V81.5
        during derailment V81.7
          with antecedent collision
            - *see* Accident, transport,
            railway vehicle occupant,
            collision
        from railway vehicle V81.6
          during derailment V81.7
            with antecedent collision
              - *see* Accident, transport,
              railway vehicle
              occupant, collision
          while boarding or alighting
            V81.4
      fire V81.81
      object falling onto train V81.82
      specified type NEC V81.89
      while boarding or alighting V81.4
    ski lift V98.3
    snowmobile occupant (nontraffic)
      V86.92
      driver V86.52
      hanger-on V86.72
      passenger V86.62
      traffic V86.32
        driver V86.02
        hanger-on V86.22
        passenger V86.12
      while boarding or alighting
        V86.42
    specified NEC V98.8
    sport utility vehicle occupant - *see*
      also Accident, transport, car
      occupant

Accident *(Continued)*
  transport *(Continued)*
    sport utility vehicle occupant
      (Continued)
      collision (with)
        stationary object (traffic)
          V47.91
          nontraffic V47.31
      driver
        collision (with)
          stationary object (traffic)
            V47.51
            nontraffic V47.01
      passenger
        collision (with)
          stationary object (traffic)
            V47.61
            nontraffic V47.11
    streetcar occupant V82.9
      collision (with) V82.3
        motor vehicle (traffic) V82.1
          nontraffic V82.0
        rolling stock V82.2
      during derailment V82.7
        with antecedent collision
          - *see* Accident, transport,
          streetcar occupant, collision
      fall (in streetcar) V82.5
        during derailment V82.7
          with antecedent collision
            - *see* Accident, transport,
            streetcar occupant, collision
        from streetcar V82.6
          during derailment V82.7
            with antecedent collision
              - *see* Accident, transport,
              streetcar occupant,
              collision
          while boarding or alighting
            V82.4
        while boarding or alighting
          V82.4
      specified type NEC V82.8
      while boarding or alighting
        V82.4
    three-wheeled motor vehicle
      occupant V39.9
      collision (with)
        animal (traffic) V30.9
          being ridden (traffic) V36.9
            nontraffic V36.3
            while boarding or alighting
              V36.4
          nontraffic V30.3
          while boarding or alighting
            V30.4
        animal-drawn vehicle (traffic)
          V36.9
          nontraffic V36.3
          while boarding or alighting
            V36.4
        bus (traffic) V34.9
          nontraffic V34.3
          while boarding or alighting
            V34.4
        car (traffic) V33.9
          nontraffic V33.3
          while boarding or alighting
            V33.4
        motor vehicle NOS (traffic)
          V39.60
          nontraffic V39.20
            specified type NEC (traffic)
              V39.69
              nontraffic V39.29

Accident *(Continued)*
  transport *(Continued)*
    three-wheeled motor vehicle
      occupant *(Continued)*
        collision *(Continued)*
          pedal cycle (traffic) V31.9
            nontraffic V31.3
              while boarding or alighting
                V31.4
          pickup truck (traffic) V33.9
            nontraffic V33.3
              while boarding or alighting
                V33.4
          railway vehicle (traffic) V35.9
            nontraffic V35.3
              while boarding or alighting
                V35.4
          specified vehicle NEC (traffic)
            V36.9
            nontraffic V36.3
              while boarding or alighting
                V36.4
          stationary object (traffic) V37.9
            nontraffic V37.3
              while boarding or alighting
                V37.4
          streetcar (traffic) V36.9
            nontraffic V36.3
              while boarding or alighting
                V36.4
          three wheeled motor vehicle
            (traffic) V32.9
            nontraffic V32.3
              while boarding or alighting
                V32.4
          truck (traffic) V34.9
            nontraffic V34.3
              while boarding or alighting
                V34.4
          two wheeled motor vehicle
            (traffic) V32.9
            nontraffic V32.3
              while boarding or alighting
                V32.4
          van (traffic) V33.9
            nontraffic V33.3
              while boarding or alighting V33.4
      driver
        collision (with)
          animal (traffic) V30.5
            being ridden (traffic) V36.5
              nontraffic V36.0
            nontraffic V30.0
          animal-drawn vehicle (traffic)
            V36.5
            nontraffic V36.0
          bus (traffic) V34.5
            nontraffic V34.0
          car (traffic) V33.5
            nontraffic V33.0
          motor vehicle NOS (traffic)
            V39.40
            nontraffic V39.00
              specified type NEC (traffic)
                V39.49
                nontraffic V39.09
          pedal cycle (traffic) V31.5
            nontraffic V31.0
          pickup truck (traffic) V33.5
            nontraffic V33.0
          railway vehicle (traffic) V35.5
            nontraffic V35.0
          specified vehicle NEC (traffic)
            V36.5
            nontraffic V36.0

Accident *(Continued)*
  transport *(Continued)*
    three-wheeled motor vehicle
      occupant *(Continued)*
        driver *(Continued)*
          collision *(Continued)*
            stationary object (traffic) V37.5
              nontraffic V37.0
            streetcar (traffic) V36.5
              nontraffic V36.0
            three wheeled motor vehicle
              (traffic) V32.5
              nontraffic V32.0
            truck (traffic) V34.5
              nontraffic V34.0
            two wheeled motor vehicle
              (traffic) V32.5
              nontraffic V32.0
            van (traffic) V33.5
              nontraffic V33.0
          noncollision accident (traffic)
            V38.5
            nontraffic V38.0
        noncollision accident (traffic)
          V38.9
          nontraffic V38.3
            while boarding or alighting
              V38.4
        nontraffic V39.3
        hanger-on
          collision (with)
            animal (traffic) V30.7
              being ridden (traffic)
                V36.7
                nontraffic V36.2
              nontraffic V30.2
            animal-drawn vehicle (traffic)
              V36.7
              nontraffic V36.2
            bus (traffic) V34.7
              nontraffic V34.2
            car (traffic) V33.7
              nontraffic V33.2
            pedal cycle (traffic) V31.7
              nontraffic V31.2
            pickup truck (traffic) V33.7
              nontraffic V33.2
            railway vehicle (traffic) V35.7
              nontraffic V35.2
            specified vehicle NEC (traffic)
              V36.7
              nontraffic V36.2
            stationary object (traffic) V37.7
              nontraffic V37.2
            streetcar (traffic) V36.7
              nontraffic V36.2
            three wheeled motor vehicle
              (traffic) V32.7
              nontraffic V32.2
            truck (traffic) V34.7
              nontraffic V34.2
            two wheeled motor vehicle
              (traffic) V32.7
              nontraffic V32.2
            van (traffic) V33.7
              nontraffic V33.2
          noncollision accident (traffic)
            V38.7
            nontraffic V38.2
        passenger
          collision (with)
            animal (traffic) V30.6
              being ridden (traffic) V36.6
                nontraffic V36.1
              nontraffic V30.1

Accident *(Continued)*
  transport *(Continued)*
    three-wheeled motor vehicle
      occupant *(Continued)*
        passenger *(Continued)*
          collision *(Continued)*
            animal-drawn vehicle (traffic)
              V36.6
              nontraffic V36.1
            bus (traffic) V34.6
              nontraffic V34.1
            car (traffic) V33.6
              nontraffic V33.1
            motor vehicle NOS (traffic)
              V39.50
              nontraffic V39.10
                specified type NEC (traffic)
                  V39.59
                  nontraffic V39.19
            pedal cycle (traffic) V31.6
              nontraffic V31.1
            pickup truck (traffic) V33.6
              nontraffic V33.1
            railway vehicle (traffic) V35.6
              nontraffic V35.1
            specified vehicle NEC (traffic)
              V36.6
              nontraffic V36.1
            stationary object (traffic) V37.6
              nontraffic V37.1
            streetcar (traffic) V36.6
              nontraffic V36.1
            three wheeled motor vehicle
              (traffic) V32.6
              nontraffic V32.1
            truck (traffic) V34.6
              nontraffic V34.1
            two wheeled motor vehicle
              (traffic) V32.6
              nontraffic V32.1
            van (traffic) V33.6
              nontraffic V33.1
          noncollision accident (traffic)
            V38.6
            nontraffic V38.1
        specified type NEC V39.89
          military vehicle V39.81
    tractor (farm) (and trailer) - *see*
        Accident, transport, agricultural
        vehicle occupant
    tram - *see* Accident, transport,
        streetcar
      in mine or quarry - *see* Accident,
        transport, industrial vehicle
        occupant
    trolley - *see* Accident, transport,
        streetcar
      in mine or quarry - *see* Accident,
        transport, industrial vehicle
        occupant
    truck (heavy) occupant V69.9
      collision (with)
        animal (traffic) V60.9
          being ridden (traffic) V66.9
            nontraffic V66.3
              while boarding or alighting
                V66.4
          nontraffic V60.3
            while boarding or alighting
              V60.4
        animal-drawn vehicle (traffic)
          V66.9
          nontraffic V66.3
            while boarding or alighting
              V66.4

Accident (Continued)
transport (Continued)
truck (heavy) occupant (Continued)
collision (Continued)
bus (traffic) V64.9
nontraffic V64.3
while boarding or alighting
V64.4
car (traffic) V63.9
nontraffic V63.3
while boarding or alighting
V63.4
motor vehicle NOS (traffic)
V69.60
nontraffic V69.20
specified type NEC (traffic)
V69.69
nontraffic V69.29
pedal cycle (traffic) V61.9
nontraffic V61.3
while boarding or alighting
V61.4
pickup truck (traffic) V63.9
nontraffic V63.3
while boarding or alighting
V63.4
railway vehicle (traffic) V65.9
nontraffic V65.3
while boarding or alighting
V65.4
specified vehicle NEC (traffic)
V66.9
nontraffic V66.3
while boarding or alighting
V66.4
stationary object (traffic) V67.9
nontraffic V67.3
while boarding or alighting
V67.4
streetcar (traffic) V66.9
nontraffic V66.3
while boarding or alighting
V66.4
three wheeled motor vehicle
(traffic) V62.9
nontraffic V62.3
while boarding or alighting
V62.4
truck (traffic) V64.9
nontraffic V64.3
while boarding or alighting
V64.4
two wheeled motor vehicle
(traffic) V62.9
nontraffic V62.3
while boarding or alighting
V62.4
van (traffic) V63.9
nontraffic V63.3
while boarding or alighting
V63.4
driver
collision (with)
animal (traffic) V60.5
being ridden (traffic)
V66.5
nontraffic V66.0
nontraffic V60.0
animal-drawn vehicle (traffic)
V66.5
nontraffic V66.0
bus (traffic) V64.5
nontraffic V64.0
car (traffic) V63.5
nontraffic V63.0

Accident (Continued)
transport (Continued)
truck (heavy) occupant (Continued)
driver (Continued)
collision (Continued)
motor vehicle NOS (traffic)
V69.40
nontraffic V69.00
specified type NEC (traffic)
V69.49
nontraffic V69.09
pedal cycle (traffic) V61.5
nontraffic V61.0
pickup truck (traffic) V63.5
nontraffic V63.0
railway vehicle (traffic) V65.5
nontraffic V65.0
specified vehicle NEC (traffic)
V66.5
nontraffic V66.0
stationary object (traffic) V67.5
nontraffic V67.0
streetcar (traffic) V66.5
nontraffic V66.0
three wheeled motor vehicle
(traffic) V62.5
nontraffic V62.0
truck (traffic) V64.5
nontraffic V64.0
two wheeled motor vehicle
(traffic) V62.5
nontraffic V62.0
van (traffic) V63.5
nontraffic V63.0
noncollision accident (traffic)
V68.5
nontraffic V68.0
dump - see Accident, transport,
construction vehicle occupant
hanger-on
collision (with)
animal (traffic) V60.7
being ridden (traffic) V66.7
nontraffic V66.2
nontraffic V60.2
animal-drawn vehicle (traffic)
V66.7
nontraffic V66.2
bus (traffic) V64.7
nontraffic V64.2
car (traffic) V63.7
nontraffic V63.2
pedal cycle (traffic) V61.7
nontraffic V61.2
pickup truck (traffic) V63.7
nontraffic V63.2
railway vehicle (traffic) V65.7
nontraffic V65.2
specified vehicle NEC (traffic)
V66.7
nontraffic V66.2
stationary object (traffic) V67.7
nontraffic V67.2
streetcar (traffic) V66.7
nontraffic V66.2
three wheeled motor vehicle
(traffic) V62.7
nontraffic V62.2
truck (traffic) V64.7
nontraffic V64.2
two wheeled motor vehicle
(traffic) V62.7
nontraffic V62.2
van (traffic) V63.7
nontraffic V63.2

Accident (Continued)
transport (Continued)
truck (heavy) occupant (Continued)
hanger-on (Continued)
noncollision accident (traffic)
V68.7
nontraffic V68.2
noncollision accident (traffic)
V68.9
nontraffic V68.3
while boarding or alighting
V68.4
nontraffic V69.3
passenger
collision (with)
animal (traffic) V60.6
being ridden (traffic)
V66.6
nontraffic V66.1
nontraffic V60.1
animal-drawn vehicle (traffic)
V66.6
nontraffic V66.1
bus (traffic) V64.6
nontraffic V64.1
car (traffic) V63.6
nontraffic V63.1
motor vehicle NOS (traffic)
V69.50
nontraffic V69.10
specified type NEC (traffic)
V69.59
nontraffic V69.19
pedal cycle (traffic) V61.6
nontraffic V61.1
pickup truck (traffic) V63.6
nontraffic V63.1
railway vehicle (traffic)
V65.6
nontraffic V65.1
specified vehicle NEC (traffic)
V66.6
nontraffic V66.1
stationary object (traffic)
V67.6
nontraffic V67.1
streetcar (traffic) V66.6
nontraffic V66.1
three wheeled motor vehicle
(traffic) V62.6
nontraffic V62.1
truck (traffic) V64.6
nontraffic V64.1
two wheeled motor vehicle
(traffic) V62.6
nontraffic V62.1
van (traffic) V63.6
nontraffic V63.1
noncollision accident (traffic)
V68.6
nontraffic V68.1
pickup - see Accident, transport,
pickup truck occupant
specified type NEC V69.88
military vehicle V69.81
van occupant V59.9
collision (with)
animal (traffic) V50.9
being ridden (traffic) V56.9
nontraffic V56.3
while boarding or alighting
V56.4
nontraffic V50.3
while boarding or alighting
V50.4

Accident *(Continued)*
  transport *(Continued)*
    van occupant *(Continued)*
      collision *(Continued)*
        animal-drawn vehicle (traffic)
          V56.9
          nontraffic V56.3
          while boarding or alighting
            V56.4
        bus (traffic) V54.9
          nontraffic V54.3
          while boarding or alighting
            V54.4
        car (traffic) V53.9
          nontraffic V53.3
          while boarding or alighting
            V53.4
        motor vehicle NOS (traffic) V59.60
          nontraffic V59.20
          specified type NEC (traffic)
            V59.69
            nontraffic V59.29
        pedal cycle (traffic) V51.9
          nontraffic V51.3
          while boarding or alighting
            V51.4
        pickup truck (traffic) V53.9
          nontraffic V53.3
          while boarding or alighting
            V53.4
        railway vehicle (traffic) V55.9
          nontraffic V55.3
          while boarding or alighting
            V55.4
        specified vehicle NEC (traffic)
          V56.9
          nontraffic V56.3
          while boarding or alighting
            V56.4
        stationary object (traffic) V57.9
          nontraffic V57.3
          while boarding or alighting
            V57.4
        streetcar (traffic) V56.9
          nontraffic V56.3
          while boarding or alighting
            V56.4
        three wheeled motor vehicle
          (traffic) V52.9
          nontraffic V52.3
          while boarding or alighting
            V52.4
        truck (traffic) V54.9
          nontraffic V54.3
          while boarding or alighting
            V54.4
        two wheeled motor vehicle
          (traffic) V52.9
          nontraffic V52.3
          while boarding or alighting
            V52.4
        van (traffic) V53.9
          nontraffic V53.3
          while boarding or alighting
            V53.4
      driver
        collision (with)
          animal (traffic) V50.5
            being ridden (traffic)
              V56.5
              nontraffic V56.0
            nontraffic V50.0
          animal-drawn vehicle (traffic)
            V56.5
            nontraffic V56.0

Accident *(Continued)*
  transport *(Continued)*
    van occupant *(Continued)*
      driver *(Continued)*
        collision *(Continued)*
          bus (traffic) V54.5
            nontraffic V54.0
          car (traffic) V53.5
            nontraffic V53.0
          motor vehicle NOS (traffic)
            V59.40
            nontraffic V59.00
            specified type NEC (traffic)
              V59.49
              nontraffic V59.09
          pedal cycle (traffic) V51.5
            nontraffic V51.0
          pickup truck (traffic) V53.5
            nontraffic V53.0
          railway vehicle (traffic) V55.5
            nontraffic V55.0
          specified vehicle NEC (traffic)
            V56.5
            nontraffic V56.0
          stationary object (traffic) V57.5
            nontraffic V57.0
          streetcar (traffic) V56.5
            nontraffic V56.0
          three wheeled motor vehicle
            (traffic) V52.5
            nontraffic V52.0
          truck (traffic) V54.5
            nontraffic V54.0
          two wheeled motor vehicle
            (traffic) V52.5
            nontraffic V52.0
          van (traffic) V53.5
            nontraffic V53.0
        noncollision accident (traffic)
          V58.5
          nontraffic V58.0
        noncollision accident (traffic) V58.9
          nontraffic V58.3
          while boarding or alighting
            V58.4
        nontraffic V59.3
      hanger-on
        collision (with)
          animal (traffic) V50.7
            being ridden (traffic) V56.7
              nontraffic V56.2
            nontraffic V50.2
          animal-drawn vehicle (traffic)
            V56.7
            nontraffic V56.2
          bus (traffic) V54.7
            nontraffic V54.2
          car (traffic) V53.7
            nontraffic V53.2
          pedal cycle (traffic) V51.7
            nontraffic V51.2
          pickup truck (traffic) V53.7
            nontraffic V53.2
          railway vehicle (traffic) V55.7
            nontraffic V55.2
          specified vehicle NEC (traffic)
            V56.7
            nontraffic V56.2
          stationary object (traffic) V57.7
            nontraffic V57.2
          streetcar (traffic) V56.7
            nontraffic V56.2
          three wheeled motor vehicle
            (traffic) V52.7
            nontraffic V52.2

Accident *(Continued)*
  transport *(Continued)*
    van occupant *(Continued)*
      hanger-on *(Continued)*
        collision *(Continued)*
          truck (traffic) V54.7
            nontraffic V54.2
          two wheeled motor vehicle
            (traffic) V52.7
            nontraffic V52.2
          van (traffic) V53.7
            nontraffic V53.2
        noncollision accident (traffic)
          V58.7
          nontraffic V58.2
      passenger
        collision (with)
          animal (traffic) V50.6
            being ridden (traffic) V56.6
              nontraffic V56.1
            nontraffic V50.1
          animal-drawn vehicle (traffic)
            V56.6
            nontraffic V56.1
          bus (traffic) V54.6
            nontraffic V54.1
          car (traffic) V53.6
            nontraffic V53.1
          motor vehicle NOS (traffic)
            V59.50
            nontraffic V59.10
            specified type NEC (traffic)
              V59.59
              nontraffic V59.19
          pedal cycle (traffic) V51.6
            nontraffic V51.1
          pickup truck (traffic) V53.6
            nontraffic V53.1
          railway vehicle (traffic) V55.6
            nontraffic V55.1
          specified vehicle NEC (traffic)
            V56.6
            nontraffic V56.1
          stationary object (traffic) V57.6
            nontraffic V57.1
          streetcar (traffic) V56.6
            nontraffic V56.1
          three wheeled motor vehicle
            (traffic) V52.6
            nontraffic V52.1
          truck (traffic) V54.6
            nontraffic V54.1
          two wheeled motor vehicle
            (traffic) V52.6
            nontraffic V52.1
          van (traffic) V53.6
            nontraffic V53.1
        noncollision accident (traffic)
          V58.6
          nontraffic V58.1
      specified type NEC V59.88
        military vehicle V59.81
    watercraft occupant - *see* Accident,
      watercraft
    vehicle NEC V89.9
      animal-drawn NEC - *see* Accident,
        transport, animal-drawn vehicle
        occupant
      special
        agricultural - *see* Accident,
          transport, agricultural vehicle
          occupant
        construction - *see* Accident,
          transport, construction vehicle
          occupant

Accident *(Continued)*
vehicle NEC *(Continued)*
special *(Continued)*
industrial - *see* Accident, transport,
industrial vehicle occupant
three-wheeled NEC (motorized)
- *see* Accident, transport, three-
wheeled motor vehicle occupant
watercraft V94.9
causing
drowning - *see* Drowning, due to,
accident to, watercraft
injury NEC V91.89
crushed between craft and object
V91.19
powered craft V91.13
ferry boat V91.11
fishing boat V91.12
jetskis V91.13
liner V91.11
merchant ship V91.10
passenger ship V91.11
unpowered craft V91.18
canoe V91.15
inflatable V91.16
kayak V91.15
sailboat V91.14
surf-board V91.18
windsurfer V91.18
fall on board V91.29
powered craft V91.23
ferry boat V91.21
fishing boat V91.22
jetskis V91.23
liner V91.21
merchant ship V91.20
passenger ship V91.21
unpowered craft
canoe V91.25
inflatable V91.26
kayak V91.25
sailboat V91.24
fire on board causing burn
V91.09
powered craft V91.03
ferry boat V91.01
fishing boat V91.02
jetskis V91.03
liner V91.01
merchant ship V91.00
passenger ship V91.01
unpowered craft V91.08
canoe V91.05
inflatable V91.06
kayak V91.05
sailboat V91.04
surf-board V91.08
water skis V91.07
windsurfer V91.08
hit by falling object V91.39
powered craft V91.33
ferry boat V91.31
fishing boat V91.32
jetskis V91.33
liner V91.31
merchant ship V91.30
passenger ship V91.31
unpowered craft V91.38
canoe V91.35
inflatable V91.36
kayak V91.35
sailboat V91.34
surf-board V91.38
water skis V91.37
windsurfer V91.38

Accident *(Continued)*
watercraft *(Continued)*
causing *(Continued)*
injury NEC *(Continued)*
specified type NEC V91.8
powered craft V91.83
ferry boat V91.81
fishing boat V91.82
jetskis V91.83
liner V91.81
merchant ship V91.80
passenger ship V91.81
unpowered craft V91.88
canoe V91.85
inflatable V91.86
kayak V91.85
sailboat V91.84
surf-board V91.88
water skis V91.87
windsurfer V91.88
due to, caused by cataclysm-*see*
Forces of nature, by type
military NEC V94.818
with civilian watercraft V94.810
civilian in water injured by
V94.811
nonpowered, struck by
nonpowered vessel V94.22
powered vessel V94.21
specified type NEC V94.89
striking swimmer
powered V94.11
unpowered V94.12
Acid throwing (assault) Y08.89
Activity (involving) (of victim at time of
event) Y93.9
aerobic and step exercise (class) Y93.a3
alpine skiing Y93.23
animal care NEC Y93.k9
arts and handcrafts NEC Y93.d9
athletics NEC Y93.79
athletics played as a team or group
NEC Y93.69
athletics played individually NEC
Y93.59
baking Y93.g3
ballet Y93.41
barbells Y93.b3
BASE (Building, Antenna, Span, Earth)
jumping Y93.33
baseball Y93.64
basketball Y93.67
bathing (personal) Y93.e1
beach volleyball Y93.68
bike riding Y93.55
boogie boarding Y93.18
bowling Y93.54
boxing Y93.71
brass instrument playing Y93.j4
building construction Y93.h3
bungee jumping Y93.34
calisthenics Y93.a2
canoeing (in calm and turbulent water)
Y93.16
capture the flag Y93.68
cardiorespiratory exercise NEC Y93.a9
caregiving (providing) NEC Y93.f9
bathing Y93.f1
lifting Y93.f2
cellular
communication device Y93.c2
telephone Y93.c2
challenge course Y93.a5
cheerleading Y93.45
circuit training Y93.a4

Activity *(Continued)*
cleaning
floor Y93.e5
climbing NEC Y93.39
mountain Y93.31
rock Y93.31
wall Y93.31
cool down exercises Y93.a2
combatives Y93.75
computer
keyboarding Y93.c1
technology NEC Y93.c9
computer keyboarding Y93.c1
computer technology NEC Y93.c9
confidence course Y93.a5
construction (building) Y93.h3
cooking and baking Y93.g3
cricket Y93.69
crocheting Y93.d1
cross country skiing Y93.24
dancing (all types) Y93.41
digging
dirt Y93.h1
dirt digging Y93.h1
dishwashing Y93.g1
diving (platform) (springboard)
Y93.12
underwater Y93.15
dodge ball Y93.68
downhill skiing Y93.23
drum playing Y93.j2
dumbbells Y93.b3
electronic
devices NEC Y93.c9
hand held interactive Y93.c2
game playing (using) (with)
keyboard or other stationary device
Y93.c1
interactive device Y93.c2
elliptical machine Y93.a1
exercise(s)
machines ((primarily) for)
cardiorespiratory conditioning
Y93.a1
muscle strengthening Y93.b1
muscle strengthening (non-machine)
NEC Y93.b9
external motion NEC Y93.i9
rollercoaster Y93.i1
field hockey Y93.65
figure skating (pairs) (singles) Y93.21
flag football Y93.62
floor mopping and cleaning Y93.e5
food preparation and clean up Y93.g1
football (American) NOS Y93.61
flag Y93.62
tackle Y93.61
touch Y93.62
four square Y93.68
free weights Y93.b3
frisbee (ultimate) Y93.74
furniture
building Y93.d3
finishing Y93.d3
repair Y93.d3
game playing (electronic)
using keyboard or other stationary
device Y93.c1
using interactive device Y93.c2
gardening Y93.h2
golf Y93.53
grass drills Y93.a6
grilling and smoking food Y93.g2
grooming and shearing an animal
Y93.k3

Activity *(Continued)*
  guerilla drills Y93.a6
  gymnastics (rhythmic) Y93.43
  handball Y93.73
  handcrafts NEC Y93.d9
  hand held interactive electronic device
    Y93.c2
  hang gliding Y93.35
  hiking (on level or elevated terrain)
    Y93.01
  hockey (ice) Y93.22
    field Y93.65
  horseback riding Y93.52
  household maintenance NEC Y93.e9
  ice NEC Y93.29
    dancing Y93.21
    hockey Y93.22
    skating Y93.21
  inline roller skating Y93.51
  ironing Y93.e4
  judo Y93.75
  jumping (off) NEC Y93.39
    BASE (Building, Antenna, Span,
      Earth) Y93.33
    bungee Y93.34
    jacks Y93.a2
    rope Y93.56
  jumping jacks Y93.a2
  jumping rope Y93.56
  karate Y93.75
  kayaking (in calm and turbulent water)
    Y93.16
  keyboarding (computer) Y93.c1
  kickball Y93.68
  knitting Y93.d1
  lacrosse Y93.65
  land maintenance NEC Y93.h9
  landscaping Y93.h2
  laundry Y93.e2
  machines (exercise)
    primarily for cardiorespiratory
      conditioning Y93.a1
    primarily for muscle strengthening
      Y93.b1
  maintenance
    building NEC Y93.h9
    household NEC Y93.e9
    land Y93.h9
    property Y93.h9
  marching (on level or elevated terrain)
    Y93.01
  martial arts Y93.75
  microwave oven Y93.g3
  mopping (floor) Y93.e5
  mountain climbing Y93.31
  milking an animal Y93.k2
  muscle strengthening
    exercises (non-machine) NEC Y93.b9
    machines Y93.b1
  musical keyboard (electronic) playing
    Y93.j1
  nordic skiing Y93.24
  obstacle course Y93.a5
  oven (microwave) Y93.g3
  packing up and unpacking in moving to
    a new residence Y93.e6
  parasailing Y93.19
  percussion instrument playing NEC Y93.j2
  personal
    bathing and showering Y93.e1
    hygiene NEC Y93.e8
    showering Y93.e1
  physical games generally associated
    with school recess, summer camp
    and children Y93.68

Activity *(Continued)*
  physical training NEC Y93.a9
  piano playing Y93.j1
  pilates Y93.b4
  platform diving Y93.12
  playing musical instrument
    brass instrument Y93.j4
    drum Y93.j2
    musical keyboard (electronic) Y93.j1
    percussion instrument NEC Y93.j2
    piano Y93.j1
    string instrument Y93.j3
    winds instrument Y93.j4
  property maintenance NE Y93.h9
  pruning (garden and lawn) Y93.h2
  pull-ups Y93.b2
  push-ups Y93.b2
  racquetball Y93.73
  rafting (in calm and turbulent water)
    Y93.16
  raking (leaves) Y93.h1
  rappelling Y93.32
  refereeing a sports activity Y93.81
  residential relocation Y93.e6
  rhythmic gymnastics Y93.43
  rhythmic movement NEC Y93.49
  riding
    horseback Y93.52
    rollercoaster Y93.i1
  rock climbing Y93.31
  rollercoaster riding Y93.i1
  roller skating (inline) Y93.51
  rough housing and horseplay Y93.83
  rowing (in calm and turbulent water)
    Y93.16
  rugby Y93.63
  running Y93.02
  SCUBA diving Y93.15
  sewing Y93.d2
  shoveling Y93.h1
    dirt Y93.h1
    snow Y93.h1
  showering (personal) Y93.e1
  sit-ups Y93.b2
  skateboarding Y93.51
  skating (ice) Y93.21
    roller Y93.51
  skiing (alpine) (downhill) Y93.23
    cross country Y93.24
    nordic Y93.24
    water Y93.17
  sledding (snow) Y93.23
  sleeping (sleep) Y93.84
  smoking and grilling food Y93.g2
  snorkeling Y93.15
  snow NEC Y93.29
    boarding Y93.23
    shoveling Y93.h1
    sledding Y93.23
    tubing Y93.23
  soccer Y93.66
  softball Y93.64
  specified NEC Y93.89
  spectator at an event Y93.82
  sports NEC Y93.79
    sports played as a team or group
      NEC Y93.69
    sports played individually NEC
      Y93.59
  springboard diving Y93.12
  squash Y93.73
  stationary bike Y93.a1
  step (stepping) exercise (class)
    Y93.a3
  stepper machine Y93.a1

Activity *(Continued)*
  stove Y93.g3
  string instrument playing Y93.j3
  surfing Y93.18
    wind Y93.18
  swimming Y93.11
  tackle football Y93.61
  tap dancing Y93.41
  tennis Y93.73
  tobogganing Y93.23
  touch football Y93.62
  track and field events (non-running)
    Y93.57
    running Y93.02
  trampoline Y93.44
  treadmill Y93.a1
  trimming shrubs Y93.h2
  tubing (in calm and turbulent water)
    Y93.16
    snow Y93.23
  ultimate frisbee Y93.74
  underwater diving Y93.15
  unpacking in moving to a new
    residence Y93.e6
  use of stove, oven and microwave oven
    Y93.g3
  vacuuming Y93.e3
  volleyball (beach) (court) Y93.68
  wake boarding Y93.17
  walking an animal Y93.k1
  walking (on level or elevated terrain)
    Y93.01
    an animal Y93.k1
  wall climbing Y93.31
  warm up and cool down exercises
    Y93.a2
  water NEC Y93.19
    aerobics Y93.14
    craft NEC Y93.19
    exercise Y93.14
    polo Y93.13
    skiing Y93.17
    sliding Y93.18
    survival training and testing
      Y93.19
  weeding (garden and lawn) Y93.h2
  wind instrument playing Y93.j4
  windsurfing Y93.18
  wrestling Y93.72
  yoga Y93.42
Adverse effect of drugs - *see* Table of
  Drugs and Chemicals
Aerosinusitis - *see* Air, pressure
After-effect, late - *see* Sequelae
Air
  blast in war operations - *see* War
    operations, air blast
  pressure
    change, rapid
      during
        ascent W94.29
          while (in) (surfacing from)
            aircraft W94.23
            deep water diving
              W94.21
            underground W94.22
        descent W94.39
        in
          aircraft W94.31
          water W94.32
    high, prolonged W94.0
    low, prolonged W94.12
      due to residence or long visit at
        high altitude W94.11
  sickness X51.0

Alpine sickness W94.11
Altitude sickness W94.11
Anaphylactic shock, anaphylaxis - *see*
    Table of drugs and chemicals
Andes disease W94.11
Arachnidism, arachnoidism X58.8
Arson (with intent to injure or kill)
    X97
Asphyxia, asphyxiation
    by
        food (bone) (seed) - *see* categories
            T17 and T18
        gas - *see also* Table of drugs and
            chemicals
            legal
                execution Y35.91
                intervention - *see* Legal,
                    intervention, gas
        from
            fire - *see also* Exposure, fire
                in war operations - *see* War
                    operations, fire
            ignition - *see* Ignition
            vomitus - *see* subcategories T17.81,
                T18.81.
        in war operations - *see* War operations,
            restriction of airway
Aspiration
    food (any type) (into respiratory
        tract) (with asphyxia, obstruction
        respiratory tract, suffocation) - *see*
        categories T17 and T18
    foreign body - *see* Foreign body,
        aspiration
    vomitus (with asphyxia, obstruction
        respiratory tract, suffocation) - *see*
        subcategories T17.81, T18.81.
Assassination (attempt) - *see* Assault
Assault (homicidal) (by) (in) Y09
    arson X97
    bite (of human being) Y04.1
    bodily force Y04.8
        bite Y04.1
        bumping into Y04.2
        sexual - *see* subcategories T74.0,
            T76.0
        unarmed fight Y04.0
    bomb X96.9
        antipersonnel X96.0
        fertilizer X96.3
        gasoline X96.1
        letter X96.2
        petrol X96.1
        pipe X96.3
        specified NEC X96.8
    brawl (hand) (fists) (foot) (unarmed)
        Y04.0

Assault *(Continued)*
    burning, burns (by fire) NEC X97
        acid Y08.89
        caustic, corrosive substance Y08.89
        chemical from swallowing caustic,
            corrosive substance - *see* Table of
            drugs and chemicals
        cigarette(s) X97
        hot object X98.9
            fluid NEC X98.2
            household appliance X98.3
            specified NEC X98.8
            steam X98.0
            tap water X98.1
            vapors X98.0
        scalding - *see* Assault, burning
        steam X98.0
        vitriol Y08.89
    caustic, corrosive substance (gas)
        Y08.89
    crashing of
        aircraft Y08.81
        motor vehicle Y03.8
            pushed in front of Y03.1
            run over Y03.0
            specified NEC Y03.8
    cutting or piercing instrument X99.9
        dagger X99.2
        glass X99.0
        knife X99.1
        specified NEC X99.8
        sword X99.2
    dagger X99.2
    drowning (in) X92.9
        bathtub X92.0
        natural water X92.3
        specified NEC X92.8
        swimming pool X92.1
            following fall X92.2
    dynamite X96.8
    explosive(s) (material) X96.9
    fight (hand) (fists) (foot) (unarmed) Y04.0
        with weapon - *see* Assault, by type of
            weapon
    fire X97
    firearm X95.9
        airgun X95.01
        handgun X93
        hunting rifle X94.1
        larger X94.9
            specified NEC X94.8
        machine gun X94.2
        shotgun X94.0
        specified NEC X95.8
    gunshot (wound) NEC - *see* Assault,
        firearm, by type
    incendiary device X97

Assault *(Continued)*
    injury Y09
        to child due to criminal abortion
            attempt NEC Y08.89
    knife X99.1
    late effect of - *see* X92-Y08 with q as
        terminal character
    placing before moving object Y02
        motor vehicle Y03.1
    poisoning - *see* categories T36-T65 with
        terminal digit 3
    puncture, any part of body - *see* Assault,
        cutting or piercing instrument
    pushing
        before moving object Y02
            motor vehicle Y03.1
        from high place Y01
    rape Y05
    scalding - *see* Assault, burning
    sequelae of - *see* X92-Y08 with q as
        terminal character
    sexual (by bodily force) Y05
    shooting - *see* Assault, firearm
    specified means NEC Y08.89
    stab, any part of body - *see* Assault,
        cutting or piercing instrument
    steam X98.0
    striking against
        other person Y04.2
        sports equipment Y08.09
            baseball bat Y08.02
            hockey stick Y08.01
    struck by
        sports equipment Y08.09
            baseball bat Y08.02
            hockey stick Y08.01
    submersion - *see* Assault, drowning
    violence Y09
    weapon Y09
        blunt Y00
        cutting or piercing - *see* Assault,
            cutting or piercing instrument
        firearm - *see* Assault, firearm
    wound Y09
        cutting - *see* Assault, cutting or
            piercing instrument
        gunshot - *see* Assault, firearm
        knife X99.1
        piercing - *see* Assault, cutting or
            piercing instrument
        puncture - *see* Assault, cutting or
            piercing instrument
        stab - *see* Assault, cutting or piercing
            instrument
Attack by mammals NEC W55.89
Avalanche - *see* Landslide
Aviator's disease - *see* Air, pressure

B

Barotitis, barodontalgia, barosinusitis, barotrauma (otitic) (sinus) - *see* Air, pressure
Battered (baby) (child) (person) (syndrome) X58
Bayonet wound W26.1
  in
    legal intervention - *see* Legal, intervention, sharp object, bayonet
    war operations - *see* War operations, combat
  stated as undetermined whether accidental or intentional Y28.8
  suicide (attempt) X78.2
Bean in nose - *see* categories T17 and T18
Bed set on fire NEC - *see* Exposure, fire, uncontrolled, building, bed
Beheading (by guillotine)
  homicide X99.9
  legal execution Y35.91
Bending, injury in - *see* Overexertion
Bends - *see* Air, pressure, change
Bite, bitten by
  alligator W58.01
  arthropod (nonvenomous) NEC W57
  bull W55.21
  cat W55.01
  cow W55.21
  crocodile W58.11
  dog W54.0
  goat W55.31
  hoof stock NEC W55.31
  horse W55.11
  human being (accidentally) W50.3
    with intent to injure or kill Y04.1
    as, or caused by, a crowd or human stampede (with fall) W52
    assault Y04.1
    homicide (attempt) Y04.1
    in
      fight Y04.1
  insect (nonvenomous) W57
  lizard (nonvenomous) W59.01
  mammal NEC W55.89
    marine W56.89
  marine animal (nonvenomous) W56.89
  millipede W57
  mammal NEC W55.81
  moray eel W56.51
  mouse W53.01
  person(s) (accidentally) W50.3
    with intent to injure or kill Y04.1
    as, or caused by, a crowd or human stampede (with fall) W52
    assault Y04.1
    homicide (attempt) Y04.1
    in
      fight Y04.1
  pig W55.41
  raccoon W55.51
  rat W53.11
  reptile W59.81
    lizard W59.01
    snake W59.11
    turtle W59.21
      terrestrial W59.81
  rodent W53.81
    mouse W53.01
    rat W53.11
    specified NEC W53.81
    squirrel W53.21

Bite, bitten by *(Continued)*
  shark W56.41
  sheep W55.31
  snake (nonvenomous) W59.11
  spider (nonvenomous) - *see* subcategory T73.9
  squirrel W53.21
Blast (air) in war operations - *see* War operations, blast
Blizzard X37.2
Blood alcohol level Y90.9
  less than 20mg/100ml Y90.0
  presence in blood, level not specified Y90.9
  20-39mg/100ml Y90.1
  40-59mg/100ml Y90.2
  60-79mg/100ml Y90.3
  80-99mg/100ml Y90.4
  100-119mg/100ml Y90.5
  120-199mg/100ml Y90.6
  200-239mg/100ml Y90.7
Blow X58
  by law-enforcing agent, police (on duty) - *see* Legal, intervention, manhandling
    blunt object - *see* Legal, intervention, blunt object
Blowing up - *see* Explosion
Brawl (hand) (fists) (foot) Y04.0
Breakage (accidental) (part of)
  ladder (causing fall) W11
  scaffolding (causing fall) W12
Broken
  glass, contact with - *see* Contact, with, glass
  power line (causing electric shock) W85
Bumping against, into (accidentally)
  object NEC W22.8
    with fall - *see* Fall, due to, bumping against, object
    caused by crowd or human stampede (with fall) W52
    sports equipment W21.9
  person(s) W51
    with fall W03
      due to ice or snow W00.0
    assault Y04.2
    caused by, a crowd or human stampede (with fall) W52
    homicide (attempt) Y04.2
  sports equipment W21.9
Burn, burned, burning (accidental) (by) (from) (on)
  acid NEC - *see* Table of drugs and chemicals
  bed linen - *see* Exposure, fire, uncontrolled, in building, bed
  blowtorch X08.8
    with ignition of clothing NEC X06.2
    nightwear X05
  bonfire, campfire (controlled) - *see also* Exposure, fire, controlled, not in building
    uncontrolled - *see* Exposure, fire, uncontrolled, not in building
  candle X08.8
    with ignition of clothing NEC X06.2
    nightwear X05
  caustic liquid, substance (external) (internal) NEC - *see* Table of drugs and chemicals

Burn, burned, burning *(Continued)*
  chemical (external) (internal) - *see also* Table of drugs and chemicals
    in war operations - *see* War operations, fire
  cigar(s) or cigarette(s) X08.8
    with ignition of clothing NEC X06.2
    nightwear X05
  clothes, clothing NEC (from controlled fire) X06.2
    with conflagration - *see* Exposure, fire, uncontrolled, building
    not in building or structure - *see* Exposure, fire, uncontrolled, not in building
  cooker (hot) X15.8
    stated as undetermined whether accidental or intentional Y27.3
    suicide (attempt) X77.3
  electric blanket X16
  engine (hot) X17
  fire, flames - *see* Exposure, fire
  flare, Very pistol - *see* Discharge, firearm NEC
  heat
    from appliance (electrical) (household) X15.8
      cooker X15.8
      hotplate X15.2
      kettle X15.8
      light bulb X15.8
      saucepan X15.3
      skillet X15.3
      stove X15.0
      stated as undetermined whether accidental or intentional Y27.3
      suicide (attempt) X77.3
      toaster X15.1
    in local application or packing during medical or surgical procedure Y63.5
  heating
    appliance, radiator or pipe X16
  homicide (attempt) - *see* Assault, burning
  hot
    air X14.1
    cooker X15.8
    drink X10.0
    engine X17
    fat X10.2
    fluid NEC X12
    food X10.1
    gases X14.1
    heating appliance X16
    household appliance NEC X15.8
    kettle X15.8
    liquid NEC X12
    machinery X17
    metal (molten) (liquid) NEC X18
    object (not producing fire or flames) NEC X19
    oil (cooking) X10.2
    pipe(s) X16
    radiator X16
    saucepan (glass) (metal) X15.3
    stove (kitchen) X15.0
    substance NEC X19
      caustic or corrosive NEC - *see* Table of drugs and chemicals
    toaster X15.1
    tool X17
    vapor X13.1
    water (tap) - *see* Contact, with, hot, tap water

Burn, burned, burning (*Continued*)
hotplate X15.2
   suicide (attempt) X77.3
ignition - *see* Ignition
in war operations - *see also* War
   operations, fire
inflicted by other person X97
   by hot objects, hot vapor, and steam
      - *see* Assault, burning, hot object
internal, from swallowed caustic,
   corrosive liquid, substance - *see*
   Table of drugs and chemicals
iron (hot) X15.8
   stated as undetermined whether
      accidental or intentional Y27.3
   suicide (attempt) X77.3
kettle (hot) X15.8
   stated as undetermined whether
      accidental or intentional Y27.3
   suicide (attempt) X77.3
lamp (flame) X08.8
   with ignition of clothing NEC X06.2
      nightwear X05
lighter (cigar) (cigarette) X08.8
   with ignition of clothing NEC X06.2
      nightwear X05
lightning X33
   causing fire - *see* Exposure, fire
liquid (boiling) (hot) NEC X12
   stated as undetermined whether
      accidental or intentional Y27.2
   suicide (attempt) X77.2
local application of externally applied
   substance in medical or surgical
   care Y63.5
on board watercraft
   due to
      accident to watercraft V91.09
         powered craft V91.03
            ferry boat V91.01
            fishing boat V91.02
            jetskis V91.03
            liner V91.01
            merchant ship V91.00
            passenger ship V91.01
         unpowered craft V91.08
            canoe V91.05
            inflatable V91.06
            kayak V91.05
            sailboat V91.04
            surf-board V91.08
            water skis V91.07
            windsurfer V91.08

Burn, burned, burning (*Continued*)
on board watercraft (*Continued*)
   due to (*Continued*)
      fire on board V93.09
         ferry boat V93.01
         fishing boat V93.02
         jetskis V93.03
         liner V93.01
         merchant ship V93.00
         passenger ship V93.01
         powered craft NEC V93.03
         sailboat V93.04
      specified heat source NEC on
         board V93.19
         ferry boat V93.11
         fishing boat V93.12
         jetskis V93.13
         liner V93.11
         merchant ship V93.10
         passenger ship V93.11
         powered craft NEC V93.13
         sailboat V93.14
machinery (hot) X17
matches X08.8
   with ignition of clothing NEC X06.2
      nightwear X05
mattress - *see* Exposure, fire,
   uncontrolled, building, bed
medicament, externally applied Y63.5
metal (hot) (liquid) (molten) NEC X18
nightwear (nightclothes, nightdress,
   gown, pajamas, robe) X05
object (hot) NEC X19
pipe (hot) X16
   smoking X08.8
      with ignition of clothing NEC X06.2
         nightwear X05
powder - *see* Powder burn
radiator (hot) X16
saucepan (hot) (glass) (metal) X15.3
   stated as undetermined whether
      accidental or intentional Y27.3
   suicide (attempt) X77.3
self-inflicted X76
   stated as undetermined whether
      accidental or intentional Y26
steam X13.1
   pipe X16
      stated as undetermined whether
         accidental or intentional Y27.8
   stated as undetermined whether
      accidental or intentional Y27.0
   suicide (attempt) X77.0

Burn, burned, burning (*Continued*)
stove (hot) (kitchen) X15.0
   stated as undetermined whether
      accidental or intentional Y27.3
   suicide (attempt) X77.3
substance (hot) NEC X19
   boiling X12
      stated as undetermined whether
         accidental or intentional Y27.2
      suicide (attempt) X77.2
   molten (metal) X18
suicide (attempt) NEC X76
   hot
      household appliance X77.3
      object X77.9
stated as undetermined whether
   accidental or intentional Y27.0
therapeutic misadventure
   heat in local application or packing
      during medical or surgical
      procedure Y63.5
   overdose of radiation Y63.2
toaster (hot) X15.1
   stated as undetermined whether
      accidental or intentional Y27.3
   suicide (attempt) X77.3
tool (hot) X17
torch, welding X08.8
   with ignition of clothing NEC X06.2
      nightwear X05
trash fire (controlled) - *see* Exposure,
   fire, controlled, not in building
   uncontrolled - *see* Exposure, fire,
      uncontrolled, not in building
vapor (hot) X13.1
   stated as undetermined whether
      accidental or intentional Y27.0
   suicide (attempt) X77.0
Very pistol - *see* Discharge, firearm NEC
Butted by animal W55.89
bull W55.22
cow W55.22
goat W55.32
horse W55.12
pig W55.42
sheep W55.32

C

Caisson disease - *see* Air, pressure, change
Campfire (exposure to) (controlled) - *see*
    also Exposure, fire, controlled, not in
    building
    uncontrolled - *see* Exposure, fire,
        uncontrolled, not in building
Capital punishment (any means)
    Y35.91
Car sickness T75.3
Casualty (not due to war) NEC X58
    war - *see* War operations
Cat
    bite W55.01
    scratch W55.03
Cataclysm, cataclysmic (any injury) NEC
    see Forces of nature
Catching fire - *see* Exposure, fire
Caught
    between
        folding object W23.0
        objects (moving) (stationary and
            moving) W23.0
        and machinery - *see* Contact, with,
            by type of machine
        stationary W23.1
        sliding door and door frame W23.0
    by, in
        machinery (moving parts of) - *see*
            Contact, with, by type of machine
        object NEC W23.2
        washing-machine wringer W23.0
        under packing crate (due to losing grip)
            W23.1
Cave-in caused by cataclysmic earth
    surface movement or eruption - *see*
    Landslide
Change(s) in air pressure - *see* Air, pres-
    sure, change
Choked, choking (on) (any object except
    food or vomitus)
    food (bone) (seed) - *see* categories T17
        and T18
    vomitus - *see* subcategories T17.81,
        T18.81
Civil insurrection - *see* War operations
Cloudburst (any injury) X37.8
Cold, exposure to (accidental) (excessive)
    (extreme) (natural) (place) NEC - *see*
    Exposure, cold
Collapse
    building W20.1
        burning (uncontrolled fire) X00.2
    dam or man-made structure (causing
        earth movement) X36.0
    machinery - *see* Contact, with, by type
        of machine
    structure W20.1
        burning (uncontrolled fire) X00.2
Collision (accidental) NEC (*see* also
    Accident, transport) V89.9
    pedestrian W51
        with fall W03
            due to ice or snow W00.0
            involving pedestrian conveyance
                - *see* Accident, transport,
                pedestrian, conveyance
        and
            crowd or human stampede (with
                fall) W52
            object W22.8
                with fall - *see* Fall, due to,
                    bumping against, object
        person(s) - *see* Collision, pedestrian

Collision *(Continued)*
    transport vehicle NEC V89.9
    and
        avalanche, fallen or not moving
            - *see* Accident, transport
        falling or moving - *see* Landslide
        landslide, fallen or not moving - *see*
            Accident, transport
        falling or moving - *see* Landslide
    due to cataclysm - *see* Forces of
        nature, by type
    intentional, purposeful suicide
        (attempt) - *see* Suicide, collision
Combustion, spontaneous - *see* Ignition
Complication (delayed) of or following
    (medical or surgical procedure) Y84.9
    with misadventure - *see* Misadventure
    amputation of limb(s) Y83.5
    anastomosis (arteriovenous) (blood
        vessel) (gastrojejunal) (tendon)
        (natural or artificial material) Y83.2
    aspiration (of fluid) Y84.4
        tissue Y84.8
    biopsy Y84.8
    blood
        sampling Y84.7
        transfusion
            procedure Y84.8
    bypass Y83.2
    catheterization (urinary) Y84.6
        cardiac Y84.0
    colostomy Y83.3
    cystostomy Y83.3
    dialysis (kidney) Y84.1
    drug - *see* Table of drugs and chemicals
    due to misadventure - *see* Misadventure
    duodenostomy Y83.3
    electroshock therapy Y84.3
    external stoma, creation of Y83.3
    formation of external stoma Y83.3
    gastrostomy Y83.3
    graft Y83.2
    hypothermia (medically-induced)
        Y84.8
    implant, implantation (of)
        artificial
            internal device (cardiac pacemaker)
                (electrodes in brain) (heart
                valve prosthesis) (orthopedic)
                Y83.1
            material or tissue (for anastomosis
                or bypass) Y83.2
                with creation of external stoma
                    Y83.3
            natural tissues (for anastomosis or
                bypass) Y83.2
                with creation of external stoma
                    Y83.3
    infusion
        procedure Y84.8
    injection - *see* Table of drugs and
        chemicals
        procedure Y84.8
    insertion of gastric or duodenal sound
        Y84.5
    insulin-shock therapy Y84.3
    paracentesis (abdominal) (thoracic)
        (aspirative) Y84.4
    procedures other than surgical
        operation - *see* Complication of or
        following, by type of procedure
    radiological procedure or therapy
        Y84.2
    removal of organ (partial) (total) NEC
        Y83.6

Complication *(Continued)*
    sampling
        blood Y84.7
        fluid NEC Y84.4
        tissue Y84.8
    shock therapy Y84.3
    surgical operation NEC (*see* also
        Complication of or following, by
        type of operation) Y83.9
        reconstructive NEC Y83.4
            with
                anastomosis, bypass or graft
                    Y83.2
                formation of external stoma Y83.3
        specified NEC Y83.8
    transfusion - *see* also Table of drugs and
        chemicals
        procedure Y84.8
    transplant, transplantation (heart)
        (kidney) (liver) (whole organ, any)
        Y83.0
        partial organ Y83.4
    ureterostomy Y83.3
    vaccination- *see* also Table of drugs and
        chemicals
        procedure Y84.8
Compression
    divers' squeeze - *see* Air, pressure, change
    trachea by
        food (lodged in esophagus) - *see*
            categories T17 and T18
        vomitus (lodged in esophagus) - *see*
            subcategories T17.81, T18.81
Conflagration - *see* Exposure, fire,
    uncontrolled
Contact (accidental)
    with
        abrasive wheel (metalworking) W31.1
        alligator
            bite W58.01
            crushing W58.03
            strike W58.02
        amphibian W62.9
            frog W62.0
            toad W62.1
        animal (nonvenomous) NEC W64
            marine W56.89
                bite W56.81
                dolphin - *see* Contact, with,
                    dolphin
                fish NEC - *see* Contact, with, fish
                mammal - *see* Contact, with,
                    mammal, marine
                orca - *see* Contact, with, orca
                sea lion - *see* Contact, with, sea
                    lion
                shark - *see* Contact, with, shark
                strike W56.82
        animate mechanical force NEC W64
        arrow W21.89
            not thrown, projected or falling
                W45.8
        arthropods (nonvenomous) W57
        axe W27.0
        band-saw (industrial) W31.2
        bayonet - *see* Bayonet wound
        bee(s) X58
        bench-saw (industrial) W31.2
        bird W61.99
            bite W61.91
            chicken - *see* Contact, with, chicken
            duck - *see* Contact, with, duck
            goose - *see* Contact, with, goose
            macaw - *see* Contact, with, macaw
            parrot - *see* Contact, with, parrot

Contact *(Continued)*
with *(Continued)*
bird *(Continued)*
psittacine - *see* Contact, with, psittacine
strike W61.92
turkey - *see* Contact, with, turkey
blender W29.0
boiling water X12
stated as undetermined whether accidental or intentional Y27.2
suicide (attempt) X77.2
bore, earth-drilling or mining (land) (seabed) W31.0
buffalo - *see* Contact, with, hoof stock NEC
bull W55.29
bite W55.21
strike W55.22
bumper cars W31.81
camel - *see* Contact, with, hoof stock NEC
can
lid W45.2
opener W27.5
powered W29.0
cat W55.09
bite W55.01
scratch W55.03
caterpillar (venomous) X58
centipede (venomous) X58
chain
hoist W24.0
agricultural operations W30.89
saw W29.3
chicken W61.39
peck W61.33
strike W61.32
chisel W27.0
circular saw W31.2
cobra X58
combine (harvester) W30.0
conveyer belt W24.1
cooker (hot) X15.8
stated as undetermined whether accidental or intentional Y27.3
suicide (attempt) X77.3
coral X58
cotton gin W31.82
cow W55.29
bite W55.21
strike W55.22
crane W24.0
agricultural operations W30.89
crocodile
bite W58.11
crushing W58.13
strike W58.12
dagger W26.1
stated as undetermined whether accidental or intentional Y28.2
suicide (attempt) X78.2
dairy equipment W31.82
dart W21.89
not thrown, projected or falling W45.8
deer - *see* Contact, with, hoof stock NEC
derrick W24.0
agricultural operations W30.89
hay W30.2

Contact *(Continued)*
with *(Continued)*
dog W54.8
bite W54.0
strike W54.1
dolphin W56.09
bite W56.01
strike W56.02
donkey - *see* Contact, with, hoof stock NEC
drill (powered) W29.8
earth (land) (seabed) W31.0
nonpowered W27.8
drive belt W24.0
agricultural operations W30.89
dry ice - *see* Exposure, cold, man-made
dryer (spin) (clothes) (powered) W29.2
duck W61.69
bite W61.61
strike W61.62
earth(-)
drilling machine (industrial) W31.0
scraping machine in stationary use W31.83
edge of stiff paper W45.1
electric
beater W29.0
blanket X16
fan W29.2
commercial W31.82
knife W29.1
mixer W29.0
elevator (building) W24.0
agricultural operations W30.89
grain W30.3
engine(s), hot NEC X17
excavating machine W31.0
farm machine W30.9
feces - *see* Contact, with, by type of animal
fer de lance X58
fish W56.59
bite W56.51
shark - *see* Contact, with, shark
strike W56.52
flying horses W31.81
forging (metalworking) machine W31.1
fork W27.5
forklift (truck) W24.0
agricultural operations W30.89
frog W62.0
garden
cultivator (powered) W29.3
riding W30.89
fork W27.1
gas turbine W31.3
Gila monster X58
giraffe - *see* Contact, with, hoof stock NEC
glass (sharp) (broken) W25
with subsequent fall W18.02
assault X99.0
due to fall - *see* Fall, by type
stated as undetermined whether accidental or intentional Y28. 0
suicide (attempt) X78.0
goat W55.39
bite W55.31
strike W55.32

Contact *(Continued)*
with *(Continued)*
goose W61.59
bite W61.51
strike W61.52
hand
saw W27.0
tool (not powered) NEC W27.8
powered W29.8
harvester W30.0
hay-derrick W30.2
heat NEC X19
from appliance (electrical) (household) - *see* Contact, with, hot, household appliance
heating appliance X16
heating
appliance (hot) X16
pad (electric) X16
hedge-trimmer (powered) W29.3
hoe W27.1
hoist (chain) (shaft) NEC W24.0
agricultural W30.89
hoof stock NEC W55.39
bite W55.31
strike W55.32
hornet(s) X58
horse W55.19
bite W55.11
strike W55.12
hot
air X14.1
inhalation X14.0
cooker X15.8
drinks X10.0
engine X17
fats X10.2
fluids NEC X12
assault X98.2
suicide (attempt) X77.2
undetermined whether accidental or intentional Y27.2
food X10.1
gases X14.1
inhalation X14.0
heating appliance X16
household appliance X15.8
assault X98.3
cooker X15.8
hotplate X15.2
kettle X15.8
light bulb X15.8
object NEC X19
assault X98.8
stated as undetermined whether accidental or intentional Y27.9
suicide (attempt) X77.8
saucepan X15.3
skillet X15.3
stove X15.0
stated as undetermined whether accidental or intentional Y27.3
suicide (attempt) X77.3
toaster X15.1
kettle X15.8
light bulb X15.8
liquid NEC (*see also* Burning) X12
drinks X10.0
stated as undetermined whether accidental or intentional Y27.2
suicide (attempt) X77.2

Contact *(Continued)*
  with *(Continued)*
    hot *(Continued)*
      liquid NEC *(Continued)*
        tap water X11.8
          stated as undetermined
            whether accidental or
              intentional Y27.1
          suicide (attempt) X77.1
      machinery X17
      metal (molten) (liquid) NEC X18
      object (not producing fire or
        flames) NEC X19
      oil (cooking) X10.2
      pipe X16
      plate X15.2
      radiator X16
      saucepan (glass) (metal) X15.3
      skillet X15.3
      stove (kitchen) X15.0
      substance NEC X19
      tap-water X11.8
        assault X98.1
        heated on stove X12
          stated as undetermined
            whether accidental or
              intentional Y27.2
          suicide (attempt) X77.2
        in bathtub X11.0
        running X11.1
          stated as undetermined whether
            accidental or intentional Y27.1
          suicide (attempt) X77.1
      toaster X15.1
      tool X17
      vapors X13.1
        inhalation X13.0
      water (tap) X11.8
        boiling X12
          stated as undetermined
            whether accidental or
              intentional Y27.2
          suicide (attempt) X77.2
        heated on stove X12
          stated as undetermined
            whether accidental or
              intentional Y27.2
          suicide (attempt) X77.2
        in bathtub X11.0
        running X11.1
          stated as undetermined whether
            accidental or intentional
              Y27.1
          suicide (attempt) X77.1
    hotplate X15.2
    ice-pick W27.5
    insect (nonvenomous) NEC W57
    kettle (hot) X15.8
    knife W26.0
      assault X99.1
      electric W29.1
      stated as undetermined whether
        accidental or intentional
          Y28.1
      suicide (attempt) X78.1
    lathe (metalworking) W31.1
      turnings W45.8
      woodworking W31.2
    lawnmower (powered) (ridden) W28
      causing electrocution W86.8
      suicide (attempt) X83.1
      unpowered W27.1
    lift, lifting (devices) W24.0
      agricultural operations W30.89
      shaft W24.0

Contact *(Continued)*
  with *(Continued)*
    liquefied gas - *see* Exposure, cold,
      man-made
    liquid air, hydrogen, nitrogen - *see*
      Exposure, cold, man-made
    lizard (nonvenomous) W59.09
      bite W59.01
      strike W59.02
    llama - *see* Contact, with, hoof stock
      NEC
    macaw W61.19
      bite W61.11
      strike W61.12
    machine, machinery W31.9
      abrasive wheel W31.1
      agricultural including
        animal-powered W30.9
        combine harvester W30.0
        grain storage elevator W30.3
        hay derrick W30.2
        power take-off device W30.1
        reaper W30.0
        specified NEC W30.89
        thresher W30.0
        transport vehicle, stationary
          W30.81
      band saw W31.2
      bench saw W31.2
      circular saw W31.2
      commercial NEC W31.82
      drilling, metal (industrial) W31.1
      earth-drilling W31.0
      earthmoving or scraping W31.89
      excavating W31.89
      forging machine W31.1
      gas turbine W31.3
      hot X17
      internal combustion engine
        W31.3
      land drill W31.0
      lathe W31.1
      lifting (devices) W24.0
      metal drill W31.1
      metalworking (industrial) W31.1
      milling, metal W31.1
      mining W31.0
      molding W31.2
      overhead plane W31.2
      power press, metal W31.1
      prime mover W31.3
      printing W31.89
      radial saw W31.2
      recreational W31.81
      roller-coaster W31.81
      rolling mill, metal W31.1
      sander W31.2
      seabed drill W31.0
      shaft
        hoist W31.0
        lift W31.0
      specified NEC W31.89
      spinning W31.89
      steam engine W31.3
      transmission W24.1
      undercutter W31.0
      water driven turbine W31.3
      weaving W31.89
      woodworking or forming
        (industrial) W31.2
    mammal (feces) (urine) W55.89
      bull - *see* Contact, with, bull
      cat - *see* Contact, with, cat
      cow - *see* Contact, with, cow
      goat - *see* Contact, with, goat

Contact *(Continued)*
  with *(Continued)*
    mammal *(Continued)*
      hoof stock - *see* Contact, with, hoof
        stock
      horse - *see* Contact, with, horse
      marine W56.39
        dolphin - *see* Contact, with,
          dolphin
        orca - *see* Contact, with, orca
        sea lion - *see* Contact, with, sea lion
        specified NEC W56.39
          bite W56.31
          strike W56.32
      pig - *see* Contact, with, pig
      raccoon - *see* Contact, with, raccoon
      rodent - *see* Contact, with, rodent
      sheep - *see* Contact, with, sheep
      specified NEC W55.89
        bite W55.81
        strike W55.82
    marine
      animal W56.89
        bite W56.81
        dolphin - *see* Contact, with,
          dolphin
        fish NEC - *see* Contact, with, fish
        mammal - *see* Contact, with,
          mammal, marine
        orca - *see* Contact, with, orca
        sea lion - *see* Contact, with, sea lion
        shark - *see* Contact, with, shark
        strike W56.82
    meat
      grinder (domestic) W29.0
        industrial W31.82
        nonpowered W27.5
      slicer (domestic) W29.0
        industrial W31.82
    merry go round W31.81
    metal (hot) (liquid) (molten) NEC X18
    millipede W57
    nail W45.0
      gun W29.4
    needle (sewing) W27.4
      hypodermic W46.0
        contaminated W46.1
    object (blunt) NEC
      hot NEC X19
      legal intervention - *see* Legal,
        intervention, blunt object
      sharp NEC W45.8
        inflicted by other person NEC
          W45.8
          stated as
            intentional homicide (attempt)
              - *see* Assault, cutting or
                piercing instrument
          legal intervention - *see* Legal,
            intervention, sharp object
          self-inflicted X78.9
    orca W56.29
      bite W56.21
      strike W56.22
    overhead plane W31.2
    paper (as sharp object) W45.1
    paper-cutter W27.6
    parrot W61.09
      bite W61.01
      strike W61.02
    pig W55.49
      bite W55.41
      strike W55.42
    pipe, hot X16
    pitchfork W27.1

Contact *(Continued)*
  with *(Continued)*
    plane (metal) (wood) W27.0
      overhead W31.2
    plant thorns, spines, sharp leaves or
      other mechanisms W60
    powered
      garden cultivator W29.3
      household appliance, implement,
        or machine W29.8
      saw (industrial) W31.2
        hand W29.8
    printing machine W31.89
    psittacine bird W61.29
      bite W61.21
      macaw - *see* Contace, with, macaw
      parrot - *see* Contact, with, parrot
      strike W61.22
    pulley (block) (transmission) W24.0
      agricultural operations W30.89
    raccoon W55.59
      bite W55.51
      strike W55.52
    radial-saw (industrial) W31.2
    radiator (hot) X16
    rake W27.1
    rattlesnake X58
    reaper W30.0
    reptile W59.89
      lizard - *see* Contact, with, lizard
      snake - *see* Contact, with, snake
      specified NEC W59.89
        bite W59.81
        crushing W59.83
        strike W59.82
      turtle - *see* Contact, with, turtle
    rivet gun (powered) W29.4
    road scraper - *see* Accident, transport,
      construction vehicle
    rodent (feces) (urine) W53.89
      bite W53.81
      mouse W53.09
        bite W53.01
      rat W53.19
        bite W53.11
      specified NEC W53.89
        bite W53.81
      squirrel W53.29
        bite W53.21
    roller coaster W31.81
    rope NEC W24.0
      agricultural operations W30.89
    saliva - *see* Contact, with, by type of
      animal
    sander W29.8
      industrial W31.2
    saucepan (hot) (glass) (metal) X15.3
    saw W27.0
      band (industrial) W31.2
      bench (industrial) W31.2
      chain W29.3
      hand W27.0
    sawing machine, metal W31.1
    scissors W27.2
    scorpion X58
    screwdriver W27.0
      powered W29.8
    sea
      anemone, cucumber or urchin
        (spine) X58
      lion W56.19
        bite W56.11
        strike W56.12
    serpent - *see* Contact, with, snake,
      by type

Contact *(Continued)*
  with *(Continued)*
    sewing-machine (electric) (powered)
      W29.2
      not powered W27.8
    shaft (hoist) (lift) (transmission) NEC
      W24.0
      agricultural W30.89
    shark W56.49
      bite W56.41
      strike W56.42
    shears (hand) W27.2
      powered (industrial) W31.1
      domestic W29.2
    sheep W55.39
      bite W55.31
      strike W55.32
    shovel W27.8
      steam - *see* Accident, transport,
        construction vehicle
    snake (nonvenomous) W59.19
      bite W59.11
      crushing W59.13
      strike W59.12
    spade W27.1
    spider (venomous) X58
    spin-drier W29.2
    spinning machine W31.89
    splinter W45.8
    sports equipment W21.9
    staple gun (powered) W29.8
    steam X13.1
      engine W31.3
      inhalation X13.0
      pipe X16
      shovel W31.89
    stove (hot) (kitchen) X15.0
    substance, hot NEC X19
      molten (metal) X18
    sword W26.1
      assault X99.2
      stated as undetermined whether
        accidental or intentional Y28.2
      suicide (attempt) X78.2
    tarantula X58
    thresher W30.0
    tin can lid W45.2
    toad W62.1
    toaster (hot) X15.1
    tool W27.8
      hand (not powered) W27.8
        auger W27.0
        axe W27.0
        can opener W27.5
        chisel W27.0
        fork W27.5
        garden W27.1
        handsaw W27.0
        hoe W27.1
        ice-pick W27.5
        kitchen utensil W27.5
        manual
          lawn mower W27.1
          sewing machine W27.1
        meat grinder W27.5
        needle (sewing) W27.4
          hypodermic (contaminated)
            W27.3
        paper cutter W27.6
        pitchfork W27.1
        rake W27.1
        scissors W27.2
        screwdriver W27.0
        specified NEC W27.8
        workbench W27.0

Contact *(Continued)*
  with *(Continued)*
    tool *(Continued)*
      hot X17
      powered W29.8
        blender W29.0
          commercial W31.82
        can opener W29.0
          commercial W31.82
        chainsaw W29.3
        clothes dryer W29.2
          commercial W31.82
        dishwasher W29.2
          commercial W31.82
        edger W29.3
        electric fan W29.2
          commercial W31.82
        electric knife W29.1
        food processor W29.0
          commercial W31.82
        garbage disposal W29.0
          commercial W31.82
        garden tool W29.3
        hedge trimmer W29.3
        ice maker W29.0
          commercial W31.82
        kitchen appliance W29.0
          commercial W31.82
        lawn mower W28
        meat grinder W29.0
          commercial W31.82
        mixer W29.0
          commercial W31.82
        rototiller W29.3
        sewing machine W29.2
          commercial W31.82
        washing machine W29.2
          commercial W31.82
    transmission device (belt, cable,
      chain, gear, pinion, shaft) W24.1
      agricultural operations W30.89
    turbine (gas) (water-driven) W31.3
    turkey W61.49
      peck W61.43
      strike W61.42
    turtle (nonvenomous) W59.29
      bite W59.21
      strike W59.22
      terrestrial W59.89
        bite W59.81
        crushing W59.83
        strike W59.82
    under-cutter W31.0
    urine - *see* Contact, with, by type of
      animal
    vehicle
      agricultural use (transport)
        - *see* Accident, transport,
        agricultural vehicle
        not on public highway W30.81
      industrial use (transport) - *see*
        Accident, transport, industrial
        vehicle
        not on public highway W31.83
      off-road use (transport) - *see*
        Accident, transport, all-terrain
        or off-road vehicle
        not on public highway W31.83
      special construction use (transport)
        - *see* Accident, transport,
        construction vehicle
        not on public highway W31.83
    venomous
      animal X58
      arthropods X58

Contact *(Continued)*
  with *(Continued)*
    venomous *(Continued)*
      lizard X58
      marine animal NEC X58
      marine plant NEC X58
      millipedes (tropical) X58
      plant(s) X58
      snake X58
      spider X58
      viper X58
      washing-machine (powered) W29.2
      wasp X58
      weaving-machine W31.89
      winch W24.0
        agricultural operations W30.89
      wire NEC W24.0
        agricultural operations W30.89
      wood slivers W45.8
      yellow jacket X58
      zebra - *see* Contact, with, hoof stock
        NEC
Coup de soleil X32
Crash
  aircraft (in transit) (powered) V95.9
    balloon V96.01
    fixed wing NEC (private) V95.21
      commercial V95.31
    glider V96.21
      hang V96.11
      powered V95.11
    helicopter V95.01
    in war operations - *see* War
      operations, destruction of aircraft
    microlight V95.11
    nonpowered V96.9
      specified NEC V96.8

Crash *(Continued)*
  aircraft *(Continued)*
    powered NEC V95.8
    stated as
      homicide (attempt) Y08.81
      suicide (attempt) X83.0
    ultralight V95.11
  spacecraft V95.41
  transport vehicle NEC (*see also*
    Accident, transport) V89.9
    homicide (attempt) Y03.8
    motor NEC (traffic) V89.2
      homicide (attempt) Y03.8
    suicide (attempt) - *see* Suicide,
      collision
Cruelty (mental) (physical) (sexual) X58
Crushed (accidentally) X58
  between objects (moving) (stationary
    and moving) W23.0
    stationary W23.1
  by
    alligator W58.03
    avalanche NEC - *see* Landslide
    cave-in W20.0
      caused by cataclysmic earth surface
        movement - *see* Landslide
    crocodile W58.13
    crowd or human stampede W52
    falling
      aircraft V97.39
        in war operations - *see* War
          operations, destruction of
          aircraft
      earth, material W20.0
        caused by cataclysmic earth surface
          movement - *see* Landslide
      object NEC W20.8

Crushed *(Continued)*
  by *(Continued)*
    landslide NEC - *see* Landslide
    lizard (nonvenomous) W59.09
    machinery - *see* Contact, with, by type
      of machine
    reptile NEC W59.89
    snake (nonvenomous) W59.13
  in
    machinery - *see* Contact, with, by type
      of machine
    object W23.2
Cut, cutting (any part of body) (accidental) - *see also* Contact, with, by object
  or machine
  during medical or surgical treatment as
    misadventure - *see* Misadventure,
    cut, by type of procedure
  homicide (attempt) - *see* Assault, cutting
    or piercing instrument
  inflicted by other person - *see* Assault,
    cutting or piercing instrument
  legal
    execution Y35.91
    intervention - *see* Legal, intervention,
      sharp object
  machine NEC (*see also* Contact, with, by
    type of machine) W31.9
  self-inflicted - *see* Suicide, cutting or
    piercing instrument
  suicide (attempt) - *see* Suicide, cutting
    or piercing instrument
Cyclone (any injury) X37.1

D

Decapitation (accidental circumstances)
  NEC X58
  homicide X99.9
  legal execution (by guillotine) Y35.91
Dehydration from lack of water X58
Deprivation X58
  homicidal intent - *see* Maltreatment
Derailment (accidental)
  railway (rolling stock) (train) (vehicle)
    (without antecedent collision)
    V81.7
    with antecedent collision - *see*
      Accident, transport, railway
      vehicle occupant
  streetcar (without antecedent collision)
    V82.7
    with antecedent collision - *see*
      Accident, transport, streetcar
      occupant
Descent
  parachute (voluntary) (without accident
    to aircraft) V97.29
  due to accident to aircraft - *see*
    Accident, transport, aircraft
Desertion X58
Destitution X58
Disability, late effect or sequela of injury
  - *see* Sequelae
Discharge (accidental)
  airgun W34.010
    assault X95.01
    homicide (attempt) X95.01
    stated as undetermined whether
      accidental or intentional Y24.0
    suicide (attempt) X74.01
  BB gun - *see* Discharge, airgun
  firearm (accidental) W34.00
    assault X95.9
    handgun (pistol) (revolver) W32.0
      assault X93
      homicide (attempt) X93
      legal intervention - *see* Legal,
        intervention, firearm,
        handgun
      stated as undetermined whether
        accidental or intentional
        Y22
      suicide (attempt) X72
    homicide (attempt) X95.9
    hunting rifle W33.02
      assault X94.1
      homicide (attempt) X94.1
      legal intervention Y35.034
        injuring
          bystander Y35.033
          law enforcement personnel
            Y35.032
          suspect Y35.031
      stated as undetermined whether
        accidental or intentional
        Y23.1
      suicide (attempt) X73.1
    larger W33.00
      assault X94.9
      homicide (attempt) X94.9
      hunting rifle - *see* Discharge,
        firearm, hunting rifle
      legal intervention - *see* Legal,
        intervention, firearm by type
        of firearm
      machine gun - *see* Discharge,
        firearm, machine gun

Discharge *(Continued)*
  firearm *(Continued)*
    larger *(Continued)*
      shotgun - *see* Discharge, firearm,
        shotgun
      specified NEC W33.09
        assault X94.8
        homicide (attempt) X94.8
        legal intervention Y35.094
          injuring
            bystander Y35.093
            law enforcement personnel
              Y35.092
            suspect Y35.091
        stated as undetermined whether
          accidental or intentional
          Y23.8
        suicide (attempt) X73.8
      stated as undetermined whether
        accidental or intentional
        Y23.9
      suicide (attempt) X73.9
    legal intervention Y35.004
      injuring
        bystander Y35.003
        law enforcement personnel
          Y35.002
        suspect Y35.001
      using rubber bullet Y35.044
        injuring
          bystander Y35.043
          law enforcement personnel
            Y35.042
          suspect Y35.041
    machine gun W33.03
      assault X94.2
      homicide (attempt) X94.2
      legal intervention - *see* Legal,
        intervention, firearm, machine
        gun
      stated as undetermined whether
        accidental or intentional Y23.3
      suicide (attempt) X73.2
    pellet gun - *see* Discharge, airgun
    shotgun W33.01
      assault X94.0
      homicide (attempt) X94.0
      legal intervention - *see* Legal,
        intervention, firearm, specified
        NEC
      stated as undetermined whether
        accidental or intentional Y23.0
      suicide (attempt) X73.0
    specified NEC W34.09
      assault X95.8
      homicide (attempt) X95.8
      legal intervention - *see* Legal,
        intervention, firearm, specified
        NEC
      stated as undetermined whether
        accidental or intentional Y24.8
      suicide (attempt) X74.8
      stated as undetermined whether
        accidental or intentional Y24.9
    suicide (attempt) X74.9
    Very pistol W34.09
      assault X95.8
      homicide (attempt) X95.8
      stated as undetermined whether
        accidental or intentional Y24.8
      suicide (attempt) X74.8
  firework(s) W39
    stated as undetermined whether
      accidental or intentional Y25

Discharge *(Continued)*
  gas-operated gun NEC W34.018
    airgun - *see* Discharge, airgun
    assault X95.09
    homicide (attempt) X95.09
    paintball gun - *see* Discharge,
      paintball gun
    stated as undetermined whether
      accidental or intentional Y24.8
    suicide (attempt) X74.09
  gun NEC - *see also* Discharge, firearm
    NEC
    air - *see* Discharge, airgun
    BB - *see* Discharge, airgun
    for single hand use - *see* Discharge,
      firearm, handgun
    hand - *see* Discharge, firearm,
      handgun
    machine - *see* Discharge, firearm,
      machine gun
    other specified - *see* Discharge,
      firearm NEC
    paintball - *see* Discharge, paintball
      gun
    pellet - *see* Discharge, airgun
  handgun - *see* Discharge, firearm,
    handgun
  machine gun - *see* Discharge, firearm,
    machine gun
  paintball gun W34.011
    assault X95.02
    homicide (attempt) X95.02
    stated as undetermined whether
      accidental or intentional
      Y24.8
    suicide (attempt) X74.02
  pistol - *see* Discharge, firearm, handgun
    flare - *see* Discharge, firearm, Very
      pistol
    pellet - *see* Discharge, airgun
    Very - *see* Discharge, firearm, Very
      pistol
  revolver - *see* Discharge, firearm,
    handgun
  rifle (hunting) - *see* Discharge, firearm,
    hunting rifle
  shotgun - *see* Discharge, firearm,
    shotgun
  spring-operated gun NEC W34.018
    assault X95.09
    homicide (attempt) X95.09
    stated as undetermined whether
      accidental or intentional Y24.8
    suicide (attempt) X74.09
Disease
  Andes W94.11
  aviator's - *see* Air, pressure
  range W94.11
Diver's disease, palsy, paralysis, squeeze
  - *see* Air, pressure
Diving (into water) - *see* Accident, diving
Dog bite W54.0
Dragged by transport vehicle NEC (*see
  also* Accident, transport) V09.9
Drinking poison (accidental) - *see* Table of
  drugs and chemicals
Dropped (accidentally) **while being carried
  or supported by other person** W04
Drowning (accidental) W74
  assault X92.9
  due to
    accident (to)
      machinery - *see* Contact, with, by
        type of machine

Drowning *(Continued)*
  in *(Continued)*
    natural water *(Continued)*
      stated as undetermined whether
        accidental or intentional
        Y21.4
      suicide (attempt) X71.3
    quarry - *see* Drowning, in, specified
      place NEC
    quenching tank - *see* Drowning, in,
      specified place NEC
    reservoir - *see* Drowning, in, specified
      place NEC
    river - *see* Drowning, in, natural
      water
    sea - *see* Drowning, in, natural water
    specified place NEC W73
      assault X92.8
      following
        dive or jump W16.811
          striking
            bottom W16.821
            wall W16.831

Drowning *(Continued)*
  in *(Continued)*
    specified place *(Continued)*
      following *(Continued)*
        fall W16.311
          striking
            bottom W16.321
            wall W16.331
      stated as undetermined whether
        accidental or intentional
        Y21.8
      suicide (attempt) X71.8
    stream - *see* Drowning, in, natural
      water
    swimming-pool W67
      assault X92.1
        following fall X92.2
      following
        dive or jump W16.511
          striking
            bottom W16.521
            wall W16.531

Drowning *(Continued)*
  in *(Continued)*
    swimming-pool *(Continued)*
      following *(Continued)*
        fall W16.011
          striking
            bottom W16.021
            wall W16.031
      stated as undetermined whether
        accidental or intentional Y21.2
      following fall Y21.3
      suicide (attempt) X71.1
        following fall X71.2
    war operations - *see* War operations,
      restriction of airway
  resulting from accident to watercraft
    - *see* Drowning, due to, accident,
    watercraft
  self-inflicted X71.9
  stated as undetermined whether
    accidental or intentional Y21.9
  suicide (attempt) X71.9

E

Earth (surface) movement NEC - *see*
    Forces of nature, earth movement
Earth falling (on) W20.0
    caused by cataclysmic earth surface
        movement or eruption - *see*
        Landslide
Earthquake (any injury) X34
Effect(s) (adverse) of
    air pressure (any) - *see* Air, pressure
    cold, excessive (exposure to) - *see*
        Exposure, cold
    heat (excessive) - *see* Heat
    hot place (weather) - *see* Heat
    insolation X30
    late - *see* Sequelae
    motion - *see* Motion
    nuclear explosion or weapon in war
        operations - *see* War operations,
        nuclear weapon
    radiation - *see* Radiation
    travel - *see* Travel
Electric shock (accidental) (by) (in) - *see*
    Exposure, electric current
Electrocution (accidental) - *see* Exposure,
    electric current
Endotracheal tube wrongly placed dur-
    ing anesthetic procedure Y65.3
Entanglement
    in
        bed linen, causing suffocation - *see*
           category T71
        wheel of pedal cycle V19.88
Entry of foreign body or material - *see*
    Foreign body
Environmental pollution related condi-
    tion - *see* Z57, Z58
Execution, legal (any method) Y35.91
Exhaustion
    cold - *see* Exposure, cold
    due to excessive exertion - *see*
        Overexertion
    heat - *see* Heat
Explosion (accidental) (of) (with second-
    ary fire) W40.9
    acetylene W40.1
    aerosol can W36.1
    air tank (compressed) (in machinery)
        W36.2
    aircraft (in transit) (powered) NEC
        V95.9
        balloon V96.05
        fixed wing NEC (private) V95.25
           commercial V95.35
        glider V96.25
           hang V96.15
           powered V95.15
        helicopter V95.05
        in war operations - *see* War operations,
           destruction of aircraft
        microlight V95.15
        nonpowered V96.9
           specified NEC V96.8
        powered NEC V95.8
        stated as
           homicide (attempt) Y03.8
           suicide (attempt) X83.0
        ultralight V95.15
    anesthetic gas in operating room
        W40.1
    antipersonnel bomb W40.8
        assault X96.0
        homicide (attempt) X96.0
        suicide (attempt) X75

Explosion *(Continued)*
    assault X96.9
    bicycle tire W37.0
    blasting (cap) (materials) W40.0
    boiler (machinery), not on transport
        vehicle W35
        on watercraft - *see* Explosion, in,
           watercraft
    butane W40.1
    caused by other person X96.9
    coal gas W40.1
    detonator W40.0
    dump (munitions) W40.8
    dynamite W40.0
        in
           assault X96.8
           homicide (attempt) X96.8
           legal intervention Y35.114
               injuring
                   bystander Y35.113
                   law enforcement personnel
                      Y35.112
                   suspect Y35.111
           suicide (attempt) X75
    explosive (material) W40.9
        gas W40.1
        in blasting operation W40.0
        specified NEC W40.8
           in
              assault X96.8
              homicide (attempt) X96.8
              legal intervention Y35.194
                  injuring
                     bystander Y35.193
                     law enforcement personnel
                      Y35.192
                   suspect Y35.191
             suicide (attempt) X75
    factory (munitions) W40.8
    fertilizer bomb W40.8
        assault X96.3
        homicide (attempt) X96.3
        suicide (attempt) X75
    firearm (parts) NEC W34.19
        airgun W34.110
        BB gun W34.110
        gas, air or spring-operated gun NEC
           W34.118
        handgun W32.1
        hunting rifle W33.12
        larger firearm W33.10
           specified NEC W33.19
        machine gun W33.13
        paintball gun W34.111
        pellet gun W34.110
        shotgun W33.11
        Very pistol [flare] W34.19
    fire-damp W40.1
    fireworks W39
    gas (coal) (explosive) W40.1
        cylinder W36.9
           aerosol can W36.1
           air tank W36.2
           pressurized W36.3
           specified NEC W36.8
    gasoline (fumes) (tank) not in moving
        motor vehicle W40.1
        bomb W40.8
           assault X96.1
           homicide (attempt) X96.1
           suicide (attempt) X75
        in motor vehicle - *see* Accident,
           transport, by type of
           vehicle
    grain store W40.8

Explosion *(Continued)*
    grenade W40.8
        in
           assault X96.8
           homicide (attempt) X96.8
           legal intervention Y35.194
               injuring
                   bystander Y35.193
                   law enforcement personnel
                      Y35.192
                   suspect Y35.191
           suicide (attempt) X75
    handgun (parts) - *see* Explosion,
        firearm, handgun (parts)
    homicide (attempt) X96.9
        antipersonnel bomb - *see* Explosion,
           antipersonnel bomb
        fertilizer bomb - *see* Explosion,
           fertilizer bomb
        gasoline bomb - *see* Explosion,
           gasoline bomb
        letter bomb - *see* Explosion, letter
           bomb
        pipe bomb - *see* Explosion, pipe
           bomb
        specified NEC X96.8
    hose, pressurized W37.8
    hot water heater, tank (in machinery)
        W35
        on watercraft - *see* Explosion, in,
           watercraft
    in, on
        dump W40.8
        factory W40.8
        mine (of explosive gases) NEC
           W40.1
        watercraft V93.59
           powered craft V93.53
              ferry boat V93.51
              fishing boat V93.52
              jetskis V93.53
              liner V93.51
              merchant ship V93.50
              passenger ship V93.51
              sailboat V93.54
    letter bomb W40.8
        assault X96.2
        homicide (attempt) X96.2
        suicide (attempt) X75
    machinery - *see also* Contact, with, by
        type of machine
        on board watercraft - *see* Explosion,
           in, watercraft
        pressure vessel - *see* Explosion, by
           type of vessel
    methane W40.1
    mine W40.1
    missile NEC W40.8
    mortar bomb W40.8
        in
           assault X96.8
           homicide (attempt) X96.8
           legal intervention Y35.194
               injuring
                   bystander Y35.193
                   law enforcement personnel
                      Y35.192
                   suspect Y35.191
           suicide (attempt) X75
    munitions (dump) (factory) W40.8
    pipe, pressurized W37.8
        bomb W40.8
        assault X96.4
        homicide (attempt) X96.4
        suicide (attempt) X75

Explosion *(Continued)*
  pressure, pressurized
    cooker W38
    gas tank (in machinery) W36.3
    hose W37.8
    pipe W37.8
    specified device NEC W38
    tire W37.8
      bicycle W37.0
    vessel (in machinery) W38
  propane W40.1
  self-inflicted X75
  shell (artillery) NEC W40.8
    during war operations - *see* War
        operations, explosion
    in
      legal intervention Y35.124
        injuring
          bystander Y35.123
          law enforcement personnel
              Y35.122
          suspect Y35.121
      war - *see* War operations, explosion
  spacecraft V95.45
  steam or water lines (in machinery)
      W37.8
  stove W40.9
  stated as undetermined whether
      accidental or intentional Y25
  suicide (attempt) X75
  tire, pressurized W37.8
    bicycle W37.0
  undetermined whether accidental or
      intentional Y25
  vehicle tire NEC W37.8
    bicycle W37.0
  war operations - *see* War operations,
      explosion
Exposure (to) X58
  air pressure change - *see* Air, pressure
  cold (accidental) (excessive) (extreme)
      (natural) (place) X31
    assault Y08.89
    due to
      man-made conditions W93.8
        dry ice (contact) W93.01
          inhalation W93.02
        liquid air (contact) (hydrogen)
            (nitrogen) W93.11
          inhalation W93.12
        refrigeration unit (deep freeze)
            W93.2
        suicide (attempt) X83.2
        weather (conditions) X31
    homicide (attempt) Y08.89
    self-inflicted X83.2
  due to abandonment or neglect X58
  electric current W86.8
    appliance (faulty) W86.8
      domestic W86.0
    caused by other person Y08.89
    conductor (faulty) W86.1
    control apparatus (faulty) W86.1
    electric power generating plant,
        distribution station W86.1
    electroshock gun - *see* Exposure,
        electric current, taser
    high-voltage cable W85
    homicide (attempt) Y08.89
    legal execution Y35.91
    lightning X33
    live rail W86.8
    misadventure in medical or surgical
        procedure in electroshock
        therapy Y63.4

Exposure *(Continued)*
  electric current *(Continued)*
    motor (electric) (faulty) W86.8
      domestic W86.0
    self-inflicted X83.1
    specified NEC W86.8
      domestic W86.0
    stun gun - *see* Exposure, electric
        current, taser
    suicide (attempt) X83.1
    taser W86.8
      assault Y08.89
      legal intervention Y35.89-
      self-harm (intentional) X83.8
      undetermined intent Y33
    third rail W86.8
    transformer (faulty) W86.1
    transmission lines W85
  environmental tobacco smoke X58
  excessive
    cold - *see* Exposure, cold
    heat (natural) NEC X30
      man-made W92
  factor(s) NOS X58
    environmental NEC X58
      man-made NEC W99
      natural NEC - *see* Forces of nature
    specified NEC X58
  fire, flames (accidental) X08.8
    assault X97
    campfire - *see* Exposure, fire,
        controlled, not in building
    controlled (in)
      with ignition (of) clothing (*see* also
          Ignition, clothes) X06.2
        nightwear X05
      bonfire - *see* Exposure, fire,
          controlled, not in building
      brazier (in building or structure)
          - *see* also Exposure, fire,
          controlled, building
        not in building or structure - *see*
            Exposure, fire, controlled,
            not in building
      building or structure X02.0
        with
          fall from building X02.3
          injury due to building collapse
              X02.2
          from building X02.5
          smoke inhalation X02.1
        hit by object from building
            X02.4
        specified mode of injury NEC
            X02.8
      fireplace, furnace or stove - *see*
          Exposure, fire, controlled,
          building
      not in building or structure X03.0
        with
          fall X03.3
          smoke inhalation X03.1
        hit by object X03.4
        specified mode of injury NEC
            X03.8
      trash - *see* Exposure, fire,
          controlled, not in building
    fireplace - *see* Exposure, fire,
        controlled, building
    fittings or furniture (in building or
        structure) (uncontrolled) - *see*
        Exposure, fire, uncontrolled,
        building
    forest (uncontrolled) - *see* Exposure,
        fire, uncontrolled, not in building

Exposure *(Continued)*
  fire, flames *(Continued)*
    grass (uncontrolled) - *see* Exposure,
        fire, uncontrolled, not in
        building
    hay (uncontrolled) - *see* Exposure,
        fire, uncontrolled, not in
        building
    homicide (attempt) X97
    ignition of highly flammable material
        X04
    in, of, on, starting in
      machinery - *see* Contact, with, by
          type of machine
      motor vehicle (in motion) (*see* also
          Accident, transport, occupant
          by type of vehicle) V87.8
        with collision - *see* Collision
      railway rolling stock, train, vehicle
          V81.81
        with collision - *see* Accident,
            transport, railway vehicle
            occupant
      street car (in motion) V82.8
        with collision - *see* Accident,
            transport, streetcar
            occupant
      transport vehicle NEC - *see* also
          Accident, transport
        with collision - *see* Collision
      war operations - *see* also War
          operations, fire
        from nuclear explosion - *see* War
            operation, nuclear weapons
      watercraft (in transit) (not in
          transit) V91.09
    localized-ee Burn, on board
        watercraft, due to, fire on
        board
      powered craft V91.03
        ferry boat V91.01
        fishing boat V91.02
        jet skis V91.03
        liner V91.01
        merchant ship V91.00
        passenger ship V91.01
      unpowered craft V91.08
        canoe V91.05
        inflatable V91.06
        kayak V91.05
        sailboat V91.04
        surf-board V91.08
        waterskis V91.07
        windsurfer V91.08
    lumber (uncontrolled) - *see* Exposure,
        fire, uncontrolled, not in building
    mine (uncontrolled) - *see* Exposure,
        fire, uncontrolled, not in building
    prairie (uncontrolled) - *see* Exposure,
        fire, uncontrolled, not in
        building
    resulting from
      explosion - *see* Explosion
      lightning X08.8
    self-inflicted X76
    specified NEC X08.8
    started by other person X97
    stove - *see* Exposure, fire, controlled,
        building
    stated as undetermined whether
        accidental or intentional Y26
    suicide (attempt) X76
    tunnel (uncontrolled) - *see* Exposure,
        fire, uncontrolled, not in
        building

Exposure *(Continued)*
  fire, flames *(Continued)*
    uncontrolled
      in building or structure X00.0
        with
          fall from building X00.3
          injury due to building collapse
            X00.2
          jump from building X00.5
          smoke inhalation X00.1
        bed X08.00
          due to
            cigarette X08.01
            specified material NEC
              X08.09
        furniture NEC X08.20
          due to
            cigarette X08.21
            specified material NEC
              X08.29
        hit by object from building
          X00.4
        sofa X08.10
          due to
            cigarette X08.11
            specified material NEC
              X08.19
        specified mode of injury NEC
          X00.8
      not in building or structure (any)
        X01.0
        with
          fall X01.3
          smoke inhalation X01.1

Exposure *(Continued)*
  fire, flames *(Continued)*
    uncontrolled *(Continued)*
      not in building or structure
        (Continued)
        hit by object X01.4
        specified mode of injury NEC
          X01.8
      undetermined whether accidental or
        intentional Y26
  forces of nature NEC - *see* Forces of
    nature
  G-forces (abnormal) W49
  gravitational forces (abnormal) W49
  heat (natural) NEC - *see* Heat
  high-pressure jet (hydraulic)
    (pneumatic) W49
  hydraulic jet W49
  inanimate mechanical force W49
  jet, high-pressure (hydraulic)
    (pneumatic) W49
  lightning X33
    causing fire - *see* Exposure, fire
  mechanical forces NEC W49
    animate NEC W64
    inanimate NEC W49
  noise W42.9
    supersonic W42.0
  noxious substance - *see* Table of drugs
    and chemical
  pneumatic jet W49
  prolonged in deep-freeze unit or
    refrigerator W93.2

Exposure *(Continued)*
  radiation - *see* Radiation
  smoke - *see* also Exposure, fire
    tobacco, second hand X58.1
  specified factors NEC X58
  sunlight X32
    man-made (sun lamp) W89.8
      tanning bed W89.1
  supersonic waves W42.0
  transmission line(s), electric W85
  vibration W49
  waves
    infrasound W49
    sound W42.9
    supersonic W42.0
  weather NEC - *see* Forces of nature
External cause status Y99.9
  civilian activity done for financial or
    other compensation Y99.0
  civilian activity done for income or pay
    Y99.0
  hobby not done for income Y99.8
  leisure activity Y99.8
  military activity Y99.1
  off-duty activity of military personnel
    Y99.8
  recreation or sport not for income or
    while a student Y99.8
  specified NEC Y99.8
  student activity Y99.8
  volunteer activity Y99.8

F

Factors, supplemental
  alcohol
    blood level
      less than 20mg/100ml Y90.0
      presence in blood, level not
        specified Y90.9
      20-39mg/100ml Y90.1
      40-59mg/100ml Y90.2
      60-79mg/100ml Y90.3
      80-99mg/100ml Y90.4
      100-119mg/100ml Y90.5
      120-199mg/100ml Y90.6
      200-239mg/100ml Y90.7
      240mg/100ml or more Y90.8
      presence in blood, but level not
        specified Y90.9
  environmental-pollution-related
    condition - *see* Z57, Z58
  nosocomial condition Y95
  work-related condition - use Y3 with
    extension 2

Failure
  in suture or ligature during surgical
    procedure Y65.2
  mechanical, of instrument or apparatus
    (any) (during any medical or
    surgical procedure) Y65.8
  sterile precautions (during medical and
    surgical care) - *see* Misadventure,
    failure, sterile precautions, by type
    of procedure
  to
    introduce tube or instrument Y65.4
    endotracheal tube during
      anesthesia Y65.3
    make curve (transport vehicle) NEC
      - *see* Accident, transport
    remove tube or instrument Y65.4

Fall, falling (accidental) W19
  building W20.1
    burning (uncontrolled fire) X00.3
  down
    embankment W17.8
    escalator W10.0
    hill W17.8
    ladder W11
    ramp W10.3
    stairs, steps W10.9
  due to
    bumping against
      object W18.00
        sharp glass W18.02
        specified NEC W18.09
        sports equipment W18.01
      person W03
        due to ice or snow W00.0
        on pedestrian conveyance
          - *see* Accident, transport,
          pedestrian, conveyance
    collision with another person W03
      due to ice or snow W00.0
      involving pedestrian conveyance
        - *see* Accident, transport,
        pedestrian, conveyance
    ice or snow W00.9
      from one level to another W00.2
      on stairs or steps W00.1
      involving pedestrian conveyance
        - *see* Accident, transport,
        pedestrian, conveyance
      on same level W00.0
    slipping (on moving sidewalk)
      W01.0

Fall, falling (Continued)
  due to (Continued)
    slipping (Continued)
      with subsequent striking against
        object W01.10
        furniture W01.190
        sharp object W01.119
          glass W01.110
          power tool or machine
            W01.111
          specified NEC W01.118
        specified NEC W01.198
    striking against
      object W18.00
        sharp glass W18.02
        specified NEC W18.09
        sports equipment W18.01
      person W03
        due to ice or snow W00.0
        on pedestrian conveyance
          - *see* Accident, transport,
          pedestrian, conveyance
  earth (with asphyxia or suffocation (by
    pressure)) - *see* Earth, falling
  from, off
    aircraft NEC (with accident to aircraft
      NEC) V97.0
      while boarding or alighting V97.1
    balcony W13.0
    bed W06
    boat, ship, watercraft NEC (with
      drowning or submersion) - *see*
      Drowning, due to, fall overboard
      with hitting bottom or object V94.0
    bridge W13.1
    building W13.9
      burning (uncontrolled fire) X00.3
    cavity W17.2
    chair W07
    cliff W15
    dock W17.4
    embankment W17.8
    escalator W10.0
    flagpole W13.8
    furniture NEC W08
    haystack W17.8
    high place NEC W17.8
      stated as undetermined whether
        accidental or intentional Y30
    hole W17.2
    incline W10.3
    ladder W11
    machine, machinery - *see* also
      Contact, with, by type of
      machine
    not in operation W17.8
    manhole W17.1
    one level to another NEC W17.8
      intentional, purposeful, suicide
        (attempt) X80
      stated as undetermined whether
        accidental or intentional Y30
    pit W17.2
    playground equipment W09.8
      jungle gym W09.2
      slide W09.0
      swing W09.1
    quarry W17.8
    railing W13.9
    ramp W10.3
    roof W13.2
    scaffolding W12
    stairs, steps W10.9
      curb W10.1
      due to ice or snow W00.1

Fall, falling (Continued)
  from, off (Continued)
    stairs, steps (Continued)
      escalator W10.0
      incline W10.3
      ramp W10.3
      sidewalk curb W10.1
      specified NEC W10.8
    stepladder W11
    storm drain W17.1
    streetcar NEC V82.6
      with antecedent collision - *see*
        Accident, transport, streetcar
        occupant
      while boarding or alighting V82.4
    structure NEC W13.8
      burning (uncontrolled fire) X00.3
    table W08
    toilet W18.11
      with subsequent striking against
        object W18.12
    train NEC V81.6
      during derailment (without
        antecedent collision) V81.7
      with antecedent collision - *see*
        Accident, transport, railway
        vehicle occupant
      while boarding or alighting V81.4
    transport vehicle after collision - *see*
      Accident, transport, by type of
      vehicle, collision
    tree W14
    vehicle (in motion) NEC (*see* also
      Accident, transport) V89.9
      motor NEC (*see* also Accident,
        transport, occupant, by type of
        vehicle) V87.8
      stationary W17.8
        while boarding or alighting - *see*
          Accident, transport, by type
          of vehicle, while boarding or
          alighting
    viaduct W13.8
    wall W13.8
    watercraft - *see* also Drowning, due
      to, fall overboard
      with hitting bottom or object
        V94.0
    well W17.0
    wheelchair W05
      powered - *see* Accident, transport,
        pedestrian, conveyance
        occupant, specified type
        NEC
    window W13.4
  in, on
    aircraft NEC V97.0
      with accident to aircraft V97.0
      while boarding or alighting V97.1
    bathtub (empty) W18.2
      filled W16.212
        causing drowning W16.211
    escalator W10.0
    incline W10.3
    ladder W11
    machine, machinery - *see* Contact,
      with, by type of machine
    object, edged, pointed or sharp (with
      cut) - *see* Fall, by type
    playground equipment W09.8
      jungle gym W09.2
      slide W09.0
      swing W09.1
    ramp W10.3
    scaffolding W12

Forces of nature X39.8
  avalanche X36.1
    causing transport accident - *see*
      Accident, transport, by type of
      vehicle
  blizzard X37.2
  cataclysmic storm X37.9
    with flood X38
    blizzard X37.2
    cloudburst X37.8
    cyclone X37.1
    dust storm X37.3
    hurricane X37.0
    specified storm NEC X37.8
    storm surge X37.0
    tornado X37.1
    twister X37.1
    typhoon X37.0
  cloudburst X37.8
  cold (natural) X31
  cyclone X37.1
  dam collapse causing earth movement
    X36.0
  dust storm X37.3
  earth movement X36.1
    earthquake X34
    caused by dam or structure collapse
      X36.0
  earthquake X34

Forces of nature *(Continued)*
  flood (caused by) X38
    dam collapse X36.0
    tidal wave - *see* Forces of nature, tidal
      wave
  heat (natural) X30
  hurricane X37.0
  landslide X36.1
    causing transport accident - *see* Acci-
      dent, transport, by type of vehicle
  lightning X33
    causing fire - *see* Exposure, fire
  mudslide X36.1
    causing transport accident - *see* Acci-
      dent, transport, by type of vehicle
  radiation (natural) X39.08
    radon X39.01
  radon X39.01
  specified force NEC X39.8
  storm surge X37.0
  structure collapse causing earth
    movement X36.0
  sunlight X32
  tidal wave X37.41
    due to
      earthquake X37.41
      landslide X37.43
      storm X37.42
      volcanic eruption X37.41

Forces of nature *(Continued)*
  tornado X37.1
  tsunami X37.41
  twister X37.1
  typhoon X37.0
  volcanic eruption X35
Foreign body entering through skin
  W45.8
  can lid W45.2
  nail W45.0
  paper W45.1
  specified NEC W45.8
  splinter W45.8
Forest fire (exposure to) - *see* Exposure,
  fire, uncontrolled, not in building
Found injured X58
  from exposure (to) - *see* Exposure
  on
    highway, road(way), street V89.9
    railway right of way V81.9
Fracture (circumstances unknown or
  unspecified) X58
  due to specified cause NEC X58
Freezing - *see* Exposure, cold
Frostbite X31
  due to man-made conditions - *see*
    Exposure, cold, man-made
Frozen - *see* Exposure, cold

G

Gored by bull W55.29
Gunshot wound W34.00

H

Hailstones, injured by X39.8
Hanged herself or himself - *see* Hanging, self-inflicted
Hanging (accidental) - *see also* category T71
  legal execution Y35.91
Heat (effects of) (excessive) X30
  due to
    man-made conditions W92
      on board watercraft V93.29
        fishing boat V93.22
        merchant ship V93.20
        passenger ship V93.21
        sailboat V93.24
        specified powered craft NEC V93.23
    weather (conditions) X30
  from
    electric heating apparatus causing burning X16

Heat *(Continued)*
  from *(Continued)*
    nuclear explosion in war operations - *see* War operations, nuclear weapons
    inappropriate in local application or packing in medical or surgical procedure Y63.5
Hemorrhage
  delayed following medical or surgical treatment without mention of misadventure - *see* Complication of or following, by type of procedure
  during medical or surgical treatment as misadventure - *see* Misadventure, cut, by type of procedure
High
  altitude (effects) - *see* Air, pressure, low
  level of radioactivity, effects - *see* Radiation
  pressure (effects) - *see* Air, pressure, high
  temperature, effects *see* Heat

Hit, hitting (accidental) by - *see* Struck by
Hitting against - *see* Striking against
Homicide (attempt) (justifiable) - *see* Assault
Hot
  place, effects - *see also* Heat
  weather, effects X30
House fire (uncontrolled) - *see* Exposure, fire, uncontrolled, building
Humidity, causing problem X39.8
Hunger X58
Hurricane (any injury) X37.0
Hypobarism, hypobaropathy - *see* Air, pressure, low

I

Ictus
  caloris - *see also* Heat
  solaris X30
Ignition (accidental) (*see also* Exposure,
    fire) X08.8
  anesthetic gas in operating room
    W40.1
  apparel X06.2
    from highly flammable material
      X04
    nightwear X05
  bed linen (sheets) (spreads) (pillows)
    (mattress) - *see* Exposure, fire,
    uncontrolled, building, bed
  benzine X04
  clothes, clothing NEC (from controlled
    fire) X06.2
    from
      highly flammable material X04
  ether X04
    in operating room W40.1
  explosive material - *see* Explosion
  gasoline X04
  jewelry (plastic) (any) X06.0
  kerosene X04
  material
    explosive - *see* Explosion
    highly flammable with secondary
      explosion X04
  nightwear X05
  paraffin X04
  petrol X04
Immersion (accidental) - *see also*
    Drowning
  hand or foot due to cold (excessive)
    X31
Implantation of quills of porcupine
    W55.89
Inanition (from) (hunger) X58
  thirst X58.8
Inappropriate operation performed
    Y65.5
Inattention after, at birth (homicidal
    intent) (infanticidal intent) X58
Incident, adverse
  device
    anesthesiology Y70.8
      accessory Y70.2
      diagnostic Y70.0
      miscellaneous Y70.8
      monitoring Y70.0
      prosthetic Y70.2
      rehabilitative Y70.1
      surgical Y70.3
      therapeutic Y70.1
    cardiovascular Y71.8
      accessory Y71.2
      diagnostic Y71.0
      miscellaneous Y71.8
      monitoring Y71.0
      prosthetic Y71.2
      rehabilitative Y71.1
      surgical Y71.3
      therapeutic Y71.1
    gastroenterology Y73.8
      accessory Y73.2
      diagnostic Y73.0
      miscellaneous Y73.8
      monitoring Y73.0
      prosthetic Y73.2
      rehabilitative Y73.1
      surgical Y73.3
      therapeutic Y73.1

Incident, adverse (*Continued*)
  device (*Continued*)
    general
      hospital Y74.8
        accessory Y74.2
        diagnostic Y74.0
        miscellaneous Y74.8
        monitoring Y74.0
        prosthetic Y74.2
        rehabilitative Y74.1
        surgical Y74.3
        therapeutic Y74.1
      surgical Y81.8
        accessory Y81.2
        diagnostic Y81.0
        miscellaneous Y81.8
        monitoring Y81.0
        prosthetic Y81.2
        rehabilitative Y81.1
        surgical Y81.3
        therapeutic Y81.1
    gynecological Y76.8
      accessory Y76.2
      diagnostic Y76.0
      miscellaneous Y76.8
      monitoring Y76.0
      prosthetic Y76.2
      rehabilitative Y76.1
      surgical Y76.3
      therapeutic Y76.1
    medical Y82.9
      specified type NEC Y82.0
    neurological Y75.8
      accessory Y75.2
      diagnostic Y75.0
      miscellaneous Y75.8
      monitoring Y75.0
      prosthetic Y75.2
      rehabilitative Y75.1
      surgical Y75.3
      therapeutic Y75.1
    obstetrical Y76.8
      accessory Y76.2
      diagnostic Y76.0
      miscellaneous Y76.8
      monitoring Y76.0
      prosthetic Y76.2
      rehabilitative Y76.1
      surgical Y76.3
      therapeutic Y76.1
    ophthalmic Y77.8
      accessory Y77.2
      diagnostic Y77.0
      miscellaneous Y77.8
      monitoring Y77.0
      prosthetic Y77.2
      rehabilitative Y77.1
      surgical Y77.3
      therapeutic Y77.1
    orthopedic Y79.8
      accessory Y79.2
      diagnostic Y79.0
      miscellaneous Y79.8
      monitoring Y79.0
      prosthetic Y79.2
      rehabilitative Y79.1
      surgical Y79.3
      therapeutic Y79.1
    otorhinolaryngological Y72.8
      accessory Y72.2
      diagnostic Y72.0
      miscellaneous Y72.8
      monitoring Y72.0
      prosthetic Y72.2
      rehabilitative Y72.1

Incident, adverse (*Continued*)
  device (*Continued*)
    otorhinolaryngological (*Continued*)
      surgical Y72.3
      therapeutic Y72.1
    personal use Y74.8
      accessory Y74.2
      diagnostic Y74.0
      miscellaneous Y74.8
      monitoring Y74.0
      prosthetic Y74.2
      rehabilitative Y74.1
      surgical Y74.3
      therapeutic Y74.1
    physical medicine Y80.8
      accessory Y80.2
      diagnostic Y80.0
      miscellaneous Y80.8
      monitoring Y80.0
      prosthetic Y80.2
      rehabilitative Y80.1
      surgical Y80.3
      therapeutic Y80.1
    plastic surgical Y81.8
      accessory Y81.2
      diagnostic Y81.0
      miscellaneous Y81.8
      monitoring Y81.0
      prosthetic Y81.2
      rehabilitative Y81.1
      surgical Y81.3
      therapeutic Y81.1
    radiological Y78.8
      accessory Y78.2
      diagnostic Y78.0
      miscellaneous Y78.8
      monitoring Y78.0
      prosthetic Y78.2
      rehabilitative Y78.1
      surgical Y78.3
      therapeutic Y78.1
    urology Y73.8
      accessory Y73.2
      diagnostic Y73.0
      miscellaneous Y73.8
      monitoring Y73.0
      prosthetic Y73.2
      rehabilitative Y73.1
      surgical Y73.3
      therapeutic Y73.1
Incineration (accidental) - *see* Exposure,
    fire
Infanticide - *see* Assault
Infrasound waves (causing injury) W49
Ingestion
  foreign body (causing injury) (with
    obstruction) - *see* Foreign body,
    alimentary canal
  poisonous
    plant(s) X58
    substance NEC - *see* Table of drugs
      and chemicals
Inhalation
  excessively cold substance, man-made
    - *see* Exposure, cold, man-made
  food (any type) (into respiratory
    tract) (with asphyxia, obstruction
    respiratory tract, suffocation) - *see*
    categories T17 and T18
  foreign body - *see* Foreign body, aspiration
  gastric contents (with asphyxia,
    obstruction respiratory passage,
    suffocation) - *see* subcategories
    T17.81, T18.81
  hot air or gases X14.0

Inhalation *(Continued)*
    liquid air, hydrogen, nitrogen W93.12
        suicide (attempt) X83.2
    steam X13.0
        assault X98.0
        stated as undetermined whether
            accidental or intentional Y27.0
        suicide (attempt) X77.0
    toxic gas - *see* Table of drugs and
        chemicals
    vomitus (with asphyxia, obstruction
        respiratory passage, suffocation)
        - *see* subcategories T17.81, T18.81
Injury, injured (accidental(ly)) **NOS** X58
    by, caused by, from
        assault - *see* Assault
        law-enforcing agent, police, in course
            of legal intervention - *see* legal
            intervention
        suicide (attempt) X83.8

Injury, injured *(Continued)*
    due to, in
        civil insurrection - *see* War operations
        fight (*see* also Assault, fight) Y04.0
        war operations - *see* War operations
    homicide (*see* also Assault) Y09
    inflicted (by)
        in course of arrest (attempted),
            suppression of disturbance,
            maintenance of order, by
            law-enforcing agents - *see* Legal
            intervention
        other person
            stated as
                accidental X58
                intentional, homicide (attempt)
                    - *see* Assault
                undetermined whether
                    accidental or intentional
                    Y33

Injury, injured *(Continued)*
    purposely (inflicted) by other person(s)
        - *see* Assault
    self-inflicted X83.8
        stated as accidental X58
    specified cause NEC X58
    undetermined whether accidental or
        intentional Y33
Insolation, effects X30
Insufficient nourishment X58
    homicidal intent - *see* Maltreatment
Interruption of respiration (by)
    food (lodged in esophagus) - *see*
        categories T17 and T18
    vomitus (lodged in esophagus) - *see*
        subcategories T17.81, T18.81
Intervention, legal - *see* Legal intervention
Intoxication
    drug - *see* Table of drugs and chemicals
    poison - *see* Table of drugs and chemicals

J

Jammed (accidentally)
  between objects (moving) (stationary
    and moving) W23.0
    stationary W23.1
Jumped, jumping
  before moving object X81
    motor vehicle X81.0
    undetermined whether accidental or
      intentional Y31
  from
    boat (into water) voluntarily, without
      accident (to or on boat) W16.712
      with
        accident to or on boat - *see*
          Accident, watercraft
        drowning or submersion W16.711
          suicide (attempt) X71.3
        striking bottom W16.722
          causing drowning W16.721

Jumped, jumping *(Continued)*
  from *(Continued)*
    building (*see* also Jumped, from, high
      place) W13.9
      burning (uncontrolled fire)
        X00.5
    high place NEC W17.8
      suicide (attempt) X80
      undetermined whether accidental
        or intentional Y30
    structure (*see* also Jumped, from, high
      place) W13.9
      burning (uncontrolled fire)
        X00.5
  into water W16.92
    causing drowning W16.91
    from, off watercraft - *see* Jumped,
      from, boat
    in
      natural body W16.612
        causing drowning W16.611

Jumped, jumping *(Continued)*
  into water *(Continued)*
    in *(Continued)*
      natural body *(Continued)*
        striking bottom W16.622
          causing drowning W16.621
      specified place NEC W16.812
        causing drowning W16.811
        striking
          bottom W16.822
            causing drowning W16.821
          wall W16.832
            causing drowning W16.831
      swimming pool W16.512
        causing drowning W16.511
        striking
          bottom W16.522
            causing drowning W16.521
          wall W16.532
            causing drowning W16.531
  suicide (attempt) X71.3

K

Kicked by
  animal NEC W55.89
  person(s) (accidentally) W50.1
    with intent to injure or kill Y04.0
    as, or caused by, a crowd or human
      stampede (with fall) W52
    assault Y04.0
    homicide (attempt) Y04.0
    in
      fight Y04.0
      legal intervention Y35.814
        injuring
          bystander Y35.813
          law enforcement personnel
            Y35.812
          suspect Y35.811

Kicking against
  object W22.8
    sports equipment W21.9
    stationary W22.09
      sports equipment W21.89
  person - *see* Striking against, person
  sports equipment W21.9
Killed, killing (accidentally) NOS (*see*
  also Injury) X58
  in
    action - *see* War operations
    brawl, fight (hand) (fists) (foot)
      Y04.0
      by weapon - *see* also Assault
      cutting, piercing - *see* Assault,
        cutting or piercing instrument
      firearm - *see* Discharge, firearm, by
        type, homicide

Killed, killing (*Continued*)
  self
    stated as
      accident NOS X58
      suicide - *see* Suicide
      undetermined whether accidental
        or intentional Y33
Knocked down (accidentally) (by) NOS
  X58
  animal (not being ridden) NEC - *see* also
    Struck by, by type of animal
    being ridden V06
  crowd or human stampede W52
  person W51
    in brawl, fight Y04.0
  transport vehicle NEC (*see* also
    Accident, transport) V09.9

L

Laceration NEC - *see* Injury
Lack of
  care (helpless person) (infant)
    (newborn) X58
  food except as result of abandonment
    or neglect X58
    due to abandonment or neglect
      X58
  water except as result of transport
    accident X58
    due to transport accident - *see*
      Accident, transport, by type
  helpless person, infant, newborn
    X58
Landslide (falling on transport vehicle)
  X36.1
  caused by collapse of man-made
    structure X36.0
Late effect - *see* Sequelae
Legal
  execution Y35.91
  intervention (by) Y35.99
    baton - *see* Legal, intervention, blunt
      object, baton
    bayonet - *see* Legal, intervention,
      sharp object, bayonet
    blow - *see* Legal, intervention,
      manhandling
    blunt object Y35.304
      baton Y35.314
        injuring
          bystander Y35.313
          law enforcement personnel
            Y35.312
          suspect Y35.311
      specified NEC Y35.394
        injuring
          bystander Y35.393
          law enforcement personnel
            Y35.392
          suspect Y35.391
      stave Y35.394
        injuring
          bystander Y35.393
          law enforcement personnel
            Y35.392
          suspect Y35.391
    bomb - *see* Legal, intervention,
      explosive
    cutting or piercing instrument - *see*
      Legal, intervention, sharp object
    dynamite - *see* Legal, intervention,
      explosive, dynamite
    execution, any method Y35.91
    explosive(s) Y35.104
      dynamite Y35.114
        injuring
          bystander Y35.113
          law enforcement personnel
            Y35.112
          suspect Y35.111
      grenade Y35.194
        injuring
          bystander Y35.193
          law enforcement personnel
            Y35.192
          suspect Y35.191

Legal (*Continued*)
  intervention (*Continued*)
    explosive (*Continued*)
      injuring
        bystander Y35.103
        law enforcement personnel
          Y35.102
        suspect Y35.101
      mortar bomb Y35.194
        injuring
          bystander Y35.193
          law enforcement personnel
            Y35.192
          suspect Y35.191
      shell Y35.124
        injuring
          bystander Y35.123
          law enforcement personnel
            Y35.122
          suspect Y35.121
      specified NEC Y35.194
        injuring
          bystander Y35.193
          law enforcement personnel
            Y35.192
          suspect Y35.191
    firearm(s) (discharge) Y35.004
      handgun Y35.024
        injuring
          bystander Y35.023
          law enforcement personnel
            Y35.022
          suspect Y35.021
      injuring
        bystander Y35.003
        law enforcement personnel Y35.002
        suspect Y35.001
      machine gun Y35.014
        injuring
          bystander Y35.013
          law enforcement personnel
            Y35.012
          suspect Y35.011
      rifle pellet Y35.034
        injuring
          bystander Y35.033
          law enforcement personnel
            Y35.032
          suspect Y35.031
      rubber bullet Y35.044
        injuring
          bystander Y35.043
          law enforcement personnel
            Y35.042
          suspect Y35.041
      shotgun - *see* Legal, intervention,
        firearm, specified NEC
      specified NEC Y35.094
        injuring
          bystander Y35.093
          law enforcement personnel
            Y35.092
          suspect Y35.091
    gas (asphyxiation) (poisoning) Y35.204
      injuring
        bystander Y35.203
        law enforcement personnel
          Y35.202
        suspect Y35.201
      specified NEC Y35.294
        injuring
          bystander Y35.293
          law enforcement personnel
            Y35.292
          suspect Y35.291

Legal (*Continued*)
  intervention (*Continued*)
    gas (*Continued*)
      tear gas Y35.214
        injuring
          bystander Y35.213
          law enforcement personnel
            Y35.212
          suspect Y35.211
      grenade - *see* Legal, intervention,
        explosive, grenade
      injuring
        bystander Y35.93
        law enforcement personnel
          Y35.92
        suspect Y35.91
    late effect (of) - *see* Y35 with q as
      terminal character
    manhandling Y35.814
      injuring
        bystander Y35.813
        law enforcement personnel
          Y35.812
        suspect Y35.811
    sequelae (of) - *see* Y35 with q as
      terminal character
    sharp objects Y35.404
      bayonet Y35.414
        injuring
          bystander Y35.413
          law enforcement personnel
            Y35.412
          suspect Y35.411
      injuring
        bystander Y35.403
        law enforcement personnel
          Y35.402
        suspect Y35.401
      specified NEC Y35.494
        injuring
          bystander Y35.493
          law enforcement personnel
            Y35.492
          suspect Y35.491
    specified means NEC Y35.894
      injuring
        bystander Y35.892
        law enforcement personnel
          Y35.891
        suspect Y35.890
    stabbing - *see* Legal, intervention,
      sharp object
    stave - *see* Legal, intervention, blunt
      object, stave
    tear gas - *see* Legal, intervention, gas,
      tear gas
    truncheon - *see* Legal, intervention,
      blunt object, stave
Lightning (shock) (stroke) (struck by)
  X33
  causing fire - *see* Exposure, fire
Loss of control (transport vehicle) NEC
  - *see* Accident, transport
Lost at sea NOS - *see* Drowning, due to,
  fall overboard
Low
  pressure (effects) - *see* Air, pressure, low
  temperature (effects) - *see* Exposure,
    cold
Lying before train, vehicle or other
  moving object X81
  undetermined whether accidental or
    intentional Y31
Lynching - *see* Assault

M

Malfunction (mechanism or component)
(of)
firearm
airgun W34.110
BB gun W34.110
gas, air or spring-operated gun NEC
W34.118
handgun W32.1
hunting rifle W33.12
larger firearm W33.10
specified NEC W33.19
machine gun W33.13
paintball gun W34.111
pellet gun W34.110
shotgun W33.11
specified NEC W34.19
Very pistol [flare] W34.19
handgun - see Malfunction, firearm,
handgun
Maltreatment - see Perpetrator
Mangled (accidentally) NOS X58
Manhandling (in brawl, fight) Y04.0
legal intervention - see Legal,
intervention, manhandling
Manslaughter (nonaccidental) - see
Assault
Mauled by animal NEC W55.89
Medical procedure, complication of
(delayed or as an abnormal
reaction without mention of
misadventure) - see Complication
of or following, by specified type of
procedure
due to or as a result of misadventure
- see Misadventure
Melting (due to fire) (see also Exposure,
fire)
apparel NEC X06.3
clothes, clothing NEC X06.3
nightwear X05
fittings or furniture (burning building)
(uncontrolled fire) X00.8
nightwear X05
plastic jewelry X06.1
Mental cruelty X58
Military operations (injuries to military and civilians occuring during
peacetime on military property and
during routine military exercises and
operations) (by) (from) (involving)
Y37.90-
air blast Y37.20-
aircraft
destruction- see Military operations,
destruction of aircraft
airway restriction - see Military
operations, restriction of airways
asphyxiation - see Military operations,
restriction of airways
biological weapons Y37.6x-
blast Y37.20-
blast fragments Y37.20-
blast wave Y37.20-
blast wind Y37.20-
bomb Y37.20-
dirty Y37.50-
gasoline Y37.31-
incendiary Y37.31-
petrol Y37.31-
bullet Y37.43-
incendiary Y37.32-
rubber Y37.41-
chemical weapons Y37.7x-

Military operations (Continued)
combat
hand to hand (unarmed) combat
Y37.44-
using blunt or piercing object
Y37.45-
conflagration - see Military operations,
fire
conventional warfare NEC Y37.49-
depth-charge Y37.01-
destruction of aircraft Y37.10-
due to
air to air missile Y37.11-
collision with other aircraft Y37.12-
detonation (accidental) of onboard
munitions and explosives
Y37.14-
enemy fire or explosives Y37.11-
explosive placed on aircraft Y37.11-
onboard fire Y37.13-
rocket propelled grenade [RPG]
Y37.11-
small arms fire Y37.11-
surface to air missile Y37.11-
specified NEC Y37.19-
detonation (accidental) of
onboard marine weapons Y37.05-
own munitions or munitions launch
device Y37.24-
dirty bomb Y37.50-
explosion (of) Y37.20-
aerial bomb Y37.21-
bomb NOS Y37.20 - see also Military
operations, bomb(s)
own munitions or munitions launch
device (accidental) Y37.24-
fragments Y37.20-
grenade Y37.29-
guided missile Y37.22-
improvised explosive device [IED]
(person-borne) (roadside)
(vehicle-borne) Y37.23-
land mine Y37.29-
marine mine (at sea) (in harbor)
Y37.02-
marine weapon Y37.00-
specified NEC Y37.09-
sea-based artillery shell Y37.03-
specified NEC Y37.29-
torpedo Y37.04-
fire Y37.30-
firearms
discharge Y37.43-
pellets Y37.42-
flamethrower Y37.33-
fragments (from) (of)
improvised explosive device [IED]
(person-borne) (roadside)
(vehicle-borne) Y37.26-
munitions Y37.25-
specified NEC Y37.29-
weapons Y37.27-
friendly fire Y37.92-
hand to hand (unarmed) combat
Y37.44-
hot substances - see Military operations,
fire
incendiary bullet Y37.32-
nuclear weapon (effects of) Y37.50-
acute radiation exposure Y37.54-
blast pressure Y37.51-
direct blast Y37.51-
direct heat Y37.53-
fallout exposure Y37.54-
fireball Y37.53-

Military operations (Continued)
nuclear weapon (effects of) (Continued)
indirect blast (struck or crushed by
blast debris) (being thrown by
blast) Y37.52-
ionizing radiation (immediate
exposure) Y37.54-
nuclear radiation Y37.54-
radiation
ionizing (immediate exposure)
Y37.54-
nuclear Y37.54-
thermal Y37.53-
specified NEC Y37.59-
secondary effects Y37.54-
thermal radiation Y37.53-
restriction of air (airway)
intentional Y37.46-
unintentional Y37.47-
rubber bullets Y37.41-
shrapnel NOS Y37.29-
suffocation - see Military operations,
restriction of airways
unconventional warfare NEC Y37.7x-
underwater blast NOS Y37.00-
warfare
conventional NEC Y37.49-
unconventional NEC Y37.7x-
weapons
biological weapons Y37.6x-
chemical Y37.7x-
nuclear (effects of) Y37.50-
acute radiation exposure Y37.54-
blast pressure Y37.51-
direct blast Y37.51-
direct heat Y37.53-
fallout exposure Y37.54-
fireball Y37.53-
indirect blast (struck or crushed by
blast debris) (being thrown by
blast) Y37.52-
radiation
ionizing (immediate exposure)
Y37.54-
nuclear Y37.54-
thermal Y37.53-
secondary effects Y37.54-
specified NEC Y37.59-
indirect blast (struck or crushed by
blast debris) (being thrown by
blast) Y37.52-
of mass destruction [WMD] Y37.91-
weapon of mass destruction [WMD]
Y37.91-
volunteer activity Y99.8
Misadventure(s) to patient(s) during
surgical or medical care Y69
contaminated medical or biological
substance (blood, drug, fluid) Y64.9
administered (by) NEC Y64.9
immunization Y64.1
infusion Y64.0
injection Y64.1
specified means NEC Y64.8
transfusion Y64.0
vaccination Y64.1
excessive amount of blood or other
fluid during transfusion or infusion
Y63.0
failure
in dosage Y63.9
electroshock therapy Y63.4
inappropriate temperature (too hot
or too cold) in local application
and packing Y63.5

Misadventure(s) to patient(s) during
surgical or medical care *(Continued)*
failure *(Continued)*
in dosage *(Continued)*
infusion
excessive amount of fluid Y63.0
incorrect dilution of fluid Y63.1
insulin-shock therapy Y63.4
nonadministration of necessary
drug or biological substance
Y63.6
overdose - *see* Table of drugs and
chemicals
radiation, in therapy Y63.2
radiation
overdose Y63.2
specified procedure NEC Y63.8
transfusion
excessive amount of blood
Y63.0
mechanical, of instrument or
apparatus (any) (during any
procedure) Y65.8
sterile precautions (during
procedure) Y62.9
aspiration of fluid or tissue (by
puncture or catheterization,
except heart) Y62.6
biopsy (except needle aspiration)
Y62.8
needle (aspirating) Y62.6
blood sampling Y62.6
catheterization Y62.6
heart Y62.5
dialysis (kidney) Y62.2
endoscopic examination Y62.4
enema Y62.8
immunization Y62.3
infusion Y62.1
injection Y62.3

Misadventure(s) to patient(s) during
surgical or medical care *(Continued)*
failure *(Continued)*
sterile precautions *(Continued)*
needle biopsy Y62.6
paracentesis (abdominal) (thoracic)
Y62.6
perfusion Y62.2
puncture (lumbar) Y62.6
removal of catheter or packing Y62.8
specified procedure NEC Y62.8
surgical operation Y62.0
transfusion Y62.1
vaccination Y62.3
suture or ligature during surgical
procedure Y65.2
to introduce or to remove tube or
instrument - *see* Failure, to
hemorrhage - *see* Misadventure, cut, by
type of procedure
inadvertent exposure of patient to
radiation Y63.3
inappropriate
operation performed Y65.5
temperature (too hot or too cold)
in local application or packing
Y63.5
infusion (*see also* Misadventure, by
type, infusion) Y69
excessive amount of fluid Y63.0
incorrect dilution of fluid Y63.1
wrong fluid Y65.1
mismatched blood in transfusion Y65.0
nonadministration of necessary drug or
biological substance Y63.6
overdose - *see* Table of drugs and
chemicals
radiation (in therapy) Y63.2
perforation - *see* Misadventure, cut, by
type of procedure

Misadventure(s) to patient(s) during
surgical or medical care *(Continued)*
performance of inappropriate operation
Y65.5
puncture - *see* Misadventure, cut, by
type of procedure
specified type NEC Y65.8
failure
suture or ligature during surgical
operation Y65.2
to introduce or to remove tube or
instrument - *see* Failure, to
infusion of wrong fluid Y65.1
performance of inappropriate
operation Y65.5
transfusion of mismatched blood
Y65.0
wrong
fluid in infusion Y65.1
placement of endotracheal tube
during anesthetic procedure
Y65.3
transfusion - *see* Misadventure, by type,
transfusion
excessive amount of blood Y63.0
mismatched blood Y65.0
wrong
drug given in error - *see* Table of
drugs and chemicals
fluid in infusion Y65.1
placement of endotracheal tube
during anesthetic procedure
Y65.3
Mismatched blood in transfusion Y65.0
Motion T75.3
Mountain sickness W94.11
Mudslide (of cataclysmic nature) - *see*
Landslide
Murder (attempt) - *see* Assault

N

Nail, contact with W45.0
  gun W29.4
Neglect (criminal) (homicidal intent) X58
Noise (causing injury) (pollution) W42.9
  supersonic W42.0

Nonadministration (of)
  drug or biological substance (necessary)
    Y63.6
  surgical and medical care Y66
Nosocomial condition Y95

O

Object
  falling
    from, in, on, hitting
      machinery - *see* Contact, with, by
        type of machine
  set in motion by
    accidental explosion or rupture of
      pressure vessel W38
    firearm - *see* Discharge, firearm, by
      type
    machine(ry) - *see* Contact, with, by
      type of machine

Overdose (drug) - *see* Table of drugs and
  chemicals
  radiation Y63.2
Overexertion - *see* category Y93
Overexposure (accidental) (to)
  cold (*see* also Exposure, cold) X31
    due to man-made conditions *see*
      Exposure, cold, man-made
  heat (*see* also Heat) X30
  radiation - *see* Radiation
  radioactivity W88.0
  sun (sunburn) X32
  weather NEC - *see* Forces of nature
  wind NEC - *see* Forces of nature

Overheated - *see* Heat
Overturning (accidental)
  machinery - *see* Contact, with, by type
    of machine
  transport vehicle NEC (*see* also
    Accident, transport) V89.9
  watercraft (causing drowning,
    submersion) - *see* also Drowning,
    due to, accident to, watercraft,
    overturning
    causing injury except drowning
      or submersion - *see* Accident,
      watercraft, causing, injury NEC

P

Parachute descent (voluntary) (without accident to aircraft) V97.29
  due to accident to aircraft - *see* Accident, transport, aircraft
Pecked by bird W64
Perforation during medical or surgical treatment as misadventure - *see* Misadventure, cut, by type of procedure
Perpetrator, perpetration, of assault, mal-treatment and neglect (by) Y07.50
  boyfriend Y07.432
  brother Y07.410
    stepbrother Y07.435
  coach Y07.53
  cousin
    female Y07.491
    male Y07.490
  daycare provider Y07.519
    at-home
      adult care Y07.512
      childcare Y07.510
    care center
      adult care Y07.513
      childcare Y07.511
  family member NEC Y07.499
  father Y07.11
    adoptive Y07.13
    foster Y07.420
    stepfather Y07.430
  girl friend Y07.434
  healthcare provider Y07.529
    mental health Y07.521
    specified NEC Y07.528
  husband Y07.01
  instructor Y07.53
  mother Y07.12
    adoptive Y07.14
    foster Y07.421
    stepmother Y07.433
  nonfamily member NEC Y07.59
  nurse Y07.528
  occupational therapist Y07.528
  partner of parent
    female Y07.04
    male Y07.03
  physical therapist Y07.528
  sister Y07.411
  speech therapist Y07.528
  stepbrother Y07.435
  stepfather Y07.430
  stepmother Y07.433
  stepsister Y07.436
  teacher Y07.53
  wife Y07.02
Piercing - *see* Contact, with, by type of object or machine
Pinched
  between objects (moving) (stationary and moving) W23.0
    stationary W23.1
Pinned under machine(ry) - *see* Contact, with, by type of machine
Place of occurrence Y92.9
  abandoned house Y92.89
  airplane Y92.813
  airport Y92.520
  amusement park Y92.831
  apartment (co-op) - *see* Place of occurrence, residence, apartment
  assembly hall Y92.29
  bank Y92.510
  barn Y92.71

Place of occurrence *(Continued)*
  baseball field Y92.320
  basketball court Y92.310
  beach Y92.832
  boarding house - *see* Place of occurrence, residence, boarding house
  boat Y92.814
  bowling alley Y92.39
  bridge Y92.89
  building under construction Y92.61
  bus Y92.811
    station Y92.521
  cafe Y92.511
  campsite Y92.833
  campus - *see* Place of occurrence, school
  canal Y92.89
  car Y92.810
  casino Y92.59
  children's home - *see* Place of occurrence, residence, institutional, orphanage
  church Y92.22
  cinema Y92.26
  clubhouse Y92.29
  coal pit Y92.64
  college (community) Y92.214
  condominium - *see* Place of occurrence, residence, apartment
  construction area - *see* Place of occurrence, industrial and construction area
  convalescent home - *see* Place of occurrence, residence, institutional, nursing home
  court-house Y92.240
  cricket ground Y92.328
  cultural building Y92.258
    art gallery Y92.250
    museum Y92.251
    music hall Y92.252
    opera house Y92.253
    specified NEC Y92.258
    theater Y92.254
  dancehall Y92.252
  day nursery Y92.210
  derelict house Y92.89
  desert Y92.820
  dock NOS Y92.89
  dockyard Y92.62
  dormitory - *see* Place of occurrence, residence, institutional, school dormitory
  dry dock Y92.62
  factory (building) (premises) Y92.63
  farm (land under cultivation) (outbuildings) Y92.79
    barn Y92.71
    chicken coop Y92.72
    field Y92.73
    hen house Y92.72
    house - *see* Place of occurrence, residence, house
    orchard Y92.74
    specified NEC Y92.79
  football field Y92.321
  forest Y92.821
  freeway Y92.411
  gallery Y92.250
  garage (commercial) Y92.59
    boarding house Y92.044
    military base Y92.135
    mobile home Y92.025
    nursing home Y92.124
    orphanage Y92.114
    private house Y92.015
    reform school Y92.155

Place of occurrence *(Continued)*
  gas station Y92.524
  gasworks Y92.69
  golf course Y92.39
  gravel pit Y92.64
  grocery Y92.512
  gymnasium Y92.39
  handball court Y92.318
  harbor Y92.89
  harness racing course Y92.39
  highway (interstate) Y92.411
  hill Y92.828
  hockey rink Y92.330
  home - *see* Place of occurrence, residence
  hospice - *see* Place of occurrence, residence, institutional, nursing home
  hospital Y92.239
    cafeteria Y92.233
    corridor Y92.232
    operating room Y92.234
    patient
      bathroom Y92.231
      room Y92.230
    specified NEC Y92.238
  hotel Y92.59
  house - *see also* Place of occurrence, residence
    abandoned Y92.89
    under construction Y92.61
  industrial and construction area (yard) Y92.69
    building under construction Y92.61
    dock Y92.62
    dry dock Y92.62
    factory Y92.63
    gasworks Y92.69
    mine Y92.64
    oil rig Y92.65
    pit Y92.64
    power station Y92.69
    shipyard Y92.62
    specified NEC Y92.69
    tunnel under construction Y92.69
    workshop Y92.69
  kindergarten Y92.211
  lacrosse field Y92.328
  lake Y92.828
  library Y92.241
  mall Y92.59
  market Y92.512
  marsh Y92.828
  military
    base - *see* Place of occurrence, residence, institutional, military base
    training ground Y92.84
  mine Y92.64
  mosque Y92.22
  motel Y92.59
  motorway (interstate) Y92.411
  mountain Y92.828
  movie-house Y92.26
  museum Y92.251
  music-hall Y92.252
  nuclear power station Y92.69
  nursing home - *see* Place of occurrence, residence, institutional, nursing home
  office building Y92.59
  offshore installation Y92.65
  oil rig Y92.65
  old people's home - *see* Place of occurrence, residence, institutional, specified NEC
  opera-house Y92.253

Place of occurrence *(Continued)*
  orphanage - *see* Place of occurrence,
      residence, institutional, orphanage
  park (public) Y92.830
    amusement Y92.831
  parking garage Y92.89
    lot Y92.481
  pavement Y92.480
  polo field Y92.328
  pond Y92.828
  post office Y92.242
  power station Y92.69
  prairie Y92.828
  prison - *see* Place of occurrence,
      residence, institutional, prison
  public
    administration building Y92.248
      city hall Y92.243
      courthouse Y92.240
      library Y92.241
      post office Y92.242
      specified NEC Y92.248
    building NEC Y92.29
    hall Y92.29
    place NOS Y92.89
  race course Y92.39
  radio station Y92.59
  railway line (bridge) Y92.85
  ranch (outbuildings) - *see* Place of
      occurrence, farm
  recreation area Y92.838
    amusement park Y92.831
    beach Y92.832
    campsite Y92.833
    park (public) Y92.830
    seashore Y92.832
    specified NEC Y92.838
  religious institution Y92.22
  reform school - *see* Place of occurrence,
      residence, institutional, reform school
  residence (non-institutional) (private)
    Y92.00
    apartment Y92.039
      bathroom Y92.031
      bedroom Y92.032
      kitchen Y92.030
      specified NEC Y92.038
    boarding house Y92.049
      bathroom Y92.041
      bedroom Y92.042
      driveway Y92.043
      garage Y92.044
      garden Y92.046
      kitchen Y92.040
      specified NEC Y92.048
      swimming pool Y92.045
      yard Y92.046
    house, single family Y92.019
      bathroom Y92.012
      bedroom Y92.013
      dining room Y92.011
      driveway Y92.014
      garage Y92.015
      garden Y92.017
      kitchen Y92.010
      specified NEC Y92.018
      swimming pool Y92.016
      yard Y92.017
    institutional Y92.10
      children's home - *see* Place of
        occurrence, residence,
        institutional, orphanage
      hospice - *see* Place of occurrence,
        residence, institutional,
        nursing home

Place of occurrence *(Continued)*
  residence *(Continued)*
    institutional *(Continued)*
      military base Y92.139
        barracks Y92.133
        garage Y92.135
        garden Y92.137
        kitchen Y92.130
        mess hall Y92.131
        specified NEC Y92.138
        swimming pool Y92.136
        yard Y92.137
      nursing home Y92.129
        bathroom Y92.121
        bedroom Y92.122
        driveway Y92.123
        garage Y92.124
        garden Y92.126
        kitchen Y92.120
        specified NEC Y92.128
        swimming pool Y92.125
        yard Y92.126
      orphanage Y92.119
        bathroom Y92.111
        bedroom Y92.112
        driveway Y92.113
        garage Y92.114
        garden Y92.116
        kitchen Y92.110
        specified NEC Y92.118
        swimming pool Y92.115
        yard Y92.116
      prison Y92.149
        bathroom Y92.142
        cell Y92.143
        courtyard Y92.147
        dining room Y92.141
        kitchen Y92.140
        specified NEC Y92.148
        swimming pool Y92.146
      reform school Y92.159
        bathroom Y92.152
        bedroom Y92.153
        dining room Y92.151
        driveway Y92.154
        garage Y92.155
        garden Y92.157
        kitchen Y92.150
        specified NEC Y92.158
        swimming pool Y92.156
        yard Y92.157
      school dormitory Y92.169
        bathroom Y92.162
        bedroom Y92.163
        dining room Y92.161
        kitchen Y92.160
        specified NEC Y92.168
      specified NEC Y92.199
        bathroom Y92.192
        bedroom Y92.193
        dining room Y92.191
        driveway Y92.194
        garage Y92.195
        garden Y92.197
        kitchen Y92.190
        specified NEC Y92.198
        swimming pool Y92.196
        yard Y92.197
    mobile home Y92.029
      bathroom Y92.022
      bedroom Y92.023
      dining room Y92.021
      driveway Y92.024
      garage Y92.025
      garden Y92.027

Place of occurrence *(Continued)*
  residence *(Continued)*
    institutional *(Continued)*
      kitchen Y92.020
      specified NEC Y92.028
      swimming pool Y92.026
      yard Y92.027
    specified NEC Y92.099
      bathroom Y92.091
      bedroom Y92.092
      driveway Y92.093
      garage Y92.094
      garden Y92.096
      kitchen Y92.090
      specified NEC Y92.098
      swimming pool Y92.095
      yard Y92.096
  restaurant Y92.511
  riding school Y92.39
  river Y92.828
  road Y92.488
  rodeo ring Y92.39
  rugby field Y92.328
  sand pit Y92.64
  school (private) (public) (state) Y92.219
    college Y92.214
    daycare center Y92.210
    elementary school Y92.211
    high school Y92.213
    kindergarten Y92.211
    middle school Y92.212
    specified NEC Y92.218
    trace school Y92.215
    university Y92.214
    vocational school Y92.215
  sea (shore) Y92.832
  senior citizen center Y92.29
  service area
    airport Y92.520
    bus station Y92.521
    gas station Y92.524
    highway rest stop Y92.523
    railway station Y92.522
  shipyard Y92.62
  shop(commercial) Y92.513
  sidewalk Y92.480
  silo Y92.79
  skating rink (roller) Y92.331
    ice Y92.330
  slaughter house Y92.86
  soccer field Y92.322
  specified place NEC Y92.89
  sports area Y92.39
    athletic
      court Y92.318
        basketball Y92.310
        specified NEC Y92.318
        squash Y92.311
        tennis Y92.312
      field Y92.328
        baseball Y92.320
        cricket ground Y92.328
        football Y92.321
        hockey Y92.328
        soccer Y92.322
        specified NEC Y92.328
    golf course Y92.39
    gymnasium Y92.39
    riding school Y92.39
    skating rink (roller) Y92.331
      ice Y92.330
    stadium Y92.39
    swimming pool Y92.34
  squash court Y92.311
  stadium Y92.39

R

Radiation (exposure to)
  arc lamps W89.0
  atomic power plant (malfunction) NEC
    W88.1
  complication of or abnormal reaction to
    medical radiotherapy Y84.2
  electromagnetic, ionizing W88.0
  gamma rays W88.1
  in
    war operations (from or following
      nuclear explosion) - *see* also War
      operations
  inadvertent exposure of patient
    (receiving test or therapy) Y63.3
  infrared (heaters and lamps) W90.1
    excessive heat from W92
  ionized, ionizing (particles, artificially
    accelerated)
    radioisotopes W88.1
    x-rays W88.0
  isotopes, radioactive - *see* Radiation,
    radioactive isotopes
  laser(s) W90.2
    in war operations - *see* War
      operations
    misadventure in medical care Y63.2
  light sources (man-made visible and
    ultraviolet) W89.9
    natural X32
    specified NEC W89.8
    tanning bed W89.1
    welding light W89.0
  man-made visible light W89.9
    specified NEC W89.8
    tanning bed W89.1
    welding light W89.0
  microwave W90.8
  misadventure in medical or surgical
    procedure Y63.2

Radiation *(Continued)*
  natural NEC X39.08
    radon X39.01
  overdose (in medical or surgical
    procedure) Y63.2
  radar W90.0
  radioactive isotopes (any) W88.1
    atomic power plant malfunction
      W88.1
    misadventure in medical or surgical
      treatment Y63.2
  radiofrequency W90.0
  radium NEC W88.1
  sun X32
  ultraviolet (light) (man-made) W89.9
    natural X32
    specified NEC W89.8
    tanning bed W89.1
    welding light W89.0
  welding arc, torch, or light W89.0
    excessive heat from W92
  x-rays (hard) (soft) W88.0
Range disease W94.11
Rape (attempted) Y05
Rat bite W53.11
Reaction, abnormal to medical procedure
  (*see* also Complication of or following,
  by type of procedure) Y84.9
  with misadventure - *see* Misadventure
  biologicals - *see* Table of drugs and
    chemicals
  drugs - *see* Table of drugs and
    chemicals
  vaccine - *see* Table of drugs and
    chemicals
Recoil
  airgun W34.110
  BB gun W34.110
  firearm NEC W34.19
  gas, air or spring-operated gun NEC
    W34.118

Recoil *(Continued)*
  handgun W32.1
  hunting rifle W33.12
  larger firearm W33.10
    specified NEC W33.19
  machine gun W33.13
  paintball gun W34.111
  pellet W34.110
  shotgun W33.11
  Very pistol [flare] W34.19
Reduction in
  atmospheric pressure - *see* Air, pressure,
    change
Rock falling on or hitting (accidentally)
  (person) W20.8
  in cave-in W20.0
Run over (accidentally) (by)
  animal (not being ridden) NEC W55.89
    being ridden V06
  machinery - *see* Contact, with, by
    specified type of machine
  transport vehicle NEC (*see* also
    Accident, transport) V09.9
    intentional homicide (attempt) Y03.0
    motor NEC V09.20
      intentional homicide (attempt)
        Y03.0
Running
  before moving object X81
    motor vehicle X81.0
Running off, away
  animal (being ridden) (*see* also
    Accident, transport) V80.918
    not being ridden W55.89
  animal-drawn vehicle NEC (*see* also
    Accident, transport) V80.928
  highway, road(way), street
    transport vehicle NEC (*see* also
      Accident, transport) V89.9
Rupture pressurized devices - *see*
  Explosion, by type of device

S

Saturnism - *see* Table of drugs and chemicals, lead
Scald, scalding (accidental) (by) (from) (in) X19
air (hot) X14.1
gases (hot) X14.1
homicide (attempt) - *see* Assault, burning, hot object
inflicted by other person
stated as intentional, homicide (attempt) - *see* Assault, burning, hot object
liquid (boiling) (hot) NEC X12
stated as undetermined whether accidental or intentional Y27.2
suicide (attempt) X77.2
local application of externally applied substance in medical or surgical care Y63.5
metal (molten) (liquid) (hot) NEC X18
self-inflicted X77.9
stated as undetermined whether accidental or intentional Y27.8
steam X13.1
assault X98.0
stated as undetermined whether accidental or intentional Y27.0
suicide (attempt) X77.0
suicide (attempt) X77.9
vapor (hot) X13.1
assault X98.0
stated as undetermined whether accidental or intentional Y27.0
suicide (attempt) X77.0
Scratched by
cat W55.03
person(s) (accidentally) W50.4
with intent to injure or kill Y04.0
as, or caused by, a crowd or human stampede (with fall) W52
assault Y04.0
homicide (attempt) Y04.0
in
fight Y04.0
legal intervention Y35.894
injuring
bystander Y35.892
law enforcement personnel Y35.891
suspect Y35.890
Seasickness T75.3
Self-harm NEC - *see also* External cause by type, undetermined whether accidental or intentional
intentional - *see* Suicide
poisoning NEC - *see* Table of drugs and biologicals, accident
Self-inflicted (injury) NEC - *see also* External cause by type, undetermined whether accidental or intentional
intentional - *see* Suicide
poisoning NEC - *see* Table of drugs and biologicals, accident
Sequelae (of)
accident NEC - *see* W00-X58 with q as terminal character
assault (homicidal) (any means) - *see* X92-Y08 with q as terminal character

Sequelae (Continued)
homicide, attempt (any means) - *see* X92-Y08 with q as terminal character
injury undetermined whether accidentally or purposely inflicted - *see* Y21-Y33 with q as terminal character
intentional self-harm (classifiable to X71-X83) - *see* X71-X83 with q as terminal character
legal intervention - *see* Y35 with q as terminal character
motor vehicle accident - *see* V00-V99 with q as terminal character
suicide, attempt (any means) - *see* X71-X83 with q as terminal character
transport accident - *see* V00-V99 with q as terminal character
war operations - *see* War operations
Shock
electric - *see* Exposure, electric current
from electric appliance (any) (faulty) W86.8
domestic W86.0
suicide (attempt) X83.1
Shooting, shot (accidental(ly)) - *see also* Discharge, firearm, by type
herself or himself - *see* Discharge, firearm by type, self-inflicted
homicide (attempt) - *see* Discharge, firearm by type, homicide
in war operations - *see* War operations
inflicted by other person - *see* Discharge, firearm by type, homicide
accidental - *see* Discharge, firearm, by type of firearm
legal
execution Y35.91
intervention - *see* Legal, intervention, firearm
self-inflicted - *see* Discharge, firearm by type, suicide
accidental - *see* Discharge, firearm, by type of firearm
suicide (attempt) - *see* Discharge, firearm by type, suicide
Shoving (accidentally) by other person - *see* Pushing, by other person
Sickness
alpine W94.11
motion - *see* Motion
mountain W94.11
Sinking (accidental)
watercraft (causing drowning, submersion) - *see also* Drowning, due to, accident to, watercraft, sinking
causing injury except drowning or submersion - *see* Accident, watercraft, causing, injury NEC
Siriasis X32
Slashed wrists - *see* Cut, self-inflicted
Slipping (accidental) (on same level) (with fall) W01.0
on
ice W00.0
with skates - *see* Accident, transport, pedestrian, conveyance
mud W01.0
oil W01.0

Slipping (Continued)
on (Continued)
snow W00.0
with skis - *see* Accident, transport, pedestrian, conveyance
surface (slippery) (wet) NEC W01.0
Sliver, wood, contact with W45.8
Smoldering (due to fire) - *see* Exposure, fire
Sodomy (attempted) by force Y05
Sound waves (causing injury) W42.9
supersonic W42.0
Splinter, contact with W45.8
Stab, stabbing - *see* Cut
Starvation X58
Status of external cause Y99.9
civilian activity done for financial or other compensation Y99.0
civilian activity done for income or pay Y99.0
hobby not done for income Y99.8
leisure activity Y99.8
military activity Y99.1
off-duty activity of military personnel Y99.8
recreation or sport not for income or while a student Y99.8
specified NEC Y99.8
student activity Y99.8
volunteer activity Y99.8
Stepped on
by
animal (not being ridden) NEC W55.89
being ridden V06
crowd or human stampede W52
person W50.0
Stepping on
object W22.8
with fall W18.9
sports equipment W21.9
stationary W22.09
sports equipment W21.89
person W51
by crowd or human stampede W52
sports equipment W21.9
Sting
arthropod, nonvenomous W57
insect, nonvenomous W57
Storm (cataclysmic) - *see* Forces of nature, cataclysmic storm
Straining, excessive - *see* Overexertion
Strangling - *see* Strangulation
Strangulation (accidental) - *see* category T71
Strenuous movements - *see* Repetitive movements
Striking against
airbag (automobile) W22.10
driver side W22.11
front passenger side W22.12
specified NEC W22.19
bottom when
diving or jumping into water (in) W16.822
causing drowning W16.821
from boat W16.722
causing drowning W16.721
natural body W16.622
causing drowning W16.821
swimming pool W16.522
causing drowning W16.521
falling into water (in) W16.322
causing drowning W16.321

Striking against (*Continued*)
  bottom when (*Continued*)
    falling into water (*Continued*)
      fountain - *see* Striking against,
          bottom when, falling into
          water, specified NEC
      natural body W16.122
        causing drowning W16.121
      reservoir - *see* Striking against,
          bottom when, falling into
          water, specified NEC
      specified NEC W16.322
        causing drowning W16.321
      swimming pool W16.022
        causing drowning W16.021
  diving board (swimming-pool) W21.4
  object W22.8
    with
      drowning or submersion - *see*
          Drowning
      fall - *see* Fall, due to, bumping
          against, object
      caused by crowd or human stampede
          (with fall) W52
      furniture W22.03
      lamppost W22.02
      sports equipment W21.9
      stationary W22.09
        sports equipment W21.89
      wall W22.01
    person(s) W51
      with fall W03
        due to ice or snow W00.0
      as, or caused by, a crowd or human
          stampede (with fall) W52
      assault Y04.2
      homicide (attempt) Y04.2
  sports equipment W21.9
  wall (when) W22.01
    diving or jumping into water (in)
        W16.832
      causing drowning W16.831
      swimming pool W16.532
        causing drowning W16.531
    falling into water (in) W16.332
      causing drowning W16.331
      fountain - *see* Striking against,
          wall when, falling into water,
          specified NEC
      natural body W16.132
        causing drowning W16.131
      reservoir - *see* Striking against,
          wall when, falling into water,
          specified NEC
      specified NEC W16.332
        causing drowning W16.331
      swimming pool W16.032
        causing drowning W16.031
    swimming pool (when) W22.042
      causing drowning W22.041
      diving or jumping into water
          W16.532
        causing drowning W16.531
      falling into water W16.032
        causing drowning W16.031
Struck (accidentally) **by**
  airbag (automobile) W22.10
    driver side W22.11
    front passenger side W22.12
    specified NEC W22.19
  alligator W58.02
  animal (not being ridden) NEC
      W55.89
    being ridden V06

Struck (*Continued*)
  avalanche - *see* Landslide
  ball (hit) (thrown) W21.00
    assault Y08.09
    baseball W21.03
    basketball W21.05
    golf ball W21.04
    football W21.01
    soccer W21.02
    softball W21.07
    specified NEC W21.09
    volleyball W21.06
  bat or racquet
    baseball bat W21.11
      assault Y08.02
    golf club W21.13
      assault Y08.09
    specified NEC W21.19
      assault Y08.09
    tennis racquet W21.12
      assault Y08.09
  bullet - *see also* Discharge, firearm by
      type
    in war operations - *see* War
        operations
  crocodile W58.12
  dog W54.1
  flare, Very pistol - *see* Discharge, firearm
      NEC
  hailstones X39.8
  hockey (ice)
    field
      puck W21.221
      stick W21.211
    puck W21.220
    stick W21.210
      assault Y08.01
  landslide - *see* Landslide
  law-enforcement agent (on duty) -
      see Legal, intervention,
      manhandling
    with blunt object - *see* Legal,
        intervention, blunt object
  lightning X33
    causing fire - *see* Exposure,
        fire
  machine - *see* Contact, with, by type of
      machine
  mammal NEC W55.89
    marine W56.89
  marine animal W56.89
  missile
    firearm - *see* Discharge, firearm by
        type
    in war operations - *see* War
        operations, missile
  object W22.8
    blunt W22.8
      assault Y00
      suicide (attempt) X79
      undetermined whether accidental
          or intentional Y29
    falling W20.8
      from, in, on
        building W20.1
          burning (uncontrolled fire)
              X00.4
        cataclysmic
          earth surface movement NEC
              - *see* Landslide
          storm - *see* Forces of nature,
              cataclysmic storm
        cave-in W20.0
        earthquake X34

Struck (*Continued*)
  object (*Continued*)
    falling (*Continued*)
      from, in, on (*Continued*)
        machine (in operation) - *see*
            Contact, with, by type of
            machine
        structure W20.1
          burning X00.4
        transport vehicle (in motion)*see*
            Accident, transport, by type
            of vehicle
        watercraft V93.49
          due to
            accident to craft V91.39
              powered craft V91.33
                ferry boat V91.31
                fishing boat V91.32
                jetskis V91.33
                liner V91.31
                merchant ship V91.30
                passenger ship V91.31
              unpowered craft V91.38
                canoe V91.35
                inflatable V91.36
                kayak V91.35
                sailboat V91.34
                surf-board V91.38
                windsurfer V91.38
            powered craft V93.43
              ferry boat V93.41
              fishing boat V93.42
              jetskis V93.43
              liner V93.41
              merchant ship V93.40
              passenger ship V93.41
            unpowered craft V93.48
              sailboat V93.44
              surf-board V93.48
              windsurfer V93.48
    moving NEC W20.8
    projected W20.8
      assault Y00
      in sports W21.9
        assault Y08.09
        ball W21.00
          baseball W21.03
          basketball W21.05
          football W21.01
          golf ball W21.04
          soccer W21.02
          softball W21.07
          specified NEC W21.09
          volleyball W21.06
        bat or racquet
          baseball bat W21.11
            assault Y08.02
          golf club W21.13
            assault Y08.09-
          specified NEC W21.19
            assault Y08.09
          tennis racquet W21.12
            assault Y08.09
        hockey (ice)
          field
            puck W21.221
            stick W21.211
          puck W21.220
          stick W21.210
            assault Y08.01
        specified NEC W21.89
      set in motion by explosion - *see*
          Explosion
      thrown W20.8

Struck *(Continued)*
  object *(Continued)*
    thrown *(Continued)*
      assault Y00
      in sports W21.9
        assault Y08.09
        ball W21.00
          baseball W21.03
          basketball W21.05
          football W21.01
          golf ball W21.04
          soccer W21.02
          soft ball W21.07
          specified NEC W21.09
          volleyball W21.06
        bat or racquet
          baseball bat W21.11
            assault Y08.02
          golf club W21.13
            assault Y08.09
          specified NEC W21.19
            assault Y08.09
          tennis racquet W21.12
            assault Y08.09
        hockey (ice)
          field
            puck W21.221
            stick W21.211
          puck W21.220
          stick W21.210
            assault Y08.01
        specified NEC W21.89
  other person(s) W50.0
    with
      blunt object W22.8
        intentional, homicide (attempt) Y00
        sports equipment W21.9
        undetermined whether accidental or intentional Y29
      fall W03
        due to ice or snow W00.0
    as, or caused by, a crowd or human stampede (with fall) W52
    assault Y04.2
    homicide (attempt) Y04.2
    in legal intervention Y35.814
      injuring
        bystander Y35.813
        law enforcement personnel Y35.812
        suspect Y35.811
      sports equipment W21.9
  police (on duty) - *see* Legal, intervention, manhandling
    with blunt object - *see* Legal, intervention, blunt object
  sports equipment W21.9
    assault Y08.09
    ball W21.00
      baseball W21.03
      basketball W21.05
      football W21.01
      golf ball W21.04
      soccer W21.02
      soft ball W21.07
      specified NEC W21.09
      volleyball W21.06
    bat or racquet
      baseball bat W21.11
        assault Y08.02
      golf club W21.13
        assault Y08.09

Struck *(Continued)*
  sports equipment *(Continued)*
    bat or racquet *(Continued)*
      specified NEC W21.19
      tennis racquet W21.12
        assault Y08.09
    cleats (shoe) W21.31
    foot wear NEC W21.39
    football helmet W21.81
    hockey (ice)
      field
        puck W21.221
        stick W21.211
      puck W21.220
      stick W21.210
        assault Y08.01
    skate blades W21.32
    specified NEC W21.89
      assault Y08.09
  thunderbolt X33
    causing fire - *see* Exposure, fire
  transport vehicle NEC *(see also* Accident, transport) V09.9
    intentional, homicide (attempt) Y03.0
    motor NEC *(see also* Accident, transport) V09.20
    homicide Y03.0
  vehicle (transport) NEC - *see* Accident, transport, by type of vehicle
    stationary (falling from jack, hydraulic lift, ramp) W20.8
Stumbling
  over
    animal NEC W64
      with fall W18.09
    carpet, rug or (small) object W22.8
      with fall W18.09
    person W51
      with fall W03
        due to ice or snow W00.0
Submersion (accidental) - *see* Drowning
Suffocation (accidental) (by external means) (by pressure) (mechanical) - *see also* category T71
  due to, by
    avalanche - *see* Landslide
    explosion - *see* Explosion
    fire - *see* Exposure, fire
    food, any type (aspiration) (ingestion) (inhalation) - *see* categories T17 and T18
    ignition - *see* Ignition
    landslide - *see* Landslide
    machine(ry) - *see* Contact, with, by type of machine
    vomitus (aspiration) (inhalation) - *see* subcategories T17.81, T18.81
  in
    burning building X00.8
Suicide, suicidal (attempted) (by) X83.8
  blunt object X79
  burning, burns X76
    hot object X77.9
      fluid NEC X77.2
      household appliance X77.3
      specified NEC X77.8
      steam X77.0
      tap water X77.1
      vapors X77.0
  caustic substance - *see* Table of drugs and chemicals
  cold, extreme X83.2

Suicide, suicidal *(Continued)*
  collision of motor vehicle with
    motor vehicle X82.0
    specified NEC X82.8
    train X82.1
    tree X82.2
  crashing of aircraft X83.0
  cut (any part of body) X78.9
  cutting or piercing instrument X78.9
    dagger X78.2
    glass X78.0
    knife X78.1
    specified NEC X78.8
    sword X78.2
  drowning (in) X71.9
    bathtub X71.0
    natural water X71.3
    specified NEC X71.8
    swimming pool X71.1
      following fall X71.2
  electrocution X83.1
  explosive(s) (material) X75
  fire, flames X76
  firearm X74.9
    airgun X74.01
    handgun X72
    hunting rifle X73.1
    larger X73.9
      specified NEC X73.8
    machine gun X73.2
    shotgun X73.0
    specified NEC X74.8
  hanging X83.8
  hot object - *see* Suicide, burning, hot object
  jumping
    before moving object X81
      motor vehicle X81.0
    from high place X80
  late effect of attempt - *see* X71-X83 with q as terminal character
  lying before moving object, train, vehicle X81
  poisoning - *see* Table of drugs and chemicals
  puncture (any part of body) - *see* Suicide, cutting or piercing instrument
  scald - *see* Suicide, burning, hot object
  sequelae of attempt - *see* X71-X83 with q as terminal character
  sharp object (any) - *see* Suicide, cutting or piercing instrument
  shooting - *see* Suicide, firearm
  specified means NEC X83.8
  stab (any part of body) - *see* Suicide, cutting or piercing instrument
  steam, hot vapors X77.0
  strangulation X83.8
  submersion - *see* Suicide, drowning
  suffocation X83.8
  wound NEC X83.8
Sunstroke X32
Supersonic waves (causing injury) W42.0
Surgical procedure, complication of (delayed or as an abnormal reaction without mention of misadventure) - *see also* Complication of or following, by type of procedure
  due to or as a result of misadventure - *see* Misadventure

Swallowed, swallowing
  foreign body - *see* Foreign body,
    alimentary canal
  poison - *see* Table of drugs and
    chemicals

Swallowed, swallowing *(Continued)*
  substance
    caustic or corrosive - *see* Table of
      drugs and chemicals

Swallowed, swallowing *(Continued)*
  substance *(Continued)*
    poisonous - *see* Table of drugs and
      chemicals

T

Tackle in sport W03
Terrorism (involving) Y38.9
  biological weapons Y38.6
  chemical weapons Y38.7
  conflagration Y38.3
  explosion Y38.2
    destruction of aircraft Y38.1
    marine weapons Y38.0
  fire Y38.3
  firearms Y38.4
  hot substances Y38.3
  nuclear weapons Y38.5
  specified method NEC Y38.8
Thirst X58.8
Threat to breathing
  aspiration - *see* Aspiration
  due to cave-in, falling earth or
    substance NEC - *see* category T71
Thrown (accidentally)
  against part (any) of or object in
    transport vehicle (in motion) NEC
    (*see* also Accident, transport)
  from
    high place, homicide (attempt) Y01
    machinery - *see* Contact, with, by type
      of machine

Thrown (*Continued*)
  from (*Continued*)
    transport vehicle NEC (*see* also
      Accident, transport) V89.9
  off - *see* Thrown, from
Thunderbolt X33
  causing fire - *see* Exposure, fire
Tidal wave (any injury) NEC - *see* Forces
  of nature, tidal wave
Took
  overdose (drug) - *see* Table of drugs and
    chemicals
  poison - *see* Table of drugs and
    chemicals
Tornado (any injury) X37.1
Torrential rain (any injury) X37.8
Torture X58
Trampled by animal NEC W55.89
  being ridden V06
Trapped (accidentally)
  between objects (moving) (stationary
    and moving) - *see* Caught
  by part (any) of
    motorcycle V29.88
    pedal cycle V19.88
    transport vehicle NEC (*see* also
      Accident, transport) V89.9

Travel (effects) (sickness) T75.3
Tree falling on or hitting (accidentally)
  (person) W20.8
Tripping
  over
    animal W64
      with fall W01.0
    carpet, rug or (small) object W22.8
      with fall W18.09
    person W51
      with fall W03
        due to ice or snow W00.0
Twisted by person(s) (accidentally)
  W50.2
  with intent to injure or kill Y04.0
  as, or caused by, a crowd or human
    stampede (with fall) W52
  assault Y04.0
  homicide (attempt) Y04.0
  in
    fight Y04.0
    legal intervention - *see* Legal,
      intervention, manhandling
Twisting, excessive - *see*
  Overexertion

U

Undetermined intent (contact)
    (exposure)
  automobile collision Y32
  blunt object Y29
  drowning (submersion) (in) Y21.9
    bathtub Y21.0
      after fall Y21.1
    natural water (lake) (ocean) (pond)
        (river) (stream) Y21.4
    specified place NEC Y21.8
    swimming pool Y21.2
      after fall Y21.3
  explosive material Y25
  fall, jump or push from high place Y30
  falling, lying or running before moving
      object Y31
  fire Y26
  firearm discharge Y24.9
    airgun (BB) (pellet) Y24.0
    handgun (pistol) (revolver) Y22

Undetermined intent *(Continued)*
  firearm discharge *(Continued)*
    hunting rifle Y23.1
    larger Y23.9
      hunting rifle Y23.1
      machine fun Y23.3
      military Y23.2
      shotgun Y23.0
      specified type NEC Y23.8
    machine fun Y23.3
    military Y23.2
    shotgun Y23.0
    specified type NEC Y24.8
    Very pistol Y24.8
  hot object Y27.9
    fluid NEC Y27.2
    household appliance Y27.3
    specified object NEC Y27.8
    steam Y27.0
    tap water Y27.1
    vapor Y27.0

Undetermined intent *(Continued)*
  jump, fall or push from high
      place Y30
  lying, falling or running before moving
      object Y31
  motor vehicle crash Y32
  push, fall or jump from high
      place Y30
  running, falling or lying before moving
      object Y31
  sharp object Y28.9
    dagger Y28.2
    glass Y28.0
    knife Y28.1
    specified object NEC Y28.8
    sword Y28.2
  smoke Y26
  specified event NEC Y33

V

Vibration (causing injury) W49
Victim (of)
    avalanche - *see* Landslide
    earth movements NEC - *see* Forces of
        nature, earth movement
    earthquake X34
    flood - *see* Flood
    landslide - *see* Landslide

Victim *(Continued)*
    lightning X33
        causing fire - *see* Exposure, fire
    storm (cataclysmic) NEC - *see* Forces of
        nature, cataclysmic storm
    volcanic eruption X35-
Volcanic eruption (any injury) X35-
Vomitus, gastric contents in air passages
    (with asphyxia, obstruction or suffoca-
    tion) - *see* subcategories T17.81, T18.81

W

Walked into stationary object (any) W22.09
  furniture W22.03
  lamppost W22.02
  wall W22.01
War operations (injuries to military personnel and civilians during war, civil insurrection and peacekeeping missions)
  (by) (from) (involving) Y36.90-
  after cessation of hostilities Y36.89-
    explosion (of)
      bomb placed during war
        operations Y36.82-
      mine placed during war operations
        Y36.81-
    specified NEC Y36.88-
  air blast Y36.20-
  aircraft
    destruction- *see* War operations,
      destruction of aircraft
  airway restriction - *see* War operations,
    restriction of airways
  asphyxiation - *see* War operations,
    restriction of airways
  biological weapons Y36.6x-
  blast Y36.20-
  blast fragments Y36.20-
  blast wave Y36.20-
  blast wind Y36.20-
  bomb Y36.20-
    dirty Y36.50-
    gasoline Y36.31-
    incendiary Y36.31-
    petrol Y36.31-
  bullet Y36.43-
    incendiary Y36.32-
    rubber Y36.41-
  chemical weapons Y36.7x-
  combat
    hand to hand (unarmed) combat
      Y36.44-
    using blunt or piercing object Y36.45-
  conflagration - *see* War operations, fire
  conventional warfare NEC Y36.49-
  depth-charge Y36.01-
  destruction of aircraft Y36.10-
    due to
      air to air missile Y36.11-
      collision with other aircraft Y36.12-
      detonation (accidental) of onboard
        munitions and explosives
        Y36.14-
      enemy fire or explosives Y36.11-
      explosive placed on aircraft Y36.11-
      onboard fire Y36.13-
      rocket propelled grenade [RPG]
        Y36.11-
      small arms fire Y36.11-
      surface to air missile Y36.11-
    specified NEC Y36.19-
  detonation (accidental) of
    onboard marine weapons Y36.05-
    own munitions or munitions launch
      device Y36.24-

War operations *(Continued)*
  dirty bomb Y36.50-
  explosion (of) Y36.20-
    after cessation of hostilities
      bomb placed during war
        operations Y36.82-
      mine placed during war operations
        Y36.81-
    aerial bomb Y36.21-
    bomb NOS Y36.20- - *see also* War
      operations, bomb(s)
    own munitions or munitions launch
      device (accidental) Y36.24-
    fragments Y36.20-
    grenade Y36.29-
    guided missile Y36.22-
    improvised explosive device [IED]
      (person-borne) (roadside)
      (vehicle-borne) Y36.23-
    land mine Y36.29-
    marine mine (at sea) (in harbor)
      Y36.02-
    marine weapon Y36.00-
      specified NEC Y36.09-
    sea-based artillery shell Y36.03-
    specified NEC Y36.29-
    torpedo Y36.04-
  fire Y36.30-
  firearms
    discharge Y36.43-
    pellets Y36.42-
  flamethrower Y36.33-
  fragments (from) (of)
    improvised explosive device [IED]
      (person-borne) (roadside)
      (vehicle-borne)Y36.26-
    munitions Y36.25-
    specified NEC Y36.29-
    weapons Y36.27-
  friendly fire Y36.92-
  hand to hand (unarmed) combat Y36.44-
  hot substances - *see* War operations, fire
  incendiary bullet Y36.32-
  nuclear weapon (effects of) Y36.50-
    acute radiation exposure Y36.54-
    blast pressure Y36.51-
    direct blast Y36.51-
    direct heat Y36.53-
    fallout exposure Y36.54-
    fireball Y36.53-
    indirect blast (struck or crushed by
      blast debris) (being thrown by
      blast) Y36.52-
    ionizing radiation (immediate
      exposure) Y36.54-
    nuclear radiation Y36.54-
    radiation
      ionizing (immediate exposure)
        Y36.54-
      nuclear Y36.54-
      thermal Y36.53-
    specified NEC Y36.59-
    secondary effects Y36.54-
    thermal radiation Y36.53-

War operations *(Continued)*
  restriction of air (airway)
    intentional Y36.46-
    unintentional Y36.47-
  rubber bullets Y36.41-
  shrapnel NOS Y36.29-
  suffocation - *see* War operations,
    restriction of airways
  unconventional warfare NEC Y36.7x-
  underwater blast NOS Y36.00-
  warfare
    conventional NEC Y36.49-
    unconventional NEC Y36.7x-
  weapons
    biological weapons Y36.6x-
    chemical Y36.7x-
    nuclear (effects of) Y36.50-
      acute radiation exposure Y36.54-
      blast pressure Y36.51-
      direct blast Y36.51-
      direct heat Y36.53-
      fallout exposure Y36.54-
      fireball Y36.53-
      indirect blast (struck or crushed by
        blast debris) (being thrown by
        blast) Y36.52-
      radiation
        ionizing (immediate exposure)
          Y36.54-
        nuclear Y36.54-
        thermal Y36.53-
      secondary effects Y36.54-
      specified NEC Y36.59-
      indirect blast (struck or crushed by
        blast debris) (being thrown by
        blast) Y36.52-
  of mass destruction [WMD] Y36.91-
  weapon of mass destruction [WMD]
    Y36.91-
Washed
  away by flood - *see* Flood
  off road by storm (transport vehicle)
    - *see* Forces of nature, cataclysmic
    storm
Weather exposure NEC - *see* Forces of
  nature
Weightlessness (causing injury) (effects of)
  (in spacecraft, real or simulated) X52
Work related condition Y99.0
Wound (accidental) NEC (*see also* Injury)
  X58
  battle (*see also* War operations) Y36.9
  gunshot - *see* Discharge, firearm by
    type
Wreck transport vehicle NEC (*see* also
  Accident, transport) V89.9
Wrong
  device implanted into correct surgical
    site Y65.51
  fluid in infusion Y65.1
  procedure (operation) on correct patient
    Y65.51
  patient, procedure performed on Y65.52

PART III

ICD-10-CM
Tabular List of Diseases
and Injuries

CHAPTER 1

CERTAIN INFECTIOUS AND PARASITIC DISEASES (A00-B99)

Includes diseases generally recognized as communicable or transmissible
Use additional code for any associated drug resistance (Z16)

Excludes1 carrier or suspected carrier of infectious disease (Z22.-)
certain localized infections - see body system-related chapters
infectious and parasitic diseases complicating pregnancy, childbirth and the puerperium (O98.-)
influenza and other acute respiratory infections (J00-J22)

Excludes2 infectious and parasitic diseases specific to the perinatal period (P35-P39)

This chapter contains the following blocks:

A00-A09	Intestinal infectious diseases
A15-A19	Tuberculosis
A20-A28	Certain zoonotic bacterial diseases
A30-A49	Other bacterial diseases
A50-A64	Infections with a predominantly sexual mode of transmission
A65-A69	Other spirochetal diseases
A70-A74	Other diseases caused by chlamydiae
A75-A79	Rickettsioses
A80-A89	Viral infections of the central nervous system
A90-A99	Arthropod-borne viral fevers and viral hemorrhagic fevers
B00-B09	Viral infections characterized by skin and mucous membrane lesions
B10	Other human herpesviruses
B15-B19	Viral hepatitis
B20	Human immunodeficiency virus [HIV] disease
B25-B34	Other viral diseases
B35-B49	Mycoses
B50-B64	Protozoal diseases
B65-B83	Helminthiases
B85-B89	Pediculosis, acariasis and other infestations
B90-B94	Sequelae of infectious and parasitic diseases
B95-B97	Bacterial, viral and other infectious agents
B99	Other infectious diseases

INTESTINAL INFECTIOUS DISEASES (A00-A09)

● **A00 Cholera**
A serious, often deadly, infectious disease of the small intestine

  A00.0 Cholera due to Vibrio cholerae 01, biovar cholerae 🦠
  Classical cholera

  A00.1 Cholera due to Vibrio cholerae 01, biovar eltor 🦠
  Cholera eltor

  ■**A00.9 Cholera, unspecified** 🦠

● **A01 Typhoid and paratyphoid fevers**
Caused by Salmonella typhi and Salmonella paratyphi A, B, and C bacteria

  ● **A01.0 Typhoid fever**
  Infection due to Salmonella typhi

  ■ **A01.00 Typhoid fever, unspecified** 🦠
  A01.01 Typhoid meningitis 🦠
  A01.02 Typhoid fever with heart involvement 🦠
  Typhoid endocarditis
  Typhoid myocarditis
  A01.03 Typhoid pneumonia 🦠
  A01.04 Typhoid arthritis 🦠
  A01.05 Typhoid osteomyelitis 🦠
  A01.09 Typhoid fever with other complications 🦠

  A01.1 Paratyphoid fever A 🦠
  A01.2 Paratyphoid fever B 🦠
  A01.3 Paratyphoid fever C 🦠
  ■**A01.4 Paratyphoid fever, unspecified** 🦠
  Infection due to Salmonella paratyphi NOS

● **A02 Other salmonella infections**
  Includes infection or foodborne intoxication due to any Salmonella species other than S. typhi and S. paratyphi

  A02.0 Salmonella enteritis 🦠
  Salmonellosis

  A02.1 Salmonella sepsis 🦠

  ● **A02.2 Localized salmonella infections**
    ■**A02.20 Localized salmonella infection, unspecified**
    Specified in the documentation as localized, but unspecified as to type

    A02.21 Salmonella meningitis 🦠
    Specified as localized in the meninges

    A02.22 Salmonella pneumonia 🦠
    Specified as localized in the lungs

    A02.23 Salmonella arthritis 🦠
    Specified as localized in the joints

    A02.24 Salmonella osteomyelitis 🦠
    Specified as localized in bone

    A02.25 Salmonella pyelonephritis 🦠
    Salmonella tubulo-interstitial nephropathy

    A02.29 Salmonella with other localized infection 🦠
    Specified as localized (because it is still under localized heading) but does not assign into any of the above codes

  A02.8 Other specified salmonella infections 🦠
  Any specified salmonella infection which does NOT assign into any of the above codes (not specified as localized)

  ■**A02.9 Salmonella infection, unspecified** 🦠
  Unspecified in the documentation as to specific type of salmonella

Item 1-1 Salmonella is a bacterium that lives in the intestines of fowl and mammals and can spread to humans through improper food preparation and cooking. Salmonellosis is an infection with the bacterium. Symptoms include diarrhea, fever, and abdominal cramps 12 to 72 hours after infection. The illness usually lasts 4 to 7 days, and most persons recover without treatment. The diarrhea may be so severe that the patient needs to be hospitalized. Patients with immunocompromised systems in chronic, ill health are more likely to have the infection invade their bloodstream with life-threatening results. For example, patients with sickle cell disease are more prone to salmonella osteomyelitis than others.

● Unacceptable First-Listed Diagnosis   ● Use Additional Character(s)   ■ Unspecified   **OGCR** Official Guidelines for Coding and Reporting
🦠 Complication\Comorbidity   🦠 Major C\C   Excludes 1   Excludes 2   Includes   Use additional   Code first   Code also

CHAPTER 1 (A00-B99)

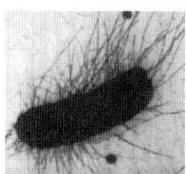

Figure 1-1 Electron micrograh of escherichia coli *(E. coli)* expressing P fimbriae. (From Mandell, Bennett, & Dolin: Principles and Practice of Infectious Diseases, 6th ed. 2005, Churchill Livingstone, An Imprint of Elsevier.)

Item 1-2   Escherichia coli [E. coli] is a gram-negative bacterium found in the intestinal tracts of humans and animals and is usually non-pathogenic. Pathogenic strains can cause diarrhea or pyogenic (pus-producing) infections. Can be a threat to food safety.

● **A03   Shigellosis**
An infectious disease caused by bacteria (Shigella)

A03.0   Shigellosis due to Shigella dysenteriae 🦠
Group A shigellosis [Shiga-Kruse dysentery]

A03.1   Shigellosis due to Shigella flexneri
Group B shigellosis

A03.2   Shigellosis due to Shigella boydii
Group C shigellosis

A03.3   Shigellosis due to Shigella sonnei
Group D shigellosis

A03.8   Other shigellosis

■ **A03.9   Shigellosis, unspecified**
Bacillary dysentery NOS

● **A04   Other bacterial intestinal infections**

> **Excludes1**   bacterial foodborne intoxications, NEC (A05.-)
> tuberculous enteritis (A18.32)

A04.0   Enteropathogenic Escherichia coli infection 🦠
Pertaining to or producing intestinal disease

A04.1   Enterotoxigenic Escherichia coli infection 🦠
Producing or containing intestinal toxin

A04.2   Enteroinvasive Escherichia coli infection 🦠
Capable of penetrating and spreading through intestinal mucosal epithelium

A04.3   Enterohemorrhagic Escherichia coli infection 🦠
Causing bloody diarrhea, resulting from microorganisms

A04.4   Other intestinal Escherichia coli infections 🦠
Escherichia coli enteritis NOS

A04.5   Campylobacter enteritis 🦠
Spiral shaped bacterium

A04.6   Enteritis due to Yersinia enterocolitica 🦠

> **Excludes1**   extraintestinal yersiniosis (A28.2)

Transmitted by infected food /water and person-to-person contact, affecting intestinal tract

A04.7   Enterocolitis due to Clostridium difficile
Foodborne intoxication by Clostridium difficile
Pseudomembraneous colitis 🦠
Marked by fibrinous deposit (false membrane) with enmeshed necrotic cells

A04.8   Other specified bacterial intestinal infections 🦠

■ **A04.9   Bacterial intestinal infection, unspecified** 🦠
Bacterial enteritis NOS

● **A05   Other bacterial foodborne intoxications, not elsewhere classified**

> **Excludes1**   Escherichia coli infection (A04.0-A04.4)
> foodborne intoxication by Clostridium difficile (A04.7)
> listeriosis (A32.-)
> salmonella foodborne intoxication and infection (A02.-)
> toxic effect of noxious foodstuffs (T61-T62)

A05.0   Foodborne staphylococcal intoxication 🦠

A05.1   Botulism food poisoning 🦠
Botulism NOS
Classical foodborne intoxication due to Clostridium botulinum

> **Excludes1**   infant botulism (A48.51)
> wound botulism (A48.52)

A05.2   Foodborne Clostridium perfringens [Clostridium welchii] intoxication 🦠
Type A causes gas gangrene and necrotizing colitis; major cause of food poisoning in humans
Enteritis necroticans
Pig-bel

A05.3   Foodborne Vibrio parahaemolyticus intoxication 🦠
Organism that survives only in high salt environment (halophilic), major cause of gastroenteritis due to consumption of raw or improperly cooked fish/seafood

A05.4   Foodborne Bacillus cereus intoxication 🦠
Spore-forming species commonly found in soil, causes food poisoning from formation of intestinal toxins in contaminated foods

A05.5   Foodborne Vibrio vulnificus intoxication 🦠
Species that survives in high salt environment (halophilic) with infection by eating raw seafood causes septicemia and cellulitis

A05.8   Other specified bacterial foodborne intoxications 🦠

■ **A05.9   Bacterial foodborne intoxication, unspecified**

● **A06   Amebiasis**
An intestinal illness caused by the microscopic parasite Entamoeba histolytica

> **Includes**   infection due to Entamoeba histolytica
> **Excludes1**   other protozoal intestinal diseases (A07.-)
> **Excludes2**   acanthamebiasis (B60.1-)
> Naegleriasis (B60.2)

A06.0   Acute amebic dysentery 🦠
Acute amebiasis
Intestinal amebiasis NOS

A06.1   Chronic intestinal amebiasis 🦠

A06.2   Amebic nondysenteric colitis 🦠
Pertaining to single cell microorganism

A06.3   Ameboma of intestine 🦠
Tumorlike mass produced by localized inflammation often in intestine
Ameboma NOS

A06.4   Amebic liver abscess 🦠
Hepatic amebiasis

A06.5   Amebic lung abscess 🦠
Amebic abscess of lung (and liver)

A06.6   Amebic brain abscess 🦠
Amebic abscess of brain (and liver) (and lung)

A06.7   Cutaneous amebiasis

● Unacceptable First-Listed Diagnosis   ● Use Additional Character(s)   ■ Unspecified   **OGCR** Official Guidelines for Coding and Reporting
🦠 Complication\Comorbidity   🦠 Major C\C   Excludes 1   Excludes 2   Includes   Use additional   Code first   Code also

CHAPTER 1 (A00-B99)

● **A06.8 Amebic infection of other sites**

    A06.81 Amebic cystitis 🦠

    A06.82 Other amebic genitourinary infections 🦠
        Amebic balanitis
        Amebic vesiculitis
        Amebic vulvovaginitis

    A06.89 Other amebic infections 🦠
        Amebic appendicitis
        Amebic splenic abscess

■ **A06.9 Amebiasis, unspecified**

● **A07 Other protozoal intestinal diseases**

    A07.0 Balantidiasis
        Balantidial dysentery
        Infection by protozoa that may cause diarrhea and dysentery, with ulceration of colonic mucous membranes

    A07.1 Giardiasis [lambliasis] 🦠
        Common infection in small intestine spread by contaminated food, water, or direct person-to-person contact

    A07.2 Cryptosporidiosis 🦠
        Human infection with protozoa usually seen as self-limited diarrhea in those who work with cattle

    A07.3 Isosporiasis 🦠
        Human intestinal disease caused by protozoa
        Infection due to Isospora belli and Isospora hominis
        Intestinal coccidiosis
        Isosporosis

    A07.4 Cyclosporiasis 🦠
        Infection by protozoa with most common species infecting humans being C cayetanensis

    A07.8 Other specified protozoal intestinal diseases 🦠
        Intestinal microsporidiosis
        Intestinal trichomoniasis
        Sarcocystosis
        Sarcosporidiosis

■ **A07.9 Protozoal intestinal disease, unspecified** 🦠
        Flagellate diarrhea
        Protozoal colitis
        Protozoal diarrhea
        Protozoal dysentery

● **A08 Viral and other specified intestinal infections**

    | Excludes1 | influenza with involvement of gastrointestinal tract (J10.81) |

    A08.0 Rotaviral enteritis 🦠

●   **A08.1 Acute gastroenteropathy due to Norwalk agent and other small round viruses**

    A08.11 Acute gastroenteropathy due to Norwalk 🦠
        Acute gastroenteropathy due to Norovirus
        Acute gastroenteropathy due to Norwalk-like agent

    A08.19 Acute gastroenteropathy due to other small round viruses 🦠
        Acute gastroenteropathy due to small round virus [SRV] NOS

    A08.2 Adenoviral enteritis 🦠

●   **A08.3 Other viral enteritis**

    A08.31 Calicivirus enteritis 🦠

    A08.32 Astrovirus enteritis 🦠

    A08.39 Other viral enteritis 🦠
        Coxsackie virus enteritis
        Echovirus enteritis
        Enterovirus enteritis NEC
        Torovirus enteritis

■ **A08.4 Viral intestinal infection, unspecified**
    Viral enteritis NOS
    Viral gastroenteritis NOS
    Viral gastroenteropathy NOS

  A08.8 Other specified intestinal infections

■ **A09 Infectious gastroenteritis and colitis, unspecified** 🦠
    Infectious colitis NOS
    Infectious enteritis NOS
    Infectious gastroenteritis NOS

    | Excludes1 | colitis NOS (K52.9) |
        diarrhea NOS (R19.7)
        enteritis NOS (K52.9)
        gastroenteritis NOS (K52.9)
        noninfective gastroenteritis and colitis, unspecified (K52.9)

TUBERCULOSIS (A15-A19)

    | Includes | infections due to Mycobacterium tuberculosis and Mycobacterium bovis |
    | Excludes1 | congenital tuberculosis (P37.0) |
        pneumoconiosis associated with tuberculosis, any type in A15 (J65)
        sequelae of tuberculosis (B90.-)
        silicotuberculosis (J65)

● **A15 Respiratory tuberculosis**

    A15.0 Tuberculosis of lung 🦠
        Tuberculous bronchiectasis
        Chronic dilatation of bronchi
        Tuberculous fibrosis of lung
        Tuberculous pneumonia
        Tuberculous pneumothorax

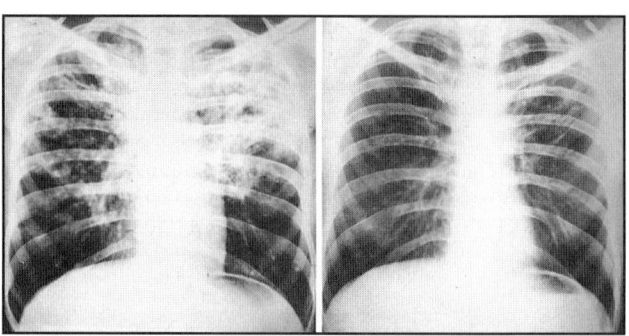

Figure 1-2 Far advanced bilteral pulmonary tuberculosis before and after 8 months of treatment with streptomycin, PAS, and isoniazid. (From Hinshaw HC, Garland LH: Diseases of the Chest, 2nd ed. Philadelphia, WB Saunders, 1963, p. 538.)

Item 1-3 Tuberculosis is a common and deadly infectious disease caused by the Mycobacterium tuberculosis organism. The first tuberculosis infection is called the **primary infection** and most commonly attacks the lungs but can affect the central nervous system, lymphatic system, circulatory system, genitourinary system, bones, joints, and even the skin. A **Ghon** lesion is the **initial lesion.** A **secondary lesion** occurs when the tubercle bacilli are carried to other areas.

Item 1-4 Although it primarily affects the lungs, the bacteria *Mycobacterium tuberculosis* can travel from the pulmonary circulation to virtually any organ in the body, much as a cancer metastasizes to a secondary site. If the immune system becomes compromised by age or disease, what would otherwise be a self-limiting primary tuberculosis in the lungs will develop in other organs. These are known as extrapulmonary sites.

CHAPTER 1 (A00-B99)

● Unacceptable First-Listed Diagnosis   ● Use Additional Character(s)   ■ Unspecified   **OGCR** Official Guidelines for Coding and Reporting
🦠 Complication\Comorbidity   🦠 Major C\C | Excludes 1 | | Excludes 2 | Includes   Use additional   Code first   Code also

A15.4　Tuberculosis of intrathoracic lymph nodes 🦠
　　Tuberculosis of hilar lymph nodes
　　Tuberculosis of mediastinal lymph nodes
　　Tuberculosis of tracheobronchial lymph nodes
　　| Excludes1 | tuberculosis specified as primary (A15.7)

A15.5　Tuberculosis of larynx, trachea and bronchus 🦠
　　Tuberculosis of bronchus
　　Tuberculosis of glottis
　　Tuberculosis of larynx
　　Tuberculosis of trachea

A15.6　Tuberculous pleurisy 🦠
　　Tuberculosis of pleura
　　Tuberculous empyema
　　| Excludes1 | primary respiratory tuberculosis (A15.7)

A15.7　Primary respiratory tuberculosis 🦠

A15.8　Other respiratory tuberculosis 🦠
　　Mediastinal tuberculosis
　　Nasopharyngeal tuberculosis
　　Tuberculosis of nose
　　Tuberculosis of sinus [any nasal]

A15.9　Respiratory tuberculosis unspecified 🦠

● **A17　Tuberculosis of nervous system**

A17.0　Tuberculous meningitis 🦠
　　Tuberculosis of meninges (cerebral) (spinal)
　　Tuberculous leptomeningitis
　　| Excludes1 | tuberculous meningoencephalitis (A17.82)

A17.1　Meningeal tuberculoma 🦠
　　Tuberculoma of meninges (cerebral) (spinal)
　　| Excludes2 | tuberculoma of brain and spinal cord (A17.81)

● **A17.8　Other tuberculosis of nervous system**

A17.81　Tuberculoma of brain and spinal cord 🦠
　　Tuberculous abscess of brain and spinal cord

A17.82　Tuberculous meningoencephalitis 🦠
　　Inflammation of brain and meninges; AKA cerebromeningitis and encephalomeningitis
　　Tuberculous myelitis

A17.83　Tuberculous neuritis 🦠
　　Tuberculous mononeuropathy

A17.89　Other tuberculosis of nervous system 🦠
　　Tuberculous polyneuropathy

A17.9　Tuberculosis of nervous system, unspecified 🦠

● **A18　Tuberculosis of other organs**

● **A18.0　Tuberculosis of bones and joints**

A18.01　Tuberculosis of spine 🦠
　　Pott's disease or curvature of spine
　　Tuberculous arthritis
　　Tuberculous osteomyelitis of spine
　　Tuberculous spondylitis

A18.02　Tuberculous arthritis of other joints 🦠
　　Tuberculosis of hip (joint)
　　Tuberculosis of knee (joint)

A18.03　Tuberculosis of other bones 🦠
　　Tuberculous mastoiditis
　　Tuberculous osteomyelitis

A18.09　Other musculoskeletal tuberculosis 🦠
　　Tuberculous myositis
　　Tuberculous synovitis
　　Tuberculous tenosynovitis

● **A18.1　Tuberculosis of genitourinary system**

A18.10　Tuberculosis of genitourinary system, unspecified 🦠

A18.11　Tuberculosis of kidney and ureter 🦠

A18.12　Tuberculosis of bladder 🦠

A18.13　Tuberculosis of other urinary organs 🦠
　　Tuberculous urethritis

A18.14　Tuberculosis of prostate 🦠

A18.15　Tuberculosis of other male genital organs 🦠

A18.16　Tuberculosis of cervix 🦠

A18.17　Tuberculous female pelvic inflammatory disease 🦠
　　Tuberculous endometritis
　　Tuberculous oophoritis and salpingitis
　　Oophoritis = inflammation of ovary
　　Salpingitis = inflammation of fallopian tube

A18.18　Tuberculosis of other female genital organs 🦠
　　Tuberculous ulceration of vulva

● **A18.2　Tuberculous peripheral lymphadenopathy** 🦠
　　Tuberculous adenitis
　　| Excludes2 | tuberculosis of bronchial and mediastinal lymph nodes (A15.4)
　　tuberculosis of mesenteric and retroperitoneal lymph nodes (A18.39)
　　tuberculous tracheobronchial adenopathy (A15.4)

● **A18.3　Tuberculosis of intestines, peritoneum and mesenteric glands**

A18.31　Tuberculous peritonitis 🦠
　　Tuberculous ascites

A18.32　Tuberculous enteritis 🦠
　　Tuberculosis of anus and rectum
　　Tuberculosis of intestine (large) (small)

A18.39　Retroperitoneal tuberculosis 🦠
　　Tuberculosis of mesenteric glands
　　Tuberculosis of retroperitoneal (lymph glands)

● **A18.4　Tuberculosis of skin and subcutaneous tissue** 🦠
　　Erythema induratum, tuberculous
　　Lupus excedens
　　Lupus vulgaris NOS
　　Lupus vulgaris of eyelid
　　Cutaneous tuberculosis characterized by reddish brown plaque on skin surrounded by papules and nodules
　　Scrofuloderma
　　Type of cutaneous tuberculosis, with direct extension of tuberculosis into skin from underlying structures; AKA tuberculosis colliquativa
　　Tuberculosis of external ear
　　| Excludes2 | lupus erythematosus (L93.-)
　　lupus NOS (M32.9)
　　systemic (M32.-)

● **A18.5　Tuberculosis of eye**
　　| Excludes2 | lupus vulgaris of eyelid (A18.4)

A18.50　Tuberculosis of eye, unspecified 🦠

A18.51　Tuberculous episcleritis 🦠
　　Inflammation of episclera and adjacent tissues

● Unacceptable First-Listed Diagnosis　　● Use Additional Character(s)　　▨ Unspecified　　**OGCR** Official Guidelines for Coding and Reporting
🦠 Complication\Comorbidity　🦠 Major C\C　| Excludes 1 |　| Excludes 2 |　Includes　Use additional　Code first　Code also

793

CHAPTER 1 (A00-B99)

A18.52 **Tuberculous keratitis** 🕭
    Tuberculous interstitial keratitis
    Tuberculous keratoconjunctivitis
      (interstitial) (phlyctenular)
    Inflammation of cornea and conjunctiva

A18.53 **Tuberculous chorioretinitis** 🕭
    Inflammation of choroid and retina; retino-
    * choroiditis*

A18.54 **Tuberculous iridocyclitis** 🕭
    Inflammation of iris and ciliary body

A18.59 **Other tuberculosis of eye** 🕭
    Tuberculous conjunctivitis

A18.6 **Tuberculosis of (inner) (middle) ear** 🕭
    Tuberculous otitis media

    | Excludes2 | tuberculosis of external ear (A18.4)
                         tuberculous mastoiditis (A18.03)

A18.7 **Tuberculosis of adrenal glands** 🕭
    Tuberculous Addison's disease

● A18.8 **Tuberculosis of other specified organs**

A18.81 **Tuberculosis of thyroid gland** 🕭

A18.82 **Tuberculosis of other endocrine glands** 🕭
    Tuberculosis of pituitary gland
    Tuberculosis of thymus gland

A18.83 **Tuberculosis of digestive tract organs, not elsewhere classified** 🕭

    | Excludes1 | tuberculosis of intestine
                        (A18.32)

A18.84 **Tuberculosis of heart** 🕭
    Tuberculous cardiomyopathy
    Tuberculous endocarditis
    Tuberculous myocarditis
    Tuberculous pericarditis

A18.85 **Tuberculosis of spleen** 🕭

A18.89 **Tuberculosis of other sites** 🕭
    Tuberculosis of muscle
    Tuberculous cerebral arteritis

● A19 **Miliary tuberculosis**

    | Includes | disseminated tuberculosis
               generalized tuberculosis
               tuberculous polyserositis

A19.0 **Acute miliary tuberculosis of a single specified site** 🕭

A19.1 **Acute miliary tuberculosis of multiple sites** 🕭

■ A19.2 **Acute miliary tuberculosis, unspecified** 🕭

A19.8 **Other miliary tuberculosis** 🕭

■ A19.9 **Miliary tuberculosis, unspecified** 🕭

CERTAIN ZOONOTIC BACTERIAL DISEASES (A20-A28)

● A20 **Plague**
    Infectious disease caused by a Yersinia pestis bacterium,
    * transmitted by a rodent flea bite or handling of infected*
    * animal*

    | Includes | infection due to Yersinia pestis

A20.0 **Bubonic plague** 🕭

A20.1 **Cellulocutaneous plague** 🕭
    Skin and subcutaneous tissue plague

A20.2 **Pneumonic plague** 🕭

A20.3 **Plague meningitis** 🕭

A20.7 **Septicemic plague** 🕭

A20.8 **Other forms of plague** 🕭
    Abortive plague
    Asymptomatic plague
    Pestis minor
    Systemic bacterial disease

■ A20.9 **Plague, unspecified** 🕭

● A21 **Tularemia**
    Caused by Francisella tularensis bacterium found in rodents,
    * rabbits, and hares and transmitted to humans by contact*
    * with infected animal tissues or by ticks, biting flies, or*
    * mosquitoes*

    | Includes | deer-fly fever
               infection due to Francisella tularensis
               rabbit fever

A21.0 **Ulceroglandular tularemia** 🕭
    Most common form of tularemia in humans is painful,
    * swollen, erythematous papule at point of inoculation*
    * that ruptures to form shallow ulcer*

A21.1 **Oculoglandular tularemia** 🕭
    Primary site of entry is conjunctival sac, results in
    * granulomatous corneal lesions*
    Ophthalmic tularemia

A21.2 **Pulmonary tularemia** 🕭

A21.3 **Gastrointestinal tularemia** 🕭
    Abdominal tularemia

A21.7 **Generalized tularemia** 🕭

A21.8 **Other forms of tularemia** 🕭

■ A21.9 **Tularemia, unspecified** 🕭

● A22 **Anthrax**
    An acute infectious disease caused by the spore-forming
    * Bacillus anthracis; occurs in humans exposed to infected*
    * animals or tissue from infected animals*

    | Includes | infection due to Bacillus anthracis

A22.0 **Cutaneous anthrax** 🕭
    Malignant carbuncle
    Malignant pustule

A22.1 **Pulmonary anthrax** 🕭
    Inhalation anthrax
    Ragpicker's disease
    Woolsorter's disease

A22.2 **Gastrointestinal anthrax** 🕭

A22.7 **Anthrax sepsis** 🕭
    Infectious bacterial disease

A22.8 **Other forms of anthrax** 🕭
    Anthrax meningitis

■ A22.9 **Anthrax, unspecified** 🕭

Item 1-6 Brucellosis: An infectious disease caused by the bacterium Brucella. Humans are infected by contact with contaminated animals or animal products. In humans brucellosis symptoms that are similar to the flu include fever, sweats, headaches, back pains, and physical weakness. Severe infections of the central nervous system or lining of the heart may occur. Brucellosis can also cause chronic symptoms that include recurrent fevers, joint pain, and fatigue.

Item 1-5 Miliary tuberculosis can be a life-threatening condition. If a tuberculous lesion enters a blood vessel, immense dissemination of tuberculous organisms can occur if the immune system is weak. High-risk populations—children under 4 years of age, the elderly, or the immunocompromised—are particularly prone to this type of infection. The lesions will have a millet seedlike appearance on chest x-ray. Bronchial washings and biopsy may aid in diagnosis.

● Unacceptable First-Listed Diagnosis   ● Use Additional Character(s)   ■ Unspecified   **OGCR** Official Guidelines for Coding and Reporting
🕭 Complication\Comorbidity   🕭 Major C\C | Excludes 1 | | Excludes 2 | Includes   Use additional   Code first   Code also

● **A23 Brucellosis**

> **Includes**   Malta fever
> Mediterranean fever
> undulant fever

    A23.0 Brucellosis due to Brucella melitensis
> *Resulting in flu-like symptoms that may lead to chronic symptoms that include recurrent fevers, joint pain, and fatigue*

    A23.1 Brucellosis due to Brucella abortus
> *Most common cause of brucellosis in humans; AKA Bang bacillus*

    A23.2 Brucellosis due to Brucella suis
> *Species found primarily in pigs, rabbits, and reindeer*

    A23.3 Brucellosis due to Brucella canis
> *Species that causes respiratory tract infection in humans*

    A23.8 Other brucellosis 🦠

    🔲**A23.9 Brucellosis, unspecified** 🦠

● **A24 Glanders and melioidosis**
> *Infection, usually of rodents, which spreads to other animals and humans, caused by Burkholderia pseudomallei through break in skin contaminated with infested soil or water*

    A24.0 Glanders 🦠
> Infection due to Pseudomonas mallei
> Malleus

    A24.1 Acute and fulminating melioidosis 🦠
> Melioidosis pneumonia
> Melioidosis sepsis

    A24.2 Subacute and chronic melioidosis 🦠

    A24.3 Other melioidosis 🦠

    🔲**A24.9 Melioidosis, unspecified** 🦠
> Infection due to Pseudomonas pseudomallei NOS
> Whitmore's disease

● **A25 Rat-bite fevers**
> *RBF, infectious disease caused by Streptobacillus moniliformis or Spirillum minus.*

    A25.0 Spirillosis 🦠
> *Any disease condition caused by spirilla*
> Sodoku

    A25.1 Streptobacillosis 🦠
> *Acute, febrile human illness caused by bacteria transmitted by rats in most cases, passed from rodent to human via rodent's urine or mucous secretions; AKA rat fever*
> Epidemic arthritic erythema
> Haverhill fever
> Streptobacillary rat-bite fever

    🔲**A25.9 Rat-bite fever, unspecified** 🦠

● **A26 Erysipeloid**
> *Infection with Erysipelothrix rhusiopathiae, occurring often as occupational disease resulting from handling infected fish, shellfish, meat, or poultry*

    A26.0 Cutaneous erysipeloid
> Erythema migrans

    A26.7 Erysipelothrix sepsis

    A26.8 Other forms of erysipeloid

    🔲**A26.9 Erysipeloid, unspecified**

● **A27 Leptospirosis**
> *Occurs most commonly in the tropics*

    A27.0 Leptospirosis icterohemorrhagica 🦠
> Leptospiral or spirochetal jaundice (hemorrhagic)
> Weil's disease

    ● **A27.8 Other forms of leptospirosis**

      A27.81 Aseptic meningitis in leptospirosis 🦠

      A27.89 Other forms of leptospirosis 🦠

    🔲**A27.9 Leptospirosis, unspecified** 🦠

● **A28 Other zoonotic bacterial diseases, not elsewhere classified**

    A28.0 Pasteurellosis 🦠
> *Infection of humans or other animals by species of Pasteurella*

    A28.1 Cat-scratch disease 🦠
> Cat-scratch fever

    A28.2 Extraintestinal yersiniosis 🦠
> *Infection from Yersinia enterocolitica; AKA enteric yersiniosis, intestinal yersiniosis, Yersinia enteritis*

> **Excludes1**   enteritis due to Yersinia enterocolitica (A04.6)
> plague (A20.-)

    A28.8 Other specified zoonotic bacterial diseases, not elsewhere classified 🦠

    🔲**A28.9 Zoonotic bacterial disease, unspecified** 🦠

OTHER BACTERIAL DISEASES (A30-A49)

● **A30 Leprosy [Hansen's disease]**
> *Chronic infectious disease attacking the skin, peripheral nerves, and mucous membranes*

> **Includes**   infection due to Mycobacterium leprae
> **Excludes1**   sequelae of leprosy (B92)

    A30.0 Indeterminate leprosy 🦠
> I leprosy

    A30.1 Tuberculoid leprosy 🦠
> TT leprosy

    A30.2 Borderline tuberculoid leprosy 🦠
> BT leprosy

    A30.3 Borderline leprosy 🦠
> BB leprosy

    A30.4 Borderline lepromatous leprosy 🦠
> BL leprosy

    A30.5 Lepromatous leprosy 🦠
> LL leprosy

    A30.8 Other forms of leprosy 🦠

    🔲**A30.9 Leprosy, unspecified** 🦠

● **A31 Infection due to other mycobacteria**

> **Excludes2**   leprosy (A30.-)
> tuberculosis (A15-A19)

    A31.0 Pulmonary mycobacterial infection 🦠
> Infection due to Mycobacterium avium
> Infection due to Mycobacterium intracellulare [Battey bacillus]
> Infection due to Mycobacterium kansasii

    A31.1 Cutaneous mycobacterial infection 🦠
> Buruli ulcer
> Infection due to Mycobacterium marinum
> Infection due to Mycobacterium ulcerans

    A31.2 Disseminated mycobacterium avium-intracellulare complex (DMAC) 🦠
> MAC sepsis

    A31.8 Other mycobacterial infections 🦠

    🔲**A31.9 Mycobacterial infection, unspecified** 🦠
> Atypical mycobacterial infection NOS
> Mycobacteriosis NOS

CHAPTER 1 (A00-B99)

● Unacceptable First-Listed Diagnosis   ● Use Additional Character(s)   🔲 Unspecified   **OGCR** Official Guidelines for Coding and Reporting

🦠 Complication\Comorbidity   🦠 Major C\C   Excludes 1   Excludes 2   Includes   Use additional   Code first   Code also

795

● **A32 Listeriosis**
Infection caused by Listeria monocytogenes

> **Includes**   listerial foodborne infection
>
> **Excludes1**   neonatal (disseminated) listeriosis (P37.2)

    A32.0 Cutaneous listeriosis 🍗

●   **A32.1 Listerial meningitis and meningoencephalitis**

        A32.11 Listerial meningitis 🍗

        A32.12 Listerial meningoencephalitis 🍗

    A32.7 Listerial sepsis 🍗

●   **A32.8 Other forms of listeriosis**

        A32.81 Oculoglandular listeriosis 🍗
Primary infection site is conjunctival sac, which if untreated may result in perforation of cornea and optic atrophy

        A32.82 Listerial endocarditis 🍗
Exudative and proliferative inflammatory condition of endocardium caused by listeria bacteria

        A32.89 Other forms of listeriosis 🍗
Listerial cerebral arteritis

    ■**A32.9 Listeriosis, unspecified** 🍗

  A33 Tetanus neonatorum 🍗
Neonate = newborn

  A34 Obstetrical tetanus 🍗

  A35 Other tetanus 🍗
Tetanus NOS

> **Excludes1**   tetanus neonatorum (A33):
>   obstetrical tetanus (A34)

● **A36 Diphtheria**

    A36.0 Pharyngeal diphtheria 🍗
Diphtheritic membranous angina
Tonsillar diphtheria

    A36.1 Nasopharyngeal diphtheria 🍗

    A36.2 Laryngeal diphtheria 🍗
Diphtheritic laryngotracheitis

    A36.3 Cutaneous diphtheria 🍗

> **Excludes2**   erythrasma (L08.1)

●   **A36.8 Other diphtheria**

        A36.81 Diphtheritic cardiomyopathy 🍗
Diphtheritic myocarditis

        A36.82 Diphtheritic radiculomyelitis 🍗

        A36.83 Diphtheritic polyneuritis 🍗

        A36.84 Diphtheritic tubulo-interstitial nephropathy 🍗

        A36.85 Diphtheritic cystitis 🍗

        A36.86 Diphtheritic conjunctivitis 🍗

        A36.89 Other diphtheritic complications 🍗
Diphtheritic peritonitis

    ■**A36.9 Diphtheria, unspecified** 🍗

● **A37 Whooping cough**
Pertussis is a highly contagious disease caused by the bacterium Bordetella pertussis and results in a whooping sounding cough.

Item 1-7 Diptheria: A highly contagious bacterial disease that results in the formation of an adherent membrane in the throat that may lead to suffocation. In its most poisonous form, it attacks the heart and lungs. It is spread by direct physical contact or breathing the aerosolized secretions of infected individuals. The exact location is specified in the codes.

● **A37.0 Whooping cough due to Bordetella pertussis**

    A37.00 Whooping cough due to Bordetella pertussis without pneumonia 🍗

    A37.01 Whooping cough due to Bordetella pertussis with pneumonia 🍗

● **A37.1 Whooping cough due to Bordetella parapertussis**

    A37.10 Whooping cough due to Bordetella parapertussis without pneumonia 🍗

    A37.11 Whooping cough due to Bordetella parapertussis with pneumonia 🍗

● **A37.8 Whooping cough due to other Bordetella species**

    A37.80 Whooping cough due to other Bordetella species without pneumonia 🍗

    A37.81 Whooping cough due to other Bordetella species with pneumonia 🍗

● **A37.9 Whooping cough, unspecified species**

    ■**A37.90 Whooping cough, unspecified species without pneumonia** 🍗

    ■**A37.91 Whooping cough, unspecified species with pneumonia** 🍗

● **A38 Scarlet fever**
Most commonly caused by the bacteria Streptococcus pneumoniae and Neisseria meningitides

> **Includes**   scarlatina
>
> **Excludes2**   streptococcal sore throat (J02.0)

  A38.0 Scarlet fever with otitis media 🍗

  A38.1 Scarlet fever with myocarditis 🍗

  A38.8 Scarlet fever with other complications 🍗

  A38.9 Scarlet fever, uncomplicated 🍗
Scarlet fever, NOS

● **A39 Meningococcal infection**
Most commonly caused by the bacteria Streptococcus pneumoniae and Neisseria meningitides

  A39.0 Meningococcal meningitis 🍗

  A39.1 Waterhouse-Friderichsen syndrome 🍗
Fulminating complication of meningococcemia
Meningococcal hemorrhagic adrenalitis
Meningococcic adrenal syndrome

  A39.2 Acute meningococcemia 🍗

  A39.3 Chronic meningococcemia 🍗

  ■**A39.4 Meningococcemia, unspecified** 🍗

● **A39.5 Meningococcal heart disease**

    ■**A39.50 Meningococcal carditis, unspecified** 🍗

    A39.51 Meningococcal endocarditis 🍗

    A39.52 Meningococcal myocarditis 🍗

    A39.53 Meningococcal pericarditis 🍗

● **A39.8 Other meningococcal infections**

    A39.81 Meningococcal encephalitis 🍗

    A39.82 Meningococcal retrobulbar neuritis 🍗
Optic neuritis in portion of optic nerve posterior to eyeball; AKA postocular optic neuritis

    A39.83 Meningococcal arthritis 🍗

    A39.84 Postmeningococcal arthritis 🍗

    A39.89 Other meningococcal infections 🍗
Meningococcal conjunctivitis

■**A39.9 Meningococcal infection, unspecified** 🍗
Meningococcal disease NOS

● Unacceptable First-Listed Diagnosis   ● Use Additional Character(s)   ■ Unspecified   **OGCR** Official Guidelines for Coding and Reporting
🍗 Complication\Comorbidity   🍗 Major C\C   Excludes 1   Excludes 2   Includes   Use additional   Code first   Code also

● **A40   Streptococcal sepsis**

> *Code first:* postprocedural streptococcal sepsis (T81.4)
> streptococcal sepsis during labor (O75.3)
> streptococcal sepsis following abortion or ectopic
>   or molar pregnancy (O03-O07, O08.0)
> streptococcal sepsis following immunization
>   (T88.0)
> streptococcal sepsis following infusion,
>   transfusion or therapeutic injection (T80.2-)

> | **Excludes1** | neonatal (P36.0-P36.1)
> puerperal sepsis (O85)
> sepsis due to Streptococcus, group D (A41.81)

A40.0   **Sepsis due to streptococcus, group A** 🔗

A40.1   **Sepsis due to streptococcus, group B** 🔗

A40.3   **Sepsis due to Streptococcus pneumoniae** 🔗
    Pneumococcal sepsis

A40.8   **Other streptococcal sepsis** 🔗

⬛A40.9   **Streptococcal sepsis, unspecified** 🔗

● **A41   Other sepsis**

> *Code first:* postprocedural sepsis (T81.4)
> sepsis during labor (O75.3)
> sepsis following abortion, ectopic or molar
>   pregnancy (O03-O07, O08.0)
> sepsis following immunization (T88.0)
> sepsis following infusion, transfusion or
>   therapeutic injection (T80.2-)

> | **Excludes1** | bacteremia NOS (R78.81)
> neonatal (P36.-)
> puerperal sepsis (O85)
> sepsis NOS (A41.9)
> streptococcal sepsis (A40.-)

> | **Excludes2** | sepsis (due to) (in):
>   actinomycotic (A42.7)
>   anthrax (A22.7)
>   candidal (B37.7)
>   Erysipelothrix (A26.7)
>   extraintestinal yersiniosis (A28.2)
>   gonococcal (A54.86)
>   herpesviral (B00.7)
>   listerial (A32.7)
>   meningococcal (A39.2-A39.4)
>   melioidosis (A24.1)
>   plague (A20.7)
>   tularemia (A21.7)
> toxic shock syndrome (A48.3)

A41.0   **Sepsis due to Staphylococcus aureus** 🔗

A41.1   **Sepsis due to other specified staphylococcus** 🔗
    Coagulase negative staphylococcus sepsis
    Sepsis due to other specified staphylococcus

⬛A41.2   **Sepsis due to unspecified staphylococcus** 🔗

A41.3   **Sepsis due to Hemophilus influenzae** 🔗

A41.4   **Sepsis due to anaerobes** 🔗

> | **Excludes1** | gas gangrene (A48.0)

● A41.5   **Sepsis due to other Gram-negative organisms**

⬛A41.50   **Gram-negative sepsis, unspecified** 🔗
    Gram-negative sepsis NOS

A41.51   **Sepsis due to Escherichia coli [E. coli]** 🔗

A41.52   **Sepsis due to Pseudomonas** 🔗
    Pseudomonas aeroginosa

A41.53   **Sepsis due to Serratia** 🔗

A41.59   **Other Gram-negative sepsis** 🔗

● A41.8   **Other specified sepsis**

A41.81   **Sepsis due to Enterococcus** 🔗

A41.89   **Other specified sepsis** 🔗

⬛A41.9   **Sepsis, unspecified** 🔗
    Septicemia NOS

● **A42   Actinomycosis**

> | **Excludes1** | actinomycetoma (B47.1)

A42.0   **Pulmonary actinomycosis** 🔗

A42.1   **Abdominal actinomycosis** 🔗

A42.2   **Cervicofacial actinomycosis** 🔗

A42.7   **Actinomycotic sepsis** 🔗

● A42.8   **Other forms of actinomycosis**

A42.81   **Actinomycotic meningitis** 🔗

A42.82   **Actinomycotic encephalitis** 🔗

A42.89   **Other forms of actinomycosis** 🔗

⬛A42.9   **Actinomycosis, unspecified** 🔗

● **A43   Nocardiosis**

A43.0   **Pulmonary nocardiosis** 🔗

A43.1   **Cutaneous nocardiosis** 🔗

A43.8   **Other forms of nocardiosis** 🔗

⬛A43.9   **Nocardiosis, unspecified** 🔗

● **A44   Bartonellosis**

A44.0   **Systemic bartonellosis** 🔗
    Oroya fever

A44.1   **Cutaneous and mucocutaneous bartonellosis** 🔗
    Verruga peruana

A44.8   **Other forms of bartonellosis** 🔗

⬛A44.9   **Bartonellosis, unspecified** 🔗

A46   Erysipelas

> | **Excludes1** | postpartum or puerperal erysipelas (O86.89)

● **A48   Other bacterial diseases, not elsewhere classified**

> | **Excludes1** | actinomycetoma (B47.1)

A48.0   **Gas gangrene** 🔗
    Clostridial cellulitis
    Clostridial myonecrosis

A48.1   **Legionnaires' disease** 🔗

A48.2   **Nonpneumonic Legionnaires' disease [Pontiac fever]**

A48.3   **Toxic shock syndrome** 🔗

> Use additional code to identify the organism
>   (B95, B96)

> | **Excludes1** | endotoxic shock NOS (R57.8)
> sepsis NOS (A41.9)

A48.4   **Brazilian purpuric fever**
    Systemic Hemophilus aegyptius infection

● A48.5   **Other specified botulism**
    Non-foodborne intoxication due to toxins of
    Clostridium botulinum [C. botulinum]

> | **Excludes1** | food poisoning due to toxins of
>   Clostridium botulinum (A05.1)

A48.51   **Infant botulism** 🔗

A48.52   **Wound botulism** 🔗
    Non-foodborne botulism NOS
    Use additional code for associated wound

A48.8   **Other specified bacterial diseases** 🔗

Item 1–8   Gas gangrene is a necrotizing subcutaneous infection that will cause tissue death. Patients with poor circulation (e.g., diabetes, peripheral nephropathy) will have low oxygen content in their tissues (hypoxia), which allows the Clostridium bacteria to flourish. Gas gangrene often occurs at the site of a surgical wound or trauma. Onset is sudden and dramatic. Treatment can include debridement, amputation, and/or hyperbaric oxygen treatments.

● Unacceptable First-Listed Diagnosis   ● Use Additional Character(s)   ⬛ Unspecified   **OGCR** Official Guidelines for Coding and Reporting

🔗 Complication\Comorbidity   🔗 Major C\C | Excludes 1 | | Excludes 2 | Includes   Use additional   Code first   Code also

797

CHAPTER 1 (A00-B99)

● **A49 Bacterial infection of unspecified site**

> Excludes1 bacterial agents as the cause of diseases
> classified elsewhere (B95-B96)
> chlamydial infection NOS (A74.9)
> meningococcal infection NOS (A39.9)
> rickettsial infection NOS (A79.9)
> spirochetal infection NOS (A69.9)

▣ **A49.0 Staphylococcal infection, unspecified site**

▣ **A49.1 Streptococcal infection, unspecified site**

▣ **A49.2 Hemophilus influenzae infection, unspecified site**
> *Any of seven bacterium of genus Haemophilus*

▣ **A49.3 Mycoplasma infection, unspecified site**
> *Bacterium of class Mollicutes, unusual group of
> bacteria distinguished by absence of cell wall*

▣ **A49.8 Other bacterial infections of unspecified site**

▣ **A49.9 Bacterial infection, unspecified**
> Excludes1 bacteremia NOS (R78.81)

INFECTIONS WITH A PREDOMINANTLY SEXUAL MODE OF TRANSMISSION (A50-A64)

> Excludes1 human immunodeficiency virus [HIV]
> disease (B20)
> nonspecific and nongonococcal urethritis
> (N34.1)
> Reiter's disease (M02.3-)

● **A50 Congenital syphilis**

● **A50.0 Early congenital syphilis, symptomatic**
> Any congenital syphilitic condition specified as
> early or manifest less than two years after birth

A50.01 **Early congenital syphilitic oculopathy** 🦠

A50.02 **Early congenital syphilitic osteochondropathy** 🦠

A50.03 **Early congenital syphilitic pharyngitis** 🦠
> Early congenital syphilitic laryngitis

A50.04 **Early congenital syphilitic pneumonia** 🦠

A50.05 **Early congenital syphilitic rhinitis** 🦠

A50.06 **Early cutaneous congenital syphilis** 🦠

A50.07 **Early mucocutaneous congenital syphilis** 🦠

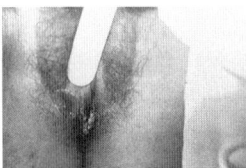

Figure 1-3 Chancre of primary syphilis. (From Mandell, Bennrtt, & Dolin: Principles and Practice of Infectious Diseases, 6th ed. 2005, Churchill Livingstone, An Imprint of Elsevir)

Item 1-9 Syphilis, also known as lues, is the most serious of the venereal diseases caused by *Treponema pallidum*. The **primary** stage is characterized by an ulceration known as **chancre,** which usually appears on the genitals but can also develop on the anus, lips, tonsils, breasts, or fingers. Syphilis is easy to cure in its early stages. A single intramuscular injection of penicillin will usually cure a person who has had syphilis for less than a year.

The **secondary** stage is characterized by a rash that can affect any area of the body. **Latent** syphilis is divided into **early,** which is diagnosed within two years of infection, and **late,** which is diagnosed two years or more after infection. Additional doses of penicillin or another antibiotic are needed to treat someone who has had syphilis for longer than a year. For those allergic to penicillin, there are other antibiotic treatments. **Congenital** syphilis is also labeled **early** or **late** based on the time of diagnosis.

A50.08 **Early visceral congenital syphilis** 🦠

A50.09 **Other early congenital syphilis, symptomatic** 🦠

A50.1 Early congenital syphilis, latent
> Congenital syphilis without clinical manifestations, with positive serological reaction and negative spinal fluid test, less than two years after birth

▣ **A50.2 Early congenital syphilis, unspecified** 🦠
> Congenital syphilis NOS less than two years after birth

● **A50.3 Late congenital syphilitic oculopathy**
> Excludes1 Hutchinson's triad (A50.53)

▣ A50.30 **Late congenital syphilitic oculopathy, unspecified** 🦠

A50.31 **Late congenital syphilitic interstitial keratitis** 🦠

A50.32 **Late congenital syphilitic chorioretinitis** 🦠

A50.39 **Other late congenital syphilitic oculopathy** 🦠

● **A50.4 Late congenital neurosyphilis [juvenile neurosyphilis]**
> Use additional code to identify any associated mental disorder
> Excludes1 Hutchinson's triad (A50.53)

▣ A50.40 **Late congenital neurosyphilis, unspecified** 🦠
> Juvenile neurosyphilis NOS

A50.41 **Late congenital syphilitic meningitis** 🦠

A50.42 **Late congenital syphilitic encephalitis** 🦠

A50.43 **Late congenital syphilitic polyneuropathy** 🦠

A50.44 **Late congenital syphilitic optic nerve atrophy** 🦠

A50.45 **Juvenile general paresis** 🦠
> Dementia paralytica juvenilis
> Juvenile tabetoparetic neurosyphilis

A50.49 **Other late congenital neurosyphilis** 🦠
> Juvenile tabes dorsalis

● **A50.5 Other late congenital syphilis, symptomatic**
> Any congenital syphilitic condition specified as late or manifest two years or more after birth

A50.51 **Clutton's joints** 🦠

A50.52 **Hutchinson's teeth** 🦠

A50.53 **Hutchinson's triad** 🦠

A50.54 **Late congenital cardiovascular syphilis** 🦠

A50.55 **Late congenital syphilitic arthropathy** 🦠

A50.56 **Late congenital syphilitic osteochondropathy** 🦠

A50.57 **Syphilitic saddle nose** 🦠

A50.59 **Other late congenital syphilis, symptomatic** 🦠

A50.6 Late congenital syphilis, latent
> Congenital syphilis without clinical manifestations, with positive serological reaction and negative spinal fluid test, two years or more after birth.

▣ **A50.7 Late congenital syphilis, unspecified**
> Congenital syphilis NOS two years or more after birth.

▣ **A50.9 Congenital syphilis, unspecified**

● **A51 Early syphilis**

A51.0 Primary genital syphilis
> Syphilitic chancre NOS

● Unacceptable First-Listed Diagnosis   ● Use Additional Character(s)   ▣ Unspecified   **OGCR** Official Guidelines for Coding and Reporting

🦠 Complication\Comorbidity   🦠 Major C\C   Excludes 1   Excludes 2   Includes   Use additional   Code first   Code also

CHAPTER 1 (A00-B99)

798

A51.1   Primary anal syphilis

A51.2   Primary syphilis of other sites

● **A51.3**   Secondary syphilis of skin and mucous membranes

     A51.31   Condyloma latum 🦠

     A51.32   Syphilitic alopecia 🦠

     A51.39   Other secondary syphilis of skin 🦠
         Syphilitic leukoderma
         Syphilitic mucous patch

         | Excludes1 | late syphilitic leukoderma (A52.79)

● **A51.4**   Other secondary syphilis

     A51.41   Secondary syphilitic meningitis 🦠

     A51.42   Secondary syphilitic female pelvic disease 🦠

     A51.43   Secondary syphilitic oculopathy 🦠
         Secondary syphilitic chorioretinitis
         Secondary syphilitic iridocyclitis, iritis
         Secondary syphilitic uveitis

     A51.44   Secondary syphilitic nephritis 🦠

     A51.45   Secondary syphilitic hepatitis 🦠

     A51.46   Secondary syphilitic osteopathy 🦠

     A51.49   Other secondary syphilitic conditions 🦠
         Secondary syphilitic lymphadenopathy
         Secondary syphilitic myositis

A51.5   Early syphilis, latent
     Syphilis (acquired) without clinical manifestations, with positive serological reaction and negative spinal fluid test, less than two years after infection.

◼ **A51.9**   Early syphilis, unspecified

● **A52**   Late syphilis

   ● **A52.0**   Cardiovascular and cerebrovascular syphilis

     ◼ **A52.00**   Cardiovascular syphilis, unspecified 🦠

     A52.01   Syphilitic aneurysm of aorta 🦠

     A52.02   Syphilitic aortitis 🦠

     A52.03   Syphilitic endocarditis 🦠
         Syphilitic aortic valve incompetence or stenosis
         Syphilitic mitral valve stenosis
         Syphilitic pulmonary valve regurgitation

     A52.04   Syphilitic cerebral arteritis 🦠

     A52.05   Other cerebrovascular syphilis 🦠
         Syphilitic cerebral aneurysm (ruptured) (non-ruptured)
         Syphilitic cerebral thrombosis

     A52.06   Other syphilitic heart involvement 🦠
         Syphilitic coronary artery disease
         Syphilitic myocarditis
         Syphilitic pericarditis

     A52.09   Other cardiovascular syphilis 🦠

   ● **A52.1**   Symptomatic neurosyphilis

     ◼ **A52.10**   Symptomatic neurosyphilis, unspecified 🦠

     A52.11   Tabes dorsalis 🦠
         Cognitive decline with progressive degeneration of posterior columns, roots, and ganglia of spinal cord, occur 15-20 years after initial infection of syphilis; AKA Duchenne disease
         Locomotor ataxia (progressive)
         Tabetic neurosyphilis

     A52.12   Other cerebrospinal syphilis 🦠

A52.13   Late syphilitic meningitis 🦠

A52.14   Late syphilitic encephalitis 🦠

A52.15   Late syphilitic neuropathy 🦠
     Late syphilitic acoustic neuritis
     Late syphilitic optic (nerve) atrophy
     Late syphilitic polyneuropathy
     Late syphilitic retrobulbar neuritis

A52.16   Charcot's arthropathy (diabetic) 🦠
     Progressive musculoskeletal condition characterized by joint dislocation, fractures, and deformities, results in progressive destruction of bone and soft tissue of weight-bearing joints

A52.17   General paresis 🦠
     Chronic meningoencephalitis results in loss of cortical function, or progressive dementia and generalized paralysis, occurring 10-20 years after initial infection of syphilis; AKA Bayle disease, dementia paralytica, paralytic dementiaparetic neurosyphilis, syphilitic meningoencephalitis
     Dementia paralytica

A52.19   Other symptomatic neurosyphilis 🦠
     Syphilitic parkinsonism

A52.2   Asymptomatic neurosyphilis 🦠

◼ **A52.3**   Neurosyphilis, unspecified 🦠
     Gumma (syphilitic)
     Destructive lesions of syphilis
     Syphilis (late)
     Syphiloma

● **A52.7**   Other symptomatic late syphilis

     A52.71   Late syphilitic oculopathy 🦠
         Late syphilitic chorioretinitis
         Late syphilitic episcleritis

     A52.72   Syphilis of lung and bronchus 🦠

     A52.73   Symptomatic late syphilis of other respiratory organs 🦠

     A52.74   Syphilis of liver and other viscera 🦠
         Late syphilitic peritonitis

     A52.75   Syphilis of kidney and ureter 🦠
         Syphilitic glomerular disease

     A52.76   Other genitourinary symptomatic late syphilis 🦠
         Late syphilitic female pelvic inflammatory disease

     A52.77   Syphilis of bone and joint 🦠

     A52.78   Syphilis of other musculoskeletal tissue 🦠
         Late syphilitic bursitis
         Syphilis [stage unspecified] of bursa
         Syphilis [stage unspecified] of muscle
         Syphilis [stage unspecified] of synovium
         Syphilis [stage unspecified] of tendon

     A52.79   Other symptomatic late syphilis 🦠
         Late syphilitic leukoderma
         Syphilis of adrenal gland
         Syphilis of pituitary gland
         Syphilis of thyroid gland
         Syphilitic splenomegaly

         | Excludes1 | syphilitic leukoderma (secondary) (A51.39)

A52.8   Late syphilis, latent
     Syphilis (acquired) without clinical manifestations, with positive serological reaction and negative spinal fluid test, two years or more after infection

◼ **A52.9**   Late syphilis, unspecified

● Unacceptable First-Listed Diagnosis   ● Use Additional Character(s)   ◼ Unspecified   **OGCR** Official Guidelines for Coding and Reporting

🦠 Complication\Comorbidity   🦠 Major C\C | Excludes 1 | | Excludes 2 | Includes   Use additional   Code first   Code also

799

● **A53　Other and unspecified syphilis**

■ **A53.0　Latent syphilis, unspecified as early or late**
Latent syphilis NOS
Positive serological reaction for syphilis

■ **A53.9　Syphilis, unspecified**
Infection due to Treponema pallidum NOS
Syphilis (acquired) NOS

> **Excludes1**　syphilis NOS under two years of age (A50.2)

● **A54　Gonococcal infection**

● **A54.0　Gonococcal infection of lower genitourinary tract without periurethral or accessory gland abscess**

> **Excludes1**　gonococcal infection with genitourinary gland abscess (A54.1)
> gonococcal infection with periurethral abscess (A54.1)

■ **A54.00　Gonococcal infection of lower genitourinary tract, unspecified** 🕮

■ **A54.01　Gonococcal cystitis and urethritis, unspecified** 🕮

■ **A54.02　Gonococcal vulvovaginitis, unspecified** 🕮

■ **A54.03　Gonococcal cervicitis, unspecified** 🕮

A54.09　Other gonococcal infection of lower genitourinary tract 🕮

A54.1　Gonococcal infection of lower genitourinary tract with periurethral and accessory gland abscess 🕮
Gonococcal Bartholin's gland abscess

● **A54.2　Gonococcal pelviperitonitis and other gonococcal genitourinary infection**

A54.21　Gonococcal infection of kidney and ureter 🕮

A54.22　Gonococcal prostatitis 🕮

A54.23　Gonococcal infection of other male genital organs 🕮
Gonococcal epididymitis
Gonococcal orchitis

A54.24　Gonococcal female pelvic inflammatory disease 🕮
Gonococcal pelviperitonitis

> **Excludes1**　gonococcal peritonitis (A54.85)

A54.29　Other gonococcal genitourinary infections 🕮

● **A54.3　Gonococcal infection of eye**

■ **A54.30　Gonococcal infection of eye, unspecified** 🕮

A54.31　Gonococcal conjunctivitis 🕮
Form of bacterial conjunctivitis contracted by newborns during delivery; AKA neonatal conjunctivitis
Ophthalmia neonatorum due to gonococcus

A54.32　Gonococcal iridocyclitis 🕮
Inflammation of iris and of ciliary body due to gonococcal infection

A54.33　Gonococcal keratitis 🕮
Inflammation of cornea due to gonococcal infection; AKA keratoconjunctivitis, keratopathy

A54.39　Other gonococcal eye infection 🕮
Gonococcal endophthalmia

Item 1-10 An STD (sexually transmitted disease) caused by **Neisseria gonorrhoeae** that flourishes in the warm, moist areas of the reproductive tract. Untreated gonorrhea spreads to other parts of the body, causing inflammation of the testes or prostate or pelvic inflammatory disease (PID).

● **A54.4　Gonococcal infection of musculoskeletal system**

■ **A54.40　Gonococcal infection of musculoskeletal system, unspecified** 🕮

A54.41　Gonococcal spondylopathy 🕮
Disorder of vertebrae due to gonococcal infection; AKA rachiopathy

A54.42　Gonococcal arthritis 🕮
> **Excludes2**　gonococcal infection of spine (A54.41)

A54.43　Gonococcal osteomyelitis 🕮
> **Excludes2**　gonococcal infection of spine (A54.41)

A54.49　Gonococcal infection of other musculoskeletal tissue 🕮
Gonococcal bursitis
Gonococcal myositis
Gonococcal synovitis
Gonococcal tenosynovitis

A54.5　Gonococcal pharyngitis

A54.6　Gonococcal infection of anus and rectum

● **A54.8　Other gonococcal infections**

A54.81　Gonococcal meningitis 🕮

A54.82　Gonococcal brain abscess 🕮

A54.83　Gonococcal heart infection 🕮
Gonococcal endocarditis
Gonococcal myocarditis
Gonococcal pericarditis

A54.84　Gonococcal pneumonia 🕮

A54.85　Gonococcal peritonitis 🕮
> **Excludes1**　gonococcal pelviperitonitis (A54.24)

A54.86　Gonococcal sepsis 🕮

A54.89　Other gonococcal infections 🕮
Gonococcal keratoderma
Gonococcal lymphadenitis

■ **A54.9　Gonococcal infection, unspecified** 🕮

A55　Chlamydial lymphogranuloma (venereum)

> **Includes**　climatic or tropical bubo
> Durand-Nicolas-Favre disease
> Esthiomene
> lymphogranuloma inguinale

● **A56　Other sexually transmitted chlamydial diseases**

> **Includes**　sexually transmitted diseases due to Chlamydia trachomatis
> **Excludes1**　neonatal chlamydial conjunctivitis (P39.1)
> neonatal chlamydial pneumonia (P23.1)
> **Excludes2**　chlamydial lymphogranuloma (A55)
> conditions classified to A74.-

● **A56.0　Chlamydial infection of lower genitourinary tract**

■ **A56.00　Chlamydial infection of lower genitourinary tract, unspecified**

A56.01　Chlamydial cystitis and urethritis

A56.02　Chlamydial vulvovaginitis

A56.09　Other chlamydial infection of lower genitourinary tract
Chlamydial cervicitis

● **A56.1　Chlamydial infection of pelviperitoneum and other genitourinary organs**

A56.11　Chlamydial female pelvic inflammatory disease

● Unacceptable First-Listed Diagnosis　● Use Additional Character(s)　■ Unspecified　**OGCR** Official Guidelines for Coding and Reporting
🕮 Complication\Comorbidity　🕮 Major C\C　Excludes 1　Excludes 2　Includes　Use additional　Code first　Code also

A56.19   **Other chlamydial genitourinary infection**
Chlamydial epididymitis
Chlamydial orchitis

◻ A56.2   **Chlamydial infection of genitourinary tract, unspecified**

A56.3   **Chlamydial infection of anus and rectum**

A56.4   **Chlamydial infection of pharynx**

A56.8   **Sexually transmitted chlamydial infection of other sites**

A57   **Chancroid**
Ulcus molle
Sexually transmitted infection caused by bacteria, Haemophilus ducreyi

A58   **Granuloma inguinale**
Chronic, progressive, ulcerative granulomatous disease
Donovanosis

● A59   **Trichomoniasis**

Excludes2   intestinal trichomoniasis (A07.8)

A common STD caused by a parasite, Trichomonas vaginalis

● A59.0   **Urogenital trichomoniasis**

◻ A59.00   **Urogenital trichomoniasis, unspecified**
Fluor (vaginalis) due to Trichomonas
Leukorrhea (vaginalis) due to Trichomonas

A59.01   **Trichomonal vulvovaginitis**

A59.02   **Trichomonal prostatitis**

A59.03   **Trichomonal cystitis and urethritis**

A59.09   **Other urogenital trichomoniasis**
Common sexually transmitted disease (STD) caused by single-celled protozoan parasite; AKA trich
Trichomonas cervicitis

A59.8   **Trichomoniasis of other sites**

◻ A59.9   **Trichomoniasis, unspecified**

● A60   **Anogenital herpesviral [herpes simplex] infections**

● A60.0   **Herpesviral infection of genitalia and urogenital tract**

◻ A60.00   **Herpesviral infection of urogenital system, unspecified**

A60.01   **Herpesviral infection of penis**

A60.02   **Herpesviral infection of other male genital organs**

A60.03   **Herpesviral cervicitis**

A60.04   **Herpesviral vulvovaginitis**
Herpesviral [herpes simplex] ulceration
Herpesviral [herpes simplex] vaginitis
Herpesviral [herpes simplex] vulvitis

A60.09   **Herpesviral infection of other urogenital tract**

A60.1   **Herpesviral infection of perianal skin and rectum**

◻ A60.9   **Anogenital herpesviral infection, unspecified**

● A63   **Other predominantly sexually transmitted diseases, not elsewhere classified**

Excludes2   molluscum contagiosum (B08.1)
papilloma of cervix (D26.0)

A63.0   **Anogenital (venereal) warts**
Anogenital warts due to (human) papillomavirus [HPV]

Condyloma acuminatum

A63.8   **Other specified predominantly sexually transmitted diseases**

◻ A64   **Unspecified sexually transmitted disease**

OTHER SPIROCHETAL DISEASES (A65-A69)

Excludes2   leptospirosis (A27.-)
syphilis (A50-A53)

A65   **Nonvenereal syphilis**
Bejel
Endemic syphilis
Njovera

● A66   **Yaws**
Endemic, infectious, tropical disease caused by spirochete, spread by direct contact; AKA frambesia, framboesia, frambesia tropica

Includes   bouba
frambesia (tropica)
pian

A66.0   **Initial lesions of yaws**
Chancre of yaws
Frambesia, initial or primary
Initial frambesial ulcer
Mother yaw

A66.1   **Multiple papillomata and wet crab yaws**
Frambesioma
Pianoma
Plantar or palmar papilloma of yaws

A66.2   **Other early skin lesions of yaws**
Cutaneous yaws, less than five years after infection
Early yaws (cutaneous)(macular)(maculopapular) (micropapular)(papular)
Frambeside of early yaws

A66.3   **Hyperkeratosis of yaws**
Hypertrophy of stratum corneum of skin in which there are small, hard, verrucous scales
Ghoul hand
Hyperkeratosis, palmar or plantar (early) (late) due to yaws
Worm-eaten soles

A66.4   **Gummata and ulcers of yaws**
Small, rubbery granuloma with necrotic center and inflamed characteristic of advanced stage of syphilis; AKA syphiloma
Gummatous frambeside
Nodular late yaws (ulcerated)

A66.5   **Gangosa**
Manifestation of yaws that develops in the soft palate and spreads eroding bone, cartilage, and soft tissue
Rhinopharyngitis mutilans

A66.6   **Bone and joint lesions of yaws**
Yaws ganglion
Yaws goundou
Yaws gumma, bone
Yaws gummatous osteitis or periostitis
Yaws hydrarthrosis
Yaws osteitis
Yaws periostitis (hypertrophic)

A66.7   **Other manifestations of yaws**
Juxta-articular nodules of yaws
Mucosal yaws

A66.8   **Latent yaws**
Yaws without clinical manifestations, with positive serology

◻ A66.9   **Yaws, unspecified**

● Unacceptable First-Listed Diagnosis   ● Use Additional Character(s)   ◻ Unspecified   **OGCR** Official Guidelines for Coding and Reporting

 Complication\Comorbidity    Major C\C   Excludes 1   Excludes 2   Includes   Use additional   Code first   Code also

801

CHAPTER 1 (A00-B99)

● **A67   Pinta [carate]**
Group of nonvenereal diseases caused by Treponema species

     A67.0   Primary lesions of pinta
         Chancre (primary) of pinta
         Papule (primary) of pinta

     A67.1   Intermediate lesions of pinta
         Erythematous plaques of pinta
         Hyperchromic lesions of pinta
         Hyperkeratosis of pinta
         Pintids

     A67.2   Late lesions of pinta
         Achromic skin lesions of pinta
         Cicatricial skin lesions of pinta
         Dyschromic skin lesions of pinta

     A67.3   Mixed lesions of pinta
         Achromic with hyperchromic skin lesions of pinta [carate]

     ▨ **A67.9   Pinta, unspecified**

● **A68   Relapsing fevers**
     Includes   recurrent fever
     Excludes2   Lyme disease (A69.2-)

     A68.0   Louse-borne relapsing fever 🕷
         Relapsing fever due to Borrelia recurrentis

     A68.1   Tick-borne relapsing fever 🕷
         Relapsing fever due to any Borrelia species other than Borrelia recurrentis

     ▨ **A68.9   Relapsing fever, unspecified** 🕷

● **A69   Other spirochetal infections**

     A69.0   Necrotizing ulcerative stomatitis
         Cancrum oris
         Fusospirochetal gangrene
         Noma
         Stomatitis gangrenosa

     A69.1   Other Vincent's infections 🕷
         Fusospirochetal pharyngitis
         Necrotizing ulcerative (acute) gingivitis
         Necrotizing ulcerative (acute) gingivostomatitis
         Spirochetal stomatitis
         Trench mouth
         Vincent's angina
         Vincent's gingivitis

     ● **A69.2   Lyme disease**
         Erythema chronicum migrans due to Borrelia burgdorferi

       ▨ **A69.20   Lyme disease, unspecified** 🕷

       A69.21   Meningitis due to Lyme disease 🕷

       A69.22   Other neurologic disorders in Lyme disease 🕷
         Cranial neuritis
         Meningoencephalitis
         Polyneuropathy

       A69.23   Arthritis due to Lyme disease 🕷

       A69.29   Other conditions associated with Lyme disease 🕷
         Myopericarditis due to Lyme disease

     A69.8   Other specified spirochetal infections

     ▨ **A69.9   Spirochetal infection, unspecified**

Item 1-11 Cancrum oris, also known as **noma** or **gangrenous stomatitis,** begins as an ulcer of the gingiva and results in a progressive gangrenous process.

OTHER DISEASES CAUSED BY CHLAMYDIAE (A70-A74)

     Excludes1   sexually transmitted chlamydial diseases (A55-A56)

     A70   Chlamydia psittaci infections 🕷
         Ornithosis
         Parrot fever
         Psittacosis

● **A71   Trachoma**
     Excludes1   sequelae of trachoma (B94.0)

     A71.0   Initial stage of trachoma
         Trachoma dubium

     A71.1   Active stage of trachoma
         Granular conjunctivitis (trachomatous)
         Trachomatous follicular conjunctivitis
         Trachomatous pannus

     ▨ **A71.9   Trachoma, unspecified**

● **A74   Other diseases caused by chlamydiae**
     Excludes1   neonatal chlamydial conjunctivitis (P39.1)
                 neonatal chlamydial pneumonia (P23.1)
                 Reiter's disease (M02.3-)
                 sexually transmitted chlamydial diseases (A55-A56)
     Excludes2   chlamydial pneumonia (J16.0)

     A74.0   Chlamydial conjunctivitis
         Paratrachoma

     ● **A74.8   Other chlamydial diseases**

       A74.81   Chlamydial peritonitis

       A74.89   Other chlamydial diseases

     ▨ **A74.9   Chlamydial infection, unspecified**
         Chlamydiosis NOS

RICKETTSIOSES (A75-A79)

● **A75   Typhus fever**
     Excludes1   rickettsiosis due to Ehrlichia sennetsu (A79.2)

     A75.0   Epidemic louse-borne typhus fever due to Rickettsia prowazekii 🕷
         Organisms transmitted between humans via louse
         Classical typhus (fever)
         Epidemic (louse-borne) typhus

     A75.1   Recrudescent typhus [Brill's disease] 🕷
         Brill-Zinsser disease

     A75.2   Typhus fever due to Rickettsia typhi 🕷
         Murine (flea-borne) typhus

     A75.3   Typhus fever due to Rickettsia tsutsugamushi 🕷
         Scrub (mite-borne) typhus
         Tsutsugamushi fever

     ▨ **A75.9   Typhus fever, unspecified** 🕷
         Typhus (fever) NOS

Item 1-12   Rickettsioses are diseases spread from ticks, lice, fleas, or mites to humans.

Typhus is spread to humans chiefly by the fleas of rats.

Endemic identifies a disease as being present in low numbers of humans at all times, whereas **epidemic** identifies a disease as being present in high numbers of humans at a specific time. Morbidity (death) is higher in epidemic diseases.

Brill's disease, also known as **Brill-Zinsser disease,** is spread from human to human by body lice and also from the lice of flying squirrels. **Scrub typhus** is spread in the same ways as Brill's disease.

Malaria is spread to humans by mosquitoes.

● A77 Spotted fever [tick-borne rickettsioses]

    A77.0 Spotted fever due to Rickettsia rickettsii 🗫
        Rocky Mountain spotted fever
        Sao Paulo fever

    A77.1 Spotted fever due to Rickettsia conorii 🗫
        African tick typhus
        Boutonneuse fever
        India tick typhus
        Kenya tick typhus
        Marseilles fever
        Mediterranean tick fever

    A77.2 Spotted fever due to Rickettsia siberica 🗫
        North Asian tick fever
        Siberian tick typhus

    A77.3 Spotted fever due to Rickettsia australis 🗫
        Queensland tick typhus

  ● A77.4 Ehrlichiosis
      Type of tick-borne fever caused by bacteria infection
      Excludes1 Rickettsiosis due to Ehrlichia
          sennetsu (A79.81)

      ▪A77.40 Ehrlichiosis, unspecified 🗫

      A77.41 Ehrlichiosis chafeensis [E. chafeensis] 🗫

      A77.49 Other ehrlichiosis 🗫

    A77.8 Other spotted fevers 🗫

  ▪A77.9 Spotted fever, unspecified 🗫
      Tick-borne typhus NOS

A78 Q fever 🗫
    Infection due to Coxiella burnetii
    Nine Mile fever
    Quadrilateral fever

● A79 Other rickettsioses

    A79.0 Trench fever 🗫
        Quintan fever
        Wolhynian fever

    A79.1 Rickettsialpox due to Rickettsia akari 🗫
        Kew Garden fever
        Vesicular rickettsiosis

  ● A79.8 Other specified rickettsioses

      A79.81 Rickettsiosis due to Ehrlichia sennetsu 🗫

      A79.89 Other specified rickettsioses 🗫

  ▪A79.9 Rickettsiosis, unspecified 🗫
      Rickettsial infection NOS

VIRAL AND PRION INFECTIONS OF THE CENTRAL NERVOUS SYSTEM (A80-A89)

    Excludes1 postpolio syndrome (G14)
        sequelae of poliomyelitis (B91)
        sequelae of viral encephalitis (B94.1)

● A80 Acute poliomyelitis

    A80.0 Acute paralytic poliomyelitis, vaccine-associated 🗫

    A80.1 Acute paralytic poliomyelitis, wild virus, imported 🗫

    A80.2 Acute paralytic poliomyelitis, wild virus, indigenous 🗫

  ● A80.3 Acute paralytic poliomyelitis, other and unspecified

      ▪A80.30 Acute paralytic poliomyelitis, unspecified 🗫

      A80.39 Other acute paralytic poliomyelitis 🗫

Item 1-13 Acute Poliomyelitis: Also called infantile paralysis and is caused by the poliovirus, which enters the body orally and infects the intestinal wall and then enters the blood stream and central nervous system, causing muscle weakness and paralysis. This disease has been nearly eradicated with the polio vaccine.

    A80.4 Acute nonparalytic poliomyelitis

  ▪A80.9 Acute poliomyelitis, unspecified

● A81 Atypical virus infections of central nervous system
    Includes diseases of the central nervous system caused by prions
    Use additional code to identify:
      dementia with behavioral disturbance (F02.81)
      dementia without behavioral disturbance (F02.80)

  ● A81.0 Creutzfeldt-Jakob disease

      ▪A81.00 Creutzfeldt-Jakob disease, unspecified 🗫
        Jakob-Creutzfeldt disease, unspecified

      A81.01 Variant Creutzfeldt-Jakob disease 🗫
        vCJD

      A81.09 Other Creutzfeldt-Jakob disease 🗫
        CJD
        Familial Creutzfeldt-Jakob disease
        Iatrogenic Creutzfeldt-Jakob disease
        Sporadic Creutzfeldt-Jakob disease
        Subacute spongiform encephalopathy (with dementia)

    A81.1 Subacute sclerosing panencephalitis 🗫
      Type of viral encephalitis that causes parenchymatous lesions in gray and white matter of brain
      Dawson's inclusion body encephalitis
      Van Bogaert's sclerosing leukoencephalopathy

    A81.2 Progressive multifocal leukoencephalopathy 🗫
      Group of diseases affecting white matter of brain
      Multifocal leukoencephalopathy NOS

  ● A81.8 Other atypical virus infections of central nervous system

      A81.81 Kuru 🗫

      A81.82 Gerstmann-Sträussler-Scheinker syndrome 🗫
        GSS syndrome

      A81.83 Fatal familial insomnia 🗫
        FFI

      A81.89 Other atypical virus infections of central nervous system 🗫

  ▪A81.9 Atypical virus infection of central nervous system, unspecified 🗫
      Prion diseases of the central nervous system NOS

● A82 Rabies
    Viral disease affecting the central nervous system and transmitted from infected mammals to man.

    A82.0 Sylvatic rabies

    A82.1 Urban rabies

  ▪A82.9 Rabies, unspecified

● A83 Mosquito-borne viral encephalitis
    Inflammation of the brain caused most commonly by Herpes Simplex virus.
    Includes mosquito-borne viral meningoencephalitis
    Excludes2 Venezuelan equine encephalitis (A92.2)
        West Nile fever (A92.3-)
        West Nile virus (A92.3-)

    A83.0 Japanese encephalitis 🗫

    A83.1 Western equine encephalitis 🗫

    A83.2 Eastern equine encephalitis 🗫

    A83.3 St. Louis encephalitis 🗫

    A83.4 Australian encephalitis 🗫
      Kunjin virus disease

| ● Unacceptable First-Listed Diagnosis | ● Use Additional Character(s) | ▪ Unspecified | **OGCR** Official Guidelines for Coding and Reporting |
| 🗫 Complication\Comorbidity | 🗫 Major C\C | Excludes 1 / Excludes 2 | Includes / Use additional / Code first / Code also |

CHAPTER 1 (A00-B99)

803

A83.5 **California encephalitis** 🦟
California meningoencephalitis
La Crosse encephalitis

A83.6 **Rocio virus disease** 🦟
Mosquito-borne virus

A83.8 **Other mosquito-borne viral encephalitis** 🦟

◾A83.9 **Mosquito-borne viral encephalitis, unspecified** 🦟

● A84 **Tick-borne viral encephalitis**

> **Includes**   tick-borne viral meningoencephalitis

A84.0 **Far Eastern tick-borne encephalitis [Russian spring-summer encephalitis]** 🦟

A84.1 **Central European tick-borne encephalitis** 🦟

A84.8 **Other tick-borne viral encephalitis** 🦟
Louping ill
Powassan virus disease

◾A84.9 **Tick-borne viral encephalitis, unspecified** 🦟

● A85 **Other viral encephalitis, not elsewhere classified**

> **Includes**   specified viral encephalomyelitis NEC
>   specified viral meningoencephalitis NEC

> **Excludes1**   benign myalgic encephalomyelitis (G93.3)
>   encephalitis due to:
>   cytomegalovirus (B25.8)
>   herpesvirus NEC (B10.0-)
>   herpesvirus [herpes simplex] (B00.4)
>   measles virus (B05.0) mumps virus (B26.2)
>   poliomyelitis virus (A80.-)
>   zoster (B02.0)
>   lymphocytic choriomeningitis (A87.2)

A85.0 **Enteroviral encephalitis** 🦠
Enteroviral encephalomyelitis

A85.1 **Adenoviral encephalitis** 🦠
Adenoviral meningoencephalitis

◾A85.2 **Arthropod-borne viral encephalitis, unspecified** 🦠

> **Excludes1**   West nile virus with encephalitis (A92.31)

A85.8 **Other specified viral encephalitis** 🦠
Encephalitis lethargica
Von Economo-Cruchet disease

◾A86 **Unspecified viral encephalitis** 🦠

> **Includes**   viral encephalomyelitis NOS
>   viral meningoencephalitis NOS

● A87 **Viral meningitis**

> **Excludes1**   meningitis due to:
>   herpesvirus [herpes simplex] (B00.3)
>   measles virus (B05.1)
>   mumps virus (B26.1)
>   poliomyelitis virus (A80.-)
>   zoster (B02.1)

A87.0 **Enteroviral meningitis** 🦠
Group of common viruses responsible for the majority of viral meningitis
Coxsackievirus meningitis
Echovirus meningitis

A87.1 **Adenoviral meningitis** 🦠

A87.2 **Lymphocytic choriomeningitis** 🦠
Lymphocytic meningoencephalitis

A87.8 **Other viral meningitis** 🦠

◾A87.9 **Viral meningitis, unspecified** 🦠

● A88 **Other viral infections of central nervous system, not elsewhere classified**

> **Excludes1**   viral encephalitis NOS (A86)
>   viral meningitis NOS (A87.9)

A88.0 **Enteroviral exanthematous fever [Boston exanthem]** 🦠
Infectious skin eruption

A88.1 **Epidemic vertigo**

A88.8 **Other specified viral infections of central nervous system** 🦠

◾A89 **Unspecified viral infection of central nervous system** 🦠

ARTHROPOD-BORNE VIRAL FEVERS AND VIRAL HEMORRHAGIC FEVERS (A90-A99)

A90 **Dengue fever [classical dengue]** 🦠
Acute, self-limited disease, characterized by fever, prostration, severe muscle pains, headache, rash, lymphadenopathy, and leukopenia, caused by dengue virus; AKA breakbone, dandy

> **Excludes1**   dengue hemorrhagic fever (A91)

A91 **Dengue hemorrhagic fever** 🦠
Serious follow-up to regular dengue, with symptoms of hemorrhage

● A92 **Other mosquito-borne viral fevers**

> **Excludes1**   Ross River disease (B33.1)

A92.0 **Chikungunya virus disease** 🦠
Transmitted by mosquitoes
Chikungunya (hemorrhagic) fever

A92.1 **O'nyong-nyong fever** 🦠
Acute, nonfatal febrile disease transmitted by mosquitoes, which clinically resembles dengue and chikungunya

A92.2 **Venezuelan equine fever** 🦠
Venezuelan equine encephalitis
Venezuelan equine encephalomyelitis virus disease

● A92.3 **West Nile virus infection**
West Nile fever

◾A92.30 **West Nile virus infection, unspecified** 🦠
West Nile fever NOS
West Nile fever without complications
West Nile virus NOS

A92.31 **West Nile virus infection with encephalitis** 🦠
West Nile encephalitis
West Nile encephalomyelitis

A92.32 **West Nile virus infection with other neurologic manifestation** 🦠
Use additional code to specify the neurologic manifestation

A92.39 **West Nile virus infection with other complications** 🦠
Use additional code to specify the other conditions

A92.4 **Rift Valley fever** 🦠

A92.8 **Other specified mosquito-borne viral fevers** 🦠

◾A92.9 **Mosquito-borne viral fever, unspecified** 🦠

Item 1-14   **Encephalitis** is an inflammation of the brain most often caused by a virus but may also be caused by a bacteria and most commonly transmitted by a mosquito. **Myelitis** is an inflammation of the spinal cord that may disrupt CNS function. Untreated myelitis may rapidly lead to permanent damage to the spinal cord. **Encephalomyelitis** is a general term for an inflammation of the brain and spinal cord.

● Unacceptable First-Listed Diagnosis   ● Use Additional Character(s)   ◾ Unspecified   **OGCR** Official Guidelines for Coding and Reporting
🦠 Complication\Comorbidity   🦟 Major C\C   Excludes 1   Excludes 2   Includes   Use additional   Code first   Code also

● **A93   Other arthropod-borne viral fevers, not elsewhere classified**

     A93.0   Oropouche virus disease 🦠
          Tropical viral infection
          Oropouche fever

     A93.1   Sandfly fever 🦠
          Pappataci fever
          Phlebotomus fever

     A93.2   Colorado tick fever 🦠

     A93.8   Other specified arthropod-borne viral fevers 🦠
          Piry virus disease
          Vesicular stomatitis virus disease [Indiana fever]

■ **A94   Unspecified arthropod-borne viral fever** 🦠

     | **Includes** | arboviral fever NOS |
                      arbovirus infection NOS

● **A95   Yellow fever**
     Acute infectious disease transmitted by mosquitoes

     A95.0   Sylvatic yellow fever 🦠
          Jungle yellow fever

     A95.1   Urban yellow fever 🦠

     ■ **A95.9   Yellow fever, unspecified** 🦠

● **A96   Arenaviral hemorrhagic fever**
     Virus that causes various hemorrhagic fevers

     A96.0   Junin hemorrhagic fever 🦠
          Argentinian hemorrhagic fever

     A96.1   Machupo hemorrhagic fever 🦠
          Transmitted by contact with infected rodents
          Bolivian hemorrhagic fever

     A96.2   Lassa fever 🦠
          Acute type of hemorrhagic fever caused by contact with disease carrying mouse or person

     A96.8   Other arenaviral hemorrhagic fevers 🦠

     ■ **A96.9   Arenaviral hemorrhagic fever, unspecified** 🦠

● **A98   Other viral hemorrhagic fevers, not elsewhere classified**

     | **Excludes1** | chikungunya hemorrhagic fever (A92.0) |
                      dengue hemorrhagic fever (A91)

     A98.0   Crimean-Congo hemorrhagic fever 🦠
          Virus transmitted by ticks and contact with blood, secretions, or fluids from infected humans or animals
          Central Asian hemorrhagic fever

     A98.1   Omsk hemorrhagic fever 🦠
          Transmitted to humans by bites of infected ticks or contact with infected muskrats

     A98.2   Kyasanur Forest disease 🦠
          Transmitted via infected monkeys, voles, ticks

     A98.3   Marburg virus disease
          Rare, acute, often fatal type of hemorrhagic fever

     A98.4   Ebola virus disease

     A98.5   Hemorrhagic fever with renal syndrome 🦠
          Epidemic hemorrhagic fever
          Korean hemorrhagic fever
          Russian hemorrhagic fever
          Hantaan virus disease
          Hantavirus disease with renal manifestations
          Nephropathia epidemica
          Songo fever

         | **Excludes1** | hantavirus (cardio)-pulmonary syndrome (B33.4) |

     A98.8   Other specified viral hemorrhagic fevers 🦠

■ **A99   Unspecified viral hemorrhagic fever** 🦠

● Unacceptable First-Listed Diagnosis   ● Use Additional Character(s)   ■ Unspecified   **OGCR** Official Guidelines for Coding and Reporting

🦠 Complication\Comorbidity   🦠 Major C\C | Excludes 1 | | Excludes 2 | Includes   Use additional   Code first   Code also

805

VIRAL INFECTIONS CHARACTERIZED BY SKIN AND MUCOUS MEMBRANE LESIONS (B00-B09)

● **B00   Herpesviral [herpes simplex] infections**

> **Excludes1**   congenital herpesviral infections (P35.2)
>
> **Excludes2**   anogenital herpesviral infection (A60.-)
> gammaherpesviral mononucleosis (B27.0-)
> herpangina (B08.5)

B00.0   Eczema herpeticum
> *Cutaneous eruption caused by herpes simplex virus (HSV) type 1, HSV-2, coxsackievirus A16, or vaccinia virus*
> Kaposi's varicelliform eruption

B00.1   Herpesviral vesicular dermatitis
> *Vesicle formation; characteristics include formation of blisters and scabs on feet and legs*
> Herpes simplex facialis
> Herpes simplex labialis
> Herpes simplex otitis externa
> Vesicular dermatitis of ear
> Vesicular dermatitis of lip

B00.2   Herpesviral gingivostomatitis and pharyngotonsillitis 🗲
> *Inflammation involving both gingivae and oral mucosa*
> Herpesviral pharyngitis
> *Inflammation of pharynx and tonsils; AKA tonsillopharyngitis*

B00.3   Herpesviral meningitis 🗲

B00.4   Herpesviral encephalitis 🗲
> Herpesviral meningoencephalitis
> Simian B disease
>
> > **Excludes1**   herpesviral encephalitis due to herpesvirus 6 and 7 (B10.01, B10.09)
> > non-simplex herpesviral encephalitis (B10.0-)

● **B00.5   Herpesviral ocular disease**
> ▪ **B00.50   Herpesviral ocular disease, unspecified** 🗲
>
> **B00.51   Herpesviral iridocyclitis** 🗲
> > Herpesviral iritis
> > Herpesviral uveitis, anterior
>
> **B00.52   Herpesviral keratitis** 🗲
> > Herpesviral keratoconjunctivitis
>
> **B00.53   Herpesviral conjunctivitis** 🗲
>
> **B00.59   Other herpesviral disease of eye** 🗲
> > Herpesviral dermatitis of eyelid

B00.7   Disseminated herpesviral disease 🗲
> Herpesviral sepsis

● **B00.8   Other forms of herpesviral infections**
> **B00.81   Herpesviral hepatitis** 🗲
>
> **B00.82   Herpes simplex myelitis** 🗲
>
> **B00.89   Other herpesviral infection** 🗲
> > Herpesviral whitlow

▪ **B00.9   Herpesviral infection, unspecified**
> Herpes simplex infection NOS

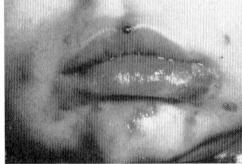

Figure 1-4   Primary herpes simplex in and around the mouth. The infection is usually acquired from siblings or parents and is readily transmitted to other direct contacts. (From Forbes, Jackson: Colour Atlas and Text of Clinical Medicine, International Edition. 2002, Mosby)

Item 1-15   Herpes is a viral disease for which there is no cure. There are two types of the herpes simplex virus: **Type I** causes **cold sores** or **fever blisters**, and **Type II** causes **genital herpes.** The virus can be spread from a sore on the lips to the genitals or from the genitals to the lips.

● **B01   Varicella [chickenpox]**
> *Very contagious disease caused by the varicella zoster virus that results in an itchy outbreak of skin blisters (varicella). The same virus causes shingles (zoster).*

B01.0   Varicella meningitis 🗲

● **B01.1   Varicella encephalitis, myelitis and encephalomyelitis**
> Postchickenpox encephalitis, myelitis and encephalomyelitis
>
> **B01.11   Varicella encephalitis and encephalomyelitis** 🗲
> > Postchickenpox encephalitis and encephalomyelitis
>
> **B01.12   Varicella myelitis** 🗲
> > Postchickenpox myelitis

B01.2   Varicella pneumonia 🗲

● **B01.8   Varicella with other complications**
> **B01.81   Varicella keratitis** 🗲
>
> **B01.89   Other varicella complications** 🗲

B01.9   Varicella without complication 🗲
> Varicella NOS

● **B02   Zoster [herpes zoster]**
> **Includes**   shingles
>   zona

B02.0   Zoster encephalitis 🗲
> Zoster meningoencephalitis

B02.1   Zoster meningitis 🗲

● **B02.2   Zoster with other nervous system involvement**
> **B02.21   Postherpetic geniculate ganglionitis** 🗲
>
> **B02.22   Postherpetic trigeminal neuralgia** 🗲
>
> **B02.23   Postherpetic polyneuropathy** 🗲
>
> **B02.24   Postherpetic myelitis** 🗲
> > Herpes zoster myelitis
>
> **B02.29   Other postherpetic nervous system involvement** 🗲
> > Postherpetic radiculopathy

● **B02.3   Zoster ocular disease**
> ▪ **B02.30   Zoster ocular disease, unspecified** 🗲
>
> **B02.31   Zoster conjunctivitis** 🗲
>
> **B02.32   Zoster iridocyclitis** 🗲
>
> **B02.33   Zoster keratitis** 🗲
> > Herpes zoster keratoconjunctivitis
>
> **B02.34   Zoster scleritis** 🗲
>
> **B02.39   Other herpes zoster eye disease** 🗲
> > Zoster blepharitis

Item 1-16   Zoster: Also known as *shingles* and is caused by the same virus as chickenpox. After exposure, the virus lies dormant in nerve tissue and is activated by factors including aging, stress, suppression of the immune system, and certain medication. It begins as a unilateral rash that leads to blisters and sores on the skin. It may involve the nerve pathways of the eye, forehead, nose, and eyelids and may be very painful with long term systemic effects.

● Unacceptable First-Listed Diagnosis   ● Use Additional Character(s)   ▪ Unspecified   **OGCR** Official Guidelines for Coding and Reporting
🗲 Complication\Comorbidity   🗲 Major C\C   [Excludes 1]   [Excludes 2]   Includes   Use additional   Code first   Code also

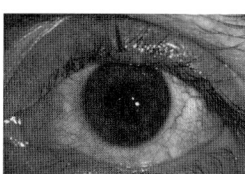

Figure 1-5 Photograph of eyelids with marginal blepharitis. (From Mandell, Bennett, & Dolin Principles and Practice of Infectious Diseases, 6th ed. 2005, Churchill Livingstone, An Imprint of Elsevier)

Item 1-17 Blepharitis is a common condition in which the eyelid is swollen and yellow scaling and conjunctivitis develop. Usually the hair on the scalp and brow is involved.

B02.7 Disseminated zoster 🏷

B02.8 Zoster with other complications 🏷
Herpes zoster otitis externa

B02.9 Zoster without complications
Zoster NOS

B03 Smallpox 🏷
In 1980 the 33rd World Health Assembly declared that smallpox had been eradicated. The classification is maintained for surveillance purposes.

B04 Monkeypox 🏷
Disease occurring in captive monkeys and other mammals that may be transmitted to humans, clinically similar to smallpox

● **B05 Measles**
  Includes   morbilli
  Excludes1   subacute sclerosing panencephalitis (A81.1)

B05.0 Measles complicated by encephalitis 🏷
Postmeasles encephalitis

B05.1 Measles complicated by meningitis 🏷
Postmeasles meningitis

B05.2 Measles complicated by pneumonia 🏷
Postmeasles pneumonia

B05.3 Measles complicated by otitis media
Postmeasles otitis media

B05.4 Measles with intestinal complications 🏷

● **B05.8 Measles with other complications**

  B05.81 Measles keratitis and keratoconjunctivitis 🏷

  B05.89 Other measles complications 🏷

B05.9 Measles without complication
Measles NOS

● **B06 Rubella [German measles]**
  Excludes1   congenital rubella (P35.0)

● **B06.0 Rubella with neurological complications**

  ■ **B06.00 Rubella with neurological complication, unspecified** 🏷

  B06.01 Rubella encephalitis 🏷
  Rubella meningoencephalitis

  B06.02 Rubella meningitis 🏷

  B06.09 Other neurological complications of rubella 🏷

● **B06.8 Rubella with other complications**

  B06.81 Rubella pneumonia 🏷

  B06.82 Rubella arthritis 🏷

  B06.89 Other rubella complications 🏷

B06.9 Rubella without complication
Rubella NOS

● **B07 Viral warts**
  Includes   verruca simplex
                  verruca vulgaris
                  viral warts due to human papillomavirus
  Excludes2   anogenital (venereal) warts (A63.0)
                   papilloma of bladder (D41.4)
                   papilloma of cervix (D26.0)
                   papilloma larynx (D14.1)

B07.0 Plantar wart
Verruca plantaris

B07.8 Other viralwarts
Common wart
Flat wart
Verruca plana

■ **B07.9 Viral wart, unspecified**

● **B08 Other viral infections characterized by skin and mucous membrane lesions, not elsewhere classified**
  Excludes1   vesicular stomatitis virus disease (A93.8)

● **B08.0 Other orthopoxvirus infections**
  Excludes2   monkeypox (B04)

  ● **B08.01 Cowpox and vaccinia not from vaccine**

    B08.010 Cowpox

    B08.011 Vaccinia not from vaccine
    Excludes1   vaccinia (from vaccination) (generalized) (T88.1)

  B08.02 Orf virus disease
  Contagious pustular dermatitis
  Ecthyma contagiosum

  B08.03 Pseudocowpox [milker's node]

  ■ **B08.04 Paravaccinia, unspecified**

  B08.09 Other orthopoxvirus infections
  Orthopoxvirus infection NOS

B08.1 Molluscum contagiosum
Various skin diseases characterized by soft, rounded, cutaneous lesions

● **B08.2 Exanthema subitum [sixth disease] Roseola infantum**
Acute, short-lived high fever in infants and young children followed by a rash mainly on the trunk, caused by human herpesvirus 6

  ■ **B08.20 Exanthema subitum [sixth disease], unspecified Roseola infantum, unspecified**

  B08.21 Exanthema subitum [sixth disease] due to human herpesvirus 6 Roseola infantum due to human herpesvirus 6
  Virus results in sudden rash; infection results in lifelong persistence

  B08.22 Exanthema subitum [sixth disease] due to human herpesvirus 7 Roseola infantum due to human herpesvirus 7

B08.3 Erythema infectiosum [fifth disease] 🏷
Moderately contagious, epidemic disease in children caused by B19 virus; onset of rash that begins as redness of cheeks, later there is rash on trunk and limbs; when this fades, there may be central clearing that leaves lacelike pattern

B08.4 Enteroviral vesicular stomatitis with exanthem
Hand, foot and mouth disease
Check your documentation—this code is HAND, foot, and mouth disease. Code B08.8 is foot and mouth disease.

B08.5 Enteroviral vesicular pharyngitis
Herpangina

● Unacceptable First-Listed Diagnosis   ● Use Additional Character(s)   ■ Unspecified   **OGCR** Official Guidelines for Coding and Reporting
🏷 Complication\Comorbidity   🏷 Major C\C   Excludes 1   Excludes 2   Includes   Use additional   Code first   Code also

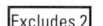

- **B08.6**   **Parapoxvirus infections**
  - ◻ **B08.60**   **Parapoxvirus infection, unspecified**
  - **B08.61**   **Bovine stomatitis**
  - **B08.62**   **Sealpox**
  - **B08.69**   **Other parapoxvirus infections**
- **B08.7**   **Yatapoxvirus infections**
  - ◻ **B08.70**   **Yatapoxvirus infection, unspecified**
  - **B08.71**   **Tanapox virus disease**
  - **B08.72**   **Yaba pox virus disease**
    - Yaba monkey tumor disease
  - **B08.79**   **Other yatapoxvirus infections**
- **B08.8**   **Other specified viral infections characterized by skin and mucous membrane lesions** 🔖
  - Enteroviral lymphonodular pharyngitis
  - Foot-and-mouth disease
    - *Check your documentation. Code B08.4 is for HAND, foot, and mouth disease.*
  - Poxvirus NEC

- ◻ **B09**   **Unspecified viral infection characterized by skin and mucous membrane lesions**

Includes	viral enanthema NOS
	viral exanthema NOS

OTHER HUMAN HERPESVIRUSES (B10)

- ● **B10**   **Other human herpesviruses**

Excludes2	cytomegalovirus (B25.9)
	Epstein-Barr virus (B27.0-)
	herpes NOS (B00.9)
	herpes simplex (B00.-)
	herpes zoster (B02.-)
	human herpesvirus NOS (B00.-)
	human herpesvirus 1 and 2 (B00.-)
	human herpesvirus 3 (B01.-, B02.-)
	human herpesvirus 4 (B27.0-)
	human herpesvirus 5 (B25.-)
	varicella (B01.-)
	zoster (B02.-)

  - ● **B10.0**   **Other human herpesvirus encephalitis**

Excludes2	herpes encephalitis NOS (B00.4)
	herpes simplex encephalitis (B00.4)
	human herpesvirus encephalitis (B00.4)
	simian B herpes virus encephalitis (B00.4)

    - **B10.01**   **Human herpesvirus 6 encephalitis** 🔖
      - *Sudden rash or roseola*
    - **B10.09**   **Other human herpesvirus encephalitis** 🔖
      - Human herpesvirus 7 encephalitis
      - *Virus closely related to human herpesvirus 6, but not known to cause any disease*
  - ● **B10.8**   **Other human herpesvirus infection**
    - **B10.81**   **Human herpesvirus 6 infection**
      - *Causative agent of exanthema subitum that results in sudden rash*
    - **B10.82**   **Human herpesvirus 7 infection**
      - *Closely related to human herpesvirus 6, but not known cause any disease*
    - **B10.89**   **Other human herpesvirus infection**
      - Human herpesvirus 8 infection
      - *May be the cause of Kaposi sarcoma, a malignant tumor*
      - Kaposi's sarcoma-associated herpesvirus infection

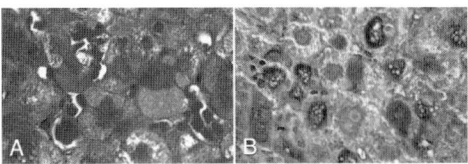

Figure 1-6   Hepatitis B viral infection. **A.** Liver parenchyma showing hepatocytes with diffuse granular cytoplasm, so-called ground glass hepatocytes (H&E). **B.** Immunoperoxidase stains from the same case, showing cytoplasmic inclusions of viral particles. (From Kumar: Robbins and Cotran: Pathologic Basis of Disease, 7th ed. 2005, Saunders, An Imprint of Elsevier)

Item 1–18   Hepatitis A (HAV) was formerly called epidemic, infectious, short-incubation, or acute catarrhal jaundice hepatitis. The primary transmission mode is the oral–fecal route. **Hepatitis B (HBV)** was formerly called long-incubation period, serum, or homologous serum hepatitis. Transmission modes are through blood from infected persons and from body fluids of infected mother to neonate. **Hepatitis C (HCV),** caused by the hepatitis C virus, is primarily transfusion associated. **Hepatitis D (HDV),** also called delta hepatitis, is caused by the hepatitis D virus in patients formerly or currently infected with hepatitis B. **Hepatitis E (HEV)** is also called enterically transmitted non-A, non-B hepatitis. The primary transmission mode is the oral–fecal route, usually through contaminated water.

VIRAL HEPATITIS (B15-B19)

Excludes1	sequelae of viral hepatitis (B94.2)
Excludes2	cytomegaloviral hepatitis (B25.1)
	herpesviral [herpes simplex] hepatitis (B00.81)

- ● **B15**   **Acute hepatitis A**
  - **B15.0**   **Hepatitis A with hepatic coma** 🔖
  - **B15.9**   **Hepatitis A without hepatic coma** 🔖
    - Hepatitis A (acute) (viral) NOS
- ● **B16**   **Acute hepatitis B**
  - **B16.0**   **Acute hepatitis B with delta-agent with hepatic coma** 🔖
  - **B16.1**   **Acute hepatitis B with delta-agent without hepatic coma** 🔖
  - **B16.2**   **Acute hepatitis B without delta-agent with hepatic coma** 🔖
  - **B16.9**   **Acute hepatitis B without delta-agent and without hepatic coma** 🔖
    - Hepatitis B (acute) (viral) NOS
- ● **B17**   **Other acute viral hepatitis**
  - **B17.0**   **Acute delta-(super) infection of hepatitis B carrier** 🔖
  - ● **B17.1**   **Acute hepatitis C**
    - **B17.10**   **Acute hepatitis C without hepatic coma** 🔖
      - Acute hepatitis C NOS
    - **B17.11**   **Acute hepatitis C with hepatic coma** 🔖
  - **B17.2**   **Acute hepatitis E** 🔖
  - **B17.8**   **Other specified acute viral hepatitis** 🔖
    - Hepatitis non-A non-B (acute) (viral) NEC
  - ◻ **B17.9**   **Acute viral hepatitis, unspecified** 🔖
    - Acute hepatitis NOS
- ● **B18**   **Chronic viral hepatitis**
  - **B18.0**   **Chronic viral hepatitis B with delta-agent** 🔖
  - **B18.1**   **Chronic viral hepatitis B without delta-agent** 🔖
    - Chronic (viral) hepatitis B

● Unacceptable First-Listed Diagnosis   ● Use Additional Character(s)   ◻ Unspecified   **OGCR** Official Guidelines for Coding and Reporting

🔖 Complication\Comorbidity   🔖 Major C\C   Excludes 1   Excludes 2   Includes   Use additional   Code first   Code also

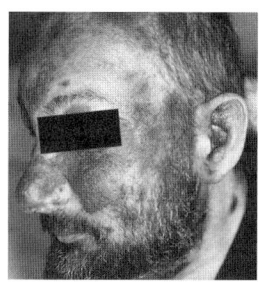

Figure 1-7   Kaposi's sarcoma. There are large confluent hyperpigmented patch-stage lesions with lymphedema. (From Cahen & Powderly: Infectious Disease, 2nd ed 2004, Mosby, An imprint of Elsevier)

Item 1–19   AIDS (acquired immune deficiency syndrome) is caused by **HIV** (human immunodeficiency virus). HIV affects certain white blood cells (T-4 lymphocytes) and destroys the ability of the cells to fight infections, making patients susceptible to a host of infectious diseases (e.g., **Pneumocystis carinii pneumonia (PCP), Kaposi's sarcoma,** and **lymphoma). AIDS-related complex (ARC)** is an early stage of AIDS in which tests for HIV are positive but the symptoms are mild.

     B18.2   Chronic viral hepatitis C

     B18.8   Other chronic viral hepatitis 🦠

     ▣ B18.9   Chronic viral hepatitis, unspecified 🦠

● **B19**   Unspecified viral hepatitis

     ▣ **B19.0**   Unspecified viral hepatitis with hepatic coma 🦠

     ● **B19.1**   Unspecified viral hepatitis B

         ▣ **B19.10**   Unspecified viral hepatitis B without hepatic coma 🦠
                 Unspecified viral hepatitis B NOS

         ▣ **B19.11**   Unspecified viral hepatitis B with hepatic coma 🦠

     ● **B19.2**   Unspecified viral hepatitis C

         ▣ **B19.20**   Unspecified viral hepatitis C without hepatic coma 🦠
                 Viral hepatitis C NOS

         ▣ **B19.21**   Unspecified viral hepatitis C with hepatic coma 🦠

     ▣ **B19.9**   Unspecified viral hepatitis without hepatic coma 🦠
            Viral hepatitis NOS

OGCR   Section I. C.1.a

     Certain Infectious and Parasitic Diseases (A00-B99)
     a. Human Immunodeficiency Virus (HIV) Infections
       1) Code only confirmed cases
          Code only confirmed cases of HIV infection illness. This is an exception to the hospital inpatient guideline Section II, H.

          In this context, "confirmation" does not require documentation of positive serology or culture for HIV; the provider's diagnostic statement that the patient is HIV positive, or has an HIV-related illness is sufficient.

HUMAN IMMUNODEFICIENCY VIRUS [HIV] DISEASE (B20)

B20   Human immunodeficiency virus [HIV] disease 🦠

     | Includes | acquired immune deficiency syndrome [AIDS]
                  AIDS-related complex [ARC]
                  HIV infection, symptomatic

     Code first: Human immunodeficiency [HIV] disease complicating pregnancy, childbirth and the puerperium, if applicable (O98.7-)

     Use additional code(s) to identify all manifestations of HIV infection.

     | Excludes1 | asymptomatic human immunodeficiency virus [HIV] infection status (Z21)
                    exposure to HIV virus (Z20.6)
                    inconclusive serologic evidence of HIV (R75)

OTHER VIRAL DISEASES (B25-B34)

● **B25   Cytomegaloviral disease**
     AKA: HCMV or Human Herpesvirus 5 (HHV-5)

     | Excludes1 | congenital cytomegalovirus infection (P35.1)
                    cytomegaloviral mononucleosis (B27.1-)

     B25.0   Cytomegaloviral pneumonitis 🦠

     B25.1   Cytomegaloviral hepatitis 🦠

     B25.2   Cytomegaloviral pancreatitis 🦠

     B25.8   Other cytomegaloviral diseases 🦠
              Cytomegaloviral encephalitis

     ▣ B25.9   Cytomegaloviral disease, unspecified 🦠

● **B26   Mumps**

     | Includes | epidemic parotitis
                  infectious parotitis
     Acute, contagious, viral disease

     B26.0   Mumps orchitis 🦠

     B26.1   Mumps meningitis 🦠

     B26.2   Mumps encephalitis 🦠

     B26.3   Mumps pancreatitis 🦠

     ● B26.8   Mumps with other complications

         B26.81   Mumps hepatitis 🦠
         B26.82   Mumps myocarditis 🦠
         B26.83   Mumps nephritis 🦠
         B26.84   Mumps polyneuropathy 🦠
         B26.85   Mumps arthritis 🦠
         B26.89   Other mumps complications 🦠

     B26.9   Mumps without complication
              Mumps NOS
              Mumps parotitis NOS

● **B27   Infectious mononucleosis**

     | Includes | glandular fever
                  monocytic angina
                  Pfeiffer's disease

     ● B27.0   Gammaherpesviral mononucleosis
              AKA: Pfeiffer's disease, infective mononucleosis
              Mononucleosis due to Epstein-Barr virus

         B27.00   Gammaherpesviral mononucleosis without complication
                 Infective mononucleosis

         B27.01   Gammaherpesviral mononucleosis with polyneuropathy

         B27.02   Gammaherpesviral mononucleosis with meningitis

         B27.09   Gammaherpesviral mononucleosis with other complications
                 Hepatomegaly in gammaherpesviral mononucleosis

     ● B27.1   Cytomegaloviral mononucleosis
              Infectious disease resembling infectious mononucleosis

         B27.10   Cytomegaloviral mononucleosis without complications

● Unacceptable First-Listed Diagnosis   ● Use Additional Character(s)   ▣ Unspecified   **OGCR** Official Guidelines for Coding and Reporting

🦠 Complication\Comorbidity   🦠 Major C\C | Excludes 1 | | Excludes 2 | Includes   Use additional   Code first   Code also

809

CHAPTER 1 (A00-B99)

B27.11   **Cytomegaloviral mononucleosis with polyneuropathy**

B27.12   **Cytomegaloviral mononucleosis with meningitis**

B27.19   **Cytomegaloviral mononucleosis with other complication**
    Hepatomegaly in cytomegaloviral mononucleosis

● B27.8   **Other infectious mononucleosis**

B27.80   **Other infectious mononucleosis without complication**

B27.81   **Other infectious mononucleosis with polyneuropathy**

B27.82   **Other infectious mononucleosis with meningitis**

B27.89   **Other infectious mononucleosis with other complication**
    Hepatomegaly in other infectious mononucleosis

● B27.9   **Infectious mononucleosis, unspecified**

B27.90   **Infectious mononucleosis, unspecified without complication**

B27.91   **Infectious mononucleosis, unspecified with polyneuropathy**

B27.92   **Infectious mononucleosis, unspecified with meningitis**

B27.99   **Infectious mononucleosis, unspecified with other complication**
    Hepatomegaly in unspecified infectious mononucleosis

● **B30   Viral conjunctivitis**

| **Excludes1** | herpesviral [herpes simplex] ocular disease (B00.5)
ocular zoster (B02.3) |

B30.0   **Keratoconjunctivitis due to adenovirus**
    Epidemic keratoconjunctivitis
    Shipyard eye

B30.1   **Conjunctivitis due to adenovirus**
    Acute adenoviral follicular conjunctivitis
    Swimming-pool conjunctivitis

B30.2   **Viral pharyngoconjunctivitis**

B30.3   **Acute epidemic hemorrhagic conjunctivitis (enteroviral)**
    Conjunctivitis due to coxsackievirus 24
    Conjunctivitis due to enterovirus 70
    Hemorrhagic conjunctivitis (acute)(epidemic)

B30.8   **Other viral conjunctivitis**
    Newcastle conjunctivitis

B30.9   **Viral conjunctivitis, unspecified**

● **B33   Other viral diseases, not elsewhere classified**

B33.0   **Epidemic myalgia**
    Acute infectious disease, caused by group A coxsackie viruses or other enteroviruses with symptoms that include sudden pain in chest or upper abdomen with fever
    Bornholm disease

B33.1   **Ross River disease** 🔖
    Epidemic polyarthritis and exanthema
    Ross River fever

● B33.2   **Viral carditis**
    Coxsackie (virus) carditis

B33.20   **Viral carditis, unspecified** 🔖

B33.21   **Viral endocarditis** 🔖

B33.22   **Viral myocarditis** 🔖

B33.23   **Viral pericarditis** 🔖

B33.24   **Viral cardiomyopathy**

B33.3   **Retrovirus infections, not elsewhere classified**
    Retrovirus infection NOS

B33.4   **Hantavirus (cardio)-pulmonary syndrome [HPS] [HCPS]** 🔖
    Hantavirus disease with pulmonary manifestations
    Sin nombre virus disease

    Use additional code to identify any associated acute kidney failure (N17.9)

| **Excludes1** | hantavirus disease with renal manifestations (A98.5)
hemorrhagic fever with renal manifestations (A98.5) |

B33.8   **Other specified viral diseases**

| **Excludes1** | anogenital human papillomavirus infection (A63.0)
viral warts due to human papillomavirus infection (B07) |

● **B34   Viral infection of unspecified site**

| **Excludes1** | anogenital human papillomavirus infection (A63.0)
cytomegaloviral disease NOS (B25.9)
herpesvirus [herpes simplex] infection NOS (B00.9)
retrovirus infection NOS (B33.3)
viral agents as the cause of diseases classified elsewhere (B97.-)
viral warts due to human papillomavirus infection (B07) |

B34.0   **Adenovirus infection, unspecified**

B34.1   **Enterovirus infection, unspecified**
    Intestinal tract infection
    Coxsackievirus infection NOS
    Echovirus infection NOS

B34.2   **Coronavirus infection, unspecified**

| **Excludes1** | pneumonia due to SARS-associated coronavirus (J12.3) |

B34.3   **Parvovirus infection, unspecified** 🔖

B34.4   **Papovavirus infection, unspecified**

B34.8   **Other viral infections of unspecified site**

B34.9   **Viral infection, unspecified**
    Viremia NOS

MYCOSES (B35-B49)

| **Excludes2** | hypersensitivity pneumonitis due to organic dust (J67.-)
mycosis fungoides (C84.0-) |

● **B35   Dermatophytosis**
    AKA tinea or ringworm

| **Includes** | favus
infections due to species of Epidermophyton, Micro-sporum and Trichophyton
tinea, any type except those in B36. |

B35.0   **Tinea barbae and tinea capitis**
    Beard ringworm
    Kerion
    Scalp ringworm
    Sycosis, mycotic

● Unacceptable First-Listed Diagnosis   ● Use Additional Character(s)   ■ Unspecified   **OGCR** Official Guidelines for Coding and Reporting
🔖 Complication\Comorbidity   🔖 Major C\C   Excludes 1   Excludes 2   Includes   Use additional   Code first   Code also

B35.1 Tinea unguium
White patches or pits on surface or edges of nails, followed by infection under nail plate
Dermatophytic onychia
Dermatophytosis of nail
Onychomycosis
Ringworm of nails

B35.2 Tinea manuum
Tinea of hands
Dermatophytosis of hand
Hand ringworm

B35.3 Tinea pedis
Tinea affecting feet
Athlete's foot
Dermatophytosis of foot
Foot ringworm

B35.4 Tinea corporis
Infecting skin areas other than hands
Ringworm of the body

B35.5 Tinea imbricata
Chronic tropical tinea corporis; AKA Oriental ringworm, tinea inguinalis, tinea cruris
Tokelau

B35.6 Tinea cruris
In groin or perineal area, spreading to adjacent regions; AKA jock itch, eczema marginatum, ringworm of groin, or t inguinalis
Dhobi itch
Groin ringworm
Jock itch

B35.8 Other dermatophytoses
Disseminated dermatophytosis
Granulomatous dermatophytosis

◼B35.9 Dermatophytosis, unspecified
Ringworm NOS

● B36 Other superficial mycoses

B36.0 Pityriasis versicolor
Common, chronic, symptomless disorder that includes macular patches of various sizes and shapes; AKA liver spots
Tinea flava
Tinea versicolor

B36.1 Tinea nigra
Minor fungal infection, with dark lesions, usually on skin of hands
Keratomycosis nigricans palmaris
Microsporosis nigra
Pityriasis nigra

B36.2 White piedra
White to light brown nodules on hair of beard, axilla, or groin; AKA trichosporosis
Tinea blanca

B36.3 Black piedra
Characterized by small black or brown nodules on shafts of scalp hair

B36.8 Other specified superficial mycoses

◼B36.9 Superficial mycosis, unspecified

● B37 Candidiasis

> **Includes**   candidosis
>   moniliasis

> **Excludes1**   neonatal candidiasis (P37.5)

B37.0 Candidal stomatitis ✇
Oral thrush

Figure 1-8 Oral candidiasis (thrush). *(Courtesy of Stephen Raffanti, MD, MPH).* (From Mandell, Bennett, & Dolin: Principles and Practice of Infectious Diseases, 6th ed, 2005, Churchill Livingstone, An Imprint of Elsevier)

Item 1–20 Candidiasis, also called oidiomycosis or moniliasis, is a fungal infection. It most often appears on moist cutaneous areas of the body but can also be responsible for a variety of systemic infections such as endocarditis, meningitis, arthritis, and myositis. Antifungal medications cure most yeast infections.

B37.1 Pulmonary candidiasis ✇
Candidal bronchitis
Candidal pneumonia

B37.2 Candidiasis of skin and nail
Candidal onychia
Candidal paronychia

> **Excludes2**   diaper dermatitis (L22)

B37.3 Candidiasis of vulva and vagina
Candidal vulvovaginitis
Monilial vulvovaginitis
Vaginal thrush

● B37.4 Candidiasis of other urogenital sites

     B37.41 Candidal cystitis and urethritis ✇

     B37.42 Candidal balanitis
            Male condition only

     B37.49 Other urogenital candidiasis ✇
            Candidal pyelonephritis

B37.5 Candidal meningitis ✇

B37.6 Candidal endocarditis ✇

B37.7 Candidal sepsis ✇
Disseminated candidiasis systemic candidiasis

● B37.8 Candidiasis of other sites

     B37.81 Candidal esophagitis ✇

     B37.82 Candidal enteritis ✇
            Candidal proctitis

     B37.83 Candidal cheilitis ✇
            Inflammation affecting lip

     B37.84 Candidal otitis externa ✇
            Inflammation of external auditory canal

     B37.89 Other sites of candidiasis ✇
            Infection manifested by invasive candidiasis
            Candidal osteomyelitis

◼B37.9 Candidiasis, unspecified
Thrush NOS

● B38 Coccidioidomycosis
Fungal disease; AKA coccidioidosis, coccidioidal granuloma, Posadas, or Posadas-Wernicke disease

B38.0 Acute pulmonary coccidioidomycosis ✇

B38.1 Chronic pulmonary coccidioidomycosis ✇

◼B38.2 Pulmonary coccidioidomycosis, unspecified ✇

B38.3 Cutaneous coccidioidomycosis ✇

B38.4 Coccidioidomycosis meningitis ✇

B38.7 Disseminated coccidioidomycosis ✇
Generalized coccidioidomycosis

● B38.8 Other forms of coccidioidomycosis

     B38.81 Prostatic coccidioidomycosis ✇

     B38.89 Other forms of coccidioidomycosis ✇

◼B38.9 Coccidioidomycosis, unspecified ✇

● Unacceptable First-Listed Diagnosis   ● Use Additional Character(s)   ◼ Unspecified   **OGCR** Official Guidelines for Coding and Reporting

✇ Complication\Comorbidity   ✇ Major C\C   Excludes 1   Excludes 2   Includes   Use additional   Code first   Code also

811

Item 1–21 Bird and bat droppings that fall into the soil give rise to a fungus that can spread airborne spores. When inhaled into the lungs, these spores divide and multiply into lesions. Histoplasmosis capsulatum takes three forms: primary (lodged in the lungs only), chronic (resembles TB), and disseminated (infection has moved to other organs). This is an opportunistic infection in immunosuppressed patients.

● **B39 Histoplasmosis**
>   *Infection resulting from inhalation or ingestion of spores; AKA Darling disease*
>
>   Code first *associated AIDS (B20)*
>
>   Use additional code for any associated manifestations, such as:
>   endocarditis (I39)
>   meningitis (G02)
>   pericarditis (I32)
>   retinitis (H32)

   B39.0 Acute pulmonary histoplasmosis capsulati 🩸

   B39.1 Chronic pulmonary histoplasmosis capsulati 🩸

■ **B39.2 Pulmonary histoplasmosis capsulati, unspecified** 🩸

   B39.3 Disseminated histoplasmosis capsulati 🩸
>   Generalized histoplasmosis capsulati

■ **B39.4 Histoplasmosis capsulati, unspecified**
>   American histoplasmosis

   B39.5 Histoplasmosis duboisii
>   African histoplasmosis

■ **B39.9 Histoplasmosis, unspecified**

● **B40 Blastomycosis**
>   *Rare and potentially fatal infection caused by inhaling fungus found in moist soil in temperate climates.*
>
>   **Excludes1** Brazilian blastomycosis (B41.-)
>   keloidal blastomycosis (B48.0)

   B40.0 Acute pulmonary blastomycosis 🩸

   B40.1 Chronic pulmonary blastomycosis 🩸

■ **B40.2 Pulmonary blastomycosis, unspecified** 🩸

   B40.3 Cutaneous blastomycosis 🩸

   B40.7 Disseminated blastomycosis 🩸
>   Generalized blastomycosis

● **B40.8 Other forms of blastomycosis**

      B40.81 Blastomycotic meningoencephalitis 🩸
>   Meningomyelitis due to blastomycosis

      B40.89 Other forms of blastomycosis 🩸

■ **B40.9 Blastomycosis, unspecified** 🩸

● **B41 Paracoccidioidomycosis**
>   *Fungal infection usually chronic that begins in lungs, spreads to mucocutaneous areas which may extend to skin, tonsils, gastrointestinal lymphatics, liver, and spleen; AKA Almeida or Lutz-Splendore-Almeida disease, Brazilian or South American blastomycosis, or paracoccidioidal granuloma*
>
>   **Includes** Brazilian blastomycosis
>   Lutz' disease

   B41.0 Pulmonary paracoccidioidomycosis 🩸

   B41.7 Disseminated paracoccidioidomycosis 🩸
>   Generalized paracoccidioidomycosis

   B41.8 Other forms of paracoccidioidomycosis 🩸

■ **B41.9 Paracoccidioidomycosis, unspecified** 🩸

● **B42 Sporotrichosis**
>   *Chronic fungal infection with nodular lesions*

   B42.0 Pulmonary sporotrichosis

   B42.1 Lymphocutaneous sporotrichosis

   B42.7 Disseminated sporotrichosis
>   Generalized sporotrichosis

● **B42.8 Other forms of sporotrichosis**

      B42.81 Cerebral sporotrichosis
>   Meningitis due to sporotrichosis

      B42.82 Sporotrichosis arthritis

      B42.89 Other forms of sporotrichosis

■ **B42.9 Sporotrichosis, unspecified**

● **B43 Chromomycosis and pheomycotic abscess**
>   *Chronic fungal infection of skin, initiated at site of puncture affecting lower limb or foot (mossy foot)*

   B43.0 Cutaneous chromomycosis
>   Dermatitis verrucosa

   B43.1 Pheomycotic brain abscess
>   Cerebral chromomycosis

   B43.2 Subcutaneous pheomycotic abscess and cyst

   B43.8 Other forms of chromomycosis

■ **B43.9 Chromomycosis, unspecified**

● **B44 Aspergillosis**
>   *Infection marked by inflammatory lesions in skin, ear, orbit, nasal sinuses, lungs, and occasionally bones and meninges*
>
>   **Includes** aspergilloma

   B44.0 Invasive pulmonary aspergillosis 🩸

   B44.1 Other pulmonary aspergillosis 🩸

   B44.2 Tonsillar aspergillosis 🩸

   B44.7 Disseminated aspergillosis 🩸
>   Generalized aspergillosis

● **B44.8 Other forms of aspergillosis**

      B44.81 Allergic bronchopulmonary aspergillosis 🩸

      B44.89 Other forms of aspergillosis 🩸

■ **B44.9 Aspergillosis, unspecified** 🩸

● **B45 Cryptococcosis**
>   *Infection in the immunocompromised and fatal if left untreated; AKA torulosis, Buschke, or Busse-Buschke disease*

   B45.0 Pulmonary cryptococcosis 🩸

   B45.1 Cerebral cryptococcosis 🩸
>   Cryptococcal meningitis
>   Cryptococcosis meningocerebralis

   B45.2 Cutaneous cryptococcosis 🩸

   B45.3 Osseous cryptococcosis 🩸

   B45.7 Disseminated cryptococcosis 🩸
>   Generalized cryptococcosis

   B45.8 Other forms of cryptococcosis 🩸

■ **B45.9 Cryptococcosis, unspecified** 🩸

● **B46 Zygomycosis**
>   *Fungal infections including subcutaneous lesions and infection of sinuses, brain, or lungs*

   B46.0 Pulmonary mucormycosis 🩸
>   *Fungal infection affecting lung*

   B46.1 Rhinocerebral mucormycosis 🩸

   B46.2 Gastrointestinal mucormycosis 🩸

   B46.3 Cutaneous mucormycosis 🩸
>   Subcutaneous mucormycosis

   B46.4 Disseminated mucormycosis 🩸
>   Generalized mucormycosis

■ **B46.5 Mucormycosis, unspecified** 🩸

   B46.8 Other zygomycoses 🩸
>   Entomophthoromycosis

■ **B46.9 Zygomycosis, unspecified** 🩸
>   Phycomycosis NOS

● Unacceptable First-Listed Diagnosis   ● Use Additional Character(s)   ■ Unspecified   **OGCR** Official Guidelines for Coding and Reporting
🩸 Complication\Comorbidity   🩸 Major C\C   Excludes 1   Excludes 2   Includes   Use additional   Code first   Code also

● B47 **Mycetoma**
Slow progressive, destructive fungal infection of cutaneous and subcutaneous tissues, fascia, and bone, primarily seen in foot (Madura foot) or leg

B47.0 **Eumycetoma** 🦠
Madura foot, mycotic Maduromycosis

B47.1 **Actinomycetoma** 🦠

■ B47.9 **Mycetoma, unspecified** 🦠
Madura foot NOS

● B48 **Other mycoses, not elsewhere classified**

B48.0 **Lobomycosis**
Infection with symptoms of red, smooth, hard cutaneous nodules resembling keloids
Keloidal blastomycosis
Lobo's disease

B48.1 **Rhinosporidiosis**
Chronic, localized granulomatous fungal infection, affecting mucocutaneous tissues, usually of nose characterized by polyps, papillomas, and wartlike lesions

B48.2 **Allescheriasis** 🦠
Fungal infection
Infection due to Pseudallescheria boydii
Excludes1 eumycetoma (B47.0)

B48.3 **Geotrichosis** 🦠
Fungal infection usually of bronchi, lungs, mouth, or intestinal tract
Geotrichum stomatitis

B48.4 **Penicillosis** 🦠
Fungal infection

B48.8 **Other specified mycoses** 🦠
Adiaspiromycosis
Infection of tissue and organs by Alternaria
Infection of tissue and organs by Drechslera
Infection of tissue and organs by Fusarium
Infection of tissue and organs by saprophytic fungi NEC

■ B49 **Unspecified mycosis** 🦠
Fungemia NOS

PROTOZOAL DISEASES (B50-B64)

Excludes1 amebiasis (A06.-)
other protozoal intestinal diseases (A07.-)

● B50 **Plasmodium falciparum malaria**
Severe form of malaria that can be fatal
Includes mixed infections of Plasmodium falciparum with any other Plasmodium species

B50.0 **Plasmodium falciparum malaria with cerebral complications** 🦠
Cerebral malaria NOS

B50.8 **Other severe and complicated Plasmodium falciparum malaria** 🦠
Severe or complicated Plasmodium falciparum malaria NOS

■ B50.9 **Plasmodium falciparum malaria, unspecified** 🦠

● B51 **Plasmodium vivax malaria**
Includes mixed infections of Plasmodium vivax with other Plasmodium species, except Plasmodium falciparum
Excludes1 plasmodium vivav with Plasmodium falciparum (B50.-)

B51.0 **Plasmodium vivax malaria with rupture of spleen** 🦠
B51.8 **Plasmodium vivax malaria with other complications** 🦠
B51.9 **Plasmodium vivax malaria without complication** 🦠
Plasmodium vivax malaria NOS

● B52 **Plasmodium malariae malaria**
Causes fever that recurs at approximately three-day intervals (quartan fever), longer than two-day (tertian) intervals of other malarial parasites
Includes mixed infections of Plasmodium malariae with other Plasmodium species, except Plasmodium falciparum and Plasmodium vivax
Excludes1 plasmodium falciparum (B50.-)
plasmodium vivax (B51.-)

B52.0 **Plasmodium malariae malaria with nephropathy** 🦠
B52.8 **Plasmodium malariae malaria with other complications** 🦠
B52.9 **Plasmodium malariae malaria without complication** 🦠
Plasmodium malariae malaria NOS

● B53 **Other specified malaria**

B53.0 **Plasmodium ovale malaria** 🦠
Least diagnosed type of malaria spread by female mosquitoes of rare species
Excludes1 plasmodium ovale with Plasmodium falciparum (B50.-)
plasmodium ovale with Plasmodium malariae (B52.-)
plasmodium ovale with Plasmodium vivax (B51.-)

B53.1 **Malaria due to simian plasmodia** 🦠
Malaria-like disease (parasite infection)
Excludes1 malaria due to simian plasmodia with Plasmodium falciparum (B50.-)
malaria due to simian plasmodia with Plasmodium malariae (B52.-)
malaria due to simian plasmodia with Plasmodium ovale (B53.0)
malaria due to simian plasmodia with Plasmodium vivax (B51.-)

B53.8 **Other malaria, not elsewhere classified** 🦠

■ B54 **Unspecified malaria** 🦠

● B55 **Leishmaniasis**
Protozoal infection

B55.0 **Visceral leishmaniasis** 🦠
Kala-azar
Post-kala-azar dermal leishmaniasis

B55.1 **Cutaneous leishmaniasis** 🦠
B55.2 **Mucocutaneous leishmaniasis** 🦠
■ B55.9 **Leishmaniasis, unspecified** 🦠

● B56 **African trypanosomiasis**
Human African trypanosomiasis (HAT) is transmitted by fly bites

B56.0 **Gambiense trypanosomiasis** 🦠
Infection due to Trypanosoma brucei gambiense
West African sleeping sickness

B56.1 **Rhodesiense trypanosomiasis** 🦠
East African sleeping sickness
Infection due to Trypanosoma brucei rhodesiense

■ B56.9 **African trypanosomiasis, unspecified** 🦠
Sleeping sickness NOS

● B57 **Chagas' disease**
Tropical parasitic disease
Includes American trypanosomiasis
infection due to Trypanosoma cruzi

B57.0 **Acute Chagas' disease with heart involvement** 🦠
Acute Chagas' disease with myocarditis

● Unacceptable First-Listed Diagnosis   ● Use Additional Character(s)   ■ Unspecified   **OGCR** Official Guidelines for Coding and Reporting
🦠 Complication\Comorbidity   🦠 Major C\C   Excludes 1   Excludes 2   Includes   Use additional   Code first   Code also
813
CHAPTER 1 (A00-B99)

Item 1–22   **Toxoplasmosis** is caused by the protozoa **Toxoplasma gondii,** of which the house cat can be a host. Human infection occurs when contact is made with materials containing the pathogen, such as feces, contaminated soil, or ingestion of infected lamb, goat, or pork. Of the infected, very few have symptoms because a healthy person's immune system keeps the parasite from causing illness. When the immune system is compromised, symptoms may occur. Clinical symptoms include flu-like symptoms, but the disease progresses to include the eyes and the brain in babies.

B57.1   **Acute Chagas' disease without heart involvement** 🦠
     Acute Chagas' disease NOS

B57.2   **Chagas' disease (chronic) with heart involvement** 🦠
     American trypanosomiasis NOS
     Chagas' disease (chronic) NOS
     Chagas' disease (chronic) with myocarditis
     Trypanosomiasis NOS

● B57.3   **Chagas' disease (chronic) with digestive system involvement**
     ▨ B57.30   **Chagas' disease with digestive system involvement, unspecified** 🦠
     B57.31   **Megaesophagus in Chagas' disease** 🦠
     B57.32   **Megacolon in Chagas' disease** 🦠
     B57.39   **Other digestive system involvement in Chagas' disease** 🦠

● B57.4   **Chagas' disease (chronic) with nervous system involvement**
     ▨ B57.40   **Chagas' disease with nervous system involvement, unspecified** 🦠
     B57.41   **Meningitis in Chagas' disease** 🦠
     B57.42   **Meningoencephalitis in Chagas' disease** 🦠
     B57.49   **Other nervous system involvement in Chagas' disease** 🦠

B57.5   **Chagas' disease (chronic) with other organ involvement** 🦠

● B58   **Toxoplasmosis**
     Infection by protozoon transmitted in cysts in feces of cats
     Includes   infection due to Toxoplasma gondii
     Excludes1   congenital toxoplasmosis (P37.1)

   ● B58.0   **Toxoplasma oculopathy**
     ▨ B58.00   **Toxoplasma oculopathy, unspecified** 🦠
     B58.01   **Toxoplasma chorioretinitis** 🦠
     B58.09   **Other toxoplasma oculopathy** 🦠
         Toxoplasma uveitis

   B58.1   **Toxoplasma hepatitis** 🦠
   B58.2   **Toxoplasma meningoencephalitis** 🦠
   B58.3   **Pulmonary toxoplasmosis** 🦠

   ● B58.8   **Toxoplasmosis with other organ involvement**
     B58.81   **Toxoplasma myocarditis** 🦠
     B58.82   **Toxoplasma myositis** 🦠
     B58.83   **Toxoplasma tubulo-interstitial nephropathy** 🦠
         Toxoplasma pyelonephritis
     B58.89   **Toxoplasmosis with other organ involvement** 🦠

   ▨ B58.9   **Toxoplasmosis, unspecified** 🦠

B59   **Pneumocystosis** 🦠
     Caused by fungus
     Pneumonia due to Pneumocystis carinii
     Pneumonia due to Pneumocystis jiroveci

● B60   **Other protozoal diseases, not elsewhere classified**
     Excludes1   cryptosporidiosis (A07.2)
         intestinal microsporidiosis (A07.8)
         isosporiasis (A07.3)

   B60.0   **Babesiosis** 🦠
     Tickborne disease caused by microscopic organisms
     Piroplasmosis

   ● B60.1   **Acanthamebiasis**
     ▨ B60.10   **Acanthamebiasis, unspecified** 🦠
     B60.11   **Meningoencephalitis due to Acanthamoeba (culbertsoni)**
     B60.12   **Conjunctivitis due to Acanthamoeba**
     B60.13   **Keratoconjunctivitis due to Acanthamoeba**
     B60.19   **Other acanthamebic disease** 🦠

   B60.2   **Naegleriasis** 🦠
     Infection with microscopic organisms
     Primary amebic meningoencephalitis

   B60.8   **Other specified protozoal diseases**
     Microsporidiosis

▨ B64   **Unspecified protozoal disease**

HELMINTHIASES (B65-B83)

Diseases or infestations caused by parasitic worms

● B65   **Schistosomiasis [bilharziasis]**
     Infection with flukes (flat parasitic worms)
     Includes   snail fever

   B65.0   **Schistosomiasis due to Schistosoma haematobium [urinary schistosomiasis]** 🦠

   B65.1   **Schistosomiasis due to Schistosoma mansoni [intestinal schistosomiasis]** 🦠

   B65.2   **Schistosomiasis due to Schistosoma japonicum** 🦠
     Asiatic schistosomiasis

   B65.3   **Cercarial dermatitis** 🦠
     Swimmer's itch

   B65.8   **Other schistosomiasis** 🦠
     Infection due to Schistosoma intercalatum
     Infection due to Schistosoma mattheei
     Infection due to Schistosoma mekongi

   ▨ B65.9   **Schistosomiasis, unspecified**

● B66   **Other fluke infections**
     Trematode (parasitic worms)

   B66.0   **Opisthorchiasis** 🦠
     Infection due to cat liver fluke
     Infection due to Opisthorchis (felineus)(viverrini)

   B66.1   **Clonorchiasis** 🦠
     Chinese liver fluke disease
     Infection due to Clonorchis sinensis
     Oriental liver fluke disease

   B66.2   **Dicroceliasis** 🦠
     Liver fluke
     Infection due to Dicrocoelium dendriticum
     Lancet fluke infection

   B66.3   **Fascioliasis** 🦠
     Infection due to Fasciola gigantica
     Infection due to Fasciola hepatica
     Infection due to Fasciola indica
     Sheep liver fluke disease

   B66.4   **Paragonimiasis** 🦠
     Infection due to Paragonimus species
     Lung fluke disease
     Pulmonary distomiasis

   B66.5   **Fasciolopsiasis** 🦠
     Largest intestinal fluke in humans
     Infection due to Fasciolopsis buski
     Intestinal distomiasis

● Unacceptable First-Listed Diagnosis   ● Use Additional Character(s)   ▨ Unspecified   **OGCR** Official Guidelines for Coding and Reporting
🦠 Complication\Comorbidity   🦠 Major C\C   Excludes 1   Excludes 2   Includes   Use additional   Code first   Code also

Item 1-23 Echinococcosis: Also known as hydatid disease; is caused by Echinococcus granulosus, E. multilocularis, and E. vogeli tapeworms; and is contracted from infected food. Found in southern South America, the Mediterranean, the Middle East, central Asia, and Africa and uncommon in the United States but has been reported in California, New Mexico, Arizona and Utah. The disease is treated with medication over a long course as it is resistive.

B66.8   **Other specified fluke infections** 🐛
     Echinostomiasis
     Heterophyiasis
     Metagonimiasis
     Nanophyetiasis
     Watsoniasis

▨ B66.9   **Fluke infection, unspecified**

● **B67   Echinococcosis**
   Larval forms of tapeworms usually of liver or lungs
   Includes   hydatidosis

B67.0   **Echinococcus granulosus infection of liver** 🐛

B67.1   **Echinococcus granulosus infection of lung** 🐛

B67.2   **Echinococcus granulosus infection of bone** 🐛

● B67.3   **Echinococcus granulosus infection, other and multiple sites**

     B67.31   **Echinococcus granulosus infection, thyroid gland** 🐛

     B67.32   **Echinococcus granulosus infection, multiple sites** 🐛

     B67.39   **Echinococcus granulosus infection, other sites** 🐛

▨ B67.4   **Echinococcus granulosus infection, unspecified** 🐛
     Dog tapeworm (infection)

B67.5   **Echinococcus multilocularis infection of liver** 🐛

● B67.6   **Echinococcus multilocularis infection, other and multiple sites**

     B67.61   **Echinococcus multilocularis infection, multiple sites** 🐛

     B67.69   **Echinococcus multilocularis infection, other sites** 🐛

▨ B67.7   **Echinococcus multilocularis infection, unspecified** 🐛

▨ B67.8   **Echinococcosis, unspecified, of liver** 🐛

● B67.9   **Echinococcosis, other and unspecified**

     ▨ B67.90   **Echinococcosis, unspecified** 🐛
         Echinococcosis NOS

     B67.99   **Other echinococcosis** 🐛

● **B68   Taeniasis**
   Intestinal tapeworm (cestode) infection from raw or under-cooked meat of infected animal
   Excludes1   cysticercosis (B69.-)

B68.0   **Taenia solium taeniasis** 🐛
     Pork tapeworm (infection)

B68.1   **Taenia saginata taeniasis** 🐛
     Beef tapeworm (infection)
     Infection due to adult tapeworm Taenia saginata

▨ B68.9   **Taeniasis, unspecified** 🐛

● **B69   Cysticercosis**
   Systemic illness caused by the larvae of pork tapeworm
   Includes   cysticerciasis infection due to larval form of Taenia solium

B69.0   **Cysticercosis of central nervous system** 🐛

B69.1   **Cysticercosis of eye** 🐛

● B69.8   **Cysticercosis of other sites**

     B69.81   **Myositis in cysticercosis** 🐛

     B69.89   **Cysticercosis of other sites** 🐛

▨ B69.9   **Cysticercosis, unspecified** 🐛

● **B70   Diphyllobothriasis and sparganosis**
   Infection with tapeworms seen most often from inadequately cooked fish

B70.0   **Diphyllobothriasis** 🐛
     Diphyllobothrium (adult) (latum) (pacificum) infection
     Fish tapeworm (infection)
     Excludes2   larval diphyllobothriasis (B70.1)

B70.1   **Sparganosis** 🐛
   Infection with migrating tapeworm larvae, which invade subcutaneous tissues, causing inflammation and fibrosis that resembles cellulitis
     Infection due to Sparganum (mansoni) (proliferum)
     Infection due to Spirometra larva
     Larval diphyllobothriasis
     Spirometrosis

● **B71   Other cestode infections**

B71.0   **Hymenolepiasis** 🐛
   Intestinal infestation with tapeworms
     Dwarf tapeworm infection
     Rat tapeworm (infection)

B71.1   **Dipylidiasis** 🐛
   Infection with tapeworm common to dogs and cats and seen in children having close contact with infected pets

B71.8   **Other specified cestode infections** 🐛
   Infection by the larval stage of a tapeworm, usually through fruit or vegetables
     Coenurosis

▨ B71.9   **Cestode infection, unspecified**
     Tapeworm (infection) NOS

B72   Dracunculiasis 🐛
   Infection with roundworms
   Includes   guinea worm infection
             infection due to Dracunculus medinensis

● **B73   Onchocerciasis**
   Infection with parasitic worm
   Includes   onchocerca volvulus infection
             onchocercosis
             river blindness

● B73.0   **Onchocerciasis with eye disease**

     ▨ B73.00   **Onchocerciasis with eye involvement, unspecified** 🐛

     B73.01   **Onchocerciasis with endophthalmitis** 🐛

     B73.02   **Onchocerciasis with glaucoma** 🐛

     B73.09   **Onchocerciasis with other eye involvement** 🐛
         Infestation of eyelid due to onchocerciasis

B73.1   **Onchocerciasis without eye disease** 🐛

● **B74   Filariasis**
   Infestation with slender threadlike worms
   Excludes2   onchocerciasis (B73)
             tropical (pulmonary) eosinophilia NOS (J82)

B74.0   **Filariasis due to Wuchereria bancrofti** 🐛
     Bancroftian elephantiasis
     Bancroftian filariasis

● Unacceptable First-Listed Diagnosis   ● Use Additional Character(s)   ▨ Unspecified   **OGCR** Official Guidelines for Coding and Reporting
🐛 Complication\Comorbidity   🐛 Major C\C   Excludes 1   Excludes 2   Includes   Use additional   Code first   Code also

B74.1 **Filariasis due to Brugia malayi** 🦠

B74.2 **Filariasis due to Brugia timori** 🦠

B74.3 **Loiasis** 🦠
  Infection with round worms growing in subcutaneous connective tissue
  Calabar swelling
  Eyeworm disease of Africa
  Loa loa infection

B74.4 **Mansonelliasis** 🦠
  Infection with filarial parasite
  Infection due to Mansonella ozzardi
  Infection due to Mansonella perstans
  Infection due to Mansonella streptocerca

B74.8 **Other filariases** 🦠
  Dirofilariasis

🔲 B74.9 **Filariasis, unspecified** 🦠

● B75 **Trichinellosis** 🦠
  Infestation with parasitic roundworms ingested in undercooked contaminated meat
  Includes infection due to Trichinella species
  trichiniasis

● B76 **Hookworm diseases**
  Occurs in hot, humid parts of world where larvae are soil borne, enter digestive tract through skin of feet/legs or in contaminated food/water; AKA ground itch
  Includes uncinariasis

B76.0 **Ancylostomiasis** 🦠
  Infection due to Ancylostoma species

B76.1 **Necatoriasis** 🦠
  Infection due to Necator americanus

B76.8 **Other hookworm diseases**

🔲 B76.9 **Hookworm disease, unspecified** 🦠
  Cutaneous larva migrans NOS

● B77 **Ascariasis**
  Infection by roundworm in small intestine
  Includes ascaridiasis
  roundworm infection

B77.0 **Ascariasis with intestinal complications** 🦠

● B77.8 **Ascariasis with other complications**

  B77.81 **Ascariasis pneumonia** 🦠

  B77.89 **Ascariasis with other complications** 🦠

🔲 B77.9 **Ascariasis, unspecified** 🦠

● B78 **Strongyloidiasis**
  Infection with adult female roundworms
  Excludes1 trichostrongyliasis (B81.2)

B78.0 **Intestinal strongyloidiasis** 🦠

B78.1 **Cutaneous strongyloidiasis**

B78.7 **Disseminated strongyloidiasis** 🦠

🔲 B78.9 **Strongyloidiasis, unspecified** 🦠

B79 **Trichuriasis** 🦠
  Intestinal infection with roundworms
  Includes trichocephaliasis
  whipworm (disease)(infection)

B80 **Enterobiasis** 🦠
  Intestinal infection with pinworms
  Includes oxyuriasis
  pinworm infection
  threadworm infection

● B81 **Other intestinal helminthiases, not elsewhere classified**
  Diseases or infestations caused by parasitic worms
  Excludes1 angiostrongyliasis due to Parastrongylus cantonensis (B83.2)

B81.0 **Anisakiasis** 🦠
  Roundworm infection via contaminated undercooked infected fish or marine mammals
  Infection due to Anisakis larva

B81.1 **Intestinal capillariasis** 🦠
  Infestation with of parasites (nematodes)
  Capillariasis NOS
  Infection due to Capillaria philippinensis
  Excludes2 hepatic capillariasis (B83.8)

B81.2 **Trichostrongyliasis** 🦠

B81.3 **Intestinal angiostrongyliasis** 🦠
  Angiostrongyliasis due to Parastrongylus costaricensis

B81.4 **Mixed intestinal helminthiases** 🦠
  Infection due to intestinal helminths classified to more than one of the categories B65.0-B81.3 and B81.8
  Mixed helminthiasis NOS

B81.8 **Other specified intestinal helminthiases** 🦠
  Infection due to Oesophagostomum species [esophagostomiasis]
  Infection due to Ternidens diminutus [ternidensiasis]

● B82 **Unspecified intestinal parasitism**

🔲 B82.0 **Intestinal helminthiasis, unspecified** 🦠
  Infected with worms

🔲 B82.9 **Intestinal parasitism, unspecified**

● B83 **Other helminthiases**
  Caused by parasitic worms
  Excludes1 capillariasis NOS (B81.1)
  Excludes2 intestinal capillariasis (B81.1)

B83.0 **Visceral larva migrans**
  Prolonged migration of nematode larvae
  Toxocariasis

B83.1 **Gnathostomiasis**
  Infection with nematode occurring from ingested undercooked fish contaminated with larvae; larvae migrate to subcutaneous tissue or deeper tissues, results are abscesses
  Wandering swelling

B83.2 **Angiostrongyliasis due to Parastrongylus cantonensis**
  Nematode infection caused by eating contaminated raw snails, slugs, or paratenic hosts such as prawns or crabs; larval worms migrate to central nervous system resulting in eosinophilic meningitis
  Eosinophilic meningoencephalitis due to Parastrongylus cantonensis
  Excludes2 intestinal angiostrongyliasis (B81.3)

B83.3 **Syngamiasis**
  Infestation with gapeworm from turkey, pheasant, guinea fowl, goose, and wild birds
  Syngamosis

B83.4 **Internal hirudiniasis**
  Infestation by leeches
  Excludes2 external hirudiniasis (B88.3)

B83.8   Other specified helminthiases
Parasitic worm infestation
Acanthocephaliasis
Gongylonemiasis
Hepatic capillariasis
Metastrongyliasis
Thelaziasis

■**B83.9   Helminthiasis, unspecified**
Worms NOS

> | Excludes1 | intestinal helminthiasis NOS (B82.0)

PEDICULOSIS, ACARIASIS AND OTHER INFESTATIONS (B85-B89)

Infestation of lice

● **B85   Pediculosis and phthiriasis**

B85.0   Pediculosis due to Pediculus humanus capitis
Head-louse infestation

B85.1   Pediculosis due to Pediculus humanus corporis
Body-louse infestation

■**B85.2   Pediculosis, unspecified**

B85.3   Phthiriasis
Crab or pubic lice

Infestation by crab-louse
Infestation by Phthirus pubis

B85.4   Mixed pediculosis and phthiriasis
Infestation classifiable to more than one of the categories B85.0-B85.3

B86   Scabies
Contagious dermatitis caused by mites

> | Includes | sarcoptic itch

● **B87   Myiasis**
Infestation by fly maggots

> | Includes | infestation by larva of flies

B87.0   Cutaneous myiasis
Creeping myiasis

B87.1   Wound myiasis
Traumatic myiasis

B87.2   Ocular myiasis

B87.3   Nasopharyngeal myiasis
Laryngeal myiasis

B87.4   Aural myiasis

● **B87.8   Myiasis of other sites**

B87.81   Genitourinary myiasis

B87.82   Intestinal myiasis

B87.89   Myiasis of other sites

■**B87.9   Myiasis, unspecified**

● **B88   Other infestations**

B88.0   Other acariasis
Acarine dermatitis
Dermatitis due to Demodex species
Dermatitis due to Dermanyssus gallinae
Dermatitis due to Liponyssoides sanguineus
Trombiculosis

> | Excludes2 | scabies (B86)

B88.1   Tungiasis [sandflea infestation]
Inflammatory skin disease caused by infestation of fleas

B88.2   Other arthropod infestations
Scarabiasis

B88.3   External hirudiniasis
Leech infestation NOS

> | Excludes2 | internal hirudiniasis (B83.4)

B88.8   Other specified infestations
Infection of topical fresh water fish parasite
Ichthyoparasitism due to Vandellia cirrhosa
Linguatulosis
Porocephaliasis

■**B88.9   Infestation, unspecified**
Infestation (skin) NOS
Infestation by mites NOS
Skin parasites NOS

■**B89   Unspecified parasitic disease**

SEQUELAE OF INFECTIOUS AND PARASITIC DISEASES (B90-B94)

Note: Categories B90-B94 are to be used to indicate conditions in categories A00-B89 as the cause of sequelae, which are themselves classified elsewhere. The "sequelae" include conditions specified as such; they also include residuals of diseases classifiable to the above categories if there is evidence that the disease itself is no longer present. Codes from these categories are not to be used for chronic infections. Code chronic current infections to active infectious disease as appropriate.

Code first condition resulting from (sequela) the infectious or parasitic disease

● **B90   Sequelae of tuberculosis**
Condition resulting from tuberculosis

B90.0   Sequelae of central nervous system tuberculosis

B90.1   Sequelae of genitourinary tuberculosis

B90.2   Sequelae of tuberculosis of bones and joints

B90.8   Sequelae of tuberculosis of other organs

> | Excludes2 | sequelae of respiratory tuberculosis (B90.9)

B90.9   Sequelae of respiratory and unspecified tuberculosis
Sequelae of tuberculosis NOS

B91   Sequelae of poliomyelitis

> | Excludes1 | postpolio syndrome (G14)

B92   Sequelae of leprosy

● **B94   Sequelae of other and unspecified infectious and parasitic diseases**

B94.0   Sequelae of trachoma

B94.1   Sequelae of viral encephalitis

B94.2   Sequelae of viral hepatitis

B94.8   Sequelae of other specified infectious and parasitic diseases

■**B94.9   Sequelae of unspecified infectious and parasitic disease**

OGCR   Section I.C.1.b

Certain infectious and parasitic diseases

Infectious agents as the cause of diseases classified to other chapters

Certain infections are classified in chapters other than Chapter 1 and no organism is identified as part of the infection code. In these instances, it is necessary to use an additional code from Chapter 1 to identify the organism. A code from category B95, Streptococcus, Staphylococcus, and Enterococcus as the cause of diseases classified to other chapters, B96, Other bacterial agents as the cause of diseases classified to other chapters, or B97, Viral agents as the cause of diseases classified to other chapters, is to be used as an additional code to identify the organism. An instructional not will be found at the infection code advising that an additional organism code is required.

● Unacceptable First-Listed Diagnosis   ● Use Additional Character(s)   ■ Unspecified   **OGCR** Official Guidelines for Coding and Reporting

🅒 Complication\Comorbidity   🅜 Major C\C | Excludes 1 | | Excludes 2 | Includes   Use additional   Code first   Code also

817

BACTERIAL AND VIRAL INFECTIOUS AGENTS (B95-B97)

Note: These categories are provided for use as supplementary or additional codes to identify the infectious agent(s) in diseases classified elsewhere.

Code the disease first, then the bacterium.

● B95   **Streptococcus, Staphylococcus, and Enterococcus as the cause of diseases classified elsewhere**

    ● B95.0   Streptococcus, group A, as the cause of diseases classified elsewhere

    ● B95.1   Streptococcus, group B, as the cause of diseases classified elsewhere

    ● B95.2   Enterococcus as the cause of diseases classified elsewhere

    ● B95.3   Streptococcus pneumoniae as the cause of diseases classified elsewhere

    ● B95.4   Other streptococcus as the cause of diseases classified elsewhere

    ● ■ B95.5   Unspecified streptococcus as the cause of diseases classified elsewhere

    ● B95.6   Staphylococcus aureus as the cause of diseases classified elsewhere

    ● B95.7   Other staphylococcus as the cause of diseases classified elsewhere

    ● ■ B95.8   Unspecified staphylococcus as the cause of diseases classified elsewhere

● B96   **Other bacterial agents as the cause of diseases classified elsewhere**

    ● B96.0   Mycoplasma pneumoniae [M. pneumoniae] as the cause of diseases classified elsewhere
                Pleuro-pneumonia-like-organism [PPLO]

    ● B96.1   Klebsiella pneumoniae [K. pneumoniae] as the cause of diseases classified elsewhere

    ● B96.2   Escherichia coli [E. coli] as the cause of diseases classified elsewhere

    ● B96.3   Hemophilus influenzae [H. influenzae] as the cause of diseases classified elsewhere

    ● B96.4   Proteus (mirabilis) (morganii) as the cause of diseases classified elsewhere

    ● B96.5   Pseudomonas (aeruginosa) (mallei) (pseudomallei) as the cause of diseases classified elsewhere

    ● B96.6   Bacteroides fragilis [B. fragilis] as the cause of diseases classified elsewhere

    ● B96.7   Clostridium perfringens [C. perfringens] as the cause of diseases classified elsewhere

    ● B96.8   Other specified bacterial agents as the cause of diseases classified elsewhere

       ● B96.81   Helicobacter pylori [H. pylori] as the cause of diseases classified elsewhere

       ● B96.82   Vibrio vulnificus as the cause of diseases classified elsewhere

       ● B96.89   Other specified bacterial agents as the cause of diseases classified elsewhere

● B97   **Viral agents as the cause of diseases classified elsewhere**

    ● B97.0   Adenovirus as the cause of diseases classified elsewhere

    ● B97.1   Enterovirus as the cause of diseases classified elsewhere

       ● ■ B97.10   Unspecified enterovirus as the cause of diseases classified elsewhere

       ● B97.11   Coxsackievirus as the cause of diseases classified elsewhere

Item 1–24   Retrovirus develops by copying its RNA, genetic materials, into the DNA, which then produces new virus particles. It is from the Retroviridae virus family. **Human T-cell lymphotropic virus, Type I (HTLV-I)** is also called human T-cell leukemia virus, Type I, and is a retrovirus thought to cause T-cell leukemia/lymphoma. **Human T-cell lymphotropic virus, Type II (HTLV-II),** is also called human T-cell leukemia virus, Type II, and is a retrovirus associated with hematologic disorders.

    HIV-2 is one of the serotypes of HIV and is usually confined to West Africa, whereas HIV-1 is found worldwide.

       ● B97.12   Echovirus as the cause of diseases classified elsewhere

       ● B97.19   Other enterovirus as the cause of diseases classified elsewhere

    ● B97.2   Coronavirus as the cause of diseases classified elsewhere

       ● B97.21   SARS-associated coronavirus as the cause of diseases classified elsewhere 🏥

          | **Excludes1** | pneumonia due to SARS-associated coronavirus (J12.3) |

       ● B97.29   Other coronavirus as the cause of diseases classified elsewhere

    ● B97.3   Retrovirus as the cause of diseases classified elsewhere

          | **Excludes1** | human immunodeficiency virus [HIV} disease (B20) |

       ● ■ B97.30   Unspecified retrovirus as the cause of diseases classified elsewhere

       ● B97.31   Lentivirus as the cause of diseases classified elsewhere

       ● B97.32   Oncovirus as the cause of diseases classified elsewhere

       ● B97.33   Human T-cell lymphotrophic virus, type I [HTLV-I] as the cause of diseases classified elsewhere 🏥

       ● B97.34   Human T-cell lymphotrophic virus, type II [HTLV-II] as the cause of diseases classified elsewhere 🏥

       ● B97.35   Human immunodeficiency virus, type 2 [HIV 2] as the cause of diseases classified elsewhere 🏥

       ● B97.39   Other retrovirus as the cause of diseases classified elsewhere

    ● B97.4   Respiratory syncytial virus as the cause of diseases classified elsewhere

    ● B97.5   Reovirus as the cause of diseases classified elsewhere

    ● B97.6   Parvovirus as the cause of diseases classified elsewhere

    ● B97.7   Papillomavirus as the cause of diseases classified elsewhere

    ● B97.8   Other viral agents as the cause of diseases classified elsewhere

       ● B97.81   Human metapneumovirus as the cause of diseases classified elsewhere

       ● B97.89   Other viral agents as the cause of diseases classified elsewhere

OTHER INFECTIOUS DISEASES (B99)

● B99   Other and unspecified infectious diseases

    B99.8   Other infectious disease

    ■ B99.9   Unspecified infectious disease

| ● Unacceptable First-Listed Diagnosis | ● Use Additional Character(s) | ■ Unspecified | **OGCR** Official Guidelines for Coding and Reporting |
| 🏥 Complication\Comorbidity | 🏥 Major C\C | Excludes 1 | Excludes 2 | Includes | Use additional | Code first | Code also |

818

Item 2–1 Neoplasm: Neo = new, plasm = growth, development, formation. This new growth (mass, tumor) can be malignant or benign, which is confirmed by the pathology report. Do not assign a code to a neoplasm until you review the pathology report. Certain CPT codes will specify benign or malignant lesion, so be certain the diagnosis code supports the procedure code.

OGCR Section I.C.2

General Guidelines

Chapter 2 of the ICD-10-CM contains the codes for the most benign and all malignant neoplasms. Certain benign neoplasms, such as prostatic adenomas, may be found in the specific body system chapters. To properly code a neoplasm, it is necessary to determine from the record if the neoplasm is benign, in-situ, malignant, or, of uncertain histologic behavior. If malignant, any secondary (metastatic) sites should also be determined.

CHAPTER 2

NEOPLASMS (C00-D49)

This chapter contains the following broad groups of neoplasms:

C00-C75	Malignant neoplasms, stated or presumed to be primary (of specified sites), and certain specified histologies, except neuroendocrine, and of lymphoid, hematopoietic and related tissue
C00-C14	Malignant neoplasms of lip, oral cavity and pharynx
C15-C26	Malignant neoplasms of digestive organs
C30-C39	Malignant neoplasms of respiratory and intrathoracic organs
C40-C41	Malignant neoplasms of bone and articular cartilage
C43-C44	Malignant neoplasms of skin
C45-C49	Malignant neoplasms of mesothelial and soft tissue
C50	Malignant neoplasms of breast
C51-C58	Malignant neoplasms of female genital organs
C60-C63	Malignant neoplasms of male genital organs
C64-C68	Malignant neoplasms of urinary tract
C69-C72	Malignant neoplasms of eye, brain and other parts of central nervous system
C73-C75	Malignant neoplasms of thyroid and other endocrine glands
C7a	Malignant neuroendocrine tumors
C7b	Secondary neuroendocrine tumors
C76-C80	Malignant neoplasms of ill-defined, other secondary and unspecified sites
C81-C96	Malignant neoplasms of lymphoid, hematopoietic and related tissue
D00-D09	In situ neoplasms
D10-D36	Benign neoplasms, except benign neuroendocrine tumors
D3a	Benign neuroendocrine tumors
D37-D48	Neoplasms of uncertain behavior
D49	Neoplasms of unspecified behavior

Notes: Functional activity

All neoplasms are classified in this chapter, whether they are functionally active or not. An additional code from Chapter 4 may be used, to identify functional activity associated with any neoplasm.

Morphology [Histology]

Chapter 2 classifies neoplasms primarily by site (topography), with broad groupings for behavior, malignant, in situ, benign, etc. The Table of Neoplasms should be used to identify the correct topography code. In a few cases, such as for malignant melanoma and certain neuroendocrine tumors, the morphology (histologic type) is included in the category and codes. To identify the morphology for the majority of Chapter 2 codes that do not include the histologic type, comprehensive separate morphology codes are provided. These morphology codes are derived from the International Classification of Diseases for Oncology (ICD-O).

Primary malignant neoplasms overlapping site boundaries

A primary malignant neoplasm that overlaps two or more contiguous (next to each other) sites should be classified to the subcategory/code .8 ("overlapping lesion"), unless the combination is specifically indexed elsewhere. For multiple neoplasms of the same site that are not contiguous, such as tumors in different quadrants of the same breast, codes for each site should be assigned.

Malignant neoplasm of ectopic tissue

Malignant neoplasms of ectopic tissue are to be coded to the site mentioned, e.g., ectopic pancreatic malignant neoplasms are coded to pancreas, unspecified (C25.9).

MALIGNANT NEOPLASMS (C00-C96)

Use additional morphology codes with behavior code /3

MALIGNANT NEOPLASMS, STATED OR PRESUMED TO BE PRIMARY (OF SPECIFIED SITES), AND CERTAIN SPECIFIED HISTOLOGIES, EXCEPT NEUROENDOCRINE, AND OF LYMPHOID, HEMATOPOIETIC AND RELATED TISSUE (C00-C75)

MALIGNANT NEOPLASM OF LIP, ORAL CAVITY AND PHARYNX (C00-C14)

● **C00 Malignant neoplasm of lip**

　　Excludes1　malignant neoplasm of skin of lip (C43.0, C44.0)
　　　　　　　Merkel cell carcinoma of lip (C4a.0)

　　Use additional code to identify:
　　　alcohol abuse and dependence (F10.-)
　　　history of tobacco use (Z87.891)
　　　tobacco dependence (F17.-)
　　　tobacco use (Z72.0)

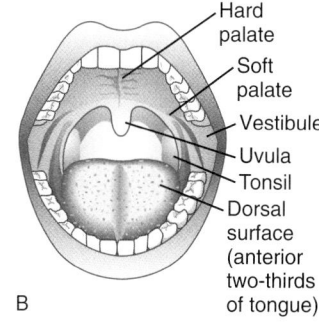

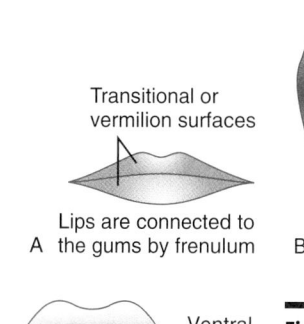

Transitional or vermilion surfaces

Lips are connected to
A the gums by frenulum

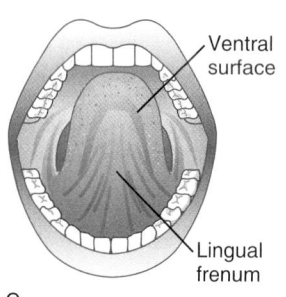

Ventral surface

Lingual frenum

C

Figure 2-1 Anatomical structures of the mouth and lips. **A.** Transitional or vermilion borders. Lips are connected to the gums by frenulum. **B.** Dorsal surface. **C.** Ventral surface.

● Unacceptable First-Listed Diagnosis　　● Use Additional Character(s)　　■ Unspecified　　**OGCR** Official Guidelines for Coding and Reporting

🩺 Complication\Comorbidity　　🩺 Major C\C　　Excludes 1　　Excludes 2　　Includes　　Use additional　　Code first　　Code also

CHAPTER 2 (C00-D49)

819

C00.0 Malignant neoplasm of external upper lip
Malignant neoplasm of lipstick area of upper lip
Malignant neoplasm of upper lip NOS
Malignant neoplasm of vermilion border of upper lip

C00.1 Malignant neoplasm of external lower lip
Malignant neoplasm of lower lip NOS
Malignant neoplasm of lipstick area of lower lip
Malignant neoplasm of vermilion border of lower lip

C00.2 Malignant neoplasm of external lip, unspecified
Malignant neoplasm of vermilion border of lip NOS

C00.3 Malignant neoplasm of upper lip, inner aspect
Malignant neoplasm of buccal aspect of upper lip
Malignant neoplasm of frenulum of upper lip
Malignant neoplasm of mucosa of upper lip
Malignant neoplasm of oral aspect of upper lip

C00.4 Malignant neoplasm of lower lip, inner aspect
Malignant neoplasm of buccal aspect of lower lip
Malignant neoplasm of frenulum of lower lip
Malignant neoplasm of mucosa of lower lip
Malignant neoplasm of oral aspect of lower lip

C00.5 Malignant neoplasm of lip, unspecified, inner aspect
Malignant neoplasm of buccal aspect of lip, unspecified
Malignant neoplasm of frenulum of lip, unspecified
Malignant neoplasm of mucosa of lip, unspecified
Malignant neoplasm of oral aspect of lip, unspecified

C00.6 Malignant neoplasm of commissure of lip, unspecified
Commissure: Site of union of corresponding parts

C00.8 Malignant neoplasm of overlapping sites of lip

C00.9 Malignant neoplasm of lip, unspecified

C01 Malignant neoplasm of base of tongue
> **Includes**   malignant neoplasm of dorsal surface of base of tongue
> malignant neoplasm of fixed part of tongue NOS
> malignant neoplasm of posterior third of tongue

Use additional code to identify:
alcohol abuse and dependence (F10.-)
history of tobacco use (Z87.891)
tobacco dependence (F17.-)
tobacco use (Z72.0)

C02 Malignant neoplasm of other and unspecified parts of tongue
Use additional code to identify:
alcohol abuse and dependence (F10.-)
history of tobacco use (Z87.891)
tobacco dependence (F17.-)
tobacco use (Z72.0)

C02.0 Malignant neoplasm of dorsal surface of tongue
Malignant neoplasm of anterior two-thirds of tongue, dorsal surface
> **Excludes2**   malignant neoplasm of dorsal surface of base of tongue (C01)

C02.1 Malignant neoplasm of border of tongue
Malignant neoplasm of tip of tongue

C02.2 Malignant neoplasm of ventral surface of tongue
Malignant neoplasm of anterior two-thirds of tongue, ventral surface
Malignant neoplasm of frenulum linguae

C02.3 Malignant neoplasm of anterior two-thirds of tongue, part unspecified
Malignant neoplasm of middle third of tongue NOS
Malignant neoplasm of mobile part of tongue NOS

C02.4 Malignant neoplasm of lingual tonsil
Lingual tonsil: Aggregation of lymph follicles at root of tongue
> **Excludes2**   malignant neoplasm of tonsil NOS (C09.9)

C02.8 Malignant neoplasm of overlapping sites of tongue
Malignant neoplasm of two or more contiguous sites of tongue

C02.9 Malignant neoplasm of tongue, unspecified

C03 Malignant neoplasm of gum
> **Includes**   malignant neoplasm of alveolar (ridge) mucosa
> malignant neoplasm of gingival
> **Excludes2**   malignant odontogenic neoplasms (C41.0-C41.1)

Use additional code to identify:
alcohol abuse and dependence (F10.-)
history of tobacco use (Z87.891)
tobacco dependence (F17.-)
tobacco use (Z72.0)

C03.0 Malignant neoplasm of upper gum

C03.1 Malignant neoplasm of lower gum

C03.9 Malignant neoplasm of gum, unspecified

C04 Malignant neoplasm of floor of mouth
Use additional code to identify:
alcohol abuse and dependence (F10.-)
history of tobacco use (Z87.891)
tobacco dependence (F17.-)
tobacco use (Z72.0)

C04.0 Malignant neoplasm of anterior floor of mouth
Malignant neoplasm of anterior to the premolar-canine junction

C04.1 Malignant neoplasm of lateral floor of mouth

C04.8 Malignant neoplasm of overlapping sites of floor of mouth

C04.9 Malignant neoplasm of floor of mouth, unspecified

C05 Malignant neoplasm of palate
> **Excludes1**   Kaposi's sarcoma of palate (C46.2)

Use additional code to identify:
alcohol abuse and dependence (F10.-)
history of tobacco use (Z87.891)
tobacco dependence (F17.-)
tobacco use (Z72.0)

C05.0 Malignant neoplasm of hard palate

C05.1 Malignant neoplasm of soft palate
> **Excludes2**   malignant neoplasm of nasopharyngeal surface of soft palate (C11.3)

C05.2 Malignant neoplasm of uvula

C05.8 Malignant neoplasm of overlapping sites of palate

C05.9 Malignant neoplasm of palate, unspecified
Malignant neoplasm of roof of mouth

C06 Malignant neoplasm of other and unspecified parts of mouth
Use additional code to identify:
alcohol abuse and dependence (F10.-)
history of tobacco use (Z87.891)
tobacco dependence (F17.-)
tobacco use (Z72.0)

CHAPTER 2 (C00-D49)

820

● Unacceptable First-Listed Diagnosis   ● Use Additional Character(s)   ▣ Unspecified   **OGCR** Official Guidelines for Coding and Reporting
 Complication\Comorbidity    Major C\C   Excludes 1   Excludes 2   Includes   Use additional   Code first   Code also

C06.0   **Malignant neoplasm of cheek mucosa**
    Malignant neoplasm of buccal mucosa NOS
    Malignant neoplasm of internal cheek

C06.1   **Malignant neoplasm of vestibule of mouth**
    Malignant neoplasm of buccal sulcus (upper)
      (lower)
    Malignant neoplasm of labial sulcus (upper) (lower)

C06.2   **Malignant neoplasm of retromolar area**

● C06.8   **Malignant neoplasm of overlapping sites of other and unspecified parts of mouth**

    ▨ C06.80   **Malignant neoplasm of overlapping sites of unspecified parts of mouth**

    C06.89   **Malignant neoplasm of overlapping sites of other parts of mouth "book leaf" neoplasm [ventral surface of tongue and floor of mouth]**

▨ C06.9   **Malignant neoplasm of mouth, unspecified**
    Malignant neoplasm of minor salivary gland, unspecified side
    Malignant neoplasm of oral cavity NOS

C07   **Malignant neoplasm of parotid gland**
    Use additional code to identify:
    alcohol abuse and dependence (F10.-)
    exposure to environmental tobacco smoke (Z77.22)
    exposure to tobacco smoke in the perinatal period (P96.81)
    history of tobacco use (Z87.891)
    occupational exposure to environmental tobacco smoke (Z57.31)
    tobacco dependence (F17.-)
    tobacco use (Z72.0)

● C08   **Malignant neoplasm of other and unspecified major salivary glands**

    Includes   malignant neoplasm of salivary ducts

    Excludes1   malignant neoplasms of specified minor salivary glands which are classified according to their anatomical location

    Excludes2   malignant neoplasms of minor salivary glands NOS (C06.9)
      malignant neoplasm of parotid gland (C07)

    Use additional code to identify:
    alcohol abuse and dependence (F10.-)
    exposure to environmental tobacco smoke (Z77.22)
    exposure to tobacco smoke in the perinatal period (P96.81)
    history of tobacco use (Z87.891)
    occupational exposure to environmental tobacco smoke (Z57.31)
    tobacco dependence (F17.-)
    tobacco use (Z72.0)

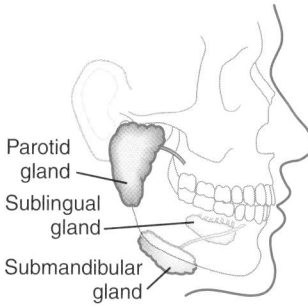

Figure 2-2   Major salivary glands.

C08.0   **Malignant neoplasm of submandibular gland**
    Malignant neoplasm of submaxillary gland

C08.1   **Malignant neoplasm of sublingual gland**

▨ C08.9   **Malignant neoplasm of major salivary gland, unspecified**
    Malignant neoplasm of salivary gland (major) NOS

(See Plate 61 on page NAP-25.)

● C09   **Malignant neoplasm of tonsil**

    Excludes2   malignant neoplasm of lingual tonsil (C02.4)
      malignant neoplasm of pharyngeal tonsil (C11.1)

    Use additional code to identify:
    alcohol abuse and dependence (F10.-)
    exposure to environmental tobacco smoke (Z77.22)
    exposure to tobacco smoke in the perinatal period (P96.81)
    history of tobacco use (Z87.891)
    occupational exposure to environmental tobacco smoke (Z57.31)
    tobacco dependence (F17.-)
    tobacco use (Z72.0)

C09.0   **Malignant neoplasm of tonsillar fossa**
    Surface of palatine (two masses of lymphatic tissue on sides of throat) tonsils

C09.1   **Malignant neoplasm of tonsillar pillar (anterior) (posterior)**
    Extension from palatine (two masses of lymphatic tissue on sides of throat) tonsils

C09.8   **Malignant neoplasm of overlapping sites of tonsil**

▨ C09.9   **Malignant neoplasm of tonsil, unspecified**
    Malignant neoplasm of tonsil NOS
    Malignant neoplasm of faucial tonsils
    Malignant neoplasm of palatine tonsils

● C10   **Malignant neoplasm of oropharynx**
    Area of throat at back of mouth

    Excludes2   malignant neoplasm of tonsil (C09.-)

    Use additional code to identify:
    alcohol abuse and dependence (F10.-)
    exposure to environmental tobacco smoke (Z77.22)
    exposure to tobacco smoke in the perinatal period (P96.81)
    history of tobacco use (Z87.891)
    occupational exposure to environmental tobacco smoke (Z57.31)
    tobacco dependence (F17.-)
    tobacco use (Z72.0)

C10.0   **Malignant neoplasm of vallecula**
    Vallecula, depression or furrow

C10.1   **Malignant neoplasm of anterior surface of epiglottis**
    Malignant neoplasm of epiglottis, free border [margin]
    Malignant neoplasm of glossoepiglottic fold(s)

    Excludes2   malignant neoplasm of epiglottis (suprahyoid portion) NOS (C32.1)

C10.2   **Malignant neoplasm of lateral wall of oropharynx**

C10.3   **Malignant neoplasm of posterior wall of oropharynx**

C10.4   **Malignant neoplasm of branchial cleft**
    Congenital slitlike openings formed between branchial arches pharyngeal groove
    Malignant neoplasm of branchial cyst [site of neoplasm]

● Unacceptable First-Listed Diagnosis   ● Use Additional Character(s)   ▨ Unspecified   **OGCR** Official Guidelines for Coding and Reporting

🗞 Complication\Comorbidity   🗞 Major C\C   Excludes 1   Excludes 2   Includes   Use additional   Code first   Code also

821

CHAPTER 2 (C00-D49)

C10.8 **Malignant neoplasm of overlapping sites of oropharynx**
Malignant neoplasm of junctional region of oropharynx

C10.9 **Malignant neoplasm of oropharynx, unspecified**

● C11 **Malignant neoplasm of nasopharynx**
Use additional code to identify:
exposure to environmental tobacco smoke (Z77.22)
exposure to tobacco smoke in the perinatal period (P96.81)
history of tobacco use (Z87.891)
occupational exposure to environmental tobacco smoke (Z57.31)
tobacco dependence (F17.-)
tobacco use (Z72.0)

C11.0 **Malignant neoplasm of superior wall of nasopharynx**
Part of pharynx that lies above soft palate
Malignant neoplasm of roof of nasopharynx

C11.1 **Malignant neoplasm of posterior wall of nasopharynx**
Malignant neoplasm of adenoid
Malignant neoplasm of pharyngeal tonsil

C11.2 **Malignant neoplasm of lateral wall of nasopharynx**
Malignant neoplasm of fossa of Rosenmüller
Malignant neoplasm of opening of auditory tube
Malignant neoplasm of pharyngeal recess

C11.3 **Malignant neoplasm of anterior wall of nasopharynx**
Malignant neoplasm of floor of nasopharynx
Malignant neoplasm of nasopharyngeal (anterior) (posterior) surface of soft palate
Malignant neoplasm of posterior margin of nasal choana
Malignant neoplasm of posterior margin of nasal septum

C11.8 **Malignant neoplasm of overlapping sites of nasopharynx**

C11.9 **Malignant neoplasm of nasopharynx, unspecified**
Malignant neoplasm of nasopharyngeal wall NOS

C12 **Malignant neoplasm of pyriform sinus**
Includes malignant neoplasm of pyriform fossa
Use additional code to identify:
exposure to environmental tobacco smoke (Z77.22)
exposure to tobacco smoke in the perinatal period (P96.81)
history of tobacco use (Z87.891)
occupational exposure to environmental tobacco smoke (Z57.31)
tobacco dependence (F17.-)
tobacco use (Z72.0)

● C13 **Malignant neoplasm of hypopharynx**
Excludes2 malignant neoplasm of pyriform sinus (C12)
Use additional code to identify:
exposure to environmental tobacco smoke (Z77.22)
exposure to tobacco smoke in the perinatal period (P96.81)
history of tobacco use (Z87.891)
occupational exposure to environmental tobacco smoke (Z57.31)
tobacco dependence (F17.-)
tobacco use (Z72.0)

C13.0 **Malignant neoplasm of postcricoid region**
Behind the cricoid cartilage of neck

C13.1 **Malignant neoplasm of aryepiglottic fold, hypopharyngeal aspect**
Arytenoepiglottic fold, triangular opening between side of epiglottis and apex of arytenoid cartilage
Malignant neoplasm of aryepiglottic fold NOS
Malignant neoplasm of interarytenoid fold NOS
Malignant neoplasm of aryepiglottic fold marginal zone
Malignant neoplasm of interarytenoid fold marginal zone
Excludes2 malignant neoplasm of aryepiglottic fold or interarytenoid fold, laryngeal aspect (C32.1)

C13.2 **Malignant neoplasm of posterior wall of hypopharynx**

C13.8 **Malignant neoplasm of overlapping sites of hypopharynx**

C13.9 **Malignant neoplasm of hypopharynx, unspecified**
Malignant neoplasm of hypopharyngeal wall NOS

● C14 **Malignant neoplasm of other and ill-defined sites in the lip, oral cavity and pharynx**
Excludes1 malignant neoplasm of oral cavity NOS (C06.9)
Use additional code to identify:
alcohol abuse and dependence (F10.-)
exposure to environmental tobacco smoke (Z77.22)
exposure to tobacco smoke in the perinatal period (P96.81)
history of tobacco use (Z87.891)
occupational exposure to environmental tobacco smoke (Z57.31)
tobacco dependence (F17.-)
tobacco use (Z72.0)

C14.0 **Malignant neoplasm of pharynx, unspecified**

C14.2 **Malignant neoplasm of Waldeyer's ring**

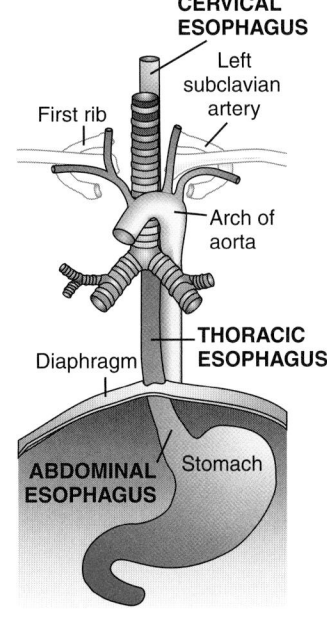

Figure 2-3 The esophagus is the muscular tube that connects the pharynx and the stomach. The 10 inch (25 cm) long esophagus is divided into three parts: **cervical, thoracic,** and **abdominal.**

● Unacceptable First-Listed Diagnosis ● Use Additional Character(s) ▉ Unspecified OGCR Official Guidelines for Coding and Reporting
Complication\Comorbidity Major C\C Excludes 1 Excludes 2 Includes Use additional Code first Code also

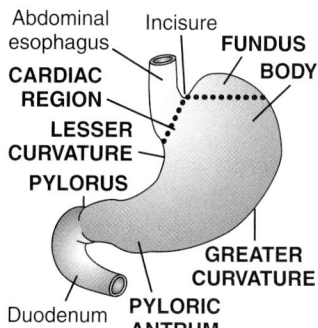

Figure 2-4   Parts of the stomach.

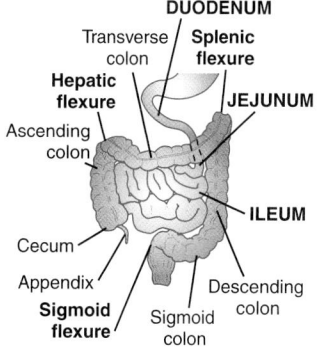

Figure 2-5   Smal intestine and colon.

Item 2–2   The esophagus opens into the stomach through the **cardiac orifice,** also called the **cardioesophageal junction.** The **cardia** is adjacent to the cardiac orifice. The stomach widens into the **greater** and **lesser curvatures.** The **pyloric antrum** precedes the **pylorus,** which opens to the duodenum.

C14.8   **Malignant neoplasm of overlapping sites of lip, oral cavity and pharynx**
> Primary malignant neoplasm of two or more contiguous sites of lip, oral cavity and pharynx
>
> | Excludes1 | "book leaf" neoplasm [ventral surface of tongue and floor of mouth] (C06.89) |

MALIGNANT NEOPLASM OF DIGESTIVE ORGANS (C15-C26)

| Excludes1 | Kaposi's sarcoma of gastrointestinal sites (C46.4) |

● C15   **Malignant neoplasm of esophagus**
> Use additional code to identify:
> alcohol abuse and dependence (F10.-)

C15.3   **Malignant neoplasm of upper third of esophagus** 🦠

C15.4   **Malignant neoplasm of middle third of esophagus** 🦠

C15.5   **Malignant neoplasm of lower third of esophagus** 🦠
> | Excludes1 | malignant neoplasm of cardio-esophageal junction (C16.0) |

C15.8   **Malignant neoplasm of overlapping sites of esophagus** 🦠

■ C15.9   **Malignant neoplasm of esophagus, unspecified** 🦠

● C16   **Malignant neoplasm of stomach**
> Use additional code to identify:
> alcohol abuse and dependence (F10.-)
>
> | Excludes2 | malignant carcinoid tumor of the stomach (C7a.092) |

C16.0   **Malignant neoplasm of cardia** 🦠
> Malignant neoplasm of cardiac orifice
> Malignant neoplasm of cardio-esophageal junction
> Malignant neoplasm of esophagus and stomach
> Malignant neoplasm of gastro-esophageal junction

C16.1   **Malignant neoplasm of fundus of stomach** 🦠

C16.2   **Malignant neoplasm of body of stomach** 🦠

C16.3   **Malignant neoplasm of pyloric antrum** 🦠
> Malignant neoplasm of gastric antrum

C16.4   **Malignant neoplasm of pylorus** 🦠
> Malignant neoplasm of prepylorus
> Malignant neoplasm of pyloric canal

■ C16.5   **Malignant neoplasm of lesser curvature of stomach, unspecified** 🦠
> Malignant neoplasm of lesser curvature of stomach, not classifiable to C16.1-C16.4

■ C16.6   **Malignant neoplasm of greater curvature of stomach, unspecified** 🦠
> Malignant neoplasm of greater curvature of stomach, not classifiable to C16.0-C16.4

C16.8   **Malignant neoplasm of overlapping sites of stomach** 🦠

■ C16.9   **Malignant neoplasm of stomach, unspecified** 🦠
> Gastric cancer NOS

● C17   **Malignant neoplasm of small intestine**
> | Excludes1 | malignant carcinoid tumor of the small intestine (C7a.01) |

C17.0   **Malignant neoplasm of duodenum** 🦠
> *First or proximal portion of small intestine, extending from pylorus to jejunum*

C17.1   **Malignant neoplasm of jejunum** 🦠
> *Second section of small intestine, extending from duodenum to ileum*

C17.2   **Malignant neoplasm of ileum** 🦠
> *Distal and longest portion of small intestine, extending from jejunum to cecum*
>
> | Excludes1 | malignant neoplasm of ileocecal valve (C18.0) |

C17.3   **Meckel's diverticulum** 🦠
> *Appendage of ileum*

C17.8   **Malignant neoplasm of overlapping sites of small intestine** 🦠

■ C17.9   **Malignant neoplasm of small intestine, unspecified** 🦠

● C18   **Malignant neoplasm of colon**
> | Excludes1 | malignant carcinoid tumors of the colon (C7a.02) |

C18.0   **Malignant neoplasm of cecum** 🦠
> *First section of large intestine*
> Malignant neoplasm of ileocecal valve

C18.1   **Malignant neoplasm of appendix** 🦠
> *Blind ended tube connected to the cecum; AKA vermiform appendix*

C18.2   **Malignant neoplasm of ascending colon** 🦠
> *Ascending colon is between cecum and right colic flexure*

C18.3   **Malignant neoplasm of hepatic flexure** 🦠
> *A flexure is a bending in a structure or organ. Note the three flexures illustrated in Figure 2–5.*

C18.4   **Malignant neoplasm of transverse colon** 🦠
> *Portion of colon that runs transversely across upper part of abdomen, between right and left colic flexures*

C18.5   **Malignant neoplasm of splenic flexure** 🦠
> *Bend at junction of transverse and descending colon*

●   Unacceptable First-Listed Diagnosis   ●   Use Additional Character(s)   ■ Unspecified   **OGCR** Official Guidelines for Coding and Reporting

🦠 Complication\Comorbidity   🦠 Major C\C | Excludes 1 | | Excludes 2 | Includes   Use additional   Code first   Code also

CHAPTER 2 (C00-D49)

C18.6 **Malignant neoplasm of descending colon** 🕱
Portion between left colic flexure and sigmoid colon at pelvic brim; AKA iliac colon

C18.7 **Malignant neoplasm of sigmoid colon** 🕱
S-shaped part of colon extending from pelvic brim to third segment of sacrum
Malignant neoplasm of sigmoid (flexure)

   Excludes1   malignant neoplasm of rectosigmoid junction (C19)

C18.8 **Malignant neoplasm of overlapping sites of colon** 🕱

◼ **C18.9** **Malignant neoplasm of colon, unspecified** 🕱
Malignant neoplasm of large intestine NOS

C19 **Malignant neoplasm of rectosigmoid junction** 🕱

   Includes   malignant neoplasm of colon with rectum
malignant neoplasm of rectosigmoid (colon)

   Excludes1   malignant carcinoid tumors of the colon (C7a.02-)

C20 **Malignant neoplasm of rectum** 🕱

   Includes   malignant neoplasm of rectal ampulla

   Excludes1   malignant carcinoid tumor of the rectum (C7a.026)

● **C21** **Malignant neoplasm of anus and anal canal**

   Excludes2   malignant carcinoid tumors of the colon (C7a.02-)
malignant melanoma of anal margin (C43.51)
malignant melanoma of anal skin (C43.51)
malignant melanoma of perianal skin (C43.51)
malignant neoplasm of anal margin (C44.51)
malignant neoplasm of anal skin (C44.51)
malignant neoplasm of perianal skin (C44.51)

◼ **C21.0** **Malignant neoplasm of anus, unspecified** 🕱

C21.1 **Malignant neoplasm of anal canal** 🕱
Terminal part of large intestine
Malignant neoplasm of anal sphincter

C21.2 **Malignant neoplasm of cloacogenic zone** 🕱

C21.8 **Malignant neoplasm of overlapping sites of rectum, anus and anal canal** 🕱
Malignant neoplasm of anorectal junction
Malignant neoplasm of anorectum
Primary malignant neoplasm of two or more contiguous sites of rectum, anus and anal canal

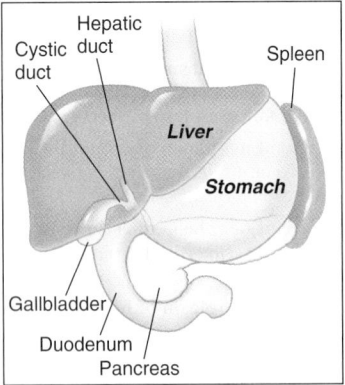

Figure 2-6 Diagram of liver, gallbladder, hepatic duct, pancreas, and spleen. (From Thibodeau and Patton: Anatomy and Physiology, 6th ed. 2007. Mosby)

● **C22** **Malignant neoplasm of liver and intrahepatic bile ducts**
Intrahepatic: Within liver

   Excludes1   malignant neoplasm of biliary tract NOS (C24.9)
secondary malignant neoplasm of liver and intrahepatic bile duct (C78.7)

Use additional code to identify:
alcohol abuse and dependence (F10.-)
hepatitis B (B16.-, B18.0-B18.1) hepatitis C (B17.1-, B18.2)

C22.0 **Liver cell carcinoma** 🕱
Hepatocellular carcinoma
Hepatoma

C22.1 **Intrahepatic bile duct carcinoma** 🕱
Adenocarcinoma (cancer that originates in glandular tissue) arising from epithelium of intrahepatic bile ducts
Cholangiocarcinoma

   Excludes1   malignant neoplasm of hepatic duct (C24.0)

C22.2 **Hepatoblastoma** 🕱
Malignant intrahepatic tumor

C22.3 **Angiosarcoma of liver** 🕱
Kupffer cell sarcoma

C22.4 **Other sarcomas of liver** 🕱

C22.7 **Other specified carcinomas of liver** 🕱

◼ **C22.8** **Malignant neoplasm of liver, primary, unspecified as to type** 🕱

C22.9 **Malignant neoplasm of liver, not specified as primary or secondary** 🕱

C23 **Malignant neoplasm of gallbladder** 🕱

● **C24** **Malignant neoplasm of other and unspecified parts of biliary tract**

   Excludes1   malignant neoplasm of intrahepatic bile duct (C22.1)

C24.0 **Malignant neoplasm of extrahepatic bile duct** 🕱
Extrahepatic = outside the liver
Malignant neoplasm of biliary duct or passage NOS
Malignant neoplasm of common bile duct
Malignant neoplasm of cystic duct
Malignant neoplasm of hepatic duct

C24.1 **Malignant neoplasm of ampulla of Vater** 🕱
Union of pancreatic duct and common bile duct

C24.8 **Malignant neoplasm of overlapping sites of biliary tract** 🕱
Malignant neoplasm involving both intrahepatic and extrahepatic bile ducts
Primary malignant neoplasm of two or more contiguous sites of biliary tract

◼ **C24.9** **Malignant neoplasm of biliary tract, unspecified** 🕱

● **C25** **Malignant neoplasm of pancreas**
Check documentation for specific site.

Use additional code to identify:
alcohol abuse and dependence (F10.-)

Item 2–3 **Islets** of Langerhans (endocrine producing cells comprising 1% to 2% of the pancreatic mass) make and secrete hormones that regulate the body's production of insulin, glucagon, and stomach acid. Breakdown of the insulin-producing cells can cause diabetes mellitus. Islet cell tumors can be benign or malignant and include glucagonomas, insulinomas, gastrinomas, and neuroendocrine tumor. The neoplasm table must be consulted for the correct neoplasm code.

● Unacceptable First-Listed Diagnosis   ● Use Additional Character(s)   ◼ Unspecified   **OGCR** Official Guidelines for Coding and Reporting
🕱 Complication\Comorbidity   🕱 Major C\C   Excludes 1   Excludes 2   Includes   Use additional   Code first   Code also

C25.0   **Malignant neoplasm of head of pancreas** 🝔

C25.1   **Malignant neoplasm of body of pancreas** 🝔

C25.2   **Malignant neoplasm of tail of pancreas** 🝔

C25.3   **Malignant neoplasm of pancreatic duct** 🝔

C25.4   **Malignant neoplasm of endocrine pancreas** 🝔
> *That part of the pancreas that acts as endocrine gland and consists of islets of Langerhans*
> Malignant neoplasm of islets of Langerhans
>
> Use additional code to identify any functional activity.

C25.7   **Malignant neoplasm of other parts of pancreas** 🝔
> Malignant neoplasm of neck of pancreas

C25.8   **Malignant neoplasm of overlapping sites of pancreas** 🝔

◼ C25.9   **Malignant neoplasm of pancreas, unspecified** 🝔

● **C26   Malignant neoplasm of other and ill-defined digestive organs**
> **Excludes1**   malignant neoplasm of peritoneum and retroperitoneum (C48.-)

◼ **C26.0   Malignant neoplasm of intestinal tract, part unspecified**
> Malignant neoplasm of intestine NOS

C26.1   **Malignant neoplasm of spleen**
> **Excludes1**   Hodgkin lymphoma (C81.-)
> non-Hodgkin lymphoma (C82-C85)

C26.9   **Malignant neoplasm of ill-defined sites within the digestive system**
> Malignant neoplasm of alimentary canal or tract NOS
> Malignant neoplasm of gastrointestinal tract NOS
> **Excludes1**   malignant neoplasm of abdominal NOS (C76.2)
> malignant neoplasm of intra-abdominal NOS (C76.2)

MALIGNANT NEOPLASM OF RESPIRATORY AND INTRATHORACIC ORGANS (C30-C39)

> **Includes**   malignant neoplasm of middle ear
> **Excludes1**   mesothelioma (C45.-)

● **C30   Malignant neoplasm of nasal cavity and middle ear**

C30.0   **Malignant neoplasm of nasal cavity**
> Malignant neoplasm of cartilage of nose
> Malignant neoplasm of nasal concha
> Malignant neoplasm of internal nose
> Malignant neoplasm of septum of nose
> Malignant neoplasm of vestibule of nose
> *Anterior part of nasal cavity*
> **Excludes1**   malignant neoplasm of nasal bone (C41.0)
> malignant neoplasm of nose NOS (C76.0)
> malignant neoplasm of olfactory bulb (C72.2-)
> malignant neoplasm of posterior margin of nasal septum and choana (C11.3)
> malignant neoplasm of skin of nose (C43.31, C44.31)
> malignant neoplasm of turbinates (C41.0)

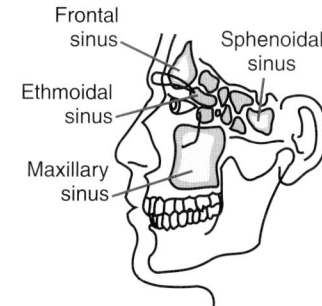

Figure 2-7 *Paranasal sinuses. (From Buck CJ: Step-by-Step Medica Coding. 2006 ed. Philadelphia, WB Saunders, 2006.*

C30.1   **Malignant neoplasm of middle ear**
> Malignant neoplasm of antrum tympanicum
> *Boney cavity or chamber*
> Malignant neoplasm of auditory tube
> Malignant neoplasm of eustachian tube
> Malignant neoplasm of inner ear
> Malignant neoplasm of mastoid air cells
> Malignant neoplasm of tympanic cavity
> **Excludes1**   malignant neoplasm of auricular canal (external) (C43.2-, C44.2-)
> malignant neoplasm of bone of ear (meatus) (C41.0)
> malignant neoplasm of cartilage of ear (C49.0)
> malignant neoplasm of skin of (external) ear (C43.2-, C44.2-)

● **C31   Malignant neoplasm of accessory sinuses**
> *Paired sinuses in bones of face*

C31.0   **Malignant neoplasm of maxillary sinus**
> Malignant neoplasm of antrum (Highmore) (maxillary)

C31.1   **Malignant neoplasm of ethmoidal sinus**

C31.2   **Malignant neoplasm of frontal sinus**

C31.3   **Malignant neoplasm of sphenoid sinus**

C31.8   **Malignant neoplasm of overlapping sites of accessory sinuses**

◼ C31.9   **Malignant neoplasm of accessory sinus, unspecified**

● **C32   Malignant neoplasm of larynx**
> Use additional code to identify:
> alcohol abuse and dependence (F10.-)
> exposure to environmental tobacco smoke (Z77.22)
> exposure to tobacco smoke in the perinatal period (P96.81)
> history of tobacco use (Z87.891)
> occupational exposure to environmental tobacco smoke (Z57.31)
> tobacco dependence (F17.-)
> tobacco use (Z72.0)

C32.0   **Malignant neoplasm of glottis**
> *Vocal apparatus of larynx, consisting of true vocal cords (plicae vocales) and opening between them (rima glottidis)*
> Malignant neoplasm of intrinsic larynx
> Malignant neoplasm of laryngeal commissure (anterior)(posterior)
> Malignant neoplasm of vocal cord (true) NOS
> ***True*** *vocal cords ("lower vocal folds") produce vocalization when air from the lungs passes between them. Check your documentation. Code C32.1 is for malignant neoplasm of the **false** vocal cords.*

● Unacceptable First-Listed Diagnosis   ● Use Additional Character(s)   ◼ Unspecified   **OGCR** Official Guidelines for Coding and Reporting

🝔 Complication\Comorbidity   🝔 Major C\C   Excludes 1   Excludes 2   Includes   Use additional   Code first   Code also

825

CHAPTER 2 (C00-D49)

C32.1 Malignant neoplasm of supraglottis
Area of pharynx above glottis
Malignant neoplasm of aryepiglottic fold or interarytenoid fold, laryngeal aspect
Malignant neoplasm of epiglottis (suprahyoid portion) NOS
Malignant neoplasm of extrinsic larynx
Malignant neoplasm of false vocal cord
__False__ vocal cords ("upper vocal folds") are not involved in vocalization. Check your documentation. Code C32.0 is for true vocal cords.
Malignant neoplasm of posterior (laryngeal) surface of epiglottis
Malignant neoplasm of ventricular bands

> **Excludes2**　malignant neoplasm of anterior surface of epiglottis (C10.1)
> malignant neoplasm of aryepiglottic fold or interarytenoid fold:
> NOS (C13.1)
> hypopharyngeal aspect (C13.1)
> marginal zone (C13.1)

C32.2 Malignant neoplasm of subglottis
Lowest part of larynx from just below vocal cords down to top of trachea

C32.3 Malignant neoplasm of laryngeal cartilage
Cartilages of larynx, including cricoid, thyroid, and epiglottic, and two each of arytenoid, corniculate, and cuneiform

C32.8 Malignant neoplasm of overlapping sites of larynx

C32.9 Malignant neoplasm of larynx, unspecified

C33　Malignant neoplasm of trachea 🕭

　　Use additional code to identify:
　　exposure to environmental tobacco smoke (Z77.22)
　　exposure to tobacco smoke in the perinatal period (P96.81)
　　history of tobacco use (Z87.891)
　　occupational exposure to environmental tobacco smoke (Z57.31)
　　tobacco dependence (F17.-)
　　tobacco use (Z72.0)

● **C34　Malignant neoplasm of bronchus and lung**

> **Excludes1**　Kaposi's sarcoma of lung (C46.5-)
> malignant carcinoid tumor of the bronchus and lung (C7a.090)

　　Use additional code to identify:
　　exposure to environmental tobacco smoke (Z77.22)
　　exposure to tobacco smoke in the perinatal period (P96.81)
　　history of tobacco use (Z87.891)
　　occupational exposure to environmental tobacco smoke (Z57.31)
　　tobacco dependence (F17.-)
　　tobacco use (Z72.0)

● **C34.0　Malignant neoplasm of main bronchus**
Malignant neoplasm of carina
Ridgelike structure
Malignant neoplasm of hilus (of lung)
Anatomic depression or pit

　　C34.00　Malignant neoplasm of main bronchus, unspecified side 🕭

　　C34.01　Malignant neoplasm of right main bronchus 🕭

　　C34.02　Malignant neoplasm of left main bronchus 🕭

● **C34.1　Malignant neoplasm of upper lobe, bronchus or lung**

　　C34.10　Malignant neoplasm of upper lobe, bronchus or lung, unspecified side 🕭

　　C34.11　Malignant neoplasm of upper lobe, right bronchus or lung 🕭

　　C34.12　Malignant neoplasm of upper lobe, left bronchus or lung 🕭

C34.2　Malignant neoplasm of middle lobe, right bronchus or lung 🕭

● **C34.3　Malignant neoplasm of lower lobe, bronchus or lung**

　　C34.30　Malignant neoplasm of lower lobe, bronchus or lung, unspecified side 🕭

　　C34.31　Malignant neoplasm of lower lobe, right bronchus or lung 🕭

　　C34.32　Malignant neoplasm of lower lobe, left bronchus or lung 🕭

● **C34.8　Malignant neoplasm of overlapping sites of bronchus and lung**

　　C34.80　Malignant neoplasm of overlapping sites of bronchus and lung, unspecified side 🕭

　　C34.81　Malignant neoplasm of overlapping sites of right bronchus and lung 🕭

　　C34.82　Malignant neoplasm of overlapping sites of left bronchus and lung 🕭

● **C34.9　Malignant neoplasm of bronchus or lung, unspecified**

　　C34.90　Malignant neoplasm of bronchus or lung, unspecified, unspecified side 🕭

　　C34.91　Malignant neoplasm of right bronchus or lung, unspecified 🕭

　　C34.92　Malignant neoplasm of left bronchus or lung, unspecified 🕭

C37　Malignant neoplasm of thymus 🕭

> **Excludes1**　malignant carcinoid tumor of the thymus (C7a.091)

● **C38　Malignant neoplasm of heart, mediastinum and pleura**

> **Excludes1**　mesothelioma (C45.-)

C38.0　Malignant neoplasm of heart 🕭
Malignant neoplasm of pericardium

> **Excludes1**　malignant neoplasm of great vessels (C49.3)

C38.1　Malignant neoplasm of anterior mediastinum 🕭

C38.2　Malignant neoplasm of posterior mediastinum 🕭

C38.3　Malignant neoplasm of mediastinum, part unspecified 🕭

C38.4　Malignant neoplasm of pleura 🕭

C38.8　Malignant neoplasm of overlapping sites of heart, mediastinum and pleura 🕭
Pleura are comprised of serous membrane that lines the thoracic cavity (parietal) and covers the lungs (visceral).

● **C39　Malignant neoplasm of other and ill-defined sites in the respiratory system**
Intrathoracic: within thorax/chest

> **Excludes1**　intrathoracic malignant neoplasm NOS (C76.1)
> thoracic malignant neoplasm NOS (C76.1)

　　Use additional code to identify:
　　exposure to environmental tobacco smoke (Z77.22)
　　exposure to tobacco smoke in the perinatal period (P96.81)
　　history of tobacco use (Z87.891)
　　occupational exposure to environmental tobacco smoke (Z57.31)
　　tobacco dependence (F17.-)
　　tobacco use (Z72.0)

C39.0　Malignant neoplasm of upper respiratory tract, part unspecified

C39.9　Malignant neoplasm of lower respiratory tract, part unspecified
Malignant neoplasm of respiratory tract NOS

● Unacceptable First-Listed Diagnosis　　● Use Additional Character(s)　　▪ Unspecified　　**OGCR** Official Guidelines for Coding and Reporting
🕭 Complication\Comorbidity　🕭 Major C\C　| Excludes 1 |　| Excludes 2 |　Includes　Use additional　Code first　Code also

CHAPTER 2 (C00-D49)

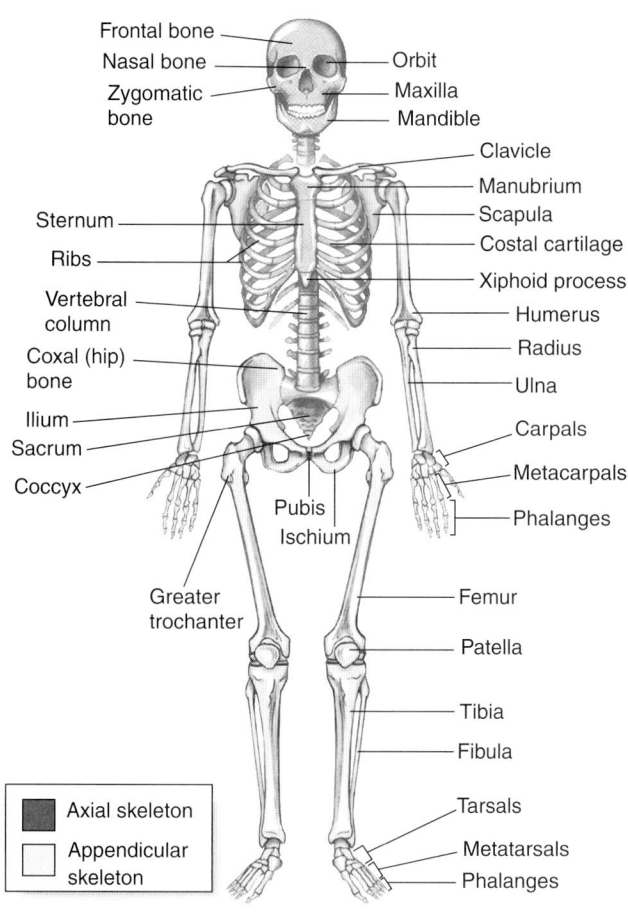

Figure 2-8   Diagram of skeleton of trunk and limbs with bones labled. (From Thibodeau and Patton: Anatomy and Physiology, 6th ed. 2007, Mosby)

MALIGNANT NEOPLASM OF BONE AND ARTICULAR CARTILAGE (C40-C41)

Includes	malignant neoplasm of cartilage (articular) (joint)
	malignant neoplasm of periosteum
Excludes1	malignant neoplasm of bone marrow NOS (C96.8)
	malignant neoplasm of synovia (C49.-)

● **C40   Malignant neoplasm of bone and articular cartilage of limbs**

     Use additional code to identify major osseous defect, if applicable (M89.7-)

   ● **C40.0   Malignant neoplasm of scapula and long bones of upper limb**

       ◼ C40.00   Malignant neoplasm of scapula and long bones of upper limb, unspecified side 🐾

       C40.01   Malignant neoplasm of scapula and long bones of right upper limb 🐾

       C40.02   Malignant neoplasm of scapula and long bones of left upper limb 🐾

   ● **C40.1   Malignant neoplasm of short bones of upper limb**

       ◼ C40.10   Malignant neoplasm of short bones of upper limb, unspecified side 🐾

       C40.11   Malignant neoplasm of short bones of right upper limb 🐾

       C40.12   Malignant neoplasm of short bones of left upper limb 🐾

● **C40.2   Malignant neoplasm of long bones of lower limb**

   ◼ C40.20   Malignant neoplasm of long bones of lower limb, unspecified side 🐾

   C40.21   Malignant neoplasm of long bones of right lower limb 🐾

   C40.22   Malignant neoplasm of long bones of left lower limb 🐾

● **C40.3   Malignant neoplasm of short bones of lower limb**

   ◼ C40.30   Malignant neoplasm of short bones of lower limb, unspecified side 🐾

   C40.31   Malignant neoplasm of short bones of right lower limb 🐾

   C40.32   Malignant neoplasm of short bones of left lower limb 🐾

● **C40.8   Malignant neoplasm of overlapping sites of bone and articular cartilage of limb**

   ◼ C40.80   Malignant neoplasm of overlapping sites of bone and articular cartilage of limb, unspecified side 🐾

   C40.81   Malignant neoplasm of overlapping sites of bone and articular cartilage of right limb 🐾

   C40.82   Malignant neoplasm of overlapping sites of bone and articular cartilage of left limb 🐾

● **C40.9   Malignant neoplasm of bones and articular cartilage of limb, unspecified**

   ◼ C40.90   Malignant neoplasm of bones and articular cartilage of limb, unspecified, unspecified side 🐾

   ◼ C40.91   Malignant neoplasm of bones and articular cartilage of right limb, unspecified 🐾

   ◼ C40.92   Malignant neoplasm of bones and articular cartilage of left limb, unspecified 🐾

● **C41   Malignant neoplasm of bone and articular cartilage of other and unspecified sites**

Excludes1	malignant neoplasm of bones of limbs (C40.-)
	malignant neoplasm of cartilage of:
	ear (C49.0)
	eyelid (C49.0)
	larynx (C32.3)
	limbs (C40.-)
	nose (C30.0)

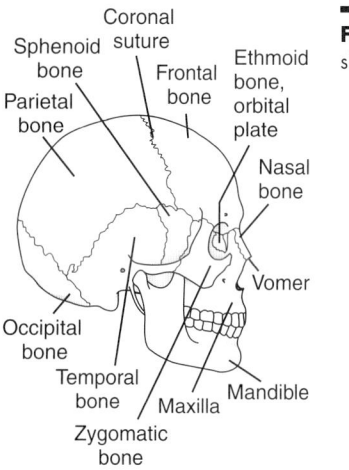

Figure 2-9   Bones of the skull.

●   Unacceptable First-Listed Diagnosis   ●   Use Additional Character(s)   ◼   Unspecified   **OGCR**   Official Guidelines for Coding and Reporting

🐾 Complication\Comorbidity   🐾 Major C\C   Excludes 1   Excludes 2   Includes   Use additional   Code first   Code also

827

CHAPTER 2 (C00-D49)

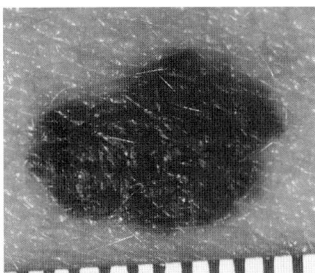

Figure 2-10   Malignant melanoma of skin. (From Goldman: Cecil Textbook of Medicine, 22nd ed. 2004, Saunders)

Item 2–4   Malignant melanoma is a serious form of skin cancer that affects the melanocytes (pigment-forming cells) and is caused by ultraviolet (UV) rays from the sun that damage skin. It is most commonly seen in the 40- to 60-year-olds with fair skin, blue or green eyes, and red or blond hair who sunburn easily.

Melanoma can spread very rapidly and is the most deadly form of skin cancer. It is less common than other types of skin cancer. The rate of melanoma is increasing and currently is the leading cause of death from skin disease.

C41.0   Malignant neoplasm of bones of skull and face 🦠
     Malignant neoplasm of maxilla (superior)
     Malignant neoplasm of orbital bone

     | **Excludes2** | carcinoma, any type except intraosseous or odontogenic of:
                   maxillary sinus (C31.0)
                   upper jaw (C03.0)
                   malignant neoplasm of jaw bone
                     (lower) (C41.1)

C41.1   Malignant neoplasm of mandible 🦠
     Malignant neoplasm of inferior maxilla
     Malignant neoplasm of lower jaw bone

     | **Excludes2** | carcinoma, any type except intraosseous or odontogenic of:
                   jaw NOS (C03.9)
                   lower (C03.1)
                   malignant neoplasm of upper jaw
                   bone (C41.0)

C41.2   Malignant neoplasm of vertebral column 🦠

     | **Excludes1** | malignant neoplasm of sacrum and coccyx (C41.4)

C41.3   Malignant neoplasm of ribs, sternum and clavicle 🦠

C41.4   Malignant neoplasm of pelvic bones, sacrum and coccyx 🦠

C41.9   Malignant neoplasm of bone and articular cartilage, unspecified 🦠

MELANOMA AND OTHER MALIGNANT NEOPLASMS OF SKIN (C43-C44)

     | **Excludes1** | melanoma in situ (D03.-)

● **C43   Malignant melanoma of skin**

     | **Excludes1** | melanoma in situ (D03.-)
     | **Excludes2** | malignant melanoma of skin of genital organs (C51-C52, C60.-, C63.-)
                   Merkel cell carcinoma (C4a.-)
                   sites other than skin-code to malignant neoplasm of the site

C43.0   Malignant melanoma of lip

     | **Excludes1** | malignant neoplasm of vermilion border of lip (C00.0-C00.2)

● **C43.1   Malignant melanoma of eyelid, including canthus**
     Canthus: Either corner of eye where upper and lower eyelids meet

     C43.10   Malignant melanoma of eyelid, including canthus, unspecified side

     C43.11   Malignant melanoma of right eyelid, including canthus

     C43.12   Malignant melanoma of left eyelid, including canthus

● **C43.2   Malignant melanoma of ear and external auricular canal**

     C43.20   Malignant melanoma of ear and external auricular canal, unspecified side

     C43.21   Malignant melanoma of right ear and external auricular canal

     C43.22   Malignant melanoma of left ear and external auricular canal

● **C43.3   Malignant melanoma of other and unspecified parts of face**

     C43.30   Malignant melanoma of unspecified part of face

     C43.31   Malignant melanoma of nose

     C43.39   Malignant melanoma of other parts of face

C43.4   Malignant melanoma of scalp and neck

● **C43.5   Malignant melanoma of trunk**

     | **Excludes2** | malignant neoplasm of anus NOS (C21.0)
                   malignant neoplasm of scrotum (C63.2)

     C43.51   Malignant melanoma of anal skin
           Malignant melanoma of anal margin
           Malignant melanoma of perianal skin

     C43.52   Malignant melanoma of skin of breast

     C43.59   Malignant melanoma of other part of trunk

● **C43.6   Malignant melanoma of upper limb, including shoulder**

     C43.60   Malignant melanoma of upper limb, including shoulder, unspecified side

     C43.61   Malignant melanoma of right upper limb, including shoulder

     C43.62   Malignant melanoma of left upper limb, including shoulder

● **C43.7   Malignant melanoma of lower limb, including hip**

     C43.70   Malignant melanoma of lower limb, including hip, unspecified side

     C43.71   Malignant melanoma of right lower limb, including hip

     C43.72   Malignant melanoma of left lower limb, including hip

C43.8   Overlapping malignant melanoma of skin

C43.9   Malignant melanoma of skin, unspecified
     Melanoma (malignant) NOS

C4a   Merkel cell carcinoma

     C4a.0   Merkel cell carcinoma of lip

         | **Excludes1** | malignant neoplasm of vermilion border of lip (C00.0-C00.2)

● **C4a.1   Merkel cell carcinoma of eyelid, including canthus**

     C4a.10   Merkel cell carcinoma of eyelid, including canthus, unspecified side

     C4a.11   Merkel cell carcinoma of right eyelid, including canthus

     C4a.12   Merkel cell carcinoma of left eyelid, including canthus

---

● Unacceptable First-Listed Diagnosis   ● Use Additional Character(s)   ■ Unspecified   **OGCR** Official Guidelines for Coding and Reporting

🦠 Complication\Comorbidity   🦠 Major C\C | Excludes 1 | | Excludes 2 | Includes   Use additional   Code first   Code also

● **C4a.2 Merkel cell carcinoma of ear and external auricular canal**
- ▪ **C4a.20 Merkel cell carcinoma of ear and external auricular canal, unspecified side**
- **C4a.21 Merkel cell carcinoma of right ear and external auricular canal**
- **C4a.22 Merkel cell carcinoma of left ear and external auricular canal**

● **C4a.3 Merkel cell carcinoma of other and unspecified parts of face**
- ▪ **C4a.30 Merkel cell carcinoma of unspecified part of face**
- **C4a.31 Merkel cell carcinoma of nose**
- **C4a.39 Merkel cell carcinoma of other parts of face**

C4a.4 Merkel cell carcinoma of scalp and neck

● **C4a.5 Merkel cell carcinoma of trunk**
> Excludes2   malignant neoplasm of anus NOS (C21.0)
> malignant neoplasm of scrotum (C63.2)
- **C4a.51 Merkel cell carcinoma of anal skin**
  Merkel cell carcinoma of anal margin
  Merkel cell carcinoma of perianal skin
- **C4a.52 Merkel cell carcinoma of skin of breast**
- **C4a.59 Merkel cell carcinoma of other part of trunk**

● **C4a.6 Merkel cell carcinoma of upper limb, including shoulder**
- ▪ **C4a.60 Merkel cell carcinoma of upper limb, including shoulder, unspecified side**
- **C4a.61 Merkel cell carcinoma of right upper limb, including shoulder**
- **C4a.62 Merkel cell carcinoma of left upper limb, including shoulder**

● **C4a.7 Merkel cell carcinoma of lower limb, including hip**
- ▪ **C4a.70 Merkel cell carcinoma of lower limb, including hip, unspecified side**
- **C4a.71 Merkel cell carcinoma of right lower limb, including hip**
- **C4a.72 Merkel cell carcinoma of left lower limb, including hip**

C4a.8 Merkel cell carcinoma of overlapping sites

▪ **C4a.9 Merkel cell carcinoma, unspecified**
Merkel cell carcinoma NOS

● **C44 Other malignant neoplasm of skin**
> Includes   malignant neoplasm of sebaceous glands
> malignant neoplasm of sweat glands
> Excludes1   Kaposi's sarcoma of skin (C46.0)
> malignant melanoma of skin (C43.-)
> malignant neoplasm of skin of genital organs (C51-C52, C60.-, C63.2)
> Merkel cell carcinoma (C4a.-)

C44.0 Malignant neoplasm of skin of lip
Malignant neoplasm of basal cell carcinoma of lip
> Excludes1   malignant neoplasm of lip (C00.-)

● **C44.1 Malignant neoplasm of skin of eyelid, including canthus**
> Excludes1   connective tissue of eyelid (C49.0)
- ▪ **C44.10 Malignant neoplasm of skin of eyelid, including canthus, unspecified side**
- **C44.11 Malignant neoplasm of skin of right eyelid, including canthus**
- **C44.12 Malignant neoplasm of skin of left eyelid, including canthus**

● **C44.2 Malignant neoplasm of skin of ear and external auricular canal**
> Excludes1   connective tissue of ear (C49.0)
- ▪ **C44.20 Malignant neoplasm of skin of ear and external auricular canal, unspecified side**
- **C44.21 Malignant neoplasm of skin of right ear and external auricular canal**
- **C44.22 Malignant neoplasm of skin of left ear and external auricular canal**

● **C44.3 Malignant neoplasm of skin of other and unspecified parts of face**
- ▪ **C44.30 Malignant neoplasm of skin of unspecified part of face**
- **C44.31 Malignant neoplasm of skin of nose**
- **C44.39 Malignant neoplasm of skin of other parts of face**

C44.4 Malignant neoplasm of skin of scalp and neck

● **C44.5 Malignant neoplasm of skin of trunk**
> Excludes1   anus NOS (C21.0)
> scrotum (C63.2)
- **C44.51 Malignant neoplasm of anal skin**
  Malignant neoplasm of anal margin
  Malignant neoplasm of perianal skin
- **C44.52 Malignant neoplasm of skin of breast**
- **C44.59 Malignant neoplasm of other part of trunk**

● **C44.6 Malignant neoplasm of skin of upper limb, including shoulder**
- ▪ **C44.60 Malignant neoplasm of skin of upper limb, including shoulder, unspecified side**
- **C44.61 Malignant neoplasm of skin of right upper limb, including shoulder**
- **C44.62 Malignant neoplasm of skin of left upper limb, including shoulder**

● **C44.7 Malignant neoplasm of skin of lower limb, including hip**
- ▪ **C44.70 Malignant neoplasm of skin of lower limb, including hip, unspecified side**
- **C44.71 Malignant neoplasm of skin of right lower limb, including hip**
- **C44.72 Malignant neoplasm of skin of left lower limb, including hip**

C44.8 Malignant neoplasm of overlapping sites of skin

▪ **C44.9 Malignant neoplasm of skin, unspecified**

MALIGNANT NEOPLASMS OF MESOTHELIAL AND SOFT TISSUE (C45-C49)

● **C45 Mesothelioma**
Malignant cells develop in protective lining that covers internal organs (mesothelium) caused by exposure to asbestos

C45.0 Mesothelioma of pleura 🕭
> Excludes1   other malignant neoplasm of pleura (C38.4)

C45.1 Mesothelioma of peritoneum 🕭
Mesothelioma of cul-de-sac
Mesothelioma of mesentery
Mesothelioma of mesocolon
Mesothelioma of omentum
Mesothelioma of peritoneum (parietal) (pelvic)
> Excludes1   other malignant neoplasm of soft tissue of peritoneum (C48.-)

● Unacceptable First-Listed Diagnosis   ● Use Additional Character(s)   ▪ Unspecified   **OGCR** Official Guidelines for Coding and Reporting

🕭 Complication\Comorbidity   🕭 Major C\C   Excludes 1   Excludes 2   Includes   Use additional   Code first   Code also   **829**

C45.2 **Mesothelioma of pericardium**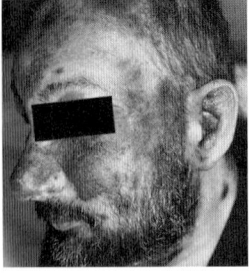

> | Excludes1 | other malignant neoplasm of
> pericardium (C38.0)

C45.7 **Mesothelioma of other sites**

C45.9 **Mesothelioma, unspecified**

● C46 **Kaposi's sarcoma**

> *Code first any human immunodeficiency virus [HIV]
> disease (B20)*

C46.0 **Kaposi's sarcoma of skin**

C46.1 **Kaposi's sarcoma of soft tissue**
Kaposi's sarcoma of blood vessel
Kaposi's sarcoma of connective tissue
Kaposi's sarcoma of fascia
Kaposi's sarcoma of ligament
Kaposi's sarcoma of lymphatic(s) NEC
Kaposi's sarcoma of muscle

> | Excludes2 | Kaposi's sarcoma of lymph glands
> and nodes (C46.3)

C46.2 **Kaposi's sarcoma of palate**

C46.3 **Kaposi's sarcoma of lymph nodes**

C46.4 **Kaposi's sarcoma of gastrointestinal sites**

● C46.5 **Kaposi's sarcoma of lung**

    C46.50 **Kaposi's sarcoma of lung, unspecified side**

    C46.51 **Kaposi's sarcoma of right lung**

    C46.52 **Kaposi's sarcoma of left lung**

C46.7 **Kaposi's sarcoma of other sites**

C46.9 **Kaposi's sarcoma, unspecified**

● C47 **Malignant neoplasm of peripheral nerves and autonomic nervous system**

> | Includes | malignant neoplasm of sympathetic and
> parasympathetic nerves and ganglia
>
> | Excludes1 | Kaposi's sarcoma of soft tissue (C46.1)

C47.0 **Malignant neoplasm of peripheral nerves of head, face and neck**

> | Excludes1 | malignant neoplasm of peripheral
> nerves of orbit (C69.6-)

● C47.1 **Malignant neoplasm of peripheral nerves of upper limb, including shoulder**

    C47.10 **Malignant neoplasm of peripheral nerves of upper limb, including shoulder, unspecified side**

    C47.11 **Malignant neoplasm of peripheral nerves of right upper limb, including shoulder**

    C47.12 **Malignant neoplasm of peripheral nerves of left upper limb, including shoulder**

● C47.2 **Malignant neoplasm of peripheral nerves of lower limb, including hip**

    C47.20 **Malignant neoplasm of peripheral nerves of lower limb, including hip, unspecified side**

    C47.21 **Malignant neoplasm of peripheral nerves of right lower limb, including hip**

    C47.22 **Malignant neoplasm of peripheral nerves of left lower limb, including hip**

C47.3 **Malignant neoplasm of peripheral nerves of thorax**

C47.4 **Malignant neoplasm of peripheral nerves of abdomen**

C47.5 **Malignant neoplasm of peripheral nerves of pelvis**

C47.6 **Malignant neoplasm of peripheral nerves of trunk, unspecified**

C47.8 **Malignant neoplasm of overlapping sites of peripheral nerves and autonomic nervous system**

C47.9 **Malignant neoplasm of peripheral nerves and autonomic nervous system, unspecified**

● C48 **Malignant neoplasm of retroperitoneum and peritoneum**

> | Excludes1 | Kaposi's sarcoma of connective tissue
> (C46.1)
> mesothelioma (C45.-)

C48.0 **Malignant neoplasm of retroperitoneum**
Behind/outside of peritoneum

C48.1 **Malignant neoplasm of specified parts of peritoneum**
Serous membrane lining abdominopelvic walls and covering viscera
Malignant neoplasm of cul-de-sac
Malignant neoplasm of mesentery
Malignant neoplasm of mesocolon
Malignant neoplasm of omentum
Malignant neoplasm of parietal peritoneum
Malignant neoplasm of pelvic peritoneum

C48.2 **Malignant neoplasm of peritoneum, unspecified**

C48.8 **Malignant neoplasm of overlapping sites of retroperitoneum and peritoneum**

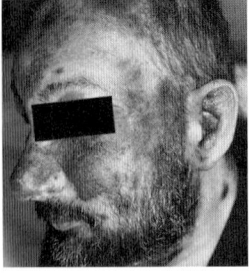

Figure 2-11 Kaposi's sarcoma. There are large confluent hyperpigmented patch-stage lesions with lymphedema. (From Cohen & Powderly: Infectious Diseases, 2nd ed. 2004, Mosby, An Imprint of Elsevier)

Item 2–5 Kaposi's sarcoma is a cancer that causes patches of abnormal tissue to grow under the skin; in the lining of the mouth, nose, and throat; or in other organs, often beginning and spreading to other organs. Patients who have had organ transplants or patients with AIDS are at high risk for this malignancy.

● Unacceptable First-Listed Diagnosis   ● Use Additional Character(s)   ■ Unspecified   **OGCR** Official Guidelines for Coding and Reporting
Complication\Comorbidity   Major C\C | Excludes 1 | | Excludes 2 | Includes   Use additional   Code first   Code also

● **C49 Malignant neoplasm of other connective and soft tissue**

Includes	malignant neoplasm of blood vessel

Includes
malignant neoplasm of blood vessel
malignant neoplasm of bursa
malignant neoplasm of cartilage
malignant neoplasm of fascia
malignant neoplasm of fat
malignant neoplasm of ligament, except uterine
malignant neoplasm of lymphatic vessel
malignant neoplasm of muscle
malignant neoplasm of synovia
malignant neoplasm of tendon (sheath)

Excludes1
malignant neoplasm of cartilage (of):
    articular (C40-C41)
    larynx (C32.3)
    nose (C30.0)
malignant neoplasm of connective tissue
    of internal organs-code to malignant
    neoplasm of the site
malignant stromal tumors-code to
    malignant neoplasm of the site

Excludes2
Kaposi's sarcoma of soft tissue (C46.1)
malignant neoplasm of heart (C38.0)
malignant neoplasm of peripheral nerves
    and autonomic nervous system (C47.-)
malignant neoplasm of peritoneum (C48.2)
malignant neoplasm of retroperitoneum
    (C48.0)
malignant neoplasm of uterine ligament
    (C57.3)
mesothelioma (C45.-)

C49.0 Malignant neoplasm of connective and soft tissue of head, face and neck 🅒
Malignant neoplasm of connective tissue of ear
Malignant neoplasm of connective tissue of eyelid

> **Excludes1** connective tissue of orbit (C69.6-)

● **C49.1 Malignant neoplasm of connective and soft tissue of upper limb, including shoulder**

◻ **C49.10 Malignant neoplasm of connective and soft tissue of upper limb, including shoulder, unspecified side** 🅒

C49.11 Malignant neoplasm of connective and soft tissue of right upper limb, including shoulder 🅒

C49.12 Malignant neoplasm of connective and soft tissue of left upper limb, including shoulder 🅒

● **C49.2 Malignant neoplasm of connective and soft tissue of lower limb, including hip**

◻ **C49.20 Malignant neoplasm of connective and soft tissue of lower limb, including hip, unspecified side** 🅒

C49.21 Malignant neoplasm of connective and soft tissue of right lower limb, including hip 🅒

C49.22 Malignant neoplasm of connective and soft tissue of left lower limb, including hip 🅒

C49.3 Malignant neoplasm of connective and soft tissue of thorax 🅒
Malignant neoplasm of axilla
Malignant neoplasm of diaphragm
Malignant neoplasm of great vessels

> **Excludes1** malignant neoplasm of breast (C50.-)
> malignant neoplasm of heart (C38.0)
> malignant neoplasm of mediastinum (C38.1-C38.3)
> malignant neoplasm of thymus (C37)

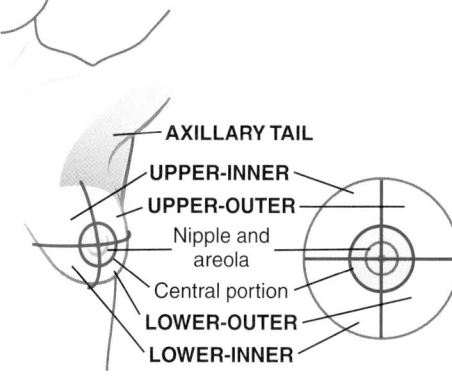

Figure 2-12 Femal Breast quadrants and axillary tail.

C49.4 Malignant neoplasm of connective and soft tissue of abdomen 🅒
Malignant neoplasm of abdominal wall
Malignant neoplasm of hypochondrium

C49.5 Malignant neoplasm of connective and soft tissue of pelvis 🅒
Malignant neoplasm of buttock
Malignant neoplasm of groin
Malignant neoplasm of perineum

◻ **C49.6 Malignant neoplasm of connective and soft tissue of trunk, unspecified** 🅒
Malignant neoplasm of back NOS

C49.8 Malignant neoplasm of overlapping sites of connective and soft tissue 🅒
Primary malignant neoplasm of two or more contiguous sites of connective and soft tissue

◻ **C49.9 Malignant neoplasm of connective and soft tissue, unspecified** 🅒

MALIGNANT NEOPLASM OF BREAST (C50)

● **C50 Malignant neoplasm of breast**

Includes
connective tissue of breast
Paget's disease of breast
Paget's disease of nipple
Intraductal carcinoma of breast characterized by eczema-like inflammatory skin changes
Use additional code to identify estrogen receptor status (Z17.0, Z17.1)

> **Excludes1** skin of breast (C43.5, C44.5)

● **C50.0 Malignant neoplasm of nipple and areola**

● **C50.01 Malignant neoplasm of nipple and areola, female**

C50.011 Malignant neoplasm of nipple and areola, right female breast

C50.012 Malignant neoplasm of nipple and areola, left female breast

◻ **C50.019 Malignant neoplasm of nipple and areola, unspecified female breast**

● **C50.02 Malignant neoplasm of nipple and areola, male**

C50.021 Malignant neoplasm of nipple and areola, right male breast

C50.022 Malignant neoplasm of nipple and areola, left male breast

◻ **C50.029 Malignant neoplasm of nipple and areola, unspecified male breast**

● Unacceptable First-Listed Diagnosis   ● Use Additional Character(s)   ◻ Unspecified   **OGCR** Official Guidelines for Coding and Reporting

🅒 Complication\Comorbidity 🅒 Major C\C | Excludes 1 | | Excludes 2 | | Includes | Use additional   Code first   Code also

831

CHAPTER 2 (C00-D49)

- **C50.1**   **Malignant neoplasm of central portion of breast**
  - **C50.11**   **Malignant neoplasm of central portion of breast, female**
    - C50.111   Malignant neoplasm of central portion of right female breast
    - C50.112   Malignant neoplasm of central portion of left female breast
    - C50.119   Malignant neoplasm of central portion of unspecified female breast
  - **C50.12**   **Malignant neoplasm of central portion of breast, male**
    - C50.121   Malignant neoplasm of central portion of right male breast
    - C50.122   Malignant neoplasm of central portion of left male breast
    - C50.129   Malignant neoplasm of central portion of unspecified male breast
- **C50.2**   **Malignant neoplasm of upper-inner quadrant of breast**
  - **C50.21**   **Malignant neoplasm of upper-inner quadrant of breast, female**
    - C50.211   Malignant neoplasm of upper-inner quadrant of right female breast
    - C50.212   Malignant neoplasm of upper-inner quadrant of left female breast
    - C50.219   Malignant neoplasm of upper-inner quadrant of unspecified female breast
  - **C50.22**   **Malignant neoplasm of upper-inner quadrant of breast, male**
    - C50.221   Malignant neoplasm of upper-inner quadrant of right male breast
    - C50.222   Malignant neoplasm of upper-inner quadrant of left male breast
    - C50.229   Malignant neoplasm of upper-inner quadrant of unspecified male breast
- **C50.3**   **Malignant neoplasm of lower-inner quadrant of breast**
  - **C50.31**   **Malignant neoplasm of lower-inner quadrant of breast, female**
    - C50.311   Malignant neoplasm of lower-inner quadrant of right female breast
    - C50.312   Malignant neoplasm of lower-inner quadrant of left female breast
    - C50.319   Malignant neoplasm of lower-inner quadrant of unspecified female breast
  - **C50.32**   **Malignant neoplasm of lower-inner quadrant of breast, male**
    - C50.321   Malignant neoplasm of lower-inner quadrant of right male breast
    - C50.322   Malignant neoplasm of lower-inner quadrant of left male breast
    - C50.329   Malignant neoplasm of lower-inner quadrant of unspecified male breast

- **C50.4**   **Malignant neoplasm of upper-outer quadrant of breast**
  - **C50.41**   **Malignant neoplasm of upper-outer quadrant of breast, female**
    - C50.411   Malignant neoplasm of upper-outer quadrant of right female breast
    - C50.412   Malignant neoplasm of upper-outer quadrant of left female breast
    - C50.419   Malignant neoplasm of upper-outer quadrant of unspecified female breast
  - **C50.42**   **Malignant neoplasm of upper-outer quadrant of breast, male**
    - C50.421   Malignant neoplasm of upper-outer quadrant of right male breast
    - C50.422   Malignant neoplasm of upper-outer quadrant of left male breast
    - C50.429   Malignant neoplasm of upper-outer quadrant of unspecified male breast
- **C50.5**   **Malignant neoplasm of lower-outer quadrant of breast**
  - **C50.51**   **Malignant neoplasm of lower-outer quadrant of breast, female**
    - C50.511   Malignant neoplasm of lower-outer quadrant of right female breast
    - C50.512   Malignant neoplasm of lower-outer quadrant of left female breast
    - C50.519   Malignant neoplasm of lower-outer quadrant of unspecified female breast
  - **C50.52**   **Malignant neoplasm of lower-outer quadrant of breast, male**
    - C50.521   Malignant neoplasm of lower-outer quadrant of right male breast
    - C50.522   Malignant neoplasm of lower-outer quadrant of left male breast
    - C50.529   Malignant neoplasm of lower-outer quadrant of unspecified male breast
- **C50.6**   **Malignant neoplasm of axillary tail of breast**
  - **C50.61**   **Malignant neoplasm of axillary tail of breast, female**
    - C50.611   Malignant neoplasm of axillary tail of right female breast
    - C50.612   Malignant neoplasm of axillary tail of left female breast
    - C50.619   Malignant neoplasm of axillary tail of unspecified female breast
  - **C50.62**   **Malignant neoplasm of axillary tail of breast, male**
    - C50.621   Malignant neoplasm of axillary tail of right male breast
    - C50.622   Malignant neoplasm of axillary tail of left male breast
    - C50.629   Malignant neoplasm of axillary tail of unspecified male breast

● Unacceptable First-Listed Diagnosis   ● Use Additional Character(s)   ▨ Unspecified   **OGCR** Official Guidelines for Coding and Reporting
🅒 Complication\Comorbidity   🅒 Major C\C   Excludes 1   Excludes 2   Includes   Use additional   Code first   Code also

● C50.8 Malignant neoplasm of overlapping sites of breast
- ● C50.81 Malignant neoplasm of overlapping sites of breast, female
  - C50.811 Malignant neoplasm of overlapping sites of right female breast
  - C50.812 Malignant neoplasm of overlapping sites of left female breast
  - ▢C50.819 Malignant neoplasm of overlapping sites of unspecified female breast
- ● C50.82 Malignant neoplasm of overlapping sites of breast, male
  - C50.821 Malignant neoplasm of overlapping sites of right male breast
  - C50.822 Malignant neoplasm of overlapping sites of left male breast
  - ▢C50.829 Malignant neoplasm of overlapping sites of unspecified male breast

● C50.9 Malignant neoplasm of breast of unspecified site
- ● C50.91 Malignant neoplasm of breast of unspecified site, female
  - ▢C50.911 Malignant neoplasm of unspecified site of right female breast
  - ▢C50.912 Malignant neoplasm of unspecified site of left female breast
  - ▢C50.919 Malignant neoplasm of unspecified site of unspecified female breast
- ● C50.92 Malignant neoplasm of breast of unspecified site, male
  - ▢C50.921 Malignant neoplasm of unspecified site of right male breast
  - ▢C50.922 Malignant neoplasm of unspecified site of left male breast
  - ▢C50.929 Malignant neoplasm of unspecified site of unspecified male breast

MALIGNANT NEOPLASM OF FEMALE GENITAL ORGANS (C51-C58)

Includes   malignant neoplasm of skin of female genital organs

● C51 Malignant neoplasm of vulva
> **Excludes1**   carcinoma in situ of vulva (D07.1)

C51.0 Malignant neoplasm of labium majus
Outer folds of skin external female genitalia
Malignant neoplasm of Bartholin's [greater vestibular] gland

C51.1 Malignant neoplasm of labium minus
Two inner folds surrounding vulva in female genitalia

C51.2 Malignant neoplasm of clitoris

C51.8 Malignant neoplasm of overlapping sites of vulva

▢C51.9 Malignant neoplasm of vulva, unspecified
Malignant neoplasm of external female genitalia NOS
Malignant neoplasm of pudendum

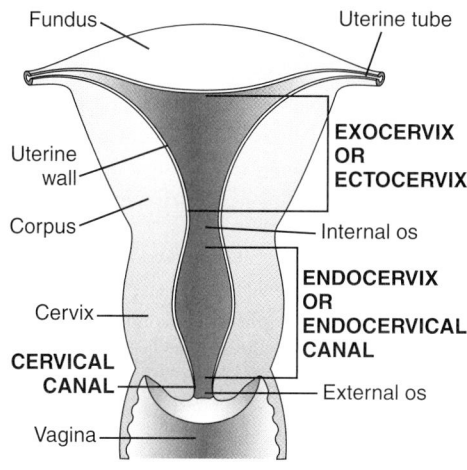

Figure 2-13   Cervix uteri.

C52 Malignant neoplasm of vagina
> **Excludes1**   carcinoma in situ of vagina (D07.2)

● C53 Malignant neoplasm of cervix uteri
> **Excludes1**   carcinoma in situ of cervix uteri (D06.-)

C53.0 Malignant neoplasm of endocervix
Inside the cervix

C53.1 Malignant neoplasm of exocervix
Outside the cervix

C53.8 Malignant neoplasm of overlapping sites of cervix uteri

▢C53.9 Malignant neoplasm of cervix uteri, unspecified

● C54 Malignant neoplasm of corpus uteri
C54.0 Malignant neoplasm of isthmus uteri
Constricted part of uterus between cervix and body
Malignant neoplasm of lower uterine segment

C54.1 Malignant neoplasm of endometrium
Lining of uterus

C54.2 Malignant neoplasm of myometrium
Middle layer of uterine wall consisting of smooth muscle supporting stromal and vascular tissue

C54.3 Malignant neoplasm of fundus uteri
Top rounded portion of uterus

C54.8 Malignant neoplasm of overlapping sites of corpus uteri
Main body of uterus

▢C54.9 Malignant neoplasm of corpus uteri, unspecified

▢C55 Malignant neoplasm of uterus, part unspecified

● C56 Malignant neoplasm of ovary
Use additional code to identify any functional activity
C56.0 Malignant neoplasm of right ovary 🅒
C56.1 Malignant neoplasm of left ovary 🅒
▢C56.9 Malignant neoplasm of ovary, unspecified side 🅒

● C57 Malignant neoplasm of other and unspecified female genital organs
- ● C57.0 Malignant neoplasm of fallopian tube
  Malignant neoplasm of oviduct
  Malignant neoplasm of uterine tube
  - ▢C57.00 Malignant neoplasm of fallopian tube, unspecified side
  - C57.01 Malignant neoplasm of right fallopian tube
  - C57.02 Malignant neoplasm of left fallopian tube

● Unacceptable First-Listed Diagnosis   ● Use Additional Character(s)   ▢ Unspecified   **OGCR** Official Guidelines for Coding and Reporting
🅒 Complication\Comorbidity   🅒 Major C\C   Excludes 1   Excludes 2   Includes   Use additional   Code first   Code also   833
CHAPTER 2 (C00-D49)

● C57.1 Malignant neoplasm of broad ligament

■ C57.10 Malignant neoplasm of broad ligament, unspecified side

C57.11 Malignant neoplasm of right broad ligament

C57.12 Malignant neoplasm of left broad ligament

● C57.2 Malignant neoplasm of round ligament

■ C57.20 Malignant neoplasm of round ligament, unspecified side

C57.21 Malignant neoplasm of right round ligament

C57.22 Malignant neoplasm of left round ligament

C57.3 Malignant neoplasm of parametrium
Malignant neoplasm of uterine ligament NOS

■ C57.4 Malignant neoplasm of uterine adnexa, unspecified

C57.7 Malignant neoplasm of other specified female genital organs
Malignant neoplasm of wolffian body or duct

C57.8 Malignant neoplasm of overlapping sites of female genital organs
Primary malignant neoplams of two or more contiguous sites of the female genital organs whose point of origin cannot be determined
Primary tubo-ovarian malignant neoplasm whose point of origin cannot be determined
Primary utero-ovarian malignant neoplasm whose point of origin cannot be determined

■ C57.9 Malignant neoplasm of female genital organ, unspecified
Malignant neoplasm of female genitourinary tract NOS

C58 Malignant neoplasm of placenta

> **Includes**   choriocarcinoma NOS
> chorionepithelioma NOS

> **Excludes1**   chorioadenoma (destruens) (D39.2)
> hydatidiform mole NOS (O01.9)
> invasive hydatidiform mole (D39.2)
> male choriocarcinoma NOS (C62.9-)
> malignant hydatidiform mole (D39.2)

MALIGNANT NEOPLASMS OF MALE GENITAL ORGANS (C60-C63)

> **Includes**   malignant neoplasm of skin of male genital organs

● C60 Malignant neoplasm of penis

C60.0 Malignant neoplasm of prepuce
Malignant neoplasm of foreskin

C60.1 Malignant neoplasm of glans penis

C60.2 Malignant neoplasm of body of penis
Malignant neoplasm of corpus cavernosum

C60.8 Malignant neoplasm of overlapping sites of penis

■ C60.9 Malignant neoplasm of penis, unspecified
Malignant neoplasm of skin of penis NOS

C61 Malignant neoplasm of prostate

> **Excludes1**   malignant neoplasm of seminal vesicle (C63.7)

● C62 Malignant neoplasm of testis
Use additional code to identify any functional activity.

● C62.0 Malignant neoplasm of undescended testis
Malignant neoplasm of ectopic testis
Malignant neoplasm of retained testis

■ C62.00 Malignant neoplasm of undescended testis, unspecified side

C62.01 Malignant neoplasm of undescended right testis

C62.02 Malignant neoplasm of undescended left testis

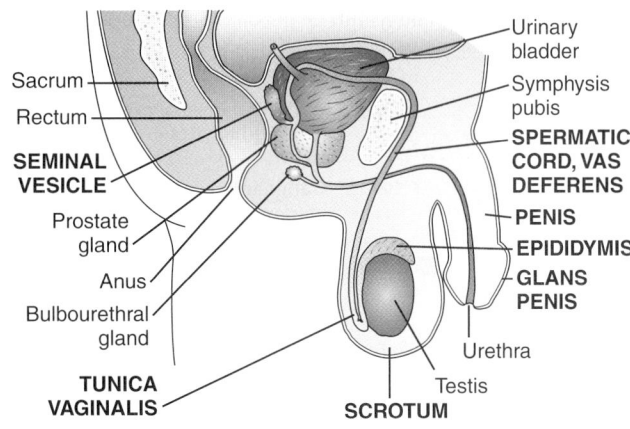

Figure 2-14 Penis and other male genital organs.

● C62.1 Malignant neoplasm of descended testis
Malignant neoplasm of scrotal testis

■ C62.10 Malignant neoplasm of descended testis, unspecified side

C62.11 Malignant neoplasm of descended right testis

C62.12 Malignant neoplasm of descended left testis

● C62.9 Malignant neoplasm of testis, unspecified

■ C62.90 Malignant neoplasm of testis, unspecified, unspecified side

■ C62.91 Malignant neoplasm of right testis, unspecified

■ C62.92 Malignant neoplasm of left testis, unspecified

● C63 Malignant neoplasm of other and unspecified male genital organs

● C63.0 Malignant neoplasm of epididymis

■ C63.00 Malignant neoplasm of epididymis, unspecified side

C63.01 Malignant neoplasm of right epididymis

C63.02 Malignant neoplasm of left epididymis

● C63.1 Malignant neoplasm of spermatic cord

■ C63.10 Malignant neoplasm of spermatic cord, unspecified side

C63.11 Malignant neoplasm of right spermatic cord

C63.12 Malignant neoplasm of left spermatic cord

C63.2 Malignant neoplasm of scrotum
Malignant neoplasm of skin of scrotum

C63.7 Malignant neoplasm of other specified male genital organs
Malignant neoplasm of seminal vesicle
Malignant neoplasm of tunica vaginalis

C63.8 Malignant neoplasm of overlapping sites of male genital organs
Primary malignant neoplasm of two or more contiguous sites of male genital organs whose point of origin cannot be determined

■ C63.9 Malignant neoplasm of male genital organ, unspecified
Malignant neoplasm of male genitourinary tract NOS

● Unacceptable First-Listed Diagnosis   ● Use Additional Character(s)   ■ Unspecified   **OGCR** Official Guidelines for Coding and Reporting
 Complication\Comorbidity   Major C\C   Excludes 1   Excludes 2   Includes   Use additional   Code first   Code also

MALIGNANT NEOPLASM OF URINARY TRACT (C64-C68)

● **C64 Malignant neoplasm of kidney, except renal pelvis**

    Excludes1   malignant carcinoid tumor of the kidney (C7a.093)
        malignant neoplasm of renal calyces (C65.-)
        malignant neoplasm of renal pelvis (C65.-)

   C64.0   Malignant neoplasm of right kidney, except renal pelvis 🗘

   C64.1   Malignant neoplasm of left kidney, except renal pelvis 🗘

   C64.9   Malignant neoplasm of kidney, except renal pelvis, unspecified side 🗘

● **C65 Malignant neoplasm of renal pelvis**

    Includes   malignant neoplasm of pelviureteric junction
        malignant neoplasm of renal calyces

   C65.0   Malignant neoplasm of right renal pelvis 🗘

   C65.1   Malignant neoplasm of left renal pelvis 🗘

   C65.9   Malignant neoplasm of renal pelvis, unspecified side 🗘

● **C66 Malignant neoplasm of ureter**

    Excludes1   malignant neoplasm of ureteric orifice of bladder (C67.6)

   C66.0   Malignant neoplasm of right ureter 🗘

   C66.1   Malignant neoplasm of left ureter 🗘

   C66.9   Malignant neoplasm of ureter, unspecified side 🗘

● **C67 Malignant neoplasm of bladder**

   C67.0   Malignant neoplasm of trigone of bladder
       Triangular area formed by three openings in the floor of urinary bladder

   C67.1   Malignant neoplasm of dome of bladder
       Vaulted roof

   C67.2   Malignant neoplasm of lateral wall of bladder
       Side walls

   C67.3   Malignant neoplasm of anterior wall of bladder
       Front wall

   C67.4   Malignant neoplasm of posterior wall of bladder
       Back wall

   C67.5   Malignant neoplasm of bladder neck
       Joining of bladder and urethra
       Malignant neoplasm of internal urethral orifice

   C67.6   Malignant neoplasm of ureteric orifice
       Opening from bladder to ureters

   C67.7   Malignant neoplasm of urachus
       Embryonic canal that connects the urinary bladder with the structure that forms the umbilical cord (allantois)

   C67.8   Malignant neoplasm of overlapping sites of bladder

   C67.9   Malignant neoplasm of bladder, unspecified

● **C68 Malignant neoplasm of other and unspecified urinary organs**

    Excludes1   malignant neoplasm of female genitourinary tract NOS (C57.9)
        malignant neoplasm of male genitourinary tract NOS (C63.9)

   C68.0   Malignant neoplasm of urethra 🗘
      Excludes1   malignant neoplasm of urethral orifice of bladder (C67.5)

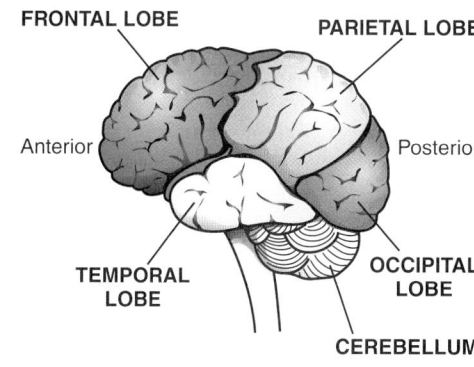

Figure 2-15 The brain.

   C68.1   Malignant neoplasm of paraurethral glands 🗘
       Group of glands of female urethra drained by paraurethral ducts; AKA Skene glands, female prostate

   C68.8   Malignant neoplasm of overlapping sites of urinary organs 🗘
       Primary malignant neoplasm of two or more contiguous sites of urinary organs whose point of origin cannot be determined

   C68.9   Malignant neoplasm of urinary organ, unspecified 🗘
       Malignant neoplasm of urinary system NOS

MALIGNANT NEOPLASMS OF EYE, BRAIN AND OTHER PARTS OF CENTRAL NERVOUS SYSTEM (C69-C72)

● **C69 Malignant neoplasm of eye and adnexa**

    Excludes1   malignant neoplasm of connective tissue of eyelid (C49.0)
        malignant neoplasm of eyelid (skin) (C43.1-, C44.1-)
        malignant neoplasm of optic nerve (C72.3-)

●   C69.0   Malignant neoplasm of conjunctiva

    C69.00   Malignant neoplasm of conjunctiva, unspecified side

    C69.01   Malignant neoplasm of right conjunctiva

    C69.02   Malignant neoplasm of left conjunctiva

●   C69.1   Malignant neoplasm of cornea

    C69.10   Malignant neoplasm of cornea, unspecified side

    C69.11   Malignant neoplasm of right cornea

    C69.12   Malignant neoplasm of left cornea

●   C69.2   Malignant neoplasm of retina

    Excludes1   dark area on retina (D49.81)
        neoplasm of unspecified behavior of retina and choroid (D49.81)
        retinal freckle (D49.81)

    C69.20   Malignant neoplasm of retina, unspecified side

    C69.21   Malignant neoplasm of right retina

    C69.22   Malignant neoplasm of left retina

●   C69.3   Malignant neoplasm of choroid

    C69.30   Malignant neoplasm of choroid, unspecified side

    C69.31   Malignant neoplasm of right choroid

    C69.32   Malignant neoplasm of left choroid

● Unacceptable First-Listed Diagnosis   ● Use Additional Character(s)   ▨ Unspecified   **OGCR** Official Guidelines for Coding and Reporting
🗘 Complication\Comorbidity   🗘 Major C\C   Excludes 1   Excludes 2   Includes   Use additional   Code first   Code also

CHAPTER 2 (C00-D49)   835

● **C69.4 Malignant neoplasm of ciliary body**
    Malignant neoplasm of eyeball

    ■**C69.40 Malignant neoplasm of ciliary body, unspecified side**

    C69.41 Malignant neoplasm of right ciliary body

    C69.42 Malignant neoplasm of left ciliary body

● **C69.5 Malignant neoplasm of lacrimal gland and duct**
    Malignant neoplasm of lacrimal sac
    Malignant neoplasm of nasolacrimal duct

    ■**C69.50 Malignant neoplasm of lacrimal gland and duct, unspecified side**

    C69.51 Malignant neoplasm of right lacrimal gland and duct

    C69.52 Malignant neoplasm of left lacrimal gland and duct

● **C69.6 Malignant neoplasm of orbit**
    Malignant neoplasm of connective tissue of orbit
    Malignant neoplasm of extraocular muscle
    Malignant neoplasm of peripheral nerves of orbit
    Malignant neoplasm of retrobulbar tissue
    Malignant neoplasm of retro-ocular tissue

    Excludes1 malignant neoplasm of orbital bone (C41.0)

    ■**C69.60 Malignant neoplasm of orbit, unspecified side**

    C69.61 Malignant neoplasm of right orbit

    C69.62 Malignant neoplasm of left orbit

● **C69.8 Malignant neoplasm of overlapping sites of eye and adnexa**

    ■**C69.80 Malignant neoplasm of overlapping sites of eye and adnexa, unspecified side**

    C69.81 Malignant neoplasm of overlapping sites of right eye and adnexa

    C69.82 Malignant neoplasm of overlapping sites of left eye and adnexa

● **C69.9 Malignant neoplasm of eye, unspecified**

    ■**C69.90 Malignant neoplasm of eye, unspecified, unspecified side**

    ■**C69.91 Malignant neoplasm of right eye, unspecified**

    ■**C69.92 Malignant neoplasm of left eye, unspecified**

● **C70 Malignant neoplasm of meninges**

    C70.0 Malignant neoplasm of cerebral meninges &

    C70.1 Malignant neoplasm of spinal meninges &

    ■**C70.9 Malignant neoplasm of meninges, unspecified** &

● **C71 Malignant neoplasm of brain**

    Excludes1 malignant neoplasm of cranial nerves (C72.2-C72.5)
       retrobulbar malignant neoplasm (C69.6-)

    C71.0 Malignant neoplasm of cerebrum, except lobes and ventricles &
    Malignant neoplasm of supratentorial NOS

    C71.1 Malignant neoplasm of frontal lobe &

    C71.2 Malignant neoplasm of temporal lobe &

    C71.3 Malignant neoplasm of parietal lobe &

    C71.4 Malignant neoplasm of occipital lobe &

    C71.5 Malignant neoplasm of cerebral ventricle &

    Excludes1 malignant neoplasm of fourth cerebral ventricle (C71.7)

    C71.6 Malignant neoplasm of cerebellum &

C71.7 Malignant neoplasm of brain stem &
    Malignant neoplasm of fourth cerebral ventricle
    Infratentorial malignant neoplasm NOS

C71.8 Malignant neoplasm of overlapping sites of brain &

■**C71.9 Malignant neoplasm of brain, unspecified** &

● **C72 Malignant neoplasm of spinal cord, cranial nerves and other parts of central nervous system**

    Excludes1 malignant neoplasm of meninges (C70.-)
       malignant neoplasm of peripheral nerves and autonomic nervous system (C47.-)

C72.0 Malignant neoplasm of spinal cord &

C72.1 Malignant neoplasm of cauda equina &
    Lower end of spinal column

● **C72.2 Malignant neoplasm of olfactory nerve**
    Malignant neoplasm of olfactory bulb

    ■**C72.20 Malignant neoplasm of olfactory nerve, unspecified side** &

    C72.21 Malignant neoplasm of right olfactory nerve &

    C72.22 Malignant neoplasm of left olfactory nerve &

● **C72.3 Malignant neoplasm of optic nerve**

    ■**C72.30 Malignant neoplasm of optic nerve, unspecified side** &

    C72.31 Malignant neoplasm of right optic nerve &

    C72.32 Malignant neoplasm of left optic nerve &

● **C72.4 Malignant neoplasm of acoustic nerve**

    ■**C72.40 Malignant neoplasm of acoustic nerve, unspecified side** &

    C72.41 Malignant neoplasm of right acoustic nerve &

    C72.42 Malignant neoplasm of left acoustic nerve &

● **C72.5 Malignant neoplasm of other and unspecified cranial nerves**

    ■**C72.50 Malignant neoplasm of unspecified cranial nerve** &
    Malignant neoplasm of cranial nerve NOS

    C72.59 Malignant neoplasm of other cranial nerves &

■**C72.9 Malignant neoplasm of central nervous system, unspecified** &
    Malignant neoplasm of nervous system NOS

MALIGNANT NEOPLASM OF THYROID AND OTHER ENDOCRINE GLANDS (C73-C75)

C73 Malignant neoplasm of thyroid gland
    Use additional code to identify any functional activity

● **C74 Malignant neoplasm of adrenal gland**

    ● **C74.0 Malignant neoplasm of cortex of adrenal gland**

       ■**C74.00 Malignant neoplasm of cortex of adrenal gland, unspecified side** &

       C74.01 Malignant neoplasm of cortex of right adrenal gland &

       C74.02 Malignant neoplasm of cortex of left adrenal gland &

    ● **C74.1 Malignant neoplasm of medulla of adrenal gland**
    Pair of glands situated on top of or above each kidney ("suprarenal")

       ■**C74.10 Malignant neoplasm of medulla of adrenal gland, unspecified side** &

       C74.11 Malignant neoplasm of medulla of right adrenal gland &

       C74.12 Malignant neoplasm of medulla of left adrenal gland &

CHAPTER 2 (C00-D49)

● Unacceptable First-Listed Diagnosis　● Use Additional Character(s)　■ Unspecified　OGCR Official Guidelines for Coding and Reporting
& Complication\Comorbidity　& Major C\C　Excludes 1　Excludes 2　Includes　Use additional　Code first　Code also

● C74.9   Malignant neoplasm of adrenal gland, unspecified

    ■ C74.90   Malignant neoplasm of adrenal gland, unspecified, unspecified side 🕭

    ■ C74.91   Malignant neoplasm of right adrenal gland, unspecified 🕭

    ■ C74.92   Malignant neoplasm of left adrenal gland, unspecified 🕭

● C75   Malignant neoplasm of other endocrine glands and related structures

    | Excludes1 | malignant carcinoid tumors (C7a.0-)
                    malignant neoplasm of adrenal gland (C74.-)
                    malignant neoplasm of endocrine pancreas (C25.4)
                    malignant neoplasm of islets of Langerhans (C25.4)
                    malignant neoplasm of ovary (C56-)
                    malignant neoplasm of testis (C62.-)
                    malignant neoplasm of thymus (C37)
                    malignant neoplasm of thyroid gland (C73)
                    malignant neuroendocrine tumors (C7a.-)

    C75.0   Malignant neoplasm of parathyroid gland 🕭

    C75.1   Malignant neoplasm of pituitary gland 🕭

    C75.2   Malignant neoplasm of craniopharyngeal duct 🕭

    C75.3   Malignant neoplasm of pineal gland 🕭

    C75.4   Malignant neoplasm of carotid body 🕭

    C75.5   Malignant neoplasm of aortic body and other paraganglia 🕭

    ■ C75.8   Malignant neoplasm with pluriglandular involvement, unspecified 🕭

    ■ C75.9   Malignant neoplasm of endocrine gland, unspecified 🕭

MALIGNANT NEUROENDOCRINE TUMORS (C7A)

● C7a   Malignant neuroendocrine tumors

    Code also any associated multiple endocrine neoplasia [MEN] syndromes (E31.2-)

    Use additional code to identify any associated endocrine syndrome, such as:
      carcinoid syndrome (E34.0)

    | Excludes2 | malignant pancreatic islet cell tumors (C25.4)
                    Merkel cell carcinoma (C4a.-)

    ● C7a.0   Malignant carcinoid tumors

       ■ C7a.00   Malignant carcinoid tumor of unspecified site

       ● C7a.01   Malignant carcinoid tumors of the small intestine

         C7a.010   Malignant carcinoid tumor of the duodenum

         C7a.011   Malignant carcinoid tumor of the jejunum

         C7a.012   Malignant carcinoid tumor of the ileum

         ■ C7a.019   Malignant carcinoid tumor of the small intestine, unspecified portion

       ● C7a.02   Malignant carcinoid tumors of the appendix, large intestine, and rectum

         C7a.020   Malignant carcinoid tumor of the appendix

         C7a.021   Malignant carcinoid tumor of the cecum

         C7a.022   Malignant carcinoid tumor of the ascending colon

         C7a.023   Malignant carcinoid tumor of the transverse colon

         C7a.024   Malignant carcinoid tumor of the descending colon

         C7a.025   Malignant carcinoid tumor of the sigmoid colon

         C7a.026   Malignant carcinoid tumor of the rectum

         ■ C7a.029   Malignant carcinoid tumor of the large intestine, unspecified portion
                Malignant carcinoid tumor of the colon NOS

       ● C7a.09   Malignant carcinoid tumors of other sites

         C7a.090   Malignant carcinoid tumor of the bronchus and lung

         C7a.091   Malignant carcinoid tumor of the thymus

         C7a.092   Malignant carcinoid tumor of the stomach

         C7a.093   Malignant carcinoid tumor of the kidney

         C7a.094   Malignant carcinoid tumor of the foregut NOS

         C7a.095   Malignant carcinoid tumor of the midgut NOS

         C7a.096   Malignant carcinoid tumor of the hindgut NOS

         C7a.098   Malignant carcinoid tumors of other sites

    C7a.1   Malignant poorly differentiated neuroendocrine tumors
       Malignant poorly differentiated neuroendocrine tumor NOS
       Malignant poorly differentiated neuroendocrine carcinoma, any site
       High grade neuroendocrine carcinoma, any site

    C7a.8   Other malignant neuroendocrine tumors
       Secondary neuroendocrine tumors (C7b)

● C7b   Secondary neuroendocrine tumors

    Use additional code to identify any functional activity

    ● C7b.0   Secondary carcinoid tumors

       ■ C7b.00   Secondary carcinoid tumors, unspecified site

       C7b.01   Secondary carcinoid tumors of distant lymph nodes
         Mesentary metastasis of carcinoid tumor

       C7b.02   Secondary carcinoid tumors of liver

       C7b.03   Secondary carcinoid tumors of bone

       C7b.04   Secondary carcinoid tumors of peritoneum

       C7b.09   Secondary carcinoid tumors of other sites

    C7b.1   Secondary Merkel cell carcinoma
       Merkel cell carcinoma nodal presentation
       Merkel cell carcinoma visceral metastatic presentation

    C7b.8   Other secondary neuroendocrine tumors

● Unacceptable First-Listed Diagnosis   ● Use Additional Character(s)   ■ Unspecified   **OGCR** Official Guidelines for Coding and Reporting

🕭 Complication\Comorbidity   🕭 Major C\C | Excludes 1 | | Excludes 2 | Includes   Use additional   Code first   Code also   837

MALIGNANT NEOPLASMS OF ILL-DEFINED, SECONDARY AND UNSPECIFIED SITES (C76-C80)

● **C76 Malignant neoplasm of other and ill-defined sites**

> **Excludes1**   malignant neoplasm of female genitourinary tract NOS (C57.9)
> malignant neoplasm of male genitourinary tract NOS (C63.9)
> malignant neoplasm of lymphoid, hematopoietic and related tissue (C81-C96)
> malignant neoplasm of skin (C44.-)
> malignant neoplasm of unspecified site NOS (C80.1)

C76.0 Malignant neoplasm of head, face and neck
Malignant neoplasm of cheek NOS
Malignant neoplasm of nose NOS

C76.1 Malignant neoplasm of thorax
Intrathoracic malignant neoplasm NOS
Malignant neoplasm of axilla NOS
Thoracic malignant neoplasm NOS

C76.2 Malignant neoplasm of abdomen

C76.3 Malignant neoplasm of pelvis
Malignant neoplasm of groin NOS
Malignant neoplasm of sites overlapping systems within the pelvis
Rectovaginal (septum) malignant neoplasm
Between rectum and vagina
Rectovesical (septum) malignant neoplasm
Between rectum and urinary bladder; AKA vesicorectal

● **C76.4 Malignant neoplasm of upper limb**

■ **C76.40 Malignant neoplasm of upper limb, unspecified side**

C76.41 Malignant neoplasm of right upper limb

C76.42 Malignant neoplasm of left upper limb

● **C76.5 Malignant neoplasm of lower limb**

■ **C76.50 Malignant neoplasm of lower limb, unspecified side**

C76.51 Malignant neoplasm of right lower limb

C76.52 Malignant neoplasm of left lower limb

C76.7 Malignant neoplasm of other ill-defined sites

● **C77 Secondary and unspecified malignant neoplasm of lymph nodes**

> **Excludes1**   malignant neoplasm of lymph nodes, specified as primary (C81-C88, C96.-)
> mesentery metastasis of carcinoid tumor (C7b.01)
> secondary carcinoid tumors of distant lymph nodes (C7b.01)

■ **C77.0 Secondary and unspecified malignant neoplasm of lymph nodes of head, face and neck** 🧬
Secondary and unspecified malignant neoplasm of supraclavicular lymph nodes

■ **C77.1 Secondary and unspecified malignant neoplasm of intrathoracic lymph nodes** 🧬

■ **C77.2 Secondary and unspecified malignant neoplasm of intra-abdominal lymph nodes** 🧬

■ **C77.3 Secondary and unspecified malignant neoplasm of axilla and upper limb lymph nodes** 🧬
Secondary and unspecified malignant neoplasm of pectoral lymph nodes

■ **C77.4 Secondary and unspecified malignant neoplasm of inguinal and lower limb lymph nodes** 🧬

■ **C77.5 Secondary and unspecified malignant neoplasm of intrapelvic lymph nodes** 🧬

■ **C77.8 Secondary and unspecified malignant neoplasm of lymph nodes of multiple regions** 🧬

■ **C77.9 Secondary and unspecified malignant neoplasm of lymph node, unspecified** 🧬

● **C78 Secondary malignant neoplasm of respiratory and digestive organs**

> **Excludes1**   lymph node metastases (C77.0)
> secondary carcinoid tumors of liver (C7b.02)
> secondary carcinoid tumors of peritoneum (C7b.04)

● **C78.0 Secondary malignant neoplasm of lung**

■ **C78.00 Secondary malignant neoplasm of lung, unspecified side** 🧬

C78.01 Secondary malignant neoplasm of right lung 🧬

C78.02 Secondary malignant neoplasm of left lung 🧬

C78.1 Secondary malignant neoplasm of mediastinum 🧬
Thoracic cavity between pleural cavities

C78.2 Secondary malignant neoplasm of pleura 🧬
Serous membrane covering lungs and lining thoracic cavity

● **C78.3 Secondary malignant neoplasm of other and unspecified respiratory organs**

■ **C78.30 Secondary malignant neoplasm of unspecified respiratory organ** 🧬

C78.39 Secondary malignant neoplasm of other respiratory organs 🧬

C78.4 Secondary malignant neoplasm of small intestine 🧬

C78.5 Secondary malignant neoplasm of large intestine and rectum 🧬

C78.6 Secondary malignant neoplasm of retroperitoneum and peritoneum 🧬

C78.7 Secondary malignant neoplasm of liver and intrahepatic bile duct 🧬

● **C78.8 Secondary malignant neoplasm of other and unspecified digestive organs**

■ **C78.80 Secondary malignant neoplasm of unspecified digestive organ** 🧬

C78.89 Secondary malignant neoplasm of other digestive organs 🧬

● **C79 Secondary malignant neoplasm of other sites**

> **Excludes1**   lymph node metastases (C77.0)
> secondary carcinoid tumors (C7b.-)
> secondary neuroendocrine tumors (C7b.-)

● **C79.0 Secondary malignant neoplasm of kidney and renal pelvis**

■ **C79.00 Secondary malignant neoplasm of kidney and renal pelvis, unspecified side** 🧬

C79.01 Secondary malignant neoplasm of right kidney and renal pelvis 🧬

C79.02 Secondary malignant neoplasm of left kidney and renal pelvis 🧬

● **C79.1 Secondary malignant neoplasm of bladder and other and unspecified urinary organs**

■ **C79.10 Secondary malignant neoplasm of unspecified urinary organs** 🧬

C79.11 Secondary malignant neoplasm of bladder 🧬

C79.19 Secondary malignant neoplasm of other urinary organs 🧬

● Unacceptable First-Listed Diagnosis   ● Use Additional Character(s)   ■ Unspecified   **OGCR** Official Guidelines for Coding and Reporting
🧬 Complication\Comorbidity   🧬 Major C\C   Excludes 1   Excludes 2   Includes   Use additional   Code first   Code also

Item 2–6　The adrenal glands are a pair of glands situated on top of or above each kidney ("suprarenal") and chiefly responsible for regulating the stress response through the synthesis of corticosteroids and catecholamines, including cortisol and adrenaline.

C79.2　**Secondary malignant neoplasm of skin** 🗲
> **Excludes1**　secondary Merkel cell carcinoma (C7b.1)

● **C79.3**　**Secondary malignant neoplasm of brain and cerebral meninges**

　　C79.31　Secondary malignant neoplasm of brain 🗲

　　C79.32　Secondary malignant neoplasm of cerebral meninges 🗲

● **C79.4**　**Secondary malignant neoplasm of other and unspecified parts of nervous system**

　　■ **C79.40**　Secondary malignant neoplasm of unspecified part of nervous system 🗲

　　C79.49　Secondary malignant neoplasm of other parts of nervous system 🗲

● **C79.5**　**Secondary malignant neoplasm of bone and bone marrow**
> **Excludes1**　secondary carcinoid tumors of bone (C7b.03)

　　C79.51　Secondary malignant neoplasm of bone 🗲

　　C79.52　Secondary malignant neoplasm of bone marrow 🗲

● **C79.6**　**Secondary malignant neoplasm of ovary**

　　■ **C79.60**　Secondary malignant neoplasm of ovary, unspecified side 🗲

　　C79.61　Secondary malignant neoplasm of right ovary 🗲

　　C79.62　Secondary malignant neoplasm of left ovary 🗲

● **C79.7**　**Secondary malignant neoplasm of adrenal gland**

　　■ **C79.70**　Secondary malignant neoplasm of adrenal gland, unspecified side 🗲

　　C79.71　Secondary malignant neoplasm of right adrenal gland 🗲

　　C79.72　Secondary malignant neoplasm of left adrenal gland 🗲

● **C79.8**　**Secondary malignant neoplasm of other specified sites**

　　C79.81　Secondary malignant neoplasm of breast 🗲

　　C79.82　Secondary malignant neoplasm of genital organs 🗲

　　C79.89　Secondary malignant neoplasm of other specified sites 🗲

■ **C79.9**　**Secondary malignant neoplasm of unspecified site** 🗲
　　Metastatic cancer NOS
　　Metastatic disease NOS
> **Excludes1**　carcinomatosis NOS (C80.0)
> generalized cancer NOS (C80.0)
> malignant (primary) neoplasm of unspecified site (C80.1)

OGCR　Section I.C.2.j and k

Disseminated malignant neoplasm, unspecified

j. Code C80.0, Disseminated malignant neoplasm, unspecified, is for use only in those cases where the patient has advanced metastatic disease and no known primary or secondary sites are specified. It should not be used in place of assigning codes for the primary site and all known secondary sites.

Malignant neoplasm without specification of site

k. Code C80.1, Malignant neoplasm, unspecified, equates to Cancer, unspecified. This code should only be used when no determination can be made as to the primary site of a malignancy. This code should rarely be used in the inpatient setting.

● **C80**　**Malignant neoplasm without specification of site**
> **Excludes1**　malignant carcinoid tumor of unspecified site (C7a.00)
> malignant neoplasm of specified multiple sites-code to each site

　■ **C80.0**　**Disseminated malignant neoplasm, unspecified** 🗲
　　Carcinomatosis NOS
　　Generalized cancer, unspecified site (primary) (secondary)
　　Generalized malignancy, unspecified site (primary) (secondary)

　■ **C80.1**　**Malignant (primary) neoplasm, unspecified**
　　Cancer NOS
　　Cancer unspecified site (primary)
　　Carcinoma unspecified site (primary)
　　Malignancy unspecified site (primary)
> **Excludes1**　secondary malignant neoplasm of unspecified site (C79.9)

　C80.2　**Malignant neoplasm associated with transplanted organ**
　　Code first complication of transplanted organ (T86.-)
　　Use additional code to identify the specific malignancy

(See Plate 315 on page NAP-1.)

MALIGNANT NEOPLASMS OF LYMPHOID, HEMATOPOIETIC AND RELATED TISSUE (C81-C96)

> **Excludes2**　Kaposi's sarcoma of lymph nodes (C46.3)
> secondary and unspecified neoplasm of lymph nodes (C77.-)
> secondary neoplasm of bone marrow (C79.52)
> secondary neoplasm of spleen (C78.89)

● **C81**　**Hodgkin lymphoma**
　　Form of malignant lymphoma with four types, nodular sclerosis, mixed cellularity, lymphocyte depleted, and lymphocyte predominant
> **Excludes1**　personal history of Hodgkin lymphoma (Z85.71)

● **C81.0**　**Nodular lymphocyte predominant Hodgkin lymphoma**
　　Least aggressive, least common, typically no symptoms
　　Lymphocytic-histiocytic predominance Hodgkin's disease

　　■ **C81.00**　Nodular lymphocyte predominant Hodgkin lymphoma, unspecified site 🗲

　　C81.01　Nodular lymphocyte predominant Hodgkin lymphoma, lymph nodes of head, face, and neck 🗲

　　C81.02　Nodular lymphocyte predominant Hodgkin lymphoma, intrathoracic lymph nodes 🗲

● Unacceptable First-Listed Diagnosis　　● Use Additional Character(s)　　■ Unspecified　　**OGCR** Official Guidelines for Coding and Reporting

🗲 Complication\Comorbidity　　🗲 Major C\C　　Excludes 1　　Excludes 2　　Includes　　Use additional　　Code first　　Code also

839

C81.03 Nodular lymphocyte predominant Hodgkin lymphoma, intra-abdominal lymph nodes 🦀

C81.04 Nodular lymphocyte predominant Hodgkin lymphoma, lymph nodes of axilla and upper limb 🦀

C81.05 Nodular lymphocyte predominant Hodgkin lymphoma, lymph nodes of inguinal region and lower limb 🦀

C81.06 Nodular lymphocyte predominant Hodgkin lymphoma, intrapelvic lymph nodes 🦀

C81.07 Nodular lymphocyte predominant Hodgkin lymphoma, spleen 🦀

C81.08 Nodular lymphocyte predominant Hodgkin lymphoma, lymph nodes of multiple sites 🦀

C81.09 Nodular lymphocyte predominant Hodgkin lymphoma, extranodal and solid organ sites 🦀

● C81.1 Nodular sclerosis classical Hodgkin lymphoma
Moderately aggressive; most common in young adults

▪ C81.10 Nodular sclerosis classical Hodgkin lymphoma, unspecified site 🦀

C81.11 Nodular sclerosis classical Hodgkin lymphoma, lymph nodes of head, face, and neck 🦀

C81.12 Nodular sclerosis classical Hodgkin lymphoma, intrathoracic lymph nodes 🦀

C81.13 Nodular sclerosis classical Hodgkin lymphoma, intra-abdominal lymph nodes 🦀

C81.14 Nodular sclerosis classical Hodgkin lymphoma, lymph nodes of axilla and upper limb 🦀

C81.15 Nodular sclerosis classical Hodgkin lymphoma, lymph nodes of inguinal region and lower limb 🦀

C81.16 Nodular sclerosis classical Hodgkin lymphoma, intrapelvic lymph nodes 🦀

C81.17 Nodular sclerosis classical Hodgkin lymphoma, spleen 🦀

C81.18 Nodular sclerosis classical Hodgkin lymphoma, lymph nodes of multiple sites 🦀

C81.19 Nodular sclerosis classical Hodgkin lymphoma, extranodal and solid organ sites 🦀

● C81.2 Mixed cellularity classical Hodgkin lymphoma
A type of Hodgkin's that is moderately aggressive with mixed cell types

▪ C81.20 Mixed cellularity classical Hodgkin lymphoma, unspecified site 🦀

C81.21 Mixed cellularity classical Hodgkin lymphoma, lymph nodes of head, face, and neck 🦀

C81.22 Mixed cellularity classical Hodgkin lymphoma, intrathoracic lymph nodes 🦀

C81.23 Mixed cellularity classical Hodgkin lymphoma, intra-abdominal lymph nodes 🦀

C81.24 Mixed cellularity classical Hodgkin lymphoma, lymph nodes of axilla and upper limb 🦀

C81.25 Mixed cellularity classical Hodgkin lymphoma, lymph nodes of inguinal region and lower limb 🦀

C81.26 Mixed cellularity classical Hodgkin lymphoma, intrapelvic lymph nodes 🦀

C81.27 Mixed cellularity classical Hodgkin lymphoma, spleen 🦀

C81.28 Mixed cellularity classical Hodgkin lymphoma, lymph nodes of multiple sites 🦀

C81.29 Mixed cellularity classical Hodgkin lymphoma, extranodal and solid organ sites 🦀

● C81.3 Lymphocytic depletion classical Hodgkin lymphoma
Most aggressive type with poor prognosis

▪ C81.30 Lymphocytic depletion classical Hodgkin lymphoma, unspecified site 🦀

C81.31 Lymphocytic depletion classical Hodgkin lymphoma, lymph nodes of head, face, and neck 🦀

C81.32 Lymphocytic depletion classical Hodgkin lymphoma, intrathoracic lymph nodes 🦀

C81.33 Lymphocytic depletion classical Hodgkin lymphoma, intra-abdominal lymph nodes 🦀

C81.34 Lymphocytic depletion classical Hodgkin lymphoma, lymph nodes of axilla and upper limb 🦀

C81.35 Lymphocytic depletion classical Hodgkin lymphoma, lymph nodes of inguinal region and lower limb 🦀

C81.36 Lymphocytic depletion classical Hodgkin lymphoma, intrapelvic lymph nodes 🦀

C81.37 Lymphocytic depletion classical Hodgkin lymphoma, spleen 🦀

C81.38 Lymphocytic depletion classical Hodgkin lymphoma, lymph nodes of multiple sites 🦀

C81.39 Lymphocytic depletion classical Hodgkin lymphoma, extranodal and solid organ sites 🦀

● C81.4 Lymphocyte-rich classical Hodgkin lymphoma
| Excludes1 | nodular lymphocyte predominant Hodgkin lymphoma (C81.0-) |

▪ C81.40 Lymphocyte-rich classical Hodgkin lymphoma, unspecified site 🦀

C81.41 Lymphocyte-rich classical Hodgkin lymphoma, lymph nodes of head, face, and neck 🦀

C81.42 Lymphocyte-rich classical Hodgkin lymphoma, intrathoracic lymph nodes 🦀

C81.43 Lymphocyte-rich classical Hodgkin lymphoma, intra-abdominal lymph nodes 🦀

C81.44 Lymphocyte-rich classical Hodgkin lymphoma, lymph nodes of axilla and upper limb 🦀

C81.45 Lymphocyte-rich classical Hodgkin lymphoma, lymph nodes of inguinal region and lower limb 🦀

C81.46 Lymphocyte-rich classical Hodgkin lymphoma, intrapelvic lymph nodes 🦀

C81.47 Lymphocyte-rich classical Hodgkin lymphoma, spleen 🦀

C81.48 Lymphocyte-rich classical Hodgkin lymphoma, lymph nodes of multiple sites 🦀

C81.49 Lymphocyte-rich classical Hodgkin lymphoma, extranodal and solid organ sites 🦀

840

CHAPTER 2 (C00-D49)

● Unacceptable First-Listed Diagnosis   ● Use Additional Character(s)   ▪ Unspecified   **OGCR** Official Guidelines for Coding and Reporting
🦀 Complication\Comorbidity   🦀 Major C\C | Excludes 1 | | Excludes 2 | Includes   Use additional   Code first   Code also

● C81.7   **Other classical Hodgkin lymphoma**
       Classical Hodgkin lymphoma NOS

◻ C81.70   Other classical Hodgkin lymphoma, unspecified site ⚕

     C81.71   Other classical Hodgkin lymphoma, lymph nodes of head, face, and neck ⚕

     C81.72   Other classical Hodgkin lymphoma, intrathoracic lymph nodes ⚕

     C81.73   Other classical Hodgkin lymphoma, intra-abdominal lymph nodes ⚕

     C81.74   Other classical Hodgkin lymphoma, lymph nodes of axilla and upper limb ⚕

     C81.75   Other classical Hodgkin lymphoma, lymph nodes of inguinal region and lower limb ⚕

     C81.76   Other classical Hodgkin lymphoma, intrapelvic lymph nodes ⚕

     C81.77   Other classical Hodgkin lymphoma, spleen ⚕

     C81.78   Other classical Hodgkin lymphoma, lymph nodes of multiple sites ⚕

     C81.79   Other classical Hodgkin lymphoma, extranodal and solid organ sites ⚕

● C81.9   **Hodgkin lymphoma, unspecified**

◻ C81.90   Hodgkin lymphoma, unspecified, unspecified site ⚕

◻ C81.91   Hodgkin lymphoma, unspecified, lymph nodes of head, face, and neck ⚕

◻ C81.92   Hodgkin lymphoma, unspecified, intrathoracic lymph nodes ⚕

◻ C81.93   Hodgkin lymphoma, unspecified, intra-abdominal lymph nodes ⚕

◻ C81.94   Hodgkin lymphoma, unspecified, lymph nodes of axilla and upper limb ⚕

◻ C81.95   Hodgkin lymphoma, unspecified, lymph nodes of inguinal region and lower limb ⚕

◻ C81.96   Hodgkin lymphoma, unspecified, intrapelvic lymph nodes ⚕

◻ C81.97   Hodgkin lymphoma, unspecified, spleen ⚕

◻ C81.98   Hodgkin lymphoma, unspecified, lymph nodes of multiple sites ⚕

◻ C81.99   Hodgkin lymphoma, unspecified, extranodal and solid organ sites ⚕

● C82   **Follicular lymphoma**
     Group of malignant lymphomas

> **Includes**   follicular lymphoma with or without diffuse areas
>
> **Excludes1**   personal history of non-Hodgkin lymphoma (Z85.72)
>   T-cell lymphoma (C84.-)

● C82.0   **Follicular lymphoma grade I**

◻ C82.00   Follicular lymphoma grade I, unspecified site ⚕

     C82.01   Follicular lymphoma grade I, lymph nodes of head, face, and neck ⚕

     C82.02   Follicular lymphoma grade I, intrathoracic lymph nodes ⚕

     C82.03   Follicular lymphoma grade I, intra-abdominal lymph nodes ⚕

     C82.04   Follicular lymphoma grade I, lymph nodes of axilla and upper limb ⚕

     C82.05   Follicular lymphoma grade I, lymph nodes of inguinal region and lower limb ⚕

     C82.06   Follicular lymphoma grade I, intrapelvic lymph nodes ⚕

     C82.07   Follicular lymphoma grade I, spleen ⚕

     C82.08   Follicular lymphoma grade I, lymph nodes of multiple sites ⚕

     C82.09   Follicular lymphoma grade I, extranodal and solid organ sites ⚕

● C82.1   **Follicular lymphoma grade II**

◻ C82.10   Follicular lymphoma grade II, unspecified site ⚕

     C82.11   Follicular lymphoma grade II, lymph nodes of head, face, and neck ⚕

     C82.12   Follicular lymphoma grade II, intrathoracic lymph nodes ⚕

     C82.13   Follicular lymphoma grade II, intra-abdominal lymph nodes ⚕

     C82.14   Follicular lymphoma grade II, lymph nodes of axilla and upper limb ⚕

     C82.15   Follicular lymphoma grade II, lymph nodes of inguinal region and lower limb ⚕

     C82.16   Follicular lymphoma grade II, intrapelvic lymph nodes ⚕

     C82.17   Follicular lymphoma grade II, spleen ⚕

     C82.18   Follicular lymphoma grade II, lymph nodes of multiple sites ⚕

     C82.19   Follicular lymphoma grade II, extranodal and solid organ sites ⚕

● C82.2   **Follicular lymphoma grade III, unspecified**

◻ C82.20   Follicular lymphoma grade III, unspecified, unspecified site ⚕

◻ C82.21   Follicular lymphoma grade III, unspecified, lymph nodes of head, face, and neck ⚕

◻ C82.22   Follicular lymphoma grade III, unspecified, intrathoracic lymph nodes ⚕

◻ C82.23   Follicular lymphoma grade III, unspecified, intra-abdominal lymph nodes ⚕

◻ C82.24   Follicular lymphoma grade III, unspecified, lymph nodes of axilla and upper limb ⚕

◻ C82.25   Follicular lymphoma grade III, unspecified, lymph nodes of inguinal region and lower limb ⚕

◻ C82.26   Follicular lymphoma grade III, unspecified, intrapelvic lymph nodes ⚕

◻ C82.27   Follicular lymphoma grade III, unspecified, spleen ⚕

◻ C82.28   Follicular lymphoma grade III, unspecified, lymph nodes of multiple sites ⚕

◻ C82.29   Follicular lymphoma grade III, unspecified, extranodal and solid organ sites ⚕

● C82.3   **Follicular lymphoma grade IIIa**

◻ C82.30   Follicular lymphoma grade IIIa, unspecified site ⚕

     C82.31   Follicular lymphoma grade IIIa, lymph nodes of head, face, and neck ⚕

     C82.32   Follicular lymphoma grade IIIa, intrathoracic lymph nodes ⚕

     C82.33   Follicular lymphoma grade IIIa, intra-abdominal lymph nodes ⚕

● Unacceptable First-Listed Diagnosis   ● Use Additional Character(s)   ◻ Unspecified   **OGCR** Official Guidelines for Coding and Reporting

⚕ Complication\Comorbidity   ⚕ Major C\C   Excludes 1   Excludes 2   Includes   Use additional   Code first   Code also

841

CHAPTER 2 (C00-D49)

C82.34 Follicular lymphoma grade IIIa, lymph nodes of axilla and upper limb

C82.35 Follicular lymphoma grade IIIa, lymph nodes of inguinal region and lower limb

C82.36 Follicular lymphoma grade IIIa, intrapelvic lymph nodes

C82.37 Follicular lymphoma grade IIIa, spleen

C82.38 Follicular lymphoma grade IIIa, lymph nodes of multiple sites

C82.39 Follicular lymphoma grade IIIa, extranodal and solid organ sites

● C82.4 Follicular lymphoma grade IIIb

C82.40 Follicular lymphoma grade IIIb, unspecified site

C82.41 Follicular lymphoma grade IIIb, lymph nodes of head, face, and neck

C82.42 Follicular lymphoma grade IIIb, intrathoracic lymph nodes

C82.43 Follicular lymphoma grade IIIb, intra-abdominal lymph nodes

C82.44 Follicular lymphoma grade IIIb, lymph nodes of axilla and upper limb

C82.45 Follicular lymphoma grade IIIb, lymph nodes of inguinal region and lower limb

C82.46 Follicular lymphoma grade IIIb, intrapelvic lymph nodes

C82.47 Follicular lymphoma grade IIIb, spleen

C82.48 Follicular lymphoma grade IIIb, lymph nodes of multiple sites

C82.49 Follicular lymphoma grade IIIb, extranodal and solid organ sites

● C82.5 Diffuse follicle center lymphoma

C82.50 Diffuse follicle center lymphoma, unspecified site

C82.51 Diffuse follicle center lymphoma, lymph nodes of head, face, and neck

C82.52 Diffuse follicle center lymphoma, intrathoracic lymph nodes

C82.53 Diffuse follicle center lymphoma, intra-abdominal lymph nodes

C82.54 Diffuse follicle center lymphoma, lymph nodes of axilla and upper limb

C82.55 Diffuse follicle center lymphoma, lymph nodes of inguinal region and lower limb

C82.56 Diffuse follicle center lymphoma, intrapelvic lymph nodes

C82.57 Diffuse follicle center lymphoma, spleen

C82.58 Diffuse follicle center lymphoma, lymph nodes of multiple sites

C82.59 Diffuse follicle center lymphoma, extranodal and solid organ sites

● C82.6 Cutaneous follicle center lymphoma

C82.60 Cutaneous follicle center lymphoma, unspecified site

C82.61 Cutaneous follicle center lymphoma, lymph nodes of head, face, and neck

C82.62 Cutaneous follicle center lymphoma, intrathoracic lymph nodes

C82.63 Cutaneous follicle center lymphoma, intra-abdominal lymph nodes

C82.64 Cutaneous follicle center lymphoma, lymph nodes of axilla and upper limb

C82.65 Cutaneous follicle center lymphoma, lymph nodes of inguinal region and lower limb

C82.66 Cutaneous follicle center lymphoma, intrapelvic lymph nodes

C82.67 Cutaneous follicle center lymphoma, spleen

C82.68 Cutaneous follicle center lymphoma, lymph nodes of multiple sites

C82.69 Cutaneous follicle center lymphoma, extranodal and solid organ sites

● C82.8 Other types of follicular lymphoma

C82.80 Other types of follicular lymphoma, unspecified site

C82.81 Other types of follicular lymphoma, lymph nodes of head, face, and neck

C82.82 Other types of follicular lymphoma, intrathoracic lymph nodes

C82.83 Other types of follicular lymphoma, intra-abdominal lymph nodes

C82.84 Other types of follicular lymphoma, lymph nodes of axilla and upper limb

C82.85 Other types of follicular lymphoma, lymph nodes of inguinal region and lower limb

C82.86 Other types of follicular lymphoma, intrapelvic lymph nodes

C82.87 Other types of follicular lymphoma, spleen

C82.88 Other types of follicular lymphoma, lymph nodes of multiple sites

C82.89 Other types of follicular lymphoma, extranodal and solid organ sites

● C82.9 Follicular lymphoma, unspecified

C82.90 Follicular lymphoma, unspecified, unspecified site

C82.91 Follicular lymphoma, unspecified, lymph nodes of head, face, and neck

C82.92 Follicular lymphoma, unspecified, intrathoracic lymph nodes

C82.93 Follicular lymphoma, unspecified, unspecified, intra-abdominal lymph nodes

C82.94 Follicular lymphoma, unspecified, lymph nodes of axilla and upper limb

C82.95 Follicular lymphoma, unspecified, lymph nodes of inguinal region and lower limb

C82.96 Follicular lymphoma, unspecified, intrapelvic lymph nodes

C82.97 Follicular lymphoma, unspecified, spleen

C82.98 Follicular lymphoma, unspecified, lymph nodes of multiple sites

C82.99 Follicular lymphoma, unspecified, extranodal and solid organ sites

● C83 Non-follicular lymphoma

Excludes1   personal history of non-Hodgkin lymphoma (Z85.72)

● C83.0 Small cell B-cell lymphoma
Lymphoplasmacytic lymphoma
Nodal marginal zone lymphoma
Non-leukemic variant of B-CLL
Splenic marginal zone lymphoma

Excludes1   chronic lymphocytic leukemia (C91.1)
T-cell lymphoma (C84.0-)
Waldenström's macroglobulinemia (C88.0)

● Unacceptable First-Listed Diagnosis   ● Use Additional Character(s)   ■ Unspecified   OGCR Official Guidelines for Coding and Reporting
 Complication\Comorbidity   Major C\C   Excludes 1   Excludes 2   Includes   Use additional   Code first   Code also

C83.00 Small cell B-cell lymphoma, unspecified site 🐾

C83.01 Small cell B-cell lymphoma, lymph nodes of head, face, and neck 🐾

C83.02 Small cell B-cell lymphoma, intrathoracic lymph nodes 🐾

C83.03 Small cell B-cell lymphoma, intra-abdominal lymph nodes 🐾

C83.04 Small cell B-cell lymphoma, lymph nodes of axilla and upper limb 🐾

C83.05 Small cell B-cell lymphoma, lymph nodes of inguinal region and lower limb 🐾

C83.06 Small cell B-cell lymphoma, intrapelvic lymph nodes 🐾

C83.07 Small cell B-cell lymphoma, spleen 🐾

C83.08 Small cell B-cell lymphoma, lymph nodes of multiple sites 🐾

C83.09 Small cell B-cell lymphoma, extranodal and solid organ sites 🐾

● C83.1 Mantle cell lymphoma
    Centrocytic lymphoma
    Malignant lymphomatous polyposis

C83.10 Mantle cell lymphoma, unspecified site 🐾

C83.11 Mantle cell lymphoma, lymph nodes of head, face, and neck 🐾

C83.12 Mantle cell lymphoma, intrathoracic lymph nodes 🐾

C83.13 Mantle cell lymphoma, intra-abdominal lymph nodes 🐾

C83.14 Mantle cell lymphoma, lymph nodes of axilla and upper limb 🐾

C83.15 Mantle cell lymphoma, lymph nodes of inguinal region and lower limb 🐾

C83.16 Mantle cell lymphoma, intrapelvic lymph nodes 🐾

C83.17 Mantle cell lymphoma, spleen 🐾

C83.18 Mantle cell lymphoma, lymph nodes of multiple sites 🐾

C83.19 Mantle cell lymphoma, extranodal and solid organ sites 🐾

● C83.3 Diffuse large B-cell lymphoma
    Anaplastic diffuse large B-cell lymphoma
    CD30-positive diffuse large B-cell lymphoma
    Centroblastic diffuse large B-cell lymphoma
    Diffuse large B-cell lymphoma, subtype not specified
    Immunoblastic diffuse large B-cell lymphoma
    Plasmablastic diffuse large B-cell lymphoma
    Diffuse large B-cell lymphoma, subtype not specified
    T-cell rich diffuse large B-cell lymphoma

Excludes1	mediastinal (thymic) large B-cell lymphoma (C85.2-)
	T-cell lymphoma (C84.-)

C83.30 Diffuse large B-cell lymphoma, unspecified site 🐾

C83.31 Diffuse large B-cell lymphoma, lymph nodes of head, face, and neck 🐾

C83.32 Diffuse large B-cell lymphoma, intrathoracic lymph nodes 🐾

C83.33 Diffuse large B-cell lymphoma, intra-abdominal lymph nodes 🐾

C83.34 Diffuse large B-cell lymphoma, lymph nodes of axilla and upper limb 🐾

C83.35 Diffuse large B-cell lymphoma, lymph nodes of inguinal region and lower limb 🐾

C83.36 Diffuse large B-cell lymphoma, intrapelvic lymph nodes 🐾

C83.37 Diffuse large B-cell lymphoma, spleen 🐾

C83.38 Diffuse large B-cell lymphoma, lymph nodes of multiple sites 🐾

C83.39 Diffuse large B-cell lymphoma, extranodal and solid organ sites 🐾

● C83.5 Lymphoblastic (diffuse) lymphoma
    Highly malignant type of non-Hodgkin lymphoma with diffuse infiltration
    B-precursor lymphoma
    Lymphoblastic B-cell lymphoma
    Lymphoblastic lymphoma NOS
    Lymphoblastic T-cell lymphoma
    T-precursor lymphoma

C83.50 Lymphoblastic (diffuse) lymphoma, unspecified site 🐾

C83.51 Lymphoblastic (diffuse) lymphoma, lymph nodes of head, face, and neck 🐾

C83.52 Lymphoblastic (diffuse) lymphoma, intrathoracic lymph nodes 🐾

C83.53 Lymphoblastic (diffuse) lymphoma, intra-abdominal lymph nodes 🐾

C83.54 Lymphoblastic (diffuse) lymphoma, lymph nodes of axilla and upper limb 🐾

C83.55 Lymphoblastic (diffuse) lymphoma, lymph nodes of inguinal region and lower limb 🐾

C83.56 Lymphoblastic (diffuse) lymphoma, intrapelvic lymph nodes 🐾

C83.57 Lymphoblastic (diffuse) lymphoma, spleen 🐾

C83.58 Lymphoblastic (diffuse) lymphoma, lymph nodes of multiple sites 🐾

C83.59 Lymphoblastic (diffuse) lymphoma, extranodal and solid organ sites 🐾

● C83.7 Burkitt lymphoma
    Form of small cell lymphoma
    Atypical Burkitt lymphoma
    Burkitt-like lymphoma

Excludes1	mature B-cell leukemia Burkitt type (C91.a-)

C83.70 Burkitt lymphoma, unspecified site 🐾

C83.71 Burkitt lymphoma, lymph nodes of head, face, and neck 🐾

C83.72 Burkitt lymphoma, intrathoracic lymph nodes 🐾

C83.73 Burkitt lymphoma, intra-abdominal lymph nodes 🐾

C83.74 Burkitt lymphoma, lymph nodes of axilla and upper limb 🐾

C83.75 Burkitt lymphoma, lymph nodes of inguinal region and lower limb 🐾

C83.76 Burkitt lymphoma, intrapelvic lymph nodes 🐾

C83.77 Burkitt lymphoma, spleen 🐾

C83.78 Burkitt lymphoma, lymph nodes of multiple sites 🐾

C83.79 Burkitt lymphoma, extranodal and solid organ sites 🐾

● Unacceptable First-Listed Diagnosis   ● Use Additional Character(s)   ▪ Unspecified   **OGCR** Official Guidelines for Coding and Reporting

🐾 Complication\Comorbidity   🐾 Major C\C   Excludes 1   Excludes 2   Includes   Use additional   Code first   Code also   843

CHAPTER 2 (C00–D49)

● **C83.8   Other non-follicular lymphoma**
     Intravascular large B-cell lymphoma
     Lymphoid granulomatosis
     Primary effusion B-cell lymphoma

     | Excludes1 | mediastinal (thymic) large B-cell lymphoma (C85.2-)
                 T-cell rich B-cell lymphoma (C83.3-)

   ◼ **C83.80   Other non-follicular lymphoma, unspecified site** 🦠

     C83.81   Other non-follicular lymphoma, lymph nodes of head, face, and neck 🦠

     C83.82   Other non-follicular lymphoma, intrathoracic lymph nodes 🦠

     C83.83   Other non-follicular lymphoma, intra-abdominal lymph nodes 🦠

     C83.84   Other non-follicular lymphoma, lymph nodes of axilla and upper limb 🦠

     C83.85   Other non-follicular lymphoma, lymph nodes of inguinal region and lower limb 🦠

     C83.86   Other non-follicular lymphoma, intrapelvic lymph nodes 🦠

     C83.87   Other non-follicular lymphoma of spleen 🦠

     C83.88   Other non-follicular lymphoma, lymph nodes of multiple sites 🦠

     C83.89   Other non-follicular lymphoma, extranodal and solid organ sites 🦠

● **C83.9   Non-follicular lymphoma, unspecified**

   ◼ **C83.90   Non-follicular lymphoma, unspecified, unspecified site** 🦠

   ◼ **C83.91   Non-follicular lymphoma, unspecified, lymph nodes of head, face, and neck** 🦠

   ◼ **C83.92   Non-follicular lymphoma, unspecified, intrathoracic lymph nodes** 🦠

   ◼ **C83.93   Non-follicular lymphoma, unspecified, intra-abdominal lymph nodes** 🦠

   ◼ **C83.94   Non-follicular lymphoma, unspecified, lymph nodes of axilla and upper limb** 🦠

   ◼ **C83.95   Non-follicular lymphoma, unspecified, lymph nodes of inguinal region and lower limb** 🦠

   ◼ **C83.96   Non-follicular lymphoma, unspecified, intrapelvic lymph nodes** 🦠

   ◼ **C83.97   Non-follicular lymphoma, unspecified, spleen** 🦠

   ◼ **C83.98   Non-follicular lymphoma, unspecified, lymph nodes of multiple sites** 🦠

   ◼ **C83.99   Non-follicular lymphoma, unspecified, extranodal and solid organ sites** 🦠

● **C84   Mature T/NK-cell lymphomas**

   | Excludes1 | personal history of non-Hodgkin lymphoma (Z85.72)

● **C84.0   Mycosis fungoides**
     Chronic or rapidly progressive form of cutaneous T-cell lymphoma; AKA granuloma fungoides

   ◼ **C84.00   Mycosis fungoides, unspecified site** 🦠

     C84.01   Mycosis fungoides, lymph nodes of head, face, and neck 🦠

     C84.02   Mycosis fungoides, intrathoracic lymph nodes 🦠

     C84.03   Mycosis fungoides, intra-abdominal lymph nodes 🦠

     C84.04   Mycosis fungoides, lymph nodes of axilla and upper limb 🦠

     C84.05   Mycosis fungoides, lymph nodes of inguinal region and lower limb 🦠

     C84.06   Mycosis fungoides, intrapelvic lymph nodes 🦠

     C84.07   Mycosis fungoides, spleen 🦠

     C84.08   Mycosis fungoides, lymph nodes of multiple sites 🦠

     C84.09   Mycosis fungoides, extranodal and solid organ sites 🦠

● **C84.1   Sézary disease**
     Type of cutaneous lymphoma affecting T-cells

   ◼ **C84.10   Sézary disease, unspecified site** 🦠

     C84.11   Sézary disease, lymph nodes of head, face, and neck 🦠

     C84.12   Sézary disease, intrathoracic lymph nodes 🦠

     C84.13   Sézary disease, intra-abdominal lymph nodes 🦠

     C84.14   Sézary disease, lymph nodes of axilla and upper limb 🦠

     C84.15   Sézary disease, lymph nodes of inguinal region and lower limb 🦠

     C84.16   Sézary disease, intrapelvic lymph nodes 🦠

     C84.17   Sézary disease, spleen 🦠

     C84.18   Sézary disease, lymph nodes of multiple sites 🦠

     C84.19   Sézary disease, extranodal and solid organ sites 🦠

● **C84.4   Peripheral T-cell lymphoma, not classified**
     Diverse group of blood carcinomas originating from T-cells, requiring aggressive chemotherapy
     Lennert's lymphoma
     Lymphoepithelioid lymphoma
     Mature T-cell lymphoma, not elsewhere classified

   ◼ **C84.40   Peripheral T-cell lymphoma, not classified, unspecified site** 🦠

     C84.41   Peripheral T-cell lymphoma, not classified, lymph nodes of head, face, and neck 🦠

     C84.42   Peripheral T-cell lymphoma, not classified, intrathoracic lymph nodes 🦠

     C84.43   Peripheral T-cell lymphoma, not classified, intra-abdominal lymph nodes 🦠

     C84.44   Peripheral T-cell lymphoma, not classified, lymph nodes of axilla and upper limb 🦠

     C84.45   Peripheral T-cell lymphoma, not classified, lymph nodes of inguinal region and lower limb 🦠

     C84.46   Peripheral T-cell lymphoma, not classified, intrapelvic lymph nodes 🦠

     C84.47   Peripheral T-cell lymphoma, not classified, spleen 🦠

     C84.48   Peripheral T-cell lymphoma, not classified, lymph nodes of multiple sites 🦠

     C84.49   Peripheral T-cell lymphoma, not classified, extranodal and solid organ sites 🦠

Item 2–7 Lymphosarcoma, also known as malignant lymphoma, is a cancer of the lymph system exhibiting abnormal cells encompassing an entire lymph node creating a diffuse pattern without any definite organization. Diffuse pattern lymphoma has a more unfavorable survival outlook than those with a follicular or nodular pattern. Reticulosarcoma is the most common aggressive form of non-Hodgkin's lymphoma.

● Unacceptable First-Listed Diagnosis   ● Use Additional Character(s)   ◼ Unspecified   **OGCR** Official Guidelines for Coding and Reporting
🦠 Complication\Comorbidity   🦠 Major C\C | Excludes 1 | | Excludes 2 | Includes   Use additional   Code first   Code also

● C84.6   Anaplastic large cell lymphoma, ALK-positive
     Anaplastic large cell lymphoma, CD30-positive

◼ C84.60   Anaplastic large cell lymphoma, ALK-positive, unspecified site 🔖

C84.61   Anaplastic large cell lymphoma, ALK-positive, lymph nodes of head, face, and neck 🔖

C84.62   Anaplastic large cell lymphoma, ALK-positive, intrathoracic lymph nodes 🔖

C84.63   Anaplastic large cell lymphoma, ALK-positive, intra-abdominal lymph nodes 🔖

C84.64   Anaplastic large cell lymphoma, ALK-positive, lymph nodes of axilla and upper limb 🔖

C84.65   Anaplastic large cell lymphoma, ALK-positive, lymph nodes of inguinal region and lower limb 🔖

C84.66   Anaplastic large cell lymphoma, ALK-positive, intrapelvic lymph nodes 🔖

C84.67   Anaplastic large cell lymphoma, ALK-positive, spleen 🔖

C84.68   Anaplastic large cell lymphoma, ALK-positive, lymph nodes of multiple sites 🔖

C84.69   Anaplastic large cell lymphoma, ALK-positive, extranodal and solid organ sites 🔖

● C84.7   Anaplastic large cell lymphoma, ALK-negative
     Excludes1   primary cutaneous CD30-positive T-cell proliferations (C86.6-)

◼ C84.70   Anaplastic large cell lymphoma, ALK-negative, unspecified site 🔖

C84.71   Anaplastic large cell lymphoma, ALK-negative, lymph nodes of head, face, and neck 🔖

C84.72   Anaplastic large cell lymphoma, ALK-negative, intrathoracic lymph nodes 🔖

C84.73   Anaplastic large cell lymphoma, ALK-negative, intra-abdominal lymph nodes 🔖

C84.74   Anaplastic large cell lymphoma, ALK-negative, lymph nodes of axilla and upper limb 🔖

C84.75   Anaplastic large cell lymphoma, ALK-negative, lymph nodes of inguinal region and lower limb 🔖

C84.76   Anaplastic large cell lymphoma, ALK-negative, intrapelvic lymph nodes 🔖

C84.77   Anaplastic large cell lymphoma, ALK-negative, spleen 🔖

C84.78   Anaplastic large cell lymphoma, ALK-negative, lymph nodes of multiple sites 🔖

C84.79   Anaplastic large cell lymphoma, ALK-negative, extranodal and solid organ sites 🔖

● C84.a   Cutaneous T-cell lymphoma, unspecified

◼ C84.a0   Cutaneous T-cell lymphoma, unspecified, unspecified site 🔖

◼ C84.a1   Cutaneous T-cell lymphoma, unspecified lymph nodes of head, face, and neck 🔖

◼ C84.a2   Cutaneous T-cell lymphoma, unspecified, intrathoracic lymph nodes 🔖

◼ C84.a3   Cutaneous T-cell lymphoma, unspecified, intra-abdominal lymph nodes 🔖

◼ C84.a4   Cutaneous T-cell lymphoma, unspecified, lymph nodes of axilla and upper limb 🔖

◼ C84.a5   Cutaneous T-cell lymphoma, unspecified, lymph nodes of inguinal region and lower limb 🔖

◼ C84.a6   Cutaneous T-cell lymphoma, unspecified, intrapelvic lymph nodes 🔖

◼ C84.a7   Cutaneous T-cell lymphoma, unspecified, spleen 🔖

◼ C84.a8   Cutaneous T-cell lymphoma, unspecified, lymph nodes of multiple sites 🔖

◼ C84.a9   Cutaneous T-cell lymphoma, unspecified, extranodal and solid organ sites 🔖

● C84.z   Other mature T/NK-cell lymphomas
     Note: If T-cell lineage or involvement is mentioned in conjunction with a specific lymphoma, code to the more specific description.

     Excludes1   angioimmunoblastic T-cell lymphoma (C86.5)
       blastic NK-cell lymphoma (C86.4)
       enteropathy-type T-cell lymphoma (C86.2)
       extranodal NK-cell lymphoma, nasal type (C86.0)
       hepatosplenic T-cell lymphoma (C86.1)
       primary cutaneous CD30-positive T-cell proliferations (C86.6)
       subcutaneous panniculitis-like T-cell lymphoma (C86.3)
       T-cell leukemia (C91.1-)

◼ C84.z0   Other mature T/NK-cell lymphomas, unspecified site 🔖

C84.z1   Other mature T/NK-cell lymphomas, lymph nodes of head, face, and neck 🔖

C84.z2   Other mature T/NK-cell lymphomas, intrathoracic lymph nodes 🔖

C84.z3   Other mature T/NK-cell lymphomas, intra-abdominal lymph nodes 🔖

C84.z4   Other mature T/NK-cell lymphomas, lymph nodes of axilla and upper limb 🔖

C84.z5   Other mature T/NK-cell lymphomas, lymph nodes of inguinal region and lower limb 🔖

C84.z6   Other mature T/NK-cell lymphomas, intrapelvic lymph nodes 🔖

C84.z7   Other mature T/NK-cell lymphomas, spleen 🔖

C84.z8   Other mature T/NK-cell lymphomas, lymph nodes of multiple sites 🔖

C84.z9   Other mature T/NK-cell lymphomas, extranodal and solid organ sites 🔖

● C84.9   Mature T/NK-cell lymphomas, unspecified
     NK/T cell lymphoma NOS
     Excludes1   mature T-cell lymphoma, not elsewhere classified (C84.4-)

◼ C84.90   Mature T/NK-cell lymphomas, unspecified, unspecified site 🔖

◼ C84.91   Mature T/NK-cell lymphomas, unspecified, lymph nodes of head, face, and neck 🔖

◼ C84.92   Mature T/NK-cell lymphomas, unspecified, intrathoracic lymph nodes 🔖

◼ C84.93   Mature T/NK-cell lymphomas, unspecified, intra-abdominal lymph nodes 🔖

◼ C84.94   Mature T/NK-cell lymphomas, unspecified, lymph nodes of axilla and upper limb 🔖

● Unacceptable First-Listed Diagnosis   ● Use Additional Character(s)   ◻ Unspecified   **OGCR** Official Guidelines for Coding and Reporting

🔖 Complication\Comorbidity   🔖 Major C\C   Excludes 1   Excludes 2   Includes   Use additional   Code first   Code also   845

CHAPTER 2 (C00-D49)

■ C84.95   Mature T/NK-cell lymphomas, unspecified, lymph nodes of inguinal region and lower limb ✎

■ C84.96   Mature T/NK-cell lymphomas, unspecified, intrapelvic lymph nodes ✎

■ C84.97   Mature T/NK-cell lymphomas, unspecified, spleen ✎

■ C84.98   Mature T/NK-cell lymphomas, unspecified, lymph nodes of multiple sites ✎

■ C84.99   Mature T/NK-cell lymphomas, unspecified, extranodal and solid organ sites ✎

● C85   Other and unspecified types of non-Hodgkin's lymphoma

> Excludes1   other specified types of T/NK-cell lymphoma (C86.-)
> personal history of non-Hodgkin's lymphoma (Z85.72)

● C85.0   Lymphosarcoma
Diffuse lymphoma

■ C85.00   Lymphosarcoma, unspecified site ✎

C85.01   Lymphosarcoma, lymph nodes of head, face, and neck ✎

C85.02   Lymphosarcoma, intrathoracic lymph nodes ✎

C85.03   Lymphosarcoma, intra-abdominal lymph nodes ✎

C85.04   Lymphosarcoma, lymph nodes of axilla and upper limb ✎

C85.05   Lymphosarcoma, lymph nodes of inguinal region and lower limb ✎

C85.06   Lymphosarcoma, intrapelvic lymph nodes ✎

C85.07   Lymphosarcoma, spleen ✎

C85.08   Lymphosarcoma, lymph nodes of multiple sites ✎

C85.09   Lymphosarcoma, extranodal and solid organ sites ✎

● C85.1   Unspecified B-cell lymphoma

> **Note:** If B-cell lineage or involvement is mentioned in conjunction with a specific lymphoma, code to the more specific description.

■ C85.10   Unspecified B-cell lymphoma, unspecified site ✎

■ C85.11   Unspecified B-cell lymphoma, lymph nodes of head, face, and neck ✎

■ C85.12   Unspecified B-cell lymphoma, intrathoracic lymph nodes ✎

■ C85.13   Unspecified B-cell lymphoma, intra-abdominal lymph nodes ✎

■ C85.14   Unspecified B-cell lymphoma, lymph nodes of axilla and upper limb ✎

■ C85.15   Unspecified B-cell lymphoma, lymph nodes of inguinal region and lower limb ✎

■ C85.16   Unspecified B-cell lymphoma, intrapelvic lymph nodes ✎

■ C85.17   Unspecified B-cell lymphoma, spleen ✎

■ C85.18   Unspecified B-cell lymphoma, lymph nodes of multiple sites ✎

■ C85.19   Unspecified B-cell lymphoma, extranodal and solid organ sites ✎

● C85.2   Mediastinal (thymic) large B-cell lymphoma

■ C85.20   Mediastinal (thymic) large B-cell lymphoma, unspecified site ✎

C85.21   Mediastinal (thymic) large B-cell lymphoma, lymph nodes of head, face, and neck ✎

C85.22   Mediastinal (thymic) large B-cell lymphoma, intrathoracic lymph nodes ✎

C85.23   Mediastinal (thymic) large B-cell lymphoma, intra-abdominal lymph nodes ✎

C85.24   Mediastinal (thymic) large B-cell lymphoma, lymph nodes of axilla and upper limb ✎

C85.25   Mediastinal (thymic) large B-cell lymphoma, lymph nodes of inguinal region and lower limb ✎

C85.26   Mediastinal (thymic) large B-cell lymphoma, intrapelvic lymph nodes ✎

C85.27   Mediastinal (thymic) large B-cell lymphoma, spleen ✎

C85.28   Mediastinal (thymic) large B-cell lymphoma, lymph nodes of multiple sites ✎

C85.29   Mediastinal (thymic) large B-cell lymphoma, extranodal and solid organ sites ✎

● C85.8   Other specified types of non-Hodgkin lymphoma
Malignant reticuloendotheliosis
Malignant reticulosis
Microglioma

■ C85.80   Other specified types of non-Hodgkin lymphoma, unspecified site ✎

C85.81   Other specified types of non-Hodgkin lymphoma, lymph nodes of head, face, and neck ✎

C85.82   Other specified types of non-Hodgkin lymphoma, intrathoracic lymph nodes ✎

C85.83   Other specified types of non-Hodgkin lymphoma, intra-abdominal lymph nodes ✎

C85.84   Other specified types of non-Hodgkin lymphoma, lymph nodes of axilla and upper limb ✎

C85.85   Other specified types of non-Hodgkin lymphoma, lymph nodes of inguinal region and lower limb ✎

C85.86   Other specified types of non-Hodgkin lymphoma, intrapelvic lymph nodes ✎

C85.87   Other specified types of non-Hodgkin lymphoma, spleen ✎

C85.88   Other specified types of non-Hodgkin lymphoma, lymph nodes of multiple sites ✎

C85.89   Other specified types of non-Hodgkin lymphoma, extranodal and solid organ sites ✎

● C85.9   Non-Hodgkin lymphoma, unspecified
Lymphoma NOS
Malignant lymphoma NOS
Non-Hodgkin lymphoma NOS

■ C85.90   Non-Hodgkin lymphoma, unspecified, unspecified site ✎

■ C85.91   Non-Hodgkin lymphoma, unspecified, lymph nodes of head, face, and neck ✎

■ C85.92   Non-Hodgkin lymphoma, unspecified, intrathoracic lymph nodes ✎

■ C85.93   Non-Hodgkin lymphoma, unspecified, intra-abdominal lymph nodes ✎

■ C85.94   Non-Hodgkin lymphoma, unspecified, lymph nodes of axilla and upper limb ✎

■ C85.95   Non-Hodgkin lymphoma, unspecified, lymph nodes of inguinal region and lower limb ✎

● Unacceptable First-Listed Diagnosis   ● Use Additional Character(s)   ■ Unspecified   **OGCR** Official Guidelines for Coding and Reporting
✎ Complication\Comorbidity   ✎ Major C\C   Excludes 1   Excludes 2   Includes   Use additional   Code first   Code also

■ **C85.96** **Non-Hodgkin lymphoma, unspecified, intrapelvic lymph nodes** 🅒

■ **C85.97** **Non-Hodgkin lymphoma, unspecified, spleen** 🅒

■ **C85.98** **Non-Hodgkin lymphoma, unspecified, lymph nodes of multiple sites** 🅒

■ **C85.99** **Non-Hodgkin lymphoma, unspecified, extranodal and solid organ sites** 🅒

C86 **Other specified types of T/NK-cell lymphoma**

> Excludes1   anaplastic large cell lymphoma, ALK negative (C84.7-)
> anaplastic large cell lymphoma, ALK positive (C84.6-)
> mature T/NK-cell lymphomas (C84.-)
> other specified types of non-Hodgkin lymphoma (C85.8-)

C86.0 **Extranodal NK/T-cell lymphoma, nasal type**

C86.1 **Hepatosplenic T-cell lymphoma**
> Alpha-beta and gamma delta types

C86.2 **Enteropathy-type (intestinal) T-cell lymphoma**
> Enteropathy associated T-cell lymphoma

C86.3 **Subcutaneous panniculitis-like T-cell lymphoma**

C86.4 **Blastic NK-cell lymphoma**

C86.5 **Angioimmunoblastic T-cell lymphoma**
> Angioimmunoblastic lymphadenopathy with dysproteinemia {AILD}

C86.6 **Primary cutaneous CD30-positive T-cell proliferations**
> Lymphomatoid papulosis
> Primary cutaneous anaplastic large cell lymphoma
> Primary cutaneous CD30-positive T-cell lymphoma

Item 2–8   **Multiple myeloma** is a cancer of a plasma cell (a type of white blood cell) and is an incurable but treatable disease. Immunoproliferative neoplasm is a term for diseases (mostly cancers) in which the immune system cells proliferate.

● **C88** **Malignant immunoproliferative diseases and certain other B-cell lymphomas**
> *Diseases involving immune system*
> Excludes1   B-cell lymphoma, unspecified C85.1-
> personal history of other malignant neoplasms of lymphoid, hematopoietic and related tissues (Z85.79)

C88.0 **Waldenström's macroglobulinemia**
> Lymphoplasmacytic lymphoma with IgM-production
> Macroglobulinemia (idiopathic) (primary)
> Excludes1   small cell B-cell lymphoma (C83.0)

C88.1 **Other heavy chain disease** 🅒

C88.2 **Gamma heavy chain disease** 🅒
> Franklin's disease
> Gamma heavy chain disease
> Mu heavy chain disease

C88.3 **Immunoproliferative small intestinal disease** 🅒
> Alpha heavy chain disease
> Mediterranean disease

C88.4 **Extranodal marginal zone B-cell lymphoma of mucosa-associated lymphoid tissue [MALT-lymphoma]**
> Lymphoma of skin-associated lymphoid tissue [SALT-lymphoma]
> Lymphoma of bronchial-associated lymphoid tissue [BALT-lymphoma]
> Excludes1   high malignant (diffuse large B-cell) lymphoma (C83.3-)

C88.8 **Other malignant immunoproliferative diseases** 🅒

■ **C88.9** **Malignant immunoproliferative disease, unspecified** 🅒
> Immunoproliferative disease NOS

● **C90** **Multiple myeloma and malignant plasma cell neoplasms**
> Excludes1   personal history of other malignant neoplasms of lymphoid, hematopoietic and related tissues (Z85.79)

● **C90.0** **Multiple myeloma**
> Kahler's disease
> Medullary plasmacytoma
> Myelomatosis
> Plasma cell myeloma
> Excludes1   solitary myeloma (C90.2-)
> solitary plasmacytoma (C90.3-)

C90.00 **Multiple myeloma not in remission** 🅒
> Multiple myeloma with failed remission
> Multiple myeloma NOS

C90.01 **Multiple myeloma in remission** 🅒

C90.02 **Multiple myeloma in relapse**

● **C90.1** **Plasma cell leukemia**
> *Rare type of acute leukemia*
> Plasmacytic leukemia

C90.10 **Plasma cell leukemia not in remission** 🅒
> Plasma cell leukemia NOS
> Plasma cell leukemia with failed remission

C90.11 **Plasma cell leukemia in remission** 🅒

C90.12 **Plasma cell leukemia in relapse**

● **C90.2** **Extramedullary plasmacytoma**
> *Malignant monoclonal plasma cell tumor growing in soft tissue; AKA plasma cell dyscrasias*

C90.20 **Extramedullary plasmacytoma not having achieved remission** 🅒
> Extramedullary plasmacytoma with failed remission
> Extramedullary plasmacytoma NOS

C90.21 **Extramedullary plasmacytoma in remission** 🅒

C90.22 **Extramedullary plasmacytoma in relapse** 🅒

C90.3 **Solitary plasmacytoma**
> Localized malignant plasma cell tumor NOS
> Plasmacytoma NOS
> Solitary myeloma

C90.30 **Solitary plasmacytoma not having achieved remission** 🅒
> Solitary plasmacytoma with failed remission
> Solitary plasmacytoma NOS

C90.31 **Solitary plasmacytoma in remission** 🅒

C90.32 **Solitary plasmacytoma in relapse** 🅒

● **C91** **Lymphoid leukemia**
> *Type of leukemia affecting circulating cells of lymphoid origin*
> Excludes1   personal history of leukemia (Z85.6)

● **C91.0** **Acute lymphoblastic leukemia [ALL]**
> **Note:** Code C91.0 should only be used for T-cell and B-cell precursor leukemia

C91.00 **Acute lymphoblastic leukemia, not having achieved remission** 🅒
> Acute lymphoblastic leukemia with failed remission
> Acute lymphoblastic leukemia NOS

C91.01 **Acute lymphoblastic leukemia, in remission**

C91.02 **Acute lymphoblastic leukemia, in relapse** 🅒

● Unacceptable First-Listed Diagnosis   ● Use Additional Character(s)   ■ Unspecified   **OGCR** Official Guidelines for Coding and Reporting

🅒 Complication\Comorbidity   🅒 Major C\C   Excludes 1   Excludes 2   Includes   Use additional   Code first   Code also

847

CHAPTER 2 (C00–D49)

Item 2–9 Leukemia is a cancer (acute or chronic) of the blood-forming tissues of the bone marrow. Blood cells all start out as stem cells. They mature and become red cells, white cells, or platelets. There are three main types of leukocytes (white cells that fight infection): monocytes, lymphocytes, and granulocytes. **Acute monocytic leukemia** (AML) affects monocytes. **Acute lymphoid leukemia** (ALL) affects lymphocytes, and **acute myeloid leukemia** (AML) affects cells that typically develop into white blood cells (not lymphocytes), though it may develop in other blood cells.

● **C91.1 Chronic lymphocytic leukemia of B-cell type**
Lymphoplasmacyticleukemia
Richter syndrome

> **Excludes1** lymphoplasmacytic lymphoma (C83.0-)

   C91.10 Chronic lymphocytic leukemia of B-cell type not having achieved remission 🗪
Chronic lymphocytic leukemia of B-cell type with failed remission
Chronic lymphocytic leukemia of B-cell type NOS

   C91.11 Chronic lymphocytic leukemia of B-cell type in remission 🗪

   C91.12 Chronic lymphocytic leukemia of B-cell type in relapse 🗪

● **C91.3 Prolymphocytic leukemia of B-cell type**
Chronic leukemia with symptoms of large number of circulating lymphocytes

   C91.30 Prolymphocytic leukemia of B-cell type not having achieved remission 🗪
Prolymphocytic leukemia of B-cell type with failed remission
Prolymphocytic leukemia of B-cell type NOS

   C91.31 Prolymphocytic leukemia of B-cell type, in remission 🗪

   C91.32 Prolymphocytic leukemia of B-cell type, in relapse 🗪

● **C91.4 Hairy-cell leukemia**
Chronic leukemia with splenomegaly and excessive number of abnormal large mononuclear cells covered by hairlike villi
Leukemic reticuloendotheliosis

   C91.40 Hairy-cell leukemia not having achieved remission 🗪
Hairy-cell leukemia with failed remission
Hairy-cell leukemia NOS

   C91.41 Hairy-cell leukemia, in remission 🗪

   C91.42 Hairy-cell leukemia, in relapse 🗪

● **C91.5 Adult T-cell lymphoma/leukemia (HTLV-1-associated)**
Acute variant of adult T-cell lymphoma/leukemia (HTLV-1-associated)
Chronic variant of adult T-cell lymphoma/leukemia (HTLV-1-associated)
Lymphomatoid variant of adult T-cell lymphoma/leukemia (HTLV-1-associated)
Smouldering variant of adult T-cell lymphoma/leukemia (HTLV-1-associated)

   C91.50 Adult T-cell lymphoma/leukemia (HTLV-1-associated) not having achieved remission 🗪
Adult T-cell lymphoma/leukemia (HTLV-1-associated) with failed remission
Adult T-cell lymphoma/leukemia (HTLV-1-associated) NOS

   C91.51 Adult T-cell lymphoma/leukemia (HTLV-1-associated), in remission 🗪

   C91.52 Adult T-cell lymphoma/leukemia (HTLV-1-associated), in relapse 🗪

● **C91.6 Prolymphocytic leukemia of T-cell type**

   C91.60 Prolymphocytic leukemia of T-cell type not having achieved remission 🗪
Prolymophocytic leukemia of T-cell type with failed remission
Prolymphocytic leukemia of T-cell type NOS

   C91.61 Prolymophocytic leukemia of T-cell type, in remission 🗪

   C91.62 Prolymphocytic leukemia of T-cell type, in relapse 🗪

● **C91.a Mature B-cell leukemia Burkitt-type**

> **Excludes1** Burkitt lymphoma (C83.7-)

   C91.a0 Mature B-cell leukemia Burkitt-type not having achieved remission 🗪
Mature B-cell leukemia Burkitt-type with failed remission
Mature B-cell leukemia Burkitt-type NOS

   C91.a1 Mature B-cell leukemia Burkitt-type, in remission 🗪

   C91.a2 Mature B-cell leukemia Burkitt-type, in relapse 🗪

● **C91.z Other lymphoid leukemia**
T-cell large granular lymphocytic leukemia

   C91.z0 Other lymphoid leukemia not having achieved remission 🗪
Other lymphoid leukemia with failed remission
Other lymphoid leukemia NOS

   C91.z1 Other lymphoid leukemia, in remission 🗪

   C91.z2 Other lymphoid leukemia, in relapse 🗪

● **C91.9 Lymphoid leukemia, unspecified**

   ■**C91.90 Lymphoid leukemia, unspecified not having achieved remission** 🗪
Lymphoid leukemia with failed remission
Lymphoid leukemia NOS

   ■**C91.91 Lymphoid leukemia, unspecified, in remission** 🗪

   ■**C91.92 Lymphoid leukemia, unspecified, in relapse** 🗪

● **C92 Myeloid leukemia**

> **Includes** granulocytic leukemia
> myelogenous leukemia

> **Excludes1** personal history of leukemia (Z85.6)

● **C92.0 Acute myeloblastic leukemia**
Acute myeloblastic leukemia, minimal differentiation
Acute myeloblastic leukemia (with maturation)
Acute myeloblastic leukemia 1/ETO
Acute myeloblastic leukemia M0
Acute myeloblastic leukemia M1
Acute myeloblastic leukemia M2
Acute myeloblastic leukemia with t(8;21)
Acute myeloblastic leukemia (without a FAB classification) NOS
Refractory anemia with excess blasts in transformation [RAEB T]

> **Excludes1** acute exacerbation of chronic myeloid leukemia (C92.10)
> refractory anemia with excess of blasts not in transformation (D46.2-)

● Unacceptable First-Listed Diagnosis   ● Use Additional Character(s)   ■ Unspecified   **OGCR** Official Guidelines for Coding and Reporting
🗪 Complication\Comorbidity   🗪 Major C\C   Excludes 1   Excludes 2   Includes   Use additional   Code first   Code also

C92.00　**Acute myeloblastic leukemia, not having achieved remission** ℗
　　　　Acute myeloblastic leukemia with failed remission
　　　　Acute myeloblastic leukemia NOS

C92.01　**Acute myeloblastic leukemia, in remission** ℗

C92.02　**Acute myeloblastic leukemia, in relapse** ℗

● C92.1　**Chronic myeloid leukemia, BCR/ABL-positive**
　　　Chronic myelogenous leukemia, Philadelphia chromosome (Ph1) positive
　　　Chronic myelogenous leukemia, t(9:22) (q34;q11)
　　　Chronic myelogenous leukemia with crisis of blast cells

　　　| Excludes1 | atypical chronic myeloid leukemia (C92.2-)
　　　chronic myelomonocytic leukemia (C93.1-)
　　　chronic myeloproliferative disease (D47.1)

C92.10　**Chronic myeloid leukemia, BCR/ABL-positive, not having achieved remission** ℗
　　　　Chronic myeloid leukemia, BCR/ABL-positive with failed remission
　　　　Chronic myeloid leukemia, BCR/ABL-positive NOS

C92.11　**Chronic myeloid leukemia, BCR/ABL-positive, in remission** ℗

C92.12　**Chronic myeloid leukemia, BCR/ABL-positive, in relapse** ℗

● C92.2　**Atypical chronic myeloid leukemia, BCR/ABL-negative**

C92.20　**Atypical chronic myeloid leukemia, BCR/ABL-negative, not having achieved remission** ℗
　　　　Atypical chronic myeloid leukemia, BCR/ABL-negative with failed remission
　　　　Atypical chronic myeloid leukemia, BCR/ABL-negative NOS

C92.21　**Atypical chronic myeloid leukemia, BCR/ABL-negative, in remission** ℗

C92.22　**Atypical chronic myeloid leukemia, BCR/ABL-negative, in relapse** ℗

● C92.3　**Myeloid sarcoma**
　　　A malignant tumor of immature myeloid cells
　　　Chloroma
　　　Granulocytic sarcoma

C92.30　**Myeloid sarcoma, not having achieved remission** ℗
　　　　Myeloid sarcoma with failed remission
　　　　Myeloid sarcoma NOS

C92.31　**Myeloid sarcoma, in remission** ℗

C92.32　**Myeloid sarcoma, in relapse** ℗

● C92.4　**Acute promyelocytic leukemia**
　　　AML M3
　　　AML Me with t(15;17) and variants

C92.40　**Acute promyelocytic leukemia, not having achieved remission** ℗
　　　　Acute promyelocytic leukemia with failed remission
　　　　Acute promyelocytic leukemia NOS

C92.41　**Acute promyelocytic leukemia, in remission** ℗

C92.42　**Acute promyelocytic leukemia, in relapse** ℗

● C92.5　**Acute myelomonocytic leukemia**
　　　AML M4
　　　AML M4 Eo with inv(16) or t(16;16)

C92.50　**Acute myelomonocytic leukemia, not having achieved remission** ℗
　　　　Acute myelomonocytic leukemia with failed remission
　　　　Acute myelomonocytic leukemia NOS

C92.51　**Acute myelomonocytic leukemia, in remission** ℗

C92.52　**Acute myelomonocytic leukemia, in relapse** ℗

● C92.6　**Acute myeloid leukemia with 11q23-abnormality**
　　　Acute myeloid leukemia with variation of MLL-gene

C92.60　**Acute myeloid leukemia with 11q23-abnormality not having achieved remission** ℗
　　　　Acute myeloid leukemia with 11q23-abnormality with failed remission
　　　　Acute myeloid leukemia with 11q23-abnormality NOS

C92.61　**Acute myeloid leukemia with 11q23-abnormality in remission** ℗

C92.62　**Acute myeloid leukemia with 11q23-abnormality in relapse** ℗

● C92.a　**Acute myeloid leukemia with multilineage dysplasia**
　　　Acute myeloid leukemia with dysplasia of remaining hematopoesis and/or myelodysplastic disease in its history

C92.a0　**Acute myeloid leukemia with multilineage dysplasia, not having achieved remission** ℗
　　　　Acute myeloid leukemia with multilineage dysplasia with failed remission
　　　　Acute myeloid leukemia with multilineage dysplasia NOS

C92.a1　**Acute myeloid leukemia with multilineage dysplasia, in remission** ℗

C92.a2　**Acute myeloid leukemia with multilineage dysplasia, in relapse** ℗

● C92.z　**Other myeloid leukemia**

C92.z0　**Other myeloid leukemia not having achieved remission** ℗
　　　　Myeloid leukemia NEC with failed remission
　　　　Myeloid leukemia NEC

C92.z1　**Other myeloid leukemia, in remission** ℗

C92.z2　**Other myeloid leukemia, in relapse** ℗

● C92.9　**Myeloid leukemia, unspecified**

■ C92.90　**Myeloid leukemia, unspecified, not having achieved remission** ℗
　　　　Myeloid leukemia, unspecified with failed remission
　　　　Myeloid leukemia, unspecified NOS

■ C92.91　**Myeloid leukemia, unspecified in remission** ℗

■ C92.92　**Myeloid leukemia, unspecified in relapse** ℗

● Unacceptable First-Listed Diagnosis　　　● Use Additional Character(s)　　■ Unspecified　　**OGCR** Official Guidelines for Coding and Reporting
℗ Complication\Comorbidity　℗ Major C\C　| Excludes 1 |　| Excludes 2 |　Includes　Use additional　Code first　Code also

CHAPTER 2 (C00–D49)

849

● **C93   Monocytic leukemia**
> **Includes**   monocytoid leukemia
> **Excludes1**   personal history of leukemia (Z85.6)

  ● **C93.0   Acute monoblastic/monocytic leukemia**
      AML M5
      AML M5a
      AML M5b

     C93.00   Acute monoblastic/monocytic leukemia, not having achieved remission 🔖
        Acute monoblastic/monocytic leukemia with failed remission
        Acute monoblastic/monocytic leukemia NOS

     C93.01   Acute monoblastic/monocytic leukemia, in remission 🔖

     C93.02   Acute monoblastic/monocytic leukemia, in relapse 🔖

  ● **C93.1   Chronic myelomonocytic leukemia**
      Chronic monocytic leukemia
      CMML-1
      CMML-2
      CMML with eosinophilia

     C93.10   Chronic myelomonocytic leukemia not having achieved remission 🔖
        Chronic myelomonocytic leukemia with failed remission
        Chronic myelomonocytic leukemia NOS

     C93.11   Chronic myelomonocytic leukemia, in remission 🔖

     C93.12   Chronic myelomonocytic leukemia, in relapse 🔖

  ● **C93.3   Juvenile myelomonocytic leukemia**

     C93.30   Juvenile myelomonocytic leukemia, not having achieved remission 🔖
        Juvenile myelomonocytic leukemia with failed remission
        Juvenile myelomonocytic leukemia NOS

     C93.31   Juvenile myelomonocytic leukemia, in remission 🔖

     C93.32   Juvenile myelomonocytic leukemia, in relapse 🔖

  ● **C93.z   Other monocytic leukemia**

     C93.z0   Other monocytic leukemia, not in remission 🔖
        Other monocytic leukemia NOS

     C93.z1   Other monocytic leukemia, in remission 🔖

  ● **C93.9   Monocytic leukemia, unspecified**

     ■ **C93.90   Monocytic leukemia, unspecified, not having achieved remission** 🔖
        Monocytic leukemia, unspecified with failed remission
        Monocytic leukemia, unspecified NOS

     ■ **C93.91   Monocytic leukemia, unspecified in remission** 🔖

     ■ **C93.92   Monocytic leukemia, unspecified in relapse** 🔖

● **C94   Other leukemias of specified cell type**
> **Excludes1**   leukemic reticuloendotheliosis (C91.4-)
>   myelodysplastic syndromes (D46.-)
>   personal history of leukemia (Z85.6)
>   plasma cell leukemia (C90.1-)

  ● **C94.0   Acute erythoid leukemia**
      Acute myeloid leukemia M6(a)(b)
      Erythroleukemia

     C94.00   Acute erythoid leukemia, not having achieved remission 🔖
        Acute erythoid leukemia with failed remission
        Acute erythoid leukemia NOS

     C94.01   Acute erythoid leukemia, in remission 🔖

     C94.02   Acute erythoid leukemia, in relapse 🔖

  ● **C94.2   Acute megakaryoblastic leukemia**
      Acute myeloid leukemia M7
      Acute megakaryocytic leukemia

     C94.20   Acute megakaryoblastic leukemia not having achieved remission 🔖
        Acute megakaryoblastic leukemia with failed remission
        Acute megakaryoblastic leukemia NOS

     C94.21   Acute megakaryoblastic leukemia, in remission 🔖

     C94.22   Acute megakaryoblastic leukemia, in relapse 🔖

  ● **C94.3   Mast cell leukemia**

     C94.30   Mast cell leukemia not having achieved remission 🔖
        Mast cell leukemia with failed remission
        Mast cell leukemia NOS

     C94.31   Mast cell leukemia, in remission 🔖

     C94.32   Mast cell leukemia, in relapse 🔖

  ● **C94.4   Acute panmyelosis with myelofibrosis**
      Acute myelofibrosis
> **Excludes1**   myelofibrosis NOS (D75.81)
>   secondary myelofibrosis NOS (D75.81)

     C94.40   Acute panmyelosis with myelofibrosis not having achieved remission 🔖
        Acute myelofibrosis NOS
        Acute panmyelosis with myelofibrosis with failed remission
        Acute panmyelosis NOS

     C94.41   Acute panmyelosis with myelofibrosis, in remission 🔖

     C94.42   Acute panmyelosis with myelofibrosis, in relapse 🔖

  ● **C94.6   Myelodysplastic disease, not classified** 🔖
      Myeloproliferative diease, not classified

  ● **C94.8   Other specified leukemias**
      Aggressive NK-cell leukemia
      Acute basophilic leukemia

     C94.80   Other specified leukemias not having achieved remission 🔖
        Other specified leukemia with failed remission
        Other specified leukemias NOS

     C94.81   Other specified leukemias, in remission 🔖

     C94.82   Other specified leukemias, in relapse 🔖

● Unacceptable First-Listed Diagnosis   ● Use Additional Character(s)   ■ Unspecified   **OGCR** Official Guidelines for Coding and Reporting
🔖 Complication\Comorbidity   🔖 Major C\C   Excludes 1   Excludes 2   Includes   Use additional   Code first   Code also

● **C95 Leukemia of unspecified cell type**

> **Excludes1**   personal history of leukemia (Z85.6)

  ● **C95.0 Acute leukemia of unspecified cell type**
Acute bilineal leukemia
Acute mixed lineage leukemia
Biphenotypic acute leukemia
Stem cell leukemia of unclear lineage

> **Excludes1**   acute exacerbation of unspecified
> chronic leukemia (C95.10)

    ◪ **C95.00 Acute leukemia of unspecified cell type
not having achieved remission** 🕿
Acute leukemia of unspecified cell type
with failed remission
Acute leukemia NOS

    ◪ **C95.01 Acute leukemia of unspecified cell type, in
remission** 🕿

    ◪ **C95.02 Acute leukemia of unspecified cell type, in
relapse** 🕿

  ● **C95.1 Chronic leukemia of unspecified cell type**

    ◪ **C95.10 Chronic leukemia of unspecified cell type
not having achieved remission** 🕿
Chronic leukemia of unspecified cell type
with failed remission
Chronic leukemia NOS

    ◪ **C95.11 Chronic leukemia of unspecified cell type,
in remission** 🕿

    ◪ **C95.12 Chronic leukemia of unspecified cell type,
in relapse** 🕿

  ● **C95.9 Leukemia, unspecified**

    ◪ **C95.90 Leukemia, unspecified not having
achieved remission** 🕿
Leukemia, unspecified with failed
remission
Leukemia NOS

    ◪ **C95.91 Leukemia, unspecified, in remission** 🕿

    ◪ **C95.92 Leukemia, unspecified, in relapse** 🕿

● **C96 Other and unspecified malignant neoplasms of lymphoid,
hematopoietic and related tissue**

> **Excludes1**   personal history of other malignant
> neoplasms of lymphoid, hematopoietic
> and related tissues (Z85.79)

  **C96.0 Multifocal and multisysemic (disseminated)
Langerhans-cell histiocytosis** 🕿
Histiocytosis X, multisystemic
Letterer-Siwe disease

> **Excludes1**   multifocal and unisystemic
> Langerhans-cell histiocytosis
> (C96.5)
> unifocal Langerhans-cell
> histiocytosis (C96.6)

C96.2 Malignant mast cell tumor 🕿
Aggressive systemic mastocytosis
Mast cell sarcoma

> **Excludes1**   indolent mastocytosis (D47.0)
> mast cell leukemia (C94.30)
> mastocytosis (congenital) (cutaneous)
> (Q82.2)

C96.4 Sarcoma of dendritic cells (accessory cells) 🕿
Follicular dendritic cell sarcoma
Interdigitating dendritic cell sarcoma
Langerhans cell sarcoma

**C96.5 Multifocal and unisystemic Langerhans-cell
histiocytosis** 🕿
Hand-Schüller-Christian disease
Histiocytosis X, multifocal

> **Excludes1**   multifocal and multisysemic
> (disseminated) Langerhans-cell
> histiocytosis (C96.0)
> unifocal Langerhans-cell
> histiocytosis (C96.6)

C96.6 Unifocal Langerhans-cell histiocytosis 🕿
Eosinophilic granuloma
Histiocytosis X, unifocal
Histiocytosis X NOS
Langerhans-cell histiocytosis NOS

> **Excludes1**   multifocal and multisysemic
> (disseminated) Langerhans-cell
> histiocytosis (C96.0)
> multifocal and unisystemic
> Langerhans-cell histiocytosis
> (C96.5)

C96.a Histiocytic sarcoma 🕿
Malignant histiocytosis

**C96.z Other specified malignant neoplasms of lymphoid,
hematopoietic and related tissue** 🕿

◪ **C96.9 Malignant neoplasm of lymphoid, hematopoietic
and related tissue, unspecified** 🕿

● Unacceptable First-Listed Diagnosis   ● Use Additional Character(s)   ◪ Unspecified   **OGCR** Official Guidelines for Coding and Reporting

🕿 Complication\Comorbidity   🕿 Major C\C   Excludes 1   Excludes 2   Includes   Use additional   Code first   Code also

851

In situ is carcinoma involving cells in localized tissues that has not spread to nearby tissues

IN SITU NEOPLASMS (D00-D09)

Includes Bowen's disease
erythroplasia
grade III intraepithelial neoplasia
Queyrat's erythroplasia

Use additional morphology codes with behavior code /2

● **D00** **Carcinoma in situ of oral cavity, esophagus and stomach**
      Excludes1 melanoma in situ (D03.-)

● **D00.0** **Carcinoma in situ of lip, oral cavity and pharynx**
      Excludes1 carcinoma in situ of aryepiglottic fold or interarytenoid fold, laryngeal aspect (D02.0)
        carcinoma in situ of epiglottis:
          NOS (D02.0)
          suprahyoid portion (D02.0)
        carcinoma in situ of skin of lip (D03.0, D04.0)

Use additional code to identify:
exposure to environmental tobacco smoke (Z77.22)
exposure to tobacco smoke in the perinatal period (P96.81)
history of tobacco use (Z87.891)
occupational exposure to environmental tobacco smoke (Z57.31)
tobacco dependence (F17.-)
tobacco use (Z72.0)

    ■ **D00.00** **Carcinoma in situ of oral cavity, unspecified site**

    D00.01 **Carcinoma in situ of labial mucosa and vermilion border**

    D00.02 **Carcinoma in situ of buccal mucosa**

    D00.03 **Carcinoma in situ of gingiva and edentulous alveolar ridge**

    D00.04 **Carcinoma in situ of soft palate**

    D00.05 **Carcinoma in situ of hard palate**

    D00.06 **Carcinoma in situ of floor of mouth**

    D00.07 **Carcinoma in situ of tongue**

    D00.08 **Carcinoma in situ of pharynx**
        Carcinoma in situ of aryepiglottic fold NOS
        Carcinoma in situ of hypopharyngeal aspect of aryepiglottic fold
        Carcinoma in situ of marginal zone of aryepiglottic fold

  D00.1 **Carcinoma in situ of esophagus**

  D00.2 **Carcinoma in situ of stomach**

● **D01** **Carcinoma in situ of other and unspecified digestive organs**
      Excludes1 melanoma in situ (D03.-)

  D01.0 **Carcinoma in situ of colon**
      Excludes1 carcinoma in situ of rectosigmoid junction (D01.1)

  D01.1 **Carcinoma in situ of rectosigmoid junction**

  D01.2 **Carcinoma in situ of rectum**

  D01.3 **Carcinoma in situ of anus and anal canal**
      Excludes1 carcinoma in situ of anal margin (D04.5)
        carcinoma in situ of anal skin (D04.5)
        carcinoma in situ of perianal skin (D04.5)

● **D01.4** **Carcinoma in situ of other and unspecified parts of intestine**
      Excludes1 carcinoma in situ of ampulla of Vater (D01.5)

    D01.40 **Carcinoma in situ of inspecified part of intestine**

    D01.49 **Carcinoma in situ of other parts of intestine**

  D01.5 **Carcinoma in situ of liver, gallbladder and bile ducts**
    Carcinoma in situ of ampulla of Vater

  D01.7 **Carcinoma in situ of other specified digestive organs**
    Carcinoma in situ of pancreas

■ **D01.9** **Carcinoma in situ of digestive organ, unspecified**

● **D02** **Carcinoma in situ of middle ear and respiratory system**
      Excludes1 melanoma in situ (D03.-)

Use additional code to identify:
exposure to environmental tobacco smoke (Z77.22)
exposure to tobacco smoke in the perinatal period (P96.81)
history of tobacco use (Z87.891)
occupational exposure to environmental tobacco smoke (Z57.31)
tobacco dependence (F17.-)
tobacco use (Z72.0)

  D02.0 **Carcinoma in situ of larynx**
    Carcinoma in situ of aryepiglottic fold or interarytenoid fold, laryngeal aspect
    Carcinoma in situ of epiglottis (suprahyoid portion)
      Excludes1 carcinoma in situ of aryepiglottic fold or interarytenoid fold NOS (D00.08)
        carcinoma in situ of hypopharyngeal aspect (D00.08)
        carcinoma in situ of marginal zone (D00.08)

  D02.1 **Carcinoma in situ of trachea**

● **D02.2** **Carcinoma in situ of bronchus and lung**
    ■ **D02.20** **Carcinoma in situ of bronchus and lung, unspecified side**

    D02.21 **Carcinoma in situ of right bronchus and lung**

    D02.22 **Carcinoma in situ of left bronchus and lung**

  D02.3 **Carcinoma in situ of other parts of respiratory system**
    Carcinoma in situ of accessory sinuses
    Carcinoma in situ of middle ear
    Carcinoma in situ of nasal cavities
      Excludes1 carcinoma in situ of ear (external) (skin) (D04.2-)
        carcinoma in situ of nose NOS (D09.7)
        carcinoma in situ of skin of nose (D04.3)

■ **D02.4** **Carcinoma in situ of respiratory system, unspecified**

● **D03** **Melanoma in situ**

  D03.0 **Melanoma in situ of lip**

● **D03.1** **Melanoma in situ of eyelid, including canthus**
    ■ **D03.10** **Melanoma in situ of eyelid, including canthus, unspecified side**

    D03.11 **Melanoma in situ of right eyelid, including canthus**

    D03.12 **Melanoma in situ of left eyelid, including canthus**

● Unacceptable First-Listed Diagnosis   ● Use Additional Character(s)   ■ Unspecified   **OGCR** Official Guidelines for Coding and Reporting
🔁 Complication\Comorbidity   🔁 Major C\C   Excludes 1   Excludes 2   Includes   Use additional   Code first   Code also

● **D03.2** Melanoma in situ of ear and external auricular canal

　■ **D03.20** Melanoma in situ of ear and external auricular canal, unspecified side

　　D03.21 Melanoma in situ of right ear and external auricular canal

　　D03.22 Melanoma in situ of left ear and external auricular canal

● **D03.3** Melanoma in situ of other and unspecified parts of face

　■ **D03.30** Melanoma in situ of unspecified part of face

　　D03.39 Melanoma in situ of other parts of face

　D03.4 Melanoma in situ of scalp and neck

● **D03.5** Melanoma in situ of trunk

　　D03.51 Melanoma in situ of anal skin
　　　　　Melanoma in situ of anal margin
　　　　　Melanoma in situ of perianal skin

　　D03.52 Melanoma in situ of breast (skin) (soft tissue)

　　D03.59 Melanoma in situ of other part of trunk

● **D03.6** Melanoma in situ of upper limb, including shoulder

　■ **D03.60** Melanoma in situ of upper limb, including shoulder, unspecified side

　　D03.61 Melanoma in situ of right upper limb, including shoulder

　　D03.62 Melanoma in situ of left upper limb, including shoulder

● **D03.7** Melanoma in situ of lower limb, including hip

　■ **D03.70** Melanoma in situ of lower limb, including hip, unspecified side

　　D03.71 Melanoma in situ of right lower limb, including hip

　　D03.72 Melanoma in situ of left lower limb, including hip

　D03.8 Melanoma in situ of other sites
　　　Melanoma in situ of scrotum

　　　| Excludes1 | carcinoma in situ of scrotum (D07.61)

■ **D03.9** Melanoma in situ, unspecified

● **D04** Carcinoma in situ of skin

　| Excludes1 | erythroplasia of Queyrat (penis) NOS (D07.4)
　　　　　　melanoma in situ (D03.-)

　D04.0 Carcinoma in situ of skin of lip

　| Excludes1 | carcinoma in situ of vermilion border of lip (D00.01)

● **D04.1** Carcinoma in situ of skin of eyelid, including canthus

　■ **D04.10** Carcinoma in situ of skin of eyelid, including canthus, unspecified side

　　D04.11 Carcinoma in situ of skin of right eyelid, including canthus

　　D04.12 Carcinoma in situ of skin of left eyelid, including canthus

● **D04.2** Carcinoma in situ of skin of ear and external auricular canal

　■ **D04.20** Carcinoma in situ of skin of ear and external auricular canal, unspecified side

　　D04.21 Carcinoma in situ of skin of right ear and external auricular canal

　　D04.22 Carcinoma in situ of skin of left ear and external auricular canal

● **D04.3** Carcinoma in situ of skin of other and unspecified parts of face

　■ **D04.30** Carcinoma in situ of skin of unspecified part of face

　　D04.39 Carcinoma in situ of skin of other parts of face

　D04.4 Carcinoma in situ of skin of scalp and neck

　D04.5 Carcinoma in situ of skin of trunk
　　　Carcinoma in situ of anal margin
　　　Carcinoma in situ of anal skin
　　　Carcinoma in situ of perianal skin
　　　Carcinoma in situ of skin of breast

　　| Excludes1 | carcinoma in situ of anus NOS (D01.3)
　　　　　　carcinoma in situ of scrotum (D07.61)
　　　　　　carcinoma in situ of skin of genital organs (D07.-)

● **D04.6** Carcinoma in situ of skin of upper limb, including shoulder

　■ **D04.60** Carcinoma in situ of skin of upper limb, including shoulder, unspecified side

　　D04.61 Carcinoma in situ of skin of right upper limb, including shoulder

　　D04.62 Carcinoma in situ of skin of left upper limb, including shoulder

● **D04.7** Carcinoma in situ of skin of lower limb, including hip

　■ **D04.70** Carcinoma in situ of skin of lower limb, including hip, unspecified side

　　D04.71 Carcinoma in situ of skin of right lower limb, including hip

　　D04.72 Carcinoma in situ of skin of left lower limb, including hip

　D04.8 Carcinoma in situ of skin of other sites

■ **D04.9** Carcinoma in situ of skin, unspecified

● **D05** Carcinoma in situ of breast

　| Excludes1 | carcinoma in situ of skin of breast (D04.5)
　　　　　　melanoma in situ of breast (skin) (D03.5)
　　　　　　Paget's disease of breast or nipple (C50.-)

● **D05.0** Lobular carcinoma in situ of breast

　　D05.01 Lobular carcinoma in situ of right breast

　　D05.02 Lobular carcinoma in situ of left breast

　■ **D05.09** Lobular carcinoma in situ of unspecified breast

● **D05.1** Intraductal carcinoma in situ of breast

　　D05.11 Intraductal carcinoma in situ of right breast

　　D05.12 Intraductal carcinoma in situ of left breast

　■ **D05.19** Intraductal carcinoma in situ of unspecified breast

● **D05.7** Other carcinoma in situ of breast

　　D05.71 Other carcinoma in situ of right breast

　　D05.72 Other carcinoma in situ of left breast

　■ **D05.79** Other carcinoma in situ of unspecified breast

● **D05.9** Unspecified carcinoma in situ of breast

　■ **D05.91** Unspecified carcinoma in situ of right breast

　■ **D05.92** Unspecified carcinoma in situ of left breast

　■ **D05.99** Unspecified carcinoma in situ of unspecified breast

---

● Unacceptable First-Listed Diagnosis　　● Use Additional Character(s)　　■ Unspecified　　**OGCR** Official Guidelines for Coding and Reporting

🄒 Complication\Comorbidity　🄒 Major C\C　| Excludes 1 |　| Excludes 2 |　Includes　Use additional　Code first　Code also

CHAPTER 2 (C00-D49)

853

● **D06** **Carcinoma in situ of cervix uteri**

     Includes   cervical adenocarcinoma in situ
                     cervical intraepithelial glandular neoplasia
                     cervical intraepithelial neoplasia III [CIN III]
                     severe dysplasia of cervix uteri

     Excludes1   cervical intraepithelial neoplasia II [CIN II]
                     (N87.1)
                     cytologic evidence of malignancy of cervix
                         without histologic confirmation (R87.614)
                     high grade squamous intraepithelial lesion
                         (HGSIL) of cervix (R87.613)
                     melanoma in situ of cervix (D03.5)
                     moderate cervical dysplasia (N87.1)

     D06.0 **Carcinoma in situ of endocervix**

     D06.1 **Carcinoma in situ of exocervix**

     D06.7 **Carcinoma in situ of other parts of cervix**

  ■ **D06.9** **Carcinoma in situ of cervix, unspecified**

● **D07** **Carcinoma in situ of other and unspecified genital organs**

     Excludes1   melanoma in situ of trunk (D03.5)

     D07.0 **Carcinoma in situ of endometrium**

     D07.1 **Carcinoma in situ of vulva**
           Severe dysplasia of vulva
           Vulvar intraepithelial neoplasia III [VIN III]

         Excludes1   moderate dysplasia of vulva (N90.1
                       vulvar intraepithelial neoplasia II
                         [VIN II] (N90.1)

     D07.2 **Carcinoma in situ of vagina**
           Severe dysplasia of vagina
           Vaginal intraepithelial neoplasia III [VAIN III]

         Excludes1   moderate dysplasia of vagina
                       (N89.1)
                     vaginal intraepithelial neoplasia II
                       [VIN II] (N89.1)

  ● **D07.3** **Carcinoma in situ of other and unspecified female genital organs**

    ■ **D07.30** **Carcinoma in situ of unspecified female genital organs**

     D07.39 **Carcinoma in situ of other female genital organs**

     D07.4 **Carcinoma in situ of penis**
           Erythroplasia of Queyrat NOS

     D07.5 **Carcinoma in situ of prostate**
           Severe dysplasia of prostate

         Excludes1   dysplasia (mild) (moderate) of
                       prostate (N42.3)
                     prostatic intraepithelial neoplasia III
                       (PIN III) (N42.3)

  ● **D07.6** **Carcinoma in situ of other and unspecified male genital organs**

    ■ **D07.60** **Carcinoma in situ of unspecified male genital organs**

     D07.61 **Carcinoma in situ of scrotum**

     D07.69 **Carcinoma in situ of other male genital organs**

● **D09** **Carcinoma in situ of other and unspecified sites**

     Excludes1   melanoma in situ (D03.-)

     D09.0 **Carcinoma in situ of bladder**

  ● **D09.1** **Carcinoma in situ of other and unspecified urinary organs**

    ■ **D09.10** **Carcinoma in situ of unspecified urinary organ**

     D09.19 **Carcinoma in situ of other urinary organs**

  ● **D09.2** **Carcinoma in situ of eye**

     Excludes1   carcinoma in situ of skin of eyelid
                     (D04.1-)

    ■ **D09.20** **Carcinoma in situ of eye, unspecified side**

     D09.21 **Carcinoma in situ of right eye**

     D09.22 **Carcinoma in situ of left eye**

     D09.3 **Carcinoma in situ of thyroid and other endocrine glands**

         Excludes1   carcinoma in situ of endocrine
                       pancreas (D01.7)
                     carcinoma in situ of ovary (D07.39)
                     carcinoma in situ of testis (D07.69)

     D09.7 **Carcinoma in situ of other specified sites**

  ■ **D09.9** **Carcinoma in situ, unspecified**

BENIGN NEOPLASMS, EXCEPT BENIGN NEUROENDOCRINE TUMORS (D10-D36)

     Use additional morphology codes with behavior
     code /0

● **D10** **Benign neoplasm of mouth and pharynx**

     D10.0 **Benign neoplasm of lip**
           Benign neoplasm of lip (frenulum) (inner aspect)
             (mucosa) (vermilion border)

         Excludes1   benign neoplasm of skin of lip
                     (D22.0, D23.0)

     D10.1 **Benign neoplasm of tongue**
           Benign neoplasm of lingual tonsil

     D10.2 **Benign neoplasm of floor of mouth**

  ● **D10.3** **Other and unspecified parts of mouth**

    ■ **D10.30** **Benign neoplasm of unspecified part of mouth**

     D10.39 **Benign neoplasm of other parts of mouth**
              Benign neoplasm of minor salivary gland
                NOS

           Excludes1   benign odontogenic
                        neoplasms (D16.4-D16.5)
                      benign neoplasm of mucosa
                        of lip (D10.0)
                      benign neoplasm of
                        nasopharyngeal surface
                        of soft palate (D10.6)

     D10.4 **Benign neoplasm of tonsil**
           Benign neoplasm of tonsil (faucial) (palatine)

         Excludes1   benign neoplasm of lingual tonsil
                     (D10.1)
                     benign neoplasm of pharyngeal
                        tonsil (D10.6)
                     benign neoplasm of tonsillar fossa
                        (D10.5)
                     benign neoplasm of tonsillar pillars
                        (D10.5)

     D10.5 **Benign neoplasm of other parts of oropharynx**
           Division of pharynx lying between soft palate and
             upper edge of epiglottis
           Benign neoplasm of epiglottis, anterior aspect
           Benign neoplasm of tonsillar fossa
           Benign neoplasm of tonsillar pillars
           Benign neoplasm of vallecula

         Excludes1   benign neoplasm of epiglottis NOS
                     (D14.1)
                     benign neoplasm of epiglottis,
                        suprahyoid portion (D14.1)

     D10.6 **Benign neoplasm of nasopharynx**
           Segment of pharynx that lies above soft palate
           Benign neoplasm of pharyngeal tonsil
           Benign neoplasm of posterior margin of septum
             and choanae

● Unacceptable First-Listed Diagnosis   ● Use Additional Character(s)   ■ Unspecified   **OGCR** Official Guidelines for Coding and Reporting

854   🝔 Complication\Comorbidity   🝔 Major C\C   Excludes 1   Excludes 2   Includes   Use additional   Code first   Code also

CHAPTER 2 (C00-D49)

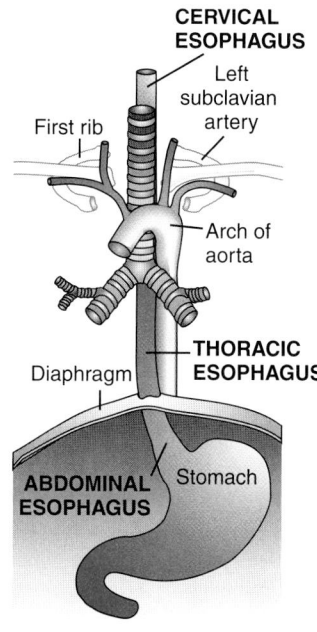

Figure 2-16 The esophagus is the muscular tube that connects the pharynx and the tomatch. The 10 inch (25 cm) long esophagus is divided into three parts: **cervical, thoracic,** and **abdominal.**

D10.7 Benign neoplasm of hypopharynx
Segment of pharynx that lies below upper edge of epiglottis and opens into larynx and esophagus

■**D10.9 Benign neoplasm of pharynx, unspecified**

●**D11 Benign neoplasm of major salivary glands**
Excludes1 benign neoplasms of specified minor salivary glands which are classified according to their anatomical location benign neoplasms of minor salivary glands NOS (D10.39)

D11.0 Benign neoplasm of parotid gland

D11.7 Benign neoplasm of other major salivary glands
Benign neoplasm of sublingual salivary gland
Benign neoplasm of submandibular salivary gland

■**D11.9 Benign neoplasm of major salivary gland, unspecified**

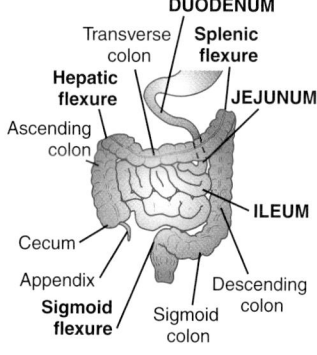

Figure 2-17 Small intestine and colon.

●**D12 Benign neoplasm of colon, rectum, anus and anal canal**
Excludes1 benign carcinoid tumors of the large intestine, and rectum (D3a.02-)

D12.0 Benign neoplasm of cecum
Benign neoplasm of ileocecal valve

D12.1 Benign neoplasm of appendix
Excludes1 benign carcinoid tumor of the appendix (D3a.020)

D12.2 Benign neoplasm of ascending colon

D12.3 Benign neoplasm of transverse colon
Benign neoplasm of hepatic flexure
Benign neoplasm of splenic flexure
Flexure is a bending in a structure or organ. Note the three flexures illustrated in Figure 2–17. Hepatic = liver, sigmoid = colon, splenic = spleen.

D12.4 Benign neoplasm of descending colon

D12.5 Benign neoplasm of sigmoid colon

■**D12.6 Benign neoplasm of colon, unspecified**
Adenomatosis of colon
Benign neoplasm of large intestine NOS
Polyposis (hereditary) of colon
Excludes1 inflammatory polyp of colon (K51.4-) polyp of colon NOS (K63.5)

D12.7 Benign neoplasm of rectosigmoid junction
Angle where sigmoid colon becomes rectum

D12.8 Benign neoplasm of rectum
Excludes1 benign carcinoid tumor of the rectum (D3a.026)

D12.9 Benign neoplasm of anus and anal canal
Benign neoplasm of anus NOS
Excludes1 benign neoplasm of anal margin (D22.5, D23.5)
benign neoplasm of anal skin (D22.5, D23.5)
benign neoplasm of perianal skin (D22.5, D23.5)

●**D13 Benign neoplasm of other and ill-defined parts of digestive system**
Excludes1 benign stromal tumors of digestive system (D21.4)

D13.0 Benign neoplasm of esophagus

D13.1 Benign neoplasm of stomach
Excludes1 benign carcinoid tumor of the stomach (D3a.092)

D13.2 Benign neoplasm of duodenum
Excludes1 benign carcinoid tumor of the duodenum (D3a.010)

●**D13.3 Benign neoplasm of other and unspecified parts of small intestine**
Excludes1 benign carcinoid tumors of the small intestine (D3a.01-)
benign neoplasm of ileocecal valve (D12.0)

■**D13.30 Benign neoplasm of unspecified part of small intestine**

D13.39 Benign neoplasm of other parts of small intestine

D13.4 Benign neoplasm of liver
Benign neoplasm of intrahepatic bile ducts

D13.5 Benign neoplasm of extrahepatic bile ducts
Extensions of common hepatic bile duct (tube that collects bile from liver)

● Unacceptable First-Listed Diagnosis   ● Use Additional Character(s)   ■ Unspecified   **OGCR** Official Guidelines for Coding and Reporting
🦠 Complication\Comorbidity   Major C\C   Excludes 1   Excludes 2   Includes   Use additional   Code first   Code also   855

CHAPTER 2 (C00-D49)

D13.6 **Benign neoplasm of pancreas**

> **Excludes1** benign neoplasm of endocrine pancreas (D13.7)

D13.7 **Benign neoplasm of endocrine pancreas**
Pancreatic islets: Cells scattered throughout pancreas
Islet cell tumor
Benign neoplasm of islets of Langerhans

> Use additional code to identify any functional activity.

D13.9 **Benign neoplasm of ill-defined sites within the digestive system**
Benign neoplasm of digestive system NOS
Benign neoplasm of intestine NOS
Benign neoplasm of spleen

● D14 **Benign neoplasm of middle ear and respiratory system**

D14.0 **Benign neoplasm of middle ear, nasal cavity and accessory sinuses**
Benign neoplasm of cartilage of nose

> **Excludes1** benign neoplasm of auricular canal (external) (D22.2-, D23.2-)
> benign neoplasm of bone of ear (D16.4)
> benign neoplasm of bone of nose (D16.4)
> benign neoplasm of cartilage of ear (D21.0)
> benign neoplasm of ear (external)(skin) (D22.2-, D23.2-)
> benign neoplasm of nose NOS (D36.7)
> benign neoplasm of skin of nose (D22.39, D23.39)
> benign neoplasm of olfactory bulb (D33.3)
> benign neoplasm of posterior margin of septum and choanae (D10.6)
> polyp of accessory sinus (J33.8)
> polyp of ear (middle) (H74.4)
> polyp of nasal (cavity) (J33.-)

D14.1 **Benign neoplasm of larynx**
Adenomatous polyp of larynx
Benign neoplasm of epiglottis (suprahyoid portion)
Horseshoe shaped bone in anterior midline of neck between chin and thyroid cartilage

> **Excludes1** benign neoplasm of epiglottis, anterior aspect (D10.5)
> polyp (nonadenomatous) of vocal cord or larynx (J38.1)

D14.2 **Benign neoplasm of trachea**

● D14.3 **Benign neoplasm of bronchus and lung**

> **Excludes1** benign carcinoid tumor of the bronchus and lung (D3a.090)

◻ D14.30 **Benign neoplasm of bronchus and lung, unspecified side**

D14.31 **Benign neoplasm of right bronchus and lung**

D14.32 **Benign neoplasm of left bronchus and lung**

◻ D14.4 **Benign neoplasm of respiratory system, unspecified**

● D15 **Benign neoplasm of other and unspecified intrathoracic organs**

> **Excludes1** benign neoplasm of mesothelial tissue (D19.-)

D15.0 **Benign neoplasm of thymus**

> **Excludes1** benign carcinoid tumor of the thymus (D3a.091)

D15.1 **Benign neoplasm of heart**

> **Excludes1** benign neoplasm of great vessels (D21.3)

D15.2 **Benign neoplasm of mediastinum**

D15.7 **Benign neoplasm of other specified intrathoracic organs**

◻ D15.9 **Benign neoplasm of intrathoracic organ, unspecified**

● D16 **Benign neoplasm of bone and articular cartilage**

> **Excludes1** benign neoplasm of connective tissue of ear (D21.0)
> benign neoplasm of connective tissue of eyelid (D21.0)
> benign neoplasm of connective tissue of larynx (D14.1)
> benign neoplasm of connective tissue of nose (D14.0)
> benign neoplasm of synovia (D21.-)

● D16.0 **Benign neoplasm of scapula and long bones of upper limb**

◻ D16.00 **Benign neoplasm of scapula and long bones of upper limb, unspecified side**

D16.01 **Benign neoplasm of scapula and long bones of right upper limb**

D16.02 **Benign neoplasm of scapula and long bones of left upper limb**

● D16.1 **Benign neoplasm of short bones of upper limb**

◻ D16.10 **Benign neoplasm of short bones of upper limb, unspecified side**

D16.11 **Benign neoplasm of short bones of right upper limb**

D16.12 **Benign neoplasm of short bones of left upper limb**

● D16.2 **Benign neoplasm of long bones of lower limb**

◻ D16.20 **Benign neoplasm of long bones of lower limb, unspecified side**

D16.21 **Benign neoplasm of long bones of right lower limb**

D16.22 **Benign neoplasm of long bones of left lower limb**

● D16.3 **Benign neoplasm of short bones of lower limb**

◻ D16.30 **Benign neoplasm of short bones of lower limb, unspecified side**

D16.31 **Benign neoplasm of short bones of right lower limb**

D16.32 **Benign neoplasm of short bones of left lower limb**

D16.4 **Benign neoplasm of bones of skull and face**
Benign neoplasm of maxilla (superior)
Benign neoplasm of orbital bone
Cavity or socket of skull in which eye and its appendages are located
Keratocyst of maxilla
Keratocystic odontogenictumor of maxilla

> **Excludes1** benign neoplasm of lower jaw bone (D16.5)

CHAPTER 2 (C00-D49)

● Unacceptable First-Listed Diagnosis ● Use Additional Character(s) ◻ Unspecified **OGCR** Official Guidelines for Coding and Reporting
🎗 Complication\Comorbidity 🎗 Major C\C Excludes 1 Excludes 2 Includes Use additional Code first Code also
856

D16.5 Benign neoplasm of lower jaw bone
Keratocyst of mandible
Keratocystic odontogenic tumor of mandible

D16.6 Benign neoplasm of vertebral column
| Excludes1 | benign neoplasm of sacrum and coccyx (D16.8)

D16.7 Benign neoplasm of ribs, sternum and clavicle

D16.8 Benign neoplasm of pelvic bones, sacrum and coccyx

▣D16.9 Benign neoplasm of bone and articular cartilage, unspecified

● **D17 Benign lipomatous neoplasm**
Slow growing benign tumors (rubbery masses) of mature fat cells enclosed in a thin fibrous capsule

D17.0 Benign lipomatous neoplasm of skin and subcutaneous tissue of head, face and neck

D17.1 Benign lipomatous neoplasm of skin and subcutaneous tissue of trunk

● **D17.2 Benign lipomatous neoplasm of skin and subcutaneous tissue of limb**

    ▣D17.20 Benign lipomatous neoplasm of skin and subcutaneous tissue of unspecified limb

    D17.21 Benign lipomatous neoplasm of skin and subcutaneous tissue of right arm

    D17.22 Benign lipomatous neoplasm of skin and subcutaneous tissue of left arm

    D17.23 Benign lipomatous neoplasm of skin and subcutaneous tissue of right leg

    D17.24 Benign lipomatous neoplasm of skin and subcutaneous tissue of left leg

● **D17.3 Benign lipomatous neoplasm of skin and subcutaneous tissue of other and unspecified sites**

    ▣D17.30 Benign lipomatous neoplasm of skin and subcutaneous tissue of unspecified sites

    D17.39 Benign lipomatous neoplasm of skin and subcutaneous tissue of other sites

D17.4 Benign lipomatous neoplasm of intrathoracic organs

D17.5 Benign lipomatous neoplasm of intra-abdominal organs
| Excludes1 | benign lipomatous neoplasm of peritoneum and retroperitoneum (D17.7)

D17.6 Benign lipomatous neoplasm of spermatic cord

D17.7 Benign lipomatous neoplasm of other sites
Benign lipomatous neoplasm of peritoneum
Benign lipomatous neoplasm of retroperitoneum

▣D17.9 Benign lipomatous neoplasm, unspecified
Lipoma NOS

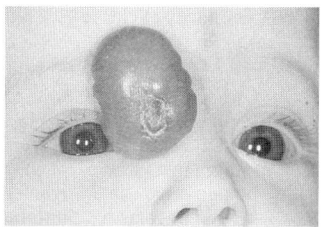

Figure 2-18 Hemangioma of skin and subcutaneous tissue. (From Yanoff: Ophthalmology, 2nd ed. 2004, Mosby, Inc.)

Item 2–10 Hemangiomas are abnormally dense collections of dilated capillaries that occur on the skin or in internal organs. Hemangiomas are both deep and superficial and undergo a rapid growth phase when the size increases rapidly, followed by a rest phase, in which the tumor changes very little, followed by an involutional phase in which the tumor begins to and can disappear altogether. **Lymphangiomas** or cystic hygroma are benign collections of overgrown lymph vessels and, although rare, may occur anywhere but most commonly on the head and neck of children and infants. Visceral organs, lungs, and gastrointestinal tract may also be involved.

● **D18 Hemangioma and lymphangioma, any site**
| Excludes1 | benign neoplasm of glomus jugulare (D35.6)
blue or pigmented nevus (D22.-)
nevus NOS (D22.-)
vascular nevus (Q82.5)

● **D18.0 Hemangioma**
Common type of vascular malformation
Angioma NOS
Cavernous nevus

    ▣D18.00 Hemangioma unspecified site

    D18.01 Hemangioma of skin and subcutaneous tissue

    D18.02 Hemangioma of intracranial structures

    D18.03 Hemangioma of intra-abdominal structures

    D18.09 Hemangioma of other sites

D18.1 Lymphangioma, any site

● **D19 Benign neoplasm of mesothelial tissue**
Mesothelial tissue is the membrane lining several body cavities

D19.0 Benign neoplasm of mesothelial tissue of pleura

D19.1 Benign neoplasm of mesothelial tissue of peritoneum

D19.7 Benign neoplasm of mesothelial tissue of other sites

▣D19.9 Benign neoplasm of mesothelial tissue, unspecified
Benign mesothelioma NOS

● **D20 Benign neoplasm of soft tissue of retroperitoneum and peritoneum**
| Excludes1 | benign lipomatous neoplasm of peritoneum and retroperitoneum (D17.7)
benign neoplasm of mesothelial tissue (D19.-)

D20.0 Benign neoplasm of soft tissue of retroperitoneum

D20.1 Benign neoplasm of soft tissue of peritoneum

● Unacceptable First-Listed Diagnosis   ● Use Additional Character(s)   ▣ Unspecified   **OGCR** Official Guidelines for Coding and Reporting
🐾 Complication\Comorbidity   🐾 Major C\C   Excludes 1   Excludes 2   Includes   Use additional   Code first   Code also

CHAPTER 2 (C00-D49)

857

● **D21**   **Other benign neoplasms of connective and other soft tissue**

> **Includes**   benign neoplasm of blood vessel
> benign neoplasm of bursa
> benign neoplasm of cartilage
> benign neoplasm of fascia
> benign neoplasm of fat
> benign neoplasm of ligament, except uterine
> benign neoplasm of lymphatic channel
> benign neoplasm of muscle
> benign neoplasm of synovia
> benign neoplasm of tendon (sheath)
> benign stromal tumors

> **Excludes1**   benign neoplasm of articular cartilage (D16.-)
> benign neoplasm of cartilage of larynx (D14.1)
> benign neoplasm of cartilage of nose (D14.0)
> benign neoplasm of connective tissue of breast (D24.-)
> benign neoplasm of peripheral nerves and autonomic nervous system (D36.1-)
> benign neoplasm of peritoneum (D20.1)
> benign neoplasm of retroperitoneum (D20.0)
> benign neoplasm of uterine ligament, any (D28.2)
> benign neoplasm of vascular tissue (D18.-)
> hemangioma (D18.0-)
> lipomatous neoplasm (D17.-)
> lymphangioma (D18.1)
> uterine leiomyoma (D25.-)

D21.0   **Benign neoplasm of connective and other soft tissue of head, face and neck**
> Benign neoplasm of connective tissue of ear
> Benign neoplasm of connective tissue of eyelid

> **Excludes1**   benign neoplasm of connective tissue of orbit (D31.6-)

● **D21.1**   **Benign neoplasm of connective and other soft tissue of upper limb, including shoulder**

    D21.10   **Benign neoplasm of connective and other soft tissue of upper limb, including shoulder, unspecified side**

    D21.11   **Benign neoplasm of connective and other soft tissue of right upper limb, including shoulder**

    D21.12   **Benign neoplasm of connective and other soft tissue of left upper limb, including shoulder**

● **D21.2**   **Benign neoplasm of connective and other soft tissue of lower limb, including hip**

    D21.20   **Benign neoplasm of connective and other soft tissue of lower limb, including hip, unspecified side**

    D21.21   **Benign neoplasm of connective and other soft tissue of right lower limb, including hip**

    D21.22   **Benign neoplasm of connective and other soft tissue of left lower limb, including hip**

D21.3   **Benign neoplasm of connective and other soft tissue of thorax**
> Benign neoplasm of axilla
> Benign neoplasm of diaphragm
> Benign neoplasm of great vessels

> **Excludes1**   benign neoplasm of heart (D15.1)
> benign neoplasm of mediastinum (D15.2)
> benign neoplasm of thymus (D15.0)

D21.4   **Benign neoplasm of connective and other soft tissue of abdomen Benign stromal tumors of abdomen**

D21.5   **Benign neoplasm of connective and other soft tissue of pelvis**

> **Excludes1**   benign neoplasm of any uterine ligament (D28.2)
> uterine leiomyoma (D25.-)

D21.6   **Benign neoplasm of connective and other soft tissue of trunk, unspecified**
> Benign neoplasm of back NOS

D21.9   **Benign neoplasm of connective and other soft tissue, unspecified**

● **D22**   **Melanocytic nevi**

> **Includes**   atypical nevus
> blue hairy pigmented nevus
> nevus NOS

D22.0   **Melanocytic nevi of lip**
> *Skin lesions composed of nests of nevus cells with macules/papules*

● **D22.1**   **Melanocytic nevi of eyelid, including canthus**

    D22.10   **Melanocytic nevi of eyelid, including canthus, unspecified side**

    D22.11   **Melanocytic nevi of right eyelid, including canthus**

    D22.12   **Melanocytic nevi of left eyelid, including canthus**

● **D22.2**   **Melanocytic nevi of ear and external auricular canal**

    D22.20   **Melanocytic nevi of ear and external auricular canal, unspecified side**

    D22.21   **Melanocytic nevi of right ear and external auricular canal**

    D22.22   **Melanocytic nevi of left ear and external auricular canal**

● **D22.3**   **Melanocytic nevi of other and unspecified parts of face**

    D22.30   **Melanocytic nevi of unspecified part of face**

    D22.39   **Melanocytic nevi of other parts of face**

D22.4   **Melanocytic nevi of scalp and neck**

D22.5   **Melanocytic nevi of trunk**
> Melanocytic nevi of anal margin
> Melanocytic nevi of anal skin
> Melanocytic nevi of perianal skin
> Melanocytic nevi of skin of breast

● **D22.6**   **Melanocytic nevi of upper limb, including shoulder**

    D22.60   **Melanocytic nevi of upper limb, including shoulder, unspecified side**

    D22.61   **Melanocytic nevi of right upper limb, including shoulder**

    D22.62   **Melanocytic nevi of left upper limb, including shoulder**

● **D22.7**   **Melanocytic nevi of lower limb, including hip**

    D22.70   **Melanocytic nevi of lower limb, including hip, unspecified side**

CHAPTER 2 (C00-D49)

858

● Unacceptable First-Listed Diagnosis   ● Use Additional Character(s)   ■ Unspecified   **OGCR** Official Guidelines for Coding and Reporting

🔾 Complication\Comorbidity   🔾 Major C\C   Excludes 1   Excludes 2   Includes   Use additional   Code first   Code also

D22.71   Melanocytic nevi of right lower limb, including hip

D22.72   Melanocytic nevi of left lower limb, including hip

◼ D22.9   Melanocytic nevi, unspecified

● D23   Other benign neoplasms of skin

> **Includes**   benign neoplasm of hair follicles
> benign neoplasm of sebaceous glands
> benign neoplasm of sweat glands

> **Excludes1**   benign lipomatous neoplasms of skin (D17.0-D17.3)
> melanocytic nevi (D22.-)

D23.0   Other benign neoplasm of skin of lip

> **Excludes1**   benign neoplasm of vermilion border of lip (D10.0)

● D23.1   Other benign neoplasm of skin of eyelid, including canthus

◼ D23.10   Other benign neoplasm of skin of eyelid, including canthus, unspecified side

D23.11   Other benign neoplasm of skin of right eyelid, including canthus

D23.12   Other benign neoplasm of skin of left eyelid, including canthus

● D23.2   Other benign neoplasm of skin of ear and external auricular canal

◼ D23.20   Other benign neoplasm of skin of ear and external auricular canal, unspecified side

D23.21   Other benign neoplasm of skin of right ear and external auricular canal

D23.22   Other benign neoplasm of skin of left ear and external auricular canal

● D23.3   Other benign neoplasm of skin of other and unspecified parts of face

◼ D23.30   Other benign neoplasm of skin of unspecified part of face

D23.39   Other benign neoplasm of skin of other parts of face

D23.4   Other benign neoplasm of skin of scalp and neck

D23.5   Other benign neoplasm of skin of trunk
Other benign neoplasm of anal margin
Other benign neoplasm of anal skin
Other benign neoplasm of perianal skin
Other benign neoplasm of skin of breast

> **Excludes1**   benign neoplasm of anus NOS (D12.9)

● D23.6   Other benign neoplasm of skin of upper limb, including shoulder

◼ D23.60   Other benign neoplasm of skin of upper limb, including shoulder, unspecified side

D23.61   Other benign neoplasm of skin of right upper limb, including shoulder

D23.62   Other benign neoplasm of skin of left upper limb, including shoulder

● D23.7   Other benign neoplasm of skin of lower limb, including hip

◼ D23.70   Other benign neoplasm of skin of lower limb, including hip, unspecified side

D23.71   Other benign neoplasm of skin of right lower limb, including hip

D23.72   Other benign neoplasm of skin of left lower limb, including hip

◼ D23.9   Other benign neoplasm of skin, unspecified

● D24   Benign neoplasm of breast

> **Includes**   benign neoplasm of connective tissue of breast
> benign neoplasm of soft parts of breast
> fibroadenoma of breast

> **Excludes2**   adenofibrosis of breast (N60.2)
> benign cyst of breast (N60.-)
> benign mammary dysplasia (N60.-)
> benign neoplasm of skin of breast (D22.5, D23.5)
> fibrocystic disease of breast (N60.-)

● D24.0   Benign neoplasm of female breast

◼ D24.00   Benign neoplasm of female breast, unspecified side

D24.01   Benign neoplasm of right female breast

D24.02   Benign neoplasm of left female breast

● D24.1   Benign neoplasm of male breast

◼ D24.10   Benign neoplasm of male breast, unspecified side

D24.11   Benign neoplasm of right male breast

D24.12   Benign neoplasm of left male breast

● D25   Leiomyoma of uterus
Benign tumors or nodules of the uterine wall

> **Includes**   uterine fibroid
> uterine fibromyoma
> uterine myoma

D25.0   Submucous leiomyoma of uterus

D25.1   Intramural leiomyoma of uterus
Interstitial leiomyoma of uterus

D25.2   Subserosal leiomyoma of uterus
Subperitoneal leiomyoma of uterus

◼ D25.9   Leiomyoma of uterus, unspecified

● D26   Other benign neoplasms of uterus

D26.0   Other benign neoplasm of cervix uteri

D26.1   Other benign neoplasm of corpus uteri

D26.7   Other benign neoplasm of other parts of uterus

◼ D26.9   Other benign neoplasm of uterus, unspecified

Item 2–11   Teratoma: terat = monster, oma = mass, tumor. Alternate terms: dermoid cyst of the ovary, ovarian teratoma. Teratomas are neoplasms and arise from germ cells (ovaries in female and testes in male) and can be benign or malignant. Teratomas have been known to contain hair, nails, and teeth, giving them a bizarre ("monster") appearance.

● Unacceptable First-Listed Diagnosis   ● Use Additional Character(s)   ◼ Unspecified   **OGCR** Official Guidelines for Coding and Reporting

 Complication\Comorbidity   Major C\C   Excludes 1   Excludes 2   Includes   Use additional   Code first   Code also

CHAPTER 2 (C00-D49)

● **D27   Benign neoplasm of ovary**

    Use additional code to identify any functional activity.

    Excludes2   corpus albicans cyst (N83.2)
                corpus luteum cyst (N83.1)
                endometrial cyst (N80.1)
                follicular (atretic) cyst (N83.0)
                graafian follicle cyst (N83.0)
                ovarian cyst NEC (N83.2)
                ovarian retention cyst (N83.2)

    D27.0   Benign neoplasm of right ovary

    D27.1   Benign neoplasm of left ovary

    ■ **D27.9   Benign neoplasm of ovary, unspecified side**

● **D28   Benign neoplasm of other and unspecified female genital organs**

    Includes   adenomatous polyp
              benign neoplasm of skin of female genital organs
              benign teratoma

    Excludes1   epoophoron cyst (Q50.5)
                fimbrial cyst (Q50.4)
                Gartner's duct cyst (Q52.4)
                parovarian cyst (Q50.5)

    D28.0   Benign neoplasm of vulva

    D28.1   Benign neoplasm of vagina

    D28.2   Benign neoplasm of uterine tubes and ligaments
         Benign neoplasm of fallopian tube
         Benign neoplasm of uterine ligament (broad) (round)

    D28.7   Benign neoplasm of other specified female genital organs

    ■ **D28.9   Benign neoplasm of female genital organ, unspecified**

● **D29   Benign neoplasm of male genital organs**

    Includes   benign neoplasm of skin of male genital organs

    D29.0   Benign neoplasm of penis

    D29.1   Benign neoplasm of prostate

        Excludes1   enlarged prostate (N40.-)

    ● **D29.2   Benign neoplasm of testis**

        Use additional code to identify any functional activity.

        ■ **D29.20   Benign neoplasm of testis, unspecified side**

        D29.21   Benign neoplasm of right testis

        D29.22   Benign neoplasm of left testis

    ● **D29.3   Benign neoplasm of epididymis**

        ■ **D29.30   Benign neoplasm of epididymis, unspecified side**

        D29.31   Benign neoplasm of right epididymis

        D29.32   Benign neoplasm of left epididymis

    D29.4   Benign neoplasm of scrotum
         Benign neoplasm of skin of scrotum

    D29.7   Benign neoplasm of other male genital organs
         Benign neoplasm of seminal vesicle
         Benign neoplasm of spermatic cord
         Benign neoplasm of tunica vaginalis

    ■ **D29.9   Benign neoplasm of male genital organ, unspecified**

● **D30   Benign neoplasm of urinary organs**

    ● **D30.0   Benign neoplasm of kidney**

        Excludes1   benign carcinoid tumor of the kidney (D3a.093)
                benign neoplasm of renal calyces (D30.1-)
                benign neoplasm of renal pelvis (D30.1-)

        ■ **D30.00   Benign neoplasm of kidney, unspecified side**

        D30.01   Benign neoplasm of right kidney

        D30.02   Benign neoplasm of left kidney

    ● **D30.1   Benign neoplasm of renal pelvis**

        ■ **D30.10   Benign neoplasm of renal pelvis, unspecified side**

        D30.11   Benign neoplasm of right renal pelvis

        D30.12   Benign neoplasm of left renal pelvis

    ● **D30.2   Benign neoplasm of ureter**

        Excludes1   benign neoplasm of ureteric orifice of bladder (D30.3)

        ■ **D30.20   Benign neoplasm of ureter, unspecified side**

        D30.21   Benign neoplasm of right ureter

        D30.22   Benign neoplasm of left ureter

    D30.3   Benign neoplasm of bladder
         Benign neoplasm of ureteric orifice of bladder
         Benign neoplasm of urethral orifice of bladder

    D30.4   Benign neoplasm of urethra

        Excludes1   benign neoplasm of urethral orifice of bladder (D30.3)

    D30.7   Benign neoplasm of other urinary organs
         Benign neoplasm of paraurethral glands

    ■ **D30.9   Benign neoplasm of urinary organ, unspecified**
         Benign neoplasm of urinary system NOS

● **D31   Benign neoplasm of eye and adnexa**

    Excludes1   benign neoplasm of connective tissue of eyelid (D21.0)
                benign neoplasm of optic nerve (D33.3)
                benign neoplasm of skin of eyelid (D22.1-, D23.1-)

    ● **D31.0   Benign neoplasm of conjunctiva**

        ■ **D31.00   Benign neoplasm of conjunctiva, unspecified side**

        D31.01   Benign neoplasm of right conjunctiva

        D31.02   Benign neoplasm of left conjunctiva

    ● **D31.1   Benign neoplasm of cornea**

        ■ **D31.10   Benign neoplasm of cornea, unspecified side**

        D31.11   Benign neoplasm of right cornea

        D31.12   Benign neoplasm of left cornea

    ● **D31.2   Benign neoplasm of retina**

        Excludes1   dark area on retina (D49.81)
                hemangioma of retina (D18.09)
                neoplasm of unspecified behavior of retina and choroid (D49.81)
                retinal freckle (D49.81)

        ■ **D31.20   Benign neoplasm of retina, unspecified side**

        D31.21   Benign neoplasm of right retina

        D31.22   Benign neoplasm of left retina

● Unacceptable First-Listed Diagnosis   ● Use Additional Character(s)   ■ Unspecified   **OGCR** Official Guidelines for Coding and Reporting

🔹 Complication\Comorbidity   🔹 Major C\C   Excludes 1   Excludes 2   Includes   Use additional   Code first   Code also

● D31.3   Benign neoplasm of choroid

     D31.30   Benign neoplasm of choroid, unspecified side

     D31.31   Benign neoplasm of right choroid

     D31.32   Benign neoplasm of left choroid

● D31.4   Benign neoplasm of ciliary body

     ■ D31.40   Benign neoplasm of ciliary body, unspecified side

     D31.41   Benign neoplasm of right ciliary body

     D31.42   Benign neoplasm of left ciliary body

● D31.5   Benign neoplasm of lacrimal gland and duct
     Benign neoplasm of lacrimal sac
     Benign neoplasm of nasolacrimal duct

     ■ D31.50   Benign neoplasm of lacrimal gland and duct, unspecified side

     D31.51   Benign neoplasm of right lacrimal gland and duct

     D31.52   Benign neoplasm of left lacrimal gland and duct

● D31.6   Benign neoplasm of orbit, unspecified
     Benign neoplasm of connective tissue of orbit
     Benign neoplasm of extraocular muscle
     Benign neoplasm of peripheral nerves of orbit
     Benign neoplasm of retrobulbar tissue
     Benign neoplasm of retro-ocular tissue

     Excludes1   benign neoplasm of orbital bone (D16.4)

     ■ D31.60   Benign neoplasm of orbit, unspecified, unspecified side

     ■ D31.61   Benign neoplasm of right orbit, unspecified

     ■ D31.62   Benign neoplasm of left orbit, unspecified

● D31.9   Benign neoplasm of eye, unspecified

     ■ D31.90   Benign neoplasm of eye, unspecified, unspecified side

     ■ D31.91   Benign neoplasm of right eye, unspecified

     ■ D31.92   Benign neoplasm of left eye, unspecified

● D32   Benign neoplasm of meninges

     D32.0   Benign neoplasm of cerebral meninges

     D32.1   Benign neoplasm of spinal meninges

     ■ D32.9   Benign neoplasm of meninges, unspecified
         Meningioma NOS

● D33   Benign neoplasm of brain and other parts of central nervous system

     Excludes1   angioma (D18.0-)
         benign neoplasm of meninges (D32.-)
         benign neoplasm of peripheral nerves and autonomic nervous system (D36.1-)
         hemangioma (D18.0-)
         neurofibromatosis (Q85.0)
         retro-ocular benign neoplasm (D31.6-)

     D33.0   Benign neoplasm of brain, supratentorial
     Benign neoplasm of cerebral ventricle
     Benign neoplasm of cerebrum
     Benign neoplasm of frontal lobe
     Benign neoplasm of occipital lobe
     Benign neoplasm of parietal lobe
     Benign neoplasm of temporal lobe

     Excludes1   benign neoplasm of fourth ventricle (D33.1)

D33.1   Benign neoplasm of brain, infratentorial
     Benign neoplasm of brain stem
     Benign neoplasm of cerebellum
     Benign neoplasm of fourth ventricle

■ D33.2   Benign neoplasm of brain, unspecified

D33.3   Benign neoplasm of cranial nerves
     Benign neoplasm of olfactory bulb

D33.4   Benign neoplasm of spinal cord

D33.7   Benign neoplasm of other specified parts of central nervous system

■ D33.9   Benign neoplasm of central nervous system, unspecified
     Benign neoplasm of nervous system (central) NOS

D34   Benign neoplasm of thyroid gland
     Use additional code to identify any functional activity.

● D35   Benign neoplasm of other and unspecified endocrine glands

     Use additional code to identify any functional activity.

     Excludes1   benign neoplasm of endocrine pancreas (D13.7)
         benign neoplasm of ovary (D27.-)
         benign neoplasm of testis (D29.2.-)
         benign neoplasm of thymus (D15.0)

     ● D35.0   Benign neoplasm of adrenal gland

         ■ D35.00   Benign neoplasm of adrenal gland, unspecified side

         D35.01   Benign neoplasm of right adrenal gland

         D35.02   Benign neoplasm of left adrenal gland

     D35.1   Benign neoplasm of parathyroid gland

     D35.2   Benign neoplasm of pituitary gland

     D35.3   Benign neoplasm of craniopharyngeal duct

     D35.4   Benign neoplasm of pineal gland

     D35.5   Benign neoplasm of carotid body

     D35.6   Benign neoplasm of aortic body and other paraganglia
     Benign tumor of glomus jugulare

     D35.7   Benign neoplasm of other specified endocrine glands

     D35.8   Benign neoplasm with pluriglandular involvement

     ■ D35.9   Benign neoplasm of endocrine gland, unspecified

● D36   Benign neoplasm of other and unspecified sites

     D36.0   Benign neoplasm of lymph nodes

     Excludes1   lymphangioma (D18.1)

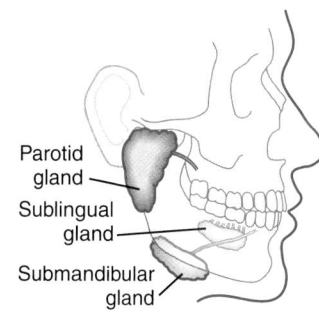

Figure 2-19   Major salivary glands.

Parotid gland
Sublingual gland
Submandibular gland

● Unacceptable First-Listed Diagnosis   ● Use Additional Character(s)   ■ Unspecified   **OGCR** Official Guidelines for Coding and Reporting

🔖 Complication\Comorbidity   🔖 Major C\C   Excludes 1   Excludes 2   Includes   Use additional   Code first   Code also

861

CHAPTER 2 (C00-D49)

● **D36.1 Benign neoplasm of peripheral nerves and autonomic nervous system**

> **Excludes1**   benign neoplasm of peripheral nerves of orbit (D31.6-)
> neurofibromatosis (Q85.0)

◼ **D36.10 Benign neoplasm of peripheral nerves and autonomic nervous system, unspecified**

D36.11 Benign neoplasm of peripheral nerves and autonomic nervous system of face, head, and neck

D36.12 Benign neoplasm of peripheral nerves and autonomic nervous system, upper limb, including shoulder

D36.13 Benign neoplasm of peripheral nerves and autonomic nervous system of lower limb, including hip

D36.14 Benign neoplasm of peripheral nerves and autonomic nervous system of thorax

D36.15 Benign neoplasm of peripheral nerves and autonomic nervous system of abdomen

D36.16 Benign neoplasm of peripheral nerves and autonomic nervous system of pelvis

◼ **D36.17 Benign neoplasm of peripheral nerves and autonomic nervous system of trunk, unspecified**

D36.7 Benign neoplasm of other specified sites
Benign neoplasm of nose NOS

◼ **D36.9 Benign neoplasm, unspecified site**

BENIGN NEUROENDOCRINE TUMORS (D3A)

● **D3a Benign neuroendocrine tumors**

> Code also any associated multiple endocrine neoplasia [MEN] syndromes (E31.2-)

> Use additional code to identify any associated endocrine syndrome, such as:
> carcinoid syndrome (E34.0)

> **Excludes2**   benign pancreatic islet cell tumors (D13.7)

● **D3a.0 Benign carcinoid tumors**

◼ **D3a.00 Benign carcinoid tumor of unspecified site**
Carcinoid tumor NOS

● **D3a.01 Benign carcinoid tumors of the small intestine**

D3a.010 Benign carcinoid tumor of the duodenum

D3a.011 Benign carcinoid tumor of the jejunum

D3a.012 Benign carcinoid tumor of the ileum

◼ **D3a.019 Benign carcinoid tumor of the small intestine, unspecified portion**

● **D3a.02 Benign carcinoid tumors of the appendix, large intestine, and rectum**

D3a.020 Benign carcinoid tumor of the appendix

D3a.021 Benign carcinoid tumor of the cecum

D3a.022 Benign carcinoid tumor of the ascending colon

D3a.023 Benign carcinoid tumor of the transverse colon

D3a.024 Benign carcinoid tumor of the descending colon

D3a.025 Benign carcinoid tumor of the sigmoid colon

D3a.026 Benign carcinoid tumor of the rectum

◼ **D3a.029 Benign carcinoid tumor of the large intestine, unspecified portion**
Benign carcinoid tumor of the colon NOS

● **D3a.09 Benign carcinoid tumors of other sites**

D3a.090 Benign carcinoid tumor of the bronchus and lung

D3a.091 Benign carcinoid tumor of the thymus

D3a.092 Benign carcinoid tumor of the stomach

D3a.093 Benign carcinoid tumor of the kidney

D3a.094 Benign carcinoid tumor of the foregut NOS

D3a.095 Benign carcinoid tumor of the midgut NOS

D3a.096 Benign carcinoid tumor of the hindgut NOS

D3a.098 Benign carcinoid tumors of other sites

D3a.8 Other benign neuroendocrine tumors
Neuroendocrine tumor NOS

NEOPLASMS OF UNCERTAIN BEHAVIOR, POLYCYTHEMIA VERA AND MYELODYSPLASTIC SYNDROMES (D37-D48)

Note: Categories D37-D44, and D48 classify by site neoplasms of uncertain behavior, i.e., histologic confirmation whether the neoplasm is malignant or benign cannot be made. Use additional morphology codes with behavior code /1.

> **Excludes1**   neoplasms of unspecified behavior (D49-)

● **D37 Neoplasm of uncertain behavior of oral cavity and digestive organs**

> **Excludes1**   stromal tumors of uncertain behavior of digestive system (D48.1)

● **D37.0 Neoplasm of uncertain behavior of lip, oral cavity and pharynx**

> **Excludes1**   neoplasm of uncertain behavior of aryepiglottic fold or interarytenoid fold, laryngeal aspect (D38.0)
> neoplasm of uncertain behavior of epiglottis NOS (D38.0)
> neoplasm of uncertain behavior of skin of lip (D48.5)
> neoplasm of uncertain behavior of suprahyoid portion of epiglottis (D38.0)

D37.01 Neoplasm of uncertain behavior of lip
Neoplasm of uncertain behavior of vermilion border of lip

D37.02 Neoplasm of uncertain behavior of tongue

● **D37.03 Neoplasm of uncertain behavior of the major salivary glands**

D37.030 Neoplasm of uncertain behavior of the parotid salivary glands

● Unacceptable First-Listed Diagnosis	● Use Additional Character(s)	◼ Unspecified	**OGCR** Official Guidelines for Coding and Reporting
🩺 Complication\Comorbidity 🩺 Major C\C	Excludes 1 Excludes 2	Includes Use additional	Code first Code also

D37.031 Neoplasm of uncertain behavior of the sublingual salivary glands

D37.032 Neoplasm of uncertain behavior of the submandibular salivary glands

■ D37.039 Neoplasm of uncertain behavior of the major salivary glands, unspecified

D37.04 Neoplasm of uncertain behavior of the minor salivary glands

Neoplasm of uncertain behavior of submucosal salivary glands of lip
Neoplasm of uncertain behavior of submucosal salivary glands of cheek
Neoplasm of uncertain behavior of submucosal salivary glands of hard palate
Neoplasm of uncertain behavior of submucosal salivary glands of soft palate

D37.05 Neoplasm of uncertain behavior of pharynx

Neoplasm of uncertain behavior of aryepiglottic fold of pharynx NOS
Neoplasm of uncertain behavior of hypopharyngeal aspect of aryepiglottic fold of pharynx
Neoplasm of uncertain behavior of marginal zone of aryepiglottic fold of pharynx

■ D37.09 Neoplasm of uncertain behavior of other specified sites of the oral cavity

D37.1 Neoplasm of uncertain behavior of stomach

D37.2 Neoplasm of uncertain behavior of small intestine

D37.3 Neoplasm of uncertain behavior of appendix

D37.4 Neoplasm of uncertain behavior of colon

D37.5 Neoplasm of uncertain behavior of rectum

Neoplasm of uncertain behavior of rectosigmoid junction
Rectosigmoid junction: Angle where sigmoid colon becomes rectum

■ D37.6 Neoplasm of uncertain behavior of liver, gallbladder and bile ducts

Neoplasm of uncertain behavior of ampulla of Vater
Ampulla of Vater: Enlarged segment of ducts from liver and pancreas at entry point to small intestine

D37.7 Neoplasm of uncertain behavior of other digestive organs

Neoplasm of uncertain behavior of anal canal
Neoplasm of uncertain behavior of anal sphincter
Neoplasm of uncertain behavior of anus NOS
Neoplasm of uncertain behavior of esophagus
Neoplasm of uncertain behavior of intestine NOS
Neoplasm of uncertain behavior of pancreas

Excludes1	neoplasm of uncertain behavior of anal margin (D48.5)
	neoplasm of uncertain behavior of anal skin (D48.5)
	neoplasm of uncertain behavior of perianal skin (D48.5)

D37.9 Neoplasm of uncertain behavior of digestive organ, unspecified

● D38 Neoplasm of uncertain behavior of middle ear and respiratory and intrathoracic organs

| Excludes1 | neoplasm of uncertain behavior of heart (D48.7) |

D38.0 Neoplasm of uncertain behavior of larynx

Neoplasm of uncertain behavior of aryepiglottic fold or interarytenoid fold, laryngeal aspect
Neoplasm of uncertain behavior of epiglottis (suprahyoid portion)

Excludes1	neoplasm of uncertain behavior of aryepiglottic fold or interarytenoid fold NOS (D37.05)
	neoplasm of uncertain behavior of hypopharyngeal aspect of aryepiglottic fold (D37.05)
	neoplasm of uncertain behavior of marginal zone of aryepiglottic fold (D37.05)

D38.1 Neoplasm of uncertain behavior of trachea, bronchus and lung

D38.2 Neoplasm of uncertain behavior of pleura

D38.3 Neoplasm of uncertain behavior of mediastinum

D38.4 Neoplasm of uncertain behavior of thymus

D38.5 Neoplasm of uncertain behavior of other respiratory organs

Neoplasm of uncertain behavior of accessory sinuses
Neoplasm of uncertain behavior of cartilage of nose
Neoplasm of uncertain behavior of middle ear
Neoplasm of uncertain behavior of nasal cavities

Excludes1	neoplasm of uncertain behavior of ear (external) (skin) (D48.5)
	neoplasm of uncertain behavior of nose NOS (D48.7)
	neoplasm of uncertain behavior of skin of nose (D48.5)

D38.6 Neoplasm of uncertain behavior of respiratory organ, unspecified

● D39 Neoplasm of uncertain behavior of female genital organs

D39.0 Neoplasm of uncertain behavior of uterus

● D39.1 Neoplasm of uncertain behavior of ovary

Use additional code to identify any functional activity.

■ D39.10 Neoplasm of uncertain behavior of ovary, unspecified side

D39.11 Neoplasm of uncertain behavior of right ovary

D39.12 Neoplasm of uncertain behavior of left ovary

D39.2 Neoplasm of uncertain behavior of placenta

Chorioadenoma destruens
Invasive hydatidiform mole
Malignant hydatidiform mole

| Excludes1 | hydatidiform mole NOS (O01.9) |

D39.7 Neoplasm of uncertain behavior of other female genital organs

Neoplasm of uncertain behavior of skin of female genital organs

■ D39.9 Neoplasm of uncertain behavior of female genital organ, unspecified

● Unacceptable First-Listed Diagnosis   ● Use Additional Character(s)   ■ Unspecified   **OGCR** Official Guidelines for Coding and Reporting

🅒 Complication\Comorbidity   🅜 Major C\C   Excludes 1   Excludes 2   Includes   Use additional   Code first   Code also

863

CHAPTER 2 (C00-D49)

● **D40   Neoplasm of uncertain behavior of male genital organs**

    D40.0   Neoplasm of uncertain behavior of prostate

    ● **D40.1   Neoplasm of uncertain behavior of testis**

        ■ **D40.10   Neoplasm of uncertain behavior of testis, unspecified side**

        D40.11   Neoplasm of uncertain behavior of right testis

        D40.12   Neoplasm of uncertain behavior of left testis

    D40.7   Neoplasm of uncertain behavior of other male genital organs

        Neoplasm of uncertain behavior of skin of male genital organs

    ■ **D40.9   Neoplasm of uncertain behavior of male genital organ, unspecified**

● **D41   Neoplasm of uncertain behavior of urinary organs**

    ● **D41.0   Neoplasm of uncertain behavior of kidney**

        Excludes1   neoplasm of uncertain behavior of renal pelvis (D41.1-)

        ■ **D41.00   Neoplasm of uncertain behavior of kidney, unspecified side**

        D41.01   Neoplasm of uncertain behavior of right kidney

        D41.02   Neoplasm of uncertain behavior of left kidney

    ● **D41.1   Neoplasm of uncertain behavior of renal pelvis**

        ■ **D41.10   Neoplasm of uncertain behavior of renal pelvis, unspecified side**

        D41.11   Neoplasm of uncertain behavior of right renal pelvis

        D41.12   Neoplasm of uncertain behavior of left renal pelvis

    ● **D41.2   Neoplasm of uncertain behavior of ureter**

        ■ **D41.20   Neoplasm of uncertain behavior of ureter, unspecified side**

        D41.21   Neoplasm of uncertain behavior of right ureter

        D41.22   Neoplasm of uncertain behavior of left ureter

    D41.3   Neoplasm of uncertain behavior of urethra

    D41.4   Neoplasm of uncertain behavior of bladder

    D41.7   Neoplasm of uncertain behavior of other urinary organs

    ■ **D41.9   Neoplasm of uncertain behavior of urinary organ, unspecified**

● **D42   Neoplasm of uncertain behavior of meninges**

    D42.0   Neoplasm of uncertain behavior of cerebral meninges

    D42.1   Neoplasm of uncertain behavior of spinal meninges

    ■ **D42.9   Neoplasm of uncertain behavior of meninges, unspecified**

● **D43   Neoplasm of uncertain behavior of brain and central nervous system**

    Excludes1   neoplasm of uncertain behavior of peripheral nerves and autonomic nervous system (D48.2)

    D43.0   Neoplasm of uncertain behavior of brain, supratentorial

        Superior to tentorium of cerebellum
        Neoplasm of uncertain behavior of cerebral ventricle
        Neoplasm of uncertain behavior of cerebrum
        Neoplasm of uncertain behavior of frontal lobe
        Neoplasm of uncertain behavior of occipital lobe
        Neoplasm of uncertain behavior of parietal lobe
        Neoplasm of uncertain behavior of temporal lobe

        Excludes1   neoplasm of uncertain behavior of fourth ventricle (D43.1)

    D43.1   Neoplasm of uncertain behavior of brain, infratentorial

        Beneath the tentorium of cerebellum
        Neoplasm of uncertain behavior of brain stem
        Neoplasm of uncertain behavior of cerebellum
        Neoplasm of uncertain behavior of fourth ventricle

    ■ **D43.2   Neoplasm of uncertain behavior of brain, unspecified**

    D43.3   Neoplasm of uncertain behavior of cranial nerves

    D43.4   Neoplasm of uncertain behavior of spinal cord

    D43.7   Neoplasm of uncertain behavior of other parts of central nervous system

    ■ **D43.9   Neoplasm of uncertain behavior of central nervous system, unspecified**

        Neoplasm of uncertain behavior of nervous system (central) NOS

● **D44   Neoplasm of uncertain behavior of endocrine glands**

    Excludes1   neoplasm of uncertain behavior of endocrine pancreas (D37.7)
        neoplasm of uncertain behavior of ovary (D39.1-)
        neoplasm of uncertain behavior of testis (D40.1-)
        neoplasm of uncertain behavior of thymus (D38.4)

    D44.0   Neoplasm of uncertain behavior of thyroid gland

    ● **D44.1   Neoplasm of uncertain behavior of adrenal gland**

        Use additional code to identify any functional activity.

        ■ **D44.10   Neoplasm of uncertain behavior of adrenal gland, unspecified side**

        D44.11   Neoplasm of uncertain behavior of right adrenal gland

        D44.12   Neoplasm of uncertain behavior of left adrenal gland

    D44.2   Neoplasm of uncertain behavior of parathyroid gland

    D44.3   Neoplasm of uncertain behavior of pituitary gland

        Use additional code to identify any functional activity.

    D44.4   Neoplasm of uncertain behavior of craniopharyngeal duct

    D44.5   Neoplasm of uncertain behavior of pineal gland

● Unacceptable First-Listed Diagnosis   ● Use Additional Character(s)   ■ Unspecified   **OGCR** Official Guidelines for Coding and Reporting

🗫 Complication\Comorbidity   🗫 Major C\C   Excludes 1   Excludes 2   Includes   Use additional   Code first   Code also

D44.6 Neoplasm of uncertain behavior of carotid body

D44.7 Neoplasm of uncertain behavior of aortic body and other paraganglia

D44.8 Neoplasm of uncertain behavior with pluriglandular involvement

> Excludes1   multiple endocrine adenomatosis (E31.2-)
>
>   multiple endocrine neoplasia (E31.2-)

D44.9 Neoplasm of uncertain behavior of endocrine gland, unspecified

D45 Polycythemia vera

> Excludes1   familial polycythemia (D75.0)
>
>   secondary polycythemia (D75.1)

Primary polycythemia. Secondary polycythemia is D75.1. Check your documentation. Polycythemia is caused by too many red blood cells, which increase the thickness of blood (viscosity). This can cause engorgement of the spleen (splenomegaly) with extra RBCs and potential clot formation.

● D46 Myelodysplastic syndromes

> *Code first (T36-T50) to identify drug, if drug induced*
>
> Excludes2   drug-induced aplastic anemia (D61.1)

D46.0 Refractory anemia without ring sideroblasts, so stated

> Refractory anemia without sideroblasts, without excess of blasts

D46.1 Refractory anemia with ring sideroblasts RARS

● D46.2 Refractory anemia with excess of blasts

> *Form of myelodysplasia with increased immature white blood cells (blasts) in bone marrow*

> **■ D46.20 Refractory anemia with excess of blasts, unspecified RAEB NOS 🔧**

> **D46.21 Refractory anemia with excess of blasts 1 RAEB 1 🔧**
>
> *Bone marrow disease which results in insufficient RBC's (anemia) in which level of blasts is less than 10%*

> **D46.22 Refractory anemia with excess of blasts 2 RAEB 2 🔧**
>
> *Bone marrow disease manifested by insufficient numbers of RBC's (anemia) with level of blasts 10-20%*

D46.a Refractory cytopenia with multilineage dysplasia

D46.b Refractory cytopenia with multilineage dysplasia and ringed sideroblasts
> RCMD RS

D46.c Myelodysplastic syndrome with isolated del(5q) chromosomal abnormality
> Myelodysplastic syndrome with 5q deletion
> 5q minus syndrome NOS

■ D46.4 Refractory anemia, unspecified

D46.z Other myelodysplastic syndromes

> Excludes1   chronic myelomonocytic leukemia (C93.1-)

■ D46.9 Myelodysplastic syndrome, unspecified
> Myelodysplasia NOS
> Preleukemia (syndrome) NOS

● D47 Other neoplasms of uncertain behavior of lymphoid, hematopoietic and related tissue

D47.0 Histiocytic and mast cell tumors of uncertain behavior 🔧
> Indolent systemic mastocytosis
> Mast cell tumor NOS
> Mastocytoma NOS

> Excludes1   malignant mast cell tumor (C96.2)
>
>   mastocytosis (congenital) (cutaneous) (Q82.2)

D47.1 Chronic myeloproliferative disease 🔧
> Chronic neutrophilic leukemia
> Myeloproliferative disease, unspecified

> Excludes1   atypical chronic myeloid leukemia (C92.2-)
>
>   chronic myeloid leukemia BCR/ABL-positive (C92.1-)
>
>   myelofibrosis NOS (D75.81)
>
>   myelophthisic anemia (D61.82)
>
>   myelophthisis (D61.82)
>
>   secondary myelofibrosis NOS (D75.81)

D47.2 Monoclonal gammopathy
> Monoclonal gammopathy of undetermined significance [MGUS]

D47.3 Essential (hemorrhagic) thrombocythemia
> Essential thrombocytosis
> Idiopathic hemorrhagic thrombocythemia

D47.4 Osteomyelofibrosis
> Chronic idiopathic myelofibrosis
> Myelofibrosis (idiopathic) (with myeloid metaplasia)
> Myelosclerosis (megakaryocytic) with myeloid metaplasia
> Secondary myelofibrosis in myeloproliferative disease

> Excludes1   acute myelofibrosis (C94.4-)

● D47.z Other specified neoplasms of uncertain behavior of lymphoid, hematopoietic and related tissue

> **D47.z1 Post-transplant lymphoproliferative disorder (PTLD)**
>
> *Code first complications of transplanted organs and tissue (T86.-)*

> **D47.z9 Other specified neoplasms of uncertain behavior of lymphoid, hematopoietic and related tissue**
> > Histiocytic tumors of uncertain behavior

■ D47.9 Neoplasm of uncertain behavior of lymphoid, hematopoietic and related tissue, unspecified 🔧
> Lymphoproliferative disease NOS

● D48 Neoplasm of uncertain behavior of other and unspecified sites

> Excludes1   neurofibromatosis (nonmalignant) (Q85.0)

D48.0 Neoplasm of uncertain behavior of bone and articular cartilage

> Excludes1   neoplasm of uncertain behavior of cartilage of ear (D48.1)
>
>   neoplasm of uncertain behavior of cartilage of larynx (D38.0)
>
>   neoplasm of uncertain behavior of cartilage of nose (D38.5)
>
>   neoplasm of uncertain behavior of connective tissue of eyelid (D48.1)
>
>   neoplasm of uncertain behavior of synovia (D48.1)

● Unacceptable First-Listed Diagnosis   ● Use Additional Character(s)   ■ Unspecified   **OGCR** Official Guidelines for Coding and Reporting

🔧 Complication\Comorbidity   🔧 Major C\C   Excludes 1   Excludes 2   Includes   Use additional   Code first   Code also

865

CHAPTER 2 (C00-D49)

D48.1 Neoplasm of uncertain behavior of connective and other soft tissue
  Neoplasm of uncertain behavior of connective tissue of ear
  Neoplasm of uncertain behavior of connective tissue of eyelid
  Stromal tumors of uncertain behavior of digestive system

  | Excludes1 | neoplasm of uncertain behavior of articular cartilage (D48.0)
  neoplasm of uncertain behavior of cartilage of larynx (D38.0)
  neoplasm of uncertain behavior of cartilage of nose (D38.5)
  neoplasm of uncertain behavior of connective tissue of breast (D48.6-)

D48.2 Neoplasm of uncertain behavior of peripheral nerves and autonomic nervous system

  | Excludes1 | neoplasm of uncertain behavior of peripheral nerves of orbit (D48.7)

D48.3 Neoplasm of uncertain behavior of retroperitoneum

D48.4 Neoplasm of uncertain behavior of peritoneum

D48.5 Neoplasm of uncertain behavior of skin
  Neoplasm of uncertain behavior of anal margin
  Neoplasm of uncertain behavior of anal skin
  Neoplasm of uncertain behavior of perianal skin
  Neoplasm of uncertain behavior of skin of breast

  | Excludes1 | neoplasm of uncertain behavior of anus NOS (D37.7)
  neoplasm of uncertain behavior of skin of genital organs (D39.7, D40.7)
  neoplasm of uncertain behavior of vermilion border of lip (D37.0)

● **D48.6 Neoplasm of uncertain behavior of breast**
  Neoplasm of uncertain behavior of connective tissue of breast
  Cystosarcoma phyllodes

  | Excludes1 | neoplasm of uncertain behavior of skin of breast (D48.5)

  D48.61 Neoplasm of uncertain behavior of right breast

  D48.62 Neoplasm of uncertain behavior of left breast

  D48.69 Neoplasm of uncertain behavior of unspecified breast

D48.7 Neoplasm of uncertain behavior of other specified sites
  Neoplasm of uncertain behavior of eye
  Neoplasm of uncertain behavior of heart
  Neoplasm of uncertain behavior of peripheral nerves of orbit

  | Excludes1 | neoplasm of uncertain behavior of connective tissue (D48.1)
  neoplasm of uncertain behavior of skin of eyelid (D48.5)

D48.9 Neoplasm of uncertain behavior, unspecified

● **D49 Neoplasms of unspecified behavior**
  Note: Category D49 classifies by site neoplasms of unspecified morphology and behavior. The term "mass", unless otherwise stated, is not to be regarded as a neoplastic growth.

  | Includes | "growth" NOS
  neoplasm NOS
  new growth NOS
  tumor NOS

  | Excludes1 | neoplasms of uncertain behavior (D37-D44, D48)

D49.0 Neoplasm of unspecified behavior of digestive system

  | Excludes1 | neoplasm of unspecified behavior of margin of anus (D49.2)
  neoplasm of unspecified behavior of perianal skin (D49.2)
  neoplasm of unspecified behavior of skin of anus (D49.2)

D49.1 Neoplasm of unspecified behavior of respiratory system

D49.2 Neoplasm of unspecified behavior of bone, soft tissue, and skin

  | Excludes1 | neoplasm of unspecified behavior of anal canal (D49.0)
  neoplasm of unspecified behavior of anus NOS (D49.0)
  neoplasm of unspecified behavior of bone marrow (D49.9)
  neoplasm of unspecified behavior of cartilage of larynx (D49.1)
  neoplasm of unspecified behavior of cartilage of nose (D49.1)
  neoplasm of unspecified behavior of connective tissue of breast (D49.3)
  neoplasm of unspecified behavior of skin of genital organs (D49.5)
  neoplasm of unspecified behavior of vermilion border of lip (D49.0)

D49.3 Neoplasm of unspecified behavior of breast

  | Excludes1 | neoplasm of unspecified behavior of skin of breast (D49.2)

D49.4 Neoplasm of unspecified behavior of bladder

D49.5 Neoplasm of unspecified behavior of other genitourinary organs

D49.6 Neoplasm of unspecified behavior of brain

  | Excludes1 | neoplasm of unspecified behavior of cerebral meninges (D49.7)
  neoplasm of unspecified behavior of cranial nerves (D49.7)

● **D49.7 Neoplasm of unspecified behavior of endocrine glands and other parts of nervous system**

  | Excludes1 | neoplasm of unspecified behavior of peripheral, sympathetic, and parasympathetic nerves and ganglia (D49.2)

● D49.8 **Neoplasm of unspecified behavior of other specified sites**

Excludes1 neoplasm of unspecified behavior of eyelid (skin) (D49.2)

neoplasm of unspecified behavior of eyelid cartilage (D49.2)

neoplasm of unspecified behavior of great vessels (D49.2)

neoplasm of unspecified behavior of optic nerve (D49.7)

■ D49.81 **Neoplasm of unspecified behavior of retina and choroid**

Dark area on retina

Retinal freckle

■ D49.89 **Neoplasm of unspecified behavior of other specified sites**

■ D49.9 **Neoplasm of unspecified behavior of unspecified site**

● Unacceptable First-Listed Diagnosis   ● Use Additional Character(s)   ■ Unspecified   **OGCR** Official Guidelines for Coding and Reporting

🔗 Complication\Comorbidity   🔗 Major C\C   Excludes 1   Excludes 2   Includes   Use additional   Code first   Code also

867

CHAPTER 2 (C00-D49)

CHAPTER 3

DISEASES OF THE BLOOD AND BLOOD-FORMING ORGANS AND CERTAIN DISORDERS INVOLVING THE IMMUNE MECHANISM (D50-D89)

Excludes2   autoimmune disease (systemic) NOS (M35.9)
certain conditions originating in the perinatal period (P00-P96)
complications of pregnancy, childbirth and the puerperium (O00-O99)
congenital malformations, deformations and chromosomal abnormalities (Q00-Q99)
endocrine, nutritional and metabolic diseases (E00-E90)
human immunodeficiency virus [HIV] disease (B20)
injury, poisoning and certain other consequences of external causes (S00-T98)
neoplasms (C00-D49)
symptoms, signs and abnormal clinical and laboratory findings, not elsewhere classified (R00-R94)

This chapter contains the following blocks:

D50-D53	Nutritional anemias
D55-D59	Hemolytic anemias
D60-D64	Aplastic and other anemias and other bone marrow failure syndromes
D65-D69	Coagulation defects, purpura and other hemorrhagic conditions
D70-D77	Other disorders of blood and blood-forming organs
D78	Intraoperative and postprocedural complications of spleen
D80-D89	Certain disorders involving the immune mechanism

NUTRITIONAL ANEMIAS (D50-D53)

● **D50   Iron deficiency anemia**
A disease characterized by a decrease in the number of red cells (hemoglobin) in the blood.

   Includes   asiderotic anemia
hypochromic anemia

D50.0   Iron deficiency anemia secondary to blood loss (chronic)
Posthemorrhagic anemia (chronic)

   Excludes1   acute posthemorrhagic anemia (D62)
congenital anemia from fetal blood loss (P61.3)

D50.1   Sideropenic dysphagia
Web-like growth of membranes in throat that makes swallowing difficult

Kelly-Paterson syndrome
Plummer-Vinson syndrome

D50.8   Other iron deficiency anemias
Iron deficiency anemia due to inadequate dietary iron intake

◼ **D50.9   Iron deficiency anemia, unspecified**

● **D51   Vitamin B12 deficiency anemia**

   Excludes1   vitamin B12 deficiency (E53.8)

D51.0   Vitamin B12 deficiency anemia due to intrinsic factor deficiency
Addison anemia
Biermer anemia
Pernicious (congenital) anemia
Congenital intrinsic factor deficiency

D51.1   Vitamin B12 deficiency anemia due to selective vitamin B12 malabsorption with proteinuria
Imerslund (-Gräsbeck) syndrome
Megaloblastic hereditary anemia

D51.2   Transcobalamin II deficiency

D51.3   Other dietary vitamin B12 deficiency anemia
Vegan anemia

D51.8   Other vitamin B12 deficiency anemias

◼ **D51.9   Vitamin B12 deficiency anemia, unspecified**

● **D52   Folate deficiency anemia**

   Excludes1   folate deficiency without anemia (E53.8)

D52.0   Dietary folate deficiency anemia
Nutritional megaloblastic anemia

● **D52.1   Drug-induced folate deficiency anemia**
Code first (T36-T50) to identify drug

D52.8   Other folate deficiency anemias

◼ **D52.9   Folate deficiency anemia, unspecified**
Folic acid deficiency anemia NOS

● **D53   Other nutritional anemias**

   Includes   megaloblastic anemia unresponsive to vitamin B12 or folate therapy

D53.0   Protein deficiency anemia
Amino-acid deficiency anemia
Orotaciduric anemia

   Excludes1   Lesch-Nyhan syndrome (E79.1)

D53.1   Other megaloblastic anemias, not elsewhere classified
Megaloblastic anemia NOS

   Excludes1   Di Guglielmo's disease (C94.0)

D53.2   Scorbutic anemia
Anemia resulting from deficiency of ascorbic acid (vitamin C)

   Excludes1   scurvy (E54)

D53.8   Other specified nutritional anemias
Anemia associated with deficiency of copper
Anemia associated with deficiency of molybdenum
Anemia associated with deficiency of zinc

   Excludes1   nutritional deficiencies without anemia, such as:
copper deficiency NOS (E61.0)
molybdenum deficiency NOS (E61.5)
zinc deficiency NOS (E60)

◼ **D53.9   Nutritional anemia, unspecified**
Simple chronic anemia

   Excludes1   anemia NOS (D64.9)

● Unacceptable First-Listed Diagnosis   ● Use Additional Character(s)   ◼ Unspecified   **OGCR** Official Guidelines for Coding and Reporting

🟊 Complication\Comorbidity   🟊 Major C\C   Excludes 1   Excludes 2   Includes   Use additional   Code first   Code also

868

HEMOLYTIC ANEMIAS (D55-D59)

● **D55 Anemia due to enzyme disorders**

> **Excludes1**   drug-induced enzyme deficiency anemia (D59.2)

D55.0 Anemia due to glucose-6-phosphate dehydrogenase [G6PD] deficiency
> Favism
> G6PD deficiency anemia

D55.1 Anemia due to other disorders of glutathione metabolism
> Anemia (due to) enzyme deficiencies, except G6PD, related to the hexose monophosphate [HMP] shunt pathway
> Anemia (due to) hemolytic nonspherocytic (hereditary), type I

D55.2 Anemia due to disorders of glycolytic enzymes
> Hemolytic nonspherocytic (hereditary) anemia, type II
> Hexokinase deficiency anemia
> Pyruvate kinase [PK] deficiency anemia
> Triose-phosphate isomerase deficiency anemia
>
> > **Excludes1**   disorders of glycolysis not associated with anemia (E74.8)

D55.3 Anemia due to disorders of nucleotide metabolism

D55.8 Other anemias due to enzyme disorders

■ **D55.9 Anemia due to enzyme disorder, unspecified**

● **D56 Thalassemia**
> *Hereditary disorders characterized by low production of hemoglobin or excessive destruction of red blood cells*
>
> > **Excludes1**   sickle-cell thalassemia (D57.4-)

D56.0 Alpha thalassemia
> Alpha thalassemia major
> Hemoglobin H disease
> Severe alpha thalassemia
> Triple gene defect alpha thalassemia
>
> > **Excludes1**   alpha thalassemia minor (D56.3)
> > asymptomatic alpha thalassemia (D56.3)
> > hydrops fetalis due to hemolytic disease (P56.-)

D56.1 Beta thalassemia
> Beta thalassemia major
> Cooley's anemia
> Homozygous beta thalassemia
> Severe beta thalassemia
> Thalassemia intermedia
>
> > **Excludes1**   beta thalassemia minor (D56.3)
> > delta-beta thalassemia (D56.2)
> > sickle-cell beta thalassemia (D57.4-)

D56.2 Delta-beta thalassemia
> Homozygous delta-beta thalassemia
>
> > **Excludes1**   delta-beta thalassemia minor (D56.3)

D56.3 Thalassemia minor
> *Genetic disorders that have in common defective production of hemoglobin*
> Alpha thalassemia minor
> Alpha thalassemia trait
> Beta thalassemia minor
> Delta-beta thalassemia minor
>
> > **Excludes1**   alpha thalassemia (D56.0)
> > beta thalassemia (D56.1)
> > delta-beta thalassemia (D56.2)

D56.4 Hereditary persistence of fetal hemoglobin [HPFH]
> *Persistent production of hemoglobin*

D56.8 Other thalassemias Hb-Bart's disease
> > **Excludes1**   sickle cell anemia (D57.-)
> > sickle-cell thalassemia (D57.4)

■ **D56.9 Thalassemia, unspecified**
> Mediterranean anemia (with other hemoglobinopathy)
> Thalassemia (minor) (mixed) (with other hemoglobinopathy)

● **D57 Sickle-cell disorders**
> *Inherited disease in which red blood cells, normally disc-shaped, become crescent shaped.*
>
> Use additional code for any associated fever (R50.81)
>
> > **Excludes1**   other hemoglobinopathies (D58.-)

● **D57.0 Hb-SS disease with crisis**
> Sickle-cell disease NOS with crisis
> Hb-SS disease with vasoocclusive pain

> ■ **D57.00 Hb-SS disease with crisis, unspecified** 🏷
>
> **D57.01 Hb-SS disease with acute chest syndrome** 🏷
>
> **D57.02 Hb-SS disease with splenic sequestration** 🏷

D57.1 Sickle-cell disease without crisis Hb-SS disease without crisis
> Sickle-cell anemia NOS
> Sickle-cell disease NOS
> Sickle-cell disorder NOS

● **D57.2 Sickle-cell/Hb-C disease**
> Hb-SC disease
> Hb-S/Hb-C disease

> **D57.20 Sickle-cell/Hb-C disease without crisis**

> ● **D57.21 Sickle-cell/Hb-C disease with crisis**
>
> > **D57.211 Sickle-cell/Hb-C disease with acute chest syndrome** 🏷
> >
> > **D57.212 Sickle-cell/Hb-C disease with splenic sequestration** 🏷
> >
> > ■ **D57.219 Sickle-cell/Hb-C disease with crisis, unspecified** 🏷
> > > Sickle-cell/Hb-C disease with crisis NOS

D57.3 Sickle-cell trait
> Hb-S trait
> Heterozygous hemoglobin S

● **D57.4 Sickle-cell thalassemia**
> Sickle-cell beta thalassemia
> Thalassemia Hb-S disease

> **D57.40 Sickle-cell thalassemia without crisis**
> > Sickle-cell thalassemia NOS
>
> ● **D57.41 Sickle-cell thalassemia with crisis**
> > *Sickle-cell "crisis" is precipitated when abnormally crescent-shaped red blood cells form clots and interrupt blood flow to major organs, causing severe pain and organ damage.*
> > Sickle-cell thalassemia with vasoocclusive pain
> >
> > > **D57.411 Sickle-cell thalassemia with acute chest syndrome** 🏷
> > >
> > > **D57.412 Sickle-cell thalassemia with splenic sequestration** 🏷
> > >
> > > ■ **D57.419 Sickle-cell thalassemia with crisis, unspecified** 🏷
> > > > Sickle-cell thalassemia with crisis NOS

● **D57.8 Other sickle-cell disorders**
> Hb-SD disease
> Hb-SE disease

> **D57.80 Other sickle-cell disorders without crisis**

● Unacceptable First-Listed Diagnosis   ● Use Additional Character(s)   ■ Unspecified   **OGCR** Official Guidelines for Coding and Reporting

🏷 Complication\Comorbidity   🏷 Major C\C   Excludes 1   Excludes 2   Includes   Use additional   Code first   Code also

869

CHAPTER 3 (D50-D89)

- **D57.81 Other sickle-cell disorders with crisis**
  - **D57.811 Other sickle-cell disorders with acute chest syndrome** 🔵
  - **D57.812 Other sickle-cell disorders with splenic sequestration** 🔵
  - ◼**D57.819 Other sickle-cell disorders with crisis, unspecified** 🔵
    Other sickle-cell disorders with crisis NOS

- **D58 Other hereditary hemolytic anemias**
  Genetic condition in which bone marrow is unable to compensate for premature destruction of red blood cells
  | **Excludes1** | hemolytic anemia of the newborn (P55.-)

  - **D58.0 Hereditary spherocytosis**
    Presence of spherocytes (spherically shaped red blood cells)
    Acholuric (familial) jaundice
    Congenital (spherocytic) hemolytic icterus
    Minkowski-Chauffard syndrome

  - **D58.1 Hereditary elliptocytosis**
    Presence of large numbers of elliptocytes in blood
    Elliptocytosis (congenital)
    Ovalocytosis (congenital) (hereditary)

  - **D58.2 Other hemoglobinopathies**
    Abnormal hemoglobin NOS
    Congenital Heinz body anemia
    Hb-C disease
    Hb-D disease
    Hb-E disease
    Hemoglobinopathy NOS
    Unstable hemoglobin hemolytic disease
    | **Excludes1** | familial polycythemia (D75.0)
    Hb-M disease (D74.0)
    hereditary persistence of fetal hemoglobin [HPFH] (D56.4)
    high-altitude polycythemia (D75.1)
    methemoglobinemia (D74.-)

  - **D58.8 Other specified hereditary hemolytic anemias** 🔵
    Stomatocytosis

  - ◼**D58.9 Hereditary hemolytic anemia, unspecified** 🔵

- **D59 Acquired hemolytic anemia**
  - **D59.0 Drug-induced autoimmune hemolytic anemia** 🔵
    Code first (T36-T50) to identify drug

  - **D59.1 Other autoimmune hemolytic anemias** 🔵
    Autoimmune hemolytic disease (cold type) (warm type)
    Chronic cold hemagglutinin disease
    Cold agglutinin disease
    Cold agglutinin hemoglobinuria
    Cold type (secondary) (symptomatic) hemolytic anemia
    Warm type (secondary) (symptomatic) hemolytic anemia
    | **Excludes1** | Evans syndrome (D69.41)
    hemolytic disease of newborn (P55.-)
    paroxysmal cold hemoglobinuria (D59.6)

  - **D59.2 Drug-induced nonautoimmune hemolytic anemia**🔵
    Drug-induced enzyme deficiency anemia
    Code first (T36-T50) to identify drug

  - **D59.3 Hemolytic-uremic syndrome** 🔵

- **D59.4 Other nonautoimmune hemolytic anemias** 🔵
  Mechanical hemolytic anemia
  Microangiopathic hemolytic anemia
  Toxic hemolytic anemia

- **D59.5 Paroxysmal nocturnal hemoglobinuria [Marchiafava-Micheli]**
  | **Excludes1** | hemoglobinuria NOS (R82.3)

- **D59.6 Hemoglobinuria due to hemolysis from other external causes**
  Hemoglobinuria from exertion
  March hemoglobinuria
  Paroxysmal cold hemoglobinuria
  Use additional code (Chapter 20) to identify external cause
  | **Excludes1** | hemoglobinuria NOS (R82.3)

- **D59.8 Other acquired hemolytic anemias**

- ◼**D59.9 Acquired hemolytic anemia, unspecified** 🔵
  Idiopathic hemolytic anemia, chronic

APLASTIC AND OTHER ANEMIAS AND OTHER BONE MARROW FAILURE SYNDROMES (D60-D64)

- **D60 Acquired pure red cell aplasia [erythroblastopenia]**
  Deficiency of erythroblasts
  | **Includes** | red cell aplasia (acquired) (adult) (with thymoma)
  | **Excludes1** | congenital red cell aplasia (D61.01)

  - **D60.0 Chronic acquired pure red cell aplasia** 🔵
    Lack of development of blood cell

  - **D60.1 Transient acquired pure red cell aplasia** 🔵

  - **D60.8 Other acquired pure red cell aplasias** 🔵

  - ◼**D60.9 Acquired pure red cell aplasia, unspecified** 🔵

- **D61 Other aplastic anemias and other bone marrow failure syndromes**
  | **Excludes1** | neutropenia (D70.-)

  - **D61.0 Constitutional aplastic anemia**
    Condition where bone marrow is unable to produce blood cells
    - **D61.01 Constitutional (pure) red blood cell aplasia** 🔵
      | **Excludes1** | acquired red cell aplasia (D60.9)
      Blackfan-Diamond syndrome
      congenital (pure) red cell aplasia
      familial hypoplastic anemia
      primary (pure) red cell aplasia
      red cell (pure) aplasia of infants

    - **D61.09 Other constitutional aplastic anemia** 🔵
      Fanconi's anemia
      Pancytopenia with malformations

  - **D61.1 Drug-induced aplastic anemia** 🔵
    Code first (T36-T50) to identify drug

  - **D61.2 Aplastic anemia due to other external agents** 🔵
    Code first (T51-T65) to identify cause

  - **D61.3 Idiopathic aplastic anemia** 🔵

● **D61.8 Other specified aplastic anemias and other bone marrow failure syndromes**

    D61.81 Pancytopenia 🅒

Marked deficiency of all the blood elements: Red blood cells (erythrocytes), white blood cells (leukocytes), and platelets (thrombocytes). Check laboratory results.

Excludes1	pancytopenia (due to) (with):
	aplastic anemia (D61.-)
	bone marrow infiltration (D61.82)
	congenital (pure) red cell aplasia (D61.01)
	drug induced (D61.1)
	hairy cell leukemia (C91.4-)
	human immunodeficiency virus disease (B20.-)
	leukoerythroblastic anemia (M61.82)
	myelodysplastic syndromes (D46.-)
	myeloproliferative disease (D47.1)

    D61.82 Myelophthisis 🅒

Leukoerythroblastic anemia
Myelophthisic anemia
Panmyelophthisis

Code also the underlying disorder, such as:

malignant neoplasm of breast (C50.-)
tuberculosis (A15.-)

Excludes1	idiopathic myelofibrosis (D47.1)
	myelofibrosis NOS (D75.81)
	myelofibrosis with myeloid metaplasia (D47.4)
	primary myelofibrosis (D47.1)
	secondary myelofibrosis (D75.81)

    D61.89 Other specified aplastic anemias and other bone marrow failure syndromes 🅜🅒

■ **D61.9 Aplastic anemia, unspecified** 🅒
Hypoplastic anemia NOS
Medullary hypoplasia

D62 Acute posthemorrhagic anemia 🅒

Excludes1	anemia due to chronic blood loss (D50.0)
	blood loss anemia NOS (D50.0)
	congenital anemia from fetal blood loss (P61.3)

● **D63 Anemia in chronic diseases classified elsewhere**

   ● **D63.0 Anemia in neoplastic disease**

Code first neoplasm (C00-D49)

Excludes1	anemia due to antineoplastic chemotherapy (D64.81)

OGCR Section I.C.2.e.2.

2) Anemia associated with chemotherapy, immunotherapy and radiation therapy

When the admission/encounter is for management of an anemia associated with an adverse effect of chemotherapy, immunotherapy or radiotherapy and the only treatment is for the anemia, the appropriate adverse effect code should be sequenced first, followed by the appropriate codes for the anemia and neoplasm

   ● **D63.1 Anemia in chronic kidney disease**
Erythropoietin resistant anemia (EPO resistant anemia)

Code first underlying chronic kidney disease (CKD) (N18.-)

● **D63.8 Anemia in other chronic diseases classified elsewhere**

Code first underlying disease, such as:
diphyllobothriasis (B70.0)
hookworm disease (B76.0-B76.9)
hypothyroidism (E00.0-E03.9)
malaria (B50.0-B54)
symptomatic late syphilis (A52.79)
tuberculosis (A18.89)

● **D64 Other anemias**

Excludes1	refractory anemia (D46.-)

    D64.0 Hereditary sideroblastic anemia
Abnormal production RBCs (erythrocytes)
Sex-linked hypochromic sideroblastic anemia

● **D64.1 Secondary sideroblastic anemia due to disease**

Code first underlying disease

● **D64.2 Secondary sideroblastic anemia due to drugs and toxins**

Code first (T36-T65) to identify drug or toxin

    D64.3 Other sideroblastic anemias
Sideroblastic anemia NOS
Pyridoxine-responsive sideroblastic anemia NEC

    D64.4 Congenital dyserythropoietic anemia
Any of several rare hereditary anemias, mostly types of macrocytic anemia
Dyshematopoietic anemia (congenital)

Excludes1	Blackfan-Diamond syndrome (D61.01)
	Di Guglielmo's disease (C94.0)

● **D64.8 Other specified anemias**

    D64.81 Anemia due to antineoplastic chemotherapy
Antineoplastic chemotherapy induced anemia

Excludes1	anemia in neoplastic disease (D63.0)
	aplastic anemia due to antineoplastic chemotherapy (D61.1)

    D64.89 Other specified anemias
Infantile pseudoleukemia

■ **D64.9 Anemia, unspecified**

COAGULATION DEFECTS, PURPURA AND OTHER HEMORRHAGIC CONDITIONS (D65-D69)

D65 Disseminated intravascular coagulation [defibrination syndrome] 🅜🅒
Blood clots form and consume all coagulation proteins and platelets and disrupt normal coagulation, resulting in abnormal bleeding

Includes	afibrinogenemia, acquired
	consumption coagulopathy
	diffuse or disseminated intravascular coagulation [DIC]
	fibrinolytic hemorrhage, acquired
	fibrinolytic purpura
	purpura fulminans

Excludes1	disseminated intravascular coagulation (complicating):
	abortion or ectopic or molar pregnancy (O00-O07, O08.1)
	in newborn (P60)
	pregnancy, childbirth and the puerperium (O45.0, O46.0, O67.0, O72.3)

● Unacceptable First-Listed Diagnosis   ● Use Additional Character(s)   ■ Unspecified   **OGCR** Official Guidelines for Coding and Reporting

🅒 Complication\Comorbidity   🅜 Major C\C   Excludes 1   Excludes 2   Includes   Use additional   Code first   Code also

871

D66   Hereditary factor VIII deficiency 🐾
Inherited coagulation disorder carried by females but most often affecting males

Includes   classical hemophilia
deficiency factor VIII (with functional defect)
hemophilia NOS
hemophilia A

Excludes1   factor VIII deficiency with vascular defect (D68.0)

D67   Hereditary factor IX deficiency 🐾

Includes   christmas disease
factor IX deficiency (with functional defect)
hemophilia B
plasma thromboplastin component [PTC] deficiency

● **D68   Other coagulation defects**

Excludes1   abnormal coagulation profile (R79.1)
coagulation defects complicating:
abortion or ectopic or molar pregnancy (O00-O07, O08.1)
pregnancy, childbirth and the puerperium (O45.0, O46.0, O67.0, O72.3)

D68.0   Von Willebrand's disease 🐾
Congenital bleeding disorder
Angiohemophilia
Factor VIII deficiency with vascular defect
Vascular hemophilia

Excludes1   capillary fragility (hereditary) (D69.8)
factor VIII deficiency NOS (D66)
factor VIII deficiency with functional defect (D66)

D68.1   Hereditary factor XI deficiency 🐾
Deficiency of blood coagulation resulting in systemic blood-clotting defect
Hemophilia C
Plasma thromboplastin antecedent [PTA] deficiency
Rosenthal's disease

D68.2   Hereditary deficiency of other clotting factors 🐾
Blood clotting disorders caused by hereditary deficiencies of one or more clotting factors
AC globulin deficiency
Congenital afibrinogenemia
Deficiency of factor I [fibrinogen]
Deficiency of factor II [prothrombin]
Deficiency of factor V [labile]
Deficiency of factor VII [stable]
Deficiency of factor X [Stuart-Prower]
Deficiency of factor XII [Hageman]
Deficiency of factor XIII [fibrin stabilizing]
Dysfibrinogenemia (congenital)
Hypoproconvertinemia
Owren's disease
Proaccelerin deficiency

● **D68.3   Hemorrhagic disorder due to circulating anticoagulants**
Blood clotting disorders caused by anticoagulants (warfarin and heparin)

D68.31   Hemorrhagic disorder due to intrinsic circulating anticoagulants 🐾
Hemorrhagic disorder due to intrinsic increase in antithrombin
Hemorrhagic disorder due to intrinsic increase in anti-VIIIa
Hemorrhagic disorder due to intrinsic increase in anti-IXa
Hemorrhagic disorder due to intrinsic increase in anti-Xa
Hemorrhagic disorder due to intrinsic increase in anti-XIa
Hyperheparinemia

● **D68.32   Hemorrhagic disorder due to extrinsic circulating anticoagulants** 🐾
Drug-induced hemorrhagic disorder
Code first (T45.5-) to identify any administered anticoagulant

D68.4   Acquired coagulation factor deficiency 🐾
Deficiency of coagulation factor due to liver disease
Deficiency of coagulation factor due to vitamin K deficiency

Excludes1   vitamin K deficiency of newborn (P53)

● **D68.5   Primary thrombophilia**
AKA idiopathic thrombocytopenia, may be acquired or congenital and is a common cause of coagulation disorders.
Primary hypercoagulable states

Excludes1   lupus anticoagulant (D68.62)
thrombotic thrombocytopenic purpura (M31.1)

D68.51   Activated protein C resistance 🐾
Factor V Leiden mutation

D68.52   Prothrombin gene mutation 🐾

D68.59   Other primary thrombophilia 🐾
Antithrombin III deficiency
Hypercoagulable state NOS
Primary hypercoagulable state NEC
Primary thrombophilia NEC
Protein C deficiency
Protein S deficiency
Thrombophilia NOS

● **D68.6   Other thrombophilia**
Other hypercoagulable states

Excludes1   diffuse or disseminated heparin induced thrombocytopenia (HIT) (D75.82)
hyperhomocysteinemia (E72.11)

D68.61   Anticardiolipin syndrome 🐾
Antiphospholipid syndrome
Excludes1   lupus anticoagulant syndrome (D68.62)

D68.62   Lupus anticoagulant syndrome 🐾
Lupus anticoagulant
Presence of systemic lupus erythematosus [SLE] inhibitor
Excludes1   anticardiolipin syndrome (D68.61)
antiphospholipid syndrome (D68.61)

D68.69   Other thrombophilia 🐾
Hypercoagulable states NEC
Secondary hypercoagulable state NOS

D68.8   Other specified coagulation defects 🐾
Excludes1   hemorrhagic disease of newborn (P53)

■ **D68.9   Coagulation defect, unspecified** 🐾

● Unacceptable First-Listed Diagnosis   ● Use Additional Character(s)   ■ Unspecified   **OGCR** Official Guidelines for Coding and Reporting
🐾 Complication\Comorbidity   🐾 Major C\C   Excludes 1   Excludes 2   Includes   Use additional   Code first   Code also

● **D69　Purpura and other hemorrhagic conditions**
Group of conditions characterized by small hemorrhages in skin, mucous membranes, or serosal surfaces

| Excludes1 | benign hypergammaglobulinemic purpura (D89.0)
cryoglobulinemic purpura (D89.1)
essential (hemorrhagic) thrombocythemia (D47.3)
hemorrhagic thrombocythemia (D47.3)
purpura fulminans (D65)
thrombotic thrombocytopenic purpura (M31.1)
Waldenström's hypergammaglobulinemic purpura (D89.0)

D69.0　Allergic purpura 🅒
Allergic vasculitis
Nonthrombocytopenic hemorrhagic purpura
Nonthrombocytopenic idiopathic purpura
Purpura anaphylactoid
Purpura Henoch(-Schönlein)
Purpura rheumatica
Vascular purpura

| Excludes1 | thrombocytopenic hemorrhagic purpura (D69.3)

D69.1　Qualitative platelet defects
Bernard-Soulier [giant platelet] syndrome
Glanzmann's disease
Grey platelet syndrome
Thromboasthenia (hemorrhagic) (hereditary)
Thrombocytopathy

| Excludes1 | von Willebrand's disease (D68.0)

D69.2　Other nonthrombocytopenic purpura
Purpura NOS
Purpura simplex
Senile purpura

D69.3　Immune thrombocytopenic purpura 🅒
Hemorrhagic (thrombocytopenic) purpura
Idiopathic thrombocytopenic purpura
Tidal platelet dysgenesis

● **D69.4　Other primary thrombocytopenia**

| Excludes1 | transient neonatal thrombocytopenia (P61.0)
Wiskott-Aldrich syndrome (D82.0)

D69.41　Evans syndrome 🅒
Acquired hemolytic anemia and thrombocytopenia

● **D69.42　Congenital and hereditary thrombocytopenia purpura** 🅒
Congenital thrombocytopenia
Hereditary thrombocytopenia

Code first: congential or hereditary disorder, such as:
thrombocytopenia with absent radius (TAR syndrome) (Q87.2)

D69.49　Other primary thrombocytopenia
Megakaryocytic hypoplasia
Primary thrombocytopenia NOS

D69.5　Secondary thrombocytopenia
Acquired reduction of number of platelets required for blood clotting

| Excludes1 | heparin induced thrombocytopenia (HIT) (D75.82)
transient thrombocytopenia of newborn (P61.0)

▨ **D69.6　Thrombocytopenia, unspecified**

D69.8　Other specified hemorrhagic conditions
Capillary fragility (hereditary)
Vascular pseudohemophilia

▨ **D69.9　Hemorrhagic condition, unspecified**

OTHER DISORDERS OF BLOOD AND BLOOD-FORMING ORGANS (D70-D77)

● **D70　Neutropenia**
Decrease in number of neutrophils (type of white blood cell)

| Includes | agranulocytosis
decreased absolute neurophile count (ANC)

Use additional code for any associated:
fever (R50.81)
mucositis (J34.81, K12.3-, K12.4, K92.81, N76.81)

| Excludes1 | neutropenic splenomegaly (D73.81)
transient neonatal neutropenia (P61.5)

D70.0　Congenital agranulocytosis
Reduced numbers of neutrophils (type of white blood cell)
Congenital neutropenia
Infantile genetic agranulocytosis
Kostmann's disease

● **D70.1　Agranulocytosis secondary to cancer chemotherapy**
Decreased numbers of granulocytes (type of white blood cell)

Code first (T45.1-) to identify drug

Code also underlying neoplasm

● **D70.2　Other drug-induced agranulocytosis**
Code first (T36-T50) to identify drug

D70.3　Neutropenia due to infection

D70.4　Cyclic neutropenia
Chronic neutropenia (low number of type of white blood cell)
Cyclic hematopoiesis
Periodic neutropenia

D70.8　Other neutropenia

▨ **D70.9　Neutropenia, unspecified**

D71　Functional disorders of polymorphonuclear neutrophils
Polymorphonuclear: varying shapes of nucleus; AKA PMNs

| Includes | cell membrane receptor complex [CR3] defect
chronic (childhood) granulomatous disease
congenital dysphagocytosis
progressive septic granulomatosis

● **D72　Other disorders of white blood cells**

| Excludes1 | basophilia (D72.824)
immunity disorders (D80-D89)
neutropenia (D70)
preleukemia (syndrome) (D46.9)

D72.0　Genetic anomalies of leukocytes
Alder (granulation) (granulocyte) anomaly
Alder syndrome
Hereditary leukocytic hypersegmentation
Hereditary leukocytic hyposegmentation
Hereditary leukomelanopathy
May-Hegglin (granulation) (granulocyte) anomaly
May-Hegglin syndrome
Pelger-Huët (granulation) (granulocyte) anomaly
Pelger-Huët syndrome

| Excludes1 | Chediak (-Steinbrinck)-Higashi syndrome (E70.330)

D72.1　Eosinophilia
Formation and accumulation of high number of white cells in blood/tissue
Allergic eosinophilia
Hereditary eosinophilia

| Excludes1 | Löffler's syndrome (J82)
pulmonary eosinophilia (J82)

● **D72.8　Other specified disorders of white blood cells**

| Excludes1 | leukemia (C91-C95)

● Unacceptable First-Listed Diagnosis　　　● Use Additional Character(s)　　　▨ Unspecified　　　**OGCR** Official Guidelines for Coding and Reporting

🅒 Complication\Comorbidity　　🅒 Major C\C　　Excludes 1　　Excludes 2　　Includes　　Use additional　　Code first　　Code also

873

CHAPTER 3 (D50-D89)

● **D72.81 Decreased white blood cell count**
> **Excludes1**   neutropenia (D70.-)

D72.810 Lymphocytopenia
> Decreased lymphocytes
> *Reduction in number of lympho cytes in blood*

D72.818 Other decreased white blood cell count
> Basophilic leukopenia
> Eosinophilic leukopenia
> Monocytopenia
> Other decreased leukocytes
> Plasmacytopenia

■ **D72.819 Decreased white blood cell count, unspecified**
> Decreased leukocytes, unspecified
> Leukocytopenia, unspecified
> Leukopenia
> > **Excludes1**   malignant leukope-nia (D70.9)

● **D72.82 Elevated white blood cell count**
> **Excludes1**   eosinophilia (D72.1)

D72.820 Lymphocytosis (symptomatic)
> Elevated lymphocytes
> *Excess of normal lymphocytes*

D72.821 Monocytosis (symptomatic)
> > **Excludes1**   infectious mono-nucleosis (B27.-)

D72.822 Plasmacytosis
> *Presence of excess plasma cells*

D72.823 Leukemoid reaction
> Basophilic leukemoid reaction
> Leukemoid reaction NOS
> Lymphocytic leukemoid reaction
> Monocytic leukemoid reaction
> Myelocytic leukemoid reaction
> Neutrophilic leukemoid reaction

D72.824 Basophilia
> *Increase of basophils in blood*

D72.825 Bandemia
> Bandemia without diagnosis of specific infection
> *Excess number of band cells (immature white blood cells) released by bone marrow*
> > **Excludes1**   confirmed infection -code to infection leukemia (C91.-, C92.-, C93.-, C94.-, C95.-)

D72.828 Ether elevated white blood cell count

■ **D72.829 Elevated white blood cell count, unspecified**
> Elevated leukocytes, unspecified
> Leukocytosis, unspecified

D72.89 Other specified disorders of white blood cells
> Abnormality of white blood cells NEC

■ **D72.9 Disorder of white blood cells, unspecified**
> Abnormal leukocyte differential NOS

● **D73 Diseases of spleen**

D73.0 Hyposplenism
> *Diminished functioning of spleen*
> Atrophy of spleen
> > **Excludes1**   asplenia (congenital) (Q89.01)
> > postsurgical absence of spleen (Z90.81)

D73.1 Hypersplenism
> *Accelerated function of spleen*
> > **Excludes1**   neutropenic splenomegaly (D73.81)
> > primary splenic neutropenia (D73.81)
> > splenitis, splenomegaly in late syphilis (A52.79)
> > splenitis, splenomegaly in tuberculosis (A18.85)
> > splenomegaly NOS (R16.1)
> > splenomegaly congenital (Q89.0)

D73.2 Chronic congestive splenomegaly
> *Enlargement of spleen*

D73.3 Abscess of spleen

D73.4 Cyst of spleen

D73.5 Infarction of spleen
> Splenic rupture, nontraumatic
> Torsion of spleen
> > **Excludes1**   rupture of spleen due to Plasmodium vivax malaria (B51.0)
> > traumatic rupture of spleen (S36.03-)

● **D73.8 Other diseases of spleen**

D73.81 Neutropenic splenomegaly
> Werner-Schultz disease
> *Enlarged spleen responding to inadequate number of neutrophils*

D73.89 Other diseases of spleen
> Fibrosis of spleen NOS
> Perisplenitis
> Splenitis NOS

■ **D73.9 Disease of spleen, unspecified**

● **D74 Methemoglobinemia**
> *Excessive methemoglobin (form of hemoglobin)*

D74.0 Congenital methemoglobinemia 🔖
> Congenital NADH-methemoglobin reductase deficiency
> Hemoglobin-M [Hb-M] disease
> Methemoglobinemia, hereditary

D74.8 Other methemoglobinemias 🔖
> Acquired methemoglobinemia (with sulfhemoglobinemia)
> Toxic methemoglobinemia

■ **D74.9 Methemoglobinemia, unspecified** 🔖

● **D75 Other and unspecified diseases of blood and blood-forming organs**
> **Excludes2**   acute lymphadenitis (L04.-)
> chronic lymphadenitis (I88.1)
> enlarged lymph nodes (R59.-)
> hypergammaglobulinemia NOS (D89.2)
> lymphadenitis NOS (I88.9)
> mesenteric lymphadenitis (acute) (chronic) (I88.0)

D75.0 Familial erythrocytosis
> *Genetic mutation of gene that results in increased circulating RBCs*
> Benign polycythemia
> Familial polycythemia
> > **Excludes1**   hereditary ovalocytosis (D58.1)

CHAPTER 3 (D50-D89)

874

● Unacceptable First-Listed Diagnosis   ● Use Additional Character(s)   ■ Unspecified   **OGCR** Official Guidelines for Coding and Reporting
🔖 Complication\Comorbidity   🔖 Major C\C   Excludes 1   Excludes 2   Includes   Use additional   Code first   Code also

D75.1 **Secondary polycythemia**
Increase in total red cell mass
Acquired polycythemia
Emotional polycythemia
Erythrocytosis NOS
Hypoxemic polycythemia
Nephrogenous polycythemia
Polycythemia due to erythropoietin
Polycythemia due to fall in plasma volume
Polycythemia due to high altitude
Polycythemia due to stress
Polycythemia NOS
Relative polycythemia

> **Excludes1**   polycythemia neonatorum (P61.1)
> polycythemia vera (D45)

● D75.8 **Other specified diseases of blood and blood-forming organs**

D75.81 **Myelofibrosis** 🔾
Replacing bone marrow by fibrous tissue
Myelofibrosis NOS
Secondary myelofibrosis NOS

Code first the underlying disorder, such as:
malignant neoplasm of breast (C50.-)

Use additional code, if applicable, for associated therapy-related myelodysplastic syndrome (D46.-)

Use additional external cause code, if due to antineoplastic chemotherapy (T45.1-)

> **Excludes1**   acute myelofibrosis (C94.4-)
> idiopathic myelofibrosis (D47.1)
> leukoerythroblastic anemia (D61.82)
> myelofibrosis with myeloid metaplasia (D47.4)
> myelophthisic anemia (D61.82)
> myelophthisis (D61.82)
> primary myelofibrosis (D47.1)

D75.82 **Heparin induced thrombocytopenia (HIT)**

D75.89 **Other specified diseases of blood and blood-forming organs**

▣ D75.9 **Disease of blood and blood-forming organs, unspecified**

● D76 **Other specified diseases with participation of lymphoreticular and reticulohistiocytic tissue**

> **Excludes1**   (Abt-) Letterer-Siwe disease (C96.0)
> eosinophilic granuloma (C96.6)
> Hand-Schüller-Christian disease (C96.5)
> histiocytic sarcoma (C96.a)
> histiocytosis X, multifocal (C96.5)
> histiocytosis X, unifocal (C96.6)
> malignant histiocytosis (C96.a)
> Langerhans-cell histiocytosis, multifocal (C96.5)
> Langerhans-cell histiocytosis NOS (C96.6)
> Langerhans-cell histiocytosis, unifocal (C96.6)

> **Excludes1**   leukemic reticuloendotheliosis or reticulosis (C91.4-)
> lipomelanotic reticuloendotheliosis or reticulosis (I89.8)

D76.1 **Hemophagocytic lymphohistiocytosis** 🔾
Familial hemophagocytic reticulosis
Histiocytoses of mononuclear phagocytes

D76.2 **Hemophagocytic syndrome, infection-associated** 🔾

Use additional code to identify infectious agent or disease.

D76.3 **Other histiocytosis syndromes** 🔾
Reticulohistiocytoma (giant-cell)
Sinus histiocytosis with massive lymphadenopathy
Xanthogranuloma

● D77 **Other disorders of blood and blood-forming organs in diseases classified elsewhere**

Code first underlying disease, such as:
amyloidosis (E85.-)
congenital early syphilis (A50.0)
echinococcosis (B67.0-B67.9)
malaria (B50.0-B54)
schistosomiasis [bilharziasis] (B65.0-B65.9)
vitamin C deficiency (E54)

> **Excludes1**   rupture of spleen due to Plasmodium vivax malaria (B51.0)
> splenitis, splenomegaly in:
> late syphilis (A52.79)
> tuberculosis (A18.85)

INTRAOPERATIVE AND POSTPROCEDURAL COMPLICATIONS OF THE SPLEEN (D78)

● D78 **Intraoperative and postprocedural complications of the spleen**

● D78.0 **Intraoperative hemorrhage and hematoma of spleen complicating a procedure**

> **Excludes1**   intraoperative hemorrhage and hematoma of spleen due to accidental puncture or laceration during a procedure (D78.1-)

D78.01 **Intraoperative hemorrhage and hematoma of spleen complicating a procedure on the spleen** 🔾

D78.02 **Intraoperative hemorrhage and hematoma of spleen complicating other procedure** 🔾

● D78.1 **Accidental puncture and laceration of spleen during a procedure**

D78.11 **Accidental puncture and laceration of spleen during a procedure on the spleen** 🔾

D78.12 **Accidental puncture and laceration of spleen during other procedure** 🔾

● D78.2 **Postprocedural hemorrhage and hematoma of spleen following a procedure**

D78.21 **Postprocedural hemorrhage and hematoma of spleen following a procedure on the spleen** 🔾

D78.22 **Postprocedural hemorrhage and hematoma of spleen following other procedure** 🔾

● D78.8 **Other intraoperative and postprocedural complications of spleen**

Use additional code, if applicable, to further specify disorder

D78.81 **Other intraoperative complications of spleen** 🔾

D78.89 **Other postprocedural complications of spleen** 🔾

CERTAIN DISORDERS INVOLVING THE IMMUNE MECHANISM (D80-D89)

> **Includes**   defects in the complement system
> immunodeficiency disorders, except human immunodeficiency virus [HIV] disease
> sarcoidosis

> **Excludes1**   autoimmune disease (systemic) NOS (M35.9)
> functional disorders of polymorphonuclear neutrophils (D71)
> human immunodeficiency virus [HIV] disease (B20)

CHAPTER 3 (D50-D89)

● **D80 Immunodeficiency with predominantly antibody defects**

D80.0 Hereditary hypogammaglobulinemia 🦠
Autosomal recessive agammaglobulinemia (Swiss type)
X-linked agammaglobulinemia [Bruton] (with growth hormone deficiency)

D80.1 Nonfamilial hypogammaglobulinemia 🦠
Abnormally low levels of all classes of immunoglobulins
Agammaglobulinemia with immunoglobulin-bearing B-lymphocytes
Common variable agammaglobulinemia [CVAgamma]
Hypogammaglobulinemia NOS

D80.2 Selective deficiency of immunoglobulin A [IgA] 🦠

D80.3 Selective deficiency of immunoglobulin G [IgG] subclasses 🦠

D80.4 Selective deficiency of immunoglobulin M [IgM] 🦠

D80.5 Immunodeficiency with increased immunoglobulin M [IgM] 🦠

D80.6 Antibody deficiency with near-normal immuno-globulins or with hyperimmunoglobulinemia 🦠
Abnormally high levels of immunoglobulins in serum

D80.7 Transient hypogammaglobulinemia of infancy 🦠

D80.8 Other immunodeficiencies with predominantly antibody defects 🦠
Kappa light chain deficiency

■ **D80.9 Immunodeficiency with predominantly antibody defects, unspecified** 🦠

● **D81 Combined immunodeficiencies**
Excludes1 autosomal recessive agammaglobulinemia (Swiss type) (D80.0)

D81.0 Severe combined immunodeficiency [SCID] with reticular dysgenesis 🦠

D81.1 Severe combined immunodeficiency [SCID] with low T- and B-cell numbers 🦠

D81.2 Severe combined immunodeficiency [SCID] with low or normal B-cell numbers 🦠

D81.3 Adenosine deaminase [ADA] deficiency 🦠

D81.4 Nezelof's syndrome 🦠

D81.5 Purine nucleoside phosphorylase [PNP] deficiency 🦠

D81.6 Major histocompatibility complex class I deficiency 🦠
Bare lymphocyte syndrome

D81.7 Major histocompatibility complex class II deficiency 🦠

● **D81.8 Other combined immunodeficiencies**

● **D81.81 Biotin-dependent carboxylase deficiency**
Multiple carboxylase deficiency
Excludes1 biotin-dependent carboxyl-ase deficiency due to dietary deficiency of biotin (E53.8)

D81.810 Biotinidase deficiency

D81.818 Other biotin-dependent carboxylase deficiency
Holocarboxylase synthetase deficiency
Other multiple carboxylase deficiency

■ **D81.819 Biotin-dependent carboxylase deficiency, unspecified**
Multiple carboxylase deficiency, unspecified

D81.89 Other combined immunodeficiencies 🦠

■ **D81.9 Combined immunodeficiency, unspecified** 🦠
Severe combined immunodeficiency disorder [SCID] NOS

● **D82 Immunodeficiency associated with other major defects**
Excludes1 ataxia telangiectasia [Louis-Bar] (G11.3)

D82.0 Wiskott-Aldrich syndrome 🦠
X-linked immunodeficiency
Immunodeficiency with thrombocytopenia and eczema

D82.1 Di George's syndrome 🦠
Congenital disorder with defective development of third and fourth pharyngeal pouches
Pharyngeal pouch syndrome
Thymic alymphoplasia
Thymic aplasia or hypoplasia with immunodeficiency

D82.2 Immunodeficiency with short-limbed stature

D82.3 Immunodeficiency following hereditary defective response to Epstein-Barr virus
X-linked lymphoproliferative disease

D82.4 Hyperimmunoglobulin E [IgE] syndrome
Suspected genetic defect that produces high levels of antibody immunoglobulin (IgE) that causes skin and lung infections and eczema

D82.8 Immunodeficiency associated with other specified major defects

■ **D82.9 Immunodeficiency associated with major defect, unspecified**

● **D83 Common variable immunodeficiency**

D83.0 Common variable immunodeficiency with predominant abnormalities of B-cell numbers and function 🦠

D83.1 Common variable immunodeficiency with predominant immunoregulatory T-cell disorders 🦠

D83.2 Common variable immunodeficiency with autoantibodies to B- or T-cells 🦠

D83.8 Other common variable immunodeficiencies 🦠

■ **D83.9 Common variable immunodeficiency, unspecified** 🦠

● **D84 Other immunodeficiencies**

D84.0 Lymphocyte function antigen-1 [LFA-1] defect

D84.1 Defects in the complement system
C1 esterase inhibitor [C1-INH] deficiency

D84.8 Other specified immunodeficiencies 🦠

■ **D84.9 Immunodeficiency, unspecified** 🦠

● **D86 Sarcoidosis**

D86.0 Sarcoidosis of lung

D86.1 Sarcoidosis of lymph nodes

D86.2 Sarcoidosis of lung with sarcoidosis of lymph nodes

D86.3 Sarcoidosis of skin

● **D86.8 Sarcoidosis of other sites**

D86.81 Sarcoid meningitis

D86.82 Multiple cranial nerve palsies in sarcoidosis

D86.83 Sarcoid iridocyclitis
Rare large tumor with irregular surface of iris

● Unacceptable First-Listed Diagnosis ● Use Additional Character(s) ■ Unspecified **OGCR** Official Guidelines for Coding and Reporting
🦠 Complication\Comorbidity 🦠 Major C\C Excludes 1 Excludes 2 Includes Use additional Code first Code also

Item 3-1 Sarcoidosis: A symptom of an inflammation producing tiny lumps of cells (granulomas) in various organs, most commonly the lungs and lymph nodes, that affect organ function. Cause is unknown occurring primarily in 20- to 40-year-olds, African-American, especially women, and those of Asian, German, Irish Scandinavian, and Puerto Rican heritage.

     D86.84   Sarcoid pyelonephritis
            Systemic disease of unknown etiology characterized by chronic granulomatous inflammation with tissue destruction of pelvis kidney
            Tubulo-interstitial nephropathy in sarcoidosis

     D86.85   Sarcoid myocarditis
     D86.86   Sarcoid arthropathy
            Polyarthritis in sarcoidosis

     D86.87   Sarcoid myositis
            Granumloma of muscle

     D86.89   Sarcoidosis of other sites
            Hepatic granuloma
            Uveoparotid fever [Heerfordt]

   ▨ **D86.9   Sarcoidosis, unspecified**

● **D89   Other disorders involving the immune mechanism, not elsewhere classified**

     | **Excludes1** | hyperglobulinemia NOS (R77.1)
            monoclonal gammopathy (of undetermined significance) (D47.2)

     | **Excludes2** | transplant failure and rejection (T86.-)

     D89.0   Polyclonal hypergammaglobulinemia
            Benign hypergammaglobulinemic purpura
            Polyclonal gammopathy NOS

     D89.1   Cryoglobulinemia
            Cryoglobulin (proteins) in blood that precipitate temperatures below 98.6 F; usually symptomatic of underlying disease
            Cryoglobulinemic purpura
            Cryoglobulinemic vasculitis
            Essential cryoglobulinemia
            Idiopathic cryoglobulinemia
            Mixed cryoglobulinemia
            Primary cryoglobulinemia
            Secondary cryoglobulinemia

▨ **D89.2   Hypergammaglobulinemia, unspecified**

     D89.3   Immune reconstitution syndrome
            Code first (T36-T50) to identify drug, if drug induced

● **D89.8   Other specified disorders involving the immune mechanism, not elsewhere classified**

    ● **D89.81   Graft-versus-host disease**
            Code first underlying cause, such as:
            complications of transplanted organs and tissue (T86.-)
            complications of blood transfusion (T80.89)

            Use additional code to identify associated manifestations, such as:
            desquamative dermatitis (L30.8)
            diarrhea (R19.7)
            elevated bilirubin (R17)
            hair loss (L65.9)

       D89.810   Acute graft-versus-host disease

       D89.811   Chronic graft-versus-host disease

       D89.812   Acute on chronic graft-versus-host disease

      ▨ **D89.813   Graft-versus-host disease, unspecified**

     D89.82   Autoimmune lymphoproliferative syndrome [ALPS]

     D89.89   Other specified disorders involving the immune mechanism, not elsewhere classified

       | **Excludes1** | human immunodeficiency virus disease (B20)

▨ **D89.9   Disorder involving the immune mechanism, unspecified**
            Immune disease NOS

● Unacceptable First-Listed Diagnosis   ● Use Additional Character(s)   ▨ Unspecified   **OGCR** Official Guidelines for Coding and Reporting

🅒 Complication\Comorbidity   🅒 Major C\C | Excludes 1 | | Excludes 2 | Includes   Use additional   Code first   Code also

877

CHAPTER 3 (D50-D89)

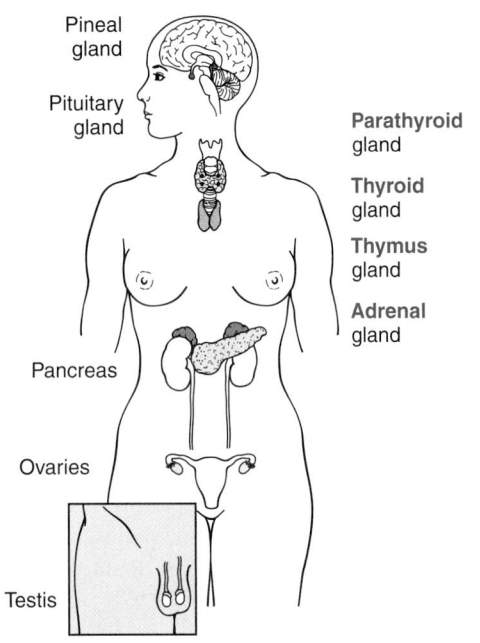

Figure 4-1 The endocrine system. (From Buck CJ: Step-by-Step Medical coding, 2010 ed. Philadelphia, WB Saunders, 2010.)

CHAPTER 4

ENDOCRINE, NUTRITIONAL AND METABOLIC DISEASES (E00-E90)

All neoplasms, whether functionally active or not, are classified in Chapter 2. Appropriate codes in this chapter (i.e., E05.8, E07.0, E16-E31, E34.-) may be used as additional codes to indicate either functional activity by neoplasms and ectopic endocrine tissue or hyperfunction and hypofunction of endocrine glands associated with neoplasms and other conditions classified elsewhere.

Excludes1 transitory endocrine and metabolic disorders specific to newborn (P70-P74)

This chapter contains the following blocks:

E00-E07	Disorders of thyroid gland
E08-E13	Diabetes mellitus
E15-E16	Other disorders of glucose regulation and pancreatic internal secretion
E20-E35	Disorders of other endocrine glands
E36	Intraoperative complications of endocrine system
E40-E46	Malnutrition
E50-E64	Other nutritional deficiencies
E65-E68	Overweight, obesity and other hyperalimentation
E70-E88	Metabolic disorders
E89	Postprocedural endocrine and metabolic complications and disorders, not elsewhere classified

DISORDERS OF THYROID GLAND (E00-E07)

● E00 **Congenital iodine-deficiency syndrome**
Use additional code (F70-F79) to identify associated mental retardation.
Excludes1 subclinical iodine-deficiency hypothyroidism (E02)

E00.0 **Congenital iodine-deficiency syndrome, neurological type**
Endemic cretinism, neurological type

E00.1 **Congenital iodine-deficiency syndrome, myxedematous type**
Dry, waxy type of swelling (nonpitting edema) with abnormal deposits of mucin in skin (mucinosis) and other tissues
Endemic hypothyroid cretinism
Endemic cretinism, myxedematous type

E00.2 **Congenital iodine-deficiency syndrome, mixed type**
Endemic cretinism, mixed type

■E00.9 **Congenital iodine-deficiency syndrome, unspecified**
Congenital iodine-deficiency hypothyroidism NOS
Endemic cretinism NOS

● E01 **Iodine-deficiency related thyroid disorders and allied conditions**
Excludes1 congenital iodine-deficiency syndrome (E00.-) subclinical iodine-deficiency hypothyroidism (E02)

E01.0 **Iodine-deficiency related diffuse (endemic) goiter**
Thyroid gland is enlarged

E01.1 **Iodine-deficiency related multinodular (endemic) goiter**
Iodine-deficiency related nodular goiter

■E01.2 **Iodine-deficiency related (endemic) goiter, unspecified**
Endemic goiter NOS

E01.8 **Other iodine-deficiency related thyroid disorders and allied conditions**
Acquired iodine-deficiency hypothyroidism NOS

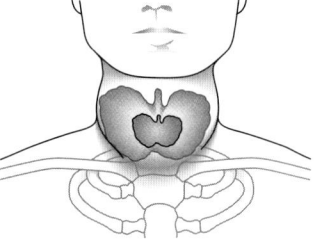

Figure 4-2 Goiter is an enlargement of the thyroid gland.

Item 4-1 Simple goiter indicates no nodules are present. The most common type of goiter is a **diffuse colloidal,** also called a **nontoxic** or **endemic** goiter.

Item 4-2 Hypothyroidism is a condition in which there are insufficient levels of thyroxine. **Cretinism** is congenital hypothyroidism, which can result in mental and physical retardation.

● Unacceptable First-Listed Diagnosis   ● Use Additional Character(s)   ■ Unspecified   OGCR Official Guidelines for Coding and Reporting
🔒 Complication\Comorbidity   🔒 Major C\C   Excludes 1   Excludes 2   Includes   Use additional   Code first   Code also
878
CHAPTER 4 (E00-E90)

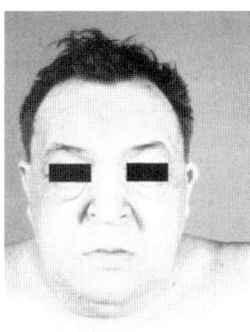

Figure 4-3 Typical appearance of patients with moderately severe primary hypothyroidism or myxedema. (From Larsen: Williams Textbook of Endocrinology, 10th ed. 2003, Saunders, An Imprint of Elsevier)

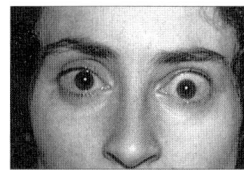

Figure 4-4 Graves' disease. In Graves' disease, exophthalmos often looks more pronounced than it actually is because of the extreme lid retraction that may occur. This patient, for instance, had minimal proptosis of the left eye but marked lid retraction.(Courtesy Dr. HG Scheie. From Yanoff M, Fine BS: Ocular Pathology, ed 5. St. Louis, Mosby, 2002.)

Item 4–3 Thyrotoxicosis is a condition caused by excessive amounts of the thyroid hormone thyroxine production or hyperthyroidism. **Graves' disease is associated with hyperthyroidism** (known as **Basedow's disease** in Europe).

E02   **Subclinical iodine-deficiency hypothyroidism**

● **E03**   **Other hypothyroidism**
     Excludes1   iodine-deficiency related hypothyroidism (E00-E02)
                  postprocedural hypothyroidism (E89.0)

   E03.0   **Congenital hypothyroidism with diffuse goiter**
           Congenital parenchymatous goiter (nontoxic)
           Congenital goiter (nontoxic) NOS
       Excludes1   transitory congenital goiter with normal function (P72.0)

   E03.1   **Congenital hypothyroidism without goiter**
           Aplasia of thyroid (with myxedema)
           Congenital atrophy of thyroid
           Congenital hypothyroidism NOS

   E03.2   **Hypothyroidism due to medicaments and other exogenous substances**
           Code first (T36-T65) to identify drug or substance

   E03.3   **Postinfectious hypothyroidism**

   E03.4   **Atrophy of thyroid (acquired)**
       Excludes1   congenital atrophy of thyroid (E03.1)

   E03.5   **Myxedema coma** 🔾
           Often fatal complication of long-term hypothyroidism

   E03.8   **Other specified hypothyroidism**

   ▪ **E03.9**   **Hypothyroidism, unspecified**
           Myxedema NOS

● **E04**   **Other nontoxic goiter**
     Excludes1   congenital goiter (NOS) (diffuse) (parenchymatous) (E03.0)
                  iodine-deficiency related goiter (E00-E02)

   E04.0   **Nontoxic diffuse goiter**
           Thyroid gland is enlarged
           Diffuse (colloid) nontoxic goiter
           Simple nontoxic goiter

   E04.1   **Nontoxic single thyroid nodule**
           Colloid nodule (cystic) (thyroid)
           Nontoxic uninodular goiter
           Thyroid (cystic) nodule NOS

   E04.2   **Nontoxic multinodular goiter**
           Enlarged thyroid gland with multiple nodules
           Cystic goiter NOS
           Multinodular (cystic) goiter NOS

   E04.8   **Other specified nontoxic goiter**

   ▪ **E04.9**   **Nontoxic goiter, unspecified**
           Goiter NOS
           Nodular goiter (nontoxic) NOS

● **E05**   **Thyrotoxicosis [hyperthyroidism]**
     Enlarged thyroid gland with multiple nodules
     Excludes1   chronic thyroiditis with transient thyrotoxicosis (E06.2)
                  neonatal thyrotoxicosis (P72.1)

● **E05.0**   **Thyrotoxicosis with diffuse goiter**
           Exophthalmic or toxic goiter NOS
           Graves' disease
           Toxic diffuse goiter

     E05.00   **Thyrotoxicosis with diffuse goiter without thyrotoxic crisis or storm**

     E05.01   **Thyrotoxicosis with diffuse goiter with thyrotoxic crisis or storm** 🔾

● **E05.1**   **Thyrotoxicosis with toxic single thyroid nodule**
           Thyrotoxicosis with toxic uninodular goiter

     E05.10   **Thyrotoxicosis with toxic single thyroid nodule without thyrotoxic crisis or storm**

     E05.11   **Thyrotoxicosis with toxic single thyroid nodule with thyrotoxic crisis or storm** 🔾

● **E05.2**   **Thyrotoxicosis with toxic multinodular goiter**
           Toxic nodular goiter NOS

     E05.20   **Thyrotoxicosis with toxic multinodular goiter without thyrotoxic crisis or storm**

     E05.21   **Thyrotoxicosis with toxic multinodular goiter with thyrotoxic crisis or storm** 🔾

● **E05.3**   **Thyrotoxicosis from ectopic thyroid tissue**

     E05.30   **Thyrotoxicosis from ectopic thyroid tissue without thyrotoxic crisis or storm**

     E05.31   **Thyrotoxicosis from ectopic thyroid tissue with thyrotoxic crisis or storm** 🔾

● **E05.4**   **Thyrotoxicosis factitia**

     E05.40   **Thyrotoxicosis factitia without thyrotoxic crisis or storm**

     E05.41   **Thyrotoxicosis factitia with thyrotoxic crisis or storm** 🔾

● **E05.8**   **Other thyrotoxicosis**
           Overproduction of thyroid-stimulating hormone

     E05.80   **Other thyrotoxicosis without thyrotoxic crisis or storm**

     E05.81   **Other thyrotoxicosis with thyrotoxic crisis or storm** 🔾

● **E05.9**   **Thyrotoxicosis, unspecified**
           Hyperthyroidism NOS

     ▪ **E05.90**   **Thyrotoxicosis, unspecified without thyrotoxic crisis or storm**

     ▪ **E05.91**   **Thyrotoxicosis, unspecified with thyrotoxic crisis or storm** 🔾

● Unacceptable First-Listed Diagnosis   ● Use Additional Character(s)   ▪ Unspecified   **OGCR** Official Guidelines for Coding and Reporting
🔾 Complication\Comorbidity   🔾 Major C\C   Excludes 1   Excludes 2   Includes   Use additional   Code first   Code also

CHAPTER 4 (E00-E90)

● **E06 Thyroiditis**
An inflammation of the thyroid gland which results in an inability to convert iodine into thyroid hormone

> **Excludes1**   postpartum thyroiditis (O90.5)

  E06.0 Acute thyroiditis 🦠
    Abscess of thyroid
    Pyogenic thyroiditis
    Suppurative thyroiditis

> Use additional code (B95-B97) to identify infectious agent.

  E06.1 Subacute thyroiditis
Inflammation of thyroid gland following viral upper respiratory infection
    de Quervain thyroiditis
    Giant-cell thyroiditis
    Granulomatous thyroiditis
    Nonsuppurative thyroiditis
    Viral thyroiditis

> **Excludes1**   autoimmune thyroiditis (E06.3)

  E06.2 Chronic thyroiditis with transient thyrotoxicosis
Chronic inflammation of thyroid gland with intermittent overproduction of thyroid hormone

> **Excludes1**   autoimmune thyroiditis (E06.3)

  E06.3 Autoimmune thyroiditis
    Hashimoto's thyroiditis
    Hashitoxicosis (transient)
    Lymphadenoid goiter
    Lymphocytic thyroiditis
    Struma lymphomatosa

●   **E06.4 Drug-induced thyroiditis**

> Code first (T36-T50) to identify drug

  E06.5 Other chronic thyroiditis
    Chronic fibrous thyroiditis
    Chronic thyroiditis NOS
    Ligneous thyroiditis
    Riedel thyroiditis

■   **E06.9 Thyroiditis, unspecified**

● **E07 Other disorders of thyroid**

  E07.0 Hypersecretion of calcitonin
    C-cell hyperplasia of thyroid
    Hypersecretion of thyrocalcitonin

  E07.1 Dyshormogenetic goiter
Group of several types of goiter resulting from enzyme defects in hormone synthesis
    Familial dyshormogenetic goiter
    Pendred's syndrome

> **Excludes1**   transitory congenital goiter with normal function (P72.0)

●   **E07.8 Other specified disorders of thyroid**

    E07.81 Sick-euthyroid syndrome
      Euthyroid sick-syndrome

    E07.89 Other specified disorders of thyroid
      Abnormality of thyroid-binding globulin
      Hemorrhage of thyroid
      Infarction of thyroid

■ **E07.9 Disorder of thyroid, unspecified**

OGCR Section I.C.4.a

4.1 Diabetes mellitus
The diabetes mellitus codes are combination codes that include the type of DM, body system affected, and the complications affecting that body system. As many codes within a particular category as are necessary to describe all of the complications of the disease may be used. They should be sequenced based on the reason for a particular visit. Assign as many codes from categories E08–E13 as needed to identify all of the associated conditions that the patient has.

DIABETES MELLITUS (E08-E13)

A metabolic disease that results in persistent hyperglycemia.

● **E08 Diabetes mellitus due to underlying condition**

> *Code first the underlying condition, such as:*
> Congenital rubella (P35.0)
> Cushing's syndrome (E24.-)
> Cystic fibrosis (E84.-)
> Malignant neoplasm (C00-C96)
> Malnutrition (E40-E46)
> Pancreatitis and other diseases of the pancreas (K85-K86.-)

> Use additional code to identify any insulin use (Z79.4)

> **Excludes1**   drug or chemical induced diabetes mellitus (E09.-)
>   gestational diabetes (O24.4-)
>   neonatal diabetes mellitus (P70.2)
>   type 1 diabetes mellitus (E10.-)
>   type 2 diabetes mellitus (E11.-)

● **E08.0 Diabetes mellitus due to underlying condition with hyperosmolarity**

  ● **E08.00 Diabetes mellitus due to underlying condition with hyperosmolarity without nonketotic hyperglycemic-hyperosmolar coma (NKHHC)**

  ● **E08.01 Diabetes mellitus due to underlying condition with hyperosmolarity with coma**

● **E08.1 Diabetes mellitus due to underlying condition with ketoacidosis**

  ● **E08.10 Diabetes mellitus due to underlying condition with ketoacidosis without coma**

  ● **E08.11 Diabetes mellitus due to underlying condition with ketoacidosis with coma**

● **E08.2 Diabetes mellitus due to underlying condition with kidney complications**

  ● **E08.21 Diabetes mellitus due to underlying condition with diabetic nephropathy**
    Diabetes mellitus due to underlying condition with intercapillary glomerulosclerosis
    Diabetes mellitus due to underlying condition with intracapillary glomerulonephrosis
    Diabetes mellitus due to underlying condition with Kimmelstiel-Wilson disease

  ● **E08.22 Diabetes mellitus due to underlying condition with diabetic chronic kidney disease**
    Diabetes mellitus due to underlying condition with chronic kidney disease due to conditions classified to .21 and .22

> Use additional code to identify stage of chronic kidney disease (N18.1-N18.6)

  ● **E08.29 Diabetes mellitus due to underlying condition with other diabetic kidney complication**
    Renal tubular degeneration in diabetes mellitus due to underlying condition

● **E08.3 Diabetes mellitus due to underlying condition with ophthalmic complications**
Changes in blood vessels of retina in which blood vessels swell and leak fluid into retinal surface.

  ● **E08.31 Diabetes mellitus due to underlying condition with unspecified diabetic retinopathy**

● Unacceptable First-Listed Diagnosis   ● Use Additional Character(s)   ■ Unspecified   **OGCR** Official Guidelines for Coding and Reporting

880   🦠 Complication\Comorbidity   🦠 Major C\C   Excludes 1   Excludes 2   Includes   Use additional   Code first   Code also

CHAPTER 4 (E00-E90)

● ■ **E08.311** **Diabetes mellitus due to underlying condition with unspecified diabetic retinopathy with macular edema**

● ■ **E08.319** **Diabetes mellitus due to underlying condition with unspecified diabetic retinopathy without macular edema**

● **E08.32** **Diabetes mellitus due to underlying condition with mild nonproliferative diabetic retinopathy**
Diabetes mellitus due to underlying condition with nonproliferative diabetic retinopathy NOS

● **E08.321** **Diabetes mellitus due to underlying condition with mild nonproliferative diabetic retinopathy with macular edema**

● **E08.329** **Diabetes mellitus due to underlying condition with mild nonproliferative diabetic retinopathy without macular edema**

● **E08.33** **Diabetes mellitus due to underlying condition with moderate nonproliferative diabetic retinopathy**

● **E08.331** **Diabetes mellitus due to underlying condition with moderate nonproliferative diabetic retinopathy with macular edema**

● **E08.339** **Diabetes mellitus due to underlying condition with moderate nonproliferative diabetic retinopathy without macular edema**

● **E08.34** **Diabetes mellitus due to underlying condition with severe nonproliferative diabetic retinopathy**

● **E08.341** **Diabetes mellitus due to underlying condition with severe nonproliferative diabetic retinopathy with macular edema**

● **E08.349** **Diabetes mellitus due to underlying condition with severe nonproliferative diabetic retinopathy without macular edema**

● **E08.35** **Diabetes mellitus due to underlying condition with proliferative diabetic retinopathy**

● **E08.351** **Diabetes mellitus due to underlying condition with proliferative diabetic retinopathy with macular edema**

● **E08.359** **Diabetes mellitus due to underlying condition with proliferative diabetic retinopathy without macular edema**

● **E08.36** **Diabetes mellitus due to underlying condition with diabetic cataract**

● **E08.39** **Diabetes mellitus due to underlying condition with other diabetic ophthalmic complication**

● **E08.4** **Diabetes mellitus due to underlying condition with neurological complications**

● ■ **E08.40 Diabetes mellitus due to underlying condition with diabetic neuropathy, unspecified**

● **E08.41** **Diabetes mellitus due to underlying condition with diabetic mononeuropathy**

● **E08.42** **Diabetes mellitus due to underlying condition with diabetic polyneuropathy**
Diabetes mellitus due to underlying condition with diabetic neuralgia

● **E08.43** **Diabetes mellitus due to underlying condition with diabetic autonomic (poly)neuropathy**
Diabetes mellitus due to underlying condition with diabetic gastroparesis

● **E08.44** **Diabetes mellitus due to underlying condition with diabetic amyotrophy**

● **E08.49** **Diabetes mellitus due to underlying condition with other diabetic neurological complication**

● **E08.5** **Diabetes mellitus due to underlying condition with circulatory complications**

● **E08.51** **Diabetes mellitus due to underlying condition with diabetic peripheral angiopathy without gangrene**

● **E08.52** **Diabetes mellitus due to underlying condition with diabetic peripheral angiopathy with gangrene**
Diabetes mellitus due to underlying condition with diabetic gangrene

● **E08.59** **Diabetes mellitus due to underlying condition with other circulatory complications**

● **E08.6** **Diabetes mellitus due to underlying condition with other specified complications**

● **E08.61** **Diabetes mellitus due to underlying condition with diabetic arthropathy**

● **E08.610** **Diabetes mellitus due to underlying condition with diabetic neuropathic arthropathy**
Diabetes mellitus due to underlying condition with Charcot's joints

● **E08.618** **Diabetes mellitus due to underlying condition with other diabetic arthropathy**

● **E08.62** **Diabetes mellitus due to underlying condition with skin complications**

● **E08.620** **Diabetes mellitus due to underlying condition with diabetic dermatitis**
Diabetes mellitus due to underlying condition with diabetic necrobiosis lipoidica

● **E08.621** **Diabetes mellitus due to underlying condition with foot ulcer**
Use additional code to identify site of ulcer (L97.4-, L97.5-)

● **E08.622** **Diabetes mellitus due to underlying condition with other skin ulcer**
Use additional code to identify site of ulcer (L97.1-L97.9, L98.41-L98.49)

● **E08.628** **Diabetes mellitus due to underlying condition with other skin complications**

● Unacceptable First-Listed Diagnosis   ● Use Additional Character(s)   ■ Unspecified   **OGCR** Official Guidelines for Coding and Reporting

🏷 Complication\Comorbidity   🏷 Major C\C   [Excludes 1]   [Excludes 2]   Includes   Use additional   Code first   Code also

881

CHAPTER 4 (E00-E90)

- ● E08.63   Diabetes mellitus due to underlying condition with oral complications
    - ● E08.630   Diabetes mellitus due to underlying condition with periodontal disease
    - ● E08.638   Diabetes mellitus due to underlying condition with other oral complications
- ● E08.64   Diabetes mellitus due to underlying condition with hypoglycemia
    - ● E08.641   Diabetes mellitus due to underlying condition with hypoglycemia with coma
    - ● E08.649   Diabetes mellitus due to underlying condition with hypoglycemia without coma
- ● E08.65   Diabetes mellitus due to underlying condition with hyperglycemia
- ● E08.69   Diabetes mellitus due to underlying condition with other specified complication
    - Use additional code to identify complication
- ●■ E08.8   Diabetes mellitus due to underlying condition with unspecified complications
- ● E08.9   Diabetes mellitus due to underlying condition without complications

- ● E09   Drug or chemical induced diabetes mellitus
    - *Code first (T36-T65) to identify drug or chemical*
    - Use additional code to identify any insulin use (Z79.4)
    - **Excludes1**   diabetes mellitus due to underlying condition (E08.-)
        - gestational diabetes (O24.4-)
        - neonatal diabetes mellitus (P70.2)
        - type 1 diabetes mellitus (E10.-)
        - type 2 diabetes mellitus (E11.-)
    - ● E09.0   Drug or chemical induced diabetes mellitus with hyperosmolarity
        - ● E09.00   Drug or chemical induced diabetes mellitus with hyperosmolarity without nonketotic hyperglycemic-hyperosmolar coma (NKHHC)
        - ● E09.01   Drug or chemical induced diabetes mellitus with hyperosmolarity with coma
    - ● E09.1   Drug or chemical induced diabetes mellitus with ketoacidosis
        - ● E09.10   Drug or chemical induced diabetes mellitus with ketoacidosis without coma
        - ● E09.11   Drug or chemical induced diabetes mellitus with ketoacidosis with coma
    - ● E09.2   Drug or chemical induced diabetes mellitus with kidney complications
        - ● E09.21   Drug or chemical induced diabetes mellitus with diabetic nephropathy
            - Drug or chemical induced diabetes mellitus with intercapillary glomerulosclerosis
            - Drug or chemical induced diabetes mellitus with intracapillary glomerulonephrosis
            - Drug or chemical induced diabetes mellitus with Kimmelstiel-Wilson disease

- ● E09.22   Drug or chemical induced diabetes mellitus with diabetic chronic kidney disease
    - Drug or chemical induced diabetes mellitus with chronic kidney disease due to conditions classified to .21 and .22
    - Use additional code to identify stage of chronic kidney disease (N18.1-N18.6)
- ● E09.29   Drug or chemical induced diabetes mellitus with other diabetic kidney complication
    - Drug or chemical induced diabetes mellitus with renal tubular degeneration
- ● E09.3   Drug or chemical induced diabetes mellitus with ophthalmic complications
    - ● E09.31   Drug or chemical induced diabetes mellitus with unspecified diabetic retinopathy
        - ●■ E09.311   Drug or chemical induced diabetes mellitus with unspecified diabetic retinopathy with macular edema
        - ●■ E09.319   Drug or chemical induced diabetes mellitus with unspecified diabetic retinopathy without macular edema
    - ● E09.32   Drug or chemical induced diabetes mellitus with mild nonproliferative diabetic retinopathy
        - Drug or chemical induced diabetes mellitus with nonproliferative diabetic retinopathy NOS
        - ● E09.321   Drug or chemical induced diabetes mellitus with mild nonproliferative diabetic retinopathy with macular edema
        - ● E09.329   Drug or chemical induced diabetes mellitus with mild nonproliferative diabetic retinopathy without macular edema
    - ● E09.33   Drug or chemical induced diabetes mellitus with moderate nonproliferative diabetic retinopathy
        - ● E09.331   Drug or chemical induced diabetes mellitus with moderate nonproliferative diabetic retinopathy with macular edema
        - ● E09.339   Drug or chemical induced diabetes mellitus with moderate nonproliferative diabetic retinopathy without macular edema
    - ● E09.34   Drug or chemical induced diabetes mellitus with severe nonproliferative diabetic retinopathy
        - ● E09.341   Drug or chemical induced diabetes mellitus with severe nonproliferative diabetic retinopathy with macular edema
        - ● E09.349   4 ou or chemical induced diabetes mellitus with severe nonproliferative diabetic retinopathy without macular edema

● Unacceptable First-Listed Diagnosis   ● Use Additional Character(s)   ■ Unspecified   **OGCR** Official Guidelines for Coding and Reporting
Complication\Comorbidity   Major C\C   Excludes 1   Excludes 2   Includes   Use additional   Code first   Code also

● E09.35   Drug or chemical induced diabetes mellitus with proliferative diabetic retinopathy

     ● E09.351   Drug or chemical induced diabetes mellitus with proliferative diabetic retinopathy with macular edema

     ● E09.359   Drug or chemical induced diabetes mellitus with proliferative diabetic retinopathy without macular edema

● E09.36   Drug or chemical induced diabetes mellitus with diabetic cataract

● E09.39   Drug or chemical induced diabetes mellitus with other diabetic ophthalmic complication

● E09.4   Drug or chemical induced diabetes mellitus with neurological complications

     ●🔲 E09.40   Drug or chemical induced diabetes mellitus with neurological complications with diabetic neuropathy, unspecified

     ● E09.41   Drug or chemical induced diabetes mellitus with neurological complications with diabetic mononeuropathy

     ● E09.42   Drug or chemical induced diabetes mellitus with neurological complications with diabetic polyneuropathy
         Drug or chemical induced diabetes mellitus with diabetic neuralgia

     ● E09.43   Drug or chemical induced diabetes mellitus with neurological complications with diabetic autonomic (poly)neuropathy
         Drug or chemical induced diabetes mellitus with diabetic gastroparesis

     ● E09.44   Drug or chemical induced diabetes mellitus with neurological complications with diabetic amyotrophy

     ● E09.49   Drug or chemical induced diabetes mellitus with neurological complications with other diabetic neurological complication

● E09.5   Drug or chemical induced diabetes mellitus with circulatory complications

     ● E09.51   Drug or chemical induced diabetes mellitus with diabetic peripheral angiopathy without gangrene

     ● E09.52   Drug or chemical induced diabetes mellitus with diabetic peripheral angiopathy with gangrene
         Drug or chemical induced diabetes mellitus with diabetic gangrene

     ● E09.59   Drug or chemical induced diabetes mellitus with other circulatory complications

● E09.6   Drug or chemical induced diabetes mellitus with other specified complications

     ● E09.61   Drug or chemical induced diabetes mellitus with diabetic arthropathy

         ● E09.610   Drug or chemical induced diabetes mellitus with diabetic neuropathic arthropathy
             Drug or chemical induced diabetes mellitus with Charcot's joints
             Progressive degeneration of weight bearing joint

         ● E09.618   Drug or chemical induced diabetes mellitus with other diabetic arthropathy

     ● E09.62   Drug or chemical induced diabetes mellitus with skin complications

         ● E09.620   Drug or chemical induced diabetes mellitus with diabetic dermatitis
             Drug or chemical induced diabetes mellitus with diabetic necrobiosis lipoidica
             Necrotizing skin condition

         ● E09.621   Drug or chemical induced diabetes mellitus with foot ulcer
             Use additional code to identify site of ulcer (L97.4-, L97.5-)

         ● E09.622   Drug or chemical induced diabetes mellitus with other skin ulcer
             Use additional code to identify site of ulcer (L97.1-L97.9, L98.41-L98.49)

         ● E09.628   Drug or chemical induced diabetes mellitus with other skin complications

     ● E09.63   Drug or chemical induced diabetes mellitus with oral complications

         ● E09.630   Drug or chemical induced diabetes mellitus with periodontal disease

         ● E09.638   Drug or chemical induced diabetes mellitus with other oral complications

     ● E09.64   Drug or chemical induced diabetes mellitus with hypoglycemia

         ● E09.641   Drug or chemical induced diabetes mellitus with hypoglycemia with coma 🅠

         ● E09.649   Drug or chemical induced diabetes mellitus with hypoglycemia without coma

     ● E09.65   Drug or chemical induced diabetes mellitus with hyperglycemia

     ● E09.69   Drug or chemical induced diabetes mellitus with other specified complication
         Use additional code to identify complication

●🔲 E09.8   Drug or chemical induced diabetes mellitus with unspecified complications

● E09.9   Drug or chemical induced diabetes mellitus without complications

● E10   Type 1 diabetes mellitus

     Includes   brittle diabetes (mellitus)
             diabetes (mellitus) due to autoimmune process
             diabetes (mellitus) due to immune mediated pancreatic islet beta-cell destruction
             idiopathic diabetes (mellitus)
             juvenile onset diabetes (mellitus)
             ketosis-prone diabetes (mellitus)

     Excludes1   diabetes mellitus due to underlying condition (E08.-)
             drug or chemical induced diabetes mellitus (E09.-)
             gestational diabetes (O24.4-)
             neonatal diabetes mellitus (P70.2)
             hyperglycemia NOS (R73.9)
             type 2 diabetes mellitus (E11.-)

● Unacceptable First-Listed Diagnosis   ● Use Additional Character(s)   🔲 Unspecified   **OGCR** Official Guidelines for Coding and Reporting

🅠 Complication\Comorbidity   🅠 Major C\C   Excludes 1   Excludes 2   Includes   Use additional   Code first   Code also

CHAPTER 4 (E00-E90)

883

● **E10.1 Type 1 diabetes mellitus with ketoacidosis**
Acidosis accompanied by accumulation of ketone bodies (ketosis) in body tissues and fluids

     E10.10 Type 1 diabetes mellitus with ketoacidosis without coma 🔖

     E10.11 Type 1 diabetes mellitus with ketoacidosis with coma 🔖

● **E10.2 Type 1 diabetes mellitus with kidney complications**

     E10.21 Type 1 diabetes mellitus with diabetic nephropathy
         Type 1 diabetes mellitus with intercapillary glomerulosclerosis
         Type 1 diabetes mellitus with intracapillary glomerulonephrosis
         Type 1 diabetes mellitus with Kimmelstiel-Wilson disease

     E10.22 Type 1 diabetes mellitus with diabetic chronic kidney disease
         Type 1 diabetes mellitus with chronic kidney disease due to conditions classified to .21 and .22
         Use additional code to identify stage of chronic kidney disease (N18.1-N18.6)

     E10.29 Type 1 diabetes mellitus with other diabetic kidney complication
         Type 1 diabetes mellitus with renal tubular degeneration

● **E10.3 Type 1 diabetes mellitus with ophthalmic complications**

  ● **E10.31 Type 1 diabetes mellitus with unspecified diabetic retinopathy**

     ■ **E10.311 Type 1 diabetes mellitus with unspecified diabetic retinopathy with macular edema**

     ■ **E10.319 Type 1 diabetes mellitus with unspecified diabetic retinopathy without macular edema**

  ● **E10.32 Type 1 diabetes mellitus with mild nonproliferative diabetic retinopathy**
         Type 1 diabetes mellitus with nonproliferative diabetic retinopathy NOS

     E10.321 Type 1 diabetes mellitus with mild nonproliferative diabetic retinopathy with macular edema

     E10.329 Type 1 diabetes mellitus with mild nonproliferative diabetic retinopathy without macular edema

  ● **E10.33 Type 1 diabetes mellitus with moderate nonproliferative diabetic retinopathy**

     E10.331 Type 1 diabetes mellitus with moderate nonproliferative diabetic retinopathy with macular edema

     E10.339 Type 1 diabetes mellitus with moderate nonproliferative diabetic retinopathy without macular edema

  ● **E10.34 Type 1 diabetes mellitus with severe nonproliferative diabetic retinopathy**

     E10.341 Type 1 diabetes mellitus with severe nonproliferative diabetic retinopathy with macular edema

     E10.349 Type 1 diabetes mellitus with severe nonproliferative diabetic retinopathy without macular edema

● **E10.35 Type 1 diabetes mellitus with proliferative diabetic retinopathy**

     E10.351 Type 1 diabetes mellitus with proliferative diabetic retinopathy with macular edema

     E10.359 Type 1 diabetes mellitus with proliferative diabetic retinopathy without macular edema

     E10.36 Type 1 diabetes mellitus with diabetic cataract

     E10.39 Type 1 diabetes mellitus with other diabetic ophthalmic complication

● **E10.4 Type 1 diabetes mellitus with neurological complications**

  ■ **E10.40 Type 1 diabetes mellitus with diabetic neuropathy, unspecified**

     E10.41 Type 1 diabetes mellitus with diabetic mononeuropathy

     E10.42 Type 1 diabetes mellitus with diabetic polyneuropathy
         Type 1 diabetes mellitus with diabetic neuralgia

     E10.43 Type 1 diabetes mellitus with diabetic autonomic (poly)neuropathy
         Type 1 diabetes mellitus with diabetic gastroparesis

     E10.44 Type 1 diabetes mellitus with diabetic amyotrophy

     E10.49 Type 1 diabetes mellitus with other diabetic neurological complication

● **E10.5 Type 1 diabetes mellitus with circulatory complications**

     E10.51 Type 1 diabetes mellitus with diabetic peripheral angiopathy without gangrene

     E10.52 Type 1 diabetes mellitus with diabetic peripheral angiopathy with gangrene
         Type 1 diabetes mellitus with diabetic gangrene

     E10.59 Type 1 diabetes mellitus with other circulatory complications

● **E10.6 Type 1 diabetes mellitus with other specified complications**

  ● **E10.61 Type 1 diabetes mellitus with diabetic arthropathy**

     E10.610 Type 1 diabetes mellitus with diabetic neuropathic arthropathy
         Type 1 diabetes mellitus with Charcot's joints

     E10.618 Type 1 diabetes mellitus with other diabetic arthropathy

  ● **E10.62 Type 1 diabetes mellitus with skin complications**

     E10.620 Type 1 diabetes mellitus with diabetic dermatitis
         Type 1 diabetes mellitus with diabetic necrobiosis lipoidica

     E10.621 Type 1 diabetes mellitus with foot ulcer
         Use additional code to identify site of ulcer (L97.4-, L97.5-)

● Unacceptable First-Listed Diagnosis   ● Use Additional Character(s)   ■ Unspecified   **OGCR** Official Guidelines for Coding and Reporting
🔖 Complication\Comorbidity   🔖 Major C\C   Excludes 1   Excludes 2   Includes   Use additional   Code first   Code also

E10.622 Type 1 diabetes mellitus with other skin ulcer

> Use additional code to identify site of ulcer (L97.1-L97.9, L98.41-L98.49)

E10.628 Type 1 diabetes mellitus with other skin complications

● E10.63 Type 1 diabetes mellitus with oral complications

E10.630 Type 1 diabetes mellitus with periodontal disease

E10.638 Type 1 diabetes mellitus with other oral complications

● E10.64 Type 1 diabetes mellitus with hypoglycemia

E10.641 Type 1 diabetes mellitus with hypoglycemia with coma 🗞

E10.649 Type 1 diabetes mellitus with hypoglycemia without coma

E10.65 Type 1 diabetes mellitus with hyperglycemia

E10.69 Type 1 diabetes mellitus with other specified complication

> Use additional code to identify complication

■ E10.8 Type 1 diabetes mellitus with unspecified complications

E10.9 Type 1 diabetes mellitus without complications

● E11 **Type 2 diabetes mellitus**

Includes diabetes (mellitus) due to insulin secretory defect
diabetes NOS
insulin resistant diabetes (mellitus)

Use additional code to identify any insulin use (Z79.4)

Excludes1 diabetes mellitus due to underlying condition (E08.-)
drug or chemical induced diabetes mellitus (E09.-)
gestational diabetes (O24.4-)
neonatal diabetes mellitus (P70.2)
type 1 diabetes mellitus (E10.-)

● E11.0 Type 2 diabetes mellitus with hyperosmolarity

E11.00 Type 2 diabetes mellitus with hyperosmolarity without nonketotic hyperglycemic-hyperosmolar coma (NKHHC) 🗞

E11.01 Type 2 diabetes mellitus with hyperosmolarity with coma 🗞

● E11.2 Type 2 diabetes mellitus with kidney complications

E11.21 Type 2 diabetes mellitus with diabetic nephropathy
Type 2 diabetes mellitus with intercapillary glomerulosclerosis
Type 2 diabetes mellitus with intracapillary glomerulonephrosis
Type 2 diabetes mellitus with Kimmelstiel-Wilson disease

E11.22 Type 2 diabetes mellitus with diabetic chronic kidney disease
Type 2 diabetes mellitus with chronic kidney disease due to conditions classified to .21 and .22
Use additional code to identify stage of chronic kidney disease (N18.1-N18.6)

E11.29 Type 2 diabetes mellitus with other diabetic kidney complication
Type 2 diabetes mellitus with renal tubular degeneration

● E11.3 Type 2 diabetes mellitus with ophthalmic complications

● E11.31 Type 2 diabetes mellitus with unspecified diabetic retinopathy

■ E11.311 Type 2 diabetes mellitus with unspecified diabetic retinopathy with macular edema

■ E11.319 Type 2 diabetes mellitus with unspecified diabetic retinopathy without macular edema

● E11.32 Type 2 diabetes mellitus with mild nonproliferative diabetic retinopathy
Type 2 diabetes mellitus with nonproliferative diabetic retinopathy NOS

E11.321 Type 2 diabetes mellitus with mild nonproliferative diabetic retinopathy with macular edema

E11.329 Type 2 diabetes mellitus with mild nonproliferative diabetic retinopathy without macular edema

● E11.33 Type 2 diabetes mellitus with moderate nonproliferative diabetic retinopathy

E11.331 Type 2 diabetes mellitus with moderate nonproliferative diabetic retinopathy with macular edema

E11.339 Type 2 diabetes mellitus with moderate nonproliferative diabetic retinopathy without macular edema

● E11.34 Type 2 diabetes mellitus with severe nonproliferative diabetic retinopathy

E11.341 Type 2 diabetes mellitus with severe nonproliferative diabetic retinopathy with macular edema

E11.349 Type 2 diabetes mellitus with severe nonproliferative diabetic retinopathy without macular edema

● E11.35 Type 2 diabetes mellitus with proliferative diabetic retinopathy

E11.351 Type 2 diabetes mellitus with proliferative diabetic retinopathy with macular edema

E11.359 Type 2 diabetes mellitus with proliferative diabetic retinopathy without macular edema

E11.36 Type 2 diabetes mellitus with diabetic cataract

E11.39 Type 2 diabetes mellitus with other diabetic ophthalmic complication

● E11.4 Type 2 diabetes mellitus with neurological complications

■ E11.40 Type 2 diabetes mellitus with diabetic neuropathy, unspecified

E11.41 Type 2 diabetes mellitus with diabetic mononeuropathy

E11.42 Type 2 diabetes mellitus with diabetic polyneuropathy
Type 2 diabetes mellitus with diabetic neuralgia

● Unacceptable First-Listed Diagnosis   ● Use Additional Character(s)   ■ Unspecified   **OGCR** Official Guidelines for Coding and Reporting
🗞 Complication\Comorbidity   🗞 Major C\C   Excludes 1   Excludes 2   Includes   Use additional   Code first   Code also

885

CHAPTER 4 (E00-E90)

E11.43   **Type 2 diabetes mellitus with diabetic autonomic (poly)neuropathy**
     Type 2 diabetes mellitus with diabetic gastroparesis

E11.44   **Type 2 diabetes mellitus with diabetic amyotrophy**

E11.49   **Type 2 diabetes mellitus with other diabetic neurological complication**

● **E11.5**   **Type 2 diabetes mellitus with circulatory complications**

     E11.51   **Type 2 diabetes mellitus with diabetic peripheral angiopathy without gangrene**

     E11.52   **Type 2 diabetes mellitus with diabetic peripheral angiopathy with gangrene**
         Type 2 diabetes mellitus with diabetic gangrene

     E11.59   **Type 2 diabetes mellitus with other circulatory complications**

● **E11.6**   **Type 2 diabetes mellitus with other specified complications**

     ● **E11.61**   **Type 2 diabetes mellitus with diabetic arthropathy**

         E11.610   **Type 2 diabetes mellitus with diabetic neuropathic arthropathy**
           Type 2 diabetes mellitus with Charcot's joints

         E11.618   **Type 2 diabetes mellitus with other diabetic arthropathy**

     ● **E11.62**   **Type 2 diabetes mellitus with skin complications**

         E11.620   **Type 2 diabetes mellitus with diabetic dermatitis**
           Type 2 diabetes mellitus with diabetic necrobiosis lipoidica

         E11.621   **Type 2 diabetes mellitus with foot ulcer**
           Use additional code to identify site of ulcer (L97.4-, L97.5-)

         E11.622   **Type 2 diabetes mellitus with other skin ulcer**
           Use additional code to identify site of ulcer (L97.1-L97.9, L98.41-L98.49)

         E11.628   **Type 2 diabetes mellitus with other skin complications**

     ● **E11.63**   **Type 2 diabetes mellitus with oral complications**

         E11.630   **Type 2 diabetes mellitus with periodontal disease**

         E11.638   **Type 2 diabetes mellitus with other oral complications**

     ● **E11.64**   **Type 2 diabetes mellitus with hypoglycemia**

         E11.641   **Type 2 diabetes mellitus with hypoglycemia with coma** 🦠

         E11.649   **Type 2 diabetes mellitus with hypoglycemia without coma**

     E11.65   **Type 2 diabetes mellitus with hyperglycemia**

     E11.69   **Type 2 diabetes mellitus with other specified complication**
         Use additional code to identify complication

■ **E11.8**   **Type 2 diabetes mellitus with unspecified complications**

     E11.9   **Type 2 diabetes mellitus without complications**

● **E13**   **Other specified diabetes mellitus**

     `Includes`   diabetes mellitus due to genetic defects of beta-cell function
         diabetes mellitus due to genetic defects in insulin action

     Use additional code to identify any insulin use (Z79.4)

     Excludes1   diabetes (mellitus) due to autoimmune process (E10.-)
         diabetes (mellitus) due to immune mediated pancreatic islet beta-cell destruction (E10.-)
         diabetes mellitus due to underlying condition (E08.-)
         drug or chemical induced diabetes mellitus (E09.-)
         gestational diabetes (O24.44)
         neonatal diabetes mellitus (P70.2)
         type 2 diabetes mellitus (E11.-)

● **E13.0**   **Other specified diabetes mellitus with hyperosmolarity**

     E13.00   **Other specified diabetes mellitus with hyperosmolarity without nonketotic hyperglycemic-hyperosmolar coma (NKHHC)**

     E13.01   **Other specified diabetes mellitus with hyperosmolarity with coma** 🦠

● **E13.1**   **Other specified diabetes mellitus with ketoacidosis**

     E13.10   **Other specified diabetes mellitus with ketoacidosis without coma** 🦠

     E13.11   **Other specified diabetes mellitus with ketoacidosis with coma** 🦠

● **E13.2**   **Other specified diabetes mellitus with kidney complications**

     E13.21   **Other specified diabetes mellitus with diabetic nephropathy**
         Other specified diabetes mellitus with intercapillary glomerulosclerosis
         Other specified diabetes mellitus with intracapillary glomerulonephrosis
         Other specified diabetes mellitus with Kimmelstiel-Wilson disease

     E13.22   **Other specified diabetes mellitus with diabetic chronic kidney disease**
         Other specified diabetes mellitus with chronic kidney disease due to conditions classified to .21 and .22
         Use additional code to identify stage of chronic kidney disease (N18.1-N18.6)

     E13.29   **Other specified diabetes mellitus with other diabetic kidney complication**
         Other specified diabetes mellitus with renal tubular degeneration

● **E13.3**   **Other specified diabetes mellitus with ophthalmic complications**

     ● **E13.31**   **Other specified diabetes mellitus with unspecified diabetic retinopathy**

         ■ **E13.311**   **Other specified diabetes mellitus with unspecified diabetic retinopathy with macular edema**

         ■ **E13.319**   **Other specified diabetes mellitus with unspecified diabetic retinopathy without macular edema**

CHAPTER 4 (E00-E90)

● E13.32 **Other specified diabetes mellitus with mild nonproliferative diabetic retinopathy**
Other specified diabetes mellitus with nonproliferative diabetic retinopathy NOS

    E13.321 **Other specified diabetes mellitus with mild nonproliferative diabetic retinopathy with macular edema**

    E13.329 **Other specified diabetes mellitus with mild nonproliferative diabetic retinopathy without macular edema**

● E13.33 **Other specified diabetes mellitus with moderate nonproliferative diabetic retinopathy**

    E13.331 **Other specified diabetes mellitus with moderate nonproliferative diabetic retinopathy with macular edema**

    E13.339 **Other specified diabetes mellitus with moderate nonproliferative diabetic retinopathy without macular edema**

● E13.34 **Other specified diabetes mellitus with severe nonproliferative diabetic retinopathy**

    E13.341 **Other specified diabetes mellitus with severe nonproliferative diabetic retinopathy with macular edema**

    E13.349 **Other specified diabetes mellitus with severe nonproliferative diabetic retinopathy without macular edema**

● E13.35 **Other specified diabetes mellitus with proliferative diabetic retinopathy**

    E13.351 **Other specified diabetes mellitus with proliferative diabetic retinopathy with macular edema**

    E13.359 **Other specified diabetes mellitus with proliferative diabetic retinopathy without macular edema**

  E13.36 **Other specified diabetes mellitus with diabetic cataract**

  E13.39 **Other specified diabetes mellitus with other diabetic ophthalmic complication**

● E13.4 **Other specified diabetes mellitus with neurological complications**

  ■E13.40 **Other specified diabetes mellitus with diabetic neuropathy, unspecified**

  E13.41 **Other specified diabetes mellitus with diabetic mononeuropathy**

  E13.42 **Other specified diabetes mellitus with diabetic polyneuropathy**
Other specified diabetes mellitus with diabetic neuralgia

  E13.43 **Other specified diabetes mellitus with diabetic autonomic (poly)neuropathy**
Other specified diabetes mellitus with diabetic gastroparesis

  E13.44 **Other specified diabetes mellitus with diabetic amyotrophy**

  E13.49 **Other specified diabetes mellitus with other diabetic neurological complication**

● E13.5 **Other specified diabetes mellitus with circulatory complications**

  E13.51 **Other specified diabetes mellitus with diabetic peripheral angiopathy without gangrene**

  E13.52 **Other specified diabetes mellitus with diabetic peripheral angiopathy with gangrene**
Other specified diabetes mellitus with diabetic gangrene

  E13.59 **Other specified diabetes mellitus with other circulatory complications**

● E13.6 **Other specified diabetes mellitus with other specified complications**

  ● E13.61 **Other specified diabetes mellitus with diabetic arthropathy**

    E13.610 **Other specified diabetes mellitus with diabetic neuropathic arthropathy**
Other specified diabetes mellitus with Charcot's joints

    E13.618 **Other specified diabetes mellitus with other diabetic arthropathy**

  ● E13.62 **Other specified diabetes mellitus with skin complications**

    E13.620 **Other specified diabetes mellitus with diabetic dermatitis**
Other specified diabetes mellitus with diabetic necrobiosis lipoidica

    E13.621 **Other specified diabetes mellitus with foot ulcer**
Use additional code to identify site of ulcer (L97.4-, L97.5-)

    E13.622 **Other specified diabetes mellitus with other skin ulcer**
Use additional code to identify site of ulcer (L97.1-L97.9, L98.41-L98.49)

    E13.628 **Other specified diabetes mellitus with other skin complications**

  ● E13.63 **Other specified diabetes mellitus with oral complications**

    E13.630 **Other specified diabetes mellitus with periodontal disease**

    E13.638 **Other specified diabetes mellitus with other oral complications**

  ● E13.64 **Other specified diabetes mellitus with hypoglycemia**

    E13.641 **Other specified diabetes mellitus with hypoglycemia with coma**

    E13.649 **Other specified diabetes mellitus with hypoglycemia without coma**

  E13.65 **Other specified diabetes mellitus with hyperglycemia**

  E13.69 **Other specified diabetes mellitus with other specified complication**
Use additional code to identify complication

■E13.8 **Other specified diabetes mellitus with unspecified complications**

  E13.9 **Other specified diabetes mellitus without complications**

● Unacceptable First-Listed Diagnosis   ● Use Additional Character(s)   ■ Unspecified   **OGCR** Official Guidelines for Coding and Reporting

🦠 Complication\Comorbidity   🦠 Major C\C   Excludes 1   Excludes 2   Includes   Use additional   Code first   Code also

887

OTHER DISORDERS OF GLUCOSE REGULATION AND PANCREATIC INTERNAL SECRETION (E15-E16)

E15   Nondiabetic hypoglycemic coma 🗝

> **Includes**   drug-induced insulin coma in nondiabetic
> hyperinsulinism with hypoglycemic coma
> hypoglycemic coma NOS

● **E16   Other disorders of pancreatic internal secretion**

  ● **E16.0   Drug-induced hypoglycemia without coma**
> *Code first (T36-T50) to identify drug*

  E16.1   Other hypoglycemia
> Functional hyperinsulinism
> Functional nonhyperinsulinemic hypoglycemia
> Hyperinsulinism NOS
> Hyperplasia of pancreatic islet beta cells NOS
>
> > **Excludes1**   hypoglycemia in infant of diabetic
> > mother (P70.1)
> > neonatal hypoglycemia (P70.4)

  ■ **E16.2   Hypoglycemia, unspecified**

  E16.3   Increased secretion of glucagon
> Hyperplasia of pancreatic endocrine cells with
> glucagon excess

  E16.4   Increased secretion of gastrin
> Hypergastrinemia
> Hyperplasia of pancreatic endocrine cells with
> gastrin excess
> Zollinger-Ellison syndrome

  E16.8   Other specified disorders of pancreatic internal secretion
> Increased secretion from endocrine pancreas of
> growth hormone-releasing hormone
> Increased secretion from endocrine pancreas of
> pancreatic polypeptide
> Increased secretion from endocrine pancreas of
> somatostatin
> Increased secretion from endocrine pancreas of
> vasoactive-intestinal polypeptide

  ■ **E16.9   Disorder of pancreatic internal secretion, unspecified**
> Islet-cell hyperplasia NOS
> Pancreatic endocrine cell hyperplasia NOS

DISORDERS OF OTHER ENDOCRINE GLANDS (E20-E35)

> **Excludes1**   galactorrhea (N64.3)
> gynecomastia (N62)

● **E20   Hypoparathyroidism**
> *Greatly reduced function of parathyroid glands; AKA parathyroid insufficiency*
>
> > **Excludes1**   Di George's syndrome (D82.1)
> > postprocedural hypoparathyroidism (E89.2)
> > tetany NOS (R29.0)
> > transitory neonatal hypoparathyroidism
> > (P71.4)

  E20.0   Idiopathic hypoparathyroidism
> *Rare condition, unknown cause; short dwarf-like with round face*

Item 4–4   Hyperparathyroidism is an overactive parathyroid gland that secretes excessive parathormone, causing increased levels of circulating calcium. This results in a loss of calcium in the bone (osteoporosis).

   Hypoparathyroidism is an underactive parathyroid gland that results in decreased levels of circulating calcium. The primary manifestation is **tetany,** a continuous muscle spasm.

Figure 4-5   Tetany caused by hypoparathyroidism.

  E20.1   Pseudohypoparathyroidism
> *Hereditary condition resembling hypoparathyroidism, but caused by inability to respond to parathyroid hormone*

  E20.8   Other hypoparathyroidism

  ■ **E20.9   Hypoparathyroidism, unspecified**
> Parathyroid tetany

● **E21   Hyperparathyroidism and other disorders of parathyroid gland**

> > **Excludes1**   adult osteomalacia (M83.-)
> > ectopic hyperparathyroidism (E34.2)
> > familial hypocalciuric hypercalcemia (E83.52)
> > hungry bone syndrome (E83.81)
> > infantile and juvenile osteomalacia (E55.0)

  E21.0   Primary hyperparathyroidism
> Hyperplasia of parathyroid
> Osteitis fibrosa cystica generalisata [von
> Recklinghausen's disease of bone]

  E21.1   Secondary hyperparathyroidism, not elsewhere classified
> > **Excludes1**   secondary hyperparathyroidism of
> > renal origin (N25.81)

  E21.2   Other hyperparathyroidism
> Tertiary hyperparathyroidism
> > **Excludes1**   familial hypocalciuric hypercalcemia
> > (E83.52)

  ■ **E21.3   Hyperparathyroidism, unspecified**

  E21.4   Other specified disorders of parathyroid gland

  ■ **E21.5   Disorder of parathyroid gland, unspecified**

● **E22   Hyperfunction of pituitary gland**

> > **Excludes1**   Cushing's syndrome (E24.-)
> > Nelson's syndrome (E24.1)
> > overproduction of ACTH not associated
> > with Cushing's disease (E27.0)
> > overproduction of pituitary ACTH (E24.0)
> > overproduction of thyroid-stimulating
> > hormone (E05.8-)

  E22.0   Acromegaly and pituitary gigantism
> *Chronic disease caused by hypersecretion of growth hormone*
> Overproduction of growth hormone
> > **Excludes1**   constitutional gigantism (E34.4)
> > constitutional tall stature (E34.4)
> > increased secretion from endocrine
> > pancreas of growth hormone-
> > releasing hormone (E16.8)

  E22.1   Hyperprolactinemia 🗝
> *Increased levels of prolactin*

  E22.2   Syndrome of inappropriate secretion of antidiuretic hormone 🗝

  E22.8   Other hyperfunction of pituitary gland 🗝
> Central precocious puberty

  ■ **E22.9   Hyperfunction of pituitary gland, unspecified** 🗝

● **E23   Hypofunction and other disorders of the pituitary gland**

> **Includes**   the listed conditions whether the disorder is
> in the pituitary or the hypothalamus
> **Excludes1**   postprocedural hypopituitarism (E89.3)

CHAPTER 4 (E00-E90)

●   Unacceptable First-Listed Diagnosis   ●   Use Additional Character(s)   ■   Unspecified   **OGCR**   Official Guidelines for Coding and Reporting

🗝 Complication\Comorbidity   🗝 Major C\C   Excludes 1   Excludes 2   Includes   Use additional   Code first   Code also

888

Item 4-5 **Hyperadrenalism** is overactivity of the adrenal cortex, which secretes corticosteroid hormones. Excessive glucocorticoid hormone results in hyperglycemia **(Cushing's syndrome)**, and excessive aldosterone results in **Conn's syndrome. Adrenogenital syndrome** is the result of excessive secretion of androgens, male hormones, which stimulates premature sexual development. **Hypoadrenalism, Addison's disease**, is a condition in which the adrenal glands atrophy.

E23.0 **Hypopituitarism** 🦠
Fertile eunuch syndrome
Hypogonadotropic hypogonadism
Idiopathic growth hormone deficiency
Isolated deficiency of gonadotropin
Isolated deficiency of growth hormone
Isolated deficiency of pituitary hormone
Kallmann's syndrome
Lorain-Levi short stature
Necrosis of pituitary gland (postpartum)
Panhypopituitarism
Pituitary cachexia
Pituitary insufficiency NOS
Pituitary short stature
Sheehan's syndrome
Simmonds' disease

● E23.1 **Drug-induced hypopituitarism**
Code first (T36-T50) to identify drug

E23.2 **Diabetes insipidus** 🦠
Excludes1 nephrogenic diabetes insipidus (N25.1)

E23.3 **Hypothalamic dysfunction, not elsewhere classified**
Excludes1 Prader-Willi syndrome (Q87.1)
Russell-Silver syndrome (Q87.1)

E23.6 **Other disorders of pituitary gland**
Abscess of pituitary
Adiposogenital dystrophy

■ E23.7 **Disorder of pituitary gland, unspecified**

● E24 **Cushing's syndrome**
Excludes1 congenital adrenal hyperplasia (E25.0)

E24.0 **Pituitary-dependent Cushing's disease** 🦠
Overproduction of pituitary ACTH
Pituitary-dependent hypercorticalism

E24.1 **Nelson's syndrome**

● E24.2 **Drug-induced Cushing's syndrome** 🦠
Code first (T36-T50) to identify drug

E24.3 **Ectopic ACTH syndrome** 🦠

E24.4 **Alcohol-induced pseudo-Cushing's syndrome** 🦠

E24.8 **Other Cushing's syndrome** 🦠

■ E24.9 **Cushing's syndrome, unspecified** 🦠

Figure 4-6 Centripetal and generalized obesity and dorsal kyphosis in a 30-year-old woman with Cushing's disease. (From Larsen: Williams Textbook of Endocrinology, 10th ed. 2003, Saunders, An Imprint of Elsevier)

● E25 **Adrenogenital disorders**
Disorder of production of steroid hormone in adrenal gland
Includes adrenogenital syndromes, virilizing or feminizing, whether acquired or due to adrenal hyperplasia consequent on inborn enzyme defects in hormone synthesis
female:
adrenal pseudohermaphroditism
heterosexual precocious pseudopuberty
male:
isosexual precocious pseudopuberty
macrogenitosomia praecox
sexual precocity with adrenal hyperplasia
virilization (female)
Excludes1 indeterminate sex and pseudohermaphroditism (Q56)
chromosomal abnormalities (Q90-Q99)

E25.0 **Congenital adrenogenital disorders associated with enzyme deficiency**
Congenital adrenal hyperplasia
21-Hydroxylase deficiency
Salt-losing congenital adrenal hyperplasia

E25.8 **Other adrenogenital disorders**
Idiopathic adrenogenital disorder

■ E25.9 **Adrenogenital disorder, unspecified**
Adrenogenital syndrome NOS

● E26 **Hyperaldosteronism**
Abnormality of electrolyte metabolism caused by excessive secretion of aldosterone

● E26.0 **Primary hyperaldosteronism**

E26.01 **Conn's syndrome**
Code also adrenal adenoma (D35.0)

E26.02 **Glucocorticoid-remediable aldosteronism**
Familial aldosteronism type I

E26.09 **Other primary hyperaldosteronism**
Primary aldosteronism due to adrenal hyperplasia (bilateral)

E26.1 **Secondary hyperaldosteronism**

● E26.8 **Other hyperaldosteronism**

E26.81 **Bartter's syndrome**

E26.89 **Other hyperaldosteronism**

■ E26.9 **Hyperaldosteronism, unspecified**
Aldosteronism NOS
Hyperaldosteronism NOS

● E27 **Other disorders of adrenal gland**

E27.0 **Other adrenocortical overactivity** 🦠
Overproduction of ACTH, not associated with Cushing's disease
Premature adrenarche
Excludes1 Cushing's syndrome (E24.-)

E27.1 **Primary adrenocortical insufficiency** 🦠
Addison's disease
Autoimmune adrenalitis
Excludes1 Addison only phenotype adrenoleukodystrophy (E71.428)
amyloidosis (E85.-)
tuberculous Addison's disease (A18.7)
Waterhouse-Friderichsen syndrome (A39.1)

E27.2 **Addisonian crisis** 🦠
Acute onset of adrenocortical insufficiency
Adrenal crisis
Adrenocortical crisis

● Unacceptable First-Listed Diagnosis ● Use Additional Character(s) ■ Unspecified OGCR Official Guidelines for Coding and Reporting
🦠 Complication\Comorbidity 🦠 Major C\C Excludes 1 Excludes 2 Includes Use additional Code first Code also
CHAPTER 4 (E00-E90) 889

● **E27.3** **Drug-induced adrenocortical insufficiency** 🅒
Code first (T36-T50) to identify drug

● **E27.4** **Other and unspecified adrenocortical insufficiency**
> **Excludes1**   adrenoleukodystrophy [Addison-Schilder] (E71.3-)
> Waterhouse-Friderichsen syndrome (A39.1)

■ **E27.40** **Unspecified adrenocortical insufficiency** 🅒
Adrenocortical insufficiency NOS
Hypoaldosteronism

     E27.49 **Other adrenocortical insufficiency** 🅒
Adrenal hemorrhage
Adrenal infarction

   E27.5 **Adrenomedullary hyperfunction** 🅒
Adrenomedullary hyperplasia
Catecholamine hypersecretion

   E27.8 **Other specified disorders of adrenal gland**
Abnormality of cortisol-binding globulin

■ **E27.9** **Disorder of adrenal gland, unspecified**

● **E28** **Ovarian dysfunction**
> **Excludes1**   isolated gonadotropin deficiency (E23.0)
> postprocedural ovarian failure (E89.4-)

   E28.0 **Estrogen excess**

   E28.1 **Androgen excess**
Hypersecretion of ovarian androgens

   E28.2 **Polycystic ovarian syndrome**
Sclerocystic ovary syndrome
Stein-Leventhal syndrome

● **E28.3** **Primary ovarian failure**
> **Excludes1**   pure gonadal dysgenesis (Q99.1)
> Turner's syndrome (Q96.-)

● **E28.31** **Premature menopause**

     E28.310 **Symptomatic premature menopause**
Symptoms such as flushing, sleeplessness, headache, lack of concentration, associated with premature menopause

     E28.319 **Asymptomatic premature menopause**
Premature menopause NOS

   E28.39 **Other primary ovarian failure**
Decreased estrogen
Resistant ovary syndrome

   E28.8 **Other ovarian dysfunction**
Ovarian hyperfunction NOS
> **Excludes1**   postprocedural ovarian failure (E89.4-)

■ **E28.9** **Ovarian dysfunction, unspecified**

● **E29** **Testicular dysfunction**
> **Excludes1**   androgen insensitivity syndrome (E34.5-)
> azoospermia or oligospermia NOS (N46.0-N46.1)
> isolated gonadotropin deficiency (E23.0)
> Klinefelter's syndrome (Q98.0-Q98.2, Q98.4)

   E29.0 **Testicular hyperfunction**
Hypersecretion of testicular hormones

   E29.1 **Testicular hypofunction**
Defective biosynthesis of testicular androgen NOS
5-delta-Reductase deficiency (with male pseudohermaphroditism)
Testicular hypogonadism NOS
> **Excludes1**   postprocedural testicular hypofunction (E89.5)

   E29.8 **Other testicular dysfunction**

■ **E29.9** **Testicular dysfunction, unspecified**

● **E30** **Disorders of puberty, not elsewhere classified**

   E30.0 **Delayed puberty**
Constitutional delay of puberty
Delayed sexual development

   E30.1 **Precocious puberty**
Sexual maturation at earlier age than normal, or before age 8 in girls and 9 in boys, usually hormonal; AKA sexual precocity or pubertas praecox
Precocious menstruation
> **Excludes1**   Albright (-McCune) (-Sternberg) syndrome (Q78.1)
> central precocious puberty (E22.8)
> congenital adrenal hyperplasia (E25.0)
> female heterosexual precocious pseudopuberty (E25.-)
> male isosexual precocious pseudopuberty (E25.-)

   E30.8 **Other disorders of puberty**
Premature thelarche

■ **E30.9** **Disorder of puberty, unspecified**

● **E31** **Polyglandular dysfunction**
> **Excludes1**   ataxia telangiectasia [Louis-Bar] (G11.3)
> dystrophia myotonica [Steinert] (G71.11)
> pseudohypoparathyroidism (E20.1)

   E31.0 **Autoimmune polyglandular failure**
Schmidt's syndrome

   E31.1 **Polyglandular hyperfunction**
> **Excludes1**   multiple endocrine adenomatosis (E31.2-)
> multiple endocrine neoplasia (E31.2-)

● **E31.2** **Multiple endocrine neoplasia [MEN] syndromes**
Adenomatous hyperplasia and malignant tumors in endocrine glands
Multiple endocrine adenomatosis
Code also any associated malignancies and other conditions associated with the syndromes

■ **E31.20** **Multiple endocrine neoplasia [MEN] syndrome, unspecified**
Multiple endocrine adenomatosis NOS
Multiple endocrine neoplasia [MEN] syndrome NOS

     E31.21 **Multiple endocrine neoplasia [MEN] type I**
Wermer's syndrome

     E31.22 **Multiple endocrine neoplasia [MEN] type IIA**
Sipple's syndrome

     E31.23 **Multiple endocrine neoplasia [MEN] type IIB**

   E31.8 **Other polyglandular dysfunction**

■ **E31.9** **Polyglandular dysfunction, unspecified**

● **E32** **Diseases of thymus**
> **Excludes1**   aplasia or hypoplasia of thymus with immunodeficiency (D82.1)
> myasthenia gravis (G70.0)

   E32.0 **Persistent hyperplasia of thymus**
Hypertrophy of thymus

   E32.1 **Abscess of thymus** 🅒

● Unacceptable First-Listed Diagnosis   ● Use Additional Character(s)   ■ Unspecified   **OGCR** Official Guidelines for Coding and Reporting
🅒 Complication\Comorbidity   🅒 Major C\C   Excludes 1   Excludes 2   Includes   Use additional   Code first   Code also

E32.8   Other diseases of thymus

> Excludes1   aplasia or hypoplasia with immunodeficiency (D82.1)
> thymoma (D15.0)

◼ E32.9   Disease of thymus, unspecified

● **E34   Other endocrine disorders**

> Excludes1   pseudohypoparathyroidism (E20.1)

E34.0   Carcinoid syndrome 🖢

> **Note:** May be used as an additional code to identify functional activity associated with a carcinoid tumor.

E34.1   Other hypersecretion of intestinal hormones

E34.2   Ectopic hormone secretion, not elsewhere classified

> Excludes1   ectopic ACTH syndrome (E24.3)

E34.3   Short stature due to endocrine disorder
     Constitutional short stature
     Laron-type short stature

> Excludes1   achondroplastic short stature (Q77.4)
> hypochondroplastic short stature (Q77.4)
> nutritional short stature (E45)
> pituitary short stature (E23.0)
> progeria (E34.8)
> renal short stature (N25.0)
> Russell-Silver syndrome (Q87.1)
> short-limbed stature with immunodeficiency (D82.2)
> short stature in specific dysmorphic syndromes - code to syndrome - see Alphabetical Index
> short stature NOS (R62.52)

E34.4   Constitutional tall stature
     Constitutional gigantism

● **E34.5   Androgen insensitivity syndrome**

> ◼ **E34.50   Androgen insensitivity syndrome, unspecified**
>   Androgen insensitivity NOS
>
> **E34.51   Complete androgen insensitivity syndrome**
>   Complete androgen insensitivity
>   de Quervain syndrome
>   Goldberg-Maxwell syndrome
>
> **E34.52   Partial androgen insensitivity syndrome**
>   Partial androgen insensitivity
>   Reifenstein syndrome

E34.8   Other specified endocrine disorders
     Pineal gland dysfunction
     Progeria

> Excludes2   pseudohypoparathyroidism (E20.1)

◼ E34.9   Endocrine disorder, unspecified
     Endocrine disturbance NOS
     Hormone disturbance NOS

● **E35   Disorders of endocrine glands in diseases classified elsewhere**

> *Code first underlying disease, such as:*
>
> late congenital syphilis of thymus gland [Dubois disease] (A50.5)
> tuberculous calcification of adrenal gland (B90.8)

> Excludes1   Echinococcus granulosus infection of thyroid gland (B67.3)
> meningococcal hemorrhagic adrenalitis (A39.1)
> syphilis of endocrine gland (A52.79)
> tuberculosis of:
>   adrenal gland, except calcification (A18.7)
>   endocrine gland NEC (A18.82)
>   thyroid gland (A18.81)
> Waterhouse-Friderichsen syndrome (A39.1)

● **E36   Intraoperative complications of endocrine system**

> Excludes2   postprocedural endocrine and metabolic complications and disorders, not elsewhere classified (E89.-)

● **E36.0   Intraoperative hemorrhage and hematoma of an endocrine system organ or structure complicating a procedure**

> Excludes1   intraoperative hemorrhage and hematoma of an endocrine system organ or structure due to accidental puncture or laceration during a procedure (E36.1-)

> **E36.01   Intraoperative hemorrhage and hematoma of an endocrine system organ or structure complicating an endocrine system procedure 🖢**
>
> **E36.02   Intraoperative hemorrhage and hematoma of an endocrine system organ or structure complicating other procedure 🖢**

● **E36.1   Accidental puncture and laceration of an endocrine system organ or structure during a procedure**

> **E36.11   Accidental puncture and laceration of an endocrine system organ or structure during an endocrine system procedure 🖢**
>
> **E36.12   Accidental puncture and laceration of an endocrine system organ or structure during other procedure 🖢**

E36.8   Other intraoperative complications of endocrine system 🖢

> Use additional code, if applicable, to further specify disorder

MALNUTRITION (E40-E46)

> Excludes1   intestinal malabsorption (K90.-)
> sequelae of protein-calorie malnutrition (E64.0)

> Excludes2   nutritional anemias (D50-D53)
> starvation (T73.0)

E40   Kwashiorkor 🖢
Malnutrition produced by severe protein deficiency

> Includes   severe malnutrition with nutritional edema with dyspigmentation of skin and hair

> Excludes1   marasmic kwashiorkor (E42)

E41   Nutritional marasmus 🖢

> Includes   severe malnutrition with marasmus

> Excludes1   marasmic kwashiorkor (E42)

E42   Marasmic kwashiorkor 🖢
Severe protein malnutrition

> Includes   severe protein-calorie malnutrition with signs of both kwashiorkor and marasmus
> intermediate form severe protein-calorie malnutrition

◼ E43   Unspecified severe protein-calorie malnutrition 🖢

> Includes   starvation edema

● **E44   Protein-calorie malnutrition of moderate and mild degree**

E44.0   Moderate protein-calorie malnutrition

E44.1   Mild protein-calorie malnutrition

E45   Retarded development following protein-calorie malnutrition 🖢

> Includes   nutritional short stature
> nutritional stunting
> physical retardation due to malnutrition

● Unacceptable First-Listed Diagnosis   ● Use Additional Character(s)   ◼ Unspecified   **OGCR** Official Guidelines for Coding and Reporting
🖢 Complication\Comorbidity   🖢 Major C\C   Excludes 1   Excludes 2   Includes   Use additional   Code first   Code also

Item 4–6 **Bitot's spots** are the result of a buildup of keratin debris found on the superficial surface the conjunctiva; oval, triangular, or irregular in shape; and a sign of vitamin A deficiency and associated with night blindness. The disease may progress to **keratomalacia**, which can result in eventual prolapse of the iris and loss of the lens.

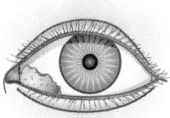

Figure 4-7 Bitot's spot on the conjunctiva.

🔲●E46   **Unspecified protein-calorie malnutrition** 🦠

> **Includes**   malnutrition NOS
> protein-calorie imbalance NOS

> **Excludes1**   nutritional deficiency NOS (E63.9)

OTHER NUTRITIONAL DEFICIENCIES (E50-E64)

> **Excludes2**   nutritional anemias (D50-D53)

● **E50   Vitamin A deficiency**

> **Excludes1**   sequelae of vitamin A deficiency (E64.1)

E50.0   Vitamin A deficiency with conjunctival xerosis

E50.1   Vitamin A deficiency with Bitot's spot and conjunctival xerosis
Bitot's spot in the young child

E50.2   Vitamin A deficiency with corneal xerosis

E50.3   Vitamin A deficiency with corneal ulceration and xerosis

E50.4   Vitamin A deficiency with keratomalacia
Eye disorder that results in dry cornea caused by vitamin A deficiency

E50.5   Vitamin A deficiency with night blindness

E50.6   Vitamin A deficiency with xerophthalmic scars of cornea
Abnormal dryness and thickening of conjunctiva and cornea due to vitamin A deficiency

E50.7   Other ocular manifestations of vitamin A deficiency
Xerophthalmia NOS

E50.8   Other manifestations of vitamin A deficiency
Follicular keratosis
Xeroderma

🔲**E50.9   Vitamin A deficiency, unspecified**
Hypovitaminosis A NOS

● **E51   Thiamine deficiency**

> **Excludes1**   sequelae of thiamine deficiency (E64.8)

● **E51.1   Beriberi**

E51.11   Dry beriberi 🦠
Thiamine deficiency with nervous system manifestation most often caused by excessive alcohol consumption
Beriberi NOS
Beriberi with polyneuropathy

E51.12   Wet beriberi 🦠
Thiamine deficiency with cardiovascular manifestation most often caused by excessive alcohol consumption
Beriberi with cardiovascular manifestations
Cardiovascular beriberi
Shoshin disease

E51.2   Wernicke's encephalopathy 🦠
Acute disease of brain due to thiamine deficiency most often associated with excessive alcohol consumption

E51.8   Other manifestations of thiamine deficiency 🦠

🔲**E51.9   Thiamine deficiency, unspecified** 🦠

Item 4–7 **Pellagra** is associated with a deficiency of niacin and its precursor, **tryptophan.** Characteristics of the condition include diarrhea, dermatitis on exposed skin surfaces, dementia, and death. It is prevalent in developing countries where nutrition is inadequate. **Beriberi** is associated with thiamine deficiency.

E52   Niacin deficiency [pellagra]

> **Includes**   niacin (-tryptophan) deficiency
> nicotinamide deficiency
> pellagra (alcoholic)

> **Excludes1**   sequelae of niacin deficiency (E64.8)

● **E53   Deficiency of other B group vitamins**

> **Excludes1**   sequelae of vitamin B deficiency (E64.8)

E53.0   Riboflavin deficiency 🦠
Ariboflavinosis
Vitamin B_2 deficiency

E53.1   Pyridoxine deficiency
Vitamin B_6 deficiency

> **Excludes1**   pyridoxine-responsive sideroblastic anemia (D64.3)

E53.8   Deficiency of other specified B group vitamins
Biotin deficiency
Cyanocobalamin deficiency
Folate deficiency
Folic acid deficiency
Pantothenic acid deficiency
Vitamin B_{12} deficiency

> **Excludes1**   folate deficiency anemia (D52.-)
> vitamin B_{12} deficiency anemia (D51.-)

🔲**E53.9   Vitamin B deficiency, unspecified**

E54   Ascorbic acid deficiency

> **Includes**   deficiency of vitamin C
> scurvy

> **Excludes1**   scorbutic anemia (D53.2)
> sequelae of vitamin C deficiency (E64.2)

● **E55   Vitamin D deficiency**

> **Excludes1**   adult osteomalacia (M83.-)
> osteoporosis (M80-)
> sequelae of rickets (E64.3)

E55.0   Rickets, active 🦠
Infantile osteomalacia
Juvenile osteomalacia
Softening of bone

> **Excludes1**   celiac rickets (K90.0)
> Crohn's rickets (K50.-)
> hereditary vitamin D-dependent rickets (E83.32)
> inactive rickets (E64.3)
> renal rickets (N25.0)
> sequelae of rickets (E64.3)
> vitamin D-resistant rickets (E83.31)

🔲**E55.9   Vitamin D deficiency, unspecified**
Avitaminosis D

● Unacceptable First-Listed Diagnosis   ● Use Additional Character(s)   🔲 Unspecified   **OGCR** Official Guidelines for Coding and Reporting
🦠 Complication\Comorbidity   🦠 Major C\C   Excludes 1   Excludes 2   Includes   Use additional   Code first   Code also

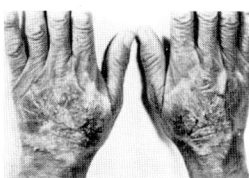

Figure 4-8 The sharply demarcated, characterstic scaling dermatitis of pellagra. (From Kumar: Robbins and Cotran: Pathologic Basis of Disease, 7th ed. 2005, Saunders, An Imprint of Elsevier)

● **E56 Other vitamin deficiencies**
    Excludes1 sequelae of other vitamin deficiencies (E64.8)

    E56.0 Deficiency of vitamin E

    E56.1 Deficiency of vitamin K
        Excludes1 deficiency of coagulation factor due to vitamin K deficiency (D68.4)
                vitamin K deficiency of newborn (P53)

    E56.8 Deficiency of other vitamins

   ■ **E56.9 Vitamin deficiency, unspecified**

  E58 Dietary calcium deficiency
    Excludes1 disorders of calcium metabolism (E83.5)
              sequelae of calcium deficiency (E64.8)

  E59 Dietary selenium deficiency
    Includes Keshan disease
    Excludes1 sequelae of selenium deficiency (E64.8)

  E60 Dietary zinc deficiency

● **E61 Deficiency of other nutrient elements**
    Excludes1 disorders of mineral metabolism (E83.-)
              iodine deficiency related thyroid disorders (E00-E02)
              sequelae of malnutrition and other nutritional deficiencies (E64.-)

    E61.0 Copper deficiency

    E61.1 Iron deficiency
        Excludes1 iron deficiency anemia (D50.-)

    E61.2 Magnesium deficiency

    E61.3 Manganese deficiency

    E61.4 Chromium deficiency

    E61.5 Molybdenum deficiency

    E61.6 Vanadium deficiency

    E61.7 Deficiency of multiple nutrient elements

    E61.8 Deficiency of other specified nutrient elements

  ■ **E61.9 Deficiency of nutrient element, unspecified**

● **E63 Other nutritional deficiencies**
    Excludes1 dehydration (E86.0)
              failure to thrive, adult (R62.7)
              failure to thrive, child (R62.51)
              feeding problems in newborn (P92.-)
              sequelae of malnutrition and other nutritional deficiencies (E64.-)

    E63.0 Essential fatty acid [EFA] deficiency

    E63.1 Imbalance of constituents of food intake

    E63.8 Other specified nutritional deficiencies

  ■ **E63.9 Nutritional deficiency, unspecified**

● **E64 Sequelae of malnutrition and other nutritional deficiencies**
    Pathological condition resulting from disease, injury, or other trauma

    This category is to be used to indicate conditions in categories E43, E44, E46, E50-E63 as the cause of sequelae, which are themselves classified elsewhere. The "sequelae" include conditions specified as such; they also include the late effects of diseases classifiable to the above categories if the disease itself is no longer present

    Code first condition resulting from (sequela) of malnutrition and other nutritional deficiencies

  ● **E64.0 Sequelae of protein-calorie malnutrition** 🅒
        Excludes2 retarded development following protein-calorie malnutrition (E45)

  ● **E64.1 Sequelae of vitamin A deficiency**

  ● **E64.2 Sequelae of vitamin C deficiency**

  ● **E64.3 Sequelae of rickets**

  ● **E64.8 Sequelae of other nutritional deficiencies**

  ● ■ **E64.9 Sequelae of unspecified nutritional deficiency**

OVERWEIGHT, OBESITY AND OTHER HYPERALIMENTATION (E65-E68)

  E65 Localized adiposity
    Fat pad

● **E66 Overweight and obesity**
    Code first: obesity complicating pregnancy, childbirth and the puerperium, if applicable (O99.21-)

    Use additional code to identify body mass index (BMI), if known (Z68.-)

    Excludes1 adiposogenital dystrophy (E23.6)
              lipomatosis NOS (E88.2)
              lipomatosis dolorosa [Dercum] (E88.2)
              Prader-Willi syndrome (Q87.1)

  ● **E66.0 Obesity due to excess calories**
      E66.01 Morbid (severe) obesity due to excess calories
          Excludes1 morbid (severe) obesity with alveolar hypoventilation (E66.2)

      E66.09 Other obesity due to excess calories

  ● **E66.1 Drug-induced obesity**
      Code first (T36-T50) to identify drug

    E66.2 Morbid (severe) obesity with alveolar hypoventilation
      Uncommon condition of unknown cause leading to inadequate ventilation in lungs, even though lungs and airways are normal
      Pickwickian syndrome

    E66.3 Overweight

    E66.8 Other obesity

  ■ **E66.9 Obesity, unspecified**
      Obesity NOS

● **E67 Other hyperalimentation**
    Ingestion of more than optimal amount of nutrients

    Excludes1 hyperalimentation NOS (R63.2)
              sequelae of hyperalimentation (E68)

    E67.0 Hypervitaminosis A

    E67.1 Hypercarotinemia

    E67.2 Megavitamin-B_6 syndrome

    E67.3 Hypervitaminosis D

    E67.8 Other specified hyperalimentation

● Unacceptable First-Listed Diagnosis   ● Use Additional Character(s)   ■ Unspecified   **OGCR** Official Guidelines for Coding and Reporting
🅒 Complication\Comorbidity 🅒 Major C\C Excludes 1 Excludes 2 Includes Use additional Code first Code also

● **E68**   **Sequelae of hyperalimentation**

Code first condition resulting from (sequela) of hyperalimentation

METABOLIC DISORDERS (E70-E90)

Excludes1	androgen insensitivity syndrome (E34.5-)
	congenital adrenal hyperplasia (E25.0)
	Ehlers-Danlos syndrome (Q79.6)
	hemolytic anemias attributable to enzyme disorders (D55.-)
	Marfan's syndrome (Q87.4)
	5-alpha-reductase deficiency (E29.1)

● **E70**   **Disorders of aromatic amino-acid metabolism**

    E70.0   **Classical phenylketonuria**

Inherited disorder that increases to harmful levels amino acid phenylalanine

    E70.1   **Other hyperphenylalaninemias**

● **E70.2**   **Disorders of tyrosine metabolism**

Excludes1	transitory tyrosinemia of newborn (P74.5)

      E70.20   **Disorder of tyrosine metabolism, unspecified**

Tyrosine: Nonessential amino acid occurring in most proteins

      E70.21   **Tyrosinemia**

Congenital amino acid metabolism

Hypertyrosinemia

      E70.29   **Other disorders of tyrosine metabolism**

Alkaptonuria

Ochronosis

● **E70.3**   **Albinism**

Congenital condition of reduced or absent pigment in eyes, skin, and hair

      E70.30   **Albinism, unspecified**

● **E70.31**   **Ocular albinism**

      E70.310   **X-linked ocular albinism**

      E70.311   **Autosomal recessive ocular albinism**

      E70.318   **Other ocular albinism**

      E70.319   **Ocular albinism, unspecified**

● **E70.32**   **Oculocutaneous albinism**

Partial or total lack of melanin pigment in eyes

Excludes1	Chediak-Higashi syndrome (E70.330)
	Hermansky-Pudlak syndrome (E70.331)

      E70.320   **Tyrosinase negative oculocutaneous albinism**

Albinism I

Oculocutaneous albinism ty-neg

      E70.321   **Tyrosinase positive oculocutaneous albinism**

Albinism II

Oculocutaneous albinism ty-pos

      E70.328   **Other oculocutaneous albinism**

Cross syndrome

      E70.329   **Oculocutaneous albinism, unspecified**

● **E70.33**   **Albinism with hematologic abnormality**

      E70.330   **Chediak-Higashi syndrome**

      E70.331   **Hermansky-Pudlak syndrome**

      E70.338   **Other albinism with hematologic abnormality**

      E70.339   **Albinism with hematologic abnormality, unspecified**

    E70.39   **Other specified albinism**

Piebaldism

● **E70.4**   **Disorders of histidine metabolism**

      E70.40   **Disorders of histidine metabolism, unspecified**

      E70.41   **Histidinemia**

      E70.49   **Other disorders of histidine metabolism**

    E70.5   **Disorders of tryptophan metabolism**

    E70.8   **Other disorders of aromatic amino-acid metabolism**

    E70.9   **Disorder of aromatic amino-acid metabolism, unspecified**

● **E71**   **Disorders of branched-chain amino-acid metabolism and fatty-acid metabolism**

    E71.0   **Maple-syrup-urine disease**

Due to defect in amino acid catabolism, causing severe ketoacidosis with smell of maple syrup in urine and on body

● **E71.1**   **Other disorders of branched-chain amino-acid metabolism**

● **E71.11**   **Branched-chain organic acidurias**

      E71.110   **Isovaleric acidemia**

      E71.111   **3-methylglutaconic aciduria**

      E71.118   **Other branched-chain organic acidurias**

● **E71.12**   **Disorders of propionate metabolism**

      E71.120   **Methylmalonic acidemia**

      E71.121   **Propionic acidemia**

      E71.128   **Other disorders of propionate metabolism**

      E71.19   **Other disorders of branched-chain amino-acid metabolism**

Hyperleucine-isoleucinemia

Hypervalinemia

    E71.2   **Disorder of branched-chain amino-acid metabolism, unspecified**

● **E71.3**   **Disorders of fatty-acid metabolism**

Excludes1	peroxisomal disorders (E71.5)
	Refsum's disease (G60.1)
	Schilder's disease (G37.0)

Excludes2	carnitine deficiency due to inborn error of metabolism (E71.42)

      E71.30   **Disorder of fatty-acid metabolism, unspecified**

● **E71.31**   **Disorders of fatty-acid oxidation**

      E71.310   **Long chain/very long chain acyl CoA dehydrogenase deficiency**

LCAD

VLCAD

      E71.311   **Medium chain acyl CoA dehydrogenase deficiency**

MCAD

      E71.312   **Short chain acyl CoA dehydrogenase deficiency**

SCAD

      E71.313   **Glutaric aciduria type II**

Glutaric aciduria type II A

Glutaric aciduria type II B

Glutaric aciduria type II C

Excludes1	glutaric aciduria (type 1) NOS (E72.3)

● Unacceptable First-Listed Diagnosis   ● Use Additional Character(s)   ■ Unspecified   **OGCR** Official Guidelines for Coding and Reporting

Complication\Comorbidity   Major C\C   Excludes 1   Excludes 2   Includes   Use additional   Code first   Code also

E71.314 **Muscle carnitine palmitoyltransferase deficiency**

E71.318 **Other disorders of fatty-acid oxidation**

E71.32 **Disorders of ketone metabolism** 🗝

E71.39 **Other disorders of fatty-acid metabolism** 🗝

● E71.4 **Disorders of carnitine metabolism**

> **Excludes1** muscle carnitine palmitoyltransferase deficiency (E71.314)

◼ E71.40 **Disorder of carnitine metabolism, unspecified**

E71.41 **Primary carnitine deficiency**

E71.42 **Carnitine deficiency due to inborn errors of metabolism**
> Code also associated inborn error or metabolism

E71.43 **Iatrogenic carnitine deficiency**
> *Iatrogenic: Outcomes from activity of physicians*
> Carnitine deficiency due to:
> hemodialysis
> Valproic acid therapy

● E71.44 **Other secondary carnitine deficiency**

E71.440 **Ruvalcaba-Myhre-Smith syndrome**

E71.448 **Other secondary carnitine deficiency**

● E71.5 **Peroxisomal disorders**
> *Class of conditions which lead to disorders of lipid metabolism*

> **Excludes1** Schilder's disease (G37.0)

◼ E71.50 **Peroxisomal disorder, unspecified** 🗝

● E71.51 **Disorders of peroxisome biogenesis**
> Group 1 peroxisomal disorders

> **Excludes1** Refsum's disease (G60.1)

E71.510 **Zellweger syndrome** 🗝

E71.511 **Neonatal adrenoleukodystrophy** 🗝

> **Excludes1** X-linked adrenoleukodystrophy (E71.42-)

E71.518 **Other disorders of peroxisome biogenesis** 🗝

● E71.52 **X-linked adrenoleukodystrophy**

E71.520 **Childhood cerebral X-linked adrenoleukodystrophy** 🗝

E71.521 **Adolescent X-linked adrenoleukodystrophy** 🗝

E71.522 **Adrenomyeloneuropathy** 🗝

E71.528 **Other X-linked adrenoleukodystrophy** 🗝
> Addison only phenotype adrenoleukodystrophy
> Addison-Schilder adrenoleukodystrophy

◼ E71.529 **X-linked adrenoleukodystrophy, unspecified** 🗝

E71.53 **Other group 2 peroxisomal disorders** 🗝

● E71.54 **Other peroxisomal disorders**

E71.540 **Rhizomelic chondrodysplasia punctata** 🗝
> *Rare, severe, inherited disorder with limb shortening, bone and cartilage abnormalities, abnormal facial appearance, severe mental retardation, psychomotor retardation, and cataracts*

> **Excludes1** chondrodysplasia punctata NOS (Q77.3)

E71.541 **Zellweger-like syndrome** 🗝

E71.542 **Other group 3 peroxisomal disorders** 🗝

E71.548 **Other peroxisomal disorders** 🗝

● E72 **Other disorders of amino-acid metabolism**

> **Excludes1** disorders of:
> aromatic amino-acid metabolism (E70.-)
> branched-chain amino-acid metabolism (E71.0-E71.2)
> fatty-acid metabolism (E71.3)
> purine and pyrimidine metabolism (E79.-)
> gout (M1a-, M10.-)

● E72.0 **Disorders of amino-acid transport**

> **Excludes1** disorders of tryptophan metabolism (E70.5)

◼ E72.00 **Disorders of amino-acid transport, unspecified** 🗝

E72.01 **Cystinuria** 🗝
> *Hereditary aminoaciduria due to impairment of renal transport with predominant symptom of urinary cystine calculi*

E72.02 **Hartnup's disease** 🗝
> *Inborn error of metabolism*

E72.03 **Lowe's syndrome** 🗝
> *X-linked disorder with rickets, hydrophthalmia, congenital glaucoma, cataracts, mental retardation, and renal tubule dysfunction*
> Use additional code for associated glaucoma (H42)

E72.04 **Cystinosis** 🗝
> *Genetic disease with excessive depostits of amino acid cystine in cells*
> Fanconi (-de Toni) (-Debré) syndrome with cystinosis

> **Excludes1** Fanconi (-de Toni) (-Debré) syndrome without cystinosis (E72.09)

E72.09 **Other disorders of amino-acid transport** 🗝
> Fanconi (-de Toni) (-Debré) syndrome, unspecified

● E72.1 **Disorders of sulfur-bearing amino-acid metabolism**

> **Excludes1** cystinosis (E72.04)
> cystinuria (E72.01)
> transcobalamin II deficiency (D51.2)

◼ E72.10 **Disorders of sulfur-bearing amino-acid metabolism, unspecified** 🗝

E72.11 **Homocystinuria** 🗝
> Cystathionine synthase deficiency

E72.12 **Methylenetetrahydrofolate reductase deficiency** 🗝

● Unacceptable First-Listed Diagnosis ● Use Additional Character(s) ◼ Unspecified OGCR Official Guidelines for Coding and Reporting
🗝 Complication\Comorbidity 🗝 Major C\C [Excludes 1] [Excludes 2] Includes Use additional Code first Code also

CHAPTER 4 (E00-E90)

895

E72.19   Other disorders of sulfur-bearing amino-acid metabolism 🗝
  Cystathioninuria
  Methioninemia
  Sulfite oxidase deficiency

● **E72.2   Disorders of urea cycle metabolism**
  Excludes1   disorders of ornithine metabolism (E72.4)

■ **E72.20   Disorder of urea cycle metabolism, unspecified** 🗝
  Hyperammonemia
  Elevated levels of ammonia

  Excludes1   hyperammonemia-hyperornithinemia-homocitrullinemia syndrome E72.4
      transient hyperammonemia of newborn (P74.6)

E72.21   Argininemia 🗝
  Disorder in which deficiency of enzyme arginase causes build up of arginine and ammonia in blood

E72.22   Arginosuccinic aciduria 🗝
  Gene disorder of urea cycle resulting accumulation of ammonia

E72.23   Citrullinemia 🗝
  Urea cycle disorder that causes ammonia and other toxic substances to accumulate in blood

E72.29   Other disorders of urea cycle metabolism 🗝

E72.3   Disorders of lysine and hydroxylysine metabolism 🗝
  Glutaric aciduria NOS
  Glutaric aciduria (type I)
  Hydroxylysinemia
  Hyperlysinemia

  Excludes1   glutaric aciduria type II (E71.313)
      Refsum's disease (G60.1)
      Zellweger syndrome (E71.510)

E72.4   Disorders of ornithine metabolism 🗝
  Hyperammonemia-Hyperornithinemia-Homocitrullinemia syndrome
  Ornithinemia (types I, II)
  Ornithine transcarbamylase deficiency

  Excludes1   hereditary choroidal dystrophy (H31.2-)

● **E72.5   Disorders of glycine metabolism**

■ **E72.50   Disorder of glycine metabolism, unspecified** 🗝

E72.51   Non-ketotic hyperglycinemia 🗝

E72.52   Trimethylaminuria 🗝

E72.53   Hyperoxaluria 🗝
  Oxalosis
  Oxaluria

E72.59   Other disorders of glycine metabolism 🗝
  D-glycericacidemia
  Hyperhydroxyprolinemia
  Hyperprolinemia (types I, II)
  Sarcosinemia

E72.8   Other specified disorders of amino-acid metabolism 🗝
  Disorders of beta-amino-acid metabolism
  Disorders of gamma-glutamyl cycle

■ **E72.9   Disorder of amino-acid metabolism, unspecified** 🗝

● **E73   Lactose intolerance**
  Intolerance for lactose, due to inherited deficiency of lactase activity in intestinal mucosa

E73.0   Congenital lactase deficiency

E73.1   Secondary lactase deficiency

E73.8   Other lactose intolerance

■ **E73.9   Lactose intolerance, unspecified**

● **E74   Other disorders of carbohydrate metabolism**
  Excludes1   diabetes mellitus (E09-E13)
      hypoglycemia NOS (E16.2)
      increased secretion of glucagon (E16.3)
      mucopolysaccharidosis (E76.0-E76.3)

● **E74.0   Glycogen storage disease**

■ **E74.00   Glycogen storage disease, unspecified** 🗝

E74.01   von Gierke's disease 🗝
  Type I glycogen storage disease

E74.02   Pompe disease 🗝
  Cardiac glycogenosis
  Type II glycogen storage disease

E74.03   Cori disease 🗝
  Forbes' disease
  Type III glycogen storage disease

E74.04   McArdle disease 🗝
  Type V glycogen storage disease

E74.09   Other glycogen storage disease 🗝
  Andersen disease
  Hers disease
  Tauri disease
  Glycogen storage disease, types 0, IV, VI-XI
  Liver phosphorylase deficiency
  Muscle phosphofructokinase deficiency

● **E74.1   Disorders of fructose metabolism**
  Excludes1   muscle phosphofructokinase deficiency (E74.09)

■ **E74.10   Disorder of fructose metabolism, unspecified**

E74.11   Essential fructosuria
  Fructokinase deficiency

E74.12   Hereditary fructose intolerance
  Fructosemia

E74.19   Other disorders of fructose metabolism
  Fructose-1, 6-diphosphatase deficiency

● **E74.2   Disorders of galactose metabolism**

■ **E74.20   Disorders of galactose metabolism, unspecified** 🗝

E74.21   Galactosemia 🗝
  Genetic disorders resulting from defective simple sugar (galactose) metabolism

E74.29   Other disorders of galactose metabolism 🗝
  Galactokinase deficiency

● **E74.3   Other disorders of intestinal carbohydrate absorption**
  Excludes2   lactose intolerance (E73.-)

E74.31   Sucrase-isomaltase deficiency
  Deficiency in metabolism in intestinal mucosa results in malabsorption of sucrose and starch

E74.39   Other disorders of intestinal carbohydrate absorption
  Disorder of intestinal carbohydrate absorption NOS
  Glucose-galactose malabsorption
  Sucrase deficiency

● Unacceptable First-Listed Diagnosis   ● Use Additional Character(s)   ■ Unspecified   **OGCR** Official Guidelines for Coding and Reporting
🗝 Complication\Comorbidity   🗝 Major C\C   Excludes 1   Excludes 2   Includes   Use additional   Code first   Code also

E74.4   **Disorders of pyruvate metabolism and gluconeogenesis** 🕮
     Deficiency of phosphoenolpyruvate carboxykinase
     Deficiency of pyruvate carboxylase
     Deficiency of pyruvate dehydrogenase

     | Excludes1 | disorders of pyruvate metabolism and gluconeogenesis with anemia (D55.-)
         Leigh's syndrome (G31.82)

E74.8   **Other specified disorders of carbohydrate metabolism** 🕮
     Essential pentosuria
     Renal glycosuria

◾E74.9   **Disorder of carbohydrate metabolism, unspecified**

● E75   **Disorders of sphingolipid metabolism and other lipid storage disorders**
     | Excludes1 | mucolipidosis, types I-III (E77.0-E77.1)
         Refsum's disease (G60.1)

● E75.0   **GM$_2$ gangliosidosis**
     Rare metabolic disorder that causes destruction of nerve cells of brain and spinal cord

     ◾E75.00   **GM$_2$ gangliosidosis, unspecified** 🕮

     E75.01   **Sandhoff disease** 🕮

     E75.02   **Tay-Sachs disease** 🕮

     E75.09   **Other GM$_2$ gangliosidosis** 🕮
         Adult GM$_2$ gangliosidosis
         Juvenile GM$_2$ gangliosidosis

● E75.1   **Other and unspecified gangliosidosis**

     ◾E75.10   **Unspecified gangliosidosis** 🕮
         Gangliosidosis NOS

     E75.11   **Mucolipidosis IV** 🕮
         Disorder with symptoms of psychomotor retardation and severe visual impairment

     E75.19   **Other gangliosidosis** 🕮
         GM$_1$ gangliosidosis
         GM$_3$ gangliosidosis

● E75.2   **Other sphingolipidosis**
     Lysosomal (a particle in a cytoplasm cell that contains digestive enzymes) storage diseases with symptoms of abnormal storage of amino acids

     | Excludes1 | adrenoleukodystrophy [Addison-Schilder] (E71.30)

     E75.21   **Fabry (-Anderson) disease**

     E75.22   **Gaucher disease**

     E75.23   **Krabbe disease** 🕮

     ● E75.24   **Niemann-Pick disease**

         E75.240   **Niemann-Pick disease type A**

         E75.241   **Niemann-Pick disease type B**

         E75.242   **Niemann-Pick disease type C**

         E75.243   **Niemann-Pick disease type D**

         E75.248   **Other Niemann-Pick disease**

         ◾ E75.249   **Niemann-Pick disease, unspecified**

     E75.25   **Metachromatic leukodystrophy** 🕮

     E75.29   **Other sphingolipidosis** 🕮
         Farber's syndrome
         Sulfatase deficiency
         Sulfatide lipidosis

Item 4–8 Leukodystrophy is characterized by degeneration and/or failure of the myelin formation of the central nervous system and sometimes of the peripheral nervous system. The disease is inherited and progressive.

◾E75.3   **Sphingolipidosis, unspecified**

E75.4   **Neuronal ceroid lipofuscinosis** 🕮
     Batten disease
     Bielschowsky-Jansky disease
     Kufs disease
     Spielmeyer-Vogt disease

E75.5   **Other lipid storage disorders**
     Cerebrotendinous cholesterosis [van Bogaert-Scherer-Epstein]
     Wolman's disease

◾E75.6   **Lipid storage disorder, unspecified**

● E76   **Disorders of glycosaminoglycan metabolism**

● E76.0   **Mucopolysaccharidosis, type I**
     Inborn metabolic disorder of enzymes that break down carbohydrates

     E76.01   **Hurler's syndrome** 🕮

     E76.02   **Hurler-Scheie syndrome** 🕮

     E76.03   **Scheie's syndrome** 🕮

E76.1   **Mucopolysaccharidosis, type II** 🕮
     Inborn metabolic disorder of enzymes that break down carbohydrates occurs in 2-4 year old males

     Hunter's syndrome

● E76.2   **Other mucopolysaccharides**

     ● E76.21   **Morquio mucopolysaccharidoses**

         E76.210   **Morquio A mucopolysaccharidoses** 🕮
             Classic Morquio syndrome
             Morquio syndrome A
             Mucopolysaccharidosis, type IVA

         E76.211   **Morquio B mucopolysaccharidoses** 🕮
             Morquio-like mucopolysaccharidoses
             Morquio-like syndrome
             Morquio syndrome B
             Mucopolysaccharidosis, type IVB

         ◾E76.219   **Morquio mucopolysaccharidoses, unspecified** 🕮
             Morquio syndrome
             Mucopolysaccharidosis, type IV

     E76.22   **Sanfilippo mucopolysaccharidoses** 🕮
         Mucopolysaccharidosis, type III (A) (B) (C) (D)
         Sanfilippo A syndrome
         Sanfilippo B syndrome
         Sanfilippo C syndrome
         Sanfilippo D syndrome

     ◾E76.29   **Other mucopolysaccharides** 🕮
         beta-Glucuronidase deficiency
         Maroteaux-Lamy (mild) (severe) syndrome
         Mucopolysaccharidosis, types VI, VII

E76.3   **Mucopolysaccharidosis, unspecified** 🕮

E76.8   **Other disorders of glucosaminoglycan metabolism** 🕮

◾E76.9   **Glucosaminoglycan metabolism disorder, unspecified** 🕮

● E77   **Disorders of glycoprotein metabolism**

E77.0   **Defects in post-translational modification of lysosomal enzymes**
     Mucolipidosis II [I-cell disease]
     Mucolipidosis III [pseudo-Hurler polydystrophy]

● Unacceptable First-Listed Diagnosis   ● Use Additional Character(s)   ◾ Unspecified   **OGCR** Official Guidelines for Coding and Reporting

🕮 Complication\Comorbidity   🕮 Major C\C | Excludes 1 | | Excludes 2 | Includes   Use additional   Code first   Code also

E77.1 Defects in glycoprotein degradation
Aspartylglucosaminuria
Fucosidosis
Mannosidosis
Sialidosis [mucolipidosis I]

E77.8 Other disorders of glycoprotein metabolism

E77.9 Disorder of glycoprotein metabolism, unspecified

E78 Disorders of lipoprotein metabolism and other lipidemias
Excludes1   sphingolipidosis (E75.0-E75.3)

E78.0 Pure hypercholesterolemia
Familial hypercholesterolemia
Fredrickson's hyperlipoproteinemia, type IIa
Hyperbetalipoproteinemia
Hyperlipidemia, Group A
Low-density-lipoprotein-type [LDL]
   hyperlipoproteinemia

E78.1 Pure hyperglyceridemia
Elevated fasting triglycerides
Endogenous hyperglyceridemia
Fredrickson's hyperlipoproteinemia, type IV
Hyperlipidemia, group B
Hyperprebetalipoproteinemia
Very-low-density-lipoprotein-type [VLDL]
   hyperlipoproteinemia

E78.2 Mixed hyperlipidemia
Broad- or floating-betalipoproteinemia
Combined hyperlipidemia NOS
Elevated cholesterol with elevated triglycerides NEC
Fredrickson's hyperlipoproteinemia, type IIb or III
Hyperbetalipoproteinemia with
   prebetalipoproteinemia
Hypercholesteremia with endogenous
   hyperglyceridemia
Hyperlipidemia, group C
Tubo-eruptive xanthoma
Xanthoma tuberosum

Excludes1   cerebrotendinous cholesterosis [van
   Bogaert-Scherer-Epstein] (E75.5)
   familial combined hyperlipidemia
   (E78.4)

E78.3 Hyperchylomicronemia
Chylomicron retention disease
Fredrickson's hyperlipoproteinemia, type I or V
Hyperlipidemia, group D
Mixed hyperglyceridemia

E78.4 Other hyperlipidemia
Familial combined hyperlipidemia

E78.5 Hyperlipidemia, unspecified

E78.6 Lipoprotein deficiency
Abetalipoproteinemia
Depressed HDL cholesterol
High-density lipoprotein deficiency
Hypoalphalipoproteinemia
Hypobetalipoproteinemia (familial)
Lecithin cholesterol acyltransferase deficiency
Tangier disease

E78.7 Disorders of bile acid and cholesterol metabolism
Excludes1   Niemann-Pick disease type C (E75.242)

E78.70 Disorder of bile acid and cholesterol metabolism, unspecified

E78.71 Barth syndrome 🦠

E78.72 Smith-Lemli-Opitz syndrome 🦠

E78.79 Other disorders of bile acid and cholesterol metabolism

E78.8 Other disorders of lipoprotein metabolism

E78.81 Lipoid dermatoarthritis

E78.89 Other lipoprotein metabolism disorders

E78.9 Disorder of lipoprotein metabolism, unspecified

E79 Disorders of purine and pyrimidine metabolism
Purines, along with pyrimidines, signal RNA and DNA production
Excludes1   Ataxia-telangiectasia (Q87.1)
   Bloom's syndrome (Q82.8)
   Cockayne's syndrome (Q87.1)
   calculus of kidney (N20.0)
   combined immunodeficiency disorders
   (D81.-)
   Fanconi's anemia (D61.09)
   gout (M1a-M10.-)
   orotaciduric anemia (D53.0)
   progeria (E34.8)
   Werner's syndrome (E34.8)
   xeroderma pigmentosum (Q82.1)

E79.0 Hyperuricemia without signs of inflammatory arthritis and tophaceous disease
Asymptomatic hyperuricemia

E79.1 Lesch-Nyhan syndrome 🦠
HGPRT deficiency

E79.2 Myoadenylate deaminase deficiency 🦠

E79.8 Other disorders of purine and pyrimidine metabolism 🦠
Hereditary xanthinuria

E79.9 Disorder of purine and pyrimidine metabolism, unspecified 🦠

E80 Disorders of porphyrin and bilirubin metabolism
Group of chemical compounds in RBC's that combine with iron to form heme
Includes   defects of catalase and peroxidase

E80.0 Hereditary erythropoietic porphyria 🦠
Congenital erythropoietic porphyria
Erythropoietic protoporphyria

E80.1 Porphyria cutanea tarda 🦠

E80.2 Other and unspecified porphyria

E80.20 Unspecified porphyria 🦠
Porphyria NOS

E80.21 Acute intermittent (hepatic) porphyria 🦠

E80.29 Other porphyria 🦠
Hereditary coproporphyria

E80.3 Defects of catalase and peroxidase 🦠
Acatalasia [Takahara]

E80.4 Gilbert's syndrome

E80.5 Crigler-Najjar syndrome

E80.6 Other disorders of bilirubin metabolism
Dubin-Johnson syndrome
Rotor's syndrome

E80.7 Disorder of bilirubin metabolism, unspecified

E83 Disorders of mineral metabolism
Excludes1   dietary mineral deficiency (E58-E61)
   parathyroid disorders (E20-E21)
   vitamin D deficiency (E55.-)

E83.0 Disorders of copper metabolism

E83.00 Disorder of copper metabolism, unspecified

E83.01 Wilson's disease
Code also associated Kayser Fleischer ring (H18.04-)

E83.09 Other disorders of copper metabolism
Menkes' (kinky hair) (steely hair) disease

E83.1 Disorders of iron metabolism
Excludes1   iron deficiency anemia (D50.-)
   sideroblastic anemia (D64.0-D64.3)

CHAPTER 4 (E00-E90)

● Unacceptable First-Listed Diagnosis   ● Use Additional Character(s)   ■ Unspecified   OGCR Official Guidelines for Coding and Reporting
🦠 Complication\Comorbidity   🦠 Major C\C   Excludes 1   Excludes 2   Includes   Use additional   Code first   Code also

898

- ▪ **E83.10 Disorder of iron metabolism, unspecified**
- **E83.11 Hemochromatosis**
- **E83.19 Other disorders of iron metabolism**
- **E83.2 Disorders of zinc metabolism**
  Acrodermatitis enteropathica
- ● **E83.3 Disorders of phosphorus metabolism and phosphatases**
  - Excludes1   adult osteomalacia (M83.-)
    osteoporosis (M80-)
  - ▪ **E83.30 Disorder of phosphorus metabolism, unspecified**
  - **E83.31 Familial hypophosphatemia**
    Vitamin D-resistant osteomalacia
    Vitamin D-resistant rickets
    - Excludes1   vitamin D-deficiency rickets (E55.0)
  - **E83.32 Hereditary vitamin D-dependent rickets (type 1) (type 2)**
    25-hydroxyvitamin D 1-alpha-hydroxylase deficiency
    Pseudovitamin D deficiency
    Vitamin D receptor defect
  - **E83.39 Other disorders of phosphorus metabolism**
    Acid phosphatase deficiency
    Hypophosphatasia
- ● **E83.4 Disorders of magnesium metabolism**
  - ▪ **E83.40 Disorders of magnesium metabolism, unspecified**
  - **E83.41 Hypermagnesemia**
  - **E83.42 Hypomagnesemia**
  - **E83.49 Other disorders of magnesium metabolism**
- ● **E83.5 Disorders of calcium metabolism**
  - Excludes1   chondrocalcinosis (M11.1-M11.2)
    hungry bone syndrome (E83.81)
    hyperparathyroidism (E21.0-E21.3)
  - ▪ **E83.50 Unspecified disorder of calcium metabolism**
  - **E83.51 Hypocalcemia**
  - **E83.52 Hypercalcemia**
    Familial hypocalciuric hypercalcemia
  - **E83.59 Other disorders of calcium metabolism**
    Idiopathic hypercalciuria
- ● **E83.8 Other disorders of mineral metabolism**
  - **E83.81 Hungry bone syndrome**
  - **E83.89 Other disorders of mineral metabolism**
- ▪ **E83.9 Disorder of mineral metabolism, unspecified**
- ● **E84 Cystic fibrosis**
  - Includes   mucoviscidosis
  - **E84.0 Cystic fibrosis with pulmonary manifestations** 🕭
    Use additional code to identify any infectious organism present, such as:
    Pseudomonas (B96.5)
  - ● **E84.1 Cystic fibrosis with intestinal manifestations**
    - **E84.11 Meconium ileus in cystic fibrosis** 🕭
      - Excludes1   meconium ileus not due to cystic fibrosis (P76.0)
    - **E84.19 Cystic fibrosis with other intestinal manifestations** 🕭
      Distal intestinal obstruction syndrome
  - **E84.8 Cystic fibrosis with other manifestations** 🕭
- ▪ **E84.9 Cystic fibrosis, unspecified** 🕭

Item 4–9 Circulating fluid volume is regulated by the amount of water and sodium ingested, excreted by the kidneys into the urine, and lost through the gastrointestinal tract, lungs, and skin. To maintain blood volume within a normal range, the kidneys regulate the amount of water and sodium lost into the urine. Too much (**fluid overload**) or too little fluid volume (**volume depletion**) will affect blood pressure. Severe cases of vomiting, diarrhea, bleeding, and burns (fluid loss through exposed burn surface area) can contribute to fluid loss. Internal body environment must maintain a precise balance (homeostasis) between too much fluid and too little fluid. This complex balancing mechanism is critical to good health.

- ● **E85 Amyloidosis**
  A disorder resulting from the abnormal deposition of a particular protein (amyloid) into tissues of the body.
  - Excludes1   Alzheimer's disease (G30.0-)
  - **E85.0 Non-neuropathic heredofamilial amyloidosis** 🕭
    Familial Mediterranean fever
    Hereditary amyloid nephropathy
  - **E85.1 Neuropathic heredofamilial amyloidosis** 🕭
    Amyloid polyneuropathy (Portuguese)
  - ▪ **E85.2 Heredofamilial amyloidosis, unspecified** 🕭
  - **E85.3 Secondary systemic amyloidosis** 🕭
    Hemodialysis-associated amyloidosis
  - **E85.4 Organ-limited amyloidosis** 🕭
    Localized amyloidosis
  - **E85.8 Other amyloidosis** 🕭
  - ▪ **E85.9 Amyloidosis, unspecified** 🕭
- ● **E86 Volume depletion**
  - Excludes1   dehydration of newborn (P74.1)
    hypovolemic shock NOS (R57.1)
    postprocedural hypovolemic shock (T81.1)
    traumatic hypovolemic shock (T79.4)
  - **E86.0 Dehydration**
    Excessive loss of body water
  - **E86.1 Hypovolemia**
    Diminished volume of circulating blood
    Depletion of volume of plasma
  - ▪ **E86.9 Volume depletion, unspecified**
- ● **E87 Other disorders of fluid, electrolyte and acid-base balance**
  - Excludes1   diabetes insipidus (E23.2)
    electrolyte imbalance associated with hyperemesis gravidarum (O21.1)
    electrolyte imbalance following ectopic or molar pregnancy (O08.5)
    familial periodic paralysis (G72.3)
  - **E87.0 Hyperosmolality and hypernatremia** 🕭
    Sodium [Na] excess
    Sodium [Na] overload
  - **E87.1 Hypo-osmolality and hyponatremia** 🕭
    Sodium [Na] deficiency
    - Excludes1   syndrome of inappropriate secretion of antidiuretic hormone (E22.2)
  - **E87.2 Acidosis** 🕭
    Acidosis NOS
    Lactic acidosis
    Metabolic acidosis
    Respiratory acidosis
    - Excludes1   diabetic acidosis - see categories E10-E13 with ketoacidosis
  - **E87.3 Alkalosis** 🕭
    Alkalosis NOS
    Metabolic alkalosis
    Respiratory alkalosis

● Unacceptable First-Listed Diagnosis   ● Use Additional Character(s)   ▪ Unspecified   **OGCR** Official Guidelines for Coding and Reporting
🕭 Complication\Comorbidity   🕭 Major C\C   Excludes 1   Excludes 2   Includes   Use additional   Code first   Code also

E87.4 Mixed disorder of acid-base balance 🗝

E87.5 Hyperkalemia
Potassium [K] excess
Potass`ium [K] overload

E87.6 Hypokalemia
Potassium [K] deficiency

E87.7 Fluid overload
| Excludes1 | edema NOS (R60.-)

E87.8 Other disorders of electrolyte and fluid balance, not elsewhere classified
Electrolyte imbalance NOS
Hyperchloremia
Hypochloremia

● **E88 Other and unspecified metabolic disorders**
Use additional codes for associated conditions
| Excludes1 | histiocytosis X (chronic) (C96.6)

● **E88.0 Disorders of plasma-protein metabolism, not elsewhere classified**
| Excludes1 | disorder of lipoprotein metabolism
(E78.-)
monoclonal gammopathy (of
undetermined significance)
(D47.2)
polyclonal hypergammaglobulinemia
(D89.0)
Waldenström macroglobulinemia
(C88.0)

E88.01 Alpha-1-antitrypsin deficiency AAT deficiency

E88.09 Other disorders of plasma-protein metabolism, not elsewhere classified
Bisalbuminemia

E88.1 Lipodystrophy, not elsewhere classified
Defective fat metabolism resulting in absence of subcutaneous fat
Lipodystrophy NOS
| Excludes1 | Whipple's disease (K90.81)

E88.2 Lipomatosis, not elsewhere classified
Abnormal tumorlike accumulations of fat in tissue
Lipomatosis NOS
Lipomatosis (Check) dolorosa [Dercum]

E88.3 Tumor lysis syndrome
Tumor lysis syndrome (spontaneous)
Tumor lysis syndrome following antineoplastic
drug chemotherapy
Code first (T45.1-) to identify drug, if drug induced

● **E88.4 Mitochondrial metabolism disorders**
Congenital disorder of metabolism
| Excludes1 | disorders of pyruvate metabolism
(E74.4)
Kearns-Sayre syndrome (H49.81)
Leber's disease (H47.22)
Leigh's encephalopathy (G31.82)
Mitochondrial myopathy, NEC (G71.3)
Reye's syndrome (G93.7)

■ **E88.40 Mitochondrial metabolism disorder, unspecified** 🗝

E88.41 MELAS syndrome 🗝
Mitochondrial myopathy,
encephalopathy, lactic acidosis and
stroke-like episodes

E88.42 MERRF syndrome 🗝
Myoclonic epilepsy associated with
ragged-red fibers
Code also myoclonic epilepsy (G40.3-)

E88.49 Other mitochondrial metabolism disorders 🗝

● **E88.8 Other specified metabolic disorders**

E88.81 Metabolic syndrome
Dysmetabolic syndrome X

E88.89 Other specified metabolic disorders
Launois-Bensaude adenolipomatosis

■ **E88.9 Metabolic disorder, unspecified**

● **E89 Postprocedural endocrine and metabolic complications and disorders, not elsewhere classified**
| Excludes2 | intraoperative complications of endocrine
system organ or structure (E36.0-,
E36.1-, E36.8)

E89.0 Postprocedural hypothyroidism
Postirradiation hypothyroidism
Postsurgical hypothyroidism

E89.1 Postprocedural hypoinsulinemia 🗝
Postpancreatectomy hyperglycemia
Postsurgical hypoinsulinemia
Use additional code, if applicable, to identify:
acquired absence of pancreas (Z90.89)
diabetes mellitus (E11.-)
insulin use (Z79.4)
| Excludes1 | transient postprocedural
hyperglycemia (R73.9)
transient postprocedural
hypoglycemia (E16.2)

E89.2 Postprocedural hypoparathyroidism
Parathyroprival tetany

E89.3 Postprocedural hypopituitarism
Postirradiation hypopituitarism

● **E89.4 Postprocedural ovarian failure**

E89.40 Asymptomatic postprocedural ovarian failure
Postprocedural ovarian failure NOS

E89.41 Symptomatic postprocedural ovarian failure
Symptoms such as flushing, sleeplessness,
headache, lack of concentration,
associated with postprocedural
menopause

E89.5 Postprocedural testicular hypofunction

E89.6 Postprocedural adrenocortical (-medullary) hypofunction 🗝

● **E89.8 Other postprocedural endocrine and metabolic complications and disorders**

● **E89.81 Postprocedural hemorrhage and hematoma of an endocrine system organ or structure following a procedure**

E89.810 Postprocedural hemorrhage and hematoma of an endocrine system organ or structure following an endocrine system procedure 🗝

E89.811 Postprocedural hemorrhage and hematoma of an endocrine system organ or structure following other procedure 🗝

E89.89 Other postprocedural endocrine and metabolic complications and disorders 🗝
Use additional code, if applicable, to
further specify disorder

● Unacceptable First-Listed Diagnosis   ● Use Additional Character(s)   ■ Unspecified   **OGCR** Official Guidelines for Coding and Reporting
🗝 Complication\Comorbidity   🗝 Major C\C | Excludes 1 | | Excludes 2 | Includes   Use additional   Code first   Code also

CHAPTER 5

MENTAL AND BEHAVIORAL DISORDERS (F01-F99)

Includes   disorders of psychological development

Excludes2   symptoms, signs and abnormal clinical laboratory findings, not elsewhere classified (R00-R99)

This chapter contains the following blocks:

F01-F09	Mental disorders due to known physiological conditions
F10-F19	Mental and behavioral disorders due to psychoactive substance use
F20-F29	Schizophrenia, schizotypal and delusional, and other non-mood psychotic disorders
F30-F39	Mood [affective] disorders
F40-F48	Anxiety, dissociative, stress-related, somatoform and other nonpsychotic mental disorders
F50-F59	Behavioral syndromes associated with physiological disturbances and physical factors
F60-F69	Disorders of adult personality and behavior
F70-F79	Mental retardation
F80-F89	Pervasive and specific developmental disorders
F90-F98	Behavioral and emotional disorders with onset usually occurring in childhood and adolescence
F99	Unspecified mental disorder

MENTAL DISORDERS DUE TO KNOWN PHYSIOLOGICAL CONDITIONS (F01-F09)

This block comprises a range of mental disorders grouped together on the basis of their having in common a demonstrable etiology in cerebral disease, brain injury, or other insult leading to cerebral dysfunction. The dysfunction may be primary, as in diseases, injuries, and insults that affect the brain directly and selectively; or secondary, as in systemic diseases and disorders that attack the brain only as one of the multiple organs or systems of the body that are involved.

● **F01**   **Vascular dementia**

Vascular dementia as a result of infarction of the brain due to vascular disease, including hypertensive cerebrovascular disease.

Includes   arteriosclerotic dementia

Code first the underlying physiological condition or sequelae of cerebrovascular disease.

● **F01.5**   **Vascular dementia**

● **F01.50**   **Vascular dementia without behavioral disturbance**

● **F01.51**   **Vascular dementia with behavioral disturbance** 🔖

Vascular dementia with aggressive behavior

Vascular dementia with combative behavior

Vascular dementia with violent behavior

Vascular dementia with wandering off

● **F02**   **Dementia in other diseases classified elsewhere**

Code first the underlying physiological condition, such as:

Alzheimer's (G30.-)
cerebral lipidosis (E75.4)
Creutzfeldt-Jakob disease (A81.0-)
dementia with Lewy bodies (G31.83)
epilepsy and recurrent seizures (G40.-)
frontotemporal dementia (G31.09)
hepatolenticular degeneration (E83.0)
human immunodeficiency virus [HIV] disease (B20)
hypercalcemia (E83.52)
hypothyroidism, acquired (E00-E03.-)
intoxications (T36-T65)
Jakob-Creutzfeldt disease (A81.0-)
multiple sclerosis (G35)
neurosyphilis (A52.17)
niacin deficiency [pellagra] (E52)
Parkinson's disease (G20)
Pick's disease (G31.01)
polyarteritis nodosa (M30.0)
systemic lupus erythematosus (M32.-)
trypanosomiasis (B56.-, B57.-)
vitamin B deficiency (E53.8)

Excludes1   dementia with Parkinsonism (G31.83)

Excludes2   dementia in alcohol and psychoactive substance disorders (F10-F19, with .17, .27, .97)

vascular dementia (F01.5-)

● **F02.8**   **Dementia in other diseases classified elsewhere**

● **F02.80**   **Dementia in other diseases classified elsewhere, without behavioral disturbance**

Dementia in other diseases classified elsewhere NOS

● **F02.81**   **Dementia in other diseases classified elsewhere, with behavioral disturbance** 🔖

Dementia in other diseases classified elsewhere with aggressive behavior

Dementia in other diseases classified elsewhere with combative behavior

Dementia in other diseases classified elsewhere with violent behavior

Dementia in other diseases classified elsewhere with wandering off

◼ **F03**   **Unspecified dementia** 🔖

Includes   presenile dementia NOS
presenile psychosis NOS
primary degenerative dementia NOS
senile dementia NOS
senile dementia depressed or paranoid type
senile psychosis NOS

Excludes1   senility NOS (R41.81)

Excludes2   senile dementia with delirium or acute confusional state (F05)

Item 5-1 Psychosis was a term formerly applied to any mental disorder but is now restricted to disturbances of a great magnitude in which there is a personality disintegration and loss of contact with reality.

● Unacceptable First-Listed Diagnosis   ● Use Additional Character(s)   ◼ Unspecified   **OGCR** Official Guidelines for Coding and Reporting

🔖 Complication\Comorbidity   🔖 Major C\C   Excludes 1   Excludes 2   Includes   Use additional   Code first   Code also

● **F04   Amnestic disorder due to known physiological condition**

     Includes   Korsakov's psychosis or syndrome, nonalcoholic

     Code first the underlying physiological condition

     Excludes1   amnesia NOS (R41.3)
                         anterograde amnesia (R41.1)
                         dissociative amnesia (F44.0)
                         retrograde amnesia (R41.2)

     Excludes2   alcohol-induced or unspecified Korsakov's syndrome (F10.26, F10.96)
                         Korsakov's syndrome induced by other psychoactive substances (F13.26, F13.96, F19.16, F19.26, F19.96)

● **F05   Delirium due to known physiological condition 🗝**

     Includes   acute or subacute brain syndrome
                         acute or subacute confusional state (nonalcoholic)
                         acute or subacute infective psychosis
                         acute or subacute organic reaction
                         acute or subacute psycho-organic syndrome
                         delirium of mixed etiology
                         delirium superimposed on dementia
                         sundowning

     Code first the underlying physiological condition

     Excludes1   delirium NOS (R41.0)
     Excludes2   delirium tremens alcohol-induced or unspecified (F10.231, F10.931)

● **F06   Other mental disorders due to known physiological condition**

     Includes   mental disorders due to endocrine disorder
                         mental disorders due to exogenous hormone
                         mental disorders due to exogenous toxic substance
                         mental disorders due to primary cerebral disease
                         mental disorders due to somatic illness
                         mental disorders due to systemic disease affecting the brain

     Code first the underlying physiological condition

     Excludes1   unspecified dementia (F03)
     Excludes2   delirium due to known physiological condition (F05)
                         dementia as classified in F01-F02
                         other mental disorders associated with alcohol and other psychoactive substances (F10-F19)

● **F06.0   Psychotic disorder with hallucinations due to known physiological condition 🗝**
         Organic hallucinatory state (nonalcoholic)

     Excludes2   hallucinations and perceptual disturbance induced by alcohol and other psychoactive substances (F10-F19 with .151, .251, .951)
                         schizophrenia (F20.-)

● **F06.1   Catatonic disorder due to known physiological condition**

     Excludes1   catatonic stupor (R40.1)
                         stupor NOS (R40.1)
     Excludes2   catatonic schizophrenia (F20.2)
                         dissociative stupor (F44.2)

● **F06.2   Psychotic disorder with delusions due to known physiological condition 🗝**
         Paranoid and paranoid-hallucinatory organic states
         Schizophrenia-like psychosis in epilepsy

     Excludes2   alcohol and drug-induced psychotic disorder (F10-F19 with .150, .250, .950)
                         brief psychotic disorder (F23)
                         delusional disorder (F22)
                         schizophrenia (F20.-)

● **F06.3   Mood disorder due to known physiological condition**

     Excludes2   mood disorders due to alcohol and other psychoactive substances (F10-F19 with .14, .24, .94)
                         mood disorders, not due to known physiological condition or unspecified (F30-F39)

     ● ▪ **F06.30   Mood disorder due to known physiological condition, unspecified**
     ● **F06.31   Mood disorder due to known physiological condition with depressive features**
     ● **F06.32   Mood disorder due to known physiological condition with major depressive-like episode**
     ● **F06.33   Mood disorder due to known physiological condition with manic features**
     ● **F06.34   Mood disorder due to known physiological condition with mixed features**

● **F06.4   Anxiety disorder due to known physiological condition**

     Excludes2   anxiety disorders due to alcohol and other psychoactive substances (F10-F19 with .180, .280, .980)
                         anxiety disorders, not due to known physiological condition or unspecified (F40.-, F41.-)

● **F06.8   Other specified mental disorders due to known physiological condition**
         Epileptic psychosis NOS
         Organic dissociative disorder
         Organic emotionally labile [asthenic] disorder

● ▪ **F06.9   Unspecified mental disorder due to known physiological condition**
         Mental disorder NOS due to known physiological condition

● **F07   Personality and behavioral disorders due to known physiological condition**

     Code first the underlying physiological condition

● **F07.0   Personality change due to known physiological condition**
         Frontal lobe syndrome
         Limbic epilepsy personality syndrome
         Lobotomy syndrome
         Organic personality disorder
         Organic pseudopsychopathic personality
         Organic pseudoretarded personality
         Postleucotomy syndrome

     Code first underlying physiological condition

     Excludes1   mild cognitive impairment (G31.84)
                         postconcussional syndrome (F07.81)
                         postencephalitic syndrome (F07.89)
                         signs and symptoms involving emotional state (R45.-)

     Excludes2   specific personality disorder (F60.-)

● Unacceptable First-Listed Diagnosis   ● Use Additional Character(s)   ▪ Unspecified   **OGCR** Official Guidelines for Coding and Reporting
🗝 Complication\Comorbidity   🗝 Major C\C   Excludes 1   Excludes 2   Includes   Use additional   Code first   Code also

● **F07.8** **Other personality and behavioral disorders due to known physiological condition**

  ● **F07.81** **Postconcussional syndrome**
Postcontusional syndrome (encephalopathy)
Post-traumatic brain syndrome, nonpsychotic
Use additional code to identify associated post-traumatic headache (G44.3-)
     Excludes1   current concussion (brain) (S06.0-)

  ● **F07.89** **Other personality and behavioral disorders due to known physiological condition**
Postencephalitic syndrome
Damage to temporal brain lobes with memory loss and abnormal behavior
Right hemispheric organic affective disorder

● ■**F07.9** **Unspecified personality and behavioral disorder due to known physiological condition**
Organic psychosyndrome
Due to exposure to organic solvents

● **F09** **Unspecified mental disorder due to known physiological condition**
     Includes   organic brain syndrome NOS
                 organic mental disorder NOS
                 organic psychosis NOS
                 symptomatic psychosis NOS

Code first the underlying physiological condition
     Excludes1   psychosis NOS (F29)

MENTAL AND BEHAVIORAL DISORDERS DUE TO PSYCHOACTIVE SUBSTANCE USE (F10-F19)

● **F10** **Alcohol related disorders**
Use additional code for blood alcohol level, if applicable (Y90.-)

  ● **F10.1** **Alcohol abuse**
     Excludes1   alcohol dependence (F10.2-)
                 alcohol use, unspecified (F10.9-)

     F10.10   Alcohol abuse, uncomplicated

  ● **F10.12** **Alcohol abuse with intoxication**
     F10.120   Alcohol abuse with intoxication, uncomplicated
     F10.121   Alcohol abuse with intoxication, delirium 🗣
     ■**F10.129**   Alcohol abuse with intoxication, unspecified

     F10.14   Alcohol abuse with alcohol-induced mood disorder

  ● **F10.15** **Alcohol abuse with alcohol-induced psychotic disorder**
     F10.150   Alcohol abuse with alcohol-induced psychotic disorder with delusions
     F10.151   Alcohol abuse with alcohol-induced psychotic disorder with hallucinations 🗣
     ■**F10.159**   Alcohol abuse with alcohol-induced psychotic disorder, unspecified

  ● **F10.18** **Alcohol abuse with other alcohol-induced disorders**
     F10.180   Alcohol abuse with alcohol-induced anxiety disorder
     F10.181   Alcohol abuse with alcohol-induced sexual dysfunction

     F10.182   Alcohol abuse with alcohol-induced sleep disorder
     F10.188   Alcohol abuse with other alcohol-induced disorder

  ■**F10.19**   Alcohol abuse with unspecified alcohol-induced disorder

● **F10.2** **Alcohol dependence**
     Excludes1   alcohol abuse (F10.1-)
                 alcohol use, unspecified (F10.9-)
     Excludes2   toxic effect of alcohol (T51.0-)

     F10.20   Alcohol dependence, uncomplicated
     F10.21   Alcohol dependence, in remission

  ● **F10.22** **Alcohol dependence with intoxication**
Acute drunkenness (in alcoholism)
     Excludes1   alcohol dependence with withdrawal (F10.23-)
     F10.220   Alcohol dependence with intoxication, uncomplicated
     F10.221   Alcohol dependence with intoxication delirium 🗣
     ■**F10.229**   Alcohol dependence with intoxication, unspecified

  ● **F10.23** **Alcohol dependence with withdrawal**
     Excludes1   alcohol dependence with intoxication (F10.22-)
     F10.230   Alcohol dependence with withdrawal, uncomplicated 🗣
     F10.231   Alcohol dependence with withdrawal delirium 🗣
     F10.232   Alcohol dependence with withdrawal with perceptual disturbance 🗣
     ■**F10.239**   Alcohol dependence with withdrawal, unspecified 🗣

     F10.24   Alcohol dependence with alcohol-induced mood disorder

  ● **F10.25** **Alcohol dependence with alcohol-induced psychotic disorder**
     F10.250   Alcohol dependence with alcohol-induced psychotic disorder with delusions
     F10.251   Alcohol dependence with alcohol-induced psychotic disorder with hallucinations 🗣
     ■**F10.259**   Alcohol dependence with alcohol-induced psychotic disorder, unspecified

     F10.26   Alcohol dependence with alcohol-induced persisting amnestic disorder
     F10.27   Alcohol dependence with alcohol-induced persisting dementia 🗣

  ● **F10.28** **Alcohol dependence with other alcohol-induced disorders**
     F10.280   Alcohol dependence with alcohol-induced anxiety disorder
     F10.281   Alcohol dependence with alcohol-induced sexual dysfunction
     F10.282   Alcohol dependence with alcohol-induced sleep disorder
     F10.288   Alcohol dependence with other alcohol-induced disorder

  ■**F10.29**   Alcohol dependence with unspecified alcohol-induced disorder

---

● Unacceptable First-Listed Diagnosis   ● Use Additional Character(s)   ■ Unspecified   **OGCR** Official Guidelines for Coding and Reporting
🗣 Complication\Comorbidity   🗣 Major C\C   Excludes 1   Excludes 2   Includes   Use additional   Code first   Code also

● F10.9   Alcohol use, unspecified
>   **Excludes1**   alcohol abuse (F10.1)
>   alcohol dependence (F10.2-)

  ● F10.92   Alcohol use, unspecified with intoxication
    ■ F10.920   Alcohol use, unspecified with intoxication, uncomplicated
    ■ F10.921   Alcohol use, unspecified with intoxication delirium ●
    ■ F10.929   Alcohol use, unspecified with intoxication, unspecified

  F10.94   Alcohol use, unspecified with alcohol-induced mood disorder ●

  ● F10.95   Alcohol use, unspecified with alcohol-induced psychotic disorder
    ■ F10.950   Alcohol use, unspecified with alcohol-induced psychotic disorder with delusions
    ■ F10.951   Alcohol use, unspecified with alcohol-induced psychotic disorder with hallucinations ●
    ■ F10.959   Alcohol use, unspecified with alcohol-induced psychotic disorder, unspecified

  ■ F10.96   Alcohol use, unspecified with alcohol-induced persisting amnestic disorder

  ■ F10.97   Alcohol use, unspecified with alcohol-induced persisting dementia ●

  ● F10.98   Alcohol use, unspecified with other alcohol-induced disorders
    ■ F10.980   Alcohol use, unspecified with alcohol-induced anxiety disorder ●
    ■ F10.981   Alcohol use, unspecified with alcohol-induced sexual dysfunction ●
    ■ F10.982   Alcohol use, unspecified with alcohol-induced sleep disorder
    ■ F10.988   Alcohol use, unspecified with other alcohol-induced disorder ●

  ■ F10.99   Alcohol use, unspecified with unspecified alcohol-induced disorder ●

● F11   Opioid related disorders
  ● F11.1   Opioid abuse
>   **Excludes1**   opioid dependence (F11.2-)
>   opioid use, unspecified (F11.9-)

    F11.10   Opioid abuse, uncomplicated

    ● F11.12   Opioid abuse with intoxication
      F11.120   Opioid abuse with intoxication, uncomplicated
      F11.121   Opioid abuse with intoxication delirium ●
      F11.122   Opioid abuse with intoxication with perceptual disturbance ●
      ■ F11.129   Opioid abuse with intoxication, unspecified

    F11.14   Opioid abuse with opioid-induced mood disorder

    ● F11.15   Opioid abuse with opioid-induced psychotic disorder
      F11.150   Opioid abuse with opioid-induced psychotic disorder with delusions ●

      F11.151   Opioid abuse with opioid-induced psychotic disorder with hallucinations ●
      ■ F11.159   Opioid abuse with opioid-induced psychotic disorder, unspecified

    ● F11.18   Opioid abuse with other opioid-induced disorder
      F11.181   Opioid abuse with opioid-induced sexual dysfunction
      F11.182   Opioid abuse with opioid-induced sleep disorder
      F11.188   Opioid abuse with other opioid-induced disorder

    ■ F11.19   Opioid abuse with unspecified opioid-induced disorder

  ● F11.2   Opioid dependence
>   **Excludes1**   opioid abuse (F11.1-)
>   opioid use, unspecified (F11.9-)
>   **Excludes2**   opioid poisoning (T40.0--T40.2-)

    F11.20   Opioid dependence, uncomplicated
    F11.21   Opioid dependence, in remission

    ● F11.22   Opioid dependence with intoxication
>   **Excludes1**   opioid dependence with withdrawal (F11.23)
      F11.220   Opioid dependence with intoxication, uncomplicated
      F11.221   Opioid dependence with intoxication delirium ●
      F11.222   Opioid dependence with intoxication with perceptual disturbance
      ■ F11.229   Opioid dependence with intoxication, unspecified

    F11.23   Opioid dependence with withdrawal ●
>   **Excludes1**   opioid dependence with intoxication (F11.22-)

    F11.24   Opioid dependence with opioid-induced mood disorder

    ● F11.25   Opioid dependence with opioid-induced psychotic disorder
      F11.250   Opioid dependence with opioid-induced psychotic disorder with delusions
      F11.251   Opioid dependence with opioid-induced psychotic disorder with hallucinations ●
      ■ F11.259   Opioid dependence with opioid-induced psychotic disorder, unspecified

    ● F11.28   Opioid dependence with other opioid-induced disorder
      F11.281   Opioid dependence with opioid-induced sexual dysfunction
      F11.282   Opioid dependence with opioid-induced sleep disorder
      F11.288   Opioid dependence with other opioid-induced disorder

    ■ F11.29   Opioid dependence with unspecified opioid-induced disorder

  ● F11.9   Opioid use, unspecified
>   **Excludes1**   opioid abuse (F11.1-)
>   opioid dependence (F11.2-)

● Unacceptable First-Listed Diagnosis   ● Use Additional Character(s)   ■ Unspecified   **OGCR** Official Guidelines for Coding and Reporting

CHAPTER 5 (F01-F99)

904   ● Complication\Comorbidity   ● Major C\C   Excludes 1   Excludes 2   Includes   Use additional   Code first   Code also

■ **F11.90** Opioid use, unspecified, uncomplicated

● **F11.92** Opioid use, unspecified with intoxication

> **Excludes1** opioid use, unspecified with withdrawal (F11.93)

> ■ **F11.920** Opioid use, unspecified with intoxication, uncomplicated

> ■ **F11.921** Opioid use, unspecified with intoxication delirium 🔗

> ■ **F11.922** Opioid use, unspecified with intoxication with perceptual disturbance

> ■ **F11.929** Opioid use, unspecified with intoxication, unspecified

■ **F11.93** Opioid use, unspecified with withdrawal 🔗

> **Excludes1** opioid use, unspecified with intoxication (F11.92-)

■ **F11.94** Opioid use, unspecified with opioid-induced mood disorder

● **F11.95** Opioid use, unspecified with opioid-induced psychotic disorder

> ■ **F11.950** Opioid use, unspecified with opioid-induced psychotic disorder with delusions 🔗

> ■ **F11.951** Opioid use, unspecified with opioid-induced psychotic disorder with hallucinations 🔗

> ■ **F11.959** Opioid use, unspecified with opioid-induced psychotic disorder, unspecified

● **F11.98** Opioid use, unspecified with other specified opioid-induced disorder

> ■ **F11.981** Opioid use, unspecified with opioid-induced sexual dysfunction

> ■ **F11.982** Opioid use, unspecified with opioid-induced sleep disorder

> ■ **F11.988** Opioid use, unspecified with other opioid-induced disorder

■ **F11.99** Opioid use, unspecified with unspecified opioid-induced disorder

● **F12** Cannabis related disorders

> **Includes** marijuana

● **F12.1** Cannabis abuse

> **Excludes1** cannabis dependence (F12.2-)
> cannabis use, unspecified (F12.9-)

> **F12.10** Cannabis abuse, uncomplicated

● **F12.12** Cannabis abuse with intoxication

> **F12.120** Cannabis abuse with intoxication, uncomplicated

> **F12.121** Cannabis abuse with intoxication delirium 🔗

> **F12.122** Cannabis abuse with intoxication with perceptual disturbance

> ■ **F12.129** Cannabis abuse with intoxication, unspecified

● **F12.15** Cannabis abuse with psychotic disorder

> **F12.150** Cannabis abuse with psychotic disorder with delusions 🔗

> **F12.151** Cannabis abuse with psychotic disorder with hallucinations 🔗

> ■ **F12.159** Cannabis abuse with psychotic disorder, unspecified

● **F12.18** Cannabis abuse with other cannabis-induced disorder

> **F12.180** Cannabis abuse with cannabis-induced anxiety disorder

> **F12.188** Cannabis abuse with other cannabis-induced disorder

■ **F12.19** Cannabis abuse with unspecified cannabis-induced disorder

● **F12.2** Cannabis dependence

> **Excludes1** cannabis abuse (F12.1-)
> cannabis use, unspecified (F12.9-)

> **Excludes2** cannabis poisoning (T40.7-)

> **F12.20** Cannabis dependence, uncomplicated

> **F12.21** Cannabis dependence, in remission

● **F12.22** Cannabis dependence with intoxication

> **F12.220** Cannabis dependence with intoxication, uncomplicated

> **F12.221** Cannabis dependence with intoxication delirium 🔗

> **F12.222** Cannabis dependence with intoxication with perceptual disturbance

> ■ **F12.229** Cannabis dependence with intoxication, unspecified

● **F12.25** Cannabis dependence with psychotic disorder

> **F12.250** Cannabis dependence with psychotic disorder with delusions 🔗

> **F12.251** Cannabis dependence with psychotic disorder with hallucinations 🔗

> ■ **F12.259** Cannabis dependence with psychotic disorder, unspecified

● **F12.28** Cannabis dependence with other cannabis-induced disorder

> **F12.280** Cannabis dependence with cannabis-induced anxiety disorder

> **F12.288** Cannabis dependence with other cannabis-induced disorder

■ **F12.29** Cannabis dependence with unspecified cannabis-induced disorder

● **F12.9** Cannabis use, unspecified

> **Excludes1** cannabis abuse (F12.1-)
> cannabis dependence (F12.2-)

■ **F12.90** Cannabis use, unspecified, uncomplicated

● **F12.92** Cannabis use, unspecified with intoxication

> ■ **F12.920** Cannabis use, unspecified with intoxication, uncomplicated

> ■ **F12.921** Cannabis use, unspecified with intoxication delirium 🔗

> ■ **F12.922** Cannabis use, unspecified with intoxication with perceptual disturbance

> ■ **F12.929** Cannabis use, unspecified with intoxication, unspecified

● **F12.95** Cannabis use, unspecified with psychotic disorder

> ■ **F12.950** Cannabis use, unspecified with psychotic disorder with delusions 🔗

● Unacceptable First-Listed Diagnosis   ● Use Additional Character(s)   ■ Unspecified   **OGCR** Official Guidelines for Coding and Reporting

🔗 Complication\Comorbidity   🔗 Major C\C   **Excludes 1**   **Excludes 2**   **Includes**   Use additional   Code first   Code also

CHAPTER 5 (F01-F99)

905

F12.951   Cannabis use, unspecified with psychotic disorder with hallucinations ✆

F12.959   Cannabis use, unspecified with psychotic disorder, unspecified

● F12.98   Cannabis use, unspecified with other cannabis-induced disorder

F12.980   Cannabis use, unspecified with anxiety disorder

F12.988   Cannabis use, unspecified with other cannabis-induced disorder

■ F12.99   Cannabis use, unspecified with unspecified cannabis-induced disorder

● F13   Sedative, hypnotic, or anxiolytic related disorders

● F13.1   Sedative, hypnotic or anxiolytic-related abuse

> **Excludes1**   sedative, hypnotic or anxiolytic-related dependence (F13.2-)
> sedative, hypnotic, or anxiolytic use, unspecified (F13.9-)

F13.10   Sedative, hypnotic or anxiolytic abuse, uncomplicated

● F13.12   Sedative, hypnotic or anxiolytic abuse with intoxication

F13.120   Sedative, hypnotic or anxiolytic abuse with intoxication, uncomplicated

F13.121   Sedative, hypnotic or anxiolytic abuse with intoxication delirium ✆

■ F13.129   Sedative, hypnotic or anxiolytic abuse with intoxication, unspecified

F13.14   Sedative, hypnotic or anxiolytic abuse with sedative, hypnotic or anxiolytic-induced mood disorder

● F13.15   Sedative, hypnotic or anxiolytic abuse with sedative, hypnotic or anxiolytic-induced psychotic disorder

F13.150   Sedative, hypnotic or anxiolytic abuse with sedative, hypnotic or anxiolytic-induced psychotic disorder with delusions ✆

F13.151   Sedative, hypnotic or anxiolytic abuse with sedative, hypnotic or anxiolytic-induced psychotic disorder with hallucinations ✆

■ F13.159   Sedative, hypnotic or anxiolytic abuse with sedative, hypnotic or anxiolytic-induced psychotic disorder, unspecified

● F13.18   Sedative, hypnotic or anxiolytic abuse with other sedative, hypnotic or anxiolytic-induced disorders

F13.180   Sedative, hypnotic or anxiolytic abuse with sedative, hypnotic or anxiolytic-induced anxiety disorder

F13.181   Sedative, hypnotic or anxiolytic abuse with sedative, hypnotic or anxiolytic-induced sexual dysfunction

F13.182   Sedative, hypnotic or anxiolytic abuse with sedative, hypnotic or anxiolytic-induced sleep disorder

F13.188   Sedative, hypnotic or anxiolytic abuse with other sedative, hypnotic or anxiolytic-induced disorder

■ F13.19   Sedative, hypnotic or anxiolytic abuse with unspecified sedative, hypnotic or anxiolyticinduced disorder

● F13.2   Sedative, hypnotic or anxiolytic-related dependence

> **Excludes1**   sedative, hypnotic or anxiolytic-related abuse (F13.1-)
> sedative, hypnotic, or anxiolytic use, unspecified (F13.9-)

> **Excludes2**   sedative, hypnotic, or anxiolytic poisoning (T42.-)

F13.20   Sedative, hypnotic or anxiolytic dependence, uncomplicated

F13.21   Sedative, hypnotic or anxiolytic dependence, in remission

● F13.22   Sedative, hypnotic or anxiolytic dependence with intoxication

> **Excludes1**   sedative, hypnotic or anxiolytic dependence with withdrawal (F13.23-)

F13.220   Sedative, hypnotic or anxiolytic dependence with intoxication, uncomplicated

F13.221   Sedative, hypnotic or anxiolytic dependence with intoxication delirium ✆

■ F13.229   Sedative, hypnotic or anxiolytic dependence with intoxication, unspecified

● F13.23   Sedative, hypnotic or anxiolytic dependence with withdrawal

> **Excludes1**   sedative, hypnotic or anxiolytic dependence with intoxication (F13.22-)

F13.230   Sedative, hypnotic or anxiolytic dependence with withdrawal, uncomplicated ✆

F13.231   Sedative, hypnotic or anxiolytic dependence with withdrawal delirium ✆

F13.232   Sedative, hypnotic or anxiolytic dependence with withdrawal with perceptual disturbance ✆

■ F13.239   Sedative, hypnotic or anxiolytic dependence with withdrawal, unspecified ✆

F13.24   Sedative, hypnotic or anxiolytic dependence with sedative, hypnotic or anxiolytic-induced mood disorder

● F13.25   Sedative, hypnotic or anxiolytic dependence with sedative, hypnotic or anxiolytic-induced psychotic disorder

F13.250   Sedative, hypnotic or anxiolytic dependence with sedative, hypnotic or anxiolytic-induced psychotic disorder with delusions ✆

F13.251   Sedative, hypnotic or anxiolytic dependence with sedative, hypnotic or anxiolytic-induced psychotic disorder with hallucinations ✆

■ F13.259   Sedative, hypnotic or anxiolytic dependence with sedative, hypnotic or anxiolytic-induced psychotic disorder, unspecified

● Unacceptable First-Listed Diagnosis   ● Use Additional Character(s)   ■ Unspecified   **OGCR** Official Guidelines for Coding and Reporting
✆ Complication\Comorbidity   ✆ Major C\C   Excludes 1   Excludes 2   Includes   Use additional   Code first   Code also

F13.26 Sedative, hypnotic or anxiolytic dependence with sedative, hypnotic or anxiolytic-induced persisting amnestic disorder

F13.27 Sedative, hypnotic or anxiolytic dependence with sedative, hypnotic or anxiolytic-induced persisting dementia 🦠

● F13.28 Sedative, hypnotic or anxiolytic dependence with other sedative, hypnotic or anxiolytic-induced disorders

  F13.280 Sedative, hypnotic or anxiolytic dependence with sedative, hypnotic or anxiolytic-induced anxiety disorder

  F13.281 Sedative, hypnotic or anxiolytic dependence with sedative, hypnotic or anxiolytic-induced sexual dysfunction

  F13.282 Sedative, hypnotic or anxiolytic dependence with sedative, hypnotic or anxiolytic-induced sleep disorder

  F13.288 Sedative, hypnotic or anxiolytic dependence with other sedative, hypnotic or anxiolytic-induced disorder

  ◻F13.29 Sedative, hypnotic or anxiolytic dependence with unspecified sedative, hypnotic or anxiolytic-induced disorder

● F13.9 Sedative, hypnotic or anxiolytic-related use, unspecified

  | Excludes1 | sedative, hypnotic or anxiolytic-related abuse (F13.1-) sedative, hypnotic or anxiolytic-related dependence (F13.2-) |

  ◻F13.90 Sedative, hypnotic, or anxiolytic use, unspecified, uncomplicated

● F13.92 Sedative, hypnotic or anxiolytic use, unspecified with intoxication

  | Excludes1 | sedative, hypnotic or anxiolytic use, unspecified with withdrawal (F13.93-) |

  ◻ F13.920 Sedative, hypnotic or anxiolytic use, unspecified with intoxication, uncomplicated

  ◻ F13.921 Sedative, hypnotic or anxiolytic use, unspecified with intoxication delirium 🦠

  ◻ F13.929 Sedative, hypnotic or anxiolytic use, unspecified with intoxication, unspecified

● F13.93 Sedative, hypnotic or anxiolytic use, unspecified with withdrawal

  | Excludes1 | sedative, hypnotic or anxiolytic use, unspecified with intoxication (F13.92-) |

  ◻ F13.930 Sedative, hypnotic or anxiolytic use, unspecified with withdrawal, uncomplicated 🦠

  ◻ F13.931 Sedative, hypnotic or anxiolytic use, unspecified with withdrawal delirium 🦠

  ◻ F13.932 Sedative, hypnotic or anxiolytic use, unspecified with withdrawal with perceptual disturbances 🦠

  ◻ F13.939 Sedative, hypnotic or anxiolytic use, unspecified with withdrawal, unspecified 🦠

◻F13.94 Sedative, hypnotic or anxiolytic use, unspecified with sedative, hypnotic or anxiolytic-induced mood disorder

● F13.95 Sedative, hypnotic or anxiolytic use, unspecified with sedative, hypnotic or anxiolytic-induced psychotic disorder

  ◻ F13.950 Sedative, hypnotic or anxiolytic use, unspecified with sedative, hypnotic or anxiolytic-induced psychotic disorder with delusions 🦠

  ◻ F13.951 Sedative, hypnotic or anxiolytic use, unspecified with sedative, hypnotic or anxiolytic-induced psychotic disorder with hallucinations 🦠

  ◻ F13.959 Sedative, hypnotic or anxiolytic use, unspecified with sedative, hypnotic or anxiolytic-induced psychotic disorder, unspecified

◻F13.96 Sedative, hypnotic or anxiolytic use, unspecified with sedative, hypnotic or anxiolytic-induced persisting amnestic disorder

◻F13.97 Sedative, hypnotic or anxiolytic use, unspecified with sedative, hypnotic or anxiolytic-induced persisting dementia 🦠

● F13.98 Sedative, hypnotic or anxiolytic use, unspecified with other sedative, hypnotic or anxiolytic-induced disorders

  ◻ F13.980 Sedative, hypnotic or anxiolytic use, unspecified with sedative, hypnotic or anxiolytic-induced anxiety disorder

  ◻ F13.981 Sedative, hypnotic or anxiolytic use, unspecified with sedative, hypnotic or anxiolytic-induced sexual dysfunction

  ◻ F13.982 Sedative, hypnotic or anxiolytic use, unspecified with sedative, hypnotic or anxiolytic-induced sleep disorder

  ◻ F13.988 Sedative, hypnotic or anxiolytic use, unspecified with other sedative, hypnotic or anxiolytic-induced disorder

◻F13.99 Sedative, hypnotic or anxiolytic use, unspecified with unspecified sedative, hypnotic or anxiolytic-induced disorder

● F14 Cocaine related disorders

  | Excludes2 | other stimulant-related disorders (F15.-) |

● F14.1 Cocaine abuse

  | Excludes1 | cocaine dependence (F14.2-) cocaine use, unspecified (F14.9-) |

  F14.10 Cocaine abuse, uncomplicated

● F14.12 Cocaine abuse with intoxication

  F14.120 Cocaine abuse with intoxication, uncomplicated

  F14.121 Cocaine abuse with intoxication with delirium 🦠

  F14.122 Cocaine abuse with intoxication with perceptual disturbance

  ◻ F14.129 Cocaine abuse with intoxication, unspecified

  F14.14 Cocaine abuse with cocaine-induced mood disorder

● Unacceptable First-Listed Diagnosis   ● Use Additional Character(s)   ◻ Unspecified   **OGCR** Official Guidelines for Coding and Reporting

🦠 Complication\Comorbidity   🦠 Major C\C | Excludes 1 | | Excludes 2 | Includes   Use additional   Code first   Code also

907

CHAPTER 5 (F01-F99)

- **F14.15** Cocaine abuse with cocaine-induced psychotic disorder
  - F14.150 Cocaine abuse with cocaine-induced psychotic disorder with delusions
  - F14.151 Cocaine abuse with cocaine-induced psychotic disorder with hallucinations
  - ▪ F14.159 Cocaine abuse with cocaine-induced psychotic disorder, unspecified
- **F14.18** Cocaine abuse with other cocaine-induced disorder
  - F14.180 Cocaine abuse with cocaine-induced anxiety disorder
  - F14.181 Cocaine abuse with cocaine-induced sexual dysfunction
  - F14.182 Cocaine abuse with cocaine-induced sleep disorder
  - F14.188 Cocaine abuse with other cocaine-induced disorder
- ▪ **F14.19** Cocaine abuse with unspecified cocaine-induced disorder
- ● **F14.2 Cocaine dependence**
  - **Excludes1** cocaine abuse (F14.1-)
    cocaine use, unspecified (F14.9-)
  - **Excludes2** cocaine poisoning (T40.5-)
  - F14.20 Cocaine dependence, uncomplicated
  - F14.21 Cocaine dependence, in remission
  - ● F14.22 Cocaine dependence with intoxication
    - **Excludes1** cocaine dependence with withdrawal (F14.23)
    - F14.220 Cocaine dependence with intoxication, uncomplicated
    - F14.221 Cocaine dependence with intoxication delirium
    - F14.222 Cocaine dependence with intoxication with perceptual disturbance
    - ▪ F14.229 Cocaine dependence with intoxication, unspecified
  - F14.23 Cocaine dependence with withdrawal
    - **Excludes1** cocaine dependence with intoxication (F14.22-)
  - F14.24 Cocaine dependence with cocaine-induced mood disorder
  - ● F14.25 Cocaine dependence with cocaine-induced psychotic disorder
    - F14.250 Cocaine dependence with cocaine-induced psychotic disorder with delusions
    - F14.251 Cocaine dependence with cocaine-induced psychotic disorder with hallucinations
    - ▪ F14.259 Cocaine dependence with cocaine-induced psychotic disorder, unspecified
  - ● F14.28 Cocaine dependence with other cocaine-induced disorder
    - F14.280 Cocaine dependence with cocaine-induced anxiety disorder
    - F14.281 Cocaine dependence with cocaine-induced sexual dysfunction

- F14.282 Cocaine dependence with cocaine-induced sleep disorder
- F14.288 Cocaine dependence with other cocaine-induced disorder
- ▪ **F14.29** Cocaine dependence with unspecified cocaine-induced disorder
- ● **F14.9 Cocaine use, unspecified**
  - **Excludes1** cocaine abuse (F14.1-)
    cocaine dependence (F14.2-)
  - ▪ F14.90 Cocaine use, unspecified, uncomplicated
  - ● F14.92 Cocaine use, unspecified with intoxication
    - ▪ F14.920 Cocaine use, unspecified with intoxication, uncomplicated
    - ▪ F14.921 Cocaine use, unspecified with intoxication delirium
    - ▪ F14.922 Cocaine use, unspecified with intoxication with perceptual disturbance
    - ▪ F14.929 Cocaine use, unspecified with intoxication, unspecified
  - ▪ F14.94 Cocaine use, unspecified with cocaine-induced mood disorder
  - ● F14.95 Cocaine use, unspecified with cocaine-induced psychotic disorder
    - ▪ F14.950 Cocaine use, unspecified with cocaine-induced psychotic disorder with delusions
    - ▪ F14.951 Cocaine use, unspecified with cocaine-induced psychotic disorder with hallucinations
    - ▪ F14.959 Cocaine use, unspecified with cocaine-induced psychotic disorder, unspecified
  - ● F14.98 Cocaine use, unspecified with other specified cocaine-induced disorder
    - ▪ F14.980 Cocaine use, unspecified with cocaine-induced anxiety disorder
    - ▪ F14.981 Cocaine use, unspecified with cocaine-induced sexual dysfunction
    - ▪ F14.982 Cocaine use, unspecified with cocaine-induced sleep disorder
    - ▪ F14.988 Cocaine use, unspecified with other cocaine-induced disorder
  - ▪ F14.99 Cocaine use, unspecified with unspecified cocaine-induced disorder
- ● **F15 Other stimulant related disorders**
  - **Includes** amphetamine-related disorders
    caffeine
  - **Excludes2** cocaine-related disorders (F14.-)
  - ● **F15.1 Other stimulant abuse**
    - **Excludes1** other stimulant dependence (F15.2-)
      other stimulant use, unspecified (F15.9-)
    - F15.10 Other stimulant abuse, uncomplicated
    - ● F15.12 Other stimulant abuse with intoxication
      - F15.120 Other stimulant abuse with intoxication, uncomplicated
      - F15.121 Other stimulant abuse with intoxication delirium
      - F15.122 Other stimulant abuse with intoxication with perceptual disturbance

● Unacceptable First-Listed Diagnosis   ● Use Additional Character(s)   ▪ Unspecified   **OGCR** Official Guidelines for Coding and Reporting

 Complication\Comorbidity   Major C\C   Excludes 1   Excludes 2   Includes   Use additional   Code first   Code also

908

F15.129   Other stimulant abuse with intoxication, unspecified

F15.14   Other stimulant abuse with stimulant-induced mood disorder

F15.15   Other stimulant abuse with stimulant-induced psychotic disorder

    F15.150   Other stimulant abuse with stimulant-induced psychotic disorder with delusions

    F15.151   Other stimulant abuse with stimulant-induced psychotic disorder with hallucinations

    F15.159   Other stimulant abuse with stimulant-induced psychotic disorder, unspecified

F15.18   Other stimulant abuse with other stimulant-induced disorder

    F15.180   Other stimulant abuse with stimulant-induced anxiety disorder

    F15.181   Other stimulant abuse with stimulant-induced sexual dysfunction

    F15.182   Other stimulant abuse with stimulant-induced sleep disorder

    F15.188   Other stimulant abuse with other stimulant-induced disorder

F15.19   Other stimulant abuse with unspecified stimulant-induced disorder

F15.2   Other stimulant dependence

> **Excludes1**   other stimulant abuse (F15.1-)
> other stimulant use, unspecified (F15.9-)

F15.20   Other stimulant dependence, uncomplicated

F15.21   Other stimulant dependence, in remission

F15.22   Other stimulant dependence with intoxication

> **Excludes1**   other stimulant dependence with withdrawal (F15.23)

    F15.220   Other stimulant dependence with intoxication, uncomplicated

    F15.221   Other stimulant dependence with intoxication delirium

    F15.222   Other stimulant dependence with intoxication with perceptual disturbance

    F15.229   Other stimulant dependence with intoxication, unspecified

F15.23   Other stimulant dependence with withdrawal

> **Excludes1**   other stimulant dependence with intoxication (F15.22-)

F15.24   Other stimulant dependence with stimulant-induced mood disorder

F15.25   Other stimulant dependence with stimulant-induced psychotic disorder

    F15.250   Other stimulant dependence with stimulant-induced psychotic disorder with delusions

    F15.251   Other stimulant dependence with stimulant-induced psychotic disorder with hallucinations

    F15.259   Other stimulant dependence with stimulant-induced psychotic disorder, unspecified

F15.28   Other stimulant dependence with other stimulant-induced disorder

    F15.280   Other stimulant dependence with stimulant-induced anxiety disorder

    F15.281   Other stimulant dependence with stimulant-induced sexual dysfunction

    F15.282   Other stimulant dependence with stimulant-induced sleep disorder

    F15.288   Other stimulant dependence with other stimulant-induced disorder

F15.29   Other stimulant dependence with unspecified stimulant-induced disorder

F15.9   Other stimulant use, unspecified

> **Excludes1**   other stimulant abuse (F15.1-)
> other stimulant dependence (F15.2-)

F15.90   Other stimulant use, unspecified, uncomplicated

F15.92   Other stimulant use, unspecified with intoxication

> **Excludes1**   other stimulant use, unspecified with withdrawal (F15.93)

    F15.920   Other stimulant use, unspecified with intoxication, uncomplicated

    F15.921   Other stimulant use, unspecified with intoxication delirium

    F15.922   Other stimulant use, unspecified with intoxication with perceptual disturbance

    F15.929   Other stimulant use, unspecified with intoxication, unspecified

F15.93   Other stimulant use, unspecified with withdrawal

> **Excludes1**   other stimulant use, unspecified with intoxication (F15.92-)

F15.94   Other stimulant use, unspecified with stimulant-induced mood disorder

F15.95   Other stimulant use, unspecified with stimulant-induced psychotic disorder

    F15.950   Other stimulant use, unspecified with stimulant-induced psychotic disorder with delusions

    F15.951   Other stimulant use, unspecified with stimulant-induced psychotic disorder with hallucinations

    F15.959   Other stimulant use, unspecified with stimulant-induced psychotic disorder, unspecified

F15.98   Other stimulant use, unspecified with other stimulant-induced disorder

    F15.980   Other stimulant use, unspecified with stimulant-induced anxiety disorder

    F15.981   Other stimulant use, unspecified with stimulant-induced sexual dysfunction

    F15.982   Other stimulant use, unspecified with stimulant-induced sleep disorder

● Unacceptable First-Listed Diagnosis   ● Use Additional Character(s)   ■ Unspecified   **OGCR** Official Guidelines for Coding and Reporting

Complication\Comorbidity   Major C\C   Excludes 1    Excludes 2   Includes   Use additional   Code first   Code also

909

CHAPTER 5 (F01-F99)

● **F15.988** Other stimulant use, unspecified with other stimulant-induced disorder

▧ **F15.99** Other stimulant use, unspecified with unspecified stimulant-induced disorder

● **F16**   Hallucinogen related disorders

     Includes   ecstasy
                  PCP
                  phencyclidine

● **F16.1**   Hallucinogen abuse

     Excludes1   hallucinogen dependence (F16.2-)
                    hallucinogen use, unspecified (F16.9-)

     F16.10   Hallucinogen abuse, uncomplicated

● **F16.12**   Hallucinogen abuse with intoxication

     F16.120   Hallucinogen abuse with intoxication, uncomplicated

     F16.121   Hallucinogen abuse with intoxication with delirium 🍬

     F16.122   Hallucinogen abuse with intoxication with perceptual disturbance

     ▧ **F16.129**   Hallucinogen abuse with intoxication, unspecified

     F16.14   Hallucinogen abuse with hallucinogen-induced mood disorder

● **F16.15**   Hallucinogen abuse with hallucinogen-induced psychotic disorder

     F16.150   Hallucinogen abuse with hallucinogen-induced psychotic disorder with delusions 🍬

     F16.151   Hallucinogen abuse with hallucinogen-induced psychotic disorder with hallucinations 🍬

     ▧ **F16.159**   Hallucinogen abuse with hallucinogen-induced psychotic disorder, unspecified

● **F16.18**   Hallucinogen abuse with other hallucinogen-induced disorder

     F16.180   Hallucinogen abuse with hallucinogen-induced anxiety disorder

     F16.183   Hallucinogen abuse with hallucinogen persisting perception disorder (flashbacks)

     F16.188   Hallucinogen abuse with other hallucinogen-induced disorder

▧ **F16.19**   Hallucinogen abuse with unspecified hallucinogen-induced disorder

● **F16.2**   Hallucinogen dependence

     Excludes1   hallucinogen abuse (F16.1-)
                    hallucinogen use, unspecified (F16.9-)

     F16.20   Hallucinogen dependence, uncomplicated

     F16.21   Hallucinogen dependence, in remission

● **F16.22**   Hallucinogen dependence with intoxication

     F16.220   Hallucinogen dependence with intoxication, uncomplicated

     F16.221   Hallucinogen dependence with intoxication with delirium 🍬

     ▧ **F16.229**   Hallucinogen dependence with intoxication, unspecified

F16.24   Hallucinogen dependence with hallucinogen-induced mood disorder

● **F16.25**   Hallucinogen dependence with hallucinogen-induced psychotic disorder

     F16.250   Hallucinogen dependence with hallucinogen-induced psychotic disorder with delusions 🍬

     F16.251   Hallucinogen dependence with hallucinogen-induced psychotic disorder with hallucinations 🍬

     ▧ **F16.259**   Hallucinogen dependence with hallucinogen-induced psychotic disorder, unspecified

● **F16.28**   Hallucinogen dependence with other hallucinogen-induced disorder

     F16.280   Hallucinogen dependence with hallucinogen-induced anxiety disorder

     F16.283   Hallucinogen dependence with hallucinogen persisting perception disorder (flashbacks)

     F16.288   Hallucinogen dependence with other hallucinogen-induced disorder

▧ **F16.29**   Hallucinogen dependence with unspecified hallucinogen-induced disorder

● **F16.9**   Hallucinogen use, unspecified

     Excludes1   hallucinogen abuse (F16.1-)
                    hallucinogen dependence (F16.2-)

▧ **F16.90**   Hallucinogen use, unspecified, uncomplicated

● **F16.92**   Hallucinogen use, unspecified with intoxication

     ▧ **F16.920**   Hallucinogen use, unspecified with intoxication, uncomplicated

     ▧ **F16.921**   Hallucinogen use, unspecified with intoxication with delirium 🍬

     ▧ **F16.929**   Hallucinogen use, unspecified with intoxication, unspecified

▧ **F16.94**   Hallucinogen use, unspecified with hallucinogen-induced mood disorder

● **F16.95**   Hallucinogen use, unspecified with hallucinogen-induced psychotic disorder

     ▧ **F16.950**   Hallucinogen use, unspecified with hallucinogen-induced psychotic disorder with delusions 🍬

     ▧ **F16.951**   Hallucinogen use, unspecified with hallucinogen-induced psychotic disorder with hallucinations 🍬

     ▧ **F16.959**   Hallucinogen use, unspecified with hallucinogen-induced psychotic disorder, unspecified

● **F16.98**   Hallucinogen use, unspecified with other specified hallucinogen-induced disorder

     ▧ **F16.980**   Hallucinogen use, unspecified with hallucinogen-induced anxiety disorder

     ▧ **F16.983**   Hallucinogen use, unspecified with hallucinogen persisting perception disorder (flashbacks)

     ▧ **F16.988**   Hallucinogen use, unspecified with other hallucinogen-induced disorder

● Unacceptable First-Listed Diagnosis   ● Use Additional Character(s)   ▧ Unspecified   **OGCR** Official Guidelines for Coding and Reporting
🍬 Complication\Comorbidity   🍬 Major C\C   Excludes 1   Excludes 2   Includes   Use additional   Code first   Code also

910

F16.99   Hallucinogen use, unspecified with
          unspecified hallucinogen-induced
          disorder

● F17   Nicotine dependence
    Excludes1   history of tobacco dependence (Z87.891)
                 tobacco use NOS (Z72.0)
    Excludes2   tobacco use (smoking) during pregnancy,
                 childbirth and the puerperium (O99.33-)
                 toxic effect of nicotine (T65.2-)

  ● F17.2   Nicotine dependence
    ● F17.20   Nicotine dependence, unspecified
        F17.200   Nicotine dependence,
                   unspecified, uncomplicated
        F17.201   Nicotine dependence,
                   unspecified, in remission
        F17.203   Nicotine dependence unspecified,
                   with withdrawal 🅒
        F17.208   Nicotine dependence,
                   unspecified, with other nicotine-
                   induced disorders
        F17.209   Nicotine dependence,
                   unspecified, with unspecified
                   nicotine-induced disorders
    ● F17.21   Nicotine dependence, cigarettes
        F17.210   Nicotine dependence, cigarettes,
                   uncomplicated
        F17.211   Nicotine dependence, cigarettes,
                   in remission
        F17.213   Nicotine dependence, cigarettes,
                   with withdrawal 🅒
        F17.218   Nicotine dependence, cigarettes,
                   with other nicotine-induced
                   disorders
        F17.219   Nicotine dependence, cigarettes,
                   with unspecified nicotine-induced
                   disorders
    ● F17.22   Nicotine dependence, chewing tobacco
        F17.220   Nicotine dependence, chewing
                   tobacco, uncomplicated
        F17.221   Nicotine dependence, chewing
                   tobacco, in remission
        F17.223   Nicotine dependence, chewing
                   tobacco, with withdrawal 🅒
        F17.228   Nicotine dependence, chewing
                   tobacco, with other nicotine-
                   induced disorders
        F17.229   Nicotine dependence, chewing
                   tobacco, with unspecified
                   nicotine-induced disorders
    ● F17.29   Nicotine dependence, other tobacco product
        F17.290   Nicotine dependence, other
                   tobacco product, uncomplicated
        F17.291   Nicotine dependence, other
                   tobacco product, in remission
        F17.293   Nicotine dependence, other
                   tobacco product, with
                   withdrawal 🅒
        F17.298   Nicotine dependence, other
                   tobacco product, with other
                   nicotine-induced disorders
        F17.299   Nicotine dependence, other
                   tobacco product, with unspecified
                   nicotine-induced disorders

● F18   Inhalant related disorders
    Includes   volatile solvents
  ● F18.1   Inhalant abuse
    Excludes1   inhalant dependence (F18.2-)
                 inhalant use, unspecified (F18.9-)
        F18.10   Inhalant abuse, uncomplicated
    ● F18.12   Inhalant abuse with intoxication
        F18.120   Inhalant abuse with intoxication,
                   uncomplicated
        F18.121   Inhalant abuse with intoxication
                   delirium 🅒
        F18.129   Inhalant abuse with intoxication,
                   unspecified
        F18.14   Inhalant abuse with inhalant-induced
                  mood disorder
    ● F18.15   Inhalant abuse with inhalant-induced
                psychotic disorder
        F18.150   Inhalant abuse with inhalant-
                   induced psychotic disorder with
                   delusions 🅒
        F18.151   Inhalant abuse with inhalant-
                   induced psychotic disorder with
                   hallucinations 🅒
        F18.159   Inhalant abuse with inhalant-
                   induced psychotic disorder,
                   unspecified
        F18.17   Inhalant abuse with inhalant-induced
                  dementia 🅒
    ● F18.18   Inhalant abuse with other inhalant-
                induced disorders
        F18.180   Inhalant abuse with inhalant-
                   induced anxiety disorder
        F18.188   Inhalant abuse with other
                   inhalant-induced disorder
        F18.19   Inhalant abuse with unspecified inhalant-
                  induced disorder
  ● F18.2   Inhalant dependence
    Excludes1   inhalant abuse (F18.1-)
                 inhalant use, unspecified (F18.9-)
        F18.20   Inhalant dependence, uncomplicated
        F18.21   Inhalant dependence, in remission
    ● F18.22   Inhalant dependence with intoxication
        F18.220   Inhalant dependence with
                   intoxication, uncomplicated
        F18.221   Inhalant dependence with
                   intoxication delirium 🅒
        F18.229   Inhalant dependence with
                   intoxication, unspecified
        F18.24   Inhalant dependence with inhalant-
                  induced mood disorder
    ● F18.25   Inhalant dependence with inhalant-
                induced psychotic disorder
        F18.250   Inhalant dependence with
                   inhalant-induced psychotic
                   disorder with delusions 🅒
        F18.251   Inhalant dependence with
                   inhalant-induced psychotic
                   disorder with hallucinations 🅒
        F18.259   Inhalant dependence with
                   inhalant-induced psychotic
                   disorder, unspecified
        F18.27   Inhalant dependence with inhalant-
                  induced dementia 🅒

● Unacceptable First-Listed Diagnosis   ● Use Additional Character(s)   ▪ Unspecified   OGCR Official Guidelines for Coding and Reporting
🅒 Complication\Comorbidity   🅒 Major C\C   Excludes 1   Excludes 2   Includes   Use additional   Code first   Code also

911

● F18.28 Inhalant dependence with other inhalant-
           induced disorders

    F18.280 Inhalant dependence with
                  inhalant-induced anxiety
                  disorder

    F18.288 Inhalant dependence with other
                  inhalant-induced disorder

■ F18.29 Inhalant dependence with unspecified
           inhalant-induced disorder

● F18.9 Inhalant use, unspecified

    Excludes1 inhalant abuse (F18.1-)
                        inhalant dependence (F18.2-)

■ F18.90 Inhalant use, unspecified, uncomplicated

● F18.92 Inhalant use, unspecified with intoxication

    ■ F18.920 Inhalant use, unspecified with
                    intoxication, uncomplicated

    ■ F18.921 Inhalant use, unspecified with
                    intoxication with delirium 🗲

    ■ F18.929 Inhalant use, unspecified with
                    intoxication, unspecified

■ F18.94 Inhalant use, unspecified with inhalant-
           induced mood disorder

● F18.95 Inhalant use, unspecified with inhalant-
           induced psychotic disorder

    ■ F18.950 Inhalant use, unspecified with
                    inhalant-induced psychotic
                    disorder with delusions 🗲

    ■ F18.951 Inhalant use, unspecified with
                    inhalant-induced psychotic
                    disorder with hallucinations 🗲

    ■ F18.959 Inhalant use, unspecified with
                    inhalant-induced psychotic
                    disorder, unspecified

■ F18.97 Inhalant use, unspecified with inhalant-
           induced persisting dementia 🗲

● F18.98 Inhalant use, unspecified with other
           inhalant-induced disorders

    ■ F18.980 Inhalant use, unspecified with
                    inhalant-induced anxiety disorder

    ■ F18.988 Inhalant use, unspecified with
                    other inhalant-induced disorder

■ F18.99 Inhalant use, unspecified with unspecified
           inhalant-induced disorder

● F19 Other psychoactive substance related disorders

    Includes polysubstance drug use (indiscriminate
                      drug use)

● F19.1 Other psychoactive substance abuse

    Excludes1 other psychoactive substance
                        dependence (F19.2-)
                        other psychoactive substance use,
                        unspecified (F19.9-)

F19.10 Other psychoactive substance abuse,
         uncomplicated

● F19.12 Other psychoactive substance abuse with
           intoxication

    F19.120 Other psychoactive substance
                  abuse with intoxication,
                  uncomplicated

    F19.121 Other psychoactive substance
                  abuse with intoxication
                  delirium 🗲

    F19.122 Other psychoactive substance
                  abuse with intoxication with
                  perceptual disturbances

■ F19.129 Other psychoactive substance
           abuse with intoxication,
           unspecified

F19.14 Other psychoactive substance abuse with
         psychoactive substance-induced mood
         disorder

● F19.15 Other psychoactive substance abuse with
           psychoactive substance-induced psychotic
           disorder

    F19.150 Other psychoactive substance
                  abuse with psychoactive
                  substance-induced psychotic
                  disorder with delusions 🗲

    F19.151 Other psychoactive substance
                  abuse with psychoactive
                  substance-induced psychotic
                  disorder with hallucinations 🗲

    ■ F19.159 Other psychoactive substance
                    abuse with psychoactive
                    substance-induced psychotic
                    disorder, unspecified

F19.16 Other psychoactive substance abuse with
         psychoactive substance-induced persisting
         amnestic disorder

F19.17 Other psychoactive substance abuse with
         psychoactive substance-induced persisting
         dementia 🗲

● F19.18 Other psychoactive substance abuse with
           other psychoactive substance-induced
           disorders

    F19.180 Other psychoactive substance
                  abuse with psychoactive
                  substance-induced anxiety
                  disorder

    F19.181 Other psychoactive substance
                  abuse with psychoactive
                  substance-induced sexual
                  dysfunction

    F19.182 Other psychoactive substance
                  abuse with psychoactive
                  substance-induced sleep
                  disorder

    F19.188 Other psychoactive substance
                  abuse with other psychoactive
                  substance-induced disorder

■ F19.19 Other psychoactive substance abuse with
           unspecified psychoactive substance-
           induced disorder

● F19.2 Other psychoactive substance dependence

    Excludes1 other psychoactive substance abuse
                        (F19.1-)
                        other psychoactive substance use,
                        unspecified (F19.9-)

F19.20 Other psychoactive substance dependence,
         uncomplicated

F19.21 Other psychoactive substance dependence,
         in remission

● F19.22 Other psychoactive substance dependence
           with intoxication

    Excludes1 other psychoactive substance
                        dependence with
                        withdrawal (F19.23-)

    F19.220 Other psychoactive substance
                  dependence with intoxication,
                  uncomplicated

● Unacceptable First-Listed Diagnosis   ● Use Additional Character(s)   ■ Unspecified   **OGCR** Official Guidelines for Coding and Reporting
🗲 Complication\Comorbidity   🗲 Major C\C   Excludes 1   Excludes 2   Includes   Use additional   Code first   Code also

F19.221 Other psychoactive substance dependence with intoxication delirium 🅒

F19.222 Other psychoactive substance dependence with intoxication with perceptual disturbance

■F19.229 Other psychoactive substance dependence with intoxication, unspecified

●F19.23 Other psychoactive substance dependence with withdrawal

Excludes1 other psychoactive substance dependence with intoxication (F19.22-)

F19.230 Other psychoactive substance dependence with withdrawal, uncomplicated 🅒

F19.231 Other psychoactive substance dependence with withdrawal delirium 🅒

F19.232 Other psychoactive substance dependence with withdrawal with perceptual disturbance 🅒

■F19.239 Other psychoactive substance dependence with withdrawal, unspecified 🅒

F19.24 Other psychoactive substance dependence with psychoactive substance-induced mood disorder

●F19.25 Other psychoactive substance dependence with psychoactive substance-induced psychotic disorder

F19.250 Other psychoactive substance dependence with psychoactive substance-induced psychotic disorder with delusions 🅒

F19.251 Other psychoactive substance dependence with psychoactive substance-induced psychotic disorder with hallucinations 🅒

■F19.259 Other psychoactive substance dependence with psychoactive substance-induced psychotic disorder, unspecified

F19.26 Other psychoactive substance dependence with psychoactive substance-induced persisting amnestic disorder

F19.27 Other psychoactive substance dependence with psychoactive substance-induced persisting dementia 🅒

●F19.28 Other psychoactive substance dependence with other psychoactive substance-induced disorders

F19.280 Other psychoactive substance dependence with psychoactive substance-induced anxiety disorder

F19.281 Other psychoactive substance dependence with psychoactive substance-induced sexual dysfunction

F19.282 Other psychoactive substance dependence with psychoactive substance-induced sleep disorder

F19.288 Other psychoactive substance dependence with other psychoactive substance-induced disorder

■F19.29 Other psychoactive substance dependence with unspecified psychoactive substance-induced disorder

●F19.9 Other psychoactive substance use, unspecified

Excludes1 other psychoactive substance abuse (F19.1-)
other psychoactive substance dependence (F19.2-)

F19.90 Other psychoactive substance use, unspecified, uncomplicated

●F19.92 Other psychoactive substance use, unspecified with intoxication

Excludes1 other psychoactive substance use, unspecified with withdrawal (F19.93)

■F19.920 Other psychoactive substance use, unspecified with intoxication, uncomplicated

■F19.921 Other psychoactive substance use, unspecified with intoxication with delirium 🅒

■F19.922 Other psychoactive substance use, unspecified with intoxication with perceptual disturbance

■F19.929 Other psychoactive substance use, unspecified with intoxication, unspecified

●F19.93 Other psychoactive substance use, unspecified with withdrawal

Excludes1 other psychoactive substance use, unspecified with intoxication (F19.92-)

■F19.930 Other psychoactive substance use, unspecified with withdrawal, uncomplicated 🅒

■F19.931 Other psychoactive substance use, unspecified with withdrawal delirium 🅒

■F19.932 Other psychoactive substance use, unspecified with withdrawal with perceptual disturbance 🅒

■F19.939 Other psychoactive substance use, unspecified with withdrawal, unspecified 🅒

■F19.94 Other psychoactive substance use, unspecified with psychoactive substance-induced mood disorder

●F19.95 Other psychoactive substance use, unspecified with psychoactive substance-induced psychotic disorder

■F19.950 Other psychoactive substance use, unspecified with psychoactive substance-induced psychotic disorder with delusions 🅒

■F19.951 Other psychoactive substance use, unspecified with psychoactive substance-induced psychotic disorder with hallucinations 🅒

■F19.959 Other psychoactive substance use, unspecified with psychoactive substance-induced psychotic disorder, unspecified

■F19.96 Other psychoactive substance use, unspecified with psychoactive substance-induced persisting amnestic disorder

● Unacceptable First-Listed Diagnosis   ● Use Additional Character(s)   ■ Unspecified   OGCR Official Guidelines for Coding and Reporting
🅒 Complication\Comorbidity 🅒 Major C\C Excludes 1 Excludes 2 Includes Use additional Code first Code also   913

CHAPTER 5 (F01-F99)

■ F19.97   Other psychoactive substance use, unspecified with psychoactive substance-induced persisting dementia 🦴

● F19.98   Other psychoactive substance use, unspecified with other psychoactive substance-induced disorders

     ■ F19.980   Other psychoactive substance use, unspecified with psychoactive substance-induced anxiety disorder

     ■ F19.981   Other psychoactive substance use, unspecified with psychoactive substance-induced sexual dysfunction

     ■ F19.982   Other psychoactive substance use, unspecified with psychoactive substance-induced sleep disorder

     ■ F19.988   Other psychoactive substance use, unspecified with other psychoactive substance-induced disorder

■ F19.99   Other psychoactive substance use, unspecified with unspecified psychoactive substance-induced disorder

---

SCHIZOPHRENIA, SCHIZOTYPAL, DELUSIONAL, AND OTHER NON-MOOD PSYCHOTIC DISORDERS (F20-F29)

● F20   **Schizophrenia**

Personality disorders characterized by multiple mental and behavioral irregularities (may exhibit disorganized thinking, delusions, and auditory hallucinations.)

Excludes1   brief psychotic disorder (F23)
cyclic schizophrenia (F25.0)
mood [affective] disorders with psychotic symptoms (F30.2, F31.2, F31.5, F31.64, F32.3, F33.3)
schizoaffective disorder (F25.-)
schizophrenic reaction NOS (F23)

Excludes2   schizophrenic reaction in:
     alcoholism (F10.15-, F10.25-, F10.95-)
     brain disease (F06.2)
     epilepsy (F06.2)
     psychoactive drug use (F11-F19 with .15, .25, .95)
     schizotypal disorder (F21)

F20.0   **Paranoid schizophrenia** 🦴
Paraphrenic schizophrenia

     Excludes1   involutional paranoid state (F22)
               paranoia (F22)

F20.1   **Disorganized schizophrenia** 🦴
Hebephrenic schizophrenia
Hebephrenia

F20.2   **Catatonic schizophrenia** 🦴

     Excludes1   catatonic stupor (R40.1)
               Schizophrenic catalepsy
               Schizophrenic catatonia
               Schizophrenic flexibilitas cerea

F20.3   **Undifferentiated schizophrenia**
Atypical schizophrenia

     Excludes1   acute schizophrenia-like psychotic disorder (F23)

     Excludes2   post-schizophrenic depression (F32.8)

F20.5   **Residual schizophrenia** 🦴
Restzustand (schizophrenic)
Schizophrenic residual state

● F20.8   **Other schizophrenia**

     F20.81   **Schizophreniform disorder** 🦴
               Schizophreniform psychosis NOS

     F20.89   **Other schizophrenia** 🦴
               Cenesthopathic schizophrenia
               Simple schizophrenia

■ F20.9   **Schizophrenia, unspecified**

F21   **Schizotypal disorder**

Personality disorder characterized by need for social isolation, odd behavior and thinking, and often unconventional beliefs

     Includes   borderline schizophrenia
               latent schizophrenia
               latent schizophrenic reaction
               prepsychotic schizophrenia
               prodromal schizophrenia
               pseudoneurotic schizophrenia
               pseudopsychopathic schizophrenia
               schizotypal personality disorder

     Excludes2   Asperger's syndrome (F84.5)
               schizoid personality disorder (F60.1)

F22   **Delusional disorders**

     Includes   delusional dysmorphophobia
               involutional paranoid state
               paranoia
               paranoia querulans
               paranoid psychosis
               paranoid state
               paraphrenia (late)
               Sensitiver Beziehungswahn

     Excludes1   mood [affective] disorders with psychotic symptoms (F30.2, F31.2, F31.5, F31.64, F32.3, F33.3)
               paranoid schizophrenia (F20.0)

     Excludes2   paranoid personality disorder (F60.0)
               paranoid psychosis, psychogenic (F23)
               paranoid reaction (F23)

F23   **Brief psychotic disorder** 🦴

     Includes   paranoid reaction
               psychogenic paranoid psychosis

     Excludes2   mood [affective] disorders with psychotic symptoms (F30.2, F31.2, F31.5, F31.64, F32.3, F33.3)

F24   **Shared psychotic disorder**

     Includes   folie à deux
               induced paranoid disorder
               induced psychotic disorder

● F25   **Schizoaffective disorders**

Mental disorder exhibiting major depressive episode, manic episode, or mixed episode occurs with symptoms of schizophrenia, and mood disorder

     Excludes1   mood [affective] disorders with psychotic symptoms (F30.2, F31.2, F31.5, F31.64, F32.3, F33.3)
               schizophrenia (F20.-)

F25.0   **Schizoaffective disorder, bipolar type**
Cyclic schizophrenia
Schizoaffective disorder, manic type
Schizoaffective disorder, mixed type
Schizoaffective psychosis, bipolar type
Schizophreniform psychosis, manic type

F25.1   **Schizoaffective disorder, depressive type**
Schizoaffective psychosis, depressive type
Schizophreniform psychosis, depressive type

● Unacceptable First-Listed Diagnosis   ● Use Additional Character(s)   ■ Unspecified   **OGCR** Official Guidelines for Coding and Reporting
🦴 Complication\Comorbidity   🦴 Major C\C   Excludes 1   Excludes 2   Includes   Use additional   Code first   Code also

F25.8   Other schizoaffective disorders

■**F25.9**   Schizoaffective disorder, unspecified
Schizoaffective psychosis NOS

F28   Other psychotic disorder not due to a substance or known physiological condition

> **Includes**   chronic hallucinatory psychosis

■**F29**   Unspecified psychosis not due to a substance or known physiological condition

> **Includes**   psychosis NOS

> **Excludes1**   mental disorder NOS (F99)
> unspecified mental disorder due to known physiological condition (F09)

MOOD [AFFECTIVE] DISORDERS (F30-F39)

●**F30**   Manic episode
Elevated, expansive, or irritable mood

> **Includes**   bipolar disorder, single manic episode
> mixed affective episode

> **Excludes1**   bipolar disorder (F31.-)
> major depressive disorder, single episode (F32.-)
> major depressive disorder, recurrent (F33.-)

●**F30.1**   Manic episode without psychotic symptoms

   ■**F30.10**   Manic episode without psychotic symptoms, unspecified

   F30.11   Manic episode without psychotic symptoms, mild

   F30.12   Manic episode without psychotic symptoms, moderate

   F30.13   Manic episode, severe, without psychotic symptoms

F30.2   Manic episode, severe with psychotic symptoms
Manic stupor
Mania with mood-congruent psychotic symptoms
Mania with mood-incongruent psychotic symptoms

F30.3   Manic episode in partial remission

F30.4   Manic episode in full remission

F30.8   Other manic episodes
Abnormality of mood resembling mania but less intense
Hypomania

■**F30.9**   Manic episode, unspecified
Mania NOS

●**F31**   Bipolar disorder
Mood disorders with history of manic, mixed, or hypomanic episodes

> **Includes**   manic-depressive illness
> manic-depressive psychosis
> manic-depressive reaction

> **Excludes1**   bipolar disorder, single manic episode (F30.-)
> major depressive disorder, single episode (F32.-)
> major depressive disorder, recurrent (F33.-)

> **Excludes2**   cyclothymia (F34.0)

F31.0   Bipolar disorder, current episode hypomanic

●**F31.1**   Bipolar disorder, current episode manic without psychotic features

   ■**F31.10**   Bipolar disorder, current episode manic without psychotic features, unspecified

   F31.11   Bipolar disorder, current episode manic without psychotic features, mild

F31.12   Bipolar disorder, current episode manic without psychotic features, moderate

F31.13   Bipolar disorder, current episode manic without psychotic features, severe

F31.2   Bipolar disorder, current episode manic severe with psychotic features
Bipolar disorder, current episode manic with mood-congruent psychotic symptoms
Bipolar disorder, current episode manic with mood-incongruent psychotic symptoms

●**F31.3**   Bipolar disorder, current episode depressed, mild or moderate severity

   ■**F31.30**   Bipolar disorder, current episode depressed, mild or moderate severity, unspecified

   F31.31   Bipolar disorder, current episode depressed, mild

   F31.32   Bipolar disorder, current episode depressed, moderate

F31.4   Bipolar disorder, current episode depressed, severe, without psychotic features

F31.5   Bipolar disorder, current episode depressed, severe, with psychotic features
Bipolar disorder, current episode depressed with mood-incongruent psychotic symptoms
Bipolar disorder, current episode depressed with mood-congruent psychotic symptoms

●**F31.6**   Bipolar disorder, current episode mixed

   ■**F31.60**   Bipolar disorder, current episode mixed, unspecified

   F31.61   Bipolar disorder, current episode mixed, mild

   F31.62   Bipolar disorder, current episode mixed, moderate

   F31.63   Bipolar disorder, current episode mixed, severe, without psychotic features

   F31.64   Bipolar disorder, current episode mixed, severe, with psychotic features
Bipolar disorder, current episode mixed with mood-congruent psychotic symptoms
Bipolar disorder, current episode mixed with mood-incongruent psychotic symptoms

●**F31.7**   Bipolar disorder, currently in remission

   ■**F31.70**   Bipolar disorder, currently in remission, most recent episode unspecified

   F31.71   Bipolar disorder, in partial remission, most recent episode hypomanic

   F31.72   Bipolar disorder, in full remission, most recent episode hypomanic

   F31.73   Bipolar disorder, in partial remission, most recent episode manic

   F31.74   Bipolar disorder, in full remission, most recent episode manic

   F31.75   Bipolar disorder, in partial remission, most recent episode depressed

   F31.76   Bipolar disorder, in full remission, most recent episode depressed

   F31.77   Bipolar disorder, in partial remission, most recent episode mixed

   F31.78   Bipolar disorder, in full remission, most recent episode mixed

---

● Unacceptable First-Listed Diagnosis   ● Use Additional Character(s)   ■ Unspecified   **OGCR** Official Guidelines for Coding and Reporting
🦠 Complication\Comorbidity   🦠 Major C\C   Excludes 1   Excludes 2   Includes   Use additional   Code first   Code also

● **F31.8 Other bipolar disorders**

    F31.81 Bipolar II disorder 🦠

    F31.89 Other bipolar disorder
        Recurrent manic episodes NOS

■ **F31.9 Bipolar disorder, unspecified**

● **F32 Major depressive disorder, single episode**

  Includes   single episode of agitated depression
          single episode of depressive reaction
          single episode of major depression
          single episode of psychogenic depression
          single episode of reactive depression
          single episode of vital depression

  Excludes1   bipolar disorder (F31.-)
          manic episode (F30-)
          recurrent depressive disorder (F33.-)

  Excludes2   adjustment disorder (F43.2)

  F32.0 Major depressive disorder, single episode, mild 🦠

  F32.1 Major depressive disorder, single episode, moderate 🦠

  F32.2 Major depressive disorder, single episode, severe without psychotic features 🦠

  F32.3 Major depressive disorder, single episode, severe with psychotic features 🦠
      Single episode of major depression with mood-congruent psychotic symptoms
      Single episode of major depression with mood-incongruent psychotic symptoms
      Single episode of major depression with psychotic symptoms
      Single episode of psychogenic depressive psychosis
      Single episode of psychotic depression
      Single episode of reactive depressive psychosis

  F32.4 Major depressive disorder, single episode, in partial remission

  F32.5 Major depressive disorder, single episode, in full remission

  F32.8 Other depressive episodes
      Atypical depression
      Post-schizophrenic depression
      Single episode of "masked" depression NOS

■ **F32.9 Major depressive disorder, single episode, unspecified** 🦠
      Depression NOS
      Depressive disorder NOS
      Major depression NOS

● **F33 Major depressive disorder, recurrent**

  Includes   recurrent episodes of:
          depressive reaction
          endogenous depression
          major depression
          psychogenic depression
          reactive depression
          seasonal depressive disorder
          vital depression

  Excludes1   bipolar disorder (F31.-)
          manic episode (F30.-)

  F33.0 Major depressive disorder, recurrent, mild 🦠

  F33.1 Major depressive disorder, recurrent, moderate 🦠

  F33.2 Major depressive disorder, recurrent severe without psychotic features 🦠

  F33.3 Major depressive disorder, recurrent, severe with psychotic symptoms 🦠
      Endogenous depression with psychotic symptoms
      Recurrent severe episodes of major depression with mood-congruent psychotic symptoms
      Recurrent severe episodes of major depression with mood-incongruent psychotic symptoms
      Recurrent severe episodes of major depression with psychotic symptoms
      Recurrent severe episodes of psychogenic depressive psychosis
      Recurrent severe episodes of psychotic depression
      Recurrent severe episodes of reactive depressive psychosis

● **F33.4 Major depressive disorder, recurrent, in remission**

  ■ **F33.40 Major depressive disorder, recurrent, in remission, unspecified** 🦠

    F33.41 Major depressive disorder, recurrent, in partial remission

    F33.42 Major depressive disorder, recurrent, in full remission

  F33.8 Other recurrent depressive disorders 🦠
      Recurrent brief depressive episodes

■ **F33.9 Major depressive disorder, recurrent, unspecified** 🦠
      Monopolar depression NOS

● **F34 Persistent mood [affective] disorders**

  F34.0 Cyclothymic disorder
      Affective personality disorder
      Cycloid personality
      Cyclothymia
      Cyclothymic personality

  F34.1 Dysthymic disorder
      Depressive neurosis
      Depressive personality disorder
      Dysthymia
      Neurotic depression
      Persistent anxiety depression

    Excludes2   anxiety depression (mild or not persistent) (F41.8)

  F34.8 Other persistent mood [affective] disorders 🦠

  ■ **F34.9 Persistent mood [affective] disorder, unspecified** 🦠

■ **F39 Unspecified mood [affective] disorder**

  Includes   affective psychosis NOS

ANXIETY, DISSOCIATIVE, STRESS-RELATED, SOMATOFORM AND OTHER NONPSYCHOTIC MENTAL DISORDERS (F40-F48)

● **F40 Phobic anxiety disorders**
  Irrational fear with avoidance of the feared subject, activity, or situation even though the individual knows that the reaction is excessive.

● **F40.0 Agoraphobia**
  Intense, irrational fear of open spaces

  ■ **F40.00 Agoraphobia, unspecified**

    F40.01 Agoraphobia with panic disorder
      Panic disorder with agoraphobia

    Excludes1   panic disorder without agoraphobia (F41.0)

    F40.02 Agoraphobia without panic disorder

● Unacceptable First-Listed Diagnosis   ● Use Additional Character(s)   ■ Unspecified   **OGCR** Official Guidelines for Coding and Reporting

🦠 Complication\Comorbidity   🦠 Major C\C   Excludes 1   Excludes 2   Includes   Use additional   Code first   Code also

● F40.1   **Social phobias**
          Anthropophobia
          Social anxiety disorder of childhood
          Social neurosis

   ■ F40.10   **Social phobia, unspecified**

   F40.11   **Social phobia, generalized**

● F40.2   **Specific (isolated) phobias**

   Excludes2   dysmorphophobia (nondelusional)
                   (F45.22)
                   nosophobia (F45.22)

   ● F40.21   **Animal type phobia**

      F40.210   **Arachnophobia**
                Fear of spiders

      F40.218   **Other animal type phobia**

   ● F40.22   **Natural environment type phobia**

      F40.220   **Fear of thunderstorms**

      F40.228   **Other natural environment type
                phobia**

   ● F40.23   **Blood, injection, injury type phobia**

      F40.230   **Fear of blood**

      F40.231   **Fear of injections and transfusions**

      F40.232   **Fear of other medical care**

      F40.233   **Fear of injury**

   ● F40.24   **Situational type phobia**

      F40.240   **Claustrophobia**
                Fear of closed spaces

      F40.241   **Acrophobia**
                Fear of heights

      F40.242   **Fear of bridges**

      F40.243   **Fear of flying**

      F40.248   **Other situational type phobia**

   ● F40.29   **Other specified phobia**

      F40.290   **Androphobia**
                Fear of men

      F40.291   **Gynephobia**
                Fear of women

      F40.298   **Other specified phobia**

   F40.8   **Other phobic anxiety disorders**
           Phobic anxiety disorder of childhood

   ■ F40.9   **Phobic anxiety disorder, unspecified**
             Phobia NOS
             Phobic state NOS

● F41   **Other anxiety disorders**

   Excludes2   anxiety in:
                   acute stress reaction (F43.0)
                   transient adjustment reaction (F43.2)
                   neurasthenia (F48.8)
                   psychophysiologic disorders (F45.-)
                   separation anxiety (F93.0)

   F41.0   **Panic disorder [episodic paroxysmal anxiety]
           without agoraphobia**
           Panic attack
           Panic state

      Excludes1   panic disorder with agoraphobia
                      (F40.01)

   F41.1   **Generalized anxiety disorder**
           Anxiety neurosis
           Anxiety reaction
           Anxiety state
           Overanxious disorder

      Excludes2   neurasthenia (F48.8)

F41.3   **Other mixed anxiety disorders**

F41.8   **Other specified anxiety disorders**
        Anxiety depression (mild or not persistent)
        Anxiety hysteria
        Mixed anxiety and depressive disorder

   ■ F41.9   **Anxiety disorder, unspecified**
             Anxiety NOS

F42   **Obsessive-compulsive disorder (OCD)**
      Anxiety disorder with recurrent obsessions or compulsions

   Includes   anancastic neurosis
                  obsessive-compulsive neurosis

   Excludes2   obsessive-compulsive personality (disorder)
                   (F60.5)
                   obsessive-compulsive symptoms occurring in:
                   depression (F32-F33)
                   schizophrenia (F20.-)

● F43   **Reaction to severe stress and adjustment disorders**

   F43.0   **Acute stress reaction**
           Acute crisis reaction
           Acute reaction to stress
           Combat fatigue
           Crisis state
           Psychic shock

   ● F43.1   **Post-traumatic stress disorder (PTSD)**
             Traumatic neurosis

      ■ F43.10   **Post-traumatic stress disorder, unspecified**

      F43.11   **Post-traumatic stress disorder, acute**

      F43.12   **Post-traumatic stress disorder, chronic**

   ● F43.2   **Adjustment disorders**
             Culture shock
             Grief reaction
             Hospitalism in children

      Excludes2   separation anxiety disorder of
                      childhood (F93.0)

      ■ F43.20   **Adjustment disorder, unspecified**

      F43.21   **Adjustment disorder with depressed mood**

      F43.22   **Adjustment disorder with anxiety**

      F43.23   **Adjustment disorder with mixed anxiety
               and depressed mood**

      F43.24   **Adjustment disorder with disturbance of
               conduct**

      F43.25   **Adjustment disorder with mixed
               disturbance of emotions and conduct**

      F43.29   **Adjustment disorder with other symptoms**

   F44.9   **Other reactions to severe stress**

   ■ F43.9   **Reaction to severe stress, unspecified**

● F44   **Dissociative and conversion disorders**

   Includes   conversion hysteria
                  conversion reaction
                  hysteria
                  hysterical psychosis

   Excludes2   malingering [conscious simulation] (Z76.5)

   F44.0   **Dissociative amnesia**
           Sudden loss of memory for personal information

      Excludes1   amnesia NOS (R41.3)
                      anterograde amnesia (R41.1)
                      retrograde amnesia (R41.2)

      Excludes2   alcohol-or other psychoactive
                      substance-induced amnestic
                      disorder (F10, F13, F19 with
                      .26, .96)
                      amnestic disorder due to known
                      physiological condition (F04)
                      postictal amnesia in epilepsy (G40.-)

● Unacceptable First-Listed Diagnosis   ● Use Additional Character(s)   ■ Unspecified   **OGCR** Official Guidelines for Coding and Reporting

🝮 Complication\Comorbidity   🝮 Major C\C   Excludes 1   Excludes 2   Includes   Use additional   Code first   Code also   917

CHAPTER 5 (F01-F99)

F44.1   Dissociative fugue
Characterized by episode of sudden, unexpected travel with amnesia for past and partial to total confusion about identity or assumption of new identity

> **Excludes2**   postictal fugue in epilepsy (G40.-)

F44.2   Dissociative stupor
Profound diminution or absence of voluntary movement and responsiveness to external stimuli

> **Excludes1**   catatonic stupor (R40.1)
> stupor NOS (R40.1)

> **Excludes2**   catatonic disorder due to known physiological condition (F06.1)
> depressive stupor (F32, F33)
> manic stupor (F30, F31)

F44.4   Conversion disorder with motor symptom or deficit
Dissociative motor disorders
Psychogenic aphonia
Psychogenic dysphonia

F44.5   Conversion disorder with seizures or convulsions
Dissociative convulsions

F44.6   Conversion disorder with sensory symptom or deficit
Dissociative anesthesia and sensory loss
Psychogenic deafness

F44.7   Conversion disorder with mixed symptom presentation

● **F44.8   Other dissociative and conversion disorders**

     F44.81   Dissociative identity disorder
         Multiple personality disorder

     F44.89   Other dissociative and conversion disorders
         Ganser's syndrome
         Psychogenic confusion
         Psychogenic twilight state
         Trance and possession disorders

■ **F44.9   Dissociative and conversion disorder, unspecified**
Dissociative disorder NOS

● **F45   Somatoform disorders**
Mental disorders characterized by symptoms suggesting general medical condition

> **Excludes2**   dissociative and conversion disorders (F44.-)
> factitious disorders (F68.1-)
> hair-plucking (F63.3)
> lalling (F80.0)
> lisping (F80.0)
> malingering [conscious simulation] (Z76.5)
> nail-biting (F98.8)
> psychological or behavioral factors associated with disorders or diseases classified elsewhere (F54)
> sexual dysfunction, not due to a substance or known physiological condition (F52.-)
> thumb-sucking (F98.8)
> tic disorders (in childhood and adolescence) (F95.-)
> Tourette's syndrome (F95.2)
> trichotillomania (F63.3)

F45.0   Somatization disorder
Briquet's disorder
Multiple psychosomatic disorder

F45.1   Undifferentiated somatoform disorder
Undifferentiated psychosomatic disorder

● **F45.2   Hypochondriacal disorders**
Persistent, unrealistic preoccupation with possibility of having serious disease

> **Excludes2**   delusional dysmorphophobia (F22)
> fixed delusions about bodily functions or shape (F22)

■ **F45.20   Hypochondriacal disorder, unspecified**

F45.21   Hypochondriasis
Hypochondriacal neurosis

F45.22   Body dysmorphic disorder
Dysmorphophobia (nondelusional)
Nosophobia

F45.29   Other hypochondriacal disorders

● **F45.4   Pain disorders related to psychological factors**

> **Excludes1**   pain NOS (R52)

F45.41   Pain disorder exclusively related to psychological factors
Somatoform pain disorder (persistent)

F45.42   Pain disorder with related psychological factors
Code also associated acute or chronic pain (G89.-)

F45.8   Other somatoform disorders
Psychogenic dysmenorrhea
Psychogenic dysphagia, including "globus hystericus"
Psychogenic pruritus
Psychogenic torticollis
Somatoform autonomic dysfunction
Teeth grinding

> **Excludes1**   sleep related teeth grinding (G47.63)

■ **F45.9   Somatoform disorder, unspecified**
Psychosomatic disorder NOS

● **F48   Other nonpsychotic mental disorders**

F48.1   Depersonalization-derealization syndrome

F48.8   Other specified nonpsychotic mental disorders
Dhat syndrome
Neurasthenia
Occupational neurosis, including writer's cramp
Psychasthenia
Psychasthenic neurosis
Psychogenic syncope

■ **F48.9   Nonpsychotic mental disorder, unspecified**
Neurosis NOS

BEHAVIORAL SYNDROMES ASSOCIATED WITH PHYSIOLOGICAL DISTURBANCES AND PHYSICAL FACTORS (F50-F59)

● **F50   Eating disorders**

> **Excludes1**   anorexia NOS (R63.0)
> feeding difficulties (R63.3)
> polyphagia (R63.2)

> **Excludes2**   feeding disorder in infancy or childhood (F98.2-)

OGCR Section I.C.5.a

Pain disorders related to psychological factors

Assign code F45.41, for pain that is exclusively psychological. Code F45.41, Pain disorder with related psychological factors, should be used following the appropriate code from category G89, Pain, not elsewhere classified, if there is documentation of a psychological component for a patient with acute or chronic pain.

See Section I.C.6. Pain

● Unacceptable First-Listed Diagnosis   ● Use Additional Character(s)   ■ Unspecified   **OGCR** Official Guidelines for Coding and Reporting

918   🅒 Complication\Comorbidity   🅜 Major C\C   Excludes 1   Excludes 2   Includes   Use additional   Code first   Code also

CHAPTER 5 (F01-F99)

● **F50.0 Anorexia nervosa**
    | Excludes1 | loss of appetite (R63.0)
             psychogenic loss of appetite (F50.8)

  ■ **F50.00 Anorexia nervosa, unspecified** 🕮

  F50.01 Anorexia nervosa, restricting type 🕮

  F50.02 Anorexia nervosa, binge eating/purging type 🕮
    | Excludes1 | bulimia nervosa (F50.2)

F50.2 Bulimia nervosa 🕮
  Bulimia NOS
  Hyperorexia nervosa
  | Excludes1 | anorexia nervosa, binge eating/purging type (F50.02)

F50.8 Other eating disorders
  Pica in adults
  Psychogenic loss of appetite
  | Excludes2 | pica of infancy and childhood (F98.3)

■ **F50.9 Eating disorder, unspecified**
  Atypical anorexia nervosa
  Atypical bulimia nervosa

● **F51 Sleep disorders not due to a substance or known physiological condition**
  | Excludes2 | organic sleep disorders (G47.-)

● **F51.0 Insomnia not due to a substance or known physiological condition**
  | Excludes2 | alcohol related insomnia (F10.182, F10.282, F10.982)
           drug related insomnia (F11.182, F11.282, F11.982, F13.182, F13.282, F13.982, F14.182, F14.282, F14.982, F15.182, F15.282, F15.982, F19.182, F19.282, F19.982)
           insomnia NOS (G47.0-)
           insomnia due to known physiological condition (G47.0-)
           organic insomnia (G47.0-)
           sleep deprivation (Z72.820)

  F51.01 Primary insomnia
    Idiopathic insomnia

  F51.02 Adjustment insomnia

  F51.03 Paradoxical insomnia

  F51.04 Psychophysiologic insomnia

  F51.05 Insomnia due to other mental disorder
    Code also associated mental disorder

  F51.09 Other insomnia not due to a substance or known physiological condition

● **F51.1 Hypersomnia not due to a substance or known physiological condition**
  Hypersomnia: Excessive sleeping/sleepiness
  | Excludes2 | alcohol related hypersomnia (F10.182, F10.282, F10.982)
           drug related hypersomnia (F11.182, F11.282, F11.982, F13.182, F13.282, F13.982, F14.182, F14.282, F14.982, F15.182, F15.282, F15.982, F19.182, F19.282, F19.982)
           hypersomnia NOS (G47.10)
           hypersomnia due to known physiological condition (G47.10)
           idiopathic hypersomnia (G47.11, G47.12)
           narcolepsy (G47.4-)

  F51.11 Primary hypersomnia

F51.12 Insufficient sleep syndrome
  | Excludes1 | sleep deprivation (Z72.820)

F51.13 Hypersomnia due to other mental disorder

F51.19 Other hypersomnia not due to a substance or known physiological condition

F51.3 Sleepwalking [somnambulism]

F51.4 Sleep terrors [night terrors]

F51.5 Nightmare disorder
  Dream anxiety disorder

F51.8 Other sleep disorders not due to a substance or known physiological condition

■ **F51.9 Sleep disorder not due to a substance or known physiological condition, unspecified**
  Emotional sleep disorder NOS

● **F52 Sexual dysfunction not due to a substance or known physiological condition**
  | Excludes2 | Dhat syndrome (F48.8)

F52.0 Hypoactive sexual desire disorder
  Anhedonia (sexual)
  Total loss of feeling of sexual pleasure
  Lack or loss of sexual desire
  | Excludes1 | decreased libido (R68.82)

F52.1 Sexual aversion disorder
  Sexual aversion and lack of sexual enjoyment

● **F52.2 Sexual arousal disorders**
  Failure of genital response

  F52.21 Male erectile disorder
    Psychogenic impotence
    | Excludes1 | impotence of organic origin (N52.-)
           impotence NOS (N52.-)

  F52.22 Female sexual arousal disorder
    Frigidity

● **F52.3 Orgasmic disorder**
  Inhibited orgasm
  Psychogenic anorgasmy

  F52.31 Female orgasmic disorder

  F52.32 Male orgasmic disorder

F52.4 Premature ejaculation

F52.5 Vaginismus not due to a substance or known physiological condition
  Psychogenic vaginismus
  | Excludes2 | vaginismus (due to a known physiological condition) (N94.2)

F52.6 Dyspareunia not due to a substance or known physiological condition
  Dyspareunia: Difficult or painful sexual intercourse
  Psychogenic dyspareunia
  | Excludes2 | dyspareunia (due to a known physiological condition) (N94.1)

F52.8 Other sexual dysfunction not due to a substance or known physiological condition
  Excessive sexual drive
  Nymphomania
  Satyriasis

■ **F52.9 Unspecified sexual dysfunction not due to a substance or known physiological condition**
  Sexual dysfunction NOS

● Unacceptable First-Listed Diagnosis   ● Use Additional Character(s)   ■ Unspecified   **OGCR** Official Guidelines for Coding and Reporting

🕮 Complication\Comorbidity   🕮 Major C\C | Excludes 1 | | Excludes 2 | Includes   Use additional   Code first   Code also   **919**

CHAPTER 5 (F01-F99)

F53 Puerperal psychosis
Acute mental illness with sudden onset following childbirth with symptoms of affective psychosis, disorientation, and confusion are prevalent

> **Includes** postpartum depression
> **Excludes1** mood disorders with psychotic features (F30.2, F31.2, F31.5, F31.64, F32.3, F33.3)
> postpartum dysphoria (O90.6)
> psychosis in schizophrenia, schizotypal, delusional, and other psychotic disorders (F20-F29)

● **F54 Psychological and behavioral factors associated with disorders or diseases classified elsewhere**
Psychological factors affecting physical conditions

> *Code first the associated physical disorder, such as:*
> asthma (J45.-)
> dermatitis (L23-L25)
> gastric ulcer (K25.-)
> mucous colitis (K58.-)
> ulcerative colitis (K51.-)
> urticaria (L50.-)
> **Excludes2** tension-type headache (G44.2)

● **F55 Abuse of non-psychoactive substances**
> **Excludes2** abuse of psychoactive substances (F10-F19)

F55.0 Abuse of antacids
F55.1 Abuse of herbal or folk remedies
F55.2 Abuse of laxatives
F55.3 Abuse of steroids or hormones
F55.4 Abuse of vitamins
F55.8 Abuse of other non-psychoactive substances

■ **F59 Unspecified behavioral syndromes associated with physiological disturbances and physical factors**
> **Includes** psychogenic physiological dysfunction NOS

DISORDERS OF ADULT PERSONALITY AND BEHAVIOR (F60-F69)

● **F60 Specific personality disorders**
Long-term patterns of thoughts and behaviors causing serious problems with relationships and work.

F60.0 Paranoid personality disorder
Hostile, devious, and combative response to disappointments
Expansive paranoid personality (disorder)
Fanatic personality (disorder)
Querulant personality (disorder)
Paranoid personality (disorder)
Sensitive paranoid personality (disorder)
> **Excludes2** paranoia (F22)
> paranoia querulans (F22)
> paranoid psychosis (F22)
> paranoid schizophrenia (F20.0)
> paranoid state (F22)

F60.1 Schizoid personality disorder
Detachment from social relationships with minimal emotional experiences and expressions
> **Excludes2** Asperger's syndrome (F84.5)
> delusional disorder (F22)
> schizoid disorder of childhood (F84.5)
> schizophrenia (F20.-)
> schizotypal disorder (F21)

F60.2 Antisocial personality disorder
Continuous and chronic antisocial behavior
Amoral personality (disorder)
Asocial personality (disorder)
Dissocial personality disorder
Psychopathic personality (disorder)
Sociopathic personality (disorder)
> **Excludes1** conduct disorders (F91.-)
> **Excludes2** borderline personality disorder (F60.3)

F60.3 Borderline personality disorder
Instability of mood, self-image or sense of self, and interpersonal relationships
Aggressive personality (disorder)
Emotionally unstable personality disorder
Explosive personality (disorder)
> **Excludes2** antisocial personality disorder (F60.2)

F60.4 Histrionic personality disorder
Personality disorder with excessive emotional and attention-seeking behavior
Hysterical personality (disorder)
Psychoinfantile personality (disorder)

F60.5 Obsessive-compulsive personality disorder
Anankastic personality (disorder)
Compulsive personality (disorder)
Obsessional personality (disorder)
> **Excludes2** obsessive-compulsive disorder (F42)

F60.6 Avoidant personality disorder
Anxious personality disorder

F60.7 Dependent personality disorder
Asthenic personality (disorder)
Inadequate personality (disorder)
Passive personality (disorder)

● **F60.8 Other specific personality disorders**

F60.81 Narcissistic personality disorder
Vanity, conceit, egotism or indifference to plight of others

F60.89 Other specific personality disorders
Eccentric personality disorder
"Haltlose" type personality disorder
Immature personality disorder
Passive-aggressive personality disorder
Psychoneurotic personality disorder
Self-defeating personality disorder

■ **F60.9 Personality disorder, unspecified**
Character disorder NOS
Character neurosis NOS
Pathological personality NOS

● **F63 Impulse disorders**
> **Excludes2** habitual excessive use of alcohol or psychoactive substances (F10-F19)
> impulse disorders involving sexual behavior (F65.-)

F63.0 Pathological gambling
Compulsive gambling
> **Excludes1** gambling and betting NOS (Z72.6)
> **Excludes2** excessive gambling by manic patients (F30, F31)
> gambling in antisocial personality disorder (F60.2)

CHAPTER 5 (F01-F99)

● Unacceptable First-Listed Diagnosis ● Use Additional Character(s) ■ Unspecified **OGCR** Official Guidelines for Coding and Reporting
🖘 Complication\Comorbidity 🖘 Major C\C Excludes 1 Excludes 2 Includes Use additional Code first Code also

F63.1   **Pyromania**
Pathological fire-setting

> **Excludes2**   fire-setting (by) (in):
> adult with antisocial personality
> disorder (F60.2)
> alcohol or psychoactive substance
> intoxication (F10-F19)
> conduct disorders (F91.-)
> mental disorders due to known
> physiological condition
> (F01-F09)
> schizophrenia (F20.-)

F63.2   **Kleptomania**
Pathological stealing

> **Excludes1**   shoplifting as the reason for
> observation for suspected
> mental disorder (Z03.8)

> **Excludes2**   depressive disorder with stealing
> (F31-F33)
> stealing due to underlying mental
> condition-code to mental
> condition
> stealing in mental disorders due to
> known physiological condition
> (F01-F09)

F63.3   **Trichotillomania**
Hair plucking

> **Excludes2**   other stereotyped movement
> disorder (F98.4)

● F63.8   **Other impulse disorders**

     F63.81   **Intermittent explosive disorder**

     F63.89   **Other impulse disorders**

▪ F63.9   **Impulse disorder, unspecified**
Impulse control disorder NOS

● **F64 Gender identity disorders**

F64.1   **Gender identity disorder in adolescence and
adulthood**
Dual role transvestism
Transsexualism

Use additional code to identify sex reassignment
status (Z87.890)

> **Excludes1**   gender identity disorder in
> childhood (F64.2)

> **Excludes2**   fetishistic transvestism (F65.1)

F64.2   **Gender identity disorder of childhood**

> **Excludes1**   gender identity disorder in adolescence
> and adulthood (F64.1)

> **Excludes2**   sexual maturation disorder (F66)

F64.8   **Other gender identity disorders**

▪ F64.9   **Gender identity disorder, unspecified**
Gender-role disorder NOS

● **F65**   **Paraphilias**

F65.0   **Fetishism**
*Intense sexual urges and arousing fantasies using
inanimate objects*

F65.1   **Transvestic fetishism**
*Intense sexual urges, arousal, or orgasm associated
with fantasized/actual cross-dressing*
Fetishistic transvestism

F65.2   **Exhibitionism**

F65.3   **Voyeurism**
*Sexual urges or arousal involving real or fantasized
observation of unsuspecting people who are naked,
disrobing, or engaging in sexual activity*

F65.4   **Pedophilia**

● F65.5   **Sadomasochism**

     ▪ F65.50   **Sadomasochism, unspecified**

     F65.51   **Sexual masochism**

     F65.52   **Sexual sadism**

● F65.8   **Other paraphilias**

     F65.81   **Frotteurism**
     *Sexual arousal or orgasm is achieved by
     rubbing up against another person (or
     fantasies of), in crowded place with
     unsuspecting victim*

     F65.89   **Other paraphilias**
     Necrophilia

▪ F65.9   **Paraphilia, unspecified**
Sexual deviation NOS

F66   **Other sexual disorders**

> **Includes**   sexual maturation disorder
> sexual relationship disorder

● **F68**   **Other disorders of adult personality and behavior**

● F68.1   **Factitious disorder**
Compensation neurosis
Elaboration of physical symptoms for
psychological reasons
Hospital hopper syndrome
Münchhausen's syndrome
Peregrinating patient

> **Excludes2**   factitial dermatitis (L98.1)
> person feigning illness (with obvious
> motivation) (Z76.5)

     ▪ F68.10   **Factitious disorder, unspecified** 🔾

     F68.11   **Factitious disorder with predominantly
psychological signs and symptoms**

     F68.12   **Factitious disorder with predominantly
physical signs and symptoms** 🔾

     F68.13   **Factitious disorder with combined psycho-
logical and physical signs and symptoms**

F68.8   **Other specified disorders of adult personality and
behavior**

▪ F69   **Unspecified disorder of adult personality and behavior**

MENTAL RETARDATION (F70-F79)

Code first any associated physical or developmental disorders

> **Excludes1**   borderline intellectual functioning, IQ above
> 70 to 84 (R41.83)

F70   **Mild mental retardation**

> **Includes**   IQ level 50-55 to approximately 70
> mild mental subnormality

F71   **Moderate mental retardation**

> **Includes**   IQ level 35-40 to 50-55
> moderate mental subnormality

F72   **Severe mental retardation** 🔾

> **Includes**   IQ 20-25 to 35-40
> severe mental subnormality

F73   **Profound mental retardation** 🔾

> **Includes**   IQ level below 20-25
> profound mental subnormality

F78   **Other mental retardation**

▪ F79   **Unspecified mental retardation**

> **Includes**   mental deficiency NOS
> mental subnormality NOS

● Unacceptable First-Listed Diagnosis   ● Use Additional Character(s)   ▪ Unspecified   **OGCR** Official Guidelines for Coding and Reporting
🔾 Complication\Comorbidity   🔾 Major C\C   Excludes 1   Excludes 2   Includes   Use additional   Code first   Code also

921

PERVASIVE AND SPECIFIC DEVELOPMENTAL DISORDERS (F80-F89)

● **F80**   **Specific developmental disorders of speech and language**

     F80.0   **Phonological disorder**
         Communication disorder of unknown cause,
         characterized by failure to use age-appropriate
         sounds
         Dyslalia
         Functional speech articulation disorder
         Lalling
         Lisping
         Phonological developmental disorder
         Speech articulation developmental disorder

         Excludes1   speech articulation impairment due
                      to aphasia NOS (R47.01)
                      speech articulation impairment due
                      to apraxia (R48.2)

         Excludes2   speech articulation impairment due
                      to hearing loss (F80.4)
                      speech articulation impairment due
                      to mental retardation (F70-F79)
                      speech articulation impairment
                      with expressive language
                      developmental disorder (F80.1)
                      speech articulation impairment with
                      mixed receptive
                      expressive language developmental
                      disorder (F80.2)

     F80.1   **Expressive language disorder**
         Developmental dysphasia or aphasia, expressive
         type
         Excludes1   mixed receptive-expressive language
                      disorder (F80.2)
                      dysphasia and aphasia NOS (R47.-)
         Excludes2   acquired aphasia with epilepsy
                      [Landau-Kleffner] (F80.3)
                      selective mutism (F94.0)
                      mental retardation (F70-F79)
                      pervasive developmental disorders
                      (F84.-)

     F80.2   **Mixed receptive-expressive language disorder**
         Developmental dysphasia or aphasia, receptive
         type
         Developmental Wernicke's aphasia
         Excludes1   central auditory processing disorder
                      (H93.25)
                      dysphasia or aphasia NOS (R47.-)
                      expressive language disorder
                      (F80.1)
                      expressive type dysphasia or aphasia
                      (F80.1)
                      word deafness (H93.25)
         Excludes2   acquired aphasia with epilepsy
                      [Landau-Kleffner] (F80.3)
                      pervasive developmental disorders
                      (F84.-)
                      selective mutism (F94.0)
                      mental retardation (F70-F79)

     F80.3   **Acquired aphasia with epilepsy [Landau-Kleffner]**
         Loss of ability to produce and/or comprehend language,
         caused by injury to brain
         Excludes1   aphasia NOS (R47.01)
         Excludes2   pervasive developmental disorders
                      (F84.-)

     F80.4   **Speech and language development delay due to**
         hearing loss
         Code also type of hearing loss (H90.-, H91.-)

     F80.8   **Other developmental disorders of speech or**
         language

     ■**F80.9**   **Developmental disorder of speech or language,**
         unspecified
         Communication disorder NOS
         Language disorder NOS

● **F81**   **Specific developmental disorders of scholastic skills**

     F81.0   **Specific reading disorder**
         "Backward reading"
         Developmental dyslexia
         Specific reading retardation
         Excludes1   alexia NOS (R48.0)
                      dyslexia NOS (R48.0)

     F81.2   **Mathematics disorder**
         Developmental acalculia
         Developmental arithmetical disorder
         Developmental Gerstmann's syndrome
         Excludes1   acalculia NOS (R48.8)
         Excludes2   arithmetical difficulties associated
                      with a reading disorder
                      (F81.0)
                      arithmetical difficulties associated
                      with a spelling disorder
                      (F81.81)
                      arithmetical difficulties due to
                      inadequate teaching (Z55.8)

● **F81.8**   **Other developmental disorders of scholastic**
         skills
         F81.81   **Disorder of written expression**
                 Specific spelling disorder
         F81.89   **Other developmental disorders of**
                 scholastic skills

     ■**F81.9**   **Developmental disorder of scholastic skills,**
         unspecified
         Knowledge acquisition disability NOS
         Learning disability NOS
         Learning disorder NOS

   F82   **Specific developmental disorder of motor function**
         Includes   clumsy child syndrome
                      developmental coordination disorder
                      developmental dyspraxia
         Excludes1   abnormalities of gait and mobility (R26.-)
                      lack of coordination (R27.-)
         Excludes2   lack of coordination secondary to mental
                      retardation (F70-F79)

● **F84**   **Pervasive developmental disorders**
         Use additional code to identify any associated medical
         condition and mental retardation.

     F84.0   **Autistic disorder** 🔖
         Infantile autism
         Infantile psychosis
         Kanner's syndrome
         Excludes1   Asperger's syndrome (F84.5)

     F84.2   **Rett's syndrome** 🔖
         Neurodevelopmental disorder
         Excludes1   Asperger's syndrome (F84.5)
                      Autistic disorder (F84.0)
                      other childhood disintegrative
                      disorder (F84.3)

● Unacceptable First-Listed Diagnosis   ● Use Additional Character(s)   ■ Unspecified   **OGCR** Official Guidelines for Coding and Reporting
🔖 Complication\Comorbidity   🔖 Major C\C   Excludes 1   Excludes 2   Includes   Use additional   Code first   Code also

F84.3   Other childhood disintegrative disorder 🍀
Dementia infantilis
At least two years of normal development followed by significant loss of language abilities, social skills, bowel/bladder control, motor skills
Disintegrative psychosis
Heller's syndrome
At least two years of normal development followed by significant loss of language abilities, social skills, bowel/bladder control, motor skills
Symbiotic psychosis
Abnormal relationship to mothering figure, characterized by intense separation anxiety, severe regression, giving up of useful speech, and autism

Use additional code to identify any associated neurological condition.

| Excludes1 | Asperger's syndrome (F84.5)
Autistic disorder (F84.0)
Rett's syndrome (F84.2) |

F84.5   Asperger's syndrome 🍀
Developmental disorder
Asperger's disorder
Autistic psychopathy
Schizoid disorder of childhood

F84.8   Other pervasive developmental disorders 🍀
Overactive disorder associated with mental retardation and stereotyped movements

F84.9   Pervasive developmental disorder, unspecified 🍀
Atypical autism

F88   Other disorders of psychological development

| Includes | developmental agnosia |

F89   Unspecified disorder of psychological development

| Includes | developmental disorder NOS |

BEHAVIORAL AND EMOTIONAL DISORDERS WITH ONSET USUALLY OCCURRING IN CHILDHOOD AND ADOLESCENCE (F90-F98)

Note: Codes within categories F90-F98 may be used regardless of the age of a patient. These disorders generally have onset within the childhood or adolescent years, but may continue throughout life or not be diagnosed until adulthood.

F90   Attention-deficit hyperactivity disorders (ADD)

| Includes | attention deficit disorder with hyperactivity
attention deficit syndrome with hyperactivity |

| Excludes2 | anxiety disorders (F40.-, F41.-)
mood [affective] disorders (F30-F39)
pervasive developmental disorders (F84.-)
schizophrenia (F20.-) |

Attention deficit disorder with hyperactivity=ADHD

F90.0   Attention-deficit hyperactivity disorder, predominantly inattentive type

F90.1   Attention-deficit hyperactivity disorder, predominantly hyperactive type

F90.2   Attention-deficit hyperactivity disorder, combined type

F90.8   Attention-deficit hyperactivity disorder, other type

F90.9   Attention-deficit hyperactivity disorder, unspecified type
Attention-deficit hyperactivity disorder of childhood or adolescence NOS
Attention-deficit hyperactivity disorder NOS

F91   Conduct disorders
Childhood/adolescence disruptive behavior disorder

| Excludes1 | antisocial behavior (Z72.81-)
antisocial personality disorder (F60.2) |

| Excludes2 | conduct problems associated with attention-deficit hyperactivity disorder (F90.-)
mood [affective] disorders (F30-F39)
pervasive developmental disorders (F84.-)
schizophrenia (F20.-) |

F91.0   Conduct disorder confined to family context

F91.1   Conduct disorder, childhood-onset type
Unsocialized conduct disorder
Conduct disorder, solitary aggressive type
Unsocialized aggressive disorder

F91.2   Conduct disorder, adolescent-onset type
Socialized conduct disorder
Conduct disorder, group type

F91.3   Oppositional defiant disorder

F91.8   Other conduct disorders

F91.9   Conduct disorder, unspecified
Behavioral disorder NOS
Conduct disorder NOS
Disruptive behavior disorder NOS

F93   Emotional disorders with onset specific to childhood

F93.0   Separation anxiety disorder of childhood

| Excludes2 | mood [affective] disorders (F30-F39)
nonpsychotic mental disorders (F40-F48)
phobic anxiety disorder of childhood (F40.8)
social phobia (F40.1) |

F93.8   Other childhood emotional disorders
Identity disorder

| Excludes2 | gender identity disorder of childhood (F64.2) |

F93.9   Childhood emotional disorder, unspecified

F94   Disorders of social functioning with onset specific to childhood and adolescence

F94.0   Selective mutism
Elective mutism

| Excludes2 | pervasive developmental disorders (F84.-)
schizophrenia (F20.-)
specific developmental disorders of speech and language (F80.-)
transient mutism as part of separation anxiety in young children (F93.0) |

F94.1   Reactive attachment disorder of childhood

Use additional code to identify any associated failure to thrive or growth retardation

| Excludes1 | disinhibited attachment disorder of childhood (F94.2)
normal variation in pattern of selective attachment |

| Excludes2 | Asperger's syndrome (F84.5)
maltreatment syndromes (T74.-)
sexual or physical abuse in childhood, resulting in psychosocial problems (Z62.81-) |

● Unacceptable First-Listed Diagnosis   ● Use Additional Character(s)   ■ Unspecified   **OGCR** Official Guidelines for Coding and Reporting
🍀 Complication\Comorbidity   🍀 Major C\C   Excludes 1   Excludes 2   Includes   Use additional   Code first   Code also

CHAPTER 5 (F01-F99)

923

F94.2   **Disinhibited attachment disorder of childhood**
Affectionless psychopathy
Institutional syndrome

> **Excludes1**   reactive attachment disorder of
> childhood (F94.l)

> **Excludes2**   Asperger's syndrome (F84.5)
> attention-deficit hyperactivity
> disorders (F90.-)
> hospitalism in children (F43.2-)

F94.8   **Other childhood disorders of social functioning**

F94.9   **Childhood disorder of social functioning, unspecified**

● F95   **Tic disorder**
Involuntary twitch

F95.0   **Transient tic disorder**

F95.1   **Chronic motor or vocal tic disorder**

F95.2   **Tourette's disorder**
Combined vocal and multiple motor tic disorder
[de la Tourette]
Tourette's syndrome

F95.8   **Other tic disorders**

F95.9   **Tic disorder, unspecified**
Tic NOS

● F98   **Other behavioral and emotional disorders with onset usually occurring in childhood and adolescence**

> **Excludes2**   breath-holding spells (R06.89)
> gender identity disorder of childhood
> (F64.2)
> Kleine-Levin syndrome (G47.13)
> obsessive-compulsive disorder (F42)
> sleep disorders not due to a substance or
> known physiological condition (F51.-)

F98.0   **Enuresis not due to a substance or known physiological condition**
Enuresis: Urinary incontinence
Enuresis (primary) (secondary) of nonorganic
origin
Functional enuresis
Psychogenic enuresis
Urinary incontinence of nonorganic origin

> **Excludes1**   enuresis NOS (R32)

F98.1   **Encopresis not due to a substance or known physiological condition**
Encopresis: Fecal incontinence
Functional encopresis
Incontinence of feces of nonorganic origin
Psychogenic encopresis

> Use additional code to identify the cause of any
> coexisting constipation.

> **Excludes1**   encopresis NOS (R15)

Item 5-2 Enuresis: Bed wetting by children at night. Causes can be either psychological or medical (diabetes, urinary tract infections, or abnormalities). **Encopresis:** Overflow incontinence of bowels sometimes resulting from chronic constipation or fecal impaction. Check the documentation for additional diagnoses.

● F98.2   **Other feeding disorders of infancy and childhood**

> **Excludes1**   feeding difficulties (R63.3)

> **Excludes2**   anorexia nervosa and other eating
> disorders (F50.-)
> feeding problems of newborn
> (P92.-)
> pica of infancy or childhood (F98.3)

F98.21   **Rumination disorder of infancy**

F98.29   **Other feeding disorders of infancy and early childhood**

F98.3   **Pica of infancy and childhood**
*Craving and eating substances such as paint, clay, or
dirt to replace a nutritional deficit in the body.*

F98.4   **Stereotyped movement disorders**
Stereotype/habit disorder

> **Excludes1**   abnormal involuntary movements
> (R25.-)

> **Excludes2**   compulsions in obsessive-
> compulsive disorder (F42)
> hair plucking (F63.3)
> movement disorders of organic
> origin (G20-G25)
> nail-biting (F98.8)
> nose-picking (F98.8)
> stereotypies that are part of a
> broader psychiatric condition
> (F01-F95)
> thumb-sucking (F98.8)
> tic disorders (F95.-)
> trichotillomania (F63.3)

F98.5   **Stuttering [stammering]**
Fluency disorder

> **Excludes2**   cluttering (F98.8)
> dysphasia (R47.02)
> stuttering (fluency disorder) following
> cerebrovascular disease (I69. with
> final characters -23)
> tic disorders (F95.-)

F98.8   **Other specified behavioral and emotional disorders with onset usually occurring in childhood and adolescence**
Cluttering
Excessive masturbation
Nail-biting
Nose-picking
Thumb-sucking

F98.9   **Unspecified behavioral and emotional disorders with onset usually occurring in childhood and adolescence**

UNSPECIFIED MENTAL DISORDER (F99)

F99   **Mental disorder, not otherwise specified**

> **Includes**   mental illness NOS

> **Excludes1**   unspecified mental disorder due to known
> physiological condition (F06.9)

● Unacceptable First-Listed Diagnosis   ● Use Additional Character(s)   ■ Unspecified   **OGCR** Official Guidelines for Coding and Reporting
🅒 Complication\Comorbidity   🅜 Major C\C   Excludes 1   Excludes 2   Includes   Use additional   Code first   Code also

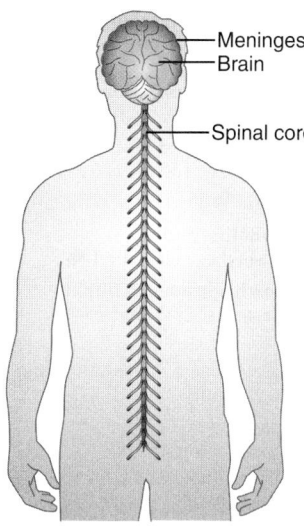

Meninges
Brain
Spinal cord

Figure 6-1 The brain and spinal cord make up the central nervous system.

Item 6-1 The two major classifications of the nervous system are the peripheral nervous system and the central nervous system (CNS). The central nervous system is comprised of the brain and the spinal cord. The peripheral nervous system is comprised of the parasympathetic and sympathetic systems. **Encephalitis** is the swelling of the brain. **Meningitis** is swelling of the covering of the brain, the meninges. Types and causes of brain infections are:

Type Cause
purulent bacterial
aseptic/abacterial viral
chronic meningitis mycobacterial and fungal

CHAPTER 6
DISEASES OF THE NERVOUS SYSTEM (G00-G99)

Excludes2	certain conditions originating in the perinatal period (P04-P96)
	certain infectious and parasitic diseases (A00-B99)
	complications of pregnancy, childbirth and the puerperium (O00-O99)
	congenital malformations, deformations, and chromosomal abnormalities (Q00-Q99)
	endocrine, nutritional and metabolic diseases (E00-E90)
	injury, poisoning and certain other consequences of external causes (S00-T98)
	neoplasms (C00-D48)
	symptoms, signs and abnormal clinical and laboratory findings, not elsewhere classified (R00-R94)

This chapter contains the following blocks:

G00-G09	Inflammatory diseases of the central nervous system
G10-G14	Systemic atrophies primarily affecting the central nervous system
G20-G26	Extrapyramidal and movement disorders
G30-G32	Other degenerative diseases of the nervous system
G35-G37	Demyelinating diseases of the central nervous system

G40-G47	Episodic and paroxysmal disorders
G50-G59	Nerve, nerve root and plexus disorders
G60-G64	Polyneuropathies and other disorders of the peripheral nervous system
G70-G73	Diseases of myoneural junction and muscle
G80-G83	Cerebral palsy and other paralytic syndromes
G89-G99	Other disorders of the nervous system

INFLAMMATORY DISEASES OF THE CENTRAL NERVOUS SYSTEM (G00-G09)

● **G00 Bacterial meningitis, not elsewhere classified**
An infection of the cerebrospinal fluid surrounding the spinal cord and brain.

Includes	bacterial arachnoiditis
	bacterial leptomeningitis
	bacterial meningitis
	bacterial pachymeningitis

Excludes1	bacterial:
	meningoencephalitis (G04.2)
	meningomyelitis (G04.2)

G00.0 Hemophilus meningitis 🗝
Meningitis due to Hemophilus influenzae

G00.1 Pneumococcal meningitis 🗝

G00.2 Streptococcal meningitis 🗝
Use additional code to further identify organism (B95.0-B95.5)

G00.3 Staphylococcal meningitis 🗝
Use additional code to further identify organism (B95.6-B95.8)

G00.8 Other bacterial meningitis 🗝
Meningitis due to Escherichia coli
Meningitis due to Friedländer bacillus
Meningitis due to Klebsiella
Use additional code to further identify organism (B96.-)

▪ **G00.9 Bacterial meningitis, unspecified** 🗝
Meningitis due to gram-negative bacteria, unspecified
Purulent meningitis NOS
Pyogenic meningitis NOS
Suppurative meningitis NOS

● **G01 Meningitis in bacterial diseases classified elsewhere** 🗝
Code first underlying disease

Excludes1	meningitis (in):
	gonococcal (A54.81)
	leptospirosis (A27.81)
	listeriosis (A32.11)
	Lyme disease (A69.21)
	meningococcal (A39.0)
	neurosyphilis (A52.13)
	tuberculosis (A17.0)
	meningoencephalitis and meningomyelitis in bacterial diseases classified elsewhere (G05)

● Unacceptable First-Listed Diagnosis   ● Use Additional Character(s)   ▪ Unspecified   **OGCR** Official Guidelines for Coding and Reporting

🗝 Complication\Comorbidity   🗝 Major C\C   Excludes 1   Excludes 2   Includes   Use additional   Code first   Code also

925

CHAPTER 6 (G00-G99)

● **G02 Meningitis in other infectious and parasitic diseases classified elsewhere** 🔖

> *Code first underlying disease, such as:*
> poliovirus infection (A80.-)

> | Excludes1 | meningitis (due to):
> candidal (B37.5)
> coccidioidomycosis (B38.4)
> cryptococcal meningitis (B45.1)
> herpesviral [herpes simplex] (B00.3)
> infectious mononucleosis (B27.-2)
> measles (B05.1)
> mumps (B26.1)
> rubella (B06.02)
> varicella [chickenpox] (B01.0)
> zoster (B02.1)
> meningoencephalitis and meningomyelitis
> in other infectious and parasitic diseases
> classified elsewhere (G05)

● **G03 Meningitis due to other and unspecified causes**

> | Includes | arachnoiditis NOS
> leptomeningitis NOS
> meningitis NOS
> pachymeningitis NOS

> | Excludes1 | meningoencephalitis (G04.-)
> meningomyelitis (G04.-)

G03.0 Nonpyogenic meningitis 🔖
> Aseptic meningitis
> Nonbacterial meningitis

G03.1 Chronic meningitis 🔖

G03.2 Benign recurrent meningitis [Mollaret] 🔖

G03.8 Meningitis due to other specified causes 🔖

■ **G03.9 Meningitis, unspecified** 🔖
> Arachnoiditis (spinal) NOS

● **G04 Encephalitis, myelitis and encephalomyelitis**

> | Includes | acute ascending myelitis
> meningoencephalitis
> meningomyelitis

> | Excludes1 | encephalopathy NOS (G93.40)
> | Excludes2 | acute transverse myelitis (G37.3-)
> alcoholic encephalopathy (G31.2)
> benign myalgic encephalomyelitis (G93.3)
> multiple sclerosis (G35)
> subacute necrotizing myelitis (G37.4)
> toxic encephalitis (G92)
> toxic encephalopathy (G92)

● **G04.0 Acute disseminated encephalitis and encephalomyelitis (ADEM)**

> | Excludes1 | acute necrotizing hemorrhagic
> encephalopathy (G04.3-)

G04.00 Postinfectious acute disseminated encephalitis and encephalomyelitis (postinfectious ADEM) 🔖
> Acute disseminated encephalitis and
> encephalomyelitis NOS

> | Excludes1 | noninfectious acute
> disseminated
> encephalomyelitis
> (noninfectious ADEM)
> (G04.81)
> postchickenpox encephalitis
> (B01.1)
> postmeasles encephalitis
> (B05.0)
> postmeasles myelitis (B05.1)

G04.01 Postimmunization acute disseminated encephalitis, myelitis and encephalomyelitis 🔖
> Encephalitis, postimmunization
> Encephalomyelitis, postimmunization

> Use additional code to identify the
> vaccine (T50.A-, T50.B-, T50.Z-)

G04.1 Tropical spastic paraplegia 🔖

G04.2 Bacterial meningoencephalitis and meningomyelitis, not elsewhere classified 🔖

● **G04.3 Acute necrotizing hemorrhagic encephalopathy**
> *Sudden and severe CNS disease with pathology of*
> *hemorrhages and necrosis of white matter*

> | Excludes1 | acute disseminated encephalitis and
> encephalomyelitis (G04.0-)

G04.30 Postinfectious acute necrotizing hemorrhagic encephalopathy 🔖
> Acute necrotizing hemorrhagic
> encephalopathy NOS

G04.31 Postimmunization acute necrotizing hemorrhagic encephalopathy 🔖
> Use additional code to identify the
> vaccine (T50.A-, T50.B-, T50.Z-)

● **G04.8 Other encephalitis, myelitis and encephalomyelitis**

G04.81 Other encephalitis and encephalomyelitis 🔖
> Noninfectious acute disseminated
> encephalomyelitis (noninfectious
> ADEM)

G04.89 Other myelitis 🔖

● **G04.9 Encephalitis, myelitis and encephalomyelitis, unspecified**

■ **G04.90 Encephalitis and encephalomyelitis, unspecified** 🔖
> Ventriculitis (cerebral) NOS

■ **G04.91 Myelitis, unspecified** 🔖

● **G05 Encephalitis, myelitis and encephalomyelitis in diseases classified elsewhere**

> *Code first underlying disease, such as:*
> poliovirus (A80.-)
> suppurative otitis media (H66.01-H66.4)
> trichinellosis (B75)

> | Excludes1 | encephalitis, myelitis and encephalomyelitis
> (in):
> adenoviral (A85.1)
> cytomegaloviral (B25.8)
> enteroviral (A85.0)
> herpesviral [herpes simplex] (B00.4)
> listerial (A32.12)
> measles (B05.0)
> meningococcal (A39.81)
> mumps (B26.2)
> postchickenpox (B01.1)
> rubella (B06.01)
> systemic lupus erythematosus (M32.19)
> toxoplasmosis (B58.2)
> congenital (P37.1)
> zoster (B02.0)
> eosinophilic meningoencephalitis (B83.2)

● **G05.3 Encephalitis and encephalomyelitis in diseases classified elsewhere** 🔖
> Meningoencephalitis in diseases classified
> elsewhere

● **G05.4 Myelitis in diseases classified elsewhere** 🔖
> Meningomyelitis in diseases classified elsewhere

● Unacceptable First-Listed Diagnosis   ● Use Additional Character(s)   ■ Unspecified   **OGCR** Official Guidelines for Coding and Reporting

🔖 Complication\Comorbidity   🔖 Major C\C | Excludes 1 | | Excludes 2 | Includes   Use additional   Code first   Code also

● **G06 Intracranial and intraspinal abscess and granuloma**
   An accumulation of pus in either the brain or spinal cord

   Use additional code (B95-B97) to identify infectious
   agent.

   G06.0 Intracranial abscess and granuloma 🔖
      Brain [any part] abscess (embolic)
      Cerebellar abscess (embolic)
      Cerebral abscess (embolic)
      Intracranial epidural abscess or granuloma
      Intracranial extradural abscess or granuloma
      Intracranial subdural abscess or granuloma
      Otogenic abscess (embolic)
      Excludes1   tuberculous intracranial abscess and
                      granuloma (A17.81)

   G06.1 Intraspinal abscess and granuloma 🔖
      Abscess (embolic) of spinal cord [any part]
      Intraspinal epidural abscess or granuloma
      Intraspinal extradural abscess or granuloma
      Intraspinal subdural abscess or granuloma
      Excludes1   tuberculous intraspinal abscess and
                      granuloma (A17.81)

   ■ **G06.2 Extradural and subdural abscess, unspecified** 🔖

● **G07 Intracranial and intraspinal abscess and granuloma in
         diseases classified elsewhere** 🔖

   Code first underlying disease, such as:
      schistosomiasis granuloma of brain (B65.-)
      Excludes1   abscess of brain:
                      amebic (A06.6)
                      chromomycotic (B43.1)
                      gonococcal (A54.82)
                      tuberculous (A17.81)
                      tuberculoma of meninges (A17.1)

**G08 Intracranial and intraspinal phlebitis and
       thrombophlebitis** 🔖

   Includes   septic embolism of intracranial or
                     intraspinal venous sinuses and veins
                  septic endophlebitis of intracranial or
                     intraspinal venous sinuses and veins
                  septic phlebitis of intracranial or intraspinal
                     venous sinuses and veins
                  septic thrombophlebitis of intracranial or
                     intraspinal venous sinuses and veins
                  septic thrombosis of intracranial or
                     intraspinal venous sinuses and veins

   Excludes1   intracranial phlebitis and thrombophlebitis
                   complicating:
                      abortion, ectopic or molar pregnancy
                         (O00-O07, O08.7)
                      pregnancy, childbirth and the puerperium
                         (O22.5, O87.3)
                      nonpyogenic intracranial phlebitis and
                         thrombophlebitis (I67.6)
                      nonpyogenic intraspinal phlebitis and
                         thrombophlebitis (G95.1)

● **G09 Sequelae of inflammatory diseases of central nervous
         system**
   Note: Category 609 is to be used to indicate conditions
             whose primary classification is to G00-G08 as the
             cause of sequelae, themselves classifiable else-
             where. The "sequelae" include conditions specified
             as residuals.

   *Code first condition resulting from (sequela) of inflammatory
    diseases of central nervous system*

Item 6–2 Huntington's chorea is an inherited degenerative disorder
of the central nervous system and is characterized by ceaseless, jerky
movements and progressive cognitive and behavioral deterioration.

SYSTEMIC ATROPHIES PRIMARILY AFFECTING THE CENTRAL NERVOUS SYSTEM (G10-G14)

G10 Huntington's disease 🔖
   *Genetic disease with degeneration of cells of the nervous
    system, including brain*
      Includes   Huntington's chorea
                     Huntington's dementia

● **G11 Hereditary ataxia**
   Genetic neurological disorder affecting coordination
      Excludes2   cerebral palsy (G80.-)
                      hereditary and idiopathic neuropathy (G60.-)
                      metabolic disorders (E70-E90)

   G11.0 Congenital nonprogressive ataxia 🔖

   G11.1 Early-onset cerebellar ataxia 🔖
      Early-onset cerebellar ataxia with essential tremor
      Early-onset cerebellar ataxia with myoclonus
         [Hunt's ataxia]
      Early-onset cerebellar ataxia with retained tendon
         reflexes
      Friedreich's ataxia (autosomal recessive)
      X-linked recessive spinocerebellar ataxia

   G11.2 Late-onset cerebellar ataxia 🔖

   G11.3 Cerebellar ataxia with defective DNA repair 🔖
      Ataxia telangiectasia [Louis-Bar]
      Excludes2   Cockayne's syndrome (Q87.1)
                      other disorders of purine and
                         pyrimidine metabolism (E79.-)
                      xeroderma pigmentosum (Q82.1)

   G11.4 Hereditary spastic paraplegia 🔖

   G11.8 Other hereditary ataxias 🔖

   ■ **G11.9 Hereditary ataxia, unspecified** 🔖
      Hereditary cerebellar ataxia NOS
      Hereditary cerebellar degeneration
      Hereditary cerebellar disease
      Hereditary cerebellar syndrome

● **G12 Spinal muscular atrophy and related syndromes**

   **G12.0 Infantile spinal muscular atrophy, type I
            [Werdnig-Hoffman]** 🔖

   G12.1 Other inherited spinal muscular atrophy 🔖
      Adult form spinal muscular atrophy
      Childhood form, type II spinal muscular atrophy
      Distal spinal muscular atrophy
      Juvenile form, type III spinal muscular atrophy
         [Kugelberg-Welander]
      Progressive bulbar palsy of childhood [Fazio-
         Londe]
      Scapuloperoneal form spinal muscular atrophy

● **G12.2 Motor neuron disease**
   *Progressive disease of motor neurons that carry
    impulses to muscles to move*

   ■ **G12.20 Motor neuron disease, unspecified** 🔖

   G12.21 Amyotrophic lateral sclerosis 🔖
      Lou Gehrig's disease (ALS)
      Progressive spinal muscle atrophy

   G12.22 Progressive bulbar palsy 🔖

   G12.29 Other motor neuron disease 🔖
      Familial motor neuron disease
      Primary lateral sclerosis

   **G12.8 Other spinal muscular atrophies and related
            syndromes** 🔖

   ■ **G12.9 Spinal muscular atrophy, unspecified** 🔖

● Unacceptable First-Listed Diagnosis   ● Use Additional Character(s)   ■ Unspecified   **OGCR** Official Guidelines for Coding and Reporting

🔖 Complication\Comorbidity   🔖 Major C\C   Excludes 1   Excludes 2   Includes   Use additional   Code first   Code also   **927**

CHAPTER 6 (G00-G99)

● **G13 Systemic atrophies primarily affecting central nervous system in diseases classified elsewhere**

● **G13.0 Paraneoplastic neuromyopathy and neuropathy**
Carcinomatous neuromyopathy
Sensorial paraneoplastic neuropathy [Denny Brown]

Code first underlying neoplasm (C00-D48)

● **G13.1 Other systemic atrophy primarily affecting central nervous system in neoplastic disease**
Paraneoplastic limbic encephalopathy

Code first underlying neoplasm (C00-D48)

● **G13.8 Systemic atrophy primarily affecting central nervous system in other diseases classified elsewhere**

Code first underlying disease, such as:
cerebellar ataxia (in):
hypothyroidism (E03.-)
myxedematous congenital iodine deficiency (E00.1)

G14 Postpolio syndrome
Postpolio myelitic syndrome

| **Excludes1** | sequelae of poliomyelitis (B91) |

EXTRAPYRAMIDAL AND MOVEMENT DISORDERS (G20-G26)

G20 Parkinson's disease
Progressive disease of the nervous system that affects muscle coordination

| **Includes** | hemiparkinsonism |
idiopathic Parkinsonism or Parkinson's disease
paralysis agitans
Parkinsonism or Parkinson's disease NOS
primary Parkinsonism or Parkinson's disease

| **Excludes1** | dementia with Parkinsonism (G31.83) |

● **G21 Secondary parkinsonism**
Symptoms of Parkinson's caused by medicines, illness, or other nervous system disorder

| **Excludes1** | dementia with Parkinsonism (G31.83) |
Huntington's disease (G10)
Shy-Drager syndrome (G90.3)
syphilitic Parkinsonism (A52.19)

● **G21.0 Malignant neuroleptic syndrome** 🦠

Code first (T43.3-T43.5) to identify drug

| **Excludes1** | neuroleptic induced parkinsonism (G21.11) |

● **G21.1 Other drug-induced secondary parkinsonism**

● **G21.11 Neuroleptic induced parkinsonism** 🦠

Code first (T43.3-T43.5) to identify drug

| **Excludes1** | malignant neuroleptic syndrome (G21.0) |

● **G21.19 Other drug induced secondary parkinsonism** 🦠

Code first (T36-T50) to identify drug

● **G21.2 Secondary parkinsonism due to other external agents** 🦠

Code first (T51-T65) to identify external agent

G21.3 Postencephalitic parkinsonism 🦠

G21.4 Vascular parkinsonism

G21.8 Other secondary parkinsonism 🦠

■ **G21.9 Secondary parkinsonism, unspecified** 🦠

● **G23 Other degenerative diseases of basal ganglia**

| **Excludes2** | multi-system degeneration of the autonomic nervous system (G90.3) |

G23.0 Hallervorden-Spatz disease 🦠
Pigmentary pallidal degeneration

G23.1 Progressive supranuclear ophthalmoplegia [Steele-Richardson-Olszewski] 🦠

G23.2 Striatonigral degeneration 🦠

G23.8 Other specified degenerative diseases of basal ganglia 🦠
Calcification of basal ganglia

■ **G23.9 Degenerative disease of basal ganglia, unspecified** 🦠

● **G24 Dystonia**
Involuntary movements

| **Includes** | dyskinesia |

| **Excludes2** | athetoid cerebral palsy (G80.3) |

● **G24.0 Drug induced dystonia**

Code first (T36-T50) to identify drug

● **G24.01 Drug induced subacute dyskinesia**
Drug induced blepharospasm
Drug induced orofacial dyskinesia
Neuroleptic induced tardive dyskinesia
Tardive dyskinesia

● **G24.02 Drug induced acute dystonia** 🦠
Acute dystonic reaction to drugs
Neuroleptic induced acute dystonia

● **G24.09 Other drug induced dystonia** 🦠

G24.1 Genetic torsion dystonia
Dystonia deformans progressiva
Dystonia musculorum deformans
Familial torsion dystonia
Idiopathic familial dystonia
Idiopathic (torsion) dystonia NOS
(Schwalbe-) Ziehen-Oppenheim disease

G24.2 Idiopathic nonfamilial dystonia 🦠

G24.3 Spasmodic torticollis
Head tilts toward one side and chin is elevated and turned toward opposite side (wry neck)

| **Excludes1** | congenital torticollis (Q68.0) |
hysterical torticollis (F44.4)
ocular torticollis (R29.891)
psychogenic torticollis (F45.8)
torticollis NOS (M43.6)
traumatic recurrent torticollis (S13.4)

G24.4 Idiopathic orofacial dystonia
Orofacial dyskinesia

| **Excludes1** | drug induced orofacial dyskinesia (G24.01) |

G24.5 Blepharospasm
Tonic spasm of orbicularis oculi muscle, producing closure of eyelids

| **Excludes1** | drug induced blepharospasm (G24.01) |

G24.8 Other dystonia 🦠
Acquired torsion dystonia NOS

■ **G24.9 Dystonia, unspecified**
Dyskinesia NOS

● **G25 Other extrapyramidal and movement disorders**
Extrapyramidal: Other than pyramidal tracts

| **Excludes2** | sleep related movement disorders (G47.6-) |

G25.0 Essential tremor
Familial tremor

| **Excludes1** | tremor NOS (R25.1) |

● Unacceptable First-Listed Diagnosis   ● Use Additional Character(s)   ■ Unspecified   **OGCR** Official Guidelines for Coding and Reporting
🦠 Complication\Comorbidity   🦠 Major C\C | Excludes 1 | | Excludes 2 | Includes   Use additional   Code first   Code also

● **G25.1 Drug-induced tremor**

> *Code first (T36-T50) to identify drug*

G25.2 Other specified forms of tremor
Intention tremor

G25.3 Myoclonus
> *Shocklike contractions muscle(s)*
Drug-induced myoclonus
Palatal myoclonus

> *Code first (T36-T50) to identify drug, if drug-induced*
> | **Excludes1** | facial myokymia (G51.4)
> | | myoclonic epilepsy (G40.-)

● **G25.4 Drug-induced chorea**

> *Code first (T36-T50) to identify drug*

G25.5 Other chorea
> *Continual, involuntary, jerky, movements*
Chorea NOS

> | **Excludes1** | chorea NOS with heart involvement
> | | (I02.0)
> | | Huntington's chorea (G10)
> | | rheumatic chorea (I02.-)
> | | Sydenham's chorea (I02.-)

● **G25.6 Drug induced tics and other tics of organic origin**

  ● **G25.61 Drug induced tics**

> *Code first (T36-T50) to identify drug*

  G25.69 Other tics of organic origin

> | **Excludes1** | habit spasm (F95.9)
> | | tic NOS (F95.9)
> | | Tourette's syndrome (F95.2)

● **G25.7 Other and unspecified drug induced movement disorders**

> *Code first (T36-T50) to identify drug*

  ● ▪ **G25.70 Drug induced movement disorder, unspecified**

  ● **G25.71 Drug induced akathisia**
      Drug induced acathisia
      Neuroleptic induced acute akathisia

  ● **G25.79 Other drug induced movement disorders**

● **G25.8 Other specified extrapyramidal and movement disorders**

  G25.81 Restless legs syndrome

  G25.82 Stiff-man syndrome 🗝

  G25.89 Other specified extrapyramidal and movement disorders

▪ **G25.9 Extrapyramidal and movement disorder, unspecified** 🗝

● **G26 Extrapyramidal and movement disorders in diseases classified elsewhere**

> *Code first underlying disease*

OTHER DEGENERATIVE DISEASES OF THE NERVOUS SYSTEM (G30-G32)

● **G30 Alzheimer's disease**
> *Progressive central neurodegenerative disorder*

> | **Includes** | Alzheimer's dementia senile and presenile
> | | forms
> Use additional code to identify:
> delirium, if applicable (F05)
> dementia with behavioral disturbance (F02.81)
> dementia without behavioral disturbance (F02.80)

> | **Excludes1** | senile degeneration of brain NEC (G31.1)
> | | senile dementia NOS (F03)
> | | senility NOS (R41.81)

G30.0 Alzheimer's disease with early onset

G30.1 Alzheimer's disease with late onset

G30.8 Other Alzheimer's disease

▪ **G30.9 Alzheimer's disease, unspecified**

● **G31 Other degenerative diseases of nervous system, not elsewhere classified**

> Use additional code to identify:
> dementia with behavioral disturbance (F02.81)
> dementia without behavioral disturbance (F02.80)

> | **Excludes2** | Reye's syndrome (G93.7)

● **G31.0 Frontotemporal dementia**

  G31.01 Pick's disease
      Circumscribed brain atrophy
      Progressive isolated aphasia

  G31.09 Other frontotemporal dementia
      Frontal dementia

G31.1 Senile degeneration of brain, not elsewhere classified

> | **Excludes1** | Alzheimer's disease (G30.-)
> | | senility NOS (R41.81)

G31.2 Degeneration of nervous system due to alcohol
Alcoholic cerebellar ataxia
Alcoholic cerebellar degeneration
Alcoholic cerebral degeneration
Alcoholic encephalopathy
Dysfunction of the autonomic nervous system due to alcohol
Code also associated alcoholism (F10.-)

● **G31.8 Other specified degenerative diseases of nervous system**

  G31.81 Alpers' disease 🗝
    Rare neuronal degeneration of cerebral cortex disease of young children
    Grey-matter degeneration

  G31.82 Leigh's disease 🗝
    Rare neurometabolic disorder that affects central nervous system
    Subacute necrotizing encephalopathy

  G31.83 Dementia with Lewy bodies
    Closely allied to Parkinson's Disease
    Dementia with Parkinsonism
    Lewy body dementia
    Lewy body disease

  G31.84 Mild cognitive impairment, so stated

> | **Excludes1** | age related cognitive decline
> | | (R41.81)
> | | altered mental status (R41.82)
> | | cerebral degeneration (G31.9)
> | | change in mental status
> | | (R41.82)
> | | cognitive deficits following
> | | (sequelae of) cerebral
> | | hemorrhage or infarction
> | | (I69.01, I69.11, I69.21,
> | | I69.31, I69.81, I69.91)
> | | cognitive impairment due
> | | to intracranial or head
> | | injury (S06.-)
> | | dementia (F01.-, F02.-, F03)
> | | mild memory disturbance
> | | (F06.8)
> | | neurologic neglect syndrome
> | | (R41.4)
> | | personality change,
> | | nonpsychotic (F68.8)

  G31.89 Other specified degenerative diseases of nervous system

▪ **G31.9 Degenerative disease of nervous system, unspecified**

● Unacceptable First-Listed Diagnosis   ● Use Additional Character(s)   ▪ Unspecified   **OGCR** Official Guidelines for Coding and Reporting
🗝 Complication\Comorbidity   🗝 Major C\C | Excludes 1 | | Excludes 2 | Includes   Use additional   Code first   Code also

929

CHAPTER 6 (G00-G99)

● G32 **Other degenerative disorders of nervous system in diseases classified elsewhere**

   ● G32.0 **Subacute combined degeneration of spinal cord in diseases classified elsewhere** 💊

Dana-Putnam syndrome
Sclerosis of spinal cord (combined) (dorsolateral) (posterolateral)

Code first underlying disease, such as:
vitamin B$_{12}$ deficiency (E53.8)
anemia (D51.9)
dietary (D51.3)
pernicious (D51.0)

Excludes1   syphilitic combined degeneration of spinal cord (A52.11)

   ● G32.8 **Other specified degenerative disorders of nervous system in diseases classified elsewhere** 💊

Degenerative encephalopathy in diseases classified elsewhere

Code first underlying disease, such as:
cerebral degeneration (due to):
amyloid (E85.-)
hypothyroidism (E00.-, E03.-)
neoplasm (C00-D48)
vitamin B deficiency, except thiamine (E52-E53.-)

Excludes1   superior hemorrhagic polioencephalitis [Wernicke's encephalopathy] (E51.2)

DEMYELINATING DISEASES OF THE CENTRAL NERVOUS SYSTEM (G35-G37)

G35 **Multiple sclerosis**

Destruction of central nervous system; four types: relapsing remitting, secondary progressive, primary progressive, and progressive relapsing

Includes   disseminated multiple sclerosis
generalized multiple sclerosis
multiple sclerosis NOS
multiple sclerosis of brain stem
multiple sclerosis of cord

● G36 **Other acute disseminated demyelination**

Excludes1   postinfectious encephalitis and encephalomyelitis NOS (G04.020)

   G36.0 **Neuromyelitis optica [Devic]** 💊

Inflammatory disorder in which immune system attacks optic nerves and spinal cord producing inflammation of optic nerve (optic neuritis) and spinal cord (myelitis)

Demyelination in optic neuritis

Excludes1   optic neuritis NOS (H46)

   G36.1 **Acute and subacute hemorrhagic leukoencephalitis [Hurst]** 💊

   G36.8 **Other specified acute disseminated demyelination** 💊

   G36.9 **Acute disseminated demyelination, unspecified** 💊

Item 6–3   Multiple sclerosis (MS) is a nervous system disease affecting the brain and spinal cord by damaging the myelin sheath surrounding and protecting nerve cells. The damage slows down/blocks messages between the brain and body. Symptoms are: visual disturbances, muscle weakness, coordination and balance issues, numbness, prickling, thinking and memory problems. The cause is unknown, though it is thought that it may be an autoimmune disease. It affects women more than men, between 20 and 40 years of age. MS can be mild, but it may cause the loss of ability to write, walk, and speak. There is no cure, but medication may slow or control symptoms.

● G37 **Other demyelinating diseases of central nervous system**

Destruction of central nervous system

   G37.0 **Diffuse sclerosis of central nervous system** 💊

Periaxial encephalitis
Schilder's disease

Excludes1   X linked adrenoleukodystrophy (E71.42-)

   G37.1 **Central demyelination of corpus callosum** 💊

   G37.2 **Central pontine myelinolysis** 💊

   G37.3 **Acute transverse myelitis in demyelinating disease of central nervous system** 💊

Acute transverse myelitis NOS
Acute transverse myelopathy

Excludes1   multiple sclerosis (G35)
neuromyelitis optica [Devic] (G36.0)

   G37.4 **Subacute necrotizing myelitis of central nervous system** 💊

   G37.5 **Concentric sclerosis [Baló] of central nervous system** 💊

   G37.8 **Other specified demyelinating diseases of central nervous system** 💊

   G37.9 **Demyelinating disease of central nervous system, unspecified** 💊

EPISODIC AND PAROXYSMAL DISORDERS (G40-G47)

● G40 **Epilepsy and recurrent seizures**

Note: The following terms are to be considered equivalent to intractable: pharmacoresistant (pharmacologically resistant), treatment resistant, refractory (medically) and poorly controlled

Excludes1   conversion disorder with seizures (F44.5)
convulsions NOS (R56.9)
hippocampal sclerosis (G93.81)
Landau-Kleffner syndrome (F80.3)
mesial temporal sclerosis (G93.81)
seizure (convulsive) NOS (R56.9)
seizure of newborn (P90)
temporal sclerosis (G93.81)
Todd's paralysis (G83.8)

   ● G40.0 **Localization-related (focal) (partial) idiopathic epilepsy and epileptic syndromes with seizures of localized onset**

Benign childhood epilepsy with centrotemporal EEG spikes
Childhood epilepsy with occipital EEG paroxysms

Excludes1   adult onset localization-related epilepsy (G40.1-, G40.2-)

     ● G40.00 **Localization-related (focal) (partial) idiopathic epilepsy and epileptic syndromes with seizures of localized onset, not intractable**

Localization-related (focal) (partial) idiopathic epilepsy and epileptic syndromes with seizures of localized onset without intractability

       G40.001 **Localization-related (focal) (partial) idiopathic epilepsy and epileptic syndromes with seizures of localized onset, not intractable, with status epilepticus** 💊

G40.009 Localization-related (focal) (partial) idiopathic epilepsy and epileptic syndromes with seizures of localized onset, not intractable, without status epilepticus 🦠
> Localization-related (focal) (partial) idiopathic epilepsy and epileptic syndromes with seizures of localized onset NOS

● G40.01 Localization-related (focal) (partial) idiopathic epilepsy and epileptic syndromes with seizures of localized onset, intractable

G40.011 Localization-related (focal) (partial) idiopathic epilepsy and epileptic syndromes with seizures of localized onset, intractable, with status epilepticus 🦠

G40.019 Localization-related (focal) (partial) idiopathic epilepsy and epileptic syndromes with seizures of localized onset, intractable, without status epilepticus 🦠

● G40.1 Localization-related (focal) (partial) symptomatic epilepsy and epileptic syndromes with simple partial seizures
> Attacks without alteration of consciousness
> Simple partial seizures developing into secondarily generalized seizures

● G40.10 Localization-related (focal) (partial) symptomatic epilepsy and epileptic syndromes with simple partial seizures, not intractable
> Localization-related (focal) (partial) symptomatic epilepsy and epileptic syndromes with simple partial seizures without intractability

G40.101 Localization-related (focal) (partial) symptomatic epilepsy and epileptic syndromes with simple partial seizures, not intractable, with status epilepticus 🦠

G40.109 Localization-related (focal) (partial) symptomatic epilepsy and epileptic syndromes with simple partial seizures, not intractable, without status epilepticus 🦠
> Localization-related (focal) (partial) symptomatic epilepsy and epileptic syndromes with simple partial seizures NOS

● G40.11 Localization-related (focal) (partial) symptomatic epilepsy and epileptic syndromes with simple partial seizures, intractable

G40.111 Localization-related (focal) (partial) symptomatic epilepsy and epileptic syndromes with simple partial seizures, intractable, with status epilepticus 🦠

G40.119 Localization-related (focal) (partial) symptomatic epilepsy and epileptic syndromes with simple partial seizures, intractable, without status epilepticus 🦠

● G40.2 Localization-related (focal) (partial) symptomatic epilepsy and epileptic syndromes with complex partial seizures
> Attacks with alteration of consciousness, often with automatisms
> Complex partial seizures developing into secondarily generalized seizures

● G40.20 Localization-related (focal) (partial) symptomatic epilepsy and epileptic syndromes with complex partial seizures, not intractable
> Localization-related (focal) (partial) symptomatic epilepsy and epileptic syndromes with complex partial seizures without intractability

G40.201 Localization-related (focal) (partial) symptomatic epilepsy and epileptic syndromes with complex partial seizures, not intractable, with status epilepticus 🦠

G40.209 Localization-related (focal) (partial) symptomatic epilepsy and epileptic syndromes with complex partial seizures, not intractable, without status epilepticus 🦠
> Localization-related (focal) (partial) symptomatic epilepsy and epileptic syndromes with complex partial seizures NOS

● G40.21 Localization-related (focal) (partial) symptomatic epilepsy and epileptic syndromes with complex partial seizures, intractable

G40.211 Localization-related (focal) (partial) symptomatic epilepsy and epileptic syndromes with complex partial seizures, intractable, with status epilepticus 🦠

G40.219 Localization-related (focal) (partial) symptomatic epilepsy and epileptic syndromes with complex partial seizures, intractable, without status epilepticus 🦠

● G40.3 Generalized idiopathic epilepsy and epileptic syndromes
> Benign myoclonic epilepsy in infancy
> Benign neonatal convulsions (familial)
> Childhood absence epilepsy [pyknolepsy]
> Epilepsy with grand mal seizures on awakening
> Grand mal seizure NOS
> *Generalized tonic-clonic seizure involving entire body.*
> Juvenile absence epilepsy
> Juvenile myoclonic epilepsy [impulsive petit mal]
> Nonspecific atonic epileptic seizures
> Nonspecific clonic epileptic seizures
> Nonspecific myoclonic epileptic seizures
> Nonspecific tonic epileptic seizures
> Nonspecific tonic-clonic epileptic seizures
> Petit mal seizure NOS
> *Temporary disturbance of brain function caused by abnormal electrical activity in brain.*

Code also: MERRF syndrome, if applicable, (M88.32)

● Unacceptable First-Listed Diagnosis   ● Use Additional Character(s)   ■ Unspecified   OGCR Official Guidelines for Coding and Reporting

🦠 Complication\Comorbidity 🦠 Major C\C Excludes 1 Excludes 2 Includes Use additional Code first Code also   931

CHAPTER 6 (G00-G99)

- **G40.30 Generalized idiopathic epilepsy and epileptic syndromes, not intractable**
  Generalized idiopathic epilepsy and epileptic syndromes without intractability

  - G40.301 Generalized idiopathic epilepsy and epileptic syndromes, not intractable, with status epilepticus 🦠

  - G40.309 Generalized idiopathic epilepsy and epileptic syndromes, not intractable, without status epilepticus 🦠
    Generalized idiopathic epilepsy and epileptic syndromes NOS

- **G40.31 Generalized idiopathic epilepsy and epileptic syndromes, intractable**

  - G40.311 Generalized idiopathic epilepsy and epileptic syndromes, intractable, with status epilepticus 🦠

  - G40.319 Generalized idiopathic epilepsy and epileptic syndromes, intractable, without status epilepticus 🦠

- **G40.4 Other generalized epilepsy and epileptic syndromes**
  Epilepsy with myoclonic absences
  Epilepsy with myoclonic-astatic seizures
  Infantile spasms
  Lennox-Gastaut syndrome
  Salaam attacks
  Symptomatic early myoclonic encephalopathy
  West's syndrome

  - **G40.40 Other generalized epilepsy and epileptic syndromes, not intractable**
    Other generalized epilepsy and epileptic syndromes without intractability
    Other generalized epilepsy and epileptic syndromes NOS

    - G40.401 Other generalized epilepsy and epileptic syndromes, not intractable, with status epilepticus 🦠

    - G40.409 Other generalized epilepsy and epileptic syndromes, not intractable, without status epilepticus 🦠

  - **G40.41 Other generalized epilepsy and epileptic syndromes, intractable**

    - G40.411 Other generalized epilepsy and epileptic syndromes, intractable, with status epilepticus 🦠

    - G40.419 Other generalized epilepsy and epileptic syndromes, intractable, without status epilepticus 🦠

- **G40.5 Special epileptic syndromes**
  Epilepsia partialis continua [Kozhevnikof]
  Epileptic seizures related to alcohol
  Epileptic seizures related to drugs
  Epileptic seizures related to hormonal changes
  Epileptic seizures related to sleep deprivation
  Epileptic seizures related to stress

  - **G40.50 Special epileptic syndromes, not intractable**
    Special epileptic syndromes without intractability

    - G40.501 Special epileptic syndromes, not intractable, with status epilepticus 🦠

  - G40.509 Special epileptic syndromes, not intractable, without status epilepticus 🦠
    Special epileptic syndromes NOS

  - **G40.51 Special epileptic syndromes, intractable**

    - G40.511 Special epileptic syndromes, intractable, with status epilepticus 🦠

    - G40.519 Special epileptic syndromes, intractable, without status epilepticus 🦠

- **G40.8 Other epilepsy and seizures**
  Epilepsies and epileptic syndromes undetermined as to whether they are focal or generalized

  - **G40.80 Other epilepsy, not intractable**
    Other epilepsy without intractability

    - G40.801 Other epilepsy, not intractable, with status epilepticus 🦠

    - G40.809 Other epilepsy, not intractable, without status epilepticus 🦠
      Other epilepsy NOS

  - **G40.81 Other epilepsy, intractable**

    - G40.811 Other epilepsy, intractable, with status epilepticus 🦠

    - G40.819 Other epilepsy, intractable, without status epilepticus 🦠

  - G40.89 Other seizures 🦠

Excludes1	recurrent seizures NOS (G40.909)
	seizure NOS (R56.9)

- **G40.9 Epilepsy, unspecified**

  - **G40.90 Epilepsy, unspecified, not intractable**
    Epilepsy, unspecified, without intractability

    - G40.901 Epilepsy, unspecified, not intractable, with status epilepticus

    - G40.909 Epilepsy, unspecified, not intractable, without status epilepticus
      Epilepsy NOS
      Epileptic convulsions NOS
      Epileptic fits NOS
      Epileptic seizures NOS
      Recurrent seizures NOS

  - **G40.91 Epilepsy, unspecified, intractable**
    Intractable seizure disorder NOS

    - G40.911 Epilepsy, unspecified, intractable, with status epilepticus 🦠

    - G40.919 Epilepsy, unspecified, intractable, without status epilepticus 🦠

- **G43 Migraine**

  Note: The following terms are to be considered equivalent to intractable: pharmacoresistant (pharmacologically resistant), treatment resistant, refractory (medically) and poorly controlled

Excludes1	headache NOS (R51)
	headache syndromes (G44.-)
	lower half migraine (G44.00)

- **G43.0 Migraine without aura**
  Neurological disorder, generally recurring headaches without early symptom (aura)
  Common migraine

Excludes1	chronic migraine without aura (G43.7)

● **G43.00**   **Migraine without aura, not intractable**
Neurological disorder, generally recurring headaches without early symptom (aura); resistant to cure, relief, or control

     G43.001   **Migraine without aura, not intractable, with status migrainosus**

     G43.009   **Migraine without aura, not intractable, without status migrainosus**

● **G43.01**   **Migraine without aura, intractable**
Intractable migraine: Not easily cured or managed; relentless pain from a migraine

     G43.011   **Migraine without aura, intractable, with status migrainosus**

     G43.019   **Migraine without aura, intractable, without status migrainosus**

● **G43.1**   **Migraine with aura**
Basilar migraine
Classical migraine
Migraine equivalents
Migraine preceded or accompanied by transient focal neurological phenomena
Migraine triggered seizures
Migraine with acute-onset aura
Migraine with aura without headache (migraine equivalents)
Migraine with prolonged aura
Migraine with typical aura
Retinal migraine
Code also any associated seizure (G40.-, R56.9)
| **Excludes1** | persistent migraine aura (G43.5-, G43.6-) |

● **G43.10**   **Migraine with aura, not intractable**

     G43.101   **Migraine with aura, not intractable, with status migrainosus**

     G43.109   **Migraine with aura, not intractable, without status migrainosus**
Migraine with aura NOS

● **G43.11**   **Migraine with aura, intractable**

     G43.111   **Migraine with aura, intractable, with status migrainosus**

     G43.119   **Migraine with aura, intractable, without status migrainosus**

G43.2   **Status migrainosus**
Debilitating migraine lasting for >72 hours

Use additional code to identify the type of migraine (G43.0-, G43.1-, G43.4-, G43.5-, G43.6-, G43.7-. G48.3-, G43.9-)

Item 6–4 Migraine headache is described as an intense pulsing or throbbing pain in one area of the head. It can be accompanied by extreme sensitivity to light (photophobic) and sound and is three times more common in women than in men. Symptoms include nausea and vomiting. Research indicates migraine headaches are caused by inherited abnormalities in genes that control the activities of certain cell populations in the brain.

● **G43.4**   **Hemiplegic migraine**
Inherited migraine disorder causing temporary paralysis of one side of body followed by severe headache and nausea
Familial migraine
Sporadic migraine

● **G43.40**   **Hemiplegic migraine, not intractable**

     G43.401   **Hemiplegic migraine, not intractable, with status migrainosus**

     G43.409   **Hemiplegic migraine, not intractable, without status migrainosus**
Hemiplegic migraine NOS

● **G43.41**   **Hemiplegic migraine, intractable**

     G43.411   **Hemiplegic migraine, intractable, with status migrainosus**

     G43.419   **Hemiplegic migraine, intractable, without status migrainosus**

● **G43.5**   **Persistent migraine aura without cerebral infarction**

● **G43.50**   **Persistent migraine aura without cerebral infarction, not intractable**

     G43.501   **Persistent migraine aura without cerebral infarction, not intractable, with status migrainosus**

     G43.509   **Persistent migraine aura without cerebral infarction, not intractable, without status migrainosus**
Persistent migraine aura NOS

● **G43.51**   **Persistent migraine aura without cerebral infarction, intractable**

     G43.511   **Persistent migraine aura without cerebral infarction, intractable, with status migrainosus**

     G43.519   **Persistent migraine aura without cerebral infarction, intractable, without status migrainosus**

● **G43.6**   **Persistent migraine aura with cerebral infarction**
Visual, motor, or psychic disturbances, paresthesias, and related neurologic abnormalities accompanying migraine

Code also the type of cerebral infarction (I63.-)

● **G43.60**   **Persistent migraine aura with cerebral infarction, not intractable**

     G43.601   **Persistent migraine aura with cerebral infarction, not intractable, with status migrainosus** 🔗

     G43.609   **Persistent migraine aura with cerebral infarction, not intractable, without status migrainosus**

● **G43.61**   **Persistent migraine aura with cerebral infarction, intractable**

     G43.611   **Persistent migraine aura with cerebral infarction, intractable, with status migrainosus** 🔗

     G43.619   **Persistent migraine aura with cerebral infarction, intractable, without status migrainosus**

● **G43.7**   **Chronic migraine without aura**
Transformed migraine
| **Excludes1** | migraine without aura (G43.0-) |

● Unacceptable First-Listed Diagnosis   ● Use Additional Character(s)   ▪ Unspecified   **OGCR** Official Guidelines for Coding and Reporting
🔗 Complication\Comorbidity   Major C\C   Excludes 1   Excludes 2   Includes   Use additional   Code first   Code also   933

CHAPTER 6 (G00-G99)

● **G43.70   Chronic migraine without aura, not intractable**

     G43.701   Chronic migraine without aura, not intractable, with status migrainosus

     G43.709   Chronic migraine without aura, not intractable, without status migrainosus

         Chronic migraine without aura NOS

● **G43.71   Chronic migraine without aura, intractable**

     G43.711   Chronic migraine without aura, intractable, with status migrainosus

     G43.719   Chronic migraine without aura, intractable, without status migrainosus

● **G43.a   Cyclical vomiting**

   ● **G43.a0   Cyclical vomiting, not intractable**

     G43.a01   Cyclical vomiting, not intractable, with status migrainosus

     G43.a09   Cyclical vomiting, not intractable, without status migrainosus

         Cyclical vomiting NOS

   ● **G43.a1   Cyclical vomiting, intractable**

     G43.a11   Cyclical vomiting, intractable, with status migrainosus

     G43.a19   Cyclical vomiting, intractable, without status migrainosus

● **G43.b   Ophthalmoplegic migraine**

   ● **G43.b0   Ophthalmoplegic migraine, not intractable**

     G43.b01   Ophthalmoplegic migraine, not intractable, with status migrainosus

     G43.b09   Ophthalmoplegic migraine, not intractable, without status migrainosus

         Ophthalmoplegic migraine NOS

   ● **G43.b1   Ophthalmoplegic migraine, intractable**

     G43.b11   Ophthalmoplegic migraine, intractable, with status migrainosus

     G43.b19   Ophthalmoplegic migraine, intractable, without status migrainosus

● **G43.c   Periodic headache syndromes in child or adult**

   ● **G43.c0   Periodic headache syndromes in child or adult, not intractable**

     G43.c01   Periodic headache syndromes in child or adult, not intractable, with status migrainosus

     G43.c09   Periodic headache syndromes in child or adult, not intractable, without status migrainosus

         Periodic headache syndromes in child or adult NOS

   ● **G43.c1   Periodic headache syndromes in child or adult, intractable**

     G43.c11   Periodic headache syndromes in child or adult, intractable, with status migrainosus

     G43.c19   Periodic headache syndromes in child or adult, intractable, without status migrainosus

● **G43.d   Menstrual migraine**

     Menstrual headache
     Menstrually related migraine
     Pre-menstrual headache
     Pre-menstrual migraine
     Pure menstrual migarine

     Code also associated premenstrual tension syndrome (N94.3)

   ● **G43.d0   Menstrual migraine, not intractable**

     G43.d01   Menstrual migraine, not intractable, with status migrainosus

     G43.d09   Menstrual migraine, not intractable, without status migrainosus

         Menstrual migraine NOS

   ● **G43.d1   Menstrual migraine, intractable**

     G43.d11   Menstrual migraine, intractable, with status migrainosus

     G43.d19   Menstrual migraine, intractable, without status migrainosus

● **G43.8   Other migraine**

   ● **G43.80   Other migraine, not intractable**

     G43.801   Other migraine, not intractable, with status migrainosus

     G43.809   Other migraine, not intractable, without status migrainosus

   ● **G43.81   Other migraine, intractable**

     G43.811   Other migraine, intractable, with status migrainosus

     G43.819   Other migraine, intractable, without status migrainosus

● **G43.9   Migraine, unspecified**

   ● **G43.90   Migraine, unspecified, not intractable**

     ▪ **G43.901   Migraine, unspecified, not intractable, with status migrainosus**

         Status migrainosus NOS

     ▪ **G43.909   Migraine, unspecified, not intractable, without status migrainosus**

         Migraine NOS

   ● **G43.91   Migraine, unspecified, intractable**

     ▪ **G43.911   Migraine, unspecified, not intractable, with status migrainosus**

     ▪ **G43.919   Migraine, unspecified, not intractable, without status migrainosus**

● **G44   Other headache syndromes**

     Excludes1   headache NOS (R51)

     Excludes2   atypical facial pain (G50.1)
         headache due to lumbar puncture (G97.1)
         migraines (G43.-)
         trigeminal neuralgia (G50.0)

CHAPTER 6 (G00-G99)

● Unacceptable First-Listed Diagnosis   ● Use Additional Character(s)   ▪ Unspecified   **OGCR** Official Guidelines for Coding and Reporting

🗲 Complication\Comorbidity   🗲 Major C\C   Excludes 1   Excludes 2   Includes   Use additional   Code first   Code also

934

● G44.0   **Cluster headaches and other trigeminal autonomic cephalgias (TAC)**

  ● G44.00   **Cluster headache syndrome, unspecified**
      Ciliary neuralgia
      Cluster headache NOS
      Histamine cephalgia
      Lower half migraine
      Migrainous neuralgia

   ■ G44.001 **Cluster headache syndrome, unspecified, intractable**

   ■ G44.009 **Cluster headache syndrome, unspecified, not intractable**
      Cluster headache syndrome NOS

  ● G44.01   **Episodic cluster headache**

    G44.011 **Episodic cluster headache, intractable**

    G44.019 **Episodic cluster headache, not intractable**
      Episodic cluster headache NOS

  ● G44.02   **Chronic cluster headache**

   ■ G44.021 **Chronic cluster headache, intractable**

    G44.029 **Chronic cluster headache, not intractable**
      Chronic cluster headache NOS

  ● G44.03   **Episodic paroxysmal hemicrania**
      Paroxysmal hemicrania NOS

    G44.031 **Episodic paroxysmal hemicrania, intractable**

    G44.039 **Episodic paroxysmal hemicrania, not intractable**
      Episodic paroxysmal hemicrania NOS

  ● G44.04   **Chronic paroxysmal hemicrania**
      Unilateral headache

    G44.041 **Chronic paroxysmal hemicrania, intractable**

    G44.049 **Chronic paroxysmal hemicrania, not intractable**
      Chronic paroxysmal hemicrania NOS

  ● G44.05   **Short lasting unilateral neuralgiform headache with conjunctival injection and tearing (SUNCT)**

    G44.051 **Short lasting unilateral neuralgiform headache with conjunctival injection and tearing (SUNCT), intractable**

    G44.059 **Short lasting unilateral neuralgiform headache with conjunctival injection and tearing (SUNCT), not intractable**
      Short lasting unilateral neuralgiform headache with conjunctival injection and tearing (SUNCT) NOS

  ● G44.09   **Other trigeminal autonomic cephalgias (TAC)**
      Cluster headaches

    G44.091 **Other trigeminal autonomic cephalgias (TAC), intractable**

    G44.099 **Other trigeminal autonomic cephalgias (TAC), not intractable**

● G44.1   **Vascular headache, not elsewhere classified**

    G44.10   **Vascular headache, not elsewhere classified, not intractable**
      Vascular headache NOS

    G44.11   **Vascular headache, not elsewhere classified, intractable**

● G44.2   **Tension-type headache**

  ● G44.20   **Tension-type headache, unspecified**

    G44.201 **Tension-type headache, unspecified, intractable**

   ■ G44.209 **Tension-type headache, unspecified, not intractable**
      Tension headache NOS

  ● G44.21   **Episodic tension-type headache**

    G44.211 **Episodic tension-type headache, intractable**

    G44.219 **Episodic tension-type headache, not intractable**
      Episodic tension-type headache NOS

  ● G44.22   **Chronic tension-type headache**

    G44.221 **Chronic tension-type headache, intractable**

    G44.229 **Chronic tension-type headache, not intractable**
      Chronic tension-type headache NOS

● G44.3   **Post-traumatic headache**
      Code first postconcussional syndrome (F07.81)

  ● G44.30   **Post-traumatic headache, unspecified**

   ● ■ G44.301 **Post-traumatic headache, unspecified, intractable**

   ● ■ G44.309 **Post-traumatic headache, unspecified, not intractable**
      Post-traumatic headache NOS

  ● G44.31   **Acute post-traumatic headache**

   ● G44.311 **Acute post-traumatic headache, intractable**

   ● G44.319 **Acute post-traumatic headache, not intractable**
      Acute post-traumatic headache NOS

  ● G44.32   **Chronic post-traumatic headache**

   ● G44.321 **Chronic post-traumatic headache, intractable**

   ● G44.329 **Chronic post-traumatic headache, not intractable**
      Chronic post-traumatic headache NOS

● G44.4   **Drug-induced headache, not elsewhere classified**
      Medication overuse headache
      Code first (T36-T50) to identify drug

  ● G44.40   **Drug-induced headache, not elsewhere classified, not intractable**

  ● G44.41   **Drug-induced headache, not elsewhere classified, intractable**

● Unacceptable First-Listed Diagnosis   ● Use Additional Character(s)   ■ Unspecified   **OGCR** Official Guidelines for Coding and Reporting

🔖 Complication\Comorbidity   🔖 Major C\C   Excludes 1   Excludes 2   Includes   Use additional   Code first   Code also

935

CHAPTER 6 (G00-G99)

- **G44.5   Complicated headache syndromes**
  - **G44.51   Hemicrania continua**
    - *Persistent unilateral headache*
  - **G44.52   New daily persistent headache (NDPH)**
  - **G44.53   Primary thunderclap headache**
  - **G44.59   Other complicated headache syndrome**
- **G44.8   Other specified headache syndromes**
  - **G44.81   Hypnic headache**
    - *Benign primary headaches*
  - **G44.82   Headache associated with sexual activity**
    - Orgasmic headache
    - Preorgasmic headache
  - **G44.83   Primary cough headache**
  - **G44.84   Primary exertional headache**
  - **G44.85   Primary stabbing headache**
  - **G44.89   Other headache syndrome**

- **G45   Transient cerebral ischemic attacks and related syndromes**
  - **Excludes1**   neonatal cerebral ischemia (P91.0)
    - transient retinal artery occlusion (H34.0-)
  - **G45.0   Vertebro-basilar artery syndrome** 🄫
  - **G45.1   Carotid artery syndrome (hemispheric)** 🄫
  - **G45.2   Multiple and bilateral precerebral artery syndromes** 🄫
  - **G45.3   Amaurosis fugax** 🄫
    - *Transient visual loss in one eye*
  - **G45.4   Transient global amnesia**
    - *Episode of short-term memory loss, nonrecurrent, lasting few hours*
    - **Excludes1**   amnesia NOS (R41.3)
  - **G45.8   Other transient cerebral ischemic attacks and related syndromes** 🄫
  - **G45.9   Transient cerebral ischemic attack, unspecified** 🄫
    - Spasm of cerebral artery
    - TIA
    - Transient cerebral ischemia NOS

- **G46   Vascular syndromes of brain in cerebrovascular diseases**
  - *Code first underlying cerebrovascular disease (I60-I69)*
  - **G46.0   Middle cerebral artery syndrome** 🄫
  - **G46.1   Anterior cerebral artery syndrome** 🄫
  - **G46.2   Posterior cerebral artery syndrome** 🄫
  - **G46.3   Brain stem stroke syndrome**
    - Benedikt syndrome
    - Claude syndrome
    - Foville syndrome
    - Millard-Gubler syndrome
    - Wallenberg syndrome
    - Weber syndrome
  - **G46.4   Cerebellar stroke syndrome**
  - **G46.5   Pure motor lacunar syndrome**
    - *Occlusion of single deep penetrating artery*
  - **G46.6   Pure sensory lacunar syndrome**
  - **G46.7   Other lacunar syndromes**
  - **G46.8   Other vascular syndromes of brain in cerebrovascular diseases**

- **G47   Sleep disorders**
  - **Excludes2**   nightmares (F51.5)
    - nonorganic sleep disorders (F51.-)
    - sleep terrors (F51.4)
    - sleepwalking (F51.3)

- **G47.0   Insomnia**
  - **Excludes2**   alcohol related insomnia (F10.182, F10.282, F10.982)
    - drug related insomnia (F11.182, F11.282, F11.982, F13.182, F13.282, F13.982, F14.182, F14.282, F14.982, F15.182, F15.282, F15.982, F19.182, F19.282, F19.982)
    - idiopathic insomnia (F51.01)
    - insomnia due to a mental disorder (F51.05)
    - insomnia not due to a substance or known physiological condition (F51.0-)
    - nonorganic insomnia (F51.0-)
    - primary insomnia (F51.01)
    - sleep apnea (G47.3-)
  - **G47.00   Insomnia, unspecified**
    - Insomnia NOS
  - **G47.01   Insomnia due to medical condition**
    - Code also associated medical condition
  - **G47.09   Other insomnia**
- **G47.1   Hypersomnia**
  - **Excludes2**   alcohol-related hypersomnia (F10.182, F10.282, F10.982)
    - drug-related hypersomnia (F11.182, F11.282, F11.982, F13.182, F13.282, F13.982, F14.182, F14.282, F14.982, F15.182, F15.282, F15.982, F19.182, F19.282, F19.982)
    - hypersomnia due to a mental disorder (F51.13)
    - hypersomnia not due to a substance or known physiological condition (F51.11)
    - primary hypersomnia (F51.11)
    - sleep apnea (G47.3-)
  - **G47.10   Hypersomnia, unspecified**
    - Hypersomnia NOS
  - **G47.11   Idiopathic hypersomnia with long sleep time**
    - Idiopathic hypersomnia NOS
  - **G47.12   Idiopathic hypersomnia without long sleep time**
  - **G47.13   Recurrent hypersomnia**
    - Kleine-Levin syndrome
    - Menstrual related hypersomnia
  - **G47.14   Hypersomnia due to medical condition**
    - Code also associated medical condition
  - **G47.19   Other hypersomnia**
- **G47.2   Circadian rhythm sleep disorders**
  - Disorders of the sleep wake schedule
  - Inversion of nyctohemeral rhythm
  - Inversion of sleep rhythm
  - **G47.20   Circadian rhythm sleep disorder, unspecified type**
    - Sleep wake schedule disorder NOS
  - **G47.21   Circadian rhythm sleep disorder, delayed sleep phase type**
    - Delayed sleep phase syndrome
  - **G47.22   Circadian rhythm sleep disorder, advanced sleep phase type**

CHAPTER 6 (G00-G99)

● Unacceptable First-Listed Diagnosis   ● Use Additional Character(s)   ▪ Unspecified   **OGCR** Official Guidelines for Coding and Reporting

🄫 Complication\Comorbidity   🄫 Major C\C   Excludes 1   Excludes 2   Includes   Use additional   Code first   Code also

G47.23 Circadian rhythm sleep disorder, irregular sleep wake type
Irregular sleep-wake pattern

G47.24 Circadian rhythm sleep disorder, free running type

G47.25 Circadian rhythm sleep disorder, jet lag type

G47.26 Circadian rhythm sleep disorder, shift work type

● **G47.27 Circadian rhythm sleep disorder in conditions classified elsewhere**
Code first underlying condition

G47.29 Other circadian rhythm sleep disorder

● **G47.3 Sleep apnea**
Characterized by episodes in which breathing stops during sleep
Code also any associated underlying condition
| Excludes1 | apnea NOS R06.81
Cheyne-Stokes breathing (R06.3)
pickwickian syndrome (E66.2)
sleep apnea of newborn (P28.3) |

▪ **G47.30 Sleep apnea, unspecified**
Sleep apnea NOS

G47.31 Primary central sleep apnea

G47.32 High altitude periodic breathing

G47.33 Obstructive sleep apnea (adult) (pediatric)

G47.34 Idiopathic sleep related nonobstructive alveolar hypoventilation
Sleep related hypoxia

G47.35 Congenital central alveolar hypoventilation syndrome

● **G47.36 Sleep related hypoventilation in conditions classified elsewhere**
Sleep related hypoxemia in conditions classified elsewhere
Code first underlying condition

● **G47.37 Central sleep apnea in conditions classified elsewhere**
Code first underlying condition

G47.39 Other sleep apnea

● **G47.4 Narcolepsy and cataplexy**
*Cataplexy is a disorder evidenced by seizures including minor slacking of the facial muscles to complete collapse and often affects people who have **narcolepsy**, a disorder in which there is great difficulty remaining awake during the daytime.*

● **G47.41 Narcolepsy**

G47.411 Narcolepsy with cataplexy

G47.419 Narcolepsy without cataplexy
Narcolepsy NOS

● **G47.42 Narcolepsy in conditions classified elsewhere**

G47.421 Narcolepsy in conditions classified elsewhere with cataplexy

G47.429 Narcolepsy in conditions classified elsewhere without cataplexy

● **G47.5 Parasomnia**
| Excludes1 | alcohol induced parasomnia (F10.182, F10.282, F10.982)
drug induced parasomnia (F11.182, F11.282, F11.982, F13.182, F13.282, F13.982, F14.182, F14.282, F14.982, F15.182, F15.282, F15.982, F19.182, F19.282, F19.982)
parasomnia not due to a substance or known physiological condition (F51.8) |

▪ **G47.50 Parasomnia, unspecified**
Parasomnia NOS

G47.51 Confusional arousals

G47.52 REM sleep behavior disorder

G47.53 Recurrent isolated sleep paralysis

● **G47.54 Parasomnia in conditions classified elsewhere**
Code first underlying condition

G47.59 Other parasomnia

● **G47.6 Sleep related movement disorders**
| Excludes2 | restless legs syndrome (G25.81) |

G47.61 Periodic limb movement disorder
Periodic limb movement disorder

G47.62 Sleep related leg cramps

G47.63 Sleep related bruxism
| Excludes1 | psychogenic bruxism (F45.8) |

G47.69 Other sleep related movement disorders

G47.8 Other sleep disorders

▪ **G47.9 Sleep disorder, unspecified**
Sleep disorder NOS

(See Plate 118 on page NAP-6.)

NERVE, NERVE ROOT AND PLEXUS DISORDERS (G50-G59)

| Excludes1 | current traumatic nerve, nerve root and plexus disorders - see Injury, nerve by body region
neuralgia NOS (M79.2)
neuritis NOS (M79.2)
peripheral neuritis in pregnancy (O26.82-)
radiculitis NOS (M54.1-) |

● **G50 Disorders of trigeminal nerve**
| Includes | disorders of 5th cranial nerve |

G50.0 Trigeminal neuralgia
Syndrome of paroxysmal facial pain
Tic douloureux

G50.1 Atypical facial pain

G50.8 Other disorders of trigeminal nerve

▪ **G50.9 Disorder of trigeminal nerve, unspecified**

● **G51 Facial nerve disorders**
| Includes | disorders of 7th cranial nerve |

G51.0 Bell's palsy
Facial palsy

Item 6–5   Trigeminal neuralgia, tic douloureux, is a pain syndrome diagnosed from the patient's history alone. The condition is characterized by pain and a brief facial spasm or tic. Pain is unilateral and follows the sensory distribution of cranial nerve V, typically radiating to the maxillary (V2) or mandibular (V3) area.

● Unacceptable First-Listed Diagnosis   ● Use Additional Character(s)   ▪ Unspecified   OGCR Official Guidelines for Coding and Reporting
🗫 Complication\Comorbidity   🗫 Major C\C   Excludes 1   Excludes 2   Includes   Use additional   Code first   Code also

937

CHAPTER 6 (G00-G99)

G51.1 **Geniculate ganglionitis**
Rare disorder with symptoms of severe pain deep in ear, spreading to ear canal, outer ear, mastoid or eye regions

> Excludes1 postherpetic geniculate ganglionitis (B02.21)

G51.2 **Melkersson's syndrome**
Melkersson-Rosenthal syndrome

G51.3 **Clonic hemifacial spasm**

G51.4 **Facial myokymia**
Involuntary facial muscle movement

G51.8 **Other disorders of facial nerve**

G51.9 **Disorder of facial nerve, unspecified**

● G52 **Disorders of other cranial nerves**

> Excludes2 disorders of acoustic [8th] nerve (H93.3)
> disorders of optic [2nd] nerve (H46, H47.0)
> paralytic strabismus due to nerve palsy (H49.0-H49.2)

G52.0 **Disorders of olfactory nerve**
Disorders of 1st cranial nerve

G52.1 **Disorders of glossopharyngeal nerve**
Disorder of 9th cranial nerve
Glossopharyngeal neuralgia

G52.2 **Disorders of vagus nerve**
Disorders of pneumogastric [10th] nerve

G52.3 **Disorders of hypoglossal nerve**
Disorders of 12th cranial nerve

G52.7 **Disorders of multiple cranial nerves**
Polyneuritis cranialis

G52.8 **Disorders of other specified cranial nerves**

G52.9 **Cranial nerve disorder, unspecified**

● G53 **Cranial nerve disorders in diseases classified elsewhere**

> *Code first underlying disease, such as:*
> neoplasm (C00-D48)

> Excludes1 multiple cranial nerve palsy in sarcoidosis (D86.82)
> multiple cranial nerve palsy in syphilis (A52.15)
> postherpetic geniculate ganglionitis (B02.21)
> postherpetic trigeminal neuralgia (B02.22)

● G54 **Nerve root and plexus disorders**
Raiculopathy (nerve root disorder) caused by pressure on nerve root, most common cause is herniation of intervertebral disk. Plexus disorders (plexopathies) are due to compression or injury.

> Excludes1 current traumatic nerve root and plexus disorders - see nerve injury by body region
> intervertebral disc disorders (M50-M51)
> neuralgia or neuritis NOS (M79.2)
> neuritis or radiculitis:
> brachial NOS (M54.13)
> lumbar NOS (M54.16)
> lumbosacral NOS (M54.17)
> thoracic NOS (M54.14)
> radiculitis NOS (M54.10)
> radiculopathy NOS (M54.10)
> spondylosis (M47.-)

G54.0 **Brachial plexus disorders**
Thoracic outlet syndrome

G54.1 **Lumbosacral plexus disorders**

G54.2 **Cervical root disorders, not elsewhere classified**

G54.3 **Thoracic root disorders, not elsewhere classified**

G54.4 **Lumbosacral root disorders, not elsewhere classified**

G54.5 **Neuralgic amyotrophy**
Parsonage-Aldren-Turner syndrome
Shoulder-girdle neuritis

> Excludes1 neuralgic amyotrophy in diabetes mellitus (E09-E13 with .44)

G54.6 **Phantom limb syndrome with pain**
Sensations (cramping, itching) in a limb that no longer exists.

G54.7 **Phantom limb syndrome without pain**
Phantom limb syndrome NOS

G54.8 **Other nerve root and plexus disorders**

G54.9 **Nerve root and plexus disorder, unspecified**

● G55 **Nerve root and plexus compressions in diseases classified elsewhere**

> *Code first underlying disease, such as:*
> neoplasm (C00-D48)

> Excludes1 nerve root compression (due to) (in):
> ankylosing spondylitis (M45.-)
> dorsopathies (M53.-, M54.-)
> intervertebral disc disorders (M50.1.-, M51.1.-)
> spondylopathies (M46.-, M48.-)
> spondylosis (M47.0-M47.2.-)

(See Plates 472 and 473 on pages NAP-8 and NAP-9.)

● G56 **Mononeuropathies of upper limb**

> Excludes1 current traumatic nerve disorder - see nerve injury by body region

● G56.0 **Carpal tunnel syndrome**

G56.00 **Carpal tunnel syndrome, unspecified side**

G56.01 **Carpal tunnel syndrome, right side**

G56.02 **Carpal tunnel syndrome, left side**

● G56.1 **Other lesions of median nerve**

G56.10 **Other lesions of median nerve, unspecified side**

G56.11 **Other lesions of median nerve, right side**

G56.12 **Other lesions of median nerve, left side**

● G56.2 **Lesion of ulnar nerve**
Tardy ulnar nerve palsy

G56.20 **Lesion of ulnar nerve, unspecified side**

G56.21 **Lesion of ulnar nerve, right side**

G56.22 **Lesion of ulnar nerve, left side**

● G56.3 **Lesion of radial nerve**

G56.30 **Lesion of radial nerve, unspecified side**

G56.31 **Lesion of radial nerve, right side**

G56.32 **Lesion of radial nerve, left side**

Item 6-6 The most common facial nerve disorder is **Bell's Palsy,** which occurs suddenly and results in facial drooping unilaterally. This disorder is the result of a reaction to a virus that causes the facial nerve in the ear to swell resulting in pressure in the bony canal.

CHAPTER 6 (G00-G99)

938

● Unacceptable First-Listed Diagnosis   ● Use Additional Character(s)   ■ Unspecified   OGCR Official Guidelines for Coding and Reporting
🔧 Complication\Comorbidity   Major C\C   Excludes 1   Excludes 2   Includes   Use additional   Code first   Code also

● G56.4   **Causalgia of upper limb**
     Intense burning pain and sensitivity to slight touch
     Complex regional pain syndrome II of upper limb

     | Excludes1 | complex regional pain syndrome I of lower limb (G90.52-)
         complex regional pain syndrome I of upper limb (G90.51-)
         complex regional pain syndrome II of lower limb (G57.7-)
         reflex sympathetic dystrophy of lower limb (G90.52-)
         reflex sympathetic dystrophy (G90.51-)

     ■ G56.40   Causalgia of upper limb, unspecified side
     G56.41   Causalgia of upper limb, right side
     G56.42   Causalgia of upper limb, left side

● G56.8   **Other mononeuropathies of upper limb**
     Disease of a single nerve
     Interdigital neuroma of upper limb

     ■ G56.80   Other mononeuropathies of upper limb, unspecified side
     G56.81   Other mononeuropathies of upper limb, right side
     G56.82   Other mononeuropathies of upper limb, left side

● G56.9   **Mononeuropathy of upper limb, unspecified**
     Disease of a single nerve

     ■ G56.90   Mononeuropathy of upper limb, unspecified, unspecified side
     ■ G56.91   Mononeuropathy of upper limb, unspecified, right side
     ■ G56.92   Mononeuropathy of upper limb, unspecified, left side

● G57   **Mononeuropathies of lower limb**

     | Excludes1 | current traumatic nerve disorder - see nerve injury by body region

(See Plates 544 and 545 on pages NAP-10 and NAP-11.)

● G57.0   **Lesion of sciatic nerve**

     | Excludes1 | sciatica NOS (M54.3-)
     | Excludes2 | sciatica attributed to intervertebral disc disorder (M51.1.-)

     ■ G57.00   Lesion of sciatic nerve, unspecified side
     G57.01   Lesion of sciatic nerve, right side
     G57.02   Lesion of sciatic nerve, left side

● G57.1   **Meralgia paresthetica**
     Numbness or pain in outer thigh caused by injury to nerve
     Lateral cutaneous nerve of thigh syndrome

     ■ G57.10   Meralgia paresthetica, unspecified side
     G57.11   Meralgia paresthetica, right side
     G57.12   Meralgia paresthetica, left side

● G57.2   **Lesion of femoral nerve**

     ■ G57.20   Lesion of femoral nerve, unspecified side
     G57.21   Lesion of femoral nerve, right side
     G57.22   Lesion of femoral nerve, left side

● G57.3   **Lesion of lateral popliteal nerve**
     Peroneal nerve palsy

     ■ G57.30   Lesion of lateral popliteal nerve, unspecified side
     G57.31   Lesion of lateral popliteal nerve, right side
     G57.32   Lesion of lateral popliteal nerve, left side

● G57.4   **Lesion of medial popliteal nerve**

     ■ G57.40   Lesion of medial popliteal nerve, unspecified side
     G57.41   Lesion of medial popliteal nerve, right side
     G57.42   Lesion of medial popliteal nerve, left side

● G57.5   **Tarsal tunnel syndrome**

     ■ G57.50   Tarsal tunnel syndrome, unspecified side
     G57.51   Tarsal tunnel syndrome, right side
     G57.52   Tarsal tunnel syndrome, left side

● G57.6   **Lesion of plantar nerve**
     Morton's metatarsalgia

     ■ G57.60   Lesion of plantar nerve, unspecified side
     G57.61   Lesion of plantar nerve, right side
     G57.62   Lesion of plantar nerve, left side

● G57.7   **Causalgia of lower limb**
     Complex regional pain syndrome II of lower limb

     | Excludes1 | complex regional pain syndrome I of lower limb (G90.52-)
         complex regional pain syndrome I of upper limb (G90.51-)
         complex regional pain syndrome II of upper limb (G56.4-)
         reflex sympathetic dystrophy of lower limb (G90.52-)
         reflex sympathetic dystrophy of upper limb (G90.51-)

     ■ G57.70   Causalgia of lower limb, unspecified side
     G57.71   Causalgia of lower limb, right side
     G57.72   Causalgia of lower limb, left side

● G57.8   **Other mononeuropathies of lower limb**
     Interdigital neuroma of lower limb

     ■ G57.80   Other mononeuropathies of lower limb, unspecified side
     G57.81   Other mononeuropathies of lower limb, right side
     G57.82   Other mononeuropathies of lower limb, left side

● G57.9   **Mononeuropathy of lower limb, unspecified**

     ■ G57.90   Mononeuropathy of lower limb, unspecified, unspecified side
     ■ G57.91   Mononeuropathy of lower limb, unspecified, right side
     ■ G57.92   Mononeuropathy of lower limb, unspecified, left side

● G58   **Other mononeuropathies**

     G58.0   Intercostal neuropathy
     G58.7   Mononeuritis multiplex
     G58.8   Other specified mononeuropathies
     ■ G58.9   Mononeuropathy, unspecified

● G59   **Mononeuropathy in diseases classified elsewhere**

     Code first underlying disease

     | Excludes1 | diabetic mononeuropathy (E09-E14 with .41)
         syphilitic nerve paralysis (A52.19)
         syphilitic neuritis (A52.15)
         tuberculous mononeuropathy (A17.83)

Item 6-7 The **peripheral nervous system** consists of 31 pairs of spinal nerves, 12 pairs of cranial nerves, and the autonomic nerves, which are divided into the parasympathetic and sympathetic nerves. The cranial nerves are: olfactory (I), optic (II), oculomotor (III), trochlear (IV), trigeminal (V), abducens (VI), facial (VII), vestibulocochlear (VIII), glossopharyngeal (IX), vagus (X), accessory (XI), and hypoglossal (XII).

CHAPTER 6 (G00-G99)

● Unacceptable First-Listed Diagnosis   ● Use Additional Character(s)   ■ Unspecified   **OGCR** Official Guidelines for Coding and Reporting

🔾 Complication\Comorbidity   🔾 Major C\C | Excludes 1 | | Excludes 2 | Includes   Use additional   Code first   Code also

939

POLYNEUROPATHIES AND OTHER DISORDERS OF THE PERIPHERAL NERVOUS SYSTEM (G60-G64)

Excludes1   neuralgia NOS (M79.2)
neuritis NOS (M79.2)
peripheral neuritis in pregnancy (O26.82-)
radiculitis NOS (M54.10)

● **G60   Hereditary and idiopathic neuropathy**

    G60.0   Hereditary motor and sensory neuropathy
Charcot-Marie-Tooth disease
Déjerine-Sottas disease
Hereditary motor and sensory neuropathy, types I-IV
Hypertrophic neuropathy of infancy
Peroneal muscular atrophy (axonal type) (hypertrophic type)
Roussy-Lévy syndrome

    G60.1   Refsum's disease 🗲
Genetic disorder affecting fatty acid metabolism
Infantile Refsum disease

    G60.2   Neuropathy in association with hereditary ataxia

    G60.3   Idiopathic progressive neuropathy

    G60.8   Other hereditary and idiopathic neuropathies
Dominantly inherited sensory neuropathy
Morvan's disease
Nelaton's syndrome
Recessively inherited sensory neuropathy

    ■ **G60.9   Hereditary and idiopathic neuropathy, unspecified**

● **G61   Inflammatory polyneuropathy**

    G61.0   Guillain-Barré syndrome 🗲
Autoimmune disease affecting peripheral nervous system
Acute (post-)infective polyneuritis
Miller Fisher Syndrome

    ● **G61.1   Serum neuropathy**
Code first (T50.9-) to identify serum

    ● **G61.8   Other inflammatory polyneuropathies**

      G61.81   Chronic inflammatory demyelinating polyneuritis 🗲

      G61.89   Other inflammatory polyneuropathies

    ■ **G61.9   Inflammatory polyneuropathy, unspecified**

● **G62   Other and unspecified polyneuropathies**

    ● **G62.0   Drug-induced polyneuropathy**
Code first (T36-T50) to identify drug

    G62.1   Alcoholic polyneuropathy
Malfunction of many peripheral nerves throughout the body

    ● **G62.2   Polyneuropathy due to other toxic agents**
Code first (T51-T65) to identify toxic agent.

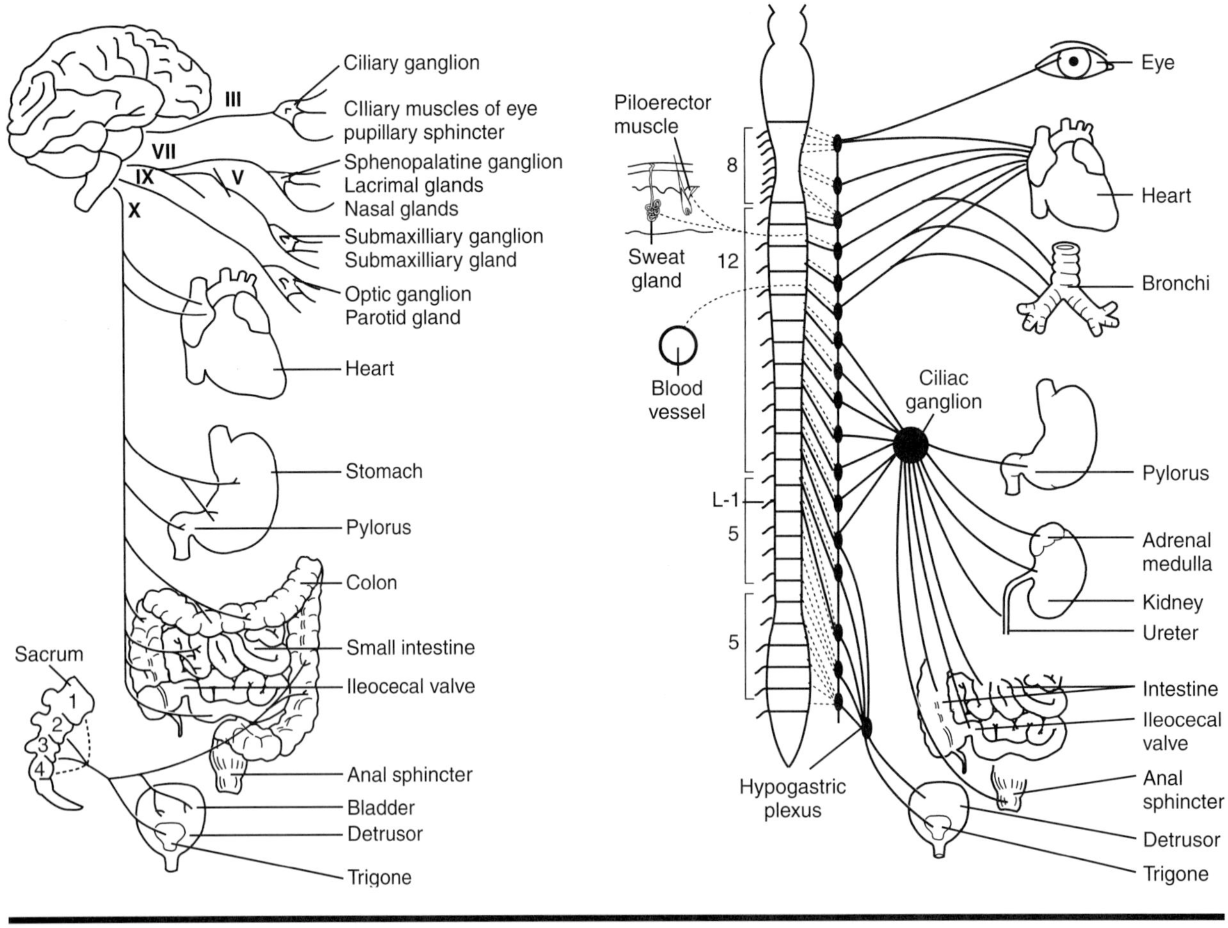

Figure 6-2   **A.** Parasympathetic nervous system. **B.** Sympathetic nervous system. (From Buck CJ: Step-by-Step Medical Coding, 2nd ed. Philadelphia, WB Saunders, 1998, pp 186 and 187.)

● Unacceptable First-Listed Diagnosis   ● Use Additional Character(s)   ■ Unspecified   **OGCR** Official Guidelines for Coding and Reporting
🗲 Complication\Comorbidity   🗲 Major C\C   Excludes 1   Excludes 2   Includes   Use additional   Code first   Code also

● **G62.8 Other specified polyneuropathies**

    G62.81 Critical illness polyneuropathy 🗣
        Acute motor neuropathy

    G62.82 Radiation-induced polyneuropathy
        Use additional external cause code
           (W88-W90, X39.0-) to identify cause

    G62.89 Other specified polyneuropathies

◾ **G62.9 Polyneuropathy, unspecified**
    Neuropathy NOS

● **G63 Polyneuropathy in diseases classified elsewhere**

    Code first underlying disease, such as:
      amyloidosis (E85.-)
      endocrine disease, except diabetes (E00-E07, E15-E16,
        E20-E34)
      metabolic diseases (E70-E89)
      neoplasm (C00-D48)
      nutritional deficiency (E40-E64)

    | Excludes1 | polyneuropathy (in):
          diabetes mellitus (E09-E13 with .42)
          diphtheria (A36.83)
          infectious mononucleosis (B27.0-B27.9
            with 1)
          Lyme disease (A69.22)
          mumps (B26.84)
          postherpetic (B02.23)
          rheumatoid arthritis (M05.33)
          scleroderma (M34.83)
          systemic lupus erythematosus (M32.19)

G64 Other disorders of peripheral nervous system
    Disorder of peripheral nervous system NOS

● **G65 Sequelae of inflammatory and toxic polyneuropathies**

    *Code first condition resulting from (sequela) of inflammatory
    and toxic polyneuropathies*

  ● **G65.0 Sequelae of Guillain-Barré syndrome**

  ● **G65.1 Sequelae of other inflammatory polyneuropathy**

  ● **G65.2 Sequelae of toxic polyneuropathy**

DISEASES OF MYONEURAL JUNCTION AND MUSCLE (G70-G73)

● **G70 Myasthenia gravis and other myoneural disorders**
    | Excludes1 | botulism food poisoning (A05.1, A48.51-
          A48.52)
         transient neonatal myasthenia gravis (P94.0)

● **G70.0 Myasthenia gravis**
    *Acquired and results in fatigable muscle weakness
      exacerbated by activity and improved with rest.*

    **G70.00 Myasthenia gravis without (acute)
           exacerbation**
        Myasthenia gravis NOS

    G70.01 Myasthenia gravis with (acute) exacerbation 🗣
        Myasthenia gravis in crisis

● **G70.1 Toxic myoneural disorders**
    *Dysfunction at junction of muscle and motor nerve
      (myoneural junction)*

    Code first (T51-T65) to identify toxic agent.

  G70.2 Congenital and developmental myasthenia

Item 6–8 Muscular dystrophies (MD) are a group of rare inherited muscle diseases. Voluntary muscles become progressively weaker. In the late stages of MD, fat and connective tissue replace muscle fibers. In some types of muscular dystrophy, heart muscles, other involuntary muscles, and other organs are affected. **Myopathies** is a general term for neuromuscular diseases in which the muscle fibers dysfunction for any one of many reasons, resulting in muscular weakness.

G70.8 Other specified myoneural disorders

◾ **G70.9 Myoneural disorder, unspecified**

● **G71 Primary disorders of muscles**
    | Excludes2 | arthrogryposis multiplex congenita (Q74.3)
         metabolic disorders (E70-E90)
         myositis (M60.-)

  G71.0 Muscular dystrophy 🗣
    Autosomal recessive, childhood type, muscular
      dystrophy resembling Duchenne or Becker
      muscular dystrophy
    Benign [Becker] muscular dystrophy
    Benign scapuloperoneal muscular dystrophy with
      early contractures [Emery-Dreifuss]
    Distal muscular dystrophy
    Facioscapulohumeral muscular dystrophy
    Limb-girdle muscular dystrophy
    Ocular muscular dystrophy
    Oculopharyngeal muscular dystrophy
    Scapuloperoneal muscular dystrophy
    Severe [Duchenne] muscular dystrophy

    | Excludes1 | congenital muscular dystrophy NOS
         (G71.2)
         congenital muscular dystrophy
           with specific morphological
           abnormalities of the muscle fiber
           (G71.2)

● **G71.1 Myo tonic disorders**
    Inherited disorder that affects muscles tone

    G71.11 Myotonic muscular dystrophy
        Dystrophia myotonica [Steinert]
        Myotonia atrophica
        Myotonic dystrophy
        Proximal myotonic myopathy (PROMM)
        Steinert disease

    G71.12 Myotonia congenita
        Acetazolamide responsive myotonia
          congenita
        Dominant myotonia congenita [Thomsen
          disease]
        Myotonia levior
        Recessive myotonia congenita [Becker
          disease]

    G71.13 Myotonic chondrodystrophy
        Chondrodystrophic myotonia
        Congenital myotonic chondrodystrophy
        Schwartz-Jampel disease

  ● **G71.14 Drug induced myotonia**

      Code first (T36-T50) to identify drug

    G71.19 Other specified myotonic disorders
        Myotonia fluctuans
        Myotonia permanens
        Neuromyotonia [Isaacs]
        Paramyotonia congenita (of von
          Eulenburg)
        Pseudomyotonia
        Symptomatic myotonia

  G71.2 Congenital myopathies 🗣
    Central core disease
    Congenital muscular dystrophy NOS
    Congenital muscular dystrophy with specific
      morphological abnormalities of the muscle
      fiber
    Fiber-type disproportion
    Minicore disease
    Multicore disease
    Myotubular (centronuclear) myopathy
    Nemaline myopathy

    | Excludes1 | arthrogryposis multiplex congenita
         (Q74.3)

● Unacceptable First-Listed Diagnosis   ● Use Additional Character(s)   ◾ Unspecified   **OGCR** Official Guidelines for Coding and Reporting

🗣 Complication\Comorbidity   🗣 Major C\C | Excludes 1 | | Excludes 2 | Includes   Use additional   Code first   Code also   **941**

CHAPTER 6 (G00-G99)

G71.3   Mitochondrial myopathy, not elsewhere classified
Myopathies associated with increased number of enlarged, often abnormal, mitochondria in muscle fibers

Excludes1   Kearns-Sayre syndrome (H49.81)
Leber's disease (H47.21)
Leigh's encephalopathy (G31.82)
mitochondrial metabolism disorders (E88.4.-)
Reye's syndrome (G93.7)

G71.8   Other primary disorders of muscles

G71.9   Primary disorder of muscle, unspecified
Hereditary myopathy NOS

● **G72   Other and unspecified myopathies**

Excludes1   arthrogryposis multiplex congenita (Q74.3)
dermatopolymyositis (M33.-)
ischemic infarction of muscle (M62.2-)
myositis (M60.-)
polymyositis (M33.2.-)

● **G72.0   Drug-induced myopathy**
Code first (T36-T50) to identify drug

G72.1   Alcoholic myopathy
Use additional code to identify alcoholism (F10.-)

● **G72.2   Myopathy due to other toxic agents**
Code first (T51-T65) to identify toxic agent.

G72.3   Periodic paralysis
Familial periodic paralysis
Hyperkalemic periodic paralysis (familial)
Hypokalemic periodic paralysis (familial)
Myotonic periodic paralysis (familial)
Normokalemic paralysis (familial)
Potassium sensitive periodic paralysis

Excludes1   paramyotonia congenita (of von Eulenburg) (G71.19)

● **G72.4   Inflammatory and immune myopathies, not elsewhere classified**

G72.41   Inclusion body myositis [IBM]

G72.49   Other inflammatory and immune myopathies, not elsewhere classified
Inflammatory myopathy NOS

● **G72.8   Other specified myopathies**

G72.81   Critical illness myopathy
Acute necrotizing myopathy
Acute quadriplegic myopathy
Intensive care (ICU) myopathy
Myopathy of critical illness

G72.89   Other specified myopathies

G72.9   Myopathy, unspecified

● **G73   Disorders of myoneural junction and muscle in diseases classified elsewhere**

● **G73.1   Lambert-Eaton syndrome**
Rare autoimmune disorder affecting calcium channels of nerve-muscle (neuromuscular) junction

Code first underlying disease, such as:
malignant neoplasm of lung (C34.-)
other neoplastic disease (C00-D48)

Excludes1   Lambert-Eaton syndrome not associated with neoplasm (G70.8)

● **G73.3   Myasthenic syndromes in other diseases classified elsewhere**
Code first underlying disease, such as:
neoplasm (C00-D498)
thyrotoxicosis (E05.-)

● **G73.7   Myopathy in diseases classified elsewhere**
Code first underlying disease, such as:
hyperparathyroidism (E21.0, E21.3)
hypoparathyroidism (E20.-)
glycogen storage disease (E74.0)
lipid storage disorders (E75.-)

Excludes1   myopathy in:
rheumatoid arthritis (M05.32)
sarcoidosis (D86.87)
scleroderma (M34.82)
sicca syndrome [Sjögren] (M35.03)
systemic lupus erythematosus (M32.19)

CEREBRAL PALSY AND OTHER PARALYTIC SYNDROMES (G80-G83)

● **G80   Cerebral palsy**

Excludes1   hereditary spastic paraplegia (G11.4)

G80.0   Spastic quadriplegic cerebral palsy
Congenital spastic paralysis (cerebral)

G80.1   Spastic diplegic cerebral palsy
Spastic cerebral palsy NOS

G80.2   Spastic hemiplegic cerebral palsy

G80.3   Athetoid cerebral palsy
Result of damage to cerebellum or basal ganglia responsible for processing neuromuscular signals
Double athetosis (syndrome)
Dyskinetic cerebral palsy
Dystonic cerebral palsy
Vogt disease

G80.4   Ataxic cerebral palsy
Poor muscle tone and coordination

G80.8   Other cerebral palsy
Mixed cerebral palsy syndromes

G80.9   Cerebral palsy, unspecified
Cerebral palsy NOS

OGCR   Section I.C.6.a.

Dominant/nondominant side

Codes from category G81, Hemiplegia and hemiparesis, and subcategories, G83.1, Monoplegia of lower limb, G83.2, Monoplegia of upper limb, and G83.3, Monoplegia, unspecified, identify whether the dominant and nondominant side is affected. Should this information not be available in the record, and the classification system does not indicate a default the default should be dominant. For ambidextrous patient, the default should also be dominant.

● **G81   Hemiplegia and hemiparesis**
Note: This category is to be used only when hemiplegia (complete)(incomplete) is reported without further specification, or is stated to be old or longstanding but of unspecified cause. The category is also for use in multiple coding to identify these types of hemiplegia resulting from any cause.

Excludes1   congenital cerebral palsy (G80.-)
hemiplegia and hemiparesis due to sequela of cerebrovascular disease (I69.05-, I69.15-, I69.25-, I69.35-, I69.45-, I69.85-, I69.95-)

● **G81.0   Flaccid hemiplegia**
Paralysis of half of body with loss of tone of muscles of paralyzed part and absence of tendon reflexes

G81.00   Flaccid hemiplegia affecting unspecified side

G81.01   Flaccid hemiplegia affecting right dominant side

● Unacceptable First-Listed Diagnosis   ● Use Additional Character(s)   ▉ Unspecified   **OGCR** Official Guidelines for Coding and Reporting
Complication\Comorbidity   Major C\C   Excludes 1   Excludes 2   Includes   Use additional   Code first   Code also

Item 6–9   **Hemiplegia** is complete paralysis of one side of the body—arm, leg, and trunk. **Hemiparesis** is a generalized weakness or incomplete paralysis of one side of the body. If most activities (eating, writing) are performed with the right hand, the right is the dominant side, and the left is the nondominant side. **Quadriplegia,** also called tetraplegia, is the complete paralysis of all four limbs. **Quadriparesis** is the incomplete paralysis of all four limbs. Nerve damage in C1–C4 is associated with lower limb paralysis, and C5–C7 damage is associated with upper limb paralysis. **Diplegia** is the paralysis of the upper limbs. **Monoplegia** is the complete paralysis of one limb.

     G81.02   **Flaccid hemiplegia affecting left dominant side**

     G81.03   **Flaccid hemiplegia affecting right nondominant side**

     G81.04   **Flaccid hemiplegia affecting left nondominant side**

● G81.1   **Spastic hemiplegia**
Paralysis of half of body with spasticity of muscles of paralyzed part and increased tendon reflexes

     G81.10   **Spastic hemiplegia affecting unspecified side**

     G81.11   **Spastic hemiplegia affecting right dominant side**

     G81.12   **Spastic hemiplegia affecting left dominant side**

     G81.13   **Spastic hemiplegia affecting right nondominant side**

     G81.14   **Spastic hemiplegia affecting left nondominant side**

● G81.9   **Hemiplegia, unspecified**

     G81.90   **Hemiplegia, unspecified affecting unspecified side**

     G81.91   **Hemiplegia, unspecified affecting right dominant side**

     G81.92   **Hemiplegia, unspecified affecting left dominant side**

     G81.93   **Hemiplegia, unspecified affecting right nondominant side**

     G81.94   **Hemiplegia, unspecified affecting left nondominant side**

● G82   **Paraplegia (paraparesis) and quadriplegia (quadriparesis)**
     Note: This category is to be used only when the listed conditions are reported without further specification, or are stated to be old or longstanding but of unspecified cause. The category is also for use in multiple coding to identify these conditions resulting from any cause.

     Excludes1   congenital cerebral palsy (G80.-)
              functional quadriplegia (R53.2)
              hysterical paralysis (F44.4)

● G82.2   **Paraplegia**
     Paralysis of both lower limbs NOS
     Paraparesis (lower) NOS
     Paraplegia (lower) NOS

     G82.20   **Paraplegia, unspecified**

     G82.21   **Paraplegia, complete**

     G82.22   **Paraplegia, incomplete**

● G82.5   **Quadriplegia**
Paralysis of all limbs; AKA tetraplegia

     G82.50   **Quadriplegia, unspecified**

     G82.51   **Quadriplegia, C1-C4 complete**

     G82.52   **Quadriplegia, C1-C4 incomplete**

     G82.53   **Quadriplegia, C5-C7 complete**

     G82.54   **Quadriplegia, C5-C7 incomplete**

● G83   **Other paralytic syndromes**
     Note: This category is to be used only when the listed conditions are reported without further specification, or are stated to be old or longstanding but of unspecified cause. The category is also for use in multiple coding to identify these conditions resulting from any cause.

     Includes   paralysis (complete) (incomplete), except as in G80-G82

● G83.0   **Diplegia of upper limbs**
Paralysis affecting limbs on both sides; AKA bilateral paralysis
     Diplegia (upper)
     Paralysis of both upper limbs

● G83.1   **Monoplegia of lower limb**
Paralysis of limb on one side
     Paralysis of lower limb

     Excludes1   monoplegia of lower limbs due to sequela of cerebrovascular disease (I69.04-, I69.14-, I69.24-, I69.34-, I69.44-, I69.84-, I69.94-)

     G83.10   **Monoplegia of lower limb affecting unspecified side**

     G83.11   **Monoplegia of lower limb affecting right dominant side**

     G83.12   **Monoplegia of lower limb affecting left dominant side**

     G83.13   **Monoplegia of lower limb affecting right nondominant side**

     G83.14   **Monoplegia of lower limb affecting left nondominant side**

● G83.2   **Monoplegia of upper limb**
     Paralysis of upper limb

     Excludes1   monoplegia of upper limbs due to sequela of cerebrovascular disease (I69.03-, I69.13-, I69.23-, I69.33-, I69.43-, I69.83-, I69.93-)

     G83.20   **Monoplegia of upper limb affecting unspecified side**

     G83.21   **Monoplegia of upper limb affecting right dominant side**

     G83.22   **Monoplegia of upper limb affecting left dominant side**

     G83.23   **Monoplegia of upper limb affecting right nondominant side**

     G83.24   **Monoplegia of upper limb affecting left nondominant side**

● G83.3   **Monoplegia, unspecified**

     G83.30   **Monoplegia, unspecified affecting unspecified side**

     G83.31   **Monoplegia, unspecified affecting right dominant side**

     G83.32   **Monoplegia, unspecified affecting left dominant side**

● Unacceptable First-Listed Diagnosis   ● Use Additional Character(s)   ▪ Unspecified   **OGCR** Official Guidelines for Coding and Reporting

 Complication\Comorbidity   Major C\C   Excludes 1   Excludes 2   Includes   Use additional   Code first   Code also

CHAPTER 6 (G00-G99)

943

■ **G83.33** **Monoplegia, unspecified affecting right nondominant side**

■ **G83.34** **Monoplegia, unspecified affecting left nondominant side**

G83.4 **Cauda equina syndrome** 🕭
Aching pain due to compression of spinal nerve roots
Neurogenic bladder due to cauda equina syndrome

> **Excludes1**   cord bladder NOS (G95.8)
> neurogenic bladder NOS (N31.9)

G83.5 **Locked-in state** 🕭

● **G83.8** **Other specified paralytic syndromes**

> **Excludes1**   paralytic syndromes due to current spinal cord injury-code to spinal cord injury (S14, S24, S34)

G83.81 **Brown-Sequard syndrome**

G83.82 **Anterior cord syndrome**

G83.83 **Posterior cord syndrome**

G83.84 **Todd's paralysis (postepileptic)**

G83.89 **Other specified paralytic syndromes**

■ **G83.9** **Paralytic syndrome, unspecified**

OTHER DISORDERS OF THE NERVOUS SYSTEM (G89-G99)

● **G89** **Pain, not elsewhere classified**
Code also related psychological factors associated with pain (F45.42)

> **Excludes1**   generalized pain NOS (R52)
> pain disorders exclusively related to psychological factors (F45.41)
> pain NOS (R52)

> **Excludes2**   atypical face pain (G50.1)
> headache syndromes (G44.-)
> localized pain, unspecified type - code to pain by site, such as:
> abdomen pain (R10.-)
> back pain (M54.9)
> breast pain (N64.4)
> chest pain (R07.1-R07.9)
> ear pain (H92.0-)
> eye pain (H57.1)
> headache (R51)
> joint pain (M25.5-)
> limb pain (M79.6-)
> lumbar region pain (M54.57)
> painful urination (R30.9)
> pelvic and perineal pain (R10.2)
> shoulder pain (M25.51-)
> spine pain (M54.-)
> throat pain (R07.0)
> tongue pain (K14.6)
> tooth pain (K08.8)
> renal colic (N23)
> migraines (G43.-)
> myalgia (M79.1)
> pain from prosthetic devices, implants, and grafts (T82.84, T83.84, T84.84, T85.84)
> phantom limb syndrome with pain (G54.6)
> vulvar vestibulitis (N94.810)
> vulvodynia (N94.81-)

G89.0 **Central pain syndrome**
Neurological condition causing intractable pain resulting from damage to CNS
Déjérine-Roussy syndrome
Myelopathic pain syndrome
Thalamic pain syndrome (hyperesthetic)

● **G89.1** **Acute pain, not elsewhere classified**

G89.11 **Acute pain due to trauma**

G89.12 **Acute post-thoracotomy pain**
Post-thoracotomy pain NOS

G89.18 **Other acute postprocedural pain**
Postoperative pain NOS
Postprocedural pain NOS

● **G89.2** **Chronic pain, not elsewhere classified**

> **Excludes1**   causalgia, lower limb (G57.7-)
> causalgia, upper limb (G56.4-)
> central pain syndrome (G89.0)
> chronic pain syndrome (G89.4)
> complex regional pain syndrome II, lower limb (G57.7-)
> complex regional pain syndrome II, upper limb (G56.4-)
> neoplasm related chronic pain (G89.3)
> reflex sympathetic dystrophy (G90.5-)

G89.21 **Chronic pain due to trauma**

G89.22 **Chronic post-thoracotomy pain**

G89.28 **Other chronic postprocedural pain**
Other chronic postoperative pain

G89.3 **Neoplasm related pain (acute) (chronic)**
Cancer associated pain
Pain due to malignancy (primary) (secondary)
Tumor associated pain

G89.4 **Chronic pain syndrome**
Chronic pain associated with significant psychosocial dysfunction

● **G90** **Disorders of autonomic nervous system**

> **Excludes1**   dysfunction of the autonomic nervous system due to alcohol (G31.2)

● **G90.0** **Idiopathic peripheral autonomic neuropathy**

G90.01 **Carotid sinus syncope**
Carotid sinus syndrome

G90.09 **Other idiopathic peripheral autonomic neuropathy**
Idiopathic peripheral autonomic neuropathy NOS

G90.1 **Familial dysautonomia [Riley-Day]**
Inherited disorder that affects nerve function

G90.2 **Horner's syndrome**
Due to damage of the sympathetic nervous system
Bernard(-Horner) syndrome
Cervical sympathetic dystrophy or paralysis

G90.3 **Multi-system degeneration of the autonomic nervous system** 🕭
Neurogenic orthostatic hypotension [Shy-Drager]

> **Excludes1**   orthostatic hypotension NOS (I95.1)

G90.4 **Autonomic dysreflexia**
Syndrome resulting from lesions of spinal cord

Use additional code to identify the cause, such as:
pressure ulcer (pressure area) (L89.-)
fecal impaction (K56.4)
urinary tract infection (N39.0)

● **G90.5   Complex regional pain syndrome I (CRPS I)**
     Reflex sympathetic dystrophy

     | Excludes1 | causalgia of lower limb (G57.7-)
                    causalgia of upper limb (G56.4-)
                    complex regional pain syndrome II
                       of lower limb (G57.7-)
                    complex regional pain syndrome II
                       of upper limb (G56.4-)

     G90.50   Complex regional pain syndrome I, unspecified

● **G90.51   Complex regional pain syndrome I of upper limb**

     G90.511   Complex regional pain syndrome I of right upper limb 🕮

     G90.512   Complex regional pain syndrome I of left upper limb 🕮

     G90.513   Complex regional pain syndrome I of upper limb, bilateral 🕮

     ▪ **G90.519   Complex regional pain syndrome I of unspecified upper limb** 🕮

● **G90.52   Complex regional pain syndrome I of lower limb**

     G90.521   Complex regional pain syndrome I of right lower limb 🕮

     G90.522   Complex regional pain syndrome I of left lower limb 🕮

     G90.523   Complex regional pain syndrome I of lower limb, bilateral 🕮

     ▪ **G90.529   Complex regional pain syndrome I of unspecified lower limb** 🕮

     G90.59   Complex regional pain syndrome I of other specified site 🕮

G90.8   Other disorders of autonomic nervous system

▪ **G90.9   Disorder of the autonomic nervous system, unspecified**

● **G91   Hydrocephalus**
     Dilatation of cerebral ventricles, accompanied by accumulation of cerebrospinal fluid

     | Includes | acquired hydrocephalus

     | Excludes1 | Arnold-Chiari syndrome with
                    hydrocephalus (Q07.-)
                    congenital hydrocephalus (Q03.-)
                    spina bifida with hydrocephalus (Q05.-)

G91.0   Communicating hydrocephalus 🕮
     Secondary normal pressure hydrocephalus

G91.1   Obstructive hydrocephalus 🕮

G91.2   (Idiopathic) normal pressure hydrocephalus 🕮
     Normal pressure hydrocephalus NOS

▪ **G91.3   Post-traumatic hydrocephalus, unspecified** 🕮

● **G91.4   Hydrocephalus in diseases classified elsewhere**

     Code first underlying condition, such as:
     congenital syphilis (A50.4-)
     neoplasm (C00-D48)

     | Excludes1 | hydrocephalus due to congenital
                    toxoplasmosis (P37.1)

G91.8   Other hydrocephalus 🕮

▪ **G91.9   Hydrocephalus, unspecified** 🕮

G92   Toxic encephalopathy 🕮
     Disorder or disease of brain caused by chemicals
     Toxic encephalitis
     Toxic metabolic encephalopathy

     Code first (T51-T65) to identify toxic agent.

● **G93   Other disorders of brain**

     G93.0   Cerebral cysts
         Arachnoid cyst
         Porencephalic cyst, acquired

         | Excludes1 | acquired periventricular cysts of
                         newborn (P91.1)
                        congenital cerebral cysts (Q04.6)

     G93.1   Anoxic brain damage, not elsewhere classified 🕮
         Permanent brain damage by lack of oxygen perfusion through brain tissues.

         | Excludes1 | cerebral anoxia due to anesthesia
                         during labor and delivery
                         (O74.3)
                      cerebral anoxia due to anesthesia
                         during the puerperium (O89.2)
                      neonatal anoxia (P28.9)

     G93.2   Benign intracranial hypertension

         | Excludes1 | hypertensive encephalopathy (I67.4)

     G93.3   Postviral fatigue syndrome
         Benign myalgic encephalomyelitis

         | Excludes1 | chronic fatigue syndrome NOS
                         (R53.82)

● **G93.4   Other and unspecified encephalopathy**

         | Excludes1 | alcoholic encephalopathy (G31.2)
                        hypertensive encephalopathy (I67.4)
                        toxic (metabolic) encephalopathy
                         (G92)

     ▪ **G93.40   Encephalopathy, unspecified** 🕮

     G93.41   Metabolic encephalopathy 🕮
         Septic encephalopathy

     G93.49   Other encephalopathy 🕮
         Encephalopathy NEC

     G93.5   Compression of brain 🕮
         Arnold-Chiari type 1 compression of brain
         Compression of brain (stem)
         Herniation of brain (stem)

         | Excludes1 | diffuse traumatic compression of
                        brain (S06.2-)
                      focal traumatic compression of brain
                      (S06.3-)

     G93.6   Cerebral edema 🕮

         | Excludes1 | cerebral edema due to birth injury
                        (P11.0)
                      traumatic cerebral edema (S06.1-)

     G93.7   Reye's syndrome 🕮
         Life-threatening neurological condition, usually follows viral illness

         Code first (T39.0-), if salicylates-induced

● **G93.8   Other specified disorders of brain**

     G93.81   Temporal sclerosis
         Hippocampal sclerosis
         Mesial temporal sclerosis

     G93.89   Other specified disorders of brain
         Postradiation encephalopathy

▪ **G93.9   Disorder of brain, unspecified**

● **G94   Other disorders of brain in diseases classified elsewhere**

     Code first underlying disease

     | Excludes1 | encephalopathy in congenital syphilis
                    (A50.49)
                   encephalopathy in influenza (J10.89)
                   encephalopathy in syphilis (A52.19)
                   hydrocephalus in diseases classified
                      elsewhere (G91.4)

● Unacceptable First-Listed Diagnosis   ● Use Additional Character(s)   ▪ Unspecified   **OGCR** Official Guidelines for Coding and Reporting

🕮 Complication\Comorbidity   🕮 Major C\C | Excludes 1 | | Excludes 2 | Includes   Use additional   Code first   Code also

945

● **G95 Other and unspecified diseases of spinal cord**
    Excludes2 myelitis (G04.-)
    G95.0 Syringomyelia and syringobulbia 🦠

● **G95.1 Vascular myelopathies**
      Excludes2 intraspinal phlebitis and thrombophlebitis, except non-pyogenic (G08)

    G95.11 Acute infarction of spinal cord (embolic) (nonembolic) 🦠
        Anoxia of spinal cord
        Arterial thrombosis of spinal cord

    G95.19 Other vascular myelopathies 🦠
        Edema of spinal cord
        Hematomyelia
        Nonpyogenic intraspinal phlebitis and thrombophlebitis
        Subacute necrotic myelopathy

● **G95.2 Other and unspecified cord compression**
    ■**G95.20 Unspecified cord compression** 🦠
    G95.29 Other cord compression 🦠

● **G95.8 Other specified diseases of spinal cord**
      Excludes1 neurogenic bladder NOS (N31.9)
           neurogenic bladder due to cauda equina syndrome (G83.4)
           neuromuscular dysfunction of bladder without spinal cord lesion (N31.-)

    G95.81 Conus medullaris syndrome 🦠
        Damage to gray matter and/or nerve roots in lower end of spinal cord

    G95.89 Other specified diseases of spinal cord 🦠
        Cord bladder NOS
        Drug-induced myelopathy
        Radiation-induced myelopathy
      Excludes1 myelopathy NOS (G95.9)

   ■**G95.9 Disease of spinal cord, unspecified** 🦠
      Myelopathy NOS

● **G96 Other disorders of central nervous system**
    G96.0 Cerebrospinal fluid leak 🦠
      Excludes1 cerebrospinal fluid leak from spinal puncture (G97.0)

● **G96.1 Disorders of meninges, not elsewhere classified**
    G96.11 Dural tear
      Excludes1 accidental puncture or laceration of dura during a procedure (G97.41)

    G96.12 Meningeal adhesions (cerebral) (spinal)

    G96.19 Other disorders of meninges, not elsewhere classified

    G96.8 Other specified disorders of central nervous system
   ■**G96.9 Disorder of central nervous system, unspecified**

● **G97 Intraoperative and postprocedural complications and disorders of nervous system, not elsewhere classified**
    Excludes2 intraoperative and postprocedural cerebrovascular infarction (I97.81-, I97.82-)

    G97.0 Cerebrospinal fluid leak from spinal puncture 🦠

    G97.1 Other reaction to spinal and lumbar puncture
      Headache due to lumbar puncture

    G97.2 Intracranial hypotension following ventricular shunting 🦠

● **G97.3 Intraoperative hemorrhage and hematoma of a nervous system organ or structure complicating a procedure**
      Excludes1 intraoperative hemorrhage and hematoma of a nervous system organ or structure due to accidental puncture and laceration during a procedure (G97.4-)

    G97.31 Intraoperative hemorrhage and hematoma of a nervous system organ or structure complicating a nervous system procedure 🦠

    G97.32 Intraoperative hemorrhage and hematoma of a nervous system organ or structure complicating other procedure 🦠

● **G97.4 Accidental puncture and laceration of a nervous system organ or structure during a procedure**
    G97.41 Accidental puncture or laceration of dura during a procedure
      Incidental (inadvertent) durotomy

    G97.48 Accidental puncture and laceration of other nervous system organ or structure during other procedure 🦠

    G97.49 Accidental puncture and laceration of other nervous system organ or structure during other procedure 🦠

● **G97.5 Postprocedural hemorrhage and hematoma of a nervous system organ or structure following a procedure**
    G97.51 Postprocedural hemorrhage and hematoma of a nervous system organ or structure following a nervous system procedure 🦠

    G97.52 Postprocedural hemorrhage and hematoma of a nervous system organ or structure following other procedure 🦠

● **G97.8 Other intraoperative and postprocedural complications and disorders of nervous system**
    Use additional code to further specify disorder

    G97.81 Other intraoperative complications of nervous system 🦠

    G97.82 Other postprocedural complications and disorders of nervous system 🦠

● **G98 Other disorders of nervous system not elsewhere classified**
    Includes nervous system disorder NOS

    G98.0 Neurogenic arthritis, not elsewhere classified
      Nonsyphilitic neurogenic arthropathy NEC
      Nonsyphilitic neurogenic spondylopathy NEC
      Excludes1 spondylopathy (in):
          syringomyelia and syringobulbia (G95.0)
          tabes dorsalis (A52.11)

    G98.8 Other disorders of nervous system
      Nervous system disorder NOS

● **G99 Other disorders of nervous system in diseases classified elsewhere**
  ● **G99.0 Autonomic neuropathy in diseases classified elsewhere** 🦠
      Code first underlying disease, such as:
        amyloidosis (E85.-)
        gout (M1a-, M10.-)
        hyperthyroidism (E05.-)
      Excludes1 diabetic autonomic neuropathy (E09-14 with .43)

● Unacceptable First-Listed Diagnosis   ● Use Additional Character(s)   ■ Unspecified   **OGCR** Official Guidelines for Coding and Reporting
🦠 Complication\Comorbidity   🦠 Major C\C   Excludes 1   Excludes 2   Includes   Use additional   Code first   Code also

● **G99.2 Myelopathy in diseases classified elsewhere** 🔗
   Code first underlying disease, such as:
      neoplasm (C00-D48)

   | **Excludes1** | myelopathy in:
      intervertebral disease (M50.0-, M51.0-)
      spondylosis (M47.0-, M47.1-)

● **G99.8 Other specified disorders of nervous system in diseases classified elsewhere**
   Code first underlying disorder, such as:
      amyloidosis (E85.-)
      avitaminosis (E56.9)

   | **Excludes1** | nervous system involvement in:
      cysticercosis (B69.0)
      rubella (B06.0-)
      syphilis (A52.1-)

● Unacceptable First-Listed Diagnosis   ● Use Additional Character(s)   Unspecified   **OGCR** Official Guidelines for Coding and Reporting

🔗 Complication\Comorbidity   🔗 Major C\C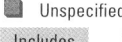

947

CHAPTER 6 (G00-G99)

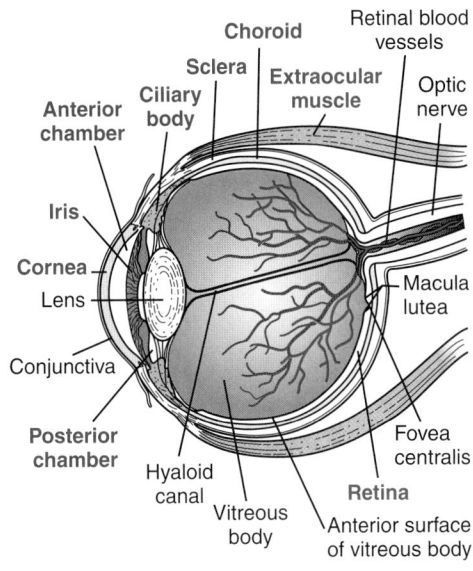

Figure 7-1 Eye and ocular adnexa. (From Buck CJ: Step-by-Step Medical Coding, 2010 ed. Philadelphia, WB Saunders, 2010.)

(See Plate 87 on page NAP-15.)

CHAPTER 7

DISEASES OF THE EYE AND ADNEXA (H00-H59)

Note: Use an external cause code following the code for the eye condition, if applicable, to identify the cause of the eye condition

Excludes2 certain conditions originating in the perinatal period (P04-P96)
certain infectious and parasitic diseases (A00-B99)
complications of pregnancy, childbirth and the puerperium (O00-O99)
congenital malformations, deformations, and chromosomal abnormalities (Q00-Q99)
diabetes mellitus related eye conditions (E09.3-, E10.3-, E11.3-, E13.3-)
endocrine, nutritional and metabolic diseases (E00-E90)
injury (trauma) of eye and orbit (S05.-)
injury, poisoning and certain other consequences of external causes (S00-T98)
neoplasms (C00-D48)
symptoms, signs and abnormal clinical and laboratory findings, not elsewhere classified (R00-R94)
syphilis related eye disorders (A50.01, A50.3-, A51.43, A52.71)

This chapter contains the following blocks:

H00-H05	Disorders of eyelid, lacrimal system and orbit
H10-H11	Disorders of conjunctiva
H15-H22	Disorders of sclera, cornea, iris and ciliary body
H25-H28	Disorders of lens
H30-H36	Disorders of choroid and retina

H40-H42	Glaucoma
H43-H44	Disorders of vitreous body and globe
H46-H47	Disorders of optic nerve and visual pathways
H49-H52	Disorders of ocular muscles, binocular movement, accommodation and refraction
H53-H54	Visual disturbances and blindness
H55-H57	Other disorders of eye and adnexa
H59	Intraoperative and postprocedural complications and disorders of eye and adnexa, not elsewhere classified

DISORDERS OF EYELID, LACRIMAL SYSTEM AND ORBIT (H00-H05)

Excludes2 open wound of eyelid (S01.1-)
superficial injury of eyelid (S00.1-, S00.2-)

● **H00 Hordeolum and chalazion**
Hordeolum: inflammatory staphylococcal infection of sebaceous glands of eyelids; AKA stye. Chalazion: eyelid mass

● **H00.0 Hordeolum (externum) (internum) of eyelid**
Bacterial infection (staphylococcus) of the sebaceous gland of the eyelid (stye)

● **H00.01 Hordeolum externum**
Hordeolum NOS
Stye

     H00.011 Hordeolum externum right upper eyelid
     H00.012 Hordeolum externum right lower eyelid
     H00.013 Hordeolum externum right eye, unspecified eyelid
     H00.014 Hordeolum externum left upper eyelid
     H00.015 Hordeolum externum left lower eyelid
     H00.016 Hordeolum externum left eye, unspecified eyelid
     H00.019 Hordeolum externum unspecified eye, unspecified eyelid

● **H00.02 Hordeolum internum**
Infection of meibomian gland (tarsal)

     H00.021 Hordeolum internum right upper eyelid
     H00.022 Hordeolum internum right lower eyelid
     H00.023 Hordeolum internum right eye, unspecified eyelid
     H00.024 Hordeolum internum left upper eyelid
     H00.025 Hordeolum internum left lower eyelid
     H00.026 Hordeolum internum left eye, unspecified eyelid
     H00.029 Hordeolum internum unspecified eye, unspecified eyelid

● **H00.03 Abscess of eyelid**
Furuncle of eyelid

     H00.031 Abscess of right upper eyelid
     H00.032 Abscess of right lower eyelid
     H00.033 Abscess of eyelid right eye, unspecified eyelid

● Unacceptable First-Listed Diagnosis   ● Use Additional Character(s)   ▨ Unspecified   **OGCR** Official Guidelines for Coding and Reporting
🔖 Complication\Comorbidity   🔖 Major C\C   Excludes 1   Excludes 2   Includes   Use additional   Code first   Code also

CHAPTER 7 (H00-H59)

H00.034   Abscess of left upper eyelid

H00.035   Abscess of left lower eyelid

 H00.036   Abscess of eyelid left eye, unspecified eyelid

 H00.039   Abscess of eyelid unspecified eye, unspecified eyelid

● **H00.1   Chalazion**

Often caused by accumulation of meibomian gland secretions resulting from a blockage of duct.

Meibomian (gland) cyst

Excludes2   infected meibomian gland (H00.02-)

H00.11   Chalazion right upper eyelid

H00.12   Chalazion right lower eyelid

 H00.13   Chalazion right eye, unspecified eyelid

H00.14   Chalazion left upper eyelid

H00.15   Chalazion left lower eyelid

 H00.16   Chalazion left eye, unspecified eyelid

 H00.19   Chalazion unspecified eye, unspecified eyelid

● **H01   Other inflammation of eyelid**

● **H01.0   Blepharitis**

Inflammation of eyelids

Excludes1   blepharoconjunctivitis (H10.5-)

● **H01.00   Unspecified blepharitis**

 H01.001   Unspecified blepharitis right upper eyelid

 H01.002   Unspecified blepharitis right lower eyelid

 H01.003   Unspecified blepharitis right eye, unspecified eyelid

 H01.004   Unspecified blepharitis left upper eyelid

 H01.005   Unspecified blepharitis left lower eyelid

 H01.006   Unspecified blepharitis left eye, unspecified eyelid

 H01.009   Unspecified blepharitis unspecified eye, unspecified eyelid

● **H01.01   Ulcerative blepharitis**

H01.011   Ulcerative blepharitis right upper eyelid

H01.012   Ulcerative blepharitis right lower eyelid

 H01.013   Ulcerative blepharitis right eye, unspecified eyelid

H01.014   Ulcerative blepharitis left upper eyelid

H01.015   Ulcerative blepharitis left lower eyelid

 H01.016   Ulcerative blepharitis left eye, unspecified eyelid

 H01.019   Ulcerative blepharitis unspecified eye, unspecified eyelid

● **H01.02   Squamous blepharitis**

H01.021   Squamous blepharitis right upper eyelid

H01.022   Squamous blepharitis right lower eyelid

 H01.023   Squamous blepharitis right eye, unspecified eyelid

H01.024   Squamous blepharitis left upper eyelid

H01.025   Squamous blepharitis left lower eyelid

 H01.026   Squamous blepharitis left eye, unspecified eyelid

 H01.029   Squamous blepharitis unspecified eye, unspecified eyelid

● **H01.1   Noninfectious dermatoses of eyelid**

● **H01.11   Allergic dermatitis of eyelid**

Contact dermatitis of eyelid

H01.111   Allergic dermatitis of right upper eyelid

H01.112   Allergic dermatitis of right lower eyelid

 H01.113   Allergic dermatitis of right eye, unspecified eyelid

H01.114   Allergic dermatitis of left upper eyelid

H01.115   Allergic dermatitis of left lower eyelid

 H01.116   Allergic dermatitis of left eye, unspecified eyelid

 H01.119   Allergic dermatitis of unspecified eye, unspecified eyelid

● **H01.12   Discoid lupus erythematosus of eyelid**

H01.121   Discoid lupus erythematosus of right upper eyelid

H01.122   Discoid lupus erythematosus of right lower eyelid

 H01.123   Discoid lupus erythematosus of right eye, unspecified eyelid

H01.124   Discoid lupus erythematosus of left upper eyelid

H01.125   Discoid lupus erythematosus of left lower eyelid

 H01.126   Discoid lupus erythematosus of left eye, unspecified eyelid

 H01.129   Discoid lupus erythematosus of unspecified eye, unspecified eyelid

● **H01.13   Eczematous dermatitis of eyelid**

H01.131   Eczematous dermatitis of right upper eyelid

H01.132   Eczematous dermatitis of right lower eyelid

 H01.133   Eczematous dermatitis of right eye, unspecified eyelid

H01.134   Eczematous dermatitis of left upper eyelid

H01.135   Eczematous dermatitis of left lower eyelid

 H01.136   Eczematous dermatitis of left eye, unspecified eyelid

 H01.139   Eczematous dermatitis of unspecified eye, unspecified eyelid

● **H01.14   Xeroderma of eyelid**

Abnormally dry

H01.141   Xeroderma of right upper eyelid

H01.142   Xeroderma of right lower eyelid

 H01.143   Xeroderma of right eye, unspecified eyelid

---

● Unacceptable First-Listed Diagnosis   ● Use Additional Character(s)   Unspecified   **OGCR** Official Guidelines for Coding and Reporting

🐾 Complication\Comorbidity   🐾 Major C\C   Excludes 1   Excludes 2   Includes   Use additional   Code first   Code also

949

CHAPTER 7 (H00-H59)

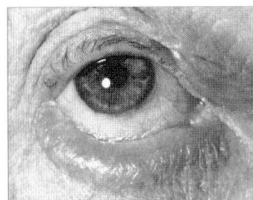

Figure 7-2 Right lower eyelid entropion. Note the inward rotation of the tarsal plate about the horizontal axis and the resultant contact between the mucocutaneous junction and ocular surface. (From Yanoff: Ophthalmology, 2nd ed. 2004, Mosby, Inc.)

H01.144 Xeroderma of left upper eyelid

H01.145 Xeroderma of left lower eyelid

H01.146 Xeroderma of left eye, unspecified eyelid

H01.149 Xeroderma of unspecified eye, unspecified eyelid

H01.8 Other specified inflammations of eyelid

H01.9 Unspecified inflammation of eyelid
Inflammation of eyelid NOS

● H02 Other disorders of eyelid
Turning inward (inversion) of eyelid margin and ingrowing eyelashes

> Excludes1 congenital malformations of eyelid (Q10.0-Q10.3)

● H02.0 Entropion and trichiasis of eyelid

● H02.00 Unspecified entropion of eyelid

H02.001 Unspecified entropion of right upper eyelid

H02.002 Unspecified entropion of right lower eyelid

H02.003 Unspecified entropion of right eye, unspecified eyelid

H02.004 Unspecified entropion of left upper eyelid

H02.005 Unspecified entropion of left lower eyelid

H02.006 Unspecified entropion of left eye, unspecified eyelid

H02.009 Unspecified entropion of unspecified eye, unspecified eyelid

● H02.01 Cicatricial entropion of eyelid
Scar

H02.011 Cicatricial entropion of right upper eyelid

H02.012 Cicatricial entropion of right lower eyelid

H02.013 Cicatricial entropion of right eye, unspecified eyelid

H02.014 Cicatricial entropion of left upper eyelid

H02.015 Cicatricial entropion of left lower eyelid

H02.016 Cicatricial entropion of left eye, unspecified eyelid

H02.019 Cicatricial entropion of unspecified eye, unspecified eyelid

● H02.02 Mechanical entropion of eyelid
Turning inward (inversion) of eyelid margin due to lack of support

H02.021 Mechanical entropion of right upper eyelid

H02.022 Mechanical entropion of right lower eyelid

H02.023 Mechanical entropion of right eye, unspecified eyelid

H02.024 Mechanical entropion of left upper eyelid

H02.025 Mechanical entropion of left lower eyelid

H02.026 Mechanical entropion of left eye, unspecified eyelid

H02.029 Mechanical entropion of unspecified eye, unspecified eyelid

● H02.03 Senile entropion of eyelid
Turning inward (inversion) of eyelid margin due to aging

H02.031 Senile entropion of right upper eyelid

H02.032 Senile entropion of right lower eyelid

H02.033 Senile entropion of right eye, unspecified eyelid

H02.034 Senile entropion of left upper eyelid

H02.035 Senile entropion of left lower eyelid

H02.036 Senile entropion of left eye, unspecified eyelid

H02.039 Senile entropion of unspecified eye, unspecified eyelid

● H02.04 Spastic entropion of eyelid
Turning inward (inversion) of eyelid margin caused by spasm of muscle

H02.041 Spastic entropion of right upper eyelid

H02.042 Spastic entropion of right lower eyelid

H02.043 Spastic entropion of right eye, unspecified eyelid

H02.044 Spastic entropion of left upper eyelid

H02.045 Spastic entropion of left lower eyelid

H02.046 Spastic entropion of left eye, unspecified eyelid

H02.049 Spastic entropion of unspecified eye, unspecified eyelid

● H02.05 Trichiasis without entropian
Ingrowing hairs of eyelashes

H02.051 Trichiasis without entropian right upper eyelid

H02.052 Trichiasis without entropian right lower eyelid

H02.053 Trichiasis without entropian right eye, unspecified eyelid

H02.054 Trichiasis without entropian left upper eyelid

H02.055 Trichiasis without entropian left lower eyelid

H02.056 Trichiasis without entropian left eye, unspecified eyelid

H02.059 Trichiasis without entropian unspecified eye, unspecified eyelid

950

● Unacceptable First-Listed Diagnosis   ● Use Additional Character(s)   ▢ Unspecified   **OGCR** Official Guidelines for Coding and Reporting
🅒 Complication\Comorbidity   🅜 Major C\C   Excludes 1   Excludes 2   Includes   Use additional   Code first   Code also

CHAPTER 7 (H00-H59)

● **H02.1　Ectropion of eyelid**
　　　Eversion (pulling away) of eyelid

　● **H02.10　Unspecified ectropion of eyelid**

　　　▪ H02.101　Unspecified ectropion of right upper eyelid

　　　▪ H02.102　Unspecified ectropion of right lower eyelid

　　　▪ H02.103　Unspecified ectropion of right eye, unspecified eyelid

　　　▪ H02.104　Unspecified ectropion of left upper eyelid

　　　▪ H02.105　Unspecified ectropion of left lower eyelid

　　　▪ H02.106　Unspecified ectropion of left eye, unspecified eyelid

　　　▪ H02.109　Unspecified ectropion of unspecified eye, unspecified eyelid

　● **H02.11　Cicatricial ectropion of eyelid**
　　　　Pulling of eyelid down and away from eye due to scar or tightening

　　　H02.111　Cicatricial ectropion of right upper eyelid

　　　H02.112　Cicatricial ectropion of right lower eyelid

　　　▪ H02.113　Cicatricial ectropion of right eye, unspecified eyelid

　　　H02.114　Cicatricial ectropion of left upper eyelid

　　　H02.115　Cicatricial ectropion of left lower eyelid

　　　▪ H02.116　Cicatricial ectropion of left eye, unspecified eyelid

　　　▪ H02.119　Cicatricial ectropion of unspecified eye, unspecified eyelid

　● **H02.12　Mechanical ectropion of eyelid**
　　　　Eversion (pulling away) of eyelid due to lack of support

　　　H02.121　Mechanical ectropion of right upper eyelid

　　　H02.122　Mechanical ectropion of right lower eyelid

　　　▪ H02.123　Mechanical ectropion of right eye, unspecified eyelid

　　　H02.124　Mechanical ectropion of left upper eyelid

　　　H02.125　Mechanical ectropion of left lower eyelid

　　　▪ H02.126　Mechanical ectropion of left eye, unspecified eyelid

　　　▪ H02.129　Mechanical ectropion of unspecified eye, unspecified eyelid

　● **H02.13　Senile ectropion of eyelid**
　　　　Eversion (pulling away) of eyelid due to age

　　　H02.131　Senile ectropion of right upper eyelid

　　　H02.132　Senile ectropion of right lower eyelid

　　　▪ H02.133　Senile ectropion of right eye, unspecified eyelid

　　　H02.134　Senile ectropion of left upper eyelid

　　　H02.135　Senile ectropion of left lower eyelid

　　　▪ H02.136　Senile ectropion of left eye, unspecified eyelid

　　　▪ H02.139　Senile ectropion of unspecified eye, unspecified eyelid

　● **H02.14　Spastic ectropion of eyelid**
　　　　Eversion (pulling away) of eyelid due to tonic muscle spasm

　　　H02.141　Spastic ectropion of right upper eyelid

　　　H02.142　Spastic ectropion of right lower eyelid

　　　▪ H02.143　Spastic ectropion of right eye, unspecified eyelid

　　　H02.144　Spastic ectropion of left upper eyelid

　　　H02.145　Spastic ectropion of left lower eyelid

　　　▪ H02.146　Spastic ectropion of left eye, unspecified eyelid

　　　▪ H02.149　Spastic ectropion of unspecified eye, unspecified eyelid

● **H02.2　Lagophthalmos**
　　　Condition in which eye cannot completely close

　● **H02.20　Unspecified lagophthalmos**

　　　▪ H02.201　Unspecified lagophthalmos right upper eyelid

　　　▪ H02.202　Unspecified lagophthalmos right lower eyelid

　　　▪ H02.203　Unspecified lagophthalmos right eye, unspecified eyelid

　　　▪ H02.204　Unspecified lagophthalmos left upper eyelid

　　　▪ H02.205　Unspecified lagophthalmos left lower eyelid

　　　▪ H02.206　Unspecified lagophthalmos left eye, unspecified eyelid

　　　▪ H02.209　Unspecified lagophthalmos unspecified eye, unspecified eyelid

　● **H02.21　Cicatricial lagophthalmos**
　　　　Upper or lower eyelid does not close due to scar or tightening
　　　　Acute chemical conjunctivitis

　　　　Code first (T51-T65) to identify chemical and intent

　　　　| **Excludes1** | burn and corrosion of eye and adnexa (T26.-) |

　　　H02.211　Cicatricial lagophthalmos right upper eyelid

　　　H02.212　Cicatricial lagophthalmos right lower eyelid

　　　▪ H02.213　Cicatricial lagophthalmos right eye, unspecified eyelid

　　　H02.214　Cicatricial lagophthalmos left upper eyelid

　　　H02.215　Cicatricial lagophthalmos left lower eyelid

　　　▪ H02.216　Cicatricial lagophthalmos left eye, unspecified eyelid

　　　▪ H02.219　Cicatricial lagophthalmos unspecified eye, unspecified eyelid

　● **H02.22　Mechanical lagophthalmos**
　　　　Inability to close lids due to structural disorder

　　　H02.221　Mechanical lagophthalmos right upper eyelid

● Unacceptable First-Listed Diagnosis　　　● Use Additional Character(s)　　　▪ Unspecified　　　**OGCR** Official Guidelines for Coding and Reporting

🔖 Complication\Comorbidity　　🔖 Major C\C　　| Excludes 1 |　| Excludes 2 |　　▪ Includes　　Use additional　　Code first　　Code also

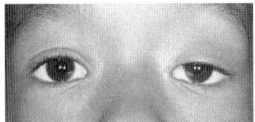

Figure 7-3 Piosis of eyelid. (From Yanoff: Ophthalmology, 2nd ed. 2004, Mosby, Inc.)

Item 7—1 Ptosis of eyelid is drooping of the upper eyelid over the pupil when the eyes are fully opened resulting from nerve or muscle damage, which may require surgical correction.

H02.222 Mechanical lagophthalmos right lower eyelid

H02.223 Mechanical lagophthalmos right eye, unspecified eyelid

H02.224 Mechanical lagophthalmos left upper eyelid

H02.225 Mechanical lagophthalmos left lower eyelid

H02.226 Mechanical lagophthalmos left eye, unspecified eyelid

H02.229 Mechanical lagophthalmos unspecified eye, unspecified eyelid

● H02.23 Paralytic lagophthalmos
Eyelids do not close due to paralysis

H02.231 Paralytic lagophthalmos right upper eyelid

H02.232 Paralytic lagophthalmos right lower eyelid

H02.233 Paralytic lagophthalmos right eye, unspecified eyelid

H02.234 Paralytic lagophthalmos left upper eyelid

H02.235 Paralytic lagophthalmos left lower eyelid

H02.236 Paralytic lagophthalmos left eye, unspecified eyelid

H02.239 Paralytic lagophthalmos unspecified eye, unspecified eyelid

(See Plate 81, middle, on page NAP-17.)

● H02.3 Blepharochalasis
Relaxation of skin of eyelid, due to atrophy of intercellular tissue
Pseudoptosis

H02.30 Blepharochalasis unspecified eye, unspecified eyelid

H02.31 Blepharochalasis right upper eyelid

H02.32 Blepharochalasis right lower eyelid

H02.33 Blepharochalasis right eye, unspecified eyelid

H02.34 Blepharochalasis left upper eyelid

H02.35 Blepharochalasis left lower eyelid

H02.36 Blepharochalasis left eye, unspecified eyelid

● H02.4 Ptosis of eyelid
Falling forward, drooping, sagging of eyelid

● H02.40 Unspecified ptosis of eyelid

H02.401 Unspecified ptosis of right eyelid

H02.402 Unspecified ptosis of left eyelid

H02.403 Unspecified ptosis of bilateral eyelids

H02.409 Unspecified ptosis of unspecified eyelid

● H02.41 Mechanical ptosis of eyelid

H02.411 Mechanical ptosis of right eyelid

H02.412 Mechanical ptosis of left eyelid

H02.413 Mechanical ptosis of bilateral eyelids

H02.419 Mechanical ptosis of unspecified eyelid

● H02.42 Myogenic ptosis of eyelid

H02.421 Myogenic ptosis of right eyelid

H02.422 Myogenic ptosis of left eyelid

H02.423 Myogenic ptosis of bilateral eyelids

H02.429 Myogenic ptosis of unspecified eyelid

● H02.43 Paralytic ptosis of eyelid
Neurogenic ptosis of eyelid

H02.431 Paralytic ptosis of right eyelid

H02.432 Paralytic ptosis of left eyelid

H02.433 Paralytic ptosis of bilateral eyelids

H02.439 Paralytic ptosis unspecified eyelid

● H02.5 Other disorders affecting eyelid function

Excludes2 blepharospasm (G24.5)
organic tic (G25.69)
psychogenic tic (F95.-)

● H02.51 Abnormal innervation syndrome

H02.511 Abnormal innervation syndrome right upper eyelid

H02.512 Abnormal innervation syndrome right lower eyelid

H02.513 Abnormal innervation syndrome right eye, unspecified eyelid

H02.514 Abnormal innervation syndrome left upper eyelid

H02.515 Abnormal innervation syndrome left lower eyelid

H02.516 Abnormal innervation syndrome left eye, unspecified eyelid

H02.519 Abnormal innervation syndrome unspecified eye, unspecified eyelid

● H02.52 Blepharophimosis
Drooping of eyelid with reduced lid size
Ankyloblepharon

H02.521 Blepharophimosis right upper eyelid

H02.522 Blepharophimosis right lower eyelid

H02.523 Blepharophimosis right eye, unspecified eyelid

H02.524 Blepharophimosis left upper eyelid

H02.525 Blepharophimosis left lower eyelid

H02.526 Blepharophimosis left eye, unspecified eyelid

H02.529 Blepharophimosis unspecified eye, unspecified lid

● Unacceptable First-Listed Diagnosis   ● Use Additional Character(s)   ▪ Unspecified   **OGCR** Official Guidelines for Coding and Reporting
🖙 Complication\Comorbidity   🖙 Major C\C   Excludes 1   Excludes 2   Includes   Use additional   Code first   Code also

- H02.53 **Eyelid retraction**
  Eyelid lag

  H02.531 **Eyelid retraction right upper eyelid**

  H02.532 **Eyelid retraction right lower eyelid**

  H02.533 **Eyelid retraction right eye, unspecified eyelid**

  H02.534 **Eyelid retraction left upper eyelid**

  H02.535 **Eyelid retraction left lower eyelid**

  H02.536 **Eyelid retraction left eye, unspecified eyelid**

  H02.539 **Eyelid retraction unspecified eye, unspecified lid**

  H02.59 **Other disorders affecting eyelid function**
  Deficient blink reflex
  Sensory disorders

- H02.6 **Xanthelasma of eyelid**
  Yellow-to-orange patches or pimples clustered together on eyelid

  H02.60 **Xanthelasma of unspecified eye, unspecified eyelid**

  H02.61 **Xanthelasma of right upper eyelid**

  H02.62 **Xanthelasma of right lower eyelid**

  H02.63 **Xanthelasma of right eye, unspecified eyelid**

  H02.64 **Xanthelasma of left upper eyelid**

  H02.65 **Xanthelasma of left lower eyelid**

  H02.66 **Xanthelasma of left eye, unspecified eyelid**

- H02.7 **Other and unspecified degenerative disorders of eyelid and periocular area**

  H02.70 **Unspecified degenerative disorders of eyelid and periocular area**

  - H02.71 **Chloasma of eyelid and periocular area**
    Dyspigmentation of eyelid
    Hyperpigmentation of eyelid

    H02.711 **Chloasma of right upper eyelid and periocular area**

    H02.712 **Chloasma of right lower eyelid and periocular area**

    H02.713 **Chloasma of right eye, unspecified eyelid and periocular area**

    H02.714 **Chloasma of left upper eyelid and periocular area**

    H02.715 **Chloasma of left lower eyelid and periocular area**

    H02.716 **Chloasma of left eye, unspecified eyelid and periocular area**

    H02.719 **Chloasma of unspecified eye, unspecified eyelid and periocular area**

  - H02.72 **Madarosis of eyelid and periocular area**
    Loss of eyelashes and/or eyebrows
    Hypotrichosis of eyelid

    H02.721 **Madarosis of right upper eyelid and periocular area**

    H02.722 **Madarosis of right lower eyelid and periocular area**

    H02.723 **Madarosis of right eye, unspecified eyelid and periocular area**

    H02.724 **Madarosis of left upper eyelid and periocular area**

    H02.725 **Madarosis of left lower eyelid and periocular area**

    H02.726 **Madarosis of left eye, unspecified eyelid and periocular area**

    H02.729 **Madarosis of unspecified eye, unspecified eyelid and periocular area**

- H02.73 **Vitiligo of eyelid and periocular area**
  Skin pigmentation disease characterized by white patches
  Hypopigmentation of eyelid

  H02.731 **Vitiligo of right upper eyelid and periocular area**

  H02.732 **Vitiligo of right lower eyelid and periocular area**

  H02.733 **Vitiligo of right eye, unspecified eyelid and periocular area**

  H02.734 **Vitiligo of left upper eyelid and periocular area**

  H02.735 **Vitiligo of left lower eyelid and periocular area**

  H02.736 **Vitiligo of left eye, unspecified eyelid and periocular area**

  H02.739 **Vitiligo of unspecified eye, unspecified eyelid and periocular area**

- H02.79 **Other degenerative disorders of eyelid and periocular area**

- H02.8 **Other specified disorders of eyelid**

  - H02.81 **Retained foreign body in eyelid**

    Excludes1 laceration of eyelid with foreign body (S01.12-)
    retained intraocular foreign body (H44.6-, H44.7-)
    superficial foreign body of eyelid and periocular area (S00.25-)

    H02.811 **Retained foreign body in right upper eyelid**

    H02.812 **Retained foreign body in right lower eyelid**

    H02.813 **Retained foreign body in right eye, unspecified eyelid**

    H02.814 **Retained foreign body in left upper eyelid**

    H02.815 **Retained foreign body in left lower eyelid**

    H02.816 **Retained foreign body in left eye, unspecified eyelid**

    H02.819 **Retained foreign body in unspecified eye, unspecified eyelid**

  - H02.82 **Cysts of eyelid**
    Sebaceous cyst of eyelid

    H02.821 **Cysts of right upper eyelid**

    H02.822 **Cysts of right lower eyelid**

    H02.823 **Cysts of right eye, unspecified eyelid**

    H02.824 **Cysts of left upper eyelid**

    H02.825 **Cysts of left lower eyelid**

    H02.826 **Cysts of left eye, unspecified eyelid**

    H02.829 **Cysts of unspecified eye, unspecified eyelid**

- Unacceptable First-Listed Diagnosis ● Use Additional Character(s) ▪ Unspecified **OGCR** Official Guidelines for Coding and Reporting

▸ Complication\Comorbidity ▹ Major C\C [Excludes 1] [Excludes 2] Includes Use additional Code first Code also

CHAPTER 7 (H00-H59)

953

● **H02.83 Dermatochalasis of eyelid**
   Skin is inelastic and hangs loosely in folds

　　H02.831 Dermatochalasis of right upper eyelid

　　H02.832 Dermatochalasis of right lower eyelid

　　H02.833 Dermatochalasis of right eye, unspecified eyelid

　　H02.834 Dermatochalasis of left upper eyelid

　　H02.835 Dermatochalasis of left lower eyelid

　　H02.836 Dermatochalasis of left eye, unspecified eyelid

　　H02.839 Dermatochalasis of unspecified eye, unspecified eyelid

● **H02.84 Edema of eyelid**
   Hyperemia of eyelid

　　H02.841 Edema of right upper eyelid

　　H02.842 Edema of right lower eyelid

　　H02.843 Edema of right eye, unspecified eyelid

　　H02.844 Edema of left upper eyelid

　　H02.845 Edema of left lower eyelid

　　H02.846 Edema of left eye, unspecified eyelid

　　H02.849 Edema of unspecified eye, unspecified eyelid

● **H02.85 Elephantiasis of eyelid**
   Massive secondary lymphedema with hypertrophy of skin and subcutaneous tissues (pachyderma)

　　H02.851 Elephantiasis of right upper eyelid

　　H02.852 Elephantiasis of right lower eyelid

　　H02.853 Elephantiasis of right eye, unspecified eyelid

　　H02.854 Elephantiasis of left upper eyelid

　　H02.855 Elephantiasis of left lower eyelid

　　H02.856 Elephantiasis of left eye, unspecified eyelid

　　H02.859 Elephantiasis of unspecified eye, unspecified eyelid

● **H02.86 Hypertrichosis of eyelid**
   Excessive growth of hair

　　H02.861 Hypertrichosis of right upper eyelid

　　H02.862 Hypertrichosis of right lower eyelid

　　H02.863 Hypertrichosis of right eye, unspecified eyelid

　　H02.864 Hypertrichosis of left upper eyelid

　　H02.865 Hypertrichosis of left lower eyelid

　　H02.866 Hypertrichosis of left eye, unspecified eyelid

　　H02.869 Hypertrichosis of unspecified eye, unspecified eyelid

● **H02.87 Vascular anomalies of eyelid**

　　H02.871 Vascular anomalies of right upper eyelid

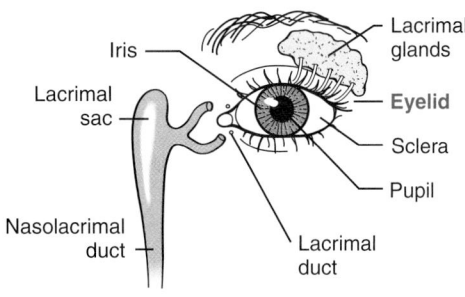

Figure 7-4 Lacrimal apparatus. (From Buck CJ: Step-by-Step Medical Coding. St. Louis, WB Saunders, 2010, p 645.)

(See Plate 82 on page NAP-19.)

　　H02.872 Vascular anomalies of right lower eyelid

　　H02.873 Vascular anomalies of right eye, unspecified eyelid

　　H02.874 Vascular anomalies of left upper eyelid

　　H02.875 Vascular anomalies of left lower eyelid

　　H02.876 Vascular anomalies of left eye, unspecified eyelid

　　H02.879 Vascular anomalies of unspecified eye, unspecified eyelid

　H02.89 Other specified disorders of eyelid
   Hemorrhage of eyelid

H02.9 Unspecified disorder of eyelid
   Disorder of eyelid NOS

● **H04 Disorders of lacrimal system**

　　Excludes1　congenital malformations of lacrimal system (Q10.4-Q10.6)

● **H04.0 Dacryoadenitis**
   Inflammation of lacrimal gland

● **H04.00 Unspecified dacryoadenitis**

　　H04.001 Unspecified dacryoadenitis, right lacrimal gland

　　H04.002 Unspecified dacryoadenitis, left lacrimal gland

　　H04.003 Unspecified dacryoadenitis, bilateral lacrimal glands

　　H04.009 Unspecified dacryoadenitis, unspecified lacrimal gland

● **H04.01 Acute dacryoadenitis**

　　H04.011 Acute dacryoadenitis, right lacrimal gland

　　H04.012 Acute dacryoadenitis, left lacrimal gland

　　H04.013 Acute dacryoadenitis, bilateral lacrimal glands

　　H04.019 Acute dacryoadenitis, unspecified lacrimal gland

● **H04.02 Chronic dacryoadenitis**

　　H04.021 Chronic dacryoadenitis, right lacrimal gland

　　H04.022 Chronic dacryoadenitis, left lacrimal gland

CHAPTER 7 (H00-H59)

954

● Unacceptable First-Listed Diagnosis　　● Use Additional Character(s)　　■ Unspecified　　**OGCR** Official Guidelines for Coding and Reporting
🅒 Complication\Comorbidity　🅜 Major C\C　 Excludes 1 　 Excludes 2 　 Includes 　 Use additional 　 Code first 　 Code also

H04.023   Chronic dacryoadenitis, bilateral lacrimal gland

■H04.029   Chronic dacryoadenitis, unspecified lacrimal gland

● H04.03   Chronic enlargement of lacrimal gland

H04.031   Chronic enlargement of right lacrimal gland

H04.032   Chronic enlargement of left lacrimal gland

H04.033   Chronic enlargement of bilateral lacrimal glands

■H04.039   Chronic enlargement of unspecified lacrimal gland

● H04.1   Other disorders of lacrimal gland

● H04.11   Dacryops
Watery eye or distention of lacrimal duct due to fluid

H04.111   Dacryops of right lacrimal gland

H04.112   Dacryops of left lacrimal gland

H04.113   Dacryops of bilateral lacrimal glands

■H04.119   Dacryops of unspecified lacrimal gland

● H04.12   Dry eye syndrome
Tear film insufficiency, NOS

H04.121   Dry eye syndrome of right lacrimal gland

H04.122   Dry eye syndrome of left lacrimal gland

H04.123   Dry eye syndrome of bilateral lacrimal glands

■H04.129   Dry eye syndrome of unspecified lacrimal gland

● H04.13   Lacrimal cyst
Lacrimal cystic degeneration

H04.131   Lacrimal cyst right lacrimal gland

H04.132   Lacrimal cyst left lacrimal gland

H04.133   Lacrimal cyst bilateral lacrimal glands

■H04.139   Lacrimal cyst unspecified lacrimal gland

● H04.14   Primary lacrimal gland atrophy

H04.141   Right primary lacrimal gland atrophy

H04.142   Left primary lacrimal gland atrophy

H04.143   Bilateral primary lacrimal gland atrophy

■H04.149   Unspecified primary lacrimal gland atrophy

● H04.15   Secondary lacrimal gland atrophy

H04.151   Right secondary lacrimal gland atrophy

H04.152   Left secondary lacrimal gland atrophy

H04.153   Bilateral secondary lacrimal gland atrophy

■H04.159   Unspecified secondary lacrimal gland atrophy

● H04.16   Lacrimal gland dislocation

H04.161   Right lacrimal gland dislocation

H04.162   Left lacrimal gland dislocation

H04.163   Bilateral lacrimal gland dislocation

■H04.169   Unspecified lacrimal gland dislocation

H04.19   Other disorders of lacrimal gland

● H04.2   Epiphora
Overflow of tears due to stricture of lacrimal passages; AKA lacrimation

● H04.20   Unspecified epiphora

H04.201   Epiphora, right side

H04.202   Epiphora, left side

H04.203   Epiphora, bilateral

■H04.209   Epiphora, unspecified side

● H04.21   Epiphora due to excess lacrimation

H04.211   Epiphora due to excess lacrimation, right side

H04.212   Epiphora due to excess lacrimation, left side

H04.213   Epiphora due to excess lacrimation, bilateral

■H04.219   Epiphora due to excess lacrimation, unspecified side

● H04.22   Epiphora due to insufficient drainage

H04.221   Epiphora due to insufficient drainage, right side

H04.222   Epiphora due to insufficient drainage, left side

H04.223   Epiphora due to insufficient drainage, bilateral

■H04.229   Epiphora due to insufficient drainage, unspecified side

● H04.3   Acute and unspecified inflammation of lacrimal passages

Excludes 1   neonatal dacryocystitis (P39.1)

● H04.30   Unspecified dacryocystitis

■H04.301   Unspecified dacryocystitis of right lacrimal passage

■H04.302   Unspecified dacryocystitis of left lacrimal passage

■H04.303   Unspecified dacryocystitis of bilateral lacrimal passages

■H04.309   Unspecified dacryocystitis of unspecified lacrimal passage

● H04.31   Phlegmonous dacryocystitis
Cellulites of lacrimal sac

H04.311   Phlegmonous dacryocystitis of right lacrimal passage

H04.312   Phlegmonous dacryocystitis of left lacrimal passage

H04.313   Phlegmonous dacryocystitis of bilateral lacrimal passages

■H04.319   Phlegmonous dacryocystitis of unspecified lacrimal passage

● H04.32   Acute dacryocystitis
Acute dacryopericystitis

H04.321   Acute dacryocystitis of right lacrimal passage

H04.322   Acute dacryocystitis of left lacrimal passage

H04.323   Acute dacryocystitis of bilateral lacrimal passages

■H04.329   Acute dacryocystitis of unspecified lacrimal passage

● Unacceptable First-Listed Diagnosis   ● Use Additional Character(s)   ■ Unspecified   **OGCR** Official Guidelines for Coding and Reporting

🐾 Complication\Comorbidity   🐾 Major C\C   Excludes 1   Excludes 2   Includes   Use additional   Code first   Code also   955

CHAPTER 7 (H00-H59)

- **H04.33**   Acute lacrimal canaliculitis
  - H04.331   Acute lacrimal canaliculitis of right lacrimal passage
  - H04.332   Acute lacrimal canaliculitis of left lacrimal passage
  - H04.333   Acute lacrimal canaliculitis of bilateral lacrimal passages
  - H04.339   Acute lacrimal canaliculitis of unspecified lacrimal passage
- **H04.4**   Chronic inflammation of lacrimal passages
  - **H04.41**   Chronic dacryocystitis
    - *Inflammation of lacrimal sac*
    - H04.411   Chronic dacryocystitis of right lacrimal passage
    - H04.412   Chronic dacryocystitis of left lacrimal passage
    - H04.413   Chronic dacryocystitis of bilateral lacrimal passages
    - H04.419   Chronic dacryocystitis of unspecified lacrimal passage
  - **H04.42**   Chronic lacrimal canaliculitis
    - *Inflammation of lacrimal ducts*
    - H04.421   Chronic lacrimal canaliculitis of right lacrimal passage
    - H04.422   Chronic lacrimal canaliculitis of left lacrimal passage
    - H04.423   Chronic lacrimal canaliculitis of bilateral lacrimal passages
    - H04.429   Chronic lacrimal canaliculitis of unspecified lacrimal passage
  - **H04.43**   Chronic lacrimal mucocele
    - *Accumulation of mucous secretion*
    - H04.431   Chronic lacrimal mucocele of right lacrimal passage
    - H04.432   Chronic lacrimal mucocele of left lacrimal passage
    - H04.433   Chronic lacrimal mucocele of bilateral lacrimal passages
    - H04.439   Chronic lacrimal mucocele of unspecified lacrimal passage
- **H04.5**   Stenosis and insufficiency of lacrimal passages
  - **H04.51**   Dacryolith
    - *Concretion in lacrimal sac/duct; AKA lacrimal calculus*
    - H04.511   Dacryolith of right lacrimal passage
    - H04.512   Dacryolith of left lacrimal passage
    - H04.513   Dacryolith of bilateral lacrimal passages
    - H04.519   Dacryolith of unspecified lacrimal passage
  - **H04.52**   Eversion of lacrimal punctum
    - *Turning out of lacrimal drainage opening*
    - H04.521   Eversion of right lacrimal punctum
    - H04.522   Eversion of left lacrimal punctum
    - H04.523   Eversion of bilateral lacrimal punctum
    - H04.529   Eversion of unspecified lacrimal punctum

- **H04.53**   Neonatal obstruction of nasolacrimal duct
  - **Excludes1**   congenital stenosis and stricture of lacrimal duct (Q10.5)
  - H04.531   Neonatal obstruction of right nasolacrimal duct
  - H04.532   Neonatal obstruction of left nasolacrimal duct
  - H04.533   Neonatal obstruction of bilateral nasolacrimal duct
  - H04.539   Neonatal obstruction of unspecified nasolacrimal duct
- **H04.54**   Stenosis of lacrimal canaliculi
  - H04.541   Stenosis of right lacrimal canaliculi
  - H04.542   Stenosis of left lacrimal canaliculi
  - H04.543   Stenosis of bilateral lacrimal canaliculi
  - H04.549   Stenosis of unspecified lacrimal canaliculi
- **H04.55**   Acquired stenosis of nasolacrimal duct
  - H04.551   Acquired stenosis of right nasolacrimal duct
  - H04.552   Acquired stenosis of left nasolacrimal duct
  - H04.553   Acquired stenosis of bilateral nasolacrimal duct
  - H04.559   Acquired stenosis of unspecified nasolacrimal duct
- **H04.56**   Stenosis of lacrimal punctum
  - H04.561   Stenosis of right lacrimal punctum
  - H04.562   Stenosis of left lacrimal punctum
  - H04.563   Stenosis of bilateral lacrimal punctum
  - H04.569   Stenosis of unspecified lacrimal punctum
- **H04.57**   Stenosis of lacrimal sac
  - H04.571   Stenosis of right lacrimal sac
  - H04.572   Stenosis of left lacrimal sac
  - H04.573   Stenosis of bilateral lacrimal sac
  - H04.579   Stenosis of unspecified lacrimal sac
- **H04.6**   Other changes of lacrimal passages
  - **H04.61**   Lacrimal fistula
    - H04.611   Lacrimal fistula right lacrimal passage
    - H04.612   Lacrimal fistula left lacrimal passage
    - H04.613   Lacrimal fistula bilateral lacrimal passages
    - H04.619   Lacrimal fistula unspecified lacrimal passage
  - H04.69   Other changes of lacrimal passages
- **H04.8**   Other disorders of lacrimal system
  - **H04.81**   Granuloma of lacrimal passages
    - *Inflammatory response due to infectious or noninfectious agents*
    - H04.811   Granuloma of right lacrimal passage
    - H04.812   Granuloma of left lacrimal passage

● Unacceptable First-Listed Diagnosis   ● Use Additional Character(s)   ▣ Unspecified   **OGCR** Official Guidelines for Coding and Reporting
🝖 Complication\Comorbidity   🝖 Major C\C   Excludes 1   Excludes 2   Includes   Use additional   Code first   Code also

CHAPTER 7 (H00-H59)

H04.813 **Granuloma of bilateral lacrimal passages**

H04.819 **Granuloma of unspecified lacrimal passage**

H04.89 **Other disorders of lacrimal system**

H04.9 **Disorder of lacrimal system, unspecified**

● H05 **Disorders of orbit**
> **Excludes1** congenital malformation of orbit (Q10.7)

● H05.0 **Acute inflammation of orbit**

H05.00 **Unspecified acute inflammation of orbit**

● H05.01 **Cellulitis of orbit**
> *Infection of soft tissue of orbit*
> Abscess of orbit

H05.011 **Cellulitis of right orbit** 🦠

H05.012 **Cellulitis of left orbit** 🦠

H05.013 **Cellulitis of bilateral orbits** 🦠

H05.019 **Cellulitis of unspecified orbit** 🦠

● H05.02 **Osteomyelitis of orbit**
> *Infection of boney orbit of eye*

H05.021 **Osteomyelitis of right orbit** 🦠

H05.022 **Osteomyelitis of left orbit** 🦠

H05.023 **Osteomyelitis of bilateral orbits** 🦠

H05.029 **Osteomyelitis of unspecified orbit** 🦠

● H05.03 **Periostitis of orbit**
> *Inflammation of periosteum (membrane covering bone surface)*

H05.031 **Periostitis of right orbit** 🦠

H05.032 **Periostitis of left orbit** 🦠

H05.033 **Periostitis of bilateral orbits** 🦠

H05.039 **Periostitis of unspecified orbit** 🦠

● H05.04 **Tenonitis of orbit**
> *Inflammation of tenon capsule (space enclosing fascia of Tenon between eyeball and fat of orbit)*

H05.041 **Tenonitis of right orbit**

H05.042 **Tenonitis of left orbit**

H05.043 **Tenonitis of bilateral orbits**

H05.049 **Tenonitis of unspecified orbit**

● H05.1 **Chronic inflammatory disorders of orbit**

H05.10 **Unspecified chronic inflammatory disorders of orbit**

● H05.11 **Granuloma of orbit**
> Pseudotumor (inflammatory) of orbit

H05.111 **Granuloma of right orbit**

H05.112 **Granuloma of left orbit**

H05.113 **Granuloma of bilateral orbits**

H05.119 **Granuloma of unspecified orbit**

● H05.12 **Orbital myositis**
> *Inflammation of extraocular muscles of orbit*

H05.121 **Orbital myositis, right orbit**

H05.122 **Orbital myositis, left orbit**

H05.123 **Orbital myositis, bilateral**

H05.129 **Orbital myositis, unspecified orbit**

● H05.2 **Exophthalmic conditions**
> *Bulging eyes*

H05.20 **Unspecified exophthalmos**

● H05.21 **Displacement (lateral) of globe**

H05.211 **Displacement (lateral) of globe, right eye**

H05.212 **Displacement (lateral) of globe, left eye**

H05.213 **Displacement (lateral) of globe, bilateral**

H05.219 **Displacement (lateral) of globe, unspecified eye**

● H05.22 **Edema of orbit**
> Orbital congestion

H05.221 **Edema of right orbit**

H05.222 **Edema of left orbit**

H05.223 **Edema of bilateral orbit**

H05.229 **Edema of unspecified orbit**

● H05.23 **Hemorrhage of orbit**

H05.231 **Hemorrhage of right orbit**

H05.232 **Hemorrhage of left orbit**

H05.233 **Hemorrhage of bilateral orbit**

H05.239 **Hemorrhage of unspecified orbit**

● H05.24 **Constant exophthalmos**
> *Constant bulging eyes, often symptom of Graves disease*

H05.241 **Constant exophthalmos, right eye**

H05.242 **Constant exophthalmos, left eye**

H05.243 **Constant exophthalmos, bilateral**

H05.249 **Constant exophthalmos, unspecified eye**

● H05.25 **Intermittent exophthalmos**
> *Intermittent bulging eye occurring with bending forward or sharp turning of head*

H05.251 **Intermittent exophthalmos, right eye**

H05.252 **Intermittent exophthalmos, left eye**

H05.253 **Intermittent exophthalmos, bilateral**

H05.259 **Intermittent exophthalmos, unspecified eye**

● H05.26 **Pulsating exophthalmos**
> *Bulging eyes with pulsation and bruit, often due to aneurysm pushing eye forward*

H05.261 **Pulsating exophthalmos, right eye**

H05.262 **Pulsating exophthalmos, left eye**

H05.263 **Pulsating exophthalmos, bilateral**

H05.269 **Pulsating exophthalmos, unspecified eye**

● H05.3 **Deformity of orbit**
> **Excludes1** congenital deformity of orbit (Q10.7)
> hypertelorism (Q75.2)

H05.30 **Unspecified deformity of orbit**

● H05.31 **Atrophy of orbit**

H05.311 **Atrophy of right orbit**

H05.312 **Atrophy of left orbit**

H05.313 **Atrophy of bilateral orbit**

H05.319 **Atrophy of unspecified orbit**

● H05.32 **Deformity of orbit due to bone disease**
> Code also associated bone disease

H05.321 **Deformity of right orbit due to bone disease**

● Unacceptable First-Listed Diagnosis   ● Use Additional Character(s)   ▪ Unspecified   **OGCR** Official Guidelines for Coding and Reporting
🦠 Complication\Comorbidity   🦠 Major C\C   Excludes 1   Excludes 2   Includes   Use additional   Code first   Code also

CHAPTER 7 (H00-H59)

957

           H05.322   Deformity of left orbit due to bone disease

           H05.323   Deformity of bilateral orbits due to bone disease

           H05.329   Deformity of unspecified orbit due to bone disease

      ● H05.33   Deformity of orbit due to trauma or surgery

           H05.331   Deformity of right orbit due to trauma or surgery

           H05.332   Deformity of left orbit due to trauma or surgery

           H05.333   Deformity of bilateral orbits due to trauma or surgery

           H05.339   Deformity of unspecified orbit due to trauma or surgery

      ● H05.34   Enlargement of orbit

           H05.341   Enlargement of right orbit

           H05.342   Enlargement of left orbit

           H05.343   Enlargement of bilateral orbits

           H05.349   Enlargement of unspecified orbit

      ● H05.35   Exostosis of orbit

           H05.351   Exostosis of right orbit

           H05.352   Exostosis of left orbit

           H05.353   Exostosis of bilateral orbits

           H05.359   Exostosis of unspecified orbit

    ● H05.4   Enophthalmos
         Recessed eyeball into orbit

      ● H05.40   Unspecified enophthalmos

           H05.401   Unspecified enophthalmos, right eye

           H05.402   Unspecified enophthalmos, left eye

           H05.403   Unspecified enophthalmos, bilateral

           H05.409   Unspecified enophthalmos, unspecified eye

      ● H05.41   Enophthalmos due to atrophy of orbital tissue

           H05.411   Enophthalmos due to atrophy of orbital tissue, right eye

           H05.412   Enophthalmos due to atrophy of orbital tissue, left eye

           H05.413   Enophthalmos due to atrophy of orbital tissue, bilateral

           H05.419   Enophthalmos due to atrophy of orbital tissue, unspecified eye

      ● H05.42   Enophthalmos due to trauma or surgery

           H05.421   Enophthalmos due to trauma or surgery, right eye

           H05.422   Enophthalmos due to trauma or surgery, left eye

           H05.423   Enophthalmos due to trauma or surgery, bilateral

           H05.429   Enophthalmos due to trauma or surgery, unspecified eye

    ● H05.5   Retained (old) foreign body following penetrating wound of orbit
         Retrobulbar foreign body

         | Excludes1 | current penetrating wound of orbit (S05.4-)

         | Excludes2 | retained foreign body of eyelid (H02.81-)
                   retained intraocular foreign body (H44.6-, H44.7-)

           H05.50   Retained (old) foreign body following penetrating wound of unspecified orbit

           H05.51   Retained (old) foreign body following penetrating wound of right orbit

           H05.52   Retained (old) foreign body following penetrating wound of left orbit

           H05.53   Retained (old) foreign body following penetrating wound of bilateral orbits

    ● H05.8   Other disorders of orbit

      ● H05.81   Cyst of orbit
           Encephalocele of orbit

           H05.811   Cyst of right orbit

           H05.812   Cyst of left orbit

           H05.813   Cyst of bilateral orbits

           H05.819   Cyst of unspecified orbit

      ● H05.82   Myopathy of extraocular muscles
           Weakness of muscles of eye

           H05.821   Myopathy of extraocular muscles, right orbit

           H05.822   Myopathy of extraocular muscles, left orbit

           H05.823   Myopathy of extraocular muscles, bilateral

           H05.829   Myopathy of extraocular muscles, unspecified orbit

      H05.89   Other disorders of orbit

    H05.9   Unspecified disorder of orbit

DISORDERS OF CONJUNCTIVA (H10-H11)

(See Plate 81, upper, on page NAP-18.)

● **H10   Conjunctivitis**
    Inflammation of membrane of the inside of the eyelid or on surface of eye (conjunctiva)

    | Excludes1 | keratoconjunctivitis (H16.2-)

    ● H10.0   Mucopurulent conjunctivitis

      ● H10.01   Acute follicular conjunctivitis

           H10.011   Acute follicular conjunctivitis, right eye

           H10.012   Acute follicular conjunctivitis, left eye

           H10.013   Acute follicular conjunctivitis, bilateral

           H10.019   Acute follicular conjunctivitis, unspecified eye

      ● H10.02   Other mucopurulent conjunctivitis

           H10.021   Other mucopurulent conjunctivitis, right eye

           H10.022   Other mucopurulent conjunctivitis, left eye

           H10.023   Other mucopurulent conjunctivitis, bilateral

           H10.029   Other mucopurulent conjunctivitis, unspecified eye

    ● H10.1   Acute atopic conjunctivitis
         Acute papillary conjunctivitis

      H10.10   Acute atopic conjunctivitis, unspecified eye

      H10.11   Acute atopic conjunctivitis, right eye

      H10.12   Acute atopic conjunctivitis, left eye

      H10.13   Acute atopic conjunctivitis, bilateral

● Unacceptable First-Listed Diagnosis   ● Use Additional Character(s)   ■ Unspecified   **OGCR** Official Guidelines for Coding and Reporting
🅒 Complication\Comorbidity   🅒 Major C\C | Excludes 1 | | Excludes 2 | Includes   Use additional   Code first   Code also

- H10.2　Other acute conjunctivitis
  - H10.21　Acute toxic conjunctivitis
    - Acute chemical conjunctivitis
    - *Code first (T51-T65) to identify chemical and intent*
    - **Excludes1**　burn and corrosion of eye and adnexa (T26.-)
    - H10.211　Acute toxic conjunctivitis, right eye
    - H10.212　Acute toxic conjunctivitis, left eye
    - H10.213　Acute toxic conjunctivitis, bilateral
    - ■H10.219　Acute toxic conjunctivitis, unspecified eye
  - H10.22　Pseudomembranous conjunctivitis
    - H10.221　Pseudomembranous conjunctivitis, right eye
    - H10.222　Pseudomembranous conjunctivitis, left eye
    - H10.223　Pseudomembranous conjunctivitis, bilateral
    - ■H10.229　Pseudomembranous conjunctivitis, unspecified eye
  - H10.23　Serous conjunctivitis, except viral
    - **Excludes1**　viral conjunctivitis (B30.-)
    - H10.231　Serous conjunctivitis, except viral, right eye
    - H10.232　Serous conjunctivitis, except viral, left eye
    - H10.233　Serous conjunctivitis, except viral, bilateral
    - ■H10.239　Serous conjunctivitis, except viral, unspecified eye
- H10.3　Unspecified acute conjunctivitis
  - **Excludes1**　ophthalmia neonatorum NOS (P39.1)
  - ■H10.30　Unspecified acute conjunctivitis, unspecified eye
  - ■H10.31　Unspecified acute conjunctivitis, right eye
  - ■H10.32　Unspecified acute conjunctivitis, left eye
  - ■H10.33　Unspecified acute conjunctivitis, bilateral
- H10.4　Chronic conjunctivitis
  - H10.40　Unspecified chronic conjunctivitis
    - ■H10.401　Unspecified chronic conjunctivitis, right eye
    - ■H10.402　Unspecified chronic conjunctivitis, left eye
    - ■H10.403　Unspecified chronic conjunctivitis, bilateral
    - ■H10.409　Unspecified chronic conjunctivitis, unspecified eye
  - H10.41　Chronic giant papillary conjunctivitis
    - *Inflammation of membrane of the inside of the eyelid or on surface of eye often associated with contact lens wear*
    - H10.411　Chronic giant papillary conjunctivitis, right eye
    - H10.412　Chronic giant papillary conjunctivitis, left eye
    - H10.413　Chronic giant papillary conjunctivitis, bilateral
    - ■H10.419　Chronic giant papillary conjunctivitis, unspecified eye
  - H10.42　Simple chronic conjunctivitis
    - H10.421　Simple chronic conjunctivitis, right eye
    - H10.422　Simple chronic conjunctivitis, left eye
    - H10.423　Simple chronic conjunctivitis, bilateral
    - ■H10.429　Simple chronic conjunctivitis, unspecified eye
  - H10.43　Chronic follicular conjunctivitis
    - *Inflammation of membrane of the inside of the eyelid or on surface of eye due to topical medications or infection*
    - H10.431　Chronic follicular conjunctivitis, right eye
    - H10.432　Chronic follicular conjunctivitis, left eye
    - H10.433　Chronic follicular conjunctivitis, bilateral
    - ■H10.439　Chronic follicular conjunctivitis, unspecified eye
  - H10.44　Vernal conjunctivitis
    - *Affecting children, especially boys in which there are flattened papules with thick, gelatinous exudate on conjunctivae on inside of upper lid*
    - **Excludes1**　vernal keratoconjunctivitis with limbar and corneal involvement (H16.26-)
  - H10.45　Other chronic allergic conjunctivitis
- H10.5　Blepharoconjunctivitis
  - *Inflammation of eyelids and conjunctiva*
  - H10.50　Unspecified blepharoconjunctivitis
    - ■H10.501　Unspecified blepharoconjunctivitis, right eye
    - ■H10.502　Unspecified blepharoconjunctivitis, left eye
    - ■H10.503　Unspecified blepharoconjunctivitis, bilateral
    - ■H10.509　Unspecified blepharoconjunctivitis, unspecified eye
  - H10.51　Ligneous conjunctivitis
    - H10.511　Ligneous conjunctivitis, right eye
    - H10.512　Ligneous conjunctivitis, left eye
    - H10.513　Ligneous conjunctivitis, bilateral
    - ■H10.519　Ligneous conjunctivitis, unspecified eye
  - H10.52　Angular blepharoconjunctivitis
    - H10.521　Angular blepharoconjunctivitis, right eye
    - H10.522　Angular blepharoconjunctivitis, left eye
    - H10.523　Angular blepharoconjunctivitis, bilateral
    - ■H10.529　Angular blepharoconjunctivitis, unspecified eye
  - H10.53　Contact blepharoconjunctivitis
    - H10.531　Contact blepharoconjunctivitis, right eye
    - H10.532　Contact blepharoconjunctivitis, left eye
    - H10.533　Contact blepharoconjunctivitis, bilateral
    - ■H10.539　Contact blepharoconjunctivitis, unspecified eye

● Unacceptable First-Listed Diagnosis　　　● Use Additional Character(s)　　　■ Unspecified　　　**OGCR** Official Guidelines for Coding and Reporting

🜚 Complication\Comorbidity　　🜚 Major C\C　　Excludes 1　　Excludes 2　　Includes　　Use additional　　Code first　　Code also

959

CHAPTER 7 (H00-H59)

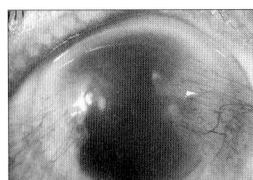

Figure 7-5   Double pterygium. Not both nasal and temporal pterygia in a 57-year-old farmer. (From Yanoff: Ophthalmology, 2nd ed. 2004, Mosby, Inc.)

Item 7–2   **Pterygium** is Greek for batlike. The condition is characterized by a membrane that extends from the limbus to the center of the cornea and resembles a wing.

● **H10.8   Other conjunctivitis**
    ● **H10.81   Pingueculitis**
       Inflammation of a yellow, raised thickening on the white of the eye associated with chronic dry eyes

       | Excludes1 | pinguecula (H11.15-)

       H10.811   Pingueculitis, right eye
       H10.812   Pingueculitis, left eye
       H10.813   Pingueculitis, bilateral
       ▪ H10.819   Pingueculitis, unspecified eye
    H10.89   Other conjunctivitis
    ▪ H10.9   Unspecified conjunctivitis

● **H11   Other disorders of conjunctiva**
    | Excludes1 | keratoconjunctivitis (H16.2-)

    ● **H11.0   Pterygium of eye**
       | Excludes1 | pseudopterygium (H11.81-)

       ● **H11.00   Unspecified pterygium of eye**
          ▪ H11.001   Unspecified pterygium of right eye
          ▪ H11.002   Unspecified pterygium of left eye
          ▪ H11.003   Unspecified pterygium of eye, bilateral
          ▪ H11.009   Unspecified pterygium of unspecified eye

       ● **H11.01   Amyloid pterygium**
          H11.011   Amyloid pterygium of right eye
          H11.012   Amyloid pterygium of left eye
          H11.013   Amyloid pterygium of eye, bilateral
          ▪ H11.019   Amyloid pterygium of unspecified eye

       ● **H11.02   Central pterygium of eye**
          H11.021   Central pterygium of right eye
          H11.022   Central pterygium of left eye
          H11.023   Central pterygium of eye, bilateral
          ▪ H11.029   Central pterygium of unspecified eye

       ● **H11.03   Double pterygium of eye**
          H11.031   Double pterygium of right eye
          H11.032   Double pterygium of left eye
          H11.033   Double pterygium of eye, bilateral
          ▪ H11.039   Double pterygium of unspecified eye

       ● **H11.04   Peripheral pterygium of eye, stationary**
          H11.041   Peripheral pterygium, stationary, right eye
          H11.042   Peripheral pterygium, stationary, left eye
          H11.043   Peripheral pterygium, stationary, bilateral

          ▪ H11.049   Peripheral pterygium, stationary, unspecified eye

       ● **H11.05   Peripheral pterygium of eye, progressive**
          H11.051   Peripheral pterygium, progressive, right eye
          H11.052   Peripheral pterygium, progressive, left eye
          H11.053   Peripheral pterygium, progressive, bilateral
          ▪ H11.059   Peripheral pterygium, progressive, unspecified eye

       ● **H11.06   Recurrent pterygium of eye**
          H11.061   Recurrent pterygium of right eye
          H11.062   Recurrent pterygium of left eye
          H11.063   Recurrent pterygium of eye, bilateral
          ▪ H11.069   Recurrent pterygium of unspecified eye

    ● **H11.1   Conjunctival degenerations and deposits**
       | Excludes2 | pseudopterygium (H11.81)

       ▪ **H11.10   Unspecified conjunctival degenerations**
       ● **H11.11   Conjunctival deposits**
          H11.111   Conjunctival deposits, right eye
          H11.112   Conjunctival deposits, left eye
          H11.113   Conjunctival deposits, bilateral
          ▪ H11.119   Conjunctival deposits, unspecified eye

       ● **H11.12   Conjunctival concretions**
          White to yellow nodules within or beneath conjunctiva

          H11.121   Conjunctival concretions, right eye
          H11.122   Conjunctival concretions, left eye
          H11.123   Conjunctival concretions, bilateral
          ▪ H11.129   Conjunctival concretions, unspecified eye

       ● **H11.13   Conjunctival pigmentations**
          Conjunctival argyrosis [argyria]
          H11.131   Conjunctival pigmentations, right eye
          H11.132   Conjunctival pigmentations, left eye
          H11.133   Conjunctival pigmentations, bilateral
          ▪ H11.139   Conjunctival pigmentations, unspecified eye

       ● **H11.14   Conjunctival xerosis NOS**
          | Excludes1 | xerosis of conjunctiva due to vitamin A deficiency (E50.0, E50.1)

          H11.141   Conjunctival xerosis NOS, right eye
          H11.142   Conjunctival xerosis NOS, left eye
          H11.143   Conjunctival xerosis NOS, bilateral
          ▪ H11.149   Conjunctival xerosis NOS, unspecified eye

       ● **H11.15   Pinguecula**
          Yellowish spot near sclerocorneal junction, usually on nasal side; associated with aging

          | Excludes1 | pingueculitis (H10.81-)

          H11.151   Pinguecula, right eye

● Unacceptable First-Listed Diagnosis   ● Use Additional Character(s)   ▪ Unspecified   **OGCR** Official Guidelines for Coding and Reporting
🔧 Complication\Comorbidity   🔧 Major C\C | Excludes 1 | | Excludes 2 | Includes   Use additional   Code first   Code also

CHAPTER 7 (H00-H59)

        H11.152   Pinguecula, left eye

        H11.153   Pinguecula, bilateral

        ▨H11.159   Pinguecula, unspecified eye

● H11.2   Conjunctival scars

   ● H11.21   Conjunctival adhesions and strands (localized)

        H11.211   Conjunctival adhesions and strands (localized), right eye

        H11.212   Conjunctival adhesions and strands (localized), left eye

        H11.213   Conjunctival adhesions and strands (localized), bilateral

        ▨H11.219   Conjunctival adhesions and strands (localized), unspecified eye

   ● H11.22   Conjunctival granuloma

        H11.221   Conjunctival granuloma, right eye

        H11.222   Conjunctival granuloma, left eye

        H11.223   Conjunctival granuloma, bilateral

        ▨H11.229   Conjunctival granuloma, unspecified

   ● H11.23   Symblepharon
        Adhesion between tarsal conjunctiva and bulbar conjunctiva

        H11.231   Symblepharon, right eye

        H11.232   Symblepharon, left eye

        H11.233   Symblepharon, bilateral

        ▨H11.239   Symblepharon, unspecified eye

   ● H11.24   Scarring of conjunctiva

        H11.241   Scarring of conjunctiva, right eye

        H11.242   Scarring of conjunctiva, left eye

        H11.243   Scarring of conjunctiva, bilateral

        ▨H11.249   Scarring of conjunctiva, unspecified eye

● H11.3   Conjunctival hemorrhage
    Subconjunctival hemorrhage

     ▨H11.30   Conjunctival hemorrhage, unspecified eye

     H11.31   Conjunctival hemorrhage, right eye

     H11.32   Conjunctival hemorrhage, left eye

     H11.33   Conjunctival hemorrhage, bilateral

● H11.4   Other conjunctival vascular disorders and cysts

   ● H11.41   Vascular abnormalities of conjunctiva
        Conjunctival aneurysm

        H11.411   Vascular abnormalities of conjunctiva, right eye

        H11.412   Vascular abnormalities of conjunctiva, left eye

        H11.413   Vascular abnormalities of conjunctiva, bilateral

        ▨H11.419   Vascular abnormalities of conjunctiva, unspecified eye

   ● H11.42   Conjunctival edema

        H11.421   Conjunctival edema, right eye

        H11.422   Conjunctival edema, left eye

        H11.423   Conjunctival edema, bilateral

        ▨H11.429   Conjunctival edema, unspecified eye

   ● H11.43   Conjunctival hyperemia

        H11.431   Conjunctival hyperemia, right eye

        H11.432   Conjunctival hyperemia, left eye

        H11.433   Conjunctival hyperemia, bilateral

        ▨H11.439   Conjunctival hyperemia, unspecified eye

   ● H11.44   Conjunctival cysts

        H11.441   Conjunctival cysts, right eye

        H11.442   Conjunctival cysts, left eye

        H11.443   Conjunctival cysts, bilateral

        ▨H11.449   Conjunctival cysts, unspecified eye

● H11.8   Other specified disorders of conjunctiva

   ● H11.81   Pseudopterygium of conjunctiva
        Conjunctival scar attached to cornea

        H11.811   Pseudopterygium of conjunctiva, right eye

        H11.812   Pseudopterygium of conjunctiva, left eye

        H11.813   Pseudopterygium of conjunctiva, bilateral

        ▨H11.819   Pseudopterygium of conjunctiva, unspecified eye

   ● H11.82   Conjunctivochalasis
        Conjunctiva bulges over eyelid margin or covers lower punctum

        H11.821   Conjunctivochalasis, right eye

        H11.822   Conjunctivochalasis, left eye

        H11.823   Conjunctivochalasis, bilateral

        ▨H11.829   Conjunctivochalasis, unspecified eye

     H11.89   Other specified disorders of conjunctiva

▨H11.9   Unspecified disorder of conjunctiva

DISORDERS OF SCLERA, CORNEA, IRIS AND CILIARY BODY (H15-H22)

● H15   Disorders of sclera

   ● H15.0   Scleritis
        Inflammation of the white (sclera and episclera) of the eye.

     ● H15.00   Unspecified scleritis

        ▨H15.001   Unspecified scleritis, right eye

        ▨H15.002   Unspecified scleritis, left eye

        ▨H15.003   Unspecified scleritis, bilateral

        ▨H15.009   Unspecified scleritis, unspecified eye

     ● H15.01   Anterior scleritis

        H15.011   Anterior scleritis, right eye

        H15.012   Anterior scleritis, left eye

        H15.013   Anterior scleritis, bilateral

        ▨H15.019   Anterior scleritis, unspecified eye

     ● H15.02   Brawny scleritis
        Swelling around the cornea that is gelantinous in appearance

        H15.021   Brawny scleritis, right eye

        H15.022   Brawny scleritis, left eye

        H15.023   Brawny scleritis, bilateral

        ▨H15.029   Brawny scleritis, unspecified eye

     ● H15.03   Posterior scleritis
        Sclerotenonitis

        H15.031   Posterior scleritis, right eye

        H15.032   Posterior scleritis, left eye

● Unacceptable First-Listed Diagnosis   ● Use Additional Character(s)   ▨ Unspecified   **OGCR** Official Guidelines for Coding and Reporting

🄒 Complication\Comorbidity   🄜 Major C\C   Excludes 1   Excludes 2   Includes   Use additional   Code first   Code also

961

CHAPTER 7 (H00-H59)

H15.033 Posterior scleritis, bilateral

H15.039 Posterior scleritis, unspecified eye

● H15.04 Scleritis with corneal involvement

H15.041 Scleritis with corneal involvement, right eye

H15.042 Scleritis with corneal involvement, left eye

H15.043 Scleritis with corneal involvement, bilateral

H15.049 Scleritis with corneal involvement, unspecified eye

● H15.05 Scleromalacia perforans

Necrotic without inflammation; usually associated with rheumatoid arthritis

H15.051 Scleromalacia perforans, right eye

H15.052 Scleromalacia perforans, left eye

H15.053 Scleromalacia perforans, bilateral

H15.059 Scleromalacia perforans, unspecified eye

● H15.09 Other scleritis

Scleral abscess

H15.091 Other scleritis, right eye

H15.092 Other scleritis, left eye

H15.093 Other scleritis, bilateral

H15.099 Other scleritis, unspecified eye

● H15.1 Episcleritis

Inflammation of the white (sclera and episclera) of the eye.

● H15.10 Unspecified episcleritis

H15.101 Unspecified episcleritis, right eye

H15.102 Unspecified episcleritis, left eye

H15.103 Unspecified episcleritis, bilateral

H15.109 Unspecified episcleritis, unspecified eye

● H15.11 Episcleritis periodica fugax

Transient, recurrent inflammation of portion of episclera (connective tissue on the surface of the sclera)

H15.111 Episcleritis periodica fugax, right eye

H15.112 Episcleritis periodica fugax, left eye

H15.113 Episcleritis periodica fugax, bilateral

H15.119 Episcleritis periodica fugax, unspecified eye

● H15.12 Nodular episcleritis

Characterized by tender, localized, moveable nodule within inflamed area

H15.121 Nodular episcleritis, right eye

H15.122 Nodular episcleritis, left eye

H15.123 Nodular episcleritis, bilateral

H15.129 Nodular episcleritis, unspecified eye

● H15.8 Other disorders of sclera

Excludes2   blue sclera (Q13.5)
                degenerative myopia (H44.2-)

● H15.81 Equatorial staphyloma

H15.811 Equatorial staphyloma, right eye

H15.812 Equatorial staphyloma, left eye

H15.813 Equatorial staphyloma, bilateral

H15.819 Equatorial staphyloma, unspecified eye

● H15.82 Localized anterior staphyloma

H15.821 Localized anterior staphyloma, right eye

H15.822 Localized anterior staphyloma, left eye

H15.823 Localized anterior staphyloma, bilateral

H15.829 Localized anterior staphyloma, unspecified eye

● H15.83 Staphyloma posticum

H15.831 Staphyloma posticum, right eye

H15.832 Staphyloma posticum, left eye

H15.833 Staphyloma posticum, bilateral

H15.839 Staphyloma posticum, unspecified eye

● H15.84 Scleral ectasia

H15.841 Scleral ectasia, right eye

H15.842 Scleral ectasia, left eye

H15.843 Scleral ectasia, bilateral

H15.849 Scleral ectasia, unspecified eye

● H15.85 Ring staphyloma

H15.851 Ring staphyloma, right eye

H15.852 Ring staphyloma, left eye

H15.853 Ring staphyloma, bilateral

H15.859 Ring staphyloma, unspecified eye

H15.89 Other disorders of sclera

H15.9 Unspecified disorder of sclera

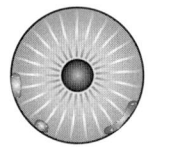
Marginal (catarrhal) ulcer

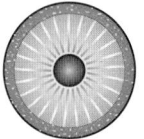
Ring ulcer

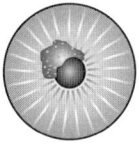
Central corneal ulcer

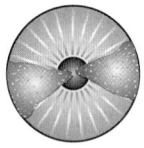
Rosacea ulcer

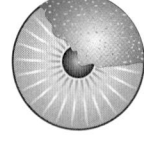
Mooren's (rodent) ulcer

Figure 7-6 Corneal ulcers: marginal, ring, central corneal, rosacea, and Mooren's.

CHAPTER 7 (H00-H59)

● Unacceptable First-Listed Diagnosis   ● Use Additional Character(s)   ▦ Unspecified   **OGCR** Official Guidelines for Coding and Reporting

962   ◔ Complication\Comorbidity   ◔ Major C\C   [Excludes 1]   [Excludes 2]   Includes   Use additional   Code first   Code also

Item 7–3 An infected ulcer is usually called a **serpiginous** or **hypopyon** ulcer which is a pus sac in the anterior chamber of the eye. **Marginal** ulcers are usually asymptomatic, not primary, and are often superficial and simple. More severe marginal ulcers spread to form a ring ulcer. **Ring** ulcers can extend around the entire corneal periphery. **Central corneal** ulcers develop when there is an abrasion to the epithelium and an infection develops in the eroded area. The **pyocyaneal** ulcer is the most serious corneal infection, which, if left untreated, can lead to loss of the eye.

● H16 Keratitis

　● H16.0 Corneal ulcer

　　● H16.00 Unspecified corneal ulcer

　　　■ H16.001 Unspecified corneal ulcer, right eye

　　　■ H16.002 Unspecified corneal ulcer, left eye

　　　■ H16.003 Unspecified corneal ulcer, bilateral

　　　■ H16.009 Unspecified corneal ulcer, unspecified eye

　　● H16.01 Central corneal ulcer

　　　H16.011 Central corneal ulcer, right eye

　　　H16.012 Central corneal ulcer, left eye

　　　H16.013 Central corneal ulcer, bilateral

　　　■ H16.019 Central corneal ulcer, unspecified eye

　　● H16.02 Ring corneal ulcer

　　　H16.021 Ring corneal ulcer, right eye

　　　H16.022 Ring corneal ulcer, left eye

　　　H16.023 Ring corneal ulcer, bilateral

　　　■ H16.029 Ring corneal ulcer, unspecified eye

　　● H16.03 Corneal ulcer with hypopyon

　　　H16.031 Corneal ulcer with hypopyon, right eye

　　　H16.032 Corneal ulcer with hypopyon, left eye

　　　H16.033 Corneal ulcer with hypopyon, bilateral

　　　■ H16.039 Corneal ulcer with hypopyon, unspecified eye

　　● H16.04 Marginal corneal ulcer

　　　H16.041 Marginal corneal ulcer, right eye

　　　H16.042 Marginal corneal ulcer, left eye

　　　H16.043 Marginal corneal ulcer, bilateral

　　　■ H16.049 Marginal corneal ulcer, unspecified eye

　　● H16.05 Mooren's corneal ulcer

　　　H16.051 Mooren's corneal ulcer, right eye

　　　H16.052 Mooren's corneal ulcer, left eye

　　　H16.053 Mooren's corneal ulcer, bilateral

　　　■ H16.059 Mooren's corneal ulcer, unspecified eye

　　● H16.06 Mycotic corneal ulcer

　　　H16.061 Mycotic corneal ulcer, right eye

　　　H16.062 Mycotic corneal ulcer, left eye

　　　H16.063 Mycotic corneal ulcer, bilateral

　　　■ H16.069 Mycotic corneal ulcer, unspecified eye

　　● H16.07 Perforated corneal ulcer

　　　H16.071 Perforated corneal ulcer, right eye

　　　H16.072 Perforated corneal ulcer, left eye

　　　H16.073 Perforated corneal ulcer, bilateral

　　　■ H16.079 Perforated corneal ulcer, unspecified eye

　● H16.1 Other and unspecified superficial keratitis without conjunctivitis

　　● H16.10 Unspecified superficial keratitis

　　　■ H16.101 Unspecified superficial keratitis, right eye

　　　■ H16.102 Unspecified superficial keratitis, left eye

　　　■ H16.103 Unspecified superficial keratitis, bilateral

　　　■ H16.109 Unspecified superficial keratitis, unspecified eye

　　● H16.11 Macular keratitis
　　　Areolar keratitis
　　　Nummular keratitis
　　　Stellate keratitis
　　　Striate keratitis

　　　H16.111 Macular keratitis, right eye

　　　H16.112 Macular keratitis, left eye

　　　H16.113 Macular keratitis, bilateral

　　　■ H16.119 Macular keratitis, unspecified eye

　　● H16.12 Filamentary keratitis

　　　H16.121 Filamentary keratitis, right eye

　　　H16.122 Filamentary keratitis, left eye

　　　H16.123 Filamentary keratitis, bilateral

　　　■ H16.129 Filamentary keratitis, unspecified eye

　　● H16.13 Photokeratitis
　　　Snow blindness
　　　Welders' keratitis

　　　H16.131 Photokeratitis, right eye

　　　H16.132 Photokeratitis, left eye

　　　H16.133 Photokeratitis, bilateral

　　　■ H16.139 Photokeratitis, unspecified eye

　　● H16.14 Punctate keratitis

　　　H16.141 Punctate keratitis, right eye

　　　H16.142 Punctate keratitis, left eye

　　　H16.143 Punctate keratitis, bilateral

　　　■ H16.149 Punctate keratitis, unspecified eye

　● H16.2 Keratoconjunctivitis

　　● H16.20 Unspecified keratoconjunctivitis
　　　Superficial keratitis with conjunctivitis NOS

　　　■ H16.201 Unspecified keratoconjunctivitis, right eye

　　　■ H16.202 Unspecified keratoconjunctivitis, left eye

　　　■ H16.203 Unspecified keratoconjunctivitis, bilateral

　　　■ H16.209 Unspecified keratoconjunctivitis, unspecified eye

　　● H16.21 Exposure keratoconjunctivitis

　　　H16.211 Exposure keratoconjunctivitis, right eye

　　　H16.212 Exposure keratoconjunctivitis, left eye

　　　H16.213 Exposure keratoconjunctivitis, bilateral

　　　■ H16.219 Exposure keratoconjunctivitis, unspecified eye

● Unacceptable First-Listed Diagnosis　　● Use Additional Character(s)　　■ Unspecified　　**OGCR** Official Guidelines for Coding and Reporting

🄲 Complication\Comorbidity　🄼 Major C\C　[Excludes 1]　[Excludes 2]　Includes　Use additional　Code first　Code also

963

CHAPTER 7 (H00–H59)

● H16.22 Keratoconjunctivitis sicca, not specified as Sjögren's

> **Excludes1** Sjogren's syndrome (M35.01)

H16.221 Keratoconjunctivitis sicca, not specified as Sjögren's, right eye

H16.222 Keratoconjunctivitis sicca, not specified as Sjögren's, left eye

H16.223 Keratoconjunctivitis sicca, not specified as Sjögren's, bilateral

■ H16.229 Keratoconjunctivitis sicca, not specified as Sjögren's, unspecified eye

● H16.23 Neurotrophic keratoconjunctivitis

H16.231 Neurotrophic keratoconjunctivitis, right eye

H16.232 Neurotrophic keratoconjunctivitis, left eye

H16.233 Neurotrophic keratoconjunctivitis, bilateral

■ H16.239 Neurotrophic keratoconjunctivitis, unspecified eye

● H16.24 Ophthalmia nodosa

H16.241 Ophthalmia nodosa, right eye

H16.242 Ophthalmia nodosa, left eye

H16.243 Ophthalmia nodosa, bilateral

■ H16.249 Ophthalmia nodosa, unspecified eye

● H16.25 Phlyctenular keratoconjunctivitis

H16.251 Phlyctenular keratoconjunctivitis, right eye

H16.252 Phlyctenular keratoconjunctivitis, left eye

H16.253 Phlyctenular keratoconjunctivitis, bilateral

■ H16.259 Phlyctenular keratoconjunctivitis, unspecified eye

● H16.26 Vernal keratoconjunctivitis, with limbar and corneal involvement

> **Excludes1** vernal conjunctivitis without limbar and corneal involvement (H10.44)

H16.261 Vernal keratoconjunctivitis, with limbar and corneal involvement, right eye

H16.262 Vernal keratoconjunctivitis, with limbar and corneal involvement, left eye

H16.263 Vernal keratoconjunctivitis, with limbar and corneal involvement, bilateral

■ H16.269 Vernal keratoconjunctivitis, with limbar and corneal involvement, unspecified eye

● H16.29 Other keratoconjunctivitis

H16.291 Other keratoconjunctivitis, right eye

H16.292 Other keratoconjunctivitis, left eye

H16.293 Other keratoconjunctivitis, bilateral

■ H16.299 Other keratoconjunctivitis, unspecified eye

● H16.3 Interstitial and deep keratitis

● H16.30 Unspecified interstitial keratitis

■ H16.301 Unspecified interstitial keratitis, right eye

■ H16.302 Unspecified interstitial keratitis, left eye

■ H16.303 Unspecified interstitial keratitis, bilateral

■ H16.309 Unspecified interstitial keratitis, unspecified eye

● H16.31 Corneal abscess

H16.311 Corneal abscess, right eye

H16.312 Corneal abscess, left eye

H16.313 Corneal abscess, bilateral

■ H16.319 Corneal abscess, unspecified eye

● H16.32 Diffuse interstitial keratitis
Cogan's syndrome

H16.321 Diffuse interstitial keratitis, right eye

H16.322 Diffuse interstitial keratitis, left eye

H16.323 Diffuse interstitial keratitis, bilateral

■ H16.329 Diffuse interstitial keratitis, unspecified eye

● H16.33 Sclerosing keratitis

H16.331 Sclerosing keratitis, right eye

H16.332 Sclerosing keratitis, left eye

H16.333 Sclerosing keratitis, bilateral

■ H16.339 Sclerosing keratitis, unspecified eye

● H16.39 Other interstitial and deep keratitis

H16.391 Other interstitial and deep keratitis, right eye

H16.392 Other interstitial and deep keratitis, left eye

H16.393 Other interstitial and deep keratitis, bilateral

■ H16.399 Other interstitial and deep keratitis, unspecified eye

● H16.4 Corneal neovascularization

● H16.40 Unspecified corneal neovascularization

■ H16.401 Unspecified corneal neovascularization, right eye

■ H16.402 Unspecified corneal neovascularization, left eye

■ H16.403 Unspecified corneal neovascularization, bilateral

■ H16.409 Unspecified corneal neovascularization, unspecified eye

● H16.41 Ghost vessels (corneal)

H16.411 Ghost vessels (corneal), right eye

H16.412 Ghost vessels (corneal), left eye

H16.413 Ghost vessels (corneal), bilateral

■ H16.419 Ghost vessels (corneal), unspecified eye

● H16.42 Pannus (corneal)

H16.421 Pannus (corneal), right eye

● Unacceptable First-Listed Diagnosis   ● Use Additional Character(s)   ■ Unspecified   **OGCR** Official Guidelines for Coding and Reporting

🅒 Complication\Comorbidity   🅒ₓ Major C\C   Excludes 1   Excludes 2   Includes   Use additional   Code first   Code also

H16.422　Pannus (corneal), left eye

H16.423　Pannus (corneal), bilateral

◼H16.429　Pannus (corneal), unspecified eye

●H16.43　Localized vascularization of cornea

H16.431　Localized vascularization of cornea, right eye

H16.432　Localized vascularization of cornea, left eye

H16.433　Localized vascularization of cornea, bilateral

◼H16.439　Localized vascularization of cornea, unspecified eye

●H16.44　Deep vascularization of cornea

H16.441　Deep vascularization of cornea, right eye

H16.442　Deep vascularization of cornea, left eye

H16.443　Deep vascularization of cornea, bilateral

◼H16.449　Deep vascularization of cornea, unspecified eye

H16.8　Other keratitis

◼H16.9　Unspecified keratitis

●H17　Corneal scars and opacities

●H17.0　Adherent leukoma

◼H17.00　Adherent leukoma, unspecified eye

H17.01　Adherent leukoma, right eye

H17.02　Adherent leukoma, left eye

H17.03　Adherent leukoma, bilateral

●H17.1　Central corneal opacity

◼H17.10　Central corneal opacity, unspecified eye

H17.11　Central corneal opacity, right eye

H17.12　Central corneal opacity, left eye

H17.13　Central corneal opacity, bilateral

●H17.8　Other corneal scars and opacities

●H17.81　Minor opacity of cornea
　　　Corneal nebula

H17.811　Minor opacity of cornea, right eye

H17.812　Minor opacity of cornea, left eye

H17.813　Minor opacity of cornea, bilateral

◼H17.819　Minor opacity of cornea, unspecified eye

●H17.82　Peripheral opacity of cornea

H17.821　Peripheral opacity of cornea, right eye

H17.822　Peripheral opacity of cornea, left eye

H17.823　Peripheral opacity of cornea, bilateral

◼H17.829　Peripheral opacity of cornea, unspecified eye

H17.89　Other corneal scars and opacities

◼H17.9　Unspecified corneal scar and opacity

●H18　Other disorders of cornea

●H18.0　Corneal pigmentations and deposits

●H18.00　Unspecified corneal deposit

◼H18.001　Unspecified corneal deposit, right eye

◼H18.002　Unspecified corneal deposit, left eye

◼H18.003　Unspecified corneal deposit, bilateral

◼H18.009　Unspecified corneal deposit, unspecified eye

●H18.01　Anterior corneal pigmentations
　　　Staehli's line

H18.011　Anterior corneal pigmentations, right eye

H18.012　Anterior corneal pigmentations, left eye

H18.013　Anterior corneal pigmentations, bilateral

◼H18.019　Anterior corneal pigmentations, unspecified eye

●H18.02　Argentous corneal deposits

H18.021　Argentous corneal deposits, right eye

H18.022　Argentous corneal deposits, left eye

H18.023　Argentous corneal deposits, bilateral

◼H18.029　Argentous corneal deposits, unspecified eye

●H18.03　Corneal deposits in metabolic disorders
　　　Code also associated metabolic disorder

H18.031　Corneal deposits in metabolic disorders, right eye

H18.032　Corneal deposits in metabolic disorders, left eye

H18.033　Corneal deposits in metabolic disorders, bilateral

◼H18.039　Corneal deposits in metabolic disorders, unspecified eye

●H18.04　Kayser-Fleischer ring
　　　Code also associated Wilson's disease (E83.01)

H18.041　Kayser-Fleischer ring, right eye

H18.042　Kayser-Fleischer ring, left eye

H18.043　Kayser-Fleischer ring, bilateral

◼H18.049　Kayser-Fleischer ring, unspecified eye

●H18.05　Posterior corneal pigmentations
　　　Krukenberg's spindle

H18.051　Posterior corneal pigmentations, right eye

H18.052　Posterior corneal pigmentations, left eye

H18.053　Posterior corneal pigmentations, bilateral

◼H18.059　Posterior corneal pigmentations, unspecified eye

●H18.06　Stromal corneal pigmentations
　　　Hematocornea

H18.061　Stromal corneal pigmentations, right eye

H18.062　Stromal corneal pigmentations, left eye

H18.063　Stromal corneal pigmentations, bilateral

◼H18.069　Stromal corneal pigmentations, unspecified eye

●H18.1　Bullous keratopathy

◼H18.10　Bullous keratopathy, unspecified eye

●　Unacceptable First-Listed Diagnosis　　　●　Use Additional Character(s)　　　◼　Unspecified　　　**OGCR**　Official Guidelines for Coding and Reporting

🅒 Complication\Comorbidity　　🅒 Major C\C　　Excludes 1　　Excludes 2　　Includes　　Use additional　　Code first　　Code also

965

CHAPTER 7 (H00-H59)

H18.11 Bullous keratopathy, right eye

H18.12 Bullous keratopathy, left eye

H18.13 Bullous keratopathy, bilateral

● H18.2 Other and unspecified corneal edema

■ H18.20 Unspecified corneal edema

● H18.21 Corneal edema secondary to contact lens

| Excludes2 | other corneal disorders due to contact lens (H18.82-) |

H18.211 Corneal edema secondary to contact lens, right eye

H18.212 Corneal edema secondary to contact lens, left eye

H18.213 Corneal edema secondary to contact lens, bilateral

■ H18.219 Corneal edema secondary to contact lens, unspecified eye

● H18.22 Idiopathic corneal edema

H18.221 Idiopathic corneal edema, right eye

H18.222 Idiopathic corneal edema, left eye

H18.223 Idiopathic corneal edema, bilateral

■ H18.229 Idiopathic corneal edema, unspecified eye

● H18.23 Secondary corneal edema

H18.231 Secondary corneal edema, right eye

H18.232 Secondary corneal edema, left eye

H18.233 Secondary corneal edema, bilateral

■ H18.239 Secondary corneal edema, unspecified eye

● H18.3 Changes of corneal membranes

■ H18.30 Unspecified corneal membrane change

● H18.31 Folds and rupture in Bowman's membrane

H18.311 Folds and rupture in Bowman's membrane, right eye

H18.312 Folds and rupture in Bowman's membrane, left eye

H18.313 Folds and rupture in Bowman's membrane, bilateral

■ H18.319 Folds and rupture in Bowman's membrane, unspecified eye

● H18.32 Folds in Descemet's membrane

H18.321 Folds in Descemet's membrane, right eye

H18.322 Folds in Descemet's membrane, left eye

H18.323 Folds in Descemet's membrane, bilateral

■ H18.329 Folds in Descemet's membrane, unspecified eye

● H18.33 Rupture in Descemet's membrane

H18.331 Rupture in Descemet's membrane, right eye

H18.332 Rupture in Descemet's membrane, left eye

H18.333 Rupture in Descemet's membrane, bilateral

■ H18.339 Rupture in Descemet's membrane, unspecified eye

● H18.4 Corneal degeneration

| Excludes1 | Mooren's ulcer (H16.0-) recurrent erosion of cornea (H18.83-) |

■ H18.40 Unspecified corneal degeneration

● H18.41 Arcus senilis
        Senile corneal changes

H18.411 Arcus senilis, right eye

H18.412 Arcus senilis, left eye

H18.413 Arcus senilis, bilateral

■ H18.419 Arcus senilis, unspecified eye

● H18.42 Band keratopathy

H18.421 Band keratopathy, right eye

H18.422 Band keratopathy, left eye

H18.423 Band keratopathy, bilateral

■ H18.429 Band keratopathy, unspecified eye

H18.43 Other calcerous corneal degeneration

● H18.44 Keratomalacia

| Excludes1 | keratomalacia due to vitamin A deficiency (E50.4) |

H18.441 Keratomalacia, right eye

H18.442 Keratomalacia, left eye

H18.443 Keratomalacia, bilateral

■ H18.449 Keratomalacia, unspecified eye

● H18.45 Nodular corneal degeneration

H18.451 Nodular corneal degeneration, right eye

H18.452 Nodular corneal degeneration, left eye

H18.453 Nodular corneal degeneration, bilateral

■ H18.459 Nodular corneal degeneration, unspecified eye

● H18.46 Peripheral corneal degeneration

H18.461 Peripheral corneal degeneration, right eye

H18.462 Peripheral corneal degeneration, left eye

H18.463 Peripheral corneal degeneration, bilateral

■ H18.469 Peripheral corneal degeneration, unspecified eye

H18.49 Other corneal degeneration

● H18.5 Hereditary corneal dystrophies

■ H18.50 Unspecified hereditary corneal dystrophies

H18.51 Endothelial corneal dystrophy
        Fuchs' dystrophy

H18.52 Epithelial (juvenile) corneal dystrophy

H18.53 Granular corneal dystrophy

H18.54 Lattice corneal dystrophy

H18.55 Macular corneal dystrophy

H18.59 Other hereditary corneal dystrophies

Figure 7-7 Lateral view of the displacement of the cone apex in keratoconus. (From Yanoff: Ophthalmology, 2nd ed. 2004, Mosby, Inc.)

● Unacceptable First-Listed Diagnosis   ● Use Additional Character(s)   ■ Unspecified   **OGCR** Official Guidelines for Coding and Reporting

🔖 Complication\Comorbidity   🔖 Major C\C | Excludes 1 | | Excludes 2 | Includes   Use additional   Code first   Code also

Item 7–4 Keratoconus results in corneal degeneration that begins in childhood, gradually changes the cornea from a round to cone shape, decreasing visual acuity. Treatment includes contact lenses. In severe cases the need for corneal transplant may be the treatment of choice; however, newer technologies may use high frequency radio energy to shrink the edges of the cornea, pulling the central area back to a more normal shape. It can help delay or avoid the need for a corneal transplantation.

- ● H18.6   **Keratoconus**
  - ● H18.60   **Keratoconus, unspecified**
    - ■ H18.601   Keratoconus, unspecified, right eye
    - ■ H18.602   Keratoconus, unspecified, left eye
    - ■ H18.603   Keratoconus, unspecified, bilateral
    - ■ H18.609   Keratoconus, unspecified, unspecified eye
  - ● H18.61   **Keratoconus, stable**
    - H18.611   Keratoconus, stable, right eye
    - H18.612   Keratoconus, stable, left eye
    - H18.613   Keratoconus, stable, bilateral
    - ■ H18.619   Keratoconus, stable, unspecified eye
  - ● H18.62   **Keratoconus, unstable**
    Acute hydrops
    - H18.621   Keratoconus, unstable, right eye
    - H18.622   Keratoconus, unstable, left eye
    - H18.623   Keratoconus, unstable, bilateral
    - ■ H18.629   Keratoconus, unstable, unspecified eye
- ● H18.7   **Other and unspecified corneal deformities**
  - **Excludes1**   congenital malformations of cornea (Q13.3-Q13.4)
  - ■ H18.70   **Unspecified corneal deformity**
  - ● H18.71   **Corneal ectasia**
    - H18.711   Corneal ectasia, right eye
    - H18.712   Corneal ectasia, left eye
    - H18.713   Corneal ectasia, bilateral
    - ■ H18.719   Corneal ectasia, unspecified eye
  - ● H18.72   **Corneal staphyloma**
    - H18.721   Corneal staphyloma, right eye
    - H18.722   Corneal staphyloma, left eye
    - H18.723   Corneal staphyloma, bilateral
    - ■ H18.729   Corneal staphyloma, unspecified eye
  - ● H18.73   **Descemetocele**
    - H18.731   Descemetocele, right eye
    - H18.732   Descemetocele, left eye
    - H18.733   Descemetocele, bilateral
    - ■ H18.739   Descemetocele, unspecified eye
  - ● H18.79   **Other corneal deformities**
    - H18.791   Other corneal deformities, right eye
    - H18.792   Other corneal deformities, left eye
    - H18.793   Other corneal deformities, bilateral
    - ■ H18.799   Other corneal deformities, unspecified eye
- ● H18.8   **Other specified disorders of cornea**
  - ● H18.81   **Anesthesia and hypoesthesia of cornea**
    - H18.811   Anesthesia and hypoesthesia of cornea, right eye

- H18.812   Anesthesia and hypoesthesia of cornea, left eye
- H18.813   Anesthesia and hypoesthesia of cornea, bilateral
- ■ H18.819   Anesthesia and hypoesthesia of cornea, unspecified eye
- ● H18.82   **Corneal disorder due to contact lens**
  - **Excludes2**   corneal edema due to contact lens (H18.21-)
  - H18.821   Corneal disorder due to contact lens, right eye
  - H18.822   Corneal disorder due to contact lens, left eye
  - H18.823   Corneal disorder due to contact lens, bilateral
  - ■ H18.829   Corneal disorder due to contact lens, unspecified eye
- ● H18.83   **Recurrent erosion of cornea**
  - H18.831   Recurrent erosion of cornea, right eye
  - H18.832   Recurrent erosion of cornea, left eye
  - H18.833   Recurrent erosion of cornea, bilateral
  - ■ H18.839   Recurrent erosion of cornea, unspecified eye
- ● H18.89   **Other specified disorders of cornea**
  - H18.891   Other specified disorders of cornea, right eye
  - H18.892   Other specified disorders of cornea, left eye
  - H18.893   Other specified disorders of cornea, bilateral
  - ■ H18.899   Other specified disorders of cornea, unspecified eye
- ■ H18.9   **Unspecified disorder of cornea**

- ● H20   **Iridocyclitis**
  - ● H20.0   **Acute and subacute iridocyclitis**
    Acute anterior uveitis
    Acute cyclitis
    Acute iritis
    Subacute anterior uveitis
    Subacute cyclitis
    Subacute iritis
    - **Excludes1**   iridocyclitis, iritis, uveitis (due to) (in):
      diabetes mellitus (E08-E13 with .39)
      diphtheria (A36.89)
      gonococcal (A54.32)
      herpes (simplex) (B00.51)
      herpes zoster (B02.32)
      late congenital syphilis (A50.39)
      late syphilis (A52.71)
      sarcoidosis (D86.83)
      syphilis (A51.43)
      toxoplasmosis (B58.09)
      tuberculosis (A18.54)
    - ■ H20.00   **Unspecified acute and subacute iridocyclitis** 🗗
    - ● H20.01   **Primary iridocyclitis**
      - H20.011   Primary iridocyclitis, right eye 🗗
      - H20.012   Primary iridocyclitis, left eye 🗗
      - H20.013   Primary iridocyclitis, bilateral 🗗
      - ■ H20.019   Primary iridocyclitis, unspecified eye 🗗

●   Unacceptable First-Listed Diagnosis   ●   Use Additional Character(s)   ■   Unspecified   **OGCR** Official Guidelines for Coding and Reporting

🗗 Complication\Comorbidity   🗗 Major C\C   Excludes 1   Excludes 2   Includes   Use additional   Code first   Code also

967

CHAPTER 7 (H00-H59)

- H20.02 **Recurrent acute iridocyclitis**
  - H20.021 Recurrent acute iridocyclitits, right eye
  - H20.022 Recurrent acute iridocyclitits, left eye
  - H20.023 Recurrent acute iridocyclitits, bilateral
  - H20.029 Recurrent acute iridocyclitits, unspecified eye
- H20.03 **Secondary infectious iridocyclitis**
  - H20.031 Secondary infectious iridocyclitis, right eye
  - H20.032 Secondary infectious iridocyclitis, left eye
  - H20.033 Secondary infectious iridocyclitis, bilateral
  - H20.039 Secondary infectious iridocyclitis, unspecified eye
- H20.04 **Secondary noninfectious iridocyclitis**
  - H20.041 Secondary noninfectious iridocyclitis, right eye
  - H20.042 Secondary noninfectious iridocyclitis, left eye
  - H20.043 Secondary noninfectious iridocyclitis, bilateral
  - H20.049 Secondary noninfectious iridocyclitis, unspecified eye
- H20.05 **Hypopyon**
  - H20.051 Hypopyon, right eye
  - H20.052 Hypopyon, left eye
  - H20.053 Hypopyon, bilateral
  - H20.059 Hypopyon, unspecified eye
- H20.1 **Chronic iridocyclitis**

  Use additional code for any associated cataract (H26.21-)

  Excludes2   posterior cyclitis (H30.2-)
  - H20.10 Chronic iridocyclitis, unspecified eye
  - H20.11 Chronic iridocyclitis, right eye
  - H20.12 Chronic iridocyclitis, left eye
  - H20.13 Chronic iridocyclitis, bilateral
- H20.2 **Lens-induced iridocyclitis**
  - H20.20 Lens-induced iridocyclitis, unspecified eye
  - H20.21 Lens-induced iridocyclitis, right eye
  - H20.22 Lens-induced iridocyclitis, left eye
  - H20.23 Lens-induced iridocyclitis, bilateral
- H20.8 **Other iridocyclitis**

  Excludes2   glaucomatocyclitic crises (H40.4-)
  posterior cyclitis (H30.2-)
  sympathetic uveitis (H44.13-)
  - H20.81 **Fuchs' heterochromic cyclitis**
    - H20.811 Fuchs' heterochromic cyclitis, right eye
    - H20.812 Fuchs' heterochromic cyclitis, left eye
    - H20.813 Fuchs' heterochromic cyclitis, bilateral
    - H20.819 Fuchs' heterochromic cyclitis, unspecified eye
  - H20.82 **Vogt-Koyanagi syndrome**
    - H20.821 Vogt-Koyanagi syndrome, right eye
    - H20.822 Vogt-Koyanagi syndrome, left eye
    - H20.823 Vogt-Koyanagi syndrome, bilateral
    - H20.829 Vogt-Koyanagi syndrome, unspecified eye
- H20.9 **Unspecified iridocyclitis**
  Uveitis NOS
- H21 **Other disorders of iris and ciliary body**

  Excludes2   sympathetic uveitis (H44.1-)
  - H21.0 **Hyphema**

    Excludes1   traumatic hyphema (S05.1-)
    - H21.00 Hyphema, unspecified eye
    - H21.01 Hyphema, right eye
    - H21.02 Hyphema, left eye
    - H21.03 Hyphema, bilateral
  - H21.1 **Other vascular disorders of iris and ciliary body**
    Neovascularization of iris or ciliary body
    Rubeosis iridis
    Rubeosis of iris
    - H21.1x **Other vascular disorders of iris and ciliary body**
      - H21.1x1 Other vascular disorders of iris and ciliary body, right eye
      - H21.1x2 Other vascular disorders of iris and ciliary body, left eye
      - H21.1x3 Other vascular disorders of iris and ciliary body, bilateral
      - H21.1x9 Other vascular disorders of iris and ciliary body, unspecified eye
  - H21.2 **Degeneration of iris and ciliary body**
    - H21.21 **Degeneration of chamber angle**
      - H21.211 Degeneration of chamber angle, right eye
      - H21.212 Degeneration of chamber angle, left eye
      - H21.213 Degeneration of chamber angle, bilateral
      - H21.219 Degeneration of chamber angle, unspecified eye
    - H21.22 **Degeneration of ciliary body**
      - H21.221 Degeneration of ciliary body, right eye
      - H21.222 Degeneration of ciliary body, left eye
      - H21.223 Degeneration of ciliary body, bilateral
      - H21.229 Degeneration of ciliary body, unspecified eye
    - H21.23 **Degeneration of iris (pigmentary)**
      Translucency of iris
      - H21.231 Degeneration of iris (pigmentary), right eye
      - H21.232 Degeneration of iris (pigmentary), left eye
      - H21.233 Degeneration of iris (pigmentary), bilateral
      - H21.239 Degeneration of iris (pigmentary), unspecified eye
    - H21.24 **Degeneration of pupillary margin**
      - H21.241 Degeneration of pupillary margin, right eye
      - H21.242 Degeneration of pupillary margin, left eye

- Unacceptable First-Listed Diagnosis   • Use Additional Character(s)   ■ Unspecified   **OGCR** Official Guidelines for Coding and Reporting
- Complication\Comorbidity   Major C\C   Excludes 1   Excludes 2   Includes   Use additional   Code first   Code also

H21.243 Degeneration of pupillary margin, bilateral

🔲 H21.249 Degeneration of pupillary margin, unspecified eye

● H21.25 Iridoschisis

H21.251 Iridoschisis, right eye

H21.252 Iridoschisis, left eye

H21.253 Iridoschisis, bilateral

🔲 H21.259 Iridoschisis, unspecified eye

● H21.26 Iris atrophy (essential) (progressive)

H21.261 Iris atrophy (essential) (progressive), right eye

H21.262 Iris atrophy (essential) (progressive), left eye

H21.263 Iris atrophy (essential) (progressive), bilateral

🔲 H21.269 Iris atrophy (essential) (progressive), unspecified eye

● H21.27 Miotic pupillary cyst

H21.271 Miotic pupillary cyst, right eye

H21.272 Miotic pupillary cyst, left eye

H21.273 Miotic pupillary cyst, bilateral

🔲 H21.279 Miotic pupillary cyst, unspecified eye

H21.29 Other iris atrophy

● H21.3 Cyst of iris, ciliary body and anterior chamber

Excludes2 miotic pupillary cyst (H21.27-)

● H21.30 Idiopathic cysts of iris, ciliary body or anterior chamber

Cyst of iris, ciliary body or anterior chamber NOS

H21.301 Idiopathic cysts of iris, ciliary body or anterior chamber, right eye

H21.302 Idiopathic cysts of iris, ciliary body or anterior chamber, left eye

H21.303 Idiopathic cysts of iris, ciliary body or anterior chamber, bilateral

🔲 H21.309 Idiopathic cysts of iris, ciliary body or anterior chamber, unspecified eye

● H21.31 Exudative cysts of iris or anterior chamber

H21.311 Exudative cysts of iris or anterior chamber, right eye

H21.312 Exudative cysts of iris or anterior chamber, left eye

H21.313 Exudative cysts of iris or anterior chamber, bilateral

🔲 H21.319 Exudative cysts of iris or anterior chamber, unspecified eye

● H21.32 Implantation cysts of iris, ciliary body or anterior chamber

H21.321 Implantation cysts of iris, ciliary body or anterior chamber, right eye

H21.322 Implantation cysts of iris, ciliary body or anterior chamber, left eye

H21.323 Implantation cysts of iris, ciliary body or anterior chamber, bilateral

🔲 H21.329 Implantation cysts of iris, ciliary body or anterior chamber, unspecified eye

● H21.33 Parasitic cyst of iris, ciliary body or anterior chamber

H21.331 Parasitic cyst of iris, ciliary body or anterior chamber, right eye 🏵

H21.332 Parasitic cyst of iris, ciliary body or anterior chamber, left eye 🏵

H21.333 Parasitic cyst of iris, ciliary body or anterior chamber, bilateral 🏵

🔲 H21.339 Parasitic cyst of iris, ciliary body or anterior chamber, unspecified eye 🏵

● H21.34 Primary cyst of pars plana

H21.341 Primary cyst of pars plana, right eye

H21.342 Primary cyst of pars plana, left eye

H21.343 Primary cyst of pars plana, bilateral

🔲 H21.349 Primary cyst of pars plana, unspecified eye

● H21.35 Exudative cyst of pars plana

H21.351 Exudative cyst of pars plana, right eye

H21.352 Exudative cyst of pars plana, left eye

H21.353 Exudative cyst of pars plana, bilateral

🔲 H21.359 Exudative cyst of pars plana, unspecified eye

● H21.4 Pupillary membranes

Iris bombé
Pupillary occlusion
Pupillary seclusion

Excludes1 congenital pupillary membranes (Q13.8)

🔲 H21.40 Pupillary membranes, unspecified eye

H21.41 Pupillary membranes, right eye

H21.42 Pupillary membranes, left eye

H21.43 Pupillary membranes, bilateral

● H21.5 Other and unspecified adhesions and disruptions of iris and ciliary body

Excludes1 corectopia (Q13.2)

● H21.50 Unspecified adhesions of iris

Synechia (iris) NOS

🔲 H21.501 Unspecified adhesions of iris, right eye

🔲 H21.502 Unspecified adhesions of iris, left eye

🔲 H21.503 Unspecified adhesions of iris, bilateral

🔲 H21.509 Unspecified adhesions of iris and ciliary body, unspecified eye

● H21.51 Anterior synechiae (iris)

H21.511 Anterior synechiae (iris), right eye

H21.512 Anterior synechiae (iris), left eye

H21.513 Anterior synechiae (iris), bilateral

🔲 H21.519 Anterior synechiae (iris), unspecified eye

● H21.52 Goniosynechiae

H21.521 Goniosynechiae, right eye

H21.522 Goniosynechiae, left eye

H21.523 Goniosynechiae, bilateral

🔲 H21.529 Goniosynechiae, unspecified eye

● Unacceptable First-Listed Diagnosis   ● Use Additional Character(s)   🔲 Unspecified   **OGCR** Official Guidelines for Coding and Reporting

🏵 Complication\Comorbidity   🏵 Major C\C   Excludes 1   Excludes 2   Includes   Use additional   Code first   Code also   969

CHAPTER 7 (H00-H59)

● **H21.53 Iridodialysis**
　　H21.531 Iridodialysis, right eye
　　H21.532 Iridodialysis, left eye
　　H21.533 Iridodialysis, bilateral
　■H21.539 Iridodialysis, unspecified eye
● **H21.54 Posterior synechiae (iris)**
　　H21.541 Posterior synechiae (iris), right eye
　　H21.542 Posterior synechiae (iris), left eye
　　H21.543 Posterior synechiae (iris), bilateral
　■H21.549 Posterior synechiae (iris), unspecified eye
● **H21.55 Recession of chamber angle**
　　H21.551 Recession of chamber angle, right eye
　　H21.552 Recession of chamber angle, left eye
　　H21.553 Recession of chamber angle, bilateral
　■H21.559 Recession of chamber angle, unspecified eye
● **H21.56 Pupillary abnormalities**
　　Deformed pupil
　　Ectopic pupil
　　Rupture of sphincter,pupil
　　Excludes1　congenital deformity of pupil (Q13.2-)
　　H21.561 Pupillary abnormality, right eye
　　H21.562 Pupillary abnormality, left eye
　　H21.563 Pupillary abnormality, bilateral
　■H21.569 Pupillary abnormality, unspecified eye
● **H21.8 Other specified disorders of iris and ciliary body**
　● **H21.81 Floppy iris syndrome**
　　　Intraoperative floppy iris syndrome (IFIS)
　　　Code first (T36-T50) to identify drug
　　H21.82 Plateau iris syndrome (post-iridectomy) (postprocedural)
　　H21.89 Other specified disorders of iris and ciliary body
■ **H21.9 Unspecified disorder of iris and ciliary body**

H22 Disorders of iris and ciliary body in diseases classified elsewhere
　　Code first underlying disease, such as:
　　gout (M1a-, M10.-)

Item 7–5 Senile cataracts are linked to the aging process. The most common area for the formation of a cataract is the cortical area of the lens. **Polar cataracts** can be either anterior or posterior. **Anterior polar cataracts** are more common and are small, white, capsular cataracts located on the anterior portion of the lens. **Total cataracts,** also called **complete** or **mature,** cause an opacity of all fibers of the lens. **Hypermature** describes a mature cataract with a swollen, milky cortex that covers the entire lens. **Immature,** also called **incipient,** cataracts have a clear cortex and are only slightly opaque. Treatment for all cataracts is the removal of the lens.

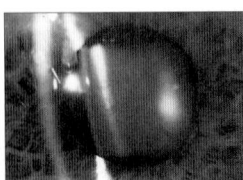

Figure 7-8 Age-related cataract. Nuclear sclerosis and cortical lens opacities are present. (From Yanoff: Ophthalmology, 2nd ed. 2004, Mosby, Inc.)

DISORDERS OF LENS (H25-H28)

● **H25 Age-related cataract**
　　Senile cataract
　　Excludes2　capsular glaucoma with pseudoexfoliation of lens (H40.1-)
● **H25.0 Age-related incipient cataract**
　● **H25.01 Cortical age-related cataract**
　　　H25.011 Cortical age-related cataract, right eye
　　　H25.012 Cortical age-related cataract, left eye
　　　H25.013 Cortical age-related cataract, bilateral
　　■H25.019 Cortical age-related cataract, unspecified eye
　● **H25.03 Anterior subcapsular polar age-related cataract**
　　　H25.031 Anterior subcapsular polar age-related cataract, right eye
　　　H25.032 Anterior subcapsular polar age-related cataract, left eye
　　　H25.033 Anterior subcapsular polar age-related cataract, bilateral
　　■H25.039 Anterior subcapsular polar age-related cataract, unspecified eye
　● **H25.04 Posterior subcapsular polar age-related cataract**
　　　H25.041 Posterior subcapsular polar age-related cataract, right eye
　　　H25.042 Posterior subcapsular polar age-related cataract, left eye
　　　H25.043 Posterior subcapsular polar age-related cataract, bilateral
　　■H25.049 Posterior subcapsular polar age-related cataract, unspecified eye
　● **H25.09 Other age-related incipient cataract**
　　　Coronary age-related cataract
　　　Punctate age-related cataract
　　　Water clefts
　　　H25.091 Other age-related incipient cataract, right eye
　　　H25.092 Other age-related incipient cataract, left eye
　　　H25.093 Other age-related incipient cataract, bilateral
　　■H25.099 Other age-related incipient cataract, unspecified eye
● **H25.1 Age-related nuclear cataract**
　　Cataracta brunescens
　　Nuclear sclerosis cataract
　■H25.10 Age-related nuclear cataract, unspecified eye
　　H25.11 Age-related nuclear cataract, right eye
　　H25.12 Age-related nuclear cataract, left eye
　　H25.13 Age-related nuclear cataract, bilateral
● **H25.2 Age-related cataract, morgagnian type**
　　Age-related hypermature cataract
　■H25.20 Age-related cataract, morgagnian type, unspecified eye
　　H25.21 Age-related cataract, morgagnian type, right eye

● Unacceptable First-Listed Diagnosis　● Use Additional Character(s)　■ Unspecified　**OGCR** Official Guidelines for Coding and Reporting　🅒 Complication\Comorbidity　🅜 Major C\C　Excludes 1　Excludes 2　Includes　Use additional　Code first　Code also

H25.22   Age-related cataract, morgagnian type, left eye

H25.23   Age-related cataract, morgagnian type, bilateral

● H25.8   Other age-related cataract

  ● H25.81   Combined forms of age-related cataract

     H25.811   Combined forms of age-related cataract, right eye

     H25.812   Combined forms of age-related cataract, left eye

     H25.813   Combined forms of age-related cataract, bilateral

     ■ H25.819   Combined forms of age-related cataract, unspecified eye

   H25.89   Other age-related cataract

■ H25.9   Unspecified age-related cataract

● H26   Other cataract

   Excludes1   congenital cataract (Q12.0)

  ● H26.0   Infantile and juvenile cataract

    ● H26.00   Unspecified infantile and juvenile cataract

       ■ H26.001   Unspecified infantile and juvenile cataract, right eye

       ■ H26.002   Unspecified infantile and juvenile cataract, left eye

       ■ H26.003   Unspecified infantile and juvenile cataract, bilateral

       ■ H26.009   Unspecified infantile and juvenile cataract, unspecified eye

    ● H26.01   Infantile and juvenile cortical, lamellar, or zonular cataract

       H26.011   Infantile and juvenile cortical, lamellar, or zonular cataract, right eye

       H26.012   Infantile and juvenile cortical, lamellar, or zonular cataract, left eye

       H26.013   Infantile and juvenile cortical, lamellar, or zonular cataract, bilateral

       ■ H26.019   Infantile and juvenile cortical, lamellar, or zonular cataract, unspecified eye

    ● H26.03   Infantile and juvenile nuclear cataract

       H26.031   Infantile and juvenile nuclear cataract, right eye

       H26.032   Infantile and juvenile nuclear cataract, left eye

       H26.033   Infantile and juvenile nuclear cataract, bilateral

       ■ H26.039   Infantile and juvenile nuclear cataract, unspecified eye

    ● H26.04   Anterior subcapsular polar infantile and juvenile cataract

       H26.041   Anterior subcapsular polar infantile and juvenile cataract, right eye

       H26.042   Anterior subcapsular polar infantile and juvenile cataract, left eye

       H26.043   Anterior subcapsular polar infantile and juvenile cataract, bilateral

       ■ H26.049   Anterior subcapsular polar infantile and juvenile cataract, unspecified eye

    ● H26.05   Posterior subcapsular polar infantile and juvenile cataract

       H26.051   Posterior subcapsular polar infantile and juvenile cataract, right eye

       H26.052   Posterior subcapsular polar infantile and juvenile cataract, left eye

       H26.053   Posterior subcapsular polar infantile and juvenile cataract, bilateral

       ■ H26.059   Posterior subcapsular polar infantile and juvenile cataract, unspecified eye

    ● H26.06   Combined forms of infantile and juvenile cataract

       H26.061   Combined forms of infantile and juvenile cataract, right eye

       H26.062   Combined forms of infantile and juvenile cataract, left eye

       H26.063   Combined forms of infantile and juvenile cataract bilateral

       ■ H26.069   Combined forms of infantile and juvenile cataract, unspecified eye

     H26.09   Other infantile and juvenile cataract

  ● H26.1   Traumatic cataract

     Use additional code (Chapter 20) to identify external cause

    ● H26.10   Unspecified traumatic cataract

       ■ H26.101   Unspecified traumatic cataract, right eye

       ■ H26.102   Unspecified traumatic cataract, left eye

       ■ H26.103   Unspecified traumatic cataract, bilateral

       ■ H26.109   Unspecified traumatic cataract, unspecified eye

    ● H26.11   Localized traumatic opacities

       H26.111   Localized traumatic opacities, right eye

       H26.112   Localized traumatic opacities, left eye

       H26.113   Localized traumatic opacities, bilateral

       ■ H26.119   Localized traumatic opacities, unspecified eye

    ● H26.12   Partially resolved traumatic cataract

       H26.121   Partially resolved traumatic cataract, right eye

       H26.122   Partially resolved traumatic cataract, left eye

       H26.123   Partially resolved traumatic cataract, bilateral

       ■ H26.129   Partially resolved traumatic cataract, unspecified eye

    ● H26.13   Total traumatic cataract

       H26.131   Total traumatic cataract, right eye

       H26.132   Total traumatic cataract, left eye

       H26.133   Total traumatic cataract, bilateral

● Unacceptable First-Listed Diagnosis   ● Use Additional Character(s)   ■ Unspecified   **OGCR** Official Guidelines for Coding and Reporting

Ⓒ Complication\Comorbidity   Ⓜ Major C\C   Excludes 1   Excludes 2   Includes   Use additional   Code first   Code also

971

CHAPTER 7 (H00–H59)

H26.139 **Total traumatic cataract, unspecified eye**

● H26.2 **Complicated cataract**

■ H26.20 **Unspecified complicated cataract**
Cataracta complicata NOS

● H26.21 **Cataract with neovascularization**
Code also associated condition, such as:
chronic iridocyclitis (H20.1-)

H26.211 **Cataract with neovascularization, right eye**

H26.212 **Cataract with neovascularization, left eye**

H26.213 **Cataract with neovascularization, bilateral**

■ H26.219 **Cataract with neovascularization, unspecified eye**

● H26.22 **Cataract secondary to ocular disorders (degenerative) (inflammatory)**
Code also associated ocular disorder

H26.221 **Cataract secondary to ocular disorders (degenerative) (inflammatory), right eye**

H26.222 **Cataract secondary to ocular disorders (degenerative) (inflammatory), left eye**

H26.223 **Cataract secondary to ocular disorders (degenerative) (inflammatory), bilateral**

■ H26.229 **Cataract secondary to ocular disorders (degenerative) (inflammatory), unspecified eye**

● H26.23 **Glaucomatous flecks (subcapsular)**

Code first underlying glaucoma (H40-H42)

● H26.231 **Glaucomatous flecks (subcapsular), right eye**

● H26.232 **Glaucomatous flecks (subcapsular), left eye**

● H26.233 **Glaucomatous flecks (subcapsular), bilateral**

● ■ H26.239 **Glaucomatous flecks (subcapsular), unspecified eye**

● H26.3 **Drug-induced cataract**
Toxic cataract

Code first (T36-T50) to identify drug

● ■ H26.30 **Drug-induced cataract, unspecified eye**

● H26.31 **Drug-induced cataract, right eye**

● H26.32 **Drug-induced cataract, left eye**

● H26.33 **Drug-induced cataract, bilateral**

● H26.4 **Secondary cataract**

■ H26.40 **Unspecified secondary cataract**

● H26.41 **Soemmering's ring**

H26.411 **Soemmering's ring, right eye**

H26.412 **Soemmering's ring, left eye**

H26.413 **Soemmering's ring, bilateral**

■ H26.419 **Soemmering's ring, unspecified eye**

● H26.49 **Other secondary cataract**

H26.491 **Other secondary cataract, right eye**

H26.492 **Other secondary cataract, left eye**

H26.493 **Other secondary cataract, bilateral**

■ H26.499 **Other secondary cataract, unspecified eye**

H26.8 **Other specified cataract**

■ H26.9 **Unspecified cataract**

● H27 **Other disorders of lens**

Excludes1   congenital lens malformations (Q12.-)
mechanical complications of intraocular lens implant (T85.2)
pseudophakia (Z96.1)

● H27.0 **Aphakia**
Acquired absence of lens
Acquired aphakia
Aphakia due to trauma

Excludes1   cataract extraction status (Z98.4-)
congenital absence of lens (Q12.3)
congenital aphakia (Q12.3)

■ H27.00 **Aphakia, unspecified eye**

H27.01 **Aphakia, right eye**

H27.02 **Aphakia, left eye**

H27.03 **Aphakia, bilateral**

● H27.1 **Dislocation of lens**

■ H27.10 **Unspecified dislocation of lens**

● H27.11 **Subluxation of lens**

H27.111 **Subluxation of lens, right eye**

H27.112 **Subluxation of lens, left eye**

H27.113 **Subluxation of lens, bilateral**

■ H27.119 **Subluxation of lens, unspecified eye**

● H27.12 **Anterior dislocation of lens**

H27.121 **Anterior dislocation of lens, right eye**

H27.122 **Anterior dislocation of lens, left eye**

H27.123 **Anterior dislocation of lens, bilateral**

■ H27.129 **Anterior dislocation of lens, unspecified eye**

● H27.13 **Posterior dislocation of lens**

H27.131 **Posterior dislocation of lens, right eye**

H27.132 **Posterior dislocation of lens, left eye**

H27.133 **Posterior dislocation of lens, bilateral**

■ H27.139 **Posterior dislocation of lens, unspecified eye**

H27.8 **Other specified disorders of lens**

■ H27.9 **Unspecified disorder of lens**

● H28 **Cataract in diseases classified elsewhere**

Code first underlying disease, such as:
hypoparathyroidism (E20.-)
myotonia (G71.1-)
myxedema (E03.-)
protein-calorie malnutrition (E40-E46)

Excludes1   cataract in diabetes mellitus (E08.33, E09.33, E10.33, E11.33, E13.33)

CHAPTER 7 (H00-H59)

972

● Unacceptable First-Listed Diagnosis   ● Use Additional Character(s)   ■ Unspecified   **OGCR** Official Guidelines for Coding and Reporting
🗲 Complication\Comorbidity   🗲 Major C\C   Excludes 1   Excludes 2   Includes   Use additional   Code first   Code also

DISORDERS OF CHOROID AND RETINA (H30-H36)

(See Plate 90 on page NAP-16.)

● H30 Chorioretinal inflammation
  ● H30.0 Focal chorioretinal inflammation
    Focal chorioretinitis
    Focal choroiditis
    Focal retinitis
    Focal retinochoroiditis
    ● H30.00 Unspecified focal chorioretinal
      inflammation
      Focal chorioretinitis NOS
      Focal choroiditis NOS
      Focal retinitis NOS
      Focal retinochoroiditis NOS
      ▨ H30.001 Unspecified focal chorioretinal
        inflammation, right eye
      ▨ H30.002 Unspecified focal chorioretinal
        inflammation, left eye
      ▨ H30.003 Unspecified focal chorioretinal
        inflammation, bilateral
      ▨ H30.009 Unspecified focal chorioretinal
        inflammation, unspecified eye
    ● H30.01 Focal chorioretinal inflammation,
      juxtapapillary
      H30.011 Focal chorioretinal inflammation,
        juxtapapillary, right eye
      H30.012 Focal chorioretinal inflammation,
        juxtapapillary, left eye
      H30.013 Focal chorioretinal inflammation,
        juxtapapillary, bilateral
      ▨ H30.019 Focal chorioretinal inflammation,
        juxtapapillary, unspecified eye
    ● H30.02 Focal chorioretinal inflammation of
      posterior pole
      H30.021 Focal chorioretinal inflammation
        of posterior pole, right eye
      H30.022 Focal chorioretinal inflammation
        of posterior pole, left eye
      H30.023 Focal chorioretinal inflammation
        of posterior pole, bilateral
      ▨ H30.029 Focal chorioretinal inflammation
        of posterior pole, unspecified eye
    ● H30.03 Focal chorioretinal inflammation,
      peripheral
      H30.031 Focal chorioretinal inflammation,
        peripheral, right eye
      H30.032 Focal chorioretinal inflammation,
        peripheral, left eye
      H30.033 Focal chorioretinal inflammation,
        peripheral, bilateral
      ▨ H30.039 Focal chorioretinal inflammation,
        peripheral, unspecified eye
    ● H30.04 Focal chorioretinal inflammation, macular
      or paramacular
      H30.041 Focal chorioretinal inflammation,
        macular or paramacular, right eye
      H30.042 Focal chorioretinal inflammation,
        macular or paramacular, left eye
      H30.043 Focal chorioretinal inflammation,
        macular or paramacular, bilateral
      ▨ H30.049 Focal chorioretinal inflammation,
        macular or paramacular,
        unspecified eye

● H30.1 Disseminated chorioretinal inflammation
    Disseminated chorioretinitis
    Disseminated choroiditis
    Disseminated retinitis
    Disseminated retinochoroiditis
    Excludes2 exudative retinopathy (H35.02-)
  ● H30.10 Unspecified disseminated chorioretinal
    inflammation
    Disseminated chorioretinitis NOS
    Disseminated choroiditis NOS
    Disseminated retinitis NOS
    Disseminated retinochoroiditis NOS
    ▨ H30.101 Unspecified disseminated
      chorioretinal inflammation, right
      eye 🔗
    ▨ H30.102 Unspecified disseminated
      chorioretinal inflammation, left
      eye 🔗
    ▨ H30.103 Unspecified disseminated
      chorioretinal inflammation,
      bilateral 🔗
    ▨ H30.109 Unspecified disseminated
      chorioretinal inflammation,
      unspecified eye 🔗
  ● H30.11 Disseminated chorioretinal inflammation
    of posterior pole
    H30.111 Disseminated chorioretinal
      inflammation of posterior pole,
      right eye 🔗
    H30.112 Disseminated chorioretinal
      inflammation of posterior pole,
      left eye 🔗
    H30.113 Disseminated chorioretinal
      inflammation of posterior pole,
      bilateral 🔗
    ▨ H30.119 Disseminated chorioretinal
      inflammation of posterior pole,
      unspecified eye 🔗
  ● H30.12 Disseminated chorioretinal inflammation,
    peripheral
    H30.121 Disseminated chorioretinal
      inflammation, peripheral right
      eye 🔗
    H30.122 Disseminated chorioretinal
      inflammation, peripheral, left
      eye 🔗
    H30.123 Disseminated chorioretinal
      inflammation, peripheral,
      bilateral 🔗
    ▨ H30.129 Disseminated chorioretinal
      inflammation, peripheral,
      unspecified eye 🔗
  ● H30.13 Disseminated chorioretinal inflammation,
    generalized
    H30.131 Disseminated chorioretinal
      inflammation, generalized, right
      eye 🔗
    H30.132 Disseminated chorioretinal
      inflammation, generalized, left
      eye 🔗
    H30.133 Disseminated chorioretinal
      inflammation, generalized,
      bilateral 🔗
    ▨ H30.139 Disseminated chorioretinal
      inflammation, generalized,
      unspecified eye 🔗

CHAPTER 7 (H00-H59)

● Unacceptable First-Listed Diagnosis   ● Use Additional Character(s)   ▨ Unspecified   **OGCR** Official Guidelines for Coding and Reporting
🔗 Complication\Comorbidity   🔗 Major C\C   Excludes 1   Excludes 2   Includes   Use additional   Code first   Code also

● H30.14   **Acute posterior multifocal placoid pigment epitheliopathy**

    H30.141   Acute posterior multifocal placoid pigment epitheliopathy, right eye 🦠

    H30.142   Acute posterior multifocal placoid pigment epitheliopathy, left eye 🦠

    H30.143   Acute posterior multifocal placoid pigment epitheliopathy, bilateral 🦠

    ▨ H30.149   Acute posterior multifocal placoid pigment epitheliopathy, unspecified eye 🦠

● H30.2   **Posterior cyclitis**
   Pars planitis

    ▨ H30.20   Posterior cyclitis, unspecified eye

    H30.21   Posterior cyclitis, right eye

    H30.22   Posterior cyclitis, left eye

    H30.23   Posterior cyclitis, bilateral

● H30.8   **Other chorioretinal inflammations**

   ● H30.81   Harada's disease

    H30.811   Harada's disease, right eye

    H30.812   Harada's disease, left eye

    H30.813   Harada's disease, bilateral

    ▨ H30.819   Harada's disease, unspecified eye

   ● H30.89   Other chorioretinal inflammations

    H30.891   Other chorioretinal inflammations, right eye

    H30.892   Other chorioretinal inflammations, left eye

    H30.893   Other chorioretinal inflammations, bilateral

    ▨ H30.899   Other chorioretinal inflammations, unspecified eye

● H30.9   **Unspecified chorioretinal inflammation**
   Chorioretinitis NOS
   Choroiditis NOS
   Neuroretinitis NOS
   Retinitis NOS
   Retinochoroiditis NOS

    ▨ H30.90   Unspecified chorioretinal inflammation, unspecified eye 🦠

    ▨ H30.91   Unspecified chorioretinal inflammation, right eye 🦠

    ▨ H30.92   Unspecified chorioretinal inflammation, left eye 🦠

    ▨ H30.93   Unspecified chorioretinal inflammation, bilateral 🦠

● H31   **Other disorders of choroid**

● H31.0   **Chorioretinal scars**

    | Excludes2 | postsurgical chorioretinal scars (H59.81-)

   ● H31.00   Unspecified chorioretinal scars

    ▨ H31.001   Unspecified chorioretinal scars, right eye

    ▨ H31.002   Unspecified chorioretinal scars, left eye

    ▨ H31.003   Unspecified chorioretinal scars, bilateral

    ▨ H31.009   Unspecified chorioretinal scars, unspecified eye

● H31.01   **Macula scars of posterior pole (postinflammatory) (post-traumatic)**

    | Excludes1 | postprocedural chorioretinal scar (H59.81-)

    H31.011   Macula scars of posterior pole (postinflammatory) (post-traumatic), right eye

    H31.012   Macula scars of posterior pole (postinflammatory) (post-traumatic), left eye

    H31.013   Macula scars of posterior pole (postinflammatory) (post-traumatic), bilateral

    ▨ H31.019   Macula scars of posterior pole (postinflammatory) (post-traumatic), unspecified eye

● H31.02   **Solar retinopathy**

    H31.021   Solar retinopathy, right eye

    H31.022   Solar retinopathy, left eye

    H31.023   Solar retinopathy, bilateral

    ▨ H31.029   Solar retinopathy, unspecified eye

● H31.09   **Other chorioretinal scars**

    H31.091   Other chorioretinal scars, right eye

    H31.092   Other chorioretinal scars, left eye

    H31.093   Other chorioretinal scars, bilateral

    ▨ H31.099   Other chorioretinal scars, unspecified eye

● H31.1   **Choroidal degeneration**

    | Excludes2 | angioid streaks of macula (H35.33)

   ● H31.10   Unspecified choroidal degeneration
    Choroidal sclerosis NOS

    ▨ H31.101   Choroidal degeneration, unspecified, right eye

    ▨ H31.102   Choroidal degeneration, unspecified, left eye

    ▨ H31.103   Choroidal degeneration, unspecified, bilateral

    ▨ H31.109   Choroidal degeneration, unspecified, unspecified eye

   ● H31.11   Age-related choroidal atrophy

    H31.111   Age-related choroidal atrophy, right eye

    H31.112   Age-related choroidal atrophy, left eye

    H31.113   Age-related choroidal atrophy, bilateral

    ▨ H31.119   Age-related choroidal atrophy, unspecified eye

   ● H31.12   Diffuse secondary atrophy of choroid

    H31.121   Diffuse secondary atrophy of choroid, right eye

    H31.122   Diffuse secondary atrophy of choroid, left eye

    H31.123   Diffuse secondary atrophy of choroid, bilateral

    ▨ H31.129   Diffuse secondary atrophy of choroid, unspecified eye

● H31.2   **Hereditary choroidal dystrophy**

    | Excludes2 | hyperornithinemia (E72.4)
               ornithinemia (E72.4)

    ▨ H31.20   Hereditary choroidal dystrophy, unspecified

● Unacceptable First-Listed Diagnosis   ● Use Additional Character(s)   ▨ Unspecified   **OGCR** Official Guidelines for Coding and Reporting

🦠 Complication\Comorbidity   🦠 Major C\C | Excludes 1 | | Excludes 2 | Includes   Use additional   Code first   Code also

974

H31.21 Choroideremia

H31.22 Choroidal dystrophy (central areolar) (generalized) (peripapillary)

H31.23 Gyrate atrophy, choroid

H31.29 Other hereditary choroidal dystrophy

● H31.3 Choroidal hemorrhage and rupture

  ● H31.30 Unspecified choroidal hemorrhage

     ▣ H31.301 Unspecified choroidal hemorrhage, right eye

     ▣ H31.302 Unspecified choroidal hemorrhage, left eye

     ▣ H31.303 Unspecified choroidal hemorrhage, bilateral

     ▣ H31.309 Unspecified choroidal hemorrhage, unspecified eye

  ● H31.31 Expulsive choroidal hemorrhage

     H31.311 Expulsive choroidal hemorrhage, right eye

     H31.312 Expulsive choroidal hemorrhage, left eye

     H31.313 Expulsive choroidal hemorrhage, bilateral

     ▣ H31.319 Expulsive choroidal hemorrhage, unspecified eye

  ● H31.32 Choroidal rupture

     H31.321 Choroidal rupture, right eye 🅒

     H31.322 Choroidal rupture, left eye 🅒

     H31.323 Choroidal rupture, bilateral 🅒

     ▣ H31.329 Choroidal rupture, unspecified eye 🅒

● H31.4 Choroidal detachment

  ● H31.40 Unspecified choroidal detachment

     ▣ H31.401 Unspecified choroidal detachment, right eye 🅒

     ▣ H31.402 Unspecified choroidal detachment, left eye 🅒

     ▣ H31.403 Unspecified choroidal detachment, bilateral 🅒

     ▣ H31.409 Unspecified choroidal detachment, unspecified eye 🅒

  ● H31.41 Hemorrhagic choroidal detachment

     H31.411 Hemorrhagic choroidal detachment, right eye 🅒

     H31.412 Hemorrhagic choroidal detachment, left eye 🅒

     H31.413 Hemorrhagic choroidal detachment, bilateral 🅒

     ▣ H31.419 Hemorrhagic choroidal detachment, unspecified eye 🅒

  ● H31.42 Serous choroidal detachment

     H31.421 Serous choroidal detachment, right eye 🅒

     H31.422 Serous choroidal detachment, left eye 🅒

     H31.423 Serous choroidal detachment, bilateral 🅒

     ▣ H31.429 Serous choroidal detachment, unspecified eye 🅒

H31.8 Other specified disorders of choroid

▣ H31.9 Unspecified disorder of choroid

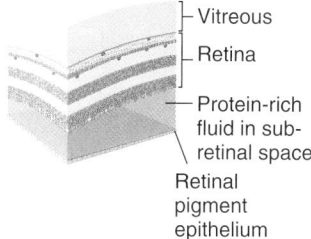

NON-RHEGMATOGENOUS RETINAL DETACHMENT

— Vitreous
— Retina
— Protein-rich fluid in sub-retinal space
Retinal pigment epithelium

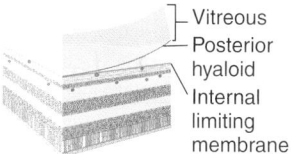

VITREOUS DETACHMENT

— Vitreous
— Posterior hyaloid
Internal limiting membrane

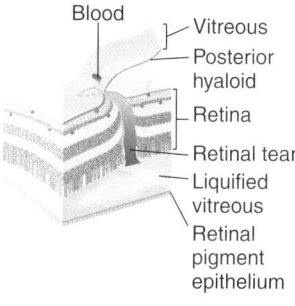

RHEGMATOGENOUS RETINAL DETACHMENT

Blood
— Vitreous
— Posterior hyaloid
— Retina
— Retinal tear
— Liquified vitreous
Retinal pigment epithelium

Figure 7-9   Rential detachment. (From Kumar: Robbins and Cotran: Pathologic Basis of Disease, 7th ed. 2005, Saunders)

● H32 Chorioretinal disorders in diseases classified elsewhere

Code first underlying disease, such as:
  congenital toxoplasmosis (P37.1)
  histoplasmosis (B39.-)
  leprosy (A30.-)

  Excludes1   chorioretinitis (in):
      toxoplasmosis (acquired) (B58.01)
      tuberculosis (A18.53)

● H33 Retinal detachments and breaks

  Excludes1   detachment of retinal pigment epithelium (H35.72-, H35.73-)

  ● H33.0 Retinal detachment with retinal break
    Rhegmatogenous retinal detachment

    Excludes1   serous retinal detachment (without retinal break) (H33.2-)

    ● H33.00 Unspecified retinal detachment with retinal break

       ▣ H33.001 Unspecified retinal detachment with retinal break, right eye

       ▣ H33.002 Unspecified retinal detachment with retinal break, left eye

● Unacceptable First-Listed Diagnosis   ● Use Additional Character(s)   ▣ Unspecified   **OGCR** Official Guidelines for Coding and Reporting
🅒 Complication\Comorbidity 🅒 Major C\C Excludes 1 Excludes 2 Includes Use additional Code first Code also

975

CHAPTER 7 (H00-H59)

Item 7-6 Retinal detachments and defects are conditions of the eye in which the retina separates from the underlying tissue. Initial detachment may be localized, requiring rapid treatment (medical emergency) to avoid the entire retina from detaching which leads to vision loss and blindness.

■ H33.003   Unspecified retinal detachment with retinal break, bilateral

■ H33.009   Unspecified retinal detachment with retinal break, unspecified eye

● H33.01   Retinal detachment with single break

    H33.011   Retinal detachment with single break, right eye

    H33.012   Retinal detachment with single break, left eye

    H33.013   Retinal detachment with single break, bilateral

    ■ H33.019   Retinal detachment with single break, unspecified eye

● H33.02   Retinal detachment with multiple breaks

    H33.021   Retinal detachment with multiple breaks, right eye

    H33.022   Retinal detachment with multiple breaks, left eye

    H33.023   Retinal detachment with multiple breaks, bilateral

    ■ H33.029   Retinal detachment with multiple breaks, unspecified eye

● H33.03   Retinal detachment with giant retinal tear

    H33.031   Retinal detachment with giant retinal tear, right eye

    H33.032   Retinal detachment with giant retinal tear, left eye

    H33.033   Retinal detachment with giant retinal tear, bilateral

    ■ H33.039   Retinal detachment with giant retinal tear, unspecified eye

● H33.04   Retinal detachment with retinal dialysis

    H33.041   Retinal detachment with retinal dialysis, right eye

    H33.042   Retinal detachment with retinal dialysis, left eye

    H33.043   Retinal detachment with retinal dialysis, bilateral

    ■ H33.049   Retinal detachment with retinal dialysis, unspecified eye

● H33.05   Total retinal detachment

    H33.051   Total retinal detachment, right eye

    H33.052   Total retinal detachment, left eye

    H33.053   Total retinal detachment, bilateral

    ■ H33.059   Total retinal detachment, unspecified eye

● H33.1   Retinoschisis and retinal cysts

    Excludes1   congenital retinoschisis (Q14.1)
            microcystoid degeneration of retina (H35.42-)

● H33.10   Unspecified retinoschisis

    ■ H33.101   Unspecified retinoschisis, right eye

    ■ H33.102   Unspecified retinoschisis, left eye

    ■ H33.103   Unspecified retinoschisis, bilateral

    ■ H33.109   Unspecified retinoschisis, unspecified eye

● H33.11   Cyst of ora serrata

    H33.111   Cyst of ora serrata, right eye

    H33.112   Cyst of ora serrata, left eye

    H33.113   Cyst of ora serrata, bilateral

    ■ H33.119   Cyst of ora serrata, unspecified eye

● H33.12   Parasitic cyst of retina

    H33.121   Parasitic cyst of retina, right eye 🦠

    H33.122   Parasitic cyst of retina, left eye 🦠

    H33.123   Parasitic cyst of retina, bilateral 🦠

    ■ H33.129   Parasitic cyst of retina, unspecified eye 🦠

● H33.19   Other retinoschisis and retinal cysts
        Pseudocyst of retina

    H33.191   Other retinoschisis and retinal cysts, right eye

    H33.192   Other retinoschisis and retinal cysts, left eye

    H33.193   Other retinoschisis and retinal cysts, bilateral

    ■ H33.199   Other retinoschisis and retinal cysts, unspecified eye

● H33.2   Serous retinal detachment
        Retinal detachment NOS
        Retinal detachment without retinal break

    Excludes1   central serous chorioretinopathy (H35.71-)

    ■ H33.20   Serous retinal detachment, unspecified eye 🦠

    H33.21   Serous retinal detachment, right eye 🦠

    H33.22   Serous retinal detachment, left eye 🦠

    H33.23   Serous retinal detachment, bilateral 🦠

● H33.3   Retinal breaks without detachment

    Excludes1   chorioretinal scars after surgery for detachment (H59.81-)
            peripheral retinal degeneration without break (H35.4-)

    ● H33.30   Unspecified retinal break

       ■ H33.301   Unspecified retinal break, right eye

       ■ H33.302   Unspecified retinal break, left eye

       ■ H33.303   Unspecified retinal break, bilateral

       ■ H33.309   Unspecified retinal break, unspecified eye

    ● H33.31   Horseshoe tear of retina without detachment
            Operculum of retina without detachment

       H33.311   Horseshoe tear of retina without detachment, right eye

       H33.312   Horseshoe tear of retina without detachment, left eye

       H33.313   Horseshoe tear of retina without detachment, bilateral

       ■ H33.319   Horseshoe tear of retina without detachment, unspecified eye

    ● H33.32   Round hole of retina without detachment

       H33.321   Round hole, right eye

       H33.322   Round hole, left eye

       H33.323   Round hole, bilateral

       ■ H33.329   Round hole, unspecified eye

● Unacceptable First-Listed Diagnosis   ● Use Additional Character(s)   ■ Unspecified   **OGCR** Official Guidelines for Coding and Reporting
🦠 Complication\Comorbidity   🦠 Major C\C   Excludes 1   Excludes 2   Includes   Use additional   Code first   Code also

- ● H33.33 **Multiple defects of retina without detachment**
  - H33.331 Multiple defects of retina without detachment, right eye
  - H33.332 Multiple defects of retina without detachment, left eye
  - H33.333 Multiple defects of retina without detachment, bilateral
  - ◼ H33.339 Multiple defects of retina without detachment, unspecified eye
- ● H33.4 **Traction detachment of retina**
  Proliferative vitreo-retinopathy with retinal detachment
  - ◼ H33.40 Traction detachment of retina, unspecified eye 🦠
  - H33.41 Traction detachment of retina, right eye 🦠
  - H33.42 Traction detachment of retina, left eye 🦠
  - H33.43 Traction detachment of retina, bilateral 🦠
- H33.8 **Other retinal detachments** 🦠

- ● H34 **Retinal vascular occlusions**
  Blockage in vessel of the retina
  Excludes1 amaurosis fugax (G45.3)
  - ● H34.0 **Transient retinal artery occlusion**
    - ◼ H34.00 Transient retinal artery occlusion, unspecified eye 🦠
    - H34.01 Transient retinal artery occlusion, right eye 🦠
    - H34.02 Transient retinal artery occlusion, left eye 🦠
    - H34.03 Transient retinal artery occlusion, bilateral 🦠
  - ● H34.1 **Central retinal artery occlusion**
    - ◼ H34.10 Central retinal artery occlusion, unspecified eye 🦠
    - H34.11 Central retinal artery occlusion, right eye 🦠
    - H34.12 Central retinal artery occlusion, left eye 🦠
    - H34.13 Central retinal artery occlusion, bilateral 🦠
  - ● H34.2 **Other retinal artery occlusions**
    - ● H34.21 **Partial retinal artery occlusion**
      Hollenhorst's plaque
      Retinal microembolism
      - H34.211 Partial retinal artery occlusion, right eye 🦠
      - H34.212 Partial retinal artery occlusion, left eye 🦠
      - H34.213 Partial retinal artery occlusion, bilateral 🦠
      - ◼ H34.219 Partial retinal artery occlusion, unspecified eye 🦠
    - ● H34.23 **Retinal artery branch occlusion**
      - H34.231 Retinal artery branch occlusion, right eye 🦠
      - H34.232 Retinal artery branch occlusion, left eye 🦠
      - H34.233 Retinal artery branch occlusion, bilateral 🦠
      - ◼ H34.239 Retinal artery branch occlusion, unspecified eye 🦠
  - ● H34.8 **Other retinal vascular occlusions**
    - ● H34.81 **Central retinal vein occlusion**
      - H34.811 Central retinal vein occlusion, right eye 🦠
      - H34.812 Central retinal vein occlusion, left eye 🦠

- H34.813 Central retinal vein occlusion, bilateral 🦠
- ◼ H34.819 Central retinal vein occlusion, unspecified eye 🦠
- ● H34.82 **Venous engorgement**
  Incipient retinal vein occlusion
  Partial retinal vein occlusion
  - H34.821 Venous engorgement, right eye
  - H34.822 Venous engorgement, left eye
  - H34.823 Venous engorgement, bilateral
  - ◼ H34.829 Venous engorgement, unspecified eye
- ● H34.83 **Tributary (branch) retinal vein occlusion**
  - H34.831 Tributary (branch) retinal vein occlusion, right eye
  - H34.832 Tributary (branch) retinal vein occlusion, left eye
  - H34.833 Tributary (branch) retinal vein occlusion, bilateral
  - ◼ H34.839 Tributary (branch) retinal vein occlusion, unspecified eye
- ◼ H34.9 **Unspecified retinal vascular occlusion** 🦠
  OGCR Section I. C.9.a.5.
  Hypertensive Retinopathy
  Code H35.0, Hypertensive retinopathy, should be used with code I10, Essential (primary) hypertension, to include the systemic hypertension. The sequencing is based on the reason for the encounter.
- ● H35 **Other retinal disorders**
  Excludes2 diabetic retinal disorders (E08.311- E08.359, E09.311- E09.359, E10.311- E10.359, E11.311- E11.359, E13.311- E13.359)
  - ● H35.0 **Background retinopathy and retinal vascular changes**
    Code also any associated hypertension (I10-)
    - ◼ H35.00 Unspecified background retinopathy
    - ● H35.01 **Changes in retinal vascular appearance**
      Retinal vascular sheathing
      - H35.011 Changes in retinal vascular appearance, right eye
      - H35.012 Changes in retinal vascular appearance, left eye
      - H35.013 Changes in retinal vascular appearance, bilateral
      - ◼ H35.019 Changes in retinal vascular appearance, unspecified eye
    - ● H35.02 **Exudative retinopathy**
      Coats retinopathy
      - H35.021 Exudative retinopathy, right eye
      - H35.022 Exudative retinopathy, left eye
      - H35.023 Exudative retinopathy, bilateral
      - ◼ H35.029 Exudative retinopathy, unspecified eye
    - ● H35.03 **Hypertensive retinopathy**
      - H35.031 Hypertensive retinopathy, right eye
      - H35.032 Hypertensive retinopathy, left eye
      - H35.033 Hypertensive retinopathy, bilateral
      - ◼ H35.039 Hypertensive retinopathy, unspecified eye

● Unacceptable First-Listed Diagnosis　● Use Additional Character(s)　◼ Unspecified　**OGCR** Official Guidelines for Coding and Reporting
🦠 Complication\Comorbidity　🦠 Major C\C　Excludes 1　Excludes 2　Includes　Use additional　Code first　Code also　977

CHAPTER 7 (H00-H59)

● **H35.04 Retinal micro-aneurysms NOS**

     H35.041 Retinal micro-aneurysms NOS, right eye

     H35.042 Retinal micro-aneurysms NOS, left eye

     H35.043 Retinal micro-aneurysms NOS, bilateral

     ▣ **H35.049 Retinal micro-aneurysms NOS, unspecified eye**

● **H35.05 Retinal neovascularization NOS**

     H35.051 Retinal neovascularization NOS, right eye

     H35.052 Retinal neovascularization NOS, left eye

     H35.053 Retinal neovascularization NOS, bilateral

     ▣ **H35.059 Retinal neovascularization NOS, unspecified eye**

● **H35.06 Retinal vasculitis**

     Eales disease

     Retinal perivasculitis

     H35.061 Retinal vasculitis, right eye

     H35.062 Retinal vasculitis, left eye

     H35.063 Retinal vasculitis, bilateral

     ▣ **H35.069 Retinal vasculitis, unspecified eye**

● **H35.07 Retinal telangiectasis**

     H35.071 Retinal telangiectasis, right eye

     H35.072 Retinal telangiectasis, left eye

     H35.073 Retinal telangiectasis, bilateral

     ▣ **H35.079 Retinal telangiectasis, unspecified eye**

H35.09 Other intraretinal microvascular abnormalities

     Retinal varices

H35.1 Retinopathy of prematurity

● **H35.10 Retinopathy of prematurity, unspecified**

     Retinopathy of prematurity NOS

     ▣ **H35.101 Retinopathy of prematurity, unspecified, right eye**

     ▣ **H35.102 Retinopathy of prematurity, unspecified, left eye**

     ▣ **H35.103 Retinopathy of prematurity, unspecified, bilateral**

     ▣ **H35.109 Retinopathy of prematurity, unspecified, unspecified eye**

● **H35.11 Retinopathy of prematurity, stage 0**

     H35.111 Retinopathy of prematurity, stage 0, right eye

     H35.112 Retinopathy of prematurity, stage 0, left eye

     H35.113 Retinopathy of prematurity, stage 0, bilateral

     ▣ **H35.119 Retinopathy of prematurity, stage 0, unspecified eye**

● **H35.12 Retinopathy of prematurity, stage 1**

     H35.121 Retinopathy of prematurity, stage 1, right eye

     H35.122 Retinopathy of prematurity, stage 1, left eye

     H35.123 Retinopathy of prematurity, stage 1, bilateral

     ▣ **H35.129 Retinopathy of prematurity, stage 1, unspecified eye**

● **H35.13 Retinopathy of prematurity, stage 2**

     H35.131 Retinopathy of prematurity, stage 2, right eye

     H35.132 Retinopathy of prematurity, stage 2, left eye

     H35.133 Retinopathy of prematurity, stage 2, bilateral

     ▣ **H35.139 Retinopathy of prematurity, stage 2, unspecified eye**

● **H35.14 Retinopathy of prematurity, stage 3**

     H35.141 Retinopathy of prematurity, stage 3, right eye

     H35.142 Retinopathy of prematurity, stage 3, left eye

     H35.143 Retinopathy of prematurity, stage 3, bilateral

     ▣ **H35.149 Retinopathy of prematurity, stage 3, unspecified eye**

● **H35.15 Retinopathy of prematurity, stage 4**

     H35.151 Retinopathy of prematurity, stage 4, right eye

     H35.152 Retinopathy of prematurity, stage 4, left eye

     H35.153 Retinopathy of prematurity, stage 4, bilateral

     ▣ **H35.159 Retinopathy of prematurity, stage 4, unspecified eye**

● **H35.16 Retinopathy of prematurity, stage 5**

     H35.161 Retinopathy of prematurity, stage 5, right eye

     H35.162 Retinopathy of prematurity, stage 5, left eye

     H35.163 Retinopathy of prematurity, stage 5, bilateral

     ▣ **H35.169 Retinopathy of prematurity, stage 5, unspecified eye**

● **H35.17 Retrolental fibroplasia**

     H35.171 Retrolental fibroplasia, right eye

     H35.172 Retrolental fibroplasia, left eye

     H35.173 Retrolental fibroplasia, bilateral

     ▣ **H35.179 Retrolental fibroplasia, unspecified eye**

● **H35.2 Other non-diabetic proliferative retinopathy**

     Proliferative vitreo-retinopathy

     Excludes1   proliferative vitreo-retinopathy with retinal detachment (H33.4-)

     ▣ **H35.20 Other non-diabetic proliferative retinopathy, unspecified eye**

     H35.21 Other non-diabetic proliferative retinopathy, right eye

     H35.22 Other non-diabetic proliferative retinopathy, left eye

     H35.23 Other non-diabetic proliferative retinopathy, bilateral

● **H35.3 Degeneration of macula and posterior pole**

     ▣ **H35.30 Unspecified macular degeneration (age-related)**

     H35.31 Nonexudative age-related macular degeneration

         Atrophic age-related macular degeneration

     H35.32 Exudative age-related macular degeneration

     H35.33 Angioid streaks of macula

● Unacceptable First-Listed Diagnosis   ● Use Additional Character(s)   ▣ Unspecified   **OGCR** Official Guidelines for Coding and Reporting

🕭 Complication\Comorbidity   🕭 Major C\C   Excludes 1   Excludes 2   Includes   Use additional   Code first   Code also

Item 7-7 Macular degeneration is typically age-related, chronic, and is evidenced by deterioration of the macula (the part of the retina that provides for central field vision), resulting in blurred vision or a blind spot in the center of visual field while not affecting peripheral vision.

● H35.34　Macular cyst, hole, or pseudohole

　　　H35.341　Macular cyst, hole, or pseudohole, right eye

　　　H35.342　Macular cyst, hole, or pseudohole, left eye

　　　H35.343　Macular cyst, hole, or pseudohole, bilateral

　　■ H35.349　Macular cyst, hole, or pseudohole, unspecified eye

● H35.35　Cystoid macular degeneration

　　　Excludes1　cystoid macular edema following cataract surgery (H59.03-)

　　　H35.351　Cystoid macular degeneration, right eye

　　　H35.352　Cystoid macular degeneration, left eye

　　　H35.353　Cystoid macular degeneration, bilateral

　　■ H35.359　Cystoid macular degeneration, unspecified eye

● H35.36　Drusen (degenerative) of macula

　　　H35.361　Drusen (degenerative) of macula, right eye

　　　H35.362　Drusen (degenerative) of macula, left eye

　　　H35.363　Drusen (degenerative) of macula, bilateral

　　■ H35.369　Drusen (degenerative) of macula, unspecified eye

● H35.37　Puckering of macula

　　　H35.371　Puckering of macula, right eye

　　　H35.372　Puckering of macula, left eye

　　　H35.373　Puckering of macula, bilateral

　　■ H35.379　Puckering of macula, unspecified eye

● H35.38　Toxic maculopathy

　　　H35.381　Toxic maculopathy, right eye

　　　H35.382　Toxic maculopathy, left eye

　　　H35.383　Toxic maculopathy, bilateral

　　■ H35.389　Toxic maculopathy, unspecified eye

● H35.4　Peripheral retinal degeneration

　　　Excludes1　hereditary retinal degeneration (dystrophy) (H35.5-)
　　　　　　peripheral retinal degeneration with retinal break (H33.3-)

　　■ H35.40　Unspecified peripheral retinal degeneration

● H35.41　Lattice degeneration of retina
　　　　　Palisade degeneration of retina

　　　H35.411　Lattice degeneration of retina, right eye

　　　H35.412　Lattice degeneration of retina, left eye

　　　H35.413　Lattice degeneration of retina, bilateral

　　■ H35.419　Lattice degeneration of retina, unspecified eye

● H35.42　Microcystoid degeneration of retina

　　　H35.421　Microcystoid degeneration of retina, right eye

　　　H35.422　Microcystoid degeneration of retina, left eye

　　　H35.423　Microcystoid degeneration of retina, bilateral

　　■ H35.429　Microcystoid degeneration of retina, unspecified eye

● H35.43　Paving stone degeneration of retina

　　　H35.431　Paving stone degeneration of retina, right eye

　　　H35.432　Paving stone degeneration of retina, left eye

　　　H35.433　Paving stone degeneration of retina, bilateral

　　■ H35.439　Paving stone degeneration of retina, unspecified eye

● H35.44　Age-related reticular degeneration of retina

　　　H35.441　Age-related reticular degeneration of retina, right eye

　　　H35.442　Age-related reticular degeneration of retina, left eye

　　　H35.443　Age-related reticular degeneration of retina, bilateral

　　■ H35.449　Age-related reticular degeneration of retina, unspecified eye

● H35.45　Secondary pigmentary degeneration

　　　H35.451　Secondary pigmentary degeneration, right eye

　　　H35.452　Secondary pigmentary degeneration, left eye

　　　H35.453　Secondary pigmentary degeneration, bilateral

　　■ H35.459　Secondary pigmentary degeneration, unspecified eye

● H35.46　Secondary vitreoretinal degeneration

　　　H35.461　Secondary vitreoretinal degeneration, right eye

　　　H35.462　Secondary vitreoretinal degeneration, left eye

　　　H35.463　Secondary vitreoretinal degeneration, bilateral

　　■ H35.469　Secondary vitreoretinal degeneration, unspecified eye

● H35.5　Hereditary retinal dystrophy

　　　Excludes1　dystrophies primarily involving Bruch's membrane (H31.1-)

　　■ H35.50　Unspecified hereditary retinal dystrophy

　　　H35.51　Vitreoretinal dystrophy

　　　H35.52　Pigmentary retinal dystrophy
　　　　　　Albipunctate retinal dystrophy
　　　　　　Retinitis pigmentosa
　　　　　　Tapetoretinal dystrophy

　　　H35.53　Other dystrophies primarily involving the sensory retina
　　　　　　Stargardt's disease

　　　H35.54　Dystrophies primarily involving the retinal pigment epithelium
　　　　　　Vitelliform retinal dystrophy

● Unacceptable First-Listed Diagnosis　　● Use Additional Character(s)　　■ Unspecified　　**OGCR** Official Guidelines for Coding and Reporting

🅒 Complication\Comorbidity　🅒 Major C\C　Excludes 1　Excludes 2　Includes　Use additional　Code first　Code also

CHAPTER 7 (H00-H59)

979

● H35.6   Retinal hemorrhage

■ H35.60   Retinal hemorrhage, unspecified eye

H35.61   Retinal hemorrhage, right eye

H35.62   Retinal hemorrhage, left eye

H35.63   Retinal hemorrhage, bilateral

● H35.7   Separation of retinal layers

> **Excludes1**   retinal detachment (serous) (H33.2-)
> rhegmatogenous retinal detachment (H33.0-)

■ H35.70   Unspecified separation of retinal layers 🅒

● H35.71   Central serous chorioretinopathy

H35.711   Central serous chorioretinopathy, right eye

H35.712   Central serous chorioretinopathy, left eye

H35.713   Central serous chorioretinopathy, bilateral

■ H35.719   Central serous chorioretinopathy, unspecified eye

● H35.72   Serous detachment of retinal pigment epithelium

H35.721   Serous detachment of retinal pigment epithelium, right eye 🅒

H35.722   Serous detachment of retinal pigment epithelium, left eye 🅒

H35.723   Serous detachment of retinal pigment epithelium, bilateral 🅒

■ H35.729   Serous detachment of retinal pigment epithelium, unspecified eye 🅒

● H35.73   Hemorrhagic detachment of retinal pigment epithelium

H35.731   Hemorrhagic detachment of retinal pigment epithelium, right eye 🅒

H35.732   Hemorrhagic detachment of retinal pigment epithelium, left eye 🅒

H35.733   Hemorrhagic detachment of retinal pigment epithelium, bilateral 🅒

■ H35.739   Hemorrhagic detachment of retinal pigment epithelium, unspecified eye 🅒

● H35.8   Other specified retinal disorders

> **Excludes2**   retinal hemorrhage (H35.6-)

H35.81   Retinal edema
> Retinal cotton wool spots

H35.82   Retinal ischemia 🅒

H35.89   Other specified retinal disorders

■ H35.9   Unspecified retinal disorder

● H36   Retinal disorders in diseases classified elsewhere

> *Code first underlying disease, such as:*
> lipid storage disorders (E75.-)
> sickle-cell disorders (D57.-)

> **Excludes1**   arteriosclerotic retinopathy (H35.0-)
> diabetic retinopathy (E08.3-, E09.3-, E10.3-, E11.3-, E13.3-)

● H40   Glaucoma

> *Intraocular pressure (IOP) that is too high results from too much aqueous humor and because of excess production or inadequate drainage, optic nerve damage and vision loss may occur.*

> **Excludes1**   absolute glaucoma (H44.51-)
> congenital glaucoma (Q15.0)
> traumatic glaucoma due to birth injury (P15.3)

H40.0   Glaucoma suspect
> Ocular hypertension

● H40.1   Open-angle glaucoma

■ H40.10   Unspecified open-angle glaucoma

H40.11   Primary open-angle glaucoma
> Chronic simple glaucoma

● H40.12   Low-tension glaucoma

H40.121   Low-tension glaucoma, right eye

H40.122   Low-tension glaucoma, left eye

H40.123   Low-tension glaucoma, bilateral

■ H40.129   Low-tension glaucoma, unspecified eye

● H40.13   Pigmentary glaucoma

H40.131   Pigmentary glaucoma, right eye

H40.132   Pigmentary glaucoma, left eye

H40.133   Pigmentary glaucoma, bilateral

■ H40.139   Pigmentary glaucoma, unspecified eye

● H40.14   Capsular glaucoma with pseudoexfoliation of lens

H40.141   Capsular glaucoma with pseudoexfoliation of lens, right eye

H40.142   Capsular glaucoma with pseudoexfoliation of lens, left eye

H40.143   Capsular glaucoma with pseudoexfoliation of lens, bilateral

■ H40.149   Capsular glaucoma with pseudoexfoliation of lens, unspecified eye

● H40.15   Residual stage of open-angle glaucoma

H40.151   Residual stage of open-angle glaucoma, right eye

H40.152   Residual stage of open-angle glaucoma, left eye

H40.153   Residual stage of open-angle glaucoma, bilateral

■ H40.159   Residual stage of open-angle glaucoma, unspecified eye

● H40.2   Primary angle-closure glaucoma

> **Excludes1**   aqueous misdirection (H40.83-)
> malignant glaucoma (H40.83-)

■ H40.20   Unspecified primary angle-closure glaucoma

● H40.21   Acute angle-closure glaucoma

H40.211   Acute angle-closure glaucoma, right eye 🅒

H40.212   Acute angle-closure glaucoma, left eye 🅒

H40.213   Acute angle-closure glaucoma, bilateral 🅒

■ H40.219   Acute angle-closure glaucoma, unspecified eye 🅒

● Unacceptable First-Listed Diagnosis   ● Use Additional Character(s)   ■ Unspecified   **OGCR** Official Guidelines for Coding and Reporting
🅒 Complication\Comorbidity   🅒 Major C\C   Excludes 1   Excludes 2   Includes   Use additional   Code first   Code also

● H40.22   Chronic angle-closure glaucoma

     H40.221   Chronic angle-closure glaucoma, right eye

     H40.222   Chronic angle-closure glaucoma, left eye

     H40.223   Chronic angle-closure glaucoma, bilateral

     ▨ H40.229   Chronic angle-closure glaucoma, unspecified eye

● H40.23   Intermittent angle-closure glaucoma

     H40.231   Intermittent angle-closure glaucoma, right eye

     H40.232   Intermittent angle-closure glaucoma, left eye

     H40.233   Intermittent angle-closure glaucoma, bilateral

     ▨ H40.239   Intermittent angle-closure glaucoma, unspecified eye

● H40.24   Residual stage of angle-closure glaucoma

     H40.241   Residual stage of angle-closure glaucoma, right eye

     H40.242   Residual stage of angle-closure glaucoma, let eye

     H40.243   Residual stage of angle-closure glaucoma, bilateral

     ▨ H40.249   Residual stage of angle-closure glaucoma, unspecified eye

● H40.3   Glaucoma secondary to eye trauma
Code also underlying condition

     ▨ H40.30   Glaucoma secondary to eye trauma, unspecified eye

     H40.31   Glaucoma secondary to eye trauma, right eye

     H40.32   Glaucoma secondary to eye trauma, left eye

     H40.33   Glaucoma secondary to eye trauma, bilateral

● H40.4   Glaucoma secondary to eye inflammation
Code also underlying condition

     ▨ H40.40   Glaucoma secondary to eye inflammation, unspecified eye

     H40.41   Glaucoma secondary to eye inflammation, right eye

     H40.42   Glaucoma secondary to eye inflammation, left eye

     H40.43   Glaucoma secondary to eye inflammation, bilateral

● H40.5   Glaucoma secondary to other eye disorders
Code also underlying eye disorder

     ▨ H40.50   Glaucoma secondary to other eye disorders, unspecified eye

     H40.51   Glaucoma secondary to other eye disorders, right eye

     H40.52   Glaucoma secondary to other eye disorders, left eye

     H40.53   Glaucoma secondary to other eye disorders, bilateral

● H40.6   Glaucoma secondary to drugs
Code first (T36-T50) to identify drug

     ● ▨ H40.60   Glaucoma secondary to drugs, unspecified eye

     ● H40.61   Glaucoma secondary to drugs, right eye

     ● H40.62   Glaucoma secondary to drugs, left eye

     ● H40.63   Glaucoma secondary to drugs, bilateral

● H40.8   Other glaucoma

     ● H40.81   Glaucoma with increased episcleral venous pressure

         H40.811   Glaucoma with increased episcleral venous pressure, right eye

         H40.812   Glaucoma with increased episcleral venous pressure, left eye

         H40.813   Glaucoma with increased episcleral venous pressure, bilateral

         ▨ H40.819   Glaucoma with increased episcleral venous pressure, unspecified eye

     ● H40.82   Hypersecretion glaucoma

         H40.821   Hypersecretion glaucoma, right eye

         H40.822   Hypersecretion glaucoma, left eye

         H40.823   Hypersecretion glaucoma, bilateral

         ▨ H40.829   Hypersecretion glaucoma, unspecified eye

     ● H40.83   Aqueous misdirection
         Malignant glaucoma

         H40.831   Aqueous misdirection, right eye

         H40.832   Aqueous misdirection, left eye

         H40.833   Aqueous misdirection, bilateral

         ▨ H40.839   Aqueous misdirection, unspecified eye

     H40.89   Other specified glaucoma

     ▨ H40.9   Unspecified glaucoma

● H42   Glaucoma in diseases classified elsewhere

Code first underlying condition, such as:
     amyloidosis (E85.-)
     aniridia (Q13.1)
     Lowe's syndrome (E72.03)
     Reiger's anomaly (Q13.81)
     specified metabolic disorder (E70-E90)

     Excludes1   glaucoma (in):
         diabetes mellitus (E08.39, E09.39, E10.39, E11.39, E13.39)
         onchocerciasis (B73.02)
         syphilis (A52.71)
         tuberculous (A18.59)

DISORDERS OF VITREOUS BODY AND GLOBE (H43-H44)

● H43   Disorders of vitreous body

     ● H43.0   Vitreous prolapse

         Excludes1   vitreous syndrome following cataract surgery (H59.0-)
             traumatic vitreous prolapse (S05.2-)

         ▨ H43.00   Vitreous prolapse, unspecified eye

         H43.01   Vitreous prolapse, right eye

         H43.02   Vitreous prolapse, left eye

         H43.03   Vitreous prolapse, bilateral

     ● H43.1   Vitreous hemorrhage

         ▨ H43.10   Vitreous hemorrhage, unspecified eye

         H43.11   Vitreous hemorrhage, right eye

         H43.12   Vitreous hemorrhage, left eye

         H43.13   Vitreous hemorrhage, bilateral

● Unacceptable First-Listed Diagnosis   ● Use Additional Character(s)   ▨ Unspecified   **OGCR** Official Guidelines for Coding and Reporting

🗗 Complication\Comorbidity   🗗 Major C\C   Excludes 1   Excludes 2   Includes   Use additional   Code first   Code also

981

- H43.2 Crystalline deposits in vitreous body
  - ▪ H43.20 Crystalline deposits in vitreous body, unspecified eye
  - H43.21 Crystalline deposits in vitreous body, right eye
  - H43.22 Crystalline deposits in vitreous body, left eye
  - H43.23 Crystalline deposits in vitreous body, bilateral
- H43.3 Other vitreous opacities
  - ● H43.31 Vitreous membranes and strands
    - H43.311 Vitreous membranes and strands, right eye
    - H43.312 Vitreous membranes and strands, left eye
    - H43.313 Vitreous membranes and strands, bilateral
    - ▪ H43.319 Vitreous membranes and strands, unspecified eye
  - ● H43.39 Other vitreous opacities
    Vitreous floaters
    Small clumps of cells that float in the vitreous of the eye, appearing as black specks or dots in the field of vision and common in the aging eye.
    - H43.391 Other vitreous opacities, right eye
    - H43.392 Other vitreous opacities, left eye
    - H43.393 Other vitreous opacities, bilateral
    - ▪ H43.399 Other vitreous opacities, unspecified eye
- ● H43.8 Other disorders of vitreous body
  - Excludes1 proliferative vitreo-retinopathy with retinal detachment (H33.4)
  - Excludes2 vitreous abscess (H44.02-)
  - ● H43.81 Vitreous degeneration
    Vitreous detachment
    - H43.811 Vitreous degeneration, right eye
    - H43.812 Vitreous degeneration, left eye
    - H43.813 Vitreous degeneration, bilateral
    - ▪ H43.819 Vitreous degeneration, unspecified eye
  - H43.89 Other disorders of vitreous body
  - ▪ H43.9 Unspecified disorder of vitreous body

- ● H44 Disorders of globe
  - Includes disorders affecting multiple structures of eye
  - ● H44.0 Purulent endophthalmitis
    Use additional code to identify organism
    - Excludes1 bleb associated endophthalmitis (H59.4-)
    - ● H44.00 Unspecified purulent endophthalmitis
      - ▪ H44.001 Unspecified purulent endophthalmitis, right eye 🦠
      - ▪ H44.002 Unspecified purulent endophthalmitis, left eye 🦠
      - ▪ H44.003 Unspecified purulent endophthalmitis, bilateral 🦠
      - ▪ H44.009 Unspecified purulent endophthalmitis, unspecified eye 🦠

- ● H44.01 Panophthalmitis (acute)
  - H44.011 Panophthalmitis (acute), right eye 🦠
  - H44.012 Panophthalmitis (acute), left eye 🦠
  - H44.013 Panophthalmitis (acute), bilateral 🦠
  - ▪ H44.019 Panophthalmitis (acute), unspecified eye 🦠
- ● H44.02 Vitreous abscess (chronic)
  - H44.021 Vitreous abscess (chronic), right eye 🦠
  - H44.022 Vitreous abscess (chronic), left eye 🦠
  - H44.023 Vitreous abscess (chronic), bilateral 🦠
  - ▪ H44.029 Vitreous abscess (chronic), unspecified eye 🦠
- ● H44.1 Other endophthalmitis
  - Excludes1 bleb associated endophthalmitis (H59.4-)
  - Excludes2 ophthalmia nodosa (H16.2-)
  - ● H44.11 Panuveitis
    - H44.111 Panuveitis, right eye 🦠
    - H44.112 Panuveitis, left eye 🦠
    - H44.113 Panuveitis, bilateral 🦠
    - ▪ H44.119 Panuveitis, unspecified eye 🦠
  - ● H44.12 Parasitic endophthalmitis NOS
    - H44.121 Parasitic endophthalmitis NOS, right eye 🦠
    - H44.122 Parasitic endophthalmitis NOS, left eye 🦠
    - H44.123 Parasitic endophthalmitis NOS, bilateral 🦠
    - ▪ H44.129 Parasitic endophthalmitis NOS, unspecified eye 🦠
  - ● H44.13 Sympathetic uveitis
    - H44.131 Sympathetic uveitis, right eye 🦠
    - H44.132 Sympathetic uveitis, left eye 🦠
    - H44.133 Sympathetic uveitis, bilateral 🦠
    - ▪ H44.139 Sympathetic uveitis, unspecified eye 🦠
  - H44.19 Other endophthalmitis 🦠
- ● H44.2 Degenerative myopia
  Malignant myopia
  - ▪ H44.20 Degenerative myopia, unspecified eye
  - H44.21 Degenerative myopia, right eye
  - H44.22 Degenerative myopia, left eye
  - H44.23 Degenerative myopia, bilateral
- ● H44.3 Other and unspecified degenerative disorders of globe
  - ▪ H44.30 Unspecified degenerative disorder of globe
  - ● H44.31 Chalcosis
    - H44.311 Chalcosis, right eye
    - H44.312 Chalcosis, left eye
    - H44.313 Chalcosis, bilateral
    - ▪ H44.319 Chalcosis, unspecified eye

● Unacceptable First-Listed Diagnosis   ● Use Additional Character(s)   ▪ Unspecified   OGCR Official Guidelines for Coding and Reporting
🦠 Complication\Comorbidity   🦠 Major C\C   Excludes 1   Excludes 2   Includes   Use additional   Code first   Code also

● H44.32   Siderosis of eye

     H44.321   Siderosis of eye, right eye

     H44.322   Siderosis of eye, left eye

     H44.323   Siderosis of eye, bilateral

     ■ H44.329   Siderosis of eye, unspecified eye

● H44.39   Other degenerative disorders of globe

     H44.391   Other degenerative disorders of globe, right eye

     H44.392   Other degenerative disorders of globe, left eye

     H44.393   Other degenerative disorders of globe, bilateral

     ■ H44.399   Other degenerative disorders of globe, unspecified eye

● H44.4   Hypotony of eye

     ■ H44.40   Unspecified hypotony of eye

     ● H44.41   Flat anterior chamber hypotony of eye

         H44.411   Flat anterior chamber hypotony of right eye

         H44.412   Flat anterior chamber hypotony of left eye

         H44.413   Flat anterior chamber hypotony of eye, bilateral

         ■ H44.419   Flat anterior chamber hypotony of unspecified eye

     ● H44.42   Hypotony of eye due to ocular fistula

         H44.421   Hypotony of right eye due to ocular fistula

         H44.422   Hypotony of left eye due to ocular fistula

         H44.423   Hypotony of eye due to ocular fistula, bilateral

         ■ H44.429   Hypotony of unspecified eye due to ocular fistula

     ● H44.43   Hypotony of eye due to other ocular disorders

         H44.431   Hypotony of eye due to other ocular disorders, right eye

         H44.432   Hypotony of eye due to other ocular disorders, left eye

         H44.433   Hypotony of eye due to other ocular disorders, bilateral

         ■ H44.439   Hypotony of eye due to other ocular disorders, unspecified eye

     ● H44.44   Primary hypotony of eye

         H44.441   Primary hypotony of right eye

         H44.442   Primary hypotony of left eye

         H44.443   Primary hypotony of eye, bilateral

         ■ H44.449   Primary hypotony of unspecified eye

● H44.5   Degenerated conditions of globe

     ■ H44.50   Unspecified degenerated conditions of globe

     ● H44.51   Absolute glaucoma

         H44.511   Absolute glaucoma, right eye

         H44.512   Absolute glaucoma, left eye

         H44.513   Absolute glaucoma, bilateral

         ■ H44.519   Absolute glaucoma, unspecified eye

● H44.52   Atrophy of globe

     Phthisis bulbi

     H44.521   Atrophy of globe, right eye

     H44.522   Atrophy of globe, left eye

     H44.523   Atrophy of globe, bilateral

     ■ H44.529   Atrophy of globe, unspecified eye

● H44.53   Leucocoria

     H44.531   Leucocoria, right eye

     H44.532   Leucocoria, left eye

     H44.533   Leucocoria, bilateral

     ■ H44.539   Leucocoria, unspecified eye

● H44.6   Retained (old) intraocular foreign body, magnetic

     | Excludes1 | current intraocular foreign body (S05.-)

     | Excludes2 | retained foreign body in eyelid (H02.81-)

         retained (old) foreign body following penetrating wound of orbit (H05.5-)

     ● H44.60   Unspecified retained (old) intraocular foreign body, magnetic

         ■ H44.601   Unspecified retained (old) intraocular foreign body, magnetic, right eye

         ■ H44.602   Unspecified retained (old) intraocular foreign body, magnetic, left eye

         ■ H44.603   Unspecified retained (old) intraocular foreign body, magnetic, bilateral

         ■ H44.609   Unspecified retained (old) intraocular foreign body, magnetic, unspecified eye

     ● H44.61   Retained (old) magnetic foreign body in anterior chamber

         H44.611   Retained (old) magnetic foreign body in anterior chamber, right eye

         H44.612   Retained (old) magnetic foreign body in anterior chamber, left eye

         H44.613   Retained (old) magnetic foreign body in anterior chamber, bilateral

         ■ H44.619   Retained (old) magnetic foreign body in anterior chamber, unspecified eye

     ● H44.62   Retained (old) magnetic foreign body in iris or ciliary body

         H44.621   Retained (old) magnetic foreign body in iris or ciliary body, right eye

         H44.622   Retained (old) magnetic foreign body in iris or ciliary body, left eye

         H44.623   Retained (old) magnetic foreign body in iris or ciliary body, bilateral

         ■ H44.629   Retained (old) magnetic foreign body in iris or ciliary body, unspecified eye

● Unacceptable First-Listed Diagnosis   ● Use Additional Character(s)   ■ Unspecified   **OGCR** Official Guidelines for Coding and Reporting

🗣 Complication\Comorbidity   🗣 Major C\C | Excludes 1 | | Excludes 2 | Includes   Use additional   Code first   Code also

983

CHAPTER 7 (H00-H59)

● H44.63   Retained (old) magnetic foreign body in lens

     H44.631   Retained (old) magnetic foreign body in lens, right eye

     H44.632   Retained (old) magnetic foreign body in lens, left eye

     H44.633   Retained (old) magnetic foreign body in lens, bilateral

     ▪ H44.639   Retained (old) magnetic foreign body in lens, unspecified eye

● H44.64   Retained (old) magnetic foreign body in posterior wall of globe

     H44.641   Retained (old) magnetic foreign body in posterior wall of globe, right eye

     H44.642   Retained (old) magnetic foreign body in posterior wall of globe, left eye

     H44.643   Retained (old) magnetic foreign body in posterior wall of globe, bilateral

     ▪ H44.649   Retained (old) magnetic foreign body in posterior wall of globe, unspecified eye

● H44.65   Retained (old) magnetic foreign body in vitreous body

     H44.651   Retained (old) magnetic foreign body in vitreous body, right eye

     H44.652   Retained (old) magnetic foreign body in vitreous body, left eye

     H44.653   Retained (old) magnetic foreign body in vitreous body, bilateral

     ▪ H44.659   Retained (old) magnetic foreign body in vitreous body, unspecified eye

● H44.69   Retained (old) intraocular foreign body, magnetic, in other or multiple sites

     H44.691   Retained (old) intraocular foreign body, magnetic, in other or multiple sites, right eye

     H44.692   Retained (old) intraocular foreign body, magnetic, in other or multiple sites, left eye

     H44.693   Retained (old) intraocular foreign body, magnetic, in other or multiple sites, bilateral

     ▪ H44.699   Retained (old) intraocular foreign body, magnetic, in other or multiple sites, unspecified eye

● H44.7   Retained (old) intraocular foreign body, nonmagnetic

     Excludes1   current intraocular foreign body (S05.-)

     Excludes2   retained foreign body in eyelid (H02.81-)
                  retained (old) foreign body following penetrating wound of orbit (H05.5-)

   ● H44.70   Unspecified retained (old) intraocular foreign body, nonmagnetic

     ▪ H44.701   Unspecified retained (old) intraocular foreign body, nonmagnetic, right eye

     ▪ H44.702   Unspecified retained (old) intraocular foreign body, nonmagnetic, left eye

     ▪ H44.703   Unspecified retained (old) intraocular foreign body, nonmagnetic, bilateral

     ▪ H44.709   Unspecified retained (old) intraocular foreign body, nonmagnetic, unspecified eye
                  Retained (old) intraocular foreign body NOS

● H44.71   Retained (nonmagnetic) (old) foreign body in anterior chamber

     H44.711   Retained (nonmagnetic) (old) foreign body in anterior chamber, right eye

     H44.712   Retained (nonmagnetic) (old) foreign body in anterior chamber, left eye

     H44.713   Retained (nonmagnetic) (old) foreign body in anterior chamber, bilateral

     ▪ H44.719   Retained (nonmagnetic) (old) foreign body in anterior chamber, unspecified eye

● H44.72   Retained (nonmagnetic) (old) foreign body in iris or ciliary body

     H44.721   Retained (nonmagnetic) (old) foreign body in iris or ciliary body, right eye

     H44.722   Retained (nonmagnetic) (old) foreign body in iris or ciliary body, left eye

     H44.723   Retained (nonmagnetic) (old) foreign body in iris or ciliary body, bilateral

     ▪ H44.729   Retained (nonmagnetic) (old) foreign body in iris or ciliary body, unspecified eye

● H44.73   Retained (nonmagnetic) (old) foreign body in lens

     H44.731   Retained (nonmagnetic) (old) foreign body in lens, right eye

     H44.732   Retained (nonmagnetic) (old) foreign body in lens, left eye

     H44.733   Retained (nonmagnetic) (old) foreign body in lens, bilateral

     ▪ H44.739   Retained (nonmagnetic) (old) foreign body in lens, unspecified eye

● H44.74   Retained (nonmagnetic) (old) foreign body in posterior wall of globe

     H44.741   Retained (nonmagnetic) (old) foreign body in posterior wall of globe, right eye

     H44.742   Retained (nonmagnetic) (old) foreign body in posterior wall of globe, left eye

     H44.743   Retained (nonmagnetic) (old) foreign body in posterior wall of globe, bilateral

     ▪ H44.749   Retained (nonmagnetic) (old) foreign body in posterior wall of globe, unspecified eye

● H44.75   Retained (nonmagnetic) (old) foreign body in vitreous body

     H44.751   Retained (nonmagnetic) (old) foreign body in vitreous body, right eye

     H44.752   Retained (nonmagnetic) (old) foreign body in vitreous body, left eye

     H44.753   Retained (nonmagnetic) (old) foreign body in vitreous body, bilateral

     ▣ H44.759   Retained (nonmagnetic) (old) foreign body in vitreous body, unspecified eye

● H44.79   Retained (old) intraocular foreign body, nonmagnetic, in other or multiple sites

     H44.791   Retained (old) intraocular foreign body, nonmagnetic, in other or multiple sites, right eye

     H44.792   Retained (old) intraocular foreign body, nonmagnetic, in other or multiple sites, left eye

     H44.793   Retained (old) intraocular foreign body, nonmagnetic, in other or multiple sites, bilateral

     ▣ H44.799   Retained (old) intraocular foreign body, nonmagnetic, in other or multiple sites, unspecified eye

● H44.8   Other disorders of globe

     ● H44.81   Hemophthalmos

         H44.811   Hemophthalmos, right eye

         H44.812   Hemophthalmos, left eye

         H44.813   Hemophthalmos, bilateral

         ▣ H44.819   Hemophthalmos, unspecified eye

     ● H44.82   Luxation of globe

         H44.821   Luxation of globe, right eye

         H44.822   Luxation of globe, left eye

         H44.823   Luxation of globe, bilateral

         ▣ H44.829   Luxation of globe, unspecified eye

     H44.89   Other disorders of globe

▣ H44.9   Unspecified disorder of globe

(See Plate 86 on page NAP-7.)

DISORDERS OF OPTIC NERVE AND VISUAL PATHWAYS (H46-H47)

● H46   Optic neuritis

     Excludes2   ischemic optic neuropathy (H47.01-)
                neuromyelitis optica [Devic] (G36.0)

     ● H46.0   Optic papillitis

         ▣ H46.00   Optic papillitis, unspecified eye 🗝

         H46.01   Optic papillitis, right eye 🗝

         H46.02   Optic papillitis, left eye 🗝

         H46.03   Optic papillitis, bilateral 🗝

     ● H46.1   Retrobulbar neuritis

         Retrobulbar neuritis NOS

         Excludes1   syphilitic retrobulbar neuritis (A52.15)

         ▣ H46.10   Retrobulbar neuritis, unspecified eye 🗝

         H46.11   Retrobulbar neuritis, right eye 🗝

         H46.12   Retrobulbar neuritis, left eye 🗝

         H46.13   Retrobulbar neuritis, bilateral 🗝

     H46.2   Nutritional optic neuropathy

     ● H46.3   Toxic optic neuropathy

         Code first (T51-T65) to identify cause

     H46.8   Other optic neuritis 🗝

     ▣ H46.9   Unspecified optic neuritis 🗝

● H47   Other disorders of optic [2nd] nerve and visual pathways

     ● H47.0   Disorders of optic nerve, not elsewhere classified

         ● H47.01   Ischemic optic neuropathy

             H47.011   Ischemic optic neuropathy, right eye

             H47.012   Ischemic optic neuropathy, left eye

             H47.013   Ischemic optic neuropathy, bilateral

             ▣ H47.019   Ischemic optic neuropathy, unspecified eye

         ● H47.02   Hemorrhage in optic nerve sheath

             H47.021   Hemorrhage in optic nerve sheath, right eye

             H47.022   Hemorrhage in optic nerve sheath, left eye

             H47.023   Hemorrhage in optic nerve sheath, bilateral

             ▣ H47.029   Hemorrhage in optic nerve sheath, unspecified eye

Item 7–8   Papilledema is swelling of the optic disc caused by increased intracranial pressure. It is most often bilateral and occurs quickly (hours) or over weeks of time. It is a common symptom of a brain tumor. The term should not be used to describe optic disc swelling with underlying infectious, infiltrative, or inflammatory etiologies.

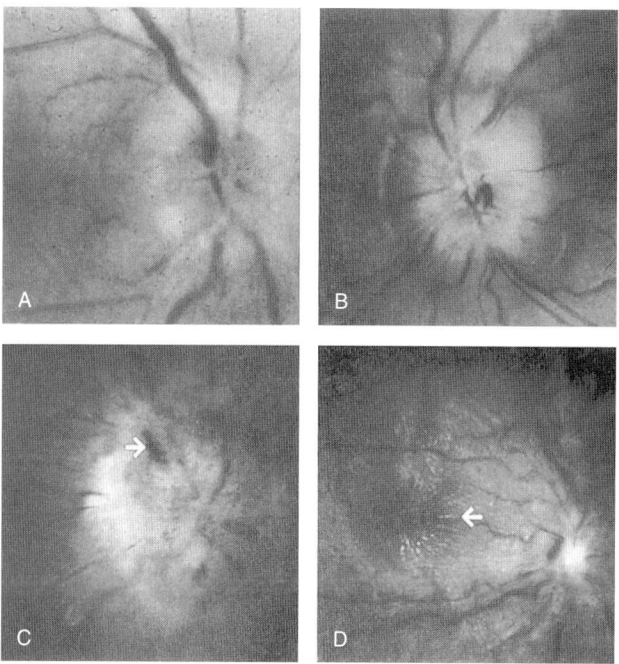

Figure 7-10   Papilledema. (From Behrma: Nelson Textbook of Pediatrics, 17th ed. 2004, Saunders)

● Unacceptable First-Listed Diagnosis   ● Use Additional Character(s)   ▣ Unspecified   **OGCR** Official Guidelines for Coding and Reporting

🗝 Complication\Comorbidity   🗝 Major C\C   Excludes 1   Excludes 2   Includes   Use additional   Code first   Code also

985

● H47.03   Optic nerve hypoplasia

     H47.031   Optic nerve hypoplasia, right eye

     H47.032   Optic nerve hypoplasia, left eye

     H47.033   Optic nerve hypoplasia, bilateral

     ■H47.039   Optic nerve hypoplasia, unspecified eye

● H47.09   Other disorders of optic nerve, not elsewhere classified
       Compression of optic nerve

     H47.091   Other disorders of optic nerve, not elsewhere classified, right eye

     H47.092   Other disorders of optic nerve, not elsewhere classified, left eye

     H47.093   Other disorders of optic nerve, not elsewhere classified, bilateral

     ■H47.099   Other disorders of optic nerve, not elsewhere classified, unspecified eye

● H47.1   Papilledema

     ■ H47.10   Unspecified papilledema 🦠

     H47.11   Papilledema associated with increased intracranial pressure 🦠

     H47.12   Papilledema associated with decreased ocular pressure

     H47.13   Papilledema associated with retinal disorder

     ● H47.14   Foster-Kennedy syndrome

         H47.141   Foster-Kennedy syndrome, right eye

         H47.142   Foster-Kennedy syndrome, left eye

         H47.143   Foster-Kennedy syndrome, bilateral

         ■H47.149   Foster-Kennedy syndrome, unspecified eye

● H47.2   Optic atrophy

     ■H47.20   Unspecified optic atrophy

     ● H47.21   Primary optic atrophy

         H47.211   Primary optic atrophy, right eye

         H47.212   Primary optic atrophy, left eye

         H47.213   Primary optic atrophy, bilateral

         ■H47.219   Primary optic atrophy, unspecified eye

     H47.22   Hereditary optic atrophy
         Leber's optic atrophy

     ● H47.23   Glaucomatous optic atrophy

         H47.231   Glaucomatous optic atrophy, right eye

         H47.232   Glaucomatous optic atrophy, left eye

         H47.233   Glaucomatous optic atrophy, bilateral

         ■H47.239   Glaucomatous optic atrophy, unspecified eye

     ● H47.29   Other optic atrophy
         Temporal pallor of optic disc

         H47.291   Other optic atrophy, right eye

         H47.292   Other optic atrophy, left eye

         H47.293   Other optic atrophy, bilateral

         ■H47.299   Other optic atrophy, unspecified eye

● H47.3   Other disorders of optic disc

● H47.31   Coloboma of optic disc

     H47.311   Coloboma of optic disc, right eye

     H47.312   Coloboma of optic disc, left eye

     H47.313   Coloboma of optic disc, bilateral

     ■H47.319   Coloboma of optic disc, unspecified eye

● H47.32   Drusen of optic disc

     H47.321   Drusen of optic disc, right eye

     H47.322   Drusen of optic disc, left eye

     H47.323   Drusen of optic disc, bilateral

     ■H47.329   Drusen of optic disc, unspecified eye

● H47.33   Pseudopapilledema of optic disc

     H47.331   Pseudopapilledema of optic disc, right eye

     H47.332   Pseudopapilledema of optic disc, left eye

     H47.333   Pseudopapilledema of optic disc, bilateral

     ■H47.339   Pseudopapilledema of optic disc, unspecified eye

● H47.39   Other disorders of optic disc

     H47.391   Other disorders of optic disc, right eye

     H47.392   Other disorders of optic disc, left eye

     H47.393   Other disorders of optic disc, bilateral

     ■H47.399   Other disorders of optic disc, unspecified eye

● H47.4   Disorders of optic chiasm
     Code also   underlying condition

     H47.41   Disorders of optic chiasm in (due to) inflammatory disorders 🦠

     H47.42   Disorders of optic chiasm in (due to) neoplasm 🦠

     H47.43   Disorders of optic chiasm in (due to) vascular disorders 🦠

     H47.49   Disorders of optic chiasm in (due to) other disorders 🦠

● H47.5   Disorders of other visual pathways
     Disorders of optic tracts, geniculate nuclei and optic radiations
     Code also   underlying condition

     ● H47.51   Disorders of visual pathways in (due to) inflammatory disorders

         H47.511   Disorders of visual pathways in (due to) inflammatory disorders, right side 🦠

         H47.512   Disorders of visual pathways in (due to) inflammatory disorders, left side 🦠

         ■H47.519   Disorders of visual pathways in (due to) inflammatory disorders, unspecified side 🦠

     ● H47.52   Disorders of visual pathways in (due to) neoplasm

         H47.521   Disorders of visual pathways in (due to) neoplasm, right side 🦠

         H47.522   Disorders of visual pathways in (due to) neoplasm, left side 🦠

         ■H47.529   Disorders of visual pathways in (due to) neoplasm, unspecified side 🦠

● **H47.53** Disorders of visual pathways in (due to) vascular disorders

     H47.531 Disorders of visual pathways in (due to) vascular disorders, right side 🗪

     H47.532 Disorders of visual pathways in (due to) vascular disorders, left side 🗪

     🔲 H47.539 Disorders of visual pathways in (due to) vascular disorders, unspecified side 🗪

● **H47.6** Disorders of visual cortex

     Code also underlying condition

     Excludes1   injury to visual cortex S04.04

● **H47.61** Cortical blindness

     H47.611 Cortical blindness, right side of brain

     H47.612 Cortical blindness, left side of brain

     🔲 H47.619 Cortical blindness, unspecified side of brain

● **H47.62** Disorders of visual cortex in (due to) inflammatory disorders

     H47.621 Disorders of visual cortex in (due to) inflammatory disorders, right side of brain 🗪

     H47.622 Disorders of visual cortex in (due to) inflammatory disorders, left side of brain 🗪

     🔲 H47.629 Disorders of visual cortex in (due to) inflammatory disorders, unspecified side of brain 🗪

● **H47.63** Disorders of visual cortex in (due to) neoplasm

     H47.631 Disorders of visual cortex in (due to) neoplasm, right side of brain 🗪

     H47.632 Disorders of visual cortex in (due to) neoplasm, left side of brain 🗪

     🔲 H47.639 Disorders of visual cortex in (due to) neoplasm, unspecified side of brain 🗪

Item 7–9 Strabismus or esotropia (crossed eyes) is a condition of the extraocular eye muscles, resulting in an inability of the eyes to focus and also affects depth perception.

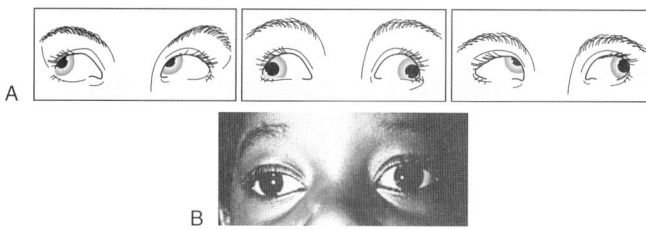

Figure 7-11 **A.** Image of strabismus. **B.** Exotropia. (**A** from Yanoff: Ophthalmology, 2nd ed. 2004, Mosby, Inc. **B** from Rakel: Textbook of Family Practice, 7th ed. 2007, Saunders)

● **H47.64** Disorders of visual cortex in (due to) vascular disorders

     H47.641 Disorders of visual cortex in (due to) vascular disorders, right side of brain 🗪

     H47.642 Disorders of visual cortex in (due to) vascular disorders, left side of brain 🗪

     🔲 H47.649 Disorders of visual cortex in (due to) vascular disorders, unspecified side of brain 🗪

🔲 **H47.9** Unspecified disorder of visual pathways

DISORDERS OF OCULAR MUSCLES, BINOCULAR MOVEMENT, ACCOMMODATION AND REFRACTION (H49-H52)

Excludes2   nystagmus and other irregular eye movements (H55)

● **H49** Paralytic strabismus

Excludes2   internal ophthalmoplegia (H52.51-)
                 internuclear ophthalmoplegia (H51.2-)
                 progressive supranuclear ophthalmoplegia (G23.1)

● **H49.0** Third [oculomotor] nerve palsy

     🔲 H49.00 Third [oculomotor] nerve palsy, unspecified eye

     H49.01 Third [oculomotor] nerve palsy, right eye

     H49.02 Third [oculomotor] nerve palsy, left eye

     H49.03 Third [oculomotor] nerve palsy, bilateral

● **H49.1** Fourth [trochlear] nerve palsy

     🔲 H49.10 Fourth [trochlear] nerve palsy, unspecified eye

     H49.11 Fourth [trochlear] nerve palsy, right eye

     H49.12 Fourth [trochlear] nerve palsy, left eye

     H49.13 Fourth [trochlear] nerve palsy, bilateral

● **H49.2** Sixth [abducent] nerve palsy

     🔲 H49.20 Sixth [abducent] nerve palsy, unspecified eye

     H49.21 Sixth [abducent] nerve palsy, right eye

     H49.22 Sixth [abducent] nerve palsy, left eye

     H49.23 Sixth [abducent] nerve palsy, bilateral

● **H49.3** Total (external) ophthalmoplegia

     🔲 H49.30 Total (external) ophthalmoplegia, unspecified eye

     H49.31 Total (external) ophthalmoplegia, right eye

     H49.32 Total (external) ophthalmoplegia, left eye

     H49.33 Total (external) ophthalmoplegia, bilateral

● **H49.4** Progressive external ophthalmoplegia

     Excludes1   Kearns-Sayre syndrome (H49.81-)

     🔲 H49.40 Progressive external ophthalmoplegia, unspecified eye

     H49.41 Progressive external ophthalmoplegia, right eye

     H49.42 Progressive external ophthalmoplegia, left eye

     H49.43 Progressive external ophthalmoplegia, bilateral

● Unacceptable First-Listed Diagnosis   ● Use Additional Character(s)   🔲 Unspecified   **OGCR** Official Guidelines for Coding and Reporting

🗪 Complication\Comorbidity   🗪 Major C\C   Excludes 1   Excludes 2   Includes   Use additional   Code first   Code also

● H49.8   **Other paralytic strabismus**

   ● H49.81   **Kearns-Sayre syndrome**
      Progressive external ophthalmoplegia with pigmentary retinopathy

      Use additional code for other manifestation, such as:
        heart block (I45.9)

      H49.811   Kearns-Sayre syndrome, right eye 🅒

      H49.812   Kearns-Sayre syndrome, left eye 🅒

      H49.813   Kearns-Sayre syndrome, bilateral 🅒

      ■ H49.819   Kearns-Sayre syndrome, unspecified eye 🅒

   ● H49.88   **Other paralytic strabismus**
      External ophthalmoplegia NOS

      H49.881   Other paralytic strabismus, right eye

      H49.882   Other paralytic strabismus, left eye

      H49.883   Other paralytic strabismus, bilateral

      ■ H49.889   Other paralytic strabismus, unspecified eye

  ■ H49.9   **Unspecified paralytic strabismus**

● H50   **Other strabismus**

   ● H50.0   **Esotropia**
      Convergent concomitant strabismus

      Excludes1   intermittent esotropia (H50.31-, H50.32)

    ■ H50.00   **Unspecified esotropia**

   ● H50.01   **Monocular esotropia**

      H50.011   Monocular esotropia, right eye

      H50.012   Monocular esotropia, left eye

   ● H50.02   **Monocular esotropia with A pattern**

      H50.021   Monocular esotropia with A pattern, right eye

      H50.022   Monocular esotropia with A pattern, left eye

   ● H50.03   **Monocular esotropia with V pattern**

      H50.031   Monocular esotropia with V pattern, right eye

      H50.032   Monocular esotropia with V pattern, left eye

   ● H50.04   **Monocular esotropia with other noncomitancies**

      H50.041   Monocular esotropia with other noncomitancies, right eye

      H50.042   Monocular esotropia with other noncomitancies, left eye

   H50.05   **Alternating esotropia**

   H50.06   **Alternating esotropia with A pattern**

   H50.07   **Alternating esotropia with V pattern**

   H50.08   **Alternating esotropia with other noncomitancies**

   ● H50.1   **Exotropia**
      Misalignment in which one eye deviates outward (away from nose) while the other fixates normally
      Divergent concomitant strabismus

      Excludes1   intermittent exotropia (H50.33-, H50.34)

    ■ H50.10   **Unspecified exotropia**

   ● H50.11   **Monocular exotropia**

      H50.111   Monocular exotropia, right eye

      H50.112   Monocular exotropia, left eye

   ● H50.12   **Monocular exotropia with A pattern**

      H50.121   Monocular exotropia with A pattern, right eye

      H50.122   Monocular exotropia with A pattern, left eye

   ● H50.13   **Monocular exotropia with V pattern**

      H50.131   Monocular exotropia with V pattern, right eye

      H50.132   Monocular exotropia with V pattern, left eye

   ● H50.14   **Monocular exotropia with other noncomitancies**

      H50.141   Monocular exotropia with other noncomitancies, right eye

      H50.142   Monocular exotropia with other noncomitancies, left eye

   H50.15   **Alternating exotropia**

   H50.16   **Alternating exotropia with A pattern**

   H50.17   **Alternating exotropia with V pattern**

   H50.18   **Alternating exotropia with other noncomitancies**

  ● H50.2   **Vertical strabismus**
     Hypertropia

   H50.21   **Vertical strabismus, right eye**

   H50.22   **Vertical strabismus, left eye**

  ● H50.3   **Intermittent heterotropia**
     Displacement of an organ or part of an organ from its normal position

    ■ H50.30   **Unspecified intermittent heterotropia**

   ● H50.31   **Intermittent monocular esotropia**

      H50.311   Intermittent monocular esotropia, right eye

      H50.312   Intermittent monocular esotropia, left eye

   H50.32   **Intermittent alternating esotropia**

   ● H50.33   **Intermittent monocular exotropia**

      H50.331   Intermittent monocular exotropia, right eye

      H50.332   Intermittent monocular exotropia, left eye

   H50.34   **Intermittent alternating exotropia**

  ● H50.4   **Other and unspecified heterotropia**

    ■ H50.40   **Unspecified heterotropia**

   ● H50.41   **Cyclotropia**

      H50.411   Cyclotropia, right eye

      H50.412   Cyclotropia, left eye

   H50.42   **Monofixation syndrome**

   H50.43   **Accommodative component in esotropia**

  ● H50.5   **Heterophoria**
     One or both eyes wander away from the position where both eyes are looking together in the same direction

    ■ H50.50   **Unspecified heterophoria**

   H50.51   **Esophoria**
     Eye deviates inward (toward the nose)

   H50.52   **Exophoria**
     Eye deviates outward (toward the ear)

H50.53   Vertical heterophoria

H50.54   Cyclophoria

H50.55   Alternating heterophoria

● H50.6   Mechanical strabismus

    ▪ H50.60   Mechanical strabismus, unspecified

    ● H50.61   Brown's sheath syndrome

       H50.611   Brown's sheath syndrome, right eye

       H50.612   Brown's sheath syndrome, left eye

    H50.69   Other mechanical strabismus

       Strabismus due to adhesions

       Traumatic limitation of duction of eye muscle

● H50.8   Other specified strabismus

    ● H50.81   Duane's syndrome

       H50.811   Duane's syndrome, right eye

       H50.812   Duane's syndrome, left eye

    H50.89   Other specified strabismus

▪ H50.9   Unspecified strabismus

● H51   Other disorders of binocular movement

    H51.0   Palsy (spasm) of conjugate gaze

    ● H51.1   Convergence insufficiency and excess

       H51.11   Convergence insufficiency

       H51.12   Convergence excess

    ● H51.2   Internuclear ophthalmoplegia

       ▪ H51.20   Internuclear ophthalmoplegia, unspecified eye

       H51.21   Internuclear ophthalmoplegia, right eye

       H51.22   Internuclear ophthalmoplegia, left eye

       H51.23   Internuclear ophthalmoplegia, bilateral

    H51.8   Other specified disorders of binocular movement

    ▪ H51.9   Unspecified disorder of binocular movement

● H52   Disorders of refraction and accommodation

    ● H52.0   Hypermetropia

       ▪ H52.00   Hypermetropia, unspecified eye

       H52.01   Hypermetropia, right eye

       H52.02   Hypermetropia, left eye

       H52.03   Hypermetropia, bilateral

    ● H52.1   Myopia

       | Excludes1 | degenerative myopia (H44.2-)

       ▪ H52.10   Myopia, unspecified eye

       H52.11   Myopia, right eye

       H52.12   Myopia, left eye

       H52.13   Myopia, bilateral

Item 7–10   Disorders of refraction: **Hypermetropia,** or farsightedness, means focus at a distance is adequate but not on close objects. **Myopia** is near-sightedness or short-sightedness and means the focus on nearby objects is clear but distant objects appear blurred. **Astigmatism** is warping of the curvature of the cornea so light rays entering do not meet a single focal point, resulting in a distorted image. **Anisometropia** is unequal refractive power in which one eye may be myopic (near-sighted) and the other hyperopic (far-sighted). **Presbyopia** is the loss of focus on near objects, which occurs with age because the lens loses elasticity.

● H52.2   Astigmatism

    ● H52.20   Unspecified astigmatism

       ▪ H52.201   Unspecified astigmatism, right eye

       ▪ H52.202   Unspecified astigmatism, left eye

       ▪ H52.203   Unspecified astigmatism, bilateral

       ▪ H52.209   Unspecified astigmatism, unspecified eye

    ● H52.21   Irregular astigmatism

       H52.211   Irregular astigmatism, right eye

       H52.212   Irregular astigmatism, left eye

       H52.213   Irregular astigmatism, bilateral

       ▪ H52.219   Irregular astigmatism, unspecified eye

    ● H52.22   Regular astigmatism

       H52.221   Regular astigmatism, right eye

       H52.222   Regular astigmatism, left eye

       H52.223   Regular astigmatism, bilateral

       ▪ H52.229   Regular astigmatism, unspecified eye

● H52.3   Anisometropia and aniseikonia

    H52.31   Anisometropia

    H52.32   Aniseikonia

    H52.4   Presbyopia

● H52.5   Disorders of accommodation

    ● H52.51   Internal ophthalmoplegia (complete) (total)

       H52.511   Internal ophthalmoplegia (complete) (total), right eye

       H52.512   Internal ophthalmoplegia (complete) (total), left eye

       H52.513   Internal ophthalmoplegia (complete) (total), bilateral

       ▪ H52.519   Internal ophthalmoplegia (complete) (total), unspecified eye

    ● H52.52   Paresis of accommodation

       H52.521   Paresis of accommodation, right eye

       H52.522   Paresis of accommodation, left eye

       H52.523   Paresis of accommodation, bilateral

       ▪ H52.529   Paresis of accommodation, unspecified eye

    ● H52.53   Spasm of accommodation

       H52.531   Spasm of accommodation, right eye

       H52.532   Spasm of accommodation, left eye

       H52.533   Spasm of accommodation, bilateral

       ▪ H52.539   Spasm of accommodation, unspecified eye

    H52.6   Other disorders of refraction

▪ H52.7   Unspecified disorder of refraction

● Unacceptable First-Listed Diagnosis   ● Use Additional Character(s)   ▪ Unspecified   **OGCR** Official Guidelines for Coding and Reporting

🏷 Complication\Comorbidity   🏷 Major C\C | Excludes 1 | | Excludes 2 | Includes   Use additional   Code first   Code also

CHAPTER 7 (H00-H59)

989

VISUAL DISTURBANCES AND BLINDNESS (H53-H54)

● H53   Visual disturbances
  ● H53.0   Amblyopia ex anopsia
      Excludes1   amblyopia due to vitamin A
                   deficiency (E50.5)
    ● H53.00   Unspecified amblyopia
        ■ H53.001   Unspecified amblyopia, right eye
        ■ H53.002   Unspecified amblyopia, left eye
        ■ H53.003   Unspecified amblyopia, bilateral
        ■ H53.009   Unspecified amblyopia,
                    unspecified eye
    ● H53.01   Deprivation amblyopia
          H53.011   Deprivation amblyopia, right eye
          H53.012   Deprivation amblyopia, left eye
          H53.013   Deprivation amblyopia, bilateral
        ■ H53.019   Deprivation amblyopia,
                    unspecified eye
    ● H53.02   Refractive amblyopia
          H53.021   Refractive amblyopia, right eye
          H53.022   Refractive amblyopia, left eye
          H53.023   Refractive amblyopia, bilateral
        ■ H53.029   Refractive amblyopia,
                    unspecified eye
    ● H53.03   Strabismic amblyopia
          Excludes1   strabismus (H50.-)
          H53.031   Strabismic amblyopia, right eye
          H53.032   Strabismic amblyopia, left eye
          H53.033   Strabismic amblyopia, bilateral
        ■ H53.039   Strabismic amblyopia,
                    unspecified eye
  ● H53.1   Subjective visual disturbances
      Excludes1   subjective visual disturbances due to
                   vitamin A deficiency (E50.5)
                   visual hallucinations (R44.1)
    ■ H53.10   Unspecified subjective visual disturbances
      H53.11   Day blindness
               Hemeralopia
    ● H53.12   Transient visual loss
               Scintillating scotoma
          Excludes1   amaurosis fugax (G45.3-)
                       transient retinal artery
                       occlusion (H34.0-)
          H53.121   Transient visual loss, right eye 🗲
          H53.122   Transient visual loss, left eye 🗲
          H53.123   Transient visual loss, bilateral 🗲
        ■ H53.129   Transient visual loss, unspecified
                    eye 🗲
    ● H53.13   Sudden visual loss
          H53.131   Sudden visual loss, right eye 🗲
          H53.132   Sudden visual loss, left eye 🗲
          H53.133   Sudden visual loss, bilateral 🗲
        ■ H53.139   Sudden visual loss, unspecified
                    eye 🗲
    ● H53.14   Visual discomfort
               Asthenopia
               Photophobia
          H53.141   Visual discomfort, right eye
          H53.142   Visual discomfort, left eye
          H53.143   Visual discomfort, bilateral

        ■ H53.149   Visual discomfort, unspecified
      H53.15   Visual distortions of shape and size
               Metamorphopsia
      H53.16   Psychophysical visual disturbances
               Prosopagnosia
               Visual object agnosia
      H53.19   Other subjective visual disturbances
               Visual halos
  H53.2   Diplopia
          Double vision
  ● H53.3   Other and unspecified disorders of binocular
            vision
        ■ H53.30   Unspecified disorder of binocular vision
      H53.31   Abnormal retinal correspondence
      H53.32   Fusion with defective stereopsis
      H53.33   Simultaneous visual perception without
               fusion
      H53.34   Suppression of binocular vision
  ● H53.4   Visual field defects
        ■ H53.40   Unspecified visual field defects
    ● H53.41   Scotoma involving central area
               Central scotoma
          H53.411   Scotoma involving central area,
                    right eye
          H53.412   Scotoma involving central area,
                    left eye
          H53.413   Scotoma involving central area,
                    bilateral
        ■ H53.419   Scotoma involving central area,
                    unspecified eye
    ● H53.42   Scotoma of blind spot area
               Enlarged blind spot
          H53.421   Scotoma of blind spot area, right
                    eye
          H53.422   Scotoma of blind spot area, left eye
          H53.423   Scotoma of blind spot area, bilateral
        ■ H53.429   Scotoma of blind spot area,
                    unspecified eye
    ● H53.43   Sector or arcuate defects
               Arcuate scotoma
               Bjerrum scotoma
          H53.431   Sector or arcuate defects, right eye
          H53.432   Sector or arcuate defects, left eye
          H53.433   Sector or arcuate defects, bilateral
        ■ H53.439   Sector or arcuate defects,
                    unspecified eye
    ● H53.45   Other localized visual field defect
               Peripheral visual field defect
               Ring scotoma NOS
               Scotoma NOS
          H53.451   Other localized visual field
                    defect, right eye
          H53.452   Other localized visual field
                    defect, left eye
          H53.453   Other localized visual field
                    defect, bilateral
        ■ H53.459   Other localized visual field
                    defect, unspecified eye

● H53.46 **Homonymous bilateral field defects**
Homonymous hemianop(s)ia
Quadrant anop(s)ia

    H53.461 **Homonymous bilateral field defects, right side**

    H53.462 **Homonymous bilateral field defects, left side**

    ■H53.469 **Homonymous bilateral field defects, unspecified side**
Homonymous bilateral field defects NOS

    H53.47 **Heteronymous bilateral field defects**
Heteronymous hemianop(s)ia

● H53.48 **Generalized contraction of visual field**

    H53.481 **Generalized contraction of visual field, right eye**

    H53.482 **Generalized contraction of visual field, left eye**

    H53.483 **Generalized contraction of visual field, bilateral**

    ■H53.489 **Generalized contraction of visual field, unspecified eye**

● H53.5 **Color vision deficiencies**
Color blindness

    Excludes2   day blindness (H53.11)

    ■H53.50 **Unspecified color vision deficiencies**
Color blindness NOS

    H53.51 **Achromatopsia**

    H53.52 **Acquired color vision deficiency**

    H53.53 **Deuteranomaly**
Deuteranopia

    H53.54 **Protanomaly**
Protanopia

    H53.55 **Tritanomaly**
Tritanopia

    H53.59 **Other color vision deficiencies**

● H53.6 **Night blindness**

    Excludes1   night blindness due to vitamin A deficiency (E50.5)

    ■H53.60 **Unspecified night blindness**

    H53.61 **Abnormal dark adaptation curve**

    H53.62 **Acquired night blindness**

    H53.63 **Congenital night blindness**

    H53.69 **Other night blindness**

    H53.7 **Vision sensitivity deficiencies**

    H53.71 **Glare sensitivity**

    H53.72 **Impaired contrast sensitivity**

    H53.8 **Other visual disturbances**

    ■H53.9 **Unspecified visual disturbance**

● H54 **Blindness and low vision**

    Note: For definition of visual impairment categories see table below.

    Code first any associated underlying cause of the blindness

    Excludes1   amaurosis fugax (G45.3)

    H54.0 **Blindness, both eyes**
Visual impairment categories 3, 4, 5 in both eyes.

● H54.1 **Blindness, one eye, low vision other eye**
Visual impairment categories 3, 4, 5 in one eye, with categories 1 or 2 in the other eye.

    ■H54.10 **Blindness, one eye, low vision other eye, unspecified eyes**

    H54.11 **Blindness, right eye, low vision left eye**

    H54.12 **Blindness, left eye, low vision right eye**

    H54.2 **Low vision, both eyes**
Visual impairment categories 1 or 2 in both eyes.

    H54.3 **Unqualified visual loss, both eyes**
Visual impairment category 9 in both eyes.

● H54.4 **Blindness, one eye**
Visual impairment categories 3, 4, 5 in one eye [normal vision in other eye]

    ■H54.40 **Blindness, one eye, unspecified eye**

    H54.41 **Blindness, right eye, normal vision left eye**

    H54.42 **Blindness, left eye, normal vision right eye**

● H54.5 **Low vision, one eye**
Visual impairment categories 1 or 2 in one eye [normal vision in other eye].

    ■H54.50 **Low vision, one eye, unspecified eye**

    H54.51 **Low vision, right eye, normal vision left eye**

    H54.52 **Low vision, left eye, normal vision right eye**

● H54.6 **Unqualified visual loss, one eye**
Visual impairment category 9 in one eye [normal vision in other eye].

    ■H54.60 **Unqualified visual loss, one eye, unspecified**

    H54.61 **Unqualified visual loss, right eye, normal vision left eye**

    H54.62 **Unqualified visual loss, left eye, normal vision right eye**

■H54.7 **Unqualified visual loss**
Visual impairment category 9 NOS

    H54.8 **Legal blindness, as defined in USA**
Blindness NOS according to USA definition

    Excludes1   legal blindness with specification of impairment level (H54.0-H54.7)

OTHER DISORDERS OF EYE AND ADNEXA (H55-H59)

● H55 **Nystagmus and other irregular eye movements**

● H55.0 **Nystagmus**
Rapid, involuntary movements of the eyes in the horizontal or vertical direction.

    ■H55.00 **Unspecified nystagmus**

    H55.01 **Congenital nystagmus**

    H55.02 **Latent nystagmus**

    H55.03 **Visual deprivation nystagmus**

    H55.04 **Dissociated nystagmus**

    H55.09 **Other forms of nystagmus**

● H55.8 **Other irregular eye movements**

    H55.81 **Saccadic eye movements**

    H55.89 **Other irregular eye movements**

● Unacceptable First-Listed Diagnosis   ● Use Additional Character(s)   ■ Unspecified   **OGCR** Official Guidelines for Coding and Reporting

🗨 Complication\Comorbidity   🗨 Major C\C   Excludes 1   Excludes 2   Includes   Use additional   Code first   Code also

991

CHAPTER 7 (H00-H59)

● **H57   Other disorders of eye and adnexa**

  ● **H57.0   Anomalies of pupillary function**

    ■ **H57.00   Unspecified anomaly of pupillary function**

    Note: The table below gives a classification of severity of visual impairment recommended by a WHO Study Group on the Prevention of Blindness, Geneva, 6-10 November l972.

    The term "low vision" in category H54 comprises categories 1 and 2 of the table, the term "blindness" categories 3, 4 and 5, and the term "unqualified visual loss" category 9.

    If the extent of the visual field is taken into account, patients with a field no greater than 10 but greater than 5 around central fixation should be placed in category 3 and patients with a field no greater than 5 around central fixation should be placed in category 4, even if the central acuity is not impaired.

Category of visual impairment	Visual acuity with best possible correction	
	Maximum less than:	**Minimum equal to or better than:**
1	6/18 3/10 (0.3) 20/70	6/60 1/10 (0.1) 20/200
2	6/60 1/10 (0.1) 20/200	3/60 1/20 (0.05) 20/400
3	3/60 1/20 (0.05) 20/400	1/60 (finger counting at 1 meter) 1/50 (0.02) 5/300 (20/1200)
4	1/60 (finger counting at 1 meter) 1/50 (0.02) 5/300	Light perception
5	No light perception	
9	Undetermined or unspecified	

    H57.01   Argyll Robertson pupil, atypical

       Excludes1   syphilitic Argyll Robertson pupil (A52.19)

    H57.02   Anisocoria

    H57.03   Miosis

    H57.04   Mydriasis

    ● **H57.05   Tonic pupil**

       H57.051   Tonic pupil, right eye

       H57.052   Tonic pupil, left eye

       H57.053   Tonic pupil, bilateral

      ■ **H57.059   Tonic pupil, unspecified eye**

    H57.09   Other anomalies of pupillary function

  ● **H57.1   Ocular pain**

    ■ **H57.10   Ocular pain, unspecified eye**

    H57.11   Ocular pain, right eye

    H57.12   Ocular pain, left eye

    H57.13   Ocular pain, bilateral

  H57.8   Other specified disorders of eye and adnexa

  ■ **H57.9   Unspecified disorder of eye and adnexa**

● **H59   Intraoperative and postprocedural complications and disorders of eye and adnexa, not elsewhere classified**

  Excludes1   mechanical complication of intraocular lens (T85.2)

       mechanical complication of other ocular prosthetic devices, implants and grafts (T85.3)

       pseudophakia (Z96.1)

       secondary cataracts (H26.4-)

  ● **H59.0   Disorders of the eye following cataract surgery**

    ● **H59.01   Keratopathy (bullous aphakic) following cataract surgery**

       Vitreal corneal syndrome

       Vitreous (touch) syndrome

       H59.011   Keratopathy (bullous aphakic) following cataract surgery, right eye

       H59.012   Keratopathy (bullous aphakic) following cataract surgery, left eye

       H59.013   Keratopathy (bullous aphakic) following cataract surgery, bilateral

      ■ **H59.019   Keratopathy (bullous aphakic) following cataract surgery, unspecified eye**

    ● **H59.02   Cataract (lens) fragments in eye following cataract surgery**

       H59.021   Cataract (lens) fragments in eye following cataract surgery, right eye

       H59.022   Cataract (lens) fragments in eye following cataract surgery, left eye

       H59.023   Cataract (lens) fragments in eye following cataract surgery, bilateral

      ■ **H59.029   Cataract (lens) fragments in eye following cataract surgery, unspecified eye**

    ● **H59.03   Cystoid macular edema following cataract surgery**

       H59.031   Cystoid macular edema following cataract surgery, right eye

       H59.032   Cystoid macular edema following cataract surgery, left eye

       H59.033   Cystoid macular edema following cataract surgery, bilateral

      ■ **H59.039   Cystoid macular edema following cataract surgery, unspecified eye**

    ● **H59.09   Other disorders of the eye following cataract surgery**

       H59.091   Other disorders of the right eye following cataract surgery

       H59.092   Other disorders of the left eye following cataract surgery

       H59.093   Other disorders of the eye following cataract surgery, bilateral

      ■ **H59.099   Other disorders of unspecified eye following cataract surgery**

● Unacceptable First-Listed Diagnosis   ● Use Additional Character(s)   ■ Unspecified   **OGCR** Official Guidelines for Coding and Reporting

   Complication\Comorbidity   Major C\C   Excludes 1   Excludes 2   Includes   Use additional   Code first   Code also

● H59.1　Intraoperative hemorrhage and hematoma of eye and adnexa complicating a procedure

> **Excludes1**　intraoperative hemorrhage and hematoma of eye and adnexa due to accidental puncture or laceration during a procedure (H59.2-)

● H59.11　Intraoperative hemorrhage and hematoma of eye and adnexa complicating an ophthalmic procedure

　　H59.111　Intraoperative hemorrhage and hematoma of right eye and adnexa complicating an ophthalmic procedure 🦠

　　H59.112　Intraoperative hemorrhage and hematoma of left eye and adnexa complicating an ophthalmic procedure 🦠

　　H59.113　Intraoperative hemorrhage and hematoma of eye and adnexa complicating an ophthalmic procedure, bilateral 🦠

　　H59.119　Intraoperative hemorrhage and hematoma of unspecified eye and adnexa complicating an ophthalmic procedure 🦠

● H59.12　Intraoperative hemorrhage and hematoma of eye and adnexa complicating other procedure

　　H59.121　Intraoperative hemorrhage and hematoma of right eye and adnexa complicating other procedure 🦠

　　H59.122　Intraoperative hemorrhage and hematoma of left eye and adnexa complicating other procedure 🦠

　　H59.123　Intraoperative hemorrhage and hematoma of eye and adnexa complicating other procedure, bilateral 🦠

　　H59.129　Intraoperative hemorrhage and hematoma of unspecified eye and adnexa complicating other procedure 🦠

● H59.2　Accidental puncture and laceration of eye and adnexa during a procedure

● H59.21　Accidental puncture and laceration of eye and adnexa during an ophthalmic procedure

　　H59.211　Accidental puncture and laceration of right eye and adnexa during an ophthalmic procedure 🦠

　　H59.212　Accidental puncture and laceration of left eye and adnexa during an ophthalmic procedure 🦠

　　H59.213　Accidental puncture and laceration of eye and adnexa during an ophthalmic procedure, bilateral 🦠

　　H59.219　Accidental puncture and laceration of unspecified eye and adnexa during an ophthalmic procedure 🦠

● H59.22　Accidental puncture and laceration of eye and adnexa during other procedure

　　H59.221　Accidental puncture and laceration of right eye and adnexa during other procedure 🦠

　　H59.222　Accidental puncture and laceration of left eye and adnexa during other procedure 🦠

　　H59.223　Accidental puncture and laceration of eye and adnexa during other procedure, bilateral 🦠

　　H59.229　Accidental puncture and laceration of unspecified eye and adnexa during other procedure 🦠

● H59.3　Postprocedural hemorrhage and hematoma of eye and adnexa following a procedure

● H59.31　Postprocedural hemorrhage and hematoma of eye and adnexa following an ophthalmic procedure

　　H59.311　Postprocedural hemorrhage and hematoma of right eye and adnexa following an ophthalmic procedure 🦠

　　H59.312　Postprocedural hemorrhage and hematoma of left eye and adnexa following an ophthalmic procedure 🦠

　　H59.313　Postprocedural hemorrhage and hematoma of eye and adnexa following an ophthalmic procedure, bilateral 🦠

　　H59.319　Postprocedural hemorrhage and hematoma of unspecified eye and adnexa following an ophthalmic procedure 🦠

● H59.32　Postprocedural hemorrhage and hematoma of eye and adnexa following other procedure

　　H59.321　Postprocedural hemorrhage and hematoma of right eye and adnexa following other procedure 🦠

　　H59.322　Postprocedural hemorrhage and hematoma of left eye and adnexa following other procedure 🦠

　　H59.323　Postprocedural hemorrhage and hematoma of eye and adnexa following other procedure, bilateral 🦠

　　H59.329　Postprocedural hemorrhage and hematoma of unspecified eye and adnexa following other procedure 🦠

● H59.4　Inflammation (infection) of postprocedural bleb
　　Postprocedural blebitis

> **Excludes1**　filtering (vitreous) bleb after glaucoma surgery status (Z98.83)

　H59.40　Inflammation (infection) of postprocedural bleb, unspecified

　H59.41　Inflammation (infection) of postprocedural bleb, stage 1

　H59.42　Inflammation (infection) of postprocedural bleb, stage 2

　H59.43　Inflammation (infection) of postprocedural bleb, stage 3
　　　Bleb endophthalmitis

● Unacceptable First-Listed Diagnosis　　● Use Additional Character(s)　　🔲 Unspecified　　**OGCR** Official Guidelines for Coding and Reporting

🦠 Complication\Comorbidity　🦠 Major C\C　 Excludes 1 　 Excludes 2 　 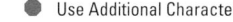 Includes　 Use additional　 Code first　 Code also

993

● H59.8   **Other intraoperative and postprocedural complications and disorders of eye and adnexa, not elsewhere classified**

   ● H59.81   **Chorioretinal scars after surgery for detachment**

       H59.811   Chorioretinal scars after surgery for detachment, right eye 🗲

       H59.812   Chorioretinal scars after surgery for detachment, left eye 🗲

       H59.813   Chorioretinal scars after surgery for detachment, bilateral 🗲

    ■ H59.819   Chorioretinal scars after surgery for detachment, unspecified eye 🗲

H59.88   Other intraoperative complications of eye and adnexa, not elsewhere classified 🗲

H59.89   Other postprocedural complications and disorders of eye and adnexa, not elsewhere classified 🗲

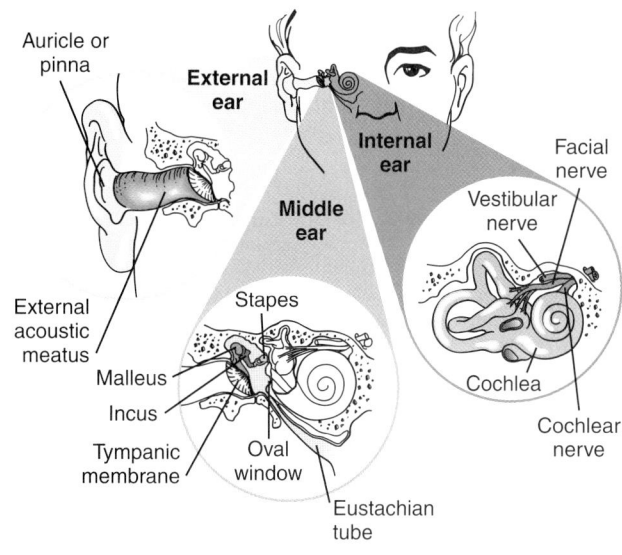

Figure 8-1 Auditory system. (From Buck CJ: Step-by-Step Medical Coding, 2010 ed. Philadelphia, WB Saunders, 2010.)

(See Plate 92 on page NAP-20.)

CHAPTER 8

DISEASES OF THE EAR AND MASTOID PROCESS (H60-H95)

Note: Use an external cause code following the code for the ear condition, if applicable, to identify the cause of the ear condition

Excludes2	certain conditions originating in the perinatal period (P04-P96)

certain conditions originating in the
    perinatal period (P04-P96)
certain infectious and parasitic diseases
    (A00-B99)
complications of pregnancy, childbirth and
    the puerperium (O00-O99)
congenital malformations, deformations
    and chromosomal abnormalities
    (Q00-Q99)
endocrine, nutritional and metabolic
    diseases (E00-E90)
injury, poisoning and certain other
    consequences of external causes
    (S00-T98)
neoplasms (C00-D48)
symptoms, signs and abnormal clinical
    and laboratory findings, not elsewhere
    classified (R00-R94)

This chapter contains the following blocks:

H60-H62	Diseases of external ear
H65-H75	Diseases of middle ear and mastoid
H80-H83	Diseases of inner ear
H90-H94	Other disorders of ear
H95	Intraoperative and postprocedural complications and disorders of ear and mastoid process, not elsewhere classified

● **H60 Otitis externa**

● **H60.0 Abscess of external ear**
    Boil of external ear
    Carbuncle of auricle or external auditory canal
    Furuncle of external ear

    ▢ H60.00 Abscess of external ear, unspecified ear
    H60.01 Abscess of right external ear
    H60.02 Abscess of left external ear
    H60.03 Abscess of external ear, bilateral

● **H60.1 Cellulitis of external ear**
    Cellulitis of auricle
    Cellulitis of external auditory canal

    ▢ H60.10 Cellulitis of external ear, unspecified ear
    H60.11 Cellulitis of right external ear
    H60.12 Cellulitis of left external ear
    H60.13 Cellulitis of external ear, bilateral

● **H60.2 Malignant otitis externa**
    ▢ H60.20 Malignant otitis externa, unspecified ear 🦠
    H60.21 Malignant otitis externa, right ear 🦠
    H60.22 Malignant otitis externa, left ear 🦠
    H60.23 Malignant otitis externa, bilateral 🦠

● **H60.3 Other infective otitis externa**
    ● H60.31 Diffuse otitis externa
        H60.311 Diffuse otitis externa, right ear
        H60.312 Diffuse otitis externa, left ear
        H60.313 Diffuse otitis externa, bilateral
        ▢ H60.319 Diffuse otitis externa, unspecified ear

    ● H60.32 Hemorrhagic otitis externa
        H60.321 Hemorrhagic otitis externa, right ear
        H60.322 Hemorrhagic otitis externa, left ear
        H60.323 Hemorrhagic otitis externa, bilateral
        ▢ H60.329 Hemorrhagic otitis externa, unspecified ear

    ● H60.33 Swimmer's ear
        H60.331 Swimmer's ear, right ear
        H60.332 Swimmer's ear, left ear
        H60.333 Swimmer's ear, bilateral
        ▢ H60.339 Swimmer's ear, unspecified ear

    ● H60.39 Other infective otitis externa
        H60.391 Other infective otitis externa, right ear
        H60.392 Other infective otitis externa, left ear
        H60.393 Other infective otitis externa, bilateral
        ▢ H60.399 Other infective otitis externa, unspecified ear

● **H60.4 Cholesteatoma of external ear**
    Keratosis obturans of external ear (canal)

Excludes2	cholesteatoma of middle ear (H71.-)

    cholesteatoma of middle ear
        (H71.-)
    recurrent cholesteatoma of
        postmastoidectomy cavity
        (H95.0-)

● Unacceptable First-Listed Diagnosis   ● Use Additional Character(s)   ▢ Unspecified   **OGCR** Official Guidelines for Coding and Reporting
🦠 Complication\Comorbidity   🦠 Major C\C   Excludes 1   Excludes 2   Includes   Use additional   Code first   Code also

H60.40 Cholesteatoma of external ear, unspecified ear

H60.41 Cholesteatoma of right external ear

H60.42 Cholesteatoma of left external ear

H60.43 Cholesteatoma of external ear, bilateral

● H60.5 Acute noninfective otitis externa

● H60.50 Unspecified acute noninfective otitis externa
Acute otitis externa NOS

H60.501 Unspecified acute noninfective otitis externa, right ear

H60.502 Unspecified acute noninfective otitis externa, left ear

H60.503 Unspecified acute noninfective otitis externa, bilateral

H60.509 Unspecified acute noninfective otitis externa, unspecified ear

● H60.51 Acute actinic otitis externa

H60.511 Acute actinic otitis externa, right ear

H60.512 Acute actinic otitis externa, left ear

H60.513 Acute actinic otitis externa, bilateral

H60.519 Acute actinic otitis externa, unspecified ear

● H60.52 Acute chemical otitis externa

H60.521 Acute chemical otitis externa, right ear

H60.522 Acute chemical otitis externa, left ear

H60.523 Acute chemical otitis externa, bilateral

H60.529 Acute chemical otitis externa, unspecified ear

● H60.53 Acute contact otitis externa

H60.531 Acute contact otitis externa, right ear

H60.532 Acute contact otitis externa, left ear

H60.533 Acute contact otitis externa, bilateral

H60.539 Acute contact otitis externa, unspecified ear

● H60.54 Acute eczematoid otitis externa

H60.541 Acute eczematoid otitis externa, right ear

H60.542 Acute eczematoid otitis externa, left ear

H60.543 Acute eczematoid otitis externa, bilateral

H60.549 Acute eczematoid otitis externa, unspecified ear

● H60.55 Acute reactive otitis externa

H60.551 Acute reactive otitis externa, right ear

H60.552 Acute reactive otitis externa, left ear

H60.553 Acute reactive otitis externa, bilateral

H60.559 Acute reactive otitis externa, unspecified ear

● H60.59 Other noninfective acute otitis externa

H60.591 Other noninfective acute otitis externa, right ear

H60.592 Other noninfective acute otitis externa, left ear

H60.593 Other noninfective acute otitis externa, bilateral

H60.599 Other noninfective acute otitis externa, unspecified ear

● H60.6 Unspecified chronic otitis externa

H60.60 Unspecified chronic otitis externa, unspecified ear

H60.61 Unspecified chronic otitis externa, right ear

H60.62 Unspecified chronic otitis externa, left ear

H60.63 Unspecified chronic otitis externa, bilateral

● H60.8 Other otitis externa

● H60.8x Other otitis externa

H60.8x1 Other otitis externa, right ear

H60.8x2 Other otitis externa, left ear

H60.8x3 Other otitis externa, bilateral

H60.8x9 Other otitis externa, unspecified ear

● H60.9 Unspecified otitis externa

H60.90 Unspecified otitis externa, unspecified ear

H60.91 Unspecified otitis externa, right ear

H60.92 Unspecified otitis externa, left ear

H60.93 Unspecified otitis externa, bilateral

● H61 Other disorders of external ear

● H61.0 Chondritis and perichondritis of external ear
Chondrodermatitis nodularis chronica helicis
Perichondritis of auricle
Perichondritis of pinna

● H61.00 Unspecified perichondritis of external ear

H61.001 Unspecified perichondritis of right external ear

H61.002 Unspecified perichondritis of left external ear

H61.003 Unspecified perichondritis of external ear, bilateral

H61.009 Unspecified perichondritis of external ear, unspecified ear

● H61.01 Acute perichondritis of external ear

H61.011 Acute perichondritis of right external ear

H61.012 Acute perichondritis of left external ear

H61.013 Acute perichondritis of external ear, bilateral

H61.019 Acute perichondritis of external ear, unspecified ear

● H61.02 Chronic perichondritis of external ear

H61.021 Chronic perichondritis of right external ear

H61.022 Chronic perichondritis of left external ear

H61.023 Chronic perichondritis of external ear, bilateral

H61.029 Chronic perichondritis of external ear, unspecified ear

● Unacceptable First-Listed Diagnosis   ● Use Additional Character(s)   ▪ Unspecified   OGCR Official Guidelines for Coding and Reporting
🝆 Complication\Comorbidity   🝆 Major C\C   Excludes 1   Excludes 2   Includes   Use additional   Code first   Code also

● H61.03   Chondritis of external ear
     Chondritis of auricle
     Chondritis of pinna

   H61.031   Chondritis of right external ear

   H61.032   Chondritis of left external ear

   H61.033   Chondritis of external ear, bilateral

   ■ H61.039   Chondritis of external ear, unspecified ear

● H61.1   Noninfective disorders of pinna

   Excludes2   cauliflower ear (M95.1-)
                gouty tophi of ear (M1a-, M10.-)

● H61.10   Unspecified noninfective disorders of pinna
     Disorder of pinna NOS

   ■ H61.101   Unspecified noninfective disorders of pinna, right ear

   ■ H61.102   Unspecified noninfective disorders of pinna, left ear

   ■ H61.103   Unspecified noninfective disorders of pinna, bilateral

   ■ H61.109   Unspecified noninfective disorders of pinna, unspecified ear

● H61.11   Acquired deformity of pinna
     Acquired deformity of auricle

     Excludes2   cauliflower ear (M95.1-)

   H61.111   Acquired deformity of pinna, right ear

   H61.112   Acquired deformity of pinna, left ear

   H61.113   Acquired deformity of pinna, bilateral

   ■ H61.119   Acquired deformity of pinna, unspecified ear

● H61.12   Hematoma of pinna
     Hematoma of auricle

   H61.121   Hematoma of pinna, right ear

   H61.122   Hematoma of pinna, left ear

   H61.123   Hematoma of pinna, bilateral

   ■ H61.129   Hematoma of pinna, unspecified ear

● H61.19   Other noninfective disorders of pinna

   H61.191   Noninfective disorders of pinna, right ear

   H61.192   Noninfective disorders of pinna, left ear

   H61.193   Noninfective disorders of pinna, bilateral

   ■ H61.199   Noninfective disorders of pinna, unspecified ear

● H61.2   Impacted cerumen
     Wax in ear

   ■ H61.20   Impacted cerumen, unspecified ear

   H61.21   Impacted cerumen, right ear

   H61.22   Impacted cerumen, left ear

   H61.23   Impacted cerumen, bilateral

● H61.3   Acquired stenosis of external ear canal
     Collapse of external ear canal

     Excludes1   postprocedural stenosis of external ear canal (H95.81-)

● H61.30   Acquired stenosis of external ear canal, unspecified

   ■ H61.301   Acquired stenosis of right external ear canal, unspecified

   ■ H61.302   Acquired stenosis of left external ear canal, unspecified

   ■ H61.303   Acquired stenosis of external ear canal, unspecified, bilateral

   ■ H61.309   Acquired stenosis of external ear canal, unspecified, unspecified ear

● H61.31   Acquired stenosis of external ear canal secondary to trauma

   H61.311   Acquired stenosis of right external ear canal secondary to trauma

   H61.312   Acquired stenosis of left external ear canal secondary to trauma

   H61.313   Acquired stenosis of external ear canal secondary to trauma, bilateral

   ■ H61.319   Acquired stenosis of external ear canal secondary to trauma, unspecified ear

● H61.32   Acquired stenosis of external ear canal secondary to inflammation and infection

   H61.321   Acquired stenosis of right external ear canal secondary to inflammation and infection

   H61.322   Acquired stenosis of left external ear canal secondary to inflammation and infection

   H61.323   Acquired stenosis of external ear canal secondary to inflammation and infection, bilateral

   ■ H61.329   Acquired stenosis of external ear canal secondary to inflammation and infection, unspecified ear

● H61.39   Other acquired stenosis of external ear canal

   H61.391   Other acquired stenosis of right external ear canal

   H61.392   Other acquired stenosis of left external ear canal

   H61.393   Other acquired stenosis of external ear canal, bilateral

   ■ H61.399   Other acquired stenosis of external ear canal, unspecified ear

● H61.8   Other specified disorders of external ear

● H61.81   Exostosis of external canal

   H61.811   Exostosis of right external canal

   H61.812   Exostosis of left external canal

   H61.813   Exostosis of external canal, bilateral

   ■ H61.819   Exostosis of external canal, unspecified ear

● H61.89   Other specified disorders of external ear

   H61.891   Other specified disorders of right external ear

   H61.892   Other specified disorders of left external ear

   H61.893   Other specified disorders of external ear, bilateral

   ■ H61.899   Other specified disorders of external ear, unspecified ear

● H61.9   Disorder of external ear, unspecified

   ■ H61.90   Disorder of external ear, unspecified, unspecified ear

   ■ H61.91   Disorder of right external ear, unspecified

● Unacceptable First-Listed Diagnosis   ● Use Additional Character(s)   ■ Unspecified   **OGCR** Official Guidelines for Coding and Reporting
   🅒 Complication\Comorbidity   🅒 Major C\C   Excludes 1   Excludes 2   Includes   Use additional   Code first   Code also

997

CHAPTER 8 (H60–H95)

H61.92   Disorder of left external ear, unspecified

H61.93   Disorder of external ear, unspecified, bilateral

● H62   Disorders of external ear in diseases classified elsewhere

    ● H62.4   Otitis externa in other diseases classified elsewhere

      Code first underlying disease, such as:
      erysipelas (A46)
      impetigo (L01.0)

      Excludes1   otitis externa (in):
           candidiasis (B37.84)
           herpes viral [herpes simplex]
             (B00.1)
           herpes zoster (B02.8)

      ● H62.40   Otitis externa in other diseases classified elsewhere, unspecified ear

      ● H62.41   Otitis externa in other diseases classified elsewhere, right ear

      ● H62.42   Otitis externa in other diseases classified elsewhere, left ear

      ● H62.43   Otitis externa in other diseases classified elsewhere, bilateral

    ● H62.8   Other disorders of external ear in diseases classified elsewhere

      Code first underlying disease, such as:
      gout (M1a-, M10.-)

      ● H62.8x   Other disorders of external ear in diseases classified elsewhere

        ● H62.8x1   Other disorders of right external ear in diseases classified elsewhere

        ● H62.8x2   Other disorders of left external ear in diseases classified elsewhere

        ● H62.8x3   Other disorders of external ear in diseases classified elsewhere, bilateral

        ● H62.8x9   Other disorders of external ear in diseases classified elsewhere, unspecified ear

---

DISEASES OF MIDDLE EAR AND MASTOID (H65-H75)

(See Plate 94 on page NAP-21.)

● H65   Nonsuppurative otitis media

    Bacterial or viral infection or inflammation of the middle ear; may result in fluid accumulation with pain and temporary hearing loss.

    Includes   nonsuppurative otitis media with myringitis

    Use additional code for any associated perforated tympanic membrane (H72.-)

    Use additional code to identify:
    exposure to environmental tobacco smoke (Z77.22)
    exposure to tobacco smoke in the perinatal period (P96.81)
    history of tobacco use (Z87.891)
    occupational exposure to environmental tobacco smoke (Z57.31)
    tobacco dependence (F17.-)
    tobacco use (Z72.0)

    ● H65.0   Acute serous otitis media
      Acute and subacute secretory otitis

      H65.00   Acute serous otitis media, unspecified ear

      H65.01   Acute serous otitis media, right ear

      H65.02   Acute serous otitis media, left ear

      H65.03   Acute serous otitis media, bilateral

H65.04   Acute serous otitis media, recurrent, right ear

H65.05   Acute serous otitis media, recurrent, left ear

H65.06   Acute serous otitis media, recurrent, bilateral

H65.07   Acute serous otitis media, recurrent, unspecified ear

● H65.1   Other acute nonsuppurative otitis media

    Excludes1   otitic barotrauma (T70.0)
           otitis media (acute) NOS (H66.9)

    ● H65.11   Acute and subacute allergic otitis media (mucoid) (sanguinous) (serous)

      H65.111   Acute and subacute allergic otitis media (mucoid) (sanguinous) (serous), right ear

      H65.112   Acute and subacute allergic otitis media (mucoid) (sanguinous) (serous), left ear

      H65.113   Acute and subacute allergic otitis media (mucoid) (sanguinous) (serous), bilateral

      H65.114   Acute and subacute allergic otitis media (mucoid) (sanguinous) (serous), recurrent, right ear

      H65.115   Acute and subacute allergic otitis media (mucoid) (sanguinous) (serous), recurrent, left ear

      H65.116   Acute and subacute allergic otitis media (mucoid) (sanguinous) (serous), recurrent, bilateral

      H65.117   Acute and subacute allergic otitis media (mucoid) (sanguinous) (serous), recurrent, unspecified ear

      H65.119   Acute and subacute allergic otitis media (mucoid) (sanguinous) (serous), unspecified ear

    ● H65.19   Other acute nonsuppurative otitis media
      Acute and subacute mucoid otitis media
      Acute and subacute nonsuppurative otitis media NOS
      Acute and subacute sanguinous otitis media
      Acute and subacute seromucinous otitis media

      H65.191   Other acute nonsuppurative otitis media, right ear

      H65.192   Other acute nonsuppurative otitis media, left ear

      H65.193   Other acute nonsuppurative otitis media, bilateral

      H65.194   Other acute nonsuppurative otitis media, recurrent, right ear

      H65.195   Other acute nonsuppurative otitis media, recurrent, left ear

      H65.196   Other acute nonsuppurative otitis media, recurrent, bilateral

      H65.197   Other acute nonsuppurative otitis media recurrent, unspecified ear

      H65.199   Other acute nonsuppurative otitis media, unspecified ear

● H65.2   Chronic serous otitis media
    Chronic tubotympanal catarrh

    H65.20   Chronic serous otitis media, unspecified ear

    H65.21   Chronic serous otitis media, right ear

H65.22   Chronic serous otitis media, left ear

H65.23   Chronic serous otitis media, bilateral

● H65.3   **Chronic mucoid otitis media**
     Chronic mucinous otitis media
     Chronic secretory otitis media
     Chronic transudative otitis media
     Glue ear

     Excludes1   adhesive middle ear disease (H74.1)

     ■H65.30   Chronic mucoid otitis media, unspecified ear

     H65.31   Chronic mucoid otitis media, right ear

     H65.32   Chronic mucoid otitis media, left ear

     H65.33   Chronic mucoid otitis media, bilateral

● H65.4   **Other chronic nonsuppurative otitis media**

     ● H65.41   **Chronic allergic otitis media**

         H65.411   Chronic allergic otitis media, right ear

         H65.412   Chronic allergic otitis media, left ear

         H65.413   Chronic allergic otitis media, bilateral

         ■H65.419   Chronic allergic otitis media, unspecified ear

     ● H65.49   **Other chronic nonsuppurative otitis media**
         Chronic exudative otitis media
         Chronic nonsuppurative otitis media NOS
         Chronic otitis media with effusion (nonpurulent)
         Chronic seromucinous otitis media

         H65.491   Other chronic nonsuppurative otitis media, right ear

         H65.492   Other chronic nonsuppurative otitis media, left ear

         H65.493   Other chronic nonsuppurative otitis media, bilateral

         ■H65.499   Other chronic nonsuppurative otitis media, unspecified ear

● H65.9   **Unspecified nonsuppurative otitis media**
     Allergic otitis media NOS
     Catarrhal otitis media NOS
     Exudative otitis media NOS
     Mucoid otitis media NOS
     Otitis media with effusion (nonpurulent) NOS
     Secretory otitis media NOS
     Seromucinous otitis media NOS
     Serous otitis media NOS
     Transudative otitis media NOS

     ■H65.90   Unspecified nonsuppurative otitis media, unspecified ear

     ■H65.91   Unspecified nonsuppurative otitis media, right ear

     ■H65.92   Unspecified nonsuppurative otitis media, left ear

     ■H65.93   Unspecified nonsuppurative otitis media, bilateral

● H66   **Suppurative and unspecified otitis media**
     Suppurative: Discharging pus

     Includes   suppurative and unspecified otitis media with myringitis

     Use additional code for any associated perforated tympanic membrane (H72.-)

     Use additional code to identify:
         exposure to environmental tobacco smoke (Z77.22)
         exposure to tobacco smoke in the perinatal period (P96.81)
         history of tobacco use (Z87.891)
         occupational exposure to environmental tobacco smoke (Z57.31)
         tobacco dependence (F17.-)
         tobacco use (Z72.0)

● H66.0   **Acute suppurative otitis media**

     ● H66.00   **Acute suppurative otitis media without spontaneous rupture of ear drum**

         H66.001   Acute suppurative otitis media without spontaneous rupture of ear drum, right ear

         H66.002   Acute suppurative otitis media without spontaneous rupture of ear drum, left ear

         H66.003   Acute suppurative otitis media without spontaneous rupture of ear drum, bilateral

         H66.004   Acute suppurative otitis media without spontaneous rupture of ear drum, recurrent, right ear

         H66.005   Acute suppurative otitis media without spontaneous rupture of ear drum, recurrent, left ear

         H66.006   Acute suppurative otitis media without spontaneous rupture of ear drum, recurrent, bilateral

         ■H66.007   Acute suppurative otitis media without spontaneous rupture of ear drum, recurrent, unspecified ear

         ■H66.009   Acute suppurative otitis media without spontaneous rupture of ear drum, unspecified ear

     ● H66.01   **Acute suppurative otitis media with spontaneous rupture of ear drum**

         H66.011   Acute suppurative otitis media with spontaneous rupture of ear drum, right ear

         H66.012   Acute suppurative otitis media with spontaneous rupture of ear drum, left ear

         H66.013   Acute suppurative otitis media with spontaneous rupture of ear drum, bilateral

         H66.014   Acute suppurative otitis media with spontaneous rupture of ear drum, recurrent, right ear

         H66.015   Acute suppurative otitis media with spontaneous rupture of ear drum, recurrent, left ear

         H66.016   Acute suppurative otitis media with spontaneous rupture of ear drum, recurrent, bilateral

         ■H66.017   Acute suppurative otitis media with spontaneous rupture of ear drum, recurrent, unspecified ear

         ■H66.019   Acute suppurative otitis media with spontaneous rupture of ear drum, unspecified ear

● Unacceptable First-Listed Diagnosis   ● Use Additional Character(s)   ■ Unspecified   **OGCR** Official Guidelines for Coding and Reporting

🝔 Complication\Comorbidity   🝔 Major C\C   Excludes 1   Excludes 2   Includes   Use additional   Code first   Code also

999

CHAPTER 8 (H60–H95)

- **H66.1 Chronic tubotympanic suppurative otitis media**
  Benign chronic suppurative otitis media
  Chronic tubotympanic disease
  - **H66.10 Chronic tubotympanic suppurative otitis media, unspecified**
  - **H66.11 Chronic tubotympanic suppurative otitis media, right ear**
  - **H66.12 Chronic tubotympanic suppurative otitis media, left ear**
  - **H66.13 Chronic tubotympanic suppurative otitis media, bilateral**
- **H66.2 Chronic atticoantral suppurative otitis media**
  Chronic atticoantral disease
  - **H66.20 Chronic atticoantral suppurative otitis media, unspecified ear**
  - **H66.21 Chronic atticoantral suppurative otitis media, right ear**
  - **H66.22 Chronic atticoantral suppurative otitis media, left ear**
  - **H66.23 Chronic atticoantral suppurative otitis media, bilateral**
- **H66.3 Other chronic suppurative otitis media**
  Chronic suppurative otitis media NOS
  - **Excludes1**   tuberculous otitis media (A18.6)
  - **H66.3x Other chronic suppurative otitis media**
    - **H66.3x1 Other chronic suppurative otitis media, right ear**
    - **H66.3x2 Other chronic suppurative otitis media, left ear**
    - **H66.3x3 Other chronic suppurative otitis media, bilateral**
    - **H66.3x9 Other chronic suppurative otitis media, unspecified ear**
- **H66.4 Suppurative otitis media, unspecified**
  Purulent otitis media NOS
  - **H66.40 Suppurative otitis media, unspecified, unspecified ear**
  - **H66.41 Suppurative otitis media, unspecified, right ear**
  - **H66.42 Suppurative otitis media, unspecified, left ear**
  - **H66.43 Suppurative otitis media, unspecified, bilateral**
- **H66.9 Otitis media, unspecified**
  Otitis media NOS
  Acute otitis media NOS
  Chronic otitis media NOS
  - **H66.90 Otitis media, unspecified, unspecified ear**
  - **H66.91 Otitis media, unspecified, right ear**
  - **H66.92 Otitis media, unspecified, left ear**
  - **H66.93 Otitis media, unspecified, bilateral**
- **H67 Otitis media in diseases classified elsewhere**
  Code first underlying disease, such as:
  viral disease NEC (B00-B34)
  Use additional code for any associated perforated tympanic membrane (H72.-)
  - **Excludes1**   otitis media in:
    influenza (J10.89)
    measles (B05.3)
    scarlet fever (A38.0)
    tuberculosis (A18.6)

- **H67.1 Otitis media in diseases classified elsewhere, right ear**
- **H67.2 Otitis media in diseases classified elsewhere, left ear**
- **H67.3 Otitis media in diseases classified elsewhere, bilateral**
- **H67.9 Otitis media in diseases classified elsewhere, unspecified ear**
- **H68 Eustachian salpingitis and obstruction**
  - **H68.0 Eustachian salpingitis**
    - **H68.00 Unspecified Eustachian salpingitis**
      - **H68.001 Unspecified Eustachian salpingitis, right ear**
      - **H68.002 Unspecified Eustachian salpingitis, left ear**
      - **H68.003 Unspecified Eustachian salpingitis, bilateral**
      - **H68.009 Unspecified Eustachian salpingitis, unspecified ear**
    - **H68.01 Acute Eustachian salpingitis**
      - **H68.011 Acute Eustachian salpingitis, right ear**
      - **H68.012 Acute Eustachian salpingitis, left ear**
      - **H68.013 Acute Eustachian salpingitis, bilateral**
      - **H68.019 Acute Eustachian salpingitis, unspecified ear**
    - **H68.02 Chronic Eustachian salpingitis**
      - **H68.021 Chronic Eustachian salpingitis, right ear**
      - **H68.022 Chronic Eustachian salpingitis, left ear**
      - **H68.023 Chronic Eustachian salpingitis, bilateral**
      - **H68.029 Chronic Eustachian salpingitis, unspecified ear**
  - **H68.1 Obstruction of Eustachian tube**
    Stenosis of Eustachian tube
    Stricture of Eustachian tube
    - **H68.10 Unspecified obstruction of Eustachian tube**
      - **H68.101 Unspecified obstruction of Eustachian tube, right ear**
      - **H68.102 Unspecified obstruction of Eustachian tube, left ear**
      - **H68.103 Unspecified obstruction of Eustachian tube, bilateral**
      - **H68.109 Unspecified obstruction of Eustachian tube, unspecified ear**
    - **H68.11 Osseous obstruction of Eustachian tube**
      - **H68.111 Osseous obstruction of Eustachian tube, right ear**
      - **H68.112 Osseous obstruction of Eustachian tube, left ear**
      - **H68.113 Osseous obstruction of Eustachian tube, bilateral**
      - **H68.119 Osseous obstruction of Eustachian tube, unspecified ear**
    - **H68.12 Intrinsic cartilagenous obstruction of Eustachian tube**
      - **H68.121 Intrinsic cartilagenous obstruction of Eustachian tube, right ear**

H68.122   Intrinsic cartilagenous obstruction of Eustachian tube, left ear

H68.123   Intrinsic cartilagenous obstruction of Eustachian tube, bilateral

H68.129   Intrinsic cartilagenous obstruction of Eustachian tube, unspecified ear

● H68.13   Extrinsic cartilagenous obstruction of Eustachian tube
     Compression of Eustachian tube

H68.131   Extrinsic cartilagenous obstruction of Eustachian tube, right ear

H68.132   Extrinsic cartilagenous obstruction of Eustachian tube, left ear

H68.133   Extrinsic cartilagenous obstruction of Eustachian tube, bilateral

H68.139   Extrinsic cartilagenous obstruction of Eustachian tube, unspecified ear

● **H69   Other and unspecified disorders of Eustachian tube**

   ● H69.0   Patulous Eustachian tube

H69.00   Patulous Eustachian tube, unspecified ear

H69.01   Patulous Eustachian tube, right ear

H69.02   Patulous Eustachian tube, left ear

H69.03   Patulous Eustachian tube, bilateral

   ● H69.8   Other specified disorders of Eustachian tube

H69.80   Other specified disorders of Eustachian tube, unspecified ear

H69.81   Other specified disorders of Eustachian tube, right ear

H69.82   Other specified disorders of Eustachian tube, left ear

H69.83   Other specified disorders of Eustachian tube, bilateral

   ● H69.9   Unspecified Eustachian tube disorder

H69.90   Unspecified Eustachian tube disorder, unspecified ear

H69.91   Unspecified Eustachian tube disorder, right ear

H69.92   Unspecified Eustachian tube disorder, left ear

H69.93   Unspecified Eustachian tube disorder, bilateral

● **H70   Mastoiditis and related conditions**

   ● H70.0   Acute mastoiditis
     Abscess of mastoid
     Empyema of mastoid

     ● H70.00   Acute mastoiditis without complications

H70.001   Acute mastoiditis without complications, right ear 🦠

H70.002   Acute mastoiditis without complications, left ear 🦠

Item 8–1   Mastoiditis is an infection of the portion of the temporal bone of the skull that is behind the ear (mastoid process) caused by an untreated otitis media, leading to an infection of the surrounding structures which may include the brain.

H70.003   Acute mastoiditis without complications, bilateral 🦠

H70.009   Acute mastoiditis without complications, unspecified ear 🦠

   ● H70.01   Subperiosteal abscess of mastoid

H70.011   Subperiosteal abscess of mastoid, right ear 🦠

H70.012   Subperiosteal abscess of mastoid, left ear 🦠

H70.013   Subperiosteal abscess of mastoid, bilateral 🦠

H70.019   Subperiosteal abscess of mastoid, unspecified ear 🦠

   ● H70.09   Acute mastoiditis with other complications

H70.091   Acute mastoiditis with other complications, right ear 🦠

H70.092   Acute mastoiditis with other complications, left ear 🦠

H70.093   Acute mastoiditis with other complications, bilateral 🦠

H70.099   Acute mastoiditis with other complications, unspecified ear 🦠

   ● H70.1   Chronic mastoiditis
     Caries of mastoid
     Fistula of mastoid

     | Excludes1 | tuberculous mastoiditis (A18.03)

H70.10   Chronic mastoiditis, unspecified ear

H70.11   Chronic mastoiditis, right ear

H70.12   Chronic mastoiditis, left ear

H70.13   Chronic mastoiditis, bilateral

   ● H70.2   Petrositis
     Inflammation of petrous bone

     ● H70.20   Unspecified petrositis

H70.201   Unspecified petrositis, right ear

H70.202   Unspecified petrositis, left ear

H70.203   Unspecified petrositis, bilateral

H70.209   Unspecified petrositis, unspecified ear

   ● H70.21   Acute petrositis

H70.211   Acute petrositis, right ear

H70.212   Acute petrositis, left ear

H70.213   Acute petrositis, bilateral

H70.219   Acute petrositis, unspecified ear

   ● H70.22   Chronic petrositis

H70.221   Chronic petrositis, right ear

H70.222   Chronic petrositis, left ear

H70.223   Chronic petrositis, bilateral

H70.229   Chronic petrositis, unspecified ear

   ● H70.8   Other mastoiditis and related conditions

     | Excludes1 | preauricular sinus and cyst (Q18.1)
     sinus, fistula, and cyst of branchial cleft (Q18.0)

   ● H70.81   Postauricular fistula

H70.811   Postauricular fistula, right ear

H70.812   Postauricular fistula, left ear

H70.813   Postauricular fistula, bilateral

H70.819   Postauricular fistula, unspecified ear

   ● H70.89   Other mastoiditis and related conditions

H70.891   Other mastoiditis and related conditions, right ear

---

● Unaccceptable First-Listed Diagnosis   ● Use Additional Character(s)   ▣ Unspecified   **OGCR** Official Guidelines for Coding and Reporting

🦠 Complication\Comorbidity   🦠 Major C\C | Excludes 1 | | Excludes 2 | Includes   Use additional   Code first   Code also

H70.892   Other mastoiditis and related conditions, left ear

H70.893   Other mastoiditis and related conditions, bilateral

H70.899   Other mastoiditis and related conditions, unspecified ear

● H70.9   Unspecified mastoiditis

H70.90   Unspecified mastoiditis, unspecified ear

H70.91   Unspecified mastoiditis, right ear

H70.92   Unspecified mastoiditis, left ear

H70.93   Unspecified mastoiditis, bilateral

● H71   Cholesteatoma of middle ear

Excludes2   cholesteatoma of external ear (H60.4-)
recurrent cholesteatoma of postmastoidectomy cavity (H95.0-)

● H71.0   Cholesteatoma of attic

H71.00   Cholesteatoma of attic, unspecified ear

H71.01   Cholesteatoma of attic, right ear

H71.02   Cholesteatoma of attic, left ear

H71.03   Cholesteatoma of attic, bilateral

● H71.1   Cholesteatoma of tympanum

H71.10   Cholesteatoma of tympanum, unspecified ear

H71.11   Cholesteatoma of tympanum, right ear

H71.12   Cholesteatoma of tympanum, left ear

H71.13   Cholesteatoma of tympanum, bilateral

● H71.2   Cholesteatoma of mastoid

H71.20   Cholesteatoma of mastoid, unspecified ear

H71.21   Cholesteatoma of mastoid, right ear

H71.22   Cholesteatoma of mastoid, left ear

H71.23   Cholesteatoma of mastoid, bilateral

● H71.3   Diffuse cholesteatosis

H71.30   Diffuse cholesteatosis, unspecified ear

H71.31   Diffuse cholesteatosis, right ear

H71.32   Diffuse cholesteatosis, left ear

H71.33   Diffuse cholesteatosis, bilateral

● H71.9   Unspecified cholesteatoma

H71.90   Unspecified cholesteatoma, unspecified ear

H71.91   Unspecified cholesteatoma, right ear

H71.92   Unspecified cholesteatoma, left ear

H71.93   Unspecified cholesteatoma, bilateral

(See Plate 93 on page NAP-21.)

● H72   Perforation of tympanic membrane
Hole or rupture in ear drum

Includes   persistent post-traumatic perforation of ear drum
postinflammatory perforation of ear drum

Code first any associated otitis media (H65.-, H66.1-, H66.2-, H66.3-, H66.4-, H66.9-, H67.-)

Excludes1   acute suppurative otitis media with rupture of the tympanic membrane (H66.01-)
traumatic rupture of ear drum (S09.2-)

● H72.0   Central perforation of tympanic membrane

H72.00   Central perforation of tympanic membrane, unspecified ear

H72.01   Central perforation of tympanic membrane, right ear

H72.02   Central perforation of tympanic membrane, left ear

H72.03   Central perforation of tympanic membrane, bilateral

● H72.1   Attic perforation of tympanic membrane
Perforation of pars flaccida

H72.10   Attic perforation of tympanic membrane, unspecified ear

H72.11   Attic perforation of tympanic membrane, right ear

H72.12   Attic perforation of tympanic membrane, left ear

H72.13   Attic perforation of tympanic membrane, bilateral

● H72.2   Other marginal perforations of tympanic membrane

● H72.2x   Other marginal perforations of tympanic membrane

H72.2x1   Other marginal perforations of tympanic membrane, right ear

H72.2x2   Other marginal perforations of tympanic membrane, left ear

H72.2x3   Other marginal perforations of tympanic membrane, bilateral

H72.2x9   Other marginal perforations of tympanic membrane, unspecified ear

● H72.8   Other perforations of tympanic membrane

● H72.81   Multiple perforations of tympanic membrane

H72.811   Multiple perforations of tympanic membrane, right ear

H72.812   Multiple perforations of tympanic membrane, left ear

H72.813   Multiple perforations of tympanic membrane, bilateral

H72.819   Multiple perforations of tympanic membrane, unspecified ear

● H72.82   Total perforations of tympanic membrane

H72.821   Total perforations of tympanic membrane, right ear

H72.822   Total perforations of tympanic membrane, left ear

H72.823   Total perforations of tympanic membrane, bilateral

H72.829   Total perforations of tympanic membrane, unspecified ear

● H72.9   Unspecified perforation of tympanic membrane

H72.90   Unspecified perforation of tympanic membrane, unspecified ear

H72.91   Unspecified perforation of tympanic membrane, right ear

H72.92   Unspecified perforation of tympanic membrane, left ear

H72.93   Unspecified perforation of tympanic membrane, bilateral

● H73   Other disorders of tympanic membrane

● H73.0   Acute myringitis

Excludes1   acute myringitis with otitis media (H65, H66)

● H73.00   Unspecified acute myringitis
Acute tympanitis NOS

H73.001   Acute myringitis, right ear

● Unacceptable First-Listed Diagnosis   ● Use Additional Character(s)   ■ Unspecified   **OGCR** Official Guidelines for Coding and Reporting

🔗 Complication\Comorbidity   🔗 Major C\C   Excludes 1   Excludes 2   Includes   Use additional   Code first   Code also

H73.002   Acute myringitis, left ear

H73.003   Acute myringitis, bilateral

H73.009   Acute myringitis, unspecified ear

● H73.01   Bullous myringitis

H73.011   Bullous myringitis, right ear

H73.012   Bullous myringitis, left ear

H73.013   Bullous myringitis, bilateral

H73.019   Bullous myringitis, unspecified ear

● H73.09   Other acute myringitis

H73.091   Other acute myringitis, right ear

H73.092   Other acute myringitis, left ear

H73.093   Other acute myringitis, bilateral

H73.099   Other acute myringitis, unspecified ear

● H73.1   Chronic myringitis

Chronic tympanitis

Excludes1   chronic myringitis with otitis media (H65, H66)

H73.10   Chronic myringitis, unspecified ear

H73.11   Chronic myringitis, right ear

H73.12   Chronic myringitis, left ear

H73.13   Chronic myringitis, bilateral

● H73.2   Unspecified myringitis

H73.20   Unspecified myringitis, unspecified ear

H73.21   Unspecified myringitis, right ear

H73.22   Unspecified myringitis, left ear

H73.23   Unspecified myringitis, bilateral

● H73.8   Other specified disorders of tympanic membrane

● H73.81   Atrophic flaccid tympanic membrane

H73.811   Atrophic flaccid tympanic membrane, right ear

H73.812   Atrophic flaccid tympanic membrane, left ear

H73.813   Atrophic flaccid tympanic membrane, bilateral

H73.819   Atrophic flaccid tympanic membrane, unspecified ear

● H73.82   Atrophic nonflaccid tympanic membrane

H73.821   Atrophic nonflaccid tympanic membrane, right ear

H73.822   Atrophic nonflaccid tympanic membrane, left ear

H73.823   Atrophic nonflaccid tympanic membrane, bilateral

H73.829   Atrophic nonflaccid tympanic membrane, unspecified ear

● H73.89   Other specified disorders of tympanic membrane

H73.891   Other specified disorders of tympanic membrane, right ear

H73.892   Other specified disorders of tympanic membrane, left ear

H73.893   Other specified disorders of tympanic membrane, bilateral

H73.899   Other specified disorders of tympanic membrane, unspecified ear

● H73.9   Unspecified disorder of tympanic membrane

H73.90   Unspecified disorder of tympanic membrane, unspecified ear

H73.91   Unspecified disorder of tympanic membrane, right ear

H73.92   Unspecified disorder of tympanic membrane, left ear

H73.93   Unspecified disorder of tympanic membrane, bilateral

● H74   Other disorders of middle ear mastoid

Excludes2   mastoiditis (H70.-)

● H74.0   Tympanosclerosis

H74.01   Tympanosclerosis, right ear

H74.02   Tympanosclerosis, left ear

H74.03   Tympanosclerosis, bilateral

H74.09   Tympanosclerosis, unspecified ear

● H74.1   Adhesive middle ear disease

Adhesive otitis

Excludes1   glue ear (H65.3-)

H74.11   Adhesive right middle ear disease

H74.12   Adhesive left middle ear disease

H74.13   Adhesive middle ear disease, bilateral

H74.19   Adhesive middle ear disease, unspecified ear

● H74.2   Discontinuity and dislocation of ear ossicles

H74.20   Discontinuity and dislocation of ear ossicles, unspecified ear

H74.21   Discontinuity and dislocation of right ear ossicles

H74.22   Discontinuity and dislocation of left ear ossicles

H74.23   Discontinuity and dislocation of ear ossicles, bilateral

● H74.3   Other acquired abnormalities of ear ossicles

● H74.31   Ankylosis of ear ossicles

H74.311   Ankylosis of ear ossicles, right ear

H74.312   Ankylosis of ear ossicles, left ear

H74.313   Ankylosis of ear ossicles, bilateral

H74.319   Ankylosis of ear ossicles, unspecified ear

● H74.32   Partial loss of ear ossicles

H74.321   Partial loss of ear ossicles, right ear

H74.322   Partial loss of ear ossicles, left ear

H74.323   Partial loss of ear ossicles, bilateral

H74.329   Partial loss of ear ossicles, unspecified ear

● H74.39   Other acquired abnormalities of ear ossicles

H74.391   Other acquired abnormalities of right ear ossicles

H74.392   Other acquired abnormalities of left ear ossicles

H74.393   Other acquired abnormalities of ear ossicles, bilateral

H74.399   Other acquired abnormalities of ear ossicles, unspecified ear

● Unacceptable First-Listed Diagnosis   ● Use Additional Character(s)   ▣ Unspecified   **OGCR** Official Guidelines for Coding and Reporting

🕭 Complication\Comorbidity   🕭 Major C\C   Excludes 1   Excludes 2    Includes   Use additional   Code first   Code also   1003

CHAPTER 8 (H60-H95)

- H74.4   Polyp of middle ear
  - ▪ H74.40   Polyp of middle ear, unspecified ear
  - H74.41   Polyp of right middle ear
  - H74.42   Polyp of left middle ear
  - H74.43   Polyp of middle ear, bilateral
- H74.8   Other specified disorders of middle ear and mastoid
  - H74.8x   Other specified disorders of middle ear and mastoid
    - H74.8x1   Other specified disorders of right middle ear and mastoid
    - H74.8x2   Other specified disorders of left middle ear and mastoid
    - H74.8x3   Other specified disorders of middle ear and mastoid, bilateral
    - ▪ H74.8x9   Other specified disorders of middle ear and mastoid, unspecified ear
- H74.9   Unspecified disorder of middle ear and mastoid
  - ▪ H74.90   Unspecified disorder of middle ear and mastoid, unspecified ear
  - ▪ H74.91   Unspecified disorder of right middle ear and mastoid
  - ▪ H74.92   Unspecified disorder of left middle ear and mastoid
  - ▪ H74.93   Unspecified disorder of middle ear and mastoid, bilateral
- H75   Other disorders of middle ear and mastoid in diseases classified elsewhere

  Code first underlying disease

  - H75.0   Mastoiditis in infectious and parasitic diseases classified elsewhere

    Excludes1   mastoiditis (in):
    syphilis (A52.77)
    tuberculosis (A18.03)

    - ● ▪ H75.00   Mastoiditis in infectious and parasitic diseases classified elsewhere, unspecified ear
    - ● H75.01   Mastoiditis in infectious and parasitic diseases classified elsewhere, right ear
    - ● H75.02   Mastoiditis in infectious and parasitic diseases classified elsewhere, left ear
    - ● H75.03   Mastoiditis in infectious and parasitic diseases classified elsewhere, bilateral
  - H75.8   Other specified disorders of middle ear and mastoid in diseases classified elsewhere
    - ● ▪ H75.80   Other specified disorders of middle ear and mastoid in diseases classified elsewhere, unspecified ear
    - ● H75.81   Other specified disorders of right middle ear and mastoid in diseases classified elsewhere
    - ● H75.82   Other specified disorders of left middle ear and mastoid in diseases classified elsewhere
    - ● H75.83   Other specified disorders of middle ear and mastoid in diseases classified elsewhere, bilateral

DISEASES OF INNER EAR (H80-H83)

(See Plate 95 on page NAP-21.)

- H80   Otosclerosis

  Inherited middle ear spongelike bone growth causing hearing loss

  Includes   Otospongiosis

  - H80.0   Otosclerosis involving oval window, nonobliterative
    - ▪ H80.00   Otosclerosis involving oval window, nonobliterative, unspecified ear
    - H80.01   Otosclerosis involving oval window, nonobliterative, right ear
    - H80.02   Otosclerosis involving oval window, nonobliterative, left ear
    - H80.03   Otosclerosis involving oval window, nonobliterative, bilateral
  - H80.1   Otosclerosis involving oval window, obliterative
    - ▪ H80.10   Otosclerosis involving oval window, obliterative, unspecified ear
    - H80.11   Otosclerosis involving oval window, obliterative, right ear
    - H80.12   Otosclerosis involving oval window, obliterative, left ear
    - H80.13   Otosclerosis involving oval window, obliterative, bilateral
  - H80.2   Cochlear otosclerosis

    Otosclerosis involving otic capsule
    Otosclerosis involving round window

    - ▪ H80.20   Cochlear otosclerosis, unspecified ear
    - H80.21   Cochlear otosclerosis, right ear
    - H80.22   Cochlear otosclerosis, left ear
    - H80.23   Cochlear otosclerosis, bilateral
  - H80.8   Other otosclerosis
    - ▪ H80.80   Other otosclerosis, unspecified ear
    - H80.81   Other otosclerosis, right ear
    - H80.82   Other otosclerosis, left ear
    - H80.83   Other otosclerosis, bilateral
  - H80.9   Unspecified otosclerosis
    - ▪ H80.90   Unspecified otosclerosis, unspecified ear
    - ▪ H80.91   Unspecified otosclerosis, right ear
    - ▪ H80.92   Unspecified otosclerosis, left ear
    - ▪ H80.93   Unspecified otosclerosis, bilateral
- H81   Disorders of vestibular function

  Excludes1   epidemic vertigo (A88.1)
  vertigo NOS (R42)

  - H81.0   Ménière's disease

    Vestibular disorder that produces recurring symptoms including severe and intermittent hearing loss including the feeling of ear pressure or pain.
    Labyrinthine hydrops
    Ménière's syndrome or vertigo

    - H81.01   Ménière's disease, right ear
    - H81.02   Ménière's disease, left ear
    - H81.03   Ménière's disease, bilateral
    - ▪ H81.09   Ménière's disease, unspecified ear

●   Unacceptable First-Listed Diagnosis   ●   Use Additional Character(s)   ▪   Unspecified   **OGCR**   Official Guidelines for Coding and Reporting

🖰 Complication\Comorbidity   🖰 Major C\C   Excludes 1   Excludes 2   Includes   Use additional   Code first   Code also

● H81.1   Benign paroxysmal vertigo

    ▨ H81.10   Benign paroxysmal vertigo, unspecified ear

    H81.11   Benign paroxysmal vertigo, right ear

    H81.12   Benign paroxysmal vertigo, left ear

    H81.13   Benign paroxysmal vertigo, bilateral

● H81.2   Vestibular neuronitis

    ▨ H81.20   Vestibular neuronitis, unspecified ear

    H81.21   Vestibular neuronitis, right ear

    H81.22   Vestibular neuronitis, left ear

    H81.23   Vestibular neuronitis, bilateral

● H81.3   Other peripheral vertigo

    ● H81.31   Aural vertigo

       H81.311   Aural vertigo, right ear

       H81.312   Aural vertigo, left ear

       H81.313   Aural vertigo, bilateral

       ▨ H81.319   Aural vertigo, unspecified ear

    ● H81.39   Other peripheral vertigo

       Lermoyez' syndrome

       Otogenic vertigo

       Peripheral vertigo NOS

       H81.391   Other peripheral vertigo, right ear

       H81.392   Other peripheral vertigo, left ear

       H81.393   Other peripheral vertigo, bilateral

       ▨ H81.399   Other peripheral vertigo, unspecified ear

● H81.4   Vertigo of central origin

    Central positional nystagmus

    H81.41   Vertigo of central origin, right ear

    H81.42   Vertigo of central origin, left ear

    H81.43   Vertigo of central origin, bilateral

    ▨ H81.49   Vertigo of central origin, unspecified ear

● H81.8   Other disorders of vestibular function

    ● H81.8x   Other disorders of vestibular function

       H81.8x1   Other disorders of vestibular function, right ear

       H81.8x2   Other disorders of vestibular function, left ear

       H81.8x3   Other disorders of vestibular function, bilateral

       ▨ H81.8x9   Other disorders of vestibular function, unspecified ear

● H81.9   Unspecified disorder of vestibular function

    Vertiginous syndrome NOS

    ▨ H81.90   Unspecified disorder of vestibular function, unspecified ear

    ▨ H81.91   Unspecified disorder of vestibular function, right ear

    ▨ H81.92   Unspecified disorder of vestibular function, left ear

    ▨ H81.93   Unspecified disorder of vestibular function, bilateral

● H82   **Vertiginous syndromes in diseases classified elsewhere**

    Code first underlying disease

    Excludes1   epidemic vertigo (A88.1)

    ● H82.1   Vertiginous syndromes in diseases classified elsewhere, right ear

● H82.2   Vertiginous syndromes in diseases classified elsewhere, left ear

● H82.3   Vertiginous syndromes in diseases classified elsewhere, bilateral

● ▨ H82.9   Vertiginous syndromes in diseases classified elsewhere, unspecified ear

● H83   Other diseases of inner ear

    ● H83.0   Labyrinthitis

       Balance disorder that follows URI or head injury.

       H83.01   Labyrinthitis, right ear

       H83.02   Labyrinthitis, left ear

       H83.03   Labyrinthitis, bilateral

       ▨ H83.09   Labyrinthitis, unspecified ear

    ● H83.1   Labyrinthine fistula

       H83.11   Labyrinthine fistula, right ear

       H83.12   Labyrinthine fistula, left ear

       H83.13   Labyrinthine fistula, bilateral

       ▨ H83.19   Labyrinthine fistula, unspecified ear

    ● H83.2   Labyrinthine dysfunction

       Labyrinthine hypersensitivity

       Labyrinthine hypofunction

       Labyrinthine loss of function

       ● H83.2x   Labyrinthine dysfunction

          H83.2x1   Labyrinthine dysfunction, right ear

          H83.2x2   Labyrinthine dysfunction, left ear

          H83.2x3   Labyrinthine dysfunction, bilateral

          ▨ H83.2x9   Labyrinthine dysfunction, unspecified ear

    ● H83.3   Noise effects on inner ear

       Acoustic trauma of inner ear

       Noise-induced hearing loss of inner ear

       ● H83.3x   Noise effects on inner ear

          H83.3x1   Noise effects on right inner ear

          H83.3x2   Noise effects on left inner ear

          H83.3x3   Noise effects on inner ear, bilateral

          ▨ H83.3x9   Noise effects on inner ear, unspecified ear

    ● H83.8   Other specified diseases of inner ear

       ● H83.8x   Other specified diseases of inner ear

          H83.8x1   Other specified diseases of right inner ear

          H83.8x2   Other specified diseases of left inner ear

          H83.8x3   Other specified diseases of inner ear, bilateral

          ▨ H83.8x9   Other specified diseases of inner ear, unspecified ear

    ● H83.9   Unspecified disease of inner ear

       ▨ H83.90   Unspecified disease of inner ear, unspecified ear

       ▨ H83.91   Unspecified disease of right inner ear

       ▨ H83.92   Unspecified disease of left inner ear

       ▨ H83.93   Unspecified disease of inner ear, bilateral

● Unacceptable First-Listed Diagnosis   ● Use Additional Character(s)   ▨ Unspecified   **OGCR** Official Guidelines for Coding and Reporting

🏵 Complication\Comorbidity   🏵 Major C\C | Excludes 1 | | Excludes 2 | | Includes | Use additional   Code first   Code also

1005

CHAPTER 8 (H60–H95)

OTHER DISORDERS OF EAR (H90-H95)

● **H90   Conductive and sensorineural hearing loss**

> **Excludes1**   deaf nonspeaking NEC (H91.3)
> deafness NOS (H91.9-)
> hearing loss NOS (H91.9-)
> noise-induced hearing loss (H83.3-)
> ototoxic hearing loss (H91.0-)
> sudden (idiopathic) hearing loss (H91.2-)

   H90.0   Conductive hearing loss, bilateral

● **H90.1   Conductive hearing loss, unilateral with unrestricted hearing on the contralateral side**

     H90.11   Conductive hearing loss, unilateral, right ear, with unrestricted hearing on the contralateral side

     H90.12   Conductive hearing loss, unilateral, left ear, with unrestricted hearing on the contralateral side

   ▪ **H90.2   Conductive hearing loss, unspecified**
       Conductive deafness NOS

   H90.3   Sensorineural hearing loss, bilateral

● **H90.4   Sensorineural hearing loss, unilateral with unrestricted hearing on the contralateral side**

     H90.41   Sensorineural hearing loss, unilateral, right ear, with unrestricted hearing on the contralateral side

     H90.42   Sensorineural hearing loss, unilateral, left ear, with unrestricted hearing on the contralateral side

▪ **H90.5   Unspecified sensorineural hearing loss**
     Central hearing loss NOS
     Congenital deafness NOS
     Neural hearing loss NOS
     Perceptive hearing loss NOS
     Sensorineural deafness NOS
     Sensory hearing loss NOS

> **Excludes1**   abnormal auditory perception (H93.2-)
> psychogenic deafness (F44.6)

   H90.6   Mixed conductive and sensorineural hearing loss, bilateral

● **H90.7   Mixed conductive and sensorineural hearing loss, unilateral with unrestricted hearing on the contralateral side**

     H90.71   Mixed conductive and sensorineural hearing loss, unilateral, right ear, with unrestricted hearing on the contralateral side

     H90.72   Mixed conductive and sensorineural hearing loss, unilateral, left ear, with unrestricted hearing on the contralateral side

▪ **H90.8   Mixed conductive and sensorineural hearing loss, unspecified**

● **H91   Other and unspecified hearing loss**

> **Excludes1**   abnormal auditory perception (H93.2-)
> hearing loss as classified in H90.-
> impacted cerumen (H61.2-)
> noise-induced hearing loss (H83.3-)
> psychogenic deafness (F44.6)
> transient ischemic deafness (H93.01-)

● **H91.0   Ototoxic hearing loss**

     Code first (T36-T65) to identify toxic agent

   ● **H91.01   Ototoxic hearing loss, right ear**

   ● **H91.02   Ototoxic hearing loss, left ear**

   ● **H91.03   Ototoxic hearing loss, bilateral**

   ● ▪ **H91.09   Ototoxic hearing loss, unspecified ear**

● **H91.1   Presbycusis**
     Presbyacusia

   ▪ **H91.10   Presbycusis, unspecified ear**

   H91.11   Presbycusis, right ear

   H91.12   Presbycusis, left ear

   H91.13   Presbycusis, bilateral

● **H91.2   Sudden idiopathic hearing loss**
     Sudden hearing loss NOS

   ▪ **H91.20   Sudden idiopathic hearing loss, unspecified ear**

   H91.21   Sudden idiopathic hearing loss, right ear

   H91.22   Sudden idiopathic hearing loss, left ear

   H91.23   Sudden idiopathic hearing loss, bilateral

   H91.3   Deaf nonspeaking, not elsewhere classified

● **H91.8   Other specified hearing loss**

   ● **H91.8x   Other specified hearing loss**

     H91.8x1   Other specified hearing loss, right ear

     H91.8x2   Other specified hearing loss, left ear

     H91.8x3   Other specified hearing loss, bilateral

     ▪ **H91.8x9   Other specified hearing loss, unspecified ear**

● **H91.9   Unspecified hearing loss**
     Congenital deafness NOS
     Deafness NOS
     High frequency deafness
     Low frequency deafness

   ▪ **H91.90   Unspecified hearing loss, unspecified ear**

   ▪ **H91.91   Unspecified hearing loss, right ear**

   ▪ **H91.92   Unspecified hearing loss, left ear**

   ▪ **H91.93   Unspecified hearing loss, bilateral**

● **H92   Otalgia and effusion of ear**

   ● **H92.0   Otalgia**

     H92.01   Otalgia, right ear

     H92.02   Otalgia, left ear

     H92.03   Otalgia, bilateral

     ▪ **H92.09   Otalgia, unspecified ear**

   ● **H92.1   Otorrhea**

> **Excludes1**   leakage of cerebrospinal fluid through ear (G96.0)

     ▪ **H92.10   Otorrhea, unspecified ear**

     H92.11   Otorrhea, right ear

     H92.12   Otorrhea, left ear

     H92.13   Otorrhea, bilateral

   ● **H92.2   Otorrhagia**

> **Excludes1**   traumatic otorrhagia - code to injury

     ▪ **H92.20   Otorrhagia, unspecified ear**

     H92.21   Otorrhagia, right ear

     H92.22   Otorrhagia, left ear

     H92.23   Otorrhagia, bilateral

● **H93   Other disorders of ear, not elsewhere classified**

   ● **H93.0   Degenerative and vascular disorders of ear**

> **Excludes1**   presbycusis (H91.1)

   ● **H93.01   Transient ischemic deafness**

     H93.011   Transient ischemic deafness, right ear

     H93.012   Transient ischemic deafness, left ear

H93.013 **Transient ischemic deafness, bilateral**

H93.019 **Transient ischemic deafness, unspecified ear**

● H93.09 **Unspecified degenerative and vascular disorders of ear**

H93.091 **Unspecified degenerative and vascular disorders of right ear**

H93.092 **Unspecified degenerative and vascular disorders of left ear**

H93.093 **Unspecified degenerative and vascular disorders of ear, bilateral**

H93.099 **Unspecified degenerative and vascular disorders of unspecified ear**

● H93.1 **Tinnitus**

Perception of sound (ringing, buzzing, humming, whistling tunes, or singing)

H93.11 **Tinnitus, right ear**

H93.12 **Tinnitus, left ear**

H93.13 **Tinnitus, bilateral**

H93.19 **Tinnitus, unspecified ear**

● H93.2 **Other abnormal auditory perceptions**

     Excludes2   auditory hallucinations (R44.0)

● H93.21 **Auditory recruitment**

H93.211 **Auditory recruitment, right ear**

H93.212 **Auditory recruitment, left ear**

H93.213 **Auditory recruitment, bilateral**

H93.219 **Auditory recruitment, unspecified ear**

● H93.22 **Diplacusis**

H93.221 **Diplacusis, right ear**

H93.222 **Diplacusis, left ear**

H93.223 **Diplacusis, bilateral**

H93.229 **Diplacusis, unspecified ear**

● H93.23 **Hyperacusis**

H93.231 **Hyperacusis, right ear**

H93.232 **Hyperacusis, left ear**

H93.233 **Hyperacusis, bilateral**

H93.239 **Hyperacusis, unspecified ear**

● H93.24 **Temporary auditory threshold shift**

H93.241 **Temporary auditory threshold shift, right ear**

H93.242 **Temporary auditory threshold shift, left ear**

H93.243 **Temporary auditory threshold shift, bilateral**

H93.249 **Temporary auditory threshold shift, unspecified ear**

H93.25 **Central auditory processing disorder**

Congenital auditory imperception
Word deafness

     Excludes1   mixed receptive-expressive language disorder (F80.2)

● H93.29 **Other abnormal auditory perceptions**

H93.291 **Other abnormal auditory perceptions, right ear**

H93.292 **Other abnormal auditory perceptions, left ear**

H93.293 **Other abnormal auditory perceptions, bilateral**

H93.299 **Other abnormal auditory perceptions, unspecified ear**

● H93.3 **Disorders of acoustic nerve**

Disorder of 8th cranial nerve

     Excludes1   acoustic neuroma (D33.3)
               syphilitic acoustic neuritis (A52.15)

● H93.3x **Disorders of acoustic nerve**

H93.3x1 **Disorders of right acoustic nerve**

H93.3x2 **Disorders of left acoustic nerve**

H93.3x3 **Disorders of bilateral acoustic nerves**

H93.3x9 **Disorders of unspecified acoustic nerve**

● H93.8 **Other specified disorders of ear**

● H93.8x **Other specified disorders of ear**

H93.8x1 **Other specified disorders of right ear**

H93.8x2 **Other specified disorders of left ear**

H93.8x3 **Other specified disorders of ear, bilateral**

H93.8x9 **Other specified disorders of ear, unspecified ear**

● H93.9 **Unspecified disorder of ear**

H93.90 **Unspecified disorder of ear, unspecified ear**

H93.91 **Unspecified disorder of right ear**

H93.92 **Unspecified disorder of left ear**

H93.93 **Unspecified disorder of ear, bilateral**

● H94 **Other disorders of ear in diseases classified elsewhere**

● H94.0 **Acoustic neuritis in infectious and parasitic diseases classified elsewhere**

Code first underlying disease, such as:
parasitic disease (B65-B89)

     Excludes1   acoustic neuritis (in):
               herpes zoster (B02.29)
               syphilis (A52.15)

● H94.00 **Acoustic neuritis in infectious and parasitic diseases classified elsewhere, unspecified ear**

● H94.01 **Acoustic neuritis in infectious and parasitic diseases classified elsewhere, right ear**

● H94.02 **Acoustic neuritis in infectious and parasitic diseases classified elsewhere, left ear**

● H94.03 **Acoustic neuritis in infectious and parasitic diseases classified elsewhere, bilateral**

● H94.8 **Other specified disorders of ear in diseases classified elsewhere**

Code first underlying disease, such as:
congenital syphilis (A50.0)

     Excludes1   aural myiasis (B87.4)
               syphilitic labyrinthitis (A52.79)

● H94.80 **Other specified disorders of ear in diseases classified elsewhere, unspecified ear**

● H94.81 **Other specified disorders of right ear in diseases classified elsewhere**

● H94.82 **Other specified disorders of left ear in diseases classified elsewhere**

● H94.83 **Other specified disorders of ear in diseases classified elsewhere, bilateral**

CHAPTER 8 (H60-H95)

● Unacceptable First-Listed Diagnosis   ● Use Additional Character(s)   ▪ Unspecified   **OGCR** Official Guidelines for Coding and Reporting

🅒 Complication\Comorbidity   🅒 Major C\C   Excludes 1   Excludes 2   Includes   Use additional   Code first   Code also

● H95 **Intraoperative and postprocedural complications and disorders of ear and mastoid process, not elsewhere classified**

   ● H95.0 **Recurrent cholesteatoma of postmastoidectomy cavity**

      ■ H95.00 Recurrent cholesteatoma of postmastoidectomy cavity, unspecified side

      H95.01 Recurrent cholesteatoma of postmastoidectomy cavity, right side

      H95.02 Recurrent cholesteatoma of postmastoidectomy cavity, left side

      H95.03 Recurrent cholesteatoma of postmastoidectomy cavity, bilateral

   ● H95.1 **Other disorders of ear and mastoid process following mastoidectomy**

      ● H95.11 **Chronic inflammation of postmastoidectomy cavity**

         H95.111 Chronic inflammation of postmastoidectomy cavity, right side

         H95.112 Chronic inflammation of postmastoidectomy cavity, left side

         H95.113 Chronic inflammation of postmastoidectomy cavity, bilateral

        ■ H95.119 Chronic inflammation of postmastoidectomy cavity, unspecified side

      ● H95.12 **Granulation of postmastoidectomy cavity**

         H95.121 Granulation of postmastoidectomy cavity, right side

         H95.122 Granulation of postmastoidectomy cavity, left side

         H95.123 Granulation of postmastoidectomy cavity, bilateral

        ■ H95.129 Granulation of postmastoidectomy cavity, unspecified side

      ● H95.13 **Mucosal cyst of postmastoidectomy cavity**

         H95.131 Mucosal cyst of postmastoidectomy cavity, right side

         H95.132 Mucosal cyst of postmastoidectomy cavity, left side

         H95.133 Mucosal cyst of postmastoidectomy cavity, bilateral

        ■ H95.139 Mucosal cyst of postmastoidectomy cavity, unspecified side

      ● H95.19 **Other disorders following mastoidectomy**

         H95.191 Other disorders following mastoidectomy, right side

         H95.192 Other disorders following mastoidectomy, left side

         H95.193 Other disorders following mastoidectomy, bilateral

        ■ H95.199 Other disorders following mastoidectomy, unspecified side

   ● H95.2 **Intraoperative hemorrhage and hematoma of ear and mastoid process complicating a procedure**

      | Excludes1 | intraoperative hemorrhage and hematoma of ear and mastoid process due to accidental puncture or laceration during a procedure (H95.3-) |

      H95.21 Intraoperative hemorrhage and hematoma of ear and mastoid process complicating a procedure on the ear and mastoid process 🗝

      H95.22 Intraoperative hemorrhage and hematoma of ear and mastoid process complicating other procedure 🗝

   ● H95.3 **Accidental puncture and laceration of ear and mastoid process during a procedure**

      H95.31 Accidental puncture and laceration of the ear and mastoid process during a procedure on the ear and mastoid process 🗝

      H95.32 Accidental puncture and laceration of the ear and mastoid process during other procedure 🗝

   ● H95.4 **Postprocedural hemorrhage and hematoma of ear and mastoid process following a procedure**

      H95.41 Postprocedural hemorrhage and hematoma of ear and mastoid process following a procedure on the ear and mastoid process 🗝

      H95.42 Postprocedural hemorrhage and hematoma of ear and mastoid process following other procedure 🗝

   ● H95.8 **Other intraoperative and postprocedural complications and disorders of the ear and mastoid process, not elsewhere classified**

      | Excludes2 | postprocedural complications and disorders following mastoidectomy (H95.0-, H95.1-) |

      ● H95.81 **Postprocedural stenosis of external ear canal**

         H95.811 Postprocedural stenosis of right external ear canal 🗝

         H95.812 Postprocedural stenosis of left external ear canal 🗝

         H95.813 Postprocedural stenosis of external ear canal, bilateral 🗝

        ■ H95.819 Postprocedural stenosis of unspecified external ear canal 🗝

      H95.88 Other intraoperative complications and disorders of the ear and mastoid process, not elsewhere classified 🗝

         Use additional code, if applicable, to further specify disorder

      H95.89 Other postprocedural complications and disorders of the ear and mastoid process, not elsewhere classified 🗝

         Use additional code, if applicable, to further specify disorder

● Unacceptable First-Listed Diagnosis   ● Use Additional Character(s)   ■ Unspecified   **OGCR** Official Guidelines for Coding and Reporting
🗝 Complication\Comorbidity   🗝 Major C\C   Excludes 1   Excludes 2   Includes   Use additional   Code first   Code also

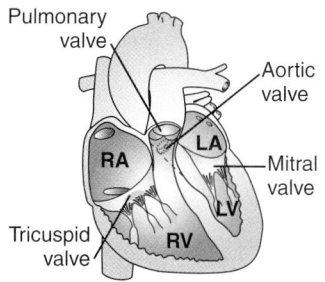

Figure 9-1 Cardiovascular valves.

Pulmonary valve
Aortic valve
Mitral valve
Tricuspid valve
RA LA LV RV

Item 9–1 Rheumatic fever is the inflammation of the valve(s) of the heart, usually the mitral or aortic, which leads to valve damage. Rheumatic heart inflammations are usually **pericarditis** (sac surrounding heart), **endocarditis** (heart cavity), or **myocarditis** (heart muscle).

CHAPTER 9   DISEASES OF THE CIRCULATORY SYSTEM (I00-I99)

Excludes2   certain conditions originating in the perinatal period (P04-P96)

certain infectious and parasitic diseases (A00-B99)

complications of pregnancy, childbirth and the puerperium (O00-O99)

congenital malformations, deformations, and chromosomal abnormalities (Q00-Q99)

endocrine, nutritional and metabolic diseases (E00-E90)

injury, poisoning and certain other consequences of external causes (S00-T98)

neoplasms (C00-D48)

symptoms, signs and abnormal clinical and laboratory findings, not elsewhere classified (R00-R94)

systemic connective tissue disorders (M30-M36)

transient cerebral ischemic attacks and related syndromes (G45.-)

This chapter contains the following blocks:

I00-I02	Acute rheumatic fever
I05-I09	Chronic rheumatic heart diseases
I10-I15	Hypertensive diseases
I20-I25	Ischemic heart diseases
I26-I28	Pulmonary heart disease and diseases of pulmonary circulation
I30-I52	Other forms of heart disease
I60-I69	Cerebrovascular diseases
I70-I79	Diseases of arteries, arterioles and capillaries
I80-I89	Diseases of veins, lymphatic vessels and lymph nodes, not elsewhere classified
I95-I99	Other and unspecified disorders of the circulatory system

ACUTE RHEUMATIC FEVER (I00-I02)

I00   **Rheumatic fever without heart involvement**

Includes   arthritis, rheumatic, acute or subacute

Excludes1   rheumatic fever with heart involvement (I01.0 - I01.9)

Item 9–2 Rheumatic chorea, also called Sydenham's, juvenile, minor, simple, or St. Vitus' dance, is a major symptom of rheumatic fever and is characterized by ceaseless, involuntary, jerky, purposeless movements.

● I01   **Rheumatic fever with heart involvement**

Excludes1   chronic diseases of rheumatic origin (I05-I09) unless rheumatic fever is also present or there is evidence of reactivation or activity of the rheumatic process.

I01.0   **Acute rheumatic pericarditis** 🗝
Any condition in I00 with pericarditis
Rheumatic pericarditis (acute)

Excludes1   acute pericarditis not specified as rheumatic (I30.-)

I01.1   **Acute rheumatic endocarditis** 🗝
Any condition in I00 with endocarditis or valvulitis
Acute rheumatic valvulitis

I01.2   **Acute rheumatic myocarditis** 🗝
Any condition in I00 with myocarditis

I01.8   **Other acute rheumatic heart disease** 🗝
Any condition in I00 with other or multiple types of heart involvement
Acute rheumatic pancarditis

■ I01.9   **Acute rheumatic heart disease, unspecified** 🗝
Any condition in I00 with unspecified type of heart involvement
Rheumatic carditis, acute
Rheumatic heart disease, active or acute

● I02   **Rheumatic chorea**

Includes   Sydenham's chorea

Excludes1   chorea NOS (G25.5)
Huntington's chorea (G10)

I02.0   **Rheumatic chorea with heart involvement** 🗝
Chorea NOS with heart involvement
Rheumatic chorea with heart involvement of any type classifiable under I01.-

I02.9   **Rheumatic chorea without heart involvement** 🗝
Rheumatic chorea NOS

CHRONIC RHEUMATIC HEART DISEASES (I05-I09)

● I05   **Rheumatic mitral valve diseases**

Includes   conditions classifiable to both I05.0 and I05.2-I05.9, whether specified as rheumatic or not

Excludes1   mitral valve disease specified as nonrheumatic (I34.-)
mitral valve disease with aortic and/or tricuspid valve involvement (I08.-)

I05.0   **Rheumatic mitral stenosis**
Mitral (valve) obstruction (rheumatic)

I05.1   **Rheumatic mitral insufficiency**
Rheumatic mitral incompetence
Rheumatic mitral regurgitation

Excludes1   mitral insufficiency not specified as rheumatic (I34.0)

(See Plate 244 on page NAP-30.)

Item 9–3 Mitral stenosis is the narrowing of the mitral valve separating the left atrium from the left ventricle. **Mitral insufficiency** is the improper closure of the mitral valve which may lead to enlargement (hypertrophy) of the left atrium.

● Unacceptable First-Listed Diagnosis   ● Use Additional Character(s)   ■ Unspecified   OGCR Official Guidelines for Coding and Reporting
🗝 Complication\Comorbidity   🗝 Major C\C   Excludes 1   Excludes 2   Includes   Use additional   Code first   Code also   1009

CHAPTER 9 (I00-I99)

Item 9–4 Aortic stenosis is the narrowing of the aortic valve located between the left ventricle and the aorta. **Aortic insufficiency** is the improper closure of the aortic valve which may lead to enlargement (hypertrophy) of the left ventricle.

I05.2 Rheumatic mitral stenosis with insufficiency
Rheumatic mitral stenosis with incompetence or regurgitation

I05.8 Other rheumatic mitral valve diseases
Rheumatic mitral (valve) failure

I05.9 Rheumatic mitral valve disease, unspecified
Rheumatic mitral (valve) disorder (chronic) NOS

● **I06 Rheumatic aortic valve diseases**
Excludes1   aortic valve disease not specified as rheumatic (I35.-)
aortic valve disease with mitral and/or tricuspid valve involvement (I08.-)

I06.0 Rheumatic aortic stenosis
Rheumatic aortic (valve) obstruction

I06.1 Rheumatic aortic insufficiency
Rheumatic aortic incompetence
Rheumatic aortic regurgitation

I06.2 Rheumatic aortic stenosis with insufficiency
Rheumatic aortic stenosis with incompetence or regurgitation

I06.8 Other rheumatic aortic valve diseases

I06.9 Rheumatic aortic valve disease, unspecified
Rheumatic aortic (valve) disease NOS

● **I07 Rheumatic tricuspid valve diseases**
Includes   rheumatic tricuspid valve diseases specified as rheumatic or unspecified
Excludes1   tricuspid valve disease specified as nonrheumatic (I36.-)
tricuspid valve disease with aortic and/or mitral valve involvement (I08.-)

I07.0 Rheumatic tricuspid stenosis
Tricuspid (valve) stenosis (rheumatic)

I07.1 Rheumatic tricuspid insufficiency
Tricuspid (valve) insufficiency (rheumatic)

I07.2 Rheumatic tricuspid stenosis and insufficiency

I07.8 Other rheumatic tricuspid valve diseases

I07.9 Rheumatic tricuspid valve disease, unspecified
Rheumatic tricuspid valve disorder NOS

● **I08 Multiple valve diseases**
Includes   multiple valve diseases specified as rheumatic or unspecified
Excludes1   endocarditis, valve unspecified (I38)
multiple valve disease specified a nonrheumatic (I34.-, I35.-, I36.-, I37.-, I38.-, Q22.-, Q23.-, Q24.8-)
rheumatic valve disease NOS (I09.1)

I08.0 Rheumatic disorders of both mitral and aortic valves
Involvement of both mitral and aortic valves specified as rheumatic or unspecified

I08.1 Rheumatic disorders of both mitral and tricuspid valves

I08.2 Rheumatic disorders of both aortic and tricuspid valves

I08.3 Combined rheumatic disorders of mitral, aortic and tricuspid valves

I08.8 Other rheumatic multiple valve diseases

I08.9 Rheumatic multiple valve disease, unspecified

Item 9–5 Hypertension is caused by high arterial blood pressure in the arteries. **Essential, primary,** or **idiopathic** hypertension occurs without identifiable organic cause. **Secondary** hypertension is that which has an organic cause. **Malignant** hypertension is severely elevated blood pressure. **Benign** hypertension is mildly elevated blood pressure.

● **I09 Other rheumatic heart diseases**

I09.0 Rheumatic myocarditis 🖉
Excludes1   myocarditis not specified as rheumatic (I51.4)

I09.1 Rheumatic diseases of endocardium, valve unspecified
Rheumatic endocarditis (chronic)
Rheumatic valvulitis (chronic)
Excludes1   endocarditis, valve unspecified (I38)

I09.2 Chronic rheumatic pericarditis 🖉
Adherent pericardium, rheumatic
Chronic rheumatic mediastinopericarditis
Chronic rheumatic myopericarditis
Excludes1   chronic pericarditis not specified as rheumatic (I31.-)

● **I09.8 Other specified rheumatic heart diseases**

I09.81 Rheumatic heart failure 🖉
Use additional code to identify type of heart failure (I50.-)

I09.89 Other specified rheumatic heart diseases
Rheumatic disease of pulmonary valve

I09.9 Rheumatic heart disease, unspecified
Rheumatic carditis
Excludes1   rheumatoid carditis (M05.31)

HYPERTENSIVE DISEASES (I10-I15)

Use additional code to identify:
exposure to environmental tobacco smoke (Z77.22)
history of tobacco use (Z87.891)
occupational exposure to environmental tobacco smoke (Z57.31)
tobacco dependence (F17.-)
tobacco use (Z72.0)
Excludes1   hypertensive disease complicating pregnancy, childbirth and the puerperium (O10-O11, O13-O16)
neonatal hypertension (P29.2)
primary pulmonary hypertension (I27.0)

● **I10 Essential (primary) hypertension**
Includes   high blood pressure
hypertension (arterial) (benign) (essential) (malignant) (primary) (systemic)
Excludes1   hypertensive disease complicating pregnancy, childbirth and the puerperium (O10-O11, O13-O16)
Excludes2   essential (primary) hypertension involving vessels of brain (I60-I69)
essential (primary) hypertension involving vessels of eye (H35.0)

● **I11 Hypertensive heart disease**
Includes   any condition in I51.4-I51.9 due to hypertension

I11.0 Hypertensive heart disease with heart failure
Hypertensive heart failure
Use additional code to identify type of heart failure (I50.-)

I11.9 Hypertensive heart disease without heart failure
Hypertensive heart disease NOS

CHAPTER 9 (I00-I99)

1010

● Unacceptable First-Listed Diagnosis   ● Use Additional Character(s)   ■ Unspecified   OGCR Official Guidelines for Coding and Reporting
🖉 Complication\Comorbidity   🖉 Major C\C   Excludes 1   Excludes 2   Includes   Use additional   Code first   Code also

OGCR Section I.C.9.a.2

Hypertensive Chronic Kidney Disease

Assign codes from category I12, Hypertensive chronic kidney disease, when both hypertension and a condition classifiable to category N18, Chronic kidney disease (CKD), are present. Unlike hypertension with heart disease, ICD-10-CM presumes a cause-and-effect relationship and classifies chronic kidney disease with hypertension as hypertensive chronic kidney disease.
The appropriate code from category N18 should be used as a secondary code with a code from category I12 to identify the stage of chronic kidney disease.

See Section I.C.14. Chronic kidney disease.

If a patient has hypertensive chronic kidney disease and acute renal failure, an additional code for the acute renal failure is required.

● **I12　Hypertensive chronic kidney disease**

> **Includes**　any condition in N18.- due to hypertension
> arteriosclerosis of kidney
> arteriosclerotic nephritis (chronic)
> (interstitial)
> hypertensive nephropathy
> nephrosclerosis

> **Excludes1**　hypertension due to kidney disease (I15.0, I15.1)
> renovascular hypertension (I15.0)
> secondary hypertension (I15.-)

> **Excludes2**　acute kidney failure (N17.-)

I12.0　Hypertensive chronic kidney disease with stage 5 chronic kidney disease or end stage renal disease 🖢

> Use additional code to identify the stage of chronic kidney disease (N18.5, N18.6)

■**I12.9　Hypertensive chronic kidney disease with stage 1 through stage 4 chronic kidney disease, or unspecified chronic kidney disease**
> Hypertensive chronic kidney disease NOS
> Hypertensive renal disease NOS

> Use additional code to identify the stage of chronic kidney disease (N18.1-N18.4, N18.9)

OGCR Section I.c.9.a.6

Hypertensive Heart and Chronic Kidney Disease

Assign codes from combination category I13, Hypertensive heart and chronic kidney disease, when both hypertensive kidney disease and hypertensive heart disease are stated in the diagnosis. Assume a relationship between the hypertension and the chronic kidney disease, whether or not the condition is so designated. If heart failure is present, assign an additional code from category I50 to identify the type of heart failure.

The appropriate code from category N18, Chronic kidney disease, should be used as a secondary code with a code from category I13 to identify the stage of chronic kidney disease.

See Section I.C.14. Chronic kidney disease.

The codes in category I13, Hypertensive heart and chronic kidney disease, are combination codes that include hypertension, heart disease and chronic kidney disease. The Includes note at I13 specifies that the conditions included at I11 and I12 are included together in I13. If a patient has hypertension, heart disease and chronic kidney disease then a code from I13 should be used, not individual codes for hypertension, heart disease and chronic kidney disease, or codes from I11 or I12.

For patients with both acute renal failure and chronic kidney disease an additional code for acute renal failure is required.

● **I13　Hypertensive heart and chronic kidney disease**

> **Includes**　any condition in I11.- with any condition in I12.- cardiorenal disease
> cardiovascular renal disease

■**I13.0　Hypertensive heart and chronic kidney disease with heart failure and stage I through stage IV chronic kidney disease, or unspecified chronic kidney disease** 🖢

> Use additional code to identify type of heart failure (I50.-)

> Use additional code to identify stage of chronic kidney disease (N18.1-N18.4, N18.9)

● **I13.1　Hypertensive heart and chronic kidney disease without heart failure**

> ■**I13.10　Hypertensive heart and chronic kidney disease without heart failure, with stage 1 through stage 4 chronic kidney disease, or unspecified chronic kidney disease**
> Hypertensive heart disease and hypertensive chronic kidney disease NOS

> Use additional code to identify the stage of chronic kidney disease (N18.1-N18.4, N18.9)

> **I13.11　Hypertensive heart and chronic kidney disease without heart failure, with stage 5 chronic kidney disease, or end stage renal disease** 🖢

> Use additional code to identify the stage of chronic kidney disease (N18.5, N18.6)

I13.2　Hypertensive heart and chronic kidney disease with heart failure and with stage 5 chronic kidney disease, or end stage renal disease 🖢

> Use additional code to identify type of heart failure (I50.-)

> Use additional code to identify the stage of chronic kidney disease (N18.5, N18.6)

OGCR Section I.9.a.6
Hypertension, Secondary

Secondary hypertension is due to an underlying condition. Two codes are required: one to identify the underlying etiology and one from category I15 to identify the hypertension. Sequencing of codes is determined by the reason for admission/encounter.

● **I15　Secondary hypertension**
　　Code also underlying condition

> **Excludes1**　postprocedural hypertension (I97.3)
> **Excludes2**　secondary hypertension involving vessels of brain (I60-I69)
> secondary hypertension involving vessels of eye (H35.0)

I15.0　Renovascular hypertension
I15.1　Hypertension secondary to other renal disorders
I15.2　Hypertension secondary to endocrine disorders
I15.8　Other secondary hypertension
■**I15.9　Secondary hypertension, unspecified**

● Unacceptable First-Listed Diagnosis　　　● Use Additional Character(s)　　　■ Unspecified　　　**OGCR** Official Guidelines for Coding and Reporting
🖢 Complication\Comorbidity　　🖢 Major C\C　　Excludes 1　　Excludes 2　　Includes　　Use additional　　Code first　　Code also　　1011

CHAPTER 9 (I00-I99)

ISCHEMIC HEART DISEASES (I20-I25)

Use additional code to identify presence of hypertension (I10-I15)

● **I20   Angina pectoris**
Chest pain/discomfort due to lack of oxygen to the heart muscle. Principal symptom of myocardial infarction.

Use additional code to identify:
  exposure to environmental tobacco smoke (Z77.22)
  history of tobacco use (Z87.891)
  occupational exposure to environmental tobacco smoke (Z57.31)
  tobacco dependence (F17.-)
  tobacco use (Z72.0)

Excludes1 | angina pectoris with atherosclerotic heart disease of native coronary arteries (I25.1-)
atherosclerosis of coronary artery bypass graft(s) and coronary artery of transplanted heart with angina pectoris (I25.7-)
postinfarction angina (I23.7)

I20.0   Unstable angina 🖘
  Accelerated angina
  Crescendo angina
  De novo effort angina
  Intermediate coronary syndrome
  Preinfarction syndrome
  Worsening effort angina

I20.1   Angina pectoris with documented spasm 🖘
  Angiospastic angina
  Prinzmetal angina
  Spasm-induced angina
  Variant angina

I20.8   Other forms of angina pectoris
  Angina equivalent
  Angina of effort
  Stenocardia

  Use additional code(s) for symptoms associated with angina equivalent

■**I20.9   Angina pectoris, unspecified**
  Angina NOS
  Anginal syndrome
  Cardiac angina
  Ischemic chest pain

OGCR   See Section I.c.9.e.3

Acute myocardial infarction, unspecified

Code I21.3, ST elevation (STEMI) myocardial infarction of unspecified site, is the default for the unspecified term acute myocardial infarction. If only STEMI or transmural MI without the site is documented, query the provider as to the site, or assign I21.3.

● **I21   ST elevation (STEMI) and non-ST elevation (NSTEMI) myocardial infarction**
Includes | cardiac infarction
coronary (artery) embolism
coronary (artery) occlusion
coronary (artery) rupture
coronary (artery) thrombosis
infarction of heart, myocardium, or ventricle
myocardial infarction specified as acute or with a stated duration of 4 weeks (28 days) or less from onset

Use additional code, if applicable, to identify:
  exposure to environmental tobacco smoke (Z77.22)
  history of tobacco use (Z87.891)
  occupational exposure to environmental tobacco smoke (Z57.31)
  status post administration of tPA (rtPA) in a different facility within the last 24 hours prior to admission to current facility (Z92.82)
  tobacco dependence (F17.-)
  tobacco use (Z72.0)

Use additional code, if known, to identify:
  body mass index (BMI) (Z68.-)

Excludes2 | old myocardial infarction (I25.2)
postmyocardial infarction syndrome (I24.1)
subsequent myocardial infarction (I22.-)

● **I21.0   ST elevation (STEMI) myocardial infarction of anterior wall**

  I21.01   ST elevation (STEMI) myocardial infarction involving left main coronary artery 🖘

  I21.02   ST elevation (STEMI) myocardial infarction involving left anterior descending coronary artery 🖘
    ST elevation (STEMI) myocardial infarction involving diagonal coronary artery

  I21.09   ST elevation (STEMI) myocardial infarction involving other coronary artery of anterior wall 🖘
    Acute transmural myocardial infarction of anterior wall
    Anteroapical transmural (Q wave) infarction (acute)
    Anterolateral transmural (Q wave) infarction (acute)
    Anteroseptal transmural (Q wave) infarction (acute)
    Transmural (Q wave) infarction (acute) (of) anterior (wall) NOS

● **I21.1   ST elevation (STEMI) myocardial infarction of inferior wall**

  I21.11   ST elevation (STEMI) myocardial infarction involving right coronary artery 🖘
    Inferoposterior transmural (Q wave) infarction (acute)

  I21.19   ST elevation (STEMI) myocardial infarction involving other coronary artery of inferior wall 🖘
    Acute transmural myocardial infarction of inferior wall
    Inferolateral transmural (Q wave) infarction (acute)
    Transmural (Q wave) infarction (acute) (of) diaphragmatic wall
    Transmural (Q wave) infarction (acute) (of) inferior (wall) NOS

    Excludes2 | ST elevation (STEMI) myocardial infarction involving left circumflex coronary artery (I21.21)

● **I21.2**   **ST elevation (STEMI) myocardial infarction of other sites**

     I21.21   **ST elevation (STEMI) myocardial infarction involving left circumflex coronary artery** 🔗
         ST elevation (STEMI) myocardial infarction involving oblique marginal coronary artery

     I21.29   **ST elevation (STEMI) myocardial infarction involving other sites** 🔗
         Acute transmural myocardial infarction of other sites
         Apical-lateral transmural (Q wave) infarction (acute)
         Basal-lateral transmural (Q wave) infarction (acute)
         High lateral transmural (Q wave) infarction (acute)
         Lateral (wall) NOS transmural (Q wave) infarction (acute)
         Posterior (true) transmural (Q wave) infarction (acute)
         Posterobasal transmural (Q wave) infarction (acute)
         Posterolateral transmural (Q wave) infarction (acute)
         Posteroseptal transmural (Q wave) infarction (acute)
         Septal transmural (Q wave) infarction (acute) NOS

◼ **I21.3**   **ST elevation (STEMI) myocardial infarction of unspecified site** 🔗
     Acute transmural myocardial infarction of unspecified site
     Myocardial infarction (acute) NOS
     Transmural (Q wave) myocardial infarction NOS

     I21.4   **Non-ST elevation (NSTEMI) myocardial infarction** 🔗
     Acute subendocardial myocardial infarction
     Non-Q wave myocardial infarction NOS
     Nontransmural myocardial infarction NOS

● **I22**   **Subsequent ST elevation (STEMI) and non-ST elevation (NSTEMI) myocardial infarction**

     Includes   acute myocardial infarction occurring within four weeks (28 days) of a previous acute myocardial infarction, regardless of site
         cardiac infarction
         coronary (artery) embolism
         coronary (artery) occlusion
         coronary (artery) rupture
         coronary (artery) thrombosis
         infarction of heart, myocardium, or ventricle
         recurrent myocardial infarction
         reinfarction of myocardium
         rupture of heart, myocardium, or ventricle

     Note: A code from category I22 must be used in conjunction with a code from category I21. The I22 code should be sequenced first, if it the reason for encounter, or, it should be sequenced after the I21 code if the subsequent MI occurs during the encounter for the initial MI.

     Use additional code, if applicable, to identify:
     exposure to environmental tobacco smoke (Z77.22)
     history of tobacco use (Z87.891)
     occupational exposure to environmental tobacco smoke (Z57.31)
     status post administration of tPA (rtPA) in a different facility within the last 24 hours prior to admission to current facility (Z92.82)
     tobacco dependence (F17.-)
     tobacco use (Z72.0)

     Use additional code, if known, to identify:
     body mass index (BMI) (Z68.-)

I22.0   **Subsequent ST elevation (STEMI) myocardial infarction of anterior wall** 🔗
     Subsequent acute transmural myocardial infarction of anterior wall
     Subsequent transmural (Q wave) infarction (acute)(of) anterior (wall) NOS
     Subsequent anteroapical transmural (Q wave) infarction (acute)
     Subsequent anterolateral transmural (Q wave) infarction (acute)
     Subsequent anteroseptal transmural (Q wave) infarction (acute)

I22.1   **Subsequent ST elevation (STEMI) myocardial infarction of inferior wall** 🔗
     Subsequent acute transmural myocardial infarction of inferior wall
     Subsequent transmural (Q wave) infarction (acute)(of) diaphragmatic wall
     Subsequent transmural (Q wave) infarction (acute)(of) inferior (wall) NOS
     Subsequent inferolateral transmural (Q wave) infarction (acute)
     Subsequent inferoposterior transmural (Q wave) infarction (acute)

I22.2   **Subsequent non-ST elevation (NSTEMI) myocardial infarction** 🔗
     Subsequent acute subendocardial myocardial infarction
     Subsequent non-Q wave myocardial infarction NOS
     Subsequent nontransmural myocardial infarction NOS

I22.8   **Subsequent ST elevation (STEMI) myocardial infarction of other sites** 🔗
     Subsequent acute transmural myocardial infarction of other sites
     Subsequent apical-lateral transmural (Q wave) myocardial infarction (acute)
     Subsequent basal-lateral transmural (Q wave) myocardial infarction (acute)
     Subsequent high lateral transmural (Q wave) myocardial infarction (acute)
     Subsequent transmural (Q wave) myocardial infarction (acute)(of) lateral (wall) NOS
     Subsequent posterior (true) transmural (Q wave) myocardial infarction (acute)
     Subsequent posterobasal transmural (Q wave) myocardial infarction (acute)
     Subsequent posterolateral transmural (Q wave) myocardial infarction (acute)
     Subsequent posteroseptal transmural (Q wave) myocardial infarction (acute)
     Subsequent septal NOS transmural (Q wave) myocardial infarction (acute)

◼ **I22.9**   **Subsequent ST elevation (STEMI) myocardial infarction of unspecified site** 🔗
     Subsequent acute myocardial infarction of unspecified site
     Subsequent myocardial infarction (acute) NOS

● **I23**   **Certain current complications following ST elevation (STEMI) and non-ST elevation (NSTEMI) myocardial infarction (within the 28 day period)**

     Note: A code from category I23 must be used in conjunction with a code from category I21 or category I22. The I23 code should be sequenced first, if it is the reason for encounter, or, it should be sequenced after the I21 or I22 code if the complication of the MI occurs during the encounter for the MI.

     I23.0   **Hemopericardium as current complication following acute myocardial infarction** 🔗
         Excludes1   hemopericardium not specified as current complication following acute myocardial infarction (I31.2)

● Unacceptable First-Listed Diagnosis   ● Use Additional Character(s)   ◼ Unspecified   **OGCR** Official Guidelines for Coding and Reporting
🔗 Complication\Comorbidity   🔗 Major C\C   Excludes 1   Excludes 2   Includes   Use additional   Code first   Code also   1013

CHAPTER 9 (I00-I99)

I23.1   Atrial septal defect as current complication following acute myocardial infarction 🅒

> **Excludes1**   acquired atrial septal defect not specified as current complication following acute myocardial infarction (I51.0)

I23.2   Ventricular septal defect as current complication following acute myocardial infarction 🅒

> **Excludes1**   acquired ventricular septal defect not specified as current complication following acute myocardial infarction (I51.0)

I23.3   Rupture of cardiac wall without hemopericardium as current complication following acute myocardial infarction 🅒

I23.4   Rupture of chordae tendineae as current complication following acute myocardial infarction 🅒

> **Excludes1**   rupture of chordae tendineae not specified as current complication following acute myocardial infarction (I51.1)

I23.5   Rupture of papillary muscle as current complication following acute myocardial infarction 🅒

> **Excludes1**   rupture of papillary muscle not specified as current complication following acute myocardial infarction (I51.2)

I23.6   Thrombosis of atrium, auricular appendage, and ventricle as current complications following acute myocardial infarction 🅒

> **Excludes1**   thrombosis of atrium, auricular appendage, and ventricle not specified as current complication following acute myocardial infarction (I51.3)

I23.7   Postinfarction angina 🅒

I23.8   Other current complications following acute myocardial infarction 🅒

● **I24   Other acute ischemic heart diseases**

> **Excludes1**   angina pectoris (I20.-)
> transient myocardial ischemia in newborn (P29.4)

I24.0   Acute coronary thrombosis not resulting in myocardial infarction 🅒

> Acute coronary (artery) (vein) embolism not resulting in myocardial infarction
> Acute coronary (artery) (vein) occlusion not resulting in myocardial infarction
> Acute coronary (artery) (vein) thromboembolism not resulting in myocardial infarction

> **Excludes1**   atherosclerotic heart disease (I25.1-)

I24.1   Dressler's syndrome 🅒

> Postmyocardial infarction syndrome

> **Excludes1**   postinfarction angina (I23.7)

I24.8   Other forms of acute ischemic heart disease 🅒

■ **I24.9   Acute ischemic heart disease, unspecified** 🅒

> **Excludes1**   ischemic heart disease (chronic) NOS (I25.9)

● **I25   Chronic ischemic heart disease**

> Use additional code to identify:
> chronic total occlusion of coronary artery (I25.82)
> exposure to environmental tobacco smoke (Z77.22)
> history of tobacco use (Z87.891)
> occupational exposure to environmental tobacco smoke (Z57.31)
> tobacco dependence (F17.-)
> tobacco use (Z72.0)

OGCR   See Section I.9.b.

Atherosclerotic coronary artery disease and angina

ICD-10-CM has combination codes for atherosclerotic heart disease with angina pectoris. The subcategories for these codes are I25.11, Atherosclerotic heart disease of native coronary artery with angina pectoris and I25.7, Atherosclerosis of coronary artery bypass graft(s) and coronary artery of transplanted heart with angina pectoris.

When using one of these combination codes it is not necessary to use an additional code for angina pectoris. A causal relationship can be assumed in a patient with both atherosclerosis and angina pectoris, unless the documentation indicates the angina is due to something other than the atherosclerosis.

If a patient with coronary artery disease is admitted due to an acute myocardial infarction (AMI), the AMI should be sequenced before the coronary artery disease.

See Section I.C.9. Acute myocardial infarction (AMI)

(See Plates 218 and 219 on pages NAP-26 and NAP-27.)

● **I25.1   Atherosclerotic heart disease of native coronary artery**

> *Disease in which fatty deposits form on the walls of arteries*
> Atherosclerotic cardiovascular disease
> Coronary (artery) atheroma
> Coronary (artery) atherosclerosis
> Coronary (artery) disease
> Coronary (artery) sclerosis

> Use additional code, if applicable, to identify coronary atherosclerosis due to lipid rich plaque (I25.83)

> **Excludes2**   atheroembolism (I75.-)
> atherosclerosis of coronary artery bypass graft(s) and transplanted heart (I25.7-)

I25.10   Atherosclerotic heart disease of native coronary artery without angina pectoris
> Atherosclerotic heart disease NOS

● **I25.11   Atherosclerotic heart disease of native coronary artery with angina pectoris**

> **I25.110   Atherosclerotic heart disease of native coronary artery with unstable angina pectoris**

> > **Excludes1**   unstable angina without atherosclerotic heart disease (I20.0)

Item 9–6   Classification is based on the location of the atherosclerosis. **"Of native coronary artery"** indicates the atherosclerosis is within an original heart artery. **"Of autologous vein bypass graft"** indicates that the atherosclerosis is within a vein graft that was taken from within the patient. **"Of nonautologous biological bypass graft"** indicates the atherosclerosis is within a vessel grafted from other than the patient. **"Of artery bypass graft"** indicates the atherosclerosis is within an artery that was grafted from within the patient.

● Unacceptable First-Listed Diagnosis   ● Use Additional Character(s)   ■ Unspecified   **OGCR** Official Guidelines for Coding and Reporting
🅒 Complication\Comorbidity   🅒 Major C\C   Excludes 1   Excludes 2   Includes   Use additional   Code first   Code also

I25.111   **Atherosclerotic heart disease of native coronary artery with angina pectoris with documented spasm**

> | Excludes1 | angina pectoris with documented spasm without atherosclerotic heart disease (I20.1) |

I25.118   **Atherosclerotic heart disease of native coronary artery with other forms of angina pectoris**

> | Excludes1 | other forms of angina pectoris without atherosclerotic heart disease (I20.8) |

■ **I25.119**   **Atherosclerotic heart disease of native coronary artery with unspecified angina pectoris**
Atherosclerotic heart disease with angina NOS
Atherosclerotic heart disease with ischemic chest pain

> | Excludes1 | unspecified angina pectoris without atherosclerotic heart disease (I20.9) |

I25.2   **Old myocardial infarction**
Healed myocardial infarction
Past myocardial infarction diagnosed by ECG or other investigation, but currently presenting no symptoms

I25.3   **Aneurysm of heart** 🗲
Mural aneurysm
Ventricular aneurysm

● **I25.4**   **Coronary artery aneurysm and dissection**

     I25.41   **Coronary artery aneurysm**
        Coronary arteriovenous fistula, acquired

> | Excludes1 | congenital coronary (artery) aneurysm (Q24.5) |

     I25.42   **Coronary artery dissection** 🗲

I25.5   **Ischemic cardiomyopathy**

> | Excludes2 | coronary atherosclerosis (I25.1-, I25.7-) |

I25.6   **Silent myocardial ischemia**

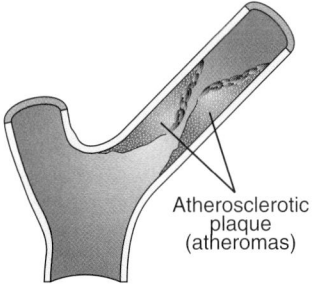

Figure 9-2 Atherosclerotic plaque.

Atherosclerotic plaque (atheromas)

● **I25.7**   **Atherosclerosis of coronary artery bypass graft(s) and coronary artery of transplanted heart with angina pectoris**
Use additional code, if applicable, to identify coronary atherosclerosis due to lipid rich plaque (I25.83)

> | Excludes1 | atherosclerosis of bypass graft(s) of transplanted heart without angina pectoris (I25.812) atherosclerosis of coronary artery bypass graft(s) without angina pectoris (I25.810) atherosclerosis of native coronary artery of transplanted heart without angina pectoris (I25.811) embolism or thrombus of coronary artery bypass graft(s) (T82.8-) |

● **I25.70**   **Atherosclerosis of coronary artery bypass graft(s), unspecified, with angina pectoris**

     ■ **I25.700**   **Atherosclerosis of coronary artery bypass graft(s), unspecified, with unstable angina pectoris**

> | Excludes1 | unstable angina pectoris without atherosclerosis of coronary artery bypass graft (I20.0) |

     ■ **I25.701**   **Atherosclerosis of coronary artery bypass graft(s), unspecified, with angina pectoris with documented spasm**

> | Excludes1 | angina pectoris with documented spasm without atherosclerosis of coronary artery bypass graft (I20.1) |

     ■ **I25.708**   **Atherosclerosis of coronary artery bypass graft(s), unspecified, with other forms of angina pectoris**

> | Excludes1 | other forms of angina pectoris without atherosclerosis of coronary artery bypass graft (I20.8) |

     ■ **I25.709**   **Atherosclerosis of coronary artery bypass graft(s), unspecified, with unspecified angina pectoris**

> | Excludes1 | unspecified angina pectoris without atherosclerosis of coronary artery bypass graft (I20.9) |

● Unacceptable First-Listed Diagnosis   ● Use Additional Character(s)   ■ Unspecified   **OGCR** Official Guidelines for Coding and Reporting

🗲 Complication\Comorbidity   🗲 Major C\C   Excludes 1   Excludes 2   Includes   Use additional   Code first   Code also

CHAPTER 9 (I00-I99)

1015

● **I25.71** **Atherosclerosis of autologous vein coronary artery bypass graft(s) with angina pectoris**

   I25.710 **Atherosclerosis of autologous vein coronary artery bypass graft(s) with unstable angina pectoris** 🏥

      | Excludes1 | unstable angina without atherosclerosis of autologous vein coronary artery bypass graft(s) (I20.0)

   I25.711 **Atherosclerosis of autologous vein coronary artery bypass graft(s) with angina pectoris with documented spasm** 🏥

      | Excludes1 | angina pectoris with documented spasm without atherosclerosis of autologous vein coronary artery bypass graft(s) (I20.1)

   I25.718 **Atherosclerosis of autologous vein coronary artery bypass graft(s) with other forms of angina pectoris** 🏥

      | Excludes1 | other forms of angina pectoris without atherosclerosis of autologous vein coronary artery bypass graft(s) (I20.8)

   ▪ **I25.719** **Atherosclerosis of autologous vein coronary artery bypass graft(s) with unspecified angina pectoris** 🏥

      | Excludes1 | unspecified angina pectoris without atherosclerosis of autologous vein coronary artery bypass graft(s) (I20.9)

● **I25.72** **Atherosclerosis of autologous artery coronary artery bypass graft(s) with angina pectoris**
   Atherosclerosis of internal mammary artery graft with angina pectoris

   I25.720 **Atherosclerosis of autologous artery coronary artery bypass graft(s) with unstable angina pectoris** 🏥

      | Excludes1 | unstable angina without atherosclerosis of autologous artery coronary artery bypass graft(s) (I20.0)

I25.721 **Atherosclerosis of autologous artery coronary artery bypass graft(s) with angina pectoris with documented spasm** 🏥

   | Excludes1 | angina pectoris with documented spasm without atherosclerosis of autologous artery coronary artery bypass graft(s) (I20.1)

I25.728 **Atherosclerosis of autologous artery coronary artery bypass graft(s) with other forms of angina pectoris** 🏥

   | Excludes1 | other forms of angina pectoris without atherosclerosis of autologous artery coronary artery bypass graft(s) (I20.8)

▪ **I25.729** **Atherosclerosis of autologous artery coronary artery bypass graft(s) with unspecified angina pectoris** 🏥

   | Excludes1 | unspecified angina pectoris without atherosclerosis of autologous artery coronary artery bypass graft(s) (I20.9)

● **I25.73** **Atherosclerosis of nonautologous biological coronary artery bypass graft(s) with angina pectoris**

   I25.730 **Atherosclerosis of nonautologous biological coronary artery bypass graft(s) with unstable angina pectoris** 🏥

      | Excludes1 | unstable angina without atherosclerosis of nonautologous biological coronary artery bypass graft(s) (I20.0)

   I25.731 **Atherosclerosis of nonautologous biological coronary artery bypass graft(s) with angina pectoris with documented spasm** 🏥

      | Excludes1 | angina pectoris with documented spasm without atherosclerosis of nonautologous biological coronary artery bypass graft(s) (I20.1)

● Unacceptable First-Listed Diagnosis   ● Use Additional Character(s)   ▪ Unspecified   **OGCR** Official Guidelines for Coding and Reporting
🏥 Complication\Comorbidity   🏥 Major C\C | Excludes 1 | | Excludes 2 | Includes   Use additional   Code first   Code also

I25.738   **Atherosclerosis of nonautologous biological coronary artery bypass graft(s) with other forms of angina pectoris** 🅒

> | Excludes1 | other forms of angina pectoris without atherosclerosis of nonautologous biological coronary artery bypass graft(s) (I20.8) |

I25.739   **Atherosclerosis of nonautologous biological coronary artery bypass graft(s) with unspecified angina pectoris** 🅒

> | Excludes1 | unspecified angina pectoris without atherosclerosis of nonautologous biological coronary artery bypass graft(s) (I20.9) |

● **I25.75**   **Atherosclerosis of native coronary artery of transplanted heart with angina pectoris**

> | Excludes1 | atherosclerosis of native coronary artery of transplanted heart without angina pectoris (I25.811) |

I25.750   **Atherosclerosis of native coronary artery of transplanted heart with unstable angina** 🅒

I25.751   **Atherosclerosis of native coronary artery of transplanted heart with angina pectoris with documented spasm** 🅒

I25.758   **Atherosclerosis of native coronary artery of transplanted heart with other forms of angina pectoris** 🅒

I25.759   **Atherosclerosis of native coronary artery of transplanted heart with unspecified angina pectoris** 🅒

● **I25.76**   **Atherosclerosis of bypass graft of coronary artery of transplanted heart with angina pectoris**

> | Excludes1 | atherosclerosis of bypass graft of coronary artery of transplanted heart without angina pectoris (I25.812) |

I25.760   **Atherosclerosis of bypass graft of coronary artery of transplanted heart with unstable angina** 🅒

I25.761   **Atherosclerosis of bypass graft of coronary artery of transplanted heart with angina pectoris with documented spasm** 🅒

I25.768   **Atherosclerosis of bypass graft of coronary artery of transplanted heart with other forms of angina pectoris** 🅒

I25.769   **Atherosclerosis of bypass graft of coronary artery of transplanted heart with unspecified angina pectoris** 🅒

● **I25.79**   **Atherosclerosis of other coronary artery bypass graft(s) with angina pectoris**

I25.790   **Atherosclerosis of other coronary artery bypass graft(s) with unstable angina pectoris** 🅒

> | Excludes1 | unstable angina without atherosclerosis of other coronary artery bypass graft(s) (I20.0) |

I25.791   **Atherosclerosis of other coronary artery bypass graft(s) with angina pectoris with documented spasm** 🅒

> | Excludes1 | angina pectoris with documented spasm without atherosclerosis of other coronary artery bypass graft(s) (I20.1) |

I25.798   **Atherosclerosis of other coronary artery bypass graft(s) with other forms of angina pectoris** 🅒

> | Excludes1 | other forms of angina pectoris without atherosclerosis of other coronary artery bypass graft(s) (I20.8) |

I25.799   **Atherosclerosis of other coronary artery bypass graft(s) with unspecified angina pectoris** 🅒

> | Excludes1 | unspecified angina pectoris without atherosclerosis of other coronary artery bypass graft(s) (I20.9) |

● **I25.8**   **Other forms of chronic ischemic heart disease**

● **I25.81**   **Atherosclerosis of other coronary vessels without angina pectoris**

> Use additional code, if applicable, to identify coronary atherosclerosis due to lipid rich plaque (I25.83)

> | Excludes1 | atherosclerotic heart disease of native coronary artery without angina pectoris (I25.10) |

Item 9–7 Pulmonary heart disease or **cor pulmonale** is right ventricle hypertrophy or RVH as a result of a respiratory disorder increasing back flow pressure to the right ventricle. Left untreated, cor pulmonale leads to right-heart failure and death.

● Unacceptable First-Listed Diagnosis   ● Use Additional Character(s)   ▪ Unspecified   **OGCR** Official Guidelines for Coding and Reporting

🅒 Complication\Comorbidity   🅒 Major C\C   Excludes 1   Excludes 2   Includes   Use additional   Code first   Code also

1017

CHAPTER 9 (I00–I99)

I25.810   **Atherosclerosis of coronary artery bypass graft(s) without angina pectoris**
Atherosclerosis of coronary artery bypass graft NOS

> **Excludes1**   atherosclerosis of coronary bypass graft(s) with angina pectoris (I25.70- -I25.73-, I25.79-)

I25.811   **Atherosclerosis of native coronary artery of transplanted heart without angina pectoris** 🗝
Atherosclerosis of native coronary artery of transplanted heart NOS

> **Excludes1**   atherosclerosis of native coronary artery of transplanted heart with angina pectoris (I25.75-)

I25.812   **Atherosclerosis of bypass graft of coronary artery of transplanted heart without angina pectoris** 🗝
Atherosclerosis of bypass graft of transplanted heart NOS

> **Excludes1**   atherosclerosis of bypass graft of transplanted heart with angina pectoris (I25.76)

● **I25.82**   **Chronic total occlusion of coronary artery**
Complete occlusion of coronary artery
Total occlusion of coronary artery

Code first coronary atherosclerosis (I25.1-, I25.7-, I25.81-)

> **Excludes1**   acute coronary occlusion with myocardial infarction (I21.-, I22.-)
> acute coronary occlusion without myocardial infarction (I24.0)

I25.83   **Coronary atherosclerosis due to lipid rich plaque**

Code first coronary atherosclerosis (I25.1-, I25.7-, I25.81-)

I25.89   **Other forms of chronic ischemic heart disease**

■**I25.9**   **Chronic ischemic heart disease, unspecified**
Ischemic heart disease (chronic) NOS

PULMONARY HEART DISEASE AND DISEASES OF PULMONARY CIRCULATION (I26-I28)

● **I26**   **Pulmonary embolism**

> **Includes**   (acute) pulmonary (artery)(vein) infarction
> (acute) pulmonary (artery)(vein) thromboembolism
> (acute) pulmonary (artery)(vein) thrombosis

> **Excludes2**   chronic pulmonary embolism (I27.82)
> personal history of pulmonary embolism (Z86.71)
> pulmonary embolism due to trauma (T79.0, T79.1)
> pulmonary embolism due to complications of surgical and medical care (T80.0, T81.7-, T82.8-)
> pulmonary embolism complicating:
> abortion, ectopic or molar pregnancy (O00-O07, O08.2)
> pregnancy, childbirth and the puerperium (O88.-)
> septic (non-pulmonary) arterial embolism (I76)

● **I26.0**   **Pulmonary embolism with acute cor pulmonale**

● **I26.01**   **Septic pulmonary embolism with acute cor pulmonale** 🗝

Code first underlying infection

I26.09   **Other pulmonary embolism with acute cor pulmonale** 🗝
Acute cor pulmonale NOS

● **I26.9**   **Pulmonary embolism without acute cor pulmonale**

● **I26.90**   **Septic pulmonary embolism without acute cor pulmonale** 🗝

Code first underlying infection

I26.99   **Other pulmonary embolism without acute cor pulmonale** 🗝
Acute pulmonary embolism NOS
Pulmonary embolism NOS

● **I27**   **Other pulmonary heart diseases**

I27.0   **Primary pulmonary hypertension** 🗝

I27.1   **Kyphoscoliotic heart disease** 🗝

I27.2   **Other secondary pulmonary hypertension**
Code also associated underlying condition

● **I27.8**   **Other specified pulmonary heart diseases**

I27.81   **Cor pulmonale (chronic)**
Cor pulmonale NOS

> **Excludes1**   acute cor pulmonale (I26.0-)

I27.82   **Chronic pulmonary embolism**

Use additional code, if applicable, for associated long-term (current) use of anticoagulants (Z79.01)

> **Excludes1**   personal history of pulmonary embolism (Z86.71)

I27.89   **Other specified pulmonary heart diseases**
Eisenmenger's complex
Eisenmenger's syndrome

> **Excludes1**   Eisenmenger's defect (Q21.8)

■**I27.9**   **Pulmonary heart disease, unspecified**
Chronic cardiopulmonary disease

● **I28**   **Other diseases of pulmonary vessels**

I28.0   **Arteriovenous fistula of pulmonary vessels** 🗝

> **Excludes1**   congenital arteriovenous fistula (Q25.7)

I28.1   **Aneurysm of pulmonary artery** 🗝

> **Excludes1**   congenital aneurysm (Q25.7)

CHAPTER 9 (I00-I99)

1018

● Unacceptable First-Listed Diagnosis   ● Use Additional Character(s)   ■ Unspecified   **OGCR** Official Guidelines for Coding and Reporting
🗝 Complication\Comorbidity   🗝 Major C\C   Excludes 1   Excludes 2   Includes   Use additional   Code first   Code also

I28.8   Other diseases of pulmonary vessels
Pulmonary arteritis
Pulmonary endarteritis
Rupture of pulmonary vessels
Stenosis of pulmonary vessels
Stricture of pulmonary vessels

I28.9   Disease of pulmonary vessels, unspecified

OTHER FORMS OF HEART DISEASE (I30-I52)

● **I30   Acute pericarditis**
Inflammation of pericardium (sac surrounding the heart) caused by an infection.

Includes   acute mediastinopericarditis
acute myopericarditis
acute pericardial effusion
acute pleuropericarditis
acute pneumopericarditis

Excludes1   Dressler's syndrome (I24.1)
rheumatic pericarditis (acute) (I01.0)

I30.0   Acute nonspecific idiopathic pericarditis 🗗

I30.1   Infective pericarditis 🗗
Pneumococcal pericarditis
Pneumopyopericardium
Purulent pericarditis
Pyopericarditis
Pyopericardium
Pyopneumopericardium
Staphylococcal pericarditis
Streptococcal pericarditis
Suppurative pericarditis
Viral pericarditis

Use additional code (B95-B97) to identify infectious agent

I30.8   Other forms of acute pericarditis 🗗

I30.9   Acute pericarditis, unspecified 🗗

● **I31   Other diseases of pericardium**

Excludes1   diseases of pericardium specified as rheumatic (I09.2)
postcardiotomy syndrome (I97.0)
traumatic injury to pericardium (S26.-)

I31.0   Chronic adhesive pericarditis 🗗
Accretio cordis
Adherent pericardium
Adhesive mediastinopericarditis

I31.1   Chronic constrictive pericarditis 🗗
Concretio cordis
Pericardial calcification

I31.2   Hemopericardium, not elsewhere classified 🗗

Excludes1   hemopericardium as current complication following acute myocardial infarction (I23.0)

I31.3   Pericardial effusion (noninflammatory) 🗗
Chylopericardium

Excludes1   acute pericardial effusion (I30.9)

● **I31.4   Cardiac tamponade** 🗗
Code first underlying cause

I31.8   Other specified diseases of pericardium 🗗
Epicardial plaques
Focal pericardial adhesions

I31.9   Disease of pericardium, unspecified 🗗
Pericarditis (chronic) NOS

● **I32   Pericarditis in diseases classified elsewhere** 🗗
Code first underlying disease

Excludes1   pericarditis (in):
coxsackie (virus) (B33.23)
gonococcal (A54.83)
meningococcal (A39.53)
rheumatoid (arthritis) (M05.31)
syphilitic (A52.06)
systemic lupus erythematosus (M32.12)
tuberculosis (A18.84)

● **I33   Acute and subacute endocarditis**
Inflammation/infection of lining of heart, affecting heart valves including replacement valves and is usually caused by a bacterial infection

Excludes1   acute rheumatic endocarditis (I01.1)
endocarditis NOS (I38)

I33.0   Acute and subacute infective endocarditis 🗗
Bacterial endocarditis (acute) (subacute)
Infective endocarditis (acute) (subacute) NOS
Endocarditis lenta (acute) (subacute)
Malignant endocarditis (acute) (subacute)
Purulent endocarditis (acute) (subacute)
Septic endocarditis (acute) (subacute)
Ulcerative endocarditis (acute) (subacute)
Vegetative endocarditis (acute) (subacute)

Use additional code (B95-B97) to identify infectious agent

I33.9   Acute and subacute endocarditis, unspecified 🗗
Acute endocarditis NOS
Acute myoendocarditis NOS
Acute periendocarditis NOS
Subacute endocarditis NOS
Subacute myoendocarditis NOS
Subacute periendocarditis NOS

● **I34   Nonrheumatic mitral valve disorders**

Excludes1   mitral valve disease (I05.9)
mitral valve failure (I05.8)
mitral valve stenosis (I05.0)
mitral valve disorder of unspecified cause with diseases of aortic and/or tricuspid valve(s) (I08.-)
mitral valve disorder of unspecified cause with mitral stenosis or obstruction (I05.0)
mitral valve disorder specified as congenital (Q23.2, Q23.3)
mitral valve disorder specified as rheumatic (I05.-)

I34.0   Nonrheumatic mitral (valve) insufficiency
Nonrheumatic mitral (valve) incompetence NOS
Nonrheumatic mitral (valve) regurgitation NOS

I34.1   Nonrheumatic mitral (valve) prolapse
Floppy nonrheumatic mitral valve syndrome

Excludes1   Marfan's syndrome (Q87.4-)

I34.2   Nonrheumatic mitral (valve) stenosis

I34.8   Other nonrheumatic mitral valve disorders

I34.9   Nonrheumatic mitral valve disorder, unspecified

● **I35   Nonrheumatic aortic valve disorders**

Excludes1   aortic valve disorder of unspecified cause but with diseases of mitral and/or tricuspid valve(s) (I08.-)
aortic valve disorder specified as congenital (Q23.0, Q23.1)
aortic valve disorder specified as rheumatic (I06.-)
hypertrophic subaortic stenosis (I42.1)

● Unacceptable First-Listed Diagnosis   ● Use Additional Character(s)   ■ Unspecified   **OGCR** Official Guidelines for Coding and Reporting

🗗 Complication\Comorbidity   🗗 Major C\C   Excludes 1   Excludes 2    Includes   Use additional   Code first   Code also   1019

CHAPTER 9 (I00-I99)

I35.0   **Nonrheumatic aortic (valve) stenosis**

I35.1   **Nonrheumatic aortic (valve) insufficiency**
     Nonrheumatic aortic (valve) incompetence NOS
     Nonrheumatic aortic (valve) regurgitation NOS

I35.2   **Nonrheumatic aortic (valve) stenosis with insufficiency**

I35.8   **Other nonrheumatic aortic valve disorders**

I35.9   **Nonrheumatic aortic valve disorder, unspecified**

● **I36**   **Nonrheumatic tricuspid valve disorders**

   Excludes1   tricuspid valve disorders of unspecified
          cause (I07.-)
        tricuspid valve disorders specified as
          congenital (Q22.4, Q22.8, Q22.9)
        tricuspid valve disorders specified as
          rheumatic (I07.-)
        tricuspid valve disorders with aortic and/or
          mitral valve involvement (I08.-)

I36.0   **Nonrheumatic tricuspid (valve) stenosis**

I36.1   **Nonrheumatic tricuspid (valve) insufficiency**
     Nonrheumatic tricuspid (valve) incompetence
     Nonrheumatic tricuspid (valve) regurgitation

I36.2   **Nonrheumatic tricuspid (valve) stenosis with insufficiency**

I36.8   **Other nonrheumatic tricuspid valve disorders**

I36.9   **Nonrheumatic tricuspid valve disorder, unspecified**

● **I37**   **Nonrheumatic pulmonary valve disorders**

   Excludes1   pulmonary valve disorder specified as
          congenital (Q22.1, Q22.2, Q22.3)
        pulmonary valve disorder specified as
          rheumatic (I09.89)

I37.0   **Nonrheumatic pulmonary valve stenosis**

I37.1   **Nonrheumatic pulmonary valve insufficiency**
     Nonrheumatic pulmonary valve incompetence
     Nonrheumatic pulmonary valve regurgitation

I37.2   **Nonrheumatic pulmonary valve stenosis with insufficiency**

I37.8   **Other nonrheumatic pulmonary valve disorders**

I37.9   **Nonrheumatic pulmonary valve disorder, unspecified**

■ **I38**   **Endocarditis, valve unspecified** 🔗

   Includes   endocarditis (chronic) NOS
        valvular incompetence NOS
        valvular insufficiency NOS
        valvular regurgitation NOS
        valvular stenosis NOS
        valvulitis (chronic) NOS

   Excludes1   congenital insufficiency of cardiac valve
          NOS (Q24.8)
        congenital stenosis of cardiac valve NOS
          (Q24.8)
        endocardial fibroelastosis (I42.4)
        endocarditis specified as rheumatic (I09.1)

● **I39**   **Endocarditis and heart valve disorders in diseases classified elsewhere** 🔗

   Code first underlying disease, such as:
     Q fever (A78)

   Excludes1   endocardial involvement in:
        candidiasis (B37.6)
        gonococcal infection (A54.83)
        Libman-Sacks disease (M32.11)
        listerosis (A32.82)
        meningococcal infection (A39.51)
        rheumatoid arthritis (M05.31)
        syphilis (A52.03)
        tuberculosis (A18.84)
        typhoid fever (A01.02)

● **I40**   **Acute myocarditis**
   Inflammation of heart muscle due to infection (viral/bacterial).

   Includes   subacute myocarditis

   Excludes1   acute rheumatic myocarditis (I01.2)

I40.0   **Infective myocarditis** 🔗
     Septic myocarditis

     Use additional code (B95-B97) to identify
       infectious agent

I40.1   **Isolated myocarditis** 🔗
     Fiedler's myocarditis
     Giant cell myocarditis
     Idiopathic myocarditis

I40.8   **Other acute myocarditis** 🔗

I40.9   **Acute myocarditis, unspecified** 🔗

● **I41**   **Myocarditis in diseases classified elsewhere** 🔗

   Code first underlying disease, such as:
     typhus (A75.0-A75.9)

   Excludes1   myocarditis (in):
        Chagas' disease (chronic) (B57.2)
        acute (B57.0)
        coxsackie (virus) infection (B33.22)
        diphtheritic (A36.81)
        gonococcal (A54.83)
        influenzal (J10.89)
        meningococcal (A39.52)
        mumps (B26.82)
        rheumatoid arthritis (M05.31)
        sarcoid (D86.85)
        syphilis (A52.06)
        toxoplasmosis (B58.81)
        tuberculous (A18.84)

● **I42**   **Cardiomyopathy**
   Disease of the heart muscle resulting in an abnormally enlarged, weakened, thickened, and/or stiffened muscles

   Includes   myocardiopathy

   Code first cardiomyopathy complicating pregnancy and puerperium (O99.4)

   Excludes1   ischemic cardiomyopathy (I25.5)
        peripartum cardiomyopathy (O90.3)

I42.0   **Dilated cardiomyopathy** 🔗
     Congestive cardiomyopathy

I42.1   **Obstructive hypertrophic cardiomyopathy** 🔗
     Hypertrophic subaortic stenosis

I42.2   **Other hypertrophic cardiomyopathy** 🔗
     Nonobstructive hypertrophic cardiomyopathy

I42.3   **Endomyocardial (eosinophilic) disease** 🔗
     Endomyocardial (tropical) fibrosis
     Löffler's endocarditis

I42.4   **Endocardial fibroelastosis** 🔗
     Congenital cardiomyopathy
     Elastomyofibrosis

I42.5   **Other restrictive cardiomyopathy** 🔗
     Constrictive cardiomyopathy NOS

I42.6   **Alcoholic cardiomyopathy** 🔗
     Code also presence of alcoholism (F10.-)

I42.7   **Cardiomyopathy due to drug and external agent** 🔗
     Code first (T36-T65) to identify cause

I42.8   **Other cardiomyopathies** 🔗

I42.9   **Cardiomyopathy, unspecified** 🔗
     Cardiomyopathy (primary) (secondary) NOS

● Unacceptable First-Listed Diagnosis   ● Use Additional Character(s)   ■ Unspecified   **OGCR** Official Guidelines for Coding and Reporting
🔗 Complication\Comorbidity   🔗 Major C\C   Excludes 1   Excludes 2   Includes   Use additional   Code first   Code also

● **I43　Cardiomyopathy in diseases classified elsewhere** 🔖

　　Code first underlying disease, such as:
　　　　amyloidosis (E85.-)
　　　　glycogen storage disease (E74.0)
　　　　gout (M10.0-)
　　　　thyrotoxicosis (E05.0--E05.9-)

　　　Excludes1　cardiomyopathy (in):
　　　　　　　　coxsackie (virus) (B33.24)
　　　　　　　　diphtheria (A36.81)
　　　　　　　　sarcoidosis (D86.85)
　　　　　　　　tuberculosis (A18.84)

● **I44　Atrioventricular and left bundle-branch block**

　　Conduction problem resulting in arrhythmias/dysrhythmias due to a lack of electrical impulses being transmitted normally through the heart.

　　I44.0　Atrioventricular block, first degree

　　I44.1　Atrioventricular block, second degree
　　　　Atrioventricular block, type I and II
　　　　Möbitz block, type I and II
　　　　Second degree block, type I and II
　　　　Wenckebach's block

　　I44.2　Atrioventricular block, complete 🔖
　　　　Complete heart block NOS
　　　　Third degree block

　● **I44.3　Other and unspecified atrioventricular block**
　　　　Atrioventricular block NOS

　　　■ **I44.30　Unspecified atrioventricular block**

　　　I44.39　Other atrioventricular block

　　I44.4　Left anterior fascicular block

　　I44.5　Left posterior fascicular block

　● **I44.6　Other and unspecified fascicular block**

　　　■ **I44.60　Unspecified fascicular block**
　　　　　Left bundle-branch hemiblock NOS

　　　I44.69　Other fascicular block

　■ **I44.7　Left bundle-branch block, unspecified**

● **I45　Other conduction disorders**

　　I45.0　Right fascicular block

　● **I45.1　Other and unspecified right bundle-branch block**

　　　■ **I45.10　Unspecified right bundle-branch block**
　　　　　Right bundle-branch block NOS

　　　I45.19　Other right bundle-branch block

　　I45.2　Bifascicular block

　　I45.3　Trifascicular block 🔖

　　I45.4　Nonspecific intraventricular block
　　　　Bundle-branch block NOS

　　I45.5　Other specified heart block
　　　　Sinoatrial block
　　　　Sinoauricular block
　　　　Excludes1　heart block NOS (I45.9)

　　I45.6　Pre-excitation syndrome
　　　　Accelerated atrioventricular conduction
　　　　Accessory atrioventricular conduction
　　　　Anomalous atrioventricular excitation
　　　　Lown-Ganong-Levine syndrome
　　　　Pre-excitation atrioventricular conduction
　　　　Wolff-Parkinson-White syndrome

　● **I45.8　Other specified conduction disorders**

　　　I45.81　Long QT syndrome

　　　I45.89　Other specified conduction disorders 🔖
　　　　　Atrioventricular [AV] dissociation
　　　　　Interference dissociation
　　　　　Isorhythmic dissociation
　　　　　Nonparoxysmal AV nodal tachycardia

　■ **I45.9　Conduction disorder, unspecified**
　　　Heart block NOS
　　　Stokes-Adams syndrome

● **I46　Cardiac arrest**
　　　Excludes1　cardiogenic shock (R57.0)

　● **I46.2　Cardiac arrest due to underlying cardiac condition** 🔖
　　　Code first underlying cardiac condition
　　　MCC: Only if patient discharged alive

　● **I46.8　Cardiac arrest due to other underlying condition** 🔖
　　　Code first underlying condition
　　　MCC: Only if patient discharged alive

　■ **I46.9　Cardiac arrest, cause unspecified** 🔖
　　　MCC: Only if patient discharged alive

● **I47　Paroxysmal tachycardia**
　　Code first tachycardia complicating:
　　　　abortion or ectopic or molar pregnancy (O00-O07, O08.8)
　　　　obstetric surgery and procedures (O75.4)
　　　Excludes1　tachycardia:
　　　　　　　NOS (R00.0)
　　　　　　　sinoauricular NOS (R00.0)
　　　　　　　sinus [sinusal] NOS (R00.0)

　　I47.0　Re-entry ventricular arrhythmia 🔖

　　I47.1　Supraventricular tachycardia 🔖
　　　　Atrial paroxysmal tachycardia
　　　　Atrioventricular [AV] paroxysmal tachycardia
　　　　Junctional paroxysmal tachycardia
　　　　Nodal paroxysmal tachycardia

　　I47.2　Ventricular tachycardia 🔖

　■ **I47.9　Paroxysmal tachycardia, unspecified**
　　　Bouveret (-Hoffman) syndrome

● **I48　Atrial fibrillation and flutter**
　　Most common abnormal heart rhythm (arrhythmia) presenting as irregular, rapid beating (tachycardia) of the heart's upper chamber.

　　I48.0　Atrial fibrillation

　　I48.1　Atrial flutter 🔖
　　　　Rapid contractions of the upper heart chamber

● **I49　Other cardiac arrhythmias**
　　Code first cardiac arrhythmia complicating:
　　　　abortion or ectopic or molar pregnancy (O00-O07, O08.8)
　　　　obstetric surgery and procedures (O75.4)
　　　Excludes1　bradycardia:
　　　　　　　NOS (R00.1)
　　　　　　　sinoatrial (R00.1)
　　　　　　　sinus (R00.1)
　　　　　　　vagal (R00.1)
　　　　　　　neonatal dysrhythmia (P29.1)

　● **I49.0　Ventricular fibrillation and flutter**

　　　I49.01　Ventricular fibrillation 🔖
　　　　　MCC: Only if patient discharged alive

　　　I49.02　Ventricular flutter 🔖

　　I49.1　Atrial premature depolarization
　　　　Atrial premature beats

　　I49.2　Junctional premature depolarization 🔖

　　I49.3　Ventricular premature depolarization 🔖

　● **I49.4　Other and unspecified premature depolarization**

　　　■ **I49.40　Unspecified premature depolarization**
　　　　　Premature beats NOS

　　　I49.49　Other premature depolarization
　　　　　Ectopic beats
　　　　　Extrasystoles
　　　　　Extrasystolic arrhythmias
　　　　　Premature contractions

● Unacceptable First-Listed Diagnosis　　● Use Additional Character(s)　　　■ Unspecified　　**OGCR** Official Guidelines for Coding and Reporting

🔖 Complication\Comorbidity　　🔖 Major C\C　　Excludes 1　　Excludes 2　　 Includes　　 Use additional　　 Code first　　 Code also

CHAPTER 9 (I00-I99)

Item 9–8 Congestive heart failure (CHF) is a condition in which the left ventricle of the heart cannot pump enough blood to the body. The blood flow from the heart slows or returns to the heart from the venous system back flow resulting in congestion (fluid accumulation) particularly in the abdomen. Most commonly, fluid collects in the lungs and results in shortness of breath, especially when in a reclining position.

I49.5   Sick sinus syndrome
Tachycardia-bradycardia syndrome

I49.8   Other specified cardiac arrhythmias
Coronary sinus rhythm disorder
Ectopic rhythm disorder
Nodal rhythm disorder

■ **I49.9   Cardiac arrhythmia, unspecified**
Arrhythmia (cardiac) NOS

● **I50   Heart failure**
Code first: heart failure complicating abortion or ectopic or molar pregnancy (O00-O07, O08.8)
heart failure following surgery (I97.13-)
heart failure due to hypertension (I11.0)
heart failure due to hypertension with chronic kidney disease (I13.-)
obstetric surgery and procedures (O75.4)
rheumatic heart failure (I09.81)

Excludes1   cardiac arrest (I46.-)
neonatal cardiac failure (P29.0)

I50.1   Left ventricular failure
Cardiac asthma
Edema of lung with heart disease NOS
Edema of lung with heart failure
Left heart failure
Pulmonary edema with heart disease NOS
Pulmonary edema with heart failure

Excludes1   edema of lung without heart disease or heart failure (J81.-)
pulmonary edema without heart disease or failure (J81.-)

● **I50.2   Systolic (congestive) heart failure**

Excludes1   combined systolic (congestive) and diastolic (congestive) heart failure (I50.4-)

■ **I50.20   Unspecified systolic (congestive) heart failure**

I50.21   Acute systolic (congestive) heart failure
Presenting a short and relatively severe episode

I50.22   Chronic systolic (congestive) heart failure
Long-lasting, presenting over time

I50.23   Acute on chronic systolic (congestive) heart failure
Combination code. What was a chronic condition now has an acute exacerbation (to make more severe).

● **I50.3   Diastolic (congestive) heart failure**

Excludes1   combined systolic (congestive) and diastolic (congestive) heart failure (I50.4-)

■ **I50.30   Unspecified diastolic (congestive) heart failure**

I50.31   Acute diastolic (congestive) heart failure

I50.32   Chronic diastolic (congestive) heart failure

I50.33   Acute on chronic diastolic (congestive) heart failure

● **I50.4   Combined systolic (congestive) and diastolic (congestive) heart failure**

■ **I50.40   Unspecified combined systolic (congestive) and diastolic (congestive) heart failure**

I50.41   Acute combined systolic (congestive) and diastolic (congestive) heart failure

I50.42   Chronic combined systolic (congestive) and diastolic (congestive) heart failure

I50.43   Acute on chronic combined systolic (congestive) and diastolic (congestive) heart failure

■ **I50.9   Heart failure, unspecified**
Biventricular (heart) failure NOS
Cardiac, heart or myocardial failure NOS
Congestive heart disease
Congestive heart failure NOS
Right ventricular failure (secondary to left heart failure)

Excludes1   fluid overload (E87.7)

● **I51   Complications and ill-defined descriptions of heart disease**

Excludes1   any condition in I51.4-I51.9 due to hypertension (I11.-)
any condition in I51.4-I51.9 due to hypertension and chronic kidney disease (I13.-)
heart disease specified as rheumatic (I00-I09)

I51.0   Cardiac septal defect, acquired
Acquired septal atrial defect (old)
Acquired septal auricular defect (old)
Acquired septal ventricular defect (old)

Excludes1   cardiac septal defect as current complication following acute myocardial infarction (I23.1, I23.2)

I51.1   Rupture of chordae tendineae, not elsewhere classified

Excludes1   rupture of chordae tendineae as current complication following acute myocardial infarction (I23.4)

I51.2   Rupture of papillary muscle, not elsewhere classified

Excludes1   rupture of papillary muscle as current complication following acute myocardial infarction (I23.5)

I51.3   Intracardiac thrombosis, not elsewhere classified
Apical thrombosis (old)
Atrial thrombosis (old)
Auricular thrombosis (old)
Mural thrombosis (old)
Ventricular thrombosis (old)

Excludes1   intracardiac thrombosis as current complication following acute myocardial infarction (I23.6)

■ **I51.4   Myocarditis, unspecified**
Chronic (interstitial) myocarditis
Myocardial fibrosis
Myocarditis NOS

Excludes1   acute or subacute myocarditis (I40.-)

I51.5   Myocardial degeneration
Fatty degeneration of heart or myocardium
Myocardial disease
Senile degeneration of heart or myocardium

● Unacceptable First-Listed Diagnosis   ● Use Additional Character(s)   ■ Unspecified   **OGCR** Official Guidelines for Coding and Reporting
🜋 Complication\Comorbidity   🜋 Major C\C   Excludes 1   Excludes 2   Includes   Use additional   Code first   Code also

I51.7   Cardiomegaly
     Cardiac dilatation
     Cardiac hypertrophy
     Ventricular dilatation

● **I51.8   Other ill-defined heart diseases**

     I51.81   Takotsubo syndrome 🅒
        Reversible left ventricular dysfunction
          following sudden emotional stress
        Stress induced cardiomyopathy
        Takotsubo cardiomyopathy
        Transient left ventricular apical
          ballooning syndrome

     I51.89   Other ill-defined heart diseases
        Carditis (acute)(chronic)
        Pancarditis (acute)(chronic)

▪ **I51.9   Heart disease, unspecified**

● **I52   Other heart disorders in diseases classified elsewhere**

     Code first underlying disease, such as:
     congenital syphilis (A50.5)
     mucopolysaccharidosis (E76.3)
     schistosomiasis (B65.0-B65.9)

     Excludes1   heart disease (in):
           gonococcal infection (A54.83)
           meningococcal infection (A39.50)
           rheumatoid arthritis (M05.31)
           syphilis (A52.06)

CEREBROVASCULAR DISEASES (I60-I69)

Use additional code to identify presence of:
     alcohol abuse and dependence (F10.-)
     exposure to environmental tobacco smoke (Z77.22)
     history of tobacco use (Z87.891)
     hypertension (I10-I15)
     occupational exposure to environmental tobacco
        smoke (Z57.31)
     tobacco dependence (F17.-)
     tobacco use (Z72.0)

     Excludes1   transient cerebral ischemic attacks and
           related syndromes (G45.-)
           traumatic intracranial hemorrhage (S06.-)

● **I60   Nontraumatic subarachnoid hemorrhage**

     Includes   ruptured cerebral aneurysm

     Excludes1   sequelae of subarachnoid hemorrhage
           (I69.0-)
           syphilitic ruptured cerebral aneurysm
           (A52.05)

● **I60.0   Nontraumatic subarachnoid hemorrhage from
        carotid siphon and bifurcation**

     ▪ **I60.00   Nontraumatic subarachnoid hemorrhage
          from unspecified carotid siphon and
          bifurcation** 🅒

     **I60.01   Nontraumatic subarachnoid hemorrhage
          from right carotid siphon and bifurcation** 🅒

     **I60.02   Nontraumatic subarachnoid hemorrhage
          from left carotid siphon and bifurcation** 🅒

● **I60.1   Nontraumatic subarachnoid hemorrhage from
        middle cerebral artery**

     ▪ **I60.10   Nontraumatic subarachnoid hemorrhage
          from unspecified middle cerebral artery** 🅒

     **I60.11   Nontraumatic subarachnoid hemorrhage
          from right middle cerebral artery** 🅒

     **I60.12   Nontraumatic subarachnoid hemorrhage
          from left middle cerebral artery** 🅒

● **I60.2   Nontraumatic subarachnoid hemorrhage from
        anterior communicating artery**

     ▪ **I60.20   Nontraumatic subarachnoid hemorrhage
          from unspecified anterior communicating
          artery** 🅒

     **I60.21   Nontraumatic subarachnoid hemorrhage
          from right anterior communicating artery** 🅒

     **I60.22   Nontraumatic subarachnoid hemorrhage
          from left anterior communicating artery** 🅒

● **I60.3   Nontraumatic subarachnoid hemorrhage from
        posterior communicating artery**

     ▪ **I60.30   Nontraumatic subarachnoid hemorrhage
          from unspecified posterior communicating
          artery** 🅒

     **I60.31   Nontraumatic subarachnoid hemorrhage
          from right posterior communicating artery** 🅒

     **I60.32   Nontraumatic subarachnoid hemorrhage
          from left posterior communicating artery** 🅒

**I60.4   Nontraumatic subarachnoid hemorrhage from
        basilar artery** 🅒

● **I60.5   Nontraumatic subarachnoid hemorrhage from
        vertebral artery**

     ▪ **I60.50   Nontraumatic subarachnoid hemorrhage
          from unspecified vertebral artery** 🅒

     **I60.51   Nontraumatic subarachnoid hemorrhage
          from right vertebral artery** 🅒

     **I60.52   Nontraumatic subarachnoid hemorrhage
          from left vertebral artery** 🅒

**I60.6   Nontraumatic subarachnoid hemorrhage from
        other intracranial arteries** 🅒

▪ **I60.7   Nontraumatic subarachnoid hemorrhage from
        unspecified intracranial artery** 🅒
        Ruptured (congenital) berry aneurysm
        Ruptured (congenital) cerebral aneurysm
        Subarachnoid hemorrhage (nontraumatic) from
          cerebral artery NOS
        Subarachnoid hemorrhage (nontraumatic) from
          communicating artery NOS

I60.8   Other nontraumatic subarachnoid hemorrhage 🅒
        Meningeal hemorrhage
        Rupture of cerebral arteriovenous malformation

▪ **I60.9   Nontraumatic subarachnoid hemorrhage,
        unspecified** 🅒

● **I61   Nontraumatic intracerebral hemorrhage**

     Excludes1   sequelae of intracerebral hemorrhage (I69.1-)

**I61.0   Nontraumatic intracerebral hemorrhage in
        hemisphere, subcortical** 🅒
        Deep intracerebral hemorrhage (nontraumatic)

**I61.1   Nontraumatic intracerebral hemorrhage in
        hemisphere, cortical** 🅒
        Cerebral lobe hemorrhage (nontraumatic)
        Superficial intracerebral hemorrhage
          (nontraumatic)

▪ **I61.2   Nontraumatic intracerebral hemorrhage in
        hemisphere, unspecified** 🅒

**I61.3   Nontraumatic intracerebral hemorrhage in brain
        stem** 🅒

**I61.4   Nontraumatic intracerebral hemorrhage in
        cerebellum** 🅒

**I61.5   Nontraumatic intracerebral hemorrhage,
        intraventricular** 🅒

**I61.6   Nontraumatic intracerebral hemorrhage, multiple
        localized** 🅒

● Unacceptable First-Listed Diagnosis   ● Use Additional Character(s)   ▪ Unspecified   **OGCR** Official Guidelines for Coding and Reporting

🅒 Complication\Comorbidity   🅒 Major C\C   Excludes 1   Excludes 2   Includes   Use additional   Code first   Code also   1023

I61.8   Other nontraumatic intracerebral hemorrhage 🦠

■I61.9   Nontraumatic intracerebral hemorrhage, unspecified 🦠

●I62   Other and unspecified nontraumatic intracranial hemorrhage

   Excludes1   sequelae of intracranial hemorrhage (I69.2)

●I62.0   Nontraumatic subdural hemorrhage

    ■I62.00   Nontraumatic subdural hemorrhage, unspecified 🦠

    I62.01   Nontraumatic acute subdural hemorrhage 🦠

    I62.02   Nontraumatic subacute subdural hemorrhage 🦠

    I62.03   Nontraumatic chronic subdural hemorrhage 🦠

   I62.1   Nontraumatic extradural hemorrhage 🦠
       Nontraumatic epidural hemorrhage

   ■I62.9   Nontraumatic intracranial hemorrhage, unspecified 🦠

(See Plate 141 on page NAP-28.)

●I63   Cerebral infarction

   Includes   occlusion and stenosis of cerebral and precerebral arteries, resulting in cerebral infarction

   Use additional code, if applicable, to identify status post administration of tPA (rtPA) in a different facility within the last 24 hours prior to admission to current facility (Z92.82)

   Excludes1   sequelae of cerebral infarction (I69.3-)

●I63.0   Cerebral infarction due to thrombosis of precerebral arteries

    ■I63.00   Cerebral infarction due to thrombosis of unspecified precerebral artery 🦠

    ●I63.01   Cerebral infarction due to thrombosis of vertebral artery

      I63.011   Cerebral infarction due to thrombosis of right vertebral artery 🦠

      I63.012   Cerebral infarction due to thrombosis of left vertebral artery 🦠

      ■I63.019   Cerebral infarction due to thrombosis of unspecified vertebral artery 🦠

    I63.02   Cerebral infarction due to thrombosis of basilar artery 🦠

    ●I63.03   Cerebral infarction due to thrombosis of carotid artery

      I63.031   Cerebral infarction due to thrombosis of right carotid artery 🦠

      I63.032   Cerebral infarction due to thrombosis of left carotid artery 🦠

      ■I63.039   Cerebral infarction due to thrombosis of unspecified carotid artery 🦠

    I63.09   Cerebral infarction due to thrombosis of other precerebral artery 🦠

   ●I63.1   Cerebral infarction due to embolism of precerebral arteries

    ■I63.10   Cerebral infarction due to embolism of unspecified precerebral artery 🦠

   ●I63.11   Cerebral infarction due to embolism of vertebral artery

      I63.111   Cerebral infarction due to embolism of left vertebral artery 🦠

      I63.112   Cerebral infarction due to embolism of right vertebral artery 🦠

      ■I63.119   Cerebral infarction due to embolism of unspecified vertebral artery 🦠

    I63.12   Cerebral infarction due to embolism of basilar artery 🦠

   ●I63.13   Cerebral infarction due to embolism of carotid artery

      I63.131   Cerebral infarction due to embolism of right carotid artery 🦠

      I63.132   Cerebral infarction due to embolism of left carotid artery 🦠

      ■I63.139   Cerebral infarction due to embolism of unspecified carotid artery 🦠

    I63.19   Cerebral infarction due to embolism of other precerebral artery 🦠

   ●I63.2   Cerebral infarction due to unspecified occlusion or stenosis of precerebral arteries

    ■I63.20   Cerebral infarction due to unspecified occlusion or stenosis of unspecified precerebral arteries 🦠

    ●I63.21   Cerebral infarction due to unspecified occlusion or stenosis of vertebral arteries

      ■I63.211   Cerebral infarction due to unspecified occlusion or stenosis of right vertebral arteries 🦠

      ■I63.212   Cerebral infarction due to unspecified occlusion or stenosis of left vertebral arteries 🦠

      ■I63.219   Cerebral infarction due to unspecified occlusion or stenosis of unspecified vertebral arteries 🦠

    ■I63.22   Cerebral infarction due to unspecified occlusion or stenosis of basilar arteries 🦠

    ●I63.23   Cerebral infarction due to unspecified occlusion or stenosis of carotid arteries

      ■I63.231   Cerebral infarction due to unspecified occlusion or stenosis of right carotid arteries 🦠

      ■I63.232   Cerebral infarction due to unspecified occlusion or stenosis of left carotid arteries 🦠

      ■I63.239   Cerebral infarction due to unspecified occlusion or stenosis of unspecified carotid arteries 🦠

    ■I63.29   Cerebral infarction due to unspecified occlusion or stenosis of other precerebral arteries 🦠

   ●I63.3   Cerebral infarction due to thrombosis of cerebral arteries

    ■I63.30   Cerebral infarction due to thrombosis of unspecified cerebral artery 🦠

    ●I63.31   Cerebral infarction due to thrombosis of middle cerebral artery

      I63.311   Cerebral infarction due to thrombosis of right middle cerebral artery 🦠

CHAPTER 9 (I00-I99)

   ● Unacceptable First-Listed Diagnosis   ● Use Additional Character(s)   ■ Unspecified   **OGCR** Official Guidelines for Coding and Reporting
   🦠 Complication\Comorbidity   🦠 Major C\C   Excludes 1   Excludes 2   Includes   Use additional   Code first   Code also

       I63.312   Cerebral infarction due to thrombosis of left middle cerebral artery 🗞

       🔲 I63.319   Cerebral infarction due to thrombosis of unspecified middle cerebral artery 🗞

   ● I63.32   Cerebral infarction due to thrombosis of anterior cerebral artery

       I63.321   Cerebral infarction due to thrombosis of right anterior cerebral artery 🗞

       I63.322   Cerebral infarction due to thrombosis of left anterior cerebral artery 🗞

       🔲 I63.329   Cerebral infarction due to thrombosis of unspecified anterior cerebral artery 🗞

   ● I63.33   Cerebral infarction due to thrombosis of posterior cerebral artery

       I63.331   Cerebral infarction due to thrombosis of right posterior cerebral artery 🗞

       I63.332   Cerebral infarction due to thrombosis of left posterior cerebral artery 🗞

       🔲 I63.339   Cerebral infarction due to thrombosis of unspecified posterior cerebral artery 🗞

   ● I63.34   Cerebral infarction due to thrombosis of cerebellar artery

       I63.341   Cerebral infarction due to thrombosis of right cerebellar artery 🗞

       I63.342   Cerebral infarction due to thrombosis of left cerebellar artery 🗞

       🔲 I63.349   Cerebral infarction due to thrombosis of unspecified cerebellar artery 🗞

      I63.39   Cerebral infarction due to thrombosis of other cerebral artery 🗞

● I63.4   Cerebral infarction due to embolism of cerebral arteries

   🔲 I63.40   Cerebral infarction due to embolism of unspecified cerebral artery 🗞

   ● I63.41   Cerebral infarction due to embolism of middle cerebral artery

       I63.411   Cerebral infarction due to embolism of right middle cerebral artery 🗞

       I63.412   Cerebral infarction due to embolism of left middle cerebral artery 🗞

       🔲 I63.419   Cerebral infarction due to embolism of unspecified middle cerebral artery 🗞

   ● I63.42   Cerebral infarction due to embolism of anterior cerebral artery

       I63.421   Cerebral infarction due to embolism of right anterior cerebral artery 🗞

       I63.422   Cerebral infarction due to embolism of left anterior cerebral artery 🗞

       🔲 I63.429   Cerebral infarction due to embolism of unspecified anterior cerebral artery 🗞

   ● I63.43   Cerebral infarction due to embolism of posterior cerebral artery

       I63.431   Cerebral infarction due to embolism of right posterior cerebral artery 🗞

       I63.432   Cerebral infarction due to embolism of left posterior cerebral artery 🗞

       🔲 I63.439   Cerebral infarction due to embolism of unspecified posterior cerebral artery 🗞

   ● I63.44   Cerebral infarction due to embolism of cerebellar artery

       I63.441   Cerebral infarction due to embolism of right cerebellar artery 🗞

       I63.442   Cerebral infarction due to embolism of left cerebellar artery 🗞

       🔲 I63.449   Cerebral infarction due to embolism of unspecified cerebellar artery 🗞

      I63.49   Cerebral infarction due to embolism of other cerebral artery 🗞

● I63.5   Cerebral infarction due to unspecified occlusion or stenosis of cerebral arteries

   🔲 I63.50   Cerebral infarction due to unspecified occlusion or stenosis of unspecified cerebral artery 🗞

   ● I63.51   Cerebral infarction due to unspecified occlusion or stenosis of middle cerebral artery

       🔲 I63.511   Cerebral infarction due to unspecified occlusion or stenosis of right middle cerebral artery 🗞

       🔲 I63.512   Cerebral infarction due to unspecified occlusion or stenosis of left middle cerebral artery 🗞

       🔲 I63.519   Cerebral infarction due to unspecified occlusion or stenosis of unspecified middle cerebral artery 🗞

   ● I63.52   Cerebral infarction due to unspecified occlusion or stenosis of anterior cerebral artery

       🔲 I63.521   Cerebral infarction due to unspecified occlusion or stenosis of right anterior cerebral artery 🗞

       🔲 I63.522   Cerebral infarction due to unspecified occlusion or stenosis of left anterior cerebral artery 🗞

       🔲 I63.529   Cerebral infarction due to unspecified occlusion or stenosis of unspecified anterior cerebral artery 🗞

   ● I63.53   Cerebral infarction due to unspecified occlusion or stenosis of posterior cerebral artery

       🔲 I63.531   Cerebral infarction due to unspecified occlusion or stenosis of left posterior cerebral artery 🗞

       🔲 I63.532   Cerebral infarction due to unspecified occlusion or stenosis of right posterior cerebral artery 🗞

● Unacceptable First-Listed Diagnosis   ● Use Additional Character(s)   🔲 Unspecified   **OGCR** Official Guidelines for Coding and Reporting

🗞 Complication\Comorbidity 🗞 Major C\C Excludes 1 Excludes 2 Includes Use additional Code first Code also

■ I63.539   Cerebral infarction due to unspecified occlusion or stenosis of unspecified posterior cerebral artery 🖉

● I63.54   Cerebral infarction due to unspecified occlusion or stenosis of cerebellar artery

■ I63.541   Cerebral infarction due to unspecified occlusion or stenosis of left cerebellar artery 🖉

■ I63.542   Cerebral infarction due to unspecified occlusion or stenosis of right cerebellar artery 🖉

■ I63.549   Cerebral infarction due to unspecified occlusion or stenosis of unspecified cerebellar artery 🖉

■ I63.59   Cerebral infarction due to unspecified occlusion or stenosis of other cerebral artery 🖉

I63.6   Cerebral infarction due to cerebral venous thrombosis, nonpyogenic 🖉

I63.8   Other cerebral infarction 🖉

■ I63.9   Cerebral infarction, unspecified 🖉
     Stroke NOS

● **I65**   **Occlusion and stenosis of precerebral arteries, not resulting in cerebral infarction**

Includes	embolism of precerebral artery

     narrowing of precerebral artery
     obstruction (complete) (partial) of precerebral artery
     thrombosis of precerebral artery

Excludes1	insufficiency, NOS, of precerebral artery (G45.-)

     insufficiency of precerebral arteries causing cerebral infarction (I63.0-I63.2)

● I65.0   Occlusion and stenosis of vertebral artery

I65.01   Occlusion and stenosis of right vertebral artery

I65.02   Occlusion and stenosis of left vertebral artery

I65.03   Occlusion and stenosis of bilateral vertebral arteries

■ I65.09   Occlusion and stenosis of unspecified vertebral artery

I65.1   Occlusion and stenosis of basilar artery

● I65.2   Occlusion and stenosis of carotid artery

I65.21   Occlusion and stenosis of right carotid artery

I65.22   Occlusion and stenosis of left carotid artery

I65.23   Occlusion and stenosis of bilateral carotid arteries

■ I65.29   Occlusion and stenosis of unspecified carotid artery

I65.8   Occlusion and stenosis of other precerebral arteries

■ I65.9   Occlusion and stenosis of unspecified precerebral artery
     Occlusion and stenosis of precerebral artery NOS

● **I66**   **Occlusion and stenosis of cerebral arteries, not resulting in cerebral infarction**

Includes	embolism of cerebral artery

     narrowing of cerebral artery
     obstruction (complete) (partial) of cerebral artery
     thrombosis of cerebral artery

Excludes1	occlusion and stenosis of cerebral artery causing cerebral infarction (I63.3-I63.5)

● I66.0   Occlusion and stenosis of middle cerebral artery

I66.01   Occlusion and stenosis of right middle cerebral artery

I66.02   Occlusion and stenosis of left middle cerebral artery

I66.03   Occlusion and stenosis of bilateral middle cerebral arteries

■ I66.09   Occlusion and stenosis of unspecified middle cerebral artery

● I66.1   Occlusion and stenosis of anterior cerebral artery

I66.11   Occlusion and stenosis of right anterior cerebral artery

I66.12   Occlusion and stenosis of left anterior cerebral artery

I66.13   Occlusion and stenosis of bilateral anterior cerebral arteries

■ I66.19   Occlusion and stenosis of unspecified anterior cerebral artery

● I66.2   Occlusion and stenosis of posterior cerebral artery

I66.21   Occlusion and stenosis of right posterior cerebral artery

I66.22   Occlusion and stenosis of left posterior cerebral artery

I66.23   Occlusion and stenosis of bilateral posterior cerebral arteries

■ I66.29   Occlusion and stenosis of unspecified posterior cerebral artery

I66.3   Occlusion and stenosis of cerebellar arteries

I66.8   Occlusion and stenosis of other cerebral arteries
     Occlusion and stenosis of perforating arteries

■ I66.9   Occlusion and stenosis of unspecified cerebral artery

● **I67**   **Other cerebrovascular diseases**

Excludes1	sequelae of the listed conditions (I69.8)

I67.0   **Dissection of cerebral arteries, nonruptured**

Excludes1	ruptured cerebral arteries (I60.7)

I67.1   **Cerebral aneurysm, nonruptured**
     Cerebral aneurysm NOS
     Cerebral arteriovenous fistula, acquired
     Internal carotid artery aneurysm, intracranial portion
     Internal carotid artery aneurysm, NOS

Excludes1	congenital cerebral aneurysm, nonruptured (Q28.-)

     ruptured cerebral aneurysm (I60.7)

I67.2   **Cerebral atherosclerosis**
     Atheroma of cerebral and precerebral arteries

I67.3   **Progressive vascular leukoencephalopathy** 🖉
     Binswanger's disease

I67.4   **Hypertensive encephalopathy** 🖉

I67.5   **Moyamoya disease** 🖉

I67.6   **Nonpyogenic thrombosis of intracranial venous system** 🖉
     Nonpyogenic thrombosis of cerebral vein
     Nonpyogenic thrombosis of intracranial venous sinus

Excludes1	nonpyogenic thrombosis of intracranial venous system causing infarction (I63.6)

I67.7   **Cerebral arteritis, not elsewhere classified** 🖉
     Granulomatous angiitis of the nervous system

Excludes1	allergic granulomatous angiitis (M30.1)

I67.8   **Other specified cerebrovascular diseases** 🖉
     Acute cerebrovascular insufficiency NOS
     Cerebral ischemia (chronic)

■ I67.9   **Cerebrovascular disease, unspecified**

● Unacceptable First-Listed Diagnosis   ● Use Additional Character(s)   ■ Unspecified   **OGCR** Official Guidelines for Coding and Reporting

🖉 Complication\Comorbidity   🖉 Major C\C   Excludes 1   Excludes 2   Includes   Use additional   Code first   Code also

- **I68　Cerebrovascular disorders in diseases classified elsewhere**
  - **I68.0　Cerebral amyloid angiopathy**

    Code first underlying amyloidosis (E85.-)
  - **I68.2　Cerebral arteritis in other diseases classified elsewhere 🐾**

    Code first underlying disease

Excludes1	cerebral arteritis (in): 　listerosis (A32.89) 　systemic lupus erythematosus 　　(M32.19) 　syphilis (A52.04) 　tuberculosis (A18.89)
  - **I68.8　Other cerebrovascular disorders in diseases classified elsewhere**

    Code first underlying disease

Excludes1	syphilitic cerebral aneurysm (A52.05)

OGCR Section I.c.9.b.

Sequelae of Cerebrovascular Disease
1) Category I69, Sequelae of Cerebrovascular disease
Category 169 is used to indicate conditions classifiable to categories I60-I67 as the causes of late effects (neurologic deficits), themselves classified elsewhere. These "late effects" include neurologic deficits that persist after initial onset of conditions classifiable to categories I60-I67. The neurologic deficits caused by cerebrovascular disease may be present from the onset of may arise at any time after the onset of the condition classifiable to categories I60-I67.

2) Codes from category I69 with codes from I60-I67
Codes from category I69 may be assigned on a health care record with codes from I60-I67, if the patient has a current cerebrovascular accident (CVA) and deficits from an old CVA.

- **I69　Sequelae of cerebrovascular disease**

  Note: Category I69 is to be used to indicate conditions in I60-I67 as the cause of sequelae. The "sequelae" include conditions specified as such or as residuals which may occur at any time after the onset of the causal condition.

Excludes1	personal history of cerebral infarction 　without residual deficit (Z86.73) personal history of prolonged reversible 　ischemic neurologic deficit (PRIND) 　(Z86.73) personal history of reversible ischemic 　neurologcial deficit (RIND) (Z86.73) sequelae of traumatic intracranial injury (S06.-) transient ischemic attack (TIA) (G45.9)

  - **I69.0　Sequelae of nontraumatic subarachnoid hemorrhage**
    - **I69.00　Unspecified sequelae of nontraumatic subarachnoid hemorrhage**
    - **I69.01　Cognitive deficits following nontraumatic subarachnoid hemorrhage**
    - **I69.02　Speech and language deficits following nontraumatic subarachnoid hemorrhage**
      - **I69.020　Aphasia following nontraumatic subarachnoid hemorrhage**
      - **I69.021　Dysphasia following nontraumatic subarachnoid hemorrhage**
      - **I69.022　Dysarthria following nontraumatic subarachnoid hemorrhage**
      - **I69.023　Fluency disorder following nontraumatic subarachnoid hemorrhage**

        Stuttering following nontraumatic subarachnoid hemorrhage
      - **I69.028　Other speech and language deficits following nontraumatic subarachnoid hemorrhage**
  - **I69.03　Monoplegia of upper limb following nontraumatic subarachnoid hemorrhage**
    - **I69.031　Monoplegia of upper limb following nontraumatic subarachnoid hemorrhage affecting right dominant side**
    - **I69.032　Monoplegia of upper limb following nontraumatic subarachnoid hemorrhage affecting left dominant side**
    - **I69.033　Monoplegia of upper limb following nontraumatic subarachnoid hemorrhage affecting right non-dominant side**
    - **I69.034　Monoplegia of upper limb following nontraumatic subarachnoid hemorrhage affecting left non-dominant side**
    - **I69.039　Monoplegia of upper limb following nontraumatic subarachnoid hemorrhage affecting unspecified side**
  - **I69.04　Monoplegia of lower limb following nontraumatic subarachnoid hemorrhage**
    - **I69.041　Monoplegia of lower limb following nontraumatic subarachnoid hemorrhage affecting right dominant side**
    - **I69.042　Monoplegia of lower limb following nontraumatic subarachnoid hemorrhage affecting left dominant side**
    - **I69.043　Monoplegia of lower limb following nontraumatic subarachnoid hemorrhage affecting right non-dominant side**
    - **I69.044　Monoplegia of lower limb following nontraumatic subarachnoid hemorrhage affecting left non-dominant side**
    - **I69.049　Monoplegia of lower limb following nontraumatic subarachnoid hemorrhage affecting unspecified side**
  - **I69.05　Hemiplegia and hemiparesis following nontraumatic subarachnoid hemorrhage**
    - **I69.051　Hemiplegia and hemiparesis following nontraumatic subarachnoid hemorrhage affecting right dominant side**
    - **I69.052　Hemiplegia and hemiparesis following nontraumatic subarachnoid hemorrhage affecting left dominant side**
    - **I69.053　Hemiplegia and hemiparesis following nontraumatic subarachnoid hemorrhage affecting right non-dominant side**
    - **I69.054　Hemiplegia and hemiparesis following nontraumatic subarachnoid hemorrhage affecting left non-dominant side**

● Unacceptable First-Listed Diagnosis　　● Use Additional Character(s)　　▨ Unspecified　　**OGCR** Official Guidelines for Coding and Reporting

🐾 Complication\Comorbidity　🐾 Major C\C　 Excludes 1 　 Excludes 2 　 Includes 　 Use additional 　 Code first 　 Code also

◼ **I69.059 Hemiplegia and hemiparesis following nontraumatic subarachnoid hemorrhage affecting unspecified side**

● **I69.06 Other paralytic syndrome following nontraumatic subarachnoid hemorrhage**

Use additional code to identify type of paralytic syndrome, such as:
Locked-in state (G83.5)
Quadriplegia (G82.39, G82.49, G82.8)

Excludes1 hemiplegia/hemiparesis following nontraumatic subarachnoid hemorrhage (I69.05-)
monoplegia of lower limb following nontraumatic subarachnoid hemorrhage (I69.04-)
monoplegia of upper limb following nontraumatic subarachnoid hemorrhage (I69.03-)

I69.061 Other paralytic syndrome following nontraumatic subarachnoid hemorrhage affecting right dominant side

I69.062 Other paralytic syndrome following nontraumatic subarachnoid hemorrhage affecting left dominant side

I69.063 Other paralytic syndrome following nontraumatic subarachnoid hemorrhage affecting right non-dominant side

I69.064 Other paralytic syndrome following nontraumatic subarachnoid hemorrhage affecting left non-dominant side

I69.065 Other paralytic syndrome following nontraumatic subarachnoid hemorrhage, bilateral

◼ **I69.069 Other paralytic syndrome following nontraumatic subarachnoid hemorrhage affecting unspecified side**

● **I69.09 Other sequelae of nontraumatic subarachnoid hemorrhage**

I69.090 Apraxia following nontraumatic subarachnoid hemorrhage

I69.091 Dysphagia following nontraumatic subarachnoid hemorrhage

Use additional code to identify the type of dysphagia, if known (R13.1-)

I69.092 Facial weakness following nontraumatic subarachnoid hemorrhage
Facial droop following nontraumatic subarachnoid hemorrhage

I69.093 Ataxia following nontraumatic subarachnoid hemorrhage

I69.098 Other sequelae following nontraumatic subarachnoid hemorrhage
Alterations of sensation following nontraumatic subarachnoid hemorrhage
Disturbance of vision following nontraumatic subarachnoid hemorrhage

Use additional code to identify the sequelae

● **I69.1 Sequelae of nontraumatic intracerebral hemorrhage**

◼ **I69.10 Unspecified sequelae of nontraumatic intracerebral hemorrhage**

I69.11 Cognitive deficits following nontraumatic intracerebral hemorrhage

● **I69.12 Speech and language deficits following nontraumatic intracerebral hemorrhage**

I69.120 Aphasia following nontraumatic intracerebral hemorrhage

I69.121 Dysphasia following nontraumatic intracerebral hemorrhage

I69.122 Dysarthria following nontraumatic intracerebral hemorrhage

I69.123 Fluency disorder following nontraumatic intracerebral hemorrhage
Stuttering following nontraumatic subarachnoid hemorrhage

I69.128 Other speech and language deficits following nontraumatic intracerebral hemorrhage

● **I69.13 Monoplegia of upper limb following nontraumatic intracerebral hemorrhage**

I69.131 Monoplegia of upper limb following nontraumatic intracerebral hemorrhage affecting right dominant side

I69.132 Monoplegia of upper limb following nontraumatic intracerebral hemorrhage affecting left dominant side

I69.133 Monoplegia of upper limb following nontraumatic intracerebral hemorrhage affecting right non-dominant side

I69.134 Monoplegia of upper limb following nontraumatic intracerebral hemorrhage affecting left non-dominant side

◼ **I69.139 Monoplegia of upper limb following nontraumatic intracerebral hemorrhage affecting unspecified side**

● **I69.14 Monoplegia of lower limb following nontraumatic intracerebral hemorrhage**

I69.141 Monoplegia of lower limb following nontraumatic intracerebral hemorrhage affecting right dominant side

I69.142 Monoplegia of lower limb following nontraumatic intracerebral hemorrhage affecting left dominant side

I69.143 Monoplegia of lower limb following nontraumatic intracerebral hemorrhage affecting right non-dominant side

I69.144 Monoplegia of lower limb following nontraumatic intracerebral hemorrhage affecting left non-dominant side

■ **I69.149 Monoplegia of lower limb following nontraumatic intracerebral hemorrhage affecting unspecified side**

● **I69.15 Hemiplegia and hemiparesis following nontraumatic intracerebral hemorrhage**

I69.151 Hemiplegia and hemiparesis following nontraumatic intracerebral hemorrhage affecting right dominant side

I69.152 Hemiplegia and hemiparesis following nontraumatic intracerebral hemorrhage affecting left dominant side

I69.153 Hemiplegia and hemiparesis following nontraumatic intracerebral hemorrhage affecting right non-dominant side

I69.154 Hemiplegia and hemiparesis following nontraumatic intracerebral hemorrhage affecting left non-dominant side

■ **I69.159 Hemiplegia and hemiparesis following nontraumatic intracerebral hemorrhage affecting unspecified side**

● **I69.16 Other paralytic syndrome following nontraumatic intracerebral hemorrhage**

Use additional code to identify type of paralytic syndrome, such as:
Locked-in state (G83.5)
Quadriplegia (G82.39, G82.49, G82.8)

Excludes1	hemiplegia/hemiparesis following nontraumatic intracerebral hemorrhage (I69.15-)
	monoplegia of lower limb following nontraumatic intracerebral hemorrhage (I69.14-)
	monoplegia of upper limb following nontraumatic intracerebral hemorrhage (I69.13-)

I69.161 Other paralytic syndrome following nontraumatic intracerebral hemorrhage affecting right dominant side

I69.162 Other paralytic syndrome following nontraumatic intracerebral hemorrhage affecting left dominant side

I69.163 Other paralytic syndrome following nontraumatic intracerebral hemorrhage affecting right non-dominant side

I69.164 Other paralytic syndrome following nontraumatic intracerebral hemorrhage affecting left non-dominant side

I69.165 Other paralytic syndrome following nontraumatic intracerebral hemorrhage, bilateral

■ **I69.169 Other paralytic syndrome following nontraumatic intracerebral hemorrhage affecting unspecified side**

● **I69.19 Other sequelae of nontraumatic intracerebral hemorrhage**

I69.190 Apraxia following nontraumatic intracerebral hemorrhage

I69.191 Dysphagia following nontraumatic intracerebral hemorrhage

Use additional code to identify the type of dysphagia, if known (R13.1-)

I69.192 Facial weakness following nontraumatic intracerebral hemorrhage

Facial droop following nontraumatic intracerebral hemorrhage

I69.193 Ataxia following nontraumatic intracerebral hemorrhage

I69.198 Other sequelae of nontraumatic intracerebral hemorrhage

Alteration of sensations following nontraumatic intracerebral hemorrhage
Disturbance of vision following nontraumatic intracerebral hemorrhage

Use additional code to identify the sequelae

● **I69.2 Sequelae of other nontraumatic intracranial hemorrhage**

■ **I69.20 Unspecified sequelae of other nontraumatic intracranial hemorrhage**

I69.21 Cognitive deficits following other nontraumatic intracranial hemorrhage

● **I69.22 Speech and language deficits following other nontraumatic intracranial hemorrhage**

I69.220 Aphasia following other nontraumatic intracranial hemorrhage

I69.221 Dysphasia following other nontraumatic intracranial hemorrhage

I69.222 Dysarthria following other nontraumatic intracranial hemorrhage

I69.223 Fluency disorder following other nontraumatic intracranial hemorrhage

Stuttering following nontraumatic subarachnoid hemorrhage

I69.228 Other speech and language deficits following other nontraumatic intracranial hemorrhage

● **I69.23 Monoplegia of upper limb following other nontraumatic intracranial hemorrhage**

I69.231 Monoplegia of upper limb following other nontraumatic intracranial hemorrhage affecting right dominant side

● Unacceptable First-Listed Diagnosis   ● Use Additional Character(s)   ■ Unspecified   OGCR Official Guidelines for Coding and Reporting
🏷 Complication\Comorbidity   🏷 Major C\C   Excludes 1   Excludes 2   Includes   Use additional   Code first   Code also

CHAPTER 9 (I00-I99)

1029

I69.232   Monoplegia of upper limb
following other nontraumatic
intracranial hemorrhage affecting
left dominant side

I69.233   Monoplegia of upper limb
following other nontraumatic
intracranial hemorrhage affecting
right non-dominant side

I69.234   Monoplegia of upper limb
following other nontraumatic
intracranial hemorrhage affecting
left non-dominant side

■ I69.239   Monoplegia of upper limb
following other nontraumatic
intracranial hemorrhage affecting
unspecified side

● I69.24   Monoplegia of lower limb following other
nontraumatic intracranial hemorrhage

I69.241   Monoplegia of lower limb
following other nontraumatic
intracranial hemorrhage affecting
right dominant side

I69.242   Monoplegia of lower limb
following other nontraumatic
intracranial hemorrhage affecting
left dominant side

I69.243   Monoplegia of lower limb
following other nontraumatic
intracranial hemorrhage affecting
right non-dominant side

I69.244   Monoplegia of lower limb
following other nontraumatic
intracranial hemorrhage affecting
left non-dominant side

■ I69.249   Monoplegia of lower limb
following other nontraumatic
intracranial hemorrhage affecting
unspecified side

● I69.25   Hemiplegia and hemiparesis following
other nontraumatic intracranial
hemorrhage

I69.251   Hemiplegia and hemiparesis
following other nontraumatic
intracranial hemorrhage affecting
right dominant side

I69.252   Hemiplegia and hemiparesis
following other nontraumatic
intracranial hemorrhage affecting
left dominant side

I69.253   Hemiplegia and hemiparesis
following other nontraumatic
intracranial hemorrhage affecting
right non-dominant side

I69.254   Hemiplegia and hemiparesis
following other nontraumatic
intracranial hemorrhage affecting
left non-dominant side

■ I69.259   Hemiplegia and hemiparesis
following other nontraumatic
intracranial hemorrhage affecting
unspecified side

● I69.26   Other paralytic syndrome following other
nontraumatic intracranial hemorrhage

Use additional code to identify type of
paralytic syndrome, such as:
Locked-in state (G83.5)
Quadriplegia (G82.39, G82.49, G82.8)

Excludes 1   hemiplegia/hemiparesis
following other
nontraumatic
intracranial hemorrhage
(I69.25-)
monoplegia of lower
limb following
other nontraumatic
intracranial hemorrhage
(I69.24-)
monoplegia of upper
limb following
other nontraumatic
intracranial hemorrhage
(I69.23-)

I69.261   Other paralytic syndrome
following other nontraumatic
intracranial hemorrhage affecting
right dominant side

I69.262   Other paralytic syndrome
following other nontraumatic
intracranial hemorrhage affecting
left dominant side

I69.263   Other paralytic syndrome
following other nontraumatic
intracranial hemorrhage affecting
right non-dominant side

I69.264   Other paralytic syndrome
following other nontraumatic
intracranial hemorrhage affecting
left non-dominant side

I69.265   Other paralytic syndrome
following other nontraumatic
intracranial hemorrhage, bilateral

■ I69.269   Other paralytic syndrome
following other nontraumatic
intracranial hemorrhage affecting
unspecified side

● I69.29   Other sequelae of other nontraumatic
intracranial hemorrhage

I69.290   Apraxia following other
nontraumatic intracranial
hemorrhage

I69.291   Dysphagia following other
nontraumatic intracranial
hemorrhage

Use additional code to identify
the type of dysphagia, if
known (R13.1-)

I69.292   Facial weakness following
other nontraumatic intracranial
hemorrhage
Facial droop following other
nontraumatic intracranial
hemorrhage

I69.293   Ataxia following other
nontraumatic intracranial
hemorrhage

● Unacceptable First-Listed Diagnosis   ● Use Additional Character(s)   ■ Unspecified   OGCR Official Guidelines for Coding and Reporting
🦠 Complication\Comorbidity   🦠 Major C\C   Excludes 1   Excludes 2   Includes   Use additional   Code first   Code also

I69.298   Other sequelae of other nontraumatic intracranial hemorrhage

    Alteration of sensation following other nontraumatic intracranial hemorrhage

    Disturbance of vision following other nontraumatic intracranial hemorrhage

    Use additional code to identify the sequelae

● I69.3   **Sequelae of cerebral infarction**
    Sequelae of stroke NOS

▪ I69.30   Unspecified sequelae of cerebral infarction

I69.31   Cognitive deficits following cerebral infarction

● I69.32   Speech and language deficits following cerebral infarction

    I69.320   Aphasia following cerebral infarction

    I69.321   Dysphasia following cerebral infarction

    I69.322   Dysarthria following cerebral infarction

    I69.323   Fluency disorder following cerebral infarction
       Stuttering following nontraumatic subarachnoid hemorrhage

    I69.328   Other speech and language deficits following cerebral infarction

● I69.33   Monoplegia of upper limb following cerebral infarction

    I69.331   Monoplegia of upper limb following cerebral infarction affecting right dominant side

    I69.332   Monoplegia of upper limb following cerebral infarction affecting left dominant side

    I69.333   Monoplegia of upper limb following cerebral infarction affecting right non-dominant side

    I69.334   Monoplegia of upper limb following cerebral infarction affecting left non-dominant side

    ▪ I69.339   Monoplegia of upper limb following cerebral infarction affecting unspecified side

● I69.34   Monoplegia of lower limb following cerebral infarction

    I69.341   Monoplegia of lower limb following cerebral infarction affecting right dominant side

    I69.342   Monoplegia of lower limb following cerebral infarction affecting left dominant side

    I69.343   Monoplegia of lower limb following cerebral infarction affecting right non-dominant side

    I69.344   Monoplegia of lower limb following cerebral infarction affecting left non-dominant side

    ▪ I69.349   Monoplegia of lower limb following cerebral infarction affecting unspecified side

● I69.35   Hemiplegia and hemiparesis following cerebral infarction

    I69.351   Hemiplegia and hemiparesis following cerebral infarction affecting right dominant side

    I69.352   Hemiplegia and hemiparesis following cerebral infarction affecting left dominant side

    I69.353   Hemiplegia and hemiparesis following cerebral infarction affecting right non-dominant side

    I69.354   Hemiplegia and hemiparesis following cerebral infarction affecting left non-dominant side

    ▪ I69.359   Hemiplegia and hemiparesis following cerebral infarction affecting unspecified side

● I69.36   Other paralytic syndrome following cerebral infarction

    Use additional code to identify type of paralytic syndrome, such as:
    Locked-in state (G83.5)
    Quadriplegia (G82.39, G82.49, G82.8)

    Excludes1   hemiplegia/hemiparesis following cerebral infarction (I69.35-)
       monoplegia of lower limb following cerebral infarction (I69.34-)
       monoplegia of upper limb following cerebral infarction (I69.33-)

    I69.361   Other paralytic syndrome following cerebral infarction affecting right dominant side

    I69.362   Other paralytic syndrome following cerebral infarction affecting left dominant side

    I69.363   Other paralytic syndrome following cerebral infarction affecting right non-dominant side

    I69.364   Other paralytic syndrome following cerebral infarction affecting left non-dominant side

    I69.365   Other paralytic syndrome following cerebral infarction, bilateral

    ▪ I69.369   Other paralytic syndrome following cerebral infarction affecting unspecified side

● I69.39   Other sequelae of cerebral infarction

    I69.390   Apraxia following cerebral infarction

    I69.391   Dysphagia following cerebral infarction
       Use additional code to identify the type of dysphagia, if known (R13.1-)

    I69.392   Facial weakness following cerebral infarction
       Facial droop following cerebral infarction

    I69.393   Ataxia following cerebral infarction

● Unacceptable First-Listed Diagnosis   ● Use Additional Character(s)   ▪ Unspecified   **OGCR** Official Guidelines for Coding and Reporting

🔗 Complication\Comorbidity   🔗 Major C\C   Excludes 1   Excludes 2   Includes   Use additional   Code first   Code also

1031

CHAPTER 9 (I00-I99)

I69.398   **Other sequelae of cerebral infarction**
Alteration of sensation following cerebral infarction
Disturbance of vision following cerebral infarction
Use additional code to identify the sequelae

● I69.8   **Sequelae of other cerebrovascular diseases**
Excludes1   sequelae of traumatic intracranial injury (S06.-)

◻ I69.80   **Unspecified sequelae of other cerebrovascular disease**

I69.81   **Cognitive deficits following other cerebrovascular disease**

● I69.82   **Speech and language deficits following other cerebrovascular disease**

◻ I69.820   **Aphasia following other cerebrovascular disease**

I69.821   **Dysphasia following other cerebrovascular disease**

I69.822   **Dysarthria following other cerebrovascular disease**

I69.823   **Fluency disorder following other cerebrovascular disease**
Stuttering following nontraumatic subarachnoid hemorrhage

I69.828   **Other speech and language deficits following other cerebrovascular disease**

● I69.83   **Monoplegia of upper limb following other cerebrovascular disease**

I69.831   **Monoplegia of upper limb following other cerebrovascular disease affecting right dominant side**

I69.832   **Monoplegia of upper limb following other cerebrovascular disease affecting left dominant side**

I69.833   **Monoplegia of upper limb following other cerebrovascular disease affecting right non-dominant side**

I69.834   **Monoplegia of upper limb following other cerebrovascular disease affecting left non-dominant side**

◻ I69.839   **Monoplegia of upper limb following other cerebrovascular disease affecting unspecified side**

● I69.84   **Monoplegia of lower limb following other cerebrovascular disease**

I69.841   **Monoplegia of lower limb following other cerebrovascular disease affecting right dominant side**

I69.842   **Monoplegia of lower limb following other cerebrovascular disease affecting left dominant side**

I69.843   **Monoplegia of lower limb following other cerebrovascular disease affecting right non-dominant side**

I69.844   **Monoplegia of lower limb following other cerebrovascular disease affecting left non-dominant side**

◻ I69.849   **Monoplegia of lower limb following other cerebrovascular disease affecting unspecified side**

● I69.85   **Hemiplegia and hemiparesis following other cerebrovascular disease**

I69.851   **Hemiplegia and hemiparesis following other cerebrovascular disease affecting right dominant side**

I69.852   **Hemiplegia and hemiparesis following other cerebrovascular disease affecting left dominant side**

I69.853   **Hemiplegia and hemiparesis following other cerebrovascular disease affecting right non-dominant side**

I69.854   **Hemiplegia and hemiparesis following other cerebrovascular disease affecting left non-dominant side**

◻ I69.859   **Hemiplegia and hemiparesis following other cerebrovascular disease affecting unspecified side**

● I69.86   **Other paralytic syndrome following other cerebrovascular disease**
Use additional code to identify type of paralytic syndrome, such as:
Locked-in state (G83.5)
Quadriplegia (G82.39, G82.49, G82.8)
Excludes1   hemiplegia/hemiparesis following other cerebrovascular disease (I69.85-)
monoplegia of lower limb following other cerebrovascular disease (I69.84-)
monoplegia of upper limb following other cerebrovascular disease (I69.83-)

I69.861   **Other paralytic syndrome following other cerebrovascular disease affecting right dominant side**

I69.862   **Other paralytic syndrome following other cerebrovascular disease affecting left dominant side**

I69.863   **Other paralytic syndrome following other cerebrovascular disease affecting right non-dominant side**

I69.864   **Other paralytic syndrome following other cerebrovascular disease affecting left non-dominant side**

I69.865   **Other paralytic syndrome following other cerebrovascular disease, bilateral**

◻ I69.869   **Other paralytic syndrome following other cerebrovascular disease affecting unspecified side**

● Unacceptable First-Listed Diagnosis   ● Use Additional Character(s)   ◻ Unspecified   **OGCR** Official Guidelines for Coding and Reporting
🅲 Complication\Comorbidity   🅜 Major C\C   Excludes 1   Excludes 2   Includes   Use additional   Code first   Code also

● I69.89 **Other sequelae of other cerebrovascular disease**

I69.890 **Apraxia following other cerebrovascular disease**

I69.891 **Dysphagia following other cerebrovascular disease**

> Use additional code to identify the type of dysphagia, if known (R13.1-)

I69.892 **Facial weakness following other cerebrovascular disease**

> Facial droop following other cerebrovascular disease

I69.893 **Ataxia following other cerebrovascular disease**

I69.898 **Other sequelae of other cerebrovascular disease**

> Alteration of sensation following other cerebrovascular disease
> Disturbance of vision following other cerebrovascular disease
> Use additional code to identify the sequelae

● I69.9 **Sequelae of unspecified cerebrovascular diseases**

> | Excludes 1 | sequelae of stroke (I63.3) |
> |---|---|
> | | sequelae of traumatic intracranial injury (S06.-) |

■ I69.90 **Unspecified sequelae of unspecified cerebrovascular disease**

■ I69.91 **Cognitive deficits following unspecified cerebrovascular disease**

● I69.92 **Speech and language deficits following unspecified cerebrovascular disease**

■ I69.920 **Aphasia following unspecified cerebrovascular disease**

■ I69.921 **Dysphasia following unspecified cerebrovascular disease**

■ I69.922 **Dysarthria following unspecified cerebrovascular disease**

■ I69.923 **Fluency disorder following unspecified cerebrovascular disease**

> Stuttering following nontraumatic subarachnoid hemorrhage

■ I69.928 **Other speech and language deficits following unspecified cerebrovascular disease**

● I69.93 **Monoplegia of upper limb following unspecified cerebrovascular disease**

■ I69.931 **Monoplegia of upper limb following unspecified cerebrovascular disease affecting right dominant side**

■ I69.932 **Monoplegia of upper limb following unspecified cerebrovascular disease affecting left dominant side**

■ I69.933 **Monoplegia of upper limb following unspecified cerebrovascular disease affecting right non-dominant side**

■ I69.934 **Monoplegia of upper limb following unspecified cerebrovascular disease affecting left non-dominant side**

■ I69.939 **Monoplegia of upper limb following unspecified cerebrovascular disease affecting unspecified side**

● I69.94 **Monoplegia of lower limb following unspecified cerebrovascular disease**

■ I69.941 **Monoplegia of lower limb following unspecified cerebrovascular disease affecting right dominant side**

■ I69.942 **Monoplegia of lower limb following unspecified cerebrovascular disease affecting left dominant side**

■ I69.943 **Monoplegia of lower limb following unspecified cerebrovascular disease affecting right non-dominant side**

■ I69.944 **Monoplegia of lower limb following unspecified cerebrovascular disease affecting left non-dominant side**

■ I69.949 **Monoplegia of lower limb following unspecified cerebrovascular disease affecting unspecified side**

● I69.95 **Hemiplegia and hemiparesis following unspecified cerebrovascular disease**

■ I69.951 **Hemiplegia and hemiparesis following unspecified cerebrovascular disease affecting right dominant side** ✪

■ I69.952 **Hemiplegia and hemiparesis following unspecified cerebrovascular disease affecting left dominant side** ✪

■ I69.953 **Hemiplegia and hemiparesis following unspecified cerebrovascular disease affecting right non-dominant side** ✪

■ I69.954 **Hemiplegia and hemiparesis following unspecified cerebrovascular disease affecting left non-dominant side** ✪

■ I69.959 **Hemiplegia and hemiparesis following unspecified cerebrovascular disease affecting unspecified side** ✪

● Unacceptable First-Listed Diagnosis   ● Use Additional Character(s)   ■ Unspecified   **OGCR** Official Guidelines for Coding and Reporting

✪ Complication\Comorbidity   ✪ Major C\C | Excludes 1 | | Excludes 2 | Includes   Use additional   Code first   Code also

1033

CHAPTER 9 (I00-I99)

- **I69.96** Other paralytic syndrome following unspecified cerebrovascular disease

  Use additional code to identify type of paralytic syndrome, such as:
  Locked-in state (G83.5)
  Quadriplegia (G82.39, G82.49, G82.8)

  Excludes1 hemiplegia/hemiparesis following unspecified cerebrovascular disease (I69.95-)
  monoplegia of lower limb following unspecified cerebrovascular disease (I69.94-)
  monoplegia of upper limb following unspecified cerebrovascular disease (I69.93-)

  - I69.961 Other paralytic syndrome following unspecified cerebrovascular disease affecting right dominant side
  - I69.962 Other paralytic syndrome following unspecified cerebrovascular disease affecting left dominant side
  - I69.963 Other paralytic syndrome following unspecified cerebrovascular disease affecting right non-dominant side
  - I69.964 Other paralytic syndrome following unspecified cerebrovascular disease affecting left non-dominant side
  - I69.965 Other paralytic syndrome following unspecified cerebrovascular disease, bilateral
  - I69.969 Other paralytic syndrome following unspecified cerebrovascular disease affecting unspecified side

- **I69.99** Other sequelae of unspecified cerebrovascular disease

  - I69.990 Apraxia following unspecified cerebrovascular disease
  - I69.991 Dysphagia following unspecified cerebrovascular disease

    Use additional code to identify the type of dysphagia, if known (R13.1-)

  - I69.992 Facial weakness following unspecified cerebrovascular disease

    Facial droop following unspecified cerebrovascular disease

  - I69.993 Ataxia following unspecified cerebrovascular disease
  - I69.998 Other sequelae following unspecified cerebrovascular disease

    Alteration in sensation following unspecified cerebrovascular disease
    Disturbance of vision following unspecified cerebrovascular disease

    Use additional code to identify the sequelae

DISEASES OF ARTERIES, ARTERIOLES AND CAPILLARIES (I70-I79)

- **I70** Atherosclerosis

  Includes arteriolosclerosis
  arterial degeneration
  arteriosclerosis
  arteriosclerotic vascular disease
  arteriovascular degeneration
  atheroma
  endarteritis deformans or obliterans
  senile arteritis
  senile endarteritis
  vascular degeneration

  Use additional code to identify:
  exposure to environmental tobacco smoke (Z77.22)
  history of tobacco use (Z87.891)
  occupational exposure to environmental tobacco smoke (Z57.31)
  tobacco dependence (F17.-)
  tobacco use (Z72.0)

  Excludes2 arteriosclerotic cardiovascular disease (I25.1-)
  arteriosclerotic heart disease (I25.1-)
  atheroembolism (I75.-)
  cerebral atherosclerosis (I67.2)
  coronary atherosclerosis (I25.1-)
  mesenteric atherosclerosis (K55.1)
  precerebral atherosclerosis (I67.2)
  primary pulmonary atherosclerosis (I27.0)

  - **I70.0** Atherosclerosis of aorta
  - **I70.1** Atherosclerosis of renal artery
    Goldblatt's kidney

    Excludes2 atherosclerosis of renal arterioles (I12.-)

(See Plates 500, 501, and 502 on pages NAP-12 – NAP-14.)

  - **I70.2** Atherosclerosis of native arteries of the extremities
    Mönckeberg's (medial) sclerosis

    Use additional code, if applicable, to identify chronic total occlusion of artery of extremity (I70.92)

    Excludes2 atherosclerosis of bypass graft of extremities (I70.30-I70.79)

    - **I70.20** Unspecified atherosclerosis of native arteries of extremities

      - I70.201 Unspecified atherosclerosis of native arteries of extremities, right leg
      - I70.202 Unspecified atherosclerosis of native arteries of extremities, left leg
      - I70.203 Unspecified atherosclerosis of native arteries of extremities, bilateral legs
      - I70.208 Unspecified atherosclerosis of native arteries of extremities, other extremity
      - I70.209 Unspecified atherosclerosis of native arteries of extremities, unspecified extremity

    - **I70.21** Atherosclerosis of native arteries of extremities with intermittent claudication

      - I70.211 Atherosclerosis of native arteries of extremities with intermittent claudication, right leg

- Unacceptable First-Listed Diagnosis
- Use Additional Character(s)
- Unspecified
- **OGCR** Official Guidelines for Coding and Reporting

- Complication\Comorbidity
- Major C\C
- Excludes 1
- Excludes 2
- Includes
- Use additional
- Code first
- Code also

I70.212 Atherosclerosis of native arteries of extremities with intermittent claudication, left leg

I70.213 Atherosclerosis of native arteries of extremities with intermittent claudication, bilateral legs

I70.218 Atherosclerosis of native arteries of extremities with intermittent claudication, other extremity

■ **I70.219** Atherosclerosis of native arteries of extremities with intermittent claudication, unspecified extremity

● **I70.22** Atherosclerosis of native arteries of extremities with rest pain

Includes   any condition classifiable to I70.21-

I70.221 Atherosclerosis of native arteries of extremities with rest pain, right leg

I70.222 Atherosclerosis of native arteries of extremities with rest pain, left leg

I70.223 Atherosclerosis of native arteries of extremities with rest pain, bilateral legs

I70.228 Atherosclerosis of native arteries of extremities with rest pain, other extremity

■ **I70.229** Atherosclerosis of native arteries of extremities with rest pain, unspecified extremity

● **I70.23** Atherosclerosis of native arteries of right leg with ulceration

Includes   any condition classifiable to I70.211 and I70.221

Use additional code to identify severity of ulcer (L97.- with fifth character 1)

I70.231 Atherosclerosis of native arteries of right leg with ulceration of thigh

I70.232 Atherosclerosis of native arteries of right leg with ulceration of calf

I70.233 Atherosclerosis of native arteries of right leg with ulceration of ankle

I70.234 Atherosclerosis of native arteries of right leg with ulceration of heel and midfoot
    Atherosclerosis of native arteries of right leg with ulceration of plantar surface of midfoot

I70.235 Atherosclerosis of native arteries of right leg with ulceration of other part of foot
    Atherosclerosis of native arteries of right leg extremities with ulceration of toe

I70.238 Atherosclerosis of native arteries of right leg with ulceration of other part of lower right leg

■ **I70.239** Atherosclerosis of native arteries of right leg with ulceration of unspecified site

● **I70.24** Atherosclerosis of native arteries of left leg with ulceration

Includes   any condition classifiable to I70.212 and I70.222

Use additional code to identify severity of ulcer (L97.- with fifth character 2)

I70.241 Atherosclerosis of native arteries of left leg with ulceration of thigh

I70.242 Atherosclerosis of native arteries of left leg with ulceration of calf

I70.243 Atherosclerosis of native arteries of left leg with ulceration of ankle

I70.244 Atherosclerosis of native arteries of left leg with ulceration of heel and midfoot
    Atherosclerosis of native arteries of left leg with ulceration of plantar surface of midfoot

I70.245 Atherosclerosis of native arteries of left leg with ulceration of other part of foot
    Atherosclerosis of native arteries of left leg extremities with ulceration of toe

I70.248 Atherosclerosis of native arteries of left leg with ulceration of other part of lower left leg

■ **I70.249** Atherosclerosis of native arteries of left leg with ulceration of unspecified site

I70.25 Atherosclerosis of native arteries of other extremities with ulceration

Includes   any condition classifiable to I70.218 and I70.228

Use additional code to identify the severity of the ulcer (L98.49-)

● **I70.26** Atherosclerosis of native arteries of extremities with gangrene

Includes   any condition classifiable to I70.21-, I70.22-, I70.23-, I70.24-, and I70.25-

Use additional code to identify the severity of any ulcer (L98.49-), if applicable

I70.261 Atherosclerosis of native arteries of extremities with gangrene, right leg 🔹

I70.262 Atherosclerosis of native arteries of extremities with gangrene, left leg 🔹

I70.263 Atherosclerosis of native arteries of extremities with gangrene, bilateral legs 🔹

I70.268 Atherosclerosis of native arteries of extremities with gangrene, other extremity 🔹

■ **I70.269** Atherosclerosis of native arteries of extremities with gangrene, unspecified extremity 🔹

● **I70.29** Other atherosclerosis of native arteries of extremities

I70.291 Other atherosclerosis of native arteries of extremities, right leg

I70.292 Other atherosclerosis of native arteries of extremities, left leg

● Unacceptable First-Listed Diagnosis   ● Use Additional Character(s)   ■ Unspecified   **OGCR** Official Guidelines for Coding and Reporting
🔹 Complication\Comorbidity   🔸 Major C\C   Excludes 1   Excludes 2   Includes   Use additional   Code first   Code also

CHAPTER 9 (I00-I99)

1035

I70.293 Other atherosclerosis of native arteries of extremities, bilateral legs

I70.298 Other atherosclerosis of native arteries of extremities, other extremity

I70.299 Other atherosclerosis of native arteries of extremities, unspecified extremity

● I70.3 Atherosclerosis of unspecified type of bypass graft(s) of the extremities

Use additional code, if applicable, to identify chronic total occlusion of artery of extremity (I70.92)

Excludes1 embolism or thrombus of bypass graft(s) of extremities (T82.8-)

● I70.30 Unspecified atherosclerosis of unspecified type of bypass graft(s) of the extremities

70.301 Unspecified atherosclerosis of unspecified type of bypass graft(s) of the extremities, right leg

I70.302 Unspecified atherosclerosis of unspecified type of bypass graft(s) of the extremities, left leg

I70.303 Unspecified atherosclerosis of unspecified type of bypass graft(s) of the extremities, bilateral legs

I70.308 Unspecified atherosclerosis of unspecified type of bypass graft(s) of the extremities, other extremity

I70.309 Unspecified atherosclerosis of unspecified type of bypass graft(s) of the extremities, unspecified extremity

● I70.31 Atherosclerosis of unspecified type of bypass graft(s) of the extremities with intermittent claudication

I70.311 Atherosclerosis of unspecified type of bypass graft(s) of the extremities with intermittent claudication, right leg

I70.312 Atherosclerosis of unspecified type of bypass graft(s) of the extremities with intermittent claudication, left leg

I70.313 Atherosclerosis of unspecified type of bypass graft(s) of the extremities with intermittent claudication, bilateral legs

I70.318 Atherosclerosis of unspecified type of bypass graft(s) of the extremities with intermittent claudication, other extremity

I70.319 Atherosclerosis of unspecified type of bypass graft(s) of the extremities with intermittent claudication, unspecified extremity

● I70.32 Atherosclerosis of unspecified type of bypass graft(s) of the extremities with rest pain

Includes any condition classifiable to I70.31-

I70.321 Atherosclerosis of unspecified type of bypass graft(s) of the extremities with rest pain, right leg

I70.322 Atherosclerosis of unspecified type of bypass graft(s) of the extremities with rest pain, left leg

I70.323 Atherosclerosis of unspecified type of bypass graft(s) of the extremities with rest pain, bilateral legs

I70.328 Atherosclerosis of unspecified type of bypass graft(s) of the extremities with rest pain, other extremity

I70.329 Atherosclerosis of unspecified type of bypass graft(s) of the extremities with rest pain, unspecified extremity

● I70.33 Atherosclerosis of unspecified type of bypass graft(s) of the right leg with ulceration

Includes any condition classifiable to I70.311 and I70.321

Use additional code to identify severity of ulcer (L97.- with fifth character 1)

I70.331 Atherosclerosis of unspecified type of bypass graft(s) of the right leg with ulceration of thigh

I70.332 Atherosclerosis of unspecified type of bypass graft(s) of the right leg with ulceration of calf

I70.333 Atherosclerosis of unspecified type of bypass graft(s) of the right leg with ulceration of ankle

I70.334 Atherosclerosis of unspecified type of bypass graft(s) of the right leg with ulceration of heel and midfoot
Atherosclerosis of unspecified type of bypass graft(s) of right leg with ulceration of plantar surface of midfoot

I70.335 Atherosclerosis of unspecified type of bypass graft(s) of the right leg with ulceration of other part of foot
Atherosclerosis of unspecified type of bypass graft(s) of the right leg with ulceration of toe

I70.338 Atherosclerosis of unspecified type of bypass graft(s) of the right leg with ulceration of other part of lower leg

I70.339 Atherosclerosis of unspecified type of bypass graft(s) of the right leg with ulceration of unspecified site

● I70.34 Atherosclerosis of unspecified type of bypass graft(s) of the left leg with ulceration

Includes any condition classifiable to I70.312 and I70.322

Use additional code to identify severity of ulcer (L97.- with fifth character 2)

I70.341 Atherosclerosis of unspecified type of bypass graft(s) of the left leg with ulceration of thigh

I70.342 Atherosclerosis of unspecified type of bypass graft(s) of the left leg with ulceration of calf

● Unacceptable First-Listed Diagnosis ● Use Additional Character(s) Unspecified OGCR Official Guidelines for Coding and Reporting
Complication\Comorbidity Major C\C Excludes 1 Excludes 2 Includes Use additional Code first Code also

■ I70.343   Atherosclerosis of unspecified type of bypass graft(s) of the left leg with ulceration of ankle

■ I70.344   Atherosclerosis of unspecified type of bypass graft(s) of the left leg with ulceration of heel and midfoot
> Atherosclerosis of unspecified type of bypass graft(s) of left leg with ulceration of plantar surface of midfoot

■ I70.345   Atherosclerosis of unspecified type of bypass graft(s) of the left leg with ulceration of other part of foot
> Atherosclerosis of unspecified type of bypass graft(s) of the left leg with ulceration of toe

■ I70.348   Atherosclerosis of unspecified type of bypass graft(s) of the left leg with ulceration of other part of lower leg

■ I70.349   Atherosclerosis of unspecified type of bypass graft(s) of the left leg with ulceration of unspecified site

■ I70.35   Atherosclerosis of unspecified type of bypass graft(s) of other extremity with ulceration

> **Includes**   any condition classifiable to I70.318 and I70.328

> Use additional code to identify severity of ulcer (L98.49-)

● I70.36   Atherosclerosis of unspecified type of bypass graft(s) of the extremities with gangrene

> **Includes**   any condition classifiable to I70.31-, I70.32-, I70.33-, I70.34-, I70.35

> Use additional code to identify the severity of any ulcer (L98.49-), if applicable

■ I70.361   Atherosclerosis of unspecified type of bypass graft(s) of the extremities with gangrene, right leg

■ I70.362   Atherosclerosis of unspecified type of bypass graft(s) of the extremities with gangrene, left leg

■ I70.363   Atherosclerosis of unspecified type of bypass graft(s) of the extremities with gangrene, bilateral legs

■ I70.368   Atherosclerosis of unspecified type of bypass graft(s) of the extremities with gangrene, other extremity

■ I70.369   Atherosclerosis of unspecified type of bypass graft(s) of the extremities with gangrene, unspecified extremity

● I70.39   Other atherosclerosis of unspecified type of bypass graft(s) of the extremities

■ I70.391   Other atherosclerosis of unspecified type of bypass graft(s) of the extremities, right leg

■ I70.392   Other atherosclerosis of unspecified type of bypass graft(s) of the extremities, left leg

■ I70.393   Other atherosclerosis of unspecified type of bypass graft(s) of the extremities, bilateral legs

■ I70.398   Other atherosclerosis of unspecified type of bypass graft(s) of the extremities, other extremity

■ I70.399   Other atherosclerosis of unspecified type of bypass graft(s) of the extremities, unspecified extremity

● I70.4   Atherosclerosis of autologous vein bypass graft(s) of the extremities

> Use additional code, if applicable, to identify chronic total occlusion of artery of extremity (I70.92)

■ I70.40   Unspecified atherosclerosis of autologous vein bypass graft(s) of the extremities

■ I70.401   Unspecified atherosclerosis of autologous vein bypass graft(s) of the extremities, right leg

■ I70.402   Unspecified atherosclerosis of autologous vein bypass graft(s) of the extremities, left leg

■ I70.403   Unspecified atherosclerosis of autologous vein bypass graft(s) of the extremities, bilateral legs

■ I70.408   Unspecified atherosclerosis of autologous vein bypass graft(s) of the extremities, other extremity

■ I70.409   Unspecified atherosclerosis of autologous vein bypass graft(s) of the extremities, unspecified extremity

● I70.41   Atherosclerosis of autologous vein bypass graft(s) of the extremities with intermittent claudication

   I70.411   Atherosclerosis of autologous vein bypass graft(s) of the extremities with intermittent claudication, right leg

   I70.412   Atherosclerosis of autologous vein bypass graft(s) of the extremities with intermittent claudication, left leg

   I70.413   Atherosclerosis of autologous vein bypass graft(s) of the extremities with intermittent claudication, bilateral legs

   I70.418   Atherosclerosis of autologous vein bypass graft(s) of the extremities with intermittent claudication, other extremity

■ I70.419   Atherosclerosis of autologous vein bypass graft(s) of the extremities with intermittent claudication, unspecified extremity

● I70.42   Atherosclerosis of autologous vein bypass graft(s) of the extremities with rest pain

> **Includes**   any condition classifiable to I70.41-

   I70.421   Atherosclerosis of autologous vein bypass graft(s) of the extremities with rest pain, right leg

● Unacceptable First-Listed Diagnosis   ● Use Additional Character(s)   ■ Unspecified   **OGCR** Official Guidelines for Coding and Reporting

🍂 Complication\Comorbidity   🍂 Major C\C   Excludes 1   Excludes 2   Includes   Use additional   Code first   Code also

1037

CHAPTER 9 (I00-I99)

I70.422   Atherosclerosis of autologous vein bypass graft(s) of the extremities with rest pain, left leg

I70.423   Atherosclerosis of autologous vein bypass graft(s) of the extremities with rest pain, bilateral legs

I70.428   Atherosclerosis of autologous vein bypass graft(s) of the extremities with rest pain, other extremity

■ I70.429   Atherosclerosis of autologous vein bypass graft(s) of the extremities with rest pain, unspecified extremity

● I70.43   Atherosclerosis of autologous vein bypass graft(s) of the right leg with ulceration

     Includes   any condition classifiable to I70.411 and I70.421

     Use additional code to identify severity of ulcer (L97.- with fifth character 1)

I70.431   Atherosclerosis of autologous vein bypass graft(s) of the right leg with ulceration of thigh

I70.432   Atherosclerosis of autologous vein bypass graft(s) of the right leg with ulceration of calf

I70.433   Atherosclerosis of autologous vein bypass graft(s) of the right leg with ulceration of ankle

I70.434   Atherosclerosis of autologous vein bypass graft(s) of the right leg with ulceration of heel and midfoot

     Atherosclerosis of autologous vein bypass graft(s) of right leg with ulceration of plantar surface of midfoot

I70.435   Atherosclerosis of autologous vein bypass graft(s) of the right leg with ulceration of other part of foot

     Atherosclerosis of autologous vein bypass graft(s) of right leg with ulceration of toe

I70.438   Atherosclerosis of autologous vein bypass graft(s) of the right leg with ulceration of other part of lower leg

■ I70.439   Atherosclerosis of autologous vein bypass graft(s) of the right leg with ulceration of unspecified site

● I70.44   Atherosclerosis of autologous vein bypass graft(s) of the left leg with ulceration

     Includes   any condition classifiable to I70.412 and I70.422

     Use additional code to identify severity of ulcer (L97.- with fifth character 2)

I70.441   Atherosclerosis of autologous vein bypass graft(s) of the left leg with ulceration of thigh

I70.442   Atherosclerosis of autologous vein bypass graft(s) of the left leg with ulceration of calf

I70.443   Atherosclerosis of autologous vein bypass graft(s) of the left leg with ulceration of ankle

I70.444   Atherosclerosis of autologous vein bypass graft(s) of the left leg with ulceration of heel and midfoot

     Atherosclerosis of autologous vein bypass graft(s) of left leg with ulceration of plantar surface of midfoot

I70.445   Atherosclerosis of autologous vein bypass graft(s) of the left leg with ulceration of other part of foot

     Atherosclerosis of autologous vein bypass graft(s) of left leg with ulceration of toe

I70.448   Atherosclerosis of autologous vein bypass graft(s) of the left leg with ulceration of other part of lower leg

■ I70.449   Atherosclerosis of autologous vein bypass graft(s) of the left leg with ulceration of unspecified site

I70.45   Atherosclerosis of autologous vein bypass graft(s) of other extremity with ulceration

     Includes   any condition classifiable to I70.418, I70.428, and I70.438

     Use additional code to identify severity of ulcer (L98.49-)

● I70.46   Atherosclerosis of autologous vein bypass graft(s) of the extremities with gangrene

     Includes   any condition classifiable to I70.41-, I70.42-, and I70.43-, I70.44-, I70.45

     Use additional code to identify the severity of any ulcer (L98.49-), if applicable

I70.461   Atherosclerosis of autologous vein bypass graft(s) of the extremities with gangrene, right leg

I70.462   Atherosclerosis of autologous vein bypass graft(s) of the extremities with gangrene, left leg

I70.463   Atherosclerosis of autologous vein bypass graft(s) of the extremities with gangrene, bilateral legs

I70.468   Atherosclerosis of autologous vein bypass graft(s) of the extremities with gangrene, other extremity

■ I70.469   Atherosclerosis of autologous vein bypass graft(s) of the extremities with gangrene, unspecified extremity

● I70.49   Other atherosclerosis of autologous vein bypass graft(s) of the extremities

I70.491   Other atherosclerosis of autologous vein bypass graft(s) of the extremities, right leg

I70.492   Other atherosclerosis of autologous vein bypass graft(s) of the extremities, left leg

I70.493   Other atherosclerosis of autologous vein bypass graft(s) of the extremities, bilateral legs

● Unacceptable First-Listed Diagnosis   ● Use Additional Character(s)   ■ Unspecified   **OGCR** Official Guidelines for Coding and Reporting

⚙ Complication\Comorbidity   ⚙ Major C\C   Excludes 1   Excludes 2   Includes   Use additional   Code first   Code also

I70.498   Other atherosclerosis of autologous vein bypass graft(s) of the extremities, other extremity

◻ I70.499   Other atherosclerosis of autologous vein bypass graft(s) of the extremities, unspecified extremity

● I70.5   Atherosclerosis of nonautologous biological bypass graft(s) of the extremities

Use additional code, if applicable, to identify chronic total occlusion of artery of extremity (I70.92)

◻ I70.50   Unspecified atherosclerosis of nonautologous biological bypass graft(s) of the extremities

◻ I70.501   Unspecified atherosclerosis of nonautologous biological bypass graft(s) of the extremities, right leg

◻ I70.502   Unspecified atherosclerosis of nonautologous biological bypass graft(s) of the extremities, left leg

◻ I70.503   Unspecified atherosclerosis of nonautologous biological bypass graft(s) of the extremities, bilateral legs

◻ I70.508   Unspecified atherosclerosis of nonautologous biological bypass graft(s) of the extremities, other extremity

◻ I70.509   Unspecified atherosclerosis of nonautologous biological bypass graft(s) of the extremities, unspecified extremity

● I70.51   Atherosclerosis of nonautologous biological bypass graft(s) of the extremities intermittent claudication

I70.511   Atherosclerosis of nonautologous biological bypass graft(s) of the extremities intermittent claudication, right leg

I70.512   Atherosclerosis of nonautologous biological bypass graft(s) of the extremities intermittent claudication, left leg

I70.513   Atherosclerosis of nonautologous biological bypass graft(s) of the extremities intermittent claudication, bilateral legs

I70.518   Atherosclerosis of nonautologous biological bypass graft(s) of the extremities intermittent claudication, other extremity

◻ I70.519   Atherosclerosis of nonautologous biological bypass graft(s) of the extremities intermittent claudication, unspecified extremity

● I70.52   Atherosclerosis of nonautologous biological bypass graft(s) of the extremities with rest pain

    Includes   any condition classifiable to I70.51-

I70.521   Atherosclerosis of nonautologous biological bypass graft(s) of the extremities with rest pain, right leg

I70.522   Atherosclerosis of nonautologous biological bypass graft(s) of the extremities with rest pain, left leg

I70.523   Atherosclerosis of nonautologous biological bypass graft(s) of the extremities with rest pain, bilateral legs

I70.528   Atherosclerosis of nonautologous biological bypass graft(s) of the extremities with rest pain, other extremity

◻ I70.529   Atherosclerosis of nonautologous biological bypass graft(s) of the extremities with rest pain, unspecified extremity

● I70.53   Atherosclerosis of nonautologous biological bypass graft(s) of the right leg with ulceration

    Includes   any condition classifiable to I70.511 and I70.521

Use additional code to identify severity of ulcer (L97.- with fifth character 1)

I70.531   Atherosclerosis of nonautologous biological bypass graft(s) of the right leg with ulceration of thigh

I70.532   Atherosclerosis of nonautologous biological bypass graft(s) of the right leg with ulceration of calf

I70.533   Atherosclerosis of nonautologous biological bypass graft(s) of the right leg with ulceration of ankle

I70.534   Atherosclerosis of nonautologous biological bypass graft(s) of the right leg with ulceration of heel and midfoot

Atherosclerosis of nonautologous biological bypass graft(s) of right leg with ulceration of plantar surface of midfoot

I70.535   Atherosclerosis of nonautologous biological bypass graft(s) of the right leg with ulceration of other part of foot

Atherosclerosis of nonautologous biological bypass graft(s) of the right leg with ulceration of toe

I70.538   Atherosclerosis of nonautologous biological bypass graft(s) of the right leg with ulceration of other part of lower leg

◻ I70.539   Atherosclerosis of nonautologous biological bypass graft(s) of the right leg with ulceration of unspecified site

● I70.54   Atherosclerosis of nonautologous biological bypass graft(s) of the left leg with ulceration

    Includes   any condition classifiable to I70.512 and I70.522

Use additional code to identify severity of ulcer (L97.- with fifth character 2)

I70.541   Atherosclerosis of nonautologous biological bypass graft(s) of the left leg with ulceration of thigh

I70.542   Atherosclerosis of nonautologous biological bypass graft(s) of the left leg with ulceration of calf

---

● Unacceptable First-Listed Diagnosis   ● Use Additional Character(s)   ◻ Unspecified   **OGCR** Official Guidelines for Coding and Reporting

🖉 Complication\Comorbidity   🖉 Major C\C   Excludes 1   Excludes 2   Includes   Use additional   Code first   Code also

I70.543 Atherosclerosis of nonautologous biological bypass graft(s) of the left leg with ulceration of ankle

I70.544 Atherosclerosis of nonautologous biological bypass graft(s) of the left leg with ulceration of heel and midfoot

    Atherosclerosis of nonautologous biological bypass graft(s) of left leg with ulceration of plantar surface of midfoot

I70.545 Atherosclerosis of nonautologous biological bypass graft(s) of the left leg with ulceration of other part of foot

    Atherosclerosis of nonautologous biological bypass graft(s) of the left leg with ulceration of toe

I70.548 Atherosclerosis of nonautologous biological bypass graft(s) of the left leg with ulceration of other part of lower leg

■ I70.549 Atherosclerosis of nonautologous biological bypass graft(s) of the left leg with ulceration of unspecified site

I70.55 Atherosclerosis of nonautologous biological bypass graft(s) of other extremity with ulceration

    Includes any condition classifiable to I70.518, I70.528, and I70.538

    Use additional code to identify severity of ulcer (L98.49)

● I70.56 Atherosclerosis of nonautologous biological bypass graft(s) of the extremities with gangrene

    Includes any condition classifiable to I70.51-, I70.52-, and I70.53-, I70.54-, I70.55

    Use additional code to identify the severity of any ulcer (L98.49-), if applicable

I70.561 Atherosclerosis of nonautologous biological bypass graft(s) of the extremities with gangrene, right leg

I70.562 Atherosclerosis of nonautologous biological bypass graft(s) of the extremities with gangrene, left leg

I70.563 Atherosclerosis of nonautologous biological bypass graft(s) of the extremities with gangrene, bilateral legs

I70.568 Atherosclerosis of nonautologous biological bypass graft(s) of the extremities with gangrene, other extremity

■ I70.569 Atherosclerosis of nonautologous biological bypass graft(s) of the extremities with gangrene, unspecified extremity

● I70.59 Other atherosclerosis of nonautologous biological bypass graft(s) of the extremities

I70.591 Other atherosclerosis of nonautologous biological bypass graft(s) of the extremities, right leg

I70.592 Other atherosclerosis of nonautologous biological bypass graft(s) of the extremities, left leg

I70.593 Other atherosclerosis of nonautologous biological bypass graft(s) of the extremities, bilateral legs

I70.598 Other atherosclerosis of nonautologous biological bypass graft(s) of the extremities, other extremity

■ I70.599 Other atherosclerosis of nonautologous biological bypass graft(s) of the extremities, unspecified extremity

● I70.6 Atherosclerosis of nonbiological bypass graft(s) of the extremities

    Use additional code, if applicable, to identify chronic total occlusion of artery of extremity (I70.92)

● I70.60 Unspecified atherosclerosis of nonbiological bypass graft(s) of the extremities

■ I70.601 Unspecified atherosclerosis of nonbiological bypass graft(s) of the extremities, right leg

■ I70.602 Unspecified atherosclerosis of nonbiological bypass graft(s) of the extremities, left leg

■ I70.603 Unspecified atherosclerosis of nonbiological bypass graft(s) of the extremities, bilateral legs

■ I70.608 Unspecified atherosclerosis of nonbiological bypass graft(s) of the extremities, other extremity

■ I70.609 Unspecified atherosclerosis of nonbiological bypass graft(s) of the extremities, unspecified extremity

● I70.61 Atherosclerosis of nonbiological bypass graft(s) of the extremities with intermittent claudication

I70.611 Atherosclerosis of nonbiological bypass graft(s) of the extremities with intermittent claudication, right leg

I70.612 Atherosclerosis of nonbiological bypass graft(s) of the extremities with intermittent claudication, left leg

I70.613 Atherosclerosis of nonbiological bypass graft(s) of the extremities with intermittent claudication, bilateral legs

I70.618 Atherosclerosis of nonbiological bypass graft(s) of the extremities with intermittent claudication, other extremity

■ I70.619 Atherosclerosis of nonbiological bypass graft(s) of the extremities with intermittent claudication, unspecified extremity

● I70.62 Atherosclerosis of nonbiological bypass graft(s) of the extremities with rest pain

    Includes any condition classifiable to I70.61-

I70.621 Atherosclerosis of nonbiological bypass graft(s) of the extremities with rest pain, right leg

● Unacceptable First-Listed Diagnosis   ● Use Additional Character(s)   ■ Unspecified   **OGCR** Official Guidelines for Coding and Reporting

🗬 Complication\Comorbidity   🗬 Major C\C   Excludes 1   Excludes 2   Includes   Use additional   Code first   Code also

I70.622   Atherosclerosis of nonbiological bypass graft(s) of the extremities with rest pain, left leg

I70.623   Atherosclerosis of nonbiological bypass graft(s) of the extremities with rest pain, bilateral legs

I70.628   Atherosclerosis of nonbiological bypass graft(s) of the extremities with rest pain, other extremity

■ I70.629   Atherosclerosis of nonbiological bypass graft(s) of the extremities with rest pain, unspecified extremity

● I70.63   Atherosclerosis of nonbiological bypass graft(s) of the right leg with ulceration

   Includes   any condition classifiable to I70.611 and I70.621

   Use additional code to identify severity of ulcer (L97.- with fifth character 1)

   I70.631   Atherosclerosis of nonbiological bypass graft(s) of the right leg with ulceration of thigh

   I70.632   Atherosclerosis of nonbiological bypass graft(s) of the right leg with ulceration of calf

   I70.633   Atherosclerosis of nonbiological bypass graft(s) of the right leg with ulceration of ankle

   I70.634   Atherosclerosis of nonbiological bypass graft(s) of the right leg with ulceration of heel and midfoot
      Atherosclerosis of nonbiological bypass graft(s) of right leg with ulceration of plantar surface of midfoot

   I70.635   Atherosclerosis of nonbiological bypass graft(s) of the right leg with ulceration of other part of foot
      Atherosclerosis of nonbiological bypass graft(s) of the right leg with ulceration of toe

   I70.638   Atherosclerosis of nonbiological bypass graft(s) of the right leg with ulceration of other part of lower leg

   ■ I70.639   Atherosclerosis of nonbiological bypass graft(s) of the right leg with ulceration of unspecified site

● I70.64   Atherosclerosis of nonbiological bypass graft(s) of the left leg with ulceration

   Includes   any condition classifiable to I70.612 and I70.622

   Use additional code to identify severity of ulcer (L97.- with fifth character 2)

   I70.641   Atherosclerosis of nonbiological bypass graft(s) of the left leg with ulceration of thigh

   I70.642   Atherosclerosis of nonbiological bypass graft(s) of the left leg with ulceration of calf

   I70.643   Atherosclerosis of nonbiological bypass graft(s) of the left leg with ulceration of ankle

I70.644   Atherosclerosis of nonbiological bypass graft(s) of the left leg with ulceration of heel and midfoot
      Atherosclerosis of nonbiological bypass graft(s) of left leg with ulceration of plantar surface of midfoot

I70.645   Atherosclerosis of nonbiological bypass graft(s) of the left leg with ulceration of other part of foot
      Atherosclerosis of nonbiological bypass graft(s) of the left leg with ulceration of toe

I70.648   Atherosclerosis of nonbiological bypass graft(s) of the left leg with ulceration of other part of lower leg

■ I70.649   Atherosclerosis of nonbiological bypass graft(s) of the left leg with ulceration of unspecified site

I70.65   Atherosclerosis of nonbiological bypass graft(s) of other extremity with ulceration

   Includes   any condition classifiable to I70.618 and I70.628

   Use additional code to identify severity of ulcer (L98.49-)

● I70.66   Atherosclerosis of nonbiological bypass graft(s) of the extremities with gangrene

   Includes   any condition classifiable to I70.61-, I70.62-, I70.63-, I70.64-, I70.65

   Use additional code to identify the severity of any ulcer (L98.49-), if applicable

   I70.661   Atherosclerosis of nonbiological bypass graft(s) of the extremities with gangrene, right leg

   I70.662   Atherosclerosis of nonbiological bypass graft(s) of the extremities with gangrene, left leg

   I70.663   Atherosclerosis of nonbiological bypass graft(s) of the extremities with gangrene, bilateral legs

   I70.668   Atherosclerosis of nonbiological bypass graft(s) of the extremities with gangrene, other extremity

   ■ I70.669   Atherosclerosis of nonbiological bypass graft(s) of the extremities with gangrene, unspecified extremity

● I70.69   Other atherosclerosis of nonbiological bypass graft(s) of the extremities

   I70.691   Other atherosclerosis of nonbiological bypass graft(s) of the extremities, right leg

   I70.692   Other atherosclerosis of nonbiological bypass graft(s) of the extremities, left leg

   I70.693   Other atherosclerosis of nonbiological bypass graft(s) of the extremities, bilateral legs

   I70.698   Other atherosclerosis of nonbiological bypass graft(s) of the extremities, other extremity

   ■ I70.699   Other atherosclerosis of nonbiological bypass graft(s) of the extremities, unspecified extremity

CHAPTER 9 (I00-I99)

● Unacceptable First-Listed Diagnosis   ● Use Additional Character(s)   ■ Unspecified   **OGCR** Official Guidelines for Coding and Reporting

🔗 Complication\Comorbidity   🔍 Major C\C    Excludes 1   Excludes 2    Includes   Use additional   Code first   Code also   **1041**

● **I70.7   Atherosclerosis of other type of bypass graft(s) of the extremities**

Use additional code, if applicable, to identify chronic total occlusion of artery of extremity (I70.92)

● **I70.70   Unspecified atherosclerosis of other type of bypass graft(s) of the extremities**

◼ **I70.701   Unspecified atherosclerosis of other type of bypass graft(s) of the extremities, right leg**

◼ **I70.702   Unspecified atherosclerosis of other type of bypass graft(s) of the extremities, left leg**

◼ **I70.703   Unspecified atherosclerosis of other type of bypass graft(s) of the extremities, bilateral legs**

◼ **I70.708   Unspecified atherosclerosis of other type of bypass graft(s) of the extremities, other extremity**

◼ **I70.709   Unspecified atherosclerosis of other type of bypass graft(s) of the extremities, unspecified extremity**

● **I70.71   Atherosclerosis of other type of bypass graft(s) of the extremities with intermittent claudication**

I70.711   Atherosclerosis of other type of bypass graft(s) of the extremities with intermittent claudication, right leg

I70.712   Atherosclerosis of other type of bypass graft(s) of the extremities with intermittent claudication, left leg

I70.713   Atherosclerosis of other type of bypass graft(s) of the extremities with intermittent claudication, bilateral legs

I70.718   Atherosclerosis of other type of bypass graft(s) of the extremities with intermittent claudication, other extremity

◼ **I70.719   Atherosclerosis of other type of bypass graft(s) of the extremities with intermittent claudication, unspecified extremity**

● **I70.72   Atherosclerosis of other type of bypass graft(s) of the extremities with rest pain**

Includes   any condition classifiable to I70.71-

I70.721   Atherosclerosis of other type of bypass graft(s) of the extremities with rest pain, right leg

I70.722   Atherosclerosis of other type of bypass graft(s) of the extremities with rest pain, left leg

I70.723   Atherosclerosis of other type of bypass graft(s) of the extremities with rest pain, bilateral legs

I70.728   Atherosclerosis of other type of bypass graft(s) of the extremities with rest pain, other extremity

◼ **I70.729   Atherosclerosis of other type of bypass graft(s) of the extremities with rest pain, unspecified extremity**

● **I70.73   Atherosclerosis of other type of bypass graft(s) of the right leg with ulceration**

Includes   any condition classifiable to I70.711 and I70.721

Use additional code to identify severity of ulcer (L97.- with fifth character 1)

I70.731   Atherosclerosis of other type of bypass graft(s) of the right leg with ulceration of thigh

I70.732   Atherosclerosis of other type of bypass graft(s) of the right leg with ulceration of calf

I70.733   Atherosclerosis of other type of bypass graft(s) of the right leg with ulceration of ankle

I70.734   Atherosclerosis of other type of bypass graft(s) of the right leg with ulceration of heel and midfoot

Atherosclerosis of other type of bypass graft(s) of right leg with ulceration of plantar surface of midfoot

I70.735   Atherosclerosis of other type of bypass graft(s) of the right leg with ulceration of other part of foot

Atherosclerosis of other type of bypass graft(s) of right leg with ulceration of toe

I70.738   Atherosclerosis of other type of bypass graft(s) of the right leg with ulceration of other part of lower leg

◼ **I70.739   Atherosclerosis of other type of bypass graft(s) of the right leg with ulceration of unspecified site**

● **I70.74   Atherosclerosis of other type of bypass graft(s) of the left leg with ulceration**

Includes   any condition classifiable to I70.712 and I70.722

Use additional code to identify severity of ulcer (L97.- with fifth character 2)

I70.741   Atherosclerosis of other type of bypass graft(s) of the left leg with ulceration of thigh

I70.742   Atherosclerosis of other type of bypass graft(s) of the left leg with ulceration of calf

I70.743   Atherosclerosis of other type of bypass graft(s) of the left leg with ulceration of ankle

I70.744   Atherosclerosis of other type of bypass graft(s) of the left leg with ulceration of heel and midfoot

Atherosclerosis of other type of bypass graft(s) of left leg with ulceration of plantar surface of midfoot

I70.745   Atherosclerosis of other type of bypass graft(s) of the left leg with ulceration of other part of foot

Atherosclerosis of other type of bypass graft(s) of left leg with ulceration of toe

I70.748   Atherosclerosis of other type of bypass graft(s) of the left leg with ulceration of other part of lower leg

● Unacceptable First-Listed Diagnosis   ● Use Additional Character(s)   ◼ Unspecified   **OGCR** Official Guidelines for Coding and Reporting

🔖 Complication\Comorbidity   🔖 Major C\C   Excludes 1   Excludes 2   Includes   Use additional   Code first   Code also

⬛ **I70.749   Atherosclerosis of other type of bypass graft(s) of the left leg with ulceration of unspecified site**

I70.75   Atherosclerosis of other type of bypass graft(s) of other extremity with ulceration

> Includes   any condition classifiable to I70.718 and I70.728

> Use additional code to identify severity of ulcer (L98.49)

⬤ **I70.76   Atherosclerosis of other type of bypass graft(s) of the extremities with gangrene**

> Includes   any condition classifiable to I70.71-, I70.72-, I70.73-, I70.74-, I70.75

> Use additional code to identify the severity of any ulcer (L98.49-), if applicable

I70.761   Atherosclerosis of other type of bypass graft(s) of the extremities with gangrene, right leg

I70.762   Atherosclerosis of other type of bypass graft(s) of the extremities with gangrene, left leg

I70.763   Atherosclerosis of other type of bypass graft(s) of the extremities with gangrene, bilateral legs

I70.768   Atherosclerosis of other type of bypass graft(s) of the extremities with gangrene, other extremity

⬛ **I70.769   Atherosclerosis of other type of bypass graft(s) of the extremities with gangrene, unspecified extremity**

⬤ **I70.79   Other atherosclerosis of other type of bypass graft(s) of the extremities**

I70.791   Other atherosclerosis of other type of bypass graft(s) of the extremities, right leg

I70.792   Other atherosclerosis of other type of bypass graft(s) of the extremities, left leg

I70.793   Other atherosclerosis of other type of bypass graft(s) of the extremities, bilateral legs

I70.798   Other atherosclerosis of other type of bypass graft(s) of the extremities, other extremity

⬛ **I70.799   Other atherosclerosis of other type of bypass graft(s) of the extremities, unspecified extremity**

I70.8   Atherosclerosis of other arteries

⬤ **I70.9   Other and unspecified atherosclerosis**

⬛ **I70.90   Unspecified atherosclerosis**

I70.91   Generalized atherosclerosis

I70.92   Chronic total occlusion of artery of the extremities

> Complete occlusion of artery of the extremities
> Total occlusion of artery of the extremities

> *Code first atherosclerosis of arteries of the extremities (I70.2-, I70.3-, I70.4-, I70.5-, I70.6-, I70.7-)*

> Excludes1   acute occlusion of artery of the extremity (I74.2-, I74.3-, I74.4-)

⬤ **I71   Aortic aneurysm and dissection**

> Excludes1   syphilitic aortic aneurysm (A52.01)
> traumatic aortic aneurysm (S25.09, S35.09)

⬤ **I71.0   Dissection of aorta**

⬛ **I71.00   Dissection of unspecified site of aorta** 🏷

I71.01   Dissection of thoracic aorta 🏷

I71.02   Dissection of abdominal aorta 🏷

I71.03   Dissection of thoracoabdominal aorta 🏷

I71.1   Thoracic aortic aneurysm, ruptured 🏷

I71.2   Thoracic aortic aneurysm, without rupture

I71.3   Abdominal aortic aneurysm, ruptured 🏷

I71.4   Abdominal aortic aneurysm, without rupture

I71.5   Thoracoabdominal aortic aneurysm, ruptured 🏷

I71.6   Thoracoabdominal aortic aneurysm, without rupture

⬛ **I71.8   Aortic aneurysm of unspecified site, ruptured** 🏷
> Rupture of aorta NOS

⬛ **I71.9   Aortic aneurysm of unspecified site, without rupture**
> Aneurysm of aorta
> Dilatation of aorta
> Hyaline necrosis of aorta

⬤ **I72   Other aneurysm**

> Includes   aneurysm (cirsoid) (false) (ruptured)

> Excludes2   acquired aneurysm (I77.0)
> aneurysm (of) aorta (I71.-)
> aneurysm (of) arteriovenous NOS (Q27.3-)
> carotid artery dissection (I77.71)
> cerebral (nonruptured) aneurysm (I67.1)
> coronary aneurysm (I25.4)
> coronary artery dissection (I25.42)
> dissection of artery NEC (I77.79)
> heart aneurysm (I25.3)
> iliac artery dissection (I77.72)
> pulmonary artery aneurysm (I28.1)
> renal artery dissection (I77.73)
> retinal aneurysm (H35.0)
> ruptured cerebral aneurysm (I60.7)
> varicose aneurysm (I77.0)
> vertebral artery dissection (I77.74)

I72.0   Aneurysm of carotid artery (common) (external) (internal, extracranial portion)

> Excludes1   aneurysm of internal carotid artery, intracranial portion (I67.1)
> aneurysm of internal carotid artery NOS (I67.1)

I72.1   Aneurysm of artery of upper extremity

I72.2   Aneurysm of renal artery

I72.3   Aneurysm of iliac artery

I72.4   Aneurysm of artery of lower extremity

I72.8   Aneurysm of other specified arteries

⬛ **I72.9   Aneurysm of unspecified site**

⬤ **I73   Other peripheral vascular diseases**

> Excludes2   chilblains (T69.1)
> frostbite (T33- T34)
> immersion hand or foot (T69.0-)
> spasm of cerebral artery (G45.9)

⬤ **I73.0   Raynaud's syndrome**

> *Diminishing oxygen supply to fingers, toes, nose, and ears when exposed to temperature changes or stress*

> Raynaud's disease
> Raynaud's phenomenon (secondary)

I73.00   Raynaud's syndrome without gangrene

I73.01   Raynaud's syndrome with gangrene

⬤ Unacceptable First-Listed Diagnosis   ⬤ Use Additional Character(s)   ⬛ Unspecified   OGCR Official Guidelines for Coding and Reporting

🏷 Complication\Comorbidity   🏷 Major C\C   Excludes 1   Excludes 2   Includes   Use additional   Code first   Code also

I73.1   **Thromboangiitis obliterans [Buerger's disease]**
Inflammatory occlusive disease resulting in poor circulation to the legs, feet, and sometimes the hands due to progressive inflammatory narrowing and eventually obliteration of the small arteries

● **I73.8**   **Other specified peripheral vascular diseases**
| Excludes1 | diabetic (peripheral) angiopathy (E08-E13 with .51-.52) |

     I73.81   **Erythromelalgia**

     I73.89   **Other specified peripheral vascular diseases**
         Acrocyanosis
         Erythrocyanosis
         Simple acroparesthesia [Schultze's type]
         Vasomotor acroparesthesia [Nothnagel's type]

■ **I73.9**   **Peripheral vascular disease, unspecified**
     Intermittent claudication
     Peripheral angiopathy NOS
     Spasm of artery
| Excludes1 | atherosclerosis of the extremities (I70.2--I70.7-) |

● **I74**   **Arterial embolism and thrombosis**
Includes	embolic infarction
	thrombotic infarction
	embolic occlusion
	thrombotic occlusion

Code first embolism and thrombosis complicating:
     abortion or ectopic or molar pregnancy (O00-O07, O08.2)
     pregnancy, childbirth and the puerperium (O88.-)
Excludes2	atheroembolism (I75.-)
	embolism and thrombosis:
	basilar (I63.0-I63.2, I65.1)
	carotid (I63.0-I63.2, I65.2)
	cerebral (I63.3-I63.5, I66.-)
	coronary (I21-I25)
	mesenteric (K55.0)
	ophthalmic (H34.-)
	precerebral NOS (I63.0-I63.2, I65.9)
	pulmonary (I26.-)
	renal (N28.0)
	retinal (H34.-)
	septic (I76)
	vertebral (I63.0-I63.2, I65.0)

     I74.0   **Embolism and thrombosis of abdominal aorta** 🦠
         Aortic bifurcation syndrome
         Aortoiliac obstruction
         Leriche's syndrome
         Saddle embolus

Item 9–9   An **embolus** is a mass of undissolved matter present in the blood that is transported by the blood current. A **thrombus** is a blood clot that occludes or shuts off a vessel. When a thrombus is dislodged, it becomes an embolus.

● **I74.1**   **Embolism and thrombosis of other and unspecified parts of aorta**

     ■ **I74.10**   **Embolism and thrombosis of unspecified parts of aorta** 🦠

     I74.11   **Embolism and thrombosis of thoracic aorta** 🦠

     I74.19   **Embolism and thrombosis of other parts of aorta** 🦠

     I74.2   **Embolism and thrombosis of arteries of the upper extremities** 🦠

     I74.3   **Embolism and thrombosis of arteries of the lower extremities** 🦠

■ **I74.4**   **Embolism and thrombosis of arteries of extremities, unspecified** 🦠
         Peripheral arterial embolism NOS

     I74.5   **Embolism and thrombosis of iliac artery** 🦠

     I74.8   **Embolism and thrombosis of other arteries** 🦠

■ **I74.9**   **Embolism and thrombosis of unspecified artery** 🦠

● **I75**   **Atheroembolism**
| Includes | Atherothrombotic microembolism |
| | Cholesterol embolism |

● **I75.0**   **Atheroembolism of extremities**

     ● **I75.01**   **Atheroembolism of upper extremity**

         I75.011   **Atheroembolism of right upper extremity** 🦠

         I75.012   **Atheroembolism of left upper extremity** 🦠

         I75.013   **Atheroembolism of bilateral upper extremities** 🦠

         ■ **I75.019**   **Atheroembolism of unspecified upper extremity** 🦠

     ● **I75.02**   **Atheroembolism of lower extremity**

         I75.021   **Atheroembolism of right lower extremity** 🦠

         I75.022   **Atheroembolism of left lower extremity** 🦠

         I75.023   **Atheroembolism of bilateral lower extremities** 🦠

         I75.029   **Atheroembolism of unspecified lower extremity** 🦠

● **I75.8**   **Atheroembolism of other sites**

     I75.81   **Atheroembolism of kidney** 🦠
         Use additional code for any associated acute kidney failure and chronic kidney disease (N17.-, N18.-)

     I75.89   **Atheroembolism of other site** 🦠

● **I76**   **Septic arterial embolism** 🦠
Code first underlying infection, such as:
     infective endocarditis (I33.0)
     lung abscess (J85.-)
Use additional code to identify the site of the embolism (I74.-)
| Excludes2 | septic pulmonary embolism (I26.01, I26.90) |

● **I77**   **Other disorders of arteries and arterioles**
Excludes2	collagen (vascular) diseases (M30-M36)
	hypersensitivity angiitis (M31.0)
	pulmonary artery (I28.-)

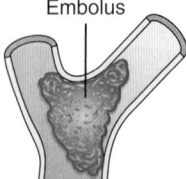
Embolus

Figure 9-3   An arterial embolus.

1044

● Unacceptable First-Listed Diagnosis   ● Use Additional Character(s)   ■ Unspecified   **OGCR** Official Guidelines for Coding and Reporting
🦠 Complication\Comorbidity   🦠 Major C\C | Excludes 1 | | Excludes 2 | Includes   Use additional   Code first   Code also

CHAPTER 9 (I00-I99)

I77.0 **Arteriovenous fistula, acquired**
Aneurysmal varix
Arteriovenous aneurysm, acquired
> **Excludes1**   arteriovenous aneurysm NOS (Q27.3-)
> presence of arteriovenous shunt (fistula) for dialysis (Z99.2)
> traumatic - see injury of blood vessel by body region

> **Excludes2**   cerebral (I67.1)
> coronary (I25.4)

I77.1 **Stricture of artery**
Narrowing of artery

I77.2 **Rupture of artery** 🔗
Erosion of artery
Fistula of artery
Ulcer of artery
> **Excludes1**   traumatic rupture of artery - see injury of blood vessel by body region

I77.3 **Arterial fibromuscular dysplasia**
Fibromuscular hyperplasia (of) carotid artery
Fibromuscular hyperplasia (of) renal artery

I77.4 **Celiac artery compression syndrome** 🔗

I77.5 **Necrosis of artery** 🔗

I77.6 **Arteritis, unspecified**
Aortitis NOS
Endarteritis NOS
> **Excludes1**   arteritis or endarteritis:
> aortic arch (M31.4)
> cerebral NEC (I67.7)
> coronary (I25.89)
> deformans (I70.-)
> giant cell (M31.5., M31.6)
> obliterans (I70.-)
> senile (I70.-)

● I77.7 **Other arterial dissection**
> **Excludes2**   dissection of aorta (I71.0-)
> dissection of coronary artery (I25.42)

     I77.71 **Dissection of carotid artery** 🔗
     I77.72 **Dissection of iliac artery** 🔗
     I77.73 **Dissection of renal artery** 🔗
     I77.74 **Dissection of vertebral artery** 🔗
     I77.79 **Dissection of other artery** 🔗

I77.8 **Other specified disorders of arteries and arterioles**

I77.9 **Disorder of arteries and arterioles, unspecified**

● I78 **Diseases of capillaries**

I78.0 **Hereditary hemorrhagic telangiectasia**
Rendu-Osler-Weber disease

I78.1 **Nevus, non-neoplastic**
Araneus nevus
Senile nevus
Spider nevus
Stellar nevus
> **Excludes1**   nevus NOS (D22.-)
> vascular NOS (Q82.5)

> **Excludes2**   blue nevus (D22.-)
> flammeus nevus (Q82.5)
> hairy nevus (D22.-)
> melanocytic nevus (D22.-)
> pigmented nevus (D22.-)
> portwine nevus (Q82.5)
> sanguineous nevus (Q82.5)
> strawberry nevus (Q82.5)
> verrucous nevus (Q82.5)

I78.8 **Other diseases of capillaries**

I78.9 **Disease of capillaries, unspecified**

● I79 **Disorders of arteries, arterioles and capillaries in diseases classified elsewhere**

● I79.0 **Aneurysm of aorta in diseases classified elsewhere**
Code first underlying disease
> **Excludes1**   syphilitic aneurysm (A52.01)

● I79.1 **Aortitis in diseases classified elsewhere**
Code first underlying disease
> **Excludes1**   syphilitic aortitis (A52.02)

● I79.8 **Other disorders of arteries, arterioles and capillaries in diseases classified elsewhere**
Code first underlying disease, such as:
amyloidosis (E85.-)
> **Excludes1**   diabetic (peripheral) angiopathy (E08-E13 with .51-.52) endarteritis:
> syphilitic (A52.09)
> tuberculous (A18.89)

DISEASES OF VEINS, LYMPHATIC VESSELS AND LYMPH NODES, NOT ELSEWHERE CLASSIFIED (I80-I89)

● I80 **Phlebitis and thrombophlebitis**
Inflammation of a vein with infiltration of walls (phlebitis).
> **Includes**   endophlebitis
> inflammation, vein
> periphlebitis
> suppurative phlebitis

Code first phlebitis and thrombophlebitis complicating:
abortion, ectopic or molar pregnancy (O00-O07, O08.7)
pregnancy, childbirth and the puerperium (O22.-, O87.-)
> **Excludes1**   venous embolism and thrombosis of lower extremities (I82.4-, I82.81-)

> **Excludes2**   phlebitis and thrombophlebitis (of):
> intracranial and intraspinal, septic or NOS (G08)
> intracranial, nonpyogenic (I67.6)
> intraspinal, nonpyogenic (G95.1)
> portal (vein) (K75.1)
> postphlebitic syndrome (I87.0)
> postthrombotic syndrome (I87.0)
> thrombophlebitis migrans (I82.1)

● I80.0 **Phlebitis and thrombophlebitis of superficial vessels of lower extremities**
Phlebitis and thrombophlebitis of femoropopliteal vein

     I80.00 **Phlebitis and thrombophlebitis of superficial vessels of unspecified lower extremity**

     I80.01 **Phlebitis and thrombophlebitis of superficial vessels of right lower extremity**

     I80.02 **Phlebitis and thrombophlebitis of superficial vessels of left lower extremity**

     I80.03 **Phlebitis and thrombophlebitis of superficial vessels of lower extremities, bilateral**

● I80.1 **Phlebitis and thrombophlebitis of femoral vein**

     I80.10 **Phlebitis and thrombophlebitis of unspecified femoral vein** 🔗

     I80.11 **Phlebitis and thrombophlebitis of right femoral vein** 🔗

     I80.12 **Phlebitis and thrombophlebitis of left femoral vein** 🔗

     I80.13 **Phlebitis and thrombophlebitis of femoral vein, bilateral** 🔗

● Unacceptable First-Listed Diagnosis   ● Use Additional Character(s)   ■ Unspecified   **OGCR** Official Guidelines for Coding and Reporting
🔗 Complication\Comorbidity   🔗 Major C\C   Excludes 1   Excludes 2   Includes   Use additional   Code first   Code also

1045

CHAPTER 9 (I00-I99)

● **I80.2 Phlebitis and thrombophlebitis of other and unspecified deep vessels of lower extremities**

  ● **I80.20 Phlebitis and thrombophlebitis of unspecified deep vessels of lower extremities**

    ▪ **I80.201 Phlebitis and thrombophlebitis of unspecified deep vessels of right lower extremity** 🦠

    ▪ **I80.202 Phlebitis and thrombophlebitis of unspecified deep vessels of left lower extremity** 🦠

    ▪ **I80.203 Phlebitis and thrombophlebitis of unspecified deep vessels of lower extremities, bilateral** 🦠

    ▪ **I80.209 Phlebitis and thrombophlebitis of unspecified deep vessels of unspecified lower extremity** 🦠

  ● **I80.21 Phlebitis and thrombophlebitis of iliac vein**

    I80.211 Phlebitis and thrombophlebitis of right iliac vein 🦠

    I80.212 Phlebitis and thrombophlebitis of left iliac vein 🦠

    I80.213 Phlebitis and thrombophlebitis of iliac vein, bilateral 🦠

    ▪ **I80.219 Phlebitis and thrombophlebitis of unspecified iliac vein** 🦠

  ● **I80.22 Phlebitis and thrombophlebitis of popliteal vein**

    I80.221 Phlebitis and thrombophlebitis of right popliteal vein 🦠

    I80.222 Phlebitis and thrombophlebitis of left popliteal vein 🦠

    I80.223 Phlebitis and thrombophlebitis of popliteal vein, bilateral 🦠

    ▪ **I80.229 Phlebitis and thrombophlebitis of unspecified popliteal vein** 🦠

  ● **I80.23 Phlebitis and thrombophlebitis of tibial vein**

    I80.231 Phlebitis and thrombophlebitis of right tibial vein 🦠

    I80.232 Phlebitis and thrombophlebitis of left tibial vein 🦠

    I80.233 Phlebitis and thrombophlebitis of tibial vein, bilateral 🦠

    ▪ **I80.239 Phlebitis and thrombophlebitis of unspecified tibial vein** 🦠

  ● **I80.29 Phlebitis and thrombophlebitis of other deep vessels of lower extremities**

    I80.291 Phlebitis and thrombophlebitis of other deep vessels of right lower extremity 🦠

    I80.292 Phlebitis and thrombophlebitis of other deep vessels of left lower extremity 🦠

    I80.293 Phlebitis and thrombophlebitis of other deep vessels of lower extremity, bilateral 🦠

    ▪ **I80.299 Phlebitis and thrombophlebitis of other deep vessels of unspecified lower extremity** 🦠

 ▪ **I80.3 Phlebitis and thrombophlebitis of lower extremities, unspecified**

 I80.8 Phlebitis and thrombophlebitis of other sites 🦠

 ▪ **I80.9 Phlebitis and thrombophlebitis of unspecified site**

● **I81 Portal vein thrombosis** 🦠

Includes	portal (vein) obstruction
Excludes2	hepatic vein thrombosis (I82.0)
	phlebitis of portal vein (K75.1)

● **I82 Other venous embolism and thrombosis**

  Code first venous embolism and thrombosis complicating:
  abortion, ectopic or molar pregnancy (O00-O07, O08.7)
  pregnancy, childbirth and the puerperium (O22.-, O87.-)

Excludes2	venous embolism and thrombosis (of)
	cerebral (I63.6, I67.6)
	coronary (I21-I25)
	intracranial and intraspinal, septic or NOS (G08)
	intracranial, nonpyogenic (I67.6)
	intraspinal, nonpyogenic (G95.1)
	mesenteric (K55.0)
	portal (I81)
	pulmonary (I26.-)

 I82.0 Budd-Chiari syndrome 🦠
  Hepatic vein thrombosis

 I82.1 Thrombophlebitis migrans 🦠
  "White leg" is the other term to describe a migrating thrombus.

● **I82.2 Embolism and thrombosis of vena cava and other thoracic veins** 🦠

  ● **I82.21 Embolism and thrombosis of superior vena cava**

    I82.210 Acute embolism and thrombosis of superior vena cava
      Embolism and thrombosis of superior vena cava NOS

    I82.211 Chronic embolism and thrombosis of superior vena cava

  ● **I82.22 Embolism and thrombosis of inferior vena cava**

    I82.220 Acute embolism and thrombosis of inferior vena cava
      Embolism and thrombosis of inferior vena cava NOS

    I82.221 Chronic embolism and thrombosis of inferior vena cava

  ● **I82.29 Embolism and thrombosis of other thoracic veins**
    Embolism and thrombosis of brachiocephalic (innominate) vein

    I82.290 Acute embolism and thrombosis of other thoracic veins

    I82.291 Chronic embolism and thrombosis of other thoracic veins

 I82.3 Embolism and thrombosis of renal vein 🦠

● **I82.4 Acute embolism and thrombosis of deep veins of lower extremity**

  ▪ **I82.40 Acute embolism and thrombosis of unspecified deep veins of lower extremity** 🦠
    Deep vein thrombosis NOS
    DVT NOS

  ● **I82.41 Acute embolism and thrombosis of femoral vein**

    I82.411 Acute embolism and thrombosis of right femoral vein 🦠

    I82.412 Acute embolism and thrombosis of left femoral vein 🦠

    I82.413 Acute embolism and thrombosis of femoral vein, bilateral 🦠

    ▪ **I82.419 Acute embolism and thrombosis of unspecified femoral vein** 🦠

● **I82.42**   Acute embolism and thrombosis of iliac vein

    I82.421   Acute embolism and thrombosis of right iliac vein 🦠

    I82.422   Acute embolism and thrombosis of left iliac vein 🦠

    I82.423   Acute embolism and thrombosis of iliac vein, bilateral 🦠

    ▣**I82.429**   Acute embolism and thrombosis of unspecified iliac vein 🦠

● **I82.43**   Acute embolism and thrombosis of popliteal vein

    I82.431   Acute embolism and thrombosis of right popliteal vein 🦠

    I82.432   Acute embolism and thrombosis of left popliteal vein 🦠

    I82.433   Acute embolism and thrombosis of popliteal vein, bilateral 🦠

    ▣**I82.439**   Acute embolism and thrombosis of unspecified popliteal vein 🦠

● **I82.44**   Acute embolism and thrombosis of tibial vein

    I82.441   Acute embolism and thrombosis of right tibial vein 🦠

    I82.442   Acute embolism and thrombosis of left tibial vein 🦠

    I82.443   Acute embolism and thrombosis of tibial vein, bilateral 🦠

    ▣**I82.449**   Acute embolism and thrombosis of unspecified tibial vein 🦠

● **I82.49**   Acute embolism and thrombosis of other deep vein of lower extremity

    I82.491   Acute embolism and thrombosis of other deep vein of right lower extremity 🦠

    I82.492   Acute embolism and thrombosis of other deep vein of left lower extremity 🦠

    I82.493   Acute embolism and thrombosis of other deep vein of lower extremity, bilateral 🦠

    ▣**I82.499**   Acute embolism and thrombosis of other deep vein of unspecified lower extremity 🦠

Item 9–10 Varicose/Varicosities (varix = singular, varices = plural): Enlarged, engorged, tortuous, twisted vascular vessels (veins, arteries, lymphatics). As such, the condition can present in various parts of the body, although the most familiar locations are the lower extremities. A common complication of varices is thrombophlebitis. Varicosities of the anus and rectum are called hemorrhoids.

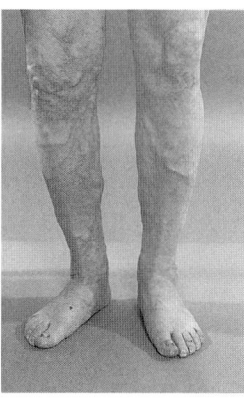

Figure 9-4 Varicose veins of the legs. (From Goldman: *Cecil Medicine*, 23rd ed. 2008, Saunders)

● **I82.5**   Chronic embolism and thrombosis of deep veins of lower extremity

    Use additional code, if applicable, for associated long-term (current) use of anticoagulants (Z79.01)

    | Excludes1 | personal history of venous embolism and thrombosis (Z86.71) |

  ▣**I82.50**   Chronic embolism and thrombosis of unspecified deep veins of lower extremity

● **I82.51**   Chronic embolism and thrombosis of femoral vein

    I82.511   Chronic embolism and thrombosis of right femoral vein

    I82.512   Chronic embolism and thrombosis of left femoral vein

    I82.513   Chronic embolism and thrombosis of femoral vein, bilateral

    ▣**I82.519**   Chronic embolism and thrombosis of unspecified femoral vein

●**I82.52**   Chronic embolism and thrombosis of iliac vein

    I82.521   Chronic embolism and thrombosis of right iliac vein

    I82.522   Chronic embolism and thrombosis of left iliac vein

    I82.523   Chronic embolism and thrombosis of iliac vein, bilateral

    ▣**I82.529**   Chronic embolism and thrombosis of unspecified iliac vein

●**I82.53**   Chronic embolism and thrombosis of popliteal vein

    I82.531   Chronic embolism and thrombosis of right popliteal vein

    I82.532   Chronic embolism and thrombosis of left popliteal vein

    I82.533   Chronic embolism and thrombosis of popliteal vein, bilateral

    ▣**I82.539**   Chronic embolism and thrombosis of unspecified popliteal vein

●**I82.54**   Chronic embolism and thrombosis of tibial vein

    I82.541   Chronic embolism and thrombosis of right tibial vein

    I82.542   Chronic embolism and thrombosis of left tibial vein

    I82.543   Chronic embolism and thrombosis of tibial vein, bilateral

    ▣**I82.549**   Chronic embolism and thrombosis of unspecified tibial vein

●**I82.59**   Chronic embolism and thrombosis of other deep vein of lower extremity

    I82.591   Chronic embolism and thrombosis of other deep vein of right lower extremity

---

● Unaccceptable First-Listed Diagnosis   ● Use Additional Character(s)   ▣ Unspecified   **OGCR** Official Guidelines for Coding and Reporting

🦠 Complication\Comorbidity   🦠 Major C\C       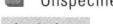 Includes   Use additional   Code first   Code also

I82.592   Chronic embolism and thrombosis of other deep vein of left lower extremity

I82.593   Chronic embolism and thrombosis of other deep vein of lower extremity, bilateral

■ I82.599   Chronic embolism and thrombosis of other deep vein of unspecified lower extremity

● I82.6   **Acute embolism and thrombosis of veins of upper extremity**

   ● I82.60   Acute embolism and thrombosis of unspecified veins of upper extremity

     ■ I82.601   Acute embolism and thrombosis of unspecified veins of right upper extremity

     ■ I82.602   Acute embolism and thrombosis of unspecified veins of left upper extremity

     ■ I82.603   Acute embolism and thrombosis of unspecified veins of upper extremity, bilateral

     ■ I82.609   Acute embolism and thrombosis of unspecified veins of unspecified upper extremity

   ● I82.61   Acute embolism and thrombosis of superficial veins of upper extremity
       Acute embolism and thrombosis of antecubital vein
       Acute embolism and thrombosis of basilic vein
       Acute embolism and thrombosis of cephalic vein

     I82.611   Acute embolism and thrombosis of superficial veins of right upper extremity

     I82.612   Acute embolism and thrombosis of superficial veins of left upper extremity

     I82.613   Acute embolism and thrombosis of superficial veins of upper extremity, bilateral

     ■ I82.619   Acute embolism and thrombosis of superficial veins of unspecified upper extremity

   ● I82.62   Acute embolism and thrombosis of deep veins of upper extremity
       Acute embolism and thrombosis of brachial vein
       Acute embolism and thrombosis of radial vein
       Acute embolism and thrombosis of ulnar vein

     I82.621   Acute embolism and thrombosis of deep veins of right upper extremity

     I82.622   Acute embolism and thrombosis of deep veins of left upper extremity

     I82.623   Acute embolism and thrombosis of deep veins of upper extremity, bilateral

     ■ I82.629   Acute embolism and thrombosis of deep veins of unspecified upper extremity

● I82.7   **Chronic embolism and thrombosis of veins of upper extremity**

   Use additional code, if applicable, for associated long-term (current) use of anticoagulants (Z79.01)

   Excludes1   personal history of venous embolism and thrombosis (Z86.71)

   ● I82.70   Chronic embolism and thrombosis of unspecified veins of upper extremity

     ■ I82.701   Chronic embolism and thrombosis of unspecified veins of right upper extremity

     ■ I82.702   Chronic embolism and thrombosis of unspecified veins of left upper extremity

     ■ I82.703   Chronic embolism and thrombosis of unspecified veins of upper extremity, bilateral

     ■ I82.709   Chronic embolism and thrombosis of unspecified veins of unspecified upper extremity

   ● I82.71   Chronic embolism and thrombosis of superficial veins of upper extremity
       Chronic embolism and thrombosis of antecubital vein
       Chronic embolism and thrombosis of basilic vein
       Chronic embolism and thrombosis of cephalic vein

     I82.711   Chronic embolism and thrombosis of superficial veins of right upper extremity

     I82.712   Chronic embolism and thrombosis of superficial veins of left upper extremity

     I82.713   Chronic embolism and thrombosis of superficial veins of upper extremity, bilateral

     ■ I82.719   Chronic embolism and thrombosis of superficial veins of unspecified upper extremity

   ● I82.72   Chronic embolism and thrombosis of deep veins of upper extremity
       Chronic embolism and thrombosis of brachial vein
       Chronic embolism and thrombosis of radial vein
       Chronic embolism and thrombosis of ulnar vein

     I82.721   Chronic embolism and thrombosis of deep veins of right upper extremity

     I82.722   Chronic embolism and thrombosis of deep veins of left upper extremity

     I82.723   Chronic embolism and thrombosis of deep veins of upper extremity, bilateral

     ■ I82.729   Chronic embolism and thrombosis of deep veins of unspecified upper extremity

CHAPTER 9 (I00-I99)

1048

● Unacceptable First-Listed Diagnosis   ● Use Additional Character(s)   ■ Unspecified   **OGCR** Official Guidelines for Coding and Reporting
🞕 Complication\Comorbidity   🞕 Major C\C   Excludes 1   Excludes 2   Includes   Use additional   Code first   Code also

● **I82.a**   Embolism and thrombosis of axillary vein

  ● **I82.a1**   Acute embolism and thrombosis of axillary vein

    I82.a11   Acute embolism and thrombosis of right axillary vein

    I82.a12   Acute embolism and thrombosis of left axillary vein

    I82.a13   Acute embolism and thrombosis of axillary vein, bilateral

    ■**I82.a19**   Acute embolism and thrombosis of unspecified axillary vein

  ● **I82.a2**   Chronic embolism and thrombosis of axillary vein

    I82.a21   Chronic embolism and thrombosis of right axillary vein

    I82.a22   Chronic embolism and thrombosis of left axillary vein

    I82.a23   Chronic embolism and thrombosis of axillary vein, bilateral

    ■**I82.a29**   Chronic embolism and thrombosis of unspecified axillary vein

● **I82.b**   Embolism and thrombosis of subclavian vein

  ● **I82.b1**   Acute embolism and thrombosis of subclavian vein

    I82.b11   Acute embolism and thrombosis of right subclavian vein

    I82.b12   Acute embolism and thrombosis of left subclavian vein

    I82.b13   Acute embolism and thrombosis of subclavian vein, bilateral

    ■**I82.b19**   Acute embolism and thrombosis of unspecified subclavian vein

  ● **I82.b2**   Chronic embolism and thrombosis of subclavian vein

    I82.b21   Chronic embolism and thrombosis of right subclavian vein

    I82.b22   Chronic embolism and thrombosis of left subclavian vein

    I82.b23   Chronic embolism and thrombosis of subclavian vein, bilateral

    ■**I82.b29**   Chronic embolism and thrombosis of unspecified subclavian vein

● **I82.c**   Embolism and thrombosis of internal jugular vein

  ● **I82.c1**   Acute embolism and thrombosis of internal jugular vein

    I82.c11   Acute embolism and thrombosis of right internal jugular vein

    I82.c12   Acute embolism and thrombosis of left internal jugular vein

    I82.c13   Acute embolism and thrombosis of internal jugular vein, bilateral

    ■**I82.c19**   Acute embolism and thrombosis of unspecified internal jugular vein

  ● **I82.c2**   Chronic embolism and thrombosis of internal jugular vein

    I82.c21   Chronic embolism and thrombosis of right internal jugular vein

    I82.c22   Chronic embolism and thrombosis of left internal jugular vein

    I82.c23   Chronic embolism and thrombosis of internal jugular vein, bilateral

    ■**I82.c29**   Chronic embolism and thrombosis of unspecified internal jugular vein

● **I82.8**   Embolism and thrombosis of other specified veins

  ● **I82.81**   Embolism and thrombosis of superficial veins of lower extremities

      Embolism and thrombosis of saphenous vein (greater) (lesser)

    I82.811   Embolism and thrombosis of superficial veins of right lower extremities ◐

    I82.812   Embolism and thrombosis of superficial veins of left lower extremities ◐

    I82.813   Embolism and thrombosis of superficial veins of lower extremities, bilateral ◐

    ■**I82.819**   Embolism and thrombosis of superficial veins of unspecified lower extremities ◐

  ● **I82.89**   Embolism and thrombosis of other specified veins

    I82.890   Acute embolism and thrombosis of other specified veins ◐

    I82.891   Chronic embolism and thrombosis of other specified veins ◐

● **I82.9**   Embolism and thrombosis of unspecified vein

  ■**I82.90**   Acute embolism and thrombosis of unspecified vein ◐

      Embolism of vein NOS

      Thrombosis (vein) NOS

  ■**I82.91**   Chronic embolism and thrombosis of unspecified vein ◐

● **I83**   Varicose veins of lower extremities

    Excludes1   varicose veins complicating pregnancy (O22.0-)

           varicose veins complicating the puerperium (O87.4)

● **I83.0**   Varicose veins of lower extremities with ulcer

    Use additional code to identify severity of ulcer (L97.-)

  ● **I83.00**   Varicose veins of unspecified lower extremity with ulcer

    ■**I83.001**   Varicose veins of unspecified lower extremity with ulcer of thigh

    ■**I83.002**   Varicose veins of unspecified lower extremity with ulcer of calf

    ■**I83.003**   Varicose veins of unspecified lower extremity with ulcer of ankle

    ■**I83.004**   Varicose veins of unspecified lower extremity with ulcer of heel and midfoot

         Varicose veins of unspecified lower extremity with ulcer of plantar surface of midfoot

---

●   Unacceptable First-Listed Diagnosis   ●   Use Additional Character(s)   ■ Unspecified   **OGCR** Official Guidelines for Coding and Reporting

◐ Complication\Comorbidity   ◐ Major C\C   Excludes 1   Excludes 2   Includes   Use additional   Code first   Code also

1049

CHAPTER 9 (I00-I99)

■ I83.005   Varicose veins of unspecified lower extremity with ulcer other part of foot
> Varicose veins of unspecified lower extremity with ulcer of toe

■ I83.008   Varicose veins of unspecified lower extremity with ulcer other part of lower leg

■ I83.009   Varicose veins of unspecified lower extremity with ulcer of unspecified site

● I83.01   Varicose veins of right lower extremity with ulcer

I83.011   Varicose veins of right lower extremity with ulcer of thigh

I83.012   Varicose veins of right lower extremity with ulcer of calf

I83.013   Varicose veins of right lower extremity with ulcer of ankle

I83.014   Varicose veins of right lower extremity with ulcer of heel and midfoot
> Varicose veins of right lower extremity with ulcer of plantar surface of midfoot

I83.015   Varicose veins of right lower extremity with ulcer other part of foot
> Varicose veins of right lower extremity with ulcer of toe

I83.018   Varicose veins of right lower extremity with ulcer other part of lower leg

■ I83.019   Varicose veins of right lower extremity with ulcer of unspecified site

● I83.02   Varicose veins of left lower extremity with ulcer

I83.021   Varicose veins of left lower extremity with ulcer of thigh

I83.022   Varicose veins of left lower extremity with ulcer of calf

I83.023   Varicose veins of left lower extremity with ulcer of ankle

I83.024   Varicose veins of left lower extremity with ulcer of heel and midfoot
> Varicose veins of left lower extremity with ulcer of plantar surface of midfoot

I83.025   Varicose veins of left lower extremity with ulcer other part of foot
> Varicose veins of left lower extremity with ulcer of toe

I83.028   Varicose veins of left lower extremity with ulcer other part of lower leg

■ I83.029   Varicose veins of left lower extremity with ulcer of unspecified site

● I83.1   Varicose veins of lower extremities with inflammation
> Stasis dermatitis

■ I83.10   Varicose veins of unspecified lower extremity with inflammation

I83.11   Varicose veins of right lower extremity with inflammation

I83.12   Varicose veins of left lower extremity with inflammation

● I83.2   Varicose veins of lower extremities with both ulcer and inflammation
> Use additional code to identify severity of ulcer (L97.-)

● I83.20   Varicose veins of unspecified lower extremity with both ulcer and inflammation

■ I83.201   Varicose veins of unspecified lower extremity with both ulcer of thigh and inflammation 🗫

■ I83.202   Varicose veins of unspecified lower extremity with both ulcer of calf and inflammation 🗫

■ I83.203   Varicose veins of unspecified lower extremity with both ulcer of ankle and inflammation 🗫

■ I83.204   Varicose veins of unspecified lower extremity with both ulcer of heel and midfoot and inflammation 🗫
> Varicose veins of unspecified lower extremity with both ulcer of plantar surface of midfoot and inflammation

■ I83.205   Varicose veins of unspecified lower extremity with both ulcer other part of foot and inflammation 🗫
> Varicose veins of unspecified lower extremity with both ulcer of toe and inflammation

■ I83.208   Varicose veins of unspecified lower extremity with both ulcer of other part of lower extremity and inflammation 🗫

■ I83.209   Varicose veins of unspecified lower extremity with both ulcer of unspecified site and inflammation 🗫

● I83.21   Varicose veins of right lower extremity with both ulcer and inflammation

I83.211   Varicose veins of right lower extremity with both ulcer of thigh and inflammation 🗫

I83.212   Varicose veins of right lower extremity with both ulcer of calf and inflammation 🗫

I83.213   Varicose veins of right lower extremity with both ulcer of ankle and inflammation 🗫

I83.214　Varicose veins of right lower extremity with both ulcer of heel and midfoot and inflammation 🅒
　　　Varicose veins of right lower extremity with both ulcer of plantar surface of midfoot and inflammation

I83.215　Varicose veins of right lower extremity with both ulcer other part of foot and inflammation 🅒
　　　Varicose veins of right lower extremity with both ulcer of toe and inflammation

I83.218　Varicose veins of right lower extremity with both ulcer of other part of lower extremity and inflammation 🅒

I83.219　Varicose veins of right lower extremity with both ulcer of unspecified site and inflammation 🅒

● I83.22　Varicose veins of left lower extremity with both ulcer and inflammation

I83.221　Varicose veins of left lower extremity with both ulcer of thigh and inflammation 🅒

I83.222　Varicose veins of left lower extremity with both ulcer of calf and inflammation 🅒

I83.223　Varicose veins of left lower extremity with both ulcer of ankle and inflammation 🅒

I83.224　Varicose veins of left lower extremity with both ulcer of heel and midfoot and inflammation 🅒
　　　Varicose veins of left lower extremity with both ulcer of plantar surface of midfoot and inflammation

I83.225　Varicose veins of left lower extremity with both ulcer other part of foot and inflammation 🅒
　　　Varicose veins of left lower extremity with both ulcer of toe and inflammation

I83.228　Varicose veins of left lower extremity with both ulcer of other part of lower extremity and inflammation 🅒

I83.229　Varicose veins of left lower extremity with both ulcer of unspecified site and inflammation 🅒

● I83.8　Varicose veins of lower extremities with other complications

● I83.81　Varicose veins of lower extremities with pain

I83.811　Varicose veins of right lower extremities with pain

I83.812　Varicose veins of left lower extremities with pain

I83.813　Varicose veins of bilateral lower extremities with pain

I83.819　Varicose veins of unspecified lower extremities with pain

● I83.89　Varicose veins of lower extremities with other complications
　　　Varicose veins of lower extremities with edema
　　　Varicose veins of lower extremities with swelling

I83.891　Varicose veins of right lower extremities with other complications

I83.892　Varicose veins of left lower extremities with other complications

I83.893　Varicose veins of bilateral lower extremities with other complications

I83.899　Varicose veins of unspecified lower extremities with other complications

● I83.9　Asymptomatic varicose veins of lower extremities
　　　Phlebectasia of lower extremities
　　　Varicose veins of lower extremities
　　　Varix of lower extremities

I83.90　Asymptomatic varicose veins of unspecified lower extremity
　　　Varicose veins NOS

I83.91　Asymptomatic varicose veins of right lower extremity

I83.92　Asymptomatic varicose veins of left lower extremity

I83.93　Asymptomatic varicose veins of bilateral lower extremities

● I84　Hemorrhoids

| **Includes** | piles |
| | varicose veins of anus and rectum |

| **Excludes 1** | hemorrhoids complicating childbirth and the puerperium (O87.2) |
| | hemorrhoids complicating pregnancy (O22.4) |

● I84.0　Thrombosed hemorrhoids

I84.00　Unspecified thrombosed hemorrhoids
　　　Thrombosed hemorrhoids, unspecified whether internal or external

I84.01　Internal thrombosed hemorrhoids

I84.02　External thrombosed hemorrhoids

I84.03　Internal and external thrombosed hemorrhoids

● I84.1　Hemorrhoids with other complications

● I84.10　Unspecified hemorrhoids with other complications

I84.101　Unspecified bleeding hemorrhoids

I84.102　Unspecified prolapsed hemorrhoids

I84.103　Unspecified strangulated hemorrhoids

I84.104　Unspecified ulcerated hemorrhoids

● I84.11　Internal hemorrhoids with other complications

I84.111　Internal bleeding hemorrhoids

I84.112　Internal prolapsed hemorrhoids

I84.113　Internal strangulated hemorrhoids

I84.114　Internal ulcerated hemorrhoids

● Unacceptable First-Listed Diagnosis　　　● Use Additional Character(s)　　　■ Unspecified　　　**OGCR** Official Guidelines for Coding and Reporting

🅒 Complication\Comorbidity　🅜 Major C\C　Excludes 1　Excludes 2　Includes　Use additional　Code first　Code also

CHAPTER 9 (I00-I99)

1051

● **I84.12**   **External hemorrhoids with other complications**

     I84.121   **External bleeding hemorrhoids**

     I84.122   **External prolapsed hemorrhoids**

     I84.123   **External strangulated hemorrhoids**

     I84.124   **External ulcerated hemorrhoids**

● **I84.13**   **Internal and external hemorrhoids with other complications**

     I84.131   **Internal and external bleeding hemorrhoids**

     I84.132   **Internal and external prolapsed hemorrhoids**

     I84.133   **Internal and external strangulated hemorrhoids**

     I84.134   **Internal and external ulcerated hemorrhoids**

● **I84.2**   **Hemorrhoids without complication**

   ▣ **I84.20**   **Unspecified hemorrhoids without complication**
       Hemorrhoids NOS

   I84.21   **Internal hemorrhoids without complication**
       Internal hemorrhoids NOS

   I84.22   **External hemorrhoids without complication**
       External hemorrhoids NOS

   I84.23   **Internal and external hemorrhoids without complication**
       Internal and external hemorrhoids NOS

I84.6   **Residual hemorrhoidal skin tags**
     Skin tags of anus or rectum

● **I85**   **Esophageal varices**

   Use additional code to identify:
     alcohol abuse and dependence (F10.-)

● **I85.0**   **Esophageal varices**
     Idiopathic esophageal varices
     Primary esophageal varices

   I85.00   **Esophageal varices without bleeding** 🦴
       Esophageal varices NOS

   I85.01   **Esophageal varices with bleeding** 🦴

● **I85.1**   **Secondary esophageal varices**
     Esophageal varices secondary to alcoholic liver disease
     Esophageal varices secondary to cirrhosis of liver
     Esophageal varices secondary to schistosomiasis
     Esophageal varices secondary to toxic liver disease

     Code first underlying disease

   ● **I85.10**   **Secondary esophageal varices without bleeding** 🦴

   ● **I85.11**   **Secondary esophageal varices with bleeding** 🦴

● **I86**   **Varicose veins of other sites**

   Excludes1   varicose veins of unspecified site (I83.9-)
   Excludes2   retinal varices (H35.0-)

I86.0   **Sublingual varices**

I86.1   **Scrotal varices**
     Varicocele

I86.2   **Pelvic varices**

I86.3   **Vulval varices**

   Excludes1   vulval varices complicating childbirth and the puerperium (O87.8)
       vulval varices complicating pregnancy (O22.1-)

I86.4   **Gastric varices**

I86.8   **Varicose veins of other specified sites**
     Varicose ulcer of nasal septum

● **I87**   **Other disorders of veins**

   ● **I87.0**   **Postthrombotic syndrome**
     Chronic venous hypertension due to deep vein thrombosis
     Postphlebitic syndrome

     Excludes1   chronic venous hypertension without deep vein thrombosis (I87.3-)

   ● **I87.00**   **Postthrombotic syndrome without complications**
       Asymptomatic postphlebitic syndrome

     I87.001   **Postthrombotic syndrome without complications of right lower extremity**

     I87.002   **Postthrombotic syndrome without complications of left lower extremity**

     I87.003   **Postthrombotic syndrome without complications of bilateral lower extremity**

     ▣ I87.009   **Postthrombotic syndrome without complications of unspecified extremity**
       Postphlebitic syndrome NOS

   ● **I87.01**   **Postthrombotic syndrome with ulcer**

     Use additional code to specify site and severity of ulcer (L97.-)

     I87.011   **Postthrombotic syndrome with ulcer of right lower extremity** 🦴

     I87.012   **Postthrombotic syndrome with ulcer of left lower extremity** 🦴

     I87.013   **Postthrombotic syndrome with ulcer of bilateral lower extremity** 🦴

     ▣ I87.019   **Postthrombotic syndrome with ulcer of unspecified lower extremity** 🦴

   ● **I87.02**   **Postthrombotic syndrome with inflammation**

     I87.021   **Postthrombotic syndrome with inflammation of right lower extremity**

     I87.022   **Postthrombotic syndrome with inflammation of left lower extremity**

     I87.023   **Postthrombotic syndrome with inflammation of bilateral lower extremity**

     ▣ I87.029   **Postthrombotic syndrome with inflammation of unspecified lower extremity**

●   Unacceptable First-Listed Diagnosis   ●   Use Additional Character(s)   ▣   Unspecified   **OGCR**   Official Guidelines for Coding and Reporting

🦴 Complication\Comorbidity   🦴 Major C\C   Excludes 1   Excludes 2   Includes   Use additional   Code first   Code also

● I87.03   Postthrombotic syndrome with ulcer and inflammation

    Use additional code to specify site and severity of ulcer (L97.-)

    I87.031   Postthrombotic syndrome with ulcer and inflammation of right lower extremity 🔗

    I87.032   Postthrombotic syndrome with ulcer and inflammation of left lower extremity 🔗

    I87.033   Postthrombotic syndrome with ulcer and inflammation of bilateral lower extremity 🔗

    ◼ I87.039   Postthrombotic syndrome with ulcer and inflammation of unspecified lower extremity 🔗

● I87.09   Postthrombotic syndrome with other complications

    I87.091   Postthrombotic syndrome with other complications of right lower extremity

    I87.092   Postthrombotic syndrome with other complications of left lower extremity

    I87.093   Postthrombotic syndrome with other complications of bilateral lower extremity

    ◼ I87.099   Postthrombotic syndrome with other complications of unspecified lower extremity

I87.1   Compression of vein 🔗
    Stricture of vein
    Vena cava syndrome (inferior) (superior)
    Excludes2   compression of pulmonary vein (I28.8)

I87.2   Venous insufficiency (chronic) (peripheral)

● I87.3   Chronic venous hypertension (idiopathic)
    Stasis edema
    Excludes1   chronic venous hypertension due to deep vein thrombosis (I87.0-)
        varicose veins of lower extremities (I83.-)

    ● I87.30   Chronic venous hypertension (idiopathic) without complications
        Asymptomatic chronic venous hypertension (idiopathic)

        I87.301   Chronic venous hypertension (idiopathic) without complications of right lower extremity

        I87.302   Chronic venous hypertension (idiopathic) without complications of left lower extremity

        I87.303   Chronic venous hypertension (idiopathic) without complications of bilateral lower extremity

        ◼ I87.309   Chronic venous hypertension (idiopathic) without complications of unspecified lower extremity
            Chronic venous hypertension NOS

● I87.31   Chronic venous hypertension (idiopathic) with ulcer

    Use additional code to specify site and severity of ulcer (L97.-)

    I87.311   Chronic venous hypertension (idiopathic) with ulcer of right lower extremity 🔗

    I87.312   Chronic venous hypertension (idiopathic) with ulcer of left lower extremity 🔗

    I87.313   Chronic venous hypertension (idiopathic) with ulcer of bilateral lower extremity 🔗

    ◼ I87.319   Chronic venous hypertension (idiopathic) with ulcer of unspecified lower extremity 🔗

● I87.32   Chronic venous hypertension (idiopathic) with inflammation

    I87.321   Chronic venous hypertension (idiopathic) with inflammation of right lower extremity

    I87.322   Chronic venous hypertension (idiopathic) with inflammation of left lower extremity

    I87.323   Chronic venous hypertension (idiopathic) with inflammation of bilateral lower extremity

    ◼ I87.329   Chronic venous hypertension (idiopathic) with inflammation of unspecified lower extremity

● I87.33   Chronic venous hypertension (idiopathic) with ulcer and inflammation

    Use additional code to specify site and severity of ulcer (L97.-)

    I87.331   Chronic venous hypertension (idiopathic) with ulcer and inflammation of right lower extremity 🔗

    I87.332   Chronic venous hypertension (idiopathic) with ulcer and inflammation of left lower extremity 🔗

    I87.333   Chronic venous hypertension (idiopathic) with ulcer and inflammation of bilateral lower extremity 🔗

    ◼ I87.339   Chronic venous hypertension (idiopathic) with ulcer and inflammation of unspecified lower extremity 🔗

● I87.39   Chronic venous hypertension (idiopathic) with other complications

    I87.391   Chronic venous hypertension (idiopathic) with other complications of right lower extremity

    I87.392   Chronic venous hypertension (idiopathic) with other complications of left lower extremity

    I87.393   Chronic venous hypertension (idiopathic) with other complications of bilateral lower extremity

    ◼ I87.399   Chronic venous hypertension (idiopathic) with other complications of unspecified lower extremity

● Unacceptable First-Listed Diagnosis   ● Use Additional Character(s)   ◼ Unspecified   **OGCR** Official Guidelines for Coding and Reporting

🔗 Complication\Comorbidity  Major C\C   Excludes 1  Excludes 2 Includes Use additional Code first   Code also

1053

CHAPTER 9 (I00-I99)

I87.8   **Other specified disorders of veins**
     Phlebosclerosis
     Venofibrosis

■ **I87.9**   **Disorder of vein, unspecified**

● **I88**   **Nonspecific lymphadenitis**

     | **Excludes1** | acute lymphadenitis, except mesenteric (L04.-)
                enlarged lymph nodes NOS (R59.-)
                human immunodeficiency virus [HIV] disease resulting in generalized lymphadenopathy (B20)

I88.0   **Nonspecific mesenteric lymphadenitis**
     Mesenteric lymphadenitis (acute)(chronic)

I88.1   **Chronic lymphadenitis, except mesenteric**
     Adenitis
     Lymphadenitis

I88.8   **Other nonspecific lymphadenitis**

■ **I88.9**   **Nonspecific lymphadenitis, unspecified**
     Lymphadenitis NOS

● **I89**   **Other noninfective disorders of lymphatic vessels and lymph nodes**

     | **Excludes1** | chylocele, tunica vaginalis (nonfilarial) NOS (N50.8)
                enlarged lymph nodes NOS (R59.-)
                filarial chylocele (B74.-)
                hereditary lymphedema (Q82.0)

I89.0   **Lymphedema, not elsewhere classified**
     Elephantiasis (nonfilarial) NOS
     Lymphangiectasis
     Obliteration, lymphatic vessel
     Praecox lymphedema
     Secondary lymphedema

       | **Excludes1** | postmastectomy lymphedema (I97.2)

I89.1   **Lymphangitis**
     Chronic lymphangitis
     Lymphangitis NOS
     Subacute lymphangitis

       | **Excludes1** | acute lymphangitis (L03.-)

I89.8   **Other specified noninfective disorders of lymphatic vessels and lymph nodes**
     Chylocele (nonfilarial)
     Chylous ascites
     Chylous cyst
     Lipomelanotic reticulosis
     Lymph node or vessel fistula
     Lymph node or vessel infarction
     Lymph node or vessel rupture

■ **I89.9**   **Noninfective disorder of lymphatic vessels and lymph nodes, unspecified**
     Disease of lymphatic vessels NOS

OTHER AND UNSPECIFIED DISORDERS OF THE CIRCULATORY SYSTEM (I95-I99)

● **I95**   **Hypotension**
     Subnormal arterial blood pressure

     | **Excludes1** | cardiovascular collapse (R57.9)
                maternal hypotension syndrome (O26.5-)
                nonspecific low blood pressure reading NOS (R03.1)

I95.0   **Idiopathic hypotension**

I95.1   **Orthostatic hypotension**
     Hypotension, postural
     Moving from a sitting or reclining position to a standing position precipitates a sudden drop in blood pressure (hypotension).

       | **Excludes1** | neurogenic orthostatic hypotension [Shy-Drager] (G90.3)
                    orthostatic hypotension due to drugs (I95.2)

I95.2   **Hypotension due to drugs**
     Orthostatic hypotension due to drugs
     Code first (T36-T50) to identify drug

I95.3   **Hypotension of hemodialysis**
     Intra-dialytic hypotension

● **I95.8**   **Other hypotension**

     I95.81   **Postprocedural hypotension**

     I95.89   **Other hypotension**
         Chronic hypotension

■ **I95.9**   **Hypotension, unspecified**

I96   **Gangrene, not elsewhere classified** 🏷

     | **Includes** | gangrenous cellulitis

     | **Excludes1** | gangrene in:
                atherosclerosis of native arteries of the extremities (I70.24)
                diabetes mellitus (E08-E13)
                hernia (K40.1, K40.4, K41.1, K41.4, K42.1, K43.1-, K44.1, K45.1, K46.1)
                other peripheral vascular diseases (I73.-)
                gangrene of certain specified sites - see Alphabetical Index
                gas gangrene (A48.0)
                pyoderma gangrenosum (L88)

● **I97**   **Intraoperative and postprocedural complications and disorders of circulatory system, not elsewhere classified**

     | **Excludes2** | postprocedural shock (T81.1)

I97.0   **Postcardiotomy syndrome**

● **I97.1**   **Other postprocedural cardiac functional disturbances**

       | **Excludes2** | acute pulmonary insufficiency following thoracic surgery (J95.1)
                    intraoperative cardiac functional disturbances (I97.7-)

     ● **I97.11**   **Postprocedural cardiac insufficiency**

         I97.110   **Postprocedural cardiac insufficiency following cardiac surgery**

         I97.111   **Postprocedural cardiac insufficiency following other surgery**

     ● **I97.12**   **Postprocedural cardiac arrest**

         I97.120   **Postprocedural cardiac arrest following cardiac surgery**

         I97.121   **Postprocedural cardiac arrest following other surgery**

     ● **I97.13**   **Postprocedural heart failure**
         Use additional code to identify the heart failure (I50.-)

● Unacceptable First-Listed Diagnosis   ● Use Additional Character(s)   ■ Unspecified   **OGCR** Official Guidelines for Coding and Reporting
🏷 Complication\Comorbidity   🏷 Major C\C | Excludes 1 | | Excludes 2 | Includes   Use additional   Code first   Code also

    I97.130   **Postprocedural heart failure following cardiac surgery**

    I97.131   **Postprocedural heart failure following other surgery**

● I97.19   **Other postprocedural cardiac functional disturbances**

    Use additional code, if applicable, to further specify disorder

    I97.190   **Other postprocedural cardiac functional disturbances following cardiac surgery**

    I97.191   **Other postprocedural cardiac functional disturbances following other surgery**

I97.2   **Postmastectomy lymphedema syndrome**
    Elephantiasis due to mastectomy
    Obliteration of lymphatic vessels

I97.3   **Postprocedural hypertension**

● I97.4   **Intraoperative hemorrhage and hematoma of a circulatory system organ or structure complicating a procedure**

    Excludes1   intraoperative hemorrhage and hematoma of a circulatory system organ or structure due to accidental puncture and laceration during a procedure (I97.5-)

    Excludes2   intraoperative cerebrovascular hemorrhage complicating a procedure (G97.3-)

  ● I97.41   **Intraoperative hemorrhage and hematoma of a circulatory system organ or structure complicating a circulatory system procedure**

    I97.410   **Intraoperative hemorrhage and hematoma of a circulatory system organ or structure complicating a cardiac catheterization** 🅒

    I97.411   **Intraoperative hemorrhage and hematoma of a circulatory system organ or structure complicating a cardiac bypass** 🅒

    I97.418   **Intraoperative hemorrhage and hematoma of a circulatory system organ or structure complicating other circulatory system procedure** 🅒

  I97.42   **Intraoperative hemorrhage and hematoma of a circulatory system organ or structure complicating other procedure** 🅒

● I97.5   **Accidental puncture and laceration of a circulatory system organ or structure during a procedure**

    Excludes2   accidental puncture and laceration of brain during a procedure (G97.4-)

  I97.51   **Accidental puncture and laceration of a circulatory system organ or structure during a circulatory system procedure** 🅒

  I97.52   **Accidental puncture and laceration of a circulatory system organ or structure during other procedure** 🅒

● I97.6   **Postprocedural hemorrhage and hematoma of a circulatory system organ or structure following a procedure**

    Excludes2   postprocedural cerebrovascular hemorrhage complicating a procedure (G97.5-)

  ● I97.61   **Postprocedural hemorrhage and hematoma of a circulatory system organ or structure following a circulatory system procedure**

    I97.610   **Postprocedural hemorrhage and hematoma of a circulatory system organ or structure following a cardiac catheterization** 🅒

    I97.611   **Postprocedural hemorrhage and hematoma of a circulatory system organ or structure following cardiac bypass** 🅒

    I97.618   **Postprocedural hemorrhage and hematoma of a circulatory system organ or structure following other circulatory system procedure** 🅒

  I97.62   **Postprocedural hemorrhage and hematoma of a circulatory system organ or structure following a other procedure** 🅒

● I97.7   **Intraoperative cardiac functional disturbances**

    Excludes2   acute pulmonary insufficiency following thoracic surgery (J95.1)
    postprocedural cardiac functional disturbances (I97.1-)

  ● I97.71   **Intraoperative cardiac arrest**

    I97.710   **Intraoperative cardiac arrest during cardiac surgery** 🅒

    I97.711   **Intraoperative cardiac arrest during other surgery** 🅒

  ● I97.79   **Other intraoperative cardiac functional disturbances**

    Use additional code, if applicable, to further specify disorder

    I97.790   **Other intraoperative cardiac functional disturbances during cardiac surgery** 🅒

    I97.791   **Other intraoperative cardiac functional disturbances during other surgery** 🅒

● I97.8   **Other intraoperative and postprocedural complications and disorders of the circulatory system, not elsewhere classified**

    Use additional code, if applicable, to further specify disorder

  ● I97.81   **Intraoperative cerebrovascular infarction**

    I97.810   **Intraoperative cerebrovascular infarction during cardiac surgery** 🅒

    I97.811   **Intraoperative cerebrovascular infarction during other surgery** 🅒

● Unacceptable First-Listed Diagnosis   ● Use Additional Character(s)   ▢ Unspecified   **OGCR** Official Guidelines for Coding and Reporting

 Complication\Comorbidity   🅒 Major C\C   Excludes 1   Excludes 2   Includes   Use additional   Code first   Code also

● **I97.82** **Postprocedural cerebrovascular infarction**

    I97.820 Postprocedural cerebrovascular infarction during cardiac surgery 🔏

    I97.821 Postprocedural cerebrovascular infarction during other surgery 🔏

  I97.88 Other intraoperative complications of the circulatory system, not elsewhere classified 🔏

  I97.89 Other postprocedural complications and disorders of the circulatory system, not elsewhere classified 🔏

● **I99** **Other and unspecified disorders of circulatory system**

  I99.8 Other disorder of circulatory system

  ◼I99.9 Unspecified disorder of circulatory system

● Unacceptable First-Listed Diagnosis   ● Use Additional Character(s)   ◼ Unspecified   **OGCR** Official Guidelines for Coding and Reporting

🔏 Complication\Comorbidity   🔏 Major C\C   Excludes 1   Excludes 2   Includes   Use additional   Code first   Code also

CHAPTER 9 (I00-I99)

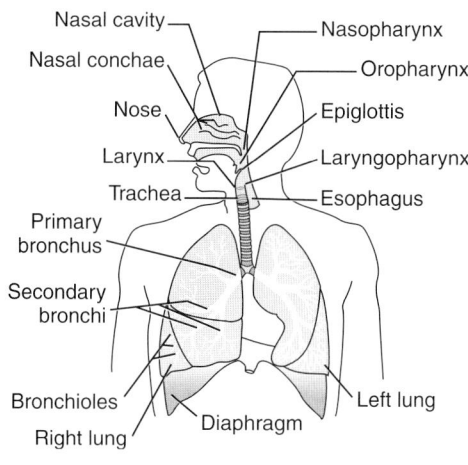

Figure 10–1 Respiratory system. (From Buck CJ: Step-by-Step Medical Coding, 2006 ed. Philadelphia, WB Saunders, 2006.)

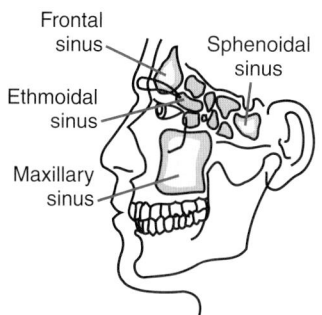

Figure 10-2 Paranasal sinuses. (From Buck CJ: Step-by-Step Medical Coding. 2006 ed. Philadelphia, WB Saunders, 2006.

Item 10–1 Pharyngitis is painful inflammation of the pharynx (sore throat). Ninety percent of the infections are caused by a virus with the remaining being bacterial and rarely a fungus (candidiasis). Other irritants such as pollutants, chemicals, or smoke may cause similar symptoms.

OGCR Section I.C.10.a.1
   10.1 Chronic Obstructive Pulmonary Disease (COPD) and Asthma

CHAPTER 10

DISEASES OF THE RESPIRATORY SYSTEM (J00-J99)

Note: When a respiratory condition is described as occurring in more than one site and is not specifically indexed, it should be classified to the lower anatomic site (e.g. tracheobronchitis to bronchitis in J40).

Use additional code, where applicable, to identify:
   exposure to environmental tobacco smoke (Z77.22)
   exposure to tobacco smoke in the perinatal period (P96.81)
   history of tobacco use (Z87.891)
   occupational exposure to environmental tobacco smoke (Z57.31)
   tobacco dependence (F17.-)
   tobacco use (Z72.0)

Excludes2 certain conditions originating in the
                perinatal period (P04-P96)
           certain infectious and parasitic diseases
                (A00-B99)
           complications of pregnancy, childbirth and
                the puerperium (O00-O99)
           congenital malformations, deformations and
                chromosomal abnormalities (Q00-Q99)
           endocrine, nutritional and metabolic
                diseases (E00-E90)
           injury, poisoning and certain other
                consequences of external causes
                (S00-T98)
           neoplasms (C00-D48)
           smoke inhalation (T59.81-)
           symptoms, signs and abnormal clinical
                and laboratory findings, not elsewhere
                classified (R00-R94)

This chapter contains the following blocks:

J00-J06	Acute upper respiratory infections
J09-J18	Influenza and pneumonia
J20-J22	Other acute lower respiratory infections
J30-J39	Other diseases of upper respiratory tract
J40-J47	Chronic lower respiratory diseases
J60-J70	Lung diseases due to external agents
J80-J84	Other respiratory diseases principally affecting the interstitium
J85-J86	Suppurative and necrotic conditions of the lower respiratory tract
J90-J94	Other diseases of the pleura
J95	Intraoperative and postprocedural complications and disorders of respiratory system, not elsewhere classified
J96-J99	Other diseases of the respiratory system

● Unacceptable First-Listed Diagnosis   ● Use Additional Character(s)   ▣ Unspecified   **OGCR** Official Guidelines for Coding and Reporting

🗞 Complication\Comorbidity   🗞 Major C\C   Excludes 1   Excludes 2   Includes   Use additional   Code first   Code also   1057

ACUTE UPPER RESPIRATORY INFECTIONS (J00-J06)

Excludes1 chronic obstructive pulmonary disease with acute lower respiratory infection (J44.0)

J00 Acute nasopharyngitis [common cold]

Includes acute rhinitis
coryza (acute)
infective nasopharyngitis NOS
infective rhinitis
nasal catarrh, acute
nasopharyngitis NOS

Excludes1 acute pharyngitis (J02.-)
acute sore throat NOS (J02.9)
pharyngitis NOS (J02.9)
rhinitis NOS (J31.0)
sore throat NOS (J02.9)

Excludes2 allergic rhinitis (J30.1-J30.9)
chronic pharyngitis (J31.2)
chronic rhinitis (J31.0)
chronic sore throat (J31.2)
nasopharyngitis, chronic (J31.1)
vasomotor rhinitis (J30.0)

(See Plate 49 on page NAP-24.)

J01 Acute sinusitis

Includes acute abscess of sinus
acute empyema of sinus
acute infection of sinus
acute inflammation of sinus
acute suppuration of sinus

Use additional code (B95-B97) to identify infectious agent.

Excludes1 sinusitis NOS (J32.9)
Excludes2 chronic sinusitis (J32.0-J32.8)

- **J01.0 Acute maxillary sinusitis**
  Acute antritis
  - J01.00 **Acute maxillary sinusitis, unspecified**
  - J01.01 **Acute recurrent maxillary sinusitis**
- **J01.1 Acute frontal sinusitis**
  - J01.10 **Acute frontal sinusitis, unspecified**
  - J01.11 **Acute recurrent frontal sinusitis**
- **J01.2 Acute ethmoidal sinusitis**
  - J01.20 **Acute ethmoidal sinusitis, unspecified**
  - J01.21 **Acute recurrent ethmoidal sinusitis**
- **J01.3 Acute sphenoidal sinusitis**
  - J01.30 **Acute sphenoidal sinusitis, unspecified**
  - J01.31 **Acute recurrent sphenoidal sinusitis**
- **J01.4 Acute pansinusitis**
  - J01.40 **Acute pansinusitis, unspecified**
  - J01.41 **Acute recurrent pansinusitis**
- **J01.8 Other acute sinusitis**
  - J01.80 **Other acute sinusitis**
    Acute sinusitis involving more than one sinus but not pansinusitis
  - J01.81 **Other acute recurrent sinusitis**
    Acute recurrent sinusitis involving more than one sinus but not pansinusitis
- **J01.9 Acute sinusitis, unspecified**
  - J01.90 **Acute sinusitis, unspecified**
  - J01.91 **Acute recurrent sinusitis, unspecified**

J02 Acute pharyngitis

Includes acute sore throat

Excludes1 acute laryngopharyngitis (J06.0)
peritonsillar abscess (J36)
pharyngeal abscess (J39.1)
pharyngitis due to coxsackie virus (B08.5)
pharyngitis due to gonococcus (A54.5)
retropharyngeal abscess (J39.0)

Excludes2 chronic pharyngitis (J31.2)

- **J02.0 Streptococcal pharyngitis**
  Septic pharyngitis
  Streptococcal sore throat
  Excludes1 scarlet fever (A38.-)
- **J02.8 Acute pharyngitis due to other specified organisms**
  Use additional code (B95-B97) to identify infectious agent
  Excludes1 acute pharyngitis due to herpes [simplex] virus (B00.2)
  acute pharyngitis due to infectious mononucleosis (B27.-)
  acute pharyngitis due to influenza virus (J10.1)
  enteroviral vesicular pharyngitis (B08.5)
- **J02.9 Acute pharyngitis, unspecified**
  Gangrenous pharyngitis (acute)
  Infective pharyngitis (acute) NOS
  Pharyngitis (acute) NOS
  Sore throat (acute) NOS
  Suppurative pharyngitis (acute)
  Ulcerative pharyngitis (acute)

J03 Acute tonsillitis
Inflammation of pharyngeal tonsils caused by virus or bacteria

Excludes1 acute sore throat (J02.-)
hypertrophy of tonsils (J35.1)
peritonsillar abscess (J36)
sore throat NOS (J02.9)
streptococcal sore throat (J02.0)

Excludes2 chronic tonsillitis (J35.0)

- **J03.0 Streptococcal tonsillitis**
  - J03.00 **Acute streptococcal tonsillitis, unspecified**
  - J03.01 **Acute recurrent streptococcal tonsillitis**
- **J03.8 Acute tonsillitis due to other specified organisms**
  Use additional code (B95-B97) to identify infectious agent.
  Excludes1 diphtheritic tonsillitis (A36.0)
  herpesviral pharyngotonsillitis (B00.2)
  streptococcal tonsillitis (J03.0)
  tuberculous tonsillitis (A15.8)
  Vincent's tonsillitis (A69.1)
  - J03.80 **Acute tonsillitis due to other specified organisms**
  - J03.81 **Acute recurrent tonsillitis due to other specified organisms**
- **J03.9 Acute tonsillitis, unspecified**
  Follicular tonsillitis (acute)
  Gangrenous tonsillitis (acute)
  Infective tonsillitis (acute)
  Tonsillitis (acute) NOS
  Ulcerative tonsillitis (acute)
  - J03.90 **Acute tonsillitis, unspecified**
  - J03.91 **Acute recurrent tonsillitis, unspecified**

CHAPTER 10 (J00-J99)

1058

● Unacceptable First-Listed Diagnosis   ● Use Additional Character(s)   ■ Unspecified   OGCR Official Guidelines for Coding and Reporting
Complication\Comorbidity   Major C\C   Excludes 1   Excludes 2   Includes   Use additional   Code first   Code also

Item 10–2 **Laryngitis** is an inflammation of the larynx (voice box) resulting in hoarse voice or the complete loss of the voice. **Tracheitis** is an inflammation of the trachea (often following a URI) commonly caused by *staphylococcus aureus* resulting in inspiratory stridor (crowing sound on inspiration) and a croup like cough.

● **J04   Acute laryngitis and tracheitis**

     Use additional code (B95-B97) to identify infectious agent.

     Excludes1   acute obstructive laryngitis [croup] and epiglottitis (J05.-)

     Excludes2   laryngismus (stridulus) (J38.5)

   J04.0   Acute laryngitis

      Edematous laryngitis (acute)
      Laryngitis (acute) NOS
      Subglottic laryngitis (acute)
      Suppurative laryngitis (acute)
      Ulcerative laryngitis (acute)

      Excludes1   acute obstructive laryngitis (J05.0)
                   influenzal laryngitis (J10.1)

      Excludes2   chronic laryngitis (J37.0)

● **J04.1   Acute tracheitis**

      Acute viral tracheitis
      Catarrhal tracheitis (acute)
      Tracheitis (acute) NOS

      Excludes2   chronic tracheitis (J42)

   J04.10   Acute tracheitis without obstruction

   J04.11   Acute tracheitis with obstruction 🕸

   J04.2   Acute laryngotracheitis

      Laryngotracheitis NOS
      Tracheitis (acute) with laryngitis (acute)

      Excludes1   acute obstructive laryngotracheitis (J05.0)

      Excludes2   chronic laryngotracheitis (J37.1)

● **J04.3   Supraglottitis, unspecified**

   ▣**J04.30   Supraglottitis, unspecified, without obstruction**

   ▣**J04.31   Supraglottitis, unspecified, with obstruction** 🕸

● **J05   Acute obstructive laryngitis [croup] and epiglottitis**

     Use additional code (B95-B97) to identify infectious agent.

   J05.0   Acute obstructive laryngitis [croup]

      Obstructive laryngitis (acute) NOS
      Obstructive laryngotracheitis NOS

   J05.1   Acute epiglottitis

      Excludes2   epiglottitis, chronic (J37.0)

   J05.10   Acute epiglottitis without obstruction 🕸
       Epiglottitis NOS

   J05.11   Acute epiglottitis with obstruction 🕸

● **J06   Acute upper respiratory infections of multiple and unspecified sites**

     Excludes1   acute respiratory infection NOS (J22)
                   influenza virus (J09.1, J10.1)
                   streptococcal pharyngitis (J02.0)

   J06.0   Acute laryngopharyngitis

   ▣**J06.9   Acute upper respiratory infection, unspecified**

      Upper respiratory disease, acute
      Upper respiratory infection NOS

INFLUENZA AND PNEUMONIA (J09-J18)

   Excludes1   allergic or eosinophilic pneumonia (J82)
                   aspiration pneumonia NOS (J69.0)
                   meconium pneumonia (P24.01)
                   neonatal aspiration pneumonia (P24.-)
                   pneumonia due to solids and liquids (J69-)
                   pneumonia with abscess of lung (J85.1)
                   congenital pneumonia (P23.9)
                   lipid pneumonia (J69.1)
                   rheumatic pneumonia (I00)
                   ventilator associated pneumonia (J95.851)

● **J09   Influenza due to certain identified influenza viruses**

     Excludes1   influenza due to other and unspecified influenza viruses (J10.-)

● **J09.0   Influenza due to identified avian influenza virus**

      Avian influenza
      Bird flu
      Influenza A/H5N1

   J09.01   Influenza due to identified avian influenza virus with respiratory manifestations

      Acute influenzal upper respiratory infection due to identified avian influenza virus
      Influenzal laryngitis due to due to identified avian influenza virus
      Influenzal pharyngitis due to due to identified avian influenza virus
      Influenzal pleural effusion due to due to identified avian influenza virus
      Code also any associated pneumonia (J12-J18)

● **J09.09   Influenza due to identified avian influenza virus with other manifestations**

   J09.090   Influenza due to identified avian influenza virus gastroenteritis

      Excludes1   "intestinal flu" [viral gastroenteritis] (A08.-)

   J09.098 Influenza due to identified avian influenza virus with other manifestations

      Influenza due to identified avian influenza virus encephalopathy
      Influenza due to identified avian influenza virus myocarditis
      Influenza due to identified avian influenza virus otitis media

● **J09.1   Influenza due to identified novel H1N1 influenza virus**

      2009 H1N1 [swine] influenza virus
      Novel 2009 influenza H1N1
      Novel H1N1 influenza
      Novel influenza A/H1N1
      Swine flu

   J09.11   Influenza due to identified novel H1N1 influenza virus with respiratory manifestations

      Acute influenzal upper respiratory infection due to identified novel H1N1 influenza virus
      Influenzal laryngitis due to due to identified novel H1N1 influenza virus
      Influenzal pharyngitis due to due to identified novel H1N1 influenza virus
      Influenzal pleural effusion due to due to identified novel H1N1 influenza virus
      Code also any associated pneumonia (J12-J18)

● Unacceptable First-Listed Diagnosis   ● Use Additional Character(s)   ▣ Unspecified   **OGCR** Official Guidelines for Coding and Reporting

🕸 Complication\Comorbidity   🕸 Major C\C   Excludes 1   Excludes 2   Includes   Use additional   Code first   Code also

1059

CHAPTER 10 (J00-J99)

● **J09.19**   **Influenza due to identified novel H1N1 influenza virus with other manifestations**

     J09.190   **Influenza due to identified novel H1N1 influenza virus gastroenteritis**

         Excludes1   "intestinal flu" [viral gastroenteritis] (A08.-)

     J09.198   **Influenza due to identified novel H1N1 influenza virus with other manifestations**

         Influenza due to identified novel H1N1 influenza virus encephalopathy

         Influenza due to identified novel H1N1 influenza virus myocarditis

         Influenza due to identified novel H1N1 influenza virus otitis media

● **J10**   **Influenza due to other influenza virus**

     Influenza due to unspecified influenza virus

     Code first any associated lung abscess (J85.1)

     Use additional code to identify the virus (B97.-)

     Excludes2   Hemophilus influenzae [H. influenzae] infection NOS (A49.2)

         Hemophilus influenzae [H. influenzae] laryngitis (J04.0)

         Hemophilus influenzae [H. influenzae] meningitis (G00.0)

         Influenza due to avian influenza virus (J09.0-)

         Influenza due to novel H1N1 influenza virus (J09.1-)

         Influenza due to swine flu (J09.1-)

     J10.1   **Influenza due to other influenza virus with respiratory manifestations**

         Acute influenzal upper respiratory infection due to other influenza virus

         Influenza NOS

         Influenzal laryngitis due to other influenza virus

         Influenzal pharyngitis due to other influenza virus

         Influenzal pleural effusion due to other influenza Vvirus

         Code also any associated pneumonia (J12-J18)

● **J10.8**   **Influenza due to other influenza virus with other manifestations**

     J10.81   **Influenzal gastroenteritis**

         Excludes1   "intestinal flu" [viral gastroenteritis] (A08.-)

     J10.89   **Influenza due to other influenza virus with other manifestations**

         Influenzal encephalopathy

         Influenzal myocarditis

         Influenzal otitis media

Item 10–3   Pneumonia is an infection of the lungs, caused by a variety of microorganisms, including viruses, most commonly the *Streptococcus pneumoniae* (pneumococcus) bacteria, fungi, and parasites. Pneumonia occurs when the immune system is weakened, often by a URI or influenza.

● **J12**   **Viral pneumonia, not elsewhere classified**

     Includes   bronchopneumonia due to viruses other than influenza viruses

     Code first any associated lung abscess (J85.1)

     Excludes1   aspiration pneumonia due to anesthesia during labor and delivery (O74.0)

         aspiration pneumonia due to anesthesia during pregnancy (O29)

         aspiration pneumonia due to anesthesia during puerperium (O89.0)

         aspiration pneumonia due to solids and liquids (J69.-)

         aspiration pneumonia NOS (J69.0)

         congenital pneumonia (P23.0)

         congenital rubella pneumonitis (P35.0)

         interstitial pneumonia NOS (J84.9)

         lipid pneumonia (J69.1)

         neonatal aspiration pneumonia (P24.-)

     J12.0   **Adenoviral pneumonia** 🏷

     J12.1   **Respiratory syncytial virus pneumonia** 🏷

     J12.2   **Parainfluenza virus pneumonia** 🏷

     J12.3   **Human metapneumovirus pneumonia** 🏷

● **J12.8**   **Other viral pneumonia**

     J12.81   **Pneumonia due to SARS-associated coronavirus** 🏷

         Severe acute respiratory syndrome NOS

     J12.89   **Other viral pneumonia** 🏷

■ **J12.9**   **Viral pneumonia, unspecified** 🏷

■ **J13**   **Pneumonia due to Streptococcus pneumoniae** 🏷

     Includes   bronchopneumonia due to S. pneumoniae

     Code first any associated lung abscess (J85.1)

     Excludes1   congenital pneumonia due to S. pneumoniae (P23.6)

         lobar pneumonia, unspecified organism (J18.1)

         pneumonia due to other streptococci (J15.3-J15.4)

J14   **Pneumonia due to Hemophilus influenzae** 🏷

     Includes   bronchopneumonia due to H. influenzae

     Code first any associated lung abscess (J85.1)

     Excludes1   congenital pneumonia due to H. influenzae (P23.6)

● **J15**   **Bacterial pneumonia, not elsewhere classified**

     Includes   bronchopneumonia due to bacteria other than S. pneumoniae and H. influenzae

     Code first any associated lung abscess (J85.1)

     Excludes1   chlamydial pneumonia (J16.0)

         congenital pneumonia (P23.-)

         Legionnaires' disease (A48.1)

         spirochetal pneumonia (A69.8)

     J15.0   **Pneumonia due to Klebsiella pneumoniae** 🏷

     J15.1   **Pneumonia due to Pseudomonas** 🏷

● **J15.2**   **Pneumonia due to staphylococcus**

     ■ **J15.20**   **Pneumonia due to staphylococcus, unspecified** 🏷

     J15.21   **Pneumonia due to staphylococcus aureus** 🏷

     J15.29   **Pneumonia due to other staphylococcus** 🏷

     J15.3   **Pneumonia due to streptococcus, group B** 🏷

● Unacceptable First-Listed Diagnosis   ● Use Additional Character(s)   ■ Unspecified   **OGCR** Official Guidelines for Coding and Reporting
🏷 Complication\Comorbidity   🏷 Major C\C   Excludes 1   Excludes 2   Includes   Use additional   Code first   Code also

J15.4   Pneumonia due to other streptococci 🦠

> **Excludes1**   pneumonia due to streptococcus,
> group B (J15.3)
> pneumonia due to Streptococcus
> pneumoniae (J13)

J15.5   Pneumonia due to Escherichia coli 🦠

**J15.6   Pneumonia due to other aerobic Gram-negative
bacteria** 🦠
> Pneumonia due to Serratia marcescens

J15.7   Pneumonia due to Mycoplasma pneumoniae 🦠

J15.8   Pneumonia due to other specified bacteria 🦠

▨J15.9   Unspecified bacterial pneumonia 🦠
> Pneumonia due to gram-positive bacteria

● **J16   Pneumonia due to other infectious organisms, not
elsewhere classified**

> *Code first any associated lung abscess (J85.1)*

> **Excludes1**   congenital pneumonia (P23.-)
> ornithosis (A70)
> pneumocystosis (B59)
> pneumonia NOS (J18.9)

J16.0   Chlamydial pneumonia 🦠

**J16.8   Pneumonia due to other specified infectious
organisms** 🦠

● **J17   Pneumonia in diseases classified elsewhere** 🦠

> *Code first underlying disease, such as:*
> Q fever (A78)
> rheumatic fever (I00)
> schistosomiasis (B65.0-B65.9)

> **Excludes1**   candidial pneumonia (B37.1)
> chlamydial pneumonia (J16.0)
> gonorrheal pneumonia (A54.84)
> histoplasmosis pneumonia (B39.0-B39.2)
> measles pneumonia (B05.2)
> nocardiosis pneumonia (A43.0)
> pneumocystosis (B59)
> pneumonia due to Pneumocystis carinii
> (B59)
> pneumonia due to Pneumocystis jiroveci
> (B59)
> pneumonia in actinomycosis (A42.0)
> pneumonia in anthrax (A22.1)
> pneumonia in ascariasis (B77.81)
> pneumonia in aspergillosis (B44.0-B44.1)
> pneumonia in coccidioidomycosis (B38.0-
> B38.2)
> pneumonia in cytomegalovirus disease
> (B25.0)
> pneumonia in toxoplasmosis (B58.3)
> rubella pneumonia (B06.81)
> salmonella pneumonia (A02.22)
> spirochetal infection NEC with pneumonia
> (A69.8)
> tularemia pneumonia (A21.2)
> typhoid fever with pneumonia (A01.03)
> varicella pneumonia (B01.2)
> whooping cough with pneumonia (A37.81)

● **J18   Pneumonia, unspecified organism**

> **Excludes1**   abscess of lung with pneumonia (J85.1)
> aspiration pneumonia due to anesthesia
> during labor and delivery (O74.0)
> aspiration pneumonia due to anesthesia
> during pregnancy (O29)
> aspiration pneumonia due to anesthesia
> during puerperium (O89.0)
> aspiration pneumonia due to solids and
> liquids (J69.-)
> aspiration pneumonia NOS (J69.0)
> congenital pneumonia (P23.0)
> drug-induced interstitial lung disorder
> (J70.2-J70.4)
> interstitial pneumonia NOS (J84.9)
> lipid pneumonia (J69.1)
> neonatal aspiration pneumonia (P24.-)
> pneumonitis due to external agents (J67-J70)
> pneumonitis due to fumes and vapors
> (J68.0)
> usual interstitial pneumonia (J84.1)

▨J18.0   Bronchopneumonia, unspecified organism 🦠

> **Excludes1**   hypostatic bronchopneumonia
> (J18.2)
> lipid pneumonia (J69.1)

> **Excludes2**   acute bronchiolitis (J21.-)
> chronic bronchiolitis (J44.9)

▨J18.1   Lobar pneumonia, unspecified organism 🦠

▨J18.2   Hypostatic pneumonia, unspecified organism 🦠
> Hypostatic bronchopneumonia
> Passive pneumonia

▨J18.8   Other pneumonia, unspecified organism 🦠

▨J18.9   Pneumonia, unspecified organism 🦠

OTHER ACUTE LOWER RESPIRATORY INFECTIONS (J20-J22)

> **Excludes1**   chronic obstructive pulmonary disease with
> acute lower respiratory infection (J44.0)

● **J20   Acute bronchitis**
> *Inflammation/irritation of the bronchial tubes lasting 2-3 weeks,
> most commonly caused by a virus.*

> **Includes**   acute and subacute bronchitis (with)
> bronchospasm
> acute and subacute bronchitis (with)
> tracheitis
> acute and subacute bronchitis (with)
> tracheobronchitis, acute
> acute and subacute fibrinous bronchitis
> acute and subacute membranous bronchitis
> acute and subacute purulent bronchitis
> acute and subacute septic bronchitis

> **Excludes2**   acute bronchitis with bronchiectasis (J47.0)
> acute bronchitis with chronic obstructive
> asthma (J44.0)
> acute bronchitis with chronic obstructive
> pulmonary disease (J44.0)
> allergic bronchitis NOS (J45.909-)
> bronchitis due to chemicals, fumes and
> vapors (J68.0)
> bronchitis NOS (J40)
> chronic bronchitis NOS (J42)
> chronic mucopurulent bronchitis (J41.1)
> chronic obstructive bronchitis (J44.-)
> chronic obstructive tracheobronchitis (J44.-)
> chronic simple bronchitis (J41.0)
> chronic tracheobronchitis (J42)
> tracheobronchitis NOS (J40)

● Unacceptable First-Listed Diagnosis   ● Use Additional Character(s)   ▨ Unspecified   **OGCR** Official Guidelines for Coding and Reporting

🦠 Complication\Comorbidity   🦠 Major C\C   Excludes 1   Excludes 2   Includes   Use additional   Code first   Code also   **1061**

CHAPTER 10 (J00-J99)

J20.0   Acute bronchitis due to Mycoplasma pneumoniae

J20.1   Acute bronchitis due to Hemophilus influenzae

J20.2   Acute bronchitis due to streptococcus

J20.3   Acute bronchitis due to coxsackievirus

J20.4   Acute bronchitis due to parainfluenza virus

J20.5   Acute bronchitis due to respiratory syncytial virus

J20.6   Acute bronchitis due to rhinovirus

J20.7   Acute bronchitis due to echovirus

J20.8   Acute bronchitis due to other specified organisms

■ **J20.9**   Acute bronchitis, unspecified

● **J21**   **Acute bronchiolitis**

Bronchiolitis obliterans with organizing pneumonia (BOOP) inflammation of bronchioles and surrounding tissue in lung.

> **Includes**   with bronchospasm

J21.0   Acute bronchiolitis due to respiratory syncytial virus 🦠

J21.1   Acute bronchiolitis due to human metapneumovirus 🦠

J21.8   Acute bronchiolitis due to other specified organisms 🦠

■ **J21.9**   Acute bronchiolitis, unspecified 🦠
     Bronchiolitis (acute)

> **Excludes1**   chronic bronchitis (J44.-)

■ **J22**   **Unspecified acute lower respiratory infection**

> **Includes**   acute (lower) respiratory (tract) infection NOS

> **Excludes1**   upper respiratory infection (acute) (J06.9)

OTHER DISEASES OF UPPER RESPIRATORY TRACT (J30-J39)

● **J30**   **Vasomotor and allergic rhinitis**

> **Includes**   spasmodic rhinorrhea

> **Excludes1**   allergic rhinitis with asthma (bronchial) (J45.909)
>   rhinitis NOS (J31.0)

J30.0   Vasomotor rhinitis

J30.1   Allergic rhinitis due to pollen
     Allergy NOS due to pollen
     Hay fever
     Pollinosis

J30.2   Other seasonal allergic rhinitis

J30.5   Allergic rhinitis due to food

● **J30.8**   Other allergic rhinitis

     J30.81   Allergic rhinitis due to animal (cat) (dog) hair and dander

     J30.89   Other allergic rhinitis
           Perennial allergic rhinitis

■ **J30.9**   Allergic rhinitis, unspecified

● **J31**   **Chronic rhinitis, nasopharyngitis and pharyngitis**

Use additional code to identify:
     exposure to environmental tobacco smoke (Z77.22)
     exposure to tobacco smoke in the perinatal period (P96.81)
     history of tobacco use (Z87.891)
     occupational exposure to environmental tobacco smoke (Z57.31)
     tobacco dependence (F17.-)
     tobacco use (Z72.0)

J31.0   Chronic rhinitis
     Atrophic rhinitis (chronic)
     Granulomatous rhinitis (chronic)
     Hypertrophic rhinitis (chronic)
     Obstructive rhinitis (chronic)
     Ozena
     Purulent rhinitis (chronic)
     Rhinitis (chronic) NOS
     Ulcerative rhinitis (chronic)

> **Excludes1**   allergic rhinitis (J30.1-J30.9)
>   vasomotor rhinitis (J30.0)

J31.1   Chronic nasopharyngitis

> **Excludes2**   acute nasopharyngitis (J00)

J31.2   Chronic pharyngitis
     Chronic sore throat
     Atrophic pharyngitis (chronic)
     Granular pharyngitis (chronic)
     Hypertrophic pharyngitis (chronic)

> **Excludes2**   acute pharyngitis (J02.9)

● **J32**   **Chronic sinusitis**

> **Includes**   sinus abscess
>   sinus empyema
>   sinus infection
>   sinus suppuration

Use additional code to identify:
     exposure to environmental tobacco smoke (Z77.22)
     exposure to tobacco smoke in the perinatal period (P96.81)
     history of tobacco use (Z87.891)
     infectious agent (B95-B97)
     occupational exposure to environmental tobacco smoke (Z57.31)
     tobacco dependence (F17.-)
     tobacco use (Z72.0)

> **Excludes2**   acute sinusitis (J01.-)

J32.0   Chronic maxillary sinusitis
     Antritis (chronic)
     Maxillary sinusitis NOS

J32.1   Chronic frontal sinusitis
     Frontal sinusitis NOS

J32.2   Chronic ethmoidal sinusitis
     Ethmoidal sinusitis NOS

> **Excludes1**   Woakes' ethmoiditis (J33.1)

J32.3   Chronic sphenoidal sinusitis
     Sphenoidal sinusitis NOS

J32.4   Chronic pansinusitis
     Pansinusitis NOS

J32.8   Other chronic sinusitis
     Sinusitis (chronic) involving more than one sinus but not pansinusitis

■ **J32.9**   Chronic sinusitis, unspecified
     Sinusitis (chronic) NOS

Item 10–4   Nasal polyps are an abnormal growth of tissue (tumor) projecting from a mucous membrane and attached to the surface by a narrow elongated stalk (pedunculated). Nasal polyps usually originate in the ethmoid sinus but also may occur in the maxillary sinus. Symptoms are nasal block, sinusitis, anosmia, and secondary infections.

● Unacceptable First-Listed Diagnosis   ● Use Additional Character(s)   ■ Unspecified   **OGCR** Official Guidelines for Coding and Reporting

🦠 Complication\Comorbidity   🦠 Major C\C   Excludes 1   Excludes 2   Includes   Use additional   Code first   Code also

● **J33   Nasal polyp**
  Use additional code to identify:
    exposure to environmental tobacco smoke (Z77.22)
    exposure to tobacco smoke in the perinatal period (P96.81)
    history of tobacco use (Z87.891)
    occupational exposure to environmental tobacco smoke
       (Z57.31)
    tobacco dependence (F17.-)
    tobacco use (Z72.0)
  Excludes1 adenomatous polyps (D14.0)

  J33.0   Polyp of nasal cavity
    Choanal polyp
    Nasopharyngeal polyp

  J33.1   Polypoid sinus degeneration
    Woakes' syndrome or ethmoiditis

  J33.8   Other polyp of sinus
    Accessory polyp of sinus
    Ethmoidal polyp of sinus
    Maxillary polyp of sinus
    Sphenoidal polyp of sinus

  J33.9   Nasal polyp, unspecified

● **J34   Other and unspecified disorders of nose and nasal sinuses**
  Excludes2 varicose ulcer of nasal septum (I86.8)

  J34.0   Abscess, furuncle and carbuncle of nose
    Cellulitis of nose
    Necrosis of nose
    Ulceration of nose

  J34.1   Cyst and mucocele of nose and nasal sinus

  J34.2   Deviated nasal septum

    Deflection or deviation of septum (nasal) (acquired)
    Excludes1 congenital deviated nasal septum
               (Q67.4)

  J34.3   Hypertrophy of nasal turbinates

● **J34.8   Other specified disorders of nose and nasal sinuses**

    J34.81   Nasal mucositis (ulcerative)
       Code also type of associated therapy,
         such as:

         antineoplastic and immunosuppressive
            drugs (T45.1x-)
         radiological procedure and
            radiotherapy (Y84.2)
         Excludes2 gastrointestinal mucositis
                    (ulcerative) (K92.81)
                    mucositis (ulcerative) of
                      vagina and vulva
                      (N76.81)
                    oral mucositis (ulcerative)
                      (K12.3-)

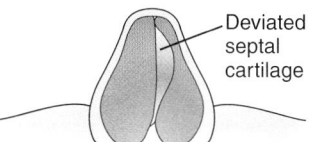
Deviated
septal
cartilage

Figure 10-3 Deviated
nasal septum.

Item 10–5 A **deviated nasal septum** is the displacement of the septal cartilage that separates the nares. This displacement causes obstructed air flow through the nasal passages. A child can be born with this displacement (congenital), or the condition may be acquired through trauma, such as a sports injury. Symptoms include nasal block, sinusitis, and related secondary infections. Septoplasty is surgical repair of this condition.

    **J34.89   Other specified disorders of nose and
              nasal sinuses**
       Perforation of nasal septum NOS
       Rhinolith

  J34.9 Unspecified disorder of nose and nasal sinuses

● **J35   Chronic diseases of tonsils and adenoids**
  Use additional code to identify:
    exposure to environmental tobacco smoke (Z77.22)
    exposure to tobacco smoke in the perinatal period (P96.81)
    history of tobacco use (Z87.891)
    occupational exposure to environmental tobacco smoke
       (Z57.31)
    tobacco dependence (F17.-)
    tobacco use (Z72.0)

● **J35.0   Chronic tonsillitis and adenoiditis**
    Excludes2 acute tonsillitis (J03.-)

    J35.01   Chronic tonsillitis

    J35.02   Chronic adenoiditis

    J35.03   Chronic tonsillitis and adenoiditis

  J35.1   Hypertrophy of tonsils
    Enlargement of tonsils
    Excludes1 hypertrophy of tonsils with tonsillitis
               (J35.0-)

  J35.2   Hypertrophy of adenoids
    Enlargement of adenoids
    Excludes1 hypertrophy of adenoids with
               adenoiditis (J35.0-)

  J35.3   Hypertrophy of tonsils with hypertrophy of adenoids
    Excludes1 hypertrophy of tonsils and adenoids
               with tonsillitis and adenoiditis
               (J35.03)

  J35.8   Other chronic diseases of tonsils and adenoids
    Adenoid vegetations
    Amygdalolith
    Calculus, tonsil
    Cicatrix of tonsil (and adenoid)
    Tonsillar tag
    Ulcer of tonsil

  **J35.9 Chronic disease of tonsils and adenoids,
           unspecified**
    Disease (chronic) of tonsils and adenoids NOS

  J36   Peritonsillar abscess 🖝
    Includes   abscess of tonsil
               peritonsillar cellulitis
               quinsy
    Use additional code (B95-B97) to identify infectious
      agent.
    Excludes1 acute tonsillitis (J03.-)
               chronic tonsillitis (J35.0)
               retropharyngeal abscess (J39.0)
               tonsillitis NOS (J03.9-)

● **J37   Chronic laryngitis and laryngotracheitis**
  Use additional code to identify:
    exposure to environmental tobacco smoke (Z77.22)
    exposure to tobacco smoke in the perinatal period
       (P96.81)
    history of tobacco use (Z87.891)
    infectious agent (B95-B97)
    occupational exposure to environmental tobacco smoke
       (Z57.31)
    tobacco dependence (F17.-)
    tobacco use (Z72.0)

● Unacceptable First-Listed Diagnosis   ● Use Additional Character(s)   ▦ Unspecified   **OGCR** Official Guidelines for Coding and Reporting
  🖝 Complication\Comorbidity   🖝 Major C\C   Excludes 1   Excludes 2   Includes   Use additional   Code first   Code also

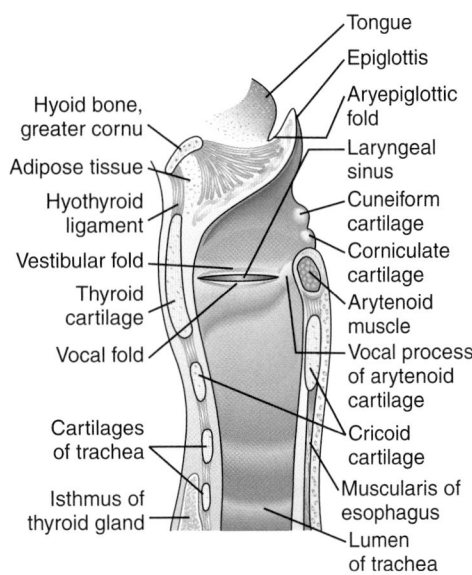

Figure 10-4 Coronal section of the larynx.

Item 10–6 The **larynx** extends from the tongue to the trachea and is divided into an upper and lower portion separated by folds. The framework of the larynx is cartilage composed of the single cricoid, thyroid, and epiglottic cartilages, and the paired arytenoid, cuneiform, and corniculate cartilages.

J37.0   Chronic laryngitis
　　　　Catarrhal laryngitis
　　　　Hypertrophic laryngitis
　　　　Sicca laryngitis
　　　　Excludes2　acute laryngitis (J04.0)
　　　　　　　　　　　obstructive (acute) laryngitis (J05.0)

J37.1   Chronic laryngotracheitis
　　　　Laryngitis, chronic, with tracheitis (chronic)
　　　　Tracheitis, chronic, with laryngitis
　　　　Excludes1　chronic tracheitis (J42)
　　　　Excludes2　acute laryngotracheitis (J04.2)
　　　　　　　　　　　acute tracheitis (J04.1)

● **J38   Diseases of vocal cords and larynx, not elsewhere classified**
　　　　Use additional code to identify:
　　　　exposure to environmental tobacco smoke (Z77.22)
　　　　exposure to tobacco smoke in the perinatal period (P96.81)
　　　　history of tobacco use (Z87.891)
　　　　occupational exposure to environmental tobacco smoke (Z57.31)
　　　　tobacco dependence (F17.-)
　　　　tobacco use (Z72.0)
　　　　Excludes1　congenital laryngeal stridor (P28.89)
　　　　　　　　　　　obstructive laryngitis (acute) (J05.0)
　　　　　　　　　　　postprocedural subglottic stenosis (J95.5)
　　　　　　　　　　　stridor (R06.1)
　　　　　　　　　　　ulcerative laryngitis (J04.0)

● **J38.0   Paralysis of vocal cords and larynx**
　　　　Laryngoplegia
　　　　Paralysis of glottis

　■ **J38.00   Paralysis of vocal cords and larynx, unspecified**

　　J38.01   Paralysis of vocal cords and larynx, unilateral

　　J38.02   Paralysis of vocal cords and larynx, bilateral

J38.1   Polyp of vocal cord and larynx
　　　　Excludes1　adenomatous polyps (D14.1)

J38.2   Nodules of vocal cords
　　　　Chorditis (fibrinous)(nodosa)(tuberosa)
　　　　Singer's nodes
　　　　Teacher's nodes

J38.3   Other diseases of vocal cords
　　　　Abscess of vocal cords
　　　　Cellulitis of vocal cords
　　　　Granuloma of vocal cords
　　　　Leukokeratosis of vocal cords
　　　　Leukoplakia of vocal cords

J38.4   Edema of larynx
　　　　Edema (of) glottis
　　　　Subglottic edema
　　　　Supraglottic edema
　　　　Excludes1　acute obstructive laryngitis [croup] (J05.0)
　　　　　　　　　　　edematous laryngitis (J04.0)

J38.5   Laryngeal spasm
　　　　Laryngismus (stridulus)

J38.6   Stenosis of larynx

J38.7   Other diseases of larynx
　　　　Abscess of larynx
　　　　Cellulitis of larynx
　　　　Disease of larynx NOS
　　　　Necrosis of larynx
　　　　Pachyderma of larynx
　　　　Perichondritis of larynx
　　　　Ulcer of larynx

● **J39   Other diseases of upper respiratory tract**
　　　　Excludes1　acute respiratory infection NOS (J22)
　　　　　　　　　　　acute upper respiratory infection (J06.9)
　　　　　　　　　　　upper respiratory inflammation due to chemicals, gases, fumes or vapors (J68.2)

J39.0   Retropharyngeal and parapharyngeal abscess 🞐
　　　　Peripharyngeal abscess
　　　　Excludes1　peritonsillar abscess (J36)

J39.1   Other abscess of pharynx 🞐
　　　　Cellulitis of pharynx
　　　　Nasopharyngeal abscess

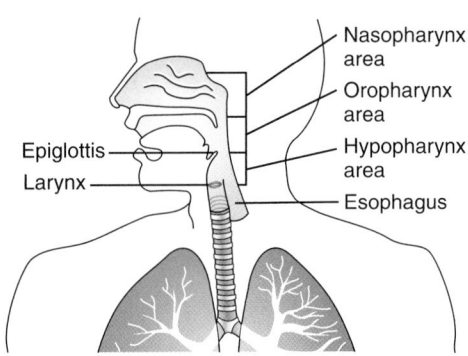

Figure 10-5 The pharynx.

Item 10–7 The **pharynx** is the passage for both food and air between the mouth and the esophagus and is divided into three areas: nasopharynx, oropharynx, and hypopharynx. The hypopharynx branches into the esophagus and the voice box.

● Unacceptable First-Listed Diagnosis   ● Use Additional Character(s)   ■ Unspecified   **OGCR** Official Guidelines for Coding and Reporting

1064   🞐 Complication\Comorbidity   🞐 Major C\C   Excludes 1   Excludes 2   Includes   Use additional   Code first   Code also

J39.2   **Other diseases of pharynx**
Cyst of pharynx
Edema of pharynx
> **Excludes2**   chronic pharyngitis (J31.2)
> ulcerative pharyngitis (J02.9)

J39.3   **Upper respiratory tract hypersensitivity reaction, site unspecified**
> **Excludes1**   hypersensitivity reaction of upper respiratory tract, such as:
> extrinsic allergic alveolitis (J67.9)
> pneumoconiosis (J60-J67.9)

J39.8   **Other specified diseases of upper respiratory tract**

J39.9   **Disease of upper respiratory tract, unspecified**

CHRONIC LOWER RESPIRATORY DISEASES (J40-J47)

> **Excludes1**   bronchitis due to chemicals, gases, fumes and vapors (J68.0)

> **Excludes2**   cystic fibrosis (E84.-)

J40   **Bronchitis, not specified as acute or chronic**
> **Includes**   bronchitis NOS
> catarrhal bronchitis
> bronchitis with tracheitis NOS
> tracheobronchitis NOS

Use additional code to identify:
exposure to environmental tobacco smoke (Z77.22)
exposure to tobacco smoke in the perinatal period (P96.81)
history of tobacco use (Z87.891)
occupational exposure to environmental tobacco smoke (Z57.31)
tobacco dependence (F17.-)
tobacco use (Z72.0)
> **Excludes1**   allergic bronchitis NOS (J45.909-)
> asthmatic bronchitis NOS (J45.9-)
> bronchitis due to chemicals, gases, fumes and vapors (J68.0)

J41   **Simple and mucopurulent chronic bronchitis**
Use additional code to identify:
exposure to environmental tobacco smoke (Z77.22)
exposure to tobacco smoke in the perinatal period (P96.81)
history of tobacco use (Z87.891)
occupational exposure to environmental tobacco smoke (Z57.31)
tobacco dependence (F17.-)
tobacco use (Z72.0)
> **Excludes1**   chronic bronchitis NOS (J42)
> chronic obstructive bronchitis (J44.-)

J41.0   **Simple chronic bronchitis**

J41.1   **Mucopurulent chronic bronchitis**

J41.8   **Mixed simple and mucopurulent chronic bronchitis**

J42   **Unspecified chronic bronchitis**
> **Includes**   chronic bronchitis NOS
> chronic tracheitis
> chronic tracheobronchitis

Use additional code to identify:
exposure to environmental tobacco smoke (Z77.22)
exposure to tobacco smoke in the perinatal period (P96.81)
history of tobacco use (Z87.891)
occupational exposure to environmental tobacco smoke (Z57.31)
tobacco dependence (F17.-)
tobacco use (Z72.0)
> **Excludes1**   chronic asthmatic bronchitis (J44.-)
> chronic bronchitis with airways obstruction (J44.-)
> chronic emphysematous bronchitis (J44.-)
> chronic obstructive pulmonary disease NOS (J44.9)
> simple and mucopurulent chronic bronchitis (J41.-)

J43   **Emphysema**
Use additional code to identify:
exposure to environmental tobacco smoke (Z77.22)
history of tobacco use (Z87.891)
occupational exposure to environmental tobacco smoke (Z57.31)
tobacco dependence (F17.-)
tobacco use (Z72.0)
> **Excludes1**   compensatory emphysema (J98.3)
> emphysema due to inhalation of chemicals, gases, fumes or vapors (J68.4)
> emphysema with chronic (obstructive) bronchitis (J44.-)
> emphysematous (obstructive) bronchitis (J44.-)
> interstitial emphysema (J98.2)
> mediastinal emphysema (J98.2)
> neonatal interstitial emphysema (P25.0)
> surgical (subcutaneous) emphysema (T81.82)
> traumatic subcutaneous emphysema (T79.7)

J43.0   **Unilateral pulmonary emphysema [MacLeod's syndrome]**
Swyer-James syndrome
Unilateral emphysema
Unilateral hyperlucent lung
Unilateral pulmonary artery functional hypoplasia
Unilateral transparency of lung

J43.1   **Panlobular emphysema**
Panacinar emphysema

J43.2   **Centrilobular emphysema**

J43.8   **Other emphysema**

Item 10–8   **Chronic bronchitis** is usually defined as being present in any patient who has persistent cough with sputum production for at least three months in at least two consecutive years. **Simple chronic bronchitis** is marked by a productive cough but no pathological airflow obstruction. **Chronic obstructive pulmonary disease (COPD)** is a group of conditions—bronchitis, emphysema, asthma, bronchiectasis, allergic alveolitis—marked by dyspnea. **Catarrhal** bronchitis is an acute form of bronchitis marked by profuse mucus and pus production (**mucopurulent** discharge). **Croupous** bronchitis, also known as pseudomembranous, fibrinous, plastic, exudative, or membranous, is marked by a violent cough and dyspnea.

● Unacceptable First-Listed Diagnosis   ● Use Additional Character(s)   Unspecified   **OGCR** Official Guidelines for Coding and Reporting
Complication\Comorbidity   Major C\C   Excludes 1   Excludes 2   Includes   Use additional   Code first   Code also
CHAPTER 10 (J00-J99)   1065

◼ **J43.9**   **Emphysema, unspecified**
Bullous emphysema (lung)(pulmonary)
Emphysema (lung)(pulmonary) NOS
Emphysematous bleb
Vesicular emphysema (lung)(pulmonary)

● **J44**   **Other chronic obstructive pulmonary disease**
    Includes   asthma with chronic obstructive pulmonary disease
chronic asthmatic (obstructive) bronchitis
chronic bronchitis with airways obstruction
chronic bronchitis with emphysema
chronic emphysematous bronchitis
chronic obstructive asthma
chronic obstructive bronchitis
chronic obstructive tracheobronchitis

   Code also type of asthma, if applicable (J45.-)

   Use additional code to identify:
exposure to environmental tobacco smoke (Z77.22)
history of tobacco use (Z87.891)
occupational exposure to environmental tobacco smoke (Z57.31)
tobacco dependence (F17.-)
tobacco use (Z72.0)

   Excludes1   bronchiectasis (J47.-)
chronic bronchitis NOS (J42)
chronic simple and mucopurulent bronchitis (J41.-)
chronic tracheitis (J42)
chronic tracheobronchitis (J42)
emphysema without chronic bronchitis (J43.-)
lung diseases due to external agents (J60-J70)

   J44.0   **Chronic obstructive pulmonary disease with acute lower respiratory infection** %
Use additional code to identify the infection

   J44.1   **Chronic obstructive pulmonary disease with (acute) exacerbation** %
Decompensated COPD
Decompensated COPD with (acute) exacerbation
    Excludes2   chronic obstructive pulmonary disease [COPD] with acute bronchitis (J44.0)

◼ **J44.9**   **Chronic obstructive pulmonary disease, unspecified**
Chronic obstructive airway disease NOS
Chronic obstructive lung disease NOS

Item 10–9   Asthma is a bronchial condition marked by airway obstruction, hyper-responsiveness, and inflammation. **Extrinsic** asthma, also known as allergic asthma, is characterized by the same symptoms that occur with exposure to allergens and is divided into the following types: **atopic, occupational, and allergic bronchopulmonary aspergillosis. Intrinsic** asthma occurs in patients who have no history of allergy or sensitivities to allergens and is divided into the following types: **nonreaginic and pharmacologic. Status asthmaticus** is the most severe form of asthma attack and can last for days or weeks.

● **J45**   **Asthma**
    Includes   allergic (predominantly) asthma
allergic bronchitis NOS
allergic rhinitis with asthma
atopic asthma
extrinsic allergic asthma
hay fever with asthma
idiosyncratic asthma
intrinsic nonallergic asthma
nonallergic asthma

   Use additional code to identify:
exposure to environmental tobacco smoke (Z77.22)
exposure to tobacco smoke in the perinatal period (P96.81)
history of tobacco use (Z87.891)
occupational exposure to environmental tobacco smoke (Z57.31)
tobacco dependence (F17.-)
tobacco use (Z72.0)

   Excludes1   detergent asthma (J69.8)
eosinophilic asthma (J82)
lung diseases due to external agents (J60-J70)
miner's asthma (J60)
wheezing NOS (R06.2)
wood asthma (J67.8)

   Excludes2   asthma with chronic obstructive pulmonary disease
chronic asthmatic (obstructive) bronchitis
chronic obstructive asthma

● **J45.2**   **Mild intermittent asthma**
   J45.20   **Mild intermittent asthma, uncomplicated**
Mild intermittent asthma NOS
   J45.21   **Mild intermittent asthma with (acute) exacerbation** %
   J45.22   **Mild intermittent asthma with status asthmaticus** %

● **J45.3**   **Mild persistent asthma**
   J45.30   **Mild persistent asthma, uncomplicated**
Mild persistent asthma NOS
   J45.31   **Mild persistent asthma with (acute) exacerbation** %
   J45.32   **Mild persistent asthma with status asthmaticus** %

● **J45.4**   **Moderate persistent**
   J45.40   **Moderate persistent, uncomplicated**
Moderate persistent asthma NOS
   J45.41   **Moderate persistent with (acute) exacerbation** %
   J45.42   **Moderate persistent with status asthmaticus** %

● **J45.5**   **Severe persistent**
   J45.50   **Severe persistent, uncomplicated**
Severe persistent asthma NOS
   J45.51   **Severe persistent with (acute) exacerbation** %
   J45.52   **Severe persistent with status asthmaticus** %

● **J45.9**   **Other and unspecified asthma**
   ● **J45.90**   **Unspecified asthma**
Asthmatic bronchitis NOS
Childhood asthma NOS
Late onset asthma
     ◼ **J45.901**   **Unspecified asthma with (acute) exacerbation** %
     ◼ **J45.902**   **Unspecified asthma with status asthmaticus** %

● Unacceptable First-Listed Diagnosis   ● Use Additional Character(s)   ◼ Unspecified   **OGCR** Official Guidelines for Coding and Reporting
% Complication\Comorbidity   % Major C\C   Excludes 1   Excludes 2   Includes   Use additional   Code first   Code also

Figure 10-6 Progressive massive fibrosis superimposed on coal workers' pneumoconiosis. The large, blackened scars are located principally in the upper lobe. (From Cotran R, Kumar V, Collins T: Robbins Pathologic Basis of Disease, 6th ed. Philadelphia, WB Saunders, 1999, p 730. Courtesy of Dr. Warner Laquer, Dr. Jerome Kleinerman, and the National Institute of Occupational Safety and Health, Morgantown. WV.)

Item 10–10   Pneumoconiosis refers to a lung condition resulting from exposure to inorganic or organic airborne particles, such as coal dust or moldy hay, as well as chemical fumes and vapors, such as insecticides. In this condition, the lungs retain the airborne particles.

■ **J45.909   Unspecified asthma, uncomplicated**
Asthma NOS

● **J45.99   Other asthma**

     J45.990   Exercise induced bronchospasm

     J45.991   Cough variant asthma

     J45.998   Other asthma

● **J47   Bronchiectasis**

     Includes   bronchiolectasis

     Use additional code to identify:
       exposure to environmental tobacco smoke (Z77.22)
       exposure to tobacco smoke in the perinatal period (P96.81)
       history of tobacco use (Z87.891)
       occupational exposure to environmental tobacco smoke (Z57.31)
       tobacco dependence (F17.-)
       tobacco use (Z72.0)

     Excludes1   congenital bronchiectasis (Q33.4)
         tuberculous bronchiectasis (current disease) (A15.0)

J47.0   Bronchiectasis with acute lower respiratory infection 🔗
Bronchiectasis with acute bronchitis

J47.1   Bronchiectasis with (acute) exacerbation 🔗

J47.9   Bronchiectasis, uncomplicated
Bronchiectasis NOS

LUNG DISEASES DUE TO EXTERNAL AGENTS (J60-J70)

     Excludes2   asthma (J45.-)
         malignant neoplasm of bronchus and lung (C34.-)

J60   Coalworker's pneumoconiosis

     Includes   anthracosilicosis
         anthracosis
         black lung disease
         coalworker's lung

     Excludes1   coalworker pneumoconiosis with tuberculosis, any type in A15 (J65)

J61   Pneumoconiosis due to asbestos and other mineral fibers

     Includes   asbestosis

     Excludes1   pleural plaque with asbestosis (J92.0)
         pneumoconiosis with tuberculosis, any type in A15 (J65)

● **J62   Pneumoconiosis due to dust containing silica**

     Includes   silicotic fibrosis (massive) of lung

     Excludes1   pneumoconiosis with tuberculosis, any type in A15 (J65)

J62.0   Pneumoconiosis due to talc dust

J62.8   Pneumoconiosis due to other dust containing silica
Silicosis NOS

● **J63   Pneumoconiosis due to other inorganic dusts**

     Excludes1   pneumoconiosis with tuberculosis, any type in A15 (J65)

J63.0   Aluminosis (of lung)

J63.1   Bauxite fibrosis (of lung)

J63.2   Berylliosis

J63.3   Graphite fibrosis (of lung)

J63.4   Siderosis

J63.5   Stannosis

J63.6   Pneumoconiosis due to other specified inorganic dusts

■ **J64   Unspecified pneumoconiosis**

     Excludes1   pneumonoconiosis with tuberculosis, any type in A15 (J65)

J65   Pneumoconiosis associated with tuberculosis

     Includes   any condition in J60-J64 with tuberculosis, any type in A15
         silicotuberculosis

● **J66   Airway disease due to specific organic dust**

     Excludes2   allergic alveolitis (J67.-)
         asbestosis (J61)
         bagassosis (J67.1)
         farmer's lung (J67.0)
         hypersensitivity pneumonitis due to organic dust (J67.-)
         reactive airways dysfunction syndrome (J68.3)

J66.0   Byssinosis
Airway disease due to cotton dust

J66.1   Flax-dressers' disease

J66.2   Cannabinosis

J66.8   Airway disease due to other specific organic dusts

● **J67   Hypersensitivity pneumonitis due to organic dust**

     Includes   allergic alveolitis and pneumonitis due to inhaled organic dust and particles of fungal, actinomycetic or other origin

     Excludes1   pneumonitis due to inhalation of chemicals, gases, fumes or vapors (J68.0)

J67.0   Farmer's lung
Harvester's lung
Haymaker's lung
Moldy hay disease

J67.1   Bagassosis
Bagasse disease
Bagasse pneumonitis

J67.2   Bird fancier's lung
Budgerigar fancier's disease or lung
Pigeon fancier's disease or lung

J67.3   Suberosis
Corkhandler's disease or lung
Corkworker's disease or lung

J67.4   Maltworker's lung
Alveolitis due to Aspergillus clavatus

CHAPTER 10 (J00-J99)

J67.5   **Mushroom-worker's lung**

J67.6   **Maple-bark-stripper's lung**
Alveolitis due to Cryptostroma corticale
Cryptostromosis

J67.7   **Air conditioner and humidifier lung** 🔵
Allergic alveolitis due to fungal, thermophilic
actinomycetes and other organisms growing
in ventilation [air conditioning] systems

J67.8   **Hypersensitivity pneumonitis due to other organic dusts** 🔵
Cheese-washer's lung
Coffee-worker's lung
Fish-meal worker's lung
Furrier's lung
Sequoiosis

◻J67.9   **Hypersensitivity pneumonitis due to unspecified organic dust** 🔵
Allergic alveolitis (extrinsic) NOS
Hypersensitivity pneumonitis NOS

● **J68**   **Respiratory conditions due to inhalation of chemicals, gases, fumes and vapors**

Code first (T51-T65) to identify cause

● **J68.0**   **Bronchitis and pneumonitis due to chemicals, gases, fumes and vapors** 🔵
Chemical bronchitis (acute)

● **J68.1**   **Pulmonary edema due to chemicals, gases, fumes and vapors** 🔵
Chemical pulmonary edema (acute) (chronic)

    Excludes1   pulmonary edema (acute) (chronic) NOS (J81.-)

● **J68.2**   **Upper respiratory inflammation due to chemicals, gases, fumes and vapors, not elsewhere classified**

● **J68.3**   **Other acute and subacute respiratory conditions due to chemicals, gases, fumes and vapors**
Reactive airways dysfunction syndrome

J68.4   **Chronic respiratory conditions due to chemicals, gases, fumes and vapors**
Emphysema (diffuse) (chronic) due to inhalation
of chemicals, gases, fumes and vapors
Obliterative bronchiolitis (chronic) (subacute) due
to inhalation of chemicals, gases, fumes and
vapors
Pulmonary fibrosis (chronic) due to inhalation of
chemicals, gases, fumes and vapors

    Excludes1   chronic pulmonary edema due to
chemicals, gases, fumes and
vapors (J68.1)

● **J68.8**   **Other respiratory conditions due to chemicals, gases, fumes and vapors**

● ◻ **J68.9**   **Unspecified respiratory condition due to chemicals, gases, fumes and vapors**

● **J69**   **Pneumonitis due to solids and liquids**

    Excludes1   neonatal aspiration syndromes (P24.-)

J69.0   **Pneumonitis due to inhalation of food and vomit** 🔵
Aspiration pneumonia NOS
Aspiration pneumonia (due to) food (regurgitated)
Aspiration pneumonia (due to) gastric secretions
Aspiration pneumonia (due to) milk
Aspiration pneumonia (due to) vomit

Code also any associated foreign body in
respiratory tract (T17.-)

    Excludes1   chemical pneumonitis due to
anesthesia [Mendelson's
syndrome] (J95.4)
obstetric aspiration pneumonitis
(O74.0)

● **J69.1**   **Pneumonitis due to inhalation of oils and essences** 🔵
Exogenous lipoid pneumonia
Lipid pneumonia NOS

Code first (T51-T65) to identify substance

    Excludes1   endogenous lipoid pneumonia
(J84.2)

● **J69.8**   **Pneumonitis due to inhalation of other solids and liquids** 🔵
Pneumonitis due to aspiration of blood
Pneumonitis due to aspiration of detergent

Code first (T51-T65) to identify substance

● **J70**   **Respiratory conditions due to other external agents**

J70.0   **Acute pulmonary manifestations due to radiation** 🔵
Radiation pneumonitis

Use additional code (W88-W90, X39.0-) to identify
the external cause

J70.1   **Chronic and other pulmonary manifestations due to radiation** 🔵
Fibrosis of lung following radiation

Use additional code (W88-W90, X39.0-) to identify
the external cause

● **J70.2**   **Acute drug-induced interstitial lung disorders**

Code first (T36-T50) to identify drug

    Excludes1   interstitial pneumonia NOS (J84.9)
lymphoid interstitial pneumonia
(J84.2)

● **J70.3**   **Chronic drug-induced interstitial lung disorders**

Code first (T36-T50 with 7th character S) to identify drug

    Excludes1   interstitial pneumonia NOS (J84.9)
lymphoid interstitial pneumonia
(J84.2)

● ◻ **J70.4**   **Drug-induced interstitial lung disorders, unspecified**

Code first (T36-T50) to identify drug

    Excludes1   interstitial pneumonia NOS (J84.9)
lymphoid interstitial pneumonia
(J84.2)

● **J70.8**   **Respiratory conditions due to other specified external agents**

Code first (T51-T65) to identify the external agent

● ◻ **J70.9**   **Respiratory conditions due to unspecified external agent**

Code first (T51-T65) to identify the external agent

OTHER RESPIRATORY DISEASES PRINCIPALLY AFFECTING THE INTERSTITIUM (J80-J84)

J80   **Acute respiratory distress syndrome** 🔵

    Includes   acute respiratory distress syndrome in
adult or child adult hyaline membrane
disease

    Excludes1   respiratory distress syndrome in newborn
(perinatal) (P22.0)

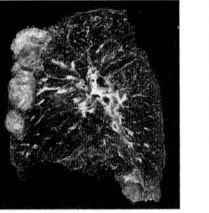

Figure 10-7   Bullous emphysema with large subpleural bullae *(upper left)*. (From Kumar: Robbins and Cotran: Pathologic Basis of Disease, 7th ed. 2005, Saunders, An Imprint of Elsevier)

1068

● Unacceptable First-Listed Diagnosis   ● Use Additional Character(s)   ◻ Unspecified   **OGCR** Official Guidelines for Coding and Reporting

🔵 Complication\Comorbidity   🔵 Major C\C   Excludes 1   Excludes 2   Includes   Use additional   Code first   Code also

CHAPTER 10 (J00-J99)

● **J81**   **Pulmonary edema**

     Use additional code to identify:
       exposure to environmental tobacco smoke (Z77.22)
       history of tobacco use (Z87.891)
       occupational exposure to environmental tobacco smoke
         (Z57.31)
       tobacco dependence (F17.-)
       tobacco use (Z72.0)

     Excludes1   chemical (acute) pulmonary edema (J68.1)
               hypostatic pneumonia (J18.2)
               passive pneumonia (J18.2)
               pulmonary edema due to external agents
                 (J60-J70)
               pulmonary edema with heart disease NOS
                 (I50.1)
               pulmonary edema with heart failure (I50.1)

   J81.0   **Acute pulmonary edema** 🦠
        Acute edema of lung

   J81.1   **Chronic pulmonary edema** 🦠
        Pulmonary congestion (chronic) (passive)
        Pulmonary edema NOS

J82   **Pulmonary eosinophilia, not elsewhere classified** 🦠

     Includes   allergic pneumonia
               eosinophilic asthma
               eosinophilic pneumonia
               Löffler's pneumonia
               tropical (pulmonary) eosinophilia NOS

     Excludes1   pulmonary eosinophilia due to aspergillosis
                 (B44.-)
               pulmonary eosinophilia due to drugs (J70.2-
                 J70.4)
               pulmonary eosinophilia due to specified
                 parasitic infection (B50-B83)
               pulmonary eosinophilia due to systemic
                 connective tissue disorders (M30-M36)

● **J84**   **Other interstitial pulmonary diseases**

     Excludes1   drug-induced interstitial lung disorders
                 (J70.2-J70.4)
               interstitial emphysema (J98.2)
               lung diseases due to external agents (J60-
                 J70)

   J84.0   **Alveolar and parieto-alveolar conditions** 🦠
        Alveolar proteinosis
        Pulmonary alveolar microlithiasis

   J84.1   **Other interstitial pulmonary diseases with
          fibrosis**
        Cirrhosis of lung
        Diffuse pulmonary fibrosis
        Fibrosing alveolitis (cryptogenic)
        Hamman-Rich syndrome
        Idiopathic pulmonary fibrosis
        Induration of lung
        Usual interstitial pneumonia

       Excludes1   pulmonary fibrosis (chronic) due to
                   inhalation of chemicals, gases,
                   fumes or vapors (J68.4)
                 pulmonary fibrosis (chronic)
                   following radiation (J70.1)

   J84.2   **Lymphoid interstitial pneumonia** 🦠
        Endogenous lipoid pneumonia
        Lymphoid interstitial pneumonitis

       Excludes1   exogenous lipoid pneumonia (J69.1)
                 unspecified lipoid pneumonia (J69.1)

Item 10–11   **Empyema** is a condition in which pus accumulates in a body cavity. Empyema **with fistula** occurs when the pus passes from one cavity to another organ or structure.

   J84.8   **Other specified interstitial pulmonary diseases** 🦠
   🔲 **J84.9**   **Interstitial pulmonary disease, unspecified** 🦠
        Interstitial pneumonia NOS

SUPPURATIVE AND NECROTIC CONDITIONS OF THE LOWER RESPIRATORY TRACT (J85-J86)

● **J85**   **Abscess of lung and mediastinum**

     Use additional code (B95-B97) to identify infectious
     agent.

   J85.0   **Gangrene and necrosis of lung** 🦠

   J85.1   **Abscess of lung with pneumonia** 🦠

       Use additional code to identify the type of
         pneumonia (J09-J16)

   J85.2   **Abscess of lung without pneumonia** 🦠
        Abscess of lung NOS

   J85.3   **Abscess of mediastinum** 🦠

● **J86**   **Pyothorax**

     Use additional code (B95-B97) to identify infectious
     agent.

     Excludes1   abscess of lung (J85.-)
               pyothorax due to tuberculosis (A15.6)

   J86.0   **Pyothorax with fistula** 🦠
        Bronchocutaneous fistula
        Bronchopleural fistula
        Hepatopleural fistula
        Mediastinal fistula
        Pleural fistula
        Thoracic fistula
        Any condition classifiable to J86.9 with fistula

   J86.9   **Pyothorax without fistula** 🦠
        Abscess of pleura
        Abscess of thorax
        Empyema (chest) (lung) (pleura)
        Fibrinopurulent pleurisy
        Purulent pleurisy
        Pyopneumothorax
        Septic pleurisy
        Seropurulent pleurisy
        Suppurative pleurisy

OTHER DISEASES OF THE PLEURA (J90-J94)

● **J90**   **Pleural effusion, not elsewhere classified** 🦠

     Includes   encysted pleurisy
               pleural effusion NOS
               pleurisy with effusion (exudative) (serous)

     Excludes1   chylous (pleural) effusion (J94.0)
               malignant pleural effusion (J91.0))
               pleurisy NOS (R09.1)
               tuberculous pleural effusion (A15.6)

● **J91**   **Pleural effusion in conditions classified elsewhere**

     Excludes2   pleural effusion in heart failure (I50.-)
               pleural effusion in systemic lupus
                 erythematosus (M32.13)

   ● **J91.0**   **Malignant pleural effusion** 🦠
        Code first underlying neoplasm

● Unacceptable First-Listed Diagnosis   ● Use Additional Character(s)   🔲 Unspecified   **OGCR** Official Guidelines for Coding and Reporting

🦠 Complication\Comorbidity   🦠 Major C\C   Excludes 1   Excludes 2   Includes   Use additional   Code first   Code also

1069

CHAPTER 10 (J00-J99)

● J91.8   **Pleural effusion in other conditions classified elsewhere** 🅒

> *Code first underlying disease, such as:*
>   filariasis (B74.0-B74.9)

● J92   **Pleural plaque**

| Includes | pleural thickening |

J92.0   **Pleural plaque with presence of asbestos**

J92.9   **Pleural plaque without asbestos**
          Pleural plaque NOS

● J93   **Pneumothorax**
          Collapsed lung

| Excludes1 | congenital or perinatal pneumothorax (P25.1)
postprocedural pneumothorax (J95.81)
traumatic pneumothorax (S27.0)
tuberculous (current disease) pneumothorax (A15.-)
pyopneumothorax (J86.-) |

J93.0   **Spontaneous tension pneumothorax** 🅒
          Tension pneumothorax (most serious type) occurs when air (positive pressure) collects in the pleural space

J93.1   **Other spontaneous pneumothorax** 🅒

J93.8   **Other pneumothorax** 🅒

| Excludes1 | postprocedural pneumothorax (J95.81) |

■ J93.9   **Pneumothorax, unspecified** 🅒

● J94   **Other pleural conditions**

| Excludes1 | pleurisy NOS (R09.1)
traumatic hemopneumothorax (S27.2)
traumatic hemothorax (S27.1)
tuberculous pleural conditions (current disease) (A15.-) |

J94.0   **Chylous effusion** 🅒
          Chyliform effusion

J94.1   **Fibrothorax**

J94.2   **Hemothorax** 🅒
          Hemopneumothorax

J94.8   **Other specified pleural conditions** 🅒
          Hydropneumothorax
          Hydrothorax

■ J94.9   **Pleural condition, unspecified**

INTRAOPERATIVE AND POSTPROCEDURAL COMPLICATIONS AND DISORDERS OF RESPIRATORY SYSTEM, NOT ELSEWHERE CLASSIFIED (J95)

● J95   **Intraoperative and postprocedural complications and disorders of respiratory system, not elsewhere classified**

| Excludes2 | aspiration pneumonia (J69.-)
emphysema (subcutaneous) resulting from a procedure (T81.82)
hypostatic pneumonia (J18.2)
pulmonary manifestations due to radiation (J70.0- J70.1) |

● J95.0   **Tracheostomy complications**

■ J95.00   **Unspecified tracheostomy complication** 🅒

J95.01   **Hemorrhage from tracheostomy stoma** 🅒

J95.02   **Infection of tracheostomy stoma** 🅒

> Use additional code to identify type of infection, such as:
>   cellulitis of neck (L03.8)
>   sepsis (A40, A41.-)

J95.03   **Malfunction of tracheostomy stoma** 🅒
          Mechanical complication of tracheostomy stoma
          Obstruction of tracheostomy airway
          Tracheal stenosis due to tracheostomy

J95.04   **Tracheo-esophageal fistula following tracheostomy** 🅒

J95.09   **Other tracheostomy complication** 🅒

J95.1   **Acute pulmonary insufficiency following thoracic surgery** 🅒

| Excludes2 | functional disturbances following cardiac surgery (I97.0, I97.1-) |

J95.2   **Acute pulmonary insufficiency following nonthoracic surgery** 🅒

| Excludes2 | functional disturbances following cardiac surgery (I97.0, I97.1-) |

J95.3   **Chronic pulmonary insufficiency following surgery** 🅒

| Excludes2 | functional disturbances following cardiac surgery (I97.0, I97.1-) |

● J95.4   **Chemical pneumonitis due to anesthesia [Mendelson's syndrome]** 🅒

> *Code first appropriate code from category T41*

| Excludes1 | aspiration pneumonitis due to anesthesia complicating labor and delivery (O74.0)
aspiration pneumonitis due to anesthesia complicating pregnancy (O29)
aspiration pneumonitis due to anesthesia complicating the puerperium (O89.01) |

J95.5   **Postprocedural subglottic stenosis** 🅒

● J95.6   **Intraoperative hemorrhage and hematoma of a respiratory system organ or structure complicating a procedure**

| Excludes1 | intraoperative hemorrhage and hematoma of a respiratory system organ or structure due to accidental puncture and laceration during procedure (J95.7-) |

J95.61   **Intraoperative hemorrhage and hematoma of a respiratory system organ or structure complicating a respiratory system procedure** 🅒

J95.62   **Intraoperative hemorrhage and hematoma of a respiratory system organ or structure complicating other procedure** 🅒

● J95.7   **Accidental puncture and laceration of a respiratory system organ or structure during a procedure**

| Excludes2 | postprocedural pneumothorax (J95.8) |

J95.71   **Accidental puncture and laceration of a respiratory system organ or structure during a respiratory system procedure** 🅒

J95.72   **Accidental puncture and laceration of a respiratory system organ or structure during other procedure** 🅒

● Unacceptable First-Listed Diagnosis   ● Use Additional Character(s)   ■ Unspecified   **OGCR** Official Guidelines for Coding and Reporting
🅒 Complication\Comorbidity   🅒 Major C\C | Excludes 1 | | Excludes 2 | | Includes | Use additional   Code first   Code also

● J95.8   Other intraoperative and postprocedural
           complications and disorders of respiratory system,
           not elsewhere classified

     J95.81   Postprocedural pneumothorax 🕮

     J95.82   Postprocedural respiratory failure 🕮

   ● J95.83   Postprocedural hemorrhage and hematoma
               of a respiratory system organ or structure
               following a procedure

          J95.830   Postprocedural hemorrhage and
                     hematoma of a respiratory system
                     organ or structure following a
                     respiratory system procedure 🕮

          J95.831   Postprocedural hemorrhage and
                     hematoma of a respiratory system
                     organ or structure following
                     other procedure 🕮

     J95.84   Transfusion-related acute lung injury
               (TRALI) 🕮

   ● J95.85   Complication of respirator [ventilator] 🕮

          J95.850   Mechanical complication of
                     respirator

                     | Excludes1 | encounter for
                                   respirator
                                   [ventilator]
                                   dependence
                                   during
                                   power failure
                                   (Z99.12)

          J95.851   Ventilator associated pneumonia
                     Ventilator associated
                          pneumonitis

                     Code also type of pneumonia
                          (J09-J18)

                     | Excludes1 | ventilator lung
                                   in newborn
                                   (P27.8)

          J95.859   Other complication of respirator
                     [ventilator]

     J95.88   Other intraoperative complications of
               respiratory system, not elsewhere
               classified 🕮

     J95.89   Other postprocedural complications
               and disorders of respiratory system, not
               elsewhere classified 🕮

               Use additional code to identify disorder,
                    such as:
                 aspiration pneumonia (J69.-)
                 bacterial or viral pneumonia (J12-J18)

               | Excludes2 | acute pulmonary
                             insufficiency following
                             thoracic surgery (J95.1)
                             postprocedural subglottic
                             stenosis (J95.5)

OTHER DISEASES OF THE RESPIRATORY SYSTEM (J96-J99)

● J96   Respiratory failure, not elsewhere classified

     | Excludes1 | acute respiratory distress syndrome (J80)
                   cardiorespiratory failure (R09.2)
                   newborn respiratory distress syndrome (P22.0)
                   postprocedural respiratory failure (J95.82)
                   respiratory arrest (R09.2)
                   respiratory arrest of newborn (P28.81)
                   respiratory failure of newborn (P28.5)

     J96.0   Acute respiratory failure 🕮

     J96.1   Chronic respiratory failure 🕮

     J96.2   Acute and chronic respiratory failure 🕮
              Acute on chronic respiratory failure

   ▨ J96.9   Respiratory failure, unspecified 🕮

● J98   Other respiratory disorders

         Use additional code to identify:
           exposure to environmental tobacco smoke (Z77.22)
           exposure to tobacco smoke in the perinatal period (P96.81)
           history of tobacco use (Z87.891)
           occupational exposure to environmental tobacco smoke
             (Z57.31)
           tobacco dependence (F17.-)
           tobacco use (Z72.0)

         | Excludes1 | newborn apnea (P28.4)
                       newborn sleep apnea (P28.3)

         | Excludes2 | apnea NOS (R06.81)
                       sleep apnea (G47.3-)

   ● J98.0   Diseases of bronchus, not elsewhere classified

          J98.01   Acute bronchospasm

                    | Excludes1 | acute bronchiolitis with
                                   bronchospasm (J21.-)
                                   acute bronchitis with
                                   bronchospasm (J20.-)
                                   asthma (J45.-)
                                   exercise induced
                                   bronchospasm (J45.990)

          J98.09   Other diseases of bronchus, not elsewhere
                    classified
                    Broncholithiasis
                    Calcification of bronchus
                    Stenosis of bronchus
                    Tracheobronchial collapse
                    Tracheobronchial dyskinesia
                    Ulcer of bronchus

   ● J98.1   Pulmonary collapse

              | Excludes1 | therapeutic collapse of lung status
                            (Z98.3)

          J98.11   Atelectasis 🕮

                    | Excludes1 | newborn atelectasis
                                   tuberculous atelectasis
                                   (current disease) (A15)

          J98.19   Other pulmonary collapse 🕮

     J98.2   Interstitial emphysema
              Mediastinal emphysema

              | Excludes1 | emphysema NOS (J43.9)
                            emphysema in fetus and newborn
                            (P25.0)
                            surgical emphysema (subcutaneous)
                            (T81.82)
                            traumatic subcutaneous emphysema
                            (T79.7)

     J98.3   Compensatory emphysema

     J98.4   Other disorders of lung
              Calcification of lung
              Cystic lung disease (acquired)
              Lung disease NOS
              Pulmolithiasis

● Unacceptable First-Listed Diagnosis   ● Use Additional Character(s)   ▨ Unspecified   OGCR Official Guidelines for Coding and Reporting
🕮 Complication\Comorbidity   🕮 Major C\C | Excludes 1 | | Excludes 2 | | Includes | | Use additional | | Code first | | Code also |

J98.5 **Diseases of mediastinum, not elsewhere classified**
Fibrosis of mediastinum
Hernia of mediastinum
Retraction of mediastinum
Mediastinitis

Excludes2   abscess of mediastinum (J85.3)

J98.6 **Disorders of diaphragm**
Diaphragmatitis
Paralysis of diaphragm
Relaxation of diaphragm

Excludes1   congenital malformation of diaphragm NEC (Q79.1)
congenital diaphragmatic hernia (Q79.0)

Excludes2   diaphragmatic hernia (K44.-)

J98.8 **Other specified respiratory disorders**

J98.9 **Respiratory disorder, unspecified**
Respiratory disease (chronic) NOS

● **J99** **Respiratory disorders in diseases classified elsewhere**
Code first underlying disease, such as:
amyloidosis (E85.-)
ankylosing spondylitis (M45)
congenital syphilis (A50.5)
cryoglobulinemia (D89.1)
early congenital syphilis (A50.0)
hemosiderosis (E83.1)
schistosomiasis (B65.0-B65.9)

Excludes1   respiratory disorders in:
amebiasis (A06.5)
blastomycosis (B40.0-B40.2)
candidiasis (B37.1)
coccidioidomycosis (B38.0-B38.2)
cystic fibrosis with pulmonary manifestations (E84.0)
dermatomyositis (M33.01, M33.11)
histoplasmosis (B39.0-B39.2)
late syphilis (A52.72, A52.73)
polymyositis (M33.21)
sicca syndrome (M35.02)
systemic lupus erythematosus (M32.13)
systemic sclerosis (M34.81)
Wegener's granulomatosis (M31.30-M31.31)

● Unacceptable First-Listed Diagnosis   ● Use Additional Character(s)   ■ Unspecified   **OGCR** Official Guidelines for Coding and Reporting
 Complication\Comorbidity   Major C\C   Excludes 1   Excludes 2   Includes   Use additional   Code first   Code also

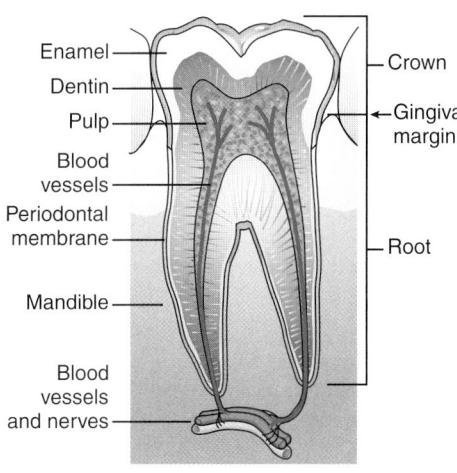

Figure 11-1   Anatomy of a tooth.

Item 11–1 Anodontia is the congenital absence of teeth. **Hypodontia** is partial anodontia. **Oligodontia** is the congenital absence of some teeth, whereas **supernumerary** is having more teeth than the normal number. **Mesiodens** are small extra teeth that often appear in pairs, although single small teeth are not uncommon.

CHAPTER 11
DISEASES OF THE DIGESTIVE SYSTEM (K00–K94)

| Excludes2 | certain conditions originating in the perinatal period (P04-P96) |

certain conditions originating in the
    perinatal period (P04-P96)
certain infectious and parasitic diseases
    (A00-B99)
complications of pregnancy, childbirth and
    the puerperium (O00-O99)
congenital malformations, deformations and
    chromosomal abnormalities (Q00-Q99)
endocrine, nutritional and metabolic
    diseases (E00-E90)
injury, poisoning and certain other
    consequences of external causes (S00-T98)
neoplasms (C00-D48)
symptoms, signs and abnormal clinical
    and laboratory findings, not elsewhere
    classified (R00-R94)

This chapter contains the following blocks:

K00-K14	Diseases of oral cavity and salivary glands
K20-K31	Diseases of esophagus, stomach and duodenum
K35-K38	Diseases of appendix
K40-K46	Hernia
K50-K52	Noninfective enteritis and colitis
K55-K63	Other diseases of intestines
K65-K68	Diseases of peritoneum and retroperitoneum
K70-K77	Diseases of liver
K80-K87	Disorders of gallbladder, biliary tract and pancreas
K90-K94	Other diseases of the digestive system

DISEASES OF ORAL CAVITY AND SALIVARY GLANDS (K00-K14)

● **K00**   **Disorders of tooth development and eruption**
    Excludes2   embedded and impacted teeth (K01.-)

    K00.0   Anodontia
         Hypodontia
         Oligodontia
         Excludes1   acquired absence of teeth (K08.1-)

    K00.1   Supernumerary teeth
         Distomolar
         Fourth molar
         Mesiodens
         Paramolar
         Supplementary teeth
         Excludes2   supernumerary roots (K00.2)

    K00.2   Abnormalities of size and form of teeth
         Concrescence of teeth
         Fusion of teeth
         Gemination of teeth
         Dens evaginatus
         Dens in dente
         Dens invaginatus
         Enamel pearls
         Macrodontia
         Microdontia
         Peg-shaped [conical] teeth
         Supernumerary roots
         Taurodontism
         Tuberculum paramolare
         Excludes1   abnormalities of teeth due to congenital syphilis (A50.5)
                  tuberculum Carabelli, which is regarded as a normal variation and should not be coded

    K00.3   Mottled teeth
         Dental fluorosis
         Mottling of enamel
         Nonfluoride enamel opacities
         Excludes2   deposits [accretions] on teeth (K03.6)

    K00.4   Disturbances in tooth formation
         Aplasia and hypoplasia of cementum
         Dilaceration of tooth
         Enamel hypoplasia (neonatal) (postnatal) (prenatal)
         Regional odontodysplasia
         Turner's tooth
         Excludes1   Hutchinson's teeth and mulberry molars in congenital syphilis (A50.5)
         Excludes2   mottled teeth (K00.3)

    K00.5   Hereditary disturbances in tooth structure, not elsewhere classified
         Amelogenesis imperfecta
         Dentinogenesis imperfecta
         Odontogenesis imperfecta
         Dentinal dysplasia
         Shell teeth

    K00.6   Disturbances in tooth eruption
         Dentia praecox
         Natal tooth
         Neonatal tooth
         Premature eruption of tooth
         Premature shedding of primary [deciduous] tooth
         Prenatal teeth
         Retained [persistent] primary tooth
         Excludes2   embedded and impacted teeth (K01.-)

● Unacceptable First-Listed Diagnosis   ● Use Additional Character(s)   ▢ Unspecified   **OGCR** Official Guidelines for Coding and Reporting
🕭 Complication\Comorbidity   🕭 Major C\C   Excludes 1   Excludes 2   Includes   Use additional   Code first   Code also
1073

CHAPTER 11 (K00-K94)

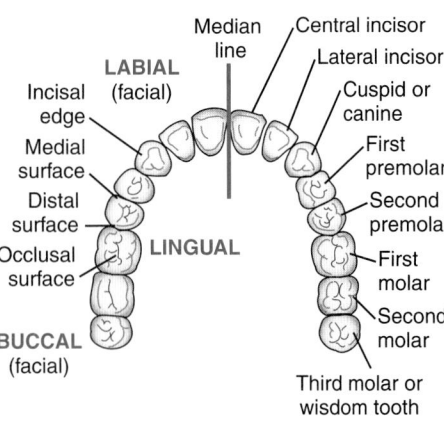

Figure 11-2   The permanent teeth within the dental arch.

Item 11–2 Each dental arch (jaw) normally contains 16 teeth. Tooth decay or **dental caries** is a disease of the enamel, dentin, and cementum of the tooth and can result in a cavity.

K00.7 Teething syndrome

K00.8 Other disorders of tooth development
Color changes during tooth formation
Intrinsic staining of teeth NOS
| **Excludes2** | posteruptive color changes (K03.7) |

K00.9 Disorder of tooth development, unspecified
Disorder of odontogenesis NOS

● **K01 Embedded and impacted teeth**
| **Excludes1** | abnormal position of fully erupted teeth (M26.3-) |

K01.0 Embedded teeth

K01.1 Impacted teeth

● **K02 Dental caries**
| **Includes** | dental cavities, tooth decay |

K02.3 Arrested dental caries
Arrested coronal and root caries

● **K02.5 Dental caries on pit and fissure surface**
Dental caries on chewing surface of tooth

     K02.51 Dental caries on pit and fissure surface limited to enamel
White spot lesions [initial caries] on pit and fissure surface of tooth

     K02.52 Dental caries on pit and fissure surface penetrating into dentin

     K02.53 Dental caries on pit and fissure surface penetrating into pulp

● **K02.6 Dental caries on smooth surface**

     K02.61 Dental caries on smooth surface limited to enamel
White spot lesions [initial caries] on smooth surface of tooth

     K02.62 Dental caries on smooth surface penetrating into dentin

     K02.63 Dental caries on smooth surface penetrating into pulp

K02.7 Dental root caries

K02.9 Dental caries, unspecified

● **K03 Other diseases of hard tissues of teeth**
Excludes2	bruxism (F45.8)
	dental caries (K02.-)
	teeth-grinding NOS (F45.8)

K03.0 Excessive attrition of teeth
Approximal wear of teeth
Occlusal wear of teeth

K03.1 Abrasion of teeth
Dentifrice abrasion of teeth
Habitual abrasion of teeth
Occupational abrasion of teeth
Ritual abrasion of teeth
Traditional abrasion of teeth
Wedge defect NOS

K03.2 Erosion of teeth
Erosion of teeth due to diet
Erosion of teeth due to drugs and medicaments
Erosion of teeth due to persistent vomiting
Erosion of teeth NOS
Idiopathic erosion of teeth
Occupational erosion of teeth

K03.3 Pathological resorption of teeth
Internal granuloma of pulp
Resorption of teeth (external)

K03.4 Hypercementosis
Cementation hyperplasia

K03.5 Ankylosis of teeth

K03.6 Deposits [accretions] on teeth
Betel deposits [accretions] on teeth
Black deposits [accretions] on teeth
Extrinsic staining of teeth NOS
Green deposits [accretions] on teeth
Materia alba deposits [accretions] on teeth
Orange deposits [accretions] on teeth
Staining of teeth NOS
Subgingival dental calculus
Supragingival dental calculus
Tobacco deposits [accretions] on teeth

K03.7 Posteruptive color changes of dental hard tissues
| **Excludes2** | deposits [accretions] on teeth (K03.6) |

● **K03.8 Other specified diseases of hard tissues of teeth**

     K03.81 Cracked tooth
| **Excludes1** | asymptomatic craze lines in enamel - omit code |
| | *broken or fractured tooth due to trauma (S02.5)* |

     K03.89 Other specified diseases of hard tissues of teeth

K03.9 Disease of hard tissues of teeth, unspecified

K04 Diseases of pulp and periapical tissues

K04.0 Pulpitis 🏷
Acute pulpitis
Chronic (hyperplastic) (ulcerative) pulpitis
Irreversible pulpitis
Reversible pulpitis

K04.1 Necrosis of pulp
Pulpal gangrene

K04.2 Pulp degeneration
Denticles
Pulpal calcifications
Pulpal stones

K04.3 Abnormal hard tissue formation in pulp
Secondary or irregular dentine

● Unacceptable First-Listed Diagnosis   ● Use Additional Character(s)   ■ Unspecified   **OGCR** Official Guidelines for Coding and Reporting
🏷 Complication\Comorbidity   🏷 Major C\C   Excludes 1   Excludes 2   Includes   Use additional   Code first   Code also

1074

Item 11–3 **Acute gingivitis,** also known as orilitis or ulitis, is the short-term, severe inflammation of the gums (gingiva) caused by bacteria. **Chronic gingivitis** is persistent inflammation of the gums. When the gingivitis moves into the periodontium it is called periodontitis, also known as paradentitis.

K04.4 Acute apical periodontitis of pulpal origin 🔾
Acute apical periodontitis NOS
> **Excludes1**   acute periodontitis (K05.2-)

K04.5 Chronic apical periodontitis
Apical or periapical granuloma
Apical periodontitis NOS
> **Excludes1**   chronic periodontitis (K05.3-)

K04.6 Periapical abscess with sinus
Dental abscess with sinus
Dentoalveolar abscess with sinus

K04.7 Periapical abscess without sinus
Dental abscess without sinus
Dentoalveolar abscess without sinus
Periapical abscess without sinus

K04.8 Radicular cyst
Apical (periodontal) cyst
Periapical cyst
Residual radicular cyst
> **Excludes2**   lateral periodontal cyst (K09.0)

● **K04.9 Other and unspecified diseases of pulp and periapical tissues**

◾ **K04.90 Unspecified diseases of pulp and periapical tissues**

K04.99 Other diseases of pulp and periapical tissues
● **K05 Gingivitis and periodontal diseases**
Use additional code to identify:
alcohol abuse and dependence (F10.-)
exposure to environmental tobacco smoke (Z77.22)
exposure to tobacco smoke in the perinatal period (P96.81)
history of tobacco use (Z87.891)
occupational exposure to environmental tobacco smoke (Z57.31)
tobacco dependence (F17.-)
tobacco use (Z72.0)

● **K05.0 Acute gingivitis**
> **Excludes1**   acute necrotizing ulcerative gingivitis (A69.1)
> herpesviral [herpes simplex] gingivostomatitis (B00.2)

K05.00 Acute gingivitis, plaque induced
Acute gingivitis NOS

K05.01 Acute gingivitis, non-plaque induced

● **K05.1 Chronic gingivitis**
Desquamative gingivitis (chronic)
Gingivitis (chronic) NOS
Hyperplastic gingivitis (chronic)
Simple marginal gingivitis (chronic)
Ulcerative gingivitis (chronic)

K05.10 Chronic gingivitis, plaque induced
Chronic gingivitis NOS
Gingivitis NOS

K05.11 Chronic gingivitis, non-plaque induced
● **K05.2 Aggressive periodontitis**
Acute pericoronitis
> **Excludes1**   acute apical periodontitis (K04.4)
> periapical abscess (K04.7)
> periapical abscess with sinus (K04.6)

◾ **K05.20 Aggressive periodontitis, unspecified**

K05.21 Aggressive periodontitis, localized
Periodontal abscess

K05.22 Aggressive periodontitis, generalized

● **K05.3 Chronic periodontitis**
Chronic pericoronitis
Complex periodontitis
Periodontitis NOS
Simplex periodontitis
> **Excludes1**   chronic apical periodontitis (K04.5)

◾ **K05.30 Chronic periodontitis, unspecified**

K05.31 Chronic periodontitis, localized

K05.32 Chronic periodontitis, generalized

K05.4 Periodontosis
Juvenile periodontosis

K05.5 Other periodontal diseases
> **Excludes2**   leukoplakia of gingiva (K13.21)
◾ **K05.6 Periodontal disease, unspecified**

● **K06 Other disorders of gingiva and edentulous alveolar ridge**
> **Excludes2**   acute gingivitis (K05.0)
> atrophy of edentulous alveolar ridge (K08.2)
> chronic gingivitis (K05.1)
> gingivitis NOS (K05.1)

K06.0 Gingival recession
Gingival recession (generalized) (localized) (postinfective) (postprocedural)

K06.1 Gingival enlargement
Gingival fibromatosis

K06.2 Gingival and edentulous alveolar ridge lesions associated with trauma
Irritative hyperplasia of edentulous ridge [denture hyperplasia]
Use additional code (Chapter 20) to identify external cause or denture status (Z97.2)

K06.8 Other specified disorders of gingiva and edentulous alveolar ridge
Fibrous epulis
Flabby alveolar ridge
Giant cell epulis
Peripheral giant cell granuloma of gingiva
Pyogenic granuloma of gingiva
> **Excludes2**   gingival cyst (K09.0)
◾ **K06.9 Disorder of gingiva and edentulous alveolar ridge, unspecified**

● **K08 Other disorders of teeth and supporting structures**
> **Excludes2**   dentofacial anomalies [including malocclusion] (M26.-)
> disorders of jaw (M27.-)

K08.0 Exfoliation of teeth due to systemic causes
Code also underlying systemic condition
● **K08.1 Complete loss of teeth**
Acquired loss of teeth, complete
> **Excludes1**   congenital absence of teeth (K00.0)
> exfoliation of teeth due to systemic causes (K08.0)
> partial loss of teeth (K08.4-)

● **K08.10 Complete loss of teeth, unspecified cause**

◾ **K08.101 Complete loss of teeth, unspecified cause, class I**
◾ **K08.102 Complete loss of teeth, unspecified cause, class II**
◾ **K08.103 Complete loss of teeth, unspecified cause, class III**
◾ **K08.104 Complete loss of teeth, unspecified cause, class IV**

● Unacceptable First-Listed Diagnosis   ● Use Additional Character(s)   ◾ Unspecified   OGCR Official Guidelines for Coding and Reporting
🔾 Complication\Comorbidity   🔾 Major C\C   Excludes 1   Excludes 2   Includes   Use additional   Code first   Code also   1075

CHAPTER 11 (K00-K94)

K08.109 **Complete loss of teeth, unspecified cause, unspecified class**
Edentulism NOS

● K08.11 **Complete loss of teeth due to trauma**
K08.111 Complete loss of teeth due to trauma, class I
K08.112 Complete loss of teeth due to trauma, class II
K08.113 Complete loss of teeth due to trauma, class III
K08.114 Complete loss of teeth due to trauma, class IV
K08.119 Complete loss of teeth due to trauma, unspecified class

● K08.12 **Complete loss of teeth due to periodontal diseases**
K08.121 Complete loss of teeth due to periodontal diseases, class I
K08.122 Complete loss of teeth due to periodontal diseases, class II
K08.123 Complete loss of teeth due to periodontal diseases, class III
K08.124 Complete loss of teeth due to periodontal diseases, class IV
K08.129 Complete loss of teeth due to periodontal diseases, unspecified class

● K08.13 **Complete loss of teeth due to caries**
K08.131 Complete loss of teeth due to caries, class I
K08.132 Complete loss of teeth due to caries, class II
K08.133 Complete loss of teeth due to caries, class III
K08.134 Complete loss of teeth due to caries, class IV
K08.139 Complete loss of teeth due to caries, unspecified class

● K08.19 **Complete loss of teeth due to other specified cause**
K08.191 Complete loss of teeth due to other specified cause, class I
K08.192 Complete loss of teeth due to other specified cause, class II
K08.193 Complete loss of teeth due to other specified cause, class III
K08.194 Complete loss of teeth due to other specified cause, class IV
K08.199 Complete loss of teeth due to other specified cause, unspecified class

● K08.2 **Atrophy of edentulous alveolar ridge**
K08.20 **Unspecified atrophy of edentulous alveolar ridge**
Atrophy of the mandible NOS
Atrophy of the maxilla NOS

K08.21 **Minimal atrophy of the mandible**
Minimal atrophy of the edentulous mandible

K08.22 **Moderate atrophy of the mandible**
Moderate atrophy of the edentulous mandible

K08.23 **Severe atrophy of the mandible**
Severe atrophy of the edentulous mandible

K08.24 **Minimal atrophy of maxilla**
Minimal atrophy of the edentulous maxilla

K08.25 **Moderate atrophy of the maxilla**
Moderate atrophy of the edentulous maxilla

K08.26 **Severe atrophy of the maxilla**
Severe atrophy of the edentulous maxilla

K08.3 **Retained dental root**

● K08.4 **Partial loss of teeth**
Acquired loss of teeth, partial

Excludes1 complete loss of teeth (K08.1-)
congenital absence of teeth (K00.0)

Excludes2 exfoliation of teeth due to systemic causes (K08.0)

● K08.40 **Partial loss of teeth, unspecified cause**
K08.401 Partial loss of teeth, unspecified cause, class I
K08.402 Partial loss of teeth, unspecified cause, class II
K08.403 Partial loss of teeth, unspecified cause, class III
K08.404 Partial loss of teeth, unspecified cause, class IV
K08.409 Partial loss of teeth, unspecified cause, unspecified class
Tooth extraction status NOS

● K08.41 **Partial loss of teeth due to trauma**
K08.411 Partial loss of teeth due to trauma, class I
K08.412 Partial loss of teeth due to trauma, class II
K08.413 Partial loss of teeth due to trauma, class III
K08.414 Partial loss of teeth due to trauma, class IV
K08.419 Partial loss of teeth due to trauma, unspecified class

● K08.42 **Partial loss of teeth due to periodontal diseases**
K08.421 Partial loss of teeth due to periodontal diseases, class I
K08.422 Partial loss of teeth due to periodontal diseases, class II
K08.423 Partial loss of teeth due to periodontal diseases, class III
K08.424 Partial loss of teeth due to periodontal diseases, class IV
K08.429 Partial loss of teeth due to periodontal diseases, unspecified class

● K08.43 **Partial loss of teeth due to caries**
K08.431 Partial loss of teeth due to caries, class I
K08.432 Partial loss of teeth due to caries, class II
K08.433 Partial loss of teeth due to caries, class III
K08.434 Partial loss of teeth due to caries, class IV
K08.439 Partial loss of teeth due to caries, unspecified class

● K08.49 **Partial loss of teeth due to other specified cause**
K08.491 Partial loss of teeth due to other specified cause, class I
K08.492 Partial loss of teeth due to other specified cause, class II

● Unacceptable First-Listed Diagnosis   ● Use Additional Character(s)   ▪ Unspecified   **OGCR** Official Guidelines for Coding and Reporting
🝏 Complication\Comorbidity   🝏 Major C\C   Excludes 1   Excludes 2   Includes   Use additional   Code first   Code also

K08.493　Partial loss of teeth due to other specified cause, class III

K08.494　Partial loss of teeth due to other specified cause, class IV

■**K08.499　Partial loss of teeth due to other specified cause, unspecified class**

●**K08.5　Unsatisfactory restoration of tooth**
Defective bridge, crown, filling
Defective dental restoration
Excludes1	dental restoration status (Z98.811)
Excludes2	endosseous dental implant failure (M27.6-)
	unsatisfactory endodontic treatment (M27.5-)

■**K08.50　Unsatisfactory restoration of tooth, unspecified**
Defective dental restoration NOS

K08.51　Open restoration margins of tooth
Dental restoration failure of marginal integrity
Open margin on tooth restoration
Poor gingival margin to tooth restoration

K08.52　Unrepairable overhanging of dental restorative materials
Overhanging of tooth restoration

●**K08.53　Fractured dental restorative material**
| Excludes1 | cracked tooth (K03.81) |
| | *traumatic fracture of tooth (S02.5)* |

K08.530　Fractured dental restorative material without loss of material

K08.531　Fractured dental restorative material with loss of material

■**K08.539　Fractured dental restorative material, unspecified**

K08.54　Contour of existing restoration of tooth biologically incompatible with oral health
Dental restoration failure of periodontal anatomical integrity
Unacceptable contours of existing restoration of tooth
Unacceptable morphology of existing restoration of tooth

K08.55　Allergy to existing dental restorative material
Use additional code to identify the specific type of allergy

K08.56　Poor aesthetic of existing restoration of tooth
Dental restoration aesthetically inadequate or displeasing

K08.59　Other unsatisfactory restoration of tooth
Other defective dental restoration

K08.8　Other specified disorders of teeth and supporting structures
Enlargement of alveolar ridge NOS
Irregular alveolar process
Toothache NOS

■**K08.9　Disorder of teeth and supporting structures, unspecified**

●**K09　Cysts of oral region, not elsewhere classified**
Includes	lesions showing histological features both of aneurysmal cyst and of another fibro-osseous lesion
Excludes2	cysts of jaw (M27.0-, M27.4-)
	radicular cyst (K04.8)

K09.0　Developmental odontogenic cysts
Dentigerous cyst
Eruption cyst
Follicular cyst
Gingival cyst
Lateral periodontal cyst
Primordial cyst
| Excludes2 | keratocysts D16.4, D16.5 |
| | odontogenic keratocystic tumors D16.4, D16.5 |

K09.1　Developmental (nonodontogenic) cysts of oral region
Cyst (of) incisive canal
Cyst (of) palatine of papilla
Globulomaxillary cyst
Median palatal cyst
Nasopalatine cyst

K09.8　Other cysts of oral region, not elsewhere classified
Dermoid cyst
Epidermoid cyst
Lymphoepithelial cyst
Epstein's pearl
Nasoalveolar cyst
Nasolabial cyst

■**K09.9　Cyst of oral region, unspecified**

●**K11　Diseases of salivary glands**
Use additional code to identify:
alcohol abuse and dependence (F10.-)
exposure to environmental tobacco smoke (Z77.22)
exposure to tobacco smoke in the perinatal period (P96.81)
history of tobacco use (Z87.891)
occupational exposure to environmental tobacco smoke (Z57.31)
tobacco dependence (F17.-)
tobacco use (Z72.0)

K11.0　Atrophy of salivary gland

K11.1　Hypertrophy of salivary gland

●**K11.2　Sialoadenitis**
Parotitis
Excludes1	epidemic parotitis (B26.-)
	mumps (B26.-)
	uveoparotid fever [Heerfordt] (D86.89)

■**K11.20　Sialoadenitis, unspecified**

K11.21　Acute sialoadenitis
| Excludes1 | acute recurrent sialoadenitis (K11.22) |

K11.22　Acute recurrent sialoadenitis

K11.23　Chronic sialoadenitis

K11.3　Abscess of salivary gland 🗪

K11.4　Fistula of salivary gland 🗪
| Excludes1 | congenital fistula of salivary gland (Q38.4) |

(See Plate 61 on page NAP-25.)

K11.5　Sialolithiasis
Calculus of salivary gland or duct
Stone of salivary gland or duct

K11.6　Mucocele of salivary gland
Mucous extravasation cyst of salivary gland
Mucous retention cyst of salivary gland
Ranula

Item 11–4　Atrophy is wasting away of a tissue or organ, whereas **hypertrophy** is overdevelopment or enlargement of a tissue or organ. **Sialoadenitis** is salivary gland inflammation. **Parotitis** is the inflammation of the parotid gland. In the epidemic form, parotitis is also known as mumps. **Sialolithiasis** is the formation of calculus within a salivary gland. **Mucocele** is a polyp composed of mucus.

● Unacceptable First-Listed Diagnosis　　　● Use Additional Character(s)　　　■ Unspecified　　　**OGCR** Official Guidelines for Coding and Reporting
🗪 Complication\Comorbidity　　🗪 Major C\C　　 Excludes 1 　 Excludes 2 　　 Includes 　　 Use additional 　　 Code first 　　 Code also

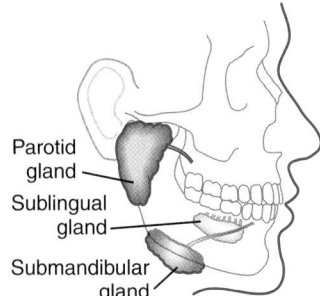

Figure 11-3 Major salivary glands.

Parotid gland
Sublingual gland
Submandibular gland

K11.7   Disturbances of salivary secretion
Hypoptyalism
Ptyalism
Xerostomia
> **Excludes2**   dry mouth NOS (R68.2)

K11.8   Other diseases of salivary glands
Benign lymphoepithelial lesion of salivary gland
Mikulicz' disease
Necrotizing sialometaplasia
Sialectasia
Stenosis of salivary duct
Stricture of salivary duct
> **Excludes1**   sicca syndrome [Sjögren] (M35.0-)

■**K11.9   Disease of salivary gland, unspecified**
Sialoadenopathy NOS

●**K12   Stomatitis and related lesions**
Use additional code to identify:
  alcohol abuse and dependence (F10.-)
  exposure to environmental tobacco smoke (Z77.22)
  exposure to tobacco smoke in the perinatal period (P96.81)
  history of tobacco use (Z87.891)
  occupational exposure to environmental tobacco smoke (Z57.31)
  tobacco dependence (F17.-)
  tobacco use (Z72.0)
> **Excludes1**   cancrum oris (A69.0)
>   cheilitis (K13.0)
>   gangrenous stomatitis (A69.0)
>   herpesviral [herpes simplex]
>   gingivostomatitis (B00.2)
>   noma (A69.0)

K12.0   Recurrent oral aphthae
Aphthous stomatitis (major) (minor)
Bednar's aphthae
Periadenitis mucosa necrotica recurrens
Recurrent aphthous ulcer
Stomatitis herpetiformis

K12.1   Other forms of stomatitis
Stomatitis NOS
Denture stomatitis
Ulcerative stomatitis
Vesicular stomatitis
> **Excludes1**   acute necrotizing ulcerative
>   stomatitis (A69.1)
>   Vincent's stomatitis (A69.1)

Item 11-5 Stomatitis is the inflammation of the oral mucosa. **Mucositis** is the inflammation of the mucous membranes lining the digestive tract from the mouth to the anus. It is a common side effect of chemotherapy and of radiotherapy that involves any part of the digestive tract.

K12.2 Cellulitis and abscess of mouth 🔗
Cellulitis of mouth (floor)
Submandibular abscess
> **Excludes2**   abscess of salivary gland (K11.3)
>   abscess of tongue (K14.0)
>   periapical abscess (K04.6-K04.7)
>   periodontal abscess (K05.21)
>   peritonsillar abscess (J36)

●**K12.3   Oral mucositis (ulcerative)**
Mucositis (oral) (oropharyneal)
> **Excludes2**   gastrointestinal mucositis
>   (ulcerative) (K92.81)
>   mucositis (ulcerative) of vagina and
>   vulva (N76.81)
>   nasal mucositis (ulcerative) (J34.81)

■**K12.30   Oral mucositis (ulcerative), unspecified**

K12.31   Oral mucositis (ulcerative) due to antineoplastic therapy
Code also type of associated therapy, such as:
  antineoplastic and immunosuppressive drugs (T45.1x-)
  radiological procedure and radiotherapy (Y84.2)

K12.32   Oral mucositis (ulcerative) due to other drugs
Code also drug (T36-T50)

K12.33   Oral mucositis (ulcerative) due to radiation
Use additional external cause code (W88-W90, X39.0-) to identify cause

K12.39   Other oral mucositis (ulcerative)
Viral oral mucositis (ulcerative)

●**K13   Other diseases of lip and oral mucosa**
> **Includes**   epithelial disturbances of tongue

Use additional code to identify:
  alcohol abuse and dependence (F10.-)
  exposure to environmental tobacco smoke (Z77.22)
  exposure to tobacco smoke in the perinatal period (P96.81)
  history of tobacco use (Z87.891)
  occupational exposure to environmental tobacco smoke (Z57.31)
  tobacco dependence (F17.-)
  tobacco use (Z72.0)
> **Excludes2**   certain disorders of gingiva and edentulous
>   alveolar ridge (K05-K06)
>   cysts of oral region (K09.-)
>   diseases of tongue (K14.-)
>   stomatitis and related lesions (K12.-)

K13.0   Diseases of lips
Abscess of lips
Angular cheilitis
Cellulitis of lips
Cheilitis NOS
Cheilodynia
Cheilosis
Exfoliative cheilitis
Fistula of lips
Glandular cheilitis
Hypertrophy of lips
Perlèche NEC
> **Excludes1**   ariboflavinosis (E53.0)
>   cheilitis due to radiation-related
>   disorders (L55-L59)
>   congenital fistula of lips (Q38.0)
>   congenital hypertrophy of lips (Q18.6)
>   perlèche due to candidiasis (B37.83)
>   perlèche due to riboflavin deficiency
>   (E53.0)

CHAPTER 11 (K00-K94)

● Unacceptable First-Listed Diagnosis   ● Use Additional Character(s)   ■ Unspecified   **OGCR** Official Guidelines for Coding and Reporting
🔗 Complication\Comorbidity   🔗 Major C\C   Excludes 1   Excludes 2   Includes   Use additional   Code first   Code also

1078

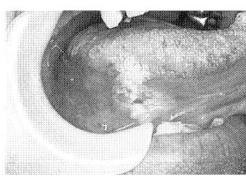

Figure 11-5 Oral leukoplakia and associated squamous carcinoma. (From Feldman: Sleisenger & Fordtran's Gastrointestinal and Liver Disease 8th ed. 2006, Saunders, An Imprint of Elsevier)

K13.1   **Cheek and lip biting**

● K13.2   **Leukoplakia and other disturbances of oral epithelium, including tongue**

> **Excludes1**   carcinoma in situ of oral epithelium (D00.0-)
> hairy leukoplakia (K13.3)

   K13.21   **Leukoplakia of oral mucosa, including tongue**
Considered precancerous and evidenced by thickened white patches of epithelium on mucous membranes
Leukokeratosis of oral mucosa
Leukoplakia of gingiva, lips, tongue

> **Excludes1**   hairy leukoplakia (K13.3)
> *leukokeratosis nicotina palati* (K13.24)

   K13.22   **Minimal keratinized residual ridge mucosa**
Minimal keratinization of alveolar ridge mucosa

   K13.23   **Excessive keratinized residual ridge mucosa**
Excessive keratinization of alveolar ridge mucosa

   K13.24   **Leukokeratosis nicotina palati**
Smoker's palate

   K13.29   **Other disturbances of oral epithelium, including tongue**
Erythroplakia of mouth or tongue
Focal epithelial hyperplasia of mouth or tongue
Leukoedema of mouth or tongue
Other oral epithelium disturbances

K13.3   **Hairy leukoplakia**

K13.4   **Granuloma and granuloma-like lesions of oral mucosa**
Eosinophilic granuloma
Granuloma pyogenicum
Verrucous xanthoma

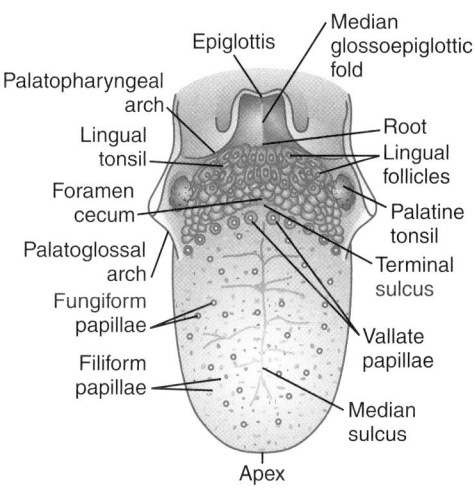

Figure 11-6   Structure of the tongue.

K13.5   **Oral submucous fibrosis**
Submucous fibrosis of tongue

K13.6   **Irritative hyperplasia of oral mucosa**

> **Excludes2**   irritative hyperplasia of edentulous ridge [denture hyperplasia] (K06.2)

● K13.7   **Other and unspecified lesions of oral mucosa**

(See Plate 58 on page NAP-23.)

   ▇K13.70   **Unspecified lesions of oral mucosa**

   K13.79   **Other lesions of oral mucosa**
Focal oral mucinosis

● K14   **Diseases of tongue**
Use additional code to identify:
alcohol abuse and dependence (F10.-)
exposure to environmental tobacco smoke (Z77.22)
history of tobacco use (Z87.891)
occupational exposure to environmental tobacco smoke (Z57.31)
tobacco dependence (F17.-)
tobacco use (Z72.0)

> **Excludes2**   erythroplakia (K13.29)
> focal epithelial hyperplasia (K13.29)
> leukedema of tongue (K13.29)
> leukoplakia of tongue (K13.21)
> hairy leukoplakia (K13.3)
> macroglossia (congenital) (Q38.2)
> submucous fibrosis of tongue (K13.5)

K14.0   **Glossitis**
Abscess of tongue
Ulceration (traumatic) of tongue

> **Excludes1**   atrophic glossitis (K14.4)

K14.1   **Geographic tongue**
Benign migratory glossitis
Glossitis areata exfoliativa

K14.2   **Median rhomboid glossitis**

K14.3   **Hypertrophy of tongue papillae**
Black hairy tongue
Coated tongue
Hypertrophy of foliate papillae
Lingua villosa nigra

K14.4   **Atrophy of tongue papillae**
Atrophic glossitis

K14.5   **Plicated tongue**
Fissured tongue
Furrowed tongue
Scrotal tongue

> **Excludes1**   fissured tongue, congenital (Q38.3)

K14.6   **Glossodynia**
Glossopyrosis
Painful tongue

K14.8   **Other diseases of tongue**
Atrophy of tongue
Crenated tongue
Enlargement of tongue
Glossocele
Glossoptosis
Hypertrophy of tongue

▇K14.9   **Disease of tongue, unspecified**
Glossopathy NOS

Item 11–6   **Esophageal reflux** is the return flow of the contents of the stomach to the esophagus and is referred to as GERD and/or "heartburn." **Gastroesophageal reflux** is the return flow of the contents of the stomach and duodenum to the esophagus. **Esophageal leukoplakia** are white areas on the mucous membrane of the esophagus for which no specific cause can be identified.

● Unacceptable First-Listed Diagnosis   ● Use Additional Character(s)

🗝 Complication\Comorbidity   🗝 Major C\C   Excludes 1   Excludes 2

▇ Unspecified   **OGCR** Official Guidelines for Coding and Reporting

Includes   Use additional   Code first   Code also

DISEASES OF ESOPHAGUS, STOMACH AND DUODENUM (K20-K31)

> Excludes2   hiatus hernia (K44.-)

● **K20   Esophagitis**

> Use additional code to identify:
> alcohol abuse and dependence (F10.-)
>
> Excludes1   erosion of esophagus (K22.1-)
> esophagitis with gastro-esophageal reflux
> disease (K21.0)
> reflux esophagitis (K21.0)
> ulcerative esophagitis (K22.1-)
>
> Excludes2   eosinophilic gastritis or gastroenteritis (K52.81)

  K20.0   Eosinophilic esophagitis

  K20.8   Other esophagitis
       Abscess of esophagus

  ■ **K20.9   Esophagitis, unspecified**
       Esophagitis NOS

● **K21   Gastro-esophageal reflux disease**

> Excludes1   newborn esophageal reflux (P78.83)

  K21.0   Gastro-esophageal reflux disease with esophagitis
       Reflux esophagitis

  K21.9   Gastro-esophageal reflux disease without esophagitis
       Esophageal reflux NOS

● **K22   Other diseases of esophagus**

> Excludes2   esophageal varices (I85.-)

  K22.0   Achalasia of cardia
       Achalasia NOS
       Cardiospasm

> Excludes1   congenital cardiospasm (Q39.5)

● **K22.1   Ulcer of esophagus**
       Barrett's ulcer
       Erosion of esophagus
       Fungal ulcer of esophagus
       Peptic ulcer of esophagus
       Ulcer of esophagus due to ingestion of chemicals
       Ulcer of esophagus due to ingestion of drugs and
       medicaments
       Ulcerative esophagitis

> *Code first (T36-T65) to identify drug or chemical*
>
> Excludes1   Barrett's esophagus (K22.81)

  K22.10   Ulcer of esophagus without bleeding 🔊
          Ulcer of esophagus NOS

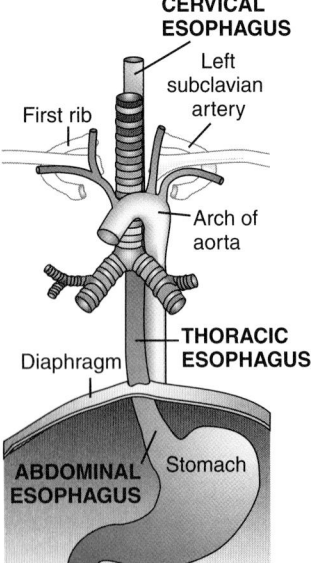

CERVICAL ESOPHAGUS
Left subclavian artery
First rib
Arch of aorta
Diaphragm
THORACIC ESOPHAGUS
ABDOMINAL ESOPHAGUS   Stomach

Figure 11-7   Figure 9–8
The esophagus is the muscular tube that connects the pharynx and the stomach. The 10 inch (25 cm) long esophagus is divided into three parts: cervical, thoracic, and abdominal.

  K22.11   Ulcer of esophagus with bleeding 🔊

> Excludes2   bleeding esophageal varices
> (I85.01, I85.11)

  K22.2   Esophageal obstruction
       Compression of esophagus
       Constriction of esophagus
       Stenosis of esophagus
       Stricture of esophagus

> Excludes1   congenital stenosis or stricture of
> esophagus (Q39.3)

  K22.3   Perforation of esophagus 🔊
       Rupture of esophagus

> Excludes1   traumatic perforation of (thoracic)
> esophagus (S27.8-)

  K22.4   Dyskinesia of esophagus
       Difficulty in moving
       Corkscrew esophagus
       Diffuse esophageal spasm
       Spasm of esophagus

> Excludes1   cardiospasm (K22.0)

  K22.5   Diverticulum of esophagus, acquired
       Esophageal pouch, acquired

> Excludes1   diverticulum of esophagus
> (congenital) (Q39.6)

  K22.6   Gastro-esophageal laceration-hemorrhage syndrome 🔊
       Mallory-Weiss syndrome

● **K22.7   Barrett's esophagus**
       Barrett's disease
       Barrett's syndrome

> Excludes1   Barrett's ulcer (K22.1)
> malignant neoplasm of esophagus
> (C15.-)

  K22.70   Barrett's esophagus without dysplasia
          Barrett's esophagus NOS

  ● **K22.71   Barrett's esophagus with dysplasia**

      K22.710   Barrett's esophagus with low grade dysplasia

      K22.711   Barrett's esophagus with high grade dysplasia

      ■ **K22.719   Barrett's esophagus with dysplasia, unspecified**

  K22.8   Other specified diseases of esophagus
       Hemorrhage of esophagus NOS

> Excludes2   esophageal varices (I85.-)
> Paterson-Kelly syndrome (D50.1)

■ **K22.9   Disease of esophagus, unspecified**

● **K23   Disorders of esophagus in diseases classified elsewhere**

> *Code first underlying disease, such as:*
> congenital syphilis (A50.5)
>
> Excludes1   late syphilis (A52.79)
> megaesophagus due to Chagas' disease
> (B57.31)
> tuberculosis (A18.83)

● **K25   Gastric ulcer**

> Includes   erosion (acute) of stomach
> pylorus ulcer (peptic)
> stomach ulcer (peptic)
>
> Use additional code to identify:
> alcohol abuse and dependence (F10.-)
>
> Excludes1   acute gastritis (K29.0-)
> peptic ulcer NOS (K27.-)

  K25.0   Acute gastric ulcer with hemorrhage 🔊

  K25.1   Acute gastric ulcer with perforation 🔊

  K25.2   Acute gastric ulcer with both hemorrhage and perforation 🔊

● Unacceptable First-Listed Diagnosis   ● Use Additional Character(s)   ■ Unspecified   **OGCR** Official Guidelines for Coding and Reporting
🔊 Complication\Comorbidity   🔊 Major C\C   Excludes 1   Excludes 2   Includes   Use additional   Code first   Code also

Item 11–7 **Achalasia** is a condition in which the smooth muscle fibers of the esophagus do not relax. Most frequently, this condition occurs at the esophagogastric sphincter. **Cardiospasm,** also known as **megaesophagus,** is achalasia of the thoracic esophagus.

> **K25.3** Acute gastric ulcer without hemorrhage or perforation 🦠
>
> ■**K25.4** Chronic or unspecified gastric ulcer with hemorrhage 🦠
>
> ■**K25.5** Chronic or unspecified gastric ulcer with perforation 🦠
>
> ■**K25.6** Chronic or unspecified gastric ulcer with both hemorrhage and perforation 🦠
>
> **K25.7** Chronic gastric ulcer without hemorrhage or perforation
>
> ■**K25.9** Gastric ulcer, unspecified as acute or chronic, without hemorrhage or perforation

● **K26** Duodenal ulcer

>   **Includes**   erosion (acute) of duodenum
>   duodenum ulcer (peptic)
>   postpyloric ulcer (peptic)
>
>   Use additional code to identify:
>   alcohol abuse and dependence (F10.-)
>
>   **Excludes1**   peptic ulcer NOS (K27.-)
>
> **K26.0** Acute duodenal ulcer with hemorrhage 🦠
>
> **K26.1** Acute duodenal ulcer with perforation 🦠
>
> **K26.2** Acute duodenal ulcer with both hemorrhage and perforation 🦠
>
> **K26.3** Acute duodenal ulcer without hemorrhage or perforation 🦠
>
> ■**K26.4** Chronic or unspecified duodenal ulcer with hemorrhage 🦠
>
> ■**K26.5** Chronic or unspecified duodenal ulcer with perforation 🦠
>
> ■**K26.6** Chronic or unspecified duodenal ulcer with both hemorrhage and perforation 🦠
>
> **K26.7** Chronic duodenal ulcer without hemorrhage or perforation
>
> ■**K26.9** Duodenal ulcer, unspecified as acute or chronic, without hemorrhage or perforation

Item 11–8 **Gastric ulcers** are lesions of the stomach that result in the death of the tissue and a defect of the surface. **Perforated ulcers** are those in which the lesion penetrates the gastric wall, leaving a hole. **Peptic ulcers** are lesions of the stomach or the duodenum. **Peptic** refers to the gastric juice, pepsin.

● **K27** Peptic ulcer, site unspecified

>   **Includes**   gastroduodenal ulcer NOS
>   peptic ulcer NOS
>
>   Use additional code to identify:
>   alcohol abuse and dependence (F10.-)
>
>   **Excludes1**   peptic ulcer of newborn (P78.82)
>
> ■**K27.0** Acute peptic ulcer, site unspecified, with hemorrhage 🦠
>
> ■**K27.1** Acute peptic ulcer, site unspecified, with perforation 🦠
>
> ■**K27.2** Acute peptic ulcer, site unspecified, with both hemorrhage and perforation 🦠
>
> ■**K27.3** Acute peptic ulcer, site unspecified, without hemorrhage or perforation 🦠
>
> ■**K27.4** Chronic or unspecified peptic ulcer, site unspecified, with hemorrhage 🦠
>
> ■**K27.5** Chronic or unspecified peptic ulcer, site unspecified, with perforation 🦠
>
> ■**K27.6** Chronic or unspecified peptic ulcer, site unspecified, with both hemorrhage and perforation 🦠
>
> ■**K27.7** Chronic peptic ulcer, site unspecified, without hemorrhage or perforation
>
> ■**K27.9** Peptic ulcer, site unspecified, unspecified as acute or chronic, without hemorrhage or perforation

● **K28** Gastrojejunal ulcer

>   **Includes**   anastomotic ulcer (peptic) or erosion
>   gastrocolic ulcer (peptic) or erosion
>   gastrointestinal ulcer (peptic) or erosion
>   gastrojejunal ulcer (peptic) or erosion
>   jejunal ulcer (peptic) or erosion
>   marginal ulcer (peptic) or erosion
>   stomal ulcer (peptic) or erosion
>
>   Use additional code to identify:
>   alcohol abuse and dependence (F10.-)
>
>   **Excludes1**   primary ulcer of small intestine (K63.3)
>
> **K28.0** Acute gastrojejunal ulcer with hemorrhage 🦠
>
> **K28.1** Acute gastrojejunal ulcer with perforation 🦠
>
> **K28.2** Acute gastrojejunal ulcer with both hemorrhage and perforation 🦠
>
> ■**K28.3** Acute gastrojejunal ulcer without hemorrhage or perforation 🦠
>
> ■**K28.4** Chronic or unspecified gastrojejunal ulcer with hemorrhage 🦠
>
> ■**K28.5** Chronic or unspecified gastrojejunal ulcer with perforation 🦠
>
> **K28.6** Chronic or unspecified gastrojejunal ulcer with both hemorrhage and perforation 🦠
>
> **K28.7** Chronic gastrojejunal ulcer without hemorrhage or perforation
>
> ■**K28.9** Gastrojejunal ulcer, unspecified as acute or chronic, without hemorrhage or perforation

● **K29** Gastritis and duodenitis

>   **Excludes1**   eosinophilic gastritis or gastroenteritis
>   (K52.81)
>   Zollinger-Ellison syndrome (E16.4)

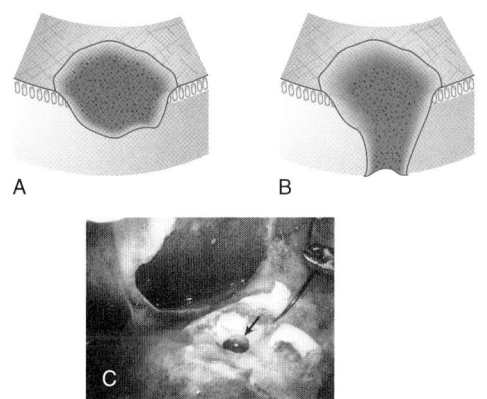

Figure 11-8 **A.** Ulcer. **B.** Perforated ulcer. **C.** Laparoscopic view of a perforated duodenal ulcer *(arrow)* with fibrinous exudate on the adjacent peritoneum. (**C** from Feldman: Sleisenger & Fordtran's Gastrointestinal and Liver Disease, 8th ed. 2006, Saunders, An Imprint of Elsevier)

● Unacceptable First-Listed Diagnosis   ● Use Additional Character(s)   ■ Unspecified   **OGCR** Official Guidelines for Coding and Reporting

🦠 Complication\Comorbidity   🦠 Major C\C   Excludes 1   Excludes 2   Includes   Use additional   Code first   Code also

● **K29.0   Acute gastritis**
>   Use additional code to identify:
>   alcohol abuse and dependence (F10.-)
>
> | Excludes1 | erosion (acute) of stomach (K25.-)

   K29.00   Acute gastritis without bleeding

   K29.01   Acute gastritis with bleeding 🗘

● **K29.2   Alcoholic gastritis**
>   Use additional code to identify:
>   alcohol abuse and dependence (F10.-)

   K29.20   Alcoholic gastritis without bleeding

   K29.21   Alcoholic gastritis with bleeding 🗘

● **K29.3   Chronic superficial gastritis**

   K29.30   Chronic superficial gastritis without bleeding

   K29.31   Chronic superficial gastritis with bleeding 🗘

● **K29.4   Chronic atrophic gastritis**
>   Gastric atrophy

   K29.40   Chronic atrophic gastritis without bleeding

   K29.41   Chronic atrophic gastritis with bleeding 🗘

● **K29.5   Unspecified chronic gastritis**
>   Chronic antral gastritis
>   Chronic fundal gastritis

   ▪ **K29.50   Unspecified chronic gastritis without bleeding**

   ▪ **K29.51   Unspecified chronic gastritis with bleeding** 🗘

● **K29.6   Other gastritis**
>   Giant hypertrophic gastritis
>   Granulomatous gastritis
>   Ménétrier's disease

   K29.60   Other gastritis without bleeding

   K29.61   Other gastritis with bleeding 🗘

● **K29.7   Gastritis, unspecified**

   ▪ **K29.70   Gastritis, unspecified, without bleeding**

   ▪ **K29.71   Gastritis, unspecified, with bleeding** 🗘

● **K29.8   Duodenitis**

   K29.80   Duodenitis without bleeding

   K29.81   Duodenitis with bleeding 🗘

● **K29.9   Gastroduodenitis, unspecified**

   ▪ **K29.90   Gastroduodenitis, unspecified, without bleeding**

   ▪ **K29.91   Gastroduodenitis, unspecified, with bleeding** 🗘

K30   Dyspepsia
> | Includes | indigestion
> | Excludes1 | heartburn (R12)
>   nervous dyspepsia (F45.8)
>   neurotic dyspepsia (F45.8)
>   psychogenic dyspepsia (F45.8)

● **K31   Other diseases of stomach and duodenum**
> | Includes | functional disorders of stomach
> | Excludes2 | diabetic gastroparesis (E08.43, E09.43,
>   E10.43, E11.43, E13.43)
>   diverticulum of duodenum (K57.00-K57.11)

   K31.0   Acute dilatation of stomach 🗘
>   Acute distention of stomach

   K31.1   Adult hypertrophic pyloric stenosis 🗘
>   Pyloric stenosis NOS
>
> | Excludes1 | congenital or infantile pyloric
>   stenosis (Q40.0)

   K31.2   Hourglass stricture and stenosis of stomach
> | Excludes1 | congenital hourglass stomach (Q40.2)
>   hourglass contraction of stomach
>   (K31.89)

Item 11-9 Gastritis is a severe inflammation of the stomach. **Atrophic gastritis** is a chronic inflammation of the stomach that results in destruction of the cells of the mucosa of the stomach. Duodenitis is an inflammation of the duodenum, the first section of the small intestine.

   K31.3   Pylorospasm, not elsewhere classified
> | Excludes1 | congenital or infantile pylorospasm
>   (Q40.0)
>   neurotic pylorospasm (F45.8)
>   psychogenic pylorospasm (F45.8)

   K31.4   Gastric diverticulum
> | Excludes1 | congenital diverticulum of stomach
>   (Q40.2)

   K31.5   Obstruction of duodenum 🗘
>   Constriction of duodenum
>   Duodenal ileus (chronic)
>   Stenosis of duodenum
>   *Narrowing*
>   Stricture of duodenum
>   *Narrowing*
>   Volvulus of duodenum
>   *Twisting/knotting*
>
> | Excludes1 | congenital stenosis of duodenum (Q41.0)

   K31.6   Fistula of stomach and duodenum 🗘
>   Gastrocolic fistula
>   Gastrojejunocolic fistula

   K31.7   Polyp of stomach and duodenum
> | Excludes1 | adenomatous polyp of stomach (D13.1)

● **K31.8   Other specified diseases of stomach and duodenum**

   ● **K31.81   Angiodysplasia of stomach and duodenum**

      K31.811   Angiodysplasia of stomach and duodenum with bleeding 🗘

      K31.819   Angiodysplasia of stomach and duodenum without bleeding
>   Angiodysplasia of stomach and duodenum NOS

   K31.82   Dieulafoy lesion (hemorrhagic) of stomach and duodenum 🗘
> | Excludes2 | Dieulafoy lesion of intestine (K63.81)

   K31.83   Achlorhydria

   K31.89   Other diseases of stomach and duodenum

▪ **K31.9   Disease of stomach and duodenum, unspecified**

DISEASES OF APPENDIX (K35-K38)

● **K35   Acute appendicitis**

   K35.2   Acute appendicitis with generalized peritonitis 🗘
>   Appendicitis (acute) with generalized (diffuse)
>   peritonitis following rupture or perforation of
>   appendix
>   Appendicitis with peritonitis NOS
>   Perforated appendix NOS
>   Ruptured appendix NOS

   K35.3   Acute appendicitis with localized peritonitis 🗘
>   Acute appendicitis with localized peritonitis with
>   or without rupture or perforation of appendix
>   Acute appendicitis with peritoneal abscess

● **K35.8   Other and unspecified acute appendicitis**

   ▪ **K35.80   Unspecified acute appendicitis** 🗘
>   Acute appendicitis NOS
>   Acute appendicitis without (localized)
>   (generalized) peritonitis

   K35.89   Other acute appendicitis

K36   Other appendicitis
> | Includes | chronic appendicitis
>   recurrent appendicitis

● Unacceptable First-Listed Diagnosis   ● Use Additional Character(s)   ▪ Unspecified   **OGCR** Official Guidelines for Coding and Reporting
🗘 Complication\Comorbidity   🗘 Major C\C | Excludes 1 | | Excludes 2 | | Includes | Use additional   Code first   Code also

Item 11–10 Achlorhydria, also known as gastric anacidity, is the absence of gastric acid.

▩ **K37 Unspecified appendicitis**

> **Excludes1** -unspecified appendicitis with peritonitis (K35.2-K35.3)

● **K38 Other diseases of appendix**

     K38.0 Hyperplasia of appendix

     K38.1 Appendicular concretions
         Fecalith of appendix
         Stercolith of appendix

     K38.2 Diverticulum of appendix

     K38.3 Fistula of appendix

     K38.8 Other specified diseases of appendix
         Intussusception of appendix

     ▩ **K38.9 Disease of appendix, unspecified**

HERNIA (K40-K46)

> **Note:** Hernia with both gangrene and obstruction is classified to hernia with gangrene.

> **Includes**   acquired hernia
>   congenital [except diaphragmatic or hiatus] hernia
>   recurrent hernia

● **K40 Inguinal hernia**

> **Includes**   bubonocele
>   direct inguinal hernia
>   double inguinal hernia
>   indirect inguinal hernia
>   inguinal hernia NOS
>   oblique inguinal hernia
>   scrotal hernia

   ● **K40.0 Bilateral inguinal hernia, with obstruction, without gangrene**
         Inguinal hernia (bilateral) causing obstruction without gangrene
         Incarcerated inguinal hernia (bilateral) without gangrene
         Irreducible inguinal hernia (bilateral) without gangrene
         Strangulated inguinal hernia (bilateral) without gangrene

     K40.00 Bilateral inguinal hernia, with obstruction, without gangrene, not specified as recurrent ✿
         Bilateral inguinal hernia, with obstruction, without gangrene NOS

     K40.01 Bilateral inguinal hernia, with obstruction, without gangrene, recurrent ✿

   ● **K40.1 Bilateral inguinal hernia, with gangrene**

     K40.10 Bilateral inguinal hernia, with gangrene, not specified as recurrent ✿
         Bilateral inguinal hernia, with gangrene NOS

     K40.11 Bilateral inguinal hernia, with gangrene, recurrent ✿

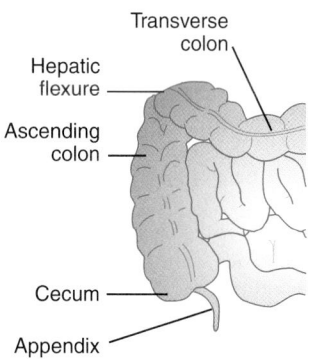

Transverse colon
Hepatic flexure
Ascending colon
Cecum
Appendix

Figure 11-9 Acute appendicitis is the inflammation of the appendix, usually associated with obstruction. Most often this is a disease of adolescents and young adults.

Item 11–11 Hernias of the groin are the most common type, accounting for 80 percent of all hernias. There are two major types of inguinal hernias: indirect (oblique) affecting men only and direct. **Indirect inguinal hernias** result when the intestines emerge through the abdominal wall in an indirect fashion through the inguinal canal. **Direct inguinal hernias** penetrate through the abdominal wall in a direct fashion. **Femoral hernias** occur at the femoral ring where the femoral vessels enter the thigh and is most common in women. An abdominal wall hernia is also called a ventral or epigastric hernia and occurs in both sexes. Classification is based on location of the hernia and whether there is obstruction or gangrene.

Ventral, epigastric, or incisional hernia occurs on the abdominal surface caused by musculature weakness or a tear at a previous surgical site and is evidenced by a bulge that changes in size, becoming larger with exertion. An **incarcerated** hernia is one in which the intestines become trapped in the hernia. A **strangulated** hernia is one in which the blood supply to the intestines is lost. Hiatal hernia occurs when a loop of the stomach protrudes upward through the small opening in the diaphragm through which the esophagus passes, leaving the abdominal cavity and entering the chest. It occurs in both sexes.

   ● **K40.2 Bilateral inguinal hernia, without obstruction or gangrene**

     K40.20 Bilateral inguinal hernia, without obstruction or gangrene, not specified as recurrent
         Bilateral inguinal hernia NOS

     K40.21 Bilateral inguinal hernia, without obstruction or gangrene, recurrent

   ● **K40.3 Unilateral inguinal hernia, with obstruction, without gangrene**
         Inguinal hernia (unilateral) causing obstruction without gangrene
         Incarcerated inguinal hernia (unilateral) without gangrene
         Irreducible inguinal hernia (unilateral) without gangrene
         Strangulated inguinal hernia (unilateral) without gangrene

     K40.30 Unilateral inguinal hernia, with obstruction, without gangrene, not specified as recurrent ✿
         Inguinal hernia, with obstruction NOS
         Unilateral inguinal hernia, with obstruction, without gangrene NOS

     K40.31 Unilateral inguinal hernia, with obstruction, without gangrene, recurrent ✿

   ● **K40.4 Unilateral inguinal hernia, with gangrene**

     K40.40 Unilateral inguinal hernia, with gangrene, not specified as recurrent ✿
         Inguinal hernia with gangrene NOS
         Unilateral inguinal hernia with gangrene NOS

     K40.41 Unilateral inguinal hernia, with gangrene, recurrent ✿

   ● **K40.9 Unilateral inguinal hernia, without obstruction or gangrene**

     K40.90 Unilateral inguinal hernia, without obstruction or gangrene, not specified as recurrent
         Inguinal hernia NOS
         Unilateral inguinal hernia NOS

     K40.91 Unilateral inguinal hernia, without obstruction or gangrene, recurrent

● Unacceptable First-Listed Diagnosis   ● Use Additional Character(s)   ▩ Unspecified   **OGCR** Official Guidelines for Coding and Reporting
✿ Complication\Comorbidity   ✿ Major C\C   [Excludes 1]   [Excludes 2]   Includes   Use additional   Code first   Code also

● **K41   Femoral hernia**

   ● **K41.0   Bilateral femoral hernia, with obstruction, without gangrene**
      Femoral hernia (bilateral) causing obstruction, without gangrene
      Incarcerated femoral hernia (bilateral), without gangrene
      Irreducible femoral hernia (bilateral), without gangrene
      Strangulated femoral hernia (bilateral), without gangrene

     K41.00   Bilateral femoral hernia, with obstruction, without gangrene, not specified as recurrent 🦠
        Bilateral femoral hernia, with obstruction, without gangrene NOS

     K41.01   Bilateral femoral hernia, with obstruction, without gangrene, recurrent 🦠

   ● **K41.1   Bilateral femoral hernia, with gangrene**

     K41.10   Bilateral femoral hernia, with gangrene, not specified as recurrent 🦠
        Bilateral femoral hernia, with gangrene NOS

     K41.11   Bilateral femoral hernia, with gangrene, recurrent 🦠

   ● **K41.2   Bilateral femoral hernia, without obstruction or gangrene**

     K41.20   Bilateral femoral hernia, without obstruction or gangrene, not specified as recurrent
        Bilateral femoral hernia NOS

     K41.21   Bilateral femoral hernia, without obstruction or gangrene, recurrent

   ● **K41.3   Unilateral femoral hernia, with obstruction, without gangrene**
      Femoral hernia (unilateral) causing obstruction, without gangrene
      Incarcerated femoral hernia (unilateral), without gangrene
      Irreducible femoral hernia (unilateral), without gangrene
      Strangulated femoral hernia (unilateral), without gangrene

     K41.30   Unilateral femoral hernia, with obstruction, without gangrene, not specified as recurrent 🦠
        Femoral hernia, with obstruction NOS
        Unilateral femoral hernia, with obstruction NOS

     K41.31   Unilateral femoral hernia, with obstruction, without gangrene, recurrent 🦠

   ● **K41.4   Unilateral femoral hernia, with gangrene**

     K41.40   Unilateral femoral hernia, with gangrene, not specified as recurrent 🦠
        Femoral hernia, with gangrene NOS
        Unilateral femoral hernia, with gangrene NOS

     K41.41   Unilateral femoral hernia, with gangrene, recurrent 🦠

   ● **K41.9   Unilateral femoral hernia, without obstruction or gangrene**

     K41.90   Unilateral femoral hernia, without obstruction or gangrene, not specified as recurrent
        Femoral hernia NOS
        Unilateral femoral hernia NOS

     K41.91   Unilateral femoral hernia, without obstruction or gangrene, recurrent

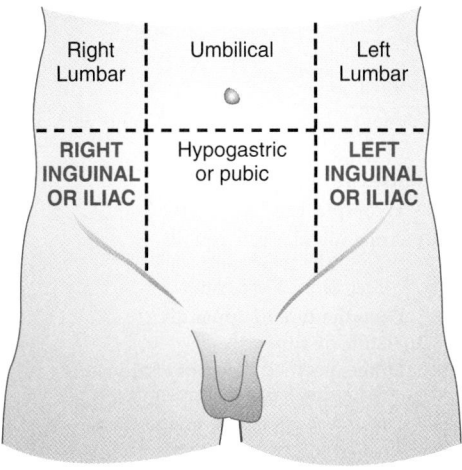

Right Lumbar	Umbilical	Left Lumbar
RIGHT INGUINAL OR ILIAC	Hypogastric or pubic	**LEFT INGUINAL OR ILIAC**

Figure 11-10   Inguinal hernias are those are located in the inguinal or iliac areas of the abdomen.

Item 11–12   Crohn's disease, also known as **regional enteritis,** is a chronic inflammatory disease of the intestines. Classification is based on location in the small (duodenum, ileum, jejunum) or large (cecum, colon, rectum, anal canal) intestine.

● **K42   Umbilical hernia**

   | **Includes** | paraumbilical hernia |
   | **Excludes1** | omphalocele (Q79.2) |

   K42.0   Umbilical hernia with obstruction, without gangrene 🦠
      Umbilical hernia causing obstruction, without gangrene
      Incarcerated umbilical hernia, without gangrene
      Irreducible umbilical hernia, without gangrene
      Strangulated umbilical hernia, without gangrene

   K42.1   Umbilical hernia with gangrene 🦠
      Gangrenous umbilical hernia

   K42.9   Umbilical hernia without obstruction or gangrene
      Umbilical hernia NOS

● **K43   Ventral hernia**

   ● **K43.0   Ventral hernia with obstruction, without gangrene**
      Ventral hernia causing obstruction, without gangrene
      Incarcerated ventral hernia, without gangrene
      Irreducible ventral hernia, without gangrene
      Strangulated ventral hernia, without gangrene

     ■ **K43.00   Ventral hernia, unspecified, with obstruction, without gangrene** 🦠

     K43.01   Incisional hernia, with obstruction, without gangrene 🦠

     K43.09   Other ventral hernia, with obstruction, without gangrene 🦠
        Epigastric hernia

   ● **K43.1   Ventral hernia with gangrene**
      Gangrenous ventral hernia

     ■ **K43.10   Ventral hernia, unspecified, with gangrene** 🦠

     K43.11   Incisional hernia, with gangrene 🦠

     K43.19   Other ventral hernia, with gangrene 🦠
        Epigastric hernia

   ● **K43.9   Ventral hernia without obstruction or gangrene**

● Unacceptable First-Listed Diagnosis   ● Use Additional Character(s)   ■ Unspecified   **OGCR** Official Guidelines for Coding and Reporting

🦠 Complication\Comorbidity   🦠 Major C\C   Excludes 1   Excludes 2   Includes   Use additional   Code first   Code also

1084

CHAPTER 11 (K00-K94)

◼ K43.90   Ventral hernia, unspecified, without obstruction or gangrene
     Ventral hernia NOS

   K43.91   Incisional hernia, without obstruction or gangrene

   K43.99   Other ventral hernia, without obstruction or gangrene
     Epigastric hernia

● K44   Diaphragmatic hernia

   | **Includes** | hiatus hernia (esophageal) (sliding) |

              paraesophageal hernia

   Excludes1   congenital diaphragmatic hernia (Q79.0)
          congenital hiatus hernia (Q40.1)

   K44.0   Diaphragmatic hernia with obstruction, without gangrene 🕮
     Diaphragmatic hernia causing obstruction
     Incarcerated diaphragmatic hernia
     Irreducible diaphragmatic hernia
     Strangulated diaphragmatic hernia

   K44.1   Diaphragmatic hernia with gangrene 🕮
     Gangrenous diaphragmatic hernia

   K44.9   Diaphragmatic hernia without obstruction or gangrene
     Diaphragmatic hernia NOS

● K45   Other abdominal hernia

   Includes   abdominal hernia, specified site NEC
          lumbar hernia
          obturator hernia
          pudendal hernia
          retroperitoneal hernia
          sciatic hernia

   K45.0   Other specified abdominal hernia with obstruction, without gangrene 🕮
     Other specified abdominal hernia causing obstruction
     Other specified incarcerated abdominal hernia
     Other specified irreducible abdominal hernia
     Other specified strangulated abdominal hernia

     Excludes2   hernia due to adhesions with obstruction (K56.5)

   K45.1   Other specified abdominal hernia with gangrene 🕮
     Any condition listed under K45 specified as gangrenous

   K45.8   Other specified abdominal hernia without obstruction or gangrene

● K46   Unspecified abdominal hernia

   Includes   enterocele
          epiplocele
          hernia NOS
          interstitial hernia
          intestinal hernia
          intra-abdominal hernia

   Excludes1   vaginal enterocele (N81.5)

◼ K46.0   Unspecified abdominal hernia with obstruction, without gangrene 🕮
     Unspecified abdominal hernia causing obstruction
     Unspecified incarcerated abdominal hernia
     Unspecified irreducible abdominal hernia
     Unspecified strangulated abdominal hernia

◼ K46.1   Unspecified abdominal hernia with gangrene 🕮
     Any condition listed under K46 specified as gangrenous

◼ K46.9   Unspecified abdominal hernia without obstruction or gangrene
     Abdominal hernia NOS

(See Plate 284 on page NAP-29.)

NONINFECTIVE ENTERITIS AND COLITIS (K50-K52)

   Includes   noninfective inflammatory bowel disease

   Excludes1   irritable bowel syndrome (K58.-)
          megacolon (K59.3)

● K50   Crohn's disease [regional enteritis]

   Includes   granulomatous enteritis

   Excludes1   ulcerative colitis (K51.-)

   Use additional code to identify manifestations, such as:
   pyoderma gangrenosum (L88)

● K50.0   Crohn's disease of small intestine
     Crohn's disease [regional enteritis] of duodenum
     Crohn's disease [regional enteritis] of ileum
     Crohn's disease [regional enteritis] of jejunum
     Regional ileitis
     Terminal ileitis

     Excludes1   Crohn's disease of both small and large intestine (K50.8-)

     K50.00   Crohn's disease of small intestine without complications 🕮

   ● K50.01   Crohn's disease of small intestine with complications

     K50.011   Crohn's disease of small intestine with rectal bleeding 🕮

     K50.012   Crohn's disease of small intestine with intestinal obstruction 🕮

     K50.013   Crohn's disease of small intestine with fistula 🕮

     K50.014   Crohn's disease of small intestine with abscess 🕮

     K50.018   Crohn's disease of small intestine with other complication 🕮

     ◼ K50.019   Crohn's disease of small intestine with unspecified complications 🕮

   ● K50.1   Crohn's disease of large intestine
     Crohn's disease [regional enteritis] of colon
     Crohn's disease [regional enteritis] of large bowel
     Crohn's disease [regional enteritis] of rectum
     Granulomatous colitis
     Regional colitis

     Excludes1   Crohn's disease of both small and large intestine (K50.8)

     K50.10   Crohn's disease of large intestine without complications 🕮

   ● K50.11   Crohn's disease of large intestine with complications

     K50.111   Crohn's disease of large intestine with rectal bleeding 🕮

     K50.112   Crohn's disease of large intestine with intestinal obstruction 🕮

     K50.113   Crohn's disease of large intestine with fistula 🕮

     K50.114   Crohn's disease of large intestine with abscess 🕮

     K50.118   Crohn's disease of large intestine with other complication 🕮

     ◼ K50.119   Crohn's disease of large intestine with unspecified complications 🕮

   ● K50.8   Crohn's disease of both small and large intestine

     K50.80   Crohn's disease of both small and large intestine without complications 🕮

● Unacceptable First-Listed Diagnosis   ● Use Additional Character(s)   ◼ Unspecified   **OGCR** Official Guidelines for Coding and Reporting

🕮 Complication\Comorbidity   🕮 Major C\C   Excludes 1   Excludes 2   Includes   Use additional   Code first   Code also

● **K50.81** **Crohn's disease of both small and large intestine with complications**

   K50.811 **Crohn's disease of both small and large intestine with rectal bleeding** 🦠

   K50.812 **Crohn's disease of both small and large intestine with intestinal obstruction** 🦠

   K50.813 **Crohn's disease of both small and large intestine with fistula** 🦠

   K50.814 **Crohn's disease of both small and large intestine with abscess** 🦠

   K50.818 **Crohn's disease of both small and large intestine with other complication** 🦠

   ▪ **K50.819** **Crohn's disease of both small and large intestine with unspecified complications** 🦠

● **K50.9** Crohn's disease, unspecified

   ▪ **K50.90** **Crohn's disease, unspecified, without complications** 🦠
      Crohn's disease NOS
      Regional enteritis NOS

   ● **K50.91** **Crohn's disease, unspecified, with complications**

      ▪ **K50.911** **Crohn's disease, unspecified, with rectal bleeding** 🦠

      ▪ **K50.912** **Crohn's disease, unspecified, with intestinal obstruction** 🦠

      ▪ **K50.913** **Crohn's disease, unspecified, with fistula** 🦠

      ▪ **K50.914** **Crohn's disease, unspecified, with abscess** 🦠

      ▪ **K50.918** **Crohn's disease, unspecified, with other complication** 🦠

      ▪ **K50.919** **Crohn's disease, unspecified, with unspecified complications** 🦠

● **K51** **Ulcerative colitis**

   Use additional code to identify manifestations, such as: pyoderma gangrenosum (L88)

   Excludes1 Crohn's disease [regional enteritis] (K50.-)

   ● **K51.0** **Ulcerative (chronic) pancolitis**
      Backwash ileitis

      K51.00 **Ulcerative (chronic) pancolitis without complications** 🦠
         Ulcerative (chronic) panocolitis NOS

      ● **K51.01** **Ulcerative (chronic) panocolitis with complications**

         K51.011 **Ulcerative (chronic) pancolitis with rectal bleeding**

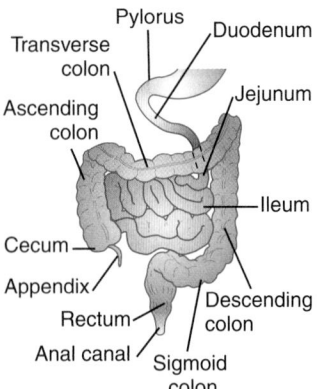

Pylorus
Duodenum
Transverse colon
Jejunum
Ascending colon
Ileum
Cecum
Appendix
Descending colon
Rectum
Anal canal
Sigmoid colon

Figure 11-11 Small and large intestines.

Item 11–13 Ulcerative colitis attacks the colonic mucosa and forms abscesses. The disease involves the intestines. Classification is based on the location:
- Enterocolitis: large and small intestine
- Ileocolitis: ileum and colon
- Proctitis: rectum
- Proctosigmoiditis: sigmoid colon and rectum

   K51.012 **Ulcerative (chronic) pancolitis with intestinal obstruction** 🦠

   K51.013 **Ulcerative (chronic) pancolitis with fistula** 🦠

   K51.014 **Ulcerative (chronic) panocolitis with abscess** 🦠

   K51.018 **Ulcerative (chronic) pancolitis with other complication** 🦠

   ▪ **K51.019** **Ulcerative (chronic) panocolitis with unspecified complications** 🦠

● **K51.2** Ulcerative (chronic) proctitis

   K51.20 **Ulcerative (chronic) proctitis without complications** 🦠
      Ulcerative (chronic) proctitis NOS

   ● **K51.21** **Ulcerative (chronic) proctitis with complications**

      K51.211 **Ulcerative (chronic) proctitis with rectal bleeding** 🦠

      K51.212 **Ulcerative (chronic) proctitis with intestinal obstruction** 🦠

      K51.213 **Ulcerative (chronic) proctitis with fistula** 🦠

      K51.214 **Ulcerative (chronic) proctitis with abscess** 🦠

      K51.218 **Ulcerative (chronic) proctitis with other complication** 🦠

      ▪ **K51.219** **Ulcerative (chronic) proctitis with unspecified complications** 🦠

● **K51.3** Ulcerative (chronic) rectosigmoiditis

   K51.30 **Ulcerative (chronic) rectosigmoiditis without complications** 🦠
      Ulcerative (chronic) rectosigmoiditis NOS

   ● **K51.31** **Ulcerative (chronic) rectosigmoiditis with complications**

      K51.311 **Ulcerative (chronic) rectosigmoiditis with rectal bleeding** 🦠

      K51.312 **Ulcerative (chronic) rectosigmoiditis with intestinal obstruction** 🦠

      K51.313 **Ulcerative (chronic) rectosigmoiditis with fistula** 🦠

      K51.314 **Ulcerative (chronic) rectosigmoiditis with abscess** 🦠

      K51.318 **Ulcerative (chronic) rectosigmoiditis with other complication** 🦠

      ▪ **K51.319** **Ulcerative (chronic) rectosigmoiditis with unspecified complications** 🦠

● **K51.4** **Inflammatory polyps of colon**

   Excludes1 adenomatous polyp of colon (D12.6)
   polyposis of colon (D12.6)
   polyps of colon NOS (K63.5)

   K51.40 **Inflammatory polyps of colon without complications** 🦠
      Inflammatory polyps of colon NOS

● Unacceptable First-Listed Diagnosis   ● Use Additional Character(s)   ▪ Unspecified   OGCR Official Guidelines for Coding and Reporting

🦠 Complication\Comorbidity   🦠 Major C\C   [Excludes 1]   [Excludes 2]   Includes   Use additional   Code first   Code also

1086

CHAPTER 11 (K00-K94)

● **K51.41   Inflammatory polyps of colon with complications**

K51.411   Inflammatory polyps of colon with rectal bleeding 🦠

K51.412   Inflammatory polyps of colon with intestinal obstruction 🦠

K51.413   Inflammatory polyps of colon with fistula 🦠

K51.414   Inflammatory polyps of colon with abscess 🦠

K51.418   Inflammatory polyps of colon with other complication 🦠

🔲K51.419   Inflammatory polyps of colon with unspecified complications 🦠

● **K51.5   Left sided colitis**
Left hemicolitis

K51.50   Left sided colitis without complications 🦠
Left sided colitis NOS

● **K51.51   Left sided colitis with complications**

K51.511   Left sided colitis with rectal bleeding 🦠

K51.512   Left sided colitis with intestinal obstruction 🦠

K51.513   Left sided colitis with fistula 🦠

K51.514   Left sided colitis with abscess 🦠

K51.518   Left sided colitis with other complication 🦠

🔲K51.519   Left sided colitis with unspecified complications 🦠

● **K51.8   Other ulcerative colitis**

K51.80   Other ulcerative colitis without complications 🦠

● **K51.81   Other ulcerative colitis with complications**

K51.811   Other ulcerative colitis with rectal bleeding 🦠

K51.812   Other ulcerative colitis with intestinal obstruction 🦠

K51.813   Other ulcerative colitis with fistula 🦠

K51.814   Other ulcerative colitis with abscess 🦠

K51.818   Other ulcerative colitis with other complication 🦠

🔲K51.819   Other ulcerative colitis with unspecified complications 🦠

● **K51.9   Ulcerative colitis, unspecified**

🔲K51.90   Ulcerative colitis, unspecified, without complications 🦠

● **K51.91   Ulcerative colitis, unspecified, with complications**

🔲K51.911   Ulcerative colitis, unspecified with rectal bleeding 🦠
🔲K51.912   Ulcerative colitis, unspecified with intestinal obstruction 🦠
🔲K51.913   Ulcerative colitis, unspecified with fistula 🦠
🔲K51.914   Ulcerative colitis, unspecified with abscess 🦠
🔲K51.918   Ulcerative colitis, unspecified with other complication 🦠
🔲K51.919   Ulcerative colitis, unspecified with unspecified complications 🦠

● **K52   Other and unspecified noninfective gastroenteritis and colitis**

K52.0   Gastroenteritis and colitis due to radiation 🦠

● **K52.1   Toxic gastroenteritis and colitis 🦠**
Code first (T51-T65) to identify toxic agent.

K52.2   Allergic and dietetic gastroenteritis and colitis
Food hypersensitivity gastroenteritis or colitis

Use additional code to identify type of food allergy (Z91.01-, Z91.02-)

● **K52.8   Other specified noninfective gastroenteritis and colitis**

K52.81   Eosinophilic gastritis or gastroenteritis
Eosinophilic enteritis

| Excludes1 | eosinophilic esophagitis (K20.0) |

K52.82   Eosinophilic colitis

K52.89   Other specified noninfective gastroenteritis and colitis
Collagenous colitis
Lymphocytic colitis
Microscopic colitis (collagenous or lymphocytic)

🔲**K52.9   Noninfective gastroenteritis and colitis, unspecified**
Colitis NOS
Enteritis NOS
Gastroenteritis NOS
Ileitis NOS
Jejunitis NOS
Sigmoiditis NOS

| Excludes1 | diarrhea NOS (R19.7) |

functional diarrhea (K59.1)
infectious gastroenteritis and colitis NOS (A09)
neonatal diarrhea (noninfective) (P78.3)
psychogenic diarrhea (F45.8)

OTHER DISEASES OF INTESTINES (K55-K63)

● **K55   Vascular disorders of intestine**

| Excludes1 | necrotizing enterocolitis of newborn (P77.-) |

K55.0   Acute vascular disorders of intestine 🦠
Acute fulminant ischemic colitis
Acute intestinal infarction
Acute small intestine ischemia
Infarction of appendices epiploicae
Mesenteric (artery) (vein) embolism
Mesenteric (artery) (vein) infarction
Mesenteric (artery) (vein) thrombosis
Necrosis of intestine
Subacute ischemic colitis

K55.1   Chronic vascular disorders of intestine 🦠
Chronic ischemic colitis
Chronic ischemic enteritis
Chronic ischemic enterocolitis
Ischemic stricture of intestine
Mesenteric atherosclerosis
Mesenteric vascular insufficiency

● **K55.2   Angiodysplasia of colon**

K55.20   Angiodysplasia of colon without hemorrhage

K55.21   Angiodysplasia of colon with hemorrhage 🦠

K55.8   Other vascular disorders of intestine 🦠

🔲**K55.9   Vascular disorder of intestine, unspecified 🦠**
Ischemic colitis
Ischemic enteritis
Ischemic enterocolitis

Item 11–14 Intussusception is the prolapse (telescoping) of a part of the intestine into another adjacent part of the intestine. Intussusception may be enteric (ileoileal, jejunoileal, jejunojejunal), colic (colocolic), or intracolic (ileocecal, ileocolic).

● Unacceptable First-Listed Diagnosis	● Use Additional Character(s)	🔲 Unspecified	**OGCR** Official Guidelines for Coding and Reporting
🦠 Complication\Comorbidity	🦠 Major C\C Excludes 1 Excludes 2	Includes Use additional Code first Code also	

● **K56 Paralytic ileus and intestinal obstruction without hernia**

> | Excludes1 | congenital stricture or stenosis of intestine (Q41-Q42)
> cystic fibrosis with meconium ileus (E84.11)
> ischemic stricture of intestine (K55.1)
> meconium ileus NOS (P76.0)
> neonatal intestinal obstructions classifiable to P76.-
> obstruction of duodenum (K31.5)
> postprocedural intestinal obstruction (K91.3)
> stenosis of anus or rectum (K62.4)
> intestinal obstruction with hernia (K40-K46)

   K56.0 Paralytic ileus 🔾
> Paralysis of bowel
> Paralysis of colon
> Paralysis of intestine
>
> | Excludes1 | gallstone ileus (K56.3)
> ileus NOS (K56.7)
> obstructive ileus NOS (K56.69)

   K56.1 Intussusception 🔾
> Intussusception or invagination of bowel
> Intussusception or invagination of colon
> Intussusception or invagination of intestine
> Intussusception or invagination of rectum
>
> | Excludes2 | intussusception of appendix (K38.8)

   K56.2 Volvulus 🔾
> Strangulation of colon or intestine
> Torsion of colon or intestine
> Twist of colon or intestine
>
> | Excludes2 | volvulus of duodenum (K31.5)

   K56.3 Gallstone ileus 🔾
> Obstruction of intestine by gallstone

   K56.4 Other impaction of intestine 🔾
> Enterolith
> Fecal impaction
> Impaction (of) colon

   K56.5 Intestinal adhesions [bands] with obstruction (postprocedural) (postinfection) 🔾
> Abdominal hernia due to adhesions with obstruction
> Peritoneal adhesions [bands] with intestinal obstruction (postprocedural) (postinfection)

● **K56.6 Other and unspecified intestinal obstruction**

   ▪ **K56.60 Unspecified intestinal obstruction**
> **Intestinal obstruction NOS** 🔾
>
> | Excludes1 | intestinal obstruction due to specified condition-code to condition

   K56.69 Other intestinal obstruction 🔾
> Enterostenosis NOS
> Obstructive ileus NOS
> Occlusion of colon or intestine NOS
> Stenosis of colon or intestine NOS
> Stricture of colon or intestine NOS
>
> | Excludes1 | intestinal obstruction due to specified condition-code to condition

   ▪ **K56.7 Ileus, unspecified** 🔾
> | Excludes1 | obstructive ileus (K56.69)

Item 11-15 Volvulus is the twisting of a segment of the intestine, resulting in obstruction. Paralytic ileus is paralysis of the intestine. It need not be a complete paralysis, but it must prohibit the passage of food through the intestine and lead to intestinal blockage. It is a common aftermath of some types of surgery.

Item 11-16 **Diverticula** of the intestines are acquired herniations of the mucosa. Diverticulum (singular): Pocket or pouch that bulges outward through a weak spot (herniation) in the colon. Diverticula (plural). **Diverticulosis** is the condition of having diverticula. **Diverticulitis** is inflammation of these pouches or herniations. Classification is based on location (small intestine or colon) and whether it occurs with or without hemorrhage.

● **K57 Diverticular disease of intestine**

> | Excludes1 | congenital diverticulum of intestine (Q43.8)
> Meckel's diverticulum (Q43.0)
>
> | Excludes2 | diverticulum of appendix (K38.2)

● **K57.0 Diverticulitis of small intestine with perforation and abscess**
> Diverticulitis of small intestine with peritonitis
>
> | Excludes1 | diverticulitis of both small and large intestine with perforation and abscess (K57.4-)

   K57.00 Diverticulitis of small intestine with perforation and abscess without bleeding 🔾

   K57.01 Diverticulitis of small intestine with perforation and abscess with bleeding 🔾

● **K57.1 Diverticular disease of small intestine without perforation or abscess**

> | Excludes1 | diverticular disease of both small and large intestine without perforation or abscess (K57.5-)

   K57.10 Diverticulosis of small intestine without perforation or abscess without bleeding
> Diverticular disease of small intestine NOS

   K57.11 Diverticulosis of small intestine without perforation or abscess with bleeding 🔾

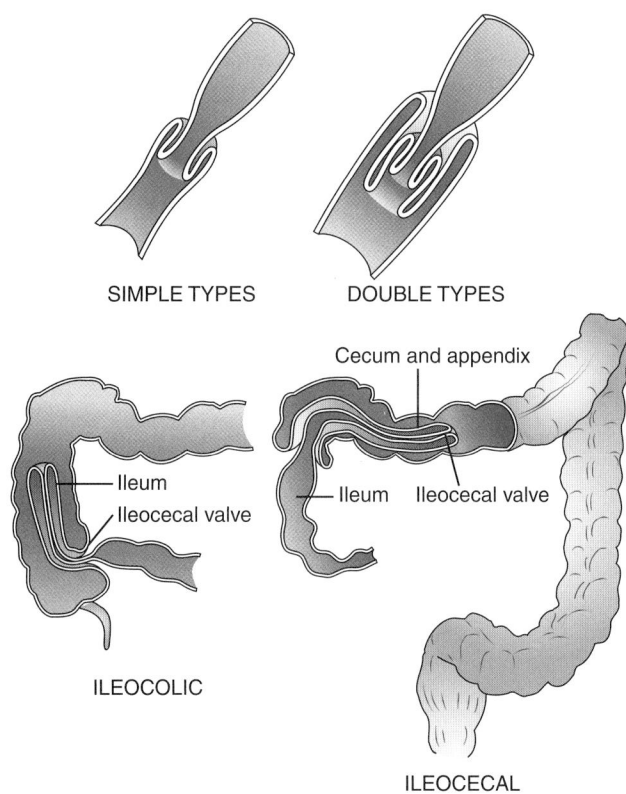

SIMPLE TYPES   DOUBLE TYPES

ILEOCOLIC

ILEOCECAL

Cecum and appendix

Ileum

Ileocecal valve

Figure 11-12 Types of intussusception.

● Unacceptable First-Listed Diagnosis   ● Use Additional Character(s)   ▪ Unspecified   **OGCR** Official Guidelines for Coding and Reporting
🔾 Complication\Comorbidity   🔾 Major C\C | Excludes 1 | | Excludes 2 | Includes   Use additional   Code first   Code also

K57.12 **Diverticulitis of small intestine without perforation or abscess without bleeding** 🅒

K57.13 **Diverticulitis of small intestine without perforation or abscess with bleeding** 🅜

● K57.2 **Diverticulitis of large intestine with perforation and abscess**
Diverticulitis of colon with peritonitis

| Excludes1 | diverticulitis of both small and large intestine with perforation and abscess (K57.4-) |

K57.20 **Diverticulitis of large intestine with perforation and abscess without bleeding** 🅒

K57.21 **Diverticulitis of large intestine with perforation and abscess with bleeding** 🅜

● K57.3 **Diverticular disease of large intestine without perforation or abscess**

| Excludes1 | diverticular disease of both small and large intestine without perforation or abscess (K57.5-) |

K57.30 **Diverticulosis of large intestine without perforation or abscess without bleeding**
Diverticular disease of colon NOS

K57.31 **Diverticulosis of large intestine without perforation or abscess with bleeding** 🅜

K57.32 **Diverticulitis of large intestine without perforation or abscess without bleeding** 🅒

K57.33 **Diverticulitis of large intestine without perforation or abscess with bleeding** 🅜

● K57.4 **Diverticulitis of both small and large intestine with perforation and abscess**
Diverticulitis of both small and large intestine with peritonitis

K57.40 **Diverticulitis of both small and large intestine with perforation and abscess without bleeding** 🅒

K57.41 **Diverticulitis of both small and large intestine with perforation and abscess with bleeding** 🅜

● K57.5 **Diverticular disease of both small and large intestine without perforation or abscess**

K57.50 **Diverticulosis of both small and large intestine without perforation or abscess without bleeding**
Diverticular disease of both small and large intestine NOS

K57.51 **Diverticulosis of both small and large intestine without perforation or abscess with bleeding** 🅜

K57.52 **Diverticulitis of both small and large intestine without perforation or abscess without bleeding** 🅒

K57.53 **Diverticulitis of both small and large intestine without perforation or abscess with bleeding** 🅜

● K57.8 **Diverticulitis of intestine, part unspecified, with perforation and abscess**
Diverticulitis of intestine NOS with peritonitis

◼ K57.80 **Diverticulitis of intestine, part unspecified, with perforation and abscess without bleeding** 🅒

◼ K57.81 **Diverticulitis of intestine, part unspecified, with perforation and abscess with bleeding** 🅜

● K57.9 **Diverticular disease of intestine, part unspecified, without perforation or abscess**

◼ K57.90 **Diverticulosis of intestine, part unspecified, without perforation or abscess without bleeding**
Diverticular disease of intestine NOS

◼ K57.91 **Diverticulosis of intestine, part unspecified, without perforation or abscess with bleeding** 🅜

◼ K57.92 **Diverticulitis of intestine, part unspecified, without perforation or abscess without bleeding** 🅒

◼ K57.93 **Diverticulitis of intestine, part unspecified, without perforation or abscess with bleeding** 🅜

● K58 **Irritable bowel syndrome**

| Includes | irritable colon |
| | spastic colon |

K58.0 **Irritable bowel syndrome with diarrhea**

K58.9 **Irritable bowel syndrome without diarrhea**
Irritable bowel syndrome NOS

● K59 **Other functional intestinal disorders**

Excludes1	change in bowel habit NOS (R19.4)
	intestinal malabsorption (K90.-)
	psychogenic intestinal disorders (F45.8)

| Excludes2 | functional disorders of stomach (K31.-) |

● K59.0 **Constipation**

◼ K59.00 **Constipation, unspecified**

K59.01 **Slow transit constipation**

K59.02 **Outlet dysfunction constipation**

K59.09 **Other constipation**

K59.1 **Functional diarrhea**

| Excludes1 | diarrhea NOS (R19.7) |
| | irritable bowel syndrome with diarrhea (K58.0) |

K59.2 **Neurogenic bowel, not elsewhere classified** 🅒

K59.3 **Megacolon, not elsewhere classified** 🅒
Dilatation of colon
Toxic megacolon

Code first (T51-T65) to identify toxic agent

Excludes1	congenital megacolon (aganglionic) (Q43.1)
	Hirschsprung's disease (Q43.1)
	megacolon in Chagas' disease (B57.32)

K59.4 **Anal spasm**
Proctalgia fugax

K59.8 **Other specified functional intestinal disorders**
Atony of colon Pseudo-obstruction (acute) (chronic) of intestine

◼ K59.9 **Functional intestinal disorder, unspecified**

● K60 **Fissure and fistula of anal and rectal regions**

| Excludes1 | fissure and fistula of anal and rectal regions with abscess or cellulitis (K61.-) |

| Excludes2 | anal sphincter tear (healed) (nontraumatic) (old) (K62.81) |

K60.0 **Acute anal fissure**

K60.1 **Chronic anal fissure**

◼ K60.2 **Anal fissure, unspecified**

K60.3 **Anal fistula**

K60.4 **Rectal fistula**
Fistula of rectum to skin

| Excludes1 | rectovaginal fistula (N82.3) |
| | vesicorectal fistula (N32.1) |

K60.5 **Anorectal fistula**

● Unaccceptable First-Listed Diagnosis   ● Use Additional Character(s)   ◼ Unspecified   **OGCR** Official Guidelines for Coding and Reporting

🅒 Complication\Comorbidity   🅜 Major C\C   Excludes 1   Excludes 2   Includes   Use additional   Code first   Code also   1089

CHAPTER 11 (K00-K94)

Item 11–17   A **fissure** is a groove in the surface, whereas a **fistula** is an abnormal passage. An **abscess** is an accumulation of pus in a tissue cavity resulting from a bacterial or parasitic infection.

● **K61   Abscess of anal and rectal regions**

> **Includes**   abscess of anal and rectal regions
> cellulitis of anal and rectal regions

K61.0   Anal abscess 🔖
> Perianal abscess
> > **Excludes1**   intrasphincteric abscess (K61.4)

K61.1   Rectal abscess 🔖
> Perirectal abscess
> > **Excludes1**   ischiorectal abscess (K61.3)

K61.2   Anorectal abscess 🔖

K61.3   Ischiorectal abscess 🔖
> Abscess of ischiorectal fossa

K61.4   Intrasphincteric abscess 🔖

● **K62   Other diseases of anus and rectum**

> **Includes**   anal canal
> **Excludes2**   colostomy and enterostomy malfunction (K91.4-)
> fecal incontinence (R15)
> hemorrhoids (I84.-)

K62.0   Anal polyp

K62.1   Rectal polyp
> > **Excludes1**   adenomatous polyp (D12.8)

K62.2   Anal prolapse
> Prolapse of anal canal

K62.3   Rectal prolapse
> Prolapse of rectal mucosa

K62.4   Stenosis of anus and rectum
> Stricture of anus (sphincter)

K62.5   Hemorrhage of anus and rectum 🔖
> > **Excludes1**   gastrointestinal bleeding NOS (K92.2)
> > melena (K92.1)
> > neonatal rectal hemorrhage (P54.2)

K62.6   Ulcer of anus and rectum 🔖
> Solitary ulcer of anus and rectum
> Stercoral ulcer of anus and rectum
> > **Excludes1**   fissure and fistula of anus and rectum (K60.-)
> > ulcerative colitis (K51.-)

K62.7   Radiation proctitis
> Use additional code to identify the type of radiation (W90.-)

● **K62.8   Other specified diseases of anus and rectum**
> > **Excludes2**   ulcerative proctitis (K51.2)

K62.81   Anal sphincter tear (healed) (nontraumatic) (old)
> Tear of anus, nontraumatic
> Use additional code for any associated fecal incontinence (R15)
> > **Excludes2**   anal fissure (K60.-)
> > anal sphincter tear (healed) (old) complicating delivery (O34.7-)
> > traumatic tear of anal sphincter (S31.831)

Item 11–18   **Peritonitis** is an inflammation of the lining (peritoneum) of the abdominal cavity and surface of the intestines.

K62.82   Dysplasia of anus 🔖
> Anal intraepithelial neoplasia I and II (AIN I and II) (histologically confirmed)
> Dysplasia of anus NOS
> Mild and moderate dysplasia of anus (histologically confirmed)
> > **Excludes1**   abnormal results from anal cytologic examination without histologic confirmation (R85.61-)
> > anal intraepithelial neoplasia III (D01.3)
> > carcinoma in situ of anus (D01.3)
> > HGSIL of anus (R85.613)
> > severe dysplasia of anus (D01.3)

K62.89   Other specified diseases of anus and rectum
> Proctitis NOS

■ **K62.9   Disease of anus and rectum, unspecified**

● **K63   Other diseases of intestine**

K63.0   Abscess of intestine 🔖
> > **Excludes1**   abscess of intestine with Crohn's disease (K50.04, K50.14, K50.84, K50.94,)
> > abscess of intestine with diverticular disease (K57.0, K57.2, K57.4, K57.8)
> > abscess of intestine with ulcerative colitis (K51.04, K51.14, K51.24, K51.34, K51.44, K51.54, K51.84, K51.94)
> > **Excludes2**   abscess of anal and rectal regions (K61.-)
> > abscess of appendix (K35.2)

K63.1   Perforation of intestine (nontraumatic) 🔖
> Perforation (nontraumatic) of rectum
> > **Excludes1**   perforation (nontraumatic) of duodenum (K26.-)
> > perforation (nontraumatic) of intestine with diverticular disease (K57.0, K57.2, K57.4, K57.8)
> > **Excludes2**   perforation (nontraumatic) of appendix (K35.2, K35.3)

K63.2   Fistula of intestine 🔖
> > **Excludes1**   fistula of duodenum (K31.6)
> > fistula of intestine with Crohn's disease (K50.03, K50.13, K50.83, K50.93,)
> > fistula of intestine with ulcerative colitis (K51.03, K51.13, K51.23, K51.33, K51.43, K51.53, K51.83, K51.93)
> > **Excludes2**   fistula of anal and rectal regions (K60.-)
> > fistula of appendix (K38.3)
> > intestinal-genital fistula, female (N82.2-N82.4)
> > vesicointestinal fistula (N32.1)

● Unacceptable First-Listed Diagnosis   ● Use Additional Character(s)   ■ Unspecified   **OGCR** Official Guidelines for Coding and Reporting
🔖 Complication\Comorbidity   🔖 Major C\C   Excludes 1   Excludes 2   Includes   Use additional   Code first   Code also

Item 11-19 Retroperitoneal infections occur between the posterior parietal peritoneum and posterior abdominal wall where the kidneys, adrenal glands, ureters, duodenum, ascending colon, descending colon, pancreas, and the large vessels and nerves are located.

    K63.3 Ulcer of intestine 🔖
      Primary ulcer of small intestine
      Excludes1 duodenal ulcer (K26.-)
          gastrointestinal ulcer (K28.-)
          gastrojejunal ulcer (K28.-)
          jejunal ulcer (K28.-)
          peptic ulcer, site unspecified (K27.-)
          ulcer of intestine with perforation (K63.1)
          ulcer of anus or rectum (K62.6)
          ulcerative colitis (K51.-)

    K63.4 Enteroptosis

    K63.5 Polyp of colon
      Excludes1 adenomatous polyp of colon (D12.6)
          inflammatory polyp of colon (K51.4-)
          polyposis of colon (D12.6)

  ● **K63.8 Other specified diseases of intestine**
      K63.81 Dieulafoy lesion of intestine 🔖
        Excludes2 Dieulafoy lesion of stomach and duodenum (K31.82)
      K63.89 Other specified diseases of intestine

  ■ **K63.9 Disease of intestine, unspecified**

DISEASES OF PERITONEUM AND RETROPERITONEUM (K65-K68)

● **K65 Peritonitis**
    Use additional code (B95-B97), to identify infectious agent
    Excludes1 acute appendicitis with generalized peritonitis (K35.2)
      aseptic peritonitis (T81.6)
      benign paroxysmal peritonitis (E85.0)
      chemical peritonitis (T81.6)
      diverticulitis of both small and large intestine with peritonitis (K57.4-)
      diverticulitis of colon with peritonitis (K57.2-)
      diverticulitis of intestine, NOS, with peritonitis (K57.8-)
      diverticulitis of small intestine with peritonitis (K57.0-)
      gonococcal peritonitis (A54.85)
      neonatal peritonitis (P78.0-P78.1)
      pelvic peritonitis, female (N73.3-N73.5)
      periodic familial peritonitis (E85.0)
      peritonitis due to talc or other foreign substance (T81.6)
      peritonitis in chlamydia (A74.81)
      peritonitis in diphtheria (A36.89)
      peritonitis in syphilis (late) (A52.74)
      peritonitis in tuberculosis (A18.31)
      peritonitis with or following abortion or ectopic or molar pregnancy (O00-O07, O08.0)
      peritonitis with or following appendicitis (K35.-)
      peritonitis with or following diverticular disease of intestine (K57.-)
      puerperal peritonitis (O85)
      retroperitoneal infections (K68.-)

    K65.0 Generalized (acute) peritonitis 🔖
      Pelvic peritonitis (acute), male
      Subphrenic peritonitis (acute)
      Suppurative peritonitis (acute)

Item 11-20 Cirrhosis is the progressive fibrosis of the liver resulting in loss of liver function. The main causes of cirrhosis of the liver are alcohol abuse, chronic hepatitis (inflammation of the liver), biliary disease, and excessive amounts of iron. **Alcoholic cirrhosis of the liver** is also called portal, Laënnec's, or fatty nutritional cirrhosis.

    K65.1 Peritoneal abscess 🔖
      Abdominopelvic abscess
      Abscess (of) omentum
      Abscess (of) peritoneum
      Mesenteric abscess
      Retrocecal abscess
      Subdiaphragmatic abscess
      Subhepatic abscess
      Subphrenic abscess

    K65.2 Spontaneous bacterial peritonitis 🔖
      Excludes1 bacterial peritonitis NOS K65.9

    K65.3 Choleperitonitis 🔖
      Peritonitis due to bile

    K65.4 Sclerosing mesenteritis 🔖
      Fat necrosis of peritoneum
      (Idiopathic) sclerosing mesenteric fibrosis
      Mesenteric lipodystrophy
      Mesenteric panniculitis
      Retractile mesenteritis

    K65.8 Other peritonitis 🔖
      Chronic proliferative peritonitis
      Peritonitis due to urine

  ■ **K65.9 Peritonitis, unspecified** 🔖
      Bacterial peritonitis NOS

● **K66 Other disorders of peritoneum**
    Excludes2 ascites (R18.-)
      peritoneal effusion (chronic) (R18.8)

    K66.0 Peritoneal adhesions (postprocedural) (postinfection)
      Adhesions (of) abdominal (wall)
      Adhesions (of) diaphragm
      Adhesions (of) intestine
      Adhesions (of) male pelvis
      Adhesions (of) omentum
      Adhesions (of) stomach
      Adhesive bands
      Mesenteric adhesions
      Excludes1 female pelvic adhesions [bands] (N73.6)
          peritoneal adhesions with intestinal obstruction (K56.5)

    K66.1 Hemoperitoneum 🔖
      Excludes1 traumatic hemoperitoneum (S36.8-)

    K66.8 Other specified disorders of peritoneum
  ■ **K66.9 Disorder of peritoneum, unspecified**

● **K67 Disorders of peritoneum in infectious diseases classified elsewhere** 🔖
    Code first underlying disease, such as :
      congenital syphilis (A50.0)
      helminthiasis (B65.0 - B83.9)
    Excludes1 peritonitis in chlamydia (A74.81)
      peritonitis in diphtheria (A36.89)
      peritonitis in gonococcal (A54.85)
      peritonitis in syphilis (late) (A52.74)
      peritonitis in tuberculosis (A18.31)

● **K68 Disorders of retroperitoneum**
  ● **K68.1 Retroperitoneal abscess**
      K68.11 Postprocedural retroperitoneal abscess 🔖
      K68.12 Psoas muscle abscess 🔖
      K68.19 Other retroperitoneal abscess 🔖
    K68.9 Other disorders of retroperitoneum 🔖

● Unacceptable First-Listed Diagnosis   ● Use Additional Character(s)   ■ Unspecified   **OGCR** Official Guidelines for Coding and Reporting
🔖 Complication\Comorbidity   🔖 Major C\C   Excludes 1   Excludes 2   Includes   Use additional   Code first   Code also

1091

CHAPTER 11 (K00-K94)

DISEASES OF LIVER (K70-K77)

> **Excludes1**   jaundice NOS (R17)
>
> **Excludes2**   hemochromatosis (E83.1)
> Reye's syndrome (G93.7)
> viral hepatitis (B15-B19)
> Wilson's disease (E83.0)

● **K70**   **Alcoholic liver disease**

> Use additional code to identify:
> alcohol abuse and dependence (F10.-)

   K70.0   Alcoholic fatty liver

● **K70.1**   Alcoholic hepatitis

     K70.10   Alcoholic hepatitis without ascites

     K70.11   Alcoholic hepatitis with ascites

   K70.2   Alcoholic fibrosis and sclerosis of liver

● **K70.3**   Alcoholic cirrhosis of liver
> Alcoholic cirrhosis NOS

     K70.30   Alcoholic cirrhosis of liver without ascites

     K70.31   Alcoholic cirrhosis of liver with ascites

● **K70.4**   Alcoholic hepatic failure
> Acute alcoholic hepatic failure
> Alcoholic hepatic failure NOS
> Chronic alcoholic hepatic failure
> Subacute alcoholic hepatic failure

     K70.40   Alcoholic hepatic failure without coma

     K70.41   Alcoholic hepatic failure with coma

■ **K70.9**   Alcoholic liver disease, unspecified

● **K71**   **Toxic liver disease**

> **Includes**   drug-induced idiosyncratic (unpredictable) liver disease
> drug-induced toxic (predictable) liver disease
>
> *Code first (T36-T65) to identify drug or toxic agent*
>
> **Excludes2**   alcoholic liver disease (K70.-)
> Budd-Chiari syndrome (I82.0)

● **K71.0**   Toxic liver disease with cholestasis
> Cholestasis with hepatocyte injury
> "Pure" cholestasis

● **K71.1**   Toxic liver disease with hepatic necrosis
> Hepatic failure (acute) (chronic) due to drugs

     ● **K71.10**   Toxic liver disease with hepatic necrosis, without coma

     ● **K71.11**   Toxic liver disease with hepatic necrosis, with coma

● **K71.2**   Toxic liver disease with acute hepatitis

● **K71.3**   Toxic liver disease with chronic persistent hepatitis

● **K71.4**   Toxic liver disease with chronic lobular hepatitis

● **K71.5**   Toxic liver disease with chronic active hepatitis
> Toxic liver disease with lupoid hepatitis

     ● **K71.50**   Toxic liver disease with chronic active hepatitis without ascites

     ● **K71.51**   Toxic liver disease with chronic active hepatitis with ascites

● **K71.6**   Toxic liver disease with hepatitis, not elsewhere classified

● **K71.7**   Toxic liver disease with fibrosis and cirrhosis of liver

● **K71.8**   Toxic liver disease with other disorders of liver
> Toxic liver disease with focal nodular hyperplasia
> Toxic liver disease with hepatic granulomas
> Toxic liver disease with peliosis hepatis
> Toxic liver disease with veno-occlusive disease of liver

● ■ **K71.9**   Toxic liver disease, unspecified

● **K72**   **Hepatic failure, not elsewhere classified**

> **Includes**   acute hepatitis NEC, with hepatic failure
> fulminant hepatitis NEC, with hepatic failure
> hepatic encephalopathy NOS
> liver (cell) necrosis with hepatic failure
> malignant hepatitis NEC, with hepatic failure
> yellow liver atrophy or dystrophy
>
> **Excludes1**   alcoholic hepatic failure (K70.4)
> hepatic failure complicating abortion or ectopic or molar pregnancy (O00-O07, O08.8)
> hepatic failure complicating pregnancy, childbirth and the puerperium (O26.6)
> hepatic failure with toxic liver disease (K71.1-)
> icterus of newborn (P55-P59)
> postprocedural hepatic failure (K91.81)
> viral hepatitis with hepatic coma (B15-B19)

● **K72.0**   Acute and subacute hepatic failure

     K72.00   Acute and subacute hepatic failure without coma 🗬

     K72.01   Acute and subacute hepatic failure with coma 🗬

● **K72.1**   Chronic hepatic failure

     K72.10   Chronic hepatic failure without coma

     K72.11   Chronic hepatic failure with coma

● **K72.9**   Hepatic failure, unspecified

     ■ **K72.90**   Hepatic failure, unspecified without coma

     ■ **K72.91**   Hepatic failure, unspecified with coma 🗬
> Hepatic coma NOS

● **K73**   **Chronic hepatitis, not elsewhere classified**

> **Excludes1**   alcoholic hepatitis (chronic) (K70.1-)
> drug-induced hepatitis (chronic) (K71.-)
> granulomatous hepatitis (chronic) NEC (K75.3)
> reactive, nonspecific hepatitis (chronic) (K75.2)
> viral hepatitis (chronic) (B15-B19)

   K73.0   Chronic persistent hepatitis, not elsewhere classified

   K73.1   Chronic lobular hepatitis, not elsewhere classified

   K73.2   Chronic active hepatitis, not elsewhere classified
> Lupoid hepatitis NEC

   K73.8   Other chronic hepatitis, not elsewhere classified

■ **K73.9**   Chronic hepatitis, unspecified

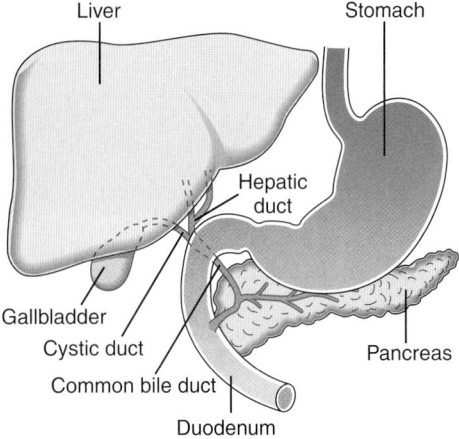

Figure 11-13   Liver and bile ducts.

● Unacceptable First-Listed Diagnosis   ● Use Additional Character(s)   ■ Unspecified   **OGCR** Official Guidelines for Coding and Reporting
🗬 Complication\Comorbidity   🗬 Major C\C   Excludes 1   Excludes 2   Includes   Use additional   Code first   Code also

CHAPTER 11 (K00-K94)

● **K74   Fibrosis and cirrhosis of liver**

> **Code also**, if applicable, viral hepatitis (acute) (chronic) (B15-B19)
>
> Excludes1   alcoholic cirrhosis (of liver) (K70.3)
> alcoholic fibrosis of liver (K70.2)
> cardiac sclerosis of liver (K76.1)
> cirrhosis (of liver) with toxic liver disease (K71.7)
> congenital cirrhosis (of liver) (P78.81)

K74.0   **Hepatic fibrosis**

K74.1   **Hepatic sclerosis**

K74.2   **Hepatic fibrosis with hepatic sclerosis**

K74.3   **Primary biliary cirrhosis**
> Chronic nonsuppurative destructive cholangitis

K74.4   **Secondary biliary cirrhosis**

■ K74.5   **Biliary cirrhosis, unspecified**

● K74.6   **Other and unspecified cirrhosis of liver**

> ■ K74.60   **Unspecified cirrhosis of liver**
> Cirrhosis (of liver) NOS

> K74.69   **Other cirrhosis of liver**
> Cryptogenic cirrhosis (of liver)
> Macronodular cirrhosis (of liver)
> Micronodular cirrhosis (of liver)
> Mixed type cirrhosis (of liver)
> Portal cirrhosis (of liver)
> Postnecrotic cirrhosis (of liver)

● **K75   Other inflammatory liver diseases**

> Excludes2   toxic liver disease (K71.-)

K75.0   **Abscess of liver** 🔗
> Cholangitic hepatic abscess
> Hematogenic hepatic abscess
> Hepatic abscess NOS
> Lymphogenic hepatic abscess
> Pylephlebitic hepatic abscess

> Excludes1   amebic liver abscess (A06.4)
> cholangitis without liver abscess (K83.0)
> pylephlebitis without liver abscess (K75.1)

K75.1   **Phlebitis of portal vein** 🔗
> Pylephlebitis

> Excludes1   pylephlebitic liver abscess (K75.0)

K75.2   **Nonspecific reactive hepatitis**

> Excludes1   acute or subacute hepatitis (K72.0-)
> chronic hepatitis NEC (K73.-)
> viral hepatitis (B15-B19)

K75.3   **Granulomatous hepatitis, not elsewhere classified**

> Excludes1   acute or subacute hepatitis (K72.0-)
> chronic hepatitis NEC (K73.-)
> viral hepatitis (B15-B19)

K75.4   **Autoimmune hepatitis**

● K75.8   **Other specified inflammatory liver diseases**

> K75.81   **Nonalcoholic steatohepatitis (NASH)**

> K75.89   **Other specified inflammatory liver diseases**

■ K75.9   **Inflammatory liver disease, unspecified**
> Hepatitis NOS

> Excludes1   acute or subacute hepatitis (K72.0-)
> chronic hepatitis NEC (K73.-)
> viral hepatitis (B15-B19)

● **K76   Other diseases of liver**

> Excludes2   alcoholic liver disease (K70.-)
> amyloid degeneration of liver (E85.-)
> cystic disease of liver (congenital) (Q44.6)
> hepatic vein thrombosis (I82.0)
> hepatomegaly NOS (R16.0)
> portal vein thrombosis (I81)
> toxic liver disease (K71.-)

K76.0   **Fatty (change of) liver, not elsewhere classified**
> Nonalcoholic fatty liver disease (NAFLD)

> Excludes1   nonalcoholic steatohepatitis (NASH) (K75.81)

K76.1   **Chronic passive congestion of liver**
> Cardiac cirrhosis
> Cardiac sclerosis

K76.2   **Central hemorrhagic necrosis of liver** 🔗

> Excludes1   liver necrosis with hepatic failure (K72.-)

K76.3   **Infarction of liver** 🔗

K76.4   **Peliosis hepatis**
> Hepatic angiomatosis

K76.5   **Hepatic veno-occlusive disease**

> Excludes1   Budd-Chiari syndrome (I82.0)

K76.6   **Portal hypertension** 🔗

K76.7   **Hepatorenal syndrome** 🔗

> Excludes1   hepatorenal syndrome following labor and delivery (O90.4)
> postprocedural hepatorenal syndrome (K91.82)

K76.8   **Other specified diseases of liver**
> Cyst (simple) of liver
> Focal nodular hyperplasia of liver
> Hepatoptosis

■ K76.9   **Liver disease, unspecified**

● **K77   Liver disorders in diseases classified elsewhere** 🔗

> *Code first underlying disease, such as:*
> amyloidosis (E85.-)
> congenital syphilis (A50.0, A50.5)
> congenital toxoplasmosis (P37.1)
> schistosomiasis (B65.0-B65.9)

> Excludes1   alcoholic hepatitis (K70.1-)
> alcoholic liver disease (K70.-)
> cytomegaloviral hepatitis (B25.1)
> herpesviral [herpes simplex] hepatitis (B00.81)
> infectious mononucleosis with liver disease (B27.0-B27.9 with .9)
> mumps hepatitis (B26.81)
> sarcoidosis with liver disease (D86.89)
> secondary syphilis with liver disease (A51.45)
> syphilis (late) with liver disease (A52.74)
> toxoplasmosis (acquired) hepatitis (B58.1)
> tuberculosis with liver disease (A18.83)

DISORDERS OF GALLBLADDER, BILIARY TRACT AND PANCREAS (K80–K87)

● **K80   Cholelithiasis**
> *Presence or formation of gallstones*

● K80.0   **Calculus of gallbladder with acute cholecystitis**
> Any condition listed in K80.2 with acute cholecystitis
> *Check documentation for acute/chronic gallbladder/ common bile duct either with or without obstruction.*

● Unacceptable First-Listed Diagnosis   ● Use Additional Character(s)   ■ Unspecified   **OGCR** Official Guidelines for Coding and Reporting

🔗 Complication\Comorbidity   🔗 Major C\C   Excludes 1   Excludes 2   Includes   Use additional   Code first   Code also

CHAPTER 11 (K00-K94)

1093

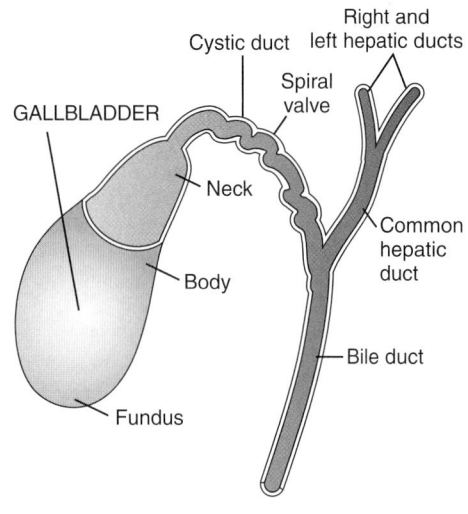

Figure 11-14   Gallbladder and bile ducts.

K80.00   **Calculus of gallbladder with acute cholecystitis without obstruction** 🕭

K80.01   **Calculus of gallbladder with acute cholecystitis with obstruction** 🕭

● K80.1   **Calculus of gallbladder with other cholecystitis**

K80.10   **Calculus of gallbladder with chronic cholecystitis without obstruction** 🕭
      Cholelithiasis with cholecystitis NOS

K80.11   **Calculus of gallbladder with chronic cholecystitis with obstruction** 🕭

K80.12   **Calculus of gallbladder with acute and chronic cholecystitis without obstruction** 🕭

K80.13   **Calculus of gallbladder with acute and chronic cholecystitis with obstruction** 🕭

K80.18   **Calculus of gallbladder with other cholecystitis without obstruction** 🕭

K80.19   **Calculus of gallbladder with other cholecystitis with obstruction** 🕭

● K80.2   **Calculus of gallbladder without cholecystitis**
      Cholecystolithiasis without cholecystitis
      Cholelithiasis (without cholecystitis)
      Colic (recurrent) of gallbladder (without cholecystitis)
      Gallstone (impacted) of cystic duct (without cholecystitis)
      Gallstone (impacted) of gallbladder (without cholecystitis)

K80.20   **Calculus of gallbladder without cholecystitis without obstruction**

K80.21   **Calculus of gallbladder without cholecystitis with obstruction** 🕭

● K80.3   **Calculus of bile duct with cholangitis**
      Any condition listed in K80.5 with cholangitis

■ K80.30   **Calculus of bile duct with cholangitis, unspecified, without obstruction**

■ K80.31   **Calculus of bile duct with cholangitis, unspecified, with obstruction** 🕭

K80.32   **Calculus of bile duct with acute cholangitis without obstruction**

K80.33   **Calculus of bile duct with acute cholangitis with obstruction** 🕭

K80.34   **Calculus of bile duct with chronic cholangitis without obstruction**

K80.35   **Calculus of bile duct with chronic cholangitis with obstruction** 🕭

K80.36   **Calculus of bile duct with acute and chronic cholangitis without obstruction**

K80.37   **Calculus of bile duct with acute and chronic cholangitis with obstruction** 🕭

● K80.4   **Calculus of bile duct with cholecystitis**
      Any condition listed in K80.5 with cholecystitis (with cholangitis)

■ K80.40   **Calculus of bile duct with cholecystitis, unspecified, without obstruction** 🕭

■ K80.41   **Calculus of bile duct with cholecystitis, unspecified, with obstruction** 🕭

K80.42   **Calculus of bile duct with acute cholecystitis without obstruction** 🕭

K80.43   **Calculus of bile duct with acute cholecystitis with obstruction** 🕭

K80.44   **Calculus of bile duct with chronic cholecystitis without obstruction** 🕭

K80.45   **Calculus of bile duct with chronic cholecystitis with obstruction** 🕭

K80.46   **Calculus of bile duct with acute and chronic cholecystitis without obstruction** 🕭

K80.47   **Calculus of bile duct with acute and chronic cholecystitis with obstruction** 🕭

● K80.5   **Calculus of bile duct without cholangitis or cholecystitis**
      Choledocholithiasis (without cholangitis or cholecystitis)
      Gallstone (impacted) of bile duct NOS (without cholangitis or cholecystitis)
      Gallstone (impacted) of common duct (without cholangitis or cholecystitis)
      Gallstone (impacted) of hepatic duct (without cholangitis or cholecystitis)
      Hepatic cholelithiasis (without cholangitis or cholecystitis)
      Hepatic colic (recurrent) (without cholangitis or cholecystitis)

K80.50   **Calculus of bile duct without cholangitis or cholecystitis without obstruction**

K80.51   **Calculus of bile duct without cholangitis or cholecystitis with obstruction** 🕭

● K80.6   **Calculus of gallbladder and bile duct with cholecystitis**

■ K80.60   **Calculus of gallbladder and bile duct with cholecystitis, unspecified, without obstruction** 🕭

■ K80.61   **Calculus of gallbladder and bile duct with cholecystitis, unspecified, with obstruction** 🕭

K80.62   **Calculus of gallbladder and bile duct with acute cholecystitis without obstruction** 🕭

K80.63   **Calculus of gallbladder and bile duct with acute cholecystitis with obstruction** 🕭

K80.64   **Calculus of gallbladder and bile duct with chronic cholecystitis without obstruction** 🕭

K80.65   **Calculus of gallbladder and bile duct with chronic cholecystitis with obstruction** 🕭

K80.66   **Calculus of gallbladder and bile duct with acute and chronic cholecystitis without obstruction** 🕭

K80.67   **Calculus of gallbladder and bile duct with acute and chronic cholecystitis with obstruction** 🕭

● Unacceptable First-Listed Diagnosis   ● Use Additional Character(s)   ■ Unspecified   **OGCR** Official Guidelines for Coding and Reporting

🕭 Complication\Comorbidity   🕭 Major C\C   Excludes 1   Excludes 2   Includes   Use additional   Code first   Code also

1094

CHAPTER 11 (K00-K94)

● K80.7 **Calculus of gallbladder and bile duct without cholecystitis**

　　K80.70 **Calculus of gallbladder and bile duct without cholecystitis without obstruction**

　　K80.71 **Calculus of gallbladder and bile duct without cholecystitis with obstruction** 🗝

● K80.8 **Other cholelithiasis**

　　K80.80 **Other cholelithiasis without obstruction**

　　K80.81 **Other cholelithiasis with obstruction** 🗝

● **K81 Cholecystitis**
　　Chronic or acute inflammation of the gallbladder.

　　| Excludes1 | cholecystitis with cholelithiasis (K80.-)

　　K81.0 **Acute cholecystitis** 🗝
　　　　Abscess of gallbladder
　　　　Angiocholecystitis
　　　　Emphysematous (acute) cholecystitis
　　　　Empyema of gallbladder
　　　　Gangrene of gallbladder
　　　　Gangrenous cholecystitis
　　　　Suppurative cholecystitis

　　K81.1 **Chronic cholecystitis**

　　K81.2 **Acute cholecystitis with chronic cholecystitis** 🗝

　　■ K81.9 **Cholecystitis, unspecified**

● **K82 Other diseases of gallbladder**

　　| Excludes1 | nonvisualization of gallbladder (R93.2)
　　　　postcholecystectomy syndrome (K91.5)

　　K82.0 **Obstruction of gallbladder** 🗝
　　　　Occlusion of cystic duct or gallbladder without
　　　　　cholelithiasis
　　　　Stenosis of cystic duct or gallbladder without
　　　　　cholelithiasis
　　　　Stricture of cystic duct or gallbladder without
　　　　　cholelithiasis

　　　　| Excludes1 | obstruction of gallbladder with
　　　　　cholelithiasis (K80.-)

　　K82.1 **Hydrops of gallbladder** 🗝
　　　　Mucocele of gallbladder

　　K82.2 **Perforation of gallbladder** 🗝
　　　　Rupture of cystic duct or gallbladder

　　K82.3 **Fistula of gallbladder** 🗝
　　　　Cholecystocolic fistula
　　　　Cholecystoduodenal fistula

　　K82.4 **Cholesterolosis of gallbladder**
　　　　Strawberry gallbladder

　　　　| Excludes1 | cholesterolosis of gallbladder with
　　　　　cholecystitis (K81.-)
　　　　　cholesterolosis of gallbladder with
　　　　　cholelithiasis (K80.-)

　　K82.8 **Other specified diseases of gallbladder**
　　　　Adhesions of cystic duct or gallbladder
　　　　Atrophy of cystic duct or gallbladder
　　　　Cyst of cystic duct or gallbladder
　　　　Dyskinesia of cystic duct or gallbladder
　　　　Hypertrophy of cystic duct or gallbladder
　　　　Nonfunctioning of cystic duct or gallbladder
　　　　Ulcer of cystic duct or gallbladder

　　■ K82.9 **Disease of gallbladder, unspecified**

● **K83 Other diseases of biliary tract**

　　| Excludes1 | postcholecystectomy syndrome (K91.5)
　　| Excludes2 | conditions involving the gallbladder
　　　　(K81-K82)
　　　　conditions involving the cystic duct
　　　　(K81-K82)

K83.0 **Cholangitis** 🗝
　　Ascending cholangitis
　　Cholangitis NOS
　　Primary cholangitis
　　Recurrent cholangitis
　　Sclerosing cholangitis
　　Secondary cholangitis
　　Stenosing cholangitis
　　Suppurative cholangitis

　　| Excludes1 | cholangitic liver abscess (K75.0)
　　　　cholangitis with choledocholithiasis
　　　　(K80.3-, K80.4-)
　　　　chronic nonsuppurative destructive
　　　　cholangitis (K74.3)

K83.1 **Obstruction of bile duct** 🗝
　　Occlusion of bile duct without cholelithiasis
　　Stenosis of bile duct without cholelithiasis
　　Stricture of bile duct without cholelithiasis

　　| Excludes1 | congenital obstruction of bile duct
　　　　(Q44.3)
　　　　obstruction of bile duct with
　　　　cholelithiasis (K80.-)

K83.2 **Perforation of bile duct** 🗝
　　Rupture of bile duct

K83.3 **Fistula of bile duct** 🗝
　　Choledochoduodenal fistula

K83.4 **Spasm of sphincter of Oddi**

K83.5 **Biliary cyst**

K83.8 **Other specified diseases of biliary tract**
　　Adhesions of biliary tract
　　Atrophy of biliary tract
　　Hypertrophy of biliary tract
　　Ulcer of biliary tract

■ K83.9 **Disease of biliary tract, unspecified**

● **K85 Acute pancreatitis**
　　*Inflammatory process in which pancreatic enzymes autodigest
　　the gland.*
　　Abscess of pancreas
　　Acute necrosis of pancreas
　　Acute (recurrent) pancreatitis
　　Gangrene of (gangrenous) pancreas
　　Hemorrhagic pancreatitis
　　Infective necrosis of pancreas
　　Subacute pancreatitis
　　Suppurative pancreatitis

K85.0 **Idiopathic acute pancreatitis** 🗝

K85.1 **Biliary acute pancreatitis** 🗝
　　Gallstone pancreatitis

K85.2 **Alcohol induced acute pancreatitis** 🗝
　　| Excludes2 | alcohol induced chronic pancreatitis
　　　　(K86.0)

K85.3 **Drug induced acute pancreatitis** 🗝
　　Use additional code to identify:
　　　drug abuse and dependence (F11.-- F17.-)

K85.8 **Other acute pancreatitis** 🗝

■ K85.9 **Acute pancreatitis, unspecified** 🗝
　　Pancreatitis NOS

● **K86 Other diseases of pancreas**

　　| Excludes2 | fibrocystic disease of pancreas (E84.-)
　　　　islet cell tumor (of pancreas) (D13.7)
　　　　pancreatic steatorrhea (K90.3)

K86.0 **Alcohol-induced chronic pancreatitis** 🗝

　　Use additional code to identify:
　　　alcohol abuse and dependence (F10.-)

　　| Excludes2 | alcohol induced acute pancreatitis
　　　　(K85.2)

● Unacceptable First-Listed Diagnosis　● Use Additional Character(s)　■ Unspecified　OGCR Official Guidelines for Coding and Reporting
🗝 Complication\Comorbidity　🗝 Major C\C　| Excludes 1 |　| Excludes 2 |　Includes　Use additional　Code first　Code also

1095

CHAPTER 11 (K00-K94)

K86.1 Other chronic pancreatitis 🐾
Chronic pancreatitis NOS
Infectious chronic pancreatitis
Recurrent chronic pancreatitis
Relapsing chronic pancreatitis

K86.2 Cyst of pancreas 🐾

K86.3 Pseudocyst of pancreas 🐾

K86.8 Other specified diseases of pancreas
Aseptic pancreatic necrosis
Atrophy of pancreas
Calculus of pancreas
Cirrhosis of pancreas
Fibrosis of pancreas
Pancreatic fat necrosis
Pancreatic infantilism
Pancreatic necrosis NOS

K86.9 Disease of pancreas, unspecified

● **K87 Disorders of gallbladder, biliary tract and pancreas in diseases classified elsewhere**

Code first underlying disease

| Excludes1 | cytomegaloviral pancreatitis(B25.2)
mumps pancreatitis (B26.3)
syphilitic gallbladder (A52.74)
syphilitic pancreas (A52.74)
tuberculosis of gallbladder (A18.83)
tuberculosis of pancreas (A18.83) |

OTHER DISEASES OF THE DIGESTIVE SYSTEM (K90-K94)

● **K90 Intestinal malabsorption**

| Excludes1 | intestinal malabsorption following gastrointestinal surgery (K91.2) |

K90.0 Celiac disease
Gluten-sensitive enteropathy
Idiopathic steatorrhea
Nontropical sprue

K90.1 Tropical sprue 🐾
Sprue NOS
Tropical steatorrhea

K90.2 Blind loop syndrome, not elsewhere classified 🐾
Blind loop syndrome NOS

| Excludes1 | congenital blind loop syndrome (Q43.8)
postsurgical blind loop syndrome (K91.2) |

K90.3 Pancreatic steatorrhea 🐾

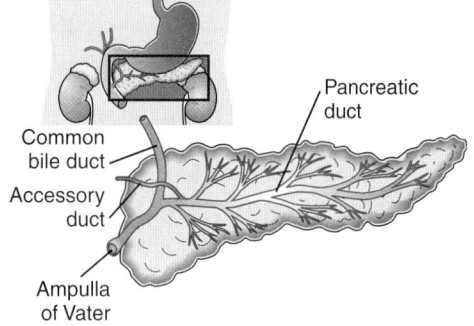

Common bile duct
Accessory duct
Pancreatic duct
Ampulla of Vater

Figure 11-15 Pancreatic ductal system.

K90.4 Malabsorption due to intolerance, not elsewhere classified 🐾
Malabsorption due to intolerance to carbohydrate
Malabsorption due to intolerance to fat
Malabsorption due to intolerance to protein
Malabsorption due to intolerance to starch

| Excludes2 | gluten-sensitive enteropathy (K90.0)
lactose intolerance (E73.-) |

● **K90.8 Other intestinal malabsorption**

K90.81 Whipple's disease 🐾

K90.89 Other intestinal malabsorption 🐾

■ **K90.9 Intestinal malabsorption, unspecified** 🐾

● **K91 Intraoperative and postprocedural complications and disorders of digestive system, not elsewhere classified**

| Excludes2 | complications of artificial opening of digestive system (K94.-)
gastrojejunal ulcer (K28.-)
postprocedural (radiation) retroperitoneal abscess (K68.11)
radiation colitis (K52.0)
radiation gastroenteritis (K52.0)
radiation proctitis (K62.7) |

K91.0 Vomiting following gastrointestinal surgery

K91.1 Postgastric surgery syndromes
Dumping syndrome
Postgastrectomy syndrome
Postvagotomy syndrome

■ **K91.2 Postsurgical malabsorption, not elsewhere classified** 🐾
Postsurgical blind loop syndrome

| Excludes1 | malabsorption osteomalacia in adults (M83.2)
malabsorption osteoporosis, postsurgical (M81.3) |

K91.3 Postprocedural intestinal obstruction 🐾

K91.5 Postcholecystectomy syndrome 🐾

● **K91.6 Intraoperative hemorrhage and hematoma of a digestive system organ or structure complicating a procedure**

| Excludes1 | intraoperative hemorrhage and hematoma of a digestive system organ or structure due to accidental puncture and laceration during a procedure (K91.7-) |

K91.61 Intraoperative hemorrhage and hematoma of a digestive system organ or structure complicating a digestive sytem procedure 🐾

K91.62 Intraoperative hemorrhage and hematoma of a digestive system organ or structure complicating other procedure 🐾

● **K91.7 Accidental puncture and laceration of a digestive system organ or structure during a procedure**

K91.71 Accidental puncture and laceration of a digestive system organ or structure during a digestive system procedure 🐾

K91.72 Accidental puncture and laceration of a digestive system organ or structure during other procedure 🐾

● **K91.8 Other intraoperative and postprocedural complications and disorders of digestive system**

K91.81 Other intraoperative complications of digestive system 🐾

K91.82 Postprocedural hepatic failure 🐾

CHAPTER 11 (K00-K94)

1096

● Unacceptable First-Listed Diagnosis   ● Use Additional Character(s)   ■ Unspecified   **OGCR** Official Guidelines for Coding and Reporting
🐾 Complication\Comorbidity   🐾 Major C\C | Excludes 1 | | Excludes 2 | Includes   Use additional   Code first   Code also

K91.83   Postprocedural hepatorenal syndrome 🔗

● K91.84   Postprocedural hemorrhage and hematoma of a digestive system organ or structure following a procedure

    K91.840   Postprocedural hemorrhage and hematoma of a digestive system organ or structure following a digestive system procedure 🔗

    K91.841   Postprocedural hemorrhage and hematoma of a digestive system organ or structure following other procedure 🔗

● K91.85   Complications of intestinal pouch

    K91.850   Pouchitis 🔗
       Inflammation of internal ileoanal pouch

    K91.858   Other complications of intestinal pouch 🔗

    K91.89   Other postprocedural complications and disorders of digestive system 🔗
       Use additional code, if applicable, to further specify disorder
       Excludes2   postprocedural retroperitoneal abscess (K68.11)

● K92   Other diseases of digestive system
    Excludes1   neonatal gastrointestinal hemorrhage (P54.0-P54.3)

    K92.0   Hematemesis 🔗

    K92.1   Melena 🔗
       Excludes1   occult blood in feces (R19.5)

    K92.2   Gastrointestinal hemorrhage, unspecified 🔗
       Gastric hemorrhage NOS
       Intestinal hemorrhage NOS
       Excludes1   acute hemorrhagic gastritis (K29.01)
           hemorrhage of anus and rectum (K62.5)
           angiodysplasia of stomach with hemorrhage (K31.811)
           diverticular disease with hemorrhage (K57.-)
           gastritis and duodenitis with hemorrhage (K29.-)
           peptic ulcer with hemorrhage (K25-K28)

● K92.8   Other specified diseases of the digestive system

    K92.81   Gastrointestinal mucositis (ulcerative)
       Code also type of associated therapy, such as:
       antineoplastic and immunosuppressive drugs (T45.1x-)
       radiological procedure and radiotherapy (Y84.2)
       Excludes2   mucositis (ulcerative) of vagina and vulva (N76.81)
           nasal mucositis (ulcerative) (J34.81)
           oral mucositis (ulcerative) (K12.3-)

    K92.89   Other specified diseases of the digestive system

■ K92.9   Disease of digestive system, unspecified

● K94   Complications of artificial openings of the digestive system

● K94.0   Colostomy complications

    ■ K94.00   Colostomy complication, unspecified

    K94.01   Colostomy hemorrhage 🔗

    K94.02   Colostomy infection 🔗
       Use additional code to specify type of infection, such as:
       cellulitis of abdominal wall (L03.32)
       sepsis (A40.-, A41.-)

    K94.03   Colostomy malfunction 🔗
       Mechanical complication of colostomy

    K94.09   Other complications of colostomy 🔗

● K94.1   Enterostomy complications

    ■ K94.10   Enterostomy complication, unspecified

    K94.11   Enterostomy hemorrhage 🔗

    K94.12   Enterostomy infection 🔗
       Use additional code to specify type of infection, such as:
       cellulitis of abdominal wall (L03.32)
       sepsis (A40.-, A41.-)

    K94.13   Enterostomy malfunction 🔗
       Mechanical complication of enterostomy

    K94.19   Other complications of enterostomy 🔗

● K94.2   Gastrostomy complications

    ■ K94.20   Gastrostomy complication, unspecified

    K94.21   Gastrostomy hemorrhage

    K94.22   Gastrostomy infection 🔗
       Use additional code to specify type of infection, such as:
       cellulitis of abdominal wall (L03.32)
       sepsis (A40.-, A41.-)

    K94.23   Gastrostomy malfunction 🔗
       Mechanical complication of gastrostomy

    K94.29   Other complications of gastrostomy

● K94.3   Esophagostomy complications

    ■ K94.30   Esophagostomy complications, unspecified 🔗

    K94.31   Esophagostomy hemorrhage 🔗

    K94.32   Esophagostomy infection 🔗
       Use additional code to identify the infection

    K94.33   Esophagostomy malfunction 🔗
       Mechanical complication of esophagostomy

    K94.39   Other complications of esophagostomy 🔗

● Unacceptable First-Listed Diagnosis   ● Use Additional Character(s)   ■ Unspecified   **OGCR** Official Guidelines for Coding and Reporting
🔗 Complication\Comorbidity   🔗 Major C\C   Excludes 1   Excludes 2   Includes   Use additional   Code first   Code also

1097

CHAPTER 11 (K00-K94)

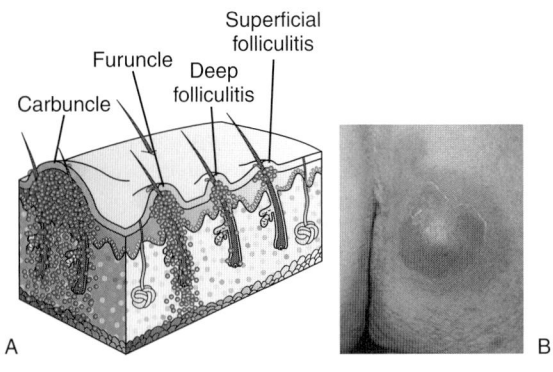

Figure 12-1 Furuncle, also known as a boil, is a staphylococcal infection. The organism enters the body through a hair follicle and so furuncles usually appear in hairy areas of the body. A cluster of furuncles is known as a carbuncle and involves infection into the deep subcutaneous fascia. These usually appear on the back and neck. (**B** from Habif: Clinical Dermatology, 4th ed. 2004, Mosby.)

CHAPTER 12
DISEASES OF THE SKIN AND SUBCUTANEOUS TISSUE (L00-L99)

Excludes2	certain conditions originating in the perinatal period (P04-P96)

certain conditions originating in the perinatal period (P04-P96)
certain infectious and parasitic diseases (A00-B99)
complications of pregnancy, childbirth and the puerperium (O00-O99)
congenital malformations, deformations, and chromosomal abnormalities (Q00-Q99)
endocrine, nutritional and metabolic diseases (E00-E90)
lipomelanotic reticulosis (I89.8)
neoplasms (C00-D48)
symptoms, signs and abnormal clinical and laboratory findings, not elsewhere classified (R00-R94)
systemic connective tissue disorders (M30-M36)
viral warts (B07.-)

This chapter contains the following blocks:

L00-L08	Infections of the skin and subcutaneous tissue
L10-L14	Bullous disorders
L20-L30	Dermatitis and eczema
L40-L45	Papulosquamous disorders
L49-L54	Urticaria and erythema
L55-L59	Radiation-related disorders of the skin and subcutaneous tissue
L60-L75	Disorders of skin appendages
L76	Intraoperative and postprocedural complications of skin and subcutaneous tissue
L80-L99	Other disorders of the skin and subcutaneous tissue

INFECTIONS OF THE SKIN AND SUBCUTANEOUS TISSUE (L00-L08)

Use additional code (B95-B97) to identify infectious agent.

Excludes2	hordeolum (H00.0)

hordeolum (H00.0)
infective dermatitis (L30.3)
local infections of skin classified in Chapter 1
lupus panniculitis (L93.2)
panniculitis NOS (M79.3)
panniculitis of neck and back (M54.0-)
perl che NOS (K13.0)
perl che due to candidiasis (B37.0)
perl che due to riboflavin deficiency (E53.0)
pyogenic granuloma (L98.0)
relapsing panniculitis [Weber-Christian] (M35.6)
viral warts (B07.-)
zoster (B02.-)

L00   Staphylococcal scalded skin syndrome
Ritter's disease

Use additional code to identify percentage of skin exfoliation (L49-)

Excludes1	bullous impetigo (L01.03)

bullous impetigo (L01.03)
pemphigus neonatorum (L01.03)
toxic epidermal necrolysis [Lyell] (L51.2)

● **L01   Impetigo**
Contagious skin infection caused by a streptococcus or staphylococcus aureus, common skin infections among children.

Excludes1	impetigo herpetiformis (L40.1)

● **L01.0   Impetigo**
Impetigo contagiosa
Impetigo vulgaris

■ **L01.00   Impetigo, unspecified**
Impetigo NOS

L01.01   Non-bullous impetigo

L01.02   Bockhart's impetigo
Impetigo follicularis
Perifolliculitis NOS
Superficial pustular perifolliculitis

L01.03   Bullous impetigo
Impetigo neonatorum
Pemphigus neonatorum
Neonate = newborn

L01.09   Other impetigo
Ulcerative impetigo

L01.1   Impetiginization of other dermatoses

● **L02   Cutaneous abscess, furuncle and carbuncle**

Use additional code to identify organism (B95-B96)

Excludes2	abscess of anus and rectal regions (K61.-)

abscess of anus and rectal regions (K61.-)
abscess of female genital organs (external) (N76.4)
abscess of male genital organs (external) (N48.2, N49.-)

● **L02.0   Cutaneous abscess, furuncle and carbuncle of face**

Excludes1	abscess of ear, external (H60.0)

abscess of ear, external (H60.0)
abscess of eyelid (H00.0)
abscess of head [any part, except face] (L02.8)
abscess of lacrimal gland (H04.0)
abscess of lacrimal passages (H04.3)
abscess of mouth (K12.2)
abscess of nose (J34.0)
abscess of orbit (H05.0)
submandibular abscess (K12.2)

L02.01   Cutaneous abscess of face 🅲🅲

L02.02   Furuncle of face
Boil of face
Folliculitis of face

L02.03   Carbuncle of face

● Unacceptable First-Listed Diagnosis   ● Use Additional Character(s)   ■ Unspecified   **OGCR** Official Guidelines for Coding and Reporting
🅲🅲 Complication\Comorbidity   🅲🅲 Major C\C   Excludes 1   Excludes 2   Includes   Use additional   Code first   Code also

CHAPTER 12 (L00-L99)

● **L02.1 Cutaneous abscess, furuncle and carbuncle of neck**

    L02.11 Cutaneous abscess of neck 🕭

    L02.12 Furuncle of neck
        Boil of neck
        Folliculitis of neck

    L02.13 Carbuncle of neck

● **L02.2 Cutaneous abscess, furuncle and carbuncle of trunk**

    | Excludes1 | non-newborn omphalitis (L08.82) |
    omphalitis of newborn (P38.-)

    | Excludes2 | abscess of breast (N61) |
    abscess of buttocks (L02.3)
    abscess of female external genital
        organs (N76.4)
    abscess of male external genital
        organs (N48.2, N49.-)
    abscess of hip (L02.4)

  ● **L02.21 Cutaneous abscess of trunk**

    L02.211 Cutaneous abscess of abdominal wall 🕭

    L02.212 Cutaneous abscess of back [any part, except buttock] 🕭

    L02.213 Cutaneous abscess of chest wall 🕭

    L02.214 Cutaneous abscess of groin 🕭

    L02.215 Cutaneous abscess of perineum 🕭

    L02.216 Cutaneous abscess of umbilicus 🕭

    ▨ **L02.219 Cutaneous abscess of trunk, unspecified** 🕭

  ● **L02.22 Furuncle of trunk**
    Boil of trunk
    Folliculitis of trunk

    L02.221 Furuncle of abdominal wall

    L02.222 Furuncle of back [any part, except buttock]

    L02.223 Furuncle of chest wall

    L02.224 Furuncle of groin

    L02.225 Furuncle of perineum

    L02.226 Furuncle of umbilicus

    ▨ **L02.229 Furuncle of trunk, unspecified**

  ● **L02.23 Carbuncle of trunk**

    L02.231 Carbuncle of abdominal wall

    L02.232 Carbuncle of back [any part, except buttock]

    L02.233 Carbuncle of chest wall

    L02.234 Carbuncle of groin

    L02.235 Carbuncle of perineum

    L02.236 Carbuncle of umbilicus

    ▨ **L02.239 Carbuncle of trunk, unspecified**

● **L02.3 Cutaneous abscess, furuncle and carbuncle of buttock**

    | Excludes1 | pilonidal cyst with abscess (L05.01) |

    L02.31 Cutaneous abscess of buttock 🕭
        Cutaneous abscess of gluteal region

    L02.32 Furuncle of buttock
        Boil of buttock
        Folliculitis of buttock
        Furuncle of gluteal region

    L02.33 Carbuncle of buttock
        Carbuncle of gluteal region

● **L02.4 Cutaneous abscess, furuncle and carbuncle of limb**

    | Excludes2 | Cutaneous abscess, furuncle and carbuncle of groin (L02.214, L02.224, L02.234) |
    Cutaneous abscess, furuncle and carbuncle of hand (L02.5-)
    Cutaneous abscess, furuncle and carbuncle of foot (L02.6-)

  ● **L02.41 Cutaneous abscess of limb**

    L02.411 Cutaneous abscess of right axilla 🕭

    L02.412 Cutaneous abscess of left axilla 🕭

    L02.413 Cutaneous abscess of right upper limb 🕭

    L02.414 Cutaneous abscess of left upper limb 🕭

    L02.415 Cutaneous abscess of right lower limb 🕭

    L02.416 Cutaneous abscess of left lower limb 🕭

    ▨ **L02.419 Cutaneous abscess of limb, unspecified** 🕭

  ● **L02.42 Furuncle of limb**
    Boil of limb
    Folliculitis of limb

    L02.421 Furuncle of right axilla

    L02.422 Furuncle of left axilla

    L02.423 Furuncle of right upper limb

    L02.424 Furuncle of left upper limb

    L02.425 Furuncle of right lower limb

    L02.426 Furuncle of left lower limb

    ▨ **L02.429 Furuncle of limb, unspecified**

  ● **L02.43 Carbuncle of limb**

    L02.431 Carbuncle of right axilla

    L02.432 Carbuncle of left axilla

    L02.433 Carbuncle of right upper limb

    L02.434 Carbuncle of left upper limb

    L02.435 Carbuncle of right lower limb

    L02.436 Carbuncle of left lower limb

    ▨ **L02.439 Carbuncle of limb, unspecified**

● **L02.5 Cutaneous abscess, furuncle and carbuncle of hand**

  ● **L02.51 Cutaneous abscess of hand**

    L02.511 Cutaneous abscess of right hand 🕭

    L02.512 Cutaneous abscess of left hand 🕭

    ▨ **L02.519 Cutaneous abscess of unspecified hand** 🕭

  ● **L02.52 Furuncle hand**
    Boil of hand
    Folliculitis of hand

    L02.521 Furuncle right hand

    L02.522 Furuncle left hand

    ▨ **L02.529 Furuncle unspecified hand**

  ● **L02.53 Carbuncle of hand**

    L02.531 Carbuncle of right hand

    L02.532 Carbuncle of left hand

    ▨ **L02.539 Carbuncle of unspecified hand**

● Unacceptable First-Listed Diagnosis   ● Use Additional Character(s)   ▨ Unspecified   **OGCR** Official Guidelines for Coding and Reporting

🕭 Complication\Comorbidity   🕭 Major C\C | Excludes 1 | | Excludes 2 | Includes   Use additional   Code first   Code also

1099

- **L02.6**   **Cutaneous abscess, furuncle and carbuncle of foot**
  - **L02.61**   **Cutaneous abscess of foot**
    - L02.611   Cutaneous abscess of right foot 🗇
    - L02.612   Cutaneous abscess of left foot 🗇
    - ▪ L02.619   Cutaneous abscess of unspecified foot 🗇
  - **L02.62**   **Furuncle of foot**
    Boil of foot
    Folliculitis of foot
    - L02.621   Furuncle of right foot
    - L02.622   Furuncle of left foot
    - ▪ L02.629   Furuncle of unspecified foot
  - **L02.63**   **Carbuncle of foot**
    - L02.631   Carbuncle of right foot
    - L02.632   Carbuncle of left foot
    - ▪ L02.639   Carbuncle of unspecified foot
- **L02.8**   **Cutaneous abscess, furuncle and carbuncle of other sites**
  - **L02.81**   **Cutaneous abscess of other sites**
    - L02.811   Cutaneous abscess of head [any part, except face] 🗇
    - L02.818   Cutaneous abscess of other sites 🗇
  - **L02.82**   **Furuncle of other sites**
    Boil of other sites
    Folliculitis of other sites
    - L02.821   Furuncle of head [any part, except face]
    - L02.828   Furuncle of other sites
  - **L02.83**   **Carbuncle of other sites**
    - L02.831   Carbuncle of head [any part, except face]
    - L02.838   Carbuncle of other sites
- **L02.9**   **Cutaneous abscess, furuncle and carbuncle, unspecified**
  - ▪ **L02.91**   **Cutaneous abscess, unspecified** 🗇
  - ▪ **L02.92**   **Furuncle, unspecified**
    Boil NOS
    Furunculosis NOS
  - ▪ **L02.93**   **Carbuncle, unspecified**
- **L03**   **Cellulitis and acute lymphangitis**
  - Excludes2   cellulitis of anal and rectal region (K61.-)
    cellulitis of external auditory canal (H60.1)
    cellulitis of eyelid (H00.0)
    cellulitis of female external genital organs (N76.4)
    cellulitis of lacrimal apparatus (H04.3)
    cellulitis of male external genital organs (N48.2, N49.-)
    cellulitis of mouth (K12.2)
    cellulitis of nose (J34.0)
    eosinophilic cellulitis [Wells] (L98.3)
    febrile neutrophilic dermatosis [Sweet] (L98.2)
    lymphangitis (chronic) (subacute) (I89.1)
  - **L03.0**   **Cellulitis and acute lymphangitis of finger and toe**
    Infection of nail
    Onychia
    Paronychia
    Perionychia

Item 12-1   **Onychia** is an inflammation of the tissue surrounding the nail with pus accumulation and loss of the nail, resulting from microscopic pathogens entering through small wounds. **Paronychia** is a nail disease also known as felon or whitlow and is a bacterial or fungal infection.

- **L03.01**   **Cellulitis of finger**
  Felon
  Whitlow
  - Excludes1   herpetic whitlow (B00.89)
  - L03.011   Cellulitis of right finger
  - L03.012   Cellulitis of left finger
  - ▪ L03.019   Cellulitis of unspecified finger
- **L03.02**   **Acute lymphangitis of finger**
  Hangnail with lymphangitis of finger
  - L03.021   Acute lymphangitis of right finger
  - L03.022   Acute lymphangitis of left finger
  - ▪ L03.029   Acute lymphangitis of unspecified finger
- **L03.03**   **Cellulitis of toe**
  - L03.031   Cellulitis of right toe
  - L03.032   Cellulitis of left toe
  - ▪ L03.039   Cellulitis of unspecified toe
- **L03.04**   **Acute lymphangitis of toe**
  Hangnail with lymphangitis of toe
  - L03.041   Acute lymphangitis of right toe
  - L03.042   Acute lymphangitis of left toe
  - ▪ L03.049   Acute lymphangitis of unspecified toe
- **L03.1**   **Cellulitis and acute lymphangitis of other parts of limb**
  - **L03.11**   **Cellulitis of other parts of limb**
    - Excludes2   cellulitis of fingers (L03.01-)
      cellulitis of toes (L03.03-)
      groin (L03.314)
    - L03.111   Cellulitis of right axilla 🗇
    - L03.112   Cellulitis of left axilla 🗇
    - L03.113   Cellulitis of right upper limb 🗇
    - L03.114   Cellulitis of left upper limb 🗇
    - L03.115   Cellulitis of right lower limb 🗇
    - L03.116   Cellulitis of left lower limb 🗇
    - ▪ L03.119   Cellulitis of unspecified part of limb 🗇
  - **L03.12**   **Acute lymphangitis of other parts of limb**
    - Excludes2   acute lymphangitis of fingers (L03.2-)
      acute lymphangitis of toes (L03.4-)
      acute lymphangitis of groin (L03.324)
    - L03.121   Acute lymphangitis of right axilla 🗇
    - L03.122   Acute lymphangitis of left axilla 🗇
    - L03.123   Acute lymphangitis of right upper limb 🗇
    - L03.124   Acute lymphangitis of left upper limb 🗇

● Unacceptable First-Listed Diagnosis   ● Use Additional Character(s)   ▪ Unspecified   **OGCR** Official Guidelines for Coding and Reporting
🗇 Complication\Comorbidity   🗇 Major C\C   Excludes 1   Excludes 2   Includes   Use additional   Code first   Code also

● L03.125   Acute lymphangitis of right lower limb 🦠

● L03.126   Acute lymphangitis of left lower limb 🦠

◼ L03.129   Acute lymphangitis of unspecified part of limb 🦠

● L03.2   Cellulitis and acute lymphangitis of face and neck

  ● L03.21   Cellulitis and acute lymphangitis of face

     L03.211   Cellulitis of face 🦠

       | Excludes2 | cellulitis of ear (H60.1-)
cellulitis of eyelid (H00.0-)
cellulitis of head (L03.81)
cellulitis of lacrimal apparatus (H04.3)
cellulitis of lip (K13.0)
cellulitis of mouth (K12.2)
cellulitis of nose (internal) (J34.0)
cellulitis of orbit (H05.0)
cellulitis of scalp (L03.81)

     L03.212   Acute lymphangitis of face 🦠

  ● L03.22   Cellulitis and acute lymphangitis of neck

     L03.221   Cellulitis of neck 🦠

     L03.222   Acute lymphangitis of neck 🦠

● L03.3   Cellulitis and acute lymphangitis of trunk

  ● L03.31   Cellulitis of trunk

     | Excludes2 | cellulitis of anal and rectal regions (K61.-)
cellulitis of breast NOS (N61)
cellulitis of female external genital organs (N76.4)
cellulitis of male external genital organs (N48.2, N49.-)
omphalitis of newborn (P38.-)
puerperal cellulitis of breast (O91.2)

     L03.311   Cellulitis of abdominal wall 🦠

       | Excludes2 | cellulitis of umbilicus (L03.316)
cellulitis of groin (L03.314)

     L03.312   Cellulitis of back [any part except buttock] 🦠

     L03.313   Cellulitis of chest wall 🦠

     L03.314   Cellulitis of groin 🦠

     L03.315   Cellulitis of perineum 🦠

     L03.316   Cellulitis of umbilicus 🦠

     L03.317   Cellulitis of buttock 🦠

  ◼ L03.319   Cellulitis of trunk, unspecified 🦠

Item 12-2   Cellulitis is an acute spreading bacterial infection below the surface of the skin characterized by redness (erythema), warmth, swelling, pain, fever, chills, and enlarged lymph nodes ("swollen glands").

● L03.32   Acute lymphangitis of trunk

     L03.321   Acute lymphangitis of abdominal wall 🦠

     L03.322   Acute lymphangitis of back [any part except buttock] 🦠

     L03.323   Acute lymphangitis of chest wall 🦠

     L03.324   Acute lymphangitis of groin 🦠

     L03.325   Acute lymphangitis of perineum 🦠

     L03.326   Acute lymphangitis of umbilicus 🦠

     L03.327   Acute lymphangitis of buttock 🦠

  ◼ L03.329   Acute lymphangitis of trunk, unspecified 🦠

● L03.8   Cellulitis and acute lymphangitis of other sites

  ● L03.81   Cellulitis of other sites

     L03.811   Cellulitis of head [any part, except face] 🦠
         Cellulitis of scalp

       | Excludes2 | cellulitis of face (L03.211)

     L03.818   Cellulitis of other sites 🦠

  ● L03.89   Acute lymphangitis of other sites

     L03.891   Acute lymphangitis of head [any part, except face] 🦠

     L03.898   Acute lymphangitis of other sites 🦠

● L03.9   Cellulitis and acute lymphangitis, unspecified

  ◼ L03.90   Cellulitis, unspecified 🦠

  ◼ L03.91   Acute lymphangitis, unspecified 🦠

     | Excludes1 | lymphangitis NOS (I89.1)

● L04   **Acute lymphadenitis**
Short-term inflammation of lymph nodes which can be regionalized to involve a given area of the lymph system or systemic involving much of the body

   | Includes | abscess (acute) of lymph nodes, except mesenteric
acute lymphadenitis, except mesenteric

   | Excludes1 | chronic or subacute lymphadenitis, except mesenteric (I88.1)
enlarged lymph nodes (R59.-)
human immunodeficiency virus [HIV] disease resulting in generalized lymphadenopathy (B20)
lymphadenitis NOS (I88.9)
nonspecific mesenteric lymphadenitis (I88.0)

L04.0   **Acute lymphadenitis of face, head and neck**

L04.1   **Acute lymphadenitis of trunk**

L04.2   **Acute lymphadenitis of upper limb**
     Acute lymphadenitis of axilla
     Acute lymphadenitis of shoulder

L04.3   **Acute lymphadenitis of lower limb**
     Acute lymphadenitis of hip

     | Excludes2 | acute lymphadenitis of groin (L04.1)

L04.8   **Acute lymphadenitis of other sites**

◼ L04.9   **Acute lymphadenitis, unspecified**

Item 12-2   Abscess is a localized collection of pus in tissues or organs and is a sign of infection resulting in swelling and inflammation.

● Unacceptable First-Listed Diagnosis   ● Use Additional Character(s)   ◼ Unspecified   **OGCR** Official Guidelines for Coding and Reporting

🦠 Complication\Comorbidity   🦠 Major C\C | Excludes 1 | | Excludes 2 | Includes   Use additional   Code first   Code also   **1101**

CHAPTER 12 (L00-L99)

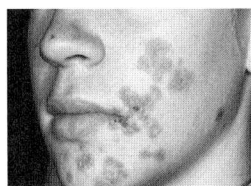

Figure 12-2 Impetigo. A thick, honey-yellow adherent crust covers the entire eroded surface. (From Habif: Clinical Dermatology, 4th ed. 2004, Mosby, Inc.)

Item 12–2 Pilonidal cyst, also called a coccygeal cyst, is the result of a disorder called pilonidal disease. The cyst usually contains hair and pus.

● **L05   Pilonidal cyst and sinus**
    ● **L05.0   Pilonidal cyst and sinus with abscess**
       L05.01   Pilonidal cyst with abscess 🦠
           Parasacral dimple with abscess
           Pilonidal abscess
           Pilonidal dimple with abscess
           Postanal dimple with abscess

       L05.02   Pilonidal sinus with abscess 🦠
           Coccygeal fistula with abscess
           Coccygeal sinus with abscess
           Pilonidal fistula with abscess

    ● **L05.9   Pilonidal cyst and sinus without abscess**
       L05.91   Pilonidal cyst without abscess
           Parasacral dimple
           Pilonidal dimple
           Postanal dimple
           Pilonidal cyst NOS

       L05.92   Pilonidal sinus without abscess
           Coccygeal fistula
           Coccygeal sinus without abscess
           Pilonidal fistula

● **L08   Other local infections of skin and subcutaneous tissue**
    L08.0   Pyoderma
       Purulent dermatitis
       Septic dermatitis
       Suppurative dermatitis
       | Excludes1 | pyoderma gangrenosum (L88)
                   pyoderma vegetans (L08.81)

    L08.1   Erythrasma 🦠
    ● **L08.8   Other specified local infections of the skin and subcutaneous tissue**
       L08.81   Pyoderma vegetans
          | Excludes1 | pyoderma gangrenosum (L88)
                   pyoderma NOS (L08.0)

       L08.82   Omphalitis not of newborn
          | Excludes1 | omphalitis of newborn (P38.-)

       L08.89   Other specified local infections of the skin and subcutaneous tissue

    ■ **L08.9   Local infection of the skin and subcutaneous tissue, unspecified**

BULLOUS DISORDERS (L10-L14)

| Excludes1 | benign familial pemphigus [Hailey-Hailey] (Q82.8)
               staphylococcal scalded skin syndrome (L00)
               toxic epidermal necrolysis [Lyell] (L51.2)

● **L10   Pemphigus**
    | Excludes1 | pemphigus neonatorum (L01.03)
    L10.0   Pemphigus vulgaris 🦠
    L10.1   Pemphigus vegetans 🦠
    L10.2   Pemphigus foliaceous 🦠
    L10.3   Brazilian pemphigus [fogo selvagem] 🦠
    L10.4   Pemphigus erythematosus 🦠
       Senear-Usher syndrome
    ● **L10.5   Drug-induced pemphigus** 🦠
       Code first (T36-T50) to identify drug
    ● **L10.8   Other pemphigus**
       L10.81   Paraneoplastic pemphigus 🦠
       L10.89   Other pemphigus 🦠
    ■ **L10.9   Pemphigus, unspecified** 🦠

● **L11   Other acantholytic disorders**
    L11.0   Acquired keratosis follicularis
       | Excludes1 | keratosis follicularis (congenital) [Darier-White] (Q82.8)
    L11.1   Transient acantholytic dermatosis [Grover]
    L11.8   Other specified acantholytic disorders
    ■ **L11.9   Acantholytic disorder, unspecified**

● **L12   Pemphigoid**
    | Excludes1 | herpes gestationis (O26.4-)
                impetigo herpetiformis (L40.1)
    L12.0   Bullous pemphigoid 🦠
    L12.1   Cicatricial pemphigoid
       Benign mucous membrane pemphigoid
    L12.2   Chronic bullous disease of childhood
       Juvenile dermatitis herpetiformis
    ● **L12.3   Acquired epidermolysis bullosa**
       | Excludes1 | epidermolysis bullosa (congenital) (Q81.-)
       ■ **L12.30   Acquired epidermolysis bullosa, unspecified** 🦠
       ● **L12.31   Epidermolysis bullosa due to drug** 🦠
          Code first (T36-T50) to identify drug
       L12.35   Other acquired epidermolysis bullosa 🦠
    L12.8   Other pemphigoid 🦠
    ■ **L12.9   Pemphigoid, unspecified** 🦠

● **L13   Other bullous disorders**
    L13.0   Dermatitis herpetiformis
       Duhring's disease
       Hydroa herpetiformis
       | Excludes1 | juvenile dermatitis herpetiformis (L12.2)
                senile dermatitis herpetiformis (L12.0)
    L13.1   Subcorneal pustular dermatitis
       Sneddon-Wilkinson disease
    L13.8   Other specified bullous disorders
    ■ **L13.9   Bullous disorder, unspecified**

● **L14   Bullous disorders in diseases classified elsewhere**
    Code first underlying disease

Item 12–3 Dermatitis herpetiformis, also known as Duhring's disease, is a systemic disease characterized by small blisters (3 to 5 mm) and occasionally large bullae (> 5 mm).

● Unacceptable First-Listed Diagnosis   ● Use Additional Character(s)   ■ Unspecified   **OGCR** Official Guidelines for Coding and Reporting

1102   🦠 Complication\Comorbidity   🦠 Major C\C | Excludes 1 | | Excludes 2 | Includes   Use additional   Code first   Code also

CHAPTER 12 (L00-L99)

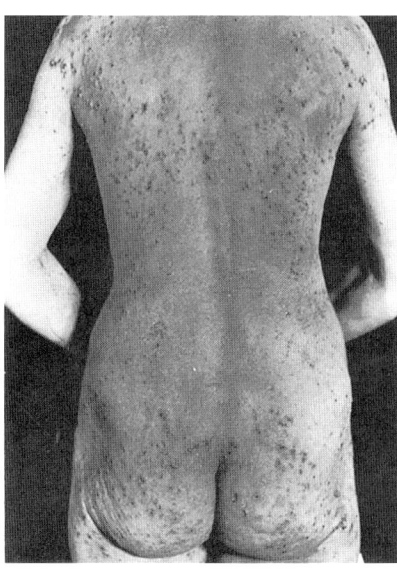

Figure 12-3 Dermatitis herpetiformis. (From Arnold HL, Odom RB, James WD: Andrews' Diseases of the skin, Clinical Dermatology, 8th ed. Philadelphia, WB Saunders, 1990, p 553.)

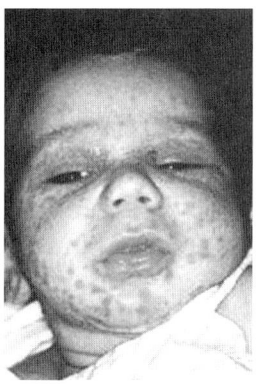

Figure 12-4 Seborrheic dermatitis. (From Cohen BA: Atlas of Pediatric Dermatology. St. Louis, Mosby, 1993.)

Item 12–4 Seborrheic dermatitis is characterized by greasy, scaly, red patches and is associated with oily skin and scalp.

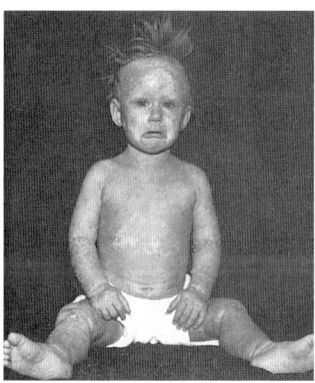

Figure 12-5 Atopic dermatitis. (From Moschella SL, Hurley HJ: Dermatology, 2nd ed. Philadelphia, WB Saunders, 1985, p 336.)

Item 12–5 Atopic dermatitis, also known as atopic eczema, infantile eczema, disseminated neuro dermatitis, flexural eczema, and *prurigo diathesique* (Besnier), is characterized by intense itching and is often hereditary.

DERMATITIS AND ECZEMA (L20-L30)

Note: In this block the terms dermatitis and eczema are used synonymously and interchangeably.

Excludes2 chronic (childhood) granulomatous disease (D71)
dermatitis gangrenosa (L88)
dermatitis herpetiformis (L13.0)
dry skin dermatitis (L85.3)
factitial dermatitis (L98.1)
perioral dermatitis (L71.0)
radiation-related disorders of the skin and subcutaneous tissue (L55-L59)
stasis dermatitis (I83.1-I83.2)

● **L20 Atopic dermatitis**
   L20.0 Besnier's prurigo
   ● **L20.8 Other atopic dermatitis**
     Excludes2 circumscribed neurodermatitis (L28.0)
     L20.81 Atopic neurodermatitis
       Diffuse neurodermatitis
     L20.82 Flexural eczema
     L20.83 Infantile (acute) (chronic) eczema
     L20.84 Intrinsic (allergic) eczema
     L20.89 Other atopic dermatitis
   ▣ **L20.9 Atopic dermatitis, unspecified**

● **L21 Seborrheic dermatitis**
   Excludes2 infective dermatitis (L30.3)
     seborrheic keratosis (L82.-)
   L21.0 Seborrhea capitis
     Cradle cap
   L21.1 Seborrheic infantile dermatitis
   L21.8 Other seborrheic dermatitis
   ▣ **L21.9 Seborrheic dermatitis, unspecified**
     Seborrhea NOS

L22 Diaper dermatitis
   Includes Diaper erythema
     Diaper rash
     Psoriasiform diaper rash

● **L23 Allergic contact dermatitis**
   Code first (T36-T65), to identify drug or substance
   Excludes1 allergy NOS (T78.40)
     contact dermatitis NOS (L25.9)
     dermatitis NOS (L30.9)
   Excludes2 dermatitis due to substances taken internally (L27.-)
     dermatitis of eyelid (H01.1-)
     diaper dermatitis (L22)
     eczema of external ear (H60.5-)
     irritant contact dermatitis (L24.-)
     perioral dermatitis (L71.0)
     radiation-related disorders of the skin and subcutaneous tissue (L55-L59)
   ● **L23.0 Allergic contact dermatitis due to metals**
     Allergic contact dermatitis due to chromium
     Allergic contact dermatitis due to nickel
   ● **L23.1 Allergic contact dermatitis due to adhesives**
   ● **L23.2 Allergic contact dermatitis due to cosmetics**
   ● **L23.3 Allergic contact dermatitis due to drugs in contact with skin**
     Excludes2 dermatitis due to ingested drugs and medicaments (L27.0-L27.1)
   ● **L23.4 Allergic contact dermatitis due to dyes**

● **L23.5 Allergic contact dermatitis due to other chemical products**
Allergic contact dermatitis due to cement
Allergic contact dermatitis due to insecticide
Allergic contact dermatitis due to plastic
Allergic contact dermatitis due to rubber

● **L23.6 Allergic contact dermatitis due to food in contact with the skin**
> Excludes2   dermatitis due to ingested food (L27.2)

● **L23.7 Allergic contact dermatitis due to plants, except food**
> Excludes2   allergy NOS due to pollen (J30.1)

● **L23.8 Allergic contact dermatitis due to other agents**

   ● **L23.81 Allergic contact dermatitis due to animal (cat) (dog) dander**
Allergic contact dermatitis due to animal (cat) (dog) hair

   ● **L23.89 Allergic contact dermatitis due to other agents**

● ■ **L23.9 Allergic contact dermatitis, unspecified cause**
Allergic contact eczema NOS

● **L24 Irritant contact dermatitis**
Code first (T36-T65) to identify drug or substance
> Excludes1   allergy NOS (T78.40)
> contact dermatitis NOS (L25.9)
> dermatitis NOS (L30.9)

> Excludes2   allergic contact dermatitis (L23.-)
> dermatitis due to substances taken internally (L27.-)
> dermatitis of eyelid (H01.1-)
> diaper dermatitis (L22)
> eczema of external ear (H60.5-)
> perioral dermatitis (L71.0)
> radiation-related disorders of the skin and subcutaneous tissue (L55-L59)

● **L24.0 Irritant contact dermatitis due to detergents**

● **L24.1 Irritant contact dermatitis due to oils and greases**

● **L24.2 Irritant contact dermatitis due to solvents**
Irritant contact dermatitis due to chlorocompound
Irritant contact dermatitis due to cyclohexane
Irritant contact dermatitis due to ester
Irritant contact dermatitis due to glycol
Irritant contact dermatitis due to hydrocarbon
Irritant contact dermatitis due to ketone

● **L24.3 Irritant contact dermatitis due to cosmetics**

● **L24.4 Irritant contact dermatitis due to drugs in contact with skin**

● **L24.5 Irritant contact dermatitis due to other chemical products**
Irritant contact dermatitis due to cement
Irritant contact dermatitis due to insecticide
Irritant contact dermatitis due to plastic
Irritant contact dermatitis due to rubber

● **L24.6 Irritant contact dermatitis due to food in contact with skin**
> Excludes2   dermatitis due to ingested food (L27.2)

● **L24.7 Irritant contact dermatitis due to plants, except food**
> Excludes2   allergy NOS to pollen (J30.1)

● **L24.8 Irritant contact dermatitis due to other agents**

   ● **L24.81 Irritant contact dermatitis due to metals**
Irritant contact dermatitis due to chromium
Irritant contact dermatitis due to nickel

   ● **L24.89 Irritant contact dermatitis due to other agents**
Irritant contact dermatitis due to dyes

● ■ **L24.9 Irritant contact dermatitis, unspecified cause**
Irritant contact eczema NOS

● **L25 Unspecified contact dermatitis**
Code first (T36-T65), to identify drug or substance
> Excludes1   allergic contact dermatitis (L23.-)
> allergy NOS (T78.40)
> dermatitis NOS (L30.9)
> irritant contact dermatitis (L24.-)

> Excludes2   dermatitis due to ingested substances (L27.-)
> dermatitis of eyelid (H01.1-)
> eczema of external ear (H60.5-)
> perioral dermatitis (L71.0)
> radiation-related disorders of the skin and subcutaneous tissue (L55-L59)

● ■ **L25.0 Unspecified contact dermatitis due to cosmetics**

● ■ **L25.1 Unspecified contact dermatitis due to drugs in contact with skin**
> Excludes2   dermatitis due to ingested drugs and medicaments (L27.0-L27.1)

● ■ **L25.2 Unspecified contact dermatitis due to dyes**

● ■ **L25.3 Unspecified contact dermatitis due to other chemical products**
Unspecified contact dermatitis due to cement
Unspecified contact dermatitis due to insecticide

● ■ **L25.4 Unspecified contact dermatitis due to food in contact with skin**
> Excludes2   dermatitis due to ingested food (L27.2)

● ■ **L25.5 Unspecified contact dermatitis due to plants, except food**
> Excludes1   nettle rash (L50.9)
> Excludes2   allergy NOS due to pollen (J30.1)

● ■ **L25.8 Unspecified contact dermatitis due to other agents**

● ■ **L25.9 Unspecified contact dermatitis, unspecified cause**
Contact dermatitis (occupational) NOS
Contact eczema (occupational) NOS

L26 Exfoliative dermatitis
> Includes   hebra's pityriasis
> Excludes1   Ritter's disease (L00)

● **L27 Dermatitis due to substances taken internally**
Code first (T36-T65), to identify drug or substance
> Excludes1   allergy NOS (T78.40)
> Excludes2   adverse food reaction, except dermatitis (T78.0-T78.1)
> contact dermatitis (L23-L25)
> drug photoallergic response (L56.1)
> drug phototoxic response (L56.0)
> urticaria (L50.-)

● **L27.0 Generalized skin eruption due to drugs and medicaments taken internally**

● **L27.1 Localized skin eruption due to drugs and medicaments taken internally**

● **L27.2 Dermatitis due to ingested food**
> Excludes2   dermatitis due to food in contact with skin (L23.6, L24.6, L25.4)

● **L27.8 Dermatitis due to other substances taken internally**

● ■ **L27.9 Dermatitis due to unspecified substance taken internally**

● Unacceptable First-Listed Diagnosis   ● Use Additional Character(s)   ■ Unspecified   **OGCR** Official Guidelines for Coding and Reporting

1104   🔹 Complication\Comorbidity   🔹 Major C\C   Excludes 1   Excludes 2   Includes   Use additional   Code first   Code also

CHAPTER 12 (L00-L99)

● **L28   Lichen simplex chronicus and prurigo**

    L28.0   Lichen simplex chronicus
         Circumscribed neurodermatitis
         Lichen NOS

    L28.1   Prurigo nodularis

    L28.2   Other prurigo
         Prurigo NOS   Prurigo mitis
         Prurigo Hebra   Urticaria papulosa

● **L29   Pruritus**

    Excludes1   neurotic excoriation (L98.1)
               psychogenic pruritus (F45.8)

    L29.0   Pruritus ani

    L29.1   Pruritus scroti

    L29.2   Pruritus vulvae

    ■ **L29.3   Anogenital pruritus, unspecified**

    L29.8   Other pruritus

    ■ **L29.9   Pruritus, unspecified**
         Itch NOS

● **L30   Other and unspecified dermatitis**

    Excludes2   contact dermatitis (L23-L25)
               dry skin dermatitis (L85.3)
               small plaque parapsoriasis (L41.3)
               stasis dermatitis (I83.1-.2)

    L30.0   Nummular dermatitis

    L30.1   Dyshidrosis [pompholyx]

    L30.2   Cutaneous autosensitization
         Candidid [levurid]   Eczematid
         Dermatophytid

    L30.3   Infective dermatitis
         Infectious eczematoid dermatitis

    L30.4   Erythema intertrigo

    L30.5   Pityriasis alba

    L30.8   Other specified dermatitis

    ■ **L30.9   Dermatitis, unspecified**
         Eczema NOS

PAPULOSQUAMOUS DISORDERS (L40-L45)

● **L40   Psoriasis**

    L40.0   Psoriasis vulgaris
         Nummular psoriasis   Plaque psoriasis

    L40.1   Generalized pustular psoriasis
         Impetigo herpetiformis
         Von Zumbusch's disease

    L40.2   Acrodermatitis continua

    L40.3   Pustulosis palmaris et plantaris

    L40.4   Guttate psoriasis

    ● **L40.5   Arthropathic psoriasis**

      ■ **L40.50   Arthropathic psoriasis, unspecified**

      **L40.51   Distal interphalangeal psoriatic
              arthropathy**

      L40.52   Psoriatic arthritis mutilans

      L40.53   Psoriatic spondylitis

      L40.54   Psoriatic juvenile arthropathy

      L40.59   Other psoriatic arthropathy

    L40.8   Other psoriasis
         Flexural psoriasis

    ■ **L40.9   Psoriasis, unspecified**

● **L41   Parapsoriasis**

    Excludes1   poikiloderma vasculare atrophicans
               (L94.5)

    L41.0   Pityriasis lichenoides et varioliformis acuta
         Mucha-Habermann disease

    L41.1   Pityriasis lichenoides chronica

    L41.2   Lymphomatoid papulosis

    L41.3   Small plaque parapsoriasis

    L41.4   Large plaque parapsoriasis

    L41.5   Retiform parapsoriasis

    L41.8   Other parapsoriasis

    ■ **L41.9   Parapsoriasis, unspecified**

  L42   Pityriasis rosea

● **L43   Lichen planus**

    Excludes1   lichen planopilaris (L66.1)

    L43.0   Hypertrophic lichen planus

    L43.1   Bullous lichen planus

    ● **L43.2   Lichenoid drug reaction**
         Code first (T36-T50) to identify drug

    L43.3   Subacute (active) lichen planus
         Lichen planus tropicus

    L43.8   Other lichen planus

    ■ **L43.9   Lichen planus, unspecified**

● **L44   Other papulosquamous disorders**

    L44.0   Pityriasis rubra pilaris

    L44.1   Lichen nitidus

    L44.2   Lichen striatus

    L44.3   Lichen ruber moniliformis

    **L44.4   Infantile papular acrodermatitis
         [Gianotti-Crosti]**

    L44.8   Other specified papulosquamous disorders

    ■ **L44.9   Papulosquamous disorder, unspecified**

● **L45   Papulosquamous disorders in diseases classified
    elsewhere**

    Code first underlying disease

Item 12–6   Psoriasis is a chronic, recurrent inflammatory skin disease characterized by small patches covered with thick silvery scales. **Parapsoriasis** is a treatment-resistant erythroderma. **Pityriasis rosea** is characterized by a herald patch that is a single large lesion and that usually appears on the trunk and is followed by scattered, smaller lesions.

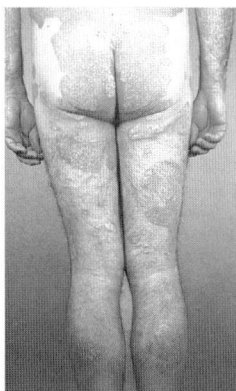

Figure 12-6 Erythematous plaques with silvery scales in a patient with psoriasis. (From Goldman: Cecil Textbook of Medicine, 22nd ed. 2004, Saunders.)

● Unacceptable First-Listed Diagnosis   ● Use Additional Character(s)   ■ Unspecified   **OGCR** Official Guidelines for Coding and Reporting
🅒 Complication\Comorbidity   🅜 Major C\C   Excludes 1   Excludes 2   Includes   Use additional   Code first   Code also

CHAPTER 12 (L00-L99)

1105

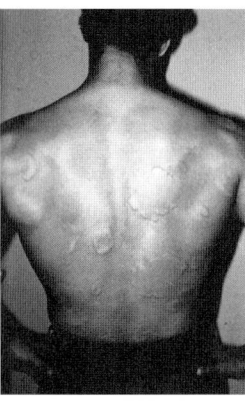

Figure 12-7 Urticaria (hives). *(Courtesy of Davis Effron, MD.)* (From Marx: Rosen's Emergency Medicine: Concepts and Clinical Practice, 6th ed. 2006, Mosby, Inc.)

Item 12–7 Urticaria is a vascular reaction in which wheals surrounded by a red halo appear and cause severe itching. The causes of urticaria or hives are extensive and varied (e.g., food, heat, cold, drugs, stress, infections).

URTICARIA AND ERYTHEMA (L49-L54)

Excludes1   Lyme disease (A69.2-)
     rosacea (L71.-)

● **L49 Exfoliation due to erythematous conditions according to extent of body surface involved**
Code first erythematous condition causing exfoliation, such as:
Ritter's disease (L00)
(Staphylococcal) scalded skin syndrome (L00)
Stevens-Johnson syndrome (L51.1)
Stevens-Johnson syndrome-toxic epidermal necrolysis overlap syndrome (L51.3)
Toxic epidermal necrolysis (L51.2)

L49.0 Exfoliation due to erythematous condition involving less than 10 percent of body surface
Exfoliation due to erythematous condition NOS

L49.1 Exfoliation due to erythematous condition involving 10-19 percent of body surface

L49.2 Exfoliation due to erythematous condition involving 20-29 percent of body surface

L49.3 Exfoliation due to erythematous condition involving 30-39 percent of body surface

L49.4 Exfoliation due to erythematous condition involving 40-49 percent of body surface

L49.5 Exfoliation due to erythematous condition involving 50-59 percent of body surface

L49.6 Exfoliation due to erythematous condition involving 60-69 percent of body surface

L49.7 Exfoliation due to erythematous condition involving 70-79 percent of body surface

L49.8 Exfoliation due to erythematous condition involving 80-89 percent of body surface

L49.9 Exfoliation due to erythematous condition involving 90 or more percent of body surface

● **L50 Urticaria**
Excludes1   allergic contact dermatitis (L23.-)
angioneurotic edema (T78.3)
giant urticaria (T78.3)
hereditary angio-edema (D84.1)
Quincke's edema (T78.3)
serum urticaria (T80.6)
solar urticaria (L56.3)
urticaria neonatorum (P83.8)
urticaria papulosa (L28.2)
urticaria pigmentosa (Q82.2)

L50.0 Allergic urticaria
L50.1 Idiopathic urticaria
L50.2 Urticaria due to cold and heat
L50.3 Dermatographic urticaria
L50.4 Vibratory urticaria
L50.5 Cholinergic urticaria
L50.6 Contact urticaria
L50.8 Other urticaria
Chronic urticaria
Recurrent periodic urticaria
L50.9 Urticaria, unspecified

● **L51 Erythema multiforme**
Code first (T36-T50) to identify drug, if drug-induced
Use additional code to identify associated manifestations, such as:
arthropathy associated with dermatological disorders (M14.8-)
conjunctival edema (H11.42)
conjunctivitis (H10.22-)
corneal scars and opacities (H17.-)
corneal ulcer (H16.0-)
edema of eyelid (H02.84)
inflammation of eyelid (H01.8)
keratoconjunctivitis sicca (H16.22-)
mechanical lagophthalmos (H02.22-)
mucositis (J34.81, K12.3-, K12.4, K92.81, N76.81)
stomatitis (K12.-)
symblepharon (H11.23-)
Use additional code to identify percentage of skin exfoliation (L49-)
Excludes1   staphylococcal scalded skin syndrome (L00)
     Ritter's disease (L00)

L51.0 Nonbullous erythema multiforme
L51.1 Bullous erythema multiforme
L51.2 Toxic epidermal necrolysis [Lyell]
L51.3 Stevens-Johnson syndrome-toxic epidermal necrolysis overlap syndrome
SJS-TEN overlap syndrome
L51.8 Other erythema multiforme
L51.9 Erythema multiforme, unspecified
Erythema iris
Erythema multiforme major NOS
Erythema multiforme minor NOS
Herpes iris

L52 Erythema nodosum
Excludes1   tuberculous erythema nodosum (A18.4)

● **L53 Other erythematous conditions**
Excludes1   erythema ab igne (L59.0)
erythema due to external agents in contact with skin (L23-L25)
erythema intertrigo (L30.4)

● **L53.0 Toxic erythema**
Code first (T36-T65) to identify external agent
Excludes1   neonatal erythema toxicum (P83.1)

L53.1 Erythema annulare centrifugum
L53.2 Erythema marginatum
L53.3 Other chronic figurate erythema
L53.8 Other specified erythematous conditions
L53.9 Erythematous condition, unspecified
Erythema NOS
Erythroderma NOS

● **L54 Erythema in diseases classified elsewhere**
Code first underlying disease

● Unacceptable First-Listed Diagnosis   ● Use Additional Character(s)   ■ Unspecified   OGCR Official Guidelines for Coding and Reporting
Complication\Comorbidity   Major C\C   Excludes 1   Excludes 2   Includes   Use additional   Code first   Code also

CHAPTER 12 (L00-L99)

RADIATION-RELATED DISORDERS OF THE SKIN AND SUBCUTANEOUS TISSUE (L55-L59)

- **L55**   **Sunburn**
  - L55.0   Sunburn of first degree
  - L55.1   Sunburn of second degree
  - L55.2   Sunburn of third degree
  - L55.9   Sunburn, unspecified

- **L56**   **Other acute skin changes due to ultraviolet radiation**

  Use additional code to identify the source of the ultraviolet radiation (W89, X32)

  - **L56.0**   **Drug phototoxic response**

    Code first (T36-T50) to identify drug

  - **L56.1**   **Drug photoallergic response**

    Code first (T36-T50) to identify drug

  - L56.2   Photocontact dermatitis [berloque dermatitis]
  - L56.3   Solar urticaria
  - L56.4   Polymorphous light eruption
  - L56.5   Disseminated superficial actinic porokeratosis (DSAP)
  - L56.8   Other specified acute skin changes due to ultraviolet radiation
  - L56.9   Acute skin change due to ultraviolet radiation, unspecified

- **L57**   **Skin changes due to chronic exposure to nonionizing radiation**

  Use additional code to identify the source of the ultraviolet radiation (W89, X32)

  - L57.0   Actinic keratosis
    - Keratosis NOS   Solar keratosis
    - Senile keratosis
  - L57.1   Actinic reticuloid
  - L57.2   Cutis rhomboidalis nuchae
  - L57.3   Poikiloderma of Civatte
  - L57.4   Cutis laxa senilis
    - Elastosis senilis
  - L57.5   Actinic granuloma
  - L57.8   Other skin changes due to chronic exposure to nonionizing radiation
    - Farmer's skin   Solar dermatitis
    - Sailor's skin
  - L57.9   Skin changes due to chronic exposure to nonionizing radiation, unspecified

- **L58**   **Radiodermatitis**

  Use additional code to identify the source of the radiation (W88, W90)

  - L58.0   Acute radiodermatitis
  - L58.1   Chronic radiodermatitis
  - L58.9   Radiodermatitis, unspecified

- **L59**   **Other disorders of skin and subcutaneous tissue related to radiation**
  - L59.0   Erythema ab igne [dermatitis ab igne]
  - L59.8   Other specified disorders of the skin and subcutaneous tissue related to radiation
  - L59.9   Disorder of the skin and subcutaneous tissue related to radiation, unspecified

DISORDERS OF SKIN APPENDAGES (L60-L75)

> **Excludes1**   congenital malformations of integument (Q84.-)

- **L60**   **Nail disorders**

  > **Excludes2**   clubbing of nails (R68.3)
  > onychia and paronychia (L03.0-)

  - L60.0   Ingrowing nail
  - L60.1   Onycholysis
  - L60.2   Onychogryphosis
  - L60.3   Nail dystrophy
  - L60.4   Beau's lines
  - L60.5   Yellow nail syndrome
  - L60.8   Other nail disorders
  - L60.9   Nail disorder, unspecified

- **L62**   **Nail disorders in diseases classified elsewhere**

  Code first underlying disease, such as:
  pachydermoperiostosis (M89.4-)

- **L63**   **Alopecia areata**
  - L63.0   Alopecia (capitis) totalis
  - L63.1   Alopecia universalis
  - L63.2   Ophiasis
  - L63.8   Other alopecia areata
  - L63.9   Alopecia areata, unspecified

- **L64**   **Androgenic alopecia**

  > **Includes**   male-pattern baldness

  - **L64.0**   **Drug-induced androgenic alopecia**

    Code first (T36-T50) to identify drug

  - L64.8   Other androgenic alopecia
  - L64.9   Androgenic alopecia, unspecified

Item 12–8 Alopecia is lack of hair and takes many forms. The most common is male pattern alopecia, also known as **androgenetic alopecia. Telogen effluvium** is early and excessive loss of hair resulting from a trauma to the hair follicle (fever, drugs, surgery, etc.).

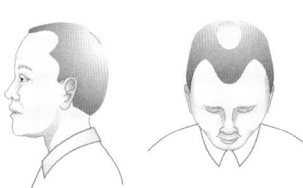

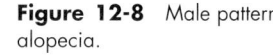
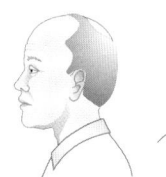

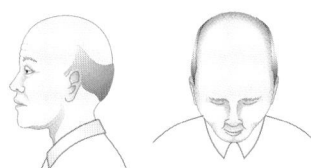

Figure 12-8 Male pattern alopecia.

● Unacceptable First-Listed Diagnosis   ● Use Additional Character(s)   ▣ Unspecified   **OGCR** Official Guidelines for Coding and Reporting

🔗 Complication\Comorbidity   🔗 Major C\C   Excludes 1   Excludes 2   Includes   Use additional   Code first   Code also

1107

CHAPTER 12 (L00-L99)

● **L65   Other nonscarring hair loss**
     Excludes1   trichotillomania (F63.3)
     L65.0   Telogen effluvium
     L65.1   Anagen effluvium
     L65.2   Alopecia mucinosa
     L65.8   Other specified nonscarring hair loss
     ■L65.9   Nonscarring hair loss, unspecified
          Alopecia NOS

● **L66   Cicatricial alopecia [scarring hair loss]**
     L66.0   Pseudopelade
     L66.1   Lichen planopilaris
          Follicular lichen planus
     L66.2   Folliculitis decalvans
     L66.3   Perifolliculitis capitis abscedens
     L66.4   Folliculitis ulerythematosa reticulata
     L66.8   Other cicatricial alopecia
     ■L66.9   Cicatricial alopecia, unspecified

● **L67   Hair color and hair shaft abnormalities**
     Excludes1   monilethrix (Q84.1)
          pili annulati (Q84.1)
          telogen effluvium (L65.0)
     L67.0   Trichorrhexis nodosa
     L67.1   Variations in hair color
          Canities
          Greyness, hair (premature)
          Heterochromia of hair
          Poliosis circumscripta, acquired
          Poliosis NOS
     L67.8   Other hair color and hair shaft abnormalities
          Fragilitas crinium
     ■L67.9   Hair color and hair shaft abnormality, unspecified

● **L68   Hypertrichosis**
     Includes   excess hair
     Excludes1   congenital hypertrichosis (Q84.2)
          persistent lanugo (Q84.2)
     L68.0   Hirsutism
          Excessive growth of hair
     L68.1   Acquired hypertrichosis lanuginosa
     L68.2   Localized hypertrichosis
     L68.3   Polytrichia
     L68.8   Other hypertrichosis
     ■L68.9   Hypertrichosis, unspecified

● **L70   Acne**
     Excludes2   acne keloid (L73.0)
     L70.0   Acne vulgaris
     L70.1   Acne conglobata
     L70.2   Acne varioliformis
          Acne necrotica miliaris
     L70.3   Acne tropica
     L70.4   Infantile acne
     L70.5   Acné excoriée des jeunes filles
          Picker's acne
     L70.8   Other acne
     ■L70.9   Acne, unspecified

● **L71   Rosacea**
     L71.0   Perioral dermatitis
     L71.1   Rhinophyma
     L71.8   Other rosacea
     ■L71.9   Rosacea, unspecified

● **L72   Follicular cysts of skin and subcutaneous tissue**
     L72.0   Epidermal cyst
     L72.1   Trichodermal cyst
          Pilar cyst
          Sebaceous cyst
     L72.2   Steatocystoma multiplex
     L72.8   Other follicular cysts of the skin and subcutaneous tissue
     ■L72.9   Follicular cyst of the skin and subcutaneous tissue, unspecified

● **L73   Other follicular disorders**
     L73.0   Acne keloid
     L73.1   Pseudofolliculitis barbae
     L73.2   Hidradenitis suppurativa
     L73.8   Other specified follicular disorders
          Sycosis barbae
     ■L73.9   Follicular disorder, unspecified

● **L74   Eccrine sweat disorders**
     Excludes2   generalized hyperhidrosis (R61)
     L74.0   Miliaria rubra
     L74.1   Miliaria crystallina
     L74.2   Miliaria profunda
          Miliaria tropicalis
     ■L74.3   Miliaria, unspecified
     L74.4   Anhidrosis
          Hypohidrosis
     ● L74.5   Focal hyperhidrosis
         ● L74.51   Primary focal hyperhidrosis
            L74.510   Primary focal hyperhidrosis, axilla
            L74.511   Primary focal hyperhidrosis, face
            L74.512   Primary focal hyperhidrosis, palms
            L74.513   Primary focal hyperhidrosis, soles
            ■L74.519   Primary focal hyperhidrosis, unspecified
         L74.52   Secondary focal hyperhidrosis
            Frey's syndrome
     L74.8   Other eccrine sweat disorders
     ■L74.9   Eccrine sweat disorder, unspecified
          Sweat gland disorder NOS

● **L75   Apocrine sweat disorders**
     Excludes1   dyshidrosis (L30.1)
          hidradenitis suppurativa (L73.2)
     L75.0   Bromhidrosis
     L75.1   Chromhidrosis
     L75.2   Apocrine miliaria
          Fox-Fordyce disease
     L75.8   Other apocrine sweat disorders
     ■L75.9   Apocrine sweat disorder, unspecified
          Intraoperative and postprocedural complications of skin and subcutaneous tissue (L76)

● **L76   Intraoperative and postprocedural complications of skin and subcutaneous tissue**

● Unacceptable First-Listed Diagnosis   ● Use Additional Character(s)   ■ Unspecified   **OGCR** Official Guidelines for Coding and Reporting
🔾 Complication\Comorbidity   🔾 Major C\C   Excludes 1   Excludes 2   Includes   Use additional   Code first   Code also

CHAPTER 12 (L00-L99)

● **L76.0** **Intraoperative hemorrhage and hematoma of skin and subcutaneous tissue complicating a procedure**

　　Excludes1　intraoperative hemorrhage and hematoma of skin and subcutaneous tissue due to accidental puncture and laceration during a procedure (L76.1-)

　　L76.01 Intraoperative hemorrhage and hematoma of skin and subcutaneous tissue complicating a dermatologic procedure 🖐

　　L76.02 Intraoperative hemorrhage and hematoma of skin and subcutaneous tissue complicating other procedure 🖐

● **L76.1** **Accidental puncture and laceration of skin and subcutaneous tissue during a procedure**

　　L76.11 Accidental puncture and laceration of skin and subcutaneous tissue during a dermatologic procedure 🖐

　　L76.12 Accidental puncture and laceration of skin and subcutaneous tissue during other procedure 🖐

● **L76.2** **Postprocedural hemorrhage and hematoma of skin and subcutaneous tissue following a procedure**

　　L76.21 Postprocedural hemorrhage and hematoma of skin and subcutaneous tissue following a dermatologic procedure 🖐

　　L76.22 Postprocedural hemorrhage and hematoma of skin and subcutaneous tissue following other procedure 🖐

● **L76.8** **Other intraoperative and postprocedural complications of skin and subcutaneous tissue**

　　Use additional code, if applicable, to further specify disorder

　　L76.81 Other intraoperative complications of skin and subcutaneous tissue

　　L76.82 Other postprocedural complications of skin and subcutaneous tissue

OTHER DISORDERS OF THE SKIN AND SUBCUTANEOUS TISSUE (L80-L99)

L80 **Vitiligo**

　　Excludes2　vitiligo of eyelids (H02.73-)
　　　　　　　　vitiligo of vulva (N90.8)

● **L81** **Other disorders of pigmentation**

　　Excludes1　birthmark NOS (Q82.5)
　　　　　　　　Peutz-Jeghers syndrome (Q85.8)

　　Excludes2　nevus - see Alphabetical Index

　　L81.0 Postinflammatory hyperpigmentation

　　L81.1 Chloasma

　　L81.2 Freckles

　　L81.3 Café au lait spots

　　L81.4 Other melanin hyperpigmentation
　　　　　　Lentigo

　　L81.5 Leukoderma, not elsewhere classified

　　L81.6 Other disorders of diminished melanin formation

　　L81.7 Pigmented purpuric dermatosis
　　　　　　Angioma serpiginosum

　　L81.8 Other specified disorders of pigmentation
　　　　　　Iron pigmentation
　　　　　　Tattoo pigmentation

　　■ **L81.9** Disorder of pigmentation, unspecified

● **L82** **Seborrheic keratosis**

　　Includes　dermatosis papulosa nigra
　　　　　　　Leser-Trélat disease

　　Excludes2　seborrheic dermatitis (L21.-)

　　L82.0 Inflamed seborrheic keratosis

　　L82.1 Other seborrheic keratosis
　　　　　　Seborrheic keratosis NOS

L83 **Acanthosis nigricans**

　　Includes　confluent and reticulated papillomatosis

L84 **Corns and callosities**

　　Includes　callus
　　　　　　　clavus

● **L85** **Other epidermal thickening**

　　Excludes2　hypertrophic disorders of the skin (L91.-)

　　L85.0 Acquired ichthyosis

　　　　Excludes1　congenital ichthyosis (Q80.-)

　　L85.1 Acquired keratosis [keratoderma] palmaris et plantaris

　　　　Excludes1　inherited keratosis palmaris et plantaris (Q82.8)

　　L85.2 Keratosis punctata (palmaris et plantaris) L85.3
　　　　　　Xerosis cutis
　　　　　　Dry skin dermatitis

　　L85.8 Other specified epidermal thickening
　　　　　　Cutaneous horn

　　■ **L85.9** Epidermal thickening, unspecified

● **L86** **Keratoderma in diseases classified elsewhere**

　　Firm horny papules that have a cobblestone appearance.

　　Code first underlying disease, such as:
　　　　Reiter's disease (M02.3-)

　　Excludes1　gonococcal keratoderma (A54.89)
　　　　　　　gonococcal keratosis (A54.89)
　　　　　　　keratoderma due to vitamin A deficiency (E50.8)
　　　　　　　keratosis due to vitamin A deficiency (E50.8)
　　　　　　　xeroderma due to vitamin A deficiency (E50.8)

● **L87** **Transepidermal elimination disorders**

　　Excludes1　granuloma annulare (perforating) (L92.0)

　　L87.0 Keratosis follicularis et parafollicularis in cutem penetrans [Kyrle]
　　　　　　Hyperkeratosis follicularis penetrans

　　L87.1 Reactive perforating collagenosis

　　L87.2 Elastosis perforans serpiginosa

　　L87.8 Other transepidermal elimination disorders

　　■ **L87.9** Transepidermal elimination disorder, unspecified

L88 **Pyoderma gangrenosum** 🖐

　　Includes　dermatitis gangrenosa
　　　　　　　phagedenic pyoderma

● **L89** **Pressure ulcer**

　　Includes　bed sore　　　　pressure area
　　　　　　　decubitus ulcer　pressure sore
　　　　　　　plaster ulcer

　　Code first any associated gangrene (I96)

　　Excludes2　decubitus (trophic) ulcer of cervix (uteri) (N86)
　　　　　　　diabetic ulcers (E08.621, E08.622, E09.621, E09.622, E10.621, E10.622, E11.621, E11.622, E13.621, E13.622)
　　　　　　　non-pressure chronic ulcer of skin (L97.-)
　　　　　　　skin infections (L00-L08)
　　　　　　　varicose ulcer (I83.0, I83.2)

● Unacceptable First-Listed Diagnosis　　● Use Additional Character(s)　　■ Unspecified　　**OGCR** Official Guidelines for Coding and Reporting
🖐 Complication\Comorbidity　🖐 Major C\C　Excludes 1　Excludes 2　Includes　Use additional　Code first　Code also

1109

CHAPTER 12 (L00-L99)

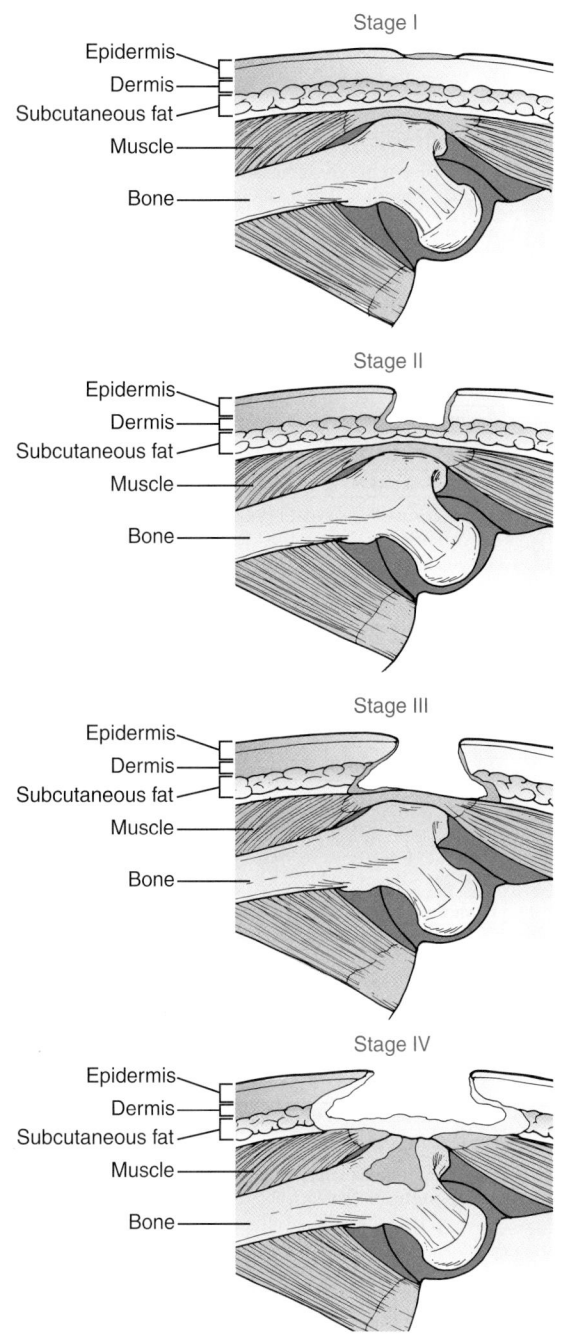

Figure 12-10   Stage I, II, III, and IV of pressure ulcers.

● **L89.0   Pressure ulcer of elbow**

  ● **L89.00   Pressure ulcer of unspecified elbow**

    ▪ **L89.000   Pressure ulcer of unspecified elbow, unstageable**

    ▪ **L89.001   Pressure ulcer of unspecified elbow, stage 1**
         Healing pressure ulcer of unspecified elbow, stage 1
         Pressure pre-ulcer skin changes limited to persistent focal edema, unspecified elbow

▪ **L89.002   Pressure ulcer of unspecified elbow, stage 2**
     Pressure ulcer with abrasion, blister, partial thickness skin loss involving epidermis and/or dermis, unspecified elbow

▪ **L89.003   Pressure ulcer of unspecified elbow, stage 3** 🔖
     Pressure ulcer with full thickness skin loss involving damage or necrosis of subcutaneous tissue, unspecified elbow

▪ **L89.004   Pressure ulcer of unspecified elbow, stage 4** 🔖
     Healing pressure ulcer of unspecified elbow, stage 4
     Pressure ulcer with necrosis of soft tissues through to underlying muscle, tendon, or bone, unspecified elbow

▪ **L89.009   Pressure ulcer of unspecified elbow, unspecified stage**
     Healing pressure ulcer of elbow NOS
     Healing pressure ulcer of unspecified elbow, unspecified stage

● **L89.01   Pressure ulcer of right elbow**

  L89.010   Pressure ulcer of right elbow, unstageable

  L89.011   Pressure ulcer of right elbow, stage I
     Healing pressure ulcer of right elbow, stage I
     Pressure pre-ulcer skin changes limited to persistent focal edema, right elbow

  L89.012   Pressure ulcer of right elbow, stage II
     Healing pressure ulcer of right elbow, stage II
     Pressure ulcer with abrasion, blister, partial thickness skin loss involving epidermis and/or dermis, right elbow

  L89.013   Pressure ulcer of right elbow, stage III 🔖
     Healing pressure ulcer of right elbow, stage III
     Pressure ulcer with full thickness skin loss involving damage or necrosis of subcutaneous tissue, right elbow

  L89.014   Pressure ulcer of right elbow, stage IV 🔖
     Healing pressure ulcer of right elbow, stage IV
     Pressure ulcer with necrosis of soft tissues through to underlying muscle, tendon, or bone, right elbow

●   Unacceptable First-Listed Diagnosis   ●   Use Additional Character(s)   ▪ Unspecified   **OGCR** Official Guidelines for Coding and Reporting
🔖 Complication\Comorbidity   🔖 Major C\C   Excludes 1   Excludes 2   Includes   Use additional   Code first   Code also

1110

L89.019 Pressure ulcer of right elbow, unspecified stage
Healing pressure right of elbow NOS
Healing pressure ulcer of unspecified elbow, unspecified stage

● **L89.02 Pressure ulcer of left elbow**

L89.020 Pressure ulcer of left elbow, unstageable

L89.021 Pressure ulcer of left elbow, stage I
Healing pressure ulcer of left elbow, stage I
Pressure pre-ulcer skin changes limited to persistent focal edema, left elbow

L89.022 Pressure ulcer of left elbow, stage II
Healing pressure ulcer of left elbow, stage II
Pressure ulcer with abrasion, blister, partial thickness skin loss involving epidermis and/or dermis, left elbow

L89.023 Pressure ulcer of left elbow, stage III 🦠
Healing pressure ulcer of left elbow, stage III
Pressure ulcer with full thickness skin loss involving damage or necrosis of subcutaneous tissue, left elbow

L89.024 Pressure ulcer of left elbow, stage IV 🦠
Healing pressure ulcer of left elbow, stage IV
Pressure ulcer with necrosis of soft tissues through to underlying muscle, tendon, or bone, left elbow

L89.029 Pressure ulcer of left elbow, unspecified stage
Healing pressure ulcer of left of elbow NOS
Healing pressure ulcer of unspecified elbow, unspecified stage

● **L89.1 Pressure ulcer of back**

● **L89.10 Pressure ulcer of unspecified part of back**

L89.100 Pressure ulcer of unspecified part of back, unstageable

L89.101 Pressure ulcer of unspecified part of back, stage I
Healing pressure ulcer of unspecified part of back, stage I
Pressure pre-ulcer skin changes limited to persistent focal edema, unspecified part of back

L89.102 Pressure ulcer of unspecified part of back, stage II
Healing pressure ulcer of unspecified part of back, stage II
Pressure ulcer with abrasion, blister, partial thickness skin loss involving epidermis and/or dermis, unspecified part of back

L89.103 Pressure ulcer of unspecified part of back, stage III 🦠
Healing pressure ulcer of unspecified part of back, stage III
Pressure ulcer with full thickness skin loss involving damage or necrosis of subcutaneous tissue, unspecified part of back

L89.104 Pressure ulcer of unspecified part of back, stage IV 🦠
Healing pressure ulcer of unspecified part of back, stage IV
Pressure ulcer with necrosis of soft tissues through to underlying muscle, tendon, or bone, unspecified part of back

L89.109 Pressure ulcer of unspecified part of back, unspecified stage
Healing pressure ulcer of unspecified part of back NOS
Healing pressure ulcer of unspecified part of back, unspecified stage

● **L89.11 Pressure ulcer of right upper back**
Pressure ulcer of right shoulder blade

L89.110 Pressure ulcer of right upper back, unstageable

L89.111 Pressure ulcer of right upper back, stage I
Healing pressure ulcer of right upper back, stage I
Pressure pre-ulcer skin changes limited to persistent focal edema, right upper back

L89.112 Pressure ulcer of right upper back, stage II
Healing pressure ulcer of right upper back, stage II
Pressure ulcer with abrasion, blister, partial thickness skin loss involving epidermis and/or dermis, right upper back

L89.113 Pressure ulcer of right upper back, stage III 🦠
Healing pressure ulcer of right upper back, stage III
Pressure ulcer with full thickness skin loss involving damage or necrosis of subcutaneous tissue, right upper back

L89.114 Pressure ulcer of right upper back, stage IV 🦠
Healing pressure ulcer of right upper back, stage IV
Pressure ulcer with necrosis of soft tissues through to underlying muscle, tendon, or bone, right upper back

● Unacceptable First-Listed Diagnosis   ● Use Additional Character(s)    Unspecified   **OGCR** Official Guidelines for Coding and Reporting
🦠 Complication\Comorbidity   🦠 Major C\C   [Excludes 1]   [Excludes 2]    Includes   Use additional   Code first   Code also

CHAPTER 12 (L00-L99)

1111

◻ **L89.119**   **Pressure ulcer of right upper back, unspecified stage**
    Healing pressure ulcer of right upper back NOS
    Healing pressure ulcer of right upper back, unspecified stage

● **L89.12**   **Pressure ulcer of left upper back**
    Pressure ulcer of left shoulder blade

    L89.120   **Pressure ulcer of left upper back, unstageable**

    L89.121   **Pressure ulcer of left upper back, stage I**
      Healing pressure ulcer of left upper back, stage I
      Pressure pre-ulcer skin changes limited to persistent focal edema, left upper back

    L89.122   **Pressure ulcer of left upper back, stage II**
      Healing pressure ulcer of left upper back, stage II
      Pressure ulcer with abrasion, blister, partial thickness skin loss involving epidermis and/or dermis, left upper back

    L89.123   **Pressure ulcer of left upper back, stage III** 🐾
      Healing pressure ulcer of left upper back, stage III
      Pressure ulcer with full thickness skin loss involving damage or necrosis of subcutaneous tissue, left upper back

    L89.124   **Pressure ulcer of left upper back, stage IV** 🐾
      Healing pressure ulcer of left upper back, stage IV
      Pressure ulcer with necrosis of soft tissues through to underlying muscle, tendon, or bone, left upper back

◻ **L89.129**   **Pressure ulcer of left upper back, unspecified stage**
    Healing pressure ulcer of left upper back NOS
    Healing pressure ulcer of left upper back, unspecified stage

● **L89.13 Pressure ulcer of right lower back**

    L89.130   **Pressure ulcer of right lower back, unstageable**

    L89.131   **Pressure ulcer of right lower back, stage I**
      Healing pressure ulcer of right lower back, stage I
      Pressure pre-ulcer skin changes limited to persistent focal edema, right lower back

    L89.132   **Pressure ulcer of right lower back, stage II**
      Healing pressure ulcer of right lower back, stage II
      Pressure ulcer with abrasion, blister, partial thickness skin loss involving epidermis and/or dermis, right lower back

    L89.133   **Pressure ulcer of right lower back, stage III** 🐾
      Healing pressure ulcer of right lower back, stage III
      Pressure ulcer with full thickness skin loss involving damage or necrosis of subcutaneous tissue, right lower back

    L89.134   **Pressure ulcer of right lower back, stage IV** 🐾
      Healing pressure ulcer of right lower back, stage IV
      Pressure ulcer with necrosis of soft tissues through to underlying muscle, tendon, or bone, right lower back

◻ **L89.139**   **Pressure ulcer of right lower back, unspecified stage**
    Healing pressure ulcer of right lower back NOS
    Healing pressure ulcer of right lower back, unspecified stage

● **L89.14**   **Pressure ulcer of left lower back**

    L89.140   **Pressure ulcer of left lower back, unstageable**

    L89.141   **Pressure ulcer of left lower back, stage I**
      Healing pressure ulcer of left lower back, stage I
      Pressure pre-ulcer skin changes limited to persistent focal edema, left lower back

    L89.142   **Pressure ulcer of left lower back, stage II**
      Healing pressure ulcer of left lower back, stage II
      Pressure ulcer with abrasion, blister, partial thickness skin loss involving epidermis and/or dermis, left lower back

    L89.143   **Pressure ulcer of left lower back, stage III** 🐾
      Healing pressure ulcer of left lower back, stage III
      Pressure ulcer with full thickness skin loss involving damage or necrosis of subcutaneous tissue, left lower back

● Unacceptable First-Listed Diagnosis   ● Use Additional Character(s)   ◻ Unspecified   **OGCR** Official Guidelines for Coding and Reporting
🐾 Complication\Comorbidity   🐾 Major C\C   Excludes 1   Excludes 2   Includes   Use additional   Code first   Code also

L89.144   Pressure ulcer of left lower back, stage IV 🗲
  Healing pressure ulcer of left lower back, stage IV
  Pressure ulcer with necrosis of soft tissues through to underlying muscle, tendon, or bone, left lower back

L89.149   Pressure ulcer of left lower back, unspecified stage
  Healing pressure ulcer of left lower back NOS
  Healing pressure ulcer of left lower back, unspecified stage

● **L89.15   Pressure ulcer of sacral region**
  Pressure ulcer of coccyx
  Pressure ulcer of tailbone

L89.150   Pressure ulcer of sacral region, unstageable

L89.151   Pressure ulcer of sacral region, stage I
  Healing pressure ulcer of sacral region, stage I
  Pressure pre-ulcer skin changes limited to persistent focal edema, sacral region

L89.152   Pressure ulcer of sacral region, stage II
  Healing pressure ulcer of sacral region, stage II
  Pressure ulcer with abrasion, blister, partial thickness skin loss involving epidermis and/or dermis, sacral region

L89.153   Pressure ulcer of sacral region, stage III 🗲
  Healing pressure ulcer of sacral region, stage III
  Pressure ulcer with full thickness skin loss involving damage or necrosis of subcutaneous tissue, sacral region

L89.154   Pressure ulcer of sacral region, stage IV 🗲
  Healing pressure ulcer of sacral region, stage IV
  Pressure ulcer with necrosis of soft tissues through to underlying muscle, tendon, or bone, sacral region

L89.159   Pressure ulcer of sacral region, unspecified stage
  Healing pressure ulcer of sacral region NOS
  Healing pressure ulcer of sacral region, unspecified stage

● **L89.2   Pressure ulcer of hip**

● **L89.20   Pressure ulcer of unspecified hip**

L89.200   Pressure ulcer of unspecified hip, unstageable

L89.201   Pressure ulcer of unspecified hip, stage I
  Healing pressure ulcer of unspecified hip back, stage I
  Pressure pre-ulcer skin changes limited to persistent focal edema, unspecified hip

L89.202   Pressure ulcer of unspecified hip, stage II
  Healing pressure ulcer of unspecified hip, stage II Pressure ulcer with abrasion, blister, partial thickness skin loss involving epidermis and/or dermis, unspecified hip

L89.203   Pressure ulcer of unspecified hip, stage III 🗲
  Healing pressure ulcer of unspecified hip, stage III
  Pressure ulcer with full thickness skin loss involving damage or necrosis of subcutaneous tissue, unspecified hip

L89.204   Pressure ulcer of unspecified hip, stage IV 🗲
  Healing pressure ulcer of unspecified hip, stage IV
  Pressure ulcer with necrosis of soft tissues through to underlying muscle, tendon, or bone, unspecified hip

L89.209   Pressure ulcer of unspecified hip, unspecified stage
  Healing pressure ulcer of unspecified hip NOS
  Healing pressure ulcer of unspecified hip, unspecified stage

■ **L89.21   Pressure ulcer of right hip**

L89.210   Pressure ulcer of right hip, unstageable

L89.211   Pressure ulcer of right hip, stage I
  Healing pressure ulcer of right hip back, stage I
  Pressure pre-ulcer skin changes limited to persistent focal edema, right hip

L89.212   Pressure ulcer of right hip, stage II
  Healing pressure ulcer of right hip, stage II
  Pressure ulcer with abrasion, blister, partial thickness skin loss involving epidermis and/or dermis, right hip

L89.213   Pressure ulcer of right hip, stage III 🗲
  Healing pressure ulcer of right hip, stage III
  Pressure ulcer with full thickness skin loss involving damage or necrosis of subcutaneous tissue, right hip

● Unacceptable First-Listed Diagnosis   ● Use Additional Character(s)   ■ Unspecified   **OGCR** Official Guidelines for Coding and Reporting
🗲 Complication\Comorbidity   🗲 Major C\C   Excludes 1   Excludes 2   Includes   Use additional   Code first   Code also

1113

CHAPTER 12 (L00-L99)

L89.214 Pressure ulcer of right hip, stage IV 🔖
> Healing pressure ulcer of right hip, stage IV
> Pressure ulcer with necrosis of soft tissues through to underlying muscle, tendon, or bone, right hip

◼ **L89.219 Pressure ulcer of right hip, unspecified stage**
> Healing pressure ulcer of right hip NOS
> Healing pressure ulcer of right hip, unspecified stage

● **L89.22 Pressure ulcer of left hip**

L89.220 Pressure ulcer of left hip, unstageable

L89.221 Pressure ulcer of left hip, stage I
> Healing pressure ulcer of left hip back, stage I
> Pressure pre-ulcer skin changes limited to persistent focal edema, left hip

L89.222 Pressure ulcer of left hip, stage II
> Healing pressure ulcer of left hip, stage II
> Pressure ulcer with abrasion, blister, partial thickness skin loss involving epidermis and/or dermis, left hip

L89.223 Pressure ulcer of left hip, stage III 🔖
> Healing pressure ulcer of left hip, stage III
> Pressure ulcer with full thickness skin loss involving damage or necrosis of subcutaneous tissue, left hip

L89.224 Pressure ulcer of left hip, stage IV 🔖
> Healing pressure ulcer of left hip, stage IV
> Pressure ulcer with necrosis of soft tissues through to underlying muscle, tendon, or bone, left hip

◼ **L89.229 Pressure ulcer of left hip, unspecified stage**
> Healing pressure ulcer of left hip NOS
> Healing pressure ulcer of left hip, unspecified stage

● **L89.3 Pressure ulcer of buttock**

● **L89.30 Pressure ulcer of unspecified buttock**

◼ **L89.300 Pressure ulcer of unspecified buttock, unstageable**

◼ **L89.301 Pressure ulcer of unspecified buttock, stage I**
> Healing pressure ulcer of unspecified buttock, stage I
> Pressure pre-ulcer skin changes limited to persistent focal edema, unspecified buttock

◼ **L89.302 Pressure ulcer of unspecified buttock, stage II**
> Healing pressure ulcer of unspecified buttock, stage II
> Pressure ulcer with abrasion, blister, partial thickness skin loss involving epidermis and/or dermis, unspecified buttock

◼ **L89.303 Pressure ulcer of unspecified buttock, stage III** 🔖
> Healing pressure ulcer of unspecified buttock, stage III
> Pressure ulcer with full thickness skin loss involving damage or necrosis of subcutaneous tissue, unspecified buttock

◼ **L89.304 Pressure ulcer of unspecified buttock, stage IV** 🔖
> Healing pressure ulcer of unspecified buttock, stage IV Pressure ulcer with necrosis of soft tissues through to underlying muscle, tendon, or bone, unspecified buttock

◼ **L89.309 Pressure ulcer of unspecified buttock, unspecified stage**
> Healing pressure ulcer of unspecified buttock NOS
> Healing pressure ulcer of unspecified buttock, unspecified stage

● **L89.31 Pressure ulcer of right buttock**

L89.310 Pressure ulcer of right buttock, unstageable

L89.311 Pressure ulcer of right buttock, stage I
> Healing pressure ulcer of right buttock, stage I
> Pressure pre-ulcer skin changes limited to persistent focal edema, right buttock

L89.312 Pressure ulcer of right buttock, stage II
> Healing pressure ulcer of right buttock, stage II
> Pressure ulcer with abrasion, blister, partial thickness skin loss involving epidermis and/or dermis, right buttock

L89.313 Pressure ulcer of right buttock, stage III 🔖
> Healing pressure ulcer of right buttock, stage III
> Pressure ulcer with full thickness skin loss involving damage or necrosis of subcutaneous tissue, right buttock

L89.314 Pressure ulcer of right buttock, stage IV 🔖
> Healing pressure ulcer of right buttock, stage IV
> Pressure ulcer with necrosis of soft tissues through to underlying muscle, tendon, or bone, right buttock

CHAPTER 12 (L00-L99)

1114

● Unacceptable First-Listed Diagnosis   ● Use Additional Character(s)   ◼ Unspecified   **OGCR** Official Guidelines for Coding and Reporting
🔖 Complication\Comorbidity   🔖 Major C\C   Excludes 1   Excludes 2   Includes   Use additional   Code first   Code also

■ **L89.319 Pressure ulcer of right buttock, unspecified stage**
> Healing pressure ulcer of right buttock NOS
> Healing pressure ulcer of right buttock, unspecified stage

● **L89.32 Pressure ulcer of left buttock**

L89.320 Pressure ulcer of left buttock, unstageable

L89.321 Pressure ulcer of left buttock, stage I
> Healing pressure ulcer of left buttock, stage I
> Pressure pre-ulcer skin changes limited to persistent focal edema, left buttock

L89.322 Pressure ulcer of left buttock, stage II
> Healing pressure ulcer of left buttock, stage II
> Pressure ulcer with abrasion, blister, partial thickness skin loss involving epidermis and/or dermis, left buttock

L89.323 Pressure ulcer of left buttock, stage III 🗞
> Healing pressure ulcer of left buttock, stage III
> Pressure ulcer with full thickness skin loss involving damage or necrosis of subcutaneous tissue, left buttock

L89.324 Pressure ulcer of left buttock, stage IV 🗞
> Healing pressure ulcer of left buttock, stage IV
> Pressure ulcer with necrosis of soft tissues through to underlying muscle, tendon, or bone, left buttock

■ **L89.329 Pressure ulcer of left buttock, unspecified stage**
> Healing pressure ulcer of left buttock NOS
> Healing pressure ulcer of left buttock, unspecified stage

● **L89.4 Pressure ulcer of contiguous site of back, buttock and hip**

■ **L89.40 Pressure ulcer of contiguous site of back, buttock and hip, unspecified stage**
> Healing pressure ulcer of contiguous site of back, buttock and hip NOS
> Healing pressure ulcer of contiguous site of back, buttock and hip, unspecified stage

L89.41 Pressure ulcer of contiguous site of back, buttock and hip, stage I
> Healing pressure ulcer of contiguous site of back, buttock and hip, stage I
> Pressure pre-ulcer skin changes limited to persistent focal edema, contiguous site of back, buttock and hip

L89.42 Pressure ulcer of contiguous site of back, buttock and hip, stage II
> Healing pressure ulcer of contiguous site of back, buttock and hip, stage II
> Pressure ulcer with abrasion, blister, partial thickness skin loss involving epidermis and/or dermis, contiguous site of back, buttock and hip

L89.43 Pressure ulcer of contiguous site of back, buttock and hip, stage III 🗞
> Healing pressure ulcer of contiguous site of back, buttock and hip, stage III
> Pressure ulcer with full thickness skin loss involving damage or necrosis of subcutaneous tissue, contiguous site of back, buttock and hip

L89.44 Pressure ulcer of contiguous site of back, buttock and hip, stage IV 🗞
> Healing pressure ulcer of contiguous site of back, buttock and hip, stage IV
> Pressure ulcer with necrosis of soft tissues through to underlying muscle, tendon, or bone, contiguous site of back, buttock and hip

L89.45 Pressure ulcer of contiguous site of back, buttock and hip, unstageable

● **L89.5 Pressure ulcer of ankle**

● **L89.50 Pressure ulcer of unspecified ankle**

■ **L89.500 Pressure ulcer of unspecified ankle, unstageable**

■ **L89.501 Pressure ulcer of unspecified ankle, stage I**
> Healing pressure ulcer of unspecified ankle, stage I
> Pressure pre-ulcer skin changes limited to persistent focal edema, unspecified ankle

■ **L89.502 Pressure ulcer of unspecified ankle, stage II**
> Healing pressure ulcer of unspecified ankle, stage II
> Pressure ulcer with abrasion, blister, partial thickness skin loss involving epidermis and/or dermis, unspecified ankle

■ **L89.503 Pressure ulcer of unspecified ankle, stage III** 🗞
> Healing pressure ulcer of unspecified ankle, stage III
> Pressure ulcer with full thickness skin loss involving damage or necrosis of subcutaneous tissue, unspecified ankle

■ **L89.504 Pressure ulcer of unspecified ankle, stage IV** 🗞
> Healing pressure ulcer of unspecified ankle, stage IV
> Pressure ulcer with necrosis of soft tissues through to underlying muscle, tendon, or bone, unspecified ankle

■ **L89.509 Pressure ulcer of unspecified ankle, unspecified stage**
> Healing pressure ulcer of unspecified ankle NOS
> Healing pressure ulcer of unspecified ankle, unspecified stage

● Unacceptable First-Listed Diagnosis   ● Use Additional Character(s)   ■ Unspecified   **OGCR** Official Guidelines for Coding and Reporting

🗞 Complication\Comorbidity   🗞 Major C\C   Excludes 1   Excludes 2   Includes   Use additional   Code first   Code also

1115

CHAPTER 12 (L00-L99)

● **L89.51   Pressure ulcer of right ankle**

     L89.510   Pressure ulcer of right ankle, unstageable

     L89.511   Pressure ulcer of right ankle, stage I
         Healing pressure ulcer of right ankle, stage I
         Pressure pre-ulcer skin changes limited to persistent focal edema, right ankle

     L89.512   Pressure ulcer of right ankle, stage II
         Healing pressure ulcer of right ankle, stage II
         Pressure ulcer with abrasion, blister, partial thickness skin loss involving epidermis and/or dermis, right ankle

     L89.513   Pressure ulcer of right ankle, stage III 🝙
         Healing pressure ulcer of right ankle, stage III
         Pressure ulcer with full thickness skin loss involving damage or necrosis of subcutaneous tissue, right ankle

     L89.514   Pressure ulcer of right ankle, stage IV 🝙
         Healing pressure ulcer of right ankle, stage IV
         Pressure ulcer with necrosis of soft tissues through to underlying muscle, tendon, or bone, right ankle

     ■ **L89.519   Pressure ulcer of right ankle, unspecified stage**
         Healing pressure ulcer of right ankle NOS
         Healing pressure ulcer of right ankle, unspecified stage

● **L89.52   Pressure ulcer of left ankle**

     L89.520   Pressure ulcer of left ankle, unstageable

     L89.521   Pressure ulcer of left ankle, stage I
         Healing pressure ulcer of left ankle, stage I
         Pressure pre-ulcer skin changes limited to persistent focal edema, left ankle

     L89.522   Pressure ulcer of left ankle, stage II
         Healing pressure ulcer of left ankle, stage II
         Pressure ulcer with abrasion, blister, partial thickness skin loss involving epidermis and/or dermis, left ankle

     L89.523   Pressure ulcer of left ankle, stage III 🝙
         Healing pressure ulcer of left ankle, stage III
         Pressure ulcer with full thickness skin loss involving damage or necrosis of subcutaneous tissue, left ankle

     L89.524   Pressure ulcer of left ankle, stage IV 🝙
         Healing pressure ulcer of left ankle, stage IV
         Pressure ulcer with necrosis of soft tissues through to underlying muscle, tendon, or bone, left ankle

     ■ **L89.529   Pressure ulcer of left ankle, unspecified stage**
         Healing pressure ulcer of left ankle NOS
         Healing pressure ulcer of left ankle, unspecified stage

● **L89.6   Pressure ulcer of heel**

   ● **L89.60   Pressure ulcer of unspecified heel**

     ■ **L89.600   Pressure ulcer of unspecified heel, unstageable**

     ■ **L89.601   Pressure ulcer of unspecified heel, stage I**
         Healing pressure ulcer of unspecified heel, stage I Pressure pre-ulcer skin changes limited to persistent focal edema, unspecified heel

     ■ **L89.602   Pressure ulcer of unspecified heel, stage II**
         Healing pressure ulcer of unspecified heel, stage II
         Pressure ulcer with abrasion, blister, partial thickness skin loss involving epidermis and/or dermis, unspecified heel

     ■ **L89.603   Pressure ulcer of unspecified heel, stage III** 🝙
         Healing pressure ulcer of unspecified heel, stage III
         Pressure ulcer with full thickness skin loss involving damage or necrosis of subcutaneous tissue, unspecified heel

     ■ **L89.604   Pressure ulcer of unspecified heel, stage IV** 🝙
         Healing pressure ulcer of unspecified heel, stage IV
         Pressure ulcer with necrosis of soft tissues through to underlying muscle, tendon, or bone, unspecified heel

     ■ **L89.609   Pressure ulcer of unspecified heel, unspecified stage**
         Healing pressure ulcer of unspecified heel NOS
         Healing pressure ulcer of unspecified heel, unspecified stage

   ● **L89.61   Pressure ulcer of right heel**

     L89.610   Pressure ulcer of right heel, unstageable

     L89.611   Pressure ulcer of right heel, stage I
         Healing pressure ulcer of right heel, stage I
         Pressure pre-ulcer skin changes limited to persistent focal edema, right heel

CHAPTER 12 (L00-L99)

● Unacceptable First-Listed Diagnosis   ● Use Additional Character(s)   ■ Unspecified   **OGCR** Official Guidelines for Coding and Reporting
🝙 Complication\Comorbidity   🝙 Major C\C   Excludes 1   Excludes 2   Includes   Use additional   Code first   Code also

L89.612   **Pressure ulcer of right heel, stage II**
Healing pressure ulcer of right heel, stage II
Pressure ulcer with abrasion, blister, partial thickness skin loss involving epidermis and/or dermis, right heel

L89.613   **Pressure ulcer of right heel, stage III**
Healing pressure ulcer of right heel, stage III
Pressure ulcer with full thickness skin loss involving damage or necrosis of subcutaneous tissue, right heel

L89.614   **Pressure ulcer of right heel, stage IV**
Healing pressure ulcer of right heel, stage IV
Pressure ulcer with necrosis of soft tissues through to underlying muscle, tendon, or bone, right heel

▨ L89.619   **Pressure ulcer of right heel, unspecified stage**
Healing pressure ulcer of right heel NOS
Healing pressure ulcer of unspecified heel, right stage

● **L89.62   Pressure ulcer of left heel**

L89.620   **Pressure ulcer of left heel, unstageable**

L89.621   **Pressure ulcer of left heel, stage I**
Healing pressure ulcer of left heel, stage I
Pressure pre-ulcer skin changes limited to persistent focal edema, left heel

L89.622   **Pressure ulcer of left heel, stage II**
Healing pressure ulcer of left heel, stage II
Pressure ulcer with abrasion, blister, partial thickness skin loss involving epidermis and/or dermis, left heel

L89.623   **Pressure ulcer of left heel, stage III**
Healing pressure ulcer of left heel, stage III
Pressure ulcer with full thickness skin loss involving damage or necrosis of subcutaneous tissue, left heel

L89.624   **Pressure ulcer of left heel, stage IV**
Healing pressure ulcer of left heel, stage IV
Pressure ulcer with necrosis of soft tissues through to underlying muscle, tendon, or bone, left heel

▨ L89.629   **Pressure ulcer of left heel, unspecified stage**
Healing pressure ulcer of left heel NOS
Healing pressure ulcer of left heel, unspecified stage

● **L89.8   Pressure ulcer of other site**

● **L89.81   Pressure ulcer of head**
Pressure ulcer of face

L89.810   **Pressure ulcer of head, unstageable**

L89.811   **Pressure ulcer of head, stage I**
Healing pressure ulcer of head, stage I
Pressure pre-ulcer skin changes limited to persistent focal edema, head

L89.812   **Pressure ulcer of head, stage II**
Healing pressure ulcer of head, stage II
Pressure ulcer with abrasion, blister, partial thickness skin loss involving epidermis and/or dermis, head

L89.813   **Pressure ulcer of head, stage III**
Healing pressure ulcer of head, stage III
Pressure ulcer with full thickness skin loss involving damage or necrosis of subcutaneous tissue, head

L89.814   **Pressure ulcer of head, stage IV**
Healing pressure ulcer of head, stage IV
Pressure ulcer with necrosis of soft tissues through to underlying muscle, tendon, or bone, head

▨ L89.819   **Pressure ulcer of head, unspecified stage**
Healing pressure ulcer of head NOS
Healing pressure ulcer of head, unspecified stage

● **L89.89   Pressure ulcer of other site**

L89.890   **Pressure ulcer of other site, unstageable**

L89.891   **Pressure ulcer of other site, stage I**
Healing pressure ulcer of other site, stage I
Pressure pre-ulcer skin changes limited to persistent focal edema, other site

L89.892   **Pressure ulcer of other site, stage II**
Healing pressure ulcer of other site, stage II
Pressure ulcer with abrasion, blister, partial thickness skin loss involving epidermis and/or dermis, other site

L89.893   **Pressure ulcer of other site, stage III**
Healing pressure ulcer of other site, stage III
Pressure ulcer with full thickness skin loss involving damage or necrosis of subcutaneous tissue, other site

● Unacceptable First-Listed Diagnosis   ● Use Additional Character(s)   ▨ Unspecified   **OGCR** Official Guidelines for Coding and Reporting

🝾 Complication\Comorbidity   🝾 Major C\C   Excludes 1   Excludes 2   Includes   Use additional   Code first   Code also   **1117**

CHAPTER 12 (L00-L99)

L89.894 **Pressure ulcer of other site, stage IV** 🦠
Healing pressure ulcer of other site, stage IV
Pressure ulcer with necrosis of soft tissues through to underlying muscle, tendon, or bone, other site

● L89.899 **Pressure ulcer of other site, unspecified stage**
Healing pressure ulcer of other site NOS
Healing pressure ulcer of other site, unspecified stage

● L89.9 **Pressure ulcer of unspecified site**

◼ L89.90 **Pressure ulcer of unspecified site, unspecified stage**
Healing pressure ulcer of unspecified site NOS
Healing pressure ulcer of unspecified site, unspecified stage

◼ L89.91 **Pressure ulcer of unspecified site, stage I**
Healing pressure ulcer of unspecified site, stage I
Pressure pre-ulcer skin changes limited to persistent focal edema, unspecified site

◼ L89.92 **Pressure ulcer of unspecified site, stage II**
Healing pressure ulcer of unspecified site, stage II
Pressure ulcer with abrasion, blister, partial thickness skin loss involving epidermis and/or dermis, unspecified site

◼ L89.93 **Pressure ulcer of unspecified site, stage III** 🦠
Healing pressure ulcer of unspecified site, stage III
Pressure ulcer with full thickness skin loss involving damage or necrosis of subcutaneous tissue, unspecified site

◼ L89.94 **Pressure ulcer of unspecified site, stage IV** 🦠
Healing pressure ulcer of unspecified site, stage IV
Pressure ulcer with necrosis of soft tissues through to underlying muscle, tendon, or bone, unspecified site

● L89.95 **Pressure ulcer of unspecified site, unstageable**

● L90 **Atrophic disorders of skin**

L90.0 **Lichen sclerosus et atrophicus**
Excludes2 lichen sclerosus of external female genital organs (N90.4)
lichen sclerosus of external male genital organs (N48.0)

L90.1 **Anetoderma of Schweninger-Buzzi**

L90.2 **Anetoderma of Jadassohn-Pellizzari**

L90.3 **Atrophoderma of Pasini and Pierini**

L90.4 **Acrodermatitis chronica atrophicans**

L90.5 **Scar conditions and fibrosis of skin**
Adherent scar (skin)
Cicatrix
Disfigurement of skin due to scar
Fibrosis of skin NOS
Scar NOS
Excludes2 hypertrophic scar (L91.0)
keloid scar (L91.0)

L90.6 **Striae atrophicae**

L90.8 **Other atrophic disorders of skin**

◼ L90.9 **Atrophic disorder of skin, unspecified**

● L91 **Hypertrophic disorders of skin**

L91.0 **Keloid scar**
Hypertrophic scar
Keloid
Excludes2 acne keloid (L73.0)
scar NOS (L90.5)

L91.8 **Other hypertrophic disorders of the skin**

◼ L91.9 **Hypertrophic disorder of the skin, unspecified**

● L92 **Granulomatous disorders of skin and subcutaneous tissue**
Excludes2 actinic granuloma (L57.5)

L92.0 **Granuloma annulare**
Perforating granuloma annulare

L92.1 **Necrobiosis lipoidica, not elsewhere classified**
Excludes1 necrobiosis lipoidica associated with diabetes mellitus (E08-E13 with .620)

L92.2 **Granuloma faciale [eosinophilic granuloma of skin]**

L92.3 **Foreign body granuloma of the skin and subcutaneous tissue**

L92.8 **Other granulomatous disorders of the skin and subcutaneous tissue**

◼ L92.9 **Granulomatous disorder of the skin and subcutaneous tissue, unspecified**

● L93 **Lupus erythematosus**
Excludes1 lupus exedens (A18.4)
lupus vulgaris (A18.4)
scleroderma (M34.-)
systemic lupus erythematosus (M32.-)

L93.0 **Discoid lupus erythematosus**
Lupus erythematosus NOS

L93.1 **Subacute cutaneous lupus erythematosus**

L93.2 **Other local lupus erythematosus**
Lupus erythematosus profundus
Lupus panniculitis

● L94 **Other localized connective tissue disorders**
Excludes1 systemic connective tissue disorders (M30-M36)

L94.0 **Localized scleroderma [morphea]**
Circumscribed scleroderma

L94.1 **Linear scleroderma**
En coup de sabre lesion

L94.2 **Calcinosis cutis**

L94.3 **Sclerodactyly**

L94.4 **Gottron's papules**

L94.5 **Poikiloderma vasculare atrophicans**

L94.6 **Ainhum**

L94.8 **Other specified localized connective tissue disorders**

◼ L94.9 **Localized connective tissue disorder, unspecified**

Item 12–9 Scleroderma means hard skin. It is a group of diseases that causes abnormal growth of connective tissues that support the skin and organs. There are two types: localized scleroderma affecting the skin and systemic scleroderma affecting blood vessels and internal organs and the skin.

CHAPTER 12 (L00-L99)

● Unacceptable First-Listed Diagnosis ● Use Additional Character(s) ◼ Unspecified **OGCR** Official Guidelines for Coding and Reporting

1118 🦠 Complication\Comorbidity 🦠 Major C\C Excludes 1 Excludes 2 Includes Use additional Code first Code also

● **L95** **Vasculitis limited to skin, not elsewhere classified**

    Excludes1   angioma serpiginosum (L81.7)
                Henoch(-Schönlein) purpura (D69.0)
                hypersensitivity angiitis (M31.0)
                lupus panniculitis (L93.2)
                panniculitis NOS (M79.3)
                panniculitis of neck and back (M54.0-)
                polyarteritis nodosa (M30.0)
                relapsing panniculitis (M35.6)
                rheumatoid vasculitis (M05.2)
                serum sickness (T80.6)
                urticaria (L50.-)
                Wegener's granulomatosis (M31.3-)

  L95.0 **Livedoid vasculitis**
        Atrophie blanche (en plaque)

  L95.1 **Erythema elevatum diutinum**

  L95.8 **Other vasculitis limited to the skin**

  ▪ **L95.9** **Vasculitis limited to the skin, unspecified**

● **L97** **Non-pressure chronic ulcer of lower limb, not elsewhere classified**

    Includes   Chronic ulcer of skin NOS
              Non-healing ulcer of skin
              Non-infected sinus of skin
               Trophic ulcer NOS
               Tropical ulcer NOS
               Ulcer of skin NOS

    Code first any associated underlying condition:

    Note: A code from L97 may be used as a principal or first listed code if no underlying condition is documented as the cause of the ulcer. If one of the underlying conditions listed below is documented with a lower extremity ulcer, a causal condition should be assumed.

        Atherosclerosis of the lower extremities (I70.23-, I70.24-, I70.33-, I70.34-, I70.43-, I70.44-, I70.53-, I70.54-, I70.63-, I70.64-, I70.73-, I70.74-)
        Chronic venous hypertension (I87.31-, I87.33-)
        Diabetic ulcers (E08.621, E08.622, E09.621, E09.622, E10.621, E10.622, E11.621, E11.622, E13.621, E13.622)
        Postphlebitic syndrome (I87.01-, I87.03-)
        Postthrombotic syndrome (I87.01-, I87.03-)
        Varicose ulcer (I83.0-, I83.2-)

    Code first any associated gangrene (I96)

    Excludes2   pressure ulcer (pressure area) (L89.-)
                skin infections (L00-L08)
                specific infections classified to A00-B99

  ● **L97.1** **Non-pressure chronic ulcer of thigh**

    ● **L97.10** **Non-pressure chronic ulcer of unspecified thigh**

      ▪ **L97.101** **Non-pressure chronic ulcer of unspecified thigh limited to breakdown of skin** 🦠

      ▪ **L97.102** **Non-pressure chronic ulcer of unspecified thigh with fat layer exposed** 🦠

      ▪ **L97.103** **Non-pressure chronic ulcer of unspecified thigh with necrosis of muscle** 🦠

      ▪ **L97.104** **Non-pressure chronic ulcer of unspecified thigh with necrosis of bone** 🦠

      ▪ **L97.109** **Non-pressure chronic ulcer of unspecified thigh with unspecified severity** 🦠

  ● **L97.11** **Non-pressure chronic ulcer of right thigh**

    L97.111 **Non-pressure chronic ulcer of right thigh limited to breakdown of skin** 🦠

    L97.112 **Non-pressure chronic ulcer of right thigh with fat layer exposed** 🦠

    L97.113 **Non-pressure chronic ulcer of right thigh with necrosis of muscle** 🦠

    L97.114 **Non-pressure chronic ulcer of right thigh with necrosis of bone** 🦠

    ▪ **L97.119** **Non-pressure chronic ulcer of righthigh with unspecified severity** 🦠

  ● **L97.12** **Non-pressure chronic ulcer of left thigh**

    L97.121 **Non-pressure chronic ulcer of left thigh limited to breakdown of skin** 🦠

    L97.122 **Non-pressure chronic ulcer of left thigh with fat layer exposed** 🦠

    L97.123 **Non-pressure chronic ulcer of left thigh with necrosis of muscle** 🦠

    L97.124 **Non-pressure chronic ulcer of left thigh with necrosis of bone** 🦠

    ▪ **L97.129** **Non-pressure chronic ulcer of left thigh with unspecified severity** 🦠

  ● **L97.2** **Non-pressure chronic ulcer of calf**

    ● **L97.20** **Non-pressure chronic ulcer of unspecified calf**

      ▪ **L97.201** **Non-pressure chronic ulcer of unspecified calf limited to breakdown of skin** 🦠

      ▪ **L97.202** **Non-pressure chronic ulcer of unspecified calf with fat layer exposed** 🦠

      ▪ **L97.203** **Non-pressure chronic ulcer of unspecified calf with necrosis of muscle** 🦠

      ▪ **L97.204** **Non-pressure chronic ulcer of unspecified calf with necrosis of bone** 🦠

      ▪ **L97.209** **Non-pressure chronic ulcer of unspecified calf with unspecified severity** 🦠

    ● **L97.21** **Non-pressure chronic ulcer of right calf**

      L97.211 **Non-pressure chronic ulcer of right calf limited to breakdown of skin** 🦠

      L97.212 **Non-pressure chronic ulcer of right calf with fat layer exposed** 🦠

      L97.213 **Non-pressure chronic ulcer of right calf with necrosis of muscle** 🦠

● Unacceptable First-Listed Diagnosis   ● Use Additional Character(s)   ▪ Unspecified   **OGCR** Official Guidelines for Coding and Reporting

 Complication\Comorbidity  Major C\C Excludes 1 Excludes 2 Includes Use additional Code first Code also

1119

CHAPTER 12 (L00-L99)

L97.214 Non-pressure chronic ulcer of right calf with necrosis of bone 🗫

■ **L97.219** Non-pressure chronic ulcer of right calf with unspecified severity 🗫

● **L97.22** Non-pressure chronic ulcer of left calf

L97.221 Non-pressure chronic ulcer of left calf limited to breakdown of skin 🗫

L97.222 Non-pressure chronic ulcer of left calf with fat layer exposed 🗫

L97.223 Non-pressure chronic ulcer of left calf with necrosis of muscle 🗫

L97.224 Non-pressure chronic ulcer of left calf with necrosis of bone 🗫

■ **L97.229** Non-pressure chronic ulcer of left calf with unspecified severity 🗫

● **L97.3** Non-pressure chronic ulcer of ankle

● **L97.30** Non-pressure chronic ulcer of unspecified ankle

■ **L97.301** Non-pressure chronic ulcer of unspecified ankle limited to breakdown of skin 🗫

■ **L97.302** Non-pressure chronic ulcer of unspecified ankle with fat layer exposed 🗫

■ **L97.303** Non-pressure chronic ulcer of unspecified ankle with necrosis of muscle 🗫

■ **L97.304** Non-pressure chronic ulcer of unspecified ankle with necrosis of bone 🗫

■ **L97.309** Non-pressure chronic ulcer of unspecified ankle with unspecified severity 🗫

● **L97.31** Non-pressure chronic ulcer of right ankle

L97.311 Non-pressure chronic ulcer of right ankle limited to breakdown of skin 🗫

L97.312 Non-pressure chronic ulcer of right ankle with fat layer exposed 🗫

L97.313 Non-pressure chronic ulcer of right ankle with necrosis of muscle 🗫

L97.314 Non-pressure chronic ulcer of right ankle with necrosis of bone 🗫

■ **L97.319** Non-pressure chronic ulcer of right ankle with unspecified severity 🗫

● **L97.32** Non-pressure chronic ulcer of left ankle

L97.321 Non-pressure chronic ulcer of left ankle limited to breakdown of skin 🗫

L97.322 Non-pressure chronic ulcer of left ankle with fat layer exposed 🗫

L97.323 Non-pressure chronic ulcer of left ankle with necrosis of muscle 🗫

L97.324 Non-pressure chronic ulcer of left ankle with necrosis of bone 🗫

■ **L97.329** Non-pressure chronic ulcer of left ankle with unspecified severity 🗫

● **L97.4** Non-pressure chronic ulcer of heel and midfoot
Non-pressure chronic ulcer of plantar surface of midfoot

● **L97.40** Non-pressure chronic ulcer of unspecified heel and midfoot

■ **L97.401** Non-pressure chronic ulcer of unspecified heel and midfoot limited to breakdown of skin 🗫

■ **L97.402** Non-pressure chronic ulcer of unspecified heel and midfoot with fat layer exposed 🗫

■ **L97.403** Non-pressure chronic ulcer of unspecified heel and midfoot with necrosis of muscle 🗫

■ **L97.404** Non-pressure chronic ulcer of unspecified heel and midfoot with necrosis of bone 🗫

■ **L97.409** Non-pressure chronic ulcer of unspecified heel and midfoot with unspecified severity 🗫

● **L97.41** Non-pressure chronic ulcer of right heel and midfoot

L97.411 Non-pressure chronic ulcer of right heel and midfoot limited to breakdown of skin 🗫

L97.412 Non-pressure chronic ulcer of right heel and midfoot with fat layer exposed 🗫

L97.413 Non-pressure chronic ulcer of right heel and midfoot with necrosis of muscle 🗫

L97.414 Non-pressure chronic ulcer of right heel and midfoot with necrosis of bone 🗫

■ **L97.419** Non-pressure chronic ulcer of right heel and midfoot with unspecified severity 🗫

● **L97.42** Non-pressure chronic ulcer of left heel and midfoot

L97.421 Non-pressure chronic ulcer of left heel and midfoot limited to breakdown of skin 🗫

L97.422 Non-pressure chronic ulcer of left heel and midfoot with fat layer exposed 🗫

L97.423 Non-pressure chronic ulcer of left heel and midfoot with necrosis of muscle 🗫

L97.424 Non-pressure chronic ulcer of left heel and midfoot with necrosis of bone 🗫

■ **L97.429** Non-pressure chronic ulcer of left heel and midfoot with unspecified severity 🗫

● **L97.5** Non-pressure chronic ulcer of other part of foot
Non-pressure chronic ulcer of toe

● **L97.50** Non-pressure chronic ulcer of other part of unspecified foot

■ **L97.501** Non-pressure chronic ulcer of other part of unspecified foot limited to breakdown of skin

■ **L97.502** Non-pressure chronic ulcer of other part of unspecified foot with fat layer exposed

■ **L97.503** Non-pressure chronic ulcer of other part of unspecified foot with necrosis of muscle

■ **L97.504** Non-pressure chronic ulcer of other part of unspecified foot with necrosis of bone

● Unacceptable First-Listed Diagnosis   ● Use Additional Character(s)   ■ Unspecified   **OGCR** Official Guidelines for Coding and Reporting
🗫 Complication\Comorbidity   🗫 Major C\C   Excludes 1   Excludes 2   Includes   Use additional   Code first   Code also

L97.509   Non-pressure chronic ulcer of other part of unspecified foot with unspecified severity

● L97.51   Non-pressure chronic ulcer of other part of right foot

L97.511   Non-pressure chronic ulcer of other part of right foot limited to breakdown of skin

L97.512   Non-pressure chronic ulcer of other part of right foot with fat layer exposed

L97.513   Non-pressure chronic ulcer of other part of right foot with necrosis of muscle

L97.514   Non-pressure chronic ulcer of other part of right foot with necrosis of bone

L97.519   Non-pressure chronic ulcer of other part of right foot with unspecified severity

● L97.52   Non-pressure chronic ulcer of other part of left foot

L97.521   Non-pressure chronic ulcer of other part of left foot limited to breakdown of skin

L97.522   Non-pressure chronic ulcer of other part of left foot with fat layer exposed

L97.523   Non-pressure chronic ulcer of other part of left foot with necrosis of muscle

L97.524   Non-pressure chronic ulcer of other part of left foot with necrosis of bone

L97.529   Non-pressure chronic ulcer of other part of left foot with unspecified severity

● L97.8   Non-pressure chronic ulcer of other part of lower leg

● L97.80   Non-pressure chronic ulcer of other part of unspecified lower leg

L97.801   Non-pressure chronic ulcer of other part of unspecified lower leg limited to breakdown of skin

L97.802   Non-pressure chronic ulcer of other part of unspecified lower leg with fat layer exposed

L97.803   Non-pressure chronic ulcer of other part of unspecified lower leg with necrosis of muscle

L97.804   Non-pressure chronic ulcer of other part of unspecified lower leg with necrosis of bone

L97.809   Non-pressure chronic ulcer of other part of unspecified lower leg with unspecified severity

● L97.81   Non-pressure chronic ulcer of other part of right lower leg

L97.811   Non-pressure chronic ulcer of other part of right lower leg limited to breakdown of skin

L97.812   Non-pressure chronic ulcer of other part of right lower leg with fat layer exposed

L97.813   Non-pressure chronic ulcer of other part of right lower leg with necrosis of muscle

L97.814   Non-pressure chronic ulcer of other part of right lower leg with necrosis of bone

L97.819   Non-pressure chronic ulcer of other part of right lower leg with unspecified severity

● L97.82   Non-pressure chronic ulcer of other part of left lower leg

L97.821   Non-pressure chronic ulcer of other part of left lower leg limited to breakdown of skin

L97.822   Non-pressure chronic ulcer of other part of left lower leg with fat layer exposed

L97.823   Non-pressure chronic ulcer of other part of left lower leg with necrosis of muscle

L97.824   Non-pressure chronic ulcer of other part of left lower leg with necrosis of bone

L97.829   Non-pressure chronic ulcer of other part of left lower leg with unspecified severity

● L97.9   Non-pressure chronic ulcer of unspecified part of lower leg

● L97.90   Non-pressure chronic ulcer of unspecified part of unspecified lower leg

L97.901   Non-pressure chronic ulcer of unspecified part of unspecified lower leg limited to breakdown of skin

L97.902   Non-pressure chronic ulcer of unspecified part of unspecified lower leg with fat layer exposed

L97.903   Non-pressure chronic ulcer of unspecified part of unspecified lower leg with necrosis of muscle

L97.904   Non-pressure chronic ulcer of unspecified part of unspecified lower leg with necrosis of bone

L97.909   Non-pressure chronic ulcer of unspecified part of unspecified lower leg with unspecified severity

● L97.91   Non-pressure chronic ulcer of unspecified part of right lower leg

L97.911   Non-pressure chronic ulcer of unspecified part of right lower leg limited to breakdown of skin

L97.912   Non-pressure chronic ulcer of unspecified part of right lower leg with fat layer exposed

L97.913   Non-pressure chronic ulcer of unspecified part of right lower leg with necrosis of muscle

L97.914   Non-pressure chronic ulcer of unspecified part of right lower leg with necrosis of bone

●   Unacceptable First-Listed Diagnosis   ●   Use Additional Character(s)   ▥   Unspecified   **OGCR**   Official Guidelines for Coding and Reporting

🦠 Complication\Comorbidity   🦠 Major C\C   Excludes 1   Excludes 2   Includes   Use additional   Code first   Code also

1121

CHAPTER 12 (L00-L99)

L97.919   Non-pressure chronic ulcer of unspecified part of right lower leg with unspecified severity 🦠

● L97.92   Non-pressure chronic ulcer of unspecified part of left lower leg

L97.921   Non-pressure chronic ulcer of unspecified part of left lower leg limited to breakdown of skin 🦠

L97.922   Non-pressure chronic ulcer of unspecified part of left lower leg with fat layer exposed 🦠

L97.923   Non-pressure chronic ulcer of unspecified part of left lower leg with necrosis of muscle 🦠

L97.924   Non-pressure chronic ulcer of unspecified part of left lower leg with necrosis of bone 🦠

L97.929   Non-pressure chronic ulcer of unspecified part of left lower leg with unspecified severity 🦠

● L98   Other disorders of skin and subcutaneous tissue, not elsewhere classified

L98.0   Pyogenic granuloma

> **Excludes2**   pyogenic granuloma of gingiva (K06.8)
> pyogenic granuloma of maxillary alveolar ridge (K04.5)
> pyogenic granuloma of oral mucosa (K13.4)

L98.1   Factitial dermatitis
Neurotic excoriation

L98.2   Febrile neutrophilic dermatosis [Sweet]

L98.3   Eosinophilic cellulitis [Wells] 🦠

● L98.4   Non-pressure chronic ulcer of skin, not elsewhere classified
Chronic ulcer of skin NOS
Tropical ulcer NOS
Ulcer of skin NOS

> **Excludes2**   pressure ulcer (pressure area) (L89.-)
> gangrene (I96)
> skin infections (L00-L08)
> specific infections classified to A00-B99
> ulcer of lower limb NEC (L97.-)
> varicose ulcer (I83.0-I82.2)

● L98.41   Non-pressure chronic ulcer of buttock

L98.411   Non-pressure chronic ulcer of buttock limited to breakdown of skin

L98.412   Non-pressure chronic ulcer of buttock with fat layer exposed

L98.413   Non-pressure chronic ulcer of buttock with necrosis of muscle

L98.414   Non-pressure chronic ulcer of buttock with necrosis of bone

L98.419   Non-pressure chronic ulcer of buttock with unspecified severity

● L98.42   Non-pressure chronic ulcer of back

L98.421   Non-pressure chronic ulcer of back limited to breakdown of skin

L98.422   Non-pressure chronic ulcer of back with fat layer exposed

L98.423   Non-pressure chronic ulcer of back with necrosis of muscle

L98.424   Non-pressure chronic ulcer of back with necrosis of bone

L98.429   Non-pressure chronic ulcer of back with unspecified severity

● L98.49   Non-pressure chronic ulcer of skin of other sites
Non-pressure chronic ulcer of skin NOS

L98.491   Non-pressure chronic ulcer of skin of other sites limited to breakdown of skin

L98.492   Non-pressure chronic ulcer of skin of other sites with fat layer exposed

L98.493   Non-pressure chronic ulcer of skin of other sites with necrosis of muscle

L98.494   Non-pressure chronic ulcer of skin of other sites with necrosis of bone

L98.499   Non-pressure chronic ulcer of skin of other sites with unspecified severity

L98.5   Mucinosis of the skin
Focal mucinosis
Lichen myxedematosus

> **Excludes1**   focal oral mucinosis (K13.79)
> myxedema (E03.9)

L98.6   Other infiltrative disorders of the skin and subcutaneous tissue

> **Excludes1**   hyalinosis cutis et mucosae (E78.89)

L98.8   Other specified disorders of the skin and subcutaneous tissue

L98.9   Disorder of the skin and subcutaneous tissue, unspecified

● L99   Other disorders of skin and subcutaneous tissue in diseases classified elsewhere

Code first underlying disease, such as:
amyloidosis (E85.-)

> **Excludes1**   skin disorders in diabetes (E08-E13 with .62)
> skin disorders in gonorrhea (A54.89)
> skin disorders in syphilis (A51.31, A52.79)

● Unacceptable First-Listed Diagnosis   ● Use Additional Character(s)   ■ Unspecified   **OGCR** Official Guidelines for Coding and Reporting
🦠 Complication\Comorbidity   🦠 Major C\C   Excludes 1   Excludes 2   Includes   Use additional   Code first   Code also

OGCR Section I.C.a.-c.

a. Site and laterality

Most of the codes within Chapter 13 have site and laterality designations. The site represents either the bone, joint or the muscle involved. For some conditions where more than one bone, joint or muscle is usually involved, such as osteoarthritis, there is a "multiple sites" code available. For categories where no multiple site code is provided and more than one bone, joint or muscle is involved, multiple codes should be used to indicate the different sites involved.

1) Bone versus joint

For certain conditions, the bone may be affected at the upper or lower end, (e.g., avascular necrosis of bone, M87, Osteoporosis, M80, M81). Though the portion of the bone affected may be at the joint, the site designation will be the bone, not the joint.

b. Acute traumatic versus chronic or recurrent musculoskeletal conditions

Many musculoskeletal conditions are a result of previous injury or trauma to a site, or are recurrent conditions. Bone, joint or muscle conditions that are the result of a healed injury are usually found in chapter 13. Recurrent bone, joint or muscle conditions are also usually found in chapter 13. Any current, acute injury should be coded to the appropriate injury code from chapter 19. Chronic or recurrent conditions should generally be coded with a code from chapter 13. If it is difficult to determine from the documentation in the record which code is best to describe a condition, query the provider.

c. Coding of Pathologic Fractures

7th character A is for use as long as the patient is receiving active treatment for the fracture. Examples of active treatment are: surgical treatment, emergency department encounter, evaluation and treatment by a new physician. 7th character, D is to be used for encounters after the patient has completed active treatment. The other 7th characters, listed under each subcategory in the Tabular List, are to be used for subsequent encounters for treatment of problems associated with the healing, such as malunions and nonunions, and sequelae.

Care for complications of surgical treatment for fracture repairs during the healing or recovery phase should be coded with the appropriate complication codes.

See Section I.C.19. Coding of traumatic fractures.

CHAPTER 13

DISEASES OF THE MUSCULOSKELETAL SYSTEM AND CONNECTIVE TISSUE (M00-M99)

Note: Use an external cause code following the code for the musculoskeletal condition, if applicable, to identify the cause of the musculoskeletal condition

Excludes2   arthropathic psoriasis (L40.5-)

certain conditions originating in the perinatal period (P04-P96)

certain infectious and parasitic diseases (A00-B99)

compartment syndrome (traumatic) (T79.A-)

complications of pregnancy, childbirth and the puerperium (O00-O99)

congenital malformations, deformations, and chromosomal abnormalities (Q00-Q99)

endocrine, nutritional and metabolic diseases (E00-E90)

injury, poisoning and certain other consequences of external causes (S00-T98)

neoplasms (C00-D48)

symptoms, signs and abnormal clinical and laboratory findings, not elsewhere classified (R00-R94)

This chapter contains the following blocks:

M00-M02	Infectious arthropathies
M05-M14	Inflammatory polyarthropathies
M15-M19	Osteoarthritis
M20-M25	Other joint disorders
M26-M27	Dentofacial anomalies [including malocclusion] and other disorders of jaw
M30-M36	Systemic connective tissue disorders
M40-M43	Deforming dorsopathies
M45-M49	Spondylopathies
M50-M54	Other dorsopathies
M60-M63	Disorders of muscles
M65-M67	Disorders of synovium and tendon
M70-M79	Other soft tissue disorders
M80-M85	Disorders of bone density and structure
M86-M90	Other osteopathies
M91-M94	Chondropathies
M95	Other disorders of the musculoskeletal system and connective tissue
M96	Intraoperative and postprocedural complications and disorders of musculoskeletal system, not elsewhere classified
M99	Biomechanical lesions, not elsewhere classified

ARTHROPATHIES (M00-M25)

Disorders affecting predominantly peripheral (limb) joints

INFECTIOUS ARTHROPATHIES (M00-M02)

This block comprises arthropathies due to microbiological agents.

Distinction is made between the following types of etiological relationship:

a) direct infection of joint, where organisms invade synovial tissue and microbial antigen is present in the joint;

b) indirect infection, which may be of two types: a reactive arthropathy, where microbial infection of the body is established but neither organisms nor antigens can be identified in the joint, and a postinfective arthropathy, where microbial antigen is present but recovery of an organism is inconstant and evidence of local multiplication is lacking.

● **M00 Pyogenic arthritis**

   ● **M00.0 Staphylococcal arthritis and polyarthritis**

     Use additional code (B95.6-B95.7) to identify bacterial agent

     ▪ **M00.00 Staphylococcal arthritis, unspecified joint** 🔖

     ● **M00.01 Staphylococcal arthritis, shoulder**

       M00.011 Staphylococcal arthritis, right shoulder 🔖

       M00.012 Staphylococcal arthritis, left shoulder 🔖

       ▪ **M00.019 Staphylococcal arthritis, unspecified shoulder** 🔖

     ● **M00.02 Staphylococcal arthritis, elbow**

       M00.021 Staphylococcal arthritis, right elbow

● Unacceptable First-Listed Diagnosis	● Use Additional Character(s)	▪ Unspecified	**OGCR** Official Guidelines for Coding and Reporting
🔖 Complication\Comorbidity	🔖 Major C\C	Excludes 1 Excludes 2	
		Includes Use additional Code first Code also	

    M00.022 Staphylococcal arthritis, left elbow 🦠

■ M00.029 Staphylococcal arthritis, unspecified elbow 🦠

● M00.03 Staphylococcal arthritis, wrist
    Staphylococcal arthritis of carpal bones

    M00.031 Staphylococcal arthritis, right wrist 🦠

    M00.032 Staphylococcal arthritis, left wrist 🦠

■ M00.039 Staphylococcal arthritis, unspecified wrist 🦠

● M00.04 Staphylococcal arthritis, hand
    Staphylococcal arthritis of metacarpus and phalanges

    M00.041 Staphylococcal arthritis, right hand 🦠

    M00.042 Staphylococcal arthritis, left hand 🦠

■ M00.049 Staphylococcal arthritis, unspecified hand 🦠

● M00.05 Staphylococcal arthritis, hip

    M00.051 Staphylococcal arthritis, right hip 🦠

    M00.052 Staphylococcal arthritis, left hip 🦠

■ M00.059 Staphylococcal arthritis, unspecified hip 🦠

● M00.06 Staphylococcal arthritis, knee

    M00.061 Staphylococcal arthritis, right knee 🦠

    M00.062 Staphylococcal arthritis, left knee 🦠

■ M00.069 Staphylococcal arthritis, unspecified knee 🦠

● M00.07 Staphylococcal arthritis, ankle and foot
    Staphylococcal arthritis, tarsus, metatarsus and phalanges

    M00.071 Staphylococcal arthritis, right ankle and foot 🦠

    M00.072 Staphylococcal arthritis, left ankle and foot 🦠

■ M00.079 Staphylococcal arthritis, unspecified ankle and foot 🦠

    M00.08 Staphylococcal arthritis, vertebrae 🦠

    M00.09 Staphylococcal polyarthritis 🦠

● M00.1 Pneumococcal arthritis and polyarthritis

■ M00.10 Pneumococcal arthritis, unspecified joint 🦠

● M00.11 Pneumococcal arthritis, shoulder

    M00.111 Pneumococcal arthritis, right shoulder 🦠

    M00.112 Pneumococcal arthritis, left shoulder 🦠

■ M00.119 Pneumococcal arthritis, unspecified shoulder 🦠

● M00.12 Pneumococcal arthritis, elbow

    M00.121 Pneumococcal arthritis, right elbow 🦠

    M00.122 Pneumococcal arthritis, left elbow 🦠

■ M00.129 Pneumococcal arthritis, unspecified elbow 🦠

● M00.13 Pneumococcal arthritis, wrist
    Pneumococcal arthritis of carpal bones

    M00.131 Pneumococcal arthritis, right wrist 🦠

    M00.132 Pneumococcal arthritis, left wrist 🦠

■ M00.139 Pneumococcal arthritis, unspecified wrist 🦠

● M00.14 Pneumococcal arthritis, hand
    Pneumococcal arthritis of metacarpus and phalanges

    M00.141 Pneumococcal arthritis, right hand 🦠

    M00.142 Pneumococcal arthritis, left hand 🦠

■ M00.149 Pneumococcal arthritis, unspecified hand 🦠

● M00.15 Pneumococcal arthritis, hip

    M00.151 Pneumococcal arthritis, right hip 🦠

    M00.152 Pneumococcal arthritis, left hip 🦠

■ M00.159 Pneumococcal arthritis, unspecified hip 🦠

● M00.16 Pneumococcal arthritis, knee

    M00.161 Pneumococcal arthritis, right knee 🦠

    M00.162 Pneumococcal arthritis, left knee 🦠

■ M00.169 Pneumococcal arthritis, unspecified knee 🦠

● M00.17 Pneumococcal arthritis, ankle and foot
    Pneumococcal arthritis, tarsus, metatarsus and phalanges

    M00.171 Pneumococcal arthritis, right ankle and foot 🦠

    M00.172 Pneumococcal arthritis, left ankle and foot 🦠

■ M00.179 Pneumococcal arthritis, unspecified ankle and foot 🦠

    M00.18 Pneumococcal arthritis, vertebrae 🦠

    M00.19 Pneumococcal polyarthritis 🦠

● M00.2 Other streptococcal arthritis and polyarthritis
    Use additional code (B95.0-B95.2, B95.4-B95.5) to identify bacterial agent

■ M00.20 Other streptococcal arthritis, unspecified joint 🦠

● M00.21 Other streptococcal arthritis, shoulder

    M00.211 Other streptococcal arthritis, right shoulder 🦠

    M00.212 Other streptococcal arthritis, left shoulder 🦠

■ M00.219 Other streptococcal arthritis, unspecified shoulder 🦠

● M00.22 Other streptococcal arthritis, elbow

    M00.221 Other streptococcal arthritis, right elbow 🦠

    M00.222 Other streptococcal arthritis, left elbow 🦠

■ M00.229 Other streptococcal arthritis, unspecified elbow 🦠

● M00.23 **Other streptococcal arthritis, wrist**
Other streptococcal arthritis of carpal bones

     M00.231 Other streptococcal arthritis, right wrist 🦠

     M00.232 Other streptococcal arthritis, left wrist 🦠

     ◻M00.239 Other streptococcal arthritis, unspecified wrist 🦠

● M00.24 **Other streptococcal arthritis, hand**
Other streptococcal arthritis metacarpus and phalanges

     M00.241 Other streptococcal arthritis, right hand 🦠

     M00.242 Other streptococcal arthritis, left hand 🦠

     ◻M00.249 Other streptococcal arthritis, unspecified hand 🦠

● M00.25 **Other streptococcal arthritis, hip**

     M00.251 Other streptococcal arthritis, right hip 🦠

     M00.252 Other streptococcal arthritis, left hip 🦠

     ◻M00.259 Other streptococcal arthritis, unspecified hip 🦠

● M00.26 **Other streptococcal arthritis, knee**

     M00.261 Other streptococcal arthritis, right knee 🦠

     M00.262 Other streptococcal arthritis, left knee 🦠

     ◻M00.269 Other streptococcal arthritis, unspecified knee 🦠

● M00.27 **Other streptococcal arthritis, ankle and foot**
Other streptococcal arthritis, tarsus, metatarsus and phalanges

     M00.271 Other streptococcal arthritis, right ankle and foot 🦠

     M00.272 Other streptococcal arthritis, left ankle and foot 🦠

     ◻M00.279 Other streptococcal arthritis, unspecified ankle and foot 🦠

   M00.28 Other streptococcal arthritis, vertebrae 🦠

   M00.29 Other streptococcal polyarthritis 🦠

● M00.8 **Arthritis and polyarthritis due to other bacteria**
Use additional code (B96) to identify bacteria

   ◻M00.80 Arthritis due to other bacteria, unspecified joint 🦠

● M00.81 **Arthritis due to other bacteria, shoulder**

     M00.811 Arthritis due to other bacteria, right shoulder 🦠

     M00.812 Arthritis due to other bacteria, left shoulder 🦠

     ◻M00.819 Arthritis due to other bacteria, unspecified shoulder 🦠

● M00.82 **Arthritis due to other bacteria, elbow**

     M00.821 Arthritis due to other bacteria, right elbow 🦠

     M00.822 Arthritis due to other bacteria, left elbow 🦠

     ◻M00.829 Arthritis due to other bacteria, unspecified elbow 🦠

● M00.83 **Arthritis due to other bacteria, wrist**
Arthritis due to other bacteria, carpal bones

     M00.831 Arthritis due to other bacteria, right wrist 🦠

     M00.832 Arthritis due to other bacteria, left wrist 🦠

     ◻M00.839 Arthritis due to other bacteria, unspecified wrist 🦠

● M00.84 **Arthritis due to other bacteria, hand**
Arthritis due to other bacteria, metacarpus and phalanges

     M00.841 Arthritis due to other bacteria, right hand 🦠

     M00.842 Arthritis due to other bacteria, left hand 🦠

     ◻M00.849 Arthritis due to other bacteria, unspecified hand 🦠

● M00.85 **Arthritis due to other bacteria, hip**

     M00.851 Arthritis due to other bacteria, right hip 🦠

     M00.852 Arthritis due to other bacteria, left hip 🦠

     ◻M00.859 Arthritis due to other bacteria, unspecified hip 🦠

● M00.86 **Arthritis due to other bacteria, knee**

     M00.861 Arthritis due to other bacteria, right knee 🦠

     M00.862 Arthritis due to other bacteria, left knee 🦠

     ◻M00.869 Arthritis due to other bacteria, unspecified knee 🦠

● M00.87 **Arthritis due to other bacteria, ankle and foot**
Arthritis due to other bacteria, tarsus, metatarsus, and phalanges

     M00.871 Arthritis due to other bacteria, right ankle and foot 🦠

     M00.872 Arthritis due to other bacteria, left ankle and foot 🦠

     ◻M00.879 Arthritis due to other bacteria, unspecified ankle and foot 🦠

   M00.88 Arthritis due to other bacteria, vertebrae 🦠

   M00.89 Polyarthritis due to other bacteria 🦠

◻M00.9 **Pyogenic arthritis, unspecified** 🦠
Infective arthritis NOS

● **M01 Direct infections of joint in infectious and parasitic diseases classified elsewhere**

   Code first underlying disease, such as:
leprosy [Hansen's disease] (A30.-)
mycoses (B35-B49)
O'nyong-nyong fever (A92.1)
paratyphoid fever (A01.1-A01.4)

   Excludes1   arthritis, arthropathy (in):
     gonococcal (A54.42)
     Lyme disease (A69.23)
     meningococcal (A39.83)
     postmeningococcal (A39.84)
     mumps (B26.85)
     postinfective (M02.-)
     reactive (M04.0-)
     rubella (B06.82)
     sarcoidosis (D86.86)
     typhoid fever (A01.04)
     tuberculosis (A18.02)
     spine (A18.01)

● Unacceptable First-Listed Diagnosis   ● Use Additional Character(s)   ◻ Unspecified   **OGCR** Official Guidelines for Coding and Reporting

🦠 Complication\Comorbidity   🦠 Major C\C   Excludes 1   Excludes 2   Includes   Use additional   Code first   Code also

1125

CHAPTER 13 (M00-M99)

● ■ **M01.x0**   **Direct infection of unspecified joint in infectious and parasitic diseases classified elsewhere** 🗝

● **M01.x1**   **Direct infection of shoulder joint in infectious and parasitic diseases classified elsewhere**

     ● **M01.x11**   Direct infection of right shoulder in infectious and parasitic diseases classified elsewhere 🗝

     ● **M01.x12**   Direct infection of left shoulder in infectious and parasitic diseases classified elsewhere 🗝

     ● ■ **M01.x19**   Direct infection of unspecified shoulder in infectious and parasitic diseases classified elsewhere 🗝

● **M01.x2**   **Direct infection of elbow in infectious and parasitic diseases classified elsewhere**

     ● **M01.x21**   Direct infection of right elbow in infectious and parasitic diseases classified elsewhere 🗝

     ● **M01.x22**   Direct infection of left elbow in infectious and parasitic diseases classified elsewhere 🗝

     ● ■ **M01.x29**   Direct infection of unspecified elbow in infectious and parasitic diseases classified elsewhere 🗝

● **M01.x3**   **Direct infection of wrist in infectious and parasitic diseases classified elsewhere**
       Direct infection of carpal bones in infectious and parasitic diseases classified elsewhere

     ● **M01.x31**   Direct infection of right wrist in infectious and parasitic diseases classified elsewhere 🗝

     ● **M01.x32**   Direct infection of left wrist in infectious and parasitic diseases classified elsewhere 🗝

     ● ■ **M01.x39**   Direct infection of unspecified wrist in infectious and parasitic diseases classified elsewhere 🗝

● **M01.x4**   **Direct infection of hand in infectious and parasitic diseases classified elsewhere**
       Direct infection of metacarpus and phalanges in infectious and parasitic diseases classified elsewhere

     ● **M01.x41**   Direct infection of right hand in infectious and parasitic diseases classified elsewhere 🗝

     ● **M01.x42**   Direct infection of left hand in infectious and parasitic diseases classified elsewhere 🗝

     ● ■ **M01.x49**   Direct infection of unspecified hand in infectious and parasitic diseases classified elsewhere 🗝

● **M01.x5**   **Direct infection of hip in infectious and parasitic diseases classified elsewhere**

     ● **M01.x51**   Direct infection of right hip in infectious and parasitic diseases classified elsewhere 🗝

     ● **M01.x52**   Direct infection of left hip in infectious and parasitic diseases classified elsewhere 🗝

     ● ■ **M01.x59**   Direct infection of unspecified hip in infectious and parasitic diseases classified elsewhere 🗝

● **M01.x6**   **Direct infection of knee in infectious and parasitic diseases classified elsewhere**

     ● **M01.x61**   Direct infection of right knee in infectious and parasitic diseases classified elsewhere 🗝

     ● **M01.x62**   Direct infection of left knee in infectious and parasitic diseases classified elsewhere 🗝

     ● ■ **M01.x69**   Direct infection of unspecified knee in infectious and parasitic diseases classified elsewhere 🗝

● **M01.x7**   **Direct infection of ankle and foot in infectious and parasitic diseases classified elsewhere**
       Direct infection of tarsus, metatarsus and phalanges in infectious and parasitic diseases classified elsewhere

     ● **M01.x71**   Direct infection of right ankle and foot in infectious and parasitic diseases classified elsewhere 🗝

     ● **M01.x72**   Direct infection of left ankle and foot in infectious and parasitic diseases classified elsewhere 🗝

     ● ■ **M01.x79**   Direct infection of unspecified ankle and foot in infectious and parasitic diseases classified elsewhere 🗝

● **M01.x8**   **Direct infection of vertebrae in infectious and parasitic diseases classified elsewhere** 🗝

● **M01.x9**   **Direct infection of multiple joints in infectious and parasitic diseases classified elsewhere** 🗝

● **M02**   **Postinfective and reactive arthropathies**

     Code first underlying disease, such as:
       congenital syphilis [Clutton's joints] (A50.5)
       enteritis due to Yersinia enterocolitica (A04.6)
       infective endocarditis (I33.0)
       viral hepatitis (B15-B19)

     | Excludes1 | Behçet's disease (M35.2)
       direct infections of joints in diseases classified elsewhere (M01.0-)
       postinfectious arthritis (in):
         meningococcal (A39.84)
         mumps (B26.85)
         rubella (B06.82)
         syphilis (late) (A52.77)
       rheumatic fever (I00)
       tabetic arthropathy [Charcot's] (A52.16)

● **M02.0**   **Arthropathy following intestinal bypass**

     ■ **M02.00**   Arthropathy following intestinal bypass, unspecified site

     ● **M02.01**   Arthropathy following intestinal bypass, shoulder

       M02.011   Arthropathy following intestinal bypass, right shoulder

       M02.012   Arthropathy following intestinal bypass, left shoulder

       ■ **M02.019**   Arthropathy following intestinal bypass, unspecified shoulder

     ● **M02.02**   Arthropathy following intestinal bypass, elbow

       M02.021   Arthropathy following intestinal bypass, right elbow

       M02.022   Arthropathy following intestinal bypass, left elbow

       ■ **M02.029**   Arthropathy following intestinal bypass, unspecified elbow

- M02.03 Arthropathy following intestinal bypass, wrist
  Arthropathy following intestinal bypass, carpal bones
  - M02.031 Arthropathy following intestinal bypass, right wrist
  - M02.032 Arthropathy following intestinal bypass, left wrist
  - M02.039 Arthropathy following intestinal bypass, unspecified wrist
- M02.04 Arthropathy following intestinal bypass, hand
  Arthropathy following intestinal bypass, metacarpals and phalanges
  - M02.041 Arthropathy following intestinal bypass, right hand
  - M02.042 Arthropathy following intestinal bypass, left hand
  - M02.049 Arthropathy following intestinal bypass, unspecified hand
- M02.05 Arthropathy following intestinal bypass, hip
  - M02.051 Arthropathy following intestinal bypass, right hip
  - M02.052 Arthropathy following intestinal bypass, left hip
  - M02.059 Arthropathy following intestinal bypass, unspecified hip
- M02.06 Arthropathy following intestinal bypass, knee
  - M02.061 Arthropathy following intestinal bypass, right knee
  - M02.062 Arthropathy following intestinal bypass, left knee
  - M02.069 Arthropathy following intestinal bypass, unspecified knee
- M02.07 Arthropathy following intestinal bypass, ankle and foot
  Arthropathy following intestinal bypass, tarsus, metatarsus and phalanges
  - M02.071 Arthropathy following intestinal bypass, right ankle and foot
  - M02.072 Arthropathy following intestinal bypass, left ankle and foot
  - M02.079 Arthropathy following intestinal bypass, unspecified ankle and foot
  - M02.08 Arthropathy following intestinal bypass, vertebrae
  - M02.09 Arthropathy following intestinal bypass, multiple sites
- M02.1 Postdysenteric arthropathy
  - M02.10 Postdysenteric arthropathy, unspecified site 🗞
- M02.11 Postdysenteric arthropathy, shoulder
  - M02.111 Postdysenteric arthropathy, right shoulder 🗞
  - M02.112 Postdysenteric arthropathy, left shoulder 🗞
  - M02.119 Postdysenteric arthropathy, unspecified shoulder 🗞
- M02.12 Postdysenteric arthropathy, elbow
  - M02.121 Postdysenteric arthropathy, right elbow 🗞
  - M02.122 Postdysenteric arthropathy, left elbow 🗞
  - M02.129 Postdysenteric arthropathy, unspecified elbow 🗞

- M02.13 Postdysenteric arthropathy, wrist
  Postdysenteric arthropathy, carpal bones
  - M02.131 Postdysenteric arthropathy, right wrist 🗞
  - M02.132 Postdysenteric arthropathy, left wrist 🗞
  - M02.139 Postdysenteric arthropathy, unspecified wrist 🗞
- M02.14 Postdysenteric arthropathy, hand
  Postdysenteric arthropathy, metacarpus and phalanges
  - M02.141 Postdysenteric arthropathy, right hand 🗞
  - M02.142 Postdysenteric arthropathy, left hand 🗞
  - M02.149 Postdysenteric arthropathy, unspecified hand 🗞
- M02.15 Postdysenteric arthropathy, hip
  - M02.151 Postdysenteric arthropathy, right hip 🗞
  - M02.152 Postdysenteric arthropathy, left hip 🗞
  - M02.159 Postdysenteric arthropathy, unspecified hip 🗞
- M02.16 Postdysenteric arthropathy, knee
  - M02.161 Postdysenteric arthropathy, right knee 🗞
  - M02.162 Postdysenteric arthropathy, left knee 🗞
  - M02.169 Postdysenteric arthropathy, unspecified knee 🗞
- M02.17 Postdysenteric arthropathy, ankle and foot
  Postdysenteric arthropathy, tarsus, metatarsus and phalanges
  - M02.171 Postdysenteric arthropathy, right ankle and foot 🗞
  - M02.172 Postdysenteric arthropathy, left ankle and foot 🗞
  - M02.179 Postdysenteric arthropathy, unspecified ankle and foot 🗞
  - M02.18 Postdysenteric arthropathy, vertebrae 🗞
  - M02.19 Postdysenteric arthropathy, multiple sites 🗞
- M02.2 Postimmunization arthropathy
  - M02.20 Postimmunization arthropathy, unspecified site
- M02.21 Postimmunization arthropathy, shoulder
  - M02.211 Postimmunization arthropathy, right shoulder
  - M02.212 Postimmunization arthropathy, left shoulder
  - M02.219 Postimmunization arthropathy, unspecified shoulder
- M02.22 Postimmunization arthropathy, elbow
  - M02.221 Postimmunization arthropathy, right elbow
  - M02.222 Postimmunization arthropathy, left elbow
  - M02.229 Postimmunization arthropathy, unspecified elbow

● Unacceptable First-Listed Diagnosis   ● Use Additional Character(s)   🗆 Unspecified   **OGCR** Official Guidelines for Coding and Reporting

🗞 Complication\Comorbidity   🗞 Major C\C   Excludes 1   Excludes 2   Includes   Use additional   Code first   Code also   1127

CHAPTER 13 (M00-M99)

● **M02.23 Postimmunization arthropathy, wrist**
  Postimmunization arthropathy, carpal bones
  M02.231 Postimmunization arthropathy, right wrist
  M02.232 Postimmunization arthropathy, left wrist
  ■ **M02.239 Postimmunization arthropathy, unspecified wrist**

● **M02.24 Postimmunization arthropathy, hand**
  Postimmunization arthropathy, metacarpus and phalanges
  M02.241 Postimmunization arthropathy, right hand
  M02.242 Postimmunization arthropathy, left hand
  ■ **M02.249 Postimmunization arthropathy, unspecified hand**

● **M02.25 Postimmunization arthropathy, hip**
  M02.251 Postimmunization arthropathy, right hip
  M02.252 Postimmunization arthropathy, left hip
  ■ **M02.259 Postimmunization arthropathy, unspecified hip**

● **M02.26 Postimmunization arthropathy, knee**
  M02.261 Postimmunization arthropathy, right knee
  M02.262 Postimmunization arthropathy, left knee
  ■ **M02.269 Postimmunization arthropathy, unspecified knee**

● **M02.27 Postimmunization arthropathy, ankle and foot**
  Postimmunization arthropathy, tarsus, metatarsus and phalanges
  M02.271 Postimmunization arthropathy, right ankle and foot
  M02.272 Postimmunization arthropathy, left ankle and foot
  ■ **M02.279 Postimmunization arthropathy, unspecified ankle and foot**

  M02.28 Postimmunization arthropathy, vertebrae
  M02.29 Postimmunization arthropathy, multiple sites

● **M02.3 Reiter's disease**
  ■ **M02.30 Reiter's disease, unspecified site** %

● **M02.31 Reiter's disease, shoulder**
  M02.311 Reiter's disease, right shoulder
  M02.312 Reiter's disease, left shoulder
  ■ **M02.319 Reiter's disease, unspecified shoulder** %

● **M02.32 Reiter's disease, elbow**
  M02.321 Reiter's disease, right elbow
  M02.322 Reiter's disease, left elbow
  ■ **M02.329 Reiter's disease, unspecified elbow** %

● **M02.33 Reiter's disease, wrist**
  Reiter's disease, carpal bones
  M02.331 Reiter's disease, right wrist
  M02.332 Reiter's disease, left wrist
  ■ **M02.339 Reiter's disease, unspecified wrist** %

● **M02.34 Reiter's disease, hand**
  Reiter's disease, metacarpus and phalanges
  M02.341 Reiter's disease, right hand
  M02.342 Reiter's disease, left hand
  ■ **M02.349 Reiter's disease, unspecified hand** %

● **M02.35 Reiter's disease, hip**
  M02.351 Reiter's disease, right hip
  M02.352 Reiter's disease, left hip
  ■ **M02.359 Reiter's disease, unspecified hip** %

● **M02.36 Reiter's disease, knee**
  M02.361 Reiter's disease, right knee
  M02.362 Reiter's disease, left knee
  ■ **M02.369 Reiter's disease, unspecified knee** %

● **M02.37 Reiter's disease, ankle and foot**
  Reiter's disease, tarsus, metatarsus and phalanges
  M02.371 Reiter's disease, right ankle and foot
  M02.372 Reiter's disease, left ankle and foot
  ■ **M02.379 Reiter's disease, unspecified ankle and foot** %

  M02.38 Reiter's disease, vertebrae %
  M02.39 Reiter's disease, multiple sites %

● **M02.8 Other reactive arthropathies**
  ■ **M02.80 Other reactive arthropathies, unspecified site** %

● **M02.81 Other reactive arthropathies, shoulder**
  M02.811 Other reactive arthropathies, right shoulder %
  M02.812 Other reactive arthropathies, left shoulder %
  ■ **M02.819 Other reactive arthropathies, unspecified shoulder** %

● **M02.82 Other reactive arthropathies, elbow**
  M02.821 Other reactive arthropathies, right elbow %
  M02.822 Other reactive arthropathies, left elbow %
  ■ **M02.829 Other reactive arthropathies, unspecified elbow** %

● **M02.83 Other reactive arthropathies, wrist**
  Other reactive arthropathies, carpal bones
  M02.831 Other reactive arthropathies, right wrist %
  M02.832 Other reactive arthropathies, left wrist %
  ■ **M02.839 Other reactive arthropathies, unspecified wrist** %

● **M02.84 Other reactive arthropathies, hand**
  Other reactive arthropathies, metacarpus and phalanges
  M02.841 Other reactive arthropathies, right hand %
  M02.842 Other reactive arthropathies, left hand %
  ■ **M02.849 Other reactive arthropathies, unspecified hand** %

● Unacceptable First-Listed Diagnosis   ● Use Additional Character(s)   ■ Unspecified   **OGCR** Official Guidelines for Coding and Reporting
% Complication\Comorbidity   % Major C\C   Excludes 1   Excludes 2   Includes   Use additional   Code first   Code also

● M02.85 Other reactive arthropathies, hip

    M02.851 Other reactive arthropathies, right hip 🍂

    M02.852 Other reactive arthropathies, left hip 🍂

    ◻M02.859 Other reactive arthropathies, unspecified hip 🍂

● M02.86 Other reactive arthropathies, knee

    M02.861 Other reactive arthropathies, right knee 🍂

    M02.862 Other reactive arthropathies, left knee 🍂

    ◻M02.869 Other reactive arthropathies, unspecified knee 🍂

● M02.87 Other reactive arthropathies, ankle and foot
    Other reactive arthropathies, tarsus, metatarsus and phalanges

    M02.871 Other reactive arthropathies, right ankle and foot 🍂

    M02.872 Other reactive arthropathies, left ankle and foot 🍂

    ◻M02.879 Other reactive arthropathies, unspecified ankle and foot 🍂

  M02.88 Other reactive arthropathies, vertebrae 🍂

  M02.89 Other reactive arthropathies, multiple sites 🍂

◻M02.9 Reactive arthopathy, unspecified

Item 13–1 Rheumatoid arthritis (RA) is a chronic systemic inflammatory disease of undetermined etiology involving primarily the synovial membranes and articular structures of multiple joints. The disease is often progressive and results in pain, stiffness, and swelling of joints. In late stages, deformity, ankylosis, and other **inflammatory polyarthropathies** develop.

INFLAMMATORY POLYARTHROPATHIES (M05-M14)

● **M05 Rheumatoid arthritis with rheumatoid factor**

    Excludes1 rheumatic fever (I00)
                juvenile rheumatoid arthritis (M08.-)
                rheumatoid arthritis of spine (M45.-)

● M05.0 Felty's syndrome
    Rheumatoid arthritis with splenoadenomegaly and leukopenia

  ◻M05.00 Felty's syndrome, unspecified site

  ● M05.01 Felty's syndrome, shoulder

    M05.011 Felty's syndrome, right shoulder

    M05.012 Felty's syndrome, left shoulder

    ◻M05.019 Felty's syndrome, unspecified shoulder

  ● M05.02 Felty's syndrome, elbow

    M05.021 Felty's syndrome, right elbow

    M05.022 Felty's syndrome, left elbow

    ◻M05.029 Felty's syndrome, unspecified elbow

  ● M05.03 Felty's syndrome, wrist
    Felty's syndrome, carpal bones

    M05.031 Felty's syndrome, right wrist

    M05.032 Felty's syndrome, left wrist

    ◻M05.039 Felty's syndrome, unspecified wrist

● M05.04 Felty's syndrome, hand
    Felty's syndrome, metacarpus and phalanges

    M05.041 Felty's syndrome, right hand

    M05.042 Felty's syndrome, left hand

    ◻M05.049 Felty's syndrome, unspecified hand

● M05.05 Felty's syndrome, hip

    M05.051 Felty's syndrome, right hip

    M05.052 Felty's syndrome, left hip

    ◻M05.059 Felty's syndrome, unspecified hip

● M05.06 Felty's syndrome, knee

    M05.061 Felty's syndrome, right knee

    M05.062 Felty's syndrome, left knee

    ◻M05.069 Felty's syndrome, unspecified knee

● M05.07 Felty's syndrome, ankle and foot
    Felty's syndrome, tarsus, metatarsus and phalanges

    M05.071 Felty's syndrome, right ankle and foot

    M05.072 Felty's syndrome, left ankle and foot

    ◻M05.079 Felty's syndrome, unspecified ankle and foot

  M05.09 Felty's syndrome, multiple sites

● M05.1 Rheumatoid lung disease with rheumatoid arthritis

  ◻M05.10 Rheumatoid lung disease with rheumatoid arthritis of unspecified site

  ● M05.11 Rheumatoid lung disease with rheumatoid arthritis of shoulder

    M05.111 Rheumatoid lung disease with rheumatoid arthritis of right shoulder

    M05.112 Rheumatoid lung disease with rheumatoid arthritis of left shoulder

    ◻M05.119 Rheumatoid lung disease with rheumatoid arthritis of unspecified shoulder

  ● M05.12 Rheumatoid lung disease with rheumatoid arthritis of elbow

    M05.121 Rheumatoid lung disease with rheumatoid arthritis of right elbow

    M05.122 Rheumatoid lung disease with rheumatoid arthritis of left elbow

    ◻M05.129 Rheumatoid lung disease with rheumatoid arthritis of unspecified elbow

  ● M05.13 Rheumatoid lung disease with rheumatoid arthritis of wrist
    Rheumatoid lung disease with rheumatoid arthritis, carpal bones

    M05.131 Rheumatoid lung disease with rheumatoid arthritis of right wrist

    M05.132 Rheumatoid lung disease with rheumatoid arthritis of left wrist

    ◻M05.139 Rheumatoid lung disease with rheumatoid arthritis of unspecified wrist

  ● M05.14 Rheumatoid lung disease with rheumatoid arthritis of hand
    Rheumatoid lung disease with rheumatoid arthritis, metacarpus and phalanges

    M05.141 Rheumatoid lung disease with rheumatoid arthritis of right hand

---

● Unacceptable First-Listed Diagnosis   ● Use Additional Character(s)   ◻ Unspecified   **OGCR** Official Guidelines for Coding and Reporting

🍂 Complication\Comorbidity   🍂 Major C\C   Excludes 1   Excludes 2   Includes   Use additional   Code first   Code also

1129

CHAPTER 13 (M00-M99)

M05.142 Rheumatoid lung disease with rheumatoid arthritis of left hand

■ M05.149 Rheumatoid lung disease with rheumatoid arthritis of unspecified hand

● M05.15 Rheumatoid lung disease with rheumatoid arthritis of hip

M05.151 Rheumatoid lung disease with rheumatoid arthritis of right hip

M05.152 Rheumatoid lung disease with rheumatoid arthritis of left hip

■ M05.159 Rheumatoid lung disease with rheumatoid arthritis of unspecified hip

● M05.16 Rheumatoid lung disease with rheumatoid arthritis of knee

M05.161 Rheumatoid lung disease with rheumatoid arthritis of right knee

M05.162 Rheumatoid lung disease with rheumatoid arthritis of left knee

■ M05.169 Rheumatoid lung disease with rheumatoid arthritis of unspecified knee

● M05.17 Rheumatoid lung disease with rheumatoid arthritis of ankle and foot
Rheumatoid lung disease with rheumatoid arthritis, tarsus, metatarsus and phalanges

M05.171 Rheumatoid lung disease with rheumatoid arthritis of right ankle and foot

M05.172 Rheumatoid lung disease with rheumatoid arthritis of left ankle and foot

■ M05.179 Rheumatoid lung disease with rheumatoid arthritis of unspecified ankle and foot

M05.19 Rheumatoid lung disease with rheumatoid arthritis of multiple sites

● M05.2 Rheumatoid vasculitis with rheumatoid arthritis

■ M05.20 Rheumatoid vasculitis with rheumatoid arthritis of unspecified site

● M05.21 Rheumatoid vasculitis with rheumatoid arthritis of shoulder

M05.211 Rheumatoid vasculitis with rheumatoid arthritis of right shoulder

M05.212 Rheumatoid vasculitis with rheumatoid arthritis of left shoulder

■ M05.219 Rheumatoid vasculitis with rheumatoid arthritis of unspecified shoulder

● M05.22 Rheumatoid vasculitis with rheumatoid arthritis of elbow

M05.221 Rheumatoid vasculitis with rheumatoid arthritis of right elbow

M05.222 Rheumatoid vasculitis with rheumatoid arthritis of left elbow

■ M05.229 Rheumatoid vasculitis with rheumatoid arthritis of unspecified elbow

● M05.23 Rheumatoid vasculitis with rheumatoid arthritis of wrist
Rheumatoid vasculitis with rheumatoid arthritis, carpal bones

M05.231 Rheumatoid vasculitis with rheumatoid arthritis of right wrist

M05.232 Rheumatoid vasculitis with rheumatoid arthritis of left wrist

■ M05.239 Rheumatoid vasculitis with rheumatoid arthritis of unspecified wrist

● M05.24 Rheumatoid vasculitis with rheumatoid arthritis of hand
Rheumatoid vasculitis with rheumatoid arthritis, metacarpus and phalanges

M05.241 Rheumatoid vasculitis with rheumatoid arthritis of right hand

M05.242 Rheumatoid vasculitis with rheumatoid arthritis of left hand

■ M05.249 Rheumatoid vasculitis with rheumatoid arthritis of unspecified hand

● M05.25 Rheumatoid vasculitis with rheumatoid arthritis of hip

M05.251 Rheumatoid vasculitis with rheumatoid arthritis of right hip

M05.252 Rheumatoid vasculitis with rheumatoid arthritis of left hip

■ M05.259 Rheumatoid vasculitis with rheumatoid arthritis of unspecified hip

● M05.26 Rheumatoid vasculitis with rheumatoid arthritis of knee

M05.261 Rheumatoid vasculitis with rheumatoid arthritis of right knee

M05.262 Rheumatoid vasculitis with rheumatoid arthritis of left knee

■ M05.269 Rheumatoid vasculitis with rheumatoid arthritis of unspecified knee

● M05.27 Rheumatoid vasculitis with rheumatoid arthritis of ankle and foot
Rheumatoid vasculitis with rheumatoid arthritis, tarsus, metatarsus and phalanges

M05.271 Rheumatoid vasculitis with rheumatoid arthritis of right ankle and foot

M05.272 Rheumatoid vasculitis with rheumatoid arthritis of left ankle and foot

■ M05.279 Rheumatoid vasculitis with rheumatoid arthritis of unspecified ankle and foot

M05.29 Rheumatoid vasculitis with rheumatoid arthritis of multiple sites

● M05.3 Rheumatoid heart disease with rheumatoid arthritis
Rheumatoid carditis
Rheumatoid endocarditis
Rheumatoid myocarditis
Rheumatoid pericarditis

■ M05.30 Rheumatoid heart disease with rheumatoid arthritis of unspecified site

● Unacceptable First-Listed Diagnosis   ● Use Additional Character(s)   ■ Unspecified   OGCR Official Guidelines for Coding and Reporting

1130   🅒 Complication\Comorbidity   🅒 Major C\C   Excludes 1   Excludes 2   Includes   Use additional   Code first   Code also

● M05.31 Rheumatoid heart disease with rheumatoid arthritis of shoulder

　　M05.311 Rheumatoid heart disease with rheumatoid arthritis of right shoulder

　　M05.312 Rheumatoid heart disease with rheumatoid arthritis of left shoulder

　　■M05.319 Rheumatoid heart disease with rheumatoid arthritis of unspecified shoulder

● M05.32 Rheumatoid heart disease with rheumatoid arthritis of elbow

　　M05.321 Rheumatoid heart disease with rheumatoid arthritis of right elbow

　　M05.322 Rheumatoid heart disease with rheumatoid arthritis of left elbow

　　■M05.329 Rheumatoid heart disease with rheumatoid arthritis of unspecified elbow

● M05.33 Rheumatoid heart disease with rheumatoid arthritis of wrist
　　　Rheumatoid heart disease with rheumatoid arthritis, carpal bones

　　M05.331 Rheumatoid heart disease with rheumatoid arthritis of right wrist

　　M05.332 Rheumatoid heart disease with rheumatoid arthritis of left wrist

　　■M05.339 Rheumatoid heart disease with rheumatoid arthritis of unspecified wrist

● M05.34 Rheumatoid heart disease with rheumatoid arthritis of hand
　　　Rheumatoid heart disease with rheumatoid arthritis, metacarpus and phalanges

　　M05.341 Rheumatoid heart disease with rheumatoid arthritis of right hand

　　M05.342 Rheumatoid heart disease with rheumatoid arthritis of left hand

　　■M05.349 Rheumatoid heart disease with rheumatoid arthritis of unspecified hand

● M05.35 Rheumatoid heart disease with rheumatoid arthritis of hip

　　M05.351 Rheumatoid heart disease with rheumatoid arthritis of right hip

　　M05.352 Rheumatoid heart disease with rheumatoid arthritis of left hip

　　■M05.359 Rheumatoid heart disease with rheumatoid arthritis of unspecified hip

● M05.36 Rheumatoid heart disease with rheumatoid arthritis of knee

　　M05.361 Rheumatoid heart disease with rheumatoid arthritis of right knee

　　M05.362 Rheumatoid heart disease with rheumatoid arthritis of left knee

　　■M05.369 Rheumatoid heart disease with rheumatoid arthritis of unspecified knee

● M05.37 Rheumatoid heart disease with rheumatoid arthritis of ankle and foot
　　　Rheumatoid heart disease with rheumatoid arthritis, tarsus, metatarsus and phalanges

　　M05.371 Rheumatoid heart disease with rheumatoid arthritis of right ankle and foot

　　M05.372 Rheumatoid heart disease with rheumatoid arthritis of left ankle and foot

　　■M05.379 Rheumatoid heart disease with rheumatoid arthritis of unspecified ankle and foot

　M05.39 Rheumatoid heart disease with rheumatoid arthritis of multiple sites

● M05.4 Rheumatoid myopathy with rheumatoid arthritis

　　■M05.40 Rheumatoid myopathy with rheumatoid arthritis of unspecified site

● M05.41 Rheumatoid myopathy with rheumatoid arthritis of shoulder

　　M05.411 Rheumatoid myopathy with rheumatoid arthritis of right shoulder

　　M05.412 Rheumatoid myopathy with rheumatoid arthritis of left shoulder

　　■M05.419 Rheumatoid myopathy with rheumatoid arthritis of unspecified shoulder

● M05.42 Rheumatoid myopathy with rheumatoid arthritis of elbow

　　M05.421 Rheumatoid myopathy with rheumatoid arthritis of right elbow

　　M05.422 Rheumatoid myopathy with rheumatoid arthritis of left elbow

　　■M05.429 Rheumatoid myopathy with rheumatoid arthritis of unspecified elbow

● M05.43 Rheumatoid myopathy with rheumatoid arthritis of wrist
　　　Rheumatoid myopathy with rheumatoid arthritis, carpal bones

　　M05.431 Rheumatoid myopathy with rheumatoid arthritis of right wrist

　　M05.432 Rheumatoid myopathy with rheumatoid arthritis of left wrist

　　■M05.439 Rheumatoid myopathy with rheumatoid arthritis of unspecified wrist

● M05.44 Rheumatoid myopathy with rheumatoid arthritis of hand
　　　Rheumatoid myopathy with rheumatoid arthritis, metacarpus and phalanges

　　M05.441 Rheumatoid myopathy with rheumatoid arthritis of right hand

　　M05.442 Rheumatoid myopathy with rheumatoid arthritis of left hand

　　■M05.449 Rheumatoid myopathy with rheumatoid arthritis of unspecified hand

● Unacceptable First-Listed Diagnosis　　● Use Additional Character(s)　　■ Unspecified　　**OGCR** Official Guidelines for Coding and Reporting

🧷 Complication\Comorbidity　🧷 Major C\C　 Excludes 1　 Excludes 2　■ Includes　　Use additional　　Code first　　Code also

1131

CHAPTER 13 (M00-M99)

● M05.45 **Rheumatoid myopathy with rheumatoid arthritis of hip**

     M05.451 **Rheumatoid myopathy with rheumatoid arthritis of right hip**

     M05.452 **Rheumatoid myopathy with rheumatoid arthritis of left hip**

     ▣ M05.459 **Rheumatoid myopathy with rheumatoid arthritis of unspecified hip**

● M05.46 **Rheumatoid myopathy with rheumatoid arthritis of knee**

     M05.461 **Rheumatoid myopathy with rheumatoid arthritis of right knee**

     M05.462 **Rheumatoid myopathy with rheumatoid arthritis of left knee**

     ▣ M05.469 **Rheumatoid myopathy with rheumatoid arthritis of unspecified knee**

● M05.47 **Rheumatoid myopathy with rheumatoid arthritis of ankle and foot**

     Rheumatoid myopathy with rheumatoid arthritis, tarsus, metatarsus and phalanges

     M05.471 **Rheumatoid myopathy with rheumatoid arthritis of right ankle and foot**

     M05.472 **Rheumatoid myopathy with rheumatoid arthritis of left ankle and foot**

     ▣ M05.479 **Rheumatoid myopathy with rheumatoid arthritis of unspecified ankle and foot**

     M05.49 **Rheumatoid myopathy with rheumatoid arthritis of multiple sites**

● M05.5 **Rheumatoid polyneuropathy with rheumatoid arthritis**

     ▣ M05.50 **Rheumatoid polyneuropathy with rheumatoid arthritis of unspecified site**

● M05.51 **Rheumatoid polyneuropathy with rheumatoid arthritis of shoulder**

     M05.511 **Rheumatoid polyneuropathy with rheumatoid arthritis of right shoulder**

     M05.512 **Rheumatoid polyneuropathy with rheumatoid arthritis of left shoulder**

     ▣ M05.519 **Rheumatoid polyneuropathy with rheumatoid arthritis of unspecified shoulder**

● M05.52 **Rheumatoid polyneuropathy with rheumatoid arthritis of elbow**

     M05.521 **Rheumatoid polyneuropathy with rheumatoid arthritis of right elbow**

     M05.522 **Rheumatoid polyneuropathy with rheumatoid arthritis of left elbow**

     ▣ M05.529 **Rheumatoid polyneuropathy with rheumatoid arthritis of unspecified elbow**

● M05.53 **Rheumatoid polyneuropathy with rheumatoid arthritis of wrist**

     Rheumatoid polyneuropathy with rheumatoid arthritis, carpal bones

     M05.531 **Rheumatoid polyneuropathy with rheumatoid arthritis of right wrist**

     M05.532 **Rheumatoid polyneuropathy with rheumatoid arthritis of left wrist**

     ▣ M05.539 **Rheumatoid polyneuropathy with rheumatoid arthritis of unspecified wrist**

● M05.54 **Rheumatoid polyneuropathy with rheumatoid arthritis of hand**

     Rheumatoid polyneuropathy with rheumatoid arthritis, metacarpus and phalanges

     M05.541 **Rheumatoid polyneuropathy with rheumatoid arthritis of right hand**

     M05.542 **Rheumatoid polyneuropathy with rheumatoid arthritis of left hand**

     ▣ M05.549 **Rheumatoid polyneuropathy with rheumatoid arthritis of unspecified hand**

● M05.55 **Rheumatoid polyneuropathy with rheumatoid arthritis of hip**

     M05.551 **Rheumatoid polyneuropathy with rheumatoid arthritis of right hip**

     M05.552 **Rheumatoid polyneuropathy with rheumatoid arthritis of left hip**

     ▣ M05.559 **Rheumatoid polyneuropathy with rheumatoid arthritis of unspecified hip**

● M05.56 **Rheumatoid polyneuropathy with rheumatoid arthritis of knee**

     M05.561 **Rheumatoid polyneuropathy with rheumatoid arthritis of right knee**

     M05.562 **Rheumatoid polyneuropathy with rheumatoid arthritis of left knee**

     ▣ M05.569 **Rheumatoid polyneuropathy with rheumatoid arthritis of unspecified knee**

● M05.57 **Rheumatoid polyneuropathy with rheumatoid arthritis of ankle and foot**

     Rheumatoid polyneuropathy with rheumatoid arthritis, tarsus, metatarsus and phalanges

     M05.571 **Rheumatoid polyneuropathy with rheumatoid arthritis of right ankle and foot**

     M05.572 **Rheumatoid polyneuropathy with rheumatoid arthritis of left ankle and foot**

     ▣ M05.579 **Rheumatoid polyneuropathy with rheumatoid arthritis of unspecified ankle and foot**

     M05.59 **Rheumatoid polyneuropathy with rheumatoid arthritis of multiple sites**

● M05.6 **Rheumatoid arthritis with involvement of other organs and systems**

     ▣ M05.60 **Rheumatoid arthritis of unspecified site with involvement of other organs and systems**

● Unacceptable First-Listed Diagnosis   ● Use Additional Character(s)   ▣ Unspecified   **OGCR** Official Guidelines for Coding and Reporting

🔗 Complication\Comorbidity   🔗 Major C\C   [Excludes 1]   [Excludes 2]   Includes   Use additional   Code first   Code also

● **M05.61 Rheumatoid arthritis of shoulder with involvement of other organs and systems**

     M05.611 Rheumatoid arthritis of right shoulder with involvement of other organs and systems

     M05.612 Rheumatoid arthritis of left shoulder with involvement of other organs and systems

     ▪ M05.619 Rheumatoid arthritis of unspecified shoulder with involvement of other organs and systems

● **M05.62 Rheumatoid arthritis of elbow with involvement of other organs and systems**

     M05.621 Rheumatoid arthritis of right elbow with involvement of other organs and systems

     M05.622 Rheumatoid arthritis of left elbow with involvement of other organs and systems

     ▪ M05.629 Rheumatoid arthritis of unspecified elbow with involvement of other organs and systems

● **M05.63 Rheumatoid arthritis of wrist with involvement of other organs and systems**
       Rheumatoid arthritis of carpal bones with involvement of other organs and systems

     M05.631 Rheumatoid arthritis of right wrist with involvement of other organs and systems

     M05.632 Rheumatoid arthritis of left wrist with involvement of other organs and systems

     ▪ M05.639 Rheumatoid arthritis of unspecified wrist with involvement of other organs and systems

● **M05.64 Rheumatoid arthritis of hand with involvement of other organs and systems**
       Rheumatoid arthritis of metacarpus and phalanges with involvement of other organs and systems

     M05.641 Rheumatoid arthritis of right hand with involvement of other organs and systems

     M05.642 Rheumatoid arthritis of left hand with involvement of other organs and systems

     ▪ M05.649 Rheumatoid arthritis of unspecified hand with involvement of other organs and systems

● **M05.65 Rheumatoid arthritis of hip with involvement of other organs and systems**

     M05.651 Rheumatoid arthritis of right hip with involvement of other organs and systems

     M05.652 Rheumatoid arthritis of left hip with involvement of other organs and systems

     ▪ M05.659 Rheumatoid arthritis of unspecified hip with involvement of other organs and systems

● **M05.66 Rheumatoid arthritis of knee with involvement of other organs and systems**

     M05.661 Rheumatoid arthritis of right knee with involvement of other organs and systems

     M05.662 Rheumatoid arthritis of left knee with involvement of other organs and systems

     ▪ M05.669 Rheumatoid arthritis of unspecified knee with involvement of other organs and systems

● **M05.67 Rheumatoid arthritis of ankle and foot with involvement of other organs and systems**
       Rheumatoid arthritis of tarsus, metatarsus and phalanges with involvement of other organs and systems

     M05.671 Rheumatoid arthritis of right ankle and foot with involvement of other organs and systems

     M05.672 Rheumatoid arthritis of left ankle and foot with involvement of other organs and systems

     ▪ M05.679 Rheumatoid arthritis of unspecified ankle and foot with involvement of other organs and systems

     M05.69 Rheumatoid arthritis of multiple sites with involvement of other organs and systems

● **M05.7 Rheumatoid arthritis with rheumatoid factor without organ or systems involvement**

     ▪ M05.70 Rheumatoid arthritis with rheumatoid factor of unspecified site without organ or systems involvement

     ● **M05.71 Rheumatoid arthritis with rheumatoid factor of shoulder without organ or systems involvement**

         M05.711 Rheumatoid arthritis with rheumatoid factor of right shoulder without organ or systems involvement

         M05.712 Rheumatoid arthritis with rheumatoid factor of left shoulder without organ or systems involvement

         ▪ M05.719 Rheumatoid arthritis with rheumatoid factor of unspecified shoulder without organ or systems involvement

     ● **M05.72 Rheumatoid arthritis with rheumatoid factor of elbow without organ or systems involvement**

         M05.721 Rheumatoid arthritis with rheumatoid factor of right elbow without organ or systems involvement

         M05.722 Rheumatoid arthritis with rheumatoid factor of left elbow without organ or systems involvement

         ▪ M05.729 Rheumatoid arthritis with rheumatoid factor of unspecified elbow without organ or systems involvement

● Unacceptable First-Listed Diagnosis   ● Use Additional Character(s)   ▪ Unspecified   **OGCR** Official Guidelines for Coding and Reporting

 Complication\Comorbidity   Major C\C   Excludes 1   Excludes 2   Includes   Use additional   Code first   Code also   **1133**

CHAPTER 13 (M00-M99)

● **M05.73** Rheumatoid arthritis with rheumatoid factor of wrist without organ or systems involvement

   M05.731 Rheumatoid arthritis with rheumatoid factor of right wrist without organ or systems involvement

   M05.732 Rheumatoid arthritis with rheumatoid factor of left wrist without organ or systems involvement

   ■ **M05.739** Rheumatoid arthritis with rheumatoid factor of unspecified wrist without organ or systems involvement

● **M05.74** Rheumatoid arthritis with rheumatoid factor of hand without organ or systems involvement

   M05.741 Rheumatoid arthritis with rheumatoid factor of right hand without organ or systems involvement

   M05.742 Rheumatoid arthritis with rheumatoid factor of left hand without organ or systems involvement

   ■ **M05.749** Rheumatoid arthritis with rheumatoid factor of unspecified hand without organ or systems involvement

● **M05.75** Rheumatoid arthritis with rheumatoid factor of hip without organ or systems involvement

   M05.751 Rheumatoid arthritis with rheumatoid factor of right hip without organ or systems involvement

   M05.752 Rheumatoid arthritis with rheumatoid factor of left hip without organ or systems involvement

   ■ **M05.759** Rheumatoid arthritis with rheumatoid factor of unspecified hip without organ or systems involvement

● **M05.76** Rheumatoid arthritis with rheumatoid factor of knee without organ or systems involvement

   M05.761 Rheumatoid arthritis with rheumatoid factor of right knee without organ or systems involvement

   M05.762 Rheumatoid arthritis with rheumatoid factor of left knee without organ or systems involvement

   ■ **M05.769** Rheumatoid arthritis with rheumatoid factor of unspecified knee without organ or systems involvement

● **M05.77** Rheumatoid arthritis with rheumatoid factor of ankle and foot without organ or systems involvement

   M05.771 Rheumatoid arthritis with rheumatoid factor of right ankle and foot without organ or systems involvement

   M05.772 Rheumatoid arthritis with rheumatoid factor of left ankle and foot without organ or systems involvement

   ■ **M05.779** Rheumatoid arthritis with rheumatoid factor of unspecified ankle and foot without organ or systems involvement

 M05.79 Rheumatoid arthritis with rheumatoid factor of multiple sites without organ or systems involvement

● **M05.8** Other rheumatoid arthritis with rheumatoid factor

  ■ **M05.80** Other rheumatoid arthritis with rheumatoid factor of unspecified site

  ● **M05.81** Other rheumatoid arthritis with rheumatoid factor of shoulder

   M05.811 Other rheumatoid arthritis with rheumatoid factor of right shoulder

   M05.812 Other rheumatoid arthritis with rheumatoid factor of left shoulder

   ■ **M05.819** Other rheumatoid arthritis with rheumatoid factor of unspecified shoulder

  ● **M05.82** Other rheumatoid arthritis with rheumatoid factor of elbow

   M05.821 Other rheumatoid arthritis with rheumatoid factor of right elbow

   M05.822 Other rheumatoid arthritis with rheumatoid factor of left elbow

   ■ **M05.829** Other rheumatoid arthritis with rheumatoid factor of unspecified elbow

  ● **M05.83** Other rheumatoid arthritis with rheumatoid factor of wrist

   M05.831 Other rheumatoid arthritis with rheumatoid factor of right wrist

   M05.832 Other rheumatoid arthritis with rheumatoid factor of left wrist

   ■ **M05.839** Other rheumatoid arthritis with rheumatoid factor of unspecified wrist

  ● **M05.84** Other rheumatoid arthritis with rheumatoid factor of hand

   M05.841 Other rheumatoid arthritis with rheumatoid factor of right hand

   M05.842 Other rheumatoid arthritis with rheumatoid factor of left hand

   ■ **M05.849** Other rheumatoid arthritis with rheumatoid factor of unspecified hand

  ● **M05.85** Other rheumatoid arthritis with rheumatoid factor of hip

   M05.851 Other rheumatoid arthritis with rheumatoid factor of right hip

   M05.852 Other rheumatoid arthritis with rheumatoid factor of left hip

   ■ **M05.859** Other rheumatoid arthritis with rheumatoid factor of unspecified hip

  ● **M05.86** Other rheumatoid arthritis with rheumatoid factor of knee

   M05.861 Other rheumatoid arthritis with rheumatoid factor of right knee

● Unacceptable First-Listed Diagnosis   ● Use Additional Character(s)   ■ Unspecified   **OGCR** Official Guidelines for Coding and Reporting
🖉 Complication\Comorbidity   🖉 Major C\C   Excludes 1   Excludes 2   Includes   Use additional   Code first   Code also

M05.862 Other rheumatoid arthritis with rheumatoid factor of left knee

■ M05.869 Other rheumatoid arthritis with rheumatoid factor of unspecified knee

● M05.87 Other rheumatoid arthritis with rheumatoid factor of ankle and foot

M05.871 Other rheumatoid arthritis with rheumatoid factor of right ankle and foot

M05.872 Other rheumatoid arthritis with rheumatoid factor of left ankle and foot

■ M05.879 Other rheumatoid arthritis with rheumatoid factor of unspecified ankle and foot

M05.89 Other rheumatoid arthritis with rheumatoid factor of multiple sites

■ M05.9 Rheumatoid arthritis with rheumatoid factor, unspecified

● M06 Other rheumatoid arthritis

● M06.0 Rheumatoid arthritis without rheumatoid factor

■ M06.00 Rheumatoid arthritis without rheumatoid factor, unspecified site

● M06.01 Rheumatoid arthritis without rheumatoid factor, shoulder

M06.011 Rheumatoid arthritis without rheumatoid factor, right shoulder

M06.012 Rheumatoid arthritis without rheumatoid factor, left shoulder

■ M06.019 Rheumatoid arthritis without rheumatoid factor, unspecified shoulder

● M06.02 Rheumatoid arthritis without rheumatoid factor, elbow

M06.021 Rheumatoid arthritis without rheumatoid factor, right elbow

M06.022 Rheumatoid arthritis without rheumatoid factor, left elbow

■ M06.029 Rheumatoid arthritis without rheumatoid factor, unspecified elbow

● M06.03 Rheumatoid arthritis without rheumatoid factor, wrist

M06.031 Rheumatoid arthritis without rheumatoid factor, right wrist

M06.032 Rheumatoid arthritis without rheumatoid factor, left wrist

■ M06.039 Rheumatoid arthritis without rheumatoid factor, unspecified wrist

● M06.04 Rheumatoid arthritis without rheumatoid factor, hand

M06.041 Rheumatoid arthritis without rheumatoid factor, right hand

M06.042 Rheumatoid arthritis without rheumatoid factor, left hand

■ M06.049 Rheumatoid arthritis without rheumatoid factor, unspecified hand

● M06.05 Rheumatoid arthritis without rheumatoid factor, hip

M06.051 Rheumatoid arthritis without rheumatoid factor, right hip

M06.052 Rheumatoid arthritis without rheumatoid factor, left hip

■ M06.059 Rheumatoid arthritis without rheumatoid factor, unspecified hip

● M06.06 Rheumatoid arthritis without rheumatoid factor, knee

M06.061 Rheumatoid arthritis without rheumatoid factor, right knee

M06.062 Rheumatoid arthritis without rheumatoid factor, left knee

■ M06.069 Rheumatoid arthritis without rheumatoid factor, unspecified knee

● M06.07 Rheumatoid arthritis without rheumatoid factor, ankle and foot

M06.071 Rheumatoid arthritis without rheumatoid factor, right ankle and foot

M06.072 Rheumatoid arthritis without rheumatoid factor, left ankle and foot

■ M06.079 Rheumatoid arthritis without rheumatoid factor, unspecified ankle and foot

M06.08 Rheumatoid arthritis without rheumatoid factor, vertebrae

M06.09 Rheumatoid arthritis without rheumatoid factor, multiple sites

M06.1 Adult-onset Still's disease

> **Excludes1**   Still's disease NOS (M08.2-)

● M06.2 Rheumatoid bursitis

■ M06.20 Rheumatoid bursitis, unspecified site

● M06.21 Rheumatoid bursitis, shoulder

M06.211 Rheumatoid bursitis, right shoulder

M06.212 Rheumatoid bursitis, left shoulder

■ M06.219 Rheumatoid bursitis, unspecified shoulder

● M06.22 Rheumatoid bursitis, elbow

M06.221 Rheumatoid bursitis, right elbow

M06.222 Rheumatoid bursitis, left elbow

■ M06.229 Rheumatoid bursitis, unspecified elbow

● M06.23 Rheumatoid bursitis, wrist

M06.231 Rheumatoid bursitis, right wrist

M06.232 Rheumatoid bursitis, left wrist

■ M06.239 Rheumatoid bursitis, unspecified wrist

● M06.24 Rheumatoid bursitis, hand

M06.241 Rheumatoid bursitis, right hand

M06.242 Rheumatoid bursitis, left hand

■ M06.249 Rheumatoid bursitis, unspecified hand

● M06.25 Rheumatoid bursitis, hip

M06.251 Rheumatoid bursitis, right hip

M06.252 Rheumatoid bursitis, left hip

■ M06.259 Rheumatoid bursitis, unspecified hip

● Unacceptable First-Listed Diagnosis   ● Use Additional Character(s)   ■ Unspecified   **OGCR** Official Guidelines for Coding and Reporting

🗪 Complication\Comorbidity   🗪 Major C\C   Excludes 1   Excludes 2   Includes   Use additional   Code first   Code also

1135

● M06.26 Rheumatoid bursitis, knee

    M06.261 Rheumatoid bursitis, right knee

    M06.262 Rheumatoid bursitis, left knee

    ■ M06.269 Rheumatoid bursitis, unspecified knee

● M06.27 Rheumatoid bursitis, ankle and foot

    M06.271 Rheumatoid bursitis, right ankle and foot

    M06.272 Rheumatoid bursitis, left ankle and foot

    ■ M06.279 Rheumatoid bursitis, unspecified ankle and foot

  M06.28 Rheumatoid bursitis, vertebrae

  M06.29 Rheumatoid bursitis, multiple sites

● M06.3 Rheumatoid nodule

  ■ M06.30 Rheumatoid nodule, unspecified site

● M06.31 Rheumatoid nodule, shoulder

    M06.311 Rheumatoid nodule, right shoulder

    M06.312 Rheumatoid nodule, left shoulder

    ■ M06.319 Rheumatoid nodule, unspecified shoulder

● M06.32 Rheumatoid nodule, elbow

    M06.321 Rheumatoid nodule, right elbow

    M06.322 Rheumatoid nodule, left elbow

    ■ M06.329 Rheumatoid nodule, unspecified elbow

● M06.33 Rheumatoid nodule, wrist

    M06.331 Rheumatoid nodule, right wrist

    M06.332 Rheumatoid nodule, left wrist

    ■ M06.339 Rheumatoid nodule, unspecified wrist

● M06.34 Rheumatoid nodule, hand

    M06.341 Rheumatoid nodule, right hand

    M06.342 Rheumatoid nodule, left hand

    ■ M06.349 Rheumatoid nodule, unspecified hand

● M06.35 Rheumatoid nodule, hip

    M06.351 Rheumatoid nodule, right hip

    M06.352 Rheumatoid nodule, left hip

    ■ M06.359 Rheumatoid nodule, unspecified hip

● M06.36 Rheumatoid nodule, knee

    M06.361 Rheumatoid nodule, right knee

    M06.362 Rheumatoid nodule, left knee

    ■ M06.369 Rheumatoid nodule, unspecified knee

● M06.37 Rheumatoid nodule, ankle and foot

    M06.371 Rheumatoid nodule, right ankle and foot

    M06.372 Rheumatoid nodule, left ankle and foot

    ■ M06.379 Rheumatoid nodule, unspecified ankle and foot

  M06.38 Rheumatoid nodule, vertebrae

  M06.39 Rheumatoid nodule, multiple sites

M06.4 Inflammatory polyarthropathy

    Excludes1 polyarthritis NOS (M13.0)

● M06.8 Other specified rheumatoid arthritis

  ■ M06.80 Other specified rheumatoid arthritis, unspecified site

● M06.81 Other specified rheumatoid arthritis, shoulder

    M06.811 Other specified rheumatoid arthritis, right shoulder

    M06.812 Other specified rheumatoid arthritis, left shoulder

    ■ M06.819 Other specified rheumatoid arthritis, unspecified shoulder

● M06.82 Other specified rheumatoid arthritis, elbow

    M06.821 Other specified rheumatoid arthritis, right elbow

    M06.822 Other specified rheumatoid arthritis, left elbow

    ■ M06.829 Other specified rheumatoid arthritis, unspecified elbow

● M06.83 Other specified rheumatoid arthritis, wrist

    M06.831 Other specified rheumatoid arthritis, right wrist

    M06.832 Other specified rheumatoid arthritis, left wrist

    ■ M06.839 Other specified rheumatoid arthritis, unspecified wrist

● M06.84 Other specified rheumatoid arthritis, hand

    M06.841 Other specified rheumatoid arthritis, right hand

    M06.842 Other specified rheumatoid arthritis, left hand

    ■ M06.849 Other specified rheumatoid arthritis, unspecified hand

● M06.85 Other specified rheumatoid arthritis, hip

    M06.851 Other specified rheumatoid arthritis, right hip

    M06.852 Other specified rheumatoid arthritis, left hip

    ■ M06.859 Other specified rheumatoid arthritis, unspecified hip

● M06.86 Other specified rheumatoid arthritis, knee

    M06.861 Other specified rheumatoid arthritis, right knee

    M06.862 Other specified rheumatoid arthritis, left knee

    ■ M06.869 Other specified rheumatoid arthritis, unspecified knee

● M06.87 Other specified rheumatoid arthritis, ankle and foot

    M06.871 Other specified rheumatoid arthritis, right ankle and foot

    M06.872 Other specified rheumatoid arthritis, left ankle and foot

    ■ M06.879 Other specified rheumatoid arthritis, unspecified ankle and foot

  M06.88 Other specified rheumatoid arthritis, vertebrae

  M06.89 Other specified rheumatoid arthritis, multiple sites

■ M06.9 Rheumatoid arthritis, unspecified

● Unacceptable First-Listed Diagnosis   ● Use Additional Character(s)   ■ Unspecified   **OGCR** Official Guidelines for Coding and Reporting

🄲 Complication\Comorbidity   🄲 Major C\C   Excludes 1   Excludes 2   Includes   Use additional   Code first   Code also

● **M07 Enteropathic arthropathies**
    Code also associated enteropathy, such as:
      regional enteritis [Crohn's disease] (K50.-)
      ulcerative colitis (K51.-)
    Excludes1   psoriatic arthropathies (L40.5-)

● **M07.6 Enteropathic arthropathies**

  ◼ **M07.60**   Enteropathic arthropathies, unspecified site

  ● **M07.61**   Enteropathic arthropathies, shoulder

    M07.611   Enteropathic arthropathies, right shoulder

    M07.612   Enteropathic arthropathies, left shoulder

    ◼ **M07.619**   Enteropathic arthropathies, unspecified shoulder

  ● **M07.62**   Enteropathic arthropathies, elbow

    M07.621   Enteropathic arthropathies, right elbow

    M07.622   Enteropathic arthropathies, left elbow

    ◼ **M07.629**   Enteropathic arthropathies, unspecified elbow

  ● **M07.63**   Enteropathic arthropathies, wrist

    M07.631   Enteropathic arthropathies, right wrist

    M07.632   Enteropathic arthropathies, left wrist

    ◼ **M07.639**   Enteropathic arthropathies, unspecified wrist

  ● **M07.64**   Enteropathic arthropathies, hand

    M07.641   Enteropathic arthropathies, right hand

    M07.642   Enteropathic arthropathies, left hand

    ◼ **M07.649**   Enteropathic arthropathies, unspecified hand

  ● **M07.65**   Enteropathic arthropathies, hip

    M07.651   Enteropathic arthropathies, right hip

    M07.652   Enteropathic arthropathies, left hip

    ◼ **M07.659**   Enteropathic arthropathies, unspecified hip

  ● **M07.66**   Enteropathic arthropathies, knee

    M07.661   Enteropathic arthropathies, right knee

    M07.662   Enteropathic arthropathies, left knee

    ◼ **M07.669**   Enteropathic arthropathies, unspecified knee

  ● **M07.67**   Enteropathic arthropathies, ankle and foot

    M07.671   Enteropathic arthropathies, right ankle and foot

    M07.672   Enteropathic arthropathies, left ankle and foot

    ◼ **M07.679**   Enteropathic arthropathies, unspecified ankle and foot

    M07.68   Enteropathic arthropathies, vertebrae

    M07.69   Enteropathic arthropathies, multiple sites

● **M08 Juvenile arthritis**
    Code also any associated underlying condition, such as:
      regional enteritis [Crohn's disease] (K50.-)
      ulcerative colitis (K51.-)
    Excludes1   arthropathy in Whipple's disease (M14.8)
      Felty's syndrome (M05.0)
      juvenile dermatomyositis (M33.0-)
      psoriatic juvenile arthropathy (L40.54)

● **M08.0 Unspecified juvenile rheumatoid arthritis**
    Juvenile rheumatoid arthritis with or without rheumatoid factor

  ◼ **M08.00**   Unspecified juvenile rheumatoid arthritis of unspecified site

  ● **M08.01**   Unspecified juvenile rheumatoid arthritis, shoulder

    ◼ **M08.011**   Unspecified juvenile rheumatoid arthritis, right shoulder

    ◼ **M08.012**   Unspecified juvenile rheumatoid arthritis, left shoulder

    ◼ **M08.019**   Unspecified juvenile rheumatoid arthritis, unspecified shoulder

  ● **M08.02**   Unspecified juvenile rheumatoid arthritis of elbow

    ◼ **M08.021**   Unspecified juvenile rheumatoid arthritis, right elbow

    ◼ **M08.022**   Unspecified juvenile rheumatoid arthritis, left elbow

    ◼ **M08.029**   Unspecified juvenile rheumatoid arthritis, unspecified elbow

  ● **M08.03**   Unspecified juvenile rheumatoid arthritis, wrist

    ◼ **M08.031**   Unspecified juvenile rheumatoid arthritis, right wrist

    ◼ **M08.032**   Unspecified juvenile rheumatoid arthritis, left wrist

    ◼ **M08.039**   Unspecified juvenile rheumatoid arthritis, unspecified wrist

  ● **M08.04**   Unspecified juvenile rheumatoid arthritis, hand

    ◼ **M08.041**   Unspecified juvenile rheumatoid arthritis, right hand

    ◼ **M08.042**   Unspecified juvenile rheumatoid arthritis, left hand

    ◼ **M08.049**   Unspecified juvenile rheumatoid arthritis, unspecified hand

  ● **M08.05**   Unspecified juvenile rheumatoid arthritis, hip

    ◼ **M08.051**   Unspecified juvenile rheumatoid arthritis, right hip

    ◼ **M08.052**   Unspecified juvenile rheumatoid arthritis, left hip

    ◼ **M08.059**   Unspecified juvenile rheumatoid arthritis, unspecified hip

  ● **M08.06**   Unspecified juvenile rheumatoid arthritis, knee

    ◼ **M08.061**   Unspecified juvenile rheumatoid arthritis, right knee

    ◼ **M08.062**   Unspecified juvenile rheumatoid arthritis, left knee

    ◼ **M08.069**   Unspecified juvenile rheumatoid arthritis, unspecified knee

● Unacceptable First-Listed Diagnosis   ● Use Additional Character(s)   ◼ Unspecified   **OGCR** Official Guidelines for Coding and Reporting

 Complication\Comorbidity   Major C\C   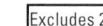Excludes 1   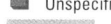Excludes 2   Includes   Use additional   Code first   Code also

1137

- **M08.07** Unspecified juvenile rheumatoid arthritis, ankle and foot
  - **M08.071** Unspecified juvenile rheumatoid arthritis, right ankle and foot
  - **M08.072** Unspecified juvenile rheumatoid arthritis, left ankle and foot
  - **M08.079** Unspecified juvenile rheumatoid arthritis, unspecified ankle and foot
- **M08.08** Unspecified juvenile rheumatoid arthritis, vertebrae
- **M08.09** Unspecified juvenile rheumatoid arthritis, multiple sites

M08.1 Juvenile ankylosing spondylitis

> **Excludes1**   ankylosing spondylitis in adults (M45.0-)

- **M08.2** Juvenile rheumatoid arthritis with systemic onset
  Still's disease NOS

  > **Excludes1**   adult-onset Still's disease (M06.1-)

  - **M08.20** Juvenile rheumatoid arthritis with systemic onset, unspecified site
  - **M08.21** Juvenile rheumatoid arthritis with systemic onset, shoulder
    - **M08.211** Juvenile rheumatoid arthritis with systemic onset, right shoulder
    - **M08.212** Juvenile rheumatoid arthritis with systemic onset, left shoulder
    - **M08.219** Juvenile rheumatoid arthritis with systemic onset, unspecified shoulder
  - **M08.22** Juvenile rheumatoid arthritis with systemic onset, elbow
    - **M08.221** Juvenile rheumatoid arthritis with systemic onset, right elbow
    - **M08.222** Juvenile rheumatoid arthritis with systemic onset, left elbow
    - **M08.229** Juvenile rheumatoid arthritis with systemic onset, unspecified elbow
  - **M08.23** Juvenile rheumatoid arthritis with systemic onset, wrist
    - **M08.231** Juvenile rheumatoid arthritis with systemic onset, right wrist
    - **M08.232** Juvenile rheumatoid arthritis with systemic onset, left wrist
    - **M08.239** Juvenile rheumatoid arthritis with systemic onset, unspecified wrist
  - **M08.24** Juvenile rheumatoid arthritis with systemic onset, hand
    - **M08.241** Juvenile rheumatoid arthritis with systemic onset, right hand
    - **M08.242** Juvenile rheumatoid arthritis with systemic onset, left hand
    - **M08.249** Juvenile rheumatoid arthritis with systemic onset, unspecified hand
  - **M08.25** Juvenile rheumatoid arthritis with systemic onset, hip
    - **M08.251** Juvenile rheumatoid arthritis with systemic onset, right hip

  - **M08.252** Juvenile rheumatoid arthritis with systemic onset, left hip
    - **M08.259** Juvenile rheumatoid arthritis with systemic onset, unspecified hip
  - **M08.26** Juvenile rheumatoid arthritis with systemic onset, knee
    - **M08.261** Juvenile rheumatoid arthritis with systemic onset, right knee
    - **M08.262** Juvenile rheumatoid arthritis with systemic onset, left knee
    - **M08.269** Juvenile rheumatoid arthritis with systemic onset, unspecified knee
  - **M08.27** Juvenile rheumatoid arthritis with systemic onset, ankle and foot
    - **M08.271** Juvenile rheumatoid arthritis with systemic onset, right ankle and foot
    - **M08.272** Juvenile rheumatoid arthritis with systemic onset, left ankle and foot
    - **M08.279** Juvenile rheumatoid arthritis with systemic onset, unspecified ankle and foot
  - **M08.28** Juvenile rheumatoid arthritis with systemic onset, vertebrae
  - **M08.29** Juvenile rheumatoid arthritis with systemic onset, multiple sites

M08.3 Juvenile rheumatoid polyarthritis (seronegative)

- **M08.4** Pauciarticular juvenile rheumatoid arthritis
  - **M08.40** Pauciarticular juvenile rheumatoid arthritis, unspecified site
  - **M08.41** Pauciarticular juvenile rheumatoid arthritis, shoulder
    - **M08.411** Pauciarticular juvenile rheumatoid arthritis, right shoulder
    - **M08.412** Pauciarticular juvenile rheumatoid arthritis, left shoulder
    - **M08.419** Pauciarticular juvenile rheumatoid arthritis, unspecified shoulder
  - **M08.42** Pauciarticular juvenile rheumatoid arthritis, elbow
    - **M08.421** Pauciarticular juvenile rheumatoid arthritis, right elbow
    - **M08.422** Pauciarticular juvenile rheumatoid arthritis, left elbow
    - **M08.429** Pauciarticular juvenile rheumatoid arthritis, unspecified elbow
  - **M08.43** Pauciarticular juvenile rheumatoid arthritis, wrist
    - **M08.431** Pauciarticular juvenile rheumatoid arthritis, right wrist
    - **M08.432** Pauciarticular juvenile rheumatoid arthritis, left wrist
    - **M08.439** Pauciarticular juvenile rheumatoid arthritis, unspecified wrist
  - **M08.44** Pauciarticular juvenile rheumatoid arthritis, hand
    - **M08.441** Pauciarticular juvenile rheumatoid arthritis, right hand

CHAPTER 13 (M00-M99)

M08.442 Pauciarticular juvenile rheumatoid arthritis, left hand

M08.449 Pauciarticular juvenile rheumatoid arthritis, unspecified hand

● M08.45 Pauciarticular juvenile rheumatoid arthritis, hip

M08.451 Pauciarticular juvenile rheumatoid arthritis, right hip

M08.452 Pauciarticular juvenile rheumatoid arthritis, left hip

M08.459 Pauciarticular juvenile rheumatoid arthritis, unspecified hip

● M08.46 Pauciarticular juvenile rheumatoid arthritis, knee

M08.461 Pauciarticular juvenile rheumatoid arthritis, right knee

M08.462 Pauciarticular juvenile rheumatoid arthritis, left knee

M08.469 Pauciarticular juvenile rheumatoid arthritis, unspecified knee

● M08.47 Pauciarticular juvenile rheumatoid arthritis, ankle and foot

M08.471 Pauciarticular juvenile rheumatoid arthritis, right ankle and foot

M08.472 Pauciarticular juvenile rheumatoid arthritis, left ankle and foot

M08.479 Pauciarticular juvenile rheumatoid arthritis, unspecified ankle and foot

M08.48 Pauciarticular juvenile rheumatoid arthritis, vertebrae

● M08.8 Other juvenile arthritis

M08.80 Other juvenile arthritis, unspecified site

● M08.81 Other juvenile arthritis, shoulder

M08.811 Other juvenile arthritis, right shoulder

M08.812 Other juvenile arthritis, left shoulder

M08.819 Other juvenile arthritis, unspecified shoulder

● M08.82 Other juvenile arthritis, elbow

M08.821 Other juvenile arthritis, right elbow

M08.822 Other juvenile arthritis, left elbow

M08.829 Other juvenile arthritis, unspecified elbow

● M08.83 Other juvenile arthritis, wrist

M08.831 Other juvenile arthritis, right wrist

M08.832 Other juvenile arthritis, left wrist

M08.839 Other juvenile arthritis, unspecified wrist

● M08.84 Other juvenile arthritis, hand

M08.841 Other juvenile arthritis, right hand

M08.842 Other juvenile arthritis, left hand

M08.849 Other juvenile arthritis, unspecified hand

● M08.85 Other juvenile arthritis, hip

M08.851 Other juvenile arthritis, right hip

M08.852 Other juvenile arthritis, left hip

M08.859 Other juvenile arthritis, unspecified hip

● M08.86 Other juvenile arthritis, knee

M08.861 Other juvenile arthritis, right knee

M08.862 Other juvenile arthritis, left knee

M08.869 Other juvenile arthritis, unspecified knee

● M08.87 Other juvenile arthritis, ankle and foot

M08.871 Other juvenile arthritis, right ankle and foot

M08.872 Other juvenile arthritis, left ankle and foot

M08.879 Other juvenile arthritis, unspecified ankle and foot

M08.88 Other juvenile arthritis, vertebrae

M08.89 Other juvenile arthritis, multiple sites

● M08.9 Juvenile arthritis, unspecified

Excludes1   juvenile rheumatoid arthritis, unspecified (M08.0-)

M08.90 Juvenile arthritis, unspecified, unspecified site

● M08.91 Juvenile arthritis, unspecified, shoulder

M08.911 Juvenile arthritis, unspecified, right shoulder

M08.912 Juvenile arthritis, unspecified, left shoulder

M08.919 Juvenile arthritis, unspecified, unspecified shoulder

● M08.92 Juvenile arthritis, unspecified, elbow

M08.921 Juvenile arthritis, unspecified, right elbow

M08.922 Juvenile arthritis, unspecified, left elbow

M08.929 Juvenile arthritis, unspecified, unspecified elbow

● M08.93 Juvenile arthritis, unspecified, wrist

M08.931 Juvenile arthritis, unspecified, right wrist

M08.932 Juvenile arthritis, unspecified, left wrist

M08.939 Juvenile arthritis, unspecified, unspecified wrist

● M08.94 Juvenile arthritis, unspecified, hand

M08.941 Juvenile arthritis, unspecified, right hand

M08.942 Juvenile arthritis, unspecified, left hand

M08.949 Juvenile arthritis, unspecified, unspecified hand

● M08.95 Juvenile arthritis, unspecified, hip

M08.951 Juvenile arthritis, unspecified, right hip

M08.952 Juvenile arthritis, unspecified, left hip

M08.959 Juvenile arthritis, unspecified, unspecified hip

● M08.96 Juvenile arthritis, unspecified, knee

M08.961 Juvenile arthritis, unspecified, right knee

M08.962 Juvenile arthritis, unspecified, left knee

● Unacceptable First-Listed Diagnosis   ● Use Additional Character(s)   Unspecified   OGCR Official Guidelines for Coding and Reporting   Complication\Comorbidity   Major C\C   Excludes 1   Excludes 2   Includes   Use additional   Code first   Code also   1139

CHAPTER 13 (M00-M99)

       M08.969 Juvenile arthritis, unspecified, unspecified knee

● M08.97 Juvenile arthritis, unspecified, ankle and foot

       M08.971 Juvenile arthritis, unspecified, right ankle and foot

       M08.972 Juvenile arthritis, unspecified, left ankle and foot

       M08.979 Juvenile arthritis, unspecified, unspecified ankle and foot

■ M08.98 Juvenile arthritis, unspecified, vertebrae

■ M08.99 Juvenile arthritis, unspecified, multiple sites

● **M1a**   **Chronic gout**

     Use additional code to identify:

       Autonomic neuropathy in diseases classified elsewhere (G99.0)

       Calculus of urinary tract in diseases classified elsewhere (N22)

       Cardiomyopathy in diseases classified elsewhere (I43)

       Disorders of external ear in diseases classified elsewhere (H61.1-, H62.8-)

       Disorders of iris and ciliary body in diseases classified elsewhere (H22)

       Glomerular disorders in diseases classified elsewhere (N08)

> The appropriate 7th character is to be added to each code from category M1a
> 0   without tophus (tophi)
> 1   with tophus (tophi)

Excludes1   acute gout (M10-)
           gout NOS (M10.-)

● **M1a.0 Idiopathic chronic gout**
     Chronic gouty bursitis
     Primary chronic gout

■ M1a.00 Idiopathic chronic gout, unspecified site

● M1a.01 Idiopathic chronic gout, shoulder

       M1a.011 Idiopathic chronic gout, right shoulder

       M1a.012 Idiopathic chronic gout, left shoulder

       M1a.019 Idiopathic chronic gout, unspecified shoulder

● M1a.02 Idiopathic chronic gout, elbow

       M1a.021 Idiopathic chronic gout, right elbow

       M1a.022 Idiopathic chronic gout, left elbow

       M1a.029 Idiopathic chronic gout, unspecified elbow

● M1a.03 Idiopathic chronic gout, wrist

       M1a.031 Idiopathic chronic gout, right wrist

       M1a.032 Idiopathic chronic gout, left wrist

       M1a.039 Idiopathic chronic gout, unspecified wrist

● M1a.04 Idiopathic chronic gout, hand

       M1a.041 Idiopathic chronic gout, right hand

       M1a.042 Idiopathic chronic gout, left hand

       M1a.049 Idiopathic chronic gout, unspecified hand

● M1a.05 Idiopathic chronic gout, hip

       M1a.051 Idiopathic chronic gout, right hip

       M1a.052 Idiopathic chronic gout, left hip

       M1a.059 Idiopathic chronic gout, unspecified hip

● M1a.06 Idiopathic chronic gout, knee

       M1a.061 Idiopathic chronic gout, right knee

       M1a.062 Idiopathic chronic gout, left knee

       M1a.069 Idiopathic chronic gout, unspecified knee

● M1a.07 Idiopathic chronic gout, ankle and foot

       M1a.071 Idiopathic chronic gout, right ankle and foot

       M1a.072 Idiopathic chronic gout, left ankle and foot

       M1a.079 Idiopathic chronic gout, unspecified ankle and foot

     M1a.08 Idiopathic chronic gout, vertebrae

     M1a.09 Idiopathic chronic gout, multiple sites

M1a.1 Lead-induced chronic gout
     Code first toxic effects of lead and its compounds (T56.0-)

■ M1a.10 Lead-induced chronic gout, unspecified site

● M1a.11 Lead-induced chronic gout, shoulder

       M1a.111 Lead-induced chronic gout, right shoulder

       M1a.112 Lead-induced chronic gout, left shoulder

       M1a.119 Lead-induced chronic gout, unspecified shoulder

● M1a.12 Lead-induced chronic gout, elbow

       M1a.121 Lead-induced chronic gout, right elbow

       M1a.122 Lead-induced chronic gout, left elbow

       M1a.129 Lead-induced chronic gout, unspecified elbow

● M1a.13 Lead-induced chronic gout, wrist

       M1a.131 Lead-induced chronic gout, right wrist

       M1a.132 Lead-induced chronic gout, left wrist

       M1a.139 Lead-induced chronic gout, unspecified wrist

● M1a.14 Lead-induced chronic gout, hand

       M1a.141 Lead-induced chronic gout, right hand

       M1a.142 Lead-induced chronic gout, left hand

       M1a.149 Lead-induced chronic gout, unspecified hand

● M1a.15 Lead-induced chronic gout, hip

       M1a.151 Lead-induced chronic gout, right hip

       M1a.152 Lead-induced chronic gout, left hip

       M1a.159 Lead-induced chronic gout, unspecified hip

● M1a.16 Lead-induced chronic gout, knee

       M1a.161 Lead-induced chronic gout, right knee

M1a.162   Lead-induced chronic gout, left knee

M1a.169   Lead-induced chronic gout, unspecified knee

● M1a.17   Lead-induced chronic gout, ankle and foot

M1a.171   Lead-induced chronic gout, right ankle and foot

M1a.172   Lead-induced chronic gout, left ankle and foot

M1a.179   Lead-induced chronic gout, unspecified ankle and foot

M1a.18   Lead-induced chronic gout, vertebrae

M1a.19   Lead-induced chronic gout, multiple sites

● M1a.2   Drug-induced chronic gout
Code first (T36-T50) to identify drug

M1a.20   Drug-induced chronic gout, unspecified site

● M1a.21   Drug-induced chronic gout, shoulder

M1a.211   Drug-induced chronic gout, right shoulder

M1a.212   Drug-induced chronic gout, left shoulder

M1a.219   Drug-induced chronic gout, unspecified shoulder

● M1a.22   Drug-induced chronic gout, elbow

M1a.221   Drug-induced chronic gout, right elbow

M1a.222   Drug-induced chronic gout, left elbow

M1a.229   Drug-induced chronic gout, unspecified elbow

● M1a.23   Drug-induced chronic gout, wrist

M1a.231   Drug-induced chronic gout, right wrist

M1a.232   Drug-induced chronic gout, left wrist

M1a.239   Drug-induced chronic gout, unspecified wrist

● M1a.24   Drug-induced chronic gout, hand

M1a.241   Drug-induced chronic gout, right hand

M1a.242   Drug-induced chronic gout, left hand

M1a.249   Drug-induced chronic gout, unspecified hand

● M1a.25   Drug-induced chronic gout, hip

M1a.251   Drug-induced chronic gout, right hip

M1a.252   Drug-induced chronic gout, left hip

M1a.259   Drug-induced chronic gout, unspecified hip

● M1a.26   Drug-induced chronic gout, knee

M1a.261   Drug-induced chronic gout, right knee

M1a.262   Drug-induced chronic gout, left knee

M1a.269   Drug-induced chronic gout, unspecified knee

● M1a.27   Drug-induced chronic gout, ankle and foot

M1a.271   Drug-induced chronic gout, right ankle and foot

M1a.272   Drug-induced chronic gout, left ankle and foot

M1a.279   Drug-induced chronic gout, unspecified ankle and foot

M1a.28   Drug-induced chronic gout, vertebrae

M1a.29   Drug-induced chronic gout, multiple sites

● M1a.3   Chronic gout due to renal impairment
Code first associated renal disease

M1a.30   Chronic gout due to renal impairment, unspecified site

● M1a.31   Chronic gout due to renal impairment, shoulder

M1a.311   Chronic gout due to renal impairment, right shoulder

M1a.312   Chronic gout due to renal impairment, left shoulder

M1a.319   Chronic gout due to renal impairment, unspecified shoulder

● M1a.32   Chronic gout due to renal impairment, elbow

M1a.321   Chronic gout due to renal impairment, right elbow

M1a.322   Chronic gout due to renal impairment, left elbow

M1a.329   Chronic gout due to renal impairment, unspecified elbow

M1a.33   Chronic gout due to renal impairment, wrist

M1a.331   Chronic gout due to renal impairment, right wrist

M1a.332   Chronic gout due to renal impairment, left wrist

M1a.339   Chronic gout due to renal impairment, unspecified wrist

● M1a.34   Chronic gout due to renal impairment, hand

M1a.341   Chronic gout due to renal impairment, right hand

M1a.342   Chronic gout due to renal impairment, left hand

M1a.349   Chronic gout due to renal impairment, unspecified hand

● M1a.35   Chronic gout due to renal impairment, hip

M1a.351   Chronic gout due to renal impairment, right hip

M1a.352   Chronic gout due to renal impairment, left hip

M1a.359   Chronic gout due to renal impairment, unspecified hip

● M1a.36   Chronic gout due to renal impairment, knee

M1a.361   Chronic gout due to renal impairment, right knee

M1a.362   Chronic gout due to renal impairment, left knee

M1a.369   Chronic gout due to renal impairment, unspecified knee

● M1a.37   Chronic gout due to renal impairment, ankle and foot

M1a.371   Chronic gout due to renal impairment, right ankle and foot

M1a.372   Chronic gout due to renal impairment, left ankle and foot

M1a.379   Chronic gout due to renal impairment, unspecified ankle and foot

● Unacceptable First-Listed Diagnosis   ● Use Additional Character(s)   ■ Unspecified   **OGCR** Official Guidelines for Coding and Reporting

🗣 Complication\Comorbidity   🗣 Major C\C         Use additional   Code first   Code also

1141

CHAPTER 13 (M00-M99)

M1a.38 Chronic gout due to renal impairment, vertebrae

M1a.39 Chronic gout due to renal impairment, multiple sites

● M1a.4 Other secondary chronic gout
Code first associated condition

◼ M1a.40 Other secondary chronic gout, unspecified site

● M1a.41 Other secondary chronic gout, shoulder

M1a.411 Other secondary chronic gout, right shoulder

M1a.412 Other secondary chronic gout, left shoulder

◼ M1a.419 Other secondary chronic gout, unspecified shoulder

● M1a.42 Other secondary chronic gout, elbow

M1a.421 Other secondary chronic gout, right elbow

M1a.422 Other secondary chronic gout, left elbow

◼ M1a.429 Other secondary chronic gout, unspecified elbow

● M1a.43 Other secondary chronic gout, wrist

M1a.431 Other secondary chronic gout, right wrist

M1a.432 Other secondary chronic gout, left wrist

◼ M1a.439 Other secondary chronic gout, unspecified wrist

● M1a.44 Other secondary chronic gout, hand

M1a.441 Other secondary chronic gout, right hand

M1a.442 Other secondary chronic gout, left hand

◼ M1a.449 Other secondary chronic gout, unspecified hand

● M1a.45 Other secondary chronic gout, hip

M1a.451 Other secondary chronic gout, right hip

M1a.452 Other secondary chronic gout, left hip

◼ M1a.459 Other secondary chronic gout, unspecified hip

● M1a.46 Other secondary chronic gout, knee

M1a.461 Other secondary chronic gout, right knee

M1a.462 Other secondary chronic gout, left knee

◼ M1a.469 Other secondary chronic gout, unspecified knee

● M1a.47 Other secondary chronic gout, ankle and foot

M1a.471 Other secondary chronic gout, right ankle and foot

M1a.472 Other secondary chronic gout, left ankle and foot

◼ M1a.479 Other secondary chronic gout, unspecified ankle and foot

M1a.48 Other secondary chronic gout, vertebrae

M1a.49 Other secondary chronic gout, multiple sites

● M1a.9 Chronic gout, unspecified

● M10 Gout
Accumulation of uric acid that results in swollen, red, hot, painful, stiff joints.
Acute gout
Gout attack
Gout flare
Gout NOS
Podagra

Use additional code to identify:
Autonomic neuropathy in diseases classified elsewhere (G99.0)
Calculus of urinary tract in diseases classified elsewhere (N22)
Cardiomyopathy in diseases classified elsewhere (I43)
Disorders of external ear in diseases classified elsewhere (H61.1-, H62.8-)
Disorders of iris and ciliary body in diseases classified elsewhere (H22)
Glomerular disorders in diseases classified elsewhere (N08)

Excludes1 chronic gout (M1a-)

● M10.0 Idiopathic gout
Gouty bursitis
Primary gout

◼ M10.00 Idiopathic gout, unspecified site

● M10.01 Idiopathic gout, shoulder

M10.011 Idiopathic gout, right shoulder

M10.012 Idiopathic gout, left shoulder

◼ M10.019 Idiopathic gout, unspecified shoulder

● M10.02 Idiopathic gout, elbow

M10.021 Idiopathic gout, right elbow

M10.022 Idiopathic gout, left elbow

◼ M10.029 Idiopathic gout, unspecified elbow

● M10.03 Idiopathic gout, wrist

M10.031 Idiopathic gout, right wrist

M10.032 Idiopathic gout, left wrist

◼ M10.039 Idiopathic gout, unspecified wrist

● M10.04 Idiopathic gout, hand

M10.041 Idiopathic gout, right hand

M10.042 Idiopathic gout, left hand

◼ M10.049 Idiopathic gout, unspecified hand

● M10.05 Idiopathic gout, hip

M10.051 Idiopathic gout, right hip

M10.052 Idiopathic gout, left hip

◼ M10.059 Idiopathic gout, unspecified hip

● M10.06 Idiopathic gout, knee

M10.061 Idiopathic gout, right knee

M10.062 Idiopathic gout, left knee

◼ M10.069 Idiopathic gout, unspecified knee

● M10.07 Idiopathic gout, ankle and foot

M10.071 Idiopathic gout, right ankle and foot

M10.072 Idiopathic gout, left ankle and foot

◼ M10.079 Idiopathic gout, unspecified ankle and foot

M10.08 Idiopathic gout, vertebrae

M10.09 Idiopathic gout, multiple sites

● M10.1 Lead-induced gout
   Code first toxic effects of lead and its compounds (T56.0-)
▪ M10.10 Lead-induced gout, unspecified site
● M10.11 Lead-induced gout, shoulder
   M10.111 Lead-induced gout, right shoulder
   M10.112 Lead-induced gout, left shoulder
   ▪ M10.119 Lead-induced gout, unspecified shoulder
● M10.12 Lead-induced gout, elbow
   M10.121 Lead-induced gout, right elbow
   M10.122 Lead-induced gout, left elbow
   ▪ M10.129 Lead-induced gout, unspecified elbow
● M10.13 Lead-induced gout, wrist
   M10.131 Lead-induced gout, right wrist
   M10.132 Lead-induced gout, left wrist
   ▪ M10.139 Lead-induced gout, unspecified wrist
● M10.14 Lead-induced gout, hand
   M10.141 Lead-induced gout, right hand
   M10.142 Lead-induced gout, left hand
   ▪ M10.149 Lead-induced gout, unspecified hand
● M10.15 Lead-induced gout, hip
   M10.151 Lead-induced gout, right hip
   M10.152 Lead-induced gout, left hip
   ▪ M10.159 Lead-induced gout, unspecified hip
● M10.16 Lead-induced gout, knee
   M10.161 Lead-induced gout, right knee
   M10.162 Lead-induced gout, left knee
   ▪ M10.169 Lead-induced gout, unspecified knee
● M10.17 Lead-induced gout, ankle and foot
   M10.171 Lead-induced gout, right ankle and foot
   M10.172 Lead-induced gout, left ankle and foot
   ▪ M10.179 Lead-induced gout, unspecified ankle and foot
   M10.18 Lead-induced gout, vertebrae
   M10.19 Lead-induced gout, multiple sites
● M10.2 Drug-induced gout
   Code first (T36-T50) to identify drug
● ▪ M10.20 Drug-induced gout, unspecified site
● M10.21 Drug-induced gout, shoulder
   ● M10.211 Drug-induced gout, right shoulder
   ● M10.212 Drug-induced gout, left shoulder
   ● ▪ M10.219 Drug-induced gout, unspecified shoulder
● M10.22 Drug-induced gout, elbow
   ● M10.221 Drug-induced gout, right elbow
   ● M10.222 Drug-induced gout, left elbow
   ● ▪ M10.229 Drug-induced gout, unspecified elbow
● M10.23 Drug-induced gout, wrist
   ● M10.231 Drug-induced gout, right wrist
   ● M10.232 Drug-induced gout, left wrist

● ▪ M10.239 Drug-induced gout, unspecified wrist
● M10.24 Drug-induced gout, hand
   ● M10.241 Drug-induced gout, right hand
   ● M10.242 Drug-induced gout, left hand
   ● ▪ M10.249 Drug-induced gout, unspecified hand
● M10.25 Drug-induced gout, hip
   ● M10.251 Drug-induced gout, right hip
   ● M10.252 Drug-induced gout, left hip
   ● ▪ M10.259 Drug-induced gout, unspecified hip
● M10.26 Drug-induced gout, knee
   ● M10.261 Drug-induced gout, right knee
   ● M10.262 Drug-induced gout, left knee
   ● ▪ M10.269 Drug-induced gout, unspecified knee
● M10.27 Drug-induced gout, ankle and foot
   ● M10.271 Drug-induced gout, right ankle and foot
   ● M10.272 Drug-induced gout, left ankle and foot
   ● ▪ M10.279 Drug-induced gout, unspecified ankle and foot
● M10.28 Drug-induced gout, vertebrae
● M10.29 Drug-induced gout, multiple sites
● M10.3 Gout due to renal impairment
   Code also associated renal disease
▪ M10.30 Gout due to renal impairment, unspecified site
● M10.31 Gout due to renal impairment, shoulder
   M10.311 Gout due to renal impairment, right shoulder
   M10.312 Gout due to renal impairment, left shoulder
   ▪ M10.319 Gout due to renal impairment, unspecified shoulder
● M10.32 Gout due to renal impairment, elbow
   M10.321 Gout due to renal impairment, right elbow
   M10.322 Gout due to renal impairment, left elbow
   ▪ M10.329 Gout due to renal impairment, unspecified elbow
● M10.33 Gout due to renal impairment, wrist
   M10.331 Gout due to renal impairment, right wrist
   M10.332 Gout due to renal impairment, left wrist
   ▪ M10.339 Gout due to renal impairment, unspecified wrist
● M10.34 Gout due to renal impairment, hand
   M10.341 Gout due to renal impairment, right hand
   M10.342 Gout due to renal impairment, left hand
   ▪ M10.349 Gout due to renal impairment, unspecified hand
● M10.35 Gout due to renal impairment, hip
   M10.351 Gout due to renal impairment, right hip

● Unacceptable First-Listed Diagnosis   ● Use Additional Character(s)   ▪ Unspecified   **OGCR** Official Guidelines for Coding and Reporting
🗲 Complication\Comorbidity   🗲 Major C\C   Excludes 1   Excludes 2   Includes   Use additional   Code first   Code also
1143

CHAPTER 13 (M00-M99)

M10.352 Gout due to renal impairment, left hip

M10.359 Gout due to renal impairment, unspecified hip

M10.36 Gout due to renal impairment, knee

M10.361 Gout due to renal impairment, right knee

M10.362 Gout due to renal impairment, left knee

M10.369 Gout due to renal impairment, unspecified knee

M10.37 Gout due to renal impairment, ankle and foot

M10.371 Gout due to renal impairment, right ankle and foot

M10.372 Gout due to renal impairment, left ankle and foot

M10.379 Gout due to renal impairment, unspecified ankle and foot

M10.38 Gout due to renal impairment, vertebrae

M10.39 Gout due to renal impairment, multiple sites

M10.4 Other secondary gout

Code first associated condition

M10.40 Other secondary gout, unspecified site

M10.41 Other secondary gout, shoulder

M10.411 Other secondary gout, right shoulder

M10.412 Other secondary gout, left shoulder

M10.419 Other secondary gout, unspecified shoulder

M10.42 Other secondary gout, elbow

M10.421 Other secondary gout, right elbow

M10.422 Other secondary gout, left elbow

M10.429 Other secondary gout, unspecified elbow

M10.43 Other secondary gout, wrist

M10.431 Other secondary gout, right wrist

M10.432 Other secondary gout, left wrist

M10.439 Other secondary gout, unspecified wrist

M10.44 Other secondary gout, hand

M10.441 Other secondary gout, right hand

M10.442 Other secondary gout, left hand

M10.449 Other secondary gout, unspecified hand

M10.45 Other secondary gout, hip

M10.451 Other secondary gout, right hip

M10.452 Other secondary gout, left hip

M10.459 Other secondary gout, unspecified hip

M10.46 Other secondary gout, knee

M10.461 Other secondary gout, right knee

M10.462 Other secondary gout, left knee

M10.469 Other secondary gout, unspecified knee

M10.47 Other secondary gout, ankle and foot

M10.471 Other secondary gout, right ankle and foot

M10.472 Other secondary gout, left ankle and foot

M10.479 Other secondary gout, unspecified ankle and foot

M10.48 Other secondary gout, vertebrae

M10.49 Other secondary gout, multiple sites

M10.9 Gout, unspecified
Gout NOS

M11 Other crystal arthropathies

M11.0 Hydroxyapatite deposition disease

M11.00 Hydroxyapatite deposition disease, unspecified site

M11.01 Hydroxyapatite deposition disease, shoulder

M11.011 Hydroxyapatite deposition disease, right shoulder

M11.012 Hydroxyapatite deposition disease, left shoulder

M11.019 Hydroxyapatite deposition disease, unspecified shoulder

M11.02 Hydroxyapatite deposition disease, elbow

M11.021 Hydroxyapatite deposition disease, right elbow

M11.022 Hydroxyapatite deposition disease, left elbow

M11.029 Hydroxyapatite deposition disease, unspecified elbow

M11.03 Hydroxyapatite deposition disease, wrist

M11.031 Hydroxyapatite deposition disease, right wrist

M11.032 Hydroxyapatite deposition disease, left wrist

M11.039 Hydroxyapatite deposition disease, unspecified wrist

M11.04 Hydroxyapatite deposition disease, hand

M11.041 Hydroxyapatite deposition disease, right hand

M11.042 Hydroxyapatite deposition disease, left hand

M11.049 Hydroxyapatite deposition disease, unspecified hand

M11.05 Hydroxyapatite deposition disease, hip

M11.051 Hydroxyapatite deposition disease, right hip

M11.052 Hydroxyapatite deposition disease, left hip

M11.059 Hydroxyapatite deposition disease, unspecified hip

M11.06 Hydroxyapatite deposition disease, knee

M11.061 Hydroxyapatite deposition disease, right knee

M11.062 Hydroxyapatite deposition disease, left knee

M11.069 Hydroxyapatite deposition disease, unspecified knee

M11.07 Hydroxyapatite deposition disease, ankle and foot

M11.071 Hydroxyapatite deposition disease, right ankle and foot

M11.072 Hydroxyapatite deposition disease, left ankle and foot

M11.079 Hydroxyapatite deposition disease, unspecified ankle and foot

● Unacceptable First-Listed Diagnosis   ● Use Additional Character(s)   ▣ Unspecified   **OGCR** Official Guidelines for Coding and Reporting
🔗 Complication\Comorbidity   🔗 Major C\C   Excludes 1   Excludes 2   Includes   Use additional   Code first   Code also

M11.08 Hydroxyapatite deposition disease, vertebrae

M11.09 Hydroxyapatite deposition disease, multiple sites

● M11.1 Familial chondrocalcinosis

◼ M11.10 Familial chondrocalcinosis, unspecified site

● M11.11 Familial chondrocalcinosis, shoulder

M11.111 Familial chondrocalcinosis, right shoulder

M11.112 Familial chondrocalcinosis, left shoulder

◼ M11.119 Familial chondrocalcinosis, unspecified shoulder

● M11.12 Familial chondrocalcinosis, elbow

M11.121 Familial chondrocalcinosis, right elbow

M11.122 Familial chondrocalcinosis, left elbow

◼ M11.129 Familial chondrocalcinosis, unspecified elbow

● M11.13 Familial chondrocalcinosis, wrist

M11.131 Familial chondrocalcinosis, right wrist

M11.132 Familial chondrocalcinosis, left wrist

◼ M11.139 Familial chondrocalcinosis, unspecified wrist

● M11.14 Familial chondrocalcinosis, hand

M11.141 Familial chondrocalcinosis, right hand

M11.142 Familial chondrocalcinosis, left hand

◼ M11.149 Familial chondrocalcinosis, unspecified hand

● M11.15 Familial chondrocalcinosis, hip

M11.151 Familial chondrocalcinosis, right hip

M11.152 Familial chondrocalcinosis, left hip

◼ M11.159 Familial chondrocalcinosis, unspecified hip

● M11.16 Familial chondrocalcinosis, knee

M11.161 Familial chondrocalcinosis, right knee

M11.162 Familial chondrocalcinosis, left knee

◼ M11.169 Familial chondrocalcinosis, unspecified knee

● M11.17 Familial chondrocalcinosis, ankle and foot

M11.171 Familial chondrocalcinosis, right ankle and foot

M11.172 Familial chondrocalcinosis, left ankle and foot

◼ M11.179 Familial chondrocalcinosis, unspecified ankle and foot

M11.18 Familial chondrocalcinosis, vertebrae

M11.19 Familial chondrocalcinosis, multiple sites

● M11.2 Other chondrocalcinosis
Chondrocalcinosis NOS

◼ M11.20 Other chondrocalcinosis, unspecified site

● M11.21 Other chondrocalcinosis, shoulder

M11.211 Other chondrocalcinosis, right shoulder

M11.212 Other chondrocalcinosis, left shoulder

◼ M11.219 Other chondrocalcinosis, unspecified shoulder

● M11.22 Other chondrocalcinosis, elbow

M11.221 Other chondrocalcinosis, right elbow

M11.222 Other chondrocalcinosis, left elbow

◼ M11.229 Other chondrocalcinosis, unspecified elbow

● M11.23 Other chondrocalcinosis, wrist

M11.231 Other chondrocalcinosis, right wrist

M11.232 Other chondrocalcinosis, left wrist

◼ M11.239 Other chondrocalcinosis, unspecified wrist

● M11.24 Other chondrocalcinosis, hand

M11.241 Other chondrocalcinosis, right hand

M11.242 Other chondrocalcinosis, left hand

◼ M11.249 Other chondrocalcinosis, unspecified hand

● M11.25 Other chondrocalcinosis, hip

M11.251 Other chondrocalcinosis, right hip

M11.252 Other chondrocalcinosis, left hip

◼ M11.259 Other chondrocalcinosis, unspecified hip

● M11.26 Other chondrocalcinosis, knee

M11.261 Other chondrocalcinosis, right knee

M11.262 Other chondrocalcinosis, left knee

◼ M11.269 Other chondrocalcinosis, unspecified knee

● M11.27 Other chondrocalcinosis, ankle and foot

M11.271 Other chondrocalcinosis, right ankle and foot

M11.272 Other chondrocalcinosis, left ankle and foot

◼ M11.279 Other chondrocalcinosis, unspecified ankle and foot

M11.28 Other chondrocalcinosis, vertebrae

M11.29 Other chondrocalcinosis, multiple sites

● M11.8 Other specified crystal arthropathies

◼ M11.80 Other specified crystal arthropathies, unspecified site

● M11.81 Other specified crystal arthropathies, shoulder

M11.811 Other specified crystal arthropathies, right shoulder

M11.812 Other specified crystal arthropathies, left shoulder

◼ M11.819 Other specified crystal arthropathies, unspecified shoulder

● Unacceptable First-Listed Diagnosis   ● Use Additional Character(s)   ◼ Unspecified   **OGCR** Official Guidelines for Coding and Reporting

 Complication\Comorbidity   Major C\C   Excludes 1   Excludes 2   Includes   Use additional   Code first   Code also

1145

● **M11.82** Other specified crystal arthropathies, elbow

    M11.821 Other specified crystal arthropathies, right elbow

    M11.822 Other specified crystal arthropathies, left elbow

    ■**M11.829** Other specified crystal arthropathies, unspecified elbow

● **M11.83** Other specified crystal arthropathies, wrist

    M11.831 Other specified crystal arthropathies, right wrist

    M11.832 Other specified crystal arthropathies, left wrist

    ■**M11.839** Other specified crystal arthropathies, unspecified wrist

● **M11.84** Other specified crystal arthropathies, hand

    M11.841 Other specified crystal arthropathies, right hand

    M11.842 Other specified crystal arthropathies, left hand

    ■**M11.849** Other specified crystal arthropathies, unspecified hand

● **M11.85** Other specified crystal arthropathies, hip

    M11.851 Other specified crystal arthropathies, right hip

    M11.852 Other specified crystal arthropathies, left hip

    ■**M11.859** Other specified crystal arthropathies, unspecified hip

● **M11.86** Other specified crystal arthropathies, knee

    M11.861 Other specified crystal arthropathies, right knee

    M11.862 Other specified crystal arthropathies, left knee

    ■**M11.869** Other specified crystal arthropathies, unspecified knee

● **M11.87** Other specified crystal arthropathies, ankle and foot

    M11.871 Other specified crystal arthropathies, right ankle and foot

    M11.872 Other specified crystal arthropathies, left ankle and foot

    ■**M11.879** Other specified crystal arthropathies, unspecified ankle and foot

    M11.88 Other specified crystal arthropathies, vertebrae

    M11.89 Other specified crystal arthropathies, multiple sites

■**M11.9** Crystal arthropathy, unspecified

● **M12** Other and unspecified arthropathy

    Excludes1   arthrosis (M15-M19)
                 cricoarytenoid arthropathy (J38.7)

● **M12.0** Chronic postrheumatic arthropathy [Jaccoud]

    ■**M12.00** Chronic postrheumatic arthropathy [Jaccoud], unspecified site

    ● **M12.01** Chronic postrheumatic arthropathy [Jaccoud], shoulder

        M12.011 Chronic postrheumatic arthropathy [Jaccoud], right shoulder

        M12.012 Chronic postrheumatic arthropathy [Jaccoud], left shoulder

        ■**M12.019** Chronic postrheumatic arthropathy [Jaccoud], unspecified shoulder

● **M12.02** Chronic postrheumatic arthropathy [Jaccoud], elbow

    M12.021 Chronic postrheumatic arthropathy [Jaccoud], right elbow

    M12.022 Chronic postrheumatic arthropathy [Jaccoud], left elbow

    ■**M12.029** Chronic postrheumatic arthropathy [Jaccoud], unspecified elbow

● **M12.03** Chronic postrheumatic arthropathy [Jaccoud], wrist

    M12.031 Chronic postrheumatic arthropathy [Jaccoud], right wrist

    M12.032 Chronic postrheumatic arthropathy [Jaccoud], left wrist

    ■**M12.039** Chronic postrheumatic arthropathy [Jaccoud], unspecified wrist

● **M12.04** Chronic postrheumatic arthropathy [Jaccoud], hand

    M12.041 Chronic postrheumatic arthropathy [Jaccoud], right hand

    M12.042 Chronic postrheumatic arthropathy [Jaccoud], left hand

    ■**M12.049** Chronic postrheumatic arthropathy [Jaccoud], unspecified hand

● **M12.05** Chronic postrheumatic arthropathy [Jaccoud], hip

    M12.051 Chronic postrheumatic arthropathy [Jaccoud], right hip

    M12.052 Chronic postrheumatic arthropathy [Jaccoud], left hip

    ■**M12.059** Chronic postrheumatic arthropathy [Jaccoud], unspecified hip

● **M12.06** Chronic postrheumatic arthropathy [Jaccoud], knee

    M12.061 Chronic postrheumatic arthropathy [Jaccoud], right knee

    M12.062 Chronic postrheumatic arthropathy [Jaccoud], left knee

    ■**M12.069** Chronic postrheumatic arthropathy [Jaccoud], unspecified knee

● **M12.07** Chronic postrheumatic arthropathy [Jaccoud], ankle and foot

    M12.071 Chronic postrheumatic arthropathy [Jaccoud], right ankle and foot

    M12.072 Chronic postrheumatic arthropathy [Jaccoud], left ankle and foot

    ■**M12.079** Chronic postrheumatic arthropathy [Jaccoud], unspecified ankle and foot

    M12.08 Chronic postrheumatic arthropathy [Jaccoud], vertebrae

● Unacceptable First-Listed Diagnosis   ● Use Additional Character(s)   ■ Unspecified   **OGCR** Official Guidelines for Coding and Reporting

🏷 Complication\Comorbidity   🏷 Major C\C   Excludes 1   Excludes 2   Includes   Use additional   Code first   Code also

M12.09   Chronic postrheumatic arthropathy [Jaccoud], multiple sites

● M12.1   **Kaschin-Beck disease**
     Osteochondroarthrosis deformans endemica

◼ M12.10   Kaschin-Beck disease, unspecified site

● M12.11   Kaschin-Beck disease, shoulder

     M12.111   Kaschin-Beck disease, right shoulder

     M12.112   Kaschin-Beck disease, left shoulder

     ◼ M12.119   Kaschin-Beck disease, unspecified shoulder

● M12.12   Kaschin-Beck disease, elbow

     M12.121   Kaschin-Beck disease, right elbow

     M12.122   Kaschin-Beck disease, left elbow

     ◼ M12.129   Kaschin-Beck disease, unspecified elbow

● M12.13   Kaschin-Beck disease, wrist

     M12.131   Kaschin-Beck disease, right wrist

     M12.132   Kaschin-Beck disease, left wrist

     ◼ M12.139   Kaschin-Beck disease, unspecified wrist

● M12.14   Kaschin-Beck disease, hand

     M12.141   Kaschin-Beck disease, right hand

     M12.142   Kaschin-Beck disease, left hand

     ◼ M12.149   Kaschin-Beck disease, unspecified hand

● M12.15   Kaschin-Beck disease, hip

     M12.151   Kaschin-Beck disease, right hip

     M12.152   Kaschin-Beck disease, left hip

     ◼ M12.159   Kaschin-Beck disease, unspecified hip

● M12.16   Kaschin-Beck disease, knee

     M12.161   Kaschin-Beck disease, right knee

     M12.162   Kaschin-Beck disease, left knee

     ◼ M12.169   Kaschin-Beck disease, unspecified knee

● M12.17   Kaschin-Beck disease, ankle and foot

     M12.171   Kaschin-Beck disease, right ankle and foot

     M12.172   Kaschin-Beck disease, left ankle and foot

     ◼ M12.179   Kaschin-Beck disease, unspecified ankle and foot

M12.18   Kaschin-Beck disease, vertebrae

M12.19   Kaschin-Beck disease, multiple sites

● M12.2   Villonodular synovitis (pigmented)

◼ M12.20   Villonodular synovitis (pigmented), unspecified site

● M12.21   Villonodular synovitis (pigmented), shoulder

     M12.211   Villonodular synovitis (pigmented), right shoulder

     M12.212   Villonodular synovitis (pigmented), left shoulder

     ◼ M12.219   Villonodular synovitis (pigmented), unspecified shoulder

● M12.22   Villonodular synovitis (pigmented), elbow

     M12.221   Villonodular synovitis (pigmented), right elbow

     M12.222   Villonodular synovitis (pigmented), left elbow

     ◼ M12.229   Villonodular synovitis (pigmented), unspecified elbow

● M12.23   Villonodular synovitis (pigmented), wrist

     M12.231   Villonodular synovitis (pigmented), right wrist

     M12.232   Villonodular synovitis (pigmented), left wrist

     ◼ M12.239   Villonodular synovitis (pigmented), unspecified wrist

● M12.24   Villonodular synovitis (pigmented), hand

     M12.241   Villonodular synovitis (pigmented), right hand

     M12.242   Villonodular synovitis (pigmented), left hand

     ◼ M12.249   Villonodular synovitis (pigmented), unspecified hand

● M12.25   Villonodular synovitis (pigmented), hip

     M12.251   Villonodular synovitis (pigmented), right hip

     M12.252   Villonodular synovitis (pigmented), left hip

     ◼ M12.259   Villonodular synovitis (pigmented), unspecified hip

● M12.26   Villonodular synovitis (pigmented), knee

     M12.261   Villonodular synovitis (pigmented), right knee

     M12.262   Villonodular synovitis (pigmented), left knee

     ◼ M12.269   Villonodular synovitis (pigmented), unspecified knee

● M12.27   Villonodular synovitis (pigmented), ankle and foot

     M12.271   Villonodular synovitis (pigmented), right ankle and foot

     M12.272   Villonodular synovitis (pigmented), left ankle and foot

     ◼ M12.279   Villonodular synovitis (pigmented), unspecified ankle and foot

M12.28   Villonodular synovitis (pigmented), vertebrae

M12.29   Villonodular synovitis (pigmented), multiple sites

● M12.3   Palindromic rheumatism

◼ M12.30   Palindromic rheumatism, unspecified site

● M12.31   Palindromic rheumatism, shoulder

     M12.311   Palindromic rheumatism, right shoulder

     M12.312   Palindromic rheumatism, left shoulder

     ◼ M12.319   Palindromic rheumatism, unspecified shoulder

● M12.32   Palindromic rheumatism, elbow

     M12.321   Palindromic rheumatism, right elbow

● Unacceptable First-Listed Diagnosis   ● Use Additional Character(s)   ◼ Unspecified   **OGCR** Official Guidelines for Coding and Reporting

🗣 Complication\Comorbidity   🗣 Major C\C   Excludes 1   Excludes 2   Includes   Use additional   Code first   Code also

1147

M12.322 Palindromic rheumatism, left elbow

■ M12.329 Palindromic rheumatism, unspecified elbow

● M12.33 Palindromic rheumatism, wrist

M12.331 Palindromic rheumatism, right wrist

M12.332 Palindromic rheumatism, left wrist

■ M12.339 Palindromic rheumatism, unspecified wrist

● M12.34 Palindromic rheumatism, hand

M12.341 Palindromic rheumatism, right hand

M12.342 Palindromic rheumatism, left hand

■ M12.349 Palindromic rheumatism, unspecified hand

● M12.35 Palindromic rheumatism, hip

M12.351 Palindromic rheumatism, right hip

M12.352 Palindromic rheumatism, left hip

■ M12.359 Palindromic rheumatism, unspecified hip

● M12.36 Palindromic rheumatism, knee

M12.361 Palindromic rheumatism, right knee

M12.362 Palindromic rheumatism, left knee

■ M12.369 Palindromic rheumatism, unspecified knee

● M12.37 Palindromic rheumatism, ankle and foot

M12.371 Palindromic rheumatism, right ankle and foot

M12.372 Palindromic rheumatism, left ankle and foot

■ M12.379 Palindromic rheumatism, unspecified ankle and foot

M12.38 Palindromic rheumatism, vertebrae

M12.39 Palindromic rheumatism, multiple sites

● M12.4 Intermittent hydrarthrosis

■ M12.40 Intermittent hydrarthrosis, unspecified site

● M12.41 Intermittent hydrarthrosis, shoulder

M12.411 Intermittent hydrarthrosis, right shoulder

M12.412 Intermittent hydrarthrosis, left shoulder

■ M12.419 Intermittent hydrarthrosis, unspecified shoulder

● M12.42 Intermittent hydrarthrosis, elbow

M12.421 Intermittent hydrarthrosis, right elbow

M12.422 Intermittent hydrarthrosis, left elbow

■ M12.429 Intermittent hydrarthrosis, unspecified elbow

● M12.43 Intermittent hydrarthrosis, wrist

M12.431 Intermittent hydrarthrosis, right wrist

M12.432 Intermittent hydrarthrosis, left wrist

■ M12.439 Intermittent hydrarthrosis, unspecified wrist

● M12.44 Intermittent hydrarthrosis, hand

M12.441 Intermittent hydrarthrosis, right hand

M12.442 Intermittent hydrarthrosis, left hand

■ M12.449 Intermittent hydrarthrosis, unspecified hand

● M12.45 Intermittent hydrarthrosis, hip

M12.451 Intermittent hydrarthrosis, right hip

M12.452 Intermittent hydrarthrosis, left hip

■ M12.459 Intermittent hydrarthrosis, unspecified hip

● M12.46 Intermittent hydrarthrosis, knee

M12.461 Intermittent hydrarthrosis, right knee

M12.462 Intermittent hydrarthrosis, left knee

■ M12.469 Intermittent hydrarthrosis, unspecified knee

● M12.47 Intermittent hydrarthrosis, ankle and foot

M12.471 Intermittent hydrarthrosis, right ankle and foot

M12.472 Intermittent hydrarthrosis, left ankle and foot

■ M12.479 Intermittent hydrarthrosis, unspecified ankle and foot

M12.48 Intermittent hydrarthrosis, other site

M12.49 Intermittent hydrarthrosis, multiple sites

● M12.5 Traumatic arthropathy

Excludes1   current injury-see Alphabetic Index
             post-traumatic osteoarthritis (of):
                 NOS (M19.1-)
                 first carpometacarpal joint (M18.2-M18.3)
                 hip (M16.4-M16.5)
                 knee (M17.2-M17.3)
                 other single joints (M19.1-)

■ M12.50 Traumatic arthropathy, unspecified site

● M12.51 Traumatic arthropathy, shoulder

M12.511 Traumatic arthropathy, right shoulder

M12.512 Traumatic arthropathy, left shoulder

■ M12.519 Traumatic arthropathy, unspecified shoulder

● M12.52 Traumatic arthropathy, elbow

M12.521 Traumatic arthropathy, right elbow

M12.522 Traumatic arthropathy, left elbow

■ M12.529 Traumatic arthropathy, unspecified elbow

● M12.53 Traumatic arthropathy, wrist

M12.531 Traumatic arthropathy, right wrist

M12.532 Traumatic arthropathy, left wrist

■ M12.539 Traumatic arthropathy, unspecified wrist

● Unacceptable First-Listed Diagnosis   ● Use Additional Character(s)   ■ Unspecified   OGCR Official Guidelines for Coding and Reporting
🔖 Complication\Comorbidity   🔖 Major C\C   Excludes 1   Excludes 2   Includes   Use additional   Code first   Code also

● M12.54 Traumatic arthropathy, hand

    M12.541 Traumatic arthropathy, right hand

    M12.542 Traumatic arthropathy, left hand

    ■M12.549 Traumatic arthropathy, unspecified hand

● M12.55 Traumatic arthropathy, hip

    M12.551 Traumatic arthropathy, right hip

    M12.552 Traumatic arthropathy, left hip

    ■M12.559 Traumatic arthropathy, unspecified hip

● M12.56 Traumatic arthropathy, knee

    M12.561 Traumatic arthropathy, right knee

    M12.562 Traumatic arthropathy, left knee

    ■M12.569 Traumatic arthropathy, unspecified knee

● M12.57 Traumatic arthropathy, ankle and foot

    M12.571 Traumatic arthropathy, right ankle and foot

    M12.572 Traumatic arthropathy, left ankle and foot

    ■M12.579 Traumatic arthropathy, unspecified ankle and foot

  M12.58 Traumatic arthropathy, vertebrae

  M12.59 Traumatic arthropathy, multiple sites

● M12.8 Other specific arthropathies, not elsewhere classified
    Transient arthropathy

  ■M12.80 Other specific arthropathies, not elsewhere classified, unspecified site

● M12.81 Other specific arthropathies, not elsewhere classified, shoulder

    M12.811 Other specific arthropathies, not elsewhere classified, right shoulder

    M12.812 Other specific arthropathies, not elsewhere classified, left shoulder

    ■M12.819 Other specific arthropathies, not elsewhere classified, unspecified shoulder

● M12.82 Other specific arthropathies, not elsewhere classified, elbow

    M12.821 Other specific arthropathies, not elsewhere classified, right elbow

    M12.822 Other specific arthropathies, not elsewhere classified, left elbow

    ■M12.829 Other specific arthropathies, not elsewhere classified, unspecified elbow

● M12.83 Other specific arthropathies, not elsewhere classified, wrist

    M12.831 Other specific arthropathies, not elsewhere classified, right wrist

    M12.832 Other specific arthropathies, not elsewhere classified, left wrist

    ■M12.839 Other specific arthropathies, not elsewhere classified, unspecified wrist

● M12.84 Other specific arthropathies, not elsewhere classified, hand

    M12.841 Other specific arthropathies, not elsewhere classified, right hand

    M12.842 Other specific arthropathies, not elsewhere classified, left hand

    ■M12.849 Other specific arthropathies, not elsewhere classified, unspecified hand

● M12.85 Other specific arthropathies, not elsewhere classified, hip

    M12.851 Other specific arthropathies, not elsewhere classified, right hip

    M12.852 Other specific arthropathies, not elsewhere classified, left hip

    ■M12.859 Other specific arthropathies, not elsewhere classified, unspecified hip

● M12.86 Other specific arthropathies, not elsewhere classified, knee

    M12.861 Other specific arthropathies, not elsewhere classified, right knee

    M12.862 Other specific arthropathies, not elsewhere classified, left knee

    ■M12.869 Other specific arthropathies, not elsewhere classified, unspecified knee

● M12.87 Other specific arthropathies, not elsewhere classified, ankle and foot

    M12.871 Other specific arthropathies, not elsewhere classified, right ankle and foot

    M12.872 Other specific arthropathies, not elsewhere classified, left ankle and foot

    ■M12.879 Other specific arthropathies, not elsewhere classified, unspecified ankle and foot

  M12.88 Other specific arthropathies, not elsewhere classified, vertebrae

  M12.89 Other specific arthropathies, not elsewhere classified, multiple sites

■M12.9 Arthropathy, unspecified

● M13 Other arthritis

    Excludes1 arthrosis (M15-M19)
              osteoarthritis (M15-M19)

  ■M13.0 Polyarthritis, unspecified

● M13.1 Monoarthritis, not elsewhere classified

  ■M13.10 Monoarthritis, not elsewhere classified, unspecified site

● M13.11 Monoarthritis, not elsewhere classified, shoulder

    M13.111 Monoarthritis, not elsewhere classified, right shoulder

    M13.112 Monoarthritis, not elsewhere classified, left shoulder

    ■M13.119 Monoarthritis, not elsewhere classified, unspecified shoulder

● M13.12 Monoarthritis, not elsewhere classified, elbow

    M13.121 Monoarthritis, not elsewhere classified, right elbow

    M13.122 Monoarthritis, not elsewhere classified, left elbow

    ■M13.129 Monoarthritis, not elsewhere classified, unspecified elbow

● Unacceptable First-Listed Diagnosis   ● Use Additional Character(s)   ■ Unspecified   **OGCR** Official Guidelines for Coding and Reporting

  🔖 Complication\Comorbidity   🔖 Major C\C   Excludes 1   Excludes 2   Includes   Use additional   Code first   Code also

1149

CHAPTER 13 (M00-M99)

● **M13.13 Monoarthritis, not elsewhere classified, wrist**
- M13.131 Monoarthritis, not elsewhere classified, right wrist
- M13.132 Monoarthritis, not elsewhere classified, left wrist
- ◻ M13.139 Monoarthritis, not elsewhere classified, unspecified wrist

● **M13.14 Monoarthritis, not elsewhere classified, hand**
- M13.141 Monoarthritis, not elsewhere classified, right hand
- M13.142 Monoarthritis, not elsewhere classified, left hand
- ◻ M13.149 Monoarthritis, not elsewhere classified, unspecified hand

● **M13.15 Monoarthritis, not elsewhere classified, hip**
- M13.151 Monoarthritis, not elsewhere classified, right hip
- M13.152 Monoarthritis, not elsewhere classified, left hip
- ◻ M13.159 Monoarthritis, not elsewhere classified, unspecified hip

● **M13.16 Monoarthritis, not elsewhere classified, knee**
- M13.161 Monoarthritis, not elsewhere classified, right knee
- M13.162 Monoarthritis, not elsewhere classified, left knee
- ◻ M13.169 Monoarthritis, not elsewhere classified, unspecified knee

● **M13.17 Monoarthritis, not elsewhere classified, ankle and foot**
- M13.171 Monoarthritis, not elsewhere classified, right ankle and foot
- M13.172 Monoarthritis, not elsewhere classified, left ankle and foot
- ◻ M13.179 Monoarthritis, not elsewhere classified, unspecified ankle and foot

● **M13.8 Other specified arthritis**
Allergic arthritis
> **Excludes1**   osteoarthritis (M15-M19)

- ◻ M13.80 Other specified arthritis, unspecified site
- ● M13.81 Other specified arthritis, shoulder
  - M13.811 Other specified arthritis, right shoulder
  - M13.812 Other specified arthritis, left shoulder
  - ◻ M13.819 Other specified arthritis, unspecified shoulder
- ● M13.82 Other specified arthritis, elbow
  - M13.821 Other specified arthritis, right elbow
  - M13.822 Other specified arthritis, left elbow
  - ◻ M13.829 Other specified arthritis, unspecified elbow
- ● M13.83 Other specified arthritis, wrist
  - M13.831 Other specified arthritis, right wrist
  - M13.832 Other specified arthritis, left wrist
  - ◻ M13.839 Other specified arthritis, unspecified wrist

● **M13.84 Other specified arthritis, hand**
- M13.841 Other specified arthritis, right hand
- M13.842 Other specified arthritis, left hand
- ◻ M13.849 Other specified arthritis, unspecified hand

● **M13.85 Other specified arthritis, hip**
- M13.851 Other specified arthritis, right hip
- M13.852 Other specified arthritis, left hip
- ◻ M13.859 Other specified arthritis, unspecified hip

● **M13.86 Other specified arthritis, knee**
- M13.861 Other specified arthritis, right knee
- M13.862 Other specified arthritis, left knee
- ◻ M13.869 Other specified arthritis, unspecified knee

● **M13.87 Other specified arthritis, ankle and foot**
- M13.871 Other specified arthritis, right ankle and foot
- M13.872 Other specified arthritis, left ankle and foot
- ◻ M13.879 Other specified arthritis, unspecified ankle and foot

M13.88 Other specified arthritis, vertebrae

M13.89 Other specified arthritis, multiple sites

● **M14 Arthropathies in other diseases classified elsewhere**
> **Excludes1**   arthropathy in:
>   diabetes mellitus (E08-E13 with 4th character 61)
>   hematological disorders (M36.2-M36.3)
>   hypersensitivity reactions (M36.4)
>   neoplastic disease (M36.1)
>   neurosyphillis (A52.16)
>   sarcoidosis (D86.86)
> enteropathic arthropathies (M07.0-)
> juvenile psoriatic arthropathy (L40.54)
> lipoid dermatoarthritis (E78.81)

● **M14.6 Charcot's joint**
Neuropathic arthropathy
> **Excludes1**   Charcot's joint in diabetes mellitus (E08-E13 with final characters 610)
>   Charcot's joint in tabes dorsalis (A52.16)

- ● ◻ M14.60 Charcot's joint, unspecified site
- ● M14.61 Charcot's joint, shoulder
  - ● M14.611 Charcot's joint, right shoulder
  - ● M14.612 Charcot's joint, left shoulder
  - ● ◻ M14.619 Charcot's joint, unspecified shoulder
- ● M14.62 Charcot's joint, elbow
  - ● M14.621 Charcot's joint, right elbow
  - ● M14.622 Charcot's joint, left elbow
  - ● ◻ M14.629 Charcot's joint, unspecified elbow
- ● M14.63 Charcot's joint, wrist
  - ● M14.631 Charcot's joint, right wrist
  - ● M14.632 Charcot's joint, left wrist
  - ● ◻ M14.639 Charcot's joint, unspecified wrist
- ● M14.64 Charcot's joint, hand
  - ● M14.641 Charcot's joint, right hand
  - ● M14.642 Charcot's joint, left hand
  - ● ◻ M14.649 Charcot's joint, unspecified hand

● Unacceptable First-Listed Diagnosis   ● Use Additional Character(s)   ◻ Unspecified   **OGCR** Official Guidelines for Coding and Reporting

🗝 Complication\Comorbidity   🗝 Major C\C   Excludes 1   Excludes 2   Includes   Use additional   Code first   Code also

● M14.65 Charcot's joint, hip
  ● M14.651 Charcot's joint, right hip
  ● M14.652 Charcot's joint, left hip
  ●▪ M14.659 Charcot's joint, unspecified hip
● M14.66 Charcot's joint, knee
  ● M14.661 Charcot's joint, right knee
  ● M14.662 Charcot's joint, left knee
  ●▪ M14.669 Charcot's joint, unspecified knee
● M14.67 Charcot's joint, ankle and foot
  ● M14.671 Charcot's joint, right ankle and foot
  ● M14.672 Charcot's joint, left ankle and foot
  ●▪ M14.679 Charcot's joint, unspecified ankle and foot
● M14.68 Charcot's joint, vertebrae
● M14.69 Charcot's joint, multiple sites
● M14.8 Arthropathies in other specified diseases classified elsewhere

  Code first underlying disease, such as:
    amyloidosis (E85.-)
    erythema multiforme (L51.-)
    erythema nodosum (L52)
    hemochromatosis (E83.1)
    hyperparathyroidism (E21.-)
    hypothyroidism (E00-E03)
    sickle-cell disorders (D57.-)
    thyrotoxicosis [hyperthyroidism] (E05.-)
    Whipple's disease (K90.8)

  ●▪ M14.80   Arthropathies in other specified diseases classified elsewhere, unspecified site
  ● M14.81 Arthropathies in other specified diseases classified elsewhere, shoulder
    ● M14.811 Arthropathies in other specified diseases classified elsewhere, right shoulder
    ● M14.812 Arthropathies in other specified diseases classified elsewhere, left shoulder
    ●▪ M14.819 Arthropathies in other specified diseases classified elsewhere, unspecified shoulder
  ● M14.82 Arthropathies in other specified diseases classified elsewhere, elbow
    ● M14.821 Arthropathies in other specified diseases classified elsewhere, right elbow
    ● M14.822 Arthropathies in other specified diseases classified elsewhere, left elbow
    ●▪ M14.829 Arthropathies in other specified diseases classified elsewhere, unspecified elbow
  ● M14.83 Arthropathies in other specified diseases classified elsewhere, wrist
    ● M14.831 Arthropathies in other specified diseases classified elsewhere, right wrist
    ● M14.832 Arthropathies in other specified diseases classified elsewhere, left wrist
    ●▪ M14.839 Arthropathies in other specified diseases classified elsewhere, unspecified wrist

● M14.84 Arthropathies in other specified diseases classified elsewhere, hand
  ● M14.841 Arthropathies in other specified diseases classified elsewhere, right hand
  ● M14.842 Arthropathies in other specified diseases classified elsewhere, left hand
  ●▪ M14.849 Arthropathies in other specified diseases classified elsewhere, unspecified hand
● M14.85 Arthropathies in other specified diseases classified elsewhere, hip
  ● M14.851 Arthropathies in other specified diseases classified elsewhere, right hip
  ● M14.852 Arthropathies in other specified diseases classified elsewhere, left hip
  ●▪ M14.859 Arthropathies in other specified diseases classified elsewhere, unspecified hip
● M14.86 Arthropathies in other specified diseases classified elsewhere, knee
  ● M14.861 Arthropathies in other specified diseases classified elsewhere, right knee
  ● M14.862 Arthropathies in other specified diseases classified elsewhere, left knee
  ●▪ M14.869 Arthropathies in other specified diseases classified elsewhere, unspecified knee
● M14.87 Arthropathies in other specified diseases classified elsewhere, ankle and foot
  ● M14.871 Arthropathies in other specified diseases classified elsewhere, right ankle and foot
  ● M14.872 Arthropathies in other specified diseases classified elsewhere, left ankle and foot
  ●▪ M14.879 Arthropathies in other specified diseases classified elsewhere, unspecified ankle and foot
● M14.88 Arthropathies in other specified diseases classified elsewhere, vertebrae
● M14.89 Arthropathies in other specified diseases classified elsewhere, multiple sites

OSTEOARTHRITIS (M15-M19)

Osteoarthritis is the most common degenerative joint disease and form of arthritis that breaks down the cartilage causing pain, swelling, and reduced motion in the joints.

  Excludes2   osteoarthritis of spine (M47.-)

● M15 Polyosteoarthritis

  Includes   arthritis of multiple sites
  Excludes1   bilateral involvement of single joint (M16-M19)

  M15.0 Primary generalized (osteo)arthritis
  M15.1 Heberden's nodes (with arthropathy)
    Interphalangeal distal osteoarthritis
  M15.2 Bouchard's nodes (with arthropathy)
    Juxtaphalangeal distal osteoarthritis
  M15.3 Secondary multiple arthritis
    Post-traumatic polyosteoarthritis

● Unacceptable First-Listed Diagnosis   ● Use Additional Character(s)   ▪ Unspecified   **OGCR** Official Guidelines for Coding and Reporting

🔗 Complication\Comorbidity   🔗 Major C\C   [Excludes 1]   [Excludes 2]   Includes   Use additional   Code first   Code also

1151

CHAPTER 13 (M00-M99)

M15.4   Erosive (osteo)arthritis

M15.8   Other polyosteoarthritis

◨ M15.9   Polyosteoarthritis, unspecified
      Generalized osteoarthritis NOS

● M16   Osteoarthritis of hip

M16.0   Bilateral primary osteoarthritis of hip

● M16.1   Unilateral primary osteoarthritis of hip
      Primary osteoarthritis of hip NOS

    ◨ M16.10   Unilateral primary osteoarthritis,
      unspecified hip

    M16.11   Unilateral primary osteoarthritis, right hip

    M16.12   Unilateral primary osteoarthritis, left hip

M16.2   Bilateral osteoarthritis resulting from hip dysplasia

● M16.3   Unilateral osteoarthritis resulting from hip dysplasia
      Dysplastic osteoarthritis of hip NOS

    ◨ M16.30   Unilateral osteoarthritis resulting from hip
      dysplasia, unspecified hip

    M16.31   Unilateral osteoarthritis resulting from hip
      dysplasia, right hip

    M16.32   Unilateral osteoarthritis resulting from hip
      dysplasia, left hip

M16.4   Bilateral post-traumatic osteoarthritis of hip

● M16.5   Unilateral post-traumatic osteoarthritis of hip
      Post-traumatic osteoarthritis of hip NOS

    ◨ M16.50   Unilateral post-traumatic osteoarthritis,
      unspecified hip

    M16.51   Unilateral post-traumatic osteoarthritis,
      right hip

    M16.52   Unilateral post-traumatic osteoarthritis,
      left hip

M16.6   Other bilateral secondary osteoarthritis of hip

M16.7   Other unilateral secondary osteoarthritis of hip
      Secondary osteoarthritis of hip NOS

◨ M16.9   Osteoarthritis of hip, unspecified

● M17   Osteoarthritis of knee

M17.0   Bilateral primary osteoarthritis of knee

● M17.1   Unilateral primary osteoarthritis of knee
      Primary osteoarthritis of knee NOS

    ◨ M17.10   Unilateral primary osteoarthritis,
      unspecified knee

    M17.11   Unilateral primary osteoarthritis, right knee

    M17.12   Unilateral primary osteoarthritis, left knee

M17.2   Bilateral post-traumatic osteoarthritis of knee

● M17.3   Unilateral post-traumatic osteoarthritis of knee
      Post-traumatic osteoarthritis of knee NOS

    ◨ M17.30   Unilateral post-traumatic osteoarthritis,
      unspecified knee

    M17.31   Unilateral post-traumatic osteoarthritis,
      right knee

    M17.32   Unilateral post-traumatic osteoarthritis,
      left knee

M17.4   Other bilateral secondary osteoarthritis of knee

M17.5   Other unilateral secondary osteoarthritis of knee
      Secondary osteoarthritis of knee NOS

◨ M17.9   Osteoarthritis of knee, unspecified

● M18   Osteoarthritis of first carpometacarpal joint

M18.0   Bilateral primary osteoarthritis of first
      carpometacarpal joints

● M18.1   Unilateral primary osteoarthritis of first
      carpometacarpal joint
      Primary osteoarthritis of first carpometacarpal
      joint NOS

    ◨ M18.10   Unilateral primary osteoarthritis of first
      carpometacarpal joint, unspecified hand

    M18.11   Unilateral primary osteoarthritis of first
      carpometacarpal joint, right hand

    M18.12   Unilateral primary osteoarthritis of first
      carpometacarpal joint, left hand

M18.2   Bilateral post-traumatic osteoarthritis of first
      carpometacarpal joints

● M18.3   Unilateral post-traumatic osteoarthritis of first
      carpometacarpal joint
      Post-traumatic osteoarthritis of first
      carpometacarpal joint NOS

    ◨ M18.30   Unilateral post-traumatic osteoarthritis
      of first carpometacarpal joint, unspecified
      hand

    M18.31   Unilateral post-traumatic osteoarthritis of
      first carpometacarpal joint, right hand

    M18.32   Unilateral post-traumatic osteoarthritis of
      first carpometacarpal joint, left hand

M18.4   Other bilateral secondary osteoarthritis of first
      carpometacarpal joints

● M18.5   Other unilateral secondary osteoarthritis of first
      carpometacarpal joint
      Secondary osteoarthritis of first carpometacarpal
      joint NOS

    ◨ M18.50   Other unilateral secondary osteoarthritis
      of first carpometacarpal joint, unspecified
      hand

    M18.51   Other unilateral secondary osteoarthritis
      of first carpometacarpal joint, right hand

    M18.52   Other unilateral secondary osteoarthritis
      of first carpometacarpal joint, left hand

◨ M18.9   Osteoarthritis of first carpometacarpal joint,
      unspecified

● M19   Other and unspecified osteoarthritis

    Excludes1   polyarthritis (M15.-)

    Excludes2   arthrosis of spine (M47.-)
      hallux rigidus (M20.2)
      osteoarthritis of spine (M47.-)

● M19.0   Primary osteoarthritis of other joints

    ● M19.01   Primary osteoarthritis, shoulder

      M19.011   Primary osteoarthritis, right
      shoulder

      M19.012   Primary osteoarthritis, left
      shoulder

      ◨ M19.019   Primary osteoarthritis,
      unspecified shoulder

    ● M19.02   Primary osteoarthritis, elbow

      M19.021   Primary osteoarthritis, right
      elbow

      M19.022   Primary osteoarthritis, left elbow

      ◨ M19.029   Primary osteoarthritis,
      unspecified elbow

    ● M19.03   Primary osteoarthritis, wrist

      M19.031   Primary osteoarthritis, right wrist

      M19.032   Primary osteoarthritis, left wrist

      ◨ M19.039   Primary osteoarthritis,
      unspecified wrist

● Unacceptable First-Listed Diagnosis   ● Use Additional Character(s)   ◨ Unspecified   **OGCR** Official Guidelines for Coding and Reporting
🔖 Complication\Comorbidity   🔖 Major C\C   Excludes 1   Excludes 2   Includes   Use additional   Code first   Code also

● **M19.04 Primary osteoarthritis, hand**

Excludes2   primary osteoarthritis of first carpometacarpal joint (M18.0-, M18.1-)

    M19.041 Primary osteoarthritis, right hand

    M19.042 Primary osteoarthritis, left hand

    ■ M19.049 Primary osteoarthritis, unspecified hand

● **M19.07 Primary osteoarthritis ankle and foot**

    M19.071 Primary osteoarthritis, right ankle and foot

    M19.072 Primary osteoarthritis, left ankle and foot

    ■ M19.079 Primary osteoarthritis, unspecified ankle and foot

● **M19.1 Post-traumatic osteoarthritis of other joints**

  ● **M19.11 Post-traumatic osteoarthritis, shoulder**

    M19.111 Post-traumatic osteoarthritis, right shoulder

    M19.112 Post-traumatic osteoarthritis, left shoulder

    ■ M19.119 Post-traumatic osteoarthritis, unspecified shoulder

  ● **M19.12 Post-traumatic osteoarthritis, elbow**

    M19.121 Post-traumatic osteoarthritis, right elbow

    M19.122 Post-traumatic osteoarthritis, left elbow

    ■ M19.129 Post-traumatic osteoarthritis, unspecified elbow

  ● **M19.13 Post-traumatic osteoarthritis, wrist**

    M19.131 Post-traumatic osteoarthritis, right wrist

    M19.132 Post-traumatic osteoarthritis, left wrist

    ■ M19.139 Post-traumatic osteoarthritis, unspecified wrist

  ● **M19.14 Post-traumatic osteoarthritis, hand**

Excludes2   post-traumatic osteoarthritis of first carpometacarpal joint (M18.2-, M18.3-)

    M19.141 Post-traumatic osteoarthritis, right hand

    M19.142 Post-traumatic osteoarthritis, left hand

    ■ M19.149 Post-traumatic osteoarthritis, unspecified hand

  ● **M19.17 Post-traumatic osteoarthritis, ankle and foot**

    M19.171 Post-traumatic osteoarthritis, right ankle and foot

    M19.172 Post-traumatic osteoarthritis, left ankle and foot

    ■ M19.179 Post-traumatic osteoarthritis, unspecified ankle and foot

● **M19.2 Secondary osteoarthritis of other joints**

  ● **M19.21 Secondary osteoarthritis, shoulder**

    M19.211 Secondary osteoarthritis, right shoulder

    M19.212 Secondary osteoarthritis, left shoulder

    ■ M19.219 Secondary osteoarthritis, unspecified shoulder

● **M19.22 Secondary osteoarthritis, elbow**

    M19.221 Secondary osteoarthritis, right elbow

    M19.222 Secondary osteoarthritis, left elbow

    ■ M19.229 Secondary osteoarthritis, unspecified elbow

● **M19.23 Secondary osteoarthritis, wrist**

    M19.231 Secondary osteoarthritis, right wrist

    M19.232 Secondary osteoarthritis, left wrist

    ■ M19.239 Secondary osteoarthritis, unspecified wrist

● **M19.24 Secondary osteoarthritis, hand**

    M19.241 Secondary osteoarthritis, right hand

    M19.242 Secondary osteoarthritis, left hand

    ■ M19.249 Secondary osteoarthritis, unspecified hand

● **M19.27 Secondary osteoarthritis, ankle and foot**

    M19.271 Secondary osteoarthritis, right ankle and foot

    M19.272 Secondary osteoarthritis, left ankle and foot

    ■ M19.279 Secondary osteoarthritis, unspecified ankle and foot

● **M19.9 Osteoarthritis, unspecified site**

    ■ M19.90 Unspecified osteoarthritis, unspecified site
       Arthrosis NOS
       Arthritis NOS
       Osteoarthritis NOS

    ■ M19.91 Primary osteoarthritis, unspecified site
       Primary osteoarthritis NOS

    ■ M19.92 Post-traumatic osteoarthritis, unspecified site
       Post-traumatic osteoarthritis NOS

    ■ M19.93 Secondary osteoarthritis, unspecified site
       Secondary osteoarthritis NOS

OTHER JOINT DISORDERS (M20-M25)

Excludes2   joints of the spine (M40-M54)

● **M20 Acquired deformities of fingers and toes**

Excludes1   acquired absence of fingers and toes (Z89.-)
      congenital absence of fingers and toes (Q71.3-, Q72.3-)
      congenital deformities and malformations of fingers and toes (Q66.-, Q68-Q70, Q74.-)

● **M20.0 Deformity of finger(s)**

Excludes1   clubbing of fingers (R68.3)
      palmar fascial fibromatosis [Dupuytren] (M72.0)
      trigger finger (M65.3)

  ● **M20.00 Unspecified deformity of finger(s)**

    ■ M20.001 Unspecified deformity of right finger(s)

    ■ M20.002 Unspecified deformity of left finger(s)

    ■ M20.009 Unspecified deformity of unspecified finger(s)

  ● **M20.01 Mallet finger**

    M20.011 Mallet finger of right finger(s)

● Unacceptable First-Listed Diagnosis   ● Use Additional Character(s)   ■ Unspecified   **OGCR** Official Guidelines for Coding and Reporting

🗪 Complication\Comorbidity   🗪 Major C\C   Excludes 1   Excludes 2   Includes   Use additional   Code first   Code also

1153

CHAPTER 13 (M00-M99)

M20.012 Mallet finger of left finger(s)

◼ M20.019 Mallet finger of unspecified finger(s)

● M20.02 Boutonnière deformity

M20.021 Boutonnière deformity of right finger(s)

M20.022 Boutonnière deformity of left finger(s)

◼ M20.029 Boutonnière deformity of unspecified finger(s)

● M20.03 Swan-neck deformity

M20.031 Swan-neck deformity of right finger(s)

M20.032 Swan-neck deformity of left finger(s)

◼ M20.039 Swan-neck deformity of unspecified finger(s)

● M20.09 Other deformity of finger(s)

M20.091 Other deformity of right finger(s)

M20.092 Other deformity of left finger(s)

◼ M20.099 Other deformity of finger(s), unspecified finger(s)

● M20.1 Hallux valgus (acquired)
    Bunion

◼ M20.10 Hallux valgus (acquired), unspecified foot

M20.11 Hallux valgus (acquired), right foot

M20.12 Hallux valgus (acquired), left foot

● M20.2 Hallux rigidus

◼ M20.20 Hallux rigidus, unspecified foot

M20.21 Hallux rigidus, right foot

M20.22 Hallux rigidus, left foot

● M20.3 Hallux varus (acquired)

◼ M20.30 Hallux varus (acquired), unspecified foot

M20.31 Hallux varus (acquired), right foot

M20.32 Hallux varus (acquired), left foot

● M20.4 Other hammer toe(s) (acquired)

◼ M20.40 Other hammer toe(s) (acquired), unspecified foot

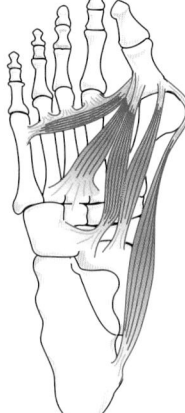

Figure 13-1   Hallux valgus or bunion.

Item 13–2   Hallux valgus or bunion is a sometimes painful structural deformity caused by an inflammation of the bursal sac at the base of the metatarsophalangeal joint (big toe). **Hallus varus** is a deviation of the great toe to the inner side of the foot or away from the next toe.

Item 13–3   Cubitus valgus is a deformity of the elbow resulting in an increased carrying angle in which the arm extends at the side and the palm faces forward, which results in the forearm and hand extended at a greater than 15 degrees.

M20.41 Other hammer toe(s) (acquired), right foot

M20.42 Other hammer toe(s) (acquired), left foot

● M20.5 Other deformities of toe(s) (acquired)

● M20.5x Other deformities of toe(s) (acquired)

M20.5x1 Other deformities of toe(s) (acquired), right foot

M20.5x2 Other deformities of toe(s) (acquired), left foot

◼ M20.5x9 Other deformities of toe(s) (acquired), unspecified foot

● M20.6 Acquired deformities of toe(s), unspecified

◼ M20.60 Acquired deformities of toe(s), unspecified, unspecified foot

◼ M20.61 Acquired deformities of toe(s), unspecified, right foot

◼ M20.62 Acquired deformities of toe(s), unspecified, left foot

● M21 Other acquired deformities of limbs

Excludes1   acquired absence of limb (Z89.-)
congenital absence of limbs (Q71-Q73)
congenital deformities and malformations of limbs (Q65-Q66, Q68-Q74)

Excludes2   acquired deformities of fingers or toes (M20.-)
coxa plana (M91.2)

● M21.0 Valgus deformity, not elsewhere classified

Excludes1   metatarsus valgus (Q66.6)
talipes calcaneovalgus (Q66.4)

◼ M21.00 Valgus deformity, not elsewhere classified, unspecified site

● M21.02 Valgus deformity, not elsewhere classified, elbow
    Cubitus valgus

M21.021 Valgus deformity, not elsewhere classified, right elbow

M21.022 Valgus deformity, not elsewhere classified, left elbow

◼ M21.029 Valgus deformity, not elsewhere classified, unspecified elbow

● M21.06 Valgus deformity, not elsewhere classified, knee
    Genu valgum
    Knock knee

M21.061 Valgus deformity, not elsewhere classified, right knee

M21.062 Valgus deformity, not elsewhere classified, left knee

◼ M21.069 Valgus deformity, not elsewhere classified, unspecified knee

● M21.07 Valgus deformity, not elsewhere classified, ankle

M21.071 Valgus deformity, not elsewhere classified, right ankle

M21.072 Valgus deformity, not elsewhere classified, left ankle

◼ M21.079 Valgus deformity, not elsewhere classified, unspecified ankle

● Unacceptable First-Listed Diagnosis   ● Use Additional Character(s)   ◼ Unspecified   **OGCR** Official Guidelines for Coding and Reporting
🔖 Complication\Comorbidity   🔖 Major C\C   Excludes 1   Excludes 2   Includes   Use additional   Code first   Code also

Item 13–4 Cubitus varus is a deformity of the elbow resulting in the arm extended at the side and the palm facing forward so that the forearm and hand are held at less than 5 degrees, decreasing the carrying angle.

● M21.1 Varus deformity, not elsewhere classified
> Excludes1   metatarsus varus (Q66.2)
> tibia vara (M92.5)

■ M21.10 Varus deformity, not elsewhere classified, unspecified site

● M21.12 Varus deformity, not elsewhere classified, elbow
> Cubitus varus, elbow

M21.121 Varus deformity, not elsewhere classified, right elbow

M21.122 Varus deformity, not elsewhere classified, left elbow

■ M21.129 Varus deformity, not elsewhere classified, unspecified elbow

● M21.16 Varus deformity, not elsewhere classified, knee
> Bow leg
> Genu varum

M21.161 Varus deformity, not elsewhere classified, right knee

M21.162 Varus deformity, not elsewhere classified, left knee

■ M21.169 Varus deformity, not elsewhere classified, unspecified knee

● M21.17 Varus deformity, not elsewhere classified, ankle

M21.171 Varus deformity, not elsewhere classified, right ankle

M21.172 Varus deformity, not elsewhere classified, left ankle

■ M21.179 Varus deformity, not elsewhere classified, unspecified ankle

● M21.2 Flexion deformity

■ M21.20 Flexion deformity, unspecified site

● M21.21 Flexion deformity, shoulder

M21.211 Flexion deformity, right shoulder

M21.212 Flexion deformity, left shoulder

■ M21.219 Flexion deformity, unspecified shoulder

● M21.22 Flexion deformity, elbow

M21.221 Flexion deformity, right elbow

M21.222 Flexion deformity, left elbow

■ M21.229 Flexion deformity, unspecified elbow

● M21.23 Flexion deformity, wrist

M21.231 Flexion deformity, right wrist

M21.232 Flexion deformity, left wrist

■ M21.239 Flexion deformity, unspecified wrist

● M21.24 Flexion deformity, finger joints

M21.241 Flexion deformity, right finger joints

M21.242 Flexion deformity, left finger joints

■ M21.249 Flexion deformity, unspecified finger joints

● M21.25 Flexion deformity, hip

M21.251 Flexion deformity, right hip

M21.252 Flexion deformity, left hip

■ M21.259 Flexion deformity, unspecified hip

● M21.26 Flexion deformity, knee

M21.261 Flexion deformity, right knee

M21.262 Flexion deformity, left knee

■ M21.269 Flexion deformity, unspecified knee

● M21.27 Flexion deformity, ankle and toes

M21.271 Flexion deformity, right ankle and toes

M21.272 Flexion deformity, left ankle and toes

■ M21.279 Flexion deformity, unspecified ankle and toes

● M21.3 Wrist or foot drop (acquired)

● M21.33 Wrist drop (acquired)

M21.331 Wrist drop, right wrist

M21.332 Wrist drop, left wrist

■ M21.339 Wrist drop, unspecified wrist

● M21.37 Foot drop (acquired)

M21.371 Foot drop, right foot

M21.372 Foot drop, left foot

■ M21.379 Foot drop, unspecified foot

● M21.4 Flat foot [pes planus] (acquired)
> Excludes1   congenital pes planus (Q66.5)

■ M21.40 Flat foot [pes planus] (acquired), unspecified foot

M21.41 Flat foot [pes planus] (acquired), right foot

M21.42 Flat foot [pes planus] (acquired), left foot

● M21.5 Acquired clawhand, clubhand, clawfoot and clubfoot
> Excludes1   clubfoot, not specified as acquired (Q66.8)

● M21.51 Acquired clawhand

M21.511 Acquired clawhand, right hand

M21.512 Acquired clawhand, left hand

■ M21.519 Acquired clawhand, unspecified hand

● M21.52 Acquired clubhand

M21.521 Acquired clubhand, right hand

M21.522 Acquired clubhand, left hand

■ M21.529 Acquired clubhand, unspecified hand

● M21.53 Acquired clawfoot

M21.531 Acquired clawfoot, right foot

M21.532 Acquired clawfoot, left foot

■ M21.539 Acquired clawfoot, unspecified foot

● M21.54 Acquired clubfoot

M21.541 Acquired clubfoot, right foot

M21.542 Acquired clubfoot, left foot

■ M21.549 Acquired clubfoot, unspecified foot

● M21.6 Other acquired deformities of foot
> Excludes2   deformities of toe (acquired) (M20.1-M20.6)

● M21.6x Other acquired deformities of foot

M21.6x1 Other acquired deformities of right foot

M21.6x2 Other acquired deformities of left foot

■ M21.6x9 Other acquired deformities of unspecified foot

● Unacceptable First-Listed Diagnosis   ● Use Additional Character(s)   ■ Unspecified   **OGCR** Official Guidelines for Coding and Reporting

🐾 Complication\Comorbidity   🐾 Major C\C   Excludes 1   Excludes 2   Includes   Use additional   Code first   Code also

- **M21.7 Unequal limb length (acquired)**
  - **Note:** The site used should correspond to the shorter limb.
  - ◻ **M21.70 Unequal limb length (acquired), unspecified site**
  - ● **M21.72 Unequal limb length (acquired), humerus**
    - **M21.721** Unequal limb length (acquired), right humerus
    - **M21.722** Unequal limb length (acquired), left humerus
    - ◻ **M21.729** Unequal limb length (acquired), unspecified humerus
  - ● **M21.73 Unequal limb length (acquired), ulna and radius**
    - **M21.731** Unequal limb length (acquired), right ulna
    - **M21.732** Unequal limb length (acquired), left ulna
    - **M21.733** Unequal limb length (acquired), right radius
    - **M21.734** Unequal limb length (acquired), left radius
    - ◻ **M21.739** Unequal limb length (acquired), unspecified ulna and radius
  - ● **M21.75 Unequal limb length (acquired), femur**
    - **M21.751** Unequal limb length (acquired), right femur
    - **M21.752** Unequal limb length (acquired), left femur
    - ◻ **M21.759** Unequal limb length (acquired), unspecified femur
  - ● **M21.76 Unequal limb length (acquired), tibia and fibula**
    - **M21.761** Unequal limb length (acquired), right tibia
    - **M21.762** Unequal limb length (acquired), left tibia
    - **M21.763** Unequal limb length (acquired), right fibula
    - **M21.764** Unequal limb length (acquired), left fibula
    - ◻ **M21.769** Unequal limb length (acquired), unspecified tibia and fibula
- ● **M21.8 Other specified acquired deformities of limbs**
  - | **Excludes2** | coxa plana (M91.2) |
  - ◻ **M21.80 Other specified acquired deformities of unspecified limb**
  - ● **M21.82 Other specified acquired deformities of upper arm**
    - **M21.821** Other specified acquired deformities of right upper arm
    - **M21.822** Other specified acquired deformities of left upper arm
    - ◻ **M21.829** Other specified acquired deformities of unspecified upper arm
  - ● **M21.83 Other specified acquired deformities of forearm**
    - **M21.831** Other specified acquired deformities of right forearm
    - **M21.832** Other specified acquired deformities of left forearm

- ◻ **M21.839** Other specified acquired deformities of unspecified forearm
- ● **M21.85 Other specified acquired deformities of thigh**
  - **M21.851** Other specified acquired deformities of right thigh
  - **M21.852** Other specified acquired deformities of left thigh
  - ◻ **M21.859** Other specified acquired deformities of unspecified thigh
- ● **M21.86 Other specified acquired deformities of lower leg**
  - **M21.861** Other specified acquired deformities of right lower leg
  - **M21.862** Other specified acquired deformities of left lower leg
  - ◻ **M21.869** Other specified acquired deformities of unspecified lower leg
- ● **M21.9 Unspecified acquired deformity of limb and hand**
  - ◻ **M21.90 Unspecified acquired deformity of unspecified limb**
  - ● **M21.92 Unspecified acquired deformity of upper arm**
    - ◻ **M21.921** Unspecified acquired deformity of right upper arm
    - ◻ **M21.922** Unspecified acquired deformity of left upper arm
    - ◻ **M21.929** Unspecified acquired deformity of unspecified upper arm
  - ● **M21.93 Unspecified acquired deformity of forearm**
    - ◻ **M21.931** Unspecified acquired deformity of right forearm
    - ◻ **M21.932** Unspecified acquired deformity of left forearm
    - ◻ **M21.939** Unspecified acquired deformity of unspecified forearm
  - ● **M21.94 Unspecified acquired deformity of hand**
    - ◻ **M21.941** Unspecified acquired deformity of hand, right hand
    - ◻ **M21.942** Unspecified acquired deformity of hand, left hand
    - ◻ **M21.949** Unspecified acquired deformity of hand, unspecified hand
  - ● **M21.95 Unspecified acquired deformity of thigh**
    - ◻ **M21.951** Unspecified acquired deformity of right thigh
    - ◻ **M21.952** Unspecified acquired deformity of left thigh
    - ◻ **M21.959** Unspecified acquired deformity of unspecified thigh
  - ● **M21.96 Unspecified acquired deformity of lower leg**
    - ◻ **M21.961** Unspecified acquired deformity of right lower leg
    - ◻ **M21.962** Unspecified acquired deformity of left lower leg
    - ◻ **M21.969** Unspecified acquired deformity of unspecified lower leg

● Unacceptable First-Listed Diagnosis   ● Use Additional Character(s)   ◻ Unspecified   **OGCR** Official Guidelines for Coding and Reporting
   🗲 Complication\Comorbidity   🗲 Major C\C | Excludes 1 | | Excludes 2 | Includes   Use additional   Code first   Code also

● **M22 Disorder of patella**

　　[Excludes1] traumatic dislocation of patella (S83.0-)

　● **M22.0 Recurrent dislocation of patella**

　　■ M22.00 Recurrent dislocation of patella, unspecified knee

　　　M22.01 Recurrent dislocation of patella, right knee

　　　M22.02 Recurrent dislocation of patella, left knee

　● **M22.1 Recurrent subluxation of patella**

　　　Incomplete dislocation of patella

　　■ M22.10 Recurrent subluxation of patella, unspecified knee

　　　M22.11 Recurrent subluxation of patella, right knee

　　　M22.12 Recurrent subluxation of patella, left knee

　● **M22.2 Patellofemoral disorders**

　　● M22.2x Patellofemoral disorders

　　　　M22.2x1 Patellofemoral disorders, right knee

　　　　M22.2x2 Patellofemoral disorders, left knee

　　　■ M22.2x9 Patellofemoral disorders, unspecified knee

　● **M22.3 Other derangements of patella**

　　● M22.3x Other derangements of patella

　　　　M22.3x1 Other derangements of patella, right knee

　　　　M22.3x2 Other derangements of patella, left knee

　　　■ M22.3x9 Other derangements of patella, unspecified knee

　● **M22.4 Chondromalacia patellae**

　　■ M22.40 Chondromalacia patellae, unspecified knee

　　　M22.41 Chondromalacia patellae, right knee

　　　M22.42 Chondromalacia patellae, left knee

　● **M22.8 Other disorders of patella**

　　● M22.8x Other disorders of patella

　　　　M22.8x1 Other disorders of patella, right knee

　　　　M22.8x2 Other disorders of patella, left knee

　　　■ M22.8x9 Other disorders of patella, unspecified knee

　● **M22.9 Unspecified disorder of patella**

　　■ M22.90 Unspecified disorder of patella, unspecified knee

　　■ M22.91 Unspecified disorder of patella, right knee

　　■ M22.92 Unspecified disorder of patella, left knee

● **M23 Internal derangement of knee**

　　[Excludes1] ankylosis (M24.66)
　　　　current injury - see injury of knee and lower leg (S80-S89)
　　　　deformity of knee (M21.-)
　　　　osteochondritis dissecans (M93.2)
　　　　recurrent dislocation or subluxation of joints (M24.4)
　　　　recurrent dislocation or subluxation of patella (M22.0-M22.1)

　● **M23.0 Cystic meniscus**

　　● **M23.00 Cystic meniscus, unspecified meniscus**
　　　　Cystic meniscus, unspecified lateral meniscus
　　　　Cystic meniscus, unspecified medial meniscus

　　■ M23.000 Cystic meniscus, unspecified lateral meniscus, right knee

　　■ M23.001 Cystic meniscus, unspecified lateral meniscus, left knee

　　■ M23.002 Cystic meniscus, unspecified lateral meniscus, unspecified knee

　　■ M23.003 Cystic meniscus, unspecified medial meniscus, right knee

　　■ M23.004 Cystic meniscus, unspecified medial meniscus, left knee

　　■ M23.005 Cystic meniscus, unspecified medial meniscus, unspecified knee

　　■ M23.006 Cystic meniscus, unspecified meniscus, right knee

　　■ M23.007 Cystic meniscus, unspecified meniscus, left knee

　　■ M23.009 Cystic meniscus, unspecified meniscus, unspecified knee

　● M23.01 Cystic meniscus, anterior horn of medial meniscus

　　　M23.011 Cystic meniscus, anterior horn of medial meniscus, right knee

　　　M23.012 Cystic meniscus, anterior horn of medial meniscus, left knee

　　■ M23.019 Cystic meniscus, anterior horn of medial meniscus, unspecified knee

　● M23.02 Cystic meniscus, posterior horn of medial meniscus

　　　M23.021 Cystic meniscus, posterior horn of medial meniscus, right knee

　　　M23.022 Cystic meniscus, posterior horn of medial meniscus, left knee

　　■ M23.029 Cystic meniscus, posterior horn of medial meniscus, unspecified knee

　● M23.03 Cystic meniscus, other medial meniscus

　　　M23.031 Cystic meniscus, other medial meniscus, right knee

　　　M23.032 Cystic meniscus, other medial meniscus, left knee

　　■ M23.039 Cystic meniscus, other medial meniscus, unspecified knee

　● M23.04 Cystic meniscus, anterior horn of lateral meniscus

　　　M23.041 Cystic meniscus, anterior horn of lateral meniscus, right knee

　　　M23.042 Cystic meniscus, anterior horn of lateral meniscus, left knee

　　■ M23.049 Cystic meniscus, anterior horn of lateral meniscus, unspecified knee

　● M23.05 Cystic meniscus, posterior horn of lateral meniscus

　　　M23.051 Cystic meniscus, posterior horn of lateral meniscus, right knee

　　　M23.052 Cystic meniscus, posterior horn of lateral meniscus, left knee

　　■ M23.059 Cystic meniscus, posterior horn of lateral meniscus, unspecified knee

● Unacceptable First-Listed Diagnosis　　● Use Additional Character(s)　　■ Unspecified　　**OGCR** Official Guidelines for Coding and Reporting

🗲 Complication\Comorbidity　　🗲 Major C\C　　[Excludes 1]　　[Excludes 2]　　Includes　　Use additional　　Code first　　Code also

1157

● **M23.06 Cystic meniscus, other lateral meniscus**

    M23.061 Cystic meniscus, other lateral meniscus, right knee

    M23.062 Cystic meniscus, other lateral meniscus, left knee

    ◾M23.069 Cystic meniscus, other lateral meniscus, unspecified knee

(See Plate 509 on page NAP-31.)

● **M23.2 Derangement of meniscus due to old tear or injury**
    Old bucket-handle tear

  ● **M23.20 Derangement of unspecified meniscus due to old tear or injury**
     Derangement of unspecified lateral meniscus due to old tear or injury
     Derangement of unspecified medial meniscus due to old tear or injury

    ◾M23.200 Derangement of unspecified lateral meniscus due to old tear or injury, right knee

    ◾M23.201 Derangement of unspecified lateral meniscus due to old tear or injury, left knee

    ◾M23.202 Derangement of unspecified lateral meniscus due to old tear or injury, unspecified knee

    ◾M23.203 Derangement of unspecified medial meniscus due to old tear or injury, right knee

    ◾M23.204 Derangement of unspecified medial meniscus due to old tear or injury, left knee

    ◾M23.205 Derangement of unspecified medial meniscus due to old tear or injury, unspecified knee

    ◾M23.206 Derangement of unspecified meniscus due to old tear or injury, right knee

    ◾M23.207 Derangement of unspecified meniscus due to old tear or injury, left knee

    ◾M23.209 Derangement of unspecified meniscus due to old tear or injury, unspecified knee

  ● **M23.21 Derangement of anterior horn of medial meniscus due to old tear or injury**

    M23.211 Derangement of anterior horn of medial meniscus due to old tear or injury, right knee

    M23.212 Derangement of anterior horn of medial meniscus due to old tear or injury, left knee

    ◾M23.219 Derangement of anterior horn of medial meniscus due to old tear or injury, unspecified knee

  ● **M23.22 Derangement of posterior horn of medial meniscus due to old tear or injury**

    M23.221 Derangement of posterior horn of medial meniscus due to old tear or injury, right knee

    M23.222 Derangement of posterior horn of medial meniscus due to old tear or injury, left knee

    ◾M23.229 Derangement of posterior horn of medial meniscus due to old tear or injury, unspecified knee

● **M23.23 Derangement of other medial meniscus due to old tear or injury**

    M23.231 Derangement of other medial meniscus due to old tear or injury, right knee

    M23.232 Derangement of other medial meniscus due to old tear or injury, left knee

    ◾M23.239 Derangement of other medial meniscus due to old tear or injury, unspecified knee

● **M23.24 Derangement of anterior horn of lateral meniscus due to old tear or injury**

    M23.241 Derangement of anterior horn of lateral meniscus due to old tear or injury, right knee

    M23.242 Derangement of anterior horn of lateral meniscus due to old tear or injury, left knee

    ◾M23.249 Derangement of anterior horn of lateral meniscus due to old tear or injury, unspecified knee

● **M23.25 Derangement of posterior horn of lateral meniscus due to old tear or injury**

    M23.251 Derangement of posterior horn of lateral meniscus due to old tear or injury, right knee

    M23.252 Derangement of posterior horn of lateral meniscus due to old tear or injury, left knee

    ◾M23.259 Derangement of posterior horn of lateral meniscus due to old tear or injury, unspecified knee

● **M23.26 Derangement of other lateral meniscus due to old tear or injury**

    M23.261 Derangement of other lateral meniscus due to old tear or injury, right knee

    M23.262 Derangement of other lateral meniscus due to old tear or injury, left knee

    ◾M23.269 Derangement of other lateral meniscus due to old tear or injury, unspecified knee

● **M23.3 Other meniscus derangements**
    Degenerate meniscus
    Detached meniscus
    Retained meniscus

  ● **M23.30 Other meniscus derangements, unspecified meniscus**
     Other meniscus derangements, unspecified lateral meniscus
     Other meniscus derangements, unspecified medial meniscus

    ◾M23.300 Other meniscus derangements, unspecified lateral meniscus, right knee

    ◾M23.301 Other meniscus derangements, unspecified lateral meniscus, left knee

    ◾M23.302 Other meniscus derangements, unspecified lateral meniscus, unspecified knee

    ◾M23.303 Other meniscus derangements, unspecified medial meniscus, right knee

M23.304 Other meniscus derangements, unspecified medial meniscus, left knee

M23.305 Other meniscus derangements, unspecified medial meniscus, unspecified knee

M23.306 Other meniscus derangements, unspecified meniscus, right knee

M23.307 Other meniscus derangements, unspecified meniscus, left knee

M23.309 Other meniscus derangements, unspecified meniscus, unspecified knee

● M23.31 Other meniscus derangements, anterior horn of medial meniscus

M23.311 Other meniscus derangements, anterior horn of medial meniscus, right knee

M23.312 Other meniscus derangements, anterior horn of medial meniscus, left knee

M23.319 Other meniscus derangements, anterior horn of medial meniscus, unspecified knee

● M23.32 Other meniscus derangements, posterior horn of medial meniscus

M23.321 Other meniscus derangements, posterior horn of medial meniscus, right knee

M23.322 Other meniscus derangements, posterior horn of medial meniscus, left knee

M23.329 Other meniscus derangements, posterior horn of medial meniscus, unspecified knee

● M23.33 Other meniscus derangements, other medial meniscus

M23.331 Other meniscus derangements, other medial meniscus, right knee

M23.332 Other meniscus derangements, other medial meniscus, left knee

M23.339 Other meniscus derangements, other medial meniscus, unspecified knee

● M23.34 Other meniscus derangements, anterior horn of lateral meniscus

M23.341 Other meniscus derangements, anterior horn of lateral meniscus, right knee

M23.342 Other meniscus derangements, anterior horn of lateral meniscus, left knee

M23.349 Other meniscus derangements, anterior horn of lateral meniscus, unspecified knee

● M23.35 Other meniscus derangements, posterior horn of lateral meniscus

M23.351 Other meniscus derangements, posterior horn of lateral meniscus, right knee

M23.352 Other meniscus derangements, posterior horn of lateral meniscus, left knee

M23.359 Other meniscus derangements, posterior horn of lateral meniscus, unspecified knee

● M23.36 Other meniscus derangements, other lateral meniscus

M23.361 Other meniscus derangements, other lateral meniscus, right knee

M23.362 Other meniscus derangements, other lateral meniscus, left knee

M23.369 Other meniscus derangements, other lateral meniscus, unspecified knee

● M23.4 Loose body in knee

M23.40 Loose body in knee, unspecified knee

M23.41 Loose body in knee, right knee

M23.42 Loose body in knee, left knee

● M23.5 Chronic instability of knee

M23.50 Chronic instability of knee, unspecified knee

M23.51 Chronic instability of knee, right knee

M23.52 Chronic instability of knee, left knee

● M23.6 Other spontaneous disruption of ligament(s) of knee

● M23.60 Other spontaneous disruption of unspecified ligament of knee

M23.601 Other spontaneous disruption of unspecified ligament of right knee

M23.602 Other spontaneous disruption of unspecified ligament of left knee

M23.609 Other spontaneous disruption of unspecified ligament of unspecified knee

● M23.61 Other spontaneous disruption of anterior cruciate ligament of knee

M23.611 Other spontaneous disruption of anterior cruciate ligament of right knee

M23.612 Other spontaneous disruption of anterior cruciate ligament of left knee

M23.619 Other spontaneous disruption of anterior cruciate ligament of unspecified knee

● M23.62 Other spontaneous disruption of posterior cruciate ligament of knee

M23.621 Other spontaneous disruption of posterior cruciate ligament of right knee

M23.622 Other spontaneous disruption of posterior cruciate ligament of left knee

M23.629 Other spontaneous disruption of posterior cruciate ligament of unspecified knee

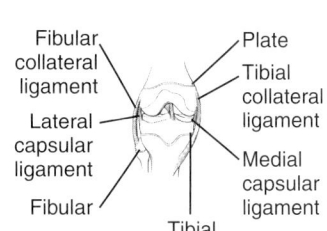

Figure 13-2 Collateral and cruciate ligament of knee. (From DeLee: DeLee and Drez's Orthopaedic Sports Medicine, 2nd ed. 2002, Saunders)

● Unacceptable First-Listed Diagnosis   ● Use Additional Character(s)   ▣ Unspecified   **OGCR** Official Guidelines for Coding and Reporting

🖉 Complication\Comorbidity   🖉 Major C\C   Excludes 1   Excludes 2   Includes   Use additional   Code first   Code also

● M23.63 Other spontaneous disruption of medial
          collateral ligament of knee

　　M23.631 Other spontaneous disruption
　　　　　　of medial collateral ligament of
　　　　　　right knee

　　M23.632 Other spontaneous disruption of
　　　　　　medial collateral ligament of left
　　　　　　knee

　■ M23.639 Other spontaneous disruption
　　　　　　of medial collateral ligament of
　　　　　　unspecified knee

● M23.64 Other spontaneous disruption of lateral
          collateral ligament of knee

　　M23.641 Other spontaneous disruption of
　　　　　　lateral collateral ligament of right
　　　　　　knee

　　M23.642 Other spontaneous disruption of
　　　　　　lateral collateral ligament of left
　　　　　　knee

　■ M23.649 Other spontaneous disruption
　　　　　　of lateral collateral ligament of
　　　　　　unspecified knee

● M23.67 Other spontaneous disruption of capsular
          ligament of knee

　　M23.671 Other spontaneous disruption of
　　　　　　capsular ligament of right knee

　　M23.672 Other spontaneous disruption of
　　　　　　capsular ligament of left knee

　■ M23.679 Other spontaneous disruption of
　　　　　　capsular ligament of unspecified
　　　　　　knee

● M23.8 Other internal derangements of knee
        Laxity of ligament of knee
        Snapping knee

　● M23.8x Other internal derangements of knee

　　　M23.8x1 Other internal derangements of
　　　　　　　right knee

　　　M23.8x2 Other internal derangements of
　　　　　　　left knee

　■　M23.8x9 Other internal derangements of
　　　　　　　unspecified knee

● M23.9 Unspecified internal derangement of knee

　■ M23.90 Unspecified internal derangement of
　　　　　　unspecified knee

　■ M23.91 Unspecified internal derangement of right
　　　　　　knee

　■ M23.92 Unspecified internal derangement of left
　　　　　　knee

● M24 Other specific joint derangements

　Excludes1 current injury - see injury of joint by body
　　　　　　region

　Excludes2 ganglion (M67.4)
　　　　　　snapping knee (M23.8-)
　　　　　　temporomandibular joint disorders (M26.6-)

● M24.0 Loose body in joint

　Excludes2 loose body in knee (M23.4)

　■ M24.00 Loose body in unspecified joint

　● M24.01 Loose body in shoulder

　　　M24.011 Loose body in right shoulder

　　　M24.012 Loose body in left shoulder

　■　M24.019 Loose body in unspecified
　　　　　　　shoulder

● M24.02 Loose body in elbow

　　M24.021 Loose body in right elbow

　　M24.022 Loose body in left elbow

　■ M24.029 Loose body in unspecified elbow

● M24.03 Loose body in wrist

　　M24.031 Loose body in right wrist

　　M24.032 Loose body in left wrist

　■ M24.039 Loose body in unspecified wrist

● M24.04 Loose body in finger joints

　　M24.041 Loose body in right finger joint(s)

　　M24.042 Loose body in left finger joint(s)

　■ M24.049 Loose body in unspecified finger
　　　　　　joint(s)

● M24.05 Loose body in hip

　　M24.051 Loose body in right hip

　　M24.052 Loose body in left hip

　■ M24.059 Loose body in unspecified hip

● M24.07 Loose body in ankle and toe joints

　　M24.071 Loose body in right ankle

　　M24.072 Loose body in left ankle

　　M24.073 Loose body in unspecified ankle

　　M24.074 Loose body in right toe joint(s)

　　M24.075 Loose body in left toe joint(s)

　■ M24.076 Loose body in unspecified toe
　　　　　　joints

　　M24.08 Loose body, other site

● M24.1 Other articular cartilage disorders

　Excludes2 chondrocalcinosis (M11.1, M11.2-)
　　　　　　internal derangement of knee (M23.-)
　　　　　　metastatic calcification (E83.5)
　　　　　　ochronosis (E70.2)

　■ M24.10 Other articular cartilage disorders,
　　　　　　unspecified site

● M24.11 Other articular cartilage disorders, shoulder

　　M24.111 Other articular cartilage
　　　　　　disorders, right shoulder

　　M24.112 Other articular cartilage
　　　　　　disorders, left shoulder

　■ M24.119 Other articular cartilage
　　　　　　disorders, unspecified shoulder

● M24.12 Other articular cartilage disorders, elbow

　　M24.121 Other articular cartilage
　　　　　　disorders, right elbow

　　M24.122 Other articular cartilage
　　　　　　disorders, left elbow

　■ M24.129 Other articular cartilage
　　　　　　disorders, unspecified elbow

● M24.13 Other articular cartilage disorders, wrist

　　M24.131 Other articular cartilage
　　　　　　disorders, right wrist

　　M24.132 Other articular cartilage
　　　　　　disorders, left wrist

　■ M24.139 Other articular cartilage
　　　　　　disorders, unspecified wrist

● M24.14 Other articular cartilage disorders, hand

　　M24.141 Other articular cartilage
　　　　　　disorders, right hand

　　M24.142 Other articular cartilage
　　　　　　disorders, left hand

　■ M24.149 Other articular cartilage
　　　　　　disorders, unspecified hand

● Unacceptable First-Listed Diagnosis   ● Use Additional Character(s)   ■ Unspecified   OGCR Official Guidelines for Coding and Reporting

1160   🅒 Complication\Comorbidity   🅒 Major C\C   Excludes 1   Excludes 2   Includes   Use additional   Code first   Code also

● M24.15 Other articular cartilage disorders, hip

    M24.151 Other articular cartilage disorders, right hip

    M24.152 Other articular cartilage disorders, left hip

    ■ M24.159 Other articular cartilage disorders, unspecified hip

● M24.17 Other articular cartilage disorders, ankle and foot

    M24.171 Other articular cartilage disorders, right ankle

    M24.172 Other articular cartilage disorders, left ankle

    ■ M24.173 Other articular cartilage disorders, unspecified ankle

    M24.174 Other articular cartilage disorders, right foot

    M24.175 Other articular cartilage disorders, left foot

    ■ M24.176 Other articular cartilage disorders, unspecified foot

● M24.2 Disorder of ligament

    Instability secondary to old ligament injury
    Ligamentous laxity NOS

    | Excludes1 | familial ligamentous laxity (M35.7) |
    | Excludes2 | internal derangement of knee (M23.5-M23.89) |

■ M24.20 Disorder of ligament, unspecified site

● M24.21 Disorder of ligament, shoulder

    M24.211 Disorder of ligament, right shoulder

    M24.212 Disorder of ligament, left shoulder

    ■ M24.219 Disorder of ligament, unspecified shoulder

● M24.22 Disorder of ligament, elbow

    M24.221 Disorder of ligament, right elbow

    M24.222 Disorder of ligament, left elbow

    ■ M24.229 Disorder of ligament, unspecified elbow

● M24.23 Disorder of ligament, wrist

    M24.231 Disorder of ligament, right wrist

    M24.232 Disorder of ligament, left wrist

    ■ M24.239 Disorder of ligament, unspecified wrist

● M24.24 Disorder of ligament, hand

    M24.241 Disorder of ligament, right hand

    M24.242 Disorder of ligament, left hand

    ■ M24.249 Disorder of ligament, unspecified hand

● M24.25 Disorder of ligament, hip

    M24.251 Disorder of ligament, right hip

    M24.252 Disorder of ligament, left hip

    ■ M24.259 Disorder of ligament, unspecified hip

● M24.27 Disorder of ligament, ankle and foot

    M24.271 Disorder of ligament, right ankle

    M24.272 Disorder of ligament, left ankle

    ■ M24.273 Disorder of ligament, unspecified ankle

    M24.274 Disorder of ligament, right foot

    M24.275 Disorder of ligament, left foot

    ■ M24.276 Disorder of ligament, unspecified foot

M24.28 Disorder of ligament, vertebrae

● M24.3 Pathological dislocation of joint, not elsewhere classified

    | Excludes1 | congenital dislocation or displacement of joint - see congenital malformations and deformations of the musculoskeletal system (Q65-Q79) |
    | | current injury - see injury of joints and ligaments by body region |
    | | recurrent dislocation of joint (M24.4-) |

■ M24.30 Pathological dislocation of unspecified joint, not elsewhere classified

● M24.31 Pathological dislocation of shoulder, not elsewhere classified

    M24.311 Pathological dislocation of right shoulder, not elsewhere classified

    M24.312 Pathological dislocation of left shoulder, not elsewhere classified

    ■ M24.319 Pathological dislocation of unspecified shoulder, not elsewhere classified

● M24.32 Pathological dislocation of elbow, not elsewhere classified

    M24.321 Pathological dislocation of right elbow, not elsewhere classified

    M24.322 Pathological dislocation of left elbow, not elsewhere classified

    ■ M24.329 Pathological dislocation of unspecified elbow, not elsewhere classified

● M24.33 Pathological dislocation of wrist, not elsewhere classified

    M24.331 Pathological dislocation of right wrist, not elsewhere classified

    M24.332 Pathological dislocation of left wrist, not elsewhere classified

    ■ M24.339 Pathological dislocation of unspecified wrist, not elsewhere classified

● M24.34 Pathological dislocation of hand, not elsewhere classified

    M24.341 Pathological dislocation of right hand, not elsewhere classified

    M24.342 Pathological dislocation of left hand, not elsewhere classified

    ■ M24.349 Pathological dislocation of unspecified hand, not elsewhere classified

● M24.35 Pathological dislocation of hip, not elsewhere classified

    M24.351 Pathological dislocation of right hip, not elsewhere classified

    M24.352 Pathological dislocation of left hip, not elsewhere classified

    ■ M24.359 Pathological dislocation of unspecified hip, not elsewhere classified

● Unacceptable First-Listed Diagnosis   ● Use Additional Character(s)   ■ Unspecified   **OGCR** Official Guidelines for Coding and Reporting

 Complication\Comorbidity    Major C\C   Excludes 1   Excludes 2   Includes   Use additional   Code first   Code also

1161

CHAPTER 13 (M00-M99)

● M24.36 Pathological dislocation of knee, not elsewhere classified

    M24.361 Pathological dislocation of right knee, not elsewhere classified

    M24.362 Pathological dislocation of left knee, not elsewhere classified

    ■M24.369 Pathological dislocation of unspecified knee, not elsewhere classified

● M24.37 Pathological dislocation of ankle and foot, not elsewhere classified

    M24.371 Pathological dislocation of right ankle, not elsewhere classified

    M24.372 Pathological dislocation of left ankle, not elsewhere classified

    ■M24.373 Pathological dislocation of unspecified ankle, not elsewhere classified

    M24.374 Pathological dislocation of right foot, not elsewhere classified

    M24.375 Pathological dislocation of left foot, not elsewhere classified

    ■M24.376 Pathological dislocation of unspecified foot, not elsewhere classified

● M24.4 Recurrent dislocation of joint
    Recurrent subluxation of joint

    Excludes2   recurrent dislocation of patella (M22.0-M22.1)
                    recurrent vertebral dislocation (M43.3-, M43.4, M43.5-)

    ■M24.40 Recurrent dislocation, unspecified joint

● M24.41 Recurrent dislocation, shoulder

    M24.411 Recurrent dislocation, right shoulder

    M24.412 Recurrent dislocation, left shoulder

    ■M24.419 Recurrent dislocation, unspecified shoulder

● M24.42 Recurrent dislocation, elbow

    M24.421 Recurrent dislocation, right elbow

    M24.422 Recurrent dislocation, left elbow

    ■M24.429 Recurrent dislocation, unspecified elbow

● M24.43 Recurrent dislocation, wrist

    M24.431 Recurrent dislocation, right wrist

    M24.432 Recurrent dislocation, left wrist

    ■M24.439 Recurrent dislocation, unspecified wrist

● M24.44 Recurrent dislocation, hand and finger(s)

    M24.441 Recurrent dislocation, right hand

    M24.442 Recurrent dislocation, left hand

    ■M24.443 Recurrent dislocation, unspecified hand

    M24.444 Recurrent dislocation, right finger

    M24.445 Recurrent dislocation, left finger

    ■M24.446 Recurrent dislocation, unspecified finger

● M24.45 Recurrent dislocation, hip

    M24.451 Recurrent dislocation, right hip

    M24.452 Recurrent dislocation, left hip

    ■M24.459 Recurrent dislocation, unspecified hip

● M24.46 Recurrent dislocation, knee

    M24.461 Recurrent dislocation, right knee

    M24.462 Recurrent dislocation, left knee

    ■M24.469 Recurrent dislocation, unspecified knee

● M24.47 Recurrent dislocation, ankle, foot and toes

    M24.471 Recurrent dislocation, right ankle

    M24.472 Recurrent dislocation, left ankle

    ■M24.473 Recurrent dislocation, unspecified ankle

    M24.474 Recurrent dislocation, right foot

    M24.475 Recurrent dislocation, left foot

    M24.476 Recurrent dislocation, unspecified foot

    M24.477 Recurrent dislocation, right toe(s)

    M24.478 Recurrent dislocation, left toe(s)

    ■M24.479 Recurrent dislocation, unspecified toe(s)

● M24.5 Contracture of joint

    Excludes1   contracture of muscle without contracture of joint (M62.4-)
                    contracture of tendon (sheath) without contracture of joint (M62.4-)
                    Dupuytren's contracture (M72.0)

    Excludes2   acquired deformities of limbs (M20-M21)

    ■M24.50 Contracture, unspecified joint

● M24.51 Contracture, shoulder

    M24.511 Contracture, right shoulder

    M24.512 Contracture, left shoulder

    ■M24.519 Contracture, unspecified shoulder

● M24.52 Contracture, elbow

    M24.521 Contracture, right elbow

    M24.522 Contracture, left elbow

    ■M24.529 Contracture, unspecified elbow

● M24.53 Contracture, wrist

    M24.531 Contracture, right wrist

    M24.532 Contracture, left wrist

    ■M24.539 Contracture, unspecified wrist

● M24.54 Contracture, hand

    M24.541 Contracture, right hand

    M24.542 Contracture, left hand

    ■M24.549 Contracture, unspecified hand

● M24.55 Contracture, hip

    M24.551 Contracture, right hip

    M24.552 Contracture, left hip

    ■M24.559 Contracture, unspecified hip

● M24.56 Contracture, knee

    M24.561 Contracture, right knee

    M24.562 Contracture, left knee

    ■M24.569 Contracture, unspecified knee

● M24.57 Contracture, ankle and foot

    M24.571 Contracture, right ankle

    M24.572 Contracture, left ankle

    ■M24.573 Contracture, unspecified ankle

    M24.574 Contracture, right foot

    M24.575 Contracture, left foot

    ■M24.576 Contracture, unspecified foot

● Unacceptable First-Listed Diagnosis   ● Use Additional Character(s)   ■ Unspecified   **OGCR** Official Guidelines for Coding and Reporting

🅒 Complication\Comorbidity   🅜 Major C\C   Excludes 1   Excludes 2   Includes   Use additional   Code first   Code also

Item 13–5 Ankylosis or arthrokleisis is a consolidation of a joint due to disease, injury, or surgical procedure. Spondylosis is the degeneration of the vertebral processes and formation of osteophytes and commonly occurs with age. **Spondylitis** or ankylosing spondylitis is a type of arthritis that affects the spine or backbone causing back pain and stiffness.

● M24.6 Ankylosis of joint
>> Excludes1   stiffness of joint without ankylosis (M25.6-)
>> Excludes2   spine (M43.2-)

> ▪ M24.60 Ankylosis, unspecified joint
> ● M24.61 Ankylosis, shoulder
>> M24.611 Ankylosis, right shoulder
>> M24.612 Ankylosis, left shoulder
>> ▪ M24.619 Ankylosis, unspecified shoulder
> ● M24.62 Ankylosis, elbow
>> M24.621 Ankylosis, right elbow
>> M24.622 Ankylosis, left elbow
>> ▪ M24.629 Ankylosis, unspecified elbow
> ● M24.63 Ankylosis, wrist
>> M24.631 Ankylosis, right wrist
>> M24.632 Ankylosis, left wrist
>> ▪ M24.639 Ankylosis, unspecified wrist
> ● M24.64 Ankylosis, hand
>> M24.641 Ankylosis, right hand
>> M24.642 Ankylosis, left hand
>> ▪ M24.649 Ankylosis, unspecified hand
> ● M24.65 Ankylosis, hip
>> M24.651 Ankylosis, right hip
>> M24.652 Ankylosis, left hip
>> ▪ M24.659 Ankylosis, unspecified hip
> ● M24.66 Ankylosis, knee
>> M24.661 Ankylosis, right knee
>> M24.662 Ankylosis, left knee
>> ▪ M24.669 Ankylosis, unspecified knee
> ● M24.67 Ankylosis, ankle and foot
>> M24.671 Ankylosis, right ankle
>> M24.672 Ankylosis, left ankle
>> ▪ M24.673 Ankylosis, unspecified ankle
>> M24.674 Ankylosis, right foot
>> M24.675 Ankylosis, left foot
>> ▪ M24.676 Ankylosis, unspecified foot

M24.7 Protrusio acetabuli

● M24.8 Other specific joint derangements, not elsewhere classified
>> Excludes2   iliotibial band syndrome (M76.3)

> ▪ M24.80 Other specific joint derangements of unspecified joint, not elsewhere classified
> ● M24.81 Other specific joint derangements of shoulder, not elsewhere classified
>> M24.811 Other specific joint derangements of right shoulder, not elsewhere classified
>> M24.812 Other specific joint derangements of left shoulder, not elsewhere classified
>> ▪ M24.819 Other specific joint derangements of unspecified shoulder, not elsewhere classified

● M24.82 Other specific joint derangements of elbow, not elsewhere classified
>> M24.821 Other specific joint derangements of right elbow, not elsewhere classified
>> M24.822 Other specific joint derangements of left elbow, not elsewhere classified
>> ▪ M24.829 Other specific joint derangements of unspecified elbow, not elsewhere classified
● M24.83 Other specific joint derangements of wrist, not elsewhere classified
>> M24.831 Other specific joint derangements of right wrist, not elsewhere classified
>> M24.832 Other specific joint derangements of left wrist, not elsewhere classified
>> ▪ M24.839 Other specific joint derangements of unspecified wrist, not elsewhere classified
● M24.84 Other specific joint derangements of hand, not elsewhere classified
>> M24.841 Other specific joint derangements of right hand, not elsewhere classified
>> M24.842 Other specific joint derangements of left hand, not elsewhere classified
>> ▪ M24.849 Other specific joint derangements of unspecified hand, not elsewhere classified
● M24.85 Other specific joint derangements of hip, not elsewhere classified
>> Irritable hip
>> M24.851 Other specific joint derangements of right hip, not elsewhere classified
>> M24.852 Other specific joint derangements of left hip, not elsewhere classified
>> ▪ M24.859 Other specific joint derangements of unspecified hip, not elsewhere classified
● M24.87 Other specific joint derangements of ankle and foot, not elsewhere classified
>> M24.871 Other specific joint derangements of right ankle, not elsewhere classified
>> M24.872 Other specific joint derangements of left ankle, not elsewhere classified
>> ▪ M24.873 Other specific joint derangements of unspecified ankle, not elsewhere classified
>> M24.874 Other specific joint derangements of right foot, not elsewhere classified
>> M24.875 Other specific joint derangements left foot, not elsewhere classified
>> ▪ M24.876 Other specific joint derangements of unspecified foot, not elsewhere classified

▪ M24.9 Joint derangement, unspecified

● Unacceptable First-Listed Diagnosis   ● Use Additional Character(s)   ▪ Unspecified   **OGCR** Official Guidelines for Coding and Reporting

🔖 Complication\Comorbidity   🔖 Major C\C   Excludes 1   Excludes 2   Includes   Use additional   Code first   Code also

● M25   **Other joint disorder, not elsewhere classified**

> **Excludes2**   abnormality of gait and mobility (R26.-)
> acquired deformities of limb (M20-M21)
> calcification of bursa (M71.4-)
> calcification of shoulder (joint) (M75.3)
> calcification of tendon (M65.2-)
> difficulty in walking (R26.2)
> temporomandibular joint disorder (M26.6-)

  ● M25.0   **Hemarthrosis**

> **Excludes1**   current injury - see injury of joint by
> body region
> hemophilic arthropathy (M36.2)

    ■ M25.00   Hemarthrosis, unspecified joint 🝆

    ● M25.01   Hemarthrosis, shoulder

       M25.011   Hemarthrosis, right shoulder 🝆

       M25.012   Hemarthrosis, left shoulder 🝆

      ■ M25.019   Hemarthrosis, unspecified
         shoulder 🝆

    ● M25.02   Hemarthrosis, elbow

       M25.021   Hemarthrosis, right elbow 🝆

       M25.022   Hemarthrosis, left elbow 🝆

      ■ M25.029   Hemarthrosis, unspecified elbow 🝆

    ● M25.03   Hemarthrosis, wrist

       M25.031   Hemarthrosis, right wrist 🝆

       M25.032   Hemarthrosis, left wrist 🝆

      ■ M25.039   Hemarthrosis, unspecified wrist 🝆

    ● M25.04   Hemarthrosis, hand

       M25.041   Hemarthrosis, right hand 🝆

       M25.042   Hemarthrosis, left hand 🝆

      ■ M25.049   Hemarthrosis, unspecified hand 🝆

    ● M25.05   Hemarthrosis, hip

       M25.051   Hemarthrosis, right hip 🝆

       M25.052   Hemarthrosis, left hip 🝆

      ■ M25.059   Hemarthrosis, unspecified hip 🝆

    ● M25.06   Hemarthrosis, knee

       M25.061   Hemarthrosis, right knee 🝆

       M25.062   Hemarthrosis, left knee 🝆

      ■ M25.069   Hemarthrosis, unspecified knee 🝆

    ● M25.07   Hemarthrosis, ankle and foot

       M25.071   Hemarthrosis, right ankle 🝆

       M25.072   Hemarthrosis, left ankle 🝆

      ■ M25.073   Hemarthrosis, unspecified ankle 🝆

       M25.074   Hemarthrosis, right foot 🝆

       M25.075   Hemarthrosis, left foot 🝆

      ■ M25.076   Hemarthrosis, unspecified foot 🝆

     M25.08   Hemarthrosis, vertebrae 🝆

  ● M25.1   **Fistula of joint**

    ■ M25.10   Fistula, unspecified joint

    ● M25.11   Fistula, shoulder

       M25.111   Fistula, right shoulder

       M25.112   Fistula, left shoulder

      ■ M25.119   Fistula, unspecified shoulder

    ● M25.12   Fistula, elbow

       M25.121   Fistula, right elbow

       M25.122   Fistula, left elbow

      ■ M25.129   Fistula, unspecified elbow

    ● M25.13   Fistula, wrist

       M25.131   Fistula, right wrist

       M25.132   Fistula, left wrist

      ■ M25.139   Fistula, unspecified wrist

  ● M25.14   Fistula, hand

     M25.141   Fistula, right hand

     M25.142   Fistula, left hand

    ■ M25.149   Fistula, unspecified hand

  ● M25.15   Fistula, hip

     M25.151   Fistula, right hip

     M25.152   Fistula, left hip

    ■ M25.159   Fistula, unspecified hip

  ● M25.16   Fistula, knee

     M25.161   Fistula, right knee

     M25.162   Fistula, left knee

    ■ M25.169   Fistula, unspecified knee

  ● M25.17   Fistula, ankle and foot

     M25.171   Fistula, right ankle

     M25.172   Fistula, left ankle

    ■ M25.173   Fistula, unspecified ankle

     M25.174   Fistula, right foot

     M25.175   Fistula, left foot

    ■ M25.176   Fistula, unspecified foot

     M25.18   Fistula, vertebrae

● M25.2   **Flail joint**

  ■ M25.20   Flail joint, unspecified joint

  ● M25.21   Flail joint, shoulder

     M25.211   Flail joint, right shoulder

     M25.212   Flail joint, left shoulder

    ■ M25.219   Flail joint, unspecified shoulder

  ● M25.22   Flail joint, elbow

     M25.221   Flail joint, right elbow

     M25.222   Flail joint, left elbow

    ■ M25.229   Flail joint, unspecified elbow

  ● M25.23   Flail joint, wrist

     M25.231   Flail joint, right wrist

     M25.232   Flail joint, left wrist

    ■ M25.239   Flail joint, unspecified wrist

  ● M25.24   Flail joint, hand

     M25.241   Flail joint, right hand

     M25.242   Flail joint, left hand

    ■ M25.249   Flail joint, unspecified hand

  ● M25.25   Flail joint, hip

     M25.251   Flail joint, right hip

     M25.252   Flail joint, left hip

    ■ M25.259   Flail joint, unspecified hip

  ● M25.26   Flail joint, knee

     M25.261   Flail joint, right knee

     M25.262   Flail joint, left knee

    ■ M25.269   Flail joint, unspecified knee

  ● M25.27   Flail joint, ankle and foot

     M25.271   Flail joint, right ankle and foot

     M25.272   Flail joint, left ankle and foot

    ■ M25.279   Flail joint, unspecified ankle and
       foot

     M25.28   Flail joint, other site

● M25.3   Other instability of joint

> **Excludes1**   instability of joint secondary to old ligament injury (M24.2-)
> instability of joint secondary to removal of joint prosthesis (M96.8-)

> **Excludes2**   spinal instabilities (M53.2-)

◼ M25.30   Other instability, unspecified joint

● M25.31   Other instability, shoulder
     M25.311   Other instability, right shoulder
     M25.312   Other instability, left shoulder
     ◼ M25.319   Other instability, unspecified shoulder

● M25.32   Other instability, elbow
     M25.321   Other instability, right elbow
     M25.322   Other instability, left elbow
     ◼ M25.329   Other instability, unspecified elbow

● M25.33   Other instability, wrist
     M25.331   Other instability, right wrist
     M25.332   Other instability, left wrist
     ◼ M25.339   Other instability, unspecified wrist

● M25.34   Other instability, hand
     M25.341   Other instability, right hand
     M25.342   Other instability, left hand
     ◼ M25.349   Other instability, unspecified hand

● M25.35   Other instability, hip
     M25.351   Other instability, right hip
     M25.352   Other instability, left hip
     ◼ M25.359   Other instability, unspecified hip

● M25.36   Other instability, knee
     M25.361   Other instability, right knee
     M25.362   Other instability, left knee
     ◼ M25.369   Other instability, unspecified knee

● M25.37   Other instability, ankle and foot
     M25.371   Other instability, right ankle
     M25.372   Other instability, left ankle
     ◼ M25.373   Other instability, unspecified ankle
     M25.374   Other instability, right foot
     M25.375   Other instability, left foot
     ◼ M25.376   Other instability, unspecified foot

● M25.4   Effusion of joint

> **Excludes1**   hydrarthrosis in yaws (A66.6)
> intermittent hydrarthrosis (M12.4-)
> other infective (teno)synovitis (M65.1-)

◼ M25.40   Effusion, unspecified joint

● M25.41   Effusion, shoulder
     M25.411   Effusion, right shoulder
     M25.412   Effusion, left shoulder
     ◼ M25.419   Effusion, unspecified shoulder

● M25.42   Effusion, elbow
     M25.421   Effusion, right elbow
     M25.422   Effusion, left elbow
     ◼ M25.429   Effusion, unspecified elbow

● M25.43   Effusion, wrist
     M25.431   Effusion, right wrist
     M25.432   Effusion, left wrist
     ◼ M25.439   Effusion, unspecified wrist

● M25.44   Effusion, hand
     M25.441   Effusion, right hand
     M25.442   Effusion, left hand
     ◼ M25.449   Effusion, unspecified hand

● M25.45   Effusion, hip
     M25.451   Effusion, right hip
     M25.452   Effusion, left hip
     ◼ M25.459   Effusion, unspecified hip

● M25.46   Effusion, knee
     M25.461   Effusion, right knee
     M25.462   Effusion, left knee
     ◼ M25.469   Effusion, unspecified knee

● M25.47   Effusion, ankle and foot
     M25.471   Effusion, right ankle
     M25.472   Effusion, left ankle
     ◼ M25.473   Effusion, unspecified ankle
     M25.474   Effusion, right foot
     M25.475   Effusion, left foot
     ◼ M25.476   Effusion, unspecified foot

M25.48   Effusion, other site

● M25.5   Pain in joint

> **Excludes2**   pain in hand (M79.64-)
> pain in fingers (M79.64-)
> pain in foot (M79.67-)
> pain in limb (M79.6-)
> pain in toes (M79.67-)

◼ M25.50   Pain in unspecified joint

● M25.51   Pain in shoulder
     M25.511   Pain in right shoulder
     M25.512   Pain in left shoulder
     ◼ M25.519   Pain in unspecified shoulder

● M25.52   Pain in elbow
     M25.521   Pain in right elbow
     M25.522   Pain in left elbow
     ◼ M25.529   Pain in unspecified elbow

● M25.53   Pain in wrist
     M25.531   Pain in right wrist
     M25.532   Pain in left wrist
     ◼ M25.539   Pain in unspecified wrist

● M25.55   Pain in hip
     M25.551   Pain in right hip
     M25.552   Pain in left hip
     ◼ M25.559   Pain in unspecified hip

● M25.56   Pain in knee
     M25.561   Pain in right knee
     M25.562   Pain in left knee
     ◼ M25.569   Pain in unspecified knee

● M25.57   Pain in ankle
     M25.571   Pain in right ankle
     M25.572   Pain in left ankle
     ◼ M25.579   Pain in unspecified ankle

● Unacceptable First-Listed Diagnosis   ● Use Additional Character(s)   ◼ Unspecified   **OGCR** Official Guidelines for Coding and Reporting

 Complication\Comorbidity   Major C\C   Excludes 1   Excludes 2   Includes   Use additional   Code first   Code also

1165

● **M25.6 Stiffness of joint, not elsewhere classified**

> **Excludes1**   ankylosis of joint (M24.6-)
> contracture of joint (M24.5-)

◻ **M25.60 Stiffness of unspecified joint, not elsewhere classified**

● **M25.61 Stiffness of shoulder, not elsewhere classified**

   M25.611 Stiffness of right shoulder, not elsewhere classified

   M25.612 Stiffness of left shoulder, not elsewhere classified

   ◻ **M25.619 Stiffness of unspecified shoulder, not elsewhere classified**

● **M25.62 Stiffness of elbow, not elsewhere classified**

   M25.621 Stiffness of right elbow, not elsewhere classified

   M25.622 Stiffness of left elbow, not elsewhere classified

   ◻ **M25.629 Stiffness of unspecified elbow, not elsewhere classified**

● **M25.63 Stiffness of wrist, not elsewhere classified**

   M25.631 Stiffness of right wrist, not elsewhere classified

   M25.632 Stiffness of left wrist, not elsewhere classified

   ◻ **M25.639 Stiffness of unspecified wrist, not elsewhere classified**

● **M25.64 Stiffness of hand, not elsewhere classified**

   M25.641 Stiffness of right hand, not elsewhere classified

   M25.642 Stiffness of left hand, not elsewhere classified

   ◻ **M25.649 Stiffness of unspecified hand, not elsewhere classified**

● **M25.65 Stiffness of hip, not elsewhere classified**

   M25.651 Stiffness of right hip, not elsewhere classified

   M25.652 Stiffness of left hip, not elsewhere classified

   ◻ **M25.659 Stiffness of unspecified hip, not elsewhere classified**

● **M25.66 Stiffness of knee, not elsewhere classified**

   M25.661 Stiffness of right knee, not elsewhere classified

   M25.662 Stiffness of left knee, not elsewhere classified

   ◻ **M25.669 Stiffness of unspecified knee, not elsewhere classified**

● **M25.67 Stiffness of ankle and foot, not elsewhere classified**

   M25.671 Stiffness of right ankle, not elsewhere classified

   M25.672 Stiffness of left ankle, not elsewhere classified

   ◻ **M25.673 Stiffness of unspecified ankle, not elsewhere classified**

   M25.674 Stiffness of right foot, not elsewhere classified

   M25.675 Stiffness of left foot, not elsewhere classified

   ◻ **M25.676 Stiffness of unspecified foot, not elsewhere classified**

● **M25.7 Osteophyte**

◻ **M25.70 Osteophyte, unspecified joint**

● **M25.71 Osteophyte, shoulder**

   M25.711 Osteophyte, right shoulder

   M25.712 Osteophyte, left shoulder

   ◻ **M25.719 Osteophyte, unspecified shoulder**

● **M25.72 Osteophyte, elbow**

   M25.721 Osteophyte, right elbow

   M25.722 Osteophyte, left elbow

   ◻ **M25.729 Osteophyte, unspecified elbow**

● **M25.73 Osteophyte, wrist**

   M25.731 Osteophyte, right wrist

   M25.732 Osteophyte, left wrist

   ◻ **M25.739 Osteophyte, unspecified wrist**

● **M25.74 Osteophyte, hand**

   M25.741 Osteophyte, right hand

   M25.742 Osteophyte, left hand

   ◻ **M25.749 Osteophyte, unspecified hand**

● **M25.75 Osteophyte, hip**

   M25.751 Osteophyte, right hip

   M25.752 Osteophyte, left hip

   ◻ **M25.759 Osteophyte, unspecified hip**

● **M25.76 Osteophyte, knee**

   M25.761 Osteophyte, right knee

   M25.762 Osteophyte, left knee

   ◻ **M25.769 Osteophyte, unspecified knee**

● **M25.77 Osteophyte, ankle and foot**

   M25.771 Osteophyte, right ankle

   M25.772 Osteophyte, left ankle

   ◻ **M25.773 Osteophyte, unspecified ankle**

   M25.774 Osteophyte, right foot

   M25.775 Osteophyte, left foot

   ◻ **M25.776 Osteophyte, unspecified foot**

   M25.78 Osteophyte, vertebrae

● **M25.8 Other specified joint disorders**

◻ **M25.80 Other specified joint disorders, unspecified joint**

● **M25.81 Other specified joint disorders, shoulder**

   M25.811 Other specified joint disorders, right shoulder

   M25.812 Other specified joint disorders, left shoulder

   ◻ **M25.819 Other specified joint disorders, unspecified shoulder**

● **M25.82 Other specified joint disorders, elbow**

   M25.821 Other specified joint disorders, right elbow

   M25.822 Other specified joint disorders, left elbow

   ◻ **M25.829 Other specified joint disorders, unspecified elbow**

● **M25.83 Other specified joint disorders, wrist**

   M25.831 Other specified joint disorders, right wrist

   M25.832 Other specified joint disorders, left wrist

   ◻ **M25.839 Other specified joint disorders, unspecified wrist**

● Unacceptable First-Listed Diagnosis   ● Use Additional Character(s)   ◻ Unspecified   **OGCR** Official Guidelines for Coding and Reporting

🅒 Complication\Comorbidity   🅒 Major C\C   Excludes 1   Excludes 2   Includes   Use additional   Code first   Code also

● M25.84 Other specified joint disorders, hand

    M25.841 Other specified joint disorders, right hand

    M25.842 Other specified joint disorders, left hand

    ◼ M25.849 Other specified joint disorders, unspecified hand

● M25.85 Other specified joint disorders, hip

    M25.851 Other specified joint disorders, right hip

    M25.852 Other specified joint disorders, left hip

    ◼ M25.859 Other specified joint disorders, unspecified hip

● M25.86 Other specified joint disorders, knee

    M25.861 Other specified joint disorders, right knee

    M25.862 Other specified joint disorders, left knee

    ◼ M25.869 Other specified joint disorders, unspecified knee

● M25.87 Other specified joint disorders, ankle and foot

    M25.871 Other specified joint disorders, right ankle and foot

    M25.872 Other specified joint disorders, left ankle and foot

    ◼ M25.879 Other specified joint disorders, unspecified ankle and foot

◼ M25.9 Joint disorder, unspecified

> **Excludes1**   hemifacial atrophy or hypertrophy (Q67.4)
> unilateral condylar hyperplasia or hypoplasia (M27.8)

DENTOFACIAL ANOMALIES [INCLUDING MALOCCLUSION] AND OTHER DISORDERS OF JAW (M26-M27)

● M26 Dentofacial anomalies [including malocclusion]

● M26.0 Major anomalies of jaw size

> **Excludes1**   acromegaly (E22.0)
> Robin's syndrome (Q87.0)

◼ M26.00 Unspecified anomaly of jaw size

M26.01 Maxillary hyperplasia

M26.02 Maxillary hypoplasia

M26.03 Mandibular hyperplasia

M26.04 Mandibular hypoplasia

M26.05 Macrogenia

M26.06 Microgenia

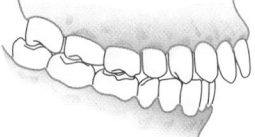

Figure 13-3   Dental malocclusion.

Item 13–6   **Hyperplasia** is a condition of overdevelopment, whereas **hypoplasia** is a condition of underdevelopment. **Macrogenia** is overdevelopment of the chin, whereas **microgenia** is underdevelopment of the chin.

M26.07 Excessive tuberosity of jaw
    Entire maxillary tuberosity

M26.09 Other specified anomalies of jaw size

● M26.1 Anomalies of jaw-cranial base relationship

  ◼ M26.10 Unspecified anomaly of jaw-cranial base relationship

M26.11 Maxillary asymmetry

M26.12 Other jaw asymmetry

M26.19 Other specified anomalies of jaw-cranial base relationship

● M26.2 Anomalies of dental arch relationship

  ◼ M26.20 Unspecified anomaly of dental arch relationship

● M26.21 Malocclusion, Angle's class

    M26.211 Malocclusion, Angle's class I
      Neutro-occlusion

    M26.212 Malocclusion, Angle's class II
      Disto-occlusion Division I
      Disto-occlusion Division II

    M26.213 Malocclusion, Angle's class III
      Mesio-occlusion

    ◼ M26.219 Malocclusion, Angle's class, unspecified

● M26.22 Open occlusal relationship

    M26.220 Open anterior occlusal relationship
      Anterior openbite

    M26.221 Open posterior occlusal relationship
      Posterior openbite

M26.23 Excessive horizontal overlap
    Excessive horizontal overjet

M26.24 Reverse articulation
    Crossbite (anterior) (posterior)

M26.25 Anomalies of interarch distance

M26.29 Other anomalies of dental arch relationship
    Midline deviation of dental arch
    Overbite (excessive) deep
    Overbite (excessive) horizontal
    Overbite (excessive) vertical
    Posterior lingual occlusion of mandibular teeth

● M26.3 Anomalies of tooth position of fully erupted tooth or teeth

> **Excludes2**   embedded and impacted teeth (K01.-)

◼ M26.30 Unspecified anomaly of tooth position of fully erupted tooth or teeth
    Abnormal spacing of fully erupted tooth or teeth NOS
    Displacement of fully erupted tooth or teeth NOS
    Transposition of fully erupted tooth or teeth NOS

M26.31 Crowding of fully erupted teeth

M26.32 Excessive spacing of fully erupted teeth
    Diastema of fully erupted tooth or teeth NOS

M26.33 Horizontal displacement of fully erupted tooth or teeth
    Tipped tooth or teeth
    Tipping of fully erupted tooth

● Unacceptable First-Listed Diagnosis   ● Use Additional Character(s)   ◼ Unspecified   **OGCR** Official Guidelines for Coding and Reporting

🏵 Complication\Comorbidity   🏵 Major C\C   Excludes 1   Excludes 2   Includes   Use additional   Code first   Code also

M26.34 Vertical displacement of fully erupted tooth or teeth
Extruded tooth
Infraeruption of tooth or teeth
Supraeruption of tooth or teeth

M26.35 Rotation of fully erupted tooth or teeth

M26.36 Insufficient interocclusal distance of fully erupted teeth (ridge)
Lack of adequate intermaxillary vertical dimension of fully erupted teeth

M26.37 Excessive interocclusal distance of fully erupted teeth
Excessive intermaxillary vertical dimension of fully erupted teeth
Loss of occlusal vertical dimension of fully erupted teeth

M26.39 Other anomalites of tooth position of fully erupted tooth or teeth

M26.4 Malocclusion, unspecified

M26.5 Dentofacial functional abnormalities

> **Excludes1** bruxism (F45.8)
> teeth-grinding NOS (F45.8)

M26.50 Dentofacial functional abnormalities, unspecified

M26.51 Abnormal jaw closure

M26.52 Limited mandibular range of motion

M26.53 Deviation in opening and closing of the mandible

M26.54 Insufficient anterior guidance
Insufficient anterior occlusal guidance

M26.55 Centric occlusion maximum intercuspation discrepancy

> **Excludes1** centric occlusion NOS (M26.59)

M26.56 Non-working side interference
Balancing side interference

M26.57 Lack of posterior occlusal support

M26.59 Other dentofacial functional abnormalities
Centric occlusion (of teeth) NOS
Malocclusion due to abnormal swallowing
Malocclusion due to mouth breathing
Malocclusion due to tongue, lip or finger habits

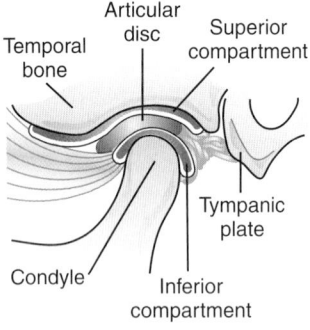

Figure 13-4 Temporomandibular joint.

Item 13-7 Dysfunction of the temporomandibular joint is termed **temporomandibular joint (TMJ) syndrome** and is characterized by pain and tenderness/spasm of the muscles of mastication, joint noise, and in the later stages, limited mandibular movement.

M26.6 Temporomandibular joint disorders

> **Excludes2** current temporomandibular joint dislocation (S03.0)
> current temporomandibular joint sprain (S03.4)

M26.60 Temporomandibular joint disorder, unspecified

M26.61 Adhesions and ankylosis of temporomandibular joint

M26.62 Arthralgia of temporomandibular joint

M26.63 Articular disc disorder of temporomandibular joint

M26.69 Other specified disorders of temporomandibular joint

M26.7 Dental alveolar anomalies

M26.70 Unspecified alveolar anomaly

M26.71 Alveolar maxillary hyperplasia

M26.72 Alveolar mandibular hyperplasia

M26.73 Alveolar maxillary hypoplasia

M26.74 Alveolar mandibular hypoplasia

M26.79 Other specified alveolar anomalies

M26.8 Other dentofacial anomalies

M26.81 Anterior soft tissue impingement
Anterior soft tissue impingement on teeth

M26.82 Posterior soft tissue impingement
Posterior soft tissue impingement on teeth

M26.89 Other dentofacial anomalies

M26.9 Dentofacial anomaly, unspecified

M27 Other diseases of jaws

M27.0 Developmental disorders of jaws
Latent bone cyst of jaw
Stafne's cyst
Torus mandibularis
Torus palatinus

M27.1 Giant cell granuloma, central
Giant cell granuloma NOS

> **Excludes1** peripheral giant cell granuloma (K06.8)

M27.2 Inflammatory conditions of jaws
Osteitis of jaw(s)
Osteomyelitis (neonatal) jaw(s)
Osteoradionecrosis jaw(s)
Periostitis jaw(s)
Sequestrum of jaw bone

Use additional code (W88-W90, X39.0) to identify radiation, if radiation-induced

> **Excludes2** osteonecrosis of jaw due to drug (M87.180)

M27.3 Alveolitis of jaws
Alveolar osteitis
Dry socket

M27.4 Other and unspecified cysts of jaw

> **Excludes1** cysts of oral region (K09.-)
> latent bone cyst of jaw (M27.0)
> Stafne's cyst (M27.0)

M27.40 Unspecified cyst of jaw
Cyst of jaw NOS

M27.49 Other cysts of jaw
Aneurysmal cyst of jaw
Hemorrhagic cyst of jaw
Traumatic cyst of jaw

CHAPTER 13 (M00-M99)

1168

● Unacceptable First-Listed Diagnosis   ● Use Additional Character(s)   ■ Unspecified   **OGCR** Official Guidelines for Coding and Reporting
🔗 Complication\Comorbidity   🔗 Major C\C   Excludes 1   Excludes 2   Includes   Use additional   Code first   Code also

● M27.5 **Periradicular pathology associated with previous endodontic treatment**

     M27.51 **Perforation of root canal space due to endodontic treatment**

     M27.52 **Endodontic overfill**

     M27.53 **Endodontic underfill**

     M27.59 **Other periradicular pathology associated with previous endodontic treatment**

● M27.6 **Endosseous dental implant failure**

     M27.61 **Osseointegration failure of dental implant**
       Hemorrhagic complications of dental implant placement
       Iatrogenic osseointegration failure of dental implant
       Osseointegration failure of dental implant due to complications of systemic disease
       Osseointegration failure of dental implant due to poor bone quality
       Pre-integration failure of dental implant NOS
       Pre-osseointegration failure of dental implant

     M27.62 **Post-osseointegration biological failure of dental implant**
       Failure of dental implant due to lack of attached gingiva
       Failure of dental implant due to occlusal trauma (caused by poor prosthetic design)
       Failure of dental implant due to parafunctional habits
       Failure of dental implant due to periodontal infection (peri–implantitis)
       Failure of dental implant due to poor oral hygiene
       Iatrogenic post-osseointegration failure of dental implant
       Post-osseointegration failure of dental implant due to complications of systemic disease

     M27.63 **Post-osseointegration mechanical failure of dental implant**
       Failure of dental prosthesis causing loss of dental implant
       Fracture of dental implant

       | Excludes2 | cracked tooth (K03.81)
                   fractured dental restorative material with loss of material (K08.531)
                   fractured dental restorative material without loss of material (K08.530)
                   fractured tooth (S02.5)

     M27.69 **Other endosseous dental implant failure**
       Dental implant failure NOS

   M27.8 **Other specified diseases of jaws**
      Cherubism
      Exostosis
      Fibrous dysplasia
      Unilateral condylar hyperplasia
      Unilateral condylar hypoplasia

▪ M27.9 **Disease of jaws, unspecified**

SYSTEMIC CONNECTIVE TISSUE DISORDERS (M30-M36)

| Includes | autoimmune disease NOS
              collagen (vascular) disease NOS
              systemic autoimmune disease
              systemic collagen (vascular) disease

| Excludes1 | autoimmune disease, single organ or single cell-type - code to relevant condition category

● M30 **Polyarteritis nodosa and related conditions**
     | Excludes1 | microscopic polyarteritis (M31.7)

   M30.0 **Polyarteritis nodosa** 🦠

   M30.1 **Polyarteritis with lung involvement [Churg-Strauss]** 🦠
      Allergic granulomatous angiitis

   M30.2 **Juvenile polyarteritis** 🦠

   M30.3 **Mucocutaneous lymph node syndrome [Kawasaki]** 🦠

   M30.8 **Other conditions related to polyarteritis nodosa** 🦠
      Polyangiitis overlap syndrome

● M31 **Other necrotizing vasculopathies**

   M31.0 **Hypersensitivity angiitis** 🦠
      Goodpasture's syndrome

   M31.1 **Thrombotic microangiopathy** 🦠
      Thrombotic thrombocytopenic purpura

   M31.2 **Lethal midline granuloma** 🦠

   M31.3 **Wegener's granulomatosis**
      Necrotizing respiratory granulomatosis

     M31.30 **Wegener's granulomatosis without renal involvement** 🦠
        Wegener's granulomatosis NOS

     M31.31 **Wegener's granulomatosis with renal involvement** 🦠

   M31.4 **Aortic arch syndrome [Takayasu]** 🦠

   M31.5 **Giant cell arteritis with polymyalgia rheumatica**

   M31.6 **Other giant cell arteritis**

   M31.7 **Microscopic polyangiitis** 🦠
      Microscopic polyarteritis
      | Excludes1 | polyarteritis nodosa (M30.0)

   M31.8 **Other specified necrotizing vasculopathies** 🦠
      Hypocomplementemic vasculitis
      Septic vasculitis

▪ M31.9 **Necrotizing vasculopathy, unspecified** 🦠

● M32 **Systemic lupus erythematosus (SLE)**
   Autoimmune inflammatory connective tissue disease of unknown cause that occurs most often in women.
   | Excludes1 | lupus erythematosus (discoid) (NOS) (L93.0)

● M32.0 **Drug-induced systemic lupus erythematosus**
   Code first (T36-T50) to identify drug

● M32.1 **Systemic lupus erythematosus with organ or system involvement**

     ▪ M32.10 **Systemic lupus erythematosus, organ or system involvement unspecified**

     M32.11 **Endocarditis in systemic lupus erythematosus**
        Libman-Sacks disease

     M32.12 **Pericarditis in systemic lupus erythematosus**
        Lupus pericarditis

     M32.13 **Lung involvement in systemic lupus erythematosus**
        Pleural effusion due to systemic lupus erythematosus

● Unacceptable First-Listed Diagnosis   ● Use Additional Character(s)   ▪ Unspecified   **OGCR** Official Guidelines for Coding and Reporting
🦠 Complication\Comorbidity   🦠 Major C\C | Excludes 1 | | Excludes 2 | Includes   Use additional   Code first   Code also

1169

CHAPTER 13 (M00-M99)

M32.14 **Glomerular disease in systemic lupus erythematosus**
Lupus renal disease NOS

M32.15 **Tubulo-interstitial nephropathy in systemic lupus erythematosus**

M32.19 **Other organ or system involvement in systemic lupus erythematosus**

M32.8 **Other forms of systemic lupus erythematosus**

M32.9 **Systemic lupus erythematosus, unspecified**
SLE NOS
Systemic lupus erythematosus NOS
Systemic lupus erythematosus without organ involvement

● M33 **Dermatopolymyositis**
● M33.0 **Juvenile dermatopolymyositis**
M33.00 **Juvenile dermatopolymyositis, organ involvement unspecified** 🅒
M33.01 **Juvenile dermatopolymyositis with respiratory involvement** 🅒
M33.02 **Juvenile dermatopolymyositis with myopathy** 🅒
M33.09 **Juvenile dermatopolymyositis with other organ involvement** 🅒
● M33.1 **Other dermatopolymyositis**
M33.10 **Other dermatopolymyositis, organ involvement unspecified** 🅒
M33.11 **Other dermatopolymyositis with respiratory involvement** 🅒
M33.12 **Other dermatopolymyositis with myopathy** 🅒
M33.19 **Other dermatopolymyositis with other organ involvement** 🅒
● M33.2 **Polymyositis**
M33.20 **Polymyositis, organ involvement unspecified** 🅒
M33.21 **Polymyositis with respiratory involvement** 🅒
M33.22 **Polymyositis with myopathy** 🅒
M33.29 **Polymyositis with other organ involvement** 🅒
● M33.9 **Dermatopolymyositis, unspecified**
M33.90 **Dermatopolymyositis, unspecified, organ involvement unspecified** 🅒
M33.91 **Dermatopolymyositis, unspecified with respiratory involvement** 🅒
M33.92 **Dermatopolymyositis, unspecified with myopathy** 🅒
M33.99 **Dermatopolymyositis, unspecified with other organ involvement** 🅒

● M34 **Systemic sclerosis [scleroderma]**
Excludes1 circumscribed scleroderma (L94.0)
neonatal scleroderma (P83.8)

M34.0 **Progressive systemic sclerosis**
M34.1 **CR(E)ST syndrome**
Combination of calcinosis, Raynaud's phenomenon, esophageal dysfunction, sclerodactyly, telangiectasia

M34.2 **Systemic sclerosis induced by drug and chemical**
Code first (T36-T65) to identify agent

● M34.8 **Other forms of systemic sclerosis**
M34.81 **Systemic sclerosis with lung involvement** 🅒
M34.82 **Systemic sclerosis with myopathy**
M34.83 **Systemic sclerosis with polyneuropathy**
M34.89 **Other systemic sclerosis**
M34.9 **Systemic sclerosis, unspecified**

● M35 **Other systemic involvement of connective tissue**
Excludes1 reactive perforating collagenosis (L87.1)
● M35.0 **Sicca syndrome [Sjögren]**
M35.00 **Sicca syndrome, unspecified**
M35.01 **Sicca syndrome with keratoconjunctivitis**
M35.02 **Sicca syndrome with lung involvement**
M35.03 **Sicca syndrome with myopathy**
M35.04 **Sicca syndrome with tubulo-interstitial nephropathy**
Renal tubular acidosis in sicca syndrome
M35.09 **Sicca syndrome with other organ involvement**

M35.1 **Other overlap syndromes** 🅒
Mixed connective tissue disease
Excludes1 polyangiitis overlap syndrome (M30.8)

M35.2 **Behçet's disease** 🅒

Item 13–3 Polymyalgia rheumatica is a syndrome characterized by aching and morning stiffness and is related to aging and hereditary predisposition.

M35.3 **Polymyalgia rheumatica**
Excludes1 polymyalgia rheumatica with giant cell arteritis (M31.5)

M35.4 **Diffuse (eosinophilic) fasciitis**
M35.5 **Multifocal fibrosclerosis** 🅒
M35.6 **Relapsing panniculitis [Weber-Christian]**
Excludes1 lupus panniculitis (L93.2)
panniculitis NOS (M79.3-)
M35.7 **Hypermobility syndrome**
Familial ligamentous laxity
Excludes1 Ehlers-Danlos syndrome (Q79.6)
ligamentous laxity, NOS (M24.2-)
M35.8 **Other specified systemic involvement of connective tissue** 🅒
M35.9 **Systemic involvement of connective tissue, unspecified**
Autoimmune disease (systemic) NOS
Collagen (vascular) disease NOS

● M36 **Systemic disorders of connective tissue in diseases classified elsewhere**
Excludes2 arthropathies in diseases classified elsewhere (M14.-)
● M36.0 **Dermato(poly)myositis in neoplastic disease** 🅒
Code first underlying neoplasm (C00-D48)
● M36.1 **Arthropathy in neoplastic disease**
Code first underlying neoplasm, such as:
leukemia (C91-C95)
malignant histiocytosis (C96.a)
multiple myeloma (C90.0)

CHAPTER 13 (M00-M99)

1170

● Unacceptable First-Listed Diagnosis   ● Use Additional Character(s)   ▪ Unspecified   **OGCR** Official Guidelines for Coding and Reporting
🅒 Complication\Comorbidity   🅒 Major C\C   Excludes 1   Excludes 2   Includes   Use additional   Code first   Code also

Item 13–8 **Kyphosis** is an abnormal curvature of the spine. **Senile kyphosis** is a result of disc degeneration causing ossification (turning to bone). **Adolescent** or **juvenile** kyphosis is also known as **Scheuermann's disease,** a condition in which the discs of the lower thoracic spine herniate, causing the disc space to narrow and the spine to tilt forward. This condition is attributed to poor posture. Lordosis or swayback is an abnormal curvature of the spine resulting in an inward curve of the lumbar spine just above the buttocks. Scoliosis causes a sideways curve to the spine. The curves are S- or C-shaped, and it is most commonly acquired in late childhood and early teen years, when growth is fast.

● **M36.2 Hemophilic arthropathy**
> Hemarthrosis in hemophilic arthropathy
>
> *Code first underlying disease, such as:*
>   factor VIII deficiency (D66)
>   with vascular defect (D68.0)
>   factor IX deficiency (D67)
>   hemophilia (classical) (D66)
>   hemophilia B (D67)
>   hemophilia C (D68.1)

● **M36.3 Arthropathy in other blood disorders**

● **M36.4 Arthropathy in hypersensitivity reactions classified elsewhere**
> *Code first underlying disease, such as:*
>   Henoch (-Schönlein) purpura (D69.0)

● **M36.8 Systemic disorders of connective tissue in other diseases classified elsewhere**
> *Code first underlying disease, such as:*
>   alkaptonuria (E70.2)
>   hypogammaglobulinemia (D80.-)
>   ochronosis (E70.2)

DORSOPATHIES (M40-M54)

DEFORMING DORSOPATHIES (M40-M43)

● **M40 Kyphosis and lordosis**
> | Excludes1 | congenital kyphosis and lordosis (Q76.4)
> kyphoscoliosis (M41.-)
> postprocedural kyphosis and lordosis (M96.-) |

● **M40.0 Postural kyphosis**
> | Excludes1 | osteochondrosis of spine (M42.-) |

   ▪ M40.00 Postural kyphosis, site unspecified

     M40.03 Postural kyphosis, cervicothoracic region

     M40.04 Postural kyphosis, thoracic region

     M40.05 Postural kyphosis, thoracolumbar region

● **M40.1 Other secondary kyphosis**

   ▪ M40.10 Other secondary kyphosis, site unspecified

     M40.12 Other secondary kyphosis, cervical region

     M40.13 Other secondary kyphosis, cervicothoracic region

     M40.14 Other secondary kyphosis, thoracic region

     M40.15 Other secondary kyphosis, thoracolumbar region

● **M40.2 Other and unspecified kyphosis**

   ● M40.20 Unspecified kyphosis

     ▪ M40.202 Unspecified kyphosis, cervical region

     ▪ M40.203 Unspecified kyphosis, cervicothoracic region

     ▪ M40.204 Unspecified kyphosis, thoracic region

     ▪ M40.205 Unspecified kyphosis, thoracolumbar region

     ▪ M40.209 Unspecified kyphosis, site unspecified

   ● M40.29 Other kyphosis

     M40.292 Other kyphosis, cervical region

     M40.293 Other kyphosis, cervicothoracic region

     M40.294 Other kyphosis, thoracic region

     M40.295 Other kyphosis, thoracolumbar region

     ▪ M40.299 Other kyphosis, site unspecified

● **M40.3 Flatback syndrome**

   ▪ M40.30 Flatback syndrome, site unspecified

     M40.35 Flatback syndrome, thoracolumbar region

     M40.36 Flatback syndrome, lumbar region

     M40.37 Flatback syndrome, lumbosacral region

● **M40.4 Postural lordosis**
> *Abnormal increase in the normal curvature of the lumbar spine (sway back)*
> Acquired lordosis

   ▪ M40.40 Postural lordosis, site unspecified

     M40.45 Postural lordosis, thoracolumbar region

     M40.46 Postural lordosis, lumbar region

     M40.47 Postural lordosis, lumbosacral region

● **M40.5 Lordosis, unspecified**

   ▪ M40.50 Lordosis, unspecified, site unspecified

   ▪ M40.55 Lordosis, unspecified, thoracolumbar region

   ▪ M40.56 Lordosis, unspecified, lumbar region

   ▪ M40.57 Lordosis, unspecified, lumbosacral region

● **M41 Scoliosis**
> | Includes | kyphoscoliosis |
> | Excludes1 | congenital scoliosis NOS (Q67.5)
> congenital scoliosis due to bony malformation (Q76.3)
> postural congenital scoliosis (Q67.5)
> kyphoscoliotic heart disease (I27.1)
> postprocedural scoliosis (M96.-) |

● **M41.0 Infantile idiopathic scoliosis**
> **Note:** Infantile is defined as birth through 4 years of age.

   ▪ M41.00 Infantile idiopathic scoliosis, site unspecified

     M41.02 Infantile idiopathic scoliosis, cervical region

     M41.03 Infantile idiopathic scoliosis, cervicothoracic region

     M41.04 Infantile idiopathic scoliosis, thoracic region

     M41.05 Infantile idiopathic scoliosis, thoracolumbar region

     M41.06 Infantile idiopathic scoliosis, lumbar region

     M41.07 Infantile idiopathic scoliosis, lumbosacral region

     M41.08 Infantile idiopathic scoliosis, sacral and sacrococcygeal region

● Unacceptable First-Listed Diagnosis   ● Use Additional Character(s)   ▪ Unspecified   **OGCR** Official Guidelines for Coding and Reporting

🅒 Complication\Comorbidity   🅒 Major C\C | Excludes 1 | | Excludes 2 | Includes   Use additional   Code first   Code also

1171

● **M41.1 Juvenile and adolescent idiopathic scoliosis**

  ● **M41.11 Juvenile idiopathic scoliosis**

    Note: Juvenile is defined as 5 through 10 years of age.

    M41.112 Juvenile idiopathic scoliosis, cervical region

    M41.113 Juvenile idiopathic scoliosis, cervicothoracic region

    M41.114 Juvenile idiopathic scoliosis, thoracic region

    M41.115 Juvenile idiopathic scoliosis, thoracolumbar region

    M41.116 Juvenile idiopathic scoliosis, lumbar region

    M41.117 Juvenile idiopathic scoliosis, lumbosacral region

    ▪**M41.119 Juvenile idiopathic scoliosis, site unspecified**

  ● **M41.12 Adolescent scoliosis**

    Note: Adolescent is defined as 11 through 17 years of age.

    M41.122 Adolescent idiopathic scoliosis, cervical region

    M41.123 Adolescent idiopathic scoliosis, cervicothoracic region

    M41.124 Adolescent idiopathic scoliosis, thoracic region

    M41.125 Adolescent idiopathic scoliosis, thoracolumbar region

    M41.126 Adolescent idiopathic scoliosis, lumbar region

    M41.127 Adolescent idiopathic scoliosis, lumbosacral region

    ▪**M41.129 Adolescent idiopathic scoliosis, site unspecified**

● **M41.2 Other idiopathic scoliosis**

  ▪**M41.20 Other idiopathic scoliosis, site unspecified**

  M41.22 Other idiopathic scoliosis, cervical region

  M41.23 Other idiopathic scoliosis, cervicothoracic region

  M41.24 Other idiopathic scoliosis, thoracic region

  M41.25 Other idiopathic scoliosis, thoracolumbar region

  M41.26 Other idiopathic scoliosis, lumbar region

  M41.27 Other idiopathic scoliosis, lumbosacral region

● **M41.3 Thoracogenic scoliosis**

  ▪**M41.30 Thoracogenic scoliosis, site unspecified**

  M41.34 Thoracogenic scoliosis, thoracic region

  M41.35 Thoracogenic scoliosis, thoracolumbar region

● **M41.4 Neuromuscular scoliosis**

  Scoliosis secondary to cerebral palsy, Friedreich's ataxia, poliomyelitis and other neuromuscular disorders

  Code also underlying condition

  ▪**M41.40 Neuromuscular scoliosis, site unspecified**

  M41.41 Neuromuscular scoliosis, occipito-atlanto-axial region

  M41.42 Neuromuscular scoliosis, cervical region

  M41.43 Neuromuscular scoliosis, cervicothoracic region

  M41.44 Neuromuscular scoliosis, thoracic region

  M41.45 Neuromuscular scoliosis, thoracolumbar region

  M41.46 Neuromuscular scoliosis, lumbar region

  M41.47 Neuromuscular scoliosis, lumbosacral region

● **M41.5 Other secondary scoliosis**

  ▪**M41.50 Other secondary scoliosis, site unspecified**

  M41.52 Other secondary scoliosis, cervical region

  M41.53 Other secondary scoliosis, cervicothoracic region

  M41.54 Other secondary scoliosis, thoracic region

  M41.55 Other secondary scoliosis, thoracolumbar region

  M41.56 Other secondary scoliosis, lumbar region

  M41.57 Other secondary scoliosis, lumbosacral region

● **M41.8 Other forms of scoliosis**

  ▪**M41.80 Other forms of scoliosis, site unspecified**

  M41.82 Other forms of scoliosis, cervical region

  M41.83 Other forms of scoliosis, cervicothoracic region

  M41.84 Other forms of scoliosis, thoracic region

  M41.85 Other forms of scoliosis, thoracolumbar region

  M41.86 Other forms of scoliosis, lumbar region

  M41.87 Other forms of scoliosis, lumbosacral region

▪**M41.9 Scoliosis, unspecified**

● **M42 Spinal osteochondrosis**

  ● **M42.0 Juvenile osteochondrosis of spine**

    Calvé's disease

    Scheuermann's disease

    Excludes1   postural kyphosis (M40.0)

    ▪**M42.00 Juvenile osteochondrosis of spine, site unspecified**

    M42.01 Juvenile osteochondrosis of spine, occipito-atlanto-axial region

    M42.02 Juvenile osteochondrosis of spine, cervical region

    M42.03 Juvenile osteochondrosis of spine, cervicothoracic region

    M42.04 Juvenile osteochondrosis of spine, thoracic region

    M42.05 Juvenile osteochondrosis of spine, thoracolumbar region

    M42.06 Juvenile osteochondrosis of spine, lumbar region

    M42.07 Juvenile osteochondrosis of spine, lumbosacral region

    M42.08 Juvenile osteochondrosis of spine, sacral and sacrococcygeal region

    M42.09 Juvenile osteochondrosis of spine, multiple sites in spine

  ● **M42.1 Adult osteochondrosis of spine**

    ▪**M42.10 Adult osteochondrosis of spine, site unspecified**

    M42.11 Adult osteochondrosis of spine, occipito-atlanto-axial region

    M42.12 Adult osteochondrosis of spine, cervical region

    M42.13 Adult osteochondrosis of spine, cervicothoracic region

● Unacceptable First-Listed Diagnosis   ● Use Additional Character(s)   ▪ Unspecified   **OGCR** Official Guidelines for Coding and Reporting

🗸 Complication\Comorbidity   🗸 Major C\C   Excludes 1   Excludes 2   Includes   Use additional   Code first   Code also

M42.14   Adult osteochondrosis of spine, thoracic region

M42.15   Adult osteochondrosis of spine, thoracolumbar region

M42.16   Adult osteochondrosis of spine, lumbar region

M42.17   Adult osteochondrosis of spine, lumbosacral region

M42.18   Adult osteochondrosis of spine, sacral and sacrococcygeal region

M42.19   Adult osteochondrosis of spine, multiple sites in spine

M42.9   Spinal osteochondrosis, unspecified

● M43   Other deforming dorsopathies

> **Excludes1**   congenital spondylolysis and spondylolisthesis (Q76.2)
> hemivertebra (Q76.3-Q76.4)
> Klippel-Feil syndrome (Q76.1)
> lumbarization and sacralization (Q76.4)
> platyspondylisis (Q76.4)
> spina bifida occulta (Q76.0)
> spinal curvature in osteoporosis (M80-)
> spinal curvature in Paget's disease of bone [osteitis deformans] (M88.-)

● M43.0   Spondylolysis

> **Excludes1**   congenital spondylolysis (Q76.2)
> spondylolisthesis (M43.1)

M43.00   Spondylolysis, site unspecified

M43.01   Spondylolysis, occipito-atlanto-axial region

M43.02   Spondylolysis, cervical region

M43.03   Spondylolysis, cervicothoracic region

M43.04   Spondylolysis, thoracic region

M43.05   Spondylolysis, thoracolumbar region

M43.06   Spondylolysis, lumbar region

M43.07   Spondylolysis, lumbosacral region

M43.08   Spondylolysis, sacral and sacrococcygeal region

M43.09   Spondylolysis, multiple sites in spine

Item 13–9   Spondylolisthesis is a condition caused by the slipping forward of one disc over another.

● M43.1   Spondylolisthesis

> **Excludes1**   acute traumatic of lumbosacral region (S33.1)
> acute traumatic of sites other than lumbosacral - code to Fracture, vertebra, by region
> congenital spondylolisthesis (Q76.2)

M43.10   Spondylolisthesis, site unspecified

M43.11   Spondylolisthesis, occipito-atlanto-axial region

M43.12   Spondylolisthesis, cervical region

M43.13   Spondylolisthesis, cervicothoracic region

M43.14   Spondylolisthesis, thoracic region

M43.15   Spondylolisthesis, thoracolumbar region

M43.16   Spondylolisthesis, lumbar region

M43.17   Spondylolisthesis, lumbosacral region

M43.18   Spondylolisthesis, sacral and sacrococcygeal region

M43.19   Spondylolisthesis, multiple sites in spine

● M43.2   Fusion of spine
Ankylosis of spinal joint

> **Excludes1**   ankylosing spondylitis (M45.0-)
> congenital fusion of spine (Q76.4)

> **Excludes2**   arthrodesis status (Z98.1)
> pseudoarthrosis after fusion or arthrodesis (M96.0)

M43.20   Fusion of spine, site unspecified

M43.21   Fusion of spine, occipito-atlanto-axial region

M43.22   Fusion of spine, cervical region

M43.23   Fusion of spine, cervicothoracic region

M43.24   Fusion of spine, thoracic region

M43.25   Fusion of spine, thoracolumbar region

M43.26   Fusion of spine, lumbar region

M43.27   Fusion of spine, lumbosacral region

M43.28   Fusion of spine, sacral and sacrococcygeal region

M43.3   Recurrent atlantoaxial dislocation with myelopathy

M43.4   Other recurrent atlantoaxial dislocation

● M43.5   Other recurrent vertebral dislocation

> **Excludes1**   biomechanical lesions NEC (M99.-)

● M43.5x   Other recurrent vertebral dislocation

M43.5x2   Other recurrent vertebral dislocation, cervical region

M43.5x3   Other recurrent vertebral dislocation, cervicothoracic region

M43.5x4   Other recurrent vertebral dislocation, thoracic region

M43.5x5   Other recurrent vertebral dislocation, thoracolumbar region

M43.5x6   Other recurrent vertebral dislocation, lumbar region

M43.5x7   Other recurrent vertebral dislocation, lumbosacral region

M43.5x8   Other recurrent vertebral dislocation, sacral and sacrococcygeal region

M43.5x9   Other recurrent vertebral dislocation, site unspecified

M43.6   Torticollis

> **Excludes1**   congenital (sternomastoid) torticollis (Q68.0)
> current injury - see Injury, of spine, by body region ocular torticollis (R29.891)
> psychogenic torticollis (F45.8)
> spasmodic torticollis (G24.3)
> torticollis due to birth injury (P15.2)

● M43.8   Other specified deforming dorsopathies

> **Excludes2**   kyphosis and lordosis (M40.-)
> scoliosis (M41.-)

● M43.8x   Other specified deforming dorsopathies

M43.8x1   Other specified deforming dorsopathies, occipito-atlanto-axial region

M43.8x2   Other specified deforming dorsopathies, cervical region

M43.8x3   Other specified deforming dorsopathies, cervicothoracic region

● Unacceptable First-Listed Diagnosis   ● Use Additional Character(s)   ▪ Unspecified   **OGCR** Official Guidelines for Coding and Reporting

 Complication\Comorbidity   Major C\C   Excludes 1   Excludes 2   Includes   Use additional   Code first   Code also

1173

CHAPTER 13 (M00-M99)

M43.8x4　Other specified deforming dorsopathies, thoracic region

M43.8x5　Other specified deforming dorsopathies, thoracolumbar region

M43.8x6　Other specified deforming dorsopathies, lumbar region

M43.8x7　Other specified deforming dorsopathies, lumbosacral region

M43.8x8　Other specified deforming dorsopathies, sacral and sacrococcygeal region

■M43.8x9　Other specified deforming dorsopathies, site unspecified

■M43.9　Deforming dorsopathy, unspecified
Curvature of spine NOS

SPONDYLOPATHIES (M45-M49)

● M45　Ankylosing spondylitis
Rheumatoid arthritis of spine

| Excludes1 | arthropathy in Reiter's disease (M02.3-) juvenile (ankylosing) spondylitis (M08.18) |

| Excludes2 | Behçet's disease (M35.2) |

M45.0　Ankylosing spondylitis of multiple sites in spine

M45.1　Ankylosing spondylitis of occipito-atlanto-axial region

M45.2　Ankylosing spondylitis of cervical region

M45.3　Ankylosing spondylitis of cervicothoracic region

M45.4　Ankylosing spondylitis of thoracic region

M45.5　Ankylosing spondylitis of thoracolumbar region

M45.6　Ankylosing spondylitis lumbar region

M45.7　Ankylosing spondylitis of lumbosacral region

M45.8　Ankylosing spondylitis sacral and sacrococcygeal region

■M45.9　Ankylosing spondylitis of unspecified sites in spine

● M46　Other inflammatory spondylopathies

● M46.0　Spinal enthesopathy
Disorder of ligamentous or muscular attachments of spine

■M46.00　Spinal enthesopathy, site unspecified

M46.01　Spinal enthesopathy, occipito-atlanto-axial region

M46.02　Spinal enthesopathy, cervical region

M46.03　Spinal enthesopathy, cervicothoracic region

M46.04　Spinal enthesopathy, thoracic region

M46.05　Spinal enthesopathy, thoracolumbar region

M46.06　Spinal enthesopathy, lumbar region

M46.07　Spinal enthesopathy, lumbosacral region

M46.08　Spinal enthesopathy, sacral and sacrococcygeal region

M46.09　Spinal enthesopathy, multiple sites in spine

M46.1　Sacroiliitis, not elsewhere classified

● M46.2　Osteomyelitis of vertebra

■M46.20　Osteomyelitis of vertebra, site unspecified ✪

M46.21　Osteomyelitis of vertebra, occipito-atlanto-axial region ✪

M46.22　Osteomyelitis of vertebra, cervical region ✪

M46.23　Osteomyelitis of vertebra, cervicothoracic region ✪

M46.24　Osteomyelitis of vertebra, thoracic region ✪

M46.25　Osteomyelitis of vertebra, thoracolumbar region ✪

M46.26　Osteomyelitis of vertebra, lumbar region ✪

M46.27　Osteomyelitis of vertebra, lumbosacral region ✪

M46.28　Osteomyelitis of vertebra, sacral and sacrococcygeal region ✪

● M46.3　Infection of intervertebral disc (pyogenic)
Use additional code (B95-B97) to identify infectious agent

■M46.30　Infection of intervertebral disc (pyogenic), site unspecified ✪

M46.31　Infection of intervertebral disc (pyogenic), occipito-atlanto-axial region ✪

M46.32　Infection of intervertebral disc (pyogenic), cervical region ✪

M46.33　Infection of intervertebral disc (pyogenic), cervicothoracic region ✪

M46.34　Infection of intervertebral disc (pyogenic), thoracic region ✪

M46.35　Infection of intervertebral disc (pyogenic), thoracolumbar region ✪

M46.36　Infection of intervertebral disc (pyogenic), lumbar region ✪

M46.37　Infection of intervertebral disc (pyogenic), lumbosacral region ✪

M46.38　Infection of intervertebral disc (pyogenic), sacral and sacrococcygeal region ✪

M46.39　Infection of intervertebral disc (pyogenic), multiple sites in spine ✪

● M46.4　Discitis, unspecified

■M46.40　Discitis, unspecified, site unspecified

■M46.41　Discitis, unspecified, occipito-atlanto-axial region

■M46.42　Discitis, unspecified, cervical region

■M46.43　Discitis, unspecified, cervicothoracic region

■M46.44　Discitis, unspecified, thoracic region

■M46.45　Discitis, unspecified, thoracolumbar region

■M46.46　Discitis, unspecified, lumbar region

■M46.47　Discitis, unspecified, lumbosacral region

■M46.48　Discitis, unspecified, sacral and sacrococcygeal region

■M46.49　Discitis, unspecified, multiple sites in spine

● M46.5　Other infective spondylopathies

■M46.50　Other infective spondylopathies, site unspecified

M46.51　Other infective spondylopathies, occipito-atlanto-axial region

M46.52　Other infective spondylopathies, cervical region

M46.53　Other infective spondylopathies, cervicothoracic region

M46.54　Other infective spondylopathies, thoracic region

M46.55　Other infective spondylopathies, thoracolumbar region

● Unacceptable First-Listed Diagnosis　　● Use Additional Character(s)　　■ Unspecified　　**OGCR** Official Guidelines for Coding and Reporting
✪ Complication\Comorbidity　✪ Major C\C　| Excludes 1 |　| Excludes 2 |　Includes　Use additional　Code first　Code also

M46.56 Other infective spondylopathies, lumbar region

M46.57 Other infective spondylopathies, lumbosacral region

M46.58 Other infective spondylopathies, sacral and sacrococcygeal region

M46.59 Other infective spondylopathies, multiple sites in spine

● M46.8 Other specified inflammatory spondylopathies

■ M46.80 Other specified inflammatory spondylopathies, site unspecified

M46.81 Other specified inflammatory spondylopathies, occipito-atlanto-axial region

M46.82 Other specified inflammatory spondylopathies, cervical region

M46.83 Other specified inflammatory spondylopathies, cervicothoracic region

M46.84 Other specified inflammatory spondylopathies, thoracic region

M46.85 Other specified inflammatory spondylopathies, thoracolumbar region

M46.86 Other specified inflammatory spondylopathies, lumbar region

M46.87 Other specified inflammatory spondylopathies, lumbosacral region

M46.88 Other specified inflammatory spondylopathies, sacral and sacrococcygeal region

M46.89 Other specified inflammatory spondylopathies, multiple sites in spine

● M46.9 Unspecified inflammatory spondylopathy

■ M46.90 Unspecified inflammatory spondylopathy, site unspecified

■ M46.91 Unspecified inflammatory spondylopathy, occipito-atlanto-axial region

■ M46.92 Unspecified inflammatory spondylopathy, cervical region

■ M46.93 Unspecified inflammatory spondylopathy, cervicothoracic region

■ M46.94 Unspecified inflammatory spondylopathy, thoracic region

■ M46.95 Unspecified inflammatory spondylopathy, thoracolumbar region

■ M46.96 Unspecified inflammatory spondylopathy, lumbar region

■ M46.97 Unspecified inflammatory spondylopathy, lumbosacral region

■ M46.98 Unspecified inflammatory spondylopathy, sacral and sacrococcygeal region

■ M46.99 Unspecified inflammatory spondylopathy, multiple sites in spine

● M47 Spondylosis

Includes arthrosis or osteoarthritis of spine degeneration of facet joints

● M47.0 Anterior spinal and vertebral artery compression syndromes

● M47.01 Anterior spinal artery compression syndromes

M47.011 Anterior spinal artery compression syndromes, occipito-atlanto-axial region

M47.012 Anterior spinal artery compression syndromes, cervical region

M47.013 Anterior spinal artery compression syndromes, cervicothoracic region

M47.014 Anterior spinal artery compression syndromes, thoracic region

M47.015 Anterior spinal artery compression syndromes, thoracolumbar region

M47.016 Anterior spinal artery compression syndromes, lumbar region

■ M47.019 Anterior spinal artery compression syndromes, site unspecified

● M47.02 Vertebral artery compression syndromes

M47.021 Vertebral artery compression syndromes, occipito-atlanto-axial region

M47.022 Vertebral artery compression syndromes, cervical region

■ M47.029 Vertebral artery compression syndromes, site unspecified

● M47.1 Other spondylosis with myelopathy
Spondylogenic compression of spinal cord

Excludes1 vertebral subluxation (M43.3-M43.59)

■ M47.10 Other spondylosis with myelopathy, site unspecified

M47.11 Other spondylosis with myelopathy, occipito-atlanto-axial region

M47.12 Other spondylosis with myelopathy, cervical region

M47.13 Other spondylosis with myelopathy, cervicothoracic region

M47.14 Other spondylosis with myelopathy, thoracic region

M47.15 Other spondylosis with myelopathy, thoracolumbar region

M47.16 Other spondylosis with myelopathy, lumbar region

M47.17 Other spondylosis with myelopathy, lumbosacral region

M47.18 Other spondylosis with myelopathy, sacral and sacrococcygeal region

● M47.2 Other spondylosis with radiculopathy

■ M47.20 Other spondylosis with radiculopathy, site unspecified

M47.21 Other spondylosis with radiculopathy, occipito-atlanto-axial region

M47.22 Other spondylosis with radiculopathy, cervical region

M47.23 Other spondylosis with radiculopathy, cervicothoracic region

M47.24 Other spondylosis with radiculopathy, thoracic region

M47.25 Other spondylosis with radiculopathy, thoracolumbar region

M47.26 Other spondylosis with radiculopathy, lumbar region

M47.27 Other spondylosis with radiculopathy, lumbosacral region

M47.28 Other spondylosis with radiculopathy, sacral and sacrococcygeal region

● Unacceptable First-Listed Diagnosis   ● Use Additional Character(s)   ■ Unspecified   **OGCR** Official Guidelines for Coding and Reporting

 Complication\Comorbidity   Major C\C   Excludes 1   Excludes 2   Includes   Use additional   Code first   Code also

1175

CHAPTER 13 (M00-M99)

- M47.8 Other spondylosis
  - M47.81 Spondylosis without myelopathy or radiculopathy
    - M47.811 Spondylosis without myelopathy or radiculopathy, occipito-atlanto-axial region
    - M47.812 Spondylosis without myelopathy or radiculopathy, cervical region
    - M47.813 Spondylosis without myelopathy or radiculopathy, cervicothoracic region
    - M47.814 Spondylosis without myelopathy or radiculopathy, thoracic region
    - M47.815 Spondylosis without myelopathy or radiculopathy, thoracolumbar region
    - M47.816 Spondylosis without myelopathy or radiculopathy, lumbar region
    - M47.817 Spondylosis without myelopathy or radiculopathy, lumbosacral region
    - M47.818 Spondylosis without myelopathy or radiculopathy, sacral and sacrococcygeal region
    - M47.819 Spondylosis without myelopathy or radiculopathy, site unspecified
  - M47.89 Other spondylosis
    - M47.891 Other spondylosis, occipito-atlanto-axial region
    - M47.892 Other spondylosis, cervical region
    - M47.893 Other spondylosis, cervicothoracic region
    - M47.894 Other spondylosis, thoracic region
    - M47.895 Other spondylosis, thoracolumbar region
    - M47.896 Other spondylosis, lumbar region
    - M47.897 Other spondylosis, lumbosacral region
    - M47.898 Other spondylosis, sacral and sacrococcygeal region
    - M47.899 Other spondylosis, site unspecified
- M47.9 Spondylosis, unspecified

- M48 Other spondylopathies
  - M48.0 Spinal stenosis
    Caudal stenosis
    - M48.00 Spinal stenosis, site unspecified
    - M48.01 Spinal stenosis, occipito-atlanto-axial region
    - M48.02 Spinal stenosis, cervical region
    - M48.03 Spinal stenosis, cervicothoracic region
    - M48.04 Spinal stenosis, thoracic region
    - M48.05 Spinal stenosis, thoracolumbar region
    - M48.06 Spinal stenosis, lumbar region
    - M48.07 Spinal stenosis, lumbosacral region
    - M48.08 Spinal stenosis, sacral and sacrococcygeal region
  - M48.1 Ankylosing hyperostosis [Forestier]
    Diffuse idiopathic skeletal hyperostosis [DISH]
    - M48.10 Ankylosing hyperostosis [Forestier], site unspecified

---

- M48.11 Ankylosing hyperostosis [Forestier], occipito-atlanto-axial region
- M48.12 Ankylosing hyperostosis [Forestier], cervical region
- M48.13 Ankylosing hyperostosis [Forestier], cervicothoracic region
- M48.14 Ankylosing hyperostosis [Forestier], thoracic region
- M48.15 Ankylosing hyperostosis [Forestier], thoracolumbar region
- M48.16 Ankylosing hyperostosis [Forestier], lumbar region
- M48.17 Ankylosing hyperostosis [Forestier], lumbosacral region
- M48.18 Ankylosing hyperostosis [Forestier], sacral and sacrococcygeal region
- M48.19 Ankylosing hyperostosis [Forestier], multiple sites in spine

- M48.2 Kissing spine
  - M48.20 Kissing spine, site unspecified
  - M48.21 Kissing spine, occipito-atlanto-axial region
  - M48.22 Kissing spine, cervical region
  - M48.23 Kissing spine, cervicothoracic region
  - M48.24 Kissing spine, thoracic region
  - M48.25 Kissing spine, thoracolumbar region
  - M48.26 Kissing spine, lumbar region
  - M48.27 Kissing spine, lumbosacral region

- M48.3 Traumatic spondylopathy
  - M48.30 Traumatic spondylopathy, site unspecified
  - M48.31 Traumatic spondylopathy, occipito-atlanto-axial region
  - M48.32 Traumatic spondylopathy, cervical region
  - M48.33 Traumatic spondylopathy, cervicothoracic region
  - M48.34 Traumatic spondylopathy, thoracic region
  - M48.35 Traumatic spondylopathy, thoracolumbar region
  - M48.36 Traumatic spondylopathy, lumbar region
  - M48.37 Traumatic spondylopathy, lumbosacral region
  - M48.38 Traumatic spondylopathy, sacral and sacrococcygeal region

- M48.4 Fatigue fracture of vertebra
  Stress fracture of vertebra

  Excludes1 pathological fracture NOS (M84.4-)
  pathological fracture of vertebra due to neoplasm (M84.58)
  pathological fracture of vertebra due to other diagnosis (M84.68)
  pathological fracture of vertebra due to osteoporosis (M80.-)
  traumatic fracture of vertebrae (S12.0--S12.3-, S22.0-, S32.0-)

  > The appropriate 7th character is to be added to each code from subcategory M48.4:
  > A   initial encounter for fracture
  > D   subsequent encounter for fracture with routine healing
  > G   subsequent encounter for fracture with delayed healing
  > S   sequela of fracture

● Unacceptable First-Listed Diagnosis   ● Use Additional Character(s)   ▪ Unspecified   **OGCR** Official Guidelines for Coding and Reporting
🦴 Complication\Comorbidity   🦴 Major C\C   Excludes 1   Excludes 2   Includes   Use additional   Code first   Code also

■ M48.40 Fatigue fracture of vertebra, site unspecified

M48.41 Fatigue fracture of vertebra, occipito-atlanto-axial region

M48.42 Fatigue fracture of vertebra, cervical region

M48.43 Fatigue fracture of vertebra, cervicothoracic region

M48.44 Fatigue fracture of vertebra, thoracic region

M48.45 Fatigue fracture of vertebra, thoracolumbar region

M48.46 Fatigue fracture of vertebra, lumbar region

M48.47 Fatigue fracture of vertebra, lumbosacral region

M48.48 Fatigue fracture of vertebra, sacral and sacrococcygeal region

● **M48.5 Collapsed vertebra, not elsewhere classified**
Collapsed vertebra NOS
Wedging of vertebra NOS

> **Excludes1**   current injury - see Injury of spine, by body region
> fatigue fracture of vertebra (M48.4)
> pathological fracture of vertebra due to neoplasm (M84.58)
> pathological fracture of vertebra due to other diagnosis (M84.68)
> pathological fracture of vertebra due to osteoporosis (M80.-)
> pathological fracture NOS (M84.4-)
> stress fracture of vertebra (M48.4-)
> traumatic fracture of vertebra (S12.-, S22.-, S32.-)

> The appropriate 7th character is to be added to each code from subcategory M48.5:
> A   initial encounter for fracture
> D   subsequent encounter for fracture with routine healing
> G   subsequent encounter for fracture with delayed healing
> S   sequela of fracture

■ M48.50 Collapsed vertebra, not elsewhere classified, site unspecified xA 🦠

M48.51 Collapsed vertebra, not elsewhere classified, occipito-atlanto-axial region xA 🦠

M48.52 Collapsed vertebra, not elsewhere classified, cervical region xA 🦠

M48.53 Collapsed vertebra, not elsewhere classified, cervicothoracic region xA 🦠

M48.54 Collapsed vertebra, not elsewhere classified, thoracic region xA 🦠

M48.55 Collapsed vertebra, not elsewhere classified, thoracolumbar region xA 🦠

M48.56 Collapsed vertebra, not elsewhere classified, lumbar region xA 🦠

M48.57 Collapsed vertebra, not elsewhere classified, lumbosacral region xA 🦠

M48.58 Collapsed vertebra, not elsewhere classified, sacral and sacrococcygeal region xA 🦠

● **M48.8 Other specified spondylopathies**
Ossification of posterior longitudinal ligament

● M48.8x Other specified spondylopathies

M48.8x1 Other specified spondylopathies, occipito-atlanto-axial region

M48.8x2 Other specified spondylopathies, cervical region

M48.8x3 Other specified spondylopathies, cervicothoracic region

M48.8x4 Other specified spondylopathies, thoracic region

M48.8x5 Other specified spondylopathies, thoracolumbar region

M48.8x6 Other specified spondylopathies, lumbar region

M48.8x7 Other specified spondylopathies, lumbosacral region

M48.8x8 Other specified spondylopathies, sacral and sacrococcygeal region

■ M48.8x9 Other specified spondylopathies, site unspecified

■ M48.9 Spondylopathy, unspecified

● **M49 Spondylopathies in diseases classified elsewhere**

> **Includes**   curvature of spine in diseases classified elsewhere
> deformity of spine in diseases classified elsewhere
> kyphosis in diseases classified elsewhere
> scoliosis in diseases classified elsewhere
> spondylopathy in diseases classified elsewhere

> **Excludes1**   curvature of spine in tuberculosis [Pott's] (A18.01)
> enteropathic arthropathies (M07.-)
> neuropathic spondylopathy (in):
>   nonsyphilitic NEC (G98.0)
>   syringomyelia (G95.0)
>   tabes dorsalis (A52.11)
> spondylitis (in):
>   gonococcal (A54.41)
>   syphilis (acquired) (A52.77)
>   neuropathic [tabes dorsalis] (A52.11)
>   tuberculosis (A18.01)
>   typhoid fever (A01.05)

Code first underlying disease, such as:
   brucellosis (A23.-)
   Charcot-Marie-Tooth disease (G60.0)
   enterobacterial infections (A01-A04)
   osteitis fibrosa cystica (E21.0)

● **M49.8 Spondylopathy in diseases classified elsewhere**

● ■ M49.80 Spondylopathy in diseases classified elsewhere, site unspecified

● M49.81 Spondylopathy in diseases classified elsewhere, occipito-atlanto-axial region

● M49.82 Spondylopathy in diseases classified elsewhere, cervical region

● M49.83 Spondylopathy in diseases classified elsewhere, cervicothoracic region

● M49.84 Spondylopathy in diseases classified elsewhere, thoracic region

● M49.85 Spondylopathy in diseases classified elsewhere, thoracolumbar region

● M49.86 Spondylopathy in diseases classified elsewhere, lumbar region

● M49.87 Spondylopathy in diseases classified elsewhere, lumbosacral region

● M49.88 Spondylopathy in diseases classified elsewhere, sacral and sacrococcygeal region

● M49.89 Spondylopathy in diseases classified elsewhere, multiple sites in spine

● Unacceptable First-Listed Diagnosis   ● Use Additional Character(s)   ■ Unspecified   **OGCR** Official Guidelines for Coding and Reporting

🦠 Complication\Comorbidity   🦠 Major C\C   Excludes 1   Excludes 2   Includes   Use additional   Code first   Code also

1177

OTHER DORSOPATHIES (M50-M54)

> **Excludes1**   current injury - see injury of spine by body region discitis NOS (M46.4-)

● **M50   Cervical disc disorders**

> **Includes**   cervicothoracic disc disorders with cervicalgia
> cervicothoracic disc disorders

Note: Code to the most superior level of disorder.

● **M50.0   Cervical disc disorder with myelopathy**

▪ **M50.00**   Cervical disc disorder with myelopathy, unspecified cervical region 🦠

M50.01   Cervical disc disorder with myelopathy, occipito-atlanto-axial region 🦠

M50.02   Cervical disc disorder with myelopathy, mid-cervical region 🦠

M50.03   Cervical disc disorder with myelopathy, cervicothoracic region 🦠

● **M50.1   Cervical disc disorder with radiculopathy**

> **Excludes2**   brachial radiculitis NOS (M54.13)

▪ **M50.10**   Cervical disc disorder with radiculopathy, unspecified cervical region

M50.11   Cervical disc disorder with radiculopathy, occipito-atlanto-axial region

M50.12   Cervical disc disorder with radiculopathy, mid-cervical region

M50.13   Cervical disc disorder with radiculopathy, cervicothoracic region

● **M50.2   Other cervical disc displacement**

▪ **M50.20**   Other cervical disc displacement, unspecified cervical region

M50.21   Other cervical disc displacement, occipitoatlanto-axial region

M50.22   Other cervical disc displacement, mid-cervical region

M50.23   Other cervical disc displacement, cervicothoracic region

● **M50.3   Other cervical disc degeneration**

▪ **M50.30**   Other cervical disc degeneration, unspecified cervical region

M50.31   Other cervical disc degeneration, occipito-atlanto-axial region

M50.32   Other cervical disc degeneration, mid-cervical region

M50.33   Other cervical disc degeneration, cervicothoracic region

● **M50.8   Other cervical disc disorders**

▪ **M50.80**   Other cervical disc disorders, unspecified cervical region

M50.81   Other cervical disc disorders, occipito-atlanto-axial region

M50.82   Other cervical disc disorders, mid-cervical region

M50.83   Other cervical disc disorders, cervicothoracic region

● **M50.9   Cervical disc disorder, unspecified**

▪ **M50.90**   Cervical disc disorder, unspecified, unspecified cervical region

▪ **M50.91**   Cervical disc disorder, unspecified, occipito-atlanto-axial region

▪ **M50.92**   Cervical disc disorder, unspecified, mid-cervical region

▪ **M50.93**   Cervical disc disorder, unspecified, cervicothoracic region

● **M51   Thoracic, thoracolumbar, and lumbosacral intervertebral disc disorders**

> **Excludes2**   cervical and cervicothoracic disc disorders (M50.-)
> sacral and sacrococcygeal disorders (M53.3)

● **M51.0   Thoracic, thoracolumbar and lumbosacral intervertebral disc disorders with myelopathy**

M51.04   Intervertebral disc disorders with myelopathy, thoracic region 🦠

M51.05   Intervertebral disc disorders with myelopathy, thoracolumbar region 🦠

M51.06   Intervertebral disc disorders with myelopathy, lumbar region 🦠

M51.07   Intervertebral disc disorders with myelopathy, lumbosacral region 🦠

● **M51.1   Thoracic, thoracolumbar and lumbosacral intervertebral disc disorders with radiculopathy**
Sciatica due to intervertebral disc disorder

> **Excludes1**   lumbar radiculitis NOS (M54.16)
> sciatica NOS (M54.3)

M51.14   Intervertebral disc disorders with radiculopathy, thoracic region

M51.15   Intervertebral disc disorders with radiculopathy, thoracolumbar region

M51.16   Intervertebral disc disorders with radiculopathy, lumbar region

M51.17   Intervertebral disc disorders with radiculopathy, lumbosacral region

● **M51.2   Other thoracic, thoracolumbar and lumbosacral intervertebral disc displacement**
Lumbago due to displacement of intervertebral disc

M51.24   Other intervertebral disc displacement, thoracic region

M51.25   Other intervertebral disc displacement, thoracolumbar region

M51.26   Other intervertebral disc displacement, lumbar region

M51.27   Other intervertebral disc displacement, lumbosacral region

● **M51.3   Other thoracic, thoracolumbar and lumbosacral intervertebral disc degeneration**

M51.34   Other intervertebral disc degeneration, thoracic region

M51.35   Other intervertebral disc degeneration, thoracolumbar region

M51.36   Other intervertebral disc degeneration, lumbar region

M51.37   Other intervertebral disc degeneration, lumbosacral region

● **M51.4   Schmorl's nodes**

M51.44   Schmorl's nodes, thoracic region

M51.45   Schmorl's nodes, thoracolumbar region

M51.46   Schmorl's nodes, lumbar region

M51.47   Schmorl's nodes, lumbosacral region

● **M51.8   Other thoracic, thoracolumbar and lumbosacral intervertebral disc disorders**

M51.84   Other intervertebral disc disorders, thoracic region

M51.85   Other intervertebral disc disorders, thoracolumbar region

● Unacceptable First-Listed Diagnosis   ● Use Additional Character(s)   ▪ Unspecified   **OGCR** Official Guidelines for Coding and Reporting
🦠 Complication\Comorbidity   🦠 Major C\C   Excludes 1   Excludes 2   Includes   Use additional   Code first   Code also

M51.86 Other intervertebral disc disorders, lumbar region

M51.87 Other intervertebral disc disorders, lumbosacral region

■ M51.9 Unspecified thoracic, thoracolumbar and lumbosacral intervertebral disc disorder

● **M53 Other and unspecified dorsopathies, not elsewhere classified**

M53.0 Cervicocranial syndrome
Posterior cervical sympathetic syndrome

M53.1 Cervicobrachial syndrome

> Excludes2   cervical disc disorder (M50.-)
> thoracic outlet syndrome (G54.0)

● M53.2 Spinal instabilities

  ● M53.2x Spinal instabilities

M53.2x1 Spinal instabilities, occipito-atlanto-axial region

M53.2x2 Spinal instabilities, cervical region

M53.2x3 Spinal instabilities, cervicothoracic region

M53.2x4 Spinal instabilities, thoracic region

M53.2x5 Spinal instabilities, thoracolumbar region

M53.2x6 Spinal instabilities, lumbar region

M53.2x7 Spinal instabilities, lumbosacral region

M53.2x8 Spinal instabilities, sacral and sacrococcygeal region

■ M53.2x9 Spinal instabilities, site unspecified

M53.3 Sacrococcygeal disorders, not elsewhere classified
Coccygodynia

● M53.8 Other specified dorsopathies

■ M53.80 Other specified dorsopathies, site unspecified

M53.81 Other specified dorsopathies, occipito-atlanto-axial region

M53.82 Other specified dorsopathies, cervical region

M53.83 Other specified dorsopathies, cervicothoracic region

M53.84 Other specified dorsopathies, thoracic region

M53.85 Other specified dorsopathies, thoracolumbar region

M53.86 Other specified dorsopathies, lumbar region

M53.87 Other specified dorsopathies, lumbosacral region

M53.88 Other specified dorsopathies, sacral and sacrococcygeal region

■ M53.9 Dorsopathy, unspecified

● **M54 Dorsalgia**

> Excludes1   psychogenic dorsalgia (F45.41)

  ● M54.0 Panniculitis affecting regions of neck and back

> Excludes1   lupus panniculitis (L93.2)
> panniculitis NOS (M79.3)
> relapsing [Weber-Christian] panniculitis (M35.6)

■ M54.00 Panniculitis affecting regions of neck and back, site unspecified

M54.01 Panniculitis affecting regions of neck and back, occipito-atlanto-axial region

M54.02 Panniculitis affecting regions of neck and back, cervical region

M54.03 Panniculitis affecting regions of neck and back, cervicothoracic region

M54.04 Panniculitis affecting regions of neck and back, thoracic region

M54.05 Panniculitis affecting regions of neck and back, thoracolumbar region

M54.06 Panniculitis affecting regions of neck and back, lumbar region

M54.07 Panniculitis affecting regions of neck and back, lumbosacral region

M54.08 Panniculitis affecting regions of neck and back, sacral and sacrococcygeal region

M54.09 Panniculitis affecting regions, neck and back, multiple sites in spine

● M54.1 Radiculopathy
Brachial neuritis or radiculitis NOS
Lumbar neuritis or radiculitis NOS
Lumbosacral neuritis or radiculitis NOS
Thoracic neuritis or radiculitis NOS
Radiculitis NOS

> Excludes1   neuralgia and neuritis NOS (M79.2)
> radiculopathy with cervical disc disorder (M50.1)
> radiculopathy with lumbar and other intervertebral disc disorder (M51.1-)
> radiculopathy with spondylosis (M47.2-)

■ M54.10 Radiculopathy, site unspecified

M54.11 Radiculopathy, occipito-atlanto-axial region

M54.12 Radiculopathy, cervical region

M54.13 Radiculopathy, cervicothoracic region

M54.14 Radiculopathy, thoracic region

M54.15 Radiculopathy, thoracolumbar region

M54.16 Radiculopathy, lumbar region

M54.17 Radiculopathy, lumbosacral region

M54.18 Radiculopathy, sacral and sacrococcygeal region

M54.2 Cervicalgia

> Excludes1   cervicalgia due to intervertebral cervical disc disorder (M50.-)

● M54.3 Sciatica

> Excludes1   lesion of sciatic nerve (G57.0)
> sciatica due to intervertebral disc disorder (M51.1-)
> sciatica with lumbago (M54.4-)

■ M54.30 Sciatica, unspecified side

M54.31 Sciatica, right side

M54.32 Sciatica, left side

● M54.4 Lumbago with sciatica

> Excludes1   lumbago with sciatica due to intervertebral disc disorder (M51.1-)

■ M54.40 Lumbago with sciatica, unspecified side

M54.41 Lumbago with sciatica, right side

M54.42 Lumbago with sciatica, left side

● Unacceptable First-Listed Diagnosis   ● Use Additional Character(s)   ■ Unspecified   **OGCR** Official Guidelines for Coding and Reporting

🝔 Complication\Comorbidity   🝔 Major C\C   Excludes 1   Excludes 2   Includes   Use additional   Code first   Code also

1179

CHAPTER 13 (M00-M99)

M54.5 Low back pain
Loin pain
Lumbago NOS
> Excludes1　low back strain S39.012
> lumbago due to intervertebral disc
> displacement (M51.2-)
> lumbago with sciatica (M54.4-)

M54.6 Pain in thoracic spine
> Excludes1　pain in thoracic spine due to
> intervertebral disc disorder (M51.)

● **M54.8 Other dorsalgia**
> Excludes1　dorsalgia in thoracic region (M54.6)
> low back pain (M54.5)

M54.81 Occipital neuralgia

M54.89 Other dorsalgia

■ **M54.9 Dorsalgia, unspecified**
Backache NOS
Back pain NOS

SOFT TISSUE DISORDERS (M60-M79)

DISORDERS OF MUSCLES (M60-M63)

> Excludes1　dermatopolymyositis (M33.-)
> muscular dystrophies and myopathies
> (G71-G72)
> myopathy in:
> amyloidosis (E85.-)
> polyarteritis nodosa (M30.0)
> rheumatoid arthritis (M05.32)
> scleroderma (M34.-)
> Sjögren's syndrome (M35.03)
> systemic lupus erythematosus (M32.-)

● **M60 Myositis**
> Excludes2　inclusion bodymyositis [IBM] (G72.41)

● **M60.0 Infective myositis**
Tropical pyomyositis
> Use additional code (B95-B97) to identify
> infectious agent

　● **M60.00 Infective myositis, unspecified site**

　　■ **M60.000 Infective myositis, unspecified
right arm** 🦠
Infective myositis, right upper
limb NOS

　　■ **M60.001 Infective myositis, unspecified
left arm** 🦠
Infective myositis, left upper
limb NOS

　　■ **M60.002 Infective myositis, unspecified
arm** 🦠
Infective myositis, upper limb
NOS

　　■ **M60.003 Infective myositis, unspecified
right leg** 🦠
Infective myositis, right lower
limb NOS

　　■ **M60.004 Infective myositis, unspecified
left leg** 🦠
Infective myositis, left lower
limb NOS

　　■ **M60.005 Infective myositis, unspecified
leg** 🦠
Infective myositis, lower limb
NOS

　　■ **M60.009 Infective myositis, unspecified
site** 🦠

● **M60.01 Infective myositis, shoulder**

M60.011 Infective myositis, right shoulder 🦠

M60.012 Infective myositis, left shoulder 🦠

■ **M60.019 Infective myositis, unspecified
shoulder** 🦠

● **M60.02 Infective myositis, upper arm**

**M60.021 Infective myositis, right upper
arm** 🦠

M60.022 Infective myositis, left upper arm 🦠

■ **M60.029 Infective myositis, unspecified
upper arm** 🦠

● **M60.03 Infective myositis, forearm**

M60.031 Infective myositis, right forearm 🦠

M60.032 Infective myositis, left forearm 🦠

■ **M60.039 Infective myositis, unspecified
forearm** 🦠

● **M60.04 Infective myositis, hand and fingers**

M60.041 Infective myositis, right hand 🦠

M60.042 Infective myositis, left hand 🦠

■ **M60.043 Infective myositis, unspecified
hand** 🦠

M60.044 Infective myositis, right finger(s) 🦠

M60.045 Infective myositis, left finger(s) 🦠

■ **M60.046 Infective myositis, unspecified
finger(s)** 🦠

● **M60.05 Infective myositis, thigh**

M60.051 Infective myositis, right thigh 🦠

M60.052 Infective myositis, left thigh 🦠

■ **M60.059 Infective myositis, unspecified
thigh** 🦠

● **M60.06 Infective myositis, lower leg**

M60.061 Infective myositis, right lower leg 🦠

M60.062 Infective myositis, left lower leg 🦠

■ **M60.069 Infective myositis, unspecified
lower leg** 🦠

● **M60.07 Infective myositis, ankle, foot and toes**

M60.070 Infective myositis, right ankle 🦠

M60.071 Infective myositis, left ankle 🦠

■ **M60.072 Infective myositis, unspecified
ankle** 🦠

M60.073 Infective myositis, right foot 🦠

M60.074 Infective myositis, left foot 🦠

■ **M60.075 Infective myositis, unspecified
foot** 🦠

M60.076 Infective myositis, right toe(s) 🦠

M60.077 Infective myositis, left toe(s) 🦠

■ **M60.078 Infective myositis, unspecified
toe(s)** 🦠

M60.08 Infective myositis, other site 🦠

M60.09 Infective myositis, multiple sites 🦠

● **M60.1 Interstitial myositis**

■ **M60.10 Interstitial myositis of unspecified site**

● **M60.11 Interstitial myositis, shoulder**

**M60.111 Interstitial myositis, right
shoulder**

M60.112 Interstitial myositis, left shoulder

■ **M60.119 Interstitial myositis, unspecified
shoulder**

● Unacceptable First-Listed Diagnosis　　● Use Additional Character(s)　　■ Unspecified　　**OGCR** Official Guidelines for Coding and Reporting
🦠 Complication\Comorbidity　　🦠 Major C\C　　[Excludes 1]　[Excludes 2]　　Includes　　Use additional　　Code first　　Code also
1180

● M60.12 Interstitial myositis, upper arm

    M60.121 Interstitial myositis, right upper arm

    M60.122 Interstitial myositis, left upper arm

    ■ M60.129 Interstitial myositis, unspecified upper arm

● M60.13 Interstitial myositis, forearm

    M60.131 Interstitial myositis, right forearm

    M60.132 Interstitial myositis, left forearm

    ■ M60.139 Interstitial myositis, unspecified forearm

● M60.14 Interstitial myositis, hand

    M60.141 Interstitial myositis, right hand

    M60.142 Interstitial myositis, left hand

    ■ M60.149 Interstitial myositis, unspecified hand

● M60.15 Interstitial myositis, thigh

    M60.151 Interstitial myositis, right thigh

    M60.152 Interstitial myositis, left thigh

    ■ M60.159 Interstitial myositis, unspecified thigh

● M60.16 Interstitial myositis, lower leg

    M60.161 Interstitial myositis, right lower leg

    M60.162 Interstitial myositis, left lower leg

    ■ M60.169 Interstitial myositis, unspecified lower leg

● M60.17 Interstitial myositis, ankle and foot

    M60.171 Interstitial myositis, right ankle and foot

    M60.172 Interstitial myositis, left ankle and foot

    ■ M60.179 Interstitial myositis, unspecified ankle and foot

    M60.18 Interstitial myositis, other site

    M60.19 Interstitial myositis, multiple sites

● M60.2 Foreign body granuloma of soft tissue, not elsewhere classified

    Excludes1   foreign body granuloma of skin and subcutaneous tissue (L92.3)

■ M60.20 Foreign body granuloma of soft tissue, not elsewhere classified, unspecified site

● M60.21 Foreign body granuloma of soft tissue, not elsewhere classified, shoulder

    M60.211 Foreign body granuloma of soft tissue, not elsewhere classified, right shoulder

    M60.212 Foreign body granuloma of soft tissue, not elsewhere classified, left shoulder

    ■ M60.219 Foreign body granuloma of soft tissue, not elsewhere classified, unspecified shoulder

● M60.22 Foreign body granuloma of soft tissue, not elsewhere classified, upper arm

    M60.221 Foreign body granuloma of soft tissue, not elsewhere classified, right upper arm

    M60.222 Foreign body granuloma of soft tissue, not elsewhere classified, left upper arm

    ■ M60.229 Foreign body granuloma of soft tissue, not elsewhere classified, unspecified upper arm

● M60.23 Foreign body granuloma of soft tissue, not elsewhere classified, forearm

    M60.231 Foreign body granuloma of soft tissue, not elsewhere classified, right forearm

    M60.232 Foreign body granuloma of soft tissue, not elsewhere classified, left forearm

    ■ M60.239 Foreign body granuloma of soft tissue, not elsewhere classified, unspecified forearm

● M60.24 Foreign body granuloma of soft tissue, not elsewhere classified, hand

    M60.241 Foreign body granuloma of soft tissue, not elsewhere classified, right hand

    M60.242 Foreign body granuloma of soft tissue, not elsewhere classified, left hand

    ■ M60.249 Foreign body granuloma of soft tissue, not elsewhere classified, unspecified hand

● M60.25 Foreign body granuloma of soft tissue, not elsewhere classified, thigh

    M60.251 Foreign body granuloma of soft tissue, not elsewhere classified, right thigh

    M60.252 Foreign body granuloma of soft tissue, not elsewhere classified, left thigh

    ■ M60.259 Foreign body granuloma of soft tissue, not elsewhere classified, unspecified thigh

● M60.26 Foreign body granuloma of soft tissue, not elsewhere classified, lower leg

    M60.261 Foreign body granuloma of soft tissue, not elsewhere classified, right lower leg

    M60.262 Foreign body granuloma of soft tissue, not elsewhere classified, left lower leg

    ■ M60.269 Foreign body granuloma of soft tissue, not elsewhere classified, unspecified lower leg

● M60.27 Foreign body granuloma of soft tissue, not elsewhere classified, ankle and foot

    M60.271 Foreign body granuloma of soft tissue, not elsewhere classified, right ankle and foot

    M60.272 Foreign body granuloma of soft tissue, not elsewhere classified, left ankle and foot

    ■ M60.279 Foreign body granuloma of soft tissue, not elsewhere classified, unspecified ankle and foot

    M60.28 Foreign body granuloma of soft tissue, not elsewhere classified, other site

● Unacceptable First-Listed Diagnosis   ● Use Additional Character(s)   ■ Unspecified   **OGCR** Official Guidelines for Coding and Reporting

 Complication\Comorbidity   Major C\C   Excludes 1   Excludes 2   Includes   Use additional   Code first   Code also

1181

- M60.8 Other myositis
  - M60.80 Other myositis, unspecified site
  - M60.81 Other myositis shoulder
    - M60.811 Other myositis, right shoulder
    - M60.812 Other myositis, left shoulder
    - M60.819 Other myositis, unspecified shoulder
  - M60.82 Other myositis, upper arm
    - M60.821 Other myositis, right upper arm
    - M60.822 Other myositis, left upper arm
    - M60.829 Other myositis, unspecified upper arm
  - M60.83 Other myositis, forearm
    - M60.831 Other myositis, right forearm
    - M60.832 Other myositis, left forearm
    - M60.839 Other myositis, unspecified forearm
  - M60.84 Other myositis, hand
    - M60.841 Other myositis, right hand
    - M60.842 Other myositis, left hand
    - M60.849 Other myositis, unspecified hand
  - M60.85 Other myositis, thigh
    - M60.851 Other myositis, right thigh
    - M60.852 Other myositis, left thigh
    - M60.859 Other myositis, unspecified thigh
  - M60.86 Other myositis, lower leg
    - M60.861 Other myositis, right lower leg
    - M60.862 Other myositis, left lower leg
    - M60.869 Other myositis, unspecified lower leg
  - M60.87 Other myositis, ankle and foot
    - M60.871 Other myositis, right ankle and foot
    - M60.872 Other myositis, left ankle and foot
    - M60.879 Other myositis, unspecified ankle and foot
  - M60.88 Other myositis, other site
  - M60.89 Other myositis, multiple sites
- M60.9 Myositis, unspecified
- M61 Calcification and ossification of muscle
  - M61.0 Myositis ossificans traumatica
    - M61.00 Myositis ossificans traumatica, unspecified site
    - M61.01 Myositis ossificans traumatica, shoulder
      - M61.011 Myositis ossificans traumatica, right shoulder
      - M61.012 Myositis ossificans traumatica, left shoulder
      - M61.019 Myositis ossificans traumatica, unspecified shoulder
    - M61.02 Myositis ossificans traumatica, upper arm
      - M61.021 Myositis ossificans traumatica, right upper arm
      - M61.022 Myositis ossificans traumatica, left upper arm
      - M61.029 Myositis ossificans traumatica, unspecified upper arm
  - M61.03 Myositis ossificans traumatica, forearm
    - M61.031 Myositis ossificans traumatica, right forearm
    - M61.032 Myositis ossificans traumatica, left forearm
    - M61.039 Myositis ossificans traumatica, unspecified forearm
  - M61.04 Myositis ossificans traumatica, hand
    - M61.041 Myositis ossificans traumatica, right hand
    - M61.042 Myositis ossificans traumatica, left hand
    - M61.049 Myositis ossificans traumatica, unspecified hand
  - M61.05 Myositis ossificans traumatica, thigh
    - M61.051 Myositis ossificans traumatica, right thigh
    - M61.052 Myositis ossificans traumatica, left thigh
    - M61.059 Myositis ossificans traumatica, unspecified thigh
  - M61.06 Myositis ossificans traumatica, lower leg
    - M61.061 Myositis ossificans traumatica, right lower leg
    - M61.062 Myositis ossificans traumatica, left lower leg
    - M61.069 Myositis ossificans traumatica, unspecified lower leg
  - M61.07 Myositis ossificans traumatica, ankle and foot
    - M61.071 Myositis ossificans traumatica, right ankle and foot
    - M61.072 Myositis ossificans traumatica, left ankle and foot
    - M61.079 Myositis ossificans traumatica, unspecified ankle and foot
  - M61.08 Myositis ossificans traumatica, other site
  - M61.09 Myositis ossificans traumatica, multiple sites
- M61.1 Myositis ossificans progressiva
  Fibrodysplasia ossificans progressiva
  - M61.10 Myositis ossificans progressiva, unspecified site
  - M61.11 Myositis ossificans progressiva, shoulder
    - M61.111 Myositis ossificans progressiva, right shoulder
    - M61.112 Myositis ossificans progressiva, left shoulder
    - M61.119 Myositis ossificans progressiva, unspecified shoulder
  - M61.12 Myositis ossificans progressiva, upper arm
    - M61.121 Myositis ossificans progressiva, right upper arm
    - M61.122 Myositis ossificans progressiva, left upper arm
    - M61.129 Myositis ossificans progressiva, unspecified arm
  - M61.13 Myositis ossificans progressiva, forearm
    - M61.131 Myositis ossificans progressiva, right forearm
    - M61.132 Myositis ossificans progressiva, left forearm
    - M61.139 Myositis ossificans progressiva, unspecified forearm

CHAPTER 13 (M00-M99)

● M61.14   Myositis ossificans progressiva, hand and finger(s)

    M61.141   Myositis ossificans progressiva, right hand

    M61.142   Myositis ossificans progressiva, left hand

    ▣ M61.143   Myositis ossificans progressiva, unspecified hand

    M61.144   Myositis ossificans progressiva, right finger(s)

    M61.145   Myositis ossificans progressiva, left finger(s)

    ▣ M61.146   Myositis ossificans progressiva, unspecified finger(s)

● M61.15   Myositis ossificans progressiva, thigh

    M61.151   Myositis ossificans progressiva, right thigh

    M61.152   Myositis ossificans progressiva, left thigh

    ▣ M61.159   Myositis ossificans progressiva, unspecified thigh

● M61.16   Myositis ossificans progressiva, lower leg

    M61.161   Myositis ossificans progressiva, right lower leg

    M61.162   Myositis ossificans progressiva, left lower leg

    ▣ M61.169   Myositis ossificans progressiva, unspecified lower leg

● M61.17   Myositis ossificans progressiva, ankle, foot and toe(s)

    M61.171   Myositis ossificans progressiva, right ankle

    M61.172   Myositis ossificans progressiva, left ankle

    ▣ M61.173   Myositis ossificans progressiva, unspecified ankle

    M61.174   Myositis ossificans progressiva, right foot

    M61.175   Myositis ossificans progressiva, left foot

    ▣ M61.176   Myositis ossificans progressiva, unspecified foot

    M61.177   Myositis ossificans progressiva, right toe(s)

    M61.178   Myositis ossificans progressiva, left toe(s)

    ▣ M61.179   Myositis ossificans progressiva, unspecified toe(s)

    M61.18   Myositis ossificans progressiva, other site

    M61.19   Myositis ossificans progressiva, multiple sites

● M61.2   Paralytic calcification and ossification of muscle
     Myositis ossificans associated with quadriplegia or paraplegia

    ▣ M61.20   Paralytic calcification and ossification of muscle, unspecified site

● M61.21   Paralytic calcification and ossification of muscle, shoulder

    M61.211   Paralytic calcification and ossification of muscle, right shoulder

    M61.212   Paralytic calcification and ossification of muscle, left shoulder

    ▣ M61.219   Paralytic calcification and ossification of muscle, unspecified shoulder

● M61.22   Paralytic calcification and ossification of muscle, upper arm

    M61.221   Paralytic calcification and ossification of muscle, right upper arm

    M61.222   Paralytic calcification and ossification of muscle, left upper arm

    ▣ M61.229   Paralytic calcification and ossification of muscle, unspecified upper arm

● M61.23   Paralytic calcification and ossification of muscle, forearm

    M61.231   Paralytic calcification and ossification of muscle, right forearm

    M61.232   Paralytic calcification and ossification of muscle, left forearm

    ▣ M61.239   Paralytic calcification and ossification of muscle, unspecified forearm

● M61.24   Paralytic calcification and ossification of muscle, hand

    M61.241   Paralytic calcification and ossification of muscle, right hand

    M61.242   Paralytic calcification and ossification of muscle, left hand

    ▣ M61.249   Paralytic calcification and ossification of muscle, unspecified hand

● M61.25   Paralytic calcification and ossification of muscle, thigh

    M61.251   Paralytic calcification and ossification of muscle, right thigh

    M61.252   Paralytic calcification and ossification of muscle, left thigh

    ▣ M61.259   Paralytic calcification and ossification of muscle, unspecified thigh

● M61.26   Paralytic calcification and ossification of muscle, lower leg

    M61.261   Paralytic calcification and ossification of muscle, right lower leg

    M61.262   Paralytic calcification and ossification of muscle, left lower leg

    ▣ M61.269   Paralytic calcification and ossification of muscle, unspecified lower leg

● M61.27   Paralytic calcification and ossification of muscle, ankle and foot

    M61.271   Paralytic calcification and ossification of muscle, right ankle and foot

    M61.272   Paralytic calcification and ossification of muscle, left ankle and foot

● Unacceptable First-Listed Diagnosis   ● Use Additional Character(s)   ▣ Unspecified   **OGCR** Official Guidelines for Coding and Reporting

 Complication\Comorbidity   Major C\C   Excludes 1   Excludes 2   Includes   Use additional   Code first   Code also

1183

CHAPTER 13 (M00-M99)

M61.279 Paralytic calcification and ossification of muscle, unspecified ankle and foot

M61.28 Paralytic calcification and ossification of muscle, other site

M61.29 Paralytic calcification and ossification of muscle, multiple sites

● M61.3 Calcification and ossification of muscles associated with burns
Myositis ossificans associated with burns

M61.30 Calcification and ossification of muscles associated with burns, unspecified site

● M61.31 Calcification and ossification of muscles associated with burns, shoulder

M61.311 Calcification and ossification of muscles associated with burns, right shoulder

M61.312 Calcification and ossification of muscles associated with burns, left shoulder

M61.319 Calcification and ossification of muscles associated with burns, unspecified shoulder

● M61.32 Calcification and ossification of muscles associated with burns, upper arm

M61.321 Calcification and ossification of muscles associated with burns, right upper arm

M61.322 Calcification and ossification of muscles associated with burns, left upper arm

M61.329 Calcification and ossification of muscles associated with burns, unspecified upper arm

● M61.33 Calcification and ossification of muscles associated with burns, forearm

M61.331 Calcification and ossification of muscles associated with burns, right forearm

M61.332 Calcification and ossification of muscles associated with burns, left forearm

M61.339 Calcification and ossification of muscles associated with burns, unspecified forearm

● M61.34 Calcification and ossification of muscles associated with burns, hand

M61.341 Calcification and ossification of muscles associated with burns, right hand

M61.342 Calcification and ossification of muscles associated with burns, left hand

M61.349 Calcification and ossification of muscles associated with burns, unspecified hand

● M61.35 Calcification and ossification of muscles associated with burns, thigh

M61.351 Calcification and ossification of muscles associated with burns, right thigh

M61.352 Calcification and ossification of muscles associated with burns, left thigh

M61.359 Calcification and ossification of muscles associated with burns, unspecified thigh

● M61.36 Calcification and ossification of muscles associated with burns, lower leg

M61.361 Calcification and ossification of muscles associated with burns, right lower leg

M61.362 Calcification and ossification of muscles associated with burns, left lower leg

M61.369 Calcification and ossification of muscles associated with burns, unspecified lower leg

● M61.37 Calcification and ossification of muscles associated with burns, ankle and foot

M61.371 Calcification and ossification of muscles associated with burns, right ankle and foot

M61.372 Calcification and ossification of muscles associated with burns, left ankle and foot

M61.379 Calcification and ossification of muscles associated with burns, unspecified ankle and foot

M61.38 Calcification and ossification of muscles associated with burns, other site

M61.39 Calcification and ossification of muscles associated with burns, multiple sites

● M61.4 Other calcification of muscle

Excludes1   calcific tendinitis NOS (M65.2-)
calcific tendinitis of shoulder (M75.3)

M61.40 Other calcification of muscle, unspecified site

● M61.41 Other calcification of muscle, shoulder

M61.411 Other calcification of muscle, right shoulder

M61.412 Other calcification of muscle, left shoulder

M61.419 Other calcification of muscle, unspecified shoulder

● M61.42 Other calcification of muscle, upper arm

M61.421 Other calcification of muscle, right upper arm

M61.422 Other calcification of muscle, left upper arm

M61.429 Other calcification of muscle, unspecified upper arm

● M61.43 Other calcification of muscle, forearm

M61.431 Other calcification of muscle, right forearm

M61.432 Other calcification of muscle, left forearm

M61.439 Other calcification of muscle, unspecified forearm

● M61.44 Other calcification of muscle, hand

M61.441 Other calcification of muscle, right hand

M61.442 Other calcification of muscle, left hand

M61.449 Other calcification of muscle, unspecified hand

● Unacceptable First-Listed Diagnosis   ● Use Additional Character(s)   ■ Unspecified   OGCR Official Guidelines for Coding and Reporting
🗲 Complication\Comorbidity   🗲 Major C\C   Excludes 1   Excludes 2   Includes   Use additional   Code first   Code also

● M61.45 Other calcification of muscle, thigh

    M61.451 Other calcification of muscle, right thigh

    M61.452 Other calcification of muscle, left thigh

    ■M61.459 Other calcification of muscle, unspecified thigh

● M61.46 Other calcification of muscle, lower leg

    M61.461 Other calcification of muscle, right lower leg

    M61.462 Other calcification of muscle, left lower leg

    ■M61.469 Other calcification of muscle, unspecified lower leg

● M61.47 Other calcification of muscle, ankle and foot

    M61.471 Other calcification of muscle, right ankle and foot

    M61.472 Other calcification of muscle, left ankle and foot

    ■M61.479 Other calcification of muscle, unspecified ankle and foot

    M61.48 Other calcification of muscle, other site

    M61.49 Other calcification of muscle, multiple sites

● M61.5 Other ossification of muscle

    ■M61.50 Other ossification of muscle, unspecified site

    ● M61.51 Other ossification of muscle, shoulder

        M61.511 Other ossification of muscle, right shoulder

        M61.512 Other ossification of muscle, left shoulder

        ■M61.519 Other ossification of muscle, unspecified shoulder

    ● M61.52 Other ossification of muscle, upper arm

        M61.521 Other ossification of muscle, right upper arm

        M61.522 Other ossification of muscle, left upper arm

        ■M61.529 Other ossification of muscle, unspecified upper arm

    ● M61.53 Other ossification of muscle, forearm

        M61.531 Other ossification of muscle, right forearm

        M61.532 Other ossification of muscle, left forearm

        ■M61.539 Other ossification of muscle, unspecified forearm

    ● M61.54 Other ossification of muscle, hand

        M61.541 Other ossification of muscle, right hand

        M61.542 Other ossification of muscle, left hand

        ■M61.549 Other ossification of muscle, unspecified hand

    ● M61.55 Other ossification of muscle, thigh

        M61.551 Other ossification of muscle, right thigh

        M61.552 Other ossification of muscle, left thigh

        ■M61.559 Other ossification of muscle, unspecified thigh

● M61.56 Other ossification of muscle, lower leg

    M61.561 Other ossification of muscle, right lower leg

    M61.562 Other ossification of muscle, left lower leg

    ■M61.569 Other ossification of muscle, unspecified lower leg

● M61.57 Other ossification of muscle, ankle and foot

    M61.571 Other ossification of muscle, right ankle and foot

    M61.572 Other ossification of muscle, left ankle and foot

    ■M61.579 Other ossification of muscle, unspecified ankle and foot

    M61.58 Other ossification of muscle, other site

    M61.59 Other ossification of muscle, multiple sites

■M61.9 Calcification and ossification of muscle, unspecified

● M62 Other disorders of muscle

    | **Excludes1** | alcoholic myopathy (G72.1) |
    cramp and spasm (R25.2)
    drug-induced myopathy (G72.0)
    myalgia (M79.1)
    stiff-man syndrome (G25.82)

    Excludes2 nontraumatic hematoma of muscle (M79.81)

  ● M62.0 Separation of muscle (nontraumatic)

    Diastasis of muscle

    Excludes1 diastasis recti complicating pregnancy, labor and delivery (O71.8)

        traumatic separation of muscle - see strain of muscle by body region

    ■M62.00 Separation of muscle (nontraumatic), unspecified site

    ● M62.01 Separation of muscle (nontraumatic), shoulder

        M62.011 Separation of muscle (nontraumatic), right shoulder

        M62.012 Separation of muscle (nontraumatic), left shoulder

        ■M62.019 Separation of muscle (nontraumatic), unspecified shoulder

    ● M62.02 Separation of muscle (nontraumatic), upper arm

        M62.021 Separation of muscle (nontraumatic), right upper arm

        M62.022 Separation of muscle (nontraumatic), left upper arm

        ■M62.029 Separation of muscle (nontraumatic), unspecified upper arm

    ● M62.03 Separation of muscle (nontraumatic), forearm

        M62.031 Separation of muscle (nontraumatic), right forearm

        M62.032 Separation of muscle (nontraumatic), left forearm

        ■M62.039 Separation of muscle (nontraumatic), unspecified forearm

    ● M62.04 Separation of muscle (nontraumatic), hand

        M62.041 Separation of muscle (nontraumatic), right hand

● Unacceptable First-Listed Diagnosis   ● Use Additional Character(s)   ■ Unspecified   **OGCR** Official Guidelines for Coding and Reporting

🅒 Complication\Comorbidity   🅒 Major C\C   Excludes 1   Excludes 2   Includes   Use additional   Code first   Code also

1185

M62.042 Separation of muscle (nontraumatic), left hand

■ M62.049 Separation of muscle (nontraumatic), unspecified hand

● M62.05 Separation of muscle (nontraumatic), thigh

M62.051 Separation of muscle (nontraumatic), right thigh

M62.052 Separation of muscle (nontraumatic), left thigh

■ M62.059 Separation of muscle (nontraumatic), unspecified thigh

● M62.06 Separation of muscle (nontraumatic), lower leg

M62.061 Separation of muscle (nontraumatic), right lower leg

M62.062 Separation of muscle (nontraumatic), left lower leg

■ M62.069 Separation of muscle (nontraumatic), unspecified lower leg

● M62.07 Separation of muscle (nontraumatic), ankle and foot

M62.071 Separation of muscle (nontraumatic), right ankle and foot

M62.072 Separation of muscle (nontraumatic), left ankle and foot

■ M62.079 Separation of muscle (nontraumatic), unspecified ankle and foot

M62.08 Separation of muscle (nontraumatic), other site

● M62.1 Other rupture of muscle (nontraumatic)

Excludes1 traumatic rupture of muscle - see strain of muscle by body region

Excludes2 rupture of tendon (M66.-)

■ M62.10 Other rupture of muscle (nontraumatic), unspecified site

● M62.11 Other rupture of muscle (nontraumatic), shoulder

M62.111 Other rupture of muscle (nontraumatic), right shoulder

M62.112 Other rupture of muscle (nontraumatic), left shoulder

■ M62.119 Other rupture of muscle (nontraumatic), unspecified shoulder

● M62.12 Other rupture of muscle (nontraumatic), upper arm

M62.121 Other rupture of muscle (nontraumatic), right upper arm

M62.122 Other rupture of muscle (nontraumatic), left upper arm

■ M62.129 Other rupture of muscle (nontraumatic), unspecified upper arm

● M62.13 Other rupture of muscle (nontraumatic), forearm

M62.131 Other rupture of muscle (nontraumatic), right forearm

M62.132 Other rupture of muscle (nontraumatic), left forearm

■ M62.139 Other rupture of muscle (nontraumatic), unspecified forearm

● M62.14 Other rupture of muscle (nontraumatic), hand

M62.141 Other rupture of muscle (nontraumatic), right hand

M62.142 Other rupture of muscle (nontraumatic), left hand

■ M62.149 Other rupture of muscle (nontraumatic), unspecified hand

● M62.15 Other rupture of muscle (nontraumatic), thigh

M62.151 Other rupture of muscle (nontraumatic), right thigh

M62.152 Other rupture of muscle (nontraumatic), left thigh

■ M62.159 Other rupture of muscle (nontraumatic), unspecified thigh

● M62.16 Other rupture of muscle (nontraumatic), lower leg

M62.161 Other rupture of muscle (nontraumatic), right lower leg

M62.162 Other rupture of muscle (nontraumatic), left lower leg

■ M62.169 Other rupture of muscle (nontraumatic), unspecified lower leg

● M62.17 Other rupture of muscle (nontraumatic), ankle and foot

M62.171 Other rupture of muscle (nontraumatic), right ankle and foot

M62.172 Other rupture of muscle (nontraumatic), left ankle and foot

■ M62.179 Other rupture of muscle (nontraumatic), unspecified ankle and foot

M62.18 Other rupture of muscle (nontraumatic), other site

● M62.2 Nontraumatic ischemic infarction of muscle

Excludes1 compartment syndrome (traumatic) (T79.A-)
nontraumatic compartment syndrome (M79.A-)
traumatic ischemia of muscle (T79.6)
rhabdomyolysis (M62.82)
Volkmann's ischemic contracture (T79.6)

■ M62.20 Nontraumatic ischemic infarction of muscle, unspecified site

● M62.21 Nontraumatic ischemic infarction of muscle, shoulder

M62.211 Nontraumatic ischemic infarction of muscle, right shoulder

M62.212 Nontraumatic ischemic infarction of muscle, left shoulder

■ M62.219 Nontraumatic ischemic infarction of muscle, unspecified shoulder

● M62.22 Nontraumatic ischemic infarction of muscle, upper arm

M62.221 Nontraumatic ischemic infarction of muscle, right upper arm

M62.222 Nontraumatic ischemic infarction of muscle, left upper arm

■ M62.229 Nontraumatic ischemic infarction of muscle, unspecified upper arm

● M62.23 Nontraumatic ischemic infarction of muscle, forearm

M62.231 Nontraumatic ischemic infarction of muscle, right forearm

M62.232 Nontraumatic ischemic infarction of muscle, left forearm

■ M62.239 Nontraumatic ischemic infarction of muscle, unspecified forearm

● M62.24 Nontraumatic ischemic infarction of muscle, hand

M62.241 Nontraumatic ischemic infarction of muscle, right hand

M62.242 Nontraumatic ischemic infarction of muscle, left hand

■ M62.249 Nontraumatic ischemic infarction of muscle, unspecified hand

● M62.25 Nontraumatic ischemic infarction of muscle, thigh

M62.251 Nontraumatic ischemic infarction of muscle, right thigh

M62.252 Nontraumatic ischemic infarction of muscle, left thigh

■ M62.259 Nontraumatic ischemic infarction of muscle, unspecified thigh

● M62.26 Nontraumatic ischemic infarction of muscle, lower leg

M62.261 Nontraumatic ischemic infarction of muscle, right lower leg

M62.262 Nontraumatic ischemic infarction of muscle, left lower leg

■ M62.269 Nontraumatic ischemic infarction of muscle, unspecified lower leg

● M62.27 Nontraumatic ischemic infarction of muscle, ankle and foot

M62.271 Nontraumatic ischemic infarction of muscle, right ankle and foot

M62.272 Nontraumatic ischemic infarction of muscle, left ankle and foot

■ M62.279 Nontraumatic ischemic infarction of muscle, unspecified ankle and foot

M62.28 Nontraumatic ischemic infarction of muscle, other site

M62.3 Immobility syndrome (paraplegic)

M62.4 Contracture of muscle

CONTRACTURE OF TENDON (SHEATH)

Excludes1   contracture of joint (M24.5-)

■ M62.40 Contracture of muscle, unspecified site

● M62.41 Contracture of muscle, shoulder

M62.411 Contracture of muscle, right shoulder

M62.412 Contracture of muscle, left shoulder

■ M62.419 Contracture of muscle, unspecified shoulder

● M62.42 Contracture of muscle, upper arm

M62.421 Contracture of muscle, right upper arm

M62.422 Contracture of muscle, left upper arm

■ M62.429 Contracture of muscle, unspecified upper arm

● M62.43 Contracture of muscle, forearm

M62.431 Contracture of muscle, right forearm

M62.432 Contracture of muscle, left forearm

■ M62.439 Contracture of muscle, unspecified forearm

● M62.44 Contracture of muscle, hand

M62.441 Contracture of muscle, right hand

M62.442 Contracture of muscle, left hand

■ M62.449 Contracture of muscle, unspecified hand

● M62.45 Contracture of muscle, thigh

M62.451 Contracture of muscle, right thigh

M62.452 Contracture of muscle, left thigh

■ M62.459 Contracture of muscle, unspecified thigh

● M62.46 Contracture of muscle, lower leg

M62.461 Contracture of muscle, right lower leg

M62.462 Contracture of muscle, left lower leg

■ M62.469 Contracture of muscle, unspecified lower leg

● M62.47 Contracture of muscle, ankle and foot

M62.471 Contracture of muscle, right ankle and foot

M62.472 Contracture of muscle, left ankle and foot

■ M62.479 Contracture of muscle, unspecified ankle and foot

M62.48 Contracture of muscle, other site

M62.49 Contracture of muscle, multiple sites

● M62.5 Muscle wasting and atrophy, not elsewhere classified

Disuse atrophy NEC

Excludes1   neuralgic amyotrophy (G54.5)
progressive muscular atrophy (G12.29)

Excludes2   pelvic muscle wasting (N81.84)

■ M62.50 Muscle wasting and atrophy, not elsewhere classified, unspecified site

● M62.51 Muscle wasting and atrophy, not elsewhere classified, shoulder

M62.511 Muscle wasting and atrophy, not elsewhere classified, right shoulder

M62.512 Muscle wasting and atrophy, not elsewhere classified, left shoulder

■ M62.519 Muscle wasting and atrophy, not elsewhere classified, unspecified shoulder

CHAPTER 13 (M00–M99)

● Unacceptable First-Listed Diagnosis   ● Use Additional Character(s)   ■ Unspecified   **OGCR** Official Guidelines for Coding and Reporting

🝂 Complication\Comorbidity   🝂 Major C\C   Excludes 1   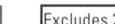 Excludes 2   Includes   Use additional   Code first   Code also

1187

● **M62.52 Muscle wasting and atrophy, not elsewhere classified, upper arm**

   M62.521 Muscle wasting and atrophy, not elsewhere classified, right upper arm

   M62.522 Muscle wasting and atrophy, not elsewhere classified, left upper arm

   ■M62.529 Muscle wasting and atrophy, not elsewhere classified, unspecified upper arm

● **M62.53 Muscle wasting and atrophy, not elsewhere classified, forearm**

   M62.531 Muscle wasting and atrophy, not elsewhere classified, right forearm

   M62.532 Muscle wasting and atrophy, not elsewhere classified, left forearm

   ■M62.539 Muscle wasting and atrophy, not elsewhere classified, unspecified forearm

● **M62.54 Muscle wasting and atrophy, not elsewhere classified, hand**

   M62.541 Muscle wasting and atrophy, not elsewhere classified, right hand

   M62.542 Muscle wasting and atrophy, not elsewhere classified, left hand

   ■M62.549 Muscle wasting and atrophy, not elsewhere classified, unspecified hand

● **M62.55 Muscle wasting and atrophy, not elsewhere classified, thigh**

   M62.551 Muscle wasting and atrophy, not elsewhere classified, right thigh

   M62.552 Muscle wasting and atrophy, not elsewhere classified, left thigh

   ■M62.559 Muscle wasting and atrophy, not elsewhere classified, unspecified thigh

● **M62.56 Muscle wasting and atrophy, not elsewhere classified, lower leg**

   M62.561 Muscle wasting and atrophy, not elsewhere classified, right lower leg

   M62.562 Muscle wasting and atrophy, not elsewhere classified, left lower leg

   ■M62.569 Muscle wasting and atrophy, not elsewhere classified, unspecified lower leg

● **M62.57 Muscle wasting and atrophy, not elsewhere classified, ankle and foot**

   M62.571 Muscle wasting and atrophy, not elsewhere classified, right ankle and foot

   M62.572 Muscle wasting and atrophy, not elsewhere classified, left ankle and foot

   ■M62.579 Muscle wasting and atrophy, not elsewhere classified, unspecified ankle and foot

M62.58 Muscle wasting and atrophy, not elsewhere classified, other site

M62.59 Muscle wasting and atrophy, not elsewhere classified, multiple sites

● **M62.8 Other specified disorders of muscle**

   Excludes2 nontraumatic hematoma of muscle (M79.81)

   M62.81 Muscle weakness (generalized)

   M62.82 Rhabdomyolysis 🝙

      Excludes1 traumatic rhabdomyolysis (T79.6)

 ● **M62.83 Muscle spasm**

   M62.830 Muscle spasm of back

   M62.831 Muscle spasm of calf
      Charley-horse

   M62.838 Other muscle spasm

   M62.89 Other specified disorders of muscle
      Muscle (sheath) hernia

■**M62.9 Disorder of muscle, unspecified**

● **M63 Disorders of muscle in diseases classified elsewhere**

   Excludes1 myopathy in:
      cysticercosis (B69.81)
      endocrine diseases (G73.7)
      metabolic diseases (G73.7)
      sarcoidosis (D86.87)
      syphilis (late) (A52.78)
      secondary (A51.49)
      toxoplasmosis (B58.82)
      tuberculosis (A18.09)

   Code first underlying disease, such as:
   leprosy (A30.-)
   neoplasm (C49.-, C79.89, D21.-, D48.1)
   schistosomiasis (B65.-)
   trichinellosis (B75)

● **M63.8 Disorders of muscle in diseases classified elsewhere**

 ● ■**M63.80 Disorders of muscle in diseases classified elsewhere, unspecified site**

 ● **M63.81 Disorders of muscle in diseases classified elsewhere, shoulder**

   ● M63.811 Disorders of muscle in diseases classified elsewhere, right shoulder

   ● M63.812 Disorders of muscle in diseases classified elsewhere, left shoulder

   ● ■ M63.819 Disorders of muscle in diseases classified elsewhere, unspecified shoulder

 ● **M63.82 Disorders of muscle in diseases classified elsewhere, upper arm**

   ● M63.821 Disorders of muscle in diseases classified elsewhere, right upper arm

   ● M63.822 Disorders of muscle in diseases classified elsewhere, left upper arm

   ● ■ M63.829 Disorders of muscle in diseases classified elsewhere, unspecified upper arm

 ● **M63.83 Disorders of muscle in diseases classified elsewhere, forearm**

   ● M63.831 Disorders of muscle in diseases classified elsewhere, right forearm

   ● M63.832 Disorders of muscle in diseases classified elsewhere, left forearm

   ● ■ M63.839 Disorders of muscle in diseases classified elsewhere, unspecified forearm

● Unacceptable First-Listed Diagnosis   ● Use Additional Character(s)   ■ Unspecified   **OGCR** Official Guidelines for Coding and Reporting
🝙 Complication\Comorbidity   🝙 Major C\C   Excludes 1   Excludes 2   Includes   Use additional   Code first   Code also

● M63.84 Disorders of muscle in diseases classified elsewhere, hand
- ● M63.841 Disorders of muscle in diseases classified elsewhere, right hand
- ● M63.842 Disorders of muscle in diseases classified elsewhere, left hand
- ● ■ M63.849 Disorders of muscle in diseases classified elsewhere, unspecified hand

● M63.85 Disorders of muscle in diseases classified elsewhere, thigh
- ● M63.851 Disorders of muscle in diseases classified elsewhere, right thigh
- ● M63.852 Disorders of muscle in diseases classified elsewhere, left thigh
- ● ■ M63.859 Disorders of muscle in diseases classified elsewhere, unspecified thigh

● M63.86 Disorders of muscle in diseases classified elsewhere, lower leg
- ● M63.861 Disorders of muscle in diseases classified elsewhere, right lower leg
- ● M63.862 Disorders of muscle in diseases classified elsewhere, left lower leg
- ● ■ M63.869 Disorders of muscle in diseases classified elsewhere, unspecified lower leg

● M63.87 Disorders of muscle in diseases classified elsewhere, ankle and foot
- ● M63.871 Disorders of muscle in diseases classified elsewhere, right ankle and foot
- ● M63.872 Disorders of muscle in diseases classified elsewhere, left ankle and foot
- ● ■ M63.879 Disorders of muscle in diseases classified elsewhere, unspecified ankle and foot

● M63.88 Disorders of muscle in diseases classified elsewhere, other site

● M63.89 Disorders of muscle in diseases classified elsewhere, multiple sites

---

DISORDERS OF SYNOVIUM AND TENDON (M65-M67)

● M65 Synovitis and tenosynovitis

Excludes1	chronic crepitant synovitis of hand and wrist (M70.0-)
	current injury - see injury of ligament or tendon by body region
	soft tissue disorders related to use, overuse and pressure (M70.-)

Item 13–10 Synovitis is an inflammation of a synovial membrane resulting in pain on motion and is characterized by fluctuating swelling due to effusion in a synovial sac. **Tenosynovitis** is an inflammation of a tendon sheath and occurs most commonly in the wrists, hands, and feet. Bursitis is inflammation of a bursa (fluid filled sac) caused by repetitive use, trauma, infection, or systemic inflammatory disease. Bursae act as protectors and facilitate movement between bones and overlapping muscles (deep bursae) or between bones and tendons/skin (superficial bursae).

● M65.0 Abscess of tendon sheath
Use additional code (B95-B96) to identify bacterial agent
- ■ M65.00 Abscess of tendon sheath, unspecified site
- ● M65.01 Abscess of tendon sheath, shoulder
  - M65.011 Abscess of tendon sheath, right shoulder
  - M65.012 Abscess of tendon sheath, left shoulder
  - ■ M65.019 Abscess of tendon sheath, unspecified shoulder
- ● M65.02 Abscess of tendon sheath, upper arm
  - M65.021 Abscess of tendon sheath, right upper arm
  - M65.022 Abscess of tendon sheath, left upper arm
  - ■ M65.029 Abscess of tendon sheath, unspecified upper arm
- ● M65.03 Abscess of tendon sheath, forearm
  - M65.031 Abscess of tendon sheath, right forearm
  - M65.032 Abscess of tendon sheath, left forearm
  - ■ M65.039 Abscess of tendon sheath, unspecified forearm
- ● M65.04 Abscess of tendon sheath, hand
  - M65.041 Abscess of tendon sheath, right hand
  - M65.042 Abscess of tendon sheath, left hand
  - ■ M65.049 Abscess of tendon sheath, unspecified hand
- ● M65.05 Abscess of tendon sheath, thigh
  - M65.051 Abscess of tendon sheath, right thigh
  - M65.052 Abscess of tendon sheath, left thigh
  - ■ M65.059 Abscess of tendon sheath, unspecified thigh
- ● M65.06 Abscess of tendon sheath, lower leg
  - M65.061 Abscess of tendon sheath, right lower leg
  - M65.062 Abscess of tendon sheath, left lower leg
  - ■ M65.069 Abscess of tendon sheath, unspecified lower leg
- ● M65.07 Abscess of tendon sheath, ankle and foot
  - M65.071 Abscess of tendon sheath, right ankle and foot
  - M65.072 Abscess of tendon sheath, left ankle and foot
  - ■ M65.079 Abscess of tendon sheath, unspecified ankle and foot
- M65.08 Abscess of tendon sheath, other site

● M65.1 Other infective (teno)synovitis
- ■ M65.10 Other infective (teno)synovitis, unspecified site
- ● M65.11 Other infective (teno)synovitis, shoulder
  - M65.111 Other infective (teno)synovitis, right shoulder
  - M65.112 Other infective (teno)synovitis, left shoulder

● Unacceptable First-Listed Diagnosis   ● Use Additional Character(s)   ■ Unspecified   **OGCR** Official Guidelines for Coding and Reporting

🏷 Complication\Comorbidity   🏷 Major C\C   Excludes 1   Excludes 2   Includes   Use additional   Code first   Code also   1189

■ M65.119 Other infective (teno)synovitis, unspecified shoulder

● M65.12 Other infective (teno)synovitis, elbow

     M65.121 Other infective (teno)synovitis, right elbow

     M65.122 Other infective (teno)synovitis, left elbow

     ■ M65.129 Other infective (teno)synovitis, unspecified elbow

● M65.13 Other infective (teno)synovitis, wrist

     M65.131 Other infective (teno)synovitis, right wrist

     M65.132 Other infective (teno)synovitis, left wrist

     ■ M65.139 Other infective (teno)synovitis, unspecified wrist

● M65.14 Other infective (teno)synovitis, hand

     M65.141 Other infective (teno)synovitis, right hand

     M65.142 Other infective (teno)synovitis, left hand

     ■ M65.149 Other infective (teno)synovitis, unspecified hand

● M65.15 Other infective (teno)synovitis, hip

     M65.151 Other infective (teno)synovitis, right hip

     M65.152 Other infective (teno)synovitis, left hip

     ■ M65.159 Other infective (teno)synovitis, unspecified hip

● M65.16 Other infective (teno)synovitis, knee

     M65.161 Other infective (teno)synovitis, right knee

     M65.162 Other infective (teno)synovitis, left knee

     ■ M65.169 Other infective (teno)synovitis, unspecified knee

● M65.17 Other infective (teno)synovitis, ankle and foot

     M65.171 Other infective (teno)synovitis, right ankle and foot

     M65.172 Other infective (teno)synovitis, left ankle and foot

     ■ M65.179 Other infective (teno)synovitis, unspecified ankle and foot

M65.18 Other infective (teno)synovitis, other site

M65.19 Other infective (teno)synovitis, multiple sites

● M65.2 Calcific tendinitis

     Excludes1   tendinitis as classified in M75-M77   calcified tendinitis of shoulder (M75.3)

■ M65.20 Calcific tendinitis, unspecified site

● M65.22 Calcific tendinitis, upper arm

     M65.221 Calcific tendinitis, right upper arm

     M65.222 Calcific tendinitis, left upper arm

     ■ M65.229 Calcific tendinitis, unspecified upper arm

● M65.23 Calcific tendinitis, forearm

     M65.231 Calcific tendinitis, right forearm

     M65.232 Calcific tendinitis, left forearm

     ■ M65.239 Calcific tendinitis, unspecified forearm

● M65.24 Calcific tendinitis, hand

     M65.241 Calcific tendinitis, right hand

     M65.242 Calcific tendinitis, left hand

     ■ M65.249 Calcific tendinitis, unspecified hand

● M65.25 Calcific tendinitis, thigh

     M65.251 Calcific tendinitis, right thigh

     M65.252 Calcific tendinitis, left thigh

     ■ M65.259 Calcific tendinitis, unspecified thigh

● M65.26 Calcific tendinitis, lower leg

     M65.261 Calcific tendinitis, right lower leg

     M65.262 Calcific tendinitis, left lower leg

     ■ M65.269 Calcific tendinitis, unspecified lower leg

● M65.27 Calcific tendinitis, ankle and foot

     M65.271 Calcific tendinitis, right ankle and foot

     M65.272 Calcific tendinitis, left ankle and foot

     ■ M65.279 Calcific tendinitis, unspecified ankle and foot

M65.28 Calcific tendinitis, other site

M65.29 Calcific tendinitis, multiple sites

● M65.3 Trigger finger
    Nodular tendinous disease

     ■ M65.30 Trigger finger, unspecified finger

● M65.31 Trigger thumb

     M65.311 Trigger thumb, right thumb

     M65.312 Trigger thumb, left thumb

     ■ M65.319 Trigger thumb, unspecified thumb

● M65.32 Trigger finger, index finger

     M65.321 Trigger finger, right index finger

     M65.322 Trigger finger, left index finger

     ■ M65.329 Trigger finger, unspecified index finger

● M65.33 Trigger finger, middle finger

     M65.331 Trigger finger, right middle finger

     M65.332 Trigger finger, left middle finger

     ■ M65.339 Trigger finger, unspecified middle finger

● M65.34 Trigger finger, ring finger

     M65.341 Trigger finger, right ring finger

     M65.342 Trigger finger, left ring finger

     ■ M65.349 Trigger finger, unspecified ring finger

● M65.35 Trigger finger, little finger

     M65.351 Trigger finger, right little finger

     M65.352 Trigger finger, left little finger

     ■ M65.359 Trigger finger, unspecified little finger

M65.4 Radial styloid tenosynovitis [de Quervain]

● M65.8 Other synovitis and tenosynovitis

     ■ M65.80 Other synovitis and tenosynovitis, unspecified site

● M65.81   Other synovitis and tenosynovitis, shoulder
    M65.811   Other synovitis and tenosynovitis, right shoulder
    M65.812   Other synovitis and tenosynovitis, left shoulder
    ■ M65.819   Other synovitis and tenosynovitis, unspecified shoulder

● M65.82   Other synovitis and tenosynovitis, upper arm
    M65.821   Other synovitis and tenosynovitis, right upper arm
    M65.822   Other synovitis and tenosynovitis, left upper arm
    ■ M65.829   Other synovitis and tenosynovitis, unspecified upper arm

● M65.83   Other synovitis and tenosynovitis, forearm
    M65.831   Other synovitis and tenosynovitis, right forearm
    M65.832   Other synovitis and tenosynovitis, left forearm
    ■ M65.839   Other synovitis and tenosynovitis, unspecified forearm

● M65.84   Other synovitis and tenosynovitis, hand
    M65.841   Other synovitis and tenosynovitis, right hand
    M65.842   Other synovitis and tenosynovitis, left hand
    ■ M65.849   Other synovitis and tenosynovitis, unspecified hand

● M65.85   Other synovitis and tenosynovitis, thigh
    M65.851   Other synovitis and tenosynovitis, right thigh
    M65.852   Other synovitis and tenosynovitis, left thigh
    ■ M65.859   Other synovitis and tenosynovitis, unspecified thigh

● M65.86   Other synovitis and tenosynovitis, lower leg
    M65.861   Other synovitis and tenosynovitis, right lower leg
    M65.862   Other synovitis and tenosynovitis, left lower leg
    ■ M65.869   Other synovitis and tenosynovitis, unspecified lower leg

● M65.87   Other synovitis and tenosynovitis, ankle and foot
    M65.871   Other synovitis and tenosynovitis, right ankle and foot
    M65.872   Other synovitis and tenosynovitis, left ankle and foot
    ■ M65.879   Other synovitis and tenosynovitis, unspecified ankle and foot

   M65.88   Other synovitis and tenosynovitis, other site

   M65.89   Other synovitis and tenosynovitis, multiple sites

■ M65.9   Synovitis and tenosynovitis, unspecified

● M66   **Spontaneous rupture of synovium and tendon**
   Note: A spontaneous rutpure is one that occurs when a normal force is applied to tissues that are inferred to have less than normal strength.
   Excludes2   rotator cuff syndrome (M75.1)
     rupture where an abnormal force is applied to normal tissue - see injury of tendon by body region

   M66.0   **Rupture of popliteal cyst**

● M66.1   **Rupture of synovium**
    Rupture of synovial cyst
    Excludes2   rupture of popliteal cyst (M66.0)

   ■ M66.10   Rupture of synovium, unspecified joint

● M66.11   Rupture of synovium, shoulder
    M66.111   Rupture of synovium, right shoulder
    M66.112   Rupture of synovium, left shoulder
    ■ M66.119   Rupture of synovium, unspecified shoulder

● M66.12   Rupture of synovium, elbow
    M66.121   Rupture of synovium, right elbow
    M66.122   Rupture of synovium, left elbow
    ■ M66.129   Rupture of synovium, unspecified elbow

● M66.13   Rupture of synovium, wrist
    M66.131   Rupture of synovium, right wrist
    M66.132   Rupture of synovium, left wrist
    ■ M66.139   Rupture of synovium, unspecified wrist

● M66.14   Rupture of synovium, hand and fingers
    M66.141   Rupture of synovium, right hand
    M66.142   Rupture of synovium, left hand
    ■ M66.143   Rupture of synovium, unspecified hand
    M66.144   Rupture of synovium, right finger(s)
    M66.145   Rupture of synovium, left finger(s)
    ■ M66.146   Rupture of synovium, unspecified finger(s)

● M66.15   Rupture of synovium, hip
    M66.151   Rupture of synovium, right hip
    M66.152   Rupture of synovium, left hip
    ■ M66.159   Rupture of synovium, unspecified hip

● M66.17   Rupture of synovium, ankle, foot and toes
    M66.171   Rupture of synovium, right ankle
    M66.172   Rupture of synovium, left ankle
    ■ M66.173   Rupture of synovium, unspecified ankle
    M66.174   Rupture of synovium, right foot
    M66.175   Rupture of synovium, left foot
    ■ M66.176   Rupture of synovium, unspecified foot
    M66.177   Rupture of synovium, right toe(s)
    M66.178   Rupture of synovium, left toe(s)
    ■ M66.179   Rupture of synovium, unspecified toe(s)

   M66.18   Rupture of synovium, other site

● Unacceptable First-Listed Diagnosis   ● Use Additional Character(s)   ■ Unspecified   **OGCR** Official Guidelines for Coding and Reporting
🅒 Complication\Comorbidity   🅜 Major C\C   Excludes 1   Excludes 2   Includes   Use additional   Code first   Code also

- ● M66.2   Spontaneous rupture of extensor tendons
  - ■ M66.20   Spontaneous rupture of extensor tendons, unspecified site
  - ● M66.21   Spontaneous rupture of extensor tendons, shoulder
    - M66.211   Spontaneous rupture of extensor tendons, right shoulder
    - M66.212   Spontaneous rupture of extensor tendons, left shoulder
    - ■ M66.219   Spontaneous rupture of extensor tendons, unspecified shoulder
  - ● M66.22   Spontaneous rupture of extensor tendons, upper arm
    - M66.221   Spontaneous rupture of extensor tendons, right upper arm
    - M66.222   Spontaneous rupture of extensor tendons, left upper arm
    - ■ M66.229   Spontaneous rupture of extensor tendons, unspecified upper arm
  - ● M66.23   Spontaneous rupture of extensor tendons, forearm
    - M66.231   Spontaneous rupture of extensor tendons, right forearm
    - M66.232   Spontaneous rupture of extensor tendons, left forearm
    - ■ M66.239   Spontaneous rupture of extensor tendons, unspecified forearm
  - ● M66.24   Spontaneous rupture of extensor tendons, hand
    - M66.241   Spontaneous rupture of extensor tendons, right hand
    - M66.242   Spontaneous rupture of extensor tendons, left hand
    - ■ M66.249   Spontaneous rupture of extensor tendons, unspecified hand
  - ● M66.25   Spontaneous rupture of extensor tendons, thigh
    - M66.251   Spontaneous rupture of extensor tendons, right thigh
    - M66.252   Spontaneous rupture of extensor tendons, left thigh
    - ■ M66.259   Spontaneous rupture of extensor tendons, unspecified thigh
  - ● M66.26   Spontaneous rupture of extensor tendons, lower leg
    - M66.261   Spontaneous rupture of extensor tendons, right lower leg
    - M66.262   Spontaneous rupture of extensor tendons, left lower leg
    - ■ M66.269   Spontaneous rupture of extensor tendons, unspecified lower leg
  - ● M66.27   Spontaneous rupture of extensor tendons, ankle and foot
    - M66.271   Spontaneous rupture of extensor tendons, right ankle and foot
    - M66.272   Spontaneous rupture of extensor tendons, left ankle and foot
    - ■ M66.279   Spontaneous rupture of extensor tendons, unspecified ankle and foot
  - M66.28   Spontaneous rupture of extensor tendons, other site
  - M66.29   Spontaneous rupture of extensor tendons, multiple sites

- ● M66.3   Spontaneous rupture of flexor tendons
  - ■ M66.30   Spontaneous rupture of flexor tendons, unspecified site
  - ● M66.31   Spontaneous rupture of flexor tendons, shoulder
    - M66.311   Spontaneous rupture of flexor tendons, right shoulder
    - M66.312   Spontaneous rupture of flexor tendons, left shoulder
    - ■ M66.319   Spontaneous rupture of flexor tendons, unspecified shoulder
  - ● M66.32   Spontaneous rupture of flexor tendons, upper arm
    - M66.321   Spontaneous rupture of flexor tendons, right upper arm
    - M66.322   Spontaneous rupture of flexor tendons, left upper arm
    - ■ M66.329   Spontaneous rupture of flexor tendons, unspecified upper arm
  - ● M66.33   Spontaneous rupture of flexor tendons, forearm
    - M66.331   Spontaneous rupture of flexor tendons, right forearm
    - M66.332   Spontaneous rupture of flexor tendons, left forearm
    - ■ M66.339   Spontaneous rupture of flexor tendons, unspecified forearm
  - ● M66.34   Spontaneous rupture of flexor tendons, hand
    - M66.341   Spontaneous rupture of flexor tendons, right hand
    - M66.342   Spontaneous rupture of flexor tendons, left hand
    - ■ M66.349   Spontaneous rupture of flexor tendons, unspecified hand
  - ● M66.35   Spontaneous rupture of flexor tendons, thigh
    - M66.351   Spontaneous rupture of flexor tendons, right thigh
    - M66.352   Spontaneous rupture of flexor tendons, left thigh
    - ■ M66.359   Spontaneous rupture of flexor tendons, unspecified thigh
  - ● M66.36   Spontaneous rupture of flexor tendons, lower leg
    - M66.361   Spontaneous rupture of flexor tendons, right lower leg
    - M66.362   Spontaneous rupture of flexor tendons, left lower leg
    - ■ M66.369   Spontaneous rupture of flexor tendons, unspecified lower leg
  - ● M66.37   Spontaneous rupture of flexor tendons, ankle and foot
    - M66.371   Spontaneous rupture of flexor tendons, right ankle and foot
    - M66.372   Spontaneous rupture of flexor tendons, left ankle and foot
    - ■ M66.379   Spontaneous rupture of flexor tendons, unspecified ankle and foot
  - M66.38   Spontaneous rupture of flexor tendons, other site
  - M66.39   Spontaneous rupture of flexor tendons, multiple sites

CHAPTER 13 (M00-M99)

● Unacceptable First-Listed Diagnosis   ● Use Additional Character(s)   ■ Unspecified   **OGCR** Official Guidelines for Coding and Reporting   🅒 Complication\Comorbidity   🅜 Major C\C | Excludes 1 | | Excludes 2 | | Includes | Use additional   Code first   Code also

● **M66.8 Spontaneous rupture of other tendons**
- ■ **M66.80** Spontaneous rupture of other tendons, unspecified site
- ● **M66.81** Spontaneous rupture of other tendons, shoulder
  - **M66.811** Spontaneous rupture of other tendons, right shoulder
  - **M66.812** Spontaneous rupture of other tendons, left shoulder
  - ■ **M66.819** Spontaneous rupture of other tendons, unspecified shoulder
- ● **M66.82** Spontaneous rupture of other tendons, upper arm
  - **M66.821** Spontaneous rupture of other tendons, right upper arm
  - **M66.822** Spontaneous rupture of other tendons, left upper arm
  - ■ **M66.829** Spontaneous rupture of other tendons, unspecified upper arm
- ● **M66.83** Spontaneous rupture of other tendons, forearm
  - **M66.831** Spontaneous rupture of other tendons, right forearm
  - **M66.832** Spontaneous rupture of other tendons, left forearm
  - ■ **M66.839** Spontaneous rupture of other tendons, unspecified forearm
- ● **M66.84** Spontaneous rupture of other tendons, hand
  - **M66.841** Spontaneous rupture of other tendons, right hand
  - **M66.842** Spontaneous rupture of other tendons, left hand
  - ■ **M66.849** Spontaneous rupture of other tendons, unspecified hand
- ● **M66.85** Spontaneous rupture of other tendons, thigh
  - **M66.851** Spontaneous rupture of other tendons, right thigh
  - **M66.852** Spontaneous rupture of other tendons, left thigh
  - ■ **M66.859** Spontaneous rupture of other tendons, unspecified thigh
- ● **M66.86** Spontaneous rupture of other tendons, lower leg
  - **M66.861** Spontaneous rupture of other tendons, right lower leg
  - **M66.862** Spontaneous rupture of other tendons, left lower leg
  - ■ **M66.869** Spontaneous rupture of other tendons, unspecified lower leg
- ● **M66.87** Spontaneous rupture of other tendons, ankle and foot
  - **M66.871** Spontaneous rupture of other tendons, right ankle and foot
  - **M66.872** Spontaneous rupture of other tendons, left ankle and foot
  - ■ **M66.879** Spontaneous rupture of other tendons, unspecified ankle and foot
- **M66.88** Spontaneous rupture of other tendons, other
- **M66.89** Spontaneous rupture of other tendons, multiple sites

■ **M66.9 Spontaneous rupture of unspecified tendon**
  Rupture at musculotendinous junction, nontraumatic

● **M67 Other disorders of synovium and tendon**
  Excludes1 palmar fascial fibromatosis [Dupuytren] (M72.0)
  tendinitis NOS (M77.9-)
  xanthomatosis localized to tendons (E78.2)
- ● **M67.0 Short Achilles tendon (acquired)**
  - ■ **M67.00** Short Achilles tendon (acquired), unspecified ankle
  - **M67.01** Short Achilles tendon (acquired), right ankle
  - **M67.02** Short Achilles tendon (acquired), left ankle
- ● **M67.2 Synovial hypertrophy, not elsewhere classified**
  Excludes1 villonodular synovitis (pigmented) (M12.2-)
  - ■ **M67.20** Synovial hypertrophy, not elsewhere classified, unspecified site
  - ● **M67.21** Synovial hypertrophy, not elsewhere classified, shoulder
    - **M67.211** Synovial hypertrophy, not elsewhere classified, right shoulder
    - **M67.212** Synovial hypertrophy, not elsewhere classified, left shoulder
    - ■ **M67.219** Synovial hypertrophy, not elsewhere classified, unspecified shoulder
  - ● **M67.22** Synovial hypertrophy, not elsewhere classified, upper arm
    - **M67.221** Synovial hypertrophy, not elsewhere classified, right upper arm
    - **M67.222** Synovial hypertrophy, not elsewhere classified, left upper arm
    - ■ **M67.229** Synovial hypertrophy, not elsewhere classified, unspecified upper arm
  - ● **M67.23** Synovial hypertrophy, not elsewhere classified, forearm
    - **M67.231** Synovial hypertrophy, not elsewhere classified, right forearm
    - **M67.232** Synovial hypertrophy, not elsewhere classified, left forearm
    - ■ **M67.239** Synovial hypertrophy, not elsewhere classified, unspecified forearm
  - ● **M67.24** Synovial hypertrophy, not elsewhere classified, hand
    - **M67.241** Synovial hypertrophy, not elsewhere classified, right hand
    - **M67.242** Synovial hypertrophy, not elsewhere classified, left hand
    - ■ **M67.249** Synovial hypertrophy, not elsewhere classified, unspecified hand
  - ● **M67.25** Synovial hypertrophy, not elsewhere classified, thigh
    - **M67.251** Synovial hypertrophy, not elsewhere classified, right thigh
    - **M67.252** Synovial hypertrophy, not elsewhere classified, left thigh
    - ■ **M67.259** Synovial hypertrophy, not elsewhere classified, unspecified thigh

● Unacceptable First-Listed Diagnosis ● Use Additional Character(s) ■ Unspecified **OGCR** Official Guidelines for Coding and Reporting
🅒 Complication\Comorbidity 🅒 Major C\C Excludes 1 Excludes 2 Includes Use additional Code first Code also
1193
CHAPTER 13 (M00-M99)

● M67.26   Synovial hypertrophy, not elsewhere classified, lower leg

     M67.261   Synovial hypertrophy, not elsewhere classified, right lower leg

     M67.262   Synovial hypertrophy, not elsewhere classified, left lower leg

     ■M67.269   Synovial hypertrophy, not elsewhere classified, unspecified lower leg

● M67.27   Synovial hypertrophy, not elsewhere classified, ankle and foot

     M67.271   Synovial hypertrophy, not elsewhere classified, right ankle and foot

     M67.272   Synovial hypertrophy, not elsewhere classified, left ankle and foot

     ■M67.279   Synovial hypertrophy, not elsewhere classified, unspecified ankle and foot

M67.28   Synovial hypertrophy, not elsewhere classified, other site

M67.29   Synovial hypertrophy, not elsewhere classified, multiple sites

● M67.3   Transient synovitis
     Toxic synovitis

     Excludes1   palindromic rheumatism (M12.3-)

■M67.30   Transient synovitis, unspecified site

● M67.31   Transient synovitis, shoulder

     M67.311   Transient synovitis, right shoulder

     M67.312   Transient synovitis, left shoulder

     ■M67.319   Transient synovitis, unspecified shoulder

● M67.32   Transient synovitis, elbow

     M67.321   Transient synovitis, right elbow

     M67.322   Transient synovitis, left elbow

     ■M67.329   Transient synovitis, unspecified elbow

● M67.33   Transient synovitis, wrist

     M67.331   Transient synovitis, right wrist

     M67.332   Transient synovitis, left wrist

     ■M67.339   Transient synovitis, unspecified wrist

● M67.34   Transient synovitis, hand

     M67.341   Transient synovitis, right hand

     M67.342   Transient synovitis, left hand

     ■M67.349   Transient synovitis, unspecified hand

● M67.35   Transient synovitis, hip

     M67.351   Transient synovitis, right hip

     M67.352   Transient synovitis, left hip

     ■M67.359   Transient synovitis, unspecified hip

● M67.36   Transient synovitis, knee

     M67.361   Transient synovitis, right knee

     M67.362   Transient synovitis, left knee

     ■M67.369   Transient synovitis, unspecified knee

● M67.37   Transient synovitis, ankle and foot

     M67.371   Transient synovitis, right ankle and foot

     M67.372   Transient synovitis, left ankle and foot

     ■M67.379   Transient synovitis, unspecified ankle and foot

M67.38   Transient synovitis, other site

M67.39   Transient synovitis, multiple sites

● M67.4   Ganglion
     Ganglion of joint or tendon (sheath)

     Excludes1   ganglion in yaws (A66.6)

     Excludes2   cyst of bursa (M71.2-M71.3)
                   cyst of synovium (M71.2-M71.3)

■M67.40   Ganglion, unspecified site

● M67.41   Ganglion, shoulder

     M67.411   Ganglion, right shoulder

     M67.412   Ganglion, left shoulder

     ■M67.419   Ganglion, unspecified shoulder

● M67.42   Ganglion, elbow

     M67.421   Ganglion, right elbow

     M67.422   Ganglion, left elbow

     ■M67.429   Ganglion, unspecified elbow

● M67.43   Ganglion, wrist

     M67.431   Ganglion, right wrist

     M67.432   Ganglion, left wrist

     ■M67.439   Ganglion, unspecified wrist

● M67.44   Ganglion, hand

     M67.441   Ganglion, right hand

     M67.442   Ganglion, left hand

     ■M67.449   Ganglion, unspecified hand

● M67.45   Ganglion, hip

     M67.451   Ganglion, right hip

     M67.452   Ganglion, left hip

     ■M67.459   Ganglion, unspecified hip

● M67.46   Ganglion, knee

     M67.461   Ganglion, right knee

     M67.462   Ganglion, left knee

     ■M67.469   Ganglion, unspecified knee

● M67.47   Ganglion, ankle and foot

     M67.471   Ganglion, right ankle and foot

     M67.472   Ganglion, left ankle and foot

     ■M67.479   Ganglion, unspecified ankle and foot

M67.48   Ganglion, other site

M67.49   Ganglion, multiple sites

● M67.5   Plica syndrome
     Plica knee

■M67.50   Plica syndrome, unspecified knee

M67.51   Plica syndrome, right knee

M67.52   Plica syndrome, left knee

● M67.8   Other specified disorders of synovium and tendon

     ■M67.80   Other specified disorders of synovium and tendon, unspecified site

     ● M67.81   Other specified disorders of synovium and tendon, shoulder

● Unacceptable First-Listed Diagnosis   ● Use Additional Character(s)   ■ Unspecified   **OGCR** Official Guidelines for Coding and Reporting

🗝 Complication\Comorbidity   🗝 Major C\C   Excludes 1   Excludes 2   Includes   Use additional   Code first   Code also

M67.811 Other specified disorders of synovium, right shoulder

M67.812 Other specified disorders of synovium, left shoulder

M67.813 Other specified disorders of tendon, right shoulder

M67.814 Other specified disorders of tendon, left shoulder

■ M67.819 Other specified disorders of synovium and tendon, unspecified shoulder

● M67.82 Other specified disorders of synovium and tendon, elbow

M67.821 Other specified disorders of synovium, right elbow

M67.822 Other specified disorders of synovium, left elbow

M67.823 Other specified disorders of tendon, right elbow

M67.824 Other specified disorders of tendon, left elbow

■ M67.829 Other specified disorders of synovium and tendon, unspecified elbow

● M67.83 Other specified disorders of synovium and tendon, wrist

M67.831 Other specified disorders of synovium, right wrist

M67.832 Other specified disorders of synovium, left wrist

M67.833 Other specified disorders of tendon, right wrist

M67.834 Other specified disorders of tendon, left wrist

■ M67.839 Other specified disorders of synovium and tendon, unspecified forearm

● M67.84 Other specified disorders of synovium and tendon, hand

M67.841 Other specified disorders of synovium, right hand

M67.842 Other specified disorders of synovium, left hand

M67.843 Other specified disorders of tendon, right hand

M67.844 Other specified disorders of tendon, left hand

■ M67.849 Other specified disorders of synovium and tendon, unspecified hand

● M67.85 Other specified disorders of synovium and tendon, hip

M67.851 Other specified disorders of synovium, right hip

M67.852 Other specified disorders of synovium, left hip

M67.853 Other specified disorders of tendon, right hip

M67.854 Other specified disorders of tendon, left hip

■ M67.859 Other specified disorders of synovium and tendon, unspecified hip

● M67.86 Other specified disorders of synovium and tendon, knee

M67.861 Other specified disorders of synovium, right knee

M67.862 Other specified disorders of synovium, left knee

M67.863 Other specified disorders of tendon, right knee

M67.864 Other specified disorders of tendon, left knee

■ M67.869 Other specified disorders of synovium and tendon, unspecified knee

● M67.87 Other specified disorders of synovium and tendon, ankle and foot

M67.871 Other specified disorders of synovium, right ankle and foot

M67.872 Other specified disorders of synovium, left ankle and foot

M67.873 Other specified disorders of tendon, right ankle and foot

M67.874 Other specified disorders of tendon, left ankle and foot

■ M67.879 Other specified disorders of synovium and tendon, unspecified ankle and foot

M67.88 Other specified disorders of synovium and tendon, other site

M67.89 Other specified disorders of synovium and tendon, multiple sites

● M67.9 Unspecified disorder of synovium and tendon

■ M67.90 Unspecified disorder of synovium and tendon, unspecified site

● M67.91 Unspecified disorder of synovium and tendon, shoulder

■ M67.911 Unspecified disorder of synovium and tendon, right shoulder

■ M67.912 Unspecified disorder of synovium and tendon, left shoulder

■ M67.919 Unspecified disorder of synovium and tendon, unspecified shoulder

● M67.92 Unspecified disorder of synovium and tendon, upper arm

■ M67.921 Unspecified disorder of synovium and tendon, right upper arm

■ M67.922 Unspecified disorder of synovium and tendon, left upper arm

■ M67.929 Unspecified disorder of synovium and tendon, unspecified upper arm

● M67.93 Unspecified disorder of synovium and tendon, forearm

■ M67.931 Unspecified disorder of synovium and tendon, right forearm

■ M67.932 Unspecified disorder of synovium and tendon, left forearm

■ M67.939 Unspecified disorder of synovium and tendon, unspecified forearm

● M67.94 Unspecified disorder of synovium and tendon, hand

■ M67.941 Unspecified disorder of synovium and tendon, right hand

■ M67.942 Unspecified disorder of synovium and tendon, left hand

■ M67.949 Unspecified disorder of synovium and tendon, unspecified hand

● Unacceptable First-Listed Diagnosis   ● Use Additional Character(s)   ■ Unspecified   **OGCR** Official Guidelines for Coding and Reporting

🗣 Complication\Comorbidity   🗣 Major C\C   Excludes 1   Excludes 2   Includes   Use additional   Code first   Code also

1195

● M67.95 Unspecified disorder of synovium and tendon, thigh
- ◻ M67.951 Unspecified disorder of synovium and tendon, right thigh
- ◻ M67.952 Unspecified disorder of synovium and tendon, left thigh
- ◻ M67.959 Unspecified disorder of synovium and tendon, unspecified thigh

● M67.96 Unspecified disorder of synovium and tendon, lower leg
- ◻ M67.961 Unspecified disorder of synovium and tendon, right lower leg
- ◻ M67.962 Unspecified disorder of synovium and tendon, left lower leg
- ◻ M67.969 Unspecified disorder of synovium and tendon, unspecified lower leg

● M67.97 Unspecified disorder of synovium and tendon, ankle and foot
- ◻ M67.971 Unspecified disorder of synovium and tendon, right ankle and foot
- ◻ M67.972 Unspecified disorder of synovium and tendon, left ankle and foot
- ◻ M67.979 Unspecified disorder of synovium and tendon, unspecified ankle and foot

◻ M67.98 Unspecified disorder of synovium and tendon, other site

◻ M67.99 Unspecified disorder of synovium and tendon, multiple sites

OTHER SOFT TISSUE DISORDERS (M70-M79)

● M70 Soft tissue disorders related to use, overuse and pressure

Includes	soft tissue disorders of occupational origin
Excludes1	bursitis NOS (M71.9-)
Excludes2	bursitis of shoulder (M75.5)
	enthesopathies (M76-M77)
	pressure ulcer (pressure area) (L89.-)

Use additional external cause code to identify activity causing disorder (Y93-)

● M70.0 Crepitant synovitis (acute) (chronic) of hand and wrist
- ● M70.03 Crepitant synovitis (acute) (chronic), wrist
  - M70.031 Crepitant synovitis (acute) (chronic), right wrist
  - M70.032 Crepitant synovitis (acute) (chronic), left wrist
  - ◻ M70.039 Crepitant synovitis (acute) (chronic), unspecified wrist
- ● M70.04 Crepitant synovitis (acute) (chronic), hand
  - M70.041 Crepitant synovitis (acute) (chronic), right hand
  - M70.042 Crepitant synovitis (acute) (chronic), left hand
  - ◻ M70.049 Crepitant synovitis (acute) (chronic), unspecified hand

● M70.1 Bursitis of hand
- ◻ M70.10 Bursitis, unspecified hand
- M70.11 Bursitis, right hand
- M70.12 Bursitis, left hand

● M70.2 Olecranon bursitis
- ◻ M70.20 Olecranon bursitis, unspecified elbow
- M70.21 Olecranon bursitis, right elbow
- M70.22 Olecranon bursitis, left elbow

● M70.3 Other bursitis of elbow
- ◻ M70.30 Other bursitis of elbow, unspecified elbow
- M70.31 Other bursitis of elbow, right elbow
- M70.32 Other bursitis of elbow, left elbow

● M70.4 Prepatellar bursitis
- ◻ M70.40 Prepatellar bursitis, unspecified knee
- M70.41 Prepatellar bursitis, right knee
- M70.42 Prepatellar bursitis, left knee

● M70.5 Other bursitis of knee
- ◻ M70.50 Other bursitis of knee, unspecified knee
- M70.51 Other bursitis of knee, right knee
- M70.52 Other bursitis of knee, left knee

● M70.6 Trochanteric bursitis
Trochanteric tendinitis
- ◻ M70.60 Trochanteric bursitis, unspecified hip
- M70.61 Trochanteric bursitis, right hip
- M70.62 Trochanteric bursitis, left hip

● M70.7 Other bursitis of hip
Ischial bursitis
- ◻ M70.70 Other bursitis of hip, unspecified hip
- M70.71 Other bursitis of hip, right hip
- M70.72 Other bursitis of hip, left hip

● M70.8 Other soft tissue disorders related to use, overuse and pressure
- ◻ M70.80 Other soft tissue disorders related to use, overuse and pressure of unspecified site
- ● M70.81 Other soft tissue disorders related to use, overuse and pressure of shoulder
  - M70.811 Other soft tissue disorders related to use, overuse and pressure, right shoulder
  - M70.812 Other soft tissue disorders related to use, overuse and pressure, left shoulder
  - ◻ M70.819 Other soft tissue disorders related to use, overuse and pressure, unspecified shoulder
- ● M70.82 Other soft tissue disorders related to use, overuse and pressure of upper arm
  - M70.821 Other soft tissue disorders related to use, overuse and pressure, right upper arm
  - M70.822 Other soft tissue disorders related to use, overuse and pressure, left upper arm
  - ◻ M70.829 Other soft tissue disorders related to use, overuse and pressure, unspecified upper arms
- ● M70.83 Other soft tissue disorders related to use, overuse and pressure of forearm
  - M70.831 Other soft tissue disorders related to use, overuse and pressure, right forearm
  - M70.832 Other soft tissue disorders related to use, overuse and pressure, left forearm

● Unacceptable First-Listed Diagnosis   ● Use Additional Character(s)   ◻ Unspecified   **OGCR** Official Guidelines for Coding and Reporting

🔖 Complication\Comorbidity   🔖 Major C\C   Excludes 1   Excludes 2   Includes   Use additional   Code first   Code also

M70.839 Other soft tissue disorders related to use, overuse and pressure, unspecified forearm

● M70.84 Other soft tissue disorders related to use, overuse and pressure of hand

M70.841 Other soft tissue disorders related to use, overuse and pressure, right hand

M70.842 Other soft tissue disorders related to use, overuse and pressure, left hand

M70.849 Other soft tissue disorders related to use, overuse and pressure, unspecified hand

● M70.85 Other soft tissue disorders related to use, overuse and pressure of thigh

M70.851 Other soft tissue disorders related to use, overuse and pressure, right thigh

M70.852 Other soft tissue disorders related to use, overuse and pressure, left thigh

M70.859 Other soft tissue disorders related to use, overuse and pressure, unspecified thigh

● M70.86 Other soft tissue disorders related to use, overuse and pressure lower leg

M70.861 Other soft tissue disorders related to use, overuse and pressure, right lower leg

M70.862 Other soft tissue disorders related to use, overuse and pressure, left lower leg

M70.869 Other soft tissue disorders related to use, overuse and pressure, unspecified leg

● M70.87 Other soft tissue disorders related to use, overuse and pressure of ankle and foot

M70.871 Other soft tissue disorders related to use, overuse and pressure, right ankle and foot

M70.872 Other soft tissue disorders related to use, overuse and pressure, left ankle and foot

M70.879 Other soft tissue disorders related to use, overuse and pressure, unspecified ankle and foot

M70.88 Other soft tissue disorders related to use, overuse and pressure other site

M70.89 Other soft tissue disorders related to use, overuse and pressure multiple sites

● M70.9 Unspecified soft tissue disorder related to use, overuse and pressure

M70.90 Unspecified soft tissue disorder related to use, overuse and pressure of unspecified site

● M70.91 Unspecified soft tissue disorder related to use, overuse and pressure of shoulder

M70.911 Unspecified soft tissue disorder related to use, overuse and pressure, right shoulder

M70.912 Unspecified soft tissue disorder related to use, overuse and pressure, left shoulder

M70.919 Unspecified soft tissue disorder related to use, overuse and pressure, unspecified shoulder

● M70.92 Unspecified soft tissue disorder related to use, overuse and pressure of upper arm

M70.921 Unspecified soft tissue disorder related to use, overuse and pressure, right upper arm

M70.922 Unspecified soft tissue disorder related to use, overuse and pressure, left upper arm

M70.929 Unspecified soft tissue disorder related to use, overuse and pressure, unspecified upper arm

● M70.93 Unspecified soft tissue disorder related to use, overuse and pressure of forearm

M70.931 Unspecified soft tissue disorder related to use, overuse and pressure, right forearm

M70.932 Unspecified soft tissue disorder related to use, overuse and pressure, left forearm

M70.939 Unspecified soft tissue disorder related to use, overuse and pressure, unspecified forearm

● M70.94 Unspecified soft tissue disorder related to use, overuse and pressure of hand

M70.941 Unspecified soft tissue disorder related to use, overuse and pressure, right hand

M70.942 Unspecified soft tissue disorder related to use, overuse and pressure, left hand

M70.949 Unspecified soft tissue disorder related to use, overuse and pressure, unspecified hand

● M70.95 Unspecified soft tissue disorder related to use, overuse and pressure of thigh

M70.951 Unspecified soft tissue disorder related to use, overuse and pressure, right thigh

M70.952 Unspecified soft tissue disorder related to use, overuse and pressure, left thigh

M70.959 Unspecified soft tissue disorder related to use, overuse and pressure, unspecified thigh

● M70.96 Unspecified soft tissue disorder related to use, overuse and pressure lower leg

M70.961 Unspecified soft tissue disorder related to use, overuse and pressure, right lower leg

M70.962 Unspecified soft tissue disorder related to use, overuse and pressure, left lower leg

M70.969 Unspecified soft tissue disorder related to use, overuse and pressure, unspecified lower leg

● M70.97 Unspecified soft tissue disorder related to use, overuse and pressure of ankle and foot

M70.971 Unspecified soft tissue disorder related to use, overuse and pressure, right ankle and foot

● Unacceptable First-Listed Diagnosis   ● Use Additional Character(s)   ■ Unspecified   **OGCR** Official Guidelines for Coding and Reporting

 Complication\Comorbidity   Major C\C   Excludes 1   Excludes 2   Includes   Use additional   Code first   Code also

1197

CHAPTER 13 (M00–M99)

M70.972 Unspecified soft tissue disorder related to use, overuse and pressure, left ankle and foot

M70.979 Unspecified soft tissue disorder related to use, overuse and pressure, unspecified ankle and foot

M70.98 Unspecified soft tissue disorder related to use, overuse and pressure other

M70.99 Unspecified soft tissue disorder related to use, overuse and pressure multiple sites

● M71 Other bursopathies

Excludes1 bunion (M20.1)
bursitis related to use, overuse or pressure (M70.-)
enthesopathies (M76-M77)

● M71.0 Abscess of bursa
Use additional code (B95.-, B96.-) to identify causative organism

M71.00 Abscess of bursa, unspecified site

● M71.01 Abscess of bursa, shoulder
M71.011 Abscess of bursa, right shoulder
M71.012 Abscess of bursa, left shoulder
M71.019 Abscess of bursa, unspecified shoulder

● M71.02 Abscess of bursa, elbow
M71.021 Abscess of bursa, right elbow
M71.022 Abscess of bursa, left elbow
M71.029 Abscess of bursa, unspecified elbow

● M71.03 Abscess of bursa, wrist
M71.031 Abscess of bursa, right wrist
M71.032 Abscess of bursa, left wrist
M71.039 Abscess of bursa, unspecified wrist

● M71.04 Abscess of bursa, hand
M71.041 Abscess of bursa, right hand
M71.042 Abscess of bursa, left hand
M71.049 Abscess of bursa, unspecified hand

● M71.05 Abscess of bursa, hip
M71.051 Abscess of bursa, right hip
M71.052 Abscess of bursa, left hip
M71.059 Abscess of bursa, unspecified hip

● M71.06 Abscess of bursa, knee
M71.061 Abscess of bursa, right knee
M71.062 Abscess of bursa, left knee
M71.069 Abscess of bursa, unspecified knee

● M71.07 Abscess of bursa, ankle and foot
M71.071 Abscess of bursa, right ankle and foot
M71.072 Abscess of bursa, left ankle and foot
M71.079 Abscess of bursa, unspecified ankle and foot

M71.08 Abscess of bursa, other site

M71.09 Abscess of bursa, multiple sites

● M71.1 Other infective bursitis
Use additional code (B95.-, B96.-) to identify causative organism

M71.10 Other infective bursitis, unspecified site

● M71.11 Other infective bursitis, shoulder
M71.111 Other infective bursitis, right shoulder
M71.112 Other infective bursitis, left shoulder
M71.119 Other infective bursitis, unspecified shoulder

● M71.12 Other infective bursitis, elbow
M71.121 Other infective bursitis, right elbow
M71.122 Other infective bursitis, left elbow
M71.129 Other infective bursitis, unspecified elbow

● M71.13 Other infective bursitis, wrist
M71.131 Other infective bursitis, right wrist
M71.132 Other infective bursitis, left wrist
M71.139 Other infective bursitis, unspecified wrist

● M71.14 Other infective bursitis, hand
M71.141 Other infective bursitis, right hand
M71.142 Other infective bursitis, left hand
M71.149 Other infective bursitis, unspecified hand

● M71.15 Other infective bursitis, hip
M71.151 Other infective bursitis, right hip
M71.152 Other infective bursitis, left hip
M71.159 Other infective bursitis, unspecified hip

● M71.16 Other infective bursitis, knee
M71.161 Other infective bursitis, right knee
M71.162 Other infective bursitis, left knee
M71.169 Other infective bursitis, unspecified knee

● M71.17 Other infective bursitis, ankle and foot
M71.171 Other infective bursitis, right ankle and foot
M71.172 Other infective bursitis, left ankle and foot
M71.179 Other infective bursitis, unspecified ankle and foot

M71.18 Other infective bursitis, other site

M71.19 Other infective bursitis, multiple sites

● M71.2 Synovial cyst of popliteal space [Baker]
Popliteal space = popliteal cavity, popliteal fossa. Depression in the posterior aspect of the knee (behind the knee).

Excludes1 synovial cyst of popliteal space with rupture (M66.0)

M71.20 Synovial cyst of popliteal space [Baker], unspecified knee

M71.21 Synovial cyst of popliteal space [Baker], right knee

M71.22 Synovial cyst of popliteal space [Baker], left knee

● Unacceptable First-Listed Diagnosis   ● Use Additional Character(s)   ▪ Unspecified   OGCR Official Guidelines for Coding and Reporting
🔖 Complication\Comorbidity   🔖 Major C\C   Excludes 1   Excludes 2   Includes   Use additional   Code first   Code also

● **M71.3 Other bursal cyst**
  Synovial cyst NOS
   Excludes1 synovial cyst with rupture (M66.1-)

■ M71.30 Other bursal cyst, unspecified site
● M71.31 Other bursal cyst, shoulder
    M71.311 Other bursal cyst, right shoulder
    M71.312 Other bursal cyst, left shoulder
    ■ M71.319 Other bursal cyst, unspecified shoulder
● M71.32 Other bursal cyst, elbow
    M71.321 Other bursal cyst, right elbow
    M71.322 Other bursal cyst, left elbow
    ■ M71.329 Other bursal cyst, unspecified elbow
● M71.33 Other bursal cyst, wrist
    M71.331 Other bursal cyst, right wrist
    M71.332 Other bursal cyst, left wrist
    ■ M71.339 Other bursal cyst, unspecified wrist
● M71.34 Other bursal cyst, hand
    M71.341 Other bursal cyst, right hand
    M71.342 Other bursal cyst, left hand
    ■ M71.349 Other bursal cyst, unspecified hand
● M71.35 Other bursal cyst, hip
    M71.351 Other bursal cyst, right hip
    M71.352 Other bursal cyst, left hip
    ■ M71.359 Other bursal cyst, unspecified hip
● M71.37 Other bursal cyst, ankle and foot
    M71.371 Other bursal cyst, right ankle and foot
    M71.372 Other bursal cyst, left ankle and foot
    ■ M71.379 Other bursal cyst, unspecified ankle and foot
M71.38 Other bursal cyst, other site
M71.39 Other bursal cyst, multiple sites
● **M71.4 Calcium deposit in bursa**
   Excludes2 calcium deposit in bursa of shoulder (M75.3)

■ M71.40 Calcium deposit in bursa, unspecified site
● M71.42 Calcium deposit in bursa, elbow
    M71.421 Calcium deposit in bursa, right elbow
    M71.422 Calcium deposit in bursa, left elbow
    ■ M71.429 Calcium deposit in bursa, unspecified elbow
● M71.43 Calcium deposit in bursa, wrist
    M71.431 Calcium deposit in bursa, right wrist
    M71.432 Calcium deposit in bursa, left wrist
    ■ M71.439 Calcium deposit in bursa, unspecified wrist
● M71.44 Calcium deposit in bursa, hand
    M71.441 Calcium deposit in bursa, right hand
    M71.442 Calcium deposit in bursa, left hand

    ■ M71.449 Calcium deposit in bursa, unspecified hand
● M71.45 Calcium deposit in bursa, hip
    M71.451 Calcium deposit in bursa, right hip
    M71.452 Calcium deposit in bursa, left hip
    ■ M71.459 Calcium deposit in bursa, unspecified hip
● M71.46 Calcium deposit in bursa, knee
    M71.461 Calcium deposit in bursa, right knee
    M71.462 Calcium deposit in bursa, left knee
    ■ M71.469 Calcium deposit in bursa, unspecified knee
● M71.47 Calcium deposit in bursa, ankle and foot
    M71.471 Calcium deposit in bursa, right ankle and foot
    M71.472 Calcium deposit in bursa, left ankle and foot
    ■ M71.479 Calcium deposit in bursa, unspecified ankle and foot
M71.48 Calcium deposit in bursa, other site
M71.49 Calcium deposit in bursa, multiple sites
● **M71.5 Other bursitis, not elsewhere classified**
   Excludes1 bursitis NOS (M71.9-)
   Excludes2 bursitis of shoulder (M75.5)
       bursitis of tibial collateral [Pellegrini-Stieda] (M76.4)

■ M71.50 Other bursitis, not elsewhere classified, unspecified site
● M71.52 Other bursitis, not elsewhere classified, elbow
    M71.521 Other bursitis, not elsewhere classified, right elbow
    M71.522 Other bursitis, not elsewhere classified, left elbow
    ■ M71.529 Other bursitis, not elsewhere classified, unspecified elbow
● M71.53 Other bursitis, not elsewhere classified, wrist
    M71.531 Other bursitis, not elsewhere classified, right wrist
    M71.532 Other bursitis, not elsewhere classified, left wrist
    ■ M71.539 Other bursitis, not elsewhere classified, unspecified wrist
● M71.54 Other bursitis, not elsewhere classified, hand
    M71.541 Other bursitis, not elsewhere classified, right hand
    M71.542 Other bursitis, not elsewhere classified, left hand
    ■ M71.549 Other bursitis, not elsewhere classified, unspecified hand
● M71.55 Other bursitis, not elsewhere classified, hip
    M71.551 Other bursitis, not elsewhere classified, right hip
    M71.552 Other bursitis, not elsewhere classified, left hip
    ■ M71.559 Other bursitis, not elsewhere classified, unspecified hip

● M71.56   Other bursitis, not elsewhere classified, knee

     M71.561   Other bursitis, not elsewhere classified, right knee

     M71.562   Other bursitis, not elsewhere classified, left knee

     ◼M71.569   Other bursitis, not elsewhere classified, unspecified knee

● M71.57   Other bursitis, not elsewhere classified, ankle and foot

     M71.571   Other bursitis, not elsewhere classified, right ankle and foot

     M71.572   Other bursitis, not elsewhere classified, left ankle and foot

     ◼M71.579   Other bursitis, not elsewhere classified, unspecified ankle and foot

   M71.58   Other bursitis, not elsewhere classified, other site

● M71.8   Other specified bursopathies

     ◼M71.80   Other specified bursopathies, unspecified site

● M71.81   Other specified bursopathies, shoulder

     M71.811   Other specified bursopathies, right shoulder

     M71.812   Other specified bursopathies, left shoulder

     ◼M71.819   Other specified bursopathies, unspecified shoulder

● M71.82   Other specified bursopathies, elbow

     M71.821   Other specified bursopathies, right elbow

     M71.822   Other specified bursopathies, left elbow

     ◼M71.829   Other specified bursopathies, unspecified elbow

● M71.83   Other specified bursopathies, wrist

     M71.831   Other specified bursopathies, right wrist

     M71.832   Other specified bursopathies, left wrist

     ◼M71.839   Other specified bursopathies, unspecified wrist

● M71.84   Other specified bursopathies, hand

     M71.841   Other specified bursopathies, right hand

     M71.842   Other specified bursopathies, left hand

     ◼M71.849   Other specified bursopathies, unspecified hand

● M71.85   Other specified bursopathies, hip

     M71.851   Other specified bursopathies, right hip

     M71.852   Other specified bursopathies, left hip

     ◼M71.859   Other specified bursopathies, unspecified hip

● M71.86   Other specified bursopathies, knee

     M71.861   Other specified bursopathies, right knee

     M71.862   Other specified bursopathies, left knee

     ◼M71.869   Other specified bursopathies, unspecified knee

● M71.87   Other specified bursopathies, ankle and foot

     M71.871   Other specified bursopathies, right ankle and foot

     M71.872   Other specified bursopathies, left ankle and foot

     ◼M71.879   Other specified bursopathies, unspecified ankle and foot

   M71.88   Other specified bursopathies, other site

   M71.89   Other specified bursopathies, multiple sites

◼M71.9   Bursopathy, unspecified
     Bursitis NOS

● M72   Fibroblastic disorders

     | Excludes2 | retroperitoneal fibromatosis (D48.3)

   M72.0   Palmar fascial fibromatosis [Dupuytren]

   M72.1   Knuckle pads

   M72.2   Plantar fascial fibromatosis
     Plantar fasciitis

   M72.4   Pseudosarcomatous fibromatosis
     Nodular fasciitis

   M72.6   Necrotizing fasciitis 🔗

     Use additional code (B95.-, B96.-) to identify causative organism

   M72.8   Other fibroblastic disorders
     Abscess of fascia
     Fasciitis NEC
     Other infective fasciitis

     Use additional code to (B95.-, B96.-) identify causative organism

     | Excludes1 | diffuse (eosinophilic) fasciitis (M35.4)
         necrotizing fasciitis (M72.6)
         nodular fasciitis (M72.4)
         perirenal fasciitis NOS (N13.5)
         perirenal fasciitis with infection (N13.6)
         plantar fasciitis (M72.2)

◼M72.9   Fibroblastic disorder, unspecified
     Fasciitis NOS
     Fibromatosis NOS

● M75   Shoulder lesions

     | Excludes2 | shoulder-hand syndrome (M89.0-)

● M75.0   Adhesive capsulitis of shoulder
     Frozen shoulder
     Periarthritis of shoulder

     ◼M75.00   Adhesive capsulitis of unspecified shoulder

     M75.01   Adhesive capsulitis of right shoulder

     M75.02   Adhesive capsulitis of left shoulder

● M75.1   Rotator cuff syndrome
     Rotator cuff or supraspinatus tear or rupture (complete) (incomplete), not specified as traumatic
     Supraspinatus syndrome

     ◼M75.10   Rotator cuff syndrome, unspecified shoulder

     M75.11   Rotator cuff syndrome, right shoulder

     M75.12   Rotator cuff syndrome, left shoulder

● M75.2   Bicipital tendinitis

     ◼M75.20   Bicipital tendinitis, unspecified shoulder

     M75.21   Bicipital tendinitis, right shoulder

     M75.22   Bicipital tendinitis, left shoulder

● M75.3   Calcific tendinitis of shoulder
     Calcified bursa of shoulder

     ◼M75.30   Calcific tendinitis of unspecified shoulder

     M75.31   Calcific tendinitis of right shoulder

     M75.32   Calcific tendinitis of left shoulder

● M75.4 Impingement syndrome of shoulder
    ▪M75.40 Impingement syndrome of unspecified shoulder
    M75.41 Impingement syndrome of right shoulder
    M75.42 Impingement syndrome of left shoulder
● M75.5 Bursitis of shoulder
    ▪M75.50 Bursitis of unspecified shoulder
    M75.51 Bursitis of right shoulder
    M75.52 Bursitis of left shoulder
● M75.8 Other shoulder lesions
    ▪M75.80 Other shoulder lesions, unspecified shoulder
    M75.81 Other shoulder lesions, right shoulder
    M75.82 Other shoulder lesions, left shoulder
● M75.9 Shoulder lesion, unspecified
    ▪M75.90 Shoulder lesion, unspecified, unspecified shoulder
    ▪M75.91 Shoulder lesion, unspecified, right shoulder
    ▪M75.92 Shoulder lesion, unspecified, left shoulder

● M76 Enthesopathies, lower limb, excluding foot
    Excludes2   bursitis due to use, overuse and pressure (M70.-)
          enthesopathies of ankle and foot (M77.5-)
● M76.0 Gluteal tendinitis
    ▪M76.00 Gluteal tendinitis, unspecified buttock
    M76.01 Gluteal tendinitis, right buttock
    M76.02 Gluteal tendinitis, left buttock
● M76.1 Psoas tendinitis
    ▪M76.10 Psoas tendinitis, unspecified side
    M76.11 Psoas tendinitis, right side
    M76.12 Psoas tendinitis, left side
● M76.2 Iliac crest spur
    ▪M76.20 Iliac crest spur, unspecified hip
    M76.21 Iliac crest spur, right hip
    M76.22 Iliac crest spur, left hip
● M76.3 Iliotibial band syndrome
    ▪M76.30 Iliotibial band syndrome, unspecified side
    M76.31 Iliotibial band syndrome, right side
    M76.32 Iliotibial band syndrome, left side
● M76.4 Tibial collateral bursitis [Pellegrini-Stieda]
    ▪M76.40 Tibial collateral bursitis [Pellegrini-Stieda], unspecified leg
    M76.41 Tibial collateral bursitis [Pellegrini-Stieda], right leg
    M76.42 Tibial collateral bursitis [Pellegrini-Stieda], left leg
● M76.5 Patellar tendinitis
    ▪M76.50 Patellar tendinitis, unspecified knee
    M76.51 Patellar tendinitis, right knee
    M76.52 Patellar tendinitis, left knee
● M76.6 Achilles tendinitis
    Achilles bursitis
    ▪M76.60 Achilles tendinitis, unspecified leg
    M76.61 Achilles tendinitis, right leg
    M76.62 Achilles tendinitis, left leg
● M76.7 Peroneal tendinitis
    ▪M76.70 Peroneal tendinitis, unspecified leg
    M76.71 Peroneal tendinitis, right leg
    M76.72 Peroneal tendinitis, left leg

● M76.8 Other enthesopathies of lower limb, excluding foot
    Anterior tibial syndrome
    Posterior tibial tendinitis
    ▪M76.80 Other enthesopathies, lower limb of unspecified site
    ● M76.85 Other enthesopathies, thigh
        M76.851 Other enthesopathies, right thigh
        M76.852 Other enthesopathies, left thigh
        ▪M76.859 Other enthesopathies, unspecified thighs
    ● M76.86 Other enthesopathies, lower leg
        M76.861 Other enthesopathies, right lower leg
        M76.862 Other enthesopathies, left lower leg
        ▪M76.869 Other enthesopathies, unspecified lower leg
    M76.89 Other enthesopathies, lower limb multiple sites
● M76.9 Unspecified enthesopathy, lower limb, excluding foot
    ▪M76.90 Unspecified enthesopathy, lower limb, excluding foot, unspecified site
    ● M76.95 Unspecified enthesopathy, thigh
        ▪M76.951 Unspecified enthesopathy, right thigh
        ▪M76.952 Unspecified enthesopathy, left thigh
        ▪M76.959 Unspecified enthesopathy, unspecified thigh
    ● M76.96 Unspecified enthesopathy, unspecified lower leg
        ▪M76.961 Unspecified enthesopathy, right lower leg
        ▪M76.962 Unspecified enthesopathy, left lower leg
        ▪M76.969 Unspecified enthesopathy, unspecified lower leg
    ▪M76.99 Unspecified enthesopathy, lower limb, multiple sites

● M77 Other enthesopathies
    Excludes1   bursitis NOS (M71.9-)
    Excludes2   bursitis due to use, overuse and pressure (M70.-)
          osteophyte (M25.7)
          spinal enthesopathy (M46.0-)
● M77.0 Medial epicondylitis
    ▪M77.00 Medial epicondylitis, unspecified elbow
    M77.01 Medial epicondylitis, right elbow
    M77.02 Medial epicondylitis, left elbow
● M77.1 Lateral epicondylitis
    Tennis elbow
    ▪M77.10 Lateral epicondylitis, unspecified elbow
    M77.11 Lateral epicondylitis, right elbow
    M77.12 Lateral epicondylitis, left elbow
● M77.2 Periarthritis of wrist
    ▪M77.20 Periarthritis, unspecified wrist
    M77.21 Periarthritis, right wrist
    M77.22 Periarthritis, left wrist

● Unacceptable First-Listed Diagnosis   ● Use Additional Character(s)   ▪ Unspecified   **OGCR** Official Guidelines for Coding and Reporting
🗣 Complication\Comorbidity   🗣 Major C\C   Excludes 1   Excludes 2   Includes   Use additional   Code first   Code also

1201

CHAPTER 13 (M00-M99)

- M77.3 Calcaneal spur
    - M77.30 Calcaneal spur, unspecified foot
    - M77.31 Calcaneal spur, right foot
    - M77.32 Calcaneal spur, left foot
- M77.4 Metatarsalgia
    - Excludes1   Morton's metatarsalgia (G57.6)
    - M77.40 Metatarsalgia, unspecified foot
    - M77.41 Metatarsalgia, right foot
    - M77.42 Metatarsalgia, left foot
- M77.5 Other enthesopathy of foot
    - M77.50 Other enthesopathy of unspecified foot
    - M77.51 Other enthesopathy of right foot
    - M77.52 Other enthesopathy of left foot
- M77.8 Other enthesopathies, not elsewhere classified
- M77.9 Enthesopathy, unspecified
    - Bone spur NOS
    - Capsulitis NOS
    - Periarthritis NOS
    - Tendinitis NOS

- M79 Other and unspecified soft tissue disorders, not elsewhere classified
    - Excludes1   psychogenic rheumatism (F45.8)
      soft tissue pain, psychogenic (F45.41)
    - M79.0 Rheumatism, unspecified
        - Excludes1   fibromyalgia (M79.7)
          palindromic rheumatism (M12.3-)
    - M79.1 Myalgia
        - Myofascial pain syndrome
        - Excludes1   fibromyalgia (M79.7)
          myositis (M60.-)
    - M79.2 Neuralgia and neuritis, unspecified
        - Excludes1   brachial radiculitis NOS (M54.1)
          lumbosacral radiculitis NOS (M54.1)
          mononeuropathies (G56-G58)
          radiculitis NOS (M54.1)
          sciatica (M54.3-M54.4)
    - M79.3 Panniculitis, unspecified
        - Excludes1   lupus panniculitis (L93.2)
          neck and back panniculitis (M54.0-)
          relapsing [Weber-Christian] panniculitis (M35.6)
    - M79.4 Hypertrophy of (infrapatellar) fat pad
    - M79.5 Residual foreign body in soft tissue
        - Excludes1   foreign body granuloma of skin and subcutaneous tissue (L92.3)
          foreign body granuloma of soft tissue (M60.2-)
    - M79.6 Pain in limb, hand, foot, fingers and toes
        - Excludes2   pain in joint (M25.5-)
        - M79.60 Pain in limb, unspecified
            - M79.601 Pain in right arm
                - Pain in right upper limb NOS
            - M79.602 Pain in left arm
                - Pain in left upper limb NOS
            - M79.603 Pain in arm, unspecified
                - Pain in upper limb NOS
            - M79.604 Pain in right leg
                - Pain in right lower limb NOS
            - M79.605 Pain in left leg
                - Pain in left lower limb NOS
            - M79.606 Pain in leg, unspecified
                - Pain in lower limb NOS

- M79.609 Pain in unspecified limb
    - Pain in limb NOS
- M79.62 Pain in upper arm
    - Pain in axillary region
    - M79.621 Pain in right upper arm
    - M79.622 Pain in left upper arm
    - M79.629 Pain in unspecified upper arm
- M79.63 Pain in forearm
    - M79.631 Pain in right forearm
    - M79.632 Pain in left forearm
    - M79.639 Pain in unspecified forearm
- M79.64 Pain in hand and fingers
    - M79.641 Pain in right hand
    - M79.642 Pain in left hand
    - M79.643 Pain in unspecified hand
    - M79.644 Pain in right finger(s)
    - M79.645 Pain in left finger(s)
    - M79.646 Pain in unspecified finger(s)
- M79.65 Pain in thigh
    - M79.651 Pain in right thigh
    - M79.652 Pain in left thigh
    - M79.659 Pain in unspecified thigh
- M79.66 Pain in lower leg
    - M79.661 Pain in right lower leg
    - M79.662 Pain in left lower leg
    - M79.669 Pain in unspecified lower leg
- M79.67 Pain in foot and toes
    - M79.671 Pain in right foot
    - M79.672 Pain in left foot
    - M79.673 Pain in unspecified foot
    - M79.674 Pain in right toe(s)
    - M79.675 Pain in left toe(s)
    - M79.676 Pain in unspecified toe(s)
- M79.7 Fibromyalgia
    - Fibromyositis
    - Fibrositis
    - Myofibrositis
- M79.A Nontraumatic compartment syndrome
    - *Code first, if applicable, associated postprocedural complication*
    - Excludes1   compartment syndrome NOS (T79.A-)
      fibromyalgia (M79.7) nontraumatic ischemic infarction of muscle (M62.2-)
      traumatic compartment syndrome (T79.A-)
    - M79.A1 Nontraumatic compartment syndrome of upper extremity
        - Nontraumatic compartment syndrome of shoulder, arm, forearm, wrist, hand, and fingers
        - M79.A11 Nontraumatic compartment syndrome of right upper extremity
        - M79.A12 Nontraumatic compartment syndrome of left upper extremity
        - M79.A19 Nontraumatic compartment syndrome of unspecified upper extremity

● Unacceptable First-Listed Diagnosis   ● Use Additional Character(s)   ▨ Unspecified   OGCR Official Guidelines for Coding and Reporting   Complication\Comorbidity   Major C\C   Excludes 1   Excludes 2   Includes   Use additional   Code first   Code also

● **M79.A2 Nontraumatic compartment syndrome of lower extremity**
  Nontraumatic compartment syndrome of hip, buttock, thigh, leg, foot, and toes

  M79.A21 Nontraumatic compartment syndrome of right lower extremity 🦴

  M79.A22 Nontraumatic compartment syndrome of left lower extremity 🦴

  ▪ **M79.A29 Nontraumatic compartment syndrome of unspecified lower extremity** 🦴

  M79.A3 Nontraumatic compartment syndrome of abdomen 🦴

  M79.A9 Nontraumatic compartment syndrome of other sites 🦴

● **M79.8 Other specified soft tissue disorders**

  M79.81 Nontraumatic hematoma of soft tissue
    Nontraumatic hematoma of muscle
    Nontraumatic seroma of muscle and soft tissue

  M79.89 Other specified soft tissue disorders
    Polyalgia

▪ **M79.9 Soft tissue disorder, unspecified**

OGCR See Section I.C., Chapter 13.d
   Osteoporosis

OSTEOPATHIES AND CHONDROPATHIES (M80-M94)

DISORDERS OF BONE DENSITY AND STRUCTURE (M80-M85)

M80 Osteoporosis with current pathological fracture
  Excessive skeletal fragility (porous bone) resulting in bone fractures

  Includes   osteoporosis with current fragility fracture

  Note: Fragility fracture is defined as a fracture sustained with trauma no more than a fall from a standing height or less that occurs under circumstances that would not cause a fracture in a normal healthy bone.

  Use additional code to identify major osseous defect, if applicable (M89.7-)

  Excludes1 collapsed vertebra NOS (M48.5)
         pathological fracture NOS (M84.4)
         wedging of vertebra NOS (M48.5)
  Excludes2 personal history of (healed) osteoporosis fracture (Z87.310)

  ┌──┐
  │ The appropriate 7th character is to be added to each │
  │   code from category M80:   │
  │ A initial encounter for fracture   │
  │ D subsequent encounter for fracture with routine │
  │   healing   │
  │ G subsequent encounter for fracture with delayed │
  │   healing   │
  │ K subsequent encounter for fracture with nonunion │
  │   *Total failure of fracture healing*   │
  │   │
  │ P subsequent encounter for fracture with malunion │
  │   *Fracture ends do not heal together correctly.* │
  │   │
  │ S sequela   │
  └──┘

● **M80.0 Age-related osteoporosis with current pathological fracture**
  Involutional osteoporosis with current pathological fracture
  Osteoporosis NOS with current pathological fracture
  Postmenopausal osteoporosis with current pathological fracture
  Senile osteoporosis with current pathological fracture

  ▪ **M80.00 Age-related osteoporosis with current pathological fracture, unspecified site** A, K, P 🦴

  ● **M80.01 Age-related osteoporosis with current pathological fracture, shoulder**

    M80.011 Age-related osteoporosis with current pathological fracture, right shoulder A, K, P 🦴

    M80.012 Age-related osteoporosis with current pathological fracture, left shoulder A, K, P 🦴

    ▪ **M80.019 Age-related osteoporosis with current pathological fracture, unspecified shoulder** A, K, P 🦴

  ● **M80.02 Age-related osteoporosis with current pathological fracture, humerus**

    M80.021 Age-related osteoporosis with current pathological fracture, right humerus A, K, P 🦴

    M80.022 Age-related osteoporosis with current pathological fracture, left humerus A, K, P 🦴

    ▪ **M80.029 Age-related osteoporosis with current pathological fracture, unspecified humerus** A, K, P 🦴

  ● **M80.03 Age-related osteoporosis with current pathological fracture, forearm**
    Age-related osteoporosis with current pathological fracture of wrist

    M80.031 Age-related osteoporosis with current pathological fracture, right forearm A, K, P 🦴

    M80.032 Age-related osteoporosis with current pathological fracture, left forearm A, K, P 🦴

    ▪ **M80.039 Age-related osteoporosis with current pathological fracture, unspecified forearm** A, K, P 🦴

  ● **M80.04 Age-related osteoporosis with current pathological fracture, hand**

    M80.041 Age-related osteoporosis with current pathological fracture, right hand A, K, P 🦴

    M80.042 Age-related osteoporosis with current pathological fracture, left hand A, K, P 🦴

    ▪ **M80.049 Age-related osteoporosis with current pathological fracture, unspecified hand** A, K, P 🦴

  ● **M80.05 Age-related osteoporosis with current pathological fracture, femur**
    Age-related osteoporosis with current pathological fracture of hip

    M80.051 Age-related osteoporosis with current pathological fracture, right femur A, K, P 🦴

    M80.052 Age-related osteoporosis with current pathological fracture, left femur A, K, P 🦴

● Unacceptable First-Listed Diagnosis   ● Use Additional Character(s)   ▪ Unspecified   **OGCR** Official Guidelines for Coding and Reporting

🦴 Complication\Comorbidity   🦴 Major C\C   Excludes 1   Excludes 2   Includes   Use additional   Code first   Code also

1203

CHAPTER 13 (M00-M99)

CHAPTER 13 (M00-M99)

◻ M80.059   Age-related osteoporosis with current pathological fracture, unspecified femur A, K, P 🦟

● M80.06   Age-related osteoporosis with current pathological fracture, lower leg

    M80.061   Age-related osteoporosis with current pathological fracture, right lower leg A, K, P 🦟

    M80.062   Age-related osteoporosis with current pathological fracture, left lower leg A, K, P 🦟

    ◻ M80.069   Age-related osteoporosis with current pathological fracture, unspecified lower leg A, K, P 🦟

● M80.07   Age-related osteoporosis with current pathological fracture, ankle and foot

    M80.071   Age-related osteoporosis with current pathological fracture, right ankle and foot A, K, P 🦟

    M80.072   Age-related osteoporosis with current pathological fracture, left ankle and foot A, K, P 🦟

    ◻ M80.079   Age-related osteoporosis with current pathological fracture, unspecified ankle and foot A, K, P 🦟

M80.08   Age-related osteoporosis with current pathological fracture, vertebra(e) A, K, P 🦟

● M80.8   Other osteoporosis with current pathological fracture
    Drug-induced osteoporosis with current pathological fracture
    Idiopathic osteoporosis with current pathological fracture
    Osteoporosis of disuse with current pathological fracture
    Postoopherectomy osteoporosis with current pathological fracture
    Postsurgical malabsorption osteoporosis with current pathological fracture
    Post-traumatic osteoporosis with current pathological fracture

◻ M80.80   Other osteoporosis with current pathological fracture, unspecified site A, K, P 🦟

● M80.81   Other osteoporosis with pathological fracture, shoulder

    M80.811   Other osteoporosis with current pathological fracture, right shoulder A, K, P 🦟

    M80.812   Other osteoporosis with current pathological fracture, left shoulder A, K, P 🦟

    ◻ M80.819   Other osteoporosis with current pathological fracture, unspecified shoulder A, K, P 🦟

● M80.82   Other osteoporosis with current pathological fracture, humerus

    M80.821   Other osteoporosis with current pathological fracture, right humerus A, K, P 🦟

    M80.822   Other osteoporosis with current pathological fracture, left humerus A, K, P 🦟

    ◻ M80.829   Other osteoporosis with current pathological fracture, unspecified humerus A, K, P 🦟

● M80.83   Other osteoporosis with current pathological fracture, forearm
    Other osteoporosis with current pathological fracture of wrist

    M80.831   Other osteoporosis with current pathological fracture, right forearm A, K, P 🦟

    M80.832   Other osteoporosis with current pathological fracture, left forearm A, K, P 🦟

    ◻ M80.839   Other osteoporosis with current pathological fracture, unspecified forearm A, K, P 🦟

● M80.84   Other osteoporosis with current pathological fracture, hand

    M80.841   Other osteoporosis with current pathological fracture, right hand A, K, P 🦟

    M80.842   Other osteoporosis with current pathological fracture, left hand A, K, P 🦟

    ◻ M80.849   Other osteoporosis with current pathological fracture, unspecified hand A, K, P 🦟

● M80.85   Other osteoporosis with current pathological fracture, femur
    Other osteoporosis with current pathological fracture of hip

    M80.851   Other osteoporosis with current pathological fracture, right femur A, K, P 🦟

    M80.852   Other osteoporosis with current pathological fracture, left femur A, K, P 🦟

    ◻ M80.859   Other osteoporosis with current pathological fracture, unspecified femur A, K, P 🦟

● M80.86   Other osteoporosis with current pathological fracture, lower leg

    M80.861   Other osteoporosis with current pathological fracture, right lower leg A, K, P 🦟

    M80.862   Other osteoporosis with current pathological fracture, left lower leg A, K, P 🦟

    ◻ M80.869   Other osteoporosis with current pathological fracture, unspecified lower leg A, K, P 🦟

● M80.87   Other osteoporosis with current pathological fracture, ankle and foot

    M80.871   Other osteoporosis with current pathological fracture, right ankle and foot A, K, P 🦟

    M80.872   Other osteoporosis with current pathological fracture, left ankle and foot A, K, P 🦟

    ◻ M80.879   Other osteoporosis with current pathological fracture, unspecified ankle and foot A, K, P 🦟

M80.88   Other osteoporosis with current pathological fracture, vertebra(e) A, K, P 🦟

● Unacceptable First-Listed Diagnosis   ● Use Additional Character(s)   ◻ Unspecified   **OGCR** Official Guidelines for Coding and Reporting
🦟 Complication\Comorbidity   🦟 Major C\C   Excludes 1   Excludes 2   Includes   Use additional   Code first   Code also

● **M81 Osteoporosis without current pathological fracture**

     Use additional code to identify:
         major osseous defect, if applicable (M89.7-)
         personal history of (healed) osteoporosis fracture,
            if applicable (Z87.310)

       | Excludes1 | osteoporosis with current pathological
                 fracture (M80.-)
                 Sudeck's atrophy (M89.0)

     **M81.0 Age-related osteoporosis without current
         pathological fracture**
         Involutional osteoporosis without current
            pathological fracture
         Osteoporosis NOS
         Postmenopausal osteoporosis without current
            pathological fracture
         Senile osteoporosis without current pathological
            fracture

     M81.6 Localized osteoporosis [Lequesne]
         | Excludes1 | Sudeck's atrophy (M89.0)

     **M81.8 Other osteoporosis without current pathological
     fracture**
         Drug-induced osteoporosis without current
            pathological fracture
         Idiopathic osteoporosis without current
            pathological fracture
         Osteoporosis of disuse without current
            pathological fracture
         Postoopherectomy osteoporosis without current
            pathological fracture
         Postsurgical malabsorption osteoporosis without
            current pathological fracture
         Post-traumatic osteoporosis without current
            pathological fracture

● **M83 Adult osteomalacia**

       | Excludes1 | infantile and juvenile osteomalacia (E55.0)
                 renal osteodystrophy (N25.0)
                 rickets (active) (E55.0)
                 rickets (active) sequelae (E64.3)
                 vitamin D-resistant osteomalacia (E83.3)
                 vitamin D-resistant rickets (active) (E83.3)

     M83.0 Puerperal osteomalacia

     M83.1 Senile osteomalacia

     M83.2 Adult osteomalacia due to malabsorption
         Postsurgical malabsorption osteomalacia in adults

     M83.3 Adult osteomalacia due to malnutrition

     M83.4 Aluminum bone disease

   ● **M83.5 Other drug-induced osteomalacia in adults**
         Code first (T36-T50) to identify drug

     M83.8 Other adult osteomalacia

     ▨**M83.9 Adult osteomalacia, unspecified**

● **M84 Disorder of continuity of bone**

       | Excludes2 | traumatic fracture of bone-see fracture, by
                 site

   ● **M84.3 Stress fracture**
         Fatigue fracture
         March fracture
         Stress fracture NOS
         Stress reaction

         Use additional external cause code(s) to identify
            the cause of the stress fracture

       | Excludes1 | pathological fracture NOS (M84.4.-)
                 pathological fracture due to
                   osteoporosis (M80.-)
                 traumatic fracture (S12.-, S22.-, S32.-,
                   S42.-, S52.-, S62.-, S72.-, S82.-,
                   S92.-)

       | Excludes2 | personal history of (healed) stress
                 (fatigue) fracture (Z87.312)
                 stress fracture of vertebra (M48.4-)

     ┌───┐
     The appropriate 7th character is to be added to
         each code from subcategory M84.3:
       A   initial encounter for fracture
       D   subsequent encounter for fracture with
          routine healing
       G   subsequent encounter for fracture with
          delayed healing
       K   subsequent encounter for fracture with
          nonunion
       P   subsequent encounter for fracture with
          malunion
       S   sequela
     └───┘

   ▨**M84.30 Stress fracture, unspecified site** K, P 🦠

   ● **M84.31 Stress fracture, shoulder**
         M84.311 Stress fracture, right shoulder K, P 🦠
         M84.312 Stress fracture, left shoulder K, P 🦠
       ▨**M84.319 Stress fracture, unspecified
            shoulder** K, P 🦠

   ● **M84.32 Stress fracture, humerus**
         M84.321 Stress fracture, right humerus K, P 🦠
         M84.322 Stress fracture, left humerus K, P 🦠
       ▨**M84.329 Stress fracture, unspecified
            humerus** K, P 🦠

   ● **M84.33 Stress fracture, ulna and radius**
         M84.331 Stress fracture, right ulna K, P 🦠
         M84.332 Stress fracture, left ulna K, P 🦠
         M84.333 Stress fracture, right radius K, P 🦠
         M84.334 Stress fracture, left radius K, P 🦠
       ▨**M84.339 Stress fracture, unspecified ulna
            and radius** K, P 🦠

   ● **M84.34 Stress fracture, hand and fingers**
         M84.341 Stress fracture, right hand K, P 🦠
         M84.342 Stress fracture, left hand K, P 🦠
       ▨**M84.343 Stress fracture, unspecified
            hand** K, P 🦠
         M84.344 Stress fracture, right finger(s) K, P 🦠
         M84.345 Stress fracture, left finger(s) K, P 🦠
       ▨**M84.346 Stress fracture, unspecified
            finger(s)** K, P 🦠

   ● **M84.35 Stress fracture, pelvis and femur**
         Stress fracture, hip
         M84.350 Stress fracture, pelvis K, P 🦠
         M84.351 Stress fracture, right femur K, P 🦠
         M84.352 Stress fracture, left femur K, P 🦠

●   Unacceptable First-Listed Diagnosis   ●   Use Additional Character(s)   ▨   Unspecified   **OGCR**   Official Guidelines for Coding and Reporting

🦠 Complication\Comorbidity   🦠 Major C\C | Excludes 1 | | Excludes 2 | Includes   Use additional   Code first   Code also

1205

　　　　　■ M84.353 Stress fracture, unspecified
　　　　　　　　femur K, P 🦴

　　　　　■ M84.359 Stress fracture, hip, unspecified
　　　　　　　　K, P 🦴

　　● M84.36 Stress fracture, tibia and fibula

　　　　　M84.361 Stress fracture, right tibia K, P 🦴

　　　　　M84.362 Stress fracture, left tibia K, P 🦴

　　　　　M84.363 Stress fracture, right fibula K, P 🦴

　　　　　M84.364 Stress fracture, left fibula K, P 🦴

　　　　　■ M84.369 Stress fracture, unspecified tibia
　　　　　　　　and fibula K, P 🦴

　　● M84.37 Stress fracture, ankle, foot and toes

　　　　　M84.371 Stress fracture, right ankle K, P 🦴

　　　　　M84.372 Stress fracture, left ankle K, P 🦴

　　　　　■ M84.373 Stress fracture, unspecified ankle
　　　　　　　　K, P 🦴

　　　　　M84.374 Stress fracture, right foot K, P 🦴

　　　　　M84.375 Stress fracture, left foot K, P 🦴

　　　　　■ M84.376 Stress fracture, unspecified foot
　　　　　　　　K, P 🦴

　　　　　M84.377 Stress fracture, right toe(s) K, P 🦴

　　　　　M84.378 Stress fracture, left toe(s) K, P 🦴

　　　　　■ M84.379 Stress fracture, unspecified toe(s)
　　　　　　　　K, P 🦴

　　M84.38 Stress fracture, other site K, P 🦴

　　　　　| Excludes2 | stress fracture of vertebra (M48.4-) |

● M84.4 Pathological fracture, not elsewhere classified
　　　Chronic fracture
　　　Pathological fracture NOS

　　| Excludes1 | collapsed vertebra NEC (M48.5) |
　　　　　　pathological fracture in neoplastic
　　　　　　　disease (M84.5-)
　　　　　　pathological fracture in osteoporosis
　　　　　　　(M80.-)
　　　　　　pathological fracture in other disease
　　　　　　　(M84.6-)
　　　　　　stress fracture (M84.3-)
　　　　　　traumatic fracture (S12.-, S22.-, S32.-,
　　　　　　　S42.-, S52.-, S62.-, S72.-, S82.-, S92.-)

　　| Excludes2 | personal history of (healed) pathological fracture (Z87.311) |

> The appropriate 7th character is to be added to
> each code from subcategory M84.4:
> A　initial encounter for fracture
> D　subsequent encounter for fracture with
> 　　routine healing
> G　subsequent encounter for fracture with
> 　　delayed healing
> K　subsequent encounter for fracture with
> 　　nonunion
> P　subsequent encounter for fracture with
> 　　malunion
> S　sequela

　■ M84.40 Pathological fracture, unspecified site
　　　　A, K, P 🦴

● M84.41 Pathological fracture, shoulder

　　　M84.411 Pathological fracture, right
　　　　　shoulder A, K, P 🦴

　　　M84.412 Pathological fracture, left
　　　　　shoulder A, K, P 🦴

　　　■ M84.419 Pathological fracture, unspecified
　　　　　shoulder A, K, P 🦴

● M84.42 Pathological fracture, humerus

　　　M84.421 Pathological fracture, right
　　　　　humerus A, K, P 🦴

　　　M84.422 Pathological fracture, left
　　　　　humerus A, K, P 🦴

　　　■ M84.429 Pathological fracture, unspecified
　　　　　humerus A, K, P 🦴

● M84.43 Pathological fracture, ulna and radius

　　　M84.431 Pathological fracture, right ulna
　　　　　A, K, P 🦴

　　　M84.432 Pathological fracture, left ulna
　　　　　A, K, P 🦴

　　　M84.433 Pathological fracture, right
　　　　　radius A, K, P 🦴

　　　M84.434 Pathological fracture, left
　　　　　radius A, K, P 🦴

　　　■ M84.439 Pathological fracture, unspecified
　　　　　ulna and radius A, K, P 🦴

● M84.44 Pathological fracture, hand and fingers

　　　M84.441 Pathological fracture, right hand
　　　　　A, K, P 🦴

　　　M84.442 Pathological fracture, left hand
　　　　　A, K, P 🦴

　　　■ M84.443 Pathological fracture, unspecified
　　　　　hand A, K, P 🦴

　　　M84.444 Pathological fracture, right
　　　　　finger(s) A, K, P 🦴

　　　M84.445 Pathological fracture, left
　　　　　finger(s) A, K, P 🦴

　　　■ M84.446 Pathological fracture, unspecified
　　　　　finger(s) A, K, P 🦴

● M84.45 Pathological fracture, femur and pelvis

　　　M84.451 Pathological fracture, right
　　　　　femur A, K, P 🦴

　　　M84.452 Pathological fracture, left femur
　　　　　A, K, P 🦴

　　　■ M84.453 Pathological fracture, unspecified
　　　　　femur A, K, P 🦴

　　　M84.454 Pathological fracture, pelvis
　　　　　A, K, P 🦴

　　　■ M84.459 Pathological fracture, hip,
　　　　　unspecified A, K, P 🦴

● M84.46 Pathological fracture, tibia and fibula

　　　M84.461 Pathological fracture, right tibia
　　　　　A, K, P 🦴

　　　M84.462 Pathological fracture, left tibia
　　　　　A, K, P 🦴

　　　M84.463 Pathological fracture, right fibula
　　　　　A, K, P 🦴

　　　M84.464 Pathological fracture, left fibula
　　　　　A, K, P 🦴

　　　■ M84.469 Pathological fracture, unspecified
　　　　　tibia and fibula A, K, P 🦴

● M84.47 Pathological fracture, ankle, foot and toes

　　　M84.471 Pathological fracture, right ankle
　　　　　A, K, P 🦴

　　　M84.472 Pathological fracture, left ankle
　　　　　A, K, P 🦴

　　　■ M84.473 Pathological fracture, unspecified
　　　　　ankle A, K, P 🦴

● Unacceptable First-Listed Diagnosis　　● Use Additional Character(s)　　■ Unspecified　　**OGCR** Official Guidelines for Coding and Reporting
🦴 Complication\Comorbidity　　🦴 Major C\C　　| Excludes 1 |　　| Excludes 2 |　　Includes　　Use additional　　Code first　　Code also

OGCR Section I.a, Chapter 13.C.
Coding of Pathologic Fractures
7th character A is for use as long as the patient is receiving active treatment for the fracture. Examples of active treatment are: surgical treatment, emergency department encounter, evaluation and treatment by a new physician. 7th character, D is to be used for encounters after the patient has completed active treatment. The other 7th characters, listed under each subcategory in the Tabular List, are to be used for subsequent encounters for treatment of problems associated with the healing, such as malunions, nonunions, and sequelae.
Care for complications of surgical treatment for fracture repairs during the healing or recovery phase should be coded with the appropriate complication codes.

See Section I.C.19. Coding of traumatic fractures.

         M84.474 Pathological fracture, right foot
                 A, K, P 🅒

         M84.475 Pathological fracture, left foot
                 A, K, P 🅒

       ▪ M84.476 Pathological fracture, unspecified
                 foot A, K, P 🅒

         M84.477 Pathological fracture, right toe(s)
                 A, K, P 🅒

         M84.478 Pathological fracture, left toe(s)
                 A, K, P 🅒

       ▪ M84.479 Pathological fracture, unspecified
                 toe(s) A, K, P 🅒

      M84.48 Pathological fracture, other site A, K, P 🅒

● **M84.5 Pathological fracture in neoplastic disease**
      Code also underlying neoplasm

> The appropriate 7th character is to be added to
>   each code from subcategory M84.5:
> A   initial encounter for fracture
> D   subsequent encounter for fracture with
>   routine healing
> G   subsequent encounter for fracture with
>   delayed healing
> K   subsequent encounter for fracture with
>   nonunion
> P   subsequent encounter for fracture with
>   malunion
> S   sequela

▪ M84.50 Pathological fracture in neoplastic disease,
         unspecified site A, K, P 🅒

● M84.51 Pathological fracture in neoplastic disease,
         shoulder

         M84.511 Pathological fracture in
                 neoplastic disease, right shoulder
                 A, K, P 🅒

         M84.512 Pathological fracture in
                 neoplastic disease, left shoulder
                 A, K, P 🅒

       ▪ M84.519 Pathological fracture in
                 neoplastic disease, unspecified
                 shoulder A, K, P 🅒

● M84.52 Pathological fracture in neoplastic disease,
         humerus

         M84.521 Pathological fracture in
                 neoplastic disease, right humerus
                 A, K, P 🅒

         M84.522 Pathological fracture in
                 neoplastic disease, left humerus
                 A, K, P 🅒

       ▪ M84.529 Pathological fracture in
                 neoplastic disease, unspecified
                 humerus A, K, P 🅒

● M84.53 Pathological fracture in neoplastic disease,
         ulna and radius

         M84.531 Pathological fracture in
                 neoplastic disease, right ulna
                 A, K, P 🅒

         M84.532 Pathological fracture in
                 neoplastic disease, left ulna
                 A, K, P 🅒

         M84.533 Pathological fracture in
                 neoplastic disease, right radius
                 A, K, P 🅒

         M84.534 Pathological fracture in
                 neoplastic disease, left radius
                 A, K, P 🅒

       ▪ M84.539 Pathological fracture in
                 neoplastic disease, unspecified
                 ulna and radius A, K, P 🅒

● M84.54 Pathological fracture in neoplastic disease,
         hand

         M84.541 Pathological fracture in
                 neoplastic disease, right hand
                 A, K, P 🅒

         M84.542 Pathological fracture in
                 neoplastic disease, left hand
                 A, K, P 🅒

       ▪ M84.549 Pathological fracture in
                 neoplastic disease, unspecified
                 hand A, K, P 🅒

● M84.55 Pathological fracture in neoplastic disease,
         pelvis and femur

         M84.550 Pathological fracture in neoplastic
                 disease, pelvis A, K, P 🅒

         M84.551 Pathological fracture in
                 neoplastic disease, right femur
                 A, K, P 🅒

         M84.552 Pathological fracture in
                 neoplastic disease, left femur
                 A, K, P 🅒

       ▪ M84.553 Pathological fracture in
                 neoplastic disease, unspecified
                 femur A, K, P 🅒

       ▪ M84.559 Pathological fracture in
                 neoplastic disease, hip,
                 unspecified A, K, P 🅒

● M84.56 Pathological fracture in neoplastic disease,
         tibia and fibula

         M84.561 Pathological fracture in
                 neoplastic disease, right tibia
                 A, K, P 🅒

         M84.562 Pathological fracture in
                 neoplastic disease, left tibia
                 A, K, P 🅒

         M84.563 Pathological fracture in
                 neoplastic disease, right fibula
                 A, K, P 🅒

         M84.564 Pathological fracture in
                 neoplastic disease, left fibula
                 A, K, P 🅒

● Unacceptable First-Listed Diagnosis   ● Use Additional Character(s)   ▪ Unspecified   **OGCR** Official Guidelines for Coding and Reporting
🅒 Complication\Comorbidity   🅒 Major C\C   [Excludes 1]   [Excludes 2]   Includes   Use additional   Code first   Code also   1207

CHAPTER 13 (M00–M99)

M84.569 Pathological fracture in neoplastic disease, unspecified tibia and fibula A, K, P 🝔

● M84.57 Pathological fracture in neoplastic disease, ankle and foot

M84.571 Pathological fracture in neoplastic disease, right ankle A, K, P 🝔

M84.572 Pathological fracture in neoplastic disease, left ankle A, K, P 🝔

M84.573 Pathological fracture in neoplastic disease, unspecified ankle A, K, P 🝔

M84.574 Pathological fracture in neoplastic disease, right foot A, K, P 🝔

M84.575 Pathological fracture in neoplastic disease, left foot A, K, P 🝔

M84.576 Pathological fracture in neoplastic disease, unspecified foot A, K, P 🝔

M84.58 Pathological fracture in neoplastic disease, vertebrae A, K, P 🝔

● M84.6 Pathological fracture in other disease
Code also underlying condition

Excludes1 pathological fracture in osteoporosis (M80.-)

The appropriate 7th character is to be added to each code from subcategory M84.6:
A   initial encounter for fracture
D   subsequent encounter for fracture with routine healing
G   subsequent encounter for fracture with delayed healing
K   subsequent encounter for fracture with nonunion
P   subsequent encounter for fracture with malunion
S   sequela

M84.60 Pathological fracture in other disease, unspecified site A, K, P 🝔

● M84.61 Pathological fracture in other disease, shoulder

M84.611 Pathological fracture in other disease, right shoulder A, K, P 🝔

M84.612 Pathological fracture in other disease, left shoulder A, K, P 🝔

M84.619 Pathological fracture in other disease, unspecified shoulder A, K, P 🝔

● M84.62 Pathological fracture in other disease, humerus

M84.621 Pathological fracture in other disease, right humerus A, K, P 🝔

M84.622 Pathological fracture in other disease, left humerus A, K, P 🝔

M84.629 Pathological fracture in other disease, unspecified humerus A, K, P 🝔

● M84.63 Pathological fracture in other disease, ulna and radius

M84.631 Pathological fracture in other disease, right ulna A, K, P 🝔

M84.632 Pathological fracture in other disease, left ulna A, K, P 🝔

M84.633 Pathological fracture in other disease, right radius A, K, P 🝔

M84.634 Pathological fracture in other disease, left radius A, K, P 🝔

M84.639 Pathological fracture in other disease, unspecified ulna and radius A, K, P 🝔

● M84.64 Pathological fracture in other disease, hand

M84.641 Pathological fracture in other disease, right hand A, K, P 🝔

M84.642 Pathological fracture in other disease, left hand A, K, P 🝔

M84.649 Pathological fracture in other disease, unspecified hand A, K, P 🝔

● M84.65 Pathological fracture in other disease, pelvis and femur

M84.650 Pathological fracture in other disease, pelvis A, K, P 🝔

M84.651 Pathological fracture in other disease, right femur A, K, P 🝔

M84.652 Pathological fracture in other disease, left femur A, K, P 🝔

M84.653 Pathological fracture in other disease, unspecified femur A, K, P 🝔

M84.659 Pathological fracture in other disease, hip, unspecified A, K, P 🝔

● M84.66 Pathological fracture in other disease, tibia and fibula

M84.661 Pathological fracture in other disease, right tibia A, K, P 🝔

M84.662 Pathological fracture in other disease, left tibia A, K, P 🝔

M84.663 Pathological fracture in other disease, right fibula A, K, P 🝔

M84.664 Pathological fracture in other disease, left fibula A, K, P 🝔

M84.669 Pathological fracture in other disease, unspecified tibia and fibula A, K, P 🝔

● M84.67 Pathological fracture in other disease, ankle and foot

M84.671 Pathological fracture in other disease, right ankle A, K, P 🝔

M84.672 Pathological fracture in other disease, left ankle A, K, P 🝔

M84.673 Pathological fracture in other disease, unspecified ankle A, K, P 🝔

M84.674 Pathological fracture in other disease, right foot A, K, P 🝔

M84.675 Pathological fracture in other disease, left foot A, K, P 🝔

M84.676 Pathological fracture in other disease, unspecified foot A, K, P 🝔

M84.68 Pathological fracture in other disease, other site A, K, P 🝔

● M84.8 Other disorders of continuity of bone

M84.80 Other disorders of continuity of bone, unspecified site

● M84.81 Other disorders of continuity of bone, shoulder

M84.811 Other disorders of continuity of bone, right shoulder

● Unacceptable First-Listed Diagnosis   ● Use Additional Character(s)   ▢ Unspecified   OGCR Official Guidelines for Coding and Reporting
🝔 Complication\Comorbidity   🝔 Major C\C   Excludes 1   Excludes 2   Includes   Use additional   Code first   Code also

M84.812 Other disorders of continuity of bone, left shoulder

■ M84.819 Other disorders of continuity of bone, unspecified shoulder

● M84.82 Other disorders of continuity of bone, humerus

M84.821 Other disorders of continuity of bone, right humerus

M84.822 Other disorders of continuity of bone, left humerus

■ M84.829 Other disorders of continuity of bone, unspecified humerus

● M84.83 Other disorders of continuity of bone, ulna and radius

M84.831 Other disorders of continuity of bone, right ulna

M84.832 Other disorders of continuity of bone, left ulna

M84.833 Other disorders of continuity of bone, right radius

M84.834 Other disorders of continuity of bone, left radius

■ M84.839 Other disorders of continuity of bone, unspecified ulna and radius

● M84.84 Other disorders of continuity of bone, hand

M84.841 Other disorders of continuity of bone, right hand

M84.842 Other disorders of continuity of bone, left hand

■ M84.849 Other disorders of continuity of bone, unspecified hand

● M84.85 Other disorders of continuity of bone, pelvic region and thigh

M84.851 Other disorders of continuity of bone, right pelvic region and thigh

M84.852 Other disorders of continuity of bone, left pelvic region and thigh

■ M84.859 Other disorders of continuity of bone, unspecified pelvic region and thigh

● M84.86 Other disorders of continuity of bone, tibia and fibula

M84.861 Other disorders of continuity of bone, right tibia

M84.862 Other disorders of continuity of bone, left tibia

M84.863 Other disorders of continuity of bone, right fibula

M84.864 Other disorders of continuity of bone, left fibula

■ M84.869 Other disorders of continuity of bone, unspecified tibia and fibula

● M84.87 Other disorders of continuity of bone, ankle and foot

M84.871 Other disorders of continuity of bone, right ankle and foot

M84.872 Other disorders of continuity of bone, left ankle and foot

■ M84.879 Other disorders of continuity of bone, unspecified ankle and foot

M84.88 Other disorders of continuity of bone, other site

■ M84.9 Disorder of continuity of bone, unspecified

● M85 Other disorders of bone density and structure

Excludes1   osteogenesis imperfecta (Q78.0)
osteopetrosis (Q78.2)
osteopoikilosis (Q78.8)
polyostotic fibrous dysplasia (Q78.1)

● M85.0 Fibrous dysplasia (monostotic)

Excludes2   fibrous dysplasia of jaw (M27.8)

■ M85.00 Fibrous dysplasia (monostotic), unspecified site

● M85.01 Fibrous dysplasia (monostotic), shoulder

M85.011 Fibrous dysplasia (monostotic), right shoulder

M85.012 Fibrous dysplasia (monostotic), left shoulder

■ M85.019 Fibrous dysplasia (monostotic), unspecified shoulder

● M85.02 Fibrous dysplasia (monostotic), upper arm

M85.021 Fibrous dysplasia (monostotic), right upper arm

M85.022 Fibrous dysplasia (monostotic), left upper arm

■ M85.029 Fibrous dysplasia (monostotic), unspecified upper arm

● M85.03 Fibrous dysplasia (monostotic), forearm

M85.031 Fibrous dysplasia (monostotic), right forearm

M85.032 Fibrous dysplasia (monostotic), left forearm

■ M85.039 Fibrous dysplasia (monostotic), unspecified forearm

● M85.04 Fibrous dysplasia (monostotic), hand

M85.041 Fibrous dysplasia (monostotic), right hand

M85.042 Fibrous dysplasia (monostotic), left hand

■ M85.049 Fibrous dysplasia (monostotic), unspecified hand

● M85.05 Fibrous dysplasia (monostotic), thigh

M85.051 Fibrous dysplasia (monostotic), right thigh

M85.052 Fibrous dysplasia (monostotic), left thigh

■ M85.059 Fibrous dysplasia (monostotic), unspecified thigh

● M85.06 Fibrous dysplasia (monostotic), lower leg

M85.061 Fibrous dysplasia (monostotic), right lower leg

M85.062 Fibrous dysplasia (monostotic), left lower leg

■ M85.069 Fibrous dysplasia (monostotic), unspecified lower leg

● M85.07 Fibrous dysplasia (monostotic), ankle and foot

M85.071 Fibrous dysplasia (monostotic), right ankle and foot

M85.072 Fibrous dysplasia (monostotic), left ankle and foot

■ M85.079 Fibrous dysplasia (monostotic), unspecified ankle and foot

M85.08 Fibrous dysplasia (monostotic), other site

M85.09 Fibrous dysplasia (monostotic), multiple sites

● Unacceptable First-Listed Diagnosis   ● Use Additional Character(s)   ■ Unspecified   **OGCR** Official Guidelines for Coding and Reporting
🗞 Complication\Comorbidity   🗞 Major C\C   Excludes 1   Excludes 2   Includes   Use additional   Code first   Code also

CHAPTER 13 (M00-M99)

1209

● M85.1   Skeletal fluorosis
- ■ M85.10   Skeletal fluorosis, unspecified site
- ● M85.11   Skeletal fluorosis, shoulder
  - M85.111   Skeletal fluorosis, right shoulder
  - M85.112   Skeletal fluorosis, left shoulder
  - ■ M85.119   Skeletal fluorosis, unspecified shoulder
- ● M85.12   Skeletal fluorosis, upper arm
  - M85.121   Skeletal fluorosis, right upper arm
  - M85.122   Skeletal fluorosis, left upper arm
  - ■ M85.129   Skeletal fluorosis, unspecified upper arm
- ● M85.13   Skeletal fluorosis, forearm
  - M85.131   Skeletal fluorosis, right forearm
  - M85.132   Skeletal fluorosis, left forearm
  - ■ M85.139   Skeletal fluorosis, unspecified forearm
- ● M85.14   Skeletal fluorosis, hand
  - M85.141   Skeletal fluorosis, right hand
  - M85.142   Skeletal fluorosis, left hand
  - ■ M85.149   Skeletal fluorosis, unspecified hand
- ● M85.15   Skeletal fluorosis, thigh
  - M85.151   Skeletal fluorosis, right thigh
  - M85.152   Skeletal fluorosis, left thigh
  - ■ M85.159   Skeletal fluorosis, unspecified thigh
- ● M85.16   Skeletal fluorosis, lower leg
  - M85.161   Skeletal fluorosis, right lower leg
  - M85.162   Skeletal fluorosis, left lower leg
  - ■ M85.169   Skeletal fluorosis, unspecified lower leg
- ● M85.17   Skeletal fluorosis, ankle and foot
  - M85.171   Skeletal fluorosis, right ankle and foot
  - M85.172   Skeletal fluorosis, left ankle and foot
  - ■ M85.179   Skeletal fluorosis, unspecified ankle and foot
- M85.18   Skeletal fluorosis, other site
- M85.19   Skeletal fluorosis, multiple sites

M85.2   Hyperostosis of skull

● M85.3   Osteitis condensans
- ■ M85.30   Osteitis condensans, unspecified site
- ● M85.31   Osteitis condensans, shoulder
  - M85.311   Osteitis condensans, right shoulder
  - M85.312   Osteitis condensans, left shoulder
  - ■ M85.319   Osteitis condensans, unspecified shoulder
- ● M85.32   Osteitis condensans, upper arm
  - M85.321   Osteitis condensans, right upper arm
  - M85.322   Osteitis condensans, left upper arm
  - ■ M85.329   Osteitis condensans, unspecified upper arm
- ● M85.33   Osteitis condensans, forearm
  - M85.331   Osteitis condensans, right forearm

- M85.332   Osteitis condensans, left forearm
- ■ M85.339   Osteitis condensans, unspecified forearm
- ● M85.34   Osteitis condensans, hand
  - M85.341   Osteitis condensans, right hand
  - M85.342   Osteitis condensans, left hand
  - ■ M85.349   Osteitis condensans, unspecified hand
- ● M85.35   Osteitis condensans, thigh
  - M85.351   Osteitis condensans, right thigh
  - M85.352   Osteitis condensans, left thigh
  - ■ M85.359   Osteitis condensans, unspecified thigh
- ● M85.36   Osteitis condensans, lower leg
  - M85.361   Osteitis condensans, right lower leg
  - M85.362   Osteitis condensans, left lower leg
  - ■ M85.369   Osteitis condensans, unspecified lower leg
- ● M85.37   Osteitis condensans, ankle and foot
  - M85.371   Osteitis condensans, right ankle and foot
  - M85.372   Osteitis condensans, left ankle and foot
  - ■ M85.379   Osteitis condensans, unspecified ankle and foot
- M85.38   Osteitis condensans, vertebrae
- M85.39   Osteitis condensans, multiple sites

● M85.4   Solitary bone cyst
- **Excludes2**   solitary cyst of jaw (M27.4)
- ■ M85.40   Solitary bone cyst, unspecified site
- ● M85.41   Solitary bone cyst, shoulder
  - M85.411   Solitary bone cyst, right shoulder
  - M85.412   Solitary bone cyst, left shoulder
  - ■ M85.419   Solitary bone cyst, unspecified shoulder
- ● M85.42   Solitary bone cyst, humerus
  - M85.421   Solitary bone cyst, right humerus
  - M85.422   Solitary bone cyst, left humerus
  - ■ M85.429   Solitary bone cyst, unspecified humerus
- ● M85.43   Solitary bone cyst, ulna and radius
  - M85.431   Solitary bone cyst, right ulna and radius
  - M85.432   Solitary bone cyst, left ulna and radius
  - ■ M85.439   Solitary bone cyst, unspecified ulna and radius
- ● M85.44   Solitary bone cyst, hand
  - M85.441   Solitary bone cyst, right hand
  - M85.442   Solitary bone cyst, left hand
  - ■ M85.449   Solitary bone cyst, unspecified hand
- ● M85.45   Solitary bone cyst, pelvis
  - M85.451   Solitary bone cyst, right pelvis
  - M85.452   Solitary bone cyst, left pelvis
  - ■ M85.459   Solitary bone cyst, unspecified pelvis

● M85.46　Solitary bone cyst, tibia and fibula

　　M85.461　Solitary bone cyst, right tibia and fibula

　　M85.462　Solitary bone cyst, left tibia and fibula

　　■ M85.469　Solitary bone cyst, unspecified tibia and fibula

● M85.47　Solitary bone cyst, ankle and foot

　　M85.471　Solitary bone cyst, right ankle and foot

　　M85.472　Solitary bone cyst, left ankle and foot

　　■ M85.479　Solitary bone cyst, unspecified ankle and foot

　M85.48　Solitary bone cyst, other site

● M85.5　Aneurysmal bone cyst

　　Excludes2　aneurysmal cyst of jaw (M27.4)

　■ M85.50　Aneurysmal bone cyst, unspecified site

● M85.51　Aneurysmal bone cyst, shoulder

　　M85.511　Aneurysmal bone cyst, right shoulder

　　M85.512　Aneurysmal bone cyst, left shoulder

　　■ M85.519　Aneurysmal bone cyst, unspecified shoulder

● M85.52　Aneurysmal bone cyst, upper arm

　　M85.521　Aneurysmal bone cyst, right upper arm

　　M85.522　Aneurysmal bone cyst, left upper arm

　　■ M85.529　Aneurysmal bone cyst, unspecified upper arm

● M85.53　Aneurysmal bone cyst, forearm

　　M85.531　Aneurysmal bone cyst, right forearm

　　M85.532　Aneurysmal bone cyst, left forearm

　　■ M85.539　Aneurysmal bone cyst, unspecified forearm

● M85.54　Aneurysmal bone cyst, hand

　　M85.541　Aneurysmal bone cyst, right hand

　　M85.542　Aneurysmal bone cyst, left hand

　　■ M85.549　Aneurysmal bone cyst, unspecified hand

● M85.55　Aneurysmal bone cyst, thigh

　　M85.551　Aneurysmal bone cyst, right thigh

　　M85.552　Aneurysmal bone cyst, left thigh

　　■ M85.559　Aneurysmal bone cyst, unspecified thigh

● M85.56　Aneurysmal bone cyst, lower leg

　　M85.561　Aneurysmal bone cyst, right lower leg

　　M85.562　Aneurysmal bone cyst, left lower leg

　　■ M85.569　Aneurysmal bone cyst, unspecified lower leg

● M85.57　Aneurysmal bone cyst, ankle and foot

　　M85.571　Aneurysmal bone cyst, right ankle and foot

　　M85.572　Aneurysmal bone cyst, left ankle and foot

　　■ M85.579　Aneurysmal bone cyst, unspecified ankle and foot

　M85.58　Aneurysmal bone cyst, other site

　M85.59　Aneurysmal bone cyst, multiple sites

● M85.6　Other cyst of bone

　　Excludes1　cyst of jaw NEC (M27.4)
　　　　　　　osteitis fibrosa cystica generalisata [von Recklinghausen's disease of bone] (E21.0)

　■ M85.60　Other cyst of bone, unspecified site

● M85.61　Other cyst of bone, shoulder

　　M85.611　Other cyst of bone, right shoulder

　　M85.612　Other cyst of bone, left shoulder

　　■ M85.619　Other cyst of bone, unspecified shoulder

● M85.62　Other cyst of bone, upper arm

　　M85.621　Other cyst of bone, right upper arm

　　M85.622　Other cyst of bone, left upper arm

　　■ M85.629　Other cyst of bone, unspecified upper arm

● M85.63　Other cyst of bone, forearm

　　M85.631　Other cyst of bone, right forearm

　　M85.632　Other cyst of bone, left forearm

　　■ M85.639　Other cyst of bone, unspecified forearm

● M85.64　Other cyst of bone, hand

　　M85.641　Other cyst of bone, right hand

　　M85.642　Other cyst of bone, left hand

　　■ M85.649　Other cyst of bone, unspecified hand

● M85.65　Other cyst of bone, thigh

　　M85.651　Other cyst of bone, right thigh

　　M85.652　Other cyst of bone, left thigh

　　■ M85.659　Other cyst of bone, unspecified thigh

● M85.66　Other cyst of bone, lower leg

　　M85.661　Other cyst of bone, right lower leg

　　M85.662　Other cyst of bone, left lower leg

　　■ M85.669　Other cyst of bone, unspecified lower leg

● M85.67　Other cyst of bone, ankle and foot

　　M85.671　Other cyst of bone, right ankle and foot

　　M85.672　Other cyst of bone, left ankle and foot

　　■ M85.679　Other cyst of bone, unspecified ankle and foot

　M85.68　Other cyst of bone, other site

　M85.69　Other cyst of bone, multiple sites

● M85.8　Other specified disorders of bone density and structure

　　Hyperostosis of bones, except skull
　　Osteosclerosis, acquired

　　Excludes1　diffuse idiopathic skeletal hyperostosis [DISH] (M48.1)
　　　　　　　osteosclerosis congenita (Q77.4)
　　　　　　　osteosclerosis fragilitas (generalista) (Q78.2)
　　　　　　　osteosclerosis myelofibrosis (D75.81)

　■ M85.80　Other specified disorders of bone density and structure, unspecified site

● Unacceptable First-Listed Diagnosis　　● Use Additional Character(s)　　■ Unspecified　　OGCR Official Guidelines for Coding and Reporting

🝊 Complication\Comorbidity　🝊 Major C\C　Excludes 1　Excludes 2　Includes　Use additional　Code first　Code also

CHAPTER 13 (M00-M99)

1211

● M85.81   Other specified disorders of bone density and structure, shoulder

     M85.811   Other specified disorders of bone density and structure, right shoulder

     M85.812   Other specified disorders of bone density and structure, left shoulder

     ■ M85.819   Other specified disorders of bone density and structure, unspecified shoulder

● M85.82   Other specified disorders of bone density and structure, upper arm

     M85.821   Other specified disorders of bone density and structure, right upper arm

     M85.822   Other specified disorders of bone density and structure, left upper arm

     ■ M85.829   Other specified disorders of bone density and structure, unspecified upper arm

● M85.83   Other specified disorders of bone density and structure, forearm

     M85.831   Other specified disorders of bone density and structure, right forearm

     M85.832   Other specified disorders of bone density and structure, left forearm

     ■ M85.839   Other specified disorders of bone density and structure, unspecified forearm

● M85.84   Other specified disorders of bone density and structure, hand

     M85.841   Other specified disorders of bone density and structure, right hand

     M85.842   Other specified disorders of bone density and structure, left hand

     ■ M85.849   Other specified disorders of bone density and structure, unspecified hand

● M85.85   Other specified disorders of bone density and structure, thigh

     M85.851   Other specified disorders of bone density and structure, right thigh

     M85.852   Other specified disorders of bone density and structure, left thigh

     ■ M85.859   Other specified disorders of bone density and structure, unspecified thigh

● M85.86   Other specified disorders of bone density and structure, lower leg

     M85.861   Other specified disorders of bone density and structure, right lower leg

     M85.862   Other specified disorders of bone density and structure, left lower leg

     ■ M85.869   Other specified disorders of bone density and structure, unspecified lower leg

● M85.87   Other specified disorders of bone density and structure, ankle and foot

Item 13-11   **Osteomyelitis** is an inflammation of the bone. **Acute osteomyelitis** is a rapidly destructive, pus-producing infection capable of causing severe bone destruction. **Chronic osteomyelitis** can remain long after the initial acute episode has passed and may lead to a recurrence of the acute phase. **Brodie's abscess** is an encapsulated focal abscess that must be surgically drained. Periostitis is an inflammation of the periosteum, a dense membrane composed of fibrous connective tissue that closely wraps all bone, except those with articulating surfaces in joints, which are covered by synovial membranes.

     M85.871   Other specified disorders of bone density and structure, right ankle and foot

     M85.872   Other specified disorders of bone density and structure, left ankle and foot

     ■ M85.879   Other specified disorders of bone density and structure, unspecified ankle and foot

   M85.88   Other specified disorders of bone density and structure, other site

   M85.89   Other specified disorders of bone density and structure, multiple sites

■ M85.9   Disorder of bone density and structure, unspecified

---

OTHER OSTEOPATHIES (M86-M90)

| Excludes1 | postprocedural osteopathies (M96.-) |

● M86   Osteomyelitis

     Use additional code (B95-B97) to identify infectious agent

     Use additional code to identify major osseous defect, if applicable (M89.7-)

| Excludes1 | osteomyelitis due to:
    echinococcus (B67.2)
    gonococcus (A54.43)
    salmonella (A02.24) |

| Excludes2 | ostemyelitis of:
    orbit (H05.0-)
    petrous bone (H70.2-)
    vertebra (M46.2-) |

● M86.0   Acute hematogenous osteomyelitis

     ■ M86.00   Acute hematogenous osteomyelitis, unspecified site 🦴

     ● M86.01   Acute hematogenous osteomyelitis, shoulder

         M86.011   Acute hematogenous osteomyelitis, right shoulder 🦴

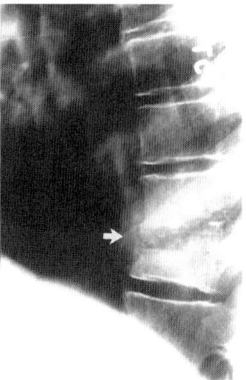

Figure 13-5   Osleomyelitis of the spine. A lateral view of the lower thoracic spine demonstrates destruction of the disk space *(arrow)* as well as destruction of the adjoining vertebral bodies. (From Mettler: Essentials of Radiology, 2nd ed. 2005, Sounders, An Imprint of Elsevier)

● Unacceptable First-Listed Diagnosis   ● Use Additional Character(s)   ■ Unspecified   **OGCR** Official Guidelines for Coding and Reporting
🦴 Complication\Comorbidity   🦴 Major C\C   Excludes 1   Excludes 2   Includes   Use additional   Code first   Code also

M86.012 Acute hematogenous osteomyelitis, left shoulder 🍂

◼ M86.019 Acute hematogenous osteomyelitis, unspecified shoulder 🍂

● M86.02 Acute hematogenous osteomyelitis, humerus

M86.021 Acute hematogenous osteomyelitis, right humerus 🍂

M86.022 Acute hematogenous osteomyelitis, left humerus 🍂

◼ M86.029 Acute hematogenous osteomyelitis, unspecified humerus 🍂

● M86.03 Acute hematogenous osteomyelitis, radius and ulna

M86.031 Acute hematogenous osteomyelitis, right radius and ulna 🍂

M86.032 Acute hematogenous osteomyelitis, left radius and ulna 🍂

◼ M86.039 Acute hematogenous osteomyelitis, unspecified radius and ulna 🍂

● M86.04 Acute hematogenous osteomyelitis, hand

M86.041 Acute hematogenous osteomyelitis, right hand 🍂

M86.042 Acute hematogenous osteomyelitis, left hand 🍂

◼ M86.049 Acute hematogenous osteomyelitis, unspecified hand 🍂

● M86.05 Acute hematogenous osteomyelitis, femur

M86.051 Acute hematogenous osteomyelitis, right femur 🍂

M86.052 Acute hematogenous osteomyelitis, left femur 🍂

◼ M86.059 Acute hematogenous osteomyelitis, unspecified femur 🍂

● M86.06 Acute hematogenous osteomyelitis, tibia and fibula

M86.061 Acute hematogenous osteomyelitis, right tibia and fibula 🍂

M86.062 Acute hematogenous osteomyelitis, left tibia and fibula 🍂

◼ M86.069 Acute hematogenous osteomyelitis, unspecified tibia and fibula 🍂

● M86.07 Acute hematogenous osteomyelitis, ankle and foot

M86.071 Acute hematogenous osteomyelitis, right ankle and foot 🍂

M86.072 Acute hematogenous osteomyelitis, left ankle and foot 🍂

◼ M86.079 Acute hematogenous osteomyelitis, unspecified ankle and foot 🍂

M86.08 Acute hematogenous osteomyelitis, other sites 🍂

M86.09 Acute hematogenous osteomyelitis, multiple sites 🍂

● M86.1 Other acute osteomyelitis

◼ M86.10 Other acute osteomyelitis, unspecified site 🍂

● M86.11 Other acute osteomyelitis, shoulder

M86.111 Other acute osteomyelitis, right shoulder 🍂

M86.112 Other acute osteomyelitis, left shoulder 🍂

◼ M86.119 Other acute osteomyelitis, unspecified shoulder 🍂

● M86.12 Other acute osteomyelitis, humerus

M86.121 Other acute osteomyelitis, right humerus 🍂

M86.122 Other acute osteomyelitis, left humerus 🍂

◼ M86.129 Other acute osteomyelitis, unspecified humerus 🍂

● M86.13 Other acute osteomyelitis, radius and ulna

M86.131 Other acute osteomyelitis, right radius and ulna 🍂

M86.132 Other acute osteomyelitis, left radius and ulna 🍂

◼ M86.139 Other acute osteomyelitis, unspecified radius and ulna 🍂

● M86.14 Other acute osteomyelitis, hand

M86.141 Other acute osteomyelitis, right hand 🍂

M86.142 Other acute osteomyelitis, left hand 🍂

◼ M86.149 Other acute osteomyelitis, unspecified hand 🍂

● M86.15 Other acute osteomyelitis, femur

M86.151 Other acute osteomyelitis, right femur 🍂

M86.152 Other acute osteomyelitis, left femur 🍂

◼ M86.159 Other acute osteomyelitis, unspecified femur 🍂

● M86.16 Other acute osteomyelitis, tibia and fibula

M86.161 Other acute osteomyelitis, right tibia and fibula 🍂

M86.162 Other acute osteomyelitis, left tibia and fibula 🍂

◼ M86.169 Other acute osteomyelitis, unspecified tibia and fibula 🍂

● M86.17 Other acute osteomyelitis, ankle and foot

M86.171 Other acute osteomyelitis, right ankle and foot 🍂

M86.172 Other acute osteomyelitis, left ankle and foot 🍂

◼ M86.179 Other acute osteomyelitis, unspecified ankle and foot 🍂

M86.18 Other acute osteomyelitis, other site 🍂

M86.19 Other acute osteomyelitis, multiple sites 🍂

● Unaccceptable First-Listed Diagnosis   ● Use Additional Character(s)   ◼ Unspecified   **OGCR** Official Guidelines for Coding and Reporting

🍂 Complication\Comorbidity   🍂 Major C\C   Excludes 1   Excludes 2   Includes   Use additional   Code first   Code also

1213

CHAPTER 13 (M00-M99)

- ● M86.2 Subacute osteomyelitis
  - ▣ M86.20 Subacute osteomyelitis, unspecified site 🦠
  - ● M86.21 Subacute osteomyelitis, shoulder
    - M86.211 Subacute osteomyelitis, right shoulder 🦠
    - M86.212 Subacute osteomyelitis, left shoulder 🦠
    - ▣ M86.219 Subacute osteomyelitis, unspecified shoulder 🦠
  - ● M86.22 Subacute osteomyelitis, humerus
    - M86.221 Subacute osteomyelitis, right humerus 🦠
    - M86.222 Subacute osteomyelitis, left humerus 🦠
    - ▣ M86.229 Subacute osteomyelitis, unspecified humerus 🦠
  - ● M86.23 Subacute osteomyelitis, radius and ulna
    - M86.231 Subacute osteomyelitis, right radius and ulna 🦠
    - M86.232 Subacute osteomyelitis, left radius and ulna 🦠
    - ▣ M86.239 Subacute osteomyelitis, unspecified radius and ulna 🦠
  - ● M86.24 Subacute osteomyelitis, hand
    - M86.241 Subacute osteomyelitis, right hand 🦠
    - M86.242 Subacute osteomyelitis, left hand 🦠
    - ▣ M86.249 Subacute osteomyelitis, unspecified hand 🦠
  - ● M86.25 Subacute osteomyelitis, femur
    - M86.251 Subacute osteomyelitis, right femur 🦠
    - M86.252 Subacute osteomyelitis, left femur 🦠
    - ▣ M86.259 Subacute osteomyelitis, unspecified femur 🦠
  - ● M86.26 Subacute osteomyelitis, tibia and fibula
    - M86.261 Subacute osteomyelitis, right tibia and fibula 🦠
    - M86.262 Subacute osteomyelitis, left tibia and fibula 🦠
    - ▣ M86.269 Subacute osteomyelitis, unspecified tibia and fibula 🦠
  - ● M86.27 Subacute osteomyelitis, ankle and foot
    - M86.271 Subacute osteomyelitis, right ankle and foot 🦠
    - M86.272 Subacute osteomyelitis, left ankle and foot 🦠
    - ▣ M86.279 Subacute osteomyelitis, unspecified ankle and foot 🦠
  - M86.28 Subacute osteomyelitis, other site 🦠
  - M86.29 Subacute osteomyelitis, multiple sites 🦠
- ● M86.3 Chronic multifocal osteomyelitis
  - ▣ M86.30 Chronic multifocal osteomyelitis, unspecified site 🦠
  - ● M86.31 Chronic multifocal osteomyelitis, shoulder
    - M86.311 Chronic multifocal osteomyelitis, right shoulder 🦠
    - M86.312 Chronic multifocal osteomyelitis, left shoulder 🦠
  - ▣ M86.319 Chronic multifocal osteomyelitis, unspecified shoulder 🦠
  - ● M86.32 Chronic multifocal osteomyelitis, humerus
    - M86.321 Chronic multifocal osteomyelitis, right humerus 🦠
    - M86.322 Chronic multifocal osteomyelitis, left humerus 🦠
    - ▣ M86.329 Chronic multifocal osteomyelitis, unspecified humerus 🦠
  - ● M86.33 Chronic multifocal osteomyelitis, radius and ulna
    - M86.331 Chronic multifocal osteomyelitis, right radius and ulna 🦠
    - M86.332 Chronic multifocal osteomyelitis, left radius and ulna 🦠
    - ▣ M86.339 Chronic multifocal osteomyelitis, unspecified radius and ulna 🦠
  - ● M86.34 Chronic multifocal osteomyelitis, hand
    - M86.341 Chronic multifocal osteomyelitis, right hand 🦠
    - M86.342 Chronic multifocal osteomyelitis, left hand 🦠
    - ▣ M86.349 Chronic multifocal osteomyelitis, unspecified hand 🦠
  - ● M86.35 Chronic multifocal osteomyelitis, femur
    - M86.351 Chronic multifocal osteomyelitis, right femur 🦠
    - M86.352 Chronic multifocal osteomyelitis, left femur 🦠
    - ▣ M86.359 Chronic multifocal osteomyelitis, unspecified femur 🦠
  - ● M86.36 Chronic multifocal osteomyelitis, tibia and fibula
    - M86.361 Chronic multifocal osteomyelitis, right tibia and fibula 🦠
    - M86.362 Chronic multifocal osteomyelitis, left tibia and fibula 🦠
    - ▣ M86.369 Chronic multifocal osteomyelitis, unspecified tibia and fibula 🦠
  - ● M86.37 Chronic multifocal osteomyelitis, ankle and foot
    - M86.371 Chronic multifocal osteomyelitis, right ankle and foot 🦠
    - M86.372 Chronic multifocal osteomyelitis, left ankle and foot 🦠
    - ▣ M86.379 Chronic multifocal osteomyelitis, unspecified ankle and foot 🦠
  - M86.38 Chronic multifocal osteomyelitis, other site 🦠
  - M86.39 Chronic multifocal osteomyelitis, multiple sites 🦠
- ● M86.4 Chronic osteomyelitis with draining sinus
  - ▣ M86.40 Chronic osteomyelitis with draining sinus, unspecified site 🦠
  - ● M86.41 Chronic osteomyelitis with draining sinus, shoulder
    - M86.411 Chronic osteomyelitis with draining sinus, right shoulder 🦠
    - M86.412 Chronic osteomyelitis with draining sinus, left shoulder 🦠
    - ▣ M86.419 Chronic osteomyelitis with draining sinus, unspecified shoulder 🦠

● Unacceptable First-Listed Diagnosis   ● Use Additional Character(s)   ▣ Unspecified   **OGCR** Official Guidelines for Coding and Reporting
🦠 Complication\Comorbidity   🦠 Major C\C   Excludes 1   Excludes 2   Includes   Use additional   Code first   Code also

● **M86.42 Chronic osteomyelitis with draining sinus, humerus**

     M86.421 Chronic osteomyelitis with draining sinus, right humerus 🦠

     M86.422 Chronic osteomyelitis with draining sinus, left humerus 🦠

     ■ M86.429 Chronic osteomyelitis with draining sinus, unspecified humerus 🦠

● **M86.43 Chronic osteomyelitis with draining sinus, forearm**

     M86.431 Chronic osteomyelitis with draining sinus, right forearm 🦠

     M86.432 Chronic osteomyelitis with draining sinus, left forearm 🦠

     ■ M86.439 Chronic osteomyelitis with draining sinus, unspecified forearm 🦠

● **M86.44 Chronic osteomyelitis with draining sinus, hand**

     M86.441 Chronic osteomyelitis with draining sinus, right hand 🦠

     M86.442 Chronic osteomyelitis with draining sinus, left hand 🦠

     ■ M86.449 Chronic osteomyelitis with draining sinus, unspecified hand 🦠

● **M86.45 Chronic osteomyelitis with draining sinus, femur**

     M86.451 Chronic osteomyelitis with draining sinus, right femur 🦠

     M86.452 Chronic osteomyelitis with draining sinus, left femur 🦠

     ■ M86.459 Chronic osteomyelitis with draining sinus, unspecified femur 🦠

● **M86.46 Chronic osteomyelitis with draining sinus, lower leg**

     M86.461 Chronic osteomyelitis with draining sinus, right lower leg 🦠

     M86.462 Chronic osteomyelitis with draining sinus, left lower leg 🦠

     ■ M86.469 Chronic osteomyelitis with draining sinus, unspecified lower leg 🦠

● **M86.47 Chronic osteomyelitis with draining sinus, ankle and foot**

     M86.471 Chronic osteomyelitis with draining sinus, right ankle and foot 🦠

     M86.472 Chronic osteomyelitis with draining sinus, left ankle and foot 🦠

     ■ M86.479 Chronic osteomyelitis with draining sinus, unspecified ankle and foot 🦠

     M86.48 Chronic osteomyelitis with draining sinus, other site 🦠

     M86.49 Chronic osteomyelitis with draining sinus, multiple sites 🦠

● **M86.5 Other chronic hematogenous osteomyelitis**

     ■ M86.50 Other chronic hematogenous osteomyelitis, unspecified site 🦠

● **M86.51 Other chronic hematogenous osteomyelitis, shoulder**

     M86.511 Other chronic hematogenous osteomyelitis, right shoulder 🦠

     M86.512 Other chronic hematogenous osteomyelitis, left shoulder 🦠

     ■ M86.519 Other chronic hematogenous osteomyelitis, unspecified shoulder 🦠

● **M86.52 Other chronic hematogenous osteomyelitis, humerus**

     M86.521 Other chronic hematogenous osteomyelitis, right humerus 🦠

     M86.522 Other chronic hematogenous osteomyelitis, left humerus 🦠

     ■ M86.529 Other chronic hematogenous osteomyelitis, unspecified humerus 🦠

● **M86.53 Other chronic hematogenous osteomyelitis, forearm**

     M86.531 Other chronic hematogenous osteomyelitis, right forearm 🦠

     M86.532 Other chronic hematogenous osteomyelitis, left forearm 🦠

     ■ M86.539 Other chronic hematogenous osteomyelitis, unspecified forearm 🦠

● **M86.54 Other chronic hematogenous osteomyelitis, hand**

     M86.541 Other chronic hematogenous osteomyelitis, right hand 🦠

     M86.542 Other chronic hematogenous osteomyelitis, left hand 🦠

     ■ M86.549 Other chronic hematogenous osteomyelitis, unspecified hand 🦠

● **M86.55 Other chronic hematogenous osteomyelitis, femur**

     M86.551 Other chronic hematogenous osteomyelitis, right femur 🦠

     M86.552 Other chronic hematogenous osteomyelitis, left femur 🦠

     ■ M86.559 Other chronic hematogenous osteomyelitis, unspecified femur 🦠

● **M86.56 Other chronic hematogenous osteomyelitis, lower leg**

     M86.561 Other chronic hematogenous osteomyelitis, right lower leg 🦠

     M86.562 Other chronic hematogenous osteomyelitis, left lower leg 🦠

     ■ M86.569 Other chronic hematogenous osteomyelitis, unspecified lower leg 🦠

● **M86.57 Other chronic hematogenous osteomyelitis, ankle and foot**

     M86.571 Other chronic hematogenous osteomyelitis, right ankle and foot 🦠

     M86.572 Other chronic hematogenous osteomyelitis, left ankle and foot 🦠

     ■ M86.579 Other chronic hematogenous osteomyelitis, unspecified ankle and foot 🦠

● Unacceptable First-Listed Diagnosis   ● Use Additional Character(s)   ■ Unspecified   **OGCR** Official Guidelines for Coding and Reporting

🦠 Complication\Comorbidity   🦠 Major C\C   Excludes 1   Excludes 2   Includes    Use additional   Code first   Code also

CHAPTER 13 (M00-M99)

M86.58   Other chronic hematogenous osteomyelitis, other site 🦴

M86.59   Other chronic hematogenous osteomyelitis, multiple sites 🦴

● M86.6   Other chronic osteomyelitis

◼ M86.60   Other chronic osteomyelitis, unspecified site 🦴

● M86.61   Other chronic osteomyelitis, shoulder

M86.611   Other chronic osteomyelitis, right shoulder 🦴

M86.612   Other chronic osteomyelitis, left shoulder 🦴

◼ M86.619   Other chronic osteomyelitis, unspecified shoulder 🦴

● M86.62   Other chronic osteomyelitis, upper arm

M86.621   Other chronic osteomyelitis, right upper arm 🦴

M86.622   Other chronic osteomyelitis, left upper arm 🦴

◼ M86.629   Other chronic osteomyelitis, unspecified upper arm 🦴

● M86.63   Other chronic osteomyelitis, forearm

M86.631   Other chronic osteomyelitis, right forearm 🦴

M86.632   Other chronic osteomyelitis, left forearm 🦴

◼ M86.639   Other chronic osteomyelitis, unspecified forearm 🦴

● M86.64   Other chronic osteomyelitis, hand

M86.641   Other chronic osteomyelitis, right hand 🦴

M86.642   Other chronic osteomyelitis, left hand 🦴

◼ M86.649   Other chronic osteomyelitis, unspecified hand 🦴

● M86.65   Other chronic osteomyelitis, thigh

M86.651   Other chronic osteomyelitis, right thigh 🦴

M86.652   Other chronic osteomyelitis, left thigh 🦴

◼ M86.659   Other chronic osteomyelitis, unspecified thigh 🦴

● M86.66   Other chronic osteomyelitis, lower leg

M86.661   Other chronic osteomyelitis, right lower leg 🦴

M86.662   Other chronic osteomyelitis, left lower leg 🦴

◼ M86.669   Other chronic osteomyelitis, unspecified lower leg 🦴

● M86.67   Other chronic osteomyelitis, ankle and foot

M86.671   Other chronic osteomyelitis, right ankle and foot 🦴

M86.672   Other chronic osteomyelitis, left ankle and foot 🦴

◼ M86.679   Other chronic osteomyelitis, unspecified ankle and foot 🦴

M86.68   Other chronic osteomyelitis, other site 🦴

M86.69   Other chronic osteomyelitis, multiple sites 🦴

● M86.8   Other osteomyelitis
Brodie's abscess

● M86.8x   Other osteomyelitis

M86.8x0   Other osteomyelitis, multiple sites 🦴

M86.8x1   Other osteomyelitis, shoulder 🦴

M86.8x2   Other osteomyelitis, upper arm 🦴

M86.8x3   Other osteomyelitis, forearm 🦴

M86.8x4   Other osteomyelitis, hand 🦴

M86.8x5   Other osteomyelitis, thigh 🦴

M86.8x6   Other osteomyelitis, lower leg 🦴

M86.8x7   Other osteomyelitis, ankle and foot 🦴

M86.8x8   Other osteomyelitis, other site 🦴

◼ M86.8x9   Other osteomyelitis, unspecified sites 🦴

◼ M86.9   Osteomyelitis, unspecified 🦴
Infection of bone NOS
Periostitis without osteomyelitis

● M87   Osteonecrosis

Includes   avascular necrosis of bone

Use additional code to identify major osseous defect, if applicable (M89.7-)

Excludes1   juvenile osteonecrosis (M91-M92)
osteochondropathies (M90-M93)

● M87.0   Idiopathic aseptic necrosis of bone

◼ M87.00   Idiopathic aseptic necrosis of unspecified bone 🦴

● M87.01   Idiopathic aseptic necrosis of shoulder
Idiopathic aseptic necrosis of clavicle and scapula

M87.011   Idiopathic aseptic necrosis of right shoulder 🦴

M87.012   Idiopathic aseptic necrosis of left shoulder 🦴

◼ M87.019   Idiopathic aseptic necrosis of unspecified shoulder 🦴

● M87.02   Idiopathic aseptic necrosis of humerus

M87.021   Idiopathic aseptic necrosis of right humerus 🦴

M87.022   Idiopathic aseptic necrosis of left humerus 🦴

◼ M87.029   Idiopathic aseptic necrosis of unspecified humerus 🦴

● M87.03   Idiopathic aseptic necrosis of radius, ulna and carpus

M87.031   Idiopathic aseptic necrosis of right radius 🦴

M87.032   Idiopathic aseptic necrosis of left radius 🦴

◼ M87.033   Idiopathic aseptic necrosis of unspecified radius 🦴

M87.034   Idiopathic aseptic necrosis of right ulna 🦴

M87.035   Idiopathic aseptic necrosis of left ulna 🦴

◼ M87.036   Idiopathic aseptic necrosis of unspecified ulna 🦴

M87.037   Idiopathic aseptic necrosis of right carpus 🦴

● Unacceptable First-Listed Diagnosis   ● Use Additional Character(s)   ◼ Unspecified   **OGCR** Official Guidelines for Coding and Reporting
🦴 Complication\Comorbidity   🦴 Major C\C   Excludes 1   Excludes 2   Includes   Use additional   Code first   Code also

M87.038 Idiopathic aseptic necrosis of left carpus 🦟

◼ M87.039 Idiopathic aseptic necrosis of unspecified carpus 🦟

● M87.04 Idiopathic aseptic necrosis of hand and fingers
    Idiopathic aseptic necrosis of metacarpals and phalanges of hands

M87.041 Idiopathic aseptic necrosis of right hand 🦟

M87.042 Idiopathic aseptic necrosis of left hand 🦟

◼ M87.043 Idiopathic aseptic necrosis of unspecified hand 🦟

M87.044 Idiopathic aseptic necrosis of right finger(s) 🦟

M87.045 Idiopathic aseptic necrosis of left finger(s) 🦟

◼ M87.046 Idiopathic aseptic necrosis of unspecified finger(s) 🦟

● M87.05 Idiopathic aseptic necrosis of pelvis and femur

M87.050 Idiopathic aseptic necrosis of pelvis 🦟

M87.051 Idiopathic aseptic necrosis of right femur 🦟

M87.052 Idiopathic aseptic necrosis of left femur 🦟

◼ M87.059 Idiopathic aseptic necrosis of unspecified femur 🦟
    Idiopathic aseptic necrosis of hip NOS

● M87.06 Idiopathic aseptic necrosis of tibia and fibula

M87.061 Idiopathic aseptic necrosis of right tibia 🦟

M87.062 Idiopathic aseptic necrosis of left tibia 🦟

◼ M87.063 Idiopathic aseptic necrosis of unspecified tibia 🦟

M87.064 Idiopathic aseptic necrosis of right fibula 🦟

M87.065 Idiopathic aseptic necrosis of left fibula 🦟

◼ M87.066 Idiopathic aseptic necrosis of unspecified fibula 🦟

● M87.07 Idiopathic aseptic necrosis of ankle, foot and toes
    Idiopathic aseptic necrosis of metatarsus, tarsus, and phalanges of toes

M87.071 Idiopathic aseptic necrosis of right ankle 🦟

M87.072 Idiopathic aseptic necrosis of left ankle 🦟

◼ M87.073 Idiopathic aseptic necrosis of unspecified ankle 🦟

M87.074 Idiopathic aseptic necrosis of right foot 🦟

M87.075 Idiopathic aseptic necrosis of left foot 🦟

◼ M87.076 Idiopathic aseptic necrosis of unspecified foot 🦟

M87.077 Idiopathic aseptic necrosis of right toe(s) 🦟

M87.078 Idiopathic aseptic necrosis of left toe(s) 🦟

◼ M87.079 Idiopathic aseptic necrosis of unspecified toe(s) 🦟

M87.08 Idiopathic aseptic necrosis of bone, other site 🦟

M87.09 Idiopathic aseptic necrosis of bone, multiple sites 🦟

● M87.1 Osteonecrosis due to drugs
    Code first (T36-T50) to identify drug

● ◼ M87.10 Osteonecrosis due to drugs, unspecified bone 🦟

● M87.11 Osteonecrosis due to drugs, shoulder

  ● M87.111 Osteonecrosis due to drugs, right shoulder 🦟

  ● M87.112 Osteonecrosis due to drugs, left shoulder 🦟

  ● ◼ M87.119 Osteonecrosis due to drugs, unspecified shoulder 🦟

● M87.12 Osteonecrosis due to drugs, humerus

  ● M87.121 Osteonecrosis due to drugs, right humerus 🦟

  ● M87.122 Osteonecrosis due to drugs, left humerus 🦟

  ● ◼ M87.129 Osteonecrosis due to drugs, unspecified humerus 🦟

● M87.13 Osteonecrosis due to drugs of radius, ulna and carpus

  ● M87.131 Osteonecrosis due to drugs of right radius 🦟

  ● M87.132 Osteonecrosis due to drugs of left radius 🦟

  ● ◼ M87.133 Osteonecrosis due to drugs of unspecified radius 🦟

  ● M87.134 Osteonecrosis due to drugs of right ulna 🦟

  ● M87.135 Osteonecrosis due to drugs of left ulna 🦟

  ● ◼ M87.136 Osteonecrosis due to drugs of unspecified ulna 🦟

  ● M87.137 Osteonecrosis due to drugs of right carpus 🦟

  ● M87.138 Osteonecrosis due to drugs of left carpus 🦟

  ● ◼ M87.139 Osteonecrosis due to drugs of unspecified carpus 🦟

● M87.14 Osteonecrosis due to drugs, hand and fingers

  ● M87.141 Osteonecrosis due to drugs, right hand 🦟

  ● M87.142 Osteonecrosis due to drugs, left hand 🦟

  ● ◼ M87.143 Osteonecrosis due to drugs, unspecified hand 🦟

  ● M87.144 Osteonecrosis due to drugs, right finger(s) 🦟

  ● M87.145 Osteonecrosis due to drugs, left finger(s) 🦟

  ● ◼ M87.146 Osteonecrosis due to drugs, unspecified finger(s) 🦟

● M87.15 Osteonecrosis due to drugs, pelvis and femur

● Unacceptable First-Listed Diagnosis   ● Use Additional Character(s)   ◼ Unspecified   **OGCR** Official Guidelines for Coding and Reporting
🦟 Complication\Comorbidity   🦟 Major C\C   Excludes 1   Excludes 2   Includes   Use additional   Code first   Code also

- ● M87.150 Osteonecrosis due to drugs, pelvis 🇶
- ● M87.151 Osteonecrosis due to drugs, right femur 🇶
- ● M87.152 Osteonecrosis due to drugs, left femur 🇶
- ● ▪ M87.159 Osteonecrosis due to drugs, unspecified femur 🇶
- ● M87.16 Osteonecrosis due to drugs, tibia and fibula
  - ● M87.161 Osteonecrosis due to drugs, right tibia 🇶
  - ● M87.162 Osteonecrosis due to drugs, left tibia 🇶
  - ● ▪ M87.163 Osteonecrosis due to drugs, unspecified tibia 🇶
  - ● M87.164 Osteonecrosis due to drugs, right fibula 🇶
  - ● M87.165 Osteonecrosis due to drugs, left fibula 🇶
  - ● ▪ M87.166 Osteonecrosis due to drugs, unspecified fibula 🇶
- ● M87.17 Osteonecrosis due to drugs, ankle, foot and toes
  - ● M87.171 Osteonecrosis due to drugs, right ankle 🇶
  - ● M87.172 Osteonecrosis due to drugs, left ankle 🇶
  - ● ▪ M87.173 Osteonecrosis due to drugs, unspecified ankle 🇶
  - ● M87.174 Osteonecrosis due to drugs, right foot 🇶
  - ● M87.175 Osteonecrosis due to drugs, left foot 🇶
  - ● ▪ M87.176 Osteonecrosis due to drugs, unspecified foot 🇶
  - ● M87.177 Osteonecrosis due to drugs, right toe(s) 🇶
  - ● M87.178 Osteonecrosis due to drugs, left toe(s) 🇶
  - ● ▪ M87.179 Osteonecrosis due to drugs, unspecified toe(s) 🇶
- ● M87.18 Osteonecrosis due to drugs, other site
  - ● M87.180 Osteonecrosis due to drugs, jaw 🇶
  - ● M87.188 Osteonecrosis due to drugs, other site 🇶
- ● M87.19 Osteonecrosis due to drugs, multiple sites 🇶
- ● M87.2 Osteonecrosis due to previous trauma
  - ▪ M87.20 Osteonecrosis due to previous trauma, unspecified bone 🇶
  - ● M87.21 Osteonecrosis due to previous trauma, shoulder
    - M87.211 Osteonecrosis due to previous trauma, right shoulder 🇶
    - M87.212 Osteonecrosis due to previous trauma, left shoulder 🇶
    - ▪ M87.219 Osteonecrosis due to previous trauma, unspecified shoulder 🇶
  - ● M87.22 Osteonecrosis due to previous trauma, humerus
    - M87.221 Osteonecrosis due to previous trauma, right humerus 🇶

- M87.222 Osteonecrosis due to previous trauma, left humerus 🇶
- ▪ M87.229 Osteonecrosis due to previous trauma, unspecified humerus 🇶
- ● M87.23 Osteonecrosis due to previous trauma of radius, ulna and carpus
  - M87.231 Osteonecrosis due to previous trauma of right radius 🇶
  - M87.232 Osteonecrosis due to previous trauma of left radius 🇶
  - ▪ M87.233 Osteonecrosis due to previous trauma of unspecified radius 🇶
  - M87.234 Osteonecrosis due to previous trauma of right ulna 🇶
  - M87.235 Osteonecrosis due to previous trauma of left ulna 🇶
  - ▪ M87.236 Osteonecrosis due to previous trauma of unspecified ulna 🇶
  - M87.237 Osteonecrosis due to previous trauma of right carpus 🇶
  - M87.238 Osteonecrosis due to previous trauma of left carpus 🇶
  - ▪ M87.239 Osteonecrosis due to previous trauma of unspecified carpus 🇶
- ● M87.24 Osteonecrosis due to previous trauma, hand and fingers
  - M87.241 Osteonecrosis due to previous trauma, right hand 🇶
  - M87.242 Osteonecrosis due to previous trauma, left hand 🇶
  - ▪ M87.243 Osteonecrosis due to previous trauma, unspecified hand 🇶
  - M87.244 Osteonecrosis due to previous trauma, right finger(s) 🇶
  - M87.245 Osteonecrosis due to previous trauma, left finger(s) 🇶
  - ▪ M87.246 Osteonecrosis due to previous trauma, unspecified finger(s) 🇶
- ● M87.25 Osteonecrosis due to previous trauma, pelvis and femur
  - M87.250 Osteonecrosis due to previous trauma, pelvis 🇶
  - M87.251 Osteonecrosis due to previous trauma, right femur 🇶
  - M87.252 Osteonecrosis due to previous trauma, left femur 🇶
  - ▪ M87.256 Osteonecrosis due to previous trauma, unspecified femur 🇶
- ● M87.26 Osteonecrosis due to previous trauma, tibia and fibula
  - M87.261 Osteonecrosis due to previous trauma, right tibia 🇶
  - M87.262 Osteonecrosis due to previous trauma, left tibia 🇶
  - ▪ M87.263 Osteonecrosis due to previous trauma, unspecified tibia 🇶
  - M87.264 Osteonecrosis due to previous trauma, right fibula 🇶
  - M87.265 Osteonecrosis due to previous trauma, left fibula 🇶
  - ▪ M87.266 Osteonecrosis due to previous trauma, unspecified fibula 🇶
- ● M87.27 Osteonecrosis due to previous trauma, ankle, foot and toes

● Unacceptable First-Listed Diagnosis   ● Use Additional Character(s)   ▪ Unspecified   **OGCR** Official Guidelines for Coding and Reporting

🇶 Complication\Comorbidity   🇶 Major C\C   Excludes 1   Excludes 2   Includes   Use additional   Code first   Code also

M87.271 Osteonecrosis due to previous trauma, right ankle 🦠

M87.272 Osteonecrosis due to previous trauma, left ankle 🦠

■ M87.273 Osteonecrosis due to previous trauma, unspecified ankle 🦠

M87.274 Osteonecrosis due to previous trauma, right foot 🦠

M87.275 Osteonecrosis due to previous trauma, left foot 🦠

■ M87.276 Osteonecrosis due to previous trauma, unspecified foot 🦠

M87.277 Osteonecrosis due to previous trauma, right toe(s) 🦠

M87.278 Osteonecrosis due to previous trauma, left toe(s) 🦠

■ M87.279 Osteonecrosis due to previous trauma, unspecified toe(s) 🦠

M87.28 Osteonecrosis due to previous trauma, other site 🦠

M87.29 Osteonecrosis due to previous trauma, multiple sites 🦠

● M87.3 Other secondary osteonecrosis

■ M87.30 Other secondary osteonecrosis, unspecified bone 🦠

● M87.31 Other secondary osteonecrosis, shoulder

M87.311 Other secondary osteonecrosis, right shoulder 🦠

M87.312 Other secondary osteonecrosis, left shoulder 🦠

■ M87.319 Other secondary osteonecrosis, unspecified shoulder 🦠

● M87.32 Other secondary osteonecrosis, humerus

M87.321 Other secondary osteonecrosis, right humerus 🦠

M87.322 Other secondary osteonecrosis, left humerus 🦠

■ M87.329 Other secondary osteonecrosis, unspecified humerus 🦠

● M87.33 Other secondary osteonecrosis of radius, ulna and carpus

M87.331 Other secondary osteonecrosis of right radius 🦠

M87.332 Other secondary osteonecrosis of left radius 🦠

■ M87.333 Other secondary osteonecrosis of unspecified radius 🦠

M87.334 Other secondary osteonecrosis of right ulna 🦠

M87.335 Other secondary osteonecrosis of left ulna 🦠

■ M87.336 Other secondary osteonecrosis of unspecified ulna 🦠

M87.337 Other secondary osteonecrosis of right carpus 🦠

M87.338 Other secondary osteonecrosis of left carpus 🦠

■ M87.339 Other secondary osteonecrosis of unspecified carpus 🦠

● M87.34 Other secondary osteonecrosis, hand and fingers

M87.341 Other secondary osteonecrosis, right hand 🦠

M87.342 Other secondary osteonecrosis, left hand 🦠

■ M87.343 Other secondary osteonecrosis, unspecified hand 🦠

M87.344 Other secondary osteonecrosis, right finger(s) 🦠

M87.345 Other secondary osteonecrosis, left finger(s) 🦠

■ M87.346 Other secondary osteonecrosis, unspecified finger(s) 🦠

● M87.35 Other secondary osteonecrosis, pelvis and femur

M87.350 Other secondary osteonecrosis, pelvis 🦠

M87.351 Other secondary osteonecrosis, right femur 🦠

M87.352 Other secondary osteonecrosis, left femur 🦠

■ M87.353 Other secondary osteonecrosis, unspecified femur 🦠

● M87.36 Other secondary osteonecrosis, tibia and fibula

M87.361 Other secondary osteonecrosis, right tibia 🦠

M87.362 Other secondary osteonecrosis, left tibia 🦠

■ M87.363 Other secondary osteonecrosis, unspecified tibia 🦠

M87.364 Other secondary osteonecrosis, right fibula 🦠

M87.365 Other secondary osteonecrosis, left fibula 🦠

■ M87.366 Other secondary osteonecrosis, unspecified fibula 🦠

● M87.37 Other secondary osteonecrosis, ankle and foot

M87.371 Other secondary osteonecrosis, right ankle 🦠

M87.372 Other secondary osteonecrosis, left ankle 🦠

■ M87.373 Other secondary osteonecrosis, unspecified ankle 🦠

M87.374 Other secondary osteonecrosis, right foot 🦠

M87.375 Other secondary osteonecrosis, left foot 🦠

■ M87.376 Other secondary osteonecrosis, unspecified foot 🦠

M87.377 Other secondary osteonecrosis, right toe(s) 🦠

M87.378 Other secondary osteonecrosis, left toe(s) 🦠

■ M87.379 Other secondary osteonecrosis, unspecified toe(s) 🦠

M87.38 Other secondary osteonecrosis, other site 🦠

M87.39 Other secondary osteonecrosis, multiple sites 🦠

● M87.8 Other osteonecrosis

■ M87.80 Other osteonecrosis, unspecified bone 🦠

● M87.81 Other osteonecrosis, shoulder

M87.811 Other osteonecrosis, right shoulder 🦠

● Unacceptable First-Listed Diagnosis   ● Use Additional Character(s)   ■ Unspecified   **OGCR** Official Guidelines for Coding and Reporting

🦠 Complication\Comorbidity   🦠 Major C\C   Excludes 1   Excludes 2   Includes   Use additional   Code first   Code also

1219

CHAPTER 13 (M00-M99)

M87.812   Other osteonecrosis, left shoulder 🗨

M87.819   Other osteonecrosis, unspecified shoulder 🗨

● M87.82   Other osteonecrosis, humerus

M87.821   Other osteonecrosis, right humerus 🗨

M87.822   Other osteonecrosis, left humerus 🗨

M87.829   Other osteonecrosis, unspecified humerus 🗨

● M87.83   Other osteonecrosis of radius, ulna and carpus

M87.831   Other osteonecrosis of right radius 🗨

M87.832   Other osteonecrosis of left radius 🗨

M87.833   Other osteonecrosis of unspecified radius 🗨

M87.834   Other osteonecrosis of right ulna 🗨

M87.835   Other osteonecrosis of left ulna 🗨

M87.836   Other osteonecrosis of unspecified ulna 🗨

M87.837   Other osteonecrosis of right carpus 🗨

M87.838   Other osteonecrosis of left carpus 🗨

M87.839   Other osteonecrosis of unspecified carpus 🗨

● M87.84   Other osteonecrosis, hand and fingers

M87.841   Other osteonecrosis, right hand 🗨

M87.842   Other osteonecrosis, left hand 🗨

M87.843   Other osteonecrosis, unspecified hand 🗨

M87.844   Other osteonecrosis, right finger(s) 🗨

M87.845   Other osteonecrosis, left finger(s) 🗨

M87.849   Other osteonecrosis, unspecified finger(s) 🗨

● M87.85   Other osteonecrosis, pelvis and femur

M87.850   Other osteonecrosis, pelvis 🗨

M87.851   Other osteonecrosis, right femur 🗨

M87.852   Other osteonecrosis, left femur 🗨

M87.859   Other osteonecrosis, unspecified femur 🗨

● M87.86   Other osteonecrosis, tibia and fibula

M87.861   Other osteonecrosis, right tibia 🗨

M87.862   Other osteonecrosis, left tibia 🗨

M87.863   Other osteonecrosis, unspecified tibia 🗨

M87.864   Other osteonecrosis, right fibula 🗨

M87.865   Other osteonecrosis, left fibula 🗨

M87.869   Other osteonecrosis, unspecified fibula 🗨

● M87.87   Other osteonecrosis, ankle, foot and toes

M87.871   Other osteonecrosis, right ankle 🗨

M87.872   Other osteonecrosis, left ankle 🗨

M87.873   Other osteonecrosis, unspecified ankle 🗨

M87.874   Other osteonecrosis, right foot 🗨

M87.875   Other osteonecrosis, left foot 🗨

M87.876   Other osteonecrosis, unspecified foot 🗨

M87.877   Other osteonecrosis, right toe(s) 🗨

M87.878   Other osteonecrosis, left toe(s) 🗨

M87.879   Other osteonecrosis, unspecified toe(s) 🗨

M87.88   Other osteonecrosis, other site 🗨

M87.89   Other osteonecrosis, multiple sites 🗨

M87.9   Osteonecrosis, unspecified 🗨
     Necrosis of bone NOS

● M88   Osteitis deformans [Paget's disease of bone]
     Chronic disorder that results in enlarged and deformed bones. The excessive breakdown and formation of bone tissue causes bones to weaken and results in bone pain, arthritis, deformities, and fractures.

> **Excludes1**   osteitis deformans in neoplastic disease (M90.6)

M88.0   Osteitis deformans of skull

M88.1   Osteitis deformans of vertebrae

● M88.8   Osteitis deformans of other bones

● M88.81   Osteitis deformans of shoulder

M88.811   Osteitis deformans of right shoulder

M88.812   Osteitis deformans of left shoulder

M88.819   Osteitis deformans of unspecified shoulder

● M88.82   Osteitis deformans of upper arm

M88.821   Osteitis deformans of right upper arm

M88.822   Osteitis deformans of left upper arm

M88.829   Osteitis deformans of unspecified upper arm

● M88.83   Osteitis deformans of forearm

M88.831   Osteitis deformans of right forearm

M88.832   Osteitis deformans of left forearm

M88.839   Osteitis deformans of unspecified forearm

● M88.84   Osteitis deformans of hand

M88.841   Osteitis deformans of right hand

M88.842   Osteitis deformans of left hand

M88.849   Osteitis deformans of unspecified hand

● M88.85   Osteitis deformans of thigh

M88.851   Osteitis deformans of right thigh

M88.852   Osteitis deformans of left thigh

M88.859   Osteitis deformans of unspecified thigh

● M88.86   Osteitis deformans of lower leg

M88.861   Osteitis deformans of right lower leg

M88.862   Osteitis deformans of left lower leg

M88.869   Osteitis deformans of unspecified lower leg

● Unacceptable First-Listed Diagnosis   ● Use Additional Character(s)   ■ Unspecified   **OGCR** Official Guidelines for Coding and Reporting

🗨 Complication\Comorbidity   🗨 Major C\C   Excludes 1   Excludes 2   Includes   Use additional   Code first   Code also

● M88.87   Osteitis deformans of ankle and foot

     M88.871   Osteitis deformans of right ankle and foot

     M88.872   Osteitis deformans of left ankle and foot

     ■ M88.879   Osteitis deformans of unspecified ankle and foot

M88.88   Osteitis deformans of other bones

     | Excludes2 | osteitis deformans of skull (M88.0) |
     | | *osteitis deformans of vertebrae (M88.1)* |

M88.89   Osteitis deformans of multiple sites

■ M88.9   Osteitis deformans of unspecified bone

● M89   Other disorders of bone

   ● M89.0   Algoneurodystrophy

     Shoulder-hand syndrome
     Sudeck's atrophy

     | Excludes1 | causalgia, lower limb (G57.7-) |
     | | causalgia, upper limb (G56.4-) |
     | | complex regional pain syndrome II, lower limb (G57.7-) |
     | | complex regional pain syndrome II, upper limb (G56.4-) |
     | | reflex sympathetic dystrophy (G90.5-) |

     ■ M89.00   Algoneurodystrophy, unspecified site

   ● M89.01   Algoneurodystrophy, shoulder

     M89.011   Algoneurodystrophy, right shoulder

     M89.012   Algoneurodystrophy, left shoulder

     ■ M89.019   Algoneurodystrophy, unspecified shoulder

   ● M89.02   Algoneurodystrophy, upper arm

     M89.021   Algoneurodystrophy, right upper arm

     M89.022   Algoneurodystrophy, left upper arm

     ■ M89.029   Algoneurodystrophy, unspecified upper arm

   ● M89.03   Algoneurodystrophy, forearm

     M89.031   Algoneurodystrophy, right forearm

     M89.032   Algoneurodystrophy, left forearm

     ■ M89.039   Algoneurodystrophy, unspecified forearm

   ● M89.04   Algoneurodystrophy, hand

     M89.041   Algoneurodystrophy, right hand

     M89.042   Algoneurodystrophy, left hand

     ■ M89.049   Algoneurodystrophy, unspecified hand

   ● M89.05   Algoneurodystrophy, thigh

     M89.051   Algoneurodystrophy, right thigh

     M89.052   Algoneurodystrophy, left thigh

     ■ M89.059   Algoneurodystrophy, unspecified thigh

   ● M89.06   Algoneurodystrophy, lower leg

     M89.061   Algoneurodystrophy, right lower leg

     M89.062   Algoneurodystrophy, left lower leg

     ■ M89.069   Algoneurodystrophy, unspecified lower leg

   ● M89.07   Algoneurodystrophy, ankle and foot

     M89.071   Algoneurodystrophy, right ankle and foot

     M89.072   Algoneurodystrophy, left ankle and foot

     ■ M89.079   Algoneurodystrophy, unspecified ankle and foot

   M89.08   Algoneurodystrophy, other site

   M89.09   Algoneurodystrophy, multiple sites

   ● M89.1   Physeal arrest

     Arrest of growth plate
     Epiphyseal arrest
     Growth plate arrest

   ● M89.12   Physeal arrest, humerus

     M89.121   Complete physeal arrest, right proximal humerus

     M89.122   Complete physeal arrest, left proximal humerus

     M89.123   Partial physeal arrest, right proximal humerus

     M89.124   Partial physeal arrest, left proximal humerus

     M89.125   Complete physeal arrest, right distal humerus

     M89.126   Complete physeal arrest, left distal humerus

     M89.127   Partial physeal arrest, right distal humerus

     M89.128   Partial physeal arrest, left distal humerus

     ■ M89.129   Physeal arrest, humerus, unspecified

   ● M89.13   Physeal arrest, forearm

     M89.131   Complete physeal arrest, right distal radius

     M89.132   Complete physeal arrest, left distal radius

     M89.133   Partial physeal arrest, right distal radius

     M89.134   Partial physeal arrest, left distal radius

     M89.138   Other physeal arrest of forearm

     ■ M89.139   Physeal arrest, forearm, unspecified

   ● M89.15   Physeal arrest, femur

     M89.151   Complete physeal arrest, right proximal femur

     M89.152   Complete physeal arrest, left proximal femur

     M89.153   Partial physeal arrest, right proximal femur

     M89.154   Partial physeal arrest, left proximal femur

     M89.155   Complete physeal arrest, right distal femur

     M89.156   Complete physeal arrest, left distal femur

     M89.157   Partial physeal arrest, right distal femur

     M89.158   Partial physeal arrest, left distal femur

     ■ M89.159   Physeal arrest, femur, unspecified

● Unacceptable First-Listed Diagnosis   ● Use Additional Character(s)   ■ Unspecified   **OGCR** Official Guidelines for Coding and Reporting

🗞 Complication\Comorbidity   🗞 Major C\C | Excludes 1 | | Excludes 2 | | Includes | Use additional   Code first   Code also

1221

● M89.16 Physeal arrest, lower leg
    M89.160 Complete physeal arrest, right proximal tibia
    M89.161 Complete physeal arrest, left proximal tibia
    M89.162 Partial physeal arrest, right proximal tibia
    M89.163 Partial physeal arrest, left proximal tibia
    M89.164 Complete physeal arrest, right distal tibia
    M89.165 Complete physeal arrest, left distal tibia
    M89.166 Partial physeal arrest, right distal tibia
    M89.167 Partial physeal arrest, left distal tibia
    M89.168 Other physeal arrest of lower leg
    ■ M89.169 Physeal arrest, lower leg, unspecified
    M89.18 Physeal arrest, other site
● M89.2 Other disorders of bone development and growth
    ■ M89.20 Other disorders of bone development and growth, unspecified site
   ● M89.21 Other disorders of bone development and growth, shoulder
    M89.211 Other disorders of bone development and growth, right shoulder
    M89.212 Other disorders of bone development and growth, left shoulder
    ■ M89.219 Other disorders of bone development and growth, unspecified shoulder
   ● M89.22 Other disorders of bone development and growth, humerus
    M89.221 Other disorders of bone development and growth, right humerus
    M89.222 Other disorders of bone development and growth, left humerus
    ■ M89.229 Other disorders of bone development and growth, unspecified humerus
   ● M89.23 Other disorders of bone development and growth, ulna and radius
    M89.231 Other disorders of bone development and growth, right ulna
    M89.232 Other disorders of bone development and growth, left ulna
    M89.233 Other disorders of bone development and growth, right radius
    M89.234 Other disorders of bone development and growth, left radius
    ■ M89.239 Other disorders of bone development and growth, unspecified ulna and radius

● M89.24 Other disorders of bone development and growth, hand
    M89.241 Other disorders of bone development and growth, right hand
    M89.242 Other disorders of bone development and growth, left hand
    ■ M89.249 Other disorders of bone development and growth, unspecified hand
● M89.25 Other disorders of bone development and growth, femur
    M89.251 Other disorders of bone development and growth, right femur
    M89.252 Other disorders of bone development and growth, left femur
    ■ M89.259 Other disorders of bone development and growth, unspecified femur
● M89.26 Other disorders of bone development and growth, tibia and fibula
    M89.261 Other disorders of bone development and growth, right tibia
    M89.262 Other disorders of bone development and growth, left tibia
    M89.263 Other disorders of bone development and growth, right fibula
    M89.264 Other disorders of bone development and growth, left fibula
    ■ M89.269 Other disorders of bone development and growth, unspecified lower leg
● M89.27 Other disorders of bone development and growth, ankle and foot
    M89.271 Other disorders of bone development and growth, right ankle and foot
    M89.272 Other disorders of bone development and growth, left ankle and foot
    ■ M89.279 Other disorders of bone development and growth, unspecified ankle and foot
    M89.28 Other disorders of bone development and growth, other site
    M89.29 Other disorders of bone development and growth, multiple sites
● M89.3 Hypertrophy of bone
    ■ M89.30 Hypertrophy of bone, unspecified site
   ● M89.31 Hypertrophy of bone, shoulder
    M89.311 Hypertrophy of bone, right shoulder
    M89.312 Hypertrophy of bone, left shoulder
    ■ M89.319 Hypertrophy of bone, unspecified shoulder
   ● M89.32 Hypertrophy of bone, humerus

M89.321 Hypertrophy of bone, right humerus

M89.322 Hypertrophy of bone, left humerus

◼M89.329 Hypertrophy of bone, unspecified humerus

●M89.33 Hypertrophy of bone, ulna and radius

M89.331 Hypertrophy of bone, right ulna

M89.332 Hypertrophy of bone, left ulna

M89.333 Hypertrophy of bone, right radius

M89.334 Hypertrophy of bone, left radius

◼M89.339 Hypertrophy of bone, unspecified ulna and radius

●M89.34 Hypertrophy of bone, hand

M89.341 Hypertrophy of bone, right hand

M89.342 Hypertrophy of bone, left hand

◼M89.349 Hypertrophy of bone, unspecified hand

●M89.35 Hypertrophy of bone, femur

M89.351 Hypertrophy of bone, right femur

M89.352 Hypertrophy of bone, left femur

◼M89.359 Hypertrophy of bone, unspecified femur

●M89.36 Hypertrophy of bone, tibia and fibula

M89.361 Hypertrophy of bone, right tibia

M89.362 Hypertrophy of bone, left tibia

M89.363 Hypertrophy of bone, right fibula

M89.364 Hypertrophy of bone, left fibula

◼M89.369 Hypertrophy of bone, unspecified tibia and fibula

●M89.37 Hypertrophy of bone, ankle and foot

M89.371 Hypertrophy of bone, right ankle and foot

M89.372 Hypertrophy of bone, left ankle and foot

◼M89.379 Hypertrophy of bone, unspecified ankle and foot

M89.38 Hypertrophy of bone, other site

M89.39 Hypertrophy of bone, multiple sites

●M89.4 Other hypertrophic osteoarthropathy
    Marie-Bamberger disease
    Pachydermoperiostosis

◼M89.40 Other hypertrophic osteoarthropathy, unspecified site

●M89.41 Other hypertrophic osteoarthropathy, shoulder

M89.411 Other hypertrophic osteoarthropathy, right shoulder

M89.412 Other hypertrophic osteoarthropathy, left shoulder

◼M89.419 Other hypertrophic osteoarthropathy, unspecified shoulder

●M89.42 Other hypertrophic osteoarthropathy, upper arm

M89.421 Other hypertrophic osteoarthropathy, right upper arm

M89.422 Other hypertrophic osteoarthropathy, left upper arm

◼M89.429 Other hypertrophic osteoarthropathy, unspecified upper arm

●M89.43 Other hypertrophic osteoarthropathy, forearm

M89.431 Other hypertrophic osteoarthropathy, right forearm

M89.432 Other hypertrophic osteoarthropathy, left forearm

◼M89.439 Other hypertrophic osteoarthropathy, unspecified forearm

●M89.44 Other hypertrophic osteoarthropathy, hand

M89.441 Other hypertrophic osteoarthropathy, right hand

M89.442 Other hypertrophic osteoarthropathy, left hand

◼M89.449 Other hypertrophic osteoarthropathy, unspecified hand

●M89.45 Other hypertrophic osteoarthropathy, thigh

M89.451 Other hypertrophic osteoarthropathy, right thigh

M89.452 Other hypertrophic osteoarthropathy, left thigh

◼M89.459 Other hypertrophic osteoarthropathy, unspecified thigh

●M89.46 Other hypertrophic osteoarthropathy, lower leg

M89.461 Other hypertrophic osteoarthropathy, right lower leg

M89.462 Other hypertrophic osteoarthropathy, left lower leg

◼M89.469 Other hypertrophic osteoarthropathy, unspecified lower leg

●M89.47 Other hypertrophic osteoarthropathy, ankle and foot

M89.471 Other hypertrophic osteoarthropathy, right ankle and foot

M89.472 Other hypertrophic osteoarthropathy, left ankle and foot

◼M89.479 Other hypertrophic osteoarthropathy, unspecified ankle and foot

M89.48 Other hypertrophic osteoarthropathy, other site

M89.49 Other hypertrophic osteoarthropathy, multiple sites

●M89.5 Osteolysis

    Use additional code to identify major osseous defect, if applicable (M89.7-)

    Excludes2   periprosthetic osteolysis of internal prosthetic joint (T84.05-)

◼M89.50 Osteolysis, unspecified site

●M89.51 Osteolysis, shoulder

M89.511 Osteolysis, right shoulder

M89.512 Osteolysis, left shoulder

◼M89.519 Osteolysis, unspecified shoulder

●M89.52 Osteolysis, upper arm

M89.521 Osteolysis, right upper arm

M89.522 Osteolysis, left upper arm

◼M89.529 Osteolysis, unspecified upper arm

● Unacceptable First-Listed Diagnosis   ● Use Additional Character(s)   ◼ Unspecified   **OGCR** Official Guidelines for Coding and Reporting
🗇 Complication\Comorbidity   🗇 Major C\C   Excludes 1   Excludes 2   Includes   Use additional   Code first   Code also
1223

● M89.53 Osteolysis, forearm

    M89.531 Osteolysis, right forearm

    M89.532 Osteolysis, left forearm

    ■ M89.539 Osteolysis, unspecified forearm

● M89.54 Osteolysis, hand

    M89.541 Osteolysis, right hand

    M89.542 Osteolysis, left hand

    ■ M89.549 Osteolysis, unspecified hand

● M89.55 Osteolysis, thigh

    M89.551 Osteolysis, right thigh

    M89.552 Osteolysis, left thigh

    ■ M89.559 Osteolysis, unspecified thigh

● M89.56 Osteolysis, lower leg

    M89.561 Osteolysis, right lower leg

    M89.562 Osteolysis, left lower leg

    ■ M89.569 Osteolysis, unspecified lower leg

● M89.57 Osteolysis, ankle and foot

    M89.571 Osteolysis, right ankle and foot

    M89.572 Osteolysis, left ankle and foot

    ■ M89.579 Osteolysis, unspecified ankle and foot

    M89.58 Osteolysis, other site site

    M89.59 Osteolysis, multiple sites

● M89.6 Osteopathy after poliomyelitis

    Use additional code (B91) to identify previous poliomyelitis

    Excludes1   postpolio syndrome (G14)

■ M89.60 Osteopathy after poliomyelitis, unspecified site

● M89.61 Osteopathy after poliomyelitis, shoulder

    M89.611 Osteopathy after poliomyelitis, right shoulder

    M89.612 Osteopathy after poliomyelitis, left shoulder

    ■ M89.619 Osteopathy after poliomyelitis, unspecified shoulder

● M89.62 Osteopathy after poliomyelitis, upper arm

    M89.621 Osteopathy after poliomyelitis, right upper arm

    M89.622 Osteopathy after poliomyelitis, left upper arm

    ■ M89.629 Osteopathy after poliomyelitis, unspecified upper arm

● M89.63 Osteopathy after poliomyelitis, forearm

    M89.631 Osteopathy after poliomyelitis, right forearm

    M89.632 Osteopathy after poliomyelitis, left forearm

    ■ M89.639 Osteopathy after poliomyelitis, unspecified forearm

● M89.64 Osteopathy after poliomyelitis, hand

    M89.641 Osteopathy after poliomyelitis, right hand

    M89.642 Osteopathy after poliomyelitis, left hand

    ■ M89.649 Osteopathy after poliomyelitis, unspecified hand

● M89.65 Osteopathy after poliomyelitis, thigh

    M89.651 Osteopathy after poliomyelitis, right thigh

    M89.652 Osteopathy after poliomyelitis, left thigh

    ■ M89.659 Osteopathy after poliomyelitis, unspecified thigh

● M89.66 Osteopathy after poliomyelitis, lower leg

    M89.661 Osteopathy after poliomyelitis, right lower leg

    M89.662 Osteopathy after poliomyelitis, left lower leg

    ■ M89.669 Osteopathy after poliomyelitis, unspecified lower leg

● M89.67 Osteopathy after poliomyelitis, ankle and foot

    M89.671 Osteopathy after poliomyelitis, right ankle and foot

    M89.672 Osteopathy after poliomyelitis, left ankle and foot

    ■ M89.679 Osteopathy after poliomyelitis, unspecified ankle and foot

    M89.68 Osteopathy after poliomyelitis, other site

    M89.69 Osteopathy after poliomyelitis, multiple sites

● M89.7 Major osseous defect

    Code first underlying disease, if known, such as:
    aseptic necrosis of bone (M87.-)
    malignant neoplasm of bone (C40.-)
    osteolysis (M89.5)
    osteomyelitis (M86.-)
    osteonecrosis (M87.-)
    osteoporosis (M80.-, M81.-)
    periprosthetic osteolysis (T84.05-)

■ M89.70 Major osseous defect, unspecified site

● M89.71 Major osseous defect, shoulder region

    Major osseous defect clavicle or scapula

    M89.711 Major osseous defect, right shoulder region

    M89.712 Major osseous defect, left shoulder region

    ■ M89.719 Major osseous defect, unspecified shoulder region

● M89.72 Major osseous defect, humerous

    M89.721 Major osseous defect, right humerous

    M89.722 Major osseous defect, left humerous

    ■ M89.729 Major osseous defect, unspecified humerous

● M89.73 Major osseous defect, forearm

    Major osseous defect of radius and ulna

    M89.731 Major osseous defect, right forearm

    M89.732 Major osseous defect, left forearm

    ■ M89.739 Major osseous defect, unspecified forearm

● M89.74 Major osseous defect, hand

    Major osseous defect of carpus, fingers, metacarpus

    M89.741 Major osseous defect, right hand

    M89.742 Major osseous defect, left hand

    ■ M89.749 Major osseous defect, unspecified hand

● Unacceptable First-Listed Diagnosis   ● Use Additional Character(s)   ■ Unspecified   **OGCR** Official Guidelines for Coding and Reporting

🅒 Complication\Comorbidity   🅒 Major C\C   Excludes 1   Excludes 2   Includes   Use additional   Code first   Code also

● M89.75　Major osseous defect, pelvic region and thigh
　　　Major osseous defect of femur and pelvis

　　　M89.751　Major osseous defect, right pelvic region and thigh

　　　M89.752　Major osseous defect, left pelvic region and thigh

　　　🔲M89.759　Major osseous defect, unspecified pelvic region and thigh

● M89.76　Major osseous defect, lower leg
　　　Major osseous defect of fibula and tibia

　　　M89.761　Major osseous defect, right lower leg

　　　M89.762　Major osseous defect, left lower leg

　　　🔲M89.769　Major osseous defect, unspecified lower leg

● M89.77　Major osseous defect, ankle and foot
　　　Major osseous defect of metatarsus, tarsus, toes

　　　M89.771　Major osseous defect, right ankle and foot

　　　M89.772　Major osseous defect, left ankle and foot

　　　🔲M89.779　Major osseous defect, unspecified ankle and foot

　　M89.78　Major osseous defect, other site

　　M89.79　Major osseous defect, multiple sites

● M89.8　Other specified disorders of bone
　　　Infantile cortical hyperostoses
　　　Post-traumatic subperiosteal ossification

● M89.8x　Other specified disorders of bone

　　　M89.8x0　Other specified disorders of bone, multiple sites

　　　M89.8x1　Other specified disorders of bone, shoulder

　　　M89.8x2　Other specified disorders of bone, upper arm

　　　M89.8x3　Other specified disorders of bone, forearm

　　　M89.8x4　Other specified disorders of bone, hand

　　　M89.8x5　Other specified disorders of bone, thigh

　　　M89.8x6　Other specified disorders of bone, lower leg

　　　M89.8x7　Other specified disorders of bone, ankle and foot

　　　M89.8x8　Other specified disorders of bone, other site

　　　🔲M89.8x9　Other specified disorders of bone, unspecified site

🔲M89.9　Disorder of bone, unspecified

● M90　Osteopathies in diseases classified elsewhere

　　Excludes1　osteochondritis, osteomyelitis, and osteopathy (in):
　　　cryptococcosis (B45.3)
　　　diabetes mellitus (E08-E13 with 4th character .61-)
　　　gonococcal (A54.43)
　　　neurogenic syphilis (A52.11)
　　　renal osteodystrophy (N25.0)
　　　salmonellosis (A02.24)
　　　secondary syphilis (A51.46)
　　　syphilis (late) (A52.77)

● M90.5　Osteonecrosis in diseases classified elsewhere
　　　Code first underlying disease, such as:
　　　caisson disease (T70.3)
　　　hemoglobinopathy (D50-D64)

● 🔲M90.50　Osteonecrosis in diseases classified elsewhere, unspecified site

● M90.51　Osteonecrosis in diseases classified elsewhere, shoulder

　　　● M90.511　Osteonecrosis in diseases classified elsewhere, right shoulder

　　　● M90.512　Osteonecrosis in diseases classified elsewhere, left shoulder

　　　● 🔲M90.519　Osteonecrosis in diseases classified elsewhere, unspecified shoulder

● M90.52　Osteonecrosis in diseases classified elsewhere, upper arm

　　　● M90.521　Osteonecrosis in diseases classified elsewhere, right upper arm

　　　● M90.522　Osteonecrosis in diseases classified elsewhere, left upper arm

　　　● 🔲M90.529　Osteonecrosis in diseases classified elsewhere, unspecified upper arm

● M90.53　Osteonecrosis in diseases classified elsewhere, forearm

　　　● M90.531　Osteonecrosis in diseases classified elsewhere, right forearm

　　　● M90.532　Osteonecrosis in diseases classified elsewhere, left forearm

　　　● 🔲M90.539　Osteonecrosis in diseases classified elsewhere, unspecified forearm

● M90.54　Osteonecrosis in diseases classified elsewhere, hand

　　　● M90.541　Osteonecrosis in diseases classified elsewhere, right hand

　　　● M90.542　Osteonecrosis in diseases classified elsewhere, left hand

　　　● 🔲M90.549　Osteonecrosis in diseases classified elsewhere, unspecified hand

● M90.55　Osteonecrosis in diseases classified elsewhere, thigh

　　　● M90.551　Osteonecrosis in diseases classified elsewhere, right thigh

　　　● M90.552　Osteonecrosis in diseases classified elsewhere, left thigh

　　　● 🔲M90.559　Osteonecrosis in diseases classified elsewhere, unspecified thigh

● M90.56　Osteonecrosis in diseases classified elsewhere, lower leg

　　　● M90.561　Osteonecrosis in diseases classified elsewhere, right lower leg

　　　● M90.562　Osteonecrosis in diseases classified elsewhere, left lower leg

　　　● 🔲M90.569　Osteonecrosis in diseases classified elsewhere, unspecified lower leg

● Unacceptable First-Listed Diagnosis　　● Use Additional Character(s)　　🔲 Unspecified　　OGCR Official Guidelines for Coding and Reporting
🅒 Complication\Comorbidity　🅜 Major C\C　Excludes 1　Excludes 2　Includes　Use additional　Code first　Code also

1225

CHAPTER 13 (M00-M99)

- M90.57 Osteonecrosis in diseases classified elsewhere, ankle and foot
  - M90.571 Osteonecrosis in diseases classified elsewhere, right ankle and foot
  - M90.572 Osteonecrosis in diseases classified elsewhere, left ankle and foot
  - M90.579 Osteonecrosis in diseases classified elsewhere, unspecified ankle and foot
- M90.58 Osteonecrosis in diseases classified elsewhere, other site
- M90.59 Osteonecrosis in diseases classified elsewhere, multiple sites

- M90.6 Osteitis deformans in neoplastic diseases
  Osteitis deformans in malignant neoplasm of bone

  Code first the neoplasm (C40.-, C41.-)

  Excludes1   osteitis deformans [Paget's disease of bone] (M88.-)

  - M90.60 Osteitis deformans in neoplastic diseases, unspecified site
  - M90.61 Osteitis deformans in neoplastic diseases, shoulder
    - M90.611 Osteitis deformans in neoplastic diseases, right shoulder
    - M90.612 Osteitis deformans in neoplastic diseases, left shoulder
    - M90.619 Osteitis deformans in neoplastic diseases, unspecified shoulder
  - M90.62 Osteitis deformans in neoplastic diseases, upper arm
    - M90.621 Osteitis deformans in neoplastic diseases, right upper arm
    - M90.622 Osteitis deformans in neoplastic diseases, left upper arm
    - M90.629 Osteitis deformans in neoplastic diseases, unspecified upper arm
  - M90.63 Osteitis deformans in neoplastic diseases, forearm
    - M90.631 Osteitis deformans in neoplastic diseases, right forearm
    - M90.632 Osteitis deformans in neoplastic diseases, left forearm
    - M90.639 Osteitis deformans in neoplastic diseases, unspecified forearm
  - M90.64 Osteitis deformans in neoplastic diseases, hand
    - M90.641 Osteitis deformans in neoplastic diseases, right hand
    - M90.642 Osteitis deformans in neoplastic diseases, left hand
    - M90.649 Osteitis deformans in neoplastic diseases, unspecified hand
  - M90.65 Osteitis deformans in neoplastic diseases, thigh
    - M90.651 Osteitis deformans in neoplastic diseases, right thigh
    - M90.652 Osteitis deformans in neoplastic diseases, left thigh
    - M90.659 Osteitis deformans in neoplastic diseases, unspecified thigh

- M90.66 Osteitis deformans in neoplastic diseases, lower leg
  - M90.661 Osteitis deformans in neoplastic diseases, right lower leg
  - M90.662 Osteitis deformans in neoplastic diseases, left lower leg
  - M90.669 Osteitis deformans in neoplastic diseases, unspecified lower leg
- M90.67 Osteitis deformans in neoplastic diseases, ankle and foot
  - M90.671 Osteitis deformans in neoplastic diseases, right ankle and foot
  - M90.672 Osteitis deformans in neoplastic diseases, left ankle and foot
  - M90.679 Osteitis deformans in neoplastic diseases, unspecified ankle and foot
- M90.68 Osteitis deformans in neoplastic diseases, other site
- M90.69 Osteitis deformans in neoplastic diseases, multiple sites

- M90.8 Osteopathy in diseases classified elsewhere

  Code first underlying disease, such as:
  rickets (E55.0)
  vitamin-D-resistant rickets (E83.3)

  - M90.80 Osteopathy in diseases classified elsewhere, unspecified site
  - M90.81 Osteopathy in diseases classified elsewhere, shoulder
    - M90.811 Osteopathy in diseases classified elsewhere, right shoulder
    - M90.812 Osteopathy in diseases classified elsewhere, left shoulder
    - M90.819 Osteopathy in diseases classified elsewhere, unspecified shoulder
  - M90.82 Osteopathy in diseases classified elsewhere, upper arm
    - M90.821 Osteopathy in diseases classified elsewhere, right upper arm
    - M90.822 Osteopathy in diseases classified elsewhere, left upper arm
    - M90.829 Osteopathy in diseases classified elsewhere, unspecified upper arm
  - M90.83 Osteopathy in diseases classified elsewhere, forearm
    - M90.831 Osteopathy in diseases classified elsewhere, right forearm
    - M90.832 Osteopathy in diseases classified elsewhere, left forearm
    - M90.839 Osteopathy in diseases classified elsewhere, unspecified forearm
  - M90.84 Osteopathy in diseases classified elsewhere, hand
    - M90.841 Osteopathy in diseases classified elsewhere, right hand
    - M90.842 Osteopathy in diseases classified elsewhere, left hand
    - M90.849 Osteopathy in diseases classified elsewhere, unspecified hand
  - M90.85 Osteopathy in diseases classified elsewhere, thigh
    - M90.851 Osteopathy in diseases classified elsewhere, right thigh
    - M90.852 Osteopathy in diseases classified elsewhere, left thigh

CHAPTER 13 (M00-M99)

1226

● Unacceptable First-Listed Diagnosis   ● Use Additional Character(s)   ■ Unspecified   **OGCR** Official Guidelines for Coding and Reporting
🅒 Complication\Comorbidity   🅜 Major C\C   Excludes 1   Excludes 2   Includes   Use additional   Code first   Code also

- ● ▨ M90.859 Osteopathy in diseases classified elsewhere, unspecified thigh
- ● M90.86 Osteopathy in diseases classified elsewhere, lower leg
  - ● M90.861 Osteopathy in diseases classified elsewhere, right lower leg
  - ● M90.862 Osteopathy in diseases classified elsewhere, left lower leg
  - ● ▨ M90.869 Osteopathy in diseases classified elsewhere, unspecified lower leg
- ● M90.87 Osteopathy in diseases classified elsewhere, ankle and foot
  - ● M90.871 Osteopathy in diseases classified elsewhere, right ankle and foot
  - ● M90.872 Osteopathy in diseases classified elsewhere, left ankle and foot
  - ● ▨ M90.879 Osteopathy in diseases classified elsewhere, unspecified ankle and foot
- ● M90.88 Osteopathy in diseases classified elsewhere, other site
- ● M90.89 Osteopathy in diseases classified elsewhere, multiple sites

CHONDROPATHIES (M91-M94)

| Excludes1 | postprocedural chondropathies (M96.-) |

- ● M91 Juvenile osteochondrosis of hip and pelvis

| Excludes1 | slipped upper femoral epiphysis (nontraumatic) (M93.0) |

- M91.0 Juvenile osteochondrosis of pelvis
  Osteochondrosis (juvenile) of:
  acetabulum
  iliac crest [Buchanan]
  ischiopubic synchondrosis [van Neck]
  symphysis pubis [Pierson]
- ● M91.1 Juvenile osteochondrosis of head of femur [Legg-Calvé-Perthes]
  - ▨ M91.10 Juvenile osteochondrosis of head of femur [Legg-Calvé-Perthes], unspecified leg
  - M91.11 Juvenile osteochondrosis of head of femur [Legg-Calvé-Perthes], right leg
  - M91.12 Juvenile osteochondrosis of head of femur [Legg-Calvé-Perthes], left leg
- ● M91.2 Coxa plana
  Hip deformity due to previous juvenile osteochondrosis
  - ▨ M91.20 Coxa plana, unspecified hip
  - M91.21 Coxa plana, right hip
  - M91.22 Coxa plana, left hip
- ● M91.3 Pseudocoxalgia
  - ▨ M91.30 Pseudocoxalgia, unspecified hip
  - M91.31 Pseudocoxalgia, right hip
  - M91.32 Pseudocoxalgia, left hip
- ● M91.4 Coxa magna
  - ▨ M91.40 Coxa magna, unspecified hip
  - M91.41 Coxa magna, right hip
  - M91.42 Coxa magna, left hip
- ● M91.8 Other juvenile osteochondrosis of hip and pelvis
  Juvenile osteochondrosis after reduction of congenital dislocation of hip
  - ▨ M91.80 Other juvenile osteochondrosis of hip and pelvis, unspecified leg

- M91.81 Other juvenile osteochondrosis of hip and pelvis, right leg
- M91.82 Other juvenile osteochondrosis of hip and pelvis, left leg
- ● M91.9 Juvenile osteochondrosis of hip and pelvis, unspecified
  - ▨ M91.90 Juvenile osteochondrosis of hip and pelvis, unspecified, unspecified leg
  - ▨ M91.91 Juvenile osteochondrosis of hip and pelvis, unspecified, right leg
  - ▨ M91.92 Juvenile osteochondrosis of hip and pelvis, unspecified, left leg
- ● M92 Other juvenile osteochondrosis
  - ● M92.0 Juvenile osteochondrosis of humerus
    Osteochondrosis (juvenile) of capitulum of humerus [Panner]
    Osteochondrosis (juvenile) of head of humerus [Haas]
    - ▨ M92.00 Juvenile osteochondrosis of humerus, unspecified arm
    - M92.01 Juvenile osteochondrosis of humerus, right arm
    - M92.02 Juvenile osteochondrosis of humerus, left arm
  - ● M92.1 Juvenile osteochondrosis of radius and ulna
    Osteochondrosis (juvenile) of lower ulna [Burns]
    Osteochondrosis (juvenile) of radial head [Brailsford]
    - ▨ M92.10 Juvenile osteochondrosis of radius and ulna, unspecified arm
    - M92.11 Juvenile osteochondrosis of radius and ulna, right arm
    - M92.12 Juvenile osteochondrosis of radius and ulna, left arm
  - ● M92.2 Juvenile osteochondrosis, hand
    - ● M92.20 Unspecified juvenile osteochondrosis, hand
      - ▨ M92.201 Unspecified juvenile osteochondrosis, right hand
      - ▨ M92.202 Unspecified juvenile osteochondrosis, left hand
      - ▨ M92.209 Unspecified juvenile osteochondrosis, unspecified hand
    - ● M92.21 Osteochondrosis (juvenile) of carpal lunate [Kienböck]
      - M92.211 Osteochondrosis (juvenile) of carpal lunate [Kienböck], right hand
      - M92.212 Osteochondrosis (juvenile) of carpal lunate [Kienböck], left hand
      - ▨ M92.219 Osteochondrosis (juvenile) of carpal lunate [Kienböck], unspecified hand
    - ● M92.22 Osteochondrosis (juvenile) of metacarpal heads [Mauclaire]
      - M92.221 Osteochondrosis (juvenile) of metacarpal heads [Mauclaire], right hand
      - M92.222 Osteochondrosis (juvenile) of metacarpal heads [Mauclaire], left hand
      - ▨ M92.229 Osteochondrosis (juvenile) of metacarpal heads [Mauclaire], unspecified hand

● Unacceptable First-Listed Diagnosis   ● Use Additional Character(s)   ▨ Unspecified   **OGCR** Official Guidelines for Coding and Reporting

🅒 Complication\Comorbidity   🅜 Major C\C

1227

CHAPTER 13 (M00-M99)

● M92.29 Other juvenile osteochondrosis, hand

  M92.291 Other juvenile osteochondrosis, right hand

  M92.292 Other juvenile osteochondrosis, left hand

  ■ M92.299 Other juvenile osteochondrosis, unspecified hand

● M92.3 Other juvenile osteochondrosis, upper limb

  ■ M92.30 Other juvenile osteochondrosis, unspecified upper limb

  M92.31 Other juvenile osteochondrosis, right upper limb

  M92.32 Other juvenile osteochondrosis, left upper limb

● M92.4 Juvenile osteochondrosis of patella

  Osteochondrosis (juvenile) of primary patellar center [Köhler]

  Osteochondrosis (juvenile) of secondary patellar center [Sinding Larsen]

  ■ M92.40 Juvenile osteochondrosis of patella, unspecified knee

  M92.41 Juvenile osteochondrosis of patella, right knee

  M92.42 Juvenile osteochondrosis of patella, left knee

● M92.5 Juvenile osteochondrosis of tibia and fibula

  Osteochondrosis (juvenile) of proximal tibia [Blount]

  Osteochondrosis (juvenile) of tibial tubercle [Osgood-Schlatter]

  Tibia vara

  ■ M92.50 Juvenile osteochondrosis of tibia and fibula, unspecified leg

  M92.51 Juvenile osteochondrosis of tibia and fibula, right leg

  M92.52 Juvenile osteochondrosis of tibia and fibula, left leg

● M92.6 Juvenile osteochondrosis of tarsus

  Osteochondrosis (juvenile) of calcaneum [Sever]

  Osteochondrosis (juvenile) of os tibiale externum [Haglund]

  Osteochondrosis (juvenile) of talus [Diaz]

  Osteochondrosis (juvenile) of tarsal navicular [Köhler]

  ■ M92.60 Juvenile osteochondrosis of tarsus, unspecified ankle

  M92.61 Juvenile osteochondrosis of tarsus, right ankle

  M92.62 Juvenile osteochondrosis of tarsus, left ankle

● M92.7 Juvenile osteochondrosis of metatarsus

  Osteochondrosis (juvenile) of fifth metatarsus [Iselin]

  Osteochondrosis (juvenile) of second metatarsus [Freiberg]

  ■ M92.70 Juvenile osteochondrosis of metatarsus, unspecified foot

  M92.71 Juvenile osteochondrosis of metatarsus, right foot

  M92.72 Juvenile osteochondrosis of metatarsus, left foot

M92.8 Other specified juvenile osteochondrosis

  Calcaneal apophysitis

■ M92.9 Juvenile osteochondrosis, unspecified

  Juvenile apophysitis NOS

  Juvenile epiphysitis NOS

  Juvenile osteochondritis NOS

  Juvenile osteochondrosis NOS

● M93 Other osteochondropathies

  Excludes2   osteochondrosis of spine (M42.-)

● M93.0 Slipped upper femoral epiphysis (nontraumatic)

  Use additional code for associated chondrolysis (M94.3)

  ● M93.00 Unspecified slipped upper femoral epiphysis (nontraumatic)

    ■ M93.001 Unspecified slipped upper femoral epiphysis (nontraumatic), right hip

    ■ M93.002 Unspecified slipped upper femoral epiphysis (nontraumatic), left hip

    ■ M93.003 Unspecified slipped upper femoral epiphysis (nontraumatic), unspecified hip

  ● M93.01 Acute slipped upper femoral epiphysis (nontraumatic)

    M93.011 Acute slipped upper femoral epiphysis (nontraumatic), right hip

    M93.012 Acute slipped upper femoral epiphysis (nontraumatic), left hip

    ■ M93.013 Acute slipped upper femoral epiphysis (nontraumatic), unspecified hip

  ● M93.02 Chronic slipped upper femoral epiphysis (nontraumatic)

    M93.021 Chronic slipped upper femoral epiphysis (nontraumatic), right hip

    M93.022 Chronic slipped upper femoral epiphysis (nontraumatic), left hip

    ■ M93.023 Chronic slipped upper femoral epiphysis (nontraumatic), unspecified hip

  ● M93.03 Acute on chronic slipped upper femoral epiphysis (nontraumatic)

    M93.031 Acute on chronic slipped upper femoral epiphysis (nontraumatic), right hip

    M93.032 Acute on chronic slipped upper femoral epiphysis (nontraumatic), left hip

    ■ M93.033 Acute on chronic slipped upper femoral epiphysis (nontraumatic), unspecified hip

M93.1 Kienböck's disease of adults

  Adult osteochondrosis of carpal lunates

● M93.2 Osteochondritis dissecans

  ■ M93.20 Osteochondritis dissecans of unspecified site

  ● M93.21 Osteochondritis dissecans of shoulder

    M93.211 Osteochondritis dissecans, right shoulder

    M93.212 Osteochondritis dissecans, left shoulder

CHAPTER 13 (M00-M99)

1228

● Unacceptable First-Listed Diagnosis   ● Use Additional Character(s)   ■ Unspecified   OGCR Official Guidelines for Coding and Reporting
🅒 Complication\Comorbidity   🅒 Major C\C   Excludes 1   Excludes 2   Includes   Use additional   Code first   Code also

◼ M93.219 Osteochondritis dissecans, unspecified shoulder

● M93.22 Osteochondritis dissecans of elbow

     M93.221 Osteochondritis dissecans, right elbow

     M93.222 Osteochondritis dissecans, left elbow

     ◼ M93.229 Osteochondritis dissecans, unspecified elbow

● M93.23 Osteochondritis dissecans of wrist

     M93.231 Osteochondritis dissecans, right wrist

     M93.232 Osteochondritis dissecans, left wrist

     ◼ M93.239 Osteochondritis dissecans, unspecified wrist

● M93.24 Osteochondritis dissecans of joints of hand

     M93.241 Osteochondritis dissecans, joints of right hand

     M93.242 Osteochondritis dissecans, joints of left hand

     ◼ M93.249 Osteochondritis dissecans, joints of unspecified hand

● M93.25 Osteochondritis dissecans of hip

     M93.251 Osteochondritis dissecans, right hip

     M93.252 Osteochondritis dissecans, left hip

     ◼ M93.259 Osteochondritis dissecans, unspecified hip

● M93.26 Osteochondritis dissecans knee

     M93.261 Osteochondritis dissecans, right knee

     M93.262 Osteochondritis dissecans, left knee

     ◼ M93.269 Osteochondritis dissecans, unspecified knee

● M93.27 Osteochondritis dissecans of ankle and joints of foot

     M93.271 Osteochondritis dissecans, right ankle and joints of right foot

     M93.272 Osteochondritis dissecans, left ankle and joints of left foot

     ◼ M93.279 Osteochondritis dissecans, unspecified ankle and joints of foot

M93.28 Osteochondritis dissecans other site

M93.29 Osteochondritis dissecans multiple sites

● M93.8 Other specified osteochondropathies

     ◼ M93.80 Other specified osteochondropathies of unspecified site

     ● M93.81 Other specified osteochondropathies of shoulder

         M93.811 Other specified osteochondropathies, right shoulder

         M93.812 Other specified osteochondropathies, left shoulder

         ◼ M93.819 Other specified osteochondropathies, unspecified shoulder

● M93.82 Other specified osteochondropathies of upper arm

     M93.821 Other specified osteochondropathies, right upper arm

     M93.822 Other specified osteochondropathies, left upper arm

     ◼ M93.829 Other specified osteochondropathies, unspecified upper arm

● M93.83 Other specified osteochondropathies of forearm

     M93.831 Other specified osteochondropathies, right forearm

     M93.832 Other specified osteochondropathies, left forearm

     ◼ M93.839 Other specified osteochondropathies, unspecified forearm

● M93.84 Other specified osteochondropathies of hand

     M93.841 Other specified osteochondropathies, right hand

     M93.842 Other specified osteochondropathies, left hand

     ◼ M93.849 Other specified osteochondropathies, unspecified hand

● M93.85 Other specified osteochondropathies of thigh

     M93.851 Other specified osteochondropathies, right thigh

     M93.852 Other specified osteochondropathies, left thigh

     ◼ M93.859 Other specified osteochondropathies, unspecified thigh

● M93.86 Other specified osteochondropathies lower leg

     M93.861 Other specified osteochondropathies, right lower leg

     M93.862 Other specified osteochondropathies, left lower leg

     ◼ M93.869 Other specified osteochondropathies, unspecified lower leg

● M93.87 Other specified osteochondropathies of ankle and foot

     M93.871 Other specified osteochondropathies, right ankle and foot

     M93.872 Other specified osteochondropathies, left ankle and foot

     ◼ M93.879 Other specified osteochondropathies, unspecified ankle and foot

M93.88 Other specified osteochondropathies other

M93.89 Other specified osteochondropathies multiple sites

● Unacceptable First-Listed Diagnosis   ● Use Additional Character(s)   ◼ Unspecified   **OGCR** Official Guidelines for Coding and Reporting

🗘 Complication\Comorbidity   🗘 Major C\C   [Excludes 1]   [Excludes 2]   Includes   Use additional   Code first   Code also

CHAPTER 13 (M00-M99)

1229

● M93.9 Osteochondropathy, unspecified
    Apophysitis NOS
    Epiphysitis NOS
    Osteochondritis NOS
    Osteochondrosis NOS

◼ M93.90 Osteochondropathy, unspecified of unspecified site

● M93.91 Osteochondropathy, unspecified of shoulder

    ◼ M93.911 Osteochondropathy, unspecified, right shoulder

    ◼ M93.912 Osteochondropathy, unspecified, left shoulder

    ◼ M93.919 Osteochondropathy, unspecified, unspecified shoulder

● M93.92 Osteochondropathy, unspecified of upper arm

    ◼ M93.921 Osteochondropathy, unspecified, right upper arm

    ◼ M93.922 Osteochondropathy, unspecified, left upper arm

    ◼ M93.929 Osteochondropathy, unspecified, unspecified upper arm

● M93.93 Osteochondropathy, unspecified of forearm

    ◼ M93.931 Osteochondropathy, unspecified, right forearm

    ◼ M93.932 Osteochondropathy, unspecified, left forearm

    ◼ M93.939 Osteochondropathy, unspecified, unspecified forearm

● M93.94 Osteochondropathy, unspecified of hand

    ◼ M93.941 Osteochondropathy, unspecified, right hand

    ◼ M93.942 Osteochondropathy, unspecified, left hand

    ◼ M93.949 Osteochondropathy, unspecified, unspecified hand

● M93.95 Osteochondropathy, unspecified of thigh

    ◼ M93.951 Osteochondropathy, unspecified, right thigh

    ◼ M93.952 Osteochondropathy, unspecified, left thigh

    ◼ M93.959 Osteochondropathy, unspecified, unspecified thigh

● M93.96 Osteochondropathy, unspecified lower leg

    ◼ M93.961 Osteochondropathy, unspecified, right lower leg

    ◼ M93.962 Osteochondropathy, unspecified, left lower leg

    ◼ M93.969 Osteochondropathy, unspecified, unspecified lower leg

● M93.97 Osteochondropathy, unspecified of ankle and foot

    ◼ M93.971 Osteochondropathy, unspecified, right ankle and foot

    ◼ M93.972 Osteochondropathy, unspecified, left ankle and foot

    ◼ M93.979 Osteochondropathy, unspecified, unspecified ankle and foot

◼ M93.98 Osteochondropathy, unspecified other

◼ M93.99 Osteochondropathy, unspecified multiple sites

● M94 Other disorders of cartilage

M94.0 Chondrocostal junction syndrome [Tietze]
    Costochondritis

M94.1 Relapsing polychondritis

● M94.2 Chondromalacia

    Excludes1   chondromalacia patellae (M22.4)

    ◼ M94.20 Chondromalacia, unspecified site

    ● M94.21 Chondromalacia, shoulder

        M94.211 Chondromalacia, right shoulder

        M94.212 Chondromalacia, left shoulder

        ◼ M94.219 Chondromalacia, unspecified shoulder

    ● M94.22 Chondromalacia, elbow

        M94.221 Chondromalacia, right elbow

        M94.222 Chondromalacia, left elbow

        ◼ M94.229 Chondromalacia, unspecified elbow

    ● M94.23 Chondromalacia, wrist

        M94.231 Chondromalacia, right wrist

        M94.232 Chondromalacia, left wrist

        ◼ M94.239 Chondromalacia, unspecified wrist

    ● M94.24 Chondromalacia, joints of hand

        M94.241 Chondromalacia, joints of right hand

        M94.242 Chondromalacia, joints of left hand

        ◼ M94.249 Chondromalacia, joints of unspecified hand

    ● M94.25 Chondromalacia, hip

        M94.251 Chondromalacia, right hip

        M94.252 Chondromalacia, left hip

        ◼ M94.259 Chondromalacia, unspecified hip

    ● M94.26 Chondromalacia, knee

        M94.261 Chondromalacia, right knee

        M94.262 Chondromalacia, left knee

        ◼ M94.269 Chondromalacia, unspecified knee

    ● M94.27 Chondromalacia, ankle and joints of foot

        M94.271 Chondromalacia, right ankle and joints of right foot

        M94.272 Chondromalacia, left ankle and joints of left foot

        ◼ M94.279 Chondromalacia, unspecified ankle and joints of foot

    M94.28 Chondromalacia, other site

    M94.29 Chondromalacia, multiple sites

● M94.3 Chondrolysis

    Code first any associated slipped upper femoral epiphysis (nontraumatic) (M93.0-)

    ● M94.35 Chondrolysis, hip

        M94.351 Chondrolysis, right hip

        M94.352 Chondrolysis, left hip

        ◼ M94.359 Chondrolysis, unspecified hip

● M94.8 Other specified disorders of cartilage

    ● M94.8x Other specified disorders of cartilage

        M94.8x0 Other specified disorders of cartilage, multiple sites

        M94.8x1 Other specified disorders of cartilage, shoulder

● Unacceptable First-Listed Diagnosis   ● Use Additional Character(s)   ◼ Unspecified   **OGCR** Official Guidelines for Coding and Reporting
🝢 Complication\Comorbidity   🝢 Major C\C   Excludes 1   Excludes 2   Includes   Use additional   Code first   Code also

M94.8x2 Other specified disorders of cartilage, upper arm

M94.8x3 Other specified disorders of cartilage, forearm

M94.8x4 Other specified disorders of cartilage, hand

M94.8x5 Other specified disorders of cartilage, thigh

M94.8x6 Other specified disorders of cartilage, lower leg

M94.8x7 Other specified disorders of cartilage, ankle and foot

M94.8x8 Other specified disorders of cartilage, other site

■M94.8x9 Other specified disorders of cartilage, unspecified sites

■M94.9 Disorder of cartilage, unspecified

OTHER DISORDERS OF THE MUSCULOSKELETAL SYSTEM AND CONNECTIVE TISSUE (M95)

● M95 Other acquired deformities of musculoskeletal system and connective tissue

> **Excludes2**   acquired absence of limbs and organs (Z89-Z90)
> acquired deformities of limbs (M20-M21)
> congenital malformations and deformations of the musculoskeletal system (Q65-Q79)
> deforming dorsopathies (M40-M43)
> dentofacial anomalies [including malocclusion] (M26.-)
> postprocedural musculoskeletal disorders (M96.-)

M95.0 Acquired deformity of nose

> **Excludes2**   deviated nasal septum (J34.2)

● M95.1 Cauliflower ear

> **Excludes2**   other acquired deformities of ear (H61.1)

■M95.10 Cauliflower ear, unspecified ear

M95.11 Cauliflower ear, right ear

M95.12 Cauliflower ear, left ear

M95.2 Other acquired deformity of head

M95.3 Acquired deformity of neck

M95.4 Acquired deformity of chest and rib

M95.5 Acquired deformity of pelvis

> **Excludes1**   maternal care for known or suspected disproportion (O33.-)

M95.8 Other specified acquired deformities of musculoskeletal system

■M95.9 Acquired deformity of musculoskeletal system, unspecified

---

INTRAOPERATIVE AND POSTPROCEDURAL COMPLICATIONS AND DISORDERS OF MUSCULOSKELETAL SYSTEM, NOT ELSEWHERE CLASSIFIED (M96)

● M96 Intraoperative and postprocedural complications and disorders of musculoskeletal system, not elsewhere classified

> **Excludes2**   arthropathy following intestinal bypass (M02.0-)
> complications of internal orthopedic prosthetic devices, implants and grafts (T84.-)
> disorders associated with osteoporosis (M80)
> presence of functional implants and other devices (Z96-Z97)

M96.0 Pseudarthrosis after fusion or arthrodesis

M96.1 Postlaminectomy syndrome, not elsewhere classified

M96.2 Postradiation kyphosis

M96.3 Postlaminectomy kyphosis

M96.4 Postsurgical lordosis

M96.5 Postradiation scoliosis

● M96.6 Fracture of bone following insertion of orthopedic implant, joint prosthesis, or bone plate

> Intraoperative fracture of bone during insertion of orthopedic implant, joint prosthesis, or bone plate

> **Excludes2**   complication of internal orthopedic devices, implants or grafts (T84.-)

● M96.62 Fracture of humerus following insertion of orthopedic implant, joint prosthesis, or bone plate

M96.621 Fracture of humerus following insertion of orthopedic implant, joint prosthesis, or bone plate, right arm 🏷

M96.622 Fracture of humerus following insertion of orthopedic implant, joint prosthesis, or bone plate, left arm 🏷

■M96.629 Fracture of humerus following insertion of orthopedic implant, joint prosthesis, or bone plate, unspecified arm 🏷

● M96.63 Fracture of radius or ulna following insertion of orthopedic implant, joint prosthesis, or bone plate

M96.631 Fracture of radius or ulna following insertion of orthopedic implant, joint prosthesis, or bone plate, right arm 🏷

M96.632 Fracture of radius or ulna following insertion of orthopedic implant, joint prosthesis, or bone plate, left arm 🏷

■M96.639 Fracture of radius or ulna following insertion of orthopedic implant, joint prosthesis, or bone plate, unspecified arm 🏷

M96.65 Fracture of pelvis following insertion of orthopedic implant, joint prosthesis, or bone plate 🏷

● Unacceptable First-Listed Diagnosis   ● Use Additional Character(s)   ■ Unspecified   **OGCR** Official Guidelines for Coding and Reporting

🏷 Complication\Comorbidity   🏷 Major C\C   Excludes 1   Excludes 2   Includes   Use additional   Code first   Code also

1231

CHAPTER 13 (M00-M99)

● M96.66 Fracture of femur following insertion of orthopedic implant, joint prosthesis, or bone plate

     M96.661 Fracture of femur following insertion of orthopedic implant, joint prosthesis, or bone plate, right leg 🍋

     M96.662 Fracture of femur following insertion of orthopedic implant, joint prosthesis, or bone plate, left leg 🍋

     ■ M96.669 Fracture of femur following insertion of orthopedic implant, joint prosthesis, or bone plate, unspecified leg 🍋

● M96.67 Fracture of tibia or fibula following insertion of orthopedic implant, joint prosthesis, or bone plate

     M96.671 Fracture of tibia or fibula following insertion of orthopedic implant, joint prosthesis, or bone plate, right leg 🍋

     M96.672 Fracture of tibia or fibula following insertion of orthopedic implant, joint prosthesis, or bone plate, left leg 🍋

     ■ M96.679 Fracture of tibia or fibula following insertion of orthopedic implant, joint prosthesis, or bone plate, unspecified leg 🍋

     M96.69 Fracture of other bone following insertion of orthopedic implant, joint prosthesis, or bone plate 🍋

● M96.8 Other intraoperative and postprocedural complications and disorders of musculoskeletal system, not elsewhere classified

     ● M96.81 Intraoperative hemorrhage and hematoma of a musculoskeletal structure complicating a procedure

         | Excludes1 | intraoperative hemorrhage and hematoma of a musculoskeletal structure due to accidental puncture and laceration during a procedure (M98.82-)

         M96.810 Intraoperative hemorrhage and hematoma of a musculoskeletal structure complicating a musculoskeletal system procedure 🍋

         M96.811 Intraoperative hemorrhage and hematoma of a musculoskeletal structure complicating other procedure 🍋

     ● M96.82 Accidental puncture and laceration of a musculoskeletal structure during a procedure

         M96.820 Accidental puncture and laceration of a musculoskeletal structure during a musculoskeletal system procedure 🍋

         M96.821 Accidental puncture and laceration of a musculoskeletal structure during other procedure 🍋

● M96.83 Postprocedural hemorrhage and hematoma of a musculoskeletal structure following a procedure

     M96.830 Postprocedural hemorrhage and hematoma of a musculoskeletal structure following a musculoskeletal system procedure 🍋

     M96.831 Postprocedural hemorrhage and hematoma of a musculoskeletal structure following other procedure 🍋

     M96.89 Other intraoperative and postprocedural complications and disorders of the musculoskeletal system 🍋

         Instability of joint secondary to removal of joint prosthesis

         Use additional code, if applicable, to further specify disorder

BIOMECHANICAL LESIONS, NOT ELSEWHERE CLASSIFIED (M99)

● M99 Biomechanical lesions, not elsewhere classified

     Note: This category should not be used if the condition can be classified elsewhere.

     ● M99.0 Segmental and somatic dysfunction

         M99.00 Segmental and somatic dysfunction of head region

         M99.01 Segmental and somatic dysfunction of cervical region

         M99.02 Segmental and somatic dysfunction of thoracic region

         M99.03 Segmental and somatic dysfunction of lumbar region

         M99.04 Segmental and somatic dysfunction of sacral region

         M99.05 Segmental and somatic dysfunction of pelvic region

         M99.06 Segmental and somatic dysfunction of lower extremity

         M99.07 Segmental and somatic dysfunction of upper extremity

         M99.08 Segmental and somatic dysfunction of rib cage

         M99.09 Segmental and somatic dysfunction of abdomen and other regions

     ● M99.1 Subluxation complex (vertebral)

         M99.10 Subluxation complex (vertebral) of head region 🍋

         M99.11 Subluxation complex (vertebral) of cervical region 🍋

         M99.12 Subluxation complex (vertebral) of thoracic region

         M99.13 Subluxation complex (vertebral) of lumbar region

         M99.14 Subluxation complex (vertebral) of sacral region

         M99.15 Subluxation complex (vertebral) of pelvic region

         M99.16 Subluxation complex (vertebral) of lower extremity

         M99.17 Subluxation complex (vertebral) of upper extremity

M99.18 Subluxation complex (vertebral) of rib cage

M99.19 Subluxation complex (vertebral) of abdomen and other regions

● M99.2 Subluxation stenosis of neural canal

M99.20 Subluxation stenosis of neural canal of head region

M99.21 Subluxation stenosis of neural canal of cervical region

M99.22 Subluxation stenosis of neural canal of thoracic region

M99.23 Subluxation stenosis of neural canal of lumbar region

M99.24 Subluxation stenosis of neural canal of sacral region

M99.25 Subluxation stenosis of neural canal of pelvic region

M99.26 Subluxation stenosis of neural canal of lower extremity

M99.27 Subluxation stenosis of neural canal of upper extremity

M99.28 Subluxation stenosis of neural canal of rib cage

M99.29 Subluxation stenosis of neural canal of abdomen and other regions

● M99.3 Osseous stenosis of neural canal

M99.30 Osseous stenosis of neural canal of head region

M99.31 Osseous stenosis of neural canal of cervical region

M99.32 Osseous stenosis of neural canal of thoracic region

M99.33 Osseous stenosis of neural canal of lumbar region

M99.34 Osseous stenosis of neural canal of sacral region

M99.35 Osseous stenosis of neural canal of pelvic region

M99.36 Osseous stenosis of neural canal of lower extremity

M99.37 Osseous stenosis of neural canal of upper extremity

M99.38 Osseous stenosis of neural canal of rib cage

M99.39 Osseous stenosis of neural canal of abdomen and other regions

● M99.4 Connective tissue stenosis of neural canal

M99.40 Connective tissue stenosis of neural canal of head region

M99.41 Connective tissue stenosis of neural canal of cervical region

M99.42 Connective tissue stenosis of neural canal of thoracic region

M99.43 Connective tissue stenosis of neural canal of lumbar region

M99.44 Connective tissue stenosis of neural canal of sacral region

M99.45 Connective tissue stenosis of neural canal of pelvic region

M99.46 Connective tissue stenosis of neural canal of lower extremity

M99.47 Connective tissue stenosis of neural canal of upper extremity

M99.48 Connective tissue stenosis of neural canal of rib cage

M99.49 Connective tissue stenosis of neural canal of abdomen and other regions

● M99.5 Intervertebral disc stenosis of neural canal

M99.50 Intervertebral disc stenosis of neural canal of head region

M99.51 Intervertebral disc stenosis of neural canal of cervical region

M99.52 Intervertebral disc stenosis of neural canal of thoracic region

M99.53 Intervertebral disc stenosis of neural canal of lumbar region

M99.54 Intervertebral disc stenosis of neural canal of sacral region

M99.55 Intervertebral disc stenosis of neural canal of pelvic region

M99.56 Intervertebral disc stenosis of neural canal of lower extremity

M99.57 Intervertebral disc stenosis of neural canal of upper extremity

M99.58 Intervertebral disc stenosis of neural canal of rib cage

M99.59 Intervertebral disc stenosis of neural canal of abdomen and other regions

● M99.6 Osseous and subluxation stenosis of intervertebral foramina

M99.60 Osseous and subluxation stenosis of intervertebral foramina of head region

M99.61 Osseous and subluxation stenosis of intervertebral foramina of cervical region

M99.62 Osseous and subluxation stenosis of intervertebral foramina of thoracic region

M99.63 Osseous and subluxation stenosis of intervertebral foramina of lumbar region

M99.64 Osseous and subluxation stenosis of intervertebral foramina of sacral region

M99.65 Osseous and subluxation stenosis of intervertebral foramina of pelvic region

M99.66 Osseous and subluxation stenosis of intervertebral foramina of lower extremity

M99.67 Osseous and subluxation stenosis of intervertebral foramina of upper extremity

M99.68 Osseous and subluxation stenosis of intervertebral foramina of rib cage

M99.69 Osseous and subluxation stenosis of intervertebral foramina of abdomen and other regions

● M99.7 Connective tissue and disc stenosis of intervertebral foramina

M99.70 Connective tissue and disc stenosis of intervertebral foramina of head region

M99.71 Connective tissue and disc stenosis of intervertebral foramina of cervical region

M99.72 Connective tissue and disc stenosis of intervertebral foramina of thoracic region

M99.73 Connective tissue and disc stenosis of intervertebral foramina of lumbar region

M99.74 Connective tissue and disc stenosis of intervertebral foramina of sacral region

---

● Unacceptable First-Listed Diagnosis   ● Use Additional Character(s)   ▨ Unspecified   **OGCR** Official Guidelines for Coding and Reporting

 Complication\Comorbidity   Major C\C   Excludes 1   Excludes 2    Includes   Use additional   Code first   Code also

M99.75   Connective tissue and disc stenosis of intervertebral foramina of pelvic region

M99.76   Connective tissue and disc stenosis of intervertebral foramina of lower extremity

M99.77   Connective tissue and disc stenosis of intervertebral foramina of upper extremity

M99.78   Connective tissue and disc stenosis of intervertebral foramina of rib cage

M99.79   Connective tissue and disc stenosis of intervertebral foramina of abdomen and other regions

● M99.8 Other biomechanical lesions

M99.80   Other biomechanical lesions of head region

M99.81   Other biomechanical lesions of cervical region

M99.82   Other biomechanical lesions of thoracic region

M99.83   Other biomechanical lesions of lumbar region

M99.84   Other biomechanical lesions of sacral region

M99.85   Other biomechanical lesions of pelvic region

M99.86   Other biomechanical lesions of lower extremity

M99.87   Other biomechanical lesions of upper extremity

M99.88   Other biomechanical lesions of rib cage

M99.89   Other biomechanical lesions of abdomen and other regions

■ M99.9 Biomechanical lesion, unspecified

Item 14–1 Nephritis (inflammation) or **nephropathy** (disease) **with lesion of proliferative glomerulonephritis** results from a streptococcal infection.

Nephritis (inflammation) or **nephropathy** (disease) **with lesion of membranous glomerulonephritis** is characterized by deposits along the epithelial side of the basement membrane.

Nephritis (inflammation) or **nephropathy** (disease) **with lesion of membranoproliferative glomerulonephritis** is characterized by alterations in the basement membranes of the kidney and the glomerular cells.

Nephritis (inflammation) or **nephropathy** (disease) **with lesion of rapidly progressive glomerulonephritis** is characterized by rapid and progressive decline in renal function.

Nephritis (inflammation) or **nephropathy** (disease) **with lesion of renal cortical necrosis** is characterized by death of the cortical tissues.

Nephritis (inflammation) or **nephropathy** (disease) **with lesion of renal medullary necrosis** is characterized by death of the tissues that collect urine.

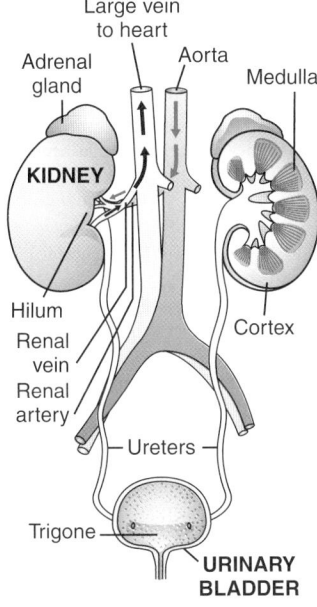

Figure 14-1   Kidneys within the urinary system.

Item 14–2 Glomerulonephritis is nephritis accompanied by inflammation of the glomeruli of the kidney, resulting in the degeneration of the glomeruli and the nephrons.

Acute glomerulonephritis primarily affects children and young adults and is usually a result of a streptococcal infection.

Proliferative glomerulonephritis is the acute form of the disease resulting from a streptococcal infection.

Rapidly progressive glomerulonephritis, also known as **crescentic** or **malignant glomerulonephritis**, is the acute form of the disease, which leads quickly to rapid and progressive decline in renal function.

CHAPTER 14

DISEASES OF THE GENITOURINARY SYSTEM (N00-N99)

| Excludes2 | certain conditions originating in the perinatal period (P04-P96)
certain infectious and parasitic diseases (A00-B99)
complications of pregnancy, childbirth and the puerperium (O00-O99)
congenital malformations, deformations and chromosomal abnormalities (Q00-Q99)
endocrine, nutritional and metabolic diseases (E00-E90)
injury, poisoning and certain other consequences of external causes (S00-T98)
neoplasms (C00-D48)
symptoms, signs and abnormal clinical and laboratory findings, not elsewhere classified (R00-R94) |

This chapter contains the following blocks:

N00-N08	Glomerular diseases
N10-N16	Renal tubulo-interstitial diseases
N17-N19	Acute kidney failure and chronic kidney disease
N20-N23	Urolithiasis
N25-N29	Other disorders of kidney and ureter
N30-N39	Other diseases of the urinary system
N40-N51	Diseases of male genital organs
N60-N65	Disorders of breast
N70-N77	Inflammatory diseases of female pelvic organs
N80-N98	Noninflammatory disorders of female genital tract
N99	Intraoperative and postprocedural complications and disorders of genitourinary system, not elsewhere classified

GLOMERULAR DISEASES (N00-N08)

Code also any associated kidney failure (N17-N19)

| Excludes1 | hypertensive chronic kidney disease (I12.-) |

● N00 **Acute nephritic syndrome**

| Includes | acute glomerular disease
acute glomerulonephritis
acute nephritis |

| Excludes1 | acute tubulo-interstitial nephritis (N10)
nephritic syndrome NOS (N05.-) |

N00.0 **Acute nephritic syndrome with minor glomerular abnormality** 🗲
  Acute nephritic syndrome with minimal change lesion

N00.1 **Acute nephritic syndrome with focal and segmental glomerular lesions** 🗲
  Acute nephritic syndrome with focal and segmental hyalinosis
  Acute nephritic syndrome with focal and segmental sclerosis
  Acute nephritic syndrome with focal glomerulonephritis

N00.2 **Acute nephritic syndrome with diffuse membranous glomerulonephritis** 🗲

● Unacceptable First-Listed Diagnosis   ● Use Additional Character(s)   ▨ Unspecified   **OGCR** Official Guidelines for Coding and Reporting

🗲 Complication\Comorbidity   🗲 Major C\C   Excludes 1   Excludes 2   Includes   Use additional   Code first   Code also

1235

CHAPTER 14 (N00-N99)

N00.3 **Acute nephritic syndrome with diffuse mesangial proliferative glomerulonephritis** 🐾

N00.4 **Acute nephritic syndrome with diffuse endocapillary proliferative glomerulonephritis** 🐾

N00.5 **Acute nephritic syndrome with diffuse mesangiocapillary glomerulonephritis** 🐾
Acute nephritic syndrome with membranoproliferative glomerulonephritis, types 1 and 3, or NOS

N00.6 **Acute nephritic syndrome with dense deposit disease** 🐾
Acute nephritic syndrome with membranoproliferative glomerulonephritis, type 2

N00.7 **Acute nephritic syndrome with diffuse crescentic glomerulonephritis** 🐾
Acute nephritic syndrome with extracapillary glomerulonephritis

N00.8 **Acute nephritic syndrome with other morphologic changes** 🐾
Acute nephritic syndrome with proliferative glomerulonephritis NOS

◼N00.9 **Acute nephritic syndrome with unspecified morphologic changes** 🐾

● N01 **Rapidly progressive nephritic syndrome**
Includes rapidly progressive glomerular disease
rapidly progressive glomerulonephritis
rapidly progressive nephritis

Excludes1 nephritic syndrome NOS (N05.-)

N01.0 **Rapidly progressive nephritic syndrome with minor glomerular abnormality** 🐾
Rapidly progressive nephritic syndrome with minimal change lesion

N01.1 **Rapidly progressive nephritic syndrome with focal and segmental glomerular lesions** 🐾
Rapidly progressive nephritic syndrome with focal and segmental hyalinosis
Rapidly progressive nephritic syndrome with focal and segmental sclerosis
Rapidly progressive nephritic syndrome with focal glomerulonephritis

N01.2 **Rapidly progressive nephritic syndrome with diffuse membranous glomerulonephritis** 🐾

N01.3 **Rapidly progressive nephritic syndrome with diffuse mesangial proliferative glomerulonephritis** 🐾

N01.4 **Rapidly progressive nephritic syndrome with diffuse endocapillary proliferative glomerulonephritis** 🐾

N01.5 **Rapidly progressive nephritic syndrome with diffuse mesangiocapillary glomerulonephritis** 🐾
Rapidly progressive nephritic syndrome with membranoproliferative glomerulonephritis, types 1 and 3, or NOS

N01.6 **Rapidly progressive nephritic syndrome with dense deposit disease** 🐾
Rapidly progressive nephritic syndrome with membranoproliferative glomerulonephritis, type 2

N01.7 **Rapidly progressive nephritic syndrome with diffuse crescentic glomerulonephritis** 🐾
Rapidly progressive nephritic syndrome with extracapillary glomerulonephritis

N01.8 **Rapidly progressive nephritic syndrome with other morphologic changes** 🐾
Rapidly progressive nephritic syndrome with proliferative glomerulonephritis NOS

◼N01.9 **Rapidly progressive nephritic syndrome with unspecified morphologic changes** 🐾

● N02 **Recurrent and persistent hematuria**
Excludes1 acute cystitis with hematuria (N30.01)
acute prostatitis with hematuria (N41.01)
chronic prostatitis with hematuria (N41.11)
hematuria NOS (R31.9)
hematuria not associated with specified morphologic lesions (R31.-)

N02.0 **Recurrent and persistent hematuria with minor glomerular abnormality** 🐾
Recurrent and persistent hematuria with minimal change lesion

N02.1 **Recurrent and persistent hematuria with focal and segmental glomerular lesions** 🐾
Recurrent and persistent hematuria with focal and segmental hyalinosis
Recurrent and persistent hematuria with focal and segmental sclerosis
Recurrent and persistent hematuria with focal glomerulonephritis

N02.2 **Recurrent and persistent hematuria with diffuse membranous glomerulonephritis** 🐾

N02.3 **Recurrent and persistent hematuria with diffuse mesangial proliferative glomerulonephritis** 🐾

N02.4 **Recurrent and persistent hematuria with diffuse endocapillary proliferative glomerulonephritis** 🐾

N02.5 **Recurrent and persistent hematuria with diffuse mesangiocapillary glomerulonephritis** 🐾
Recurrent and persistent hematuria with membranoproliferative glomerulonephritis, types 1 and 3, or NOS

N02.6 **Recurrent and persistent hematuria with dense deposit disease** 🐾
Recurrent and persistent hematuria with membranoproliferative glomerulonephritis, type 2

N02.7 **Recurrent and persistent hematuria with diffuse crescentic glomerulonephritis** 🐾
Recurrent and persistent hematuria with extracapillary glomerulonephritis

N02.8 **Recurrent and persistent hematuria with other morphologic changes** 🐾
Recurrent and persistent hematuria with proliferative glomerulonephritis NOS

◼N02.9 **Recurrent and persistent hematuria with unspecified morphologic changes** 🐾

Item 14–3 Chronic glomerulonephritis (GN) persists over a period of years, with remissions and exacerbation.
Chronic GN with lesion of proliferative glomerulonephritis results from a streptococcal infection.
Chronic GN with lesion of membranous glomerulonephritis, also known as membranous nephropathy, is characterized by deposits along the epithelial side of the basement membrane.
Chronic GN with lesion of membrano-proliferative glomerulonephritis (MPGN) is a group of disorders characterized by alterations in the basement membranes of the kidney and the glomerular cells.
Chronic GN with lesion of rapidly progressive glomerulonephritis is characterized by necrosis, endothelial proliferation, and mesangial proliferation. The condition is marked by rapid and progressive decline in renal function.

● Unacceptable First-Listed Diagnosis ● Use Additional Character(s) ◼ Unspecified **OGCR** Official Guidelines for Coding and Reporting
🐾 Complication\Comorbidity 🐾 Major C\C Excludes 1 Excludes 2 Includes Use additional Code first Code also

● **N03   Chronic nephritic syndrome**

> **Includes**   chronic glomerular disease
> chronic glomerulonephritis
> chronic nephritis

> **Excludes1**   chronic tubulo-interstitial nephritis (N11.-)
> diffuse sclerosing glomerulonephritis (N05.8-)
> nephritic syndrome NOS (N05.-)

N03.0   Chronic nephritic syndrome with minor glomerular abnormality 🗨
> Chronic nephritic syndrome with minimal change lesion

N03.1   Chronic nephritic syndrome with focal and segmental glomerular lesions 🗨
> Chronic nephritic syndrome with focal and segmental hyalinosis
> Chronic nephritic syndrome with focal and segmental sclerosis
> Chronic nephritic syndrome with focal glomerulonephritis

N03.2   Chronic nephritic syndrome with diffuse membranous glomerulonephritis 🗨

N03.3   Chronic nephritic syndrome with diffuse mesangial proliferative glomerulonephritis 🗨

N03.4   Chronic nephritic syndrome with diffuse endocapillary proliferative glomerulonephritis 🗨

N03.5   Chronic nephritic syndrome with diffuse mesangiocapillary glomerulonephritis 🗨
> Chronic nephritic syndrome with membranoproliferative glomerulonephritis, types 1 and 3, or NOS

N03.6   Chronic nephritic syndrome with dense deposit disease 🗨
> Chronic nephritic syndrome with membranoproliferative glomerulonephritis, type 2

N03.7   Chronic nephritic syndrome with diffuse crescentic glomerulonephritis 🗨
> Chronic nephritic syndrome with extracapillary glomerulonephritis

N03.8   Chronic nephritic syndrome with other morphologic changes 🗨
> Chronic nephritic syndrome with proliferative glomerulonephritis NOS

▪ **N03.9   Chronic nephritic syndrome with unspecified morphologic changes** 🗨

Item 14–4 Nephrotic syndrome (NS) is marked by massive proteinuria (protein in the urine) and water retention. Patients with NS are particularly vulnerable to staphylococcal and pneumococcal infections. NS with lesion of proliferative glomerulonephritis results from a streptococcal infection. NS with lesion of membranous glomerulonephritis results in thickening of the capillary walls. NS with lesion of minimal change glomerulonephritis is usually a benign disorder that occurs mostly in children and requires electron microscopy (biopsy) to verify changes in the glomeruli.

● **N04   Nephrotic syndrome**

> **Includes**   congenital nephrotic syndrome
> lipoid nephrosis

N04.0   Nephrotic syndrome with minor glomerular abnormality 🗨
> Nephrotic syndrome with minimal change lesion

N04.1   Nephrotic syndrome with focal and segmental glomerular lesions 🗨
> Nephrotic syndrome with focal and segmental hyalinosis
> Nephrotic syndrome with focal and segmental sclerosis
> Nephrotic syndrome with focal glomerulonephritis

N04.2   Nephrotic syndrome with diffuse membranous glomerulonephritis 🗨

N04.3   Nephrotic syndrome with diffuse mesangial proliferative glomerulonephritis 🗨

N04.4   Nephrotic syndrome with diffuse endocapillary proliferative glomerulonephritis 🗨

N04.5   Nephrotic syndrome with diffuse mesangiocapillary glomerulonephritis 🗨
> Nephrotic syndrome with membranoproliferative glomerulonephritis, types 1 and 3, or NOS

N04.6   Nephrotic syndrome with dense deposit disease 🗨
> Nephrotic syndrome with membranoproliferative glomerulonephritis, type 2

N04.7   Nephrotic syndrome with diffuse crescentic glomerulonephritis 🗨
> Nephrotic syndrome with extracapillary glomerulonephritis

N04.8   Nephrotic syndrome with other morphologic changes 🗨
> Nephrotic syndrome with proliferative glomerulonephritis NOS

▪ **N04.9   Nephrotic syndrome with unspecified morphologic changes** 🗨

● **N05   Unspecified nephritic syndrome**

> **Includes**   glomerular disease NOS
> glomerulonephritis NOS
> nephritis NOS
> nephropathy NOS and renal disease NOS with morphological lesion specified in .0-.8

> **Excludes1**   nephropathy NOS with no stated morphological lesion (N28.9)
> renal disease NOS with no stated morphological lesion (N28.9)
> tubulo-interstitial nephritis NOS (N12)

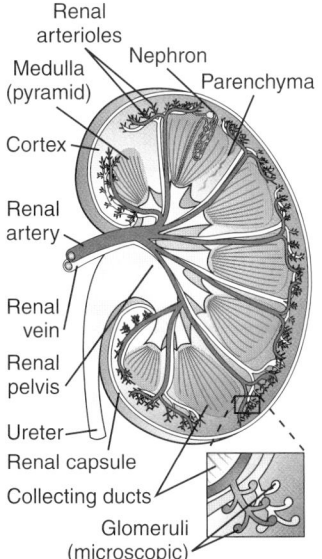

Renal arterioles
Nephron
Medulla (pyramid)
Parenchyma
Cortex
Renal artery
Renal vein
Renal pelvis
Ureter
Renal capsule
Collecting ducts
Glomeruli (microscopic)

Figure 14-2   Kidney cross section

● Unacceptable First-Listed Diagnosis   ● Use Additional Character(s)   ▪ Unspecified   **OGCR** Official Guidelines for Coding and Reporting
🗨 Complication\Comorbidity   🗨 Major C\C   Excludes 1   Excludes 2   Includes   Use additional   Code first   Code also

1237

CHAPTER 14 (N00-N99)

N05.0 Unspecified nephritic syndrome with minor glomerular abnormality
Unspecified nephritic syndrome with minimal change lesion

N05.1 Unspecified nephritic syndrome with focal and segmental glomerular lesions
Unspecified nephritic syndrome with focal and segmental hyalinosis
Unspecified nephritic syndrome with focal and segmental sclerosis
Unspecified nephritic syndrome with focal glomerulonephritis

N05.2 Unspecified nephritic syndrome with diffuse membranous glomerulonephritis

N05.3 Unspecified nephritic syndrome with diffuse mesangial proliferative glomerulonephritis

N05.4 Unspecified nephritic syndrome with diffuse endocapillary proliferative glomerulonephritis

N05.5 Unspecified nephritic syndrome with diffuse mesangiocapillary glomerulonephritis
Unspecified nephritic syndrome with membranoproliferative glomerulonephritis, types 1 and 3, or NOS

N05.6 Unspecified nephritic syndrome with dense deposit disease
Unspecified nephritic syndrome with membranoproliferative glomerulonephritis, type 2

N05.7 Unspecified nephritic syndrome with diffuse crescentic glomerulonephritis
Unspecified nephritic syndrome with extracapillary glomerulonephritis

N05.8 Unspecified nephritic syndrome with other morphologic changes
Unspecified nephritic syndrome with proliferative glomerulonephritis NOS

N05.9 Unspecified nephritic syndrome with unspecified morphologic changes

● **N06 Isolated proteinuria with specified morphological lesion**

Excludes1   proteinuria not associated with specific morphologic lesions (R80.0)

N06.0 Isolated proteinuria with minor glomerular abnormality
Isolated proteinuria with minimal change lesion

N06.1 Isolated proteinuria with focal and segmental glomerular lesions
Isolated proteinuria with focal and segmental hyalinosis
Isolated proteinuria with focal and segmental sclerosis
Isolated proteinuria with focal glomerulonephritis

N06.2 Isolated proteinuria with diffuse membranous glomerulonephritis

N06.3 Isolated proteinuria with diffuse mesangial proliferative glomerulonephritis

N06.4 Isolated proteinuria with diffuse endocapillary proliferative glomerulonephritis

N06.5 Isolated proteinuria with diffuse mesangiocapillary glomerulonephritis
Isolated proteinuria with membranoproliferative glomerulonephritis, types 1 and 3, or NOS

N06.6 Isolated proteinuria with dense deposit disease
Isolated proteinuria with membranoproliferative glomerulonephritis, type 2

N06.7 Isolated proteinuria with diffuse crescentic glomerulonephritis
Isolated proteinuria with extracapillary glomerulonephritis

N06.8 Isolated proteinuria with other morphologic lesion
Isolated proteinuria with proliferative glomerulonephritis NOS

N06.9 Isolated proteinuria with unspecified morphologic lesion

● **N07 Hereditary nephropathy, not elsewhere classified**

Excludes2   Alport's syndrome (Q87.81-)
hereditary amyloid nephropathy (E85.-)
nail patella syndrome (Q87.2)
non-neuropathic heredofamilial amyloidosis (E85.-)

N07.0 Hereditary nephropathy, not elsewhere classified with minor glomerular abnormality
Hereditary nephropathy, not elsewhere classified with minimal change lesion

N07.1 Hereditary nephropathy, not elsewhere classified with focal and segmental glomerular lesions
Hereditary nephropathy, not elsewhere classified with focal and segmental hyalinosis
Hereditary nephropathy, not elsewhere classified with focal and segmental sclerosis
Hereditary nephropathy, not elsewhere classified with focal glomerulonephritis

N07.2 Hereditary nephropathy, not elsewhere classified with diffuse membranous glomerulonephritis

N07.3 Hereditary nephropathy, not elsewhere classified with diffuse mesangial proliferative glomerulonephritis

N07.4 Hereditary nephropathy, not elsewhere classified with diffuse endocapillary proliferative glomerulonephritis

N07.5 Hereditary nephropathy, not elsewhere classified with diffuse mesangiocapillary glomerulonephritis
Hereditary nephropathy, not elsewhere classified with membranoproliferative glomerulonephritis, types 1 and 3, or NOS

N07.6 Hereditary nephropathy, not elsewhere classified with dense deposit disease
Hereditary nephropathy, not elsewhere classified with membranoproliferative glomerulonephritis, type 2

N07.7 Hereditary nephropathy, not elsewhere classified with diffuse crescentic glomerulonephritis
Hereditary nephropathy, not elsewhere classified with extracapillary glomerulonephritis

N07.8 Hereditary nephropathy, not elsewhere classified with other morphologic lesions
Hereditary nephropathy, not elsewhere classified with proliferative glomerulonephritis NOS

N07.9 Hereditary nephropathy, not elsewhere classified with unspecified morphologic lesions

CHAPTER 14 (N00-N99)

1238

● Unacceptable First-Listed Diagnosis   ● Use Additional Character(s)   ■ Unspecified   **OGCR** Official Guidelines for Coding and Reporting
Complication\Comorbidity   Major C\C   Excludes 1   Excludes 2   Includes   Use additional   Code first   Code also

● **N08 Glomerular disorders in diseases classified elsewhere**

> **Includes** glomerulonephritis
> nephritis
> nephropathy

> *Code first underlying disease, such as:*
> amyloidosis (E85.-)
> congenital syphilis (A50.5)
> cryoglobulinemia (D89.1)
> disseminated intravascular coagulation (D65)
> gout (M1a-, M10.-)
> microscopic polyangiitis (M31.7)
> multiple myeloma (C90.0-)
> sepsis (A40.0-A41.9)
> sickle-cell disease (D57.0-D57.8)

> **Excludes1** glomerulonephritis, nephritis and
> nephropathy (in):
> antiglomerular basement membrane
> disease (M31.0)
> diabetes (E09-E13 with .21)
> gonococcal (A54.21)
> Goodpasture's syndrome (M31.0)
> hemolytic-uremic syndrome (D59.3)
> lupus (M32.14)
> mumps (B26.83)
> syphilis (A52.75)
> systemic lupus erythematosus (M32.14)
> Wegener's granulomatosis (M31.31)
> pyelonephritis in diseases classified
> elsewhere (N16)
> renal tubulo-interstitial disorders classified
> elsewhere (N16)

RENAL TUBULO-INTERSTITIAL DISEASES (N10-N16)

> **Includes** pyelonephritis
> **Excludes1** pyeloureteritis cystica (N28.85)

N10 Acute tubulo-interstitial nephritis

> **Includes** acute infectious interstitial nephritis
> acute pyelitis
> acute pyelonephritis
> acute tubular necrosis
> hemoglobin nephrosis
> myoglobin nephrosis

> Use additional code (B95-B97), to identify infectious agent

● **N11 Chronic tubulo-interstitial nephritis**

> **Includes** chronic infectious interstitial nephritis
> chronic pyelitis
> chronic pyelonephritis

> Use additional code (B95-B97), to identify infectious agent

**N11.0 Nonobstructive reflux-associated chronic
pyelonephritis**
> Pyelonephritis (chronic) associated with
> (vesicoureteral) reflux
> **Excludes1** vesicoureteral reflux NOS (N13.70)

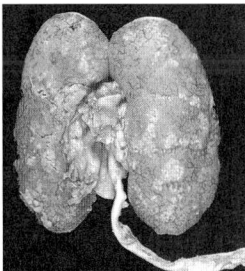

Figure 14-3 Acute pyelonephritis. Cortical surface exhibits grayish white areas of inflammation and abscess formation. (From Kumar: Robbins and Cartan: Pathologic Basis of Disease, 7th ed. 2005, Saunders, An Imprint of Elsevier)

Item 14–5 Pyelonephritis is an infection of the kidneys and ureters and may be chronic or acute in one or both kidneys.

N11.1 Chronic obstructive pyelonephritis
> Pyelonephritis (chronic) associated with anomaly
> of pelviureteric junction
> Pyelonephritis (chronic) associated with anomaly
> of pyeloureteric junction
> Pyelonephritis (chronic) associated with crossing
> of vessel
> Pyelonephritis (chronic) associated with kinking
> of ureter
> Pyelonephritis (chronic) associated with
> obstruction of ureter
> Pyelonephritis (chronic) associated with stricture
> of pelviureteric junction
> Pyelonephritis (chronic) associated with stricture
> of ureter
> **Excludes1** calculous pyelonephritis (N20.9)
> obstructive uropathy (N13.-)

N11.8 Other chronic tubulo-interstitial nephritis
> Nonobstructive chronic pyelonephritis NOS

▪**N11.9 Chronic tubulo-interstitial nephritis, unspecified**
> Chronic interstitial nephritis NOS
> Chronic pyelitis NOS
> Chronic pyelonephritis NOS

**N12 Tubulo-interstitial nephritis, not specified as acute or
chronic**
> **Includes** interstitial nephritis NOS
> pyelitis NOS
> pyelonephritis NOS
> **Excludes1** calculous pyelonephritis (N20.9)

● **N13 Obstructive and reflux uropathy.**
> **Excludes2** calculus of kidney and ureter without
> hydronephrosis (N20.-)
> congenital obstructive defects of renal pelvis
> and ureter (Q62.0-Q62.3)
> hydronephrosis with ureteropelvic junction
> obstruction (Q62.1)
> obstructive pyelonephritis (N11.1)

**N13.1 Hydronephrosis with ureteral stricture, not
elsewhere classified**
> **Excludes1** hydronephrosis with ureteral
> stricture with infection (N13.6)

**N13.2 Hydronephrosis with renal and ureteral calculous
obstruction**
> **Excludes1** hydronephrosis with renal and
> ureteral calculous obstruction
> with infection (N13.6)

● **N13.3 Other and unspecified hydronephrosis**
> **Excludes1** hydronephrosis with infection (N13.6)

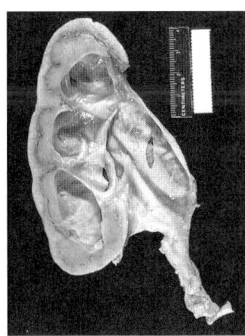

Figure 14-4 Hydronephrosis of the kidney, with marked dilation of pelvis and calyces and thinning of renal parenchyma. (From Kumar: Robbins and Cartan: Pathologic Basis of Disease, 7th ed 2005, Saundres, An Imprint of Elsevier)

● Unacceptable First-Listed Diagnosis   ● Use Additional Character(s)   ▪ Unspecified   **OGCR** Official Guidelines for Coding and Reporting
 Complication\Comorbidity   Major C\C   Excludes 1   Excludes 2   Includes   Use additional   Code first   Code also

■ N13.30　Unspecified hydronephrosis ✿

N13.39　Other hydronephrosis ✿

N13.4　Hydroureter ✿

> Excludes1 │ congenital hydroureter (Q62.3)
> hydroureter with infection (N13.6)
> vesicoureteral-reflux with
> hydroureter (N13.73-)

N13.5　Crossing vessel and stricture of ureter without hydronephrosis

> Kinking and stricture of ureter without hydronephrosis

> Excludes1 │ crossing vessel and stricture of ureter
> without hydronephrosis with
> infection (N13.6)

N13.6　Pyonephrosis ✿

> Conditions in N13.0-N13.5 with infection
> Obstructive uropathy with infection

> Use additional code (B95-B97), to identify infectious agent

● N13.7　Vesicoureteral-reflux

> Excludes1 │ reflux-associated pyelonephritis
> (N11.0)

■ N13.70　Vesicoureteral-reflux, unspecified

> *Occurs when urine flows from bladder back into ureters*
> Vesicoureteral-reflux NOS

N13.71　Vesicoureteral-reflux without reflux nephropathy

● N13.72　Vesicoureteral-reflux with reflux nephropathy without hydroureter

N13.721　Vesicoureteral-reflux with reflux nephropathy without hydroureter, unilateral

N13.722　Vesicoureteral-reflux with reflux nephropathy without hydroureter, bilateral

■ N13.729　Vesicoureteral-reflux with reflux nephropathy without hydroureter, unspecified

● N13.73　Vesicoureteral-reflux with reflux nephropathy with hydroureter

N13.731　Vesicoureteral-reflux with reflux nephropathy with hydroureter, unilateral

N13.732　Vesicoureteral-reflux with reflux nephropathy with hydroureter, bilateral

■ N13.739　Vesicoureteral-reflux with reflux nephropathy with hydroureter, unspecified

N13.8　Other obstructive and reflux uropathy ✿

> Urinary tract obstruction due to specified cause
> Code, if applicable, any causal condition first, such as:
> enlarged prostate (N40.1)

■ N13.9　Obstructive and reflux uropathy, unspecified

> Urinary tract obstruction NOS

● N14　Drug- and heavy-metal-induced tubulo-interstitial and tubular conditions

> *Code first (T36-T65) to identify drug and toxic agent*

● N14.0　Analgesic nephropathy

● N14.1　Nephropathy induced by other drugs, medicaments and biological substances

● ■ N14.2　Nephropathy induced by unspecified drug, medicament or biological substance

● N14.3　Nephropathy induced by heavy metals

● N14.4　Toxic nephropathy, not elsewhere classified

● N15　Other renal tubulo-interstitial diseases

N15.0　Balkan nephropathy

> Balkan endemic nephropathy

N15.1　Renal and perinephric abscess ✿

N15.8　Other specified renal tubulo-interstitial diseases

■ N15.9　Renal tubulo-interstitial disease, unspecified

> Infection of kidney NOS

> Excludes1 │ urinary tract infection NOS (N39.0)

● N16　Renal tubulo-interstitial disorders in diseases classified elsewhere

> Includes │ pyelonephritis
> tubulo-interstitial nephritis

> *Code first underlying disease, such as:*
> brucellosis (A23.0-A23.9)
> cryoglobulinemia (D89.1)
> glycogen storage disease (E74.0)
> leukemia (C91-C95)
> lymphoma (C81.0-C85.9, C96.0-C96.9)
> multiple myeloma (C90.0-)
> sepsis (A40.0-A41.9)
> Wilson's disease (E83.0)

> Excludes1 │ pyelonephritis and tubulo-interstitial
> nephritis (in):
> candidiasis (B37.49)
> cystinosis (E72.0)
> diphtheritic (A36.84)
> salmonella infection (A02.25)
> sarcoidosis (D86.84)
> sicca syndrome [Sjogren's] (M35.04)
> syphilitic (A52.75)
> systemic lupus erythematosus (M32.15)
> toxoplasmosis (B58.83)
> renal tubular degeneration in diabetes
> (E08-E13 with .22)

ACUTE KIDNEY FAILURE AND CHRONIC KIDNEY DISEASE (N17-N19)

> Excludes2 │ congenital renal failure (P96.0)
> drug- and heavy-metal-induced tubulo-
> interstitial and tubular conditions
> (N14.-)
> extrarenal uremia (R39.2)
> hemolytic-uremic syndrome (D59.3)
> hepatorenal syndrome (K76.7)
> postpartum hepatorenal syndrome (O90.4)
> posttraumatic renal failure (T79.5)
> prerenal uremia (R39.2)
> renal failure:
> complicating abortion or ectopic or molar
> pregnancy (O00-O07, O08.4)
> following labor and delivery (O90.4)
> postprocedural (N99.0)

● N17　Acute kidney failure

> Code also associated underlying condition

> Excludes1 │ posttraumatic renal failure (T79.5)

N17.0　Acute kidney failure with tubular necrosis ✿

> Acute tubular necrosis
> Renal tubular necrosis
> Tubular necrosis NOS

N17.1　Acute kidney failure with acute cortical necrosis ✿

> Acute cortical necrosis
> Cortical necrosis NOS
> Renal cortical necrosis

CHAPTER 14 (N00-N99)

1240

● Unacceptable First-Listed Diagnosis　　● Use Additional Character(s)　　■ Unspecified　　OGCR Official Guidelines for Coding and Reporting
✿ Complication\Comorbidity　　✿ Major C\C　　│Excludes 1│　│Excludes 2│　Includes　Use additional　Code first　Code also

Item 14–6 Decreased blood flow is the usual cause of **acute renal failure** that offers a good prognosis for recovery.
Chronic renal failure is usually the result of long-standing kidney disease and is a very serious condition that generally results in death.

N17.2 Acute kidney failure with medullary necrosis 🔖
   Medullary [papillary] necrosis NOS
   Acute medullary [papillary] necrosis
   Renal medullary [papillary] necrosis

N17.8 Other acute kidney failure 🔖

N17.9 Acute renal failure, unspecified 🔖
   Acute kidney injury (nontraumatic)
   | Excludes2 | traumatic kidney injury (S37.0-)

● **N18 Chronic kidney disease (CKD)**
   Code first any associated:
   diabetic chronic kidney disease (E08.22, E09.22, E10.22, E11.22, E13.22)
   hypertensive chronic kidney disease (I12.-, I13.-)

   Use additional code to identify kidney transplant status, if applicable, (Z94.0)

   N18.1 Chronic kidney disease, stage I

   N18.2 Chronic kidney disease, stage II (mild)

   N18.3 Chronic kidney disease, stage III (moderate)

   N18.4 Chronic kidney disease, stage IV (severe) 🔖

   N18.5 Chronic kidney disease, stage V 🔖
   | Excludes1 | chronic kidney disease, stage V requiring chronic dialysis (N18.6)

   N18.6 End stage renal disease 🔖
   Chronic kidney disease requiring chronic dialysis
   Use additional code to identify dialysis status (Z99.2)

   N18.9 Chronic kidney disease, unspecified
   Chronic renal disease
   Chronic renal failure NOS
   Chronic renal insufficieny
   Chronic uremia
   Renal disease NOS

N19 Unspecified kidney failure
   | Includes | uremia NOS
   | Excludes1 | acute kidney failure (N17.-)
   chronic kidney disease (N18.-)
   chronic uremia (N18.9)
   extrarenal uremia (R39.2)
   prerenal uremia (R39.2)
   renal insufficiency (acute) (N28.9)
   uremia of newborn (P96.0)

UROLITHIASIS (N20-N23)

● **N20 Calculus of kidney and ureter**
   Calculous pyelonephritis
   | Excludes1 | nephrocalcinosis (E83.5)
   that with hydronephrosis (N13.2)

   N20.0 Calculus of kidney
   Nephrolithiasis NOS   Staghorn calculus
   Renal calculus   Stone in kidney
   Renal stone

   N20.1 Calculus of ureter 🔖
   Ureteric stone

   N20.2 Calculus of kidney with calculus of ureter

   N20.9 Urinary calculus, unspecified

● **N21 Calculus of lower urinary tract**
   | Includes | that with cystitis and urethritis

   N21.0 Calculus in bladder
   Calculus in diverticulum of bladder
   Urinary bladder stone
   | Excludes2 | staghorn calculus (N20.0)

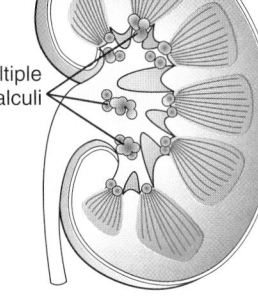

Figure 14-5 Multiple urinary calculi.

Multiple calculi

N21.1 Calculus in urethra
   | Excludes2 | calculus of prostate (N42.0)

N21.8 Other lower urinary tract calculus

N21.9 Calculus of lower urinary tract, unspecified
   | Excludes1 | calculus of urinary tract NOS (N20.9)

● **N22 Calculus of urinary tract in diseases classified elsewhere**
   Code first underlying disease, such as:
   gout (M1a-, M10.-)
   schistosomiasis (B65.0-B65.9)

N23 Unspecified renal colic

OTHER DISORDERS OF KIDNEY AND URETER (N25-N29)
   | Excludes2 | disorders of kidney and ureter with urolithiasis (N20-N23)

● **N25 Disorders resulting from impaired renal tubular function**
   | Excludes1 | metabolic disorders classifiable to E70-E90

   N25.0 Renal osteodystrophy
   Azotemic osteodystrophy
   Phosphate-losing tubular disorders
   Renal rickets
   Renal short stature

   N25.1 Nephrogenic diabetes insipidus 🔖
   | Excludes1 | diabetes insipidus NOS (E23.2)

   ● **N25.8 Other disorders resulting from impaired renal tubular function**

      N25.81 Secondary hyperparathyroidism of renal origin 🔖
      | Excludes1 | secondary hyperparathyroidism, non-renal (E21.1)

      N25.89 Other disorders resulting from impaired renal tubular function
      Hypokalemic nephropathy
      Lightwood-Albright syndrome
      Renal tubular acidosis NOS

   N25.9 Disorder resulting from impaired renal tubular function, unspecified

● **N26 Unspecified contracted kidney**
   | Excludes1 | contracted kidney due to hypertension (I12.-)
   diffuse sclerosing glomerulonephritis (N05.8.-)
   hypertensive nephrosclerosis (arteriolar) (arteriosclerotic) (I12.-)
   small kidney of unknown cause (N27.-)

● Unacceptable First-Listed Diagnosis   ● Use Additional Character(s)   ▨ Unspecified   **OGCR** Official Guidelines for Coding and Reporting
🔖 Complication\Comorbidity   🔖 Major C\C | Excludes 1 | | Excludes 2 | | Includes | Use additional   Code first   Code also

CHAPTER 14 (N00-N99)

N26.1   **Atrophy of kidney (terminal)**

N26.2   **Page kidney**

N26.9   **Renal sclerosis NOS**

● N27   **Small kidney of unknown cause**

> **Includes**   oligonephronia

N27.0   **Small kidney, unilateral**

N27.1   **Small kidney, bilateral**

◼ N27.9   **Small kidney, unspecified**

● N28   **Other disorders of kidney and ureter, not elsewhere classified**

N28.0   **Ischemia and infarction of kidney** ◍

> Renal artery embolism
> Renal artery obstruction
> Renal artery occlusion
> Renal artery thrombosis
> Renal infarct

> | Excludes1 | atherosclerosis of renal artery (extrarenal part) (I70.1)
> congenital stenosis of renal artery (Q27.1)
> Goldblatt's kidney (I70.1)

N28.1   **Cyst of kidney, acquired**

> Cyst (multiple)(solitary) of kidney, acquired

> | Excludes1 | cystic kidney disease (congenital) (Q61.-)

● N28.8   **Other specified disorders of kidney and ureter**

> | Excludes1 | hydroureter (N13.4)
> ureteric stricture with hydronephrosis (N13.1)
> ureteric stricture without hydronephrosis (N13.5)

N28.81   **Hypertrophy of kidney**

N28.82   **Megaloureter**

N28.83   **Nephroptosis**

N28.84   **Pyelitis cystica**

N28.85   **Pyeloureteritis cystica** ◍

N28.86   **Ureteritis cystica**

N28.89   **Other specified disorders of kidney and ureter**

◼ N28.9   **Disorder of kidney and ureter, unspecified**

> Nephropathy NOS
> Renal disease (acute) NOS
> Renal insufficiency (acute)

> | Excludes1 | chronic renal insufficiency (N18.9)
> unspecified nephritic syndrome (N05-)

● N29   **Other disorders of kidney and ureter in diseases classified elsewhere**

> *Code first underlying disease, such as:*
> amyloidosis (E85.-)
> nephrocalcinosis (E83.5)
> schistosomiasis (B65.0-B65.9)

> | Excludes1 | disorders of kidney and ureter in:
> cystinosis (E72.0)
> gonorrhea (A54.21)
> syphilis (A52.75)
> tuberculosis (A18.11)

OTHER DISEASES OF THE URINARY SYSTEM (N30-N39)

> | Excludes1 | urinary infection (complicating):
> abortion or ectopic or molar pregnancy (O00-O07, O08.8)
> pregnancy, childbirth and the puerperium (O23.-, O75.3, O86.2-)

● N30   **Cystitis**

> *Infection of bladder and irritation in lower urinary tract*

> Use additional code to identify infectious agent (B95-B97)

> | Excludes1 | prostatocystitis (N41.3)

● N30.0   **Acute cystitis**

> | Excludes1 | irradiation cystitis (N30.4-)
> trigonitis (N30.3-)

N30.00   **Acute cystitis without hematuria** ◍

N30.01   **Acute cystitis with hematuria** ◍

● N30.1   **Interstitial cystitis (chronic)**

> *Ongoing infection of kidney glomeruli and tubules*

N30.10   **Interstitial cystitis (chronic) without hematuria**

N30.11   **Interstitial cystitis (chronic) with hematuria**

● N30.2   **Other chronic cystitis**

N30.20   **Other chronic cystitis without hematuria**

N30.21   **Other chronic cystitis with hematuria**

● N30.3   **Trigonitis**

> *Inflammation of triangular area of bladder (where the ureters and urethra come together)*
> Urethrotrigonitis

N30.30   **Trigonitis without hematuria**

N30.31   **Trigonitis with hematuria**

● N30.4   **Irradiation cystitis**

N30.40   **Irradiation cystitis without hematuria** ◍

N30.41   **Irradiation cystitis with hematuria** ◍

● N30.8   **Other cystitis**

> Abscess of bladder

N30.80   **Other cystitis without hematuria**

N30.81   **Other cystitis with hematuria**

● N30.9   **Cystitis, unspecified**

◼ N30.90   **Cystitis, unspecified without hematuria**

◼ N30.91   **Cystitis, unspecified with hematuria**

● N31   **Neuromuscular dysfunction of bladder, not elsewhere classified**

> Use additional code to identify any associated urinary incontinence (N39.3-N39.4-)

> | Excludes1 | cord bladder NOS (G95.8)
> neurogenic bladder due to cauda equina syndrome (G83.4)
> neuromuscular dysfunction due to spinal cord lesion (G95.8)

N31.0   **Uninhibited neuropathic bladder, not elsewhere classified**

N31.1   **Reflex neuropathic bladder, not elsewhere classified**

N31.2   **Flaccid neuropathic bladder, not elsewhere classified**

> Atonic (motor) (sensory) neuropathic bladder
> *Diminished tone of bladder muscle*
> Autonomous neuropathic bladder
> Nonreflex neuropathic bladder

N31.8   **Other neuromuscular dysfunction of bladder**

◼ N31.9   **Neuromuscular dysfunction of bladder, unspecified**

> Neurogenic bladder dysfunction NOS

● N32   **Other disorders of bladder**

> | Excludes2 | calculus of bladder (N21.0)
> cystocele (N81.1-)
> hernia or prolapse of bladder, female (N81.1-)

CHAPTER 14 (N00-N99)

● Unacceptable First-Listed Diagnosis   ● Use Additional Character(s)   ◼ Unspecified   **OGCR** Official Guidelines for Coding and Reporting

1242   ◍ Complication\Comorbidity   ◍ Major C\C | Excludes 1 | | Excludes 2 | Includes   Use additional   Code first   Code also

N32.0   Bladder-neck obstruction
    Bladder-neck stenosis (acquired)
    | Excludes1 | congenital bladder-neck obstruction (Q64.3-)

N32.1   Vesicointestinal fistula 🗓
    Vesicorectal fistula

N32.2   Vesical fistula, not elsewhere classified 🗓
    | Excludes1 | fistula between bladder and female genital tract (N82.0-N82.1)

N32.3   Diverticulum of bladder
    Formation of sac from a herniation of wall of bladder
    | Excludes1 | congenital diverticulum of bladder (Q64.6)
                  diverticulitis of bladder (N30.8-)

● **N32.8   Other specified disorders of bladder**

    N32.81   Overactive bladder
         Destrusor muscle hyperactivity
         | Excludes1 | frequent urination due to specified bladder condition- code to condition

    N32.89   Other specified disorders of bladder
         Calcified bladder
         Contracted bladder

▪ **N32.9   Bladder disorder, unspecified**

● **N33   Bladder disorders in diseases classified elsewhere**
    Code first underlying disease, such as:
    schistosomiasis (B65.0-B65.9)
    | Excludes1 | bladder disorder in:
           syphilis (A52.76)
           tuberculosis (A18.12)
           cystitis (in):
              candidal infection (B37.41)
              chlamydial (A56.01)
              diphtheritic (A36.85)
              gonorrhea (A54.01)
              syphilitic (A52.76)
              trichomonal infection (A59.03)
           neurogenic bladder (N31.-)

● **N34   Urethritis and urethral syndrome**
    Use additional code (B95-B97), to identify infectious agent
    | Excludes2 | Reiter's disease (M02.3-)
           urethritis in diseases with a predominantly sexual mode of transmission (A50-A64)
           urethrotrigonitis (N30.3-)

    N34.0   Urethral abscess 🗓
         Abscess (of) Cowper's gland
         Abscess (of) Littré's gland
         Abscess (of) urethral (gland)
         Periurethral abscess
         | Excludes1 | urethral caruncle (N36.2)

    N34.1   Nonspecific urethritis
         Nongonococcal urethritis
         Nonvenereal urethritis

    N34.2   Other urethritis
         Inflammation of urethra
         Meatitis, urethral
         Postmenopausal urethritis
         Ulcer of urethra (meatus)
         Urethritis NOS

▪ **N34.3   Urethral syndrome, unspecified**

● **N35   Urethral stricture**
    Narrowing of lumen of urethra caused by scarring due to infection or injury
    | Excludes1 | congenital urethral stricture (Q64.3-)
           postprocedural urethral stricture (N99.1-)

● **N35.0   Post-traumatic urethral stricture**
    Urethral stricture due to injury
    | Excludes1 | postprocedural urethral stricture (N99.1-)

    ● **N35.01   Post-traumatic urethral stricture, male**

         N35.010   Post-traumatic urethral stricture, male, meatal

         N35.011   Post-traumatic bulbous urethral stricture

         N35.012   Post-traumatic membranous urethral stricture

         N35.013   Post-traumatic anterior urethral stricture

         ▪ **N35.014   Post-traumatic urethral stricture, male, unspecified**

    ● **N35.02   Post-traumatic urethral stricture, female**

         N35.021   Urethral stricture due to childbirth

         N35.028   Other post-traumatic urethral stricture, female

● **N35.1   Postinfective urethral stricture, not elsewhere classified**
    | Excludes1 | urethral stricture associated with schistosomiasis (B65.-, N29)
           gonococcal urethral stricture (A54.01)
           syphilitic urethral stricture (A52.76)

    ● **N35.11   Postinfective urethral stricture, not elsewhere classified, male**

         N35.111   Postinfective urethral stricture, not elsewhere classified, male, meatal

         N35.112   Postinfective bulbous urethral stricture, not elsewhere classified

         N35.113   Postinfective membranous urethral stricture, not elsewhere classified

         N35.114   Postinfective anterior urethral stricture, not elsewhere classified

         ▪ **N35.119   Postinfective urethral stricture, not elsewhere classified, male, unspecified**

    N35.12   Postinfective urethral stricture, not elsewhere classified, female

    N35.8   Other urethral stricture
         | Excludes1 | postprocedural urethral stricture (N99.1-)

▪ **N35.9   Urethral stricture, unspecified**

● **N36   Other disorders of urethra**

    N36.0   Urethral fistula 🗓
         False urethral passage
         Urethroperineal fistula
         Urethrorectal fistula
         Urinary fistula NOS
         | Excludes1 | urethroscrotal fistula (N50.8)
              urethrovaginal fistula (N82.1)
              urethrovesicovaginal fistula (N82.1)

● Unacceptable First-Listed Diagnosis   ● Use Additional Character(s)   ▪ Unspecified   **OGCR** Official Guidelines for Coding and Reporting

🗓 Complication\Comorbidity   🗓 Major C\C | Excludes 1 | Excludes 2 | | Includes | Use additional   Code first   Code also

1243

N36.1   **Urethral diverticulum**

N36.2   **Urethral caruncle**

● N36.4   **Urethral functional and muscular disorders**

> Use additional code to identify associated urinary stress incontinence (N39.3)

     N36.41   **Hypermobility of urethra**

     N36.42   **Intrinsic sphincter deficiency (ISD)**

     N36.43   **Combined hypermobility of urethra and intrinsic sphincter deficiency**

     N36.44   **Muscular disorders of urethra**
> Bladder sphincter dyssynergy

N36.8   **Other specified disorders of urethra**

■ N36.9   **Urethral disorder, unspecified**

● N37   **Urethral disorders in diseases classified elsewhere**

> *Code first underlying disease*

> **Excludes1**   urethritis (in):
> candidal infection (B37.41)
> chlamydial (A56.01)
> gonorrhea (A54.01)
> syphilis (A52.76)
> trichomonal infection (A59.03)
> tuberculosis (A18.13)

● N39   **Other disorders of urinary system**

> **Excludes2**   hematuria NOS (R31-)
> recurrent or persistent hematuria (N02.-)
> recurrent or persistent hematuria with specified morphological lesion (N02.-)
> proteinuria NOS (R80.-)

N39.0   **Urinary tract infection, site not specified** 🦠

> Use additional code (B95-B97), to identify infectious agent

> **Excludes1**   candidiasis of urinary tract (B37.4-)
> neonatal urinary tract infection (P39.3)
> urinary tract infection of specified site, such as:
> cystitis (N30.-)
> urethritis (N34.-)

N39.3   **Stress incontinence (female) (male)**
> Code also any associated overactive bladder (N32.81)

> **Excludes1**   mixed incontinence (N39.46)

● N39.4   **Other specified urinary incontinence**
> Code also any associated overactive bladder (N32.81)

> **Excludes1**   enuresis NOS (R32)
> functional urinary incontinence (R39.81)
> urinary incontinence associated with cognitive impairment (R39.81)
> urinary incontinence NOS (R32)
> urinary incontinence of nonorganic origin (F98.0)

     N39.41   **Urge incontinence**

> **Excludes1**   mixed incontinence (N39.46)

     N39.42   **Incontinence without sensory awareness**

     N39.43   **Post-void dribbling**

     N39.44   **Nocturnal enuresis**

     N39.45   **Continuous leakage**

     N39.46   **Mixed incontinence**
> Urge and stress incontinence

● N39.49   **Other specified urinary incontinence**

     N39.490   **Overflow incontinence**

     N39.498   **Other specified urinary incontinence**
> Reflex incontinence
> Total incontinence

N39.8   **Other specified disorders of urinary system**

■ N39.9   **Disorder of urinary system, unspecified**

DISEASES OF MALE GENITAL ORGANS (N40-N51)

(See Plate 387 on page NAP-5.)

● N40   **Enlarged prostate (EP)**

> **Includes**   adenofibromatous hypertrophy of prostate
> benign hypertrophy of the prostate
> *Enlargement of prostate gland usually occurring with age and causing obstructed urine flow*
> benign prostatic hyperplasia
> benign prostatic hypertrophy (BPH)
> nodular prostate
> polyp of prostate

> **Excludes2**   benign neoplasms of prostate (adenoma, benign) (fibroadenoma) (fibroma) (myoma) (D29.1)
> malignant neoplasm of prostate (C61)

N40.0   **Enlarged prostate without lower urinary tract symptoms (LUTS)**
> Enlarged prostate NOS

N40.1   **Enlarge prostate with lower urinary tract symptoms (LUTS)**

> Use additional code for associated symptoms, when specified:
> incomplete bladder emptying (R39.14)
> nocturia (R35.1)
> straining on urination (R39.16)
> urinary frequency (R35.0)
> urinary hesitancy (R39.11)
> urinary incontinence (N39.4-)
> urinary obstruction (N13.8)
> urinary retention (R33.8)
> urinary urgency (R39.15)
> weak urinary stream (R39.12)

● N41   **Inflammatory diseases of prostate**

> Use additional code (B95-B97), to identify infectious agent

● N41.0   **Acute prostatitis**

     N41.00   **Acute prostatitis without hematuria** 🦠

     N41.01   **Acute prostatitis with hematuria** 🦠

● N41.1   **Chronic prostatitis**

     N41.10   **Chronic prostatitis without hematuria**

     N41.11   **Chronic prostatitis with hematuria**

N41.2   **Abscess of prostate** 🦠

Item 14-7 Hydrocele is a sac of fluid accumulating in the testes membrane.

    N41.3 Prostatocystitis

    N41.4 Granulomatous prostatitis

    N41.8 Other inflammatory diseases of prostate

    ◼N41.9 Inflammatory disease of prostate, unspecified
            Prostatitis NOS

● N42 Other and unspecified disorders of prostate

    N42.0 Calculus of prostate
          Prostatic stone

    N42.1 Congestion and hemorrhage of prostate
        | Excludes1 | enlarged prostate (N40.-)
                 hematuria (R31.-)
                 hyperplasia of prostate (N40.-)
                 inflammatory diseases of prostate
                    (N41.-)

    N42.3 Dysplasia of prostate
          Prostatic intraepithelial neoplasia I (PIN I)
          Prostatic intraepithelial neoplasia II (PIN II)
        | Excludes1 | prostatic intraepithelial neoplasia III
                 (PIN III) (D07.5)

    ● N42.8 Other specified disorders of prostate

        N42.81 Prostatodynia syndrome
             Painful prostate syndrome

        N42.82 Prostatosis syndrome

        N42.89 Other specified disorders of prostate
             Cyst of prostate

    ◼N42.9 Disorder of prostate, unspecified

● N43 Hydrocele and spermatocele
      | Includes | hydrocele of spermatic cord, testis or tunica
               vaginalis

      | Excludes1 | congenital hydrocele (P83.5)

    N43.0 Encysted hydrocele

    N43.1 Infected hydrocele 🦠
          Use additional code (B95-B97), to identify
             infectious agent

    N43.2 Other hydrocele

    ◼N43.3 Hydrocele, unspecified

    ● N43.4 Spermatocele of epididymis
          Spermatic cyst

        ◼N43.40 Spermatocele of epididymis, unspecified

        N43.41 Spermatocele of epididymis, single

        N43.42 Spermatocele of epididymis, multiple

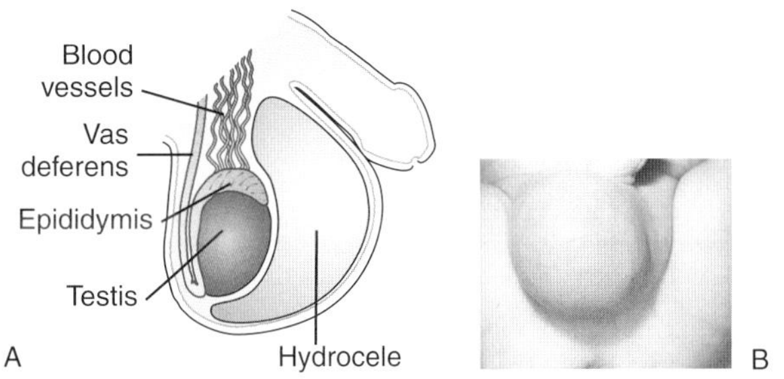

Figure 14-6 A. Hydrocele. **B.** Newborn with large right hydrocele. (**B** from Behrman. Nelson Textbook of Pediatrics, 17th ed. 2004, Saunders, An Imprint of Elsevier)

Item 14-8 Male infertility is the inability of the female sex partner to conceive after one year of unprotected intercourse.
    Azoospermia is no sperm ejaculated and **oligospermia** is few sperm ejaculated—both resulting in infertility. Extratesticular causes such as injury, infections, radiation, and chemotherapy may also cause male infertility.

● N44 Noninflammatory disorders of testis

    ● N44.0 Torsion of testis

        ◼N44.00 Torsion of testis, unspecified 🦠

        N44.01 Extravaginal torsion of spermatic cord 🦠

        N44.02 Intravaginal torsion of spermatic cord 🦠
             Torsion of spermatic cord NOS

        N44.03 Torsion of appendix testis 🦠

        N44.04 Torsion of appendix epididymis 🦠

    N44.1 Cyst of tunica albuginea testis

    N44.2 Benign cyst of testis

    N44.8 Other noninflammatory disorders of the testis

● N45 Orchitis and epididymitis
      Orchitis is inflammation of one or both of the testes as a
      result of mumps or other infection, trauma, or metastasis.
      Epididymitis is inflammation of the tubular structure that
      connects the testicle with the vas deferens.

      Use additional code (B95-B97), to identify infectious agent

    N45.1 Epididymitis

    N45.2 Orchitis

    N45.3 Epididymo-orchitis

    N45.4 Abscess of epididymis or testis 🦠

● N46 Male infertility
      | Excludes1 | vasectomy status (Z98.52)

    ● N46.0 Azoospermia
          Absolute male infertility
          Male infertility due to germinal (cell) aplasia
          Male infertility due to spermatogenic arrest
            (complete)

        N46.01 Organic azoospermia
             Azoospermia NOS

        ● N46.02 Azoospermia due to extratesticular causes
             Code also associated cause

            N46.021 Azoospermia due to drug therapy

            N46.022 Azoospermia due to infection

            N46.023 Azoospermia due to obstruction
                 of efferent ducts

            N46.024 Azoospermia due to radiation

            N46.025 Azoospermia due to systemic
                 disease

            N46.029 Azoospermia due to other
                 extratesticular causes

    ● N46.1 Oligospermia
          Male infertility due to germinal cell desquamation
          Male infertility due to hypospermatogenesis
          Male infertility due to incomplete spermatogenic
            arrest

        N46.11 Organic oligospermia
             Oligospermia NOS

        ● N46.12 Oligospermia due to extratesticular
             causes
             Code also associated cause

            N46.121 Oligospermia due to drug
                 therapy

            N46.122 Oligospermia due to infection

● Unacceptable First-Listed Diagnosis   ● Use Additional Character(s)   ◼ Unspecified   **OGCR** Official Guidelines for Coding and Reporting
🦠 Complication\Comorbidity   🦠 Major C\C | Excludes 1 | | Excludes 2 | | Includes | Use additional   Code first   Code also

N46.123　Oligospermia due to obstruction of efferent ducts

N46.124　Oligospermia due to radiation

N46.125　Oligospermia due to systemic disease

N46.129　Oligospermia due to other extratesticular causes

N46.8　Other male infertility

■ N46.9　Male infertility, unspecified

● N47　Disorders of prepuce

N47.0　Adherent prepuce, newborn

N47.1　Phimosis

N47.2　Paraphimosis

N47.3　Deficient foreskin

N47.4　Benign cyst of prepuce

N47.5　Adhesions of prepuce and glans penis

N47.6　Balanoposthitis

> **Excludes1**　balanitis (N48.1)
>
> Use additional code (B95-B97), to identify infectious agent

N47.7　Other inflammatory diseases of prepuce

> Use additional code (B95-B97), to identify infectious agent

N47.8　Other disorders of prepuce

● N48　Other disorders of penis

N48.0　Leukoplakia of penis
Balanitis xerotica obliterans
Kraurosis of penis
Lichen sclerosus of external male genital organs

> **Excludes1**　carcinoma in situ of penis (D07.4)

N48.1　Balanitis

> **Excludes1**　amebic balanitis (A06.8)
> balanitis xerotica obliterans (N48.0)
> candidal balanitis (B37.42)
> gonococcal balanitis (A54.23)
> herpesviral [herpes simplex] balanitis (A60.01)
>
> Use additional code (B95-B97), to identify infectious agent

● N48.2　Other inflammatory disorders of penis

> Use additional code (B95-B97), to identify infectious agent
>
> **Excludes1**　balanitis (N48.1)
> balanitis xerotica obliterans (N48.0)
> balanoposthitis (N47.6)

N48.21　Abscess of corpus cavernosum and penis

N48.22　Cellulitis of corpus cavernosum and penis

N48.29　Other inflammatory disorders of penis

● N48.3　Priapism
Painful erection
Code first underlying cause

■ N48.30　Priapism, unspecified 🗫

N48.31　Priapism due to trauma 🗫

Item 14–9 Seminal vesiculitis is an inflammation of the seminal vesicle. Spermatocele is a benign cystic accumulation of sperm arising from the head of the epididymis. Torsion of the testis is a medical emergency occurring most commonly in boys 7 to 12 years of age and results from a congenital abnormality of the covering of the testis allowing the testis to twist within its sac and cutting off the blood supply to the testis.

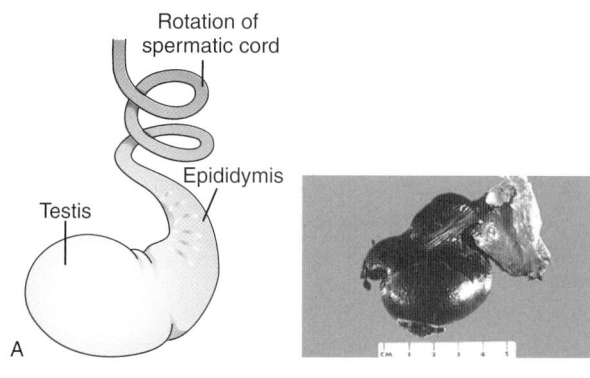

Figure 14-7　A. Torsion of testis. **B.** Torsion of testis. (**B** from Kumar: Robbins and Catran: Pathologic Basis of Disease, 7th ed. 2005, Saunders, An Imprint of Elsevier)

N48.32　Priapism due to disease classified elsewhere 🗫

N48.33　Priapism, drug-induced 🗫

N48.39　Other priapism 🗫

N48.5　Ulcer of penis

N48.6　Induration penis plastica
Peyronie's disease
Plastic induration of penis

● N48.8　Other specified disorders of penis

N48.81　Thrombosis of superficial vein of penis

N48.89　Other specified disorders of penis

■ N48.9　Disorder of penis, unspecified

● N49　Inflammatory disorders of male genital organs, not elsewhere classified

> Use additional code (B95-B97), to identify infectious agent
>
> **Excludes1**　inflammation of penis (N48.1, N48.2-)
> orchitis and epididymitis (N45.-)

N49.0　Inflammatory disorders of seminal vesicle
Vesiculitis NOS

N49.1　Inflammatory disorders of spermatic cord, tunica vaginalis and vas deferens
Vasitis

N49.2　Inflammatory disorders of scrotum

N49.3　Fournier gangrene 🗫

N49.8　Inflammatory disorders of other specified male genital organs
Inflammation of multiple sites in male genital organs

■ N49.9　Inflammatory disorder of unspecified male genital organ
Abscess of unspecified male genital organ
Boil of unspecified male genital organ
Carbuncle of unspecified male genital organ
Cellulitis of unspecified male genital organ

● N50　Other and unspecified disorders of male genital organs

> **Excludes2**　torsion of testis (N44.0-)

N50.0　Atrophy of testis

N50.1　Vascular disorders of male genital organs
Hematocele, NOS, of male genital organs
Hemorrhage of male genital organs
Thrombosis of male genital organs

CHAPTER 14 (N00-N99)

1246

● Unacceptable First-Listed Diagnosis　　● Use Additional Character(s)　　■ Unspecified　　**OGCR** Official Guidelines for Coding and Reporting
🗫 Complication\Comorbidity　🗫 Major C\C　Excludes 1　Excludes 2　Includes　Use additional　Code first　Code also

N50.8   **Other specified disorders of male genital organs**
    Atrophy of scrotum, seminal vesicle, spermatic cord, tunica vaginalis and vas deferens
    Edema of scrotum, seminal vesicle, spermatic cord, testis, tunica vaginalis and vas deferens
    Hypertrophy of scrotum, seminal vesicle, spermatic cord, testis, tunica vaginalis and vas deferens
    Ulcer of scrotum, seminal vesicle, spermatic cord, testis, tunica vaginalis and vas deferens
    Chylocele, tunica vaginalis (nonfilarial) NOS
    Urethroscrotal fistula
    Stricture of spermatic cord, tunica vaginalis, and vas deferens

◼ N50.9   **Disorder of male genital organs, unspecified**

● **N51**   **Disorders of male genital organs in diseases classified elsewhere**

    Code first underlying disease, such as:
    filariasis (B74.0-B74.9)

    Excludes1   amebic balanitis (A06.8)
                candidal balanitis (B37.42)
                gonococcal balanitis (A54.23)
                gonococcal prostatitis (A54.22)
                herpesviral [herpes simplex] balanitis (A60.01)
                trichomonal prostatitis (A59.02)
                tuberculous prostatitis (A18.14)

● **N52**   **Male erectile dysfunction**

    Excludes1   psychogenic impotence (F52.21)

● N52.0   **Vasculogenic erectile dysfunction**

    N52.01   **Erectile dysfunction due to arterial insufficiency**

    N52.02   **Corporo-venous occlusive erectile dysfunction**

    N52.03   **Combined arterial insufficiency and corporo-venous occlusive erectile dysfunction**

● N52.1   **Erectile dysfunction due to diseases classified elsewhere**

    Code first underlying disease

N52.2   **Drug-induced erectile dysfunction**

● N52.3   **Post-surgical erectile dysfunction**

    N52.31   **Erectile dysfunction following radical prostatectomy**

    N52.32   **Erectile dysfunction following radical cystectomy**

    N52.33   **Erectile dysfunction following urethral surgery**

    N52.34   **Erectile dysfunction following simple prostatectomy**

    N52.39   **Other post-surgical erectile dysfunction**

N52.8   **Other male erectile dysfunction**

◼ N52.9   **Male erectile dysfunction, unspecified**
    Impotence NOS

● **N53**   **Other male sexual dysfunction**

    Excludes1   psychogenic sexual dysfunction (F52.-)

● N53.1   **Ejaculatory dysfunction**

    Excludes1   premature ejaculation (F52.4)

    N53.11   **Retarded ejaculation**

    N53.12   **Painful ejaculation**

    N53.13   **Anejaculatory orgasm**

    N53.14   **Retrograde ejaculation**

    N53.19   **Other ejaculatory dysfunction**
          Ejaculatory dysfunction NOS

N53.8   **Other male sexual dysfunction**

◼ N53.9   **Unspecified male sexual dysfunction**

DISORDERS OF BREAST (N60-N65)

    Excludes1   disorders of breast associated with childbirth (O91-O92)

● **N60**   **Benign mammary dysplasia**
    Benign lumpiness of breast

    Includes   fibrocystic mastopathy

● N60.0   **Solitary cyst of breast**
    Cyst of breast

    N60.01   **Solitary cyst of right breast**

    N60.02   **Solitary cyst of left breast**

    ◼ N60.09   **Solitary cyst of unspecified breast**

● N60.1   **Diffuse cystic mastopathy**
    Cystic breast
    Fibrocystic disease of breast

    Excludes1   diffuse cystic mastopathy with epithelial proliferation (N60.3-)

    N60.11   **Diffuse cystic mastopathy of right breast**

    N60.12   **Diffuse cystic mastopathy of left breast**

    ◼ N60.19   **Diffuse cystic mastopathy of unspecified breast**

● N60.2   **Fibroadenosis of breast**
    Adenofibrosis of breast

    Excludes2   fibroadenoma of breast (D24.-)

    N60.21   **Fibroadenosis of right breast**

    N60.22   **Fibroadenosis of left breast**

    ◼ N60.29   **Fibroadenosis of unspecified breast**

● N60.3   **Fibrosclerosis of breast**
    Cystic mastopathy with epithelial proliferation

    N60.31   **Fibrosclerosis of right breast**

    N60.32   **Fibrosclerosis of left breast**

    ◼ N60.39   **Fibrosclerosis of unspecified breast**

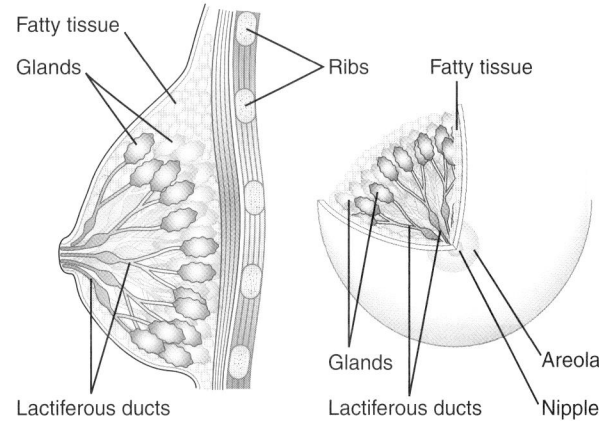

Fatty tissue — Glands — Ribs — Fatty tissue — Glands — Areola — Lactiferous ducts — Lactiferous ducts — Nipple

Figure 14-8   Breast.

● Unacceptable First-Listed Diagnosis   ● Use Additional Character(s)   ◼ Unspecified   **OGCR** Official Guidelines for Coding and Reporting

🅒 Complication\Comorbidity   🅜 Major C\C   Excludes 1   Excludes 2   Includes   Use additional   Code first   Code also

CHAPTER 14 (N00-N99)

1247

● N60.4   Mammary duct ectasia

     N60.41   Mammary duct ectasia of right breast

     N60.42   Mammary duct ectasia of left breast

     ■ N60.49   Mammary duct ectasia of unspecified breast

● N60.8   Other benign mammary dysplasias

     N60.81   Other benign mammary dysplasias of right breast

     N60.82   Other benign mammary dysplasias of left breast

     ■ N60.89   Other benign mammary dysplasias of unspecified breast

● N60.9   Unspecified benign mammary dysplasia

     ■ N60.91   Unspecified benign mammary dysplasia of right breast

     ■ N60.92   Unspecified benign mammary dysplasia of left breast

     ■ N60.99   Unspecified benign mammary dysplasia of unspecified breast

N61   **Inflammatory disorders of breast**

Includes	abscess (acute) (chronic) (nonpuerperal) of areola
	abscess (acute) (chronic) (nonpuerperal) of breast
	carbuncle of breast
	infective mastitis (acute) (subacute) (nonpuerperal)
	mastitis (acute) (subacute) (nonpuerperal) NOS

Excludes1	inflammatory carcinoma of breast (C50.9)
	inflammatory disorder of breast associated with childbirth (O91.-)
	neonatal infective mastitis (P39.0)
	thrombophlebitis of breast [Mondor's disease] (I80.8)

N62   **Hypertrophy of breast**

Includes	gynecomastia
	hypertrophy of breast NOS
	massive pubertal hypertrophy of breast

Excludes1	breast engorgement of newborn (P83.4)
	disproportion of reconstructed breast (N65.1)

■ **N63**   **Unspecified lump in breast**

Includes	nodule(s) NOS in breast

● **N64**   **Other disorders of breast**

Excludes2	mechanical complication of breast prosthesis and implant (T85.4-)

N64.0   Fissure and fistula of nipple

N64.1   Fat necrosis of breast

     Fat necrosis (segmental) of breast

     Code first breast necrosis due to breast graft (T85.89)

N64.2   Atrophy of breast

N64.3   Galactorrhea not associated with childbirth

     Excessive or spontaneous flow of milk

N64.4   Mastodynia

● **N64.5**   Other signs and symptoms in breast

Excludes2	abnormal findings on diagnostic imaging of breast (R92.-)

N64.51   Induration of breast

N64.52   Nipple discharge

Excludes1	abnormal findings in nipple discharge (R89.-)

N64.53   Retraction of nipple

N64.59   Other signs and symptoms in breast

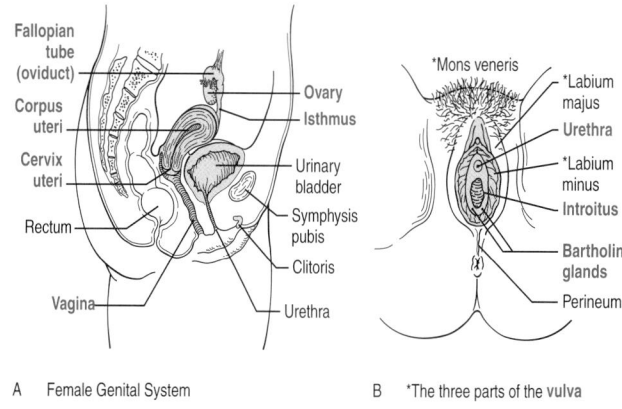

A   Female Genital System   B   *The three parts of the vulva

Figure 14-9   **A.** Female genital system. **B.** External female genital system. (From Buck CJ: Step-by-Step Medical Coding, 2010 ed. Philadelphia, WB Saunders, 2010.)

Item 14–10 Salpingitis is an infection of one or both fallopian tubes. **Oophoritis** is an infection of one or both ovaries.

● **N64.8**   Other specified disorders of breast

     N64.81   Ptosis of breast

Excludes1	ptosis of native breast in relation to reconstructed breast (N65.1)

     N64.82   Hypoplasia of breast

         Micromastia

Excludes1	congenital absence of breast (Q83.0)
	hypoplasia of native breast in relation to reconstructed breast (N65.1)

     N64.89   Other specified disorders of breast

         Galactocele

         Subinvolution of breast (postlactational)

■ **N64.9**   Disorder of breast, unspecified

● **N65**   **Deformity and disproportion of reconstructed breast**

     N65.0   Deformity of reconstructed breast

         Contour irregularity in reconstructed breast

         Excess tissue in reconstructed breast

         Misshapen reconstructed breast

     N65.1   Disproportion of reconstructed breast

         Breast asymmetry between native breast and reconstructed breast

         Disproportion between native breast and reconstructed breast

INFLAMMATORY DISEASES OF FEMALE PELVIC ORGANS (N70-N77)

Excludes1	inflammatory diseases of female pelvic organs complicating:
	abortion or ectopic or molar pregnancy (O00-O07, O08.0)
	pregnancy, childbirth and the puerperium (O23.-, O75.3, O85, O86.-)

(See Plate 360 on page NAP-32.)

CHAPTER 14 (N00-N99)

1248

●   Unacceptable First-Listed Diagnosis   ●   Use Additional Character(s)   ■   Unspecified   **OGCR**   Official Guidelines for Coding and Reporting

🔖 Complication\Comorbidity   🔖 Major C\C   Excludes 1   Excludes 2   Includes   Use additional   Code first   Code also

● **N70 Salpingitis and oophoritis**
> *Oophoritis = inflammation of ovary*
> *Salpingitis = inflammation of falloplan tube*

> | Includes | abscess (of) fallopian tube |
> |---|---|
> | | abscess (of) ovary |
> | | pyosalpinx |
> | | salpingo-oophoritis |
> | | tubo-ovarian abscess |
> | | tubo-ovarian inflammatory disease |

> Use additional code (B95-B97), to identify infectious agent

> | Excludes1 | gonococcal infection (A54.24) |
> |---|---|
> | | tuberculous infection (A18.17) |

   ● **N70.0 Acute salpingitis and oophoritis**

      N70.01   Acute salpingitis 🇶

      N70.02   Acute oophoritis 🇶

      N70.03   Acute salpingitis and oophoritis 🇶

   ● **N70.1 Chronic salpingitis and oophoritis**
> Hydrosalpinx

      N70.11   Chronic salpingitis

      N70.12   Chronic oophoritis

      N70.13   Chronic salpingitis and oophoritis

   ● **N70.9 Salpingitis and oophoritis, unspecified**

      ▪ N70.91   Salpingitis, unspecified

      ▪ N70.92   Oophoritis, unspecified

      ▪ N70.93   Salpingitis and oophoritis, unspecified

● **N71 Inflammatory disease of uterus, except cervix**

> | Includes | endo (myo) metritis |
> |---|---|
> | | metritis |
> | | myometritis |
> | | pyometra |
> | | uterine abscess |

> Use additional code (B95-B97), to identify infectious agent

> | Excludes1 | hyperplastic endometritis (N85.0-) |
> |---|---|
> | | infection of uterus following delivery (O85, O86.-) |

   N71.0   Acute inflammatory disease of uterus 🇶

   N71.1   Chronic inflammatory disease of uterus

   ▪ N71.9   Inflammatory disease of uterus, unspecified

N72 Inflammatory disease of cervix uteri

> | Includes | cervicitis (with or without erosion or ectropion) |
> |---|---|
> | | endocervicitis (with or without erosion or ectropion) |
> | | exocervicitis (with or without erosion or ectropion) |

> Use additional code (B95-B97), to identify infectious agent

> | Excludes1 | erosion and ectropion of cervix without cervicitis (N86) |
> |---|---|

● **N73 Other female pelvic inflammatory diseases**

> Use additional code (B95-B97), to identify infectious agent

   N73.0   Acute parametritis and pelvic cellulitis 🇶
> Abscess of broad ligament
> Abscess of parametrium
> Pelvic cellulitis, female

   N73.1   Chronic parametritis and pelvic cellulitis
> Any condition in N73.0 specified as chronic

> | Excludes1 | tuberculous parametritis and pelvic cellultis (A18.17) |
> |---|---|

   ▪ N73.2   Unspecified parametritis and pelvic cellulitis
> Any condition in N73.0 unspecified whether acute or chronic

   N73.3   Female acute pelvic peritonitis 🇶

   N73.4   Female chronic pelvic peritonitis 🇶

> | Excludes1 | tuberculous pelvic (female) peritonitis (A18.17) |
> |---|---|

   ▪ N73.5   Female pelvic peritonitis, unspecified

   N73.6   Female pelvic peritoneal adhesions (postinfective)

> | Excludes2 | postprocedural pelvic peritoneal adhesions (N99.4) |
> |---|---|

   N73.8   Other specified female pelvic inflammatory diseases

   ▪ N73.9   Female pelvic inflammatory disease, unspecified
> Female pelvic infection or inflammation NOS

● **N74 Female pelvic inflammatory disorders in diseases classified elsewhere**
> *Code first underlying disease*

> | Excludes1 | cervicitis: |
> |---|---|
> | | chlamydial (A56.02) |
> | | gonococcal (A54.03) |
> | | herpesviral [herpes simplex] (A60.03) |
> | | syphilitic (A52.76) |
> | | trichomonal (A59.09) |
> | | tuberculous (A18.16) |
> | | pelvic inflammatory disease: |
> | | chlamydial (A56.11) |
> | | gonococcal (A54.24) |
> | | herpesviral [herpes simplex] (A60.09) |
> | | syphilitic (A52.76) |
> | | tuberculous (A18.17) |

● **N75 Diseases of Bartholin's gland**

   N75.0   Cyst of Bartholin's gland
> *Cysts filled with liquid or semisolid material.*

   N75.1   Abscess of Bartholin's gland 🇶
> *Localized collection of pus*

   N75.8   Other diseases of Bartholin's gland
> Bartholinitis

   ▪ N75.9   Disease of Bartholin's gland, unspecified

● **N76 Other inflammation of vagina and vulva**

> Use additional code (B95-B97), to identify infectious agent

> | Excludes2 | senile (atrophic) vaginitis (N95.2) |
> |---|---|
> | | vulvar vestibulitis (N94.810) |

   N76.0   Acute vaginitis
> Acute vulvovaginitis
> Vaginitis NOS
> Vulvovaginitis NOS

   N76.1   Subacute and chronic vaginitis
> Chronic vulvovaginitis
> Subacute vulvovaginitis

   N76.2   Acute vulvitis
> Vulvitis NOS

   N76.3   Subacute and chronic vulvitis

   N76.4   Abscess of vulva 🇶
> Furuncle of vulva

   N76.5   Ulceration of vagina

   N76.6   Ulceration of vulva

● Unacceptable First-Listed Diagnosis   ● Use Additional Character(s)   ▪ Unspecified   **OGCR** Official Guidelines for Coding and Reporting

🇶 Complication\Comorbidity   🇶 Major C\C   Excludes 1   Excludes 2   Includes   Use additional   Code first   Code also

CHAPTER 14 (N00-N99)

1249

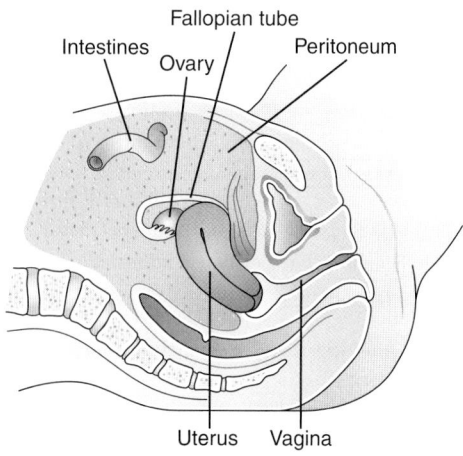

Figure 14-10 Sites of potential endometrial implants.

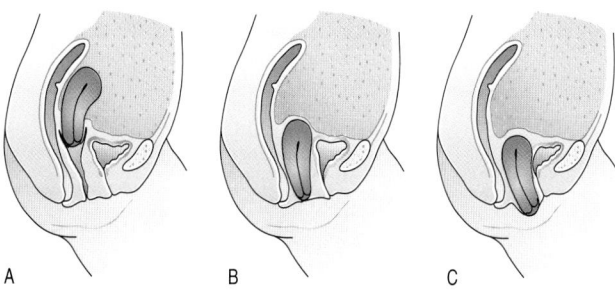

Figure 14-11 Three stages of uterine prolapse. **A.** Uterus is prolapsed. **B.** Vagina and uterus are prolapsed (incomplete uterovaginal prolapse). **C.** Vagina and uterus are completely prolapsed and are exposed through the external genitalia (complete uterovaginal prolapse).

● **N76.8   Other specified inflammation of vagina and vulva**

   N76.81   Mucositis (ulcerative) of vagina and vulva 🅒
      Code also type of associated therapy, such as:
         antineoplastic and immunosuppressive drugs (T45.1x-)
         radiological procedure and radiotherapy (Y84.2)
      | Excludes2 | gastrointestinal mucositis (ulcerative) (K92.81)
         nasal mucositis (ulcerative) (J34.81)
         oral mucositis (ulcerative) (K12.3-)

   N76.89   Other specified inflammation of vagina and vulva

● **N77   Vulvovaginal ulceration and inflammation in diseases classified elsewhere**

   ● **N77.0   Ulceration of vulva in diseases classified elsewhere**
      Code first underlying disease, such as:
         Behçet's disease (M35.2)
      | Excludes1 | ulceration of vulva in gonococcal infection (A54.02)
         ulceration of vulva in herpesviral [herpes simplex] infection (A60.04)
         ulceration of vulva in syphilis (A51.0)
         ulceration of vulva in tuberculosis (A18.18)

   ● **N77.1   Vaginitis, vulvitis and vulvovaginitis in diseases classified elsewhere**
      Code first underlying disease, such as:
         pinworm (B80)
      | Excludes1 | vaginitis, vulvitis and vulvovaginitis (in):
         candidiasis (B37.3)
         chlamydial (A56.02)
         gonococcal infection (A54.02)
         herpesviral [herpes simplex] infection (A60.04)
         syphilitic, early (A51.0)
         syphilitic, late (A52.76)
         trichomonal (A59.01)
         tuberculous (A18.18)

Item 14–11 Endometriosis is a condition for which no clear cause has been identified. Endometrial tissue is expelled from the uterus into the abdominal cavity and can implant onto a variety of organs. Classification is based on the site of implant of the endometrial tissue.

NONINFLAMMATORY DISORDERS OF FEMALE GENITAL TRACT (N80-N98)

● **N80   Endometriosis**

   N80.0   Endometriosis of uterus
      Adenomyosis
      | Excludes1 | stromal endometriosis (D39.0)

   N80.1   Endometriosis of ovary

   N80.2   Endometriosis of fallopian tube

   N80.3   Endometriosis of pelvic peritoneum

   N80.4   Endometriosis of rectovaginal septum and vagina

   N80.5   Endometriosis of intestine

   N80.6   Endometriosis in cutaneous scar

   N80.8   Other endometriosis

   ◼ **N80.9   Endometriosis, unspecified**

● **N81   Female genital prolapse**
   | Excludes1 | genital prolapse complicating pregnancy, labor or delivery (O34.5-)
      prolapse and hernia of ovary and fallopian tube (N83.4)
      prolapse of vaginal vault after hysterectomy (N99.3)

   N81.0   Urethrocele
      | Excludes1 | urethrocele with cystocele (N81.1-)
         urethrocele with prolapse of uterus (N81.2-N81.4)

   ● **N81.1   Cystocele**
      Cystocele with urethrocele
      Cystourethrocele
      | Excludes1 | cystocele with prolapse of uterus (N81.2-N81.4)

      ◼ **N81.10   Cystocele, unspecified**
         Prolapse of (anterior) vaginal wall NOS

      N81.11   Cystocele, midline

      N81.12   Cystocele, lateral
         Paravaginal cystocele

   N81.2   Incomplete uterovaginal prolapse
      First degree uterine prolapse
      Prolapse of cervix NOS
      Second degree uterine prolapse
      | Excludes1 | cervical stump prolaspe (N81.85)

   N81.3   Complete uterovaginal prolapse
      Procidential (uteri) NOS
      Third degree uterine prolapse

● Unacceptable First-Listed Diagnosis   ● Use Additional Character(s)   ◼ Unspecified   **OGCR** Official Guidelines for Coding and Reporting

1250   🅒 Complication\Comorbidity   🅒 Major C\C | Excludes 1 | | Excludes 2 | Includes   Use additional   Code first   Code also

CHAPTER 14 (N00-N99)

▪ **N81.4   Uterovaginal prolapse, unspecified**
     Prolapse of uterus NOS

N81.5   Vaginal enterocele
     Excludes1   enterocele with prolapse of uterus
                (N81.2-N81.4)

N81.6   Rectocele
     Prolapse of posterior vaginal wall
     Excludes1   perineocele N81.81
                rectal prolapse (K62.3)
                rectocele with prolapse of uterus
                    (N81.2-N81.4)

● **N81.8   Other female genital prolapse**

N81.81   Perineocele

N81.82   Incompetence or weakening of pubocervical tissue

N81.83   Incompetence or weakening of rectovaginal tissue

N81.84   Pelvic muscle wasting
     Disuse atrophy of pelvic muscles and anal sphincter

N81.85   Cervical stump prolapse

N81.89   Other female genital prolapse
     Deficient perineum
     Old laceration of muscles of pelvic floor

▪ **N81.9   Female genital prolapse, unspecified**

● **N82   Fistulae involving female genital tract**
     Excludes1   vesicointestinal fistulae (N32.1)

N82.0   Vesicovaginal fistula

N82.1   Other female urinary-genital tract fistulae
     Cervicovesical fistula
     Ureterovaginal fistula
     Urethrovaginal fistula
     Uteroureteric fistula
     Uterovesical fistula

N82.2   Fistula of vagina to small intestine 🕸

N82.3   Fistula of vagina to large intestine 🕸
     Rectovaginal fistula

N82.4   Other female intestinal-genital tract fistulae 🕸
     Intestinouterine fistula

N82.5   Female genital tract-skin fistulae 🕸
     Uterus to abdominal wall fistula
     Vaginoperineal fistula

N82.8   Other female genital tract fistulae 🕸

▪ **N82.9   Female genital tract fistula, unspecified** 🕸

● **N83   Noninflammatory disorders of ovary, fallopian tube and broad ligament**
     Excludes2   hydrosalpinx (N70.1-)

N83.0   Follicular cyst of ovary
     Cyst of graafian follicle
     Hemorrhagic follicular cyst (of ovary)

N83.1   Corpus luteum cyst
     Hemorrhagic corpus luteum cyst

● **N83.2   Other and unspecified ovarian cysts**
     Excludes1   developmental ovarian cyst (Q50.1)
                neoplastic ovarian cyst (D27.-)
                polycystic ovarian syndrome (E28.2)
                Stein-Leventhal syndrome (E28.2)

▪ **N83.20   Unspecified ovarian cysts**

N83.29   Other ovarian cysts
     Retention cyst of ovary
     Simple cyst of ovary

● **N83.3   Acquired atrophy of ovary and fallopian tube**

N83.31   Acquired atrophy of ovary

N83.32   Acquired atrophy of fallopian tube

N83.33   Acquired atrophy of ovary and fallopian tube

N83.4   Prolapse and hernia of ovary and fallopian tube

● **N83.5   Torsion of ovary, ovarian pedicle and fallopian tube**
     Torsion of accessory tube

N83.51   Torsion of ovary and ovarian pedicle 🕸

N83.52   Torsion of fallopian tube 🕸
     Torsion of hydatid of Morgagni

N83.53   Torsion of ovary, ovarian pedicle and fallopian tube 🕸

N83.6   Hematosalpinx
     Excludes1   hematosalpinx (with) (in):
                hematocolpos (N89.7)
                hematometra (N85.7)
                tubal pregnancy (O00.1)

N83.7   Hematoma of broad ligament

N83.8   Other noninflammatory disorders of ovary, fallopian tube and broad ligament
     Broad ligament laceration syndrome [Allen-Masters]

▪ **N83.9   Noninflammatory disorder of ovary, fallopian tube and broad ligament, unspecified**

● **N84   Polyp of female genital tract**
     Excludes1   adenomatous polyp (D28.-)
                placental polyp (O90.89)

N84.0   Polyp of corpus uteri
     Polyp of endometrium
     Polyp of uterus NOS
     Excludes1   polypoid endometrial hyperplasia
                (N85.0-)

N84.1   Polyp of cervix uteri
     Mucous polyp of cervix

N84.2   Polyp of vagina

N84.3   Polyp of vulva
     Polyp of labia

N84.8   Polyp of other parts of female genital tract

▪ **N84.9   Polyp of female genital tract, unspecified**

● **N85   Other noninflammatory disorders of uterus, except cervix**
     Excludes1   endometriosis (N80.-)
                inflammatory diseases of uterus (N71.-)
                noninflammatory disorders of cervix, except
                    malposition (N86-N88)
                polyp of corpus uteri (N84.0)
                uterine prolapse (N81.-)

● **N85.0   Endometrial hyperplasia**

▪ **N85.00   Endometrial hyperplasia, unspecified**
     Hyperplasia (adenomatous) (cystic) (glandular) of endometrium
     Hyperplastic endometritis

N85.01   Benign endometrial hyperplasia
     Endometrial hyperplasia (complex) (simple) without atypia

N85.02   Endometrial intraepithelial neoplasia [EIN]
     Endometrial hyperplasia with atypia
     Excludes1   malignant neoplasm
                of endometrium
                (with endometrial
                intraepithelial neoplasia
                [EIN]) (C54.1)

● Unacceptable First-Listed Diagnosis   ● Use Additional Character(s)   ▪ Unspecified   **OGCR** Official Guidelines for Coding and Reporting

🕸 Complication\Comorbidity   🕸 Major C\C   Excludes 1   Excludes 2   Includes   Use additional   Code first   Code also   1251

CHAPTER 14 (N00-N99)

N85.2 Hypertrophy of uterus
Bulky or enlarged uterus

> **Excludes1**   puerperal hypertrophy of uterus (O90.89)

N85.3 Subinvolution of uterus

> **Excludes1**   puerperal subinvolution of uterus (O90.89)

N85.4 Malposition of uterus
Anteversion of uterus
Retroflexion of uterus
Retroversion of uterus

> **Excludes1**   malposition of uterus complicating pregnancy, labor or delivery (O34.5-, O65.5)

N85.5 Inversion of uterus

> **Excludes1**   current obstetric trauma (O71.2) postpartum inversion of uterus (O71.2)

N85.6 Intrauterine synechiae

N85.7 Hematometra
Hematosalpinx with hematometra

> **Excludes1**   hematometra with hematocolpos (N89.7)

N85.8 Other specified noninflammatory disorders of uterus
Atrophy of uterus, acquired
Fibrosis of uterus NOS

▪N85.9 Noninflammatory disorder of uterus, unspecified
Disorder of uterus NOS

N86 Erosion and ectropion of cervix uteri

> **Includes**   decubitus (trophic) ulcer of cervix eversion of cervix

> **Excludes1**   erosion and ectropion of cervix with cervicitis (N72)

● N87 Dysplasia of cervix uteri

> **Excludes1**   abnormal results from cervical cytologic examination without histologic confirmation (R87.61-)
> carcinoma in situ of cervix uteri (D06.-)
> cervical intraepithelial neoplasia III [CIN III] (D06.-)
> HGSIL of cervix (R87.613)
> severe dysplasia of cervix uteri (D06.-)

N87.0 Mild cervical dysplasia
Cervical intraepithelial neoplasia I [CIN I]

N87.1 Moderate cervical dysplasia
Cervical intraepithelial neoplasia II [CIN II]

▪N87.9 Dysplasia of cervix uteri, unspecified
Anaplasia of cervix
Cervical atypism
Cervical dysplasia NOS

● N88 Other noninflammatory disorders of cervix uteri

> **Excludes2**   inflammatory disease of cervix (N72) polyp of cervix (N84.1)

N88.0 Leukoplakia of cervix uteri

N88.1 Old laceration of cervix uteri
Adhesions of cervix

> **Excludes1**   current obstetric trauma (O71.3)

N88.2 Stricture and stenosis of cervix uteri

> **Excludes1**   stricture and stenosis of cervix uteri complicating labor (O65.5)

N88.3 Incompetence of cervix uteri
Investigation and management of (suspected) cervical incompetence in a nonpregnant woman

> **Excludes1**   cervical incompetence complicating pregnancy (O34.3-)

N88.4 Hypertrophic elongation of cervix uteri

N88.8 Other specified noninflammatory disorders of cervix uteri

> **Excludes1**   current obstetric trauma (O71.3)

▪N88.9 Noninflammatory disorder of cervix uteri, unspecified

● N89 Other noninflammatory disorders of vagina

> **Excludes1**   abnormal results from vaginal cytologic examination without histologic confirmation (R87.62-)
> carcinoma in situ of vagina (D07.2)
> HGSIL of vagina (R87.623)
> inflammation of vagina (N76.-)
> senile (atrophic) vaginitis (N95.2)
> severe dysplasia of vagina (D07.2)
> trichomonal leukorrhea (A59.00)
> vaginal intraepithelial neoplasia [VAIN], grade III (D07.2)

N89.0 Mild vaginal dysplasia
Vaginal intraepithelial neoplasia [VAIN], grade I

N89.1 Moderate vaginal dysplasia
Vaginal intraepithelial neoplasia [VAIN], grade II

▪N89.3 Dysplasia of vagina, unspecified

N89.4 Leukoplakia of vagina

N89.5 Stricture and atresia of vagina
Vaginal adhesions   Vaginal stenosis

> **Excludes1**   congenital atresia or stricture (Q52.4) postprocedural adhesions of vagina (N99.2)

N89.6 Tight hymenal ring
Rigid hymen   Tight introitus

> **Excludes1**   imperforate hymen (Q52.3)

N89.7 Hematocolpos
Hematocolpos with hematometra or hematosalpinx

N89.8 Other specified noninflammatory disorders of vagina
Leukorrhea NOS
Old vaginal laceration
Pessary ulcer of vagina

> **Excludes1**   current obstetric trauma (O70.-, O71.4, O71.7-O71.8)
> old laceration involving muscles of pelvic floor (N81.8)

▪N89.9 Noninflammatory disorder of vagina, unspecified

● N90 Other noninflammatory disorders of vulva and perineum

> **Excludes1**   anogenital (venereal) warts (A63.0)
> carcinoma in situ of vulva (D07.1)
> condyloma acuminatum (A63.0)
> current obstetric trauma (O70.-, O71.7-O71.8)
> inflammation of vulva (N76.-)
> severe dysplasia of vulva (D07.1)
> vulvar intraepithelial neoplasm III [VIN III] (D07.1)

N90.0 Mild vulvar dysplasia
Vulvar intraepithelial neoplasia [VIN], grade I

N90.1 Moderate vulvar dysplasia
Vulvar intraepithelial neoplasia [VIN], grade II

CHAPTER 14 (N00-N99)

● Unacceptable First-Listed Diagnosis   ● Use Additional Character(s)   ▪ Unspecified   **OGCR** Official Guidelines for Coding and Reporting

1252   🗣 Complication\Comorbidity   🗣 Major C\C   Excludes 1   Excludes 2   Includes   Use additional   Code first   Code also

N90.3 **Dysplasia of vulva, unspecified**

N90.4 **Leukoplakia of vulva**
Dystrophy of vulva
Kraurosis of vulva
Lichen sclerosus of external female genital organs

N90.5 **Atrophy of vulva**
Stenosis of vulva

N90.6 **Hypertrophy of vulva**
Hypertrophy of labia

N90.7 **Vulvar cyst**

● N90.8 **Other specified noninflammatory disorders of vulva and perineum**

    ● N90.81 **Female genital mutilation status**
    Female genital cutting status

        ◻ N90.810 **Female genital mutilation status, unspecified**
        Female genital cutting status, unspecified
        Female genital mutilation status NOS

        N90.811 **Female genital mutilation Type I status**
        Clitorectomy status
        Female genital cutting Type I status

        N90.812 **Female genital mutilation Type II status**
        Clitorectomy with excision of labia minora status
        Female genital cutting Type II status

        N90.813 **Female genital mutilation Type III status**
        Female genital cutting Type III status
        Infibulation status

        N90.818 **Other female genital mutilation status**
        Female genital cutting Type IV status
        Female genital mutilation Type IV status
        Other female genital cutting status

    N90.89 **Other specified noninflammatory disorders of vulva and perineum**
    Adhesions of vulva
    Hypertrophy of clitoris

◻ N90.9 **Noninflammatory disorder of vulva and perineum, unspecified**

● N91 **Absent, scanty and rare menstruation**
    | **Excludes1** | ovarian dysfunction (E28.-) |

N91.0 **Primary amenorrhea**

N91.1 **Secondary amenorrhea**

◻ N91.2 **Amenorrhea, unspecified**

N91.3 **Primary oligomenorrhea**

N91.4 **Secondary oligomenorrhea**

◻ N91.5 **Oligomenorrhea, unspecified**
Hypomenorrhea NOS

● N92 **Excessive, frequent and irregular menstruation**
    | **Excludes1** | postmenopausal bleeding (N95.0) |

N92.0 **Excessive and frequent menstruation with regular cycle**
Heavy periods NOS   Polymenorrhea
Menorrhagia NOS

N92.1 **Excessive and frequent menstruation with irregular cycle**
Irregular intermenstrual bleeding
Irregular, shortened intervals between menstrual bleeding
Menometrorrhagia
Metrorrhagia

N92.2 **Excessive menstruation at puberty**
Excessive bleeding associated with onset of menstrual periods
Pubertal menorrhagia
Puberty bleeding

N92.3 **Ovulation bleeding**
Regular intermenstrual bleeding

N92.4 **Excessive bleeding in the premenopausal period**
Climacteric menorrhagia or metrorrhagia
Menopausal menorrhagia or metrorrhagia
Preclimacteric menorrhagia or metrorrhagia
Premenopausal menorrhagia or metrorrhagia

N92.5 **Other specified irregular menstruation**

◻ N92.6 **Irregular menstruation, unspecified**
Irregular bleeding NOS
Irregular periods NOS
    | **Excludes1** | irregular menstruation with: lengthened intervals or scanty bleeding (N91.3-N91.5) shortened intervals or excessive bleeding (N92.1) |

● N93 **Other abnormal uterine and vaginal bleeding**
    | **Excludes1** | neonatal vaginal hemorrhage (P54.6) pseudomenses (P54.6) |

N93.0 **Postcoital and contact bleeding**

N93.8 **Other specified abnormal uterine and vaginal bleeding**
Dysfunctional or functional uterine or vaginal bleeding NOS

◻ N93.9 **Abnormal uterine and vaginal bleeding, unspecified**

● N94 **Pain and other conditions associated with female genital organs and menstrual cycle**

N94.0 **Mittelschmerz**
Ovulation pain

N94.1 **Dyspareunia**
Painful intercourse/coitus
    | **Excludes1** | psychogenic dyspareunia (F52.6) |

N94.2 **Vaginismus**
Vagina tightness
    | **Excludes1** | psychogenic vaginismus (F52.5) |

N94.3 **Premenstrual tension syndrome**
AKA: PMS
Premenstrual dysphoric disorder
Code also associated menstrual migraine (G43.d-)

N94.4 **Primary dysmenorrhea**
Lifelong painful menstruation

N94.5 **Secondary dysmenorrhea**
Later onset of painful menstruation

◻ N94.6 **Dysmenorrhea, unspecified**
    | **Excludes1** | psychogenic dysmenorrhea (F45.8) |

● N94.8 **Other specified conditions associated with female genital organs and menstrual cycle**

    ● N94.81 **Vulvodynia**

        N94.810 **Vulvar vestibulitis**

        N94.818 **Other vulvodynia**

● Unacceptable First-Listed Diagnosis   ● Use Additional Character(s)   ◻ Unspecified   **OGCR** Official Guidelines for Coding and Reporting
⬙ Complication\Comorbidity   ⬙ Major C\C   ☐ Excludes 1   ☐ Excludes 2   Includes   Use additional   Code first   Code also

■ **N94.819**   Vulvodynia, unspecified
       Vulvodynia NOS

N94.89   Other specified conditions associated with female genital organs and menstrual cycle

■ **N94.9**   Unspecified condition associated with female genital organs and menstrual cycle

● **N95**   Menopausal and other perimenopausal disorders
      Menopausal and other perimenopausal disorders due to naturally occurring (age-related) menopause and perimenopause

> **Excludes1**   excessive bleeding in the premenopausal period (N92.4)
> menopausal and perimenopausal disorders due to artificial or premature menopause (E89.4-, E28.31-)
> premature menopause (E28.31-)

> **Excludes2**   postmenopausal osteoporosis (M81.0-)
> postmenopausal osteoporosis with current pathological fracture (M80.0-)
> postmenopausal urethritis (N34.2)

N95.0   Postmenopausal bleeding

N95.1   Menopausal and female climacteric states
     Symptoms such as flushing, sleeplessness, headache, lack of concentration, associated with natural (age-related) menopause

     Use additional code for associated symptoms

> **Excludes1**   asymptomatic menopausal state (Z78.0)
> symptoms associated with artificial menopause (E89.41)
> symptoms associated with premature menopause (E28.310)

N95.2   Postmenopausal atrophic vaginitis
     Senile (atrophic) vaginitis

N95.8   Other specified menopausal and perimenopausal disorders

■ **N95.9**   Unspecified menopausal and perimenopausal disorder

N96   Habitual aborter

> **Includes**   investigation or care in a nonpregnant woman

> **Excludes1**   habitual aborter with current pregnancy (O26.2-)

● **N97**   Female infertility

> **Includes**   inability to achieve a pregnancy
> sterility, female NOS

> **Excludes1**   female infertility associated with:
> hypopituitarism (E23.0)
> Stein-Leventhal syndrome (E28.2)

> **Excludes2**   incompetence of cervix uteri (N88.3)

N97.0   Female infertility associated with anovulation

N97.1   Female infertility of tubal origin
     Female infertility associated with congenital anomaly of tube
     Female infertility due to tubal block
     Female infertility due to tubal occlusion
     Female infertility due to tubal stenosis

N97.2   Female infertility of uterine origin
     Female infertility associated with congenital anomaly of uterus
     Female infertility due to nonimplantation of ovum

N97.8   Female infertility of other origin

■ **N97.9**   Female infertility, unspecified

● **N98**   Complications associated with artificial fertilization

N98.0   Infection associated with artificial insemination 🔖

N98.1   Hyperstimulation of ovaries 🔖
     Hyperstimulation of ovaries NOS
     Hyperstimulation of ovaries associated with induced ovulation

N98.2   Complications of attempted introduction of fertilized ovum following in vitro fertilization 🔖

N98.3   Complications of attempted introduction of embryo in embryo transfer 🔖

N98.8   Other complications associated with artificial fertilization 🔖

■ **N98.9**   Complication associated with artificial fertilization, unspecified 🔖

INTRAOPERATIVE AND POSTPROCEDURAL COMPLICATIONS AND DISORDERS OF GENITOURINARY SYSTEM, NOT ELSEWHERE CLASSIFIED (N99)

● **N99**   Intraoperative and postprocedural complications and disorders of genitourinary system, not elsewhere classified

> **Excludes2**   irradiation cystitis (N30.4-)
> postoophorectomy osteoporosis (M81.8-)
> postoophorectomy osteoporosis with current pathological fracture (M80.8-)

N99.0   Postprocedural (acute) (chronic) kidney failure
     Use additional code to type of kidney disease

● **N99.1**   Postprocedural urethral stricture
     Postcatheterization urethral stricture

   ● **N99.11**   Postprocedural urethral stricture, male

      N99.110   Postprocedural urethral stricture, male, meatal

      N99.111   Postprocedural bulbous urethral stricture

      N99.112   Postprocedural membranous urethral stricture

      N99.113   Postprocedural anterior urethral stricture

      ■ **N99.114**   Postprocedural urethral stricture, male, unspecified

    N99.12   Postprocedural urethral stricture, female

N99.2   Postprocedural adhesions of vagina

N99.3   Prolapse of vaginal vault after hysterectomy

N99.4   Postprocedural pelvic peritoneal adhesions

> **Excludes2**   pelvic peritoneal adhesions NOS (N73.6)
> postinfective pelvic peritoneal adhesions (N73.6)

● **N99.5**   Complications of stoma of urinary tract

> **Excludes2**   mechanical complication of urinary (indwelling) catheter (T83.0-)

   ● **N99.51**   Complication of cystostomy

      N99.510   Cystostomy hemorrhage

      N99.511   Cystostomy infection

      N99.512   Cystostomy malfunction

      N99.518   Other cystostomy complication

   ● **N99.52**   Complication of other external stoma of urinary tract

      N99.520   Hemorrhage of other external stoma of urinary tract

      N99.521   Infection of other external stoma of urinary tract

● Unacceptable First-Listed Diagnosis   ● Use Additional Character(s)   ■ Unspecified   **OGCR** Official Guidelines for Coding and Reporting
🔖 Complication\Comorbidity   🔖 Major C\C   Excludes 1   Excludes 2   Includes   Use additional   Code first   Code also

N99.522　Malfunction of other external stoma of urinary tract

N99.528　Other complication of other external stoma of urinary tract

● N99.53　Complication of other stoma of urinary tract

N99.530　Hemorrhage of other stoma of urinary tract

N99.531　Infection of other stoma of urinary tract

N99.532　Malfunction of other stoma of urinary tract

N99.538　Other complication of other stoma of urinary tract

● N99.6　Intraoperative hemorrhage and hematoma of a genitourinary system organ or structure complicating a procedure

> Excludes1　intraoperative hemorrhage and hematoma of a genitourinary system organ or structure due to accidental puncture or laceration during a procedure (N99.7-)

N99.61　Intraoperative hemorrhage and hematoma of a genitourinary system organ or structure complicating a genitourinary system procedure

N99.62　Intraoperative hemorrhage and hematoma of a genitourinary system organ or structure complicating other procedure

● N99.7　Accidental puncture and laceration of a genitourinary system organ or structure during a procedure

N99.71　Accidental puncture and laceration of a genitourinary system organ or structure during a genitourinary system procedure

N99.72　Accidental puncture and laceration of a genitourinary system organ or structure during other procedure

● N99.8　Other intraoperative and postprocedural complications and disorders of genitourinary system

N99.81　Other intraoperative complications of genitourinary system

● N99.82　Postprocedural hemorrhage and hematoma of a genitourinary system organ or structure following a procedure

N99.820　Postprocedural hemorrhage and hematoma of a genitourinary system organ or structure following a genitourinary system procedure

N99.821　Postprocedural hemorrhage and hematoma of a genitourinary system organ or structure following other procedure

N99.83　Residual ovary syndrome

N99.89　Other postprocedural complications and disorders of genitourinary system

> Excludes1　continuing pregnancy in multiple gestation after abortion of one fetus or more (O31.1-, O31.3-)

● Unacceptable First-Listed Diagnosis　　● Use Additional Character(s)　　▨ Unspecified　　**OGCR** Official Guidelines for Coding and Reporting

 Complication\Comorbidity　　 Major C\C　　 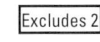　　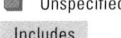 Use additional　　Code first　　Code also

1255

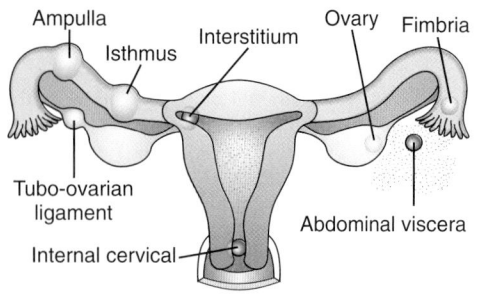

Figure 15-1 Implantation sites of ectopic pregnancy.

Item 15-1 Ectopic pregnancy most often occurs in the fallopian tube. Pregnancy outside the uterus may end in a lifethreatening rupture.

OGCR See Section I.C.15.
    Chapter 15 Pregnancy, Childbirth, and the Puerperium

(See Plate 375 on page NAP-4.)

CHAPTER 15

PREGNANCY, CHILDBIRTH AND THE PUERPERIUM (O00-O99)

Note: CODES FROM THIS CHAPTER ARE FOR USE ONLY ON MATERNAL RECORDS, NEVER ON NEWBORN RECORDS

Codes from this chapter are for use for conditions related to or aggravated by the pregnancy, childbirth, or by the puerperium (maternal causes or obstetric causes)

Note: Trimesters are counted from the first day of the last menstrual period. They are defined as follows:

1st trimester - less than 14 weeks 0 days
2nd trimester - 14 weeks 0 days to less than
       28 weeks 0 days
3rd trimester - 28 weeks 0 days until delivery

| Excludes1 | supervision of normal pregnancy (Z34.-) |
| Excludes2 | mental and behavioral disorders associated with the puerperium (F53) obstetrical tetanus (A34) postpartum necrosis of pituitary gland (E23.0) puerperal osteomalacia (M83.0) |

This chapter contains the following blocks:

O00-O08	Pregnancy with abortive outcome
O09	Supervision of high risk pregnancy
O10-O16	Edema, proteinuria and hypertensive disorders in pregnancy, childbirth and the puerperium
O20-O29	Other maternal disorders predominantly related to pregnancy
O30-O48	Maternal care related to the fetus and amniotic cavity and possible delivery problems
O60-O77	Complications of labor and delivery
O80, O82	Encounter for delivery
O85-O92	Complications predominantly related to the puerperium
O94-O9A	Other obstetric conditions, not elsewhere classified

PREGNANCY WITH ABORTIVE OUTCOME (O00-O08)

● O00 Ectopic pregnancy
    Includes   ruptured ectopic pregnancy
    Use additional code from category O08 to identify any associated complication

    O00.0 Abdominal pregnancy 🅒
        Excludes1   maternal care for viable fetus in abdominal pregnancy (O36.7-)

    O00.1 Tubal pregnancy 🅒
        Fallopian pregnancy
        Rupture of (fallopian) tube due to pregnancy
        Tubal abortion

    O00.2 Ovarian pregnancy 🅒

    O00.8 Other ectopic pregnancy 🅒
        Cervical pregnancy
        Cornual pregnancy
        Intraligamentous pregnancy
        Mural pregnancy

    ■ O00.9 Ectopic pregnancy, unspecified 🅒

Item 15-2 A **hydatidiform** mole is a benign tumor of the placenta. The tumor secretes a hormone, chorionic gonadotropic hormone (CGH), that indicates a positive pregnancy test.

● O01 Hydatidiform mole
        Use additional code from category O08 to identify any associated complication
        Excludes1   chorioadenoma (destruens) (D39.2)
                     malignant hydatidiform mole (D39.2)

    O01.0 Classical hydatidiform mole
        Complete hydatidiform mole

    O01.1 Incomplete and partial hydatidiform mole

    ■ O01.9 Hydatidiform mole, unspecified
        Trophoblastic disease NOS
        Vesicular mole NOS

● O02 Other abnormal products of conception
        Use additional code from category O08 to identify any associated complication
        Excludes1   papyraceous fetus (O31.0-)

    O02.0 Blighted ovum and nonhydatidiform mole
        Carneous mole   Molar pregnancy NEC
        Fleshy mole   Pathological ovum
        Intrauterine mole NOS

    O02.1 Missed abortion
        Early fetal death, before completion of 20 weeks of gestation, with retention of dead fetus
        Excludes1   failed induced abortion (O07.-)
                     fetal death (intrauterine) (late) (O36.4)
                     missed abortion with blighted ovum (O02.0)
                     missed abortion with hydatidiform mole (O01.-)
                     missed abortion with nonhydatidiform (O02.0)
                     missed delivery (O36.4)
                     stillbirth (P95)

    O02.8 Other specified abnormal products of conception
        Excludes1   abnormal products of conception with blighted ovum (O02.0)
                     abnormal products of conception with hydatidiform mole (O01.-)
                     abnormal products of conception with nonhydatidiform mole (O02.0)

    ■ O02.9 Abnormal product of conception, unspecified

● Unacceptable First-Listed Diagnosis   ● Use Additional Character(s)   ■ Unspecified   **OGCR** Official Guidelines for Coding and Reporting
🅒 Complication\Comorbidity 🅒 Major C\C   Excludes 1   Excludes 2   Includes   Use additional   Code first   Code also

● **O03 Spontaneous abortion**

> **Note:** Incomplete abortion includes retained products of conception following spontaneous abortion.

> **Includes** miscarriage

O03.0 Genital tract and pelvic infection following incomplete spontaneous abortion 🩸

    Endometritis following incomplete spontaneous abortion

    Oophoritis following incomplete spontaneous abortion

    Parametritis following incomplete spontaneous abortion

    Pelvic peritonitis following incomplete spontaneous abortion

    Salpingitis following incomplete spontaneous abortion

    Salpingo-oophoritis following incomplete spontaneous abortion

> **Excludes1** sepsis following incomplete spontaneous abortion (O03.37)
> urinary tract infection following incomplete spontaneous abortion (O03.38)

O03.1 Delayed or excessive hemorrhage following incomplete spontaneous abortion

    Afibrinogenemia following incomplete spontaneous abortion

    Defibrination syndrome following incomplete spontaneous abortion

    Hemolysis following incomplete spontaneous abortion

    Intravascular coagulation following incomplete spontaneous abortion

O03.2 Embolism following incomplete spontaneous abortion 🩸

    Air embolism following incomplete spontaneous abortion

    Amniotic fluid embolism following incomplete spontaneous abortion

    Blood-clot embolism following incomplete spontaneous abortion

    Embolism NOS following incomplete spontaneous abortion

    Fat embolism following incomplete spontaneous abortion

    Pulmonary embolism following incomplete spontaneous abortion

    Pyemic embolism following incomplete spontaneous abortion

    Septic or septicopyemic embolism following incomplete spontaneous abortion

    Soap embolism following incomplete spontaneous abortion

● **O03.3 Other and unspecified complications following incomplete spontaneous abortion**

■ **O03.30 Unspecified complication following incomplete spontaneous abortion** 🩸

O03.31 Shock following incomplete spontaneous abortion 🩸

    Circulatory collapse following incomplete spontaneous abortion

    Shock (postprocedural) following incomplete spontaneous abortion

> **Excludes1** shock due to infection following incomplete spontaneous abortion (O03.37)

O03.32 Renal failure following incomplete spontaneous abortion 🩸

    Kidney failure (acute) following incomplete spontaneous abortion

    Oliguria following incomplete spontaneous abortion

    Renal shutdown following incomplete spontaneous abortion

    Renal tubular necrosis following incomplete spontaneous abortion

    Uremia following incomplete spontaneous abortion

O03.33 Metabolic disorder following incomplete spontaneous abortion 🩸

O03.34 Damage to pelvic organs following incomplete spontaneous abortion 🩸

    Laceration, perforation, tear or chemical damage of bladder following incomplete spontaneous abortion

    Laceration, perforation, tear or chemical damage of bowel following incomplete spontaneous abortion

    Laceration, perforation, tear or chemical damage of broad ligament following incomplete spontaneous abortion

    Laceration, perforation, tear or chemical damage of cervix following incomplete spontaneous abortion

    Laceration, perforation, tear or chemical damage of periurethral tissue following incomplete spontaneous abortion

    Laceration, perforation, tear or chemical damage of uterus following incomplete spontaneous abortion

    Laceration, perforation, tear or chemical damage of vagina following incomplete spontaneous abortion

O03.35 Other venous complications following incomplete spontaneous abortion 🩸

O03.36 Cardiac arrest following incomplete spontaneous abortion 🩸

O03.37 Sepsis following incomplete spontaneous abortion 🩸

> Use additional code (B95-B97), to identify infectious agent

> Use additional code (R65.2-) to identify severe sepsis, if applicable

> **Excludes1** septic or septicopyemic embolism following incomplete spontaneous abortion (O03.2)

O03.38 Urinary tract infection following incomplete spontaneous abortion 🩸

    Cystitis following incomplete spontaneous abortion

O03.39 Incomplete spontaneous abortion with other complications 🩸

O03.4 Incomplete spontaneous abortion without complication

● Unacceptable First-Listed Diagnosis   ● Use Additional Character(s)   ■ Unspecified   **OGCR** Official Guidelines for Coding and Reporting

🩸 Complication\Comorbidity   🩸 Major C\C   Excludes 1   Excludes 2   Includes   Use additional   Code first   Code also

■ **O03.5** **Genital tract and pelvic infection following complete or unspecified spontaneous abortion** 🅒
Endometritis following complete or unspecified spontaneous abortion
Oophoritis following complete or unspecified spontaneous abortion
Parametritis following complete or unspecified spontaneous abortion
Pelvic peritonitis following complete or unspecified spontaneous abortion
Salpingitis following complete or unspecified spontaneous abortion
Salpingo-oophoritis following complete or unspecified spontaneous abortion

> **Excludes1** sepsis following complete or unspecified spontaneous abortion (O03.87)
> urinary tract infection following complete or unspecified spontaneous abortion (O03.88)

■ **O03.6** **Delayed or excessive hemorrhage following complete or unspecified spontaneous abortion**
Afibrinogenemia following complete or unspecified spontaneous abortion
Defibrination syndrome following complete or unspecified spontaneous abortion
Hemolysis following complete or unspecified spontaneous abortion
Intravascular coagulation following complete or unspecified spontaneous abortion

■ **O03.7** **Embolism following complete or unspecified spontaneous abortion** 🅒
Air embolism following complete or unspecified spontaneous abortion
Amniotic fluid embolism following complete or unspecified spontaneous abortion
Blood-clot embolism following complete or unspecified spontaneous abortion
Embolism NOS following complete or unspecified spontaneous abortion
Fat embolism following complete or unspecified spontaneous abortion
Pulmonary embolism following complete or unspecified spontaneous abortion
Pyemic embolism following complete or unspecified spontaneous abortion
Septic or septicopyemic embolism following complete or unspecified spontaneous abortion
Soap embolism following complete or unspecified spontaneous abortion

● **O03.8** **Other and unspecified complications following complete or unspecified spontaneous abortion**

■ **O03.80** **Unspecified complication following complete or unspecified spontaneous abortion** 🅒

■ **O03.81** **Shock following complete or unspecified spontaneous abortion** 🅒
Circulatory collapse following complete or unspecified spontaneous abortion
Shock (postprocedural) following complete or unspecified spontaneous abortion

> **Excludes1** shock due to infection following complete or unspecified spontaneous abortion (O03.87)

■ **O03.82** **Renal failure following complete or unspecified spontaneous abortion** 🅒
Kidney failure (acute) following complete or unspecified spontaneous abortion
Oliguria following complete or unspecified spontaneous abortion
Renal shutdown following complete or unspecified spontaneous abortion
Renal tubular necrosis following complete or unspecified spontaneous abortion
Uremia following complete or unspecified spontaneous abortion

■ **O03.83** **Metabolic disorder following complete or unspecified spontaneous abortion** 🅒

■ **O03.84** **Damage to pelvic organs following complete or unspecified spontaneous abortion** 🅒
Laceration, perforation, tear or chemical damage of bladder following complete or unspecified spontaneous abortion
Laceration, perforation, tear or chemical damage of bowel following complete or unspecified spontaneous abortion
Laceration, perforation, tear or chemical damage of broad ligament following complete or unspecified spontaneous abortion
Laceration, perforation, tear or chemical damage of cervix following complete or unspecified spontaneous abortion
Laceration, perforation, tear or chemical damage of periurethral tissue following complete or unspecified spontaneous abortion
Laceration, perforation, tear or chemical damage of uterus following complete or unspecified spontaneous abortion
Laceration, perforation, tear or chemical damage of vagina following complete or unspecified spontaneous abortion

■ **O03.85** **Other venous complications following complete or unspecified spontaneous abortion** 🅒

■ **O03.86** **Cardiac arrest following complete or unspecified spontaneous abortion** 🅒

■ **O03.87** **Sepsis following complete or unspecified spontaneous abortion** 🅒
Use additional code (B95-B97), to identify infectious agent
Use additional code (R65.2-) to identify severe sepsis, if applicable

> **Excludes1** septic or septicopyemic embolism following complete or unspecified spontaneous abortion (O03.7)

■ **O03.88** **Urinary tract infection following complete or unspecified spontaneous abortion** 🅒
Cystitis following complete or unspecified spontaneous abortion

■ **O03.89** **Complete or unspecified spontaneous abortion with other complications** 🅒

■ **O03.9** **Complete or unspecified spontaneous abortion without complication**
Miscarriage NOS
Spontaneous abortion NOS

● Unacceptable First-Listed Diagnosis   ● Use Additional Character(s)   ■ Unspecified   **OGCR** Official Guidelines for Coding and Reporting
🅒 Complication\Comorbidity   🅒 Major C\C   Excludes 1   Excludes 2   Includes   Use additional   Code first   Code also

CHAPTER 15 (O00-O99)

● **O04**   **Complications following (induced) termination of pregnancy**

> **Includes**   complications following (induced) termination of pregnancy
>
> **Excludes1**   encounter for elective termination of pregnancy, uncomplicated (Z33.2)
> failed attempted termination of pregnancy (O07.-)

O04.5   **Genital tract and pelvic infection following (induced) termination of pregnancy** 🜂
> Endometritis following (induced) termination of pregnancy
> Oophoritis following (induced) termination of pregnancy
> Parametritis following (induced) termination of pregnancy
> Pelvic peritonitis following (induced) termination of pregnancy
> Salpingitis following (induced) termination of pregnancy
> Salpingo-oophoritis following (induced) termination of pregnancy
>
>> **Excludes1**   sepsis following (induced) termination of pregnancy (O04.87)
>> urinary tract infection following (induced) termination of pregnancy (O04.88)

O04.6   **Delayed or excessive hemorrhage following (induced) termination of pregnancy**
> Afibrinogenemia following (induced) termination of pregnancy
> Defibrination syndrome following (induced) termination of pregnancy
> Hemolysis following (induced) termination of pregnancy
> Intravascular coagulation following (induced) termination of pregnancy

O04.7   **Embolism following (induced) termination of pregnancy** 🜂
> Air embolism following (induced) termination of pregnancy
> Amniotic fluid embolism following (induced) termination of pregnancy
> Blood-clot embolism following (induced) termination of pregnancy
> Embolism NOS following (induced) termination of pregnancy
> Fat embolism following (induced) termination of pregnancy
> Pulmonary embolism following (induced) termination of pregnancy
> Pyemic embolism following (induced) termination of pregnancy
> Septic or septicopyemic embolism following (induced) termination of pregnancy
> Soap embolism following (induced) termination of pregnancy

● **O04.8**   **(Induced) termination of pregnancy with other and unspecified complications**

▪ **O04.80**   **(Induced) termination of pregnancy with unspecified complications** 🜂

O04.81   **Shock following (induced) termination of pregnancy** 🜂
> Circulatory collapse following (induced) termination of pregnancy
> Shock due to infection following (induced) termination of pregnancy
>
>> **Excludes1**   septic shock following (induced) termination of pregnancy (O04.87)

O04.82   **Renal failure following (induced) termination of pregnancy** 🜂
> Kidney failure (acute) following (induced) termination of pregnancy
> Oliguria following (induced) termination of pregnancy
> Renal shutdown following (induced) termination of pregnancy
> Renal tubular necrosis following (induced) termination of pregnancy
> Uremia following (induced) termination of pregnancy

O04.83   **Metabolic disorder following (induced) termination of pregnancy** 🜂

O04.84   **Damage to pelvic organs following (induced) termination of pregnancy** 🜂
> Laceration, perforation, tear or chemical damage of bladder following (induced) termination of pregnancy
> Laceration, perforation, tear or chemical damage of bowel following (induced) termination of pregnancy
> Laceration, perforation, tear or chemical damage of broad ligament following (induced) termination of pregnancy
> Laceration, perforation, tear or chemical damage of cervix following (induced) termination of pregnancy
> Laceration, perforation, tear or chemical damage of periurethral tissue following (induced) termination of pregnancy
> Laceration, perforation, tear or chemical damage of uterus following (induced) termination of pregnancy
> Laceration, perforation, tear or chemical damage of vagina following (induced) termination of pregnancy

O04.85   **Other venous complications following (induced) termination of pregnancy** 🜂

O04.86   **Cardiac arrest following (induced) termination of pregnancy** 🜂

O04.87   **Sepsis following (induced) termination of pregnancy** 🜂
> Use additional code (B95-B97), to identify infectious agent
> Use additional code (R65.2-) to identify severe sepsis, if applicable
>
>> **Excludes1**   septic or septicopyemic embolism following (induced) termination of pregnancy (O04.2)

O04.88   **Urinary tract infection following (induced) termination of pregnancy** 🜂
> Cystitis following (induced) termination of pregnancy

O04.89   **(Induced) termination of pregnancy with other complications** 🜂

● **O07**   **Failed attempted termination of pregnancy**

> **Includes**   failure of attempted induction of termination of pregnancy
> incomplete elective abortion
>
> **Excludes1**   incomplete spontaneous abortion (O03.0-)

● Unacceptable First-Listed Diagnosis   ● Use Additional Character(s)   ▪ Unspecified   **OGCR** Official Guidelines for Coding and Reporting

🜂 Complication\Comorbidity   🜂 Major C\C   Excludes 1   Excludes 2   Includes   Use additional   Code first   Code also

O07.0   Genital tract and pelvic infection following failed attempted termination of pregnancy 🍇
    Endometritis following failed attempted termination of pregnancy
    Oophoritis following failed attempted termination of pregnancy
    Parametritis following failed attempted termination of pregnancy
    Pelvic peritonitis following failed attempted termination of pregnancy
    Salpingitis following failed attempted termination of pregnancy
    Salpingo-oophoritis following failed attempted termination of pregnancy

    Excludes1   sepsis following failed attempted termination of pregnancy (O07.37)
        urinary tract infection following failed attempted termination of pregnancy (O07.38)

O07.1   Delayed or excessive hemorrhage following failed attempted termination of pregnancy 🍇
    Afibrinogenemia following failed attempted termination of pregnancy
    Defibrination syndrome following failed attempted termination of pregnancy
    Hemolysis following failed attempted termination of pregnancy
    Intravascular coagulation following failed attempted termination of pregnancy

O07.2   Embolism following failed attempted termination of pregnancy 🍇
    Air embolism following failed attempted termination of pregnancy
    Amniotic fluid embolism following failed attempted termination of pregnancy
    Blood-clot embolism following failed attempted termination of pregnancy
    Embolism NOS following failed attempted termination of pregnancy
    Fat embolism following failed attempted termination of pregnancy
    Pulmonary embolism following failed attempted termination of pregnancy
    Pyemic embolism following failed attempted termination of pregnancy
    Septic or septicopyemic embolism following failed attempted termination of pregnancy
    Soap embolism following failed attempted termination of pregnancy

● **O07.3   Failed attempted termination of pregnancy with other and unspecified complications**

  ■ **O07.30   Failed attempted termination of pregnancy with unspecified complications** 🍇

  O07.31   Shock following failed attempted termination of pregnancy 🍇
    Circulatory collapse following failed attempted termination of pregnancy
    Shock (postprocedural) following failed attempted termination of pregnancy

    Excludes1   shock due to infection following failed attempted termination of pregnancy (O07.37)

O07.32   Renal failure following failed attempted termination of pregnancy 🍇
    Kidney failure (acute) following failed attempted termination of pregnancy
    Oliguria following failed attempted termination of pregnancy
    Renal shutdown following failed attempted termination of pregnancy
    Renal tubular necrosis following failed attempted termination of pregnancy
    Uremia following failed attempted termination of pregnancy

O07.33   Metabolic disorder following failed attempted termination of pregnancy 🍇

O07.34   Damage to pelvic organs following failed attempted termination of pregnancy 🍇
    Laceration, perforation, tear or chemical damage of bladder following failed attempted termination of pregnancy
    Laceration, perforation, tear or chemical damage of bowel following failed attempted termination of pregnancy
    Laceration, perforation, tear or chemical damage of broad ligament following failed attempted termination of pregnancy
    Laceration, perforation, tear or chemical damage of cervix following failed attempted termination of pregnancy
    Laceration, perforation, tear or chemical damage of periurethral tissue following failed attempted termination of pregnancy
    Laceration, perforation, tear or chemical damage of uterus following failed attempted termination of pregnancy
    Laceration, perforation, tear or chemical damage of vagina following failed attempted termination of pregnancy

O07.35   Other venous complications following failed attempted termination of pregnancy 🍇

O07.36   Cardiac arrest following failed attempted termination of pregnancy 🍇

O07.37   Sepsis following failed attempted termination of pregnancy 🍇

    Use additional code (B95-B97), to identify infectious agent
    Use additional code (R65.2-) to identify severe sepsis, if applicable

    Excludes1   septic or septicopyemic embolism following failed attempted termination of pregnancy (O07.2)

O07.38   Urinary tract infection following failed attempted termination of pregnancy 🍇
    Cystitis following failed attempted termination of pregnancy

O07.39   Failed attempted termination of pregnancy with other complications 🍇

O07.4   Failed attempted termination of pregnancy without complication

● **O08 Complications following ectopic and molar pregnancy**
This category is for use with categories O00-O02 to identify any associated complications.

O08.0 Genital tract and pelvic infection following ectopic and molar pregnancy 🍏
Endometritis following ectopic and molar pregnancy
Oophoritis following ectopic and molar pregnancy
Parametritis following ectopic and molar pregnancy
Pelvic peritonitis following ectopic and molar pregnancy
Salpingitis following ectopic and molar pregnancy
Salpingo-oophoritis following ectopic and molar pregnancy

> **Excludes1**   sepsis following ectopic and molar pregnancy (O08.82)
> urinary tract infection (O08.83)

O08.1 Delayed or excessive hemorrhage following ectopic and molar pregnancy 🍏
Afibrinogenemia following ectopic and molar pregnancy
Defibrination syndrome following ectopic and molar pregnancy
Hemolysis following ectopic and molar pregnancy
Intravascular coagulation following ectopic and molar pregnancy

> **Excludes1**   delayed or excessive hemorrhage due to incomplete abortion (O03.1)

O08.2 Embolism following ectopic and molar pregnancy 🍏
Air embolism following ectopic and molar pregnancy
Amniotic fluid embolism following ectopic and molar pregnancy
Blood-clot embolism following ectopic and molar pregnancy
Embolism NOS following ectopic and molar pregnancy
Fat embolism following ectopic and molar pregnancy
Pulmonary embolism following ectopic and molar pregnancy
Pyemic embolism following ectopic and molar pregnancy
Septic or septicopyemic embolism following ectopic and molar pregnancy
Soap embolism following ectopic and molar pregnancy

O08.3 Shock following ectopic and molar pregnancy 🍏
Circulatory collapse following ectopic and molar pregnancy
Shock (postprocedural) following ectopic and molar pregnancy

> **Excludes1**   shock due to infection following ectopic and molar pregnancy (O08.82)

O08.4 Renal failure following ectopic and molar pregnancy 🍏
Kidney failure (acute) following ectopic and molar pregnancy
Oliguria following ectopic and molar pregnancy
Renal shutdown following ectopic and molar pregnancy
Renal tubular necrosis following ectopic and molar pregnancy
Uremia following ectopic and molar pregnancy

O08.5 Metabolic disorders following an ectopic and molar pregnancy 🍏

O08.6 Damage to pelvic organs and tissues following an ectopic and molar pregnancy 🍏
Laceration, perforation, tear or chemical damage of bladder following an ectopic and molar pregnancy
Laceration, perforation, tear or chemical damage of bowel following an ectopic and molar pregnancy
Laceration, perforation, tear or chemical damage of broad ligament following an ectopic and molar pregnancy
Laceration, perforation, tear or chemical damage of cervix following an ectopic and molar pregnancy
Laceration, perforation, tear or chemical damage of periurethral tissue following an ectopic and molar pregnancy
Laceration, perforation, tear or chemical damage of uterus following an ectopic and molar pregnancy
Laceration, perforation, tear or chemical damage of vagina following an ectopic and molar pregnancy

O08.7 Other venous complications following an ectopic and molar pregnancy 🍏

● **O08.8 Other complications following an ectopic and molar pregnancy**

O08.81 Cardiac arrest following an ectopic and molar pregnancy 🍏

O08.82 Sepsis following ectopic and molar pregnancy 🍏

Use additional code (B95-B97), to identify infectious agent

Use additional code (R65.2-) to identify severe sepsis, if applicable

> **Excludes1**   septic or septicopyemic embolism following ectopic and molar pregnancy (O08.2)

O08.83 Urinary tract infection following an ectopic and molar pregnancy 🍏
Cystitis following an ectopic and molar pregnancy

O08.89 Other complications following an ectopic and molar pregnancy 🍏

■ **O08.9 Unspecified complication following an ectopic and molar pregnancy** 🍏

● **O09 Supervision of high risk pregnancy**

● **O09.0 Supervision of pregnancy with history of infertility**

■ **O09.00 Supervision of pregnancy with history of infertility, unspecified trimester**

O09.01 Supervision of pregnancy with history of infertility, first trimester

O09.02 Supervision of pregnancy with history of infertility, second trimester

O09.03 Supervision of pregnancy with history of infertility, third trimester

● **O09.1 Supervision of pregnancy with history of ectopic or molar pregnancy**

■ **O09.10 Supervision of pregnancy with history of ectopic or molar pregnancy, unspecified trimester**

O09.11 Supervision of pregnancy with history of ectopic or molar pregnancy, first trimester

● Unacceptable First-Listed Diagnosis   ● Use Additional Character(s)   ■ Unspecified   **OGCR** Official Guidelines for Coding and Reporting
🍏 Complication\Comorbidity   🍏 Major C\C   Excludes 1   Excludes 2   Includes   Use additional   Code first   Code also

1261

CHAPTER 15 (O00-O99)

O09.12   Supervision of pregnancy with history of ectopic or molar pregnancy, second trimester

O09.13   Supervision of pregnancy with history of ectopic or molar pregnancy, third trimester

● **O09.2**   Supervision of pregnancy with other poor reproductive or obstetric history

> Excludes2   pregnancy care of habitual aborter (O26.2-)

   ● **O09.21**   Supervision of pregnancy with history of pre-term labor

     O09.211   Supervision of pregnancy with history of pre-term labor, first trimester

     O09.212   Supervision of pregnancy with history of pre-term labor, second trimester

     O09.213   Supervision of pregnancy with history of pre-term labor, third trimester

     ■ **O09.219**   Supervision of pregnancy with history of pre-term labor, unspecified trimester

   ● **O09.29**   Supervision of pregnancy with other poor reproductive or obstetric history

> Supervision of pregnancy with history of neonatal death
> Supervision of pregnancy with history of stillbirth

     O09.291   Supervision of pregnancy with other poor reproductive or obstetric history, first trimester

     O09.292   Supervision of pregnancy with other poor reproductive or obstetric history, second trimester

     O09.293   Supervision of pregnancy with other poor reproductive or obstetric history, third trimester

     ■ **O09.299**   Supervision of pregnancy with other poor reproductive or obstetric history, unspecified trimester

● **O09.3**   Supervision of pregnancy with insufficient antenatal care

> Supervision of concealed pregnancy
> Supervision of hidden pregnancy

   ■ **O09.30**   Supervision of pregnancy with insufficient antenat al care, unspecified trimester

   O09.31   Supervision of pregnancy with insufficient antenatal care, first trimester

   O09.32   Supervision of pregnancy with insufficient antenatal care, second trimester

   O09.33   Supervision of pregnancy with insufficient antenatal care, third trimester

● **O09.4**   Supervision of pregnancy with grand multiparity

   ■ **O09.40**   Supervision of pregnancy with grand multiparity, unspecified trimester

   O09.41   Supervision of pregnancy with grand multiparity, first trimester

   O09.42   Supervision of pregnancy with grand multiparity, second trimester

   O09.43   Supervision of pregnancy with grand multiparity, third trimester

● **O09.5**   Supervision of elderly primigravida and multigravida

> Pregnancy for a female 35 years and older at expected date of delivery

   ● **O09.51**   Supervision of elderly primigravida

     O09.511   Supervision of elderly primigravida, first trimester

     O09.512   Supervision of elderly primigravida, second trimester

     O09.513   Supervision of elderly primigravida, third trimester

     ■ **O09.519**   Supervision of elderly primigravida, unspecified trimester

   ● **O09.52**   Supervision of elderly multigravida

     O09.521   Supervision of elderly multigravida, first trimester

     O09.522   Supervision of elderly multigravida, second trimester

     O09.523   Supervision of elderly multigravida, third trimester

     ■ **O09.529**   Supervision of elderly multigravida, unspecified trimester

● **O09.6**   Supervision of young primigravida and multigravida

> Supervision of pregnancy for a female less than 16 years old at expected date of delivery

   ● **O09.61**   Supervision of young primigravida

     O09.611   Supervision of young primigravida, first trimester

     O09.612   Supervision of young primigravida, second trimester

     O09.613   Supervision of young primigravida, third trimester

     ■ **O09.619**   Supervision of young primigravida, unspecified trimester

   ● **O09.62**   Supervision of young multigravida

     O09.621   Supervision of young multigravida, first trimester

     O09.622   Supervision of young multigravida, second trimester

     O09.623   Supervision of young multigravida, third trimester

     ■ **O09.629**   Supervision of young multigravida, unspecified trimester

● **O09.7**   Supervision of high risk pregnancy due to social problems

   ■ **O09.70**   Supervision of high risk pregnancy due to social problems, unspecified trimester

   O09.71   Supervision of high risk pregnancy due to social problems, first trimester

   O09.72   Supervision of high risk pregnancy due to social problems, second trimester

   O09.73   Supervision of high risk pregnancy due to social problems, third trimester

● **O09.8**   Supervision of other high risk pregnancies

   ● **O09.81**   Supervision of pregnancy resulting from assisted reproductive technology

> Supervision of pregnancy resulting from in-vitro fertilization

     O09.811   Supervision of pregnancy resulting from assisted reproductive technology, first trimester

     O09.812   Supervision of pregnancy resulting from assisted reproductive technology, second trimester

     O09.813   Supervision of pregnancy resulting from assisted reproductive technology, third trimester

▪ **O09.819** Supervision of pregnancy resulting from assisted reproductive technology, unspecified trimester

● **O09.82** Supervision of pregnancy with history of in utero procedure during previous pregnancy

     O09.821 Supervision of pregnancy with history of in utero procedure during previous pregnancy, first trimester

     O09.822 Supervision of pregnancy with history of in utero procedure during previous pregnancy, second trimester

     O09.823 Supervision of pregnancy with history of in utero procedure during previous pregnancy, third trimester

     ▪ **O09.829** Supervision of pregnancy with history of in utero procedure during previous pregnancy, unspecified trimester

         | Excludes1 | supervision of pregnancy affected by in utero procedure during current pregnancy (O35.7)

● **O09.89** Supervision of other high risk pregnancies

     O09.891 Supervision of other high risk pregnancies, first trimester

     O09.892 Supervision of other high risk pregnancies, second trimester

     O09.893 Supervision of other high risk pregnancies, third trimester

     ▪ **O09.899** Supervision of other high risk pregnancies, unspecified trimester

● **O09.9** Supervision of high risk pregnancy, unspecified

     ▪ **O09.90** Supervision of high risk pregnancy, unspecified, unspecified trimester

     ▪ **O09.91** Supervision of high risk pregnancy, unspecified, first trimester

     ▪ **O09.92** Supervision of high risk pregnancy, unspecified, second trimester

     ▪ **O09.93** Supervision of high risk pregnancy, unspecified, third trimester

EDEMA, PROTEINURIA AND HYPERTENSIVE DISORDERS IN PREGNANCY, CHILDBIRTH AND THE PUERPERIUM (O10-O16)

● **O10** pre-existing hypertension complicating pregnancy, childbirth and the puerperium

     | Includes | pre-existing hypertension with pre-existing proteinuria complicating pregnancy, childbirth and the puerperium

     | Excludes2 | pre-existing hypertension with increased or superimposed proteinuria complicating pregnancy, childbirth and the puerperium (O11.-)

● **O10.0** Pre-existing essential hypertension complicating pregnancy, childbirth and the puerperium

     Any condition in I10 specified as a reason for obstetric care during pregnancy, childbirth or the puerperium

● **O10.01** Pre-existing essential hypertension complicating pregnancy

     O10.011 Pre-existing essential hypertension complicating pregnancy, first trimester 🔗

     O10.012 Pre-existing essential hypertension complicating pregnancy, second trimester 🔗

     O10.013 Pre-existing essential hypertension complicating pregnancy, third trimester 🔗

     ▪ **O10.019** Pre-existing essential hypertension complicating pregnancy, unspecified trimester

     O10.02 Pre-existing essential hypertension complicating childbirth 🔗

     O10.03 Pre-existing essential hypertension complicating the puerperium 🔗

● **O10.1** Pre-existing hypertensive heart disease complicating pregnancy, childbirth and the puerperium

     Any condition in I11 specified as a reason for obstetric care during pregnancy, childbirth or the puerperium

     Use additional code from I11 to identify the type of hypertensive heart disease

● **O10.11** Pre-existing hypertensive heart disease complicating pregnancy

     O10.111 Pre-existing hypertensive heart disease complicating pregnancy, first trimester

     O10.112 Pre-existing hypertensive heart disease complicating pregnancy, second trimester

     O10.113 Pre-existing hypertensive heart disease complicating pregnancy, third trimester

     ▪ **O10.119** Pre-existing hypertensive heart disease complicating pregnancy, unspecified trimester

     O10.12 Pre-existing hypertensive heart disease complicating childbirth

     O10.13 Pre-existing hypertensive heart disease complicating the puerperium

● **O10.2** Pre-existing hypertensive chronic kidney disease complicating pregnancy, childbirth and the puerperium

     Any condition in I12 specified as a reason for obstetric care during pregnancy, childbirth or the puerperium

     Use additional code from I12 to identify the type of hypertensive chronic kidney disease

● **O10.21** Pre-existing hypertensive chronic kidney disease complicating pregnancy

     O10.211 Pre-existing hypertensive chronic kidney disease complicating pregnancy, first trimester

     O10.212 Pre-existing hypertensive chronic kidney disease complicating pregnancy, second trimester

     O10.213 Pre-existing hypertensive chronic kidney disease complicating pregnancy, third trimester

     ▪ **O10.219** Pre-existing hypertensive chronic kidney disease complicating pregnancy, unspecified trimester

     O10.22 Pre-existing hypertensive chronic kidney disease complicating childbirth

     O10.23 Pre-existing hypertensive chronic kidney disease complicating the puerperium

● Unacceptable First-Listed Diagnosis   ● Use Additional Character(s)   ▪ Unspecified   **OGCR** Official Guidelines for Coding and Reporting

🔗 Complication\Comorbidity   🔗 Major C\C | Excludes 1 | | Excludes 2 | Includes   Use additional   Code first   Code also

1263

CHAPTER 15 (O00-O99)

● **O10.3** **Pre-existing hypertensive heart and chronic kidney disease complicating pregnancy, childbirth and the puerperium**

Any condition in I13 specified as a reason for obstetric care during pregnancy, childbirth or the puerperium

Use additional code from I13 to identify the type of hypertensive heart and chronic kidney disease

     ● **O10.31** **Pre-existing hypertensive heart and chronic kidney disease complicating pregnancy**

         O10.311 **Pre-existing hypertensive heart and chronic kidney disease complicating pregnancy, first trimester**

         O10.312 **Pre-existing hypertensive heart and chronic kidney disease complicating pregnancy, second trimester**

         O10.313 **Pre-existing hypertensive heart and chronic kidney disease complicating pregnancy, third trimester**

         ■ **O10.319** **Pre-existing hypertensive heart and chronic kidney disease complicating pregnancy, unspecified trimester**

     O10.32 **Pre-existing hypertensive heart and chronic kidney disease complicating childbirth**

     O10.33 **Pre-existing hypertensive heart and chronic kidney disease complicating the puerperium**

● **O10.4** **Pre-existing secondary hypertension complicating pregnancy, childbirth and the puerperium**

Any condition in I15 specified as a reason for obstetric care during pregnancy, childbirth or the puerperium

Use additional code from I15 to identify the type of secondary hypertension

     ● **O10.41** **Pre-existing secondary hypertension complicating pregnancy**

         O10.411 **Pre-existing secondary hypertension complicating pregnancy, first trimester** 🗲

         O10.412 **Pre-existing secondary hypertension complicating pregnancy, second trimester** 🗲

         O10.413 **Pre-existing secondary hypertension complicating pregnancy, third trimester** 🗲

         ■ **O10.419** **Pre-existing secondary hypertension complicating pregnancy, unspecified trimester**

     O10.42 **Pre-existing secondary hypertension complicating childbirth** 🗲

     O10.43 **Pre-existing secondary hypertension complicating the puerperium** 🗲

● **O10.9** **Unspecified pre-existing hypertension complicating pregnancy, childbirth and the puerperium**

     ● **O10.91** **Unspecified pre-existing hypertension complicating pregnancy**

         ■ **O10.911** **Unspecified pre-existing hypertension complicating pregnancy, first trimester** 🗲

         ■ **O10.912** **Unspecified pre-existing hypertension complicating pregnancy, second trimester** 🗲

         ■ **O10.913** **Unspecified pre-existing hypertension complicating pregnancy, third trimester** 🗲

         ■ **O10.919** **Unspecified pre-existing hypertension complicating pregnancy, unspecified trimester**

     ■ **O10.92** **Unspecified pre-existing hypertension complicating childbirth** 🗲

     ■ **O10.93** **Unspecified pre-existing hypertension complicating the puerperium** 🗲

● **O11** **Pre-existing hypertensive disorder with superimposed proteinuria**

Includes	conditions in O10 complicated by increased proteinuria

         superimposed pre-eclampsia

Use additional code from O10 to identify the type of hypertension

     O11.1 **Pre-existing hypertensive disorder with superimposed proteinuria, first trimester** 🗲

     O11.2 **Pre-existing hypertensive disorder with superimposed proteinuria, second trimester** 🗲

     O11.3 **Pre-existing hypertensive disorder with superimposed proteinuria, third trimester** 🗲

     ■ **O11.9** **Pre-existing hypertensive disorder with superimposed proteinuria, unspecified trimester**

● **O12** **Gestational [pregnancy-induced] edema and proteinuria without hypertension**

     ● **O12.0** **Gestational edema**

         ■ **O12.00** **Gestational edema, unspecified trimester**

         O12.01 **Gestational edema, first trimester**

         O12.02 **Gestational edema, second trimester**

         O12.03 **Gestational edema, third trimester**

     ● **O12.1** **Gestational proteinuria**

         ■ **O12.10** **Gestational proteinuria, unspecified trimester**

         O12.11 **Gestational proteinuria, first trimester**

         O12.12 **Gestational proteinuria, second trimester**

         O12.13 **Gestational proteinuria, third trimester**

     ● **O12.2** **Gestational edema with proteinuria**

         ■ **O12.20** **Gestational edema with proteinuria, unspecified trimester**

         O12.21 **Gestational edema with proteinuria, first trimester**

         O12.22 **Gestational edema with proteinuria, second trimester**

         O12.23 **Gestational edema with proteinuria, third trimester**

● **O13** **Gestational [pregnancy-induced] hypertension without significant proteinuria**

Includes	gestational hypertension NOS

     O13.1 **Gestational [pregnancy-induced] hypertension without significant proteinuria, first trimester** 🗲

     O13.2 **Gestational [pregnancy-induced] hypertension without significant proteinuria, second trimester** 🗲

     O13.3 **Gestational [pregnancy-induced] hypertension without significant proteinuria, third trimester** 🗲

     ■ **O13.9** **Gestational [pregnancy-induced] hypertension without significant proteinuria, unspecified trimester**

● Unacceptable First-Listed Diagnosis   ● Use Additional Character(s)   ■ Unspecified   **OGCR** Official Guidelines for Coding and Reporting

🗲 Complication\Comorbidity   🗲 Major C\C   Excludes 1   Excludes 2   Includes   Use additional   Code first   Code also

● **O14   Gestational [pregnancy-induced] hypertension with significant proteinuria**
     Pre-eclampsia
     Excludes1   superimposed pre-eclampsia (O11)

  ● **O14.0   Mild pre-eclampsia**
    ■ **O14.00   Mild pre-eclampsia, unspecified trimester**
     O14.02   Mild pre-eclampsia, second trimester 🅒
     O14.03   Mild pre-eclampsia, third trimester 🅒

  ● **O14.1   Severe pre-eclampsia**
     Excludes1   HELLP syndrome (O14.2-)
     H=hemolysis, EL=elevated liver enzymes, LP=low platelet count
    ■ **O14.10   Severe pre-eclampsia, unspecified trimester**
     O14.12   Severe pre-eclampsia, second trimester 🅒
     O14.13   Severe pre-eclampsia, third trimester 🅒

  ● **O14.2   HELLP syndrome (HELLP)**
     Severe pre-eclampsia with hemolysis, elevated liver enzymes and low platelet count
    ■ **O14.20   HELLP syndrome (HELLP), unspecified trimester**
     O14.22   HELLP syndrome (HELLP), second trimester
     O14.23   HELLP syndrome (HELLP), third trimester

  ● **O14.9   Unspecified pre-eclampsia**
    ■ **O14.90   Unspecified pre-eclampsia, unspecified trimester** 🅒
    ■ **O14.92   Unspecified pre-eclampsia, second trimester** 🅒
    ■ **O14.93   Unspecified pre-eclampsia, third trimester** 🅒

● **O15   Eclampsia**
     Includes   convulsions following conditions in O10-O14 and O16

  ● **O15.0   Eclampsia in pregnancy**
    ■ **O15.00   Eclampsia in pregnancy, unspecified trimester**
     O15.02   Eclampsia in pregnancy, second trimester 🅒
     O15.03   Eclampsia in pregnancy, third trimester 🅒
     O15.1   Eclampsia in labor 🅒
     O15.2   Eclampsia in the puerperium 🅒
    ■ **O15.9   Eclampsia, unspecified as to time period**
     Eclampsia NOS

● **O16   Unspecified maternal hypertension**
    ■ **O16.1   Unspecified maternal hypertension, first trimester** 🅒
    ■ **O16.2   Unspecified maternal hypertension, second trimester** 🅒
    ■ **O16.3   Unspecified maternal hypertension, third trimester** 🅒
    ■ **O16.9   Unspecified maternal hypertension, unspecified trimester** 🅒

OTHER MATERNAL DISORDERS PREDOMINANTLY RELATED TO PREGNANCY (O20-O29)

     Excludes2   maternal care related to the fetus and amniotic cavity and possible delivery problems (O30-O48)
     maternal diseases classifiable elsewhere but complicating pregnancy, labor and delivery, and the puerperium (O98-O99)

● **O20   Hemorrhage in early pregnancy**
     Includes   before completion of 20 weeks gestation
     Excludes1   pregnancy with abortive outcome (O00-O08)
     O20.0   Threatened abortion 🅒
     Hemorrhage specified as due to threatened abortion
     O20.8   Other hemorrhage in early pregnancy
  ■ **O20.9   Hemorrhage in early pregnancy, unspecified** 🅒

● **O21   Excessive vomiting in pregnancy**
     O21.0   Mild hyperemesis gravidarum
     Hyperemesis gravidarum, mild or unspecified, starting before the end of the 20th week of gestation
     O21.1   Hyperemesis gravidarum with metabolic disturbance
     Hyperemesis gravidarum, starting before the end of the 20th week of gestation, with metabolic disturbance such as carbohydrate depletion
     Hyperemesis gravidarum, starting before the end of the 20th week of gestation, with metabolic disturbance such as dehydration
     Hyperemesis gravidarum, starting before the end of the 20th week of gestation, with metabolic disturbance such as electrolyte imbalance
     O21.2   Late vomiting of pregnancy
     Excessive vomiting starting after 20 completed weeks of gestation
     O21.8   Other vomiting complicating pregnancy
     Vomiting due to diseases classified elsewhere, complicating pregnancy
     Use additional code, to identify cause
  ■ **O21.9   Vomiting of pregnancy, unspecified**

● **O22   Venous complications in pregnancy**
     Excludes1   venous complications of:
     abortion NOS (O03.9)
     ectopic or molar pregnancy (O08.7)
     failed attempted abortion (O07.39, O07.89)
     induced abortion (O04.89, O05.89)
     spontaneous abortion (O03.89, O03.89)
     Excludes2   obstetric pulmonary embolism (O88.-)
     venous complications of childbirth and the puerperium (O87.-)

  ● **O22.0   Varicose veins of lower extremity in pregnancy**
     Varicose veins NOS in pregnancy
    ■ **O22.00   Varicose veins of lower extremity in pregnancy, unspecified trimester**
     O22.01   Varicose veins of lower extremity in pregnancy, first trimester
     O22.02   Varicose veins of lower extremity in pregnancy, second trimester
     O22.03   Varicose veins of lower extremity in pregnancy, third trimester

  ● **O22.1   Genital varices in pregnancy**
     Perineal varices in pregnancy
     Vaginal varices in pregnancy
     Vulval varices in pregnancy
    ■ **O22.10   Genital varices in pregnancy, unspecified trimester**
     O22.11   Genital varices in pregnancy, first trimester
     O22.12   Genital varices in pregnancy, second trimester
     O22.13   Genital varices in pregnancy, third trimester

● Unacceptable First-Listed Diagnosis   ● Use Additional Character(s)   ■ Unspecified   **OGCR** Official Guidelines for Coding and Reporting
🅒 Complication\Comorbidity   🅒 Major C\C   Excludes 1   Excludes 2   Includes   Use additional   Code first   Code also

1265

● **O22.2 Superficial thrombophlebitis in pregnancy**
Phlebitis in pregnancy NOS
Thrombophlebitis of legs in pregnancy
Thrombosis in pregnancy NOS

■ **O22.20 Superficial thrombophlebitis in pregnancy, unspecified trimester** 💉

O22.21 Superficial thrombophlebitis in pregnancy, first trimester 💉

O22.22 Superficial thrombophlebitis in pregnancy, second trimester 💉

O22.23 Superficial thrombophlebitis in pregnancy, third trimester 💉

● **O22.3 Deep phlebothrombosis in pregnancy**
Deep vein thrombosis, antepartum

Use additional code to identify the deep vein thrombosis (I82.4-, I82.5-, I82.62-. I82.72-)

Use additional code, if applicable, for associated long-term (current) use of anticoagulants (Z79.01)

■ **O22.30 Deep phlebothrombosis in pregnancy, unspecified trimester** 💉

O22.31 Deep phlebothrombosis in pregnancy, first trimester 💉

O22.32 Deep phlebothrombosis in pregnancy, second trimester 💉

O22.33 Deep phlebothrombosis in pregnancy, third trimester 💉

● **O22.4 Hemorrhoids in pregnancy**

■ **O22.40 Hemorrhoids in pregnancy, unspecified trimester** 💉

O22.41 Hemorrhoids in pregnancy, first trimester 💉

O22.42 Hemorrhoids in pregnancy, second trimester 💉

O22.43 Hemorrhoids in pregnancy, third trimester 💉

● **O22.5 Cerebral venous thrombosis in pregnancy**
Cerebrovenous sinus thrombosis in pregnancy

■ **O22.50 Cerebral venous thrombosis in pregnancy, unspecified trimester** 💉

O22.51 Cerebral venous thrombosis in pregnancy, first trimester 💉

O22.52 Cerebral venous thrombosis in pregnancy, second trimester 💉

O22.53 Cerebral venous thrombosis in pregnancy, third trimester 💉

● **O22.8 Other venous complications in pregnancy**

● **O22.8x Other venous complications in pregnancy**

O22.8x1 Other venous complications in pregnancy, first trimester 💉

O22.8x2 Other venous complications in pregnancy, second trimester 💉

O22.8x3 Other venous complications in pregnancy, third trimester 💉

■ **O22.8x9 Other venous complications in pregnancy, unspecified trimester** 💉

● **O22.9 Venous complication in pregnancy, unspecified**
Gestational phlebitis NOS
Gestational phlebopathy NOS
Gestational thrombosis NOS

■ **O22.90 Venous complication in pregnancy, unspecified, unspecified trimester** 💉

■ **O22.91 Venous complication in pregnancy, unspecified, first trimester** 💉

■ **O22.92 Venous complication in pregnancy, unspecified, second trimester** 💉

■ **O22.93 Venous complication in pregnancy, unspecified, third trimester** 💉

● **O23 Infections of genitourinary tract in pregnancy**
Use additional code to identify organism (B95.-, B96.-)

● **O23.0 Infections of kidney in pregnancy**
Pyelonephritis in pregnancy

■ **O23.00 Infections of kidney in pregnancy, unspecified trimester**

O23.01 Infections of kidney in pregnancy, first trimester 💉

O23.02 Infections of kidney in pregnancy, second trimester 💉

O23.03 Infections of kidney in pregnancy, third trimester 💉

● **O23.1 Infections of bladder in pregnancy**

■ **O23.10 Infections of bladder in pregnancy, unspecified trimester**

O23.11 Infections of bladder in pregnancy, first trimester 💉

O23.12 Infections of bladder in pregnancy, second trimester 💉

O23.13 Infections of bladder in pregnancy, third trimester 💉

● **O23.2 Infections of urethra in pregnancy**

■ **O23.20 Infections of urethra in pregnancy, unspecified trimester**

O23.21 Infections of urethra in pregnancy, first trimester 💉

O23.22 Infections of urethra in pregnancy, second trimester 💉

O23.23 Infections of urethra in pregnancy, third trimester 💉

● **O23.3 Infections of other parts of urinary tract in pregnancy**

■ **O23.30 Infections of other parts of urinary tract in pregnancy, unspecified trimester**

O23.31 Infections of other parts of urinary tract in pregnancy, first trimester 💉

O23.32 Infections of other parts of urinary tract in pregnancy, second trimester 💉

O23.33 Infections of other parts of urinary tract in pregnancy, third trimester 💉

● **O23.4 Unspecified infection of urinary tract in pregnancy**

■ **O23.40 Unspecified infection of urinary tract in pregnancy, unspecified trimester**

■ **O23.41 Unspecified infection of urinary tract in pregnancy, first trimester** 💉

■ **O23.42 Unspecified infection of urinary tract in pregnancy, second trimester** 💉

■ **O23.43 Unspecified infection of urinary tract in pregnancy, third trimester** 💉

● **O23.5 Infections of the genital tract in pregnancy**

● **O23.51 Infection of cervix in pregnancy**

O23.511 Infections of cervix in pregnancy, first trimester 💉

O23.512 Infections of cervix in pregnancy, second trimester 💉

O23.513 Infections of cervix in pregnancy, third trimester 💉

■ **O23.519 Infections of cervix in pregnancy, unspecified trimester**

● Unacceptable First-Listed Diagnosis   ● Use Additional Character(s)   ■ Unspecified   **OGCR** Official Guidelines for Coding and Reporting
💉 Complication\Comorbidity   💉 Major C\C   Excludes 1   Excludes 2   Includes   Use additional   Code first   Code also

● O23.52   **Salpingo-oophoritis in pregnancy**
     Oophoritis = inflammation of ovary
     Salpingitis = inflammation of fallopian tube
     Oophoritis in pregnancy
     Salpingitis in pregnancy

     O23.521   **Salpingo-oophoritis in pregnancy, first trimester** 🦠

     O23.522   **Salpingo-oophoritis in pregnancy, second trimester** 🦠

     O23.523   **Salpingo-oophoritis in pregnancy, third trimester** 🦠

     🔲 O23.529   **Salpingo-oophoritis in pregnancy, unspecified trimester**

● O23.59   **Infection of other part of genital tract in pregnancy**

     O23.591   **Infection of other part of genital tract in pregnancy, first trimester** 🦠

     O23.592   **Infection of other part of genital tract in pregnancy, second trimester** 🦠

     O23.593   **Infection of other part of genital tract in pregnancy, third trimester** 🦠

     🔲 O23.599   **Infection of other part of genital tract in pregnancy, unspecified trimester**

● O23.9   **Unspecified genitourinary tract infection in pregnancy**
     Genitourinary tract infection in pregnancy NOS

     🔲 O23.90   **Unspecified genitourinary tract infection in pregnancy, unspecified trimester**

     🔲 O23.91   **Unspecified genitourinary tract infection in pregnancy, first trimester** 🦠

     🔲 O23.92   **Unspecified genitourinary tract infection in pregnancy, second trimester** 🦠

     🔲 O23.93   **Unspecified genitourinary tract infection in pregnancy, third trimester** 🦠

OGCR   Section I.C.15.g.
g. Diabetes mellitus in pregnancy

Diabetes mellitus is a significant complicating factor in pregnancy. Pregnant women who are diabetic should be assigned a code O24, Diabetes mellitus in pregnancy, childbirth, and the puerperium, first, followed by the appropriate diabetes code(s)(E08-E13) from Chapter 4.

OGCR   Section I.C.15.i.
i. Gestational (pregnancy induced) diabetes

Gestational (pregnancy induced) diabetes can occur during the second and third trimester of pregnancy in women who were not diabetic prior to pregnancy. Gestational diabetes can cause complications in the pregnancy similar to those of pre-existing diabetes mellitus. It also puts the woman at greater risk of developing diabetes after the pregnancy. Codes for gestational diabetes are in subcategory O24.4, Gestational diabetes mellitus. No other code from category O24, Diabetes mellitus in pregnancy, childbirth, and the puerperium, should be used with a code from O24.4

The codes under subcategory O24.4 include diet controlled and insulin controlled. If a patient with gestational diabetes is treated with both diet and insulin, only the code for insulin-controlled is required. Code Z79.4, Long-term (current) use of insulin, should not be assigned with codes from subcategory O24.4.

An abnormal glucose tolerance in pregnancy is assigned a code from subcategory O99.81, Abnormal glucose complicating pregnancy, childbirth, and the puerperium.

● O24   **Diabetes mellitus in pregnancy, childbirth, and the puerperium**

     ● O24.0   **Pre-existing diabetes mellitus, type 1, in pregnancy, childbirth and the puerperium**
       Juvenile onset diabetes mellitus, in pregnancy, childbirth and the puerperium
       Ketosis-prone diabetes mellitus in pregnancy, childbirth and the puerperium

       Use additional code from category E10 to further identify any manifestations

     ● O24.01   **Pre-existing diabetes mellitus, type 1, in pregnancy**

       O24.011   **Pre-existing diabetes mellitus, type 1, in pregnancy, first trimester** 🦠

       O24.012   **Pre-existing diabetes mellitus, type 1, in pregnancy, second trimester** 🦠

       O24.013   **Pre-existing diabetes mellitus, type 1, in pregnancy, third trimester** 🦠

       🔲 O24.019   **Pre-existing diabetes mellitus, type 1, in pregnancy, unspecified trimester** 🦠

     O24.02   **Pre-existing diabetes mellitus, type 1, in childbirth** 🦠

     O24.03   **Pre-existing diabetes mellitus, type 1, in the puerperium** 🦠

     ● O24.1   **Pre-existing diabetes mellitus, type 2, in pregnancy, childbirth and the puerperium**
       Insulin-resistant diabetes mellitus in pregnancy, childbirth and the puerperium

       Use additional code (for):
       from category E11 to further identify any manifestations
       long-term (current) use of insulin (Z79.4)

     ● O24.11   **Pre-existing diabetes mellitus, type 2, in pregnancy** 🦠

       O24.111   **Pre-existing diabetes mellitus, type 2, in pregnancy, first trimester**

       O24.112   **Pre-existing diabetes mellitus, type 2, in pregnancy, second trimester**

       O24.113   **Pre-existing diabetes mellitus, type 2, in pregnancy, third trimester**

       🔲 O24.119   **Pre-existing diabetes mellitus, type 2, in pregnancy, unspecified trimester**

     O24.12   **Pre-existing diabetes mellitus, type 2, in childbirth** 🦠

     O24.13   **Pre-existing diabetes mellitus, type 2, in the puerperium** 🦠

     ● O24.3   **Unspecified pre-existing diabetes mellitus in pregnancy, childbirth and the puerperium**

       Use additional code (for):
       from category E11 to further identify any manifestation
       long-term (current) use of insulin (Z79.4)

     ● O24.31   **Unspecified pre-existing diabetes mellitus in pregnancy**

       🔲 O24.311   **Unspecified pre-existing diabetes mellitus in pregnancy, first trimester** 🦠

       🔲 O24.312   **Unspecified pre-existing diabetes mellitus in pregnancy, second trimester** 🦠

● Unacceptable First-Listed Diagnosis   ● Use Additional Character(s)   🔲 Unspecified   **OGCR** Official Guidelines for Coding and Reporting

🦠 Complication\Comorbidity   🦠 Major C\C   [Excludes 1]   [Excludes 2]   Includes   Use additional   Code first   Code also

1267

CHAPTER 15 (O00-O99)

O24.313   Unspecified pre-existing diabetes mellitus in pregnancy, third trimester 🌂

O24.319   Unspecified pre-existing diabetes mellitus in pregnancy, unspecified trimester 🌂

O24.32   Unspecified pre-existing diabetes mellitus in childbirth 🌂

O24.33   Unspecified pre-existing diabetes mellitus in the puerperium 🌂

● O24.4   Gestational diabetes mellitus
　　　Diabetes mellitus arising in pregnancy
　　　Gestational diabetes mellitus NOS

● O24.41   Gestational diabetes mellitus in pregnancy

O24.410   Gestational diabetes mellitus in pregnancy, diet-controlled

O24.414   Gestational diabetes mellitus in pregnancy, insulin controlled

O24.419   Gestational diabetes mellitus in pregnancy, unspecified control

● O24.42   Gestational diabetes mellitus in childbirth

O24.420   Gestational diabetes mellitus in childbirth, diet controlled

O24.424   Gestational diabetes mellitus in childbirth, insulin controlled

O24.429   Gestational diabetes mellitus in childbirth, unspecified control

● O24.43   Gestational diabetes mellitus in the puerperium

O24.430   Gestational diabetes mellitus in the puerperium, diet controlled

O24.434   Gestational diabetes mellitus in the puerperium, insulin controlled

O24.439   Gestational diabetes mellitus in the puerperium, unspecified control

● O24.8   Other pre-existing diabetes mellitus in pregnancy, childbirth, and the puerperium
　　　Use additional code (for):
　　　　from categories E08, E09 and E13 to further identify any manifestation
　　　long-term (current) use of insulin (Z79.4)

● O24.81   Other pre-existing diabetes mellitus in pregnancy

O24.811   Other pre-existing diabetes mellitus in pregnancy, first trimester 🌂

O24.812   Other pre-existing diabetes mellitus in pregnancy, second trimester 🌂

O24.813   Other pre-existing diabetes mellitus in pregnancy, third trimester 🌂

O24.819   Other pre-existing diabetes mellitus in pregnancy, unspecified trimester 🌂

O24.82   Other pre-existing diabetes mellitus in childbirth 🌂

O24.83   Other pre-existing diabetes mellitus in the puerperium 🌂

● O24.9   Unspecified diabetes mellitus in pregnancy, childbirth and the puerperium
　　　Use additional code for long-term (current) use of insulin (Z79.4)

● O24.91   Unspecified diabetes mellitus in pregnancy

O24.911   Unspecified diabetes mellitus in pregnancy, first trimester 🌂

O24.912   Unspecified diabetes mellitus in pregnancy, second trimester 🌂

O24.913   Unspecified diabetes mellitus in pregnancy, third trimester 🌂

O24.919   Unspecified diabetes mellitus in pregnancy, unspecified trimester 🌂

O24.92   Unspecified diabetes mellitus in childbirth

O24.93   Unspecified diabetes mellitus in the puerperium 🌂

● O25   Malnutrition in pregnancy, childbirth and the puerperium

● O25.1   Malnutrition in pregnancy

O25.10   Malnutrition in pregnancy, unspecified trimester

O25.11   Malnutrition in pregnancy, first trimester

O25.12   Malnutrition in pregnancy, second trimester

O25.13   Malnutrition in pregnancy, third trimester

O25.2   Malnutrition in childbirth

O25.3   Malnutrition in the puerperium

● O26   Maternal care for other conditions predominantly related to pregnancy

● O26.0   Excessive weight gain in pregnancy
　　　Excludes2   gestational edema (O12.0, O12.2)

O26.00   Excessive weight gain in pregnancy, unspecified trimester

O26.01   Excessive weight gain in pregnancy, first trimester

O26.02   Excessive weight gain in pregnancy, second trimester

O26.03   Excessive weight gain in pregnancy, third trimester

● O26.1   Low weight gain in pregnancy

O26.10   Low weight gain in pregnancy, unspecified trimester

O26.11   Low weight gain in pregnancy, first trimester

O26.12   Low weight gain in pregnancy, second trimester

O26.13   Low weight gain in pregnancy, third trimester

● O26.2   Pregnancy care of habitual aborter

O26.20   Pregnancy care of habitual aborter, unspecified trimester

O26.21   Pregnancy care of habitual aborter, first trimester 🌂

O26.22   Pregnancy care of habitual aborter, second trimester 🌂

O26.23   Pregnancy care of habitual aborter, third trimester 🌂

● O26.3   Retained intrauterine contraceptive device in pregnancy

O26.30   Retained intrauterine contraceptive device in pregnancy, unspecified trimester

O26.31   Retained intrauterine contraceptive device in pregnancy, first trimester

O26.32   Retained intrauterine contraceptive device in pregnancy, second trimester

O26.33   Retained intrauterine contraceptive device in pregnancy, third trimester

● Unacceptable First-Listed Diagnosis　　● Use Additional Character(s)　　　■ Unspecified　　OGCR Official Guidelines for Coding and Reporting
🌂 Complication\Comorbidity　　🌂 Major C\C　　Excludes 1　　Excludes 2　　Includes　　Use additional　　Code first　　Code also

● O26.4   Herpes gestationis

◼ O26.40   Herpes gestationis, unspecified trimester

O26.41   Herpes gestationis, first trimester

O26.42   Herpes gestationis, second trimester

O26.43   Herpes gestationis, third trimester

● O26.5   Maternal hypotension syndrome
     Supine hypotensive syndrome

◼ O26.50   Maternal hypotension syndrome, unspecified trimester

O26.51   Maternal hypotension syndrome, first trimester 🦠

O26.52   Maternal hypotension syndrome, second trimester 🦠

O26.53   Maternal hypotension syndrome, third trimester 🦠

● O26.6   Liver disorders in pregnancy, childbirth and the puerperium
     Use additional code to identify the specific disorder
     | Excludes2 | hepatorenal syndrome following labor and delivery (O90.4)

● O26.61   Liver disorders in pregnancy

O26.611   Liver disorders in pregnancy, first trimester 🦠

O26.612   Liver disorders in pregnancy, second trimester 🦠

O26.613   Liver disorders in pregnancy, third trimester 🦠

◼ O26.619   Liver disorders in pregnancy, unspecified trimester

O26.62   Liver disorders in childbirth 🦠

O26.63   Liver disorders in the puerperium

● O26.7   Subluxation of symphysis (pubis) in pregnancy, childbirth and the puerperium
     | Excludes1 | traumatic separation of symphysis (pubis) during childbirth (O71.6)

● O26.71   Subluxation of symphysis (pubis) in pregnancy

O26.711   Subluxation of symphysis (pubis) in pregnancy, first trimester

O26.712   Subluxation of symphysis (pubis) in pregnancy, second trimester

O26.713   Subluxation of symphysis (pubis) in pregnancy, third trimester

◼ O26.719   Subluxation of symphysis (pubis) in pregnancy, unspecified trimester

O26.72   Subluxation of symphysis (pubis) in childbirth

O26.73   Subluxation of symphysis (pubis) in the puerperium

● O26.8   Other specified pregnancy related conditions

● O26.81   Pregnancy related exhaustion and fatigue

O26.811   Pregnancy related exhaustion and fatigue, first trimester

O26.812   Pregnancy related exhaustion and fatigue, second trimester

O26.813   Pregnancy related exhaustion and fatigue, third trimester

◼ O26.819   Pregnancy related exhaustion and fatigue, unspecified trimester

● O26.82   Pregnancy related peripheral neuritis

O26.821   Pregnancy related peripheral neuritis, first trimester

O26.822   Pregnancy related peripheral neuritis, second trimester

O26.823   Pregnancy related peripheral neuritis, third trimester

◼ O26.829   Pregnancy related peripheral neuritis, unspecified trimester

● O26.83   Pregnancy related renal disease
     Use additional code to identify the specific disorder

O26.831   Pregnancy related renal disease, first trimester 🦠

O26.832   Pregnancy related renal disease, second trimester 🦠

O26.833   Pregnancy related renal disease, third trimester 🦠

◼ O26.839   Pregnancy related renal disease, unspecified trimester

● O26.84   Uterine size-date discrepancy complicating pregnancy
     | Excludes1 | encounter for suspected problem with fetal

O26.841   Uterine size-date discrepancy, first trimester

O26.842   Uterine size-date discrepancy, second trimester

O26.843   Uterine size-date discrepancy, third trimester

◼ O26.849   Uterine size-date discrepancy, unspecified trimester

● O26.85   Spotting complicating pregnancy

O26.851   Spotting complicating pregnancy, first trimester

O26.852   Spotting complicating pregnancy, second trimester

O26.853   Spotting complicating pregnancy, third trimester

◼ O26.859   Spotting complicating pregnancy, unspecified trimester

O26.86   Pruritic urticarial papules and plaques of pregnancy (PUPPP)
     Polymorphic eruption of pregnancy

● O26.87   Cervical shortening
     | Excludes1 | encounter for suspected cervical shortening ruled out (Z03.75)

O26.872   Cervical shortening, second trimester

O26.873   Cervical shortening, third trimester

◼ O26.879   Cervical shortening, unspecified trimester

● O26.89   Other specified pregnancy related conditions

O26.891   Other specified pregnancy related conditions, first trimester

O26.892   Other specified pregnancy related conditions, second trimester

O26.893   Other specified pregnancy related conditions, third trimester

◼ O26.899   Other specified pregnancy related conditions, unspecified trimester

---

● Unacceptable First-Listed Diagnosis   ● Use Additional Character(s)   ◼ Unspecified   **OGCR** Official Guidelines for Coding and Reporting

🦠 Complication\Comorbidity   🦠 Major C\C   Excludes 1   Excludes 2   Includes   Use additional   Code first   Code also

1269

CHAPTER 15 (O00-O99)

- O26.9 **Pregnancy related conditions, unspecified**
  - O26.90 Pregnancy related conditions, unspecified, unspecified trimester
  - O26.91 Pregnancy related conditions, unspecified, first trimester
  - O26.92 Pregnancy related conditions, unspecified, second trimester
  - O26.93 Pregnancy related conditions, unspecified, third trimester

- O28 **Abnormal findings on antenatal screening of mother**

  Excludes1 diagnostic findings classified elsewhere - see Alphabetical Index

  - O28.0 Abnormal hematological finding on antenatal screening of mother
  - O28.1 Abnormal biochemical finding on antenatal screening of mother
  - O28.2 Abnormal cytological finding on antenatal screening of mother
  - O28.3 Abnormal ultrasonic finding on antenatal screening of mother
  - O28.4 Abnormal radiological finding on antenatal screening of mother
  - O28.5 Abnormal chromosomal and genetic finding on antenatal screening of mother
  - O28.8 Other abnormal findings on antenatal screening of mother
  - O28.9 Unspecified abnormal findings on antenatal screening of mother

- O29 **Complications of anesthesia during pregnancy**

  Includes maternal complications arising from the administration of a general, regional or local anesthetic, analgesic or other sedation during pregnancy

  Use additional code, if necessary, to identify the complication

  Excludes2 complications of anesthesia during labor and delivery (O74.-)
  complications of anesthesia during the puerperium (O89.-)

  - O29.0 **Pulmonary complications of anesthesia during pregnancy**
    - O29.01 **Aspiration pneumonitis due to anesthesia during pregnancy**
      Inhalation of stomach contents or secretions NOS due to anesthesia during pregnancy
      Mendelson's syndrome due to anesthesia during pregnancy
      - O29.011 Aspiration pneumonitis due to anesthesia during pregnancy, first trimester
      - O29.012 Aspiration pneumonitis due to anesthesia during pregnancy, second trimester
      - O29.013 Aspiration pneumonitis due to anesthesia during pregnancy, third trimester
      - O29.019 Aspiration pneumonitis due to anesthesia during pregnancy, unspecified trimester
    - O29.02 **Pressure collapse of lung due to anesthesia during pregnancy**
      - O29.021 Pressure collapse of lung due to anesthesia during pregnancy, first trimester
      - O29.022 Pressure collapse of lung due to anesthesia during pregnancy, second trimester
      - O29.023 Pressure collapse of lung due to anesthesia during pregnancy, third trimester
      - O29.029 Pressure collapse of lung due to anesthesia during pregnancy, unspecified trimester
    - O29.09 **Other pulmonary complications of anesthesia during pregnancy**
      - O29.091 Other pulmonary complications of anesthesia during pregnancy, first trimester
      - O29.092 Other pulmonary complications of anesthesia during pregnancy, second trimester
      - O29.093 Other pulmonary complications of anesthesia during pregnancy, third trimester
      - O29.099 Other pulmonary complications of anesthesia during pregnancy, unspecified trimester
  - O29.1 **Cardiac complications of anesthesia during pregnancy**
    - O29.11 **Cardiac arrest due to anesthesia during pregnancy**
      - O29.111 Cardiac arrest due to anesthesia during pregnancy, first trimester
      - O29.112 Cardiac arrest due to anesthesia during pregnancy, second trimester
      - O29.113 Cardiac arrest due to anesthesia during pregnancy, third trimester
      - O29.119 Cardiac arrest due to anesthesia during pregnancy, unspecified trimester
    - O29.12 **Cardiac failure due to anesthesia during pregnancy**
      - O29.121 Cardiac failure due to anesthesia during pregnancy, first trimester
      - O29.122 Cardiac failure due to anesthesia during pregnancy, second trimester
      - O29.123 Cardiac failure due to anesthesia during pregnancy, third trimester
      - O29.129 Cardiac failure due to anesthesia during pregnancy, unspecified trimester
    - O29.19 **Other cardiac complications of anesthesia during pregnancy**
      - O29.191 Other cardiac complications of anesthesia during pregnancy, first trimester
      - O29.192 Other cardiac complications of anesthesia during pregnancy, second trimester
      - O29.193 Other cardiac complications of anesthesia during pregnancy, third trimester
      - O29.199 Other cardiac complications of anesthesia during pregnancy, unspecified trimester
  - O29.2 **Central nervous system complications of anesthesia during pregnancy**
    - O29.21 **Cerebral anoxia due to anesthesia during pregnancy**

Unacceptable First-Listed Diagnosis · Use Additional Character(s) · Complication\Comorbidity · Major C\C · Excludes 1 · Excludes 2 · Unspecified · **OGCR** Official Guidelines for Coding and Reporting · Includes · Use additional · Code first · Code also

O29.211　Cerebral anoxia due to anesthesia during pregnancy, first trimester

O29.212　Cerebral anoxia due to anesthesia during pregnancy, second trimester

O29.213　Cerebral anoxia due to anesthesia during pregnancy, third trimester

◻O29.219　Cerebral anoxia due to anesthesia during pregnancy, unspecified trimester

● O29.29　Other central nervous system complications of anesthesia during pregnancy

O29.291　Other central nervous system complications of anesthesia during pregnancy, first trimester

O29.292　Other central nervous system complications of anesthesia during pregnancy, second trimester

O29.293　Other central nervous system complications of anesthesia during pregnancy, third trimester

◻O29.299　Other central nervous system complications of anesthesia during pregnancy, unspecified trimester

● O29.3　Toxic reaction to local anesthesia during pregnancy

● O29.3x　Toxic reaction to local anesthesia during pregnancy

O29.3x1　Toxic reaction to local anesthesia during pregnancy, first trimester

O29.3x2　Toxic reaction to local anesthesia during pregnancy, second trimester

O29.3x3　Toxic reaction to local anesthesia during pregnancy, third trimester

◻O29.3x9　Toxic reaction to local anesthesia during pregnancy, unspecified trimester

● O29.4　Spinal and epidural anesthesia induced headache during pregnancy

◻O29.40　Spinal and epidural anesthesia induced headache during pregnancy, unspecified trimester

O29.41　Spinal and epidural anesthesia induced headache during pregnancy, first trimester

O29.42　Spinal and epidural anesthesia induced headache during pregnancy, second trimester

O29.43　Spinal and epidural anesthesia induced headache during pregnancy, third trimester

● O29.5　Other complications of spinal and epidural anesthesia during pregnancy

● O29.5x　Other complications of spinal and epidural anesthesia during pregnancy

O29.5x1　Other complications of spinal and epidural anesthesia during pregnancy, first trimester

O29.5x2　Other complications of spinal and epidural anesthesia during pregnancy, second trimester

O29.5x3　Other complications of spinal and epidural anesthesia during pregnancy, third trimester

◻O29.5x9　Other complications of spinal and epidural anesthesia during pregnancy, unspecified trimester

● O29.6　Failed or difficult intubation for anesthesia during pregnancy

◻O29.60　Failed or difficult intubation for anesthesia during pregnancy, unspecified trimester

O29.61　Failed or difficult intubation for anesthesia during pregnancy, first trimester

O29.62　Failed or difficult intubation for anesthesia during pregnancy, second trimester

O29.63　Failed or difficult intubation for anesthesia during pregnancy, third trimester

● O29.8　Other complications of anesthesia during pregnancy

● O29.8x　Other complications of anesthesia during pregnancy

O29.8x1　Other complications of anesthesia during pregnancy, first trimester

O29.8x2　Other complications of anesthesia during pregnancy, second trimester

O29.8x3　Other complications of anesthesia during pregnancy, third trimester

◻O29.8x9　Other complications of anesthesia during pregnancy, unspecified trimester

● O29.9　Unspecified complication of anesthesia during pregnancy

◻O29.90　Unspecified complication of anesthesia during pregnancy, unspecified trimester

◻O29.91　Unspecified complication of anesthesia during pregnancy, first trimester

◻O29.92　Unspecified complication of anesthesia during pregnancy, second trimester

◻O29.93　Unspecified complication of anesthesia during pregnancy, third trimester

---

MATERNAL CARE RELATED TO THE FETUS AND AMNIOTIC CAVITY AND POSSIBLE DELIVERY PROBLEMS (O30-O48)

● O30　Multiple gestation

Code also any complications specific to multiple gestation

● O30.0　Twin pregnancy

● O30.00　Twin pregnancy, unspecified

◻O30.001　Twin pregnancy, unspecified, first trimester 🐾

◻O30.002　Twin pregnancy, unspecified, second trimester 🐾

◻O30.003　Twin pregnancy, unspecified, third trimester 🐾

◻O30.009　Twin pregnancy, unspecified, unspecified trimester

● O30.01　Twin pregnancy, monoamniotic/monochorionic

O30.011　Twin pregnancy, monoamniotic/monochorionic, first trimester 🐾

O30.012　Twin pregnancy, monoamniotic/monochorionic, second trimester 🐾

O30.013　Twin pregnancy, monoamniotic/monochorionic, third trimester 🐾

◻O30.019　Twin pregnancy, monoamniotic/monochorionic, unspecified trimester

---

● Unacceptable First-Listed Diagnosis　　● Use Additional Character(s)　　◻ Unspecified　　**OGCR** Official Guidelines for Coding and Reporting

🐾 Complication\Comorbidity　　🐾 Major C\C　　Excludes 1　　Excludes 2　　Includes　　Use additional　　Code first　　Code also

● O30.02   Conjoined twins
> O30.021   Conjoined twins, first trimester
> O30.022   Conjoined twins, second trimester
> O30.023   Conjoined twins, third trimester
> ■ O30.029   Conjoined twins, unspecified trimester

● O30.09   Other twin pregnancy
> O30.091   Other twin pregnancy, first trimester 🦠
> O30.092   Other twin pregnancy, second trimester 🦠
> O30.093   Other twin pregnancy, third trimester 🦠
> ■ O30.099   Other twin pregnancy, unspecified trimester

● O30.1   Triplet pregnancy
> ■ O30.10   Triplet pregnancy, unspecified trimester
> O30.11   Triplet pregnancy, first trimester 🦠
> O30.12   Triplet pregnancy, second trimester 🦠
> O30.13   Triplet pregnancy, third trimester 🦠

● O30.2   Quadruplet pregnancy
> ■ O30.20   Quadruplet pregnancy, unspecified trimester
> O30.21   Quadruplet pregnancy, first trimester 🦠
> O30.22   Quadruplet pregnancy, second trimester 🦠
> O30.23   Quadruplet pregnancy, third trimester 🦠

● O30.8   Other multiple gestation
> ■ O30.80   Other multiple gestation, unspecified trimester
> O30.81   Other multiple gestation, first trimester 🦠
> O30.82   Other multiple gestation, second trimester 🦠
> O30.83   Other multiple gestation, third trimester 🦠

● O30.9   Multiple gestation, unspecified
> Multiple pregnancy NOS
> ■ O30.90   Multiple gestation, unspecified, unspecified trimester
> ■ O30.91   Multiple gestation, unspecified, first trimester
> ■ O30.92   Multiple gestation, unspecified, second trimester
> ■ O30.93   Multiple gestation, unspecified, third trimester

● O31   Complications specific to multiple gestation
> **Excludes2**   delayed delivery of second twin, triplet, etc. (O63.2)
> malpresentation of one fetus or more (O32.5)
> placental transfusion syndromes (O43.0-)

> One of the following 7th characters is to be assigned to each code under category O31. 7th character 0 is for single gestations and multiple gestations where the fetus is unspecified. 7th characters 1 through 9 are for cases of multiple gestations to identify the fetus for which the code applies. The appropriate code from category O30, Multiple gestation, must also be assigned when assigning a code from category O31 that has a 7th character of 1 through 9.

> | | |
> |---|---|
> | 0 | not applicable or unspecified |
> | 1 | fetus 1 |
> | 2 | fetus 2 |
> | 3 | fetus 3 |
> | 4 | fetus 4 |
> | 5 | fetus 5 |
> | 9 | other fetus |

● O31.0   Papyraceous fetus
> Fetus compressus
> ● ■ O31.00   Papyraceous fetus, unspecified trimester
> ● O31.01   Papyraceous fetus, first trimester
> ● O31.02   Papyraceous fetus, second trimester
> ● O31.03   Papyraceous fetus, third trimester

● O31.1   Continuing pregnancy after spontaneous abortion of one fetus or more
> ● ■ O31.10   Continuing pregnancy after spontaneous abortion of one fetus or more, unspecified trimester
> ● O31.11   Continuing pregnancy after spontaneous abortion of one fetus or more, first trimester
> ● O31.12   Continuing pregnancy after spontaneous abortion of one fetus or more, second trimester
> ● O31.13   Continuing pregnancy after spontaneous abortion of one fetus or more, third trimester

● O31.2   Continuing pregnancy after intrauterine death of one fetus or more
> ● ■ O31.20   Continuing pregnancy after intrauterine death of one fetus or more, unspecified trimester
> ● O31.21   Continuing pregnancy after intrauterine death of one fetus or more, first trimester
> ● O31.22   Continuing pregnancy after intrauterine death of one fetus or more, second trimester
> ● O31.23   Continuing pregnancy after intrauterine death of one fetus or more, third trimester

● O31.3   Continuing pregnancy after elective fetal reduction of one fetus or more
> Continuing pregnancy after selective termination of one fetus or more
> ● ■ O31.30   Continuing pregnancy after elective fetal reduction of one fetus or more, unspecified trimester
> ● O31.31   Continuing pregnancy after elective fetal reduction of one fetus or more, first trimester
> ● O31.32   Continuing pregnancy after elective fetal reduction of one fetus or more, second trimester
> ● O31.33   Continuing pregnancy after elective fetal reduction of one fetus or more, third trimester

● O31.8   Other complications specific to multiple gestation
> ● O31.8x   Other complications specific to multiple gestation
>> ● O31.8x1   Other complications specific to multiple gestation, first trimester 🦠
>> ● O31.8x2   Other complications specific to multiple gestation, second trimester 🦠
>> ● O31.8x3   Other complications specific to multiple gestation, third trimester 🦠
>> ● ■ O31.8x9   Other complications specific to multiple gestation, unspecified trimester

CHAPTER 15 (O00-O99)

1272

● Unacceptable First-Listed Diagnosis   ● Use Additional Character(s)   ■ Unspecified   **OGCR** Official Guidelines for Coding and Reporting
🦠 Complication\Comorbidity   🦠 Major C\C   Excludes 1   Excludes 2   Includes   Use additional   Code first   Code also

● **O32** **Maternal care for malpresentation of fetus**

    | Includes | the listed conditions as a reason for observation, hospitalization or other obstetric care of the mother, or for cesarean delivery before onset of labor |

    | Excludes1 | malpresentation of fetus with obstructed labor (O64.-) |

    One of the following 7th characters is to be assigned to each code under category O32. 7th character 0 is for single gestations and multiple gestations where the fetus is unspecified. 7th characters 1 through 9 are for cases of multiple gestations to identify the fetus for which the code applies. The appropriate code from category O30, Multiple gestation, must also be assigned when assigning a code from category O32 that has a 7th character of 1 through 9.

    | 0 | not applicable or unspecified |
    | 1 | fetus 1 |
    | 2 | fetus 2 |
    | 3 | fetus 3 |
    | 4 | fetus 4 |
    | 5 | fetus 5 |
    | 9 | other fetus |

● **O32.0** **Maternal care for unstable lie**

● **O32.1** **Maternal care for breech presentation**
    Maternal care for buttocks presentation
    Maternal care for complete breech
    Maternal care for frank breech

    | Excludes1 | footling presentation (O32.8) incomplete breech (O32.8) |

● **O32.2** **Maternal care for transverse and oblique lie**
    Maternal care for oblique presentation
    Maternal care for transverse presentation

● **O32.3** **Maternal care for face, brow and chin presentation**

● **O32.4** **Maternal care for high head at term**
    Maternal care for failure of head to enter pelvic brim

● **O32.6** **Maternal care for compound presentation**

● **O32.8** **Maternal care for other malpresentation of fetus**
    Maternal care for footling presentation
    Maternal care for incomplete breech

● ▨ **O32.9** **Maternal care for malpresentation of fetus, unspecified**

● **O33** **Maternal care for disproportion**

    | Includes | the listed conditions as a reason for observation, hospitalization or other obstetric care of the mother, or for cesarean delivery before onset of labor |

    | Excludes1 | disproportion with obstructed labor (O65-O66) |

O33.0 **Maternal care for disproportion due to deformity of maternal pelvic bones** 🐾
    Maternal care for disproportion due to pelvic deformity causing disproportion NOS

O33.1 **Maternal care for disproportion due to generally contracted pelvis**
    Maternal care for disproportion due to contracted pelvis NOS causing disproportion

O33.2 **Maternal care for disproportion due to inlet contraction of pelvis**
    Maternal care for disproportion due to inlet contraction (pelvis) causing disproportion

O33.3 **Maternal care for disproportion due to outlet contraction of pelvis**
    Maternal care for disproportion due to mid-cavity contraction (pelvis)
    Maternal care for disproportion due to outlet contraction (pelvis)

    One of the following 7th characters is to be assigned to code O33.4. 7th character 0 is for single gestations and multiple gestations where the fetus is unspecified. 7th characters 1 through 9 are for cases of multiple gestations to identify the fetus for which the code applies. The appropriate code from category O30, Multiple gestation, must also be assigned when assigning code O33.4 with a 7th character of 1 through 9.

    | 0 | not applicable or unspecified |
    | 1 | fetus 1 |
    | 2 | fetus 2 |
    | 3 | fetus 3 |
    | 4 | fetus 4 |
    | 5 | fetus 5 |
    | 9 | other fetus |

● **O33.4** **Maternal care for disproportion of mixed maternal and fetal origin**
    One of the following 7th characters is to be assigned to code O33.5. 7th character 0 is for single gestations and multiple gestations where the fetus is unspecified. 7th characters 1 through 9 are for cases of multiple gestations to identify the fetus for which the code applies. The appropriate code from category O30, Multiple gestation, must also be assigned when assigning code O33.5 with a 7th character of 1 through 9.

    | 0 | not applicable or unspecified |
    | 1 | fetus 1 |
    | 2 | fetus 2 |
    | 3 | fetus 3 |
    | 4 | fetus 4 |
    | 5 | fetus 5 |
    | 9 | other fetus |

● **O33.5** **Maternal care for disproportion due to unusually large fetus**
    Maternal care for disproportion due to disproportion of fetal origin with normally formed fetus
    Maternal care for disproportion due to fetal disproportion NOS

    One of the following 7th characters is to be assigned to code O33.6. 7th character 0 is for single gestations and multiple gestations where the fetus is unspecified. 7th characters 1 through 9 are for cases of multiple gestations to identify the fetus for which the code applies. The appropriate code from category O30, Multiple gestation, must also be assigned when assigning code O33.6 with a 7th character of 1 through 9.

    | 0 | not applicable or unspecified |
    | 1 | fetus 1 |
    | 2 | fetus 2 |
    | 3 | fetus 3 |
    | 4 | fetus 4 |
    | 5 | fetus 5 |
    | 9 | other fetus |

CHAPTER 15 (O00-O99)

● Unacceptable First-Listed Diagnosis   ● Use Additional Character(s)   ▨ Unspecified   **OGCR** Official Guidelines for Coding and Reporting

🐾 Complication\Comorbidity   🐾 Major C\C | Excludes 1 | | Excludes 2 | Includes   Use additional   Code first   Code also

1273

● **O33.6 Maternal care for disproportion due to hydrocephalic fetus**

One of the following 7th characters is to be assigned to code O33.7. 7th character 0 is for single gestations and multiple gestations where the fetus is unspecified. 7th characters 1 through 9 are for cases of multiple gestations to identify the fetus for which the code applies. The appropriate code from category O30, Multiple gestation, must also be assigned when assigning code O33.7 with a 7th character of 1 through 9.

```
0   not applicable or unspecified
1   fetus 1
2   fetus 2
3   fetus 3
4   fetus 4
5   fetus 5
9   other fetus
```

O33.7 Maternal care for disproportion due to other fetal deformities

Maternal care for disproportion due to fetal ascites
Maternal care for disproportion due to fetal hydrops
Maternal care for disproportion due to fetal meningomyelocele
Maternal care for disproportion due to fetal sacral teratoma
Maternal care for disproportion due to fetal tumor

Excludes1 obstructed labor due to other fetal deformities (O66.3)

O33.8 Maternal care for disproportion of other origin

■**O33.9 Maternal care for disproportion, unspecified**

Maternal care for disproportion due to cephalopelvic disproportion NOS
Maternal care for disproportion due to fetopelvic disproportion NOS

● **O34 Maternal care for abnormality of pelvic organs**

Includes the listed conditions as a reason for hospitalization or other obstetric care of the mother, or for cesarean delivery before onset of labor

Code first any associated obstructed labor (O65.5)

Use additional code for specific condition

● **O34.0 Maternal care for congenital malformation of uterus**

■**O34.00 Maternal care for unspecified congenital malformation of uterus, unspecified trimester**

■**O34.01 Maternal care for unspecified congenital malformation of uterus, first trimester**

■**O34.02 Maternal care for unspecified congenital malformation of uterus, second trimester**

■**O34.03 Maternal care for unspecified congenital malformation of uterus, third trimester**

● **O34.1 Maternal care for benign tumor of corpus uteri**

Excludes2 maternal care for benign tumor of cervix (O34.4-)
maternal care for malignant neoplasm of uterus (O94.11-)

■**O34.10 Maternal care for benign tumor of corpus uteri, unspecified trimester**

O34.11 Maternal care for benign tumor of corpus uteri, first trimester

O34.12 Maternal care for benign tumor of corpus uteri, second trimester

O34.13 Maternal care for benign tumor of corpus uteri, third trimester

● **O34.2 Maternal care due to uterine scar from previous surgery**

O34.21 Maternal care for scar from previous cesarean delivery

O34.29 Maternal care due to uterine scar from other previous surgery

● **O34.3 Maternal care for cervical incompetence**

Maternal care for cerclage with or without cervical incompetence
Maternal care for Shirodkar suture with or without cervical incompetence

■**O34.30 Maternal care for cervical incompetence, unspecified trimester**

O34.31 Maternal care for cervical incompetence, first trimester 🗫

O34.32 Maternal care for cervical incompetence, second trimester 🗫

O34.33 Maternal care for cervical incompetence, third trimester 🗫

● **O34.4 Maternal care for other abnormalities of cervix**

■**O34.40 Maternal care for other abnormalities of cervix, unspecified trimester**

O34.41 Maternal care for other abnormalities of cervix, first trimester

O34.42 Maternal care for other abnormalities of cervix, second trimester

O34.43 Maternal care for other abnormalities of cervix, third trimester

● **O34.5 Maternal care for other abnormalities of gravid uterus**

● **O34.51 Maternal care for incarceration of gravid uterus**

O34.511 Maternal care for incarceration of gravid uterus, first trimester

O34.512 Maternal care for incarceration of gravid uterus, second trimester

O34.513 Maternal care for incarceration of gravid uterus, third trimester

■**O34.519 Maternal care for incarceration of gravid uterus, unspecified trimester**

● **O34.52 Maternal care for prolapse of gravid uterus**

O34.521 Maternal care for prolapse of gravid uterus, first trimester

O34.522 Maternal care for prolapse of gravid uterus, second trimester

O34.523 Maternal care for prolapse of gravid uterus, third trimester

■**O34.529 Maternal care for prolapse of gravid uterus, unspecified trimester**

● **O34.53 Maternal care for retroversion of gravid uterus**

O34.531 Maternal care for retroversion of gravid uterus, first trimester

O34.532 Maternal care for retroversion of gravid uterus, second trimester

O34.533 Maternal care for retroversion of gravid uterus, third trimester

■**O34.539 Maternal care for retroversion of gravid uterus, unspecified trimester**

● O34.59   Maternal care for other abnormalities of gravid uterus

     O34.591   Maternal care for other abnormalities of gravid uterus, first trimester

     O34.592   Maternal care for other abnormalities of gravid uterus, second trimester

     O34.593   Maternal care for other abnormalities of gravid uterus, third trimester

     ▣ O34.599   Maternal care for other abnormalities of gravid uterus, unspecified trimester

● O34.6   Maternal care for abnormality of vagina

    Excludes2   maternal care for vaginal varices in pregnancy (O22.1-)

   ▣ O34.60   Maternal care for abnormality of vagina, unspecified trimester

     O34.61   Maternal care for abnormality of vagina, first trimester

     O34.62   Maternal care for abnormality of vagina, second trimester

     O34.63   Maternal care for abnormality of vagina, third trimester

● O34.7   Maternal care for abnormality of vulva and perineum

    Excludes2   maternal care for perineal and vulval varices in pregnancy (O22.1-)

   ▣ O34.70   Maternal care for abnormality of vulva and perineum, unspecified trimester

     O34.71   Maternal care for abnormality of vulva and perineum, first trimester

     O34.72   Maternal care for abnormality of vulva and perineum, second trimester

     O34.73   Maternal care for abnormality of vulva and perineum, third trimester

● O34.8   Maternal care for other abnormalities of pelvic organs

   ▣ O34.80   Maternal care for other abnormalities of pelvic organs, unspecified trimester

     O34.81   Maternal care for other abnormalities of pelvic organs, first trimester

     O34.82   Maternal care for other abnormalities of pelvic organs, second trimester

     O34.83   Maternal care for other abnormalities of pelvic organs, third trimester

● O34.9   Maternal care for abnormality of pelvic organ, unspecified

   ▣ O34.90   Maternal care for abnormality of pelvic organ, unspecified, unspecified trimester

   ▣ O34.91   Maternal care for abnormality of pelvic organ, unspecified, first trimester

   ▣ O34.92   Maternal care for abnormality of pelvic organ, unspecified, second trimester

   ▣ O34.93   Maternal care for abnormality of pelvic organ, unspecified, third trimester

OGCR Section I.C.15.e.l.

Fetal Conditions Affecting the Management of the Mother

1) Code from categories O35 and O36

Codes from categories O35, Maternal care for known or suspected fetal abnormality and damage, and O36, Maternal care for other fetal problems, are assigned only when the fetal condition is actually responsible for modifying the management of the mother, i.e., by requiring diagnostic studies, additional observation, special care, or termination of pregnancy. The fact that the fetal condition exists does not justify assigning a code from this series to the mother's record.

2) In utero surgery

In cases when surgery is performed on the fetus, a diagnosis code from category O35, Maternal care for known or suspected fetal abnormality and damage, should be assigned identifying the fetal condition. Assign the appropriate procedure code for the procedure performed.

No code from Chapter 16, the perinatal codes, should be used on the mother's record to identify fetal conditions. Surgery performed in utero on a fetus is still to be coded as an obstetric encounter.

● O35   Maternal care for known or suspected fetal abnormality and damage

    Includes   the listed conditions in the fetus as a reason for hospitalization or other obstetric care to the mother, or for termination of pregnancy

   Code also any associated maternal condition

    Excludes1   encounter for suspected maternal and fetal conditions ruled out (Z03.7)

One of the following 7th characters is to be assigned to each code under category O35. 7th character 0 is for single gestations and multiple gestations where the fetus is unspecified. 7th characters 1 through 9 are for cases of multiple gestations to identify the fetus for which the code applies. The appropriate code from category O30, Multiple gestation, must also be assigned when assigning a code from category O35 that has a 7th character of 1 through 9.

0	not applicable or unspecified
1	fetus 1
2	fetus 2
3	fetus 3
4	fetus 4
5	fetus 5
9	other fetus

● O35.0   Maternal care for (suspected) central nervous system malformation in fetus

    Maternal care for fetal anencephaly

    Maternal care for fetal hydrocephalus

    Maternal care for fetal spina bifida

    Excludes2   chromosomal abnormality in fetus (O35.1)

● O35.1   Maternal care for (suspected) chromosomal abnormality in fetus

● O35.2   Maternal care for (suspected) hereditary disease in fetus

    Excludes2   chromosomal abnormality in fetus (O35.1)

● O35.3   Maternal care for (suspected) damage to fetus from viral disease in mother

    Maternal care for damage to fetus from maternal cytomegalovirus infection

    Maternal care for damage to fetus from maternal rubella

● Unacceptable First-Listed Diagnosis   ● Use Additional Character(s)   ▣ Unspecified   **OGCR** Official Guidelines for Coding and Reporting

🅒 Complication\Comorbidity   🅜 Major C\C   Excludes 1   Excludes 2   Includes   Use additional   Code first   Code also

CHAPTER 15 (O00–O99)

1275

● **O35.4 Maternal care for (suspected) damage to fetus from alcohol**

● **O35.5 Maternal care for (suspected) damage to fetus by drugs**
    Maternal care for damage to fetus from drug addiction

● **O35.6 Maternal care for (suspected) damage to fetus by radiation**

● **O35.7 Maternal care for (suspected) damage to fetus by other medical procedures**
    Maternal care for damage to fetus by amniocentesis
    Maternal care for damage to fetus by biopsy procedures
    Maternal care for damage to fetus by hematological investigation
    Maternal care for damage to fetus by intrauterine contraceptive device
    Maternal care for damage to fetus by intrauterine surgery

● **O35.8 Maternal care for other (suspected) fetal abnormality and damage**
    Maternal care for damage to fetus from maternal listeriosis
    Maternal care for damage to fetus from maternal toxoplasmosis

● ■ **O35.9 Maternal care for (suspected) fetal abnormality and damage, unspecified**

● **O36 Maternal care for other fetal problems**

> **Includes**   the listed conditions in the fetus as a reason for hospitalization or other obstetric care of the mother, or for termination of pregnancy

> **Excludes1**   encounter for suspected maternal and fetal conditions ruled out (Z03.7)
>   placental transfusion syndromes (O43.0-)

> **Excludes2**   labor and delivery complicated by fetal stress (O77.-)

One of the following 7th characters is to be assigned to each code under category O36. 7th character 0 is for single gestations and multiple gestations where the fetus is unspecified. 7th characters 1 through 9 are for cases of multiple gestations to identify the fetus for which the code applies. The appropriate code from category O30, Multiple gestation, must also be assigned when assigning a code from category O36 that has a 7th character of 1 through 9.

0	not applicable or unspecified
1	fetus 1
2	fetus 2
3	fetus 3
4	fetus 4
5	fetus 5
9	other fetus

● **O36.0 Maternal care for rhesus isoimmunization**
    Maternal care for Rh incompatibility (with hydrops fetalis)

  ● **O36.01 Maternal care for anti-D [Rh] antibodies**

    ● **O36.011 Maternal care for anti-D [Rh] antibodies, first trimester** 🅒

    ● **O36.012 Maternal care for anti-D [Rh] antibodies, second trimester** 🅒

    ● **O36.013 Maternal care for anti-D [Rh] antibodies, third trimester** 🅒

    ● ■ **O36.019 Maternal care for anti-D [Rh] antibodies, unspecified trimester**

● **O36.09 Maternal care for other rhesus isoimmunization**

    ● **O36.091 Maternal care for other rhesus isoimmunization, first trimester** 🅒

    ● **O36.092 Maternal care for other rhesus isoimmunization, second trimester** 🅒

    ● **O36.093 Maternal care for other rhesus isoimmunization, third trimester** 🅒

    ● ■ **O36.099 Maternal care for other rhesus isoimmunization, unspecified trimester**

● **O36.1 Maternal care for other isoimmunization**
    Maternal care for ABO isoimmunization

  ● **O36.11 Maternal care for Anti-A sensitization**
    Maternal care for isoimmunization NOS (with hydrops fetalis)

    ● **O36.111 Maternal care for Anti-A sensitization, first trimester**

    ● **O36.112 Maternal care for Anti-A sensitization, second trimester**

    ● **O36.113 Maternal care for Anti-A sensitization, third trimester**

    ● ■ **O36.119 Maternal care for Anti-A sensitization, unspecified trimester**

  ● **O36.19 Maternal care for other isoimmunization**
    Maternal care for Anti-B sensitization

    ● **O36.191 Maternal care for other isoimmunization, first trimester**

    ● **O36.192 Maternal care for other isoimmunization, second trimester**

    ● **O36.193 Maternal care for other isoimmunization, third trimester**

    ● ■ **O36.199 Maternal care for other isoimmunization, unspecified trimester**

● **O36.2 Maternal care for hydrops fetalis**
    Maternal care for hydrops fetalis NOS
    Maternal care for hydrops fetalis not associated with isoimmunization

> **Excludes1**   hydrops fetalis associated with ABO isoimmunization (O36.1-)
>   hydrops fetalis associated with rhesus isoimmunization (O36.0-)

  ● ■ **O36.20 Maternal care for hydrops fetalis, unspecified trimester**

  ● **O36.21 Maternal care for hydrops fetalis, first trimester**

  ● **O36.22 Maternal care for hydrops fetalis, second trimester**

  ● **O36.23 Maternal care for hydrops fetalis, third trimester**

● **O36.4 Maternal care for intrauterine death** 🅒
    Maternal care for intrauterine fetal death NOS
    Maternal care for intrauterine fetal death after completion of 20 weeks of gestation
    Maternal care for late fetal death
    Maternal care for missed delivery

> **Excludes1**   missed abortion (O02.1)
>   stillbirth (P95)

● **O36.5 Maternal care for known or suspected poor fetal growth**

  ● **O36.51 Maternal care for known or suspected placental insufficiency**

CHAPTER 15 (O00-O99)

- O36.511 Maternal care for known or suspected placental insufficiency, first trimester 0, 1, 2, 3, 4, 9 ⊘
- O36.512 Maternal care for known or suspected placental insufficiency, second trimester
- O36.513 Maternal care for known or suspected placental insufficiency, third trimester ⊘
- O36.519 Maternal care for known or suspected placental insufficiency, unspecified trimester
- O36.59 Maternal care for other known or suspected poor fetal growth
  Maternal care for known or suspected light-for-dates NOS
  Maternal care for known or suspected small-for-dates NOS
  - O36.591 Maternal care for other known or suspected poor fetal growth, first trimester ⊘
  - O36.592 Maternal care for other known or suspected poor fetal growth, second trimester ⊘
  - O36.593 Maternal care for other known or suspected poor fetal growth, third trimester ⊘
  - O36.599 Maternal care for other known or suspected poor fetal growth, unspecified trimester
- O36.6 Maternal care for excessive fetal growth
  Maternal care for known or suspected large-for-dates
  - O36.60 Maternal care for excessive fetal growth, unspecified trimester
  - O36.61 Maternal care for excessive fetal growth, first trimester
  - O36.62 Maternal care for excessive fetal growth, second trimester
  - O36.63 Maternal care for excessive fetal growth, third trimester
- O36.7 Maternal care for viable fetus in abdominal pregnancy
  - O36.70 Maternal care for viable fetus in abdominal pregnancy, unspecified trimester
  - O36.71 Maternal care for viable fetus in abdominal pregnancy, first trimester
  - O36.72 Maternal care for viable fetus in abdominal pregnancy, second trimester
  - O36.73 Maternal care for viable fetus in abdominal pregnancy, third trimester
- O36.8 Maternal care for other specified fetal problems
  - O36.81 Decreased fetal movements
    - O36.812 Decreased fetal movements, second trimester
    - O36.813 Decreased fetal movements, third trimester
    - O36.819 Decreased fetal movements, unspecified trimester
  - O36.82 Fetal anemia and thrombocytopenia
    - O36.821 Fetal anemia and thrombocytopenia, first trimester
    - O36.822 Fetal anemia and thrombocytopenia, second trimester

- O36.823 Fetal anemia and thrombocytopenia, third trimester
- O36.829 Fetal anemia and thrombocytopenia, unspecified trimester
- O36.89 Maternal care for other specified fetal problems
  - O36.891 Maternal care for other specified fetal problems, first trimester
  - O36.892 Maternal care for other specified fetal problems, second trimester
  - O36.893 Maternal care for other specified fetal problems, third trimester
  - O36.899 Maternal care for other specified fetal problems, unspecified trimester
- O36.9 Maternal care for fetal problem, unspecified
  - O36.90 Maternal care for fetal problem, unspecified, unspecified trimester
  - O36.91 Maternal care for fetal problem, unspecified, first trimester
  - O36.92 Maternal care for fetal problem, unspecified, second trimester
  - O36.93 Maternal care for fetal problem, unspecified, third trimester

- O40 Polyhydramnios
  Overabundance of amniotic fluid
  Includes hydramnios
  Excludes1 encounter for suspected maternal and fetal conditions ruled out (Z03.7-)
  One of the following 7th characters is to be assigned to each code under category O40. 7th character 0 is for single gestations and multiple gestations where the fetus is unspecified. 7th characters 1 through 9 are for cases of multiple gestations to identify the fetus for which the code applies. The appropriate code from category O30, Multiple gestation, must also be assigned when assigning a code from category O40 that has a 7th character of 1 through 9.

0	not applicable or unspecified
1	fetus 1
2	fetus 2
3	fetus 3
4	fetus 4
5	fetus 5
9	other fetus

  - O40.1 Polyhydramnios, first trimester ⊘
  - O40.2 Polyhydramnios, second trimester ⊘
  - O40.3 Polyhydramnios, third trimester ⊘
  - O40.9 Polyhydramnios, unspecified trimester

● Unacceptable First-Listed Diagnosis   ● Use Additional Character(s)   ■ Unspecified   **OGCR** Official Guidelines for Coding and Reporting
⊘ Complication\Comorbidity   ⊘ Major C\C   Excludes 1   Excludes 2   Includes   Use additional   Code first   Code also

CHAPTER 15 (O00-O99)

1277

● **O41   Other disorders of amniotic fluid and membranes**

> **Excludes1**   encounter for suspected maternal and fetal conditions ruled out (Z03.7-)

One of the following 7th characters is to be assigned to each code under category O41. 7th character 0 is for single gestations and multiple gestations where the fetus is unspecified. 7th characters 1 through 9 are for cases of multiple gestations to identify the fetus for which the code applies. The appropriate code from category O30, Multiple gestation, must also be assigned when assigning a code from category O41 that has a 7th character of 1 through 9.

0	not applicable or unspecified
1	fetus 1
2	fetus 2
3	fetus 3
4	fetus 4
5	fetus 5
9	other fetus

● **O41.0   Oligohydramnios**
> *Scant volume of amniotic fluid*
> Oligohydramnios without rupture of membranes

   ● ▪ **O41.00   Oligohydramnios, unspecified trimester**

   ● **O41.01   Oligohydramnios, first trimester** 🗫

   ● **O41.02   Oligohydramnios, second trimester** 🗫

   ● **O41.03   Oligohydramnios, third trimester** 🗫

● **O41.1   Infection of amniotic sac and membranes**

   ● **O41.10   Infection of amniotic sac and membranes, unspecified**

     ● ▪ **O41.101   Infection of amniotic sac and membranes, unspecified, first trimester** 🗫

     ● ▪ **O41.102   Infection of amniotic sac and membranes, unspecified, second trimester** 🗫

     ● ▪ **O41.103   Infection of amniotic sac and membranes, unspecified, third trimester** 🗫

     ● ▪ **O41.109   Infection of amniotic sac and membranes, unspecified, unspecified trimester**

   ● **O41.12   Chorioamnionitis**

     ● **O41.121   Chorioamnionitis, first trimester** 🗫

     ● **O41.122   Chorioamnionitis, second trimester** 🗫

     ● **O41.123   Chorioamnionitis, third trimester** 🗫

     ● ▪ **O41.129   Chorioamnionitis, unspecified trimester**

   ● **O41.14   Placentitis**

     ● **O41.141   Placentitis, first trimester** 🗫

     ● **O41.142   Placentitis, second trimester** 🗫

     ● **O41.143   Placentitis, third trimester** 🗫

     ● ▪ **O41.149   Placentitis, unspecified trimester**

● **O41.8   Other specified disorders of amniotic fluid and membranes**

   ● **O41.8x   Other specified disorders of amniotic fluid and membranes**

     ● **O41.8x1   Other specified disorders of amniotic fluid and membranes, first trimester** 🗫

     ● **O41.8x2   Other specified disorders of amniotic fluid and membranes, second trimester** 🗫

     ● **O41.8x3   Other specified disorders of amniotic fluid and membranes, third trimester** 🗫

     ● ▪ **O41.8x9   Other specified disorders of amniotic fluid and membranes, unspecified trimester**

● **O41.9   Disorder of amniotic fluid and membranes, unspecified**

   ● ▪ **O41.90   Disorder of amniotic fluid and membranes, unspecified, unspecified trimester**

   ● ▪ **O41.91   Disorder of amniotic fluid and membranes, unspecified, first trimester**

   ● ▪ **O41.92   Disorder of amniotic fluid and membranes, unspecified, second trimester**

   ● ▪ **O41.93   Disorder of amniotic fluid and membranes, unspecified, third trimester**

● **O42   Premature rupture of membranes**

   ● **O42.0   Premature rupture of membranes, onset of labor within 24 hours of rupture**

     ▪ **O42.00   Premature rupture of membranes, onset of labor within 24 hours of rupture, unspecified weeks of gestation**

     ● **O42.01   Preterm premature rupture of membranes, onset of labor within 24 hours of rupture**
> Premature rupture of membranes before 37 completed weeks of gestation

       O42.011   Preterm premature rupture of membranes, onset of labor within 24 hours of rupture, first trimester

       O42.012   Preterm premature rupture of membranes, onset of labor within 24 hours of rupture, second trimester

       O42.013   Preterm premature rupture of membranes, onset of labor within 24 hours of rupture, third trimester

       ▪ **O42.019   Preterm premature rupture of membranes, onset of labor within 24 hours of rupture, unspecified trimester**

     O42.02   Full-term premature rupture of membranes, onset of labor within 24 hours of rupture
> Premature rupture of membranes after 37 completed weeks of gestation

   ● **O42.1   Premature rupture of membranes, onset of labor more than 24 hours following rupture**

     ▪ **O42.10   Premature rupture of membranes, onset of labor more than 24 hours following rupture, unspecified weeks of gestation**

     ● **O42.11   Preterm premature rupture of membranes, onset of labor more than 24 hours following rupture**
> Premature rupture of membranes before 37 completed weeks of gestation

       O42.111   Preterm premature rupture of membranes, onset of labor more than 24 hours following rupture, first trimester

       O42.112   Preterm premature rupture of membranes, onset of labor more than 24 hours following rupture, second trimester

       O42.113   Preterm premature rupture of membranes, onset of labor more than 24 hours following rupture, third trimester

1278

● Unacceptable First-Listed Diagnosis   ● Use Additional Character(s)   ▪ Unspecified   **OGCR** Official Guidelines for Coding and Reporting

🗫 Complication\Comorbidity   🗫 Major C\C   Excludes 1   Excludes 2   Includes   Use additional   Code first   Code also

CHAPTER 15 (O00-O99)

O42.119 Preterm premature rupture of membranes, onset of labor more than 24 hours following rupture, unspecified trimester

O42.12 Full-term premature rupture of membranes, onset of labor more than 24 hours following rupture
> Premature rupture of membranes after 37 completed weeks of gestation

● O42.9 Premature rupture of membranes, unspecified as to length of time between rupture and onset of labor

O42.90 Premature rupture of membranes, unspecified as to length of time between rupture and onset of labor, unspecified weeks of gestation

● O42.91 Preterm premature rupture of membranes, unspecified as to length of time between rupture and onset of labor
> Premature rupture of membranes before 37 completed weeks of gestation

O42.911 Preterm premature rupture of membranes, unspecified as to length of time between rupture and onset of labor, first trimester

O42.912 Preterm premature rupture of membranes, unspecified as to length of time between rupture and onset of labor, second trimester

O42.913 Preterm premature rupture of membranes, unspecified as to length of time between rupture and onset of labor, third trimester

O42.919 Preterm premature rupture of membranes, unspecified as to length of time between rupture and onset of labor, unspecified trimester

O42.92 Full-term premature rupture of membranes, unspecified as to length of time between rupture and onset of labor
> Premature rupture of membranes after 37 completed weeks of gestation

● O43 Placental disorders

> **Excludes2** maternal care for poor fetal growth due to placental insufficiency (O36.5-)
> placenta previa (O44.-)
> placental polyp (O90.89)
> placentitis (O41.14-)
> premature separation of placenta [abruptio placentae] (O45.-)

● O43.0 Placental transfusion syndromes

● O43.01 Fetomaternal placental transfusion syndrome
> Maternofetal placental transfusion syndrome

O43.011 Fetomaternal placental transfusion syndrome, first trimester

O43.012 Fetomaternal placental transfusion syndrome, second trimester

O43.013 Fetomaternal placental transfusion syndrome, third trimester

O43.019 Fetomaternal placental transfusion syndrome, unspecified trimester

● O43.02 Fetus-to-fetus placental transfusion syndrome

O43.021 Fetus-to-fetus placental transfusion syndrome, first trimester

O43.022 Fetus-to-fetus placental transfusion syndrome, second trimester

O43.023 Fetus-to-fetus placental transfusion syndrome, third trimester

O43.029 Fetus-to-fetus placental transfusion syndrome, unspecified trimester

● O43.1 Malformation of placenta

● O43.10 Malformation of placenta, unspecified
> Abnormal placenta NOS

O43.101 Malformation of placenta, unspecified, first trimester

O43.102 Malformation of placenta, unspecified, second trimester

O43.103 Malformation of placenta, unspecified, third trimester

O43.109 Malformation of placenta, unspecified, unspecified trimester

● O43.11 Circumvallate placenta

O43.111 Circumvallate placenta, first trimester

O43.112 Circumvallate placenta, second trimester

O43.113 Circumvallate placenta, third trimester

O43.119 Circumvallate placenta, unspecified trimester

● O43.12 Velamentous insertion of umbilical cord

O43.121 Velamentous insertion of umbilical cord, first trimester

O43.122 Velamentous insertion of umbilical cord, second trimester

O43.123 Velamentous insertion of umbilical cord, third trimester

O43.129 Velamentous insertion of umbilical cord, unspecified trimester

● O43.19 Other malformation of placenta

O43.191 Other malformation of placenta, first trimester

O43.192 Other malformation of placenta, second trimester

O43.193 Other malformation of placenta, third trimester

O43.199 Other malformation of placenta, unspecified trimester

● O43.2 Morbidly adherent placenta

> Code also associated third stage postpartum hemorrhage, if applicable (O72.0)
> **Excludes1** retained placenta (O73.-)

● O43.21 Placenta accreta

O43.211 Placenta accreta, first trimester

O43.212 Placenta accreta, second trimester

O43.213 Placenta accreta, third trimester

O43.219 Placenta accreta, unspecified trimester

● O43.22 Placenta increta

O43.221 Placenta increta, first trimester

O43.222 Placenta increta, second trimester

O43.223 Placenta increta, third trimester

O43.229 Placenta increta, unspecified trimester

● Unacceptable First-Listed Diagnosis   ● Use Additional Character(s)   ▨ Unspecified   **OGCR** Official Guidelines for Coding and Reporting

🍇 Complication\Comorbidity   🍇 Major C\C   [Excludes 1]   [Excludes 2]   Includes   Use additional   Code first   Code also   1279

CHAPTER 15 (O00-O99)

● O43.23 Placenta percreta

    O43.231 Placenta percreta, first trimester

    O43.232 Placenta percreta, second trimester

    O43.233 Placenta percreta, third trimester

    ■ O43.239 Placenta percreta, unspecified trimester

● O43.8 Other placental disorders

  ● O43.81 Placental infarction

    O43.811 Placental infarction, first trimester

    O43.812 Placental infarction, second trimester

    O43.813 Placental infarction, third trimester

    ■ O43.819 Placental infarction, unspecified trimester

  ● O43.89 Other placental disorders
    Placental dysfunction

    O43.891 Other placental disorders, first trimester

    O43.892 Other placental disorders, second trimester

    O43.893 Other placental disorders, third trimester

    ■ O43.899 Other placental disorders, unspecified trimester

● O43.9 Unspecified placental disorder

  ■ O43.90 Unspecified placental disorder, unspecified trimester

  ■ O43.91 Unspecified placental disorder, first trimester

  ■ O43.92 Unspecified placental disorder, second trimester

  ■ O43.93 Unspecified placental disorder, third trimester

● O44 Placenta previa

  ● O44.0 Placenta previa specified as without hemorrhage
    Low implantation of placenta specified as without hemorrhage

  ■ O44.00 Placenta previa specified as without hemorrhage, unspecified trimester

    O44.01 Placenta previa specified as without hemorrhage, first trimester 🔗

    O44.02 Placenta previa specified as without hemorrhage, second trimester 🔗

    O44.03 Placenta previa specified as without hemorrhage, third trimester 🔗

  ● O44.1 Placenta previa with hemorrhage
    Low implantation of placenta, NOS or with hemorrhage
    Marginal placenta previa, NOS or with hemorrhage
    Partial placenta previa, NOS or with hemorrhage
    Total placenta previa, NOS or with hemorrhage

    | Excludes1 | labor and delivery complicated by hemorrhage from vasa previa (O69.4) |

  ■ O44.10 Placenta previa with hemorrhage, unspecified trimester

    O44.11 Placenta previa with hemorrhage, first trimester 🔗

    O44.12 Placenta previa with hemorrhage, second trimester 🔗

    O44.13 Placenta previa with hemorrhage, third trimester 🔗

● O45 Premature separation of placenta [abruptio placentae]

  ● O45.0 Premature separation of placenta with coagulation defect

    ● O45.00 Premature separation of placenta with coagulation defect, unspecified

      ■ O45.001 Premature separation of placenta with coagulation defect, unspecified, first trimester 🔗

      ■ O45.002 Premature separation of placenta with coagulation defect, unspecified, second trimester 🔗

      ■ O45.003 Premature separation of placenta with coagulation defect, unspecified, third trimester 🔗

      ■ O45.009 Premature separation of placenta with coagulation defect, unspecified, unspecified trimester

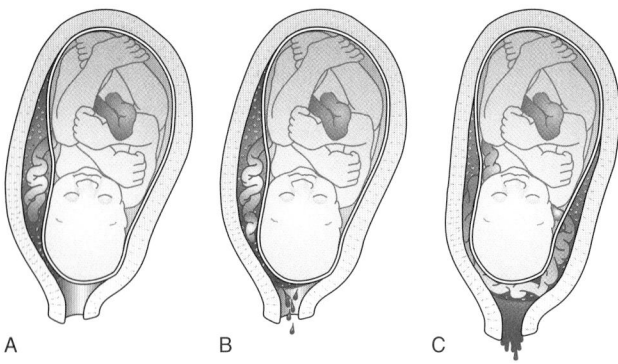

Figure 15-2 **A.** Marginal placento previa. **B.** Partial placenta previa. **C.** Total placento previa.

Item 15–3 **Placenta previa** is a condition in which the opening of the cervix is obstructed by the displaced placenta. The three types, marginal, partial, and total, are varying degrees of placenta displacement. Placenta abruption is the premature breaking away of the placenta from the site of the uterine implant before the delivery of the fetus.

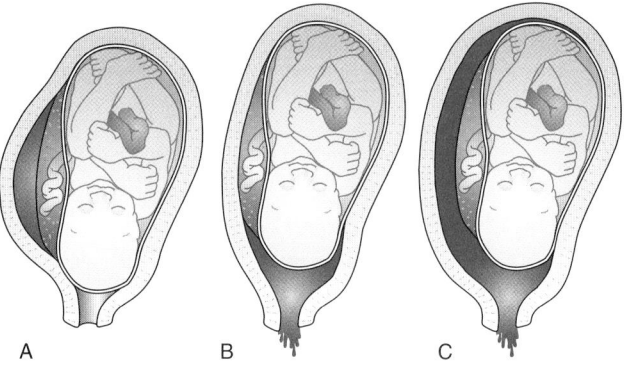

Figure 15-3 Abruptio placentae is classified according to the grade of separation of the placenta from the uterine wall. **A.** Mild separation in which hemorrhage is internal. **B.** Moderate separation in which there is external hemorrhage. **C.** Severe separation in which there is external hemorrhage and extreme separation.

● Unacceptable First-Listed Diagnosis   ● Use Additional Character(s)   ■ Unspecified   **OGCR** Official Guidelines for Coding and Reporting
🔗 Complication\Comorbidity   🔗 Major C\C | Excludes 1 | | Excludes 2 | Includes   Use additional   Code first   Code also

- ● O45.01   Premature separation of placenta with afibrinogenemia
  - Premature separation of placenta with hypofibrinogenemia
  - O45.011   Premature separation of placenta with afibrinogenemia, first trimester
  - O45.012   Premature separation of placenta with afibrinogenemia, second trimester
  - O45.013   Premature separation of placenta with afibrinogenemia, third trimester
  - ■ O45.019   Premature separation of placenta with afibrinogenemia, unspecified trimester
- ● O45.02   Premature separation of placenta with disseminated intravascular coagulation
  - O45.021   Premature separation of placenta with disseminated intravascular coagulation, first trimester
  - O45.022   Premature separation of placenta with disseminated intravascular coagulation, second trimester
  - O45.023   Premature separation of placenta with disseminated intravascular coagulation, third trimester
  - ■ O45.029   Premature separation of placenta with disseminated intravascular coagulation, unspecified trimester
- ● O45.09   Premature separation of placenta with other coagulation defect
  - O45.091   Premature separation of placenta with other coagulation defect, first trimester
  - O45.092   Premature separation of placenta with other coagulation defect, second trimester
  - O45.093   Premature separation of placenta with other coagulation defect, third trimester
  - ■ O45.099   Premature separation of placenta with other coagulation defect, unspecified trimester
- ● O45.8   Other premature separation of placenta
  - ● O45.8x   Other premature separation of placenta
    - O45.8x1   Other premature separation of placenta, first trimester
    - O45.8x2   Other premature separation of placenta, second trimester
    - O45.8x3   Other premature separation of placenta, third trimester
    - ■ O45.8x9   Other premature separation of placenta, unspecified trimester
- ● O45.9   Premature separation of placenta, unspecified
  - Abruptio placentae NOS
  - ■ O45.90   Premature separation of placenta, unspecified, unspecified trimester
  - ■ O45.91   Premature separation of placenta, unspecified, first trimester
  - ■ O45.92   Premature separation of placenta, unspecified, second trimester
  - ■ O45.93   Premature separation of placenta, unspecified, third trimester

- ● O46   Antepartum hemorrhage, not elsewhere classified
  - **Excludes1**   hemorrhage in early pregnancy (O20.-)
    - intrapartum hemorrhage NEC (O67.-)
    - placenta previa (O44.-)
    - premature separation of placenta [abruptio placentae] (O45.-)
  - ● O46.0   Antepartum hemorrhage with coagulation defect
    - ● O46.00   Antepartum hemorrhage with coagulation defect, unspecified
      - ■ O46.001   Antepartum hemorrhage with coagulation defect, unspecified, first trimester
      - ■ O46.002   Antepartum hemorrhage with coagulation defect, unspecified, second trimester
      - ■ O46.003   Antepartum hemorrhage with coagulation defect, unspecified, third trimester
      - ■ O46.009   Antepartum hemorrhage with coagulation defect, unspecified, unspecified trimester
    - ● O46.01   Antepartum hemorrhage with afibrinogenemia
      - Antepartum hemorrhage with hypofibrinogenemia
      - O46.011   Antepartum hemorrhage with afibrinogenemia, first trimester
      - O46.012   Antepartum hemorrhage with afibrinogenemia, second trimester
      - O46.013   Antepartum hemorrhage with afibrinogenemia, third trimester
      - ■ O46.019   Antepartum hemorrhage with afibrinogenemia, unspecified trimester
    - ● O46.02   Antepartum hemorrhage with disseminated intravascular coagulation
      - O46.021   Antepartum hemorrhage with disseminated intravascular coagulation, first trimester
      - O46.022   Antepartum hemorrhage with disseminated intravascular coagulation, second trimester
      - O46.023   Antepartum hemorrhage with disseminated intravascular coagulation, third trimester
      - ■ O46.029   Antepartum hemorrhage with disseminated intravascular coagulation, unspecified trimester
    - ● O46.09   Antepartum hemorrhage with other coagulation defect
      - O46.091   Antepartum hemorrhage with other coagulation defect, first trimester
      - O46.092   Antepartum hemorrhage with other coagulation defect, second trimester
      - O46.093   Antepartum hemorrhage with other coagulation defect, third trimester
      - ■ O46.099   Antepartum hemorrhage with other coagulation defect, unspecified trimester

●   Unacceptable First-Listed Diagnosis   ●   Use Additional Character(s)   ■   Unspecified   **OGCR**   Official Guidelines for Coding and Reporting

 Complication\Comorbidity    Major C\C   Excludes 1   Excludes 2   Includes   Use additional   Code first   Code also

1281

CHAPTER 15 (O00-O99)

- O46.8 Other antepartum hemorrhage
  - O46.8x Other antepartum hemorrhage
    - O46.8x1 Other antepartum hemorrhage, first trimester
    - O46.8x2 Other antepartum hemorrhage, second trimester
    - O46.8x3 Other antepartum hemorrhage, third trimester
    - O46.8x9 Other antepartum hemorrhage, unspecified trimester
  - O46.9 Antepartum hemorrhage, unspecified
    - O46.90 Antepartum hemorrhage, unspecified, unspecified trimester
    - O46.91 Antepartum hemorrhage, unspecified, first trimester
    - O46.92 Antepartum hemorrhage, unspecified, second trimester
    - O46.93 Antepartum hemorrhage, unspecified, third trimester

- O47 False labor
  | Includes | Braxton Hicks contractions |
  | | threatened labor |

  | Excludes1 | preterm labor (O60.-) |

  - O47.0 False labor before 37 completed weeks of gestation
    - O47.00 False labor before 37 completed weeks of gestation, unspecified trimester
    - O47.02 False labor before 37 completed weeks of gestation, second trimester
    - O47.03 False labor before 37 completed weeks of gestation, third trimester
  - O47.1 False labor at or after 37 completed weeks of gestation
  - O47.9 False labor, unspecified

- O48 Late pregnancy
  - O48.0 Post-term pregnancy
    Pregnancy over 40 completed weeks to 42 completed weeks gestation
  - O48.1 Prolonged pregnancy
    Pregnancy which has advanced beyond 42 completed weeks gestation

---

COMPLICATIONS OF LABOR AND DELIVERY (O60-O77)

- O60 Preterm labor
  | Includes | onset (spontaneous) of labor before 37 completed weeks of gestation |

  | Excludes1 | false labor (O47.0-) |
  | | threatened labor NOS (O47.0-) |

  - O60.0 Preterm labor without delivery
    - O60.00 Preterm labor without delivery, unspecified trimester
    - O60.02 Preterm labor without delivery, second trimester

  - O60.03 Preterm labor without delivery, third trimester

One of the following 7th characters is to be assigned to each code under subcategory O60.1. 7th character 0 is for single gestations and multiple gestations where the fetus is unspecified. 7th characters 1 through 9 are for cases of multiple gestations to identify the fetus for which the code applies. The appropriate code from category O30, Multiple gestation, must also be assigned when assigning a code from subcategory O60.1 that has a 7th character of 1 through 9.

0	not applicable or unspecified
1	fetus 1
2	fetus 2
3	fetus 3
4	fetus 4
5	fetus 5
9	other fetus

- O60.1 Preterm labor with preterm delivery
  - O60.10 Preterm labor with preterm delivery, unspecified trimester
    Preterm labor with delivery NOS
  - O60.12 Preterm labor second trimester with preterm delivery second trimester
  - O60.13 Preterm labor second trimester with preterm delivery third trimester
  - O60.14 Preterm labor third trimester with preterm delivery third trimester

One of the following 7th characters is to be assigned to each code under subcategory O60.2. 7th character 0 is for single gestations and multiple gestations where the fetus is unspecified. 7th characters 1 through 9 are for cases of multiple gestations to identify the fetus for which the code applies. The appropriate code from category O30, Multiple gestation, must also be assigned when assigning a code from subcategory O60.2 that has a 7th character of 1 through 9.

0	not applicable or unspecified
1	fetus 1
2	fetus 2
3	fetus 3
4	fetus 4
5	fetus 5
9	other fetus

- O60.2 Term delivery with preterm labor
  - O60.20 Term delivery with preterm labor, unspecified trimester
  - O60.22 Term delivery with preterm labor, second trimester
  - O60.23 Term delivery with preterm labor, third trimester

- O61 Failed induction of labor
  - O61.0 Failed medical induction of labor
    Failed induction (of labor) by oxytocin
    Failed induction (of labor) by prostaglandins
  - O61.1 Failed instrumental induction of labor
    Failed mechanical induction (of labor)
    Failed surgical induction (of labor)
  - O61.8 Other failed induction of labor
  - O61.9 Failed induction of labor, unspecified

● Unacceptable First-Listed Diagnosis   ● Use Additional Character(s)   ■ Unspecified   **OGCR** Official Guidelines for Coding and Reporting
🍷 Complication\Comorbidity   🍷 Major C\C   Excludes 1   Excludes 2   Includes   Use additional   Code first   Code also

● **O62   Abnormalities of forces of labor**

  O62.0   Primary inadequate contractions
         Failure of cervical dilatation
         Primary hypotonic uterine dysfunction
         Uterine inertia during latent phase of labor

  O62.1   Secondary uterine inertia
         Arrested active phase of labor
         Secondary hypotonic uterine dysfunction

  O62.2   Other uterine inertia
         Atony of uterus without hemorrhage
         Atony of uterus NOS
         Desultory labor
         Hypotonic uterine dysfunction NOS
         Irregular labor
         Poor contractions
         Slow slope active phase of labor
         Uterine inertia NOS

         | Excludes1 | atony of uterus with hemorrhage
                       (postpartum) (O72.1)
                       postpartum atony of uterus without
                       hemorrhage (O75.89)

  O62.3   Precipitate labor

  **O62.4   Hypertonic, incoordinate, and prolonged uterine
         contractions**
         Cervical spasm
         Contraction ring dystocia
         Dyscoordinate labor
         Hour-glass contraction of uterus
         Hypertonic uterine dysfunction
         Incoordinate uterine action
         Tetanic contractions
         Uterine dystocia NOS
         Uterine spasm

         | Excludes1 | dystocia (fetal) (maternal) NOS (O66.9)

  O62.8   Other abnormalities of forces of labor

  ■ **O62.9   Abnormality of forces of labor, unspecified**

● **O63   Long labor**

  O63.0   Prolonged first stage (of labor)

  O63.1   Prolonged second stage (of labor)

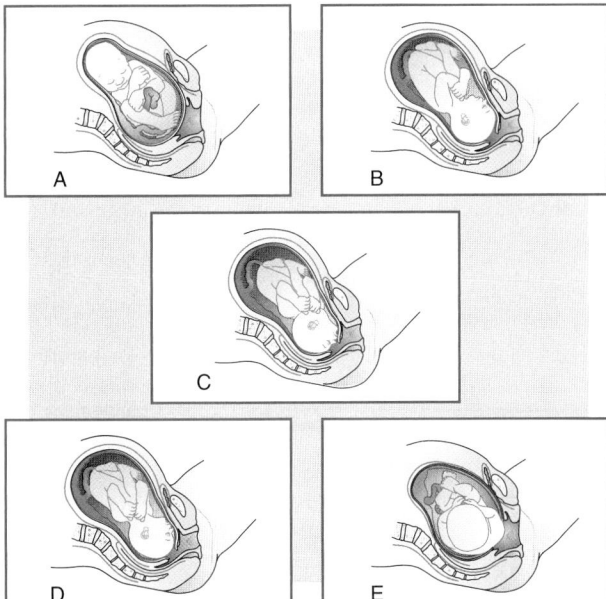

Figure 15-4 Five types of malposition and malpresentation of the fetus: **A.** Breech. **B.** Vertex. **C.** Face. **D.** Brow. **E.** Shoulder.

  O63.2   Delayed delivery of second twin, triplet, etc.

  ■ **O63.9   Long labor, unspecified** 📞
         Prolonged labor NOS

● **O64   Obstructed labor due to malposition and malpresentation
    of fetus**

  One of the following 7th characters is to be assigned to each code
  under category O64. 7th character 0 is for single gestations
  and multiple gestations where the fetus is unspecified. 7th
  characters 1 through 9 are for cases of multiple gestations
  to identify the fetus for which the code applies. The
  appropriate code from category O30, Multiple gestation,
  must also be assigned when assigning a code from category
  O64 that has a 7th character of 1 through 9.

0	not applicable or unspecified
1	fetus 1
2	fetus 2
3	fetus 3
4	fetus 4
5	fetus 5
9	other fetus

  ● **O64.0   Obstructed labor due to incomplete rotation of
         fetal head**
         Deep transverse arrest
         Obstructed labor due to persistent occipitoiliac
            (position)
         Obstructed labor due to persistent
            occipitoposterior (position)
         Obstructed labor due to persistent occipitosacral
            (position)
         Obstructed labor due to persistent
            occipitotransverse (position)

  ● **O64.1   Obstructed labor due to breech presentation**
         Obstructed labor due to buttocks presentation
         Obstructed labor due to complete breech
            presentation
         Obstructed labor due to frank breech presentation

  ● **O64.2   Obstructed labor due to face presentation**
         Obstructed labor due to chin presentation

  ● **O64.3   Obstructed labor due to brow presentation**

  ● **O64.4   Obstructed labor due to shoulder presentation**
         Prolapsed arm

         | Excludes1 | impacted shoulders (O66.0)
                       shoulder dystocia (O66.0)

  ● **O64.5   Obstructed labor due to compound presentation**

  ● **O64.8   Obstructed labor due to other malposition and
         malpresentation**
         Obstructed labor due to footling presentation
         Obstructed labor due to incomplete breech
            presentation

  ● ■ **O64.9   Obstructed labor due to malposition and
         malpresentation, unspecified**

● **O65   Obstructed labor due to maternal pelvic abnormality**

  O65.0   Obstructed labor due to deformed pelvis

  O65.1   Obstructed labor due to generally contracted pelvis

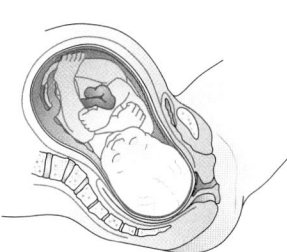

Figure 15-5 Hydrocephalic fetus causing disproportion.

● Unacceptable First-Listed Diagnosis   ● Use Additional Character(s)   ■ Unspecified   **OGCR** Official Guidelines for Coding and Reporting

📞 Complication\Comorbidity   📞 Major C\C | Excludes 1 | | Excludes 2 | Includes   Use additional   Code first   Code also   1283

CHAPTER 15 (O00-O99)

O65.2 Obstructed labor due to pelvic inlet contraction

O65.3 Obstructed labor due to pelvic outlet and mid-cavity contraction

■O65.4 Obstructed labor due to fetopelvic disproportion, unspecified

> Excludes1   dystocia due to abnormality of fetus (O66.2-O66.3)

O65.5 Obstructed labor due to abnormality of maternal pelvic organs

> Obstructed labor due to conditions listed in O34.-
>
> Use additional code to identify abnormality of pelvic organs O34.-

O65.8 Obstructed labor due to other maternal pelvic abnormalities

■O65.9 Obstructed labor due to maternal pelvic abnormality, unspecified

●O66 Other obstructed labor

O66.0 Obstructed labor due to shoulder dystocia
> Impacted shoulders

O66.1 Obstructed labor due to locked twins

O66.2 Obstructed labor due to unusually large fetus

O66.3 Obstructed labor due to other abnormalities of fetus
> Dystocia due to fetal ascites
> Dystocia due to fetal hydrops
> Dystocia due to fetal meningomyelocele
> Dystocia due to fetal sacral teratoma
> Dystocia due to fetal tumor
> Dystocia due to hydrocephalic fetus
>
> Use additional code to identify cause of obstruction

●O66.4 Failed trial of labor

■O66.40 Failed trial of labor, unspecified

O66.41 Failed attempted vaginal birth after previous cesarean delivery
> *Code first rupture of uterus, if applicable (O71.0-, O71.1)*

O66.5 Attempted application of vacuum extractor and forceps
> Attempted application of vacuum or forceps, with subsequent delivery by forceps or cesarean delivery

O66.6 Obstructed labor due to other multiple fetuses

O66.8 Other specified obstructed labor
> Use additional code to identify cause of obstruction

■O66.9 Obstructed labor, unspecified
> Dystocia NOS
> Fetal dystocia NOS
> Maternal dystocia NOS

●O67 Labor and delivery complicated by intrapartum hemorrhage, not elsewhere classified

> Excludes1   antepartum hemorrhage NEC (O46.-)
> placenta previa (O44.-)
> premature separation of placenta [abruptio placentae] (O45.-)

> Excludes2   postpartum hemorrhage (O72.-)

O67.0 Intrapartum hemorrhage with coagulation defect 🗘
> Intrapartum hemorrhage (excessive) associated with afibrinogenemia
> Intrapartum hemorrhage (excessive) associated with disseminated intravascular coagulation
> Intrapartum hemorrhage (excessive) associated with hyperfibrinolysis
> Intrapartum hemorrhage (excessive) associated with hypofibrinogenemia

O67.8 Other intrapartum hemorrhage
> Excessive intrapartum hemorrhage

■O67.9 Intrapartum hemorrhage, unspecified

O68 Labor and delivery complicated by abnormality of fetal acid-base balance 🗘

> Includes   fetal acidemia complicating labor and delivery
> fetal acidosis complicating labor and delivery
> fetal alkalosis complicating labor and delivery
> fetal metabolic acidemia complicating labor and delivery

> Excludes1   fetal stress NOS (O77.9)
> labor and delivery complicated by electrocardiographic evidence of fetal stress (O77.8)
> labor and delivery complicated by ultrasonic evidence of fetal stress (O77.8)

> Excludes2   abnormality in fetal heart rate or rhythm (O76)
> labor and delivery complicated by meconium in amniotic fluid (O77.0)

●O69 Labor and delivery complicated by umbilical cord complications

> One of the following 7th characters is to be assigned to each code under category O69. 7th character 0 is for single gestations and multiple gestations where the fetus is unspecified. 7th characters 1 through 9 are for cases of multiple gestations to identify the fetus for which the code applies. The appropriate code from category O30, Multiple gestation, must also be assigned when assigning a code from category O69 that has a 7th character of 1 through 9.

0	not applicable or unspecified
1	fetus 1
2	fetus 2
3	fetus 3
4	fetus 4
5	fetus 5
9	other fetus

●O69.0 Labor and delivery complicated by prolapse of cord

●O69.1 Labor and delivery complicated by cord around neck, with compression

> Excludes1   labor and delivery complicated by cord around neck, without compression (O69.81)

●O69.2 Labor and delivery complicated by other cord entanglement, with compression
> Labor and delivery complicated by compression of cord NOS
> Labor and delivery complicated by entanglement of cords of twins in monoamniotic sac
> Labor and delivery complicated by knot in cord

> Excludes1   labor and delivery complicated by other cord entanglement, without compression (O69.82)

●O69.3 Labor and delivery complicated by short cord

●O69.4 Labor and delivery complicated by vasa previa
> Labor and delivery complicated by hemorrhage from vasa previa

●O69.5 Labor and delivery complicated by vascular lesion of cord
> Labor and delivery complicated by cord bruising
> Labor and delivery complicated by cord hematoma
> Labor and delivery complicated by thrombosis of umbilical vessels

● Unacceptable First-Listed Diagnosis   ● Use Additional Character(s)   ■ Unspecified   **OGCR** Official Guidelines for Coding and Reporting
🗘 Complication\Comorbidity   🗘 Major C\C   Excludes 1   Excludes 2   Includes   Use additional   Code first   Code also

● O69.8   **Labor and delivery complicated by other cord complications**

    ● O69.81   **Labor and delivery complicated by cord around neck, without compression**

    ● O69.82   **Labor and delivery complicated by other cord entanglement, without compression**

    ● O69.89   **Labor and delivery complicated by other cord complications**

● ▢ O69.9   **Labor and delivery complicated by cord complication, unspecified**

● **O70   Perineal laceration during delivery**

    Includes   episiotomy extended by laceration

    Excludes1   obstetric high vaginal laceration alone (O71.4)

    O70.0   First degree perineal laceration during delivery
       Perineal laceration, rupture or tear involving fourchette during delivery
       Perineal laceration, rupture or tear involving labia during delivery
       Perineal laceration, rupture or tear involving skin during delivery
       Perineal laceration, rupture or tear involving vagina during delivery
       Perineal laceration, rupture or tear involving vulva during delivery
       Slight perineal laceration, rupture or tear during delivery

    O70.1   Second degree perineal laceration during delivery
       Perineal laceration, rupture or tear during delivery as in O70.0, also involving pelvic floor
       Perineal laceration, rupture or tear during delivery as in O70.0, also involving perineal muscles
       Perineal laceration, rupture or tear during delivery as in O70.0, also involving vaginal muscles

    Excludes1   perineal laceration involving anal sphincter (O70.2)

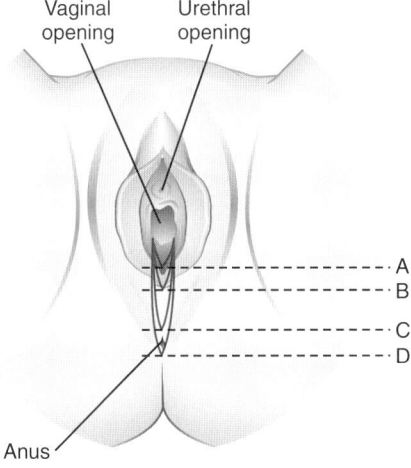

Figure 15-6   Perineal lacerations: **A.** First-degree is laceration of superficial tissues. **B.** Second-degree is limited to the pelvic floor and may involve the perineal or vaginal muscles. **C.** Third-degree involves the anal sphincter. **D.** Fourth-degree involves anal or rectal muscosa.

    O70.2   Third degree perineal laceration during delivery ◔
       Perineal laceration, rupture or tear during delivery as in O70.1, also involving anal sphincter
       Perineal laceration, rupture or tear during delivery as in O70.1, also involving rectovaginal septum
       Perineal laceration, rupture or tear during delivery as in O70.1, also involving sphincter NOS

       Excludes1   anal sphincter tear during delivery without third degree perineal laceration (O70.4)
          perineal laceration involving anal or rectal mucosa (O70.3)

    O70.3   Fourth degree perineal laceration during delivery ◔
       Perineal laceration, rupture or tear during delivery as in O70.2, also involving anal mucosa
       Perineal laceration, rupture or tear during delivery as in O70.2, also involving rectal mucosa

    O70.4   Anal sphincter tear complicating delivery, not associated with third degree laceration ◔

       Excludes1   anal sphincter tear with third degree perineal laceration (O70.2)

    ▢ **O70.9   Perineal laceration during delivery, unspecified**

● **O71   Other obstetric trauma**

    Includes   damage from instruments

    ● **O71.0   Rupture of uterus (spontaneous) before onset of labor**

       Excludes1   disruption of (current) cesarean delivery wound (O90.0)
          laceration of uterus, NEC (O71.81)

      ▢ **O71.00   Rupture of uterus before onset of labor, unspecified trimester**

      O71.02   Rupture of uterus before onset of labor, second trimester ◔

      O71.03   Rupture of uterus before onset of labor, third trimester ◔

    O71.1   Rupture of uterus during labor ◔
       Rupture of uterus not stated as occurring before onset of labor

       Excludes1   disruption of cesarean delivery wound (O90.0)
          laceration of uterus, NEC (O71.81)

    O71.2   Postpartum inversion of uterus

    O71.3   Obstetric laceration of cervix ◔
       Annular detachment of cervix

    O71.4   Obstetric high vaginal laceration alone ◔
       Laceration of vaginal wall without perineal laceration

       Excludes1   obstetric high vaginal laceration with perineal laceration (O70.-)

    O71.5   Other obstetric injury to pelvic organs ◔
       Obstetric injury to bladder
       Obstetric injury to urethra

    O71.6   Obstetric damage to pelvic joints and ligaments ◔
       Obstetric avulsion of inner symphyseal cartilage
       Obstetric damage to coccyx
       Obstetric traumatic separation of symphysis (pubis)

    O71.7   Obstetric hematoma of pelvis ◔
       Obstetric hematoma of perineum
       Obstetric hematoma of vagina
       Obstetric hematoma of vulva

    ● **O71.8   Other specified obstetric trauma**

      O71.81   Laceration of uterus, not elsewhere classified

      O71.89   Other specified obstetric trauma

    ▢ **O71.9   Obstetric trauma, unspecified**

● Unacceptable First-Listed Diagnosis   ● Use Additional Character(s)   ▢ Unspecified   **OGCR** Official Guidelines for Coding and Reporting

◔ Complication\Comorbidity   ◔ Major C\C   Excludes 1   Excludes 2   Includes   Use additional   Code first   Code also

CHAPTER 15 (O00-O99)

1285

● **O72   Postpartum hemorrhage**

    Includes   hemorrhage after delivery of fetus or infant

    O72.0   Third-stage hemorrhage 🕮
       Hemorrhage associated with retained, trapped or adherent placenta
       Retained placenta NOS

       Code also type of adherent placenta (O43.2-)

    O72.1   Other immediate postpartum hemorrhage 🕮
       Hemorrhage following delivery of placenta
       Postpartum hemorrhage (atonic) NOS
       Uterine atony with hemorrhage

       Excludes1   uterine atony NOS (O62.2)
                 uterine atony without hemorrhage (O62.2)
                 postpartum atony of uterus without hemorrhage (O75.89)

    O72.2   Delayed and secondary postpartum hemorrhage 🕮
       Hemorrhage associated with retained portions of placenta or membranes after the first 24 hours following delivery of placenta
       Retained products of conception NOS, following delivery

    O72.3   Postpartum coagulation defects
       Postpartum afibrinogenemia
       Postpartum fibrinolysis

● **O73   Retained placenta and membranes, without hemorrhage**

    Excludes1   placenta accreta (O43.21-)
                 placenta increta (O43.22-)
                 placenta percreta (O43.23-)

    O73.0   Retained placenta without hemorrhage
       Adherent placenta, without hemorrhage
       Trapped placenta without hemorrhage

    O73.1   Retained portions of placenta and membranes, without hemorrhage
       Retained products of conception following delivery, without hemorrhage

● **O74   Complications of anesthesia during labor and delivery**

    Includes   maternal complications arising from the administration of a general, regional or local anesthetic, analgesic or other sedation during labor and delivery

    Use additional code, if applicable, to identify specific complication

    O74.0   Aspiration pneumonitis due to anesthesia during labor and delivery
       Inhalation of stomach contents or secretions NOS due to anesthesia during labor and delivery
       Mendelson's syndrome due to anesthesia during labor and delivery

    O74.1   Other pulmonary complications of anesthesia during labor and delivery

    O74.2   Cardiac complications of anesthesia during labor and delivery

    O74.3   Central nervous system complications of anesthesia during labor and delivery

    O74.4   Toxic reaction to local anesthesia during labor and delivery

    O74.5   Spinal and epidural anesthesia-induced headache during labor and delivery

    O74.6   Other complications of spinal and epidural anesthesia during labor and delivery

    O74.7   Failed or difficult intubation for anesthesia during labor and delivery

    O74.8   Other complications of anesthesia during labor and delivery

◼ **O74.9   Complication of anesthesia during labor and delivery, unspecified**

● **O75   Other complications of labor and delivery, not elsewhere classified**

    Excludes2   puerperal (postpartum) infection (O86.-)
                 puerperal (postpartum) sepsis (O85)

    O75.0   Maternal distress during labor and delivery

    O75.1   Shock during or following labor and delivery 🕮
       Obstetric shock following labor and delivery

    O75.2   Pyrexia during labor, not elsewhere classified 🕮

    O75.3   Other infection during labor 🕮
       Sepsis during labor

       Use additional code (B95-B97), to identify infectious agent

    O75.4   Other complications of obstetric surgery and procedures
       Cardiac arrest following obstetric surgery or procedures
       Cardiac failure following obstetric surgery or procedures
       Cerebral anoxia following obstetric surgery or procedures
       Pulmonary edema following obstetric surgery or procedures

       Use additional code to identify specific complication

       Excludes2   complications of anesthesia during labor and delivery (O74.-)
                 disruption of obstetrical (surgical) wound (O90.0-O90.1)
                 hematoma of obstetrical (surgical) wound (O90.2)
                 infection of obstetrical (surgical) wound (O86.0)

    O75.5   Delayed delivery after artificial rupture of membranes

● **O75.8   Other specified complications of labor and delivery**

       O75.81   Maternal exhaustion complicating labor and delivery

       O75.89   Other specified complications of labor and delivery

◼ **O75.9   Complication of labor and delivery, unspecified**

O76   Abnormality in fetal heart rate and rhythm complicating labor and delivery

    Includes   depressed fetal heart rate tones complicating labor and delivery
                 fetal bradycardia complicating labor and delivery
                 fetal heart rate decelerations complicating labor and delivery
                 fetal heart rate irregularity complicating labor and delivery
                 fetal heart rate abnormal variability complicating labor and delivery
                 fetal tachycardia complicating labor and delivery
                 non-reassuring fetal heart rate or rhythm complicating labor and delivery

    Excludes1   fetal stress NOS (O77.9)
                 labor and delivery complicated by electrocardiographic evidence of fetal stress (O77.8)
                 labor and delivery complicated by ultrasonic evidence of fetal stress (O77.8)

    Excludes2   fetal metabolic acidemia (O68)
                 other fetal stress (O77.0-O77.1)

● Unacceptable First-Listed Diagnosis   ● Use Additional Character(s)   ◼ Unspecified   **OGCR** Official Guidelines for Coding and Reporting
🕮 Complication\Comorbidity   🕮 Major C\C   Excludes 1   Excludes 2   Includes   Use additional   Code first   Code also

● **O77**   **Other fetal stress complicating labor and delivery**

     O77.0   **Labor and delivery complicated by meconium in amniotic fluid**

     O77.1   **Fetal stress in labor or delivery due to drug administration**

     O77.8   **Labor and delivery complicated by other evidence of fetal stress**
         Labor and delivery complicated by electrocardiographic evidence of fetal stress
         Labor and delivery complicated by ultrasonic evidence of fetal stress

         | Excludes1 | abnormality of fetal acid-base balance (O68)
                 abnormality in fetal heart rate or rhythm (O76)
                 fetal metabolic acidemia (O68)

   ■ **O77.9**   **Labor and delivery complicated by fetal stress, unspecified**

         | Excludes1 | abnormality of fetal acid-base balance (O68)
                 abnormality in fetal heart rate or rhythm (O76)
                 fetal metabolic acidemia (O68)

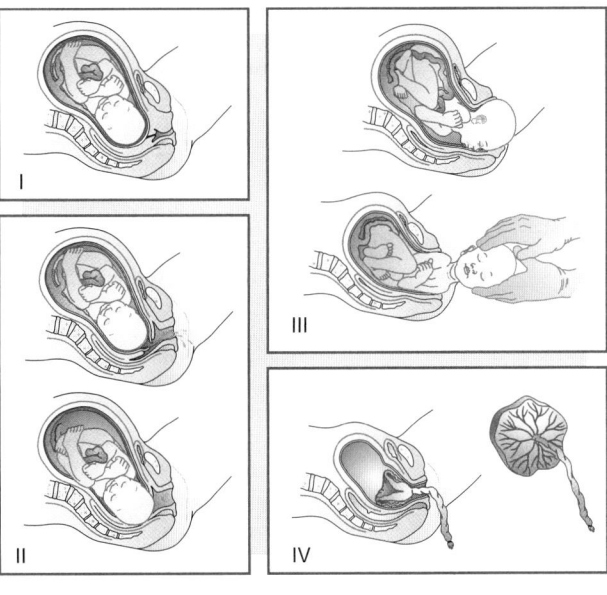

Figure 15-7   The four stages of normal delivery: **I.** Lightening, which occurs 2 to 4 weeks before birth, at which time the fetus turns with head toward the vagina. **II.** Regular contractions begin, the amniotic sac ruptures, and dilation is complete. **III.** Delivery of the head and rotation. **IV.** Expulsion of placenta.

OGCR   Section I.C., Chapter 15.m.
       Normal Delivery, Code O80

1) Encounter for full term uncomplicated delivery
Code O80 should be assigned when a woman is admitted for a full-term normal delivery and delivers a single, healthy infant without any complications antepartum, during the delivery, or postpartum during the delivery episode. Code O80 is always a principal diagnosis. It is not to be used if any other code from chapter 15 is needed to describe a current complication of the antenatal, delivery, or perinatal period. Additional codes from other chapters may be used with code O80 if they are not related to or are in any way complicating the pregnancy.

2) Uncomplicated delivery with resolved antepartum complication
Code O80 may be used if the patient had a complication at some point during the pregnancy, but the complication is not present at the time of the admission for delivery.

3) Outcome of delivery for O80
Z37.0, Single live brith, is the only outcome of delivery code ppropriate for use with O80.

ENCOUNTER FOR DELIVERY (O80, O82)

O80   **Encounter for full-term uncomplicated delivery**
         Delivery requiring minimal or no assistance, with or without episiotomy, without fetal manipulation [e.g., rotation version] or instrumentation [forceps] of a spontaneous, cephalic, vaginal, full-term, single, live-born infant. This code is for use as a single diagnosis code and is not to be used with any other code from chapter 15. This code must be accompanied by a delivery code from the appropriate procedure classification.

         Use additional code to indicate outcome of delivery (Z37.0)

O82   **Encounter for cesarean delivery without indication**
         This code must be accompanied by a delivery code from the appropriate procedure classification.

         Use additional code to indicate outcome of delivery (Z37.0)

COMPLICATIONS PREDOMINANTLY RELATED TO THE PUERPERIUM (O85-O92)

     | Excludes2 | mental and behavioral disorders associated with the puerperium (F53)
                 obstetrical tetanus (A34)
                 puerperal osteomalacia (M83.0)

O85   **Puerperal sepsis** 🔹

     | Includes | postpartum sepsis
               puerperal peritonitis
               puerperal pyemia

     Use additional code (B95-B97), to identify infectious agent

     | Excludes1 | fever of unknown origin following delivery (O86.4)
                 genital tract infection following delivery (O86.1-)
                 obstetric pyemic and septic embolism (O88.3-)
                 puerperal septic thrombophlebitis (O86.81)
                 urinary tract infection following delivery (O86.2-)

     | Excludes2 | sepsis during labor (O75.3)

● **O86**   **Other puerperal infections**

     Use additional code (B95-B97), to identify infectious agent

     | Excludes2 | infection during labor (O75.3)
                 obstetrical tetanus (A34)

     O86.0   **Infection of obstetric surgical wound**
         Infected cesarean delivery wound following delivery
         Infected perineal repair following delivery

● Unacceptable First-Listed Diagnosis   ● Use Additional Character(s)   ■ Unspecified   **OGCR** Official Guidelines for Coding and Reporting
🔹 Complication\Comorbidity   🔸 Major C\C | Excludes 1 | | Excludes 2 | | Includes | Use additional   Code first   Code also

1287

CHAPTER 15 (O00-O99)

- **O86.1 Other infection of genital tract following delivery** 🦠
  - **O86.11 Cervicitis following delivery**
  - **O86.12 Endometritis following delivery**
  - **O86.13 Vaginitis following delivery**
  - **O86.19 Other infection of genital tract following delivery**
- **O86.2 Urinary tract infection following delivery**
  - ▪**O86.20 Urinary tract infection following delivery, unspecified** 🦠
    - Puerperal urinary tract infection NOS
  - **O86.21 Infection of kidney following delivery** 🦠
  - **O86.22 Infection of bladder following delivery** 🦠
    - Infection of urethra following delivery
  - **O86.29 Other urinary tract infection following delivery** 🦠
  - **O86.4 Pyrexia of unknown origin following delivery** 🦠
    - Puerperal infection NOS following delivery
    - Puerperal pyrexia NOS following delivery
    - **Excludes2**   pyrexia during labor (O75.2)
- **O86.8 Other specified puerperal infections**
  - **O86.81 Puerperal septic thrombophlebitis** 🦠
  - **O86.89 Other specified puerperal infections** 🦠
- **O87 Venous complications in the puerperium**
  - **Includes**   those in labor, delivery and the puerperium
  - **Excludes2**   obstetric embolism (O88.-)
    - puerperal septic thrombophlebitis (O86.81)
    - venous complications in pregnancy (O22.-)
  - **O87.0 Superficial thrombophlebitis in the puerperium** 🦠
    - Puerperal phlebitis NOS
    - Puerperal thrombosis NOS
  - **O87.1 Deep phlebothrombosis in the puerperium** 🦠
    - Deep vein thrombosis, postpartum
    - Pelvic thrombophlebitis, postpartum
    - Use additional code to identify the deep vein thrombosis (I82.4-, I82.5-, I82.62-. I82.72-)
    - Use additional code, if applicable, for associated long-term (current) use of anticoagulants (Z79.01)
  - **O87.2 Hemorrhoids in the puerperium** 🦠
  - **O87.3 Cerebral venous thrombosis in the puerperium** 🦠
    - Cerebrovenous sinus thrombosis in the puerperium
  - **O87.4 Varicose veins of lower extremity in the puerperium**
  - **O87.8 Other venous complications in the puerperium** 🦠
    - Genital varices in the puerperium
  - ▪**O87.9 Venous complication in the puerperium, unspecified**
    - Puerperal phlebopathy NOS
- **O88 Obstetric embolism**
  - **Excludes1**   embolism complicating abortion NOS (O03.2)
    - embolism complicating ectopic or molar pregnancy (O08.2)
    - embolism complicating failed attempted abortion (O07.2, O07.7)
    - embolism complicating induced abortion (O04.2, O05.2)
    - embolism complicating spontaneous abortion (O03.2, O03.7)
- **O88.0 Obstetric air embolism**
  - **O88.01 Obstetric air embolism in pregnancy**
    - **O88.011 Air embolism in pregnancy, first trimester** 🦠
    - **O88.012 Air embolism in pregnancy, second trimester** 🦠
    - **O88.013 Air embolism in pregnancy, third trimester** 🦠
    - ▪**O88.019 Air embolism in pregnancy, unspecified trimester**

- **O88.02 Air embolism in childbirth** 🦠
- **O88.03 Air embolism in the puerperium** 🦠
- **O88.1 Amniotic fluid embolism**
  - Anaphylactoid syndrome in pregnancy
  - **O88.11 Amniotic fluid embolism in pregnancy**
    - **O88.111 Amniotic fluid embolism in pregnancy, first trimester** 🦠
    - **O88.112 Amniotic fluid embolism in pregnancy, second trimester** 🦠
    - **O88.113 Amniotic fluid embolism in pregnancy, third trimester** 🦠
    - ▪**O88.119 Amniotic fluid embolism in pregnancy, unspecified trimester**
  - **O88.12 Amniotic fluid embolism in childbirth** 🦠
  - **O88.13 Amniotic fluid embolism in the puerperium** 🦠
- **O88.2 Obstetric thromboembolism**
  - **O88.21 Thromboembolism in pregnancy**
    - Obstetric (pulmonary) embolism NOS
    - **O88.211 Thromboembolism in pregnancy, first trimester** 🦠
    - **O88.212 Thromboembolism in pregnancy, second trimester** 🦠
    - **O88.213 Thromboembolism in pregnancy, third trimester** 🦠
    - ▪**O88.219 Thromboembolism in pregnancy, unspecified trimester**
  - **O88.22 Thromboembolism in childbirth** 🦠
  - **O88.23 Thromboembolism in the puerperium** 🦠
    - Puerperal (pulmonary) embolism NOS
- **O88.3 Obstetric pyemic and septic embolism**
  - **O88.31 Pyemic and septic embolism in pregnancy**
    - **O88.311 Pyemic and septic embolism in pregnancy, first trimester** 🦠
    - **O88.312 Pyemic and septic embolism in pregnancy, second trimester** 🦠
    - **O88.313 Pyemic and septic embolism in pregnancy, third trimester** 🦠
    - ▪**O88.319 Pyemic and septic embolism in pregnancy, unspecified trimester** 🦠
  - **O88.32 Pyemic and septic embolism in childbirth** 🦠
  - **O88.33 Pyemic and septic embolism in the puerperium** 🦠
- **O88.8 Other obstetric embolism**
  - Obstetric fat embolism
  - **O88.81 Other embolism in pregnancy**
    - **O88.811 Other embolism in pregnancy, first trimester** 🦠
    - **O88.812 Other embolism in pregnancy, second trimester** 🦠
    - **O88.813 Other embolism in pregnancy, third trimester** 🦠
    - ▪**O88.819 Other embolism in pregnancy, unspecified trimester**
  - **O88.82 Other embolism in childbirth** 🦠
  - **O88.83 Other embolism in the puerperium** 🦠
- **O89 Complications of anesthesia during the puerperium**
  - **Includes**   maternal complications arising from the administration of a general, regional or local anesthetic, analgesic or other sedation during the puerperium
  - Use additional code, if applicable, to identify specific complication

● Unacceptable First-Listed Diagnosis   ● Use Additional Character(s)   ▪ Unspecified   **OGCR** Official Guidelines for Coding and Reporting

🦠 Complication\Comorbidity   🦠 Major C\C   Excludes 1   Excludes 2   Includes   Use additional   Code first   Code also

● **O89.0** **Pulmonary complications of anesthesia during the puerperium**

     O89.01 **Aspiration pneumonitis due to anesthesia during the puerperium**
         Inhalation of stomach contents or secretions NOS due to anesthesia during the puerperium
         Mendelson's syndrome due to anesthesia during the puerperium

     O89.09 **Other pulmonary complications of anesthesia during the puerperium**

     O89.1 **Cardiac complications of anesthesia during the puerperium**

     O89.2 **Central nervous system complications of anesthesia during the puerperium**

     O89.3 **Toxic reaction to local anesthesia during the puerperium**

     O89.4 **Spinal and epidural anesthesia-induced headache during the puerperium**

     O89.5 **Other complications of spinal and epidural anesthesia during the puerperium**

     O89.6 **Failed or difficult intubation for anesthesia during the puerperium**

     O89.8 **Other complications of anesthesia during the puerperium**

     ▣ **O89.9** **Complication of anesthesia during the puerperium, unspecified**

● **O90** **Complications of the puerperium, not elsewhere classified**

     O90.0 **Disruption of cesarean delivery wound**
         Dehiscence of cesarean delivery wound
         | **Excludes1** | rupture of uterus (spontaneous) before onset of labor (O71.0-)
         rupture of uterus during labor (O71.1)

     O90.1 **Disruption of perineal obstetric wound**
         Disruption of wound of episiotomy
         Disruption of wound of perineal laceration
         Secondary perineal tear

     O90.2 **Hematoma of obstetric wound**

     O90.3 **Peripartum cardiomyopathy** 🗞
         Conditions in I42.- arising during pregnancy and the puerperium
         | **Excludes1** | pre-existing heart disease complicating pregnancy and the puerperium (O99.4-)

     O90.4 **Postpartum acute kidney failure** 🗞
         Hepatorenal syndrome following labor and delivery

     O90.5 **Postpartum thyroiditis**

     O90.6 **Postpartum mood disturbance**
         Postpartum blues   Postpartum sadness
         Postpartum dysphoria
         | **Excludes1** | postpartum depression (F53) puerperal psychosis (F53)

● **O90.8** **Other complications of the puerperium, not elsewhere classified**

     O90.81 **Anemia of the puerperium**
         Postpartum anemia NOS
         | **Excludes1** | pre-existing anemia complicating the puerperium (O99.03)

     ▣ **O90.89** **Other complications of the puerperium, not elsewhere classified**
         Placental polyp

     O90.9 **Complication of the puerperium, unspecified**

● **O91** **Infections of breast associated with pregnancy, the puerperium and lactation**
     Use additional code to identify infection

● **O91.0** **Infection of nipple associated with pregnancy, the puerperium and lactation**

     ● **O91.01** **Infection of nipple associated with pregnancy**
         Gestational abscess of nipple

         O91.011 **Infection of nipple associated with pregnancy, first trimester**

         O91.012 **Infection of nipple associated with pregnancy, second trimester**

         O91.013 **Infection of nipple associated with pregnancy, third trimester**

         ▣ **O91.019** **Infection of nipple associated with pregnancy, unspecified trimester**

     O91.02 **Infection of nipple associated with the puerperium**
         Puerperal abscess of nipple

     O91.03 **Infection of nipple associated with lactation**
         Abscess of nipple associated with lactation

● **O91.1** **Abscess of breast associated with pregnancy, the puerperium and lactation**

     ● **O91.11** **Abscess of breast associated with pregnancy**
         Gestational mammary abscess
         Gestational purulent mastitis
         Gestational subareolar abscess

         O91.111 **Abscess of breast associated with pregnancy, first trimester** 🗞

         O91.112 **Abscess of breast associated with pregnancy, second trimester** 🗞

         O91.113 **Abscess of breast associated with pregnancy, third trimester** 🗞

         ▣ **O91.119** **Abscess of breast associated with pregnancy, unspecified trimester**

     O91.12 **Abscess of breast associated with the puerperium** 🗞
         Puerperal mammary abscess
         Puerperal purulent mastitis
         Puerperal subareolar abscess

     O91.13 **Abscess of breast associated with lactation**
         Mammary abscess associated with lactation
         Purulent mastitis associated with lactation
         Subareolar abscess associated with lactation

● **O91.2** **Nonpurulent mastitis associated with pregnancy, the puerperium and lactation**

     ● **O91.21** **Nonpurulent mastitis associated with pregnancy**
         Gestational interstitial mastitis
         Gestational lymphangitis of breast
         Gestational mastitis NOS
         Gestational parenchymatous mastitis

         O91.211 **Nonpurulent mastitis associated with pregnancy, first trimester**

         O91.212 **Nonpurulent mastitis associated with pregnancy, second trimester**

         O91.213 **Nonpurulent mastitis associated with pregnancy, third trimester**

● Unacceptable First-Listed Diagnosis   ● Use Additional Character(s)   ▣ Unspecified   **OGCR** Official Guidelines for Coding and Reporting
🗞 Complication\Comorbidity   🗞 Major C\C | Excludes 1 | | Excludes 2 | Includes   Use additional   Code first   Code also

■ O91.219   **Nonpurulent mastitis associated with pregnancy, unspecified trimester**

O91.22   **Nonpurulent mastitis associated with the puerperium**
Puerperal interstitial mastitis
Puerperal lymphangitis of breast
Puerperal mastitis NOS
Puerperal parenchymatous mastitis

O91.23   **Nonpurulent mastitis associated with lactation**
Interstitial mastitis associated with lactation
Lymphangitis of breast associated with lactation
Mastitis NOS associated with lactation
Parenchymatous mastitis associated with lactation

● O92   **Other disorders of breast and disorders of lactation associated with pregnancy and the puerperium**

  ● O92.0   **Retracted nipple associated with pregnancy, the puerperium, and lactation**

    ● O92.01   **Retracted nipple associated with pregnancy**

O92.011   **Retracted nipple associated with pregnancy, first trimester**

O92.012   **Retracted nipple associated with pregnancy, second trimester**

O92.013   **Retracted nipple associated with pregnancy, third trimester**

■ O92.019   **Retracted nipple associated with pregnancy, unspecified trimester**

O92.02   **Retracted nipple associated with the puerperium**

O92.03   **Retracted nipple associated with lactation**

  ● O92.1   **Cracked nipple associated with pregnancy, the puerperium, and lactation**
Fissure of nipple, gestational or puerperal

    ● O92.11   **Cracked nipple associated with pregnancy**

O92.111   **Cracked nipple associated with pregnancy, first trimester**

O92.112   **Cracked nipple associated with pregnancy, second trimester**

O92.113   **Cracked nipple associated with pregnancy, third trimester**

■ O92.119   **Cracked nipple associated with pregnancy, unspecified trimester**

O92.12   **Cracked nipple associated with the puerperium**

O92.13   **Cracked nipple associated with lactation**

  ● O92.2   **Other and unspecified disorders of breast associated with pregnancy and the puerperium**

■ O92.20   **Unspecified disorder of breast associated with pregnancy and the puerperium**

O92.29   **Other disorders of breast associated with pregnancy and the puerperium**

O92.3   **Agalactia**
Primary agalactia
> **Excludes1**   elective agalactia (O92.5)
> secondary agalactia (O92.5)
> therapeutic agalactia (O92.5)

O92.4   **Hypogalactia**

O92.5   **Suppressed lactation**
Elective agalactia   Therapeutic agalactia
Secondary agalactia
> **Excludes1**   primary agalactia (O92.3)

O92.6   **Galactorrhea**

● O92.7   **Other and unspecified disorders of lactation**

■ O92.70   **Unspecified disorders of lactation**

O92.79   **Other disorders of lactation**
Puerperal galactocele

OGCR   Section I.C.2.1.3.
Malignant neoplasm in a pregnant patient

Codes from chapter 15, Pregnancy, childbirth, and the puerperium, are always sequenced first on a medical record. A code from subcategory O94.1-, Malignant neoplasm complicating pregnancy, childbirth, and the puerperium, should be used first, followed by the appropriate code from Chapter 2 to indicate the type of neoplasm.

OTHER OBSTETRIC CONDITIONS, NOT ELSEWHERE CLASSIFIED (O94-O9A)

● O94   **Sequelae of complication of pregnancy, childbirth, and the puerperium**

> **Note:** This category is to be used to indicate conditions in O00-O77.-, O85-O94 and O98-O99.- as the cause of late effects. The "sequelae" include conditions specified as such, or as late effects, which may occur at any time after the puerperium.

> *Code first condition resulting from (sequela) of complication of pregnancy, childbirth, and the puerperium*

O98   **Maternal infectious and parasitic diseases classifiable elsewhere but complicating pregnancy, childbirth and the puerperium**

> **Includes**   the listed conditions when complicating the pregnant state, when aggravated by the pregnancy, or as a reason for obstetric care

> Use additional code (Chapter 1), to identify specific infectious or parasitic disease

> **Excludes2**   herpes gestationis (O26.4-)
> infectious carrier state (O99.82-, O99.83-)
> obstetrical tetanus (A34)
> puerperal infection (O86.-)
> puerperal sepsis (O85)
> when the reason for maternal care is that the disease is known or suspected to have affected the fetus (O35-O36)

  ● O98.0   **Tuberculosis complicating pregnancy, childbirth and the puerperium**
Conditions in A15-A19

    ● O98.01   **Tuberculosis complicating pregnancy**

O98.011   **Tuberculosis complicating pregnancy, first trimester** 🔖

O98.012   **Tuberculosis complicating pregnancy, second trimester** 🔖

O98.013   **Tuberculosis complicating pregnancy, third trimester** 🔖

■ O98.019   **Tuberculosis complicating pregnancy, unspecified trimester**

O98.02   **Tuberculosis complicating childbirth** 🔖

O98.03   **Tuberculosis complicating the puerperium** 🔖

  ● O98.1   **Syphilis complicating pregnancy, childbirth and the puerperium**
Conditions in A50-A53

    ● O98.11   **Syphilis complicating pregnancy**

O98.111   **Syphilis complicating pregnancy, first trimester** 🔖

O98.112   **Syphilis complicating pregnancy, second trimester** 🔖

● Unacceptable First-Listed Diagnosis   ● Use Additional Character(s)   ■ Unspecified   **OGCR** Official Guidelines for Coding and Reporting
🔖 Complication\Comorbidity   🔖 Major C\C   Excludes 1   Excludes 2   Includes   Use additional   Code first   Code also

●   O98.113   Syphilis complicating pregnancy, third trimester 🎗

        ■ O98.119   Syphilis complicating pregnancy, unspecified trimester

    O98.12   Syphilis complicating childbirth 🎗

    O98.13   Syphilis complicating the puerperium 🎗

● O98.2   Gonorrhea complicating pregnancy, childbirth and the puerperium
      Conditions in A54.-

   ● O98.21   Gonorrhea complicating pregnancy

       O98.211   Gonorrhea complicating pregnancy, first trimester 🎗

       O98.212   Gonorrhea complicating pregnancy, second trimester 🎗

       O98.213   Gonorrhea complicating pregnancy, third trimester 🎗

      ■ O98.219   Gonorrhea complicating pregnancy, unspecified trimester

    O98.22   Gonorrhea complicating childbirth 🎗

    O98.23   Gonorrhea complicating the puerperium 🎗

● O98.3   Other infections with a predominantly sexual mode of transmission complicating pregnancy, childbirth and the puerperium
      Conditions in A55-A64

   ● O98.31   Other infections with a predominantly sexual mode of transmission complicating pregnancy

       O98.311   Other infections with a predominantly sexual mode of transmission complicating pregnancy, first trimester 🎗

       O98.312   Other infections with a predominantly sexual mode of transmission complicating pregnancy, second trimester 🎗

       O98.313   Other infections with a predominantly sexual mode of transmission complicating pregnancy, third trimester 🎗

      ■ O98.319   Other infections with a predominantly sexual mode of transmission complicating pregnancy, unspecified trimester

    O98.32   Other infections with a predominantly sexual mode of transmission complicating childbirth 🎗

    O98.33   Other infections with a predominantly sexual mode of transmission complicating the puerperium 🎗

● O98.4   Viral hepatitis complicating pregnancy, childbirth and the puerperium
      Conditions in B15-B19

   ● O98.41   Viral hepatitis complicating pregnancy

       O98.411   Viral hepatitis complicating pregnancy, first trimester 🎗

       O98.412   Viral hepatitis complicating pregnancy, second trimester 🎗

       O98.413   Viral hepatitis complicating pregnancy, third trimester 🎗

      ■ O98.419   Viral hepatitis complicating pregnancy, unspecified trimester

    O98.42   Viral hepatitis complicating childbirth 🎗

    O98.43   Viral hepatitis complicating the puerperium 🎗

● O98.5   Other viral diseases complicating pregnancy, childbirth and the puerperium
      Conditions in A80-B09, B25-B34, R87.81-, R87.82-

      | **Excludes:1** | human immunodeficiency [HIV] disease complicating pregnancy, childbirth and the puerperium (O98.7-) |

   ● O98.51   Other viral diseases complicating pregnancy

       O98.511   Other viral diseases complicating pregnancy, first trimester 🎗

       O98.512   Other viral diseases complicating pregnancy, second trimester 🎗

       O98.513   Other viral diseases complicating pregnancy, third trimester 🎗

      ■ O98.519   Other viral diseases complicating pregnancy, unspecified trimester

    O98.52   Other viral diseases complicating childbirth 🎗

    O98.53   Other viral diseases complicating the puerperium 🎗

● O98.6   Protozoal diseases complicating pregnancy, childbirth and the puerperium
      Conditions in B50-B64

   ● O98.61   Protozoal diseases complicating pregnancy

       O98.611   Protozoal diseases complicating pregnancy, first trimester 🎗

       O98.612   Protozoal diseases complicating pregnancy, second trimester 🎗

       O98.613   Protozoal diseases complicating pregnancy, third trimester 🎗

      ■ O98.619   Protozoal diseases complicating pregnancy, unspecified trimester

    O98.62   Protozoal diseases complicating childbirth 🎗

    O98.63   Protozoal diseases complicating the puerperium 🎗

● O98.7   Human immunodeficiency [HIV] disease complicating pregnancy, childbirth and the puerperium

      Use additional code to identify the type of HIV disease:
        Acquired immune deficiency syndrome (AIDS) (B20)
        Asymptomatic HIV status (Z21)
        HIV positive NOS (Z21)
        Symptomatic HIV disease (B20)

OGCR   Section I.C.15.f.

HIV Infection in Pregnancy, Childbirth and the Puerperium

During pregnancy, childbirth or the puerperium, a patient admitted because of an HIV-related illness should receive a principal diagnosis from subcategory O98.7-. Human immunodeficiency [HIV] disease complicating pregnancy, childbirth and the puerperium, followed by the code(s) for the HIV-related illness(es).

Patients with asymptomatic HIV infection status admitted during pregnancy, childbirth, or the puerperium should receive codes of O98.7- and Z21, Asymptomatic human immunodeficiency virus [HIV] infection status.

   ● O98.71   Human immunodeficiency [HIV] disease complicating pregnancy

       O98.711   Human immunodeficiency [HIV] disease complicating pregnancy, first trimester 🎗

       O98.712   Human immunodeficiency [HIV] disease complicating pregnancy, second trimester 🎗

●   Unacceptable First-Listed Diagnosis   ●   Use Additional Character(s)   ■ Unspecified   **OGCR**   Official Guidelines for Coding and Reporting

🎗 Complication\Comorbidity   🎗 Major C\C   Excludes 1   Excludes 2   Includes   Use additional   Code first   Code also

1291

O98.713   Human immunodeficiency [HIV] disease complicating pregnancy, third trimester 🦠

⬜ O98.719   Human immunodeficiency [HIV] disease complicating pregnancy, unspecified trimester

O98.72   Human immunodeficiency [HIV] disease complicating childbirth 🦠

O98.73   Human immunodeficiency [HIV] disease complicating the puerperium 🦠

● O98.8   Other maternal infectious and parasitic diseases complicating pregnancy, childbirth and the puerperium

  ● O98.81   Other maternal infectious and parasitic diseases complicating pregnancy

     O98.811   Other maternal infectious and parasitic diseases complicating pregnancy, first trimester 🦠

     O98.812   Other maternal infectious and parasitic diseases complicating pregnancy, second trimester 🦠

     O98.813   Other maternal infectious and parasitic diseases complicating pregnancy, third trimester 🦠

    ⬜ O98.819   Other maternal infectious and parasitic diseases complicating pregnancy, unspecified trimester

   O98.82   Other maternal infectious and parasitic diseases complicating childbirth 🦠

   O98.83   Other maternal infectious and parasitic diseases complicating the puerperium 🦠

● O98.9   Unspecified maternal infectious and parasitic disease complicating pregnancy, childbirth and the puerperium

  ● O98.91   Unspecified maternal infectious and parasitic disease complicating pregnancy

    ⬜ O98.911   Unspecified maternal infectious and parasitic disease complicating pregnancy, first trimester 🦠

    ⬜ O98.912   Unspecified maternal infectious and parasitic disease complicating pregnancy, second trimester 🦠

    ⬜ O98.913   Unspecified maternal infectious and parasitic disease complicating pregnancy, third trimester 🦠

    ⬜ O98.919   Unspecified maternal infectious and parasitic disease complicating pregnancy, unspecified trimester

  ⬜ O98.92   Unspecified maternal infectious and parasitic disease complicating childbirth 🦠

  ⬜ O98.93   Unspecified maternal infectious and parasitic disease complicating the puerperium 🦠

● O99   Other maternal diseases classifiable elsewhere but complicating pregnancy, childbirth and the puerperium

   Note: This category includes conditions which complicate the pregnant state, are aggravated by the pregnancy or are a main reason for obstetric care.

   Use additional code to identify specific condition

   Excludes2   when the reason for maternal care is that the condition is known or suspected to have affected the fetus (O35-O36)

● O99.0   Anemia complicating pregnancy, childbirth and the puerperium
     Conditions in D50-D64

   Excludes1   anemia arising in the puerperium (O90.81)
          postpartum anemia NOS (O90.81)

  ● O99.01   Anemia complicating pregnancy

     O99.011   Anemia complicating pregnancy, first trimester

     O99.012   Anemia complicating pregnancy, second trimester

     O99.013   Anemia complicating pregnancy, third trimester

    ⬜ O99.019   Anemia complicating pregnancy, unspecified trimester

   O99.02   Anemia complicating childbirth

   O99.03   Anemia complicating the puerperium

   Excludes1   postpartum anemia not pre-existing prior to delivery (O90-.81)

● O99.1   Other diseases of the blood and blood-forming organs and certain disorders involving the immune mechanism complicating pregnancy, childbirth and the puerperium
     Conditions in D65-D89

   Excludes2   hemorrhage with coagulation defects (O45.-, O46.0-, O67.0, O72.3)

  ● O99.11   Other diseases of the blood and blood-forming organs and certain disorders involving the immune mechanism complicating pregnancy

     O99.111   Other diseases of the blood and blood-forming organs and certain disorders involving the immune mechanism complicating pregnancy, first trimester 🦠

     O99.112   Other diseases of the blood and blood-forming organs and certain disorders involving the immune mechanism complicating pregnancy, second trimester 🦠

     O99.113   Other diseases of the blood and blood-forming organs and certain disorders involving the immune mechanism complicating pregnancy, third trimester 🦠

    ⬜ O99.119   Other diseases of the blood and blood-forming organs and certain disorders involving the immune mechanism complicating pregnancy, unspecified trimester 🦠

   O99.12   Other diseases of the blood and blood-forming organs and certain disorders involving the immune mechanism complicating childbirth 🦠

   O99.13   Other diseases of the blood and blood-forming organs and certain disorders involving the immune mechanism complicating the puerperium 🦠

● O99.2   Endocrine, nutritional and metabolic diseases complicating pregnancy, childbirth and the puerperium
     Conditions in E00-E90

   Excludes2   diabetes mellitus (O24.-)
          malnutrition (O25.-)
          postpartum thyroiditis (O90.5)

● Unacceptable First-Listed Diagnosis   ● Use Additional Character(s)   ⬜ Unspecified   **OGCR** Official Guidelines for Coding and Reporting
🦠 Complication\Comorbidity   🦠 Major C\C   Excludes 1   Excludes 2   Includes   Use additional   Code first   Code also

1292

● O99.21 **Obesity complicating pregnancy, childbirth, and the puerperium**

Use additional code to identify the type of obesity (E66.-)

■ O99.210 Obesity complicating pregnancy, unspecified trimester

O99.211 Obesity complicating pregnancy, first trimester

O99.212 Obesity complicating pregnancy, second trimester

O99.213 Obesity complicating pregnancy, third trimester

O99.214 Obesity complicating childbirth

O99.215 Obesity complicating the puerperium

● O99.28 **Other endocrine, nutritional and metabolic diseases complicating pregnancy, childbirth and the puerperium**

■ O99.280 Endocrine, nutritional and metabolic diseases complicating pregnancy, unspecified trimester

O99.281 Endocrine, nutritional and metabolic diseases complicating pregnancy, first trimester

O99.282 Endocrine, nutritional and metabolic diseases complicating pregnancy, second trimester

O99.283 Endocrine, nutritional and metabolic diseases complicating pregnancy, third trimester

O99.284 Endocrine, nutritional and metabolic diseases complicating childbirth

O99.285 Endocrine, nutritional and metabolic diseases complicating the puerperium

● O99.3 **Mental disorders and diseases of the nervous system complicating pregnancy, childbirth and the puerperium**

● O99.31 **Alcohol use complicating pregnancy, childbirth, and the puerperium**

Use additional code(s) from F10 to identify manifestations of the alcohol use

■ O99.310 Alcohol use complicating pregnancy, unspecified trimester

O99.311 Alcohol use complicating pregnancy, first trimester

O99.312 Alcohol use complicating pregnancy, second trimester

O99.313 Alcohol use complicating pregnancy, third trimester

O99.314 Alcohol use complicating childbirth

O99.315 Alcohol use complicating the puerperium

● O99.32 **Drug use complicating pregnancy, childbirth, and the puerperium**

Use additional code(s) from F11-F16 and F18-F19 to identify manifestations of the drug use

■ O99.320 Drug use complicating pregnancy, unspecified trimester

O99.321 Drug use complicating pregnancy, first trimester 🦠

O99.322 Drug use complicating pregnancy, second trimester 🦠

O99.323 Drug use complicating pregnancy, third trimester 🦠

O99.324 Drug use complicating childbirth 🦠

O99.325 Drug use complicating the puerperium 🦠

● O99.33 **Smoking (tobacco) complicating pregnancy, childbirth, and the puerperium**

Use additional code from F17 to identify type of tobacco

■ O99.330 Smoking (tobacco) complicating pregnancy, unspecified trimester

O99.331 Smoking (tobacco) complicating pregnancy, first trimester

O99.332 Smoking (tobacco) complicating pregnancy, second trimester

O99.333 Smoking (tobacco) complicating pregnancy, third trimester

O99.334 Smoking (tobacco) complicating childbirth

O99.335 Smoking (tobacco) complicating the puerperium

● O99.34 **Other mental disorders complicating pregnancy, childbirth, and the puerperium**

Conditions in F00-F09 and F20-F99

Excludes2　postpartum mood disturbance (O90.6)
postnatal psychosis (F53)
puerperal psychosis (F53)

■ O99.340 Other mental disorders complicating pregnancy, unspecified trimester

O99.341 Other mental disorders complicating pregnancy, first trimester

O99.342 Other mental disorders complicating pregnancy, second trimester

O99.343 Other mental disorders complicating pregnancy, third trimester

O99.344 Other mental disorders complicating childbirth

O99.345 Other mental disorders complicating the puerperium

● O99.35 **Diseases of the nervous system complicating pregnancy, childbirth, and the puerperium**

Conditions in G00-G99

Excludes2　pregnancy related peripheral neuritis (O26.8-)

■ O99.350 Diseases of the nervous system complicating pregnancy, unspecified trimester

O99.351 Diseases of the nervous system complicating pregnancy, first trimester

O99.352 Diseases of the nervous system complicating pregnancy, second trimester

O99.353 Diseases of the nervous system complicating pregnancy, third trimester

O99.354 Diseases of the nervous system complicating childbirth 🦠

O99.355 Diseases of the nervous system complicating the puerperium 🦠

● Unacceptable First-Listed Diagnosis　　　● Use Additional Character(s)　　　■ Unspecified　　　**OGCR** Official Guidelines for Coding and Reporting

🦠 Complication\Comorbidity　　🦠 Major C\C　　Excludes 1　　Excludes 2　　Includes　　Use additional　　Code first　　Code also

1293

CHAPTER 15 (O00-O99)

● **O99.4 Diseases of the circulatory system complicating pregnancy, childbirth and the puerperium**
Conditions in I00-I99

> **Excludes1**   peripartum cardiomyopathy (O90.3)

> **Excludes2**   hypertensive disorders (O10-O16)
> obstetric embolism (O88.-)
> venous complications and cerebrovenous sinus thrombosis in:
> labor, childbirth and the puerperium (O87.-)
> pregnancy (O22.-)

  ● **O99.41 Diseases of the circulatory system complicating pregnancy**

     O99.411 Diseases of the circulatory system complicating pregnancy, first trimester 🅒

     O99.412 Diseases of the circulatory system complicating pregnancy, second trimester 🅒

     O99.413 Diseases of the circulatory system complicating pregnancy, third trimester 🅒

     ▪ **O99.419 Diseases of the circulatory system complicating pregnancy, unspecified trimester**

    O99.42 Diseases of the circulatory system complicating childbirth 🅒

    O99.43 Diseases of the circulatory system complicating the puerperium 🅒

● **O99.5 Diseases of the respiratory system complicating pregnancy, childbirth and the puerperium**
Conditions in J00-J99

  ● **O99.51 Diseases of the respiratory system complicating pregnancy**

     O99.511 Diseases of the respiratory system complicating pregnancy, first trimester

     O99.512 Diseases of the respiratory system complicating pregnancy, second trimester

     O99.513 Diseases of the respiratory system complicating pregnancy, third trimester

     ▪ **O99.519 Diseases of the respiratory system complicating pregnancy, unspecified trimester**

    O99.52 Diseases of the respiratory system complicating childbirth

    O99.53 Diseases of the respiratory system complicating the puerperium

● **O99.6 Diseases of the digestive system complicating pregnancy, childbirth and the puerperium**
Conditions in K00-K93

> **Excludes2**   liver disorders in pregnancy, childbirth and the puerperium (O26.6)

  ● **O99.61 Diseases of the digestive system complicating pregnancy**

     O99.611 Diseases of the digestive system complicating pregnancy, first trimester

     O99.612 Diseases of the digestive system complicating pregnancy, second trimester

     O99.613 Diseases of the digestive system complicating pregnancy, third trimester

     ▪ **O99.619 Diseases of the digestive system complicating pregnancy, unspecified trimester**

    O99.62 Diseases of the digestive system complicating childbirth

    O99.63 Diseases of the digestive system complicating the puerperium

● **O99.7 Diseases of the skin and subcutaneous tissue complicating pregnancy, childbirth and the puerperium**
Conditions in L00-L99

> **Excludes2**   herpes gestationis (O26.4)
> pruritic urticarial papules and plaques of pregnancy (PUPPP) (O26.86)

  ● **O99.71 Diseases of the skin and subcutaneous tissue complicating pregnancy**

     O99.711 Diseases of the skin and subcutaneous tissue complicating pregnancy, first trimester

     O99.712 Diseases of the skin and subcutaneous tissue complicating pregnancy, second trimester

     O99.713 Diseases of the skin and subcutaneous tissue complicating pregnancy, third trimester

     ▪ **O99.719 Diseases of the skin and subcutaneous tissue complicating pregnancy, unspecified trimester**

    O99.72 Diseases of the skin and subcutaneous tissue complicating childbirth

    O99.73 Diseases of the skin and subcutaneous tissue complicating the puerperium

● **O99.8 Other specified diseases and conditions complicating pregnancy, childbirth and the puerperium**
Conditions in D00-D48, H00-H95, M00-N99, and Q00-Q99

> Use additional code to identify condition

> **Excludes2**   genitourinary infections in pregnancy (O23.-)
> infection of genitourinary tract following delivery (O86.1-O86.3)
> malignant neoplasms in pregnancy (O94.1-)
> maternal care for known or suspected abnormality of maternal pelvic organs (O34.-)
> postpartum acute kidney failure (O90.4)
> traumatic injuries in pregnancy (O94.2-)

  ● **O99.81 Abnormal glucose complicating pregnancy, childbirth and the puerperium**

> **Excludes1**   gestational diabetes (O24.4-)

     O99.810 Abnormal glucose complicating pregnancy

     O99.814 Abnormal glucose complicating childbirth

     O99.815 Abnormal glucose complicating the puerperium

● Unacceptable First-Listed Diagnosis   ● Use Additional Character(s)   ▪ Unspecified   **OGCR** Official Guidelines for Coding and Reporting
🅒 Complication\Comorbidity   🅒 Major C\C   Excludes 1   Excludes 2    Includes   Use additional   Code first   Code also

● O99.82   **Streptococcus B carrier state complicating pregnancy, childbirth and the puerperium**

    O99.820   **Streptococcus B carrier state complicating pregnancy**

    O99.824   **Streptococcus B carrier state complicating childbirth**

    O99.825   **Streptococcus B carrier state complicating the puerperium** 🦠

● O99.83   **Other infection carrier state complicating pregnancy, childbirth and the puerperium**

    Use additional code to identify the carrier state (Z22.-)

    O99.830   **Other infection carrier state complicating pregnancy** 🦠

    O99.834   **Other infection carrier state complicating childbirth** 🦠

    O99.835   **Other infection carrier state complicating the puerperium** 🦠

● O99.84   **Bariatric surgery status complicating pregnancy, childbirth and the puerperium**

    Gastric banding status complicating pregnancy, childbirth and the puerperium

    Gastric bypass status for obesity complicating pregnancy, childbirth and the puerperium

    Obesity surgery status complicating pregnancy, childbirth and the puerperium

    ▨ O99.840   **Bariatric surgery status complicating pregnancy, unspecified trimester**

    O99.841   **Bariatric surgery status complicating pregnancy, first trimester**

    O99.842   **Bariatric surgery status complicating pregnancy, second trimester**

    O99.843   **Bariatric surgery status complicating pregnancy, third trimester**

    O99.844   **Bariatric surgery status complicating childbirth**

    O99.845   **Bariatric surgery status complicating the puerperium**

    O99.89   **Other specified diseases and conditions complicating pregnancy, childbirth and the puerperium**

● **O9A**   **Maternal malignant neoplasms, traumatic injuries and abuse classifiable elsewhere but complicating pregnancy, childbirth and the puerperium**

 ● **O9A.1**   **Malignant neoplasm complicating pregnancy, childbirth and the puerperium**

    Conditions in C00-C97

    Use additional code to identify neoplasm

    Excludes2   maternal care for benign tumor of corpus uteri (O34.1-)
                maternal care for benign tumor of cervix (O34.4-)

  ● **O9A.11**   **Malignant neoplasm complicating pregnancy**

    O9A.111   **Malignant neoplasm complicating pregnancy, first trimester**

    O9A.112   **Malignant neoplasm complicating pregnancy, second trimester**

    O9A.113   **Malignant neoplasm complicating pregnancy, third trimester**

    ▨ O9A.119   **Malignant neoplasm complicating pregnancy, unspecified trimester**

    O9A.12   **Malignant neoplasm complicating childbirth**

    O9A.13   **Malignant neoplasm complicating the puerperium**

 ● **O9A.2**   **Injury, poisoning and certain other consequences of external causes complicating pregnancy, childbirth and the puerperium**

    Conditions in S00-T98, except T74 and T76

    Use additional code(s) to identify the injury or poisoning

    Excludes2   physical, sexual and psychological abuse complicating pregnancy, childbirth and the puerperium (O94.3, O94.4, O94.5)

  ● **O9A.21**   **Injury, poisoning and certain other consequences of external causes complicating pregnancy**

    O9A.211   **Injury, poisoning and certain other consequences of external causes complicating pregnancy, first trimester**

    O9A.212   **Injury, poisoning and certain other consequences of external causes complicating pregnancy, second trimester**

    O9A.213   **Injury, poisoning and certain other consequences of external causes complicating pregnancy, third trimester**

    ▨ O9A.219   **Injury, poisoning and certain other consequences of external causes complicating pregnancy, unspecified trimester**

    O9A.22   **Injury, poisoning and certain other consequences of external causes complicating childbirth**

    O9A.23   **Injury, poisoning and certain other consequences of external causes complicating the puerperium**

 ● **O9A.3**   **Physical abuse complicating pregnancy, childbirth and the puerperium**

    Conditions in T74.11 or T76.11

    Use additional code (if applicable):
      to identify any associated current injury due to physical abuse
      to identify the perpetrator of abuse (Y07.-)

    Excludes2   sexual abuse complicating pregnancy, childbirth and the puerperium (O94.4-)

  ● **O9A.31**   **Physical abuse complicating pregnancy**

    O9A.311   **Physical abuse complicating pregnancy, first trimester**

    O9A.312   **Physical abuse complicating pregnancy, second trimester**

    O9A.313   **Physical abuse complicating pregnancy, third trimester**

    ▨ O9A.319   **Physical abuse complicating pregnancy, unspecified trimester**

● Unacceptable First-Listed Diagnosis   ● Use Additional Character(s)   ▨ Unspecified   **OGCR** Official Guidelines for Coding and Reporting

🦠 Complication\Comorbidity   🦠 Major C\C   Excludes 1   Excludes 2   Includes   Use additional   Code first   Code also

CHAPTER 15 (O00-O99)

1295

    O9A.32 **Physical abuse complicating childbirth**

    O9A.33 **Physical abuse complicating the puerperium**

● O9A.4 **Sexual abuse complicating pregnancy, childbirth and the puerperium**
Conditions in T74.21 or T76.21

Use additional code (if applicable):
to identify any associated current injury due to sexual abuse
to identify the perpetrator of abuse (Y07.-)

● O9A.41 **Sexual abuse complicating pregnancy**

    O9A.411 **Sexual abuse complicating pregnancy, first trimester**

    O9A.412 **Sexual abuse complicating pregnancy, second trimester**

    O9A.413 **Sexual abuse complicating pregnancy, third trimester**

    ■ O9A.419 **Sexual abuse complicating pregnancy, unspecified trimester**

    O9A.42 **Sexual abuse complicating childbirth**

    O9A.43 **Sexual abuse complicating the puerperium**

● O9A.5 **Psychological abuse complicating pregnancy, childbirth and the puerperium**
Conditions in T74.31 or T76.31

Use additional code to identify the perpetrator of abuse (Y07.-)

● O9A.51 **Psychological abuse complicating pregnancy**

    O9A.511 **Psychological abuse complicating pregnancy, first trimester**

    O9A.512 **Psychological abuse complicating pregnancy, second trimester**

    O9A.513 **Psychological abuse complicating pregnancy, third trimester**

    ■ O9A.519 **Psychological abuse complicating pregnancy, unspecified trimester**

    O9A.52 **Psychological abuse complicating childbirth**

    O9A.53 **Psychological abuse complicating the puerperium**

OGCR See Section I.C., Chapter 16
Newborn (Perinatal) Guidelines

CHAPTER 16

CERTAIN CONDITIONS ORIGINATING IN THE PERINATAL PERIOD (P00-P96)

Note: Codes from this chapter are for use on newborn records only, never on maternal records.

Includes   conditions that have their origin in the fetal or perinatal period (before birth through the first 28 days after birth) even if morbidity occurs later

Excludes1   apparent life threatening event in newborn and infant [ALTE] (R68.13)

Excludes2   congenital malformations, deformations and chromosomal abnormalities (Q00-Q99)
endocrine, nutritional and metabolic diseases (E00-E90)
injury, poisoning and certain other consequences of external causes (S00-T98)
neoplasms (C00-D48)
tetanus neonatorum (A33)

This chapter contains the following blocks:

P00-P04	Newborn affected by maternal factors and by complications of pregnancy, labor, and delivery
P05-P08	Disorders related to length of gestation and fetal growth
P09	Abnormal findings on neonatal screening
P10-P15	Birth trauma
P19-P29	Respiratory and cardiovascular disorders specific to the perinatal period
P35-P39	Infections specific to the perinatal period
P50-P61	Hemorrhagic and hematological disorders of newborn
P70-P74	Transitory endocrine and metabolic disorders specific to newborn
P76-P78	Digestive system disorders of newborn
P80-P83	Conditions involving the integument and temperature regulation of newborn
P84	Other problems with newborn
P90-P96	Other disorders originating in the perinatal period

NEWBORN AFFECTED BY MATERNAL FACTORS AND BY COMPLICATIONS OF PREGNANCY, LABOR, AND DELIVERY (P00–P04)

Note: These codes are for use when the listed maternal conditions are specified as the cause of confirmed morbidity or potential morbidity which have their origin in the perinatal period (before birth through the first 28 days after birth). Codes from these categories are also for use for newborns who are suspected of having an abnormal condition resulting from exposure from the mother or the birth process, but without signs or symptoms, and, which after examination and observation, is found not to exist. These codes may be used even if treatment is begun for a suspected condition that is ruled out.

● **P00**   **Newborn (suspected to be) affected by maternal conditions that may be unrelated to present pregnancy**

Code first any current condition in newborn

Excludes2   newborn (suspected to be) affected by maternal complications of pregnancy (P01.-)
newborn affected by maternal endocrine and metabolic disorders (P70–P74)
newborn affected by noxious substances transmitted via placenta or breast milk (P04.-)

P00.0   **Newborn (suspected to be) affected by maternal hypertensive disorders**
Newborn (suspected to be) affected by maternal conditions classifiable to O10-O11, O13-O16

P00.1   **Newborn (suspected to be) affected by maternal renal and urinary tract diseases**
Newborn (suspected to be) affected by maternal conditions classifiable to N00-N39

P00.2   **Newborn (suspected to be) affected by maternal infectious and parasitic diseases**
Newborn (suspected to be) affected by maternal infectious disease classifiable to A00-B99, J09 and J10

Excludes1   infections specific to the perinatal period (P35-P39)
maternal genital tract or other localized infections (P00.8)

P00.3   **Newborn (suspected to be) affected by other maternal circulatory and respiratory diseases**
Newborn (suspected to be) affected by maternal conditions classifiable to I00-I99, J00-J99, Q20-Q34 and not included in P00.0, P00.2

P00.4   **Newborn (suspected to be) affected by maternal nutritional disorders**
Newborn (suspected to be) affected by maternal disorders classifiable to E40-E64
Maternal malnutrition NOS

P00.5   **Newborn (suspected to be) affected by maternal injury**
Newborn (suspected to be) affected by maternal conditions classifiable to O97.2

P00.6   **Newborn (suspected to be) affected by surgical procedure on mother**
Newborn (suspected to be) affected by amniocentesis

Excludes1   Cesarean delivery for present delivery (P03.4)
damage to placenta from amniocentesis, Cesarean delivery or surgical induction (P02.1)
previous surgery to uterus or pelvic organs (P03.89)

Excludes2   newborn affected by complication of (fetal) intrauterine procedure (P96.5)

P00.7   **Newborn (suspected to be) affected by other medical procedures on mother, not elsewhere classified**
Newborn (suspected to be) affected by radiation to mother

Excludes1   damage to placenta from amniocentesis, Cesarean delivery or surgical induction (P02.1)
newborn affected by other complications of labor and delivery (P03.-)

● Unacceptable First-Listed Diagnosis   ● Use Additional Character(s)   ■ Unspecified   **OGCR** Official Guidelines for Coding and Reporting

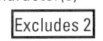 Complication\Comorbidity   Major C\C   Excludes 1   Excludes 2   Includes   Use additional   Code first   Code also   1297

CHAPTER 16 (P00-P96)

- **P00.8 Newborn (suspected to be) affected by other maternal conditions**
  - **P00.81 Newborn (suspected to be) affected by periodontal disease in mother**
  - **P00.89 Newborn (suspected to be) affected by other maternal conditions**
    Newborn (suspected to be) affected by conditions classifiable to T80-T88
    Newborn (suspected to be) affected by maternal genital tract or other localized infections
    Newborn (suspected to be) affected by maternal systemic lupus erythematosus
- **P00.9 Newborn (suspected to be) affected by unspecified maternal condition**

- **P01 Newborn (suspected to be) affected by maternal complications of pregnancy**
  Code first any current condition in newborn
  - **P01.0 Newborn (suspected to be) affected by incompetent cervix**
  - **P01.1 Newborn (suspected to be) affected by premature rupture of membranes**
  - **P01.2 Newborn (suspected to be) affected by oligohydramnios**
    Excludes1 oligohydramnios due to premature rupture of membranes (P01.1)
  - **P01.3 Newborn (suspected to be) affected by polyhydramnios**
    Excess of amniotic fluid, usually > 2000 mL
    Newborn (suspected to be) affected by hydramnios
  - **P01.4 Newborn (suspected to be) affected by ectopic pregnancy**
    Newborn (suspected to be) affected by abdominal pregnancy
  - **P01.5 Newborn (suspected to be) affected by multiple pregnancy**
    Newborn (suspected to be) affected by triplet (pregnancy)
    Newborn (suspected to be) affected by twin (pregnancy)
  - **P01.6 Newborn (suspected to be) affected by maternal death**
  - **P01.7 Newborn (suspected to be) affected by malpresentation before labor**
    Newborn (suspected to be) affected by breech presentation before labor
    Newborn (suspected to be) affected by external version before labor
    Newborn (suspected to be) affected by face presentation before labor
    Newborn (suspected to be) affected by transverse lie before labor
    Newborn (suspected to be) affected by unstable lie before labor
  - **P01.8 Newborn (suspected to be) affected by other maternal complications of pregnancy**
  - **P01.9 Newborn (suspected to be) affected by maternal complication of pregnancy, unspecified**

- **P02 Newborn (suspected to be) affected by complications of placenta, cord and membranes**
  Code first any current condition in newborn
  - **P02.0 Newborn (suspected to be) affected by placenta previa**

- **P02.1 Newborn (suspected to be) affected by other forms of placental separation and hemorrhage**
  Newborn (suspected to be) affected by abruptio placenta
  Newborn (suspected to be) affected by accidental hemorrhage
  Newborn (suspected to be) affected by antepartum hemorrhage
  Newborn (suspected to be) affected by damage to placenta from amniocentesis, cesarean delivery or surgical induction
  Newborn (suspected to be) affected by maternal blood loss
  Newborn (suspected to be) affected by premature separation of placenta
- **P02.2 Newborn (suspected to be) affected by other and unspecified morphological and functional abnormalities of placenta**
  - **P02.20 Newborn (suspected to be) affected by unspecified morphological and functional abnormalities of placenta**
  - **P02.29 Newborn (suspected to be) affected by other morphological and functional abnormalities of placenta**
    Newborn (suspected to be) affected by placental dysfunction
    Newborn (suspected to be) affected by placental infarction
    Newborn (suspected to be) affected by placental insufficiency
- **P02.3 Newborn (suspected to be) affected by placental transfusion syndromes**
  Newborn (suspected to be) affected by placental and cord abnormalities resulting in twin-to-twin or other transplacental transfusion
- **P02.4 Newborn (suspected to be) affected by prolapsed cord**
- **P02.5 Newborn (suspected to be) affected by other compression of umbilical cord**
  Newborn (suspected to be) affected by umbilical cord (tightly) around neck
  Newborn (suspected to be) affected by entanglement of umbilical cord
  Newborn (suspected to be) affected by knot in umbilical cord
- **P02.6 Newborn (suspected to be) affected by other and unspecified conditions of umbilical cord**
  - **P02.60 Newborn (suspected to be) affected by unspecified conditions of umbilical cord**
  - **P02.69 Newborn (suspected to be) affected by other conditions of umbilical cord**
    Newborn (suspected to be) affected by short umbilical cord
    Newborn (suspected to be) affected by vasa previa
    Excludes1 newborn affected by single umbilical artery (Q27.0)
- **P02.7 Newborn (suspected to be) affected by chorioamnionitis**
  Inflammation of chorion and amnion
  Newborn (suspected to be) affected by amnionitis
  Newborn (suspected to be) affected by membranitis
  Newborn (suspected to be) affected by placentitis
- **P02.8 Newborn (suspected to be) affected by other abnormalities of membranes**
- **P02.9 Newborn (suspected to be) affected by abnormality of membranes, unspecified**

CHAPTER 16 (P00-P96)

1298

● Unacceptable First-Listed Diagnosis   ● Use Additional Character(s)   ■ Unspecified   **OGCR** Official Guidelines for Coding and Reporting
Complication\Comorbidity   Major C\C   Excludes 1   Excludes 2    Includes   Use additional   Code first   Code also

● **P03** **Newborn (suspected to be) affected by other complications of labor and delivery**

Code first any current condition in newborn

P03.0 **Newborn (suspected to be) affected by breech delivery and extraction**

P03.1 **Newborn (suspected to be) affected by other malpresentation, malposition and disproportion during labor and delivery**
    Newborn (suspected to be) affected by contracted pelvis
    Newborn (suspected to be) affected by conditions classifiable to O64-O66
    Newborn (suspected to be) affected by persistent occipitoposterior
    Newborn (suspected to be) affected by transverse lie

P03.2 **Newborn (suspected to be) affected by forceps delivery**

P03.3 **Newborn (suspected to be) affected by delivery by vacuum extractor [ventouse]**

P03.4 **Newborn (suspected to be) affected by Cesarean delivery**

P03.5 **Newborn (suspected to be) affected by precipitate delivery**
    Newborn (suspected to be) affected by rapid second stage

P03.6 **Newborn (suspected to be) affected by abnormal uterine contractions**
    Newborn (suspected to be) affected by conditions classifiable to O62.-, except O62.3
    Newborn (suspected to be) affected by hypertonic labor
    Newborn (suspected to be) affected by uterine inertia

● **P03.8** **Newborn (suspected to be) affected by other specified complications of labor and delivery**

    ● **P03.81** **Newborn (suspected to be) affected by abnormality in fetal (intrauterine) heart rate or rhythm**

        Excludes1 neonatal cardiac dysrhythmia (P29.1)

        P03.810 **Newborn (suspected to be) affected by abnormality in fetal (intrauterine) heart rate or rhythm before the onset of labor**

        P03.811 **Newborn (suspected to be) affected by abnormality in fetal (intrauterine) heart rate or rhythm during labor**

        ▪ **P03.819** **Newborn (suspected to be) affected by abnormality in fetal (intrauterine) heart rate or rhythm, unspecified as to time of onset**

    P03.82 **Meconium passage during delivery**
        Excludes1 meconium aspiration (P24.00, P24.01)
        meconium staining (P96.83)

    P03.89 **Newborn (suspected to be) affected by other specified complications of labor and delivery**
        Newborn (suspected to be) affected by abnormality of maternal soft tissues
        Newborn (suspected to be) affected by conditions classifiable to O60-O75 and by procedures used in labor and delivery not included in P02.- and P03.0-P03.6
        Newborn (suspected to be) affected by induction of labor

▪ **P03.9** **Newborn (suspected to be) affected by complication of labor and delivery, unspecified**

● **P04** **Newborn (suspected to be) affected by noxious substances transmitted via placenta or breast milk**

    Includes nonteratogenic effects of substances transmitted via placenta

    Excludes2 congenital malformations (Q00-Q99)
    neonatal jaundice from excessive hemolysis due to drugs or toxins transmitted from mother (P58.4)
    newborn in contact with and (suspected) exposures hazardous to health not transmitted via placenta or breast milk (Z77.-)

● **P04.0** **Newborn (suspected to be) affected by maternal anesthesia and analgesia in pregnancy, labor and delivery**
    Newborn (suspected to be) affected by reactions and intoxications from maternal opiates and tranquilizers administered during labor and delivery

P04.1 **Newborn (suspected to be) affected by other maternal medication**
    Newborn (suspected to be) affected by cancer chemotherapy
    Newborn (suspected to be) affected by cytotoxic drugs

    Excludes1 dysmorphism due to warfarin (Q86.2)
    fetal hydantoin syndrome (Q86.1)
    maternal use of drugs of addiction (P04.4-)

P04.2 **Newborn (suspected to be) affected by maternal use of tobacco**
    Newborn (suspected to be) affected by exposure in utero to tobacco smoke

    Excludes2 newborn exposure to environmental tobacco smoke (P96.81)

P04.3 **Newborn (suspected to be) affected by maternal use of alcohol**
    Excludes1 fetal alcohol syndrome (Q86.0)

● **P04.4** **Newborn (suspected to be) affected by maternal use of drugs of addiction**

    P04.41 **Newborn (suspected to be) affected by maternal use of cocaine**
        "Crack baby"

    P04.49 **Newborn (suspected to be) affected by maternal use of other drugs of addiction**

        Excludes2 newborn (suspected to be) affected by maternal anesthesia and analgesia (P04.0)
        withdrawal symptoms from maternal use of drugs of addiction (P96.1)

P04.5 **Newborn (suspected to be) affected by maternal use of nutritional chemical substances**

P04.6 **Newborn (suspected to be) affected by maternal exposure to environmental chemical substances**

P04.8 **Newborn (suspected to be) affected by other maternal noxious substances**

▪ **P04.9** **Newborn (suspected to be) affected by maternal noxious substance, unspecified**

● Unacceptable First-Listed Diagnosis   ● Use Additional Character(s)   ▪ Unspecified   **OGCR** Official Guidelines for Coding and Reporting

🩺 Complication\Comorbidity   🩺 Major C\C   Excludes 1   Excludes 2   Includes   Use additional   Code first   Code also

1299

CHAPTER 16 (P00-P96)

OGCR Section I.C.16.d.

Prematurity and Fetal Growth Retardation

Providers utilize different criteria in determining prematurity. A code for prematurity should not be assigned unless it is documented. Assignment of codes in categories P05, Disorders of newborn related to slow fetal growth and fetal malnutrition, and P07, Disorders of newborn related to short gestation and low birth weight, not elsewhere classified, should be based on the recorded birth weight and estimated gestational age. Codes from category P05 should not be assigned with codes from category P07.

When both birth weight and gestational age are available, two codes from category P07 should be assigned, with the code for birth weight sequenced before the code for gestational age.

DISORDERS OF NEWBORN RELATED TO LENGTH OF GESTATION AND FETAL GROWTH (P05-P08)

● **P05 Disorders of newborn related to slow fetal growth and fetal malnutrition**

● **P05.0 Newborn light for gestational age**
Newborn light-for-dates

◼ P05.00 **Newborn light for gestational age, unspecified weight**

P05.01 **Newborn light for gestational age, less than 500 grams**

P05.02 **Newborn light for gestational age, 500-749 grams**

P05.03 **Newborn light for gestational age, 750-999 grams**

P05.04 **Newborn light for gestational age, 1000-1249 grams**

P05.05 **Newborn light for gestational age, 1250-1499 grams**

P05.06 **Newborn light for gestational age, 1500-1749 grams**

P05.07 **Newborn light for gestational age, 1750-1999 grams**

P05.08 **Newborn light for gestational age, 2000-2499 grams**

● **P05.1 Newborn small for gestational age**
Newborn small-and-light-for-dates
Newborn small-for-dates

◼ P05.10 **Newborn small for gestational age, unspecified weight**

P05.11 **Newborn small for gestational age, less than 500 grams**

P05.12 **Newborn small for gestational age, 500-749 grams**

P05.13 **Newborn small for gestational age, 750-999 grams**

P05.14 **Newborn small for gestational age, 1000-1249 grams**

P05.15 **Newborn small for gestational age, 1250-1499 grams**

P05.16 **Newborn small for gestational age, 1500-1749 grams**

P05.17 **Newborn small for gestational age, 1750-1999 grams**

P05.18 **Newborn small for gestational age, 2000-2499 grams**

P05.2 **Newborn affected by fetal (intrauterine) malnutrition not light or small for gestational age**
Infant, not light or small for gestational age, showing signs of fetal malnutrition, such as dry, peeling skin and loss of subcutaneous tissue

　　Excludes1 newborn affected by fetal malnutrition with light for gestational age (P05.0-)
newborn affected by fetal malnutrition with small for gestational age (P05.1-)

◼ **P05.9 Newborn affected by slow intrauterine growth, unspecified**
Newborn affected by fetal growth retardation NOS

● **P07 Disorders of newborn related to short gestation and low birth weight, not elsewhere classified**

Note: When both birth weight and gestational age of the newborn are available, both should be coded with birth weight sequenced before gestational age.

　　Includes the listed conditions, without further specification, as the cause of morbidity or additional care, in newborn

　　Excludes1 low birth weight due to slow fetal growth and fetal malnutrition (P05.-)

● **P07.0 Extremely low birth weight newborn**
Newborn birth weight 999 g. or less

◼ P07.00 **Extremely low birth weight newborn, unspecified weight**

P07.01 **Extremely low birth weight newborn, less than 500 grams**

P07.02 **Extremely low birth weight newborn, 500-749 grams**

P07.03 **Extremely low birth weight newborn, 750-999 grams**

● **P07.1 Other low birth weight newborn**
Newborn birth weight 1000-2499 g.

◼ P07.10 **Other low birth weight newborn, unspecified weight**

P07.14 **Other low birth weight newborn, 1000-1249 grams**

P07.15 **Other low birth weight newborn, 1250-1499 grams**

P07.16 **Other low birth weight newborn, 1500-1749 grams**

P07.17 **Other low birth weight newborn, 1750-1999 grams**

P07.18 **Other low birth weight newborn, 2000-2499 grams**

● **P07.2 Extreme immaturity of newborn**
Less than 28 completed weeks (less than 196 completed days) of gestation

◼ P07.20 **Extreme immaturity of newborn, unspecified weeks**

P07.21 **Extreme immaturity of newborn, less than 24 completed weeks**

P07.22 **Extreme immaturity of newborn, 24-26 completed weeks**

P07.23 **Extreme immaturity of newborn, 27 completed weeks**

● Unacceptable First-Listed Diagnosis   ● Use Additional Character(s)   ◼ Unspecified   **OGCR** Official Guidelines for Coding and Reporting
🔖 Complication\Comorbidity   🔖 Major C\C   Excludes 1   Excludes 2   Includes   Use additional   Code first   Code also

● P07.3　**Other preterm newborn**
　　　　28 completed weeks or more but less than 37
　　　　　completed weeks (196 completed days but
　　　　　less than 259 completed days) of gestation
　　　　Prematurity NOS

　　■ P07.30　**Other preterm newborn, unspecified
　　　　　　　weeks**

　　　P07.31　**Other preterm newborn, 28-31 completed
　　　　　　　weeks**

　　　P07.32　**Other preterm newborn, 32-36 completed
　　　　　　　weeks**

● P08　**Disorders of newborn related to long gestation and high
　　　birth weight**

　　Note: When both birth weight and gestational age of the
　　　　　newborn are available, priority of assignment
　　　　　should be given to birth weight.

　　　Includes　the listed conditions, without further
　　　　　　　specification, as causes of morbidity or
　　　　　　　additional care, in newborn

　　P08.0　**Exceptionally large newborn baby**
　　　　　Usually implies a birth weight of 4500 g. or more
　　　　　Excludes1　syndrome of infant of diabetic
　　　　　　　　mother (P70.1)
　　　　　　　syndrome of infant of mother with
　　　　　　　　gestational diabetes (P70.0)

　　P08.1　**Other heavy for gestational age newborn**
　　　　　Other newborn heavy- or large-for-dates
　　　　　　regardless of period of gestation
　　　　　Usually implies a birth weight of 4000 g. to 4499 g.
　　　　　Excludes1　newborn with a birth weight of 4500
　　　　　　　　or more (P08.0)
　　　　　　　syndrome of infant of diabetic
　　　　　　　　mother (P70.1)
　　　　　　　syndrome of infant of mother with
　　　　　　　　gestational diabetes (P70.0)

● P08.2　**Late newborn, not heavy for gestational age**

　　　P08.21　**Post-term newborn**
　　　　　　Newborn with gestation period over 40
　　　　　　　completed weeks to 42 completed
　　　　　　　weeks

　　　P08.22　**Prolonged gestation of newborn**
　　　　　　Newborn with gestation period over 42
　　　　　　　completed weeks (294 days or more),
　　　　　　　not heavy- or large-for-dates
　　　　　　Postmaturity NOS

ABNORMAL FINDINGS ON NEONATAL SCREENING (P09)

P09　**Abnormal findings on neonatal screening**
　　　Use additional code to identify signs, symptoms and
　　　　conditions associated with the screening
　　　Excludes2　nonspecific serologic evidence of human
　　　　　　immunodeficiency virus [HIV] (R75)

BIRTH TRAUMA (P10-P15)

● P10　**Intracranial laceration and hemorrhage due to birth
　　　injury**
　　　Excludes1　intracranial hemorrhage of newborn NOS
　　　　　　(P52.9)
　　　　　intracranial hemorrhage of newborn due to
　　　　　　anoxia or hypoxia (P52.-)
　　　　　nontraumatic intracranial hemorrhage of
　　　　　　newborn (P52.-)

P10.0　**Subdural hemorrhage due to birth injury** 🗝
　　　　Subdural hematoma (localized) due to birth
　　　　　injury
　　　　Excludes1　subdural hemorrhage accompanying
　　　　　　tentorial tear (P10.4)

P10.1　**Cerebral hemorrhage due to birth injury** 🗝

P10.2　**Intraventricular hemorrhage due to birth injury** 🗝

P10.3　**Subarachnoid hemorrhage due to birth injury** 🗝

P10.4　**Tentorial tear due to birth injury** 🗝
　　　　*Pertaining to tentorium of cerebellum (extension of
　　　　　dura mater that separates cerebellum from inferior
　　　　　portion of occipital lobes)*

P10.8　**Other intracranial lacerations and hemorrhages
　　　　due to birth injury** 🗝

■ P10.9　**Unspecified intracranial laceration and
　　　　hemorrhage due to birth injury** 🗝

● P11　**Other birth injuries to central nervous system**

P11.0　**Cerebral edema due to birth injury** 🗝

P11.1　**Other specified brain damage due to birth injury**

■ P11.2　**Unspecified brain damage due to birth injury** 🗝

P11.3　**Birth injury to facial nerve**
　　　　Facial palsy due to birth injury

P11.4　**Birth injury to other cranial nerves**

P11.5　**Birth injury to spine and spinal cord**
　　　　Fracture of spine due to birth injury

■ P11.9　**Birth injury to central nervous system,
　　　　unspecified** 🗝

● P12　**Birth injury to scalp**

P12.0　**Cephalhematoma due to birth injury**

P12.1　**Chignon (from vacuum extraction) due to birth
　　　　injury**

P12.2　**Epicranial subaponeurotic hemorrhage due to
　　　　birth injury** 🗝
　　　　Subgaleal hemorrhage

P12.3　**Bruising of scalp due to birth injury**

P12.4　**Injury of scalp of newborn due to monitoring
　　　　equipment**
　　　　Sampling incision of scalp of newborn
　　　　Scalp clip (electrode) injury of newborn

● P12.8　**Other birth injuries to scalp**

　　　P12.81　**Caput succedaneum**

　　　P12.89　**Other birth injuries to scalp**

■ P12.9　**Birth injury to scalp, unspecified**

● P13　**Birth injury to skeleton**
　　　Excludes2　birth injury to spine (P11.5)

P13.0　**Fracture of skull due to birth injury**

P13.1　**Other birth injuries to skull**
　　　　Excludes1　cephalhematoma (P12.0)

P13.2　**Birth injury to femur**

P13.3　**Birth injury to other long bones**

P13.4　**Fracture of clavicle due to birth injury**

P13.8　**Birth injuries to other parts of skeleton**

■ P13.9　**Birth injury to skeleton, unspecified**

● P14　**Birth injury to peripheral nervous system**

P14.0　**Erb's paralysis due to birth injury**

P14.1　**Klumpke's paralysis due to birth injury**

P14.2　**Phrenic nerve paralysis due to birth injury**

● Unacceptable First-Listed Diagnosis　　　● Use Additional Character(s)　　　■ Unspecified　　　**OGCR** Official Guidelines for Coding and Reporting
🗝 Complication\Comorbidity　　🗝 Major C\C　　Excludes 1　　Excludes 2　　Includes　　Use additional　　Code first　　Code also　　　1301

CHAPTER 16 (P00-P96)

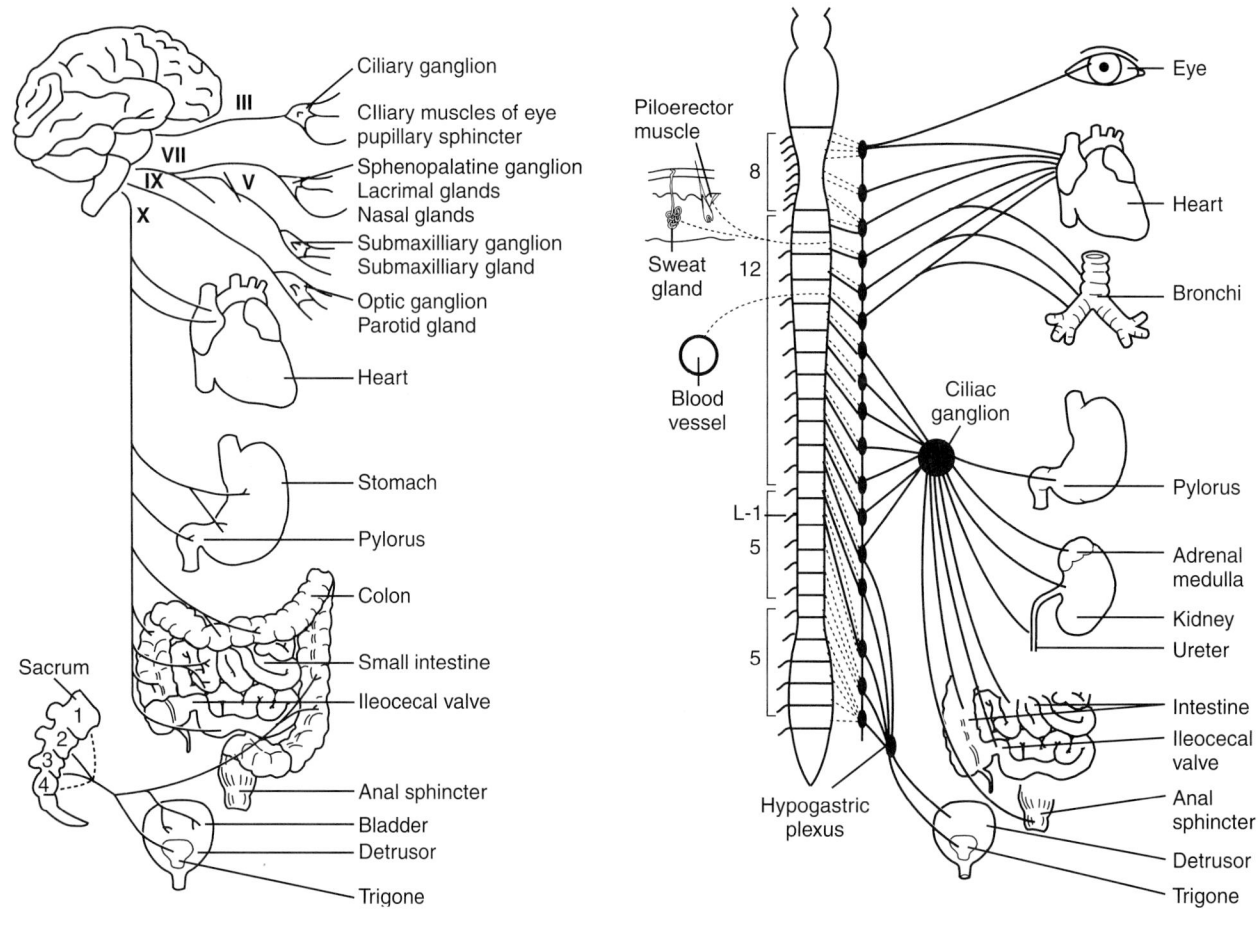

Figure 16-1 A. Parasympathetic nervous system. **B.** Sympathetic nervous system. (From Buck CJ: Step-by Step Medical Coding, Philadelphia, WB Saunders, 2010.)

Item 16–1   The **peripheral nervous system** consists of 31 pairs of spinal nerves, 12 pairs of cranial nerves, and the autonomic nerves, which are divided into the parasympathetic and sympathetic nerves. The cranial nerves are: olfactory (I), optic (II), oculomotor (III), trochlear (IV), trigeminal (V), abducens (VI), facial (VII), vestibulocochlear (VIII), glossopharyngeal (IX), vagus (X), accessory (XI), and hypoglossal (XII).

P14.3   **Other brachial plexus birth injuries**

P14.8   **Birth injuries to other parts of peripheral nervous system**

◼ P14.9   **Birth injury to peripheral nervous system, unspecified**

● P15   **Other birth injuries**

P15.0   **Birth injury to liver**
Rupture of liver due to birth injury

P15.1   **Birth injury to spleen**
Rupture of spleen due to birth injury

P15.2   **Sternomastoid injury due to birth injury**

P15.3   **Birth injury to eye**
Subconjunctival hemorrhage due to birth injury
Traumatic glaucoma due to birth injury

P15.4   **Birth injury to face**
Facial congestion due to birth injury

P15.5   **Birth injury to external genitalia**

P15.6   **Subcutaneous fat necrosis due to birth injury**

P15.8   **Other specified birth injuries**

◼ P15.9   **Birth injury, unspecified**

RESPIRATORY AND CARDIOVASCULAR DISORDERS SPECIFIC TO THE PERINATAL PERIOD (P19-P29)

● P19   **Metabolic acidemia in newborn**
Includes   (fetal) metabolic acidemia in newborn

P19.0   **Metabolic acidemia in newborn first noted before onset of labor**

P19.1   **Metabolic acidemia in newborn first noted during labor**

P19.2   **Metabolic acidemia noted at birth**

◼ P19.9   **Metabolic acidemia, unspecified**

● P22   **Respiratory distress of newborn**
Excludes1   respiratory arrest of newborn (P28.81)
respiratory failure of newborn NOS (P28.5)

P22.0   **Respiratory distress syndrome of newborn** 🐾
Cardiorespiratory distress syndrome of newborn
Hyaline membrane disease
Idiopathic respiratory distress syndrome [IRDS or RDS] of newborn
Pulmonary hypoperfusion syndrome
Respiratory distress syndrome, type I

● Unacceptable First-Listed Diagnosis   ● Use Additional Character(s)   ◼ Unspecified   **OGCR** Official Guidelines for Coding and Reporting

🐾 Complication\Comorbidity   🐾 Major C\C   Excludes 1   Excludes 2   Includes   Use additional   Code first   Code also

1302

P22.1 Transient tachypnea of newborn
Idiopathic tachypnea of newborn
Respiratory distress syndrome, type II
Wet lung syndrome

P22.8 Other respiratory distress of newborn

■ **P22.9 Respiratory distress of newborn, unspecified**

● **P23 Congenital pneumonia**

> **Includes**   infective pneumonia acquired in utero or during birth

> **Excludes1**   neonatal pneumonia resulting from aspiration (P24.-)

P23.0 Congenital pneumonia due to viral agent 🦠

> **Excludes1**   congenital rubella pneumonitis (P35.0)

P23.1 Congenital pneumonia due to Chlamydia 🦠

P23.2 Congenital pneumonia due to staphylococcus 🦠

P23.3 Congenital pneumonia due to streptococcus, group B 🦠

P23.4 Congenital pneumonia due to Escherichia coli 🦠

P23.5 Congenital pneumonia due to Pseudomonas 🦠

P23.6 Congenital pneumonia due to other bacterial agents 🦠
Congenital pneumonia due to Hemophilus influenzae
Congenital pneumonia due to Klebsiella pneumoniae
Congenital pneumonia due to Mycoplasma
Congenital pneumonia due to Streptococcus, except group B

> Use additional code (B95-B96) to identify organism

P23.8 Congenital pneumonia due to other organisms 🦠

> Use additional code (B97) to identify organism

■ **P23.9 Congenital pneumonia, unspecified** 🦠

● **P24 Neonatal aspiration**

> **Includes**   aspiration in utero and during delivery

● **P24.0 Meconium aspiration**

> **Excludes1**   meconium passage (without aspiration) during delivery (P03.82)
> meconium staining (P96.83)

P24.00 Meconium aspiration without respiratory symptoms
Meconium aspiration NOS

P24.01 Meconium aspiration with respiratory symptoms 🦠
Meconium aspiration pneumonia
Meconium aspiration pneumonitis
Meconium aspiration syndrome NOS

> Use additional code to identify any secondary pulmonary hypertension (I27.81), if applicable

● **P24.1 Neonatal aspiration of (clear) amniotic fluid and mucus**
Neonatal aspiration of liquor (amnii)

P24.10 Neonatal aspiration of (clear) amniotic fluid and mucus without respiratory symptoms
Neonatal aspiration of amniotic fluid and mucus NOS

P24.11 Neonatal aspiration of (clear) amniotic fluid and mucus with respiratory symptoms 🦠
Neonatal aspiration of amniotic fluid and mucus with pneumonia
Neonatal aspiration of amniotic fluid and mucus with pneumonitis

> Use additional code to identify any secondary pulmonary hypertension (I27.81), if applicable

● **P24.2 Neonatal aspiration of blood**

P24.20 Neonatal aspiration of blood without respiratory symptoms
Neonatal aspiration of blood NOS

P24.21 Neonatal aspiration of blood with respiratory symptoms 🦠
Neonatal aspiration of blood with pneumonia
Neonatal aspiration of blood with pneumonitis

> Use additional code to identify any secondary pulmonary hypertension (I27.81), if applicable

● **P24.3 Neonatal aspiration of milk and regurgitated food**
Neonatal aspiration of stomach contents

P24.30 Neonatal aspiration of milk and regurgitated food without respiratory symptoms
Neonatal aspiration of milk and regurgitated food NOS

P24.31 Neonatal aspiration of milk and regurgitated food with respiratory symptoms 🦠
Neonatal aspiration of milk and regurgitated food with pneumonia
Neonatal aspiration of milk and regurgitated food with pneumonitis

> Use additional code to identify any secondary pulmonary hypertension (I27.81), if applicable

● **P24.8 Other neonatal aspiration**

P24.80 Other neonatal aspiration without respiratory symptoms
Neonatal aspiration NEC

P24.81 Other neonatal aspiration with respiratory symptoms 🦠
Neonatal aspiration pneumonia NEC
Neonatal aspiration with pneumonitis NEC
Neonatal aspiration with pneumonia NOS
Neonatal aspiration with pneumonitis NOS

> Use additional code to identify any secondary pulmonary hypertension (I27.81), if applicable

■ **P24.9 Neonatal aspiration, unspecified**

● **P25 Interstitial emphysema and related conditions originating in the perinatal period**

P25.0 Interstitial emphysema originating in the perinatal period 🦠

P25.1 Pneumothorax originating in the perinatal period 🦠

P25.2 Pneumomediastinum originating in the perinatal period 🦠

P25.3 Pneumopericardium originating in the perinatal period 🦠

P25.8 Other conditions related to interstitial emphysema originating in the perinatal period 🦠

● **P26 Pulmonary hemorrhage originating in the perinatal period**

P26.0 Tracheobronchial hemorrhage originating in the perinatal period 🦠

P26.1 Massive pulmonary hemorrhage originating in the perinatal period 🦠

P26.8 Other pulmonary hemorrhages originating in the perinatal period 🦠

■ **P26.9 Unspecified pulmonary hemorrhage originating in the perinatal period** 🦠

● Unacceptable First-Listed Diagnosis   ● Use Additional Character(s)   ■ Unspecified   **OGCR** Official Guidelines for Coding and Reporting

🦠 Complication\Comorbidity   🦠 Major C\C   Excludes 1   Excludes 2   Includes   Use additional   Code first   Code also

CHAPTER 16 (P00-P96)

● **P27 Chronic respiratory disease originating in the perinatal period**

> **Excludes1** respiratory distress of newborn (P22.0-P22.9)

P27.0 Wilson-Mikity syndrome 🅱
Pulmonary dysmaturity

P27.1 Bronchopulmonary dysplasia originating in the perinatal period 🅱

P27.8 Other chronic respiratory diseases originating in the perinatal period 🅱
Congenital pulmonary fibrosis
Ventilator lung in newborn

■ **P27.9 Unspecified chronic respiratory disease originating in the perinatal period** 🅱

● **P28 Other respiratory conditions originating in the perinatal period**

> **Excludes1** congenital malformations of the respiratory system (Q30-Q34)

P28.0 Primary atelectasis of newborn 🅱
Failure of lungs to expand properly at birth
Primary failure to expand terminal respiratory units
Pulmonary hypoplasia associated with short gestation
Pulmonary immaturity NOS

● **P28.1 Other and unspecified atelectasis of newborn**

■ **P28.10 Unspecified atelectasis of newborn** 🅱
Atelectasis of newborn NOS

P28.11 Resorption atelectasis without respiratory distress syndrome 🅱
> **Excludes1** resorption atelectasis with respiratory distress syndrome (P22.0)

P28.19 Other atelectasis of newborn 🅱
Partial atelectasis of newborn
Secondary atelectasis of newborn

P28.2 Cyanotic attacks of newborn 🅱
> **Excludes1** apnea of newborn (P28.3-P28.4)

P28.3 Primary sleep apnea of newborn 🅱
Sleep apnea of newborn NOS

P28.4 Other apnea of newborn 🅱

P28.5 Respiratory failure of newborn 🅱
> **Excludes1** respiratory arrest of newborn (P28.81)
> respiratory distress of newborn (P22.0-)

● **P28.8 Other specified respiratory conditions of newborn**

P28.81 Respiratory arrest of newborn 🅱

P28.89 Other specified respiratory conditions of newborn
Congenital laryngeal stridor
Sniffles in newborn
Snuffles in newborn
> **Excludes1** early congenital syphilitic rhinitis (A50.0)

■ **P28.9 Respiratory condition of newborn, unspecified**
Respiratory depression in newborn

● **P29 Cardiovascular disorders originating in the perinatal period**
> **Excludes1** congenital malformations of the circulatory system (Q20-Q28)

P29.0 Neonatal cardiac failure

● **P29.1 Neonatal cardiac dysrhythmia**
P29.11 Neonatal tachycardia
P29.12 Neonatal bradycardia

P29.2 Neonatal hypertension

P29.3 Persistent fetal circulation 🅱
Delayed closure of ductus arteriosus
(Persistent) pulmonary hypertension of newborn

P29.4 Transient myocardial ischemia in newborn

● **P29.8 Other cardiovascular disorders originating in the perinatal period**

P29.81 Cardiac arrest of newborn 🅱

P29.89 Other cardiovascular disorders originating in the perinatal period

■ **P29.9 Cardiovascular disorder originating in the perinatal period, unspecified**

INFECTIONS SPECIFIC TO THE PERINATAL PERIOD (P35-P39)

Includes infections acquired in utero, during birth via the umbilicus, or during the first 28 days after birth

Excludes2 asymptomatic human immunodeficiency virus [HIV] infection status (Z21)
congenital gonococcal infection (A54.-)
congenital pneumonia (P23.-)
congenital syphilis (A50.-)
human immunodeficiency virus [HIV] disease (B20)
infant botulism (A48.51)
infectious diseases not specific to the perinatal period (A00-B99, J09, J10.-)
intestinal infectious disease (A00-A09)
laboratory evidence of human immunodeficiency virus [HIV] (R75)
tetanus neonatorum (A33)

● **P35 Congenital viral diseases**
Includes infections acquired in utero or during birth

P35.0 Congenital rubella syndrome 🅱
Congenital rubella pneumonitis

P35.1 Congenital cytomegalovirus infection 🅱
Viruses transmitted by multiple routes that cause mild/subclinical infection

P35.2 Congenital herpesviral [herpes simplex] infection 🅱

P35.3 Congenital viral hepatitis 🅱

P35.8 Other congenital viral diseases 🅱
Congenital varicella [chickenpox] 🅱

■ **P35.9 Congenital viral disease, unspecified** 🅱

● **P36 Bacterial sepsis of newborn**
Includes congenital sepsis
Use additional code(s), if applicable, to identify severe sepsis (R65.2-) and associated acute organ dysfunction(s)

P36.0 Sepsis of newborn due to streptococcus, group B 🅱

● **P36.1 Sepsis of newborn due to other and unspecified streptococci**

■ **P36.10 Sepsis of newborn due to unspecified streptococci** 🅱

P36.19 Sepsis of newborn due to other streptococci 🅱

P36.2   **Sepsis of newborn due to Staphylococcus aureus** 🖝

● P36.3   **Sepsis of newborn due to other and unspecified staphylococci**

◼ P36.30   **Sepsis of newborn due to unspecified staphylococci** 🖝

P36.39   **Sepsis of newborn due to other staphylococci** 🖝

P36.4   **Sepsis of newborn due to Escherichia coli** 🖝

P36.5   **Sepsis of newborn due to anaerobes** 🖝

P36.8   **Other bacterial sepsis of newborn** 🖝

Use additional code from category B96 to identify organism

◼ P36.9   **Bacterial sepsis of newborn, unspecified** 🖝

● P37   **Other congenital infectious and parasitic diseases**

   Excludes2   congenital syphilis (A50.-)
infectious neonatal diarrhea (A00-A09)
necrotizing enterocolitis in newborn (P77.-)
noninfectious neonatal diarrhea (P78.3)
ophthalmia neonatorum due to gonococcus (A54.31)
tetanus neonatorum (A33)

P37.0   **Congenital tuberculosis** 🖝

P37.1   **Congenital toxoplasmosis** 🖝
Parasitic infection, often causing mild flu-like illness
Hydrocephalus due to congenital toxoplasmosis

P37.2   **Neonatal (disseminated) listeriosis** 🖝
Acquired transplacentally or during/after parturition in which symptoms are those of sepsis

P37.3   **Congenital falciparum malaria** 🖝

P37.4   **Other congenital malaria** 🖝

P37.5   **Neonatal candidiasis**

P37.8   **Other specified congenital infectious and parasitic diseases** 🖝

◼ P37.9   **Congenital infectious or parasitic disease, unspecified** 🖝

● P38   **Omphalitis of newborn**
Inflammation of umbilicus

   Excludes1   omphalitis not of newborn (L08.82)
tetanus omphalitis (A33)
umbilical hemorrhage of newborn (P51.-)

P38.1   **Omphalitis with mild hemorrhage** 🖝

P38.9   **Omphalitis without hemorrhage** 🖝
Omphalitis of newborn NOS

● P39   **Other infections specific to the perinatal period**
Use additional code to identify organism (B95.-, B96.-)

P39.0   **Neonatal infective mastitis** 🖝

   Excludes1   breast engorgement of newborn (P83.4)
noninfective mastitis of newborn (P83.4)

P39.1   **Neonatal conjunctivitis and dacryocystitis**
Neonatal chlamydial conjunctivitis
Ophthalmia neonatorum NOS
Neonate = newborn

   Excludes1   gonococcal conjunctivitis (A54.31)

P39.2   **Intra-amniotic infection affecting newborn, not elsewhere classified** 🖝

P39.3   **Neonatal urinary tract infection** 🖝

P39.4   **Neonatal skin infection** 🖝
Neonatal pyoderma

   Excludes1   pemphigus neonatorum (L00)
staphylococcal scalded skin syndrome (L00)

P39.8   **Other specified infections specific to the perinatal period** 🖝

◼ P39.9   **Infection specific to the perinatal period, unspecified** 🖝

HEMORRHAGIC AND HEMATOLOGICAL DISORDERS OF NEWBORN (P50-P61)

   Excludes1   congenital stenosis and stricture of bile ducts (Q44.3)

Crigler-Najjar syndrome (E80.5)
Dubin-Johnson syndrome (E80.6)
Gilbert's syndrome (E80.4)
hereditary hemolytic anemias (D55-D58)

● P50   **Newborn affected by intrauterine (fetal) blood loss**

   Excludes1   congenital anemia from intrauterine (fetal) blood loss (P61.3)

P50.0   **Newborn affected by intrauterine (fetal) blood loss from vasa previa**

P50.1   **Newborn affected by intrauterine (fetal) blood loss from ruptured cord**

P50.2   **Newborn affected by intrauterine (fetal) blood loss from placenta**

P50.3   **Newborn affected by hemorrhage into co-twin**

P50.4   **Newborn affected by hemorrhage into maternal circulation**

P50.5   **Newborn affected by intrauterine (fetal) blood loss from cut end of co-twin's cord**

P50.8   **Newborn affected by other intrauterine (fetal) blood loss**

◼ P50.9   **Newborn affected by intrauterine (fetal) blood loss, unspecified**
Newborn affected by fetal hemorrhage NOS

● P51   **Umbilical hemorrhage of newborn**

   Excludes1   omphalitis with mild hemorrhage (P38.1)
umbilical hemorrhage from cut end of co-twins cord (P50.5)

P51.0   **Massive umbilical hemorrhage of newborn**

P51.8   **Other umbilical hemorrhages of newborn**
Slipped umbilical ligature NOS

◼ P51.9   **Umbilical hemorrhage of newborn, unspecified**

● P52   **Intracranial nontraumatic hemorrhage of newborn**

   Includes   intracranial hemorrhage due to anoxia or hypoxia

   Excludes1   intracranial hemorrhage due to birth injury (P10.-)
intracranial hemorrhage due to other injury (S06.-)

P52.0   **Intraventricular (nontraumatic) hemorrhage, grade 1, of newborn** 🖝
Subependymal hemorrhage (without intraventricular extension)
Bleeding into germinal matrix

P52.1   **Intraventricular (nontraumatic) hemorrhage, grade 2, of newborn** 🖝
Subependymal hemorrhage with intraventricular extension
Bleeding into ventricle

● Unacceptable First-Listed Diagnosis   ● Use Additional Character(s)   ◼ Unspecified   **OGCR** Official Guidelines for Coding and Reporting

🖝 Complication\Comorbidity   🖝 Major C\C   Excludes 1   Excludes 2    Includes   Use additional   Code first   Code also

1305

CHAPTER 16 (P00-P96)

● P52.2   **Intraventricular (nontraumatic) hemorrhage, grade 3 and grade 4, of newborn**

     P52.21   **Intraventricular (nontraumatic) hemorrhage, grade 3, of newborn** 🦠
         Subependymal hemorrhage with intraventricular extension with enlargement of ventricle

     P52.22   **Intraventricular (nontraumatic) hemorrhage, grade 4, of newborn** 🦠
         Bleeding into cerebral cortex
         Subependymal hemorrhage with intracerebral extension

■ P52.3   **Unspecified intraventricular (nontraumatic) hemorrhage of newborn** 🦠

    P52.4   **Intracerebral (nontraumatic) hemorrhage of newborn** 🦠

    P52.5   **Subarachnoid (nontraumatic) hemorrhage of newborn** 🦠

    P52.6   **Cerebellar (nontraumatic) and posterior fossa hemorrhage of newborn** 🦠

    P52.8   **Other intracranial (nontraumatic) hemorrhages and newborn** 🦠

■ P52.9   **Intracranial (nontraumatic) hemorrhage of newborn, unspecified** 🦠

P53   **Hemorrhagic disease of newborn** 🦠

    | Includes | vitamin K deficiency of newborn

● P54   **Other neonatal hemorrhages**

    | Excludes1 | newborn affected by (intrauterine) blood loss (P50.-)
         pulmonary hemorrhage originating in the perinatal period (P26.-)

    P54.0   **Neonatal hematemesis**
      Vomiting of blood

      | Excludes1 | neonatal hematemesis due to swallowed maternal blood (P78.2)

    P54.1   **Neonatal melena** 🦠
      Dark-colored feces stained with blood pigments

      | Excludes1 | neonatal melena due to swallowed maternal blood (P78.2)

    P54.2   **Neonatal rectal hemorrhage** 🦠

    P54.3   **Other neonatal gastrointestinal hemorrhage** 🦠

    P54.4   **Neonatal adrenal hemorrhage** 🦠

    P54.5   **Neonatal cutaneous hemorrhage**
      Neonatal bruising
      Neonatal ecchymoses
      Neonatal petechiae
      Neonatal superficial hematomata

      | Excludes2 | bruising of scalp due to birth injury (P12.3)
         cephalhematoma due to birth injury (P12.0)

    P54.6   **Neonatal vaginal hemorrhage**
      Neonatal pseudomenses

    P54.8   **Other specified neonatal hemorrhages**

■ P54.9   **Neonatal hemorrhage, unspecified**

● P55   **Hemolytic disease of newborn**
      AKA erythroblastosis fetalis and is due to Rh isoimmunization, result of Rh blood factor incompatibilities between mother (Rh negative) and fetus (Rh positive)

    P55.0   **Rh isoimmunization of newborn**

    P55.1   **ABO isoimmunization of newborn**

    P55.8   **Other hemolytic diseases of newborn**

■ P55.9   **Hemolytic disease of newborn, unspecified**

● P56   **Hydrops fetalis due to hemolytic disease**
      Caused by maternal sensitization to fetal blood group antigen

    | Excludes1 | hydrops fetalis NOS (P83.2)

    P56.0   **Hydrops fetalis due to isoimmunization** 🦠

● P56.9   **Hydrops fetalis due to other and unspecified hemolytic disease**

     ■ P56.90   **Hydrops fetalis due to unspecified hemolytic disease** 🦠

     P56.99   **Hydrops fetalis due to other hemolytic disease** 🦠

● P57   **Kernicterus**
      High levels of bilirubin in blood, with severe neural symptoms

    P57.0   **Kernicterus due to isoimmunization** 🦠

    P57.8   **Other specified kernicterus** 🦠

      | Excludes1 | Crigler-Najjar syndrome (E80.5)

■ P57.9   **Kernicterus, unspecified** 🦠

● P58   **Neonatal jaundice due to other excessive hemolysis**

    | Excludes1 | jaundice due to isoimmunization (P55-P57)

    P58.0   **Neonatal jaundice due to bruising**

    P58.1   **Neonatal jaundice due to bleeding**

    P58.2   **Neonatal jaundice due to infection**

    P58.3   **Neonatal jaundice due to polycythemia**

● P58.4   **Neonatal jaundice due to drugs or toxins transmitted from mother or given to newborn**
      Code first (T36-T65) to identify drug or toxin

     ● P58.41   **Neonatal jaundice due to drugs or toxins transmitted from mother**

     ● P58.42   **Neonatal jaundice due to drugs or toxins given to newborn**

    P58.5   **Neonatal jaundice due to swallowed maternal blood**

    P58.8   **Neonatal jaundice due to other specified excessive hemolysis**

■ P58.9   **Neonatal jaundice due to excessive hemolysis, unspecified**

● P59   **Neonatal jaundice from other and unspecified causes**

    | Excludes1 | jaundice due to inborn errors of metabolism (E70-E90)
         kernicterus (P57.-)

    P59.0   **Neonatal jaundice associated with preterm delivery**
      Hyperbilirubinemia of prematurity
      Jaundice due to delayed conjugation associated with preterm delivery

    P59.1   **Inspissated bile syndrome** 🦠

● P59.2   **Neonatal jaundice from other and unspecified hepatocellular damage**

      | Excludes1 | congenital viral hepatitis (P35.3)

     ■ P59.20   **Neonatal jaundice from unspecified hepatocellular damage** 🦠

     P59.29   **Neonatal jaundice from other hepatocellular damage** 🦠
         Giant cell hepatitis
         Neonatal (idiopathic) hepatitis

    P59.3   **Neonatal jaundice from breast milk inhibitor**

    P59.8   **Neonatal jaundice from other specified causes**

■ P59.9   **Neonatal jaundice, unspecified**
      Neonatal physiological jaundice (intense)(prolonged) NOS

● Unacceptable First-Listed Diagnosis   ● Use Additional Character(s)   ■ Unspecified   **OGCR** Official Guidelines for Coding and Reporting
🦠 Complication\Comorbidity   🦠 Major C\C | Excludes 1 | | Excludes 2 | Includes   Use additional   Code first   Code also

● **P60 Disseminated intravascular coagulation of newborn** 🦠
> **Includes**   defibrination syndrome of newborn

● **P61 Other perinatal hematological disorders**
> **Excludes1**   transient hypogammaglobulinemia of infancy (D80.7)

P61.0 Transient neonatal thrombocytopenia 🦠
> *Lack of sufficient numbers of circulating thrombocytes (platelets)*
> Neonatal thrombocytopenia due to exchange transfusion
> Neonatal thrombocytopenia due to idiopathic maternal thrombocytopenia
> Neonatal thrombocytopenia due to isoimmunization

P61.1 Polycythemia neonatorum
> *Neonate = newborn*

P61.2 Anemia of prematurity 🦠

P61.3 Congenital anemia from fetal blood loss 🦠

P61.4 Other congenital anemias, not elsewhere classified 🦠
> Congenital anemia NOS

P61.5 Transient neonatal neutropenia 🦠
> *Low levels of granulocytic neutrophilic white blood cells*
> > **Excludes1**   congenital neutropenia (nontransient) (D70.0)

P61.6 Other transient neonatal disorders of coagulation 🦠

P61.8 Other specified perinatal hematological disorders

▪ **P61.9 Perinatal hematological disorder, unspecified**

TRANSITORY ENDOCRINE AND METABOLIC DISORDERS SPECIFIC TO NEWBORN (P70-P74)

> **Includes**   transitory endocrine and metabolic disturbances caused by the infant's response to maternal endocrine and metabolic factors, or its adjustment to extrauterine environment

● **P70 Transitory disorders of carbohydrate metabolism specific to newborn**

P70.0 Syndrome of infant of mother with gestational diabetes
> Newborn (with hypoglycemia) affected by maternal gestational diabetes
> > **Excludes1**   newborn (with hypoglycemia) affected by maternal (pre-existing) diabetes mellitus (P70.1)
> > syndrome of infant of a diabetic mother (P70.1)

P70.1 Syndrome of infant of a diabetic mother
> Newborn (with hypoglycemia) affected by maternal (pre-existing) diabetes mellitus
> > **Excludes1**   newborn (with hypoglycemia) affected by maternal gestational diabetes (P70.0)
> > syndrome of infant of mother with gestational diabetes (P70.0)

P70.2 Neonatal diabetes mellitus 🦠

P70.3 Iatrogenic neonatal hypoglycemia

P70.4 Other neonatal hypoglycemia
> Transitory neonatal hypoglycemia

P70.8 Other transitory disorders of carbohydrate metabolism of newborn 🦠

▪ **P70.9 Transitory disorder of carbohydrate metabolism of newborn, unspecified**

● **P71 Transitory neonatal disorders of calcium and magnesium metabolism**

P71.0 Cow's milk hypocalcemia in newborn 🦠

P71.1 Other neonatal hypocalcemia 🦠
> > **Excludes1**   neonatal hypoparathyroidism (P71.4)

P71.2 Neonatal hypomagnesemia 🦠

P71.3 Neonatal tetany without calcium or magnesium deficiency 🦠
> Neonatal tetany NOS

P71.4 Transitory neonatal hypoparathyroidism 🦠

P71.8 Other transitory neonatal disorders of calcium and magnesium metabolism 🦠

▪ **P71.9 Transitory neonatal disorder of calcium and magnesium metabolism, unspecified** 🦠

● **P72 Other transitory neonatal endocrine disorders**
> **Excludes1**   congenital hypothyroidism with or without goiter (E03.0-E03.1)
> dyshormogenetic goiter (E07.1)
> Pendred's syndrome (E07.1)

P72.0 Neonatal goiter, not elsewhere classified 🦠
> Transitory congenital goiter with normal functioning

P72.1 Transitory neonatal hyperthyroidism 🦠
> Neonatal thyrotoxicosis

P72.2 Other transitory neonatal disorders of thyroid function, not elsewhere classified 🦠
> Transitory neonatal hypothyroidism

P72.8 Other specified transitory neonatal endocrine disorders 🦠

▪ **P72.9 Transitory neonatal endocrine disorder, unspecified**

● **P74 Other transitory neonatal electrolyte and metabolic disturbances**

P74.0 Late metabolic acidosis of newborn 🦠
> > **Excludes1**   (fetal) metabolic acidosis of newborn (P19)

P74.1 Dehydration of newborn

P74.2 Disturbances of sodium balance of newborn

P74.3 Disturbances of potassium balance of newborn

P74.4 Other transitory electrolyte disturbances of newborn

P74.5 Transitory tyrosinemia of newborn 🦠

P74.6 Transitory hyperammonemia of newborn 🦠

P74.8 Other transitory metabolic disturbances of newborn 🦠
> Amino-acid metabolic disorders described as transitory

▪ **P74.9 Transitory metabolic disturbance of newborn, unspecified**

● Unacceptable First-Listed Diagnosis   ● Use Additional Character(s)   ▪ Unspecified   **OGCR** Official Guidelines for Coding and Reporting

🦠 Complication\Comorbidity   🦠 Major C\C   Excludes 1   Excludes 2   Includes   Use additional   Code first   Code also

1307

DIGESTIVE SYSTEM DISORDERS OF NEWBORN (P76-P78)

● **P76　Other intestinal obstruction of newborn**

> **Excludes1**　meconium ileus in cystic fibrosis (E84.11)

P76.0　Meconium plug syndrome
Intestinal obstruction; most often seen in premature infants
Meconium ileus NOS

> **Excludes1**　meconium ileus in cystic fibrosis (E84.11)

P76.1　Transitory ileus of newborn 🕮
Temporary obstruction of ileus (small intestine)

> **Excludes1**　Hirschsprung's disease (Q43.1)

P76.2　Intestinal obstruction due to inspissated milk
Being thickened, dried, or made less fluid

P76.8　Other specified intestinal obstruction of newborn

> **Excludes1**　intestinal obstruction classifiable to K56.-

◼ **P76.9　Intestinal obstruction of newborn, unspecified**

● **P77　Necrotizing enterocolitis of newborn**

P77.1　Stage 1 necrotizing enterocolitis in newborn 🕮
Necrotizing enterocolitis without pneumatosis, without perforation

P77.2　Stage 2 necrotizing enterocolitis in newborn 🕮
Necrotizing enterocolitis with pneumatosis, without perforation

P77.3　Stage 3 necrotizing enterocolitis in newborn 🕮
Necrotizing enterocolitis with perforation
Necrotizing enterocolitis with pneumatosis and perforation

◼ **P77.9　Necrotizing enterocolitis in newborn, unspecified** 🕮
Necrotizing enterocolitis in newborn, NOS

● **P78　Other perinatal digestive system disorders**

> **Excludes1**　cystic fibrosis (E84.0-E84.9)
> neonatal gastrointestinal hemorrhages (P54.0-P54.3)

P78.0　Perinatal intestinal perforation 🕮
Meconium peritonitis

P78.1　Other neonatal peritonitis
Neonatal peritonitis NOS

P78.2　Neonatal hematemesis and melena due to swallowed maternal blood

P78.3　Noninfective neonatal diarrhea
Neonatal diarrhea NOS

● **P78.8　Other specified perinatal digestive system disorders**

P78.81　Congenital cirrhosis (of liver)

P78.82　Peptic ulcer of newborn

P78.83　Newborn esophageal reflux
Neonatal esophageal reflux

P78.89　Other specified perinatal digestive system disorders

◼ **P78.9　Perinatal digestive system disorder, unspecified**

CONDITIONS INVOLVING THE INTEGUMENT AND TEMPERATURE REGULATION OF NEWBORN (P80-P83)

● **P80　Hypothermia of newborn**

P80.0　Cold injury syndrome
Severe and usually chronic hypothermia associated with a pink flushed appearance, edema and neurological and biochemical abnormalities.

> **Excludes1**　mild hypothermia of newborn (P80.8)

P80.8　Other hypothermia of newborn
Mild hypothermia of newborn

◼ **P80.9　Hypothermia of newborn, unspecified**

● **P81　Other disturbances of temperature regulation of newborn**

P81.0　Environmental hyperthermia of newborn

P81.8　Other specified disturbances of temperature regulation of newborn

◼ **P81.9　Disturbance of temperature regulation of newborn, unspecified**
Fever of newborn NOS

● **P83　Other conditions of integument specific to newborn**

> **Excludes1**　congenital malformations of skin and integument (Q80-Q84)
> hydrops fetalis due to hemolytic disease (P56.-)
> neonatal skin infection (P39.4)
> staphylococcal scalded skin syndrome (L00)

> **Excludes2**　cradle cap (L21.0)
> diaper [napkin] dermatitis (L22)

P83.0　Sclerema neonatorum 🕮
Neonate = newborn

P83.1　Neonatal erythema toxicum
Benign, generalized, transient pustules that become firm vesicles

P83.2　Hydrops fetalis not due to hemolytic disease 🕮
Severe, life-threatening problem of severe edema (swelling) as result of too much fluid leaving blood and entering tissue
Hydrops fetalis NOS

● **P83.3　Other and unspecified edema specific to newborn**

◼ **P83.30　Unspecified edema specific to newborn** 🕮

P83.39　Other edema specific to newborn 🕮

P83.4　Breast engorgement of newborn
Noninfective mastitis of newborn

P83.5　Congenital hydrocele

P83.6　Umbilical polyp of newborn

P83.8　Other specified conditions integument specific to newborn
Bronze baby syndrome
Neonatal scleroderma
Urticaria neonatorum

◼ **P83.9　Condition of the integument specific to newborn, unspecified**

● Unacceptable First-Listed Diagnosis　　● Use Additional Character(s)　　◼ Unspecified　　**OGCR** Official Guidelines for Coding and Reporting
🕮 Complication\Comorbidity　🕮 Major C\C　Excludes 1　Excludes 2　Includes　Use additional　Code first　Code also

OTHER PROBLEMS WITH NEWBORN (P84)

P84   **Other problems with newborn**
Acidemia of newborn
Acidosis of newborn
Anoxia of newborn NOS
Asphyxia of newborn NOS
Hypercapnia of newborn
Hypoxemia of newborn
Hypoxia of newborn NOS
Mixed metabolic and respiratory acidosis of newborn

Excludes1   intracranial hemorrhage due to anoxia or
hypoxia (P52.-)
hypoxic ischemic encephalopathy [HIE]
(P91.6-)
late metabolic acidosis of newborn (P74.0)

OTHER DISORDERS ORIGINATING IN THE PERINATAL PERIOD (P90-P96)

P90   **Convulsions of newborn** 🏵

Excludes1   benign myoclonic epilepsy in infancy
(G40.3-)
benign neonatal convulsions (familial)
(G40.3-)

● P91   **Other disturbances of cerebral status of newborn**

P91.0   **Neonatal cerebral ischemia** 🏵

P91.1   **Acquired periventricular cysts of newborn** 🏵

P91.2   **Neonatal cerebral leukomalacia** 🏵
*Degeneration of white matter adjacent to cerebral
ventricles following cerebral hypoxia or brain
ischemia in neonates*
Periventricular leukomalacia

P91.3   **Neonatal cerebral irritability** 🏵

P91.4   **Neonatal cerebral depression** 🏵

P91.5   **Neonatal coma** 🏵

● P91.6   **Hypoxic ischemic encephalopathy (HIE)** 🏵

■ P91.60   **Hypoxic ischemic encephalopathy [HIE],
unspecified**

P91.61   **Mild hypoxic ischemic encephalopathy
[HIE]**

P91.62   **Moderate hypoxic ischemic
encephalopathy [HIE]**

P91.63   **Severe hypoxic ischemic encephalopathy
[HIE]**

P91.8   **Other specified disturbances of cerebral status of
newborn**

■ P91.9   **Disturbance of cerebral status of newborn,
unspecified**

● P92   **Feeding problems of newborn**
Excludes1   feeding problems in child over 28 days old
(R63.3)

● P92.0   **Vomiting of newborn**
Excludes1   vomiting of child over 28 days old
(R11.-)

P92.01   **Bilious vomiting of newborn**
Excludes1   bilious vomiting in child
over 28 days old (R11.4)

P92.09   **Other vomiting of newborn**
Excludes1   regurgitation of food in
newborn (P92.1)

P92.1   **Regurgitation and rumination of newborn**

P92.2   **Slow feeding of newborn**

P92.3   **Underfeeding of newborn**

P92.4   **Overfeeding of newborn**

P92.5   **Neonatal difficulty in feeding at breast**

P92.6   **Failure to thrive in newborn**
Excludes1   failure to thrive in child over 28 days
old (R62.51)

P92.8   **Other feeding problems of newborn**

■ P92.9   **Feeding problem of newborn, unspecified**

● P93   **Reactions and intoxications due to drugs administered to
newborn**

Includes   reactions and intoxications due to drugs
administered to fetus affecting newborn

Excludes1   jaundice due to drugs or toxins transmitted
from mother or given to newborn
(P58.4-)
reactions and intoxications from maternal
opiates, tranquilizers and other
medication (P04.0-P04.1, P04.4)
withdrawal symptoms from maternal use of
drugs of addiction (P96.1)
withdrawal symptoms from therapeutic use
of drugs in newborn (P96.2)

P93.0   **Grey baby syndrome** 🏵
Grey syndrome from chloramphenicol
administration in newborn

P93.8   **Other reactions and intoxications due to drugs
administered to newborn** 🏵
Code first (T36-T50) to identify drug

● P94   **Disorders of muscle tone of newborn**

P94.0   **Transient neonatal myasthenia gravis** 🏵
Excludes1   myasthenia gravis (G70.0)

P94.1   **Congenital hypertonia**

P94.2   **Congenital hypotonia**
Floppy baby syndrome, unspecified

P94.8   **Other disorders of muscle tone of newborn**

■ P94.9   **Disorder of muscle tone of newborn, unspecified**

P95   **Stillbirth**

Includes   deadborn fetus NOS
fetal death of unspecified cause
stillbirth NOS

Excludes1   maternal care for intrauterine death (O36.4)
missed abortion (O02.1)
outcome of delivery, stillbirth (Z37.1, Z37.3,
Z37.4, Z37.7)

OGCR   Section I.C.16.g.
Stillbirth

Code P95, Stillbirth, is only for use for institutions
that maintain separate records for stillbirths. No
other code should be used with P95. Code P95
should not be used on the mother's record.

● Unacceptable First-Listed Diagnosis   ● Use Additional Character(s)   ■ Unspecified   **OGCR** Official Guidelines for Coding and Reporting
🏵 Complication\Comorbidity   🏵 Major C\C   Excludes 1   Excludes 2   Includes   Use additional   Code first   Code also

● **P96   Other conditions originating in the perinatal period**

   P96.0   Congenital renal failure
   Uremia of newborn

   P96.1   Neonatal withdrawal symptoms from maternal use of drugs of addiction 🦠
   Drug withdrawal syndrome in infant of dependent mother
   Neonatal abstinence syndrome
   | Excludes1 | reactions and intoxications from maternal opiates and tranquilizers administered during labor and delivery (P04.0) |

   P96.2   Withdrawal symptoms from therapeutic use of drugs in newborn 🦠

   P96.3   Wide cranial sutures of newborn
   Neonatal craniotabes

   P96.5   Complication to newborn due to (fetal) intrauterine procedure
   | Excludes2 | newborn (suspected to be) affected by amniocentesis (P00.6) |

● **P96.8   Other specified conditions originating in the perinatal period**

   P96.81   Exposure to (parental) (environmental) tobacco smoke in the perinatal period
   | Excludes2 | newborn affected by in utero exposure to tobacco (P04.2)
   exposure to environmental tobacco smoke after the perinatal period (Z77.22) |

   P96.82   Delayed separation of umbilical cord

   P96.83   Meconium staining
   | Excludes1 | meconium aspiration (P24.00, P24.01)
   meconium passage during delivery (P03.82) |

   P96.89   Other specified conditions originating in the perinatal period
   Use additional code to specify condition

■ **P96.9   Condition originating in the perinatal period, unspecified**
   Congenital debility NOS

CHAPTER 16 (P00-P96)

1310

● Unacceptable First-Listed Diagnosis   ● Use Additional Character(s)   ■ Unspecified   **OGCR** Official Guidelines for Coding and Reporting
🦠 Complication\Comorbidity   🦠 Major C\C   Excludes 1   Excludes 2   Includes   Use additional   Code first   Code also

OGCR See Section III, Chapter 17

CHAPTER 17

CONGENITAL MALFORMATIONS, DEFORMATIONS AND CHROMOSOMAL ABNORMALITIES (Q00-Q99)

Note: CODES FROM THIS CHAPTER ARE NOT FOR USE ON MATERNAL OR FETAL RECORDS

Excludes1 inborn errors of metabolism (E70-E90)

This chapter contains the following blocks:

Q00-Q07	Congenital malformations of the nervous system
Q10-Q18	Congenital malformations of eye, ear, face and neck
Q20-Q28	Congenital malformations of the circulatory system
Q30-Q34	Congenital malformations of the respiratory system
Q35-Q37	Cleft lip and cleft palate
Q38-Q45	Other congenital malformations of the digestive system
Q50-Q56	Congenital malformations of genital organs
Q60-Q64	Congenital malformations of the urinary system
Q65-Q79	Congenital malformations and deformations of the musculoskeletal system
Q80-Q89	Other congenital malformations
Q90-Q99	Chromosomal abnormalities, not elsewhere classified

CONGENITAL MALFORMATIONS OF THE NERVOUS SYSTEM (Q00–Q07)

● **Q00   Anencephaly and similar malformations**

Q00.0 Anencephaly 🕲
  Absence of skull with cerebral hemispheres missing or reduced to small masses attached to base of cranium
  Acephaly
  Acrania
  Amyelencephaly
  Hemianencephaly
  Hemicephaly

Q00.1 Craniorachischisis 🕲
  Developmental anomaly consisting of fissure of cranium and vertebral column

Q00.2 Iniencephaly 🕲
  Developmental anomaly characterized by enlargement of foramen magnum and absence of laminae and spinous processes of cervical, dorsal

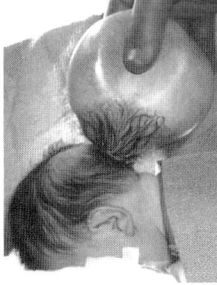

Figure 17-1 An infant with a large occipital encephalocele. The large skin-covered encephalocele is visible. (From Townsend: Sabiston Textbook of Surgery, 17th ed. 2004, Sounders, An Imprint of Elsevier.)

● **Q01   Encephalocele**
  Sac-like protrusions of brain and membranes visible through an opening in skull

  Includes   Arnold-Chiari syndrome, type III
  encephalocystocele
  encephalomyelocele
  hydroencephalocele
  hydromeningocele, cranial
  meningocele, cerebral
  meningoencephalocele

  Excludes1   Meckel-Gruber syndrome (Q61.9)

  Q01.0 Frontal encephalocele 🕲
  Q01.1 Nasofrontal encephalocele 🕲
  Q01.2 Occipital encephalocele 🕲
  Q01.8 Encephalocele of other sites 🕲
  ◼ **Q01.9 Encephalocele, unspecified** 🕲

Q02   Microcephaly
  Head size measures significantly below normal based on standardized charts

  Includes   hydromicrocephaly
  micrencephalon

  Excludes1   Meckel-Gruber syndrome (Q61.9)

● **Q03   Congenital hydrocephalus**
  Accumulation of cerebrospinal fluid in ventricles resulting in swelling and enlargement

  Includes   hydrocephalus in newborn
  Excludes1   Arnold-Chiari syndrome, type II (Q07.0-)
  acquired hydrocephalus (G91.-)
  hydrocephalus due to congenital toxoplasmosis (P37.1)
  hydrocephalus with spina bifida (Q05.0-Q05.4)

  Q03.0 Malformations of aqueduct of Sylvius
  Anomaly of aqueduct of Sylvius
  Obstruction of aqueduct of Sylvius, congenital
  Stenosis of aqueduct of Sylvius

  Q03.1 Atresia of foramina of Magendie and Luschka
  Dandy-Walker syndrome

  Q03.8 Other congenital hydrocephalus
  ◼ **Q03.9 Congenital hydrocephalus, unspecified**

● **Q04   Other congenital malformations of brain**

  Excludes1   cyclopia (Q87.0)
  macrocephaly (Q75.3)

  Q04.0 Congenital malformations of corpus callosum 🕲
  Agenesis of corpus callosum

  Q04.1 Arhinencephaly 🕲
  Congenital absence of olfactory bulbs, tract, or nerves

  Q04.2 Holoprosencephaly 🕲
  Failure of cleavage of forebrain (prosencephalon) resulting in incomplete or absent cortical separation and deficits in midline facial development

● Unacceptable First-Listed Diagnosis	● Use Additional Character(s)	◼ Unspecified	**OGCR** Official Guidelines for Coding and Reporting	
🕲 Complication\Comorbidity	🕲 Major C\C	Excludes 1 Excludes 2	Includes Use additional Code first Code also	1311

Q04.3 Other reduction deformities of brain 🔗
     Absence of part of brain   Agyria
     Agenesis of part of brain
         Cerebral cortex are not fully formed, brain surface
           is smooth
     Aplasia of part of brain
     Hydranencephaly
     Hypoplasia of part of brain
     Lissencephaly
         Congenital malformation or absence of convolutions
           of cerebral cortex
     Microgyria
         Malformation of brain characterized by excessive
           number of small convolutions (gyri) on surface
     Pachygyria
         Reduction in number of sulci of cerebrum

     | Excludes1 | congenital malformations of corpus callosum (Q04.0)

Q04.4 Septo-optic dysplasia of brain 🔗

Q04.5 Megalencephaly 🔗
     Abnormally large brain

Q04.6 Congenital cerebral cysts 🔗
     Porencephaly   Schizencephaly

     | Excludes1 | acquired porencephalic cyst (G93.0)

Q04.8 Other specified congenital malformations of brain 🔗
     Arnold-Chiari syndrome, type IV
     Macrogyria

Q04.9 Congenital malformation of brain, unspecified 🔗
     Congenital anomaly NOS of brain
     Congenital deformity NOS of brain
     Congenital disease or lesion NOS of brain
     Multiple anomalies NOS of brain, congenital

● **Q05   Spina bifida**
     Developmental anomaly characterized by defective closure of
       vertebral arch, through which spinal cord and meninges
       may protrude

     | Includes | hydromeningocele (spinal)
             meningocele (spinal)
             meningomyelocele
             myelocele
             myelomeningocele
             rachischisis
             spina bifida (aperta)(cystica)
             syringomyelocele

     Use additional code for any associated paraplegia
     (paraparesis) (G82.2-)

     | Excludes1 | Arnold-Chiari syndrome, type II (Q07.0-)
                spina bifida occulta (Q76.0)

Q05.0 Cervical spina bifida with hydrocephalus 🔗

Q05.1 Thoracic spina bifida with hydrocephalus 🔗
     Dorsal spina bifida with hydrocephalus
     Thoracolumbar spina bifida with hydrocephalus

Q05.2 Lumbar spina bifida with hydrocephalus 🔗
     Lumbosacral spina bifida with hydrocephalus

Q05.3 Sacral spina bifida with hydrocephalus 🔗

Q05.4 Unspecified spina bifida with hydrocephalus 🔗

Q05.5 Cervical spina bifida without hydrocephalus

Q05.6 Thoracic spina bifida without hydrocephalus
     Dorsal spina bifida NOS
     Thoracolumbar spina bifida NOS

Q05.7 Lumbar spina bifida without hydrocephalus
     Lumbosacral spina bifida NOS

Q05.8 Sacral spina bifida without hydrocephalus

Q05.9 Spina bifida, unspecified

● **Q06   Other congenital malformations of spinal cord**

Q06.0 Amyelia
     Congenital absence of spinal cord

Q06.1 Hypoplasia and dysplasia of spinal cord
     Underdevelopment of spinal cord
     Atelomyelia
         Congenitally incomplete development of spinal cord
     Myelatelia
     Myelodysplasia of spinal cord
         Defective development of spinal cord, especially
           lower segments

Q06.2 Diastematomyelia
     Congenital anomaly, associated with spina bifida,
       in which spinal cord is split into halves and
       surrounded by dural sac

Q06.3 Other congenital cauda equina malformations

Q06.4 Hydromyelia
     Dilation of central canal of spinal cord with increased
       fluid accumulation
     Hydrorachis

Q06.8 Other specified congenital malformations of spinal cord

Q06.9 Congenital malformation of spinal cord, unspecified
     Congenital anomaly NOS of spinal cord
     Congenital deformity NOS of spinal cord
     Congenital disease or lesion NOS of spinal cord

● **Q07   Other congenital malformations of nervous system**

     | Excludes2 | congenital central alveolar hypoventilation syndrome (G47.35)
                familial dysautonomia [Riley-Day] (G90.1)
                neurofibromatosis (nonmalignant) (Q85.0)

● **Q07.0 Arnold-Chiari syndrome**
     Herniation of cerebellar tonsils and vermis through
       foramen magnum into spinal canal
     Arnold-Chiari syndrome, type II

     | Excludes1 | Arnold-Chiari syndrome, type III (Q01.-)
                Arnold-Chiari syndrome, type IV (Q04.8)

Q07.00 Arnold-Chiari syndrome without spina bifida or hydrocephalus

Q07.01 Arnold-Chiari syndrome with spina bifida 🔗

Q07.02 Arnold-Chiari syndrome with hydrocephalus 🔗

Q07.03 Arnold-Chiari syndrome with spina bifida and hydrocephalus 🔗

Q07.8 Other specified congenital malformations of nervous system
     Agenesis of nerve
     Displacement of brachial plexus
     Jaw-winking syndrome
     Marcus Gunn's syndrome

Q07.9 Congenital malformation of nervous system, unspecified
     Congenital anomaly NOS of nervous system
     Congenital deformity NOS of nervous system
     Congenital disease or lesion NOS of nervous system

CONGENITAL MALFORMATIONS OF EYE, EAR, FACE AND NECK (Q10-Q18)

     | Excludes2 | cleft lip and cleft palate (Q35-Q37)
             congenital malformation of:
                cervical spine (Q05.0, Q05.5, Q67.5, Q76.0-Q76.4)
                larynx (Q31.-)
                lip NEC (Q38.0)
                nose (Q30.-)
                parathyroid gland (Q89.2)
                thyroid gland (Q89.2)

● Unacceptable First-Listed Diagnosis   ● Use Additional Character(s)   ■ Unspecified   **OGCR** Official Guidelines for Coding and Reporting
🔗 Complication\Comorbidity   🔗 Major C\C | Excludes 1 | | Excludes 2 | Includes   Use additional   Code first   Code also

● **Q10 Congenital malformations of eyelid, lacrimal apparatus and orbit**

  | Excludes1 | cryptophthalmos NOS (Q11.2)
  cryptophthalmos syndrome (Q87.0)

  Q10.0 Congenital ptosis
  Prolapse or drooping of upper eyelid from paralysis of third nerve or from sympathetic innervations

  Q10.1 Congenital ectropion
  Outward turning of eyelid

  Q10.2 Congenital entropion
  Inward turning of eyelid

  Q10.3 Other congenital malformations of eyelid
  Ablepharon
  Blepharophimosis, congenital
  Coloboma of eyelid
  Congenital absence or agenesis of cilia
  Congenital absence or agenesis of eyelid
  Congenital accessory eyelid
  Congenital accessory eye muscle
  Congenital malformation of eyelid NOS

  Q10.4 Absence and agenesis of lacrimal apparatus
  Congenital absence of punctum lacrimale

  Q10.5 Congenital stenosis and stricture of lacrimal duct

  Q10.6 Other congenital malformations of lacrimal apparatus
  Congenital malformation of lacrimal apparatus NOS

  Q10.7 Congenital malformation of orbit

● **Q11 Anophthalmos, microphthalmos and macrophthalmos**
  Absence of eye and optic pit

  Q11.0 Cystic eyeball

  Q11.1 Other anophthalmos
  Anophthalmos NOS
  Agenesis of eye
   Absence of eye
  Aplasia of eye

  Q11.2 Microphthalmos
  Partial absence of eye and optic pit
  Cryptophthalmos NOS
  Dysplasia of eye
  Hypoplasia of eye
  Rudimentary eye

  | Excludes1 | cryptophthalmos syndrome (Q87.0)

  Q11.3 Macrophthalmos
  Congenital enlargement of eyes

  | Excludes1 | macrophthalmos in congenital glaucoma (Q15.0)

● **Q12 Congenital lens malformations**
  Q12.0 Congenital cataract
  Q12.1 Congenital displaced lens

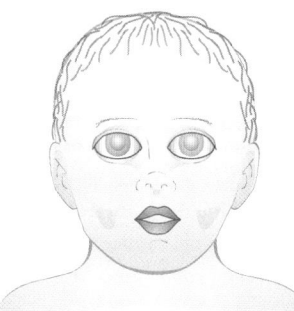

Figure 17-2 Bilateral congenital **hydrophthalmia,** in which the eyes are very large in comparison to the other facial features due to glaucoma.

Q12.2 Coloboma of lens
Q12.3 Congenital aphakia
Q12.4 Spherophakia
  Smaller, more spherical optic lens than normal
Q12.8 Other congenital lens malformations
  Microphakia
■ **Q12.9 Congenital lens malformation, unspecified**

● **Q13 Congenital malformations of anterior segment of eye**
  Q13.0 Coloboma of iris
  Coloboma NOS
  Q13.1 Absence of iris
  Aniridia
   Use additional code for associated glaucoma (H42)
  Q13.2 Other congenital malformations of iris
  Anisocoria, congenital
  Atresia of pupil
  Congenital malformation of iris NOS
  Corectopia
  Q13.3 Congenital corneal opacity
  Q13.4 Other congenital corneal malformations
  Congenital malformation of cornea NOS
  Microcornea
  Peter's anomaly
  Q13.5 Blue sclera
  Condition of unusual blueness of sclera; not harmful
  Q13.8 Other congenital malformations of anterior segment of eye
   Q13.81 Rieger's anomaly
      Use additional code for associated glaucoma (H42)
   Q13.89 Other congenital malformations of anterior segment of eye
■ **Q13.9 Congenital malformation of anterior segment of eye, unspecified**

● **Q14 Congenital malformations of posterior segment of eye**
  | Excludes2 | optic nerve hypoplasia (H47.03-)
  Q14.0 Congenital malformation of vitreous humor
  Congenital vitreous opacity
  Q14.1 Congenital malformation of retina
  Congenital retinal aneurysm
  Q14.2 Congenital malformation of optic disc
  Coloboma of optic disc
  Q14.3 Congenital malformation of choroid
  Q14.8 Other congenital malformations of posterior segment of eye
  Coloboma of the fundus
■ **Q14.9 Congenital malformation of posterior segment of eye, unspecified**

● **Q15 Other congenital malformations of eye**
  | Excludes1 | congenital nystagmus (H55.01)
  ocular albinism (E70.31-)
  optic nerve hypoplasia (H47.03-)
  retinitis pigmentosa (H35.52)
  Q15.0 Congenital glaucoma
  Axenfeld's anomaly
  Buphthalmos
   Congenital syndrome characterized by port-wine nevus covering portions of face and cranium
  Glaucoma of childhood
  Glaucoma of newborn
  Hydrophthalmos
  Keratoglobus, congenital, with glaucoma
  Macrocornea with glaucoma
  Macrophthalmos in congenital glaucoma
  Megalocornea with glaucoma

● Unacceptable First-Listed Diagnosis   ● Use Additional Character(s)   ■ Unspecified   **OGCR** Official Guidelines for Coding and Reporting

🦠 Complication\Comorbidity   🦠 Major C\C | Excludes 1 | | Excludes 2 | | Includes | | Use additional | | Code first | | Code also |

CHAPTER 17 (Q00–Q99)

1313

Q15.8 Other specified congenital malformations of eye

▪ Q15.9 Congenital malformation of eye, unspecified
Congenital anomaly of eye
Congenital deformity of eye

● Q16 Congenital malformations of ear causing impairment of hearing

| Excludes1 | congenital deafness (H90.-) |

Q16.0 Congenital absence of (ear) auricle

Q16.1 Congenital absence, atresia and stricture of auditory canal (external)
Congenital atresia or stricture of osseous meatus

Q16.2 Absence of eustachian tube

Q16.3 Congenital malformation of ear ossicles
Congenital fusion of ear ossicles

Q16.4 Other congenital malformations of middle ear
Congenital malformation of middle ear NOS

Q16.5 Congenital malformation of inner ear
Congenital anomaly of membranous labyrinth
Congenital anomaly of organ of Corti

▪ Q16.9 Congenital malformation of ear causing impairment of hearing, unspecified
Congenital absence of ear NOS

● Q17 Other congenital malformations of ear

| Excludes1 | congenital malformations of ear with impairment of hearing (Q16.0- Q16.9)
preauricular sinus (Q18.1) |

Q17.0 Accessory auricle
Accessory tragus
Polyotia
Preauricular appendage or tag
Supernumerary ear
Supernumerary lobule

Q17.1 Macrotia
Enlarged ears

Q17.2 Microtia
An abnormally small or underdeveloped external ear

Q17.3 Other misshapen ear
Pointed ear

Q17.4 Misplaced ear
Low-set ears

| Excludes1 | cervical auricle (Q18.2) |

Q17.5 Prominent ear
Bat ear

Q17.8 Other specified congenital malformations of ear
Congenital absence of lobe of ear

▪ Q17.9 Congenital malformation of ear, unspecified
Congenital anomaly of ear NOS

● Q18 Other congenital malformations of face and neck

| Excludes1 | cleft lip and cleft palate (Q35-Q37)
conditions classified to Q67.0-Q67.4
congenital malformations of skull and face bones (Q75.-)
cyclopia (Q87.0)
dentofacial anomalies [including malocclusion] (M26.-)
malformation syndromes affecting facial appearance (Q87.0)
persistent thyroglossal duct (Q89.2) |

Q18.0 Sinus, fistula and cyst of branchial cleft
Branchial vestige
Brachial remnants (cysts, fistula, skin tags) that are developmental anomalies

Q18.1 Preauricular sinus and cyst
Fistula of auricle, congenital
Cervicoaural fistula
Abnormal passage in neck originating from first branchial cleft

Q18.2 Other branchial cleft malformations
Branchial cleft malformation NOS
Cervical auricle
Otocephaly

Q18.3 Webbing of neck
Pterygium colli
Thick fold of skin on side of neck

Q18.4 Macrostomia
Results from failure of union of maxillary and mandibular processes, results in abnormally large mouth

Q18.5 Microstomia

Q18.6 Macrocheilia
Excessive size of lips
Hypertrophy of lip, congenital

Q18.7 Microcheilia
Abnormal smallness of lips

Q18.8 Other specified congenital malformations of face and neck
Medial cyst of face and neck
Medial fistula of face and neck
Medial sinus of face and neck

▪ Q18.9 Congenital malformation of face and neck, unspecified
Congenital anomaly NOS of face and neck

CONGENITAL MALFORMATIONS OF THE CIRCULATORY SYSTEM (Q20-Q28)

● Q20 Congenital malformations of cardiac chambers and connections

| Excludes1 | dextrocardia with situs inversus (Q89.3)
mirror-image atrial arrangement with situs inversus (Q89.3) |

Q20.0 Common arterial trunk 🗇
Persistent truncus arteriosus

| Excludes1 | aortic septal defect (Q21.4) |

Q20.1 Double outlet right ventricle 🗇
Taussig-Bing syndrome

Q20.2 Double outlet left ventricle

Q20.3 Discordant ventriculoarterial connection 🗇
Dextrotransposition of aorta
Transposition of great vessels (complete)

Q20.4 Double inlet ventricle 🗇
Common ventricle
Cor triloculare biatriatum
Single ventricle

Q20.5 Discordant atrioventricular connection 🗇
Corrected transposition
Levotransposition
Ventricular inversion

Q20.6 Isomerism of atrial appendages
Isomerism of atrial appendages with asplenia or polysplenia

Q20.8 Other congenital malformations of cardiac chambers and connections
Cor binoculare

▪ Q20.9 Congenital malformation of cardiac chambers and connections, unspecified 🗇

● Q21 Congenital malformations of cardiac septa

| Excludes1 | acquired cardiac septal defect (I51.0) |

Q21.0 Ventricular septal defect 🗇
Roger's disease

● Unacceptable First-Listed Diagnosis   ● Use Additional Character(s)   ▪ Unspecified   OGCR Official Guidelines for Coding and Reporting
🗇 Complication\Comorbidity   🗇 Major C\C   Excludes 1   Excludes 2   Includes   Use additional   Code first   Code also

Q21.1 Atrial septal defect 🦠
     Coronary sinus defect
     Patent or persistent foramen ovale
     Patent or persistent ostium secundum defect
       (type II)
     Patent or persistent sinus venosus defect

Q21.2 Atrioventricular septal defect 🦠
     Common atrioventricular canal
     Endocardial cushion defect
     Ostium primum atrial septal defect (type I)

Q21.3 Tetralogy of Fallot 🦠
     Ventricular septal defect with pulmonary stenosis
       or atresia, dextroposition of aorta and
       hypertrophy of right ventricle.

Q21.4 Aortopulmonary septal defect
     Aortic septal defect
     Aortopulmonary window

Q21.8 Other congenital malformations of cardiac septa
     Eisenmenger's defect
     Pentalogy of Fallot
     | Excludes1 | Eisenmenger's complex (I27.8)
                 Eisenmenger's syndrome (I27.8)

▨Q21.9 Congenital malformation of cardiac septum, unspecified
     Septal (heart) defect NOS

● **Q22 Congenital malformations of pulmonary and tricuspid valves**

Q22.0 Pulmonary valve atresia 🦠

Q22.1 Congenital pulmonary valve stenosis 🦠

Q22.2 Congenital pulmonary valve insufficiency 🦠
     Congenital pulmonary valve regurgitation

Q22.3 Other congenital malformations of pulmonary valve 🦠
     Congenital malformation of pulmonary valve
       NOS
     Supernumerary cusps of pulmonary valve

Q22.4 Congenital tricuspid stenosis 🦠
     Congenital tricuspid atresia

Q22.5 Ebstein's anomaly 🦠
     Malformation of tricuspid valve

Q22.6 Hypoplastic right heart syndrome 🦠

Q22.8 Other congenital malformations of tricuspid valve 🦠

▨Q22.9 Congenital malformation of tricuspid valve, unspecified 🦠

● **Q23 Congenital malformations of aortic and mitral valves**

Q23.0 Congenital stenosis of aortic valve 🦠
     Congenital aortic atresia
     Congenital aortic stenosis NOS
     | Excludes1 | congenital stenosis of aortic valve in
                 hypoplastic left heart syndrome
                 (Q23.4)
              congenital subaortic stenosis (Q24.4)
              supravalvular aortic stenosis
                 (congenital) (Q25.3)

Q23.1 Congenital insufficiency of aortic valve 🦠
     Bicuspid aortic valve
     Congenital aortic insufficiency

Q23.2 Congenital mitral stenosis 🦠
     Congenital mitral atresia

Q23.3 Congenital mitral insufficiency 🦠

Q23.4 Hypoplastic left heart syndrome 🦠

Q23.8 Other congenital malformations of aortic and mitral valves

▨Q23.9 Congenital malformation of aortic and mitral valves, unspecified

● **Q24 Other congenital malformations of heart**
     | Excludes1 | endocardial fibroelastosis (I42.4)

Q24.0 Dextrocardia 🦠
     Heart is located in right hemithorax
     | Excludes1 | dextrocardia with situs inversus
                 (Q89.3)
              isomerism of atrial appendages
                 (with asplenia or polysplenia)
                 (Q20.6)
              mirror-image atrial arrangement
                 with situs inversus (Q89.3)

Q24.1 Levocardia 🦠
     Normal position of heart but related structures on
       wrong side

Q24.2 Cor triatriatum 🦠
     Congenital heart defect; left atrium is subdivided

Q24.3 Pulmonary infundibular stenosis 🦠
     Subvalvular pulmonic stenosis

Q24.4 Congenital subaortic stenosis 🦠

Q24.5 Malformation of coronary vessels 🦠
     Congenital coronary (artery) aneurysm

Q24.6 Congenital heart block 🦠

Q24.8 Other specified congenital malformations of heart
     Congenital diverticulum of left ventricle
     Congenital malformation of myocardium
     Congenital malformation of pericardium
     Malposition of heart
     Uhl's disease

▨Q24.9 Congenital malformation of heart, unspecified
     Congenital anomaly of heart
     Congenital disease of heart

● **Q25 Congenital malformations of great arteries**

Q25.0 Patent ductus arteriosus 🦠
     Fetal blood vessel connecting left pulmonary artery
       directly to descending aorta
     Patent ductus Botallo
     Persistent ductus arteriosus

Q25.1 Coarctation of aorta 🦠
     Coarctation of aorta (preductal) (postductal)

Q25.2 Atresia of aorta 🦠

Q25.3 Supravalvular aortic stenosis 🦠
     | Excludes1 | congenital aortic stenosis NOS (Q23.0)
              congenital aortic valve stenosis (Q23.0)

Q25.4 Other congenital malformations of aorta 🦠
     Absence of aorta
     Aneurysm of sinus of Valsalva (ruptured)
     Aplasia of aorta
     Congenital aneurysm of aorta
     Congenital malformations of aorta
     Congenital dilatation of aorta
     Double aortic arch [vascular ring of aorta]
     Hypoplasia of aorta
     Persistent convolutions of aortic arch
     Persistent right aortic arch
     | Excludes1 | hypoplasia of aorta in hypoplastic
              left heart syndrome (Q23.4)

Q25.5 Atresia of pulmonary artery 🦠

Q25.6 Stenosis of pulmonary artery 🦠
     Supravalvular pulmonary stenosis

Q25.7 Other congenital malformations of pulmonary artery 🦠
     Aberrant pulmonary artery
     Agenesis of pulmonary artery
     Congenital aneurysm of pulmonary artery
     Congenital anomaly of pulmonary artery
     Congenital pulmonary arteriovenous aneurysm
     Hypoplasia of pulmonary artery

● Unacceptable First-Listed Diagnosis   ● Use Additional Character(s)   ▨ Unspecified   **OGCR** Official Guidelines for Coding and Reporting

🦠 Complication\Comorbidity   🦠 Major C\C | Excludes 1 | | Excludes 2 | Includes   Use additional   Code first   Code also

Q25.8 **Other congenital malformations of other great arteries** 🌑

▪Q25.9 **Congenital malformation of great arteries, unspecified** 🌑

● Q26 **Congenital malformations of great veins**

Q26.0 **Congenital stenosis of vena cava** 🌑
Congenital stenosis of vena cava (inferior)(superior)

Q26.1 **Persistent left superior vena cava** 🌑

Q26.2 **Total anomalous pulmonary venous connection** 🌑
Total anomalous pulmonary venous return [TAPVR], subdiaphragmatic
Total anomalous pulmonary venous return [TAPVR], supradiaphragmatic

Q26.3 **Partial anomalous pulmonary venous connection** 🌑
Partial anomalous pulmonary venous return

▪Q26.4 **Anomalous pulmonary venous connection, unspecified** 🌑

Q26.5 **Anomalous portal venous connection**

Q26.6 **Portal vein-hepatic artery fistula**

Q26.8 **Other congenital malformations of great veins** 🌑
Absence of vena cava (inferior) (superior)
Azygos continuation of inferior vena cava
Persistent left posterior cardinal vein
Scimitar syndrome

▪Q26.9 **Congenital malformation of great vein, unspecified** 🌑
Congenital anomaly of vena cava (inferior) (superior) NOS

● Q27 **Other congenital malformations of peripheral vascular system**

| Excludes2 | anomalies of cerebral and precerebral vessels (Q28.0-Q28.3)
anomalies of coronary vessels (Q24.5)
anomalies of pulmonary artery (Q25.5-Q25.7)
congenital retinal aneurysm (Q14.1)
hemangioma and lymphangioma (D18.-) |

Q27.0 **Congenital absence and hypoplasia of umbilical artery**
Single umbilical artery

Q27.1 **Congenital renal artery stenosis**

Q27.2 **Other congenital malformations of renal artery**
Congenital malformation of renal artery NOS
Multiple renal arteries

● Q27.3 **Arteriovenous malformation (peripheral)**
Arteriovenous aneurysm

| Excludes1 | acquired arteriovenous aneurysm (I77.0) |

| Excludes2 | arteriovenous malformation of cerebral vessels (Q28.2)
arteriovenous malformation of precerebral vessels (Q28.0) |

▪Q27.30 **Arteriovenous malformation, site unspecified** 🌑

Q27.31 **Arteriovenous malformation of vessel of upper limb**

Q27.32 **Arteriovenous malformation of vessel of lower limb**

Q27.33 **Arteriovenous malformation of digestive system vessel**

Q27.34 **Arteriovenous malformation of renal vessel**

Q27.39 **Arteriovenous malformation, other site**

Q27.4 **Congenital phlebectasia** 🌑

Q27.8 **Other specified congenital malformations of peripheral vascular system**
Absence of peripheral vascular system
Atresia of peripheral vascular system
Congenital aneurysm (peripheral)
Congenital stricture, artery
Congenital varix

| Excludes1 | arteriovenous malformation (Q27.3-) |

▪Q27.9 **Congenital malformation of peripheral vascular system, unspecified**
Anomaly of artery or vein NOS

● Q28 **Other congenital malformations of circulatory system**

| Excludes1 | congenital aneurysm NOS (Q27.8)
congenital coronary aneurysm (Q24.5)
ruptured cerebral arteriovenous malformation (I60.8)
ruptured malformation of precerebral vessels (I72.0) |

| Excludes2 | congenital peripheral aneurysm (Q27.8)
congenital pulmonary aneurysm (Q25.7)
congenital retinal aneurysm (Q14.1) |

Q28.0 **Arteriovenous malformation of precerebral vessels** 🌑
Congenital arteriovenous precerebral aneurysm (nonruptured)

Q28.1 **Other malformations of precerebral vessels** 🌑
Congenital malformation of precerebral vessels NOS
Congenital precerebral aneurysm (nonruptured)

Q28.2 **Arteriovenous malformation of cerebral vessels** 🌑
Arteriovenous malformation of brain NOS
Congenital arteriovenous cerebral aneurysm (nonruptured)

Q28.3 **Other malformations of cerebral vessels** 🌑
Congenital cerebral aneurysm (nonruptured)
Congenital malformation of cerebral vessels NOS

Q28.8 **Other specified congenital malformations of circulatory system** 🌑
Congenital aneurysm, specified site NEC
Spinal vessel anomaly

▪Q28.9 **Congenital malformation of circulatory system, unspecified** 🌑

CONGENITAL MALFORMATIONS OF THE RESPIRATORY SYSTEM (Q30-Q34)

● Q30 **Congenital malformations of nose**

| Excludes1 | congenital deviation of nasal septum (Q67.4) |

Q30.0 **Choanal atresia**
Atresia of nares (anterior) (posterior)
Congenital stenosis of nares (anterior) (posterior)

Q30.1 **Agenesis and underdevelopment of nose**
Congenital absent of nose

Q30.2 **Fissured, notched and cleft nose**

Q30.3 **Congenital perforated nasal septum**

Q30.8 **Other congenital malformations of nose**
Accessory nose
Congenital anomaly of nasal sinus wall

▪Q30.9 **Congenital malformation of nose, unspecified**

● Q31 **Congenital malformations of larynx**

| Excludes1 | congenital laryngeal stridor NOS (P28.89) |

Q31.0 **Web of larynx**
Glottic web of larynx
Subglottic web of larynx
Web of larynx NOS

Q31.1 **Congenital subglottic stenosis** 🌑

● Unacceptable First-Listed Diagnosis ● Use Additional Character(s) ▪ Unspecified **OGCR** Official Guidelines for Coding and Reporting
🌑 Complication\Comorbidity 🌑 Major C\C | Excludes 1 | Excludes 2 | Includes Use additional Code first Code also

Q31.2   **Laryngeal hypoplasia** 🩸

Q31.3   **Laryngocele** 🩸

Q31.5   **Congenital laryngomalacia** 🩸

Q31.8   **Other congenital malformations of larynx** 🩸
     Absence of larynx
     Agenesis of larynx
     Atresia of larynx
     Congenital cleft thyroid cartilage
     Congenital fissure of epiglottis
     Congenital stenosis of larynx NEC
     Posterior cleft of cricoid cartilage

◼Q31.9   **Congenital malformation of larynx, unspecified** 🩸

● **Q32**   **Congenital malformations of trachea and bronchus**
     Excludes1   congenital bronchiectasis (Q33.4)

Q32.0   **Congenital tracheomalacia** 🩸

Q32.1   **Other congenital malformations of trachea** 🩸
     Atresia of trachea
     Congenital anomaly of tracheal cartilage
     Congenital dilatation of trachea
     Congenital malformation of trachea
     Congenital stenosis of trachea
     Congenital tracheocele

Q32.2   **Congenital bronchomalacia** 🩸

Q32.3   **Congenital stenosis of bronchus** 🩸

Q32.4   **Other congenital malformations of bronchus** 🩸
     Absence of bronchus
     Agenesis of bronchus
     Atresia of bronchus
     Congenital diverticulum of bronchus
     Congenital malformation of bronchus NOS

● **Q33**   **Congenital malformations of lung**

Q33.0   **Congenital cystic lung** 🩸
     Congenital cystic lung disease
     Congenital honeycomb lung
     Congenital polycystic lung disease
     Excludes1   cystic fibrosis (E84.0)
                 cystic lung disease, acquired or
                     unspecified (J98.4)

Q33.1   **Accessory lobe of lung**
     Azygos lobe (fissured), lung

Q33.2   **Sequestration of lung**

Q33.3   **Agenesis of lung** 🩸
     Congenital absence of lung (lobe)

Q33.4   **Congenital bronchiectasis** 🩸

Q33.5   **Ectopic tissue in lung**

Q33.6   **Congenital hypoplasia and dysplasia of lung**
     Excludes1   pulmonary hypoplasia associated
                 with short gestation (P28.0)

Q33.8   **Other congenital malformations of lung**

◼Q33.9   **Congenital malformation of lung, unspecified**

● **Q34**   **Other congenital malformations of respiratory system**
     Excludes2   congenital central alveolar hypoventilation
                 syndrome (G47.35)

Q34.0   **Anomaly of pleura**

Q34.1   **Congenital cyst of mediastinum**

Q34.8   **Other specified congenital malformations of
respiratory system**
     Atresia of nasopharynx

◼Q34.9   **Congenital malformation of respiratory system,
unspecified**
     Congenital absence of respiratory system
     Congenital anomaly of respiratory system NOS

Figure 17-3   Cleft palate.

CLEFT LIP AND CLEFT PALATE (Q35-Q37)

    Use additional code to identify associated malformation
    of the nose (Q30.2)
     Excludes1   Robin's syndrome (Q87.0)

● **Q35**   **Cleft palate**
     Includes   fissure of palate
                palatoschisis
     Excludes1   cleft palate with cleft lip (Q37.-)

Q35.1   **Cleft hard palate**

Q35.3   **Cleft soft palate**

Q35.5   **Cleft hard palate with cleft soft palate**

Q35.7   **Cleft uvula**

◼Q35.9   **Cleft palate, unspecified**
     Cleft palate NOS

● **Q36**   **Cleft lip**
     Includes   cheiloschisis
                congenital fissure of lip
                harelip
                labium leporinum
     Excludes1   cleft lip with cleft palate (Q37.-)

Q36.0   **Cleft lip, bilateral**

Q36.1   **Cleft lip, median**

Q36.9   **Cleft lip, unilateral**
     Cleft lip NOS

● **Q37**   **Cleft palate with cleft lip**
     Includes   cheilopalatoschisis

Q37.0   **Cleft hard palate with bilateral cleft lip**

Q37.1   **Cleft hard palate with unilateral cleft lip**
     Cleft hard palate with cleft lip NOS

Q37.2   **Cleft soft palate with bilateral cleft lip**

Q37.3   **Cleft soft palate with unilateral cleft lip**
     Cleft soft palate with cleft lip NOS

Q37.4   **Cleft hard and soft palate with bilateral cleft lip**

Q37.5   **Cleft hard and soft palate with unilateral cleft lip**
     Cleft hard and soft palate with cleft lip NOS

◼Q37.8   **Unspecified cleft palate with bilateral cleft lip**

◼Q37.9   **Unspecified cleft palate with unilateral cleft lip**
     Cleft palate with cleft lip NOS

OTHER CONGENITAL MALFORMATIONS OF THE DIGESTIVE SYSTEM (Q38-Q45)

● **Q38**   **Other congenital malformations of tongue, mouth and
pharynx**
     Excludes1   dentofacial anomalies (M26.-)
                macrostomia (Q18.4)
                microstomia (Q18.5)

● Unacceptable First-Listed Diagnosis   ● Use Additional Character(s)   ◼ Unspecified   **OGCR** Official Guidelines for Coding and Reporting
🩸 Complication\Comorbidity   🩸 Major C\C   Excludes 1   Excludes 2   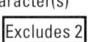 Includes   Use additional   Code first   Code also

1317

CHAPTER 17 (Q00-Q99)

Q38.0 **Congenital malformations of lips, not elsewhere classified**
Congenital fistula of lip
Congenital malformation of lip NOS
Van der Woude's syndrome
> **Excludes1**   cleft lip (Q36.-)
> cleft lip with cleft palate (Q37.-)
> macrocheilia (Q18.6)
> microcheilia (Q18.7)

Q38.1 **Ankyloglossia**
Restricted movement of tongue resulting in speech difficulty
Tongue tie

Q38.2 **Macroglossia**
Excessive size of tongue
Congenital hypertrophy of tongue

Q38.3 **Other congenital malformations of tongue**
Aglossia
Bifid tongue
Congenital adhesion of tongue
Congenital fissure of tongue
Congenital malformation of tongue NOS
Double tongue
Hypoglossia
Hypoplasia of tongue
Microglossia

Q38.4 **Congenital malformations of salivary glands and ducts**
Atresia of salivary glands and ducts
Congenital absence of salivary glands and ducts
Congenital accessory salivary glands and ducts
Congenital fistula of salivary gland

Q38.5 **Congenital malformations of palate, not elsewhere classified**
Congenital absence of uvula
Congenital malformation of palate NOS
Congenital high arched palate
> **Excludes1**   cleft palate (Q35.-)
> cleft palate with cleft lip (Q37.-)

Q38.6 **Other congenital malformations of mouth**
Congenital malformation of mouth NOS

Q38.7 **Congenital pharyngeal pouch**
Congenital diverticulum of pharynx
> **Excludes1**   pharyngeal pouch syndrome (D82.1)

Q38.8 **Other congenital malformations of pharynx**
Congenital malformation of pharynx NOS
Imperforate pharynx

● Q39 **Congenital malformations of esophagus**

Q39.0 **Atresia of esophagus without fistula** 🔖
Atresia of esophagus NOS

Q39.1 **Atresia of esophagus with tracheo-esophageal fistula** 🔖
Atresia of esophagus with broncho-esophageal fistula

Q39.2 **Congenital tracheo-esophageal fistula without atresia** 🔖
Congenital tracheo-esophageal fistula NOS

Q39.3 **Congenital stenosis and stricture of esophagus** 🔖

Q39.4 **Esophageal web** 🔖

Q39.5 **Congenital dilatation of esophagus** 🔖
Congenital cardiospasm

Q39.6 **Congenital diverticulum of esophagus** 🔖
Congenital esophageal pouch

Q39.8 **Other congenital malformations of esophagus** 🔖
Congenital absence of esophagus
Congenital displacement of esophagus
Congenital duplication of esophagus

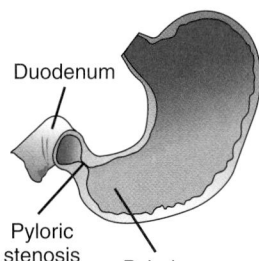

Figure 17-4   Pyloric stenosis.

Duodenum

Pyloric stenosis

Pyloric part of stomach

🔲 Q39.9 **Congenital malformation of esophagus, unspecified** 🔖

● Q40 **Other congenital malformations of upper alimentary tract**

Q40.0 **Congenital hypertrophic pyloric stenosis**
Congenital or infantile constriction
Congenital or infantile hypertrophy
Congenital or infantile spasm
Congenital or infantile stenosis
Congenital or infantile stricture

Q40.1 **Congenital hiatus hernia**
Congenital displacement of cardia through esophageal hiatus
> **Excludes1**   congenital diaphragmatic hernia (Q79.0)

Q40.2 **Other specified congenital malformations of stomach**
Congenital displacement of stomach
Congenital diverticulum of stomach
Congenital hourglass stomach
Congenital duplication of stomach
Megalogastria
Microgastria

🔲 Q40.3 **Congenital malformation of stomach, unspecified**

Q40.8 **Other specified congenital malformations of upper alimentary tract**

🔲 Q40.9 **Congenital malformation of upper alimentary tract, unspecified**
Congenital anomaly of upper alimentary tract
Congenital deformity of upper alimentary tract

● Q41 **Congenital absence, atresia and stenosis of small intestine**
> **Includes**   congenital obstruction, occlusion or stricture of small intestine or intestine NOS
> **Excludes1**   cystic fibrosis with intestinal manifestation (E84.11)
> meconium ileus NOS (without cystic fibrosis) (P76.0)

Q41.0 **Congenital absence, atresia and stenosis of duodenum** 🔖

Q41.1 **Congenital absence, atresia and stenosis of jejunum** 🔖
Apple peel syndrome
Imperforate jejunum

Q41.2 **Congenital absence, atresia and stenosis of ileum** 🔖

Q41.8 **Congenital absence, atresia and stenosis of other specified parts of small intestine** 🔖

🔲 Q41.9 **Congenital absence, atresia and stenosis of small intestine, part unspecified** 🔖
Congenital absence, atresia and stenosis of intestine NOS

● Q42 **Congenital absence, atresia and stenosis of large intestine**
> **Includes**   congenital obstruction, occlusion and stricture of large intestine

● Unacceptable First-Listed Diagnosis   ● Use Additional Character(s)   🔲 Unspecified   **OGCR** Official Guidelines for Coding and Reporting
🔖 Complication\Comorbidity   🔖 Major C\C   Excludes 1   Excludes 2   Includes   Use additional   Code first   Code also

CHAPTER 17 (Q00-Q99)

Q42.0 Congenital absence, atresia and stenosis of rectum with fistula 🦠

Q42.1 Congenital absence, atresia and stenosis of rectum without fistula 🦠
    Imperforate rectum

Q42.2 Congenital absence, atresia and stenosis of anus with fistula 🦠

Q42.3 Congenital absence, atresia and stenosis of anus without fistula 🦠
    Imperforate anus

Q42.8 Congenital absence, atresia and stenosis of other parts of large intestine 🦠

Q42.9 Congenital absence, atresia and stenosis of large intestine, part unspecified 🦠

● **Q43 Other congenital malformations of intestine**

Q43.0 Meckel's diverticulum (displaced) (hypertrophic)
    Congenital abnormality in which a pouch remains on the lower end of the small intestine
    Persistent omphalomesenteric duct
    Persistent vitelline duct

Q43.1 Hirschsprung's disease 🦠
    Developmental disorder of enteric nervous system characterized by absence of ganglion cells in distal colon resulting in functional obstruction.
    Aganglionosis
    Congenital (aganglionic) megacolon

Q43.2 Other congenital functional disorders of colon 🦠
    Congenital dilatation of colon

Q43.3 Congenital malformations of intestinal fixation 🦠
    Congenital omental, anomalous adhesions [bands]
    Congenital peritoneal adhesions [bands]
    Incomplete rotation of cecum and colon
    Insufficient rotation of cecum and colon
    Jackson's membrane
    Malrotation of colon
    Rotation failure of cecum and colon
    Universal mesentery

Q43.4 Duplication of intestine 🦠

Q43.5 Ectopic anus 🦠
    Anal opening in abnormal location

Q43.6 Congenital fistula of rectum and anus 🦠
    Excludes1   congenital fistula of anus with absence, atresia and stenosis (Q42.2)
                  congenital fistula of rectum with absence, atresia and stenosis (Q42.0)
                   congenital rectovaginal fistula (Q52.2)
                   congenital urethrorectal fistula (Q64.7)
                   pilonidal fistula or sinus (L05.-)

Q43.7 Persistent cloaca 🦠
    Malformation in which rectum, vagina, and urinary tract form one channel AKA congenital cloaca
    Cloaca NOS

Q43.8 Other specified congenital malformations of intestine 🦠
    Congenital blind loop syndrome
    Congenital diverticulitis, colon
    Congenital diverticulum, intestine
    Dolichocolon
    Megaloappendix
    Megaloduodenum
    Microcolon
    Transposition of appendix
    Transposition of colon
    Transposition of intestine

Q43.9 Congenital malformation of intestine, unspecified 🦠

● **Q44 Congenital malformations of gallbladder, bile ducts and liver**

Q44.0 Agenesis, aplasia and hypoplasia of gallbladder 🦠
    Congenital absence of gallbladder

Q44.1 Other congenital malformations of gallbladder 🦠
    Congenital malformation of gallbladder NOS
    Intrahepatic gallbladder

Q44.2 Atresia of bile ducts 🦠

Q44.3 Congenital stenosis and stricture of bile ducts 🦠

Q44.4 Choledochal cyst 🦠

Q44.5 Other congenital malformations of bile ducts 🦠
    Accessory hepatic duct
    Biliary duct duplication
    Congenital malformation of bile duct NOS
    Cystic duct duplication

Q44.6 Cystic disease of liver 🦠
    Fibrocystic disease of liver

Q44.7 Other congenital malformations of liver 🦠
    Accessory liver
    Alagille's syndrome
    Congenital absence of liver
    Congenital hepatomegaly
    Congenital malformation of liver NOS

● **Q45 Other congenital malformations of digestive system**
    Excludes2   congenital diaphragmatic hernia (Q79.0)
                  congenital hiatus hernia (Q40.1)

Q45.0 Agenesis, aplasia and hypoplasia of pancreas 🦠
    Congenital absence of pancreas

Q45.1 Annular pancreas 🦠

Q45.2 Congenital pancreatic cyst 🦠

Q45.3 Other congenital malformations of pancreas and pancreatic duct 🦠
    Accessory pancreas
    Congenital malformation of pancreas or pancreatic duct NOS
    Excludes1   congenital diabetes mellitus (E10.-)
                  cystic fibrosis (E84.0-E84.9)
                  fibrocystic disease of pancreas (E84.-)
                  neonatal diabetes mellitus (P70.2)

Q45.8 Other specified congenital malformations of digestive system
    Absence (complete) (partial) of alimentary tract NOS
    Duplication of digestive system
    Malposition, congenital of digestive system

Q45.9 Congenital malformation of digestive system, unspecified
    Congenital anomaly of digestive system
    Congenital deformity of digestive system

CONGENITAL MALFORMATIONS OF GENITAL ORGANS (Q50-Q56)

    Excludes1   androgen insensitivity syndrome (E34.5-)
                  syndromes associated with anomalies in the number and form of chromosomes (Q90-Q99)

● **Q50 Congenital malformations of ovaries, fallopian tubes and broad ligaments**

● **Q50.0 Congenital absence of ovary**
    Excludes1   Turner's syndrome (Q96.-)

    Q50.01 Congenital absence of ovary, unilateral

    Q50.02 Congenital absence of ovary, bilateral

Q50.1 Developmental ovarian cyst

Q50.2 Congenital torsion of ovary

● Unacceptable First-Listed Diagnosis   ● Use Additional Character(s)   ▧ Unspecified   **OGCR** Official Guidelines for Coding and Reporting

🦠 Complication\Comorbidity   🦠 Major C\C   Excludes 1   Excludes 2   Includes   Use additional   Code first   Code also   1319

CHAPTER 17 (Q00-Q99)

● **Q50.3   Other congenital malformations of ovary**

    Q50.31   Accessory ovary

    Q50.32   Ovarian streak
        Inadequate ovaries with absent follicular and hormonal function
        46, XX with streak gonads

    Q50.39   Other congenital malformation of ovary
        Congenital malformation of ovary NOS

Q50.4   Embryonic cyst of fallopian tube
    Fimbrial cyst

Q50.5   Embryonic cyst of broad ligament
    Epoophoron cyst
    Parovarian cyst

Q50.6   Other congenital malformations of fallopian tube and broad ligament
    Absence of fallopian tube and broad ligament
    Accessory fallopian tube and broad ligament
    Atresia of fallopian tube and broad ligament
    Congenital malformation of fallopian tube or broad ligament NOS

● **Q51   Congenital malformations of uterus and cervix**

Q51.0   Agenesis and aplasia of uterus
    Congenital absence of uterus

● **Q51.1   Doubling of uterus with doubling of cervix and vagina**

    Q51.10   Doubling of uterus with doubling of cervix and vagina without obstruction
        Doubling of uterus with doubling of cervix and vagina NOS

    Q51.11   Doubling of uterus with doubling of cervix and vagina with obstruction

Q51.2   Other doubling of uterus
    Doubling of uterus NOS

Q51.3   Bicornate uterus
    Birth defect in which uterus has two separate 'horns' that form top of uterus

Q51.4   Unicornate uterus
    Uterus with half being undeveloped

Q51.5   Agenesis and aplasia of cervix
    Congenital absence of cervix

Q51.6   Embryonic cyst of cervix

Q51.7   Congenital fistulae between uterus and digestive and urinary tracts

Q51.8   Other congenital malformations of uterus and cervix
    Hypoplasia of uterus and cervix

■ **Q51.9   Congenital malformation of uterus and cervix, unspecified**

● **Q52   Other congenital malformations of female genitalia**

Q52.0   Congenital absence of vagina

Q52.1   Doubling of vagina
    Septate vagina
    | Excludes1 | doubling of vagina with doubling of uterus and cervix (Q51.1-) |

Q52.2   Congenital rectovaginal fistula
    | Excludes1 | cloaca (Q43.7) |

Q52.3   Imperforate hymen
    Membrane (hymen) completely closes vaginal orifice

Q52.4   Other congenital malformations of vagina
    Canal of Nuck cyst, congenital
    Congenital malformation of vagina NOS
    Embryonic vaginal cyst
    Gartner's duct cyst

Q52.5   Fusion of labia

Q52.6   Congenital malformation of clitoris

Item 17–1   Testes form in the abdomen of the male and only descend into the scrotum during normal embryonic development. "Ectopic" testes are out of their normal place or "retained" (left behind) in the abdomen. Crypto (hidden) orchism (testicle) is a major risk factor for testicular cancer.

● **Q52.7   Other and unspecified congenital malformations of vulva**

   ■ **Q52.70   Unspecified congenital malformations of vulva**
        Congenital malformation of vulva NOS

    Q52.71   Congenital absence of vulva

    Q52.79   Other congenital malformations of vulva
        Congenital cyst of vulva

Q52.8   Other specified congenital malformations of female genitalia

■ **Q52.9   Congenital malformation of female genitalia, unspecified**

● **Q53   Undescended and ectopic testicle**

● **Q53.0   Ectopic testis**

   ■ **Q53.00   Ectopic testis, unspecified**

    Q53.01   Ectopic testis, unilateral

    Q53.02   Ectopic testes, bilateral

● **Q53.1   Undescended testicle, unilateral**

   ■ **Q53.10   Unspecified undescended testicle, unilateral**

    Q53.11   Abdominal testis, unilateral

    Q53.12   Ectopic perineal testis, unilateral

● **Q53.2   Undescended testicle, bilateral**

   ■ **Q53.20   Undescended testicle, unspecified, bilateral**

    Q53.21   Abdominal testis, bilateral

    Q53.22   Ectopic perineal testis, bilateral

■ **Q53.9   Undescended testicle, unspecified**
    Cryptorchism NOS

● **Q54   Hypospadias**
    Birth defect of male; urethra opens in abnormal location on shaft
    | Excludes1 | epispadias (Q64.0) |

Q54.0   Hypospadias, balanic
    Hypospadias, coronal
    Hypospadias, glandular

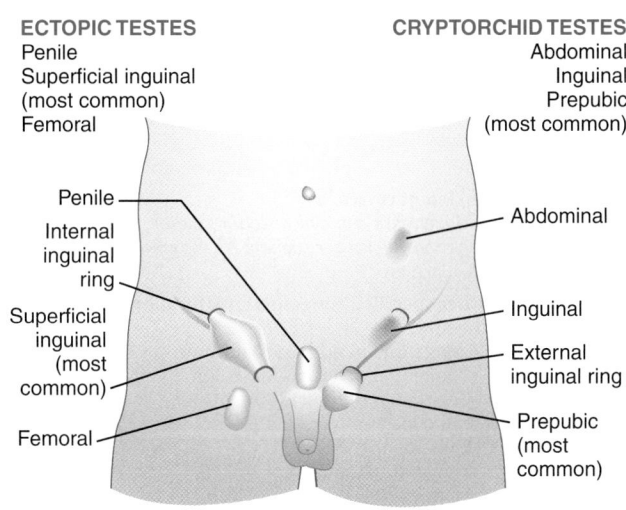

ECTOPIC TESTES
Penile
Superficial inguinal (most common)
Femoral

CRYPTORCHID TESTES
Abdominal
Inguinal
Prepubic (most common)

Penile
Internal inguinal ring
Superficial inguinal (most common)
Femoral

Abdominal
Inguinal
External inguinal ring
Prepubic (most common)

Figure 17-5   Undescended testes and the positions of the testes in various types of cryptorchidism or abnormal paths of descent.

● Unacceptable First-Listed Diagnosis   ● Use Additional Character(s)   ■ Unspecified   **OGCR** Official Guidelines for Coding and Reporting
🅒 Complication\Comorbidity   🅒 Major C\C | Excludes 1 | | Excludes 2 | Includes   Use additional   Code first   Code also

Q54.1 **Hypospadias, penile**

Q54.2 **Hypospadias, penoscrotal**

Q54.3 **Hypospadias, perineal**

Q54.4 **Congenital chordee**
Chordee without hypospadias

Q54.8 **Other hypospadias**
Hypospadias with intersex state

■ Q54.9 **Hypospadias, unspecified**

● Q55 **Other congenital malformations of male genital organs**

> | **Excludes1** | congenital hydrocele (P83.5) |
> |---|---|
> | | hypospadias (Q54.-) |

Q55.0 **Absence and aplasia of testis**
Monorchism

Q55.1 **Hypoplasia of testis and scrotum**
Fusion of testes

● Q55.2 **Other and unspecified congenital malformations of testis and scrotum**

■ Q55.20 **Unspecified congenital malformations of testis and scrotum**
Congenital malformation of testis or scrotum NOS

Q55.21 **Polyorchism**
Developmental anomaly characterized by presence of more than two testes

Q55.22 **Retractile testis**

Q55.23 **Scrotal transposition**

Q55.29 **Other congenital malformations of testis and scrotum**

Q55.3 **Atresia of vas deferens**
Code first any associated cystic fibrosis (E84.-)

Q55.4 **Other congenital malformations of vas deferens, epididymis, seminal vesicles and prostate**
Absence or aplasia of prostate
Absence or aplasia of spermatic cord
Congenital malformation of vas deferens, epididymis, seminal vesicles or prostate NOS

Q55.5 **Congenital absence and aplasia of penis**

● Q55.6 **Other congenital malformations of penis**

Q55.61 **Curvature of penis (lateral)**

Q55.62 **Hypoplasia of penis**
Underdevelopment penis
Micropenis

Q55.69 **Other congenital malformation of penis NOS**
Congenital malformation of penis NOS

Q55.7 **Congenital vasocutaneous fistula**
Abnormal opening between vas deferens and skin

Q55.8 **Other specified congenital malformations of male genital organs**

■ Q55.9 **Congenital malformation of male genital organ, unspecified**
Congenital anomaly of male genital organ
Congenital deformity of male genital organ

● Q56 **Indeterminate sex and pseudohermaphroditism**
Internal reproductive organs are opposite external physical characteristics.

> | **Excludes1** | 46,XX true hermaphrodite (Q99.1) |
> |---|---|
> | | androgen insensitivity syndrome (E34.5-) |
> | | chimera 46,XX/46,XY true hermaphrodite (Q99.0) |
> | | female pseudohermaphroditism with adrenocortical disorder (E25.-) |
> | | pseudohermaphroditism with specified chromosomal anomaly (Q96-Q99) |
> | | pure gonadal dysgenesis (Q99.1) |

Q56.0 **Hermaphroditism, not elsewhere classified**
Ovotestis

Q56.1 **Male pseudohermaphroditism, not elsewhere classified**
46, XY with streak gonads
Male pseudohermaphroditism NOS

Q56.2 **Female pseudohermaphroditism, not elsewhere classified**
Female pseudohermaphroditism NOS

■ Q56.3 **Pseudohermaphroditism, unspecified**

■ Q56.4 **Indeterminate sex, unspecified**
Ambiguous genitalia

CONGENITAL MALFORMATIONS OF THE URINARY SYSTEM (Q60-Q64)

● Q60 **Renal agenesis and other reduction defects of kidney**

> | **Includes** | congenital absence of kidney |
> |---|---|
> | | congenital atrophy of kidney |
> | | infantile atrophy of kidney |

Q60.0 **Renal agenesis, unilateral** 🦠

Q60.1 **Renal agenesis, bilateral** 🦠

■ Q60.2 **Renal agenesis, unspecified** 🦠

Q60.3 **Renal hypoplasia, unilateral** 🦠

Q60.4 **Renal hypoplasia, bilateral** 🦠

■ Q60.5 **Renal hypoplasia, unspecified** 🦠

Q60.6 **Potter's syndrome** 🦠

● Q61 **Cystic kidney disease**
Cysts that develop in failing kidney due to end-stage renal disease

> | **Excludes1** | acquired cyst of kidney (N28.1) |
> |---|---|
> | | Potter's syndrome (Q60.6) |

● Q61.0 **Congenital renal cyst**

■ Q61.00 **Congenital renal cyst, unspecified** 🦠
Cyst of kidney NOS (congenital)

Q61.01 **Congenital single renal cyst** 🦠

Q61.02 **Congenital multiple renal cysts** 🦠

● Q61.1 **Polycystic kidney, infantile type**
Polycystic kidney, autosomal recessive

Q61.11 **Cystic dilatation of collecting ducts** 🦠

Q61.19 **Other polycystic kidney, infantile type** 🦠

Q61.2 **Polycystic kidney, adult type** 🦠
Polycystic kidney, autosomal dominant

■ Q61.3 **Polycystic kidney, unspecified** 🦠

Q61.4 **Renal dysplasia** 🦠
Multicystic dysplastic kidney
Multicystic kidney (development)
Multicystic kidney disease
Multicystic renal dysplasia

> | **Excludes1** | polycystic kidney disease (Q61.11-Q61.3) |
> |---|---|

Q61.5 **Medullary cystic kidney** 🦠
Nephronopthisis
Sponge kidney NOS

Q61.8 **Other cystic kidney diseases** 🦠
Fibrocystic kidney
Fibrocystic renal degeneration or disease

■ Q61.9 **Cystic kidney disease, unspecified** 🦠
Meckel-Gruber syndrome

● Q62 **Congenital obstructive defects of renal pelvis and congenital malformations of ureter**

Q62.0 **Congenital hydronephrosis** 🦠

● Q62.1 **Congenital occlusion of ureter**
Atresia and stenosis of ureter

■ Q62.10 **Congenital occlusion of ureter, unspecified** 🦠

● Unacceptable First-Listed Diagnosis   ● Use Additional Character(s)   ■ Unspecified   **OGCR** Official Guidelines for Coding and Reporting

🦠 Complication\Comorbidity   🦠 Major C\C   Excludes 1   Excludes 2   ■ Includes   Use additional   Code first   Code also

1321

CHAPTER 17 (Q00-Q99)

Q62.11 Congenital occlusion of ureteropelvic junction 🦠

Q62.12 Congenital occlusion of ureterovesical orifice 🦠

Q62.2 Congenital megaureter 🦠
    Congenital dilatation of ureter

● Q62.3 Other obstructive defects of renal pelvis and ureter

Q62.31 Congenital ureterocele, orthotopic 🦠

Q62.32 Cecoureterocele 🦠
    Ectopic ureterocele

Q62.39 Other obstructive defects of renal pelvis and ureter 🦠
    Ureteropelvic junction obstruction NOS

Q62.4 Agenesis of ureter
    Congenital absence ureter

Q62.5 Duplication of ureter
    Accessory ureter
    Double ureter

● Q62.6 Malposition of ureter

■ Q62.60 Malposition of ureter, unspecified

Q62.61 Deviation of ureter

Q62.62 Displacement of ureter

Q62.63 Anomalous implantation of ureter
    Ectopia of ureter
    Ectopic ureter

Q62.69 Other malposition of ureter

Q62.7 Congenital vesico-uretero-renal reflux

Q62.8 Other congenital malformations of ureter
    Anomaly of ureter NOS

● Q63 Other congenital malformations of kidney
    Excludes1   congenital nephrotic syndrome (N04.-)

Q63.0 Accessory kidney

Q63.1 Lobulated, fused and horseshoe kidney

Q63.2 Ectopic kidney
    Congenital displaced kidney
    Malrotation of kidney

Q63.3 Hyperplastic and giant kidney
    Compensatory hypertrophy of kidney

Q63.8 Other specified congenital malformations of kidney
    Congenital renal calculi

■ Q63.9 Congenital malformation of kidney, unspecified

● Q64 Other congenital malformations of urinary system

Q64.0 Epispadias
    Urethral opening somewhere on dorsum of penis
    Excludes1   hypospadias (Q54.-)

● Q64.1 Exstrophy of urinary bladder
    Bladder is exposed, inside out, and protrudes through abdominal wall

■ Q64.10 Exstrophy of urinary bladder, unspecified 🦠
    Ectopia vesicae

Q64.11 Supravesical fissure of urinary bladder 🦠

Q64.12 Cloacal extrophy of urinary bladder 🦠

Q64.19 Other exstrophy of urinary bladder 🦠
    Extroversion of bladder

Q64.2 Congenital posterior urethral valves 🦠

● Q64.3 Other atresia and stenosis of urethra and bladder neck

Q64.31 Congenital bladder neck obstruction 🦠
    Congenital obstruction of vesicourethral orifice

Q64.32 Congenital stricture of urethra 🦠

Q64.33 Congenital stricture of urinary meatus 🦠

Q64.39 Other atresia and stenosis of urethra and bladder neck 🦠
    Atresia and stenosis of urethra and bladder neck NOS

Q64.4 Malformation of urachus
    Cyst of urachus
    Patent urachus
    Prolapse of urachus

Q64.5 Congenital absence of bladder and urethra

Q64.6 Congenital diverticulum of bladder

● Q64.7 Other and unspecified congenital malformations of bladder and urethra
    Excludes1   congenital prolapse of bladder (mucosa) (Q79.4)

■ Q64.70 Unspecified congenital malformation of bladder and urethra
    Malformation of bladder or urethra NOS

Q64.71 Congenital prolapse of urethra

Q64.72 Congenital prolapse of urinary meatus

Q64.73 Congenital urethrorectal fistula

Q64.74 Double urethra

Q64.75 Double urinary meatus

Q64.79 Other congenital malformations of bladder and urethra

Q64.8 Other specified congenital malformations of urinary system

■ Q64.9 Congenital malformation of urinary system, unspecified
    Congenital anomaly NOS of urinary system
    Congenital deformity NOS of urinary system

CONGENITAL MALFORMATIONS AND DEFORMATIONS OF THE MUSCULOSKELETAL SYSTEM (Q65-Q79)

● Q65 Congenital deformities of hip
    Excludes1   clicking hip (R29.4)

● Q65.0 Congenital dislocation of hip, unilateral

■ Q65.00 Congenital dislocation of hip, unilateral, unspecified side

Q65.01 Congenital dislocation of right hip

Q65.02 Congenital dislocation of left hip

Q65.1 Congenital dislocation of hip, bilateral

■ Q65.2 Congenital dislocation of hip, unspecified

● Q65.3 Congenital partial dislocation of hip, unilateral

■ Q65.30 Congenital partial dislocation of hip, unilateral, unspecified side

Q65.31 Congenital partial dislocation of right hip

Q65.32 Congenital partial dislocation of left hip

Q65.4 Congenital partial dislocation of hip, bilateral

■ Q65.5 Congenital partial dislocation of hip, unspecified

Q65.6 Congenital unstable hip
    Congenital dislocatable hip

Q65.8 Other congenital deformities of hip
    Anteversion of femoral neck
    Congenital acetabular dysplasia
    Congenital coxa valga
    Congenital coxa vara

■ Q65.9 Congenital deformity of hip, unspecified

Item 17–2 **Equinus foot** is a term referring to the hoof of a horse. The deformity is usually congenital or spastic. Talipes equinovarus is referred to as clubfoot. The foot tends to be smaller than normal, with the heel pointing downward and the forefoot turning inward. The heel cord (Achilles tendon) is tight, causing the heel to be drawn up toward the leg.

● Unacceptable First-Listed Diagnosis   ● Use Additional Character(s)   ■ Unspecified   **OGCR** Official Guidelines for Coding and Reporting
🦠 Complication\Comorbidity   🦠 Major C\C   Excludes 1   Excludes 2   Includes   Use additional   Code first   Code also

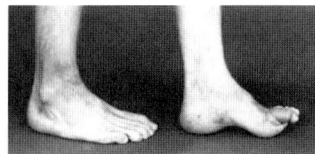

Figure 17-6 Supination and cavus deformity of forefoot. *(Courtesy Jay Cummings, MD.)* (From Canale: Campbell's Operative Orthopaedics, 10th ed. 2003, Mosby, Inc.)

● **Q66 Congenital deformities of feet**

> **Excludes1** reduction defects of feet (Q72.-)
> valgus deformities (acquired) (M21.0)
> varus deformities (acquired) (M21.1)

Q66.0 Congenital talipes equinovarus
Heel is turned inward from midline and foot is plantar flexed; AKA clubfoot

Q66.1 Congenital talipes calcaneovarus
Deformity of foot in which heel is turned toward midline of body and anterior of foot is elevated

Q66.2 Congenital metatarsus (primus) varus
Angulation of first metatarsal bone toward midline of body

Q66.3 Other congenital varus deformities of feet
Hallux varus, congenital

Q66.4 Congenital talipes calcaneovalgus

Q66.5 Congenital pes planus
Congenital flat foot
Congenital rigid flat foot
Congenital spastic (everted) flat foot

> **Excludes1** pes planus, acquired (M21.4)

Q66.6 Other congenital valgus deformities of feet
Inward angulation
Congenital metatarsus valgus

Q66.7 Congenital pes cavus

Q66.8 Other congenital deformities of feet
Congenital asymmetric talipes
Congenital clubfoot NOS
Congenital talipes NOS
Congenital tarsal coalition
Congenital vertical talus
Hammer toe, congenital

▨ **Q66.9 Congenital deformity of feet, unspecified**

● **Q67 Congenital musculoskeletal deformities of head, face, spine and chest**

> **Excludes1** congenital malformation syndromes
> classified to Q87.-
> Potter's syndrome (Q60.6)

Q67.0 Congenital facial asymmetry

Q67.1 Congenital compression facies

Q67.2 Dolichocephaly
Long head dimension

Q67.3 Plagiocephaly
Asymmetric shape of head resulting from irregular closure of cranial sutures

Q67.4 Other congenital deformities of skull, face and jaw
Congenital depressions in skull
Congenital hemifacial atrophy or hypertrophy
Deviation of nasal septum, congenital
Squashed or bent nose, congenital

> **Excludes1** dentofacial anomalies [including
> malocclusion] (M26-)
> syphilitic saddle nose (A50.5)

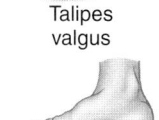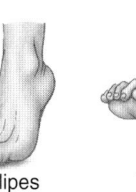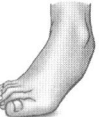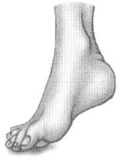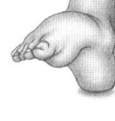

Talipes cavus Talipes equinus Talipes calcaneus

Talipes valgus Talipes equinovalgus Talipes calcaneovalgus

Talipes varus

Talipes cavovarus Talipes equinovarus Talipes calcaneocavus

Figure 17-7 Talipes. (From Dorland: Dorland's Illustrated Medical Dictionary, 31st ed. 2007, Saunders. p.1893)

Q67.5 Congenital deformity of spine ☙
Congenital postural scoliosis
Congenital scoliosis NOS

> **Excludes1** infantile idiopathic scoliosis (M41.0)
> scoliosis due to congenital bony
> malformation (Q76.3)

Q67.6 Pectus excavatum
Congenital funnel chest
Funnel-shaped chest depression

Q67.7 Pectus carinatum
Congenital pigeon chest

Q67.8 Other congenital deformities of chest ☙
Congenital deformity of chest wall NOS

● **Q68 Other congenital musculoskeletal deformities**

> **Excludes1** reduction defects of limb(s) (Q71-Q73)
> **Excludes2** congenital myotonic chondrodystrophy
> (G71.13)

Q68.0 Congenital deformity of sternocleidomastoid muscle
Congenital contracture of sternocleidomastoid (muscle)
Congenital (sternomastoid) torticollis
Sternomastoid tumor (congenital)

Q68.1 Congenital deformity of finger(s) and hand ☙
Congenital clubfinger
Spade-like hand (congenital)

Q68.2 Congenital deformity of knee
Congenital dislocation of knee
Congenital genu recurvatum
Hyperextension of knee resulting from hypermobility

Q68.3 Congenital bowing of femur

> **Excludes1** anteversion of femur (neck) (Q65.8)

Q68.4 Congenital bowing of tibia and fibula

▨ **Q68.5 Congenital bowing of long bones of leg, unspecified**

Q68.6 Discoid meniscus

● Unacceptable First-Listed Diagnosis   ● Use Additional Character(s)   ▨ Unspecified   **OGCR** Official Guidelines for Coding and Reporting
☙ Complication\Comorbidity ☙ Major C\C Excludes 1 Excludes 2   Includes   Use additional   Code first   Code also

CHAPTER 17 (Q00-Q99)

1323

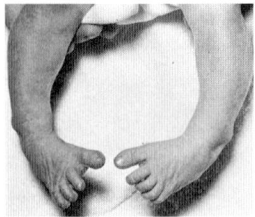

Figure 17-8 Mild to moderate inbowing of the lower leg. (From Jones KL: Smith's Recognizable Patterns of Human Malformation, 4th ed. Philadelphia, Saunders, 1988, p 671.)

Q68.8 **Other specified congenital musculoskeletal deformities**
Congenital deformity of clavicle
Congenital deformity of elbow
Congenital deformity of forearm
Congenital deformity of scapula
Congenital deformity of wrist
Congenital dislocation of elbow
Congenital dislocation of shoulder
Congenital dislocation of wrist

● Q69 **Polydactyly**
AKA hyperdactyly, consists of supernumerary fingers or toes

Q69.0 **Accessory finger(s)**

Q69.1 **Accessory thumb(s)**

Q69.2 **Accessory toe(s)**
Accessory hallux

■ Q69.9 **Polydactyly, unspecified**
Supernumerary digit(s) NOS

● Q70 **Syndactyly**
Webbing between distal phalanges of adjacent digits

● Q70.0 **Fused fingers**
Complex syndactyly of fingers with synostosis

■ Q70.00 **Fused fingers, unspecified fingers**

Q70.01 **Fused right fingers**

Q70.02 **Fused left fingers**

Q70.03 **Fused fingers, bilateral**

● Q70.1 **Webbed fingers**
Simple syndactyly of fingers without synostosis

■ Q70.10 **Webbed fingers, unspecified side**

Q70.11 **Webbed right fingers**

Q70.12 **Webbed left fingers**

Q70.13 **Webbed fingers, bilateral**

Q70.2 **Fused toes**
Complex syndactyly of toes with synostosis

Q70.3 **Webbed toes**
Simple syndactyly of toes without synostosis

Q70.4 **Polysyndactyly**
Extra and webbed digits

■ Q70.9 **Syndactyly, unspecified**
Symphalangy NOS

● Q71 **Reduction defects of upper limb**

● Q71.0 **Congenital complete absence of upper limb**

■ Q71.00 **Congenital complete absence of upper limb, unspecified side**

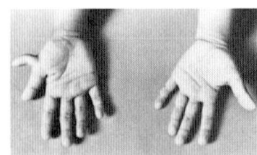

Figure 17-9 Polydactyly, congenital duplicated thumb. (From DeLee and Drez's Orthopaedic Sports Medicine, 2nd ed. 2003, Saunders, An Imprint of Elsevier.)

Q71.01 **Congenital complete absence of right upper limb**

Q71.02 **Congenital complete absence of left upper limb**

Q71.03 **Congenital complete absence of upper limb, bilateral**

● Q71.1 **Congenital absence of upper arm and forearm with hand present**

■ Q71.10 **Congenital absence of upper arm and forearm with hand present, unspecified side**

Q71.11 **Congenital absence of right upper arm and forearm with hand present**

Q71.12 **Congenital absence of left upper arm and forearm with hand present**

Q71.13 **Congenital absence of upper arm and forearm with hand present, bilateral**

● Q71.2 **Congenital absence of both forearm and hand**

■ Q71.20 **Congenital absence of both forearm and hand, unspecified side**

Q71.21 **Congenital absence of both right forearm and hand**

Q71.22 **Congenital absence of both left forearm and hand**

Q71.23 **Congenital absence of both forearm and hand, bilateral**

● Q71.3 **Congenital absence of hand and finger**

■ Q71.30 **Congenital absence of hand and finger, unspecified side**

Q71.31 **Congenital absence of right hand and finger**

Q71.32 **Congenital absence of left hand and finger**

Q71.33 **Congenital absence of hand and finger, bilateral**

● Q71.4 **Longitudinal reduction defect of radius**
Clubhand (congenital)
Radial clubhand

■ Q71.40 **Longitudinal reduction defect of radius, unspecified side**

Q71.41 **Longitudinal reduction defect of right radius**

Q71.42 **Longitudinal reduction defect of left radius**

Q71.43 **Longitudinal reduction defect of radius, bilateral**

● Q71.5 **Longitudinal reduction defect of ulna**

■ Q71.50 **Longitudinal reduction defect of ulna, unspecified side**

Q71.51 **Longitudinal reduction defect of right ulna**

Q71.52 **Longitudinal reduction defect of left ulna**

Q71.53 **Longitudinal reduction defect of ulna, bilateral**

● Q71.6 **Lobster-claw hand**

■ Q71.60 **Lobster-claw hand, unspecified side**

Q71.61 **Lobster-claw right hand**

Q71.62 **Lobster-claw left hand**

Q71.63 **Lobster-claw hand, bilateral**

● Q71.8 **Other reduction defects of upper limb**
Congenital shortening of upper limb

■ Q71.80 **Other reduction defects of upper limb, unspecified side**

Q71.81 **Other reduction defects of right upper limb**

● Unacceptable First-Listed Diagnosis   ● Use Additional Character(s)   ■ Unspecified   **OGCR** Official Guidelines for Coding and Reporting
🅒 Complication\Comorbidity   🅒 Major C\C   [Excludes 1]   [Excludes 2]   Includes   Use additional   Code first   Code also

Q71.82 Other reduction defects of left upper limb

Q71.83 Other reduction defects of upper limb, bilateral

● Q71.9 Reduction defect of upper limb, unspecified

 ▢ Q71.90 Reduction defect of upper limb, unspecified, side unspecified

 ▢ Q71.91 Reduction defect of right upper limb, unspecified

 ▢ Q71.92 Reduction defect of left upper limb, unspecified

 ▢ Q71.93 Reduction defect of upper limb, unspecified, bilateral

● Q72 Reduction defects of lower limb

 ● Q72.0 Congenital complete absence of lower limb

  ▢ Q72.00 Congenital complete absence of lower limb, unspecified side

  Q72.01 Congenital complete absence of right lower limb

  Q72.02 Congenital complete absence of left lower limb

  Q72.03 Congenital complete absence of lower limb, bilateral

 ● Q72.1 Congenital absence of thigh and lower leg with foot present

  ▢ Q72.10 Congenital absence of thigh and lower leg with foot present, unspecified side

  Q72.11 Congenital absence of right thigh and lower leg with foot present

  Q72.12 Congenital absence of left thigh and lower leg with foot present

  Q72.13 Congenital absence of thigh and lower leg with foot present, bilateral

 ● Q72.2 Congenital absence of both lower leg and foot

  ▢ Q72.20 Congenital absence of both lower leg and foot, unspecified side

  Q72.21 Congenital absence of both right lower leg and foot

  Q72.22 Congenital absence of both left lower leg and foot

  Q72.23 Congenital absence of both lower leg and foot, bilateral

 ● Q72.3 Congenital absence of foot and toe(s)

  ▢ Q72.30 Congenital absence of foot and toe(s), unspecified side

  Q72.31 Congenital absence of right foot and toe(s)

  Q72.32 Congenital absence of left foot and toe(s)

  Q72.33 Congenital absence of foot and toe(s), bilateral

 ● Q72.4 Longitudinal reduction defect of femur
   Proximal femoral focal deficiency

  ▢ Q72.40 Longitudinal reduction defect of femur, unspecified side

  Q72.41 Longitudinal reduction defect of right femur

  Q72.42 Longitudinal reduction defect of left femur

  Q72.43 Longitudinal reduction defect of femur, bilateral

 ● Q72.5 Longitudinal reduction defect of tibia

  ▢ Q72.50 Longitudinal reduction defect of tibia, unspecified side

  Q72.51 Longitudinal reduction defect of right tibia

  Q72.52 Longitudinal reduction defect of left tibia

  Q72.53 Longitudinal reduction defect of tibia, bilateral

 ● Q72.6 Longitudinal reduction defect of fibula

  ▢ Q72.60 Longitudinal reduction defect of fibula, unspecified side

  Q72.61 Longitudinal reduction defect of right fibula

  Q72.62 Longitudinal reduction defect of left fibula

  Q72.63 Longitudinal reduction defect of fibula, bilateral

 ● Q72.7 Split foot

  ▢ Q72.70 Split foot, unspecified side

  Q72.71 Right split foot

  Q72.72 Left split foot

  Q72.73 Split foot, bilateral

 ● Q72.8 Other reduction defects of lower limb
   Congenital shortening of lower limb(s)

  ▢ Q72.80 Other reduction defects of lower limb, unspecified side

  Q72.81 Other reduction defects of right lower limb

  Q72.82 Other reduction defects of left lower limb

  Q72.83 Other reduction defects of lower limb, bilateral

 ● Q72.9 Reduction defect of lower limb, unspecified

  ▢ Q72.90 Reduction defect of lower limb, unspecified, unspecified side

  ▢ Q72.91 Reduction defect of right lower limb, unspecified

  ▢ Q72.92 Reduction defect of left lower limb, unspecified

  ▢ Q72.93 Reduction defect of lower limb, unspecified, bilateral

● Q73 Reduction defects of unspecified limb

 ▢ Q73.0 Congenital absence of unspecified limb(s)
   Amelia NOS

 ▢ Q73.1 Phocomelia, unspecified limb(s)
   Phocomelia NOS
    Absence/shortening of long bones primarily as a result of thalidomide

 ▢ Q73.8 Other reduction defects of unspecified limb(s)
   Longitudinal reduction deformity of unspecified limb(s)
   Ectromelia of limb NOS
    Gross hypoplasia or aplasia of one or more long bones of limb(s)
   Hemimelia of limb NOS
    Absence of one-half of long bone
   Reduction defect of limb NOS

● Q74 Other congenital malformations of limb(s)

  | **Excludes1** | polydactyly (Q69.-) |
      reduction defect of limb (Q71-Q73)
      syndactyly (Q70.-)

 Q74.0 Other congenital malformations of upper limb(s), including shoulder girdle
   Accessory carpal bones
   Cleidocranial dysostosis
   Congenital pseudarthrosis of clavicle
   Macrodactylia (fingers)
   Madelung's deformity
   Radioulnar synostosis
   Sprengel's deformity
   Triphalangeal thumb

● Unacceptable First-Listed Diagnosis ● Use Additional Character(s) ▢ Unspecified **OGCR** Official Guidelines for Coding and Reporting

🔖 Complication\Comorbidity 🔖 Major C\C | Excludes 1 | | Excludes 2 | Includes Use additional Code first Code also 1325

CHAPTER 17 (Q00–Q99)

Item 17–3 **Anencephalus** is a congenital deformity of the cranial vault. **Craniosynostosis,** also known as craniostenosis and stenocephaly, signifies any form of congenital deformity of the skull that results from the premature closing of the sutures of the skull. **Iniencephaly** is a deformity in which the head and neck are flexed backward to a great extent and the head is very large in comparison to the shortened body.

Q74.1 **Congenital malformation of knee**
Congenital absence of patella
Congenital dislocation of patella
Congenital genu valgum
Congenital genu varum
Rudimentary patella
> **Excludes1** congenital dislocation of knee (Q68.2)
> congenital genu recurvatum (Q68.2)
> nail patella syndrome (Q87.2)

Q74.2 **Other congenital malformations of lower limb(s), including pelvic girdle**
Congenital fusion of sacroiliac joint
Congenital malformation of ankle joint
Congenital malformation of sacroiliac joint
> **Excludes1** anteversion of femur (neck) (Q65.8)

Q74.3 **Arthrogryposis multiplex congenita** 🗝

Q74.8 **Other specified congenital malformations of limb(s)**

■Q74.9 **Unspecified congenital malformation of limb(s)**
Congenital anomaly of limb(s) NOS

● Q75 **Other congenital malformations of skull and face bones**
> **Excludes1** congenital malformation of face NOS (Q18.-)
> congenital malformation syndromes classified to Q87.-
> dentofacial anomalies [including malocclusion] (M26.-)
> musculoskeletal deformities of head and face (Q67.0-Q67.4)
> skull defects associated with congenital anomalies of brain such as:
> anencephaly (Q00.0)
> encephalocele (Q01.-)
> hydrocephalus (Q03.-)
> microcephaly (Q02)

Q75.0 **Craniosynostosis**
Premature closure of sutures of skull
Acrocephaly
Imperfect fusion of skull
Oxycephaly
Trigonocephaly

Q75.1 **Craniofacial dysostosis**
Congential deformity of head
Crouzon's disease

Q75.2 **Hypertelorism**

Q75.3 **Macrocephaly**
Unusually large size of head; AKA megalocephaly

Q75.4 **Mandibulofacial dysostosis**
Franceschetti syndrome
Treacher Collins syndrome

Q75.5 **Oculomandibular dysostosis**
Ossification of occular and mandibular bones

Q75.8 **Other specified congenital malformations of skull and face bones**
Absence of skull bone, congenital
Congenital deformity of forehead
Platybasia

■Q75.9 **Congenital malformation of skull and face bones, unspecified**
Congenital anomaly of face bones NOS
Congenital anomaly of skull NOS

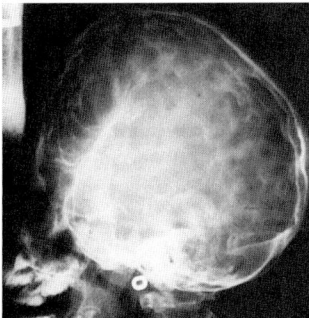

Figure 17-10 Generalized craniosynostosis in a 4-year-old girl without symptoms or signs of increased intracranial pressure. (From Bell WE, McCormick WF: Increased Intracranial Pressure in Children, 2nd ed. Philadelphia, WB Saunders, 1978, p116.)

Item 17–4 **Spina bifida** is a midline spinal defect in which one or more vertebrae fail to fuse, leaving an opening in the vertebral canal. When the defect is not visible, it is called spina bifida occulta, and when it is visible, it is called spina bifida cystica.

● Q76 **Congenital malformations of spine and bony thorax**
> **Excludes1** congenital musculoskeletal deformities of spine and chest (Q67.5-Q67.8)

Q76.0 **Spina bifida occulta**
> **Excludes1** meningocele (spinal) (Q05.-)
> spina bifida (aperta) (cystica) (Q05.-)

Q76.1 **Klippel-Feil syndrome**
Cervical fusion syndrome

Q76.2 **Congenital spondylolisthesis**
Congenital spondylolysis
> **Excludes1** spondylolisthesis (acquired) (M43.1-)
> spondylolysis (acquired) (M43.0-)

Q76.3 **Congenital scoliosis due to congenital bony malformation** 🗝
Hemivertebra fusion or failure of segmentation with scoliosis

● Q76.4 **Other congenital malformations of spine, not associated with scoliosis**
● Q76.41 **Congenital kyphosis**
Abnormal increase in convexity curvature of thoracic spinal column; AKA humpback
Q76.411 **Congenital kyphosis, occipito-atlanto-axial region** 🗝
Q76.412 **Congenital kyphosis, cervical region** 🗝
Q76.413 **Congenital kyphosis, cervicothoracic region** 🗝
Q76.414 **Congenital kyphosis, thoracic region** 🗝
Q76.415 **Congenital kyphosis, thoracolumbar region** 🗝
■Q76.419 **Congenital kyphosis, unspecified region** 🗝
● Q76.42 **Congenital lordosis**
An abnormal increase in curvature of lumbar spine (sway back)
Q76.425 **Congenital lordosis, thoracolumbar region** 🗝
Q76.426 **Congenital lordosis, lumbar region** 🗝
Q76.427 **Congenital lordosis, lumbosacral region** 🗝
Q76.428 **Congenital lordosis, sacral and sacrococcygeal region** 🗝
■Q76.429 **Congenital lordosis, unspecified region** 🗝

● Unacceptable First-Listed Diagnosis   ● Use Additional Character(s)   ■ Unspecified   **OGCR** Official Guidelines for Coding and Reporting
🗝 Complication\Comorbidity   🗝 Major C\C   Excludes 1   Excludes 2   Includes   Use additional   Code first   Code also

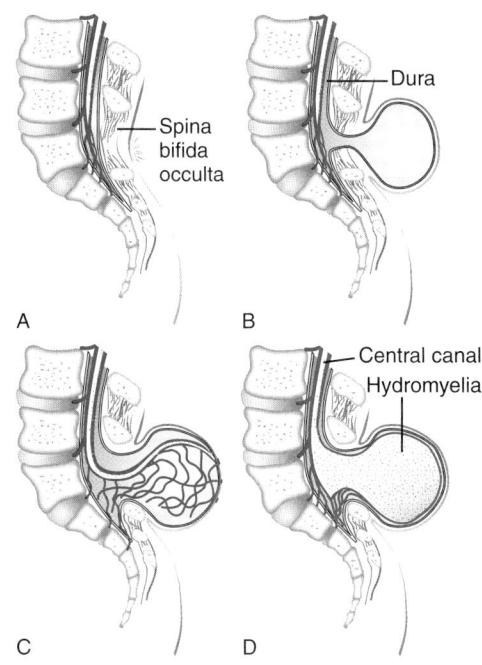

Figure 17-11 **A.** Spina bifida occulta. **B.** Meningocele.
C. Myelomeningocele. **D.** Myelocystocele (syringomyelocele)
or hydromyelia.

**Q76.49 Other congenital malformations of spine,
not associated with scoliosis**
Congenital absence of vertebra NOS
Congenital fusion of spine NOS
Congenital malformation of lumbosacral
(joint) (region) NOS
Congenital malformation of spine NOS
Hemivertebra NOS
Malformation of spine NOS
Platyspondylisis NOS
Supernumerary vertebra NOS

Q76.5 Cervical rib
Supernumerary rib in cervical region

Q76.6 Other congenital malformations of ribs 🔖
Accessory rib
Congenital absence of rib
Congenital fusion of ribs
Congenital malformation of ribs NOS
> **Excludes1**   short rib syndrome (Q77.2)

Q76.7 Congenital malformation of sternum 🔖
Congenital absence of sternum
Sternum bifidum

Q76.8 Other congenital malformations of bony thorax 🔖

🔲**Q76.9 Congenital malformation of bony thorax,
unspecified** 🔖

● **Q77 Osteochondrodysplasia with defects of growth of tubular
bones and spine**
> **Excludes1**   mucopolysaccharidosis (E76.0-E76.3)
> **Excludes2**   congenital myotonic chondrodystrophy
> (G71.13)

Q77.0 Achondrogenesis
Hypochondrogenesis

Q77.1 Thanatophoric short stature

Q77.2 Short rib syndrome
Asphyxiating thoracic dysplasia [Jeune]

Q77.3 Chondrodysplasia punctata
Benign cartilaginous neoplasms
> **Excludes1**   rhizomelic chondrodysplasia
> punctata (E71.43)

Q77.4 Achondroplasia
*Disturbance of epiphyseal chondroblastic growth and
maturation, results in dwarfism*
Hypochondroplasia
Osteosclerosis congenita

Q77.5 Diastrophic dysplasia

Q77.6 Chondroectodermal dysplasia
*Defective development of skin, hair, teeth, with
polydactyly and defect of cardiac septum*
Ellis-van Creveld syndrome

Q77.7 Spondyloepiphyseal dysplasia

**Q77.8 Other osteochondrodysplasia with defects of
growth of tubular bones and spine**

🔲**Q77.9 Osteochondrodysplasia with defects of growth of
tubular bones and spine, unspecified**

● **Q78 Other osteochondrodysplasias**
*Disorder of development of bone and cartilage; common cause
of dwarfism*
> **Excludes2**   congenital myotonic chondrodystrophy
> (G71.13)

Q78.0 Osteogenesis imperfecta 🔖
Fragilitas ossium
Osteopsathyrosis

Q78.1 Polyostotic fibrous dysplasia
Albright(-McCune)(-Sternberg) syndrome

Q78.2 Osteopetrosis 🔖
*Abnormally dense bone; AKA marble bones disease,
ivory bones*
Albers-Schönberg syndrome
Osteosclerosis NOS

Q78.3 Progressive diaphyseal dysplasia
Camurati-Engelmann syndrome

Q78.4 Enchondromatosis
*Thinning of overlying cortex of bone and distorted
length*
Maffucci's syndrome
Ollier's disease

Q78.5 Metaphyseal dysplasia
*Disturbance in enchondral bone growth, causing
ends of shafts to remain larger than normal in
circumference*
Pyle's syndrome

Q78.6 Multiple congenital exostoses
Diaphyseal aclasis

Q78.8 Other specified osteochondrodysplasias
Osteopoikilosis

🔲**Q78.9 Osteochondrodysplasia, unspecified**
Chondrodystrophy NOS
*AKA skeletal dysplasia (dwarfism) caused by genetic
mutations affecting hyaline cartilage capping
long bones and vertebrae*
Osteodystrophy NOS

● **Q79 Congenital malformations of musculoskeletal system, not
elsewhere classified**
> **Excludes2**   congenital (sternomastoid) torticollis (Q68.0)

Q79.0 Congenital diaphragmatic hernia 🔖
> **Excludes1**   congenital hiatus hernia (Q40.1)

Q79.1 Other congenital malformations of diaphragm 🔖
Absence of diaphragm
Congenital malformation of diaphragm NOS
Eventration of diaphragm

CHAPTER 17 (Q00-Q99)

● Unacceptable First-Listed Diagnosis	● Use Additional Character(s)	🔲 Unspecified	**OGCR** Official Guidelines for Coding and Reporting
🔖 Complication\Comorbidity 🔖 Major C\C	Excludes 1 Excludes 2	Includes Use additional	Code first Code also

Q79.2 **Exomphalos** 🦴
> *Abdominal hernia in which part of intestine protrudes at umbilicus; AKA exomphalos and exumbilication*
Omphalocele
> **Excludes1**   umbilical hernia (K42.-)

Q79.3 **Gastroschisis** 🦴
> *Congenital fissure of anterior abdominal wall often with protrusion of small/large intestine*

Q79.4 **Prune belly syndrome** 🦴
> Congenital prolapse of bladder mucosa
> Eagle-Barrett syndrome

● Q79.5 **Other congenital malformations of abdominal wall** 🦴
> **Excludes1**   umbilical hernia (K42.-)

     Q79.51 **Congenital hernia of bladder**

     Q79.59 **Other congenital malformations of abdominal wall**

Q79.6 **Ehlers-Danlos syndrome** 🦴
> *Group of inherited disorders of connective tissue; AKA cutis hyperelastica*

Q79.8 **Other congenital malformations of musculoskeletal system**
> Absence of muscle
> Absence of tendon
> Accessory muscle
> Amyotrophia congenita
> Congenital constricting bands
> Congenital shortening of tendon
> Poland's syndrome

■ Q79.9 **Congenital malformation of musculoskeletal system, unspecified**
> Congenital anomaly of musculoskeletal system NOS
> Congenital deformity of musculoskeletal system NOS

OTHER CONGENITAL MALFORMATIONS (Q80-Q89)

● Q80 **Congenital ichthyosis**
> *Characterized by increased keratinization, resulting in noninflammatory scaling of skin*
> **Excludes1**   Refsum's disease (G60.1)

Q80.0 **Ichthyosis vulgaris**

Q80.1 **X-linked ichthyosis**

Q80.2 **Lamellar ichthyosis**
> Collodion baby

Q80.3 **Congenital bullous ichthyosiform erythroderma**

Q80.4 **Harlequin fetus**

Q80.8 **Other congenital ichthyosis**

■ Q80.9 **Congenital ichthyosis, unspecified**

● Q81 **Epidermolysis bullosa**
> *Loosening of epidermis*

Q81.0 **Epidermolysis bullosa simplex**
> **Excludes1**   Cockayne's syndrome (Q87.1)

Q81.1 **Epidermolysis bullosa letalis**
> Herlitz' syndrome

Q81.2 **Epidermolysis bullosa dystrophica**

Q81.8 **Other epidermolysis bullosa**

■ Q81.9 **Epidermolysis bullosa, unspecified**

● Q82 **Other congenital malformations of skin**
> **Excludes1**   acrodermatitis enteropathica (E83.2)
> congenital erythropoietic porphyria (E80.0)
> pilonidal cyst or sinus (L05.-)
> Sturge-Weber (-Dimitri) syndrome (Q85.8)

Q82.0 **Hereditary lymphedema**
> *Characterized by swelling of subcutaneous tissue caused by obstruction of lymphatic vessels and resulting edema of lymph fluid*

Q82.1 **Xeroderma pigmentosum**
> *Dry, rough, discolored state of skin, and formation of scaly desquamation*

Q82.2 **Mastocytosis**
> *Characterized by infiltrates of mast cells in tissues/ organs*
> Urticaria pigmentosa
> **Excludes1**   malignant mastocytosis (C96.2)

Q82.3 **Incontinentia pigmenti**
> *Characterized by hyperpigmented cutaneous*

Q82.4 **Ectodermal dysplasia (anhidrotic)**
> *Absence/deficiency of tissues/structures, including teeth, hair, nails, and certain glands*
> **Excludes1**   Ellis-van Creveld syndrome (Q77.6)

Q82.5 **Congenital non-neoplastic nevus**
> Birthmark NOS
> Flammeus Nevus
> Portwine Nevus
> Sanguineous Nevus
> Strawberry Nevus
> Vascular Nevus NOS
> Verrucous Nevus
> **Excludes2**   café au lait spots (L81.3)
> lentigo (L81.4)
> nevus NOS (D22.-)
> araneus nevus (I78.1)
> melanocytic nevus (D22.-)
> pigmented nevus (D22.-)
> spider nevus (I78.1)
> stellar nevus (I78.1)

Q82.8 **Other specified congenital malformations of skin**
> Abnormal palmar creases
> Accessory skin tags
> Benign familial pemphigus [Hailey-Hailey]
> Congenital poikiloderma
> Cutis laxa (hyperelastica)
> Dermatoglyphic anomalies
> Inherited keratosis palmaris et plantaris
> Keratosis follicularis [Darier-White]
> **Excludes1**   Ehlers-Danlos syndrome (Q79.6)

■ Q82.9 **Congenital malformation of skin, unspecified**

● Q83 **Congenital malformations of breast**
> **Excludes2**   absence of pectoral muscle (Q79.8)
> hypoplasia of breast (N64.82)
> micromastia (N64.82)

Q83.0 **Congenital absence of breast with absent nipple**

Q83.1 **Accessory breast**
> Supernumerary breast

Q83.2 **Absent nipple**

Q83.3 **Accessory nipple**
> Supernumerary nipple

Q83.8 **Other congenital malformations of breast**

■ Q83.9 **Congenital malformation of breast, unspecified**

● Q84 **Other congenital malformations of integument**

Q84.0 **Congenital alopecia**
> Congenital atrichosis

Q84.1 **Congenital morphological disturbances of hair, not elsewhere classified**
> Beaded hair
> Monilethrix
> Pili annulati
> **Excludes1**   Menkes' kinky hair syndrome (E83.0)

● Unacceptable First-Listed Diagnosis   ● Use Additional Character(s)   ■ Unspecified   **OGCR** Official Guidelines for Coding and Reporting
🦴 Complication\Comorbidity   🦴 Major C\C   Excludes 1   Excludes 2   Includes   Use additional   Code first   Code also

Q84.2 Other congenital malformations of hair
   Congenital hypertrichosis
   Congenital malformation of hair NOS
   Persistent lanugo

Q84.3 Anonychia
   Absence of nail
   | Excludes1 | nail patella syndrome (Q87.2)

Q84.4 Congenital leukonychia
   *Opaque, whitish discoloration of nails; AKA
      leukopathia unguium*

Q84.5 Enlarged and hypertrophic nails
   Congenital onychauxis
   Pachyonychia

Q84.6 Other congenital malformations of nails
   Congenital clubnail
   Congenital koilonychia
   Congenital malformation of nail NOS

**Q84.8 Other specified congenital malformations of
   integument**
   Aplasia cutis congenita

Q84.9 Congenital malformation of integument, unspecified
   Congenital anomaly of integument NOS
   Congenital deformity of integument NOS

● **Q85 Phakomatoses, not elsewhere classified**
   | Excludes1 | ataxia telangiectasia [Louis-Bar] (G11.3)
                  familial dysautonomia [Riley-Day] (G90.1)

Q85.0 Neurofibromatosis (nonmalignant)
   *Developmental changes in nervous system and other
      structures, with formation of neurofibromas*
   Von Recklinghausen's disease

Q85.1 Tuberous sclerosis 🦠
   Bourneville's disease
   Epiloia

Q85.8 Other phakomatoses, not elsewhere classified 🦠
   Peutz-Jeghers Syndrome
   Sturge-Weber(-Dimitri) syndrome
   von Hippel-Lindau syndrome
   | Excludes1 | Meckel-Gruber syndrome (Q61.9)

Q85.9 Phakomatosis, unspecified 🦠
   Hamartosis NOS

● **Q86 Congenital malformation syndromes due to known
   exogenous causes, not elsewhere classified**
   | Excludes2 | iodine-deficiency-related hypothyroidism
                  (E00-E02)
                  nonteratogenic effects of substances
                  transmitted via placenta or breast
                  milk (P04.-)

Q86.0 Fetal alcohol syndrome (dysmorphic)

Q86.1 Fetal hydantoin syndrome
   Meadow's syndrome

Q86.2 Dysmorphism due to warfarin

**Q86.8 Other congenital malformation syndromes due to
   known exogenous causes**

● **Q87 Other specified congenital malformation syndromes
   affecting multiple systems**
   Use additional code(s) to identify all associated
      manifestations

**Q87.0 Congenital malformation syndromes
   predominantly affecting facial appearance**
   Acrocephalopolysyndactyly
   Acrocephalosyndactyly [Apert]
   Cryptophthalmos syndrome
   Cyclopia
   Goldenhar syndrome
   Moebius syndrome
   Oro-facial-digital syndrome
   Robin syndrome
   Whistling face

**Q87.1 Congenital malformation syndromes
   predominantly associated with short stature** 🦠
   Aarskog syndrome
   Cockayne syndrome
   De Lange syndrome
   Dubowitz syndrome
   Noonan syndrome
   Prader-Willi syndrome
   Robinow-Silverman-Smith syndrome
   Russell-Silver syndrome
   Seckel syndrome
   Smith-Lemli-Opitz syndrome
   | Excludes1 | Ellis-van Creveld syndrome (Q77.6)

**Q87.2 Congenital malformation syndromes
   predominantly involving limbs** 🦠
   Holt-Oram syndrome
   Klippel-Trenaunay-Weber syndrome
   Nail patella syndrome
   Rubinstein-Taybi syndrome
   Sirenomelia syndrome
   Thrombocytopenia with absent radius [TAR]
      syndrome
   VATER syndrome

**Q87.3 Congenital malformation syndromes involving
   early overgrowth** 🦠
   Beckwith-Wiedemann syndrome
   Sotos' syndrome
   Weaver syndrome

● **Q87.4 Marfan's syndrome**

   Q87.40 Marfan's syndrome, unspecified 🦠

   ● **Q87.41 Marfan's syndrome with cardiovascular
      manifestations**

      **Q87.410 Marfan's syndrome with aortic
         dilation** 🦠

      **Q87.418 Marfan's syndrome with other
         cardiovascular manifestations** 🦠

   **Q87.42 Marfan's syndrome with ocular
      manifestations** 🦠

   **Q87.43 Marfan's syndrome with skeletal
      manifestation** 🦠

**Q87.5 Other congenital malformation syndromes with
   other skeletal changes** 🦠

● **Q87.8 Other specified congenital malformation
   syndromes, not elsewhere classified**
   | Excludes1 | Zellweger syndrome (E71.510)

   Q87.81 Alport syndrome 🦠
      *Progressive sensorineural hearing loss,
         progressive pyelonephritis or
         glomerulonephritis, and ocular defects*
      Use additional code to identify stage of
         chronic kidney disease (N18.1-N18.6)

   **Q87.89 Other specified congenital malformation
      syndromes, not elsewhere classified** 🦠
      Laurence-Moon (-Bardet)-Biedl syndrome

● **Q89 Other congenital malformations, not elsewhere classified**

   ● **Q89.0 Congenital absence and malformations of spleen**
      | Excludes1 | isomerism of atrial appendages (with
                     asplenia or polysplenia) (Q20.6)

      Q89.01 Asplenia (congenital) 🦠

      Q89.09 Congenital malformations of spleen 🦠
         Congenital splenomegaly

   Q89.1 Congenital malformations of adrenal gland
      | Excludes1 | adrenogenital disorders (E25.-)
                     congenital adrenal hyperplasia
                     (E25.0)

● Unacceptable First-Listed Diagnosis   ● Use Additional Character(s)   ■ Unspecified   **OGCR** Official Guidelines for Coding and Reporting
🦠 Complication\Comorbidity   🦠 Major C\C | Excludes 1 | | Excludes 2 | Includes   Use additional   Code first   Code also

CHAPTER 17 (Q00-Q99)

1329

Q89.2 Congenital malformations of other endocrine glands
Congenital malformation of parathyroid or thyroid gland
Persistent thyroglossal duct
Thyroglossal cyst
> **Excludes1** congenital goiter (E03.0)
> congenital hypothyroidism (E03.1)

Q89.3 Situs inversus 🏷
Lateral transposition of viscera of thorax and abdomen
Dextrocardia with situs inversus
Mirror-image atrial arrangement with situs inversus
Situs inversus or transversus abdominalis
Situs inversus or transversus thoracis
Transposition of abdominal viscera
Transposition of thoracic viscera
> **Excludes1** dextrocardia NOS (Q24.0)

Q89.4 Conjoined twins 🏷
Craniopagus
Dicephaly
Pygopagus
Thoracopagus

Q89.7 Multiple congenital malformations, not elsewhere classified 🏷
Multiple congenital anomalies NOS
Multiple congenital deformities NOS
> **Excludes1** congenital malformation syndromes affecting multiple systems (Q87.-)

Q89.8 Other specified congenital malformations 🏷
Use additional code(s) to identify all associated manifestations

▪Q89.9 Congenital malformation, unspecified
Congenital anomaly NOS
Congenital deformity NOS

CHROMOSOMAL ABNORMALITIES, NOT ELSEWHERE CLASSIFIED (Q90-Q99)

> **Excludes2** mitochondrial metabolic disorders (E88.3-)

● Q90 Down syndrome
Use additional code(s) to identify any associated physical conditions and degree of mental retardation (F70-F79)

Q90.0 Trisomy 21, nonmosaicism (meiotic nondisjunction)

Q90.1 Trisomy 21, mosaicism (mitotic nondisjunction)

Q90.2 Trisomy 21, translocation

▪Q90.9 Down's syndrome, unspecified
Trisomy 21 NOS

● Q91 Trisomy 18 and Trisomy 13

Q91.0 Trisomy 18, nonmosaicism (meiotic nondisjunction) 🏷

Q91.1 Trisomy 18, mosaicism (mitotic nondisjunction) 🏷

Q91.2 Trisomy 18, translocation 🏷

▪Q91.3 Trisomy 18, unspecified 🏷

Q91.4 Trisomy 13, nonmosaicism (meiotic nondisjunction) 🏷

Q91.5 Trisomy 13, mosaicism (mitotic nondisjunction) 🏷

Q91.6 Trisomy 13, translocation 🏷

▪Q91.7 Trisomy 13, unspecified 🏷

● Q92 Other trisomies and partial trisomies of the autosomes, not elsewhere classified
> **Includes** unbalanced translocations and insertions
> **Excludes1** trisomies of chromosomes 13, 18, 21 (Q90-Q91)

Q92.0 Whole chromosome trisomy, nonmosaicism (meiotic nondisjunction)

Q92.1 Whole chromosome trisomy, mosaicism (mitotic nondisjunction)

Q92.2 Partial trisomy
Less than whole arm duplicated
Whole arm or more duplicated
> **Excludes1** partial trisomy due to unbalanced translocation (Q92.5)

Q92.5 Duplications with other complex rearrangements
Partial trisomy due to unbalanced translocations
Code also any associated deletions due to unbalanced translocations, inversions and insertions (Q93.7)

● Q92.6 Marker chromosomes
Trisomies due to dicentrics
Trisomies due to extra rings
Trisomies due to isochromosomes
Individual with marker heterochromatin

Q92.61 Marker chromosomes in normal individual

Q92.62 Marker chromosomes in abnormal individual

Q92.7 Triploidy and polyploidy

Q92.8 Other specified trisomies and partial trisomies of autosomes
Duplications identified by fluorescence in situ hybridization (FISH)
Duplications identified by in situ hybridization (ISH)
Duplications seen only at prometaphase

▪Q92.9 Trisomy and partial trisomy of autosomes, unspecified

● Q93 Monosomies and deletions from the autosomes, not elsewhere classified

Q93.0 Whole chromosome monosomy, nonmosaicism (meiotic nondisjunction)

Q93.1 Whole chromosome monosomy, mosaicism (mitotic nondisjunction)

Q93.2 Chromosome replaced with ring, dicentric or isochromosome

Q93.3 Deletion of short arm of chromosome 4 🏷
Wolff-Hirschorn syndrome

Q93.4 Deletion of short arm of chromosome 5 🏷
Cri-du-chat syndrome

Q93.5 Other deletions of part of a chromosome 🏷
Angelman syndrome

Q93.7 Deletions with other complex rearrangements 🏷
Deletions due to unbalanced translocations, inversions and insertions
Code also any associated duplications due to unbalanced translocations, inversions and insertions (Q92.5)

● Q93.8 Other deletions from the autosomes

Q93.81 Velo-cardio-facial syndrome 🏷
Deletion 22q11.2

Q93.88 Other microdeletions Miller-Dieker syndrome 🏷
Smith-Magenis syndrome

Q93.89 Other deletions from the autosomes 🏷
Deletions identified by fluorescence in situ hybridization (FISH)
Deletions identified by in situ hybridization (ISH)
Deletions seen only at prometaphase

▪Q93.9 Deletion from autosomes, unspecified 🏷

● Unacceptable First-Listed Diagnosis   ● Use Additional Character(s)   ▪ Unspecified   **OGCR** Official Guidelines for Coding and Reporting
🏷 Complication\Comorbidity   🏷 Major C\C   Excludes 1   Excludes 2   Includes   Use additional   Code first   Code also

CHAPTER 17 (Q00-Q99)

● **Q95 Balanced rearrangements and structural markers, not elsewhere classified**

> **Includes**   Robertsonian and balanced reciprocal translocations and insertions

   Q95.0 Balanced translocation and insertion in normal individual

   Q95.1 Chromosome inversion in normal individual

   Q95.2 Balanced autosomal rearrangement in abnormal individual

   Q95.3 Balanced sex/autosomal rearrangement in abnormal individuals

   Q95.5 Individual with autosomal fragile site

   Q95.8 Other balanced rearrangements and structural markers

   ▨ Q95.9 Balanced rearrangement and structural marker, unspecified

● **Q96 Turner's syndrome**

> *Caused by missing or incomplete X chromosome affected growth and sexual development*

> **Excludes1**   Noonan syndrome (Q87.1)

   Q96.0 Karyotype 45, X

   Q96.1 Karyotype 46, X iso (Xq)
      Karyotype 46, isochromosome Xq

   Q96.2 Karyotype 46, X with abnormal sex chromosome, except iso (Xq)
      Karyotype 46, X with abnormal sex chromosome, except isochromosome Xq

   Q96.3 Mosaicism, 45, X/46, XX or XY

   Q96.4 Mosaicism, 45, X/other cell line(s) with abnormal sex chromosome

   Q96.8 Other variants of Turner's syndrome

   ▨ Q96.9 Turner's syndrome, unspecified

● **Q97 Other sex chromosome abnormalities, female phenotype, not elsewhere classified**

> **Excludes1**   Turner's syndrome (Q96.-)

   Q97.0 Karyotype 47, XXX

   Q97.1 Female with more than three X chromosomes

   Q97.2 Mosaicism, lines with various numbers of X chromosomes

   Q97.3 Female with 46, XY karyotype

   Q97.8 Other specified sex chromosome abnormalities, female phenotype

   ▨ Q97.9 Sex chromosome abnormality, female phenotype, unspecified

● **Q98 Other sex chromosome abnormalities, male phenotype, not elsewhere classified**

   Q98.0 Klinefelter syndrome karyotype 47, XXY

   Q98.1 Klinefelter syndrome, male with more than two X chromosomes

   Q98.3 Other male with 46, XX karyotype

   ▨ Q98.4 Klinefelter syndrome, unspecified

   Q98.5 Karyotype 47, XYY

   Q98.6 Male with structurally abnormal sex chromosome

   Q98.7 Male with sex chromosome mosaicism

   Q98.8 Other specified sex chromosome abnormalities, male phenotype

   ▨ Q98.9 Sex chromosome abnormality, male phenotype, unspecified

● **Q99 Other chromosome abnormalities, not elsewhere classified**

   Q99.0 Chimera 46, XX/46, XY
      Chimera 46, XX/46, XY true hermaphrodite

   Q99.1 46, XX true hermaphrodite
      46, XX with streak gonads
      46, XY with streak gonads
      Pure gonadal dysgenesis

   Q99.2 Fragile X chromosome
      Fragile X syndrome

   Q99.8 Other specified chromosome abnormalities

   ▨ Q99.9 Chromosomal abnormality, unspecified

● Unacceptable First-Listed Diagnosis   ● Use Additional Character(s)   ▨ Unspecified   **OGCR** Official Guidelines for Coding and Reporting

 Complication\Comorbidity   Major C\C   Excludes 1   Excludes 2   Includes   Use additional   Code first   Code also   1331

CHAPTER 17 (Q00–Q99)

OGCR Section I.B.4.

Signs and symptoms
Codes that describe symptoms and signs, as opposed to diagnoses, are acceptable for reporting purposes when a related definitive diagnosis has not been established (confirmed) by the provider. Chapter 18 of ICD-10-CM, Symptoms, Signs, and Abnormal Clinical and Laboratory Findings, Not Elsewhere Classified (codes R00.0-R99) contains many, but not all codes for symptoms.

Section I.C.18.a. to c.
Symptoms, signs, and abnormal clinical and laboratory findings, not elsewhere classified.

Chapter 18 includes symptoms, signs, abnormal results of clinical or other investigative procedures, and ill-defined conditions regarding which no diagnosis classifiable elsewhere is recorded. Signs and symptoms that point to a specific diagnosis have been assigned to a category in other chapters of the classification.

a. Use of symptom codes
Codes that describe symptoms and signs are acceptable for reporting purposes when a related definitive diagnosis has not been established (confirmed) by the provider.

b. Use of a symptom code with a definitive diagnosis code
Codes for signs and symptoms may be reported in addition to a related definitive diagnosis when the sign or symptom is not routinely associated with that diagnosis, such as the various signs and symptoms associated with complex syndromes. The definitive diagnosis code should be sequenced before the symptom code.

Signs or symptoms that are associated routinely with a disease process should not be assigned as additional codes, unless otherwise instructed by the classification.

c. Combination codes that include symptoms
ICD-10-CM contains a number of combination codes that identify both the definitive diagnosis and common symptoms of that diagnosis. When using one of these combination codes, an additional code should not be assigned for the symptom.

CHAPTER 18

SYMPTOMS, SIGNS AND ABNORMAL CLINICAL AND LABORATORY FINDINGS, NOT ELSEWHERE CLASSIFIED (R00-R99)

This chapter includes symptoms, signs, abnormal results of clinical or other investigative procedures, and ill-defined conditions regarding which no diagnosis classifiable elsewhere is recorded.

Signs and symptoms that point rather definitely to a given diagnosis have been assigned to a category in other chapters of the classification. In general, categories in this chapter include the less well-defined conditions and symptoms that, without the necessary study of the case to establish a final diagnosis, point perhaps equally to two or more diseases or to two or more systems of the body. Practically all categories in the chapter could be designated "not otherwise specified", "unknown etiology" or "transient". The Alphabetical Index should be consulted to determine which symptoms and signs are to be allocated here and which to other chapters. The residual subcategories, numbered .8, are generally provided for other relevant symptoms that cannot be allocated elsewhere in the classification.

The conditions and signs or symptoms included in categories R00-R94 consist of: (a) cases for which no more specific diagnosis can be made even after all the facts bearing on the case have been investigated: (b) signs or symptoms existing at the time of initial encounter that proved to be transient and whose causes could not be determined; (c) provisional diagnosis in a patient who failed to return for further investigation or care;(d) cases referred elsewhere for investigation or treatment before

the diagnosis was made; (e) cases in which a more precise diagnosis was not available for any other reason; (f) certain symptoms, for which supplementary information is provided, that represent important problems in medical care in their own right.

Excludes2	abnormal findings on antenatal screening of mother (O28.-)
	certain conditions originating in the perinatal period (P04-P96)
	signs and symptoms classified in the body system chapters
	signs and symptoms of breast (N63, N64.5)

This chapter contains the following blocks:

R00-R09	Symptoms and signs involving the circulatory and respiratory systems
R10-R19	Symptoms and signs involving the digestive system and abdomen
R20-R23	Symptoms and signs involving the skin and subcutaneous tissue
R25-R29	Symptoms and signs involving the nervous and musculoskeletal systems
R30-R39	Symptoms and signs involving the urinary system
R40-R46	Symptoms and signs involving cognition, perception, emotional state and behavior
R47-R49	Symptoms and signs involving speech and voice
R50-R69	General symptoms and signs
R70-R79	Abnormal findings on examination of blood, without diagnosis
R80-R82	Abnormal findings on examination of urine, without diagnosis
R83-R89	Abnormal findings on examination of other body fluids, substances and tissues, without diagnosis
R90-R94	Abnormal findings on diagnostic imaging and in function studies, without diagnosis
R97	Abnormal tumor markers
R99	Ill-defined and unknown cause of mortality

SYMPTOMS AND SIGNS INVOLVING THE CIRCULATORY AND RESPIRATORY SYSTEMS (R00-R09)

● **R00   Abnormalities of heart beat**

| **Excludes1** | abnormalities originating in the perinatal period (P29.1) |
| | specified arrhythmias (I47-I49) |

■ **R00.0   Tachycardia, unspecified**
Rapid heart rate >100 beats
Rapid heart beat
Sinoauricular tachycardia NOS
Sinus [sinusal] tachycardia NOS

| **Excludes1** | neonatal tachycardia (P29.11) |
| | paroxysmal tachycardia (I47.-) |

■ **R00.1   Bradycardia, unspecified**
Slow heart rate, <60
Sinoatrial bradycardia
Sinus bradycardia
Slow heart beat
Vagal bradycardia

| **Excludes1** | neonatal bradycardia (P29.12) |

● Unacceptable First-Listed Diagnosis   ● Use Additional Character(s)   ■ Unspecified   **OGCR** Official Guidelines for Coding and Reporting

1332   🔖 Complication\Comorbidity   🔖 Major C\C   Excludes 1   Excludes 2   Includes   Use additional   Code first   Code also

R00.2 **Palpitations**
　　　　Awareness of heart beat

R00.8 **Other abnormalities of heart beat**

■R00.9 **Unspecified abnormalities of heart beat**

● R01 **Cardiac murmurs and other cardiac sounds**

　　　Excludes1　cardiac murmurs and sounds originating in
　　　　　　　　　　the perinatal period (P29.8)

R01.0 **Benign and innocent cardiac murmurs**
　　　　Functional cardiac murmur

■R01.1 **Cardiac murmur, unspecified**
　　　　Cardiac bruit NOS
　　　　Heart murmur NOS

R01.2 **Other cardiac sounds**
　　　　Cardiac dullness, increased or decreased
　　　　Precordial friction

OGCR Section I.C.9.a.7.
　　　Hypertension, Transient
　　　Assign code R03.0, Elevated blood pressure reading without
　　　diagnosis of hypertension, unless patient has an established
　　　diagnosis of hypertension. Assign code O13.-, Gestational
　　　[pregnancy-induced] hypertension with significant proteinuria,
　　　or O14.-, Gestational [pregnancy-induced] hypertension with
　　　significant proteinuria, for transient hypertension of pregnancy.

● R03 **Abnormal blood-pressure reading, without diagnosis**

R03.0 **Elevated blood-pressure reading, without
　　　　diagnosis of hypertension**

　　　　Note: This category is to be used to record an
　　　　　　　episode of elevated blood pressure in a patient
　　　　　　　in whom no formal diagnosis of hypertension
　　　　　　　has been made, or as an isolated incidental
　　　　　　　finding.

R03.1 **Nonspecific low blood-pressure reading**

　　　　Excludes1　hypotension (I95.-)
　　　　　　　　　　maternal hypotension syndrome
　　　　　　　　　　　　(O26.5-)
　　　　　　　　　　neurogenic orthostatic hypotension
　　　　　　　　　　　　(G90.3)

● R04 **Hemorrhage from respiratory passages**

R04.0 **Epistaxis**
　　　　Hemorrhage from nose
　　　　Nosebleed

R04.1 **Hemorrhage from throat**

　　　　Excludes2　hemoptysis (R04.2)

R04.2 **Hemoptysis** 🍂
　　　　Blood-stained sputum
　　　　Cough with hemorrhage

R04.8 **Hemorrhage from other sites in respiratory
　　　　passages** 🍂
　　　　Pulmonary hemorrhage NOS

　　　　Excludes1　perinatal pulmonary hemorrhage
　　　　　　　　　　(P26.-)

■R04.9 **Hemorrhage from respiratory passages,
　　　　unspecified** 🍂

R05 **Cough**

　　　Excludes1　cough with hemorrhage (R04.2)
　　　　　　　　　smoker's cough (J41.0)

● R06 **Abnormalities of breathing**

　　　Excludes1　acute respiratory distress syndrome (J80)
　　　　　　　　　respiratory arrest (R09.2)
　　　　　　　　　respiratory arrest of newborn (P28.81)
　　　　　　　　　respiratory distress syndrome of newborn
　　　　　　　　　　(P22.-)
　　　　　　　　　respiratory failure (J96.-)
　　　　　　　　　respiratory failure of newborn (P28.5)

● R06.0 **Dyspnea**

　　　　Excludes1　tachypnea NOS (R06.82)
　　　　　　　　　　transient tachypnea of newborn
　　　　　　　　　　　(P22.1)

R06.00 **Dyspnea NOS**

R06.01 **Orthopnea**

R06.02 **Shortness of breath**

R06.09 **Other forms of dyspnea**

R06.1 **Stridor**
　　　　Harsh, high-pitched breath sound

　　　　Excludes1　congenital laryngeal stridor (P28.89)
　　　　　　　　　　laryngismus (stridulus) (J38.5)

R06.2 **Wheezing**

　　　　Excludes1　Asthma (J45.-)

R06.3 **Periodic breathing** 🍂
　　　　Cheyne-Stokes breathing
　　　　*An abnormal pattern of breathing with gradually
　　　　　increasing and decreasing tidal volume with
　　　　　some periods of apnea*

R06.4 **Hyperventilation**

　　　　Excludes1　psychogenic hyperventilation (F45.8)

R06.5 **Mouth breathing**

　　　　Excludes2　dry mouth NOS (R68.2)

R06.6 **Hiccough**

　　　　Excludes1　psychogenic hiccough (F45.8)

R06.7 **Sneezing**

● R06.8 **Other abnormalities of breathing**

R06.81 **Apnea, not elsewhere classified**
　　　　Apnea NOS

　　　　　Excludes1　apnea (of) newborn (P28.4)
　　　　　　　　　　　sleep apnea (G47.3-)
　　　　　　　　　　　sleep apnea of newborn
　　　　　　　　　　　　(primary) (P28.3)

R06.82 **Tachypnea, not elsewhere classified**
　　　　Tachypnea NOS

　　　　　Excludes1　transitory tachypnea of
　　　　　　　　　　　newborn (P22.1)

R06.83 **Snoring**

R06.89 **Other abnormalities of breathing**
　　　　Breath-holding (spells)
　　　　Sighing

■R06.9 **Unspecified abnormalities of breathing**

● R07 **Pain in throat and chest**

　　　Excludes1　epidemic myalgia (B33.0)
　　　Excludes2　pain in breast (N64.4)

R07.0 **Pain in throat**

　　　　Excludes1　chronic sore throat (J31.2)
　　　　　　　　　　sore throat (acute) NOS (J02.9)

　　　　Excludes2　dysphagia (R13.1-)
　　　　　　　　　　pain in neck (M54.2)

R07.1 **Chest pain on breathing**
　　　　Painful respiration

R07.2 **Precordial pain**

● R07.8 **Other chest pain**

R07.81 **Pleurodynia**
　　　　Pleurodynia NOS

　　　　　Excludes1　epidemic pleurodynia
　　　　　　　　　　　(B33.0)

R07.82 **Intercostal pain**

● Unacceptable First-Listed Diagnosis　　　● Use Additional Character(s)　　　■ Unspecified　　　**OGCR** Official Guidelines for Coding and Reporting

🍂 Complication\Comorbidity　　🍂 Major C\C　　 Excludes 1 　 Excludes 2 　 Includes 　 Use additional 　 Code first 　 Code also

1333

R07.89   Other chest pain
    Anterior chest-wall pain NOS

■ **R07.9   Chest pain, unspecified**

● **R09   Other symptoms and signs involving the circulatory and respiratory system**

    Excludes1   acute respiratory distress syndrome (J80)
                respiratory arrest of newborn (P28.81)
                respiratory distress syndrome of newborn (P22.0)
                respiratory failure (J96.-)
                respiratory failure of newborn (P28.5)

● **R09.0   Asphyxia and hypoxemia**

    Excludes1   asphyxia due to carbon monoxide (T58.-)
                asphyxia due to foreign body in respiratory tract (T17.-)
                birth (intrauterine) asphyxia (P84)
                hypercapnia (R06.4)
                hyperventilation (R06.4)
                traumatic asphyxia (T71-)

    R09.01   Asphyxia 🔗

    R09.02   Hypoxemia

R09.1   Pleurisy
    Occurs when double membrane (pleura) lining chest cavity and lung surface becomes inflamed causing sharp pain on inspiration/expiration.

    Excludes1   pleurisy with effusion (J90)

R09.2   Respiratory arrest 🔗
    Cardiorespiratory failure

    Excludes1   cardiac arrest (I46.-)
                respiratory arrest of newborn (P28.81)
                respiratory distress of newborn (P22.0)
                respiratory failure (J96.-)
                respiratory failure of newborn (P28.5)
                respiratory insufficiency (R06.89)
                respiratory insufficiency of newborn (P28.5)

    MCC: Only if patient discharged alive

R09.3   Abnormal sputum
    Abnormal amount of sputum
    Abnormal color of sputum
    Abnormal odor of sputum
    Excessive sputum

    Excludes1   blood-stained sputum (R04.2)

● **R09.8   Other specified symptoms and signs involving the circulatory and respiratory systems**

    R09.81   Nasal congestion

    R09.82   Postnasal drip

    R09.89   Other specified symptoms and signs involving the circulatory and respiratory systems
        Bruit (arterial)
        Abnormal chest percussion
        Feeling of foreign body in throat
        Friction sounds in chest
        Chest tympany
        Choking sensation
        Rales
          Wet rattling, clicking, crackling sounds on auscultation
        Weak pulse

        Excludes2   foreign body in throat (T17.2-)
                  wheezing (R06.2)

SYMPTOMS AND SIGNS INVOLVING THE DIGESTIVE SYSTEM AND ABDOMEN (R10-R19)

Excludes1   congenital or infantile pylorospasm (Q40.0)
                gastrointestinal hemorrhage (K92.0-K92.2)
                intestinal obstruction (K56.-)
                newborn gastrointestinal hemorrhage (P54.0-P54.3)
                newborn intestinal obstruction (P76.-)
                pylorospasm (K31.3)
                signs and symptoms involving the urinary system (R30-R39)
                symptoms referable to female genital organs (N94.-)
                symptoms referable to male genital organs male (N48-N50)

● **R10   Abdominal and pelvic pain**

    Excludes1   renal colic (N23)
    Excludes2   dorsalgia (M54.-)
                flatulence and related conditions (R14.-)

R10.0   Acute abdomen
    Severe abdominal pain (generalized) (with abdominal rigidity)

    Excludes1   abdominal rigidity NOS (R19.3)
                generalized abdominal pain NOS (R10.84)
                localized abdominal pain (R10.1-R10.3-)

● **R10.1   Pain localized to upper abdomen**

    ■ **R10.10   Upper abdominal pain, unspecified**

    R10.11   Right upper quadrant pain

    R10.12   Left upper quadrant pain

    R10.13   Epigastric pain

R10.2   Pelvic and perineal pain
    Excludes1   vulvodynia (N94.81)

● **R10.3   Pain localized to other parts of lower abdomen**

    ■ **R10.30   Lower abdominal pain, unspecified**

    R10.31   Right lower quadrant pain

    R10.32   Left lower quadrant pain

    R10.33   Periumbilical pain

● **R10.8   Other abdominal pain**

    ● **R10.81   Abdominal tenderness**
        Abdominal tenderness NOS

        R10.811   Right upper quadrant abdominal tenderness

        R10.812   Left upper quadrant abdominal tenderness

        R10.813   Right lower quadrant abdominal tenderness

        R10.814   Left lower quadrant abdominal tenderness

        R10.815   Periumbilic abdominal tenderness

        R10.816   Epigastric abdominal tenderness

        R10.817   Generalized abdominal tenderness

        ■ **R10.819   Abdominal tenderness, unspecified site**

    ● **R10.82   Rebound abdominal tenderness**

        R10.821   Right upper quadrant rebound abdominal tenderness

        R10.822   Left upper quadrant rebound abdominal tenderness

R10.823 **Right lower quadrant rebound abdominal tenderness**

R10.824 **Left lower quadrant rebound abdominal tenderness**

R10.825 **Periumbilic rebound abdominal tenderness**

R10.826 **Epigastric rebound abdominal tenderness**

R10.827 **Generalized rebound abdominal tenderness**

■ R10.829 **Rebound abdominal tenderness, unspecified site**

R10.83 **Colic**
Colic NOS
Infantile colic
| **Excludes1** | colic in adult and child over 12 months old (R10.84) |

R10.84 **Generalized abdominal pain**
| **Excludes1** | generalized abdominal pain associated with acute abdomen (R10.0) |

■ R10.9 **Unspecified abdominal pain**

● R11 **Nausea and vomiting**
| **Excludes1** | cyclical vomiting associated with migraine (G43.a-) |
excessive vomiting in pregnancy (O21.-)
hematemesis (K92.0)
neonatal hematemesis (P54.0)
newborn vomiting (P92.0-)
psychogenic vomiting (F50.8)
vomiting associated with bulimia nervosa (F50.2)
vomiting following gastrointestinal surgery (K91.0)

● R11.0 **Nausea**
Nausea NOS
Nausea without vomiting

● R11.1 **Vomiting**
■ R11.10 **Vomiting, unspecified**
Vomiting NOS

R11.11 **Vomiting without nausea**

R11.12 **Projectile vomiting**

R11.13 **Vomiting of fecal matter**

R11.14 **Bilious vomiting**
Bilious emesis

■ R11.2 **Nausea with vomiting, unspecified**
Persistent nausea with vomiting NOS

R12 **Heartburn**
| **Excludes1** | dyspepsia (K30) |

● R13 **Aphagia and dysphagia**
R13.0 **Aphagia**
Inability to swallow
| **Excludes1** | psychogenic aphagia (F50.9) |

● R13.1 **Dysphagia**
Difficulty swallowing
Code first, if applicable, dysphagia following cerebrovascular disease (I69. with final characters -91)
| **Excludes1** | psychogenic dysphagia (F45.8) |

■ R13.10 **Dysphagia, unspecified**
Difficulty in swallowing NOS

R13.11 **Dysphagia, oral phase**

R13.12 **Dysphagia, oropharyngeal phase**

R13.13 **Dysphagia, pharyngeal phase**

R13.14 **Dysphagia, pharyngoesophageal phase**

R13.19 **Other dysphagia**
Cervical dysphagia
Neurogenic dysphagia

● R14 **Flatulence and related conditions**
| **Excludes1** | psychogenic aerophagy (F45.8) |

R14.0 **Abdominal distension (gaseous)**
Bloating
Tympanites (abdominal) (intestinal)

R14.1 **Gas pain**

R14.2 **Eructation**
Belching air from stomach through mouth

R14.3 **Flatulence**

R14.8 **Other**

R15 **Fecal incontinence**
| **Includes** | encopresis NOS |
| **Excludes1** | fecal incontinence of nonorganic origin (F98.1) |

● R16 **Hepatomegaly and splenomegaly, not elsewhere classified**
Enlargement of liver or spleen

R16.0 **Hepatomegaly, not elsewhere classified**
Hepatomegaly NOS

R16.1 **Splenomegaly, not elsewhere classified**
Splenomegaly NOS

R16.2 **Hepatomegaly with splenomegaly, not elsewhere classified**
Hepatosplenomegaly NOS

■ R17 **Unspecified jaundice** ⚕
| **Excludes1** | neonatal jaundice (P55, P57-P59) |

● R18 **Ascites**
| **Includes** | fluid in peritoneal cavity |
| **Excludes1** | ascites in alcoholic cirrhosis (K70.31) |
ascites in alcoholic hepatitis (K70.11)
ascites in toxic liver disease with chronic active hepatitis (K71.51)

R18.0 **Malignant ascites** ⚕
Code first malignancy, such as:
malignant neoplasm of ovary (C56.-)
secondary malignant neoplasm of retroperitoneum and peritoneum (C78.6)

R18.8 **Other ascites** ⚕
Ascites NOS
Peritoneal effusion (chronic)

● R19 **Other symptoms and signs involving the digestive system and abdomen**
| **Excludes1** | acute abdomen (R10.0) |

● R19.0 **Intra-abdominal and pelvic swelling, mass and lump**
| **Excludes1** | abdominal distension (gaseous) (R14.-) |
ascites (R18.-)

■ R19.00 **Intra-abdominal and pelvic swelling, mass and lump, unspecified site**

R19.01 **Right upper quadrant abdominal swelling, mass and lump**

● Unacceptable First-Listed Diagnosis   ● Use Additional Character(s)   ■ Unspecified   **OGCR** Official Guidelines for Coding and Reporting

⚕ Complication\Comorbidity   ⚕ Major C\C   Excludes 1   Excludes 2   Includes   Use additional   Code first   Code also

1335

CHAPTER 18 (R00-R99)

R19.02 **Left upper quadrant abdominal swelling, mass and lump**

R19.03 **Right lower quadrant abdominal swelling, mass and lump**

R19.04 **Left lower quadrant abdominal swelling, mass and lump**

R19.05 **Periumbilic swelling, mass or lump**
Diffuse or generalized umbilical swelling or mass

R19.06 **Epigastric swelling, mass or lump**

R19.07 **Generalized intra-abdominal and pelvic swelling, mass and lump**
Diffuse or generalized intra-abdominal swelling or mass NOS
Diffuse or generalized pelvic swelling or mass NOS

R19.09 **Other intra-abdominal and pelvic swelling, mass and lump**

● R19.1 **Abnormal bowel sounds**

R19.11 **Absent bowel sounds**

R19.12 **Hyperactive bowel sounds**

R19.15 **Other abnormal bowel sounds**
Abnormal bowel sounds NOS

R19.2 **Visible peristalsis**
Hyperperistalsis

● R19.3 **Abdominal rigidity**
Excludes1 abdominal rigidity with severe abdominal pain (R10.0)

■ R19.30 **Abdominal rigidity, unspecified site**

R19.31 **Right upper quadrant abdominal rigidity**

R19.32 **Left upper quadrant abdominal rigidity**

R19.33 **Right lower quadrant abdominal rigidity**

R19.34 **Left lower quadrant abdominal rigidity**

R19.35 **Periumbilic abdominal rigidity**

R19.36 **Epigastric abdominal rigidity**

R19.37 **Generalized abdominal rigidity**

R19.4 **Change in bowel habit**
Excludes1 constipation (K59.0-)
functional diarrhea (K59.1)

R19.5 **Other fecal abnormalities**
Abnormal stool color
Bulky stools
Mucus in stools
Occult blood in feces
Occult blood in stools
Excludes1 melena (K92.1)
neonatal melena (P54.1)

R19.6 **Halitosis**

■ R19.7 **Diarrhea, unspecified**
Diarrhea NOS
Excludes1 functional diarrhea (K59.1)
neonatal diarrhea (P78.3)
psychogenic diarrhea (F45.8)

R19.8 **Other specified symptoms and signs involving the digestive system and abdomen**

SYMPTOMS AND SIGNS INVOLVING THE SKIN AND SUBCUTANEOUS TISSUE (R20-R23)
Excludes2 symptoms relating to breast (N64.4-N64.5)

● R20 **Disturbances of skin sensation**
Excludes1 dissociative anesthesia and sensory loss (F44.6)
psychogenic disturbances (F45.8)

R20.0 **Anesthesia of skin**
Loss of sensation

R20.1 **Hypoesthesia of skin**
Unpleasant abnormal sensation

R20.2 **Paresthesia of skin**
Abnormal touch sensation, including burning, prickling, often in absence of external stimulus
Formication   Tingling skin
Pins and needles
Excludes1 acroparesthesia (I73.8)

R20.3 **Hyperesthesia**

R20.8 **Other disturbances of skin sensation**

■ R20.9 **Unspecified disturbances of skin sensation**

R21 **Rash and other nonspecific skin eruption**
Rash NOS
Excludes1 specified type of rash- code to condition
vesicular eruption (R23.8)

● R22 **Localized swelling, mass and lump of skin and subcutaneous tissue**
Includes subcutaneous nodules (localized)(superficial)
Excludes1 abnormal findings on diagnostic imaging (R90-R93)
edema (R60.-)
enlarged lymph nodes (R59.-)
localized adiposity (E65)
swelling of joint (M25.4-)

R22.0 **Localized swelling, mass and lump, head**

R22.1 **Localized swelling, mass and lump, neck**

R22.2 **Localized swelling, mass and lump, trunk**
Excludes1 intra-abdominal or pelvic mass and lump (R19.0-)
intra-abdominal or pelvic swelling (R19.0-)
Excludes2 breast mass and lump (N63)

● R22.3 **Localized swelling, mass and lump, upper limb**

■ R22.30 **Localized swelling, mass and lump, upper limb, unspecified side**

R22.31 **Localized swelling, mass and lump, right upper limb**

R22.32 **Localized swelling, mass and lump, left upper limb**

R22.33 **Localized swelling, mass and lump, upper limb, bilateral**

● R22.4 **Localized swelling, mass and lump, lower limb**

■ R22.40 **Localized swelling, mass and lump, lower limb, unspecified side**

R22.41 **Localized swelling, mass and lump, right lower limb**

R22.42 **Localized swelling, mass and lump, left lower limb**

R22.43 **Localized swelling, mass and lump, lower limb, bilateral**

■ R22.9 **Localized swelling, mass and lump, unspecified**

● R23 **Other skin changes**

R23.0 **Cyanosis**
Excludes1 acrocyanosis (I73.8)
cyanotic attacks of newborn (P28.2)

R23.1 **Pallor**
Clammy skin

CHAPTER 18 (R00-R99)

R23.2 Flushing
Excessive blushing

Code first, if applicable, menopausal and female climacteric states (N95.1)

R23.3 Spontaneous ecchymoses
Small hemorrhagic spot of skin; AKA black and blue spot
Petechiae

Excludes1	ecchymoses of newborn (P54.5)
	purpura (D69.-)

R23.4 Changes in skin texture
Desquamation of skin   Scaling of skin
Induration of skin

Excludes1	epidermal thickening NOS (L85.9)

R23.8 Other skin changes

R23.9 Unspecified skin changes

SYMPTOMS AND SIGNS INVOLVING THE NERVOUS AND MUSCULOSKELETAL SYSTEMS (R25-R29)

● **R25 Abnormal involuntary movements**

Excludes1	specific movement disorders (G20-G26)
	stereotyped movement disorders (F98.4)
	tic disorders (F95.-)

R25.0 Abnormal head movements

R25.1 Tremor, unspecified

Excludes1	chorea NOS (G25.5)
	essential tremor (G25.0)
	hysterical tremor (F44.4)
	intention tremor (G25.2)

R25.2 Cramp and spasm

Excludes2	carpopedal spasm (R29.0)
	charley-horse (M62.831)
	infantile spasms (G40.4-)
	muscle spasm of back (M62.830)
	muscle spasm of calf (M62.831)

R25.3 Fasciculation
Twitching NOS

R25.8 Other abnormal involuntary movements

R25.9 Unspecified abnormal involuntary movements

● **R26 Abnormalities of gait and mobility**

Excludes1	ataxia NOS (R27.0)
	hereditary ataxia (G11.-)
	locomotor (syphilitic) ataxia (A52.11)
	immobility syndrome (paraplegic) (M62.3)

R26.0 Ataxic gait
Staggering gait

R26.1 Paralytic gait
Spastic gait

R26.2 Difficulty in walking, not elsewhere classified

Excludes1	falling (R29.6)
	unsteadiness on feet (R26.81)

● **R26.8 Other abnormalities of gait and mobility**

     R26.81 Unsteadiness on feet

     R26.89 Other abnormalities of gait and mobility

R26.9 Unspecified abnormalities of gait and mobility

● **R27 Other lack of coordination**

Excludes1	ataxic gait (R26.0)
	hereditary ataxia (G11.-)
	vertigo NOS (R42)

R27.0 Ataxia, unspecified

Excludes1	ataxia following cerebrovascular disease (I69. with final characters -93)

R27.8 Other lack of coordination

R27.9 Unspecified lack of coordination

● **R29 Other symptoms and signs involving the nervous and musculoskeletal systems**

R29.0 Tetany 🅒
Hyperexcitability of nerves and muscles characterized by spasm, twitching, and cramps
Carpopedal spasm

Excludes1	hysterical tetany (F44.5)
	neonatal tetany (P71.3)
	parathyroid tetany (E20.9)
	post-thyroidectomy tetany (E89.2)

R29.1 Meningismus 🅒

R29.2 Abnormal reflex

Excludes2	abnormal pupillary reflex (H57.0)
	hyperactive gag reflex (J39.2)
	vasovagal reaction or syncope (R55)

R29.3 Abnormal posture

R29.4 Clicking hip

Excludes1	congenital deformities of hip (Q65.-)

R29.5 Transient paralysis 🅒
Code first any associated spinal cord injury (S14.0, S14.1-, S24.0, S24.1-, S34.0, S34.1-)

Excludes1	transient ischemic attack (G45.9)

R29.6 Repeated falls
Falling
Tendency to fall

Excludes2	at risk for falling (Z91.81)
	history of falling (Z91.81)

OGCR Section I.C.18.d.
Repeated falls
Code R29.6, Repeated falls, is for use for encounters when a patient has recently fallen and the reason for the fall is being investigated.

Code Z91.81, History of falling, is for use when a patient has fallen in the past and is at risk for future falls. When appropriate, both codes R29.6 and Z91.81 may be assigned together.

● **R29.8 Other symptoms and signs involving the nervous and musculoskeletal systems**

● **R29.81 Other symptoms and signs involving the nervous system**

     R29.810 Facial weakness
Facial droop

Excludes1	Bell's palsy (G51.0)
	facial weakness following cerebrovascular disease (I69. with final characters -92)

     R29.818 Other symptoms and signs involving the nervous system

● **R29.89 Other symptoms and signs involving the musculoskeletal system**

Excludes2	pain in limb (M79.6-)

     R29.890 Loss of height

Excludes1	osteoporosis (M80-M82)

● Unacceptable First-Listed Diagnosis   ● Use Additional Character(s)   ▪ Unspecified   **OGCR** Official Guidelines for Coding and Reporting

🅒 Complication\Comorbidity   🅒 Major C\C   Excludes 1   Excludes 2   Includes   Use additional   Code first   Code also

1337

CHAPTER 18 (R00-R99)

           R29.891   Ocular torticollis
> **Excludes1**   congenital (sternomas-toid) torticollis Q68.0
> psychogenic torticollis (F45.8)
> spasmodic torticollis (G24.3)
> torticollis due to birth injury (P15.8)
> torticollis NOS M43.6

           R29.898   Other symptoms and signs involving the musculoskeletal system

● **R29.9   Unspecified symptoms and signs involving the nervous and musculoskeletal systems**

   ■ **R29.90   Unspecified symptoms and signs involving the nervous system**

   ■ **R29.91   Unspecified symptoms and signs involving the musculoskeletal system**

SYMPTOMS AND SIGNS INVOLVING THE GENITOURINARY SYSTEM (R30-R39)

● **R30   Pain associated with micturition**
> **Excludes1**   psychogenic pain associated with micturition (F45.8)

    R30.0   Dysuria
> *Painful urination*
> Strangury

    R30.1   Vesical tenesmus
> *Straining to urinate*

   ■ **R30.9   Painful micturition, unspecified**
> Painful urination NOS

● **R31   Hematuria**
> **Excludes1**   hematuria included with underlying conditions, such as:
>   acute cystitis with hematuria (N30.01)
>   acute prostatitis with hematuria (N41.01)
>   recurrent and persistent hematuria in glomerular diseases (N02.-)

    R31.0   Gross hematuria

    R31.1   Benign essential microscopic hematuria

    R31.2   Other microscopic hematuria

   ■ **R31.9   Hematuria, unspecified**

■ **R32   Unspecified urinary incontinence**
> **Includes**   enuresis NOS
> **Excludes1**   functional urinary incontinence (R39.81)
> nonorganic enuresis (F98.0)
> stress incontinence and other specified urinary incontinence (N39.3-N39.4-)
> urinary incontinence associated with cognitive impairment (R39.81)

● **R33   Retention of urine**
> **Excludes1**   psychogenic retention of urine (F45.8)

  ● **R33.0   Drug induced retention of urine**
> *Code first (T36-T50) to identify the drug*

    R33.8   Other retention of urine
> Code, if applicable, any causal condition first, such as:
>   enlarged prostate (N40.1)

   ■ **R33.9   Retention of urine, unspecified**

● **R34   Anuria and oliguria**
> **Excludes1**   anuria and oliguria complicating abortion or ectopic or molar pregnancy (O00-O07, O08.4)
> anuria and oliguria complicating pregnancy (O26.83-)
> anuria and oliguria complicating the puerperium (O90.4)

● **R35   Polyuria**
> *Passage of excessive volume of urine*
> Code, if applicable, any causal condition first, such as:
>   enlarged prostate (N40.1)
> **Excludes1**   psychogenic polyuria (F45.8)

    R35.0   Frequency of micturition
> *Discharge or passage of urine; AKA uresis*

    R35.1   Nocturia
> *Urinary frequency at night*

    R35.8   Other polyuria
> Polyuria NOS

● **R36   Urethral discharge**

    R36.0   Urethral discharge without blood

    R36.1   Hematospermia
> *Presence of blood in semen*

   ■ **R36.9   Urethral discharge, unspecified**
> Penile discharge NOS
> Urethrorrhea

■ **R37   Sexual dysfunction, unspecified**

● **R39   Other and unspecified symptoms and signs involving the genitourinary system**

    R39.0   Extravasation of urine 🝆
> *Leakage, discharge*

  ● **R39.1   Other difficulties with micturition**
> Code, if applicable, any causal condition first, such as:
>   enlarged prostate (N40.1)

    R39.11   Hesitancy of micturition

    R39.12   Poor urinary stream
> Weak urinary steam

    R39.13   Splitting of urinary stream

    R39.14   Feeling of incomplete bladder emptying

    R39.15   Urgency of urination
> **Excludes1**   urge incontinence (N39.41, N39.46)

    R39.16   Straining to void

    R39.19   Other difficulties with micturition

    R39.2   Extrarenal uremia
> Prerenal uremia
> **Excludes1**   uremia NOS (N19)

  ● **R39.8   Other symptoms and signs involving the genitourinary system**

    R39.81   Functional urinary incontinence
> Urinary incontinence due to cognitive impairment, or severe physical disability or immobility
> **Excludes1**   stress incontinence and other specified urinary incontinence (N39.3-N39.4-)
> urinary incontinence NOS (R32)

    R39.89   Other symptoms and signs involving the genitourinary system

   ■ **R39.9   Unspecified symptoms and signs involving the genitourinary system**

SYMPTOMS AND SIGNS INVOLVING COGNITION, PERCEPTION, EMOTIONAL STATE AND BEHAVIOR (R40-R46)

Excludes1 symptoms and signs constituting part of a pattern of mental disorder (F01-F99)

● R40 Somnolence, stupor and coma

Excludes1 neonatal coma (P91.5)
somnolence, stupor and coma in diabetes (E08-E13)
somnolence, stupor and coma in hepatic failure (K72.-)
somnolence, stupor and coma in hypoglycemia (nondiabetic) (E15)

R40.0 Somnolence
Drowsiness
Excludes1 coma (R40.2-)

R40.1 Stupor
Lowered level of consciousness
Catatonic stupor
Semicoma
Excludes1 catatonic schizophrenia (F20.2)
coma (R40.2-)
depressive stupor (F31-F33)
dissociative stupor (F44.2)
manic stupor (F30.2)

Glasgow Coma Scale

Eye Opening Response	
• Spontaneous--open with blinking at baseline	4 points
• To verbal stimuli, command, speech	3 points
• To pain only (not applied to face)	2 points
• No response	1 point
Verbal Response	
• Oriented	5 points
• Confused conversation, but able to answer questions	4 points
• Inappropriate words	3 points
• Incomprehensible speech	2 points
• No response	1 point
Motor Response	
• Obeys commands for movement	6 points
• Purposeful movement to painful stimulus	5 points
• Withdraws in response to pain	4 points
• Flexion in response to pain (decorticate posturing)	3 points
• Extension response in response to pain (decerebrate posturing)	2 points
• No response	1 point
Categorization:	
Coma: No eye opening, no ability to follow commands, no word verbalizations (3-8)	
Head Injury Classification:	
Severe Head Injury--GCS score of 8 or less	
Moderate Head Injury--GCS score of 9 to 12	
Mild head injury--GCS score of 13 to 15	
(Adapted from: Advanced Trauma Life Support: Course for Physicians, American College of Surgeons, 1993). http://www.bt.cdc.gov/masscasulatires/gscale.asp	

OGCR Section I.C.18.e.
Glasgow coma scale
The Glasgow coma scale codes (R40.2-) can be used in conjunction with traumatic brain injury codes or sequelae of cerebrovascular accident codes. These codes are primarily for use by trauma registries, but they may be used in any setting where this information is collected. The coma scale codes should be sequenced after the diagnosis code(s).

These codes, one from each subcategory, are needed to complete the scale. The 7th character indicates when the scale was recorded. The 7th character should match for all three codes.

At a minimum, report the initial score documented on presentation at your facility. This may be a score from the emergency medicine technician (EMT) or in the emergency department. If desired, a facility may choose to capture multiple Glasgow coma scale scores.

R40.2 Coma
Coma NOS
Unconsciousness NOS
Code first any associated:
coma in fracture of skull (S02.-)
coma in intracranial injury (S06.-)

The appropriate 7th character is to be added to each code from subcategory R40.21-, R40.22-, R40.23-:

0	unspecified time
1	in the field [EMT or ambulance]
2	at arrival to emergency department
3	at hospital admission
4	24 hours or more after hospital admission

A code from each subcategory is required to complete the coma scale.

Note: These codes are intended primarily for trauma registry and research use but may be utilized by all users of the classification who wish to collect this information.

■ R40.20 Unspecified coma 🅒
● R40.21 Coma scale, eyes open
 ● R40.211 Coma scale, eyes open, never 🅒
 ● R40.212 Coma scale, eyes open, to pain 🅒
 ● R40.213 Coma scale, eyes open, to sound 🅒
 ● R40.214 Coma scale, eyes open, spontaneous 🅒
● R40.22 Coma scale, best verbal response
 ● R40.221 Coma scale, best verbal response, none 🅒
 ● R40.222 Coma scale, best verbal response, incomprehensible words 🅒
 ● R40.223 Coma scale, best verbal response, inappropriate words 🅒
 ● R40.224 Coma scale, best verbal response, confused conversation 🅒
 ● R40.225 Coma scale, best verbal response, oriented 🅒
● R40.23 Coma scale, best motor response
 ● R40.231 Coma scale, best motor response, none 🅒
 ● R40.232 Coma scale, best motor response, extension 🅒
 ● R40.233 Coma scale, best motor response, abnormal 🅒
 ● R40.234 Coma scale, best motor response, flexion withdrawal 🅒

● Unacceptable First-Listed Diagnosis   ● Use Additional Character(s)   ■ Unspecified   **OGCR** Official Guidelines for Coding and Reporting
🅒 Complication\Comorbidity   🅒 Major C\C   Excludes 1   Excludes 2   Includes   Use additional   Code first   Code also

CHAPTER 18 (R00-R99)

1339

● R40.235 Coma scale, best motor response, localizes pain 🔖

● R40.236 Coma scale, best motor response, obeys commands 🔖

R40.3 Persistent vegetative state 🔖

R40.4 Transient alteration of awareness

● R41 Other symptoms and signs involving cognitive functions and awareness

Excludes1 dissociative [conversion] disorders (F44.-)

■R41.0 Disorientation, unspecified
Confusion NOS   Delirium NOS

R41.1 Anterograde amnesia

R41.2 Retrograde amnesia

R41.3 Other amnesia
Amnesia NOS
Memory loss NOS

Excludes1 amnestic disorder due to known physiologic condition (F04)
amnestic syndrome due to psychoactive substance use (F10-F19 with 5th character .6)
transient global amnesia (G45.4)

R41.4 Neurologic neglect syndrome 🔖
Asomatognosia   Left-sided neglect
Hemi-akinesia   Sensory neglect
Hemi-inattention   Visuospatial neglect
Hemispatial neglect

● R41.8 Other symptoms and signs involving cognitive functions and awareness

R41.81 Age-related cognitive decline
Senility NOS

■R41.82 Altered mental status, unspecified
Change in mental status NOS

Excludes1 altered level of consciousness (R40.-)
altered mental status due to known condition - code to condition
delirium NOS (R41.0)

R41.83 Borderline intellectual functioning
IQ level 71 to 84

Excludes1 mental retardation (F70-F79)

R41.89 Other symptoms and signs involving cognitive functions and awareness
Anosognosia

■R41.9 Unspecified symptoms and signs involving cognitive functions and awareness

R42 Dizziness and giddiness

Includes light-headedness
vertigo NOS

Excludes1 vertiginous syndromes (H81.-)
vertigo from infrasound (T75.23)

● R43 Disturbances of smell and taste

R43.0 Anosmia
Absence of sense of smell; AKA anosphresia and olfactory anesthesia

R43.1 Parosmia

R43.2 Parageusia
Perversion of sense of taste or bad taste in mouth; AKA dysgeusia

R43.8 Other disturbances of smell and taste
Mixed disturbance of smell and taste

■R43.9 Unspecified disturbances of smell and taste

● R44 Other symptoms and signs involving general sensations and perceptions

Excludes1 alcoholic hallucinations (F1.5)
hallucinations in drug psychosis (F11-F19 with .5)
hallucinations in mood disorders with psychotic symptoms (F30.2, F31.5, F32.3, F33.3)
hallucinations in schizophrenia, schizotypal and delusional disorders (F20-F29)

Excludes2 disturbances of skin sensation (R20.-)

R44.0 Auditory hallucinations 🔖

R44.1 Visual hallucinations

R44.2 Other hallucinations 🔖

■R44.3 Hallucinations, unspecified 🔖

R44.8 Other symptoms and signs involving general sensations and perceptions

■R44.9 Unspecified symptoms and signs involving general sensations and perceptions

● R45 Symptoms and signs involving emotional state

R45.0 Nervousness
Nervous tension

R45.1 Restlessness and agitation

R45.2 Unhappiness

R45.3 Demoralization and apathy

Excludes1 anhedonia (R45.84)

R45.4 Irritability and anger

R45.5 Hostility

R45.6 Violent behavior

■R45.7 State of emotional shock and stress, unspecified

● R45.8 Other symptoms and signs involving emotional state

R45.81 Low self-esteem

R45.82 Worries

R45.83 Excessive crying of child, adolescent or adult

Excludes1 excessive crying of infant (baby) R68.11

R45.84 Anhedonia
Total loss of feeling of pleasure in pleasurable acts

R45.85 Suicidal ideation 🔖

Excludes1 suicide attempt (T14.91)

R45.86 Emotional lability

R45.87 Impulsiveness

R45.89 Other symptoms and signs involving emotional state

● R46 Symptoms and signs involving appearance and behavior

Excludes1 appearance and behavior in schizophrenia, schizotypal and delusional disorders (F20-F29)
mental and behavioral disorders (F01-F99)

R46.0 Very low level of personal hygiene

R46.1 Bizarre personal appearance

R46.2 Strange and inexplicable behavior

R46.3 Overactivity

● Unacceptable First-Listed Diagnosis   ● Use Additional Character(s)   ■ Unspecified   OGCR Official Guidelines for Coding and Reporting
🔖 Complication\Comorbidity   🔖 Major C\C   Excludes 1   Excludes 2   Includes   Use additional   Code first   Code also

R46.4 **Slowness and poor responsiveness**
> **Excludes1**   stupor (R40.1)

R46.5 **Suspiciousness and marked evasiveness**

R46.6 **Undue concern and preoccupation with stressful events**

R46.7 **Verbosity and circumstantial detail obscuring reason for contact**

● R46.8 **Other symptoms and signs involving appearance and behavior**

R46.81 **Obsessive-compulsive behavior**
> **Excludes1**   obsessive-compulsive disorder (F42)

R46.89 **Other symptoms and signs involving appearance and behavior**

SYMPTOMS AND SIGNS INVOLVING SPEECH AND VOICE (R47-R49)

● R47 **Speech disturbances, not elsewhere classified**
> **Excludes1**   autism (F84.0)
> cluttering (F98.8)
> specific developmental disorders of speech and language (F80.-)
> stuttering [stammering] (F98.5)

● R47.0 **Dysphasia and aphasia**

R47.01 **Aphasia**
> **Excludes1**   aphasia following cerebrovascular disease (I69. with final characters -20)
> progressive isolated aphasia (G31.01)

R47.02 **Dysphasia**
Impairment in comprehension of speech, caused by left-sided brain damage
> **Excludes1**   dysphasia following cerebrovascular disease (I69. with final characters -21)

R47.1 **Dysarthria and anarthria**
Motor speech disorder
> **Excludes1**   dyarthria following cerebrovascular disease (I69. with final characters -22)

● R47.8 **Other speech disturbances**
> **Excludes1**   dyarthria following cerebrovascular disease (I69. with final characters -28)

R47.81 **Slurred speech**

R47.89 **Other speech disturbances**

■ R47.9 **Unspecified speech disturbances**

● R48 **Dyslexia and other symbolic dysfunctions, not elsewhere classified**
> **Excludes1**   specific developmental disorders of scholastic skills (F81.-)

R48.0 **Dyslexia and alexia**

R48.1 **Agnosia**
Loss of ability to recognize objects, persons, sounds, shapes, or smells
Astereognosis (astereognosis)
Autotopagnosia
> **Excludes1**   visual object agnosia H53.16

R48.2 **Apraxia**
Loss of ability to execute or carry out learned purposeful movements
> **Excludes1**   apraxia following cerebrovascular disease (I69. with final characters -90)

R48.8 **Other symbolic dysfunctions**
Acalculia
Difficulty performing simple mathematical tasks resulting from neurological injury
Agraphia

■ R48.9 **Unspecified symbolic dysfunctions**

● R49 **Voice and resonance disorders**
> **Excludes1**   psychogenic voice and resonance disorders (F44.4)

R49.0 **Dysphonia**
Hoarseness

R49.1 **Aphonia**
Loss of voice

● R49.2 **Hypernasality and hyponasality**

R49.21 **Hypernasality**

R49.22 **Hyponasality**

R49.8 **Other voice and resonance disorders**

■ R49.9 **Unspecified voice and resonance disorders**
Change in voice NOS
Resonance disorder NOS

GENERAL SYMPTOMS AND SIGNS (R50-R69)

● R50 **Fever of other and unknown origin**
> **Excludes1**   febrile convulsions (R56.0-)
> fever of unknown origin during labor (O75.2)
> fever of unknown origin in newborn (P81.9)
> malignant hyperthermia due to anesthesia (T88.3)
> puerperal pyrexia NOS (O86.4)

● R50.2 **Drug induced fever**
Code first (T36-T50) to identify drug
> **Excludes1**   postvaccination (postimmunization) fever (R50.83)

● R50.8 **Other specified fever**

● R50.81 **Fever presenting with conditions classified elsewhere**
Code first underlying condition when associated fever is present, such as with:
leukemia (C91-C95)
neutropenia (D70.-)
sickle cell disease (D57.-)

R50.82 **Postprocedural fever**
> **Excludes1**   postprocedural infection (T81.4)
>
> postvaccination (postimmunization) fever (R50.83)

R50.83 **Postvaccination fever**
Postimmunization fever

● Unacceptable First-Listed Diagnosis   ● Use Additional Character(s)   ■ Unspecified   **OGCR** Official Guidelines for Coding and Reporting

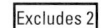 Complication\Comorbidity   Major C\C   Excludes 1   Excludes 2   Includes   Use additional   Code first   Code also

1341

CHAPTER 18 (R00-R99)

■ **R50.9**   **Fever, unspecified**
    Fever NOS
    Fever of unknown origin [FUO]
    Fever with chills
    Fever with rigors
    Hyperpyrexia NOS
    Persistent fever
    Pyrexia NOS

R51   **Headache**

> **Includes**   facial pain NOS
>
> **Excludes1**   atypical face pain (G50.1)
>   migraine and other headache syndromes
>   (G43-G44)
>   trigeminal neuralgia (G50.0)

■ **R52**   **Pain, unspecified**

Acute pain NOS	Generalized pain NOS
Chronic pain NOS	Pain NOS

> **Excludes1**   acute and chronic pain, not elsewhere
>   classified (G89.-)
>   localized pain, unspecified type - code to
>   pain by site, such as:
>   abdomen pain (R10.-)
>   back pain (M54.9)
>   breast pain (N64.4)
>   chest pain (R07.1-R07.9)
>   ear pain (H92.0-)
>   eye pain (H57.1)
>   headache (R51)
>   joint pain (M25.5-)
>   limb pain (M79.6-)
>   lumbar region pain (M54.57)
>   pelvic and perineal pain (R10.2)
>   shoulder pain (M25.51-)
>   spine pain (M54.-)
>   throat pain (R07.0)
>   tongue pain (K14.6)
>   tooth pain (K08.8)
>   renal colic (N23)
>   pain disorders exclusively related to
>   psychological factors (F45.41)

● **R53**   **Malaise and fatigue**

  ● **R53.0**   **Neoplastic (malignant) related fatigue**
      Code first associated neoplasm

  R53.1   **Weakness**
      Asthenia NOS

> **Excludes1**   age-related weakness (R54)
>   muscle weakness (M62.8-)
>   senile asthenia (R54)

  R53.2   **Functional quadriplegia** 🐾
      Complete immobility due to severe physical
      disability or frailty

> **Excludes1**   frailty NOS (R54)
>   hysterical paralysis (F44.4)
>   immobility syndrome (M62.3)
>   neurologic quadriplegia (G82.5-)
>   quadriplegia (G82.50)

  ● **R53.8**   **Other malaise and fatigue**

> **Excludes1**   combat exhaustion and fatigue (F43.0)
>   congenital debility (P96.9)
>   exhaustion and fatigue due to:
>   depressive episode (F32.-)
>   excessive exertion (T73.3)
>   exposure (T73.2)
>   heat (T67.-)
>   pregnancy (O26.8-)
>   recurrent depressive episode (F33)
>   senile debility (R54)

R53.81   **Other malaise**
    Chronic debility
    Debility NOS
    General physical deterioration
    Malaise NOS
    Nervous debility

> **Excludes1**   age-related physical debility
>   (R54)

■ **R53.82**   **Chronic fatigue, unspecified**
    Chronic fatigue syndrome NOS

> **Excludes1**   postviral fatigue syndrome
>   (G93.3)

R53.83   **Other fatigue**

Fatigue NOS	Lethargy
Lack of energy	Tiredness

R54   **Age-related physical debility**

Frailty	Senile asthenia
Old age	Senile debility
Senescence	

> **Excludes1**   age-related cognitive decline (R41.81)
>   senile psychosis (F03)
>   senility NOS (R41.81)

R55   **Syncope and collapse**

> **Includes**   blackout
>   fainting
>   vasovagal attack
>
> **Excludes1**   cardiogenic shock (R57.0)
>   carotid sinus syncope (G90.01)
>   heat syncope (T67.1)
>   neurocirculatory asthenia (F45.3)
>   neurogenic orthostatic hypotension (G90.3)
>   orthostatic hypotension (I95.1)
>   postprocedural shock (T81.1)
>   psychogenic syncope (F48.8)
>   shock NOS (R57.9)
>   shock complicating or following abortion or
>   ectopic or molar pregnancy (O00-O07,
>   O08.3)
>   shock complicating or following labor and
>   delivery (O75.1)
>   Stokes-Adams attack (I45.9)
>   unconsciousness NOS (R40.2-)

● **R56**   **Convulsions, not elsewhere classified**

> **Excludes1**   dissociative convulsions and seizures (F44.5)
>   epileptic convulsions and seizures (G40.-)
>   newborn convulsions and seizures (P90)

  ● **R56.0**   **Febrile convulsions**

  R56.00   **Simple febrile convulsions** 🐾
      Febrile convulsion NOS
      Febrile seizure NOS

  R56.01   **Complex febrile convulsions** 🐾
      Atypical febrile seizure
      Complex febrile seizure
      Complicated febrile seizure

> **Excludes1**   status epilepticus (G40.901)

■ **R56.9**   **Unspecified convulsions**

Convulsion disorder	Recurrent convulsions
Fit NOS	Seizure(s) (convulsive) NOS

● Unacceptable First-Listed Diagnosis   ● Use Additional Character(s)   ■ Unspecified   **OGCR** Official Guidelines for Coding and Reporting
🐾 Complication\Comorbidity   🐾 Major C\C   Excludes 1   Excludes 2   Includes   Use additional   Code first   Code also

CHAPTER 18 (R00-R99)

● **R57   Shock, not elsewhere classified**

> | Excludes1 | anaphylactic shock NOS (T78.2)
> anaphylactic shock (reaction) due to adverse food reaction (T78.0-)
> anaphylactic shock due to serum (T80.5)
> anesthetic shock (T88.3)
> electric shock (T75.4)
> obstetric shock (O75.1)
> postprocedural shock (T81.1)
> psychic shock (F43.0)
> septic shock (R65.21)
> shock complicating or following ectopic or molar pregnancy (O00-O07, O08.3)
> shock due to lightning (T75.0)
> traumatic shock (T79.4)
> toxic shock syndrome (A48.3)

    R57.0   Cardiogenic shock 🅒
> MCC: Only if patient discharged alive

    R57.1   Hypovolemic shock 🅒
> *Decreased blood volume (loss)*
> MCC: Only if patient discharged alive

    R57.8   Other shock 🅒
> MCC: Only if patient discharged alive

◼ **R57.9   Shock, unspecified** 🅒
> Failure of peripheral circulation NOS
> *Resulting in significant blood pressure drop*

R58   Hemorrhage, not elsewhere classified

> | Includes | hemorrhage NOS
>
> | Excludes1 | hemorrhage included with underlying conditions, such as:
> acute duodenal ulcer with hemorrhage (K26.0)
> acute gastritis with bleeding (K29.01)
> ulcerative enterocolitis with rectal bleeding (K51.01)

● **R59   Enlarged lymph nodes**

> | Includes | swollen glands
>
> | Excludes1 | lymphadenitis NOS (I88.9)
> acute lymphadenitis (L04.-)
> chronic lymphadenitis (I88.1)
> mesenteric (acute) (chronic) lymphadenitis (I88.0)

    R59.0   Localized enlarged lymph nodes

    R59.1   Generalized enlarged lymph nodes
> Lymphadenopathy NOS

◼ **R59.9   Enlarged lymph nodes, unspecified**

● **R60   Edema, not elsewhere classified**

> | Excludes1 | angioneurotic edema (T78.3)
> ascites (R18.-)
> cerebral edema (G93.6)
> cerebral edema due to birth injury (P11.0)
> edema of larynx (J38.4)
> edema of nasopharynx (J39.2)
> edema of pharynx (J39.2)
> gestational edema (O12.0-)
> hereditary edema (Q82.0)
> hydrops fetalis NOS (P83.2)
> hydrothorax (J94.8)
> nutritional edema (E40-E46)
> hydrops fetalis NOS (P83.2)
> newborn edema (P83.3)
> pulmonary edema (J81.-)

    R60.0   Localized edema

    R60.1   Generalized edema

◼ **R60.9   Edema, unspecified**
> Fluid retention NOS

● **R61   Generalized hyperhidrosis**
> Excessive sweating
> Night sweats
> Secondary hyperhidrosis
>
> *Code first, if applicable, menopausal and female climacteric states (N95.1)*
>
> | Excludes1 | focal (primary) (secondary) hyperhidrosis (L74.5-)
> Frey's syndrome (L74.52)
> localized (primary) (secondary) hyperhidrosis (L74.5-)

● **R62   Lack of expected normal physiological development in childhood and adults**

> | Excludes1 | delayed puberty (E30.0)
> gonadal dysgenesis (Q99.1)
> hypopituitarism (E23.0)

    R62.0   Delayed milestone in childhood
> Delayed attainment of expected physiological developmental stage
> Late talker
> Late walker

● **R62.5   Other and unspecified lack of expected normal physiological development in childhood**

> | Excludes1 | HIV disease resulting in failure to thrive (B20)
> physical retardation due to malnutrition (E45)

◼ **R62.50   Unspecified lack of expected normal physiological development in childhood**
> Infantilism NOS

    R62.51   Failure to thrive (child)
> Failure to gain weight
>
> | Excludes1 | failure to thrive in child under 28 days old (P92.6)

    R62.52   Short stature (child)
> Lack of growth   Short stature NOS
> Physical retardation
>
> | Excludes1 | short stature due to endocrine disorder (E34.3)

    R62.59   Other lack of expected normal physiological development in childhood

    R62.7   Adult failure to thrive

● **R63   Symptoms and signs concerning food and fluid intake**

> | Excludes1 | bulimia NOS (F50.2)
> eating disorders of nonorganic origin (F50.-)
> malnutrition (E40-E46)

    R63.0   Anorexia
> Loss of appetite
>
> | Excludes1 | anorexia nervosa (F50.0-)
> loss of appetite of nonorganic origin (F50.8)

    R63.1   Polydipsia
> Excessive thirst

    R63.2   Polyphagia
> Excessive eating   Hyperalimentation NOS

    R63.3   Feeding difficulties
> Feeding problem (elderly) (infant) NOS
>
> | Excludes1 | feeding problems of newborn (P92.-)
> infant feeding disorder of nonorganic origin (F98.2-)

● Unacceptable First-Listed Diagnosis   ● Use Additional Character(s)   ◼ Unspecified   **OGCR** Official Guidelines for Coding and Reporting
🅒 Complication\Comorbidity   🅒 Major C\C | Excludes 1 | | Excludes 2 | | Includes | Use additional   Code first   Code also

1343

CHAPTER 18 (R00-R99)

OGCR Section I.C.18.g.
SIRS due to Non-Infectious Process

The systemic inflammatory response syndrome (SIRS) can develop as a result of certain non-infectious disease processes, such as trauma, malignant neoplasm, or pancreatitis. When SIRS is documented with a noninfectious condition, and no subsequent infection is documented, the code for the underlying condition, such as an injury, should be assigned, followed by code R65.10. Systemic inflammatory response syndrome (SIRS) of non-infectious origin without acute organ dysfunction, or code R65.11, Systemic inflammatory response syndrome (SIRS) of non-infectious origin with acute organ dysfunction. If an associated acute organ dysfunction is documented, the appropriate code(s) for the specific type of organ dysfunction(s) should be assigned in addition to code R65.11. If acute organ dysfunction is documented, but it cannot be determined if the acute organ dysfunction is associated with SIRS or due to another condition (e.g., directly due to the trauma), the provider should be queried.

R63.4 Abnormal weight loss

R63.5 Abnormal weight gain
> **Excludes1** excessive weight gain in pregnancy (O26.0-)
> obesity (E66.-)

R63.6 Underweight
> Use additional code to identify body mass index (BMI), if known (Z68.-)
> **Excludes1** abnormal weight loss (R63.4)
> anorexia nervosa (F50.0-)
> malnutrition (E40-E46)

R63.8 Other symptoms and signs concerning food and fluid intake

R64 Cachexia 🍂
> **Includes** wasting syndrome
> *Code first* underlying condition, if known
> **Excludes1** abnormal weight loss (R63.4)
> nutritional marasmus (E41)

● R65 Symptoms and signs specifically associated with systemic inflammation and infection

● R65.1 Systemic inflammatory response syndrome (SIRS) of non-infectious origin
> *Code first* underlying condition
> **Excludes1** sepsis - code to infection
> severe sepsis (R65.2)

● R65.10 Systemic inflammatory response syndrome (SIRS) of non-infectious origin without acute organ dysfunction 🍂
> Systemic inflammatory response syndrome (SIRS) NOS

● R65.11 Systemic inflammatory response syndrome (SIRS) of non-infectious origin with acute organ dysfunction 🍂
> Use additional code to identify specific acute organ dysfunction, such as:
> acute kidney failure (N17.-)
> acute respiratory failure (J96.0)
> critical illness myopathy (G72.81)
> critical illness polyneuropathy (G62.81)
> disseminated intravascular coagulopathy [DIC] (D65)
> encephalopathy (metabolic) (septic) (G93.41)
> hepatic failure (K72.0-)

● R65.2 Severe sepsis
> Infection with associated acute organ dysfunction
> Sepsis with acute organ dysfunction
> Sepsis with multiple organ dysfunction
> Systemic inflammatory response syndrome due to infectious process with acute organ dysfunction
>
> *Code first* underlying infection, such as:
> Infection following a procedure (T81.4)
> Infections following infusion, transfusion and therapeutic injection (T80.2)
> Sepsis following complete or unspecified spontaneous abortion (O03.87)
> Sepsis following ectopic and molar pregnancy (O08.82)
> Sepsis following incomplete spontaneous abortion (O03.37)
> Sepsis following (induced) termination of pregnancy (O04.87)
> Sepsis NOS A41.9
>
> Use additional code to identify specific acute organ dysfunction, such as:
> acute kidney failure (N17.-)
> acute respiratory failure (J96.0)
> critical illness myopathy (G72.81)
> critical illness polyneuropathy (G62.81)
> disseminated intravascular coagulopathy [DIC] (D65)
> encephalopathy (metabolic) (septic) (G93.41)
> hepatic failure (K72.0-)

● R65.20 Severe sepsis without septic shock 🍂
> Severe sepsis NOS

● R65.21 Severe sepsis with septic shock 🍂

● R68 Other general symptoms and signs

R68.0 Hypothermia, not associated with low environmental temperature
> **Excludes1** hypothermia NOS (accidental) (T68)
> hypothermia due to anesthesia (T88.51)
> hypothermia due to low environmental temperature (T68)
> newborn hypothermia (P80.-)

● R68.1 Nonspecific symptoms peculiar to infancy
> **Excludes1** colic, infantile (R10.43)
> neonatal cerebral irritability (P91.3)
> teething syndrome (K00.7)

R68.11 Excessive crying of infant (baby)
> **Excludes1** excessive crying of child, adolescent, or adult (R45.83)

R68.12 Fussy infant (baby)
> Irritable infant

R68.13 Apparent life threatening event in infant [ALTE]
> Apparent life threatening event in newborn
> Use additional code(s) for associated signs and symptoms
> **Excludes1** signs and symptoms associated with a confirmed diagnosis - code to confirmed diagnosis

R68.19 Other nonspecific symptoms peculiar to infancy

■ R68.2   **Dry mouth, unspecified**

     Excludes1   dry mouth due to dehydration (E86.0)

                 dry mouth due to sicca syndrome [Sjögren] (M35.0-)

                 salivary gland hyposecretion (K11.7)

   R68.3   **Clubbing of fingers**

       Clubbing of nails

       Excludes1   congenital clubfinger (Q68.1)

● R68.8   **Other general symptoms and signs**

     R68.81   **Early satiety**

     R68.82   **Decreased libido**

         Decreased sexual desire

     R68.83   **Chills (without fever)**

         Chills NOS

         Excludes1   chills with fever (R50.9)

     R68.89   **Other general symptoms and signs**

■ R69   **Illness NOS**

     Includes   unknown and unspecified cases of morbidity

ABNORMAL FINDINGS ON EXAMINATION OF BLOOD, WITHOUT DIAGNOSIS (R70-R79)

     Excludes1   abnormalities (of)(on):

            abnormal findings on antenatal screening of mother (O28.-)

            coagulation hemorrhagic disorders (D65-D68)

            lipids (E78.-)

            platelets and thrombocytes (D69.-)

            white blood cells classified elsewhere (D70-D72)

            diagnostic abnormal findings classified elsewhere - see Alphabetical Index

            hemorrhagic and hematological disorders of newborn (P50-P61)

● R70   **Elevated erythrocyte sedimentation rate and abnormality of plasma viscosity**

   R70.0   **Elevated erythrocyte sedimentation rate**

   R70.1   **Abnormal plasma viscosity**

● R71   **Abnormality of red blood cells**

     Excludes1   anemias (D50-D64)

            anemia of premature infant (P61.2)

            benign (familial) polycythemia (D75.0)

            congenital anemias (P61.2-P61.4)

            newborn anemia due to isoimmunization (P55.-)

            polycythemia neonatorum (P61.1)

            polycythemia NOS (D75.1)

            polycythemia vera (D45)

            secondary polycythemia (D75.1)

   R71.0   **Precipitous drop in hematocrit** 🅒

       Drop (precipitous) in hemoglobin

       Drop in hematocrit

       Blood volume that is red blood cells

   R71.8   **Other abnormality of red blood cells**

       Abnormal red-cell morphology NOS

       Abnormal red-cell volume NOS

       Anisocytosis

         Red blood cells of unequal size

       Poikilocytosis

         Red blood cells of abnormal shape

● R73   **Elevated blood glucose level**

     Excludes1   diabetes mellitus (E08-E13)

            diabetes mellitus in pregnancy, childbirth and the puerperium (O24.-)

            neonatal disorders (P70.0-P70.2)

            postsurgical hypoinsulinemia (E89.1)

● R73.0   **Abnormal glucose**

     Excludes1   abnormal glucose in pregnancy (O99.81-)

            diabetes mellitus (E08-E13)

            dysmetabolic syndrome X (E88.81)

            gestational diabetes (O24.4)

            glycosuria (R81)

            hypoglycemia (E16.2)

     R73.01   **Impaired fasting glucose**

         Elevated fasting glucose

     R73.02   **Impaired glucose tolerance (oral)**

         Elevated glucose tolerance

     R73.09   **Other abnormal glucose**

         Abnormal glucose NOS

         Abnormal non-fasting glucose tolerance

         Latent diabetes

         Prediabetes

■ R73.9   **Hyperglycemia, unspecified**

● R74   **Abnormal serum enzyme levels**

   R74.0   **Nonspecific elevation of levels of transaminase and lactic acid dehydrogenase [LDH]**

   R74.8   **Abnormal levels of other serum enzymes**

       Abnormal level of acid phosphatase

       Abnormal level of alkaline phosphatase

       Abnormal level of amylase

       Abnormal level of lipase [triacylglycerol lipase]

■ R74.9   **Abnormal serum enzyme level, unspecified**

   R75   **Inconclusive laboratory evidence of human immunodeficiency virus [HIV]**

     Includes   nonconclusive HIV-test finding in infants

     Excludes1   asymptomatic human immunodeficiency virus [HIV] infection status (Z21)

            human immunodeficiency virus [HIV] disease (B20)

● R76   **Other abnormal immunological findings in serum**

   R76.0   **Raised antibody titer**

     Excludes1   isoimmunization in pregnancy (O36.0-O36.1)

            isoimmunization affecting newborn (P55.-)

   R76.1   **Abnormal reaction to tuberculin test**

       Abnormal result of Mantoux test

   R76.8   **Other specified abnormal immunological findings in serum**

       Raised level of immunoglobulins NOS

■ R76.9   **Abnormal immunological finding in serum, unspecified**

CHAPTER 18 (R00-R99)

● Unacceptable First-Listed Diagnosis   ● Use Additional Character(s)   ■ Unspecified   **OGCR** Official Guidelines for Coding and Reporting

🅒 Complication\Comorbidity   🅒 Major C\C   Excludes 1   Excludes 2   Includes   Use additional   Code first   Code also

1345

OGCR Section I.C.1.2.e and f.
Patients with inconclusive HIV serology

e. Patients with inconclusive HIV serology, but no definitive diagnosis or manifestations of the illness, may be assigned code R75, Inconclusive laboratory evidence of human immunodeficiency virus [HIV].

f. Previously diagnosed HIV-related illness
Patients with any known prior diagnosis of an HIV-related illness should be coded to B20. Once a patient has developed an HIV-related illness, the patient should always be assigned code B20 on every subsequent admission/encounter. Patients previously diagnosed with any HIV illness (B20) should never be assigned to R75 or Z21, Asymptomatic human immunodeficiency virus [HIV] infection status.

● R77   **Other abnormalities of plasma proteins**

     Excludes1   disorders of plasma-protein metabolism (E88.0)

     R77.0   **Abnormality of albumin**

     R77.1   **Abnormality of globulin**
          Hyperglobulinemia NOS

     R77.2   **Abnormality of alphafetoprotein**

     R77.8   **Other specified abnormalities of plasma proteins**

     ■ R77.9   **Abnormality of plasma protein, unspecified**

● R78   **Findings of drugs and other substances, not normally found in blood**

     Excludes1   mental or behavioral disorders due to psychoactive substance use (F10-F19)

     R78.0   **Finding of alcohol in blood**
          Use additional external cause code (Y90.-), for detail regarding alcohol level.

     R78.1   **Finding of opiate drug in blood**

     R78.2   **Finding of cocaine in blood**

     R78.3   **Finding of hallucinogen in blood**

     R78.4   **Finding of other drugs of addictive potential in blood**

     R78.5   **Finding of other psychotropic drug in blood**

     R78.6   **Finding of steroid agent in blood**

     ● R78.7   **Finding of abnormal level of heavy metals in blood**

         R78.71   **Abnormal lead level in blood**

            Excludes1   lead poisoning (T56.0-)

         R78.79   **Finding of abnormal level of heavy metals in blood**

     ● R78.8   **Finding of other specified substances, not normally found in blood**

         R78.81   **Bacteremia** 🦠
            Blood poisoning/bacteremia
            Excludes1   sepsis-code to specified infection (A00-B99)

         R78.89   **Finding of other specified substances, not normally found in blood**
            Finding of abnormal level of lithium in blood

     ■ R78.9   **Finding of unspecified substance, not normally found in blood**

● R79   **Other abnormal findings of blood chemistry**

     Excludes1   abnormality of fluid, electrolyte or acid-base balance (E86-E87)
          asymptomatic hyperuricemia (E79.0)
          hyperglycemia NOS (R73.9)
          hypoglycemia NOS (E16.2)
          neonatal hypoglycemia (P70.3-P70.4)
          specific findings indicating disorder of:
            amino-acid metabolism (E70-E72)
            carbohydrate metabolism (E73-E74)
            lipid metabolism (E75.-)

     R79.0   **Abnormal level of blood mineral**
          Abnormal blood level of cobalt
          Abnormal blood level of copper
          Abnormal blood level of iron
          Abnormal blood level of magnesium
          Abnormal blood level of mineral NEC
          Abnormal blood level of zinc

         Excludes1   abnormal level of lithium (R78.89)
            disorders of mineral metabolism (E83.-)
            neonatal hypomagnesemia (P71.2)
            nutritional mineral deficiency (E58-E61)

     R79.1   **Abnormal coagulation profile**
          Abnormal or prolonged bleeding time
          Abnormal or prolonged coagulation time
          Abnormal or prolonged partial thromboplastin time [PTT]
          Abnormal or prolonged prothrombin time [PT]

         Excludes1   coagulation defects (D68.-)

     ● R79.8   **Other specified abnormal findings of blood chemistry**

         R79.81   **Abnormal blood-gas level**

         R79.82   **Elevated C-reactive protein (CRP)**

         R79.89   **Other specified abnormal findings of blood chemistry**

     ■ R79.9   **Abnormal finding of blood chemistry, unspecified**

ABNORMAL FINDINGS ON EXAMINATION OF URINE, WITHOUT DIAGNOSIS (R80-R82)

     Excludes1   abnormal findings on antenatal screening of mother (O28.-)
          diagnostic abnormal findings classified elsewhere - see Alphabetical Index
          specific findings indicating disorder of:
            amino-acid metabolism (E70-E72)
            carbohydrate metabolism (E73-E74)

● R80   **Proteinuria**

     Excludes1   gestational proteinuria (O12.1-)

     R80.0   **Isolated proteinuria**
          Idiopathic proteinuria

         Excludes1   isolated proteinuria with specific morphological lesion (N06.-)

     ■ R80.1   **Persistent proteinuria, unspecified**

     ■ R80.2   **Orthostatic proteinuria, unspecified**
          Postural proteinuria

     R80.3   **Bence Jones proteinuria**

     R80.8   **Other proteinuria**

     R80.9   **Proteinuria NOS**
          Albuminuria NOS

   R81   **Glycosuria**

     Excludes1   renal glycosuria (E74.8)

● Unacceptable First-Listed Diagnosis   ● Use Additional Character(s)   ■ Unspecified   **OGCR** Official Guidelines for Coding and Reporting
🦠 Complication\Comorbidity   🦠 Major C\C    Includes   Use additional   Code first   Code also

● **R82** **Other and unspecified abnormal findings in urine**

> **Includes** chromoabnormalities in urine

> **Excludes2** hematuria (R31.-)

R82.0 **Chyluria** 🦠
> *White milky urine*
> > **Excludes1** filarial chyluria (B74.-)

R82.1 **Myoglobinuria** 🦠
> *Presence of myoglobin (iron containing protein) in urine*

R82.2 **Biliuria**
> *Presence of bile pigments/salts in urine*

R82.3 **Hemoglobinuria**
> *Presence of hemoglobin in urine*
> > **Excludes1** hemoglobinuria due to hemolysis from external causes NEC (D59.6)
> > hemoglobinuria due to paroxysmal nocturnal [Marchiafava-Micheli] (D59.5)

R82.4 **Acetonuria**
> Ketonuria

R82.5 **Elevated urine levels of drugs, medicaments and biological substances**
> Elevated urine levels of catecholamines
> Elevated urine levels of indoleacetic acid
> Elevated urine levels of 17-ketosteroids
> Elevated urine levels of steroids

R82.6 **Abnormal urine levels of substances chiefly nonmedicinal as to source**
> Abnormal urine level of heavy metals

R82.7 **Abnormal findings on microbiological examination of urine**
> Positive culture findings of urine
> > **Excludes1** colonization status (Z22.-)

R82.8 **Abnormal findings on cytological and histological examination of urine**

● **R82.9** **Other and unspecified abnormal findings in urine**

> ■ **R82.90** **Unspecified abnormal findings in urine**

> **R82.91** **Other chromoabnormalities of urine**
> > Chromoconversion (dipstick)
> > Idiopathic dipstick converts positive for blood with no cellular forms in sediment
> > > **Excludes1** hemoglobinuria (R82.3)
> > > myoglobinuria (R82.1)

> **R82.99** **Other abnormal findings in urine**
> > Cells and casts in urine
> > Crystalluria
> > Melanuria

ABNORMAL FINDINGS ON EXAMINATION OF OTHER BODY FLUIDS, SUBSTANCES AND TISSUES, WITHOUT DIAGNOSIS (R83-R89)

> **Excludes1** abnormal findings on antenatal screening of mother (O28.-)
> diagnostic abnormal findings classified elsewhere - see Alphabetical Index

> **Excludes2** abnormal findings on examination of blood, without diagnosis (R70-R79)
> abnormal findings on examination of urine, without diagnosis (R80-R82)
> abnormal tumor markers (R97.-)

● **R83** **Abnormal findings in cerebrospinal fluid**

R83.0 **Abnormal level of enzymes in cerebrospinal fluid**

R83.1 **Abnormal level of hormones in cerebrospinal fluid**

R83.2 **Abnormal level of other drugs, medicaments and biological substances in cerebrospinal fluid**

R83.3 **Abnormal level of substances chiefly nonmedicinal as to source in cerebrospinal fluid**

R83.4 **Abnormal immunological findings in cerebrospinal fluid**

R83.5 **Abnormal microbiological findings in cerebrospinal fluid**
> Positive culture findings in cerebrospinal fluid
> > **Excludes1** colonization status (Z22.-)

R83.6 **Abnormal cytological findings in cerebrospinal fluid**

R83.8 **Other abnormal findings in cerebrospinal fluid**
> Abnormal chromosomal findings in cerebrospinal fluid

■ **R83.9** **Unspecified abnormal finding in cerebrospinal fluid**

● **R84** **Abnormal findings in specimens from respiratory organs and thorax**

> **Includes** abnormal findings in bronchial washings
> abnormal findings in nasal secretions
> abnormal findings in pleural fluid
> abnormal findings in sputum
> abnormal findings in throat scrapings

> **Excludes1** blood-stained sputum (R04.2)

R84.0 **Abnormal level of enzymes in specimens from respiratory organs and thorax**

R84.1 **Abnormal level of hormones in specimens from respiratory organs and thorax**

R84.2 **Abnormal level of other drugs, medicaments and biological substances in specimens from respiratory organs and thorax**

R84.3 **Abnormal level of substances chiefly nonmedicinal as to source in specimens from respiratory organs and thorax**

R84.4 **Abnormal immunological findings in specimens from respiratory organs and thorax**

R84.5 **Abnormal microbiological findings in specimens from respiratory organs and thorax**
> Positive culture findings in specimens from respiratory organs and thorax
> > **Excludes1** colonization status (Z22.-)

R84.6 **Abnormal cytological findings in specimens from respiratory organs and thorax**

R84.7 **Abnormal histological findings in specimens from respiratory organs and thorax**

R84.8 **Other abnormal findings in specimens from respiratory organs and thorax**
> Abnormal chromosomal findings in specimens from respiratory organs and thorax

■ **R84.9** **Unspecified abnormal finding in specimens from respiratory organs and thorax**

● **R85** **Abnormal findings in specimens from digestive organs and abdominal cavity**

> **Includes** abnormal findings in peritoneal fluid
> abnormal findings in saliva

> **Excludes1** cloudy peritoneal dialysis effluent (R88.0)
> fecal abnormalities (R19.5)

R85.0 **Abnormal level of enzymes in specimens from digestive organs and abdominal cavity**

R85.1 **Abnormal level of hormones in specimens from digestive organs and abdominal cavity**

● Unacceptable First-Listed Diagnosis　　● Use Additional Character(s)　　■ Unspecified　　**OGCR** Official Guidelines for Coding and Reporting
🦠 Complication\Comorbidity　🦠 Major C\C　Excludes 1　Excludes 2　　Includes　Use additional　Code first　Code also

CHAPTER 18 (R00-R99)

1347

R85.2   **Abnormal level of other drugs, medicaments and biological substances in specimens from digestive organs and abdominal cavity**

R85.3   **Abnormal level of substances chiefly nonmedicinal as to source in specimens from digestive organs and abdominal cavity**

R85.4   **Abnormal immunological findings in specimens from digestive organs and abdominal cavity**

R85.5   **Abnormal microbiological findings in specimens from digestive organs and abdominal cavity**

> Positive culture findings in specimens from digestive organs and abdominal cavity
>
> **Excludes1**   colonization status (Z22.-)

● R85.6   **Abnormal cytological findings in specimens from digestive organs and abdominal cavity**

  ● R85.61   **Abnormal cytologic smear of anus**

> **Excludes1**   abnormal cytological findings in specimens from other digestive organs and abdominal cavity (R85.69)
> carcinoma in situ of anus (histologically confirmed) (D01.3)
> anal intraepithelial neoplasia I [AIN I] (K62.82)
> anal intraepithelial neoplasia II [AIN II] (K62.82)
> anal intraepithelial neoplasia III [AIN III] (D01.3)
> dysplasia (mild) (moderate) of anus (histologically confirmed) (K62.82)
> severe dysplasia of anus (histologically confirmed) (D01.3)
>
> **Excludes2**   anal high risk human papillomavirus (HPV) DNA test positive (R85.81)
> anal low risk human papillomavirus (HPV) DNA test positive (R85.82)

    R85.610   **Atypical squamous cells of undetermined significance on cytologic smear of anus (ASC-US)**

    R85.611   **Atypical squamous cells cannot exclude high grade squamous intraepithelial lesion on cytologic smear of anus (ASC-H)**

    R85.612   **Low grade squamous intraepithelial lesion on cytologic smear of anus (LGSIL)**

    R85.613   **High grade squamous intraepithelial lesion on cytologic smear of anus (HGSIL)**

    R85.614   **Cytologic evidence of malignancy on smear of anus**

    R85.615   **Unsatisfactory cytologic smear of anus**

> Inadequate sample of cytologic smear of anus

    R85.616   **Satisfactory anal smear but lacking transformation zone**

    R85.618   **Other abnormal cytological findings on specimens from anus**

    ■ R85.619   **Unspecified abnormal cytological findings in specimens from anus**

> Abnormal anal cytology NOS
> Atypical glandular cells of anus NOS

R85.7   **Abnormal histological findings in specimens from digestive organs and abdominal cavity**

● R85.8   **Other abnormal findings in specimens from digestive organs and abdominal cavity**

  R85.81   **Anal high risk human papillomavirus (HPV) DNA test positive**

> **Excludes1**   anogenital warts due to human papillomavirus (HPV) (A63.0)
> condyloma acuminatum (A63.0)

  R85.82   **Anal low risk human papillomavirus (HPV) DNA test positive**

> Use additional code for associated human papillomavirus (B97.7)

  R85.89   **Other abnormal findings in specimens from digestive organs and abdominal cavity**

> Abnormal chromosomal findings in specimens from digestive organs and abdominal cavity

■ R85.9   **Unspecified abnormal finding in specimens from digestive organs and abdominal cavity**

● R86   **Abnormal findings in specimens from male genital organs**

> **Includes**   abnormal findings in prostatic secretions
> abnormal findings in semen, seminal fluid
> abnormal spermatozoa
>
> **Excludes1**   azoospermia (N46.0-)
> oligospermia (N46.1-)

R86.0   **Abnormal level of enzymes in specimens from male genital organs**

R86.1   **Abnormal level of hormones in specimens from male genital organs**

R86.2   **Abnormal level of other drugs, medicaments and biological substances in specimens from male genital organs**

R86.3   **Abnormal level of substances chiefly nonmedicinal as to source in specimens from male genital organs**

R86.4   **Abnormal immunological findings in specimens from male genital organs**

R86.5   **Abnormal microbiological findings in specimens from male genital organs**

> Positive culture findings in specimens from male genital organs
>
> **Excludes1**   colonization status (Z22.-)

R86.6   **Abnormal cytological findings in specimens from male genital organs**

R86.7   **Abnormal histological findings in specimens from male genital organs**

R86.8   **Other abnormal findings in specimens from male genital organs**

> Abnormal chromosomal findings in specimens from male genital organs

■ R86.9   **Unspecified abnormal finding in specimens from male genital organs**

● R87   **Abnormal findings in specimens from female genital organs**

> **Includes**   abnormal findings in secretion and smears from cervix uteri
> abnormal findings in secretion and smears from vagina
> abnormal findings in secretion and smears from vulva

R87.0   **Abnormal level of enzymes in specimens from female genital organs**

R87.1   **Abnormal level of hormones in specimens from female genital organs**

R87.2 Abnormal level of other drugs, medicaments and biological substances in specimens from female genital organs

R87.3 Abnormal level of substances chiefly nonmedicinal as to source in specimens from female genital organs

R87.4 Abnormal immunological findings in specimens from female genital organs

R87.5 Abnormal microbiological findings in specimens from female genital organs

Positive culture findings in specimens from female genital organs

Excludes1 colonization status (Z22.-)

● R87.6 Abnormal cytological findings in specimens from female genital organs

● R87.61 Abnormal cytological findings in specimens from cervix uteri

Excludes1 abnormal cytological findings in specimens from other female genital organs (R87.69)

abnormal cytological findings in specimens from vagina (R87.62-)

carcinoma in situ of cervix uteri (histologically confirmed) (D06.-)

cervical intraepithelial neoplasia I [CIN I] (N87.0)

cervical intraepithelial neoplasia II [CIN II] (N87.1)

cervical intraepithelial neoplasia III [CIN III] (D06.-)

dysplasia (mild) (moderate) of cervix uteri (histologically confirmed) (N87.-)

severe dysplasia of cervix uteri (histologically confirmed) (D06.-)

Excludes2 cervical high risk human papillomavirus (HPV) DNA test positive (R87.810)

cervical low risk human papillomavirus (HPV) DNA test positive (R87.820)

R87.610 Atypical squamous cells of undetermined significance on cytologic smear of cervix (ASC-US)

R87.611 Atypical squamous cells cannot exclude high grade squamous intraepithelial lesion on cytologic smear of cervix (ASC-H)

R87.612 Low grade squamous intraepithelial lesion on cytologic smear of cervix (LGSIL)

R87.613 High grade squamous intraepithelial lesion on cytologic smear of cervix (HGSIL)

R87.614 Cytologic evidence of malignancy on smear of cervix

R87.615 Unsatisfactory cytologic smear of cervix

Inadequate sample of cytologic smear of cervix

R87.616 Satisfactory cervical smear but lacking transformation zone

R87.618 Other abnormal cytological findings on specimens from cervix uteri

■ R87.619 Unspecified abnormal cytological findings in specimens from cervix uteri

Abnormal cervical cytology NOS

Abnormal Papanicolaou smear of cervix NOS

Abnormal thin preparation smear of cervix NOS

Atypical endocervical cells of cervix NOS

Atypical endometrial cells of cervix NOS

Atypical glandular cells of cervix NOS

● R87.62 Abnormal cytological findings in specimens from vagina

Use additional code to identify acquired absence of uterus and cervix, if applicable (Z90.71-)

Excludes1 abnormal cytological findings in specimens from cervix uteri (R87.61-)

abnormal cytological findings in specimens from other female genital organs (R87.69)

carcinoma in situ of vagina (histologically confirmed) (D07.2)

vaginal intraepithelial neoplasia I [VAIN I] (N89.0)

vaginal intraepithelial neoplasia II [VAIN II] (N89.1)

vaginal intraepithelial neoplasia III [VAIN III] (D07.2)

dysplasia (mild) (moderate) of vagina (histologically confirmed) (N89.-)

severe dysplasia of vagina (histologically confirmed) (D07.2)

Excludes2 vaginal high risk human papillomavirus (HPV) DNA test positive (R87.811)

vaginal low risk human papillomavirus (HPV) DNA test positive (R87.821)

R87.620 Atypical squamous cells of undetermined significance on cytologic smear of vagina (ASC-US)

R87.621 Atypical squamous cells cannot exclude high grade squamous intraepithelial lesion on cytologic smear of vagina (ASC-H)

R87.622 Low grade squamous intraepithelial lesion on cyologic smear of vagina (LGSIL)

R87.623 High grade squamous intraepithelial lesion on cytologic smear of vagina (HGSIL)

R87.624 Cytologic evidence of malignancy on smear of vagina

● Unacceptable First-Listed Diagnosis   ● Use Additional Character(s)   ■ Unspecified   **OGCR** Official Guidelines for Coding and Reporting

🗣 Complication\Comorbidity   🗣 Major C\C   Excludes 1   Excludes 2   Includes   Use additional   Code first   Code also

1349

CHAPTER 18 (R00-R99)

R87.625 **Unsatisfactory cytologic smear of vagina**
Inadequate sample of cytologic smear of vagina

R87.628 **Other abnormal cytological findings on specimens from vagina**

■ R87.629 **Unspecified abnormal cytological findings in specimens from vagina**
Abnormal Papanicolaou smear of vagina NOS
Abnormal thin preparation smear of vagina NOS
Abnormal vaginal cytology NOS
Atypical endocervical cells of vagina NOS
Atypical endometrial cells of vagina NOS
Atypical glandular cells of vagina NOS

R87.69 **Abnormal cytological findings in specimens from other female genital organs**
Abnormal cytological findings in specimens from female genital organs NOS

> **Excludes1** dysplasia of vulva (histologically confirmed) (N90.0-N90.3)

R87.7 **Abnormal histological findings in specimens from female genital organs**

> **Excludes1** carcinoma in situ (histologically confirmed) of female genital organs (D06-D07.3)
> cervical intraepithelial neoplasia I [CIN I] (N87.0)
> cervical intraepithelial neoplasia II [CIN II] (N87.1)
> cervical intraepithelial neoplasia III [CIN III] (D06.-)
> dysplasia (mild) (moderate) of cervix uteri (histologically confirmed) (N87.-)
> dysplasia (mild) (moderate) of vagina (histologically confirmed) (N89.-)
> vaginal intraepithelial neoplasia I [VAIN I] (N89.0)
> vaginal intraepithelial neoplasia II [VAIN II] (N89.1)
> vaginal intraepithelial neoplasia III [VAIN III] (D07.2)
> severe dysplasia of cervix uteri (histologically confirmed) (D06.-)
> severe dysplasia of vagina (histologically confirmed) (D07.2)

● R87.8 **Other abnormal findings in specimens from female genital organs**

● R87.81 **High risk human papillomavirus (HPV) DNA test positive from female genital organs**

> **Excludes1** anogenital warts due to human papillomavirus (HPV) (A63.0)
> condyloma acuminatum (A63.0)

R87.810 **Cervical high risk human papillomavirus (HPV) DNA test positive**

R87.811 **Vaginal high risk human papillomavirus (HPV) DNA test positive**

● R87.82 **Low risk human papillomavirus (HPV) DNA test positive from female genital organs**

> Use additional code for associated human papillomavirus (B97.7)

R87.820 **Cervical low risk human papillomavirus (HPV) DNA test positive**

R87.821 **Vaginal low risk human papillomavirus (HPV) DNA test positive**

R87.89 **Other abnormal findings in specimens from female genital organs**
Abnormal chromosomal findings in specimens from female genital organs

■ R87.9 **Unspecified abnormal finding in specimens from female genital organs**

● R88 **Abnormal findings in other body fluids and substances**

R88.0 **Cloudy (hemodialysis) (peritoneal) dialysis effluent**

R88.8 **Abnormal findings in other body fluids and substances**

● R89 **Abnormal findings in specimens from other organs, systems and tissues**

> **Includes** abnormal findings in nipple discharge
> abnormal findings in synovial fluid
> abnormal findings in wound secretions

R89.0 **Abnormal level of enzymes in specimens from other organs, systems and tissues**

R89.1 **Abnormal level of hormones in specimens from other organs, systems and tissues**

R89.2 **Abnormal level of other drugs, medicaments and biological substances in specimens from other organs, systems and tissues**

R89.3 **Abnormal level of substances chiefly nonmedicinal as to source in specimens from other organs, systems and tissues**

R89.4 **Abnormal immunological findings in specimens from other organs, systems and tissues**

R89.5 **Abnormal microbiological findings in specimens from other organs, systems and tissues**
Positive culture findings in specimens from other organs, systems and tissues

> **Excludes1** colonization status (Z22.-)

R89.6 **Abnormal cytological findings in specimens from other organs, systems and tissues**

R89.7 **Abnormal histological findings in specimens from other organs, systems and tissues**

R89.8 **Other abnormal findings in specimens from other organs, systems and tissues**
Abnormal chromosomal findings in specimens from other organs, systems and tissues

■ R89.9 **Unspecified abnormal finding in specimens from other organs, systems and tissues**

● Unacceptable First-Listed Diagnosis   ● Use Additional Character(s)   ■ Unspecified   **OGCR** Official Guidelines for Coding and Reporting
1350
🦠 Complication\Comorbidity   🦠 Major C\C   Excludes 1   Excludes 2   Includes   Use additional   Code first   Code also

ABNORMAL FINDINGS ON DIAGNOSTIC IMAGING AND IN FUNCTION STUDIES, WITHOUT DIAGNOSIS (R90-R94)

| Includes | nonspecific abnormal findings on diagnostic imaging by: computerized axial tomography [CAT scan] magnetic resonance imaging [MRI][NMR] positron emission tomography [PET scan] thermography ultrasound [echogram] x-ray examination |

| Excludes1 | abnormal findings on antenatal screening of mother (O28.-) diagnostic abnormal findings classified elsewhere - see Alphabetical Index |

● R90   **Abnormal findings on diagnostic imaging of central nervous system**

     R90.0   **Intracranial space-occupying lesion found on diagnostic imaging of central nervous system**

     ● R90.8   **Other abnormal findings on diagnostic imaging of central nervous system**

         R90.81   **Abnormal echoencephalogram**

         ■ R90.82   **White matter disease, unspecified**

         R90.89   **Other abnormal findings on diagnostic imaging of central nervous system**
             Other cerebrovascular abnormality found on diagnostic imaging of central nervous system

R91   **Abnormal findings on diagnostic imaging of lung**

| Includes | coin lesion NOS found on diagnostic imaging of lung lung mass NOS found on diagnostic imaging of lung |

● R92   **Abnormal and inconclusive findings on diagnostic imaging of breast**

     R92.0   **Mammographic microcalcification found on diagnostic imaging of breast**

| Excludes2 | mammographic calcification (calculus) found on diagnostic imaging of breast (R92.1) |

     R92.1   **Mammographic calcification found on diagnostic imaging of breast**
         Mammographic calculus found on diagnostic imaging of breast

     R92.2   **Inconclusive mammogram**
         Dense breasts NOS
         Inconclusive mammogram NEC
         Inconclusive mammography due to dense breasts
         Inconclusive mammography NEC

     R92.8   **Other abnormal and inconclusive findings on diagnostic imaging of breast**

● R93   **Abnormal findings on diagnostic imaging of other body structures**

     R93.0   **Abnormal findings on diagnostic imaging of skull and head, not elsewhere classified**

| Excludes1 | intracranial space-occupying lesion found on diagnostic imaging (R90.0) |

     R93.1   **Abnormal findings on diagnostic imaging of heart and coronary circulation**
         Abnormal echocardiogram NOS
         Abnormal heart shadow

     R93.2   **Abnormal findings on diagnostic imaging of liver and biliary tract**
         Nonvisualization of gallbladder

     R93.3   **Abnormal findings on diagnostic imaging of other parts of digestive tract**

     R93.4   **Abnormal findings on diagnostic imaging of urinary organs**
         Filling defect of bladder found on diagnostic imaging
         Filling defect of kidney found on diagnostic imaging
         Filling defect of ureter found on diagnostic imaging

| Excludes1 | hypertrophy of kidney (N28.81) |

     R93.5   **Abnormal findings on diagnostic imaging of other abdominal regions, including retroperitoneum**

     R93.6   **Abnormal findings on diagnostic imaging of limbs**

| Excludes2 | abnormal finding in skin and subcutaneous tissue (R93.8) |

     R93.7   **Abnormal findings on diagnostic imaging of other parts of musculoskeletal system**

| Excludes2 | abnormal findings on diagnostic imaging of skull (R93.0) |

     R93.8   **Abnormal findings on diagnostic imaging of other specified body structures**
         Abnormal finding by radioisotope localization of placenta
         Abnormal radiological finding in skin and subcutaneous tissue
         Mediastinal shift

     R93.9   **Diagnostic imaging inconclusive due to excess body fat of patient**

● R94   **Abnormal results of function studies**

| Includes | abnormal results of radionuclide [radioisotope] uptake studies abnormal results of scintigraphy |

     ● R94.0   **Abnormal results of function studies of central nervous system**

         R94.01   **Abnormal electroencephalogram [EEG]**

         R94.02   **Abnormal brain scan**

         R94.09   **Abnormal results of other function studies of central nervous system**

     ● R94.1   **Abnormal results of function studies of peripheral nervous system and special senses**

         ● R94.11   **Abnormal results of function studies of eye**

             R94.110   **Abnormal electro-oculogram [EOG]**

             R94.111   **Abnormal electroretinogram [ERG]**
                 Abnormal retinal function study

             R94.112   **Abnormal visually evoked potential [VEP]**

             R94.113   **Abnormal oculomotor study**

             R94.118   **Abnormal results of other function studies of eye**

         ● R94.12   **Abnormal results of function studies of ear and other special senses**

             R94.120   **Abnormal auditory function study**

             R94.121   **Abnormal vestibular function study**

             R94.128   **Abnormal results of other function studies of ear and other special senses**

● Unacceptable First-Listed Diagnosis   ● Use Additional Character(s)   ■ Unspecified   **OGCR** Official Guidelines for Coding and Reporting

🗫 Complication\Comorbidity   🗫 Major C\C   Excludes 1   Excludes 2   Includes   Use additional   Code first   Code also

1351

CHAPTER 18 (R00-R99)

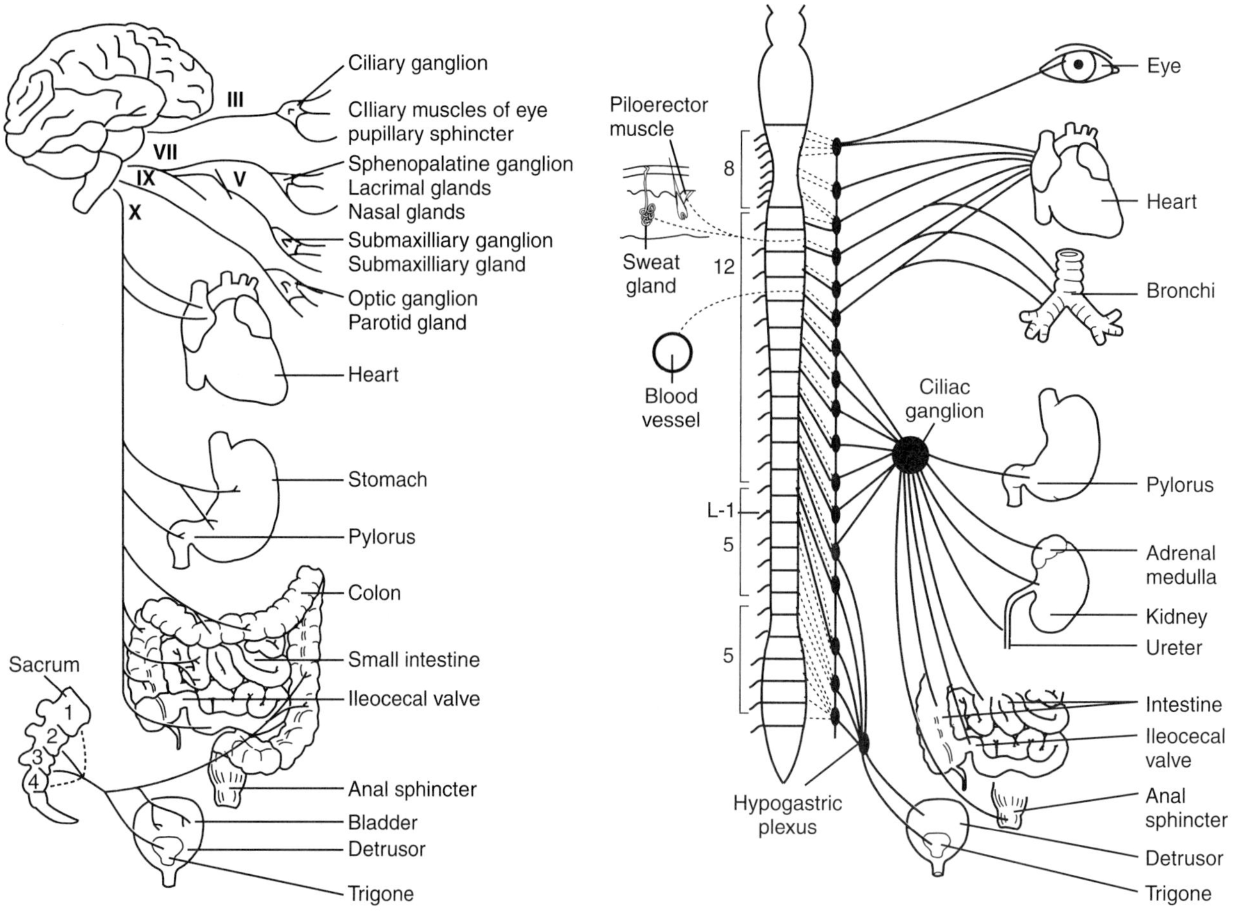

Figure 18-1 A. Parasympathetic nervous system. **B.** Sympathetic nervous system. (From Buck CJ: Step-by-Step Medical Coding, St. Louis, WB Saunders, 2010.)

Item 18-1 The **peripheral nervous system** consists of 31 pairs of spinal nerves, 12 pairs of cranial nerves, and the autonomic nerves, which are divided into the parasympathetic and sympathetic nerves. The cranial nerves are: olfactory (I), optic (II), oculomotor (III), trochlear (IV), trigeminal (V), abducens (VI), facial (VII), vestibulocochlear (VIII), glossopharyngeal (IX), vagus (X), accessory (XI), and hypoglossal (XII).

- ● R94.13   **Abnormal results of function studies of peripheral nervous system**
  - ■ R94.130   **Abnormal response to nerve stimulation, unspecified**
  - R94.131   **Abnormal electromyogram [EMG]**
    - Excludes1   electromyogram of eye (R94.113)
  - R94.138   **Abnormal results of other function studies of peripheral nervous system**
- R94.2   **Abnormal results of pulmonary function studies**
  Reduced ventilatory capacity
  Reduced vital capacity

- ● R94.3   **Abnormal results of cardiovascular function studies**
  - ■ R94.30   **Abnormal result of cardiovascular function study, unspecified**
  - R94.31   **Abnormal electrocardiogram [ECG] [EKG]**
    - Excludes1   long QT syndrome (I45.81)
  - R94.39   **Abnormal result of other cardiovascular function study**
    Abnormal electrophysiological intracardiac studies
    Abnormal phonocardiogram
    Abnormal vectorcardiogram
- R94.4   **Abnormal results of kidney function studies**
  Abnormal renal function test
- R94.5   **Abnormal results of liver function studies**
- R94.6   **Abnormal results of thyroid function studies**
- R94.7   **Abnormal results of other endocrine function studies**
  - Excludes2   abnormal glucose (R73.0-)

CHAPTER 18 (R00-R99)

● Unacceptable First-Listed Diagnosis   ● Use Additional Character(s)   ■ Unspecified   **OGCR** Official Guidelines for Coding and Reporting
🅒 Complication\Comorbidity   🅜 Major C\C   Excludes 1   Excludes 2   Includes   Use additional   Code first   Code also

R94.8   **Abnormal results of function studies of other organs and systems**
Abnormal basal metabolic rate [BMR]
Abnormal bladder function test
Abnormal splenic function test

ABNORMAL TUMOR MARKERS (R97)

● R97   **Abnormal tumor markers**
Elevated tumor associated antigens [TAA]
Elevated tumor specific antigens [TSA]

   R97.0   **Elevated carcinoembryonic antigen [CEA]**

   R97.1   **Elevated cancer antigen 125 [CA 125]**

   R97.2   **Elevated prostate specific antigen [PSA]**

   R97.8   **Other abnormal tumor markers**

ILL-DEFINED AND UNKNOWN CAUSE OF MORTALITY (R99)

■ R99   **Ill-defined and unknown cause of mortality**

   | Includes | death (unexplained) NOS
                 unspecified cause of mortality

OGCR   Section I.C.18.g.
18.6 Death NOS

Code R99, Ill-defined and unknown cause of mortality, is only for use in the very limited circumstance when a patient who has already died is brought into the emergency department or other healthcare facility and is pronounced dead upon arrival. It does not represent the discharge disposition of death.

 Unacceptable First-Listed Diagnosis   ● Use Additional Character(s)   ■ Unspecified   **OGCR** Official Guidelines for Coding and Reporting
 Complication\Comorbidity   Major C\C   Excludes 1   Excludes 2   Includes   Use additional   Code first   Code also

1353

CHAPTER 18 (R00-R99)

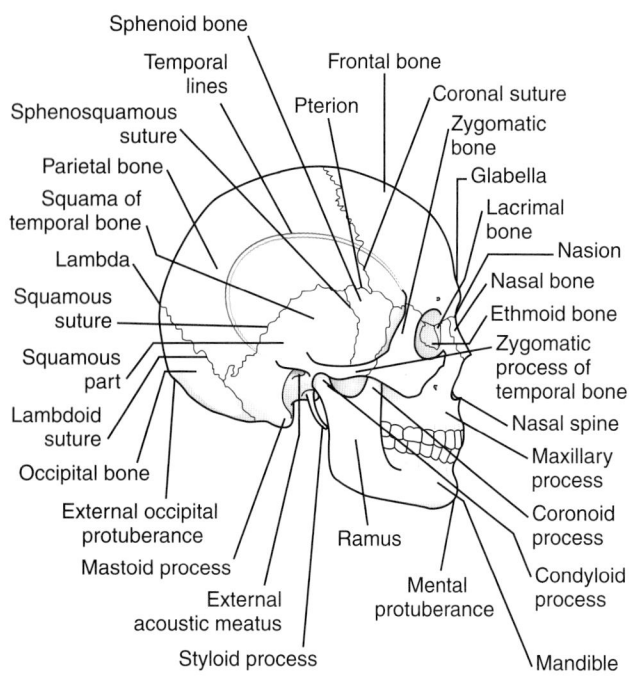

Figure 19-1 Lateral view of skull

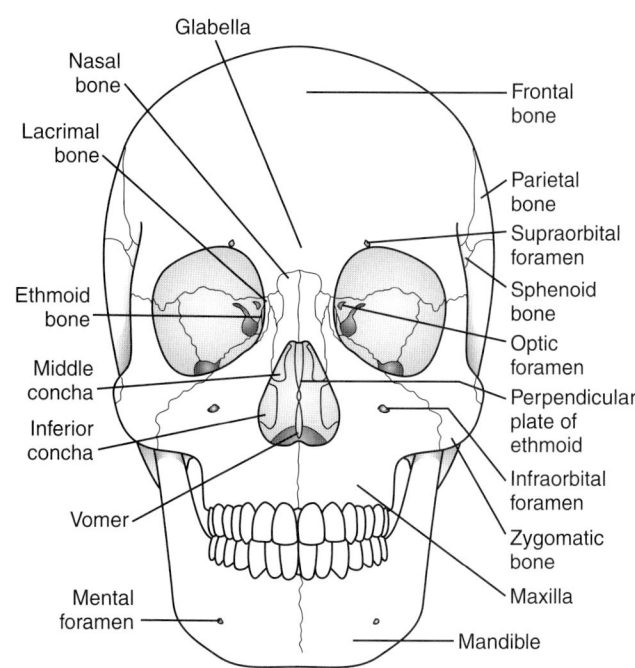

Figure 19-2 Frontal view of skull.

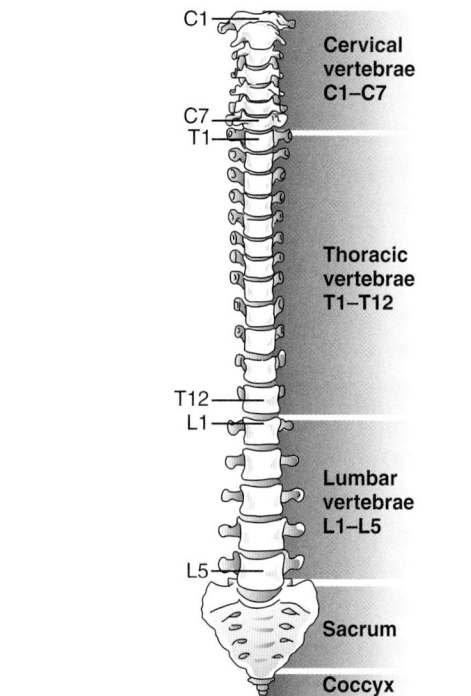

Figure 19-3 Anterior view of vertebral column.

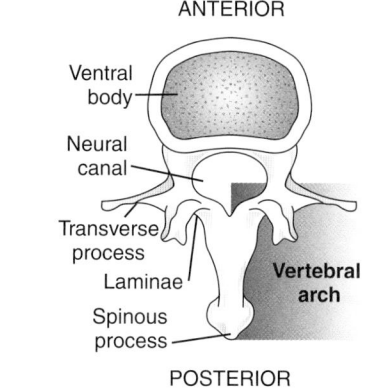

Figure 19-4 Vertebra viewed from above

● Unacceptable First-Listed Diagnosis   ● Use Additional Character(s)   ▮ Unspecified   **OGCR** Official Guidelines for Coding and Reporting

🔖 Complication\Comorbidity   🔖 Major C\C   ⬚ Excludes 1   ⬚ Excludes 2   ▮ Includes   Use additional   Code first   Code also

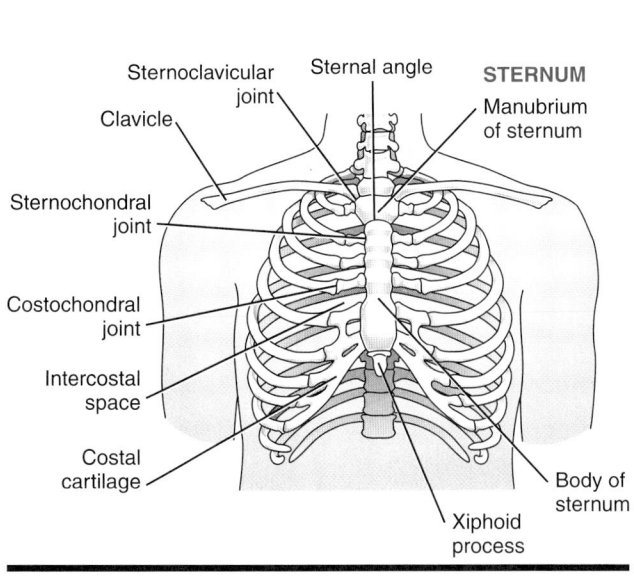

Figure 19-5 Anterior view of rib cage.

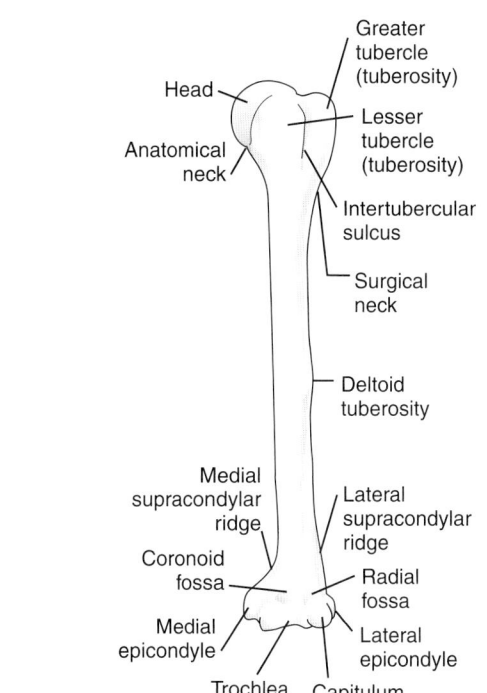

Figure 19-6 Anterior aspect of left humerus.

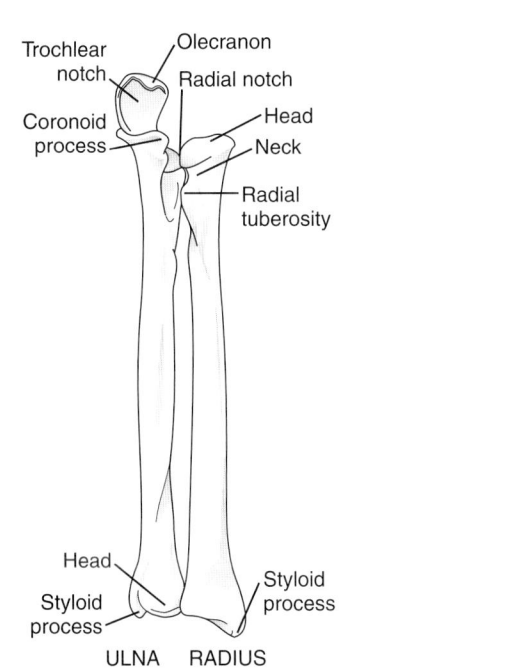

Figure 19-7 Anterior aspect of left radius and ulna.

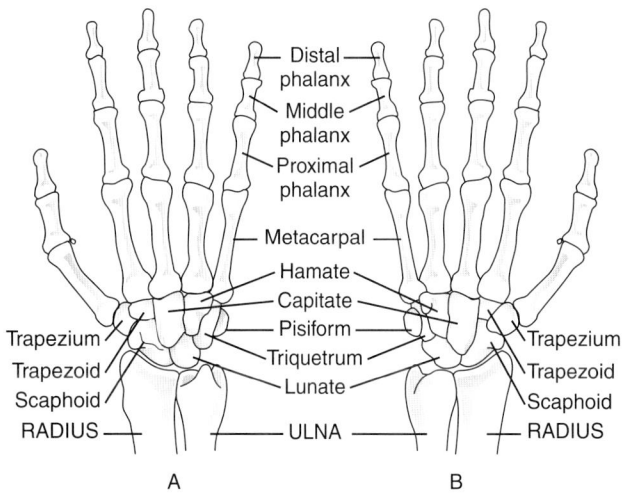

Figure 19-8 Right hand and wrist: **A.** Dorsal surface. **B.** Palmar surface.

● Unacceptable First-Listed Diagnosis   ● Use Additional Character(s)   ▪ Unspecified   **OGCR** Official Guidelines for Coding and Reporting

🔖 Complication\Comorbidity   🔖 Major C\C   Excludes 1   Excludes 2   Includes   Use additional   Code first   Code also

CHAPTER 19 (S00-T88)

1355

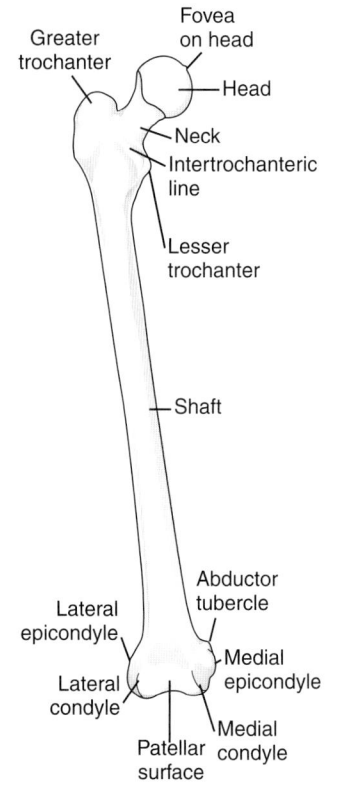

Figure 19-9   Anterior aspect of right femur.

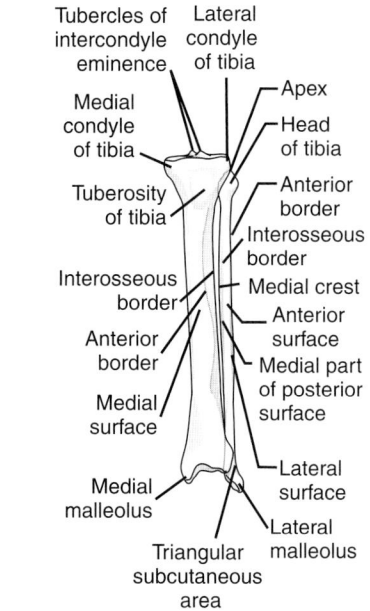

Figure 19-10   Anterior aspect of left tibia and fibula.

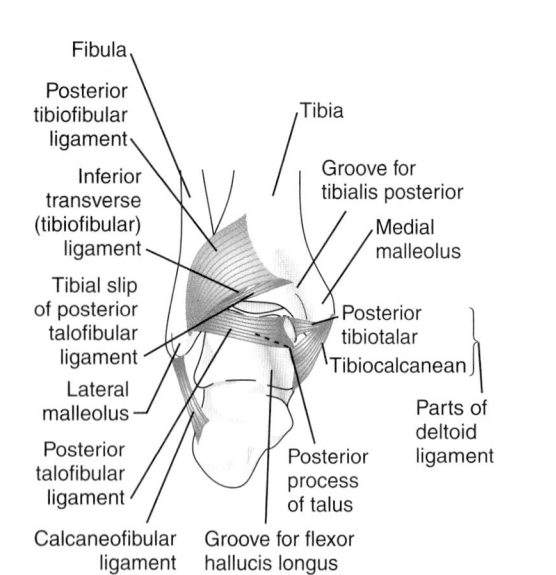

Figure 19-11   Posterior aspect of the left ankle joint.

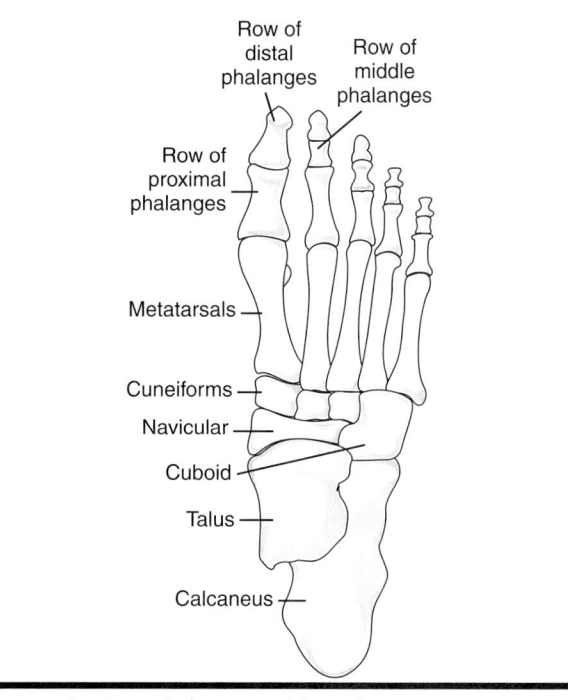

Figure 19-12   Right foot viewed from above.

CHAPTER 19 (S00-T88)

1356

● Unacceptable First-Listed Diagnosis   ● Use Additional Character(s)   ■ Unspecified   **OGCR** Official Guidelines for Coding and Reporting
🄒 Complication\Comorbidity   🄒 Major C\C   Excludes 1   Excludes 2   Includes   Use additional   Code first   Code also

OGCR Chapter Guidelines are located in **Section I.9.**

CHAPTER 19

INJURY, POISONING AND CERTAIN OTHER CONSEQUENCES OF EXTERNAL CAUSES (S00-T88)

Use secondary code(s) from Chapter 20, External causes of morbidity, to indicate cause of injury. Codes within the T section that include the external cause do not require an additional external cause code

Excludes1   birth trauma (P10-P15)
              obstetric trauma (O70-O71)

This chapter contains the following blocks:

S00-S09	Injuries to the head
S10-S19	Injuries to the neck
S20-S29	Injuries to the thorax
S30-S39	Injuries to the abdomen, lower back, lumbar spine, pelvis and external genitals
S40-S49	Injuries to the shoulder and upper arm
S50-S59	Injuries to the elbow and forearm
S60-S69	Injuries to the wrist and hand
S70-S79	Injuries to the hip and thigh
S80-S89	Injuries to the knee and lower leg
S90-S99	Injuries to the ankle and foot
T07	Unspecified multiple injuries
T14	Injury of unspecified body region
T15-T19	Effects of foreign body entering through natural orifice
T20-T32	Burns and corrosions
T33-T34	Frostbite
T36-T50	Poisoning by, adverse effect of and underdosing of drugs, medicaments and biological substances
T51-T65	Toxic effects of substances chiefly nonmedicinal as to source
T66-T78	Other and unspecified effects of external causes
T79	Certain early complications of trauma
T80-T88	Complications of surgical and medical care, not elsewhere classified

The chapter uses the S-section for coding different types of injuries related to single body regions and the T-section to cover injuries to unspecified body regions as well as poisoning and certain other consequences of external causes.

INJURIES TO THE HEAD (S00-S09)

Includes   injuries of ear
             injuries of eye
             injuries of face [any part]
             injuries of gum
             injuries of jaw
             injuries of oral cavity
             injuries of palate
             injuries of periocular area
             injuries of scalp
             injuries of temporomandibular joint area
             injuries of tongue
             injuries of tooth

Code also for any associated infection

Excludes2   burns and corrosions (T20-T32)
             effects of foreign body in ear (T16)
             effects of foreign body in larynx (T17.3)
             effects of foreign body in mouth NOS (T18.0)
             effects of foreign body in nose (T17.0-T17.1)
             effects of foreign body in pharynx (T17.2)
             effects of foreign body on external eye (T15.-)
             frostbite (T33-T34)
             insect bite or sting, venomous (T63.4)

● **S00 Superficial injury of head**

Excludes1   diffuse cerebral contusion (S06.2-)
             focal cerebral contusion (S06.3-)
             injury of eye and orbit (S05.-)
             open wound of head (S01.-)

The appropriate 7th character is to be added to each code from category S00

A	initial encounter
D	subsequent encounter
S	sequela

● **S00.0   Superficial injury of scalp**

  ● ■ **S00.00 Unspecified superficial injury of scalp**

  ● **S00.01 Abrasion of scalp**

  ● **S00.02 Blister (nonthermal) of scalp**

  ● **S00.03 Contusion of scalp**
           Bruise of scalp
           Hematoma of scalp

  ● **S00.04 External constriction of part of scalp**

  ● **S00.05 Superficial foreign body of scalp**
           Splinter in the scalp

  ● **S00.06 Insect bite (nonvenomous) of scalp**

  ● **S00.07 Other superficial bite of scalp**
           Excludes1   open bite of scalp (S01.05)

● **S00.1   Contusion of eyelid and periocular area**
         Black eye
         Excludes2   contusion of eyeball and orbital tissues (S05.1)

  ● ■ **S00.10 Contusion of unspecified eyelid and periocular area**

  ● **S00.11 Contusion of right eyelid and periocular area**

  ● **S00.12 Contusion of left eyelid and periocular area**

● **S00.2   Other and unspecified superficial injuries of eyelid and periocular area**
         Excludes2   superficial injury of conjunctiva and cornea (S05.0-)

  ● ■ **S00.20 Unspecified superficial injury of eyelid and periocular area**

       S00.201 Unspecified superficial injury of right eyelid and periocular area

---

● Unacceptable First-Listed Diagnosis   ● Use Additional Character(s)   ■ Unspecified   OGCR Official Guidelines for Coding and Reporting

🜨 Complication\Comorbidity   🜨 Major C\C   Excludes 1   Excludes 2   Includes   Use additional   Code first   Code also

CHAPTER 19 (S00-T88)

1357

● ■ **S00.202** Unspecified superficial injury of left eyelid and periocular area

● ■ **S00.209** Unspecified superficial injury of unspecified eyelid and periocular area

● **S00.21** Abrasion of eyelid and periocular area

　● **S00.211** Abrasion of right eyelid and periocular area

　● **S00.212** Abrasion of left eyelid and periocular area

　● ■ **S00.219** Abrasion of unspecified eyelid and periocular area

● **S00.22** Blister (nonthermal) of eyelid and periocular area

　● **S00.221** Blister (nonthermal) of right eyelid and periocular area

　● **S00.222** Blister (nonthermal) of left eyelid and periocular area

　● ■ **S00.229** Blister (nonthermal) of unspecified eyelid and periocular area

● **S00.24** External constriction of eyelid and periocular area

　● **S00.241** External constriction of right eyelid and periocular area

　● **S00.242** External constriction of left eyelid and periocular area

　● ■ **S00.249** External constriction of unspecified eyelid and periocular area

● **S00.25** Superficial foreign body of eyelid and periocular area
　　Splinter of eyelid and periocular area
　　Excludes2　retained foreign body in eyelid (H02.81-)

　● **S00.251** Superficial foreign body of right eyelid and periocular area

　● **S00.252** Superficial foreign body of left eyelid and periocular area

　● ■ **S00.259** Superficial foreign body of unspecified eyelid and periocular area

● **S00.26** Insect bite (nonvenomous) of eyelid and periocular area

　● **S00.261** Insect bite (nonvenomous) of right eyelid and periocular area

　● **S00.262** Insect bite (nonvenomous) of left eyelid and periocular area

　● ■ **S00.269** Insect bite (nonvenomous) of unspecified eyelid and periocular area

● **S00.27** Other superficial bite of eyelid and periocular area
　　Excludes1　open bite of eyelid and periocular area (S01.15)

　● **S00.271** Other superficial bite of right eyelid and periocular area

　● **S00.272** Other superficial bite of left eyelid and periocular area

　● ■ **S00.279** Other superficial bite of unspecified eyelid and periocular area

● **S00.3** Superficial injury of nose

　● ■ **S00.30** Unspecified superficial injury of nose

● **S00.31** Abrasion of nose

● **S00.32** Blister (nonthermal) of nose

● **S00.33** Contusion of nose
　　Bruise of nose
　　Hematoma of nose

● **S00.34** External constriction of nose

● **S00.35** Superficial foreign body of nose
　　Splinter in the nose

● **S00.36** Insect bite (nonvenomous) of nose

● **S00.37** Other superficial bite of nose
　　Excludes1　open bite of nose (S01.25)

● **S00.4** Superficial injury of ear

　● **S00.40** Unspecified superficial injury of ear

　　● ■ **S00.401** Unspecified superficial injury of right ear

　　● ■ **S00.402** Unspecified superficial injury of left ear

　　● ■ **S00.409** Unspecified superficial injury of unspecified ear

　● **S00.41** Abrasion of ear

　　● **S00.411** Abrasion of right ear

　　● **S00.412** Abrasion of left ear

　　● ■ **S00.419** Abrasion of unspecified ear

　● **S00.42** Blister (nonthermal) of ear

　　● **S00.421** Blister (nonthermal) of right ear

　　● **S00.422** Blister (nonthermal) of left ear

　　● ■ **S00.429** Blister (nonthermal) of unspecified ear

　● **S00.43** Contusion of ear
　　　Bruise of ear
　　　Hematoma of ear

　　● **S00.431** Contusion of right ear

　　● **S00.432** Contusion of left ear

　　● ■ **S00.439** Contusion of unspecified ear

　● **S00.44** External constriction of ear

　　● **S00.441** External constriction of right ear

　　● **S00.442** External constriction of left ear

　　● ■ **S00.449** External constriction of unspecified ear

　● **S00.45** Superficial foreign body of ear
　　　Splinter in the ear

　　● **S00.451** Superficial foreign body of right ear

　　● **S00.452** Superficial foreign body of left ear

　　● ■ **S00.459** Superficial foreign body of unspecified ear

　● **S00.46** Insect bite (nonvenomous) of ear

　　● **S00.461** Insect bite (nonvenomous) of right ear

　　● **S00.462** Insect bite (nonvenomous) of left ear

　　● ■ **S00.469** Insect bite (nonvenomous) of unspecified ear

　● **S00.47** Other superficial bite of ear
　　　Excludes1　open bite of ear (S01.35)

　　● **S00.471** Other superficial bite of right ear

　　● **S00.472** Other superficial bite of left ear

　　● ■ **S00.479** Other superficial bite of unspecified ear

● **S00.5**   **Superficial injury of lip and oral cavity**

  ● **S00.50**   Unspecified superficial injury of lip and oral cavity

    ● ▪ **S00.501**   Unspecified superficial injury of lip

    ● ▪ **S00.502**   Unspecified superficial injury of oral cavity

  ● **S00.51**   Abrasion of lip and oral cavity

    ● **S00.511**   Abrasion of lip

    ● **S00.512**   Abrasion of oral cavity

  ● **S00.52**   Blister (nonthermal) of lip and oral cavity

    ● **S00.521**   Blister (nonthermal) of lip

    ● **S00.522**   Blister (nonthermal) of oral cavity

  ● **S00.53**   Contusion of lip and oral cavity

    ● **S00.531**   Contusion of lip
          Bruise of lip
          Hematoma of oral cavity

    ● **S00.532**   Contusion of oral cavity
          Bruise of lip
          Hematoma of oral cavity

  ● **S00.54**   External constriction of lip and oral cavity

    ● **S00.541**   External constriction of lip

    ● **S00.542**   External constriction of oral cavity

  ● **S00.55**   Superficial foreign body of lip and oral cavity

    ● **S00.551**   Superficial foreign body of lip
          Splinter of lip and oral cavity

    ● **S00.552**   Superficial foreign body of oral cavity
          Splinter of lip and oral cavity

  ● **S00.56**   Insect bite (nonvenomous) of lip and oral cavity

    ● **S00.561**   Insect bite (nonvenomous) of lip

    ● **S00.562**   Insect bite (nonvenomous) of oral cavity

  ● **S00.57**   Other superficial bite of lip and oral cavity

    ● **S00.571**   Other superficial bite of lip

         | **Excludes1** | open bite of lip (S01.551)

    ● **S00.572**   Other superficial bite of oral cavity

         | **Excludes1** | open bite of oral cavity (S01.552)

● **S00.8**   **Superficial injury of other parts of head**

  ● ▪ **S00.80**   Unspecified superficial injury of other part of head

  ● **S00.81**   Abrasion of other part of head

  ● **S00.82**   Blister (nonthermal) of other part of head

  ● **S00.83**   Contusion of other part of head
        Bruise of other part of head
        Hematoma of other part of head

  ● **S00.84**   External constriction of other part of head

  ● **S00.85**   Superficial foreign body of other part of head
        Splinter in other part of head

  ● **S00.86**   Insect bite (nonvenomous) of other part of head

● **S00.87**   Other superficial bite of other part of head

     | **Excludes1** | open bite of other part of head (S01.87)

● **S00.9**   **Superficial injury of unspecified part of head**

  ● ▪ **S00.90**   Unspecified superficial injury of unspecified part of head

  ● ▪ **S00.91**   Abrasion of unspecified part of head

  ● ▪ **S00.92**   Blister (nonthermal) of unspecified part of head

  ● ▪ **S00.93**   Contusion of unspecified part of head
        Bruise of head
        Hematoma of head

  ● ▪ **S00.94**   External constriction of unspecified part of head

  ● ▪ **S00.95**   Superficial foreign body of unspecified part of head
        Splinter of head

  ● ▪ **S00.96**   Insect bite (nonvenomous) of unspecified part of head

  ● ▪ **S00.97**   Other superficial bite of unspecified part of head

     | **Excludes1** | open bite of head (S01.95)

● **S01**   **Open wound of head**
    Code also any associated:
      injury of cranial nerve (S04.-)
      injury of muscle and tendon of head (S09.1-)
      intracranial injury (S06.-)
      wound infection

    | **Excludes1** | open skull fracture (S02.- with 7th character B)

    | **Excludes2** | injury of eye and orbit (S05.-)
             traumatic amputation of part of head (S08.-)

    The appropriate 7th character is to be added to each code from category S01

    | A   initial encounter |
    | D   subsequent encounter |
    | S   sequela |

  ● **S01.0**   **Open wound of scalp**

     | **Excludes1** | avulsion of scalp (S08.0)

    ● ▪ **S01.00**   Unspecified open wound of scalp

    ● **S01.01**   Laceration without foreign body of scalp

    ● **S01.02**   Laceration with foreign body of scalp

    ● **S01.03**   Puncture wound without foreign body of scalp

    ● **S01.04**   Puncture wound with foreign body of scalp

    ● **S01.05**   Open bite of scalp
          Bite of scalp NOS

       | **Excludes1** | superficial bite of scalp (S00.06, S00.07-)

  ● **S01.1**   **Open wound of eyelid and periocular area**
      Open wound of eyelid and periocular area with or without involvement of lacrimal passages

    ● **S01.10**   Unspecified open wound of eyelid and periocular area

      ● ▪ **S01.101**   Unspecified open wound of right eyelid and periocular area A 🔗

      ● ▪ **S01.102**   Unspecified open wound of left eyelid and periocular area A 🔗

      ● ▪ **S01.109**   Unspecified open wound of unspecified eyelid and periocular area A 🔗

● Unacceptable First-Listed Diagnosis   ● Use Additional Character(s)   ▪ Unspecified   **OGCR** Official Guidelines for Coding and Reporting

🔗 Complication\Comorbidity   🔗 Major C\C | Excludes 1 | | Excludes 2 | Includes   Use additional   Code first   Code also

CHAPTER 19 (S00-T88)

1359

- ● S01.11   Laceration without foreign body of eyelid and periocular area
  - ● S01.111   Laceration without foreign body of right eyelid and periocular area
  - ● S01.112   Laceration without foreign body of left eyelid and periocular area
  - ● ■ S01.119   Laceration without foreign body of unspecified eyelid and periocular area
- ● S01.12   Laceration with foreign body of eyelid and periocular area
  - ● S01.121   Laceration with foreign body of right eyelid and periocular area
  - ● S01.122   Laceration with foreign body of left eyelid and periocular area
  - ● ■ S01.129   Laceration with foreign body of unspecified eyelid and periocular area
- ● S01.13   Puncture wound without foreign body of eyelid and periocular area
  - ● S01.131   Puncture wound without foreign body of right eyelid and periocular area
  - ● S01.132   Puncture wound without foreign body of left eyelid and periocular area
  - ● ■ S01.139   Puncture wound without foreign body of unspecified eyelid and periocular area
- ● S01.14   Puncture wound with foreign body of eyelid and periocular area
  - ● S01.141   Puncture wound with foreign body of right eyelid and periocular area
  - ● S01.142   Puncture wound with foreign body of left eyelid and periocular area
  - ● ■ S01.149   Puncture wound with foreign body of unspecified eyelid and periocular area
- ● S01.15   Open bite of eyelid and periocular area
  Bite of eyelid and periocular area NOS
  - Excludes1   superficial bite of eyelid and periocular area (S00.26, S00.27)
  - ● S01.151   Open bite of right eyelid and periocular area
  - ● S01.152   Open bite of left eyelid and periocular area
  - ● ■ S01.159   Open bite of unspecified eyelid and periocular area
- ● S01.2   Open wound of nose
  - ● ■ S01.20   Unspecified open wound of nose
  - ● S01.21   Laceration without foreign body of nose
  - ● S01.22   Laceration with foreign body of nose
  - ● S01.23   Puncture wound without foreign body of nose
  - ● S01.24   Puncture wound with foreign body of nose
  - ● S01.25   Open bite of nose
    Bite of nose NOS
    - Excludes1   superficial bite of nose (S00.36, S00.37)

- ● S01.3   Open wound of ear
  - ● S01.30   Unspecified open wound of ear
    - ● ■ S01.301   Unspecified open wound of right ear
    - ● ■ S01.302   Unspecified open wound of left ear
    - ● ■ S01.309   Unspecified open wound of unspecified ear
  - ● S01.31   Laceration without foreign body of ear
    - ● S01.311   Laceration without foreign body of right ear
    - ● S01.312   Laceration without foreign body of left ear
    - ● ■ S01.319   Laceration without foreign body of unspecified ear
  - ● S01.32   Laceration with foreign body of ear
    - ● S01.321   Laceration with foreign body of right ear
    - ● S01.322   Laceration with foreign body of left ear
    - ● ■ S01.329   Laceration with foreign body of unspecified ear
  - ● S01.33   Puncture wound without foreign body of ear
    - ● S01.331   Puncture wound without foreign body of right ear
    - ● S01.332   Puncture wound without foreign body of left ear
    - ● ■ S01.339   Puncture wound without foreign body of unspecified ear
  - ● S01.34   Puncture wound with foreign body of ear
    - ● S01.341   Puncture wound with foreign body of right ear
    - ● S01.342   Puncture wound with foreign body of left ear
    - ● ■ S01.349   Puncture wound with foreign body of unspecified ear
  - ● S01.35   Open bite of ear
    Bite of ear NOS
    - Excludes1   superficial bite of ear (S00.46, S00.47)
    - ● S01.351   Open bite of right ear
    - ● S01.352   Open bite of left ear
    - ● ■ S01.359   Open bite of unspecified ear
- ● S01.4   Open wound of cheek and temporomandibular area
  - ● S01.40   Unspecified open wound of cheek and temporomandibular area
    - ● ■ S01.401   Unspecified open wound of right cheek and temporomandibular area
    - ● ■ S01.402   Unspecified open wound of left cheek and temporomandibular area
    - ● ■ S01.409   Unspecified open wound of unspecified cheek and temporomandibular area
  - ● S01.41   Laceration without foreign body of cheek and temporomandibular area
    - ● S01.411   Laceration without foreign body of right cheek and temporomandibular area
    - ● S01.412   Laceration without foreign body of left cheek and temporomandibular area

● ■ S01.419   Laceration without foreign body of unspecified cheek and temporomandibular area

● S01.42   Laceration with foreign body of cheek and temporomandibular area

   ● S01.421   Laceration with foreign body of right cheek and temporomandibular area

   ● S01.422   Laceration with foreign body of left cheek and temporomandibular area

   ● ■ S01.429   Laceration with foreign body of unspecified cheek and temporomandibular area

● S01.43   Puncture wound without foreign body of cheek and temporomandibular area

   ● S01.431   Puncture wound without foreign body of right cheek and temporomandibular area

   ● S01.432   Puncture wound without foreign body of left cheek and temporomandibular area

   ● ■ S01.439   Puncture wound without foreign body of unspecified cheek and temporomandibular area

● S01.44   Puncture wound with foreign body of cheek and temporomandibular area

   ● S01.441   Puncture wound with foreign body of right cheek and temporomandibular area

   ● S01.442   Puncture wound with foreign body of left cheek and temporomandibular area

   ● ■ S01.449   Puncture wound with foreign body of unspecified cheek and temporomandibular area

● S01.45   Open bite of cheek and temporomandibular area
   Bite of cheek and temporomandibular area NOS

   Excludes2 superficial bite of cheek and temporomandibular area (S00.86, S00.87)

   ● S01.451   Open bite of right cheek and temporomandibular area

   ● S01.452   Open bite of left cheek and temporomandibular area

   ● ■ S01.459   Open bite of unspecified cheek and temporomandibular area

● S01.5   Open wound of lip and oral cavity

   Excludes2 tooth dislocation (S03.2)
   tooth fracture (S02.5)

   ● S01.50   Unspecified open wound of lip and oral cavity

   ● ■ S01.501   Unspecified open wound of lip

   ● ■ S01.502   Unspecified open wound of oral cavity

   ● S01.51   Laceration of lip and oral cavity without foreign body

   ● S01.511   Laceration without foreign body of lip

   ● S01.512   Laceration without foreign body of oral cavity

● S01.52   Laceration of lip and oral cavity with foreign body

   ● S01.521   Laceration with foreign body of lip

   ● S01.522   Laceration with foreign body of oral cavity

● S01.53   Puncture wound of lip and oral cavity without foreign body

   ● S01.531   Puncture wound without foreign body of lip

   ● S01.532   Puncture wound without foreign body of oral cavity

● S01.54   Puncture wound of lip and oral cavity with foreign body

   ● S01.541   Puncture wound with foreign body of lip

   ● S01.542   Puncture wound with foreign body of oral cavity

● S01.55   Open bite of lip and oral cavity

   ● S01.551   Open bite of lip
   Bite of lip NOS
   Excludes1 superficial bite of lip (S00.571)

   ● S01.552   Open bite of oral cavity
   Bite of oral cavity NOS
   Excludes1 superficial bite of oral cavity (S00.572)

● S01.8   Open wound of other parts of head

   ● ■ S01.80   Unspecified open wound of other part of head

   ● S01.81   Laceration without foreign body of other part of head

   ● S01.82   Laceration with foreign body of other part of head

   ● S01.83   Puncture wound without foreign body of other part of head

   ● S01.84   Puncture wound with foreign body of other part of head

   ● S01.85   Open bite of other part of head
   Bite of other part of head NOS
   Excludes1 superficial bite of other part of head (S00.85)

● S01.9   Open wound of unspecified part of head

   ● ■ S01.90   Unspecified open wound of unspecified part of head

   ● ■ S01.91   Laceration without foreign body of unspecified part of head

   ● ■ S01.92   Laceration with foreign body of unspecified part of head

   ● ■ S01.93   Puncture wound without foreign body of unspecified part of head

   ● ■ S01.94   Puncture wound with foreign body of unspecified part of head

   ● ■ S01.95   Open bite of unspecified part of head
   Bite of head NOS
   Excludes1 superficial bite of head NOS (S00.97)

● Unacceptable First-Listed Diagnosis   ● Use Additional Character(s)   ■ Unspecified   OGCR Official Guidelines for Coding and Reporting

🖏 Complication\Comorbidity   🖏 Major C\C   Excludes 1   Excludes 2    Includes    Use additional   Code first   Code also

1361

CHAPTER 19 (S00-T88)

● **S02   Fracture of skull and facial bones**
Code also any associated intracranial injury (S06.-)
The appropriate 7th character is to be added to each code
from category S02
A fracture not indicated as open or closed should be
coded to closed

> A   initial encounter for closed fracture
> B   initial encounter for open fracture
> D   subsequent encounter for fracture with routine
>   healing
> G   subsequent encounter for fracture with delayed
>   healing
> K   subsequent encounter for fracture with nonunion
> S   sequela

● **S02.0   Fracture of vault of skull A, K 🦠, B 🦠**
Fracture of frontal bone
Fracture of parietal bone

● **S02.1   Fracture of base of skull**
> **Excludes1**   orbit NOS (S02.89)
> **Excludes2**   orbital floor (S02.3-)

● ■ **S02.10   Unspecified fracture of base of
skull A, K 🦠, B 🦠**

● **S02.11   Fracture of occiput**

● **S02.110   Type I occipital condyle fracture
A, K 🦠, B 🦠**

● **S02.111   Type II occipital condyle fracture
A, K 🦠, B 🦠**

● **S02.112   Type III occipital condyle
fracture A, K 🦠, B 🦠**

● ■ **S02.113   Unspecified occipital condyle
fracture A, K 🦠, B 🦠**

● **S02.118   Other fracture of occiput A, K 🦠,
B 🦠**

● ■ **S02.119   Unspecified fracture of occiput
A, K 🦠, B 🦠**

● **S02.19   Other fracture of base of skull A, K 🦠,
B 🦠**
Fracture of anterior fossa of base of skull
Fracture of ethmoid sinus
Fracture of frontal sinus
Fracture of middle fossa of base of skull
Fracture of orbital roof
Fracture of posterior fossa of base of
skull
Fracture of sphenoid
Fracture of temporal bone

● **S02.2   Fracture of nasal bones B, X 🦠**

● **S02.3   Fracture of orbital floor A, B, K 🦠**
> **Excludes1**   orbit NOS (S02.89)
> **Excludes2**   orbital roof (S02.1-)

● **S02.4   Fracture of malar, maxillary and zygoma bones**
Fracture of superior maxilla
Fracture of upper jaw (bone)
Fracture of zygomatic process of temporal bone

● ■ **S02.40   Fracture of malar, maxillary and zygoma
bones, unspecified A, B, K 🦠**

● **S02.41   LeFort fracture**

● **S02.411   LeFort I fracture A, B, K 🦠**

● **S02.412   LeFort II fracture A, B, K 🦠**

● **S02.413   LeFort III fracture A, B, K 🦠**

● **S02.44   Fracture of zygoma A, B, K 🦠**

● **S02.5   Fracture of tooth (traumatic) Broken tooth K 🦠**
> **Excludes1**   cracked tooth (nontraumatic)
>   (K03.81)

● **S02.6   Fracture of mandible**
Fracture of lower jaw (bone)

● ■ **S02.60   Fracture of mandible of unspecified site
A, B, K 🦠**

● **S02.61   Fracture of condylar process of mandible
A, B, K 🦠**

● **S02.62   Fracture of subcondylar process of mandible
A, B, K 🦠**

● **S02.63   Fracture of coronoid process of mandible
A, B, K 🦠**

● **S02.64   Fracture of ramus of mandible A, B, K 🦠**

● **S02.65   Fracture of angle of mandible A, B, K 🦠**

● **S02.66   Fracture of symphysis of mandible A, B, K 🦠**

● ■ **S02.68   Fracture of unspecified part of body of
mandible A, B, K 🦠**

● **S02.69   Fracture of mandible of other site A, B, K 🦠**

● **S02.8   Fractures of other skull and facial bones**

● **S02.81   Fracture of alveolus, maxilla A, B, K 🦠**

● **S02.82   Fracture of alveolus, mandible A, B, K 🦠**

● ■ **S02.83   Fracture of alveolus, unspecified A, B, K 🦠**

● **S02.89   Fractures of other skull and facial bones
A, B, K 🦠**
Fracture of orbit NOS
Fracture of palate
> **Excludes1**   fracture of orbital floor (S02.3-)
>   fracture of orbital roof (S02.1-)

● **S02.9   Fracture of unspecified skull and facial bones**

● ■ **S02.91   Unspecified fracture of skull A, K 🦠, B 🦠**

● ■ **S02.92   Unspecified fracture of facial bones
A, B, K 🦠**

● **S03   Dislocation and sprain of joints and ligaments of head**
> **Includes**   avulsion of joint (capsule) or ligament of head
>   laceration of cartilage, joint (capsule) or
>   ligament of head
>   sprain of cartilage, joint (capsule) or
>   ligament of head
>   traumatic hemarthrosis of joint or ligament
>   of head
>   traumatic rupture of joint or ligament of head
>   traumatic subluxation of joint or ligament
>   of head
>   traumatic tear of joint or ligament of head

Code also any associated open wound
> **Excludes2**   Strain of muscle or tendon of head (S09.1)

The appropriate 7th character is to be added to each code
from category S03

> A   initial encounter
> D   subsequent encounter
> S   sequela

● **S03.0   Dislocation of jaw**
Dislocation of jaw (cartilage) (meniscus)
Dislocation of mandible
Dislocation of temporomandibular (joint)

● **S03.1   Dislocation of septal cartilage of nose**

● **S03.2   Dislocation of tooth**

● **S03.4   Sprain of jaw**
Sprain of temporomandibular (joint) (ligament)

● **S03.8   Sprain of joints and ligaments of other parts of
head**

● ■ **S03.9   Sprain of joints and ligaments of unspecified parts
of head**

● Unacceptable First-Listed Diagnosis   ● Use Additional Character(s)   ■ Unspecified   **OGCR** Official Guidelines for Coding and Reporting

1362   🦠 Complication\Comorbidity   🦠 Major C\C   Excludes 1   Excludes 2   Includes   Use additional   Code first   Code also

● **S04   Injury of cranial nerve**
> The selection of side should be based on the side of the body being affected
> *Code first any associated intracranial injury (S06.-)*
>
> Code also any associated:
> open wound of head (S01.-)
> skull fracture (S02.-)
>
> The appropriate 7th character is to be added to each code from category S04

> | | |
> |---|---|
> | A | initial encounter |
> | D | subsequent encounter |
> | S | sequela |

● **S04.0 Injury of optic nerve and pathways**
> Use additional code to identify any visual field defect or blindness (H53.4-, H54)

  ● **S04.01   Injury of optic nerve**
> Injury of 2nd cranial nerve

    ● S04.011   Injury of optic nerve, right eye A 🐾

    ● S04.012   Injury of optic nerve, left eye A 🐾

    ● ▪ S04.019   Injury of optic nerve, unspecified eye A 🐾
> Injury of optic nerve NOS

  ● S04.02   Injury of optic chiasm A 🐾

  ● **S04.03   Injury of optic tract and pathways**
> Injury of optic radiation

    ● S04.031   Injury of optic tract and pathways, right eye A 🐾

    ● S04.032   Injury of optic tract and pathways, left eye A 🐾

    ● ▪ S04.039   Injury of optic tract and pathways, unspecified eye A 🐾
> Injury of optic tract and pathways NOS

  ● **S04.04   Injury of visual cortex**

    ● S04.041   Injury of visual cortex, right eye A 🐾

    ● S04.042   Injury of visual cortex, left eye A 🐾

    ● ▪ S04.049   Injury of visual cortex, unspecified eye A 🐾
> Injury of visual cortex NOS

● **S04.1   Injury of oculomotor nerve**
> Injury of 3rd cranial nerve

  ● ▪ S04.10   Injury of oculomotor nerve, unspecified side A 🐾

  ● S04.11   Injury of oculomotor nerve, right side A 🐾

  ● S04.12   Injury of oculomotor nerve, left side A 🐾

● **S04.2   Injury of trochlear nerve**
> Injury of 4th cranial nerve

  ● ▪ S04.20   Injury of trochlear nerve, unspecified side A 🐾

  ● S04.21   Injury of trochlear nerve, right side A 🐾

  ● S04.22   Injury of trochlear nerve, left side A 🐾

● **S04.3   Injury of trigeminal nerve**
> Injury of 5th cranial nerve

  ● ▪ S04.30   Injury of trigeminal nerve, unspecified side A 🐾

  ● S04.31   Injury of trigeminal nerve, right side A 🐾

  ● S04.32   Injury of trigeminal nerve, left side A 🐾

● **S04.4   Injury of abducent nerve**
> Injury of 6th cranial nerve

  ● ▪ S04.40   Injury of abducent nerve, unspecified side A 🐾

  ● S04.41   Injury of abducent nerve, right side A 🐾

  ● S04.42   Injury of abducent nerve, left side A 🐾

● **S04.5   Injury of facial nerve**
> Injury of 7th cranial nerve

  ● ▪ S04.50   Injury of facial nerve, unspecified side A 🐾

  ● S04.51   Injury of facial nerve, right side A 🐾

  ● S04.52   Injury of facial nerve, left side A 🐾

● **S04.6   Injury of acoustic nerve**
> Injury of auditory nerve
> Injury of 8th cranial nerve

  ● ▪ S04.60   Injury of acoustic nerve, unspecified side A 🐾

  ● S04.61   Injury of acoustic nerve, right side A 🐾

  ● S04.62   Injury of acoustic nerve, left side A 🐾

● **S04.7   Injury of accessory nerve**
> Injury of 11th cranial nerve

  ● ▪ S04.70   Injury of accessory nerve, unspecified side A 🐾

  ● S04.71   Injury of accessory nerve, right side A 🐾

  ● S04.72   Injury of accessory nerve, left side A 🐾

● **S04.8   Injury of other cranial nerves**

  ● **S04.81   Injury of olfactory [1st] nerve**

    ● S04.811   Injury of olfactory [1st] nerve, right side A 🐾

    ● S04.812   Injury of olfactory [1st] nerve, left side A 🐾

    ● ▪ S04.819   Injury of olfactory [1st] nerve, unspecified side A 🐾

  ● **S04.89   Injury of other cranial nerves**
> Injury of vagus [10th] nerve

    ● S04.891   Injury of other cranial nerves, right side A 🐾

    ● S04.892   Injury of other cranial nerves, left side A 🐾

    ● ▪ S04.899   Injury of other cranial nerves, unspecified side A 🐾

● S04.9   Injury of unspecified cranial nerve A 🐾

● **S05   Injury of eye and orbit**
> | **Includes** | open wound of eye and orbit |
> |---|---|
> | **Excludes2** | 2nd cranial [optic] nerve injury (S04.0-) |
> | | 3rd cranial [oculomotor] nerve injury (S04.1-) |
> | | open wound of eyelid and periocular area (S01.1-) |
> | | orbital bone fracture (S02.1-, S02.3-, S02.8-) |
> | | superficial injury of eyelid (S00.1-S00.2) |

> The appropriate 7th character is to be added to each code from category S05

> | | |
> |---|---|
> | A | initial encounter |
> | D | subsequent encounter |
> | S | sequela |

● **S05.0   Injury of conjunctiva and corneal abrasion without foreign body**
> | **Excludes1** | foreign body in conjunctival sac (T15.1) |
> |---|---|
> | | foreign body in cornea (T15.0) |

● Unacceptable First-Listed Diagnosis   ● Use Additional Character(s)   ▪ Unspecified   **OGCR** Official Guidelines for Coding and Reporting

🐾 Complication\Comorbidity   🐾 Major C\C   Excludes 1   Excludes 2   Includes   Use additional   Code first   Code also

1363

- ● ▣ **S05.00** Injury of conjunctiva and corneal abrasion without foreign body, unspecified eye
- ● **S05.01** Injury of conjunctiva and corneal abrasion without foreign body, right eye
- ● **S05.02** Injury of conjunctiva and corneal abrasion without foreign body, left eye
- ● **S05.1** **Contusion of eyeball and orbital tissues**
  Traumatic hyphema
  > **Excludes2** black eye NOS (S00.1)
  > contusion of eyelid and periocular area (S00.1)
  - ● ▣ **S05.10** Contusion of eyeball and orbital tissues, unspecified eye
  - ● **S05.11** Contusion of eyeball and orbital tissues, right eye
  - ● **S05.12** Contusion of eyeball and orbital tissues, left eye
- ● **S05.2** **Ocular laceration and rupture with prolapse or loss of intraocular tissue**
  - ● ▣ **S05.20** Ocular laceration and rupture with prolapse or loss of intraocular tissue, unspecified eye A ☣
  - ● **S05.21** Ocular laceration and rupture with prolapse or loss of intraocular tissue, right eye A ☣
  - ● **S05.22** Ocular laceration and rupture with prolapse or loss of intraocular tissue, left eye A ☣
- ● **S05.3** **Ocular laceration without prolapse or loss of intraocular tissue**
  Laceration of eye NOS
  - ● ▣ **S05.30** Ocular laceration without prolapse or loss of intraocular tissue, unspecified eye A ☣
  - ● **S05.31** Ocular laceration without prolapse or loss of intraocular tissue, right eye
  - ● **S05.32** Ocular laceration without prolapse or loss of intraocular tissue, left eye A ☣
- ● **S05.4** **Penetrating wound of orbit with or without foreign body**
  > **Excludes2** retained (old) foreign body following penetrating wound in orbit (H05.5-)
  - ● ▣ **S05.40** Penetrating wound of orbit with or without foreign body, unspecified eye A ☣
  - ● **S05.41** Penetrating wound of orbit with or without foreign body, right eye A ☣
  - ● **S05.42** Penetrating wound of orbit with or without foreign body, left eye A ☣
- ● **S05.5** **Penetrating wound with foreign body of eyeball**
  > **Excludes2** retained (old) intraocular foreign body (H44.6-, H44.7)
  - ● ▣ **S05.50** Penetrating wound with foreign body of unspecified eyeball A ☣
  - ● **S05.51** Penetrating wound with foreign body of right eyeball A ☣
  - ● **S05.52** Penetrating wound with foreign body of left eyeball A ☣
- ● **S05.6** **Penetrating wound without foreign body of eyeball**
  Ocular penetration NOS
  - ● ▣ **S05.60** Penetrating wound without foreign body of unspecified eyeball
  - ● **S05.61** Penetrating wound without foreign body of right eyeball
  - ● **S05.62** Penetrating wound without foreign body of left eyeball

- ● **S05.7** **Avulsion of eye**
  Traumatic enucleation
  - ● ▣ **S05.70** Avulsion of unspecified eye A ☣
  - ● **S05.71** Avulsion of right eye A ☣
  - ● **S05.72** Avulsion of left eye A ☣
- ● **S05.8** **Other injuries of eye and orbit**
  Lacrimal duct injury
  - ● **S05.8x** Other injuries of eye and orbit
    - ● **S05.8x1** Other injuries of right eye and orbit A ☣
    - ● **S05.8x2** Other injuries of left eye and orbit A ☣
    - ● ▣ **S05.8x9** Other injuries of unspecified eye and orbit A ☣
- ● **S05.9** **Unspecified injury of eye and orbit**
  Injury of eye NOS
  - ● ▣ **S05.90** Unspecified injury of unspecified eye and orbit A ☣
  - ● ▣ **S05.91** Unspecified injury of right eye and orbit A ☣
  - ● ▣ **S05.92** Unspecified injury of left eye and orbit A ☣

- ● **S06** **Intracranial injury**
  > **Includes** traumatic brain injury
  > Code also any associated:
  >   open wound of head (S01.-)
  >   skull fracture (S02.-)
  > **Excludes1** head injury NOS (S09.90)

  The appropriate 7th character is to be added to each code from category S06

A	initial encounter
D	subsequent encounter
S	sequela

  - ● **S06.0** **Concussion**
    Commotio cerebri
    > **Excludes1** concussion with other intracranial injuries classified in category S06- code to specified intracranial injury
    - ● **S06.0x** Concussion
      - ● **S06.0x0** Concussion without loss of consciousness
      - ● **S06.0x1** Concussion with loss of consciousness of 30 minutes or less A ☣
      - ● **S06.0x2** Concussion with loss of consciousness of 31 minutes to 59 minutes A ☣
      - ● **S06.0x3** Concussion with loss of consciousness of 1 hour to 5 hours 59 minutes A ☣
      - ● **S06.0x4** Concussion with loss of consciousness of 6 hours to 24 hours A ☣
      - ● **S06.0x5** Concussion with loss of consciousness greater than 24 hours with return to pre-existing conscious level A ☣
      - ● **S06.0x6** Concussion with loss of consciousness greater than 24 hours without return to pre-existing conscious level with patient surviving A ☣

● Unacceptable First-Listed Diagnosis   ● Use Additional Character(s)   ▣ Unspecified   **OGCR** Official Guidelines for Coding and Reporting
☣ Complication\Comorbidity   ☣ Major C\C   Excludes 1   Excludes 2   Includes   Use additional   Code first   Code also

● S06.0x7   Concussion with loss of consciousness of any duration with death due to brain injury prior to regaining consciousness A 🦠

● S06.0x8   Concussion with loss of consciousness of any duration with death due to other cause prior to regaining consciousness A 🦠

● ■ S06.0x9   Concussion with loss of consciousness of unspecified duration A 🦠
Concussion NOS

● S06.1   Traumatic cerebral edema
Diffuse traumatic cerebral edema
Focal traumatic cerebral edema

● S06.1x   Traumatic cerebral edema

● S06.1x0   Traumatic cerebral edema without loss of consciousness

● S06.1x1   Traumatic cerebral edema with loss of consciousness of 30 minutes or less A 🦠

● S06.1x2   Traumatic cerebral edema with loss of consciousness of 31 minutes to 59 minutes A 🦠

● S06.1x3   Traumatic cerebral edema with loss of consciousness of 1 hour to 5 hours 59 minutes A 🦠

● S06.1x4   Traumatic cerebral edema with loss of consciousness of 6 hours to 24 hours A 🦠

● S06.1x5   Traumatic cerebral edema with loss of consciousness greater than 24 hours with return to pre-existing conscious level A 🦠

● S06.1x6   Traumatic cerebral edema with loss of consciousness greater than 24 hours without return to pre-existing conscious level with patient surviving A 🦠

● S06.1x7   Traumatic cerebral edema with loss of consciousness of any duration with death due to brain injury prior to regaining consciousness A 🦠

● S06.1x8   Traumatic cerebral edema with loss of consciousness of any duration with death due to other cause prior to regaining consciousness A 🦠

● ■ S06.1x9   Traumatic cerebral edema with loss of consciousness of unspecified duration A 🦠
Traumatic cerebral edema NOS

● S06.2   Diffuse traumatic brain injury
Diffuse axonal brain injury

| **Excludes1** | traumatic diffuse cerebral edema (S06.10-S06.18) |

● S06.2x   Diffuse traumatic brain injury

● S06.2x0   Diffuse traumatic brain injury without loss of consciousness

● S06.2x1   Diffuse traumatic brain injury with loss of consciousness of 30 minutes or less A 🦠

● S06.2x2   Diffuse traumatic brain injury with loss of consciousness of 31 minutes to 59 minutes A 🦠

● S06.2x3   Diffuse traumatic brain injury with loss of consciousness of 1 hour to 5 hours 59 minutes A 🦠

● S06.2x4   Diffuse traumatic brain injury with loss of consciousness of 6 hours to 24 hours A 🦠

● S06.2x5   Diffuse traumatic brain injury with loss of consciousness greater than 24 hours with return to pre-existing conscious levels A 🦠

● S06.2x6   Diffuse traumatic brain injury with loss of consciousness greater than 24 hours without return to pre-existing conscious level with patient surviving A 🦠

● S06.2x7   Diffuse traumatic brain injury with loss of consciousness of any duration with death due to brain injury prior to regaining consciousness A 🦠

● S06.2x8   Diffuse traumatic brain injury with loss of consciousness of any duration with death due to other cause prior to regaining consciousness A 🦠

● ■ S06.2x9   Diffuse traumatic brain injury with loss of consciousness of unspecified duration A 🦠
Diffuse traumatic brain injury NOS

● S06.3   Focal traumatic brain injury

| **Excludes1** | any condition classifiable to S06.4-S06.6 |
| | focal cerebral edema (S06.1) |

● S06.30   Unspecified focal traumatic brain injury

● ■ S06.300   Unspecified focal traumatic brain injury without loss of consciousness

● ■ S06.301   Unspecified focal traumatic brain injury with loss of consciousness of 30 minutes or less A 🦠

● ■ S06.302   Unspecified focal traumatic brain injury with loss of consciousness of 31 minutes to 59 minutes A 🦠

● ■ S06.303   Unspecified focal traumatic brain injury with loss of consciousness of 1 hour to 5 hours 59 minutes A 🦠

● ■ S06.304   Unspecified focal traumatic brain injury with loss of consciousness of 6 hours to 24 hours A 🦠

● ■ S06.305   Unspecified focal traumatic brain injury with loss of consciousness greater than 24 hours with return to pre-existing conscious level A 🦠

● ■ S06.306   Unspecified focal traumatic brain injury with loss of consciousness greater than 24 hours without return to pre-existing conscious level with patient surviving A 🦠

● ■ S06.307   Unspecified focal traumatic brain injury with loss of consciousness of any duration with death due to brain injury prior to regaining consciousness A 🦠

● Unacceptable First-Listed Diagnosis   ● Use Additional Character(s)   ■ Unspecified   **OGCR** Official Guidelines for Coding and Reporting

🦠 Complication\Comorbidity   🦠 Major C\C   Excludes 1   Excludes 2    Includes   Use additional   Code first   Code also   1365

CHAPTER 19 (S00-T88)

● ◼ **S06.308**   Unspecified focal traumatic brain injury with loss of consciousness of any duration with death due to other cause prior to regaining consciousness A 🔖

● ◼ **S06.309**   Unspecified focal traumatic brain injury with loss of consciousness of unspecified duration A 🔖
  Unspecified focal traumatic brain injury NOS

● **S06.31**   Contusion and laceration of right cerebrum

  ● **S06.310**   Contusion and laceration of right cerebrum without loss of consciousness A 🔖

  ● **S06.311**   Contusion and laceration of right cerebrum with loss of consciousness of 30 minutes or less A 🔖

  ● **S06.312**   Contusion and laceration of right cerebrum with loss of consciousness of 31 minutes to 59 minutes A 🔖

  ● **S06.313**   Contusion and laceration of right cerebrum with loss of consciousness of 1 hour to 5 hours 59 minutes A 🔖

  ● **S06.314**   Contusion and laceration of right cerebrum with loss of consciousness of 6 hours to 24 hours A 🔖

  ● **S06.315**   Contusion and laceration of right cerebrum with loss of consciousness greater than 24 hours with return to pre-existing conscious level A 🔖

  ● **S06.316**   Contusion and laceration of right cerebrum with loss of consciousness greater than 24 hours without return to pre-existing conscious level with patient surviving A 🔖

  ● **S06.317**   Contusion and laceration of right cerebrum with loss of consciousness of any duration with death due to brain injury prior to regaining consciousness A 🔖

  ● **S06.318**   Contusion and laceration of right cerebrum with loss of consciousness of any duration with death due to other cause prior to regaining consciousness A 🔖

  ● ◼ **S06.319**   Contusion and laceration of right cerebrum with loss of consciousness of unspecified duration A 🔖
  Contusion and laceration of right cerebrum NOS

● **S06.32**   Contusion and laceration of left cerebrum

  ● **S06.320**   Contusion and laceration of left cerebrum without loss of consciousness A 🔖

  ● **S06.321**   Contusion and laceration of left cerebrum with loss of consciousness of 30 minutes or less A 🔖

  ● **S06.322**   Contusion and laceration of left cerebrum with loss of consciousness of 31 minutes to 59 minutes A 🔖

● **S06.323**   Contusion and laceration of left cerebrum with loss of consciousness of 1 hour to 5 hours 59 minutes A 🔖

● **S06.324**   Contusion and laceration of left cerebrum with loss of consciousness of 6 hours to 24 hours A 🔖

● **S06.325**   Contusion and laceration of left cerebrum with loss of consciousness greater than 24 hours with return to pre-existing conscious level A 🔖

● **S06.326**   Contusion and laceration of left cerebrum with loss of consciousness greater than 24 hours without return to pre-existing conscious level with patient surviving A 🔖

● **S06.327**   Contusion and laceration of left cerebrum with loss of consciousness of any duration with death due to brain injury prior to regaining consciousness A 🔖

● **S06.328**   Contusion and laceration of left cerebrum with loss of consciousness of any duration with death due to other cause prior to regaining consciousness A 🔖

● ◼ **S06.329**   Contusion and laceration of left cerebrum with loss of consciousness of unspecified duration A 🔖
  Contusion and laceration of left cerebrum NOS

● **S06.33**   Contusion and laceration of cerebrum, unspecified

  ● ◼ **S06.330**   Contusion and laceration of cerebrum, unspecified, without loss of consciousness A 🔖

  ● ◼ **S06.331**   Contusion and laceration of cerebrum, unspecified, with loss of consciousness of 30 minutes or less A 🔖

  ● ◼ **S06.332**   Contusion and laceration of cerebrum, unspecified, with loss of consciousness of 31 minutes to 59 minutes A 🔖

  ● ◼ **S06.333**   Contusion and laceration of cerebrum, unspecified, with loss of consciousness of 1 hour to 5 hours 59 minutes A 🔖

  ● ◼ **S06.334**   Contusion and laceration of cerebrum, unspecified, with loss of consciousness of 6 hours to 24 hours A 🔖

  ● ◼ **S06.335**   Contusion and laceration of cerebrum, unspecified, with loss of consciousness greater than 24 hours with return to pre-existing conscious level A 🔖

  ● ◼ **S06.336**   Contusion and laceration of cerebrum, unspecified, with loss of consciousness greater than 24 hours without return to pre-existing conscious level with patient surviving A 🔖

● Unacceptable First-Listed Diagnosis   ● Use Additional Character(s)   ◼ Unspecified   **OGCR** Official Guidelines for Coding and Reporting
🔖 Complication\Comorbidity   🔖 Major C\C | Excludes 1 | | Excludes 2 | Includes   Use additional   Code first   Code also

● ◼ S06.337   Contusion and laceration of cerebrum, unspecified, with loss of consciousness of any duration with death due to brain injury prior to regaining consciousness A ◔

● ◼ S06.338   Contusion and laceration of cerebrum, unspecified, with loss of consciousness of any duration with death due to other cause prior to regaining consciousness A ◔

● ◼ S06.339   Contusion and laceration of cerebrum, unspecified, with loss of consciousness of unspecified duration A ◔
        Contusion and laceration of cerebrum NOS

● S06.34   Traumatic hemorrhage of right cerebrum
        Traumatic intracerebral hemorrhage and hematoma of right cerebrum

● S06.340   Traumatic hemorrhage of right cerebrum without loss of consciousness A ◔

● S06.341   Traumatic hemorrhage of right cerebrum with loss of consciousness of 30 minutes or less A ◔

● S06.342   Traumatic hemorrhage of right cerebrum with loss of consciousness of 31 minutes to 59 minutes A ◔

● S06.343   Traumatic hemorrhage of right cerebrum with loss of consciousness of 1 hours to 5 hours 59 minutes A ◔

● S06.344   Traumatic hemorrhage of right cerebrum with loss of consciousness of 6 hours to 24 hours A ◔

● S06.345   Traumatic hemorrhage of right cerebrum with loss of consciousness greater than 24 hours with return to pre-existing conscious level A ◔

● S06.346   Traumatic hemorrhage of right cerebrum with loss of consciousness greater than 24 hours without return to pre-existing conscious level with patient surviving A ◔

● S06.347   Traumatic hemorrhage of right cerebrum with loss of consciousness of any duration with death due to brain injury prior to regaining consciousness A ◔

● S06.348   Traumatic hemorrhage of right cerebrum with loss of consciousness of any duration with death due to other cause prior to regaining consciousness A ◔

● ◼ S06.349   Traumatic hemorrhage of right cerebrum with loss of consciousness of unspecified duration A ◔
        Traumatic hemorrhage of right cerebrum NOS

● S06.35   Traumatic hemorrhage of left cerebrum
        Traumatic intracerebral hemorrhage and hematoma of left cerebrum

● S06.350   Traumatic hemorrhage of left cerebrum without loss of consciousness A ◔

● S06.351   Traumatic hemorrhage of left cerebrum with loss of consciousness of 30 minutes or less A ◔

● S06.352   Traumatic hemorrhage of left cerebrum with loss of consciousness of 31 minutes to 59 minutes A ◔

● S06.353   Traumatic hemorrhage of left cerebrum with loss of consciousness of 1 hours to 5 hours 59 minutes A ◔

● S06.354   Traumatic hemorrhage of left cerebrum with loss of consciousness of 6 hours to 24 hours A ◔

● S06.355   Traumatic hemorrhage of left cerebrum with loss of consciousness greater than 24 hours with return to pre-existing conscious level A ◔

● S06.356   Traumatic hemorrhage of left cerebrum with loss of consciousness greater than 24 hours without return to pre-existing conscious level with patient surviving A ◔

● S06.357   Traumatic hemorrhage of left cerebrum with loss of consciousness of any duration with death due to brain injury prior to regaining consciousness A ◔

● S06.358   Traumatic hemorrhage of left cerebrum with loss of consciousness of any duration with death due to other cause prior to regaining consciousness A ◔

● ◼ S06.359   Traumatic hemorrhage of left cerebrum with loss of consciousness of unspecified duration A ◔
        Traumatic hemorrhage of left cerebrum NOS

● S06.36   Traumatic hemorrhage of cerebrum, unspecified
        Traumatic intracerebral hemorrhage and hematoma, unspecified

● ◼ S06.360   Traumatic hemorrhage of cerebrum, unspecified, without loss of consciousness A ◔

● ◼ S06.361   Traumatic hemorrhage of cerebrum, unspecified, with loss of consciousness of 30 minutes or less A ◔

● ◼ S06.362   Traumatic hemorrhage of cerebrum, unspecified, with loss of consciousness of 31 minutes to 59 minutes A ◔

● Unacceptable First-Listed Diagnosis   ● Use Additional Character(s)   ◼ Unspecified   OGCR Official Guidelines for Coding and Reporting
◔ Complication\Comorbidity   ◔ Major C\C   Excludes 1   Excludes 2   Includes   Use additional   Code first   Code also

1367

CHAPTER 19 (S00-T88)

● ■ **S06.363**   Traumatic hemorrhage of cerebrum, unspecified, with loss of consciousness of 1 hours to 5 hours 59 minutes A 🐾

● ■ **S06.364**   Traumatic hemorrhage of cerebrum, unspecified, with loss of consciousness of 6 hours to 24 hours A 🐾

● ■ **S06.365**   Traumatic hemorrhage of cerebrum, unspecified, with loss of consciousness greater than 24 hours with return to pre-existing conscious level A 🐾

● ■ **S06.366**   Traumatic hemorrhage of cerebrum, unspecified, with loss of consciousness greater than 24 hours without return to pre-existing conscious level with patient surviving A 🐾

● ■ **S06.367**   Traumatic hemorrhage of cerebrum, unspecified, with loss of consciousness of any duration with death due to brain injury prior to regaining consciousness A 🐾

● ■ **S06.368**   Traumatic hemorrhage of cerebrum, unspecified, with loss of consciousness of any duration with death due to other cause prior to regaining consciousness A 🐾

● ■ **S06.369**   Traumatic hemorrhage of cerebrum, unspecified, with loss of consciousness of unspecified duration A 🐾

     Traumatic hemorrhage of cerebrum NOS

● **S06.37**   Contusion, laceration, and hemorrhage of cerebellum

● **S06.370**   Contusion, laceration, and hemorrhage of cerebellum without loss of consciousness

● **S06.371**   Contusion, laceration, and hemorrhage of cerebellum with loss of consciousness of 30 minutes or less A 🐾

● **S06.372**   Contusion, laceration, and hemorrhage of cerebellum with loss of consciousness of 31 minutes to 59 minutes A 🐾

● **S06.373**   Contusion, laceration, and hemorrhage of cerebellum with loss of consciousness of 1 hour to 5 hours 59 minutes A 🐾

● **S06.374**   Contusion, laceration, and hemorrhage of cerebellum with loss of consciousness of 6 hours to 24 hours A 🐾

● **S06.375**   Contusion, laceration, and hemorrhage of cerebellum with loss of consciousness greater than 24 hours with return to pre-existing conscious level A 🐾

● **S06.376**   Contusion, laceration, and hemorrhage of cerebellum with loss of consciousness greater than 24 hours without return to pre-existing conscious level with patient surviving A 🐾

● **S06.377**   Contusion, laceration, and hemorrhage of cerebellum with loss of consciousness of any duration with death due to brain injury prior to regaining consciousness A 🐾

● **S06.378**   Contusion, laceration, and hemorrhage of cerebellum with loss of consciousness of any duration with death due to other cause prior to regaining consciousness A 🐾

● ■ **S06.379**   Contusion, laceration, and hemorrhage of cerebellum with loss of consciousness of unspecified duration A 🐾

     Contusion, laceration, and hemorrhage of cerebellum NOS

● **S06.38**   Contusion, laceration, and hemorrhage of brainstem

● **S06.380**   Contusion, laceration, and hemorrhage of brainstem without loss of consciousness

● **S06.381**   Contusion, laceration, and hemorrhage of brainstem with loss of consciousness of 30 minutes or less A 🐾

● **S06.382**   Contusion, laceration, and hemorrhage of brainstem with loss of consciousness of 31 minutes to 59 minutes A 🐾

● **S06.383**   Contusion, laceration, and hemorrhage of brainstem with loss of consciousness of 1 hour to 5 hours 59 minutes A 🐾

● **S06.384**   Contusion, laceration, and hemorrhage of brainstem with loss of consciousness of 6 hours to 24 hours A 🐾

● **S06.385**   Contusion, laceration, and hemorrhage of brainstem with loss of consciousness greater than 24 hours with return to pre-existing conscious level A 🐾

● **S06.386**   Contusion, laceration, and hemorrhage of brainstem with loss of consciousness greater than 24 hours without return to pre-existing conscious level with patient surviving A 🐾

● **S06.387**   Contusion, laceration, and hemorrhage of brainstem with loss of consciousness of any duration with death due to brain injury prior to regaining consciousness A 🐾

● **S06.388**   Contusion, laceration, and hemorrhage of brainstem with loss of consciousness of any duration with death due to other cause prior to regaining consciousness A 🐾

● ■ **S06.389**   Contusion, laceration, and hemorrhage of brainstem with loss of consciousness of unspecified duration A 🐾

     Contusion, laceration, and hemorrhage of brainstem NOS

● Unacceptable First-Listed Diagnosis   ● Use Additional Character(s)   ■ Unspecified   **OGCR** Official Guidelines for Coding and Reporting
🐾 Complication\Comorbidity   🐾 Major C\C   Excludes 1   Excludes 2   Includes   Use additional   Code first   Code also

● S06.4　Epidural hemorrhage
　　Situated outside dura mater
　　Extradural hemorrhage NOS
　　Intracranial hemorrhage due to trauma
　　Extradural hemorrhage (traumatic)

　● S06.4x　Epidural hemorrhage

　　● S06.4x0　Epidural hemorrhage without loss of consciousness A

　　● S06.4x1　Epidural hemorrhage with loss of consciousness of 30 minutes or less A

　　● S06.4x2　Epidural hemorrhage with loss of consciousness of 31 minutes to 59 minutes A

　　● S06.4x3　Epidural hemorrhage with loss of consciousness of 1 hour to 5 hours 59 minutes A

　　● S06.4x4　Epidural hemorrhage with loss of consciousness of 6 hours to 24 hours A

　　● S06.4x5　Epidural hemorrhage with loss of consciousness greater than 24 hours with return to pre-existing conscious level A

　　● S06.4x6　Epidural hemorrhage with loss of consciousness greater than 24 hours without return to pre-existing conscious level with patient surviving A

　　● S06.4x7　Epidural hemorrhage with loss of consciousness of any duration with death due to brain injury prior to regaining consciousness A

　　● S06.4x8　Epidural hemorrhage with loss of consciousness of any duration with death due to other causes prior to regaining consciousness A

　　● ■ S06.4x9　Epidural hemorrhage with loss of consciousness of unspecified duration A
　　　　Epidural hemorrhage NOS

● S06.5　Traumatic subdural hemorrhage

　● S06.5x　Traumatic subdural hemorrhage

　　● S06.5x0　Traumatic subdural hemorrhage without loss of consciousness A

　　● S06.5x1　Traumatic subdural hemorrhage with loss of consciousness of 30 minutes or less A

　　● S06.5x2　Traumatic subdural hemorrhage with loss of consciousness of 31 minutes to 59 minutes A

　　● S06.5x3　Traumatic subdural hemorrhage with loss of consciousness of 1 hour to 5 hours 59 minutes A

　　● S06.5x4　Traumatic subdural hemorrhage with loss of consciousness of 6 hours to 24 hours A

　　● S06.5x5　Traumatic subdural hemorrhage with loss of consciousness greater than 24 hours with return to pre-existing conscious level A

　　● S06.5x6　Traumatic subdural hemorrhage with loss of consciousness greater than 24 hours without return to pre-existing conscious level with patient surviving A

　　● S06.5x7　Traumatic subdural hemorrhage with loss of consciousness of any duration with death due to brain injury before regaining consciousness A

　　● S06.5x8　Traumatic subdural hemorrhage with loss of consciousness of any duration with death due to other cause before regaining consciousness A

　　● ■ S06.5x9　Traumatic subdural hemorrhage with loss of consciousness of unspecified duration A
　　　　Traumatic subdural hemorrhage NOS

● S06.6　Traumatic subarachnoid hemorrhage
　　Between arachnoid and pia mater

　● S06.6x　Traumatic subarachnoid hemorrhage

　　● S06.6x0　Traumatic subarachnoid hemorrhage without loss of consciousness A

　　● S06.6x1　Traumatic subarachnoid hemorrhage with loss of consciousness of 30 minutes or less A

　　● S06.6x2　Traumatic subarachnoid hemorrhage with loss of consciousness of 31 minutes to 59 minutes A

　　● S06.6x3　Traumatic subarachnoid hemorrhage with loss of consciousness of 1 hour to 5 hours 59 minutes A

　　● S06.6x4　Traumatic subarachnoid hemorrhage with loss of consciousness of 6 hours to 24 hours A

　　● S06.6x5　Traumatic subarachnoid hemorrhage with loss of consciousness greater than 24 hours with return to pre-existing conscious level A

　　● S06.6x6　Traumatic subarachnoid hemorrhage with loss of consciousness greater than 24 hours without return to pre-existing conscious level with patient surviving A

　　● S06.6x7　Traumatic subarachnoid hemorrhage with loss of consciousness of any duration with death due to brain injury prior to regaining consciousness A

　　● S06.6x8　Traumatic subarachnoid hemorrhage with loss of consciousness of any duration with death due to other cause prior to regaining consciousness A

● Unacceptable First-Listed Diagnosis　　● Use Additional Character(s)　　■ Unspecified　　OGCR Official Guidelines for Coding and Reporting

 Complication\Comorbidity　　Major C\C　　Excludes 1　　Excludes 2　　Includes　　Use additional　　Code first　　Code also

CHAPTER 19 (S00–T88)

1369

● ■ **S06.6x9** Traumatic subarachnoid hemorrhage with loss of consciousness of unspecified duration A 🐾

    Traumatic subarachnoid hemorrhage NOS

● **S06.8** Other intracranial injuries

  ● **S06.81** Injury of right internal carotid artery, intracranial portion, not elsewhere classified

    ● **S06.810** Injury of right internal carotid artery, intracranial portion, not elsewhere classified without loss of consciousness

    ● **S06.811** Injury of right internal carotid artery, intracranial portion, not elsewhere classified with loss of consciousness of 30 minutes or less A 🐾

    ● **S06.812** Injury of right internal carotid artery, intracranial portion, not elsewhere classified with loss of consciousness of 31 minutes to 59 minutes A 🐾

    ● **S06.813** Injury of right internal carotid artery, intracranial portion, not elsewhere classified with loss of consciousness of 1 hour to 5 hours 59 minutes A 🐾

    ● **S06.814** Injury of right internal carotid artery, intracranial portion, not elsewhere classified with loss of consciousness of 6 hours to 24 hours A 🐾

    ● **S06.815** Injury of right internal carotid artery, intracranial portion, not elsewhere classified with loss of consciousness greater than 24 hours with return to pre-existing conscious level A 🐾

    ● **S06.816** Injury of right internal carotid artery, intracranial portion, not elsewhere classified with loss of consciousness greater than 24 hours without return to pre-existing conscious level with patient surviving A 🐾

    ● **S06.817** Injury of right internal carotid artery, intracranial portion, not elsewhere classified with loss of consciousness of any duration with death due to brain injury prior to regaining consciousness A 🐾

    ● **S06.818** Injury of right internal carotid artery, intracranial portion, not elsewhere classified with loss of consciousness of any duration with death due to other cause prior to regaining consciousness A 🐾

    ● ■ **S06.819** Injury of right internal carotid artery, intracranial portion, not elsewhere classified with loss of consciousness of unspecified duration A 🐾

      Injury of right internal carotid artery, intracranial portion, not elsewhere classified NOS

● **S06.82** Injury of left internal carotid artery, intracranial portion, not elsewhere classified

  ● **S06.820** Injury of left internal carotid artery, intracranial portion, not elsewhere classified without loss of consciousness

  ● **S06.821** Injury of left internal carotid artery, intracranial portion, not elsewhere classified with loss of consciousness of 30 minutes or less A 🐾

  ● **S06.822** Injury of left internal carotid artery, intracranial portion, not elsewhere classified with loss of consciousness of 31 minutes to 59 minutes A 🐾

  ● **S06.823** Injury of left internal carotid artery, intracranial portion, not elsewhere classified with loss of consciousness of 1 hour to 5 hours 59 minutes A 🐾

  ● **S06.824** Injury of left internal carotid artery, intracranial portion, not elsewhere classified with loss of consciousness of 6 hours to 24 hours A 🐾

  ● **S06.825** Injury of left internal carotid artery, intracranial portion, not elsewhere classified with loss of consciousness greater than 24 hours with return to pre-existing conscious level A 🐾

  ● **S06.826** Injury of left internal carotid artery, intracranial portion, not elsewhere classified with loss of consciousness greater than 24 hours without return to pre-existing conscious level with patient surviving A 🐾

  ● **S06.827** Injury of left internal carotid artery, intracranial portion, not elsewhere classified with loss of consciousness of any duration with death due to brain injury prior to regaining consciousness A 🐾

  ● **S06.828** Injury of left internal carotid artery, intracranial portion, not elsewhere classified with loss of consciousness of any duration with death due to other cause prior to regaining consciousness A 🐾

  ● ■ **S06.829** Injury of left internal carotid artery, intracranial portion, not elsewhere classified with loss of consciousness of unspecified duration A 🐾

    Injury of left internal carotid artery, intracranial portion, not elsewhere classified NOS

● **S06.89** Other intracranial injury

  ● **S06.890** Other intracranial injury without loss of consciousness

  ● **S06.891** Other intracranial injury with loss of consciousness of 30 minutes or less A 🐾

● Unacceptable First-Listed Diagnosis   ● Use Additional Character(s)   ■ Unspecified   **OGCR** Official Guidelines for Coding and Reporting
🐾 Complication\Comorbidity   🐾 Major C\C   Excludes 1   Excludes 2   Includes   Use additional   Code first   Code also

CHAPTER 19 (S00-T88)

● S06.892 Other intracranial injury with loss of consciousness of 31 minutes to 59 minutes A 🝓

● S06.893 Other intracranial injury with loss of consciousness of 1 hour to 5 hours 59 minutes A 🝓

● S06.894 Other intracranial injury with loss of consciousness of 6 hours to 24 hours A 🝓

● S06.895 Other intracranial injury with loss of consciousness greater than 24 hours with return to pre-existing conscious level A 🝓

● S06.896 Other intracranial injury with loss of consciousness greater than 24 hours without return to pre-existing conscious level with patient surviving A 🝓

● S06.897 Other intracranial injury with loss of consciousness of any duration with death due to brain injury prior to regaining consciousness A 🝓

● S06.898 Other intracranial injury with loss of consciousness of any duration with death due to other cause prior to regaining consciousness A 🝓

● ■ S06.899 Other intracranial injury with loss of consciousness of unspecified duration A 🝓

● S06.9 Unspecified intracranial injury
Brain injury NOS
Head injury NOS with loss of consciousness
Excludes1 head injury NOS (S09.90)

● S06.9x Unspecified intracranial injury

● ■ S06.9x0 Unspecified intracranial injury without loss of consciousness

● ■ S06.9x1 Unspecified intracranial injury with loss of consciousness of 30 minutes or less A 🝓

● ■ S06.9x2 Unspecified intracranial injury with loss of consciousness of 31 minutes to 59 minutes A 🝓

● ■ S06.9x3 Unspecified intracranial injury with loss of consciousness of 1 hour to 5 hours 59 minutes A 🝓

● ■ S06.9x4 Unspecified intracranial injury with loss of consciousness of 6 hours to 24 hours A 🝓

● ■ S06.9x5 Unspecified intracranial injury with loss of consciousness greater than 24 hours with return to pre-existing conscious level A 🝓

● ■ S06.9x6 Unspecified intracranial injury with loss of consciousness greater than 24 hours without return to pre-existing conscious level with patient surviving A 🝓

● ■ S06.9x7 Unspecified intracranial injury with loss of consciousness of any duration with death due to brain injury prior to regaining consciousness A 🝓

● ■ S06.9x8 Unspecified intracranial injury with loss of consciousness of any duration with death due to other cause prior to regaining consciousness A 🝓

● ■ S06.9x9 Unspecified intracranial injury with loss of consciousness of unspecified duration A 🝓

● S07 Crushing injury of head
Use additional code for all associated injuries, such as:
intracranial injuries (S06-)
skull fractures (S02.-)

The appropriate 7th character is to be added to each code from category S07

A	initial encounter
D	subsequent encounter
S	sequela

● S07.0 Crushing injury of face A 🝓

● S07.1 Crushing injury of skull A 🝓

● S07.8 Crushing injury of other parts of head A 🝓

● ■ S07.9 Crushing injury of head, part unspecified A 🝓

● S08 Avulsion and traumatic amputation of part of head
An amputation not identified as partial or complete should be coded to complete
The appropriate 7th character is to be added to each code from category S08

A	initial encounter
D	subsequent encounter
S	sequela

● S08.0 Avulsion of scalp

● S08.1 Traumatic amputation of ear

● S08.11 Complete traumatic amputation of ear

● S08.111 Complete traumatic amputation of right ear

● S08.112 Complete traumatic amputation of left ear

● ■ S08.119 Complete traumatic amputation of unspecified ear

● S08.12 Partial traumatic amputation of ear

● S08.121 Partial traumatic amputation of right ear A 🝓

● S08.122 Partial traumatic amputation of left ear A 🝓

● ■ S08.129 Partial traumatic amputation of unspecified ear A 🝓

● S08.8 Traumatic amputation of other parts of head

● S08.81 Traumatic amputation of nose

● S08.811 Complete traumatic amputation of nose

● S08.812 Partial traumatic amputation of nose

● S08.89 Traumatic amputation of other parts of head

● Unacceptable First-Listed Diagnosis   ● Use Additional Character(s)   ■ Unspecified   **OGCR** Official Guidelines for Coding and Reporting

🝓 Complication\Comorbidity   Major C\C   Excludes 1   Excludes 2   Includes   Use additional   Code first   Code also   1371

CHAPTER 19 (S00–T88)

● **S09 Other and unspecified injuries of head**
The appropriate 7th character is to be added to each code from category S09

A	initial encounter
D	subsequent encounter
S	sequela

● **S09.0 Injury of blood vessels of head, not elsewhere classified A** 🏵

Excludes1 injury of cerebral blood vessels (S06.-)
injury of precerebral blood vessels (S15.-)

● **S09.1 Injury of muscle and tendon of head**
Code also any associated open wound (S01.-)

Excludes2 sprain to joints and ligament of head (S03.9)

● ■ **S09.10 Unspecified injury of muscle and tendon of head**
Injury of muscle and tendon of head NOS

● **S09.11 Strain of muscle and tendon of head**

● **S09.12 Laceration of muscle and tendon of head**

● **S09.19 Other injury of muscle and tendon of head**

● **S09.2 Traumatic rupture of ear drum**

Excludes1 traumatic rupture of ear drum due to blast injury (S09.31-)

● ■ **S09.20 Traumatic rupture of unspecified ear drum A** 🏵

● **S09.21 Traumatic rupture of right ear drum A** 🏵

● **S09.22 Traumatic rupture of left ear drum A** 🏵

● **S09.3 Other and unspecified injury of middle and inner ear**

Excludes1 injury to ear NOS (S09.91-)
Excludes2 injury to external ear (S00.4-, S01.3-, S08.1-)

● **S09.30 Unspecified injury of middle and inner ear**

● ■ **S09.301 Unspecified injury of right middle and inner ear A** 🏵

● ■ **S09.302 Unspecified injury of left middle and inner ear A** 🏵

● ■ **S09.309 Unspecified injury of unspecified middle and inner ear A** 🏵

● **S09.31 Primary blast injury of ear**
Blast injury of ear NOS

● **S09.311 Primary blast injury of right ear A** 🏵

● **S09.312 Primary blast injury of left ear A** 🏵

● **S09.313 Primary blast injury of ear, bilateral A** 🏵

● ■ **S09.319 Primary blast injury of unspecified ear A** 🏵

● **S09.39 Other injury of middle and inner ear**
Secondary blast injury to ear

● **S09.391 Other injury of right middle and inner ear A** 🏵

● **S09.392 Other injury of left middle and inner ear A** 🏵

● ■ **S09.399 Other injury of unspecified middle and inner ear A** 🏵

● **S09.8 Other specified injuries of head**

● **S09.9 Unspecified injury of face and head**

● ■ **S09.90 Unspecified injury of head**
Head injury NOS

Excludes1 brain injury NOS (S06.9-)
head injury NOS with loss of consciousness (S06.9-)
intracranial injury NOS (S06.9-)

● ■ **S09.91 Unspecified injury of ear**
Injury of ear NOS

● ■ **S09.92 Unspecified injury of nose**
Injury of nose NOS

● ■ **S09.93 Unspecified injury of face**
Injury of face NOS

INJURIES TO THE NECK (S10-S19)

Includes injuries of nape
injuries of supraclavicular region
injuries of throat

Excludes2 burns and corrosions (T20-T32)
effects of foreign body in esophagus (T18.1)
effects of foreign body in larynx (T17.3)
effects of foreign body in pharynx (T17.2)
effects of foreign body in trachea (T17.4)
frostbite (T33-T34)
insect bite or sting, venomous (T63.4)

● **S10 Superficial injury of neck**
The appropriate 7th character is to be added to each code from category S10

A	initial encounter
D	subsequent encounter
S	sequela

● **S10.0 Contusion of throat**
Contusion of cervical esophagus
Contusion of larynx
Contusion of pharynx
Contusion of trachea

● **S10.1 Other and unspecified superficial injuries of throat**

● ■ **S10.10 Unspecified superficial injuries of throat**

● **S10.11 Abrasion of throat**

● **S10.12 Blister (nonthermal) of throat**

● **S10.14 External constriction of part of throat**

● **S10.15 Superficial foreign body of throat**
Splinter in the throat

● **S10.16 Insect bite (nonvenomous) of throat**

● **S10.17 Other superficial bite of throat**

Excludes1 open bite of throat (S11.85)

● **S10.8 Superficial injury of other parts of neck**

● ■ **S10.80 Unspecified superficial injury of other part of neck**

● **S10.81 Abrasion of other part of neck**

● **S10.82 Blister (nonthermal) of other part of neck**

● **S10.83 Contusion of other part of neck**

● **S10.84 External constriction of other part of neck**

● **S10.85 Superficial foreign body of other part of neck**
Splinter in other part of neck

● **S10.86 Insect bite of other part of neck**

● **S10.87 Other superficial bite of other part of neck**

Excludes1 open bite of other parts of neck (S11.85)

● Unacceptable First-Listed Diagnosis ● Use Additional Character(s) ■ Unspecified **OGCR** Official Guidelines for Coding and Reporting
🏵 Complication\Comorbidity 🏵 Major C\C Excludes 1 Excludes 2 Includes Use additional Code first Code also

● S10.9 Superficial injury of unspecified part of neck

  ● ■ S10.90 Unspecified superficial injury of unspecified part of neck

  ● ■ S10.91 Abrasion of unspecified part of neck

  ● ■ S10.92 Blister (nonthermal) of unspecified part of neck

  ● ■ S10.93 Contusion of unspecified part of neck

  ● ■ S10.94 External constriction of unspecified part of neck

  ● ■ S10.95 Superficial foreign body of unspecified part of neck

  ● ■ S10.96 Insect bite of unspecified part of neck

  ● ■ S10.97 Other superficial bite of unspecified part of neck

● S11 Open wound of neck

  Code also any associated:
    spinal cord injury (S14.0, S14.1-)
    wound infection

  | Excludes2 | open fracture of vertebra (S12.- with 7th character B) |

  The appropriate 7th character is to be added to each code from category S11

A	initial encounter
D	subsequent encounter
S	sequela

  ● S11.0 Open wound of larynx and trachea

    ● S11.01 Open wound of larynx

    | Excludes2 | open wound of vocal cord (S11.03) |

      ● S11.011 Laceration without foreign body of larynx A 🦠

      ● S11.012 Laceration with foreign body of larynx A 🦠

      ● S11.013 Puncture wound without foreign body of larynx A 🦠

      ● S11.014 Puncture wound with foreign body of larynx A 🦠

      ● S11.015 Open bite of larynx A 🦠
        Bite of larynx NOS

      ● ■ S11.019 Unspecified open wound of larynx A 🦠

    ● S11.02 Open wound of trachea
      Open wound of cervical trachea
      Open wound of trachea NOS

    | Excludes2 | open wound of thoracic trachea (S27.5-) |

      ● S11.021 Laceration without foreign body of trachea A 🦠

      ● S11.022 Laceration with foreign body of trachea A 🦠

      ● S11.023 Puncture wound without foreign body of trachea A 🦠

      ● S11.024 Puncture wound with foreign body of trachea A 🦠

      ● S11.025 Open bite of trachea A 🦠
        Bite of trachea NOS

      ● ■ S11.029 Unspecified open wound of trachea A 🦠

    ● S11.03 Open wound of vocal cord

      ● S11.031 Laceration without foreign body of vocal cord A 🦠

      ● S11.032 Laceration with foreign body of vocal cord A 🦠

      ● S11.033 Puncture wound without foreign body of vocal cord A 🦠

      ● S11.034 Puncture wound with foreign body of vocal cord A 🦠

      ● S11.035 Open bite of vocal cord A 🦠
        Bite of vocal cord NOS

      ● ■ S11.039 Unspecified open wound of vocal cord A 🦠

  ● S11.1 Open wound of thyroid gland

    ● ■ S11.10 Unspecified open wound of thyroid gland A 🦠

    ● S11.11 Laceration without foreign body of thyroid gland A 🦠

    ● S11.12 Laceration with foreign body of thyroid gland A 🦠

    ● S11.13 Puncture wound without foreign body of thyroid gland A 🦠

    ● S11.14 Puncture wound with foreign body of thyroid gland A 🦠

    ● S11.15 Open bite of thyroid gland A 🦠
      Bite of thyroid gland NOS

  ● S11.2 Open wound of pharynx and cervical esophagus

  | Excludes1 | open wound of esophagus NOS (S27.8-) |

    ● ■ S11.20 Unspecified open wound of pharynx and cervical esophagus A 🦠

    ● S11.21 Laceration without foreign body of pharynx and cervical esophagus A 🦠

    ● S11.22 Laceration with foreign body of pharynx and cervical esophagus A 🦠

    ● S11.23 Puncture wound without foreign body of pharynx and cervical esophagus A 🦠

    ● S11.24 Puncture wound with foreign body of pharynx and cervical esophagus A 🦠

    ● S11.25 Open bite of pharynx and cervical esophagus A 🦠
      Bite of pharynx and cervical esophagus NOS

  ● S11.8 Open wound of other parts of neck

    ● ■ S11.80 Unspecified open wound of other part of neck

    ● S11.81 Laceration without foreign body of other part of neck

    ● S11.82 Laceration with foreign body of other part of neck

    ● S11.83 Puncture wound without foreign body of other part of neck

    ● S11.84 Puncture wound with foreign body of other part of neck

    ● S11.85 Open bite of other part of neck
      Bite of other part of neck NOS

    | Excludes1 | superficial bite of other part of neck (S10.87) |

    ● S11.89 Other open wound of other part of neck

  ● S11.9 Open wound of unspecified part of neck

    ● ■ S11.90 Unspecified open wound of unspecified part of neck

    ● ■ S11.91 Laceration without foreign body of unspecified part of neck

    ● ■ S11.92 Laceration with foreign body of unspecified part of neck

● Unacceptable First-Listed Diagnosis   ● Use Additional Character(s)   ■ Unspecified   **OGCR** Official Guidelines for Coding and Reporting

🦠 Complication\Comorbidity   🦠 Major C\C | Excludes 1 | | Excludes 2 | Includes   Use additional   Code first   Code also

CHAPTER 19 (S00-T88)

1373

● ■ **S11.93**   **Puncture wound without foreign body of unspecified part of neck**

● ■ **S11.94**   **Puncture wound with foreign body of unspecified part of neck**

● ■ **S11.95**   **Open bite of unspecified part of neck**
Bite of neck NOS

> | **Excludes1** | superficial bite of neck (S10.97) |

● **S12**   **Fracture of cervical vertebra and other parts of neck**
A fracture not indicated as nondisplaced or displaced should be classified to displaced

> | **Includes** | fracture of cervical neural arch |
> | | fracture of cervical spine |
> | | fracture of cervical spinous process |
> | | fracture of cervical transverse process |
> | | fracture of cervical vertebral arch |
> | | fracture of neck |

Code also any associated cervical spinal cord injury (S14.0, S14.1-)

The appropriate 7th character is to be added to all codes from subcategories S12.0-S12.6
A fracture not indicated as open or closed should be coded to closed

> | A | initial encounter for closed fracture |
> | B | initial encounter for open fracture |
> | D | subsequent encounter for fracture with routine healing |
> | G | subsequent encounter for fracture with delayed healing |
> | K | subsequent encounter for fracture with nonunion |
> | S | sequela |

● **S12.0**   **Fracture of first cervical vertebra**
Atlas

   ● **S12.00**   **Unspecified fracture of first cervical vertebra**

     ● ■ **S12.000**   **Unspecified displaced fracture of first cervical vertebra A, K 🅒, B 🅜**

     ● ■ **S12.001**   **Unspecified nondisplaced fracture of first cervical vertebra A, K 🅒, B 🅜**

   ● **S12.01**   **Stable burst fracture of first cervical vertebra A, K 🅒, B 🅜**

   ● **S12.02**   **Unstable burst fracture of first cervical vertebra A, K 🅒, B 🅜**

   ● **S12.03**   **Posterior arch fracture of first cervical vertebra**

     ● **S12.030**   **Displaced posterior arch fracture of first cervical vertebra A, K 🅒, B 🅜**

     ● **S12.031**   **Nondisplaced posterior arch fracture of first cervical vertebra A, K 🅒, B 🅜**

   ● **S12.04**   **Lateral mass fracture of first cervical vertebra**

     ● **S12.040**   **Displaced lateral mass fracture of first cervical vertebra A, K 🅒, B 🅜**

     ● **S12.041**   **Nondisplaced lateral mass fracture of first cervical vertebra A, K 🅒, B 🅜**

   ● **S12.09**   **Other fracture of first cervical vertebra**

     ● **S12.090**   **Other displaced fracture of first cervical vertebra A, K 🅒, B 🅜**

     ● **S12.091**   **Other nondisplaced fracture of first cervical vertebra A, K 🅒, B 🅜**

● **S12.1**   **Fracture of second cervical vertebra**
Axis

   ● **S12.10**   **Unspecified fracture of second cervical vertebra**

     ● ■ **S12.100**   **Unspecified displaced fracture of second cervical vertebra A, K 🅒, B 🅜**

     ● ■ **S12.101**   **Unspecified nondisplaced fracture of second cervical vertebra A, K 🅒, B 🅜**

   ● **S12.11**   **Type II dens fracture**

     ● **S12.110**   **Anterior displaced Type II dens fracture A, K 🅒, B 🅜**

     ● **S12.111**   **Posterior displaced Type II dens fracture A, K 🅒, B 🅜**

     ● **S12.112**   **Nondisplaced Type II dens fracture A, K 🅒, B 🅜**

   ● **S12.12**   **Other dens fracture**

     ● **S12.120**   **Other displaced dens fracture A, K 🅒, B 🅜**

     ● **S12.121**   **Other nondisplaced dens fracture A, K 🅒, B 🅜**

   ● **S12.13**   **Unspecified traumatic spondylolisthesis of second cervical vertebra**

     ● ■ **S12.130**   **Unspecified traumatic displaced spondylolisthesis of second cervical vertebra A, K 🅒, B 🅜**

     ● ■ **S12.131**   **Unspecified traumatic nondisplaced spondylolisthesis of second cervical vertebra A, K 🅒, B 🅜**

   ● **S12.14**   **Type III traumatic spondylolisthesis of second cervical vertebra A, K 🅒, B 🅜**

   ● **S12.15**   **Other traumatic spondylolisthesis of second cervical vertebra**

     ● **S12.150**   **Other traumatic displaced spondylolisthesis of second cervical vertebra A, K 🅒, B 🅜**

     ● **S12.151**   **Other traumatic nondisplaced spondylolisthesis of second cervical vertebra A, K 🅒, B 🅜**

   ● **S12.19**   **Other fracture of second cervical vertebra**

     ● **S12.190**   **Other displaced fracture of second cervical vertebra A, K 🅒, B 🅜**

     ● **S12.191**   **Other nondisplaced fracture of second cervical vertebra A, K 🅒, B 🅜**

● **S12.2**   **Fracture of third cervical vertebra**

   ● **S12.20**   **Unspecified fracture of third cervical vertebra**

     ● ■ **S12.200**   **Unspecified displaced fracture of third cervical vertebra A, K 🅒, B 🅜**

     ● ■ **S12.201**   **Unspecified nondisplaced fracture of third cervical vertebra A, K 🅒, B 🅜**

   ● **S12.23**   **Unspecified traumatic spondylolisthesis of third cervical vertebra**

     ● ■ **S12.230**   **Unspecified traumatic displaced spondylolisthesis of third cervical vertebra A, K 🅒, B 🅜**

● Unacceptable First-Listed Diagnosis   ● Use Additional Character(s)   ■ Unspecified   **OGCR** Official Guidelines for Coding and Reporting
🅒 Complication\Comorbidity   🅜 Major C\C | Excludes 1 | | Excludes 2 | Includes   Use additional   Code first   Code also

● ■ S12.231　Unspecified traumatic nondisplaced spondylolisthesis of third cervical vertebra A, K 🦠, B 🦠

● S12.24　Type III traumatic spondylolisthesis of third cervical vertebra A, K 🦠, B 🦠

● S12.25　Other traumatic spondylolisthesis of third cervical vertebra

　　● S12.250　Other traumatic displaced spondylolisthesis of third cervical vertebra A, K 🦠, B 🦠

　　● S12.251　Other traumatic nondisplaced spondylolisthesis of third cervical vertebra A, K 🦠, B 🦠

● S12.29　Other fracture of third cervical vertebra

　　● S12.290　Other displaced fracture of third cervical vertebra A, K 🦠, B 🦠

　　● S12.291　Other nondisplaced fracture of third cervical vertebra A, K 🦠, B 🦠

● S12.3　Fracture of fourth cervical vertebra

　● S12.30　Unspecified fracture of fourth cervical vertebra

　　● ■ S12.300　Unspecified displaced fracture of fourth cervical vertebra A, K 🦠, B 🦠

　　● ■ S12.301　Unspecified nondisplaced fracture of fourth cervical vertebra A, K 🦠, B 🦠

　● S12.33　Unspecified traumatic spondylolisthesis of fourth cervical vertebra

　　● ■ S12.330　Unspecified traumatic displaced spondylolisthesis of fourth cervical vertebra A, K 🦠, B 🦠

　　● ■ S12.331　Unspecified traumatic nondisplaced spondylolisthesis of fourth cervical vertebra A, K 🦠, B 🦠

　● S12.34　Type III traumatic spondylolisthesis of fourth cervical vertebra A, K 🦠, B 🦠

　● S12.35　Other traumatic spondylolisthesis of fourth cervical vertebra

　　● S12.350　Other traumatic displaced spondylolisthesis of fourth cervical vertebra A, K 🦠, B 🦠

　　● S12.351　Other traumatic nondisplaced spondylolisthesis of fourth cervical vertebra A, K 🦠, B 🦠

　● S12.39　Other fracture of fourth cervical vertebra

　　● S12.390　Other displaced fracture of fourth cervical vertebra A, K 🦠, B 🦠

　　● S12.391　Other nondisplaced fracture of fourth cervical vertebra A, K 🦠, B 🦠

● S12.4　Fracture of fifth cervical vertebra

　● S12.40　Unspecified fracture of fifth cervical vertebra

　　● ■ S12.400　Unspecified displaced fracture of fifth cervical vertebra A, K 🦠, B 🦠

　　● ■ S12.401　Unspecified nondisplaced fracture of fifth cervical vertebra A, K 🦠, B 🦠

　● S12.43　Unspecified traumatic spondylolisthesis of fifth cervical vertebra

● ■ S12.430　Unspecified traumatic displaced spondylolisthesis of fifth cervical vertebra A, K 🦠, B 🦠

● ■ S12.431　Unspecified traumatic nondisplaced spondylolisthesis of fifth cervical vertebra A, K 🦠, B 🦠

● S12.44　Type III traumatic spondylolisthesis of fifth cervical vertebra A, K 🦠, B 🦠

● S12.45　Other traumatic spondylolisthesis of fifth cervical vertebra

　　● S12.450　Other traumatic displaced spondylolisthesis of fifth cervical vertebra A, K 🦠, B 🦠

　　● S12.451　Other traumatic nondisplaced spondylolisthesis of fifth cervical vertebra A, K 🦠, B 🦠

● S12.49　Other fracture of fifth cervical vertebra

　　● S12.490　Other displaced fracture of fifth cervical vertebra A, K 🦠, B 🦠

　　● S12.491　Other nondisplaced fracture of fifth cervical vertebra A, K 🦠, B 🦠

● S12.5　Fracture of sixth cervical vertebra

　● S12.50　Unspecified fracture of sixth cervical vertebra

　　● ■ S12.500　Unspecified displaced fracture of sixth cervical vertebra A, K 🦠, B 🦠

　　● ■ S12.501　Unspecified nondisplaced fracture of sixth cervical vertebra A, K 🦠, B 🦠

　● S12.53　Unspecified traumatic spondylolisthesis of sixth cervical vertebra

　　● ■ S12.530　Unspecified traumatic displaced spondylolisthesis of sixth cervical vertebra A, K 🦠, B 🦠

　　● ■ S12.531　Unspecified traumatic nondisplaced spondylolisthesis of sixth cervical vertebra A, K 🦠, B 🦠

　● S12.54　Type III traumatic spondylolisthesis of sixth cervical vertebra A, K 🦠, B 🦠

　● S12.55　Other traumatic spondylolisthesis of sixth cervical vertebra

　　● S12.550　Other traumatic displaced spondylolisthesis of sixth cervical vertebra A, K 🦠, B 🦠

　　● S12.551　Other traumatic nondisplaced spondylolisthesis of sixth cervical vertebra A, K 🦠, B 🦠

　● S12.59　Other fracture of sixth cervical vertebra

　　● S12.590　Other displaced fracture of sixth cervical vertebra A, K 🦠, B 🦠

　　● S12.591　Other nondisplaced fracture of sixth cervical vertebra A, K 🦠, B 🦠

● S12.6　Fracture of seventh cervical vertebra

　S12.60　Unspecified fracture of seventh cervical vertebra

　　● ■ S12.600　Unspecified displaced fracture of seventh cervical vertebra A, K 🦠, B 🦠

　　● ■ S12.601　Unspecified nondisplaced fracture of seventh cervical vertebra A, K 🦠, B 🦠

　● S12.63　Unspecified traumatic spondylolisthesis of seventh cervical vertebra

---

● Unacceptable First-Listed Diagnosis　　● Use Additional Character(s)　　■ Unspecified　　**OGCR** Official Guidelines for Coding and Reporting

🦠 Complication\Comorbidity　🦠 Major C\C　[Excludes 1]　[Excludes 2]　Includes　Use additional　Code first　Code also　　1375

CHAPTER 19 (S00-T88)

● ■ **S12.630** **Unspecified traumatic displaced spondylolisthesis of seventh cervical vertebra A, K** 🦠**, B** 🦠

● ■ **S12.631** **Unspecified traumatic nondisplaced spondylolisthesis of seventh cervical vertebra A, K** 🦠**, B** 🦠

S12.64 **Type III traumatic spondylolisthesis of seventh cervical vertebra A, K** 🦠**, B** 🦠

● **S12.65** **Other traumatic spondylolisthesis of seventh cervical vertebra**

● **S12.650** **Other traumatic displaced spondylolisthesis of seventh cervical vertebra A, K** 🦠**, B** 🦠

● **S12.651** **Other traumatic nondisplaced spondylolisthesis of seventh cervical vertebra A, K** 🦠**, B** 🦠

● **S12.69** **Other fracture of seventh cervical vertebra**

● **S12.690** **Other displaced fracture of seventh cervical vertebra A, K** 🦠**, B** 🦠

● **S12.691** **Other nondisplaced fracture of seventh cervical vertebra B** 🦠

The appropriate 7th character is to be added to codes S12.8 and S12.9

A	initial encounter
D	subsequent encounter
S	sequela

● **S12.8** **Fracture of other parts of neck A** 🦠

Hyoid bone   Thyroid cartilage
Larynx   Trachea

● ■ **S12.9** **Fracture of neck, unspecified A** 🦠

Fracture of neck NOS
Fracture of cervical spine NOS
Fracture of cervical vertebra NOS

● **S13** **Dislocation and sprain of joints and ligaments at neck level**

Includes avulsion of joint or ligament at neck level
laceration of cartilage, joint or ligament at neck level
sprain of cartilage, joint or ligament at neck level
traumatic hemarthrosis of joint or ligament at neck level
traumatic rupture of joint or ligament at neck level
traumatic subluxation of joint or ligament at neck level
traumatic tear of joint or ligament at neck level

Code also any associated open wound

Excludes2 strain of muscle or tendon at neck level (S16.1)

The appropriate 7th character is to be added to each code from category S13

A	initial encounter
D	subsequent encounter
S	sequela

● **S13.0** **Traumatic rupture of cervical intervertebral disc A** 🦠

Excludes1 rupture or displacement (nontraumatic) of cervical intervertebral disc NOS (M50.-)

● **S13.1** **Subluxation and dislocation of cervical vertebrae**

Code also any associated:
open wound of neck (S11.-)
spinal cord injury (S14.1-)

Excludes2 fracture of cervical vertebrae (S12.0--S12.3-)

● **S13.10** **Subluxation and dislocation of unspecified cervical vertebrae**

● ■ **S13.100** **Subluxation of unspecified cervical vertebrae A** 🦠

● ■ **S13.101** **Dislocation of unspecified cervical vertebrae A** 🦠

● **S13.11** **Subluxation and dislocation of C₀/C₁ cervical vertebrae**

Subluxation and dislocation of atlantooccipital joint
Subluxation and dislocation of atloidooccipital joint
Subluxation and dislocation of occipitoatloid joint

● **S13.110** **Subluxation of C_0/C_1 cervical vertebrae A** 🦠

● **S13.111** **Dislocation of C_0/C_1 cervical vertebrae A** 🦠

● **S13.12** **Subluxation and dislocation of C_1/C_2 cervical vertebrae**

Subluxation and dislocation of atlantoaxial joint

● **S13.120** **Subluxation of C_1/C_2 cervical vertebrae A** 🦠

● **S13.121** **Dislocation of C_1/C_2 cervical vertebrae A** 🦠

● **S13.13** **Subluxation and dislocation of C_2/C_3 cervical vertebrae**

● **S13.130** **Subluxation of C_2/C_3 cervical vertebrae A** 🦠

● **S13.131** **Dislocation of C_2/C_3 cervical vertebrae**

● **S13.14** **Subluxation and dislocation of C_3/C_4 cervical vertebrae**

● **S13.140** **Subluxation of C_3/C_4 cervical vertebrae A** 🦠

● **S13.141** **Dislocation of C_3/C_4 cervical vertebrae A** 🦠

● **S13.15** **Subluxation and dislocation of C_4/C_5 cervical vertebrae**

● **S13.150** **Subluxation of C_4/C_5 cervical vertebrae A** 🦠

● **S13.151** **Dislocation of C_4/C_5 cervical vertebrae A** 🦠

● **S13.16** **Subluxation and dislocation of C_5/C_6 cervical vertebrae**

● **S13.160** **Subluxation of C_5/C_6 cervical vertebrae A** 🦠

● **S13.161** **Dislocation of C_5/C_6 cervical vertebrae A** 🦠

● **S13.17** **Subluxation and dislocation of C_6/C_7 cervical vertebrae**

● **S13.170** **Subluxation of C_6/C_7 cervical vertebrae A** 🦠

● **S13.171** **Dislocation of C_6/C_7 cervical vertebrae A** 🦠

● Unacceptable First-Listed Diagnosis   ● Use Additional Character(s)   ■ Unspecified   **OGCR** Official Guidelines for Coding and Reporting
🦠 Complication\Comorbidity   🦠 Major C\C      Includes   Use additional   Code first   Code also

● **S13.18** Subluxation and dislocation of C_7/T_1 cervical vertebrae

   ● **S13.180** Subluxation of C_7/T_1 cervical vertebrae A 🕭

   ● **S13.181** Dislocation of C_7/T_1 cervical vertebrae A 🕭

● **S13.2** Dislocation of other and unspecified parts of neck

   ● ■ **S13.20** Dislocation of unspecified parts of neck A 🕭

   ● **S13.29** Dislocation of other parts of neck A 🕭

● **S13.4** Sprain of ligaments of cervical spine
   Sprain of anterior longitudinal (ligament), cervical
   Sprain of atlanto-axial (joints)
   Sprain of atlanto-occipital (joints)
   Whiplash injury of cervical spine

● **S13.5** Sprain of thyroid region
   Sprain of cricoarytenoid (joint) (ligament)
   Sprain of cricothyroid (joint) (ligament)
   Sprain of thyroid cartilage

● **S13.8** Sprain of joints and ligaments of other parts of neck

● ■ **S13.9** Sprain of joints and ligaments of unspecified parts of neck

● **S14** **Injury of nerves and spinal cord at neck level**
   Code to highest level of cervical cord injury
   Code also any associated:
      fracture of cervical vertebra (S12.0--S12.6.-)
      open wound of neck (S11-)
      transient paralysis (R29.5)

   The appropriate 7th character is to be added to each code from category S14

   > A   initial encounter
   > D   subsequent encounter
   > S   sequela

● **S14.0** Concussion and edema of cervical spinal cord A 🕭

● **S14.1** Other and unspecified injuries of cervical spinal cord

   ● **S14.10** Unspecified injury of cervical spinal cord

      ● ■ **S14.101** Unspecified injury at C_1 level of cervical spinal cord A 🕭

      ● ■ **S14.102** Unspecified injury at C_2 level of cervical spinal cord A 🕭

      ● ■ **S14.103** Unspecified injury at C_3 level of cervical spinal cord A 🕭

      ● ■ **S14.104** Unspecified injury at C_4 level of cervical spinal cord A 🕭

      ● ■ **S14.105** Unspecified injury at C_5 level of cervical spinal cord A 🕭

      ● ■ **S14.106** Unspecified injury at C_6 level of cervical spinal cord A 🕭

      ● ■ **S14.107** Unspecified injury at C_7 level of cervical spinal cord A 🕭

      ● ■ **S14.108** Unspecified injury at C_8 level of cervical spinal cord A 🕭

      ● ■ **S14.109** Unspecified injury at unspecified level of cervical spinal cord
         Injury of cervical spinal cord NOS

   ● **S14.11** Complete lesion of cervical spinal cord

      ● **S14.111** Complete lesion at C_1 level of cervical spinal cord A 🕭

      ● **S14.112** Complete lesion at C_2 level of cervical spinal cord A 🕭

      ● **S14.113** Complete lesion at C_3 level of cervical spinal cord A 🕭

      ● **S14.114** Complete lesion at C_4 level of cervical spinal cord A 🕭

      ● **S14.115** Complete lesion at C_5 level of cervical spinal cord A 🕭

      ● **S14.116** Complete lesion at C_6 level of cervical spinal cord A 🕭

      ● **S14.117** Complete lesion at C_7 level of cervical spinal cord A 🕭

      ● **S14.118** Complete lesion at C_8 level of cervical spinal cord A 🕭

      ● ■ **S14.119** Complete lesion at unspecified level of cervical spinal cord

   ● **S14.12** Central cord syndrome of cervical spinal cord

      ● **S14.121** Central cord syndrome at C_1 level of cervical spinal cord A 🕭

      ● **S14.122** Central cord syndrome at C_2 level of cervical spinal cord A 🕭

      ● **S14.123** Central cord syndrome at C_3 level of cervical spinal cord A 🕭

      ● **S14.124** Central cord syndrome at C_4 level of cervical spinal cord A 🕭

      ● **S14.125** Central cord syndrome at C_5 level of cervical spinal cord A 🕭

      ● **S14.126** Central cord syndrome at C_6 level of cervical spinal cord A 🕭

      ● **S14.127** Central cord syndrome at C_7 level of cervical spinal cord A 🕭

      ● **S14.128** Central cord syndrome at C_8 level of cervical spinal cord A 🕭

      ● ■ **S14.129** Central cord syndrome at unspecified level of cervical spinal cord

   ● **S14.13** Anterior cord syndrome of cervical spinal cord

      ● **S14.131** Anterior cord syndrome at C_1 level of cervical spinal cord A 🕭

      ● **S14.132** Anterior cord syndrome at C_2 level of cervical spinal cord A 🕭

      ● **S14.133** Anterior cord syndrome at C_3 level of cervical spinal cord A 🕭

      ● **S14.134** Anterior cord syndrome at C_4 level of cervical spinal cord A 🕭

      ● **S14.135** Anterior cord syndrome at C_5 level of cervical spinal cord A 🕭

      ● **S14.136** Anterior cord syndrome at C_6 level of cervical spinal cord A 🕭

      ● **S14.137** Anterior cord syndrome at C_7 level of cervical spinal cord A 🕭

      ● **S14.138** Anterior cord syndrome at C_8 level of cervical spinal cord A 🕭

      ● ■ **S14.139** Anterior cord syndrome at unspecified level of cervical spinal cord

   ● **S14.14** Brown-Sequard syndrome of cervical spinal cord

      ● **S14.141** Brown-Sequard syndrome at C_1 level of cervical spinal cord A 🕭

      ● **S14.142** Brown-Sequard syndrome at C_2 level of cervical spinal cord A 🕭

      ● **S14.143** Brown-Sequard syndrome at C_3 level of cervical spinal cord A 🕭

      ● **S14.144** Brown-Sequard syndrome at C_4 level of cervical spinal cord A 🕭

● Unacceptable First-Listed Diagnosis   ● Use Additional Character(s)   ■ Unspecified   **OGCR** Official Guidelines for Coding and Reporting

🕭 Complication\Comorbidity   🕭 Major C\C   Excludes 1   Excludes 2   Includes   Use additional   Code first   Code also

CHAPTER 19 (S00-T88)

1377

● S14.145   Brown-Sequard syndrome at C_5 level of cervical spinal cord A

● S14.146   Brown-Sequard syndrome at C_6 level of cervical spinal cord A

● S14.147   Brown-Sequard syndrome at C_7 level of cervical spinal cord A

● S14.148   Brown-Sequard syndrome at C_8 level of cervical spinal cord A

● ■ S14.149   Brown-Sequard syndrome at unspecified level of cervical spinal cord

● S14.15   Other incomplete lesions of cervical spinal cord

     Incomplete lesion of cervical spinal cord NOS
     Posterior cord syndrome of cervical spinal cord

● S14.151   Other incomplete lesion at C_1 level of cervical spinal cord A

● S14.152   Other incomplete lesion at C_2 level of cervical spinal cord A

● S14.153   Other incomplete lesion at C_3 level of cervical spinal cord A

● S14.154   Other incomplete lesion at C_4 level of cervical spinal cord A

● S14.155   Other incomplete lesion at C_5 level of cervical spinal cord A

● S14.156   Other incomplete lesion at C_6 level of cervical spinal cord A

● S14.157   Other incomplete lesion at C_7 level of cervical spinal cord A

● S14.158   Other incomplete lesion at C_8 level of cervical spinal cord A

● ■ S14.159   Other incomplete lesion at unspecified level of cervical spinal cord

● S14.2   Injury of nerve root of cervical spine

● S14.3   Injury of brachial plexus

● S14.4   Injury of peripheral nerves of neck

● S14.5   Injury of cervical sympathetic nerves

● S14.8   Injury of other nerves of neck

● ■ S14.9   Injury of unspecified nerves of neck

● S15   Injury of blood vessels at neck level

     Code also any associated open wound (S11.-)

     The appropriate 7th character is to be added to each code from category S15

     A   initial encounter
     D   subsequent encounter
     S   sequela

● S15.0   Injury of carotid artery of neck

     Injury of carotid artery (common) (external) (internal, extracranial portion)
     Injury of carotid artery NOS

     Excludes1   injury of internal carotid artery, intracranial portion (S06.8)

● S15.00   Unspecified injury of carotid artery

● ■ S15.001   Unspecified injury of right carotid artery A

● ■ S15.002   Unspecified injury of left carotid artery A

● ■ S15.009   Unspecified injury of unspecified carotid artery A

● S15.01   Minor laceration of carotid artery

     Incomplete transection of carotid artery
     Laceration of carotid artery NOS
     Superficial laceration of carotid artery

● S15.011   Minor laceration of right carotid artery A

● S15.012   Minor laceration of left carotid artery A

● ■ S15.019   Minor laceration of unspecified carotid artery A

● S15.02   Major laceration of carotid artery

     Complete transection of carotid artery
     Traumatic rupture of carotid artery

● S15.021   Major laceration of right carotid artery A

● S15.022   Major laceration of left carotid artery A

● ■ S15.029   Major laceration of unspecified carotid artery A

● S15.09   Other injury of carotid artery

● S15.091   Other injury of right carotid artery A

● S15.092   Other injury of left carotid artery A

● ■ S15.099   Other injury of unspecified carotid artery A

● S15.1   Injury of vertebral artery

● S15.10   Unspecified injury of vertebral artery

● ■ S15.101   Unspecified injury of right vertebral artery A

● ■ S15.102   Unspecified injury of left vertebral artery A

● ■ S15.109   Unspecified injury of unspecified vertebral artery A

● S15.11   Minor laceration of vertebral artery

     Incomplete transection of vertebral artery
     Laceration of vertebral artery NOS
     Superficial laceration of vertebral artery

● S15.111   Minor laceration of right vertebral artery A

● S15.112   Minor laceration of left vertebral artery A

● ■ S15.119   Minor laceration of unspecified vertebral artery A

● S15.12   Major laceration of vertebral artery

     Complete transection of vertebral artery
     Traumatic rupture of vertebral artery

● S15.121   Major laceration of right vertebral artery A

● S15.122   Major laceration of left vertebral artery A

● ■ S15.129   Major laceration of unspecified vertebral artery A

● S15.19   Other injury of vertebral artery

● S15.191   Other injury of right vertebral artery A

● S15.192   Other injury of left vertebral artery A

● ■ S15.199   Other injury of unspecified vertebral artery A

● S15.2   Injury of external jugular vein

● S15.20   Unspecified injury of external jugular vein

● Unacceptable First-Listed Diagnosis   ● Use Additional Character(s)   ■ Unspecified   OGCR Official Guidelines for Coding and Reporting

 Complication\Comorbidity   Major C\C   Excludes 1   Excludes 2   Includes   Use additional   Code first   Code also

1378

CHAPTER 19 (S00-T88)

● ■ **S15.201** Unspecified injury of right external jugular vein A 🗲

● ■ **S15.202** Unspecified injury of left external jugular vein A 🗲

● ■ **S15.209** Unspecified injury of unspecified external jugular vein A 🗲

● **S15.21** Minor laceration of external jugular vein
Incomplete transection of external jugular vein
Laceration of external jugular vein NOS
Superficial laceration of external jugular vein

     ● **S15.211** Minor laceration of right external jugular vein A 🗲

     ● **S15.212** Minor laceration of left external jugular vein A 🗲

     ● ■ **S15.219** Minor laceration of unspecified external jugular vein A 🗲

● **S15.22** Major laceration of external jugular vein
Complete transection of external jugular vein
Traumatic rupture of external jugular vein

     ● **S15.221** Major laceration of right external jugular vein A 🗲

     ● **S15.222** Major laceration of left external jugular vein A 🗲

     ● ■ **S15.229** Major laceration of unspecified external jugular vein A 🗲

● **S15.29** Other injury of external jugular vein

     ● **S15.291** Other injury of right external jugular vein A 🗲

     ● **S15.292** Other injury of left external jugular vein A 🗲

     ● ■ **S15.299** Other injury of unspecified external jugular vein A 🗲

● **S15.3** Injury of internal jugular vein

     ● **S15.30** Unspecified injury of internal jugular vein

         ● ■ **S15.301** Unspecified injury of right internal jugular vein A 🗲

         ● ■ **S15.302** Unspecified injury of left internal jugular vein A 🗲

         ● ■ **S15.309** Unspecified injury of unspecified internal jugular vein A 🗲

     ● **S15.31** Minor laceration of internal jugular vein
Incomplete transection of internal jugular vein
Laceration of internal jugular vein NOS
Superficial laceration of internal jugular vein

         ● **S15.311** Minor laceration of right internal jugular vein A 🗲

         ● **S15.312** Minor laceration of left internal jugular vein A 🗲

         ● ■ **S15.319** Minor laceration of unspecified internal jugular vein A 🗲

     ● **S15.32** Major laceration of internal jugular vein
Complete transection of internal jugular vein
Traumatic rupture of internal jugular vein

         ● **S15.321** Major laceration of right internal jugular vein A 🗲

         ● **S15.322** Major laceration of left internal jugular vein A 🗲

         ● ■ **S15.329** Major laceration of unspecified internal jugular vein A 🗲

● **S15.39** Other injury of internal jugular vein

     ● **S15.391** Other injury of right internal jugular vein A 🗲

     ● **S15.392** Other injury of left internal jugular vein A 🗲

     ● ■ **S15.399** Other injury of unspecified internal jugular vein A 🗲

● **S15.8** Injury of other blood vessels at neck level A 🗲

● ■ **S15.9** Injury of unspecified blood vessel at neck level A 🗲

● **S16** Injury of muscle, fascia and tendon at neck level
Code also any associated open wound (S11.-)

     Excludes2   sprain of joint or ligament at neck level (S13.9)

The appropriate 7th character is to be added to each code from category S16

A	initial encounter
D	subsequent encounter
S	sequela

● **S16.1** Strain of muscle, fascia and tendon at neck level

● **S16.2** Laceration of muscle, fascia and tendon at neck level

● **S16.8** Other injury of muscle, fascia and tendon at neck level

● ■ **S16.9** Unspecified injury of muscle, fascia and tendon at neck level

● **S17** Crushing injury of neck
Use additional code for all associated injuries, such as:
injury of blood vessels (S15.-)
open wound of neck (S11.-)
spinal cord injury (S14.0, S14.1-)
vertebral fracture (S12.0--S12.3-)

The appropriate 7th character is to be added to each code from category S17

A	initial encounter
D	subsequent encounter
S	sequela

● **S17.0** Crushing injury of larynx and trachea A 🗲

● **S17.8** Crushing injury of other parts of neck A 🗲

● ■ **S17.9** Crushing injury of neck, part unspecified A 🗲

● **S19** Other and unspecified injuries of neck
The appropriate 7th character is to be added to each code from category S19

A	initial encounter
D	subsequent encounter
S	sequela

● **S19.8** Other specified injuries of neck

     ● ■ **S19.80** Other specified injuries of unspecified part of neck

     ● **S19.81** Other specified injuries of larynx

     ● **S19.82** Other specified injuries of cervical trachea

         Excludes2   other specified injury of thoracic trachea (S27.5-)

     ● **S19.83** Other specified injuries of vocal cord

     ● **S19.84** Other specified injuries of thyroid gland

     ● **S19.85** Other specified injuries of pharynx and cervical esophagus

     ● **S19.89** Other specified injuries of other part of neck

● ■ **S19.9** Unspecified injury of neck

● Unacceptable First-Listed Diagnosis   ● Use Additional Character(s)   ■ Unspecified   **OGCR** Official Guidelines for Coding and Reporting
🗲 Complication\Comorbidity   🗲 Major C\C   Excludes 1   Excludes 2   Includes   Use additional   Code first   Code also

INJURIES TO THE THORAX (S20-S29)

Includes   injuries of breast
injuries of chest (wall)
injuries of interscapular area

Excludes2   burns and corrosions (T20-T32)
effects of foreign body in bronchus (T17.5)
effects of foreign body in esophagus (T18.1)
effects of foreign body in lung (T17.8)
effects of foreign body in trachea (T17.4)
frostbite (T33-T34)
injuries of axilla
injuries of clavicle
injuries of scapular region
injuries of shoulder
insect bite or sting, venomous (T63.4)

● **S20   Superficial injury of thorax**
The appropriate 7th character is to be added to each code from category S20

A	initial encounter
D	subsequent encounter
S	sequela

● **S20.0   Contusion of breast**

● ■ S20.00   Contusion of breast, unspecified breast

● S20.01   Contusion of right breast

● S20.02   Contusion of left breast

● **S20.1   Other and unspecified superficial injuries of breast**

● S20.10   Unspecified superficial injuries of breast

● ■ S20.101   Unspecified superficial injuries of breast, right breast

● ■ S20.102   Unspecified superficial injuries of breast, left breast

● ■ S20.109   Unspecified superficial injuries of breast, unspecified breast

● S20.11   Abrasion of breast

● S20.111   Abrasion of breast, right breast

● S20.112   Abrasion of breast, left breast

● ■ S20.119   Abrasion of breast, unspecified breast

● S20.12   Blister (nonthermal) of breast

● S20.121   Blister (nonthermal) of breast, right breast

● S20.122   Blister (nonthermal) of breast, left breast

● ■ S20.129   Blister (nonthermal) of breast, unspecified breast

● S20.14   External constriction of part of breast

● S20.141   External constriction of part of breast, right breast

● S20.142   External constriction of part of breast, left breast

● ■ S20.149   External constriction of part of breast, unspecified breast

● S20.15   Superficial foreign body of breast
Splinter in the breast

● S20.151   Superficial foreign body of breast, right breast

● S20.152   Superficial foreign body of breast, left breast

● ■ S20.159   Superficial foreign body of breast, unspecified breast

● S20.16   Insect bite (nonvenomous) of breast

● S20.161   Insect bite (nonvenomous) of breast, right breast

● S20.162   Insect bite (nonvenomous) of breast, left breast

● ■ S20.169   Insect bite (nonvenomous) of breast, unspecified breast

● S20.17   Other superficial bite of breast

Excludes1   open bite of breast (S21.05-)

● S20.171   Other superficial bite of breast, right breast

● S20.172   Other superficial bite of breast, left breast

● ■ S20.179   Other superficial bite of breast, unspecified breast

● **S20.2   Contusion of thorax**

● ■ S20.20   Contusion of thorax, unspecified

● S20.21   Contusion of front wall of thorax

● S20.211   Contusion of right front wall of thorax

● S20.212   Contusion of left front wall of thorax

● ■ S20.219   Contusion of unspecified front wall of thorax

● S20.22   Contusion of back wall of thorax

● S20.221   Contusion of right back wall of thorax

● S20.222   Contusion of left back wall of thorax

● ■ S20.229   Contusion of unspecified back wall of thorax

● **S20.3   Other and unspecified superficial injuries of front wall of thorax**

● S20.30   Unspecified superficial injuries of front wall of thorax

● ■ S20.301   Unspecified superficial injuries of right front wall of thorax

● ■ S20.302   Unspecified superficial injuries of left front wall of thorax

● ■ S20.309   Unspecified superficial injuries of unspecified front wall of thorax

● S20.31   Abrasion of front wall of thorax

● S20.311   Abrasion of right front wall of thorax

● S20.312   Abrasion of left front wall of thorax

● ■ S20.319   Abrasion of unspecified front wall of thorax

● S20.32   Blister (nonthermal) of front wall of thorax

● S20.321   Blister (nonthermal) of right front wall of thorax

● S20.322   Blister (nonthermal) of left front wall of thorax

● ■ S20.329   Blister (nonthermal) of unspecified front wall of thorax

● S20.34   External constriction of front wall of thorax

● S20.341   External constriction of right front wall of thorax

● S20.342   External constriction of left front wall of thorax

● ■ S20.349   External constriction of unspecified front wall of thorax

● Unacceptable First-Listed Diagnosis   ● Use Additional Character(s)   ■ Unspecified   **OGCR** Official Guidelines for Coding and Reporting
Complication\Comorbidity   Major C\C   Excludes 1   Excludes 2   Includes   Use additional   Code first   Code also

- S20.35 **Superficial foreign body of front wall of thorax**
  Splinter in front wall of thorax
  - S20.351 **Superficial foreign body of right front wall of thorax**
  - S20.352 **Superficial foreign body of left front wall of thorax**
  - ■ S20.359 **Superficial foreign body of unspecified front wall of thorax**
- S20.36 **Insect bite (nonvenomous) of front wall of thorax**
  - S20.361 **Insect bite (nonvenomous) of right front wall of thorax**
  - S20.362 **Insect bite (nonvenomous) of left front wall of thorax**
  - ■ S20.369 **Insect bite (nonvenomous) of unspecified front wall of thorax**
- S20.37 **Other superficial bite of front wall of thorax**
  | Excludes1 | open bite of front wall of thorax (S21.14) |
  - S20.371 **Other superficial bite of right front wall of thorax**
  - S20.372 **Other superficial bite of left front wall of thorax**
  - ■ S20.379 **Other superficial bite of unspecified front wall of thorax**
- S20.4 **Other and unspecified superficial injuries of back wall of thorax**
  - S20.40 **Unspecified superficial injuries of back wall of thorax**
    - ■ S20.401 **Unspecified superficial injuries of right back wall of thorax**
    - ■ S20.402 **Unspecified superficial injuries of left back wall of thorax**
    - ■ S20.409 **Unspecified superficial injuries of unspecified back wall of thorax**
  - S20.41 **Abrasion of back wall of thorax**
    - S20.411 **Abrasion of right back wall of thorax**
    - S20.412 **Abrasion of left back wall of thorax**
    - ■ S20.419 **Abrasion of unspecified back wall of thorax**
  - S20.42 **Blister (nonthermal) of back wall of thorax**
    - S20.421 **Blister (nonthermal) of right back wall of thorax**
    - S20.422 **Blister (nonthermal) of left back wall of thorax**
    - ■ S20.429 **Blister (nonthermal) of unspecified back wall of thorax**
  - S20.44 **External constriction of back wall of thorax**
    - S20.441 **External constriction of right back wall of thorax**
    - S20.442 **External constriction of left back wall of thorax**
    - ■ S20.449 **External constriction of unspecified back wall of thorax**

- S20.45 **Superficial foreign body of back wall of thorax**
  Splinter of back wall of thorax
  - S20.451 **Superficial foreign body of right back wall of thorax**
  - S20.452 **Superficial foreign body of left back wall of thorax**
  - ■ S20.459 **Superficial foreign body of unspecified back wall of thorax**
- S20.46 **Insect bite (nonvenomous) of back wall of thorax**
  - S20.461 **Insect bite (nonvenomous) of right back wall of thorax**
  - S20.462 **Insect bite (nonvenomous) of left back wall of thorax**
  - ■ S20.469 **Insect bite (nonvenomous) of unspecified back wall of thorax**
- S20.47 **Other superficial bite of back wall of thorax**
  | Excludes1 | open bite of back wall of thorax (S21.24) |
  - S20.471 **Other superficial bite of right back wall of thorax**
  - S20.472 **Other superficial bite of left back wall of thorax**
  - ■ S20.479 **Other superficial bite of unspecified back wall of thorax**
- S20.9 **Superficial injury of unspecified parts of thorax**
  | Excludes1 | contusion of thorax NOS (S20.20) |
  - ■ S20.90 **Unspecified superficial injury of unspecified parts of thorax**
    Superficial injury of thoracic wall NOS
  - ■ S20.91 **Abrasion of unspecified parts of thorax**
  - ■ S20.92 **Blister (nonthermal) of unspecified parts of thorax**
  - ■ S20.94 **External constriction of unspecified parts of thorax**
  - ■ S20.95 **Superficial foreign body of unspecified parts of thorax**
    Splinter in thorax NOS
  - ■ S20.96 **Insect bite (nonvenomous) of unspecified parts of thorax**
  - ■ S20.97 **Other superficial bite of unspecified parts of thorax**
    | Excludes1 | open bite of thorax NOS (S21.95) |

Item 19-1 Pneumothorax is a collection of gas (positive air pressure) in the pleural space resulting in the lung collapsing. A tension pneumothorax is life-threatening and is a result of air in the pleural space causing a displacement in the mediastinal structures and cardiopulmonary function compromise. A traumatic pneumothorax results from blunt or penetrating injury that disrupts the parietal/visceral pleura. **Hemothorax** is blood or bloody fluid in the pleural cavity as a result of traumatic blood vessel rupture or inflammation of the lungs from pneumonia.

● Unacceptable First-Listed Diagnosis   ● Use Additional Character(s)   ■ Unspecified   **OGCR** Official Guidelines for Coding and Reporting

 Complication\Comorbidity   Major C\C | Excludes 1 | | Excludes 2 | Includes   Use additional   Code first   Code also

CHAPTER 19 (S00–T88)   1381

● **S21   Open wound of thorax**

> Code also any associated injury (to) (such as) :

> heart (S26.-)
> intrathoracic organs (S27.-)
> rib fracture (S22.3-, S22.4-)
> spinal cord injury (S24.0-, S24.1-)
> traumatic hemothorax (S27.1)
> traumatic hemopneumothorax (S27.3)
> traumatic pneumothorax (S27.0)
> wound infection

> | Excludes1 | traumatic amputation (partial) of thorax (S28.1) |

> The appropriate 7th character is to be added to each code from category S21

> A   initial encounter
> D   subsequent encounter
> S   sequela

● **S21.0   Open wound of breast**

  ● **S21.00   Unspecified open wound of breast**

    ● ■ **S21.001   Unspecified open wound of right breast**

    ● ■ **S21.002   Unspecified open wound of left breast**

    ● ■ **S21.009   Unspecified open wound of unspecified breast**

  ● **S21.01   Laceration without foreign body of breast**

    ● **S21.011   Laceration without foreign body of right breast**

    ● **S21.012   Laceration without foreign body of left breast**

    ● ■ **S21.019   Laceration without foreign body of unspecified breast**

  ● **S21.02   Laceration with foreign body of breast**

    ● **S21.021   Laceration with foreign body of right breast**

    ● **S21.022   Laceration with foreign body of left breast**

    ● ■ **S21.029   Laceration with foreign body of unspecified breast**

  ● **S21.03   Puncture wound without foreign body of breast**

    ● **S21.031   Puncture wound without foreign body of right breast**

    ● **S21.032   Puncture wound without foreign body of left breast**

    ● ■ **S21.039   Puncture wound without foreign body of unspecified breast**

  ● **S21.04   Puncture wound with foreign body of breast**

    ● **S21.041   Puncture wound with foreign body of right breast**

    ● **S21.042   Puncture wound with foreign body of left breast**

    ● ■ **S21.049   Puncture wound with foreign body of unspecified breast**

  ● **S21.05   Open bite of breast**
> Bite of breast NOS

> | Excludes1 | superficial bite of breast (S20.17) |

    ● **S21.051   Open bite of right breast**

    ● **S21.052   Open bite of left breast**

    ● ■ **S21.059   Open bite of unspecified breast**

● **S21.1   Open wound of front wall of thorax without penetration into thoracic cavity**
> Open wound of chest without penetration into thoracic cavity

  ● **S21.10   Unspecified open wound of front wall of thorax without penetration into thoracic cavity**

    ● ■ **S21.101   Unspecified open wound of right front wall of thorax without penetration into thoracic cavity A** 🗫

    ● ■ **S21.102   Unspecified open wound of left front wall of thorax without penetration into thoracic cavity A** 🗫

    ● ■ **S21.109   Unspecified open wound of unspecified front wall of thorax without penetration into thoracic cavity A** 🗫

  ● **S21.11   Laceration without foreign body of front wall of thorax without penetration into thoracic cavity**

    ● **S21.111   Laceration without foreign body of right front wall of thorax without penetration into thoracic cavity A** 🗫

    ● **S21.112   Laceration without foreign body of left front wall of thorax without penetration into thoracic cavity A** 🗫

    ● ■ **S21.119   Laceration without foreign body of unspecified front wall of thorax without penetration into thoracic cavity A** 🗫

  ● **S21.12   Laceration with foreign body of front wall of thorax without penetration into thoracic cavity**

    ● **S21.121   Laceration with foreign body of right front wall of thorax without penetration into thoracic cavity A** 🗫

    ● **S21.122   Laceration with foreign body of left front wall of thorax without penetration into thoracic cavity A** 🗫

    ● ■ **S21.129   Laceration with foreign body of unspecified front wall of thorax without penetration into thoracic cavity A** 🗫

  ● **S21.13   Puncture wound without foreign body of front wall of thorax without penetration into thoracic cavity**

    ● **S21.131   Puncture wound without foreign body of right front wall of thorax without penetration into thoracic cavity A** 🗫

    ● **S21.132   Puncture wound without foreign body of left front wall of thorax without penetration into thoracic cavity A** 🗫

    ● ■ **S21.139   Puncture wound without foreign body of unspecified front wall of thorax without penetration into thoracic cavity A** 🗫

● Unacceptable First-Listed Diagnosis   ● Use Additional Character(s)   ■ Unspecified   **OGCR** Official Guidelines for Coding and Reporting

🗫 Complication\Comorbidity   🗫 Major C\C | Excludes 1 | | Excludes 2 | Includes   Use additional   Code first   Code also

● S21.14　Puncture wound with foreign body of front wall of thorax without penetration into thoracic cavity

  ● S21.141　Puncture wound with foreign body of right front wall of thorax without penetration into thoracic cavity A 🦠

  ● S21.142　Puncture wound with foreign body of left front wall of thorax without penetration into thoracic cavity A 🦠

  ● ■ S21.149　Puncture wound with foreign body of unspecified front wall of thorax without penetration into thoracic cavity A 🦠

● S21.15　Open bite of front wall of thorax without penetration into thoracic cavity
    Bite of front wall of thorax NOS

    | Excludes1 | superficial bite of front wall of thorax (S20.37) |

  ● S21.151　Open bite of right front wall of thorax without penetration into thoracic cavity A 🦠

  ● S21.152　Open bite of left front wall of thorax without penetration into thoracic cavity A 🦠

  ● ■ S21.159　Open bite of unspecified front wall of thorax without penetration into thoracic cavity A 🦠

● S21.2　Open wound of back wall of thorax without penetration into thoracic cavity

 ● S21.20　Unspecified open wound of back wall of thorax without penetration into thoracic cavity

  ● ■ S21.201　Unspecified open wound of right back wall of thorax without penetration into thoracic cavity

  ● ■ S21.202　Unspecified open wound of left back wall of thorax without penetration into thoracic cavity

  ● ■ S21.209　Unspecified open wound of unspecified back wall of thorax without penetration into thoracic cavity

 ● S21.21　Laceration without foreign body of back wall of thorax without penetration into thoracic cavity

  ● S21.211　Laceration without foreign body of right back wall of thorax without penetration into thoracic cavity

  ● S21.212　Laceration without foreign body of left back wall of thorax without penetration into thoracic cavity

  ● ■ S21.219　Laceration without foreign body of unspecified back wall of thorax without penetration into thoracic cavity

 ● S21.22　Laceration with foreign body of back wall of thorax without penetration into thoracic cavity

  ● S21.221　Laceration with foreign body of right back wall of thorax without penetration into thoracic cavity A 🦠

  ● S21.222　Laceration with foreign body of left back wall of thorax without penetration into thoracic cavity A 🦠

  ● ■ S21.229　Laceration with foreign body of unspecified back wall of thorax without penetration into thoracic cavity A 🦠

● S21.23　Puncture wound without foreign body of back wall of thorax without penetration into thoracic cavity

  ● S21.231　Puncture wound without foreign body of right back wall of thorax without penetration into thoracic cavity

  ● S21.232　Puncture wound without foreign body of left back wall of thorax without penetration into thoracic cavity

  ● ■ S21.239　Puncture wound without foreign body of unspecified back wall of thorax without penetration into thoracic cavity

● S21.24　Puncture wound with foreign body of back wall of thorax without penetration into thoracic cavity

  ● S21.241　Puncture wound with foreign body of right back wall of thorax without penetration into thoracic cavity A 🦠

  ● S21.242　Puncture wound with foreign body of left back wall of thorax without penetration into thoracic cavity A 🦠

  ● ■ S21.249　Puncture wound with foreign body of unspecified back wall of thorax without penetration into thoracic cavity A 🦠

● S21.25　Open bite of back wall of thorax without penetration into thoracic cavity
    Bite of back wall of thorax NOS

    | Excludes1 | superficial bite of back wall of thorax (S20.47) |

  ● S21.251　Open bite of right back wall of thorax without penetration into thoracic cavity

  ● S21.252　Open bite of left back wall of thorax without penetration into thoracic cavity

  ● ■ S21.259　Open bite of unspecified back wall of thorax without penetration into thoracic cavity

● S21.3　Open wound of front wall of thorax with penetration into thoracic cavity
    Open wound of chest with penetration into thoracic cavity

 ● S21.30　Unspecified open wound of front wall of thorax with penetration into thoracic cavity

  ● ■ S21.301　Unspecified open wound of right front wall of thorax with penetration into thoracic cavity A 🦠

  ● ■ S21.302　Unspecified open wound of left front wall of thorax with penetration into thoracic cavity A 🦠

● Unacceptable First-Listed Diagnosis　　　● Use Additional Character(s)　　　■ Unspecified　　　**OGCR** Official Guidelines for Coding and Reporting

🦠 Complication\Comorbidity　　🦠 Major C\C　　| Excludes 1 |　　| Excludes 2 |　　Includes　　Use additional　　Code first　　Code also

1383

CHAPTER 19 (S00-T88)

● ▣ **S21.309** Unspecified open wound of unspecified front wall of thorax with penetration into thoracic cavity A ◐

● **S21.31** Laceration without foreign body of front wall of thorax with penetration into thoracic cavity

     ● **S21.311** Laceration without foreign body of right front wall of thorax with penetration into thoracic cavity A ◐

     ● **S21.312** Laceration without foreign body of left front wall of thorax with penetration into thoracic cavity A ◐

     ● ▣ **S21.319** Laceration without foreign body of unspecified front wall of thorax with penetration into thoracic cavity A ◐

● **S21.32** Laceration with foreign body of front wall of thorax with penetration into thoracic cavity

     ● **S21.321** Laceration with foreign body of right front wall of thorax with penetration into thoracic cavity A ◐

     ● **S21.322** Laceration with foreign body of left front wall of thorax with penetration into thoracic cavity A ◐

     ● ▣ **S21.329** Laceration with foreign body of unspecified front wall of thorax with penetration into thoracic cavity A ◐

● **S21.33** Puncture wound without foreign body of front wall of thorax with penetration into thoracic cavity

     ● **S21.331** Puncture wound without foreign body of right front wall of thorax with penetration into thoracic cavity A ◐

     ● **S21.332** Puncture wound without foreign body of left front wall of thorax with penetration into thoracic cavity A ◐

     ● ▣ **S21.339** Puncture wound without foreign body of unspecified front wall of thorax with penetration into thoracic cavity A ◐

● **S21.34** Puncture wound with foreign body of front wall of thorax with penetration into thoracic cavity

     ● **S21.341** Puncture wound with foreign body of right front wall of thorax with penetration into thoracic cavity A ◐

     ● **S21.342** Puncture wound with foreign body of left front wall of thorax with penetration into thoracic cavity A ◐

     ● ▣ **S21.349** Puncture wound with foreign body of unspecified front wall of thorax with penetration into thoracic cavity A ◐

● **S21.35** Open bite of front wall of thorax with penetration into thoracic cavity

     Excludes1   superficial bite of front wall of thorax (S20.37)

     ● **S21.351** Open bite of right front wall of thorax with penetration into thoracic cavity A ◐

     ● **S21.352** Open bite of left front wall of thorax with penetration into thoracic cavity A ◐

     ● ▣ **S21.359** Open bite of unspecified front wall of thorax with penetration into thoracic cavity A ◐

● **S21.4** Open wound of back wall of thorax with penetration into thoracic cavity

     ● **S21.40** Unspecified open wound of back wall of thorax with penetration into thoracic cavity

         ● ▣ **S21.401** Unspecified open wound of right back wall of thorax with penetration into thoracic cavity A ◐

         ● ▣ **S21.402** Unspecified open wound of left back wall of thorax with penetration into thoracic cavity A ◐

         ● ▣ **S21.409** Unspecified open wound of unspecified back wall of thorax with penetration into thoracic cavity A ◐

     ● **S21.41** Laceration without foreign body of back wall of thorax with penetration into thoracic cavity

         ● **S21.411** Laceration without foreign body of right back wall of thorax with penetration into thoracic cavity A ◐

         ● **S21.412** Laceration without foreign body of left back wall of thorax with penetration into thoracic cavity A ◐

         ● ▣ **S21.419** Laceration without foreign body of unspecified back wall of thorax with penetration into thoracic cavity A ◐

     ● **S21.42** Laceration with foreign body of back wall of thorax with penetration into thoracic cavity

         ● **S21.421** Laceration with foreign body of right back wall of thorax with penetration into thoracic cavity A ◐

         ● **S21.422** Laceration with foreign body of left back wall of thorax with penetration into thoracic cavity A ◐

         ● ▣ **S21.429** Laceration with foreign body of unspecified back wall of thorax with penetration into thoracic cavity A ◐

● **S21.43** **Puncture wound without foreign body of back wall of thorax with penetration into thoracic cavity**

   ● **S21.431** Puncture wound without foreign body of right back wall of thorax with penetration into thoracic cavity A 🗝

   ● **S21.432** Puncture wound without foreign body of left back wall of thorax with penetration into thoracic cavity A 🗝

   ● ▢ **S21.439** Puncture wound without foreign body of unspecified back wall of thorax with penetration into thoracic cavity A 🗝

● **S21.44** **Puncture wound with foreign body of back wall of thorax with penetration into thoracic cavity**

   ● **S21.441** Puncture wound with foreign body of right back wall of thorax with penetration into thoracic cavity A 🗝

   ● **S21.442** Puncture wound with foreign body of left back wall of thorax with penetration into thoracic cavity A 🗝

   ● ▢ **S21.449** Puncture wound with foreign body of unspecified back wall of thorax with penetration into thoracic cavity A 🗝

● **S21.45** **Open bite of back wall of thorax with penetration into thoracic cavity**
    Bite of back wall of thorax NOS

    | **Excludes1** | superficial bite of back wall of thorax (S20.47) |

   ● **S21.451** Open bite of right back wall of thorax with penetration into thoracic cavity A 🗝

   ● **S21.452** Open bite of left back wall of thorax with penetration into thoracic cavity A 🗝

   ● ▢ **S21.459** Open bite of unspecified back wall of thorax with penetration into thoracic cavity A 🗝

● **S21.9** **Open wound of unspecified part of thorax**
    Open wound of thoracic wall NOS

   ● ▢ **S21.90** Unspecified open wound of unspecified part of thorax A 🗝

   ● ▢ **S21.91** Laceration without foreign body of unspecified part of thorax A 🗝

   ● ▢ **S21.92** Laceration with foreign body of unspecified part of thorax A 🗝

   ● ▢ **S21.93** Puncture wound without foreign body of unspecified part of thorax A 🗝

   ● ▢ **S21.94** Puncture wound with foreign body of unspecified part of thorax

   ● ▢ **S21.95** Open bite of unspecified part of thorax A 🗝

    | **Excludes1** | superficial bite of thorax (S20.97) |

● **S22** **Fracture of rib(s), sternum and thoracic spine**
    A fracture not indicated as nondisplaced or displaced should be classified to displaced

    | **Includes** | fracture of thoracic neural arch |
                 fracture of thoracic spinous process
                 fracture of thoracic transverse process
                 fracture of thoracic vertebra
                 fracture of thoracic vertebral arch

    Code first any associated:
      injury of intrathoracic organ (S27.-)
      spinal cord injury (S24.0-, S24.1-)

    | **Excludes1** | transection of thorax (S28.1) |

    | **Excludes2** | fracture of clavicle (S42.0-) |
                      fracture of scapula (S42.1-)

    The appropriate 7th character is to be added to each code from category S22
    A fracture not identified as open or closed should be coded to closed

> A   initial encounter for closed fracture
> B   initial encounter for open fracture
> D   subsequent encounter for fracture with routine healing
> G   subsequent encounter for fracture with delayed healing
> K   subsequent encounter for fracture with nonunion
> S   sequela

● **S22.0** **Fracture of thoracic vertebra**

   ● **S22.00** **Fracture of unspecified thoracic vertebra**

     ● ▢ **S22.000** Wedge compression fracture of unspecified thoracic vertebra A, K 🗝, B 🗝

     ● ▢ **S22.001** Stable burst fracture of unspecified thoracic vertebra A, K 🗝, B 🗝

     ● ▢ **S22.002** Unstable burst fracture of unspecified thoracic vertebra A, K 🗝, B 🗝

     ● ▢ **S22.008** Other fracture of unspecified thoracic vertebra A, K 🗝, B 🗝

     ● ▢ **S22.009** Unspecified fracture of unspecified thoracic vertebra A, K 🗝, B 🗝

   ● **S22.01** **Fracture of first thoracic vertebra**

     ● **S22.010** Wedge compression fracture of first thoracic vertebra A, K 🗝, B 🗝

     ● **S22.011** Stable burst fracture of first thoracic vertebra A, K 🗝, B 🗝

     ● **S22.012** Unstable burst fracture of first thoracic vertebra A, K 🗝, B 🗝

     ● **S22.018** Other fracture of first thoracic vertebra A, K 🗝, B 🗝

     ● ▢ **S22.019** Unspecified fracture of first thoracic vertebra A, K 🗝, B 🗝

   ● **S22.02** **Fracture of second thoracic vertebra**

     ● **S22.020** Wedge compression fracture of second thoracic vertebra A, K 🗝, B 🗝

     ● **S22.021** Stable burst fracture of second thoracic vertebra A, K 🗝, B 🗝

     ● **S22.022** Unstable burst fracture of second thoracic vertebra A, K 🗝, B 🗝

     ● **S22.028** Other fracture of second thoracic vertebra A, K 🗝, B 🗝

     ● ▢ **S22.029** Unspecified fracture of second thoracic vertebra A, K 🗝, B 🗝

● Unacceptable First-Listed Diagnosis   ● Use Additional Character(s)   ▢ Unspecified   **OGCR** Official Guidelines for Coding and Reporting
🗝 Complication\Comorbidity   🗝 Major C\C | Excludes 1 | | Excludes 2 | Includes   Use additional   Code first   Code also

CHAPTER 19 (S00-T88)

1385

- S22.03 Fracture of third thoracic vertebra
  - S22.030 Wedge compression fracture of third thoracic vertebra A, K 🝖, B 🝖
  - S22.031 Stable burst fracture of third thoracic vertebra A, K 🝖, B 🝖
  - S22.032 Unstable burst fracture of third thoracic vertebra A, K 🝖, B 🝖
  - S22.038 Other fracture of third thoracic vertebra A, K 🝖, B 🝖
  - ■ S22.039 Unspecified fracture of third thoracic vertebra A, K 🝖, B 🝖
- S22.04 Fracture of fourth thoracic vertebra
  - S22.040 Wedge compression fracture of fourth thoracic vertebra A, K 🝖, B 🝖
  - S22.041 Stable burst fracture of fourth thoracic vertebra A, K 🝖, B 🝖
  - S22.042 Unstable burst fracture of fourth thoracic vertebra A, K 🝖, B 🝖
  - S22.048 Other fracture of fourth thoracic vertebra A, K 🝖, B 🝖
  - ■ S22.049 Unspecified fracture of fourth thoracic vertebra A, K 🝖, B 🝖
- S22.05 Fracture of T_5-T_6 vertebra
  - S22.050 Wedge compression fracture of T_5-T_6 vertebra A, K 🝖, B 🝖
  - S22.051 Stable burst fracture of T_5-T_6 vertebra A, K 🝖, B 🝖
  - S22.052 Unstable burst fracture of T_5-T_6 vertebra A, K 🝖, B 🝖
  - S22.058 Other fracture of T_5-T_6 vertebra A, K 🝖, B 🝖
  - ■ S22.059 Unspecified fracture of T_5-T_6 vertebra A, K 🝖, B 🝖
- S22.06 Fracture of T_7-T_8 vertebra
  - S22.060 Wedge compression fracture of T_7-T_8 vertebra A, K 🝖, B 🝖
  - S22.061 Stable burst fracture of T_7-T_8 vertebra A, K 🝖, B 🝖
  - S22.062 Unstable burst fracture of T_7-T_8 vertebra A, K 🝖, B 🝖
  - S22.068 Other fracture of T_7-T_8 thoracic vertebra A, K 🝖, B 🝖
  - ■ S22.069 Unspecified fracture of T_7-T_8 vertebra A, K 🝖, B 🝖
- S22.07 Fracture of T_9-T_{10} vertebra
  - S22.070 Wedge compression fracture of T_9-T_{10} vertebra A, K 🝖, B 🝖
  - S22.071 Stable burst fracture of T_9-T_{10} vertebra A, K 🝖, B 🝖
  - S22.072 Unstable burst fracture of T_9-T_{10} vertebra A, K 🝖, B 🝖
  - S22.078 Other fracture of T_9-T_{10} vertebra A, K 🝖, B 🝖
  - ■ S22.079 Unspecified fracture of T_9-T_{10} vertebra A, K 🝖, B 🝖
- S22.08 Fracture of T_{11}-T_{12} vertebra
  - S22.080 Wedge compression fracture of T_{11}-T_{12} vertebra A, K 🝖, B 🝖
  - S22.081 Stable burst fracture of T_{11}-T_{12} vertebra A, K 🝖, B 🝖
  - S22.082 Unstable burst fracture of T_{11}-T_{12} vertebra A, K 🝖, B 🝖
  - S22.088 Other fracture of T_{11}-T_{12} vertebra A, K 🝖, B 🝖
  - ■ S22.089 Unspecified fracture of T_{11}-T_{12} vertebra A, K 🝖, B 🝖
- S22.2 Fracture of sternum
  - ■ S22.20 Unspecified fracture of sternum A, K 🝖, B 🝖
  - S22.21 Fracture of manubrium A, K 🝖, B 🝖
  - S22.22 Fracture of body of sternum A, K 🝖, B 🝖
  - S22.23 Sternal manubrial dissociation A, K 🝖, B 🝖
  - S22.24 Fracture of xiphoid process A, K 🝖, B 🝖
- S22.3 Fracture of one rib
  - S22.31 Fracture of rib, right side A, K 🝖, B 🝖
  - S22.32 Fracture of rib, left side A, K 🝖, B 🝖
  - ■ S22.39 Fracture of rib, unspecified side A, K 🝖, B 🝖
- S22.4 Multiple fractures of ribs
  Fractures of two or more ribs
  > **Excludes1** flail chest (S22.5-)
  - S22.41 Multiple fractures of ribs, right side A, K 🝖, B 🝖
  - S22.42 Multiple fractures of ribs, left side A, K 🝖, B 🝖
  - S22.43 Multiple fractures of ribs, bilateral A, K 🝖, B 🝖
  - ■ S22.49 Multiple fractures of ribs, unspecified side A, K 🝖, B 🝖
- S22.5 Flail chest
  Unstable chest due to sternum and/or rib fracture
  - S22.51 Flail chest, right side K 🝖, A, B 🝖
  - S22.52 Flail chest, left side K 🝖, A, B 🝖
  - S22.53 Flail chest, bilateral K 🝖, A, B 🝖
  - ■ S22.59 Flail chest, unspecified side K 🝖, A, B 🝖
- ■ S22.9 Fracture of bony thorax, part unspecified A, K 🝖, B 🝖

- S23 Dislocation and sprain of joints and ligaments of thorax
  > **Includes** avulsion of joint or ligament of thorax
  > laceration of cartilage, joint or ligament of thorax
  > sprain of cartilage, joint or ligament of thorax
  > traumatic hemarthrosis of joint or ligament of thorax
  > traumatic rupture of joint or ligament of thorax
  > traumatic subluxation of joint or ligament of thorax
  > traumatic tear of joint or ligament of thorax

  Code also any associated open wound
  > **Excludes2** dislocation, sprain of sternoclavicular joint (S43.2, S43.6)
  > strain of muscle or tendon of thorax (S29.1)

  The appropriate 7th character is to be added to each code from category S23

A	initial encounter
D	subsequent encounter
S	sequela

CHAPTER 19 (S00-T88)

● Unacceptable First-Listed Diagnosis ● Use Additional Character(s) ■ Unspecified **OGCR** Official Guidelines for Coding and Reporting
🝖 Complication\Comorbidity 🝖 Major C\C Excludes 1 Excludes 2 Includes Use additional Code first Code also

● **S23.0   Traumatic rupture of thoracic intervertebral disc**

| Excludes1 | rupture or displacement (nontraumatic) of thoracic intervertebral disc NOS (M51.- with fifth character 4) |

● **S23.1   Subluxation and dislocation of thoracic vertebra**

Code also any associated
  open wound of thorax (S21.-)
  spinal cord injury (S24.0-, S24.1-)

| Excludes2 | fracture of thoracic vertebrae (S22.0-) |

  ● **S23.10   Subluxation and dislocation of unspecified thoracic vertebra**

    ● ■ **S23.100   Subluxation of unspecified thoracic vertebra**

    ● ■ **S23.101   Dislocation of unspecified thoracic vertebra**

  ● **S23.11   Subluxation and dislocation of T_1/T_2 thoracic vertebra**

    ● **S23.110   Subluxation of T_1/T_2 thoracic vertebra**

    ● **S23.111   Dislocation of T_1/T_2 thoracic vertebra**

  ● **S23.12   Subluxation and dislocation of T_2/T_3-T_3/T_4 thoracic vertebra**

    ● **S23.120   Subluxation of T_2-T_3 thoracic vertebra**

    ● **S23.121   Dislocation of T_2-T_3 thoracic vertebra**

    ● **S23.122   Subluxation of T_3/T_4 thoracic vertebra**

    ● **S23.123   Dislocation of T_3/T_4 thoracic vertebra**

  ● **S23.13   Subluxation and dislocation of T_4/T_5-T_5/T_6 thoracic vertebra**

    ● **S23.130   Subluxation of T_4/T_5 thoracic vertebra**

    ● **S23.131   Dislocation of T_4-T_5 thoracic vertebra**

    ● **S23.132   Subluxation of T_5/T_6 thoracic vertebra**

    ● **S23.133   Dislocation of T_5/T_6 thoracic vertebra**

  ● **S23.14   Subluxation and dislocation of T_6/T_7-T_7/T_8 thoracic vertebra**

    ● **S23.140   Subluxation of T_6/T_7 thoracic vertebra**

    ● **S23.141   Dislocation of T_6-T_7 thoracic vertebra**

    ● **S23.142   Subluxation of T_7-T_8 thoracic vertebra**

    ● **S23.143   Dislocation of T_7/T_8 thoracic vertebra**

  ● **S23.15   Subluxation and dislocation of T_8/T_9-T_9/T_{10} thoracic vertebra**

    ● **S23.150   Subluxation of T_8/T_9 thoracic vertebra**

    ● **S23.151   Dislocation of T_8/T_9 thoracic vertebra**

    ● **S23.152   Subluxation of T_9/T_{10} thoracic vertebra**

    ● **S23.153   Dislocation of T_9/T_{10} thoracic vertebra**

  ● **S23.16   Subluxation and dislocation of T_{10}/T_{11}-T_{11}/T_{12} thoracic vertebra**

    ● **S23.160   Subluxation of T_{10}/T_{11} thoracic vertebra**

    ● **S23.161   Dislocation of T_{10}/T_{11} thoracic vertebra**

    ● **S23.162   Subluxation of T_{11}/T_{12} thoracic vertebra**

    ● **S23.163   Dislocation of T_{11}/T_{12} thoracic vertebra**

  ● **S23.17   Subluxation and dislocation of T_{12}/L_1 thoracic vertebra**

    ● **S23.170   Subluxation of T_{12}/L_1 thoracic vertebra**

    ● **S23.171   Dislocation of T_{12}/L_1 thoracic vertebra**

● **S23.2   Dislocation of other and unspecified parts of thorax**

  ● ■ **S23.20   Dislocation of unspecified part of thorax**

  ● **S23.29   Dislocation of other parts of thorax**

● **S23.3   Sprain of ligaments of thoracic spine**

● **S23.4   Sprain of ribs and sternum**

  ● **S23.41   Sprain of ribs**

  ● **S23.42   Sprain of sternum**

    ● **S23.420   Sprain of sternoclavicular (joint) (ligament)**

    ● **S23.421   Sprain of chondrosternal joint**

    ● **S23.428   Other sprain of sternum**

    ● ■ **S23.429   Unspecified sprain of sternum**

● **S23.8   Sprain of other parts of thorax**

● ■ **S23.9   Sprain of unspecified parts of thorax**

● **S24   Injury of nerves and spinal cord at thorax level**

Note: Code to highest level of thoracic spinal cord injury.

Code also any associated:
  fracture of thoracic vertebra (S22.0-)
  open wound of thorax (S21.-)
  transient paralysis (R29.5)

| Excludes2 | injury of brachial plexus (S14.3) |

The appropriate 7th character is to be added to each code from category S24

A	initial encounter
D	subsequent encounter
S	sequela

● **S24.0   Concussion and edema of thoracic spinal cord** A 🗞

● **S24.1   Other and unspecified injuries of thoracic spinal cord**

  ● **S24.10   Unspecified injury of thoracic spinal cord**

    ● ■ **S24.101   Unspecified injury at T_1 level of thoracic spinal cord** A 🗞

    ● ■ **S24.102   Unspecified injury at T_2-T_6 level of thoracic spinal cord** A 🗞

    ● ■ **S24.103   Unspecified injury at T_7-T_{10} level of thoracic spinal cord** A 🗞

    ● ■ **S24.104   Unspecified injury at T_{11}-T_{12} level of thoracic spinal cord** A 🗞

    ● ■ **S24.109   Unspecified injury at unspecified level of thoracic spinal cord**
        Injury of thoracic spinal cord NOS

● Unacceptable First-Listed Diagnosis   ● Use Additional Character(s)   ■ Unspecified   **OGCR** Official Guidelines for Coding and Reporting

🗞 Complication\Comorbidity   🗞 Major C\C   Excludes 1   Excludes 2   Includes   Use additional   Code first   Code also

1387

CHAPTER 19 (S00-T88)

- ● S24.11   Complete lesion of thoracic spinal cord
  - ● S24.111   Complete lesion at T_1 level of thoracic spinal cord A 🗗
  - ● S24.112   Complete lesion at T_2-T_6 level of thoracic spinal cord A 🗗
  - ● S24.113   Complete lesion at T_7-T_{10} level of thoracic spinal cord A 🗗
  - ● S24.114   Complete lesion at T_{11}-T_{12} level of thoracic spinal cord A 🗗
  - ● ▢ S24.119   Complete lesion at unspecified level of thoracic spinal cord
- ● S24.13   Anterior cord syndrome of thoracic spinal cord
  - ● S24.131   Anterior cord syndrome at T_1 level of thoracic spinal cord A 🗗
  - ● S24.132   Anterior cord syndrome at T_2-T_6 level of thoracic spinal cord A 🗗
  - ● S24.133   Anterior cord syndrome at T_7-T_{10} level of thoracic spinal cord A 🗗
  - ● S24.134   Anterior cord syndrome at T_{11}-T_{12} level of thoracic spinal cord A 🗗
  - ● ▢ S24.139   Anterior cord syndrome at unspecified level of thoracic spinal cord
- ● S24.14   Brown-Sequard syndrome of thoracic spinal cord
  - ● S24.141   Brown-Sequard syndrome at T_1 level of thoracic spinal cord A 🗗
  - ● S24.142   Brown-Sequard syndrome at T_2-T_6 level of thoracic spinal cord A 🗗
  - ● S24.143   Brown-Sequard syndrome at T_7-T_{10} level of thoracic spinal cord A 🗗
  - ● S24.144   Brown-Sequard syndrome at T_{11}-T_{12} level of thoracic spinal cord A 🗗
  - ● ▢ S24.149   Brown-Sequard syndrome at unspecified level of thoracic spinal cord
- ● S24.15   Other incomplete lesions of thoracic spinal cord
  Incomplete lesion of thoracic spinal cord NOS
  Posterior cord syndrome of thoracic spinal cord
  - ● S24.151   Other incomplete lesion at T_1 level of thoracic spinal cord A 🗗
  - ● S24.152   Other incomplete lesion at T_2-T_6 level of thoracic spinal cord A 🗗
  - ● S24.153   Other incomplete lesion at T_7-T_{10} level of thoracic spinal cord A 🗗
  - ● S24.154   Other incomplete lesion at T_{11}-T_{12} level of thoracic spinal cord A 🗗
  - ● ▢ S24.159   Other incomplete lesion at unspecified level of thoracic spinal cord
- ● S24.2   Injury of nerve root of thoracic spine
- ● S24.3   Injury of peripheral nerves of thorax
- ● S24.4   Injury of thoracic sympathetic nervous system
  Injury of cardiac plexus
  Injury of esophageal plexus
  Injury of pulmonary plexus
  Injury of stellate ganglion
  Injury of thoracic sympathetic ganglion

- ● S24.8   Injury of other nerves of thorax
- ● ▢ S24.9   Injury of unspecified nerve of thorax
- ● S25   Injury of blood vessels of thorax

  Code also any associated open wound (S21.-)

  The appropriate 7th character is to be added to each code from category S25

A	initial encounter
D	subsequent encounter
S	sequela

  - ● S25.0   Injury of thoracic aorta
    Injury of aorta NOS
    - ● ▢ S25.00   Unspecified injury of thoracic aorta A 🗗
    - ● S25.01   Minor laceration of thoracic aorta A 🗗
      Incomplete transection of thoracic aorta
      Laceration of thoracic aorta NOS
      Superficial laceration of thoracic aorta
    - ● S25.02   Major laceration of thoracic aorta A 🗗
      Complete transection of thoracic aorta
      Traumatic rupture of thoracic aorta
    - ● S25.09   Other injury of thoracic aorta A 🗗
  - ● S25.1   Injury of innominate or subclavian artery
    - ● S25.10   Unspecified injury of innominate or subclavian artery
      - ● ▢ S25.101   Unspecified injury of right innominate or subclavian artery A 🗗
      - ● ▢ S25.102   Unspecified injury of left innominate or subclavian artery A 🗗
      - ● ▢ S25.109   Unspecified injury of unspecified innominate or subclavian artery A 🗗
    - ● S25.11   Minor laceration of innominate or subclavian artery
      Incomplete transection of innominate or subclavian artery
      Laceration of innominate or subclavian artery NOS
      Superficial laceration of innominate or subclavian artery
      - ● S25.111   Minor laceration of right innominate or subclavian artery A 🗗
      - ● S25.112   Minor laceration of left innominate or subclavian artery A 🗗
      - ● ▢ S25.119   Minor laceration of unspecified innominate or subclavian artery A 🗗
    - ● S25.12   Major laceration of innominate or subclavian artery
      Complete transection of innominate or subclavian artery
      Traumatic rupture of innominate or subclavian artery
      - ● S25.121   Major laceration of right innominate or subclavian artery A 🗗
      - ● S25.122   Major laceration of left innominate or subclavian artery A 🗗
      - ● ▢ S25.129   Major laceration of unspecified innominate or subclavian artery A 🗗

● Unacceptable First-Listed Diagnosis   ● Use Additional Character(s)   ▢ Unspecified   **OGCR** Official Guidelines for Coding and Reporting
🗗 Complication\Comorbidity   🗗 Major C\C   Excludes 1   Excludes 2   Includes   Use additional   Code first   Code also

● S25.19   Other specified injury of innominate or
            subclavian artery
    ● S25.191   Other specified injury of right
                innominate or subclavian artery
                A ✆
    ● S25.192   Other specified injury of left
                innominate or subclavian artery
                A ✆
    ● ■ S25.199   Other specified injury of
                  unspecified innominate or
                  subclavian artery A ✆

● S25.2   Injury of superior vena cava
           Injury of vena cava NOS
    ● ■ S25.20   Unspecified injury of superior vena
                 cava A ✆
    ● S25.21   Minor laceration of superior vena cava A ✆
                Incomplete transection of superior vena
                    cava
                Laceration of superior vena cava NOS
                Superficial laceration of superior vena cava
    ● S25.22   Major laceration of superior vena cava A ✆
                Complete transection of superior vena cava
                Traumatic rupture of superior vena cava
    ● S25.29   Other specified injury of superior vena
                cava A ✆

● S25.3   Injury of innominate or subclavian vein
    ● S25.30   Unspecified injury of innominate or
                subclavian vein
        ● ■ S25.301   Unspecified injury of right
                      innominate or subclavian
                      vein A ✆
        ● ■ S25.302   Unspecified injury of left
                      innominate or subclavian
                      vein A ✆
        ● ■ S25.309   Unspecified injury of unspecified
                      innominate or subclavian
                      vein A ✆
    ● S25.31   Minor laceration of innominate or
                subclavian vein
                Incomplete transection of innominate or
                    subclavian vein
                Laceration of innominate or subclavian
                    vein NOS
                Superficial laceration of innominate or
                    subclavian vein
        ● S25.311   Minor laceration of right
                    innominate or subclavian
                    vein A ✆
        ● S25.312   Minor laceration of left innominate
                    or subclavian vein A ✆
        ● ■ S25.319   Minor laceration of unspecified
                      innominate or subclavian
                      vein A ✆
    ● S25.32   Major laceration of innominate or
                subclavian vein
                Complete transection of innominate or
                    subclavian vein
                Traumatic rupture of innominate or
                    subclavian vein
        ● S25.321   Major laceration of right
                    innominate or subclavian
                    vein A ✆
        ● S25.322   Major laceration of left innominate
                    or subclavian vein A ✆
        ● ■ S25.329   Major laceration of unspecified
                      innominate or subclavian
                      vein A ✆

● S25.39   Other specified injury of innominate or
            subclavian vein
    ● S25.391   Other specified injury of right
                innominate or subclavian
                vein A ✆
    ● S25.392   Other specified injury of left
                innominate or subclavian
                vein A ✆
    ● ■ S25.399   Other specified injury of
                  unspecified innominate or
                  subclavian vein A ✆

● S25.4   Injury of pulmonary blood vessels
    ● S25.40   Unspecified injury of pulmonary blood
                vessels
        ● ■ S25.401   Unspecified injury of right
                      pulmonary blood vessels A ✆
        ● ■ S25.402   Unspecified injury of left
                      pulmonary blood vessels A ✆
        ● ■ S25.409   Unspecified injury of unspecified
                      pulmonary blood vessels A ✆
    ● S25.41   Minor laceration of pulmonary blood
                vessels
                Incomplete transection of pulmonary
                    blood vessels
                Laceration of pulmonary blood vessels
                    NOS
                Superficial laceration of pulmonary blood
                    vessels
        ● S25.411   Minor laceration of right
                    pulmonary blood vessels A ✆
        ● S25.412   Minor laceration of left
                    pulmonary blood vessels A ✆
        ● ■ S25.419   Minor laceration of unspecified
                      pulmonary blood vessels A ✆
    ● S25.42   Major laceration of pulmonary blood
                vessels
                Complete transection of pulmonary blood
                    vessels
                Traumatic rupture of pulmonary blood
                    vessels
        ● S25.421   Major laceration of right
                    pulmonary blood vessels A ✆
        ● S25.422   Major laceration of left
                    pulmonary blood vessels A ✆
        ● ■ S25.429   Major laceration of unspecified
                      pulmonary blood vessels A ✆
    ● S25.49   Other specified injury of pulmonary blood
                vessels
        ● S25.491   Other specified injury of right
                    pulmonary blood vessels A ✆
        ● S25.492   Other specified injury of left
                    pulmonary blood vessels A ✆
        ● ■ S25.499   Other specified injury of
                      unspecified pulmonary blood
                      vessels A ✆

● S25.5   Injury of intercostal blood vessels
    ● S25.50   Unspecified injury of intercostal blood
                vessels
        ● ■ S25.501   Unspecified injury of intercostal
                      blood vessels, right side A ✆
        ● ■ S25.502   Unspecified injury of intercostal
                      blood vessels, left side A ✆
        ● ■ S25.509   Unspecified injury of intercostal
                      blood vessels, unspecified side
                      A ✆

● Unacceptable First-Listed Diagnosis   ● Use Additional Character(s)   ■ Unspecified   **OGCR** Official Guidelines for Coding and Reporting

✆ Complication\Comorbidity   ✆ Major C\C   Excludes 1   Excludes 2   Includes   Use additional   Code first   Code also

● S25.51   Laceration of intercostal blood vessels

     ● S25.511   Laceration of intercostal blood vessels, right side A ✆

     ● S25.512   Laceration of intercostal blood vessels, left side A ✆

     ● ■ S25.519   Laceration of intercostal blood vessels, unspecified side A ✆

● S25.59   Other specified injury of intercostal blood vessels

     ● S25.591   Other specified injury of intercostal blood vessels, right side A ✆

     ● S25.592   Other specified injury of intercostal blood vessels, left side A ✆

     ● ■ S25.599   Other specified injury of intercostal blood vessels, unspecified side A ✆

● S25.8   Injury of other blood vessels of thorax
     Injury of azygos vein
     Injury of mammary artery or vein

   ● S25.80   Unspecified injury of other blood vessels of thorax

     ● ■ S25.801   Unspecified injury of other blood vessels of thorax, right side A ✆

     ● ■ S25.802   Unspecified injury of other blood vessels of thorax, left side A ✆

     ● ■ S25.809   Unspecified injury of other blood vessels of thorax, unspecified side A ✆

   ● S25.81   Laceration of other blood vessels of thorax

     ● S25.811   Laceration of other blood vessels of thorax, right side A ✆

     ● S25.812   Laceration of other blood vessels of thorax, left side A ✆

     ● ■ S25.819   Laceration of other blood vessels of thorax, unspecified side A ✆

   ● S25.89   Other specified injury of other blood vessels of thorax

     ● S25.891   Other specified injury of other blood vessels of thorax, right side A ✆

     ● S25.892   Other specified injury of other blood vessels of thorax, left side A ✆

     ● ■ S25.899   Other specified injury of other blood vessels of thorax, unspecified side A ✆

● S25.9   Injury of unspecified blood vessel of thorax

   ● ■ S25.90   Unspecified injury of unspecified blood vessel of thorax A ✆

   ● ■ S25.91   Laceration of unspecified blood vessel of thorax A ✆

   ● ■ S25.99   Other specified injury of unspecified blood vessel of thorax A ✆

Item 19-2   **Pneumothorax** is a collection of gas (positive air pressure) in the pleural space resulting in the lung collapsing. A tension pneumothorax is life-threatening and is a result of air in the pleural space causing a displacement in the mediastinal structures and cardiopulmonary function compromise. A traumatic pneumothorax results from blunt or penetrating injury that disrupts the parietal/visceral pleura. **Hemothorax** is blood or bloody fluid in the pleural cavity as a result of traumatic blood vessel rupture or inflammation of the lungs from pneumonia.

● S26   Injury of heart

     Code also any associated:
       open wound of thorax (S21.-)
       traumatic hemopneumothorax (S27.2)
       traumatic hemothorax (S27.1)
       traumatic pneumothorax (S27.0)

     The appropriate 7th character is to be added to each code from category S26

A	initial encounter
D	subsequent encounter
S	sequela

   ● S26.0   Injury of heart with hemopericardium
     Hemopericardium: effusion of blood within pericardium

     ● ■ S26.00   Unspecified injury of heart with hemopericardium A ✆

     ● S26.01   Contusion of heart with hemopericardium A ✆

     ● S26.02   Laceration of heart with hemopericardium

       ● S26.020   Mild laceration of heart with hemopericardium A ✆
         Laceration of heart without penetration of heart chamber

       ● S26.021   Moderate laceration of heart with hemopericardium A ✆
         Laceration of heart with penetration of heart chamber

       ● S26.022   Major laceration of heart with hemopericardium A ✆
         Laceration of heart with penetration of multiple heart chambers

     ● S26.09   Other injury of heart with hemopericardium A ✆

   ● S26.1   Injury of heart without hemopericardium
     Hemopericardium: effusion of blood within pericardium

     ● ■ S26.10   Unspecified injury of heart without hemopericardium A ✆

     ● S26.11   Contusion of heart without hemopericardium A ✆

     ● S26.12   Laceration of heart without hemopericardium A ✆

     ● S26.19   Other injury of heart without hemopericardium A ✆

   ● S26.9   Injury of heart, unspecified with or without hemopericardium
     Hemopericardium: effusion of blood within pericardium

     ● ■ S26.90   Unspecified injury of heart, unspecified with or without hemopericardium A ✆

     ● ■ S26.91   Contusion of heart, unspecified with or without hemopericardium A ✆

     ● ■ S26.92   Laceration of heart, unspecified with or without hemopericardium A ✆
       Laceration of heart NOS

     ● ■ S26.99   Other injury of heart, unspecified with or without hemopericardium A ✆

● S27   Injury of other and unspecified intrathoracic organs

     Code also any associated open wound of thorax (S21.-)

     Excludes2   injury of cervical esophagus (S10-S19)
                injury of trachea (cervical) (S10-S19)

     The appropriate 7th character is to be added to each code from category S27

A	initial encounter
D	subsequent encounter
S	sequela

● Unacceptable First-Listed Diagnosis   ● Use Additional Character(s)   ■ Unspecified   **OGCR** Official Guidelines for Coding and Reporting

✆ Complication\Comorbidity   ✆ Major C\C   Excludes 1   Excludes 2   Includes   Use additional   Code first   Code also

● S27.0   Traumatic pneumothorax A 🅒

     Excludes1   spontaneous pneumothorax (J93.-)

● S27.1   Traumatic hemothorax A 🅒

● S27.2   Traumatic hemopneumothorax A 🅒

● S27.3   Other and unspecified injuries of lung

   ● S27.30   Unspecified injury of lung

     ● ◻ S27.301   Unspecified injury of lung, unilateral A 🅒

     ● ◻ S27.302   Unspecified injury of lung, bilateral A 🅒

     ● ◻ S27.309   Unspecified injury of lung, unspecified A 🅒

   ● S27.31   Primary blast injury of lung
           Blast injury of lung NOS

     ● S27.311   Primary blast injury of lung, unilateral A 🅒

     ● S27.312   Primary blast injury of lung, bilateral A 🅒

     ● ◻ S27.319   Primary blast injury of lung, unspecified A 🅒

   ● S27.32   Contusion of lung

     ● S27.321   Contusion of lung, unilateral A 🅒

     ● S27.322   Contusion of lung, bilateral A 🅒

     ● ◻ S27.329   Contusion of lung, unspecified A 🅒

   ● S27.33   Laceration of lung

     ● S27.331   Laceration of lung, unilateral A 🅒

     ● S27.332   Laceration of lung, bilateral A 🅒

     ● ◻ S27.339   Laceration of lung, unspecified A 🅒

   ● S27.39   Other injuries of lung
           Secondary blast injury of lung

     ● S27.391   Other injuries of lung, unilateral A 🅒

     ● S27.392   Other injuries of lung, bilateral A 🅒

     ● ◻ S27.399   Other injuries of lung, unspecified A 🅒

● S27.4   Injury of bronchus

   ● S27.40   Unspecified injury of bronchus

     ● ◻ S27.401   Unspecified injury of bronchus, unilateral A 🅒

     ● ◻ S27.402   Unspecified injury of bronchus, bilateral A 🅒

     ● ◻ S27.409   Unspecified injury of bronchus, unspecified A 🅒

   ● S27.41   Primary blast injury of bronchus
           Blast injury of bronchus NOS

     ● S27.411   Primary blast injury of bronchus, unilateral A 🅒

     ● S27.412   Primary blast injury of bronchus, bilateral A 🅒

     ● ◻ S27.419   Primary blast injury of bronchus, unspecified A 🅒

   ● S27.42   Contusion of bronchus

     ● S27.421   Contusion of bronchus, unilateral A 🅒

     ● S27.422   Contusion of bronchus, bilateral A 🅒

     ● ◻ S27.429   Contusion of bronchus, unspecified A 🅒

   ● S27.43   Laceration of bronchus

     ● S27.431   Laceration of bronchus, unilateral A 🅒

     ● S27.432   Laceration of bronchus, bilateral A 🅒

     ● ◻ S27.439   Laceration of bronchus, unspecified A 🅒

   ● S27.49   Other injury of bronchus
           Secondary blast injury of bronchus

     ● S27.491   Other injury of bronchus, unilateral A 🅒

     ● S27.492   Other injury of bronchus, bilateral A 🅒

     ● ◻ S27.499   Other injury of bronchus, unspecified A 🅒

● S27.5   Injury of thoracic trachea

   ● ◻ S27.50   Unspecified injury of thoracic trachea A 🅒

   ● S27.51   Primary blast injury of thoracic trachea A 🅒
           Blast injury of thoracic trachea NOS

   ● S27.52   Contusion of thoracic trachea A 🅒

   ● S27.53   Laceration of thoracic trachea A 🅒

   ● S27.59   Other injury of thoracic trachea A 🅒
           Secondary blast injury of thoracic trachea

● S27.6   Injury of pleura

   ● ◻ S27.60   Unspecified injury of pleura A 🅒

   ● S27.63   Laceration of pleura A 🅒

   ● S27.69   Other injury of pleura A 🅒

● S27.8   Injury of other specified intrathoracic organs

   ● S27.80   Injury of diaphragm

     ● S27.802   Contusion of diaphragm A 🅒

     ● S27.803   Laceration of diaphragm A 🅒

     ● S27.808   Other injury of diaphragm A 🅒

     ● ◻ S27.809   Unspecified injury of diaphragm A 🅒

   ● S27.81   Injury of esophagus (thoracic part)

     ● S27.812   Contusion of esophagus (thoracic part) A 🅒

     ● S27.813   Laceration of esophagus (thoracic part) A 🅒

     ● S27.818   Other injury of esophagus (thoracic part) A 🅒

     ● ◻ S27.819   Unspecified injury of esophagus (thoracic part) A 🅒

   ● S27.89   Injury of other specified intrathoracic organs
           Injury of lymphatic thoracic duct
           Injury of thymus gland

     ● S27.892   Contusion of other specified intrathoracic organs A 🅒

     ● S27.893   Laceration of other specified intrathoracic organs A 🅒

     ● S27.898   Other injury of other specified intrathoracic organs A 🅒

     ● ◻ S27.899   Unspecified injury of other specified intrathoracic organs A 🅒

● ◻ S27.9   Injury of unspecified intrathoracic organ A 🅒

●   Unacceptable First-Listed Diagnosis   ●   Use Additional Character(s)   ◻   Unspecified   **OGCR**   Official Guidelines for Coding and Reporting

🅒 Complication\Comorbidity   🅒 Major C\C    Excludes 1   Excludes 2   Includes   Use additional   Code first   Code also

● **S28**   **Crushing injury of thorax, and traumatic amputation of part of thorax**

> The appropriate 7th character is to be added to each code from category S28

> A   initial encounter
> D   subsequent encounter
> S   sequela

● **S28.0**   **Crushed chest**

> Use additional code for all associated injuries

> **Excludes1**   flail chest (S22.5)

● **S28.1**   **Traumatic amputation (partial) of part of thorax, except breast A 🝔**

● **S28.2**   **Traumatic amputation of breast**

● **S28.21**   **Complete traumatic amputation of breast**
> Traumatic amputation of breast NOS

● **S28.211**   **Complete traumatic amputation of right breast**

● **S28.212**   **Complete traumatic amputation of left breast**

● ■ **S28.219**   **Complete traumatic amputation of unspecified breast**

● **S28.22**   **Partial traumatic amputation of breast**

● **S28.221**   **Partial traumatic amputation of right breast**

● **S28.222**   **Partial traumatic amputation of left breast**

● ■ **S28.229**   **Partial traumatic amputation of unspecified breast**

● **S29**   **Other and unspecified injuries of thorax**
> Code also any associated open wound (S21.-)

> The appropriate 7th character is to be added to each code from category S29

> A   initial encounter
> D   subsequent encounter
> S   sequela

● **S29.0**   **Injury of muscle and tendon at thorax level**

● **S29.00**   **Unspecified injury of muscle and tendon of thorax**

● ■ **S29.001**   Unspecified injury of muscle and tendon of front wall of thorax

● ■ **S29.002**   Unspecified injury of muscle and tendon of back wall of thorax

● ■ **S29.009**   Unspecified injury of muscle and tendon of unspecified wall of thorax

● **S29.01**   **Strain of muscle and tendon of thorax**

● **S29.011**   Strain of muscle and tendon of front wall of thorax

● **S29.012**   Strain of muscle and tendon of back wall of thorax

● ■ **S29.019**   Strain of muscle and tendon of unspecified wall of thorax

● **S29.02**   **Laceration of muscle and tendon of thorax**

● **S29.021**   Laceration of muscle and tendon of front wall of thorax A, K 🝔

● **S29.022**   Laceration of muscle and tendon of back wall of thorax A, K 🝔

● ■ **S29.029**   Laceration of muscle and tendon of unspecified wall of thorax A, K 🝔

● **S29.09**   **Other injury of muscle and tendon of thorax**

● **S29.091**   Other injury of muscle and tendon of front wall of thorax

● **S29.092**   Other injury of muscle and tendon of back wall of thorax

● ■ **S29.099**   Other injury of muscle and tendon of unspecified wall of thorax

● **S29.8**   **Other specified injuries of thorax**

● ■ **S29.9**   **Unspecified injury of thorax**

INJURIES TO THE ABDOMEN, LOWER BACK, LUMBAR SPINE, PELVIS AND EXTERNAL GENITALS (S30-S39)

> **Includes**   injuries to the abdominal wall
> injuries to the anus
> injuries to the buttock
> injuries to the external genitalia
> injuries to the flank
> injuries to the groin

> **Excludes2**   burns and corrosions (T20-T32)
> effects of foreign body in anus and rectum (T18.5)
> effects of foreign body in genitourinary tract (T19.-)
> effects of foreign body in stomach, small intestine and colon (T18.2-T18.4)
> frostbite (T33-T34)
> insect bite or sting, venomous (T63.4)

● **S30**   **Superficial injury of abdomen, lower back, pelvis and external genitals**

> **Excludes2**   superficial injury of hip (S70.-)

> The appropriate 7th character is to be added to each code from category S30

> A   initial encounter
> D   subsequent encounter
> S   sequela

● **S30.0**   **Contusion of lower back and pelvis**
> Contusion of buttock

● **S30.1**   **Contusion of abdominal wall**
> Contusion of flank
> Contusion of groin

● **S30.2**   **Contusion of external genital organs**

● **S30.20**   **Contusion of unspecified external genital organ**

● ■ **S30.201**   Contusion of unspecified external genital organ, male

● ■ **S30.202**   Contusion of unspecified external genital organ, female

● **S30.21**   **Contusion of penis**

● **S30.22**   **Contusion of scrotum and testes**

● **S30.23**   **Contusion of vagina and vulva**

● **S30.3**   **Contusion of anus**

● **S30.8**   **Other superficial injuries of abdomen, lower back, pelvis and external genitals**

● **S30.81**   **Abrasion of abdomen, lower back, pelvis and external genitals**

● **S30.810**   Abrasion of lower back and pelvis

● **S30.811**   Abrasion of abdominal wall

● **S30.812**   Abrasion of penis

● **S30.813**   Abrasion of scrotum and testes

● **S30.814**   Abrasion of vagina and vulva

● Unacceptable First-Listed Diagnosis   ● Use Additional Character(s)   ■ Unspecified   **OGCR** Official Guidelines for Coding and Reporting
🝔 Complication\Comorbidity   🝔 Major C\C   Excludes 1   Excludes 2   Includes   Use additional   Code first   Code also

● ■ **S30.815** **Abrasion of unspecified external genital organs, male**

● ■ **S30.816** **Abrasion of unspecified external genital organs, female**

● **S30.817** **Abrasion of anus**

● **S30.82** **Blister (nonthermal) of abdomen, lower back, pelvis and external genitals**

　● **S30.820** **Blister (nonthermal) of lower back and pelvis**

　● **S30.821** **Blister (nonthermal) of abdominal wall**

　● **S30.822** **Blister (nonthermal) of penis**

　● **S30.823** **Blister (nonthermal) of scrotum and testes**

　● **S30.824** **Blister (nonthermal) of vagina and vulva**

　● ■ **S30.825** **Blister (nonthermal) of unspecified external genital organs, male**

　● ■ **S30.826** **Blister (nonthermal) of unspecified external genital organs, female**

　● **S30.827** **Blister (nonthermal) of anus**

● **S30.84** **External constriction of abdomen, lower back, pelvis and external genitals**

　● **S30.840** **External constriction of lower back and pelvis**

　● **S30.841** **External constriction of abdominal wall**

　● **S30.842** **External constriction of penis**
　　　　　Hair tourniquet syndrome of penis

　　　　　Use additional cause code to identify the constricting item (W49.0-)

　● **S30.843** **External constriction of scrotum and testes**

　● **S30.844** **External constriction of vagina and vulva**

　● ■ **S30.845** **External constriction of unspecified external genital organs, male**

　● ■ **S30.846** **External constriction of unspecified external genital organs, female**

● **S30.85** **Superficial foreign body of abdomen, lower back, pelvis and external genitals**
　　　　　Splinter in the abdomen, lower back, pelvis and external genitals

　● **S30.850** **Superficial foreign body of lower back and pelvis**

　● **S30.851** **Superficial foreign body of abdominal wall**

　● **S30.852** **Superficial foreign body of penis**

　● **S30.853** **Superficial foreign body of scrotum and testes**

　● **S30.854** **Superficial foreign body of vagina and vulva**

　● ■ **S30.855** **Superficial foreign body of unspecified external genital organs, male**

● ■ **S30.856** **Superficial foreign body of unspecified external genital organs, female**

● **S30.857** **Superficial foreign body of anus**

● **S30.86** **Insect bite (nonvenomous) of abdomen, lower back, pelvis and external genitals**

　● **S30.860** **Insect bite (nonvenomous) of lower back and pelvis**

　● **S30.861** **Insect bite (nonvenomous) of abdominal wall**

　● **S30.862** **Insect bite (nonvenomous) of penis**

　● **S30.863** **Insect bite (nonvenomous) of scrotum and testes**

　● **S30.864** **Insect bite (nonvenomous) of vagina and vulva**

　● ■ **S30.865** **Insect bite (nonvenomous) of unspecified external genital organs, male**

　● ■ **S30.866** **Insect bite (nonvenomous) of unspecified external genital organs, female**

　● **S30.867** **Insect bite (nonvenomous) of anus**

● **S30.87** **Other superficial bite of abdomen, lower back, pelvis and external genitals**

　　| **Excludes 1** | open bite of abdomen, lower back, pelvis and external genitals (S31.05, S31.15, S31.25, S31.35, S31.45, S31.55) |

　● **S30.870** **Other superficial bite of lower back and pelvis**

　● **S30.871** **Other superficial bite of abdominal wall**

　● **S30.872** **Other superficial bite of penis**

　● **S30.873** **Other superficial bite of scrotum and testes**

　● **S30.874** **Other superficial bite of vagina and vulva**

　● ■ **S30.875** **Other superficial bite of unspecified external genital organs, male**

　● ■ **S30.876** **Other superficial bite of unspecified external genital organs, female**

　● **S30.877** **Other superficial bite of anus**

● **S30.9** **Unspecified superficial injury of abdomen, lower back, pelvis and external genitals**

　● ■ **S30.91** **Unspecified superficial injury of lower back and pelvis**

　● ■ **S30.92** **Unspecified superficial injury of abdominal wall**

　● ■ **S30.93** **Unspecified superficial injury of penis**

　● ■ **S30.94** **Unspecified superficial injury of scrotum and testes**

　● ■ **S30.95** **Unspecified superficial injury of vagina and vulva**

　● ■ **S30.96** **Unspecified superficial injury of unspecified external genital organs, male**

　● ■ **S30.97** **Unspecified superficial injury of unspecified external genital organs, female**

　● ■ **S30.98** **Unspecified superficial injury of anus**

● Unacceptable First-Listed Diagnosis　　● Use Additional Character(s)　　■ Unspecified　　**OGCR** Official Guidelines for Coding and Reporting

🗝 Complication\Comorbidity　　🗝 Major C\C　　Excludes 1　　Excludes 2　　Includes　　Use additional　　Code first　　Code also

1393

CHAPTER 19 (S00–T88)

● **S31** **Open wound of abdomen, lower back, pelvis and external genitals**

Code also any associated:
spinal cord injury (S24.0, S24.1-, S34.0, S34.1-)
wound infection

Excludes1 traumatic amputation of part of abdomen, lower back and pelvis (S38.2-, S38.3)

Excludes2 open wound of hip (S71.00-S71.02)
open fracture of pelvis (S32.1--S32.9 with 7th character B)

The appropriate 7th character is to be added to each code from category S31

> A　initial encounter
> D　subsequent encounter
> S　sequela

● **S31.0** **Open wound of lower back and pelvis**

　　● **S31.00** **Unspecified open wound of lower back and pelvis**

　　　　● ■ **S31.000** **Unspecified open wound of lower back and pelvis without penetration into retroperitoneum**
Unspecified open wound of lower back and pelvis NOS

　　　　● ■ **S31.001** **Unspecified open wound of lower back and pelvis with penetration into retroperitoneum A** 🗱

　　● **S31.01** **Laceration without foreign body of lower back and pelvis**

　　　　● **S31.010** **Laceration without foreign body of lower back and pelvis without penetration into retroperitoneum**
Laceration without foreign body of lower back and pelvis NOS

　　　　● **S31.011** **Laceration without foreign body of lower back and pelvis with penetration into retroperitoneum A** 🗱

　　● **S31.02** **Laceration with foreign body of lower back and pelvis**

　　　　● **S31.020** **Laceration with foreign body of lower back and pelvis without penetration into retroperitoneum**
Laceration with foreign body of lower back and pelvis NOS

　　　　● **S31.021** **Laceration with foreign body of lower back and pelvis with penetration into retroperitoneum A** 🗱

　　● **S31.03** **Puncture wound without foreign body of lower back and pelvis**

　　　　● **S31.030** **Puncture wound without foreign body of lower back and pelvis without penetration into retroperitoneum**
Puncture wound without foreign body of lower back and pelvis NOS

　　　　● **S31.031** **Puncture wound without foreign body of lower back and pelvis with penetration into retroperitoneum A** 🗱

● **S31.04** **Puncture wound with foreign body of lower back and pelvis**

　　● **S31.040** **Puncture wound with foreign body of lower back and pelvis without penetration into retroperitoneum**
Puncture wound with foreign body of lower back and pelvis NOS

　　● **S31.041** **Puncture wound with foreign body of lower back and pelvis with penetration into retroperitoneum A** 🗱

● **S31.05** **Open bite of lower back and pelvis**
Bite of lower back and pelvis NOS

Excludes1 superficial bite of lower back and pelvis (S30.860, S30.870)

　　● **S31.050** **Open bite of lower back and pelvis without penetration into retroperitoneum**
Open bite of lower back and pelvis NOS

　　● **S31.051** **Open bite of lower back and pelvis with penetration into retroperitoneum A** 🗱

● **S31.1** **Open wound of abdominal wall without penetration into peritoneal cavity**
Open wound of abdominal wall NOS

Excludes2 open wound of abdominal wall with penetration into peritoneal cavity (S31.6-)

● **S31.10** **Unspecified open wound of abdominal wall without penetration into peritoneal cavity**

　　● ■ **S31.100** **Unspecified open wound of abdominal wall, right upper quadrant without penetration into peritoneal cavity**

　　● ■ **S31.101** **Unspecified open wound of abdominal wall, left upper quadrant without penetration into peritoneal cavity**

　　● ■ **S31.102** **Unspecified open wound of abdominal wall, epigastric region without penetration into peritoneal cavity**

　　● ■ **S31.103** **Unspecified open wound of abdominal wall, right lower quadrant without penetration into peritoneal cavity**

　　● ■ **S31.104** **Unspecified open wound of abdominal wall, left lower quadrant without penetration into peritoneal cavity**

　　● ■ **S31.105** **Unspecified open wound of abdominal wall, periumbilic region without penetration into peritoneal cavity**

　　● ■ **S31.109** **Unspecified open wound of abdominal wall, unspecified quadrant without penetration into peritoneal cavity**
Unspecified open wound of abdominal wall NOS

● Unacceptable First-Listed Diagnosis　　● Use Additional Character(s)　　■ Unspecified　　**OGCR** Official Guidelines for Coding and Reporting
🗱 Complication\Comorbidity　　🗱 Major C\C　　Excludes 1　　Excludes 2　　Includes　　Use additional　　Code first　　Code also

● S31.11   Laceration without foreign body of abdominal wall without penetration into peritoneal cavity

    ● S31.110   Laceration without foreign body of abdominal wall, right upper quadrant without penetration into peritoneal cavity

    ● S31.111   Laceration without foreign body of abdominal wall, left upper quadrant without penetration into peritoneal cavity

    ● S31.112   Laceration without foreign body of abdominal wall, epigastric region without penetration into peritoneal cavity

    ● S31.113   Laceration without foreign body of abdominal wall, right lower quadrant without penetration into peritoneal cavity

    ● S31.114   Laceration without foreign body of abdominal wall, left lower quadrant without penetration into peritoneal cavity

    ● S31.115   Laceration without foreign body of abdominal wall, periumbilic region without penetration into peritoneal cavity

    ● ■ S31.119   Laceration without foreign body of abdominal wall, unspecified quadrant without penetration into peritoneal cavity

● S31.12   Laceration with foreign body of abdominal wall without penetration into peritoneal cavity

    ● S31.120   Laceration of abdominal wall with foreign body, right upper quadrant without penetration into peritoneal cavity

    ● S31.121   Laceration of abdominal wall with foreign body, left upper quadrant without penetration into peritoneal cavity

    ● S31.122   Laceration of abdominal wall with foreign body, epigastric region without penetration into peritoneal cavity

    ● S31.123   Laceration of abdominal wall with foreign body, right lower quadrant without penetration into peritoneal cavity

    ● S31.124   Laceration of abdominal wall with foreign body, left lower quadrant without penetration into peritoneal cavity

    ● S31.125   Laceration of abdominal wall with foreign body, periumbilic region without penetration into peritoneal cavity

    ● ■ S31.129   Laceration of abdominal wall with foreign body, unspecified quadrant without penetration into peritoneal cavity

● S31.13   Puncture wound of abdominal wall without foreign body without penetration into peritoneal cavity

    ● S31.130   Puncture wound of abdominal wall without foreign body, right upper quadrant without penetration into peritoneal cavity

    ● S31.131   Puncture wound of abdominal wall without foreign body, left upper quadrant without penetration into peritoneal cavity

    ● S31.132   Puncture wound of abdominal wall without foreign body, epigastric region without penetration into peritoneal cavity

    ● S31.133   Puncture wound of abdominal wall without foreign body, right lower quadrant without penetration into peritoneal cavity

    ● S31.134   Puncture wound of abdominal wall without foreign body, left lower quadrant without penetration into peritoneal cavity

    ● S31.135   Puncture wound of abdominal wall without foreign body, periumbilic region without penetration into peritoneal cavity

    ● ■ S31.139   Puncture wound of abdominal wall without foreign body, unspecified quadrant without penetration into peritoneal cavity

● S31.14   Puncture wound of abdominal wall with foreign body without penetration into peritoneal cavity

    ● S31.140   Puncture wound of abdominal wall with foreign body, right upper quadrant without penetration into peritoneal cavity

    ● S31.141   Puncture wound of abdominal wall with foreign body, left upper quadrant without penetration into peritoneal cavity

    ● S31.142   Puncture wound of abdominal wall with foreign body, epigastric region without penetration into peritoneal cavity

    ● S31.143   Puncture wound of abdominal wall with foreign body, right lower quadrant without penetration into peritoneal cavity

    ● S31.144   Puncture wound of abdominal wall with foreign body, left lower quadrant without penetration into peritoneal cavity

    ● S31.145   Puncture wound of abdominal wall with foreign body, periumbilic region without penetration into peritoneal cavity

    ● ■ S31.149   Puncture wound of abdominal wall with foreign body, unspecified quadrant without penetration into peritoneal cavity

CHAPTER 19 (S00-T88)

● Unacceptable First-Listed Diagnosis   ● Use Additional Character(s)   ■ Unspecified   **OGCR** Official Guidelines for Coding and Reporting

 Complication\Comorbidity   Major C\C    Excludes 1   Excludes 2   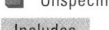 Includes   Use additional   Code first   Code also

● S31.15   **Open bite of abdominal wall without penetration into peritoneal cavity**
Bite of abdominal wall NOS

> Excludes1   superficial bite of abdominal wall (S30.871)

- ● S31.150   Open bite of abdominal wall, right upper quadrant without penetration into peritoneal cavity
- ● S31.151   Open bite of abdominal wall, left upper quadrant without penetration into peritoneal cavity
- ● S31.152   Open bite of abdominal wall, epigastric region without penetration into peritoneal cavity
- ● S31.153   Open bite of abdominal wall, right lower quadrant without penetration into peritoneal cavity
- ● S31.154   Open bite of abdominal wall, left lower quadrant without penetration into peritoneal cavity
- ● S31.155   Open bite of abdominal wall, periumbilic region without penetration into peritoneal cavity
- ●■ S31.159   Open bite of abdominal wall, unspecified quadrant without penetration into peritoneal cavity

● S31.2   **Open wound of penis**

- ●■ S31.20   Unspecified open wound of penis
- ● S31.21   Laceration without foreign body of penis
- ● S31.22   Laceration with foreign body of penis
- ● S31.23   Puncture wound without foreign body of penis
- ● S31.24   Puncture wound with foreign body of penis
- ● S31.25   Open bite of penis
Bite of penis NOS
  > Excludes1   superficial bite of penis (S30.862, S30.872)

● S31.3   **Open wound of scrotum and testes**

- ●■ S31.30   Unspecified open wound of scrotum and testes
- ● S31.31   Laceration without foreign body of scrotum and testes
- ● S31.32   Laceration with foreign body of scrotum and testes
- ● S31.33   Puncture wound without foreign body of scrotum and testes
- ● S31.34   Puncture wound with foreign body of scrotum and testes
- ● S31.35   Open bite of scrotum and testes
Bite of scrotum and testes NOS
  > Excludes1   superficial bite of scrotum and testes (S30.863, S30.873)

● S31.4   **Open wound of vagina and vulva**

> Excludes1   injury to vagina and vulva during delivery (O70.-, O71.4)

- ●■ S31.40   Unspecified open wound of vagina and vulva
- ● S31.41   Laceration without foreign body of vagina and vulva
- ● S31.42   Laceration with foreign body of vagina and vulva

- ● S31.43   Puncture wound without foreign body of vagina and vulva
- ● S31.44   Puncture wound with foreign body of vagina and vulva
- ● S31.45   Open bite of vagina and vulva
Bite of vagina and vulva NOS
  > Excludes1   superficial bite of vagina and vulva (S30.864, S30.874)

● S31.5   **Open wound of unspecified external genital organs**

> Excludes1   traumatic amputation of external genital organs (S38.21, S38.22)

- ● S31.50   Unspecified open wound of unspecified external genital organs
  - ●■ S31.501   Unspecified open wound of unspecified external genital organs, male
  - ●■ S31.502   Unspecified open wound of unspecified external genital organs, female
- ● S31.51   Laceration without foreign body of unspecified external genital organs
  - ●■ S31.511   Laceration without foreign body of unspecified external genital organs, male
  - ●■ S31.512   Laceration without foreign body of unspecified external genital organs, female
- ● S31.52   Laceration with foreign body of unspecified external genital organs
  - ●■ S31.521   Laceration with foreign body of unspecified external genital organs, male
  - ●■ S31.522   Laceration with foreign body of unspecified external genital organs, female
- ● S31.53   Puncture wound without foreign body of unspecified external genital organs
  - ●■ S31.531   Puncture wound without foreign body of unspecified external genital organs, male
  - ●■ S31.532   Puncture wound without foreign body of unspecified external genital organs, female
- ● S31.54   Puncture wound with foreign body of unspecified external genital organs
  - ●■ S31.541   Puncture wound with foreign body of unspecified external genital organs, male
  - ●■ S31.542   Puncture wound with foreign body of unspecified external genital organs, female
- ● S31.55   Open bite of unspecified external genital organs
Bite of unspecified external genital organs NOS
  > Excludes1   superficial bite of unspecified external genital organs (S30.865, S30.866, S30.875, S30.876)
  - ●■ S31.551   Open bite of unspecified external genital organs, male
  - ●■ S31.552   Open bite of unspecified external genital organs, female

● Unacceptable First-Listed Diagnosis   ● Use Additional Character(s)   ■ Unspecified   **OGCR** Official Guidelines for Coding and Reporting
🝰 Complication\Comorbidity   🝰 Major C\C   Excludes 1   Excludes 2   Includes   Use additional   Code first   Code also

● S31.6 **Open wound of abdominal wall with penetration into peritoneal cavity**

  ● S31.60 **Unspecified open wound of abdominal wall with penetration into peritoneal cavity**

    ● ▢ S31.600 Unspecified open wound of abdominal wall, right upper quadrant with penetration into peritoneal cavity A 🗞

    ● ▢ S31.601 Unspecified open wound of abdominal wall, left upper quadrant with penetration into peritoneal cavity A 🗞

    ● ▢ S31.602 Unspecified open wound of abdominal wall, epigastric region with penetration into peritoneal cavity A 🗞

    ● ▢ S31.603 Unspecified open wound of abdominal wall, right lower quadrant with penetration into peritoneal cavity A 🗞

    ● ▢ S31.604 Unspecified open wound of abdominal wall, left lower quadrant with penetration into peritoneal cavity A 🗞

    ● ▢ S31.605 Unspecified open wound of abdominal wall, periumbilic region with penetration into peritoneal cavity A 🗞

    ● ▢ S31.609 Unspecified open wound of abdominal wall, unspecified quadrant with penetration into peritoneal cavity A 🗞

  ● S31.61 **Laceration without foreign body of abdominal wall with penetration into peritoneal cavity**

    ● S31.610 Laceration without foreign body of abdominal wall, right upper quadrant with penetration into peritoneal cavity A 🗞

    ● S31.611 Laceration without foreign body of abdominal wall, left upper quadrant with penetration into peritoneal cavity A 🗞

    ● S31.612 Laceration without foreign body of abdominal wall, epigastric region with penetration into peritoneal cavity A 🗞

    ● S31.613 Laceration without foreign body of abdominal wall, right lower quadrant with penetration into peritoneal cavity A 🗞

    ● S31.614 Laceration without foreign body of abdominal wall, left lower quadrant with penetration into peritoneal cavity A 🗞

    ● S31.615 Laceration without foreign body of abdominal wall, periumbilic region with penetration into peritoneal cavity A 🗞

    ● ▢ S31.619 Laceration without foreign body of abdominal wall, unspecified quadrant with penetration into peritoneal cavity A 🗞

● S31.62 **Laceration with foreign body of abdominal wall with penetration into peritoneal cavity**

    ● S31.620 Laceration with foreign body of abdominal wall, right upper quadrant with penetration into peritoneal cavity A 🗞

    ● S31.621 Laceration with foreign body of abdominal wall, left upper quadrant with penetration into peritoneal cavity A 🗞

    ● S31.622 Laceration with foreign body of abdominal wall, epigastric region with penetration into peritoneal cavity A 🗞

    ● S31.623 Laceration with foreign body of abdominal wall, right lower quadrant with penetration into peritoneal cavity A 🗞

    ● S31.624 Laceration with foreign body of abdominal wall, left lower quadrant with penetration into peritoneal cavity A 🗞

    ● S31.625 Laceration with foreign body of abdominal wall, periumbilic region with penetration into peritoneal cavity A 🗞

    ● ▢ S31.629 Laceration with foreign body of abdominal wall, unspecified quadrant with penetration into peritoneal cavity A 🗞

  ● S31.63 **Puncture wound without foreign body of abdominal wall with penetration into peritoneal cavity**

    ● S31.630 Puncture wound without foreign body of abdominal wall, right upper quadrant with penetration into peritoneal cavity A 🗞

    ● S31.631 Puncture wound without foreign body of abdominal wall, left upper quadrant with penetration into peritoneal cavity A 🗞

    ● S31.632 Puncture wound without foreign body of abdominal wall, epigastric region with penetration into peritoneal cavity A 🗞

    ● S31.633 Puncture wound without foreign body of abdominal wall, right lower quadrant with penetration into peritoneal cavity A 🗞

    ● S31.634 Puncture wound without foreign body of abdominal wall, left lower quadrant with penetration into peritoneal cavity A 🗞

    ● S31.635 Puncture wound without foreign body of abdominal wall, periumbilic region with penetration into peritoneal cavity A 🗞

    ● ▢ S31.639 Puncture wound without foreign body of abdominal wall, unspecified quadrant with penetration into peritoneal cavity A 🗞

● Unacceptable First-Listed Diagnosis   ● Use Additional Character(s)   ▢ Unspecified   **OGCR** Official Guidelines for Coding and Reporting

🗞 Complication\Comorbidity   🗞 Major C\C   Excludes 1   Excludes 2   Includes   Use additional   Code first   Code also

1397

● **S31.64**   **Puncture wound with foreign body of abdominal wall with penetration into peritoneal cavity**

    ● **S31.640**   Puncture wound with foreign body of abdominal wall, right upper quadrant with penetration into peritoneal cavity A 🐾

    ● **S31.641**   Puncture wound with foreign body of abdominal wall, left upper quadrant with penetration into peritoneal cavity A 🐾

    ● **S31.642**   Puncture wound with foreign body of abdominal wall, epigastric region with penetration into peritoneal cavity A 🐾

    ● **S31.643**   Puncture wound with foreign body of abdominal wall, right lower quadrant with penetration into peritoneal cavity A 🐾

    ● **S31.644**   Puncture wound with foreign body of abdominal wall, left lower quadrant with penetration into peritoneal cavity A 🐾

    ● **S31.645**   Puncture wound with foreign body of abdominal wall, periumbilic region with penetration into peritoneal cavity A 🐾

    ● ■ **S31.649**   Puncture wound with foreign body of abdominal wall, unspecified quadrant with penetration into peritoneal cavity A 🐾

● **S31.65**   **Open bite of abdominal wall with penetration into peritoneal cavity**

    Excludes1   superficial bite of abdominal wall (S30.861, S30.871)

    ● **S31.650**   Open bite of abdominal wall, right upper quadrant with penetration into peritoneal cavity A 🐾

    ● **S31.651**   Open bite of abdominal wall, left upper quadrant with penetration into peritoneal cavity A 🐾

    ● **S31.652**   Open bite of abdominal wall, epigastric region with penetration into peritoneal cavity A 🐾

    ● **S31.653**   Open bite of abdominal wall, right lower quadrant with penetration into peritoneal cavity A 🐾

    ● **S31.654**   Open bite of abdominal wall, left lower quadrant with penetration into peritoneal cavity A 🐾

    ● **S31.655**   Open bite of abdominal wall, periumbilic region with penetration into peritoneal cavity A 🐾

    ● ■ **S31.659**   Open bite of abdominal wall, unspecified quadrant with penetration into peritoneal cavity A 🐾

● **S31.8**   **Open wound of other parts of abdomen, lower back and pelvis**

    ● **S31.80**   **Open wound of unspecified buttock**

      ● ■ **S31.801**   Laceration without foreign body of unspecified buttock

      ● ■ **S31.802**   Laceration with foreign body of unspecified buttock

      ● ■ **S31.803**   Puncture wound without foreign body of unspecified buttock

      ● ■ **S31.804**   Puncture wound with foreign body of unspecified buttock

      ● ■ **S31.805**   Open bite of unspecified buttock
         Bite of buttock NOS

         Excludes1   superficial bite of buttock (S30.870)

      ● ■ **S31.809**   Unspecified open wound of unspecified buttock

    ● **S31.81**   **Open wound of right buttock**

      ● **S31.811**   Laceration without foreign body of right buttock

      ● **S31.812**   Laceration with foreign body of right buttock

      ● **S31.813**   Puncture wound without foreign body of right buttock

      ● **S31.814**   Puncture wound with foreign body of right buttock

      ● **S31.815**   Open bite of right buttock
         Bite of right buttock NOS

         Excludes1   superficial bite of buttock (S30.870)

      ● ■ **S31.819**   Unspecified open wound of right buttock

    ● **S31.82**   **Open wound of left buttock**

      ● **S31.821**   Laceration without foreign body of left buttock

      ● **S31.822**   Laceration with foreign body of left buttock

      ● **S31.823**   Puncture wound without foreign body of left buttock

      ● **S31.824**   Puncture wound with foreign body of left buttock

      ● **S31.825**   Open bite of left buttock
         Bite of left buttock NOS

         Excludes1   superficial bite of buttock (S30.870)

      ● ■ **S31.829**   Unspecified open wound of left buttock

    ● **S31.83**   **Open wound of anus**

      ● **S31.831**   Laceration without foreign body of anus

      ● **S31.832**   Laceration with foreign body of anus

      ● **S31.833**   Puncture wound without foreign body of anus

      ● **S31.834**   Puncture wound with foreign body of anus

      ● **S31.835**   Open bite of anus
         Bite of anus NOS

         Excludes1   superficial bite of anus (S30.877)

      ● ■ **S31.839**   Unspecified open wound of anus

● **S32   Fracture of lumbar spine and pelvis**
　　A fracture not identified as displaced or nondisplaced should be coded to displaced

　　Includes   fracture of lumbosacral neural arch
　　　　　　　fracture of lumbosacral spinous process
　　　　　　　fracture of lumbosacral transverse process
　　　　　　　fracture of lumbosacral vertebra
　　　　　　　fracture of lumbosacral vertebral arch

　　Code first any associated spinal cord and spinal nerve injury (S34-)

　　Excludes1   transection of abdomen (S38.3)
　　Excludes2   fracture of hip NOS (S72.0-)

　　The appropriate 7th character is to be added to each code from category S32
　　A fracture not identified as opened or closed should be coded to closed

A	initial encounter for closed fracture
B	initial encounter for open fracture
D	subsequent encounter for fracture with routine healing
G	subsequent encounter for fracture with delayed healing
K	subsequent encounter for fracture with nonunion
S	sequela

● **S32.0   Fracture of lumbar vertebra**
　　Fracture of lumbar spine NOS

　● **S32.00   Fracture of unspecified lumbar vertebra**

　　● S32.000   Wedge compression fracture of unspecified lumbar vertebra A, K, B

　　● S32.001   Stable burst fracture of unspecified lumbar vertebra A, K, B

　　● S32.002   Unstable burst fracture of unspecified lumbar vertebra A, K, B

　　● S32.008   Other fracture of unspecified lumbar vertebra A, K, B

　　● S32.009   Unspecified fracture of unspecified lumbar vertebra A, K, B

　● **S32.01   Fracture of first lumbar vertebra**

　　● S32.010   Wedge compression fracture of first lumbar vertebra A, K, B

　　● S32.011   Stable burst fracture of first lumbar vertebra A, K, B

　　● S32.012   Unstable burst fracture of first lumbar vertebra A, K, B

　　● S32.018   Other fracture of first lumbar vertebra A, K, B

　　● S32.019   Unspecified fracture of first lumbar vertebra A, K, B

　● **S32.02   Fracture of second lumbar vertebra**

　　● S32.020   Wedge compression fracture of second lumbar vertebra A, K, B

　　● S32.021   Stable burst fracture of second lumbar vertebra A, K, B

　　● S32.022   Unstable burst fracture of second lumbar vertebra A, K, B

　　● S32.028   Other fracture of second lumbar vertebra A, K, B

　　● S32.029   Unspecified fracture of second lumbar vertebra A, K, B

● **S32.03   Fracture of third lumbar vertebra**

　　● S32.030   Wedge compression fracture of third lumbar vertebra A, K, B

　　● S32.031   Stable burst fracture of third lumbar vertebra A, K, B

　　● S32.032   Unstable burst fracture of third lumbar vertebra A, K, B

　　● S32.038   Other fracture of third lumbar vertebra A, K, B

　　● S32.039   Unspecified fracture of third lumbar vertebra A, K, B

● **S32.04   Fracture of fourth lumbar vertebra**

　　● S32.040   Wedge compression fracture of fourth lumbar vertebra A, K, B

　　● S32.041   Stable burst fracture of fourth lumbar vertebra A, K, B

　　● S32.042   Unstable burst fracture of fourth lumbar vertebra A, K, B

　　● S32.048   Other fracture of fourth lumbar vertebra A, K, B

　　● S32.049   Unspecified fracture of fourth lumbar vertebra A, K, B

● **S32.05   Fracture of fifth lumbar vertebra**

　　● S32.050   Wedge compression fracture of fifth lumbar vertebra A, K, B

　　● S32.051   Stable burst fracture of fifth lumbar vertebra A, K, B

　　● S32.052   Unstable burst fracture of fifth lumbar vertebra A, K, B

　　● S32.058   Other fracture of fifth lumbar vertebra A, K, B

　　● S32.059   Unspecified fracture of fifth lumbar vertebra A, K, B

● **S32.1   Fracture of sacrum**
　　For vertical fractures, code to most medial fracture extension
　　Use two codes if both a vertical and transverse fracture are present
　　Code also any associated fracture of pelvic circle (S32.8-)

　● S32.10   Unspecified fracture of sacrum A, K, B

　● **S32.11   Zone I fracture of sacrum**
　　　Vertical sacral ala fracture of sacrum

　　● S32.110   Nondisplaced Zone I fracture of sacrum A, K, B

　　● S32.111   Minimally displaced Zone I fracture of sacrum A, K, B

　　● S32.112   Severely displaced Zone I fracture of sacrum A, K, B

　　● S32.119   Unspecified Zone I fracture of sacrum A, K, B

　● **S32.12   Zone II fracture of sacrum**
　　　Vertical foraminal region fracture of sacrum

　　● S32.120   Nondisplaced Zone II fracture of sacrum A, K, B

　　● S32.121   Minimally displaced Zone II fracture of sacrum A, K, B

　　● S32.122   Severely displaced Zone II fracture of sacrum A, K, B

　　● S32.129   Unspecified Zone II fracture of sacrum A, K, B

● Unacceptable First-Listed Diagnosis　　● Use Additional Character(s)　　■ Unspecified　　**OGCR** Official Guidelines for Coding and Reporting

Complication\Comorbidity　Major C\C　Excludes 1　Excludes 2　 Includes　 Use additional　 Code first　Code also

CHAPTER 19 (S00-T88)

1399

S32.13 Zone III fracture of sacrum
Vertical fracture into spinal canal region of sacrum

- **S32.130 Nondisplaced Zone III fracture of sacrum** A, K, B
- **S32.131 Minimally displaced Zone III fracture of sacrum** A, K, B
- **S32.132 Severely displaced Zone III fracture of sacrum** A, K, B
- **S32.139 Unspecified Zone III fracture of sacrum** A, K, B

S32.14 Type 1 fracture of sacrum A, K, B
Transverse flexion fracture of sacrum without displacement

S32.15 Type 2 fracture of sacrum A, K, B
Transverse flexion fracture of sacrum with posterior displacement

S32.16 Type 3 fracture of sacrum A, K, B
Transverse extension fracture of sacrum with anterior displacement

S32.17 Type 4 fracture of sacrum A, K, B
Transverse segmental comminution of upper sacrum

S32.19 Other fracture of sacrum A, K, B

S32.2 Fracture of coccyx A, K, B

S32.3 Fracture of ilium

Excludes1: fracture of ilium with associated disruption of pelvic circle (S32.8-)

S32.30 Unspecified fracture of ilium
- **S32.301 Unspecified fracture of ilium, right side** A, K, B
- **S32.302 Unspecified fracture of ilium, left side** A, K, B
- **S32.309 Unspecified fracture of ilium, unspecified side** A, K, B

S32.31 Avulsion fracture of ilium
- **S32.311 Displaced avulsion fracture of ilium, right side** A, K, B
- **S32.312 Displaced avulsion fracture of ilium, left side** A, K, B
- **S32.313 Displaced avulsion fracture of ilium, unspecified side** A, K, B
- **S32.314 Nondisplaced avulsion fracture of ilium, right side** A, K, B
- **S32.315 Nondisplaced avulsion fracture of ilium, left side** A, K, B
- **S32.316 Nondisplaced avulsion fracture of ilium, unspecified side** A, K, B

S32.39 Other fracture of ilium
- **S32.391 Other fracture of ilium, right side** A, K, B
- **S32.392 Other fracture of ilium, left side** A, K, B
- **S32.399 Other fracture of ilium, unspecified side** A, K, B

S32.4 Fracture of acetabulum

Code also any associated fracture of pelvic circle (S32.8-)

S32.40 Unspecified fracture of acetabulum
- **S32.401 Unspecified fracture of acetabulum, right side** K, A, B

- **S32.402 Unspecified fracture of acetabulum, left side** K, A, B
- **S32.409 Unspecified fracture of acetabulum, unspecified side** K, A, B

S32.41 Fracture of anterior wall of acetabulum
- **S32.411 Displaced fracture of anterior wall of acetabulum, right side** K, A, B
- **S32.412 Displaced fracture of anterior wall of acetabulum, left side** K, A, B
- **S32.413 Displaced fracture of anterior wall of acetabulum, unspecified side** K, A, B
- **S32.414 Nondisplaced fracture of anterior wall of acetabulum, right side** K, A, B
- **S32.415 Nondisplaced fracture of anterior wall of acetabulum, left side** K, A, B
- **S32.416 Nondisplaced fracture of anterior wall of acetabulum, unspecified side** K, A, B

S32.42 Fracture of posterior wall of acetabulum
- **S32.421 Displaced fracture of posterior wall of acetabulum, right side** K, A, B
- **S32.422 Displaced fracture of posterior wall of acetabulum, left side** K, A, B
- **S32.423 Displaced fracture of posterior wall of acetabulum, unspecified side** K, A, B
- **S32.424 Nondisplaced fracture of posterior wall of acetabulum, right side** K, A, B
- **S32.425 Nondisplaced fracture of posterior wall of acetabulum, left side** K, A, B
- **S32.426 Nondisplaced fracture of posterior wall of acetabulum, unspecified side** K, A, B

S32.43 Fracture of anterior column [iliopubic] of acetabulum
- **S32.431 Displaced fracture of anterior column [iliopubic] of acetabulum, right side** K, A, B
- **S32.432 Displaced fracture of anterior column [iliopubic] of acetabulum, left side** K, A, B
- **S32.433 Displaced fracture of anterior column [iliopubic] of acetabulum, unspecified side** K, A, B
- **S32.434 Nondisplaced fracture of anterior column [iliopubic] of acetabulum, right side** K, A, B
- **S32.435 Nondisplaced fracture of anterior column [iliopubic] of acetabulum, left side** K, A, B
- **S32.436 Nondisplaced fracture of anterior column [iliopubic] of acetabulum, unspecified side** K, A, B

Unacceptable First-Listed Diagnosis   Use Additional Character(s)   Unspecified   OGCR Official Guidelines for Coding and Reporting
Complication\Comorbidity   Major C\C   Excludes 1   Excludes 2   Includes   Use additional   Code first   Code also

● S32.44   Fracture of posterior column [ilioischial] of acetabulum
  ● S32.441   Displaced fracture of posterior column [ilioischial] of acetabulum, right side K 🦠, A, B 🦠
  ● S32.442   Displaced fracture of posterior column [ilioischial] of acetabulum, left side K 🦠, A, B 🦠
  ● ◼ S32.443   Displaced fracture of posterior column [ilioischial] of acetabulum, unspecified side K 🦠, A, B 🦠
  ● S32.444   Nondisplaced fracture of posterior column [ilioischial] of acetabulum, right side K 🦠, A, B 🦠
  ● S32.445   Nondisplaced fracture of posterior column [ilioischial] of acetabulum, left side K 🦠, A, B 🦠
  ● ◼ S32.446   Nondisplaced fracture of posterior column [ilioischial] of acetabulum, unspecified side K 🦠, A, B 🦠

● S32.45   Transverse fracture of acetabulum
  ● S32.451   Displaced transverse fracture of acetabulum, right side K 🦠, A, B 🦠
  ● S32.452   Displaced transverse fracture of acetabulum, left side K 🦠, A, B 🦠
  ● ◼ S32.453   Displaced transverse fracture of acetabulum, unspecified side K 🦠, A, B 🦠
  ● S32.454   Nondisplaced transverse fracture of acetabulum, right side K 🦠, A, B 🦠
  ● S32.455   Nondisplaced transverse fracture of acetabulum, left side K 🦠, A, B 🦠
  ● ◼ S32.456   Nondisplaced transverse fracture of acetabulum, unspecified side K 🦠, A, B 🦠

● S32.46   Associated transverse-posterior fracture of acetabulum
  ● S32.461   Displaced associated transverse-posterior fracture of acetabulum, right side K 🦠, A, B 🦠
  ● S32.462   Displaced associated transverse-posterior fracture of acetabulum, left side K 🦠, A, B 🦠
  ● ◼ S32.463   Displaced associated transverse-posterior fracture of acetabulum, unspecified side K 🦠, A, B 🦠
  ● S32.464   Nondisplaced associated transverse-posterior fracture of acetabulum, right side K 🦠, A, B 🦠
  ● S32.465   Nondisplaced associated transverse-posterior fracture of acetabulum, left side K 🦠, A, B 🦠
  ● ◼ S32.466   Nondisplaced associated transverse-posterior fracture of acetabulum, unspecified side K 🦠, A, B 🦠

● S32.47   Fracture of medial wall of acetabulum
  ● S32.471   Displaced fracture of medial wall of acetabulum, right side K 🦠, A, B 🦠
  ● S32.472   Displaced fracture of medial wall of acetabulum, left side K 🦠, A, B 🦠
  ● ◼ S32.473   Displaced fracture of medial wall of acetabulum, unspecified side K 🦠, A, B 🦠
  ● S32.474   Nondisplaced fracture of medial wall of acetabulum, right side K 🦠, A, B 🦠
  ● S32.475   Nondisplaced fracture of medial wall of acetabulum, left side K 🦠, A, B 🦠
  ● ◼ S32.476   Nondisplaced fracture of medial wall of acetabulum, unspecified side K 🦠, A, B 🦠

● S32.48   Dome fracture of acetabulum
  ● S32.481   Displaced dome fracture of acetabulum, right side K 🦠, A, B 🦠
  ● S32.482   Displaced dome fracture of acetabulum, left side K 🦠, A, B 🦠
  ● ◼ S32.483   Displaced dome fracture of acetabulum, unspecified side K 🦠, A, B 🦠
  ● S32.484   Nondisplaced dome fracture of acetabulum, right side K 🦠, A, B 🦠
  ● S32.485   Nondisplaced dome fracture of acetabulum, left side K 🦠, A, B 🦠
  ● ◼ S32.486   Nondisplaced dome fracture of acetabulum, unspecified side K 🦠, A, B 🦠

● S32.49   Other fracture of acetabulum
  ● S32.491   Other fracture of acetabulum, right side K 🦠, A, B 🦠
  ● S32.492   Other fracture of acetabulum, left side K 🦠, A, B 🦠
  ● ◼ S32.499   Other fracture of acetabulum, unspecified side K 🦠, A, B 🦠

● S32.5   Fracture of pubis
  | **Excludes1** | fracture of pubis with associated disruption of pelvic circle (S32.8-) |
  ● S32.50   Fracture of pubis A, K 🦠, B 🦠
  ● S32.51   Fracture of superior rim of pubis
    ● S32.511   Fracture of right superior rim of pubis A, K 🦠, B 🦠
    ● S32.512   Fracture of left superior rim of pubis A, K 🦠, B 🦠
    ● ◼ S32.519   Fracture of unspecified superior rim of pubis A, K 🦠, B 🦠
  ● S32.59   Other fracture of pubis A, K 🦠, B 🦠

● S32.6   Fracture of ischium
  | **Excludes1** | fracture of ischium with associated disruption of pelvic circle (S32.8-) |
  ● S32.60   Unspecified fracture of ischium
    ● ◼ S32.601   Unspecified fracture of ischium, right side A, K 🦠, B 🦠
    ● ◼ S32.602   Unspecified fracture of ischium, left side A, K 🦠, B 🦠
    ● ◼ S32.609   Unspecified fracture of ischium, unspecified side A, K 🦠, B 🦠
  ● S32.61   Avulsion fracture of ischium
    ● S32.611   Displaced avulsion fracture of ischium, right side A, K 🦠, B 🦠
    ● S32.612   Displaced avulsion fracture of ischium, left side A, K 🦠, B 🦠
    ● ◼ S32.613   Displaced avulsion fracture of ischium, unspecified side A, K 🦠, B 🦠

● Unacceptable First-Listed Diagnosis   ● Use Additional Character(s)   ◼ Unspecified   **OGCR** Official Guidelines for Coding and Reporting
🦠 Complication\Comorbidity   🦠 Major C\C   Excludes 1   Excludes 2   Includes   Use additional   Code first   Code also   1401

CHAPTER 19 (S00-T88)

- ● S32.614   Nondisplaced avulsion fracture of ischium, right side A, K 🎗, B 🎗
- ● S32.615   Nondisplaced avulsion fracture of ischium, left side A, K 🎗, B 🎗
- ● ■ S32.616   Nondisplaced avulsion fracture of ischium, unspecified side A, K 🎗, B 🎗
- ● S32.69   Other fracture of ischium
  - ● S32.691   Other fracture of ischium, right side A, K 🎗, B 🎗
  - ● S32.692   Other fracture of ischium, left side A, K 🎗, B 🎗
  - ● ■ S32.699   Other fracture of ischium, unspecified side A, K 🎗, B 🎗
- ● S32.8   Fracture of other parts of pelvis

  Code also any associated:
  fracture of acetabulum (S32.4-)
  sacral fracture (S32.1-)

  - ● S32.81   Multiple fractures of pelvis with disruption of pelvic circle
    - ● S32.810   Multiple fractures of pelvis with stable disruption of pelvic circle A, K 🎗, B 🎗
    - ● S32.811   Multiple fractures of pelvis with unstable disruption of pelvic circle A, K 🎗, B 🎗
  - ● S32.89   Fracture of other parts of pelvis A, K 🎗, B 🎗
- ● ■ S32.9   Fracture of unspecified parts of lumbosacral spine and pelvis A, K 🎗, B 🎗

  Fracture of lumbosacral spine NOS
  Fracture of pelvis NOS

- ● S33   **Dislocation and sprain of joints and ligaments of lumbar spine and pelvis**

  Includes   avulsion of joint or ligament of lumbar spine and pelvis
  laceration of cartilage, joint or ligament of lumbar spine and pelvis
  sprain of cartilage, joint or ligament of lumbar spine and pelvis
  traumatic hemarthrosis of joint or ligament of lumbar spine and pelvis
  traumatic rupture of joint or ligament of lumbar spine and pelvis
  traumatic subluxation of joint or ligament of lumbar spine and pelvis
  traumatic tear of joint or ligament of lumbar spine and pelvis

  Code also any associated open wound

Excludes1	nontraumatic rupture or displacement of lumbar intervertebral disc NOS (M51.-)
	obstetric damage to pelvic joints and ligaments (O71.6)

Excludes2	dislocation and sprain of joints and ligaments of hip (S73.-)
	strain of muscle of lower back and pelvis (S39.12, S39.13)

  The appropriate 7th character is to be added to each code from category S33

A	initial encounter
D	subsequent encounter
S	sequela

  - ● S33.0   Traumatic rupture of lumbar intervertebral disc

Excludes1	rupture or displacement (nontraumatic) of lumbar intervertebral disc NOS (M51.- with fifth character 6)

  - ● S33.1   Subluxation and dislocation of lumbar vertebra

    Code also any associated:
    open wound of abdomen, lower back and pelvis (S31)
    spinal cord injury (S24.0, S24.1-, S34.0, S34.1-)

Excludes2	fracture of lumbar vertebrae (S32.0-)

    - ● S33.10   Subluxation and dislocation of unspecified lumbar vertebra
      - ● ■ S33.100   Subluxation of unspecified lumbar vertebra
      - ● ■ S33.101   Dislocation of unspecified lumbar vertebra
    - ● S33.11   Subluxation and dislocation of L_1/L_2 lumbar vertebra
      - ● S33.110   Subluxation of L_1/L_2 lumbar vertebra
      - ● S33.111   Dislocation of L_1/L_2 lumbar vertebra
    - ● S33.12   Subluxation and dislocation of L_2/L_3 lumbar vertebra
      - ● S33.120   Subluxation of L_2/L_3 lumbar vertebra
      - ● S33.121   Dislocation of L_2/L_3 lumbar vertebra
    - ● S33.13   Subluxation and dislocation of L_3/L_4 lumbar vertebra
      - ● S33.130   Subluxation of L_3/L_4 lumbar vertebra
      - ● S33.131   Dislocation of L_3/L_4 lumbar vertebra
    - ● S33.14   Subluxation and dislocation of L_4/L_5 lumbar vertebra
      - ● S33.140   Subluxation of L_4/L_5 lumbar vertebra
      - ● S33.141   Dislocation of L_4/L_5 lumbar vertebra
  - ● S33.2   Dislocation of sacroiliac and sacrococcygeal joint
  - ● S33.3   Dislocation of other and unspecified parts of lumbar spine and pelvis
    - ● ■ S33.30   Dislocation of unspecified parts of lumbar spine and pelvis
    - ● ■ S33.39   Dislocation of other parts of lumbar spine and pelvis
  - ● S33.4   Traumatic rupture of symphysis pubis
  - ● S33.5   Sprain of ligaments of lumbar spine
  - ● S33.6   Sprain of sacroiliac joint
  - ● S33.8   Sprain of other parts of lumbar spine and pelvis
  - ● ■ S33.9   Sprain of unspecified parts of lumbar spine and pelvis
- ● S34   **Injury of lumbar and sacral spinal cord and nerves at abdomen, lower back and pelvis level**

  Code to highest level of lumbar cord injury
  Code also any associated:
  fracture of vertebra (S22.0-, S32.0-)
  open wound of abdomen, lower back and pelvis (S31.-)
  transient paralysis (R29.5)

  The appropriate 7th character is to be added to each code from category S34

A	initial encounter
D	subsequent encounter
S	sequela

● Unacceptable First-Listed Diagnosis   ● Use Additional Character(s)   ■ Unspecified   **OGCR** Official Guidelines for Coding and Reporting

1402   🎗 Complication\Comorbidity   🎗 Major C\C   Excludes 1   Excludes 2   Includes   Use additional   Code first   Code also

- ● S34.0   **Concussion and edema of lumbar and sacral spinal cord**
  - ● S34.01   **Concussion and edema of lumbar spinal cord** A 🗞
  - ● S34.02   **Concussion and edema of sacral spinal cord** A 🗞
    - Concussion and edema of conus medullaris
- ● S34.1   **Other and unspecified injury of lumbar and sacral spinal cord**
  - ● S34.10   **Unspecified injury to lumbar spinal cord**
    - ● ■ S34.101   Unspecified injury to L_1 level of lumbar spinal cord A 🗞
    - ● ■ S34.102   Unspecified injury to L_2 level of lumbar spinal cord A 🗞
    - ● ■ S34.103   Unspecified injury to L_3 level of lumbar spinal cord A 🗞
    - ● ■ S34.104   Unspecified injury to L_4 level of lumbar spinal cord A 🗞
    - ● ■ S34.105   Unspecified injury to L_5 level of lumbar spinal cord A 🗞
    - ● ■ S34.109   Unspecified injury to unspecified level of lumbar spinal cord A 🗞
  - ● S34.11   **Complete lesion of lumbar spinal cord**
    - ● S34.111   Complete lesion of L_1 level of lumbar spinal cord A 🗞
    - ● S34.112   Complete lesion of L_2 level of lumbar spinal cord A 🗞
    - ● S34.113   Complete lesion of L_3 level of lumbar spinal cord A 🗞
    - ● S34.114   Complete lesion of L_4 level of lumbar spinal cord A 🗞
    - ● S34.115   Complete lesion of L_5 level of lumbar spinal cord A 🗞
    - ● ■ S34.119   Complete lesion of unspecified level of lumbar spinal cord A 🗞
  - ● S34.12   **Incomplete lesion of lumbar spinal cord**
    - ● S34.121   Incomplete lesion of L_1 level of lumbar spinal cord A 🗞
    - ● S34.122   Incomplete lesion of L_2 level of lumbar spinal cord A 🗞
    - ● S34.123   Incomplete lesion of L_3 level of lumbar spinal cord A 🗞
    - ● S34.124   Incomplete lesion of L_4 level of lumbar spinal cord A 🗞
    - ● S34.125   Incomplete lesion of L_5 level of lumbar spinal cord A 🗞
    - ● ■ S34.129   Incomplete lesion of unspecified level of lumbar spinal cord A 🗞
  - ● S34.13   **Other and unspecified injury to sacral spinal cord**
    - Other injury to conus medullaris
    - ● S34.131   Complete lesion of sacral spinal cord A 🗞
      - Complete lesion of conus medullaris
    - ● S34.132   Incomplete lesion of sacral spinal cord A 🗞
      - Incomplete lesion of conus medullaris

- ● ■ S34.139   Unspecified injury to sacral spinal cord A 🗞
  - Unspecified injury of conus medullaris
- ● S34.2   **Injury of nerve root of lumbar and sacral spine**
  - ● S34.21   **Injury of nerve root of lumbar spine**
  - ● S34.22   **Injury of nerve root of sacral spine**
- ● S34.3   **Injury of cauda equina** A 🗞
- ● S34.4   **Injury of lumbosacral plexus**
- ● S34.5   **Injury of lumbar, sacral and pelvic sympathetic nerves**
  - Injury of celiac ganglion or plexus
  - Injury of hypogastric plexus
  - Injury of mesenteric plexus (inferior) (superior)
  - Injury of splanchnic nerve
- ● S34.6   **Injury of peripheral nerve(s) at abdomen, lower back and pelvis level**
- ● S34.8   **Injury of other nerves at abdomen, lower back and pelvis level**
- ● ■ S34.9   **Injury of unspecified nerves at abdomen, lower back and pelvis level**
- ● S35   **Injury of blood vessels at abdomen, lower back and pelvis level**
  - Code also any associated open wound (S31.-)
  - The appropriate 7th character is to be added to each code from category S35

A	initial encounter
D	subsequent encounter
S	sequela

  - ● S35.0   **Injury of abdominal aorta**
    - **Excludes1**   injury of aorta NOS (S25.0)
    - ● ■ S35.00   Unspecified injury of abdominal aorta A 🗞
    - ● S35.01   Minor laceration of abdominal aorta A 🗞
      - Incomplete transection of abdominal aorta
      - Laceration of abdominal aorta NOS
      - Superficial laceration of abdominal aorta
    - ● S35.02   Major laceration of abdominal aorta A 🗞
      - Complete transection of abdominal aorta
      - Traumatic rupture of abdominal aorta
    - ● S35.09   Other injury of abdominal aorta A 🗞
  - ● S35.1   **Injury of inferior vena cava**
    - Injury of hepatic vein
    - **Excludes1**   injury of vena cava NOS (S25.2)
    - ● ■ S35.10   Unspecified injury of inferior vena cava A 🗞
    - ● S35.11   Minor laceration of inferior vena cava A 🗞
      - Incomplete transection of inferior vena cava
      - Laceration of inferior vena cava NOS
      - Superficial laceration of inferior vena cava
    - ● S35.12   Major laceration of inferior vena cava A 🗞
      - Complete transection of inferior vena cava
      - Traumatic rupture of inferior vena cava
    - ● S35.19   Other injury of inferior vena cava A 🗞
  - ● S35.2   **Injury of celiac or mesenteric artery and branches**
    - ● S35.21   **Injury of celiac artery**
      - ● S35.211   Minor laceration of celiac artery A 🗞
        - Incomplete transection of celiac artery
        - Laceration of celiac artery NOS
        - Superficial laceration of celiac artery

● Unacceptable First-Listed Diagnosis   ● Use Additional Character(s)   ■ Unspecified   **OGCR** Official Guidelines for Coding and Reporting

🗞 Complication\Comorbidity   🗞 Major C\C   Excludes 1   Excludes 2   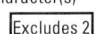 Includes   Use additional   Code first   Code also

1403

CHAPTER 19 (S00-T88)

● S35.212 **Major laceration of celiac artery** A 🐾
   Complete transection of celiac artery
   Traumatic rupture of celiac artery

● S35.218 **Other injury of celiac artery** A 🐾

● ■ S35.219 **Unspecified injury of celiac artery** A 🐾

● S35.22 **Injury of superior mesenteric artery**

● S35.221 **Minor laceration of superior mesenteric artery** A 🐾
   Incomplete transection of superior mesenteric artery
   Laceration of superior mesenteric artery NOS
   Superficial laceration of superior mesenteric artery

● S35.222 **Major laceration of superior mesenteric artery** A 🐾
   Complete transection of superior mesenteric artery
   Traumatic rupture of superior mesenteric artery

● S35.228 **Other injury of superior mesenteric artery** A 🐾

● ■ S35.229 **Unspecified injury of superior mesenteric artery** A 🐾

● S35.23 **Injury of inferior mesenteric artery**

● S35.231 **Minor laceration of inferior mesenteric artery** A 🐾
   Incomplete transection of inferior mesenteric artery
   Laceration of inferior mesenteric artery NOS
   Superficial laceration of inferior mesenteric artery

● S35.232 **Major laceration of inferior mesenteric artery** A 🐾
   Complete transection of inferior mesenteric artery
   Traumatic rupture of inferior mesenteric artery

● S35.238 **Other injury of inferior mesenteric artery** A 🐾

● ■ S35.239 **Unspecified injury of inferior mesenteric artery** A 🐾

● S35.29 **Injury of branches of celiac and mesenteric artery**
   Injury of gastric artery
   Injury of gastroduodenal artery
   Injury of hepatic artery
   Injury of splenic artery

● S35.291 **Minor laceration of branches of celiac and mesenteric artery** A 🐾
   Incomplete transection of branches of celiac and mesenteric artery
   Laceration of branches of celiac and mesenteric artery NOS
   Superficial laceration of branches of celiac and mesenteric artery

● S35.292 **Major laceration of branches of celiac and mesenteric artery** A 🐾
   Complete transection of branches of celiac and mesenteric artery
   Traumatic rupture of branches of celiac and mesenteric artery

● S35.298 **Other injury of branches of celiac and mesenteric artery** A 🐾

● ■ S35.299 **Unspecified injury of branches of celiac and mesenteric artery** A 🐾

● S35.3 **Injury of portal or splenic vein and branches**

● S35.31 **Injury of portal vein**

● S35.311 **Laceration of portal vein** A 🐾

● S35.318 **Other specified injury of portal vein** A 🐾

● ■ S35.319 **Unspecified injury of portal vein** A 🐾

● S35.32 **Injury of splenic vein**

● S35.321 **Laceration of splenic vein** A 🐾

● S35.328 **Other specified injury of splenic vein** A 🐾

● ■ S35.329 **Unspecified injury of splenic vein** A 🐾

● S35.33 **Injury of superior mesenteric vein**

● S35.331 **Laceration of superior mesenteric vein** A 🐾

● S35.338 **Other specified injury of superior mesenteric vein** A 🐾

● ■ S35.339 **Unspecified injury of superior mesenteric vein** A 🐾

● S35.34 **Injury of inferior mesenteric vein**

● S35.341 **Laceration of inferior mesenteric vein** A 🐾

● S35.348 **Other specified injury of inferior mesenteric vein** A 🐾

● ■ S35.349 **Unspecified injury of inferior mesenteric vein** A 🐾

● S35.4 **Injury of renal blood vessels**

● S35.40 **Unspecified injury of renal blood vessel**

● ■ S35.401 **Unspecified injury of right renal artery** A 🐾

● ■ S35.402 **Unspecified injury of left renal artery** A 🐾

● ■ S35.403 **Unspecified injury of unspecified renal artery** A 🐾

● ■ S35.404 **Unspecified injury of right renal vein** A 🐾

● ■ S35.405 **Unspecified injury of left renal vein** A 🐾

● ■ S35.406 **Unspecified injury of unspecified renal vein** A 🐾

● S35.41 **Laceration of renal blood vessel**

● S35.411 **Laceration of right renal artery** A 🐾

● S35.412 **Laceration of left renal artery** A 🐾

● ■ S35.413 **Laceration of unspecified renal artery** A 🐾

● S35.414 **Laceration of right renal vein** A 🐾

● S35.415 **Laceration of left renal vein** A 🐾

● ■ S35.416 **Laceration of unspecified renal vein** A 🐾

● Unacceptable First-Listed Diagnosis   ● Use Additional Character(s)   ■ Unspecified   **OGCR** Official Guidelines for Coding and Reporting
🐾 Complication\Comorbidity   🐾 Major C\C   Excludes 1   Excludes 2   Includes   Use additional   Code first   Code also

● **S35.49**   **Other specified injury of renal blood vessel**
- ● **S35.491**   **Other specified injury of right renal artery** A 🐾
- ● **S35.492**   **Other specified injury of left renal artery** A 🐾
- ● ▣ **S35.493**   **Other specified injury of unspecified renal artery** A 🐾
- ● **S35.494**   **Other specified injury of right renal vein** A 🐾
- ● **S35.495**   **Other specified injury of left renal vein** A 🐾
- ● ▣ **S35.496**   **Other specified injury of unspecified renal vein** A 🐾

● **S35.5**   **Injury of iliac blood vessels**
- ● ▣ **S35.50**   **Injury of unspecified iliac blood vessel(s)** A 🐾
- ● **S35.51**   **Injury of iliac artery or vein**
  Injury of hypogastric artery or vein
  - ● **S35.511**   **Injury of right iliac artery** A 🐾
  - ● **S35.512**   **Injury of left iliac artery** A 🐾
  - ● ▣ **S35.513**   **Injury of unspecified iliac artery** A 🐾
  - ● **S35.514**   **Injury of right iliac vein** A 🐾
  - ● **S35.515**   **Injury of left iliac vein** A 🐾
  - ● ▣ **S35.516**   **Injury of unspecified iliac vein** A 🐾
- ● **S35.53**   **Injury of uterine artery or vein**
  - ● **S35.531**   **Injury of right uterine artery** A 🐾
  - ● **S35.532**   **Injury of left uterine artery** A 🐾
  - ● ▣ **S35.533**   **Injury of unspecified uterine artery** A 🐾
  - ● **S35.534**   **Injury of right uterine vein** A 🐾
  - ● **S35.535**   **Injury of left uterine vein** A 🐾
  - ● ▣ **S35.536**   **Injury of unspecified uterine vein** A 🐾
- ● **S35.59**   **Injury of other iliac blood vessels** A 🐾

● **S35.8**   **Injury of other blood vessels at abdomen, lower back and pelvis level**
  Injury of ovarian artery or vein
- ● **S35.8x**   **Injury of other blood vessels at abdomen, lower back and pelvis level**
  - ● **S35.8x1**   **Laceration of other blood vessels at abdomen, lower back and pelvis level** A 🐾
  - ● **S35.8x8**   **Other specified injury of other blood vessels at abdomen, lower back and pelvis level** A 🐾
  - ● ▣ **S35.8x9**   **Unspecified injury of other blood vessels at abdomen, lower back and pelvis level** A 🐾

● **S35.9**   **Injury of unspecified blood vessel at abdomen, lower back and pelvis level**
- ● ▣ **S35.90**   **Unspecified injury of unspecified blood vessel at abdomen, lower back and pelvis level** A 🐾
- ● ▣ **S35.91**   **Laceration of unspecified blood vessel at abdomen, lower back and pelvis level** A 🐾
- ● ▣ **S35.99**   **Other specified injury of unspecified blood vessel at abdomen, lower back and pelvis level** A 🐾

● **S36**   **Injury of intra-abdominal organs**

Code also any associated open wound (S31.-)

The appropriate 7th character is to be added to each code from category S36

A	initial encounter
D	subsequent encounter
S	sequela

● **S36.0**   **Injury of spleen**
- ● ▣ **S36.00**   **Unspecified injury of spleen** A 🐾
- ● **S36.02**   **Contusion of spleen**
  - ● **S36.020**   **Minor contusion of spleen** A 🐾
    Contusion of spleen less than 2 cm
  - ● **S36.021**   **Major contusion of spleen** A 🐾
    Contusion of spleen greater than 2 cm
  - ● ▣ **S36.029**   **Unspecified contusion of spleen** A 🐾
- ● **S36.03**   **Laceration of spleen**
  - ● **S36.030**   **Superficial (capsular) laceration of spleen** A 🐾
    Laceration of spleen less than 1 cm
    Minor laceration of spleen
  - ● **S36.031**   **Moderate laceration of spleen** A 🐾
    Laceration of spleen 1 to 3 cm
  - ● **S36.032**   **Major laceration of spleen** A 🐾
    Avulsion of spleen
    Laceration of spleen greater than 3 cm
    Massive laceration of spleen
    Multiple moderate lacerations of spleen
    Stellate laceration of spleen
  - ● ▣ **S36.039**   **Unspecified laceration of spleen** A 🐾
- ● **S36.09**   **Other injury of spleen** A 🐾

● **S36.1**   **Injury of liver and gallbladder and bile duct**
- ● **S36.11**   **Injury of liver**
  - ● **S36.112**   **Contusion of liver** A 🐾
  - ● ▣ **S36.113**   **Laceration of liver, unspecified degree** A 🐾
  - ● **S36.114**   **Minor laceration of liver** A 🐾
    Laceration involving capsule only, or, without significant involvement of hepatic parenchyma [i.e., less than 1 cm deep]
  - ● **S36.115**   **Moderate laceration of liver** A 🐾
    Laceration involving parenchyma but without major disruption of parenchyma [i.e., less than 10 cm long and less than 3 cm deep]
  - ● **S36.116**   **Major laceration of liver** A 🐾
    Laceration with significant disruption of hepatic parenchyma [i.e., greater than 10 cm long and 3 cm deep]
    Multiple moderate lacerations, with or without hematoma
    Stellate laceration of liver
  - ● **S36.118**   **Other injury of liver** A 🐾
  - ● ▣ **S36.119**   **Unspecified injury of liver** A 🐾

● Unacceptable First-Listed Diagnosis   ● Use Additional Character(s)   ▣ Unspecified   **OGCR** Official Guidelines for Coding and Reporting

🐾 Complication\Comorbidity   🐾 Major C\C   Excludes 1   Excludes 2   Includes   Use additional   Code first   Code also

1405

CHAPTER 19 (S00-T88)

- S36.12   Injury of gallbladder
  - S36.122   Contusion of gallbladder A 🝆
  - S36.123   Laceration of gallbladder A 🝆
  - S36.128   Other injury of gallbladder A 🝆
  - ▪ S36.129   Unspecified injury of gallbladder A 🝆
- S36.13   Injury of bile duct A 🝆
- S36.2   Injury of pancreas
  - S36.20   Unspecified injury of pancreas
    - ▪ S36.200   Unspecified injury of head of pancreas A 🝆
    - ▪ S36.201   Unspecified injury of body of pancreas A 🝆
    - ▪ S36.202   Unspecified injury of tail of pancreas A 🝆
    - ▪ S36.209   Unspecified injury of unspecified part of pancreas A 🝆
  - S36.22   Contusion of pancreas
    - S36.220   Contusion of head of pancreas A 🝆
    - S36.221   Contusion of body of pancreas A 🝆
    - S36.222   Contusion of tail of pancreas A 🝆
    - ▪ S36.229   Contusion of unspecified part of pancreas A 🝆
  - S36.23   Laceration of pancreas, unspecified degree
    - ▪ S36.230   Laceration of head of pancreas, unspecified degree A 🝆
    - ▪ S36.231   Laceration of body of pancreas, unspecified degree A 🝆
    - ▪ S36.232   Laceration of tail of pancreas, unspecified degree A 🝆
    - ▪ S36.239   Laceration of unspecified part of pancreas, unspecified degree A 🝆
  - S36.24   Minor laceration of pancreas
    - S36.240   Minor laceration of head of pancreas A 🝆
    - S36.241   Minor laceration of body of pancreas A 🝆
    - S36.242   Minor laceration of tail of pancreas A 🝆
    - ▪ S36.249   Minor laceration of unspecified part of pancreas A 🝆
  - S36.25   Moderate laceration of pancreas
    - S36.250   Moderate laceration of head of pancreas A 🝆
    - S36.251   Moderate laceration of body of pancreas A 🝆
    - S36.252   Moderate laceration of tail of pancreas A 🝆
    - ▪ S36.259   Moderate laceration of unspecified part of pancreas A 🝆
  - S36.26   Major laceration of pancreas
    - S36.260   Major laceration of head of pancreas A 🝆
    - S36.261   Major laceration of body of pancreas A 🝆
    - S36.262   Major laceration of tail of pancreas A 🝆
    - ▪ S36.269   Major laceration of unspecified part of pancreas A 🝆

- S36.29   Other injury of pancreas
  - S36.290   Other injury of head of pancreas A 🝆
  - S36.291   Other injury of body of pancreas A 🝆
  - S36.292   Other injury of tail of pancreas A 🝆
  - ▪ S36.299   Other injury of unspecified part of pancreas A 🝆
- S36.3   Injury of stomach
  - ▪ S36.30   Unspecified injury of stomach A 🝆
  - S36.32   Contusion of stomach A 🝆
  - S36.33   Laceration of stomach A 🝆
  - S36.39   Other injury of stomach A 🝆
- S36.4   Injury of small intestine
  - S36.40   Unspecified injury of small intestine
    - ▪ S36.400   Unspecified injury of duodenum A 🝆
    - ▪ S36.408   Unspecified injury of other part of small intestine A 🝆
    - ▪ S36.409   Unspecified injury of unspecified part of small intestine A 🝆
  - S36.41   Primary blast injury of small intestine
    Blast injury of small intestine NOS
    - S36.410   Primary blast injury of duodenum A 🝆
    - S36.418   Primary blast injury of other part of small intestine A 🝆
    - ▪ S36.419   Primary blast injury of unspecified part of small intestine A 🝆
  - S36.42   Contusion of small intestine
    - S36.420   Contusion of duodenum A 🝆
    - S36.428   Contusion of other part of small intestine A 🝆
    - ▪ S36.429   Contusion of unspecified part of small intestine A 🝆
  - S36.43   Laceration of small intestine
    - S36.430   Laceration of duodenum A 🝆
    - S36.438   Laceration of other part of small intestine A 🝆
    - ▪ S36.439   Laceration of unspecified part of small intestine A 🝆
  - S36.49   Other injury of small intestine
    - S36.490   Other injury of duodenum A 🝆
    - S36.498   Other injury of other part of small intestine A 🝆
    - ▪ S36.499   Other injury of unspecified part of small intestine A 🝆
- S36.5   Injury of colon
  - Excludes2   injury of rectum (S36.6-)
  - S36.50   Unspecified injury of colon
    - ▪ S36.500   Unspecified injury of ascending [right] colon A 🝆
    - ▪ S36.501   Unspecified injury of transverse colon A 🝆
    - ▪ S36.502   Unspecified injury of descending [left] colon A 🝆
    - ▪ S36.503   Unspecified injury of sigmoid colon A 🝆

- ● Unacceptable First-Listed Diagnosis
- ● Use Additional Character(s)
- ▪ Unspecified
- 🝆 Complication\Comorbidity
- 🝆 Major C\C
- Excludes 1
- Excludes 2
- Includes
- OGCR Official Guidelines for Coding and Reporting
- Use additional
- Code first
- Code also

CHAPTER 19 (S00-T88)

● ■ **S36.508** Unspecified injury of other part of colon A 🦠

● ■ **S36.509** Unspecified injury of unspecified part of colon A 🦠

● **S36.51** Primary blast injury of colon
Blast injury of colon NOS

● **S36.510** Primary blast injury of ascending [right] colon A 🦠

● **S36.511** Primary blast injury of transverse colon A 🦠

● **S36.512** Primary blast injury of descending [left] colon A 🦠

● **S36.513** Primary blast injury of sigmoid colon A 🦠

● **S36.518** Primary blast injury of other part of colon A 🦠

● ■ **S36.519** Primary blast injury of unspecified part of colon A 🦠

● **S36.52** Contusion of colon

● **S36.520** Contusion of ascending [right] colon A 🦠

● **S36.521** Contusion of transverse colon A 🦠

● **S36.522** Contusion of descending [left] colon A 🦠

● **S36.523** Contusion of sigmoid colon A 🦠

● **S36.528** Contusion of other part of colon A 🦠

● ■ **S36.529** Contusion of unspecified part of colon A 🦠

● **S36.53** Laceration of colon

● **S36.530** Laceration of ascending [right] colon A 🦠

● **S36.531** Laceration of transverse colon A 🦠

● **S36.532** Laceration of descending [left] colon A 🦠

● **S36.533** Laceration of sigmoid colon A 🦠

● **S36.538** Laceration of other part of colon A 🦠

■ **S36.539** Laceration of unspecified part of colon A 🦠

● **S36.59** Other injury of colon
Secondary blast injury of colon

● **S36.590** Other injury of ascending [right] colon A 🦠

● **S36.591** Other injury of transverse colon A 🦠

● **S36.592** Other injury of descending [left] colon A 🦠

● **S36.593** Other injury of sigmoid colon A 🦠

● **S36.598** Other injury of other part of colon A 🦠

● ■ **S36.599** Other injury of unspecified part of colon A 🦠

● **S36.6** Injury of rectum

● ■ **S36.60** Unspecified injury of rectum A 🦠

● **S36.61** Primary blast injury of rectum A 🦠
Blast injury of rectum NOS

● **S36.62** Contusion of rectum A 🦠

● **S36.63** Laceration of rectum A 🦠

● **S36.69** Other injury of rectum A 🦠
Secondary blast injury of rectum

● **S36.8** Injury of other intra-abdominal organs

● **S36.81** Injury of peritoneum A 🦠

● **S36.89** Injury of other intra-abdominal organs A 🦠
Injury of retroperitoneum

● **S36.892** Contusion of other intra-abdominal organs A 🦠

● **S36.893** Laceration of other intra-abdominal organs A 🦠

● **S36.898** Other injury of other intra-abdominal organs A 🦠

■ **S36.899** Unspecified injury of other intra-abdominal organs A 🦠

● **S36.9** Injury of unspecified intra-abdominal organ

■ **S36.90** Unspecified injury of unspecified intra-abdominal organ A 🦠

● ■ **S36.92** Contusion of unspecified intra-abdominal organ A 🦠

● ■ **S36.93** Laceration of unspecified intra-abdominal organ A 🦠

● ■ **S36.99** Other injury of unspecified intra-abdominal organ A 🦠

● **S37** Injury of urinary and pelvic organs
Code also any associated open wound (S31.-)

| Excludes1 | obstetric trauma to pelvic organs (O71-) |

| Excludes2 | injury of peritoneum (S36.81) |
| | injury of retroperitoneum (S36.89-) |

The appropriate 7th character is to be added to each code from category S37

```
A   initial encounter
D   subsequent encounter
S   sequela
```

● **S37.0** Injury of kidney

| Excludes2 | acute kidney injury (nontraumatic) (N17.9) |

● **S37.00** Unspecified injury of kidney

● ■ **S37.001** Unspecified injury of right kidney A 🦠

● ■ **S37.002** Unspecified injury of left kidney A 🦠

● ■ **S37.009** Unspecified injury of unspecified kidney A 🦠

● **S37.01** Minor contusion of kidney
Contusion of kidney less than 2 cm
Contusion of kidney NOS

● **S37.011** Minor contusion of right kidney A 🦠

● **S37.012** Minor contusion of left kidney A 🦠

● ■ **S37.019** Minor contusion of unspecified kidney A 🦠

● **S37.02** Major contusion of kidney
Contusion of kidney greater than 2 cm

● **S37.021** Major contusion of right kidney A 🦠

● **S37.022** Major contusion of left kidney A 🦠

● ■ **S37.029** Major contusion of unspecified kidney A 🦠

● Unacceptable First-Listed Diagnosis   ● Use Additional Character(s)   ■ Unspecified   **OGCR** Official Guidelines for Coding and Reporting

🦠 Complication\Comorbidity   🦠 Major C\C   Excludes 1    Excludes 2   Includes   Use additional   Code first   Code also   1407

CHAPTER 19 (S00-T88)

● S37.03　Laceration of kidney, unspecified degree
 ● ■ S37.031　Laceration of right kidney, unspecified degree A ◎
 ● ■ S37.032　Laceration of left kidney, unspecified degree A ◎
 ● ■ S37.039　Laceration of unspecified kidney, unspecified degree A ◎
● S37.04　Minor laceration of kidney
  Laceration of kidney less than 1 cm
 ● S37.041　Minor laceration of right kidney A ◎
 ● S37.042　Minor laceration of left kidney A ◎
 ● ■ S37.049　Minor laceration of unspecified kidney A ◎
● S37.05　Moderate laceration of kidney
  Laceration of kidney 1 to 3 cm
 ● S37.051　Moderate laceration of right kidney A ◎
 ● S37.052　Moderate laceration of left kidney A ◎
 ● ■ S37.059　Moderate laceration of unspecified kidney A ◎
● S37.06　Major laceration of kidney
  Avulsion of kidney
  Laceration of kidney greater than 3 cm
  Massive laceration of kidney
  Multiple moderate lacerations of kidney
  Stellate laceration of kidney
 ● S37.061　Major laceration of right kidney A ◎
 ● S37.062　Major laceration of left kidney
 ● ■ S37.069　Major laceration of unspecified kidney
● S37.09　Other injury of kidney
 ● S37.091　Other injury of right kidney A ◎
 ● S37.092　Other injury of left kidney A ◎
 ● ■ S37.099　Other injury of unspecified kidney A ◎
● S37.1　Injury of ureter
 ● ■ S37.10　Unspecified injury of ureter A ◎
 ● S37.12　Contusion of ureter A ◎
 ● S37.13　Laceration of ureter A ◎
 ● S37.19　Other injury of ureter A ◎
● S37.2　Injury of bladder
 ● ■ S37.20　Unspecified injury of bladder A ◎
 ● S37.22　Contusion of bladder A ◎
 ● S37.23　Laceration of bladder A ◎
 ● S37.28　Other injury of bladder A ◎
● S37.3　Injury of urethra
 ● ■ S37.30　Unspecified injury of urethra A ◎
 ● S37.32　Contusion of urethra A ◎
 ● S37.33　Laceration of urethra A ◎
 ● S37.38　Other injury of urethra A ◎
● S37.4　Injury of ovary
 ● S37.40　Unspecified injury of ovary
  ● ■ S37.401　Unspecified injury of ovary, unilateral
  ● ■ S37.402　Unspecified injury of ovary, bilateral
  ● ■ S37.409　Unspecified injury of ovary, unspecified

● S37.42　Contusion of ovary
 ● S37.421　Contusion of ovary, unilateral
 ● S37.422　Contusion of ovary, bilateral
 ● ■ S37.429　Contusion of ovary, unspecified
● S37.43　Laceration of ovary
 ● S37.431　Laceration of ovary, unilateral
 ● S37.432　Laceration of ovary, bilateral
 ● ■ S37.439　Laceration of ovary, unspecified
● S37.49　Other injury of ovary
 ● S37.491　Other injury of ovary, unilateral
 ● S37.492　Other injury of ovary, bilateral
 ● ■ S37.499　Other injury of ovary, unspecified
● S37.5　Injury of fallopian tube
 ● S37.50　Unspecified injury of fallopian tube
  ● ■ S37.501　Unspecified injury of fallopian tube, unilateral
  ● ■ S37.502　Unspecified injury of fallopian tube, bilateral
  ● ■ S37.509　Unspecified injury of fallopian tube, unspecified
 ● S37.51　Primary blast injury of fallopian tube
  Blast injury of fallopian tube NOS
  ● S37.511　Primary blast injury of fallopian tube, unilateral
  ● S37.512　Primary blast injury of fallopian tube, bilateral
  ● ■ S37.519　Primary blast injury of fallopian tube, unspecified
 ● S37.52　Contusion of fallopian tube
  ● S37.521　Contusion of fallopian tube, unilateral
  ● S37.522　Contusion of fallopian tube, bilateral
  ● ■ S37.529　Contusion of fallopian tube, unspecified
 ● S37.53　Laceration of fallopian tube
  ● S37.531　Laceration of fallopian tube, unilateral
  ● S37.532　Laceration of fallopian tube, bilateral
  ● ■ S37.539　Laceration of fallopian tube, unspecified
 ● S37.59　Other injury of fallopian tube
  Secondary blast injury of fallopian tube
  ● S37.591　Other injury of fallopian tube, unilateral
  ● S37.592　Other injury of fallopian tube, bilateral
  ● ■ S37.599　Other injury of fallopian tube, unspecified
● S37.6　Injury of uterus
  Excludes1　injury to gravid uterus (O9A.2-)
   injury to uterus during delivery (O71.-)
 ● ■ S37.60　Unspecified injury of uterus A ◎
 ● S37.62　Contusion of uterus A ◎
 ● S37.63　Laceration of uterus A ◎
 ● S37.69　Other injury of uterus A ◎

CHAPTER 19 (S00-T88)

● Unacceptable First-Listed Diagnosis ● Use Additional Character(s) ■ Unspecified OGCR Official Guidelines for Coding and Reporting
◎ Complication\Comorbidity ◎ Major C\C Excludes 1 Excludes 2 Includes Use additional Code first Code also

● S37.8   **Injury of other urinary and pelvic organs**
   ● S37.81   **Injury of adrenal gland**
     ● S37.812   Contusion of adrenal gland A 🅒
     ● S37.813   Laceration of adrenal gland A 🅒
     ● S37.818   Other injury of adrenal gland A 🅒
     ● ■ S37.819   Unspecified injury of adrenal gland A 🅒
   ● S37.82   **Injury of prostate**
     ● S37.822   Contusion of prostate
     ● S37.823   Laceration of prostate
     ● S37.828   Other injury of prostate
     ● ■ S37.829   Unspecified injury of prostate
   ● S37.89   **Injury of other urinary and pelvic organ**
     ● S37.892   Contusion of other urinary and pelvic organ A 🅒
     ● S37.893   Laceration of other urinary and pelvic organ A 🅒
     ● S37.898   Other injury of other urinary and pelvic organ A 🅒
     ● ■ S37.899   Unspecified injury of other urinary and pelvic organ A 🅒
  ● S37.9   **Injury of unspecified urinary and pelvic organ**
   ● ■ S37.90   Unspecified injury of unspecified pelvic organ A 🅒
   ● ■ S37.92   Contusion of unspecified pelvic organ A 🅒
   ● ■ S37.93   Laceration of unspecified pelvic organ A 🅒
   ● ■ S37.99   Other injury of unspecified pelvic organ A 🅒

● **S38**   **Crushing injury and traumatic amputation of abdomen, lower back, pelvis and external genitals**
     An amputation not identified as partial or complete should be coded to complete
     The appropriate 7th character is to be added to each code from category S38

     | | |
     A   initial encounter
     D   subsequent encounter
     S   sequela

  ● S38.0   **Crushing injury of external genital organs**
     Use additional code for any associated injuries
   ● S38.00   **Crushing injury of unspecified external genital organs**
     ● ■ S38.001   Crushing injury of unspecified external genital organs, male
     ● ■ S38.002   Crushing injury of unspecified external genital organs, female
   ● S38.01   **Crushing injury of penis**
   ● S38.02   **Crushing injury of scrotum and testis**
   ● S38.03   **Crushing injury of vulva**
  ● S38.1   **Crushing injury of abdomen, lower back, and pelvis**
     Use additional code for all associated injuries, such as:
       fracture of thoracic or lumbar spine and pelvis (S22.0-, S32.-)
       injury to intra-abdominal organs (S36.-)
       injury to urinary and pelvic organs (S37.-)
       open wound of abdominal wall (S31-)
       spinal cord injury (S34.0, S34.1-)
     Excludes2   crushing injury of external genital organs (S38.2-)

● S38.2   **Traumatic amputation of external genital organs**
   ● S38.21   **Traumatic amputation of female external genital organs**
     Traumatic amputation of clitoris
     Traumatic amputation of labium (majus) (minus)
     Traumatic amputation of vulva
     ● S38.211   Complete traumatic amputation of female external genital organs
     ● S38.212   Partial traumatic amputation of female external genital organs
   ● S38.22   **Traumatic amputation of penis**
     ● S38.221   Complete traumatic amputation of penis
     ● S38.222   Partial traumatic amputation of penis
   ● S38.23   **Traumatic amputation of scrotum and testis**
     ● S38.231   Complete traumatic amputation of scrotum and testis
     ● S38.232   Partial traumatic amputation of scrotum and testis
  ● S38.3   **Transection (partial) of abdomen**

● **S39**   **Other and unspecified injuries of abdomen, lower back, pelvis and external genitals**
     Code also any associated open wound (S31.-)
     Excludes2   sprain of joints and ligaments of lumbar spine and pelvis (S33.7)
     The appropriate 7th character is to be added to each code from category S39

     | | |
     A   initial encounter
     D   subsequent encounter
     S   sequela

  ● S39.0   **Injury of muscle, fascia and tendon of abdomen, lower back and pelvis**
   ● S39.00   **Unspecified injury of muscle, fascia and tendon of abdomen, lower back and pelvis**
     ● ■ S39.001   Unspecified injury of muscle, fascia and tendon of abdomen
     ● ■ S39.002   Unspecified injury of muscle, fascia and tendon of lower back
     ● ■ S39.003   Unspecified injury of muscle, fascia and tendon of pelvis
   ● S39.01   **Strain of muscle, fascia and tendon of abdomen, lower back and pelvis**
     ● S39.011   Strain of muscle, fascia and tendon of abdomen
     ● S39.012   Strain of muscle, fascia and tendon of lower back
     ● S39.013   Strain of muscle, fascia and tendon of pelvis
   ● S39.02   **Laceration of muscle, fascia and tendon of abdomen, lower back and pelvis**
     ● S39.021   Laceration of muscle, fascia and tendon of abdomen
     ● S39.022   Laceration of muscle, fascia and tendon of lower back
     ● S39.023   Laceration of muscle, fascia and tendon of pelvis

---

● Unacceptable First-Listed Diagnosis   ● Use Additional Character(s)   ■ Unspecified   **OGCR** Official Guidelines for Coding and Reporting
🅒 Complication\Comorbidity   🅒 Major C\C   Excludes 1   Excludes 2   Includes   Use additional   Code first   Code also

● S39.09   Other injury of muscle, fascia and tendon of abdomen, lower back and pelvis

     ● S39.091   Other injury of muscle, fascia and tendon of abdomen

     ● S39.092   Other injury of muscle, fascia and tendon of lower back

     ● S39.093   Other injury of muscle, fascia and tendon of pelvis

● S39.8   Other specified injuries of abdomen, lower back, pelvis and external genitals

   ● S39.81   Other specified injuries of abdomen

   ● S39.82   Other specified injuries of lower back

   ● S39.83   Other specified injuries of pelvis

   ● S39.84   Other specified injuries of external genitals

     ● S39.840   Fracture of corpus cavernosum penis

     ● S39.848   Other specified injuries of external genitals

● S39.9   Unspecified injury of abdomen, lower back, pelvis and external genitals

   ● ■ S39.91   Unspecified injury of abdomen

   ● ■ S39.92   Unspecified injury of lower back

   ● ■ S39.93   Unspecified injury of pelvis

   ● ■ S39.94   Unspecified injury of external genitals

INJURIES TO THE SHOULDER AND UPPER ARM (S40-S49)

Includes	injuries of axilla injuries of scapular region
Excludes2	burns and corrosions (T20-T32)
	frostbite (T33-T34)
	injuries of elbow (S50-S59)
	insect bite or sting, venomous (T63.4)

● S40   **Superficial injury of shoulder and upper arm**

     The appropriate 7th character is to be added to each code from category S40

> A   initial encounter
> D   subsequent encounter
> S   sequela

   ● S40.0   Contusion of shoulder and upper arm

     ● S40.01   Contusion of shoulder

       ● S40.011   Contusion of right shoulder

       ● S40.012   Contusion of left shoulder

       ● ■ S40.019   Contusion of shoulder, unspecified side

     ● S40.02   Contusion of upper arm

       ● S40.021   Contusion of right upper arm

       ● S40.022   Contusion of left upper arm

       ● ■ S40.029   Contusion of upper arm, unspecified side

   ● S40.2   Other superficial injuries of shoulder

     ● S40.21   Abrasion of shoulder

       ● S40.211   Abrasion of right shoulder

       ● S40.212   Abrasion of left shoulder

       ● ■ S40.219   Abrasion of unspecified shoulder

     ● S40.22   Blister (nonthermal) of shoulder

       ● S40.221   Blister (nonthermal) of right shoulder

       ● S40.222   Blister (nonthermal) of left shoulder

       ● ■ S40.229   Blister (nonthermal) of unspecified shoulder

     ● S40.24   External constriction of shoulder

       ● S40.241   External constriction of right shoulder

       ● S40.242   External constriction of left shoulder

       ● ■ S40.249   External constriction of unspecified shoulder

     ● S40.25   Superficial foreign body of shoulder
         Splinter in the shoulder

       ● S40.251   Superficial foreign body of right shoulder

       ● S40.252   Superficial foreign body of left shoulder

       ● ■ S40.259   Superficial foreign body of unspecified shoulder

     ● S40.26   Insect bite (nonvenomous) of shoulder

       ● S40.261   Insect bite (nonvenomous) of right shoulder

       ● S40.262   Insect bite (nonvenomous) of left shoulder

       ● ■ S40.269   Insect bite (nonvenomous) of unspecified shoulder

     ● S40.27   Other superficial bite of shoulder

> | **Excludes1** | open bite of shoulder (S41.05) |
> |---|---|

       ● S40.271   Other superficial bite of right shoulder

       ● S40.272   Other superficial bite of left shoulder

       ● ■ S40.279   Other superficial bite of unspecified shoulder

   ● S40.8   Other superficial injuries of upper arm

     ● S40.81   Abrasion of upper arm

       ● S40.811   Abrasion of right upper arm

       ● S40.812   Abrasion of left upper arm

       ● ■ S40.819   Abrasion of unspecified upper arm

     ● S40.82   Blister (nonthermal) of upper arm

       ● S40.821   Blister (nonthermal) of right upper arm

       ● S40.822   Blister (nonthermal) of left upper arm

       ● ■ S40.829   Blister (nonthermal) of unspecified upper arm

     ● S40.84   External constriction of upper arm

       ● S40.841   External constriction of right upper arm

       ● S40.842   External constriction of left upper arm

       ● ■ S40.849   External constriction of unspecified upper arm

     ● S40.85   Superficial foreign body of upper arm
         Splinter in the upper arm

       ● S40.851   Superficial foreign body of right upper arm

       ● S40.852   Superficial foreign body of left upper arm

● ■ S40.859 Superficial foreign body of unspecified upper arm

● S40.86 Insect bite (nonvenomous) of upper arm

    ● S40.861 Insect bite (nonvenomous) of right upper arm

    ● S40.862 Insect bite (nonvenomous) of left upper arm

    ● ■ S40.869 Insect bite (nonvenomous) of unspecified upper arm

● S40.87 Other superficial bite of upper arm

    Excludes1 open bite of upper arm (S41.14)

    Excludes2 other superficial bite of shoulder (S40.27-)

    ● S40.871 Other superficial bite of right upper arm

    ● S40.872 Other superficial bite of left upper arm

    ● ■ S40.879 Other superficial bite of unspecified upper arm

● S40.9 Unspecified superficial injury of shoulder and upper arm

    ● S40.91 Unspecified superficial injury of shoulder

      ● ■ S40.911 Unspecified superficial injury of right shoulder

      ● ■ S40.912 Unspecified superficial injury of left shoulder

      ● ■ S40.919 Unspecified superficial injury of shoulder, unspecified side

    ● S40.92 Unspecified superficial injury of upper arm

      ● ■ S40.921 Unspecified superficial injury of right upper arm

      ● ■ S40.922 Unspecified superficial injury of left upper arm

      ● ■ S40.929 Unspecified superficial injury of upper arm, unspecified side

● S41 Open wound of shoulder and upper arm

    Code also any associated wound infection

    Excludes1 traumatic amputation of shoulder and upper arm (S48.-)

    Excludes2 open fracture of shoulder and upper arm (S42.- with 7th character B or C)

    The appropriate 7th character is to be added to each code from category S41

      A   initial encounter
      D   subsequent encounter
      S   sequela

● S41.0 Open wound of shoulder

    ● S41.00 Unspecified open wound of shoulder

      ● ■ S41.001 Unspecified open wound of right shoulder

      ● ■ S41.002 Unspecified open wound of left shoulder

      ● ■ S41.009 Unspecified open wound of unspecified shoulder

    ● S41.01 Laceration without foreign body of shoulder

      ● S41.011 Laceration without foreign body of right shoulder

      ● S41.012 Laceration without foreign body of left shoulder

      ● ■ S41.019 Laceration without foreign body of unspecified shoulder

● S41.02 Laceration with foreign body of shoulder

    ● S41.021 Laceration with foreign body of right shoulder

    ● S41.022 Laceration with foreign body of left shoulder

    ● ■ S41.029 Laceration with foreign body of unspecified shoulder

● S41.03 Puncture wound without foreign body of shoulder

    ● S41.031 Puncture wound without foreign body of right shoulder

    ● S41.032 Puncture wound without foreign body of left shoulder

    ● ■ S41.039 Puncture wound without foreign body of unspecified shoulder

● S41.04 Puncture wound with foreign body of shoulder

    ● S41.041 Puncture wound with foreign body of right shoulder

    ● S41.042 Puncture wound with foreign body of left shoulder

    ● ■ S41.049 Puncture wound with foreign body of unspecified shoulder

● S41.05 Open bite of shoulder
    Bite of shoulder NOS

    Excludes1 superficial bite of shoulder (S40.27)

    ● S41.051 Open bite of right shoulder

    ● S41.052 Open bite of left shoulder

    ● ■ S41.059 Open bite of unspecified shoulder

● S41.1 Open wound of upper arm

    ● S41.10 Unspecified open wound of upper arm

      ● ■ S41.101 Unspecified open wound of right upper arm

      ● ■ S41.102 Unspecified open wound of left upper arm

      ● ■ S41.109 Unspecified open wound of unspecified upper arm

    ● S41.11 Laceration without foreign body of upper arm

      ● S41.111 Laceration without foreign body of right upper arm

      ● S41.112 Laceration without foreign body of left upper arm

      ● ■ S41.119 Laceration without foreign body of unspecified upper arm

    ● S41.12 Laceration with foreign body of upper arm

      ● S41.121 Laceration with foreign body of right upper arm

      ● S41.122 Laceration with foreign body of left upper arm

      ● ■ S41.129 Laceration with foreign body of unspecified upper arm

    ● S41.13 Puncture wound without foreign body of upper arm

      ● S41.131 Puncture wound without foreign body of right upper arm

      ● S41.132 Puncture wound without foreign body of left upper arm

      ● ■ S41.139 Puncture wound without foreign body of unspecified upper arm

● Unacceptable First-Listed Diagnosis   ● Use Additional Character(s)   ■ Unspecified   OGCR Official Guidelines for Coding and Reporting

 Complication\Comorbidity   Major C\C   Excludes 1   Excludes 2   Includes   Use additional   Code first   Code also

1411

CHAPTER 19 (S00-T88)

● **S41.14**   **Puncture wound with foreign body of upper arm**

    ● **S41.141**   Puncture wound with foreign body of right upper arm

    ● **S41.142**   Puncture wound with foreign body of left upper arm

    ● ■ **S41.149**   Puncture wound with foreign body of unspecified upper arm

● **S41.15**   **Open bite of upper arm**
       Bite of upper arm NOS

       | Excludes1 | superficial bite of upper arm (S40.87) |

    ● **S41.151**   Open bite of right upper arm

    ● **S41.152**   Open bite of left upper arm

    ● ■ **S41.159**   Open bite of unspecified upper arm

● **S42**   **Fracture of shoulder and upper arm**
       A fracture not indicated as displaced or nondisplaced should be coded to displaced

       | Excludes1 | traumatic amputation of shoulder and upper arm (S48.-) |

       The appropriate 7th character is to be added to all codes from category S42
       A fracture not designated as open or closed should be coded to closed

A	initial encounter for closed fracture
B	initial encounter for open fracture
D	subsequent encounter for fracture with routine healing
G	subsequent encounter for fracture with delayed healing
K	subsequent encounter for fracture with nonunion
P	subsequent encounter for fracture with malunion
S	sequela

● **S42.0**   **Fracture of clavicle**

   ● **S42.00**   **Fracture of unspecified part of clavicle**

     ● ■ **S42.001**   Fracture of unspecified part of right clavicle B, K, P 🌕

     ● ■ **S42.002**   Fracture of unspecified part of left clavicle B, K, P 🌕

     ● ■ **S42.009**   Fracture of unspecified part of unspecified clavicle B, K, P 🌕

   ● **S42.01**   **Fracture of sternal end of clavicle**

     ● **S42.011**   Anterior displaced fracture of sternal end of right clavicle B, K, P 🌕

     ● **S42.012**   Anterior displaced fracture of sternal end of left clavicle B, K, P 🌕

     ● ■ **S42.013**   Anterior displaced fracture of sternal end of unspecified clavicle B, K, P 🌕
         Displaced fracture of sternal end of clavicle NOS

     ● **S42.014**   Posterior displaced fracture of sternal end of right clavicle B, K, P 🌕

     ● **S42.015**   Posterior displaced fracture of sternal end of left clavicle B, K, P 🌕

     ● ■ **S42.016**   Posterior displaced fracture of sternal end of unspecified clavicle B, K, P 🌕

     ● **S42.017**   Nondisplaced fracture of sternal end of right clavicle B, K, P 🌕

     ● **S42.018**   Nondisplaced fracture of sternal end of left clavicle B, K, P 🌕

     ● ■ **S42.019**   Nondisplaced fracture of sternal end of unspecified clavicle B, K, P 🌕

   ● **S42.02**   **Fracture of shaft of clavicle**

     ● **S42.021**   Displaced fracture of shaft of right clavicle B, K, P 🌕

     ● **S42.022**   Displaced fracture of shaft of left clavicle B, K, P 🌕

     ● ■ **S42.023**   Displaced fracture of shaft of unspecified clavicle B, K, P 🌕

     ● **S42.024**   Nondisplaced fracture of shaft of right clavicle B, K, P 🌕

     ● **S42.025**   Nondisplaced fracture of shaft of left clavicle B, K, P 🌕

     ● ■ **S42.026**   Nondisplaced fracture of shaft of unspecified clavicle B, K, P 🌕

   ● **S42.03**   **Fracture of lateral end of clavicle**
      Fracture of acromial end of clavicle

     ● **S42.031**   Displaced fracture of lateral end of right clavicle B, K, P 🌕

     ● **S42.032**   Displaced fracture of lateral end of left clavicle B, K, P 🌕

     ● ■ **S42.033**   Displaced fracture of lateral end of unspecified clavicle B, K, P 🌕

     ● **S42.034**   Nondisplaced fracture of lateral end of right clavicle B, K, P 🌕

     ● **S42.035**   Nondisplaced fracture of lateral end of left clavicle B, K, P 🌕

     ● ■ **S42.036**   Nondisplaced fracture of lateral end of unspecified clavicle B, K, P 🌕

● **S42.1**   **Fracture of scapula**

   ● **S42.10**   **Fracture of unspecified part of scapula**

     ● ■ **S42.101**   Fracture of unspecified part of scapula, right shoulder B, K, P 🌕

     ● ■ **S42.102**   Fracture of unspecified part of scapula, left shoulder B, K, P 🌕

     ● ■ **S42.109**   Fracture of unspecified part of scapula, unspecified shoulder B, K, P 🌕

   ● **S42.11**   **Fracture of body of scapula**

     ● **S42.111**   Displaced fracture of body of scapula, right shoulder B, K, P 🌕

     ● **S42.112**   Displaced fracture of body of scapula, left shoulder B, K, P 🌕

     ● ■ **S42.113**   Displaced fracture of body of scapula, unspecified shoulder B, K, P 🌕

     ● **S42.114**   Nondisplaced fracture of body of scapula, right shoulder B, K, P 🌕

     ● **S42.115**   Nondisplaced fracture of body of scapula, left shoulder B, K, P 🌕

     ● ■ **S42.116**   Nondisplaced fracture of body of scapula, unspecified shoulder B, K, P 🌕

● S42.12   Fracture of acromial process

    ● S42.121   Displaced fracture of acromial process, right shoulder B, K, P 🦠

    ● S42.122   Displaced fracture of acromial process, left shoulder B, K, P 🦠

    ● ▪ S42.123   Displaced fracture of acromial process, unspecified shoulder B, K, P 🦠

    ● S42.124   Nondisplaced fracture of acromial process, right shoulder B, K, P 🦠

    ● S42.125   Nondisplaced fracture of acromial process, left shoulder B, K, P 🦠

    ● ▪ S42.126   Nondisplaced fracture of acromial process, unspecified shoulder B, K, P 🦠

● S42.13   Fracture of coracoid process

    ● S42.131   Displaced fracture of coracoid process, right shoulder B, K, P 🦠

    ● S42.132   Displaced fracture of coracoid process, left shoulder B, K, P 🦠

    ● ▪ S42.133   Displaced fracture of coracoid process, unspecified shoulder B, K, P 🦠

    ● S42.134   Nondisplaced fracture of coracoid process, right shoulder B, K, P 🦠

    ● S42.135   Nondisplaced fracture of coracoid process, left shoulder B, K, P 🦠

    ● ▪ S42.136   Nondisplaced fracture of coracoid process, unspecified shoulder B, K, P 🦠

● S42.14   Fracture of glenoid cavity of scapula

    ● S42.141   Displaced fracture of glenoid cavity of scapula, right shoulder B, K, P 🦠

    ● S42.142   Displaced fracture of glenoid cavity of scapula, left shoulder B, K, P 🦠

    ● ▪ S42.143   Displaced fracture of glenoid cavity of scapula, unspecified shoulder B, K, P 🦠

    ● S42.144   Nondisplaced fracture of glenoid cavity of scapula, right shoulder B, K, P 🦠

    ● S42.145   Nondisplaced fracture of glenoid cavity of scapula, left shoulder B, K, P 🦠

    ● ▪ S42.146   Nondisplaced fracture of glenoid cavity of scapula, unspecified shoulder B, K, P 🦠

● S42.15   Fracture of neck of scapula

    ● S42.151   Displaced fracture of neck of scapula, right shoulder B, K, P 🦠

    ● S42.152   Displaced fracture of neck of scapula, left shoulder B, K, P 🦠

    ● ▪ S42.153   Displaced fracture of neck of scapula, unspecified shoulder B, K, P 🦠

    ● S42.154   Nondisplaced fracture of neck of scapula, right shoulder B, K, P 🦠

    ● S42.155   Nondisplaced fracture of neck of scapula, left shoulder B, K, P 🦠

    ● ▪ S42.156   Nondisplaced fracture of neck of scapula, unspecified shoulder B, K, P 🦠

● S42.19   Fracture of other part of scapula

    ● S42.191   Fracture of other part of scapula, right shoulder B, K, P 🦠

    ● S42.192   Fracture of other part of scapula, left shoulder B, K, P 🦠

    ● ▪ S42.199   Fracture of other part of scapula, unspecified shoulder B, K, P 🦠

● S42.2   Fracture of upper end of humerus
    Fracture of proximal end of humerus

    | **Excludes2** | fracture of shaft of humerus (S42.3-) physeal fracture of upper end of humerus (S49.0-) |

    ● S42.20   Unspecified fracture of upper end of humerus

      ● ▪ S42.201   Unspecified fracture of upper end of right humerus A, K, P 🦠, B 🦠

      ● ▪ S42.202   Unspecified fracture of upper end of left humerus A, K, P 🦠, B 🦠

      ● ▪ S42.209   Unspecified fracture of upper end of unspecified humerus A, K, P 🦠, B 🦠

    ● S42.21   Unspecified fracture of surgical neck of humerus
       Fracture of neck of humerus NOS

      ● ▪ S42.211   Unspecified displaced fracture of surgical neck of right humerus A, K, P 🦠, B 🦠

      ● ▪ S42.212   Unspecified displaced fracture of surgical neck of left humerus A, K, P 🦠, B 🦠

      ● ▪ S42.213   Unspecified displaced fracture of surgical neck of unspecified humerus A, K, P 🦠, B 🦠

      ● ▪ S42.214   Unspecified nondisplaced fracture of surgical neck of right humerus A, K, P 🦠, B 🦠

      ● ▪ S42.215   Unspecified nondisplaced fracture of surgical neck of left humerus A, K, P 🦠, B 🦠

      ● ▪ S42.216   Unspecified nondisplaced fracture of surgical neck of unspecified humerus A, K, P 🦠, B 🦠

    ● S42.22   2-part fracture of surgical neck of humerus

      ● S42.221   2-part displaced fracture of surgical neck of right humerus A, K, P 🦠, B 🦠

      ● S42.222   2-part displaced fracture of surgical neck of left humerus A, K, P 🦠, B 🦠

      ● ▪ S42.223   2-part displaced fracture of surgical neck of unspecified humerus A, K, P 🦠, B 🦠

      ● S42.224   2-part nondisplaced fracture of surgical neck of right humerus A, K, P 🦠, B 🦠

      ● S42.225   2-part nondisplaced fracture of surgical neck of left humerus A, K, P 🦠, B 🦠

      ● ▪ S42.226   2-part nondisplaced fracture of surgical neck of unspecified humerus A, K, P 🦠, B 🦠

● Unacceptable First-Listed Diagnosis   ● Use Additional Character(s)   ▪ Unspecified   **OGCR** Official Guidelines for Coding and Reporting

🦠 Complication\Comorbidity   🦠 Major C\C | Excludes 1 | | Excludes 2 | Includes   Use additional   Code first   Code also

1413

CHAPTER 19 (S00-T88)

● S42.23   3-part fracture of surgical neck of humerus
- ● S42.231   3-part fracture of surgical neck of right humerus A, K, P 🔒, B 🔒
- ● S42.232   3-part fracture of surgical neck of left humerus A, K, P 🔒, B 🔒
- ● ■ S42.239   3-part fracture of surgical neck of unspecified humerus A, K, P 🔒, B 🔒

● S42.24   4-part fracture of surgical neck of humerus
- ● S42.241   4-part fracture of surgical neck of right humerus A, K, P 🔒, B 🔒
- ● S42.242   4-part fracture of surgical neck of left humerus A, K, P 🔒, B 🔒
- ● ■ S42.249   4-part fracture of surgical neck of unspecified humerus A, K, P 🔒, B 🔒

● S42.25   Fracture of greater tuberosity of humerus
- ● S42.251   Displaced fracture of greater tuberosity of right humerus A, K, P 🔒, B 🔒
- ● S42.252   Displaced fracture of greater tuberosity of left humerus A, K, P 🔒, B 🔒
- ● ■ S42.253   Displaced fracture of greater tuberosity of unspecified humerus A, K, P 🔒, B 🔒
- ● S42.254   Nondisplaced fracture of greater tuberosity of right humerus A, K, P 🔒, B 🔒
- ● S42.255   Nondisplaced fracture of greater tuberosity of left humerus A, K, P 🔒, B 🔒
- ● ■ S42.256   Nondisplaced fracture of greater tuberosity of unspecified humerus A, K, P 🔒, B 🔒

● S42.26   Fracture of lesser tuberosity of humerus
- ● S42.261   Displaced fracture of lesser tuberosity of right humerus A, K, P 🔒, B 🔒
- ● S42.262   Displaced fracture of lesser tuberosity of left humerus A, K, P 🔒, B 🔒
- ● ■ S42.263   Displaced fracture of lesser tuberosity of unspecified humerus A, K, P 🔒, B 🔒
- ● S42.264   Nondisplaced fracture of lesser tuberosity of right humerus A, K, P 🔒, B 🔒
- ● S42.265   Nondisplaced fracture of lesser tuberosity of left humerus A, K, P 🔒, B 🔒
- ● ■ S42.266   Nondisplaced fracture of lesser tuberosity of unspecified humerus A, K, P 🔒, B 🔒

● S42.27   Torus fracture of upper end of humerus

     Note: 7th character B is not applicable to codes under subcategory S42.27.
- ● S42.271   Torus fracture of upper end of right humerus A, K, P 🔒
- ● S42.272   Torus fracture of upper end of left humerus A, K, P 🔒
- ● ■ S42.279   Torus fracture of upper end of unspecified humerus A, K, P 🔒

● S42.29   Other fracture of upper end of humerus
     Fracture of anatomical neck of humerus
     Fracture of articular head of humerus
- ● S42.291   Other displaced fracture of upper end of right humerus A, K, P 🔒, B 🔒
- ● S42.292   Other displaced fracture of upper end of left humerus A, K, P 🔒, B 🔒
- ● ■ S42.293   Other displaced fracture of upper end of unspecified humerus A, K, P 🔒, B 🔒
- ● S42.294   Other nondisplaced fracture of upper end of right humerus A, K, P 🔒, B 🔒
- ● S42.295   Other nondisplaced fracture of upper end of left humerus A, K, P 🔒, B 🔒
- ● ■ S42.296   Other nondisplaced fracture of upper end of unspecified humerus A, K, P 🔒, B 🔒

● S42.3   Fracture of shaft of humerus
     Fracture of humerus NOS
     Fracture of upper arm NOS

     | Excludes2 | physeal fractures of upper end of humerus (S49.0-)
                   physeal fractures of lower end of humerus (S49.1-)

● S42.30   Unspecified fracture of shaft of humerus
- ● ■ S42.301   Unspecified fracture of shaft of humerus, right arm A, K, P 🔒, B 🔒
- ● ■ S42.302   Unspecified fracture of shaft of humerus, left arm A, K, P 🔒, B 🔒
- ● ■ S42.309   Unspecified fracture of shaft of humerus, unspecified arm A, K, P 🔒, B 🔒

● S42.31   Greenstick fracture of shaft of humerus

     Note: 7th character B is not applicable to codes under subcategory S42.31.
- ● S42.311   Greenstick fracture of shaft of humerus, right arm A, K, P 🔒
- ● S42.312   Greenstick fracture of shaft of humerus, left arm A, K, P 🔒
- ● ■ S42.319   Greenstick fracture of shaft of humerus, unspecified arm A, K, P 🔒

● S42.32   Transverse fracture of shaft of humerus
- ● S42.321   Displaced transverse fracture of shaft of humerus, right arm A, K, P 🔒, B 🔒
- ● S42.322   Displaced transverse fracture of shaft of humerus, left arm A, K, P 🔒, B 🔒
- ● ■ S42.323   Displaced transverse fracture of shaft of humerus, unspecified arm A, K, P 🔒, B 🔒
- ● S42.324   Nondisplaced transverse fracture of shaft of humerus, right arm A, K, P 🔒, B 🔒
- ● S42.325   Nondisplaced transverse fracture of shaft of humerus, left arm A, K, P 🔒, B 🔒
- ● ■ S42.326   Nondisplaced transverse fracture of shaft of humerus, unspecified arm A, K, P 🔒, B 🔒

● Unacceptable First-Listed Diagnosis   ● Use Additional Character(s)   ■ Unspecified   **OGCR** Official Guidelines for Coding and Reporting
🔒 Complication\Comorbidity   🔒 Major C\C | Excludes 1 | | Excludes 2 | Includes   Use additional   Code first   Code also

● **S42.33**   Oblique fracture of shaft of humerus

  ● **S42.331**   Displaced oblique fracture of shaft of humerus, right arm A, K, P 🦠, B 🦠

  ● **S42.332**   Displaced oblique fracture of shaft of humerus, left arm A, K, P 🦠, B 🦠

  ● ■ **S42.333**   Displaced oblique fracture of shaft of humerus, unspecified arm A, K, P 🦠, B 🦠

  ● **S42.334**   Nondisplaced oblique fracture of shaft of humerus, right arm A, K, P 🦠, B 🦠

  ● **S42.335**   Nondisplaced oblique fracture of shaft of humerus, left arm A, K, P 🦠, B 🦠

  ● ■ **S42.336**   Nondisplaced oblique fracture of shaft of humerus, unspecified arm A, K, P 🦠, B 🦠

● **S42.34**   Spiral fracture of shaft of humerus

  ● **S42.341**   Displaced spiral fracture of shaft of humerus, right arm B 🦠

  ● **S42.342**   Displaced spiral fracture of shaft of humerus, left arm B 🦠

  ● ■ **S42.343**   Displaced spiral fracture of shaft of humerus, unspecified arm B 🦠

  ● **S42.344**   Nondisplaced spiral fracture of shaft of humerus, right arm B 🦠

  ● **S42.345**   Nondisplaced spiral fracture of shaft of humerus, left arm B 🦠

  ● ■ **S42.346**   Nondisplaced spiral fracture of shaft of humerus, unspecified arm B 🦠

● **S42.35**   Comminuted fracture of shaft of humerus

  ● **S42.351**   Displaced comminuted fracture of shaft of humerus, right arm B 🦠

  ● **S42.352**   Displaced comminuted fracture of shaft of humerus, left arm B 🦠

  ● ■ **S42.353**   Displaced comminuted fracture of shaft of humerus, unspecified arm B 🦠

  ● **S42.354**   Nondisplaced comminuted fracture of shaft of humerus, right arm B 🦠

  ● **S42.355**   Nondisplaced comminuted fracture of shaft of humerus, left arm B 🦠

  ● ■ **S42.356**   Nondisplaced comminuted fracture of shaft of humerus, unspecified arm B 🦠

● **S42.36**   Segmental fracture of shaft of humerus

  ● **S42.361**   Displaced segmental fracture of shaft of humerus, right arm B 🦠

  ● **S42.362**   Displaced segmental fracture of shaft of humerus, left arm B 🦠

  ● ■ **S42.363**   Displaced segmental fracture of shaft of humerus, unspecified arm B 🦠

  ● **S42.364**   Nondisplaced segmental fracture of shaft of humerus, right arm B 🦠

  ● **S42.365**   Nondisplaced segmental fracture of shaft of humerus, left arm B 🦠

  ● ■ **S42.366**   Nondisplaced segmental fracture of shaft of humerus, unspecified arm B 🦠

● **S42.39**   Other fracture of shaft of humerus

  ● **S42.391**   Other fracture of shaft of right humerus A, K, P 🦠, B 🦠

  ● **S42.392**   Other fracture of shaft of left humerus B 🦠

  ● ■ **S42.399**   Other fracture of shaft of unspecified humerus B 🦠

● **S42.4**   Fracture of lower end of humerus
     Fracture of distal end of humerus

     | Excludes2 | fracture of shaft of humerus (S42.3-)
         physeal fracture of lower end of humerus (S49.1-)

  ● **S42.40**   Unspecified fracture of lower end of humerus
       Fracture of elbow NOS

    ● ■ **S42.401**   Unspecified fracture of lower end of right humerus A, K, P 🦠, B 🦠

    ● ■ **S42.402**   Unspecified fracture of lower end of left humerus A, K, P 🦠, B 🦠

    ● ■ **S42.409**   Unspecified fracture of lower end of unspecified humerus A, K, P 🦠, B 🦠

  ● **S42.41**   Simple supracondylar fracture without intercondylar fracture of humerus

    ● **S42.411**   Displaced simple supracondylar fracture without intercondylar fracture of right humerus A, K, P 🦠, B 🦠

    ● **S42.412**   Displaced simple supracondylar fracture without intercondylar fracture of left humerus A, K, P 🦠, B 🦠

    ● ■ **S42.413**   Displaced simple supracondylar fracture without intercondylar fracture of unspecified humerus A, K, P 🦠, B 🦠

    ● **S42.414**   Nondisplaced simple supracondylar fracture without intercondylar fracture of right humerus A, K, P 🦠, B 🦠

    ● **S42.415**   Nondisplaced simple supracondylar fracture without intercondylar fracture of left humerus A, K, P 🦠, B 🦠

    ● ■ **S42.416**   Nondisplaced simple supracondylar fracture without intercondylar fracture of unspecified humerus A, K, P 🦠, B 🦠

  ● **S42.42**   Comminuted supracondylar fracture without intercondylar fracture of humerus

    ● **S42.421**   Displaced comminuted supracondylar fracture without intercondylar fracture of right humerus A, K, P 🦠, B 🦠

    ● **S42.422**   Displaced comminuted supracondylar fracture without intercondylar fracture of left humerus A, K, P 🦠, B 🦠

●   Unacceptable First-Listed Diagnosis   ●   Use Additional Character(s)   ■   Unspecified   **OGCR**   Official Guidelines for Coding and Reporting

🦠 Complication\Comorbidity   🦠 Major C\C | Excludes 1 | | Excludes 2 | | Includes | Use additional   Code first   Code also

1415

CHAPTER 19 (S00-T88)

● ■ S42.423 Displaced comminuted supracondylar fracture without intercondylar fracture of unspecified humerus A, K, P ☣, B ☣

● S42.424 Nondisplaced comminuted supracondylar fracture without intercondylar fracture of right humerus A, K, P ☣, B ☣

● S42.425 Nondisplaced comminuted supracondylar fracture without intercondylar fracture of left humerus A, K, P ☣, B ☣

● ■ S42.426 Nondisplaced comminuted supracondylar fracture without intercondylar fracture of unspecified humerus A, K, P ☣, B ☣

● S42.43 Fracture (avulsion) of lateral epicondyle of humerus

● S42.431 Displaced fracture (avulsion) of lateral epicondyle of right humerus A, K, P ☣, B ☣

● S42.432 Displaced fracture (avulsion) of lateral epicondyle of left humerus A, K, P ☣, B ☣

● ■ S42.433 Displaced fracture (avulsion) of lateral epicondyle of unspecified humerus A, K, P ☣, B ☣

● S42.434 Nondisplaced fracture (avulsion) of lateral epicondyle of right humerus A, K, P ☣, B ☣

● S42.435 Nondisplaced fracture (avulsion) of lateral epicondyle of left humerus A, K, P ☣, B ☣

● ■ S42.436 Nondisplaced fracture (avulsion) of lateral epicondyle of unspecified humerus A, K, P ☣, B ☣

● S42.44 Fracture (avulsion) of medial epicondyle of humerus

● S42.441 Displaced fracture (avulsion) of medial epicondyle of right humerus A, K, P ☣, B ☣

● S42.442 Displaced fracture (avulsion) of medial epicondyle of left humerus A, K, P ☣, B ☣

● ■ S42.443 Displaced fracture (avulsion) of medial epicondyle of unspecified humerus A, K, P ☣, B ☣

● S42.444 Nondisplaced fracture (avulsion) of medial epicondyle of right humerus A, K, P ☣, B ☣

● S42.445 Nondisplaced fracture (avulsion) of medial epicondyle of left humerus A, K, P ☣, B ☣

● ■ S42.446 Nondisplaced fracture (avulsion) of medial epicondyle of unspecified humerus A, K, P ☣, B ☣

● S42.447 Incarcerated fracture (avulsion) of medial epicondyle of right humerus A, K, P ☣, B ☣

● S42.448 Incarcerated fracture (avulsion) of medial epicondyle of left humerus A, K, P ☣, B ☣

● ■ S42.449 Incarcerated fracture (avulsion) of medial epicondyle of unspecified humerus A, K, P ☣, B ☣

● S42.45 Fracture of lateral condyle of humerus
Fracture of capitellum of humerus

● S42.451 Displaced fracture of lateral condyle of right humerus A, K, P ☣, B ☣

● S42.452 Displaced fracture of lateral condyle of left humerus A, K, P ☣, B ☣

● ■ S42.453 Displaced fracture of lateral condyle of unspecified humerus A, K, P ☣, B ☣

● S42.454 Nondisplaced fracture of lateral condyle of right humerus A, K, P ☣, B ☣

● S42.455 Nondisplaced fracture of lateral condyle of left humerus A, K, P ☣, B ☣

● ■ S42.456 Nondisplaced fracture of lateral condyle of unspecified humerus A, K, P ☣, B ☣

● S42.46 Fracture of medial condyle of humerus
Trochlea fracture of humerus

● S42.461 Displaced fracture of medial condyle of right humerus A, K, P ☣, B ☣

● S42.462 Displaced fracture of medial condyle of left humerus A, K, P ☣, B ☣

● ■ S42.463 Displaced fracture of medial condyle of unspecified humerus A, K, P ☣, B ☣

● S42.464 Nondisplaced fracture of medial condyle of right humerus A, K, P ☣, B ☣

● S42.465 Nondisplaced fracture of medial condyle of left humerus A, K, P ☣, B ☣

● ■ S42.466 Nondisplaced fracture of medial condyle of unspecified humerus A, K, P ☣, B ☣

● S42.47 Transcondylar fracture of humerus

● S42.471 Displaced transcondylar fracture of right humerus A, K, P ☣, B ☣

● S42.472 Displaced transcondylar fracture of left humerus A, K, P ☣, B ☣

● ■ S42.473 Displaced transcondylar fracture of unspecified humerus A, K, P ☣, B ☣

● S42.474 Nondisplaced transcondylar fracture of right humerus A, K, P ☣, B ☣

● S42.475 Nondisplaced transcondylar fracture of left humerus A, K, P ☣, B ☣

● ■ S42.476 Nondisplaced transcondylar fracture of unspecified humerus A, K, P ☣, B ☣

● Unacceptable First-Listed Diagnosis   ● Use Additional Character(s)   ■ Unspecified   **OGCR** Official Guidelines for Coding and Reporting
☣ Complication\Comorbidity   ☣ Major C\C   Excludes 1   Excludes 2   Includes   Use additional   Code first   Code also

● S42.48   Torus fracture of lower end of humerus

Note: 7th character B is not applicable to codes under subcategory S42.48.

- ● S42.481   Torus fracture of lower end of right humerus A, K, P 🔵
- ● S42.482   Torus fracture of lower end of left humerus A, K, P 🔵
- ● ▪ S42.489   Torus fracture of lower end of unspecified humerus A, K, P 🔵

● S42.49   Other fracture of lower end of humerus

- ● S42.491   Other displaced fracture of lower end of right humerus A, K, P 🔵, B 🔵
- ● S42.492   Other displaced fracture of lower end of left humerus A, K, P 🔵, B 🔵
- ● ▪ S42.493   Other displaced fracture of lower end of unspecified humerus A, K, P 🔵, B 🔵
- ● S42.494   Other nondisplaced fracture of lower end of right humerus A, K, P 🔵, B 🔵
- ● S42.495   Other nondisplaced fracture of lower end of left humerus A, K, P 🔵, B 🔵
- ● ▪ S42.496   Other nondisplaced fracture of lower end of unspecified humerus A, K, P 🔵, B 🔵

● S42.9   Fracture of shoulder girdle, part unspecified
Fracture of shoulder NOS

- ● ▪ S42.90   Fracture of unspecified shoulder girdle, part unspecified A, K, P 🔵, B 🔵
- ● ▪ S42.91   Fracture of right shoulder girdle, part unspecified A, K, P 🔵, B 🔵
- ● ▪ S42.92   Fracture of left shoulder girdle, part unspecified A, K, P 🔵, B 🔵

● S43   Dislocation and sprain of joints and ligaments of shoulder girdle

Includes	avulsion of joint or ligament of shoulder girdle

avulsion of joint or ligament of shoulder girdle
laceration of cartilage, joint or ligament of shoulder girdle
sprain of cartilage, joint or ligament of shoulder girdle
traumatic hemarthrosis of joint or ligament of shoulder girdle
traumatic rupture of joint or ligament of shoulder girdle
traumatic subluxation of joint or ligament of shoulder girdle
traumatic tear of joint or ligament of shoulder girdle

Code also any associated open wound

Excludes2	strain of muscle, fascia and tendon of shoulder and upper arm (S46.-)

The appropriate 7th character is to be added to each code from category S43

A	initial encounter
D	subsequent encounter
S	sequela

● S43.0   Subluxation and dislocation of shoulder joint
Dislocation of glenohumeral joint
Subluxation of glenohumeral joint

● S43.00   Unspecified subluxation and dislocation of shoulder joint
Dislocation of humerus NOS
Subluxation of humerus NOS

- ● ▪ S43.001   Unspecified subluxation of right shoulder joint
- ● ▪ S43.002   Unspecified subluxation of left shoulder joint
- ● ▪ S43.003   Unspecified subluxation of unspecified shoulder joint
- ● ▪ S43.004   Unspecified dislocation of right shoulder joint
- ● ▪ S43.005   Unspecified dislocation of left shoulder joint
- ● ▪ S43.006   Unspecified dislocation of unspecified shoulder joint

● S43.01   Anterior subluxation and dislocation of humerus

- ● S43.011   Anterior subluxation of right humerus
- ● S43.012   Anterior subluxation of left humerus
- ● ▪ S43.013   Anterior subluxation of unspecified humerus
- ● S43.014   Anterior dislocation of right humerus
- ● S43.015   Anterior dislocation of left humerus
- ● ▪ S43.016   Anterior dislocation of unspecified humerus

● S43.02   Posterior subluxation and dislocation of humerus

- ● S43.021   Posterior subluxation of right humerus
- ● S43.022   Posterior subluxation of left humerus
- ● ▪ S43.023   Posterior subluxation of unspecified humerus
- ● S43.024   Posterior dislocation of right humerus
- ● S43.025   Posterior dislocation of left humerus
- ● ▪ S43.026   Posterior dislocation of unspecified humerus

● S43.03   Inferior subluxation and dislocation of humerus

- ● S43.031   Inferior subluxation of right humerus
- ● S43.032   Inferior subluxation of left inferior humerus
- ● ▪ S43.033   Inferior subluxation of unspecified inferior humerus
- ● S43.034   Inferior dislocation of right inferior humerus
- ● S43.035   Inferior dislocation of left inferior humerus
- ● ▪ S43.036   Inferior dislocation of unspecified inferior humerus

● Unacceptable First-Listed Diagnosis   ● Use Additional Character(s)   ▪ Unspecified   **OGCR** Official Guidelines for Coding and Reporting
🔵 Complication\Comorbidity   🔵 Major C\C   Excludes 1   Excludes 2   Includes   Use additional   Code first   Code also   1417

CHAPTER 19 (S00-T88)

● S43.08   Other subluxation and dislocation of shoulder joint

　　● S43.081   Other subluxation of right shoulder joint

　　● S43.082   Other subluxation of left shoulder joint

　　● ■ S43.083   Other subluxation of unspecified shoulder joint

　　● S43.084   Other dislocation of right shoulder joint

　　● S43.085   Other dislocation of left shoulder joint

　　● ■ S43.086   Other dislocation of unspecified shoulder joint

● S43.1   Subluxation and dislocation of acromioclavicular joint

　● S43.10   Unspecified dislocation of acromioclavicular joint

　　● ■ S43.101   Unspecified dislocation of right acromioclavicular joint

　　● ■ S43.102   Unspecified dislocation of left acromioclavicular joint

　　● ■ S43.109   Unspecified dislocation of unspecified acromioclavicular joint

　● S43.11   Subluxation of acromioclavicular joint

　　● S43.111   Subluxation of right acromioclavicular joint

　　● S43.112   Subluxation of left acromioclavicular joint

　　● ■ S43.119   Subluxation of unspecified acromioclavicular joint

　● S43.12   Dislocation of acromioclavicular joint, 100%-200% displacement

　　● S43.121   Dislocation of right acromioclavicular joint, 100%-200% displacement

　　● S43.122   Dislocation of left acromioclavicular joint, 100%-200% displacement

　　● ■ S43.129   Dislocation of unspecified acromioclavicular joint, 100%-200% displacement

　● S43.13   Dislocation of acromioclavicular joint, greater than 200% displacement

　　● S43.131   Dislocation of right acromioclavicular joint, greater than 200% displacement

　　● S43.132   Dislocation of left acromioclavicular joint, greater than 200% displacement

　　● ■ S43.139   Dislocation of unspecified acromioclavicular joint, greater than 200% displacement

　● S43.14   Inferior dislocation of acromioclavicular joint

　　● S43.141   Inferior dislocation of right acromioclavicular joint

　　● S43.142   Inferior dislocation of left acromioclavicular joint

　　● ■ S43.149   Inferior dislocation of unspecified acromioclavicular joint

● S43.15   Posterior dislocation of acromioclavicular joint

　　● S43.151   Posterior dislocation of right acromioclavicular joint

　　● S43.152   Posterior dislocation of left acromioclavicular joint

　　● ■ S43.159   Posterior dislocation of unspecified acromioclavicular joint

● S43.2   Subluxation and dislocation of sternoclavicular joint

　● S43.20   Unspecified subluxation and dislocation of sternoclavicular joint

　　● ■ S43.201   Unspecified subluxation of right sternoclavicular joint A 🦠

　　● ■ S43.202   Unspecified subluxation of left sternoclavicular joint A 🦠

　　● ■ S43.203   Unspecified subluxation of unspecified sternoclavicular joint A 🦠

　　● ■ S43.204   Unspecified dislocation of right sternoclavicular joint A 🦠

　　● ■ S43.205   Unspecified dislocation of left sternoclavicular joint A 🦠

　　● ■ S43.206   Unspecified dislocation of unspecified sternoclavicular joint A 🦠

　● S43.21   Anterior subluxation and dislocation of sternoclavicular joint

　　● S43.211   Anterior subluxation of right sternoclavicular joint A 🦠

　　● S43.212   Anterior subluxation of left sternoclavicular joint A 🦠

　　● ■ S43.213   Anterior subluxation of unspecified sternoclavicular joint A 🦠

　　● S43.214   Anterior dislocation of right sternoclavicular joint A 🦠

　　● S43.215   Anterior dislocation of left sternoclavicular joint A 🦠

　　● ■ S43.216   Anterior dislocation of unspecified sternoclavicular joint A 🦠

　● S43.22   Posterior subluxation and dislocation of sternoclavicular joint

　　● S43.221   Posterior subluxation of right sternoclavicular joint A 🦠

　　● S43.222   Posterior subluxation of left sternoclavicular joint A 🦠

　　● ■ S43.223   Posterior subluxation of unspecified sternoclavicular joint A 🦠

　　● S43.224   Posterior dislocation of right sternoclavicular joint A 🦠

　　● S43.225   Posterior dislocation of left sternoclavicular joint A 🦠

　　● ■ S43.226   Posterior dislocation of unspecified sternoclavicular joint A 🦠

● Unacceptable First-Listed Diagnosis　　　● Use Additional Character(s)　　　■ Unspecified　　　**OGCR** Official Guidelines for Coding and Reporting

🦠 Complication\Comorbidity　　🦠 Major C\C　　Excludes 1　　Excludes 2　　Includes　　Use additional　　Code first　　Code also

● **S43.3**   **Subluxation and dislocation of other and unspecified parts of shoulder girdle**

  ● **S43.30**   **Subluxation and dislocation of unspecified parts of shoulder girdle**
     Dislocation of shoulder girdle NOS
     Subluxation of shoulder girdle NOS

    ● ■ **S43.301**   Subluxation of unspecified parts of right shoulder girdle

    ● ■ **S43.302**   Subluxation of unspecified parts of left shoulder girdle

    ● ■ **S43.303**   Subluxation of unspecified parts of unspecified shoulder girdle

    ● ■ **S43.304**   Dislocation of unspecified parts of right shoulder girdle

    ● ■ **S43.305**   Dislocation of unspecified parts of left shoulder girdle

    ● ■ **S43.306**   Dislocation of unspecified parts of unspecified shoulder girdle

  ● **S43.31**   **Subluxation and dislocation of scapula**

    ● **S43.311**   Subluxation of right scapula

    ● **S43.312**   Subluxation of left scapula

    ● ■ **S43.313**   Subluxation of unspecified scapula

    ● **S43.314**   Dislocation of right scapula

    ● **S43.315**   Dislocation of left scapula

    ● ■ **S43.316**   Dislocation of unspecified scapula

  ● **S43.39**   **Subluxation and dislocation of other parts of shoulder girdle**

    ● **S43.391**   Subluxation of other parts of right shoulder girdle

    ● **S43.392**   Subluxation of other parts of left shoulder girdle

    ● ■ **S43.393**   Subluxation of other parts of unspecified shoulder girdle

    ● **S43.394**   Dislocation of other parts of right shoulder girdle

    ● **S43.395**   Dislocation of other parts of left shoulder girdle

    ● ■ **S43.396**   Dislocation of other parts of unspecified shoulder girdle

● **S43.4**   **Sprain of shoulder joint**

  ● **S43.40**   **Unspecified sprain of shoulder joint**

    ● ■ **S43.401**   Unspecified sprain of right shoulder joint

    ● ■ **S43.402**   Unspecified sprain of left shoulder joint

    ● ■ **S43.409**   Unspecified sprain of unspecified shoulder joint

  ● **S43.41**   **Sprain of coracohumeral (ligament)**

    ● **S43.411**   Sprain of right coracohumeral (ligament)

    ● **S43.412**   Sprain of left coracohumeral (ligament)

    ● ■ **S43.419**   Sprain of unspecified coracohumeral (ligament)

  ● **S43.42**   **Sprain of rotator cuff capsule**

    | **Excludes1** | rotator cuff syndrome (complete) (incomplete), not specified as traumatic (M75.1-) |

    | **Excludes2** | injury of tendon of rotator cuff (S46.0-) |

    ● **S43.421**   Sprain of right rotator cuff capsule

    ● **S43.422**   Sprain of left rotator cuff capsule

    ● ■ **S43.429**   Sprain of unspecified rotator cuff capsule

  ● **S43.43**   **Superior glenoid labrum lesion**
     SLAP lesion

    ● **S43.431**   Superior glenoid labrum lesion of right shoulder

    ● **S43.432**   Superior glenoid labrum lesion of left shoulder

    ● ■ **S43.439**   Superior glenoid labrum lesion of unspecified shoulder

  ● **S43.49**   **Other sprain of shoulder joint**

    ● **S43.491**   Other sprain of right shoulder joint

    ● **S43.492**   Other sprain of left shoulder joint

    ● ■ **S43.499**   Other sprain of shoulder joint, unspecified side

● **S43.5**   **Sprain of acromioclavicular joint**
   Sprain of acromioclavicular ligament

  ● ■ **S43.50**   Sprain of acromioclavicular joint, unspecified side

  ● **S43.51**   Sprain of right acromioclavicular joint

  ● **S43.52**   Sprain of left acromioclavicular joint

● **S43.6**   **Sprain of sternoclavicular joint**

  ● ■ **S43.60**   Sprain of sternoclavicular joint, unspecified side

  ● **S43.61**   Sprain of right sternoclavicular joint

  ● **S43.62**   Sprain of left sternoclavicular joint

● **S43.8**   **Sprain of other parts of shoulder girdle**

  ● ■ **S43.80**   Sprain of other parts of shoulder girdle, unspecified side

  ● **S43.81**   Sprain of other parts of right shoulder girdle

  ● **S43.82**   Sprain of other parts of left shoulder girdle

● **S43.9**   **Sprain of unspecified parts of shoulder girdle**

  ● ■ **S43.90**   Sprain of unspecified parts of shoulder girdle, unspecified side
     Sprain of shoulder girdle NOS

  ● ■ **S43.91**   Sprain of unspecified parts of right shoulder girdle

  ● ■ **S43.92**   Sprain of unspecified parts of left shoulder girdle

---

● Unacceptable First-Listed Diagnosis   ● Use Additional Character(s)   ■ Unspecified   **OGCR** Official Guidelines for Coding and Reporting

🅒 Complication\Comorbidity   🅒 Major C\C | Excludes 1 | | Excludes 2 |  Includes   Use additional   Code first   Code also

1419

CHAPTER 19 (S00-T88)

● **S44   Injury of nerves at shoulder and upper arm level**
     Code also any associated open wound (S41.-)

     Excludes2   injury of brachial plexus (S14.3-)

     The appropriate 7th character is to be added to each code from category S44

     A   initial encounter
     D   subsequent encounter
     S   sequela

● **S44.0   Injury of ulnar nerve at upper arm level**

     Excludes1   ulnar nerve NOS (S54.0)

   ● **S44.00**   Injury of ulnar nerve at upper arm level, unspecified arm

   ● **S44.01**   Injury of ulnar nerve at upper arm level, right arm

   ● **S44.02**   Injury of ulnar nerve at upper arm level, left arm

● **S44.1   Injury of median nerve at upper arm level**

     Excludes1   median nerve NOS (S54.1)

   ● **S44.10**   Injury of median nerve at upper arm level, unspecified arm

   ● **S44.11**   Injury of median nerve at upper arm level, right arm

   ● **S44.12**   Injury of median nerve at upper arm level, left arm

● **S44.2   Injury of radial nerve at upper arm level**

     Excludes1   radial nerve NOS (S54.2)

   ● **S44.20**   Injury of radial nerve at upper arm level, unspecified arm

   ● **S44.21**   Injury of radial nerve at upper arm level, right arm

   ● **S44.22**   Injury of radial nerve at upper arm level, left arm

● **S44.3   Injury of axillary nerve**

   ● **S44.30**   Injury of axillary nerve, unspecified arm

   ● **S44.31**   Injury of axillary nerve, right arm

   ● **S44.32**   Injury of axillary nerve, left arm

● **S44.4   Injury of musculocutaneous nerve**

   ● **S44.40**   Injury of musculocutaneous nerve, unspecified arm

   ● **S44.41**   Injury of musculocutaneous nerve, right arm

   ● **S44.42**   Injury of musculocutaneous nerve, left arm

● **S44.5   Injury of cutaneous sensory nerve at shoulder and upper arm level**

   ● **S44.50**   Injury of cutaneous sensory nerve at shoulder and upper arm level, unspecified arm

   ● **S44.51**   Injury of cutaneous sensory nerve at shoulder and upper arm level, right arm

   ● **S44.52**   Injury of cutaneous sensory nerve at shoulder and upper arm level, left arm

● **S44.8   Injury of other nerves at shoulder and upper arm level**

   ● **S44.8x**   Injury of other nerves at shoulder and upper arm level

     ● **S44.8x1**   Injury of other nerves at shoulder and upper arm level, right arm

     ● **S44.8x2**   Injury of other nerves at shoulder and upper arm level, left arm

     ● **S44.8x9**   Injury of other nerves at shoulder and upper arm level, unspecified arm

● **S44.9   Injury of unspecified nerve at shoulder and upper arm level**

   ● **S44.90**   Injury of unspecified nerve at shoulder and upper arm level, unspecified arm

   ● **S44.91**   Injury of unspecified nerve at shoulder and upper arm level, right arm

   ● **S44.92**   Injury of unspecified nerve at shoulder and upper arm level, left arm

● **S45   Injury of blood vessels at shoulder and upper arm level**
     Code also any associated open wound (S41.-)

     Excludes2   injury of subclavian artery (S25.1)
                 injury of subclavian vein (S25.3)

     The appropriate 7th character is to be added to each code from category S45

     A   initial encounter
     D   subsequent encounter
     S   sequela

● **S45.0   Injury of axillary artery**

   ● **S45.00**   Unspecified injury of axillary artery

     ● **S45.001**   Unspecified injury of axillary artery, right side A

     ● **S45.002**   Unspecified injury of axillary artery, left side A

     ● **S45.009**   Unspecified injury of axillary artery, unspecified side A

   ● **S45.01**   Laceration of axillary artery

     ● **S45.011**   Laceration of axillary artery, right side A

     ● **S45.012**   Laceration of axillary artery, left side A

     ● **S45.019**   Laceration of axillary artery, unspecified side A

   ● **S45.09**   Other specified injury of axillary artery

     ● **S45.091**   Other specified injury of axillary artery, right side A

     ● **S45.092**   Other specified injury of axillary artery, left side A

     ● **S45.099**   Other specified injury of axillary artery, unspecified side A

● **S45.1   Injury of brachial artery**

   ● **S45.10**   Unspecified injury of brachial artery

     ● **S45.101**   Unspecified injury of brachial artery, right side A, A

     ● **S45.102**   Unspecified injury of brachial artery, left side A, A

     ● **S45.109**   Unspecified injury of brachial artery, unspecified side A, A

   ● **S45.11**   Laceration of brachial artery

     ● **S45.111**   Laceration of brachial artery, right side A, A

     ● **S45.112**   Laceration of brachial artery, left side A, A

     ● **S45.119**   Laceration of brachial artery, unspecified side A, A

   ● **S45.19**   Other specified injury of brachial artery

     ● **S45.191**   Other specified injury of brachial artery, right side A, A

     ● **S45.192**   Other specified injury of brachial artery, left side A, A

     ● **S45.199**   Other specified injury of brachial artery, unspecified side A, A

● Unacceptable First-Listed Diagnosis   ● Use Additional Character(s)   ■ Unspecified   **OGCR** Official Guidelines for Coding and Reporting

Complication\Comorbidity   Major C\C   Excludes 1   Excludes 2   Includes   Use additional   Code first   Code also

● S45.2 Injury of axillary or brachial vein
  ● S45.20 Unspecified injury of axillary or brachial vein
    ● ■ S45.201 Unspecified injury of axillary or brachial vein, right side A 🩺, A 🩺
    ● ■ S45.202 Unspecified injury of axillary or brachial vein, left side A 🩺, A 🩺
    ● ■ S45.209 Unspecified injury of axillary or brachial vein, unspecified side A 🩺, A 🩺
  ● S45.21 Laceration of axillary or brachial vein
    ● S45.211 Laceration of axillary or brachial vein, right side A 🩺, A 🩺
    ● S45.212 Laceration of axillary or brachial vein, left side A 🩺, A 🩺
    ● ■ S45.219 Laceration of axillary or brachial vein, unspecified side A 🩺, A 🩺
  ● S45.29 Other specified injury of axillary or brachial vein
    ● S45.291 Other specified injury of axillary or brachial vein, right side A 🩺, A 🩺
    ● S45.292 Other specified injury of axillary or brachial vein, left side A 🩺, A 🩺
    ● ■ S45.299 Other specified injury of axillary or brachial vein, unspecified side A 🩺, A 🩺
● S45.3 Injury of superficial vein at shoulder and upper arm level
  ● S45.30 Unspecified injury of superficial vein at shoulder and upper arm level
    ● ■ S45.301 Unspecified injury of superficial vein at shoulder and upper arm level, right side A 🩺, A 🩺
    ● ■ S45.302 Unspecified injury of superficial vein at shoulder and upper arm level, left side A 🩺, A 🩺
    ● ■ S45.309 Unspecified injury of superficial vein at shoulder and upper arm level, unspecified side A 🩺, A 🩺
  ● S45.31 Laceration of superficial vein at shoulder and upper arm level
    ● S45.311 Laceration of superficial vein at shoulder and upper arm level, right side A 🩺, A 🩺
    ● S45.312 Laceration of superficial vein at shoulder and upper arm level, left side A 🩺, A 🩺
    ● ■ S45.319 Laceration of superficial vein at shoulder and upper arm level, unspecified side A 🩺, A 🩺
  ● S45.39 Other specified injury of superficial vein at shoulder and upper arm level
    ● S45.391 Other specified injury of superficial vein at shoulder and upper arm level, right side A 🩺, A 🩺
    ● S45.392 Other specified injury of superficial vein at shoulder and upper arm level, left side A 🩺, A 🩺

    ● ■ S45.399 Other specified injury of superficial vein at shoulder and upper arm level, unspecified side A 🩺, A 🩺
● S45.8 Injury of other blood vessels at shoulder and upper arm level
  ● S45.80 Unspecified injury of other blood vessels at shoulder and upper arm level A 🩺
    ● ■ S45.801 Unspecified injury of other blood vessels at shoulder and upper arm level, right side A 🩺, A 🩺
    ● ■ S45.802 Unspecified injury of other blood vessels at shoulder and upper arm level, left side A 🩺, A 🩺
    ● ■ S45.809 Unspecified injury of other blood vessels at shoulder and upper arm level, unspecified side A 🩺, A 🩺
  ● S45.81 Laceration of other blood vessels at shoulder and upper arm level
    ● S45.811 Laceration of other blood vessels at shoulder and upper arm level, right side A 🩺, A 🩺
    ● S45.812 Laceration of other blood vessels at shoulder and upper arm level, left side A 🩺, A 🩺
    ● ■ S45.819 Laceration of other blood vessels at shoulder and upper arm level, unspecified side A 🩺, A 🩺
  ● S45.89 Other specified injury of other blood vessels at shoulder and upper arm level
    ● S45.891 Other specified injury of other blood vessels at shoulder and upper arm level, right side A 🩺, A 🩺
    ● S45.892 Other specified injury of other blood vessels at shoulder and upper arm level, left side A 🩺, A 🩺
    ● ■ S45.899 Other specified injury of other blood vessels at shoulder and upper arm level, unspecified side A 🩺, A 🩺
● S45.9 Injury of unspecified blood vessel at shoulder and upper arm level
  ● S45.90 Unspecified injury of unspecified blood vessel at shoulder and upper arm level
    ● ■ S45.901 Unspecified injury of unspecified blood vessel at shoulder and upper arm level, right side A 🩺, A 🩺
    ● ■ S45.902 Unspecified injury of unspecified blood vessel at shoulder and upper arm level, left side A 🩺, A 🩺
    ● ■ S45.909 Unspecified injury of unspecified blood vessel at shoulder and upper arm level, unspecified side A 🩺, A 🩺
  ● S45.91 Laceration of unspecified blood vessel at shoulder and upper arm level
    ● ■ S45.911 Laceration of unspecified blood vessel at shoulder and upper arm level, right side A 🩺, A 🩺

● Unacceptable First-Listed Diagnosis   ● Use Additional Character(s)   ■ Unspecified   OGCR Official Guidelines for Coding and Reporting

🩺 Complication\Comorbidity   🩺 Major C\C   [Excludes 1]   [Excludes 2]   Includes   Use additional   Code first   Code also

CHAPTER 19 (S00-T88)

1421

● ▪ S45.912 Laceration of unspecified blood vessel at shoulder and upper arm level, left side A 🬀, A 🬀

● ▪ S45.919 Laceration of unspecified blood vessel at shoulder and upper arm level, unspecified side A 🬀, A 🬀

● S45.99 Other specified injury of unspecified blood vessel at shoulder and upper arm level

● ▪ S45.991 Other specified injury of unspecified blood vessel at shoulder and upper arm level, right side A 🬀, A 🬀

● ▪ S45.992 Other specified injury of unspecified blood vessel at shoulder and upper arm level, left side A 🬀, A 🬀

● ▪ S45.999 Other specified injury of unspecified blood vessel at shoulder and upper arm level, unspecified side A 🬀, A 🬀

● S46 Injury of muscle, fascia and tendon at shoulder and upper arm level

Code also any associated open wound (S41.-)

Excludes2 injury of muscle, fascia and tendon at elbow (S56.-)
sprain of joints and ligaments of shoulder girdle (S43.9)

The appropriate 7th character is to be added to each code from category S46

A	initial encounter
D	subsequent encounter
S	sequela

● S46.0 Injury of muscle(s) and tendon(s) of the rotator cuff of shoulder

● S46.00 Unspecified injury of tendon of the rotator cuff of shoulder

● ▪ S46.001 Unspecified injury of muscle(s) and tendon(s) of the rotator cuff of right shoulder

● ▪ S46.002 Unspecified injury of muscle(s) and tendon(s) of the rotator cuff of left shoulder

● ▪ S46.009 Unspecified injury of muscle(s) and tendon(s) of the rotator cuff of unspecified shoulder

● S46.01 Strain of muscle(s) and tendon(s) of the rotator cuff of shoulder

● S46.011 Strain of muscle(s) and tendon(s) of the rotator cuff of right shoulder

● S46.012 Strain of muscle(s) and tendon(s) of the rotator cuff of left shoulder

● ▪ S46.019 Strain of muscle(s) and tendon(s) of the rotator cuff of unspecified shoulder

● S46.02 Laceration of muscle(s) and tendon(s) of the rotator cuff of shoulder

● S46.021 Laceration of muscle(s) and tendon(s) of the rotator cuff of right shoulder A 🬀

● S46.022 Laceration of muscle(s) and tendon(s) of the rotator cuff of left shoulder A 🬀

● ▪ S46.029 Laceration of muscle(s) and tendon(s) of the rotator cuff of unspecified shoulder A 🬀

● S46.09 Other injury of muscle(s) and tendon(s) of the rotator cuff of shoulder

● S46.091 Other injury of muscle(s) and tendon(s) of the rotator cuff of right shoulder

● S46.092 Other injury of muscle(s) and tendon(s) of the rotator cuff of left shoulder

● ▪ S46.099 Other injury of muscle(s) and tendon(s) of the rotator cuff of unspecified shoulder

● S46.1 Injury of muscle, fascia and tendon of long head of biceps

● S46.10 Unspecified injury of muscle, fascia and tendon of long head of biceps

● ▪ S46.101 Unspecified injury of muscle, fascia and tendon of long head of biceps, right arm

● ▪ S46.102 Unspecified injury of muscle, fascia and tendon of long head of biceps, left arm

● ▪ S46.109 Unspecified injury of muscle, fascia and tendon of long head of biceps, unspecified arm

● S46.11 Strain of muscle, fascia and tendon of long head of biceps

● S46.111 Strain of muscle, fascia and tendon of long head of biceps, right arm

● S46.112 Strain of muscle, fascia and tendon of long head of biceps, left arm

● ▪ S46.119 Strain of muscle, fascia and tendon of long head of biceps, unspecified arm

● S46.12 Laceration of muscle, fascia and tendon of long head of biceps

● S46.121 Laceration of muscle, fascia and tendon of long head of biceps, right arm A 🬀

● S46.122 Laceration of muscle, fascia and tendon of long head of biceps, left arm A 🬀

● ▪ S46.129 Laceration of muscle, fascia and tendon of long head of biceps, unspecified arm A 🬀

● S46.19 Other injury of muscle, fascia and tendon of long head of biceps

● S46.191 Other injury of muscle, fascia and tendon of long head of biceps, right arm

● S46.192 Other injury of muscle, fascia and tendon of long head of biceps, left arm

● ▪ S46.199 Other injury of muscle, fascia and tendon of long head of biceps, unspecified arm

CHAPTER 19 (S00-T88)

● S46.2   Injury of muscle, fascia and tendon of other parts of biceps

  ● S46.20   Unspecified injury of muscle, fascia and tendon of other parts of biceps

    ● ■ S46.201   Unspecified injury of muscle, fascia and tendon of other parts of biceps, right arm

    ● ■ S46.202   Unspecified injury of muscle, fascia and tendon of other parts of biceps, left arm

    ● ■ S46.209   Unspecified injury of muscle, fascia and tendon of other parts of biceps, unspecified arm

  ● S46.21   Strain of muscle, fascia and tendon of other parts of biceps

    ● S46.211   Strain of muscle, fascia and tendon of other parts of biceps, right arm

    ● S46.212   Strain of muscle, fascia and tendon of other parts of biceps, left arm

    ● ■ S46.219   Strain of muscle, fascia and tendon of other parts of biceps, unspecified arm

  ● S46.22   Laceration of muscle, fascia and tendon of other parts of biceps

    ● S46.221   Laceration of muscle, fascia and tendon of other parts of biceps, right arm A 🐾

    ● S46.222   Laceration of muscle, fascia and tendon of other parts of biceps, left arm A 🐾

    ● ■ S46.229   Laceration of muscle, fascia and tendon of other parts of biceps, unspecified arm A 🐾

  ● S46.29   Other injury of muscle, fascia and tendon of other parts of biceps

    ● S46.291   Other injury of muscle, fascia and tendon of other parts of biceps, right arm A 🐾

    ● S46.292   Other injury of muscle, fascia and tendon of other parts of biceps, left arm A 🐾

    ● ■ S46.299   Other injury of muscle, fascia and tendon of other parts of biceps, unspecified arm A 🐾

● S46.3   Injury of muscle, fascia and tendon of triceps

  ● S46.30   Unspecified injury of muscle, fascia and tendon of triceps

    ● ■ S46.301   Unspecified injury of muscle, fascia and tendon of triceps, right arm

    ● ■ S46.302   Unspecified injury of muscle, fascia and tendon of triceps, left arm

    ● ■ S46.309   Unspecified injury of muscle, fascia and tendon of triceps, unspecified arm

  ● S46.31   Strain of muscle, fascia and tendon of triceps

    ● S46.311   Strain of muscle, fascia and tendon of triceps, right arm

    ● S46.312   Strain of muscle, fascia and tendon of triceps, left arm

    ● ■ S46.319   Strain of muscle, fascia and tendon of triceps, unspecified arm

  ● S46.32   Laceration of muscle, fascia and tendon of triceps

    ● S46.321   Laceration of muscle, fascia and tendon of triceps, right arm A 🐾

    ● S46.322   Laceration of muscle, fascia and tendon of triceps, left arm A 🐾

    ● ■ S46.329   Laceration of muscle, fascia and tendon of triceps, unspecified arm A 🐾

  ● S46.39   Other injury of muscle, fascia and tendon of triceps

    ● S46.391   Other injury of muscle, fascia and tendon of triceps, right arm

    ● S46.392   Other injury of muscle, fascia and tendon of triceps, left arm

    ● ■ S46.399   Other injury of muscle, fascia and tendon of triceps, unspecified arm

● S46.8   Injury of other muscles, fascia and tendons at shoulder and upper arm level

  ● S46.80   Unspecified injury of other muscles, fascia and tendons at shoulder and upper arm level

    ● ■ S46.801   Unspecified injury of other muscles, fascia and tendons at shoulder and upper arm level, right arm

    ● ■ S46.802   Unspecified injury of other muscles, fascia and tendons at shoulder and upper arm level, left arm

    ● ■ S46.809   Unspecified injury of other muscles, fascia and tendons at shoulder and upper arm level, unspecified arm

  ● S46.81   Strain of other muscles, fascia and tendons at shoulder and upper arm level

    ● S46.811   Strain of other muscles, fascia and tendons at shoulder and upper arm level, right arm

    ● S46.812   Strain of other muscles, fascia and tendons at shoulder and upper arm level, left arm

    ● ■ S46.819   Strain of other muscles, fascia and tendons at shoulder and upper arm level, unspecified arm

  ● S46.82   Laceration of other muscles, fascia and tendons at shoulder and upper arm level

    ● S46.821   Laceration of other muscles, fascia and tendons at shoulder and upper arm level, right arm A 🐾

    ● S46.822   Laceration of other muscles, fascia and tendons at shoulder and upper arm level, left arm A 🐾

    ● ■ S46.829   Laceration of other muscles, fascia and tendons at shoulder and upper arm level, unspecified arm A 🐾

● Unacceptable First-Listed Diagnosis   ● Use Additional Character(s)   ■ Unspecified   OGCR Official Guidelines for Coding and Reporting

🐾 Complication\Comorbidity   🐾 Major C\C   Excludes 1   Excludes 2   Includes   Use additional   Code first   Code also

1423

CHAPTER 19 (S00-T88)

- S46.89 Other injury of other muscles, fascia and tendons at shoulder and upper arm level
  - S46.891 Injury of other muscles, fascia and tendons at shoulder and upper arm level, right arm
  - S46.892 Injury of other muscles, fascia and tendons at shoulder and upper arm level, left arm
  - ■S46.899 Injury of other muscles, fascia and tendons at shoulder and upper arm level, unspecified arm
- S46.9 Injury of unspecified muscle, fascia and tendon at shoulder and upper arm level
  - S46.90 Unspecified injury of unspecified muscle, fascia and tendon at shoulder and upper arm level
    - ■S46.901 Unspecified injury of unspecified muscle, fascia and tendon at shoulder and upper arm level, right arm
    - ■S46.902 Unspecified injury of unspecified muscle, fascia and tendon at shoulder and upper arm level, left arm
    - ■S46.909 Unspecified injury of unspecified muscle, fascia and tendon at shoulder and upper arm level, unspecified arm
  - S46.91 Strain of unspecified muscle, fascia and tendon at shoulder and upper arm level
    - ■S46.911 Strain of unspecified muscle, fascia and tendon at shoulder and upper arm level, right arm
    - ■S46.912 Strain of unspecified muscle, fascia and tendon at shoulder and upper arm level, left arm
    - ■S46.919 Strain of unspecified muscle, fascia and tendon at shoulder and upper arm level, unspecified arm
  - S46.92 Laceration of unspecified muscle, fascia and tendon at shoulder and upper arm level
    - ■S46.921 Laceration of unspecified muscle, fascia and tendon at shoulder and upper arm level, right arm A 🐾
    - ■S46.922 Laceration of unspecified muscle, fascia and tendon at shoulder and upper arm level, left arm A 🐾
    - ■S46.929 Laceration of unspecified muscle, fascia and tendon at shoulder and upper arm level, unspecified arm A 🐾
  - S46.99 Other injury of unspecified muscle, fascia and tendon at shoulder and upper arm level
    - ■S46.991 Other injury of unspecified muscle, fascia and tendon at shoulder and upper arm, right arm
    - ■S46.992 Other injury of unspecified muscle, fascia and tendon at shoulder and upper arm level, left arm
    - ■S46.999 Other injury of unspecified muscle, fascia and tendon at shoulder and upper arm level, unspecified arm

- S47 Crushing injury of shoulder and upper arm

  Use additional code for all associated injuries

  Excludes2 crushing injury of elbow (S57.0-)

  The appropriate 7th character is to be added to each code from category S47

A	initial encounter
D	subsequent encounter
S	sequela

  - S47.1 Crushing injury of right shoulder and upper arm
  - S47.2 Crushing injury of left shoulder and upper arm
  - ■S47.9 Crushing injury of shoulder and upper arm, unspecified arm

- S48 Traumatic amputation of shoulder and upper arm

  An amputation not identified as partial or complete should be coded to complete

  Excludes1 traumatic amputation at elbow level (S58.0)

  The appropriate 7th character is to be added to each code from category S48

A	initial encounter
D	subsequent encounter
S	sequela

  - S48.0 Traumatic amputation at shoulder joint
    - S48.01 Complete traumatic amputation at shoulder joint
      - S48.011 Complete traumatic amputation at right shoulder joint A 🐾
      - S48.012 Complete traumatic amputation at left shoulder joint A 🐾
      - ■S48.019 Complete traumatic amputation at unspecified shoulder joint A 🐾
    - S48.02 Partial traumatic amputation at shoulder joint
      - S48.021 Partial traumatic amputation at right shoulder joint A 🐾
      - S48.022 Partial traumatic amputation at left shoulder joint A 🐾
      - ■S48.029 Partial traumatic amputation at unspecified shoulder joint A 🐾
  - S48.1 Traumatic amputation at level between shoulder and elbow
    - S48.11 Complete traumatic amputation at level between shoulder and elbow
      - S48.111 Complete traumatic amputation at level between right shoulder and elbow A 🐾
      - S48.112 Complete traumatic amputation at level between left shoulder and elbow A 🐾
      - ■S48.119 Complete traumatic amputation at level between unspecified shoulder and elbow A 🐾
    - S48.12 Partial traumatic amputation at level between shoulder and elbow
      - S48.121 Partial traumatic amputation at level between right shoulder and elbow A 🐾
      - S48.122 Partial traumatic amputation at level between left shoulder and elbow A 🐾
      - ■S48.129 Partial traumatic amputation at level between unspecified shoulder and elbow A 🐾

- Unacceptable First-Listed Diagnosis   ● Use Additional Character(s)   ■ Unspecified   **OGCR** Official Guidelines for Coding and Reporting
🐾 Complication\Comorbidity   🐾 Major C\C   Excludes 1   Excludes 2   Includes   Use additional   Code first   Code also

Item 19-3   **SALTER-HARRIS TYPE 1:** epiphysis is completely separated from end of bone, or metaphysic growth plate remains attached to epiphysis

SALTER-HARRIS TYPE 2: epiphysis and growth plate are partially separated from metaphysis, which is cracked—most common type

SALTER-HARRIS TYPE 3: fracture occurring through epiphysis and separates part of epiphysis and growth plate from metaphysis fracture, usually at distal end of tibia

SALTER-HARRIS TYPE 4: fracture runs through epiphysis, across growth plate, into metaphysic, surgery is required to restore joint surface to normal and align growth plate

- ● **S48.9**   Traumatic amputation of shoulder and upper arm, level unspecified
  - ● **S48.91**   Complete traumatic amputation of shoulder and upper arm, level unspecified
    - ● ▪ **S48.911**   Complete traumatic amputation of right shoulder and upper arm, level unspecified A 🔿
    - ● ▪ **S48.912**   Complete traumatic amputation of left shoulder and upper arm, level unspecified A 🔿
    - ● ▪ **S48.919**   Complete traumatic amputation of unspecified shoulder and upper arm, level unspecified A 🔿
  - ● **S48.92**   Partial traumatic amputation of shoulder and upper arm, level unspecified
    - ● ▪ **S48.921**   Partial traumatic amputation of right shoulder and upper arm, level unspecified A 🔿
    - ● ▪ **S48.922**   Partial traumatic amputation of left shoulder and upper arm, level unspecified A 🔿
    - ● ▪ **S48.929**   Partial traumatic amputation of unspecified shoulder and upper arm, level unspecified A 🔿

- ● **S49**   Other and unspecified injuries of shoulder and upper arm

  The appropriate 7th character is to be added to each code from subcategories S49.0 and S49.1

A	initial encounter for closed fracture
D	subsequent encounter for fracture with routine healing
G	subsequent encounter for fracture with delayed healing
K	subsequent encounter for fracture with nonunion
P	subsequent encounter for fracture with malunion
S	sequela

  - ● **S49.0**   Physeal fracture of upper end of humerus
    - ● **S49.00**   Unspecified physeal fracture of upper end of humerus
      - ● ▪ **S49.001**   Unspecified physeal fracture of upper end of humerus, right arm A, K, P 🔿
      - ● ▪ **S49.002**   Unspecified physeal fracture of upper end of humerus, left arm A, K, P 🔿
      - ● ▪ **S49.009**   Unspecified physeal fracture of upper end of humerus, unspecified arm A, K, P 🔿

  - ● **S49.01**   Salter-Harris Type I physeal fracture of upper end of humerus
    - ● **S49.011**   Salter-Harris Type I physeal fracture of upper end of humerus, right arm A, K, P 🔿
    - ● **S49.012**   Salter-Harris Type I physeal fracture of upper end of humerus, left arm A, K, P 🔿
    - ● ▪ **S49.019**   Salter-Harris Type I physeal fracture of upper end of humerus, unspecified arm A, K, P 🔿
  - ● **S49.02**   Salter-Harris Type II physeal fracture of upper end of humerus
    - ● **S49.021**   Salter-Harris Type II physeal fracture of upper end of humerus, right arm A, K, P 🔿
    - ● **S49.022**   Salter-Harris Type II physeal fracture of upper end of humerus, left arm A, K, P 🔿
    - ● ▪ **S49.029**   Salter-Harris Type II physeal fracture of upper end of humerus, unspecified arm A, K, P 🔿
  - ● **S49.03**   Salter-Harris Type III physeal fracture of upper end of humerus
    - ● **S49.031**   Salter Harris Type III physeal fracture of upper end of humerus, right arm A, K, P 🔿
    - ● **S49.032**   Salter Harris Type III physeal fracture of upper end of humerus, left arm A, K, P 🔿
    - ● ▪ **S49.039**   Salter Harris Type III physeal fracture of upper end of humerus, unspecified arm A, K, P 🔿
  - ● **S49.04**   Salter-Harris Type IV physeal fracture of upper end of humerus
    - ● **S49.041**   Salter-Harris Type IV physeal fracture of upper end of humerus, right arm A, K, P 🔿
    - ● **S49.042**   Salter-Harris Type IV physeal fracture of upper end of humerus, left arm A, K, P 🔿
    - ● ▪ **S49.049**   Salter-Harris Type IV physeal fracture of upper end of humerus, unspecified arm A, K, P 🔿
  - ● **S49.09**   Other physeal fracture of upper end of humerus
    - ● **S49.091**   Other physeal fracture of upper end of humerus, right arm A, K, P 🔿
    - ● **S49.092**   Other physeal fracture of upper end of humerus, left arm A, K, P 🔿
    - ● ▪ **S49.099**   Other physeal fracture of upper end of humerus, unspecified arm A, K, P 🔿
  - ● **S49.1**   Physeal fracture of lower end of humerus
    - ● **S49.10**   Unspecified physeal fracture of lower end of humerus
      - ● ▪ **S49.101**   Unspecified physeal fracture of lower end of humerus, right arm A, K, P 🔿
      - ● ▪ **S49.102**   Unspecified physeal fracture of lower end of humerus, left arm A, K, P 🔿

● Unacceptable First-Listed Diagnosis   ● Use Additional Character(s)   ▪ Unspecified   **OGCR** Official Guidelines for Coding and Reporting

🔿 Complication\Comorbidity   🔿 Major C\C   Excludes 1   Excludes 2   Includes   Use additional   Code first   Code also

CHAPTER 19 (S00-T88)

1425

● ■ S49.109   Unspecified physeal fracture
              of lower end of humerus,
              unspecified arm A, K, P ⓒ

● S49.11   Salter-Harris Type I physeal fracture of
           lower end of humerus

  ● S49.111   Salter-Harris Type I physeal
             fracture of lower end of humerus,
             right arm A, K, P ⓒ

  ● S49.112   Salter-Harris Type I physeal
             fracture of lower end of humerus,
             left arm A, K, P ⓒ

● ■ S49.119   Salter-Harris Type I physeal
             fracture of lower end of humerus,
             unspecified arm A, K, P ⓒ

● S49.12   Salter-Harris Type II physeal fracture of
           lower end of humerus

  ● S49.121   Salter-Harris Type II physeal
             fracture of lower end of humerus,
             right arm A, K, P ⓒ

  ● S49.122   Salter-Harris Type II physeal
             fracture of lower end of humerus,
             left arm A, K, P ⓒ

● ■ S49.129   Salter-Harris Type II physeal
             fracture of lower end of humerus,
             unspecified arm A, K, P ⓒ

● S49.13   Salter Harris Type III physeal fracture of
           lower end of humerus

  ● S49.131   Salter Harris Type III physeal
             fracture of lower end of humerus,
             right arm A, K, P ⓒ

  ● S49.132   Salter Harris Type III physeal
             fracture of lower end of humerus,
             left arm A, K, P ⓒ

● ■ S49.139   Salter Harris Type III physeal
             fracture of lower end of humerus,
             unspecified arm A, K, P ⓒ

● S49.14   Salter-Harris Type IV physeal fracture of
           lower end of humerus

  ● S49.141   Salter-Harris Type IV physeal
             fracture of lower end of humerus,
             right arm A, K, P ⓒ

  ● S49.142   Salter-Harris Type IV physeal
             fracture of lower end of humerus,
             left arm A, K, P ⓒ

● ■ S49.149   Salter-Harris Type IV physeal
             fracture of lower end of humerus,
             unspecified arm A, K, P ⓒ

● S49.19   Other physeal fracture of lower end of
           humerus

  ● S49.191   Other physeal fracture of lower
             end of humerus, right arm
             A, K, P ⓒ

  ● S49.192   Other physeal fracture of lower
             end of humerus, left arm A, K, P ⓒ

  ● S49.199   Other physeal fracture of lower
             end of humerus, unspecified arm
             A, K, P ⓒ

The appropriate 7th character is to be added to
    each code from subcategories S49.8 and S49.9

    ┌─────────────────────────────┐
    │ A   initial encounter   │
    │ D   subsequent encounter   │
    │ S   sequela   │
    └─────────────────────────────┘

● S49.8   Other specified injuries of shoulder and upper arm

  ● ■ S49.80   Other specified injuries of shoulder and
             upper arm, unspecified arm

  ● S49.81   Other specified injuries of right shoulder
             and upper arm

  ● S49.82   Other specified injuries of left shoulder
             and upper arm

● S49.9   Unspecified injury of shoulder and upper arm

  ● ■ S49.90   Unspecified injury of shoulder and upper
             arm, unspecified arm

  ● ■ S49.91   Unspecified injury of right shoulder and
             upper arm

  ● ■ S49.92   Unspecified injury of left shoulder and
             upper arm

INJURIES TO THE ELBOW AND FOREARM (S50-S59)

┌──────────┐
│ Excludes2 │   burns and corrosions (T20-T32)
└──────────┘   frostbite (T33-T34)
               injuries of wrist and hand (S60-S69)
               insect bite or sting, venomous (T63.4)

● S50   Superficial injury of elbow and forearm

    ┌──────────┐
    │ Excludes2 │   superficial injury of wrist and hand (S60.-)
    └──────────┘

    The appropriate 7th character is to be added to each code
        from category S50

    ┌─────────────────────────────┐
    │ A   initial encounter   │
    │ D   subsequent encounter   │
    │ S   sequela   │
    └─────────────────────────────┘

● S50.0   Contusion of elbow

  ● ■ S50.00   Contusion of unspecified elbow

  ● S50.01   Contusion of right elbow

  ● S50.02   Contusion of left elbow

● S50.1   Contusion of forearm

  ● ■ S50.10   Contusion of unspecified forearm

  ● S50.11   Contusion of right forearm

  ● S50.12   Contusion of left forearm

● S50.3   Other superficial injuries of elbow

  ● S50.31   Abrasion of elbow

    ● S50.311   Abrasion of right elbow

    ● S50.312   Abrasion of left elbow

  ● ■ S50.319   Abrasion of unspecified elbow

  ● S50.32   Blister (nonthermal) of elbow

    ● S50.321   Blister (nonthermal) of right elbow

    ● S50.322   Blister (nonthermal) of left elbow

  ● ■ S50.329   Blister (nonthermal) of
             unspecified elbow

  ● S50.34   External constriction of elbow

    ● S50.341   External constriction of right elbow

    ● S50.342   External constriction of left elbow

  ● ■ S50.349   External constriction of
             unspecified elbow

  ● S50.35   Superficial foreign body of elbow
             Splinter in the elbow

    ● S50.351   Superficial foreign body of right
             elbow

    ● S50.352   Superficial foreign body of left
             elbow

  ● ■ S50.359   Superficial foreign body of
             unspecified elbow

● Unacceptable First-Listed Diagnosis   ● Use Additional Character(s)   ■ Unspecified   **OGCR** Official Guidelines for Coding and Reporting
ⓒ Complication\Comorbidity   ⓒ Major C\C   Excludes 1   Excludes 2   Includes   Use additional   Code first   Code also

● S50.36   Insect bite (nonvenomous) of elbow
- ● S50.361   Insect bite (nonvenomous) of right elbow
- ● S50.362   Insect bite (nonvenomous) of left elbow
- ● ▨ S50.369   Insect bite (nonvenomous) of unspecified elbow

● S50.37   Other superficial bite of elbow

Excludes1   open bite of elbow (S51.04)

- ● S50.371   Other superficial bite of right elbow
- ● S50.372   Other superficial bite of left elbow
- ● ▨ S50.379   Other superficial bite of unspecified elbow

● S50.8   Other superficial injuries of forearm
- ● S50.81   Abrasion of forearm
  - ● S50.811   Abrasion of right forearm
  - ● S50.812   Abrasion of left forearm
  - ● ▨ S50.819   Abrasion of unspecified forearm
- ● S50.82   Blister (nonthermal) of forearm
  - ● S50.821   Blister (nonthermal) of right forearm
  - ● S50.822   Blister (nonthermal) of left forearm
  - ● ▨ S50.829   Blister (nonthermal) of unspecified forearm
- ● S50.84   External constriction of forearm
  - ● S50.841   External constriction of right forearm
  - ● S50.842   External constriction of left forearm
  - ● ▨ S50.849   External constriction of unspecified forearm
- ● S50.85   Superficial foreign body of forearm
  Splinter in the forearm
  - ● S50.851   Superficial foreign body of right forearm
  - ● S50.852   Superficial foreign body of left forearm
  - ● ▨ S50.859   Superficial foreign body of unspecified forearm
- ● S50.86   Insect bite (nonvenomous) of forearm
  - ● S50.861   Insect bite (nonvenomous) of right forearm
  - ● S50.862   Insect bite (nonvenomous) of left forearm
  - ● ▨ S50.869   Insect bite (nonvenomous) of unspecified forearm
- ● S50.87   Other superficial bite of forearm

  Excludes1   open bite of forearm (S51.84)

  - ● S50.871   Other superficial bite of right forearm
  - ● S50.872   Other superficial bite of left forearm
  - ● ▨ S50.879   Other superficial bite of unspecified forearm

● S50.9   Unspecified superficial injury of elbow and forearm
- ● S50.90   Unspecified superficial injury of elbow
  - ● ▨ S50.901   Unspecified superficial injury of right elbow
  - ● ▨ S50.902   Unspecified superficial injury of left elbow
  - ● ▨ S50.909   Unspecified superficial injury of unspecified elbow
- ● S50.91   Unspecified superficial injury of forearm
  - ● ▨ S50.911   Unspecified superficial injury of right forearm
  - ● ▨ S50.912   Unspecified superficial injury of left forearm
  - ● ▨ S50.919   Unspecified superficial injury of unspecified forearm

● S51   Open wound of elbow and forearm
  Code also any associated wound infection

Excludes1   open fracture of elbow and forearm (S52.- with open fracture 7th character)
traumatic amputation of elbow and forearm (S58.-)

Excludes2   open wound of wrist and hand (S61.-)

The appropriate 7th character is to be added to each code from category S51

A   initial encounter
D   subsequent encounter
S   sequela

● S51.0   Open wound of elbow
- ● S51.00   Unspecified open wound of elbow
  - ● ▨ S51.001   Unspecified open wound of right elbow
  - ● ▨ S51.002   Unspecified open wound of left elbow
  - ● ▨ S51.009   Unspecified open wound of unspecified elbow

    Open wound of elbow NOS

- ● S51.01   Laceration without foreign body of elbow
  - ● S51.011   Laceration without foreign body of right elbow
  - ● S51.012   Laceration without foreign body of left elbow
  - ● ▨ S51.019   Laceration without foreign body of unspecified elbow
- ● S51.02   Laceration with foreign body of elbow
  - ● S51.021   Laceration with foreign body of right elbow
  - ● S51.022   Laceration with foreign body of left elbow
  - ● ▨ S51.029   Laceration with foreign body of unspecified elbow
- ● S51.03   Puncture wound without foreign body of elbow
  - ● S51.031   Puncture wound without foreign body of right elbow
  - ● S51.032   Puncture wound without foreign body of left elbow
  - ● ▨ S51.039   Puncture wound without foreign body of unspecified elbow

CHAPTER 19 (S00-T88)

● Unacceptable First-Listed Diagnosis   ● Use Additional Character(s)   ▨ Unspecified   **OGCR** Official Guidelines for Coding and Reporting

 Complication\Comorbidity   Major C\C   Excludes 1   Excludes 2   Includes   Use additional   Code first   Code also

1427

- ● S51.04 **Puncture wound with foreign body of elbow**
  - ● S51.041 **Puncture wound with foreign body of right elbow**
  - ● S51.042 **Puncture wound with foreign body of left elbow**
  - ● ■ S51.049 **Puncture wound with foreign body of unspecified elbow**
- ● S51.05 **Open bite of elbow**
  Bite of elbow NOS
  - **Excludes1**   superficial bite of elbow (S50.36, S50.37)
  - ● S51.051 **Open bite, right elbow**
  - ● S51.052 **Open bite, left elbow**
  - ● ■ S51.059 **Open bite, unspecified elbow**
- ● S51.8 **Open wound of forearm**
  - **Excludes2**   open wound of elbow (51.0-)
  - ● S51.80 **Unspecified open wound of forearm**
    - ● ■ S51.801 **Unspecified open wound of right forearm**
    - ● ■ S51.802 **Unspecified open wound of left forearm**
    - ● ■ S51.809 **Unspecified open wound of unspecified forearm**
      Open wound of forearm NOS
  - ● S51.81 **Laceration without foreign body of forearm**
    - ● S51.811 **Laceration without foreign body of right forearm**
    - ● S51.812 **Laceration without foreign body of left forearm**
    - ● ■ S51.819 **Laceration without foreign body of unspecified forearm**
  - ● S51.82 **Laceration with foreign body of forearm**
    - ● S51.821 **Laceration with foreign body of right forearm**
    - ● S51.822 **Laceration with foreign body of left forearm**
    - ● ■ S51.829 **Laceration with foreign body of unspecified forearm**
  - ● S51.83 **Puncture wound without foreign body of forearm**
    - ● S51.831 **Puncture wound without foreign body of right forearm**
    - ● S51.832 **Puncture wound without foreign body of left forearm**
    - ● ■ S51.839 **Puncture wound without foreign body of unspecified forearm**
  - ● S51.84 **Puncture wound with foreign body of forearm**
    - ● S51.841 **Puncture wound with foreign body of right forearm**
    - ● S51.842 **Puncture wound with foreign body of left forearm**
    - ● ■ S51.849 **Puncture wound with foreign body of unspecified forearm**

- ● S51.85 **Open bite of forearm**
  Bite of forearm NOS
  - **Excludes1**   superficial bite of forearm (S50.86, S50.87)
  - ● S51.851 **Open bite of right forearm**
  - ● S51.852 **Open bite of left forearm**
  - ● ■ S51.859 **Open bite of unspecified forearm**
- ● S52 **Fracture of forearm**
  A fracture not identified as displaced or nondisplaced should be coded to displaced
  - **Excludes1**   traumatic amputation of forearm (S58.-)
  - **Excludes2**   fracture at wrist and hand level (S62.-)
  The appropriate 7th character is to be added to each code from category S52
  A fracture not designated as open or closed should be coded to closed
  The open fracture designations are based on the Gustilo open fracture classification

A	initial encounter for closed fracture
B	initial encounter for open fracture type I or II initial encounter for open fracture NOS
C	initial encounter for open fracture type IIIA, IIIB, or IIIC
D	subsequent encounter for closed fracture with routine healing
E	subsequent encounter for open fracture type I or II with routine healing
F	subsequent encounter for open fracture type IIIA, IIIB, or IIIC with routine healing
G	subsequent encounter for closed fracture with delayed healing
H	subsequent encounter for open fracture type I or II with delayed healing
J	subsequent encounter for open fracture type IIIA, IIIB, or IIIC with delayed healing
K	subsequent encounter for closed fracture with nonunion
M	subsequent encounter for open fracture type I or II with nonunion
N	subsequent encounter for open fracture type IIIA, IIIB, or IIIC with nonunion
P	subsequent encounter for closed fracture with malunion
Q	subsequent encounter for open fracture type I or II with malunion
R	subsequent encounter for open fracture type IIIA, IIIB, or IIIC with malunion
S	sequela

  - ● S52.0 **Fracture of upper end of ulna**
    Fracture of proximal end of ulna
    - **Excludes2**   fracture of elbow NOS (S42.40-) fractures of shaft of ulna (S52.2-)
    - ● S52.00 **Unspecified fracture of upper end of ulna**
      - ● ■ S52.001 **Unspecified fracture of upper end of right ulna** K, M, N, P, Q, R 🐾, B, C 🐾
      - ● ■ S52.002 **Unspecified fracture of upper end of left ulna** K, M, N, P, Q, R 🐾, B, C 🐾
      - ● ■ S52.009 **Unspecified fracture of upper end of unspecified ulna** K, M, N, P, Q, R 🐾, B, C 🐾

1428

● Unacceptable First-Listed Diagnosis   ● Use Additional Character(s)   ■ Unspecified   **OGCR** Official Guidelines for Coding and Reporting
🐾 Complication\Comorbidity   🐾 Major C\C   Excludes 1   Excludes 2   Includes   Use additional   Code first   Code also

● **S52.01**   Torus fracture of upper end of ulna

> **Note:** Open fracture 7th characters do not apply to codes under subcategory S52.01.

   ● S52.011   Torus fracture of upper end of right ulna K, P 🦠

   ● S52.012   Torus fracture of upper end of left ulna K, P 🦠

   ● ▪ S52.019   Torus fracture of upper end of unspecified ulna K, P 🦠

● **S52.02**   Fracture of olecranon process without intraarticular extension of ulna

   ● S52.021   Displaced fracture of olecranon process without intraarticular extension of right ulna K, M, P, Q, R 🦠, B, C 🦠

   ● S52.022   Displaced fracture of olecranon process without intraarticular extension of left ulna K, M, P, Q, R 🦠, B, C 🦠

   ● ▪ S52.023   Displaced fracture of olecranon process without intraarticular extension of unspecified ulna K, M, P, Q, R 🦠, B, C 🦠

   ● S52.024   Nondisplaced fracture of olecranon process without intraarticular extension of right ulna K, M, P, Q, R 🦠, B, C 🦠

   ● S52.025   Nondisplaced fracture of olecranon process without intraarticular extension of left ulna K, M, P, Q, R 🦠, B, C 🦠

   ● ▪ S52.026   Nondisplaced fracture of olecranon process without intraarticular extension of unspecified ulna K, M, P, Q, R 🦠, B, C 🦠

● **S52.03**   Fracture of olecranon process with intraarticular extension of ulna

   ● S52.031   Displaced fracture of olecranon process with intraarticular extension of right ulna K, M, P, Q, R 🦠, B, C 🦠

   ● S52.032   Displaced fracture of olecranon process with intraarticular extension of left ulna K, M, P, Q, R 🦠, B, C 🦠

   ● ▪ S52.033   Displaced fracture of olecranon process with intraarticular extension of unspecified ulna K, M, P, Q, R 🦠, B, C 🦠

   ● S52.034   Nondisplaced fracture of olecranon process with intraarticular extension of right ulna K, M, P, Q, R 🦠, B, C 🦠

   ● S52.035   Nondisplaced fracture of olecranon process with intraarticular extension of left ulna K, M, P, Q, R 🦠, B, C 🦠

   ● ▪ S52.036   Nondisplaced fracture of olecranon process with intraarticular extension of unspecified ulna K, M, P, Q, R 🦠, B, C 🦠

● **S52.04**   Fracture of coronoid process of ulna

   ● S52.041   Displaced fracture of coronoid process of right ulna K, M, P, Q, R 🦠, B, C 🦠

   ● S52.042   Displaced fracture of coronoid process of left ulna K, M, P, Q, R 🦠, B, C 🦠

   ● ▪ S52.043   Displaced fracture of coronoid process of unspecified ulna K, M, P, Q, R 🦠, B, C 🦠

   ● S52.044   Nondisplaced fracture of coronoid process of right ulna K, M, P, Q, R 🦠, B, C 🦠

   ● S52.045   Nondisplaced fracture of coronoid process of left ulna K, M, P, Q, R 🦠, B, C 🦠

   ● ▪ S52.046   Nondisplaced fracture of coronoid process of unspecified ulna K, M, P, Q, R 🦠, B, C 🦠

● **S52.09**   Other fracture of upper end of ulna

   ● S52.091   Other fracture of upper end of right ulna K, M, P, Q, R 🦠, B, C 🦠

   ● S52.092   Other fracture of upper end of left ulna K, M, P, Q, R 🦠, B, C 🦠

   ● ▪ S52.099   Other fracture of upper end of unspecified ulna K, M, P, Q, R 🦠, B, C 🦠

● **S52.1**   Fracture of upper end of radius

> Fracture of proximal end of radius

> **Excludes2**   physeal fractures of upper end of radius (S59.2-)
> fracture of shaft of radius (S52.3-)

● **S52.10**   Unspecified fracture of upper end of radius

   ● ▪ S52.101   Unspecified fracture of upper end of right radius K, M, N, P, Q, R 🦠, B, C 🦠

   ● ▪ S52.102   Unspecified fracture of upper end of left radius K, M, N, P, Q, R 🦠, B, C 🦠

   ● ▪ S52.109   Unspecified fracture of upper end of unspecified radius K, M, N, P, Q, R 🦠, B, C 🦠

● **S52.11**   Torus fracture of upper end of radius

> **Note:** Open fracture 7th characters do not apply to codes under subcategory.

   ● S52.111   Torus fracture of upper end of right radius K, P 🦠

   ● S52.112   Torus fracture of upper end of left radius K, P 🦠

   ● ▪ S52.119   Torus fracture of upper end of unspecified radius K, P 🦠

● **S52.12**   Fracture of head of radius

   ● S52.121   Displaced fracture of head of right radius K, M, N, P, Q, R 🦠, B, C 🦠

   ● S52.122   Displaced fracture of head of left radius K, M, N, P, Q, R 🦠, B, C 🦠

   ● ▪ S52.123   Displaced fracture of head of unspecified radius K, M, N, P, Q, R 🦠, B, C 🦠

● Unacceptable First-Listed Diagnosis   ● Use Additional Character(s)   ▪ Unspecified   **OGCR** Official Guidelines for Coding and Reporting

🦠 Complication\Comorbidity 🦠 Major C\C Excludes 1 Excludes 2 Includes Use additional Code first Code also

1429

● ● S52.124 Nondisplaced fracture of head of right radius K, M, N, P, Q, R 🦠, B, C 🦠

● ● S52.125 Nondisplaced fracture of head of left radius K, M, N, P, Q, R 🦠, B, C 🦠

● ■ S52.126 Nondisplaced fracture of head of unspecified radius K, M, N, P, Q, R 🦠, B, C 🦠

● S52.13 Fracture of neck of radius

● ● S52.131 Displaced fracture of neck of right radius K, M, N, P, Q, R 🦠, B, C 🦠

● ● S52.132 Displaced fracture of neck of left radius K, M, N, P, Q, R 🦠, B, C 🦠

● ■ S52.133 Displaced fracture of neck of unspecified radius K, M, N, P, Q, R 🦠, B, C 🦠

● ● S52.134 Nondisplaced fracture of neck of right radius K, M, N, P, Q, R 🦠, B, C 🦠

● ● S52.135 Nondisplaced fracture of neck of left radius K, M, N, P, Q, R 🦠, B, C 🦠

● ■ S52.136 Nondisplaced fracture of neck of unspecified radius K, M, N, P, Q, R 🦠, B, C 🦠

● S52.18 Other fracture of upper end of radius

● ● S52.181 Other fracture of upper end of right radius K, M, N, P, Q, R 🦠, B, C, H, J 🦠

● ● S52.182 Other fracture of of upper end of left radius K, M, N, P, Q, R 🦠, B, C, H, J 🦠

● ■ S52.189 Other fracture of of upper end of unspecified radius K, M, N, P, Q, R 🦠, B, C, H, J 🦠

● S52.2 Fracture of shaft of ulna

● S52.20 Unspecified fracture of shaft of ulna
Fracture of ulna NOS

● ■ S52.201 Unspecified fracture of shaft of right ulna A, K, M, N, P, Q, R 🦠, B, C 🦠

● ■ S52.202 Unspecified fracture of shaft of left ulna A, K, M, N, P, Q, R 🦠, B, C 🦠

● ■ S52.209 Unspecified fracture of shaft of unspecified ulna A, K, M, N, P, Q, R 🦠, B, C 🦠

● S52.21 Greenstick fracture of shaft of ulna

● ● S52.211 Greenstick fracture of shaft of right ulna A, K, P 🦠

● ● S52.212 Greenstick fracture of shaft of left ulna A, K, P 🦠

● ■ S52.219 Greenstick fracture of shaft of unspecified ulna A, K, P 🦠

● S52.22 Transverse fracture of shaft of ulna

● ● S52.221 Displaced transverse fracture of shaft of right ulna A, K, M, N, P, Q, R 🦠, B, C 🦠

● ● S52.222 Displaced transverse fracture of shaft of left ulna A, K, M, N, P, Q, R 🦠, B, C 🦠

● ● S52.223 Displaced transverse fracture of shaft of unspecified ulna A, K, M, N, P, Q, R 🦠, B, C 🦠

● ● S52.224 Nondisplaced transverse fracture of shaft of right ulna A, K, M, N, P, Q, R 🦠, B, C 🦠

● ● S52.225 Nondisplaced transverse fracture of shaft of left ulna A, K, M, N, P, Q, R 🦠, B, C 🦠

● ■ S52.226 Nondisplaced transverse fracture of shaft of unspecified ulna A, K, M, N, P, Q, R 🦠, B, C 🦠

● S52.23 Oblique fracture of shaft of ulna

● ● S52.231 Displaced oblique fracture of shaft of right ulna A, K, M, N, P, Q, R 🦠, B, C 🦠

● ● S52.232 Displaced oblique fracture of shaft of left ulna A, K, M, N, P, Q, R 🦠, B, C 🦠

● ■ S52.233 Displaced oblique fracture of shaft of unspecified ulna A, K, M, N, P, Q, R 🦠, B, C 🦠

● ● S52.234 Nondisplaced oblique fracture of shaft of right ulna A, K, M, N, P, Q, R 🦠, B, C 🦠

● ● S52.235 Nondisplaced oblique fracture of shaft of left ulna A, K, M, N, P, Q, R 🦠, B, C 🦠

● ■ S52.236 Nondisplaced oblique fracture of shaft of unspecified ulna A, K, M, N, P, Q, R 🦠, B, C 🦠

● S52.24 Spiral fracture of shaft of ulna

● ● S52.241 Displaced spiral fracture of shaft of ulna, right arm A, K, M, N, P, Q, R 🦠, B, C 🦠

● ● S52.242 Displaced spiral fracture of shaft of ulna, left arm A, K, M, N, P, Q, R 🦠, B, C 🦠

● ■ S52.243 Displaced spiral fracture of shaft of ulna, unspecified arm A, K, M, N, P, Q, R 🦠, B, C 🦠

● ● S52.244 Nondisplaced spiral fracture of shaft of ulna, right arm A, K, M, N, P, Q, R 🦠, B, C 🦠

● ● S52.245 Nondisplaced spiral fracture of shaft of ulna, left arm A, K, M, N, P, Q, R 🦠, B, C 🦠

● ■ S52.246 Nondisplaced spiral fracture of shaft of ulna, unspecified arm A, K, M, N, P, Q, R 🦠, B, C 🦠

● S52.25 Comminuted fracture of shaft of ulna

● ● S52.251 Displaced comminuted fracture of shaft of ulna, right arm A, K, M, N, P, Q, R 🦠, B, C 🦠

● ● S52.252 Displaced comminuted fracture of shaft of ulna, left arm A, K, M, N, P, Q, R 🦠, B, C 🦠

● ■ S52.253 Displaced comminuted fracture of shaft of ulna, unspecified arm A, K, M, N, P, Q, R 🦠, B, C 🦠

● ● S52.254 Nondisplaced comminuted fracture of shaft of ulna, right arm A, K, M, N, P, Q, R 🦠, B, C 🦠

CHAPTER 19 (S00-T88)

1430

● Unacceptable First-Listed Diagnosis   ● Use Additional Character(s)   ■ Unspecified   OGCR Official Guidelines for Coding and Reporting
🦠 Complication\Comorbidity   🦠 Major C\C   Excludes 1   Excludes 2   Includes   Use additional   Code first   Code also

● S52.255   Nondisplaced comminuted fracture of shaft of ulna, left arm A, K, M, N, P, Q, R 🔖, B, C 🔖

● ▪ S52.256   Nondisplaced comminuted fracture of shaft of ulna, unspecified arm A, K, M, N, P, Q, R 🔖, B, C 🔖

● S52.26   Segmental fracture of shaft of ulna

   ● S52.261   Displaced segmental fracture of shaft of ulna, right arm A, K, M, N, P, Q, R 🔖, B, C 🔖

   ● S52.262   Displaced segmental fracture of shaft of ulna, left arm A, K, M, N, P, Q, R 🔖, B, C 🔖

   ● ▪ S52.263   Displaced segmental fracture of shaft of ulna, unspecified arm A, K, M, N, P, Q, R 🔖, B, C 🔖

   ● S52.264   Nondisplaced segmental fracture of shaft of ulna, right arm A, K, M, N, P, Q, R 🔖, B, C 🔖

   ● S52.265   Nondisplaced segmental fracture of shaft of ulna, left arm A, K, M, N, P, Q, R 🔖, B, C 🔖

   ● ▪ S52.266   Nondisplaced segmental fracture of shaft of ulna, unspecified arm A, K, M, N, P, Q, R 🔖, B, C 🔖

● S52.27   Monteggia's fracture of ulna
    Fracture of upper shaft of ulna with dislocation of radial head

   ● S52.271   Monteggia's fracture of right ulna K, M, N, P, Q, R 🔖, B, C 🔖

   ● S52.272   Monteggia's fracture of left ulna K, M, N, P, Q, R 🔖, B, C 🔖

   ● ▪ S52.279   Monteggia's fracture of unspecified ulna K, M, N, P, Q, R 🔖, B, C 🔖

● S52.28   Bent bone of ulna

   ● S52.281   Bent bone of right ulna A, K, M, N, P, Q, R 🔖, B, C, H, J 🔖

   ● S52.282   Bent bone of left ulna A, K, M, N, P, Q, R 🔖, B, C, H, J 🔖

   ● ▪ S52.283   Bent bone of unspecified ulna A, K, M, N, P, Q, R 🔖, B, C, H, J 🔖

● S52.29   Other fracture of shaft of ulna

   ● S52.291   Other fracture of shaft of right ulna A, K, M, N, P, Q, R 🔖, B, C 🔖

   ● S52.292   Other fracture of shaft of left ulna A, K, M, N, P, Q, R 🔖, B, C 🔖

   ● ▪ S52.299   Other fracture of shaft of unspecified ulna A, K, M, N, P, Q, R 🔖, B, C 🔖

● S52.3   Fracture of shaft of radius

 ● S52.30   Unspecified fracture of shaft of radius

   ● ▪ S52.301   Unspecified fracture of shaft of right radius A, K, M, N, P, Q, R 🔖, B, C 🔖

   ● ▪ S52.302   Unspecified fracture of shaft of left radius A, K, M, N, P, Q, R 🔖, B, C 🔖

   ● ▪ S52.309   Unspecified fracture of shaft of unspecified radius A, K, M, N, P, Q, R 🔖, B, C 🔖

● S52.31   Greenstick fracture of shaft of radius

   ● S52.311   Greenstick fracture of shaft of radius, right arm A, K, P 🔖

   ● S52.312   Greenstick fracture of shaft of radius, left arm A, K, P 🔖

   ● ▪ S52.319   Greenstick fracture of shaft of radius, unspecified arm A, K, P 🔖

● S52.32   Transverse fracture of shaft of radius

   ● S52.321   Displaced transverse fracture of shaft of right radius A, K, M, N, P, Q, R 🔖, B, C 🔖

   ● S52.322   Displaced transverse fracture of shaft of left radius A, K, M, N, P, Q, R 🔖, B, C 🔖

   ● ▪ S52.323   Displaced transverse fracture of shaft of unspecified radius A, K, M, N, P, Q, R 🔖, B, C 🔖

   ● S52.324   Nondisplaced transverse fracture of shaft of right radius A, K, M, N, P, Q, R 🔖, B, C 🔖

   ● S52.325   Nondisplaced transverse fracture of shaft of left radius A, K, M, N, P, Q, R 🔖, B, C 🔖

   ● ▪ S52.326   Nondisplaced transverse fracture of shaft of unspecified radius A, K, M, N, P, Q, R 🔖, B, C 🔖

● S52.33   Oblique fracture of shaft of radius

   ● S52.331   Displaced oblique fracture of shaft of right radius A, K, M, N, P, Q, R 🔖, B, C 🔖

   ● S52.332   Displaced oblique fracture of shaft of left radius A, K, M, N, P, Q, R 🔖, B, C 🔖

   ● ▪ S52.333   Displaced oblique fracture of shaft of unspecified radius A, K, M, N, P, Q, R 🔖, B, C 🔖

   ● S52.334   Nondisplaced oblique fracture of shaft of right radius A, K, M, N, P, Q, R 🔖, B, C 🔖

   ● S52.335   Nondisplaced oblique fracture of shaft of left radius A, K, M, N, P, Q, R 🔖, B, C 🔖

   ● ▪ S52.336   Nondisplaced oblique fracture of shaft of unspecified radius A, K, M, N, P, Q, R 🔖, B, C 🔖

● S52.34   Spiral fracture of shaft of radius

   ● S52.341   Displaced spiral fracture of shaft of radius, right arm A, K, M, N, P, Q, R 🔖, B, C 🔖

   ● S52.342   Displaced spiral fracture of shaft of radius, left arm A, K, M, N, P, Q, R 🔖, B, C 🔖

   ● ▪ S52.343   Displaced spiral fracture of shaft of radius, unspecified arm A, K, M, N, P, Q, R 🔖, B, C 🔖

   ● S52.344   Nondisplaced spiral fracture of shaft of radius, right arm A, K, M, N, P, Q, R 🔖, B, C 🔖

   ● S52.345   Nondisplaced spiral fracture of shaft of radius, left arm A, K, M, N, P, Q, R 🔖, B, C 🔖

● Unacceptable First-Listed Diagnosis   ● Use Additional Character(s)   ▪ Unspecified   **OGCR** Official Guidelines for Coding and Reporting

🔖 Complication\Comorbidity   🔖 Major C\C    Excludes 1   Excludes 2   Includes   Use additional   Code first   Code also

1431

CHAPTER 19 (S00-T88)

● ■ **S52.346** Nondisplaced spiral fracture of shaft of radius, unspecified arm A, K, M, N, P, Q, R 🝢, B, C 🝢

● **S52.35** Comminuted fracture of shaft of radius

  ● **S52.351** Displaced comminuted fracture of shaft of radius, right arm A, K, M, N, P, Q, R 🝢, B, C 🝢

  ● **S52.352** Displaced comminuted fracture of shaft of radius, left arm A, K, M, N, P, Q, R 🝢, B, C 🝢

  ● ■ **S52.353** Displaced comminuted fracture of shaft of radius, unspecified arm A, K, M, N, P, Q, R 🝢, B, C 🝢

  ● **S52.354** Nondisplaced comminuted fracture of shaft of radius, right arm A, K, M, N, P, Q, R 🝢, B, C 🝢

  ● **S52.355** Nondisplaced comminuted fracture of shaft of radius, left arm A, K, M, N, P, Q, R 🝢, B, C 🝢

  ● ■ **S52.356** Nondisplaced comminuted fracture of shaft of radius, unspecified arm A, K, M, N, P, Q, R 🝢, B, C 🝢

● **S52.36** Segmental fracture of shaft of radius

  ● **S52.361** Displaced segmental fracture of shaft of radius, right arm A, K, M, N, P, Q, R 🝢, B, C 🝢

  ● **S52.362** Displaced segmental fracture of shaft of radius, left arm A, K, M, N, P, Q, R 🝢, B, C 🝢

  ● ■ **S52.363** Displaced segmental fracture of shaft of radius, unspecified arm A, K, M, N, P, Q, R 🝢, B, C 🝢

  ● **S52.364** Nondisplaced segmental fracture of shaft of radius, right arm A, K, M, N, P, Q, R 🝢, B, C 🝢

  ● **S52.365** Nondisplaced segmental fracture of shaft of radius, left arm A, K, M, N, P, Q, R 🝢, B, C 🝢

  ● ■ **S52.366** Nondisplaced segmental fracture of shaft of radius, unspecified arm A, K, M, N, P, Q, R 🝢, B, C 🝢

● **S52.37** Galeazzi's fracture
    Fracture of lower shaft of radius with radioulnar joint dislocation

  ● **S52.371** Galeazzi's fracture of right radius A, K, M, N, P, Q, R 🝢, B, C 🝢

  ● **S52.372** Galeazzi's fracture of left radius A, K, M, N, P, Q, R 🝢, B, C 🝢

  ● ■ **S52.379** Galeazzi's fracture of unspecified radius A, K, M, N, P, Q, R 🝢, B, C 🝢

● **S52.38** Bent bone of radius

  ● **S52.381** Bent bone of right radius A, K, M, N, P, Q, R 🝢, B, C, H, J 🝢

  ● **S52.382** Bent bone of left radius A, K, M, N, P, Q, R 🝢, B, C, H, J 🝢

  ● ■ **S52.389** Bent bone of unspecified radius A, K, M, N, P, Q, R 🝢, B, C, H, J 🝢

● **S52.39** Other fracture of shaft of radius

  ● **S52.391** Other fracture of shaft of radius, right arm A, K, M, N, P, Q, R 🝢, B, C 🝢

  ● **S52.392** Other fracture of shaft of radius, left arm A, K, M, N, P, Q, R 🝢, B, C 🝢

  ● ■ **S52.399** Other fracture of shaft of radius, unspecified arm A, K, M, N, P, Q, R 🝢, B, C 🝢

● **S52.5** Fracture of lower end of radius
    Fracture of distal end of radius

  Excludes2 physeal fractures of lower end of radius (S59.2-)

  ● **S52.50** Unspecified fracture of the lower end of radius

    ● ■ **S52.501** Unspecified fracture of the lower end of right radius A, K, M, N, P, Q, R 🝢, B, C 🝢

    ● ■ **S52.502** Unspecified fracture of the lower end of left radius A, K, M, N, P, Q, R 🝢, B, C 🝢

    ● ■ **S52.509** Unspecified fracture of the lower end of unspecified radius A, K, M, N, P, Q, R 🝢, B, C 🝢

  ● **S52.51** Fracture of radial styloid process

    ● **S52.511** Displaced fracture of right radial styloid process A, K, M, N, P, Q, R 🝢, B, C 🝢

    ● **S52.512** Displaced fracture of left radial styloid process A, K, M, N, P, Q, R 🝢, B, C 🝢

    ● ■ **S52.513** Displaced fracture of unspecified radial styloid process A, K, M, N, P, Q, R 🝢, B, C 🝢

    ● **S52.514** Nondisplaced fracture of right radial styloid process A, K, M, N, P, Q, R 🝢, B, C 🝢

    ● **S52.515** Nondisplaced fracture of left radial styloid process A, K, M, N, P, Q, R 🝢, B, C 🝢

    ● ■ **S52.516** Nondisplaced fracture of unspecified radial styloid process A, K, M, N, P, Q, R 🝢, B, C 🝢

  ● **S52.52** Torus fracture of lower end of radius

    ● **S52.521** Torus fracture of lower end of right radius A, K, P 🝢

    ● **S52.522** Torus fracture of lower end of left radius A, K, P 🝢

    ● ■ **S52.529** Torus fracture of lower end of unspecified radius A, K, P 🝢

  ● **S52.53** Colles' fracture

    ● **S52.531** Colles' fracture of right radius A, K, M, N, P, Q, R 🝢, B, C 🝢

    ● **S52.532** Colles' fracture of left radius A, K, M, N, P, Q, R 🝢, B, C 🝢

    ● ■ **S52.539** Colles' fracture of unspecified radius A, K, M, N, P, Q, R 🝢, B, C 🝢

  ● **S52.54** Smith's fracture

    ● **S52.541** Smith's fracture of right radius A, K, M, N, P, Q, R 🝢, B, C 🝢

    ● **S52.542** Smith's fracture of left radius A, K, M, N, P, Q, R 🝢, B, C 🝢

● Unacceptable First-Listed Diagnosis   ● Use Additional Character(s)   ■ Unspecified   **OGCR** Official Guidelines for Coding and Reporting
🝢 Complication\Comorbidity 🝢 Major C\C Excludes 1 Excludes 2 Includes Use additional Code first Code also

● ▣ S52.549   Smith's fracture of unspecified radius A, K, M, N, P, Q, R 🝙, B, C 🝙

● S52.55   Other extraarticular fracture of lower end of radius

     ● S52.551   Other extraarticular fracture of lower end of right radius A, K, M, N, P, Q, R 🝙, B, C 🝙

     ● S52.552   Other extraarticular fracture of lower end of left radius A, K, M, N, P, Q, R 🝙, B, C 🝙

     ● ▣ S52.559   Other extraarticular fracture of lower end of unspecified radius A, K, M, N, P, Q, R 🝙, B, C 🝙

● S52.56   Barton's fracture

     ● S52.561   Barton's fracture of right radius A, K, M, N, P, Q, R 🝙, B, C 🝙

     ● S52.562   Barton's fracture of left radius A, K, M, N, P, Q, R 🝙, B, C 🝙

     ● ▣ S52.569   Barton's fracture of unspecified radius A, K, M, N, P, Q, R 🝙, B, C 🝙

● S52.57   Other intraarticular fracture of lower end of radius

     ● S52.571   Other intraarticular fracture of lower end of right radius A, K, M, N, P, Q, R 🝙, B, C 🝙

     ● S52.572   Other intraarticular fracture of lower end of left radius A, K, M, N, P, Q, R 🝙, B, C 🝙

     ● ▣ S52.579   Other intraarticular fracture of lower end of unspecified radius A, K, M, N, P, Q, R 🝙, B, C 🝙

● S52.59   Other fractures of lower end of radius

     ● S52.591   Other fractures of lower end of right radius A, K, M, N, P, Q, R 🝙, B, C 🝙

     ● S52.592   Other fractures of lower end of left radius A, K, M, N, P, Q, R 🝙, B, C 🝙

     ● ▣ S52.599   Other fractures of lower end of unspecified radius A, K, M, N, P, Q, R 🝙, B, C 🝙

● S52.6   Fracture of lower end of ulna

     ● S52.60   Unspecified fracture of lower end of ulna

         ● ▣ S52.601   Unspecified fracture of lower end of right ulna A, K, M, N, P, Q, R 🝙, B, C 🝙

         ● ▣ S52.602   Unspecified fracture of lower end of left ulna A, K, M, N, P, Q, R 🝙, B, C 🝙

         ● ▣ S52.609   Unspecified fracture of lower end of unspecified ulna A, K, M, N, P, Q, R 🝙, B, C 🝙

     ● S52.61   Fracture of ulna styloid process

         ● S52.611   Displaced fracture of right ulna styloid process A, K, M, N, P, Q, R 🝙, B, C 🝙

         ● S52.612   Displaced fracture of left ulna styloid process A, K, M, N, P, Q, R 🝙, B, C 🝙

         ● ▣ S52.613   Displaced fracture of unspecified ulna styloid process A, K, M, N, P, Q, R 🝙, B, C 🝙

         ● S52.614   Nondisplaced fracture of right ulna styloid process A, K, M, N, P, Q, R 🝙, B, C 🝙

         ● S52.615   Nondisplaced fracture of left ulna styloid process A, K, M, N, P, Q, R 🝙, B, C 🝙

         ● ▣ S52.616   Nondisplaced fracture of unspecified ulna styloid process A, K, M, N, P, Q, R 🝙, B, C 🝙

     ● S52.62   Torus fracture of lower end of ulna

         ● S52.621   Torus fracture of lower end of right ulna A, K, P 🝙

         ● S52.622   Torus fracture of lower end of left ulna A, K, P 🝙

         ● ▣ S52.629   Torus fracture of lower end of unspecified ulna A, K, P 🝙

     ● S52.69   Other fracture of lower end of ulna

         ● S52.691   Other fracture of lower end of right ulna A, K, M, N, P, Q, R 🝙, B, C 🝙

         ● S52.692   Other fracture of lower end of left ulna A, K, M, N, P, Q, R 🝙, B, C 🝙

         ● ▣ S52.699   Other fracture of lower end of unspecified ulna A, K, M, N, P, Q, R 🝙, B, C 🝙

● S52.9   Unspecified fracture of forearm

     ● ▣ S52.90   Unspecified fracture of unspecified forearm A, K, M, N, P, Q, R 🝙, B, C 🝙

     ● ▣ S52.91   Unspecified fracture of right forearm A, K, M, N, P, Q, R 🝙, B, C 🝙

     ● ▣ S52.92   Unspecified fracture of left forearm A, K, M, N, P, Q, R 🝙, B, C 🝙

● S53   Dislocation and sprain of joints and ligaments of elbow

     Includes   avulsion of joint or ligament of elbow

         laceration of cartilage, joint or ligament of elbow

         sprain of cartilage, joint or ligament of elbow

         traumatic hemarthrosis of joint or ligament of elbow

         traumatic rupture of joint or ligament of elbow

         traumatic subluxation of joint or ligament of elbow

         traumatic tear of joint or ligament of elbow

     Code also any associated open wound

     Excludes2   strain of muscle, fascia and tendon at forearm level (S56.-)

     The appropriate 7th character is to be added to each code from category S53

A	initial encounter
D	subsequent encounter
S	sequela

● Unacceptable First-Listed Diagnosis   ● Use Additional Character(s)   ▣ Unspecified   **OGCR** Official Guidelines for Coding and Reporting

🝙 Complication\Comorbidity   🝙 Major C\C   Excludes 1   Excludes 2   Includes   Use additional   Code first   Code also

1433

CHAPTER 19 (S00-T88)

● S53.0   **Subluxation and dislocation of radial head**
Dislocation of radiohumeral joint
Subluxation of radiohumeral joint

   Excludes1   Monteggia's fracture-dislocation
(S52.27-)

 ● S53.00   **Unspecified subluxation and dislocation of radial head**

  ● ■ S53.001   Unspecified subluxation of right radial head

  ● ■ S53.002   Unspecified subluxation of left radial head

  ● ■ S53.003   Unspecified subluxation of unspecified radial head

  ● ■ S53.004   Unspecified dislocation of right radial head

  ● ■ S53.005   Unspecified dislocation of left radial head

  ● ■ S53.006   Unspecified dislocation of unspecified radial head

 ● S53.01   **Anterior subluxation and dislocation of radial head**
Anteriomedial subluxation and dislocation of radial head

  ● S53.011   Anterior subluxation of right radial head

  ● S53.012   Anterior subluxation of left radial head

  ● ■ S53.013   Anterior subluxation of unspecified radial head

  ● S53.014   Anterior dislocation of right radial head

  ● S53.015   Anterior dislocation of left radial head

  ● ■ S53.016   Anterior dislocation of unspecified radial head

 ● S53.02   **Posterior subluxation and dislocation of radial head**
Posteriolateral subluxation and dislocation of radial head

  ● S53.021   Posterior subluxation of right radial head

  ● S53.022   Posterior subluxation of left radial head

  ● ■ S53.023   Posterior subluxation of unspecified radial head

  ● S53.024   Posterior dislocation of right radial head

  ● S53.025   Posterior dislocation of left radial head

  ● ■ S53.026   Posterior dislocation of unspecified radial head

 ● S53.03   **Nursemaid's elbow**

  ● S53.031   Nursemaid's elbow, right elbow

  ● S53.032   Nursemaid's elbow, left elbow

  ● ■ S53.033   Nursemaid's elbow, unspecified

 ● S53.09   **Other subluxation and dislocation of radial head**

  ● S53.091   Other subluxation of right radial head

  ● S53.092   Other subluxation of left radial head

  ● ■ S53.093   Other subluxation of unspecified radial head

  ● S53.094   Other dislocation of right radial head

  ● S53.095   Other dislocation of left radial head

  ● ■ S53.096   Other dislocation of unspecified radial head

● S53.1   **Subluxation and dislocation of ulnohumeral joint**
Subluxation and dislocation of elbow NOS

   Excludes1   dislocation of radial head alone
(S53.0-)

 ● S53.10   **Unspecified subluxation and dislocation of ulnohumeral joint**

  ● ■ S53.101   Unspecified subluxation of right ulnohumeral joint

  ● ■ S53.102   Unspecified subluxation of left ulnohumeral joint

  ● ■ S53.103   Unspecified subluxation of unspecified ulnohumeral joint

  ● ■ S53.104   Unspecified dislocation of right ulnohumeral joint

  ● ■ S53.105   Unspecified dislocation of left ulnohumeral joint

  ● ■ S53.106   Unspecified dislocation of unspecified ulnohumeral joint

 ● S53.11   **Anterior subluxation and dislocation of ulnohumeral joint**

  ● S53.111   Anterior subluxation of right ulnohumeral joint

  ● S53.112   Anterior subluxation of left ulnohumeral joint

  ● ■ S53.113   Anterior subluxation of unspecified ulnohumeral joint

  ● S53.114   Anterior dislocation of right ulnohumeral joint

  ● S53.115   Anterior dislocation of left ulnohumeral joint

  ● ■ S53.116   Anterior dislocation of unspecified ulnohumeral joint

 ● S53.12   **Posterior subluxation and dislocation of ulnohumeral joint**

  ● S53.121   Posterior subluxation of right ulnohumeral joint

  ● S53.122   Posterior subluxation of left ulnohumeral joint

  ● ■ S53.123   Posterior subluxation of unspecified ulnohumeral joint

  ● S53.124   Posterior dislocation of right ulnohumeral joint

  ● S53.125   Posterior dislocation of left ulnohumeral joint

  ● ■ S53.126   Posterior dislocation of unspecified ulnohumeral joint

 ● S53.13   **Medial subluxation and dislocation of ulnohumeral joint**

  ● S53.131   Medial subluxation of right ulnohumeral joint

  ● S53.132   Medial subluxation of left ulnohumeral joint

  ● ■ S53.133   Medial subluxation of unspecified ulnohumeral joint

CHAPTER 19 (S00-T88)

1434

● Unacceptable First-Listed Diagnosis   ● Use Additional Character(s)   ■ Unspecified   **OGCR** Official Guidelines for Coding and Reporting
🔣 Complication\Comorbidity   🔣 Major C\C   Excludes 1   Excludes 2   Includes   Use additional   Code first   Code also

● S53.134   Medial dislocation of right ulnohumeral joint

● S53.135   Medial dislocation of left ulnohumeral joint

● ▣ S53.136   Medial dislocation of unspecified ulnohumeral joint

● S53.14   Lateral subluxation and dislocation of ulnohumeral joint

  ● S53.141   Lateral subluxation of right ulnohumeral joint

  ● S53.142   Lateral subluxation of left ulnohumeral joint

  ● ▣ S53.143   Lateral subluxation of unspecified ulnohumeral joint

  ● S53.144   Lateral dislocation of right ulnohumeral joint

  ● S53.145   Lateral dislocation of left ulnohumeral joint

  ● ▣ S53.146   Lateral dislocation of unspecified ulnohumeral joint

● S53.19   Other subluxation and dislocation of ulnohumeral joint

  ● S53.191   Other subluxation of right ulnohumeral joint

  ● S53.192   Other subluxation of left ulnohumeral joint

  ● ▣ S53.193   Other subluxation of unspecified ulnohumeral joint

  ● S53.194   Other dislocation of right ulnohumeral joint

  ● S53.195   Other dislocation of left ulnohumeral joint

  ● ▣ S53.196   Other dislocation of unspecified ulnohumeral joint

● S53.2   Traumatic rupture of radial collateral ligament

> **Excludes1**   sprain of radial collateral ligament NOS (S53.43-)

● ▣ S53.20   Traumatic rupture of radial collateral ligament, unspecified side

● S53.21   Traumatic rupture of right radial collateral ligament

● S53.22   Traumatic rupture of left radial collateral ligament

● S53.3   Traumatic rupture of ulnar collateral ligament

> **Excludes1**   sprain of ulnar collateral ligament (S53.44-)

● ▣ S53.30   Traumatic rupture of ulnar collateral ligament, unspecified side

● S53.31   Traumatic rupture of right ulnar collateral ligament

● S53.32   Traumatic rupture of left ulnar collateral ligament

● S53.4   Sprain of elbow

> **Excludes2**   traumatic rupture of radial collateral ligament (S53.2-)
> traumatic rupture of ulnar collateral ligament (S53.3-)

● S53.40   Unspecified sprain of elbow

  ● ▣ S53.401   Unspecified sprain of right elbow

  ● ▣ S53.402   Unspecified sprain of left elbow

  ● ▣ S53.409   Unspecified sprain of unspecified elbow

      Sprain of elbow NOS

● S53.41   Radiohumeral (joint) sprain

  ● S53.411   Radiohumeral (joint) sprain of right elbow

  ● S53.412   Radiohumeral (joint) sprain of left elbow

  ● ▣ S53.419   Radiohumeral (joint) sprain of unspecified elbow

● S53.42   Ulnohumeral (joint) sprain

  ● S53.421   Ulnohumeral (joint) sprain of right elbow

  ● S53.422   Ulnohumeral (joint) sprain of left elbow

  ● ▣ S53.429   Ulnohumeral (joint) sprain of unspecified elbow

● S53.43   Radial collateral ligament sprain

  ● S53.431   Radial collateral ligament sprain of right elbow

  ● S53.432   Radial collateral ligament sprain of left elbow

  ● ▣ S53.439   Radial collateral ligament sprain of unspecified elbow

● S53.44   Ulnar collateral ligament sprain

  ● S53.441   Ulnar collateral ligament sprain of right elbow

  ● S53.442   Ulnar collateral ligament sprain of left elbow

  ● ▣ S53.449   Ulnar collateral ligament sprain of unspecified elbow

● S53.49   Other sprain of elbow

  ● S53.491   Other sprain of right elbow

  ● S53.492   Other sprain of left elbow

  ● ▣ S53.499   Other sprain of unspecified elbow

● S54   **Injury of nerves at forearm level**

   Code also any associated open wound (S51.-)

> **Excludes2**   injury of nerves at wrist and hand level (S64.-)

The appropriate 7th character is to be added to each code from category S54

> A   initial encounter
> D   subsequent encounter
> S   sequela

● S54.0   Injury of ulnar nerve at forearm level

   Injury of ulnar nerve NOS

  ● ▣ S54.00   Injury of ulnar nerve at forearm level, unspecified arm

  ● S54.01   Injury of ulnar nerve at forearm level, right arm

  ● S54.02   Injury of ulnar nerve at forearm level, left arm

● S54.1   Injury of median nerve at forearm level

   Injury of median nerve NOS

  ● ▣ S54.10   Injury of median nerve at forearm level, unspecified arm

  ● S54.11   Injury of median nerve at forearm level, right arm

  ● S54.12   Injury of median nerve at forearm level, left arm

● Unacceptable First-Listed Diagnosis   ● Use Additional Character(s)   ▣ Unspecified   **OGCR** Official Guidelines for Coding and Reporting

🏷 Complication\Comorbidity   🏷 Major C\C   Excludes 1   Excludes 2   Includes   Use additional   Code first   Code also

1435

- **S54.2** **Injury of radial nerve at forearm level**
  Injury of radial nerve NOS
  - ■ **S54.20** **Injury of radial nerve at forearm level, unspecified arm**
    - **S54.21** **Injury of radial nerve at forearm level, right arm**
    - **S54.22** **Injury of radial nerve at forearm level, left arm**
- **S54.3** **Injury of cutaneous sensory nerve at forearm level**
  - ■ **S54.30** **Injury of cutaneous sensory nerve at forearm level, unspecified arm**
    - **S54.31** **Injury of cutaneous sensory nerve at forearm level, right arm**
    - **S54.32** **Injury of cutaneous sensory nerve at forearm level, left arm**
- **S54.8** **Injury of other nerves at forearm level**
  - **S54.8x** **Injury of other nerves at forearm level**
    - ■ **S54.8x1** **Unspecified injury of other nerves at forearm level, right arm**
    - ■ **S54.8x2** **Unspecified injury of other nerves at forearm level, left arm**
    - ■ **S54.8x9** **Unspecified injury of other nerves at forearm level, unspecified arm**
- **S54.9** **Injury of unspecified nerve at forearm level**
  - ■ **S54.90** **Injury of unspecified nerve at forearm level, unspecified arm**
    - **S54.91** **Injury of unspecified nerve at forearm level, right arm**
    - **S54.92** **Injury of unspecified nerve at forearm level, left arm**
- **S55** **Injury of blood vessels at forearm level**
  Code also any associated open wound (S51.-)

  Excludes2   injury of blood vessels at wrist and hand level (S65.-)
  injury of brachial vessels (S45.1-S45.2)

  The appropriate 7th character is to be added to each code from category S55

A	initial encounter
D	subsequent encounter
S	sequela

  - **S55.0** **Injury of ulnar artery at forearm level**
    - **S55.00** **Unspecified injury of ulnar artery at forearm level**
      - ■ **S55.001** **Unspecified injury of ulnar artery at forearm level, right arm** A 🍪
      - ■ **S55.002** **Unspecified injury of ulnar artery at forearm level, left arm** A 🍪
      - ■ **S55.009** **Unspecified injury of ulnar artery at forearm level, unspecified arm** A 🍪
    - **S55.01** **Laceration of ulnar artery at forearm level**
      - **S55.011** **Laceration of ulnar artery at forearm level, right arm** A 🍪
      - **S55.012** **Laceration of ulnar artery at forearm level, left arm** A 🍪
      - ■ **S55.019** **Laceration of ulnar artery at forearm level, unspecified arm** A 🍪
    - **S55.09** **Other specified injury of ulnar artery at forearm level**
      - **S55.091** **Other specified injury of ulnar artery at forearm level, right arm** A 🍪

- **S55.092** **Other specified injury of ulnar artery at forearm level, left arm** A 🍪
  - ■ **S55.099** **Other specified injury of ulnar artery at forearm level, unspecified arm** A 🍪
- **S55.1** **Injury of radial artery at forearm level**
  - **S55.10** **Unspecified injury of radial artery at forearm level**
    - ■ **S55.101** **Unspecified injury of radial artery at forearm level, right arm** A 🍪
    - ■ **S55.102** **Unspecified injury of radial artery at forearm level, left arm** A 🍪
    - ■ **S55.109** **Unspecified injury of radial artery at forearm level, unspecified arm** A 🍪
  - **S55.11** **Laceration of radial artery at forearm level**
    - **S55.111** **Laceration of radial artery at forearm level, right arm** A 🍪
    - **S55.112** **Laceration of radial artery at forearm level, left arm** A 🍪
    - ■ **S55.119** **Laceration of radial artery at forearm level, unspecified arm** A 🍪
  - **S55.19** **Other specified injury of radial artery at forearm level**
    - **S55.191** **Other specified injury of radial artery at forearm level, right arm** A 🍪
    - **S55.192** **Other specified injury of radial artery at forearm level, left arm** A 🍪
    - ■ **S55.199** **Other specified injury of radial artery at forearm level, unspecified arm** A 🍪
- **S55.2** **Injury of vein at forearm level**
  - **S55.20** **Unspecified injury of vein at forearm level**
    - ■ **S55.201** **Unspecified injury of vein at forearm level, right arm** A 🍪
    - ■ **S55.202** **Unspecified injury of vein at forearm level, left arm** A 🍪
    - ■ **S55.209** **Unspecified injury of vein at forearm level, unspecified arm** A 🍪
  - **S55.21** **Laceration of vein at forearm level**
    - **S55.211** **Laceration of vein at forearm level, right arm** A 🍪
    - **S55.212** **Laceration of vein at forearm level, left arm** A 🍪
    - ■ **S55.219** **Laceration of vein at forearm level, unspecified arm** A 🍪
  - **S55.29** **Other specified injury of vein at forearm level**
    - **S55.291** **Other specified injury of vein at forearm level, right arm** A 🍪
    - **S55.292** **Other specified injury of vein at forearm level, left arm** A 🍪
    - ■ **S55.299** **Other specified injury of vein at forearm level, unspecified arm** A 🍪

● Unacceptable First-Listed Diagnosis   ● Use Additional Character(s)   ■ Unspecified   **OGCR** Official Guidelines for Coding and Reporting
🍪 Complication\Comorbidity   🍪 Major C\C   Excludes 1   Excludes 2   Includes   Use additional   Code first   Code also

● S55.8   **Injury of other blood vessels at forearm level**

   ● S55.80   Unspecified injury of other blood vessels at forearm level

     ● ▪ S55.801   Unspecified injury of other blood vessels at forearm level, right arm A 🅒

     ● ▪ S55.802   Unspecified injury of other blood vessels at forearm level, left arm A 🅒

     ● ▪ S55.809   Unspecified injury of other blood vessels at forearm level, unspecified arm A 🅒

   ● S55.81   Laceration of other blood vessels at forearm level

     ● S55.811   Laceration of other blood vessels at forearm level, right arm A 🅒

     ● S55.812   Laceration of other blood vessels at forearm level, left arm A 🅒

     ● ▪ S55.819   Laceration of other blood vessels at forearm level, unspecified arm A 🅒

   ● S55.89   Other specified injury of other blood vessels at forearm level

     ● S55.891   Other specified injury of other blood vessels at forearm level, right arm A 🅒

     ● S55.892   Other specified injury of other blood vessels at forearm level, left arm A 🅒

     ● ▪ S55.899   Other specified injury of other blood vessels at forearm level, unspecified arm A 🅒

● S55.9   **Injury of unspecified blood vessel at forearm level**

   ● S55.90   Unspecified injury of unspecified blood vessel at forearm level

     ● ▪ S55.901   Unspecified injury of unspecified blood vessel at forearm level, right arm A 🅒

     ● ▪ S55.902   Unspecified injury of unspecified blood vessel at forearm level, left arm A 🅒

     ● ▪ S55.909   Unspecified injury of unspecified blood vessel at forearm level, unspecified arm A 🅒

   ● S55.91   Laceration of unspecified blood vessel at forearm level

     ● ▪ S55.911   Laceration of unspecified blood vessel at forearm level, right arm A 🅒

     ● ▪ S55.912   Laceration of unspecified blood vessel at forearm level, left arm A 🅒

     ● ▪ S55.919   Laceration of unspecified blood vessel at forearm level, unspecified arm A 🅒

   ● S55.99   Other specified injury of unspecified blood vessel at forearm level

     ● ▪ S55.991   Other specified injury of unspecified blood vessel at forearm level, right arm A 🅒

     ● ▪ S55.992   Other specified injury of unspecified blood vessel at forearm level, left arm A 🅒

     ● ▪ S55.999   Other specified injury of unspecified blood vessel at forearm level, unspecified arm A 🅒

● S56   **Injury of muscle, fascia and tendon at forearm level**

   Code also any associated open wound (S51.-)

   | Excludes2 | injury of muscle, fascia and tendon at or below wrist (S66.-)

      sprain of joints and ligaments of elbow (S53.4-)

   The appropriate 7th character is to be added to each code from category S56

   | A   initial encounter
   | D   subsequent encounter
   | S   sequela |

   ● S56.0   **Injury of flexor muscle, fascia and tendon of thumb at forearm level**

     ● S56.00   Unspecified injury of flexor muscle, fascia and tendon of thumb at forearm level

       ● ▪ S56.001   Unspecified injury of flexor muscle, fascia and tendon of right thumb at forearm level

       ● ▪ S56.002   Unspecified injury of flexor muscle, fascia and tendon of left thumb at forearm level

       ● ▪ S56.009   Unspecified injury of flexor muscle, fascia and tendon of unspecified thumb at forearm level

     ● S56.01   Strain of flexor muscle, fascia and tendon of thumb at forearm level

       ● S56.011   Strain of flexor muscle, fascia and tendon of right thumb at forearm level

       ● S56.012   Strain of flexor muscle, fascia and tendon of left thumb at forearm level

       ● ▪ S56.019   Strain of flexor muscle, fascia and tendon of unspecified thumb at forearm level

     ● S56.02   Laceration of flexor muscle, fascia and tendon of thumb at forearm level

       ● S56.021   Laceration of flexor muscle, fascia and tendon of right thumb at forearm level A 🅒

       ● S56.022   Laceration of flexor muscle, fascia and tendon of left thumb at forearm level A 🅒

       ● ▪ S56.029   Laceration of flexor muscle, fascia and tendon of unspecified thumb at forearm level A 🅒

     ● S56.09   Other injury of flexor muscle, fascia and tendon of thumb at forearm level

       ● S56.091   Other injury of flexor muscle, fascia and tendon of right thumb at forearm level

       ● S56.092   Other injury of flexor muscle, fascia and tendon of left thumb at forearm level

       ● ▪ S56.099   Other injury of flexor muscle, fascia and tendon of unspecified thumb at forearm level

● Unacceptable First-Listed Diagnosis   ● Use Additional Character(s)   ▪ Unspecified   **OGCR** Official Guidelines for Coding and Reporting

🅒 Complication\Comorbidity   🅒 Major C\C   Excludes 1   Excludes 2   Includes   Use additional   Code first   Code also

1437

CHAPTER 19 (S00-T88)

- ● S56.1 **Injury of flexor muscle, fascia and tendon of other and unspecified finger at forearm level**
  - ● S56.10 Unspecified injury of flexor muscle, fascia and tendon of other and unspecified finger at forearm level
    - ● ▪ S56.101 Unspecified injury of flexor muscle, fascia and tendon of right index finger at forearm level
    - ● ▪ S56.102 Unspecified injury of flexor muscle, fascia and tendon of left index finger at forearm level
    - ● ▪ S56.103 Unspecified injury of flexor muscle, fascia and tendon of right middle finger at forearm level
    - ● ▪ S56.104 Unspecified injury of flexor muscle, fascia and tendon of left middle finger at forearm level
    - ● ▪ S56.105 Unspecified injury of flexor muscle, fascia and tendon of right ring finger at forearm level
    - ● ▪ S56.106 Unspecified injury of flexor muscle, fascia and tendon of left ring finger at forearm level
    - ● ▪ S56.107 Unspecified injury of flexor muscle, fascia and tendon of right little finger at forearm level
    - ● ▪ S56.108 Unspecified injury of flexor muscle, fascia and tendon of left little finger at forearm level
    - ● ▪ S56.109 Unspecified injury of flexor muscle, fascia and tendon of unspecified finger at forearm level
  - ● S56.11 Strain of flexor muscle, fascia and tendon of other and unspecified finger at forearm level
    - ● S56.111 Strain of flexor muscle, fascia and tendon of right index finger at forearm level
    - ● S56.112 Strain of flexor muscle, fascia and tendon of left index finger at forearm level
    - ● S56.113 Strain of flexor muscle, fascia and tendon of right middle finger at forearm level
    - ● S56.114 Strain of flexor muscle, fascia and tendon of left middle finger at forearm level
    - ● S56.115 Strain of flexor muscle, fascia and tendon of right ring finger at forearm level
    - ● S56.116 Strain of flexor muscle, fascia and tendon of left ring finger at forearm level
    - ● S56.117 Strain of flexor muscle, fascia and tendon of right little finger at forearm level
    - ● S56.118 Strain of flexor muscle, fascia and tendon of left little finger at forearm level
    - ● ▪ S56.119 Strain of flexor muscle, fascia and tendon of finger of unspecified finger at forearm level

- ● S56.12 Laceration of flexor muscle, fascia and tendon of other and unspecified finger at forearm level
  - ● S56.121 Laceration of flexor muscle, fascia and tendon of right index finger at forearm level A 🐾
  - ● S56.122 Laceration of flexor muscle, fascia and tendon of left index finger at forearm level A 🐾
  - ● S56.123 Laceration of flexor muscle, fascia and tendon of right middle finger at forearm level A 🐾
  - ● S56.124 Laceration of flexor muscle, fascia and tendon of left middle finger at forearm level A 🐾
  - ● S56.125 Laceration of flexor muscle, fascia and tendon of right ring finger at forearm level A 🐾
  - ● S56.126 Laceration of flexor muscle, fascia and tendon of left ring finger at forearm level A 🐾
  - ● S56.127 Laceration of flexor muscle, fascia and tendon of right little finger at forearm level A 🐾
  - ● S56.128 Laceration of flexor muscle, fascia and tendon of left little finger at forearm level A 🐾
  - ● ▪ S56.129 Laceration of flexor muscle, fascia and tendon of unspecified finger at forearm level A 🐾
- ● S56.19 Other injury of flexor muscle, fascia and tendon of other and unspecified finger at forearm level
  - ● S56.191 Other injury of flexor muscle, fascia and tendon of right index finger at forearm level
  - ● S56.192 Other injury of flexor muscle, fascia and tendon of left index finger at forearm level
  - ● S56.193 Other injury of flexor muscle, fascia and tendon of right middle finger at forearm level
  - ● S56.194 Other injury of flexor muscle, fascia and tendon of left middle finger at forearm level
  - ● S56.195 Other injury of flexor muscle, fascia and tendon of right ring finger at forearm level
  - ● S56.196 Other injury of flexor muscle, fascia and tendon of left ring finger at forearm level
  - ● S56.197 Other injury of flexor muscle, fascia and tendon of right little finger at forearm level
  - ● S56.198 Other injury of flexor muscle, fascia and tendon of left little finger at forearm level
  - ● ▪ S56.199 Other injury of flexor muscle, fascia and tendon of unspecified finger at forearm level

● Unacceptable First-Listed Diagnosis   ● Use Additional Character(s)   ▪ Unspecified   **OGCR** Official Guidelines for Coding and Reporting
🐾 Complication\Comorbidity   🐾 Major C\C   Excludes 1   Excludes 2   Includes   Use additional   Code first   Code also

● **S56.2**   **Injury of other flexor muscle, fascia and tendon at forearm level**

   ● **S56.20**   Unspecified injury of other flexor muscle, fascia and tendon at forearm level

     ● ■ **S56.201**   Unspecified injury of other flexor muscle, fascia and tendon at forearm level, right arm

     ● ■ **S56.202**   Unspecified injury of other flexor muscle, fascia and tendon at forearm level, left arm

     ● ■ **S56.209**   Unspecified injury of other flexor muscle, fascia and tendon at forearm level, unspecified arm

   ● **S56.21**   Strain of other flexor muscle, fascia and tendon at forearm level

     ● **S56.211**   Strain of other flexor muscle, fascia and tendon at forearm level, right arm

     ● **S56.212**   Strain of other flexor muscle, fascia and tendon at forearm level, left arm

     ● ■ **S56.219**   Strain of other flexor muscle, fascia and tendon at forearm level, unspecified arm

   ● **S56.22**   Laceration of other flexor muscle, fascia and tendon at forearm level

     ● **S56.221**   Laceration of other flexor muscle, fascia and tendon at forearm level, right arm A 🝆

     ● **S56.222**   Laceration of other flexor muscle, fascia and tendon at forearm level, left arm A 🝆

     ● ■ **S56.229**   Laceration of other flexor muscle, fascia and tendon at forearm level, unspecified arm A 🝆

   ● **S56.29**   Other injury of other flexor muscle, fascia and tendon at forearm level

     ● **S56.291**   Other injury of other flexor muscle, fascia and tendon at forearm level, right arm

     ● **S56.292**   Other injury of other flexor muscle, fascia and tendon at forearm level, left arm

     ● ■ **S56.299**   Other injury of other flexor muscle, fascia and tendon at forearm level, unspecified arm

● **S56.3**   **Injury of extensor or abductor muscles, fascia and tendons of thumb at forearm level**

   ● **S56.30**   Unspecified injury of extensor or abductor muscles, fascia and tendons of thumb at forearm level

     ● ■ **S56.301**   Unspecified injury of extensor or abductor muscles, fascia and tendons of right thumb at forearm level

     ● ■ **S56.302**   Unspecified injury of extensor or abductor muscles, fascia and tendons of left thumb at forearm level

     ● ■ **S56.309**   Unspecified injury of extensor or abductor muscles, fascia and tendons of unspecified thumb at forearm level

● **S56.31**   Strain of extensor or abductor muscles, fascia and tendons of thumb at forearm level

     ● **S56.311**   Strain of extensor or abductor muscles, fascia and tendons of right thumb at forearm level

     ● **S56.312**   Strain of extensor or abductor muscles, fascia and tendons of left thumb at forearm level

     ● ■ **S56.319**   Strain of extensor or abductor muscles, fascia and tendons of unspecified thumb at forearm level

● **S56.32**   Laceration of extensor or abductor muscles, fascia and tendons of thumb at forearm level

     ● **S56.321**   Laceration of extensor or abductor muscles, fascia and tendons of right thumb at forearm level A 🝆

     ● **S56.322**   Laceration of extensor or abductor muscles, fascia and tendons of left thumb at forearm level A 🝆

     ● ■ **S56.329**   Laceration of extensor or abductor muscles, fascia and tendons of unspecified thumb at forearm level A 🝆

● **S56.39**   Other injury of extensor or abductor muscles, fascia and tendons of thumb at forearm level

     ● **S56.391**   Other injury of extensor or abductor muscles, fascia and tendons of right thumb at forearm level

     ● **S56.392**   Other injury of extensor or abductor muscles, fascia and tendons of left thumb at forearm level

     ● ■ **S56.399**   Other injury of extensor or abductor muscles, fascia and tendons of unspecified thumb at forearm level

● **S56.4**   **Injury of extensor muscle, fascia and tendon of other and unspecified finger at forearm level**

   ● **S56.40**   Unspecified injury of extensor muscle, fascia and tendon of other and unspecified finger at forearm level

     ● ■ **S56.401**   Unspecified injury of extensor muscle, fascia and tendon of right index finger at forearm level

     ● ■ **S56.402**   Unspecified injury of extensor muscle, fascia and tendon of left index finger at forearm level

     ● ■ **S56.403**   Unspecified injury of extensor muscle, fascia and tendon of right middle finger at forearm level

     ● ■ **S56.404**   Unspecified injury of extensor muscle, fascia and tendon of left middle finger at forearm level

     ● ■ **S56.405**   Unspecified injury of extensor muscle, fascia and tendon of right ring finger at forearm level

     ● ■ **S56.406**   Unspecified injury of extensor muscle, fascia and tendon of left ring finger at forearm level

     ● ■ **S56.407**   Unspecified injury of extensor muscle, fascia and tendon of right little finger at forearm level

●   Unacceptable First-Listed Diagnosis   ●   Use Additional Character(s)   ■   Unspecified   **OGCR** Official Guidelines for Coding and Reporting

🝆 Complication\Comorbidity   🝆 Major C\C   Excludes 1   Excludes 2   Includes   Use additional   Code first   Code also

1439

CHAPTER 19 (S00-T88)

● ■ S56.408 Unspecified injury of extensor muscle, fascia and tendon of left little finger at forearm level

● ■ S56.409 Unspecified injury of extensor muscle, fascia and tendon of unspecified finger at forearm level

● S56.41 Strain of extensor muscle, fascia and tendon of other and unspecified finger at forearm level

　● S56.411 Strain of extensor muscle, fascia and tendon of right index finger at forearm level

　● S56.412 Strain of extensor muscle, fascia and tendon of left index finger at forearm level

　● S56.413 Strain of extensor muscle, fascia and tendon of right middle finger at forearm level

　● S56.414 Strain of extensor muscle, fascia and tendon of left middle finger at forearm level

　● S56.415 Strain of extensor muscle, fascia and tendon of right ring finger at forearm level

　● S56.416 Strain of extensor muscle, fascia and tendon of left ring finger at forearm level

　● S56.417 Strain of extensor muscle, fascia and tendon of right little finger at forearm level

　● S56.418 Strain of extensor muscle, fascia and tendon of left little finger at forearm level

　● ■ S56.419 Strain of extensor muscle, fascia and tendon of finger, unspecified finger at forearm level

● S56.42 Laceration of extensor muscle, fascia and tendon of other and unspecified finger at forearm level

　● S56.421 Laceration of extensor muscle, fascia and tendon of right index finger at forearm level A 🦴

　● S56.422 Laceration of extensor muscle, fascia and tendon of left index finger at forearm level A 🦴

　● S56.423 Laceration of extensor muscle, fascia and tendon of right middle finger at forearm level A 🦴

　● S56.424 Laceration of extensor muscle, fascia and tendon of left middle finger at forearm level A 🦴

　● S56.425 Laceration of extensor muscle, fascia and tendon of right ring finger at forearm level A 🦴

　● S56.426 Laceration of extensor muscle, fascia and tendon of left ring finger at forearm level A 🦴

　● S56.427 Laceration of extensor muscle, fascia and tendon of right little finger at forearm level A 🦴

　● S56.428 Laceration of extensor muscle, fascia and tendon of left little finger at forearm level A 🦴

● ■ S56.429 Laceration of extensor muscle, fascia and tendon of unspecified finger at forearm level A 🦴

● S56.49 Other injury of extensor muscle, fascia and tendon of other and unspecified finger at forearm level

　● S56.491 Other injury of extensor muscle, fascia and tendon of right index finger at forearm level

　● S56.492 Other injury of extensor muscle, fascia and tendon of left index finger at forearm level

　● S56.493 Other injury of extensor muscle, fascia and tendon of right middle finger at forearm level

　● S56.494 Other injury of extensor muscle, fascia and tendon of left middle finger at forearm level

　● S56.495 Other injury of extensor muscle, fascia and tendon of right ring finger at forearm level

　● S56.496 Other injury of extensor muscle, fascia and tendon of left ring finger at forearm level

　● S56.497 Other injury of extensor muscle, fascia and tendon of right little finger at forearm level

　● S56.498 Other injury of extensor muscle, fascia and tendon of left little finger at forearm level

　● ■ S56.499 Other injury of extensor muscle, fascia and tendon of unspecified finger at forearm level

● S56.5 Injury of other extensor muscle, fascia and tendon at forearm level

● S56.50 Unspecified injury of other extensor muscle, fascia and tendon at forearm level

　● ■ S56.501 Unspecified injury of other extensor muscle, fascia and tendon at forearm level, right arm

　● ■ S56.502 Unspecified injury of other extensor muscle, fascia and tendon at forearm level, left arm

　● ■ S56.509 Unspecified injury of other extensor muscle, fascia and tendon at forearm level, unspecified arm

● S56.51 Strain of other extensor muscle, fascia and tendon at forearm level

　● S56.511 Strain of other extensor muscle, fascia and tendon at forearm level, right arm

　● S56.512 Strain of other extensor muscle, fascia and tendon at forearm level, left arm

　● ■ S56.519 Strain of other extensor muscle, fascia and tendon at forearm level, unspecified arm

● S56.52 Laceration of other extensor muscle, fascia and tendon at forearm level

　● S56.521 Laceration of other extensor muscle, fascia and tendon at forearm level, right arm A 🦴

　● S56.522 Laceration of other extensor muscle, fascia and tendon at forearm level, left arm A 🦴

● Unacceptable First-Listed Diagnosis　　● Use Additional Character(s)　　■ Unspecified　　**OGCR** Official Guidelines for Coding and Reporting
🦴 Complication\Comorbidity　　🦴 Major C\C　　Excludes 1　　Excludes 2　　Includes　　Use additional　　Code first　　Code also

● ◼ S56.529   Laceration of other extensor muscle, fascia and tendon at forearm level, unspecified arm A 🗫

● S56.59   Other injury of other extensor muscle, fascia and tendon at forearm level

  ● S56.591   Other injury of other extensor muscle, fascia and tendon at forearm level, right arm

  ● S56.592   Other injury of other extensor muscle, fascia and tendon at forearm level, left arm

  ● ◼ S56.599   Other injury of other extensor muscle, fascia and tendon at forearm level, unspecified arm

● S56.8   Injury of other muscles, fascia and tendons at forearm level

  ● S56.80   Unspecified injury of other muscles, fascia and tendons at forearm level

    ● ◼ S56.801   Unspecified injury of other muscles, fascia and tendons at forearm level, right arm

    ● ◼ S56.802   Unspecified injury of other muscles, fascia and tendons at forearm level, left arm

    ● ◼ S56.809   Unspecified injury of other muscles, fascia and tendons at forearm level, unspecified arm

  ● S56.81   Strain of other muscles, fascia and tendons at forearm level

    ● S56.811   Strain of other muscles, fascia and tendons at forearm level, right arm

    ● S56.812   Strain of other muscles, fascia and tendons at forearm level, left arm

    ● ◼ S56.819   Strain of other muscles, fascia and tendons at forearm level, unspecified arm

  ● S56.82   Laceration of other muscles, fascia and tendons at forearm level

    ● S56.821   Laceration of other muscles, fascia and tendons at forearm level, right arm A 🗫

    ● S56.822   Laceration of other muscles, fascia and tendons at forearm level, left arm A 🗫

    ● ◼ S56.829   Laceration of other muscles, fascia and tendons at forearm level, unspecified arm A 🗫

  ● S56.89   Other injury of other muscles, fascia and tendons at forearm level

    ● S56.891   Other injury of other muscles, fascia and tendons at forearm level, right arm

    ● S56.892   Other injury of other muscles, fascia and tendons at forearm level, left arm

    ● ◼ S56.899   Other injury of other muscles, fascia and tendons at forearm level, unspecified arm

● S56.9   Injury of unspecified muscles, fascia and tendons at forearm level

  ● S56.90   Unspecified injury of unspecified muscles, fascia and tendons at forearm level

    ● ◼ S56.901   Unspecified injury of unspecified muscles, fascia and tendons at forearm level, right arm

    ● ◼ S56.902   Unspecified injury of unspecified muscles, fascia and tendons at forearm level, left arm

    ● ◼ S56.909   Unspecified injury of unspecified muscles, fascia and tendons at forearm level, unspecified arm

  ● S56.91   Strain of unspecified muscles, fascia and tendons at forearm level

    ● ◼ S56.911   Strain of unspecified muscles, fascia and tendons at forearm level, right arm

    ● ◼ S56.912   Strain of unspecified muscles, fascia and tendons at forearm level, left arm

    ● ◼ S56.919   Strain of unspecified muscles, fascia and tendons at forearm level, unspecified arm

  ● S56.92   Laceration of unspecified muscles, fascia and tendons at forearm level

    ● ◼ S56.921   Laceration of unspecified muscles, fascia and tendons at forearm level, right arm A 🗫

    ● ◼ S56.922   Laceration of unspecified muscles, fascia and tendons at forearm level, left arm A 🗫

    ● ◼ S56.929   Laceration of unspecified muscles, fascia and tendons at forearm level, unspecified arm A 🗫

  ● S56.99   Other injury of unspecified muscles, fascia and tendons at forearm level

    ● ◼ S56.991   Other injury of unspecified muscles, fascia and tendons at forearm level, right arm

    ● ◼ S56.992   Other injury of unspecified muscles, fascia and tendons at forearm level, left arm

    ● ◼ S56.999   Other injury of unspecified muscles, fascia and tendons at forearm level, unspecified arm

● S57   Crushing injury of elbow and forearm

    Use additional code(s) for all associated injuries

    Excludes2   crushing injury of wrist and hand (S67.-)

    The appropriate 7th character is to be added to each code from category S57

    A   initial encounter
    D   subsequent encounter
    S   sequela

  ● S57.0   Crushing injury of elbow

    ● ◼ S57.00   Crushing injury of elbow, unspecified side

    ● S57.01   Crushing injury of right elbow

    ● S57.02   Crushing injury of left elbow

  ● S57.8   Crushing injury of forearm

    ● ◼ S57.80   Crushing injury of forearm, unspecified side

    ● S57.81   Crushing injury of right forearm

    ● S57.82   Crushing injury of left forearm

● Unacceptable First-Listed Diagnosis   ● Use Additional Character(s)   ◼ Unspecified   **OGCR** Official Guidelines for Coding and Reporting

🗫 Complication\Comorbidity   🗫 Major C\C   Excludes 1   Excludes 2   Includes   Use additional   Code first   Code also

1441

CHAPTER 19 (S00-T88)

● **S58**   **Traumatic amputation of elbow and forearm**
An amputation not identified as partial or complete should be coded to complete

> **Excludes1**   traumatic amputation of wrist and hand (S68.-)

The appropriate 7th character is to be added to each code from category S58

A	initial encounter
D	subsequent encounter
S	sequela

● **S58.0**   **Traumatic amputation at elbow level**

    ● **S58.01**   **Complete traumatic amputation at elbow level**

       ● **S58.011**   Complete traumatic amputation at elbow level, right arm A 🕭

       ● **S58.012**   Complete traumatic amputation at elbow level, left arm A 🕭

       ● ■ **S58.019**   Complete traumatic amputation at elbow level, unspecified arm A 🕭

    ● **S58.02**   **Partial traumatic amputation at elbow level**

       ● **S58.021**   Partial traumatic amputation at elbow level, right arm A 🕭

       ● **S58.022**   Partial traumatic amputation at elbow level, left arm A 🕭

       ● ■ **S58.029**   Partial traumatic amputation at elbow level, unspecified arm A 🕭

● **S58.1**   **Traumatic amputation at level between elbow and wrist**

    ● **S58.11**   **Complete traumatic amputation at level between elbow and wrist**

       ● **S58.111**   Complete traumatic amputation at level between elbow and wrist, right arm A 🕭

       ● **S58.112**   Complete traumatic amputation at level between elbow and wrist, left arm A 🕭

       ● ■ **S58.119**   Complete traumatic amputation at level between elbow and wrist, unspecified arm A 🕭

    ● **S58.12**   **Partial traumatic amputation at level between elbow and wrist**

       ● **S58.121**   Partial traumatic amputation at level between elbow and wrist, right arm A 🕭

       ● **S58.122**   Partial traumatic amputation at level between elbow and wrist, left arm A 🕭

       ● ■ **S58.129**   Partial traumatic amputation at level between elbow and wrist, unspecified arm A 🕭

● **S58.9**   **Traumatic amputation of forearm, level unspecified**

> **Excludes1**   traumatic amputation of wrist (S68.-)

    ● **S58.91**   **Complete traumatic amputation of forearm, level unspecified**

       ● ■ **S58.911**   Complete traumatic amputation of right forearm, level unspecified A 🕭

       ● ■ **S58.912**   Complete traumatic amputation of left forearm, level unspecified A 🕭

       ● ■ **S58.919**   Complete traumatic amputation of unspecified forearm, level unspecified A 🕭

    ● **S58.92**   **Partial traumatic amputation of forearm, level unspecified**

       ● ■ **S58.921**   Partial traumatic amputation of right forearm, level unspecified

       ● ■ **S58.922**   Partial traumatic amputation of left forearm, level unspecified

       ● ■ **S58.929**   Partial traumatic amputation of unspecified forearm, level unspecified

● **S59**   **Other and unspecified injuries of elbow and forearm**

> **Excludes2**   other and unspecified injuries of wrist and hand (S69.-)

The appropriate 7th character is to be added to each code from subcategories S59.0, S59.1, and S59.2

A	initial encounter for closed fracture
D	subsequent encounter for fracture with routine healing
G	subsequent encounter for fracture with delayed healing
K	subsequent encounter for fracture with nonunion
P	subsequent encounter for fracture with malunion
S	sequela

● **S59.0**   **Physeal fracture of lower end of ulna**

    ● **S59.00**   **Unspecified physeal fracture of lower end of ulna**

       ● ■ **S59.001**   Unspecified physeal fracture of lower end of ulna, right arm A, K, P 🕭

       ● ■ **S59.002**   Unspecified physeal fracture of lower end of ulna, left arm A, K, P 🕭

       ● ■ **S59.009**   Unspecified physeal fracture of lower end of ulna, unspecified arm A, K, P 🕭

    ● **S59.01**   **Salter-Harris Type I physeal fracture of lower end of ulna**

       ● **S59.011**   Salter-Harris Type I physeal fracture of lower end of ulna, right arm A, K, P 🕭

       ● **S59.012**   Salter-Harris Type I physeal fracture of lower end of ulna, left arm A, K, P 🕭

       ● ■ **S59.019**   Salter-Harris Type I physeal fracture of lower end of ulna, unspecified arm A, K, P 🕭

    ● **S59.02**   **Salter-Harris Type II physeal fracture of lower end of ulna**

       ● **S59.021**   Salter-Harris Type II physeal fracture of lower end of ulna, right arm A, K, P 🕭

       ● **S59.022**   Salter-Harris Type II physeal fracture of lower end of ulna, left arm A, K, P 🕭

Item 19-4   **SALTER-HARRIS TYPE 1:** epiphysis is completely separated from end of bone, or metaphysic growth plate remains attached to epiphysis
SALTER-HARRIS TYPE 2: epiphysis and growth plate are partially separated from metaphysis, which is cracked—most common type
SALTER-HARRIS TYPE 3: fracture occurring through epiphysis and separates part of epiphysis and growth plate from metaphysis fracture, usually at distal end of tibia
SALTER-HARRIS TYPE 4: fracture runs through epiphysis, across growth plate, into metaphysic, surgery is required to restore joint surface to normal and align growth plate

● Unacceptable First-Listed Diagnosis   ● Use Additional Character(s)   ■ Unspecified   **OGCR** Official Guidelines for Coding and Reporting
🕭 Complication\Comorbidity   🕭 Major C\C   Excludes 1   Excludes 2   Includes   Use additional   Code first   Code also

● ■ **S59.029** Salter-Harris Type II physeal fracture of lower end of ulna, unspecified arm A, K, P 🦠

● **S59.03** Salter-Harris Type III physeal fracture of lower end of ulna

● **S59.031** Salter-Harris Type III physeal fracture of lower end of ulna, right arm A, K, P 🦠

● **S59.032** Salter-Harris Type III physeal fracture of lower end of ulna, left arm A, K, P 🦠

● ■ **S59.039** Salter-Harris Type III physeal fracture of lower end of ulna, unspecified arm A, K, P 🦠

● **S59.04** Salter-Harris Type IV physeal fracture of lower end of ulna

● **S59.041** Salter-Harris Type IV physeal fracture of lower end of ulna, right arm A, K, P 🦠

● **S59.042** Salter-Harris Type IV physeal fracture of lower end of ulna, left arm A, K, P 🦠

● ■ **S59.049** Salter-Harris Type IV physeal fracture of lower end of ulna, unspecified arm A, K, P 🦠

● **S59.09** Other physeal fracture of lower end of ulna

● **S59.091** Other physeal fracture of lower end of ulna, right arm A, K, P 🦠

● **S59.092** Other physeal fracture of lower end of ulna, left arm A, K, P 🦠

● ■ **S59.099** Other physeal fracture of lower end of ulna, unspecified arm A, K, P 🦠

● **S59.1** Physeal fracture of upper end of radius

● **S59.10** Unspecified physeal fracture of upper end of radius

● ■ **S59.101** Unspecified physeal fracture of upper end of radius, right arm K, P 🦠

● ■ **S59.102** Unspecified physeal fracture of upper end of radius, left arm K, P 🦠

● ■ **S59.109** Unspecified physeal fracture of upper end of radius, unspecified arm K, P 🦠

● **S59.11** Salter-Harris Type I physeal fracture of upper end of radius

● **S59.111** Salter-Harris Type I physeal fracture of upper end of radius, right arm K, P 🦠

● **S59.112** Salter-Harris Type I physeal fracture of upper end of radius, left arm K, P 🦠

● ■ **S59.119** Salter-Harris Type I physeal fracture of upper end of radius, unspecified arm K, P 🦠

● **S59.12** Salter-Harris Type II physeal fracture of upper end of radius

● **S59.121** Salter-Harris Type II physeal fracture of upper end of radius, right arm K, P 🦠

● **S59.122** Salter-Harris Type II physeal fracture of upper end of radius, left arm K, P 🦠

● ■ **S59.129** Salter-Harris Type II physeal fracture of upper end of radius, unspecified arm K, P 🦠

● **S59.13** Salter-Harris Type III physeal fracture of upper end of radius

● **S59.131** Salter-Harris Type III physeal fracture of upper end of radius, right arm K, P 🦠

● **S59.132** Salter-Harris Type III physeal fracture of upper end of radius, left arm K, P 🦠

● ■ **S59.139** Salter-Harris Type III physeal fracture of upper end of radius, unspecified arm K, P 🦠

● **S59.14** Salter-Harris Type IV physeal fracture of upper end of radius

● **S59.141** Salter-Harris Type IV physeal fracture of upper end of radius, right arm K, P 🦠

● **S59.142** Salter-Harris Type IV physeal fracture of upper end of radius, left arm K, P 🦠

● ■ **S59.149** Salter-Harris Type IV physeal fracture of upper end of radius, unspecified arm K, P 🦠

● **S59.19** Other physeal fracture of upper end of radius

● **S59.191** Other physeal fracture of upper end of radius, right arm K, P 🦠

● **S59.192** Other physeal fracture of upper end of radius, left arm K, P 🦠

● ■ **S59.199** Other physeal fracture of upper end of radius, unspecified arm K, P 🦠

● **S59.2** Physeal fracture of lower end of radius

● **S59.20** Unspecified physeal fracture of lower end of radius

● ■ **S59.201** Unspecified physeal fracture of lower end of radius, right arm A, K, P 🦠

● ■ **S59.202** Unspecified physeal fracture of lower end of radius, left arm A, K, P 🦠

● ■ **S59.209** Unspecified physeal fracture of lower end of radius, unspecified arm A, K, P 🦠

● **S59.21** Salter-Harris Type I physeal fracture of lower end of radius

● **S59.211** Salter-Harris Type I physeal fracture of lower end of radius, right arm A, K, P 🦠

● **S59.212** Salter-Harris Type I physeal fracture of lower end of radius, left arm A, K, P 🦠

● ■ **S59.219** Salter-Harris Type I physeal fracture of lower end of radius, unspecified arm A, K, P 🦠

● **S59.22** Salter-Harris Type II physeal fracture of lower end of radius

● **S59.221** Salter-Harris Type II physeal fracture of lower end of radius, right arm A, K, P 🦠

● **S59.222** Salter-Harris Type II physeal fracture of lower end of radius, left arm A, K, P 🦠

● Unacceptable First-Listed Diagnosis   ● Use Additional Character(s)   ■ Unspecified   **OGCR** Official Guidelines for Coding and Reporting

🦠 Complication\Comorbidity   🦠 Major C\C   [Excludes 1]   [Excludes 2]   Includes   Use additional   Code first   Code also

1443

CHAPTER 19 (S00-T88)

● ▢ **S59.229** Salter-Harris Type II physeal fracture of lower end of radius, unspecified arm A, K, P 🐾

● **S59.23** Salter-Harris Type III physeal fracture of lower end of radius

  ● **S59.231** Salter-Harris Type III physeal fracture of lower end of radius, right arm A, K, P 🐾

  ● **S59.232** Salter-Harris Type III physeal fracture of lower end of radius, left arm A, K, P 🐾

  ● ▢ **S59.239** Salter-Harris Type III physeal fracture of lower end of radius, unspecified arm A, K, P 🐾

● **S59.24** Salter-Harris Type IV physeal fracture of lower end of radius

  ● **S59.241** Salter-Harris Type IV physeal fracture of lower end of radius, right arm A, K, P 🐾

  ● **S59.242** Salter-Harris Type IV physeal fracture of lower end of radius, left arm A, K, P 🐾

  ● ▢ **S59.249** Salter-Harris Type IV physeal fracture of lower end of radius, unspecified arm A, K, P 🐾

● **S59.29** Other physeal fracture of lower end of radius

  ● **S59.291** Other physeal fracture of lower end of radius, right arm A, K, P 🐾

  ● **S59.292** Other physeal fracture of lower end of radius, left arm A, K, P 🐾

  ● ▢ **S59.299** Other physeal fracture of lower end of radius, unspecified arm A, K, P 🐾

The appropriate 7th character is to be added to each code from subcategories S59.8 and S59.9

A	initial encounter
D	subsequent encounter
S	sequela

● **S59.8** Other specified injuries of elbow and forearm

  ● **S59.80** Other specified injuries of elbow

    ● **S59.801** Other specified injuries of right elbow

    ● **S59.802** Other specified injuries of left elbow

    ● ▢ **S59.809** Other specified injuries of unspecified elbow

  ● **S59.81** Other specified injuries of forearm

    ● **S59.811** Other specified injuries right forearm

    ● **S59.812** Other specified injuries left forearm

    ● ▢ **S59.819** Other specified injuries unspecified forearm

● **S59.9** Unspecified injury of elbow and forearm

  ● **S59.90** Unspecified injury of elbow

    ● ▢ **S59.901** Unspecified injury of right elbow

    ● ▢ **S59.902** Unspecified injury of left elbow

    ● ▢ **S59.909** Unspecified injury of unspecified elbow

● **S59.91** Unspecified injury of forearm

  ● ▢ **S59.911** Unspecified injury of right forearm

  ● ▢ **S59.912** Unspecified injury of left forearm

  ● ▢ **S59.919** Unspecified injury of unspecified forearm

INJURIES TO THE WRIST, HAND AND FINGERS (S60-S69)

Excludes2	burns and corrosions (T20-T32)
	frostbite (T33-T34)
	insect bite or sting, venomous (T63.4)

● **S60** **Superficial injury of wrist, hand and fingers**

The appropriate 7th character is to be added to each code from category S60

A	initial encounter
D	subsequent encounter
S	sequela

● **S60.0** Contusion of finger without damage to nail

Excludes1	contusion involving nail (matrix) (S60.1)

  ● **S60.00** Contusion of unspecified finger without damage to nail
    Contusion of finger(s) NOS

  ● **S60.01** Contusion of thumb without damage to nail

    ● **S60.011** Contusion of right thumb without damage to nail

    ● **S60.012** Contusion of left thumb without damage to nail

    ● ▢ **S60.019** Contusion of unspecified thumb without damage to nail

  ● **S60.02** Contusion of index finger without damage to nail

    ● **S60.021** Contusion of right index finger without damage to nail

    ● **S60.022** Contusion of left index finger without damage to nail

    ● ▢ **S60.029** Contusion of unspecified index finger without damage to nail

  ● **S60.03** Contusion of middle finger without damage to nail

    ● **S60.031** Contusion of right middle finger without damage to nail

    ● **S60.032** Contusion of left middle finger without damage to nail

    ● ▢ **S60.039** Contusion of unspecified middle finger without damage to nail

  ● **S60.04** Contusion of ring finger without damage to nail

    ● **S60.041** Contusion of right ring finger without damage to nail

    ● **S60.042** Contusion of left ring finger without damage to nail

    ● ▢ **S60.049** Contusion of unspecified ring finger without damage to nail

  ● **S60.05** Contusion of little finger without damage to nail

    ● **S60.051** Contusion of right little finger without damage to nail

    ● **S60.052** Contusion of left little finger without damage to nail

    ● ▢ **S60.059** Contusion of unspecified little finger without damage to nail

● Unacceptable First-Listed Diagnosis   ● Use Additional Character(s)   ▢ Unspecified   **OGCR** Official Guidelines for Coding and Reporting
🐾 Complication\Comorbidity   🐾 Major C\C   Excludes 1   Excludes 2   Includes   Use additional   Code first   Code also

● S60.1   Contusion of finger with damage to nail

   ● S60.10   Contusion of unspecified finger with damage to nail

   ● S60.11   Contusion of thumb with damage to nail

      ● S60.111   Contusion of right thumb with damage to nail

      ● S60.112   Contusion of left thumb with damage to nail

      ● ▪ S60.119   Contusion of unspecified thumb with damage to nail

   ● S60.12   Contusion of index finger with damage to nail

      ● S60.121   Contusion of right index finger with damage to nail

      ● S60.122   Contusion of left index finger with damage to nail

      ● ▪ S60.129   Contusion of unspecified index finger with damage to nail

   ● S60.13   Contusion of middle finger with damage to nail

      ● S60.131   Contusion of right middle finger with damage to nail

      ● S60.132   Contusion of left middle finger with damage to nail

      ● ▪ S60.139   Contusion of unspecified middle finger with damage to nail

● Unacceptable First-Listed Diagnosis   ● Use Additional Character(s)   ▪ Unspecified   **OGCR** Official Guidelines for Coding and Reporting

 Complication\Comorbidity    Major C\C   Excludes 1    Excludes 2   Includes   Use additional   Code first   Code also

1445

CHAPTER 19 (S00-T88)

● **S60.14** Contusion of ring finger with damage to nail

　● **S60.141** Contusion of right ring finger with damage to nail

　● **S60.142** Contusion of left ring finger with damage to nail

　●■ **S60.149** Contusion of unspecified ring finger with damage to nail

● **S60.15** Contusion of little finger with damage to nail

　● **S60.151** Contusion of right little finger with damage to nail

　● **S60.152** Contusion of left little finger with damage to nail

　●■ **S60.159** Contusion of unspecified little finger with damage to nail

● **S60.2** Contusion of wrist and hand

　Excludes2　contusion of fingers (S60.0-, S60.1-)

● **S60.21** Contusion of wrist

　● **S60.211** Contusion of right wrist

　● **S60.212** Contusion of left wrist

　●■ **S60.219** Contusion of unspecified wrist

● **S60.22** Contusion of hand

　● **S60.221** Contusion of right hand

　● **S60.222** Contusion of left hand

　●■ **S60.229** Contusion of unspecified hand

● **S60.3** Other superficial injuries of thumb

● **S60.31** Abrasion of thumb

　● **S60.311** Abrasion of right thumb

　● **S60.312** Abrasion of left thumb

　●■ **S60.319** Abrasion of unspecified thumb

● **S60.32** Blister (nonthermal) of thumb

　● **S60.321** Blister (nonthermal) of right thumb

　● **S60.322** Blister (nonthermal) of left thumb

　●■ **S60.329** Blister (nonthermal) of unspecified thumb

● **S60.34** External constriction of thumb
　　　　Hair tourniquet syndrome of thumb
　　　　Use additional cause code to identify the constricting item (W49.0-)

　● **S60.341** External constriction of right thumb

　● **S60.342** External constriction of left thumb

　●■ **S60.349** External constriction of unspecified thumb

● **S60.35** Superficial foreign body of thumb
　　　　Splinter in the thumb

　● **S60.351** Superficial foreign body of right thumb

　● **S60.352** Superficial foreign body of left thumb

　●■ **S60.359** Superficial foreign body of unspecified thumb

● **S60.36** Insect bite (nonvenomous) of thumb

　● **S60.361** Insect bite (nonvenomous) of right thumb

　● **S60.362** Insect bite (nonvenomous) of left thumb

　●■ **S60.369** Insect bite (nonvenomous) of unspecified thumb

● **S60.37** Other superficial bite of thumb

　Excludes1　open bite of thumb (S61.05-, S61.15-)

　● **S60.371** Other superficial bite of thumb of right thumb

　● **S60.372** Other superficial bite of thumb of left thumb

　●■ **S60.379** Other superficial bite of thumb of unspecified thumb

● **S60.39** Other superficial injuries of thumb

　● **S60.391** Other superficial injuries of right thumb

　● **S60.392** Other superficial injuries of left thumb

　●■ **S60.399** Other superficial injuries of unspecified thumb

● **S60.4** Other superficial injuries of other fingers

● **S60.41** Abrasion of fingers

　● **S60.410** Abrasion of right index finger

　● **S60.411** Abrasion of left index finger

　● **S60.412** Abrasion of right middle finger

　● **S60.413** Abrasion of left middle finger

　● **S60.414** Abrasion of right ring finger

　● **S60.415** Abrasion of left ring finger

　● **S60.416** Abrasion of right little finger

　● **S60.417** Abrasion of left little finger

　● **S60.418** Abrasion of other finger
　　　　Abrasion of specified finger with unspecified laterality

　●■ **S60.419** Abrasion of unspecified finger

● **S60.42** Blister (nonthermal) of fingers

　● **S60.420** Blister (nonthermal) of right index finger

　● **S60.421** Blister (nonthermal) of left index finger

　● **S60.422** Blister (nonthermal) of right middle finger

　● **S60.423** Blister (nonthermal) of left middle finger

　● **S60.424** Blister (nonthermal) of right ring finger

　● **S60.425** Blister (nonthermal) of left ring finger

　● **S60.426** Blister (nonthermal) of right little finger

　● **S60.427** Blister (nonthermal) of left little finger

　● **S60.428** Blister (nonthermal) of other finger
　　　　Blister (nonthermal) of specified finger with unspecified laterality

　●■ **S60.429** Blister (nonthermal) of unspecified finger

● **S60.44   External constriction of fingers**
    Hair tourniquet syndrome of finger
    Use additional cause code to identify the
      constricting item (W49.0-)

   ● **S60.440   External constriction of right
             index finger**

   ● **S60.441   External constriction of left index
             finger**

   ● **S60.442   External constriction of right
             middle finger**

   ● **S60.443   External constriction of left
             middle finger**

   ● **S60.444   External constriction of right ring
             finger**

   ● **S60.445   External constriction of left ring
             finger**

   ● **S60.446   External constriction of right
             little finger**

   ● **S60.447   External constriction of left little
             finger**

   ● **S60.448   External constriction of other
             finger**
         External constriction of
            specified finger with
            unspecified laterality

   ● ▣ **S60.449   External constriction of
                unspecified finger**

● **S60.45   Superficial foreign body of fingers**
    Splinter in the finger(s)

   ● **S60.450   Superficial foreign body of right
             index finger**

   ● **S60.451   Superficial foreign body of left
             index finger**

   ● **S60.452   Superficial foreign body of right
             middle finger**

   ● **S60.453   Superficial foreign body of left
             middle finger**

   ● **S60.454   Superficial foreign body of right
             ring finger**

   ● **S60.455   Superficial foreign body of left
             ring finger**

   ● **S60.456   Superficial foreign body of right
             little finger**

   ● **S60.457   Superficial foreign body of left
             little finger**

   ● **S60.458   Superficial foreign body of other
             finger**
         Superficial foreign body of
            specified finger with
            unspecified laterality

   ● ▣ **S60.459   Superficial foreign body of
                unspecified finger**

● **S60.46   Insect bite (nonvenomous) of fingers**

   ● **S60.460   Insect bite (nonvenomous) of
             right index finger**

   ● **S60.461   Insect bite (nonvenomous) of left
             index finger**

   ● **S60.462   Insect bite (nonvenomous) of
             right middle finger**

   ● **S60.463   Insect bite (nonvenomous) of left
             middle finger**

   ● **S60.464   Insect bite (nonvenomous) of
             right ring finger**

   ● **S60.465   Insect bite (nonvenomous) of left
             ring finger**

   ● **S60.466   Insect bite (nonvenomous) of
             right little finger**

   ● **S60.467   Insect bite (nonvenomous) of left
             little finger**

   ● **S60.468   Insect bite (nonvenomous) of
             other finger**
         Insect bite (nonvenomous)
            of specified finger with
            unspecified laterality

   ● ▣ **S60.469   Insect bite (nonvenomous) of
                unspecified finger**

● **S60.47   Other superficial bite of fingers**

    | Excludes1 | open bite of fingers (S61.25-,
                S61.35-)

   ● **S60.470   Other superficial bite of right
             index finger**

   ● **S60.471   Other superficial bite of left
             index finger**

   ● **S60.472   Other superficial bite of right
             middle finger**

   ● **S60.473   Other superficial bite of left
             middle finger**

   ● **S60.474   Other superficial bite of right
             ring finger**

   ● **S60.475   Other superficial bite of left ring
             finger**

   ● **S60.476   Other superficial bite of right
             little finger**

   ● **S60.477   Other superficial bite of left little
             finger**

   ● **S60.478   Other superficial bite of other
             finger**
         Other superficial bite of
            specified finger with
            unspecified laterality

   ● ▣ **S60.479   Other superficial bite of
                unspecified finger**

● **S60.5   Other superficial injuries of hand**

    | Excludes2 | superficial injuries of fingers (S60.3-,
                S60.4-)

   ● **S60.51   Abrasion of hand**

    ● **S60.511   Abrasion of right hand**

    ● **S60.512   Abrasion of left hand**

    ● ▣ **S60.519   Abrasion of unspecified hand**

   ● **S60.52   Blister (nonthermal) of hand**

    ● **S60.521   Blister (nonthermal) of right
             hand**

    ● **S60.522   Blister (nonthermal) of left hand**

    ● ▣ **S60.529   Blister (nonthermal) of
              unspecified hand**

   ● **S60.54   External constriction of hand**

    ● **S60.541   External constriction of right
             hand**

    ● **S60.542   External constriction of left hand**

    ● ▣ **S60.549   External constriction of
              unspecified hand**

   ● **S60.55   Superficial foreign body of hand**
       Splinter in the hand

    ● **S60.551   Superficial foreign body of right
             hand**

● Unacceptable First-Listed Diagnosis   ● Use Additional Character(s)   ▣ Unspecified   **OGCR** Official Guidelines for Coding and Reporting

 Complication\Comorbidity   Major C\C | Excludes 1 | | Excludes 2 | Includes   Use additional   Code first   Code also

1447

CHAPTER 19 (S00-T98)

- S60.552   Superficial foreign body of left hand
- S60.559   Superficial foreign body of unspecified hand
- S60.56   Insect bite (nonvenomous) of hand
  - S60.561   Insect bite (nonvenomous) of right hand
  - S60.562   Insect bite (nonvenomous) of left hand
  - S60.569   Insect bite (nonvenomous) of unspecified hand
- S60.57   Other superficial bite of hand
  > **Excludes1**   open bite of hand (S61.45-)
  - S60.571   Other superficial bite of hand of right hand
  - S60.572   Other superficial bite of hand of left hand
  - S60.579   Other superficial bite of hand of unspecified hand
- S60.8   Other superficial injuries of wrist
  - S60.81   Abrasion of wrist
    - S60.811   Abrasion of right wrist
    - S60.812   Abrasion of left wrist
    - S60.819   Abrasion of unspecified wrist
  - S60.82   Blister (nonthermal) of wrist
    - S60.821   Blister (nonthermal) of right wrist
    - S60.822   Blister (nonthermal) of left wrist
    - S60.829   Blister (nonthermal) of unspecified wrist
  - S60.84   External constriction of wrist
    - S60.841   External constriction of right wrist
    - S60.842   External constriction of left wrist
    - S60.849   External constriction of unspecified wrist
  - S60.85   Superficial foreign body of wrist
    Splinter in the wrist
    - S60.851   Superficial foreign body of right wrist
    - S60.852   Superficial foreign body of left wrist
    - S60.859   Superficial foreign body of unspecified wrist
  - S60.86   Insect bite (nonvenomous) of wrist
    - S60.861   Insect bite (nonvenomous) of right wrist
    - S60.862   Insect bite (nonvenomous) of left wrist
    - S60.869   Insect bite (nonvenomous) of unspecified wrist
  - S60.87   Other superficial bite of wrist
    > **Excludes1**   open bite of wrist (S61.55)
    - S60.871   Other superficial bite of right wrist
    - S60.872   Other superficial bite of left wrist
    - S60.879   Other superficial bite of unspecified wrist
- S60.9   Unspecified superficial injury of wrist, hand and fingers
  - S60.91   Unspecified superficial injury of wrist
    - S60.911   Unspecified superficial injury of right wrist
    - S60.912   Unspecified superficial injury of left wrist
    - S60.919   Unspecified superficial injury of unspecified wrist
  - S60.92   Unspecified superficial injury of hand
    - S60.921   Unspecified superficial injury of right hand
    - S60.922   Unspecified superficial injury of left hand
    - S60.929   Unspecified superficial injury of unspecified hand
  - S60.93   Unspecified superficial injury of thumb
    - S60.931   Unspecified superficial injury of right thumb
    - S60.932   Unspecified superficial injury of left thumb
    - S60.939   Unspecified superficial injury of unspecified thumb
  - S60.94   Unspecified superficial injury of other fingers
    - S60.940   Unspecified superficial injury of right index finger
    - S60.941   Unspecified superficial injury of left index finger
    - S60.942   Unspecified superficial injury of right middle finger
    - S60.943   Unspecified superficial injury of left middle finger
    - S60.944   Unspecified superficial injury of right ring finger
    - S60.945   Unspecified superficial injury of left ring finger
    - S60.946   Unspecified superficial injury of right little finger
    - S60.947   Unspecified superficial injury of left little finger
    - S60.948   Unspecified superficial injury of other finger
      Unspecified superficial injury of specified finger with unspecified laterality
    - S60.949   Unspecified superficial injury of unspecified finger
- S61   Open wound of wrist, hand and fingers
  Code also any associated wound infection
  > **Excludes1**   open fracture of wrist, hand and finger (S62.- with 7th character B)
  > traumatic amputation of wrist and hand (S68.-)

  The appropriate 7th character is to be added to each code from category S61

A	initial encounter
D	subsequent encounter
S	sequela

  - S61.0   Open wound of thumb without damage to nail
    > **Excludes1**   open wound of thumb with damage to nail (S61.1-)
    - S61.00   Unspecified open wound of thumb without damage to nail
      - S61.001   Unspecified open wound of right thumb without damage to nail

● Unacceptable First-Listed Diagnosis   ● Use Additional Character(s)   ▪ Unspecified   **OGCR** Official Guidelines for Coding and Reporting

 Complication\Comorbidity   Major C\C   Excludes 1   Excludes 2   Includes   Use additional   Code first   Code also

CHAPTER 19 (S00-T98)

● ◻ **S61.002** Unspecified open wound of left thumb without damage to nail

● ◻ **S61.009** Unspecified open wound of unspecified thumb without damage to nail

● **S61.01** Laceration without foreign body of thumb without damage to nail

  ● **S61.011** Laceration without foreign body of right thumb without damage to nail

  ● **S61.012** Laceration without foreign body of left thumb without damage to nail

  ● ◻ **S61.019** Laceration without foreign body of unspecified thumb without damage to nail

● **S61.02** Laceration with foreign body of thumb without damage to nail

  ● **S61.021** Laceration with foreign body of right thumb without damage to nail

  ● **S61.022** Laceration with foreign body of left thumb without damage to nail

  ● ◻ **S61.029** Laceration with foreign body of unspecified thumb without damage to nail

● **S61.03** Puncture wound without foreign body of thumb without damage to nail

  ● **S61.031** Puncture wound without foreign body of right thumb without damage to nail

  ● **S61.032** Puncture wound without foreign body of left thumb without damage to nail

  ● ◻ **S61.039** Puncture wound without foreign body of unspecified thumb without damage to nail

● **S61.04** Puncture wound with foreign body of thumb without damage to nail

  ● **S61.041** Puncture wound with foreign body of right thumb without damage to nail

  ● **S61.042** Puncture wound with foreign body of left thumb without damage to nail

  ● ◻ **S61.049** Puncture wound with foreign body of unspecified thumb without damage to nail

● **S61.05** Open bite of thumb without damage to nail

     Bite of thumb NOS

     | **Excludes1** | superficial bite of thumb (S60.36-, S60.37-) |

  ● **S61.051** Open bite of right thumb without damage to nail

  ● **S61.052** Open bite of left thumb without damage to nail

  ● ◻ **S61.059** Open bite of unspecified thumb without damage

● **S61.1** Open wound of thumb with damage to nail

  ● **S61.10** Unspecified open wound of thumb with damage to nail

  ● ◻ **S61.101** Unspecified open wound of right thumb with damage to nail

● ◻ **S61.102** Unspecified open wound of left thumb with damage to nail

● ◻ **S61.109** Unspecified open wound of unspecified thumb with damage to nail

● **S61.11** Laceration without foreign body of thumb with damage to nail

  ● **S61.111** Laceration without foreign body of right thumb with damage to nail

  ● **S61.112** Laceration without foreign body of left thumb with damage to nail

  ● ◻ **S61.119** Laceration without foreign body of unspecified thumb with damage to nail

● **S61.12** Laceration with foreign body of thumb with damage to nail

  ● **S61.121** Laceration with foreign body of right thumb with damage to nail

  ● **S61.122** Laceration with foreign body of left thumb with damage to nail

  ● ◻ **S61.129** Laceration with foreign body of unspecified thumb with damage to nail

● **S61.13** Puncture wound without foreign body of thumb with damage to nail

  ● **S61.131** Puncture wound without foreign body of right thumb with damage to nail

  ● **S61.132** Puncture wound without foreign body of left thumb with damage to nail

  ● ◻ **S61.139** Puncture wound without foreign body of unspecified thumb with damage to nail

● **S61.14** Puncture wound with foreign body of thumb with damage to nail

  ● **S61.141** Puncture wound with foreign body of right thumb with damage to nail

  ● **S61.142** Puncture wound with foreign body of left thumb with damage to nail

  ● ◻ **S61.149** Puncture wound with foreign body of unspecified thumb with damage to nail

● **S61.15** Open bite of thumb with damage to nail

     Bite of thumb with damage to nail NOS

     | **Excludes1** | superficial bite of thumb (S60.36-, S60.37-) |

  ● **S61.151** Bite of right thumb with damage to nail

  ● **S61.152** Bite of left thumb with damage to nail

  ● ◻ **S61.159** Bite of unspecified thumb with damage to nail

● **S61.2** Open wound of other finger without damage to nail

     | **Excludes1** | open wound of finger involving nail (matrix) (S61.3-) |

     | **Excludes2** | open wound of thumb without damage to nail (S61.0-) |

  ● **S61.20** Unspecified open wound of other finger without damage to nail

● Unacceptable First-Listed Diagnosis   ● Use Additional Character(s)   ◻ Unspecified   **OGCR** Official Guidelines for Coding and Reporting

🗫 Complication\Comorbidity   🗫 Major C\C | Excludes 1 | | Excludes 2 | Includes   Use additional   Code first   Code also

● ■ **S61.200** Unspecified open wound of right index finger without damage to nail

● ■ **S61.201** Unspecified open wound of left index finger without damage to nail

● ■ **S61.202** Unspecified open wound of right middle finger without damage to nail

● ■ **S61.203** Unspecified open wound of left middle finger without damage to nail

● ■ **S61.204** Unspecified open wound of right ring finger without damage to nail

● ■ **S61.205** Unspecified open wound of left ring finger without damage to nail

● ■ **S61.206** Unspecified open wound of right little finger without damage to nail

● ■ **S61.207** Unspecified open wound of left little finger without damage to nail

● ■ **S61.208** Unspecified open wound of other finger without damage to nail

　　　　Unspecified open wound of specified finger with unspecified laterality without damage to nail

● ■ **S61.209** Unspecified open wound of unspecified finger without damage to nail

● **S61.21** Laceration without foreign body of finger without damage to nail

● **S61.210** Laceration without foreign body of right index finger without damage to nail

● **S61.211** Laceration without foreign body of left index finger without damage to nail

● **S61.212** Laceration without foreign body of right middle finger without damage to nail

● **S61.213** Laceration without foreign body of left middle finger without damage to nail

● **S61.214** Laceration without foreign body of right ring finger without damage to nail

● **S61.215** Laceration without foreign body of left ring finger without damage to nail

● **S61.216** Laceration without foreign body of right little finger without damage to nail

● **S61.217** Laceration without foreign body of left little finger without damage to nail

● **S61.218** Laceration without foreign body of other finger without damage to nail

　　　　Laceration without foreign body of specified finger with unspecified laterality without damage to nail

● ■ **S61.219** Laceration without foreign body of unspecified finger without damage to nail

● **S61.22** Laceration with foreign body of finger without damage to nail

● **S61.220** Laceration with foreign body of right index finger without damage to nail

● **S61.221** Laceration with foreign body of left index finger without damage to nail

● **S61.222** Laceration with foreign body of right middle finger without damage to nail

● **S61.223** Laceration with foreign body of left middle finger without damage to nail

● **S61.224** Laceration with foreign body of right ring finger without damage to nail

● **S61.225** Laceration with foreign body of left ring finger without damage to nail

● **S61.226** Laceration with foreign body of right little finger without damage to nail

● **S61.227** Laceration with foreign body of left little finger without damage to nail

● **S61.228** Laceration with foreign body of other finger without damage to nail

　　　　Laceration with foreign body of specified finger with unspecified laterality without damage to nail

● ■ **S61.229** Laceration with foreign body of unspecified finger without damage to nail

● **S61.23** Puncture wound without foreign body of finger without damage to nail

● **S61.230** Puncture wound without foreign body of right index finger without damage to nail

● **S61.231** Puncture wound without foreign body of left index finger without damage to nail

● **S61.232** Puncture wound without foreign body of right middle finger without damage to nail

● **S61.233** Puncture wound without foreign body of left middle finger without damage to nail

● **S61.234** Puncture wound without foreign body of right ring finger without damage to nail

● **S61.235** Puncture wound without foreign body of left ring finger without damage to nail

● **S61.236** Puncture wound without foreign body of right little finger without damage to nail

● **S61.237** Puncture wound without foreign body of left little finger without damage to nail

● S61.238   Puncture wound without foreign body of other finger without damage to nail
    Puncture wound without foreign body of specified finger with unspecified laterality without damage to nail

● ▨ S61.239   Puncture wound without foreign body of unspecified finger without damage to nail

● S61.24   Puncture wound with foreign body of finger without damage to nail

   ● S61.240   Puncture wound with foreign body of right index finger without damage to nail

   ● S61.241   Puncture wound with foreign body of left index finger without damage to nail

   ● S61.242   Puncture wound with foreign body of right middle finger without damage to nail

   ● S61.243   Puncture wound with foreign body of left middle finger without damage to nail

   ● S61.244   Puncture wound with foreign body of right ring finger without damage to nail

   ● S61.245   Puncture wound with foreign body of left ring finger without damage to nail

   ● S61.246   Puncture wound with foreign body of right little finger without damage to nail

   ● S61.247   Puncture wound with foreign body of left little finger without damage to nail

   ● S61.248   Puncture wound with foreign body of other finger without damage to nail
     Puncture wound with foreign body of specified finger with unspecified laterality without damage to nail

   ● ▨ S61.249   Puncture wound with foreign body of unspecified finger without damage to nail

● S61.25   Open bite of finger without damage to nail
    Bite of finger without damage to nail NOS

    | Excludes1 | superficial bite of finger (S60.46-, S60.47-)

   ● S61.250   Open bite of right index finger without damage to nail

   ● S61.251   Open bite of left index finger without damage to nail

   ● S61.252   Open bite of right middle finger without damage to nail

   ● S61.253   Open bite of left middle finger without damage to nail

   ● S61.254   Open bite of right ring finger without damage to nail

   ● S61.255   Open bite of left ring finger without damage to nail

   ● S61.256   Open bite of right little finger without damage to nail

   ● S61.257   Open bite of left little finger without damage to nail

● S61.258   Open bite of other finger without damage to nail
    Open bite of specified finger with unspecified laterality without damage to nail

● ▨ S61.259   Open bite of unspecified finger without damage to nail

● S61.3   Open wound of other finger with damage to nail

  ● S61.30   Unspecified open wound of finger with damage to nail

   ● ▨ S61.300   Unspecified open wound of right index finger with damage to nail

   ● ▨ S61.301   Unspecified open wound of left index finger with damage to nail

   ● ▨ S61.302   Unspecified open wound of right middle finger with damage to nail

   ● ▨ S61.303   Unspecified open wound of left middle finger with damage to nail

   ● ▨ S61.304   Unspecified open wound of right ring finger with damage to nail

   ● ▨ S61.305   Unspecified open wound of left ring finger with damage to nail

   ● ▨ S61.306   Unspecified open wound of right little finger with damage to nail

   ● ▨ S61.307   Unspecified open wound of left little finger with damage to nail

   ● ▨ S61.308   Unspecified open wound of other finger with damage to nail
     Unspecified open wound of specified finger with unspecified laterality with damage to nail

   ● ▨ S61.309   Unspecified open wound of unspecified finger with damage to nail

  ● S61.31   Laceration without foreign body of finger with damage to nail

   ● S61.310   Laceration without foreign body of right index finger with damage to nail

   ● S61.311   Laceration without foreign body of left index finger with damage to nail

   ● S61.312   Laceration without foreign body of right middle finger with damage to nail

   ● S61.313   Laceration without foreign body of left middle finger with damage to nail

   ● S61.314   Laceration without foreign body of right ring finger with damage to nail

   ● S61.315   Laceration without foreign body of left ring finger with damage to nail

   ● S61.316   Laceration without foreign body of right little finger with damage to nail

   ● S61.317   Laceration without foreign body of left little finger with damage to nail

● Unacceptable First-Listed Diagnosis   ● Use Additional Character(s)   ▨ Unspecified   **OGCR** Official Guidelines for Coding and Reporting

🏷 Complication\Comorbidity   🏷 Major C\C | Excludes 1 | | Excludes 2 | | Includes | Use additional   Code first   Code also

1451

CHAPTER 19 (S00-T98)

● S61.318   Laceration without foreign body of other finger with damage to nail

      Laceration without foreign body of specified finger with unspecified laterality with damage to nail

● ▪ S61.319   Laceration without foreign body of unspecified finger with damage to nail

● S61.32   Laceration with foreign body of finger with damage to nail

● S61.320   Laceration with foreign body of right index finger with damage to nail

● S61.321   Laceration with foreign body of left index finger with damage to nail

● S61.322   Laceration with foreign body of right middle finger with damage to nail

● S61.323   Laceration with foreign body of left middle finger with damage to nail

● S61.324   Laceration with foreign body of right ring finger with damage to nail

● S61.325   Laceration with foreign body of left ring finger with damage to nail

● S61.326   Laceration with foreign body of right little finger with damage to nail

● S61.327   Laceration with foreign body of left little finger with damage to nail

● S61.328   Laceration with foreign body of other finger with damage to nail

      Laceration with foreign body of specified finger with unspecified laterality with damage to nail

● ▪ S61.329   Laceration with foreign body of unspecified finger with damage to nail

● S61.33   Puncture wound without foreign body of finger with damage to nail

● S61.330   Puncture wound without foreign body of right index finger with damage to nail

● S61.331   Puncture wound without foreign body of left index finger with damage to nail

● S61.332   Puncture wound without foreign body of right middle finger with damage to nail

● S61.333   Puncture wound without foreign body of left middle finger with damage to nail

● S61.334   Puncture wound without foreign body of right ring finger with damage to nail

● S61.335   Puncture wound without foreign body of left ring finger with damage to nail

● S61.336   Puncture wound without foreign body of right little finger with damage to nail

● S61.337   Puncture wound without foreign body of left little finger with damage to nail

● S61.338   Puncture wound without foreign body of other finger with damage to nail

      Puncture wound without foreign body of specified finger with unspecified laterality with damage to nail

● ▪ S61.339   Puncture wound without foreign body of unspecified finger with damage to nail

● S61.34   Puncture wound with foreign body of finger with damage to nail

● S61.340   Puncture wound with foreign body of right index finger with damage to nail

● S61.341   Puncture wound with foreign body of left index finger with damage to nail

● S61.342   Puncture wound with foreign body of right middle finger with damage to nail

● S61.343   Puncture wound with foreign body of left middle finger with damage to nail

● S61.344   Puncture wound with foreign body of right ring finger with damage to nail

● S61.345   Puncture wound with foreign body of left ring finger with damage to nail

● S61.346   Puncture wound with foreign body of right little finger with damage to nail

● S61.347   Puncture wound with foreign body of left little finger with damage to nail

● S61.348   Puncture wound with foreign body of other finger with damage to nail

      Puncture wound with foreign body of specified finger with unspecified laterality with damage to nail

● ▪ S61.349   Puncture wound with foreign body of unspecified finger with damage to nail

● S61.35   Open bite of finger with damage to nail

      Bite of finger with damage to nail NOS

      Excludes1   superficial bite of finger (S60.46-, S60.47-)

● S61.350   Open bite of right index finger with damage to nail

● S61.351   Open bite of left index finger with damage to nail

● S61.352   Open bite of right middle finger with damage to nail

● S61.353   Open bite of left middle finger with damage to nail

● S61.354   Open bite of right ring finger with damage to nail

● S61.355   Open bite of left ring finger with damage to nail

● S61.356   Open bite of right little finger with damage to nail

● S61.357   Open bite of left little finger with damage to nail

● S61.358   Open bite of other finger with damage to nail
     Open bite of specified finger with unspecified laterality with damage to nail

● ▨ S61.359   Open bite of unspecified finger with damage to nail

● **S61.4   Open wound of hand**

   ● S61.40   Unspecified open wound of hand

     ● ▨ S61.401   Unspecified open wound of right hand

     ● ▨ S61.402   Unspecified open wound of left hand

     ● ▨ S61.409   Unspecified open wound of unspecified hand

   ● S61.41   Laceration without foreign body of hand

     ● S61.411   Laceration without foreign body of right hand

     ● S61.412   Laceration without foreign body of left hand

     ● ▨ S61.419   Laceration without foreign body of unspecified hand

   ● S61.42   Laceration with foreign body of hand

     ● S61.421   Laceration with foreign body of right hand

     ● S61.422   Laceration with foreign body of left hand

     ● ▨ S61.429   Laceration with foreign body of unspecified hand

   ● S61.43   Puncture wound without foreign body of hand

     ● S61.431   Puncture wound without foreign body of right hand

     ● S61.432   Puncture wound without foreign body of left hand

     ● ▨ S61.439   Puncture wound without foreign body of unspecified hand

   ● S61.44   Puncture wound with foreign body of hand

     ● S61.441   Puncture wound with foreign body of right hand

     ● S61.442   Puncture wound with foreign body of left hand

     ● ▨ S61.449   Puncture wound with foreign body of unspecified hand

   ● S61.45   Open bite of hand
     Bite of hand NOS

     Excludes1   superficial bite of hand (S60.56-, S60.57-)

     ● S61.451   Open bite of right hand

     ● S61.452   Open bite of left hand

     ● ▨ S61.459   Open bite of unspecified hand

● **S61.5   Open wound of wrist**

   ● S61.50   Unspecified open wound of wrist

     ● ▨ S61.501   Unspecified open wound of right wrist

     ● ▨ S61.502   Unspecified open wound of left wrist

     ● ▨ S61.509   Unspecified open wound of unspecified wrist

● S61.51   Laceration without foreign body of wrist

   ● S61.511   Laceration without foreign body of right wrist

   ● S61.512   Laceration without foreign body of left wrist

   ● ▨ S61.519   Laceration without foreign body of unspecified wrist

● S61.52   Laceration with foreign body of wrist

   ● S61.521   Laceration with foreign body of right wrist

   ● S61.522   Laceration with foreign body of left wrist

   ● ▨ S61.529   Laceration with foreign body of unspecified wrist

● S61.53   Puncture wound without foreign body of wrist

   ● S61.531   Puncture wound without foreign body of right wrist

   ● S61.532   Puncture wound without foreign body of left wrist

   ● ▨ S61.539   Puncture wound without foreign body of unspecified wrist

● S61.54   Puncture wound with foreign body of wrist

   ● S61.541   Puncture wound with foreign body of right wrist

   ● S61.542   Puncture wound with foreign body of left wrist

   ● ▨ S61.549   Puncture wound with foreign body of unspecified wrist

● S61.55   Open bite of wrist
     Bite of wrist NOS

     Excludes1   superficial bite of wrist (S60.86-, S60.87-)

   ● S61.551   Open bite of right wrist

   ● S61.552   Open bite of left wrist

   ● ▨ S61.559   Open bite of unspecified wrist

● **S62   Fracture at wrist and hand level**
     A fracture not identified as displaced or nondisplaced should be coded to displaced

     Excludes1   traumatic amputation of wrist and hand (S68.-)

     Excludes2   fracture of distal parts of ulna and radius (S52.-)

     The appropriate 7th character is to be added to each code from category S62
     A fracture not designated as open or closed should be coded to closed

A	initial encounter for closed fracture
B	initial encounter for open fracture
D	subsequent encounter for fracture with routine healing
G	subsequent encounter for fracture with delayed healing
K	subsequent encounter for fracture with nonunion
P	subsequent encounter for fracture with malunion
S	sequela

● **S62.0   Fracture of navicular [scaphoid] bone of wrist**

   ● S62.00   Unspecified fracture of navicular [scaphoid] bone of wrist

     ● ▨ S62.001   Unspecified fracture of navicular [scaphoid] bone of right wrist
       B, K, P ⟡

     ● ▨ S62.002   Unspecified fracture of navicular [scaphoid] bone of left wrist
       B, K, P ⟡

● Unacceptable First-Listed Diagnosis   ● Use Additional Character(s)   ▨ Unspecified   **OGCR** Official Guidelines for Coding and Reporting

⟡ Complication\Comorbidity   ⟡ Major C\C   Excludes 1   Excludes 2   Includes   Use additional   Code first   Code also

1453

CHAPTER 19 (S00-T98)

● ■ **S62.009**   Unspecified fracture of navicular [scaphoid] bone of unspecified wrist B, K, P 🦴

● **S62.01**   Fracture of distal pole of navicular [scaphoid] bone of wrist
     Fracture of volar tuberosity of navicular [scaphoid] bone of wrist

     ● **S62.011**   Displaced fracture of distal pole of navicular [scaphoid] bone of right wrist B, K, P 🦴

     ● **S62.012**   Displaced fracture of distal pole of navicular [scaphoid] bone of left wrist B, K, P 🦴

     ● ■ **S62.013**   Displaced fracture of distal pole of navicular [scaphoid] bone of unspecified wrist B, K, P 🦴

     ● **S62.014**   Nondisplaced fracture of distal pole of navicular [scaphoid] bone of right wrist B, K, P 🦴

     ● **S62.015**   Nondisplaced fracture of distal pole of navicular [scaphoid] bone of left wrist B, K, P 🦴

     ● ■ **S62.016**   Nondisplaced fracture of distal pole of navicular [scaphoid] bone of unspecified wrist B, K, P 🦴

● **S62.02**   Fracture of middle third of navicular [scaphoid] bone of wrist

     ● **S62.021**   Displaced fracture of middle third of navicular [scaphoid] bone of right wrist B, K, P 🦴

     ● **S62.022**   Displaced fracture of middle third of navicular [scaphoid] bone of left wrist B, K, P 🦴

     ● ■ **S62.023**   Displaced fracture of middle third of navicular [scaphoid] bone of unspecified wrist B, K, P 🦴

     ● **S62.024**   Nondisplaced fracture of middle third of navicular [scaphoid] bone of right wrist B, K, P 🦴

     ● **S62.025**   Nondisplaced fracture of middle third of navicular [scaphoid] bone of left wrist B, K, P 🦴

     ● ■ **S62.026**   Nondisplaced fracture of middle third of navicular [scaphoid] bone of unspecified wrist B, K, P 🦴

● **S62.03**   Fracture of proximal third of navicular [scaphoid] bone of wrist

     ● **S62.031**   Displaced fracture of proximal third of navicular [scaphoid] bone of right wrist B, K, P 🦴

     ● **S62.032**   Displaced fracture of proximal third of navicular [scaphoid] bone of left wrist B, K, P 🦴

     ● ■ **S62.033**   Displaced fracture of proximal third of navicular [scaphoid] bone of unspecified wrist B, K, P 🦴

     ● **S62.034**   Nondisplaced fracture of proximal third of navicular [scaphoid] bone of right wrist B, K, P 🦴

     ● **S62.035**   Nondisplaced fracture of proximal third of navicular [scaphoid] bone of left wrist B, K, P 🦴

     ● ■ **S62.036**   Nondisplaced fracture of proximal third of navicular [scaphoid] bone of unspecified wrist B, K, P 🦴

● **S62.1**   Fracture of other and unspecified carpal bone(s)
     Excludes2   fracture of scaphoid of wrist (S62.0-)

● **S62.10**   Fracture of unspecified carpal bone
     Fracture of wrist NOS

     ● ■ **S62.101**   Fracture of unspecified carpal bone, right wrist B, K, P 🦴

     ● ■ **S62.102**   Fracture of unspecified carpal bone, left wrist B, K, P 🦴

     ● ■ **S62.109**   Fracture of unspecified carpal bone, unspecified wrist B, K, P 🦴

● **S62.11**   Fracture of triquetrum [cuneiform] bone of wrist

     ● **S62.111**   Displaced fracture of triquetrum [cuneiform] bone, right wrist B, K, P 🦴

     ● **S62.112**   Displaced fracture of triquetrum [cuneiform] bone, left wrist B, K, P 🦴

     ● ■ **S62.113**   Displaced fracture of triquetrum [cuneiform] bone, unspecified wrist B, K, P 🦴

     ● **S62.114**   Nondisplaced fracture of triquetrum [cuneiform] bone, right wrist B, K, P 🦴

     ● **S62.115**   Nondisplaced fracture of triquetrum [cuneiform] bone, left wrist B, K, P 🦴

     ● ■ **S62.116**   Nondisplaced fracture of triquetrum [cuneiform] bone, unspecified wrist B, K, P 🦴

● **S62.12**   Fracture of lunate [semilunar]

     ● **S62.121**   Displaced fracture of lunate [semilunar], right wrist B, K, P 🦴

     ● **S62.122**   Displaced fracture of lunate [semilunar], left wrist B, K, P 🦴

     ● ■ **S62.123**   Displaced fracture of lunate [semilunar], unspecified wrist B, K, P 🦴

     ● **S62.124**   Nondisplaced fracture of lunate [semilunar], right wrist B, K, P 🦴

     ● **S62.125**   Nondisplaced fracture of lunate [semilunar], left wrist B, K, P 🦴

     ● ■ **S62.126**   Nondisplaced fracture of lunate [semilunar], unspecified wrist B, K, P 🦴

● **S62.13**   Fracture of capitate [os magnum] bone

     ● **S62.131**   Displaced fracture of capitate [os magnum] bone, right wrist B, K, P 🦴

     ● **S62.132**   Displaced fracture of capitate [os magnum] bone, left wrist B, K, P 🦴

     ● ■ **S62.133**   Displaced fracture of capitate [os magnum] bone, unspecified wrist B, K, P 🦴

     ● **S62.134**   Nondisplaced fracture of capitate [os magnum] bone, right wrist B, K, P 🦴

     ● **S62.135**   Nondisplaced fracture of capitate [os magnum] bone, left wrist B, K, P 🦴

     ● ■ **S62.136**   Nondisplaced fracture of capitate [os magnum] bone, unspecified wrist B, K, P 🦴

● Unacceptable First-Listed Diagnosis   ● Use Additional Character(s)   ■ Unspecified   **OGCR** Official Guidelines for Coding and Reporting
🦴 Complication\Comorbidity   🦴 Major C\C   Excludes 1   Excludes 2   Includes   Use additional   Code first   Code also

● S62.14   Fracture of body of hamate [unciform] bone
     Fracture of hamate [unciform] bone NOS

   ● S62.141   Displaced fracture of body of hamate [unciform] bone, right wrist B, K, P 🦠

   ● S62.142   Displaced fracture of body of hamate [unciform] bone, left wrist B, K, P 🦠

   ● ■ S62.143   Displaced fracture of body of hamate [unciform] bone, unspecified wrist B, K, P 🦠

   ● S62.144   Nondisplaced fracture of body of hamate [unciform] bone, right wrist B, K, P 🦠

   ● S62.145   Nondisplaced fracture of body of hamate [unciform] bone, left wrist B, K, P 🦠

   ● ■ S62.146   Nondisplaced fracture of body of hamate [unciform] bone, unspecified wrist B, K, P 🦠

● S62.15   Fracture of hook process of hamate [unciform] bone
     Fracture of unciform process of hamate [unciform] bone

   ● S62.151   Displaced fracture of hook process of hamate [unciform] bone, right wrist B, K, P 🦠

   ● S62.152   Displaced fracture of hook process of hamate [unciform] bone, left wrist B, K, P 🦠

   ● ■ S62.153   Displaced fracture of hook process of hamate [unciform] bone, unspecified wrist B, K, P 🦠

   ● S62.154   Nondisplaced fracture of hook process of hamate [unciform] bone, right wrist B, K, P 🦠

   ● S62.155   Nondisplaced fracture of hook process of hamate [unciform] bone, left wrist B, K, P 🦠

   ● ■ S62.156   Nondisplaced fracture of hook process of hamate [unciform] bone, unspecified wrist B, K, P 🦠

● S62.16   Fracture of pisiform

   ● S62.161   Displaced fracture of pisiform, right wrist B, K, P 🦠

   ● S62.162   Displaced fracture of pisiform, left wrist B, K, P 🦠

   ● ■ S62.163   Displaced fracture of pisiform, unspecified wrist B, K, P 🦠

   ● S62.164   Nondisplaced fracture of pisiform, right wrist B, K, P 🦠

   ● S62.165   Nondisplaced fracture of pisiform, left wrist B, K, P 🦠

   ● ■ S62.166   Nondisplaced fracture of pisiform, unspecified wrist B, K, P 🦠

● S62.17   Fracture of trapezium [larger multangular]

   ● S62.171   Displaced fracture of trapezium [larger multangular], right wrist B, K, P 🦠

   ● S62.172   Displaced fracture of trapezium [larger multangular], left wrist B, K, P 🦠

   ● ■ S62.173   Displaced fracture of trapezium [larger multangular], unspecified wrist B, K, P 🦠

● S62.174   Nondisplaced fracture of trapezium [larger multangular], right wrist B, K, P 🦠

   ● S62.175   Nondisplaced fracture of trapezium [larger multangular], left wrist B, K, P 🦠

   ● ■ S62.176   Nondisplaced fracture of trapezium [larger multangular], unspecified wrist B, K, P 🦠

● S62.18   Fracture of trapezoid [smaller multangular]

   ● S62.181   Displaced fracture of trapezoid [smaller multangular], right wrist B, K, P 🦠

   ● S62.182   Displaced fracture of trapezoid [smaller multangular], left wrist B, K, P 🦠

   ● ■ S62.183   Displaced fracture of trapezoid [smaller multangular], unspecified wrist B, K, P 🦠

   ● S62.184   Nondisplaced fracture of trapezoid [smaller multangular], right wrist B, K, P 🦠

   ● S62.185   Nondisplaced fracture of trapezoid [smaller multangular], left wrist B, K, P 🦠

   ● ■ S62.186   Nondisplaced fracture of trapezoid [smaller multangular], unspecified wrist B, K, P 🦠

● S62.2   Fracture of first metacarpal bone

   ● S62.20   Unspecified fracture of first metacarpal bone

     ● ■ S62.201   Unspecified fracture of first metacarpal bone, right hand B, K, P 🦠

     ● ■ S62.202   Unspecified fracture of first metacarpal bone, left hand B, K, P 🦠

     ● ■ S62.209   Unspecified fracture of first metacarpal bone, unspecified hand B, K, P 🦠

   ● S62.21   Bennett's fracture

     ● S62.211   Bennett's fracture, right hand B, K, P 🦠

     ● S62.212   Bennett's fracture, left hand B, K, P 🦠

     ● ■ S62.213   Bennett's fracture, unspecified hand B, K, P 🦠

   ● S62.22   Rolando's fracture

     ● S62.221   Displaced Rolando's fracture, right hand B, K, P 🦠

     ● S62.222   Displaced Rolando's fracture, left hand B, K, P 🦠

     ● ■ S62.223   Displaced Rolando's fracture, unspecified hand B, K, P 🦠

     ● S62.224   Nondisplaced Rolando's fracture, right hand B, K, P 🦠

     ● S62.225   Nondisplaced Rolando's fracture, left hand B, K, P 🦠

     ● ■ S62.226   Nondisplaced Rolando's fracture, unspecified hand B, K, P 🦠

   ● S62.23   Other fracture of base of first metacarpal bone

     ● S62.231   Other displaced fracture of base of first metacarpal bone, right hand B, K, P 🦠

● Unacceptable First-Listed Diagnosis   ● Use Additional Character(s)   ■ Unspecified   OGCR Official Guidelines for Coding and Reporting

🦠 Complication\Comorbidity   🦠 Major C\C   Excludes 1   Excludes 2   Includes   Use additional   Code first   Code also

CHAPTER 19 (S00-T98)

1455

● S62.232 Other displaced fracture of base of first metacarpal bone, left hand B, K, P 🦠

● ■ S62.233 Other displaced fracture of base of first metacarpal bone, unspecified hand B, K, P 🦠

● S62.234 Other nondisplaced fracture of base of first metacarpal bone, right hand B, K, P 🦠

● S62.235 Other nondisplaced fracture of base of first metacarpal bone, left hand B, K, P 🦠

● ■ S62.236 Other nondisplaced fracture of base of first metacarpal bone, unspecified hand B, K, P 🦠

● S62.24 Fracture of shaft of first metacarpal bone

● S62.241 Displaced fracture of shaft of first metacarpal bone, right hand B, K, P 🦠

● S62.242 Displaced fracture of shaft of first metacarpal bone, left hand B, K, P 🦠

● ■ S62.243 Displaced fracture of shaft of first metacarpal bone, unspecified hand B, K, P 🦠

● S62.244 Nondisplaced fracture of shaft of first metacarpal bone, right hand B, K, P 🦠

● S62.245 Nondisplaced fracture of shaft of first metacarpal bone, left hand B, K, P 🦠

● ■ S62.246 Nondisplaced fracture of shaft of first metacarpal bone, unspecified hand B, K, P 🦠

● S62.25 Fracture of neck of first metacarpal bone

● S62.251 Displaced fracture of neck of first metacarpal bone, right hand B, K, P 🦠

● S62.252 Displaced fracture of neck of first metacarpal bone, left hand B, K, P 🦠

● ■ S62.253 Displaced fracture of neck of first metacarpal bone, unspecified hand B, K, P 🦠

● S62.254 Nondisplaced fracture of neck of first metacarpal bone, right hand B, K, P 🦠

● S62.255 Nondisplaced fracture of neck of first metacarpal bone, left hand B, K, P 🦠

● ■ S62.256 Nondisplaced fracture of neck of first metacarpal bone, unspecified hand B, K, P 🦠

● S62.29 Other fracture of first metacarpal bone

● S62.291 Other fracture of first metacarpal bone, right hand B, K, P 🦠

● S62.292 Other fracture of first metacarpal bone, left hand B, K, P 🦠

● ■ S62.299 Other fracture of first metacarpal bone, unspecified hand B, K, P 🦠

● S62.3 Fracture of other and unspecified metacarpal bone

Excludes2 fracture of first metacarpal bone (S62.2-)

● S62.30 Unspecified fracture of other metacarpal bone

● ■ S62.300 Unspecified fracture of second metacarpal bone, right hand B, K, P 🦠

● ■ S62.301 Unspecified fracture of second metacarpal bone, left hand B, K, P 🦠

● ■ S62.302 Unspecified fracture of third metacarpal bone, right hand B, K, P 🦠

● ■ S62.303 Unspecified fracture of third metacarpal bone, left hand B, K, P 🦠

● ■ S62.304 Unspecified fracture of fourth metacarpal bone, right hand B, K, P 🦠

● ■ S62.305 Unspecified fracture of fourth metacarpal bone, left hand B, K, P 🦠

● ■ S62.306 Unspecified fracture of fifth metacarpal bone, right hand B, K, P 🦠

● ■ S62.307 Unspecified fracture of fifth metacarpal bone, left hand B, K, P 🦠

● ■ S62.308 Unspecified fracture of other metacarpal bone B, K, P 🦠
Unspecified fracture of specified metacarpal bone with unspecified laterality

● ■ S62.309 Unspecified fracture of unspecified metacarpal bone B, K, P 🦠

● S62.31 Displaced fracture of base of other metacarpal bone

● S62.310 Displaced fracture of base of second metacarpal bone, right hand B, K, P 🦠

● S62.311 Displaced fracture of base of second metacarpal bone, left hand B, K, P 🦠

● S62.312 Displaced fracture of base of third metacarpal bone, right hand B, K, P 🦠

● S62.313 Displaced fracture of base of third metacarpal bone, left hand B, K, P 🦠

● S62.314 Displaced fracture of base of fourth metacarpal bone, right hand B, K, P 🦠

● S62.315 Displaced fracture of base of fourth metacarpal bone, left hand B, K, P 🦠

● S62.316 Displaced fracture of base of fifth metacarpal bone, right hand B, K, P 🦠

● S62.317 Displaced fracture of base of fifth metacarpal bone, left hand B, K, P 🦠

● S62.318 Displaced fracture of base of other metacarpal bone B, K, P 🦠
Displaced fracture of base of specified metacarpal bone with unspecified laterality

● ■ S62.319 Displaced fracture of base of unspecified metacarpal bone B, K, P 🦠

● Unacceptable First-Listed Diagnosis   ● Use Additional Character(s)   ■ Unspecified   **OGCR** Official Guidelines for Coding and Reporting
🦠 Complication\Comorbidity   🦠 Major C\C   Excludes 1   Excludes 2   Includes   Use additional   Code first   Code also

● S62.32   **Displaced fracture of shaft of other metacarpal bone**

   ● S62.320   Displaced fracture of shaft of second metacarpal bone, right hand B, K, P 🐾

   ● S62.321   Displaced fracture of shaft of second metacarpal bone, left hand B, K, P 🐾

   ● S62.322   Displaced fracture of shaft of third metacarpal bone, right hand B, K, P 🐾

   ● S62.323   Displaced fracture of shaft of third metacarpal bone, left hand B, K, P 🐾

   ● S62.324   Displaced fracture of shaft of fourth metacarpal bone, right hand B, K, P 🐾

   ● S62.325   Displaced fracture of shaft of fourth metacarpal bone, left hand B, K, P 🐾

   ● S62.326   Displaced fracture of shaft of fifth metacarpal bone, right hand B, K, P 🐾

   ● S62.327   Displaced fracture of shaft of fifth metacarpal bone, left hand B, K, P 🐾

   ● S62.328   Displaced fracture of shaft of other metacarpal bone B, K, P 🐾
       Displaced fracture of shaft of specified metacarpal bone with unspecified laterality

   ● ▪ S62.329   Displaced fracture of shaft of unspecified metacarpal bone B, K, P 🐾

● S62.33   **Displaced fracture of neck of other metacarpal bone**

   ● S62.330   Displaced fracture of neck of second metacarpal bone, right hand B, K, P 🐾

   ● S62.331   Displaced fracture of neck of second metacarpal bone, left hand B, K, P 🐾

   ● S62.332   Displaced fracture of neck of third metacarpal bone, right hand B, K, P 🐾

   ● S62.333   Displaced fracture of neck of third metacarpal bone, left hand B, K, P 🐾

   ● S62.334   Displaced fracture of neck of fourth metacarpal bone, right hand B, K, P 🐾

   ● S62.335   Displaced fracture of neck of fourth metacarpal bone, left hand B, K, P 🐾

   ● S62.336   Displaced fracture of neck of fifth metacarpal bone, right hand B, K, P 🐾

   ● S62.337   Displaced fracture of neck of fifth metacarpal bone, left hand B, K, P 🐾

   ● S62.338   Displaced fracture of neck of other metacarpal bone B, K, P 🐾
       Displaced fracture of neck of specified metacarpal bone with unspecified laterality

   ● ▪ S62.339   Displaced fracture of neck of unspecified metacarpal bone B, K, P 🐾

● S62.34   **Nondisplaced fracture of base of other metacarpal bone**

   ● S62.340   Nondisplaced fracture of base of second metacarpal bone, right hand B, K, P 🐾

   ● S62.341   Nondisplaced fracture of base of second metacarpal bone, left hand B, K, P 🐾

   ● S62.342   Nondisplaced fracture of base of third metacarpal bone, right hand B, K, P 🐾

   ● S62.343   Nondisplaced fracture of base of third metacarpal bone, left hand B, K, P 🐾

   ● S62.344   Nondisplaced fracture of base of fourth metacarpal bone, right hand B, K, P 🐾

   ● S62.345   Nondisplaced fracture of base of fourth metacarpal bone, left hand B, K, P 🐾

   ● S62.346   Nondisplaced fracture of base of fifth metacarpal bone, right hand B, K, P 🐾

   ● S62.347   Nondisplaced fracture of base of fifth metacarpal bone, left hand B, K, P 🐾

   ● S62.348   Nondisplaced fracture of base of other metacarpal bone B, K, P 🐾
       Nondisplaced fracture of base of specified metacarpal bone with unspecified laterality

   ● ▪ S62.349   Nondisplaced fracture of base of unspecified metacarpal bone B, K, P 🐾

● S62.35   **Nondisplaced fracture of shaft of other metacarpal bone**

   ● S62.350   Nondisplaced fracture of shaft of second metacarpal bone, right hand B, K, P 🐾

   ● S62.351   Nondisplaced fracture of shaft of second metacarpal bone, left hand B, K, P 🐾

   ● S62.352   Nondisplaced fracture of shaft of third metacarpal bone, right hand B, K, P 🐾

   ● S62.353   Nondisplaced fracture of shaft of third metacarpal bone, left hand B, K, P 🐾

   ● S62.354   Nondisplaced fracture of shaft of fourth metacarpal bone, right hand B, K, P 🐾

   ● S62.355   Nondisplaced fracture of shaft of fourth metacarpal bone, left hand B, K, P 🐾

   ● S62.356   Nondisplaced fracture of shaft of fifth metacarpal bone, right hand B, K, P 🐾

   ● S62.357   Nondisplaced fracture of shaft of fifth metacarpal bone, left hand B, K, P 🐾

   ● S62.358   Nondisplaced fracture of shaft of other metacarpal bone B, K, P 🐾
       Nondisplaced fracture of shaft of specified metacarpal bone with unspecified laterality

● Unacceptable First-Listed Diagnosis   ● Use Additional Character(s)   ▪ Unspecified   **OGCR** Official Guidelines for Coding and Reporting

🐾 Complication\Comorbidity   🐾 Major C\C | Excludes 1 | | Excludes 2 | Includes   Use additional   Code first   Code also

1457

CHAPTER 19 (S00-T98)

● ■ **S62.359** Nondisplaced fracture of shaft of unspecified metacarpal bone B, K, P 🕭

● **S62.36** Nondisplaced fracture of neck of other metacarpal bone

　● **S62.360** Nondisplaced fracture of neck of second metacarpal bone, right hand B, K, P 🕭

　● **S62.361** Nondisplaced fracture of neck of second metacarpal bone, left hand B, K, P 🕭

　● **S62.362** Nondisplaced fracture of neck of third metacarpal bone, right hand B, K, P 🕭

　● **S62.363** Nondisplaced fracture of neck of third metacarpal bone, left hand B, K, P 🕭

　● **S62.364** Nondisplaced fracture of neck of fourth metacarpal bone, right hand B, K, P 🕭

　● **S62.365** Nondisplaced fracture of neck of fourth metacarpal bone, left hand B, K, P 🕭

　● **S62.366** Nondisplaced fracture of neck of fifth metacarpal bone, right hand B, K, P 🕭

　● **S62.367** Nondisplaced fracture of neck of fifth metacarpal bone, left hand B, K, P 🕭

　● **S62.368** Nondisplaced fracture of neck of other metacarpal bone B, K, P 🕭
　　　Nondisplaced fracture of neck of specified metacarpal bone with unspecified laterality

● ■ **S62.369** Nondisplaced fracture of neck of unspecified metacarpal bone B, K, P 🕭

● **S62.39** Other fracture of other metacarpal bone

　● **S62.390** Other fracture of second metacarpal bone, right hand B, K, P 🕭

　● **S62.391** Other fracture of second metacarpal bone, left hand B, K, P 🕭

　● **S62.392** Other fracture of third metacarpal bone, right hand B, K, P 🕭

　● **S62.393** Other fracture of third metacarpal bone, left hand B, K, P 🕭

　● **S62.394** Other fracture of fourth metacarpal bone, right hand B, K, P 🕭

　● **S62.395** Other fracture of fourth metacarpal bone, left hand B, K, P 🕭

　● **S62.396** Other fracture of fifth metacarpal bone, right hand B, K, P 🕭

　● **S62.397** Other fracture of fifth metacarpal bone, left hand B, K, P 🕭

　● **S62.398** Other fracture of other metacarpal bone B, K, P 🕭
　　　Other fracture of specified metacarpal bone with unspecified laterality

● ■ **S62.399** Other fracture of unspecified metacarpal bone B, K, P 🕭

● **S62.5** Fracture of thumb

　● **S62.50** Fracture of unspecified phalanx of thumb

　● ■ **S62.501** Fracture of unspecified phalanx of right thumb B, K, P 🕭

　● ■ **S62.502** Fracture of unspecified phalanx of left thumb B, K, P 🕭

　● ■ **S62.509** Fracture of unspecified phalanx of unspecified thumb B, K, P 🕭

　● **S62.51** Fracture of proximal phalanx of thumb

　● **S62.511** Displaced fracture of proximal phalanx of right thumb B, K, P 🕭

　● **S62.512** Displaced fracture of proximal phalanx of left thumb B, K, P 🕭

　● ■ **S62.513** Displaced fracture of proximal phalanx of unspecified thumb B, K, P 🕭

　● **S62.514** Nondisplaced fracture of proximal phalanx of right thumb B, K, P 🕭

　● **S62.515** Nondisplaced fracture of proximal phalanx of left thumb B, K, P 🕭

　● ■ **S62.516** Nondisplaced fracture of proximal phalanx of unspecified thumb B, K, P 🕭

　● **S62.52** Fracture of distal phalanx of thumb

　● **S62.521** Displaced fracture of distal phalanx of right thumb B, K, P 🕭

　● **S62.522** Displaced fracture of distal phalanx of left thumb B, K, P 🕭

　● ■ **S62.523** Displaced fracture of distal phalanx of unspecified thumb B, K, P 🕭

　● **S62.524** Nondisplaced fracture of distal phalanx of right thumb B, K, P 🕭

　● **S62.525** Nondisplaced fracture of distal phalanx of left thumb B, K, P 🕭

　● ■ **S62.526** Nondisplaced fracture of distal phalanx of unspecified thumb B, K, P 🕭

● **S62.6** Fracture of other and unspecified finger(s)
　　| Excludes2 | fracture of thumb (S62.5-)

　● **S62.60** Fracture of unspecified phalanx of finger

　● ■ **S62.600** Fracture of unspecified phalanx of right index finger B, K, P 🕭

　● ■ **S62.601** Fracture of unspecified phalanx of left index finger B, K, P 🕭

　● ■ **S62.602** Fracture of unspecified phalanx of right middle finger B, K, P 🕭

　● ■ **S62.603** Fracture of unspecified phalanx of left middle finger B, K, P 🕭

　● ■ **S62.604** Fracture of unspecified phalanx of right ring finger B, K, P 🕭

　● ■ **S62.605** Fracture of unspecified phalanx of left ring finger B, K, P 🕭

　● ■ **S62.606** Fracture of unspecified phalanx of right little finger B, K, P 🕭

　● ■ **S62.607** Fracture of unspecified phalanx of left little finger B, K, P 🕭

　● ■ **S62.608** Fracture of unspecified phalanx of other finger B, K, P 🕭
　　　Fracture of unspecified phalanx of specified finger with unspecified laterality

　● ■ **S62.609** Fracture of unspecified phalanx of unspecified finger B, K, P 🕭

● Unacceptable First-Listed Diagnosis　　● Use Additional Character(s)　　■ Unspecified　　**OGCR** Official Guidelines for Coding and Reporting
🕭 Complication\Comorbidity　　🕭 Major C\C　　| Excludes 1 |　| Excludes 2 |　Includes　　Use additional　　Code first　　Code also

● S62.61   **Displaced fracture of proximal phalanx of finger**

  ● S62.610   **Displaced fracture of proximal phalanx of right index finger B, K, P** 🞉

  ● S62.611   **Displaced fracture of proximal phalanx of left index finger B, K, P** 🞉

  ● S62.612   **Displaced fracture of proximal phalanx of right middle finger B, K, P** 🞉

  ● S62.613   **Displaced fracture of proximal phalanx of left middle finger B, K, P** 🞉

  ● S62.614   **Displaced fracture of proximal phalanx of right ring finger B, K, P** 🞉

  ● S62.615   **Displaced fracture of proximal phalanx of left ring finger B, K, P** 🞉

  ● S62.616   **Displaced fracture of proximal phalanx of right little finger B, K, P** 🞉

  ● S62.617   **Displaced fracture of proximal phalanx of left little finger B, K, P** 🞉

  ● S62.618   **Displaced fracture of proximal phalanx of other finger B, K, P** 🞉
          Displaced fracture of proximal phalanx of specified finger with unspecified laterality

  ● ▢ S62.619   **Displaced fracture of proximal phalanx of unspecified finger B, K, P** 🞉

● S62.62   **Displaced fracture of middle phalanx of finger**

  ● S62.620   **Displaced fracture of middle phalanx of right index finger B, K, P** 🞉

  ● S62.621   **Displaced fracture of middle phalanx of left index finger B, K, P** 🞉

  ● S62.622   **Displaced fracture of middle phalanx of right middle finger B, K, P** 🞉

  ● S62.623   **Displaced fracture of middle phalanx of left middle finger B, K, P** 🞉

  ● S62.624   **Displaced fracture of middle phalanx of right ring finger B, K, P** 🞉

  ● S62.625   **Displaced fracture of middle phalanx of left ring finger B, K, P** 🞉

  ● S62.626   **Displaced fracture of middle phalanx of right little finger B, K, P** 🞉

  ● S62.627   **Displaced fracture of middle phalanx of left little finger B, K, P** 🞉

  ● S62.628   **Displaced fracture of middle phalanx of other finger B, K, P** 🞉
          Displaced fracture of middle phalanx of specified finger with unspecified laterality

  ● ▢ S62.629   **Displaced fracture of middle phalanx of unspecified finger B, K, P** 🞉

● S62.63   **Displaced fracture of distal phalanx of finger**

  ● S62.630   **Displaced fracture of distal phalanx of right index finger B, K, P** 🞉

  ● S62.631   **Displaced fracture of distal phalanx of left index finger B, K, P** 🞉

  ● S62.632   **Displaced fracture of distal phalanx of right middle finger B, K, P** 🞉

  ● S62.633   **Displaced fracture of distal phalanx of left middle finger B, K, P** 🞉

  ● S62.634   **Displaced fracture of distal phalanx of right ring finger B, K, P** 🞉

  ● S62.635   **Displaced fracture of distal phalanx of left ring finger B, K, P** 🞉

  ● S62.636   **Displaced fracture of distal phalanx of right little finger B, K, P** 🞉

  ● S62.637   **Displaced fracture of distal phalanx of left little finger B, K, P** 🞉

  ● S62.638   **Displaced fracture of distal phalanx of other finger B, K, P** 🞉
          Displaced fracture of distal phalanx of specified finger with unspecified laterality

  ● ▢ S62.639   **Displaced fracture of distal phalanx of unspecified finger B, K, P** 🞉

● S62.64   **Nondisplaced fracture of proximal phalanx of finger**

  ● S62.640   **Nondisplaced fracture of proximal phalanx of right index finger B, K, P** 🞉

  ● S62.641   **Nondisplaced fracture of proximal phalanx of left index finger B, K, P** 🞉

  ● S62.642   **Nondisplaced fracture of proximal phalanx of right middle finger B, K, P** 🞉

  ● S62.643   **Nondisplaced fracture of proximal phalanx of left middle finger B, K, P** 🞉

  ● S62.644   **Nondisplaced fracture of proximal phalanx of right ring finger B, K, P** 🞉

  ● S62.645   **Nondisplaced fracture of proximal phalanx of left ring finger B, K, P** 🞉

  ● S62.646   **Nondisplaced fracture of proximal phalanx of right little finger B, K, P** 🞉

  ● S62.647   **Nondisplaced fracture of proximal phalanx of left little finger B, K, P** 🞉

  ● S62.648   **Nondisplaced fracture of proximal phalanx of other finger B, K, P** 🞉
          Nondisplaced fracture of proximal phalanx of specified finger with unspecified laterality

  ● ▢ S62.649   **Nondisplaced fracture of proximal phalanx of unspecified finger B, K, P** 🞉

● Unacceptable First-Listed Diagnosis   ● Use Additional Character(s)   ▢ Unspecified   **OGCR** Official Guidelines for Coding and Reporting
🞉 Complication\Comorbidity   Major C\C   Excludes 1   Excludes 2   Includes   Use additional   Code first   Code also

CHAPTER 19 (S00-T98)

1459

● **S62.65**   **Nondisplaced fracture of middle phalanx of finger**
- ● **S62.650**   Nondisplaced fracture of middle phalanx of right index finger B, K, P 🗲
- ● **S62.651**   Nondisplaced fracture of middle phalanx of left index finger B, K, P 🗲
- ● **S62.652**   Nondisplaced fracture of middle phalanx of right middle finger B, K, P 🗲
- ● **S62.653**   Nondisplaced fracture of middle phalanx of left middle finger B, K, P 🗲
- ● **S62.654**   Nondisplaced fracture of middle phalanx of right ring finger B, K, P 🗲
- ● **S62.655**   Nondisplaced fracture of middle phalanx of left ring finger B, K, P 🗲
- ● **S62.656**   Nondisplaced fracture of middle phalanx of right little finger B, K, P 🗲
- ● **S62.657**   Nondisplaced fracture of middle phalanx of left little finger B, K, P 🗲
- ● **S62.658**   Nondisplaced fracture of middle phalanx of other finger B, K, P 🗲
  Nondisplaced fracture of middle phalanx of specified finger with unspecified laterality
- ● ■ **S62.659**   Nondisplaced fracture of middle phalanx of unspecified finger B, K, P 🗲

● **S62.66**   **Nondisplaced fracture of distal phalanx of finger**
- ● **S62.660**   Nondisplaced fracture of distal phalanx of right index finger B, K, P 🗲
- ● **S62.661**   Nondisplaced fracture of distal phalanx of left index finger B, K, P 🗲
- ● **S62.662**   Nondisplaced fracture of distal phalanx of right middle finger B, K, P 🗲
- ● **S62.663**   Nondisplaced fracture of distal phalanx of left middle finger B, K, P 🗲
- ● **S62.664**   Nondisplaced fracture of distal phalanx of right ring finger B, K, P 🗲
- ● **S62.665**   Nondisplaced fracture of distal phalanx of left ring finger B, K, P 🗲
- ● **S62.666**   Nondisplaced fracture of distal phalanx of right little finger B, K, P 🗲
- ● **S62.667**   Nondisplaced fracture of distal phalanx of left little finger B, K, P 🗲
- ● **S62.668**   Nondisplaced fracture of distal phalanx of other finger B, K, P 🗲
  Nondisplaced fracture of distal phalanx of specified finger with unspecified laterality
- ● ■ **S62.669**   Nondisplaced fracture of distal phalanx of unspecified finger B, K, P 🗲

● **S62.9**   **Unspecified fracture of wrist and hand**
- ● ■ **S62.90**   Unspecified fracture of unspecified wrist and hand B, K, P 🗲
- ● ■ **S62.91**   Unspecified fracture of right wrist and hand B, K, P 🗲
- ● ■ **S62.92**   Unspecified fracture of left wrist and hand B, K, P 🗲

● **S63**   **Dislocation and sprain of joints and ligaments at wrist and hand level**

Includes	avulsion of joint or ligament at wrist and hand level
	laceration of cartilage, joint or ligament at wrist and hand level
	sprain of cartilage, joint or ligament at wrist and hand level
	traumatic hemarthrosis of joint or ligament at wrist and hand level
	traumatic rupture of joint or ligament at wrist and hand level
	traumatic subluxation of joint or ligament at wrist and hand level
	traumatic tear of joint or ligament at wrist and hand level

Code also any associated open wound

| **Excludes2** | strain of muscle, fascia and tendon of wrist and hand (S66.-) |

The appropriate 7th character is to be added to each code from category S63

A	initial encounter
D	subsequent encounter
S	sequela

● **S63.0**   **Subluxation and dislocation of wrist and hand joints**
- ● **S63.00**   Unspecified subluxation and dislocation of wrist and hand
  Dislocation of carpal bone NOS
  Dislocation of distal end of radius NOS
  Subluxation of carpal bone NOS
  Subluxation of distal end of radius NOS
  - ● ■ **S63.001**   Unspecified subluxation of right wrist and hand

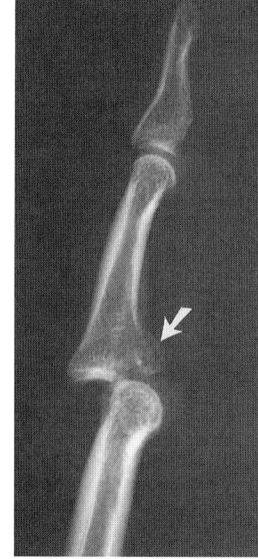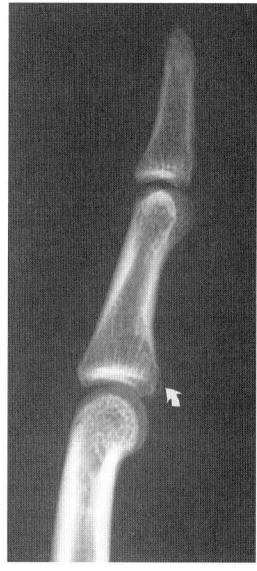

A   B

Figure 19-13 Dislocation including displacement and subluxation. (From Grainger & Allison's Diagnostic Radiology: A Textbook of Medical Imaging, 4th ed. 2001, Churchill Livingstone)

CHAPTER 19 (S00-T98)

1460

● Unacceptable First-Listed Diagnosis   ● Use Additional Character(s)   ■ Unspecified   **OGCR** Official Guidelines for Coding and Reporting

🗲 Complication\Comorbidity   🗲 Major C\C   Excludes 1   Excludes 2   Includes   Use additional   Code first   Code also

● ■ S63.002 Unspecified subluxation of left wrist and hand

● ■ S63.003 Unspecified subluxation of unspecified wrist and hand

● ■ S63.004 Unspecified dislocation of right wrist and hand

● ■ S63.005 Unspecified dislocation of left wrist and hand

● ■ S63.006 Unspecified dislocation of unspecified wrist and hand

● S63.01 Subluxation and dislocation of distal radioulnar joint

    ● S63.011 Subluxation of distal radioulnar joint of right wrist

    ● S63.012 Subluxation of distal radioulnar joint of left wrist

    ● ■ S63.013 Subluxation of distal radioulnar joint of unspecified wrist

    ● S63.014 Dislocation of distal radioulnar joint of right wrist

    ● S63.015 Dislocation of distal radioulnar joint of left wrist

    ● ■ S63.016 Dislocation of distal radioulnar joint of unspecified wrist

● S63.02 Subluxation and dislocation of radiocarpal joint

    ● S63.021 Subluxation of radiocarpal joint of right wrist

    ● S63.022 Subluxation of radiocarpal joint of left wrist

    ● ■ S63.023 Subluxation of radiocarpal joint of unspecified wrist

    ● S63.024 Dislocation of radiocarpal joint of right wrist

    ● S63.025 Dislocation of radiocarpal joint of left wrist

    ● ■ S63.026 Dislocation of radiocarpal joint of unspecified wrist

● S63.03 Subluxation and dislocation of midcarpal joint

    ● S63.031 Subluxation of midcarpal joint of right wrist

    ● S63.032 Subluxation of midcarpal joint of left wrist

    ● ■ S63.033 Subluxation of midcarpal joint of unspecified wrist

    ● S63.034 Dislocation of midcarpal joint of right wrist

    ● S63.035 Dislocation of midcarpal joint of left wrist

    ● ■ S63.036 Dislocation of midcarpal joint of unspecified wrist

● S63.04 Subluxation and dislocation of carpometacarpal joint of thumb

    Excludes2 interphalangeal subluxation and dislocation of thumb (S63.1-)

    ● S63.041 Subluxation of carpometacarpal joint of right thumb

    ● S63.042 Subluxation of carpometacarpal joint of left thumb

    ● ■ S63.043 Subluxation of carpometacarpal joint of unspecified thumb

● S63.044 Dislocation of carpometacarpal joint of right thumb

● S63.045 Dislocation of carpometacarpal joint of left thumb

● ■ S63.046 Dislocation of carpometacarpal joint of unspecified thumb

● S63.05 Subluxation and dislocation of other carpometacarpal joint

    Excludes2 subluxation and dislocation of carpometacarpal joint of thumb (S63.04-)

    ● S63.051 Subluxation of other carpometacarpal joint of right hand

    ● S63.052 Subluxation of other carpometacarpal joint of left hand

    ● ■ S63.053 Subluxation of other carpometacarpal joint of unspecified hand

    ● S63.054 Dislocation of other carpometacarpal joint of right hand

    ● S63.055 Dislocation of other carpometacarpal joint of left hand

    ● ■ S63.056 Dislocation of other carpometacarpal joint of unspecified hand

● S63.06 Subluxation and dislocation of metacarpal (bone), proximal end

    ● S63.061 Subluxation of metacarpal (bone), proximal end of right hand

    ● S63.062 Subluxation of metacarpal (bone), proximal end of left hand

    ● ■ S63.063 Subluxation of metacarpal (bone), proximal end of unspecified hand

    ● S63.064 Dislocation of metacarpal (bone), proximal end of right hand

    ● S63.065 Dislocation of metacarpal (bone), proximal end of left hand

    ● ■ S63.066 Dislocation of metacarpal (bone), proximal end of unspecified hand

● S63.07 Subluxation and dislocation of distal end of ulna

    ● S63.071 Subluxation of distal end of right ulna

    ● S63.072 Subluxation of distal end of left ulna

    ● ■ S63.073 Subluxation of distal end of unspecified ulna

    ● S63.074 Dislocation of distal end of right ulna

    ● S63.075 Dislocation of distal end of left ulna

    ● ■ S63.076 Dislocation of distal end of unspecified ulna

● S63.09 Other subluxation and dislocation of wrist and hand

    ● S63.091 Other subluxation of right wrist and hand

    ● S63.092 Other subluxation of left wrist and hand

● Unacceptable First-Listed Diagnosis   ● Use Additional Character(s)   ■ Unspecified   **OGCR** Official Guidelines for Coding and Reporting

 Complication\Comorbidity   Major C\C   Excludes 1   Excludes 2   Includes   Use additional   Code first   Code also

CHAPTER 19 (S00-T98)

● ■ **S63.093** Other subluxation of unspecified wrist and hand

● **S63.094** Other dislocation of right wrist and hand

● **S63.095** Other dislocation of left wrist and hand

● ■ **S63.096** Other dislocation of unspecified wrist and hand

● **S63.1** Subluxation and dislocation of thumb

● **S63.10** Unspecified subluxation and dislocation of thumb

● ■ **S63.101** Unspecified subluxation of right thumb

● ■ **S63.102** Unspecified subluxation of left thumb

● ■ **S63.103** Unspecified subluxation of unspecified thumb

● ■ **S63.104** Unspecified dislocation of right thumb

● ■ **S63.105** Unspecified dislocation of left thumb

● ■ **S63.106** Unspecified dislocation of unspecified thumb

● **S63.11** Subluxation and dislocation of metacarpophalangeal joint of thumb

● **S63.111** Subluxation of metacarpophalangeal joint of right thumb

● **S63.112** Subluxation of metacarpophalangeal joint of left thumb

● ■ **S63.113** Subluxation of metacarpophalangeal joint of unspecified thumb

● **S63.114** Dislocation of metacarpophalangeal joint of right thumb

● **S63.115** Dislocation of metacarpophalangeal joint of left thumb

● ■ **S63.116** Dislocation of metacarpophalangeal joint of unspecified thumb

● **S63.12** Subluxation and dislocation of unspecified interphalangeal joint of thumb

● ■ **S63.121** Subluxation of unspecified interphalangeal joint of right thumb

● ■ **S63.122** Subluxation of unspecified interphalangeal joint of left thumb

● ■ **S63.123** Subluxation of unspecified interphalangeal joint of unspecified thumb

● ■ **S63.124** Dislocation of unspecified interphalangeal joint of right thumb

● ■ **S63.125** Dislocation of unspecified interphalangeal joint of left thumb

● ■ **S63.126** Dislocation of unspecified interphalangeal joint of unspecified thumb

● **S63.13** Subluxation and dislocation of proximal interphalangeal joint of thumb

● **S63.131** Subluxation of proximal interphalangeal joint of right thumb

● **S63.132** Subluxation of proximal interphalangeal joint of left thumb

● ■ **S63.133** Subluxation of proximal interphalangeal joint of unspecified thumb

● **S63.134** Dislocation of proximal interphalangeal joint of right thumb

● **S63.135** Dislocation of proximal interphalangeal joint of left thumb

● ■ **S63.136** Dislocation of proximal interphalangeal joint of unspecified thumb

● **S63.14** Subluxation and dislocation of distal interphalangeal joint of thumb

S63.141 Subluxation of distal interphalangeal joint of right thumb

● **S63.142** Subluxation of distal interphalangeal joint of left thumb

● ■ **S63.143** Subluxation of distal interphalangeal joint of unspecified thumb

● **S63.144** Dislocation of distal interphalangeal joint of right thumb

● **S63.145** Dislocation of distal interphalangeal joint of left thumb

● ■ **S63.146** Dislocation of distal interphalangeal joint of unspecified thumb

● **S63.2** Subluxation and dislocation of other finger(s)

Excludes2 subluxation and dislocation of thumb (S63.1-)

● **S63.20** Unspecified subluxation of other finger

● ■ **S63.200** Unspecified subluxation of right index finger

● ■ **S63.201** Unspecified subluxation of left index finger

● ■ **S63.202** Unspecified subluxation of right middle finger

● ■ **S63.203** Unspecified subluxation of left middle finger

● ■ **S63.204** Unspecified subluxation of right ring finger

● ■ **S63.205** Unspecified subluxation of left ring finger

● ■ **S63.206** Unspecified subluxation of right little finger

● ■ **S63.207** Unspecified subluxation of left little finger

● ■ **S63.208** Unspecified subluxation of other finger

Unspecified subluxation of specified finger with unspecified laterality

● ■ **S63.209** Unspecified subluxation of unspecified finger

● Unacceptable First-Listed Diagnosis　　● Use Additional Character(s)　　■ Unspecified　　**OGCR** Official Guidelines for Coding and Reporting

🐾 Complication\Comorbidity　🐾 Major C\C　 Excludes 1　 Excludes 2　Includes　Use additional　Code first　Code also

● S63.21   Subluxation of metacarpophalangeal joint of finger

    ● S63.210   Subluxation of metacarpophalangeal joint of right index finger

    ● S63.211   Subluxation of metacarpophalangeal joint of left index finger

    ● S63.212   Subluxation of metacarpophalangeal joint of right middle finger

    ● S63.213   Subluxation of metacarpophalangeal joint of left middle finger

    ● S63.214   Subluxation of metacarpophalangeal joint of right ring finger

    ● S63.215   Subluxation of metacarpophalangeal joint of left ring finger

    ● S63.216   Subluxation of metacarpophalangeal joint of right little finger

    ● S63.217   Subluxation of metacarpophalangeal joint of left little finger

    ● S63.218   Subluxation of metacarpophalangeal joint of other finger

       Subluxation of metacarpophalangeal joint of specified finger with unspecified laterality

    ● ■ S63.219   Subluxation of metacarpophalangeal joint of unspecified finger

● S63.22   Subluxation of unspecified interphalangeal joint of finger

    ● ■ S63.220   Subluxation of unspecified interphalangeal joint of right index finger

    ● ■ S63.221   Subluxation of unspecified interphalangeal joint of left index finger

    ● ■ S63.222   Subluxation of unspecified interphalangeal joint of right middle finger

    ● ■ S63.223   Subluxation of unspecified interphalangeal joint of left middle finger

    ● ■ S63.224   Subluxation of unspecified interphalangeal joint of right ring finger

    ● ■ S63.225   Subluxation of unspecified interphalangeal joint of left ring finger

    ● ■ S63.226   Subluxation of unspecified interphalangeal joint of right little finger

    ● ■ S63.227   Subluxation of unspecified interphalangeal joint of left little finger

    ● ■ S63.228   Subluxation of unspecified interphalangeal joint of other finger

       Subluxation of unspecified interphalangeal joint of specified finger with unspecified laterality

    ● ■ S63.229   Subluxation of unspecified interphalangeal joint of unspecified finger

● S63.23   Subluxation of proximal interphalangeal joint of finger

    ● S63.230   Subluxation of proximal interphalangeal joint of right index finger

    ● S63.231   Subluxation of proximal interphalangeal joint of left index finger

    ● S63.232   Subluxation of proximal interphalangeal joint of right middle finger

    ● S63.233   Subluxation of proximal interphalangeal joint of left middle finger

    ● S63.234   Subluxation of proximal interphalangeal joint of right ring finger

    ● S63.235   Subluxation of proximal interphalangeal joint of left ring finger

    ● S63.236   Subluxation of proximal interphalangeal joint of right little finger

    ● S63.237   Subluxation of proximal interphalangeal joint of left little finger

    ● S63.238   Subluxation of proximal interphalangeal joint of other finger

       Subluxation of proximal interphalangeal joint of specified finger with unspecified laterality

    ● ■ S63.239   Subluxation of proximal interphalangeal joint of unspecified finger

● S63.24   Subluxation of distal interphalangeal joint of finger

    ● S63.240   Subluxation of distal interphalangeal joint of right index finger

    ● S63.241   Subluxation of distal interphalangeal joint of left index finger

    ● S63.242   Subluxation of distal interphalangeal joint of right middle finger

    ● S63.243   Subluxation of distal interphalangeal joint of left middle finger

    ● S63.244   Subluxation of distal interphalangeal joint of right ring finger

    ● S63.245   Subluxation of distal interphalangeal joint of left ring finger

● Unacceptable First-Listed Diagnosis   ● Use Additional Character(s)   ■ Unspecified   **OGCR** Official Guidelines for Coding and Reporting

⚘ Complication\Comorbidity   ⚘ Major C\C      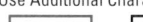

1463

CHAPTER 19 (S00-T98)

● S63.246   Subluxation of distal interphalangeal joint of right little finger

● S63.247   Subluxation of distal interphalangeal joint of left little finger

● S63.248   Subluxation of distal interphalangeal joint of other finger

     Subluxation of distal interphalangeal joint of specified finger with unspecified laterality

● ▣ S63.249   Subluxation of distal interphalangeal joint of unspecified finger

● S63.25   Unspecified dislocation of other finger

● ▣ S63.250   Unspecified dislocation of right index finger

● ▣ S63.251   Unspecified dislocation of left index finger

● ▣ S63.252   Unspecified dislocation of right middle finger

● ▣ S63.253   Unspecified dislocation of left middle finger

● ▣ S63.254   Unspecified dislocation of right ring finger

● ▣ S63.255   Unspecified dislocation of left ring finger

● ▣ S63.256   Unspecified dislocation of right little finger

● ▣ S63.257   Unspecified dislocation of left little finger

● ▣ S63.258   Unspecified dislocation of other finger

     Unspecified dislocation of specified finger with unspecified laterality

● ▣ S63.259   Unspecified dislocation of unspecified finger

     Unspecified dislocation of specified finger with unspecified laterality

● S63.26   Dislocation of metacarpophalangeal joint of finger

● S63.260   Dislocation of metacarpophalangeal joint of right index finger

● S63.261   Dislocation of metacarpophalangeal joint of left index finger

● S63.262   Dislocation of metacarpophalangeal joint of right middle finger

● S63.263   Dislocation of metacarpophalangeal joint of left middle finger

● S63.264   Dislocation of metacarpophalangeal joint of right ring finger

● S63.265   Dislocation of metacarpophalangeal joint of left ring finger

● S63.266   Dislocation of metacarpophalangeal joint of right little finger

● S63.267   Dislocation of metacarpophalangeal joint of left little finger

● S63.268   Dislocation of metacarpophalangeal joint of other finger

     Dislocation of metacarpophalangeal joint of specified finger with unspecified laterality

● ▣ S63.269   Dislocation of metacarpophalangeal joint of unspecified finger

● S63.27   Dislocation of unspecified interphalangeal joint of finger

● ▣ S63.270   Dislocation of unspecified interphalangeal joint of right index finger

● ▣ S63.271   Dislocation of unspecified interphalangeal joint of left index finger

● ▣ S63.272   Dislocation of unspecified interphalangeal joint of right middle finger

● ▣ S63.273   Dislocation of unspecified interphalangeal joint of left middle finger

● ▣ S63.274   Dislocation of unspecified interphalangeal joint of right ring finger

● ▣ S63.275   Dislocation of unspecified interphalangeal joint of left ring finger

● ▣ S63.276   Dislocation of unspecified interphalangeal joint of right little finger

● ▣ S63.277   Dislocation of unspecified interphalangeal joint of left little finger

● ▣ S63.278   Dislocation of unspecified interphalangeal joint of other finger

     Dislocation of unspecified interphalangeal joint of specified finger with unspecified laterality

● ▣ S63.279   Dislocation of unspecified interphalangeal joint of unspecified finger

     Dislocation of unspecified interphalangeal joint of specified finger without specified laterality

● S63.28   Dislocation of proximal interphalangeal joint of finger

● S63.280   Dislocation of proximal interphalangeal joint of right index finger

● S63.281   Dislocation of proximal interphalangeal joint of left index finger

● S63.282   Dislocation of proximal interphalangeal joint of right middle finger

● S63.283   Dislocation of proximal interphalangeal joint of left middle finger

● Unacceptable First-Listed Diagnosis   ● Use Additional Character(s)   ▣ Unspecified   **OGCR** Official Guidelines for Coding and Reporting

🗞 Complication\Comorbidity   🗞 Major C\C   Excludes 1   Excludes 2   Includes   Use additional   Code first   Code also

● S63.284 Dislocation of proximal interphalangeal joint of right ring finger

● S63.285 Dislocation of proximal interphalangeal joint of left ring finger

● S63.286 Dislocation of proximal interphalangeal joint of right little finger

● S63.287 Dislocation of proximal interphalangeal joint of left little finger

● S63.288 Dislocation of proximal interphalangeal joint of other finger
  Dislocation of proximal interphalangeal joint of specified finger with unspecified laterality

● ▩ S63.289 Dislocation of proximal interphalangeal joint of unspecified finger

● S63.29 Dislocation of distal interphalangeal joint of finger

● S63.290 Dislocation of distal interphalangeal joint of right index finger

● S63.291 Dislocation of distal interphalangeal joint of left index finger

● S63.292 Dislocation of distal interphalangeal joint of right middle finger

● S63.293 Dislocation of distal interphalangeal joint of left middle finger

● S63.294 Dislocation of distal interphalangeal joint of right ring finger

● S63.295 Dislocation of distal interphalangeal joint of left ring finger

● S63.296 Dislocation of distal interphalangeal joint of right little finger

● S63.297 Dislocation of distal interphalangeal joint of left little finger

● S63.298 Dislocation of distal interphalangeal joint of other finger
  Dislocation of distal interphalangeal joint of specified finger with unspecified laterality

● ▩ S63.299 Dislocation of distal interphalangeal joint of unspecified finger

● S63.3 Traumatic rupture of ligament of wrist

● S63.30 Traumatic rupture of unspecified ligament of wrist

● ▩ S63.301 Traumatic rupture of unspecified ligament of right wrist

● ▩ S63.302 Traumatic rupture of unspecified ligament of left wrist

● ▩ S63.309 Traumatic rupture of unspecified ligament of unspecified wrist

● S63.31 Traumatic rupture of collateral ligament of wrist

● S63.311 Traumatic rupture of collateral ligament of right wrist

● S63.312 Traumatic rupture of collateral ligament of left wrist

● ▩ S63.319 Traumatic rupture of collateral ligament of unspecified wrist

● S63.32 Traumatic rupture of radiocarpal ligament

● S63.321 Traumatic rupture of right radiocarpal ligament

● S63.322 Traumatic rupture of left radiocarpal ligament

● ▩ S63.329 Traumatic rupture of unspecified radiocarpal ligament

● S63.33 Traumatic rupture of ulnocarpal (palmar) ligament

● S63.331 Traumatic rupture of right ulnocarpal (palmar) ligament

● S63.332 Traumatic rupture of left ulnocarpal (palmar) ligament

● ▩ S63.339 Traumatic rupture of unspecified ulnocarpal (palmar) ligament

● S63.39 Traumatic rupture of other ligament of wrist

● S63.391 Traumatic rupture of other ligament of right wrist

● S63.392 Traumatic rupture of other ligament of left wrist

● ▩ S63.399 Traumatic rupture of other ligament of unspecified wrist

● S63.4 Traumatic rupture of ligament of finger at metacarpophalangeal and interphalangeal joint(s)

● S63.40 Traumatic rupture of unspecified ligament of finger at metacarpophalangeal and interphalangeal joint

● ▩ S63.400 Traumatic rupture of unspecified ligament of right index finger at metacarpophalangeal and interphalangeal joint

● ▩ S63.401 Traumatic rupture of unspecified ligament of left index finger at metacarpophalangeal and interphalangeal joint

● ▩ S63.402 Traumatic rupture of unspecified ligament of right middle finger at metacarpophalangeal and interphalangeal joint

● ▩ S63.403 Traumatic rupture of unspecified ligament of left middle finger at metacarpophalangeal and interphalangeal joint

● ▩ S63.404 Traumatic rupture of unspecified ligament of right ring finger at metacarpophalangeal and interphalangeal joint

● ▩ S63.405 Traumatic rupture of unspecified ligament of left ring finger at metacarpophalangeal and interphalangeal joint

● ▩ S63.406 Traumatic rupture of unspecified ligament of right little finger at metacarpophalangeal and interphalangeal joint

● Unacceptable First-Listed Diagnosis   ● Use Additional Character(s)   ▩ Unspecified   **OGCR** Official Guidelines for Coding and Reporting

 Complication\Comorbidity    Major C\C   Excludes 1   Excludes 2   Includes   Use additional   Code first   Code also

CHAPTER 19 (S00-T98)

1465

● ■ S63.407 Traumatic rupture of unspecified ligament of left little finger at metacarpophalangeal and interphalangeal joint

● ■ S63.408 Traumatic rupture of unspecified ligament of other finger at metacarpophalangeal and interphalangeal joint
Traumatic rupture of unspecified ligament of specified finger with unspecified laterality at metacarpophalangeal and interphalangeal joint

● ■ S63.409 Traumatic rupture of unspecified ligament of unspecified finger at metacarpophalangeal and interphalangeal joint

● S63.41 Traumatic rupture of collateral ligament of finger at metacarpophalangeal and interphalangeal joint

● S63.410 Traumatic rupture of collateral ligament of right index finger at metacarpophalangeal and interphalangeal joint

● S63.411 Traumatic rupture of collateral ligament of left index finger at metacarpophalangeal and interphalangeal joint

● S63.412 Traumatic rupture of collateral ligament of right middle finger at metacarpophalangeal and interphalangeal joint

● S63.413 Traumatic rupture of collateral ligament of left middle finger at metacarpophalangeal and interphalangeal joint

● S63.414 Traumatic rupture of collateral ligament of right ring finger at metacarpophalangeal and interphalangeal joint

● S63.415 Traumatic rupture of collateral ligament of left ring finger at metacarpophalangeal and interphalangeal joint

● S63.416 Traumatic rupture of collateral ligament of right little finger at metacarpophalangeal and interphalangeal joint

● S63.417 Traumatic rupture of collateral ligament of left little finger at metacarpophalangeal and interphalangeal joint

● S63.418 Traumatic rupture of collateral ligament of other finger at metacarpophalangeal and interphalangeal joint
Traumatic rupture of collateral ligament of specified finger with unspecified laterality at metacarpophalangeal and interphalangeal joint

● ■ S63.419 Traumatic rupture of collateral ligament of unspecified finger at metacarpophalangeal and interphalangeal joint

● S63.42 Traumatic rupture of palmar ligament of finger at metacarpophalangeal and interphalangeal joint

● S63.420 Traumatic rupture of palmar ligament of right index finger at metacarpophalangeal and interphalangeal joint

● S63.421 Traumatic rupture of palmar ligament of left index finger at metacarpophalangeal and interphalangeal joint

● S63.422 Traumatic rupture of palmar ligament of right middle finger at metacarpophalangeal and interphalangeal joint

● S63.423 Traumatic rupture of palmar ligament of left middle finger at metacarpophalangeal and interphalangeal joint

● S63.424 Traumatic rupture of palmar ligament of right ring finger at metacarpophalangeal and interphalangeal joint

● S63.425 Traumatic rupture of palmar ligament of left ring finger at metacarpophalangeal and interphalangeal joint

● S63.426 Traumatic rupture of palmar ligament of right little finger at metacarpophalangeal and interphalangeal joint

● S63.427 Traumatic rupture of palmar ligament of left little finger at metacarpophalangeal and interphalangeal joint

● S63.428 Traumatic rupture of palmar ligament of other finger at metacarpophalangeal and interphalangeal joint
Traumatic rupture of palmar ligament of specified finger with unspecified laterality at metacarpophalangeal and interphalangeal joint

● ■ S63.429 Traumatic rupture of palmar ligament of unspecified finger at metacarpophalangeal and interphalangeal joint

● S63.43 Traumatic rupture of volar plate of finger at metacarpophalangeal and interphalangeal joint

● S63.430 Traumatic rupture of volar plate of right index finger at metacarpophalangeal and interphalangeal joint

● S63.431 Traumatic rupture of volar plate of left index finger at metacarpophalangeal and interphalangeal joint

● S63.432 Traumatic rupture of volar plate of right middle finger at metacarpophalangeal and interphalangeal joint

● S63.433 Traumatic rupture of volar plate of left middle finger at metacarpophalangeal and interphalangeal joint

● Unacceptable First-Listed Diagnosis   ● Use Additional Character(s)   ■ Unspecified   OGCR Official Guidelines for Coding and Reporting
🗞 Complication\Comorbidity   🗞 Major C\C   Excludes 1   Excludes 2   Includes   Use additional   Code first   Code also

CHAPTER 19 (S00-T98)

- S63.434 Traumatic rupture of volar plate of right ring finger at metacarpophalangeal and interphalangeal joint
- S63.435 Traumatic rupture of volar plate of left ring finger at metacarpophalangeal and interphalangeal joint
- S63.436 Traumatic rupture of volar plate of right little finger at metacarpophalangeal and interphalangeal joint
- S63.437 Traumatic rupture of volar plate of left little finger at metacarpophalangeal and interphalangeal joint
- S63.438 Traumatic rupture of volar plate of other finger at metacarpophalangeal and interphalangeal joint
    - Traumatic rupture of volar plate of specified finger with unspecified laterality at metacarpophalangeal and interphalangeal joint
- ■ S63.439 Traumatic rupture of volar plate of unspecified finger at metacarpophalangeal and interphalangeal joint
- S63.49 Traumatic rupture of other ligament of finger at metacarpophalangeal and interphalangeal joint
    - S63.490 Traumatic rupture of other ligament of right index finger at metacarpophalangeal and interphalangeal joint
    - S63.491 Traumatic rupture of other ligament of left index finger at metacarpophalangeal and interphalangeal joint
    - S63.492 Traumatic rupture of other ligament of right middle finger at metacarpophalangeal and interphalangeal joint
    - S63.493 Traumatic rupture of other ligament of left middle finger at metacarpophalangeal and interphalangeal joint
    - S63.494 Traumatic rupture of other ligament of right ring finger at metacarpophalangeal and interphalangeal joint
    - S63.495 Traumatic rupture of other ligament of left ring finger at metacarpophalangeal and interphalangeal joint
    - S63.496 Traumatic rupture of other ligament of right little finger at metacarpophalangeal and interphalangeal joint
    - S63.497 Traumatic rupture of other ligament of left little finger at metacarpophalangeal and interphalangeal joint

- ■ S63.498 Traumatic rupture of other ligament of other finger at metacarpophalangeal and interphalangeal joint
    - Traumatic rupture of ligament of specified finger with unspecified laterality at metacarpophalangeal and interphalangeal joint
- ■ S63.499 Traumatic rupture of other ligament of unspecified finger at metacarpophalangeal and interphalangeal joint
- S63.5 Other and unspecified sprain of wrist
    - S63.50 Unspecified sprain of wrist
        - ■ S63.501 Unspecified sprain of right wrist
        - ■ S63.502 Unspecified sprain of left wrist
        - ■ S63.509 Unspecified sprain of unspecified wrist
    - S63.51 Sprain of carpal (joint)
        - S63.511 Sprain of carpal joint of right wrist
        - S63.512 Sprain of carpal joint of left wrist
        - ■ S63.519 Sprain of carpal joint of unspecified wrist
    - S63.52 Sprain of radiocarpal joint
        - **Excludes1**   traumatic rupture of radiocarpal ligament (S63.32-)
        - S63.521 Sprain of radiocarpal joint of right wrist
        - S63.522 Sprain of radiocarpal joint of left wrist
        - ■ S63.529 Sprain of radiocarpal joint of unspecified wrist
    - S63.59 Other sprain of wrist
        - S63.591 Other sprain of right wrist
        - S63.592 Other sprain of left wrist
        - ■ S63.599 Other sprain of wrist of unspecified side
- S63.6 Other and unspecified sprain of finger(s)
    - **Excludes1**   traumatic rupture of ligament of finger at metacarpophalangeal and interphalangeal joint(s) (S63.4-)
    - S63.60 Unspecified sprain of thumb
        - ■ S63.601 Unspecified sprain of right thumb
        - ■ S63.602 Unspecified sprain of left thumb
        - ■ S63.609 Unspecified sprain of unspecified thumb
    - S63.61 Unspecified sprain of other and unspecified finger(s)
        - ■ S63.610 Unspecified sprain of right index finger
        - ■ S63.611 Unspecified sprain of left index finger
        - ■ S63.612 Unspecified sprain of right middle finger
        - ■ S63.613 Unspecified sprain of left middle finger
        - ■ S63.614 Unspecified sprain of right ring finger

● Unacceptable First-Listed Diagnosis   ● Use Additional Character(s)   ■ Unspecified   **OGCR** Official Guidelines for Coding and Reporting

🗞 Complication\Comorbidity   🗞 Major C\C   Excludes 1   Excludes 2   Includes   Use additional   Code first   Code also

1467

CHAPTER 19 (S00-T98)

● ■ **S63.615** Unspecified sprain of left ring finger

● ■ **S63.616** Unspecified sprain of right little finger

● ■ **S63.617** Unspecified sprain of left little finger

● ■ **S63.618** Unspecified sprain of other finger
   Unspecified sprain of specified finger with unspecified laterality

● ■ **S63.619** Unspecified sprain of unspecified finger

● **S63.62** Sprain of interphalangeal joint of thumb

   ● **S63.621** Sprain of interphalangeal joint of right thumb

   ● **S63.622** Sprain of interphalangeal joint of left thumb

   ● ■ **S63.629** Sprain of interphalangeal joint of unspecified thumb

● **S63.63** Sprain of interphalangeal joint of other and unspecified finger(s)

   ● **S63.630** Sprain of interphalangeal joint of right index finger

   ● **S63.631** Sprain of interphalangeal joint of left index finger

   ● **S63.632** Sprain of interphalangeal joint of right middle finger

   ● **S63.633** Sprain of interphalangeal joint of left middle finger

   ● **S63.634** Sprain of interphalangeal joint of right ring finger

   ● **S63.635** Sprain of interphalangeal joint of left ring finger

   ● **S63.636** Sprain of interphalangeal joint of right little finger

   ● **S63.637** Sprain of interphalangeal joint of left little finger

   ● **S63.638** Sprain of interphalangeal joint of other finger

   ● ■ **S63.639** Sprain of interphalangeal joint of unspecified finger

● **S63.64** Sprain of metacarpophalangeal joint of thumb

   ● **S63.641** Sprain of metacarpophalangeal joint of right thumb

   ● **S63.642** Sprain of metacarpophalangeal joint of left thumb

   ● ■ **S63.649** Sprain of metacarpophalangeal joint of unspecified thumb

● **S63.65** Sprain of metacarpophalangeal joint of other and unspecified finger(s)

   ● **S63.650** Sprain of metacarpophalangeal joint of right index finger

   ● **S63.651** Sprain of metacarpophalangeal joint of left index finger

   ● **S63.652** Sprain of metacarpophalangeal joint of right middle finger

   ● **S63.653** Sprain of metacarpophalangeal joint of left middle finger

   ● **S63.654** Sprain of metacarpophalangeal joint of right ring finger

   ● **S63.655** Sprain of metacarpophalangeal joint of left ring finger

   ● **S63.656** Sprain of metacarpophalangeal joint of right little finger

   ● **S63.657** Sprain of metacarpophalangeal joint of left little finger

   ● **S63.658** Sprain of metacarpophalangeal joint of other finger
      Sprain of metacarpophalangeal joint of specified finger with unspecified laterality

   ● ■ **S63.659** Sprain of metacarpophalangeal joint of unspecified finger

● **S63.68** Other sprain of thumb

   ● **S63.681** Other sprain of right thumb

   ● **S63.682** Other sprain of left thumb

   ● ■ **S63.689** Other sprain of unspecified thumb

● **S63.69** Other sprain of other and unspecified finger(s)

   ● **S63.690** Other sprain of right index finger

   ● **S63.691** Other sprain of left index finger

   ● **S63.692** Other sprain of right middle finger

   ● **S63.693** Other sprain of left middle finger

   ● **S63.694** Other sprain of right ring finger

   ● **S63.695** Other sprain of left ring finger

   ● **S63.696** Other sprain of right little finger

   ● **S63.697** Other sprain of left little finger

   ● **S63.698** Other sprain of other finger
      Other sprain of specified finger with unspecified laterality

   ● ■ **S63.699** Other sprain of unspecified finger

● **S63.8** Sprain of other part of wrist and hand

   ● **S63.8x** Sprain of other part of wrist and hand

      ● **S63.8x1** Sprain of other part of right wrist and hand

      ● **S63.8x2** Sprain of other part of left wrist and hand

      ● ■ **S63.8x9** Sprain of other part of unspecified wrist and hand

● **S63.9** Sprain of unspecified part of wrist and hand

   ● ■ **S63.90** Sprain of unspecified part of unspecified wrist and hand

   ● ■ **S63.91** Sprain of unspecified part of right wrist and hand

   ● ■ **S63.92** Sprain of unspecified part of left wrist and hand

● **S64** **Injury of nerves at wrist and hand level**
   Code also any associated open wound (S61.-)

   The appropriate 7th character is to be added to each code from category S64

A	initial encounter
D	subsequent encounter
S	sequela

● **S64.0** Injury of ulnar nerve at wrist and hand level

   ● ■ **S64.00** Injury of ulnar nerve at wrist and hand level of unspecified arm

   ● **S64.01** Injury of ulnar nerve at wrist and hand level of right arm

   ● **S64.02** Injury of ulnar nerve at wrist and hand level of left arm

● Unacceptable First-Listed Diagnosis   ● Use Additional Character(s)   ■ Unspecified   **OGCR** Official Guidelines for Coding and Reporting
🔖 Complication\Comorbidity   🔖 Major C\C   Excludes 1   Excludes 2   Includes   Use additional   Code first   Code also

● S64.1   Injury of median nerve at wrist and hand level

   ● ▪ S64.10   Injury of median nerve at wrist and hand level of unspecified arm

   ● S64.11   Injury of median nerve at wrist and hand level of right arm

   ● S64.12   Injury of median nerve at wrist and hand level of left arm

● S64.2   Injury of radial nerve at wrist and hand level

   ● ▪ S64.20   Injury of radial nerve at wrist and hand level of unspecified arm

   ● S64.21   Injury of radial nerve at wrist and hand level of right arm

   ● S64.22   Injury of radial nerve at wrist and hand level of left arm

● S64.3   Injury of digital nerve of thumb

   ● ▪ S64.30   Injury of digital nerve of unspecified thumb

   ● S64.31   Injury of digital nerve of right thumb

   ● S64.32   Injury of digital nerve of left thumb

● S64.4   Injury of digital nerve of other and unspecified finger

   ● ▪ S64.40   Injury of digital nerve of unspecified finger

   ● S64.49   Injury of digital nerve of other finger

     ● S64.490   Injury of digital nerve of right index finger

     ● S64.491   Injury of digital nerve of left index finger

     ● S64.492   Injury of digital nerve of right middle finger

     ● S64.493   Injury of digital nerve of left middle finger

     ● S64.494   Injury of digital nerve of right ring finger

     ● S64.495   Injury of digital nerve of left ring finger

     ● S64.496   Injury of digital nerve of right little finger

     ● S64.497   Injury of digital nerve of left little finger

     ● S64.498   Injury of digital nerve of other finger
        Injury of digital nerve of specified finger with unspecified laterality

● S64.8   Injury of other nerves at wrist and hand level

   ● S64.8x   Injury of other nerves at wrist and hand level

     ● S64.8x1   Injury of other nerves at wrist and hand level of right arm

     ● S64.8x2   Injury of other nerves at wrist and hand level of left arm

     ● ▪ S64.8x9   Injury of other nerves at wrist and hand level of unspecified arm

   ● S64.9   Injury of unspecified nerve at wrist and hand level

     ● ▪ S64.90   Injury of unspecified nerve at wrist and hand level of unspecified arm

     ● ▪ S64.91   Injury of unspecified nerve at wrist and hand level of right arm

     ● ▪ S64.92   Injury of unspecified nerve at wrist and hand level of left arm

● S65   Injury of blood vessels at wrist and hand level
   Code also any associated open wound (S61.-)

   The appropriate 7th character is to be added to each code from category S65

> A   initial encounter
> D   subsequent encounter
> S   sequela

● S65.0   Injury of ulnar artery at wrist and hand level

   ● S65.00   Unspecified injury of ulnar artery at wrist and hand level

     ● ▪ S65.001   Unspecified injury of ulnar artery at wrist and hand level of right arm A 🦠

     ● ▪ S65.002   Unspecified injury of ulnar artery at wrist and hand level of left arm A 🦠

     ● ▪ S65.009   Unspecified injury of ulnar artery at wrist and hand level of unspecified arm A 🦠

   ● S65.01   Laceration of ulnar artery at wrist and hand level

     ● S65.011   Laceration of ulnar artery at wrist and hand level of right arm A 🦠

     ● S65.012   Laceration of ulnar artery at wrist and hand level of left arm A 🦠

     ● ▪ S65.019   Laceration of ulnar artery at wrist and hand level of unspecified arm A 🦠

   ● S65.09   Other specified injury of ulnar artery at wrist and hand level

     ● S65.091   Other specified injury of ulnar artery at wrist and hand level of right arm A 🦠

     ● S65.092   Other specified injury of ulnar artery at wrist and hand level of left arm A 🦠

     ● ▪ S65.099   Other specified injury of ulnar artery at wrist and hand level of unspecified arm A 🦠

● S65.1   Injury of radial artery at wrist and hand level

   ● S65.10   Unspecified injury of radial artery at wrist and hand level

     ● ▪ S65.101   Unspecified injury of radial artery at wrist and hand level of right arm A 🦠

     ● ▪ S65.102   Unspecified injury of radial artery at wrist and hand level of left arm A 🦠

     ● ▪ S65.109   Unspecified injury of radial artery at wrist and hand level of unspecified arm A 🦠

   ● S65.11   Laceration of radial artery at wrist and hand level

     ● S65.111   Laceration of radial artery at wrist and hand level of right arm A 🦠

     ● S65.112   Laceration of radial artery at wrist and hand level of left arm A 🦠

     ● ▪ S65.119   Laceration of radial artery at wrist and hand level of unspecified arm A 🦠

● Unacceptable First-Listed Diagnosis   ● Use Additional Character(s)   ▪ Unspecified   **OGCR** Official Guidelines for Coding and Reporting

 Complication\Comorbidity   🦠 Major C\C   Excludes 1   Excludes 2   Includes   Use additional   Code first   Code also

1469

CHAPTER 19 (S00-T98)

- S65.19   Other specified injury of radial artery at wrist and hand level
  - S65.191   Other specified injury of radial artery at wrist and hand level of right arm A 🅒
  - S65.192   Other specified injury of radial artery at wrist and hand level of left arm A 🅒
  - S65.199   Other specified injury of radial artery at wrist and hand level of unspecified arm A 🅒
- S65.2   Injury of superficial palmar arch
  - S65.20   Unspecified injury of superficial palmar arch
    - S65.201   Unspecified injury of superficial palmar arch of right hand A 🅒
    - S65.202   Unspecified injury of superficial palmar arch of left hand A 🅒
    - S65.209   Unspecified injury of superficial palmar arch of unspecified hand A 🅒
  - S65.21   Laceration of superficial palmar arch
    - S65.211   Laceration of superficial palmar arch of right hand A 🅒
    - S65.212   Laceration of superficial palmar arch of left hand A 🅒
    - S65.219   Laceration of superficial palmar arch of unspecified hand A 🅒
  - S65.29   Other specified injury of superficial palmar arch
    - S65.291   Other specified injury of superficial palmar arch of right hand A 🅒
    - S65.292   Other specified injury of superficial palmar arch of left hand A 🅒
    - S65.299   Other specified injury of superficial palmar arch of unspecified hand A 🅒
- S65.3   Injury of deep palmar arch
  - S65.30   Unspecified injury of deep palmar arch
    - S65.301   Unspecified injury of deep palmar arch of right hand A 🅒
    - S65.302   Unspecified injury of deep palmar arch of left hand A 🅒
    - S65.309   Unspecified injury of deep palmar arch of unspecified hand A 🅒
  - S65.31   Laceration of deep palmar arch
    - S65.311   Laceration of deep palmar arch of right hand A 🅒
    - S65.312   Laceration of deep palmar arch of left hand A 🅒
    - S65.319   Laceration of deep palmar arch of unspecified hand A 🅒
  - S65.39   Other specified injury of deep palmar arch
    - S65.391   Other specified injury of deep palmar arch of right hand A 🅒
    - S65.392   Other specified injury of deep palmar arch of left hand A 🅒
    - S65.399   Other specified injury of deep palmar arch of unspecified hand A 🅒
- S65.4   Injury of blood vessel of thumb
  - S65.40   Unspecified injury of blood vessel of thumb
    - S65.401   Unspecified injury of blood vessel of right thumb A 🅒
    - S65.402   Unspecified injury of blood vessel of left thumb A 🅒
    - S65.409   Unspecified injury of blood vessel of unspecified thumb A 🅒
  - S65.41   Laceration of blood vessel of thumb
    - S65.411   Laceration of blood vessel of right thumb A 🅒
    - S65.412   Laceration of blood vessel of left thumb A 🅒
    - S65.419   Laceration of blood vessel of unspecified thumb A 🅒
  - S65.49   Other specified injury of blood vessel of thumb
    - S65.491   Other specified injury of blood vessel of right thumb A 🅒
    - S65.492   Other specified injury of blood vessel of left thumb A 🅒
    - S65.499   Other specified injury of blood vessel of unspecified thumb A 🅒
- S65.5   Injury of blood vessel of other and unspecified finger
  - S65.50   Unspecified injury of blood vessel of other and unspecified finger
    - S65.500   Unspecified injury of blood vessel of right index finger A 🅒
    - S65.501   Unspecified injury of blood vessel of left index finger A 🅒
    - S65.502   Unspecified injury of blood vessel of right middle finger A 🅒
    - S65.503   Unspecified injury of blood vessel of left middle finger A 🅒
    - S65.504   Unspecified injury of blood vessel of right ring finger A 🅒
    - S65.505   Unspecified injury of blood vessel of left ring finger A 🅒
    - S65.506   Unspecified injury of blood vessel of right little finger A 🅒
    - S65.507   Unspecified injury of blood vessel of left little finger A 🅒
    - S65.508   Unspecified injury of blood vessel of other finger A 🅒
      Unspecified injury of blood vessel of specifed finger with unspecified laterality
    - S65.509   Unspecified injury of blood vessel of unspecified finger A 🅒
  - S65.51   Laceration of blood vessel of other and unspecified finger
    - S65.510   Laceration of blood vessel of right index finger A 🅒
    - S65.511   Laceration of blood vessel of left index finger A 🅒
    - S65.512   Laceration of blood vessel of right middle finger A 🅒
    - S65.513   Laceration of blood vessel of left middle finger A 🅒
    - S65.514   Laceration of blood vessel of right ring finger A 🅒

CHAPTER 19 (S00-T98)

● Unacceptable First-Listed Diagnosis   ● Use Additional Character(s)   ▪ Unspecified   **OGCR** Official Guidelines for Coding and Reporting   🅒 Complication\Comorbidity   🅒 Major C\C   Excludes 1   Excludes 2   Includes   Use additional   Code first   Code also

- ● S65.515 Laceration of blood vessel of left ring finger A ⬤
- ● S65.516 Laceration of blood vessel of right little finger A ⬤
- ● S65.517 Laceration of blood vessel of left little finger A ⬤
- ● S65.518 Laceration of blood vessel of other finger A ⬤
  Laceration of blood vessel of specifed finger with unspecified laterality
- ● ◼ S65.519 Laceration of blood vessel of unspecified finger A ⬤
- ● S65.59 Other specified injury of blood vessel of other and unspecified finger
  - ● S65.590 Other specified injury of blood vessel of right index finger A ⬤
  - ● S65.591 Other specified injury of blood vessel of left index finger A ⬤
  - ● S65.592 Other specified injury of blood vessel of right middle finger A ⬤
  - ● S65.593 Other specified injury of blood vessel of left middle finger A ⬤
  - ● S65.594 Other specified injury of blood vessel of right ring finger A ⬤
  - ● S65.595 Other specified injury of blood vessel of left ring finger A ⬤
  - ● S65.596 Other specified injury of blood vessel of right little finger A ⬤
  - ● S65.597 Other specified injury of blood vessel of left little finger A ⬤
  - ● S65.598 Other specified injury of blood vessel of other finger A ⬤
    Other specified injury of blood vessel of specified finger with unspecified laterality
  - ● ◼ S65.599 Other specified injury of blood vessel of unspecified finger A ⬤
- ● S65.8 Injury of other blood vessels at wrist and hand level
  - ● S65.80 Unspecified injury of other blood vessels at wrist and hand level
    - ● ◼ S65.801 Unspecified injury of other blood vessels at wrist and hand level of right arm A ⬤
    - ● ◼ S65.802 Unspecified injury of other blood vessels at wrist and hand level of left arm A ⬤
    - ● ◼ S65.809 Unspecified injury of other blood vessels at wrist and hand level of unspecified arm A ⬤
  - ● S65.81 Laceration of other blood vessels at wrist and hand level
    - ● S65.811 Laceration of other blood vessels at wrist and hand level of right arm A ⬤
    - ● S65.812 Laceration of other blood vessels at wrist and hand level of left arm A ⬤
    - ● ◼ S65.819 Laceration of other blood vessels at wrist and hand level of unspecified arm A ⬤
  - ● S65.89 Other specified injury of other blood vessels at wrist and hand level

- ● S65.891 Other specified injury of other blood vessels at wrist and hand level of right arm A ⬤
- ● S65.892 Other specified injury of other blood vessels at wrist and hand level of left arm A ⬤
- ● ◼ S65.899 Other specified injury of other blood vessels at wrist and hand level of unspecified arm A ⬤
- ● S65.9 Injury of unspecified blood vessel at wrist and hand level
  - ● S65.90 Unspecified injury of unspecified blood vessel at wrist and hand level
    - ● ◼ S65.901 Unspecified injury of unspecified blood vessel at wrist and hand level of right arm A ⬤
    - ● ◼ S65.902 Unspecified injury of unspecified blood vessel at wrist and hand level of left arm A ⬤
    - ● ◼ S65.909 Unspecified injury of unspecified blood vessel at wrist and hand level of unspecified arm A ⬤
  - ● S65.91 Laceration of unspecified blood vessel at wrist and hand level
    - ● ◼ S65.911 Laceration of unspecified blood vessel at wrist and hand level of right arm A ⬤
    - ● ◼ S65.912 Laceration of unspecified blood vessel at wrist and hand level of left arm A ⬤
    - ● ◼ S65.919 Laceration of unspecified blood vessel at wrist and hand level of unspecified arm A ⬤
  - ● S65.99 Other specified injury of unspecified blood vessel at wrist and hand level
    - ● ◼ S65.991 Other specified injury of unspecified blood vessel at wrist and hand of right arm A ⬤
    - ● ◼ S65.992 Other specified injury of unspecified blood vessel at wrist and hand of left arm A ⬤
    - ● ◼ S65.999 Other specified injury of unspecified blood vessel at wrist and hand of unspecified arm A ⬤

- ● S66 Injury of muscle, fascia and tendon at wrist and hand level
  Code also any associated open wound (S61.-)
  Excludes2 sprain of joints and ligaments of wrist and hand (S63.-)

  The appropriate 7th character is to be added to each code from category S66

A	initial encounter
D	subsequent encounter
S	sequela

  - ● S66.0 Injury of long flexor muscle, fascia and tendon of thumb at wrist and hand level
    - ● S66.00 Unspecified injury of long flexor muscle, fascia and tendon of thumb at wrist and hand level
      - ● ◼ S66.001 Unspecified injury of long flexor muscle, fascia and tendon of right thumb at wrist and hand level
      - ● ◼ S66.002 Unspecified injury of long flexor muscle, fascia and tendon of left thumb at wrist and hand level

● Unacceptable First-Listed Diagnosis   ● Use Additional Character(s)   ◼ Unspecified   **OGCR** Official Guidelines for Coding and Reporting

⬤ Complication\Comorbidity   ⬤ Major C\C   Excludes 1   Excludes 2   Includes   Use additional   Code first   Code also

1471

CHAPTER 19 (S00-T98)

● ◼ **S66.009** Unspecified injury of long flexor muscle, fascia and tendon of thumb at wrist and hand level of unspecified side

● **S66.01** Strain of long flexor muscle, fascia and tendon of thumb at wrist and hand level

　● **S66.011** Strain of long flexor muscle, fascia and tendon of right thumb at wrist and hand level

　● **S66.012** Strain of long flexor muscle, fascia and tendon of left thumb at wrist and hand level

　● ◼ **S66.019** Strain of long flexor muscle, fascia and tendon of thumb at wrist and hand level of unspecified side

● **S66.02** Laceration of long flexor muscle, fascia and tendon of thumb at wrist and hand level

　● **S66.021** Laceration of long flexor muscle, fascia and tendon of right thumb at wrist and hand level A 🔾

　● **S66.022** Laceration of long flexor muscle, fascia and tendon of left thumb at wrist and hand level A 🔾

　● ◼ **S66.029** Laceration of long flexor muscle, fascia and tendon of thumb at wrist and hand level of unspecified side A 🔾

● **S66.09** Other injury of long flexor muscle, fascia and tendon of thumb at wrist and hand level

　● **S66.091** Other injury of long flexor muscle, fascia and tendon of right thumb at wrist and hand level

　● **S66.092** Other injury of long flexor muscle, fascia and tendon of left thumb at wrist and hand level

　● ◼ **S66.099** Other injury of long flexor muscle, fascia and tendon of thumb at wrist and hand level of unspecified side

● **S66.1** Injury of flexor muscle, fascia and tendon of other and unspecified finger at wrist and hand level

　| Excludes2 | injury of long flexor muscle, fascia and tendon of thumb at wrist and hand level (S66.0-) |

　● **S66.10** Unspecified injury of flexor muscle, fascia and tendon of other and unspecified finger at wrist and hand level

　　● ◼ **S66.100** Unspecified injury of flexor muscle, fascia and tendon of right index finger at wrist and hand level

　　● ◼ **S66.101** Unspecified injury of flexor muscle, fascia and tendon of left index finger at wrist and hand level

　　● ◼ **S66.102** Unspecified injury of flexor muscle, fascia and tendon of right middle finger at wrist and hand level

　　● ◼ **S66.103** Unspecified injury of flexor muscle, fascia and tendon of left middle finger at wrist and hand level

● ◼ **S66.104** Unspecified injury of flexor muscle, fascia and tendon of right ring finger at wrist and hand level

● ◼ **S66.105** Unspecified injury of flexor muscle, fascia and tendon of left ring finger at wrist and hand level

● ◼ **S66.106** Unspecified injury of flexor muscle, fascia and tendon of right little finger at wrist and hand level

● ◼ **S66.107** Unspecified injury of flexor muscle, fascia and tendon of left little finger at wrist and hand level

● ◼ **S66.108** Unspecified injury of flexor muscle, fascia and tendon of other finger at wrist and hand level

　Unspecified injury of flexor muscle, fascia and tendon of specified finger with unspecified laterality at wrist and hand level

● ◼ **S66.109** Unspecified injury of flexor muscle, fascia and tendon of unspecified finger at wrist and hand level

● **S66.11** Strain of flexor muscle, fascia and tendon of other and unspecified finger at wrist and hand level

　● **S66.110** Strain of flexor muscle, fascia and tendon of right index finger at wrist and hand level

　● **S66.111** Strain of flexor muscle, fascia and tendon of left index finger at wrist and hand level

　● **S66.112** Strain of flexor muscle, fascia and tendon of right middle finger at wrist and hand level

　● **S66.113** Strain of flexor muscle, fascia and tendon of left middle finger at wrist and hand level

　● **S66.114** Strain of flexor muscle, fascia and tendon of right ring finger at wrist and hand level

　● **S66.115** Strain of flexor muscle, fascia and tendon of left ring finger at wrist and hand level

　● **S66.116** Strain of flexor muscle, fascia and tendon of right little finger at wrist and hand level

　● **S66.117** Strain of flexor muscle, fascia and tendon of left little finger at wrist and hand level

　● **S66.118** Strain of flexor muscle, fascia and tendon of other finger at wrist and hand level

　　Strain of flexor muscle, fascia and tendon of specified finger with unspecified laterality at wrist and hand level

　● ◼ **S66.119** Strain of flexor muscle, fascia and tendon of unspecified finger at wrist and hand level

● Unacceptable First-Listed Diagnosis　　● Use Additional Character(s)　　◼ Unspecified　　**OGCR** Official Guidelines for Coding and Reporting

🔾 Complication\Comorbidity　　🔾 Major C\C　| Excludes 1 |　| Excludes 2 |　Includes　Use additional　Code first　Code also

● S66.12 Laceration of flexor muscle, fascia and tendon of other and unspecified finger at wrist and hand level

　● S66.120 Laceration of flexor muscle, fascia and tendon of right index finger at wrist and hand level A

　● S66.121 Laceration of flexor muscle, fascia and tendon of left index finger at wrist and hand level A

　● S66.122 Laceration of flexor muscle, fascia and tendon of right middle finger at wrist and hand level A

　● S66.123 Laceration of flexor muscle, fascia and tendon of left middle finger at wrist and hand level A

　● S66.124 Laceration of flexor muscle, fascia and tendon of right ring finger at wrist and hand level A

　● S66.125 Laceration of flexor muscle, fascia and tendon of left ring finger at wrist and hand level A

　● S66.126 Laceration of flexor muscle, fascia and tendon of right little finger at wrist and hand level A

　● S66.127 Laceration of flexor muscle, fascia and tendon of left little finger at wrist and hand level A

　● S66.128 Laceration of flexor muscle, fascia and tendon of other finger at wrist and hand level A

　　Laceration of flexor muscle, fascia and tendon of specified finger with unspecified laterality at wrist and hand level

　● ■ S66.129 Laceration of flexor muscle, fascia and tendon of unspecified finger at wrist and hand level A

● S66.19 Other injury of flexor muscle, fascia and tendon of other and unspecified finger at wrist and hand level

　● S66.190 Other injury of flexor muscle, fascia and tendon of right index at wrist and hand level

　● S66.191 Other injury of flexor muscle, fascia and tendon of left index finger at wrist and hand level

　● S66.192 Other injury of flexor muscle, fascia and tendon of right middle finger at wrist and hand level

　● S66.193 Other injury of flexor muscle, fascia and tendon of left middle finger at wrist and hand level

　● S66.194 Other injury of flexor muscle, fascia and tendon of right ring finger at wrist and hand level

　● S66.195 Other injury of flexor muscle, fascia and tendon of left ring finger at wrist and hand level

　● S66.196 Other injury of flexor muscle, fascia and tendon of right little finger at wrist and hand level

　● S66.197 Other injury of flexor muscle, fascia and tendon of left little finger at wrist and hand level

● S66.198 Other injury of flexor muscle, fascia and tendon of other finger at wrist and hand level

　　Other injury of flexor muscle, fascia and tendon of specified finger with unspecified laterality at wrist and hand level

● ■ S66.199 Other injury of flexor muscle, fascia and tendon of unspecified finger at wrist and hand level

● S66.2 Injury of extensor muscle, fascia and tendon of thumb at wrist and hand level

　● S66.20 Unspecified injury of extensor muscle, fascia and tendon of thumb at wrist and hand level

　　● ■ S66.201 Unspecified injury of extensor muscle, fascia and tendon of right thumb at wrist and hand level

　　● ■ S66.202 Unspecified injury of extensor muscle, fascia and tendon of left thumb at wrist and hand level

　　● ■ S66.209 Unspecified injury of extensor muscle, fascia and tendon of thumb at wrist and hand level of unspecified side

　● S66.21 Strain of extensor muscle, fascia and tendon of thumb at wrist and hand level

　　● S66.211 Strain of extensor muscle, fascia and tendon of right thumb at wrist and hand level

　　● S66.212 Strain of extensor muscle, fascia and tendon of left thumb at wrist and hand level

　　● ■ S66.219 Strain of extensor muscle, fascia and tendon of thumb at wrist and hand level of unspecified side

　● S66.22 Laceration of extensor muscle, fascia and tendon of thumb at wrist and hand level

　　● S66.221 Laceration of extensor muscle, fascia and tendon of right thumb at wrist and hand level A

　　● S66.222 Laceration of extensor muscle, fascia and tendon of left thumb at wrist and hand level A

　　● ■ S66.229 Laceration of extensor muscle, fascia and tendon of thumb at wrist and hand level of unspecified side A

　● S66.29 Other injury of extensor muscle, fascia and tendon of thumb at wrist and hand level

　　● S66.291 Other injury of extensor muscle, fascia and tendon of right thumb at wrist and hand level

　　● S66.292 Other injury of extensor muscle, fascia and tendon of left thumb at wrist and hand level

　　● ■ S66.299 Other injury of extensor muscle, fascia and tendon of thumb at wrist and hand level of unspecified side

● Unacceptable First-Listed Diagnosis   ● Use Additional Character(s)   ■ Unspecified   OGCR Official Guidelines for Coding and Reporting
 Complication\Comorbidity    Major C\C   Excludes 1   Excludes 2   Includes   Use additional   Code first   Code also   1473

CHAPTER 19 (S00-T98)

● **S66.3** **Injury of extensor muscle, fascia and tendon of other and unspecified finger at wrist and hand level**

> **Excludes2**   injury of extensor muscle, fascia and tendon of thumb at wrist and hand level (S66.2-)

  ● **S66.30** **Unspecified injury of extensor muscle, fascia and tendon of other and unspecified finger at wrist and hand level**

    ● ◾ **S66.300** Unspecified injury of extensor muscle, fascia and tendon of right index finger at wrist and hand level

    ● ◾ **S66.301** Unspecified injury of extensor muscle, fascia and tendon of left index finger at wrist and hand level

    ● ◾ **S66.302** Unspecified injury of extensor muscle, fascia and tendon of right middle finger at wrist and hand level

    ● ◾ **S66.303** Unspecified injury of extensor muscle, fascia and tendon of left middle finger at wrist and hand level

    ● ◾ **S66.304** Unspecified injury of extensor muscle, fascia and tendon of right ring finger at wrist and hand level

    ● ◾ **S66.305** Unspecified injury of extensor muscle, fascia and tendon of left ring finger at wrist and hand level

    ● ◾ **S66.306** Unspecified injury of extensor muscle, fascia and tendon of right little finger at wrist and hand level

    ● ◾ **S66.307** Unspecified injury of extensor muscle, fascia and tendon of left little finger at wrist and hand level

    ● ◾ **S66.308** Unspecified injury of extensor muscle, fascia and tendon of other finger at wrist and hand level

> Unspecified injury of extensor muscle, fascia and tendon of specified finger with unspecified laterality at wrist and hand level

    ● ◾ **S66.309** Unspecified injury of extensor muscle, fascia and tendon of unspecified finger at wrist and hand level

  ● **S66.31** **Strain of extensor muscle, fascia and tendon of other and unspecified finger at wrist and hand level**

    ● **S66.310** Strain of extensor muscle, fascia and tendon of right index finger at wrist and hand level

    ● **S66.311** Strain of extensor muscle, fascia and tendon of left index finger at wrist and hand level

    ● **S66.312** Strain of extensor muscle, fascia and tendon of right middle finger at wrist and hand level

    ● **S66.313** Strain of extensor muscle, fascia and tendon of left middle finger at wrist and hand level

    ● **S66.314** Strain of extensor muscle, fascia and tendon of right ring finger at wrist and hand level

    ● **S66.315** Strain of extensor muscle, fascia and tendon of left ring finger at wrist and hand level

    ● **S66.316** Strain of extensor muscle, fascia and tendon of right little finger at wrist and hand level

    ● **S66.317** Strain of extensor muscle, fascia and tendon of left little finger at wrist and hand level

    ● **S66.318** Strain of extensor muscle, fascia and tendon of other finger at wrist and hand level

> Strain of extensor muscle, fascia and tendon of specified finger with unspecified laterality at wrist and hand level

    ● ◾ **S66.319** Strain of extensor muscle, fascia and tendon of unspecified finger at wrist and hand level

  ● **S66.32** **Laceration of extensor muscle, fascia and tendon of other and unspecified finger at wrist and hand level**

    ● **S66.320** Laceration of extensor muscle, fascia and tendon of right index finger at wrist and hand level A ✿

    ● **S66.321** Laceration of extensor muscle, fascia and tendon of left index finger at wrist and hand level A ✿

    ● **S66.322** Laceration of extensor muscle, fascia and tendon of right middle finger at wrist and hand level A ✿

    ● **S66.323** Laceration of extensor muscle, fascia and tendon of left middle finger at wrist and hand level A ✿

    ● **S66.324** Laceration of extensor muscle, fascia and tendon of right ring finger at wrist and hand level A ✿

    ● **S66.325** Laceration of extensor muscle, fascia and tendon of left ring finger at wrist and hand level A ✿

    ● **S66.326** Laceration of extensor muscle, fascia and tendon of right little finger at wrist and hand level A ✿

    ● **S66.327** Laceration of extensor muscle, fascia and tendon of left little finger at wrist and hand level A ✿

    ● **S66.328** Laceration of extensor muscle, fascia and tendon of other finger at wrist and hand level A ✿

> Laceration of extensor muscle, fascia and tendon of specified finger with unspecified laterality at wrist and hand level

    ● ◾ **S66.329** Laceration of extensor muscle, fascia and tendon of unspecified finger at wrist and hand level A ✿

  ● **S66.39** **Other injury of extensor muscle, fascia and tendon of other and unspecified finger at wrist and hand level**

    ● **S66.390** Other injury of extensor muscle, fascia and tendon of right index finger at wrist and hand level

● Unacceptable First-Listed Diagnosis   ● Use Additional Character(s)   ◾ Unspecified   **OGCR** Official Guidelines for Coding and Reporting

✿ Complication\Comorbidity   ✿ Major C\C   Excludes 1   Excludes 2   Includes   Use additional   Code first   Code also

● S66.391   Other injury of extensor muscle, fascia and tendon of left index finger at wrist and hand level

● S66.392   Other injury of extensor muscle, fascia and tendon of right middle finger at wrist and hand level

● S66.393   Other injury of extensor muscle, fascia and tendon of left middle finger at wrist and hand level

● S66.394   Other injury of extensor muscle, fascia and tendon of right ring finger at wrist and hand level

● S66.395   Other injury of extensor muscle, fascia and tendon of left ring finger at wrist and hand level

● S66.396   Other injury of extensor muscle, fascia and tendon of right little finger at wrist and hand level

● S66.397   Other injury of extensor muscle, fascia and tendon of left little finger at wrist and hand level

● S66.398   Other injury of extensor muscle, fascia and tendon of other finger at wrist and hand level

     Other injury of extensor muscle, fascia and tendon of specified finger with unspecified laterality at wrist and hand level

● ■ S66.399   Other injury of extensor muscle, fascia and tendon of unspecified finger at wrist and hand level

● S66.4   Injury of intrinsic muscle, fascia and tendon of thumb at wrist and hand level

   ● S66.40   Unspecified injury of intrinsic muscle, fascia and tendon of thumb at wrist and hand level

     ● ■ S66.401   Unspecified injury of intrinsic muscle, fascia and tendon of right thumb at wrist and hand level

     ● ■ S66.402   Unspecified injury of intrinsic muscle, fascia and tendon of left thumb at wrist and hand level

     ● ■ S66.409   Unspecified injury of intrinsic muscle, fascia and tendon of thumb at wrist and hand level of unspecified side

   ● S66.41   Strain of intrinsic muscle, fascia and tendon of thumb at wrist and hand level

     ● S66.411   Strain of intrinsic muscle, fascia and tendon of right thumb at wrist and hand level

     ● S66.412   Strain of intrinsic muscle, fascia and tendon of left thumb at wrist and hand level

     ● ■ S66.419   Strain of intrinsic muscle, fascia and tendon of thumb at wrist and hand level of unspecified side

   ● S66.42   Laceration of intrinsic muscle, fascia and tendon of thumb at wrist and hand level

     ● S66.421   Laceration of intrinsic muscle, fascia and tendon of right thumb at wrist and hand level A 🗣

     ● S66.422   Laceration of intrinsic muscle, fascia and tendon of left thumb at wrist and hand level A 🗣

● ■ S66.429   Laceration of intrinsic muscle, fascia and tendon of thumb at wrist and hand level of unspecified side A 🗣

   ● S66.49   Other injury of intrinsic muscle, fascia and tendon of thumb at wrist and hand level

     ● S66.491   Other injury of intrinsic muscle, fascia and tendon of right thumb at wrist and hand level

     ● S66.492   Other injury of intrinsic muscle, fascia and tendon of left thumb at wrist and hand level

     ● ■ S66.499   Other injury of intrinsic muscle, fascia and tendon of thumb at wrist and hand level of unspecified side

● S66.5   Injury of intrinsic muscle, fascia and tendon of other and unspecified finger at wrist and hand level

    Excludes2   injury of intrinsic muscle, fascia and tendon of thumb at wrist and hand level (S66.4-)

   ● S66.50   Unspecified injury of intrinsic muscle, fascia and tendon of other and unspecified finger at wrist and hand level

     ● ■ S66.500   Unspecified injury of intrinsic muscle, fascia and tendon of right index finger at wrist and hand level

     ● ■ S66.501   Unspecified injury of intrinsic muscle, fascia and tendon of left index finger at wrist and hand level

     ● ■ S66.502   Unspecified injury of intrinsic muscle, fascia and tendon of right middle finger at wrist and hand level

     ● ■ S66.503   Unspecified injury of intrinsic muscle, fascia and tendon of left middle finger at wrist and hand level

     ● ■ S66.504   Unspecified injury of intrinsic muscle, fascia and tendon of right ring finger at wrist and hand level

     ● ■ S66.505   Unspecified injury of intrinsic muscle, fascia and tendon of left ring finger at wrist and hand level

     ● ■ S66.506   Unspecified injury of intrinsic muscle, fascia and tendon of right little finger at wrist and hand level

     ● ■ S66.507   Unspecified injury of intrinsic muscle, fascia and tendon of left little finger at wrist and hand level

     ● ■ S66.508   Unspecified injury of intrinsic muscle, fascia and tendon of other finger at wrist and hand level

     Unspecified injury of intrinsic muscle, fascia and tendon of specified finger with unspecified laterality at wrist and hand level

●   Unacceptable First-Listed Diagnosis   ●   Use Additional Character(s)   ■   Unspecified   **OGCR**   Official Guidelines for Coding and Reporting

🗣 Complication\Comorbidity   🗣 Major C\C   [Excludes 1]   [Excludes 2]   [Includes]   Use additional   Code first   Code also

1475

S66.509   Unspecified injury of intrinsic muscle, fascia and tendon of unspecified finger at wrist and hand level

S66.51   Strain of intrinsic muscle, fascia and tendon of other and unspecified finger at wrist and hand level

S66.510   Strain of intrinsic muscle, fascia and tendon of right index finger at wrist and hand level

S66.511   Strain of intrinsic muscle, fascia and tendon of left index finger at wrist and hand level

S66.512   Strain of intrinsic muscle, fascia and tendon of right middle finger at wrist and hand level

S66.513   Strain of intrinsic muscle, fascia and tendon of left middle finger at wrist and hand level

S66.514   Strain of intrinsic muscle, fascia and tendon of right ring finger at wrist and hand level

S66.515   Strain of intrinsic muscle, fascia and tendon of left ring finger at wrist and hand level

S66.516   Strain of intrinsic muscle, fascia and tendon of right little finger at wrist and hand level

S66.517   Strain of intrinsic muscle, fascia and tendon of left little finger at wrist and hand level

S66.518   Strain of intrinsic muscle, fascia and tendon of other finger at wrist and hand level

Strain of intrinsic muscle, fascia and tendon of specified finger with unspecified laterality at wrist and hand level

S66.519   Strain of intrinsic muscle, fascia and tendon of unspecified finger at wrist and hand level

S66.52   Laceration of intrinsic muscle, fascia and tendon of other and unspecified finger at wrist and hand level

S66.520   Laceration of intrinsic muscle, fascia and tendon of right index finger at wrist and hand level A

S66.521   Laceration of intrinsic muscle, fascia and tendon of left index finger at wrist and hand level A

S66.522   Laceration of intrinsic muscle, fascia and tendon of right middle finger at wrist and hand level A

S66.523   Laceration of intrinsic muscle, fascia and tendon of left middle finger at wrist and hand level A

S66.524   Laceration of intrinsic muscle, fascia and tendon of right ring finger at wrist and hand level A

S66.525   Laceration of intrinsic muscle, fascia and tendon of left ring finger at wrist and hand level A

S66.526   Laceration of intrinsic muscle, fascia and tendon of right little finger at wrist and hand level A

S66.527   Laceration of intrinsic muscle, fascia and tendon of left little finger at wrist and hand level A

S66.528   Laceration of intrinsic muscle, fascia and tendon of other finger at wrist and hand level A

Laceration of intrinsic muscle, fascia and tendon of specified finger with unspecified laterality at wrist and hand level

S66.529   Laceration of intrinsic muscle, fascia and tendon of unspecified finger at wrist and hand level A

S66.59   Other injury of intrinsic muscle, fascia and tendon of other and unspecified finger at wrist and hand level

S66.590   Other injury of intrinsic muscle, fascia and tendon of right index finger at wrist and hand level

S66.591   Other injury of intrinsic muscle, fascia and tendon of left index finger at wrist and hand level

S66.592   Other injury of intrinsic muscle, fascia and tendon of right middle finger at wrist and hand level

S66.593   Other injury of intrinsic muscle, fascia and tendon of left middle finger at wrist and hand level

S66.594   Other injury of intrinsic muscle, fascia and tendon of right ring finger at wrist and hand level

S66.595   Other injury of intrinsic muscle, fascia and tendon of left ring finger at wrist and hand level

S66.596   Other injury of intrinsic muscle, fascia and tendon of right little finger at wrist and hand level

S66.597   Other injury of intrinsic muscle, fascia and tendon of left little finger at wrist and hand level

S66.598   Other injury of intrinsic muscle, fascia and tendon of other finger at wrist and hand level

Other injury of intrinsic muscle, fascia and tendon of specified finger with unspecified laterality at wrist and hand level

S66.599   Other injury of intrinsic muscle, fascia and tendon of unspecified finger at wrist and hand level

S66.8   Injury of other muscles, fascia and tendons at wrist and hand level

S66.80   Unspecified injury of other muscles, fascia and tendons at wrist and hand level

S66.801   Unspecified injury of other muscles, fascia and tendons at right wrist and hand level

S66.802   Unspecified injury of other muscles, fascia and tendons at left wrist and hand level

S66.809   Unspecified injury of other muscles, fascia and tendons at wrist and hand level of unspecified side

● S66.81 Strain of other muscles, fascia and tendons at wrist and hand level

    ● S66.811 Strain of other muscles, fascia and tendons at right wrist and hand level

    ● S66.812 Strain of other muscles, fascia and tendons at left wrist and hand level

    ● ■ S66.819 Strain of other muscles, fascia and tendons at wrist and hand level of unspecified side

● S66.82 Laceration of other muscles, fascia and tendons at wrist and hand level

    ● S66.821 Laceration of other muscles, fascia and tendons at right wrist and hand level A 🦠

    ● S66.822 Laceration of other muscles, fascia and tendons at left wrist and hand level A 🦠

    ● ■ S66.829 Laceration of other muscles, fascia and tendons at wrist and hand level of unspecified side A 🦠

● S66.89 Other injury of other muscles, fascia and tendons at wrist and hand level

    ● S66.891 Other injury of other muscles, fascia and tendons at right wrist and hand level

    ● S66.892 Other injury of other muscles, fascia and tendons at left wrist and hand level

    ● ■ S66.899 Other injury of other muscles, fascia and tendons at wrist and hand level of unspecified side

● S66.9 Injury of unspecified muscle, fascia and tendon at wrist and hand level

    ● S66.90 Unspecified injury of unspecified muscle, fascia and tendon at wrist and hand level

      ● ■ S66.901 Unspecified injury of unspecified muscle, fascia and tendon at right wrist and hand level

      ● ■ S66.902 Unspecified injury of unspecified muscle, fascia and tendon at left wrist and hand level

      ● ■ S66.909 Unspecified injury of unspecified muscle, fascia and tendon at wrist and hand level of unspecified side

    ● S66.91 Strain of unspecified muscle, fascia and tendon at wrist and hand level

      ● ■ S66.911 Strain of unspecified muscle, fascia and tendon at right wrist and hand level

      ● ■ S66.912 Strain of unspecified muscle, fascia and tendon at left wrist and hand level

      ● ■ S66.919 Strain of unspecified muscle, fascia and tendon at wrist and hand level of unspecified side

    ● S66.92 Laceration of unspecified muscle, fascia and tendon at wrist and hand level

      ● ■ S66.921 Laceration of unspecified muscle, fascia and tendon at right wrist and hand level A 🦠

      ● ■ S66.922 Laceration of unspecified muscle, fascia and tendon at left wrist and hand level A 🦠

      ● ■ S66.929 Laceration of unspecified muscle, fascia and tendon at wrist and hand level of unspecified side A 🦠

● S66.99 Other injury of unspecified muscle, fascia and tendon at wrist and hand level

    ● ■ S66.991 Other injury of unspecified muscle, fascia and tendon at right wrist and hand level

    ● ■ S66.992 Other injury of unspecified muscle, fascia and tendon at left wrist and hand level

    ● ■ S66.999 Other injury of unspecified muscle, fascia and tendon at wrist and hand level of unspecified side

● S67 Crushing injury of wrist, hand and fingers

Use additional code for all associated injuries, such as:
fracture of wrist and hand (S62.-)
open wound of wrist and hand (S61.-)

The appropriate 7th character is to be added to each code from category S67

A	initial encounter
D	subsequent encounter
S	sequela

● S67.0 Crushing injury of thumb

    ● ■ S67.00 Crushing injury of thumb of unspecified side

    ● S67.01 Crushing injury of right thumb

    ● S67.02 Crushing injury of left thumb

● S67.1 Crushing injury of other and unspecified finger(s)

    Excludes2 crushing injury of thumb (S67.0-)

    ● ■ S67.10 Crushing injury of unspecified finger(s)

    ● S67.19 Crushing injury of other finger(s)

      ● S67.190 Crushing injury of right index finger

      ● S67.191 Crushing injury of left index finger

      ● S67.192 Crushing injury of right middle finger

      ● S67.193 Crushing injury of left middle finger

      ● S67.194 Crushing injury of right ring finger

      ● S67.195 Crushing injury of left ring finger

      ● S67.196 Crushing injury of right little finger

      ● S67.197 Crushing injury of left little finger

      ● S67.198 Crushing injury of other finger
        Crushing injury of specified finger with unspecified laterality

● S67.2 Crushing injury of hand

    Excludes2 crushing injury of fingers (S67.1-)
                crushing injury of thumb (S67.0-)

    ● ■ S67.20 Crushing injury of unspecified hand

    ● S67.21 Crushing injury of right hand

    ● S67.22 Crushing injury of left hand

● S67.3 Crushing injury of wrist

    ● ■ S67.30 Crushing injury of unspecified wrist

    ● S67.31 Crushing injury of right wrist

    ● S67.32 Crushing injury of left wrist

● Unacceptable First-Listed Diagnosis   ● Use Additional Character(s)   ■ Unspecified   OGCR Official Guidelines for Coding and Reporting

🦠 Complication\Comorbidity   🦠 Major C\C   Excludes 1   Excludes 2   Includes   Use additional   Code first   Code also

CHAPTER 19 (S00-T98)

1477

- S67.4 Crushing injury of wrist and hand
  - Excludes1 crushing injury of hand alone (S67.2-)
    crushing injury of wrist alone (S67.3-)
  - Excludes2 crushing injury of fingers (S67.1-)
    crushing injury of thumb (S67.0-)
  - S67.40 Crushing injury of unspecified wrist and hand
  - S67.41 Crushing injury of right wrist and hand
  - S67.42 Crushing injury of left wrist and hand
- S67.9 Crushing injury of unspecified part(s) of wrist, hand and fingers
  - S67.90 Crushing injury of unspecified part(s) of wrist, hand and fingers of unspecified side
  - S67.91 Crushing injury of unspecified part(s) of right wrist, hand and fingers
  - S67.92 Crushing injury of unspecified part(s) of left wrist, hand and fingers
- S68 Traumatic amputation of wrist, hand and fingers
  An amputation not identified as partial or complete should be coded to complete

  The appropriate 7th character is to be added to each code from category S68
  - A initial encounter
  - D subsequent encounter
  - S sequela
- S68.0 Traumatic metacarpophalangeal amputation of thumb
  Traumatic amputation of thumb NOS
  - S68.01 Complete traumatic metacarpophalangeal amputation of thumb
    - S68.011 Complete traumatic metacarpophalangeal amputation of right thumb
    - S68.012 Complete traumatic metacarpophalangeal amputation of left thumb
    - S68.019 Complete traumatic metacarpophalangeal amputation of unspecified thumb
  - S68.02 Partial traumatic metacarpophalangeal amputation of thumb
    - S68.021 Partial traumatic metacarpophalangeal amputation of right thumb
    - S68.022 Partial traumatic metacarpophalangeal amputation of left thumb
    - S68.029 Partial traumatic metacarpophalangeal amputation of unspecified thumb
- S68.1 Traumatic metacarpophalangeal amputation of other and unspecified finger
  Traumatic amputation of finger NOS
  - Excludes2 traumatic metacarpophalangeal amputation of thumb (S68.0-)
  - S68.11 Complete traumatic metacarpophalangeal amputation of other and unspecified finger
    - S68.110 Complete traumatic metacarpophalangeal amputation of right index finger
    - S68.111 Complete traumatic metacarpophalangeal amputation of left index finger
    - S68.112 Complete traumatic metacarpophalangeal amputation of right middle finger
    - S68.113 Complete traumatic metacarpophalangeal amputation of left middle finger
    - S68.114 Complete traumatic metacarpophalangeal amputation of right ring finger
    - S68.115 Complete traumatic metacarpophalangeal amputation of left ring finger
    - S68.116 Complete traumatic metacarpophalangeal amputation of right little finger
    - S68.117 Complete traumatic metacarpophalangeal amputation of left little finger
    - S68.118 Complete traumatic metacarpophalangeal amputation of other finger
      Complete traumatic metacarpophalangeal amputation of specified finger with unspecified laterality
    - S68.119 Complete traumatic metacarpophalangeal amputation of unspecified finger
  - S68.12 Partial traumatic metacarpophalangeal amputation of other and unspecified finger
    - S68.120 Partial traumatic metacarpophalangeal amputation of right index finger
    - S68.121 Partial traumatic metacarpophalangeal amputation of left index finger
    - S68.122 Partial traumatic metacarpophalangeal amputation of right middle finger
    - S68.123 Partial traumatic metacarpophalangeal amputation of left middle finger
    - S68.124 Partial traumatic metacarpophalangeal amputation of right ring finger
    - S68.125 Partial traumatic metacarpophalangeal amputation of left ring finger
    - S68.126 Partial traumatic metacarpophalangeal amputation of right little finger
    - S68.127 Partial traumatic metacarpophalangeal amputation of left little finger
    - S68.128 Partial traumatic metacarpophalangeal amputation of other finger
      Partial traumatic metacarpophalangeal amputation of specified finger with unspecified laterality
    - S68.129 Partial traumatic metacarpophalangeal amputation of unspecified finger

● Unacceptable First-Listed Diagnosis   ● Use Additional Character(s)   ▨ Unspecified   OGCR Official Guidelines for Coding and Reporting
🖐 Complication\Comorbidity   🖐 Major C\C   Excludes 1   Excludes 2   Includes   Use additional   Code first   Code also

- ● S68.4   Traumatic amputation of hand at wrist level
  Traumatic amputation of hand NOS
  Traumatic amputation of wrist
  - ● S68.41   Complete traumatic amputation of hand at wrist level
    - ● S68.411   Complete traumatic amputation of right hand at wrist level A 🗞
    - ● S68.412   Complete traumatic amputation of left hand at wrist level A 🗞
    - ● ◼ S68.419   Complete traumatic amputation of unspecified hand at wrist level A 🗞
  - ● S68.42   Partial traumatic amputation of hand at wrist level
    - ● S68.421   Partial traumatic amputation of right hand at wrist level A 🗞
    - ● S68.422   Partial traumatic amputation of left hand at wrist level A 🗞
    - ● ◼ S68.429   Partial traumatic amputation of hand at wrist level of unspecified side A 🗞
- ● S68.5   Traumatic transphalangeal amputation of thumb
  Traumatic interphalangeal joint amputation of thumb
  - ● S68.51   Complete traumatic transphalangeal amputation of thumb
    - ● S68.511   Complete traumatic transphalangeal amputation of right thumb
    - ● S68.512   Complete traumatic transphalangeal amputation of left thumb
    - ● ◼ S68.519   Complete traumatic transphalangeal amputation of unspecified thumb
  - ● S68.52   Partial traumatic transphalangeal amputation of thumb
    - ● S68.521   Partial traumatic transphalangeal amputation of right thumb
    - ● S68.522   Partial traumatic transphalangeal amputation of left thumb
    - ● ◼ S68.529   Partial traumatic transphalangeal amputation of unspecified thumb
- ● S68.6   Traumatic transphalangeal amputation of other and unspecified finger
  - ● S68.61   Complete traumatic transphalangeal amputation of other and unspecified finger(s)
    - ● S68.610   Complete traumatic transphalangeal amputation of right index finger
    - ● S68.611   Complete traumatic transphalangeal amputation of left index finger
    - ● S68.612   Complete traumatic transphalangeal amputation of right middle finger
    - ● S68.613   Complete traumatic transphalangeal amputation of left middle finger
    - ● S68.614   Complete traumatic transphalangeal amputation of right ring finger
    - ● S68.615   Complete traumatic transphalangeal amputation of left ring finger

- ● S68.616   Complete traumatic transphalangeal amputation of right little finger
- ● S68.617   Complete traumatic transphalangeal amputation of left little finger
- ● S68.618   Complete traumatic transphalangeal amputation of other finger
  Complete traumatic transphalangeal amputation of specified finger with unspecified laterality
- ● ◼ S68.619   Complete traumatic transphalangeal amputation of unspecified finger
- ● S68.62   Partial traumatic transphalangeal amputation of other and unspecified finger
  - ● S68.620   Partial traumatic transphalangeal amputation of right index finger
  - ● S68.621   Partial traumatic transphalangeal amputation of left index finger
  - ● S68.622   Partial traumatic transphalangeal amputation of right middle finger
  - ● S68.623   Partial traumatic transphalangeal amputation of left middle finger
  - ● S68.624   Partial traumatic transphalangeal amputation of right ring finger
  - ● S68.625   Partial traumatic transphalangeal amputation of left ring finger
  - ● S68.626   Partial traumatic transphalangeal amputation of right little finger
  - ● S68.627   Partial traumatic transphalangeal amputation of left little finger
  - ● S68.628   Partial traumatic transphalangeal amputation of other finger
    Partial traumatic transphalangeal amputation of specified finger with unspecified laterality
  - ● ◼ S68.629   Partial traumatic transphalangeal amputation of unspecified finger
- ● S68.7   Traumatic transmetacarpal amputation of hand
  - ● S68.71   Complete traumatic transmetacarpal amputation of hand
    - ● S68.711   Complete traumatic transmetacarpal amputation of right hand A 🗞
    - ● S68.712   Complete traumatic transmetacarpal amputation of left hand A 🗞
    - ● ◼ S68.719   Complete traumatic transmetacarpal amputation of unspecified hand A 🗞
  - ● S68.72   Partial traumatic transmetacarpal amputation of hand
    - ● S68.721   Partial traumatic transmetacarpal amputation of right hand A 🗞
    - ● S68.722   Partial traumatic transmetacarpal amputation of left hand A 🗞
    - ● ◼ S68.729   Partial traumatic transmetacarpal amputation of unspecified hand A 🗞

● Unacceptable First-Listed Diagnosis   ● Use Additional Character(s)   ◼ Unspecified   **OGCR** Official Guidelines for Coding and Reporting

🗞 Complication\Comorbidity   🗞 Major C\C   Excludes 1   Excludes 2   Includes   Use additional   Code first   Code also

1479

● **S69**   **Other and unspecified injuries of wrist, hand and finger(s)**
> The appropriate 7th character is to be added to each code from category S69

> | A | initial encounter |
> |---|---|
> | D | subsequent encounter |
> | S | sequela |

   ● **S69.8**   **Other specified injuries of wrist, hand and finger(s)**

     ● ◻ **S69.80**   Other specified injuries of wrist, hand and finger(s) of unspecified side

     ● **S69.81**   Other specified injuries of right wrist, hand and finger(s)

     ● **S69.82**   Other specified injuries of left wrist, hand and finger(s)

   ● **S69.9**   **Unspecified injury of wrist, hand and finger(s)**

     ● ◻ **S69.90**   Unspecified injury of wrist, hand and finger(s) of unspecified side

     ● ◻ **S69.91**   Unspecified injury of right wrist, hand and finger(s)

     ● ◻ **S69.92**   Unspecified injury of left wrist, hand and finger(s)

INJURIES TO THE HIP AND THIGH (S70-S79)

> **Excludes2**   burns and corrosions (T20-T32)
> frostbite (T33-T34)
> snake bite (T63.0-)
> venomous insect bite or sting (T63.4-)

● **S70**   **Superficial injury of hip and thigh**
> The appropriate 7th character is to be added to each code from category S70

> | A | initial encounter |
> |---|---|
> | D | subsequent encounter |
> | S | sequela |

   ● **S70.0**   **Contusion of hip**

     ● ◻ **S70.00**   Contusion of unspecified hip

     ● **S70.01**   Contusion of right hip

     ● **S70.02**   Contusion of left hip

   ● **S70.1**   **Contusion of thigh**

     ● ◻ **S70.10**   Contusion of unspecified thigh

     ● **S70.11**   Contusion of right thigh

     ● **S70.12**   Contusion of left thigh

   ● **S70.2**   **Other superficial injuries of hip**

     ● **S70.21**   Abrasion of hip

       ● **S70.211**   Abrasion, right hip

       ● **S70.212**   Abrasion, left hip

       ● ◻ **S70.219**   Abrasion, unspecified hip

     ● **S70.22**   Blister (nonthermal) of hip

       ● **S70.221**   Blister (nonthermal), right hip

       ● **S70.222**   Blister (nonthermal), left hip

       ● ◻ **S70.229**   Blister (nonthermal), unspecified hip

     ● **S70.24**   External constriction of hip

       ● **S70.241**   External constriction, right hip

       ● **S70.242**   External constriction, left hip

       ● ◻ **S70.249**   External constriction, unspecified hip

     ● **S70.25**   Superficial foreign body of hip
> Splinter in the hip

       ● **S70.251**   Superficial foreign body, right hip

       ● **S70.252**   Superficial foreign body, left hip

       ● ◻ **S70.259**   Superficial foreign body, unspecified hip

     ● **S70.26**   Insect bite (nonvenomous) of hip

       ● **S70.261**   Insect bite (nonvenomous), right hip

       ● **S70.262**   Insect bite (nonvenomous), left hip

       ● ◻ **S70.269**   Insect bite (nonvenomous), unspecified hip

     ● **S70.27**   Other superficial bite of hip

> **Excludes1**   open bite of hip (S71.05-)

       ● **S70.271**   Other superficial bite of hip, right hip

       ● **S70.272**   Other superficial bite of hip, left hip

       ● ◻ **S70.279**   Other superficial bite of hip, unspecified hip

   ● **S70.3**   **Other superficial injuries of thigh**

     ● **S70.31**   Abrasion of thigh

       ● **S70.311**   Abrasion, right thigh

       ● **S70.312**   Abrasion, left thigh

       ● ◻ **S70.319**   Abrasion, unspecified thigh

     ● **S70.32**   Blister (nonthermal) of thigh

       ● **S70.321**   Blister (nonthermal), right thigh

       ● **S70.322**   Blister (nonthermal), left thigh

       ● ◻ **S70.329**   Blister (nonthermal), unspecified thigh

     ● **S70.34**   External constriction of thigh

       ● **S70.341**   External constriction, right thigh

       ● **S70.342**   External constriction, left thigh

       ● ◻ **S70.349**   External constriction, unspecified thigh

     ● **S70.35**   Superficial foreign body of thigh
> Splinter in the thigh

       ● **S70.351**   Superficial foreign body, right thigh

       ● **S70.352**   Superficial foreign body, left thigh

       ● ◻ **S70.359**   Superficial foreign body, unspecified thigh

     ● **S70.36**   Insect bite (nonvenomous) of thigh

       ● **S70.361**   Insect bite (nonvenomous), right thigh

       ● **S70.362**   Insect bite (nonvenomous), left thigh

       ● ◻ **S70.369**   Insect bite (nonvenomous), unspecified thigh

     ● **S70.37**   Other superficial bite of thigh

> **Excludes1**   open bite of thigh (S71.15)

       ● **S70.371**   Other superficial bite of right thigh

       ● **S70.372**   Other superficial bite of left thigh

       ● ◻ **S70.379**   Other superficial bite of unspecified thigh

   ● **S70.9**   **Unspecified superficial injury of hip and thigh**

     ● **S70.91**   Unspecified superficial injury of hip

       ● ◻ **S70.911**   Unspecified superficial injury of right hip

       ● ◻ **S70.912**   Unspecified superficial injury of left hip

       ● ◻ **S70.919**   Unspecified superficial injury of hip, unspecified side

● S70.92   Unspecified superficial injury of thigh

  ● ▫ S70.921   Unspecified superficial injury of right thigh

  ● ▫ S70.922   Unspecified superficial injury of left thigh

  ● ▫ S70.929   Unspecified superficial injury of thigh, unspecified side

● S71   Open wound of hip and thigh

> Code also any associated wound infection
>
> **Excludes1**   open fracture of hip and thigh (S72.-)
> traumatic amputation of hip and thigh (S78.-)
>
> **Excludes2**   bite of venomous animal (T63.-)
> open wound of ankle, foot and toes (S91.-)
> open wound of knee and lower leg (S81.-)
>
> The appropriate 7th character is to be added to each code from category S71
>
> | A | initial encounter |
> | D | subsequent encounter |
> | S | sequela |

● S71.0   Open wound of hip

  ● S71.00   Unspecified open wound of hip

    ● ▫ S71.001   Unspecified open wound, right hip

    ● ▫ S71.002   Unspecified open wound, left hip

    ● ▫ S71.009   Unspecified open wound, unspecified hip

  ● S71.01   Laceration without foreign body of hip

    ● S71.011   Laceration without foreign body, right hip

    ● S71.012   Laceration without foreign body, left hip

    ● ▫ S71.019   Laceration without foreign body, unspecified hip

  ● S71.02   Laceration with foreign body of hip

    ● S71.021   Laceration with foreign body, right hip

    ● S71.022   Laceration with foreign body, left hip

    ● ▫ S71.029   Laceration with foreign body, unspecified hip

  ● S71.03   Puncture wound without foreign body of hip

    ● S71.031   Puncture wound without foreign body, right hip

    ● S71.032   Puncture wound without foreign body, left hip

    ● ▫ S71.039   Puncture wound without foreign body, unspecified hip

  ● S71.04   Puncture wound with foreign body of hip

    ● S71.041   Puncture wound with foreign body, right hip

    ● S71.042   Puncture wound with foreign body, left hip

    ● ▫ S71.049   Puncture wound with foreign body, unspecified hip

  ● S71.05   Open bite of hip
      Bite of hip NOS

      Excludes1   superficial bite of hip (S70.26, S70.27)

    ● S71.051   Bite, right hip

    ● S71.052   Bite, left hip

    ● ▫ S71.059   Bite, unspecified hip

● S71.1   Open wound of thigh

  ● S71.10   Unspecified open wound of thigh

    ● ▫ S71.101   Unspecified open wound, right thigh

    ● ▫ S71.102   Unspecified open wound, left thigh

    ● ▫ S71.109   Unspecified open wound, unspecified thigh

  ● S71.11   Laceration without foreign body of thigh

    ● S71.111   Laceration without foreign body, right thigh

    ● S71.112   Laceration without foreign body, left thigh

    ● ▫ S71.119   Laceration without foreign body, unspecified thigh

  ● S71.12   Laceration with foreign body of thigh

    ● S71.121   Laceration with foreign body, right thigh

    ● S71.122   Laceration with foreign body, left thigh

    ● ▫ S71.129   Laceration with foreign body, unspecified thigh

  ● S71.13   Puncture wound without foreign body of thigh

    ● S71.131   Puncture wound without foreign body, right thigh

    ● S71.132   Puncture wound without foreign body, left thigh

    ● ▫ S71.139   Puncture wound without foreign body, unspecified thigh

  ● S71.14   Puncture wound with foreign body of thigh

    ● S71.141   Puncture wound with foreign body, right thigh

    ● S71.142   Puncture wound with foreign body, left thigh

    ● ▫ S71.149   Puncture wound with foreign body, unspecified thigh

  ● S71.15   Open bite of thigh
      Bite of thigh NOS

      Excludes1   superficial bite of thigh (S70.86-, S70.87-)

    ● S71.151   Bite, right thigh

    ● S71.152   Bite, left thigh

    ● ▫ S71.159   Bite, unspecified thigh

● Unacceptable First-Listed Diagnosis   ● Use Additional Character(s)   ▫ Unspecified   **OGCR** Official Guidelines for Coding and Reporting

🗞 Complication\Comorbidity   🗞 Major C\C   Excludes 1   Excludes 2   Includes   Use additional   Code first   Code also   1481

● **S72**   **Fracture of femur**

A fracture not indicated as displaced or nondisplaced should be coded to displaced

> **Excludes1**   traumatic amputation of hip and thigh (S78.-)

> **Excludes2**   fracture of lower leg and ankle (S82.-)
> fracture of foot (S92.-)
> periprosthetic fracture of prosthetic implant of hip (T84.040, T84.041)

The appropriate 7th character is to be added to each code from category S72

A fracture not designated as open or closed should be coded to closed

The open fracture designations are based on the Gustilo open fracture classification

A	initial encounter for closed fracture
B	initial encounter for open fracture type I or II
	initial encounter for open fracture NOS
C	initial encounter for open fracture type IIIA, IIIB, or IIIC
D	subsequent encounter for closed fracture with routine healing
E	subsequent encounter for open fracture type I or II with routine healing
F	subsequent encounter for open fracture type IIIA, IIIB, or IIIC with routine healing
G	subsequent encounter for closed fracture with delayed healing
H	subsequent encounter for open fracture type I or II with delayed healing
J	subsequent encounter for open fracture type IIIA, IIIB, or IIIC with delayed healing
K	subsequent encounter for closed fracture with nonunion
M	subsequent encounter for open fracture type I or II with nonunion
N	subsequent encounter for open fracture type IIIA, IIIB, or IIIC with nonunion
P	subsequent encounter for closed fracture with malunion
Q	subsequent encounter for open fracture type I or II with malunion
R	subsequent encounter for open fracture type IIIA, IIIB, or IIIC with malunion
S	sequela

● **S72.0**   **Fracture of head and neck of femur**

> **Excludes2**   physeal fracture of upper end of femur (S79.0-)

  ● **S72.00**   **Fracture of unspecified part of neck of femur**
     Fracture of hip NOS
     Fracture of neck of femur NOS

    ● ■ **S72.001**   **Fracture of unspecified part of neck of right femur** K, M, N, P, Q, R 🦠, A, B, C 🦠

    ● ■ **S72.002**   **Fracture of unspecified part of neck of left femur** K, M, N, P, Q, R 🦠, A, B, C 🦠

    ● ■ **S72.009**   **Fracture of unspecified part of neck of unspecified femur** K, M, N, P, Q, R 🦠, A, B, C 🦠

  ● **S72.01**   **Unspecified intracapsular fracture of femur**
     Subcapital fracture of femur

    ● ■ **S72.011**   **Unspecified intracapsular fracture of right femur** K, M, N, P, Q, R 🦠, A, B, C 🦠

    ● ■ **S72.012**   **Unspecified intracapsular fracture of left femur** K, M, N, P, Q, R 🦠, A, B, C 🦠

    ● ■ **S72.019**   **Unspecified intracapsular fracture of unspecified femur** K, M, N, P, Q, R 🦠, A, B, C 🦠

● **S72.02**   **Fracture of epiphysis (separation) (upper) of femur**
   Transepiphyseal fracture of femur
   Fracture and separation across growth plate

> **Excludes1**   capital femoral epiphyseal fracture (pediatric) of femur (S79.01-)
> Salter-Harris Type I physeal fracture of upper end of femur (S79.01-)

  ● **S72.021**   **Displaced fracture of epiphysis (separation) (upper) of right femur** K, M, N, P, Q, R 🦠, A, B, C 🦠

  ● **S72.022**   **Displaced fracture of epiphysis (separation) (upper) of left femur** K, M, N, P, Q, R 🦠, A, B, C 🦠

  ● ■ **S72.023**   **Displaced fracture of epiphysis (separation) (upper) of unspecified femur** K, M, N, P, Q, R 🦠, A, B, C 🦠

  ● **S72.024**   **Nondisplaced fracture of epiphysis (separation) (upper) of right femur** K, M, N, P, Q, R 🦠, A, B, C 🦠

  ● **S72.025**   **Nondisplaced fracture of epiphysis (separation) (upper) of left femur** K, M, N, P, Q, R 🦠, A, B, C 🦠

  ● ■ **S72.026**   **Nondisplaced fracture of epiphysis (separation) (upper) of unspecified femur** K, M, N, P, Q, R 🦠, A, B, C 🦠

● **S72.03**   **Midcervical fracture of femur**
   Transcervical fracture of femur NOS

  ● **S72.031**   **Displaced midcervical fracture of right femur** K, M, N, P, Q, R 🦠, A, B, C 🦠

  ● **S72.032**   **Displaced midcervical fracture of left femur** K, M, N, P, Q, R 🦠, A, B, C 🦠

  ● ■ **S72.033**   **Displaced midcervical fracture of unspecified femur** K, M, N, P, Q, R 🦠, A, B, C 🦠

  ● **S72.034**   **Nondisplaced midcervical fracture of right femur** K, M, N, P, Q, R 🦠, A, B, C 🦠

  ● **S72.035**   **Nondisplaced midcervical fracture of left femur** K, M, N, P, Q, R 🦠, A, B, C 🦠

  ● ■ **S72.036**   **Nondisplaced midcervical fracture of unspecified femur** K, M, N, P, Q, R 🦠, A, B, C 🦠

● **S72.04**   **Fracture of base of neck of femur**
   Cervicotrochanteric fracture of femur

  ● **S72.041**   **Displaced fracture of base of neck of right femur** K, M, N, P, Q, R 🦠, A, B, C 🦠

  ● **S72.042**   **Displaced fracture of base of neck of left femur** K, M, N, P, Q, R 🦠, A, B, C 🦠

  ● ■ **S72.043**   **Displaced fracture of base of neck of unspecified femur** K, M, N, P, Q, R 🦠, A, B, C 🦠

  ● **S72.044**   **Nondisplaced fracture of base of neck of right femur** K, M, N, P, Q, R 🦠, A, B, C 🦠

● S72.045   Nondisplaced fracture of base of neck of left femur K, M, N, P, Q, R 🔾, A, B, C 🔾

● S72.046   Nondisplaced fracture of base of neck of unspecified femur K, M, N, P, Q, R 🔾, A, B, C 🔾

● S72.05   Unspecified fracture of head of femur
Fracture of head of femur NOS

● S72.051   Unspecified fracture of head of right femur K, M, N, P, Q, R 🔾, A, B, C 🔾

● S72.052   Unspecified fracture of head of left femur K, M, N, P, Q, R 🔾, A, B, C 🔾

● S72.059   Unspecified fracture of head of unspecified femur K, M, N, P, Q, R 🔾, A, B, C 🔾

● S72.06   Articular fracture of head of femur

● S72.061   Displaced articular fracture of head of right femur K, M, N, P, Q, R 🔾, A, B, C 🔾

● S72.062   Displaced articular fracture of head of left femur K, M, N, P, Q, R 🔾, A, B, C 🔾

● S72.063   Displaced articular fracture of head of unspecified femur K, M, N, P, Q, R 🔾, A, B, C 🔾

● S72.064   Nondisplaced articular fracture of head of right femur K, M, N, P, Q, R 🔾, A, B, C 🔾

● S72.065   Nondisplaced articular fracture of head of left femur K, M, N, P, Q, R 🔾, A, B, C 🔾

● S72.066   Nondisplaced articular fracture of head of unspecified femur K, M, N, P, Q, R 🔾, A, B, C 🔾

● S72.09   Other fracture of head and neck of femur

● S72.091   Other fracture of head and neck of right femur K, M, N, P, Q, R 🔾, A, B, C 🔾

● S72.092   Other fracture of head and neck of left femur K, M, N, P, Q, R 🔾, A, B, C 🔾

● S72.099   Other fracture of head and neck of unspecified femur K, M, N, P, Q, R 🔾, A, B, C 🔾

● S72.1   Pertrochanteric fracture
Fracture extending close to, but not into, joint

● S72.10   Unspecified trochanteric fracture of femur
Fracture of trochanter NOS

● S72.101   Unspecified trochanteric fracture of right femur K, M, N, P, Q, R 🔾, A, B, C 🔾

● S72.102   Unspecified trochanteric fracture of left femur K, M, N, P, Q, R 🔾, A, B, C 🔾

● S72.109   Unspecified trochanteric fracture of unspecified femur K, M, N, P, Q, R 🔾, A, B, C 🔾

● S72.11   Fracture of greater trochanter of femur

● S72.111   Displaced fracture of greater trochanter of right femur K, M, N, P, Q, R 🔾, A, B, C 🔾

● S72.112   Displaced fracture of greater trochanter of left femur K, M, N, P, Q, R 🔾, A, B, C 🔾

● S72.113   Displaced fracture of greater trochanter of unspecified femur K, M, N, P, Q, R 🔾, A, B, C 🔾

● S72.114   Nondisplaced fracture of greater trochanter of right femur K, M, N, P, Q, R 🔾, A, B, C 🔾

● S72.115   Nondisplaced fracture of greater trochanter of left femur K, M, N, P, Q, R 🔾, A, B, C 🔾

● S72.116   Nondisplaced fracture of greater trochanter of unspecified femur K, M, N, P, Q, R 🔾, A, B, C 🔾

● S72.12   Fracture of lesser trochanter of femur

● S72.121   Displaced fracture of lesser trochanter of right femur K, M, N, P, Q, R 🔾, A, B, C 🔾

● S72.122   Displaced fracture of lesser trochanter of left femur K, M, N, P, Q, R 🔾, A, B, C 🔾

● S72.123   Displaced fracture of lesser trochanter of unspecified femur K, M, N, P, Q, R 🔾, A, B, C 🔾

● S72.124   Nondisplaced fracture of lesser trochanter of right femur K, M, N, P, Q, R 🔾, A, B, C 🔾

● S72.125   Nondisplaced fracture of lesser trochanter of left femur K, M, N, P, Q, R 🔾, A, B, C 🔾

● S72.126   Nondisplaced fracture of lesser trochanter of unspecified femur K, M, N, P, Q, R 🔾, A, B, C 🔾

● S72.13   Apophyseal fracture of femur
Pertaining to articulations between articular facets of adjacent vertebrae

> **Excludes1**   chronic (nontraumatic) slipped upper femoral epiphysis (M93.0-)

● S72.131   Displaced apophyseal fracture of right femur K, M, N, P, Q, R 🔾, A, B, C 🔾

● S72.132   Displaced apophyseal fracture of left femur K, M, N, P, Q, R 🔾, A, B, C 🔾

● S72.133   Displaced apophyseal fracture of unspecified femur K, M, N, P, Q, R 🔾, A, B, C 🔾

● S72.134   Nondisplaced apophyseal fracture of right femur K, M, N, P, Q, R 🔾, A, B, C 🔾

● S72.135   Nondisplaced apophyseal fracture of left femur K, M, N, P, Q, R 🔾, A, B, C 🔾

● S72.136   Nondisplaced apophyseal fracture of unspecified femur K, M, N, P, Q, R 🔾, A, B, C 🔾

● S72.14   Intertrochanteric fracture of femur

● S72.141   Displaced intertrochanteric fracture of right femur K, M, N, P, Q, R 🔾, A, B, C 🔾

● S72.142   Displaced intertrochanteric fracture of left femur K, M, N, P, Q, R 🔾, A, B, C 🔾

● S72.143   Displaced intertrochanteric fracture of unspecified femur K, M, N, P, Q, R 🔾, A, B, C 🔾

● Unacceptable First-Listed Diagnosis   ● Use Additional Character(s)   🔲 Unspecified   **OGCR** Official Guidelines for Coding and Reporting

🔾 Complication\Comorbidity   🔾 Major C\C   Excludes 1   Excludes 2   Includes   Use additional   Code first   Code also

1483

CHAPTER 19 (S00–T98)

- ● S72.144 Nondisplaced intertrochanteric fracture of right femur K, M, N, P, Q, R 🪙, A, B, C 🪙
- ● S72.145 Nondisplaced intertrochanteric fracture of left femur K, M, N, P, Q, R 🪙, A, B, C 🪙
- ● ▪ S72.146 Nondisplaced intertrochanteric fracture of unspecified femur K, M, N, P, Q, R 🪙, A, B, C 🪙

● S72.2   **Subtrochanteric fracture of femur**
  Subtrochanteric: inferior to trochanter

- ● S72.21 Displaced subtrochanteric fracture of right femur K, M, N, P, Q, R 🪙, A, B, C 🪙
- ● S72.22 Displaced subtrochanteric fracture of left femur K, M, N, P, Q, R 🪙, A, B, C 🪙
- ● ▪ S72.23 Displaced subtrochanteric fracture of unspecified femur K, M, N, P, Q, R 🪙, A, B, C 🪙
- ● S72.24 Nondisplaced subtrochanteric fracture of right femur K, M, N, P, Q, R 🪙, A, B, C 🪙
- ● S72.25 Nondisplaced subtrochanteric fracture of left femur K, M, N, P, Q, R 🪙, A, B, C 🪙
- ● ▪ S72.26 Nondisplaced subtrochanteric fracture of unspecified femur K, M, N, P, Q, R 🪙, A, B, C 🪙

● S72.3   **Fracture of shaft of femur**

- ● S72.30 Unspecified fracture of shaft of femur
  - ● ▪ S72.301 Unspecified fracture of shaft of right femur K, M, N, P, Q, R 🪙, A, B, C 🪙
  - ● ▪ S72.302 Unspecified fracture of shaft of left femur K, M, N, P, Q, R 🪙, A, B, C 🪙
  - ● ▪ S72.309 Unspecified fracture of shaft of unspecified femur K, M, N, P, Q, R 🪙, A, B, C 🪙
- ● S72.32 Transverse fracture of shaft of femur
  - ● S72.321 Displaced transverse fracture of shaft of right femur K, M, N, P, Q, R 🪙, A, B, C 🪙
  - ● S72.322 Displaced transverse fracture of shaft of left femur K, M, N, P, Q, R 🪙, A, B, C 🪙
  - ● ▪ S72.323 Displaced transverse fracture of shaft of unspecified femur K, M, N, P, Q, R 🪙, A, B, C 🪙
  - ● S72.324 Nondisplaced transverse fracture of shaft of right femur K, M, N, P, Q, R 🪙, A, B, C 🪙
  - ● S72.325 Nondisplaced transverse fracture of shaft of left femur K, M, N, P, Q, R 🪙, A, B, C 🪙
  - ● ▪ S72.326 Nondisplaced transverse fracture of shaft of unspecified femur K, M, N, P, Q, R 🪙, A, B, C 🪙
- ● S72.33 Oblique fracture of shaft of femur
  - ● S72.331 Displaced oblique fracture of shaft of right femur K, M, N, P, Q, R 🪙, A, B, C 🪙
  - ● S72.332 Displaced oblique fracture of shaft of left femur K, M, N, P, Q, R 🪙, A, B, C 🪙
  - ● ▪ S72.333 Displaced oblique fracture of shaft of unspecified femur K, M, N, P, Q, R 🪙, A, B, C 🪙

- ● S72.334 Nondisplaced oblique fracture of shaft of right femur K, M, N, P, Q, R 🪙, A, B, C 🪙
- ● S72.335 Nondisplaced oblique fracture of shaft of left femur K, M, N, P, Q, R 🪙, A, B, C 🪙
- ● ▪ S72.336 Nondisplaced oblique fracture of shaft of unspecified femur K, M, N, P, Q, R 🪙, A, B, C 🪙

● S72.34 Spiral fracture of shaft of femur

- ● S72.341 Displaced spiral fracture of shaft of right femur K, M, N, P, Q, R 🪙, A, B, C 🪙
- ● S72.342 Displaced spiral fracture of shaft of left femur K, M, N, P, Q, R 🪙, A, B, C 🪙
- ● ▪ S72.343 Displaced spiral fracture of shaft of unspecified femur K, M, N, P, Q, R 🪙, A, B, C 🪙
- ● S72.344 Nondisplaced spiral fracture of shaft of right femur K, M, N, P, Q, R 🪙, A, B, C 🪙
- ● S72.345 Nondisplaced spiral fracture of shaft of left femur K, M, N, P, Q, R 🪙, A, B, C 🪙
- ● ▪ S72.346 Nondisplaced spiral fracture of shaft of unspecified femur K, M, N, P, Q, R 🪙, A, B, C 🪙

● S72.35 Comminuted fracture of shaft of femur

- ● S72.351 Displaced comminuted fracture of shaft of right femur K, M, N, P, Q, R 🪙, A, B, C 🪙
- ● S72.352 Displaced comminuted fracture of shaft of left femur K, M, N, P, Q, R 🪙, A, B, C 🪙
- ● ▪ S72.353 Displaced comminuted fracture of shaft of unspecified femur K, M, N, P, Q, R 🪙, A, B, C 🪙
- ● S72.354 Nondisplaced comminuted fracture of shaft of right femur K, M, N, P, Q, R 🪙, A, B, C 🪙
- ● S72.355 Nondisplaced comminuted fracture of shaft of left femur K, M, N, P, Q, R 🪙, A, B, C 🪙
- ● ▪ S72.356 Nondisplaced comminuted fracture of shaft of unspecified femur K, M, N, P, Q, R 🪙, A, B, C 🪙

● S72.36 Segmental fracture of shaft of femur

- ● S72.361 Displaced segmental fracture of shaft of right femur K, M, N, P, Q, R 🪙, A, B, C 🪙
- ● S72.362 Displaced segmental fracture of shaft of left femur K, M, N, P, Q, R 🪙, A, B, C 🪙
- ● ▪ S72.363 Displaced segmental fracture of shaft of unspecified femur K, M, N, P, Q, R 🪙, A, B, C 🪙
- ● S72.364 Nondisplaced segmental fracture of shaft of right femur K, M, N, P, Q, R 🪙, A, B, C 🪙
- ● S72.365 Nondisplaced segmental fracture of shaft of left femur K, M, N, P, Q, R 🪙, A, B, C 🪙
- ● ▪ S72.366 Nondisplaced segmental fracture of shaft of unspecified femur K, M, N, P, Q, R 🪙, A, B, C 🪙

● Unacceptable First-Listed Diagnosis   ● Use Additional Character(s)   ▪ Unspecified   **OGCR** Official Guidelines for Coding and Reporting
🪙 Complication\Comorbidity   🪙 Major C\C   Excludes 1   Excludes 2   Includes   Use additional   Code first   Code also

CHAPTER 19 (S00-T98)

● S72.39   Other fracture of shaft of femur

    ● S72.391   Other fracture of shaft of right femur K, M, N, P, Q, R 🅒, A, B, C 🅜

    ● S72.392   Other fracture of shaft of left femur K, M, N, P, Q, R 🅒, A, B, C 🅜

    ● ▪ S72.399   Other fracture of shaft of unspecified femur K, M, N, P, Q, R 🅒, A, B, C 🅜

● S72.4   Fracture of lower end of femur
    Fracture of distal end of femur

    | Excludes2 | fracture of shaft of femur (S72.3-)
        physeal fracture of lower end of femur (S79.1-)

  ● S72.40   Unspecified fracture of lower end of femur

    ● ▪ S72.401   Unspecified fracture of lower end of right femur A, K, M, N, P, Q, R 🅒, B, C 🅜

    ● ▪ S72.402   Unspecified fracture of lower end of left femur A, K, M, N, P, Q, R 🅒, B, C 🅜

    ● ▪ S72.409   Unspecified fracture of lower end of unspecified femur A, K, M, N, P, Q, R 🅒, B, C 🅜

  ● S72.41   Unspecified condyle fracture of lower end of femur
    Condyle fracture of femur NOS

    ● ▪ S72.411   Displaced unspecified condyle fracture of lower end of right femur A, K, M, N, P, Q, R 🅒, B, C 🅜

    ● ▪ S72.412   Displaced unspecified condyle fracture of lower end of left femur A, K, M, N, P, Q, R 🅒, B, C 🅜

    ● ▪ S72.413   Displaced unspecified condyle fracture of lower end of unspecified femur A, K, M, N, P, Q, R 🅒, B, C 🅜

    ● ▪ S72.414   Nondisplaced unspecified condyle fracture of lower end of right femur A, K, M, N, P, Q, R 🅒, B, C 🅜

    ● ▪ S72.415   Nondisplaced unspecified condyle fracture of lower end of left femur A, K, M, N, P, Q, R 🅒, B, C 🅜

    ● ▪ S72.416   Nondisplaced unspecified condyle fracture of lower end of unspecified femur A, K, M, N, P, Q, R 🅒, B, C 🅜

  ● S72.42   Fracture of lateral condyle of femur

    ● S72.421   Displaced fracture of lateral condyle of right femur A, K, M, N, P, Q, R 🅒, B, C 🅜

    ● S72.422   Displaced fracture of lateral condyle of left femur A, K, M, N, P, Q, R 🅒, B, C 🅜

    ● ▪ S72.423   Displaced fracture of lateral condyle of unspecified femur A, K, M, N, P, Q, R 🅒, B, C 🅜

    ● S72.424   Nondisplaced fracture of lateral condyle of right femur A, K, M, N, P, Q, R 🅒, B, C 🅜

    ● S72.425   Nondisplaced fracture of lateral condyle of left femur A, K, M, N, P, Q, R 🅒, B, C 🅜

    ● ▪ S72.426   Nondisplaced fracture of lateral condyle of unspecified femur A, K, M, N, P, Q, R 🅒, B, C 🅜

  ● S72.43   Fracture of medial condyle of femur

    ● S72.431   Displaced fracture of medial condyle of right femur A, K, M, N, P, Q, R 🅒, B, C 🅜

    ● S72.432   Displaced fracture of medial condyle of left femur A, K, M, N, P, Q, R 🅒, B, C 🅜

    ● ▪ S72.433   Displaced fracture of medial condyle of unspecified femur A, K, M, N, P, Q, R 🅒, B, C 🅜

    ● S72.434   Nondisplaced fracture of medial condyle of right femur A, K, M, N, P, Q, R 🅒, B, C 🅜

    ● S72.435   Nondisplaced fracture of medial condyle of left femur A, K, M, N, P, Q, R 🅒, B, C 🅜

    ● ▪ S72.436   Nondisplaced fracture of medial condyle of unspecified femur A, K, M, N, P, Q, R 🅒, B, C 🅜

  ● S72.44   Fracture of lower epiphysis (separation) of femur

    | Excludes1 | Salter-Harris Type I physeal fracture of lower end of femur (S79.11-)

    ● S72.441   Displaced fracture of lower epiphysis (separation) of right femur A, K, M, N, P, Q, R 🅒, B, C 🅜

    ● S72.442   Displaced fracture of lower epiphysis (separation) of left femur A, K, M, N, P, Q, R 🅒, B, C 🅜

    ● ▪ S72.443   Displaced fracture of lower epiphysis (separation) of unspecified femur A, K, M, N, P, Q, R 🅒, B, C 🅜

    ● S72.444   Nondisplaced fracture of lower epiphysis (separation) of right femur A, K, M, N, P, Q, R 🅒, B, C 🅜

    ● S72.445   Nondisplaced fracture of lower epiphysis (separation) of left femur A, K, M, N, P, Q, R 🅒, B, C 🅜

    ● ▪ S72.446   Nondisplaced fracture of lower epiphysis (separation) of unspecified femur A, K, M, N, P, Q, R 🅒, B, C 🅜

  ● S72.45   Supracondylar fracture without intracondylar extension of lower end of femur
    Supracondylar fracture of lower end of femur NOS

    | Excludes1 | supracondylar fracture with intracondylar extension of lower end of femur (S72.46-)

    ● S72.451   Displaced supracondylar fracture without intracondylar extension of lower end of right femur A, K, M, N, P, Q, R 🅒, B, C 🅜

    ● S72.452   Displaced supracondylar fracture without intracondylar extension of lower end of left femur A, K, M, N, P, Q, R 🅒, B, C 🅜

● Unacceptable First-Listed Diagnosis   ● Use Additional Character(s)   ▪ Unspecified   **OGCR** Official Guidelines for Coding and Reporting

🅒 Complication\Comorbidity   🅜 Major C\C | Excludes 1 | | Excludes 2 | Includes   Use additional   Code first   Code also

1485

● ■ **S72.453** **Displaced supracondylar fracture without intracondylar extension of lower end of unspecified femur** A, K, M, N, P, Q, R 🐾, B, C 🐾

● **S72.454** **Nondisplaced supracondylar fracture without intracondylar extension of lower end of right femur** A, K, M, N, P, Q, R 🐾, B, C 🐾

● **S72.455** **Nondisplaced supracondylar fracture without intracondylar extension of lower end of left femur** A, K, M, N, P, Q, R 🐾, B, C 🐾

● ■ **S72.456** **Nondisplaced supracondylar fracture without intracondylar extension of lower end of unspecified femur** A, K, M, N, P, Q, R 🐾, B, C 🐾

● **S72.46** **Supracondylar fracture with intracondylar extension of lower end of femur**

> **Excludes1** supracondylar fracture without intracondylar extension of lower end of femur (S72.45-)

● **S72.461** **Displaced supracondylar fracture with intracondylar extension of lower end of right femur** A, K, M, N, P, Q, R 🐾, B, C 🐾

● **S72.462** **Displaced supracondylar fracture with intracondylar extension of lower end of left femur** A, K, M, N, P, Q, R 🐾, B, C 🐾

● ■ **S72.463** **Displaced supracondylar fracture with intracondylar extension of lower end of unspecified femur** A, K, M, N, P, Q, R 🐾, B, C 🐾

● **S72.464** **Nondisplaced supracondylar fracture with intracondylar extension of lower end of right femur** A, K, M, N, P, Q, R 🐾, B, C 🐾

● **S72.465** **Nondisplaced supracondylar fracture with intracondylar extension of lower end of left femur** A, K, M, N, P, Q, R 🐾, B, C 🐾

● ■ **S72.466** **Nondisplaced supracondylar fracture with intracondylar extension of lower end of unspecified femur** A, K, M, N, P, Q, R 🐾, B, C 🐾

● **S72.47** **Torus fracture of lower end of femur**

> **Note:** Open fracture 7th characters do not apply to codes under subcategory S72.47.

● **S72.471** **Torus fracture of lower end of right femur** A, K, P 🐾, B, C 🐾

● **S72.472** **Torus fracture of lower end of left femur** A, K, P 🐾, B, C 🐾

● ■ **S72.479** **Torus fracture of lower end of unspecified femur** A, K, P 🐾, B, C 🐾

● **S72.49** **Other fracture of lower end of femur**

● **S72.491** **Other fracture of lower end of right femur** A, K, M, N, P, Q, R 🐾, B, C 🐾

● **S72.492** **Other fracture of lower end of left femur** A, K, M, N, P, Q, R 🐾, B, C 🐾

● ■ **S72.499** **Other fracture of lower end of unspecified femur** A, K, M, N, P, Q, R 🐾, B, C 🐾

● **S72.8** **Other fracture of femur**

● **S72.8x** **Other fracture of femur**

● **S72.8x1** **Other fracture of right femur** K, M, N, P, Q, R 🐾, A, B, C 🐾

● **S72.8x2** **Other fracture of left femur** K, M, N, P, Q, R 🐾, A, B, C 🐾

● ■ **S72.8x9** **Other fracture of unspecified femur** K, M, N, P, Q, R 🐾, A, B, C 🐾

● **S72.9** **Unspecified fracture of femur**
Fracture of thigh NOS
Fracture of upper leg NOS

> **Excludes1** fracture of hip NOS (S72.00-, S72.01-)

● ■ **S72.90** **Unspecified fracture of unspecified femur** K, M, N, P, Q, R 🐾, A, B, C 🐾

● ■ **S72.91** **Unspecified fracture of right femur** K, M, N, P, Q, R 🐾, A, B, C 🐾

● ■ **S72.92** **Unspecified fracture of left femur** K, M, N, P, Q, R 🐾, A, B, C 🐾

● **S73** **Dislocation and sprain of joint and ligaments of hip**

> **Includes** avulsion of joint or ligament of hip
> laceration of cartilage, joint or ligament of hip
> sprain of cartilage, joint or ligament of hip
> traumatic hemarthrosis of joint or ligament of hip
> traumatic rupture of joint or ligament of hip
> traumatic subluxation of joint or ligament of hip
> traumatic tear of joint or ligament of hip

> Code also any associated open wound

> **Excludes2** strain of muscle, fascia and tendon of hip and thigh (S76.-)

The appropriate 7th character is to be added to each code from category S73

> A   initial encounter
> D   subsequent encounter
> S   sequela

● **S73.0** **Subluxation and dislocation of hip**
Out of position

> **Excludes2** dislocation and subluxation of hip prosthesis (T84.020, T84.021)

● **S73.00** **Unspecified subluxation and dislocation of hip**
Dislocation of hip NOS
Subluxation of hip NOS

● ■ **S73.001** **Unspecified subluxation of right hip** A 🐾

● ■ **S73.002** **Unspecified subluxation of left hip** A 🐾

● ■ **S73.003** **Unspecified subluxation of unspecified hip** A 🐾

● ■ **S73.004** **Unspecified dislocation of right hip** A 🐾

● Unacceptable First-Listed Diagnosis   ● Use Additional Character(s)   ■ Unspecified   **OGCR** Official Guidelines for Coding and Reporting
🐾 Complication\Comorbidity   🐾 Major C\C   Excludes 1   Excludes 2   Includes   Use additional   Code first   Code also

1486

CHAPTER 19 (S00-T98)

● ■ S73.005   Unspecified dislocation of left hip A ⬤

● ■ S73.006   Unspecified dislocation of unspecified hip A ⬤

● S73.01   Posterior subluxation and dislocation of hip

● S73.011   Posterior subluxation of right hip A ⬤

● S73.012   Posterior subluxation of left hip A ⬤

● ■ S73.013   Posterior subluxation of unspecified hip A ⬤

● S73.014   Posterior dislocation of right hip A ⬤

● S73.015   Posterior dislocation of left hip A ⬤

● ■ S73.016   Posterior dislocation of unspecified hip A ⬤

● S73.02   Obturator subluxation and dislocation of hip

● S73.021   Obturator subluxation of right hip A ⬤

● S73.022   Obturator subluxation of left hip A ⬤

● ■ S73.023   Obturator subluxation of unspecified hip A ⬤

● S73.024   Obturator dislocation of right hip A ⬤

● S73.025   Obturator dislocation of left hip A ⬤

● ■ S73.026   Obturator dislocation of unspecified hip A ⬤

● S73.03   Other anterior dislocation of hip

● S73.031   Other anterior subluxation of right hip A ⬤

● S73.032   Other anterior subluxation of left hip A ⬤

● ■ S73.033   Other anterior subluxation of unspecified hip A ⬤

● S73.034   Other anterior dislocation of right hip A ⬤

● S73.035   Other anterior dislocation of left hip A ⬤

● ■ S73.036   Other anterior dislocation of unspecified hip A ⬤

● S73.04   Central dislocation of hip

● S73.041   Central subluxation of right hip A ⬤

● S73.042   Central subluxation of left hip A ⬤

● ■ S73.043   Central subluxation of unspecified hip A ⬤

● S73.044   Central dislocation of right hip A ⬤

● S73.045   Central dislocation of left hip A ⬤

● ■ S73.046   Central dislocation of unspecified hip A ⬤

● S73.1   Sprain of hip

● S73.10   Unspecified sprain of hip

● ■ S73.101   Unspecified sprain of right hip

● ■ S73.102   Unspecified sprain of left hip

● ■ S73.109   Unspecified sprain of unspecified hip

● S73.11   Iliofemoral ligament sprain of hip

● S73.111   Iliofemoral ligament sprain of right hip

● S73.112   Iliofemoral ligament sprain of left hip

● ■ S73.119   Iliofemoral ligament sprain of unspecified hip

● S73.12   Ischiocapsular (ligament) sprain of hip

● S73.121   Ischiocapsular ligament sprain of right hip

● S73.122   Ischiocapsular ligament sprain of left hip

● ■ S73.129   Ischiocapsular ligament sprain of unspecified hip

● S73.19   Other sprain of hip

● S73.191   Other sprain of right hip

● S73.192   Other sprain of left hip

● ■ S73.199   Other sprain of unspecified hip

● S74   Injury of nerves at hip and thigh level
Code also any associated open wound (S71.-)

Excludes2	injury of nerves at ankle and foot level (S94.-)
	injury of nerves at lower leg level (S84.-)

The appropriate 7th character is to be added to each code from category S74

A   initial encounter
D   subsequent encounter
S   sequela

● S74.0   Injury of sciatic nerve at hip and thigh level

● ■ S74.00   Injury of sciatic nerve at hip and thigh level, unspecified leg

● S74.01   Injury of sciatic nerve at hip and thigh level, right leg

● S74.02   Injury of sciatic nerve at hip and thigh level, left leg

● S74.1   Injury of femoral nerve at hip and thigh level

● ■ S74.10   Injury of femoral nerve at hip and thigh level, unspecified leg

● S74.11   Injury of femoral nerve at hip and thigh level, right leg

● S74.12   Injury of femoral nerve at hip and thigh level, left leg

● S74.2   Injury of cutaneous sensory nerve at hip and thigh level

● ■ S74.20   Injury of cutaneous sensory nerve at hip and thigh level, unspecified leg

● S74.21   Injury of cutaneous sensory nerve at hip and high level, right leg

● S74.22   Injury of cutaneous sensory nerve at hip and thigh level, left leg

● S74.8   Injury of other nerves at hip and thigh level

● S74.8x   Injury of other nerves at hip and thigh level

● S74.8x1   Injury of other nerves at hip and thigh level, right leg

● S74.8x2   Injury of other nerves at hip and thigh level, left leg

● ■ S74.8x9   Injury of other nerves at hip and thigh level, unspecified leg

● Unacceptable First-Listed Diagnosis   ● Use Additional Character(s)   ■ Unspecified   **OGCR** Official Guidelines for Coding and Reporting

⬤ Complication\Comorbidity   ⬤ Major C\C   Excludes 1   Excludes 2   Includes   Use additional   Code first   Code also   1487

CHAPTER 19 (S00–T98)

- S74.9 Injury of unspecified nerve at hip and thigh level
  - S74.90 Injury of unspecified nerve at hip and thigh level, unspecified leg
  - S74.91 Injury of unspecified nerve at hip and thigh level, right leg
  - S74.92 Injury of unspecified nerve at hip and thigh level, left leg
- S75 Injury of blood vessels at hip and thigh level
  Code also any associated open wound (S71.-)

  Excludes2 injury of blood vessels at lower leg level (S85.-)
  injury of popliteal artery (S85.0)

  The appropriate 7th character is to be added to each code from category S75
  - A initial encounter
  - D subsequent encounter
  - S sequela
  - S75.0 Injury of femoral artery
    - S75.00 Unspecified injury of femoral artery
      - S75.001 Unspecified injury of femoral artery, right leg A
      - S75.002 Unspecified injury of femoral artery, left leg A
      - S75.009 Unspecified injury of femoral artery, unspecified leg A
    - S75.01 Minor laceration of femoral artery
      Incomplete transection of femoral artery
      Laceration of femoral artery NOS
      Superficial laceration of femoral artery
      - S75.011 Minor laceration of femoral artery, right leg A
      - S75.012 Minor laceration of femoral artery, left leg A
      - S75.019 Minor laceration of femoral artery, unspecified leg A
    - S75.02 Major laceration of femoral artery
      Complete transection of femoral artery
      Traumatic rupture of femoral artery
      - S75.021 Major laceration of femoral artery, right leg A
      - S75.022 Major laceration of femoral artery, left leg A
      - S75.029 Major laceration of femoral artery, unspecified leg A
    - S75.09 Other specified injury of femoral artery
      - S75.091 Other specified injury of femoral artery, right leg A
      - S75.092 Other specified injury of femoral artery, left leg A
      - S75.099 Other specified injury of femoral artery, unspecified leg A
  - S75.1 Injury of femoral vein at hip and thigh level
    - S75.10 Unspecified injury of femoral vein at hip and thigh level
      - S75.101 Unspecified injury of femoral vein at hip and thigh level, right leg A
      - S75.102 Unspecified injury of femoral vein at hip and thigh level, left leg A
      - S75.109 Unspecified injury of femoral vein at hip and thigh level, unspecified leg A

- S75.11 Minor laceration of femoral vein at hip and thigh level
  Incomplete transection of femoral vein at hip and thigh level
  Laceration of femoral vein at hip and thigh level NOS
  Superficial laceration of femoral vein at hip and thigh level
  - S75.111 Minor laceration of femoral vein at hip and thigh level, right leg A
  - S75.112 Minor laceration of femoral vein at hip and thigh level, left leg A
  - S75.119 Minor laceration of femoral vein at hip and thigh level, unspecified leg A
- S75.12 Major laceration of femoral vein at hip and thigh level
  Complete transection of femoral vein at hip and thigh level
  Traumatic rupture of femoral vein at hip and thigh level
  - S75.121 Major laceration of femoral vein at hip and thigh level, right leg A
  - S75.122 Major laceration of femoral vein at hip and thigh level, left leg A
  - S75.129 Major laceration of femoral vein at hip and thigh level, unspecified leg A
- S75.19 Other specified injury of femoral vein at hip and thigh level
  - S75.191 Other specified injury of femoral vein at hip and thigh level, right leg A
  - S75.192 Other specified injury of femoral vein at hip and thigh level, left leg A
  - S75.199 Other specified injury of femoral vein at hip and thigh level, unspecified leg A
- S75.2 Injury of greater saphenous vein at hip and thigh level

  Excludes1 greater saphenous vein NOS (S85.3)
  - S75.20 Unspecified injury of greater saphenous vein at hip and thigh level
    - S75.201 Unspecified injury of greater saphenous vein at hip and thigh level, right leg A
    - S75.202 Unspecified injury of greater saphenous vein at hip and thigh level, left leg A
    - S75.209 Unspecified injury of greater saphenous vein at hip and thigh level, unspecified leg A
  - S75.21 Minor laceration of greater saphenous vein at hip and thigh level
    Incomplete transection of greater saphenous vein at hip and thigh level
    Laceration of greater saphenous vein at hip and thigh level NOS
    Superficial laceration of greater saphenous vein at hip and thigh level

- ● S75.211 Minor laceration of greater saphenous vein at hip and thigh level, right leg A ℀
- ● S75.212 Minor laceration of greater saphenous vein at hip and thigh level, left leg A ℀
- ● ▪ S75.219 Minor laceration of greater saphenous vein at hip and thigh level, unspecified leg A ℀
- ● S75.22 Major laceration of greater saphenous vein at hip and thigh level
  Complete transection of greater saphenous vein at hip and thigh level
  Traumatic rupture of greater saphenous vein at hip and thigh level
  - ● S75.221 Major laceration of greater saphenous vein at hip and thigh level, right leg A ℀
  - ● S75.222 Major laceration of greater saphenous vein at hip and thigh level, left leg A ℀
  - ● ▪ S75.229 Major laceration of greater saphenous vein at hip and thigh level, unspecified leg A ℀
- ● S75.29 Other specified injury of greater saphenous vein at hip and thigh level
  - ● S75.291 Other specified injury of greater saphenous vein at hip and thigh level, right leg A ℀
  - ● S75.292 Other specified injury of greater saphenous vein at hip and thigh level, left leg A ℀
  - ● ▪ S75.299 Other specified injury of greater saphenous vein at hip and thigh level, unspecified leg A ℀
- ● S75.8 Injury of other blood vessels at hip and thigh level
  - ● S75.80 Unspecified injury of other blood vessels at hip and thigh level
    - ● ▪ S75.801 Unspecified injury of other blood vessels at hip and thigh level, right leg A ℀
    - ● ▪ S75.802 Unspecified injury of other blood vessels at hip and thigh level, left leg A ℀
    - ● ▪ S75.809 Unspecified injury of other blood vessels at hip and thigh level, unspecified leg A ℀
  - ● S75.81 Laceration of other blood vessels at hip and thigh level
    - ● S75.811 Laceration of other blood vessels at hip and thigh level, right leg A ℀
    - ● S75.812 Laceration of other blood vessels at hip and thigh level, left leg A ℀
    - ● ▪ S75.819 Laceration of other blood vessels at hip and thigh level, unspecified leg A ℀
  - ● S75.89 Other specified injury of other blood vessels at hip and thigh level
    - ● S75.891 Other specified injury of other blood vessels at hip and thigh level, right leg A ℀
    - ● S75.892 Other specified injury of other blood vessels at hip and thigh level, left leg A ℀
    - ● ▪ S75.899 Other specified injury of other blood vessels at hip and thigh level, unspecified leg A ℀
- ● S75.9 Injury of unspecified blood vessel at hip and thigh level
  - ● S75.90 Unspecified injury of unspecified blood vessel at hip and thigh level
    - ● ▪ S75.901 Unspecified injury of unspecified blood vessel at hip and thigh level, right leg A ℀
    - ● ▪ S75.902 Unspecified injury of unspecified blood vessel at hip and thigh level, left leg A ℀
    - ● ▪ S75.909 Unspecified injury of unspecified blood vessel at hip and thigh level, unspecified leg A ℀
  - ● S75.91 Laceration of unspecified blood vessel at hip and thigh level
    - ● ▪ S75.911 Laceration of unspecified blood vessel at hip and thigh level, right leg A ℀
    - ● ▪ S75.912 Laceration of unspecified blood vessel at hip and thigh level, left leg A ℀
    - ● ▪ S75.919 Laceration of unspecified blood vessel at hip and thigh level, unspecified leg A ℀
  - ● S75.99 Other specified injury of unspecified blood vessel at hip and thigh level
    - ● ▪ S75.991 Other specified injury of unspecified blood vessel at hip and thigh level, right leg A ℀
    - ● ▪ S75.992 Other specified injury of unspecified blood vessel at hip and thigh level, left leg A ℀
    - ● ▪ S75.999 Other specified injury of unspecified blood vessel at hip and thigh level, unspecified leg A ℀
- ● S76 Injury of muscle, fascia and tendon at hip and thigh level
  Code also any associated open wound (S71.-)
  Excludes2 injury of muscle, fascia and tendon at lower leg level (S86)
  sprain of joint and ligament of hip (S73.1)
  The appropriate 7th character is to be added to each code from category S76
A	initial encounter
D	subsequent encounter
S	sequela
  - ● S76.0 Injury of muscle, fascia and tendon of hip
    - ● S76.00 Unspecified injury of muscle, fascia and tendon of hip
      - ● ▪ S76.001 Unspecified injury of muscle, fascia and tendon of right hip
      - ● ▪ S76.002 Unspecified injury of muscle, fascia and tendon of left hip
      - ● ▪ S76.009 Unspecified injury of muscle, fascia and tendon of hip, unspecified side
    - ● S76.01 Strain of muscle, fascia and tendon of hip
      - ● S76.011 Strain of muscle, fascia and tendon of right hip
      - ● S76.012 Strain of muscle, fascia and tendon of left hip

● Unacceptable First-Listed Diagnosis   ● Use Additional Character(s)   ▪ Unspecified   **OGCR** Official Guidelines for Coding and Reporting

℀ Complication\Comorbidity   ℀ Major C\C   Excludes 1   Excludes 2   Includes   Use additional   Code first   Code also

CHAPTER 19 (S00-T98)

1489

● ▣ **S76.019** Strain of muscle, fascia and tendon of hip, unspecified side

● **S76.02** Laceration of muscle, fascia and tendon of hip

   ● **S76.021** Laceration of muscle, fascia and tendon of right hip A 🗫

   ● **S76.022** Laceration of muscle, fascia and tendon of left hip A 🗫

   ● ▣ **S76.029** Laceration of muscle, fascia and tendon of hip, unspecified side A 🗫

● **S76.09** Other injury of muscle, fascia and tendon of hip

   ● **S76.091** Other injury of muscle, fascia and tendon of right hip

   ● **S76.092** Other injury of muscle, fascia and tendon of left hip

   ● ▣ **S76.099** Other injury of muscle, fascia and tendon of hip, unspecified side

● **S76.1** Injury of quadriceps muscle, fascia and tendon
Injury of patellar ligament (tendon)

  ● **S76.10** Unspecified injury of quadriceps muscle, fascia and tendon

   ● ▣ **S76.101** Unspecified injury of right quadriceps muscle, fascia and tendon

   ● ▣ **S76.102** Unspecified injury of left quadriceps muscle, fascia and tendon

   ● ▣ **S76.109** Unspecified injury of quadriceps muscle, fascia and tendon, unspecified side

  ● **S76.11** Strain of quadriceps muscle, fascia and tendon

   ● **S76.111** Strain of right quadriceps muscle, fascia and tendon

   ● **S76.112** Strain of left quadriceps muscle, fascia and tendon

   ● ▣ **S76.119** Strain of quadriceps muscle, fascia and tendon, unspecified side

  ● **S76.12** Laceration of quadriceps muscle, fascia and tendon

   ● **S76.121** Laceration of right quadriceps muscle, fascia and tendon A 🗫

   ● **S76.122** Laceration of left quadriceps muscle, fascia and tendon A 🗫

   ● ▣ **S76.129** Laceration of quadriceps muscle, fascia and tendon, unspecified side A 🗫

  ● **S76.19** Other injury of quadriceps muscle, fascia and tendon

   ● **S76.191** Other injury of right quadriceps muscle, fascia and tendon

   ● **S76.192** Other injury of left quadriceps muscle, fascia and tendon

   ● ▣ **S76.199** Other injury of quadriceps muscle, fascia and tendon, unspecified side

● **S76.2** Injury of adductor muscle, fascia and tendon of thigh

  ● ▣ **S76.20** Unspecified injury of adductor muscle, fascia and tendon of thigh

● ▣ **S76.201** Unspecified injury of adductor muscle, fascia and tendon of right thigh

● ▣ **S76.202** Unspecified injury of adductor muscle, fascia and tendon of left thigh

● ▣ **S76.209** Unspecified injury of adductor muscle, fascia and tendon of thigh, unspecified side

● **S76.21** Strain of adductor muscle, fascia and tendon of thigh

  ● **S76.211** Strain of right adductor muscle, fascia and tendon of thigh

  ● **S76.212** Strain of left adductor muscle, fascia and tendon of thigh

  ● ▣ **S76.219** Strain of adductor muscle, fascia and tendon of thigh, unspecified side

● **S76.22** Laceration of adductor muscle, fascia and tendon of thigh

  ● **S76.221** Laceration of adductor muscle, fascia and tendon of right thigh A 🗫

  ● **S76.222** Laceration of adductor muscle, fascia and tendon of left thigh A 🗫

  ● ▣ **S76.229** Laceration of adductor muscle, fascia and tendon of thigh, unspecified side A 🗫

● **S76.29** Other injury of adductor muscle, fascia and tendon of thigh

  ● **S76.291** Other injury of adductor muscle, fascia and tendon of right thigh

  ● **S76.292** Other injury of adductor muscle, fascia and tendon of left thigh

  ● ▣ **S76.299** Other injury of adductor muscle, fascia and tendon of thigh, unspecified side

● **S76.3** Injury of muscle, fascia and tendon of the posterior muscle group at thigh level

  ● **S76.30** Unspecified injury of muscle, fascia and tendon of the posterior muscle group at thigh level

   ● ▣ **S76.301** Unspecified injury of muscle, fascia and tendon of the right posterior muscle group at thigh level

   ● ▣ **S76.302** Unspecified injury of muscle, fascia and tendon of the left posterior muscle group at thigh level

   ● ▣ **S76.309** Unspecified injury of muscle, fascia and tendon of the posterior muscle group at thigh level, unspecified side

  ● **S76.31** Strain of muscle, fascia and tendon of the posterior muscle group at thigh level

   ● **S76.311** Strain of muscle, fascia and tendon of the right posterior muscle group at thigh level

   ● **S76.312** Strain of muscle, fascia and tendon of the left posterior muscle group at thigh level

   ● ▣ **S76.319** Strain of muscle, fascia and tendon of the posterior muscle group at thigh level, unspecified side

● Unacceptable First-Listed Diagnosis   ● Use Additional Character(s)   ▣ Unspecified   **OGCR** Official Guidelines for Coding and Reporting
🗫 Complication\Comorbidity   🗫 Major C\C   Excludes 1   Excludes 2   Includes   Use additional   Code first   Code also

● S76.32   Laceration of muscle, fascia and tendon of the posterior muscle group at thigh level

    ● S76.321   Laceration of muscle, fascia and tendon of the right posterior muscle group at thigh level A ⦿

    ● S76.322   Laceration of muscle, fascia and tendon of the left posterior muscle group at thigh level A ⦿

    ● ■ S76.329   Laceration of muscle, fascia and tendon of the posterior muscle group at thigh level, unspecified side A ⦿

● S76.39   Other injury of muscle, fascia and tendon of the posterior muscle group at thigh level

    ● S76.391   Other injury of muscle, fascia and tendon of the posterior muscle group at right thigh level

    ● S76.392   Other injury of muscle, fascia and tendon of the posterior muscle group at left thigh level

    ● ■ S76.399   Other injury of muscle, fascia and tendon of the posterior muscle group at thigh level, unspecified side

● S76.8   Injury of other muscles, fasciae and tendons at thigh level

    ● S76.80   Unspecified injury of other muscles, fasciae and tendons at thigh level

      ● ■ S76.801   Unspecified injury of other muscles, fasciae and tendons at right thigh level

      ● ■ S76.802   Unspecified injury of other muscles, fasciae and tendons at left thigh level

      ● ■ S76.809   Unspecified injury of other muscles, fasciae and tendons at thigh level, unspecified side

    ● S76.81   Strain of other muscles, fasciae and tendons at thigh level

      ● S76.811   Strain of other muscles, fasciae and tendons at right thigh level

      ● S76.812   Strain of other muscles, fasciae and tendons at left thigh level

      ● ■ S76.819   Strain of other muscles, fasciae and tendons at thigh level, unspecified side

    ● S76.82   Laceration of other muscles, fasciae and tendons at thigh level

      ● S76.821   Laceration of other muscles, fasciae and tendons at right thigh level A ⦿

      ● S76.822   Laceration of other muscles, fasciae and tendons at left thigh level A ⦿

      ● ■ S76.829   Laceration of other muscles, fasciae and tendons at thigh level, unspecified side A ⦿

    ● S76.89   Other injury of other muscles, fasciae and tendons at thigh level

      ● S76.891   Other injury of other muscles, fasciae and tendons at right thigh level

      ● S76.892   Other injury of other muscles, fasciae and tendons at left thigh level

      ● ■ S76.899   Other injury of other muscles, fasciae and tendons at thigh level, unspecified side

● S76.9   Injury of unspecified muscles, fasciae and tendons at thigh level

    ● S76.90   Unspecified injury of unspecified muscles, fasciae and tendons at thigh level

      ● ■ S76.901   Unspecified injury of unspecified muscles, fasciae and tendons at right thigh level

      ● ■ S76.902   Unspecified injury of unspecified muscles, fasciae and tendons at left thigh level

      ● ■ S76.909   Unspecified injury of unspecified muscles, fasciae and tendons at thigh level, unspecified side

    ● S76.91   Strain of unspecified muscles, fasciae and tendons at thigh level

      ● ■ S76.911   Strain of unspecified muscles, fasciae and tendons at right thigh level

      ● ■ S76.912   Strain of unspecified muscles, fasciae and tendons at left thigh level

      ● ■ S76.919   Strain of unspecified muscles, fasciae and tendons at thigh level, unspecified side

    ● S76.92   Laceration of unspecified muscles, fasciae and tendons at thigh level

      ● ■ S76.921   Laceration of unspecified muscles, fasciae and tendons at right thigh level A ⦿

      ● ■ S76.922   Laceration of unspecified muscles, fasciae and tendons at left thigh level A ⦿

      ● ■ S76.929   Laceration of unspecified muscles, fasciae and tendons at thigh level, unspecified side A ⦿

    ● S76.99   Other injury of unspecified muscles, fasciae and tendons at thigh level

      ● ■ S76.991   Other injury of unspecified muscles, fasciae and tendons at right thigh level

      ● ■ S76.992   Other injury of unspecified muscles, fasciae and tendons at left thigh level

      ● ■ S76.999   Other injury of unspecified muscles, fasciae and tendons at thigh level, unspecified side

● S77   Crushing injury of hip and thigh

    Use additional code(s) for all associated injuries

    Excludes2   crushing injury of ankle and foot (S97.-)
             crushing injury of lower leg (S87.-)

    The appropriate 7th character is to be added to each code from category S77

A	initial encounter
D	subsequent encounter
S	sequela

● Unacceptable First-Listed Diagnosis   ● Use Additional Character(s)   ■ Unspecified   **OGCR** Official Guidelines for Coding and Reporting

⦿ Complication\Comorbidity   ⦿ Major C\C   Excludes 1   Excludes 2   Includes   Use additional   Code first   Code also   1491

CHAPTER 19 (S00–T98)

● S77.0   Crushing injury of hip
- ●■ S77.00   Crushing injury of hip, unspecified side A 🦠
  - ● S77.01   Crushing injury of right hip A 🦠
  - ● S77.02   Crushing injury of left hip A 🦠
- ● S77.1   Crushing injury of thigh
  - ●■ S77.10   Crushing injury of thigh, unspecified side A 🦠
  - ● S77.11   Crushing injury of right thigh A 🦠
  - ● S77.12   Crushing injury of left thigh A 🦠
- ● S77.2   Crushing injury of hip with thigh
  - ●■ S77.20   Crushing injury of hip with thigh, unspecified side
  - ● S77.21   Crushing injury of right hip with thigh
  - ● S77.22   Crushing injury of left hip with thigh

● S78   Traumatic amputation of hip and thigh

An amputation not identified and partial or complete should be coded to complete

Excludes1   traumatic amputation of knee (S88.0-)

The appropriate 7th character is to be added to each code from category S78

> A   initial encounter
> D   subsequent encounter
> S   sequela

- ● S78.0   Traumatic amputation at hip joint
  - ● S78.01   Complete traumatic amputation at hip joint
    - ● S78.011   Complete traumatic amputation at right hip joint A 🦠
    - ● S78.012   Complete traumatic amputation at left hip joint A 🦠
    - ●■ S78.019   Complete traumatic amputation at hip joint, unspecified side A 🦠
  - ● S78.02   Partial traumatic amputation at hip joint
    - ● S78.021   Partial traumatic amputation at right hip joint A 🦠
    - ● S78.022   Partial traumatic amputation at left hip joint A 🦠
    - ●■ S78.029   Partial traumatic amputation at hip joint, unspecified side A 🦠
- ● S78.1   Traumatic amputation at level between hip and knee

  Excludes1   traumatic amputation of knee (S88.0-)

  - ● S78.11   Complete traumatic amputation at level between hip and knee
    - ● S78.111   Complete traumatic amputation at level between right hip and knee A 🦠
    - ● S78.112   Complete traumatic amputation at level between left hip and knee A 🦠
    - ●■ S78.119   Complete traumatic amputation at level between hip and knee, unspecified side A 🦠
  - ● S78.12   Partial traumatic amputation at level between hip and knee
    - ● S78.121   Partial traumatic amputation at level between right hip and knee A 🦠
    - ● S78.122   Partial traumatic amputation at level between left hip and knee A 🦠

- ●■ S78.129   Partial traumatic amputation at level between hip and knee, unspecified side A 🦠
- ● S78.9   Traumatic amputation of hip and thigh, level unspecified
  - ● S78.91   Complete traumatic amputation of hip and thigh, level unspecified
    - ●■ S78.911   Complete traumatic amputation of right hip and thigh, level unspecified A 🦠
    - ●■ S78.912   Complete traumatic amputation of left hip and thigh, level unspecified A 🦠
    - ●■ S78.919   Complete traumatic amputation of hip and thigh, level unspecified, unspecified side A 🦠
  - ● S78.92   Partial traumatic amputation of hip and thigh, level unspecified
    - ●■ S78.921   Partial traumatic amputation of right hip and thigh, level unspecified A 🦠
    - ●■ S78.922   Partial traumatic amputation of left hip and thigh, level unspecified A 🦠
    - ●■ S78.929   Partial traumatic amputation of hip and thigh, level unspecified, unspecified side A 🦠

● S79   Other and unspecified injuries of hip and thigh

The appropriate 7th character is to be added to each code from subcategories S79.0 and S79.1

A fracture not designated as open or closed should be coded to closed

> A   initial encounter for closed fracture
> D   subsequent encounter for fracture with routine healing
> G   subsequent encounter for fracture with delayed healing
> K   subsequent encounter for fracture with nonunion
> P   subsequent encounter for fracture with malunion
> S   sequela

- ● S79.0   Physeal fracture of upper end of femur

  Excludes1   apophyseal fracture of upper end of femur (S72.13-)
  nontraumatic slipped upper femoral epiphysis (M93.0-)

  - ● S79.00   Unspecified physeal fracture of upper end of femur
    - ●■ S79.001   Unspecified physeal fracture of upper end of right femur K, P 🦠, A 🦠

Item 19–5   SALTER-HARRIS TYPE 1: epiphysis is completely separated from end of bone, or metaphysic growth plate remains attached to epiphysis

SALTER-HARRIS TYPE 2: epiphysis and growth plate are partially separated from metaphysis, which is cracked—most common type

SALTER-HARRIS TYPE 3: fracture occurring through epiphysis and separates part of epiphysis and growth plate from metaphysis fracture, usually at distal end of tibia

SALTER-HARRIS TYPE 4: fracture runs through epiphysis, across growth plate, into metaphysic, surgery is required to restore joint surface to normal and align growth plate

● Unacceptable First-Listed Diagnosis   ● Use Additional Character(s)   ■ Unspecified   OGCR Official Guidelines for Coding and Reporting
🦠 Complication\Comorbidity   🦠 Major C\C   Excludes 1   Excludes 2   Includes   Use additional   Code first   Code also

● ▣ **S79.002** Unspecified physeal fracture of upper end of left femur K, P 🅒, A 🅜

● ▣ **S79.009** Unspecified physeal fracture of upper end of unspecified femur K, P 🅒, A 🅜

● **S79.01** Salter-Harris Type I physeal fracture of upper end of femur
    Acute on chronic slipped capital femoral epiphysis (traumatic)
    Acute slipped capital femoral epiphysis (traumatic)
    Capital femoral epiphyseal fracture

    | Excludes1 | chronic slipped upper femoral epiphysis (nontraumatic) (M93.02-)

● **S79.011** Salter-Harris Type I physeal fracture of upper end of right femur K, P 🅒, A 🅜

● **S79.012** Salter-Harris Type I physeal fracture of upper end of left femur K, P 🅒, A 🅜

● ▣ **S79.019** Salter-Harris Type I physeal fracture of upper end of unspecified femur K, P 🅒, A 🅜

● **S79.09** Other physeal fracture of upper end of femur

● **S79.091** Other physeal fracture of upper end of right femur K, P 🅒, A 🅜

● **S79.092** Other physeal fracture of upper end of left femur K, P 🅒, A 🅜

● ▣ **S79.099** Other physeal fracture of upper end of unspecified femur K, P 🅒, A 🅜

● **S79.1** Physeal fracture of lower end of femur

● **S79.10** Unspecified physeal fracture of lower end of femur

● ▣ **S79.101** Unspecified physeal fracture of lower end of right femur A, K, P 🅒

● ▣ **S79.102** Unspecified physeal fracture of lower end of left femur A, K, P 🅒

● ▣ **S79.109** Unspecified physeal fracture of lower end of unspecified femur A, K, P 🅒

● **S79.11** Salter-Harris Type I physeal fracture of lower end of femur

● **S79.111** Salter-Harris Type I physeal fracture of lower end of right femur A, K, P 🅒

● **S79.112** Salter-Harris Type I physeal fracture of lower end of left femur A, K, P 🅒

● ▣ **S79.119** Salter-Harris Type I physeal fracture of lower end of unspecified femur A, K, P 🅒

● **S79.12** Salter-Harris Type II physeal fracture of lower end of femur

● **S79.121** Salter-Harris Type II physeal fracture of lower end of right femur A, K, P 🅒

● **S79.122** Salter-Harris Type II physeal fracture of lower end of left femur A, K, P 🅒

● ▣ **S79.129** Salter-Harris Type II physeal fracture of lower end of unspecified femur A, K, P 🅒

● **S79.13** Salter-Harris Type III physeal fracture of lower end of femur

● **S79.131** Salter-Harris Type III physeal fracture of lower end of right femur A, K, P 🅒

● **S79.132** Salter-Harris Type III physeal fracture of lower end of left femur A, K, P 🅒

● ▣ **S79.139** Salter-Harris Type III physeal fracture of lower end of unspecified femur A, K, P 🅒

● **S79.14** Salter-Harris Type IV physeal fracture of lower end of femur

● **S79.141** Salter-Harris Type IV physeal fracture of lower end of right femur A, K, P 🅒

● **S79.142** Salter-Harris Type IV physeal fracture of lower end of left femur A, K, P 🅒

● ▣ **S79.149** Salter-Harris Type IV physeal fracture of lower end of unspecified femur A, K, P 🅒

● **S79.19** Other physeal fracture of lower end of femur

● **S79.191** Other physeal fracture of lower end of right femur A, K, P 🅒

● **S79.192** Other physeal fracture of lower end of left femur A, K, P 🅒

● ▣ **S79.199** Other physeal fracture of lower end of unspecified femur A, K, P 🅒

The appropriate 7th character is to be added to each code for subcategories S79.8 and S79.9

A	initial encounter
D	subsequent encounter
S	sequela

● **S79.8** Other specified injuries of hip and thigh

● **S79.81** Other specified injuries of hip

● **S79.811** Other specified injuries of right hip

● **S79.812** Other specified injuries of left hip

● ▣ **S79.819** Other specified injuries of hip, unspecified side

● **S79.82** Other specified injuries of thigh

● **S79.821** Other specified injuries of right thigh

● **S79.822** Other specified injuries of left thigh

● ▣ **S79.829** Other specified injuries of thigh, unspecified side

● **S79.9** Unspecified injury of hip and thigh

● **S79.91** Unspecified injury of hip

● ▣ **S79.911** Unspecified injury of right hip

● ▣ **S79.912** Unspecified injury of left hip

● ▣ **S79.919** Unspecified injury of hip, unspecified side

● **S79.92** Unspecified injury of thigh

● ▣ **S79.921** Unspecified injury of right thigh

● ▣ **S79.922** Unspecified injury of left thigh

● ▣ **S79.929** Unspecified injury of thigh, unspecified side

---

● Unacceptable First-Listed Diagnosis   ● Use Additional Character(s)   ▣ Unspecified   **OGCR** Official Guidelines for Coding and Reporting

🅒 Complication\Comorbidity   🅜 Major C\C | Excludes 1 | | Excludes 2 | Includes   Use additional   Code first   Code also

INJURIES TO THE KNEE AND LOWER LEG (S80-S89)

Excludes2 burns and corrosions (T20-T32)
frostbite (T33-T34)
injuries of ankle and foot, except fracture of
ankle and malleolus (S90-S99)
insect bite or sting, venomous (T63.4)

- S80 **Superficial injury of knee and lower leg**

  Excludes2 superficial injury of ankle and foot (S90.-)

  The appropriate 7th character is to be added to each code
  from category S80

A	initial encounter
D	subsequent encounter
S	sequela

  - S80.0 **Contusion of knee**
    - S80.00 Contusion of unspecified knee
    - S80.01 Contusion of right knee
    - S80.02 Contusion of left knee
  - S80.1 **Contusion of lower leg**
    - S80.10 Contusion of unspecified lower leg
    - S80.11 Contusion of right lower leg
    - S80.12 Contusion of left lower leg
  - S80.2 **Other superficial injuries of knee**
    - S80.21 **Abrasion of knee**
      - S80.211 Abrasion, right knee
      - S80.212 Abrasion, left knee
      - S80.219 Abrasion, unspecified knee
    - S80.22 **Blister (nonthermal) of knee**
      - S80.221 Blister (nonthermal), right knee
      - S80.222 Blister (nonthermal), left knee
      - S80.229 Blister (nonthermal), unspecified knee
    - S80.24 **External constriction of knee**
      - S80.241 External constriction, right knee
      - S80.242 External constriction, left knee
      - S80.249 External constriction, unspecified knee
    - S80.25 **Superficial foreign body of knee**
      Splinter in the knee
      - S80.251 Superficial foreign body, right knee
      - S80.252 Superficial foreign body, left knee
      - S80.259 Superficial foreign body, unspecified knee
    - S80.26 **Insect bite (nonvenomous) of knee**
      - S80.261 Insect bite (nonvenomous), right knee
      - S80.262 Insect bite (nonvenomous), left knee
      - S80.269 Insect bite (nonvenomous), unspecified knee
    - S80.27 **Other superficial bite of knee**
      Excludes1 open bite of knee (S81.05-)
      - S80.271 Other superficial bite of right knee
      - S80.272 Other superficial bite of left knee
      - S80.279 Other superficial bite of unspecified knee

  - S80.8 **Other superficial injuries of lower leg**
    - S80.81 **Abrasion of lower leg**
      - S80.811 Abrasion, right lower leg
      - S80.812 Abrasion, left lower leg
      - S80.819 Abrasion, unspecified lower leg
    - S80.82 **Blister (nonthermal) of lower leg**
      - S80.821 Blister (nonthermal), right lower leg
      - S80.822 Blister (nonthermal), left lower leg
      - S80.829 Blister (nonthermal), unspecified lower leg
    - S80.84 **External constriction of lower leg**
      - S80.841 External constriction, right lower leg
      - S80.842 External constriction, left lower leg
      - S80.849 External constriction, unspecified lower leg
    - S80.85 **Superficial foreign body of lower leg**
      Splinter in the lower leg
      - S80.851 Superficial foreign body, right lower leg
      - S80.852 Superficial foreign body, left lower leg
      - S80.859 Superficial foreign body, unspecified lower leg
    - S80.86 **Insect bite (nonvenomous) of lower leg**
      - S80.861 Insect bite (nonvenomous), right lower leg
      - S80.862 Insect bite (nonvenomous), left lower leg
      - S80.869 Insect bite (nonvenomous), unspecified lower leg
    - S80.87 **Other superficial bite of lower leg**
      Excludes1 open bite of lower leg (S81.85-)
      - S80.871 Other superficial bite, right lower leg
      - S80.872 Other superficial bite, left lower leg
      - S80.879 Other superficial bite, unspecified lower leg
  - S80.9 **Unspecified superficial injury of knee and lower leg**
    - S80.91 **Unspecified superficial injury of knee**
      - S80.911 Unspecified superficial injury of right knee
      - S80.912 Unspecified superficial injury of left knee
      - S80.919 Unspecified superficial injury of unspecified knee
    - S80.92 **Unspecified superficial injury of lower leg**
      - S80.921 Unspecified superficial injury of right lower leg
      - S80.922 Unspecified superficial injury of left lower leg
      - S80.929 Unspecified superficial injury of unspecified lower leg

● Unacceptable First-Listed Diagnosis   ● Use Additional Character(s)   ■ Unspecified   **OGCR** Official Guidelines for Coding and Reporting
🅒 Complication\Comorbidity   🅜 Major C\C   Excludes 1   Excludes 2   Includes   Use additional   Code first   Code also

● **S81   Open wound of knee and lower leg**

      Code also any associated wound infection

      | **Excludes1** | open fracture of knee and lower leg (S82.-)
                                traumatic amputation of lower leg (S88.-)

      | **Excludes2** | open wound of ankle and foot (S91.-)

      The appropriate 7th character is to be added to each code from category S81

         A   initial encounter
         D   subsequent encounter
         S   sequela

   ● **S81.0   Open wound of knee**

     ● **S81.00   Unspecified open wound of knee**

       ● ▪ S81.001   Unspecified open wound, right knee

       ● ▪ S81.002   Unspecified open wound, left knee

       ● ▪ S81.009   Unspecified open wound, unspecified knee

     ● **S81.01   Laceration without foreign body of knee**

       ● S81.011   Laceration without foreign body, right knee

       ● S81.012   Laceration without foreign body, left knee

       ● ▪ S81.019   Laceration without foreign body, unspecified knee

     ● **S81.02   Laceration with foreign body of knee**

       ● S81.021   Laceration with foreign body, right knee

       ● S81.022   Laceration with foreign body, left knee

       ● ▪ S81.029   Laceration with foreign body, unspecified knee

     ● **S81.03   Puncture wound without foreign body of knee**

       ● S81.031   Puncture wound without foreign body, right knee

       ● S81.032   Puncture wound without foreign body, left knee

       ● ▪ S81.039   Puncture wound without foreign body, unspecified knee

     ● **S81.04   Puncture wound with foreign body of knee**

       ● S81.041   Puncture wound with foreign body, right knee

       ● S81.042   Puncture wound with foreign body, left knee

       ● ▪ S81.049   Puncture wound with foreign body, unspecified knee

     ● **S81.05   Open bite of knee**
          Bite of knee NOS

       | **Excludes1** | superficial bite of knee (S80.36-, S80.37-)

       ● S81.051   Open bite, right knee

       ● S81.052   Open bite, left knee

       ● ▪ S81.059   Open bite, unspecified knee

● **S81.8   Open wound of lower leg**

     ● **S81.80   Unspecified open wound of lower leg**

       ● ▪ S81.801   Unspecified open wound, right lower leg

       ● ▪ S81.802   Unspecified open wound, left lower leg

       ● ▪ S81.809   Unspecified open wound, unspecified lower leg

     ● **S81.81   Laceration without foreign body of lower leg**

       ● S81.811   Laceration without foreign body, right lower leg

       ● S81.812   Laceration without foreign body, left lower leg

       ● ▪ S81.819   Laceration without foreign body, unspecified lower leg

     ● **S81.82   Laceration with foreign body of lower leg**

       ● S81.821   Laceration with foreign body, right lower leg

       ● S81.822   Laceration with foreign body, left lower leg

       ● ▪ S81.829   Laceration with foreign body, unspecified lower leg

     ● **S81.83   Puncture wound without foreign body of lower leg**

       ● S81.831   Puncture wound without foreign body, right lower leg

       ● S81.832   Puncture wound without foreign body, left lower leg

       ● ▪ S81.839   Puncture wound without foreign body, unspecified lower leg

     ● **S81.84   Puncture wound with foreign body of lower leg**

       ● S81.841   Puncture wound with foreign body, right lower leg

       ● S81.842   Puncture wound with foreign body, left lower leg

       ● ▪ S81.849   Puncture wound with foreign body, unspecified lower leg

     ● **S81.85   Open bite of lower leg**
          Bite of lower leg NOS

       | **Excludes1** | superficial bite of lower leg (S80.86-, S80.87-)

       ● S81.851   Open bite, right lower leg

       ● S81.852   Open bite, left lower leg

       ● ▪ S81.859   Open bite, unspecified lower leg

● Unacceptable First-Listed Diagnosis   ● Use Additional Character(s)   ▪ Unspecified   **OGCR** Official Guidelines for Coding and Reporting

🔖 Complication\Comorbidity   🔖 Major C\C | Excludes 1 | | Excludes 2 | Includes   Use additional   Code first   Code also

1495

CHAPTER 19 (S00-T98)

● **S82   Fracture of lower leg, including ankle**

> A fracture not indicated as displaced or nondisplaced should be coded to displaced

> **Includes**   fracture of malleolus

> **Excludes1**   traumatic amputation of lower leg (S88.-)

> **Excludes2**   fracture of foot, except ankle (S92.-)
> periprosthetic fracture of prosthetic implant of knee (T84.042, T84.043)

> The appropriate 7th character is to be added to each code from category S82

> A fracture not designated as open or closed should be coded to closed

> The open fracture designations are based on the Gustilo open fracture classification

> | | |
> |---|---|
> | A | initial encounter for closed fracture |
> | B | initial encounter for open fracture type I or II initial encounter for open fracture NOS |
> | C | initial encounter for open fracture type IIIA, IIIB, or IIIC |
> | D | subsequent encounter for closed fracture with routine healing |
> | E | subsequent encounter for open fracture type I or II with routine healing |
> | F | subsequent encounter for open fracture type IIIA, IIIB, or IIIC with routine healing |
> | G | subsequent encounter for closed fracture with delayed healing |
> | H | subsequent encounter for open fracture type I or II with delayed healing |
> | J | subsequent encounter for open fracture type IIIA, IIIB, or IIIC with delayed healing |
> | K | subsequent encounter for closed fracture with nonunion |
> | M | subsequent encounter for open fracture type I or II with nonunion |
> | N | subsequent encounter for open fracture type IIIA, IIIB, or IIIC with nonunion |
> | P | subsequent encounter for closed fracture with malunion |
> | Q | subsequent encounter for open fracture type I or II with malunion |
> | R | subsequent encounter for open fracture type IIIA, IIIB, or IIIC with malunion |
> | S | sequela |

● **S82.0   Fracture of patella**

> *Knee cap*

> **Note:** 7th character C, F, J, N, or R do not apply to codes under subcategory S82.0.

> ● **S82.00   Unspecified fracture of patella**

>> ● ■ **S82.001   Unspecified fracture of right patella** A, B, C, K, M, N, P, Q, R 🦴

>> ● ■ **S82.002   Unspecified fracture of left patella** A, B, C, K, M, N, P, Q, R 🦴

>> ● ■ **S82.009   Unspecified fracture of unspecified patella** A, B, C, K, M, N, P, Q, R 🦴

> ● **S82.01   Osteochondral fracture of patella**

>> ● **S82.011   Displaced osteochondral fracture of right patella** A, B, C, K, M, N, P, Q, R 🦴

>> ● **S82.012   Displaced osteochondral fracture of left patella** A, B, C, K, M, N, P, Q, R 🦴

>> ● ■ **S82.013   Displaced osteochondral fracture of unspecified patella** A, B, C, K, M, N, P, Q, R 🦴

>> ● **S82.014   Nondisplaced osteochondral fracture of right patella** A, B, C, K, M, N, P, Q, R 🦴

● ■ **S82.015   Nondisplaced osteochondral fracture of left patella** A, B, C, K, M, N, P, Q, R 🦴

● ■ **S82.016   Nondisplaced osteochondral fracture of unspecified patella** A, B, C, K, M, N, P, Q, R 🦴

● **S82.02   Longitudinal fracture of patella**

> ● **S82.021   Displaced longitudinal fracture of right patella** A, B, C, K, M, N, P, Q, R 🦴

> ● **S82.022   Displaced longitudinal fracture of left patella** A, B, C, K, M, N, P, Q, R 🦴

> ● ■ **S82.023   Displaced longitudinal fracture of unspecified patella** A, B, C, K, M, N, P, Q, R 🦴

> ● **S82.024   Nondisplaced longitudinal fracture of right patella** A, B, C, K, M, N, P, Q, R 🦴

> ● **S82.025   Nondisplaced longitudinal fracture of left patella** A, B, C, K, M, N, P, Q, R 🦴

> ● ■ **S82.026   Nondisplaced longitudinal fracture of unspecified patella** A, B, C, K, M, N, P, Q, R 🦴

● **S82.03   Transverse fracture of patella**

> ● **S82.031   Displaced transverse fracture of right patella** A, B, C, K, M, N, P, Q, R 🦴

> ● **S82.032   Displaced transverse fracture of left patella** A, B, C, K, M, N, P, Q, R 🦴

> ● ■ **S82.033   Displaced transverse fracture of unspecified patella** A, B, C, K, M, N, P, Q, R 🦴

> ● **S82.034   Nondisplaced transverse fracture of right patella** A, B, C, K, M, N, P, Q, R 🦴

> ● **S82.035   Nondisplaced transverse fracture of left patella** A, B, C, K, M, N, P, Q, R 🦴

> ● ■ **S82.036   Nondisplaced transverse fracture of unspecified patella** A, B, C, K, M, N, P, Q, R 🦴

● **S82.04   Comminuted fracture of patella**

> ● **S82.041   Displaced comminuted fracture of right patella** A, B, C, K, M, N, P, Q, R 🦴

> ● **S82.042   Displaced comminuted fracture of left patella** A, B, C, K, M, N, P, Q, R 🦴

> ● ■ **S82.043   Displaced comminuted fracture of unspecified patella** A, B, C, K, M, N, P, Q, R 🦴

> ● **S82.044   Nondisplaced comminuted fracture of right patella** A, B, C, K, M, N, P, Q, R 🦴

> ● **S82.045   Nondisplaced comminuted fracture of left patella** A, B, C, K, M, N, P, Q, R 🦴

> ● ■ **S82.046   Nondisplaced comminuted fracture of unspecified patella** A, B, C, K, M, N, P, Q, R 🦴

● **S82.09   Other fracture of patella**

> ● **S82.091   Other fracture of right patella** A, B, C, K, M, N, P, Q, R 🦴

● Unacceptable First-Listed Diagnosis   ● Use Additional Character(s)   ■ Unspecified   **OGCR** Official Guidelines for Coding and Reporting

🦴 Complication\Comorbidity   🦴 Major C\C   Excludes 1   Excludes 2   Includes   Use additional   Code first   Code also

● S82.092   Other fracture of left patella A, B, C, K, M, N, P, Q, R 🦠

● ■ S82.099   Other fracture of unspecified patella A, B, C, K, M, N, P, Q, R 🦠

● S82.1   **Fracture of upper end of tibia**
Fracture of proximal end of tibia

Excludes2   fracture of shaft of tibia (S82.2-)
physeal fracture of upper end of tibia (S89.0-)

● S82.10   Unspecified fracture of upper end of tibia

● ■ S82.101   Unspecified fracture of upper end of right tibia A, K, M, N, P, Q, R 🦠, B, C 🦠

● ■ S82.102   Unspecified fracture of upper end of left tibia A, K, M, N, P, Q, R 🦠, B, C 🦠

● ■ S82.109   Unspecified fracture of upper end of unspecified tibia A, K, M, N, P, Q, R 🦠, B, C 🦠

● S82.11   Fracture of tibial spine

● S82.111   Displaced fracture of right tibial spine A, K, M, N, P, Q, R 🦠, B, C 🦠

● S82.112   Displaced fracture of left tibial spine A, K, M, N, P, Q, R 🦠, B, C 🦠

● ■ S82.113   Displaced fracture of unspecified tibial spine A, K, M, N, P, Q, R 🦠, B, C 🦠

● S82.114   Nondisplaced fracture of right tibial spine A, K, M, N, P, Q, R 🦠, B, C 🦠

● S82.115   Nondisplaced fracture of left tibial spine A, K, M, N, P, Q, R 🦠, B, C 🦠

● ■ S82.116   Nondisplaced fracture of unspecified tibial spine A, K, M, N, P, Q, R 🦠, B, C 🦠

● S82.12   Fracture of lateral condyle of tibia

● S82.121   Displaced fracture of lateral condyle of right tibia A, K, M, N, P, Q, R 🦠, B, C 🦠

● S82.122   Displaced fracture of lateral condyle of left tibia A, K, M, N, P, Q, R 🦠, B, C 🦠

● ■ S82.123   Displaced fracture of lateral condyle of unspecified tibia A, K, M, N, P, Q, R 🦠, B, C 🦠

● S82.124   Nondisplaced fracture of lateral condyle of right tibia A, K, M, N, P, Q, R 🦠, B, C 🦠

● S82.125   Nondisplaced fracture of lateral condyle of left tibia A, K, M, N, P, Q, R 🦠, B, C 🦠

● ■ S82.126   Nondisplaced fracture of lateral condyle of unspecified tibia A, K, M, N, P, Q, R 🦠, B, C 🦠

● S82.13   Fracture of medial condyle of tibia

● S82.131   Displaced fracture of medial condyle of right tibia A, K, M, N, P, Q, R 🦠, B, C 🦠

● S82.132   Displaced fracture of medial condyle of left tibia A, K, M, N, P, Q, R 🦠, B, C 🦠

● ■ S82.133   Displaced fracture of medial condyle of unspecified tibia A, K, M, N, P, Q, R 🦠, B, C 🦠

● S82.134   Nondisplaced fracture of medial condyle of right tibia A, K, M, N, P, Q, R 🦠, B, C 🦠

● S82.135   Nondisplaced fracture of medial condyle of left tibia A, K, M, N, P, Q, R 🦠, B, C 🦠

● ■ S82.136   Nondisplaced fracture of medial condyle of unspecified tibia A, K, M, N, P, Q, R 🦠, B, C 🦠

● S82.14   Bicondylar fracture of tibia
Fracture of tibial plateau NOS

● S82.141   Displaced bicondylar fracture of right tibia A, K, M, N, P, Q, R 🦠, B, C 🦠

● S82.142   Displaced bicondylar fracture of left tibia A, K, M, N, P, Q, R 🦠, B, C 🦠

● ■ S82.143   Displaced bicondylar fracture of unspecified tibia A, K, M, N, P, Q, R 🦠, B, C 🦠

● S82.144   Nondisplaced bicondylar fracture of right tibia A, K, M, N, P, Q, R 🦠, B, C 🦠

● S82.145   Nondisplaced bicondylar fracture of left tibia A, K, M, N, P, Q, R 🦠, B, C 🦠

● ■ S82.146   Nondisplaced bicondylar fracture of unspecified tibia A, K, M, N, P, Q, R 🦠, B, C 🦠

● S82.15   Fracture of tibial tuberosity

● S82.151   Displaced fracture of right tibial tuberosity A, K, M, N, P, Q, R 🦠, B, C 🦠

● S82.152   Displaced fracture of left tibial tuberosity A, K, M, N, P, Q, R 🦠, B, C 🦠

● ■ S82.153   Displaced fracture of unspecified tibial tuberosity A, K, M, N, P, Q, R 🦠, B, C 🦠

● S82.154   Nondisplaced fracture of right tibial tuberosity A, K, M, N, P, Q, R 🦠, B, C 🦠

● S82.155   Nondisplaced fracture of left tibial tuberosity A, K, M, N, P, Q, R 🦠, B, C 🦠

● ■ S82.156   Nondisplaced fracture of unspecified tibial tuberosity A, K, M, N, P, Q, R 🦠, B, C 🦠

● S82.16   Torus fracture of upper end of tibia

Note: Open fracture 7th characters do not apply to codes under subcategory S82.16.

● S82.161   Torus fracture of upper end of right tibia A, K, P 🦠

● S82.162   Torus fracture of upper end of left tibia A, K, P 🦠

● ■ S82.169   Torus fracture of upper end of unspecified tibia A, K, P 🦠

● S82.19   Other fracture of upper end of tibia

● S82.191   Other fracture of upper end of right tibia A, K, M, N, P, Q, R 🦠, B, C 🦠

● Unacceptable First-Listed Diagnosis   ● Use Additional Character(s)   ■ Unspecified   **OGCR** Official Guidelines for Coding and Reporting

🦠 Complication\Comorbidity   🦠 Major C\C   Excludes 1   Excludes 2   Includes   Use additional   Code first   Code also

1497

CHAPTER 19 (S00-T98)

● ■ S82.192   Other fracture of upper end of left tibia A, K, M, N, P, Q, R 🦠, B, C 🦠

● ■ S82.199   Other fracture of upper end of unspecified tibia A, K, M, N, P, Q, R 🦠, B, C 🦠

● S82.2   Fracture of shaft of tibia

  ● S82.20   Unspecified fracture of shaft of tibia
     Fracture of tibia NOS

    ● ■ S82.201   Unspecified fracture of shaft of right tibia A, K, M, N, P, Q, R 🦠, B, C 🦠

    ● ■ S82.202   Unspecified fracture of shaft of left tibia A, K, M, N, P, Q, R 🦠, B, C 🦠

    ● ■ S82.209   Unspecified fracture of shaft of unspecified tibia A, K, M, N, P, Q, R 🦠, B, C 🦠

  ● S82.22   Transverse fracture of shaft of tibia

    ● S82.221   Displaced transverse fracture of shaft of right tibia A, K, M, N, P, Q, R 🦠, B, C 🦠

    ● S82.222   Displaced transverse fracture of shaft of left tibia A, K, M, N, P, Q, R 🦠, B, C 🦠

    ● ■ S82.223   Displaced transverse fracture of shaft of unspecified tibia A, K, M, N, P, Q, R 🦠, B, C 🦠

    ● S82.224   Nondisplaced transverse fracture of shaft of right tibia A, K, M, N, P, Q, R 🦠, B, C 🦠

    ● S82.225   Nondisplaced transverse fracture of shaft of left tibia A, K, M, N, P, Q, R 🦠, B, C 🦠

    ● ■ S82.226   Nondisplaced transverse fracture of shaft of unspecified tibia A, K, M, N, P, Q, R 🦠, B, C 🦠

  ● S82.23   Oblique fracture of shaft of tibia

    ● S82.231   Displaced oblique fracture of shaft of right tibia A, K, M, N, P, Q, R 🦠, B, C 🦠

    ● S82.232   Displaced oblique fracture of shaft of left tibia A, K, M, N, P, Q, R 🦠, B, C 🦠

    ● ■ S82.233   Displaced oblique fracture of shaft of unspecified tibia A, K, M, N, P, Q, R 🦠, B, C 🦠

    ● S82.234   Nondisplaced oblique fracture of shaft of right tibia A, K, M, N, P, Q, R 🦠, B, C 🦠

    ● S82.235   Nondisplaced oblique fracture of shaft of left tibia A, K, M, N, P, Q, R 🦠, B, C 🦠

    ● ■ S82.236   Nondisplaced oblique fracture of shaft of unspecified tibia A, K, M, N, P, Q, R 🦠, B, C 🦠

  ● S82.24   Spiral fracture of shaft of tibia
     Toddler fracture

    ● S82.241   Displaced spiral fracture of shaft of right tibia A, K, M, N, P, Q, R 🦠, B, C 🦠

    ● S82.242   Displaced spiral fracture of shaft of left tibia A, K, M, N, P, Q, R 🦠, B, C 🦠

● ■ S82.243   Displaced spiral fracture of shaft of unspecified tibia A, K, M, N, P, Q, R 🦠, B, C 🦠

● S82.244   Nondisplaced spiral fracture of shaft of right tibia A, K, M, N, P, Q, R 🦠, B, C 🦠

● S82.245   Nondisplaced spiral fracture of shaft of left tibia A, K, M, N, P, Q, R 🦠, B, C 🦠

● ■ S82.246   Nondisplaced spiral fracture of shaft of unspecified tibia A, K, M, N, P, Q, R 🦠, B, C 🦠

● S82.25   Comminuted fracture of shaft of tibia

  ● S82.251   Displaced comminuted fracture of shaft of right tibia A, K, M, N, P, Q, R 🦠, B, C 🦠

  ● S82.252   Displaced comminuted fracture of shaft of left tibia A, K, M, N, P, Q, R 🦠, B, C 🦠

  ● ■ S82.253   Displaced comminuted fracture of shaft of unspecified tibia A, K, M, N, P, Q, R 🦠, B, C 🦠

  ● S82.254   Nondisplaced comminuted fracture of shaft of right tibia A, K, M, N, P, Q, R 🦠, B, C 🦠

  ● S82.255   Nondisplaced comminuted fracture of shaft of left tibia A, K, M, N, P, Q, R 🦠, B, C 🦠

  ● ■ S82.256   Nondisplaced comminuted fracture of shaft of unspecified tibia A, K, M, N, P, Q, R 🦠, B, C 🦠

● S82.26   Segmental fracture of shaft of tibia

  ● S82.261   Displaced segmental fracture of shaft of right tibia A, K, M, N, P, Q, R 🦠, B, C 🦠

  ● S82.262   Displaced segmental fracture of shaft of left tibia A, K, M, N, P, Q, R 🦠, B, C 🦠

  ● ■ S82.263   Displaced segmental fracture of shaft of unspecified tibia A, K, M, N, P, Q, R 🦠, B, C 🦠

  ● S82.264   Nondisplaced segmental fracture of shaft of right tibia A, K, M, N, P, Q, R 🦠, B, C 🦠

  ● S82.265   Nondisplaced segmental fracture of shaft of left tibia A, K, M, N, P, Q, R 🦠, B, C 🦠

  ● ■ S82.266   Nondisplaced segmental fracture of shaft of unspecified tibia A, K, M, N, P, Q, R 🦠, B, C 🦠

● S82.29   Other fracture of shaft of tibia

  ● S82.291   Other fracture of shaft of right tibia A, K, M, N, P, Q, R 🦠, B, C 🦠

  ● S82.292   Other fracture of shaft of left tibia A, K, M, N, P, Q, R 🦠, B, C 🦠

  ● ■ S82.299   Other fracture of shaft of unspecified tibia A, K, M, N, P, Q, R 🦠, B, C 🦠

● S82.3   Fracture of lower end of tibia

  Excludes1   bimalleolar fracture of lower leg (S82.81-)
           fracture of medial malleolus alone (S82.5-)
           Maisonneuve's fracture (S82.83-)
           pilon fracture of distal tibia (S82.84-)
           trimalleolar fractures of lower leg (S82.82-)

● Unacceptable First-Listed Diagnosis   ● Use Additional Character(s)   ■ Unspecified   **OGCR** Official Guidelines for Coding and Reporting

1498   🦠 Complication\Comorbidity   🦠 Major C\C   Excludes 1   Excludes 2   Includes   Use additional   Code first   Code also

● S82.30   Unspecified fracture of lower end of tibia

   ● ▪ S82.301   Unspecified fracture of lower end of right tibia B, C, K, M, N, P, Q, R 🍥

   ● ▪ S82.302   Unspecified fracture of lower end of left tibia B, C, K, M, N, P, Q, R 🍥

   ● ▪ S82.309   Unspecified fracture of lower end of unspecified tibia B, C, K, M, N, P, Q, R 🍥

● S82.31   Torus fracture of lower end of tibia

    Note: Open fracture 7th characters do not apply to codes under subcategory S82.31.

   ● S82.311   Torus fracture of lower end of right tibia A, K, P 🍥

   ● S82.312   Torus fracture of lower end of left tibia A, K, P 🍥

   ● ▪ S82.319   Torus fracture of lower end of unspecified tibia A, K, P 🍥

● S82.39   Other fracture of lower end of tibia

   ● S82.391   Other fracture of lower end of right tibia B, C, K, M, N, P, Q, R 🍥

   ● S82.392   Other fracture of lower end of left tibia B, C, K, M, N, P, Q, R 🍥

   ● ▪ S82.399   Other fracture of lower end of unspecified tibia B, C, K, M, N, P, Q, R 🍥

● S82.4   Fracture of shaft of fibula

   | Excludes2 | fracture of lateral malleolus alone (S82.6-) |

● S82.40   Unspecified fracture of shaft of fibula

   ● ▪ S82.401   Unspecified fracture of shaft of right fibula K, M, N, P, Q, R 🍥, B, C 🍥

   ● ▪ S82.402   Unspecified fracture of shaft of left fibula K, M, N, P, Q, R 🍥, B, C 🍥

   ● ▪ S82.409   Unspecified fracture of shaft of unspecified fibula K, M, N, P, Q, R 🍥, B, C 🍥

● S82.42   Transverse fracture of shaft of fibula

   ● S82.421   Displaced transverse fracture of shaft of right fibula K, M, N, P, Q, R 🍥, B, C 🍥

   ● S82.422   Displaced transverse fracture of shaft of left fibula K, M, N, P, Q, R 🍥, B, C 🍥

   ● ▪ S82.423   Displaced transverse fracture of shaft of unspecified fibula K, M, N, P, Q, R 🍥, B, C 🍥

   ● S82.424   Nondisplaced transverse fracture of shaft of right fibula K, M, N, P, Q, R 🍥, B, C 🍥

   ● S82.425   Nondisplaced transverse fracture of shaft of left fibula K, M, N, P, Q, R 🍥, B, C 🍥

   ● ▪ S82.426   Nondisplaced transverse fracture of shaft of unspecified fibula K, M, N, P, Q, R 🍥, B, C 🍥

● S82.43   Oblique fracture of shaft of fibula

   ● S82.431   Displaced oblique fracture of shaft of right fibula K, M, N, P, Q, R 🍥, B, C 🍥

   ● S82.432   Displaced oblique fracture of shaft of left fibula K, M, N, P, Q, R 🍥, B, C 🍥

   ● ▪ S82.433   Displaced oblique fracture of shaft of unspecified fibula K, M, N, P, Q, R 🍥, B, C 🍥

   ● S82.434   Nondisplaced oblique fracture of shaft of right fibula K, M, N, P, Q, R 🍥, B, C 🍥

   ● S82.435   Nondisplaced oblique fracture of shaft of left fibula K, M, N, P, Q, R 🍥, B, C 🍥

   ● ▪ S82.436   Nondisplaced oblique fracture of shaft of unspecified fibula K, M, N, P, Q, R 🍥, B, C 🍥

● S82.44   Spiral fracture of shaft of fibula

   ● S82.441   Displaced spiral fracture of shaft of right fibula K, M, N, P, Q, R 🍥, B, C 🍥

   ● S82.442   Displaced spiral fracture of shaft of left fibula K, M, N, P, Q, R 🍥, B, C 🍥

   ● ▪ S82.443   Displaced spiral fracture of shaft of unspecified fibula K, M, N, P, Q, R 🍥, B, C 🍥

   ● S82.444   Nondisplaced spiral fracture of shaft of right fibula K, M, N, P, Q, R 🍥, B, C 🍥

   ● S82.445   Nondisplaced spiral fracture of shaft of left fibula K, M, N, P, Q, R 🍥, B, C 🍥

   ● ▪ S82.446   Nondisplaced spiral fracture of shaft of unspecified fibula K, M, N, P, Q, R 🍥, B, C 🍥

● S82.45   Comminuted fracture of shaft of fibula

   ● S82.451   Displaced comminuted fracture of shaft of right fibula K, M, N, P, Q, R 🍥, B, C 🍥

   ● S82.452   Displaced comminuted fracture of shaft of left fibula K, M, N, P, Q, R 🍥, B, C 🍥

   ● ▪ S82.453   Displaced comminuted fracture of shaft of unspecified fibula K, M, N, P, Q, R 🍥, B, C 🍥

   ● S82.454   Nondisplaced comminuted fracture of shaft of right fibula K, M, N, P, Q, R 🍥, B, C 🍥

   ● S82.455   Nondisplaced comminuted fracture of shaft of left fibula K, M, N, P, Q, R 🍥, B, C 🍥

   ● ▪ S82.456   Nondisplaced comminuted fracture of shaft of unspecified fibula K, M, N, P, Q, R 🍥, B, C 🍥

● S82.46   Segmental fracture of shaft of fibula

   ● S82.461   Displaced segmental fracture of shaft of right fibula K, M, N, P, Q, R 🍥, B, C 🍥

   ● S82.462   Displaced segmental fracture of shaft of left fibula K, M, N, P, Q, R 🍥, B, C 🍥

   ● ▪ S82.463   Displaced segmental fracture of shaft of unspecified fibula K, M, N, P, Q, R 🍥, B, C 🍥

   ● S82.464   Nondisplaced segmental fracture of shaft of right fibula K, M, N, P, Q, R 🍥, B, C 🍥

● Unacceptable First-Listed Diagnosis   ● Use Additional Character(s)   ▪ Unspecified   **OGCR** Official Guidelines for Coding and Reporting

🍥 Complication\Comorbidity   🍥 Major C\C | Excludes 1 | | Excludes 2 | | Includes | Use additional   Code first   Code also

1499

CHAPTER 19 (S00-T98)

- S82.465   Nondisplaced segmental fracture of shaft of left fibula K, M, N, P, Q, R 🦠, B, C 🦠
- ▪ S82.466   Nondisplaced segmental fracture of shaft of unspecified fibula K, M, N, P, Q, R 🦠, B, C 🦠
- S82.49   Other fracture of shaft of fibula
  - S82.491   Other fracture of shaft of right fibula K, M, N, P, Q, R 🦠, B, C 🦠
  - S82.492   Other fracture of shaft of left fibula K, M, N, P, Q, R 🦠, B, C 🦠
  - ▪ S82.499   Other fracture of shaft of unspecified fibula K, M, N, P, Q, R 🦠, B, C 🦠
- S82.5   Fracture of medial malleolus

  Excludes1   pilon fracture of distal tibia (S82.84-)
  Salter-Harris type III of lower end of tibia (S89.13-)
  Salter-Harris type IV of lower end of tibia (S89.14-)

  - S82.51   Displaced fracture of medial malleolus of right tibia B, C, K, M, N, P, Q, R 🦠
  - S82.52   Displaced fracture of medial malleolus of left tibia B, C, K, M, N, P, Q, R 🦠
  - ▪ S82.53   Displaced fracture of medial malleolus of unspecified tibia B, C, K, M, N, P, Q, R 🦠
  - S82.54   Nondisplaced fracture of medial malleolus of right tibia B, C, K, M, N, P, Q, R 🦠
  - S82.55   Nondisplaced fracture of medial malleolus of left tibia B, C, K, M, N, P, Q, R 🦠
  - ▪ S82.56   Nondisplaced fracture of medial malleolus of unspecified tibia B, C, K, M, N, P, Q, R 🦠
- S82.6   Fracture of lateral malleolus

  Excludes1   pilon fracture of distal tibia (S82.84-)

  - S82.61   Displaced fracture of lateral malleolus of right fibula B, C, K, M, N, P, Q, R 🦠
  - S82.62   Displaced fracture of lateral malleolus of left fibula B, C, K, M, N, P, Q, R 🦠
  - ▪ S82.63   Displaced fracture of lateral malleolus of unspecified fibula B, C, K, M, N, P, Q, R 🦠
  - S82.64   Nondisplaced fracture of lateral malleolus of right fibula B, C, K, M, N, P, Q, R 🦠
  - S82.65   Nondisplaced fracture of lateral malleolus of left fibula B, C, K, M, N, P, Q, R 🦠
  - ▪ S82.66   Nondisplaced fracture of lateral malleolus of unspecified fibula B, C, K, M, N, P, Q, R 🦠
- S82.8   Other fractures of lower leg
  - S82.81   Torus fracture of upper end of fibula

    Note: Open fracture 7th characters do not apply to codes under subcategory S82.81.

    - S82.811   Torus fracture of upper end of right fibula K, P 🦠
    - S82.812   Torus fracture of upper end of left fibula K, P 🦠
    - ▪ S82.819   Torus fracture of upper end of unspecified fibula K, P 🦠
  - S82.82   Torus fracture of lower end of fibula

    Note: Open fracture 7th characters do not apply to codes under subcategory S82.82.

- S82.821   Torus fracture of lower end of right fibula K, P 🦠
- S82.822   Torus fracture of lower end of left fibula K, P 🦠
- ▪ S82.829   Torus fracture of lower end of unspecified fibula K, P 🦠
- S82.83   Other fracture of upper and lower end of fibula
  - S82.831   Other fracture of upper and lower end of right fibula K, M, N, P, Q, R 🦠, B, C
  - S82.832   Other fracture of upper and lower end of left fibula K, M, N, P, Q, R 🦠, B, C
  - ▪ S82.839   Other fracture of upper and lower end of unspecified fibula K, M, N, P, Q, R 🦠, B, C
- S82.84   Bimalleolar fracture of lower leg
  - S82.841   Displaced bimalleolar fracture of right lower leg B, C, K, M, N, P, Q, R 🦠
  - S82.842   Displaced bimalleolar fracture of left lower leg B, C, K, M, N, P, Q, R 🦠
  - ▪ S82.843   Displaced bimalleolar fracture of unspecified lower leg B, C, K, M, N, P, Q, R 🦠
  - S82.844   Nondisplaced bimalleolar fracture of right lower leg B, C, K, M, N, P, Q, R 🦠
  - S82.845   Nondisplaced bimalleolar fracture of left lower leg B, C, K, M, N, P, Q, R 🦠
  - ▪ S82.846   Nondisplaced bimalleolar fracture of unspecified lower leg B, C, K, M, N, P, Q, R 🦠
- S82.85   Trimalleolar fracture of lower leg
  - S82.851   Displaced trimalleolar fracture of right lower leg B, C, K, M, N, P, Q, R 🦠
  - S82.852   Displaced trimalleolar fracture of left lower leg B, C, K, M, N, P, Q, R 🦠
  - ▪ S82.853   Displaced trimalleolar fracture of lower leg, unspecified side B, C, K, M, N, P, Q, R 🦠
  - S82.854   Nondisplaced trimalleolar fracture of right lower leg B, C, K, M, N, P, Q, R 🦠
  - S82.855   Nondisplaced trimalleolar fracture of left lower leg B, C, K, M, N, P, Q, R 🦠
  - ▪ S82.856   Nondisplaced trimalleolar fracture of lower leg, unspecified side B, C, K, M, N, P, Q, R 🦠
- S82.86   Maisonneuve's fracture
  - S82.861   Displaced Maisonneuve's fracture of right leg K, M, N, P, Q, R 🦠, B, C 🦠
  - S82.862   Displaced Maisonneuve's fracture of left leg K, M, N, P, Q, R 🦠, B, C 🦠
  - ▪ S82.863   Displaced Maisonneuve's fracture of unspecified leg K, M, N, P, Q, R 🦠, B, C 🦠

- Unacceptable First-Listed Diagnosis   ● Use Additional Character(s)   ▪ Unspecified   **OGCR** Official Guidelines for Coding and Reporting
🦠 Complication\Comorbidity   🦠 Major C\C   Excludes 1   Excludes 2   Includes   Use additional   Code first   Code also

- **S82.864**   Nondisplaced Maisonneuve's fracture of right leg K, M, N, P, Q, R 🦠, B, C 🦠
- **S82.865**   Nondisplaced Maisonneuve's fracture of left leg K, M, N, P, Q, R 🦠, B, C 🦠
- **S82.866**   Nondisplaced Maisonneuve's fracture of unspecified leg K, M, N, P, Q, R 🦠, B, C 🦠

- **S82.87**   Pilon fracture of tibia
  - **S82.871**   Displaced pilon fracture of right tibia B, C, K, M, N, P, Q, R 🦠
  - **S82.872**   Displaced pilon fracture of left tibia B, C, K, M, N, P, Q, R 🦠
  - **S82.873**   Displaced pilon fracture of unspecified tibia B, C, K, M, N, P, Q, R 🦠
  - **S82.874**   Nondisplaced pilon fracture of right tibia B, C, K, M, N, P, Q, R 🦠
  - **S82.875**   Nondisplaced pilon fracture of left tibia B, C, K, M, N, P, Q, R 🦠
  - **S82.876**   Nondisplaced pilon fracture of unspecified tibia B, C, K, M, N, P, Q, R 🦠

- **S82.89**   Other fractures of lower leg
  Fracture of ankle NOS
  - **S82.891**   Other fracture of right lower leg B, C, K, M, N, P, Q, R 🦠
  - **S82.892**   Other fracture of left lower leg B, C, K, M, N, P, Q, R 🦠
  - **S82.899**   Other fracture of unspecified lower leg B, C, K, M, N, P, Q, R 🦠

- **S82.9**   Unspecified fracture of lower leg
  - **S82.90**   Unspecified fracture of unspecified lower leg A, K, M, N, P, Q, R 🦠, B, C 🦠
  - **S82.91**   Unspecified fracture of right lower leg A, K, M, N, P, Q, R 🦠, B, C 🦠
  - **S82.92**   Unspecified fracture of left lower leg A, K, M, N, P, Q, R 🦠, B, C 🦠

- **S83**   **Dislocation and sprain of joints and ligaments of knee**

  Includes   avulsion of joint or ligament of knee
  laceration of cartilage, joint or ligament of knee
  sprain of cartilage, joint or ligament of knee
  traumatic hemarthrosis of joint or ligament of knee
  traumatic rupture of joint or ligament of knee
  traumatic subluxation of joint or ligament of knee
  traumatic tear of joint or ligament of knee

  Code also any associated open wound

  Excludes1   derangement of patella (M22.0-M22.3)
  injury of patellar ligament (tendon) (S76.1-)
  internal derangement of knee (M23.-)
  old dislocation of knee (M24.36)
  pathological dislocation of knee (M24.36)
  recurrent dislocation of knee (M22.0)

  Excludes2   strain of muscle, fascia and tendon of lower leg (S86.-)

  The appropriate 7th character is to be added to each code from category S83

A	initial encounter
D	subsequent encounter
S	sequela

- **S83.0**   Subluxation and dislocation of patella
  - **S83.00**   Unspecified subluxation and dislocation of patella
    - **S83.001**   Unspecified subluxation of right patella
    - **S83.002**   Unspecified subluxation of left patella
    - **S83.003**   Unspecified subluxation of unspecified patella
    - **S83.004**   Unspecified dislocation of right patella
    - **S83.005**   Unspecified dislocation of left patella
    - **S83.006**   Unspecified dislocation of unspecified patella
  - **S83.01**   Lateral subluxation and dislocation of patella
    - **S83.011**   Lateral subluxation of right patella
    - **S83.012**   Lateral subluxation of left patella
    - **S83.013**   Lateral subluxation of patella, unspecified side
    - **S83.014**   Lateral dislocation of right patella
    - **S83.015**   Lateral dislocation of left patella
    - **S83.016**   Lateral dislocation of patella, unspecified side
  - **S83.09**   Other subluxation and dislocation of patella
    - **S83.091**   Other subluxation of right patella
    - **S83.092**   Other subluxation of left patella
    - **S83.093**   Other subluxation of unspecified patella
    - **S83.094**   Other dislocation of right patella
    - **S83.095**   Other dislocation of left patella
    - **S83.096**   Other dislocation of unspecified patella

- **S83.1**   Subluxation and dislocation of knee

  Excludes2   dislocation and subluxation of knee prosthesis (T84.022, T84.023)

  - **S83.10**   Unspecified subluxation and dislocation of knee
    - **S83.101**   Unspecified subluxation of right knee
    - **S83.102**   Unspecified subluxation of left knee
    - **S83.103**   Unspecified subluxation of unspecified knee
    - **S83.104**   Unspecified dislocation of right knee
    - **S83.105**   Unspecified dislocation of left knee
    - **S83.106**   Unspecified dislocation of unspecified knee
  - **S83.11**   Anterior subluxation and dislocation of proximal end of tibia
    Posterior subluxation and dislocation of distal end of femur
    - **S83.111**   Anterior subluxation of proximal end of tibia, right knee
    - **S83.112**   Anterior subluxation of proximal end of tibia, left knee

● Unacceptable First-Listed Diagnosis   ● Use Additional Character(s)   ▪ Unspecified   **OGCR** Official Guidelines for Coding and Reporting

🦠 Complication\Comorbidity   🦠 Major C\C   ⬚ Excludes 1   ▭ Excludes 2   Includes   Use additional   Code first   Code also

1501

CHAPTER 19 (S00-T98)

● ■ S83.113 Anterior subluxation of proximal end of tibia, unspecified knee

● S83.114 Anterior dislocation of proximal end of tibia, right knee

● S83.115 Anterior dislocation of proximal end of tibia, left knee

● ■ S83.116 Anterior dislocation of proximal end of tibia, unspecified knee

● S83.12 Posterior subluxation and dislocation of proximal end of tibia
Anterior dislocation of distal end of femur

● S83.121 Posterior subluxation of proximal end of tibia, right knee

● S83.122 Posterior subluxation of proximal end of tibia, left knee

● ■ S83.123 Posterior subluxation of proximal end of tibia, unspecified knee

● S83.124 Posterior dislocation of proximal end of tibia, right knee

● S83.125 Posterior dislocation of proximal end of tibia, left knee

● ■ S83.126 Posterior dislocation of proximal end of tibia, unspecified knee

● S83.13 Medial subluxation and dislocation of proximal end of tibia

● S83.131 Medial subluxation of proximal end of tibia, right knee

● S83.132 Medial subluxation of proximal end of tibia, left knee

● ■ S83.133 Medial subluxation of proximal end of tibia, unspecified knee

● S83.134 Medial dislocation of proximal end of tibia, right knee

● S83.135 Medial dislocation of proximal end of tibia, left knee

● ■ S83.136 Medial dislocation of proximal end of tibia, unspecified knee

● S83.14 Lateral subluxation and dislocation of proximal end of tibia

● S83.141 Lateral subluxation of proximal end of tibia, right knee

● S83.142 Lateral subluxation of proximal end of tibia, left knee

● ■ S83.143 Lateral subluxation of proximal end of tibia, unspecified knee

● S83.144 Lateral dislocation of proximal end of tibia, right knee

● S83.145 Lateral dislocation of proximal end of tibia, left knee

● ■ S83.146 Lateral dislocation of proximal end of tibia, unspecified knee

● S83.19 Other subluxation and dislocation of knee

● S83.191 Other subluxation of right knee

● S83.192 Other subluxation of left knee

● ■ S83.193 Other subluxation of unspecified knee

● S83.194 Other dislocation of right knee

● S83.195 Other dislocation of left knee

● ■ S83.196 Other dislocation of unspecified knee

● S83.2 Tear of meniscus, current injury
Excludes1 old bucket-handle tear (M23.2)

● S83.20 Tear of unspecified meniscus, current injury
Tear of meniscus of knee NOS

● ■ S83.200 Bucket-handle tear of unspecified meniscus, current injury, right knee

● ■ S83.201 Bucket-handle tear of unspecified meniscus, current injury, left knee

● ■ S83.202 Bucket-handle tear of unspecified meniscus, current injury, unspecified knee

● ■ S83.203 Other tear of unspecified meniscus, current injury, right knee

● ■ S83.204 Other tear of unspecified meniscus, current injury, left knee

● ■ S83.205 Other tear of unspecified meniscus, current injury, unspecified knee

● ■ S83.206 Unspecified tear of unspecified meniscus, current injury, right knee

● ■ S83.207 Unspecified tear of unspecified meniscus, current injury, left knee

● ■ S83.209 Unspecified tear of unspecified meniscus, current injury, unspecified knee

● S83.21 Bucket-handle tear of medial meniscus, current injury

● S83.211 Bucket-handle tear of medial meniscus, current injury, right knee

● S83.212 Bucket-handle tear of medial meniscus, current injury, left knee

● ■ S83.219 Bucket-handle tear of medial meniscus, current injury, unspecified knee

● S83.22 Peripheral tear of medial meniscus, current injury

● S83.221 Peripheral tear of medial meniscus, current injury, right knee

● S83.222 Peripheral tear of medial meniscus, current injury, left knee

● ■ S83.229 Peripheral tear of medial meniscus, current injury, unspecified knee

● S83.23 Complex tear of medial meniscus, current injury

● S83.231 Complex tear of medial meniscus, current injury, right knee

● S83.232 Complex tear of medial meniscus, current injury, left knee

● ■ S83.239 Complex tear of medial meniscus, current injury, unspecified knee

● S83.24 Other tear of medial meniscus, current injury

● S83.241 Other tear of medial meniscus, current injury, right knee

● S83.242 Other tear of medial meniscus, current injury, left knee

● ▣ S83.249 Other tear of medial meniscus, current injury, unspecified knee

● S83.25 Bucket-handle tear of lateral meniscus, current injury

    ● S83.251 Bucket-handle tear of lateral meniscus, current injury, right knee

    ● S83.252 Bucket-handle tear of lateral meniscus, current injury, left knee

    ● ▣ S83.259 Bucket-handle tear of lateral meniscus, current injury, unspecified knee

● S83.26 Peripheral tear of lateral meniscus, current injury

    ● S83.261 Peripheral tear of lateral meniscus, current injury, right knee

    ● S83.262 Peripheral tear of lateral meniscus, current injury, left knee

    ● ▣ S83.269 Peripheral tear of lateral meniscus, current injury, unspecified knee

● S83.27 Complex tear of lateral meniscus, current injury

    ● S83.271 Complex tear of lateral meniscus, current injury, right knee

    ● S83.272 Complex tear of lateral meniscus, current injury, left knee

    ● ▣ S83.279 Complex tear of lateral meniscus, current injury, unspecified knee

● S83.28 Other tear of lateral meniscus, current injury

    ● S83.281 Other tear of lateral meniscus, current injury, right knee

    ● S83.282 Other tear of lateral meniscus, current injury, left knee

    ● ▣ S83.289 Other tear of lateral meniscus, current injury, unspecified knee

● S83.3 Tear of articular cartilage of knee, current

  ● ▣ S83.30 Tear of articular cartilage of knee, current, unspecified side

  ● S83.31 Tear of articular cartilage of right knee, current

  ● S83.32 Tear of articular cartilage of left knee, current

● S83.4 Sprain of collateral ligament of knee

  ● S83.40 Sprain of unspecified collateral ligament of knee

    ● ▣ S83.401 Sprain of unspecified collateral ligament of right knee

    ● ▣ S83.402 Sprain of unspecified collateral ligament of left knee

    ● ▣ S83.409 Sprain of unspecified collateral ligament of unspecified knee

  ● S83.41 Sprain of medial collateral ligament of knee
        Sprain of tibial collateral ligament

● S83.411 Sprain of medial collateral ligament of right knee

● S83.412 Sprain of medial collateral ligament of left knee

● ▣ S83.419 Sprain of medial collateral ligament of unspecified knee

● S83.42 Sprain of lateral collateral ligament of knee
        Sprain of fibular collateral ligament

  ● S83.421 Sprain of lateral collateral ligament of right knee

  ● S83.422 Sprain of lateral collateral ligament of left knee

  ● ▣ S83.429 Sprain of lateral collateral ligament of unspecified knee

● S83.5 Sprain of cruciate ligament of knee

  ● S83.50 Sprain of unspecified cruciate ligament of knee

    ● ▣ S83.501 Sprain of unspecified cruciate ligament of right knee

    ● ▣ S83.502 Sprain of unspecified cruciate ligament of left knee

    ● ▣ S83.509 Sprain of unspecified cruciate ligament of unspecified knee

  ● S83.51 Sprain of anterior cruciate ligament of knee

    ● S83.511 Sprain of anterior cruciate ligament of right knee

    ● S83.512 Sprain of anterior cruciate ligament of left knee

    ● ▣ S83.519 Sprain of anterior cruciate ligament of unspecified knee

  ● S83.52 Sprain of posterior cruciate ligament of knee

    ● S83.521 Sprain of posterior cruciate ligament of right knee

    ● S83.522 Sprain of posterior cruciate ligament of left knee

    ● ▣ S83.529 Sprain of posterior cruciate ligament of unspecified knee

● S83.6 Sprain of the superior tibiofibular joint and ligament

  ● ▣ S83.60 Sprain of the superior tibiofibular joint and ligament, unspecified knee

  ● S83.61 Sprain of the superior tibiofibular joint and ligament, right knee

  ● S83.62 Sprain of the superior tibiofibular joint and ligament, left knee

● S83.8 Sprain of other sites of knee

  ● S83.8x Sprain of other sites of knee

    ● S83.8x1 Sprain of other sites of right knee

    ● S83.8x2 Sprain of other sites of left knee

    ● ▣ S83.8x9 Sprain of other sites of unspecified knee

● S83.9 Sprain of unspecified site of knee

  ● ▣ S83.90 Sprain of unspecified site of knee, unspecified side

  ● ▣ S83.91 Sprain of unspecified site of right knee

  ● ▣ S83.92 Sprain of unspecified site of left knee

● Unacceptable First-Listed Diagnosis   ● Use Additional Character(s)   ▣ Unspecified   **OGCR** Official Guidelines for Coding and Reporting

 Complication\Comorbidity   Major C\C   Excludes 1   Excludes 2   Includes   Use additional   Code first   Code also

CHAPTER 19 (S00-T98)

1503

● **S84   Injury of nerves at lower leg level**
     Code also any associated open wound (S81.-)

     Excludes2   injury of nerves at ankle and foot level (S94.-)

     The appropriate 7th character is to be added to each code from category S84

     A   initial encounter
     D   subsequent encounter
     S   sequela

  ● **S84.0   Injury of tibial nerve at lower leg level**
    ● ■ **S84.00**   Injury of tibial nerve at lower leg level, unspecified leg
    ● **S84.01**   Injury of tibial nerve at lower leg level, right leg
    ● **S84.02**   Injury of tibial nerve at lower leg level, left leg

  ● **S84.1   Injury of peroneal nerve at lower leg level**
    ● ■ **S84.10**   Injury of peroneal nerve at lower leg level, unspecified leg
    ● **S84.11**   Injury of peroneal nerve at lower leg level, right leg
    ● **S84.12**   Injury of peroneal nerve at lower leg level, left leg

  ● **S84.2   Injury of cutaneous sensory nerve at lower leg level**
    ● ■ **S84.20**   Injury of cutaneous sensory nerve at lower leg level, unspecified leg
    ● **S84.21**   Injury of cutaneous sensory nerve at lower leg level, right leg
    ● **S84.22**   Injury of cutaneous sensory nerve at lower leg level, left leg

  ● **S84.8   Injury of other nerves at lower leg level**
    ● **S84.80**   Injury of other nerves at lower leg level
      ● **S84.801**   Injury of other nerves at lower leg level, right leg
      ● **S84.802**   Injury of other nerves at lower leg level, left leg
      ● ■ **S84.809**   Injury of other nerves at lower leg level, unspecified leg

  ● **S84.9   Injury of unspecified nerve at lower leg level**
    ● ■ **S84.90**   Injury of unspecified nerve at lower leg level, unspecified leg
    ● ■ **S84.91**   Injury of unspecified nerve at lower leg level, right leg
    ● ■ **S84.92**   Injury of unspecified nerve at lower leg level, left leg

● **S85   Injury of blood vessels at lower leg level**
     Code also any associated open wound (S81.-)

     Excludes2   injury of blood vessels at ankle and foot level (S95.-)

     The appropriate 7th character is to be added to each code from category S85

     A   initial encounter
     D   subsequent encounter
     S   sequela

  ● **S85.0   Injury of popliteal artery**
    ● **S85.00**   Unspecified injury of popliteal artery
      ● ■ **S85.001**   Unspecified injury of popliteal artery, right leg A
      ● ■ **S85.002**   Unspecified injury of popliteal artery, left leg A
      ● ■ **S85.009**   Unspecified injury of popliteal artery, unspecified leg A

  ● **S85.01   Laceration of popliteal artery**
    ● **S85.011**   Laceration of popliteal artery, right leg A
    ● **S85.012**   Laceration of popliteal artery, left leg A
    ● ■ **S85.019**   Laceration of popliteal artery, unspecified leg A

  ● **S85.09   Other specified injury of popliteal artery**
    ● **S85.091**   Other specified injury of popliteal artery, right leg A
    ● **S85.092**   Other specified injury of popliteal artery, left leg A
    ● ■ **S85.099**   Other specified injury of popliteal artery, unspecified leg A

● **S85.1   Injury of tibial artery**
  ● **S85.10**   Unspecified injury of unspecified tibial artery A
     Injury of tibial artery NOS
    ● ■ **S85.101**   Unspecified injury of unspecified tibial artery, right leg A
    ● ■ **S85.102**   Unspecified injury of unspecified tibial artery, left leg A
    ● ■ **S85.109**   Unspecified injury of unspecified tibial artery, unspecified leg A

  ● **S85.11   Laceration of unspecified tibial artery**
    ● ■ **S85.111**   Laceration of unspecified tibial artery, right leg A
    ● ■ **S85.112**   Laceration of unspecified tibial artery, left leg A
    ● ■ **S85.119**   Laceration of unspecified tibial artery, unspecified leg A

  ● **S85.12   Other specified injury of unspecified tibial artery**
    ● ■ **S85.121**   Other specified injury of unspecified tibial artery, right leg A
    ● ■ **S85.122**   Other specified injury of unspecified tibial artery, left leg A
    ● ■ **S85.129**   Other specified injury of unspecified tibial artery, unspecified leg A

  ● **S85.13   Unspecified injury of anterior tibial artery**
    ● ■ **S85.131**   Unspecified injury of anterior tibial artery, right leg A
    ● ■ **S85.132**   Unspecified injury of anterior tibial artery, left leg A
    ● ■ **S85.139**   Unspecified injury of anterior tibial artery, unspecified leg A

  ● **S85.14   Laceration of anterior tibial artery**
    ● **S85.141**   Laceration of anterior tibial artery, right leg A
    ● **S85.142**   Laceration of anterior tibial artery, left leg A
    ● ■ **S85.149**   Laceration of anterior tibial artery, unspecified leg A

  ● **S85.15   Other specified injury of anterior tibial artery**
    ● **S85.151**   Other specified injury of anterior tibial artery, right leg A
    ● **S85.152**   Other specified injury of anterior tibial artery, left leg A

● ■ S85.159 Other specified injury of anterior tibial artery, unspecified leg A 🅒

● S85.16 Unspecified injury of posterior tibial artery

   ● ■ S85.161 Unspecified injury of posterior tibial artery, right leg A 🅒

   ● ■ S85.162 Unspecified injury of posterior tibial artery, left leg A 🅒

   ● ■ S85.169 Unspecified injury of posterior tibial artery, unspecified leg A 🅒

● S85.17 Laceration of posterior tibial artery

   ● S85.171 Laceration of posterior tibial artery, right leg A 🅒

   ● S85.172 Laceration of posterior tibial artery, left leg A 🅒

   ● ■ S85.179 Laceration of posterior tibial artery, unspecified leg A 🅒

● S85.18 Other specified injury of posterior tibial artery

   ● S85.181 Other specified injury of posterior tibial artery, right leg A 🅒

   ● S85.182 Other specified injury of posterior tibial artery, left leg A 🅒

   ● ■ S85.189 Other specified injury of posterior tibial artery, unspecified leg A 🅒

● S85.2 Injury of peroneal artery

   ● S85.20 Unspecified injury of peroneal artery

      ● ■ S85.201 Unspecified injury of peroneal artery, right leg A 🅒

      ● ■ S85.202 Unspecified injury of peroneal artery, left leg A 🅒

      ● ■ S85.209 Unspecified injury of peroneal artery, unspecified leg A 🅒

   ● S85.21 Laceration of peroneal artery

      ● S85.211 Laceration of peroneal artery, right leg A 🅒

      ● S85.212 Laceration of peroneal artery, left leg A 🅒

      ● ■ S85.219 Laceration of peroneal artery, unspecified leg A 🅒

   ● S85.29 Other specified injury of peroneal artery

      ● S85.291 Other specified injury of peroneal artery, right leg A 🅒

      ● S85.292 Other specified injury of peroneal artery, left leg A 🅒

      ● ■ S85.299 Other specified injury of peroneal artery, unspecified leg A 🅒

● S85.3 Injury of greater saphenous vein at lower leg level
        Injury of greater saphenous vein NOS
        Injury of saphenous vein NOS

   ● S85.30 Unspecified injury of greater saphenous vein at lower leg level

      ● ■ S85.301 Unspecified injury of greater saphenous vein at lower leg level, right leg A 🅒

      ● ■ S85.302 Unspecified injury of greater saphenous vein at lower leg level, left leg A 🅒

      ● ■ S85.309 Unspecified injury of greater saphenous vein at lower leg level, unspecified leg A 🅒

● S85.31 Laceration of greater saphenous vein at lower leg level

   ● S85.311 Laceration of greater saphenous vein at lower leg level, right leg A 🅒

   ● S85.312 Laceration of greater saphenous vein at lower leg level, left leg A 🅒

   ● ■ S85.319 Laceration of greater saphenous vein at lower leg level, unspecified leg A 🅒

● S85.39 Other specified injury of greater saphenous vein at lower leg level

   ● S85.391 Other specified injury of greater saphenous vein at lower leg level, right leg A 🅒

   ● S85.392 Other specified injury of greater saphenous vein at lower leg level, left leg A 🅒

   ● ■ S85.399 Other specified injury of greater saphenous vein at lower leg level, unspecified leg A 🅒

● S85.4 Injury of lesser saphenous vein at lower leg level

   ● S85.40 Unspecified injury of lesser saphenous vein at lower leg level

      ● ■ S85.401 Unspecified injury of lesser saphenous vein at lower leg level, right leg A 🅒

      ● ■ S85.402 Unspecified injury of lesser saphenous vein at lower leg level, left leg A 🅒

      ● ■ S85.409 Unspecified injury of lesser saphenous vein at lower leg level, unspecified leg A 🅒

   ● S85.41 Laceration of lesser saphenous vein at lower leg level

      ● S85.411 Laceration of lesser saphenous vein at lower leg level, right leg A 🅒

      ● S85.412 Laceration of lesser saphenous vein at lower leg level, left leg A 🅒

      ● ■ S85.419 Laceration of lesser saphenous vein at lower leg level, unspecified leg A 🅒

   ● S85.49 Other specified injury of lesser saphenous vein at lower leg level

      ● S85.491 Other specified injury of lesser saphenous vein at lower leg level, right leg A 🅒

      ● S85.492 Other specified injury of lesser saphenous vein at lower leg level, left leg A 🅒

      ● ■ S85.499 Other specified injury of lesser saphenous vein at lower leg level, unspecified leg A 🅒

● S85.5 Injury of popliteal vein

   ● S85.50 Unspecified injury of popliteal vein

      ● ■ S85.501 Unspecified injury of popliteal vein, right leg A 🅒

      ● ■ S85.502 Unspecified injury of popliteal vein, left leg A 🅒

      ● ■ S85.509 Unspecified injury of popliteal vein, unspecified leg A 🅒

● Unacceptable First-Listed Diagnosis   ● Use Additional Character(s)   ■ Unspecified   **OGCR** Official Guidelines for Coding and Reporting

🅒 Complication\Comorbidity   🅒 Major C\C   Excludes 1   Excludes 2   Includes   Use additional   Code first   Code also   1505

CHAPTER 19 (S00-T98)

● S85.51 Laceration of popliteal vein
  ● S85.511 Laceration of popliteal vein, right leg A 🐾
  ● S85.512 Laceration of popliteal vein, left leg A 🐾
  ● ▪ S85.519 Laceration of popliteal vein, unspecified leg A 🐾
● S85.59 Other specified injury of popliteal vein
  ● S85.591 Other specified injury of popliteal vein, right leg A 🐾
  ● S85.592 Other specified injury of popliteal vein, left leg A 🐾
  ● ▪ S85.599 Other specified injury of popliteal vein, unspecified leg A 🐾

● S85.8 Injury of other blood vessels at lower leg level
  ● S85.80 Unspecified injury of other blood vessels at lower leg level
    ● ▪ S85.801 Unspecified injury of other blood vessels at lower leg level, right leg A 🐾, A 🐾
    ● ▪ S85.802 Unspecified injury of other blood vessels at lower leg level, left leg A 🐾, A 🐾
    ● ▪ S85.809 Unspecified injury of other blood vessels at lower leg level, unspecified leg A 🐾, A 🐾
  ● S85.81 Laceration of other blood vessels at lower leg level
    ● S85.811 Laceration of other blood vessels at lower leg level, right leg A 🐾, A 🐾
    ● S85.812 Laceration of other blood vessels at lower leg level, left leg A 🐾, A 🐾
    ● ▪ S85.819 Laceration of other blood vessels at lower leg level, unspecified leg A 🐾, A 🐾
  ● S85.89 Other specified injury of other blood vessels at lower leg level
    ● S85.891 Other specified injury of other blood vessels at lower leg level, right leg A 🐾, A 🐾
    ● S85.892 Other specified injury of other blood vessels at lower leg level, left leg A 🐾, A 🐾
    ● ▪ S85.899 Other specified injury of other blood vessels at lower leg level, unspecified leg A 🐾, A 🐾

● S85.9 Injury of unspecified blood vessel at lower leg level
  ● S85.90 Unspecified injury of unspecified blood vessel at lower leg level
    ● ▪ S85.901 Unspecified injury of unspecified blood vessel at lower leg level, right leg A 🐾, A 🐾
    ● ▪ S85.902 Unspecified injury of unspecified blood vessel at lower leg level, left leg A 🐾, A 🐾
    ● ▪ S85.909 Unspecified injury of unspecified blood vessel at lower leg level, unspecified leg A 🐾, A 🐾

● S85.91 Laceration of unspecified blood vessel at lower leg level
  ● ▪ S85.911 Laceration of unspecified blood vessel at lower leg level, right leg A 🐾, A 🐾
  ● ▪ S85.912 Laceration of unspecified blood vessel at lower leg level, left leg A 🐾, A 🐾
  ● ▪ S85.919 Laceration of unspecified blood vessel at lower leg level, unspecified leg A 🐾, A 🐾
● S85.99 Other specified injury of unspecified blood vessel at lower leg level
  ● ▪ S85.991 Other specified injury of unspecified blood vessel at lower leg level, right leg A 🐾, A 🐾
  ● ▪ S85.992 Other specified injury of unspecified blood vessel at lower leg level, left leg A 🐾, A 🐾
  ● ▪ S85.999 Other specified injury of unspecified blood vessel at lower leg level, unspecified leg A 🐾, A 🐾

The appropriate 7th character is to be added to each code from category S86

A	initial encounter
D	subsequent encounter
S	sequela

● S86 Injury of muscle, fascia and tendon at lower leg level
  Code also any associated open wound (S81.-)
  Excludes2 injury of muscle, fascia and tendon at ankle (S96.-)
  injury of patellar ligament (tendon) (S76.1-)
  sprain of joints and ligaments of knee (S83.-)
  ● S86.0 Injury of Achilles tendon
    ● S86.00 Unspecified injury of Achilles tendon
      ● ▪ S86.001 Unspecified injury of right Achilles tendon
      ● ▪ S86.002 Unspecified injury of left Achilles tendon
      ● ▪ S86.009 Unspecified injury of Achilles tendon, unspecified side
    ● S86.01 Strain of Achilles tendon
      ● S86.011 Strain of right Achilles tendon
      ● S86.012 Strain of left Achilles tendon
      ● ▪ S86.019 Strain of Achilles tendon, unspecified side
    ● S86.02 Laceration of Achilles tendon
      ● S86.021 Laceration of right Achilles tendon A 🐾
      ● S86.022 Laceration of left Achilles tendon A 🐾
      ● ▪ S86.029 Laceration of Achilles tendon, unspecified side A 🐾
    ● S86.09 Other injury of Achilles tendon
      ● S86.091 Other injury of right Achilles tendon
      ● S86.092 Other injury of left Achilles tendon
      ● ▪ S86.099 Other injury of Achilles tendon, unspecified side

CHAPTER 19 (S00-T98)

1506

● Unacceptable First-Listed Diagnosis   ● Use Additional Character(s)   ▪ Unspecified   OGCR Official Guidelines for Coding and Reporting
🐾 Complication\Comorbidity   🐾 Major C\C   Excludes 1   Excludes 2   Includes   Use additional   Code first   Code also

● S86.1 Injury of other muscle(s) and tendon(s) of posterior muscle group at lower leg level

  ● S86.10 Unspecified injury of other muscle(s) and tendon(s) of posterior muscle group at lower leg level

    ● ▢ S86.101 Unspecified injury of other muscle(s) and tendon(s) of posterior muscle group at lower leg level, right leg

    ● ▢ S86.102 Unspecified injury of other muscle(s) and tendon(s) of posterior muscle group at lower leg level, left leg

    ● ▢ S86.109 Unspecified injury of other muscle(s) and tendon(s) of posterior muscle group at lower leg level, unspecified leg

  ● S86.11 Strain of other muscle(s) and tendon(s) of posterior muscle group at lower leg level

    ● S86.111 Strain of other muscle(s) and tendon(s) of posterior muscle group at lower leg level, right leg

    ● S86.112 Strain of other muscle(s) and tendon(s) of posterior muscle group at lower leg level, left leg

    ● ▢ S86.119 Strain of other muscle(s) and tendon(s) of posterior muscle group at lower leg level, unspecified leg

  ● S86.12 Laceration of other muscle(s) and tendon(s) of posterior muscle group at lower leg level

    ● S86.121 Laceration of other muscle(s) and tendon(s) of posterior muscle group at lower leg level, right leg A 🦠

    ● S86.122 Laceration of other muscle(s) and tendon(s) of posterior muscle group at lower leg level, left leg A 🦠

    ● ▢ S86.129 Laceration of other muscle(s) and tendon(s) of posterior muscle group at lower leg level, unspecified leg A 🦠

  ● S86.19 Other injury of other muscle(s) and tendon(s) of posterior muscle group at lower leg level

    ● S86.191 Other injury of other muscle(s) and tendon(s) of posterior muscle group at lower leg level, right leg

    ● S86.192 Other injury of other muscle(s) and tendon(s) of posterior muscle group at lower leg level, left leg

    ● ▢ S86.199 Other injury of other muscle(s) and tendon(s) of posterior muscle group at lower leg level, unspecified leg

● S86.2 Injury of muscle(s) and tendon(s) of anterior muscle group at lower leg level

  ● S86.20 Unspecified injury of muscle(s) and tendon(s) of anterior muscle group at lower leg level

    ● ▢ S86.201 Unspecified injury of muscle(s) and tendon(s) of anterior muscle group at lower leg level, right leg

    ● ▢ S86.202 Unspecified injury of muscle(s) and tendon(s) of anterior muscle group at lower leg level, left leg

    ● ▢ S86.209 Unspecified injury of muscle(s) and tendon(s) of anterior muscle group at lower leg level, unspecified leg

  ● S86.21 Strain of muscle(s) and tendon(s) of anterior muscle group at lower leg level

    ● S86.211 Strain of muscle(s) and tendon(s) of anterior muscle group at lower leg level, right leg

    ● S86.212 Strain of muscle(s) and tendon(s) of anterior muscle group at lower leg level, left leg

    ● ▢ S86.219 Strain of muscle(s) and tendon(s) of anterior muscle group at lower leg level, unspecified leg

  ● S86.22 Laceration of muscle(s) and tendon(s) of anterior muscle group at lower leg level

    ● S86.221 Laceration of muscle(s) and tendon(s) of anterior muscle group at lower leg level, right leg A 🦠

    ● S86.222 Laceration of muscle(s) and tendon(s) of anterior muscle group at lower leg level, left leg A 🦠

    ● ▢ S86.229 Laceration of muscle(s) and tendon(s) of anterior muscle group at lower leg level, unspecified leg A 🦠

  ● S86.29 Other injury of muscle(s) and tendon(s) of anterior muscle group at lower leg level

    ● S86.291 Other injury of muscle(s) and tendon(s) of anterior muscle group at lower leg level, right leg

    ● S86.292 Other injury of muscle(s) and tendon(s) of anterior muscle group at lower leg level, left leg

    ● ▢ S86.299 Other injury of muscle(s) and tendon(s) of anterior muscle group at lower leg level, unspecified leg

● S86.3 Injury of muscle(s) and tendon(s) of peroneal muscle group at lower leg level

  ● S86.30 Unspecified injury of muscle(s) and tendon(s) of peroneal muscle group at lower leg level

    ● ▢ S86.301 Unspecified injury of muscle(s) and tendon(s) of peroneal muscle group at lower leg level, right leg

    ● ▢ S86.302 Unspecified injury of muscle(s) and tendon(s) of peroneal muscle group at lower leg level, left leg

    ● ▢ S86.309 Unspecified injury of muscle(s) and tendon(s) of peroneal muscle group at lower leg level, unspecified leg

  ● S86.31 Strain of muscle(s) and tendon(s) of peroneal muscle group at lower leg level

    ● S86.311 Strain of muscle(s) and tendon(s) of peroneal muscle group at lower leg level, right leg

    ● S86.312 Strain of muscle(s) and tendon(s) of peroneal muscle group at lower leg level, left leg

● Unacceptable First-Listed Diagnosis   ● Use Additional Character(s)   ▢ Unspecified   OGCR Official Guidelines for Coding and Reporting

🦠 Complication\Comorbidity   🦠 Major C\C   [Excludes 1]   [Excludes 2]   Includes   Use additional   Code first   Code also

CHAPTER 19 (S00-T98)

1507

● ■ S86.319   Strain of muscle(s) and tendon(s) of peroneal muscle group at lower leg level, unspecified leg

● S86.32   Laceration of muscle(s) and tendon(s) of peroneal muscle group at lower leg level

   ● S86.321   Laceration of muscle(s) and tendon(s) of peroneal muscle group at lower leg level, right leg A ⬥

   ● S86.322   Laceration of muscle(s) and tendon(s) of peroneal muscle group at lower leg level, left leg A ⬥

   ● ■ S86.329   Laceration of muscle(s) and tendon(s) of peroneal muscle group at lower leg level, unspecified leg A ⬥

● S86.39   Other injury of muscle(s) and tendon(s) of peroneal muscle group at lower leg level

   ● S86.391   Other injury of muscle(s) and tendon(s) of peroneal muscle group at lower leg level, right leg

   ● S86.392   Other injury of muscle(s) and tendon(s) of peroneal muscle group at lower leg level, left leg

   ● ■ S86.399   Other injury of muscle(s) and tendon(s) of peroneal muscle group at lower leg level, unspecified leg

● S86.8   Injury of other muscles and tendons at lower leg level

   ● S86.80   Unspecified injury of other muscles and tendons at lower leg level

      ● ■ S86.801   Unspecified injury of other muscle(s) and tendon(s) at lower leg level, right leg

      ● ■ S86.802   Unspecified injury of other muscle(s) and tendon(s) at lower leg level, left leg

      ● ■ S86.809   Unspecified injury of other muscle(s) and tendon(s) at lower leg level, unspecified leg

   ● S86.81   Strain of other muscles and tendons at lower leg level

      ● S86.811   Strain of other muscle(s) and tendon(s) at lower leg level, right leg

      ● S86.812   Strain of other muscle(s) and tendon(s) at lower leg level, left leg

      ● ■ S86.819   Strain of other muscle(s) and tendon(s) at lower leg level, unspecified leg

   ● S86.82   Laceration of other muscles and tendons at lower leg level

      ● S86.821   Laceration of other muscle(s) and tendon(s) at lower leg level, right leg A ⬥

      ● S86.822   Laceration of other muscle(s) and tendon(s) at lower leg level, left leg A ⬥

      ● ■ S86.829   Laceration of other muscle(s) and tendon(s) at lower leg level, unspecified leg A ⬥

● S86.89   Other injury of other muscles and tendons at lower leg level

   ● S86.891   Other injury of other muscle(s) and tendon(s) at lower leg level, right leg

   ● S86.892   Other injury of other muscle(s) and tendon(s) at lower leg level, left leg

   ● ■ S86.899   Other injury of other muscle(s) and tendon(s) at lower leg level, unspecified leg

● S86.9   Injury of unspecified muscle and tendon at lower leg level

   ● S86.90   Unspecified injury of unspecified muscle and tendon at lower leg level

      ● ■ S86.901   Unspecified injury of unspecified muscle(s) and tendon(s) at lower leg level, right leg

      ● ■ S86.902   Unspecified injury of unspecified muscle(s) and tendon(s) at lower leg level, left leg

      ● ■ S86.909   Unspecified injury of unspecified muscle(s) and tendon(s) at lower leg level, unspecified leg

   ● S86.91   Strain of unspecified muscle and tendon at lower leg level

      ● ■ S86.911   Strain of unspecified muscle(s) and tendon(s) at lower leg level, right leg

      ● ■ S86.912   Strain of unspecified muscle(s) and tendon(s) at lower leg level, left leg

      ● ■ S86.919   Strain of unspecified muscle(s) and tendon(s) at lower leg level, unspecified leg

   ● S86.92   Laceration of unspecified muscle and tendon at lower leg level

      ● ■ S86.921   Laceration of unspecified muscle(s) and tendon(s) at lower leg level, right leg A ⬥

      ● ■ S86.922   Laceration of unspecified muscle(s) and tendon(s) at lower leg level, left leg A ⬥

      ● ■ S86.929   Laceration of unspecified muscle(s) and tendon(s) at lower leg level, unspecified leg A ⬥

   ● S86.99   Other injury of unspecified muscle and tendon at lower leg level

      ● ■ S86.991   Other injury of unspecified muscle(s) and tendon(s) at lower leg level, right leg

      ● ■ S86.992   Other injury of unspecified muscle(s) and tendon(s) at lower leg level, left leg

      ● ■ S86.999   Other injury of unspecified muscle(s) and tendon(s) at lower leg level, unspecified leg

The appropriate 7th character is to be added to each code from category S87

A	initial encounter
D	subsequent encounter
S	sequela

● Unacceptable First-Listed Diagnosis   ● Use Additional Character(s)   ■ Unspecified   **OGCR** Official Guidelines for Coding and Reporting
⬥ Complication\Comorbidity   ⬥ Major C\C   Excludes 1   Excludes 2   Includes   Use additional   Code first   Code also

● S87   **Crushing injury of lower leg**
     Use additional code(s) for all associated injuries
     Excludes2   crushing injury of ankle and foot (S97.-)

    ● S87.0   **Crushing injury of knee**
       ● ▪ S87.00   Crushing injury of knee, unspecified side
       ● S87.01   Crushing injury of right knee
       ● S87.02   Crushing injury of left knee

    ● S87.8   **Crushing injury of lower leg**
       ● ▪ S87.80   Crushing injury of lower leg, unspecified side
       ● S87.81   Crushing injury of right lower leg
       ● S87.82   Crushing injury of left lower leg

     The appropriate 7th character is to be added to each code from category S88

A	initial encounter
D	subsequent encounter
S	sequela

● S88   **Traumatic amputation of lower leg**
     An amputation not identified and partial or complete should be coded to complete
     Excludes1   traumatic amputation of ankle and foot (S98.-)

    ● S88.0   **Traumatic amputation at knee level**
       ● S88.01   Complete traumatic amputation at knee level
         ● S88.011   Complete traumatic amputation at right knee level A 🦠
         ● S88.012   Complete traumatic amputation at left knee level A 🦠
         ● ▪ S88.019   Complete traumatic amputation at knee level, unspecified side A 🦠
       ● S88.02   Partial traumatic amputation at knee level
         ● S88.021   Partial traumatic amputation at right knee level A 🦠
         ● S88.022   Partial traumatic amputation at left knee level A 🦠
         ● ▪ S88.029   Partial traumatic amputation at knee level, unspecified side A 🦠

    ● S88.1   **Traumatic amputation at level between knee and ankle**
       ● S88.11   Complete traumatic amputation at level between knee and ankle
         ● S88.111   Complete traumatic amputation at level between right knee and ankle A 🦠
         ● S88.112   Complete traumatic amputation at level between left knee and ankle A 🦠
         ● ▪ S88.119   Complete traumatic amputation at level between knee and ankle, unspecified side A 🦠
       ● S88.12   Partial traumatic amputation at level between knee and ankle
         ● S88.121   Partial traumatic amputation at level between right knee and ankle A 🦠
         ● S88.122   Partial traumatic amputation at level between left knee and ankle A 🦠
         ● ▪ S88.129   Partial traumatic amputation at level between knee and ankle, unspecified side A 🦠

    ● S88.9   **Traumatic amputation of lower leg, level unspecified**
       ● S88.91   Complete traumatic amputation of lower leg, level unspecified
         ● ▪ S88.911   Complete traumatic amputation of lower right leg, level unspecified A 🦠
         ● ▪ S88.912   Complete traumatic amputation of lower left leg, level unspecified A 🦠
         ● ▪ S88.919   Complete traumatic amputation of lower leg, level unspecified, unspecified side A 🦠
       ● S88.92   Partial traumatic amputation of lower leg, level unspecified
         ● ▪ S88.921   Partial traumatic amputation of lower right leg, level unspecified A 🦠
         ● ▪ S88.922   Partial traumatic amputation of lower left leg, level unspecified A 🦠
         ● ▪ S88.929   Partial traumatic amputation of lower leg, level unspecified, unspecified side A 🦠

● S89   **Other and unspecified injuries of lower leg**
     Excludes2   other and unspecified injuries of ankle and foot (S99.-)
     The appropriate 7th character is to be added to each code from subcategories S89.0, S89.1, S89.2, and S89.3
     A fracture not designated as open or closed should be coded to closed

A	initial encounter for closed fracture
D	subsequent encounter for fracture with routine healing
G	subsequent encounter for fracture with delayed healing
K	subsequent encounter for fracture with nonunion
P	subsequent encounter for fracture with malunion
S	sequela

    ● S89.0   **Physeal fracture of upper end of tibia**
       ● S89.00   Unspecified physeal fracture of upper end of tibia
         ● ▪ S89.001   Unspecified physeal fracture of upper end of right tibia A, K, P 🦠
         ● ▪ S89.002   Unspecified physeal fracture of upper end of left tibia A, K, P 🦠
         ● ▪ S89.009   Unspecified physeal fracture of upper end of unspecified tibia A, K, P 🦠
       ● S89.01   Salter-Harris Type I upper end of tibia
         ● S89.011   Salter-Harris Type I upper end of right tibia A, K, P 🦠
         ● S89.012   Salter-Harris Type I upper end of left tibia A, K, P 🦠
         ● ▪ S89.019   Salter-Harris Type I upper end of unspecified tibia A, K, P 🦠
       ● S89.02   Salter-Harris Type II upper end of tibia
         ● S89.021   Salter-Harris Type II upper end of right tibia A, K, P 🦠
         ● S89.022   Salter-Harris Type II upper end of left tibia A, K, P 🦠
         ● ▪ S89.029   Salter-Harris Type II upper end of unspecified tibia A, K, P 🦠

● Unacceptable First-Listed Diagnosis   ● Use Additional Character(s)   ▪ Unspecified   **OGCR** Official Guidelines for Coding and Reporting

🦠 Complication\Comorbidity   🦠 Major C\C   Excludes 1   Excludes 2   Includes   Use additional   Code first   Code also

1509

CHAPTER 19 (S00-T98)

- S89.03   Salter-Harris Type III upper end of tibia
  - S89.031   Salter-Harris Type III upper end of right tibia A, K, P 🍳
  - S89.032   Salter-Harris Type III upper end of left tibia A, K, P 🍳
  - ◼ S89.039   Salter-Harris Type III upper end of unspecified tibia A, K, P 🍳
- S89.04   Salter-Harris Type IV upper end of tibia
  - S89.041   Salter-Harris Type IV upper end of right tibia A, K, P 🍳
  - S89.042   Salter-Harris Type IV upper end of left tibia A, K, P 🍳
  - ◼ S89.049   Salter-Harris Type IV upper end of unspecified tibia A, K, P 🍳
- S89.09   Other physeal fracture of upper end of tibia
  - S89.091   Other physeal fracture of upper end of right tibia A, K, P 🍳
  - S89.092   Other physeal fracture of upper end of left tibia A, K, P 🍳
  - ◼ S89.099   Other physeal fracture of upper end of unspecified tibia A, K, P 🍳
- S89.1   Physeal fracture of lower end of tibia
  - S89.10   Unspecified physeal fracture of lower end of tibia
    - ◼ S89.101   Unspecified physeal fracture of lower end of right tibia K, P 🍳
    - ◼ S89.102   Unspecified physeal fracture of lower end of left tibia K, P 🍳
    - ◼ S89.109   Unspecified physeal fracture of lower end of unspecified tibia K, P 🍳
  - S89.11   Salter-Harris Type I lower end of tibia
    - S89.111   Salter-Harris Type I lower end of right tibia K, P 🍳
    - S89.112   Salter-Harris Type I lower end of left tibia K, P 🍳
    - ◼ S89.119   Salter-Harris Type I lower end of unspecified tibia K, P 🍳
  - S89.12   Salter-Harris Type II lower end of tibia
    - S89.121   Salter-Harris Type II lower end of right tibia K, P 🍳
    - S89.122   Salter-Harris Type II lower end of left tibia K, P 🍳
    - ◼ S89.129   Salter-Harris Type II lower end of unspecified tibia K, P 🍳
  - S89.13   Salter-Harris Type III lower end of tibia
    > **Excludes1**   fracture of medial malleolus (adult) (S82.5-)
    - S89.131   Salter-Harris Type III lower end of right tibia K, P 🍳
    - S89.132   Salter-Harris Type III lower end of left tibia K, P 🍳
    - ◼ S89.139   Salter-Harris Type III lower end of unspecified tibia K, P 🍳
  - S89.14   Salter-Harris Type IV lower end of tibia
    > **Excludes1**   fracture of medial malleolus (adult) (S82.5-)
    - S89.141   Salter-Harris Type IV lower end of right tibia K, P 🍳
    - S89.142   Salter-Harris Type IV lower end of left tibia K, P 🍳

- ◼ S89.149   Salter-Harris Type IV lower end of unspecified tibia K, P 🍳
- S89.19   Other physeal fracture of lower end of tibia
  - S89.191   Other physeal fracture of lower end of right tibia K, P 🍳
  - S89.192   Other physeal fracture of lower end of left tibia K, P 🍳
  - ◼ S89.199   Other physeal fracture of lower end of unspecified tibia K, P 🍳
- S89.2   Physeal fracture of upper end of fibula
  - S89.20   Unspecified physeal fracture of upper end of fibula
    - ◼ S89.201   Unspecified physeal fracture of upper end of right fibula K, P 🍳
    - ◼ S89.202   Unspecified physeal fracture of upper end of left fibula K, P 🍳
    - ◼ S89.209   Unspecified physeal fracture of upper end of unspecified fibula K, P 🍳
  - S89.21   Salter-Harris Type I upper end of fibula
    - S89.211   Salter-Harris Type I upper end of right fibula K, P 🍳
    - S89.212   Salter-Harris Type I upper end of left fibula K, P 🍳
    - ◼ S89.219   Salter-Harris Type I upper end of unspecified fibula K, P 🍳
  - S89.22   Salter-Harris Type II upper end of fibula
    - S89.221   Salter-Harris Type II upper end of right fibula K, P 🍳
    - S89.222   Salter-Harris Type II upper end of left fibula K, P 🍳
    - ◼ S89.229   Salter-Harris Type II upper end of unspecified fibula K, P 🍳
  - S89.29   Other physeal fracture of upper end of fibula
    - S89.291   Other physeal fracture of upper end of right fibula K, P 🍳
    - S89.292   Other physeal fracture of upper end of left fibula K, P 🍳
    - ◼ S89.299   Other physeal fracture of upper end of unspecified fibula K, P 🍳
- S89.3   Physeal fracture of lower end of fibula
  - S89.30   Unspecified physeal fracture of lower end of fibula
    - ◼ S89.301   Unspecified physeal fracture of lower end of right fibula K, P 🍳
    - ◼ S89.302   Unspecified physeal fracture of lower end of left fibula K, P 🍳
    - ◼ S89.309   Unspecified physeal fracture of lower end of unspecified fibula K, P 🍳
  - S89.31   Salter-Harris Type I lower end of fibula
    - S89.311   Salter-Harris Type I lower end of right fibula K, P 🍳
    - S89.312   Salter-Harris Type I lower end of left fibula K, P 🍳
    - ◼ S89.319   Salter-Harris Type I lower end of unspecified fibula K, P 🍳
  - S89.32   Salter-Harris Type II lower end of fibula
    - S89.321   Salter-Harris Type II lower end of right fibula K, P 🍳

● Unacceptable First-Listed Diagnosis   ● Use Additional Character(s)   ◼ Unspecified   **OGCR** Official Guidelines for Coding and Reporting

🍳 Complication\Comorbidity   🍳 Major C\C   Excludes 1   Excludes 2   Includes   Use additional   Code first   Code also

● S89.322   Salter-Harris Type II lower end of left fibula K, P 🔧

● ■ S89.329   Salter-Harris Type II lower end of unspecified fibula K, P 🔧

● S89.39   Other physeal fracture of lower end of fibula

    ● S89.391   Other physeal fracture of lower end of right fibula K, P 🔧

    ● S89.392   Other physeal fracture of lower end of left fibula K, P 🔧

    ● ■ S89.399   Other physeal fracture of lower end of unspecified fibula K, P 🔧

The appropriate 7th character is to be added to each code from subcategories S89.8 and S89.9

> A   initial encounter
> D   subsequent encounter
> S   sequela

● S89.8   Other specified injuries of lower leg

    ● ■ S89.80   Other specified injuries of lower leg, unspecified side

    ● S89.81   Other specified injuries of lower right leg

    ● S89.82   Other specified injuries of lower left leg

● S89.9   Unspecified injury of lower leg

    ● ■ S89.90   Unspecified injury of lower leg, unspecified side

    ● ■ S89.91   Unspecified injury of lower right leg

    ● ■ S89.92   Unspecified injury of lower left leg

INJURIES TO THE ANKLE AND FOOT (S90-S99)

| Excludes2 | burns and corrosions (T20-T32)
fracture of ankle and malleolus (S82.-)
frostbite (T33-T34)
insect bite or sting, venomous (T63.4) |

● **S90   Superficial injury of ankle, foot and toes**

The appropriate 7th character is to be added to each code from category S90

> A   initial encounter
> D   subsequent encounter
> S   sequela

● S90.0   Contusion of ankle

    ● ■ S90.00   Contusion of unspecified ankle

    ● S90.01   Contusion of right ankle

    ● S90.02   Contusion of left ankle

● S90.1   Contusion of toe without damage to nail

    ● S90.11   Contusion of great toe without damage to nail

        ● S90.111   Contusion of right great toe without damage to nail

        ● S90.112   Contusion of left great toe without damage to nail

        ● ■ S90.119   Contusion of great toe without damage to nail, unspecified side

    ● S90.12   Contusion of lesser toe without damage to nail

        ● S90.121   Contusion of lesser right toe(s) without damage to nail

        ● S90.122   Contusion of lesser left toe(s) without damage to nail

        ● ■ S90.129   Contusion of lesser toe(s) without damage to nail, unspecified side

           Contusion of toe NOS

● S90.2   Contusion of toe with damage to nail

    ● S90.21   Contusion of great toe with damage to nail

        ● S90.211   Contusion of right great toe with damage to nail

        ● S90.212   Contusion of left great toe with damage to nail

        ● ■ S90.219   Contusion of great toe with damage to nail, unspecified side

    ● S90.22   Contusion of lesser toe with damage to nail

        ● S90.221   Contusion of lesser right toe(s) with damage to nail

        ● S90.222   Contusion of lesser left toe(s) with damage to nail

        ● ■ S90.229   Contusion of lesser toe(s) with damage to nail, unspecified side

● S90.3   Contusion of foot

| Excludes2 | contusion of toes (S90.1-, S90.2-) |

    ● ■ S90.30   Contusion of unspecified foot

        Contusion of foot NOS

    ● S90.31   Contusion of right foot

    ● S90.32   Contusion of left foot

● S90.4   Other superficial injuries of toe

    ● S90.41   Abrasion of toe

        ● S90.411   Abrasion, right great toe

        ● S90.412   Abrasion, left great toe

        ● ■ S90.413   Abrasion, unspecified great toe

        ● S90.414   Abrasion, lesser right toe(s)

        ● S90.415   Abrasion, lesser left toe(s)

        ● ■ S90.416   Abrasion, unspecified lesser toe(s)

    ● S90.42   Blister (nonthermal) of toe

        ● S90.421   Blister (nonthermal), right great toe

        ● S90.422   Blister (nonthermal), left great toe

        ● ■ S90.423   Blister (nonthermal), unspecified great toe

        ● S90.424   Blister (nonthermal), lesser right toe(s)

        ● S90.425   Blister (nonthermal), lesser left toe(s)

        ● ■ S90.426   Blister (nonthermal), unspecified lesser toe(s)

    ● S90.44   External constriction of toe

        Hair tourniquet syndrome of toe

        ● S90.441   External constriction, right great toe

        ● S90.442   External constriction, left great toe

        ● ■ S90.443   External constriction, unspecified great toe

        ● S90.444   External constriction, lesser right toe(s)

        ● S90.445   External constriction, lesser left toe(s)

        ● ■ S90.446   External constriction, unspecified lesser toe(s)

● Unacceptable First-Listed Diagnosis   ● Use Additional Character(s)   ■ Unspecified   **OGCR** Official Guidelines for Coding and Reporting

🔧 Complication\Comorbidity   🔧 Major C\C | Excludes 1 | | Excludes 2 | Includes   Use additional   Code first   Code also

CHAPTER 19 (S00-T98)

1511

- ● **S90.45 Superficial foreign body of toe**
  Splinter in the toe
  - ● **S90.451 Superficial foreign body, right great toe**
  - ● **S90.452 Superficial foreign body, left great toe**
  - ● ▪ **S90.453 Superficial foreign body, unspecified great toe**
  - ● **S90.454 Superficial foreign body, lesser right toe(s)**
  - ● **S90.455 Superficial foreign body, lesser left toe(s)**
  - ● ▪ **S90.456 Superficial foreign body, unspecified lesser toe(s)**
- ● **S90.46 Insect bite (nonvenomous) of toe**
  - ● **S90.461 Insect bite (nonvenomous), right great toe**
  - ● **S90.462 Insect bite (nonvenomous), left great toe**
  - ● ▪ **S90.463 Insect bite (nonvenomous), unspecified great toe**
  - ● **S90.464 Insect bite (nonvenomous), lesser right toe(s)**
  - ● **S90.465 Insect bite (nonvenomous), lesser left toe(s)**
  - ● ▪ **S90.466 Insect bite (nonvenomous), unspecified lesser toe(s)**
- ● **S90.47 Other superficial bite of toe**
  Excludes1 open bite of toe (S91.15-, S91.25-)
  - ● **S90.471 Other superficial bite of right great toe**
  - ● **S90.472 Other superficial bite of left great toe**
  - ● ▪ **S90.473 Other superficial bite of unspecified great toe**
  - ● **S90.474 Other superficial bite of lesser right toe(s)**
  - ● **S90.475 Other superficial bite of lesser left toe(s)**
  - ● ▪ **S90.476 Other superficial bite of unspecified lesser toe(s)**
- ● **S90.5 Other superficial injuries of ankle**
  - ● **S90.51 Abrasion of ankle**
    - ● **S90.511 Abrasion, right ankle**
    - ● **S90.512 Abrasion, left ankle**
    - ● ▪ **S90.519 Abrasion, unspecified ankle**
  - ● **S90.52 Blister (nonthermal) of ankle**
    - ● **S90.521 Blister (nonthermal), right ankle**
    - ● **S90.522 Blister (nonthermal), left ankle**
    - ● ▪ **S90.529 Blister (nonthermal), unspecified ankle**
  - ● **S90.54 External constriction of ankle**
    - ● **S90.541 External constriction, right ankle**
    - ● **S90.542 External constriction, left ankle**
    - ● ▪ **S90.549 External constriction, unspecified ankle**
  - ● **S90.55 Superficial foreign body of ankle**
    Splinter in the ankle
    - ● **S90.551 Superficial foreign body, right ankle**
    - ● **S90.552 Superficial foreign body, left ankle**

- ● ▪ **S90.559 Superficial foreign body, unspecified ankle**
- ● **S90.56 Insect bite (nonvenomous) of ankle**
  - ● **S90.561 Insect bite (nonvenomous), right ankle**
  - ● **S90.562 Insect bite (nonvenomous), left ankle**
  - ● ▪ **S90.569 Insect bite (nonvenomous), unspecified ankle**
- ● **S90.57 Other superficial bite of ankle**
  Excludes1 open bite of ankle (S91.05-)
  - ● **S90.571 Other superficial bite of ankle, right ankle**
  - ● **S90.572 Other superficial bite of ankle, left ankle**
  - ● ▪ **S90.579 Other superficial bite of ankle, unspecified ankle**
- ● **S90.8 Other superficial injuries of foot**
  - ● **S90.81 Abrasion of foot**
    - ● **S90.811 Abrasion, right foot**
    - ● **S90.812 Abrasion, left foot**
    - ● ▪ **S90.819 Abrasion, unspecified foot**
  - ● **S90.82 Blister (nonthermal) of foot**
    - ● **S90.821 Blister (nonthermal), right foot**
    - ● **S90.822 Blister (nonthermal), left foot**
    - ● ▪ **S90.829 Blister (nonthermal), unspecified foot**
  - ● **S90.84 External constriction of foot**
    - ● **S90.841 External constriction, right foot**
    - ● **S90.842 External constriction, left foot**
    - ● ▪ **S90.849 External constriction, unspecified foot**
  - ● **S90.85 Superficial foreign body of foot**
    Splinter in the foot
    - ● **S90.851 Superficial foreign body, right foot**
    - ● **S90.852 Superficial foreign body, left foot**
    - ● ▪ **S90.859 Superficial foreign body, unspecified foot**
  - ● **S90.86 Insect bite (nonvenomous) of foot**
    - ● **S90.861 Insect bite (nonvenomous), right foot**
    - ● **S90.862 Insect bite (nonvenomous), left foot**
    - ● ▪ **S90.869 Insect bite (nonvenomous), unspecified foot**
  - ● **S90.87 Other superficial bite of foot**
    Excludes1 open bite of foot (S91.35-)
    - ● **S90.871 Other superficial bite of right foot**
    - ● **S90.872 Other superficial bite of left foot**
    - ● ▪ **S90.879 Other superficial bite of unspecified foot**
- ● **S90.9 Unspecified superficial injury of ankle, foot and toe**
  - ● **S90.91 Unspecified superficial injury of ankle**
    - ● ▪ **S90.911 Unspecified superficial injury of right ankle**
    - ● ▪ **S90.912 Unspecified superficial injury of left ankle**
    - ● ▪ **S90.919 Unspecified superficial injury of unspecified ankle**

● S90.92   Unspecified superficial injury of foot
    ● ▪ S90.921   Unspecified superficial injury of right foot
    ● ▪ S90.922   Unspecified superficial injury of left foot
    ● ▪ S90.929   Unspecified superficial injury of unspecified foot

   S90.93   Unspecified superficial injury of toes
    ● ▪ S90.931   Unspecified superficial injury of right great toe
    ● ▪ S90.932   Unspecified superficial injury of left great toe
    ● ▪ S90.933   Unspecified superficial injury of unspecified great toe
    ● ▪ S90.934   Unspecified superficial injury of lesser right toe(s)
    ● ▪ S90.935   Unspecified superficial injury of lesser left toe(s)
    ● ▪ S90.936   Unspecified superficial injury of unspecified lesser toe(s)

● S91   **Open wound of ankle, foot and toes**
    Code also any associated wound infection
    Excludes1   open fracture of ankle, foot and toes (S92.- with 7th character B)
            traumatic amputation of ankle and foot (S98.-)

    The appropriate 7th character is to be added to each code from category S91

     A   initial encounter
     D   subsequent encounter
     S   sequela

   ● S91.0   **Open wound of ankle**
    ● S91.00   Unspecified open wound of ankle
     ● ▪ S91.001   Unspecified open wound, right ankle
     ● ▪ S91.002   Unspecified open wound, left ankle
     ● ▪ S91.009   Unspecified open wound, unspecified ankle

    ● S91.01   Laceration without foreign body of ankle
     ● S91.011   Laceration without foreign body, right ankle
     ● S91.012   Laceration without foreign body, left ankle
     ● ▪ S91.019   Laceration without foreign body, unspecified ankle

    ● S91.02   Laceration with foreign body of ankle
     ● S91.021   Laceration with foreign body, right ankle
     ● S91.022   Laceration with foreign body, left ankle
     ● ▪ S91.029   Laceration with foreign body, unspecified ankle

    ● S91.03   Puncture wound without foreign body of ankle
     ● S91.031   Puncture wound without foreign body, right ankle
     ● S91.032   Puncture wound without foreign body, left ankle
     ● ▪ S91.039   Puncture wound without foreign body, unspecified ankle

    ● S91.04   Puncture wound with foreign body of ankle

● S91.041   Puncture wound with foreign body, right ankle
  ● S91.042   Puncture wound with foreign body, left ankle
  ● ▪ S91.049   Puncture wound with foreign body, unspecified ankle

  ● S91.05   Open bite of ankle
    Excludes1   superficial bite of ankle (S90.56-, S90.57-)
    ● S91.051   Open bite, right ankle
    ● S91.052   Open bite, left ankle
    ● ▪ S91.059   Open bite, unspecified ankle

● S91.1   **Open wound of toe without damage to nail**
  ● S91.10   Unspecified open wound of toe without damage to nail
    ● ▪ S91.101   Unspecified open wound of right great toe without damage to nail
    ● ▪ S91.102   Unspecified open wound of left great toe without damage to nail
    ● ▪ S91.103   Unspecified open wound of unspecified great toe without damage to nail
    ● ▪ S91.104   Unspecified open wound of lesser right toe(s) without damage to nail
    ● ▪ S91.105   Unspecified open wound of lesser left toe(s) without damage to nail
    ● ▪ S91.106   Unspecified open wound of unspecified lesser toe(s) without damage to nail
    ● ▪ S91.109   Unspecified open wound of unspecified toe(s) without damage to nail

  ● S91.11   Laceration without foreign body of toe without damage to nail
    ● S91.111   Laceration without foreign body of right great toe without damage to nail
    ● S91.112   Laceration without foreign body of left great toe without damage to nail
    ● ▪ S91.113   Laceration without foreign body of unspecified great toe without damage to nail
    ● S91.114   Laceration without foreign body of lesser right toe(s) without damage to nail
    ● S91.115   Laceration without foreign body of lesser left toe(s) without damage to nail
    ● ▪ S91.116   Laceration without foreign body of unspecified lesser toe(s) without damage to nail
    ● ▪ S91.119   Laceration without foreign body of unspecified toe without damage to nail

  ● S91.12   Laceration with foreign body of toe without damage to nail
    ● S91.121   Laceration with foreign body of right great toe without damage to nail
    ● S91.122   Laceration with foreign body of left great toe without damage to nail

● ▪ S91.123 Laceration with foreign body of unspecified great toe without damage to nail

  ● S91.124 Laceration with foreign body of right lesser toe(s) without damage to nail

  ● S91.125 Laceration with foreign body of left lesser toe(s) without damage to nail

● ▪ S91.126 Laceration with foreign body of unspecified lesser toe(s) without damage to nail

● ▪ S91.129 Laceration with foreign body of unspecified toe(s) without damage to nail

● S91.13 Puncture wound without foreign body of toe without damage to nail

  ● S91.131 Puncture wound without foreign body of right great toe without damage to nail

  ● S91.132 Puncture wound without foreign body of left great toe without damage to nail

● ▪ S91.133 Puncture wound without foreign body of unspecified great toe without damage to nail

  ● S91.134 Puncture wound without foreign body of right lesser toe(s) without damage to nail

  ● S91.135 Puncture wound without foreign body of left lesser toe(s) without damage to nail

● ▪ S91.136 Puncture wound without foreign body of unspecified lesser toe(s) without damage to nail

● ▪ S91.139 Puncture wound without foreign body of unspecified toe(s) without damage to nail

● S91.14 Puncture wound with foreign body of toe without damage to nail

  ● S91.141 Puncture wound with foreign body of right great toe without damage to nail

  ● S91.142 Puncture wound with foreign body of left great toe without damage to nail

● ▪ S91.143 Puncture wound with foreign body of unspecified great toe without damage to nail

  ● S91.144 Puncture wound with foreign body of right lesser toe(s) without damage to nail

  ● S91.145 Puncture wound with foreign body of left lesser toe(s) without damage to nail

● ▪ S91.146 Puncture wound with foreign body of unspecified lesser toe(s) without damage to nail

● ▪ S91.149 Puncture wound with foreign body of unspecified toe(s) without damage to nail

● S91.15 Open bite of toe without damage to nail
         Bite of toe NOS
         Excludes1 superficial bite of toe (S90.46-, S90.47-)

  ● S91.151 Open bite of right great toe without damage to nail

  ● S91.152 Open bite of left great toe without damage to nail

● ▪ S91.153 Open bite of unspecified great toe without damage to nail

  ● S91.154 Open bite of right lesser toe(s) without damage to nail

  ● S91.155 Open bite of left lesser toe(s) without damage to nail

● ▪ S91.156 Open bite of unspecified lesser toe(s) without damage to nail

● ▪ S91.159 Open bite of unspecified toe(s) without damage to nail

● S91.2 Open wound of toe with damage to nail

  ● S91.20 Unspecified open wound of toe with damage to nail

● ▪ S91.201 Unspecified open wound of right great toe with damage to nail

● ▪ S91.202 Unspecified open wound of left great toe with damage to nail

● ▪ S91.203 Unspecified open wound of unspecified great toe with damage to nail

● ▪ S91.204 Unspecified open wound of right lesser toe(s) with damage to nail

● ▪ S91.205 Unspecified open wound of left lesser toe(s) with damage to nail

● ▪ S91.206 Unspecified open wound of unspecified lesser toe(s) with damage to nail

● ▪ S91.209 Unspecified open wound of unspecified toe(s) with damage to nail

  ● S91.21 Laceration without foreign body of toe with damage to nail

  ● S91.211 Laceration without foreign body of right great toe with damage to nail

  ● S91.212 Laceration without foreign body of left great toe with damage to nail

● ▪ S91.213 Laceration without foreign body of unspecified great toe with damage to nail

  ● S91.214 Laceration without foreign body of right lesser toe(s) with damage to nail

  ● S91.215 Laceration without foreign body of left lesser toe(s) with damage to nail

● ▪ S91.216 Laceration without foreign body of unspecified lesser toe(s) with damage to nail

● ▪ S91.219 Laceration without foreign body of unspecified toe(s) with damage to nail

  ● S91.22 Laceration with foreign body of toe with damage to nail

  ● S91.221 Laceration with foreign body of right great toe with damage to nail

● Unacceptable First-Listed Diagnosis   ● Use Additional Character(s)   ▪ Unspecified   **OGCR** Official Guidelines for Coding and Reporting
🗝 Complication\Comorbidity   🗝 Major C\C   Excludes 1   Excludes 2   Includes   Use additional   Code first   Code also

● S91.222   Laceration with foreign body of left great toe with damage to nail

● ▪ S91.223   Laceration with foreign body of unspecified great toe with damage to nail

● S91.224   Laceration with foreign body of right lesser toe(s) with damage to nail

● S91.225   Laceration with foreign body of left lesser toe(s) with damage to nail

● ▪ S91.226   Laceration with foreign body of unspecified lesser toe(s) with damage to nail

● ▪ S91.229   Laceration with foreign body of unspecified toe(s) with damage to nail

● S91.23   Puncture wound without foreign body of toe with damage to nail

● S91.231   Puncture wound without foreign body of right great toe with damage to nail

● S91.232   Puncture wound without foreign body of left great toe with damage to nail

● ▪ S91.233   Puncture wound without foreign body of unspecified great toe with damage to nail

● S91.234   Puncture wound without foreign body of right lesser toe(s) with damage to nail

● S91.235   Puncture wound without foreign body of left lesser toe(s) with damage to nail

● ▪ S91.236   Puncture wound without foreign body of unspecified lesser toe(s) with damage to nail

● ▪ S91.239   Puncture wound without foreign body of unspecified toe(s) with damage to nail

● S91.24   Puncture wound with foreign body of toe with damage to nail

● S91.241   Puncture wound with foreign body of right great toe with damage to nail

● S91.242   Puncture wound with foreign body of left great toe with damage to nail

● ▪ S91.243   Puncture wound with foreign body of unspecified great toe with damage to nail

● S91.244   Puncture wound with foreign body of right lesser toe(s) with damage to nail

● S91.245   Puncture wound with foreign body of left lesser toe(s) with damage to nail

● ▪ S91.246   Puncture wound with foreign body of unspecified lesser toe(s) with damage to nail

● ▪ S91.249   Puncture wound with foreign body of unspecified toe(s) with damage to nail

● S91.25   Open bite of toe with damage to nail
    Bite of toe with damage to nail NOS
    | Excludes1 | superficial bite of toe (S90.46-, S90.47-)

● S91.251   Open bite of right great toe with damage to nail

● S91.252   Open bite of left great toe with damage to nail

● ▪ S91.253   Open bite of unspecified great toe with damage to nail

● S91.254   Open bite of right lesser toe(s) with damage to nail

● S91.255   Open bite of left lesser toe(s) with damage to nail

● ▪ S91.256   Open bite of unspecified lesser toe(s) with damage to nail

● ▪ S91.259   Open bite of unspecified toe(s) with damage to nail

● S91.3   Open wound of foot

● S91.30   Unspecified open wound of foot

● ▪ S91.301   Unspecified open wound, right foot

● ▪ S91.302   Unspecified open wound, left foot

● ▪ S91.309   Unspecified open wound, unspecified foot

● S91.31   Laceration without foreign body of foot

● S91.311   Laceration without foreign body, right foot

● S91.312   Laceration without foreign body, left foot

● ▪ S91.319   Laceration without foreign body, unspecified foot

● S91.32   Laceration with foreign body of foot

● S91.321   Laceration with foreign body, right foot

● S91.322   Laceration with foreign body, left foot

● ▪ S91.329   Laceration with foreign body, unspecified foot

● S91.33   Puncture wound without foreign body of foot

● S91.331   Puncture wound without foreign body, right foot

● S91.332   Puncture wound without foreign body, left foot

● ▪ S91.339   Puncture wound without foreign body, unspecified foot

● S91.34   Puncture wound with foreign body of foot

● S91.341   Puncture wound with foreign body, right foot

● S91.342   Puncture wound with foreign body, left foot

● ▪ S91.349   Puncture wound with foreign body, unspecified foot

● S91.35   Open bite of foot
    | Excludes1 | superficial bite of foot (S90.86-, S90.87-)

● S91.351   Open bite, right foot

● S91.352   Open bite, left foot

● ▪ S91.359   Open bite, unspecified foot

● Unacceptable First-Listed Diagnosis   ● Use Additional Character(s)   ▪ Unspecified   **OGCR** Official Guidelines for Coding and Reporting

 Complication\Comorbidity   Major C\C | Excludes 1 | | Excludes 2 | Includes   Use additional   Code first   Code also

1515

CHAPTER 19 (S00-T98)

● **S92**   **Fracture of foot and toe, except ankle**
     A fracture not identified as displaced or nondisplaced
       should be coded to displaced

     | Excludes1 | traumatic amputation of ankle and foot (S98.-)

     | Excludes2 | fracture of ankle (S82.-)
                   fracture of malleolus (S82.-)

     The appropriate 7th character is to be added to each code
       from category S92
     A fracture not designated as open or closed should be
       coded to closed

> A   initial encounter for closed fracture
> B   initial encounter for open fracture
> D   subsequent encounter for fracture with routine
>   healing
> G   subsequent encounter for fracture with delayed
>   healing
> K   subsequent encounter for fracture with nonunion
> P   subsequent encounter for fracture with malunion
> S   sequela

● **S92.0**   **Fracture of calcaneus**
     Heel bone   Os calcis

   ● **S92.00**   **Unspecified fracture of calcaneus**

     ● ■ **S92.001**   Unspecified fracture of right calcaneus B, K, P 🦠

     ● ■ **S92.002**   Unspecified fracture of left calcaneus B, K, P 🦠

     ● ■ **S92.009**   Unspecified fracture of unspecified calcaneus B, K, P 🦠

   ● **S92.01**   **Fracture of body of calcaneus**

     ● **S92.011**   Displaced fracture of body of right calcaneus B, K, P 🦠

     ● **S92.012**   Displaced fracture of body of left calcaneus B, K, P 🦠

     ● ■ **S92.013**   Displaced fracture of body of unspecified calcaneus B, K, P 🦠

     ● **S92.014**   Nondisplaced fracture of body of right calcaneus B, K, P 🦠

     ● **S92.015**   Nondisplaced fracture of body of left calcaneus B, K, P 🦠

     ● ■ **S92.016**   Nondisplaced fracture of body of unspecified calcaneus B, K, P 🦠

   ● **S92.02**   **Fracture of anterior process of calcaneus**

     ● **S92.021**   Displaced fracture of anterior process of right calcaneus B, K, P 🦠

     ● **S92.022**   Displaced fracture of anterior process of left calcaneus B, K, P 🦠

     ● ■ **S92.023**   Displaced fracture of anterior process of unspecified calcaneus B, K, P 🦠

     ● **S92.024**   Nondisplaced fracture of anterior process of right calcaneus B, K, P 🦠

     ● **S92.025**   Nondisplaced fracture of anterior process of left calcaneus B, K, P 🦠

     ● ■ **S92.026**   Nondisplaced fracture of anterior process of unspecified calcaneus B, K, P 🦠

   ● **S92.03**   **Avulsion fracture of tuberosity of calcaneus**

     ● **S92.031**   Displaced avulsion fracture of tuberosity of right calcaneus B, K, P 🦠

     ● **S92.032**   Displaced avulsion fracture of tuberosity of left calcaneus B, K, P 🦠

     ● ■ **S92.033**   Displaced avulsion fracture of tuberosity of unspecified calcaneus B, K, P 🦠

     ● **S92.034**   Nondisplaced avulsion fracture of tuberosity of right calcaneus B, K, P 🦠

     ● **S92.035**   Nondisplaced avulsion fracture of tuberosity of left calcaneus B, K, P 🦠

     ● ■ **S92.036**   Nondisplaced avulsion fracture of tuberosity of unspecified calcaneus B, K, P 🦠

   ● **S92.04**   **Other fracture of tuberosity of calcaneus**

     ● **S92.041**   Displaced other fracture of tuberosity of right calcaneus B, K, P 🦠

     ● **S92.042**   Displaced other fracture of tuberosity of left calcaneus B, K, P 🦠

     ● ■ **S92.043**   Displaced other fracture of tuberosity of unspecified calcaneus B, K, P 🦠

     ● **S92.044**   Nondisplaced other fracture of tuberosity of right calcaneus B, K, P 🦠

     ● **S92.045**   Nondisplaced other fracture of tuberosity of left calcaneus B, K, P 🦠

     ● ■ **S92.046**   Nondisplaced other fracture of tuberosity of unspecified calcaneus B, K, P 🦠

   ● **S92.05**   **Other extraarticular fracture of calcaneus**

     ● **S92.051**   Displaced other extraarticular fracture of right calcaneus B, K, P 🦠

     ● **S92.052**   Displaced other extraarticular fracture of left calcaneus B, K, P 🦠

     ● ■ **S92.053**   Displaced other extraarticular fracture of unspecified calcaneus B, K, P 🦠

     ● **S92.054**   Nondisplaced other extraarticular fracture of right calcaneus B, K, P 🦠

     ● **S92.055**   Nondisplaced other extraarticular fracture of left calcaneus B, K, P 🦠

     ● ■ **S92.056**   Nondisplaced other extraarticular fracture of unspecified calcaneus B, K, P 🦠

   ● **S92.06**   **Intraarticular fracture of calcaneus**

     ● **S92.061**   Displaced intraarticular fracture of right calcaneus B, K, P 🦠

     ● **S92.062**   Displaced intraarticular fracture of left calcaneus B, K, P 🦠

     ● ■ **S92.063**   Displaced intraarticular fracture of unspecified calcaneus B, K, P 🦠

     ● **S92.064**   Nondisplaced intraarticular fracture of right calcaneus B, K, P 🦠

     ● **S92.065**   Nondisplaced intraarticular fracture of left calcaneus B, K, P 🦠

● ■ S92.066   Nondisplaced intraarticular fracture of unspecified calcaneus B, K, P 🗞

● S92.1   **Fracture of talus**
     Astragalus

   ● S92.10   Unspecified fracture of talus

     ● ■ S92.101   Unspecified fracture of right talus B, K, P 🗞

     ● ■ S92.102   Unspecified fracture of left talus B, K, P 🗞

     ● ■ S92.109   Unspecified fracture of unspecified talus B, K, P 🗞

   ● S92.11   Fracture of neck of talus

     ● S92.111   Displaced fracture of neck of right talus B, K, P 🗞

     ● S92.112   Displaced fracture of neck of left talus B, K, P 🗞

     ● ■ S92.113   Displaced fracture of neck of unspecified talus B, K, P 🗞

     ● S92.114   Nondisplaced fracture of neck of right talus B, K, P 🗞

     ● S92.115   Nondisplaced fracture of neck of left talus B, K, P 🗞

     ● ■ S92.116   Nondisplaced fracture of neck of unspecified talus B, K, P 🗞

   ● S92.12   Fracture of body of talus

     ● S92.121   Displaced fracture of body of right talus B, K, P 🗞

     ● S92.122   Displaced fracture of body of left talus B, K, P 🗞

     ● ■ S92.123   Displaced fracture of body of unspecified talus B, K, P 🗞

     ● S92.124   Nondisplaced fracture of body of right talus B, K, P 🗞

     ● S92.125   Nondisplaced fracture of body of left talus B, K, P 🗞

     ● ■ S92.126   Nondisplaced fracture of body of unspecified talus B, K, P 🗞

   ● S92.13   Fracture of posterior process of talus

     ● S92.131   Displaced fracture of posterior process of right talus B, K, P 🗞

     ● S92.132   Displaced fracture of posterior process of left talus B, K, P 🗞

     ● ■ S92.133   Displaced fracture of posterior process of unspecified talus B, K, P 🗞

     ● S92.134   Nondisplaced fracture of posterior process of right talus B, K, P 🗞

     ● S92.135   Nondisplaced fracture of posterior process of left talus B, K, P 🗞

     ● ■ S92.136   Nondisplaced fracture of posterior process of unspecified talus B, K, P 🗞

   ● S92.14   Dome fracture of talus

     | Excludes1 | osteochondritis dissecans (M93.2) |

     ● S92.141   Displaced dome fracture of right talus B, K, P 🗞

     ● S92.142   Displaced dome fracture of left talus B, K, P 🗞

● ■ S92.143   Displaced dome fracture of unspecified talus B, K, P 🗞

● S92.144   Nondisplaced dome fracture of right talus B, K, P 🗞

● S92.145   Nondisplaced dome fracture of left talus B, K, P 🗞

● ■ S92.146   Nondisplaced dome fracture of unspecified talus B, K, P 🗞

● S92.15   Avulsion fracture (chip fracture) of talus

   ● S92.151   Displaced avulsion fracture (chip fracture) of right talus B, K, P 🗞

   ● S92.152   Displaced avulsion fracture (chip fracture) of left talus B, K, P 🗞

   ● ■ S92.153   Displaced avulsion fracture (chip fracture) of unspecified talus B, K, P 🗞

   ● S92.154   Nondisplaced avulsion fracture (chip fracture) of right talus B, K, P 🗞

   ● S92.155   Nondisplaced avulsion fracture (chip fracture) of left talus B, K, P 🗞

   ● ■ S92.156   Nondisplaced avulsion fracture (chip fracture) of unspecified talus B, K, P 🗞

● S92.19   Other fracture of talus

   ● S92.191   Other fracture of right talus B, K, P 🗞

   ● S92.192   Other fracture of left talus B, K, P 🗞

   ● ■ S92.199   Other fracture of unspecified talus B, K, P 🗞

● S92.2   **Fracture of other and unspecified tarsal bone(s)**

   ● S92.20   Fracture of unspecified tarsal bone(s)

     ● ■ S92.201   Fracture of unspecified tarsal bone(s) of right foot B, K, P 🗞

     ● ■ S92.202   Fracture of unspecified tarsal bone(s) of left foot B, K, P 🗞

     ● ■ S92.209   Fracture of unspecified tarsal bone(s) of unspecified foot B, K, P 🗞

   ● S92.21   Fracture of cuboid bone

     ● S92.211   Displaced fracture of cuboid bone of right foot B, K, P 🗞

     ● S92.212   Displaced fracture of cuboid bone of left foot B, K, P 🗞

     ● ■ S92.213   Displaced fracture of cuboid bone of unspecified foot B, K, P 🗞

     ● S92.214   Nondisplaced fracture of cuboid bone of right foot B, K, P 🗞

     ● S92.215   Nondisplaced fracture of cuboid bone of left foot B, K, P 🗞

     ● ■ S92.216   Nondisplaced fracture of cuboid bone of unspecified foot B, K, P 🗞

   ● S92.22   Fracture of lateral cuneiform

     ● S92.221   Displaced fracture of lateral cuneiform of right foot B, K, P 🗞

     ● S92.222   Displaced fracture of lateral cuneiform of left foot B, K, P 🗞

     ● ■ S92.223   Displaced fracture of lateral cuneiform of unspecified foot B, K, P 🗞

- S92.224   Nondisplaced fracture of lateral cuneiform of right foot B, K, P 🦠
- S92.225   Nondisplaced fracture of lateral cuneiform of left foot B, K, P 🦠
- ▪ S92.226   Nondisplaced fracture of lateral cuneiform of unspecified foot B, K, P 🦠
- S92.23   Fracture of intermediate cuneiform
  - S92.231   Displaced fracture of intermediate cuneiform of right foot B, K, P 🦠
  - S92.232   Displaced fracture of intermediate cuneiform of left foot B, K, P 🦠
  - ▪ S92.233   Displaced fracture of intermediate cuneiform of unspecified foot B, K, P 🦠
  - S92.234   Nondisplaced fracture of intermediate cuneiform of right foot B, K, P 🦠
  - S92.235   Nondisplaced fracture of intermediate cuneiform of left foot B, K, P 🦠
  - ▪ S92.236   Nondisplaced fracture of intermediate cuneiform of unspecified foot B, K, P 🦠
- S92.24   Fracture of medial cuneiform
  - S92.241   Displaced fracture of medial cuneiform of right foot B, K, P 🦠
  - S92.242   Displaced fracture of medial cuneiform of left foot B, K, P 🦠
  - ▪ S92.243   Displaced fracture of medial cuneiform of unspecified foot B, K, P 🦠
  - S92.244   Nondisplaced fracture of medial cuneiform of right foot B, K, P 🦠
  - S92.245   Nondisplaced fracture of medial cuneiform of left foot B, K, P 🦠
  - ▪ S92.246   Nondisplaced fracture of medial cuneiform of unspecified foot B, K, P 🦠
- S92.25   Fracture of navicular [scaphoid] of foot
  - S92.251   Displaced fracture of navicular [scaphoid] of right foot B, K, P 🦠
  - S92.252   Displaced fracture of navicular [scaphoid] of left foot B, K, P 🦠
  - ▪ S92.253   Displaced fracture of navicular [scaphoid] of unspecified foot B, K, P 🦠
  - S92.254   Nondisplaced fracture of navicular [scaphoid] of right foot B, K, P 🦠
  - S92.255   Nondisplaced fracture of navicular [scaphoid] of left foot B, K, P 🦠
  - ▪ S92.256   Nondisplaced fracture of navicular [scaphoid] of unspecified foot B, K, P 🦠
- S92.3   Fracture of metatarsal bone(s)
  - S92.30   Fracture of unspecified metatarsal bone(s)
    - ▪ S92.301   Fracture of unspecified metatarsal bone(s), right foot B, K, P 🦠
    - ▪ S92.302   Fracture of unspecified metatarsal bone(s), left foot B, K, P 🦠

- ▪ S92.309   Fracture of unspecified metatarsal bone(s), unspecified foot B, K, P 🦠
- S92.31   Fracture of first metatarsal bone
  - S92.311   Displaced fracture of first metatarsal bone, right foot B, K, P 🦠
  - S92.312   Displaced fracture of first metatarsal bone, left foot B, K, P 🦠
  - ▪ S92.313   Displaced fracture of first metatarsal bone, unspecified foot B, K, P 🦠
  - S92.314   Nondisplaced fracture of first metatarsal bone, right foot B, K, P 🦠
  - S92.315   Nondisplaced fracture of first metatarsal bone, left foot B, K, P 🦠
  - ▪ S92.316   Nondisplaced fracture of first metatarsal bone, unspecified foot B, K, P 🦠
- S92.32   Fracture of second metatarsal bone
  - S92.321   Displaced fracture of second metatarsal bone, right foot B, K, P 🦠
  - S92.322   Displaced fracture of second metatarsal bone, left foot B, K, P 🦠
  - ▪ S92.323   Displaced fracture of second metatarsal bone, unspecified foot B, K, P 🦠
  - S92.324   Nondisplaced fracture of second metatarsal bone, right foot B, K, P 🦠
  - S92.325   Nondisplaced fracture of second metatarsal bone, left foot B, K, P 🦠
  - ▪ S92.326   Nondisplaced fracture of second metatarsal bone, unspecified foot B, K, P 🦠
- S92.33   Fracture of third metatarsal bone
  - S92.331   Displaced fracture of third metatarsal bone, right foot B, K, P 🦠
  - S92.332   Displaced fracture of third metatarsal bone, left foot B, K, P 🦠
  - ▪ S92.333   Displaced fracture of third metatarsal bone, unspecified foot B, K, P 🦠
  - S92.334   Nondisplaced fracture of third metatarsal bone, right foot B, K, P 🦠
  - S92.335   Nondisplaced fracture of third metatarsal bone, left foot B, K, P 🦠
  - ▪ S92.336   Nondisplaced fracture of third metatarsal bone, unspecified foot B, K, P 🦠
- S92.34   Fracture of fourth metatarsal bone
  - S92.341   Displaced fracture of fourth metatarsal bone, right foot B, K, P 🦠

● Unacceptable First-Listed Diagnosis   ● Use Additional Character(s)   ▪ Unspecified   **OGCR** Official Guidelines for Coding and Reporting

🦠 Complication\Comorbidity   🦠 Major C\C   Excludes 1   Excludes 2   Includes   Use additional   Code first   Code also

● S92.342   Displaced fracture of fourth metatarsal bone, left foot
B, K, P 🦴

● S92.343   Displaced fracture of fourth metatarsal bone, unspecified foot
B, K, P 🦴

● ▪ S92.344   Nondisplaced fracture of fourth metatarsal bone, right foot
B, K, P 🦴

● S92.345   Nondisplaced fracture of fourth metatarsal bone, left foot
B, K, P 🦴

● ▪ S92.346   Nondisplaced fracture of fourth metatarsal bone, unspecified foot
B, K, P 🦴

● S92.35   Fracture of fifth metatarsal bone

● S92.351   Displaced fracture of fifth metatarsal bone, right foot
B, K, P 🦴

● S92.352   Displaced fracture of fifth metatarsal bone, left foot
B, K, P 🦴

● ▪ S92.353   Displaced fracture of fifth metatarsal bone, unspecified foot
B, K, P 🦴

● S92.354   Nondisplaced fracture of fifth metatarsal bone, right foot
B, K, P 🦴

● S92.355   Nondisplaced fracture of fifth metatarsal bone, left foot
B, K, P 🦴

● ▪ S92.356   Nondisplaced fracture of fifth metatarsal bone, unspecified foot
B, K, P 🦴

● S92.4   Fracture of great toe

● S92.40   Unspecified fracture of great toe

● ▪ S92.401   Displaced unspecified fracture of right great toe K, P 🦴

● ▪ S92.402   Displaced unspecified fracture of left great toe K, P 🦴

● ▪ S92.403   Displaced unspecified fracture of unspecified great toe K, P 🦴

● ▪ S92.404   Nondisplaced unspecified fracture of right great toe K, P 🦴

● ▪ S92.405   Nondisplaced unspecified fracture of left great toe K, P 🦴

● ▪ S92.406   Nondisplaced unspecified fracture of unspecified great toe K, P 🦴

● S92.41   Fracture of proximal phalanx of great toe

● S92.411   Displaced fracture of proximal phalanx of right great toe K, P 🦴

● S92.412   Displaced fracture of proximal phalanx of left great toe K, P 🦴

● ▪ S92.413   Displaced fracture of proximal phalanx of unspecified great toe K, P 🦴

● S92.414   Nondisplaced fracture of proximal phalanx of right great toe K, P 🦴

● S92.415   Nondisplaced fracture of proximal phalanx of left great toe K, P 🦴

● ▪ S92.416   Nondisplaced fracture of proximal phalanx of unspecified great toe K, P 🦴

● S92.42   Fracture of distal phalanx of great toe

● S92.421   Displaced fracture of distal phalanx of right great toe K, P 🦴

● S92.422   Displaced fracture of distal phalanx of left great toe K, P 🦴

● ▪ S92.423   Displaced fracture of distal phalanx of unspecified great toe K, P 🦴

● S92.424   Nondisplaced fracture of distal phalanx of right great toe K, P 🦴

● S92.425   Nondisplaced fracture of distal phalanx of left great toe K, P 🦴

● ▪ S92.426   Nondisplaced fracture of distal phalanx of unspecified great toe K, P 🦴

● S92.49   Other fracture of great toe

● S92.491   Other fracture of right great toe K, P 🦴

● S92.492   Other fracture of left great toe K, P 🦴

● ▪ S92.499   Other fracture of unspecified great toe K, P 🦴

● S92.5   Fracture of lesser toe(s)

● S92.50   Unspecified fracture of lesser toe(s)

● ▪ S92.501   Displaced unspecified fracture of right lesser toe(s) K, P 🦴

● ▪ S92.502   Displaced unspecified fracture of left lesser toe(s) K, P 🦴

● ▪ S92.503   Displaced unspecified fracture of unspecified lesser toe(s) K, P 🦴

● ▪ S92.504   Nondisplaced unspecified fracture of right lesser toe(s) K, P 🦴

● ▪ S92.505   Nondisplaced unspecified fracture of left lesser toe(s) K, P 🦴

● ▪ S92.506   Nondisplaced unspecified fracture of unspecified lesser toe(s) K, P 🦴

● S92.51   Fracture of proximal phalanx of lesser toe(s)

● S92.511   Displaced fracture of proximal phalanx of right lesser toe(s) K, P 🦴

● S92.512   Displaced fracture of proximal phalanx of left lesser toe(s) K, P 🦴

● ▪ S92.513   Displaced fracture of proximal phalanx of unspecified lesser toe(s) K, P 🦴

● S92.514   Nondisplaced fracture of proximal phalanx of right lesser toe(s) K, P 🦴

● S92.515   Nondisplaced fracture of proximal phalanx of left lesser toe(s) K, P 🦴

● ▪ S92.516   Nondisplaced fracture of proximal phalanx of unspecified lesser toe(s) K, P 🦴

● S92.52   Fracture of medial phalanx of lesser toe(s)

● S92.521   Displaced fracture of medial phalanx of right lesser toe(s) K, P 🦴

● S92.522   Displaced fracture of medial phalanx of left lesser toe(s) K, P 🦴

● Unacceptable First-Listed Diagnosis   ● Use Additional Character(s)   ▪ Unspecified   **OGCR** Official Guidelines for Coding and Reporting

 Complication\Comorbidity   🦴 Major C\C   [Excludes 1]   [Excludes 2]   Includes   Use additional   Code first   Code also

1519

CHAPTER 19 (S00-T98)

● ■ **S92.523**   Displaced fracture of medial phalanx of unspecified lesser toe(s) K, P 🦠

   ● **S92.524**   Nondisplaced fracture of medial phalanx of right lesser toe(s) K, P 🦠

   ● **S92.525**   Nondisplaced fracture of medial phalanx of left lesser toe(s) K, P 🦠

● ■ **S92.526**   Nondisplaced fracture of medial phalanx of unspecified lesser toe(s) K, P 🦠

● **S92.53**   Fracture of distal phalanx of lesser toe(s)

   ● **S92.531**   Displaced fracture of distal phalanx of right lesser toe(s) K, P 🦠

   ● **S92.532**   Displaced fracture of distal phalanx of left lesser toe(s) K, P 🦠

● ■ **S92.533**   Displaced fracture of distal phalanx of unspecified lesser toe(s) K, P 🦠

   ● **S92.534**   Nondisplaced fracture of distal phalanx of right lesser toe(s) K, P 🦠

   ● **S92.535**   Nondisplaced fracture of distal phalanx of left lesser toe(s) K, P 🦠

● ■ **S92.536**   Nondisplaced fracture of distal phalanx of unspecified lesser toe(s) K, P 🦠

● **S92.59**   Other fracture of lesser toe(s)

   ● **S92.591**   Other fracture of right lesser toe(s) K, P 🦠

   ● **S92.592**   Other fracture of left lesser toe(s) K, P 🦠

● ■ **S92.599**   Other fracture of unspecified lesser toe(s) K, P 🦠

● **S92.9**   Unspecified fracture of foot and toe

   ● **S92.90**   Unspecified fracture of foot

    ● ■ **S92.901**   Unspecified fracture of right foot B, K, P 🦠

    ● ■ **S92.902**   Unspecified fracture of left foot B, K, P 🦠

    ● ■ **S92.909**   Unspecified fracture of unspecified foot B, K, P 🦠

   ● **S92.91**   Unspecified fracture of toe

    ● ■ **S92.911**   Unspecified fracture of right toe(s) K, P 🦠

    ● ■ **S92.912**   Unspecified fracture of left toe(s) K, P 🦠

    ● ■ **S92.919**   Unspecified fracture of unspecified toe(s) K, P 🦠

● **S93**   **Dislocation and sprain of joints and ligaments at ankle, foot and toe level**

   Includes   avulsion of joint or ligament of ankle, foot and toe

      laceration of cartilage, joint or ligament of ankle, foot and toe

      sprain of cartilage, joint or ligament of ankle, foot and toe

      traumatic hemarthrosis of joint or ligament of ankle, foot and toe

      traumatic rupture of joint or ligament of ankle, foot and toe

      traumatic subluxation of joint or ligament of ankle, foot and toe

      traumatic tear of joint or ligament of ankle, foot and toe

   Code also any associated open wound

   Excludes2   strain of muscle and tendon of ankle and foot (S96.-)

   The appropriate 7th character is to be added to each code from category S93

     A   initial encounter
     D   subsequent encounter
     S   sequela

● **S93.0**   **Subluxation and dislocation of ankle joint**

     Subluxation and dislocation of astragalus
     Subluxation and dislocation of fibula, lower end
     Subluxation and dislocation of talus
     Subluxation and dislocation of tibia, lower end

   ● **S93.01**   Subluxation of right ankle joint

   ● **S93.02**   Subluxation of left ankle joint

   ● ■ **S93.03**   Subluxation of unspecified ankle joint

   ● **S93.04**   Dislocation of right ankle joint

   ● **S93.05**   Dislocation of left ankle joint

   ● ■ **S93.06**   Dislocation of unspecified ankle joint

● **S93.1**   **Subluxation and dislocation of toe**

   ● **S93.10**   Unspecified subluxation and dislocation of toe

     Dislocation of toe NOS
     Subluxation of toe NOS

    ● ■ **S93.101**   Unspecified subluxation of right toe(s)

    ● ■ **S93.102**   Unspecified subluxation of left toe(s)

    ● ■ **S93.103**   Unspecified subluxation of unspecified toe(s)

    ● ■ **S93.104**   Unspecified dislocation of right toe(s)

    ● ■ **S93.105**   Unspecified dislocation of left toe(s)

    ● ■ **S93.106**   Unspecified dislocation of unspecified toe(s)

   ● **S93.11**   Dislocation of interphalangeal joint

    ● **S93.111**   Dislocation of interphalangeal joint of right great toe

    ● **S93.112**   Dislocation of interphalangeal joint of left great toe

    ● ■ **S93.113**   Dislocation of interphalangeal joint of unspecified great toe

    ● **S93.114**   Dislocation of interphalangeal joint of right lesser toe(s)

    ● **S93.115**   Dislocation of interphalangeal joint of left lesser toe(s)

● ▪ S93.116　Dislocation of interphalangeal joint of unspecified lesser toe(s)

● ▪ S93.119　Dislocation of interphalangeal joint of unspecified toe(s)

● S93.12　Dislocation of metatarsophalangeal joint

　● S93.121　Dislocation of metatarsophalangeal joint of right great toe

　● S93.122　Dislocation of metatarsophalangeal joint of left great toe

　● ▪ S93.123　Dislocation of metatarsophalangeal joint of unspecified great toe

　● S93.124　Dislocation of metatarsophalangeal joint of right lesser toe(s)

　● S93.125　Dislocation of metatarsophalangeal joint of left lesser toe(s)

　● ▪ S93.126　Dislocation of metatarsophalangeal joint of unspecified lesser toe(s)

　● ▪ S93.129　Dislocation of metatarsophalangeal joint of unspecified toe(s)

● S93.13　Subluxation of interphalangeal joint

　● S93.131　Subluxation of interphalangeal joint of right great toe

　● S93.132　Subluxation of interphalangeal joint of left great toe

　● ▪ S93.133　Subluxation of interphalangeal joint of unspecified great toe

　● S93.134　Subluxation of interphalangeal joint of right lesser toe(s)

　● S93.135　Subluxation of interphalangeal joint of left lesser toe(s)

　● ▪ S93.136　Subluxation of interphalangeal joint of unspecified lesser toe(s)

　● ▪ S93.139　Subluxation of interphalangeal joint of unspecified toe(s)

● S93.14　Subluxation of metatarsophalangeal joint

　● S93.141　Subluxation of metatarsophalangeal joint of right great toe

　● S93.142　Subluxation of metatarsophalangeal joint of left great toe

　● ▪ S93.143　Subluxation of metatarsophalangeal joint of unspecified great toe

　● S93.144　Subluxation of metatarsophalangeal joint of right lesser toe(s)

　● S93.145　Subluxation of metatarsophalangeal joint of left lesser toe(s)

　● ▪ S93.146　Subluxation of metatarsophalangeal joint of unspecified lesser toe(s)

　● ▪ S93.149　Subluxation of metatarsophalangeal joint of unspecified toe(s)

● S93.3　Dislocation of foot
　　Excludes2　　dislocation of toe (S93.1-)

　● S93.30　Unspecified subluxation and dislocation of foot
　　　Dislocation of foot NOS
　　　Subluxation of foot NOS

　　● ▪ S93.301　Unspecified subluxation of right foot

　　● ▪ S93.302　Unspecified subluxation of left foot

　　● ▪ S93.303　Unspecified subluxation of unspecified foot

　　● ▪ S93.304　Unspecified dislocation of right foot

　　● ▪ S93.305　Unspecified dislocation of left foot

　　● ▪ S93.306　Unspecified dislocation of unspecified foot

　● S93.31　Subluxation and dislocation of tarsal joint

　　● S93.311　Subluxation of tarsal joint of right foot

　　● S93.312　Subluxation of tarsal joint of left foot

　　● ▪ S93.313　Subluxation of tarsal joint of unspecified foot

　　● S93.314　Dislocation of tarsal joint of right foot

　　● S93.315　Dislocation of tarsal joint of left foot

　　● ▪ S93.316　Dislocation of tarsal joint of unspecified foot

　● S93.32　Subluxation and dislocation of tarsometatarsal joint

　　● S93.321　Subluxation of tarsometatarsal joint of right foot

　　● S93.322　Subluxation of tarsometatarsal joint of left foot

　　● ▪ S93.323　Subluxation of tarsometatarsal joint of unspecified foot

　　● S93.324　Dislocation of tarsometatarsal joint of right foot

　　● S93.325　Dislocation of tarsometatarsal joint of left foot

　　● ▪ S93.326　Dislocation of tarsometatarsal joint of unspecified foot

　● S93.33　Other subluxation and dislocation of foot

　　● S93.331　Other subluxation of right foot

　　● S93.332　Other subluxation of left foot

　　● ▪ S93.333　Other subluxation of unspecified foot

　　● S93.334　Other dislocation of right foot

　　● S93.335　Other dislocation of left foot

　　● ▪ S93.336　Other dislocation of unspecified foot

● S93.4　Sprain of ankle
　　Injury to ligaments when one or more is stretched/torn
　　Excludes2　　injury of Achilles tendon (S86.0-)

　● S93.40　Sprain of unspecified ligament of ankle
　　　Sprain of ankle NOS
　　　Sprained ankle NOS

　　● ▪ S93.401　Sprain of unspecified ligament of right ankle

● Unacceptable First-Listed Diagnosis　　● Use Additional Character(s)　　▪ Unspecified　　OGCR Official Guidelines for Coding and Reporting

🗞 Complication\Comorbidity　　🗞 Major C\C　　Excludes 1　　Excludes 2　　Includes　　Use additional　　Code first　　Code also

1521

CHAPTER 19 (S00-T98)

● ■ **S93.402** Sprain of unspecified ligament of left ankle

● ■ **S93.409** Sprain of unspecified ligament of unspecified ankle

● **S93.41** Sprain of calcaneofibular ligament

  ● **S93.411** Sprain of calcaneofibular ligament of right ankle

  ● **S93.412** Sprain of calcaneofibular ligament of left ankle

  ● ■ **S93.419** Sprain of calcaneofibular ligament of unspecified ankle

● **S93.42** Sprain of deltoid ligament

  ● **S93.421** Sprain of deltoid ligament of right ankle

  ● **S93.422** Sprain of deltoid ligament of left ankle

  ● ■ **S93.429** Sprain of deltoid ligament of unspecified ankle

● **S93.43** Sprain of tibiofibular ligament

  ● **S93.431** Sprain of tibiofibular ligament of right ankle

  ● **S93.432** Sprain of tibiofibular ligament of left ankle

  ● ■ **S93.439** Sprain of tibiofibular ligament of unspecified ankle

● **S93.49** Sprain of other ligament of ankle
      Sprain of internal collateral ligament
      Sprain of talofibular ligament

  ● **S93.491** Sprain of other ligament of right ankle

  ● **S93.492** Sprain of other ligament of left ankle

  ● ■ **S93.499** Sprain of other ligament of unspecified ankle

● **S93.5** Sprain of toe

  ● **S93.50** Unspecified sprain of toe

    ● ■ **S93.501** Unspecified sprain of right great toe

    ● ■ **S93.502** Unspecified sprain of left great toe

    ● ■ **S93.503** Unspecified sprain of unspecified great toe

    ● ■ **S93.504** Unspecified sprain of right lesser toe(s)

    ● ■ **S93.505** Unspecified sprain of left lesser toe(s)

    ● ■ **S93.506** Unspecified sprain of unspecified lesser toe(s)

    ● ■ **S93.509** Unspecified sprain of unspecified toe(s)

  ● **S93.51** Sprain of interphalangeal joint of toe

    ● **S93.511** Sprain of interphalangeal joint of right great toe

    ● **S93.512** Sprain of interphalangeal joint of left great toe

    ● ■ **S93.513** Sprain of interphalangeal joint of unspecified great toe

    ● **S93.514** Sprain of interphalangeal joint of right lesser toe(s)

    ● **S93.515** Sprain of interphalangeal joint of left lesser toe(s)

    ● ■ **S93.516** Sprain of interphalangeal joint of unspecified lesser toe(s)

    ● ■ **S93.519** Sprain of interphalangeal joint of unspecified toe(s)

  ● **S93.52** Sprain of metatarsophalangeal joint of toe

    ● **S93.521** Sprain of metatarsophalangeal joint of right great toe

    ● **S93.522** Sprain of metatarsophalangeal joint of left great toe

    ● ■ **S93.523** Sprain of metatarsophalangeal joint of unspecified great toe

    ● **S93.524** Sprain of metatarsophalangeal joint of right lesser toe(s)

    ● **S93.525** Sprain of metatarsophalangeal joint of left lesser toe(s)

    ● ■ **S93.526** Sprain of metatarsophalangeal joint of unspecified lesser toe(s)

    ● ■ **S93.529** Sprain of metatarsophalangeal joint of unspecified toe(s)

● **S93.6** Sprain of foot

  Excludes2   sprain of metatarsophalangeal joint of toe (S93.52-)
              sprain of toe (S93.5-)

  ● **S93.60** Unspecified sprain of foot

    ● ■ **S93.601** Unspecified sprain of right foot

    ● ■ **S93.602** Unspecified sprain of left foot

    ● ■ **S93.609** Unspecified sprain of unspecified foot

  ● **S93.61** Sprain of tarsal ligament of foot

    ● **S93.611** Sprain of tarsal ligament of right foot

    ● **S93.612** Sprain of tarsal ligament of left foot

    ● ■ **S93.619** Sprain of tarsal ligament of unspecified foot

  ● **S93.62** Sprain of tarsometatarsal ligament of foot

    ● **S93.621** Sprain of tarsometatarsal ligament of right foot

    ● **S93.622** Sprain of tarsometatarsal ligament of left foot

    ● ■ **S93.629** Sprain of tarsometatarsal ligament of unspecified foot

  ● **S93.69** Other sprain of foot

    ● **S93.691** Other sprain of right foot

    ● **S93.692** Other sprain of left foot

    ● ■ **S93.699** Other sprain of unspecified foot

● **S94** Injury of nerves at ankle and foot level
    Code also any associated open wound (S91.-)

    The appropriate 7th character is to be added to each code from category S94

A	initial encounter
D	subsequent encounter
S	sequela

  ● **S94.0** Injury of lateral plantar nerve

    ● ■ **S94.00** Injury of lateral plantar nerve, unspecified leg

    ● **S94.01** Injury of lateral plantar nerve, right leg

    ● **S94.02** Injury of lateral plantar nerve, left leg

  ● **S94.1** Injury of medial plantar nerve

    ● ■ **S94.10** Injury of medial plantar nerve, unspecified leg

    ● **S94.11** Injury of medial plantar nerve, right leg

    ● **S94.12** Injury of medial plantar nerve, left leg

● Unacceptable First-Listed Diagnosis   ● Use Additional Character(s)   ■ Unspecified   **OGCR** Official Guidelines for Coding and Reporting
🔖 Complication\Comorbidity   🔖 Major C\C   Excludes 1   Excludes 2   Includes   Use additional   Code first   Code also

● **S94.2**   **Injury of deep peroneal nerve at ankle and foot level**
     Injury of terminal, lateral branch of deep peroneal nerve

     ● ▢ **S94.20**   Injury of deep peroneal nerve at ankle and foot level, unspecified leg

     ● **S94.21**   Injury of deep peroneal nerve at ankle and foot level, right leg

     ● **S94.22**   Injury of deep peroneal nerve at ankle and foot level, left leg

● **S94.3**   **Injury of cutaneous sensory nerve at ankle and foot level**

     ● ▢ **S94.30**   Injury of cutaneous sensory nerve at ankle and foot level, unspecified leg

     ● **S94.31**   Injury of cutaneous sensory nerve at ankle and foot level, right leg

     ● **S94.32**   Injury of cutaneous sensory nerve at ankle and foot level, left leg

● **S94.8**   **Injury of other nerves at ankle and foot level**

     ● **S94.8x**   Injury of other nerves at ankle and foot level

         ● **S94.8x1**   Injury of other nerves at ankle and foot level, right leg

         ● **S94.8x2**   Injury of other nerves at ankle and foot level, left leg

         ● ▢ **S94.8x9**   Injury of other nerves at ankle and foot level, unspecified leg

● **S94.9**   **Injury of unspecified nerve at ankle and foot level**

     ● ▢ **S94.90**   Injury of unspecified nerve at ankle and foot level, unspecified leg

     ● ▢ **S94.91**   Injury of unspecified nerve at ankle and foot level, right leg

     ● ▢ **S94.92**   Injury of unspecified nerve at ankle and foot level, left leg

● **S95**   **Injury of blood vessels at ankle and foot level**
     Code also any associated open wound (S91.-)

     ▧ **Excludes2**   injury of posterior tibial artery and vein (S85.1-, S85.8-)

     The appropriate 7th character is to be added to each code from category S95

     | A   initial encounter |
     | D   subsequent encounter |
     | S   sequela |

● **S95.0**   **Injury of dorsal artery of foot**

     ● **S95.00**   Unspecified injury of dorsal artery of foot

         ● ▢ **S95.001**   Unspecified injury of dorsal artery of right foot A 🦻

         ● ▢ **S95.002**   Unspecified injury of dorsal artery of left foot A 🦻

         ● ▢ **S95.009**   Unspecified injury of dorsal artery of unspecified foot A 🦻

     ● **S95.01**   Laceration of dorsal artery of foot

         ● **S95.011**   Laceration of dorsal artery of right foot A 🦻

         ● **S95.012**   Laceration of dorsal artery of left foot A 🦻

         ● ▢ **S95.019**   Laceration of dorsal artery of unspecified foot A 🦻

     ● **S95.09**   Other specified injury of dorsal artery of foot

         ● **S95.091**   Other specified injury of dorsal artery of right foot A 🦻

         ● **S95.092**   Other specified injury of dorsal artery of left foot A 🦻

         ● ▢ **S95.099**   Other specified injury of dorsal artery of unspecified foot A 🦻

● **S95.1**   **Injury of plantar artery of foot**

     ● **S95.10**   Unspecified injury of plantar artery of foot

         ● ▢ **S95.101**   Unspecified injury of plantar artery of right foot A 🦻

         ● ▢ **S95.102**   Unspecified injury of plantar artery of left foot A 🦻

         ● ▢ **S95.109**   Unspecified injury of plantar artery of unspecified foot A 🦻

     ● **S95.11**   Laceration of plantar artery of foot

         ● **S95.111**   Laceration of plantar artery of right foot A 🦻

         ● **S95.112**   Laceration of plantar artery of left foot A 🦻

         ● ▢ **S95.119**   Laceration of plantar artery of unspecified foot A 🦻

     ● **S95.19**   Other specified injury of plantar artery of foot

         ● **S95.191**   Other specified injury of plantar artery of right foot A 🦻

         ● **S95.192**   Other specified injury of plantar artery of left foot A 🦻

         ● ▢ **S95.199**   Other specified injury of plantar artery of unspecified foot A 🦻

● **S95.2**   **Injury of dorsal vein of foot**

     ● **S95.20**   Unspecified injury of dorsal vein of foot

         ● ▢ **S95.201**   Unspecified injury of dorsal vein of right foot A 🦻

         ● ▢ **S95.202**   Unspecified injury of dorsal vein of left foot A 🦻

         ● ▢ **S95.209**   Unspecified injury of dorsal vein of unspecified foot A 🦻

     ● **S95.21**   Laceration of dorsal vein of foot

         ● **S95.211**   Laceration of dorsal vein of right foot A 🦻

         ● **S95.212**   Laceration of dorsal vein of left foot A 🦻

         ● ▢ **S95.219**   Laceration of dorsal vein of unspecified foot A 🦻

     ● **S95.29**   Other specified injury of dorsal vein of foot

         ● **S95.291**   Other specified injury of dorsal vein of right foot A 🦻

         ● **S95.292**   Other specified injury of dorsal vein of left foot A 🦻

         ● ▢ **S95.299**   Other specified injury of dorsal vein of unspecified foot A 🦻

● **S95.8**   **Injury of other blood vessels at ankle and foot level**

     ● **S95.80**   Unspecified injury of other blood vessels at ankle and foot level

         ● ▢ **S95.801**   Unspecified injury of other blood vessels at ankle and foot level, right leg A 🦻

         ● ▢ **S95.802**   Unspecified injury of other blood vessels at ankle and foot level, left leg A 🦻

         ● ▢ **S95.809**   Unspecified injury of other blood vessels at ankle and foot level, unspecified leg A 🦻

● Unacceptable First-Listed Diagnosis   ● Use Additional Character(s)   ▢ Unspecified   **OGCR** Official Guidelines for Coding and Reporting

🦻 Complication\Comorbidity   Major C\C   Excludes 1    Excludes 2   Includes    Use additional   Code first   Code also

1523

CHAPTER 19 (S00-T98)

● S95.81   Laceration of other blood vessels at ankle and foot level

    ● S95.811   Laceration of other blood vessels at ankle and foot level, right leg A 🦠

    ● S95.812   Laceration of other blood vessels at ankle and foot level, left leg A 🦠

    ● ■ S95.819   Laceration of other blood vessels at ankle and foot level, unspecified leg A 🦠

● S95.89   Other specified injury of other blood vessels at ankle and foot level

    ● S95.891   Other specified injury of other blood vessels at ankle and foot level, right leg A 🦠

    ● S95.892   Other specified injury of other blood vessels at ankle and foot level, left leg A 🦠

    ● ■ S95.899   Other specified injury of other blood vessels at ankle and foot level, unspecified leg A 🦠

● S95.9   Injury of unspecified blood vessel at ankle and foot level

    ● S95.90   Unspecified injury of unspecified blood vessel at ankle and foot level

       ● ■ S95.901   Unspecified injury of unspecified blood vessel at ankle and foot level, right leg A 🦠

       ● ■ S95.902   Unspecified injury of unspecified blood vessel at ankle and foot level, left leg A 🦠

       ● ■ S95.909   Unspecified injury of unspecified blood vessel at ankle and foot level, unspecified leg A 🦠

    ● S95.91   Laceration of unspecified blood vessel at ankle and foot level

       ● ■ S95.911   Laceration of unspecified blood vessel at ankle and foot level, right leg A 🦠

       ● ■ S95.912   Laceration of unspecified blood vessel at ankle and foot level, left leg A 🦠

       ● ■ S95.919   Laceration of unspecified blood vessel at ankle and foot level, unspecified leg A 🦠

● S95.99   Other specified injury of unspecified blood vessel at ankle and foot level

    ● ■ S95.991   Other specified injury of unspecified blood vessel at ankle and foot level, right leg A 🦠

    ● ■ S95.992   Other specified injury of unspecified blood vessel at ankle and foot level, left leg A 🦠

    ● ■ S95.999   Other specified injury of unspecified blood vessel at ankle and foot level, unspecified leg A 🦠

● S96   Injury of muscle and tendon at ankle and foot level

Code also any associated open wound (S91.-)

Excludes2	injury of Achilles tendon (S86.0-)
	sprain of joints and ligaments of ankle and foot (S93.-)

The appropriate 7th character is to be added to each code from category S96

A	initial encounter
D	subsequent encounter
S	sequela

● S96.0   Injury of muscle and tendon of long flexor muscle of toe at ankle and foot level

    ● S96.00   Unspecified injury of muscle and tendon of long flexor muscle of toe at ankle and foot level

       ● ■ S96.001   Unspecified injury of muscle and tendon of long flexor muscle of toe at right ankle and foot level

       ● ■ S96.002   Unspecified injury of muscle and tendon of long flexor muscle of toe at left ankle and foot level

       ● ■ S96.009   Unspecified injury of muscle and tendon of long flexor muscle of toe at ankle and foot level, unspecified side

    ● S96.01   Strain of muscle and tendon of long flexor muscle of toe at ankle and foot level

       ● S96.011   Strain of muscle and tendon of long flexor muscle of toe at right ankle and foot level

       ● S96.012   Strain of muscle and tendon of long flexor muscle of toe at left ankle and foot level

       ● ■ S96.019   Strain of muscle and tendon of long flexor muscle of toe at ankle and foot level, unspecified side

    ● S96.02   Laceration of muscle and tendon of long flexor muscle of toe at ankle and foot level

       ● S96.021   Laceration of muscle and tendon of long flexor muscle of toe at right ankle and foot level A 🦠

       ● S96.022   Laceration of muscle and tendon of long flexor muscle of toe at left ankle and foot level A 🦠

       ● ■ S96.029   Laceration of muscle and tendon of long flexor muscle of toe at ankle and foot level, unspecified side A 🦠

    ● S96.09   Other injury of muscle and tendon of long flexor muscle of toe at ankle and foot level

       ● S96.091   Other injury of muscle and tendon of long flexor muscle of toe at right ankle and foot level

       ● S96.092   Other injury of muscle and tendon of long flexor muscle of toe at left ankle and foot level

       ● ■ S96.099   Other injury of muscle and tendon of long flexor muscle of toe at ankle and foot level, unspecified side

● Unacceptable First-Listed Diagnosis   ● Use Additional Character(s)   ■ Unspecified   OGCR Official Guidelines for Coding and Reporting

🦠 Complication\Comorbidity   🦠 Major C\C   Excludes 1   Excludes 2   Includes   Use additional   Code first   Code also

● S96.1   Injury of muscle and tendon of long extensor muscle of toe at ankle and foot level

  ● S96.10   Unspecified injury of muscle and tendon of long extensor muscle of toe at ankle and foot level

    ● ▣ S96.101   Unspecified injury of muscle and tendon of long extensor muscle of toe at right ankle and foot level

    ● ▣ S96.102   Unspecified injury of muscle and tendon of long extensor muscle of toe at left ankle and foot level

    ● ▣ S96.109   Unspecified injury of muscle and tendon of long extensor muscle of toe at ankle and foot level, unspecified side

  ● S96.11   Strain of muscle and tendon of long extensor muscle of toe at ankle and foot level

    ● S96.111   Strain of muscle and tendon of long extensor muscle of toe at right ankle and foot level

    ● S96.112   Strain of muscle and tendon of long extensor muscle of toe at left ankle and foot level

    ● ▣ S96.119   Strain of muscle and tendon of long extensor muscle of toe at ankle and foot level, unspecified level

  ● S96.12   Laceration of muscle and tendon of long extensor muscle of toe at ankle and foot level

    ● S96.121   Laceration of muscle and tendon of long extensor muscle of toe at right ankle and foot level A 🗇

    ● S96.122   Laceration of muscle and tendon of long extensor muscle of toe at left ankle and foot level A 🗇

    ● ▣ S96.129   Laceration of muscle and tendon of long extensor muscle of toe at ankle and foot level, unspecified side A 🗇

  ● S96.19   Other injury of muscle and tendon of long extensor muscle of toe at ankle and foot level

    ● S96.191   Other injury of muscle and tendon of long extensor muscle of toe at right ankle and foot level

    ● S96.192   Other injury of muscle and tendon of long extensor muscle of toe at left ankle and foot level

    ● ▣ S96.199   Other injury of muscle and tendon of long extensor muscle of toe at ankle and foot level, unspecified side

● S96.2   Injury of intrinsic muscle and tendon at ankle and foot level

  ● S96.20   Unspecified injury of intrinsic muscle and tendon at ankle and foot level

    ● ▣ S96.201   Unspecified injury of intrinsic muscle and tendon at right ankle and foot level

    ● ▣ S96.202   Unspecified injury of intrinsic muscle and tendon at left ankle and foot level

    ● ▣ S96.209   Unspecified injury of intrinsic muscle and tendon at ankle and foot level, unspecified side

● S96.21   Strain of intrinsic muscle and tendon at ankle and foot level

    ● S96.211   Strain of intrinsic muscle and tendon at right ankle and foot level

    ● S96.212   Strain of intrinsic muscle and tendon at left ankle and foot level

    ● ▣ S96.219   Strain of intrinsic muscle and tendon at ankle and foot level, unspecified side

  ● S96.22   Laceration of intrinsic muscle and tendon at ankle and foot level

    ● S96.221   Laceration of intrinsic muscle and tendon at right ankle and foot level A 🗇

    ● S96.222   Laceration of intrinsic muscle and tendon at left ankle and foot level A 🗇

    ● ▣ S96.229   Laceration of intrinsic muscle and tendon at ankle and foot level, unspecified side A 🗇

  ● S96.29   Other injury of intrinsic muscle and tendon at ankle and foot level

    ● S96.291   Other injury of intrinsic muscle and tendon at right ankle and foot level

    ● S96.292   Other injury of intrinsic muscle and tendon at left ankle and foot level

    ● ▣ S96.299   Other injury of intrinsic muscle and tendon at ankle and foot level, unspecified side

● S96.8   Injury of other muscles and tendons at ankle and foot level

  ● S96.80   Unspecified injury of other muscles and tendons at ankle and foot level

    ● ▣ S96.801   Unspecified injury of other muscles and tendons at right ankle and foot level

    ● ▣ S96.802   Unspecified injury of other muscles and tendons at left ankle and foot level

    ● ▣ S96.809   Unspecified injury of other muscles and tendons at ankle and foot level, unspecified side

  ● S96.81   Strain of other muscles and tendons at ankle and foot level

    ● S96.811   Strain of other muscles and tendons at right ankle and foot level

    ● S96.812   Strain of other muscles and tendons at left ankle and foot level

    ● ▣ S96.819   Strain of other muscles and tendons at ankle and foot level, unspecified side

  ● S96.82   Laceration of other muscles and tendons at ankle and foot level

    ● S96.821   Laceration of other muscles and tendons at right ankle and foot level A 🗇

    ● S96.822   Laceration of other muscles and tendons at left ankle and foot level A 🗇

● Unacceptable First-Listed Diagnosis   ● Use Additional Character(s)   ▣ Unspecified   **OGCR** Official Guidelines for Coding and Reporting

🗇 Complication\Comorbidity   🗇 Major C\C   Excludes 1   Excludes 2   Includes   Use additional   Code first   Code also

● ■ **S96.829** Laceration of other muscles and tendons at ankle and foot level, unspecified side A 🦴

● **S96.89** Other injury of other muscles and tendons at ankle and foot level

　● **S96.891** Other injury of other muscles and tendons at right ankle and foot level

　● **S96.892** Other injury of other muscles and tendons at left ankle and foot level

　● ■ **S96.899** Other injury of other muscles and tendons at ankle and foot level, unspecified side

● **S96.9** Injury of unspecified muscle and tendon at ankle and foot level

　● **S96.90** Unspecified injury of unspecified muscle and tendon at ankle and foot level

　　● ■ **S96.901** Unspecified injury of unspecified muscle and tendon at right ankle and foot level

　　● ■ **S96.902** Unspecified injury of unspecified muscle and tendon at left ankle and foot level

　　● ■ **S96.909** Unspecified injury of unspecified muscle and tendon at ankle and foot level, unspecified side

　● **S96.91** Strain of unspecified muscle and tendon at ankle and foot level

　　● ■ **S96.911** Strain of unspecified muscle and tendon at right ankle and foot level

　　● ■ **S96.912** Strain of unspecified muscle and tendon at left ankle and foot level

　　● ■ **S96.919** Strain of unspecified muscle and tendon at ankle and foot level, unspecified side

　● **S96.92** Laceration of unspecified muscle and tendon at ankle and foot level

　　● ■ **S96.921** Laceration of unspecified muscle and tendon at right ankle and foot level A 🦴

　　● ■ **S96.922** Laceration of unspecified muscle and tendon at left ankle and foot level A 🦴

　　● ■ **S96.929** Laceration of unspecified muscle and tendon at ankle and foot level, unspecified side A 🦴

　● **S96.99** Other injury of unspecified muscle and tendon at ankle and foot level

　　● ■ **S96.991** Other injury of unspecified muscle and tendon at right ankle and foot level

　　● ■ **S96.992** Other injury of unspecified muscle and tendon at left ankle and foot level

　　● ■ **S96.999** Other injury of unspecified muscle and tendon at ankle and foot level, unspecified side

● **S97** Crushing injury of ankle and foot

　Use additional code(s) for all associated injuries

　The appropriate 7th character is to be added to each code from category S97

A	initial encounter
D	subsequent encounter
S	sequela

● **S97.0** Crushing injury of ankle

　● ■ **S97.00** Crushing injury of ankle, unspecified side

　● **S97.01** Crushing injury of right ankle

　● **S97.02** Crushing injury of left ankle

● **S97.1** Crushing injury of toe

　● **S97.10** Crushing injury of unspecified toe(s)

　　● ■ **S97.101** Crushing injury of unspecified toe(s), right foot

　　● ■ **S97.102** Crushing injury of unspecified toe(s), left foot

　　● ■ **S97.109** Crushing injury of unspecified toe(s), unspecified foot

　● **S97.11** Crushing injury of great toe

　　● **S97.111** Crushing injury of great right toe

　　● **S97.112** Crushing injury of great left toe

　　● ■ **S97.119** Crushing injury of great toe, unspecified side

　● **S97.12** Crushing injury of lesser toe(s)

　　● **S97.121** Crushing injury of lesser right toe(s)

　　● **S97.122** Crushing injury of lesser left toe(s)

　　● ■ **S97.129** Crushing injury of lesser toe(s), unspecified side

● **S97.8** Crushing injury of foot

　● ■ **S97.80** Crushing injury of foot, unspecified side

　　Crushing injury of foot NOS

　● **S97.81** Crushing injury of right foot

　● **S97.82** Crushing injury of left foot

● **S98** Traumatic amputation of ankle and foot

　An amputation not identified and partial or complete should be coded to complete

　The appropriate 7th character is to be added to each code from category S98

A	initial encounter
D	subsequent encounter
S	sequela

● **S98.0** Traumatic amputation of foot at ankle level

　● **S98.01** Complete traumatic amputation of foot at ankle level

　　● **S98.011** Complete traumatic amputation of right foot at ankle level A 🦴

　　● **S98.012** Complete traumatic amputation of left foot at ankle level A 🦴

　　● ■ **S98.019** Complete traumatic amputation of foot at ankle level, unspecified side A 🦴

　● **S98.02** Partial traumatic amputation of foot at ankle level

　　● **S98.021** Partial traumatic amputation of right foot at ankle level A 🦴

　　● **S98.022** Partial traumatic amputation of left foot at ankle level A 🦴

　　● ■ **S98.029** Partial traumatic amputation of foot at ankle level, unspecified side A 🦴

● **S98.1** Traumatic amputation of one toe

　● **S98.11** Complete traumatic amputation of great toe

　　● **S98.111** Complete traumatic amputation of right great toe

● Unacceptable First-Listed Diagnosis　　● Use Additional Character(s)　　■ Unspecified　　**OGCR** Official Guidelines for Coding and Reporting

🦴 Complication\Comorbidity　🦴 Major C\C　[Excludes 1]　[Excludes 2]　Includes　Use additional　Code first　Code also

● S98.112   Complete traumatic amputation of left great toe

● ■ S98.119   Complete traumatic amputation of great toe, unspecified side

● S98.12   Partial traumatic amputation of great toe

   ● S98.121   Partial traumatic amputation of right great toe

   ● S98.122   Partial traumatic amputation of left great toe

   ● ■ S98.129   Partial traumatic amputation of great toe, unspecified side

● S98.13   Complete traumatic amputation of one lesser toe
   Traumatic amputation of toe NOS

   ● S98.131   Complete traumatic amputation of one lesser right toe(s)

   ● S98.132   Complete traumatic amputation of one lesser left toe(s)

   ● ■ S98.139   Complete traumatic amputation of one lesser toe(s), unspecified side

● S98.14   Partial traumatic amputation of one lesser toe

   ● S98.141   Partial traumatic amputation of one lesser right toe(s)

   ● S98.142   Partial traumatic amputation of one lesser left toe(s)

   ● ■ S98.149   Partial traumatic amputation of one lesser toe(s), unspecified side

● S98.2   Traumatic amputation of two or more lesser toes

   ● S98.21   Complete traumatic amputation of two or more lesser toes

      ● S98.211   Complete traumatic amputation of two or more lesser right toes

      ● S98.212   Complete traumatic amputation of two or more lesser left toes

      ● ■ S98.219   Complete traumatic amputation of two or more lesser toes, unspecified side

   ● S98.22   Partial traumatic amputation of two or more lesser toes

      ● S98.221   Partial traumatic amputation of two or more lesser right toes

      ● S98.222   Partial traumatic amputation of two or more lesser left toes

      ● ■ S98.229   Partial traumatic amputation of two or more lesser toes, unspecified side

● S98.3   Traumatic amputation of midfoot

   ● S98.31   Complete traumatic amputation of midfoot A 🌝

      ● S98.311   Complete traumatic amputation of right midfoot A 🌝

      ● S98.312   Complete traumatic amputation of left midfoot A 🌝

      ● ■ S98.319   Complete traumatic amputation of midfoot, unspecified side A 🌝

   ● S98.32   Partial traumatic amputation of midfoot

      ● S98.321   Partial traumatic amputation of right midfoot A 🌝

      ● S98.322   Partial traumatic amputation of left midfoot A 🌝

      ● ■ S98.329   Partial traumatic amputation of midfoot, unspecified side A 🌝

● S98.9   Traumatic amputation of foot, level unspecified

   ● S98.91   Complete traumatic amputation of foot, level unspecified

      ● S98.911   Complete traumatic amputation of right foot, level unspecified A 🌝

      ● S98.912   Complete traumatic amputation of left foot, level unspecified A 🌝

      ● ■ S98.919   Complete traumatic amputation of foot, level unspecified, unspecified side A 🌝

   ● S98.92   Partial traumatic amputation of foot, level unspecified

      ● ■ S98.921   Partial traumatic amputation of right foot, level unspecified A 🌝

      ● ■ S98.922   Partial traumatic amputation of left foot, level unspecified A 🌝

      ● ■ S98.929   Partial traumatic amputation of foot, level unspecified, unspecified side A 🌝

● S99   Other and unspecified injuries of ankle and foot
   The appropriate 7th character is to be added to each code from category S99

A	initial encounter
D	subsequent encounter
S	sequela

   ● S99.8   Other specified injuries of ankle and foot

      ● S99.81   Other specified injuries of ankle

         ● S99.811   Other specified injuries of right ankle

         ● S99.812   Other specified injuries of left ankle

         ● ■ S99.819   Other specified injuries of ankle, unspecified side

      ● S99.82   Other specified injuries of foot

         ● S99.821   Other specified injuries of right foot

         ● S99.822   Other specified injuries of left foot

         ● ■ S99.829   Other specified injuries of foot, unspecified side

   ● S99.9   Unspecified injury of ankle and foot

      ● S99.91   Unspecified injury of ankle

         ● ■ S99.911   Unspecified injury of right ankle

         ● ■ S99.912   Unspecified injury of left ankle

         ● ■ S99.919   Unspecified injury of ankle, unspecified side

      ● S99.92   Unspecified injury of foot

         ● ■ S99.921   Unspecified injury of right foot

         ● ■ S99.922   Unspecified injury of left foot

         ● ■ S99.929   Unspecified injury of foot, unspecified side

---

INJURY, POISONING AND CERTAIN OTHER CONSEQUENCES OF EXTERNAL CAUSES (T07-T88)

Categories T00-T06 deactivated. Code to individual injuries.

INJURIES INVOLVING MULTIPLE BODY REGIONS (T07)

Excludes1   burns and corrosions (T20-T32)
            frostbite (T33-T34)
            insect bite or sting, venomous (T63.4)
            sunburn (L55.-)

● Unacceptable First-Listed Diagnosis   ● Use Additional Character(s)   ■ Unspecified   **OGCR** Official Guidelines for Coding and Reporting

🌝 Complication\Comorbidity   🌝 Major C\C   Excludes 1   Excludes 2   Includes   Use additional   Code first   Code also   1527

CHAPTER 19 (S00-T98)

■ **T07**   **Unspecified multiple injuries**

> **Note:** This code is for use only when no documentation is available identifying the specific injuries. This code is not for use in the inpatient setting.

> **Excludes1**   injury NOS (T14)

> Categories T08-T13 deactivated

INJURY OF UNSPECIFIED BODY REGION (T14)

● **T14**   **Injury of unspecified body region**

> **Excludes1**   multiple unspecified injuries (T07)

> **T14.8**   **Other injury of suspected body region**
> > Contusion NOS   Skin injury NOS
> > Crush injury NOS   Vascular injury NOS
> > Fracture NOS

> ● **T14.9**   **Unspecified injury**

> > ■ **T14.90**   **Injury, unspecified**
> > > Injury NOS

> > > **Note:** This code is for use only when no documentation is available identifying the specific injury. This code is not for use in the inpatient setting.

> > **T14.91**   **Suicide attempt**
> > > Attempted suicide NOS

EFFECTS OF FOREIGN BODY ENTERING THROUGH NATURAL ORIFICE (T15-T19)

> **Excludes2**   foreign body accidentally left in operation wound (T81.5-)
> > foreign body in penetrating wound - see open wound by body region
> > residual foreign body in soft tissue (M79.5)
> > splinter, without open wound - see superficial injury by body region

> Codes within this section that include the external cause do not need an additional external cause code

● **T15**   **Foreign body on external eye**

> **Excludes2**   foreign body in penetrating wound of orbit and eye ball (S05.4-, S05.5-)
> > open wound of eyelid and periocular area (S01.1-)
> > retained foreign body in eyelid (H02.8-)
> > retained (old) foreign body in penetrating wound of orbit and eye ball (H05.5-, H44.6-, H44.7-)
> > superficial foreign body of eyelid and periocular area (S00.25-)

> The appropriate 7th character is to be added to each code from category T15

> | A | initial encounter |
> |---|---|
> | D | subsequent encounter |
> | S | sequela |

> ● **T15.0**   **Foreign body in cornea**

> > ● ■ **T15.00**   **Foreign body in cornea, unspecified eye**

> > ● **T15.01**   **Foreign body in cornea, right eye**

> > ● **T15.02**   **Foreign body in cornea, left eye**

> ● **T15.1**   **Foreign body in conjunctival sac**

> > ● ■ **T15.10**   **Foreign body in conjunctival sac, unspecified eye**

> > ● **T15.11**   **Foreign body in conjunctival sac, right eye**

> > ● **T15.12**   **Foreign body in conjunctival sac, left eye**

> ● **T15.8**   **Foreign body in other and multiple parts of external eye**
> > Foreign body in lacrimal punctum

> ● ■ **T15.80**   **Foreign body in other and multiple parts of external eye, unspecified eye**

> ● **T15.81**   **Foreign body in other and multiple parts of external eye, right eye**

> ● **T15.82**   **Foreign body in other and multiple parts of external eye, left eye**

● **T15.9**   **Foreign body on external eye, part unspecified**

> ● ■ **T15.90**   **Foreign body on external eye, part unspecified, unspecified eye**

> ● ■ **T15.91**   **Foreign body on external eye, part unspecified, right eye**

> ● ■ **T15.92**   **Foreign body on external eye, part unspecified, left eye**

● **T16**   **Foreign body in ear**

> **Includes**   auditory canal

> The appropriate 7th character is to be added to each code from category T16

> | A | initial encounter |
> |---|---|
> | D | subsequent encounter |
> | S | sequela |

> ● **T16.1**   **Foreign body in right ear**

> ● **T16.2**   **Foreign body in left ear**

> ● ■ **T16.9**   **Foreign body in ear, unspecified ear**

● **T17**   **Foreign body in respiratory tract**

> The appropriate 7th character is to be added to each code from category T17

> | A | initial encounter |
> |---|---|
> | D | subsequent encounter |
> | S | sequela |

> ● **T17.0**   **Foreign body in nasal sinus**

> ● **T17.1**   **Foreign body in nostril**
> > Foreign body in nose NOS

> ● **T17.2**   **Foreign body in pharynx**
> > Foreign body in nasopharynx
> > Foreign body in throat NOS

> > ● **T17.20**   **Unspecified foreign body in pharynx**

> > > ● ■ **T17.200**   **Unspecified foreign body in pharynx causing asphyxiation**

> > > ● ■ **T17.208**   **Unspecified foreign body in pharynx causing other injury**

> > ● **T17.21**   **Gastric contents in pharynx**
> > > Aspiration of gastric contents into pharynx
> > > Vomitus in pharynx

> > > ● **T17.210**   **Gastric contents in pharynx causing asphyxiation**

> > > ● **T17.218**   **Gastric contents in pharynx causing other injury**

> > ● **T17.22**   **Food in pharynx**
> > > Bones in pharynx
> > > Seeds in pharynx

> > > ● **T17.220**   **Food in pharynx causing asphyxiation**

> > > ● **T17.228**   **Food in pharynx causing other injury**

> > ● **T17.29**   **Other foreign object in pharynx**

> > > ● **T17.290**   **Other foreign object in pharynx causing asphyxiation**

> > > ● **T17.298**   **Other foreign object in pharynx causing other injury**

> ● **T17.3**   **Foreign body in larynx**

● Unacceptable First-Listed Diagnosis   ● Use Additional Character(s)   ■ Unspecified   **OGCR** Official Guidelines for Coding and Reporting

🐾 Complication\Comorbidity   🐾 Major C\C   Excludes 1   Excludes 2   Includes   Use additional   Code first   Code also

● T17.30   Unspecified foreign body in larynx

  ● ▣ T17.300   Unspecified foreign body in larynx causing asphyxiation

  ● ▣ T17.308   Unspecified foreign body in larynx causing other injury

● T17.31   Gastric contents in larynx
        Aspiration of gastric contents into larynx
        Vomitus in larynx

  ● T17.310   Gastric contents in larynx causing asphyxiation

  ● T17.318   Gastric contents in larynx causing other injury

● T17.32   Food in larynx
        Bones in larynx
        Seeds in larynx

  ● T17.320   Food in larynx causing asphyxiation

  ● T17.328   Food in larynx causing other injury

● T17.39   Other foreign object in larynx

  ● T17.390   Other foreign object in larynx causing asphyxiation

  ● T17.398   Other foreign object in larynx causing other injury

● T17.4   Foreign body in trachea

  ● T17.40   Unspecified foreign body in trachea

    ● ▣ T17.400   Unspecified foreign body in trachea causing asphyxiation A ℅

    ● ▣ T17.408   Unspecified foreign body in trachea causing other injury A ℅

  ● T17.41   Gastric contents in trachea
          Aspiration of gastric contents into trachea
          Vomitus in trachea

    ● T17.410   Gastric contents in trachea causing asphyxiation A ℅

    ● T17.418   Gastric contents in trachea causing other injury A ℅

  ● T17.42   Food in trachea
          Bones in trachea
          Seeds in trachea

    ● T17.420   Food in trachea causing asphyxiation A ℅

    ● T17.428   Food in trachea causing other injury A ℅

  ● T17.49   Other foreign object in trachea

    ● T17.490   Other foreign object in trachea causing asphyxiation A ℅

    ● T17.498   Other foreign object in trachea causing other injury A ℅

● T17.5   Foreign body in bronchus

  ● T17.50   Unspecified foreign body in bronchus

    ● ▣ T17.500   Unspecified foreign body in bronchus causing asphyxiation A ℅

    ● ▣ T17.508   Unspecified foreign body in bronchus causing other injury A ℅

  ● T17.51   Gastric contents in bronchus
          Aspiration of gastric contents into bronchus
          Vomitus in bronchus

    ● T17.510   Gastric contents in bronchus causing asphyxiation A ℅

    ● T17.518   Gastric contents in bronchus causing other injury A ℅

● T17.52   Food in bronchus
        Bones in bronchus
        Seeds in bronchus

  ● T17.520   Food in bronchus causing asphyxiation A ℅

  ● T17.528   Food in bronchus causing other injury A ℅

● T17.59   Other foreign object in bronchus

  ● T17.590   Other foreign object in bronchus causing asphyxiation A ℅

  ● T17.598   Other foreign object in bronchus causing other injury A ℅

● T17.8   Foreign body in other parts of respiratory tract
        Foreign body in bronchioles
        Foreign body in lung

  ● T17.80   Unspecified foreign body in other parts of respiratory tract

    ● ▣ T17.800   Unspecified foreign body in other parts of respiratory tract causing asphyxiation A ℅

    ● ▣ T17.808   Unspecified foreign body in other parts of respiratory tract causing other injury A ℅

  ● T17.81   Gastric contents in other parts of respiratory tract
          Aspiration of gastric contents into other parts of respiratory tract
          Vomitus in other parts of respiratory tract

    ● T17.810   Gastric contents in other parts of respiratory tract causing asphyxiation A ℅

    ● T17.818   Gastric contents in other parts of respiratory tract causing other injury A ℅

  ● T17.82   Food in other parts of respiratory tract
          Bones in other parts of respiratory tract
          Seeds in other parts of respiratory tract

    ● T17.820   Food in other parts of respiratory tract causing asphyxiation A ℅

    ● T17.828   Food in other parts of respiratory tract causing other injury A ℅

  ● T17.89   Other foreign object in other parts of respiratory tract

    ● T17.890   Other foreign object in other parts of respiratory tract causing asphyxiation A ℅

    ● T17.898   Other foreign object in other parts of respiratory tract causing other injury A ℅

● T17.9   Foreign body in respiratory tract, part unspecified

  ● T17.90   Unspecified foreign body in respiratory tract, part unspecified

    ● ▣ T17.900   Unspecified foreign body in respiratory tract, part unspecified causing asphyxiation

    ● ▣ T17.908   Unspecified foreign body in respiratory tract, part unspecified causing other injury

  ● T17.91   Gastric contents in respiratory tract, part unspecified
          Aspiration of gastric contents into respiratory tract, part unspecified
          Vomitus in trachea respiratory tract, part unspecified

● Unacceptable First-Listed Diagnosis   ● Use Additional Character(s)   ▣ Unspecified   **OGCR** Official Guidelines for Coding and Reporting

℅ Complication\Comorbidity   ℅ Major C\C   [Excludes 1]   [Excludes 2]   Includes   Use additional   Code first   Code also

1529

- ■ **T17.910** Gastric contents in respiratory tract, part unspecified causing asphyxiation
- ■ **T17.918** Gastric contents in respiratory tract, part unspecified causing other injury
- **T17.92** Food in respiratory tract, part unspecified
  Bones in respiratory tract, part unspecified
  Seeds in respiratory tract, part unspecified
  - ■ **T17.920** Food in respiratory tract, part unspecified causing asphyxiation
  - ■ **T17.928** Food in respiratory tract, part unspecified causing other injury
- **T17.99** Other foreign object in respiratory tract, part unspecified
  - ■ **T17.990** Other foreign object in respiratory tract, part unspecified in causing asphyxiation
  - ■ **T17.998** Other foreign object in respiratory tract, part unspecified causing other injury

- **T18** Foreign body in alimentary tract

  | Excludes2 | foreign body in pharynx (T17.2-) |

  The appropriate 7th character is to be added to each code from category T18

A	initial encounter
D	subsequent encounter
S	sequela

- **T18.0** Foreign body in mouth
- **T18.1** Foreign body in esophagus

  | Excludes2 | foreign body in respiratory tract (T17.-) |

  - **T18.10** Unspecified foreign body in esophagus
    - ■ **T18.100** Unspecified foreign body in esophagus causing compression of trachea
      Unspecified foreign body in esophagus causing obstruction of respiration
    - ■ **T18.108** Unspecified foreign body in esophagus causing other injury
  - **T18.11** Gastric contents in esophagus
    Vomitus in esophagus
    - **T18.110** Gastric contents in esophagus causing compression of trachea
      Gastric contents in esophagus causing obstruction of respiration
    - **T18.118** Gastric contents in esophagus causing other injury
  - **T18.12** Food in esophagus
    Bones in esophagus
    Seeds in esophagus
    - **T18.120** Food in esophagus causing compression of trachea
      Food in esophagus causing obstruction of respiration
    - **T18.128** Food in esophagus causing other injury

- **T18.19** Other foreign object in esophagus
  - **T18.190** Other foreign object in esophagus causing compression of trachea
    Other foreign body in esophagus causing obstruction of respiration
  - **T18.198** Other foreign object in esophagus causing other injury
- **T18.2** Foreign body in stomach
- **T18.3** Foreign body in small intestine
- **T18.4** Foreign body in colon
- **T18.5** Foreign body in anus and rectum
  Foreign body in rectosigmoid (junction)
- **T18.8** Foreign body in other parts of alimentary tract
- ■ **T18.9** Foreign body of alimentary tract, part unspecified
  Foreign body in digestive system NOS
  Swallowed foreign body NOS

- **T19** Foreign body in genitourinary tract

  | Excludes2 | mechanical complications of contraceptive device (intrauterine) (vaginal) (T83.3-) presence of contraceptive device (intrauterine) (vaginal) (Z97.5) |

  The appropriate 7th character is to be added to each code from category T19

A	initial encounter
D	subsequent encounter
S	sequela

- **T19.0** Foreign body in urethra
- **T19.1** Foreign body in bladder
- **T19.2** Foreign body in vulva and vagina
- **T19.3** Foreign body in uterus
- **T19.4** Foreign body in penis
- **T19.8** Foreign body in other parts of genitourinary tract
- ■ **T19.9** Foreign body in genitourinary tract, part unspecified

BURNS AND CORROSIONS (T20-T32)

| Includes | burns (thermal) from electrical heating appliances
burns (thermal) from electricity
burns (thermal) from flame
burns (thermal) from friction
burns (thermal) from hot air and hot gases
burns (thermal) from hot objects
burns (thermal) from lightning
burns (thermal) from radiation chemical
burn [corrosion] (external) (internal) scalds |

| Excludes2 | erythema [dermatitis] ab igne (L59.0)
radiation-related disorders of the skin and subcutaneous tissue (L55-L59)
sunburn (L55.-) |

● Unacceptable First-Listed Diagnosis   ● Use Additional Character(s)   ■ Unspecified   **OGCR** Official Guidelines for Coding and Reporting
🝔 Complication\Comorbidity   🝔 Major C\C | Excludes 1 | | Excludes 2 | Includes   Use additional   Code first   Code also

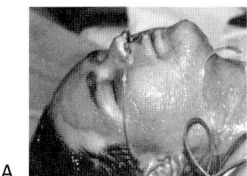
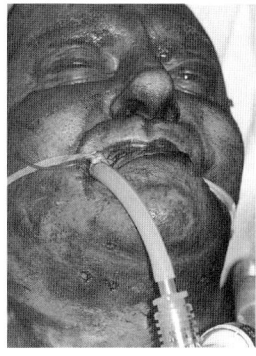

Figure 19-14 A. 2nd degree burn. B. 3rd degree burn. (From Cummings: Otolaryngology: Head & Neck Surgery, 4th ed. 2005, Mosby)

OGCR Section I.C.19.d.

Burns and Corrosions

The ICD-10-CM distinguishes between burn and corrosions. The burn codes are for thermal burns, except sunburns, that come from a heat source, such as a fire or hot appliance. The burn codes are also for burns resulting from electricity and radiation. Corrosions are burns due to chemicals. The guidelines for burns and corrosions are the same.

Current burns (T20-T25) are classified by depth, extent and by agent (X code). Burns are classified by depth as first degree (erythema), second degree (blistering), and third degree (full-thickness involvement). Burns of the eye and internal organs (T26-T28) are classified by site, but not by degree.

1) Sequencing of burn and related condition codes

Sequence first the code that reflects the highest degree of burn when more than one burn is present.

a. When the reason for the admission or encounter is for treatment of external multiple burns, sequence first the code that reflects the burn of the highest degree.

b. When a patient has both internal and external burns, the circumstances of admission govern the selection of the principal diagnosis or first-listed diagnosis.

c. When a patient is admitted for burn injuries and other related conditions such as smoke inhalation and/or respiratory failure, the circumstances of admission govern the selection of the principal or first-listed diagnosis.

2) Burns of the same local site

Classify burns of the same local site (three-digit category level, T20-T28) but of different degrees to the subcategory identifying the highest degree recorded in the diagnosis.

BURNS AND CORROSIONS OF EXTERNAL BODY SURFACE, SPECIFIED BY SITE (T20-T25)

   Includes   burns and corrosions of first degree [erythema]
                         burns and corrosions of second degree [blisters][epidermal loss]
                         burns and corrosions of third degree [deep necrosis of underlying tissue] [full-thickness skin loss]

      Use additional code from category T31 or T32 to identify extent of body surface involved

---

● **T20   Burn and corrosion of head, face, and neck**

     Excludes2   burn and corrosion of ear drum (T28.41, T28.91)
                      burn and corrosion of eye and adnexa (T26.-)
                      burn and corrosion of mouth and pharynx (T28.0)

     The appropriate 7th character is to be added to each code from category T20

       A   initial encounter
       D   subsequent encounter
       S   sequela

● **T20.0 Burn of unspecified degree of head, face, and neck**

     Use additional external cause code to identify the source, place and intent of the burn (X00-X19, X75-X77, X96-X98, Y92)

● ☐ **T20.00   Burn of unspecified degree of head, face, and neck, unspecified site**

● **T20.01   Burn of unspecified degree of ear [any part, except ear drum]**

       Excludes2   burn of ear drum (T28.41-)

   ● ☐ **T20.011 Burn of unspecified degree of right ear [any part, except ear drum]**

   ● ☐ **T20.012 Burn of unspecified degree of left ear [any part, except ear drum]**

   ● ☐ **T20.019 Burn of unspecified degree of unspecified ear [any part, except ear drum]**

● ☐ **T20.02   Burn of unspecified degree of lip(s)**

● ☐ **T20.03   Burn of unspecified degree of chin**

● ☐ **T20.04   Burn of unspecified degree of nose (septum)**

● ☐ **T20.05   Burn of unspecified degree of scalp [any part]**

● ☐ **T20.06   Burn of unspecified degree of forehead and cheek**

● ☐ **T20.07   Burn of unspecified degree of neck**

● ☐ **T20.09   Burn of unspecified degree of multiple sites of head, face, and neck**

● **T20.1 Burn of first degree of head, face, and neck**

     Use additional external cause code to identify the source, place and intent of the burn (X00-X19, X75-X77, X96-X98, Y92)

● ☐ **T20.10   Burn of first degree of head, face, and neck, unspecified site**

● **T20.11   Burn of first degree of ear [any part, except ear drum]**

       Excludes2   burn of ear drum (T28.41-)

   ● **T20.111 Burn of first degree of right ear [any part, except ear drum]**

   ● **T20.112 Burn of first degree of left ear [any part, except ear drum]**

   ● ☐ **T20.119 Burn of first degree of unspecified ear [any part, except ear drum]**

● **T20.12   Burn of first degree of lip(s)**

● **T20.13   Burn of first degree of chin**

● **T20.14   Burn of first degree of nose (septum)**

● **T20.15   Burn of first degree of scalp [any part]**

● **T20.16   Burn of first degree of forehead and cheek**

● **T20.17   Burn of first degree of neck**

● **T20.19   Burn of first degree of multiple sites of head, face, and neck**

● Unacceptable First-Listed Diagnosis   ● Use Additional Character(s)   ☐ Unspecified   **OGCR** Official Guidelines for Coding and Reporting

🞉 Complication\Comorbidity   🞉 Major C\C   Excludes 1   Excludes 2   Includes   Use additional   Code first   Code also

CHAPTER 19 (S00-T98)

- ● **T20.2**   **Burn of second degree of head, face, and neck**

  Use additional external cause code to identify the source, place and intent of the burn (X00-X19, X75-X77, X96-X98, Y92)

  - ● ◻ **T20.20**   **Burn of second degree of head, face, and neck, unspecified site**
  - ● **T20.21**   **Burn of second degree of ear [any part, except ear drum]**

    Excludes2   burn of ear drum (T28.41-)

    - ● **T20.211**   **Burn of second degree of right ear [any part, except ear drum]**
    - ● **T20.212**   **Burn of second degree of left ear [any part, except ear drum]**
    - ● ◻ **T20.219**   **Burn of second degree of unspecified ear [any part, except ear drum]**
  - ● **T20.22**   **Burn of second degree of lip(s)**
  - ● **T20.23**   **Burn of second degree of chin**
  - ● **T20.24**   **Burn of second degree of nose (septum)**
  - ● **T20.25**   **Burn of second degree of scalp [any part]**
  - ● **T20.26**   **Burn of second degree of forehead and cheek**
  - ● **T20.27**   **Burn of second degree of neck**
  - ● **T20.29**   **Burn of second degree of multiple sites of head, face, and neck**

- ● **T20.3**   **Burn of third degree of head, face, and neck**

  Use additional external cause code to identify the source, place and intent of the burn (X00-X19, X75-X77, X96-X98, Y92)

  - ● ◻ **T20.30**   **Burn of third degree of head, face, and neck, unspecified site A** 🦠
  - ● **T20.31**   **Burn of third degree of ear [any part, except ear drum]**

    Excludes2   burn of ear drum (T28.41-)

    - ● **T20.311**   **Burn of third degree of right ear [any part, except ear drum] A** 🦠
    - ● **T20.312**   **Burn of third degree of left ear [any part, except ear drum] A** 🦠
    - ● ◻ **T20.319**   **Burn of third degree of unspecified ear [any part, except ear drum] A** 🦠
  - ● **T20.32**   **Burn of third degree of lip(s) A** 🦠
  - ● **T20.33**   **Burn of third degree of chin A** 🦠
  - ● **T20.34**   **Burn of third degree of nose (septum) A** 🦠
  - ● **T20.35**   **Burn of third degree of scalp [any part] A** 🦠
  - ● **T20.36**   **Burn of third degree of forehead and cheek A** 🦠
  - ● **T20.37**   **Burn of third degree of neck A** 🦠
  - ● **T20.39**   **Burn of third degree of multiple sites of head, face, and neck A** 🦠

- ● **T20.4**   **Corrosion of unspecified degree of head, face, and neck**

  Code first (T51-T65) to identify chemical and intent

  Use additional external cause code to identify place (Y92)

  - ● ● ◻ **T20.40**   **Corrosion of unspecified degree of head, face, and neck, unspecified site**

- ● ● **T20.41**   **Corrosion of unspecified degree of ear [any part, except ear drum]**

  Excludes2   corrosion of ear drum (T28.91-)

  - ● ● ◻ **T20.411**   **Corrosion of unspecified degree of right ear [any part, except ear drum]**
  - ● ● ◻ **T20.412**   **Corrosion of unspecified degree of left ear [any part, except ear drum]**
  - ● ● ◻ **T20.419**   **Corrosion of unspecified degree of unspecified ear [any part, except ear drum]**
- ● ● ◻ **T20.42**   **Corrosion of unspecified degree of lip(s)**
- ● ● ◻ **T20.43**   **Corrosion of unspecified degree of chin**
- ● ● ◻ **T20.44**   **Corrosion of unspecified degree of nose (septum)**
- ● ● ◻ **T20.45**   **Corrosion of unspecified degree of scalp [any part]**
- ● ● ◻ **T20.46**   **Corrosion of unspecified degree of forehead and cheek**
- ● ● ◻ **T20.47**   **Corrosion of unspecified degree of neck**
- ● ● ◻ **T20.49**   **Corrosion of unspecified degree of multiple sites of head, face, and neck**

- ● **T20.5**   **Corrosion of first degree of head, face, and neck**

  Code first (T51-T65) to identify chemical and intent

  Use additional external cause code to identify place (Y92)

  - ● ● ◻ **T20.50**   **Corrosion of first degree of head, face, and neck, unspecified site**
  - ● **T20.51**   **Corrosion of first degree of ear [any part, except ear drum]**

    Excludes2   corrosion of ear drum (T28.91-)

    - ● ● **T20.511**   **Corrosion of first degree of right ear [any part, except ear drum]**
    - ● ● **T20.512**   **Corrosion of first degree of left ear [any part, except ear drum]**
    - ● ● ◻ **T20.519**   **Corrosion of first degree of unspecified ear [any part, except ear drum]**
  - ● ● **T20.52**   **Corrosion of first degree of lip(s)**
  - ● ● **T20.53**   **Corrosion of first degree of chin**
  - ● ● **T20.54**   **Corrosion of first degree of nose (septum)**
  - ● ● **T20.55**   **Corrosion of first degree of scalp [any part]**
  - ● ● **T20.56**   **Corrosion of first degree of cheek**
  - ● ● **T20.57**   **Corrosion of first degree of neck**
  - ● ● **T20.59**   **Corrosion of first degree of multiple sites of head, face, and neck**

- ● **T20.6**   **Corrosion of second degree of head, face, and neck**

  Code first (T51-T65) to identify chemical and intent

  Use additional external cause code to identify place (Y92)

  - ● ● ◻ **T20.60**   **Corrosion of second degree of head, face, and neck, unspecified site**

CHAPTER 19 (S00-T98)

● **T20.61**   **Corrosion of second degree of ear [any part, except ear drum]**
> Excludes2   corrosion of ear drum (T28.91-)

●● **T20.611**   **Corrosion of second degree of right ear [any part, except ear drum]**

●● **T20.612**   **Corrosion of second degree of left ear [any part, except ear drum]**

●●■ **T20.619**   **Corrosion of second degree of unspecified ear [any part, except ear drum]**

●● **T20.62**   **Corrosion of second degree of lip(s)**

●● **T20.63**   **Corrosion of second degree of chin**

●● **T20.64**   **Corrosion of second degree of nose (septum)**

●● **T20.65**   **Corrosion of second degree of scalp [any part]**

●● **T20.66**   **Corrosion of second degree of forehead and cheek**

●● **T20.67**   **Corrosion of second degree of neck**

●● **T20.69**   **Corrosion of second degree of multiple sites of head, face, and neck**

● **T20.7**   **Corrosion of third degree of head, face, and neck**
> *Code first (T51-T65) to identify chemical and intent*
> Use additional external cause code to identify place (Y92)

●●■ **T20.70**   **Corrosion of third degree of head, face, and neck, unspecified site A** 🗲

● **T20.71**   **Corrosion of third degree of ear [any part, except ear drum]**
> Excludes2   corrosion of ear drum (T28.91-)

●● **T20.711**   **Corrosion of third degree of right ear [any part, except ear drum] A** 🗲

●● **T20.712**   **Corrosion of third degree of left ear [any part, except ear drum] A** 🗲

●●■ **T20.719**   **Corrosion of third degree of unspecified ear [any part, except ear drum] A** 🗲

●● **T20.72**   **Corrosion of third degree of lip(s) A** 🗲

●● **T20.73**   **Corrosion of third degree of chin A** 🗲

●● **T20.74**   **Corrosion of third degree of nose (septum) A** 🗲

●● **T20.75**   **Corrosion of third degree of scalp [any part] A** 🗲

●● **T20.76**   **Corrosion of third degree of forehead and cheek A** 🗲

●● **T20.77**   **Corrosion of third degree of neck A** 🗲

●● **T20.79**   **Corrosion of third degree of multiple sites of head, face, and neck A** 🗲

● **T21**   **Burn and corrosion of trunk**
> Includes   burns and corrosion of hip region
> Excludes2   burns and corrosion of:
>   axilla (T22.- with fifth character 4)
>   scapular region (T22.- with fifth character 6)
>   shoulder (T22. with fifth character 5)

The appropriate 7th character is to be added to each code from category T21
> A   initial encounter
> D   subsequent encounter
> S   sequela

● **T21.0**   **Burn of unspecified degree of trunk**
> Use additional external cause code to identify the source, place and intent of the burn (X00-X19, X75-X77, X96-X98, Y92)

●■ **T21.00**   **Burn of unspecified degree of trunk, unspecified site**

●■ **T21.01**   **Burn of unspecified degree of chest wall**
> Burn of of unspecified degree of breast

●■ **T21.02**   **Burn of unspecified degree of abdominal wall**
> Burn of unspecified degree of flank
> Burn of unspecified degree of groin

●■ **T21.03**   **Burn of unspecified degree of upper back**
> Burn of unspecified degree of interscapular region

●■ **T21.04**   **Burn of unspecified degree of lower back**

●■ **T21.05**   **Burn of unspecified degree of buttock**
> Burn of unspecified degree of anus

●■ **T21.06**   **Burn of unspecified degree of male genital region**
> Burn of unspecified degree of penis
> Burn of unspecified degree of scrotum
> Burn of unspecified degree of testis

●■ **T21.07**   **Burn of unspecified degree of female genital region**
> Burn of unspecified degree of labium (majus) (minus)
> Burn of unspecified degree of perineum
> Burn of unspecified degree of vulva
> Excludes2   burn of vagina (T28.3)

●■ **T21.09**   **Burn of unspecified degree of other site of trunk**

● **T21.1**   **Burn of first degree of trunk**
> Use additional external cause code to identify the source, place and intent of the burn (X00-X19, X75-X77, X96-X98, Y92)

●■ **T21.10**   **Burn of first degree of trunk, unspecified site**

● **T21.11**   **Burn of first degree of chest wall**
> Burn of first degree of breast

● **T21.12**   **Burn of first degree of abdominal wall**
> Burn of first degree of flank
> Burn of first degree of groin

● **T21.13**   **Burn of first degree of upper back**
> Burn of first degree of interscapular region

● **T21.14**   **Burn of first degree of lower back**

● **T21.15**   **Burn of first degree of buttock**
> Burn of first degree of anus

● **T21.16**   **Burn of first degree of male genital region**
> Burn of first degree of penis
> Burn of first degree of scrotum
> Burn of first degree of testis

● Unacceptable First-Listed Diagnosis   ● Use Additional Character(s)   ■ Unspecified   **OGCR** Official Guidelines for Coding and Reporting

🗲 Complication\Comorbidity   🗲 Major C\C   Excludes 1   Excludes 2   Includes   Use additional   Code first   Code also

1533

CHAPTER 19 (S00-T98)

● **T21.17** **Burn of first degree of female genital region**
  Burn of first degree of labium (majus) (minus)
  Burn of first degree of perineum
  Burn of first degree of vulva
  Excludes2 burn of vagina (T28.3)

● **T21.19** **Burn of first degree of other site of trunk**

● **T21.2** **Burn of second degree of trunk**
  Use additional external cause code to identify the source, place and intent of the burn (X00-X19, X75-X77, X96-X98, Y92)

●■ **T21.20** **Burn of second degree of trunk, unspecified site**

● **T21.21** **Burn of second degree of chest wall**
  Burn of second degree of breast

● **T21.22** **Burn of second degree of abdominal wall**
  Burn of second degree of flank
  Burn of second degree of groin

● **T21.23** **Burn of second degree of upper back**
  Burn of second degree of interscapular region

● **T21.24** **Burn of second degree of lower back**

● **T21.25** **Burn of second degree of buttock**
  Burn of second degree of anus

● **T21.26** **Burn of second degree of male genital region**
  Burn of second degree of penis
  Burn of second degree of scrotum
  Burn of second degree of testis

● **T21.27** **Burn of second degree of female genital region**
  Burn of second degree of labium (majus) (minus)
  Burn of second degree of perineum
  Burn of second degree of vulva
  Excludes2 burn of vagina (T28.3)

● **T21.29** **Burn of second degree of other site of trunk**

● **T21.3** **Burn of third degree of trunk**
  Use additional external cause code to identify the source, place and intent of the burn (X00-X19, X75-X77, X96-X98, Y92)

●■ **T21.30** **Burn of third degree of trunk, unspecified site A** 🗝

● **T21.31** **Burn of third degree of chest wall A** 🗝
  Burn of third degree of breast

● **T21.32** **Burn of third degree of abdominal wall A** 🗝
  Burn of third degree of flank
  Burn of third degree of groin

● **T21.33** **Burn of third degree of upper back A** 🗝
  Burn of third degree of interscapular region

● **T21.34** **Burn of third degree of lower back A** 🗝

● **T21.35** **Burn of third degree of buttock A** 🗝
  Burn of third degree of anus

● **T21.36** **Burn of third degree of male genital region A** 🗝
  Burn of third degree of penis
  Burn of third degree of scrotum
  Burn of third degree of testis

● **T21.37** **Burn of third degree of female genital region A** 🗝
  Burn of third degree of labium (majus) (minus)
  Burn of third degree of perineum
  Burn of third degree of vulva
  Excludes2 burn of vagina (T28.3)

● **T21.39** **Burn of third degree of other site of trunk A** 🗝

● **T21.4** **Corrosion of unspecified degree of trunk**
  Code first (T51-T65) to identify chemical and intent
  Use additional external cause code to identify place (Y92)

●●■ **T21.40** **Corrosion of unspecified degree of trunk, unspecified site**

●●■ **T21.41** **Corrosion of unspecified degree of chest wall**
  Corrosion of unspecified degree of breast

●●■ **T21.42** **Corrosion of unspecified degree of abdominal wall**
  Corrosion of unspecified degree of flank
  Corrosion of unspecified degree of groin

●●■ **T21.43** **Corrosion of unspecified degree of upper back**
  Corrosion of unspecified degree of interscapular region

●●■ **T21.44** **Corrosion of unspecified degree of lower back**

●●■ **T21.45** **Corrosion of unspecified degree of buttock**
  Corrosion of unspecified degree of anus

●●■ **T21.46** **Corrosion of unspecified degree of male genital region**
  Corrosion of unspecified degree of penis
  Corrosion of unspecified degree of scrotum
  Corrosion of unspecified degree of testis

●●■ **T21.47** **Corrosion of unspecified degree of female genital region**
  Corrosion of unspecified degree of labium (majus) (minus)
  Corrosion of unspecified degree of perineum
  Corrosion of unspecified degree of vulva
  Excludes2 corrosion of vagina (T28.8)

●●■ **T21.49** **Corrosion of unspecified degree of other site of trunk**

● **T21.5** **Corrosion of first degree of trunk**
  Code first (T51-T65) to identify chemical and intent
  Use additional external cause code to identify place (Y92)

●●■ **T21.50** **Corrosion of first degree of trunk, unspecified site**

●● **T21.51** **Corrosion of first degree of chest wall**
  Corrosion of first degree of breast

●● **T21.52** **Corrosion of first degree of abdominal wall**
  Corrosion of first degree of flank
  Corrosion of first degree of groin

●● **T21.53** **Corrosion of first degree of upper back**
  Corrosion of first degree of interscapular region

●● **T21.54** **Corrosion of first degree of lower back**

●● **T21.55** **Corrosion of first degree of buttock**
  Corrosion of first degree of anus

CHAPTER 19 (S00-T98)

1534

● Unacceptable First-Listed Diagnosis   ● Use Additional Character(s)   ■ Unspecified   **OGCR** Official Guidelines for Coding and Reporting
🗝 Complication\Comorbidity   🗝 Major C\C   Excludes 1   Excludes 2   Includes   Use additional   Code first   Code also

● ● **T21.56** **Corrosion of first degree of male genital region**
     Corrosion of first degree of penis
     Corrosion of first degree of scrotum
     Corrosion of first degree of testis

● ● **T21.57** **Corrosion of first degree of female genital region**
     Corrosion of first degree of labium (majus) (minus)
     Corrosion of first degree of perineum
     Corrosion of first degree of vulva
     | Excludes2 | corrosion of vagina (T28.8)

● ● **T21.59** **Corrosion of first degree of other site of trunk**

● **T21.6** **Corrosion of second degree of trunk**
     Code first (T51-T65) to identify chemical and intent
     Use additional external cause code to identify place (Y92)

● ● ■ **T21.60** **Corrosion of second degree of trunk, unspecified site**

● ● **T21.61** **Corrosion of second degree of chest wall**
     Corrosion of second degree of breast

● ● **T21.62** **Corrosion of second degree of abdominal wall**
     Corrosion of second degree of flank
     Corrosion of second degree of groin

● ● **T21.63** **Corrosion of second degree of upper back**
     Corrosion of second degree of interscapular region

● ● **T21.64** **Corrosion of second degree of lower back**

● ● **T21.65** **Corrosion of second degree of buttock**
     Corrosion of second degree of anus

● ● **T21.66** **Corrosion of second degree of male genital region**
     Corrosion of second degree of penis
     Corrosion of second degree of scrotum
     Corrosion of second degree of testis

● ● **T21.67** **Corrosion of second degree of female genital region**
     Corrosion of second degree of labium (majus) (minus)
     Corrosion of second degree of perineum
     Corrosion of second degree of vulva
     | Excludes2 | corrosion of vagina (T28.8)

● ● **T21.69** **Corrosion of second degree of other site of trunk**

● **T21.7** **Corrosion of third degree of trunk**
     Code first (T51-T65) to identify chemical and intent
     Use additional external cause code to identify place (Y92)

● ● ■ **T21.70** **Corrosion of third degree of trunk, unspecified site A** 🔾

● ● **T21.71** **Corrosion of third degree of chest wall A** 🔾
     Corrosion of third degree of breast

● ● **T21.72** **Corrosion of third degree of abdominal wall A** 🔾
     Corrosion of third degree of flank
     Corrosion of third degree of groin

● ● **T21.73** **Corrosion of third degree of upper back A** 🔾
     Corrosion of third degree of interscapular region

● ● **T21.74** **Corrosion of third degree of lower back A** 🔾

● ● **T21.75** **Corrosion of third degree of buttock A** 🔾
     Corrosion of third degree of anus

● ● **T21.76** **Corrosion of third degree of male genital region A** 🔾
     Corrosion of third degree of penis
     Corrosion of third degree of scrotum
     Corrosion of third degree of testis

● ● **T21.77** **Corrosion of third degree of female genital region A** 🔾
     Corrosion of third degree of labium (majus) (minus)
     Corrosion of third degree of perineum
     Corrosion of third degree of vulva
     | Excludes2 | corrosion of vagina (T28.8)

● ● **T21.79** **Corrosion of third degree of other site of trunk A** 🔾

● **T22** **Burn and corrosion of shoulder and upper limb, except wrist and hand**
     | Excludes2 | burn and corrosion of interscapular region (T21.-)
     burn and corrosion of wrist and hand (T23.-)

     The appropriate 7th character is to be added to each code from category T22

     A   initial encounter
     D   subsequent encounter
     S   sequela

● ■ **T22.0** **Burn of unspecified degree of shoulder and upper limb, except wrist and hand**
     Use additional external cause code to identify the source, place and intent of the burn (X00-X19, X75-X77, X96-X98, Y92)

● ■ **T22.00** **Burn of unspecified degree of shoulder and upper limb, except wrist and hand, unspecified site**

● **T22.01** **Burn of unspecified degree of forearm**

   ● ■ **T22.011** **Burn of unspecified degree of right forearm**

   ● ■ **T22.012** **Burn of unspecified degree of left forearm**

   ● ■ **T22.019** **Burn of unspecified degree of unspecified forearm**

● **T22.02** **Burn of unspecified degree of elbow**

   ● ■ **T22.021** **Burn of unspecified degree of right elbow**

   ● ■ **T22.022** **Burn of unspecified degree of left elbow**

   ● ■ **T22.029** **Burn of unspecified degree of unspecified elbow**

● **T22.03** **Burn of unspecified degree of upper arm**

   ● ■ **T22.031** **Burn of unspecified degree of right upper arm**

   ● ■ **T22.032** **Burn of unspecified degree of left upper arm**

   ● ■ **T22.039** **Burn of unspecified degree of unspecified upper arm**

● **T22.04** **Burn of unspecified degree of axilla**

   ● ■ **T22.041** **Burn of unspecified degree of right axilla**

   ● ■ **T22.042** **Burn of unspecified degree of left axilla**

   ● ■ **T22.049** **Burn of unspecified degree of unspecified axilla**

● Unacceptable First-Listed Diagnosis   ● Use Additional Character(s)   ■ Unspecified   **OGCR** Official Guidelines for Coding and Reporting

🔾 Complication\Comorbidity   🔾 Major C\C            Use additional   Code first   Code also

1535

CHAPTER 19 (S00-T98)

● T22.05 Burn of unspecified degree of shoulder
   ● ■ T22.051 Burn of unspecified degree of right shoulder
   ● ■ T22.052 Burn of unspecified degree of left shoulder
   ● ■ T22.059 Burn of unspecified degree of unspecified shoulder
● T22.06 Burn of unspecified degree of scapular region
   ● ■ T22.061 Burn of unspecified degree of right scapular region
   ● ■ T22.062 Burn of unspecified degree of left scapular region
   ● ■ T22.069 Burn of unspecified degree of unspecified scapular region

● T22.09 Burn of unspecified degree of multiple sites of shoulder and upper limb, except wrist and hand
   ● ■ T22.091 Burn of unspecified degree of multiple sites of right shoulder and upper limb, except wrist and hand
   ● ■ T22.092 Burn of unspecified degree of multiple sites of left shoulder and upper limb, except wrist and hand
   ● ■ T22.099 Burn of unspecified degree of multiple sites of unspecified shoulder and upper limb, except wrist and hand

● Unacceptable First-Listed Diagnosis   ● Use Additional Character(s)   ■ Unspecified   **OGCR** Official Guidelines for Coding and Reporting
 Complication\Comorbidity   Major C\C   Excludes 1   Excludes 2   Includes   Use additional   Code first   Code also

● **T22.1 Burn of first degree of shoulder and upper limb, except wrist and hand**

    Use additional external cause code to identify the source, place and intent of the burn (X00-X19, X75-X77, X96-X98, Y92)

● ■ **T22.10** Burn of first degree of shoulder and upper limb, except wrist and hand, unspecified site

● **T22.11** Burn of first degree of forearm

  ● **T22.111** Burn of first degree of right forearm

  ● **T22.112** Burn of first degree of left forearm

  ● ■ **T22.119** Burn of first degree of unspecified forearm

● **T22.12** Burn of first degree of elbow

  ● **T22.121** Burn of first degree of right elbow

  ● **T22.122** Burn of first degree of left elbow

  ● ■ **T22.129** Burn of first degree of unspecified elbow

● **T22.13** Burn of first degree of upper arm

  ● **T22.131** Burn of first degree of right upper arm

  ● **T22.132** Burn of first degree of left upper arm

  ● ■ **T22.139** Burn of first degree of unspecified upper arm

● **T22.14** Burn of first degree of axilla

  ● **T22.141** Burn of first degree of right axilla

  ● **T22.142** Burn of first degree of left axilla

  ● ■ **T22.149** Burn of first degree of unspecified axilla

● **T22.15** Burn of first degree of shoulder

  ● **T22.151** Burn of first degree of right shoulder

  ● **T22.152** Burn of first degree of left shoulder

  ● ■ **T22.159** Burn of first degree of unspecified shoulder

● **T22.16** Burn of first degree of scapular region

  ● **T22.161** Burn of first degree of right scapular region

  ● **T22.162** Burn of first degree of left scapular region

  ● ■ **T22.169** Burn of first degree of unspecified scapular region

● **T22.19** Burn of first degree of multiple sites of shoulder and upper limb, except wrist and hand

  ● **T22.191** Burn of first degree of multiple sites of right shoulder and upper limb, except wrist and hand

  ● **T22.192** Burn of first degree of multiple sites of left shoulder and upper limb, except wrist and hand

  ● ■ **T22.199** Burn of first degree of multiple sites of unspecified shoulder and upper limb, except wrist and hand

● **T22.2 Burn of second degree of shoulder and upper limb, except wrist and hand**

    Use additional external cause code to identify the source, place and intent of the burn (X00-X19, X75-X77, X96-X98, Y92)

● ■ **T22.20** Burn of second degree of shoulder and upper limb, except wrist and hand, unspecified site

● **T22.21** Burn of second degree of forearm

  ● **T22.211** Burn of second degree of right forearm

  ● **T22.212** Burn of second degree of left forearm

  ● ■ **T22.219** Burn of second degree of unspecified forearm

● **T22.22** Burn of second degree of elbow

  ● **T22.221** Burn of second degree of right elbow

  ● **T22.222** Burn of second degree of left elbow

  ● ■ **T22.229** Burn of second degree of unspecified elbow

● **T22.23** Burn of second degree of upper arm

  ● **T22.231** Burn of second degree of right upper arm

  ● **T22.232** Burn of second degree of left upper arm

  ● ■ **T22.239** Burn of second degree of unspecified upper arm

● **T22.24** Burn of second degree of axilla

  ● **T22.241** Burn of second degree of right axilla

  ● **T22.242** Burn of second degree of left axilla

  ● ■ **T22.249** Burn of second degree of unspecified axilla

● **T22.25** Burn of second degree of shoulder

  ● **T22.251** Burn of second degree of right shoulder

  ● **T22.252** Burn of second degree of left shoulder

  ● ■ **T22.259** Burn of second degree of unspecified shoulder

● **T22.26** Burn of second degree of scapular region

  ● **T22.261** Burn of second degree of right scapular region

  ● **T22.262** Burn of second degree of left scapular region

  ● ■ **T22.269** Burn of second degree of unspecified scapular region

● **T22.29** Burn of second degree of multiple sites of shoulder and upper limb, except wrist and hand

  ● **T22.291** Burn of second degree of multiple sites of right shoulder and upper limb, except wrist and hand

  ● **T22.292** Burn of second degree of multiple sites of left shoulder and upper limb, except wrist and hand

CHAPTER 19 (S00-T98)

● Unacceptable First-Listed Diagnosis   ● Use Additional Character(s)   ■ Unspecified   **OGCR** Official Guidelines for Coding and Reporting

 Complication\Comorbidity    Major C\C   Excludes 1   Excludes 2   Includes   Use additional   Code first   Code also

1537

● ■ T22.299   Burn of second degree of multiple sites of unspecified shoulder and upper limb, except wrist and hand

● T22.3   **Burn of third degree of shoulder and upper limb, except wrist and hand**

Use additional external cause code to identify the source, place and intent of the burn (X00-X19, X75-X77, X96-X98, Y92)

   ● ■ T22.30   Burn of third degree of shoulder and upper limb, except wrist and hand, unspecified site A 🦠

   ● T22.31   Burn of third degree of forearm

     ● T22.311   Burn of third degree of right forearm A 🦠

     ● T22.312   Burn of third degree of left forearm A 🦠

     ● ■ T22.319   Burn of third degree of unspecified forearm A 🦠

   ● T22.32   Burn of third degree of elbow

     ● T22.321   Burn of third degree of right elbow A 🦠

     ● T22.322   Burn of third degree of left elbow A 🦠

     ● ■ T22.329   Burn of third degree of unspecified elbow A 🦠

   ● T22.33   Burn of third degree of upper arm

     ● T22.331   Burn of third degree of right upper arm A 🦠

     ● T22.332   Burn of third degree of left upper arm A 🦠

     ● ■ T22.339   Burn of third degree of unspecified upper arm A 🦠

   ● T22.34   Burn of third degree of axilla

     ● T22.341   Burn of third degree of right axilla A 🦠

     ● T22.342   Burn of third degree of left axilla A 🦠

     ● ■ T22.349   Burn of third degree of unspecified axilla A 🦠

   ● T22.35   Burn of third degree of shoulder

     ● T22.351   Burn of third degree of right shoulder A 🦠

     ● T22.352   Burn of third degree of left shoulder A 🦠

     ● ■ T22.359   Burn of third degree of unspecified shoulder A 🦠

   ● T22.36   Burn of third degree of scapular region

     ● T22.361   Burn of third degree of right scapular region A 🦠

     ● T22.362   Burn of third degree of left scapular region A 🦠

     ● ■ T22.369   Burn of third degree of unspecified scapular region A 🦠

   ● T22.39   Burn of third degree of multiple sites of shoulder and upper limb, except wrist and hand

     ● T22.391   Burn of third degree of multiple sites of right shoulder and upper limb, except wrist and hand A 🦠

     ● T22.392   Burn of third degree of multiple sites of left shoulder and upper limb, except wrist and hand A 🦠

● ■ T22.399   Burn of third degree of multiple sites of unspecified shoulder and upper limb, except wrist and hand A 🦠

● T22.4   **Corrosion of unspecified degree of shoulder and upper limb, except wrist and hand**

Code first (T51-T65) to identify chemical and intent

Use additional external cause code to identify place (Y92)

   ●● ■ T22.40   Corrosion of unspecified degree of shoulder and upper limb, except wrist and hand, unspecified site

   ● T22.41   Corrosion of unspecified degree of forearm

     ●● ■ T22.411   Corrosion of unspecified degree of right forearm

     ●● ■ T22.412   Corrosion of unspecified degree of left forearm

     ●● ■ T22.419   Corrosion of unspecified degree of unspecified forearm

   ● T22.42   Corrosion of unspecified degree of elbow

     ●● ■ T22.421   Corrosion of unspecified degree of right elbow

     ●● ■ T22.422   Corrosion of unspecified degree of left elbow

     ●● ■ T22.429   Corrosion of unspecified degree of unspecified elbow

   ● T22.43   Corrosion of unspecified degree of upper arm

     ●● ■ T22.431   Corrosion of unspecified degree of right upper arm

     ●● ■ T22.432   Corrosion of unspecified degree of left upper arm

     ●● ■ T22.439   Corrosion of unspecified degree of unspecified upper arm

   ● T22.44   Corrosion of unspecified degree of axilla

     ●● ■ T22.441   Corrosion of unspecified degree of right axilla

     ●● ■ T22.442   Corrosion of unspecified degree of left axilla

     ●● ■ T22.449   Corrosion of unspecified degree of unspecified axilla

   ● T22.45   Corrosion of unspecified degree of shoulder

     ●● ■ T22.451   Corrosion of unspecified degree of right shoulder

     ●● ■ T22.452   Corrosion of unspecified degree of left shoulder

     ●● ■ T22.459   Corrosion of unspecified degree of unspecified shoulder

   ● T22.46   Corrosion of unspecified degree of scapular region

     ●● ■ T22.461   Corrosion of unspecified degree of right scapular region

     ●● ■ T22.462   Corrosion of unspecified degree of left scapular region

     ●● ■ T22.469   Corrosion of unspecified degree of unspecified scapular region

   ● T22.49   Corrosion of unspecified degree of multiple sites of shoulder and upper limb, except wrist and hand

● Unacceptable First-Listed Diagnosis   ● Use Additional Character(s)   ■ Unspecified   **OGCR** Official Guidelines for Coding and Reporting

🦠 Complication\Comorbidity   🦠 Major C\C   Excludes 1   Excludes 2   Includes   Use additional   Code first   Code also

●● ▣ **T22.491**   Corrosion of unspecified degree of multiple sites of right shoulder and upper limb, except wrist and hand

●● ▣ **T22.492**   Corrosion of unspecified degree of multiple sites of left shoulder and upper limb, except wrist and hand

●● ▣ **T22.499**   Corrosion of unspecified degree of multiple sites of unspecified shoulder and upper limb, except wrist and hand

● **T22.5**   Corrosion of first degree of shoulder and upper limb, except wrist and hand

     Code first (T51-T65) to identify chemical and intent

     Use additional external cause code to identify place (Y92)

●● ▣ **T22.50**   Corrosion of first degree of shoulder and upper limb, except wrist and hand unspecified site

● **T22.51**   Corrosion of first degree of forearm

   ● ● **T22.511**   Corrosion of first degree of right forearm

   ● ● **T22.512**   Corrosion of first degree of left forearm

   ●● ▣ **T22.519**   Corrosion of first degree of unspecified forearm

● **T22.52**   Corrosion of first degree of elbow

   ● ● **T22.521**   Corrosion of first degree of right elbow

   ● ● **T22.522**   Corrosion of first degree of left elbow

   ●● ▣ **T22.529**   Corrosion of first degree of unspecified elbow

● **T22.53**   Corrosion of first degree of upper arm

   ● ● **T22.531**   Corrosion of first degree of right upper arm

   ● ● **T22.532**   Corrosion of first degree of left upper arm

   ●● ▣ **T22.539**   Corrosion of first degree of unspecified upper arm

● **T22.54**   Corrosion of first degree of axilla

   ● ● **T22.541**   Corrosion of first degree of right axilla

   ● ● **T22.542**   Corrosion of first degree of left axilla

   ●● ▣ **T22.549**   Corrosion of first degree of unspecified axilla

● **T22.55**   Corrosion of first degree of shoulder

   ● ● **T22.551**   Corrosion of first degree of right shoulder

   ● ● **T22.552**   Corrosion of first degree of left shoulder

   ●● ▣ **T22.559**   Corrosion of first degree of unspecified shoulder

● **T22.56**   Corrosion of first degree of scapular region

   ● ● **T22.561**   Corrosion of first degree of right scapular region

   ● ● **T22.562**   Corrosion of first degree of left scapular region

●● ▣ **T22.569**   Corrosion of first degree of unspecified scapular region

● **T22.59**   Corrosion of first degree of multiple sites of shoulder and upper limb, except wrist and hand

   ● ● **T22.591**   Corrosion of first degree of multiple sites of right shoulder and upper limb, except wrist and hand

   ● ● **T22.592**   Corrosion of first degree of multiple sites of left shoulder and upper limb, except wrist and hand

   ●● ▣ **T22.599**   Corrosion of first degree of multiple sites of unspecified shoulder and upper limb, except wrist and hand

● **T22.6**   Corrosion of second degree of shoulder and upper limb, except wrist and hand

     Code first (T51-T65) to identify chemical and intent

     Use additional external cause code to identify place (Y92)

●● ▣ **T22.60**   Corrosion of second degree of shoulder and upper limb, except wrist and hand, unspecified site

● **T22.61**   Corrosion of second degree of forearm

   ● ● **T22.611**   Corrosion of second degree of right forearm

   ● ● **T22.612**   Corrosion of second degree of left forearm

   ●● ▣ **T22.619**   Corrosion of second degree of unspecified forearm

● **T22.62**   Corrosion of second degree of elbow

   ● ● **T22.621**   Corrosion of second degree of right elbow

   ● ● **T22.622**   Corrosion of second degree of left elbow

   ●● ▣ **T22.629**   Corrosion of second degree of unspecified elbow

● **T22.63**   Corrosion of second degree of upper arm

   ● ● **T22.631**   Corrosion of second degree of right upper arm

   ● ● **T22.632**   Corrosion of second degree of left upper arm

   ●● ▣ **T22.639**   Corrosion of second degree of unspecified upper arm

● **T22.64**   Corrosion of second degree of axilla

   ● ● **T22.641**   Corrosion of second degree of right axilla

   ● ● **T22.642**   Corrosion of second degree of left axilla

   ●● ▣ **T22.649**   Corrosion of second degree of unspecified axilla

● **T22.65**   Corrosion of second degree of shoulder

   ● ● **T22.651**   Corrosion of second degree of right shoulder

   ● ● **T22.652**   Corrosion of second degree of left shoulder

   ●● ▣ **T22.659**   Corrosion of second degree of unspecified shoulder

● **T22.66**   Corrosion of second degree of scapular region

   ● ● **T22.661**   Corrosion of second degree of right scapular region

● Unacceptable First-Listed Diagnosis   ● Use Additional Character(s)   ▣ Unspecified   **OGCR** Official Guidelines for Coding and Reporting

🅒 Complication\Comorbidity   🅒 Major C\C | Excludes 1 | | Excludes 2 | | Includes | Use additional   Code first   Code also

1539

CHAPTER 19 (S00-T98)

● ● T22.662 Corrosion of second degree of left scapular region

●●■ T22.669 Corrosion of second degree of unspecified scapular region

● T22.69 Corrosion of second degree of multiple sites of shoulder and upper limb, except wrist and hand

● ● T22.691 Corrosion of second degree of multiple sites of right shoulder and upper limb, except wrist and hand

● ● T22.692 Corrosion of second degree of multiple sites of left shoulder and upper limb, except wrist and hand

●●■ T22.699 Corrosion of second degree of multiple sites of unspecified shoulder and upper limb, except wrist and hand

● T22.7 Corrosion of third degree of shoulder and upper limb, except wrist and hand

Code first (T51-T65) to identify chemical and intent

Use additional external cause code to identify place (Y92)

●●■ T22.70 Corrosion of third degree of shoulder and upper limb, except wrist and hand, unspecified site A ◔

● T22.71 Corrosion of third degree of forearm

● ● T22.711 Corrosion of third degree of right forearm A ◔

● ● T22.712 Corrosion of third degree of left forearm A ◔

●●■ T22.719 Corrosion of third degree of unspecified forearm A ◔

● T22.72 Corrosion of third degree of elbow

● ● T22.721 Corrosion of third degree of right elbow A ◔

● ● T22.722 Corrosion of third degree of left elbow A ◔

●●■ T22.729 Corrosion of third degree of unspecified elbow A ◔

● T22.73 Corrosion of third degree of upper arm

● ● T22.731 Corrosion of third degree of right upper arm A ◔

● ● T22.732 Corrosion of third degree of left upper arm A ◔

●●■ T22.739 Corrosion of third degree of unspecified upper arm A ◔

● T22.74 Corrosion of third degree of axilla

● ● T22.741 Corrosion of third degree of right axilla A ◔

● ● T22.742 Corrosion of third degree of left axilla A ◔

●●■ T22.749 Corrosion of third degree of unspecified axilla A ◔

● T22.75 Corrosion of third degree of shoulder

● ● T22.751 Corrosion of third degree of right shoulder A ◔

● ● T22.752 Corrosion of third degree of left shoulder A ◔

●●■ T22.759 Corrosion of third degree of unspecified shoulder A ◔

● T22.76 Corrosion of third degree of scapular region

● ● T22.761 Corrosion of third degree of right scapular region A ◔

● ● T22.762 Corrosion of third degree of left scapular region A ◔

●●■ T22.769 Corrosion of third degree of unspecified scapular region A ◔

● T22.79 Corrosion of third degree of multiple sites of shoulder and upper limb, except wrist and hand

● ● T22.791 Corrosion of third degree of multiple sites of right shoulder and upper limb, except wrist and hand A ◔

● ● T22.792 Corrosion of third degree of multiple sites of left shoulder and upper limb, except wrist and hand A ◔

●●■ T22.799 Corrosion of third degree of multiple sites of unspecified shoulder and upper limb, except wrist and hand A ◔

● T23 Burn and corrosion of wrist and hand

The appropriate 7th character is to be added to each code from category T23

A	initial encounter
D	subsequent encounter
S	sequela

● T23.0 Burn of unspecified degree of wrist and hand

Use additional external cause code to identify the source, place and intent of the burn (X00-X19, X75-X77, X96-X98, Y92)

● T23.00 Burn of unspecified degree of hand, unspecified site

● ■ T23.001 Burn of unspecified degree of right hand, unspecified site

● ■ T23.002 Burn of unspecified degree of left hand, unspecified site

● ■ T23.009 Burn of unspecified degree of unspecified hand, unspecified site

● T23.01 Burn of unspecified degree of thumb (nail)

● ■ T23.011 Burn of unspecified degree of right thumb (nail)

● ■ T23.012 Burn of unspecified degree of left thumb (nail)

● ■ T23.019 Burn of unspecified degree of unspecified thumb (nail)

● T23.02 Burn of unspecified degree of single finger (nail) except thumb

● ■ T23.021 Burn of unspecified degree of single right finger (nail) except thumb

● ■ T23.022 Burn of unspecified degree of single left finger (nail) except thumb

● ■ T23.029 Burn of unspecified degree of unspecified single finger (nail) except thumb

● T23.03 Burn of unspecified degree of multiple fingers (nail), not including thumb

● ■ T23.031 Burn of unspecified degree of multiple right fingers (nail), not including thumb

● Unacceptable First-Listed Diagnosis   ● Use Additional Character(s)   ■ Unspecified   OGCR Official Guidelines for Coding and Reporting
◔ Complication\Comorbidity   ◔ Major C\C   Excludes 1   Excludes 2   Includes   Use additional   Code first   Code also

● ▣ **T23.032** **Burn of unspecified degree of multiple left fingers (nail), not including thumb**

● ▣ **T23.039** **Burn of unspecified degree of unspecified multiple fingers (nail), not including thumb**

● **T23.04** **Burn of unspecified degree of multiple fingers (nail), including thumb**

  ● ▣ **T23.041** **Burn of unspecified degree of multiple right fingers (nail), including thumb**

  ● ▣ **T23.042** **Burn of unspecified degree of multiple left fingers (nail), including thumb**

  ● ▣ **T23.049** **Burn of unspecified degree of unspecified multiple fingers (nail), including thumb**

● **T23.05** **Burn of unspecified degree of palm**

  ● ▣ **T23.051** **Burn of unspecified degree of right palm**

  ● ▣ **T23.052** **Burn of unspecified degree of left palm**

  ● ▣ **T23.059** **Burn of unspecified degree of unspecified palm**

● **T23.06** **Burn of unspecified degree of back of hand**

  ● ▣ **T23.061** **Burn of unspecified degree of back of right hand**

  ● ▣ **T23.062** **Burn of unspecified degree of back of left hand**

  ● ▣ **T23.069** **Burn of unspecified degree of back of unspecified hand**

● **T23.07** **Burn of unspecified degree of wrist**

  ● ▣ **T23.071** **Burn of unspecified degree of right wrist**

  ● ▣ **T23.072** **Burn of unspecified degree of left wrist**

  ● ▣ **T23.079** **Burn of unspecified degree of unspecified wrist**

● **T23.09** **Burn of unspecified degree of multiple sites of wrist and hand**

  ● ▣ **T23.091** **Burn of unspecified degree of multiple sites of right wrist and hand**

  ● ▣ **T23.092** **Burn of unspecified degree of multiple sites of left wrist and hand**

  ● ▣ **T23.099** **Burn of unspecified degree of multiple sites of unspecified wrist and hand**

● **T23.1** **Burn of first degree of wrist and hand**

  Use additional external cause code to identify the source, place and intent of the burn (X00-X19, X75-X77, X96-X98, Y92)

  ● **T23.10** **Burn of first degree of hand, unspecified site**

    ● ▣ **T23.101** **Burn of first degree of right hand, unspecified site**

    ● ▣ **T23.102** **Burn of first degree of left hand, unspecified site**

    ● ▣ **T23.109** **Burn of first degree of unspecified hand, unspecified site**

● **T23.11** **Burn of first degree of thumb (nail)**

  ● **T23.111** **Burn of first degree of right thumb (nail)**

  ● **T23.112** **Burn of first degree of left thumb (nail)**

  ● ▣ **T23.119** **Burn of first degree of unspecified thumb (nail)**

● **T23.12** **Burn of first degree of single finger (nail) except thumb**

  ● **T23.121** **Burn of first degree of single right finger (nail) except thumb**

  ● **T23.122** **Burn of first degree of single left finger (nail) except thumb**

  ● ▣ **T23.129** **Burn of first degree of unspecified single finger (nail) except thumb**

● **T23.13** **Burn of first degree of multiple fingers (nail), not including thumb**

  ● **T23.131** **Burn of first degree of multiple right fingers (nail), not including thumb**

  ● **T23.132** **Burn of first degree of multiple left fingers (nail), not including thumb**

  ● ▣ **T23.139** **Burn of first degree of unspecified multiple fingers (nail), not including thumb**

● **T23.14** **Burn of first degree of multiple fingers (nail), including thumb**

  ● **T23.141** **Burn of first degree of multiple right fingers (nail), including thumb**

  ● **T23.142** **Burn of first degree of multiple left fingers (nail), including thumb**

  ● ▣ **T23.149** **Burn of first degree of unspecified multiple fingers (nail), including thumb**

● **T23.15** **Burn of first degree of palm**

  ● **T23.151** **Burn of first degree of right palm**

  ● **T23.152** **Burn of first degree of left palm**

  ● ▣ **T23.159** **Burn of first degree of unspecified palm**

● **T23.16** **Burn of first degree of back of hand**

  ● **T23.161** **Burn of first degree of back of right hand**

  ● **T23.162** **Burn of first degree of back of left hand**

  ● ▣ **T23.169** **Burn of first degree of back of unspecified hand**

● **T23.17** **Burn of first degree of wrist**

  ● **T23.171** **Burn of first degree of right wrist**

  ● **T23.172** **Burn of first degree of left wrist**

  ● ▣ **T23.179** **Burn of first degree of unspecified wrist**

● **T23.19** **Burn of first degree of multiple sites of wrist and hand**

  ● **T23.191** **Burn of first degree of multiple sites of right of wrist and hand**

  ● **T23.192** **Burn of first degree of multiple sites of left of wrist and hand**

  ● ▣ **T23.199** **Burn of first degree of multiple sites of unspecified of wrist and hand**

CHAPTER 19 (S00-T98)

- T23.2　Burn of second degree of wrist and hand

  Use additional external cause code to identify the source, place and intent of the burn (X00-X19, X75-X77, X96-X98, Y92)

  - T23.20　Burn of second degree of hand, unspecified site
    - ☐ T23.201　Burn of second degree of right hand, unspecified site
    - ☐ T23.202　Burn of second degree of left hand, unspecified site
    - ☐ T23.209　Burn of second degree of unspecified hand, unspecified site
  - T23.21　Burn of second degree of thumb (nail)
    - T23.211　Burn of second degree of right thumb (nail)
    - T23.212　Burn of second degree of left thumb (nail)
    - ☐ T23.219　Burn of second degree of unspecified thumb (nail)
  - T23.22　Burn of second degree of single finger (nail) except thumb
    - T23.221　Burn of second degree of single right finger (nail) except thumb
    - T23.222　Burn of second degree of single left finger (nail) except thumb
    - ☐ T23.229　Burn of second degree of unspecified single finger (nail) except thumb
  - T23.23　Burn of second degree of multiple fingers (nail), not including thumb
    - T23.231　Burn of second degree of multiple right fingers (nail), not including thumb
    - T23.232　Burn of second degree of multiple left fingers (nail), not including thumb
    - ☐ T23.239　Burn of second degree of unspecified multiple fingers (nail), not including thumb
  - T23.24　Burn of second degree of multiple fingers (nail), including thumb
    - T23.241　Burn of second degree of multiple right fingers (nail), including thumb
    - T23.242　Burn of second degree of multiple left fingers (nail), including thumb
    - ☐ T23.249　Burn of second degree of unspecified multiple fingers (nail), including thumb
  - T23.25　Burn of second degree of palm
    - T23.251　Burn of second degree of right palm
    - T23.252　Burn of second degree of left palm
    - ☐ T23.259　Burn of second degree of unspecified palm
  - T23.26　Burn of second degree of back of hand
    - T23.261　Burn of second degree of back of right hand
    - T23.262　Burn of second degree of back of left hand
    - ☐ T23.269　Burn of second degree of back of unspecified hand

- T23.27　Burn of second degree of wrist
  - T23.271　Burn of second degree of right wrist
  - T23.272　Burn of second degree of left wrist
  - ☐ T23.279　Burn of second degree of unspecified wrist
- T23.29　Burn of second degree of multiple sites of wrist and hand
  - T23.291　Burn of second degree of multiple sites of right wrist and hand
  - T23.292　Burn of second degree of multiple sites of left wrist and hand
  - ☐ T23.299　Burn of second degree of multiple sites of unspecified wrist and hand

- T23.3　Burn of third degree of wrist and hand

  Use additional external cause code to identify the source, place and intent of the burn (X00-X19, X75-X77, X96-X98, Y92)

  - T23.30　Burn of third degree of hand, unspecified site
    - ☐ T23.301　Burn of third degree of right hand, unspecified site A 🦠
    - ☐ T23.302　Burn of third degree of left hand, unspecified site A 🦠
    - ☐ T23.309　Burn of third degree of unspecified hand, unspecified site A 🦠
  - T23.31　Burn of third degree of thumb (nail)
    - T23.311　Burn of third degree of right thumb (nail) A 🦠
    - T23.312　Burn of third degree of left thumb (nail) A 🦠
    - ☐ T23.319　Burn of third degree of unspecified thumb (nail) A 🦠
  - T23.32　Burn of third degree of single finger (nail) except thumb
    - T23.321　Burn of third degree of single right finger (nail) except thumb A 🦠
    - T23.322　Burn of third degree of single left finger (nail) except thumb A 🦠
    - ☐ T23.329　Burn of third degree of unspecified single finger (nail) except thumb A 🦠
  - T23.33　Burn of third degree of multiple fingers (nail), not including thumb
    - T23.331　Burn of third degree of multiple right fingers (nail), not including thumb A 🦠
    - T23.332　Burn of third degree of multiple left fingers (nail), not including thumb A 🦠
    - ☐ T23.339　Burn of third degree of unspecified multiple fingers (nail), not including thumb A 🦠
  - T23.34　Burn of third degree of multiple fingers (nail), including thumb
    - T23.341　Burn of third degree of multiple right fingers (nail), including thumb A 🦠
    - T23.342　Burn of third degree of multiple left fingers (nail), including thumb A 🦠

● Unacceptable First-Listed Diagnosis　　● Use Additional Character(s)　　☐ Unspecified　　**OGCR** Official Guidelines for Coding and Reporting

🦠 Complication\Comorbidity　　🦠 Major C\C　　│Excludes 1│　　│Excludes 2│　　Includes　　Use additional　　Code first　　Code also

● ▣ T23.349 Burn of third degree of unspecified multiple fingers (nail), including thumb A 🅐

● T23.35 Burn of third degree of palm

● T23.351 Burn of third degree of right palm A 🅐

● T23.352 Burn of third degree of left palm A 🅐

● ▣ T23.359 Burn of third degree of unspecified palm A 🅐

● T23.36 Burn of third degree of back of hand

● T23.361 Burn of third degree of back of right hand A 🅐

● T23.362 Burn of third degree of back of left hand A 🅐

● ▣ T23.369 Burn of third degree of back of unspecified hand A 🅐

● T23.37 Burn of third degree of wrist

● T23.371 Burn of third degree of right wrist A 🅐

● T23.372 Burn of third degree of left wrist A 🅐

● ▣ T23.379 Burn of third degree of unspecified wrist A 🅐

● T23.39 Burn of third degree of multiple sites of wrist and hand

● T23.391 Burn of third degree of multiple sites of right wrist and hand A 🅐

● T23.392 Burn of third degree of multiple sites of left wrist and hand A 🅐

● ▣ T23.399 Burn of third degree of multiple sites of unspecified wrist and hand A 🅐

● T23.4 Corrosion of unspecified degree of wrist and hand

Code first (T51-T65) to identify chemical and intent

Use additional external cause code to identify place (Y92)

● T23.40 Corrosion of unspecified degree of hand, unspecified site

●● ▣ T23.401 Corrosion of unspecified degree of right hand, unspecified site

●● ▣ T23.402 Corrosion of unspecified degree of left hand, unspecified site

●● ▣ T23.409 Corrosion of unspecified degree of unspecified hand, unspecified site

● T23.41 Corrosion of unspecified degree of thumb (nail)

● ● T23.411 Corrosion of unspecified degree of right thumb (nail)

● ● T23.412 Corrosion of unspecified degree of left thumb (nail)

● ● T23.419 Corrosion of unspecified degree of unspecified thumb (nail)

● T23.42 Corrosion of unspecified degree of single finger (nail) except thumb

●● ▣ T23.421 Corrosion of unspecified degree of single right finger (nail) except thumb

●● T23.422 Corrosion of unspecified degree of single left finger (nail) except thumb

●● T23.429 Corrosion of unspecified degree of unspecified single finger (nail) except thumb

● T23.43 Corrosion of unspecified degree of multiple fingers (nail), not including thumb

●● ▣ T23.431 Corrosion of unspecified degree of multiple right fingers (nail), not including thumb

●● ▣ T23.432 Corrosion of unspecified degree of multiple left fingers (nail), not including thumb

●● ▣ T23.439 Corrosion of unspecified degree of unspecified multiple fingers (nail), not including thumb

● T23.44 Corrosion of unspecified degree of multiple fingers (nail), including thumb

●● ▣ T23.441 Corrosion of unspecified degree of multiple right fingers (nail), including thumb

●● ▣ T23.442 Corrosion of unspecified degree of multiple left fingers (nail), including thumb

●● ▣ T23.449 Corrosion of unspecified degree of unspecified multiple fingers (nail), including thumb

● T23.45 Corrosion of unspecified degree of palm

●● ▣ T23.451 Corrosion of unspecified degree of right palm

●● ▣ T23.452 Corrosion of unspecified degree of left palm

●● ▣ T23.459 Corrosion of unspecified degree of unspecified palm

● T23.46 Corrosion of unspecified degree of back of hand

●● ▣ T23.461 Corrosion of unspecified degree of back of right hand

●● ▣ T23.462 Corrosion of unspecified degree of back of left hand

●● ▣ T23.469 Corrosion of unspecified degree of back of unspecified hand

● T23.47 Corrosion of unspecified degree of wrist

●● ▣ T23.471 Corrosion of unspecified degree of right wrist

●● ▣ T23.472 Corrosion of unspecified degree of left wrist

●● ▣ T23.479 Corrosion of unspecified degree of unspecified wrist

● T23.49 Corrosion of unspecified degree of multiple sites of wrist and hand

●● ▣ T23.491 Corrosion of unspecified degree of multiple sites of right wrist and hand

●● ▣ T23.492 Corrosion of unspecified degree of multiple sites of left wrist and hand

●● ▣ T23.499 Corrosion of unspecified degree of multiple sites of unspecified wrist and hand

● T23.5 Corrosion of first degree of wrist and hand

Code first (T51-T65) to identify chemical and intent

Use additional external cause code to identify place (Y92)

● T23.50 Corrosion of first degree of hand, unspecified site

●● ▣ T23.501 Corrosion of first degree of right hand, unspecified site

● Unacceptable First-Listed Diagnosis   ● Use Additional Character(s)   ▣ Unspecified   **OGCR** Official Guidelines for Coding and Reporting

🅒 Complication\Comorbidity   🅐 Major C\C   ☐ Excludes 1   ☐ Excludes 2   ▢ Includes   Use additional   Code first   Code also   1543

●● ☐ **T23.502** Corrosion of first degree of left hand, unspecified site

●● ☐ **T23.509** Corrosion of first degree of unspecified hand, unspecified site

● **T23.51** Corrosion of first degree of thumb (nail)

   ●● **T23.511** Corrosion of first degree of right thumb (nail)

   ●● **T23.512** Corrosion of first degree of left thumb (nail)

   ●● ☐ **T23.519** Corrosion of first degree of unspecified thumb (nail)

● **T23.52** Corrosion of first degree of single finger (nail) except thumb

   ●● **T23.521** Corrosion of first degree of single right finger (nail) except thumb

   ●● **T23.522** Corrosion of first degree of single left finger (nail) except thumb

   ●● ☐ **T23.529** Corrosion of first degree of unspecified single finger (nail) except thumb

● **T23.53** Corrosion of first degree of multiple fingers (nail), not including thumb

   ●● **T23.531** Corrosion of first degree of multiple right fingers (nail), not including thumb

   ●● **T23.532** Corrosion of first degree of multiple left fingers (nail), not including thumb

   ●● ☐ **T23.539** Corrosion of first degree of unspecified multiple fingers (nail), not including thumb

● **T23.54** Corrosion of first degree of multiple fingers (nail), including thumb

   ● ● **T23.541** Corrosion of first degree of multiple right fingers (nail), including thumb

   ● ● **T23.542** Corrosion of first degree of multiple left fingers (nail), including thumb

   ●● ☐ **T23.549** Corrosion of first degree of unspecified multiple fingers (nail), including thumb

● **T23.55** Corrosion of first degree of palm

   ● ● **T23.551** Corrosion of first degree of right palm

   ● ● **T23.552** Corrosion of first degree of left palm

   ●● ☐ **T23.559** Corrosion of first degree of unspecified palm

● **T23.56** Corrosion of first degree of back of hand

   ● ● **T23.561** Corrosion of first degree of back of right hand

   ● ● **T23.562** Corrosion of first degree of back of left hand

   ●● ☐ **T23.569** Corrosion of first degree of back of unspecified hand

● **T23.57** Corrosion of first degree of wrist

   ● ● **T23.571** Corrosion of first degree of right wrist

   ● ● **T23.572** Corrosion of first degree of left wrist

   ●● ☐ **T23.579** Corrosion of first degree of unspecified wrist

● **T23.59** Corrosion of first degree of multiple sites of wrist and hand

   ● ● **T23.591** Corrosion of first degree of multiple sites of right wrist and hand

   ● ● **T23.592** Corrosion of first degree of multiple sites of left wrist and hand

   ●● ☐ **T23.599** Corrosion of first degree of multiple sites of unspecified wrist and hand

● **T23.6** Corrosion of second degree of wrist and hand

   Code first (T51-T65) *to identify chemical and intent*

   Use additional external cause code to identify place (Y92)

● **T23.60** Corrosion of second degree of hand, unspecified site

   ●● ☐ **T23.601** Corrosion of second degree of right hand, unspecified site

   ●● ☐ **T23.602** Corrosion of second degree of left hand, unspecified site

   ●● ☐ **T23.609** Corrosion of second degree of unspecified hand, unspecified site

● **T23.61** Corrosion of second degree of thumb (nail)

   ● ● **T23.611** Corrosion of second degree of right thumb (nail)

   ● ● **T23.612** Corrosion of second degree of left thumb (nail)

   ●● ☐ **T23.619** Corrosion of second degree of unspecified thumb (nail)

● **T23.62** Corrosion of second degree of single finger (nail) except thumb

   ● ● **T23.621** Corrosion of second degree of single right finger (nail) except thumb

   ● ● **T23.622** Corrosion of second degree of single left finger (nail) except thumb

   ●● ☐ **T23.629** Corrosion of second degree of unspecified single finger (nail) except thumb

● **T23.63** Corrosion of second degree of multiple fingers (nail), not including thumb

   ● ● **T23.631** Corrosion of second degree of multiple right fingers (nail), not including thumb

   ● ● **T23.632** Corrosion of second degree of multiple left fingers (nail), not including thumb

   ●● ☐ **T23.639** Corrosion of second degree of unspecified multiple fingers (nail), not including thumb

● **T23.64** Corrosion of second degree of multiple fingers (nail), including thumb

   ● ● **T23.641** Corrosion of second degree of multiple right fingers (nail), including thumb

   ● ● **T23.642** Corrosion of second degree of multiple left fingers (nail), including thumb

   ●● ☐ **T23.649** Corrosion of second degree of unspecified multiple fingers (nail), including thumb

● Unacceptable First-Listed Diagnosis   ● Use Additional Character(s)   ☐ Unspecified   **OGCR** Official Guidelines for Coding and Reporting

🝙 Complication\Comorbidity   🝙 Major C\C   Excludes 1   Excludes 2   Includes   Use additional   Code first   Code also

● T23.65   Corrosion of second degree of palm

     ● ● T23.651   Corrosion of second degree of right palm

     ● ● T23.652   Corrosion of second degree of left palm

     ●● ▢ T23.659   Corrosion of second degree of unspecified palm

● T23.66   Corrosion of second degree of back of hand

     ● ● T23.661   Corrosion of second degree of right hand

     ● ● T23.662   Corrosion of second degree of left hand

     ●● ▢ T23.669   Corrosion of second degree of unspecified hand

● T23.67   Corrosion of second degree of wrist

     ● ● T23.671   Corrosion of second degree of right wrist

     ● ● T23.672   Corrosion of second degree of left wrist

     ●● ▢ T23.679   Corrosion of second degree of unspecified wrist

● T23.69   Corrosion of second degree of multiple sites of wrist and hand

     ● ● T23.691   Corrosion of second degree of multiple sites of right wrist and hand

     ● ● T23.692   Corrosion of second degree of multiple sites of left wrist and hand

     ●● ▢ T23.699   Corrosion of second degree of multiple sites of unspecified wrist and hand

● T23.7   Corrosion of third degree of wrist and hand

     Code first (T51-T65) to identify chemical and intent

     Use additional external cause code to identify place (Y92)

   ● T23.70   Corrosion of third degree of hand, unspecified site

     ●● ▢ T23.701   Corrosion of third degree of right hand, unspecified site A 🕭

     ●● ▢ T23.702   Corrosion of third degree of left hand, unspecified site A 🕭

     ●● ▢ T23.709   Corrosion of third degree of unspecified hand, unspecified site A 🕭

   ● T23.71   Corrosion of third degree of thumb (nail)

     ● ● T23.711   Corrosion of third degree of right thumb (nail) A 🕭

     ● ● T23.712   Corrosion of third degree of left thumb (nail) A 🕭

     ●● ▢ T23.719   Corrosion of third degree of unspecified thumb (nail) A 🕭

   ● T23.72   Corrosion of third degree of single finger (nail) except thumb

     ● ● T23.721   Corrosion of third degree of single right finger (nail) except thumb A 🕭

     ● ● T23.722   Corrosion of third degree of single left finger (nail) except thumb A 🕭

     ●● ▢ T23.729   Corrosion of third degree of unspecified single finger (nail) except thumb A 🕭

   ● T23.73   Corrosion of third degree of multiple fingers (nail), not including thumb

     ● ● T23.731   Corrosion of third degree of multiple right fingers (nail), not including thumb A 🕭

     ● ● T23.732   Corrosion of third degree of multiple left fingers (nail), not including thumb A 🕭

     ●● ▢ T23.739   Corrosion of third degree of unspecified multiple fingers (nail), not including thumb A 🕭

   ● T23.74   Corrosion of third degree of multiple fingers (nail), including thumb

     ● ● T23.741   Corrosion of third degree of multiple right fingers (nail), including thumb A 🕭

     ● ● T23.742   Corrosion of third degree of multiple left fingers (nail), including thumb A 🕭

     ●● ▢ T23.749   Corrosion of third degree of unspecified multiple fingers (nail), including thumb A 🕭

   ● T23.75   Corrosion of third degree of palm

     ● ● T23.751   Corrosion of third degree of right palm A 🕭

     ● ● T23.752   Corrosion of third degree of left palm A 🕭

     ●● ▢ T23.759   Corrosion of third degree of unspecified palm A 🕭

   ● T23.76   Corrosion of third degree of back of hand

     ● ● T23.761   Corrosion of third degree of back of right hand A 🕭

     ● ● T23.762   Corrosion of third degree of back of left hand A 🕭

     ●● ▢ T23.769   Corrosion of third degree of unspecified back of hand A 🕭

   ● T23.77   Corrosion of third degree of wrist

     ● ● T23.771   Corrosion of third degree of right wrist A 🕭

     ● ● T23.772   Corrosion of third degree of left wrist A 🕭

     ●● ▢ T23.779   Corrosion of third degree of unspecified wrist A 🕭

   ● T23.79   Corrosion of third degree of multiple sites of wrist and hand

     ● ● T23.791   Corrosion of third degree of multiple sites of right wrist and hand A 🕭

     ● ● T23.792   Corrosion of third degree of multiple sites of left wrist and hand A 🕭

     ●● ▢ T23.799   Corrosion of third degree of multiple sites of unspecified wrist and hand A 🕭

● T24   Burn and corrosion of lower limb, except ankle and foot

     Excludes2   burn and corrosion of ankle and foot (T25.-)

              burn and corrosion of hip region (T21.-)

     The appropriate 7th character is to be added to each code from category T24

     | | |
     A   initial encounter
     D   subsequent encounter
     S   sequela

   ● T24.0   Burn of unspecified degree of lower limb, except ankle and foot

     Use additional external cause code to identify the source, place and intent of the burn (X00-X19, X75-X77, X96-X98, Y92)

●   Unacceptable First-Listed Diagnosis   ●   Use Additional Character(s)   ▢   Unspecified   **OGCR**   Official Guidelines for Coding and Reporting

🕭 Complication\Comorbidity   🕭 Major C\C | Excludes 1 | | Excludes 2 | | Includes | Use additional   Code first   Code also

1545

CHAPTER 19 (S00-T98)

● T24.00   Burn of unspecified degree of unspecified site of lower limb, except ankle and foot

    ● ■ T24.001   Burn of unspecified degree of unspecified site of right lower limb, except ankle and foot

    ● ■ T24.002   Burn of unspecified degree of unspecified site of left lower limb, except ankle and foot

    ● ■ T24.009   Burn of unspecified degree of unspecified site of unspecified lower limb, except ankle and foot

● T24.01   Burn of unspecified degree of thigh

    ● ■ T24.011   Burn of unspecified degree of right thigh

    ● ■ T24.012   Burn of unspecified degree of left thigh

    ● ■ T24.019   Burn of unspecified degree of unspecified thigh

● T24.02   Burn of unspecified degree of knee

    ● ■ T24.021   Burn of unspecified degree of right knee

    ● ■ T24.022   Burn of unspecified degree of left knee

    ● ■ T24.029   Burn of unspecified degree of unspecified knee

● T24.03   Burn of unspecified degree of lower leg

    ● ■ T24.031   Burn of unspecified degree of right lower leg

    ● ■ T24.032   Burn of unspecified degree of left lower leg

    ● ■ T24.039   Burn of unspecified degree of unspecified lower leg

● T24.09   Burn of unspecified degree of multiple sites of lower limb, except ankle and foot

    ● ■ T24.091   Burn of unspecified degree of multiple sites of right lower limb, except ankle and foot

    ● ■ T24.092   Burn of unspecified degree of multiple sites of left lower limb, except ankle and foot

    ● ■ T24.099   Burn of unspecified degree of multiple sites of unspecified lower limb, except ankle and foot

● T24.1   Burn of first degree of lower limb, except ankle and foot

    Use additional external cause code to identify the source, place and intent of the burn (X00-X19, X75-X77, X96-X98, Y92)

    ● T24.10   Burn of first degree of unspecified site of lower limb, except ankle and foot

       ● ■ T24.101   Burn of first degree of unspecified site of right lower limb, except ankle and foot

       ● ■ T24.102   Burn of first degree of unspecified site of left lower limb, except ankle and foot

       ● ■ T24.109   Burn of first degree of unspecified site of unspecified lower limb, except ankle and foot

    ● T24.11   Burn of first degree of thigh

       ● T24.111   Burn of first degree of right thigh

       ● T24.112   Burn of first degree of left thigh

       ● ■ T24.119   Burn of first degree of unspecified thigh

● T24.12   Burn of first degree of knee

    ● T24.121   Burn of first degree of right knee

    ● T24.122   Burn of first degree of left knee

    ● ■ T24.129   Burn of first degree of unspecified knee

● T24.13   Burn of first degree of lower leg

    ● T24.131   Burn of first degree of right lower leg

    ● T24.132   Burn of first degree of left lower leg

    ● ■ T24.139   Burn of first degree of unspecified lower leg

● T24.19   Burn of first degree of multiple sites of lower limb, except ankle and foot

    ● T24.191   Burn of first degree of multiple sites of right lower limb, except ankle and foot

    ● T24.192   Burn of first degree of multiple sites of left lower limb, except ankle and foot

    ● ■ T24.199   Burn of first degree of multiple sites of unspecified lower limb, except ankle and foot

● T24.2   Burn of second degree of lower limb, except ankle and foot

    Use additional external cause code to identify the source, place and intent of the burn (X00-X19, X75-X77, X96-X98, Y92)

    ● T24.20   Burn of second degree of unspecified site of lower limb, except ankle and foot

       ● ■ T24.201   Burn of second degree of unspecified site of right lower limb, except ankle and foot

       ● ■ T24.202   Burn of second degree of unspecified site of left lower limb, except ankle and foot

       ● ■ T24.209   Burn of second degree of unspecified site of unspecified lower limb, except ankle and foot

    ● T24.21   Burn of second degree of thigh

       ● T24.211   Burn of second degree of right thigh

       ● T24.212   Burn of second degree of left thigh

       ● ■ T24.219   Burn of second degree of unspecified thigh

    ● T24.22   Burn of second degree of knee

       ● T24.221   Burn of second degree of right knee

       ● T24.222   Burn of second degree of left knee

       ● ■ T24.229   Burn of second degree of unspecified knee

    ● T24.23   Burn of second degree of lower leg

       ● T24.231   Burn of second degree of right lower leg

       ● T24.232   Burn of second degree of left lower leg

       ● ■ T24.239   Burn of second degree of unspecified lower leg

    ● T24.29   Burn of second degree of multiple sites of lower limb, except ankle and foot

       ● T24.291   Burn of second degree of multiple sites of right lower limb, except ankle and foot

       ● T24.292   Burn of second degree of multiple sites of left lower limb, except ankle and foot

● Unacceptable First-Listed Diagnosis   ● Use Additional Character(s)   ■ Unspecified   **OGCR** Official Guidelines for Coding and Reporting

🗝 Complication\Comorbidity   🗝 Major C\C | Excludes 1 | | Excludes 2 | Includes   Use additional   Code first   Code also

● ▣ T24.299 Burn of second degree of multiple sites of unspecified lower limb, except ankle and foot

● T24.3 Burn of third degree of lower limb, except ankle and foot

> Use additional external cause code to identify the source, place and intent of the burn (X00-X19, X75-X77, X96-X98, Y92)

● T24.30 Burn of third degree of unspecified site of lower limb, except ankle and foot

● ▣ T24.301 Burn of third degree of unspecified site of right lower limb, except ankle and foot A 🍏

● ▣ T24.302 Burn of third degree of unspecified site of left lower limb, except ankle and foot A 🍏

● ▣ T24.309 Burn of third degree of unspecified site of unspecified lower limb, except ankle and foot A 🍏

● T24.31 Burn of third degree of thigh

● T24.311 Burn of third degree of right thigh A 🍏

● T24.312 Burn of third degree of left thigh A 🍏

● ▣ T24.319 Burn of third degree of unspecified thigh A 🍏

● T24.32 Burn of third degree of knee

● T24.321 Burn of third degree of right knee A 🍏

● T24.322 Burn of third degree of left knee A 🍏

● ▣ T24.329 Burn of third degree of unspecified knee A 🍏

● T24.33 Burn of third degree of lower leg

● T24.331 Burn of third degree of right lower leg A 🍏

● T24.332 Burn of third degree of left lower leg A 🍏

● ▣ T24.339 Burn of third degree of unspecified lower leg A 🍏

● T24.39 Burn of third degree of multiple sites of lower limb, except ankle and foot

● T24.391 Burn of third degree of multiple sites of right lower limb, except ankle and foot A 🍏

● T24.392 Burn of third degree of multiple sites of left lower limb, except ankle and foot A 🍏

● ▣ T24.399 Burn of third degree of multiple sites of unspecified lower limb, except ankle and foot A 🍏

● T24.4 Corrosion of unspecified degree of lower limb, except ankle and foot

> Code first (T51-T65) to identify chemical and intent

> Use additional external cause code to identify place (Y92)

● T24.40 Corrosion of unspecified degree of unspecified site of lower limb, except ankle and foot

●● ▣ T24.401 Corrosion of unspecified degree of unspecified site of right lower limb, except ankle and foot

●● ▣ T24.402 Corrosion of unspecified degree of unspecified site of left lower limb, except ankle and foot

●● ▣ T24.409 Corrosion of unspecified degree of unspecified site of unspecified lower limb, except ankle and foot

● T24.41 Corrosion of unspecified degree of thigh

●● ▣ T24.411 Corrosion of unspecified degree of right thigh

●● ▣ T24.412 Corrosion of unspecified degree of left thigh

●● ▣ T24.419 Corrosion of unspecified degree of unspecified thigh

● T24.42 Corrosion of unspecified degree of knee

●● ▣ T24.421 Corrosion of unspecified degree of right knee

●● ▣ T24.422 Corrosion of unspecified degree of left knee

●● ▣ T24.429 Corrosion of unspecified degree of unspecified knee

● T24.43 Corrosion of unspecified degree of lower leg

●● ▣ T24.431 Corrosion of unspecified degree of right lower leg

●● ▣ T24.432 Corrosion of unspecified degree of left lower leg

●● ▣ T24.439 Corrosion of unspecified degree of unspecified lower leg

● T24.49 Corrosion of unspecified degree of multiple sites of lower limb, except ankle and foot

●● ▣ T24.491 Corrosion of unspecified degree of multiple sites of right lower limb, except ankle and foot

●● ▣ T24.492 Corrosion of unspecified degree of multiple sites of left lower limb, except ankle and foot

●● ▣ T24.499 Corrosion of unspecified degree of multiple sites of unspecified lower limb, except ankle and foot

● T24.5 Corrosion of first degree of lower limb, except ankle and foot

> Code first (T51-T65) to identify chemical and intent

> Use additional external cause code to identify place (Y92)

● T24.50 Corrosion of first degree of unspecified site of lower limb, except ankle and foot

●● ▣ T24.501 Corrosion of first degree of unspecified site of right lower limb, except ankle and foot

●● ▣ T24.502 Corrosion of first degree of unspecified site of left lower limb, except ankle and foot

●● ▣ T24.509 Corrosion of first degree of unspecified site of unspecified lower limb, except ankle and foot

● T24.51 Corrosion of first degree of thigh

●● T24.511 Corrosion of first degree of right thigh

●● T24.512 Corrosion of first degree of left thigh

●● ▣ T24.519 Corrosion of first degree of unspecified thigh

● Unacceptable First-Listed Diagnosis   ● Use Additional Character(s)   ▣ Unspecified   OGCR Official Guidelines for Coding and Reporting
🍏 Complication\Comorbidity   🍏 Major C\C   [Excludes 1]   [Excludes 2]   Includes   Use additional   Code first   Code also
CHAPTER 19 (S00-T98)   1547

● **T24.52**   Corrosion of first degree of knee
  ● ● **T24.521**   Corrosion of first degree of right knee
  ● ● **T24.522**   Corrosion of first degree of left knee
  ● ● ■ **T24.529**   Corrosion of first degree of unspecified knee

● **T24.53**   Corrosion of first degree of lower leg
  ● ● **T24.531**   Corrosion of first degree of right lower leg
  ● ● **T24.532**   Corrosion of first degree of left lower leg
  ● ● ■ **T24.539**   Corrosion of first degree of unspecified lower leg

● **T24.59**   Corrosion of first degree of multiple sites of lower limb, except ankle and foot
  ● ● **T24.591**   Corrosion of first degree of multiple sites of right lower limb, except ankle and foot
  ● ● **T24.592**   Corrosion of first degree of multiple sites of left lower limb, except ankle and foot
  ● ● ■ **T24.599**   Corrosion of first degree of multiple sites of unspecified lower limb, except ankle and foot

● **T24.6**   Corrosion of second degree of lower limb, except ankle and foot

> *Code first* (T51-T65) *to identify chemical and intent*
>
> Use additional external cause code to identify place (Y92)

● **T24.60**   Corrosion of second degree of unspecified site of lower limb, except ankle and foot
  ● ● ■ **T24.601**   Corrosion of second degree of unspecified site of right lower limb, except ankle and foot
  ● ● ■ **T24.602**   Corrosion of second degree of unspecified site of left lower limb, except ankle and foot
  ● ● ■ **T24.609**   Corrosion of second degree of unspecified site of unspecified lower limb, except ankle and foot

● **T24.61**   Corrosion of second degree of thigh
  ● ● **T24.611**   Corrosion of second degree of right thigh
  ● ● **T24.612**   Corrosion of second degree of left thigh
  ● ● ■ **T24.619**   Corrosion of second degree of unspecified thigh

● **T24.62**   Corrosion of second degree of knee
  ● ● **T24.621**   Corrosion of second degree of right knee
  ● ● **T24.622**   Corrosion of second degree of left knee
  ● ● ■ **T24.629**   Corrosion of second degree of unspecified knee

● **T24.63**   Corrosion of second degree of lower leg
  ● ● **T24.631**   Corrosion of second degree of right lower leg
  ● ● **T24.632**   Corrosion of second degree of left lower leg
  ● ● ■ **T24.639**   Corrosion of second degree of unspecified lower leg

● **T24.69**   Corrosion of second degree of multiple sites of lower limb, except ankle and foot
  ● ● **T24.691**   Corrosion of second degree of multiple sites of right lower limb, except ankle and foot
  ● ● **T24.692**   Corrosion of second degree of multiple sites of left lower limb, except ankle and foot
  ● ● ■ **T24.699**   Corrosion of second degree of multiple sites of unspecified lower limb, except ankle and foot

● **T24.7**   Corrosion of third degree of lower limb, except ankle and foot

> *Code first* (T51-T65) *to identify chemical and intent*
>
> Use additional external cause code to identify place (Y92)

● **T24.70**   Corrosion of third degree of unspecified site of lower limb, except ankle and foot
  ● ● ■ **T24.701**   Corrosion of third degree of unspecified site of right lower limb, except ankle and foot A 🌎
  ● ● ■ **T24.702**   Corrosion of third degree of unspecified site of left lower limb, except ankle and foot A 🌎
  ● ● ■ **T24.709**   Corrosion of third degree of unspecified site of unspecified lower limb, except ankle and foot A 🌎

● **T24.71**   Corrosion of third degree of thigh
  ● ● **T24.711**   Corrosion of third degree of right thigh A 🌎
  ● ● **T24.712**   Corrosion of third degree of left thigh A 🌎
  ● ● ■ **T24.719**   Corrosion of third degree of unspecified thigh A 🌎

● **T24.72**   Corrosion of third degree of knee
  ● ● **T24.721**   Corrosion of third degree of right knee A 🌎
  ● ● **T24.722**   Corrosion of third degree of left knee A 🌎
  ● ● ■ **T24.729**   Corrosion of third degree of unspecified knee A 🌎

● **T24.73**   Corrosion of third degree of lower leg
  ● ● **T24.731**   Corrosion of third degree of right lower leg A 🌎
  ● ● **T24.732**   Corrosion of third degree of left lower leg A 🌎
  ● ● ■ **T24.739**   Corrosion of third degree of unspecified lower leg A 🌎

● **T24.79**   Corrosion of third degree of multiple sites of lower limb, except ankle and foot
  ● ● **T24.791**   Corrosion of third degree of multiple sites of right lower limb, except ankle and foot A 🌎
  ● ● **T24.792**   Corrosion of third degree of multiple sites of left lower limb, except ankle and foot A 🌎
  ● ● ■ **T24.799**   Corrosion of third degree of multiple sites of unspecified lower limb, except ankle and foot A 🌎

● Unacceptable First-Listed Diagnosis   ● Use Additional Character(s)   ■ Unspecified   **OGCR** Official Guidelines for Coding and Reporting
🌎 Complication\Comorbidity   🌎 Major C\C   Excludes 1   Excludes 2   Includes   Use additional   Code first   Code also

● **T25   Burn and corrosion of ankle and foot**

The appropriate 7th character is to be added to each code from category T25

> A   initial encounter
> D   subsequent encounter
> S   sequela

● **T25.0   Burn of unspecified degree of ankle and foot**

Use additional external cause code to identify the source, place and intent of the burn (X00-X19, X75-X77, X96-X98, Y92)

  ● **T25.01   Burn of unspecified degree of ankle**

    ● **T25.011   Burn of unspecified degree of right ankle**

    ● **T25.012   Burn of unspecified degree of left ankle**

    ● **T25.019   Burn of unspecified degree of unspecified ankle**

  ● **T25.02   Burn of unspecified degree of foot**

> **Excludes2**   burn of unspecified degree of toe(s) (nail) (T25.03-)

    ● **T25.021   Burn of unspecified degree of right foot**

    ● **T25.022   Burn of unspecified degree of left foot**

    ● **T25.029   Burn of unspecified degree of unspecified foot**

  ● **T25.03   Burn of unspecified degree of toe(s) (nail)**

    ● **T25.031   Burn of unspecified degree of right toe(s) (nail)**

    ● **T25.032   Burn of unspecified degree of left toe(s) (nail)**

    ● **T25.039   Burn of unspecified degree of unspecified toe(s) (nail)**

  ● **T25.09   Burn of unspecified degree of multiple sites of ankle and foot**

    ● **T25.091   Burn of unspecified degree of multiple sites of right ankle and foot**

    ● **T25.092   Burn of unspecified degree of multiple sites of left ankle and foot**

    ● **T25.099   Burn of unspecified degree of multiple sites of unspecified ankle and foot**

● **T25.1   Burn of first degree of ankle and foot**

Use additional external cause code to identify the source, place and intent of the burn (X00-X19, X75-X77, X96-X98, Y92)

  ● **T25.11   Burn of first degree of ankle**

    ● **T25.111   Burn of first degree of right ankle**

    ● **T25.112   Burn of first degree of left ankle**

    ● **T25.119   Burn of first degree of unspecified ankle**

  ● **T25.12   Burn of first degree of foot**

> **Excludes2**   burn of first degree of toe(s) (nail) (T25.13-)

    ● **T25.121   Burn of first degree of right foot**

    ● **T25.122   Burn of first degree of left foot**

    ● **T25.129   Burn of first degree of unspecified foot**

  ● **T25.13   Burn of first degree of toe(s) (nail)**

    ● **T25.131   Burn of first degree of right toe(s) (nail)**

    ● **T25.132   Burn of first degree of left toe(s) (nail)**

    ● **T25.139   Burn of first degree of unspecified toe(s) (nail)**

  ● **T25.19   Burn of first degree of multiple sites of ankle and foot**

    ● **T25.191   Burn of first degree of multiple sites of right ankle and foot**

    ● **T25.192   Burn of first degree of multiple sites of left ankle and foot**

    ● **T25.199   Burn of first degree of multiple sites of unspecified ankle and foot**

● **T25.2   Burn of second degree of ankle and foot**

Use additional external cause code to identify the source, place and intent of the burn (X00-X19, X75-X77, X96-X98, Y92)

  ● **T25.21   Burn of second degree of ankle**

    ● **T25.211   Burn of second degree of right ankle**

    ● **T25.212   Burn of second degree of left ankle**

    ● **T25.219   Burn of second degree of unspecified ankle**

  ● **T25.22   Burn of second degree of foot**

> **Excludes2**   burn of second degree of toe(s) (nail) (T25.23-)

    ● **T25.221   Burn of second degree of right foot**

    ● **T25.222   Burn of second degree of left foot**

    ● **T25.229   Burn of second degree of unspecified foot**

  ● **T25.23   Burn of second degree of toe(s) (nail)**

    ● **T25.231   Burn of second degree of right toe(s) (nail)**

    ● **T25.232   Burn of second degree of left toe(s) (nail)**

    ● **T25.239   Burn of second degree of unspecified toe(s) (nail)**

  ● **T25.29   Burn of second degree of multiple sites of ankle and foot**

    ● **T25.291   Burn of second degree of multiple sites of right ankle and foot**

    ● **T25.292   Burn of second degree of multiple sites of left ankle and foot**

    ● **T25.299   Burn of second degree of multiple sites of unspecified ankle and foot**

● **T25.3   Burn of third degree of ankle and foot**

Use additional external cause code to identify the source, place and intent of the burn (X00-X19, X75-X77, X96-X98, Y92)

  ● **T25.31   Burn of third degree of ankle**

    ● **T25.311   Burn of third degree of right ankle A** 🐾

    ● **T25.312   Burn of third degree of left ankle A** 🐾

    ● **T25.319   Burn of third degree of unspecified ankle A** 🐾

  ● **T25.32   Burn of third degree of foot**

> **Excludes2**   burn of third degree of toe(s) (nail) (T25.33-)

    ● **T25.321   Burn of third degree of right foot A** 🐾

    ● **T25.322   Burn of third degree of left foot A** 🐾

    ● **T25.329   Burn of third degree of unspecified foot A** 🐾

● Unacceptable First-Listed Diagnosis   ● Use Additional Character(s)   ▨ Unspecified   **OGCR** Official Guidelines for Coding and Reporting

🐾 Complication\Comorbidity   🐾 Major C\C   Excludes 1   Excludes 2   Includes   Use additional   Code first   Code also

1549

CHAPTER 19 (S00-T98)

● **T25.33**   Burn of third degree of toe(s) (nail)
- ● **T25.331**   Burn of third degree of right toe(s) (nail) A 🦠
- ● **T25.332**   Burn of third degree of left toe(s) (nail) A 🦠
- ● ■ **T25.339**   Burn of third degree of unspecified toe(s) (nail) A 🦠

● **T25.39**   Burn of third degree of multiple sites of ankle and foot
- ● **T25.391**   Burn of third degree of multiple sites of right ankle and foot A 🦠
- ● **T25.392**   Burn of third degree of multiple sites of left ankle and foot A 🦠
- ● **T25.399**   Burn of third degree of multiple sites of unspecified ankle and foot A 🦠

● **T25.4**   Corrosion of unspecified degree of ankle and foot
Code first (T51-T65) to identify chemical and intent
Use additional external cause code to identify place (Y92)

● **T25.41**   Corrosion of unspecified degree of ankle
- ●● ■ **T25.411**   Corrosion of unspecified degree of right ankle
- ●● ■ **T25.412**   Corrosion of unspecified degree of left ankle
- ●● ■ **T25.419**   Corrosion of unspecified degree of unspecified ankle

● **T25.42**   Corrosion of unspecified degree of foot
> **Excludes2**   corrosion of unspecified degree of toe(s) (nail) (T25.43-)
- ●● ■ **T25.421**   Corrosion of unspecified degree of right foot
- ●● ■ **T25.422**   Corrosion of unspecified degree of left foot
- ●● ■ **T25.429**   Corrosion of unspecified degree of unspecified foot

● **T25.43**   Corrosion of unspecified degree of toe(s) (nail)
- ●● ■ **T25.431**   Corrosion of unspecified degree of right toe(s) (nail)
- ●● ■ **T25.432**   Corrosion of unspecified degree of left toe(s) (nail)
- ●● ■ **T25.439**   Corrosion of unspecified degree of unspecified toe(s) (nail)

● **T25.49**   Corrosion of unspecified degree of multiple sites of ankle and foot
- ●● ■ **T25.491**   Corrosion of unspecified degree of multiple sites of right ankle and foot
- ●● ■ **T25.492**   Corrosion of unspecified degree of multiple sites of left ankle and foot
- ●● ■ **T25.499**   Corrosion of unspecified degree of multiple sites of unspecified ankle and foot

● **T25.5**   Corrosion of first degree of ankle and foot
Code first (T51-T65) to identify chemical and intent
Use additional external cause code to identify place (Y92)

● **T25.51**   Corrosion of first degree of ankle
- ● ● **T25.511**   Corrosion of first degree of right ankle

● ● **T25.512**   Corrosion of first degree of left ankle
- ●● ■ **T25.519**   Corrosion of first degree of unspecified ankle

● **T25.52**   Corrosion of first degree of foot
> **Excludes2**   corrosion of first degree of toe(s) (nail) (T25.53-)
- ● ● **T25.521**   Corrosion of first degree of right foot
- ● ● **T25.522**   Corrosion of first degree of left foot
- ●● ■ **T25.529**   Corrosion of first degree of unspecified foot

● **T25.53**   Corrosion of first degree of toe(s) (nail)
- ● ● **T25.531**   Corrosion of first degree of right toe(s) (nail)
- ● ● **T25.532**   Corrosion of first degree of left toe(s) (nail)
- ●● ■ **T25.539**   Corrosion of first degree of unspecified toe(s) (nail)

● **T25.59**   Corrosion of first degree of multiple sites of ankle and foot
- ● ● **T25.591**   Corrosion of first degree of multiple sites of right ankle and foot
- ● ● **T25.592**   Corrosion of first degree of multiple sites of left ankle and foot
- ●● ■ **T25.599**   Corrosion of first degree of multiple sites of unspecified ankle and foot

● **T25.6**   Corrosion of second degree of ankle and foot
Code first (T51-T65) to identify chemical and intent
Use additional external cause code to identify place (Y92)

● **T25.61**   Corrosion of second degree of ankle
- ● ● **T25.611**   Corrosion of second degree of right ankle
- ● ● **T25.612**   Corrosion of second degree of left ankle
- ●● ■ **T25.619**   Corrosion of second degree of unspecified ankle

● **T25.62**   Corrosion of second degree of foot
> **Excludes2**   corrosion of second degree of toe(s) (nail) (T25.63-)
- ● ● **T25.621**   Corrosion of second degree of right foot
- ● ● **T25.622**   Corrosion of second degree of left foot
- ●● ■ **T25.629**   Corrosion of second degree of unspecified foot

● **T25.63**   Corrosion of second degree of toe(s) (nail)
- ● ● **T25.631**   Corrosion of second degree of right toe(s) (nail)
- ● ● **T25.632**   Corrosion of second degree of left toe(s) (nail)
- ●● ■ **T25.639**   Corrosion of second degree of unspecified toe(s) (nail)

● **T25.69**   Corrosion of second degree of multiple sites of ankle and foot
- ● ● **T25.691**   Corrosion of second degree of right ankle and foot

● Unacceptable First-Listed Diagnosis   ● Use Additional Character(s)   ■ Unspecified   **OGCR** Official Guidelines for Coding and Reporting
🦠 Complication\Comorbidity   🦠 Major C\C   Excludes 1   Excludes 2   Includes   Use additional   Code first   Code also

- ● ● T25.692 Corrosion of second degree of left ankle and foot
- ●● ▪ T25.699 Corrosion of second degree of unspecified ankle and foot
- ● T25.7 Corrosion of third degree of ankle and foot

  Code first (T51-T65) to identify chemical and intent

  Use additional external cause code to identify place (Y92)

  - ● T25.71 Corrosion of third degree of ankle
    - ● ● T25.711 Corrosion of third degree of right ankle A 🕭
    - ● ● T25.712 Corrosion of third degree of left ankle A 🕭
    - ●● ▪ T25.719 Corrosion of third degree of unspecified ankle A 🕭
  - ● T25.72 Corrosion of third degree of foot

    Excludes2 corrosion of third degree of toe(s) (nail) (T25.73-)

    - ● ● T25.721 Corrosion of third degree of right foot A 🕭
    - ● ● T25.722 Corrosion of third degree of left foot A 🕭
    - ●● ▪ T25.729 Corrosion of third degree of unspecified foot A 🕭
  - ● T25.73 Corrosion of third degree of toe(s) (nail)
    - ● ● T25.731 Corrosion of third degree of right toe(s) (nail) A 🕭
    - ● ● T25.732 Corrosion of third degree of left toe(s) (nail) A 🕭
    - ●● ▪ T25.739 Corrosion of third degree of unspecified toe(s) (nail) A 🕭
  - ● T25.79 Corrosion of third degree of multiple sites of ankle and foot
    - ● ● T25.791 Corrosion of third degree of multiple sites of right ankle and foot A 🕭
    - ● ● T25.792 Corrosion of third degree of multiple sites of left ankle and foot A 🕭
    - ●● ▪ T25.799 Corrosion of third degree of multiple sites of unspecified ankle and foot A 🕭

BURNS AND CORROSIONS CONFINED TO EYE AND INTERNAL ORGANS (T26-T28)

- ● T26 Burn and corrosion confined to eye and adnexa

  The appropriate 7th character is to be added to each code from category T26

  > A initial encounter
  > D subsequent encounter
  > S sequela

  - ● T26.0 Burn of eyelid and periocular area

    Use additional external cause code to identify the source, place and intent of the burn (X00-X19, X75-X77, X96-X98, Y92)

    - ● ▪ T26.00 Burn of eyelid and periocular area, unspecified side
    - ● T26.01 Burn of right eyelid and periocular area
    - ● T26.02 Burn of left eyelid and periocular area
  - ● T26.1 Burn of cornea and conjunctival sac

    Use additional external cause code to identify the source, place and intent of the burn (X00-X19, X75-X77, X96-X98, Y92)

    - ● ▪ T26.10 Burn of cornea and conjunctival sac, unspecified side

- ● T26.11 Burn of cornea and conjunctival sac, right eye
- ● T26.12 Burn of cornea and conjunctival sac, left eye
- ● T26.2 Burn with resulting rupture and destruction of eyeball

  Use additional external cause code to identify the source, place and intent of the burn (X00-X19, X75-X77, X96-X98, Y92)

  - ● ▪ T26.20 Burn with resulting rupture and destruction of eyeball, unspecified side A 🕭
  - ● T26.21 Burn with resulting rupture and destruction of right eyeball A 🕭
  - ● T26.22 Burn with resulting rupture and destruction of left eyeball A 🕭
- ● T26.3 Burns of other parts of eye and adnexa

  Use additional external cause code to identify the source, place and intent of the burn (X00-X19, X75-X77, X96-X98, Y92)

  - ● ▪ T26.30 Burns of other parts of eye and adnexa, unspecified side
  - ● T26.31 Burns of other parts of right eye and adnexa
  - ● T26.32 Burns of other parts of left eye and adnexa
- ● T26.4 Burn of eye and adnexa, part unspecified

  Use additional external cause code to identify the source, place and intent of the burn (X00-X19, X75-X77, X96-X98, Y92)

  - ● ▪ T26.40 Burn of eye and adnexa, part unspecified, unspecified side
  - ● ▪ T26.41 Burn of right eye and adnexa, part unspecified
  - ● ▪ T26.42 Burn of left eye and adnexa, part unspecified
- ● T26.5 Corrosion of eyelid and periocular area

  Code first (T51-T65) to identify chemical and intent

  Use additional external cause code to identify place (Y92)

  - ●● ▪ T26.50 Corrosion of eyelid and periocular area, unspecified side
  - ● ● T26.51 Corrosion of eyelid and periocular area, right eye
  - ● ● T26.52 Corrosion of eyelid and periocular area, left eye
- ● T26.6 Corrosion of cornea and conjunctival sac

  Code first (T51-T65) to identify chemical and intent

  Use additional external cause code to identify place (Y92)

  - ●● ▪ T26.60 Corrosion of cornea and conjunctival sac, unspecified side
  - ● ● T26.61 Corrosion of cornea and conjunctival sac, right eye
  - ● ● T26.62 Corrosion of cornea and conjunctival sac, left eye
- ● T26.7 Corrosion with resulting rupture and destruction of eyeball

  Code first (T51-T65) to identify chemical and intent

  Use additional external cause code to identify place (Y92)

  - ●● ▪ T26.70 Corrosion with resulting rupture and destruction of eyeball, unspecified side A 🕭
  - ● ● T26.71 Corrosion with resulting rupture and destruction of right eyeball A 🕭
  - ● ● T26.72 Corrosion with resulting rupture and destruction of left eyeball A 🕭

● Unacceptable First-Listed Diagnosis   ● Use Additional Character(s)   ▪ Unspecified   OGCR Official Guidelines for Coding and Reporting
🕭 Complication\Comorbidity   🕭 Major C\C   Excludes 1   Excludes 2   Includes   Use additional   Code first   Code also   1551

CHAPTER 19 (S00-T98)

● T26.8 **Corrosions of other parts of eye and adnexa**
> *Code first (T51-T65) to identify chemical and intent*
>
> Use additional external cause code to identify place (Y92)

●● ■ T26.80 **Corrosions of other parts of eye and adnexa, unspecified side**

● ● T26.81 **Corrosions of other parts of right eye and adnexa**

● ● T26.82 **Corrosions of other parts of left eye and adnexa**

● T26.9 **Corrosion of eye and adnexa, part unspecified**
> *Code first (T51-T65) to identify chemical and intent*
>
> Use additional external cause code to identify place (Y92)

●● ■ T26.90 **Corrosion of eye and adnexa, part unspecified, unspecified side**

●● ■ T26.91 **Corrosion of right eye and adnexa, part unspecified**

●● ■ T26.92 **Corrosion of left eye and adnexa, part unspecified**

● T27 **Burn and corrosion of respiratory tract**
> Use additional external cause code to identify the source and intent of the burn (X00- X19, X75-X77, X96-X98)
>
> Use additional external cause code to identify place (Y92)
>
> The appropriate 7th character is to be added to each code from category T27

A	initial encounter
D	subsequent encounter
S	sequela

● T27.0 **Burn of larynx and trachea A** 🦠

● T27.1 **Burn involving larynx and trachea with lung A** 🦠

● T27.2 **Burn of other parts of respiratory tract A** 🦠
Burn of thoracic cavity

●● ■ T27.3 **Burn of respiratory tract, part unspecified A** 🦠
> *Code first (T51-T65) to identify chemical and intent for codes T27.4-T27.7*

● T27.4 **Corrosion of larynx and trachea A** 🦠

● T27.5 **Corrosion involving larynx and trachea with lung A** 🦠

● T27.6 **Corrosion of other parts of respiratory tract A** 🦠

● ■ T27.7 **Corrosion of respiratory tract, part unspecified A** 🦠

● T28 **Burn and corrosion of other internal organs**
> Use additional external cause code to identify the source and intent of the burn (X00- X19, X75-X77, X96-X98)
>
> Use additional external cause code to identify place (Y92)
>
> The appropriate 7th character is to be added to each code from category T28

A	initial encounter
D	subsequent encounter
S	sequela

● T28.0 **Burn of mouth and pharynx**

● T28.1 **Burn of esophagus A** 🦠

● T28.2 **Burn of other parts of alimentary tract A** 🦠

● T28.3 **Burn of internal genitourinary organs**

● T28.4 **Burns of other and unspecified internal organs**

●■ T28.40 **Burn of unspecified internal organ**

● T28.41 **Burn of ear drum**

● T28.411 **Burn of right ear drum**

● T28.412 **Burn of left ear drum**

●■ T28.419 **Burn of unspecified ear drum**

●● T28.49 **Burn of other internal organ**
> *Code first (T51-T65) to identify chemical and intent for T28.5-T28.9-*

● T28.5 **Corrosion of mouth and pharynx**

● T28.6 **Corrosion of esophagus A** 🦠

● T28.7 **Corrosion of other parts of alimentary tract A** 🦠

● T28.8 **Corrosion of internal genitourinary organs**

● T28.9 **Corrosions of other and unspecified internal organs**

●■ T28.90 **Corrosions of unspecified internal organs**

● T28.91 **Corrosions of ear drum**

● T28.911 **Corrosions of right ear drum**

● T28.912 **Corrosions of left ear drum**

● T28.919 **Corrosions of unspecified ear drum**

● T28.99 **Corrosions of other internal organs**

BURNS AND CORROSIONS OF MULTIPLE AND UNSPECIFIED BODY REGIONS (T30-T32)

● T30 **Burn and corrosion, body region unspecified**

■ T30.0 **Burn of unspecified body region, unspecified degree**
This code is not for inpatient use. Code to specified site and degree of burns
Burn NOS
Multiple burns NOS

■ T30.4 **Corrosion of unspecified body region, unspecified degree**
This code is not for inpatient use. Code to specified site and degree of corrosion
Corrosion NOS
Multiple corrosion NOS

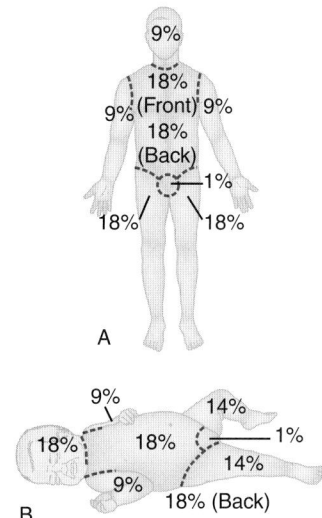

Figure 19-15 Rule of nines: percentages of total body area. (From Marx: Rosen's Emergency Medicine: Concepts and Clinical Practice, 6th ed. 2006, Mosby)

OGCR Section I.C.19.d.5.
Assign separate code for each burn site

When coding burns, assign separate codes for each burn site. Category T30, Burn and corrosion, body region unspecified is extremely vague and should rarely be used.

● Unacceptable First-Listed Diagnosis   ● Use Additional Character(s)   ■ Unspecified   **OGCR** Official Guidelines for Coding and Reporting

1552   🦠 Complication\Comorbidity   🦠 Major C\C   Excludes 1   Excludes 2   Includes   Use additional   Code first   Code also

CHAPTER 19 (S00-T98)

OGCR See Section III.C.19.d.

● **T31 Burns classified according to extent of body surface involved**
This category is to be used as the primary code only when the site of the burn is unspecified. It should be used as a supplementary code with categories T20-T25 when the site is specified.

T31.0 Burns involving less than 10% of body surface

● **T31.1 Burns involving 10-19% of body surface**

T31.10 Burns involving 10-19% of body surface with 0% to 9% third degree burns 🔹
Burns involving 10-19% of body surface NOS

T31.11 Burns involving 10-19% of body surface with 10-19% third degree burns

● **T31.2 Burns involving 20-29% of body surface**

T31.20 Burns involving 20-29% of body surface with 0% to 9% third degree burns 🔹
Burns involving 20-29% of body surface NOS

T31.21 Burns involving 20-29% of body surface with 10-19% third degree burns 🔹

T31.22 Burns involving 20-29% of body surface with 20-29% third degree burns 🔹

● **T31.3 Burns involving 30-39% of body surface**

T31.30 Burns involving 30-39% of body surface with 0% to 9% third degree burns 🔹
Burns involving 30-39% of body surface NOS

T31.31 Burns involving 30-39% of body surface with 10-19% third degree burns 🔹

T31.32 Burns involving 30-39% of body surface with 20-29% third degree burns 🔹

T31.33 Burns involving 30-39% of body surface with 30-39% third degree burns 🔹

● **T31.4 Burns involving 40-49% of body surface**

T31.40 Burns involving 40-49% of body surface with 0% to 9% third degree burns 🔹
Burns involving 40-49% of body surface NOS

T31.41 Burns involving 40-49% of body surface with 10-19% third degree burns 🔹

T31.42 Burns involving 40-49% of body surface with 20-29% third degree burns 🔹

T31.43 Burns involving 40-49% of body surface with 30-39% third degree burns 🔹

T31.44 Burns involving 40-49% of body surface with 40-49% third degree burns 🔹

● **T31.5 Burns involving 50-59% of body surface**

T31.50 Burns involving 50-59% of body surface with 0% to 9% third degree burns 🔹
Burns involving 50-59% of body surface NOS

T31.51 Burns involving 50-59% of body surface with 10-19% third degree burns 🔹

T31.52 Burns involving 50-59% of body surface with 20-29% third degree burns 🔹

T31.53 Burns involving 50-59% of body surface with 30-39% third degree burns 🔹

T31.54 Burns involving 50-59% of body surface with 40-49% third degree burns 🔹

T31.55 Burns involving 50-59% of body surface with 50-59% third degree burns 🔹

● **T31.6 Burns involving 60-69% of body surface**

T31.60 Burns involving 60-69% of body surface with 0% to 9% third degree burns 🔹
Burns involving 60-69% of body surface NOS

T31.61 Burns involving 60-69% of body surface with 10-19% third degree burns 🔹

T31.62 Burns involving 60-69% of body surface with 20-29% third degree burns 🔹

T31.63 Burns involving 60-69% of body surface with 30-39% third degree burns 🔹

T31.64 Burns involving 60-69% of body surface with 40-49% third degree burns 🔹

T31.65 Burns involving 60-69% of body surface with 50-59% third degree burns 🔹

T31.66 Burns involving 60-69% of body surface with 60-69% third degree burns 🔹

● **T31.7 Burns involving 70-79% of body surface**

T31.70 Burns involving 70-79% of body surface with 0% to 9% third degree burns 🔹
Burns involving 70-79% of body surface NOS

T31.71 Burns involving 70-79% of body surface with 10-19% third degree burns 🔹

T31.72 Burns involving 70-79% of body surface with 20-29% third degree burns 🔹

T31.73 Burns involving 70-79% of body surface with 30-39% third degree burns 🔹

T31.74 Burns involving 70-79% of body surface with 40-49% third degree burns 🔹

T31.75 Burns involving 70-79% of body surface with 50-59% third degree burns 🔹

T31.76 Burns involving 70-79% of body surface with 60-69% third degree burns 🔹

T31.77 Burns involving 70-79% of body surface with 70-79% third degree burns 🔹

● **T31.8 Burns involving 80-89% of body surface**

T31.80 Burns involving 80-89% of body surface with 0% to 9% third degree burns 🔹
Burns involving 80-89% of body surface NOS

T31.81 Burns involving 80-89% of body surface with 10-19% third degree burns 🔹

T31.82 Burns involving 80-89% of body surface with 20-29% third degree burns 🔹

T31.83 Burns involving 80-89% of body surface with 30-39% third degree burns 🔹

T31.84 Burns involving 80-89% of body surface with 40-49% third degree burns 🔹

T31.85 Burns involving 80-89% of body surface with 50-59% third degree burns 🔹

T31.86 Burns involving 80-89% of body surface with 60-69% third degree burns 🔹

T31.87 Burns involving 80-89% of body surface with 70-79% third degree burns 🔹

T31.88 Burns involving 80-89% of body surface with 80-89% third degree burns 🔹

● **T31.9 Burns involving 90% or more of body surface**

T31.90 Burns involving 90% or more of body surface with 0% to 9% third degree burns 🔹
Burns involving 90% or more of body surface NOS

T31.91 Burns involving 90% or more of body surface with 10-19% third degree burns 🔹

● Unacceptable First-Listed Diagnosis ● Use Additional Character(s) ▪ Unspecified OGCR Official Guidelines for Coding and Reporting
🔹 Complication\Comorbidity 🔹 Major C\C Excludes 1 Excludes 2 Includes Use additional Code first Code also
CHAPTER 19 (S00-T98) 1553

T31.92   Burns involving 90% or more of body surface with 20-29% third degree burns 🕸

T31.93   Burns involving 90% or more of body surface with 30-39% third degree burns 🕸

T31.94   Burns involving 90% or more of body surface with 40-49% third degree burns 🕸

T31.95   Burns involving 90% or more of body surface with 50-59% third degree burns 🕸

T31.96   Burns involving 90% or more of body surface with 60-69% third degree burns 🕸

T31.97   Burns involving 90% or more of body surface with 70-79% third degree burns 🕸

T31.98   Burns involving 90% or more of body surface with 80-89% third degree burns 🕸

T31.99   Burns involving 90% or more of body surface with 90% or more third degree burns 🕸

● **T32   Corrosions classified according to extent of body surface involved**

> **Note:** This category is to be used as the primary code only when the site of the corrosion is unspecified. It may be used as a supplementary code with categories T20-T25 when the site is specified.

   T32.0   Corrosions involving less than 10% of body surface

● **T32.1   Corrosions involving 10-19% of body surface**

T32.10   Corrosions involving 10-19% of body surface with 0% to 9% third degree corrosion 🕸

> Corrosions involving 10-19% of body surface NOS

T32.11   Corrosions involving 10-19% of body surface with 10-19% third degree corrosion 🕸

● **T32.2   Corrosions involving 20-29% of body surface**

T32.20   Corrosions involving 20-29% of body surface with 0% to 9% third degree corrosion 🕸

T32.21   Corrosions involving 20-29% of body surface with 10-19% third degree corrosion 🕸

T32.22   Corrosions involving 20-29% of body surface with 20-29% third degree corrosion 🕸

● **T32.3   Corrosions involving 30-39% of body surface**

T32.30   Corrosions involving 30-39% of body surface with 0% to 9% third degree corrosion 🕸

T32.31   Corrosions involving 30-39% of body surface with 10-19% third degree corrosion 🕸

T32.32   Corrosions involving 30-39% of body surface with 20-29% third degree corrosion 🕸

T32.33   Corrosions involving 30-39% of body surface with 30-39% third degree corrosion 🕸

● **T32.4   Corrosions involving 40-49% of body surface**

T32.40   Corrosions involving 40-49% of body surface with 0% to 9% third degree corrosion 🕸

T32.41   Corrosions involving 40-49% of body surface with 10-19% third degree corrosion 🕸

T32.42   Corrosions involving 40-49% of body surface with 20-29% third degree corrosion 🕸

T32.43   Corrosions involving 40-49% of body surface with 30-39% third degree corrosion 🕸

T32.44   Corrosions involving 40-49% of body surface with 40-49% third degree corrosion 🕸

● **T32.5   Corrosions involving 50-59% of body surface**

T32.50   Corrosions involving 50-59% of body surface with 0% to 9% third degree corrosion 🕸

T32.51   Corrosions involving 50-59% of body surface with 10-19% third degree corrosion 🕸

T32.52   Corrosions involving 50-59% of body surface with 20-29% third degree corrosion 🕸

T32.53   Corrosions involving 50-59% of body surface with 30-39% third degree corrosion 🕸

T32.54   Corrosions involving 50-59% of body surface with 40-49% third degree corrosion 🕸

T32.55   Corrosions involving 50-59% of body surface with 50-59% third degree corrosion 🕸

● **T32.6   Corrosions involving 60-69% of body surface**

T32.60   Corrosions involving 60-69% of body surface with 0% to 9% third degree corrosion 🕸

T32.61   Corrosions involving 60-69% of body surface with 10-19% third degree corrosion 🕸

T32.62   Corrosions involving 60-69% of body surface with 20-29% third degree corrosion 🕸

T32.63   Corrosions involving 60-69% of body surface with 30-39% third degree corrosion 🕸

T32.64   Corrosions involving 60-69% of body surface with 40-49% third degree corrosion 🕸

T32.65   Corrosions involving 60-69% of body surface with 50-59% third degree corrosion 🕸

T32.66   Corrosions involving 60-69% of body surface with 60-69% third degree corrosion 🕸

● **T32.7   Corrosions involving 70-79% of body surface**

T32.70   Corrosions involving 70-79% of body surface with 0% to 9% third degree corrosion 🕸

T32.71   Corrosions involving 70-79% of body surface with 10-19% third degree corrosion 🕸

T32.72   Corrosions involving 70-79% of body surface with 20-29% third degree corrosion 🕸

T32.73   Corrosions involving 70-79% of body surface with 30-39% third degree corrosion 🕸

T32.74   Corrosions involving 70-79% of body surface with 40-49% third degree corrosion 🕸

T32.75   Corrosions involving 70-79% of body surface with 50-59% third degree corrosion 🕸

T32.76   Corrosions involving 70-79% of body surface with 60-69% third degree corrosion 🕸

T32.77   Corrosions involving 70-79% of body surface with 70-79% third degree corrosion 🕸

● **T32.8   Corrosions involving 80-89% of body surface**

T32.80   Corrosions involving 80-89% of body surface with 0% to 9% third degree corrosion 🕸

T32.81   Corrosions involving 80-89% of body surface with 10-19% third degree corrosion 🕸

T32.82   Corrosions involving 80-89% of body surface with 20-29% third degree corrosion 🕸

T32.83   Corrosions involving 80-89% of body surface with 30-39% third degree corrosion 🕸

T32.84   Corrosions involving 80-89% of body surface with 40-49% third degree corrosion 🕸

T32.85   Corrosions involving 80-89% of body surface with 50-59% third degree corrosion 🕸

T32.86   Corrosions involving 80-89% of body surface with 60-69% third degree corrosion 🕸

T32.87   Corrosions involving 80-89% of body surface with 70-79% third degree corrosion 🕸

T32.88   Corrosions involving 80-89% of body surface with 80-89% third degree corrosion 🕸

● Unacceptable First-Listed Diagnosis   ● Use Additional Character(s)   ▨ Unspecified   **OGCR** Official Guidelines for Coding and Reporting

🕸 Complication\Comorbidity   🕸 Major C\C   Excludes 1   Excludes 2   Includes   Use additional   Code first   Code also

● T32.9　Corrosions involving 90% or more of body surface

　　T32.90　Corrosions involving 90% or more of body surface with 0% to 9% third degree corrosion 🦠

　　T32.91　Corrosions involving 90% or more of body surface with 10-19% third degree corrosion 🦠

　　T32.92　Corrosions involving 90% or more of body surface with 20-29% third degree corrosion 🦠

　　T32.93　Corrosions involving 90% or more of body surface with 30-39% third degree corrosion 🦠

　　T32.94　Corrosions involving 90% or more of body surface with 40-49% third degree corrosion 🦠

　　T32.95　Corrosions involving 90% or more of body surface with 50-59% third degree corrosion 🦠

　　T32.96　Corrosions involving 90% or more of body surface with 60-69% third degree corrosion 🦠

　　T32.97　Corrosions involving 90% or more of body surface with 70-79% third degree corrosion 🦠

　　T32.98　Corrosions involving 90% or more of body surface with 80-89% third degree corrosion 🦠

　　T32.99　Corrosions involving 90% or more of body surface with 90% or more third degree corrosion 🦠

FROSTBITE (T33-T34)

Excludes2　hypothermia and other effects of reduced temperature (T68, T69.-)

● **T33　Superficial frostbite**

　　Includes　frostbite with partial thickness skin loss

　　The appropriate 7th character is to be added to each code from category T33

A	initial encounter
D	subsequent encounter
S	sequela

　● T33.0　Superficial frostbite of head

　　● T33.01　Superficial frostbite of ear

　　　● T33.011　Superficial frostbite of right ear A 🦠

　　　● T33.012　Superficial frostbite of left ear A 🦠

　　　● ■ T33.019　Superficial frostbite of unspecified ear A 🦠

　　● T33.02　Superficial frostbite of nose A 🦠

　　● T33.09　Superficial frostbite of other part of head A 🦠

　● T33.1　Superficial frostbite of neck A 🦠

　● T33.2　Superficial frostbite of thorax A 🦠

　● T33.3　Superficial frostbite of abdominal wall, lower back and pelvis A 🦠

　● T33.4　Superficial frostbite of arm

　　Excludes2　superficial frostbite of wrist and hand (T33.5-)

　　● ■ T33.40　Superficial frostbite of arm, unspecified side A 🦠

　　● T33.41　Superficial frostbite of right arm A 🦠

　　● T33.42　Superficial frostbite of left arm A 🦠

　● T33.5　Superficial frostbite of wrist, hand, and fingers

　　● T33.51　Superficial frostbite of wrist

　　　● T33.511　Superficial frostbite of right wrist A 🦠

　　　● T33.512　Superficial frostbite of left wrist A 🦠

　　　● ■ T33.519　Superficial frostbite of unspecified wrist A 🦠

　　● T33.52　Superficial frostbite of hand

　　　Excludes2　superficial frostbite of fingers (T33.53-)

　　　● T33.521　Superficial frostbite of right hand A 🦠

　　　● T33.522　Superficial frostbite of left hand A 🦠

　　　● ■ T33.529　Superficial frostbite of unspecified hand A 🦠

　　● T33.53　Superficial frostbite of finger(s)

　　　● T33.531　Superficial frostbite of right finger(s) A 🦠

　　　● T33.532　Superficial frostbite of left finger(s) A 🦠

　　　● ■ T33.539　Superficial frostbite of unspecified finger(s) A 🦠

　● T33.6　Superficial frostbite of hip and thigh

　　● ■ T33.60　Superficial frostbite of hip and thigh, unspecified side A 🦠

　　● T33.61　Superficial frostbite of right hip and thigh A 🦠

　　● T33.62　Superficial frostbite of left hip and thigh A 🦠

　● T33.7　Superficial frostbite of knee and lower leg

　　Excludes2　superficial frostbite of ankle and foot (T33.8-)

　　● ■ T33.70　Superficial frostbite of knee and lower leg, unspecified side A 🦠

　　● T33.71　Superficial frostbite of right knee and lower leg A 🦠

　　● T33.72　Superficial frostbite of left knee and lower leg A 🦠

　● T33.8　Superficial frostbite of ankle, foot, and toe(s)

　　● T33.81　Superficial frostbite of ankle

　　　● T33.811　Superficial frostbite of right ankle A 🦠

　　　● T33.812　Superficial frostbite of left ankle A 🦠

　　　● ■ T33.819　Superficial frostbite of unspecified ankle A 🦠

　　● T33.82　Superficial frostbite of foot

　　　● T33.821　Superficial frostbite of right foot A 🦠

　　　● T33.822　Superficial frostbite of left foot A 🦠

　　　● ■ T33.829　Superficial frostbite of unspecified foot A 🦠

　　● T33.83　Superficial frostbite of toe(s)

　　　● T33.831　Superficial frostbite of right toe(s) A 🦠

　　　● T33.832　Superficial frostbite of left toe(s) A 🦠

　　　● ■ T33.839　Superficial frostbite of unspecified toe(s) A 🦠

　● T33.9　Superficial frostbite of other and unspecified sites

　　● ■ T33.90　Superficial frostbite of unspecified sites A 🦠
　　　　Superficial frostbite NOS

　　● T33.99　Superficial frostbite of other sites A 🦠
　　　　Superficial frostbite of leg NOS
　　　　Superficial frostbite of trunk NOS

● **T34　Frostbite with tissue necrosis**

　　The appropriate 7th character is to be added to each code from category T34

A	initial encounter
D	subsequent encounter
S	sequela

　● T34.0　Frostbite with tissue necrosis of head

　　● T34.01　Frostbite with tissue necrosis of ear

　　　● T34.011　Frostbite with tissue necrosis of right ear A 🦠

● Unacceptable First-Listed Diagnosis　　　● Use Additional Character(s)　　　■ Unspecified　　　OGCR Official Guidelines for Coding and Reporting

🦠 Complication\Comorbidity　　🦠 Major C\C　　Excludes 1　　Excludes 2　　Includes　　Use additional　　Code first　　Code also

CHAPTER 19 (S00-T98)

1555

● T34.012 Frostbite with tissue necrosis of left ear A ⦿

● ▪ T34.019 Frostbite with tissue necrosis of unspecified ear A ⦿

● T34.02 Frostbite with tissue necrosis of nose A ⦿

● T34.09 Frostbite with tissue necrosis of other part of head A ⦿

● T34.1 Frostbite with tissue necrosis of neck A ⦿

● T34.2 Frostbite with tissue necrosis of thorax A ⦿

● T34.3 Frostbite with tissue necrosis of abdominal wall, lower back and pelvis A ⦿

● T34.4 Frostbite with tissue necrosis of arm

Excludes2 frostbite with tissue necrosis of wrist and hand (T34.5-)

● ▪ T34.40 Frostbite with tissue necrosis of arm, unspecified side A ⦿

● T34.41 Frostbite with tissue necrosis of right arm A ⦿

● T34.42 Frostbite with tissue necrosis of left arm A ⦿

● T34.5 Frostbite with tissue necrosis of wrist, hand, and finger(s)

● T34.51 Frostbite with tissue necrosis of wrist

● T34.511 Frostbite with tissue necrosis of right wrist A ⦿

● T34.512 Frostbite with tissue necrosis of left wrist A ⦿

● ▪ T34.519 Frostbite with tissue necrosis of unspecified wrist A ⦿

● T34.52 Frostbite with tissue necrosis of hand

Excludes2 frostbite with tissue necrosis of finger(s) (T34.53-)

● T34.521 Frostbite with tissue necrosis of right hand A ⦿

● T34.522 Frostbite with tissue necrosis of left hand A ⦿

● ▪ T34.529 Frostbite with tissue necrosis of unspecified hand A ⦿

● T34.53 Frostbite with tissue necrosis of finger(s)

● T34.531 Frostbite with tissue necrosis of right finger(s) A ⦿

● T34.532 Frostbite with tissue necrosis of left finger(s) A ⦿

● ▪ T34.539 Frostbite with tissue necrosis of unspecified finger(s) A ⦿

● T34.6 Frostbite with tissue necrosis of hip and thigh

● ▪ T34.60 Frostbite with tissue necrosis of hip and thigh, unspecified side A ⦿

● T34.61 Frostbite with tissue necrosis of right hip and thigh A ⦿

● T34.62 Frostbite with tissue necrosis of left hip and thigh A ⦿

● T34.7 Frostbite with tissue necrosis of knee and lower leg

Excludes2 frostbite with tissue necrosis of ankle and foot (T34.8-)

● ▪ T34.70 Frostbite with tissue necrosis of knee and lower leg, unspecified side A ⦿

● T34.71 Frostbite with tissue necrosis of right knee and lower leg A ⦿

● T34.72 Frostbite with tissue necrosis of left knee and lower leg A ⦿

● T34.8 Frostbite with tissue necrosis of ankle and foot, and toe(s)

● T34.81 Frostbite with tissue necrosis of ankle

● T34.811 Frostbite with tissue necrosis of right ankle A ⦿

● T34.812 Frostbite with tissue necrosis of left ankle A ⦿

● ▪ T34.819 Frostbite with tissue necrosis of unspecified ankle A ⦿

● T34.82 Frostbite with tissue necrosis of foot

● T34.821 Frostbite with tissue necrosis of right foot A ⦿

● T34.822 Frostbite with tissue necrosis of left foot A ⦿

● ▪ T34.829 Frostbite with tissue necrosis of unspecified foot A ⦿

● T34.83 Frostbite with tissue necrosis of toe(s)

● T34.831 Frostbite with tissue necrosis of right toe(s) A ⦿

● T34.832 Frostbite with tissue necrosis of left toe(s) A ⦿

● ▪ T34.839 Frostbite with tissue necrosis of unspecified toe(s) A ⦿

● T34.9 Frostbite with tissue necrosis of other and unspecified sites

● ▪ T34.90 Frostbite with tissue necrosis of unspecified sites A ⦿
        Frostbite with tissue necrosis NOS

● T34.99 Frostbite with tissue necrosis of other sites A ⦿
        Frostbite with tissue necrosis of leg NOS
        Frostbite with tissue necrosis of trunk NOS

OGCR See Guidelines Section I.C.19.e.

POISONING BY, ADVERSE EFFECTS OF AND UNDERDOSING OF DRUGS, MEDICAMENTS AND BIOLOGICAL SUBSTANCES (T36-T50)

Includes poisoning is defined as:
        overdose of substances
        wrong substance given or taken in error
        adverse effect is defined as:
        "hypersensitivity", "reaction", etc. of correct substance properly administered
        underdosing is defined as:
        taking less of a medication than is prescribed or instructed by the manufacturer, whether inadvertently or deliberately

Use additional code(s) for all manifestations of poisoning and adverse effects

Use additional code for intent of underdosing:
        failure in dosage during medical and surgical care (Y63.61, Y63.8-Y63.9)
        patient's underdosing of medication regime (Z91.12-, Z91.13-)

Excludes1 toxic reaction to local anesthesia in pregnancy (O29.3-)

Excludes2 abuse and dependence of psychoactive substances (F10-F19)
        abuse of non-dependence-producing substances (F55.-)
        drug reaction and poisoning affecting newborn (P00-P96)
        pathological drug intoxication (inebriation) (F10-F19)

When no intent of poisoning is indicated code to accidental. Undetermined intent is only for use when there is specific documentation in the record that the intent of the poisoning cannot be determined.

● Unacceptable First-Listed Diagnosis   ● Use Additional Character(s)   ▪ Unspecified   OGCR Official Guidelines for Coding and Reporting
⦿ Complication\Comorbidity   ⦿ Major C\C   Excludes 1   Excludes 2   Includes   Use additional   Code first   Code also

● T36 Poisoning by, adverse effect of and underdosing of
        systemic antibiotics

> **Excludes1** antineoplastic antibiotics (T45.1-)
>   locally applied antibiotic NEC (T49.0)
>   topically used antibiotic for ear, nose and
>   throat (T49.6)
>   topically used antibiotic for eye (T49.5)

The appropriate 7th character is to be added to each code
from category T36

> A initial encounter
> D subsequent encounter
> S sequela

● T36.0 Poisoning by, adverse effect of and underdosing of
         penicillins

   ● T36.0x Poisoning by, adverse effect of and
             underdosing of penicillins

      ● T36.0x1 Poisoning by penicillins,
                 accidental (unintentional)
                    Poisoning by penicillins NOS

      ● T36.0x2 Poisoning by penicillins,
                 intentional self-harm

      ● T36.0x3 Poisoning by penicillins, assault

      ● T36.0x4 Poisoning by penicillins,
                 undetermined

      ● T36.0x5 Adverse effect of penicillins

      ● T36.0x6 Underdosing of penicillins

● T36.1 Poisoning by, adverse effect of and underdosing of
         cephalosporins and other betalactam antibiotics

   ● T36.1x Poisoning by, adverse effect of and
             underdosing of cephalosporins and other
             beta-lactam antibiotics

      ● T36.1x1 Poisoning by cephalosporins
                 and other betalactam antibiotics,
                 accidental (unintentional)
                    Poisoning by cephalosporins
                    and other beta-lactam
                    antibiotics NOS

      ● T36.1x2 Poisoning by cephalosporins and
                 other beta-lactam antibiotics,
                 intentional self-harm

      ● T36.1x3 Poisoning by cephalosporins and
                 other beta-lactam antibiotics,
                 assault

      ● T36.1x4 Poisoning by cephalosporins and
                 other beta-lactam antibiotics,
                 undetermined

      ● T36.1x5 Adverse effect of cephalosporins
                 and other beta-lactam antibiotics

      ● T36.1x6 Underdosing of cephalosporins
                 and other beta-lactam antibiotics

● T36.2 Poisoning by, adverse effect of and underdosing of
         chloramphenicol group

   ● T36.2x Poisoning by, adverse effect of and
             underdosing of chloramphenicol group

      ● T36.2x1 Poisoning by chloramphenicol
                 group, accidental (unintentional)
                    Poisoning by chloramphenicol
                    group NOS

      ● T36.2x2 Poisoning by chloramphenicol
                 group, intentional self-harm

      ● T36.2x3 Poisoning by chloramphenicol
                 group, assault

      ● T36.2x4 Poisoning by chloramphenicol
                 group, undetermined

      ● T36.2x5 Adverse effect of
                 chloramphenicol group

      ● T36.2x6 Underdosing of chloramphenicol
                 group

● T36.3 Poisoning by, adverse effect of and underdosing of
         macrolides

   ● T36.3x Poisoning by, adverse effect of and
             underdosing of macrolides

      ● T36.3x1 Poisoning by macrolides,
                 accidental (unintentional)
                    Poisoning by macrolides NOS

      ● T36.3x2 Poisoning by macrolides,
                 intentional self-harm

      ● T36.3x3 Poisoning by macrolides, assault

      ● T36.3x4 Poisoning by macrolides,
                 undetermined

      ● T36.3x5 Adverse effect of macrolides

      ● T36.3x6 Underdosing of macrolides

● T36.4 Poisoning by, adverse effect of and underdosing of
         tetracyclines

   ● T36.4x Poisoning by, adverse effect of and
             underdosing of tetracyclines

      ● T36.4x1 Poisoning by tetracyclines,
                 accidental (unintentional)
                    Poisoning by tetracyclines NOS

      ● T36.4x2 Poisoning by tetracyclines,
                 intentional self-harm

      ● T36.4x3 Poisoning by tetracyclines,
                 assault

      ● T36.4x4 Poisoning by tetracyclines,
                 undetermined

      ● T36.4x5 Adverse effect of tetracyclines

      ● T36.4x6 Underdosing of tetracyclines

● T36.5 Poisoning by, adverse effect of and underdosing of
         aminoglycosides
            Poisoning by, adverse effect of and underdosing
            of streptomycin

   ● T36.5x Poisoning by, adverse effect of and
             underdosing of aminoglycosides

      ● T36.5x1 Poisoning by aminoglycosides,
                 accidental (unintentional)
                    Poisoning by aminoglycosides
                    NOS

      ● T36.5x2 Poisoning by aminoglycosides,
                 intentional self-harm

      ● T36.5x3 Poisoning by aminoglycosides,
                 assault

      ● T36.5x4 Poisoning by aminoglycosides,
                 undetermined

      ● T36.5x5 Adverse effect of
                 aminoglycosides

      ● T36.5x6 Underdosing of aminoglycosides

● T36.6 Poisoning by, adverse effect of and underdosing of
         rifampicins

   ● T36.6x Poisoning by, adverse effect of and
             underdosing of rifampicins

      ● T36.6x1 Poisoning by rifampicins,
                 accidental (unintentional)
                    Poisoning by rifampicins NOS

      ● T36.6x2 Poisoning by rifampicins,
                 intentional self-harm

● Unacceptable First-Listed Diagnosis   ● Use Additional Character(s)   ■ Unspecified   **OGCR** Official Guidelines for Coding and Reporting

🗘 Complication\Comorbidity   🗘 Major C\C   Excludes 1   Excludes 2   Includes   Use additional   Code first   Code also

CHAPTER 19 (S00-T98)

1557

● T36.6x3 Poisoning by rifampicins, assault
● T36.6x4 Poisoning by rifampicins, undetermined
● T36.6x5 Adverse effect of rifampicins
● T36.6x6 Underdosing of rifampicins

● T36.7 Poisoning by, adverse effect of and underdosing of antifungal antibiotics, systemically used
  ● T36.7x Poisoning by, adverse effect of and underdosing of antifungal antibiotics, systemically used
    ● T36.7x1 Poisoning by antifungal antibiotics, systemically used, accidental (unintentional)
        Poisoning by antifungal antibiotics, systemically used NOS
    ● T36.7x2 Poisoning by antifungal antibiotics, systemically used, intentional self-harm
    ● T36.7x3 Poisoning by antifungal antibiotics, systemically used, assault
    ● T36.7x4 Poisoning by antifungal antibiotics, systemically used, undetermined
    ● T36.7x5 Adverse effect of antifungal antibiotics, systemically used
    ● T36.7x6 Underdosing of antifungal antibiotics, systemically used

● T36.8 Poisoning by, adverse effect of and underdosing of other systemic antibiotics
  ● T36.8x Poisoning by, adverse effect of and underdosing of other systemic antibiotics
    ● T36.8x1 Poisoning by other systemic antibiotics, accidental (unintentional)
        Poisoning by other systemic antibiotics NOS
    ● T36.8x2 Poisoning by other systemic antibiotics, intentional self-harm
    ● T36.8x3 Poisoning by other systemic antibiotics, assault
    ● T36.8x4 Poisoning by other systemic antibiotics, undetermined
    ● T36.8x5 Adverse effect of other systemic antibiotics
    ● T36.8x6 Underdosing of other systemic antibiotics

● T36.9 Poisoning by, adverse effect of and underdosing of unspecified systemic antibiotic
  ● ■ T36.91 Poisoning by unspecified systemic antibiotic, accidental (unintentional)
        Poisoning by systemic antibiotic NOS
  ● ■ T36.92 Poisoning by unspecified systemic antibiotic, intentional self-harm
  ● ■ T36.93 Poisoning by unspecified systemic antibiotic, assault
  ● ■ T36.94 Poisoning by unspecified systemic antibiotic, undetermined
  ● ■ T36.95 Adverse effect of unspecified systemic antibiotic
  ● ■ T36.96 Underdosing of unspecified systemic antibiotic

● T37 Poisoning by, adverse effect of and underdosing of other systemic anti-infectives and antiparasitics
    Excludes1   anti-infectives topically used for ear, nose and throat (T49.6-)
                 anti-infectives topically used for eye (T49.5-)
                 locally applied anti-infectives NEC (T49.0-)

    The appropriate 7th character is to be added to each code from category T37
    ┌─────────────────────────────────┐
    │ A   initial encounter   │
    │ D   subsequent encounter   │
    │ S   sequela   │
    └─────────────────────────────────┘

● T37.0 Poisoning by, adverse effect of and underdosing of sulfonamides
  ● T37.0x Poisoning by, adverse effect of and underdosing of sulfonamides
    ● T37.0x1 Poisoning by sulfonamides, accidental (unintentional)
        Poisoning by sulfonamides NOS
    ● T37.0x2 Poisoning by sulfonamides, intentional self-harm
    ● T37.0x3 Poisoning by sulfonamides, assault
    ● T37.0x4 Poisoning by sulfonamides, undetermined
    ● T37.0x5 Adverse effect of sulfonamides
    ● T37.0x6 Underdosing of sulfonamides

● T37.1 Poisoning by, adverse effect of and underdosing of antimycobacterial drugs
    Excludes1   rifampicins (T36.6-) streptomycin (T36.5-)
  ● T37.1x Poisoning by, adverse effect of and underdosing of antimycobacterial drugs
    ● T37.1x1 Poisoning by antimycobacterial drugs, accidental (unintentional)
        Poisoning by antimycobacterial drugs NOS
    ● T37.1x2 Poisoning by antimycobacterial drugs, intentional self-harm
    ● T37.1x3 Poisoning by antimycobacterial drugs, assault
    ● T37.1x4 Poisoning by antimycobacterial drugs, undetermined
    ● T37.1x5 Adverse effect of antimycobacterial drugs
    ● T37.1x6 Underdosing of antimycobacterial drugs

● T37.2 Poisoning by, adverse effect of and underdosing of antimalarials and drugs acting on other blood protozoa
    Excludes1   hydroxyquinoline derivatives (T37.8-)
  ● T37.2x Poisoning by, adverse effect of and underdosing of antimalarials and drugs acting on other blood protozoa
    ● T37.2x1 Poisoning by antimalarials and drugs acting on other blood protozoa, accidental (unintentional)
        Poisoning by antimalarials and drugs acting on other blood protozoa NOS
    ● T37.2x2 Poisoning by antimalarials and drugs acting on other blood protozoa, intentional self-harm
    ● T37.2x3 Poisoning by antimalarials and drugs acting on other blood protozoa, assault

● **T37.2x4** Poisoning by antimalarials and drugs acting on other blood protozoa, undetermined

● **T37.2x5** Adverse effect of antimalarials and drugs acting on other blood protozoa

● **T37.2x6** Underdosing of antimalarials and drugs acting on other blood protozoa

● **T37.3** Poisoning by, adverse effect of and underdosing of other antiprotozoal drugs

   ● **T37.3x** Poisoning by, adverse effect of and underdosing of other antiprotozoal drugs

     ● **T37.3x1** Poisoning by other antiprotozoal drugs, accidental (unintentional)
         Poisoning by other antiprotozoal drugs NOS

     ● **T37.3x2** Poisoning by other antiprotozoal drugs, intentional self-harm

     ● **T37.3x3** Poisoning by other antiprotozoal drugs, assault

     ● **T37.3x4** Poisoning by other antiprotozoal drugs, undetermined

     ● **T37.3x5** Adverse effect of other antiprotozoal drugs

     ● **T37.3x6** Underdosing of other antiprotozoal drugs

● **T37.4** Poisoning by, adverse effect of and underdosing of anthelminthics

   ● **T37.4x** Poisoning by, adverse effect of and underdosing of anthelminthics

     ● **T37.4x1** Poisoning by anthelminthics, accidental (unintentional)
         Poisoning by anthelminthics NOS

     ● **T37.4x2** Poisoning by anthelminthics, intentional self-harm

     ● **T37.4x3** Poisoning by anthelminthics, assault

     ● **T37.4x4** Poisoning by anthelminthics, undetermined

     ● **T37.4x5** Adverse effect of anthelminthics

     ● **T37.4x6** Underdosing of anthelminthics

● **T37.5** Poisoning by, adverse effect of and underdosing of antiviral drugs

     | **Excludes1** | amantadine (T42.8-) |
                   cytarabine (T45.1-)

   ● **T37.5x** Poisoning by, adverse effect of and underdosing of antiviral drugs

     ● **T37.5x1** Poisoning by antiviral drugs, accidental (unintentional)
         Poisoning by antiviral drugs NOS

     ● **T37.5x2** Poisoning by antiviral drugs, intentional self-harm

     ● **T37.5x3** Poisoning by antiviral drugs, assault

     ● **T37.5x4** Poisoning by antiviral drugs, undetermined

     ● **T37.5x5** Adverse effect of antiviral drugs

     ● **T37.5x6** Underdosing of antiviral drugs

● **T37.8** Poisoning by, adverse effect of and underdosing of other specified systemic anti-infectives and antiparasitics
     Poisoning by, adverse effect of and underdosing of hydroxyquinoline derivatives

     | **Excludes1** | antimalarial drugs (T37.2-) |

   ● **T37.8x** Poisoning by, adverse effect of and underdosing of other specified systemic anti-infectives and antiparasitics

     ● **T37.8x1** Poisoning by other specified systemic anti-infectives and antiparasitics, accidental (unintentional)
         Poisoning by other specified systemic anti-infectives and antiparasitics NOS

     ● **T37.8x2** Poisoning by other specified systemic anti-infectives and antiparasitics, intentional self-harm

     ● **T37.8x3** Poisoning by other specified systemic anti-infectives and antiparasitics, assault

     ● **T37.8x4** Poisoning by other specified systemic anti-infectives and antiparasitics, undetermined

     ● **T37.8x5** Adverse effect of other specified systemic anti-infectives and antiparasitics

     ● **T37.8x6** Underdosing of other specified systemic anti-infectives and antiparasitics

● **T37.9** Poisoning by, adverse effect of and underdosing of unspecified systemic anti-infective and antiparasitics

   ● ■ **T37.91** Poisoning by unspecified systemic anti-infective and antiparasitics, accidental (unintentional)
     Poisoning by, adverse effect of and underdosing of systemic anti-infective and antiparasitics NOS

   ● ■ **T37.92** Poisoning by unspecified systemic anti-infective and antiparasitics, intentional self-harm

   ● ■ **T37.93** Poisoning by unspecified systemic anti-infective and antiparasitics, assault

   ● ■ **T37.94** Poisoning by unspecified systemic anti-infective and antiparasitics, undetermined

   ● ■ **T37.95** Adverse effect of unspecified systemic anti-infective and antiparasitic

   ● ■ **T37.96** Underdosing of unspecified systemic anti-infectives and antiparasitics

● **T38** Poisoning by, adverse effect of and underdosing of hormones and their synthetic substitutes and antagonists, not elsewhere classified

   | **Excludes1** | mineralocorticoids and their antagonists (T50.0-) |
               oxytocic hormones (T48.0-)
               parathyroid hormones and derivatives (T50.9-)

   The appropriate 7th character is to be added to each code from category T38

     | A | initial encounter |
     | D | subsequent encounter |
     | S | sequela |

● **T38.0** Poisoning by, adverse effect of and underdosing of glucocorticoids and synthetic analogues

     | **Excludes1** | glucocorticoids, topically used (T49.-) |

● Unacceptable First-Listed Diagnosis   ● Use Additional Character(s)   ■ Unspecified   **OGCR** Official Guidelines for Coding and Reporting

🗪 Complication\Comorbidity   🗪 Major C\C   Excludes 1   Excludes 2   Includes   Use additional   Code first   Code also

1559

CHAPTER 19 (S00-T98)

- T38.0x Poisoning by, adverse effect of and underdosing of glucocorticoids and synthetic analogues
  - T38.0x1 Poisoning by glucocorticoids and synthetic analogues, accidental (unintentional)
    Poisoning by glucocorticoids and synthetic analogues NOS
  - T38.0x2 Poisoning by glucocorticoids and synthetic analogues, intentional self-harm
  - T38.0x3 Poisoning by glucocorticoids and synthetic analogues, assault
  - T38.0x4 Poisoning by glucocorticoids and synthetic analogues, undetermined
  - T38.0x5 Adverse effect of glucocorticoids and synthetic analogues
  - T38.0x6 Underdosing of glucocorticoids and synthetic analogues
- T38.1 Poisoning by, adverse effect of and underdosing of thyroid hormones and substitutes
  - T38.1x Poisoning by, adverse effect of and underdosing of thyroid hormones and substitutes
    - T38.1x1 Poisoning by thyroid hormones and substitutes, accidental (unintentional)
      Poisoning by thyroid hormones and substitutes NOS
    - T38.1x2 Poisoning by thyroid hormones and substitutes, intentional self-harm
    - T38.1x3 Poisoning by thyroid hormones and substitutes, assault
    - T38.1x4 Poisoning by thyroid hormones and substitutes, undetermined
    - T38.1x5 Adverse effect of thyroid hormones and substitutes
    - T38.1x6 Underdosing of thyroid hormones and substitutes
- T38.2 Poisoning by, adverse effect of and underdosing of antithyroid drugs
  - T38.2x Poisoning by, adverse effect of and underdosing of antithyroid drugs
    - T38.2x1 Poisoning by antithyroid drugs, accidental (unintentional)
      Poisoning by antithyroid drugs NOS
    - T38.2x2 Poisoning by antithyroid drugs, intentional self-harm
    - T38.2x3 Poisoning by antithyroid drugs, assault
    - T38.2x4 Poisoning by antithyroid drugs, undetermined
    - T38.2x5 Adverse effect of antithyroid drugs
    - T38.2x6 Underdosing of antithyroid drugs
- T38.3 Poisoning by, adverse effect of and underdosing of insulin and oral hypoglycemic [antidiabetic] drugs
  - T38.3x Poisoning by, adverse effect of and underdosing of insulin and oral hypoglycemic [antidiabetic] drugs

- T38.3x1 Poisoning by insulin and oral hypoglycemic [antidiabetic] drugs, accidental (unintentional)
  Poisoning by insulin and oral hypoglycemic [antidiabetic] drugs NOS
- T38.3x2 Poisoning by insulin and oral hypoglycemic [antidiabetic] drugs, intentional self-harm
- T38.3x3 Poisoning by insulin and oral hypoglycemic [antidiabetic] drugs, assault
- T38.3x4 Poisoning by insulin and oral hypoglycemic [antidiabetic] drugs, undetermined
- T38.3x5 Adverse effect of insulin and oral hypoglycemic [antidiabetic] drugs
- T38.3x6 Underdosing of insulin and oral hypoglycemic [antidiabetic] drugs
- T38.4 Poisoning by, adverse effect of and underdosing of oral contraceptives
  Poisoning by, adverse effect of and underdosing of multiple- and single-ingredient oral contraceptive preparations
  - T38.4x Poisoning by, adverse effect of and underdosing of oral contraceptives
    - T38.4x1 Poisoning by oral contraceptives, accidental (unintentional)
      Poisoning by oral contraceptives NOS
    - T38.4x2 Poisoning by oral contraceptives, intentional self-harm
    - T38.4x3 Poisoning by oral contraceptives, assault
    - T38.4x4 Poisoning by oral contraceptives, undetermined
    - T38.4x5 Adverse effect of oral contraceptives
    - T38.4x6 Underdosing or oral contraceptives
- T38.5 Poisoning by, adverse effect of and underdosing of other estrogens and progestogens
  Poisoning by, adverse effect of and underdosing of estrogens and progestogens mixtures and substitutes
  - T38.5x Poisoning by, adverse effect of and underdosing of other estrogens and progestogens
    - T38.5x1 Poisoning by other estrogens and progestogens, accidental (unintentional)
      Poisoning by other estrogens and progestogens NOS
    - T38.5x2 Poisoning by other estrogens and progestogens, intentional self-harm
    - T38.5x3 Poisoning by other estrogens and progestogens, assault
    - T38.5x4 Poisoning by other estrogens and progestogens, undetermined
    - T38.5x5 Adverse effect of other estrogens and progestogens
    - T38.5x6 Underdosing of other estrogens and progestogens

● Unacceptable First-Listed Diagnosis ● Use Additional Character(s) ▢ Unspecified OGCR Official Guidelines for Coding and Reporting
Ⓒ Complication\Comorbidity Ⓜ Major C\C Excludes 1 Excludes 2 Includes Use additional Code first Code also

T38.6   **Poisoning by, adverse effect of and underdosing of antigonadotrophins, antiestrogens, antiandrogens, not elsewhere classified**
> Poisoning by, adverse effect of and underdosing of tamoxifen

   T38.6x   **Poisoning by, adverse effect of and underdosing of antigonadotrophins, antiestrogens, antiandrogens, not elsewhere classified**

     T38.6x1   **Poisoning by antigonadotrophins, antiestrogens, antiandrogens, not elsewhere classified, accidental (unintentional)**
> Poisoning by antigonadotrophins, antiestrogens, antiandrogens, not elsewhere classified NOS

     T38.6x2   **Poisoning by antigonadotrophins, antiestrogens, antiandrogens, not elsewhere classified, intentional self-harm**

     T38.6x3   **Poisoning by antigonadotrophins, antiestrogens, antiandrogens, not elsewhere classified, assault**

     T38.6x4   **Poisoning by antigonadotrophins, antiestrogens, antiandrogens, not elsewhere classified, undetermined**

     T38.6x5   **Adverse effect of antigonadotrophins, antiestrogens, antiandrogens, not elsewhere classified**

     T38.6x6   **Underdosing of antigonadotrophins, antiestrogens, antiandrogens, not elsewhere classified**

T38.7   **Poisoning by, adverse effect of and underdosing of androgens and anabolic congeners**

   T38.7x   **Poisoning by, adverse effect of and underdosing of androgens and anabolic congeners**

     T38.7x1   **Poisoning by androgens and anabolic congeners, accidental (unintentional)**
> Poisoning by androgens and anabolic congeners NOS

     T38.7x2   **Poisoning by androgens and anabolic congeners, intentional self-harm**

     T38.7x3   **Poisoning by androgens and anabolic congeners, assault**

     T38.7x4   **Poisoning by androgens and anabolic congeners, undetermined**

     T38.7x5   **Adverse effect of androgens and anabolic congeners**

     T38.7x6   **Underdosing of androgens and anabolic congeners**

T38.8   **Poisoning by, adverse effect of and underdosing of other and unspecified hormones and synthetic substitutes**

   T38.80   **Poisoning by, adverse effect of and underdosing of unspecified hormones and synthetic substitutes**

     T38.801   **Poisoning by unspecified hormones and synthetic substitutes, accidental (unintentional)**
> Poisoning by unspecified hormones and synthetic substitutes NOS

     T38.802   **Poisoning by unspecified hormones and synthetic substitutes, intentional self-harm**

     T38.803   **Poisoning by unspecified hormones and synthetic substitutes, assault**

     T38.804   **Poisoning by unspecified hormones and synthetic substitutes, undetermined**

     T38.805   **Adverse effect of unspecified hormones and synthetic substitutes**

     T38.806   **Underdosing of unspecified hormones and synthetic substitutes**

   T38.81   **Poisoning by, adverse effect of and underdosing of anterior pituitary [adenohypophyseal] hormones**

     T38.811   **Poisoning by anterior pituitary [adenohypophyseal] hormones, accidental (unintentional)**
> Poisoning by anterior pituitary [adenohypophyseal] hormones NOS

     T38.812   **Poisoning by anterior pituitary [adenohypophyseal] hormones, intentional self-harm**

     T38.813   **Poisoning by anterior pituitary [adenohypophyseal] hormones, assault**

     T38.814   **Poisoning by anterior pituitary [adenohypophyseal] hormones, undetermined**

     T38.815   **Adverse effect of anterior pituitary [adenohypophyseal] hormones**

     T38.816   **Underdosing of anterior pituitary [adenohypophyseal] hormones**

   T38.89   **Poisoning by, adverse effect of and underdosing of other hormones and synthetic substitutes**

     T38.891   **Poisoning by other hormones and synthetic substitutes, accidental (unintentional)**
> Poisoning by other hormones and synthetic substitutes NOS

     T38.892   **Poisoning by other hormones and synthetic substitutes, intentional self-harm**

     T38.893   **Poisoning by other hormones and synthetic substitutes, assault**

     T38.894   **Poisoning by other hormones and synthetic substitutes, undetermined**

     T38.895   **Adverse effect of other hormones and synthetic substitutes**

     T38.896   **Underdosing of other hormones and synthetic substitutes**

● Unacceptable First-Listed Diagnosis   ● Use Additional Character(s)   ▦ Unspecified   OGCR Official Guidelines for Coding and Reporting

 Complication\Comorbidity   Major C\C   Excludes 1   Excludes 2   Includes   Use additional   Code first   Code also

1561

CHAPTER 19 (S00-T98)

● **T38.9** **Poisoning by, adverse effect of and underdosing of other and unspecified hormone antagonists**

   ● **T38.90** **Poisoning by, adverse effect of and underdosing of unspecified hormone antagonists**

      ● ■ **T38.901** **Poisoning by unspecified hormone antagonists, accidental (unintentional)**
            Poisoning by unspecified hormone antagonists NOS

      ● ■ **T38.902** **Poisoning by unspecified hormone antagonists, intentional self-harm**

      ● ■ **T38.903** **Poisoning by unspecified hormone antagonists, assault**

      ● ■ **T38.904** **Poisoning by unspecified hormone antagonists, undetermined**

      ● ■ **T38.905** **Adverse effect of unspecified hormone antagonists**

      ● ■ **T38.906** **Underdosing of unspecified hormone antagonists**

   ● **T38.99** **Poisoning by, adverse effect of and underdosing of other hormone antagonists**

      ● **T38.991** **Poisoning by other hormone antagonists, accidental (unintentional)**
            Poisoning by other hormone antagonists NOS

      ● **T38.992** **Poisoning by other hormone antagonists, intentional self-harm**

      ● **T38.993** **Poisoning by other hormone antagonists, assault**

      ● **T38.994** **Poisoning by other hormone antagonists, undetermined**

      ● **T38.995** **Adverse effect of other hormone antagonists**

      ● **T38.996** **Underdosing of other hormone antagonists**

● **T39** **Poisoning by, adverse effect of and underdosing of nonopioid analgesics, antipyretics and antirheumatics**
      The appropriate 7th character is to be added to each code from category T39

> A   initial encounter
> D   subsequent encounter
> S   sequela

  ● **T39.0** **Poisoning by, adverse effect of and underdosing of salicylates**

    ● **T39.01** **Poisoning by, adverse effect of and underdosing of aspirin**
        Poisoning by, adverse effect of and underdosing of acetylsalicylic acid

      ● **T39.011** **Poisoning by aspirin, accidental (unintentional)**

      ● **T39.012** **Poisoning by aspirin, intentional self-harm**

      ● **T39.013** **Poisoning by aspirin, assault**

      ● **T39.014** **Poisoning by aspirin, undetermined**

      ● **T39.015** **Adverse effect of aspirin**

      ● **T39.016** **Underdosing of aspirin**

    ● **T39.09** **Poisoning by, adverse effect of and underdosing of other salicylates**

      ● **T39.091** **Poisoning by salicylates, accidental (unintentional)**
          Poisoning by salicylates NOS

      ● **T39.092** **Poisoning by salicylates, intentional self-harm**

      ● **T39.093** **Poisoning by salicylates, assault**

      ● **T39.094** **Poisoning by salicylates, undetermined**

      ● **T39.095** **Adverse effect of salicylates**

      ● **T39.096** **Underdosing of salicylates**

  ● **T39.1** **Poisoning by, adverse effect of and underdosing of 4-Aminophenol derivatives**

    ● **T39.1x** **Poisoning by, adverse effect of and underdosing of 4-Aminophenol derivatives**

      ● **T39.1x1** **Poisoning by 4-Aminophenol derivatives, accidental (unintentional)**
          Poisoning by 4-Aminophenol derivatives NOS

      ● **T39.1x2** **Poisoning by 4-Aminophenol derivatives, intentional self-harm**

      ● **T39.1x3** **Poisoning by 4-Aminophenol derivatives, assault**

      ● **T39.1x4** **Poisoning by 4-Aminophenol derivatives, undetermined**

      ● **T39.1x5** **Adverse effect of 4-Aminophenol derivatives**

      ● **T39.1x6** **Underdosing of 4-Aminophenol derivatives**

  ● **T39.2** **Poisoning by, adverse effect of and underdosing of pyrazolone derivatives**

    ● **T39.2x** **Poisoning by, adverse effect of and underdosing of pyrazolone derivatives**

      ● **T39.2x1** **Poisoning by pyrazolone derivatives, accidental (unintentional)**
          Poisoning by pyrazolone derivatives NOS

      ● **T39.2x2** **Poisoning by pyrazolone derivatives, intentional self-harm**

      ● **T39.2x3** **Poisoning by pyrazolone derivatives, assault**

      ● **T39.2x4** **Poisoning by pyrazolone derivatives, undetermined**

      ● **T39.2x5** **Adverse effect of pyrazolone derivatives**

      ● **T39.2x6** **Underdosing of pyrazolone derivatives**

  ● **T39.3** **Poisoning by, adverse effect of and underdosing of other nonsteroidal anti-inflammatory drugs [NSAID]**

    ● **T39.31** **Poisoning by, adverse effect of and underdosing of propionic acid derivatives**
        Poisoning by, adverse effect of and underdosing of fenoprofen
        Poisoning by, adverse effect of and underdosing of flurbiprofen
        Poisoning by, adverse effect of and underdosing of ibuprofen
        Poisoning by, adverse effect of and underdosing of ketoprofen
        Poisoning by, adverse effect of and underdosing of naproxen
        Poisoning by, adverse effect of and underdosing of oxaprozin

      ● **T39.311** **Poisoning by propionic acid derivatives, accidental (unintentional)**

● Unacceptable First-Listed Diagnosis   ● Use Additional Character(s)   ■ Unspecified   **OGCR** Official Guidelines for Coding and Reporting
🔗 Complication\Comorbidity   🔗 Major C\C   Excludes 1   Excludes 2   Includes   Use additional   Code first   Code also

● **T39.312** Poisoning by propionic acid derivatives, intentional self-harm

● **T39.313** Poisoning by propionic acid derivatives, assault

● **T39.314** Poisoning by propionic acid derivatives, undetermined

● **T39.315** Adverse effect of propionic acid derivatives

● **T39.316** Underdosing of propionic acid derivatives

● **T39.39** Poisoning by, adverse effect of and underdosing of other nonsteroidal anti-inflammatory drugs [NSAID]

  ● **T39.391** Poisoning by other nonsteroidal anti-inflammatory drugs [NSAID], accidental (unintentional)
       Poisoning by other nonsteroidal anti-inflammatory drugs NOS

  ● **T39.392** Poisoning by other nonsteroidal anti-inflammatory drugs [NSAID], intentional self-harm

  ● **T39.393** Poisoning by other nonsteroidal anti-inflammatory drugs [NSAID], assault

  ● **T39.394** Poisoning by other nonsteroidal anti-inflammatory drugs [NSAID], undetermined

  ● **T39.395** Adverse effect of other nonsteroidal anti-inflammatory drugs [NSAID]

  ● **T39.396** Underdosing of other nonsteroidal anti-inflammatory drugs [NSAID]

● **T39.4** Poisoning by, adverse effect of and underdosing of antirheumatics, not elsewhere classified

    Excludes1   poisoning by, adverse effect of and underdosing of glucocorticoids (T38.0-)
               poisoning by, adverse effect of and underdosing of salicylates (T39.0-)

  ● **T39.4x** Poisoning by, adverse effect of and underdosing of antirheumatics, not elsewhere classified

    ● **T39.4x1** Poisoning by antirheumatics, not elsewhere classified, accidental (unintentional)
         Poisoning by antirheumatics, not elsewhere classified NOS

    ● **T39.4x2** Poisoning by antirheumatics, not elsewhere classified, intentional self-harm

    ● **T39.4x3** Poisoning by antirheumatics, not elsewhere classified, assault

    ● **T39.4x4** Poisoning by antirheumatics, not elsewhere classified, undetermined

    ● **T39.4x5** Adverse effect of antirheumatics, not elsewhere classified

    ● **T39.4x6** Underdosing of antirheumatics, not elsewhere classified

● **T39.8** Poisoning by, adverse effect of and underdosing of other nonopioid analgesics and antipyretics, not elsewhere classified

  ● **T39.8x** Poisoning by, adverse effect of and underdosing of other nonopioid analgesics and antipyretics, not elsewhere classified

    ● **T39.8x1** Poisoning by other nonopioid analgesics and antipyretics, not elsewhere classified, accidental (unintentional)
         Poisoning by other nonopioid analgesics and antipyretics, not elsewhere classified NOS

    ● **T39.8x2** Poisoning by other nonopioid analgesics and antipyretics, not elsewhere classified, intentional self-harm

    ● **T39.8x3** Poisoning by other nonopioid analgesics and antipyretics, not elsewhere classified, assault

    ● **T39.8x4** Poisoning by other nonopioid analgesics and antipyretics, not elsewhere classified, undetermined

    ● **T39.8x5** Adverse effect of other nonopioid analgesics and antipyretics, not elsewhere classified

    ● **T39.8x6** Underdosing of other nonopioid analgesics and antipyretics, not elsewhere classified

● **T39.9** Poisoning by, adverse effect of and underdosing of unspecified nonopioid analgesic, antipyretic and antirheumatic

  ●■ **T39.91** Poisoning by unspecified nonopioid analgesic, antipyretic and antirheumatic, accidental (unintentional)
       Poisoning by nonopioid analgesic, antipyretic and antirheumatic NOS

  ●■ **T39.92** Poisoning by unspecified nonopioid analgesic, antipyretic and antirheumatic, intentional self-harm

  ●■ **T39.93** Poisoning by unspecified nonopioid analgesic, antipyretic and antirheumatic, assault

  ●■ **T39.94** Poisoning by unspecified nonopioid analgesic, antipyretic and antirheumatic, undetermined

  ●■ **T39.95** Adverse effect of unspecified nonopioid analgesic, antipyretic and antirheumatic

  ●■ **T39.96** Underdosing of unspecified nonopioid analgesic, antipyretic and antirheumatic

● **T40** Poisoning by, adverse effect of and underdosing of narcotics and psychodysleptics [hallucinogens]

    Excludes2   drug dependence and related mental and behavioral disorders due to psychoactive substance use (F10.-F19.-)

    The appropriate 7th character is to be added to each code from category T40

A	initial encounter
D	subsequent encounter
S	sequela

● Unacceptable First-Listed Diagnosis   ● Use Additional Character(s)   ■ Unspecified   **OGCR** Official Guidelines for Coding and Reporting

🦠 Complication\Comorbidity   🦠 Major C\C   Excludes 1   Excludes 2   Includes   Use additional   Code first   Code also

CHAPTER 19 (S00-T98)

1563

● **T40.0**   **Poisoning by, adverse effect of and underdosing of opium**
   ● **T40.0x**   **Poisoning by, adverse effect of and underdosing of opium**
      T40.0x1   **Poisoning by opium, accidental (unintentional)**
         Poisoning by opium NOS
      ● **T40.0x2**   **Poisoning by opium, intentional self-harm**
      ● **T40.0x3**   **Poisoning by opium, assault**
      ● **T40.0x4**   **Poisoning by opium, undetermined**
      ● **T40.0x5**   **Adverse effect of opium**
      ● **T40.0x6**   **Underdosing of opium**

● **T40.1**   **Poisoning by, adverse effect of and underdosing of heroin**
   ● **T40.1x**   **Poisoning by and adverse effect of heroin**
      ● **T40.1x1**   **Poisoning by heroin, accidental (unintentional)**
         Poisoning by heroin NOS
      ● **T40.1x2**   **Poisoning by heroin, intentional self-harm**
      ● **T40.1x3**   **Poisoning by heroin, assault**
      ● **T40.1x4**   **Poisoning by heroin, undetermined**
      ● **T40.1x5**   **Adverse effect of heroin**
      ● **T40.1x6**   **Underdosing of heroin**

● **T40.2**   **Poisoning by, adverse effect of and underdosing of other opioids**
   ● **T40.2x**   **Poisoning by, adverse effect of and underdosing of other opioids**
      ● **T40.2x1**   **Poisoning by other opioids, accidental (unintentional)**
         Poisoning by other opioids NOS
      ● **T40.2x2**   **Poisoning by other opioids, intentional self-harm**
      ● **T40.2x3**   **Poisoning by other opioids, assault**
      ● **T40.2x4**   **Poisoning by other opioids, undetermined**
      ● **T40.2x5**   **Adverse effect of other opioids**
      ● **T40.2x6**   **Underdosing of other opioids**

● **T40.3**   **Poisoning by, adverse effect of and underdosing of methadone**
   ● **T40.3x**   **Poisoning by, adverse effect of and underdosing of methadone**
      ● **T40.3x1**   **Poisoning by methadone, accidental (unintentional)**
         Poisoning by methadone NOS
      ● **T40.3x2**   **Poisoning by methadone, intentional self-harm**
      ● **T40.3x3**   **Poisoning by methadone, assault**
      ● **T40.3x4**   **Poisoning by methadone, undetermined**
      ● **T40.3x5**   **Adverse effect of methadone**
      ● **T40.3x6**   **Underdosing of methadone**

● **T40.4**   **Poisoning by, adverse effect of and underdosing of other synthetic narcotics**
   ● **T40.4x**   **Poisoning by, adverse effect of and underdosing of other synthetic narcotics**

● **T40.4x1**   **Poisoning by other synthetic narcotics, accidental (unintentional)**
      Poisoning by other synthetic narcotics NOS
● **T40.4x2**   **Poisoning by other synthetic narcotics, intentional self-harm**
● **T40.4x3**   **Poisoning by other synthetic narcotics, assault**
● **T40.4x4**   **Poisoning by other synthetic narcotics, undetermined**
● **T40.4x5**   **Adverse effect of other synthetic narcotics**
● **T40.4x6**   **Underdosing of other synthetic narcotics**

● **T40.5**   **Poisoning by, adverse effect of and underdosing of cocaine**
   ● **T40.5x**   **Poisoning by, adverse effect of and underdosing of cocaine**
      ● **T40.5x1**   **Poisoning by cocaine, accidental (unintentional)**
         Poisoning by cocaine NOS
      ● **T40.5x2**   **Poisoning by cocaine, intentional self-harm**
      ● **T40.5x3**   **Poisoning by cocaine, assault**
      ● **T40.5x4**   **Poisoning by cocaine, undetermined**
      ● **T40.5x5**   **Adverse effect of cocaine**
      ● **T40.5x6**   **Underdosing of cocaine**

● **T40.6**   **Poisoning by, adverse effect of and underdosing of other and unspecified narcotics**
   ● **T40.60**   **Poisoning by, adverse effect of and underdosing of unspecified narcotics**
      ● ▣ **T40.601**   **Poisoning by unspecified narcotics, accidental (unintentional)**
         Poisoning by narcotics NOS
      ● ▣ **T40.602**   **Poisoning by unspecified narcotics, intentional self-harm**
      ● ▣ **T40.603**   **Poisoning by unspecified narcotics, assault**
      ● ▣ **T40.604**   **Poisoning by unspecified narcotics, undetermined**
      ● ▣ **T40.605**   **Adverse effect of unspecified narcotics**
      ● ▣ **T40.606**   **Underdosing of unspecified narcotics**
   ● **T40.69**   **Poisoning by, adverse effect of and underdosing of other narcotics**
      ● **T40.691**   **Poisoning by other narcotics, accidental (unintentional)**
         Poisoning by other narcotics NOS
      ● **T40.692**   **Poisoning by other narcotics, intentional self-harm**
      ● **T40.693**   **Poisoning by other narcotics, assault**
      ● **T40.694**   **Poisoning by other narcotics, undetermined**
      ● **T40.695**   **Adverse effect of other narcotics**
      ● **T40.696**   **Underdosing of other narcotics**

● Unacceptable First-Listed Diagnosis   ● Use Additional Character(s)   ▣ Unspecified   **OGCR** Official Guidelines for Coding and Reporting
🔖 Complication\Comorbidity   🔖 Major C\C   Excludes 1   Excludes 2   Includes   Use additional   Code first   Code also

● T40.7   Poisoning by, adverse effect of and underdosing of cannabis (derivatives)

    ● T40.7x   Poisoning by, adverse effect of and underdosing of cannabis (derivatives)

       ● T40.7x1   Poisoning by cannabis (derivatives), accidental (unintentional)
               Poisoning by cannabis NOS

       ● T40.7x2   Poisoning by cannabis (derivatives), intentional self-harm

       ● T40.7x3   Poisoning by cannabis (derivatives), assault

       ● T40.7x4   Poisoning by cannabis (derivatives), undetermined

       ● T40.7x5   Adverse effect of cannabis (derivatives)

       ● T40.7x6   Underdosing of cannabis (derivatives)

● T40.8   Poisoning by, adverse effect of and underdosing of lysergide [LSD]

    ● T40.8x   Poisoning by and adverse effect of lysergide [LSD]

       ● T40.8x1   Poisoning by lysergide [LSD], accidental (unintentional)
               Poisoning by lysergide [LSD] NOS

       ● T40.8x2   Poisoning by lysergide [LSD], intentional self-harm

       ● T40.8x3   Poisoning by lysergide [LSD], assault

       ● T40.8x4   Poisoning by lysergide [LSD], undetermined

       ● T40.8x5   Adverse effect of lysergide [LSD]

       ● T40.8x6   Underdosing of lysergide [LSD]

● T40.9   Poisoning by, adverse effect of and underdosing of other and unspecified psychodysleptics [hallucinogens]

    ● T40.90   Poisoning by, adverse effect of and underdosing of unspecified psychodysleptics [hallucinogens]

       ● ▢ T40.901   Poisoning by unspecified psychodysleptics [hallucinogens], accidental (unintentional)

       ● ▢ T40.902   Poisoning by unspecified psychodysleptics [hallucinogens], intentional self-harm

       ● ▢ T40.903   Poisoning by unspecified psychodysleptics [hallucinogens], assault

       ● ▢ T40.904   Poisoning by unspecified psychodysleptics [hallucinogens], undetermined

       ● ▢ T40.905   Adverse effect of unspecified psychodysleptics [hallucinogens]

       ● ▢ T40.906   Underdosing of unspecified psychodysleptics

    ● T40.99   Poisoning by, adverse effect of and underdosing of other psychodysleptics [hallucinogens]

       ● T40.991   Poisoning by other psychodysleptics [hallucinogens], accidental (unintentional)
               Poisoning by other psychodysleptics [hallucinogens] NOS

       ● T40.992   Poisoning by other psychodysleptics [hallucinogens], intentional self-harm

       ● T40.993   Poisoning by other psychodysleptics [hallucinogens], assault

       ● T40.994   Poisoning by other psychodysleptics [hallucinogens], undetermined

       ● T40.995   Adverse effect of other psychodysleptics [hallucinogens]

       ● T40.996   Underdosing of other psychodysleptics

● T41   Poisoning by, adverse effect of and underdosing of anesthetics and therapeutic gases

    Excludes1   benzodiazepines (T42.4-)
                 cocaine (T40.5-)
                 complications of anesthesia during pregnancy (O29.-)
                 complications of anesthesia during labor and delivery (O74.-)
                 complications of anesthesia during the puerperium (O89.-) opioids (T40.0-T40.2-)

    The appropriate 7th character is to be added to each code from category T41

       | | |
       A   initial encounter
       D   subsequent encounter
       S   sequela

● T41.0   Poisoning by, adverse effect of and underdosing of inhaled anesthetics

    Excludes1   oxygen (T41.5-)

    ● T41.0x   Poisoning by, adverse effect of and underdosing of inhaled anesthetics

       ● T41.0x1   Poisoning by inhaled anesthetics, accidental (unintentional)
               Poisoning by inhaled anesthetics NOS

       ● T41.0x2   Poisoning by inhaled anesthetics, intentional self-harm

       ● T41.0x3   Poisoning by inhaled anesthetics, assault

       ● T41.0x4   Poisoning by inhaled anesthetics, undetermined

       ● T41.0x5   Adverse effect of inhaled anesthetics

       ● T41.0x6   Underdosing of inhaled anesthetics

● T41.1   Poisoning by, adverse effect of and underdosing of intravenous anesthetics
       Poisoning by, adverse effect of and underdosing of thiobarbiturates

    ● T41.1x   Poisoning by, adverse effect of and underdosing of intravenous anesthetics

       ● T41.1x1   Poisoning by intravenous anesthetics, accidental (unintentional)
               Poisoning by intravenous anesthetics NOS

       ● T41.1x2   Poisoning by intravenous anesthetics, intentional self-harm

●   Unacceptable First-Listed Diagnosis   ●   Use Additional Character(s)   ▢   Unspecified   **OGCR** Official Guidelines for Coding and Reporting

🔖 Complication\Comorbidity   🔖 Major C\C   Excludes 1   Excludes 2   Includes   Use additional   Code first   Code also   **1565**

CHAPTER 19 (S00-T98)

● T41.1x3   Poisoning by intravenous anesthetics, assault

● T41.1x4   Poisoning by intravenous anesthetics, undetermined

● T41.1x5   Adverse effect of intravenous anesthetics

● T41.1x6   Underdosing of intravenous anesthetics

● T41.2   Poisoning by, adverse effect of and underdosing of other and unspecified general anesthetics

   ● T41.20   Poisoning by, adverse effect of and underdosing of unspecified general anesthetics

     ● ▢ T41.201   Poisoning by unspecified general anesthetics, accidental (unintentional)
           Poisoning by general anesthetics NOS

     ● ▢ T41.202   Poisoning by unspecified general anesthetics, intentional self-harm

     ● ▢ T41.203   Poisoning by unspecified general anesthetics, assault

     ● ▢ T41.204   Poisoning by unspecified general anesthetics, undetermined

     ● ▢ T41.205   Adverse effect of unspecified general anesthetics

     ● ▢ T41.206   Underdosing of unspecified general anesthetics

   ● T41.29   Poisoning by, adverse effect of and underdosing of other general anesthetics

     ● T41.291   Poisoning by other general anesthetics, accidental (unintentional)
           Poisoning by other general anesthetics NOS

     ● T41.292   Poisoning by other general anesthetics, intentional self-harm

     ● T41.293   Poisoning by other general anesthetics, assault

     ● T41.294   Poisoning by other general anesthetics, undetermined

     ● T41.295   Adverse effect of other general anesthetics

     ● T41.296   Underdosing of other general anesthetics

● T41.3   Poisoning by, adverse effect of and underdosing of local anesthetics

   ● T41.3x   Poisoning by, adverse effect of and underdosing of local anesthetics

     ● T41.3x1   Poisoning by local anesthetics, accidental (unintentional)
           Poisoning by local anesthetics NOS

     ● T41.3x2   Poisoning by local anesthetics, intentional self-harm

     ● T41.3x3   Poisoning by local anesthetics, assault

     ● T41.3x4   Poisoning by local anesthetics, undetermined

     ● T41.3x5   Adverse effect of local anesthetics

     ● T41.3x6   Underdosing of local anesthetics

● T41.4   Poisoning by, adverse effect of and underdosing of unspecified anesthetic

● ▢ T41.41   Poisoning by unspecified anesthetic, accidental (unintentional)
           Poisoning by anesthetic NOS

● ▢ T41.42   Poisoning by unspecified anesthetic, intentional self-harm

● ▢ T41.43   Poisoning by unspecified anesthetic, assault

● ▢ T41.44   Poisoning by unspecified anesthetic, undetermined

● ▢ T41.45   Adverse effect of unspecified anesthetic

● ▢ T41.46   Underdosing of unspecified anesthetics

● T41.5   Poisoning by, adverse effect of and underdosing of therapeutic gases

   ● T41.5x   Poisoning by, adverse effect of and underdosing of therapeutic gases

     ● T41.5x1   Poisoning by therapeutic gases, accidental (unintentional)
           Poisoning by therapeutic gases NOS

     ● T41.5x2   Poisoning by therapeutic gases, intentional self-harm

     ● T41.5x3   Poisoning by therapeutic gases, assault

     ● T41.5x4   Poisoning by therapeutic gases, undetermined

     ● T41.5x5   Adverse effect of therapeutic gases

     ● T41.5x6   Underdosing of therapeutic gases

● T42   Poisoning by, adverse effect of and underdosing of antiepileptic, sedative-hypnotic and antiparkinsonism drugs

   Excludes2   drug dependence and related mental and behavioral disorders due to psychoactive substance use (F10.--F19.-)

   The appropriate 7th character is to be added to each code from category T42

     A   initial encounter
     D   subsequent encounter
     S   sequela

● T42.0   Poisoning by, adverse effect of and underdosing of hydantoin derivatives

   ● T42.0x   Poisoning by, adverse effect of and underdosing of hydantoin derivatives

     ● T42.0x1   Poisoning by hydantoin derivatives, accidental (unintentional)
           Poisoning by hydantoin derivatives NOS

     ● T42.0x2   Poisoning by hydantoin derivatives, intentional self-harm

     ● T42.0x3   Poisoning by hydantoin derivatives, assault

     ● T42.0x4   Poisoning by hydantoin derivatives, undetermined

     ● T42.0x5   Adverse effect of hydantoin derivatives

     ● T42.0x6   Underdosing of hydantoin derivatives

● T42.1   Poisoning by, adverse effect of and underdosing of iminostilbenes
     Poisoning by, adverse effect of and underdosing of carbamazepine

   ● T42.1x   Poisoning by, adverse effect of and underdosing of iminostilbenes

● Unacceptable First-Listed Diagnosis   ● Use Additional Character(s)   ▢ Unspecified   **OGCR** Official Guidelines for Coding and Reporting
🅒 Complication\Comorbidity   🅒 Major C\C   Excludes 1   Excludes 2   Includes   Use additional   Code first   Code also

- T42.1x1 Poisoning by iminostilbenes, accidental (unintentional)
  Poisoning by iminostilbenes NOS
- T42.1x2 Poisoning by iminostilbenes, intentional self-harm
- T42.1x3 Poisoning by iminostilbenes, assault
- T42.1x4 Poisoning by iminostilbenes, undetermined
- T42.1x5 Adverse effect of iminostilbenes
- T42.1x6 Underdosing of iminostilbenes

- T42.2 Poisoning by, adverse effect of and underdosing of succinimides and oxazolidinediones
  - T42.2x Poisoning by, adverse effect of and underdosing of succinimides and oxazolidinediones
    - T42.2x1 Poisoning by succinimides and oxazolidinediones, accidental (unintentional)
      Poisoning by succinimides and oxazolidinediones NOS
    - T42.2x2 Poisoning by succinimides and oxazolidinediones, intentional self-harm
    - T42.2x3 Poisoning by succinimides and oxazolidinediones, assault
    - T42.2x4 Poisoning by succinimides and oxazolidinediones, undetermined
    - T42.2x5 Adverse effect of succinimides and oxazolidinediones
    - T42.2x6 Underdosing of succinimides and oxazolidinediones

- T42.3 Poisoning by, adverse effect of and underdosing of barbiturates
  Excludes1 poisoning by, adverse effect of and underdosing of thiobarbiturates (T41.1-)
  - T42.3x Poisoning by, adverse effect of and underdosing of barbiturates
    - T42.3x1 Poisoning by barbiturates, accidental (unintentional)
      Poisoning by barbiturates NOS
    - T42.3x2 Poisoning by barbiturates, intentional self-harm
    - T42.3x3 Poisoning by barbiturates, assault
    - T42.3x4 Poisoning by barbiturates, undetermined
    - T42.3x5 Adverse effect of barbiturates
    - T42.3x6 Underdosing of barbiturates

- T42.4 Poisoning by, adverse effect of and underdosing of benzodiazepines
  - T42.4x Poisoning by, adverse effect of and underdosing of benzodiazepines
    - T42.4x1 Poisoning by benzodiazepines, accidental (unintentional)
      Poisoning by benzodiazepines NOS
    - T42.4x2 Poisoning by benzodiazepines, intentional self-harm
    - T42.4x3 Poisoning by benzodiazepines, assault
    - T42.4x4 Poisoning by benzodiazepines, undetermined

- T42.4x5 Adverse effect of benzodiazepines
- T42.4x6 Underdosing of benzodiazepines

- T42.5 Poisoning by, adverse effect of and underdosing of mixed antiepileptics
  - T42.5x Poisoning by, adverse effect of and underdosing of antiepileptics
    - T42.5x1 Poisoning by mixed antiepileptics, accidental (unintentional)
      Poisoning by mixed antiepileptics NOS
    - T42.5x2 Poisoning by mixed antiepileptics, intentional self-harm
    - T42.5x3 Poisoning by mixed antiepileptics, assault
    - T42.5x4 Poisoning by mixed antiepileptics, undetermined
    - T42.5x5 Adverse effect of mixed antiepileptics
    - T42.5x6 Underdosing of mixed antiepileptics

- T42.6 Poisoning by, adverse effect of and underdosing of other antiepileptic and sedative-hypnotic drugs
  Poisoning by, adverse effect of and underdosing of methaqualone
  Poisoning by, adverse effect of and underdosing of valproic acid
  Excludes1 poisoning by, adverse effect of and underdosing of carbamazepine (T42.1-)
  - T42.6x Poisoning by, adverse effect of and underdosing of other antiepileptic and sedative-hypnotic drugs
    - T42.6x1 Poisoning by other antiepileptic and sedative-hypnotic drugs, accidental (unintentional)
      Poisoning by other antiepileptic and sedative-hypnotic drugs NOS
    - T42.6x2 Poisoning by other antiepileptic and sedative-hypnotic drugs, intentional self-harm
    - T42.6x3 Poisoning by other antiepileptic and sedative-hypnotic drugs, assault
    - T42.6x4 Poisoning by other antiepileptic and sedative-hypnotic drugs, undetermined
    - T42.6x5 Adverse effect of other antiepileptic and sedative-hypnotic drugs
    - T42.6x6 Underdosing of other antiepileptic and sedative-hypnotic drugs

- T42.7 Poisoning by, adverse effect of and underdosing of unspecified antiepileptic and sedative-hypnotic drugs
  - T42.71 Poisoning by unspecified antiepileptic and sedative-hypnotic drugs, accidental (unintentional)
    Poisoning by antiepileptic and sedative-hypnotic drugs NOS
  - T42.72 Poisoning by unspecified antiepileptic and sedative-hypnotic drugs, intentional self-harm
  - T42.73 Poisoning by unspecified antiepileptic and sedative-hypnotic drugs, assault

- Unacceptable First-Listed Diagnosis   ● Use Additional Character(s)   ▪ Unspecified   OGCR Official Guidelines for Coding and Reporting
🅒 Complication\Comorbidity   🅜 Major C\C   Excludes 1   Excludes 2   Includes   Use additional   Code first   Code also

CHAPTER 19 (S00-T98)

1567

● ■ **T42.74**   Poisoning by unspecified antiepileptic and sedative-hypnotic drugs, undetermined

● ■ **T42.75**   Adverse effect of unspecified antiepileptic and sedative-hypnotic drugs

● ■ **T42.76**   Underdosing of unspecified antiepileptic and sedative-hypnotic drugs

● **T42.8**   Poisoning by, adverse effect of and underdosing of antiparkinsonism drugs and other central muscle-tone depressants

     Poisoning by, adverse effect of and underdosing of amantadine

   ● **T42.8x**   Poisoning by, adverse effect of and underdosing of antiparkinsonism drugs and other central muscle-tone depressants

     ● **T42.8x1**   Poisoning by antiparkinsonism drugs and other central muscle-tone depressants, accidental (unintentional)

         Poisoning by antiparkinsonism drugs and other central muscle-tone depressants NOS

     ● **T42.8x2**   Poisoning by antiparkinsonism drugs and other central muscle-tone depressants, intentional self-harm

     ● **T42.8x3**   Poisoning by antiparkinsonism drugs and other central muscle-tone depressants, assault

     ● **T42.8x4**   Poisoning by antiparkinsonism drugs and other central muscle-tone depressants, undetermined

     ● **T42.8x5**   Adverse effect of antiparkinsonism drugs and other central muscle-tone depressants

     ● **T42.8x6**   Underdosing of antiparkinsonism drugs and other central muscle-tone depressants

● **T43**   Poisoning by, adverse effect of and underdosing of psychotropic drugs, not elsewhere classified

> **Excludes1**   appetite depressants (T50.5-)
> barbiturates (T42.3-)
> benzodiazepines (T42.4-)
> methaqualone (T42.6-)
> psychodysleptics [hallucinogens] (T40.7-T40.9-)

> **Excludes2**   drug dependence and related mental and behavioral disorders due to psychoactive substance use (F10.0--F19.-)

The appropriate 7th character is to be added to each code from category T43

> A   initial encounter
> D   subsequent encounter
> S   sequela

● **T43.0**   Poisoning by, adverse effect of and underdosing of tricyclic and tetracyclic antidepressants

   ● **T43.01**   Poisoning by, adverse effect of and underdosing of tricyclic antidepressants

     ● **T43.011**   Poisoning by tricyclic antidepressants, accidental (unintentional)

         Poisoning by tricyclic antidepressants NOS

     ● **T43.012**   Poisoning by tricyclic antidepressants, intentional self-harm

     ● **T43.013**   Poisoning by tricyclic antidepressants, assault

     ● **T43.014**   Poisoning by tricyclic antidepressants, undetermined

     ● **T43.015**   Adverse effect of tricyclic antidepressants

     ● **T43.016**   Underdosing of tricyclic antidepressants

   ● **T43.02**   Poisoning by, adverse effect of and underdosing of tetracyclic antidepressants

     ● **T43.021**   Poisoning by tetracyclic antidepressants, accidental (unintentional)

         Poisoning by tricyclic and tetracyclic antidepressants NOS

     ● **T43.022**   Poisoning by tetracyclic antidepressants, intentional self-harm

     ● **T43.023**   Poisoning by tetracyclic antidepressants, assault

     ● **T43.024**   Poisoning by tetracyclic antidepressants, undetermined

     ● **T43.025**   Adverse effect of tetracyclic antidepressants

     ● **T43.026**   Underdosing of tetracyclic antidepressants

● **T43.1**   Poisoning by, adverse effect of and underdosing of monoamine-oxidase-inhibitor antidepressants

   ● **T43.1x**   Poisoning by, adverse effect of and underdosing of monoamine-oxidase-inhibitor antidepressants

     ● **T43.1x1**   Poisoning by monoamine-oxidase-inhibitor antidepressants, accidental (unintentional)

         Poisoning by monoamine-oxidase-inhibitor antidepressants NOS

     ● **T43.1x2**   Poisoning by monoamine-oxidase-inhibitor antidepressants, intentional self-harm

     ● **T43.1x3**   Poisoning by monoamine-oxidase-inhibitor antidepressants, assault

     ● **T43.1x4**   Poisoning by monoamine-oxidase-inhibitor antidepressants, undetermined

     ● **T43.1x5**   Adverse effect of monoamine-oxidase-inhibitor antidepressants

     ● **T43.1x6**   Underdosing of monoamine-oxidase-inhibitor antidepressants

● **T43.2**   Poisoning by, adverse effect of and underdosing of other and unspecified antidepressants

   ● **T43.20**   Poisoning by, adverse effect of and underdosing of unspecified antidepressants

     ● ■ **T43.201**   Poisoning by unspecified antidepressants, accidental (unintentional)

         Poisoning by antidepressants NOS

     ● ■ **T43.202**   Poisoning by unspecified antidepressants, intentional self-harm

     ● ■ **T43.203**   Poisoning by unspecified antidepressants, assault

     ● ■ **T43.204**   Poisoning by unspecified antidepressants, undetermined

● Unacceptable First-Listed Diagnosis   ● Use Additional Character(s)   ■ Unspecified   **OGCR** Official Guidelines for Coding and Reporting

🔖 Complication\Comorbidity   🔖 Major C\C   Excludes 1   Excludes 2   Includes   Use additional   Code first   Code also

- ● ◼ T43.205   Adverse effect of unspecified antidepressants
- ● ◼ T43.206   Underdosing of unspecified antidepressants
- ● T43.21   Poisoning by, adverse effect of and underdosing of selective serotonin and norepinephrine reuptake inhibitors
  Poisoning by, adverse effect of and underdosing of SSNRI antidepressants
  - ● T43.211   Poisoning by selective serotonin and norepinephrine reuptake inhibitors, accidental (unintentional)
  - ● T43.212   Poisoning by selective serotonin and norepinephrine reuptake inhibitors, intentional self-harm
  - ● T43.213   Poisoning by selective serotonin and norepinephrine reuptake inhibitors, assault
  - ● T43.214   Poisoning by selective serotonin and norepinephrine reuptake inhibitors, undetermined
  - ● T43.215   Adverse effect of selective serotonin and norepinephrine reuptake inhibitors
  - ● T43.216   Underdosing of selective serotonin and norepinephrine reuptake inhibitors
- ● T43.22   Poisoning by, adverse effect of and underdosing of selective serotonin reuptake inhibitors
  Poisoning by, adverse effect of and underdosing of SSRI antidepressants
  - ● T43.221   Poisoning by selective serotonin reuptake inhibitors, accidental (unintentional)
  - ● T43.222   Poisoning by selective serotonin reuptake inhibitors, intentional self-harm
  - ● T43.223   Poisoning by selective serotonin reuptake inhibitors, assault
  - ● T43.224   Poisoning by selective serotonin reuptake inhibitors, undetermined
  - ● T43.225   Adverse effect of selective serotonin reuptake inhibitors
  - ● T43.226   Underdosing of selective serotonin reuptake inhibitors
- ● T43.29   Poisoning by, adverse effect of and underdosing of other antidepressants
  - ● T43.291   Poisoning by other antidepressants, accidental (unintentional)
    Poisoning by other antidepressants NOS
  - ● T43.292   Poisoning by other antidepressants, intentional self-harm
  - ● T43.293   Poisoning by other antidepressants, assault
  - ● T43.294   Poisoning by other antidepressants, undetermined
  - ● T43.295   Adverse effect of other antidepressants
  - ● T43.296   Underdosing of other antidepressants

- ● T43.3   Poisoning by, adverse effect of and underdosing of phenothiazine antipsychotics and neuroleptics
  - ● T43.3x   Poisoning by, adverse effect of and underdosing of phenothiazine antipsychotics and neuroleptics
    - ● T43.3x1   Poisoning by phenothiazine antipsychotics and neuroleptics, accidental (unintentional)
      Poisoning by phenothiazine antipsychotics and neuroleptics NOS
    - ● T43.3x2   Poisoning by phenothiazine antipsychotics and neuroleptics, intentional self-harm
    - ● T43.3x3   Poisoning by phenothiazine antipsychotics and neuroleptics, assault
    - ● T43.3x4   Poisoning by phenothiazine antipsychotics and neuroleptics, undetermined
    - ● T43.3x5   Adverse effect of phenothiazine antipsychotics and neuroleptics
    - ● T43.3x6   Underdosing of phenothiazine antipsychotics and neuroleptics
- ● T43.4   Poisoning by, adverse effect of and underdosing of butyrophenone and thiothixene neuroleptics
  - ● T43.4x   Poisoning by, adverse effect of and underdosing of butyrophenone and thiothixene neuroleptics
    - ● T43.4x1   Poisoning by butyrophenone and thiothixene neuroleptics, accidental (unintentional)
      Poisoning by butyrophenone and thiothixene neuroleptics NOS
    - ● T43.4x2   Poisoning by butyrophenone and thiothixene neuroleptics, intentional self-harm
    - ● T43.4x3   Poisoning by butyrophenone and thiothixene neuroleptics, assault
    - ● T43.4x4   Poisoning by butyrophenone and thiothixene neuroleptics, undetermined
    - ● T43.4x5   Adverse effect of butyrophenone and thiothixene neuroleptics
    - ● T43.4x6   Underdosing of butyrophenone and thiothixene neuroleptics
- ● T43.5   Poisoning by, adverse effect of and underdosing of other and unspecified antipsychotics and neuroleptics
  > **Excludes1**   poisoning by, adverse effect of and underdosing of rauwolfia (T46.5-)
  - ● T43.50   Poisoning by, adverse effect of and underdosing of unspecified antipsychotics and neuroleptics
    - ● ◼ T43.501   Poisoning by unspecified antipsychotics and neuroleptics, accidental (unintentional)
      Poisoning by antipsychotics and neuroleptics NOS
    - ● ◼ T43.502   Poisoning by unspecified antipsychotics and neuroleptics, intentional self-harm
    - ● ◼ T43.503   Poisoning by unspecified antipsychotics and neuroleptics, assault

---

●   Unacceptable First-Listed Diagnosis   ●   Use Additional Character(s)   ◼   Unspecified   **OGCR**   Official Guidelines for Coding and Reporting

 Complication\Comorbidity   🔖 Major C\C   Excludes 1   Excludes 2   Includes   Use additional   Code first   Code also

● ■ **T43.504**   Poisoning by unspecified antipsychotics and neuroleptics, undetermined

● ■ **T43.505**   Adverse effect of unspecified antipsychotics and neuroleptics

● ■ **T43.506**   Underdosing of unspecified antipsychotics and neuroleptics

● **T43.59**   Poisoning by, adverse effect of and underdosing of other antipsychotics and neuroleptics

    ● **T43.591**   Poisoning by other antipsychotics and neuroleptics, accidental (unintentional)
       Poisoning by other antipsychotics and neuroleptics NOS

    ● **T43.592**   Poisoning by other antipsychotics and neuroleptics, intentional self-harm

    ● **T43.593**   Poisoning by other antipsychotics and neuroleptics, assault

    ● **T43.594**   Poisoning by other antipsychotics and neuroleptics, undetermined

    ● **T43.595**   Adverse effect of other antipsychotics and neuroleptics

    ● **T43.596**   Underdosing of other antipsychotics and neuroleptics

● **T43.60**   Poisoning by, adverse effect of and underdosing of unspecified psychostimulant

    ● ■ **T43.601**   Poisoning by unspecified psychostimulants, accidental (unintentional)
       Poisoning by psychostimulants NOS

    ● ■ **T43.602**   Poisoning by unspecified psychostimulants, intentional self-harm

    ● ■ **T43.603**   Poisoning by unspecified psychostimulants, assault

    ● ■ **T43.604**   Poisoning by unspecified psychostimulants, undetermined

    ● ■ **T43.605**   Adverse effect of unspecified psychostimulants

    ● ■ **T43.606**   Underdosing of unspecified psychostimulants

● **T43.61**   Poisoning by, adverse effect of and underdosing of caffeine

    ● **T43.611**   Poisoning by caffeine, accidental (unintentional)
       Poisoning by caffeine NOS

    ● **T43.612**   Poisoning by caffeine, intentional self-harm

    ● **T43.613**   Poisoning by caffeine, assault

    ● **T43.614**   Poisoning by caffeine, undetermined

    ● **T43.615**   Adverse effect of caffeine

    ● **T43.616**   Underdosing of caffeine

● **T43.62**   Poisoning by, adverse effect of and underdosing of amphetamines
    Poisoning by, adverse effect of and underdosing of methamphetamines

    ● **T43.621**   Poisoning by amphetamines, accidental (unintentional)
       Poisoning by amphetamines NOS

    ● **T43.622**   Poisoning by amphetamines, intentional self-harm

    ● **T43.623**   Poisoning by amphetamines, assault

    ● **T43.624**   Poisoning by amphetamines, undetermined

    ● **T43.625**   Adverse effect of amphetamines

    ● **T43.626**   Underdosing of amphetamines

● **T43.63**   Poisoning by, adverse effect of and underdosing of methylphenidate

    ● **T43.631**   Poisoning by methylphenidate, accidental (unintentional)
       Poisoning by methylphenidate NOS

    ● **T43.632**   Poisoning by methylphenidate, intentional self-harm

    ● **T43.633**   Poisoning by methylphenidate, assault

    ● **T43.634**   Poisoning by methylphenidate, undetermined

    ● **T43.635**   Adverse effect of methylphenidate

    ● **T43.636**   Underdosing of methylphenidate

● **T43.69**   Poisoning by, adverse effect of and underdosing of other psychostimulants

    ● **T43.691**   Poisoning by other psychostimulants, accidental (unintentional)
       Poisoning by other psychostimulants NOS

    ● **T43.692**   Poisoning by other psychostimulants, intentional self-harm

    ● **T43.693**   Poisoning by other psychostimulants, assault

    ● **T43.694**   Poisoning by other psychostimulants, undetermined

    ● **T43.695**   Adverse effect of other psychostimulants

    ● **T43.696**   Underdosing of other psychostimulants

● **T43.8**   Poisoning by, adverse effect of and underdosing of other psychotropic drugs

    ● **T43.8x**   Poisoning by, adverse effect of and underdosing of other psychotropic drugs

       ● **T43.8x1**   Poisoning by other psychotropic drugs, accidental (unintentional)
          Poisoning by other psychotropic drugs NOS

       ● **T43.8x2**   Poisoning by other psychotropic drugs, intentional self-harm

       ● **T43.8x3**   Poisoning by other psychotropic drugs, assault

       ● **T43.8x4**   Poisoning by other psychotropic drugs, undetermined

       ● **T43.8x5**   Adverse effect of other psychotropic drugs

       ● **T43.8x6**   Underdosing of other psychotropic drugs

● **T43.9**   Poisoning by, adverse effect of and underdosing of unspecified psychotropic drug

    ● ■ **T43.91**   Poisoning by unspecified psychotropic drug, accidental (unintentional)
       Poisoning by psychotropic drug NOS

    ● ■ **T43.92**   Poisoning by unspecified psychotropic drug, intentional self-harm

● Unacceptable First-Listed Diagnosis   ● Use Additional Character(s)   ■ Unspecified   **OGCR** Official Guidelines for Coding and Reporting
🝢 Complication\Comorbidity   🝢 Major C\C   Excludes 1   Excludes 2   Includes   Use additional   Code first   Code also

● ■ **T43.93**   Poisoning by unspecified psychotropic drug, assault

● ■ **T43.94**   Poisoning by unspecified psychotropic drug, undetermined

● ■ **T43.95**   Adverse effect of unspecified psychotropic drug

● ■ **T43.96**   Underdosing of unspecified psychotroic drug

● **T44**   **Poisoning by, adverse effect of and underdosing of drugs primarily affecting the autonomic nervous system**

The appropriate 7th character is to be added to each code from category T44

A	initial encounter
D	subsequent encounter
S	sequela

● **T44.0**   Poisoning by, adverse effect of and underdosing of anticholinesterase agents

   ● **T44.0x**   Poisoning by, adverse effect of and underdosing of anticholinesterase agents

     ● **T44.0x1**   Poisoning by anticholinesterase agents, accidental (unintentional)
Poisoning by anticholinesterase agents NOS

     ● **T44.0x2**   Poisoning by anticholinesterase agents, intentional self-harm

     ● **T44.0x3**   Poisoning by anticholinesterase agents, assault

     ● **T44.0x4**   Poisoning by anticholinesterase agents, undetermined

     ● **T44.0x5**   Adverse effect of anticholinesterase agents

     ● **T44.0x6**   Underdosing of anticholinesterase agents

● **T44.1**   Poisoning by, adverse effect of and underdosing of other parasympathomimetics [cholinergics]

   ● **T44.1x**   Poisoning by, adverse effect of and underdosing of other parasympathomimetics [cholinergics]

     ● **T44.1x1**   Poisoning by other parasympathomimetics [cholinergics], accidental (unintentional)
Poisoning by other parasympathomimetics [cholinergics] NOS

     ● **T44.1x2**   Poisoning by other parasympathomimetics [cholinergics], intentional self-harm

     ● **T44.1x3**   Poisoning by other parasympathomimetics [cholinergics], assault

     ● **T44.1x4**   Poisoning by other parasympathomimetics [cholinergics], undetermined

     ● **T44.1x5**   Adverse effect of other parasympathomimetics [cholinergics]

     ● **T44.1x6**   Underdosing of other parasympathomimetics

● **T44.2**   Poisoning by, adverse effect of and underdosing of ganglionic blocking drugs

   ● **T44.2x**   Poisoning by, adverse effect of and underdosing of ganglionic blocking drugs

     ● **T44.2x1**   Poisoning by ganglionic blocking drugs, accidental (unintentional)
Poisoning by ganglionic blocking drugs NOS

     ● **T44.2x2**   Poisoning by ganglionic blocking drugs, intentional self-harm

     ● **T44.2x3**   Poisoning by ganglionic blocking drugs, assault

     ● **T44.2x4**   Poisoning by ganglionic blocking drugs, undetermined

     ● **T44.2x5**   Adverse effect of ganglionic blocking drugs

     ● **T44.2x6**   Underdosing of ganglionic blocking drugs

● **T44.3**   Poisoning by, adverse effect of and underdosing of other parasympatholytics [anticholinergics and antimuscarinics] and spasmolytics
Poisoning by, adverse effect of and underdosing of papaverine

   ● **T44.3x**   Poisoning by, adverse effect of and underdosing of other parasympatholytics [anticholinergics and antimuscarinics] and spasmolytics

     ● **T44.3x1**   Poisoning by other parasympatholytics [anticholinergics and antimuscarinics] and spasmolytics, accidental (unintentional)
Poisoning by other parasympatholytics [anticholinergics and antimuscarinics] and spasmolytics NOS

     ● **T44.3x2**   Poisoning by other parasympatholytics [anticholinergics and antimuscarinics] and spasmolytics, intentional self-harm

     ● **T44.3x3**   Poisoning by other parasympatholytics [anticholinergics and antimuscarinics] and spasmolytics, assault

     ● **T44.3x4**   Poisoning by other parasympatholytics [anticholinergics and antimuscarinics] and spasmolytics, undetermined

     ● **T44.3x5**   Adverse effect of other parasympatholytics [anticholinergics and antimuscarinics] and spasmolytics

     ● **T44.3x6**   Underdosing of other parasympatholytics [anticholinergics and antimuscarinics] and spasmolytics

●   Unacceptable First-Listed Diagnosis   ●   Use Additional Character(s)   ■ Unspecified   **OGCR** Official Guidelines for Coding and Reporting

 Complication\Comorbidity   Major C\C   Excludes 1   Excludes 2   Includes   Use additional   Code first   Code also

1571

CHAPTER 19 (S00-T98)

● **T44.4 Poisoning by, adverse effect of and underdosing of predominantly alpha-adrenoreceptor agonists**
   Poisoning by, adverse effect of and underdosing of metaraminol

   ● **T44.4x Poisoning by, adverse effect of and underdosing of predominantly alpha-adrenoreceptor agonists**

      ● **T44.4x1 Poisoning by predominantly alpha-adrenoreceptor agonists, accidental (unintentional)**
         Poisoning by predominantly alpha-adrenoreceptor agonists NOS

      ● **T44.4x2 Poisoning by predominantly alpha-adrenoreceptor agonists, intentional self-harm**

      ● **T44.4x3 Poisoning by predominantly alpha-adrenoreceptor agonists, assault**

      ● **T44.4x4 Poisoning by predominantly alpha-adrenoreceptor agonists, undetermined**

      ● **T44.4x5 Adverse effect of predominantly alpha-adrenoreceptor agonists**

      ● **T44.4x6 Underdosing of predominantly alpha-adrenoreceptor agonists**

● **T44.5 Poisoning by, adverse effect of and underdosing of predominantly beta-adrenoreceptor agonists**

   | **Excludes1** | poisoning by, adverse effect of and underdosing of beta-adrenoreceptor agonists used in asthma therapy (T48.6-) |

   ● **T44.5x Poisoning by, adverse effect of and underdosing of predominantly beta-adrenoreceptor agonists**

      ● **T44.5x1 Poisoning by predominantly beta-adrenoreceptor agonists, accidental (unintentional)**
         Poisoning by predominantly beta-adrenoreceptor agonists NOS

      ● **T44.5x2 Poisoning by predominantly beta-adrenoreceptor agonists, intentional self-harm**

      ● **T44.5x3 Poisoning by predominantly beta-adrenoreceptor agonists, assault**

      ● **T44.5x4 Poisoning by predominantly beta-adrenoreceptor agonists, undetermined**

      ● **T44.5x5 Adverse effect of predominantly beta-adrenoreceptor agonists**

      ● **T44.5x6 Underdosing of predominantly beta-adrenoreceptor agonists**

● **T44.6 Poisoning by, adverse effect of and underdosing of alpha-adrenoreceptor antagonists**

   | **Excludes1** | poisoning by, adverse effect of and underdosing of ergot alkaloids (T48.0) |

   ● **T44.6x Poisoning by, adverse effect of and underdosing of alpha-adrenoreceptor antagonists**

      ● **T44.6x1 Poisoning by alpha-adrenoreceptor antagonists, accidental (unintentional)**
         Poisoning by alpha-adrenoreceptor antagonists NOS

      ● **T44.6x2 Poisoning by alpha-adrenoreceptor antagonists, intentional self-harm**

      ● **T44.6x3 Poisoning by alpha-adrenoreceptor antagonists, assault**

      ● **T44.6x4 Poisoning by alpha-adrenoreceptor antagonists, undetermined**

      ● **T44.6x5 Adverse effect of alpha-adrenoreceptor antagonists**

      ● **T44.6x6 Underdosing of alpha-adrenoreceptor antagonists**

● **T44.7 Poisoning by, adverse effect of and underdosing of beta-adrenoreceptor antagonists**

   ● **T44.7x Poisoning by, adverse effect of and underdosing of beta-adrenoreceptor antagonists**

      ● **T44.7x1 Poisoning by beta-adrenoreceptor antagonists, accidental (unintentional)**
         Poisoning by beta-adrenoreceptor antagonists NOS

      ● **T44.7x2 Poisoning by beta-adrenoreceptor antagonists, intentional self-harm**

      ● **T44.7x3 Poisoning by beta-adrenoreceptor antagonists, assault**

      ● **T44.7x4 Poisoning by beta-adrenoreceptor antagonists, undetermined**

      ● **T44.7x5 Adverse effect of beta-adrenoreceptor antagonists**

      ● **T44.7x6 Underdosing of beta-adrenoreceptor antagonists**

● **T44.8 Poisoning by, adverse effect of and underdosing of centrally-acting and adrenergic-neuron- blocking agents**

   | **Excludes1** | poisoning by, adverse effect of and underdosing of clonidine (T46.5) poisoning by, adverse effect of and underdosing of guanethidine (T46.5) |

   ● **T44.8x Poisoning by, adverse effect of and underdosing of centrally-acting and adrenergic-neuron-blocking agents**

      ● **T44.8x1 Poisoning by centrally-acting and adrenergic-neuron-blocking agents, accidental (unintentional)**
         Poisoning by centrally-acting and adrenergic-neuron-blocking agents NOS

      ● **T44.8x2 Poisoning by centrally-acting and adrenergic-neuron-blocking agents, intentional self-harm**

      ● **T44.8x3 Poisoning by centrally-acting and adrenergic-neuron-blocking agents, assault**

      ● **T44.8x4 Poisoning by centrally-acting and adrenergic-neuron-blocking agents, undetermined**

      ● **T44.8x5 Adverse effect of centrally-acting and adrenergic-neuron-blocking agents**

      ● **T44.8x6 Underdosing of centrally-acting and adrenergic-neuron-blocking agents**

● Unacceptable First-Listed Diagnosis   ● Use Additional Character(s)   ■ Unspecified   **OGCR** Official Guidelines for Coding and Reporting
🔖 Complication\Comorbidity   🔖 Major C\C   Excludes 1   Excludes 2   Includes   Use additional   Code first   Code also

● **T44.9 Poisoning by, adverse effect of and underdosing of other and unspecified drugs primarily affecting the autonomic nervous system**
> Poisoning by, adverse effect of and underdosing of drug stimulating both alpha and beta-adrenoreceptors

● **T44.90 Poisoning by, adverse effect of and underdosing of unspecified drugs primarily affecting the autonomic nervous system**

● ■ **T44.901 Poisoning by unspecified drugs primarily affecting the autonomic nervous system, accidental (unintentional)**
> Poisoning by unspecified drugs primarily affecting the autonomic nervous system NOS

● ■ **T44.902 Poisoning by unspecified drugs primarily affecting the autonomic nervous system, intentional self-harm**

● ■ **T44.903 Poisoning by unspecified drugs primarily affecting the autonomic nervous system, assault**

● ■ **T44.904 Poisoning by unspecified drugs primarily affecting the autonomic nervous system, undetermined**

● ■ **T44.905 Adverse effect of unspecified drugs primarily affecting the autonomic nervous system**

● ■ **T44.906 Underdosing of unspecified drugs primarily affecting the autonomic nervous system**

● **T44.99 Poisoning by, adverse effect of and underdosing of other drugs primarily affecting the autonomic nervous system**

● **T44.991 Poisoning by other drug primarily affecting the autonomic nervous system, accidental (unintentional)**
> Poisoning by other drugs primarily affecting the autonomic nervous system NOS

● **T44.992 Poisoning by other drug primarily affecting the autonomic nervous system, intentional self-harm**

● **T44.993 Poisoning by other drug primarily affecting the autonomic nervous system, assault**

● **T44.994 Poisoning by other drug primarily affecting the autonomic nervous system, undetermined**

● **T44.995 Adverse effect of other drug primarily affecting the autonomic nervous system**

● **T44.996 Underdosing of other drug primarily affecting the autonomic nervous system**

● **T45 Poisoning by, adverse effect of and underdosing of primarily systemic and hematological agents, not elsewhere classified**
> The appropriate 7th character is to be added to each code from category T45

> | | |
> |---|---|
> | A | initial encounter |
> | D | subsequent encounter |
> | S | sequela |

● **T45.0 Poisoning by, adverse effect of and underdosing of antiallergic and antiemetic drugs**
> **Excludes1**   poisoning by, adverse effect of and underdosing of phenothiazine-based neuroleptics (T43.3)

● **T45.0x Poisoning by, adverse effect of and underdosing of antiallergic and antiemetic drugs**

● **T45.0x1 Poisoning by antiallergic and antiemetic drugs, accidental (unintentional)**
> Poisoning by antiallergic and antiemetic drugs NOS

● **T45.0x2 Poisoning by antiallergic and antiemetic drugs, intentional self-harm**

● **T45.0x3 Poisoning by antiallergic and antiemetic drugs, assault**

● **T45.0x4 Poisoning by antiallergic and antiemetic drugs, undetermined**

● **T45.0x5 Adverse effect of antiallergic and antiemetic drugs**

● **T45.0x6 Underdosing of antiallergic and antiemetic drugs**

● **T45.1 Poisoning by, adverse effect of and underdosing of antineoplastic and immunosuppressive drugs**
> **Excludes1**   poisoning by, adverse effect of and underdosing of tamoxifen (T38.6)

● **T45.1x Poisoning by, adverse effect of and underdosing of antineoplastic and immunosuppressive drugs**

● **T45.1x1 Poisoning by antineoplastic and immunosuppressive drugs, accidental (unintentional)**
> Poisoning by antineoplastic and immunosuppressive drugs NOS

● **T45.1x2 Poisoning by antineoplastic and immunosuppressive drugs, intentional self-harm**

● **T45.1x3 Poisoning by antineoplastic and immunosuppressive drugs, assault**

● **T45.1x4 Poisoning by antineoplastic and immunosuppressive drugs, undetermined**

● **T45.1x5 Adverse effect of antineoplastic and immunosuppressive drugs**

● **T45.1x6 Underdosing of antineoplastic and immunosuppressive drugs**

● Unacceptable First-Listed Diagnosis	● Use Additional Character(s)	■ Unspecified	**OGCR** Official Guidelines for Coding and Reporting	
🏷 Complication\Comorbidity	🏷 Major C\C Excludes 1 Excludes 2	Includes Use additional Code first Code also		1573

CHAPTER 19 (S00-T98)

- T45.2 **Poisoning by, adverse effect of and underdosing of vitamins**
  - Excludes2   poisoning by, adverse effect of and underdosing of nicotinic acid (derivatives) (T46.7)
    poisoning by, adverse effect of and underdosing of iron (T45.4)
    poisoning by, adverse effect of and underdosing of vitamin K (T45.7)
  - T45.2x **Poisoning by, adverse effect of and underdosing of vitamins**
    - T45.2x1 **Poisoning by vitamins, accidental (unintentional)**
      Poisoning by vitamins NOS
    - T45.2x2 **Poisoning by vitamins, intentional self-harm**
    - T45.2x3 **Poisoning by vitamins, assault**
    - T45.2x4 **Poisoning by vitamins, undetermined**
    - T45.2x5 **Adverse effect of vitamins**
    - T45.2x6 **Underdosing of vitamins**
      - Excludes1   vitamin deficiencies (E50-E56)
- T45.3 **Poisoning by, adverse effect of and underdosing of enzymes**
  - T45.3x **Poisoning by, adverse effect of and underdosing of enzymes**
    - T45.3x1 **Poisoning by enzymes, accidental (unintentional)**
      Poisoning by enzymes NOS
    - T45.3x2 **Poisoning by enzymes, intentional self-harm**
    - T45.3x3 **Poisoning by enzymes, assault**
    - T45.3x4 **Poisoning by enzymes, undetermined**
    - T45.3x5 **Adverse effect of enzymes**
    - T45.3x6 **Underdosing of enzymes**
- T45.4 **Poisoning by, adverse effect of and underdosing of iron and its compounds**
  - T45.4x **Poisoning by, adverse effect of and underdosing of iron and its compounds**
    - T45.4x1 **Poisoning by iron and its compounds, accidental (unintentional)**
      Poisoning by iron and its compounds NOS
    - T45.4x2 **Poisoning by iron and its compounds, intentional self-harm**
    - T45.4x3 **Poisoning by iron and its compounds, assault**
    - T45.4x4 **Poisoning by iron and its compounds, undetermined**
    - T45.4x5 **Adverse effect of iron and its compounds**
    - T45.4x6 **Underdosing of iron and its compounds**
      - Excludes1   iron deficiency (E61.1)
- T45.5 **Poisoning by, adverse effect of and underdosing of anticoagulants and antithrombotic drugs**
  - T45.51 **Poisoning by, adverse effect of and underdosing of anticoagulants**
    - T45.511 **Poisoning by anticoagulants, accidental (unintentional)**
      Poisoning by anticoagulants NOS

- T45.512 **Poisoning by anticoagulants, intentional self-harm**
- T45.513 **Poisoning by anticoagulants, assault**
- T45.514 **Poisoning by anticoagulants, undetermined**
- T45.515 **Adverse effect of anticoagulants**
- T45.516 **Underdosing of anticoagulants**
- T45.52 **Poisoning by, adverse effect of and underdosing of antithrombotic drugs**
  Poisoning by, adverse effect of and underdosing of antiplatelet drugs
  - Excludes2   poisoning by, adverse effect of and underdosing of aspirin (T39.01-)
    poisoning by, adverse effect of and underdosing of acetylsalicylic acid (T39.01-)
  - T45.521 **Poisoning by antithrombotic drugs, accidental (unintentional)**
    Poisoning by antithrombotic drug NOS
  - T45.522 **Poisoning by antithrombotic drugs, intentional self-harm**
  - T45.523 **Poisoning by antithrombotic drugs, assault**
  - T45.524 **Poisoning by antithrombotic drugs, undetermined**
  - T45.525 **Adverse effect of antithrombotic drugs**
  - T45.526 **Underdosing of antithrombotic drugs**
- T45.6 **Poisoning by, adverse effect of and underdosing of fibrinolysis-affecting drugs**
  - T45.60 **Poisoning by, adverse effect of and underdosing of unspecified fibrinolysis-affecting drugs**
    - T45.601 **Poisoning by unspecified fibrinolysis-affecting drugs, accidental (unintentional)**
      Poisoning by fibrinolysis-affecting drug NOS
    - T45.602 **Poisoning by unspecified fibrinolysis-affecting drugs, intentional self-harm**
    - T45.603 **Poisoning by unspecified fibrinolysis-affecting drugs, assault**
    - T45.604 **Poisoning by unspecified fibrinolysis-affecting drugs, undetermined**
    - T45.605 **Adverse effect of unspecified fibrinolysis-affecting drugs**
    - T45.606 **Underdosing of unspecified fibrinolysis-affecting drugs**
  - T45.61 **Poisoning by, adverse effect of and underdosing of thrombolytic drugs**
    - T45.611 **Poisoning by thrombolytic drug, accidental (unintentional)**
      Poisoning by thrombolytic drug NOS
    - T45.612 **Poisoning by thrombolytic drug, intentional self-harm**
    - T45.613 **Poisoning by thrombolytic drug, assault**

● Unacceptable First-Listed Diagnosis   ● Use Additional Character(s)   ■ Unspecified   **OGCR** Official Guidelines for Coding and Reporting
🝇 Complication\Comorbidity   🝆 Major C\C   Excludes 1   Excludes 2   Includes   Use additional   Code first   Code also

● T45.614　Poisoning by thrombolytic drug, undetermined

● T45.615　Adverse effect of thrombolytic drugs

● T45.616　Underdosing of thrombolytic drugs

● T45.62　Poisoning by, adverse effect of and underdosing of hemostatic drugs

● T45.621　Poisoning by hemostatic drug, accidental (unintentional)
Poisoning by hemostatic drug NOS

● T45.622　Poisoning by hemostatic drug, intentional self-harm

● T45.623　Poisoning by hemostatic drug, assault

● T45.624　Poisoning by hemostatic drug, undetermined

● T45.625　Adverse effect of hemostatic drug

● T45.626　Underdosing of hemostatic drugs

● T45.69　Poisoning by, adverse effect of and underdosing of other fibrinolysis-affecting drugs

● T45.691　Poisoning by other fibrinolysis-affecting drugs, accidental (unintentional)
Poisoning by other fibrinolysis-affecting drug NOS

● T45.692　Poisoning by other fibrinolysis-affecting drugs, intentional self-harm

● T45.693　Poisoning by other fibrinolysis-affecting drugs, assault

● T45.694　Poisoning by other fibrinolysis-affecting drugs, undetermined

● T45.695　Adverse effect of other fibrinolysis-affecting drugs

● T45.696　Underdosing of other fibrinolysis-affecting drugs

● T45.7　Poisoning by, adverse effect of and underdosing of anticoagulant antagonists, vitamin K and other coagulants

● T45.7x　Poisoning by, adverse effect of and underdosing of anticoagulant antagonists, vitamin K and other coagulants

● T45.7x1　Poisoning by anticoagulant antagonists, vitamin K and other coagulants, accidental (unintentional)
Poisoning by anticoagulant antagonists, vitamin K and other coagulants NOS

● T45.7x2　Poisoning by anticoagulant antagonists, vitamin K and other coagulants, intentional self-harm

● T45.7x3　Poisoning by anticoagulant antagonists, vitamin K and other coagulants, assault

● T45.7x4　Poisoning by anticoagulant antagonists, vitamin K and other coagulants, undetermined

● T45.7x5　Adverse effect of anticoagulant antagonists, vitamin K and other coagulants

● T45.7x6　Underdosing of anticoagulant antagonist, vitamin K and other coagulants
Excludes1　vitamin K deficiency (E56.1)

● T45.8　Poisoning by, adverse effect of and underdosing of other primarily systemic and hematological agents
Poisoning by, adverse effect of and underdosing of liver preparations and other antianemic agents
Poisoning by, adverse effect of and underdosing of natural blood and blood products
Poisoning by, adverse effect of and underdosing of plasma substitute
Excludes2　poisoning by, adverse effect of and underdosing of immunoglobulin (T50.z1)
poisoning by, adverse effect of and underdosing of iron (T45.4)

● T45.8x　Poisoning by, adverse effect of and underdosing of other primarily systemic and hematological agents

● T45.8x1　Poisoning by other primarily systemic and hematological agents, accidental (unintentional)
Poisoning by other primarily systemic and hematological agents NOS

● T45.8x2　Poisoning by other primarily systemic and hematological agents, intentional self-harm

● T45.8x3　Poisoning by other primarily systemic and hematological agents, assault

● T45.8x4　Poisoning by other primarily systemic and hematological agents, undetermined

● T45.8x5　Adverse effect of other primarily systemic and hematological agents

● T45.8x6　Underdosing of other primarily systemic and hematological agents

● T45.9　Poisoning by, adverse effect of and underdosing of unspecified primarily systemic and hematological agent

● ■ T45.91　Poisoning by unspecified primarily systemic and hematological agent, accidental (unintentional)
Poisoning by primarily systemic and hematological agent NOS

● ■ T45.92　Poisoning by unspecified primarily systemic and hematological agent, intentional self-harm

● ■ T45.93　Poisoning by unspecified primarily systemic and hematological agent, assault

● ■ T45.94　Poisoning by unspecified primarily systemic and hematological agent, undetermined

● ■ T45.95　Adverse effect of unspecified primarily systemic and hematological agent

● ■ T45.96　Underdosing of unspecified primarily systemic and hematological agent

● Unacceptable First-Listed Diagnosis　　　● Use Additional Character(s)　　　■ Unspecified　　　OGCR Official Guidelines for Coding and Reporting
🗝 Complication\Comorbidity　　🗝 Major C\C　　Excludes 1　　Excludes 2　　Includes　　Use additional　　Code first　　Code also

CHAPTER 19 (S00-T98)

1575

● **T46   Poisoning by, adverse effect of and underdosing of agents primarily affecting the cardiovascular system**

> Excludes1   poisoning by, adverse effect of and underdosing of metaraminol (T44.4)

> The appropriate 7th character is to be added to each code from category T46

> A   initial encounter
> D   subsequent encounter
> S   sequela

● **T46.0   Poisoning by, adverse effect of and underdosing of cardiac-stimulant glycosides and drugs of similar action**

  ● **T46.0x   Poisoning by, adverse effect of and underdosing of cardiac-stimulant glycosides and drugs of similar action**

    ● **T46.0x1   Poisoning by cardiac-stimulant glycosides and drugs of similar action, accidental (unintentional)**
       Poisoning by cardiac-stimulant glycosides and drugs of similar action NOS

    ● **T46.0x2   Poisoning by cardiac-stimulant glycosides and drugs of similar action, intentional self-harm**

    ● **T46.0x3   Poisoning by cardiac-stimulant glycosides and drugs of similar action, assault**

    ● **T46.0x4   Poisoning by cardiac-stimulant glycosides and drugs of similar action, undetermined**

    ● **T46.0x5   Adverse effect of cardiac-stimulant glycosides and drugs of similar action**

    ● **T46.0x6   Underdosing of cardiac-stimulant glycosides and drugs of similar action**

● **T46.1   Poisoning by, adverse effect of and underdosing of calcium-channel blockers**

  ● **T46.1x   Poisoning by, adverse effect of and underdosing of calcium-channel blockers**

    ● **T46.1x1   Poisoning by calcium-channel blockers, accidental (unintentional)**
       Poisoning by calcium-channel blockers NOS

    ● **T46.1x2   Poisoning by calcium-channel blockers, intentional self-harm**

    ● **T46.1x3   Poisoning by calcium-channel blockers, assault**

    ● **T46.1x4   Poisoning by calcium-channel blockers, undetermined**

    ● **T46.1x5   Adverse effect of calcium-channel blockers**

    ● **T46.1x6   Underdosing of calcium-channel blockers**

● **T46.2   Poisoning by, adverse effect of and underdosing of other antidysrhythmic drugs, not elsewhere classified**

> Excludes1   poisoning by, adverse effect of and underdosing of beta-adrenoreceptor antagonists (T44.7-)

● **T46.2x   Poisoning by, adverse effect of and underdosing of other antidysrhythmic drugs**

  ● **T46.2x1   Poisoning by other antidysrhythmic drugs, accidental (unintentional)**
     Poisoning by other antidysrhythmic drugs NOS

  ● **T46.2x2   Poisoning by other antidysrhythmic drugs, intentional self-harm**

  ● **T46.2x3   Poisoning by other antidysrhythmic drugs, assault**

  ● **T46.2x4   Poisoning by other antidysrhythmic drugs, undetermined**

  ● **T46.2x5   Adverse effect of other antidysrhythmic drugs**

  ● **T46.2x6   Underdosing of other antidysrhythmic drugs**

● **T46.3   Poisoning by, adverse effect of and underdosing of coronary vasodilators**

> Poisoning by, adverse effect of and underdosing of dipyridamole

> Excludes1   poisoning by, adverse effect of and underdosing of calcium-channel blockers (T46.1)

  ● **T46.3x   Poisoning by, adverse effect of and underdosing of coronary vasodilators**

    ● **T46.3x1   Poisoning by coronary vasodilators, accidental (unintentional)**
       Poisoning by coronary vasodilators NOS

    ● **T46.3x2   Poisoning by coronary vasodilators, intentional self-harm**

    ● **T46.3x3   Poisoning by coronary vasodilators, assault**

    ● **T46.3x4   Poisoning by coronary vasodilators, undetermined**

    ● **T46.3x5   Adverse effect of coronary vasodilators**

    ● **T46.3x6   Underdosing of coronary vasodilators**

● **T46.4   Poisoning by, adverse effect of and underdosing of angiotensin-converting-enzyme inhibitors**

  ● **T46.4x   Poisoning by, adverse effect of and underdosing of angiotensin-converting-enzyme inhibitors**

    ● **T46.4x1   Poisoning by angiotensin-converting-enzyme inhibitors, accidental (unintentional)**
       Poisoning by angiotensin-converting-enzyme inhibitors NOS

    ● **T46.4x2   Poisoning by angiotensin-converting-enzyme inhibitors, intentional self-harm**

    ● **T46.4x3   Poisoning by angiotensin-converting-enzyme inhibitors, assault**

    ● **T46.4x4   Poisoning by angiotensin-converting-enzyme inhibitors, undetermined**

● **T46.4x5**   **Adverse effect of angiotensin-converting-enzyme inhibitors**

● **T46.4x6**   **Underdosing of angiotensin-converting-enzyme inhibitors**

● **T46.5**   **Poisoning by, adverse effect of and underdosing of other antihypertensive drugs**

> Excludes2   poisoning by, adverse effect of and underdosing of beta-adrenoreceptor antagonists (T44.7)
>
> poisoning by, adverse effect of and underdosing of calcium-channel blockers (T46.1)
>
> poisoning by, adverse effect of and underdosing of diuretics (T50.0-T50.2)

● **T46.5x**   **Poisoning by, adverse effect of and underdosing of other antihypertensive drugs**

● **T46.5x1**   **Poisoning by other antihypertensive drugs, accidental (unintentional)**
> Poisoning by other antihypertensive drugs NOS

● **T46.5x2**   **Poisoning by other antihypertensive drugs, intentional self-harm**

● **T46.5x3**   **Poisoning by other antihypertensive drugs, assault**

● **T46.5x4**   **Poisoning by other antihypertensive drugs, undetermined**

● **T46.5x5**   **Adverse effect of other antihypertensive drugs**

● **T46.5x6**   **Underdosing of other antihypertensive drugs**

● **T46.6**   **Poisoning by, adverse effect of and underdosing of antihyperlipidemic and antiarteriosclerotic drugs**

● **T46.6x**   **Poisoning by, adverse effect of and underdosing of antihyperlipidemic and antiarteriosclerotic drugs**

● **T46.6x1**   **Poisoning by antihyperlipidemic and antiarteriosclerotic drugs, accidental (unintentional)**
> Poisoning by antihyperlipidemic and antiarteriosclerotic drugs NOS

● **T46.6x2**   **Poisoning by antihyperlipidemic and antiarteriosclerotic drugs, intentional self-harm**

● **T46.6x3**   **Poisoning by antihyperlipidemic and antiarteriosclerotic drugs, assault**

● **T46.6x4**   **Poisoning by antihyperlipidemic and antiarteriosclerotic drugs, undetermined**

● **T46.6x5**   **Adverse effect of antihyperlipidemic and antiarteriosclerotic drugs**

● **T46.6x6**   **Underdosing of antihyperlipidemic and antiarteriosclerotic drugs**

● **T46.7**   **Poisoning by, adverse effect of and underdosing of peripheral vasodilators**

> Poisoning by, adverse effect of and underdosing of nicotinic acid (derivatives)

> Excludes1   poisoning by, adverse effect of and underdosing of papaverine (T44.3)

● **T46.7x**   **Poisoning by, adverse effect of and underdosing of peripheral vasodilators**

● **T46.7x1**   **Poisoning by peripheral vasodilators, accidental (unintentional)**
> Poisoning by peripheral vasodilators NOS

● **T46.7x2**   **Poisoning by peripheral vasodilators, intentional self-harm**

● **T46.7x3**   **Poisoning by peripheral vasodilators, assault**

● **T46.7x4**   **Poisoning by peripheral vasodilators, undetermined**

● **T46.7x5**   **Adverse effect of peripheral vasodilators**

● **T46.7x6**   **Underdosing of peripheral vasodilators**

● **T46.8**   **Poisoning by, adverse effect of and underdosing of antivaricose drugs, including sclerosing agents**

● **T46.8x**   **Poisoning by, adverse effect of and underdosing of antivaricose drugs, including sclerosing agents**

● **T46.8x1**   **Poisoning by antivaricose drugs, including sclerosing agents, accidental (unintentional)**
> Poisoning by antivaricose drugs, including sclerosing agents NOS

● **T46.8x2**   **Poisoning by antivaricose drugs, including sclerosing agents, intentional self-harm**

● **T46.8x3**   **Poisoning by antivaricose drugs, including sclerosing agents, assault**

● **T46.8x4**   **Poisoning by antivaricose drugs, including sclerosing agents, undetermined**

● **T46.8x5**   **Adverse effect of antivaricose drugs, including sclerosing agents**

● **T46.8x6**   **Underdosing of antivaricose drugs, including sclerosing agents**

● **T46.9**   **Poisoning by, adverse effect of and underdosing of other and unspecified agents primarily affecting the cardiovascular system**

● **T46.90**   **Poisoning by, adverse effect of and underdosing of unspecified agents primarily affecting the cardiovascular system**

● ■ **T46.901**   **Poisoning by unspecified agents primarily affecting the cardiovascular system, accidental (unintentional)**

● ■ **T46.902**   **Poisoning by unspecified agents primarily affecting the cardiovascular system, intentional self-harm**

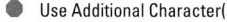

● Unacceptable First-Listed Diagnosis   ● Use Additional Character(s)   ▨ Unspecified   **OGCR** Official Guidelines for Coding and Reporting

🅒 Complication\Comorbidity   🅒 Major C\C   Excludes 1   Excludes 2   Includes   Use additional   Code first   Code also

1577

CHAPTER 19 (S00-T98)

● ■ **T46.903** Poisoning by unspecified agents primarily affecting the cardiovascular system, assault

● ■ **T46.904** Poisoning by unspecified agents primarily affecting the cardiovascular system, undetermined

● ■ **T46.905** Adverse effect of unspecified agents primarily affecting the cardiovascular system

● ■ **T46.906** Underdosing of unspecified agents primarily affecting the cardiovascular system

● **T46.99** Poisoning by, adverse effect of and underdosing of other agents primarily affecting the cardiovascular system

● **T46.991** Poisoning by other agents primarily affecting the cardiovascular system, accidental (unintentional)

● **T46.992** Poisoning by other agents primarily affecting the cardiovascular system, intentional self-harm

● **T46.993** Poisoning by other agents primarily affecting the cardiovascular system, assault

● **T46.994** Poisoning by other agents primarily affecting the cardiovascular system, undetermined

● **T46.995** Adverse effect of other agents primarily affecting the cardiovascular system

● **T46.996** Underdosing of other agents primarily affecting the cardiovascular system

● **T47** **Poisoning by, adverse effect of and underdosing of agents primarily affecting the gastrointestinal system**

The appropriate 7th character is to be added to each code from category T47

A	initial encounter
D	subsequent encounter
S	sequela

● **T47.0** Poisoning by, adverse effect of and underdosing of histamine H2-receptor blockers

● **T47.0X** Poisoning by, adverse effect of and underdosing of histamine H2-receptor blockers

● **T47.0x1** Poisoning by histamine H2-receptor blockers, accidental (unintentional)

Poisoning by histamine H2-receptor blockers NOS

● **T47.0x2** Poisoning by histamine H2-receptor blockers, intentional self-harm

● **T47.0x3** Poisoning by histamine H2-receptor blockers, assault

● **T47.0x4** Poisoning by histamine H2-receptor blockers, undetermined

● **T47.0x5** Adverse effect of histamine H2-receptor blockers

● **T47.0x6** Underdosing of histamine H2-receptor blockers

● **T47.1** Poisoning by, adverse effect of and underdosing of other antacids and anti-gastric-secretion drugs

● **T47.1x** Poisoning by, adverse effect of and underdosing of other antacids and anti-gastric-secretion drugs

● **T47.1x1** Poisoning by other antacids and anti-gastric-secretion drugs, accidental (unintentional)

Poisoning by other antacids and anti-gastric-secretion drugs NOS

● **T47.1x2** Poisoning by other antacids and anti-gastric-secretion drugs, intentional self-harm

● **T47.1x3** Poisoning by other antacids and anti-gastric-secretion drugs, assault

● **T47.1x4** Poisoning by other antacids and anti-gastric-secretion drugs, undetermined

● **T47.1x5** Adverse effect of other antacids and anti-gastric-secretion drugs

● **T47.1x6** Underdosing of other antacids and anti-gastric-secretion drugs

● **T47.2** Poisoning by, adverse effect of and underdosing of stimulant laxatives

● **T47.2x** Poisoning by, adverse effect of and underdosing of stimulant laxatives

● **T47.2x1** Poisoning by stimulant laxatives, accidental (unintentional)

Poisoning by stimulant laxatives NOS

● **T47.2x2** Poisoning by stimulant laxatives, intentional self-harm

● **T47.2x3** Poisoning by stimulant laxatives, assault

● **T47.2x4** Poisoning by stimulant laxatives, undetermined

● **T47.2x5** Adverse effect of stimulant laxatives

● **T47.2x6** Underdosing of stimulant laxatives

● **T47.3** Poisoning by, adverse effect of and underdosing of saline and osmotic laxatives

● **T47.3x** Poisoning by and adverse effect of saline and osmotic laxatives

● **T47.3x1** Poisoning by saline and osmotic laxatives, accidental (unintentional)

Poisoning by saline and osmotic laxatives NOS

● **T47.3x2** Poisoning by saline and osmotic laxatives, intentional self-harm

● **T47.3x3** Poisoning by saline and osmotic laxatives, assault

● **T47.3x4** Poisoning by saline and osmotic laxatives, undetermined

● **T47.3x5** Adverse effect of saline and osmotic laxatives

● **T47.3x6** Underdosing of saline and osmotic laxatives

● **T47.4** Poisoning by, adverse effect of and underdosing of other laxatives

● **T47.4x** Poisoning by, adverse effect of and underdosing of other laxatives

● Unacceptable First-Listed Diagnosis   ● Use Additional Character(s)   ■ Unspecified   **OGCR** Official Guidelines for Coding and Reporting

🩺 Complication\Comorbidity   🩺 Major C\C   Excludes 1   Excludes 2   Includes   Use additional   Code first   Code also

- T47.4x1   Poisoning by other laxatives, accidental (unintentional)
  - Poisoning by other laxatives NOS
- T47.4x2   Poisoning by other laxatives, intentional self-harm
- T47.4x3   Poisoning by other laxatives, assault
- T47.4x4   Poisoning by other laxatives, undetermined
- T47.4x5   Adverse effect of other laxatives
- T47.4x6   Underdosing of other laxatives
- T47.5   Poisoning by, adverse effect of and underdosing of digestants
  - T47.5x   Poisoning by, adverse effect of and underdosing of digestants
    - T47.5x1   Poisoning by digestants, accidental (unintentional)
      - Poisoning by digestants NOS
    - T47.5x2   Poisoning by digestants, intentional self-harm
    - T47.5x3   Poisoning by digestants, assault
    - T47.5x4   Poisoning by digestants, undetermined
    - T47.5x5   Adverse effect of digestants
    - T47.5x6   Underdosing of digestants
- T47.6   Poisoning by, adverse effect of and underdosing of antidiarrheal drugs

  > **Excludes2**   poisoning by, adverse effect of and underdosing of systemic antibiotics and other anti-infectives (T36-T37)

  - T47.6x   Poisoning by, adverse effect of and underdosing of antidiarrheal drugs
    - T47.6x1   Poisoning by antidiarrheal drugs, accidental (unintentional)
      - Poisoning by antidiarrheal drugs NOS
    - T47.6x2   Poisoning by antidiarrheal drugs, intentional self-harm
    - T47.6x3   Poisoning by antidiarrheal drugs, assault
    - T47.6x4   Poisoning by antidiarrheal drugs, undetermined
    - T47.6x5   Adverse effect of antidiarrheal drugs
    - T47.6x6   Underdosing of antidiarrheal drugs
- T47.7   Poisoning by, adverse effect of and underdosing of emetics
  - T47.7x   Poisoning by, adverse effect of and underdosing of emetics
    - T47.7x1   Poisoning by emetics, accidental (unintentional)
      - Poisoning by emetics NOS
    - T47.7x2   Poisoning by emetics, intentional self-harm
    - T47.7x3   Poisoning by emetics, assault
    - T47.7x4   Poisoning by emetics, undetermined
    - T47.7x5   Adverse effect of emetics
    - T47.7x6   Underdosing of emetics

- T47.8   Poisoning by, adverse effect of and underdosing of other agents primarily affecting gastrointestinal system
  - T47.8x   Poisoning by, adverse effect of and underdosing of other agents primarily affecting gastrointestinal system
    - T47.8x1   Poisoning by other agents primarily affecting gastrointestinal system, accidental (unintentional)
      - Poisoning by other agents primarily affecting gastrointestinal system NOS
    - T47.8x2   Poisoning by other agents primarily affecting gastrointestinal system, intentional self-harm
    - T47.8x3   Poisoning by other agents primarily affecting gastrointestinal system, assault
    - T47.8x4   Poisoning by other agents primarily affecting gastrointestinal system, undetermined
    - T47.8x5   Adverse effect of other agents primarily affecting gastrointestinal system
    - T47.8x6   Underdosing of other agents primarily affecting gastrointestinal system
- T47.9   Poisoning by, adverse effect of and underdosing of unspecified agents primarily affecting the gastrointestinal system
  - T47.91   Poisoning by unspecified agents primarily affecting the gastrointestinal system, accidental (unintentional)
    - Poisoning by agents primarily affecting the gastrointestinal system NOS
  - T47.92   Poisoning by unspecified agents primarily affecting the gastrointestinal system, intentional self-harm
  - T47.93   Poisoning by unspecified agents primarily affecting the gastrointestinal system, assault
  - T47.94   Poisoning by unspecified agents primarily affecting the gastrointestinal system, undetermined
  - T47.95   Adverse effect of unspecified agents primarily affecting the gastrointestinal system
  - T47.96   Underdosing of unspecified agents primarily affecting the gastrointestinal system
- T48   Poisoning by, adverse effect of and underdosing of agents primarily acting on smooth and skeletal muscles and the respiratory system

  The appropriate 7th character is to be added to each code from category T48

A	initial encounter
D	subsequent encounter
S	sequela

  - T48.0   Poisoning by, adverse effect of and underdosing of oxytocic drugs

    > **Excludes1**   poisoning by, adverse effect of and underdosing of estrogens, progestogens and antagonists (T38.4-T38.6)

- Unacceptable First-Listed Diagnosis   ● Use Additional Character(s)   ■ Unspecified   **OGCR** Official Guidelines for Coding and Reporting

🔖 Complication\Comorbidity   🔖 Major C\C   Excludes 1   Excludes 2   Includes   Use additional   Code first   Code also

1579

● T48.0x Poisoning by, adverse effect of and underdosing of oxytocic drugs

   ● T48.0x1 Poisoning by oxytocic drugs, accidental (unintentional)
      Poisoning by oxytocic drugs NOS

   ● T48.0x2 Poisoning by oxytocic drugs, intentional self-harm

   ● T48.0x3 Poisoning by oxytocic drugs, assault

   ● T48.0x4 Poisoning by oxytocic drugs, undetermined

   ● T48.0x5 Adverse effect of oxytocic drugs

   ● T48.0x6 Underdosing of oxytocic drugs

● T48.1 Poisoning by, adverse effect of and underdosing of skeletal muscle relaxants [neuromuscular blocking agents]

  ● T48.1x Poisoning by, adverse effect of and underdosing of skeletal muscle relaxants [neuromuscular blocking agents]

   ● T48.1x1 Poisoning by skeletal muscle relaxants [neuromuscular blocking agents], accidental (unintentional)
      Poisoning by skeletal muscle relaxants [neuromuscular blocking agents] NOS

   ● T48.1x2 Poisoning by skeletal muscle relaxants [neuromuscular blocking agents], intentional self-harm

   ● T48.1x3 Poisoning by skeletal muscle relaxants [neuromuscular blocking agents], assault

   ● T48.1x4 Poisoning by skeletal muscle relaxants [neuromuscular blocking agents], undetermined

   ● T48.1x5 Adverse effect of skeletal muscle relaxants [neuromuscular blocking agents]

   ● T48.1x6 Underdosing of skeletal muscle relaxants [neuromuscular blocking agents]

● T48.2 Poisoning by, adverse effect of and underdosing of other and unspecified drugs acting on muscles

  ● T48.20 Poisoning by, adverse effect of and underdosing of unspecified drugs acting on muscles

   ● ■ T48.201 Poisoning by unspecified drugs acting on muscles, accidental (unintentional)
      Poisoning by unspecified drugs acting on muscles NOS

   ● ■ T48.202 Poisoning by unspecified drugs acting on muscles, intentional self-harm

   ● ■ T48.203 Poisoning by unspecified drugs acting on muscles, assault

   ● ■ T48.204 Poisoning by unspecified drugs acting on muscles, undetermined

   ● ■ T48.205 Adverse effect of unspecified drugs acting on muscles

   ● ■ T48.206 Underdosing of unspecified drugs acting on muscles

  ● T48.29 Poisoning by, adverse effect of and underdosing of other drugs acting on muscles

   ● T48.291 Poisoning by other drugs acting on muscles, accidental (unintentional)
      Poisoning by other drugs acting on muscles NOS

   ● T48.292 Poisoning by other drugs acting on muscles, intentional self-harm

   ● T48.293 Poisoning by other drugs acting on muscles, assault

   ● T48.294 Poisoning by other drugs acting on muscles, undetermined

   ● T48.295 Adverse effect of other drugs acting on muscles

   ● T48.296 Underdosing of other drugs acting on muscles

● T48.3 Poisoning by, adverse effect of and underdosing of antitussives

  ● T48.3x Poisoning by, adverse effect of and underdosing of antitussives

   ● T48.3x1 Poisoning by antitussives, accidental (unintentional)
      Poisoning by antitussives NOS

   ● T48.3x2 Poisoning by antitussives, intentional self-harm

   ● T48.3x3 Poisoning by antitussives, assault

   ● T48.3x4 Poisoning by antitussives, undetermined

   ● T48.3x5 Adverse effect of antitussives

   ● T48.3x6 Underdosing of antitussives

● T48.4 Poisoning by, adverse effect of and underdosing of expectorants

  ● T48.4x Poisoning by, adverse effect of and underdosing of expectorants

   ● T48.4x1 Poisoning by expectorants, accidental (unintentional)
      Poisoning by expectorants NOS

   ● T48.4x2 Poisoning by expectorants, intentional self-harm

   ● T48.4x3 Poisoning by expectorants, assault

   ● T48.4x4 Poisoning by expectorants, undetermined

   ● T48.4x5 Adverse effect of expectorants

   ● T48.4x6 Underdosing of expectorants

● T48.5 Poisoning by, adverse effect of and underdosing of other anti-common-cold drugs
  Poisoning by, adverse effect of and underdosing of decongestants

  Excludes2 poisoning by, adverse effect of and underdosing of antipyretics, NEC (T39.9-)
    poisoning by, adverse effect of and underdosing of non-steroidal antiinflammatory drugs (T39.3-)
    poisoning by, adverse effect of and underdosing of salicylates (T39.0-)

  ● T48.5x Poisoning by, adverse effect of and underdosing of other anti-common-cold drugs

   ● T48.5x1 Poisoning by other anti-common-cold drugs, accidental (unintentional)
      Poisoning by other anti-common-cold drugs NOS

   ● T48.5x2 Poisoning by other anti-common-cold drugs, intentional self-harm

● Unacceptable First-Listed Diagnosis   ● Use Additional Character(s)   ■ Unspecified   OGCR Official Guidelines for Coding and Reporting
🝆 Complication\Comorbidity   🝆 Major C\C   Excludes 1   Excludes 2   Includes   Use additional   Code first   Code also

- T48.5x3   Poisoning by other anti-common-cold drugs, assault
- T48.5x4   Poisoning by other anti-common-cold drugs, undetermined
- T48.5x5   Adverse effect of other anti-common-cold drugs
- T48.5x6   Underdosing of other anti-common-cold drugs

- T48.6   **Poisoning by, adverse effect of and underdosing of antiasthmatics, not elsewhere classified**

    Poisoning by, adverse effect of and underdosing of beta-adrenoreceptor agonists used in asthma therapy

    > **Excludes1**   poisoning by, adverse effect of and underdosing of beta-adrenoreceptor agonists not used in asthma therapy (T44.5)
    > poisoning by, adverse effect of and underdosing of anterior pituitary [adenohypophyseal] hormones (T38.8)

    - T48.6x   **Poisoning by, adverse effect of and underdosing of antiasthmatics**

        - T48.6x1   Poisoning by antiasthmatics, accidental (unintentional)

            Poisoning by antiasthmatics NOS

        - T48.6x2   Poisoning by antiasthmatics, intentional self-harm
        - T48.6x3   Poisoning by antiasthmatics, assault
        - T48.6x4   Poisoning by antiasthmatics, undetermined
        - T48.6x5   Adverse effect of antiasthmatics
        - T48.6x6   Underdosing of antiasthmatics

- T48.9   **Poisoning by, adverse effect of and underdosing of other and unspecified agents primarily acting on the respiratory system**

    - T48.90   **Poisoning by, adverse effect of and underdosing of unspecified agents primarily acting on the respiratory system**

        - T48.901   Poisoning by unspecified agents primarily acting on the respiratory system, accidental (unintentional)
        - T48.902   Poisoning by unspecified agents primarily acting on the respiratory system, intentional self-harm
        - T48.903   Poisoning by unspecified agents primarily acting on the respiratory system, assault
        - T48.904   Poisoning by unspecified agents primarily acting on the respiratory system, undetermined
        - T48.905   Adverse effect of unspecified agents primarily acting on the respiratory system
        - T48.906   Underdosing of unspecified agents primarily acting on the respiratory system

    - T48.99   **Poisoning by, adverse effect of and underdosing of other agents primarily acting on the respiratory system**

        - T48.991   Poisoning by other agents primarily acting on the respiratory system, accidental (unintentional)
        - T48.992   Poisoning by other agents primarily acting on the respiratory system, intentional self-harm
        - T48.993   Poisoning by other agents primarily acting on the respiratory system, assault
        - T48.994   Poisoning by other agents primarily acting on the respiratory system, undetermined
        - T48.995   Adverse effect of other agents primarily acting on the respiratory system
        - T48.996   Underdosing of other agents primarily acting on the respiratory system

- T49   **Poisoning by, adverse effect of and underdosing of topical agents primarily affecting skin and mucous membrane and by ophthalmological, otorhinorlaryngological and dental drugs**

    > **Includes**   poisoning by, adverse effect of and underdosing of glucocorticoids, topically used

    The appropriate 7th character is to be added to each code from category T49

    > A   initial encounter
    > D   subsequent encounter
    > S   sequela

    - T49.0   **Poisoning by, adverse effect of and underdosing of local antifungal, anti-infective and anti-inflammatory drugs**

        - T49.0x   **Poisoning by, adverse effect of and underdosing of local antifungal, anti-infective and anti-inflammatory drugs**

            - T49.0x1   Poisoning by local antifungal, anti-infective and anti-inflammatory drugs, accidental (unintentional)

                Poisoning by local antifungal, anti-infective and anti-inflammatory drugs NOS

            - T49.0x2   Poisoning by local antifungal, anti-infective and anti-inflammatory drugs, intentional self-harm
            - T49.0x3   Poisoning by local antifungal, anti-infective and anti-inflammatory drugs, assault
            - T49.0x4   Poisoning by local antifungal, anti-infective and anti-inflammatory drugs, undetermined
            - T49.0x5   Adverse effect of local antifungal, anti-infective and anti-inflammatory drugs
            - T49.0x6   Underdosing of local antifungal, anti-infective and anti-inflammatory drugs

    - T49.1   **Poisoning by, adverse effect of and underdosing of antipruritics**

        - T49.1x   **Poisoning by, adverse effect of and underdosing of antipruritics**

            - T49.1x1   Poisoning by antipruritics, accidental (unintentional)

                Poisoning by antipruritics NOS

            - T49.1x2   Poisoning by antipruritics, intentional self-harm

---

● Unacceptable First-Listed Diagnosis   ● Use Additional Character(s)   ▣ Unspecified   **OGCR** Official Guidelines for Coding and Reporting

🅒 Complication\Comorbidity   🅜 Major C\C   Excludes 1   Excludes 2   Includes   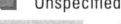 Use additional   Code first   Code also

1581

CHAPTER 19 (S00-T98)

- T49.1x3 Poisoning by antipruritics, assault
- T49.4x5 Adverse effect of keratolytics, keratoplastics, and other hair treatment drugs and preparations
- T49.4x6 Underdosing of keratolytics, keratoplastics, and other hair treatment drugs and preparations
- T49.2 Poisoning by, adverse effect of and underdosing of local astringents and local detergents
  - T49.2x Poisoning by, adverse effect of and underdosing of local astringents and local detergents
    - T49.2x1 Poisoning by local astringents and local detergents, accidental (unintentional)
      Poisoning by local astringents and local detergents NOS
    - T49.2x2 Poisoning by local astringents and local detergents, intentional self-harm
    - T49.2x3 Poisoning by local astringents and local detergents, assault
    - T49.2x4 Poisoning by local astringents and local detergents, undetermined
    - T49.2x5 Adverse effect of local astringents and local detergents
    - T49.2x6 Underdosing of local astringents and local detergents
- T49.3 Poisoning by, adverse effect of and underdosing of emollients, demulcents and protectants
  - T49.3x Poisoning by, adverse effect of and underdosing of emollients, demulcents and protectants
    - T49.3x1 Poisoning by emollients, demulcents and protectants, accidental (unintentional)
      Poisoning by emollients, demulcents and protectants NOS
    - T49.3x2 Poisoning by emollients, demulcents and protectants, intentional self-harm
    - T49.3x3 Poisoning by emollients, demulcents and protectants, assault
    - T49.3x4 Poisoning by emollients, demulcents and protectants, undetermined
    - T49.3x5 Adverse effect of emollients, demulcents and protectants
    - T49.3x6 Underdosing of emollients, demulcents and protectants
- T49.4 Poisoning by, adverse effect of and underdosing of keratolytics, keratoplastics, and other hair treatment drugs and preparations
  - T49.4x Poisoning by, adverse effect of and underdosing of keratolytics, keratoplastics, and other hair treatment drugs and preparations

- T49.4x1 Poisoning by keratolytics, keratoplastics, and other hair treatment drugs and preparations, accidental (unintentional)
  Poisoning by keratolytics, keratoplastics, and other hair treatment drugs and preparations NOS
- T49.4x2 Poisoning by keratolytics, keratoplastics, and other hair treatment drugs and preparations, intentional self-harm
- T49.4x3 Poisoning by keratolytics, keratoplastics, and other hair treatment drugs and preparations, assault
- T49.4x4 Poisoning by keratolytics, keratoplastics, and other hair treatment drugs and preparations, undetermined
- T49.4x5 Adverse effect of keratolytics, keratoplastics, and other hair treatment drugs and preparations
- T49.4x6 Underdosing of keratolytics, keratoplastics, and other hair treatment drugs and preparations
- T49.5 Poisoning by, adverse effect of and underdosing of ophthalmological drugs and preparations
  - T49.5x Poisoning by, adverse effect of and underdosing of ophthalmological drugs and preparations
    - T49.5x1 Poisoning by ophthalmological drugs and preparations, accidental (unintentional)
      Poisoning by ophthalmological drugs and preparations NOS
    - T49.5x2 Poisoning by ophthalmological drugs and preparations, intentional self-harm
    - T49.5x3 Poisoning by ophthalmological drugs and preparations, assault
    - T49.5x4 Poisoning by ophthalmological drugs and preparations, undetermined
    - T49.5x5 Adverse effect of ophthalmological drugs and preparations
    - T49.5x6 Underdosing of ophthalmological drugs and preparations
- T49.6 Poisoning by, adverse effect of and underdosing of otorhinolaryngological drugs and preparations
  - T49.6x Poisoning by, adverse effect of and underdosing of otorhinolaryngological drugs and preparations
    - T49.6x1 Poisoning by otorhinolaryngological drugs and preparations, accidental (unintentional)
      Poisoning by otorhinolaryngological drugs and preparations NOS

● Unacceptable First-Listed Diagnosis   ● Use Additional Character(s)   ■ Unspecified   OGCR Official Guidelines for Coding and Reporting
🖉 Complication\Comorbidity   🖉 Major C\C   Excludes 1   Excludes 2   Includes   Use additional   Code first   Code also

● T49.6x2   Poisoning by otorhinolaryngological drugs and preparations, intentional self-harm

● T49.6x3   Poisoning by otorhinolaryngological drugs and preparations, assault

● T49.6x4   Poisoning by otorhinolaryngological drugs and preparations, undetermined

● T49.6x5   Adverse effect of otorhinolaryngological drugs and preparations

● T49.6x6   Underdosing of otorhinolaryngological drugs and preparations

● T49.7   Poisoning by, adverse effect of and underdosing of dental drugs, topically applied

● T49.7x   Poisoning by, adverse effect of and underdosing of dental drugs, topically applied

● T49.7x1   Poisoning by dental drugs, topically applied, accidental (unintentional)
Poisoning by dental drugs, topically applied NOS

● T49.7x2   Poisoning by dental drugs, topically applied, intentional self-harm

● T49.7x3   Poisoning by dental drugs, topically applied, assault

● T49.7x4   Poisoning by dental drugs, topically applied, undetermined

● T49.7x5   Adverse effect of dental drugs, topically applied

● T49.7x6   Underdosing of dental drugs, topically applied

● T49.8   Poisoning by, adverse effect of and underdosing of other topical agents
Poisoning by, adverse effect of and underdosing of spermicides

● T49.8x   Poisoning by, adverse effect of and underdosing of other topical agents

● T49.8x1   Poisoning by other topical agents, accidental (unintentional)
Poisoning by other topical agents NOS

● T49.8x2   Poisoning by other topical agents, intentional self-harm

● T49.8x3   Poisoning by other topical agents, assault

● T49.8x4   Poisoning by other topical agents, undetermined

● T49.8x5   Adverse effect of other topical agents

● T49.8x6   Underdosing of other topical agents

● T49.9   Poisoning by, adverse effect of and underdosing of unspecified topical agent

● ▪ T49.91   Poisoning by unspecified topical agent, accidental (unintentional)

● ▪ T49.92   Poisoning by unspecified topical agent, intentional self-harm

● ▪ T49.93   Poisoning by unspecified topical agent, assault

● ▪ T49.94   Poisoning by unspecified topical agent, undetermined

● ▪ T49.95   Adverse effect of unspecified topical agent

● ▪ T49.96   Underdosing of unspecified topical agent

T50   Poisoning by, adverse effect of and underdosing of diuretics and other and unspecified drugs, medicaments and biological substances
The appropriate 7th character is to be added to each code from category T50

A	initial encounter
D	subsequent encounter
S	sequela

● T50.0   Poisoning by, adverse effect of and underdosing of mineralocorticoids and their antagonists

● T50.0x   Poisoning by, adverse effect of and underdosing of mineralocorticoids and their antagonists

● T50.0x1   Poisoning by mineralocorticoids and their antagonists, accidental (unintentional)
Poisoning by mineralocorticoids and their antagonists NOS

● T50.0x2   Poisoning by mineralocorticoids and their antagonists, intentional self-harm

● T50.0x3   Poisoning by mineralocorticoids and their antagonists, assault

● T50.0x4   Poisoning by mineralocorticoids and their antagonists, undetermined

● T50.0x5   Adverse effect of mineralocorticoids and their antagonists

● T50.0x6   Underdosing of mineralocorticoids and their antagonists

● T50.1   Poisoning by, adverse effect of and underdosing of loop [high-ceiling] diuretics

● T50.1x   Poisoning by, adverse effect of and underdosing of loop [high-ceiling] diuretics

● T50.1x1   Poisoning by loop [high-ceiling] diuretics, accidental (unintentional)
Poisoning by loop [high-ceiling] diuretics NOS

● T50.1x2   Poisoning by loop [high-ceiling] diuretics, intentional self-harm

● T50.1x3   Poisoning by loop [high-ceiling] diuretics, assault

● T50.1x4   Poisoning by loop [high-ceiling] diuretics, undetermined

● T50.1x5   Adverse effect of loop [high-ceiling] diuretics

● T50.1x6   Underdosing of loop [high-ceiling] diuretics

● T50.2   Poisoning by, adverse effect of and underdosing of carbonic-anhydrase inhibitors, benzothiadiazides and other diuretics
Poisoning by, adverse effect of and underdosing of acetazolamide

● T50.2x   Poisoning by, adverse effect of and underdosing of carbonic-anhydrase inhibitors, benzothiadiazides and other diuretics

● Unacceptable First-Listed Diagnosis   ● Use Additional Character(s)   ▪ Unspecified   **OGCR** Official Guidelines for Coding and Reporting

🦴 Complication\Comorbidity   🦴 Major C\C   Excludes 1   Excludes 2   Includes   Use additional   Code first   Code also   1583

- T50.2x1   Poisoning by carbonic-anhydrase inhibitors, benzothiadiazides and other diuretics, accidental (unintentional)

  Poisoning by carbonic-anhydrase inhibitors, benzothiadiazides and other diuretics NOS

- T50.2x2   Poisoning by carbonic-anhydrase inhibitors, benzothiadiazides and other diuretics, intentional self-harm

- T50.2x3   Poisoning by carbonic-anhydrase inhibitors, benzothiadiazides and other diuretics, assault

- T50.2x4   Poisoning by carbonic-anhydrase inhibitors, benzothiadiazides and other diuretics, undetermined

- T50.2x5   Adverse effect of carbonic-anhydrase inhibitors, benzothiadiazides and other diuretics

- T50.2x6   Underdosing of carbonic-anhydrase inhibitors, benzothiadiazides and other diuretics

- T50.3   Poisoning by, adverse effect of and underdosing of electrolytic, caloric and water-balance agents

  Poisoning by, adverse effect of and underdosing of oral rehydration salts

  - T50.3x   Poisoning by, adverse effect of and underdosing of electrolytic, caloric and water-balance agents

    - T50.3x1   Poisoning by electrolytic, caloric and water-balance agents, accidental (unintentional)

      Poisoning by electrolytic, caloric and water-balance agents NOS

    - T50.3x2   Poisoning by electrolytic, caloric and water-balance agents, intentional self-harm

    - T50.3x3   Poisoning by electrolytic, caloric and water-balance agents, assault

    - T50.3x4   Poisoning by electrolytic, caloric and water-balance agents, undetermined

    - T50.3x5   Adverse effect of electrolytic, caloric and water-balance agents

    - T50.3x6   Underdosing of electrolytic, caloric and water-balance agents

- T50.4   Poisoning by, adverse effect of and underdosing of drugs affecting uric acid metabolism

  - T50.4x   Poisoning by, adverse effect of and underdosing of drugs affecting uric acid metabolism

    - T50.4x1   Poisoning by drugs affecting uric acid metabolism, accidental (unintentional)

      Poisoning by drugs affecting uric acid metabolism NOS

    - T50.4x2   Poisoning by drugs affecting uric acid metabolism, intentional self-harm

    - T50.4x3   Poisoning by drugs affecting uric acid metabolism, assault

    - T50.4x4   Poisoning by drugs affecting uric acid metabolism, undetermined

- T50.4x5   Adverse effect of drugs affecting uric acid metabolism

- T50.4x6   Underdosing of drugs affecting uric acid metabolism

- T50.5   Poisoning by, adverse effect of and underdosing of appetite depressants

  - T50.5x   Poisoning by, adverse effect of and underdosing of appetite depressants

    - T50.5x1   Poisoning by appetite depressants, accidental (unintentional)

      Poisoning by appetite depressants NOS

    - T50.5x2   Poisoning by appetite depressants, intentional self-harm

    - T50.5x3   Poisoning by appetite depressants, assault

    - T50.5x4   Poisoning by appetite depressants, undetermined

    - T50.5x5   Adverse effect of appetite depressants

    - T50.5x6   Underdosing of appetite depressants

- T50.6   Poisoning by, adverse effect of and underdosing of antidotes and chelating agents

  Poisoning by, adverse effect of and underdosing of alcohol deterrents

  - T50.6x   Poisoning by, adverse effect of and underdosing of antidotes and chelating agents

    - T50.6x1   Poisoning by antidotes and chelating agents, accidental (unintentional)

      Poisoning by antidotes and chelating agents NOS

    - T50.6x2   Poisoning by antidotes and chelating agents, intentional self-harm

    - T50.6x3   Poisoning by antidotes and chelating agents, assault

    - T50.6x4   Poisoning by antidotes and chelating agents, undetermined

    - T50.6x5   Adverse effect of antidotes and chelating agents

    - T50.6x6   Underdosing of antidotes and chelating agents

- T50.7   Poisoning by, adverse effect of and underdosing of analeptics and opioid receptor antagonists

  - T50.7x   Poisoning by, adverse effect of and underdosing of analeptics and opioid receptor antagonists

    - T50.7x1   Poisoning by analeptics and opioid receptor antagonists, accidental (unintentional)

      Poisoning by analeptics and opioid receptor antagonists NOS

    - T50.7x2   Poisoning by analeptics and opioid receptor antagonists, intentional self-harm

    - T50.7x3   Poisoning by analeptics and opioid receptor antagonists, assault

    - T50.7x4   Poisoning by analeptics and opioid receptor antagonists, undetermined

- Unacceptable First-Listed Diagnosis   - Use Additional Character(s)   ☐ Unspecified   **OGCR** Official Guidelines for Coding and Reporting

🍁 Complication\Comorbidity   🍁 Major C\C   [Excludes 1]   [Excludes 2]   Includes   Use additional   Code first   Code also

● T50.7x5   Adverse effect of analeptics and opioid receptor antagonists

● T50.7x6   Underdosing of analeptics and opioid receptor antagonists

● T50.8   Poisoning by, adverse effect of and underdosing of diagnostic agents

   ● T50.8x   Poisoning by, adverse effect of and underdosing of diagnostic agents

     ● T50.8x1   Poisoning by diagnostic agents, accidental (unintentional)

         Poisoning by diagnostic agents NOS

     ● T50.8x2   Poisoning by diagnostic agents, intentional self-harm

     ● T50.8x3   Poisoning by diagnostic agents, assault

     ● T50.8x4   Poisoning by diagnostic agents, undetermined

     ● T50.8x5   Adverse effect of diagnostic agents

     ● T50.8x6   Underdosing of diagnostic agents

● T50.A   Poisoning by, adverse effect of and underdosing of bacterial vaccines

   ● T50.A1   Poisoning by, adverse effect of and underdosing of pertussis vaccine, including combinations with a pertussis component

     ● T50.A11   Poisoning by pertussis vaccine, including combinations with a pertussis component, accidental (unintentional)

     ● T50.A12   Poisoning by pertussis vaccine, including combinations with a pertussis component, intentional self-harm

     ● T50.A13   Poisoning by pertussis vaccine, including combinations with a pertussis component, assault

     ● T50.A14   Poisoning by pertussis vaccine, including combinations with a pertussis component, undetermined

     ● T50.A15   Adverse effect of pertussis vaccine, including combinations with a pertussis component

     ● T50.A16   Underdosing of pertussis vaccine, including combinations with a pertussis component

   ● T50.A2   Poisoning by, adverse effect of and underdosing of mixed bacterial vaccines without a pertussis component

     ● T50.A21   Poisoning by mixed bacterial vaccines without a pertussis component, accidental (unintentional)

     ● T50.A22   Poisoning by mixed bacterial vaccines without a pertussis component, intentional self-harm

     ● T50.A23   Poisoning by mixed bacterial vaccines without a pertussis component, assault

     ● T50.A24   Poisoning by mixed bacterial vaccines without a pertussis component, undetermined

     ● T50.A25   Adverse effect of mixed bacterial vaccines without a pertussis component

     ● T50.A26   Underdosing of mixed bacterial vaccines without a pertussis component

   ● T50.A9   Poisoning by, adverse effect of and underdosing of other bacterial vaccines

     ● T50.A91   Poisoning by other bacterial vaccines, accidental (unintentional)

     ● T50.A92   Poisoning by other bacterial vaccines, intentional self-harm

     ● T50.A93   Poisoning by other bacterial vaccines, assault

     ● T50.A94   Poisoning by other bacterial vaccines, undetermined

     ● T50.A95   Adverse effect of other bacterial vaccines

     ● T50.A96   Underdosing of other bacterial vaccines

● T50.B   Poisoning by, adverse effect of and underdosing of viral vaccines

   ● T50.B1   Poisoning by, adverse effect of and underdosing of smallpox vaccines

     ● T50.B11   Poisoning by smallpox vaccines, accidental (unintentional)

     ● T50.B12   Poisoning by smallpox vaccines, intentional self-harm

     ● T50.B13   Poisoning by smallpox vaccines, assault

     ● T50.B14   Poisoning by smallpox vaccines, undetermined

     ● T50.B15   Adverse effect of smallpox vaccines

     ● T50.B16   Underdosing of smallpox vaccines

   ● T50.B9   Poisoning by, adverse effect of and underdosing of other viral vaccines

     ● T50.B91   Poisoning by other viral vaccines, accidental (unintentional)

     ● T50.B92   Poisoning by other viral vaccines, intentional self-harm

     ● T50.B93   Poisoning by other viral vaccines, assault

     ● T50.B94   Poisoning by other viral vaccines, undetermined

     ● T50.B95   Adverse effect of other viral vaccines

     ● T50.B86   Underdosing of other viral vaccines

● T50.Z   Poisoning by, adverse effect of and underdosing of other vaccines and biological substances

   ● T50.Z1   Poisoning by, adverse effect of and underdosing of immunoglobulin

     ● T50.Z11   Poisoning by immunoglobulin, accidental (unintentional)

     ● T50.Z12   Poisoning by immunoglobulin, intentional self-harm

     ● T50.Z13   Poisoning by immunoglobulin, assault

● Unacceptable First-Listed Diagnosis   ● Use Additional Character(s)   ▨ Unspecified   **OGCR** Official Guidelines for Coding and Reporting

🞕 Complication\Comorbidity   🞕 Major C\C   Excludes 1   Excludes 2   Includes   Use additional   Code first   Code also

CHAPTER 19 (S00-T98)   1585

● T50.Z14   Poisoning by immunoglobulin, undetermined

● T50.Z15   Adverse effect of immunoglobulin

● T50.Z16   Underdosing of immunoglobulin

● T50.Z9   Poisoning by, adverse effect of and underdosing of other vaccines and biological substances

  ● T50.Z91   Poisoning by other vaccines and biological substances, accidental (unintentional)

  ● T50.Z92   Poisoning by other vaccines and biological substances, intentional self-harm

  ● T50.Z93   Poisoning by other vaccines and biological substances, assault

  ● T50.Z94   Poisoning by other vaccines and biological substances, undetermined

  ● T50.Z95   Adverse effect of other vaccines and biological substances

  ● T50.Z96   Underdosing of other vaccines and biological substances

● T50.9   Poisoning by, adverse effect of and underdosing of other and unspecified drugs, medicaments and biological substances

  ● T50.90   Poisoning by, adverse effect of and underdosing of unspecified drugs, medicaments and biological substances

    ● ▨ T50.901   Poisoning by unspecified drugs, medicaments and biological substances, accidental (unintentional)

    ● ▨ T50.902   Poisoning by unspecified drugs, medicaments and biological substances, intentional self-harm

    ● ▨ T50.903   Poisoning by unspecified drugs, medicaments and biological substances, assault

    ● ▨ T50.904   Poisoning by unspecified drugs, medicaments and biological substances, undetermined

    ● ▨ T50.905   Adverse effect of unspecified drugs, medicaments and biological substances

    ● ▨ T50.906   Underdosing of unspecified drugs, medicaments and biological substances

  ● T50.99   Poisoning by, adverse effect of and underdosing of other drugs, medicaments and biological substances

    ● T50.991   Poisoning by other drugs, medicaments and biological substances, accidental (unintentional)

    ● T50.992   Poisoning by other drugs, medicaments and biological substances, intentional self-harm

    ● T50.993   Poisoning by other drugs, medicaments and biological substances, assault

    ● T50.994   Poisoning by other drugs, medicaments and biological substances, undetermined

    ● T50.995   Adverse effect of other drugs, medicaments and biological substances

    ● T50.996   Underdosing of other drugs, medicaments and biological substances

---

TOXIC EFFECTS OF SUBSTANCES CHIEFLY NONMEDICINAL AS TO SOURCE (T51-T65)

Use additional code(s) for all associated manifestations of toxic effect, such as:
respiratory conditions due to external agents (J60-J70)

When no intent is indicated code to accidental. Undetermined intent is only for use when there is specific documentation in the record that the intent of the toxic effect cannot be determined

  Excludes1   contact with and (suspected) exposure to toxic substances (Z77.-)

● T51   **Toxic effect of alcohol**

The appropriate 7th character is to be added to each code from category T51

A	initial encounter
D	subsequent encounter
S	sequela

● T51.0   Toxic effect of ethanol
    Toxic effect of ethyl alcohol

  Excludes2   acute alcohol intoxication or "hangover" effects (F10.11, F10.31, F10.91)
      drunkenness (F10.11, F10.31, F10.91)
      pathological alcohol intoxication (F10.11, F10.31, F10.91)

  ● T51.0x   Toxic effect of ethanol

    ● T51.0x1   Toxic effect of ethanol, accidental (unintentional)
      Toxic effect of ethanol NOS

    ● T51.0x2   Toxic effect of ethanol, intentional self-harm

    ● T51.0x3   Toxic effect of ethanol, assault

    ● T51.0x4   Toxic effect of ethanol, undetermined

● T51.1   Toxic effect of methanol
    Toxic effect of methyl alcohol

  ● T51.1x   Toxic effect of methanol

    ● T51.1x1   Toxic effect of methanol, accidental (unintentional)
      Toxic effect of methanol NOS

    ● T51.1x2   Toxic effect of methanol, intentional self-harm

    ● T51.1x3   Toxic effect of methanol, assault

    ● T51.1x4   Toxic effect of methanol, undetermined

● T51.2   Toxic effect of 2-Propanol
    Toxic effect of isopropyl alcohol

  ● T51.2x   Toxic effect of 2-Propanol

● Unacceptable First-Listed Diagnosis   ● Use Additional Character(s)   ▨ Unspecified   **OGCR** Official Guidelines for Coding and Reporting
🖰 Complication\Comorbidity   🖰 Major C\C   Excludes 1   Excludes 2   Includes   Use additional   Code first   Code also

● T51.2x1   Toxic effect of 2-Propanol, accidental (unintentional)
    Toxic effect of 2-Propanol NOS

● T51.2x2   Toxic effect of 2-Propanol, intentional self-harm

● T51.2x3   Toxic effect of 2-Propanol, assault

● T51.2x4   Toxic effect of 2-Propanol, undetermined

● T51.3   **Toxic effect of fusel oil**
    Toxic effect of amyl alcohol
    Toxic effect of butyl [1-butanol] alcohol
    Toxic effect of propyl [1-propanol] alcohol

   ● T51.3x   **Toxic effect of fusel oil**

     ● T51.3x1   Toxic effect of fusel oil, accidental (unintentional)
      Toxic effect of fusel oil NOS

     ● T51.3x2   Toxic effect of fusel oil, intentional self-harm

     ● T51.3x3   Toxic effect of fusel oil, assault

     ● T51.3x4   Toxic effect of fusel oil, undetermined

● T51.8   **Toxic effect of other alcohols**

   ● T51.8x   **Toxic effect of other alcohols**

     ● T51.8x1   Toxic effect of other alcohols, accidental (unintentional)
      Toxic effect of other alcohols NOS

     ● T51.8x2   Toxic effect of other alcohols, intentional self-harm

     ● T51.8x3   Toxic effect of other alcohols, assault

     ● T51.8x4   Toxic effect of other alcohols, undetermined

● T51.9   **Toxic effect of unspecified alcohol**

   ● ◻ T51.91   Toxic effect of unspecified alcohol, accidental (unintentional)

   ● ◻ T51.92   Toxic effect of unspecified alcohol, intentional self-harm

   ● ◻ T51.93   Toxic effect of unspecified alcohol, assault

   ● ◻ T51.94   Toxic effect of unspecified alcohol, undetermined

● T52   **Toxic effect of organic solvents**

   | **Excludes1** | halogen derivatives of aliphatic and aromatic hydrocarbons (T53.-) |

   The appropriate 7th character is to be added to each code from category T52

    | A | initial encounter |
    | D | subsequent encounter |
    | S | sequela |

● T52.0   **Toxic effects of petroleum products**
    Toxic effects of gasoline [petrol]
    Toxic effects of kerosene [paraffin oil]
    Toxic effects of paraffin wax
    Toxic effects of ether petroleum
    Toxic effects of naphtha petroleum
    Toxic effects of spirit petroleum

   ● T52.0x   **Toxic effects of petroleum products**

     ● T52.0x1   Toxic effect of petroleum products, accidental (unintentional)
      Toxic effects of petroleum products NOS

     ● T52.0x2   Toxic effect of petroleum products, intentional self-harm

     ● T52.0x3   Toxic effect of petroleum products, assault

     ● T52.0x4   Toxic effect of petroleum products, undetermined

● T52.1   **Toxic effects of benzene**

   | **Excludes1** | homologues of benzene (T52.2) nitroderivatives and aminoderivatives of benzene and its homologues (T65.3) |

   ● T52.1x   **Toxic effects of benzene**

     ● T52.1x1   Toxic effect of benzene, accidental (unintentional)
      Toxic effects of benzene NOS

     ● T52.1x2   Toxic effect of benzene, intentional self-harm

     ● T52.1x3   Toxic effect of benzene, assault

     ● T52.1x4   Toxic effect of benzene, undetermined

● T52.2   **Toxic effects of homologues of benzene**
    Toxic effects of toluene [methylbenzene]
    Toxic effects of xylene [dimethylbenzene]

   ● T52.2x   **Toxic effects of homologues of benzene**

     ● T52.2x1   Toxic effect of homologues of benzene, accidental (unintentional)
      Toxic effects of homologues of benzene NOS

     ● T52.2x2   Toxic effect of homologues of benzene, intentional self-harm

     ● T52.2x3   Toxic effect of homologues of benzene, assault

     ● T52.2x4   Toxic effect of homologues of benzene, undetermined

● T52.3   **Toxic effects of glycols**

   ● T52.3x   **Toxic effects of glycols**

     ● T52.3x1   Toxic effect of glycols, accidental (unintentional)
      Toxic effects of glycols NOS

     ● T52.3x2   Toxic effect of glycols, intentional self-harm

     ● T52.3x3   Toxic effect of glycols, assault

     ● T52.3x4   Toxic effect of glycols, undetermined

● T52.4   **Toxic effects of ketones**

   ● T52.4x   **Toxic effects of ketones**

     ● T52.4x1   Toxic effect of ketones, accidental (unintentional)
      Toxic effects of ketones NOS

     ● T52.4x2   Toxic effect of ketones, intentional self-harm

     ● T52.4x3   Toxic effect of ketones, assault

     ● T52.4x4   Toxic effect of ketones, undetermined

● T52.8   **Toxic effects of other organic solvents**

   ● T52.8x   **Toxic effects of other organic solvents**

     ● T52.8x1   Toxic effect of other organic solvents, accidental (unintentional)
      Toxic effects of other organic solvents NOS

     ● T52.8x2   Toxic effect of other organic solvents, intentional self-harm

● Unacceptable First-Listed Diagnosis   ● Use Additional Character(s)   ◻ Unspecified   **OGCR** Official Guidelines for Coding and Reporting

🦚 Complication\Comorbidity   🦚 Major C\C | Excludes 1 | | Excludes 2 | Includes   Use additional   Code first   Code also

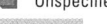

1587

CHAPTER 19 (S00-T98)

- T52.8x3   Toxic effect of other organic solvents, assault
- T52.8x4   Toxic effect of other organic solvents, undetermined
- T52.9   Toxic effects of unspecified organic solvent
  - ■ T52.91   Toxic effect of unspecified organic solvent, accidental (unintentional)
  - ■ T52.92   Toxic effect of unspecified organic solvent, intentional self-harm
  - ■ T52.93   Toxic effect of unspecified organic solvent, assault
  - ■ T52.94   Toxic effect of unspecified organic solvent, undetermined
- T53   Toxic effect of halogen derivatives of aliphatic and aromatic hydrocarbons

  The appropriate 7th character is to be added to each code from category T53

A	initial encounter
D	subsequent encounter
S	sequela

- T53.0   Toxic effects of carbon tetrachloride
  Toxic effects of tetrachloromethane
  - T53.0x   Toxic effects of carbon tetrachloride
    - T53.0x1   Toxic effect of carbon tetrachloride, accidental (unintentional)
      Toxic effects of carbon tetrachloride NOS
    - T53.0x2   Toxic effect of carbon tetrachloride, intentional self-harm
    - T53.0x3   Toxic effect of carbon tetrachloride, assault
    - T53.0x4   Toxic effect of carbon tetrachloride, undetermined
- T53.1   Toxic effects of chloroform
  Toxic effects of trichloromethane
  - T53.1x   Toxic effects of chloroform
    - T53.1x1   Toxic effect of chloroform, accidental (unintentional)
      Toxic effects of chloroform NOS
    - T53.1x2   Toxic effect of chloroform, intentional self-harm
    - T53.1x3   Toxic effect of chloroform, assault
    - T53.1x4   Toxic effect of chloroform, undetermined
- T53.2   Toxic effects of trichloroethylene
  Toxic effects of trichloroethene
  - T53.2x   Toxic effects of trichloroethylene
    - T53.2x1   Toxic effect of trichloroethylene, accidental (unintentional)
      Toxic effects of trichloroethylene NOS
    - T53.2x2   Toxic effect of trichloroethylene, intentional self-harm
    - T53.2x3   Toxic effect of trichloroethylene, assault
    - T53.2x4   Toxic effect of trichloroethylene, undetermined
- T53.3   Toxic effects of tetrachloroethylene
  Toxic effects of perchloroethylene
  Toxic effect of tetrachloroethene
  - T53.3x   Toxic effects of tetrachloroethylene

- T53.3x1   Toxic effect of tetrachloroethylene, accidental (unintentional)
  Toxic effects of tetrachloroethylene NOS
- T53.3x2   Toxic effect of tetrachloroethylene, intentional self-harm
- T53.3x3   Toxic effect of tetrachloroethylene, assault
- T53.3x4   Toxic effect of tetrachloroethylene, undetermined
- T53.4   Toxic effects of dichloromethane
  Toxic effects of methylene chloride
  - T53.4x   Toxic effects of dichloromethane
    - T53.4x1   Toxic effect of dichloromethane, accidental (unintentional)
      Toxic effects of dichloromethane NOS
    - T53.4x2   Toxic effect of dichloromethane, intentional self-harm
    - T53.4x3   Toxic effect of dichloromethane, assault
    - T53.4x4   Toxic effect of dichloromethane, undetermined
- T53.5   Toxic effects of chlorofluorocarbons
  - T53.5x   Toxic effects of chlorofluorocarbons
    - T53.5x1   Toxic effect of chlorofluorocarbons, accidental (unintentional)
      Toxic effects of chlorofluorocarbons NOS
    - T53.5x2   Toxic effect of chlorofluorocarbons, intentional self-harm
    - T53.5x3   Toxic effect of chlorofluorocarbons, assault
    - T53.5x4   Toxic effect of chlorofluorocarbons, undetermined
- T53.6   Toxic effects of other halogen derivatives of aliphatic hydrocarbons
  - T53.6x   Toxic effects of other halogen derivatives of aliphatic hydrocarbons
    - T53.6x1   Toxic effect of other halogen derivatives of aliphatic hydrocarbons, accidental (unintentional)
      Toxic effects of other halogen derivatives of aliphatic hydrocarbons NOS
    - T53.6x2   Toxic effect of other halogen derivatives of aliphatic hydrocarbons, intentional self-harm
    - T53.6x3   Toxic effect of other halogen derivatives of aliphatic hydrocarbons, assault
    - T53.6x4   Toxic effect of other halogen derivatives of aliphatic hydrocarbons, undetermined
- T53.7   Toxic effects of other halogen derivatives of aromatic hydrocarbons
  - T53.7x   Toxic effects of other halogen derivatives of aromatic hydrocarbons

● Unacceptable First-Listed Diagnosis   ● Use Additional Character(s)   ■ Unspecified   **OGCR** Official Guidelines for Coding and Reporting

🖐 Complication\Comorbidity   🖐 Major C\C   Excludes 1   Excludes 2   Includes   Use additional   Code first   Code also

● **T53.7x1** **Toxic effect of other halogen derivatives of aromatic hydrocarbons, accidental (unintentional)**
    Toxic effects of other halogen derivatives of aromatic hydrocarbons NOS

● **T53.7x2** **Toxic effect of other halogen derivatives of aromatic hydrocarbons, intentional self-harm**

● **T53.7x3** **Toxic effect of other halogen derivatives of aromatic hydrocarbons, assault**

● **T53.7x4** **Toxic effect of other halogen derivatives of aromatic hydrocarbons, undetermined**

● **T53.9** **Toxic effects of unspecified halogen derivatives of aliphatic and aromatic hydrocarbons**

● ■ **T53.91** **Toxic effect of unspecified halogen derivatives of aliphatic and aromatic hydrocarbons, accidental (unintentional)**

● ■ **T53.92** **Toxic effect of unspecified halogen derivatives of aliphatic and aromatic hydrocarbons, intentional self-harm**

● ■ **T53.93** **Toxic effect of unspecified halogen derivatives of aliphatic and aromatic hydrocarbons, assault**

● ■ **T53.94** **Toxic effect of unspecified halogen derivatives of aliphatic and aromatic hydrocarbons, undetermined**

● **T54** **Toxic effect of corrosive substances**
    The appropriate 7th character is to be added to each code from category T54

A	initial encounter
D	subsequent encounter
S	sequela

● **T54.0** **Toxic effects of phenol and phenol homologues**

● **T54.0x** **Toxic effects of phenol and phenol homologues**

● **T54.0x1** **Toxic effect of phenol and phenol homologues, accidental (unintentional)**
    Toxic effects of phenol and phenol homologues NOS

● **T54.0x2** **Toxic effect of phenol and phenol homologues, intentional self-harm**

● **T54.0x3** **Toxic effect of phenol and phenol homologues, assault**

● **T54.0x4** **Toxic effect of phenol and phenol homologues, undetermined**

● **T54.1** **Toxic effects of other corrosive organic compounds**

● **T54.1x** **Toxic effects of other corrosive organic compounds**

● **T54.1x1** **Toxic effect of other corrosive organic compounds, accidental (unintentional)**
    Toxic effects of other corrosive organic compounds NOS

● **T54.1x2** **Toxic effect of other corrosive organic compounds, intentional self-harm**

● **T54.1x3** **Toxic effect of other corrosive organic compounds, assault**

● **T54.1x4** **Toxic effect of other corrosive organic compounds, undetermined**

● **T54.2** **Toxic effects of corrosive acids and acid-like substances**
    Toxic effects of hydrochloric acid
    Toxic effects of sulfuric acid

● **T54.2x** **Toxic effects of corrosive acids and acid-like substances**

● **T54.2x1** **Toxic effect of corrosive acids and acid-like substances, accidental (unintentional)**
    Toxic effects of corrosive acids and acid-like substances NOS

● **T54.2x2** **Toxic effect of corrosive acids and acid-like substances, intentional self-harm**

● **T54.2x3** **Toxic effect of corrosive acids and acid-like substances, assault**

● **T54.2x4** **Toxic effect of corrosive acids and acid-like substances, undetermined**

● **T54.3** **Toxic effects of corrosive alkalis and alkali-like substances**
    Toxic effects of potassium hydroxide
    Toxic effects of sodium hydroxide

● **T54.3x** **Toxic effects of corrosive alkalis and alkali-like substances**

● **T54.3x1** **Toxic effect of corrosive alkalis and alkali-like substances, accidental (unintentional)**
    Toxic effects of corrosive alkalis and alkali-like substances NOS

● **T54.3x2** **Toxic effect of corrosive alkalis and alkali-like substances, intentional self-harm**

● **T54.3x3** **Toxic effect of corrosive alkalis and alkali-like substances, assault**

● **T54.3x4** **Toxic effect of corrosive alkalis and alkali-like substances, undetermined**

● **T54.9** **Toxic effects of unspecified corrosive substance**

● ■ **T54.91** **Toxic effect of unspecified corrosive substance, accidental (unintentional)**

● ■ **T54.92** **Toxic effect of unspecified corrosive substance, intentional self-harm**

● ■ **T54.93** **Toxic effect of unspecified corrosive substance, assault**

● ■ **T54.94** **Toxic effect of unspecified corrosive substance, undetermined**

● **T55** **Toxic effect of soaps and detergents**
    The appropriate 7th character is to be added to each code from category T55

A	initial encounter
D	subsequent encounter
S	sequela

● **T55.0** **Toxic effect of soaps**

● **T55.0x** **Toxic effect of soaps**

● **T55.0x1** **Toxic effect of soaps, accidental (unintentional)**
    Toxic effect of soaps NOS

● **T55.0x2** **Toxic effect of soaps, intentional self-harm**

● Unacceptable First-Listed Diagnosis   ● Use Additional Character(s)   ■ Unspecified   **OGCR** Official Guidelines for Coding and Reporting

🗪 Complication\Comorbidity   🗪 Major C\C   [Excludes 1]   [Excludes 2]   Includes   Use additional   Code first   Code also   1589

CHAPTER 19 (S00-T98)

- T55.0x3   Toxic effect of soaps, assault
- T55.0x4   Toxic effect of soaps, undetermined
- T55.1   Toxic effect of detergents
  - T55.1x   Toxic effect of detergents
    - T55.1x1   Toxic effect of detergents, accidental (unintentional)
      Toxic effect of detergents NOS
    - T55.1x2   Toxic effect of detergents, intentional self-harm
    - T55.1x3   Toxic effect of detergents, assault
    - T55.1x4   Toxic effect of detergents, undetermined

- T56   Toxic effect of metals

  Includes   toxic effects of fumes and vapors of metals
  toxic effects of metals from all sources, except medicinal substances

  Excludes1   arsenic and its compounds (T57.0)
  manganese and its compounds (T57.2)
  The appropriate 7th character is to be added to each code from category T56

A	initial encounter
D	subsequent encounter
S	sequela

  - T56.0   Toxic effects of lead and its compounds
    - T56.0x   Toxic effects of lead and its compounds
      - T56.0x1   Toxic effect of lead and its compounds, accidental (unintentional)
        Toxic effects of lead and its compounds NOS
      - T56.0x2   Toxic effect of lead and its compounds, intentional self-harm
      - T56.0x3   Toxic effect of lead and its compounds, assault
      - T56.0x4   Toxic effect of lead and its compounds, undetermined
  - T56.1   Toxic effects of mercury and its compounds
    - T56.1x   Toxic effects of mercury and its compounds
      - T56.1x1   Toxic effect of mercury and its compounds, accidental (unintentional)
        Toxic effects of mercury and its compounds NOS
      - T56.1x2   Toxic effect of mercury and its compounds, intentional self-harm
      - T56.1x3   Toxic effect of mercury and its compounds, assault
      - T56.1x4   Toxic effect of mercury and its compounds, undetermined
  - T56.2   Toxic effects of chromium and its compounds
    - T56.2x   Toxic effects of chromium and its compounds
      - T56.2x1   Toxic effect of chromium and its compounds, accidental (unintentional)
        Toxic effects of chromium and its compounds NOS

- T56.2x2   Toxic effect of chromium and its compounds, intentional self-harm
- T56.2x3   Toxic effect of chromium and its compounds, assault
- T56.2x4   Toxic effect of chromium and its compounds, undetermined
- T56.3   Toxic effects of cadmium and its compounds
  - T56.3x   Toxic effects of cadmium and its compounds
    - T56.3x1   Toxic effect of cadmium and its compounds, accidental (unintentional)
      Toxic effects of cadmium and its compounds NOS
    - T56.3x2   Toxic effect of cadmium and its compounds, intentional self-harm
    - T56.3x3   Toxic effect of cadmium and its compounds, assault
    - T56.3x4   Toxic effect of cadmium and its compounds, undetermined
- T56.4   Toxic effects of copper and its compounds
  - T56.4x   Toxic effects of copper and its compounds
    - T56.4x1   Toxic effect of copper and its compounds, accidental (unintentional)
      Toxic effects of copper and its compounds NOS
    - T56.4x2   Toxic effect of copper and its compounds, intentional self-harm
    - T56.4x3   Toxic effect of copper and its compounds, assault
    - T56.4x4   Toxic effect of copper and its compounds, undetermined
- T56.5   Toxic effects of zinc and its compounds
  - T56.5x   Toxic effects of zinc and its compounds
    - T56.5x1   Toxic effect of zinc and its compounds, accidental (unintentional)
      Toxic effects of zinc and its compounds NOS
    - T56.5x2   Toxic effect of zinc and its compounds, intentional self-harm
    - T56.5x3   Toxic effect of zinc and its compounds, assault
    - T56.5x4   Toxic effect of zinc and its compounds, undetermined
- T56.6   Toxic effects of tin and its compounds
  - T56.6x   Toxic effects of tin and its compounds
    - T56.6x1   Toxic effect of tin and its compounds, accidental (unintentional)
      Toxic effects of tin and its compounds NOS
    - T56.6x2   Toxic effect of tin and its compounds, intentional self-harm
    - T56.6x3   Toxic effect of tin and its compounds, assault
    - T56.6x4   Toxic effect of tin and its compounds, undetermined

- Unacceptable First-Listed Diagnosis   ● Use Additional Character(s)   ■ Unspecified   **OGCR** Official Guidelines for Coding and Reporting
- Complication\Comorbidity   Major C\C   Excludes 1   Excludes 2   Includes   Use additional   Code first   Code also

- **T56.7** Toxic effects of beryllium and its compounds
  - **T56.7x** Toxic effects of beryllium and its compounds
    - **T56.7x1** Toxic effect of beryllium and its compounds, accidental (unintentional)
      Toxic effects of beryllium and its compounds NOS
    - **T56.7x2** Toxic effect of beryllium and its compounds, intentional self-harm
    - **T56.7x3** Toxic effect of beryllium and its compounds, assault
    - **T56.7x4** Toxic effect of beryllium and its compounds, undetermined
- **T56.8** Toxic effects of other metals
  - **T56.81** Toxic effect of thallium
    - **T56.811** Toxic effect of thallium, accidental (unintentional)
      Toxic effect of thallium NOS
    - **T56.812** Toxic effect of thallium, intentional self-harm
    - **T56.813** Toxic effect of thallium, assault
    - **T56.814** Toxic effect of thallium, undetermined
  - **T56.89** Toxic effects of other metals
    - **T56.891** Toxic effect of other metals, accidental (unintentional)
      Toxic effects of other metals NOS
    - **T56.892** Toxic effect of other metals, intentional self-harm
    - **T56.893** Toxic effect of other metals, assault
    - **T56.894** Toxic effect of other metals, undetermined
- **T56.9** Toxic effects of unspecified metal
  - **T56.91** Toxic effect of unspecified metal, accidental (unintentional)
  - **T56.92** Toxic effect of unspecified metal, intentional self-harm
  - **T56.93** Toxic effect of unspecified metal, assault
  - **T56.94** Toxic effect of unspecified metal, undetermined
- **T57** Toxic effect of other inorganic substances
  The appropriate 7th character is to be added to each code from category T57
A	initial encounter
D	subsequent encounter
S	sequela
  - **T57.0** Toxic effect of arsenic and its compounds
    - **T57.0x** Toxic effect of arsenic and its compounds
      - **T57.0x1** Toxic effect of arsenic and its compounds, accidental (unintentional)
        Toxic effect of arsenic and its compounds NOS
      - **T57.0x2** Toxic effect of arsenic and its compounds, intentional self-harm
      - **T57.0x3** Toxic effect of arsenic and its compounds, assault
      - **T57.0x4** Toxic effect of arsenic and its compounds, undetermined

- **T57.1** Toxic effect of phosphorus and its compounds
  Excludes1 organophosphate insecticides (T60.0)
  - **T57.1x** Toxic effect of phosphorus and its compounds
    - **T57.1x1** Toxic effect of phosphorus and its compounds, accidental (unintentional)
    - **T57.1x2** Toxic effect of phosphorus and its compounds, intentional self-harm
    - **T57.1x3** Toxic effect of phosphorus and its compounds, assault
    - **T57.1x4** Toxic effect of phosphorus and its compounds, undetermined
- **T57.2** Toxic effect of manganese and its compounds
  - **T57.2x** Toxic effect of manganese and its compounds
    - **T57.2x1** Toxic effect of manganese and its compounds, accidental (unintentional)
      Toxic effect of manganese and its compounds NOS
    - **T57.2x2** Toxic effect of manganese and its compounds, intentional self-harm
    - **T57.2x3** Toxic effect of manganese and its compounds, assault
    - **T57.2x4** Toxic effect of manganese and its compounds, undetermined
- **T57.3** Toxic effect of hydrogen cyanide
  - **T57.3x** Toxic effect of hydrogen cyanide
    - **T57.3x1** Toxic effect of hydrogen cyanide, accidental (unintentional)
      Toxic effect of hydrogen cyanide NOS
    - **T57.3x2** Toxic effect of hydrogen cyanide, intentional self-harm
    - **T57.3x3** Toxic effect of hydrogen cyanide, assault
    - **T57.3x4** Toxic effect of hydrogen cyanide, undetermined
- **T57.8** Toxic effect of other specified inorganic substances
  - **T57.8x** Toxic effect of other specified inorganic substances
    - **T57.8x1** Toxic effect of other specified inorganic substances, accidental (unintentional)
      Toxic effect of other specified inorganic substances NOS
    - **T57.8x2** Toxic effect of other specified inorganic substances, intentional self-harm
    - **T57.8x3** Toxic effect of other specified inorganic substances, assault
    - **T57.8x4** Toxic effect of other specified inorganic substances, undetermined
- **T57.9** Toxic effect of unspecified inorganic substance
  - **T57.91** Toxic effect of unspecified inorganic substance, accidental (unintentional)
  - **T57.92** Toxic effect of unspecified inorganic substance, intentional self-harm
  - **T57.93** Toxic effect of unspecified inorganic substance, assault
  - **T57.94** Toxic effect of unspecified inorganic substance, undetermined

● Unacceptable First-Listed Diagnosis ● Use Additional Character(s) ▦ Unspecified **OGCR** Official Guidelines for Coding and Reporting
🗪 Complication\Comorbidity 🗪 Major C\C Excludes 1 Excludes 2 Includes Use additional Code first Code also
1591 — CHAPTER 19 (S00-T98)

● **T58** **Toxic effect of carbon monoxide**

> **Includes** asphyxiation from carbon monoxide
> toxic effect of carbon monoxide from all sources
>
> The appropriate 7th character is to be added to each code from category T58
>
> | A | initial encounter |
> |---|---|
> | D | subsequent encounter |
> | S | sequela |

● **T58.0** **Toxic effect of carbon monoxide from motor vehicle exhaust**

> Toxic effect of exhaust gas from gas engine
> Toxic effect of exhaust gas from motor pump

　● **T58.01** **Toxic effect of carbon monoxide from motor vehicle exhaust, accidental (unintentional)**

　● **T58.02** **Toxic effect of carbon monoxide from motor vehicle exhaust, intentional self-harm**

　● **T58.03** **Toxic effect of carbon monoxide from motor vehicle exhaust, assault**

　● **T58.04** **Toxic effect of carbon monoxide from motor vehicle exhaust, undetermined**

● **T58.1** **Toxic effect of carbon monoxide from utility gas**

> Toxic effect of acetylene
> Toxic effect of gas NOS used for lighting, heating, cooking
> Toxic effect of water gas

　● **T58.11** **Toxic effect of carbon monoxide from utility gas, accidental (unintentional)**

　● **T58.12** **Toxic effect of carbon monoxide from utility gas, intentional self-harm**

　● **T58.13** **Toxic effect of carbon monoxide from utility gas, assault**

　● **T58.14** **Toxic effect of carbon monoxide from utility gas, undetermined**

● **T58.2** **Toxic effect of carbon monoxide from incomplete combustion of other domestic fuels**

> Toxic effect of carbon monoxide from incomplete combustion of coal, coke, kerosene, wood

　● **T58.2x** **Toxic effect of carbon monoxide from incomplete combustion of other domestic fuels**

　　● **T58.2x1** **Toxic effect of carbon monoxide from incomplete combustion of other domestic fuels, accidental (unintentional)**

　　● **T58.2x2** **Toxic effect of carbon monoxide from incomplete combustion of other domestic fuels, intentional self-harm**

　　● **T58.2x3** **Toxic effect of carbon monoxide from incomplete combustion of other domestic fuels, assault**

　　● **T58.2x4** **Toxic effect of carbon monoxide from incomplete combustion of other domestic fuels, undetermined**

● **T58.8** **Toxic effect of carbon monoxide from other source**

> Toxic effect of carbon monoxide from blast furnace gas
> Toxic effect of carbon monoxide from fuels in industrial use
> Toxic effect of carbon monoxide from kiln vapor

● **T58.8x** **Toxic effect of carbon monoxide from other source**

　● **T58.8x1** **Toxic effect of carbon monoxide from other source, accidental (unintentional)**

　● **T58.8x2** **Toxic effect of carbon monoxide from other source, intentional self-harm**

　● **T58.8x3** **Toxic effect of carbon monoxide from other source, assault**

　● **T58.8x4** **Toxic effect of carbon monoxide from other source, undetermined**

● **T58.9** **Toxic effect of carbon monoxide from unspecified source**

　● ■ **T58.91** **Toxic effect of carbon monoxide from unspecified source, accidental (unintentional)**

　● ■ **T58.92** **Toxic effect of carbon monoxide from unspecified source, intentional self-harm**

　● ■ **T58.93** **Toxic effect of carbon monoxide from unspecified source, assault**

　● ■ **T58.94** **Toxic effect of carbon monoxide from unspecified source, undetermined**

● **T59** **Toxic effect of other gases, fumes and vapors**

> **Includes** aerosol propellants
>
> **Excludes1** chlorofluorocarbons (T53.5)
>
> The appropriate 7th character is to be added to each code from category T59
>
> | A | initial encounter |
> |---|---|
> | D | subsequent encounter |
> | S | sequela |

● **T59.0** **Toxic effect of nitrogen oxides**

　● **T59.0x** **Toxic effect of nitrogen oxides**

　　● **T59.0x1** **Toxic effect of nitrogen oxides, accidental (unintentional)**

> Toxic effect of nitrogen oxides NOS

　　● **T59.0x2** **Toxic effect of nitrogen oxides, intentional self-harm**

　　● **T59.0x3** **Toxic effect of nitrogen oxides, assault**

　　● **T59.0x4** **Toxic effect of nitrogen oxides, undetermined**

● **T59.1** **Toxic effect of sulfur dioxide**

　● **T59.1x** **Toxic effect of sulfur dioxide**

　　● **T59.1x1** **Toxic effect of sulfur dioxide, accidental (unintentional)**

> Toxic effect of sulfur dioxide NOS

　　● **T59.1x2** **Toxic effect of sulfur dioxide, intentional self-harm**

　　● **T59.1x3** **Toxic effect of sulfur dioxide, assault**

　　● **T59.1x4** **Toxic effect of sulfur dioxide, undetermined**

● **T59.2** **Toxic effect of formaldehyde**

　● **T59.2x** **Toxic effect of formaldehyde**

　　● **T59.2x1** **Toxic effect of formaldehyde, accidental (unintentional)**

> Toxic effect of formaldehyde NOS

　　● **T59.2x2** **Toxic effect of formaldehyde, intentional self-harm**

1592

● Unacceptable First-Listed Diagnosis　　● Use Additional Character(s)　　■ Unspecified　　**OGCR** Official Guidelines for Coding and Reporting

🏥 Complication\Comorbidity　　🏥 Major C\C　　Excludes 1　　Excludes 2　　Includes　　Use additional　　Code first　　Code also

CHAPTER 19 (S00-T98)

● T59.2x3 Toxic effect of formaldehyde, assault

● T59.2x4 Toxic effect of formaldehyde, undetermined

● T59.3 Toxic effect of lacrimogenic gas
   Toxic effect of tear gas

   ● T59.3x Toxic effect of lacrimogenic gas

      ● T59.3x1 Toxic effect of lacrimogenic gas, accidental (unintentional)
         Toxic effect of lacrimogenic gas NOS

      ● T59.3x2 Toxic effect of lacrimogenic gas, intentional self-harm

      ● T59.3x3 Toxic effect of lacrimogenic gas, assault

      ● T59.3x4 Toxic effect of lacrimogenic gas, undetermined

● T59.4 Toxic effect of chlorine gas

   ● T59.4x Toxic effect of chlorine gas

      ● T59.4x1 Toxic effect of chlorine gas, accidental (unintentional)
         Toxic effect of chlorine gas NOS

      ● T59.4x2 Toxic effect of chlorine gas, intentional self-harm

      ● T59.4x3 Toxic effect of chlorine gas, assault

      ● T59.4x4 Toxic effect of chlorine gas, undetermined

● T59.5 Toxic effect of fluorine gas and hydrogen fluoride

   ● T59.5x Toxic effect of fluorine gas and hydrogen fluoride

      ● T59.5x1 Toxic effect of fluorine gas and hydrogen fluoride, accidental (unintentional)
         Toxic effect of fluorine gas and hydrogen fluoride NOS

      ● T59.5x2 Toxic effect of fluorine gas and hydrogen fluoride, intentional self-harm

      ● T59.5x3 Toxic effect of fluorine gas and hydrogen fluoride, assault

      ● T59.5x4 Toxic effect of fluorine gas and hydrogen fluoride, undetermined

● T59.6 Toxic effect of hydrogen sulfide

   ● T59.6x Toxic effect of hydrogen sulfide

      ● T59.6x1 Toxic effect of hydrogen sulfide, accidental (unintentional)
         Toxic effect of hydrogen sulfide NOS

      ● T59.6x2 Toxic effect of hydrogen sulfide, intentional self-harm

      ● T59.6x3 Toxic effect of hydrogen sulfide, assault

      ● T59.6x4 Toxic effect of hydrogen sulfide, undetermined

● T59.7 Toxic effect of carbon dioxide

   ● T59.7x Toxic effect of carbon dioxide

      ● T59.7x1 Toxic effect of carbon dioxide, accidental (unintentional)
         Toxic effect of carbon dioxide NOS

      ● T59.7x2 Toxic effect of carbon dioxide, intentional self-harm

● T59.7x3 Toxic effect of carbon dioxide, assault

● T59.7x4 Toxic effect of carbon dioxide, undetermined

● T59.8 Toxic effect of other specified gases, fumes and vapors

   ● T59.81 Toxic effect of smoke
      Smoke inhalation

      Excludes2   toxic effect of cigarrette (tobacco) smoke (T65.22-)

      ● T59.811 Toxic effect of smoke, accidental (unintentional)
         Toxic effect of smoke NOS

      ● T59.812 Toxic effect of smoke, intentional self-harm

      ● T59.813 Toxic effect of smoke, assault

      ● T59.814 Toxic effect of smoke, undetermined

   ● T59.89 Toxic effect of other specified gases, fumes and vapors

      ● ■ T59.891 Toxic effect of other specified gases, fumes and vapors, accidental (unintentional)

      ● ■ T59.892 Toxic effect of other specified gases, fumes and vapors, intentional self-harm

      ● ■ T59.893 Toxic effect of other specified gases, fumes and vapors, assault

      ● ■ T59.894 Toxic effect of other specified gases, fumes and vapors, undetermined

● T59.9 Toxic effect of unspecified gases, fumes and vapors

   ● T59.91 Toxic effect of unspecified gases, fumes and vapors, accidental (unintentional)

   ● T59.92 Toxic effect of unspecified gases, fumes and vapors, intentional self-harm

   ● T59.93 Toxic effect of unspecified gases, fumes and vapors, assault

   ● T59.94 Toxic effect of unspecified gases, fumes and vapors, undetermined

● T60 Toxic effect of pesticides

   Includes   toxic effect of wood preservatives

   The appropriate 7th character is to be added to each code from category T60

A	initial encounter
D	subsequent encounter
S	sequela

● T60.0 Toxic effect of organophosphate and carbamate insecticides

   ● T60.0x Toxic effect of organophosphate and carbamate insecticides

      ● T60.0x1 Toxic effect of organophosphate and carbamate insecticides, accidental (unintentional)
         Toxic effect of organophosphate and carbamate insecticides NOS

      ● T60.0x2 Toxic effect of organophosphate and carbamate insecticides, intentional self-harm

      ● T60.0x3 Toxic effect of organophosphate and carbamate insecticides, assault

● Unacceptable First-Listed Diagnosis   ● Use Additional Character(s)   ■ Unspecified   OGCR Official Guidelines for Coding and Reporting

🕭 Complication\Comorbidity   🕭 Major C\C   Excludes 1   Excludes 2   Includes   Use additional   Code first   Code also

CHAPTER 19 (S00-T98)

1593

● T60.0x4　Toxic effect of organophosphate and carbamate insecticides, undetermined
● T60.1　Toxic effect of halogenated insecticides
　Excludes1　chlorinated hydrocarbon (T53.-)
● T60.1x　Toxic effect of halogenated insecticides
● T60.1x1　Toxic effect of halogenated insecticides, accidental (unintentional)
　　Toxic effect of halogenated insecticides NOS
● T60.1x2　Toxic effect of halogenated insecticides, intentional self-harm
● T60.1x3　Toxic effect of halogenated insecticides, assault
● T60.1x4　Toxic effect of halogenated insecticides, undetermined
● T60.2　Toxic effect of other insecticides
● T60.2x　Toxic effect of other insecticides
● T60.21　Toxic effect of other insecticides, accidental (unintentional)
　　Toxic effect of other insecticides NOS
● T60.22　Toxic effect of other insecticides, intentional self-harm
● T60.23　Toxic effect of other insecticides, assault
● T60.24　Toxic effect of other insecticides, undetermined
● T60.3　Toxic effect of herbicides and fungicides
● T60.3x　Toxic effect of herbicides and fungicides
● T60.3x1　Toxic effect of herbicides and fungicides, accidental (unintentional)
　　Toxic effect of herbicides and fungicides NOS
● T60.3x2　Toxic effect of herbicides and fungicides, intentional self-harm
● T60.3x3　Toxic effect of herbicides and fungicides, assault
● T60.3x4　Toxic effect of herbicides and fungicides, undetermined
● T60.4　Toxic effect of rodenticides
　Excludes1　strychnine and its salts (T65.1) thallium (T56.81-)
● T60.4x　Toxic effect of rodenticides
● T60.4x1　Toxic effect of rodenticides, accidental (unintentional)
　　Toxic effect of rodenticides NOS
● T60.4x2　Toxic effect of rodenticides, intentional self-harm
● T60.4x3　Toxic effect of rodenticides, assault
● T60.4x4　Toxic effect of rodenticides, undetermined
● T60.8　Toxic effect of other pesticides
● T60.8x　Toxic effect of other pesticides
● T60.8x1　Toxic effect of other pesticides, accidental (unintentional)
　　Toxic effect of other pesticides NOS
● T60.8x2　Toxic effect of other pesticides, intentional self-harm

● T60.8x3　Toxic effect of other pesticides, assault
● T60.8x4　Toxic effect of other pesticides, undetermined
● T60.9　Toxic effect of unspecified pesticide
● T60.91　Toxic effect of unspecified pesticide, accidental (unintentional)
● T60.92　Toxic effect of unspecified pesticide, intentional self-harm
● T60.93　Toxic effect of unspecified pesticide, assault
● T60.94　Toxic effect of unspecified pesticide, undetermined
● T61　Toxic effect of noxious substances eaten as seafood
　Excludes1　allergic reaction to food, such as:
　　anaphylactic shock (reaction) due to adverse food reaction (T78.0-)
　　dermatitis (L23.6, L25.4, L27.2)
　　gastroenteritis (noninfective) (K52.2)
　　anaphylactic shock (T78.02, T78.05)
　　bacterial foodborne intoxications (A05.-)
　　toxic effect of food contaminants, such as:
　　aflatoxin and other mycotoxins (T64)
　　cyanides (T65.0-)
　　harmful algae bloom (T65.82-)
　　hydrogen cyanide (T57.3-)
　　mercury (T56.1-)
　　red tide (T65.82-)
　The appropriate 7th character is to be added to each code from category T61
　A　initial encounter
　D　subsequent encounter
　S　sequela
● T61.0　Ciguatera fish poisoning
● T61.01　Ciguatera fish poisoning, accidental (unintentional)
● T61.02　Ciguatera fish poisoning, intentional self-harm
● T61.03　Ciguatera fish poisoning, assault
● T61.04　Ciguatera fish poisoning, undetermined
● T61.1　Scombroid fish poisoning
　Histamine-like syndrome
● T61.11　Scombroid fish poisoning, accidental (unintentional)
● T61.12　Scombroid fish poisoning, intentional self-harm
● T61.13　Scombroid fish poisoning, assault
● T61.14　Scombroid fish poisoning, undetermined
● T61.7　Other fish and shellfish poisoning
● T61.77　Other fish poisoning
● T61.771　Other fish poisoning, accidental (unintentional)
● T61.772　Other fish poisoning, intentional self-harm
● T61.773　Other fish poisoning, assault
● T61.774　Other fish poisoning, undetermined
● T61.78　Other shellfish poisoning
● T61.781　Other shellfish poisoning, accidental (unintentional)
● T61.782　Other shellfish poisoning, intentional self-harm

● Unacceptable First-Listed Diagnosis　● Use Additional Character(s)　■ Unspecified　OGCR Official Guidelines for Coding and Reporting
Complication\Comorbidity　Major C\C　Excludes 1　Excludes 2　Includes　Use additional　Code first　Code also

● **T61.783**   Other shellfish poisoning, assault

● **T61.784**   Other shellfish poisoning, undetermined

● **T61.8**   Toxic effect of other seafood

   ● **T61.8x**   Toxic effect of other seafood

     ● **T61.8x1**   Toxic effect of other seafood, accidental (unintentional)

     ● **T61.8x2**   Toxic effect of other seafood, intentional self-harm

     ● **T61.8x3**   Toxic effect of other seafood, assault

     ● **T61.8x4**   Toxic effect of other seafood, undetermined

● **T61.9**   Toxic effect of unspecified seafood

   ● ■ **T61.91**   Toxic effect of unspecified seafood, accidental (unintentional)

   ● ■ **T61.92**   Toxic effect of unspecified seafood, intentional self-harm

   ● ■ **T61.93**   Toxic effect of unspecified seafood, assault

   ● ■ **T61.94**   Toxic effect of unspecified seafood, undetermined

● **T62**   Toxic effect of other noxious substances eaten as food

Excludes1	allergic reaction to food, such as:

     anaphylactic shock (reaction) due to adverse food reaction (T78.0-)
     dermatitis (L23.6, L25.4, L27.2)
     gastroenteritis (noninfective) (K52.2)
     bacterial food borne intoxications (A05.-)
     toxic effect of food contaminants, such as:
     aflatoxin and other mycotoxins (T64)
     cyanides (T65.0-)
     hydrogen cyanide (T57.3-)
     mercury (T56.1-)

The appropriate 7th character is to be added to each code from category T62

   A   initial encounter
   D   subsequent encounter
   S   sequela

● **T62.0**   Toxic effect of ingested mushrooms

   ● **T62.0x**   Toxic effect of ingested mushrooms

     ● **T62.0x1**   Toxic effect of ingested mushrooms, accidental (unintentional)
       Toxic effect of ingested mushrooms NOS

     ● **T62.0x2**   Toxic effect of ingested mushrooms, intentional self-harm

     ● **T62.0x3**   Toxic effect of ingested mushrooms, assault

     ● **T62.0x4**   Toxic effect of ingested mushrooms, undetermined

● **T62.1**   Toxic effect of ingested berries

   ● **T62.1x**   Toxic effect of ingested berries

     ● **T62.1x1**   Toxic effect of ingested berries, accidental (unintentional)
       Toxic effect of ingested berries NOS

     ● **T62.1x2**   Toxic effect of ingested berries, intentional self-harm

     ● **T62.1x3**   Toxic effect of ingested berries, assault

     ● **T62.1x4**   Toxic effect of ingested berries, undetermined

● **T62.2**   Toxic effect of other ingested (parts of) plant(s)

   ● **T62.2x**   Toxic effect of other ingested (parts of) plant(s)

     ● **T62.2x1**   Toxic effect of other ingested (parts of) plant(s), accidental (unintentional)
       Toxic effect of other ingested (parts of) plant(s) NOS

     ● **T62.2x2**   Toxic effect of other ingested (parts of) plant(s), intentional self-harm

     ● **T62.2x3**   Toxic effect of other ingested (parts of) plant(s), assault

     ● **T62.2x4**   Toxic effect of other ingested (parts of) plant(s), undetermined

● **T62.8**   Toxic effect of other specified noxious substances eaten as food

   ● **T62.8x**   Toxic effect of other specified noxious substances eaten as food

     ● **T62.8x1**   Toxic effect of other specified noxious substances eaten as food, accidental (unintentional)
       Toxic effect of other specified noxious substances eaten as food NOS

     ● **T62.8x2**   Toxic effect of other specified noxious substances eaten as food, intentional self-harm

     ● **T62.8x3**   Toxic effect of other specified noxious substances eaten as food, assault

     ● **T62.8x4**   Toxic effect of other specified noxious substances eaten as food, undetermined

● **T62.9**   Toxic effect of unspecified noxious substance eaten as food

   ● ■ **T62.91**   Toxic effect of unspecified noxious substance eaten as food, accidental (unintentional)
       Toxic effect of unspecified noxious substance eaten as food NOS

   ● ■ **T62.92**   Toxic effect of unspecified noxious substance eaten as food, intentional self-harm

   ● ■ **T62.93**   Toxic effect of unspecified noxious substance eaten as food, assault

   ● ■ **T62.94**   Toxic effect of unspecified noxious substance eaten as food, undetermined

● **T63**   Toxic effect of contact with venomous animals and plants

Includes	bite or touch of venomous animal pricked or stuck by thorn or leaf

Excludes2	ingestion of toxic animal or plant (T61.-, T62.-)

The appropriate 7th character is to be added to each code from category T63

   A   initial encounter
   D   subsequent encounter
   S   sequela

● **T63.0**   Toxic effect of snake venom

   ● **T63.00**   Toxic effect of unspecified snake venom

     ● ■ **T63.001**   Toxic effect of unspecified snake venom, accidental (unintentional)
       Toxic effect of unspecified snake venom NOS

     ● ■ **T63.002**   Toxic effect of unspecified snake venom, intentional self-harm

● Unacceptable First-Listed Diagnosis   ● Use Additional Character(s)   ■ Unspecified   **OGCR** Official Guidelines for Coding and Reporting

🔗 Complication\Comorbidity   🔗 Major C\C   Excludes 1   Excludes 2   Includes   Use additional   Code first   Code also

1595

CHAPTER 19 (S00-T98)

● ▪ **T63.003** Toxic effect of unspecified snake venom, assault

● ▪ **T63.004** Toxic effect of unspecified snake venom, undetermined

● **T63.01** Toxic effect of rattlesnake venom

  ● **T63.011** Toxic effect of rattlesnake venom, accidental (unintentional)
                        Toxic effect of rattlesnake venom NOS

  ● **T63.012** Toxic effect of rattlesnake venom, intentional self-harm

  ● **T63.013** Toxic effect of rattlesnake venom, assault

  ● **T63.014** Toxic effect of rattlesnake venom, undetermined

● **T63.02** Toxic effect of coral snake venom

  ● **T63.021** Toxic effect of coral snake venom, accidental (unintentional)
                        Toxic effect of coral snake venom NOS

  ● **T63.022** Toxic effect of coral snake venom, intentional self-harm

  ● **T63.023** Toxic effect of coral snake venom, assault

  ● **T63.024** Toxic effect of coral snake venom, undetermined

● **T63.03** Toxic effect of taipan venom

  ● **T63.031** Toxic effect of taipan venom, accidental (unintentional)
                        Toxic effect of taipan venom NOS

  ● **T63.032** Toxic effect of taipan venom, intentional self-harm

  ● **T63.033** Toxic effect of taipan venom, assault

  ● **T63.034** Toxic effect of taipan venom, undetermined

● **T63.04** Toxic effect of cobra venom

  ● **T63.041** Toxic effect of cobra venom, accidental (unintentional)
                        Toxic effect of cobra venom NOS

  ● **T63.042** Toxic effect of cobra venom, intentional self-harm

  ● **T63.043** Toxic effect of cobra venom, assault

  ● **T63.044** Toxic effect of cobra venom, undetermined

● **T63.06** Toxic effect of venom of other North and South American snake

  ● **T63.061** Toxic effect of venom of other North and South American snake, accidental (unintentional)
                        Toxic effect of venom of other North and South American snake NOS

  ● **T63.062** Toxic effect of venom of other North and South American snake, intentional self-harm

  ● **T63.063** Toxic effect of venom of other North and South American snake, assault

  ● **T63.064** Toxic effect of venom of other North and South American snake, undetermined

● **T63.07** Toxic effect of venom of other Australian snake

  ● **T63.071** Toxic effect of venom of other Australian snake, accidental (unintentional)
                        Toxic effect of venom of other Australian snake NOS

  ● **T63.072** Toxic effect of venom of other Australian snake, intentional self-harm

  ● **T63.073** Toxic effect of venom of other Australian snake, assault

  ● **T63.074** Toxic effect of venom of other Australian snake, undetermined

● **T63.08** Toxic effect of venom of other African and Asian snake

  ● **T63.081** Toxic effect of venom of other African and Asian snake, accidental (unintentional)
                        Toxic effect of venom of other African and Asian snake NOS

  ● **T63.082** Toxic effect of venom of other African and Asian snake, intentional self-harm

  ● **T63.083** Toxic effect of venom of other African and Asian snake, assault

  ● **T63.084** Toxic effect of venom of other African and Asian snake, undetermined

● **T63.09** Toxic effect of venom of other snake

  ● **T63.091** Toxic effect of venom of other snake, accidental (unintentional)
                        Toxic effect of venom of other snake NOS

  ● **T63.092** Toxic effect of venom of other snake, intentional self-harm

  ● **T63.093** Toxic effect of venom of other snake, assault

  ● **T63.094** Toxic effect of venom of other snake, undetermined

● **T63.1** Toxic effect of venom of other reptiles

  ● **T63.11** Toxic effect of venom of gila monster

    ● **T63.111** Toxic effect of venom of gila monster, accidental (unintentional)
                          Toxic effect of venom of gila monster NOS

    ● **T63.112** Toxic effect of venom of gila monster, intentional self-harm

    ● **T63.113** Toxic effect of venom of gila monster, assault

    ● **T63.114** Toxic effect of venom of gila monster, undetermined

  ● **T63.12** Toxic effect of venom of other venomous lizard

    ● **T63.121** Toxic effect of venom of other venomous lizard, accidental (unintentional)
                          Toxic effect of venom of other venomous lizard NOS

    ● **T63.122** Toxic effect of venom of other venomous lizard, intentional self-harm

CHAPTER 19 (S00-T98)

1596

● Unacceptable First-Listed Diagnosis   ● Use Additional Character(s)   ▪ Unspecified   **OGCR** Official Guidelines for Coding and Reporting

🗂 Complication\Comorbidity   🗂 Major C\C | Excludes 1 | | Excludes 2 | Includes   Use additional   Code first   Code also

● T63.123 Toxic effect of venom of other venomous lizard, assault

● T63.124 Toxic effect of venom of other venomous lizard, undetermined

● T63.19 Toxic effect of venom of other reptiles

● T63.191 Toxic effect of venom of other reptiles, accidental (unintentional)
  Toxic effect of venom of other reptiles NOS

● T63.192 Toxic effect of venom of other reptiles, intentional self-harm

● T63.193 Toxic effect of venom of other reptiles, assault

● T63.194 Toxic effect of venom of other reptiles, undetermined

● T63.2 Toxic effect of venom of scorpion

● T63.2x Toxic effect of venom of scorpion

● T63.2x1 Toxic effect of venom of scorpion, accidental (unintentional)
  Toxic effect of venom of scorpion NOS

● T63.2x2 Toxic effect of venom of scorpion, intentional self-harm

● T63.2x3 Toxic effect of venom of scorpion, assault

● T63.2x4 Toxic effect of venom of scorpion, undetermined

● T63.3 Toxic effect of venom of spider

● T63.30 Toxic effect of unspecified spider venom

● ▨ T63.301 Toxic effect of unspecified spider venom, accidental (unintentional)

● ▨ T63.302 Toxic effect of unspecified spider venom, intentional self-harm

● ▨ T63.303 Toxic effect of unspecified spider venom, assault

● ▨ T63.304 Toxic effect of unspecified spider venom, undetermined

● T63.31 Toxic effect of venom of black widow spider

● T63.311 Toxic effect of venom of black widow spider, accidental (unintentional)

● T63.312 Toxic effect of venom of black widow spider, intentional self-harm

● T63.313 Toxic effect of venom of black widow spider, assault

● T63.314 Toxic effect of venom of black widow spider, undetermined

● T63.32 Toxic effect of venom of tarantula

● T63.321 Toxic effect of venom of tarantula, accidental (unintentional)

● T63.322 Toxic effect of venom of tarantula, intentional self-harm

● T63.323 Toxic effect of venom of tarantula, assault

● T63.324 Toxic effect of venom of tarantula, undetermined

● T63.33 Toxic effect of venom of brown recluse spider

● T63.331 Toxic effect of venom of brown recluse spider, accidental (unintentional)

● T63.332 Toxic effect of venom of brown recluse spider, intentional self-harm

● T63.333 Toxic effect of venom of brown recluse spider, assault

● T63.334 Toxic effect of venom of brown recluse spider, undetermined

● T63.39 Toxic effect of venom of other spider

● T63.391 Toxic effect of venom of other spider, accidental (unintentional)

● T63.392 Toxic effect of venom of other spider, intentional self-harm

● T63.393 Toxic effect of venom of other spider, assault

● T63.394 Toxic effect of venom of other spider, undetermined

● T63.4 Toxic effect of venom of other arthropods

● T63.41 Toxic effect of venom of centipedes and venomous millipedes

● T63.411 Toxic effect of venom of centipedes and venomous millipedes, accidental (unintentional)

● T63.412 Toxic effect of venom of centipedes and venomous millipedes, intentional self-harm

● T63.413 Toxic effect of venom of centipedes and venomous millipedes, assault

● T63.414 Toxic effect of venom of centipedes and venomous millipedes, undetermined

● T63.42 Toxic effect of venom of ants

● T63.421 Toxic effect of venom of ants, accidental (unintentional)

● T63.422 Toxic effect of venom of ants, intentional self-harm

● T63.423 Toxic effect of venom of ants, assault

● T63.424 Toxic effect of venom of ants, undetermined

● T63.43 Toxic effect of venom of caterpillars

● T63.431 Toxic effect of venom of caterpillars, accidental (unintentional)

● T63.432 Toxic effect of venom of caterpillars, intentional self-harm

● T63.433 Toxic effect of venom of caterpillars, assault

● T63.434 Toxic effect of venom of caterpillars, undetermined

● T63.44 Toxic effect of venom of bees

● T63.441 Toxic effect of venom of bees, accidental (unintentional)

● T63.442 Toxic effect of venom of bees, intentional self-harm

● T63.443 Toxic effect of venom of bees, assault

● T63.444 Toxic effect of venom of bees, undetermined

● T63.45 Toxic effect of venom of hornets

● T63.451 Toxic effect of venom of hornets, accidental (unintentional)

● Unacceptable First-Listed Diagnosis   ● Use Additional Character(s)   ▨ Unspecified   OGCR Official Guidelines for Coding and Reporting

🅒 Complication\Comorbidity   🅜 Major C\C   Excludes 1   Excludes 2   Includes   Use additional   Code first   Code also

1597

- ● T63.452   Toxic effect of venom of hornets, intentional self-harm
- ● T63.453   Toxic effect of venom of hornets, assault
- ● T63.454   Toxic effect of venom of hornets, undetermined
- ● T63.46   Toxic effect of venom of wasps
  Toxic effect of yellow jacket
  - ● T63.461   Toxic effect of venom of wasps, accidental (unintentional)
  - ● T63.462   Toxic effect of venom of wasps, intentional self-harm
  - ● T63.463   Toxic effect of venom of wasps, assault
  - ● T63.464   Toxic effect of venom of wasps, undetermined
- ● T63.48   Toxic effect of venom of other arthropod
  - ● T63.481   Toxic effect of venom of other arthropod, accidental (unintentional)
  - ● T63.482   Toxic effect of venom of other arthropod, intentional self-harm
  - ● T63.483   Toxic effect of venom of other arthropod, assault
  - ● T63.484   Toxic effect of venom of other arthropod, undetermined
- ● T63.5   Toxic effect of contact with venomous fish
  - **Excludes2**   poisoning by ingestion of fish (T61-)
  - ● T63.51   Toxic effect of contact with stingray
    - ● T63.511   Toxic effect of contact with stingray, accidental (unintentional)
    - ● T63.512   Toxic effect of contact with stingray, intentional self-harm
    - ● T63.513   Toxic effect of contact with stingray, assault
    - ● T63.514   Toxic effect of contact with stingray, undetermined
  - ● T63.59   Toxic effect of contact with other venomous fish
    - ● T63.591   Toxic effect of contact with other venomous fish, accidental (unintentional)
    - ● T63.592   Toxic effect of contact with other venomous fish, intentional self-harm
    - ● T63.593   Toxic effect of contact with other venomous fish, assault
    - ● T63.594   Toxic effect of contact with other venomous fish, undetermined
- ● T63.6   Toxic effect of contact with other venomous marine animals
  - **Excludes1**   sea-snake venom (T63.09)
  - **Excludes2**   poisoning by ingestion of shellfish (T61.72)
  - ● T63.61   Toxic effect of contact with Portugese Man-o-war
    Toxic effect of contact with bluebottle
    - ● T63.611   Toxic effect of contact with Portugese Man-o-war, accidental (unintentional)
    - ● T63.612   Toxic effect of contact with Portugese Man-o-war, self-harm

- ● T63.613   Toxic effect of contact with Portugese Man-o-war, assault
- ● T63.614   Toxic effect of contact with Portugese Man-o-war, undetermined
- ● T63.62   Toxic effect of contact with other jellyfish
  - ● T63.621   Toxic effect of contact with other jellyfish, accidental (unintentional)
  - ● T63.622   Toxic effect of contact with other jellyfish, intentional self-harm
  - ● T63.623   Toxic effect of contact with other jellyfish, assault
  - ● T63.624   Toxic effect of contact with other jellyfish, undetermined
- ● T63.63   Toxic effect of contact with sea anemone
  - ● T63.631   Toxic effect of contact with sea anemone, accidental (unintentional)
  - ● T63.632   Toxic effect of contact with sea anemone, intentional self-harm
  - ● T63.633   Toxic effect of contact with sea anemone, assault
  - ● T63.634   Toxic effect of contact with sea anemone, undetermined
- ● T63.69   Toxic effect of contact with other venomous marine animals
  - ● T63.691   Toxic effect of contact with other venomous marine animals, accidental (unintentional)
  - ● T63.692   Toxic effect of contact with other venomous marine animals, intentional self-harm
  - ● T63.693   Toxic effect of contact with other venomous marine animals, assault
  - ● T63.694   Toxic effect of contact with other venomous marine animals, undetermined
- ● T63.7   Toxic effect of contact with venomous plant
  - ● T63.71   Toxic effect of contact with venomous marine plant
    - ● T63.711   Toxic effect of contact with venomous marine plant, accidental (unintentional)
    - ● T63.712   Toxic effect of contact with venomous marine plant, intentional self-harm
    - ● T63.713   Toxic effect of contact with venomous marine plant, assault
    - ● T63.714   Toxic effect of contact with venomous marine plant, undetermined
  - ● T63.79   Toxic effect of contact with other venomous plant
    - ● T63.791   Toxic effect of contact with other venomous plant, accidental (unintentional)
    - ● T63.792   Toxic effect of contact with other venomous plant, intentional self-harm
    - ● T63.793   Toxic effect of contact with other venomous plant, assault
    - ● T63.794   Toxic effect of contact with other venomous plant, undetermined

CHAPTER 19 (S00-T98)

● Unacceptable First-Listed Diagnosis   ● Use Additional Character(s)   ▪ Unspecified   **OGCR** Official Guidelines for Coding and Reporting
🦠 Complication\Comorbidity   🦠 Major C\C   Excludes 1   Excludes 2   Includes   Use additional   Code first   Code also

● T63.8   Toxic effect of contact with other venomous animals

   ● T63.81   Toxic effect of contact with venomous frog

       | Excludes1 | contact with nonvenomous frog (W62.0)

      ● T63.811   Toxic effect of contact with venomous frog, accidental (unintentional)

      ● T63.812   Toxic effect of contact with venomous frog, intentional self-harm

      ● T63.813   Toxic effect of contact with venomous frog, assault

      ● T63.814   Toxic effect of contact with venomous frog, undetermined

   ● T63.82   Toxic effect of contact with venomous toad

       | Excludes1 | contact with nonvenomous toad (W62.1)

      ● T63.821   Toxic effect of contact with venomous toad, accidental (unintentional)

      ● T63.822   Toxic effect of contact with venomous toad, intentional self-harm

      ● T63.823   Toxic effect of contact with venomous toad, assault

      ● T63.824   Toxic effect of contact with venomous toad, undetermined

   ● T63.83   Toxic effect of contact with other venomous amphibian

       | Excludes1 | contact with nonvenomous amphibian (W62.9)

      ● T63.831   Toxic effect of contact with other venomous amphibian, accidental (unintentional)

      ● T63.832   Toxic effect of contact with other venomous amphibian, intentional self-harm

      ● T63.833   Toxic effect of contact with other venomous amphibian, assault

      ● T63.834   Toxic effect of contact with other venomous amphibian, undetermined

   ● T63.89   Toxic effect of contact with other venomous animals

      ● T63.891   Toxic effect of contact with other venomous animals, accidental (unintentional)

      ● T63.892   Toxic effect of contact with other venomous animals, intentional self-harm

      ● T63.893   Toxic effect of contact with other venomous animals, assault

      ● T63.894   Toxic effect of contact with other venomous animals, undetermined

● T63.9   Toxic effect of contact with unspecified venomous animal

   ● ■ T63.91   Toxic effect of contact with unspecified venomous animal, accidental (unintentional)

   ● ■ T63.92   Toxic effect of contact with unspecified venomous animal, intentional self-harm

   ● ■ T63.93   Toxic effect of contact with unspecified venomous animal, assault

   ● ■ T63.94   Toxic effect of contact with unspecified venomous animal, undetermined

● T64   Toxic effect of aflatoxin and other mycotoxin food contaminants

     The appropriate 7th character is to be added to each code from category T64

       | A   initial encounter |
       | D   subsequent encounter |
       | S   sequela |

   ● T64.0   Toxic effect of aflatoxin

      ● T64.01   Toxic effect of aflatoxin, accidental (unintentional)

      ● T64.02   Toxic effect of aflatoxin, intentional self-harm

      ● T64.03   Toxic effect of aflatoxin, assault

      ● T64.04   Toxic effect of aflatoxin, undetermined

   ● T64.8   Toxic effect of other mycotoxin food contaminants

      ● T64.81   Toxic effect of other mycotoxin food contaminants, accidental (unintentional)

      ● T64.82   Toxic effect of other mycotoxin food contaminants, intentional self-harm

      ● T64.83   Toxic effect of other mycotoxin food contaminants, assault

      ● T64.84   Toxic effect of other mycotoxin food contaminants, undetermined

● T65   Toxic effect of other and unspecified substances

     The appropriate 7th character is to be added to each code from category T65

       | A   initial encounter |
       | D   subsequent encounter |
       | S   sequela |

   ● T65.0   Toxic effect of cyanides

       | Excludes1 | hydrogen cyanide (T57.3-)

      ● T65.0x   Toxic effect of cyanides

         ● T65.0x1   Toxic effect of cyanides, accidental (unintentional)
              Toxic effect of cyanides NOS

         ● T65.0x2   Toxic effect of cyanides, intentional self-harm

         ● T65.0x3   Toxic effect of cyanides, assault

         ● T65.0x4   Toxic effect of cyanides, undetermined

   ● T65.1   Toxic effect of strychnine and its salts

      ● T65.1x   Toxic effect of strychnine and its salts

         ● T65.1x1   Toxic effect of strychnine and its salts, accidental (unintentional)
              Toxic effect of strychnine and its salts NOS

         ● T65.1x2   Toxic effect of strychnine and its salts, intentional self-harm

         ● T65.1x3   Toxic effect of strychnine and its salts, assault

         ● T65.1x4   Toxic effect of strychnine and its salts, undetermined

   ● T65.2   Toxic effect of tobacco and nicotine

       | Excludes2 | nicotine dependence (F17.-)

      ● T65.21   Toxic effect of chewing tobacco

         ● T65.211   Toxic effect of chewing tobacco, accidental (unintentional)
              Toxic effect of chewing tobacco NOS

●   Unacceptable First-Listed Diagnosis   ●   Use Additional Character(s)   ■   Unspecified   **OGCR**   Official Guidelines for Coding and Reporting

🅒 Complication\Comorbidity   🅒 Major C\C | Excludes 1 | | Excludes 2 | Includes   Use additional   Code first   Code also   **1599**

CHAPTER 19 (S00-T98)

● T65.212 Toxic effect of chewing tobacco, intentional self-harm

● T65.213 Toxic effect of chewing tobacco, assault

● T65.214 Toxic effect of chewing tobacco, undetermined

● T65.22 Toxic effect of tobacco cigarettes
Toxic effect of tobacco smoke

Use additional code for exposure to second hand tobacco smoke (Z57.31, Z77.22)

● T65.221 Toxic effect of tobacco cigarettes, accidental (unintentional)
Toxic effect of tobacco cigarettes NOS

● T65.222 Toxic effect of tobacco cigarettes, intentional self-harm

● T65.223 Toxic effect of tobacco cigarettes, assault

● T65.224 Toxic effect of tobacco cigarettes, undetermined

● T65.29 Toxic effect of other tobacco and nicotine

● T65.291 Toxic effect of other tobacco and nicotine, accidental (unintentional)
Toxic effect of other tobacco and nicotine NOS

● T65.292 Toxic effect of other tobacco and nicotine, intentional self-harm

● T65.293 Toxic effect of other tobacco and nicotine, assault

● T65.294 Toxic effect of other tobacco and nicotine, undetermined

● T65.3 Toxic effect of nitroderivatives and aminoderivatives of benzene and its homologues
Toxic effect of anilin [benzenamine]
Toxic effect of nitrobenzene
Toxic effect of trinitrotoluene

● T65.3x Toxic effect of nitroderivatives and aminoderivatives of benzene and its homologues

● T65.3x1 Toxic effect of nitroderivatives and aminoderivatives of benzene and its homologues, accidental (unintentional)
Toxic effect of nitroderivatives and aminoderivatives of benzene and its homologues NOS

● T65.3x2 Toxic effect of nitroderivatives and aminoderivatives of benzene and its homologues, intentional self-harm

● T65.3x3 Toxic effect of nitroderivatives and aminoderivatives of benzene and its homologues, assault

● T65.3x4 Toxic effect of nitroderivatives and aminoderivatives of benzene and its homologues, undetermined

● T65.4 Toxic effect of carbon disulfide

● T65.4x Toxic effect of carbon disulfide

● T65.4x1 Toxic effect of carbon disulfide, accidental (unintentional)
Toxic effect of carbon disulfide NOS

● T65.4x2 Toxic effect of carbon disulfide, intentional self-harm

● T65.4x3 Toxic effect of carbon disulfide, assault

● T65.4x4 Toxic effect of carbon disulfide, undetermined

● T65.5 Toxic effect of nitroglycerin and other nitric acids and esters
Toxic effect of 1,2,3-Propanetriol trinitrate

● T65.5x Toxic effect of nitroglycerin and other nitric acids and esters

● T65.5x1 Toxic effect of nitroglycerin and other nitric acids and esters, accidental (unintentional)
Toxic effect of nitroglycerin and other nitric acids and esters NOS

● T65.5x2 Toxic effect of nitroglycerin and other nitric acids and esters, intentional self-harm

● T65.5x3 Toxic effect of nitroglycerin and other nitric acids and esters, assault

● T65.5x4 Toxic effect of nitroglycerin and other nitric acids and esters, undetermined

● T65.6 Toxic effect of paints and dyes, not elsewhere classified

● T65.6x Toxic effect of paints and dyes, not elsewhere classified

● T65.6x1 Toxic effect of paints and dyes, not elsewhere classified, accidental (unintentional)
Toxic effect of paints and dyes NOS

● T65.6x2 Toxic effect of paints and dyes, not elsewhere classified, intentional self-harm

● T65.6x3 Toxic effect of paints and dyes, not elsewhere classified, assault

● T65.6x4 Toxic effect of paints and dyes, not elsewhere classified, undetermined

● T65.8 Toxic effect of other specified substances

● T65.81 Toxic effect of latex

● T65.811 Toxic effect of latex, accidental (unintentional)
Toxic effect of latex NOS

● T65.812 Toxic effect of latex, intentional self-harm

● T65.813 Toxic effect of latex, assault

● T65.814 Toxic effect of latex, undetermined

● T65.82 Toxic effect of harmful algae and algae toxins
Toxic effect of (harmful) algae bloom NOS
Toxic effect of blue-green algae bloom
Toxic effect of brown tide
Toxic effect of cyanobacteria bloom
Toxic effect of Florida red tide
Toxic effect of pfieteria piscicida
Toxic effect of red tide

● **T65.821**   **Toxic effect of harmful algae and algae toxins, accidental (unintentional)**
     Toxic effect of harmful algae and algae toxins NOS

● **T65.822**   **Toxic effect of harmful algae and algae toxins, intentional self-harm**

● **T65.823**   **Toxic effect of harmful algae and algae toxins, assault**

● **T65.824**   **Toxic effect of harmful algae and algae toxins, undetermined**

● **T65.83**   **Toxic effect of fiberglass**

● **T65.831**   **Toxic effect of fiberglass, accidental (unintentional)**
     Toxic effect of fiberglass NOS

● **T65.832**   **Toxic effect of fiberglass, intentional self-harm**

● **T65.833**   **Toxic effect of fiberglass, assault**

● **T65.834**   **Toxic effect of fiberglass, undetermined**

● **T65.89**   **Toxic effect of other specified substances**

● **T65.891**   **Toxic effect of other specified substances, accidental (unintentional)**
     Toxic effect of other specified substances NOS

● **T65.892**   **Toxic effect of other specified substances, intentional self-harm**

● **T65.893**   **Toxic effect of other specified substances, assault**

● **T65.894**   **Toxic effect of other specified substances, undetermined**

● **T65.9**   **Toxic effect of unspecified substance**

● ■ **T65.91**   **Toxic effect of unspecified substance, accidental (unintentional)**
     Poisoning NOS

● ■ **T65.92**   **Toxic effect of unspecified substance, intentional self-harm**

● ■ **T65.93**   **Toxic effect of unspecified substance, assault**

● ■ **T65.94**   **Toxic effect of unspecified substance, undetermined**

OTHER AND UNSPECIFIED EFFECTS OF EXTERNAL CAUSES (T66-T78)

● ■ **T66 Radiation sickness, unspecified**

   Excludes1   specified adverse effects of radiation, such as:
     burns (T20-T31)
     leukemia (C91-C95)
     radiation:
       gastroenteritis and colitis (K52.0)
       pneumonitis (J70.0)
       related disorders of the skin and subcutaneous tissue (L55-L59)
       sunburn (L55.-)

The appropriate 7th character is to be added to code T66

A	initial encounter
D	subsequent encounter
S	sequela

● **T67   Effects of heat and light**

   Excludes1   erythema [dermatitis] ab igne (L59.0)
     malignant hyperpyrexia due to anesthesia (T88.3)
     radiation-related disorders of the skin and subcutaneous tissue (L55-L59)

   Excludes2   burns (T20-T31)
     sunburn (L55.-)
     sweat disorder due to heat (L74-L75)

The appropriate 7th character is to be added to each code from category T67

A	initial encounter
D	subsequent encounter
S	sequela

● **T67.0**   **Heatstroke and sunstroke A** 🔧
     Heat apoplexy
     Heat pyrexia
     Siriasis
     Thermoplegia

● **T67.1**   **Heat syncope**
     Heat collapse

● **T67.2**   **Heat cramp**

● **T67.3**   **Heat exhaustion, anhydrotic**
     Heat prostration due to water depletion

     Excludes1   heat exhaustion due to salt depletion (T67.4)

● **T67.4**   **Heat exhaustion due to salt depletion**
     Heat prostration due to salt (and water) depletion

● ■ **T67.5**   **Heat exhaustion, unspecified**
     Heat prostration NOS

● **T67.6**   **Heat fatigue, transient**

● **T67.7**   **Heat edema**

● **T67.8**   **Other effects of heat and light**

● ■ **T67.9**   **Effect of heat and light, unspecified**

● **T68   Hypothermia**

   Includes   accidental hypothermia
     hypothermia NOS

   Excludes1   hypothermia following anesthesia (T88.51)
     hypothermia not associated with low environmental temperature (R68.0)
     hypothermia of newborn (P80.-)

   Excludes2   frostbite (T33-T34)

Use additional code to identify source of exposure:
     Exposure to excessive cold of man-made origin (W93)
     Exposure to excessive cold of natural origin (X31)

The appropriate 7th character is to be added to code T68

A	initial encounter
D	subsequent encounter
S	sequela

● **T69   Other effects of reduced temperature**

   Excludes2   frostbite (T33-T34)

Use additional code to identify source of exposure:
     Exposure to excessive cold of man-made origin (W93)
     Exposure to excessive cold of natural origin (X31)

The appropriate 7th character is to be added to each code from category T69

A	initial encounter
D	subsequent encounter
S	sequela

● Unacceptable First-Listed Diagnosis   ● Use Additional Character(s)   ■ Unspecified   **OGCR** Official Guidelines for Coding and Reporting

🔧 Complication\Comorbidity   🔧 Major C\C   Excludes 1   Excludes 2   Includes   Use additional   Code first   Code also   **1601**

- **T69.0**   **Immersion hand and foot**
  - **T69.01**   **Immersion hand**
    - **T69.011**   **Immersion hand, right hand**
    - **T69.012**   **Immersion hand, left hand**
    - **T69.019**   **Immersion hand, unspecified hand**
  - **T69.02**   **Immersion foot**
    Trench foot
    - **T69.021**   **Immersion foot, right foot A** 🦠
    - **T69.022**   **Immersion foot, left foot A** 🦠
    - **T69.029**   **Immersion foot, unspecified foot A** 🦠
- **T69.1**   **Chilblains**
- **T69.8**   **Other specified effects of reduced temperature**
- **T69.9**   **Effect of reduced temperature, unspecified**
- **T70**   **Effects of air pressure and water pressure**
  The appropriate 7th character is to be added to each code from category T70

A	initial encounter
D	subsequent encounter
S	sequela

  - **T70.0**   **Otitic barotrauma**
    Aero-otitis media
    Effects of change in ambient atmospheric pressure or water pressure on ears
  - **T70.1**   **Sinus barotrauma**
    Aerosinusitis
    Effects of change in ambient atmospheric pressure on sinuses
  - **T70.2**   **Other and unspecified effects of high altitude**

    Excludes2   polycythemia due to high altitude (D75.1)

    - **T70.20**   **Unspecified effects of high altitude**
    - **T70.29**   **Other effects of high altitude**
      Alpine sickness
      Anoxia due to high altitude
      Barotrauma NOS
      Hypobaropathy
      Mountain sickness
  - **T70.3**   **Caisson disease [decompression sickness] A** 🦠
    Compressed-air disease
    Diver's palsy or paralysis
  - **T70.4**   **Effects of high-pressure fluids**
    Hydraulic jet injection (industrial)
    Pneumatic jet injection (industrial)
    Traumatic jet injection (industrial)
  - **T70.8**   **Other effects of air pressure and water pressure**
  - **T70.9**   **Effect of air pressure and water pressure, unspecified**

- **T71**   **Asphyxiation**
  Mechanical suffocation
  Traumatic suffocation

  Excludes1   acute respiratory distress (syndrome) (J80)
  anoxia due to high altitude (T70.2)
  asphyxia NOS (R09.01)
  asphyxia from carbon monoxide (T58.-)
  asphyxia from inhalation of food or foreign body (T17.-)
  asphyxia from other gases, fumes and vapors (T59.-)
  respiratory distress (syndrome) in newborn (P22.-)

  The appropriate 7th character is to be added to each code from category T71

A	initial encounter
D	subsequent encounter
S	sequela

  - **T71.1**   **Asphyxiation due to mechanical threat to breathing**
    Suffocation due to mechanical threat to breathing
    - **T71.11**   **Asphyxiation due to smothering under pillow**
      - **T71.111**   **Asphyxiation due to smothering under pillow, accidental A** 🦠
        Asphyxiation due to smothering under pillow NOS
      - **T71.112**   **Asphyxiation due to smothering under pillow, intentional self-harm A** 🦠
      - **T71.113**   **Asphyxiation due to smothering under pillow, assault A** 🦠
      - **T71.114**   **Asphyxiation due to smothering under pillow, undetermined**
    - **T71.12**   **Asphyxiation due to plastic bag**
      - **T71.121**   **Asphyxiation due to plastic bag, accidental A** 🦠
        Asphyxiation due to plastic bag NOS
      - **T71.122**   **Asphyxiation due to plastic bag, intentional self-harm A** 🦠
      - **T71.123**   **Asphyxiation due to plastic bag, assault A** 🦠
      - **T71.124**   **Asphyxiation due to plastic bag, undetermined A** 🦠
    - **T71.13**   **Asphyxiation due to being trapped in bed linens**
      - **T71.131**   **Asphyxiation due to being trapped in bed linens, accidental A** 🦠
        Asphyxiation due to being trapped in bed linens NOS
      - **T71.132**   **Asphyxiation due to being trapped in bed linens, intentional self-harm A** 🦠
      - **T71.133**   **Asphyxiation due to being trapped in bed linens, assault A** 🦠
      - **T71.134**   **Asphyxiation due to being trapped in bed linens, undetermined A** 🦠
    - **T71.14**   **Asphyxiation due to smothering under another person's body (in bed)**
      - **T71.141**   **Asphyxiation due to smothering under another person's body (in bed), accidental A** 🦠
        Asphyxiation due to smothering under another person's body (in bed) NOS

● Unacceptable First-Listed Diagnosis   ● Use Additional Character(s)   ▪ Unspecified   **OGCR** Official Guidelines for Coding and Reporting
🦠 Complication\Comorbidity   🦠 Major C\C   Excludes 1   Excludes 2   Includes   Use additional   Code first   Code also

● **T71.143** Asphyxiation due to smothering under another person's body (in bed), assault A 🝰

● **T71.144** Asphyxiation due to smothering under another person's body (in bed), undetermined A 🝰

● **T71.15** Asphyxiation due to smothering in furniture

● **T71.151** Asphyxiation due to smothering in furniture, accidental A 🝰

● **T71.152** Asphyxiation due to smothering in furniture, intentional self-harm A 🝰

● **T71.153** Asphyxiation due to smothering in furniture, assault A 🝰

● **T71.154** Asphyxiation due to smothering in furniture, undetermined A 🝰

● **T71.16** Asphyxiation due to hanging
Hanging by window shade cord

Use additional code for any associated injuries, such as:
crushing injury of neck (S17.-)
fracture of cervical vertebrae (S12.0-S12.2-)
open wound of neck (S11.-)

● **T71.161** Asphyxiation due to hanging, accidental A 🝰
Asphyxiation due to hanging NOS
Hanging NOS

● **T71.162** Asphyxiation due to hanging, intentional self-harm A 🝰

● **T71.163** Asphyxiation due to hanging, assault A 🝰

● **T71.164** Asphyxiation due to hanging, undetermined A 🝰

● **T71.19** Asphyxiation due to mechanical
Threat to breathing due to other causes

● **T71.191** Asphyxiation due to mechanical threat to breathing due to other causes, accidental A 🝰
Asphyxiation due to other causes NOS

● **T71.192** Asphyxiation due to mechanical threat to breathing due to other causes, intentional self-harm A 🝰

● **T71.193** Asphyxiation due to mechanical threat to breathing due to other causes, assault A 🝰

● **T71.194** Asphyxiation due to mechanical threat to breathing due to other causes, undetermined A 🝰

● **T71.2** Asphyxiation due to systemic oxygen deficiency due to low oxygen content in ambient air
Suffocation due to systemic oxygen deficiency due to low oxygen content in ambient air

● ■ **T71.20** Asphyxiation due to systemic oxygen deficiency due to low oxygen content in ambient air due to unspecified cause A 🝰

● **T71.21** Asphyxiation due to cave-in or falling earth A 🝰

Use additional code for any associated cataclysm (X34-X38)

● **T71.22** Asphyxiation due to being trapped in a car trunk A 🝰

● **T71.221** Asphyxiation due to being trapped in a car trunk, accidental A 🝰

● **T71.222** Asphyxiation due to being trapped in a car trunk, intentional self-harm A 🝰

● **T71.223** Asphyxiation due to being trapped in a car trunk, assault A 🝰

● **T71.224** Asphyxiation due to being trapped in a car trunk, undetermined A 🝰

● **T71.23** Asphyxiation due to being trapped in a (discarded) refrigerator

● **T71.231** Asphyxiation due to being trapped in a (discarded) refrigerator, accidental A 🝰

● **T71.232** Asphyxiation due to being trapped in a (discarded) refrigerator, intentional self-harm A 🝰

● **T71.233** Asphyxiation due to being trapped in a (discarded) refrigerator, assault A 🝰

● **T71.234** Asphyxiation due to being trapped in a (discarded) refrigerator, undetermined A 🝰

● **T71.29** Asphyxiation due to being trapped in other low oxygen environment A 🝰

● ■ **T71.9** Asphyxiation due to unspecified cause A 🝰
Suffocation (by strangulation) due to unspecified cause
Suffocation NOS
Systemic oxygen deficiency due to low oxygen content in ambient air due to unspecified cause
Systemic oxygen deficiency due to mechanical threat to breathing due to unspecified cause
Traumatic asphyxia NOS

● **T73** Effects of other deprivation
The appropriate 7th character is to be added to each code from category T73

A	initial encounter
D	subsequent encounter
S	sequela

● **T73.0** Starvation
Deprivation of food

● **T73.1** Deprivation of water

● **T73.2** Exhaustion due to exposure

● **T73.3** Exhaustion due to excessive exertion
Exhaustion due to overexertion

● **T73.8** Other effects of deprivation

● ■ **T73.9** Effect of deprivation, unspecified

● **T74** Adult and child abuse, neglect and other maltreatment, confirmed

Excludes1 abuse and maltreatment in pregnancy (O94.3-O94.5-)
adult and child maltreatment, suspected (T76.-)

Use additional code, if applicable, to identify any associated current injury

Use additional external cause code to identify perpetrator, if known (Y07.-)

The appropriate 7th character is to be added to each code from category T74

A	initial encounter
D	subsequent encounter
S	sequela

CHAPTER 19 (S00-T98)

● Unacceptable First-Listed Diagnosis   ● Use Additional Character(s)   ■ Unspecified   **OGCR** Official Guidelines for Coding and Reporting

🝰 Complication\Comorbidity   🝰 Major C\C   Excludes 1   Excludes 2   Includes   Use additional   Code first   Code also

1603

● T74.0   Neglect or abandonment, confirmed
  - ● T74.01   Adult neglect or abandonment, confirmed A 🅒
  - ● T74.02   Child neglect or abandonment, confirmed A 🅒
- ● T74.1   Physical abuse, confirmed
  - Excludes2   sexual abuse (T74.2-)
  - ● T74.11   Adult physical abuse, confirmed A 🅒
  - ● T74.12   Child physical abuse, confirmed A 🅒
    - Excludes2   shaken infant syndrome (T74.4)
- ● T74.2   Sexual abuse, confirmed
  - Rape, confirmed
  - Sexual assault, confirmed
  - ● T74.21   Adult sexual abuse, confirmed A 🅒
  - ● T74.22   Child sexual abuse, confirmed A 🅒
- ● T74.3   Psychological abuse, confirmed
  - ● T74.31   Adult psychological abuse, confirmed A 🅒
  - ● T74.32   Child psychological abuse, confirmed A 🅒
- ● T74.4   Shaken infant syndrome A 🅒
- ● T74.9   Unspecified maltreatment, confirmed
  - ● ■ T74.91   Unspecified adult maltreatment, confirmed A 🅒
  - ● ■ T74.92   Unspecified child maltreatment, confirmed A 🅒
● T75   Other and unspecified effects of other external causes
  - Excludes1   adverse effects NEC (T78.-)
  - Excludes2   burns (electric) (T20-T31)
  - The appropriate 7th character is to be added to each code from category T75
A	initial encounter
D	subsequent encounter
S	sequela
  - ● T75.0   Effects of lightning
    - Struck by lightning
    - ● ■ T75.00   Unspecified effects of lightning
      - Struck by lightning NOS
    - ● T75.01   Shock due to being struck by lightning
    - ● T75.09   Other effects of lightning
      - Use additional code for other effects of lightning
  - ● ■ T75.1   Unspecified effects of drowning and nonfatal submersion A 🅒
    - Immersion
    - Excludes1   specified effects of drowning code to effects
  - ● T75.2   Effects of vibration
    - ● ■ T75.20   Unspecified effects of vibration
    - ● T75.21   Pneumatic hammer syndrome
    - ● T75.22   Traumatic vasospastic syndrome
    - ● T75.23   Vertigo from infrasound
      - Excludes1   vertigo NOS (R42)
    - ● T75.29   Other effects of vibration
  - ● T75.3   Motion sickness
    - Airsickness   Travel sickness
    - Seasickness
    - Use additional external cause code to identify vehicle or type of motion (Y92.81-, Y93.5-)
  - ● T75.4   Electrocution
    - Shock from electric current
    - Shock from electroshock gun (taser)

● T75.8   Other specified effects of external causes
  - ● T75.81   Effects of abnormal gravitation [G] forces
  - ● T75.82   Effects of weightlessness
  - ● T75.89   Other specified effects of external causes
● T76   Adult and child abuse, neglect and other maltreatment, suspected
  - Excludes1   adult and child maltreatment, confirmed (T74.-)
    - suspected abuse and maltreatment in pregnancy (O94.3-O94.5-)
    - suspected adult physical and sexual abuse, ruled out (Z04.71)
    - suspected child physical and sexual abuse, ruled out (Z04.72)
  - Use additional code, if applicable, to identify any associated current injury
  - The appropriate 7th character is to be added to each code from category T76
A	initial encounter
D	subsequent encounter
S	sequela
  - ● T76.0   Neglect or abandonment, suspected
    - ● T76.01   Adult neglect or abandonment, suspected A 🅒
    - ● T76.02   Child neglect or abandonment, suspected A 🅒
  - ● T76.1   Physical abuse, suspected
    - ● T76.11   Adult physical abuse, suspected A 🅒
    - ● T76.12   Child physical abuse, suspected A 🅒
  - ● T76.2   Sexual abuse, suspected
    - Rape, suspected
    - Sexual abuse, suspected
    - Excludes1   alleged abuse, ruled out (Z04.7)
    - ● T76.21   Adult sexual abuse, suspected A 🅒
    - ● T76.22   Child sexual abuse, suspected A 🅒
  - ● T76.3   Psychological abuse, suspected
    - ● T76.31   Adult psychological abuse, suspected
    - ● T76.32   Child psychological abuse, suspected A 🅒
  - ● T76.9   Unspecified maltreatment, suspected
    - ● ■ T76.91   Unspecified adult maltreatment, suspected A 🅒
    - ● ■ T76.92   Unspecified child maltreatment, suspected A 🅒
● T78   Adverse effects, not elsewhere classified
  - Excludes2   complications of surgical and medical care NEC (T80-T88)
  - The appropriate 7th character is to be added to each code from category T78
A	initial encounter
D	subsequent encounter
S	sequela
  - ● T78.0   Anaphylactic shock due to adverse food reaction
    - Anaphylactic reaction due to food
    - ● ■ T78.00   Anaphylactic shock due to unspecified food A 🅒
    - ● T78.01   Anaphylactic shock due to peanuts A 🅒
    - ● T78.02   Anaphylactic shock due to shellfish (crustaceans) A 🅒
    - ● T78.03   Anaphylactic shock due to other fish A 🅒
    - ● T78.04   Anaphylactic shock due to fruits and vegetables A 🅒

● Unacceptable First-Listed Diagnosis   ● Use Additional Character(s)   ■ Unspecified   **OGCR** Official Guidelines for Coding and Reporting
🅒 Complication\Comorbidity   🅒 Major C\C   Excludes 1   Excludes 2   Includes   Use additional   Code first   Code also

● T78.05   **Anaphylactic shock due to tree nuts and seeds A** 🦠
> Excludes1   anaphylactic shock due to peanuts (T78.01)

● T78.06   **Anaphylactic shock due to food additives A** 🦠

● T78.07   **Anaphylactic shock due to milk and dairy products A** 🦠

● T78.08   **Anaphylactic shock due to eggs A** 🦠

● T78.09   **Anaphylactic shock due to other food products A** 🦠

● T78.1   **Other adverse food reactions, not elsewhere classified**
> Use additional code to identify the type of reaction
> Excludes1   anaphylactic reaction due to food (T78.0)
> anaphylactic shock due to adverse food reaction (T78.0)
> bacterial food borne intoxications (A05.-)
> Excludes2   allergic and dietetic gastroenteritis and colitis (K52.2)
> allergic rhinitis due to food (J30.5)
> dermatitis due to food in contact with skin (L23.6, L24.6, L25.4)
> dermatitis due to ingested food (L27.2)

● ▪ **T78.2   Anaphylactic shock, unspecified A** 🦠
> *Occurs when allergic response triggers large quantities of histamines, prostaglandins, leukotrienes resulting in systemic vasodilation*
> Allergic shock
> Anaphylactic reaction
> Anaphylaxis
> Excludes1   anaphylactic shock due to:
> adverse effect of correct medicinal substance properly administered (T88.6)
> adverse food reaction (T78.0-)
> serum (T80.5)

● T78.3   **Angioneurotic edema**
> Giant urticaria
> *Vascular disorder resulting from abnormalities of autonomic nervous system fibers supplying blood vessels*
> Quincke's edema
> Excludes1   urticaria (L50.-)
> serum (T80.6)

● T78.4   **Other and unspecified allergy**
> Excludes1   specified types of allergic reaction such as:
> allergic diarrhea (K52.2)
> allergic gastroenteritis and colitis (K52.2)
> dermatitis (L23-L25, L27.-)
> hay fever (J30.1)

● T78.40   **Allergy, NOS**
> Allergic reaction NOS
> Hypersensitivity NOS

● T78.41   **Arthus phenomenon**
> Arthus reaction

● T78.49   **Other allergy**

● T78.8   **Other adverse effects, not elsewhere classified**

● T79   **Certain early complications of trauma, not elsewhere classified**
> Excludes2   acute respiratory distress syndrome (J80)
> complications occurring during or following medical procedures (T80-T88)
> complications of surgical and medical care NEC (T80-T88)
> newborn respiratory distress syndrome (P22.0)

> The appropriate 7th character is to be added to each code from category T79
> | A | initial encounter |
> | D | subsequent encounter |
> | S | sequela |

● T79.0   **Air embolism (traumatic) A** 🦠
> Excludes1   air embolism complicating:
> abortion or ectopic or molar pregnancy (O00-O07, O08.2)
> pregnancy, childbirth and the puerperium (O88.0)
> air embolism following:
> infusion, transfusion, and therapeutic injection (T80.0)
> procedure NEC (T81.7-)

● T79.1   **Fat embolism (traumatic) A** 🦠
> Excludes1   fat embolism complicating:
> abortion or ectopic or molar pregnancy (O00-O07, O08.2)
> pregnancy, childbirth and the puerperium (O88.8)

● T79.2   **Traumatic secondary and recurrent hemorrhage and seroma A** 🦠

● T79.4   **Traumatic shock A** 🦠
> Shock (immediate) (delayed) following injury
> Excludes1   anaphylactic shock due to adverse food reaction (T78.0-)
> anaphylactic shock due to correct medicinal substance properly administered (T88.6)
> anaphylactic shock due to serum (T80.5)
> anaphylactic shock NOS (T78.2)
> anesthetic shock (T88.2)
> electric shock (T75.4)
> nontraumatic shock NEC (R57.-)
> obstetric shock (O75.1)
> postprocedural shock (T81.1)
> septic shock (R65.21)
> shock complicating abortion or ectopic or molar pregnancy (O00-O07, O08.3)
> shock due to lightning (T75.01)
> shock NOS (R57.9)

● T79.5   **Traumatic anuria A** 🦠
> Crush syndrome
> Renal failure following crushing

● T79.6   **Traumatic ischemia of muscle**
> Traumatic rhabdomyolysis
> Volkmann's ischemic contracture
> Excludes2   anterior tibial syndrome (M76.8)
> compartment syndrome (traumatic) (T79.A-)
> nontraumatic ischemia of muscle (M62.2-)

● Unacceptable First-Listed Diagnosis   ● Use Additional Character(s)
🦠 Complication\Comorbidity   🦠 Major C\C   Excludes 1   Excludes 2
◼ Unspecified   **OGCR** Official Guidelines for Coding and Reporting
Includes   Use additional   Code first   Code also

CHAPTER 19 (S00-T98)

1605

● **T79.7 Traumatic subcutaneous emphysema A 🕭**
> **Excludes1** emphysema NOS (J43)
> emphysema (subcutaneous)
> resulting from a procedure
> (T81.82)

● **T79.A Traumatic compartment syndrome**
> **Excludes1** fibromyalgia (M79.7)
> nontraumatic compartment
> syndrome (M79.A-)
> traumatic ischemic infarction of
> muscle (T79.6)

● ■ **T79.A0 Compartment syndrome, unspecified A 🕭**
> Compartment syndrome NOS

● **T79.A1 Traumatic compartment syndrome of upper extremity**
> Traumatic compartment syndrome of
> shoulder, arm, forearm, wrist, hand,
> and fingers

> ● **T79.a11 Traumatic compartment syndrome of right upper extremity A 🕭**

> ● **T79.a12 Traumatic compartment syndrome of left upper extremity A 🕭**

> ● ■ **T79.a19 Traumatic compartment syndrome of unspecified upper extremity A 🕭**

● **T79.A2 Traumatic compartment syndrome of lower extremity**
> Traumatic compartment syndrome of hip,
> buttock, thigh, leg, foot, and toes

> ● **T79.a21 Traumatic compartment syndrome of right lower extremity A 🕭**

> ● **T79.a22 Traumatic compartment syndrome of left lower extremity A 🕭**

> ● ■ **T79.a29 Traumatic compartment syndrome of unspecified lower extremity A 🕭**

● **T79.A3 Traumatic compartment syndrome of abdomen A 🕭**

● **T79.A9 Traumatic compartment syndrome of other sites A 🕭**

● **T79.8 Other early complications of trauma**

● ■ **T79.9 Unspecified early complication of trauma**

COMPLICATIONS OF SURGICAL AND MEDICAL CARE, NOT ELSEWHERE CLASSIFIED (T80-T88)

Use additional code(s) to identify the specified condition
resulting from the complication.

Use additional code (Y62-Y82) to identify devices
involved and details of circumstances.

> **Excludes2** adverse effects of drugs and medicaments
> (T36-T50 with fifth or sixth character 5)
> any encounters with medical care for
> postprocedural conditions in which no
> complications are present, such as:
> artificial opening status (Z93.-)
> closure of external stoma (Z43.-)
> fitting and adjustment of external
> prosthetic device (Z44.-)
> burns and corrosions from local applications
> and irradiation (T20-T32)
> complications of surgical procedures
> during pregnancy, childbirth and the
> puerperium (O00-O99)
> mechanical complication of respirator
> [ventilator] (J95.850)
> poisoning and toxic effects of drugs and
> chemicals (T36-T65 with final characters
> 1-4)
> postprocedural fever (R50.82)
> specified complications classified elsewhere,
> such as:
> cerebrospinal fluid leak from spinal
> puncture (G97.0)
> colostomy malfunction (K94.0-)
> disorders of fluid and electrolyte
> imbalance (E86- E87)
> functional disturbances following cardiac
> surgery (I97.0-I97.1)
> intraoperative and postprocedural
> complications of specified body
> systems (D78.-, E36.-, E89.-, G97.3-,
> G97.4, H59.3-, H59.-, H95.2-, H95.3,
> I97.4-, I97.5, J95.6-, J95.7, K91.6-, L76.-,
> M96.-, N99.-)
> ostomy complications (J95.0-, K94-,
> N99.5-)
> postgastric surgery syndromes (K91.1)
> postlaminectomy syndrome NEC (M96.1)
> postmastectomy lymphedema syndrome
> (I97.2)
> postsurgical blind-loop syndrome (K91.2)
> ventilator associated pneumonia (J95.851)

● **T80 Complications following infusion, transfusion and therapeutic injection**
> **Includes** complications following perfusion
> **Excludes2** bone marrow transplant rejection (T86.01)
> transfusion related acute lung injury
> (TRALI) (J95.84)

> The appropriate 7th character is to be added to each code
> from category T80
>
> | | |
> |---|---|
> | A | initial encounter |
> | D | subsequent encounter |
> | S | sequela |

● **T80.0 Air embolism following infusion, transfusion and therapeutic injection A 🕭**

● Unacceptable First-Listed Diagnosis   ● Use Additional Character(s)   ■ Unspecified   **OGCR** Official Guidelines for Coding and Reporting
🕭 Complication\Comorbidity   🕭 Major C\C   Excludes 1   Excludes 2   Includes   Use additional   Code first   Code also

● **T80.1   Vascular complications following infusion, transfusion and therapeutic injection A** 🗲
     Phlebitis following infusion, transfusion and therapeutic injection
     Thromboembolism following infusion, transfusion and therapeutic injection
     Thrombophlebitis following infusion, transfusion and therapeutic injection

     | Excludes2 | extravasation of vesicant agent (T80.81-)
        infiltration of vesicant agent (T80.81-)
        vascular complications specified as due to prosthetic devices, implants and grafts (T82.8-T83.8, T84.8-, T85.8)
        postprocedural vascular complications (T81.7-)

● **T80.2   Infections following infusion, transfusion and therapeutic injection**
     Infection following infusion, transfusion and therapeutic injection
     Sepsis following infusion, transfusion and therapeutic injection
     Use additional code to identify the specific infection, such as:
     sepsis (A41.9)

     Use additional code (R65.2-) to identify severe sepsis, if applicable

     | Excludes2 | infections specified as due to prosthetic devices, implants and grafts (T82.6-T82.7, T83.5-T83.6, T84.5-T84.7, T85.7)
        postprocedural infections (T81.4)

● **T80.21   Infection due to central venous catheter A** 🗲
     Catheter-related bloodstream infection (CRBSI) NOS
     Infection due to portacath (port-a-cath)
     Infection due to umbilical venous catheter

● **T80.29   Infection following other infusion, transfusion and therapeutic injection A** 🗲

● **T80.3   ABO incompatibility reaction A** 🗲
     ABO incompatible blood transfusion
     Reaction to ABO blood-group incompatibility in infusion or transfusion

     | Excludes1 | minor blood group antigens reactions (Duffy) (E) (K(ell)) (Kidd) (Lewis) (M) (N) (P) (S) (T80.89)

● **T80.4   Rh incompatibility reaction A** 🗲
     Reactions due to Rh factor in infusion or transfusion

● **T80.5   Anaphylactic shock due to serum A** 🗲
     Anaphylactic reaction due to serum

     | Excludes1 | allergic shock NOS (T78.2)
        anaphylactic shock NOS (T78.2)
        anaphylactic shock due to adverse effect of correct medicinal substance properly administered (T88.6)

● **T80.6   Other serum reactions A** 🗲
     Intoxication by serum   Serum sickness
     Protein sickness   Serum urticaria
     Serum rash

     | Excludes2 | serum hepatitis (B16.-)

● **T80.8   Other complications following infusion, transfusion and therapeutic injection**

● **T80.81   Extravasation of vesicant agent**
     Infiltration of vesicant agent

● **T80.810   Extravasation of vesicant antineoplastic chemotherapy**
     Infiltration of vesicant antineoplastic chemotherapy

● **T80.818   Extravasation of other vesicant agent**
     Infiltration of other vesicant agent

● **T80.89   Other complications following infusion, transfusion and therapeutic injection**
     Use additional code to identify graft-versus-host reaction, if applicable, (D89.81-)

● ▣ **T80.9   Unspecified complication following infusion, transfusion and therapeutic injection**
     Transfusion reaction NOS

● **T81   Complications of procedures, not elsewhere classified**

     | Excludes2 | complications following immunization (T88.0-T88.1)
        complications following infusion, transfusion and therapeutic injection (T80.-)
        complications of transplanted organs and tissue (T86.-)
        specified complications classified elsewhere, such as:
        adverse effect, poisoning and toxic effects of drugs and chemicals (T36-T65)
        complication of prosthetic devices, implants and grafts (T82-T85)
        dermatitis due to drugs and medicaments (L23.3, L24.4, L25.1, L27.0-L27.1)
        endosseous dental implant failure (M27.6-)
        floppy iris syndrome (IFIS) (intraoperative) H21.81
        intraoperative and postprocedural complications of specific body system (D78.-, E36.-, E89.-, G97.3-, G97.4, H59.3-, H59.-, H95.2-, H95.3, I97.4-, I97.5, J95, K91-, L76.-, M96.-, N99.-)
        ostomy complications (J95.0-, K94.-, N99.5-)
        plateau iris syndrome (post-iridectomy) (postprocedural) H21.82

     The appropriate 7th character is to be added to each code from category T81

     | A   initial encounter
     | D   subsequent encounter
     | S   sequela

● **T81.1   Shock during or resulting from a procedure, not elsewhere classified A** 🗲
     Collapse NOS during or resulting from a procedure, not elsewhere classified
     Shock (hypovolemic) during or resulting from a procedure, not elsewhere classified
     Postprocedural shock NOS during or resulting from a procedure, not elsewhere classified

     | Excludes1 | anaphylactic shock NOS (T78.2)
        anaphylactic shock due to correct substance properly administered (T88.6)
        anaphylactic shock due to serum (T80.5)
        anesthetic shock (T88.2)
        electric shock (T75.4)
        obstetric shock (O75.1)
        septic shock (R65.21)
        shock following abortion or ectopic or molar pregnancy (O00-O07, O08.3)
        traumatic shock (T79.4)

● Unacceptable First-Listed Diagnosis   ● Use Additional Character(s)   ▣ Unspecified   **OGCR** Official Guidelines for Coding and Reporting
🗲 Complication\Comorbidity   🗲 Major C\C | Excludes 1 | | Excludes 2 | Includes   Use additional   Code first   Code also

● **T81.3**   **Disruption of wound, not elsewhere classified A** 🗇
Disruption of any suture materials or other
closure methods

> **Excludes1**   breakdown (mechanical) of
permanent sutures (T85.612)
displacement of permanent sutures
(T86.622)
disruption of cesarean delivery
wound (O90.0)
disruption of perineal obstetric
wound (O90.1)
mechanical complication of permanent
sutures NEC (T85.692)

● **T81.30**   **Disruption of wound, unspecified A** 🗇
Disruption of wound NOS

● **T81.31**   **Disruption of external operation (surgical)
wound, not elsewhere classified A** 🗇
Dehiscence of operation wound NOS
Disruption of operation wound NOS
Disruption or dehiscence of closure of
cornea
Disruption or dehiscence of closure of
mucosa
Disruption or dehiscence of closure of
skin and subcutaneous tissue
Full-thickness skin disruption or
dehiscence
Superficial disruption or dehiscence of
operation wound

● **T81.32**   **Disruption of internal operation (surgical)
wound, not elsewhere classified A** 🗇
Deep disruption or dehiscence of
operation wound NOS

● **T81.4**   **Infection following a procedure A** 🗇
Intra-abdominal abscess following a procedure
Postprocedural infection, not elsewhere classified
Sepsis following a procedure
Stitch abscess following a procedure
Subphrenic abscess following a procedure
Wound abscess following a procedure

> Use additional code to identify infection

> Use additional code (R65.2-) to identify severe
sepsis, if applicable

> **Excludes1**   obstetric surgical wound infection
(O86.0)
postprocedural fever NOS (R50.82)
postprocedural retroperitoneal
abscess (K68.11)

> **Excludes2**   bleb associated endophthalmitis (H59.4-)
infection due to infusion, transfusion
and therapeutic injection (T80.2-)
infection due to prosthetic devices,
implants and grafts (T82.6-T82.7,
T83.5-T83.6, T84.5-T84.7, T85.7)

● **T81.5**   **Complications of foreign body accidentally left in
body following procedure**

● **T81.50**   **Unspecified complication of foreign
body accidentally left in body following
procedure**

  ● ▪ **T81.500**   Unspecified complication of
foreign body accidentally left
in body following surgical
operation A 🗇

  ● ▪ **T81.501**   Unspecified complication of
foreign body accidentally left
in body following infusion or
transfusion A 🗇

  ● ▪ **T81.502**   Unspecified complication of foreign
body accidentally left in body
following kidney dialysis A 🗇

  ● ▪ **T81.503**   Unspecified complication of
foreign body accidentally left
in body following injection or
immunization A 🗇

  ● ▪ **T81.504**   Unspecified complication of
foreign body accidentally left
in body following endoscopic
examination A 🗇

  ● ▪ **T81.505**   Unspecified complication of
foreign body accidentally
left in body following heart
catheterization A 🗇

  ● ▪ **T81.506**   Unspecified complication of
foreign body accidentally
left in body following
aspiration, puncture or other
catheterization A 🗇

  ● ▪ **T81.507**   Unspecified complication of
foreign body accidentally left
in body following removal of
catheter or packing A 🗇

  ● ▪ **T81.508**   Unspecified complication of
foreign body accidentally left
in body following other
procedure A 🗇

  ● ▪ **T81.509**   Unspecified complication of
foreign body accidentally left
in body following unspecified
procedure A 🗇

● **T81.51**   **Adhesions due to foreign body
accidentally left in body following
procedure**

  ● **T81.510**   Adhesions due to foreign
body accidentally left in body
following surgical operation A 🗇

  ● **T81.511**   Adhesions due to foreign body
accidentally left in body following
infusion or transfusion A 🗇

  ● **T81.512**   Adhesions due to foreign
body accidentally left in body
following kidney dialysis A 🗇

  ● **T81.513**   Adhesions due to foreign
body accidentally left in
body following injection or
immunization A 🗇

  ● **T81.514**   Adhesions due to foreign
body accidentally left in
body following endoscopic
examination A 🗇

  ● **T81.515**   Adhesions due to foreign
body accidentally left in
body following heart
catheterization A 🗇

  ● **T81.516**   Adhesions due to foreign
body accidentally left in body
following aspiration, puncture or
other catheterization A 🗇

  ● **T81.517**   Adhesions due to foreign
body accidentally left in body
following removal of catheter or
packing A 🗇

  ● **T81.518**   Adhesions due to foreign
body accidentally left in body
following other procedure A 🗇

● ▢ T81.519　Adhesions due to foreign body accidentally left in body following unspecified procedure A 🦠

● T81.52　Obstruction due to foreign body accidentally left in body following procedure

　● T81.520　Obstruction due to foreign body accidentally left in body following surgical operation A 🦠

　● T81.521　Obstruction due to foreign body accidentally left in body following infusion or transfusion A 🦠

　● T81.522　Obstruction due to foreign body accidentally left in body following kidney dialysis A 🦠

　● T81.523　Obstruction due to foreign body accidentally left in body following injection or immunization A 🦠

　● T81.524　Obstruction due to foreign body accidentally left in body following endoscopic examination A 🦠

　● T81.525　Obstruction due to foreign body accidentally left in body following heart catheterization A 🦠

　● T81.526　Obstruction due to foreign body accidentally left in body following aspiration, puncture or other catheterization A 🦠

　● T81.527　Obstruction due to foreign body accidentally left in body following removal of catheter or packing A 🦠

　● T81.528　Obstruction due to foreign body accidentally left in body following other procedure A 🦠

　● ▢ T81.529　Obstruction due to foreign body accidentally left in body following unspecified procedure A 🦠

● T81.53　Perforation due to foreign body accidentally left in body following procedure

　● T81.530　Perforation due to foreign body accidentally left in body following surgical operation A 🦠

　● T81.531　Perforation due to foreign body accidentally left in body following infusion or transfusion A 🦠

　● T81.532　Perforation due to foreign body accidentally left in body following kidney dialysis A 🦠

　● T81.533　Perforation due to foreign body accidentally left in body following injection or immunization A 🦠

　● T81.534　Perforation due to foreign body accidentally left in body following endoscopic examination A 🦠

　● T81.535　Perforation due to foreign body accidentally left in body following heart catheterization A 🦠

　● T81.536　Perforation due to foreign body accidentally left in body following aspiration, puncture or other catheterization A 🦠

　● T81.537　Perforation due to foreign body accidentally left in body following removal of catheter or packing A 🦠

　● T81.538　Perforation due to foreign body accidentally left in body following other procedure A 🦠

　● ▢ T81.539　Perforation due to foreign body accidentally left in body following unspecified procedure A 🦠

● T81.59　Other complications of foreign body accidentally left in body following procedure

　Excludes2　obstruction or perforation due to prosthetic devices and implants intentionally left in body (T82.0-T82.5, T83.0-T83.4, T84.0-T84.4, T85.0-T85.6)

　● T81.590　Other complications of foreign body accidentally left in body following surgical operation A 🦠

　● T81.591　Other complications of foreign body accidentally left in body following infusion or transfusion A 🦠

　● T81.592　Other complications of foreign body accidentally left in body following kidney dialysis A 🦠

　● T81.593　Other complications of foreign body accidentally left in body following injection or immunization A 🦠

　● T81.594　Other complications of foreign body accidentally left in body following endoscopic examination A 🦠

　● T81.595　Other complications of foreign body accidentally left in body following heart catheterization A 🦠

　● T81.596　Other complications of foreign body accidentally left in body following aspiration, puncture or other catheterization A 🦠

　● T81.597　Other complications of foreign body accidentally left in body following removal of catheter or packing A 🦠

　● T81.598　Other complications of foreign body accidentally left in body following other procedure A 🦠

　● ▢ T81.599　Other complications of foreign body accidentally left in body following unspecified procedure A 🦠

● T81.6　Acute reaction to foreign substance accidentally left during a procedure

　Excludes2　complications of foreign body accidentally left in body cavity or operation wound following procedure (T81.5-)

　● ▢ T81.60　Unspecified acute reaction to foreign substance accidentally left during a procedure A 🦠

● Unacceptable First-Listed Diagnosis　　● Use Additional Character(s)　　▢ Unspecified　　**OGCR** Official Guidelines for Coding and Reporting

🦠 Complication\Comorbidity　　🦠 Major C\C　　 Excludes 1　　 Excludes 2　　Includes　　Use additional　　Code first　　Code also

1609

CHAPTER 19 (S00-T98)

● **T81.61** **Aseptic peritonitis due to foreign substance accidentally left during a procedure A** 🥼
   Chemical peritonitis

● **T81.69** **Other acute reaction to foreign substance accidentally left during a procedure A** 🥼

● **T81.7** **Vascular complications following a procedure, not elsewhere classified**
   Air embolism following procedure NEC
   Phlebitis or thrombophlebitis resulting from a procedure

   Excludes1   embolism complicating abortion or ectopic or molar pregnancy (O00-O07, O08.2)
   embolism complicating pregnancy, childbirth and the puerperium (O88.-)
   traumatic embolism (T79.0)

   Excludes2   embolism due to prosthetic devices, implants and grafts (T82.8, T83.8, T84.8-, T85.8)
   embolism following infusion, transfusion and therapeutic injection (T80.0)

● **T81.71** **Complication of artery following a procedure, not elsewhere classified**

   ● **T81.710** **Complication of mesenteric artery following a procedure, not elsewhere classified A** 🥼

   ● **T81.711** **Complication of renal artery following a procedure, not elsewhere classified A** 🥼

   ● **T81.718** **Complication of other artery following a procedure, not elsewhere classified A** 🥼

   ● ■ **T81.719** **Complication of unspecified artery following a procedure, not elsewhere classified A** 🥼

● **T81.72** **Complication of vein following a procedure, not elsewhere classified A** 🥼

● **T81.8** **Other complications of procedures, not elsewhere classified**

   Excludes2   hypothermia following anesthesia (T88.51)
   malignant hyperpyrexia due to anesthesia (T88.3)

● **T81.81** **Complication of inhalation therapy**

● **T81.82** **Emphysema (subcutaneous) resulting from a procedure**

● **T81.83** **Persistent postprocedural fistula A** 🥼

● **T81.89** **Other complications of procedures, not elsewhere classified**
   Use additional code to specify complication, such as:
   postprocedural delerium (F05)

● ■ **T81.9** **Unspecified complication of procedure**

● **T82** **Complications of cardiac and vascular prosthetic devices, implants and grafts**

   Excludes2   failure and rejection of transplanted organs and tissue (T86.-)
   The appropriate 7th character is to be added to each code from category T82

A	initial encounter
D	subsequent encounter
S	sequela

● **T82.0** **Mechanical complication of heart valve prosthesis**
   Mechanical complication of artificial heart valve

   Excludes1   mechanical complication of biological heart valve graft (T82.22-)

   ● **T82.01** **Breakdown (mechanical) of heart valve prosthesis**

   ● **T82.02** **Displacement of heart valve prosthesis A** 🥼
      Malposition of heart valve prosthesis

   ● **T82.03** **Leakage of heart valve prosthesis A** 🥼

   ● **T82.09** **Other mechanical complication of heart valve prosthesis A** 🥼
      Obstruction (mechanical) of heart valve prosthesis
      Perforation of heart valve prosthesis
      Protrusion of heart valve prosthesis

● **T82.1** **Mechanical complication of cardiac electronic device**

   ● **T82.11** **Breakdown (mechanical) of cardiac electronic device**

      ● **T82.110** **Breakdown (mechanical) of cardiac electrode A** 🥼

      ● **T82.111** **Breakdown (mechanical) of cardiac pulse generator (battery) A** 🥼

      ● **T82.118** **Breakdown (mechanical) of other cardiac electronic device A** 🥼

      ● ■ **T82.119** **Breakdown (mechanical) of unspecified cardiac electronic device A** 🥼

   ● **T82.12** **Displacement of cardiac electronic device**
      Malposition of cardiac electronic device

      ● **T82.120** **Displacement of cardiac electrode A** 🥼

      ● **T82.121** **Displacement of cardiac pulse generator (battery) A** 🥼

      ● **T82.128** **Displacement of other cardiac electronic device A** 🥼

      ● ■ **T82.129** **Displacement of unspecified cardiac electronic device A** 🥼

   ● **T82.19** **Other mechanical complication of cardiac electronic device**
      Leakage of cardiac electronic device
      Obstruction of cardiac electronic device
      Perforation of cardiac electronic device
      Protrusion of cardiac electronic device

      ● **T82.190** **Other mechanical complication of cardiac electrode A** 🥼

      ● **T82.191** **Other mechanical complication of cardiac pulse generator (battery) A** 🥼

● T82.198 Other mechanical complication of other cardiac electronic device A 🦴

● ◼ T82.199 Other mechanical complication of unspecified cardiac device A 🦴

● T82.2 Mechanical complication of coronary artery bypass graft and biological heart valve graft

> **Excludes1**   mechanical complication of artificial heart valve prosthesis (T82.0-)

● T82.21 Mechanical complication of coronary artery bypass graft

● T82.211 Breakdown (mechanical) of coronary artery bypass graft A 🦴

● T82.212 Displacement of coronary artery bypass graft A 🦴
> Malposition of coronary artery bypass graft

● T82.213 Leakage of coronary artery bypass graft A 🦴

● T82.218 Other mechanical complication of coronary artery bypass graft A 🦴
> Obstruction, mechanical of coronary artery bypass graft
> Perforation of coronary artery bypass graft
> Protrusion of coronary artery bypass graft

● T82.22 Mechanical complication of biological heart valve graft

● T82.221 Breakdown (mechanical) of biological heart valve graft A 🦴

● T82.222 Displacement of biological heart valve graft A 🦴
> Malposition of biological heart valve graft

● T82.223 Leakage of biological heart valve graft A 🦴

● T82.228 Other mechanical complication of biological heart valve graft A 🦴
> Obstruction of biological heart valve graft
> Perforation of biological heart valve graft
> Protrusion of biological heart valve graft

● T82.3 Mechanical complication of other vascular grafts

● T82.31 Breakdown (mechanical) of other vascular grafts

● T82.310 Breakdown (mechanical) of aortic (bifurcation) graft (replacement) A 🦴

● T82.311 Breakdown (mechanical) of carotid arterial graft (bypass) A 🦴

● T82.312 Breakdown (mechanical) of femoral arterial graft (bypass) A 🦴

● T82.318 Breakdown (mechanical) of other vascular grafts A 🦴

● ◼ T82.319 Breakdown (mechanical) of unspecified vascular grafts A 🦴

● T82.32 Displacement of other vascular grafts
> Malposition of other vascular grafts

● T82.320 Displacement of aortic (bifurcation) graft (replacement) A 🦴

● T82.321 Displacement of carotid arterial graft (bypass) A 🦴

● T82.322 Displacement of femoral arterial graft (bypass) A 🦴

● T82.328 Displacement of other vascular grafts A 🦴

● ◼ T82.329 Displacement of unspecified vascular grafts A 🦴

● T82.33 Leakage of other vascular grafts

● T82.330 Leakage of aortic (bifurcation) graft (replacement) A 🦴

● T82.331 Leakage of carotid arterial graft (bypass) A 🦴

● T82.332 Leakage of femoral arterial graft (bypass) A 🦴

● T82.338 Leakage of other vascular grafts A 🦴

● ◼ T82.339 Leakage of unspecified vascular graft A 🦴

● T82.39 Other mechanical complication of other vascular grafts
> Obstruction (mechanical) of other vascular grafts
> Perforation of other vascular grafts
> Protrusion of other vascular grafts

● T82.390 Other mechanical complication of aortic (bifurcation) graft (replacement) A 🦴

● T82.391 Other mechanical complication of carotid arterial graft (bypass) A 🦴

● T82.392 Other mechanical complication of femoral arterial graft (bypass) A 🦴

● T82.398 Other mechanical complication of other vascular grafts A 🦴

● ◼ T82.399 Other mechanical complication of unspecified vascular grafts A 🦴

● T82.4 Mechanical complication of vascular dialysis catheter
> Mechanical complication of hemodialysis catheter

> **Excludes1**   mechanical complication of intraperitoneal dialysis catheter (T85.62)

● T82.41 Breakdown (mechanical) of vascular dialysis catheter A 🦴

● T82.42 Displacement of vascular dialysis catheter A 🦴
> Malposition of vascular dialysis catheter

● T82.43 Leakage of vascular dialysis catheter A 🦴

● T82.49 Other complication of vascular dialysis catheter A 🦴
> Obstruction (mechanical) of vascular dialysis catheter
> Perforation of vascular dialysis catheter
> Protrusion of vascular dialysis catheter

● T82.5 Mechanical complication of other cardiac and vascular devices and implants

> **Excludes2**   mechanical complication of epidural and subdural infusion catheter (T85.61)

● T82.51 Breakdown (mechanical) of other cardiac and vascular devices and implants

● T82.510 Breakdown (mechanical) of surgically created arteriovenous fistula A 🦴

● Unacceptable First-Listed Diagnosis   ● Use Additional Character(s)   ◼ Unspecified   **OGCR** Official Guidelines for Coding and Reporting

🦴 Complication\Comorbidity   🦴 Major C\C   Excludes 1   Excludes 2   Includes   Use additional   Code first   Code also

CHAPTER 19 (S00-T98)

1611

● T82.511 Breakdown (mechanical) of surgically created arteriovenous shunt A 🦠

● T82.512 Breakdown (mechanical) of artificial heart A 🦠

● T82.513 Breakdown (mechanical) of balloon (counterpulsation) device A 🦠

● T82.514 Breakdown (mechanical) of infusion catheter A 🦠

● T82.515 Breakdown (mechanical) of umbrella device A 🦠

● T82.518 Breakdown (mechanical) of other cardiac and vascular devices and implants A 🦠

● ■ T82.519 Breakdown (mechanical) of unspecified cardiac and vascular devices and implants A 🦠

● T82.52 Displacement of other cardiac and vascular devices and implants
    Malposition of other cardiac and vascular devices and implants

● T82.520 Displacement of surgically created arteriovenous fistula A 🦠

● T82.521 Displacement of surgically created arteriovenous shunt A 🦠

● T82.522 Displacement of artificial heart A 🦠

● T82.523 Displacement of balloon (counterpulsation) device A 🦠

● T82.524 Displacement of infusion catheter A 🦠

● T82.525 Displacement of umbrella device A 🦠

● T82.528 Displacement of other cardiac and vascular devices and implants A 🦠

● ■ T82.529 Displacement of unspecified cardiac and vascular devices and implants A 🦠

● T82.53 Leakage of other cardiac and vascular devices and implants

● T82.530 Leakage of surgically created arteriovenous fistula A 🦠

● T82.531 Leakage of surgically created arteriovenous shunt A 🦠

● T82.532 Leakage of artificial heart A 🦠

● T82.533 Leakage of balloon (counterpulsation) device A 🦠

● T82.534 Leakage of infusion catheter A 🦠

● T82.535 Leakage of umbrella device A 🦠

● T82.538 Leakage of other cardiac and vascular devices and implants A 🦠

● ■ T82.539 Leakage of unspecified cardiac and vascular devices and implants A 🦠

● T82.59 Other mechanical complication of other cardiac and vascular devices and implants
    Obstruction (mechanical) of other cardiac and vascular devices and implants
    Perforation of other cardiac and vascular devices and implants
    Protrusion of other cardiac and vascular devices and implants

● T82.590 Other mechanical complication of surgically created arteriovenous fistula A 🦠

● T82.591 Other mechanical complication of surgically created arteriovenous shunt A 🦠

● T82.592 Other mechanical complication of artificial heart A 🦠

● T82.593 Other mechanical complication of balloon (counterpulsation) device A 🦠

● T82.594 Other mechanical complication of infusion catheter A 🦠

● T82.595 Other mechanical complication of umbrella device A 🦠

● T82.598 Other mechanical complication of other cardiac and vascular devices and implants A 🦠

● ■ T82.599 Other mechanical complication of unspecified cardiac and vascular devices and implants A 🦠

● T82.6 Infection and inflammatory reaction due to cardiac valve prosthesis A 🦠
    Use additional code to identify infection

● T82.7 Infection and inflammatory reaction due to other cardiac and vascular devices, implants and grafts A 🦠
    Use additional code to identify infection

● T82.8 Other specified complications of cardiac and vascular prosthetic devices, implants and grafts

● T82.81 Embolism of cardiac and vascular prosthetic devices, implants and grafts

● T82.817 Embolism of cardiac prosthetic devices, implants and grafts A 🦠

● T82.818 Embolism of vascular prosthetic devices, implants and grafts A 🦠

● T82.82 Fibrosis of cardiac and vascular prosthetic devices, implants and grafts

● T82.827 Fibrosis of cardiac prosthetic devices, implants and grafts A 🦠

● T82.828 Fibrosis of vascular prosthetic devices, implants and grafts A 🦠

● T82.83 Hemorrhage of cardiac and vascular prosthetic devices, implants and grafts

● T82.837 Hemorrhage of cardiac prosthetic devices, implants and grafts A 🦠

● T82.838 Hemorrhage of vascular prosthetic devices, implants and grafts A 🦠

● T82.84 Pain from cardiac and vascular prosthetic devices, implants and grafts

● T82.847 Pain from cardiac prosthetic devices, implants and grafts A 🦠

● T82.848 Pain from vascular prosthetic devices, implants and grafts A 🦠

● T82.85 Stenosis of cardiac and vascular prosthetic devices, implants and grafts

● T82.857 Stenosis of cardiac prosthetic devices, implants and grafts A 🦠

● T82.858 Stenosis of vascular prosthetic devices, implants and grafts A 🦠

● Unacceptable First-Listed Diagnosis   ● Use Additional Character(s)   ■ Unspecified   **OGCR** Official Guidelines for Coding and Reporting
🦠 Complication\Comorbidity   🦠 Major C\C   Excludes 1   Excludes 2   Includes   Use additional   Code first   Code also

● **T82.86**   Thrombosis of cardiac and vascular prosthetic devices, implants and grafts

    ● **T82.867**   Thrombosis of cardiac prosthetic devices, implants and grafts A 🦠

    ● **T82.868**   Thrombosis of vascular prosthetic devices, implants and grafts A 🦠

● **T82.89**   Other specified complication of cardiac and vascular prosthetic devices, implants and grafts

    ● **T82.897**   Other specified complication of cardiac prosthetic devices, implants and grafts A 🦠

    ● **T82.898**   Other specified complication of vascular prosthetic devices, implants and grafts A 🦠

● ■ **T82.9**   Unspecified complication of cardiac and vascular prosthetic device, implant and graft A 🦠

● **T83**   Complications of genitourinary prosthetic devices, implants and grafts

> **Excludes2**   failure and rejection of transplanted organs and tissue (T86.-)

> The appropriate 7th character is to be added to each code from category T83

> | A | initial encounter |
> |---|---|
> | D | subsequent encounter |
> | S | sequela |

● **T83.0**   Mechanical complication of urinary (indwelling) catheter

> **Excludes2**   complications of stoma of urinary tract (N99.5-)

  ● **T83.01**   Breakdown (mechanical) of urinary (indwelling) catheter

    ● **T83.010**   Breakdown (mechanical) of cystostomy catheter A 🦠

    ● **T83.018**   Breakdown (mechanical) of other indwelling urethral catheter

  ● **T83.02**   Displacement of urinary (indwelling) catheter

      Malposition of urinary (indwelling) catheter

    ● **T83.020**   Displacement of cystostomy catheter A 🦠

    ● **T83.028**   Displacement of other indwelling urethral catheter

  ● **T83.03**   Leakage of urinary (indwelling) catheter

    ● **T83.030**   Leakage of cystostomy catheter A 🦠

    ● **T83.038**   Leakage of other indwelling urethral catheter

  ● **T83.09**   Other mechanical complication of urinary (indwelling) catheter

      Obstruction (mechanical) of urinary (indwelling) catheter
      Perforation of urinary (indwelling) catheter
      Protrusion of urinary (indwelling) catheter

    ● **T83.090**   Other mechanical complication of cystostomy catheter A 🦠

    ● **T83.098**   Other mechanical complication of other indwelling urethral catheter

● **T83.1**   Mechanical complication of other urinary devices and implants

  ● **T83.11**   Breakdown (mechanical) of other urinary devices and implants

    ● **T83.110**   Breakdown (mechanical) of urinary electronic stimulator device A 🦠

    ● **T83.111**   Breakdown (mechanical) of urinary sphincter implant A 🦠

    ● **T83.112**   Breakdown (mechanical) of urinary stent A 🦠

    ● **T83.118**   Breakdown (mechanical) of other urinary devices and implants A 🦠

  ● **T83.12**   Displacement of other urinary devices and implants

      Malposition of other urinary devices and implants

    ● **T83.120**   Displacement of urinary electronic stimulator device A 🦠

    ● **T83.121**   Displacement of urinary sphincter implant A 🦠

    ● **T83.122**   Displacement of urinary stent A 🦠

    ● **T83.128**   Displacement of other urinary devices and implants A 🦠

  ● **T83.19**   Other mechanical complication of other urinary devices and implants

      Leakage of other urinary devices and implants
      Obstruction (mechanical) of other urinary devices and implants
      Perforation of other urinary devices and implants
      Protrusion of other urinary devices and implants

    ● **T83.190**   Other mechanical complication of urinary electronic stimulator device A 🦠

    ● **T83.191**   Other mechanical complication of urinary sphincter implant A 🦠

    ● **T83.192**   Other mechanical complication of urinary stent A 🦠

    ● **T83.198**   Other mechanical complication of other urinary devices and implants A 🦠

● **T83.2**   Mechanical complication of graft of urinary organ

  ● **T83.21**   Breakdown (mechanical) of graft of urinary organ A 🦠

  ● **T83.22**   Displacement of graft of urinary organ A 🦠

      Malposition of graft of urinary organ

  ● **T83.23**   Leakage of graft of urinary organ A 🦠

  ● **T83.29**   Other mechanical complication of graft of urinary organ A 🦠

      Obstruction (mechanical) of graft of urinary organ
      Perforation of graft of urinary organ
      Protrusion of graft of urinary organ

● **T83.3**   Mechanical complication of intrauterine contraceptive device

  ● **T83.31**   Breakdown (mechanical) of intrauterine contraceptive device

  ● **T83.32**   Displacement of intrauterine contraceptive device

      Malposition of intrauterine contraceptive device

● Unacceptable First-Listed Diagnosis   ● Use Additional Character(s)   ■ Unspecified   **OGCR** Official Guidelines for Coding and Reporting

🦠 Complication\Comorbidity   🦠 Major C\C | Excludes 1 | | Excludes 2 | Includes   Use additional   Code first   Code also

CHAPTER 19 (S00–T98)

1613

- **T83.39** **Other mechanical complication of intrauterine contraceptive device**
  Leakage of intrauterine contraceptive device
  Obstruction (mechanical) of intrauterine contraceptive device
  Perforation of intrauterine contraceptive device
  Protrusion of intrauterine contraceptive device

- **T83.4** **Mechanical complication of other prosthetic devices, implants and grafts of genital tract**
  - **T83.41** **Breakdown (mechanical) of other prosthetic devices, implants and grafts of genital tract**
    - **T83.410** **Breakdown (mechanical) of penile (implanted) prosthesis A** 🗫
    - **T83.418** **Breakdown (mechanical) of other prosthetic devices, implants and grafts of genital tract A** 🗫
  - **T83.42** **Displacement of other prosthetic devices, implants and grafts of genital tract**
    Malposition of other prosthetic devices, implants and grafts of genital tract
    - **T83.420** **Displacement of penile (implanted) prosthesis A** 🗫
    - **T83.428** **Displacement of other prosthetic devices, implants and grafts of genital tract A** 🗫
  - **T83.49** **Other mechanical complication of other prosthetic devices, implants and grafts of genital tract**
    Leakage of other prosthetic devices, implants and grafts of genital tract
    Obstruction, mechanical of other prosthetic devices, implants and grafts of genital tract
    Perforation of other prosthetic devices, implants and grafts of genital tract
    Protrusion of other prosthetic devices, implants and grafts of genital tract
    - **T83.490** **Other mechanical complication of penile (implanted) prosthesis A** 🗫
    - **T83.498** **Other mechanical complication of other prosthetic devices, implants and grafts of genital tract A** 🗫

- **T83.5** **Infection and inflammatory reaction due to prosthetic device, implant and graft in urinary system**
  Use additional code to identify infection
  - **T83.51** **Infection and inflammatory reaction due to indwelling urinary catheter A** 🗫
  - **T83.59** **Infection and inflammatory reaction due to prosthetic device, implant and graft in urinary system A** 🗫

- **T83.6** **Infection and inflammatory reaction due to prosthetic device, implant and graft in genital tract A** 🗫
  Use additional code to identify infection

- **T83.8** **Other specified complications of genitourinary prosthetic devices, implants and grafts**
  - **T83.81** **Embolism of genitourinary prosthetic devices, implants and grafts A** 🗫
  - **T83.82** **Fibrosis of genitourinary prosthetic devices, implants and grafts A** 🗫

- **T83.83** **Hemorrhage of genitourinary prosthetic devices, implants and grafts A** 🗫
- **T83.84** **Pain from genitourinary prosthetic devices, implants and grafts A** 🗫
- **T83.85** **Stenosis of genitourinary prosthetic devices, implants and grafts A** 🗫
- **T83.86** **Thrombosis of genitourinary prosthetic devices, implants and grafts A** 🗫
- **T83.89** **Other specified complication of genitourinary prosthetic devices, implants and grafts A** 🗫

- ■ **T83.9** **Unspecified complication of genitourinary prosthetic device, implant and graft A** 🗫

- **T84** **Complications of internal orthopedic prosthetic devices, implants and grafts**
  | **Excludes2** | failure and rejection of transplanted organs and tissues (T86.-) |
  | | fracture of bone following insertion of orthopedic implant, joint prosthesis or bone plate (M96.6) |

  The appropriate 7th character is to be added to each code from category T84

A	initial encounter
D	subsequent encounter
S	sequela

  - **T84.0** **Mechanical complication of internal joint prosthesis**
    - **T84.01** **Broken (mechanical) of internal joint prosthesis**
      Breakage (fracture) of prosthetic joint
      Broken prosthetic joint implant
      | **Excludes1** | periprosthetic joint implant fracture (T84.04) |
      - **T84.010** **Broken internal right hip prosthesis A** 🗫
      - **T84.011** **Broken internal left hip prosthesis A** 🗫
      - **T84.012** **Broken internal right knee prosthesis A** 🗫
      - **T84.013** **Broken internal left knee prosthesis A** 🗫
      - **T84.018** **Broken internal joint prosthesis, other site A** 🗫
        Use additional code to identify the joint (Z96.6-)
      - ■ **T84.019** **Broken internal joint prosthesis, unspecified site A** 🗫
    - **T84.02** **Dislocation of internal joint prosthesis**
      Instability of prosthetic joint
      Subluxation of internal joint prosthesis
      - **T84.020** **Dislocation of internal right hip prosthesis A** 🗫
      - **T84.021** **Dislocation of internal left hip prosthesis A** 🗫
      - **T84.022** **Dislocation of internal right knee prosthesis A** 🗫
      - **T84.023** **Dislocation of internal left knee prosthesis A** 🗫
      - **T84.028** **Dislocation of other internal joint prosthesis A** 🗫
        Use additional code to identify the joint (Z96.6-)
      - ■ **T84.029** **Dislocation of unspecified internal joint prosthesis A** 🗫

CHAPTER 19 (S00-T98)

● Unacceptable First-Listed Diagnosis   ● Use Additional Character(s)   ■ Unspecified   **OGCR** Official Guidelines for Coding and Reporting
🗫 Complication\Comorbidity   🗫 Major C\C   Excludes 1   Excludes 2   Includes   Use additional   Code first   Code also

1614

● **T84.03　Mechanical loosening of internal prosthetic joint**
　　　Aseptic loosening of prosthetic joint

　● T84.030　Mechanical loosening of internal right hip prosthetic joint A 🔷

　● T84.031　Mechanical loosening of internal left hip prosthetic joint A 🔷

　● T84.032　Mechanical loosening of internal right knee prosthetic joint A 🔷

　● T84.033　Mechanical loosening of internal left knee prosthetic joint A 🔷

　● T84.038　Mechanical loosening of other internal prosthetic joint A 🔷
　　　　　Use additional code to identify the joint (Z96.6-)

　● ■ T84.039　Mechanical loosening of unspecified internal prosthetic joint A 🔷

● **T84.04　Periprosthetic fracture around internal prosthetic joint**
　　　Excludes2　breakage (fracture) of prosthetic joint (T84.01)

　● T84.040　Periprosthetic fracture around internal prosthetic right hip joint A 🔷

　● T84.041　Periprosthetic fracture around internal prosthetic left hip joint A 🔷

　● T84.042　Periprosthetic fracture around internal prosthetic right knee joint A 🔷

　● T84.043　Periprosthetic fracture around internal prosthetic left knee joint A 🔷

　● T84.048　Periprosthetic fracture around other internal prosthetic joint A 🔷
　　　　　Use additional code to identify the joint (Z96.6-)

　● ■ T84.049　Periprosthetic fracture around unspecified internal prosthetic joint A 🔷

● **T84.05　Periprosthetic osteolysis of internal prosthetic joint**
　　　Use additional code to identify major osseous defect, if applicable (M89.7-)

　● T84.050　Periprosthetic osteolysis of internal prosthetic right hip joint A 🔷

　● T84.051　Periprosthetic osteolysis of internal prosthetic left hip joint A 🔷

　● T84.052　Periprosthetic osteolysis of internal prosthetic right knee joint A 🔷

　● T84.053　Periprosthetic osteolysis of internal prosthetic left knee joint A 🔷

　● T84.058　Periprosthetic osteolysis of other internal prosthetic joint A 🔷
　　　　　Use additional code to identify the joint (Z96.6-)

　● ■ T84.059　Periprosthetic osteolysis of unspecified internal prosthetic joint A 🔷

● **T84.06　Wear of articular bearing surface of internal prosthetic joint**

　● T84.060　Wear of articular bearing surface of internal prosthetic right hip joint A 🔷

　● T84.061　Wear of articular bearing surface of internal prosthetic left hip joint A 🔷

　● T84.062　Wear of articular bearing surface of internal prosthetic right knee joint A 🔷

　● T84.063　Wear of articular bearing surface of internal prosthetic left knee joint A 🔷

　● T84.068　Wear of articular bearing surface of other internal prosthetic joint A 🔷
　　　　　Use additional code to identify the joint (Z96.6-)

　● ■ T84.069　Wear of articular bearing surface of unspecified internal prosthetic joint A 🔷

● **T84.09　Other mechanical complication of internal joint prosthesis**
　　　Prosthetic joint implant failure NOS

　● T84.090　Other mechanical complication of internal right hip prosthesis A 🔷

　● T84.091　Other mechanical complication of internal left hip prosthesis A 🔷

　● T84.092　Other mechanical complication of internal right knee prosthesis A 🔷

　● T84.093　Other mechanical complication of internal left knee prosthesis A 🔷

　● T84.098　Other mechanical complication of other internal joint prosthesis A 🔷
　　　　　Use additional code to identify the joint (Z96.6-)

　● ■ T84.099　Other mechanical complication of unspecified internal joint prosthesis A 🔷

● **T84.1　Mechanical complication of internal fixation device of bones of limb**
　　　Excludes2　mechanical complication of internal fixation device of bones of feet (T84.2-)
　　　　　mechanical complication of internal fixation device of bones of fingers (T84.2-)
　　　　　mechanical complication of internal fixation device of bones of hands (T84.2-)
　　　　　mechanical complication of internal fixation device of bones of toes (T84.2-)

　● **T84.11　Breakdown (mechanical) of internal fixation device of bones of limb**

　　● T84.110　Breakdown (mechanical) of internal fixation device of right humerus A 🔷

　　● T84.111　Breakdown (mechanical) of internal fixation device of left humerus A 🔷

● Unacceptable First-Listed Diagnosis　　　● Use Additional Character(s)　　　■ Unspecified　　　**OGCR** Official Guidelines for Coding and Reporting
🔷 Complication\Comorbidity　　🔷 Major C\C　　Excludes 1　　Excludes 2　　Includes　　Use additional　　Code first　　Code also

● T84.112   Breakdown (mechanical) of internal fixation device of bone of right forearm A 🦠

● T84.113   Breakdown (mechanical) of internal fixation device of bone of left forearm A 🦠

● T84.114   Breakdown (mechanical) of internal fixation device of right femur A 🦠

● T84.115   Breakdown (mechanical) of internal fixation device of left femur A 🦠

● T84.116   Breakdown (mechanical) of internal fixation device of bone of right lower leg A 🦠

● T84.117   Breakdown (mechanical) of internal fixation device of bone of left lower leg A 🦠

● ■ T84.119   Breakdown (mechanical) of internal fixation device of unspecified bone of limb A 🦠

● T84.12   Displacement of internal fixation device of bones of limb
    Malposition of internal fixation device of bones of limb

● T84.120   Displacement of internal fixation device of right humerus A 🦠

● T84.121   Displacement of internal fixation device of left humerus A 🦠

● T84.122   Displacement of internal fixation device of bone of right forearm A 🦠

● T84.123   Displacement of internal fixation device of bone of left forearm A 🦠

● T84.124   Displacement of internal fixation device of right femur A 🦠

● T84.125   Displacement of internal fixation device of left femur A 🦠

● T84.126   Displacement of internal fixation device of bone of right lower leg A 🦠

● T84.127   Displacement of internal fixation device of bone of left lower leg A 🦠

● ■ T84.129   Displacement of internal fixation device of unspecified bone of limb A 🦠

● T84.19   Other mechanical complication of internal fixation device of bones of limb
    Obstruction (mechanical) of internal fixation device of bones of limb
    Perforation of internal fixation device of bones of limb
    Protrusion of internal fixation device of bones of limb

● T84.190   Other mechanical complication of internal fixation device of right humerus A 🦠

● T84.191   Other mechanical complication of internal fixation device of left humerus A 🦠

● T84.192   Other mechanical complication of internal fixation device of bone of right forearm A 🦠

● T84.193   Other mechanical complication of internal fixation device of bone of left forearm A 🦠

● T84.194   Other mechanical complication of internal fixation device of right femur A 🦠

● T84.195   Other mechanical complication of internal fixation device of left femur A 🦠

● T84.196   Other mechanical complication of internal fixation device of bone of right lower leg A 🦠

● T84.197   Other mechanical complication of internal fixation device of bone of left lower leg A 🦠

● ■ T84.199   Other mechanical complication of internal fixation device of unspecified bone of limb A 🦠

● T84.2   Mechanical complication of internal fixation device of other bones

● T84.21   Breakdown (mechanical) of internal fixation device of other bones

● T84.210   Breakdown (mechanical) of internal fixation device of bones of hand and fingers A 🦠

● T84.213   Breakdown (mechanical) of internal fixation device of bones of foot and toes A 🦠

● T84.216   Breakdown (mechanical) of internal fixation device of vertebrae A 🦠

● T84.218   Breakdown (mechanical) of internal fixation device of other bones A 🦠

● T84.22   Displacement of internal fixation device of other bones
    Malposition of internal fixation device of other bones

● T84.220   Displacement of internal fixation device of bones of hand and fingers A 🦠

● T84.223   Displacement of internal fixation device of bones of foot and toes A 🦠

● T84.226   Displacement of internal fixation device of vertebrae A 🦠

● T84.228   Displacement of internal fixation device of other bones A 🦠

● T84.29   Other mechanical complication of internal fixation device of other bones
    Obstruction (mechanical) of internal fixation device of other bones
    Perforation of internal fixation device of other bones
    Protrusion of internal fixation device of other bones

● T84.290   Other mechanical complication of internal fixation device of bones of hand and fingers A 🦠

● T84.293   Other mechanical complication of internal fixation device of bones of foot and toes A 🦠

● T84.296   Other mechanical complication of internal fixation device of vertebrae A 🦠

● T84.298   Other mechanical complication of internal fixation device of other bones A 🦠

● Unacceptable First-Listed Diagnosis   ● Use Additional Character(s)   ■ Unspecified   OGCR Official Guidelines for Coding and Reporting
🦠 Complication\Comorbidity   🦠 Major C\C   Excludes 1   Excludes 2   Includes   Use additional   Code first   Code also

● **T84.3   Mechanical complication of other bone devices, implants and grafts**

> | Excludes2 | other complications of bone graft (T86.83-) |

- ● **T84.31   Breakdown (mechanical) of other bone devices, implants and grafts**
  - ● **T84.310   Breakdown (mechanical) of electronic bone stimulator A** 🕭
  - ● **T84.318   Breakdown (mechanical) of other bone devices, implants and grafts A** 🕭
- ● **T84.32   Displacement of other bone devices, implants and grafts**
  > Malposition of other bone devices, implants and grafts
  - ● **T84.320   Displacement of electronic bone stimulator A** 🕭
  - ● **T84.328   Displacement of other bone devices, implants and grafts A** 🕭
- ● **T84.39   Other mechanical complication of other bone devices, implants and grafts**
  > Obstruction (mechanical) of other bone devices, implants and grafts
  > Perforation of other bone devices, implants and grafts
  > Protrusion of other bone devices, implants and grafts
  - ● **T84.390   Other mechanical complication of electronic bone stimulator A** 🕭
  - ● **T84.398   Other mechanical complication of other bone devices, implants and grafts A** 🕭

● **T84.4   Mechanical complication of other internal orthopedic devices, implants and grafts**

- ● **T84.41   Breakdown (mechanical) of other internal orthopedic devices, implants and grafts**
  - ● **T84.410   Breakdown (mechanical) of muscle and tendon graft A** 🕭
  - ● **T84.418   Breakdown (mechanical) of other internal orthopedic devices, implants and grafts A** 🕭
- ● **T84.42   Displacement of other internal orthopedic devices, implants and grafts**
  > Malposition of other internal orthopedic devices, implants and grafts
  - ● **T84.420   Displacement of muscle and tendon graft A** 🕭
  - ● **T84.428   Displacement of other internal orthopedic devices, implants and grafts A** 🕭
- ● **T84.49   Other mechanical complication of other internal orthopedic devices, implants and grafts**
  > Mechanical complication of other internal orthopedic devices, implants and grafts NOS
  > Obstruction (mechanical) of other internal orthopedic devices, implants and grafts
  > Perforation of other internal orthopedic devices, implants and grafts
  > Protrusion of other internal orthopedic devices, implants and grafts
  - ● **T84.490   Other mechanical complication of muscle and tendon graft A** 🕭
  - ● **T84.498   Other mechanical complication of other internal orthopedic devices, implants and grafts A** 🕭

● **T84.5   Infection and inflammatory reaction due to internal joint prosthesis**

> Use additional code to identify infection

- ● ■ **T84.50   Infection and inflammatory reaction due to unspecified internal joint prosthesis A** 🕭
- ● **T84.51   Infection and inflammatory reaction due to internal right hip prosthesis A** 🕭
- ● **T84.52   Infection and inflammatory reaction due to internal left hip prosthesis A** 🕭
- ● **T84.53   Infection and inflammatory reaction due to internal right knee prosthesis A** 🕭
- ● **T84.54   Infection and inflammatory reaction due to internal left knee prosthesis A** 🕭
- ● **T84.59   Infection and inflammatory reaction due to other internal joint prosthesis A** 🕭

● **T84.6   Infection and inflammatory reaction due to internal fixation device**

> Use additional code to identify infection

- ● ■ **T84.60   Infection and inflammatory reaction due to internal fixation device of unspecified site A** 🕭
- ● **T84.61   Infection and inflammatory reaction due to internal fixation device of arm**
  - ● **T84.610   Infection and inflammatory reaction due to internal fixation device of right humerus A** 🕭
  - ● **T84.611   Infection and inflammatory reaction due to internal fixation device of left humerus A** 🕭
  - ● **T84.612   Infection and inflammatory reaction due to internal fixation device of right radius A** 🕭
  - ● **T84.613   Infection and inflammatory reaction due to internal fixation device of left radius A** 🕭
  - ● **T84.614   Infection and inflammatory reaction due to internal fixation device of right ulna A** 🕭
  - ● **T84.615   Infection and inflammatory reaction due to internal fixation device of left ulna A** 🕭
  - ● ■ **T84.619   Infection and inflammatory reaction due to internal fixation device of unspecified bone of arm A** 🕭
- ● **T84.62   Infection and inflammatory reaction due to internal fixation device of leg**
  - ● **T84.620   Infection and inflammatory reaction due to internal fixation device of right femur A** 🕭
  - ● **T84.621   Infection and inflammatory reaction due to internal fixation device of left femur A** 🕭
  - ● **T84.622   Infection and inflammatory reaction due to internal fixation device of right tibia A** 🕭
  - ● **T84.623   Infection and inflammatory reaction due to internal fixation device of left tibia A** 🕭
  - ● **T84.624   Infection and inflammatory reaction due to internal fixation device of right fibula A** 🕭
  - ● **T84.625   Infection and inflammatory reaction due to internal fixation device of left fibula A** 🕭

● Unacceptable First-Listed Diagnosis   ● Use Additional Character(s)   ■ Unspecified   **OGCR** Official Guidelines for Coding and Reporting

🕭 Complication\Comorbidity   🕭 Major C\C   Excludes 1   Excludes 2   Includes   Use additional   Code first   Code also   1617

CHAPTER 19 (S00-T98)

● ■ **T84.629** Infection and inflammatory reaction due to internal fixation device of unspecified bone of leg A 🦠

  ● **T84.63** Infection and inflammatory reaction due to internal fixation device of spine A 🦠

  ● **T84.69** Infection and inflammatory reaction due to internal fixation device of other site A 🦠

● **T84.7** Infection and inflammatory reaction due to other internal orthopedic prosthetic devices, implants and grafts A 🦠

   Use additional code to identify infection

● **T84.8** Other specified complications of internal orthopedic prosthetic devices, implants and grafts

  ● **T84.81** Embolism due to internal orthopedic prosthetic devices, implants and grafts A 🦠

  ● **T84.82** Fibrosis due to internal orthopedic prosthetic devices, implants and grafts A 🦠

  ● **T84.83** Hemorrhage due to internal orthopedic prosthetic devices, implants and grafts A 🦠

  ● **T84.84** Pain due to internal orthopedic prosthetic devices, implants and grafts A 🦠

  ● **T84.85** Stenosis due to internal orthopedic prosthetic devices, implants and grafts A 🦠

  ● **T84.86** Thrombosis due to internal orthopedic prosthetic devices, implants and grafts A 🦠

  ● **T84.89** Other specified complication of internal orthopedic prosthetic devices, implants and grafts A 🦠

● ■ **T84.9** Unspecified complication of internal orthopedic prosthetic device, implant and graft A 🦠

● **T85** Complications of other internal prosthetic devices, implants and grafts

   | Excludes2 | failure and rejection of transplanted organs and tissue (T86.-) |

   The appropriate 7th character is to be added to each code from category T85

   A initial encounter
   D subsequent encounter
   S sequela

● **T85.0** Mechanical complication of ventricular intracranial (communicating) shunt

  ● **T85.01** Breakdown (mechanical) of ventricular intracranial (communicating) shunt A 🦠

  ● **T85.02** Displacement of ventricular intracranial (communicating) shunt A 🦠
     Malposition of ventricular intracranial (communicating) shunt

  ● **T85.03** Leakage of ventricular intracranial (communicating) shunt A 🦠

  ● **T85.09** Other mechanical complication of ventricular intracranial (communicating) shunt A 🦠
     Obstruction (mechanical) of ventricular intracranial (communicating) shunt
     Perforation of ventricular intracranial (communicating) shunt
     Protrusion of ventricular intracranial (communicating) shunt

● **T85.1** Mechanical complication of implanted electronic stimulator of nervous system

  ● **T85.11** Breakdown (mechanical) of implanted electronic stimulator of nervous system

   ● **T85.110** Breakdown (mechanical) of implanted electronic neurostimulator (electrode) of brain A 🦠

   ● **T85.111** Breakdown (mechanical) of implanted electronic neurostimulator (electrode) of peripheral nerve A 🦠

   ● **T85.112** Breakdown (mechanical) of implanted electronic neurostimulator (electrode) of spinal cord A 🦠

   ● **T85.118** Breakdown (mechanical) of other implanted electronic stimulator of nervous system A 🦠

  ● **T85.12** Displacement of implanted electronic stimulator of nervous system
     Malposition of implanted electronic stimulator of nervous system

   ● **T85.120** Displacement of implanted electronic neurostimulator (electrode) of brain A 🦠

   ● **T85.121** Displacement of implanted electronic neurostimulator (electrode) of peripheral nerve A 🦠

   ● **T85.122** Displacement of implanted electronic neurostimulator (electrode) of spinal cord A 🦠

   ● **T85.128** Displacement of other implanted electronic stimulator of nervous system A 🦠

  ● **T85.19** Other mechanical complication of implanted electronic stimulator of nervous system
     Leakage of implanted electronic stimulator of nervous system
     Obstruction (mechanical) of implanted electronic stimulator of nervous system
     Perforation of implanted electronic stimulator of nervous system
     Protrusion of implanted electronic stimulator of nervous system

   ● **T85.190** Other mechanical complication of implanted electronic neurostimulator (electrode) of brain A 🦠

   ● **T85.191** Other mechanical complication of implanted electronic neurostimulator (electrode) of peripheral nerve A 🦠

   ● **T85.192** Other mechanical complication of implanted electronic neurostimulator (electrode) of spinal cord A 🦠

   ● **T85.199** Other mechanical complication of other implanted electronic stimulator of nervous system A 🦠

● **T85.2** Mechanical complication of intraocular lens

  ● **T85.21** Breakdown (mechanical) of intraocular lens A 🦠

  ● **T85.22** Displacement of intraocular lens A 🦠
     Malposition of intraocular lens

● Unacceptable First-Listed Diagnosis   ● Use Additional Character(s)   ■ Unspecified   **OGCR** Official Guidelines for Coding and Reporting
🦠 Complication\Comorbidity   🦠 Major C\C   Excludes 1   Excludes 2   Includes   Use additional   Code first   Code also

● **T85.29**   **Other mechanical complication of intraocular lens A** 🔖
     Obstruction (mechanical) of intraocular lens
     Perforation of intraocular lens
     Protrusion of intraocular lens

● **T85.3**   **Mechanical complication of other ocular prosthetic devices, implants and grafts**
     Excludes2   other complications of corneal graft (T86.84-)

  ● **T85.31**   **Breakdown (mechanical) of other ocular prosthetic devices, implants and grafts**

    ● **T85.310**   **Breakdown (mechanical) of prosthetic orbit of right eye A** 🔖

    ● **T85.311**   **Breakdown (mechanical) of prosthetic orbit of left eye A** 🔖

    ● **T85.318**   **Breakdown (mechanical) of other ocular prosthetic devices, implants and grafts A** 🔖

  ● **T85.32**   **Displacement of other ocular prosthetic devices, implants and grafts**
     Malposition of other ocular prosthetic devices, implants and grafts

    ● **T85.320**   **Displacement of prosthetic orbit of right eye A** 🔖

    ● **T85.321**   **Displacement of prosthetic orbit of left eye A** 🔖

    ● **T85.328**   **Displacement of other ocular prosthetic devices, implants and grafts A** 🔖

  ● **T85.39**   **Other mechanical complication of other ocular prosthetic devices, implants and grafts**
     Obstruction (mechanical) of other ocular prosthetic devices, implants and grafts
     Perforation of other ocular prosthetic devices, implants and grafts
     Protrusion of other ocular prosthetic devices, implants and grafts

    ● **T85.390**   **Other mechanical complication of prosthetic orbit of right eye A** 🔖

    ● **T85.391**   **Other mechanical complication of prosthetic orbit of left eye A** 🔖

    ● **T85.398**   **Other mechanical complication of other ocular prosthetic devices, implants and grafts A** 🔖

● **T85.4**   **Mechanical complication of breast prosthesis and implant**

  ● **T85.41**   **Breakdown (mechanical) of breast prosthesis and implant A** 🔖

  ● **T85.42**   **Displacement of breast prosthesis and implant A** 🔖
     Malposition of breast prosthesis and implant

  ● **T85.43**   **Leakage of breast prosthesis and implant A** 🔖

  ● **T85.44**   **Capsular contracture of breast implant A** 🔖

  ● **T85.49**   **Other mechanical complication of breast prosthesis and implant A** 🔖
     Obstruction (mechanical) of breast prosthesis and implant
     Perforation of breast prosthesis and implant
     Protrusion of breast prosthesis and implant

● **T85.5**   **Mechanical complication of gastrointestinal prosthetic devices, implants and grafts**

  ● **T85.51**   **Breakdown (mechanical) of gastrointestinal prosthetic devices, implants and grafts**

    ● **T85.510**   **Breakdown (mechanical) of bile duct prosthesis A** 🔖

    ● **T85.511**   **Breakdown (mechanical) of esophageal anti-reflux device A** 🔖

    ● **T85.518**   **Breakdown (mechanical) of other gastrointestinal prosthetic devices, implants and grafts A** 🔖

  ● **T85.52**   **Displacement of gastrointestinal prosthetic devices, implants and grafts**
     Malposition of gastrointestinal prosthetic devices, implants and grafts

    ● **T85.520**   **Displacement of bile duct prosthesis A** 🔖

    ● **T85.521**   **Displacement of esophageal anti-reflux device A** 🔖

    ● **T85.528**   **Displacement of other gastrointestinal prosthetic devices, implants and grafts A** 🔖

  ● **T85.59**   **Other mechanical complication of gastrointestinal prosthetic devices, implants and**
     Obstruction, mechanical of gastrointestinal prosthetic devices, implants and grafts
     Perforation of gastrointestinal prosthetic devices, implants and grafts
     Protrusion of gastrointestinal prosthetic devices, implants and grafts

    ● **T85.590**   **Other mechanical complication of bile duct prosthesis A** 🔖

    ● **T85.591**   **Other mechanical complication of esophageal anti-reflux device A** 🔖

    ● **T85.598**   **Other mechanical complication of other gastrointestinal prosthetic devices, implants and grafts A** 🔖

● **T85.6**   **Mechanical complication of other specified internal and external prosthetic devices, implants and grafts**

  ● **T85.61**   **Breakdown (mechanical) of other specified internal prosthetic devices, implants and grafts**

    ● **T85.610**   **Breakdown (mechanical) of epidural and subdural infusion catheter A** 🔖

    ● **T85.611**   **Breakdown (mechanical) of intraperitoneal dialysis catheter A** 🔖
       Excludes1   mechanical complication of vascular dialysis catheter (T82.4-)

    ● **T85.612**   **Breakdown (mechanical) of permanent sutures A** 🔖
       Excludes1   mechanical complication of permanent (wire) suture used in bone repair (T84.1-T84.2)

● Unacceptable First-Listed Diagnosis   ● Use Additional Character(s)   ▨ Unspecified   **OGCR** Official Guidelines for Coding and Reporting

🔖 Complication\Comorbidity   🔖 Major C\C   Excludes 1   Excludes 2   Includes   Use additional   Code first   Code also   **1619**

● T85.613 **Breakdown (mechanical) of artificial skin graft and decellularized allodermis A** 🦠

Failure of artificial skin graft and decellularized allodermis

Non-adherence of artificial skin graft and decellularized allodermis

Poor incorporation of artificial skin graft and decellularized allodermis

Shearing of artificial skin graft and decellularized allodermis

● T85.614 **Breakdown (mechanical) of insulin pump A** 🦠

● T85.618 **Breakdown (mechanical) of other specified internal prosthetic devices, implants and grafts A** 🦠

● T85.62 **Displacement of other specified internal prosthetic devices, implants and grafts**

Malposition of other specified internal prosthetic devices, implants and grafts

● T85.620 **Displacement of epidural and subdural infusion catheter A** 🦠

● T85.621 **Displacement of intraperitoneal dialysis catheter A** 🦠

> Excludes1 mechanical complication of vascular dialysis catheter (T82.4-)

● T85.622 **Displacement of permanent sutures A** 🦠

> Excludes1 mechanical complication of permanent (wire) suture used in bone repair (T84.1-T84.2)

● T85.623 **Displacement of artificial skin graft and decellularized allodermis A** 🦠

Dislodgement of artificial skin graft and decellularized allodermis

Displacement of artificial skin graft and decellularized allodermis

● T85.624 **Displacement of insulin pump A** 🦠

● T85.628 **Displacement of other specified internal prosthetic devices, implants and grafts A** 🦠

● T85.63 **Leakage of other specified internal prosthetic devices, implants and grafts**

● T85.630 **Leakage of epidural and subdural infusion catheter A** 🦠

● T85.631 **Leakage of intraperitoneal dialysis catheter A** 🦠

> Excludes1 mechanical complication of vascular dialysis catheter (T82.4)

● T85.633 **Leakage of insulin pump A** 🦠

● T85.638 **Leakage of other specified internal prosthetic devices, implants and grafts A** 🦠

● T85.69 **Other mechanical complication of other specified internal prosthetic devices, implants and grafts**

Obstruction, mechanical of other specified internal prosthetic devices, implants and grafts

Perforation of other specified internal prosthetic devices, implants and grafts

Protrusion of other specified internal prosthetic devices, implants and grafts

● T85.690 **Other mechanical complication of epidural and subdural infusion catheter A** 🦠

● T85.691 **Other mechanical complication of intraperitoneal dialysis catheter A** 🦠

> Excludes1 mechanical complication of vascular dialysis catheter (T82.4)

● T85.692 **Other mechanical complication of permanent sutures A** 🦠

> Excludes1 mechanical complication of permanent (wire) suture used in bone repair (T84.1-T84.2)

● T85.693 **Other mechanical complication of artificial skin graft and decellularized allodermis A** 🦠

● T85.694 **Other mechanical complication of insulin pump A** 🦠

● T85.698 **Other mechanical complication of other specified internal prosthetic devices, implants and grafts A** 🦠

Mechanical complication of nonabsorbable surgical material NOS

● T85.7 **Infection and inflammatory reaction due to other internal prosthetic devices, implants and grafts**

Use additional code to identify infection

● T85.71 **Infection and inflammatory reaction due to peritoneal dialysis catheter** 🦠

● T85.72 **Infection and inflammatory reaction due to insulin pump** 🦠

● T85.79 **Infection and inflammatory reaction due to other internal prosthetic devices, implants and grafts** 🦠

● T85.8 **Other specified complications of internal prosthetic devices, implants and grafts, not elsewhere classified**

● T85.81 **Embolism due to internal prosthetic devices, implants and grafts, not elsewhere classified** 🦠

● T85.82 **Fibrosis due to internal prosthetic devices, implants and grafts, not elsewhere classified** 🦠

● Unacceptable First-Listed Diagnosis   ● Use Additional Character(s)   ▨ Unspecified   **OGCR** Official Guidelines for Coding and Reporting

🦠 Complication\Comorbidity   🦠 Major C\C   Excludes 1   Excludes 2   Includes   Use additional   Code first   Code also

● T85.83 **Hemorrhage due to internal prosthetic devices, implants and grafts, not elsewhere classified** 🦠

● T85.84 **Pain due to internal prosthetic devices, implants and grafts, not elsewhere classified** 🦠

● T85.85 **Stenosis due to internal prosthetic devices, implants and grafts, not elsewhere classified** 🦠

● T85.86 **Thrombosis due to internal prosthetic devices, implants and grafts, not elsewhere classified** 🦠

● T85.89 **Other specified complication of internal prosthetic devices, implants and grafts, not elsewhere classified** 🦠

● ■ **T85.9 Unspecified complication of internal prosthetic device, implant and graft** 🦠

Complication of internal prosthetic device, implant and graft NOS

● **T86 Complications of transplanted organs and tissue**

Use additional code to identify other transplant complications, such as:
graft-versus-host disease (D89.81-)
malignancy associated with organ transplant (C80.2)
post-transplant lymphoproliferative disorders (PTLD) (D47.z1)

● **T86.0 Complications of bone marrow transplant**

■ T86.00 **Unspecified complication of bone marrow transplant** 🦠

T86.01 **Bone marrow transplant rejection** 🦠

T86.02 **Bone marrow transplant failure** 🦠

T86.03 **Bone marrow transplant infection** 🦠

T86.09 **Other complications of bone marrow transplant** 🦠

● **T86.1 Complications of kidney transplant**

■ T86.10 **Unspecified complication of kidney transplant** 🦠

T86.11 **Kidney transplant rejection** 🦠

OGCR Section I.C.19.g.3.

Organ Transplant Complications

Transplant Complications
(a) Transplant complications other than kidney
Codes under category T86, Complications of transplanted organs and tissues, are for use for both complications and rejection of transplanted organs. A transplant complication code is only assigned if the complication affects the function of the transplanted organ. Two codes are required to fully describe a transplant complication: the appropriate code from category T86 and a secondary code that identifies the complication.

Pre-existing conditions or conditions that develop after the transplant are not coded as complications unless they affect the function of the transplanted organs.

See I.C.21.c.3 for transplant organ removal status

See I.C.2.r for malignant neoplasm associated with transplanted organ.

T86.12 **Kidney transplant failure** 🦠

T86.13 **Kidney transplant infection** 🦠

Use additional code to specify infection

T86.19 **Other complication of kidney transplant** 🦠

● **T86.2 Complications of heart transplant**

| Excludes1 | complication of: artificial heart device (T82.5) heart-lung transplant (T86.3) |

■ T86.20 **Unspecified complication of heart transplant** 🦠

T86.21 **Heart transplant rejection** 🦠

T86.22 **Heart transplant failure** 🦠

T86.23 **Heart transplant infection** 🦠

Use additional code to specify infection

● T86.29 **Other complications of heart transplant**

T86.290 **Cardiac allograft vasculopathy** 🦠

| Excludes1 | atherosclerosis of coronary arteries (I25.75-, I25.76-, I25.81-) |

T86.298 **Other complications of heart transplant** 🦠

● **T86.3 Complications of heart-lung transplant**

■ T86.30 **Unspecified complication of heart-lung transplant** 🦠

T86.31 **Heart-lung transplant rejection** 🦠

T86.32 **Heart-lung transplant failure** 🦠

T86.33 **Heart-lung transplant infection** 🦠

Use additional code to specify infection

T86.39 **Other complications of heart-lung transplant** 🦠

● **T86.4 Complications of liver transplant**

■ T86.40 **Unspecified complication of liver transplant** 🦠

T86.41 **Liver transplant rejection** 🦠

T86.42 **Liver transplant failure** 🦠

T86.43 **Liver transplant infection** 🦠

Use additional code to identify infection, such as:
Cytomegalovirus (CMV) infection (B25.-)

T86.49 **Other complications of liver transplant** 🦠

● **T86.8 Complications of other transplanted organs and tissues**

● T86.81 **Complications of lung transplant**

| Excludes1 | complication of heart-lung transplant (T86.3-) |

T86.810 **Lung transplant rejection** 🦠

T86.811 **Lung transplant failure** 🦠

T86.812 **Lung transplant infection** 🦠

Use additional code to specify infection

T86.818 **Other complications of lung transplant** 🦠

■ T86.819 **Unspecified complication of lung transplant** 🦠

● Unacceptable First-Listed Diagnosis   ● Use Additional Character(s)   ■ Unspecified   **OGCR** Official Guidelines for Coding and Reporting

🦠 Complication\Comorbidity   🦠 Major C\C | Excludes 1 | | Excludes 2 | ■ Includes   Use additional   Code first   Code also   1621

CHAPTER 19 (S00-T98)

● T86.82   Complications of skin graft (allograft) (autograft)

> **Excludes2**   complication of artificial skin graft (T85.64)

　　T86.820   Skin graft (allograft) rejection 🔗

　　T86.821   Skin graft (allograft) (autograft) failure 🔗

　　T86.822   Skin graft (allograft) (autograft) infection 🔗

> Use additional code to specify infection

　　T86.828   Other complications of skin graft (allograft) (autograft) 🔗

● ▪ T86.829   Unspecified complication of skin graft (allograft) (autograft) 🔗

● T86.83   Complications of bone graft

> **Excludes2**   mechanical complications of bone graft (T84.3-)

　　T86.830   Bone graft rejection 🔗

　　T86.831   Bone graft failure 🔗

　　T86.832   Bone graft infection 🔗

> Use additional code to specify infection

　　T86.838   Other complications of bone graft 🔗

　　▪ T86.839   Unspecified complication of bone graft 🔗

● T86.84   Complications of corneal transplant

> **Excludes2**   mechanical complications of corneal graft (T85.3-)

　　T86.840   Corneal transplant rejection 🔗

　　T86.841   Corneal transplant failure 🔗

　　T86.842   Corneal transplant infection 🔗

> Use additional code to specify infection

　　T86.848   Other complications of corneal transplant 🔗

　　▪ T86.849   Unspecified complication of corneal transplant 🔗

● T86.85   Complication of intestine transplant

　　T86.850   Intestine transplant rejection 🔗

　　T86.851   Intestine transplant failure 🔗

　　T86.852   Intestine transplant infection 🔗

> Use additional code to specify infection

　　T86.858   Other complications of intestine transplant 🔗

　　▪ T86.859   Unspecified complication of intestine transplant 🔗

● T86.89   Complications of other transplanted tissue
　　　　Transplant failure or rejection of pancreas

　　T86.890   Other transplanted tissue rejection 🔗

　　T86.891   Other transplanted tissue failure 🔗

　　T86.892   Other transplanted tissue infection 🔗

> Use additional code to specify infection

　　T86.898   Other complications of other transplanted tissue 🔗

　　▪ T86.899   Unspecified complication of other transplanted tissue 🔗

● T86.9   Complication of unspecified transplanted organ and tissue

　　▪ T86.90   Unspecified complication of unspecified transplanted organ and tissue 🔗

　　▪ T86.91   Unspecified transplanted organ and tissue rejection 🔗

　　▪ T86.92   Unspecified transplanted organ and tissue failure 🔗

　　▪ T86.93   Unspecified transplanted organ and tissue infection 🔗

> Use additional code to specify infection

　　▪ T86.99   Other complications of unspecified transplanted organ and tissue 🔗

● T87   Complications peculiar to reattachment and amputation

● T87.0   Complications of reattached (part of) upper extremity

● T87.0x   Complications of reattached (part of) upper extremity

　　T87.0x1   Complications of reattached (part of) right upper extremity 🔗

　　T87.0x2   Complications of reattached (part of) left upper extremity 🔗

　　▪ T87.0x9   Complications of reattached (part of) upper extremity, unspecified side 🔗

● T87.1   Complications of reattached (part of) lower extremity

● T87.1x   Complications of reattached (part of) lower extremity

　　T87.1x1   Complications of reattached (part of) right lower extremity 🔗

　　T87.1x2   Complications of reattached (part of) left lower extremity 🔗

　　▪ T87.1x9   Complications of reattached (part of) lower extremity, unspecified side 🔗

T87.2   Complications of other reattached body part 🔗

● T87.3   Neuroma of amputation stump

● ▪ T87.30   Neuroma of amputation stump, unspecified extremity

　　T87.31   Neuroma of amputation stump, right upper extremity

　　T87.32   Neuroma of amputation stump, left upper extremity

　　T87.33   Neuroma of amputation stump, right lower extremity

　　T87.34   Neuroma of amputation stump, left lower extremity

● T87.4   Infection of amputation stump

　　▪ T87.40   Infection of amputation stump, unspecified extremity 🔗

　　T87.41   Infection of amputation stump, right upper extremity 🔗

　　T87.42   Infection of amputation stump, left upper extremity 🔗

　　T87.43   Infection of amputation stump, right lower extremity 🔗

　　T87.44   Infection of amputation stump, left lower extremity 🔗

● Unacceptable First-Listed Diagnosis　　● Use Additional Character(s)　　▪ Unspecified　　**OGCR** Official Guidelines for Coding and Reporting
🔗 Complication\Comorbidity　　🔗 Major C\C　　Excludes 1　　Excludes 2　　Includes　　Use additional　　Code first　　Code also

● T87.5 **Necrosis of amputation stump**

    ▪ **T87.50 Necrosis of amputation stump, unspecified extremity**

    T87.51 Necrosis of amputation stump, right upper extremity

    T87.52 Necrosis of amputation stump, left upper extremity

    T87.53 Necrosis of amputation stump, right lower extremity

    T87.54 Necrosis of amputation stump, left lower extremity

  T87.8 Other complications of amputation stump
    Amputation stump contracture
    Amputation stump contracture of next proximal joint
    Amputation stump flexion
    Amputation stump edema
    Amputation stump hematoma

    | **Excludes2** | phantom limb syndrome (G54.6-G54.7) |

  ▪ **T87.9 Unspecified complications of amputation stump**

● **T88 Other complications of surgical and medical care, not elsewhere classified**

  | **Excludes2** | complication following: |

    infusion, transfusion and therapeutic injection (T80.-)
    procedure NEC (T81.-)
    specified complications classified elsewhere, such as:
      complication of:
        anesthesia in:
          labor and delivery (O74.-)
          pregnancy (O29.-)
          puerperium (O89.-)
      devices, implants and grafts (T82-T85)
      obstetric surgery and procedure (O75.4)
      dermatitis due to drugs and medicaments (L23.3, L24.4, L25.1, L27.0-L27.1)
      poisoning and toxic effects of drugs and chemicals (T36-T65)

  The appropriate 7th character is to be added to each code from category T88

A	initial encounter
D	subsequent encounter
S	sequela

● **T88.0 Infection following immunization A**
    Sepsis following immunization

● **T88.1 Other complications following immunization, not elsewhere classified A**
    Generalized vaccinia
    Rash following immunization

    | **Excludes1** | vaccinia not from vaccine (B08.011) |

    | **Excludes2** | anaphylactic shock due to serum (T80.5) |
    other serum reactions (T80.6)
    postimmunization:
      arthropathy (M02.2)
      encephalitis (G04.0-)
      fever (R50.83)

●● **T88.2 Shock due to anesthesia A**
    Code first appropriate code from category T41

    | **Excludes1** | complications of anesthesia (in): |
      labor and delivery (O74.-)
      pregnancy (O29.-)
      puerperium (O89.-)
      postprocedural shock NOS (T81.1)

●● **T88.3 Malignant hyperthermia due to anesthesia A**
    Code first appropriate code from category T41

● **T88.4 Failed or difficult intubation**

●● **T88.5 Other complications of anesthesia**
    Code first appropriate code from category T41

  T88.51 Hypothermia following anesthesia

  T88.52 Failed moderate sedation during procedure
    Failed conscious sedation during procedure

    | **Excludes2** | personal history of failed moderate sedation (Z92.83) |

  T88.59 Other complications of anesthesia

●● **T88.6 Anaphylactic shock due to adverse effect of correct drug or medicament properly administered A**
    Code first (T36-T50 with fifth or sixth-character 5) to identify drug

    | **Excludes1** | anaphylactic shock due to serum (T80.5) |

●● ▪ **T88.7 Unspecified adverse effect of drug or medicament**
    Code first (T36-T50 with fifth or sixth-character 5) to identify drug

    This code is not for use in the inpatient environment and is for limited use in the outpatient environment only when no sign or symptom of the adverse effect is documented

    Drug hypersensitivity NOS
    Drug reaction NOS

    | **Excludes1** | specified adverse effects of drugs and medicaments (A00-R94 and T80-T88.6, T88.8) |

● **T88.8 Other specified complications of surgical and medical care, not elsewhere classified**
    Use additional code to identify the complication

● ▪ **T88.9 Complication of surgical and medical care, unspecified**

Categories T90-T98 deactivated. Replaced with 7th character S for categories S00-T88

● Unacceptable First-Listed Diagnosis   ● Use Additional Character(s)   ▪ Unspecified   **OGCR** Official Guidelines for Coding and Reporting

 Complication\Comorbidity   Major C\C   Excludes 1   Excludes 2   Includes   Use additional   Code first   Code also

1623

CHAPTER 19 (S00-T98)

OGCR See Guidelines, Section I.20.

CHAPTER 20

EXTERNAL CAUSES OF MORBIDITY (V01-Y99)

This chapter permits the classification of environmental events and circumstances as the cause of injury, and other adverse effects. Where a code from this section is applicable, it is intended that it shall be used secondary to a code from another chapter of the Classification indicating the nature of the condition. Most often, the condition will be classifiable to Chapter 19, Injury, poisoning and certain other consequences of external causes (S00-T98). Other conditions that may be stated to be due to external causes are classified in Chapters I to XVIII. For these conditions, codes from Chapter 20 should be used to provide additional information as to the cause of the condition.

This chapter contains the following blocks:

V00-X58	Accidents
V00-V99	Transport accidents
V00-V09	Pedestrian injured in transport accident
V10-V19	Pedal cyclist injured in transport accident
V20-V29	Motorcycle rider injured in transport accident
V30-V39	Occupant of three-wheeled motor vehicle injured in transport accident
V40-V49	Car occupant injured in transport accident
V50-V59	Occupant of pick-up truck or van injured in transport accident
V60-V69	Occupant of heavy transport vehicle injured in transport accident
V70-V79	Bus occupant injured in transport accident
V80-V89	Other land transport accidents
V90-V94	Water transport accidents
V95-V97	Air and space transport accidents
V98-V99	Other and unspecified transport accidents
W00-X58	Other external causes of accidental injury
W00-W19	Slipping, tripping, stumbling and falls
W20-W49	Exposure to inanimate mechanical forces
W50-W64	Exposure to animate mechanical forces
W65-W74	Accidental drowning and submersion
W85-W99	Exposure to electric current, radiation and extreme ambient air temperature and pressure
X00-X08	Exposure to smoke, fire and flames
X10-X19	Contact with heat and hot substances
X30-X39	Exposure to forces of nature
X52, X58	Accidental exposure to other specified factors
X71-X83	Intentional self-harm
X92-Y08	Assault
Y21-Y33	Event of undetermined intent
Y35-Y38	Legal intervention, operations of war, military operations, and terrorism
Y62-Y84	Complications of medical and surgical care

Y62-Y69	Misadventures to patients during surgical and medical care
Y70-Y82	Medical devices associated with adverse incidents in diagnostic and therapeutic use
Y83-Y84	Surgical and other medical procedures as the cause of abnormal reaction of the patient, or of later complication, without mention of misadventure at the time of the procedure
Y90-Y99	Supplementary factors related to causes of morbidity classified elsewhere

TRANSPORT ACCIDENTS (V00-V99)

This section is structured in 12 groups. Those relating to land transport accidents (V01- V89) reflect the victim's mode of transport and are subdivided to identify the victim's "counterpart" or the type of event. The vehicle of which the injured person is an occupant is identified in the first two characters since it is seen as the most important factor to identify for prevention purposes. A transport accident is one in which the vehicle involved must be moving or running or in use for transport purposes at the time of the accident.

Use additional code to identify:
Airbag injury (W22.1)
Type of street or road (Y92.4-)
Use of cellular telephone and other electronic equipment at the time of the transport accident (Y93.c-)

Excludes1 agricultural vehicles in stationary use or maintenance (W31.-)
assault by crashing of motor vehicle (Y03.-)
automobile or motor cycle in stationary use or maintenance - code to type of accident
crashing of motor vehicle, undetermined intent (Y32)
intentional self-harm by crashing of motor vehicle (X82)

Excludes2 transport accidents due to cataclysm (X34-X38)

Definitions of transport vehicles:
A transport accident is any accident involving a device designed primarily for, or used at the time primarily for, conveying persons or good from one place to another

A public highway [trafficway] or street is the entire width between property lines (or other boundary lines) of land open to the public as a matter of right or custom for purposes of moving persons or property from one place to another. A roadway is that part of the public highway designed, improved and customarily used for vehicular traffic.

A traffic accident is any vehicle accident occurring on the public highway [i.e. originating on, terminating on, or involving a vehicle partially on the highway]. A vehicle accident is assumed to have occurred on the public highway unless another place is specified, except in the case of accidents involving only off-road motor vehicles, which are classified as nontraffic accidents unless the contrary is stated.

A nontraffic accident is any vehicle accident that occurs entirely in any place other than a public highway.

A pedestrian is any person involved in an accident who was not at the time of the accident riding in or on a motor vehicle, railway train, streetcar or animal-drawn or other vehicle, or on a pedal cycle or animal. This includes, a person changing a tire or working on a parked car. It also includes the use of a pedestrian conveyance such as

● Unacceptable First-Listed Diagnosis ● Use Additional Character(s) ■ Unspecified OGCR Official Guidelines for Coding and Reporting
🖉 Complication\Comorbidity 🖉 Major C\C Excludes 1 Excludes 2 Includes Use additional Code first Code also

a baby carriage, ice-skates, roller skates, a skateboard, nonmotorized wheelchair, motorized mobility scooter, or nonmotorized scooter.

A driver is an occupant of a transport vehicle who is operating or intending to operate it.

A passenger is any occupant of a transport vehicle other than the driver, except a person traveling on the outside of the vehicle.

A person on the outside of a vehicle is any person being transported by a vehicle but not occupying the space normally reserved for the driver or passengers, or the space intended for the transport of property. This includes the body, bumper, fender, roof, running board or step of a vehicle.

A pedal cycle is any land transport vehicle operated solely by nonmotorized pedals including a bicycle or tricycle.

A pedal cyclist is any person riding a pedal cycle or in a sidecar or trailer attached to a pedal cycle.

A motorcycle is a two-wheeled motor vehicle with one or two riding saddles and sometimes with a third wheel for the support of a sidecar. The sidecar is considered part of the motorcycle.

A motorcycle rider is any person riding a motorcycle or in a sidecar or trailer attached to the motorcycle.

A three-wheeled motor vehicle is a motorized tricycle designed primarily for on-road use. This includes a motor-driven tricycle, a motorized rickshaw, or a three-wheeled motor car.

A car [automobile] is a four-wheeled motor vehicle designed primarily for carrying up to 7 persons. A trailer being towed by the car is considered part of the car.

A pick-up truck or van is a four or six-wheeled motor vehicle designed for carrying passengers as well as property or cargo weighing less than the local limit for classification as a heavy goods vehicle, and not requiring a special driver's license. This includes a minivan and a sport-utility vehicle (SUV).

A heavy transport vehicle is a motor vehicle designed primarily for carrying property, meeting local criteria for classification as a heavy goods vehicle in terms of weight and requiring a special driver's license.

A bus (coach) is a motor vehicle designed or adapted primarily for carrying more than 10 passengers, and requiring a special driver's license.

A railway train or railway vehicle is any device, with or without freight or passenger cars coupled to it, designed for traffic on a railway track. This includes subterranean (subways) or elevated trains.

A streetcar is a device designed and used primarily for transporting passengers within a municipality, running on rails, usually subject to normal traffic control signals, and operated principally on a right-of-way that forms part of the roadway. This includes a tram or trolley that runs on rails. A trailer being towed by a streetcar is considered part of the streetcar.

A special vehicle mainly used on industrial premises is a motor vehicle designed primarily for use within the buildings and premises of industrial or commercial establishments. This includes battery-powered trucks, forklifts, coal-cars in a coal mine, logging cars and trucks used in mines or quarries.

A special vehicle mainly used in agriculture is a motor vehicle designed specifically for use in farming and

agriculture (horticulture), to work the land, tend and harvest crops and transport materials on the farm. This includes harvesters, farm machinery and tractor and trailers.

A special construction vehicle is a motor vehicle designed specifically for use on construction and demolition sites. This includes bulldozers, diggers, earth levellers, dump trucks, backhoes, front-end loaders, pavers, and mechanical shovels.

A special all-terrain vehicle is a motor vehicle of special design to enable it to negotiate over rough or soft terrain, snow or sand. This includes snow mobiles, all-terrain vehicles (ATV), and dune buggies. It does not include passenger vehicle designated as sport utility vehicles. (SUV)

A watercraft is any device designed for transporting passengers or goods on water. This includes motor or sail boats, ships, and hovercraft.

An aircraft is any device for transporting passengers or goods in the air. This includes hot-air balloons, gliders, helicopters and airplanes.

A military vehicle is any motorized vehicle operating on a public roadway owned by the military and being operated by a member of the military.

PEDESTRIAN INJURED IN TRANSPORT ACCIDENT (V00-V09)

Includes   person changing tire on transport vehicle
     person examining engine of vehicle broken down in (on side of) road

Excludes1   fall due to non-transport collision with other person (W03)
     pedestrian on foot falling (slipping) on ice and snow (W00.-)
     struck or bumped by another person (W51)

● **V00**   **Pedestrian conveyance accident**

Use additional place of occurrence and activity external cause codes, if known (Y92.-, Y93.-)

Excludes1   collision with another person without fall (W51)
     fall due to person on foot colliding with another person on foot (W03)
     fall from wheelchair without collision (W05)
     pedestrian (conveyance) collision with other land transport vehicle (V01-V09)
     pedestrian on foot falling (slipping) on ice and snow (W00.-)

The appropriate 7th character is to be added to each code from category V00

> A   initial encounter
> D   subsequent encounter
> S   sequela

● **V00.0**   **Pedestrian on foot injured in collision with pedestrian conveyance**

   ● **V00.01**   **Pedestrian on foot injured in collision with roller-skater**

   ● **V00.02**   **Pedestrian on foot injured in collision with skateboarder**

   ● **V00.09**   **Pedestrian on foot injured in collision with other pedestrian conveyance**

● **V00.1**   **Rolling-type pedestrian conveyance accident**

   Excludes1   accident with babystroller (V00.82-)
     accident with wheelchair (powered) (V00.81-)

● Unacceptable First-Listed Diagnosis   ● Use Additional Character(s)   ■ Unspecified   OGCR Official Guidelines for Coding and Reporting

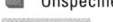 Complication\Comorbidity   🗸 Major C\C   [Excludes 1]   [Excludes 2]   Includes   Use additional   Code first   Code also

1625

- V00.11 In-line roller-skate accident
  - V00.111 Fall from in-line roller-skates
  - V00.112 In-line roller-skater colliding with stationary object
  - V00.118 Other in-line roller-skate accident

    | Excludes1 | roller-skater collision with other land transport vehicle (V01-V09 with 5th character 1) |

- V00.12 Non-in-line roller-skate accident
  - V00.121 Fall from non-in-line roller-skates
  - V00.122 Non-in-line roller-skater colliding with stationary object
  - V00.128 Other non-in-line roller-skating accident

    | Excludes1 | roller-skater collision with other land transport vehicle (V01-V09 with 5th character 1) |

- V00.13 Skateboard accident
  - V00.131 Fall from skateboard
  - V00.132 Skateboarder colliding with stationary object
  - V00.138 Other skateboard accident

    | Excludes1 | skateboarder collision with other land transport vehicle (V01-V09 with 5th character 2) |

- V00.14 Scooter (nonmotorized) accident

  | Excludes1 | motorscooter accident (V20-V29) |

  - V00.141 Fall from scooter (nonmotorized)
  - V00.142 Scooter (nonmotorized) colliding with stationary object
  - V00.148 Other scooter (nonmotorized) accident

    | Excludes1 | scooter (non-motorized) collision with other land transport vehicle (V01-V09 with fifth character 9) |

- V00.15 Heelies accident
  Wheelies accident
  - V00.151 Fall from heelies
  - V00.152 Heelies colliding with stationary object
  - V00.158 Other heelies accident
- V00.18 Accident on other rolling-type pedestrian conveyance
  - V00.181 Fall from other rolling-type pedestrian conveyance
  - V00.182 Pedestrian on other rolling-type pedestrian conveyance colliding with stationary object
  - V00.188 Other accident on other rolling-type pedestrian conveyance

- V00.2 Gliding-type pedestrian conveyance accident
  - V00.21 Ice-skates accident
    - V00.211 Fall from ice-skates
    - V00.212 Ice-skater colliding with stationary object
    - V00.218 Other ice-skates accident

      | Excludes1 | ice-skater collision with other land transport vehicle (V01-V09 with 5th digit 9) |

  - V00.22 Sled accident
    - V00.221 Fall from sled
    - V00.222 Sledder colliding with stationary object
    - V00.228 Other sled accident

      | Excludes1 | sled collision with other land transport vehicle (V01-V09 with 5th digit 9) |

  - V00.28 Other gliding-type pedestrian conveyance accident
    - V00.281 Fall from other gliding-type pedestrian conveyance
    - V00.282 Pedestrian on other gliding-type pedestrian conveyance colliding with stationary object
    - V00.288 Other accident on other gliding-type pedestrian conveyance

      | Excludes1 | gliding-type pedestrian conveyance collision with other land transport vehicle (V01-V09 with 5th digit 9) |

- V00.3 Flat-bottomed pedestrian conveyance accident
  - V00.31 Snowboard accident
    - V00.311 Fall from snowboard
    - V00.312 Snowboarder colliding with stationary object
    - V00.318 Other snowboard accident

      | Excludes1 | snowboarder collision with other land transport vehicle (V01-V09 with 5th digit 9) |

  - V00.32 Snow-ski accident
    - V00.321 Fall from snow-skis
    - V00.322 Snow-skier colliding with stationary object

- Unacceptable First-Listed Diagnosis   ● Use Additional Character(s)   ■ Unspecified   OGCR Official Guidelines for Coding and Reporting
- Complication\Comorbidity   Major C\C | Excludes 1 | | Excludes 2 | | Includes | | Use additional | | Code first | | Code also |

● V00.328   Other snow-ski accident
     Excludes1   snow-skier collision with other land transport vehicle (V01-V09 with 5th digit 9)

● V00.38   Other flat-bottomed pedestrian conveyance accident

  ● V00.381   Fall from other flat-bottomed pedestrian conveyance

  ● V00.382   Pedestrian on other flat-bottomed pedestrian conveyance colliding with stationary object

  ● V00.388   Other accident on other flat-bottomed pedestrian conveyance

● V00.8   Accident on other pedestrian conveyance

 ● V00.81   Accident with wheelchair (powered)

  ● V00.811   Fall from moving wheelchair (powered)
       Excludes1   fall from non-moving wheelchair (W05)

  ● V00.812   Wheelchair (powered) colliding with stationary object

  ● V00.818   Other accident with wheelchair (powered)

 ● V00.82   Accident with babystroller

  ● V00.821   Fall from babystroller

  ● V00.822   Babystroller colliding with stationary object

  ● V00.828   Other accident with babystroller

 ● V00.89   Accident on other pedestrian conveyance

  ● V00.891   Fall from other pedestrian conveyance

  ● V00.892   Pedestrian on other pedestrian conveyance colliding with stationary object

  ● V00.898   Other accident on other pedestrian conveyance
       Excludes1   other pedestrian (conveyance) collision with other land transport vehicle (V01-V09 with 5th digit 9)

● V01   Pedestrian injured in collision with pedal cycle
The appropriate 7th character is to be added to each code from category V01

     A   initial encounter
     D   subsequent encounter
     S   sequela

● V01.0   Pedestrian injured in collision with pedal cycle in nontraffic accident

 ● V01.00   Pedestrian on foot injured in collision with pedal cycle in nontraffic accident
     Pedestrian NOS injured in collision with pedal cycle in nontraffic accident

 ● V01.01   Pedestrian on roller-skates injured in collision with pedal cycle in nontraffic accident

● V01.02   Pedestrian on skateboard injured in collision with pedal cycle in nontraffic accident

● V01.09   Pedestrian with other conveyance injured in collision with pedal cycle in nontraffic accident
     Pedestrian with babystroller injured in collision with pedal cycle in nontraffic accident
     Pedestrian on ice-skates injured in collision with pedal cycle in nontraffic accident
     Pedestrian on sled injured in collision with pedal cycle in nontraffic accident
     Pedestrian on snowboard injured in collision with pedal cycle in nontraffic accident
     Pedestrian on snow-skis injured in collision with pedal cycle in nontraffic accident
     Pedestrian in wheelchair (powered) injured in collision with pedal cycle in nontraffic accident

● V01.1   Pedestrian injured in collision with pedal cycle in traffic accident

 ● V01.10   Pedestrian on foot injured in collision with pedal cycle in traffic accident
     Pedestrian NOS injured in collision with pedal cycle in traffic accident

 ● V01.11   Pedestrian on roller-skates injured in collision with pedal cycle in traffic accident

 ● V01.12   Pedestrian on skateboard injured in collision with pedal cycle in traffic accident

 ● V01.19   Pedestrian with other conveyance injured in collision with pedal cycle in traffic accident
     Pedestrian with babystroller injured in collision with pedal cycle in traffic accident
     Pedestrian on ice-skates injured in collision with pedal cycle in traffic accident
     Pedestrian on sled injured in collision with pedal cycle in traffic accident
     Pedestrian on snowboard injured in collision with pedal cycle in traffic accident
     Pedestrian on snow-skis injured in collision with pedal cycle in traffic accident
     Pedestrian in wheelchair (powered) injured in collision with pedal cycle in traffic accident

● V01.9   Pedestrian injured in collision with pedal cycle, unspecified whether traffic or nontraffic accident

 ● ■ V01.90   Pedestrian on foot injured in collision with pedal cycle, unspecified whether traffic or nontraffic accident
     Pedestrian NOS injured in collision with pedal cycle, unspecified whether traffic or nontraffic accident

 ● ■ V01.91   Pedestrian on roller-skates injured in collision with pedal cycle, unspecified whether traffic or nontraffic accident

 ● ■ V01.92   Pedestrian on skateboard injured in collision with pedal cycle, unspecified whether traffic or nontraffic accident

---

● Unacceptable First-Listed Diagnosis   ● Use Additional Character(s)   ■ Unspecified   **OGCR** Official Guidelines for Coding and Reporting

🗞 Complication\Comorbidity   🗞 Major C\C   Excludes 1   Excludes 2   Includes   Use additional   Code first   Code also

● ◪ **V01.99 Pedestrian with other conveyance injured in collision with pedal cycle, unspecified whether traffic or nontraffic accident**
     Pedestrian with babystroller injured in collision with pedal cycle, unspecified whether traffic or nontraffic accident
     Pedestrian on ice-skates injured in collision with pedal cycle unspecified, whether traffic or nontraffic accident
     Pedestrian on sled injured in collision with pedal cycle unspecified, whether traffic or nontraffic accident
     Pedestrian on snowboard injured in collision with pedal cycle, unspecified whether traffic or nontraffic accident
     Pedestrian on snow-skis injured in collision with pedal cycle, unspecified whether traffic or nontraffic accident
     Pedestrian in wheelchair (powered) injured in collision with pedal cycle, unspecified whether traffic or nontraffic accident

● **V02 Pedestrian injured in collision with two- or three-wheeled motor vehicle**
     The appropriate 7th character is to be added to each code from category V02

> A   initial encounter
> D   subsequent encounter
> S   sequela

● **V02.0 Pedestrian injured in collision with two- or three-wheeled motor vehicle in nontraffic accident**

● **V02.00 Pedestrian on foot injured in collision with two- or three-wheeled motor vehicle in nontraffic accident**
     Pedestrian NOS injured in collision with two- or three-wheeled motor vehicle in nontraffic accident

● **V02.01 Pedestrian on roller-skates injured in collision with two- or three-wheeled motor vehicle in nontraffic accident**

● **V02.02 Pedestrian on skateboard injured in collision with two- or three-wheeled motor vehicle in nontraffic accident**

● **V02.09 Pedestrian with other conveyance injured in collision with two- or three-wheeled motor vehicle in nontraffic accident**
     Pedestrian with babystroller injured in collision with two- or three-wheeled motor vehicle in nontraffic accident
     Pedestrian on ice-skates injured in collision with two- or three-wheeled motor vehicle in nontraffic accident
     Pedestrian on sled injured in collision with two- or three-wheeled motor vehicle in nontraffic accident
     Pedestrian on snowboard injured in collision with two- or three-wheeled motor vehicle in nontraffic accident
     Pedestrian on snow-skis injured in collision with two- or three-wheeled motor vehicle in nontraffic accident
     Pedestrian in wheelchair (powered) injured in collision with two- or three-wheeled motor vehicle in nontraffic accident

● **V02.1 Pedestrian injured in collision with two- or three-wheeled motor vehicle in traffic accident**

● **V02.10 Pedestrian on foot injured in collision with two- or three-wheeled motor vehicle in traffic accident**
     Pedestrian NOS injured in collision with two- or three-wheeled motor vehicle in traffic accident

● **V02.11 Pedestrian on roller-skates injured in collision with two- or three-wheeled motor vehicle in traffic accident**

● **V02.12 Pedestrian on skateboard injured in collision with two- or three-wheeled motor vehicle in traffic accident**

● **V02.19 Pedestrian with other conveyance injured in collision with two- or three-wheeled motor vehicle in traffic accident**
     Pedestrian with babystroller injured in collision with two- or three-wheeled motor vehicle in traffic accident
     Pedestrian on ice-skates injured in collision with two- or three-wheeled motor vehicle in traffic accident
     Pedestrian on sled injured in collision with two- or three-wheeled motor vehicle in traffic accident
     Pedestrian on snowboard injured in collision with two- or three-wheeled motor vehicle in traffic accident
     Pedestrian on snow-skis injured in collision with two- or three-wheeled motor vehicle in traffic accident
     Pedestrian in wheelchair (powered) injured in collision with two- or three-wheeled motor vehicle in traffic accident

● **V02.9 Pedestrian injured in collision with two- or three-wheeled motor vehicle, unspecified whether traffic or nontraffic accident**

● ◪ **V02.90 Pedestrian on foot injured in collision with two- or three-wheeled motor vehicle, unspecified whether traffic or nontraffic accident**
     Pedestrian NOS injured in collision with two- or three-wheeled motor vehicle, unspecified whether traffic or nontraffic accident

● ◪ **V02.91 Pedestrian on roller-skates injured in collision with two- or three-wheeled motor vehicle, unspecified whether traffic or nontraffic accident**

● ◪ **V02.92 Pedestrian on skateboard injured in collision with two- or three-wheeled motor vehicle, unspecified whether traffic or nontraffic accident**

● Unacceptable First-Listed Diagnosis   ● Use Additional Character(s)   ◪ Unspecified   **OGCR** Official Guidelines for Coding and Reporting
🖉 Complication\Comorbidity   🖉 Major C\C   Excludes 1   Excludes 2   Includes   Use additional   Code first   Code also

● ■ **V02.99 Pedestrian with other conveyance injured in collision with two- or three-wheeled motor vehicle, unspecified whether traffic or nontraffic accident**

Pedestrian with babystroller injured in collision with two- or three-wheeled motor vehicle, unspecified whether traffic or nontraffic accident

Pedestrian on ice-skates injured in collision with two- or three-wheeled motor vehicle, unspecified whether traffic or nontraffic accident

Pedestrian on sled injured in collision with two- or three-wheeled motor vehicle, unspecified whether traffic or nontraffic accident

Pedestrian on snowboard injured in collision with two- or three-wheeled motor vehicle, unspecified whether traffic or nontraffic accident

Pedestrian on snow-skis injured in collision with two- or three-wheeled motor vehicle, unspecified whether traffic or nontraffic accident

Pedestrian in wheelchair (powered) injured in collision with two- or three-wheeled motor vehicle, unspecified whether traffic or nontraffic accident

● **V03 Pedestrian injured in collision with car, pick-up truck or van**

The appropriate 7th character is to be added to each code from category V03

A initial encounter
D subsequent encounter
S sequela

● **V03.0 Pedestrian injured in collision with car, pick-up truck or van in nontraffic accident**

● **V03.00 Pedestrian on foot injured in collision with car, pick-up truck or van in nontraffic accident**

Pedestrian NOS injured in collision with car, pick-up truck or van in nontraffic accident

● **V03.01 Pedestrian on roller-skates injured in collision with car, pick-up truck or van in nontraffic accident**

● **V03.02 Pedestrian on skateboard injured in collision with car, pick-up truck or van in nontraffic accident**

● **V03.09 Pedestrian with other conveyance injured in collision with car, pick-up truck or van in nontraffic accident**

Pedestrian with babystroller injured in collision with car, pick-up truck or van in nontraffic accident

Pedestrian on ice-skates injured in collision with car, pick-up truck or van in nontraffic accident

Pedestrian on sled injured in collision with car, pick-up truck or van in nontraffic accident

Pedestrian on snowboard injured in collision with car, pick-up truck or van in nontraffic accident

Pedestrian on snow-skis injured in collision with car, pick-up truck or van in nontraffic accident

Pedestrian in wheelchair (powered) injured in collision with car, pick-up truck or van in nontraffic accident

● **V03.1 Pedestrian injured in collision with car, pick-up truck or van in traffic accident**

● **V03.10 Pedestrian on foot injured in collision with car, pick-up truck or van in traffic accident**

Pedestrian NOS injured in collision with car, pick-up truck or van in traffic accident

● **V03.11 Pedestrian on roller-skates injured in collision with car, pick-up truck or van in traffic accident**

● **V03.12 Pedestrian on skateboard injured in collision with car, pick-up truck or van in traffic accident**

● **V03.19 Pedestrian with other conveyance injured in collision with car, pick-up truck or van in traffic accident**

Pedestrian with babystroller injured in collision with car, pick-up truck or van in traffic accident

Pedestrian on ice-skates injured in collision with car, pick-up truck or van in traffic accident

Pedestrian on sled injured in collision with car, pick-up truck or van in traffic accident

Pedestrian on snowboard injured in collision with car, pick-up truck or van in traffic accident

Pedestrian on snow-skis injured in collision with car, pick-up truck or van in traffic accident

Pedestrian in wheelchair (powered) injured in collision with car, pick-up truck or van in traffic accident

● **V03.9 Pedestrian injured in collision with car, pick-up truck or van, unspecified whether traffic or nontraffic accident**

● ■ **V03.90 Pedestrian on foot injured in collision with car, pick-up truck or van, unspecified whether traffic or nontraffic accident**

Pedestrian NOS injured in collision with car, pick-up truck or van, unspecified whether traffic or nontraffic accident

● ■ **V03.91 Pedestrian on roller-skates injured in collision with car, pick-up truck or van, unspecified whether traffic or nontraffic accident**

● ■ **V03.92 Pedestrian on skateboard injured in collision with car, pick-up truck or van, unspecified whether traffic or nontraffic accident**

● Unacceptable First-Listed Diagnosis ● Use Additional Character(s) ■ Unspecified **OGCR** Official Guidelines for Coding and Reporting
🗲 Complication\Comorbidity 🗲 Major C\C Excludes 1 Excludes 2 Includes Use additional Code first Code also
CHAPTER 20 (V01-Y99) 1629

● ■● **V03.99 Pedestrian with other conveyance injured in collision with car, pick-up truck or van, unspecified whether traffic or nontraffic accident**

Pedestrian with babystroller injured in collision with car, pick-up truck or van, unspecified whether traffic or nontraffic accident

Pedestrian on ice-skates injured in collision with car, pick-up truck or van, unspecified whether traffic or nontraffic accident

Pedestrian on sled injured in collision with car, pick-up truck or van in nontraffic accident

Pedestrian on snowboard injured in collision with car, pick-up truck or van, unspecified whether traffic or nontraffic accident

Pedestrian on snow-skis injured in collision with car, pick-up truck or van, unspecified whether traffic or nontraffic accident

Pedestrian in wheelchair (powered) injured in collision with car, pick-up truck or van, unspecified whether traffic or nontraffic accident

● **V04   Pedestrian injured in collision with heavy transport vehicle or bus**

> **Excludes1** pedestrian injured in collision with military vehicle (V09.01, V09.21)

The appropriate 7th character is to be added to each code from category V04

A	initial encounter
D	subsequent encounter
S	sequela

● **V04.0 Pedestrian injured in collision with heavy transport vehicle or bus in nontraffic accident**

● **V04.00 Pedestrian on foot injured in collision with heavy transport vehicle or bus in nontraffic accident**

Pedestrian NOS injured in collision with heavy transport vehicle or bus in nontraffic accident

● **V04.01 Pedestrian on roller-skates injured in collision with heavy transport vehicle or bus in nontraffic accident**

● **V04.02 Pedestrian on skateboard injured in collision with heavy transport vehicle or bus in nontraffic accident**

● **V04.09 Pedestrian with other conveyance injured in collision with heavy transport vehicle or bus in nontraffic accident**

Pedestrian with babystroller injured in collision with heavy transport vehicle or bus in nontraffic accident

Pedestrian on ice-skates injured in collision with heavy transport vehicle or bus in nontraffic accident

Pedestrian on sled injured in collision with heavy transport vehicle or bus in nontraffic accident

Pedestrian on snowboard injured in collision with heavy transport vehicle or bus in nontraffic accident

Pedestrian on snow-skis injured in collision with heavy transport vehicle or bus in nontraffic accident

Pedestrian in wheelchair (powered) injured in collision with heavy transport vehicle or bus in nontraffic accident

● **V04.1 Pedestrian injured in collision with heavy transport vehicle or bus in traffic accident**

● **V04.10 Pedestrian on foot injured in collision with heavy transport vehicle or bus in traffic accident**

Pedestrian NOS injured in collision with heavy transport vehicle or bus in traffic accident

● **V04.11 Pedestrian on roller-skates injured in collision with heavy transport vehicle or bus in traffic accident**

● **V04.12 Pedestrian on skateboard injured in collision with heavy transport vehicle or bus in traffic accident**

● **V04.19 Pedestrian with other conveyance injured in collision with heavy transport vehicle or bus in traffic accident**

Pedestrian with babystroller injured in collision with heavy transport vehicle or bus in traffic accident

Pedestrian on ice-skates injured in collision with heavy transport vehicle or bus in traffic accident

Pedestrian on sled injured in collision with heavy transport vehicle or bus in traffic accident

Pedestrian on snowboard injured in collision with heavy transport vehicle or bus in traffic accident

Pedestrian on snow-skis injured in collision with heavy transport vehicle or bus in traffic accident

Pedestrian in wheelchair (powered) injured in collision with heavy transport vehicle or bus in traffic accident

● **V04.9 Pedestrian injured in collision with heavy transport vehicle or bus, unspecified whether traffic or nontraffic accident**

● ■ **V04.90 Pedestrian on foot injured in collision with heavy transport vehicle or bus, unspecified whether traffic or nontraffic accident**

Pedestrian NOS injured in collision with heavy transport vehicle or bus, unspecified whether traffic or nontraffic accident

● ■ **V04.91 Pedestrian on roller-skates injured in collision with heavy transport vehicle or bus, unspecified whether traffic or nontraffic accident**

● ■ **V04.92 Pedestrian on skateboard injured in collision with heavy transport vehicle or bus, unspecified whether traffic or nontraffic accident**

● Unacceptable First-Listed Diagnosis   ● Use Additional Character(s)   ■ Unspecified   **OGCR** Official Guidelines for Coding and Reporting

🗎 Complication\Comorbidity   🗎 Major C\C   Excludes 1   Excludes 2   Includes   Use additional   Code first   Code also

● ◼ **V04.99   Pedestrian with other conveyance injured in collision with heavy transport vehicle or bus, unspecified whether traffic or nontraffic accident**

Pedestrian with babystroller injured in collision with heavy transport vehicle or bus, unspecified whether traffic or nontraffic accident

Pedestrian on ice-skates injured in collision with heavy transport vehicle or bus, unspecified whether traffic or nontraffic accident

Pedestrian on sled injured in collision with heavy transport vehicle or bus, unspecified whether traffic or nontraffic accident

Pedestrian on snowboard injured in collision with heavy transport vehicle or bus, unspecified whether traffic or nontraffic accident

Pedestrian on snow-skis injured in collision with heavy transport vehicle or bus, unspecified whether traffic or nontraffic accident

Pedestrian in wheelchair (powered) injured in collision with heavy transport vehicle or bus, unspecified whether traffic or nontraffic accident

● **V05   Pedestrian injured in collision with railway train or railway vehicle**

The appropriate 7th character is to be added to each code from category V05

A	initial encounter
D	subsequent encounter
S	sequela

● **V05.0   Pedestrian injured in collision with railway train or railway vehicle in nontraffic accident**

● **V05.00   Pedestrian on foot injured in collision with railway train or railway vehicle in nontraffic accident**

Pedestrian NOS injured in collision with railway train or railway vehicle in nontraffic accident

● **V05.01   Pedestrian on roller-skates injured in collision with railway train or railway vehicle in nontraffic accident**

● **V05.02   Pedestrian on skateboard injured in collision with railway train or railway vehicle in nontraffic accident**

● **V05.09   Pedestrian with other conveyance injured in collision with railway train or railway vehicle in nontraffic accident**

Pedestrian with babystroller injured in collision with railway train or railway vehicle in nontraffic accident

Pedestrian on ice-skates injured in collision with railway train or railway vehicle in nontraffic accident

Pedestrian on sled injured in collision with railway train or railway vehicle in nontraffic accident

Pedestrian on snowboard injured in collision with railway train or railway vehicle in nontraffic accident

Pedestrian on snow-skis injured in collision with railway train or railway vehicle in nontraffic accident

Pedestrian in wheelchair (powered) injured in collision with railway train or railway vehicle in nontraffic accident

● **V05.1   Pedestrian injured in collision with railway train or railway vehicle in traffic accident**

● **V05.10   Pedestrian on foot injured in collision with railway train or railway vehicle in traffic accident**

Pedestrian NOS injured in collision with railway train or railway vehicle in traffic accident

● **V05.11   Pedestrian on roller-skates injured in collision with railway train or railway vehicle in traffic accident**

● **V05.12   Pedestrian on skateboard injured in collision with railway train or railway vehicle in traffic accident**

● **V05.19   Pedestrian with other conveyance injured in collision with railway train or railway vehicle in traffic accident**

Pedestrian with babystroller injured in collision with railway train or railway vehicle in traffic accident

Pedestrian on ice-skates injured in collision with railway train or railway vehicle in traffic accident

Pedestrian on sled injured in collision with railway train or railway vehicle in traffic accident

Pedestrian on snowboard injured in collision with railway train or railway vehicle in traffic accident

Pedestrian on snow-skis injured in collision with railway train or railway vehicle in traffic accident

Pedestrian in wheelchair (powered) injured in collision with railway train or railway vehicle in traffic accident

● **V05.9   Pedestrian injured in collision with railway train or railway vehicle, unspecified whether traffic or nontraffic accident**

● ◼ **V05.90   Pedestrian on foot injured in collision with railway train or railway vehicle, unspecified whether traffic or nontraffic accident**

Pedestrian NOS injured in collision with railway train or railway vehicle, unspecified whether traffic or nontraffic accident

● ◼ **V05.91   Pedestrian on roller-skates injured in collision with railway train or railway vehicle, unspecified whether traffic or nontraffic accident**

● ◼ **V05.92   Pedestrian on skateboard injured in collision with railway train or railway vehicle, unspecified whether traffic or nontraffic accident**

● Unacceptable First-Listed Diagnosis   ● Use Additional Character(s)   ◼ Unspecified   **OGCR** Official Guidelines for Coding and Reporting

🅒 Complication\Comorbidity   🅒 Major C\C | Excludes 1 | | Excludes 2 | Includes   Use additional   Code first   Code also

1631

CHAPTER 20 (V01-Y99)

● 🔳 **V05.99 Pedestrian with other conveyance injured in collision with railway train or railway vehicle, unspecified whether traffic or nontraffic accident**
Pedestrian with babystroller injured in collision with railway train or railway vehicle, unspecified whether traffic or nontraffic
Pedestrian on ice-skates injured in collision with railway train or railway vehicle, unspecified whether traffic or nontraffic
Pedestrian on sled injured in collision with railway train or railway vehicle, unspecified whether traffic or nontraffic
Pedestrian on snowboard injured in collision with railway train or railway vehicle, unspecified whether traffic or nontraffic
Pedestrian on snow-skis injured in collision with railway train or railway vehicle, unspecified whether traffic or nontraffic
Pedestrian in wheelchair (powered) injured in collision with railway train or railway vehicle, unspecified whether traffic or nontraffic

● **V06 Pedestrian injured in collision with other nonmotor vehicle**

> **Includes**   collision with animal-drawn vehicle, animal being ridden, nonpowered streetcar

> **Excludes1**   pedestrian injured in collision with pedestrian conveyance (V00.0-)

The appropriate 7th character is to be added to each code from category V06
> A   initial encounter
> D   subsequent encounter
> S   sequela

● **V06.0 Pedestrian injured in collision with other nonmotor vehicle in nontraffic accident**

> ● **V06.00 Pedestrian on foot injured in collision with other nonmotor vehicle in nontraffic accident**
> Pedestrian NOS injured in collision with other nonmotor vehicle in nontraffic accident

> ● **V06.01 Pedestrian on roller-skates injured in collision with other nonmotor vehicle in nontraffic accident**

> ● **V06.02 Pedestrian on skateboard injured in collision with other nonmotor vehicle in nontraffic accident**

● **V06.09 Pedestrian with other conveyance injured in collision with other nonmotor vehicle in nontraffic accident**
Pedestrian with babystroller injured in collision with other nonmotor vehicle in nontraffic accident
Pedestrian on ice-skates injured in collision with other nonmotor vehicle in nontraffic accident
Pedestrian on sled injured in collision with other nonmotor vehicle in nontraffic accident
Pedestrian on snowboard injured in collision with other nonmotor vehicle in nontraffic accident
Pedestrian on snow-skis injured in collision with other nonmotor vehicle in nontraffic accident
Pedestrian in wheelchair (powered) injured in collision with other nonmotor vehicle in nontraffic accident

● **V06.1 Pedestrian injured in collision with other nonmotor vehicle in traffic accident**

> ● **V06.10 Pedestrian on foot injured in collision with other nonmotor vehicle in traffic accident**
> Pedestrian NOS injured in collision with other nonmotor vehicle in traffic accident

> ● **V06.11 Pedestrian on roller-skates injured in collision with other nonmotor vehicle in traffic accident**

> ● **V06.12 Pedestrian on skateboard injured in collision with other nonmotor vehicle in traffic accident**

> ● **V06.19 Pedestrian with other conveyance injured in collision with other nonmotor vehicle in traffic accident**
> Pedestrian with babystroller injured in collision with other nonmotor vehicle in nontraffic accident
> Pedestrian on ice-skates injured in collision with other nonmotor vehicle in traffic accident
> Pedestrian on sled injured in collision with other nonmotor vehicle in traffic accident
> Pedestrian on snowboard injured in collision with other nonmotor vehicle in traffic accident
> Pedestrian on snow-skis injured in collision with other nonmotor vehicle in traffic accident
> Pedestrian in wheelchair (powered) injured in collision with other nonmotor vehicle in traffic accident

● **V06.9 Pedestrian injured in collision with other nonmotor vehicle, unspecified whether traffic or nontraffic accident**

> ● 🔳 **V06.90 Pedestrian on foot injured in collision with other nonmotor vehicle, unspecified whether traffic or nontraffic accident**
> Pedestrian NOS injured in collision with other nonmotor vehicle, unspecified whether traffic or nontraffic accident

> ● 🔳 **V06.91 Pedestrian on roller-skates injured in collision with other nonmotor vehicle, unspecified whether traffic or nontraffic accident**

● ▣ **V06.92**   **Pedestrian on skateboard injured in collision with other nonmotor vehicle, unspecified whether traffic or nontraffic accident**

● ▣ **V06.99**   **Pedestrian with other conveyance injured in collision with other nonmotor vehicle, unspecified whether traffic or nontraffic accident**

     Pedestrian with babystroller injured in collision with other nonmotor vehicle, unspecified whether traffic or nontraffic accident

     Pedestrian on ice-skates injured in collision with other nonmotor vehicle, unspecified whether traffic or nontraffic accident

     Pedestrian on sled injured in collision with other nonmotor vehicle, unspecified whether traffic or nontraffic accident

     Pedestrian on snowboard injured in collision with other nonmotor vehicle, unspecified whether traffic or nontraffic accident

     Pedestrian on snow-skis injured in collision with other nonmotor vehicle, unspecified whether traffic or nontraffic accident

     Pedestrian in wheelchair (powered) injured in collision with other nonmotor vehicle, unspecified whether traffic or nontraffic accident

● **V09**   **Pedestrian injured in other and unspecified transport accidents**

     The appropriate 7th character is to be added to each code from category V09

A	initial encounter
D	subsequent encounter
S	sequela

● **V09.0**   **Pedestrian injured in nontraffic accident involving other and unspecified motor vehicles**

   ● ▣ **V09.00**   **Pedestrian injured in nontraffic accident involving unspecified motor vehicles**

   ● **V09.01**   **Pedestrian injured in nontraffic accident involving military vehicle**

   ● **V09.09**   **Pedestrian injured in nontraffic accident involving other motor vehicles**

      Pedestrian injured in nontraffic accident by special vehicle

● ▣ **V09.1**   **Pedestrian injured in unspecified nontraffic accident**

● **V09.2**   **Pedestrian injured in traffic accident involving other and unspecified motor vehicles**

   ● ▣ **V09.20**   **Pedestrian injured in traffic accident involving unspecified motor vehicles**

   ● **V09.21**   **Pedestrian injured in traffic accident involving military vehicle**

   ● **V09.29**   **Pedestrian injured in traffic accident involving other motor vehicles**

● ▣ **V09.3**   **Pedestrian injured in unspecified traffic accident**

● ▣ **V09.9**   **Pedestrian injured in unspecified transport accident**

PEDAL CYCLE RIDER INJURED IN TRANSPORT ACCIDENT (V10-V19)

Includes   any non-motorized vehicle, excluding an animal-drawn vehicle, or a sidecar or trailer attached to the pedal cycle

Excludes2   rupture of pedal cycle tire (W37.0)

● **V10**   **Pedal cycle rider injured in collision with pedestrian or animal**

   Excludes1   pedal cycle rider collision with animal-drawn vehicle or animal being ridden (V16.-)

   The appropriate 7th character is to be added to each code from category V10

A	initial encounter
D	subsequent encounter
S	sequela

● **V10.0**   **Pedal cycle driver injured in collision with pedestrian or animal in nontraffic accident**

● **V10.1**   **Pedal cycle passenger injured in collision with pedestrian or animal in nontraffic accident**

● ▣ **V10.2**   **Unspecified pedal cyclist injured in collision with pedestrian or animal in nontraffic accident**

● **V10.3**   **Person boarding or alighting a pedal cycle injured in collision with pedestrian or animal**

● **V10.4**   **Pedal cycle driver injured in collision with pedestrian or animal in traffic accident**

● **V10.5**   **Pedal cycle passenger injured in collision with pedestrian or animal in traffic accident**

● ▣ **V10.9**   **Unspecified pedal cyclist injured in collision with pedestrian or animal in traffic accident**

● **V11**   **Pedal cycle rider injured in collision with other pedal cycle**

   The appropriate 7th character is to be added to each code from category V11

A	initial encounter
D	subsequent encounter
S	sequela

● **V11.0**   **Pedal cycle driver injured in collision with other pedal cycle in nontraffic accident**

● **V11.1**   **Pedal cycle passenger injured in collision with other pedal cycle in nontraffic accident**

● ▣ **V11.2**   **Unspecified pedal cyclist injured in collision with other pedal cycle in nontraffic accident**

● **V11.3**   **Person boarding or alighting a pedal cycle injured in collision with other pedal cycle**

● **V11.4**   **Pedal cycle driver injured in collision with other pedal cycle in traffic accident**

● **V11.5**   **Pedal cycle passenger injured in collision with other pedal cycle in traffic accident**

● ▣ **V11.9**   **Unspecified pedal cyclist injured in collision with other pedal cycle in traffic accident**

● **V12**   **Pedal cycle rider injured in collision with two- or three-wheeled motor vehicle**

   The appropriate 7th character is to be added to each code from category V12

A	initial encounter
D	subsequent encounter
S	sequela

● **V12.0**   **Pedal cycle driver injured in collision with two- or three-wheeled motor vehicle in nontraffic accident**

● **V12.1**   **Pedal cycle passenger injured in collision with two- or three-wheeled motor vehicle in nontraffic accident**

● ▣ **V12.2**   **Unspecified pedal cyclist injured in collision with two- or three-wheeled motor vehicle in nontraffic accident**

● **V12.3**   **Person boarding or alighting a pedal cycle injured in collision with two- or three-wheeled motor vehicle**

● **V12.4**   **Pedal cycle driver injured in collision with two- or three-wheeled motor vehicle in traffic accident**

● Unacceptable First-Listed Diagnosis   ● Use Additional Character(s)   ▣ Unspecified   **OGCR** Official Guidelines for Coding and Reporting

🅒 Complication\Comorbidity   🅒 Major C\C   Excludes 1   Excludes 2   Includes   Use additional   Code first   Code also

1633

CHAPTER 20 (V01-Y99)

● V12.5 Pedal cycle passenger injured in collision with
         two- or three-wheeled motor vehicle in traffic
         accident

● ■ V12.9 Unspecified pedal cyclist injured in collision with
           two- or three-wheeled motor vehicle in traffic
           accident

● V13 Pedal cycle rider injured in collision with car, pick-up
       truck or van
       The appropriate 7th character is to be added to each code
       from category V13

       | A | initial encounter |
       | D | subsequent encounter |
       | S | sequela |

   ● V13.0 Pedal cycle driver injured in collision with car,
            pick-up truck or van in nontraffic accident

   ● V13.1 Pedal cycle passenger injured in collision with car,
            pick-up truck or van in nontraffic accident

   ● ■ V13.2 Unspecified pedal cyclist injured in collision with
              car, pick-up truck or van in nontraffic accident

   ● V13.3 Person boarding or alighting a pedal cycle injured
            in collision with car, pick-up truck or van

   ● V13.4 Pedal cycle driver injured in collision with car,
            pick-up truck or van in traffic accident

   ● V13.5 Pedal cycle passenger injured in collision with car,
            pick-up truck or van in traffic accident

   ● ■ V13.9 Unspecified pedal cyclist injured in collision with
              car, pick-up truck or van in traffic accident

● V14 Pedal cycle rider injured in collision with heavy transport
       vehicle or bus

       Excludes1 pedal cycle rider injured in collision with
                      military vehicle (V19.81)

       The appropriate 7th character is to be added to each code
       from category V14

       | A | initial encounter |
       | D | subsequent encounter |
       | S | sequela |

   ● V14.0 Pedal cycle driver injured in collision with heavy
            transport vehicle or bus in nontraffic accident

   ● V14.1 Pedal cycle passenger injured in collision with
            heavy transport vehicle or bus in nontraffic
            accident

   ● ■ V14.2 Unspecified pedal cyclist injured in collision
              with heavy transport vehicle or bus in nontraffic
              accident

   ● V14.3 Person boarding or alighting a pedal cycle injured
            in collision with heavy transport vehicle or bus

   ● V14.4 Pedal cycle driver injured in collision with heavy
            transport vehicle or bus in traffic accident

   ● V14.5 Pedal cycle passenger injured in collision with
            heavy transport vehicle or bus in traffic accident

   ● ■ V14.9 Unspecified pedal cyclist injured in collision with
              heavy transport vehicle or bus in traffic accident

● V15 Pedal cycle rider injured in collision with railway train or
       railway vehicle
       The appropriate 7th character is to be added to each code
       from category V15

       | A | initial encounter |
       | D | subsequent encounter |
       | S | sequela |

   ● V15.0 Pedal cycle driver injured in collision with railway
            train or railway vehicle in nontraffic accident

● V15.1 Pedal cycle passenger injured in collision with
         railway train or railway vehicle in nontraffic
         accident

● ■ V15.2 Unspecified pedal cyclist injured in collision
           with railway train or railway vehicle in nontraffic
           accident

● V15.3 Person boarding or alighting a pedal cycle injured
         in collision with railway train or railway vehicle

● V15.4 Pedal cycle driver injured in collision with railway
         train or railway vehicle in traffic accident

● V15.5 Pedal cycle passenger injured in collision with
         railway train or railway vehicle in traffic accident

● ■ V15.9 Unspecified pedal cyclist injured in collision with
           railway train or railway vehicle in traffic accident

● V16 Pedal cycle rider injured in collision with other nonmotor
       vehicle

       Includes collision with animal-drawn vehicle, animal
                     being ridden, streetcar

       The appropriate 7th character is to be added to each code
       from category V16

       | A | initial encounter |
       | D | subsequent encounter |
       | S | sequela |

   ● V16.0 Pedal cycle driver injured in collision with other
            nonmotor vehicle in nontraffic accident

   ● V16.1 Pedal cycle passenger injured in collision with
            other nonmotor vehicle in nontraffic accident

   ● ■ V16.2 Unspecified pedal cyclist injured in collision with
              other nonmotor vehicle in nontraffic accident

   ● V16.3 Person boarding or alighting a pedal cycle injured
            in collision with other nonmotor vehicle in
            nontraffic accident

   ● V16.4 Pedal cycle driver injured in collision with other
            nonmotor vehicle in traffic accident

   ● V16.5 Pedal cycle passenger injured in collision with
            other nonmotor vehicle in traffic accident

   ● ■ V16.9 Unspecified pedal cyclist injured in collision with
              other nonmotor vehicle in traffic accident

● V17 Pedal cycle rider injured in collision with fixed or
       stationary object
       The appropriate 7th character is to be added to each code
       from category V17

       | A | initial encounter |
       | D | subsequent encounter |
       | S | sequela |

   ● V17.0 Pedal cycle driver injured in collision with fixed or
            stationary object in nontraffic accident

   ● V17.1 Pedal cycle passenger injured in collision with
            fixed or stationary object in nontraffic accident

   ● ■ V17.2 Unspecified pedal cyclist injured in collision with
              fixed or stationary object in nontraffic accident

   ● V17.3 Person boarding or alighting a pedal cycle injured
            in collision with fixed or stationary object

   ● V17.4 Pedal cycle driver injured in collision with fixed or
            stationary object in traffic accident

   ● V17.5 Pedal cycle passenger injured in collision with
            fixed or stationary object in traffic accident

   ● ■ V17.9 Unspecified pedal cyclist injured in collision with
              fixed or stationary object in traffic accident

● Unacceptable First-Listed Diagnosis   ● Use Additional Character(s)   ■ Unspecified   **OGCR** Official Guidelines for Coding and Reporting
🔖 Complication\Comorbidity   🔖 Major C\C   [Excludes 1]   [Excludes 2]   Includes   Use additional   Code first   Code also

● **V18**   Pedal cycle rider injured in noncollision transport accident

> | Includes | fall or thrown from pedal cycle (without antecedent collision) |
> overturning pedal cycle NOS
> overturning pedal cycle without collision

The appropriate 7th character is to be added to each code from category V18

> A   initial encounter
> D   subsequent encounter
> S   sequela

● **V18.0**   Pedal cycle driver injured in noncollision transport accident in nontraffic accident

● **V18.1**   Pedal cycle passenger injured in noncollision transport accident in nontraffic accident

● ▪ **V18.2**   Unspecified pedal cyclist injured in noncollision transport accident in nontraffic accident

● **V18.3**   Person boarding or alighting a pedal cycle injured in noncollision transport accident

● **V18.4**   Pedal cycle driver injured in noncollision transport accident in traffic accident

● **V18.5**   Pedal cycle passenger injured in noncollision transport accident in traffic accident

● ▪ **V18.9**   Unspecified pedal cyclist injured in noncollision transport accident in traffic accident

● **V19**   Pedal cycle rider injured in other and unspecified transport accidents

The appropriate 7th character is to be added to each code from category V19

> A   initial encounter
> D   subsequent encounter
> S   sequela

● **V19.0**   Pedal cycle driver injured in collision with other and unspecified motor vehicles in nontraffic accident

    ● ▪ **V19.00**   Pedal cycle driver injured in collision with unspecified motor vehicles in nontraffic accident

    ● **V19.09**   Pedal cycle driver injured in collision with other motor vehicles in nontraffic accident

● **V19.1**   Pedal cycle passenger injured in collision with other and unspecified motor vehicles in nontraffic accident

    ● ▪ **V19.10**   Pedal cycle passenger injured in collision with unspecified motor vehicles in nontraffic accident

    ● **V19.19**   Pedal cycle passenger injured in collision with other motor vehicles in nontraffic accident

● **V19.2**   Unspecified pedal cyclist injured in collision with other and unspecified motor vehicles in nontraffic accident

    ● ▪ **V19.20**   Unspecified pedal cyclist injured in collision with unspecified motor vehicles in nontraffic accident
        Pedal cycle collision NOS, nontraffic

    ● ▪ **V19.29**   Unspecified pedal cyclist injured in collision with other motor vehicles in nontraffic accident

● ▪ **V19.3**   Pedal cyclist (driver) (passenger) injured in unspecified nontraffic accident
     Pedal cycle accident NOS, nontraffic
     Pedal cyclist injured in nontraffic accident NOS

● **V19.4**   Pedal cycle driver injured in collision with other and unspecified motor vehicles in traffic accident

● ▪ **V19.40**   Pedal cycle driver injured in collision with unspecified motor vehicles in traffic accident

    ● **V19.49**   Pedal cycle driver injured in collision with other motor vehicles in traffic accident

● **V19.5**   Pedal cycle passenger injured in collision with other and unspecified motor vehicles in traffic accident

    ● ▪ **V19.50**   Pedal cycle passenger injured in collision with unspecified motor vehicles in traffic accident

    ● **V19.59**   Pedal cycle passenger injured in collision with other motor vehicles in traffic accident

● **V19.6**   Unspecified pedal cyclist injured in collision with other and unspecified motor vehicles in traffic accident

    ● ▪ **V19.60**   Unspecified pedal cyclist injured in collision with unspecified motor vehicles in traffic accident
        Pedal cycle collision NOS (traffic)

    ● ▪ **V19.69**   Unspecified pedal cyclist injured in collision with other motor vehicles in traffic accident

● **V19.8**   Pedal cyclist (driver) (passenger) injured in other specified transport accidents

    ● **V19.81**   Pedal cyclist (driver) (passenger) injured in transport accident with military vehicle

    ● **V19.88**   Pedal cyclist (driver) (passenger) injured in other specified transport accidents

● ▪ **V19.9**   Pedal cyclist (driver) (passenger) injured in unspecified traffic accident
     Pedal cycle accident NOS

MOTORCYCLE RIDER INJURED IN TRANSPORT ACCIDENT (V20-V29)

> | Includes | moped motorcycle with sidecar motorized bicycle motor scooter |

> | Excludes1 | three-wheeled motor vehicle (V30-V39) |

● **V20**   Motorcycle rider injured in collision with pedestrian or animal

> | Excludes1 | motorcycle rider collision with animal-drawn vehicle or animal being ridden (V26.-) |

The appropriate 7th character is to be added to each code from category V20

> A   initial encounter
> D   subsequent encounter
> S   sequela

● **V20.0**   Motorcycle driver injured in collision with pedestrian or animal in nontraffic accident

● **V20.1**   Motorcycle passenger injured in collision with pedestrian or animal in nontraffic accident

● ▪ **V20.2**   Unspecified motorcycle rider injured in collision with pedestrian or animal in nontraffic accident

● **V20.3**   Person boarding or alighting a motorcycle injured in collision with pedestrian or animal

● **V20.4**   Motorcycle driver injured in collision with pedestrian or animal in traffic accident

● **V20.5**   Motorcycle passenger injured in collision with pedestrian or animal in traffic accident

● ▪ **V20.9**   Unspecified motorcycle rider injured in collision with pedestrian or animal in traffic accident

● Unacceptable First-Listed Diagnosis   ● Use Additional Character(s)   ▪ Unspecified   **OGCR** Official Guidelines for Coding and Reporting

🅒 Complication\Comorbidity   🅜 Major C\C   Excludes 1   Excludes 2   Includes   Use additional   Code first   Code also

1635

CHAPTER 20 (V01-Y99)

● **V21   Motorcycle rider injured in collision with pedal cycle**
    The appropriate 7th character is to be added to each code
    from category V21

    A   initial encounter
    D   subsequent encounter
    S   sequela

● **V21.0   Motorcycle driver injured in collision with pedal cycle in nontraffic accident**

● **V21.1   Motorcycle passenger injured in collision with pedal cycle in nontraffic accident**

● ■ **V21.2   Unspecified motorcycle rider injured in collision with pedal cycle in nontraffic accident**

● **V21.3   Person boarding or alighting a motorcycle injured in collision with pedal cycle**

● **V21.4   Motorcycle driver injured in collision with pedal cycle in traffic accident**

● **V21.5   Motorcycle passenger injured in collision with pedal cycle in traffic accident**

● ■ **V21.9   Unspecified motorcycle rider injured in collision with pedal cycle in traffic accident**

● **V22   Motorcycle rider injured in collision with two- or three-wheeled motor vehicle**
    The appropriate 7th character is to be added to each code
    from category V22

    A   initial encounter
    D   subsequent encounter
    S   sequela

● **V22.0   Motorcycle driver injured in collision with two- or three-wheeled motor vehicle in nontraffic accident**

● **V22.1   Motorcycle passenger injured in collision with two- or three-wheeled motor vehicle in nontraffic accident**

● ■ **V22.2   Unspecified motorcycle rider injured in collision with two- or three-wheeled motor vehicle in nontraffic accident**

● **V22.3   Person boarding or alighting a motorcycle injured in collision with two- or three-wheeled motor vehicle**

● **V22.4   Motorcycle driver injured in collision with two- or three-wheeled motor vehicle in traffic accident**

● **V22.5   Motorcycle passenger injured in collision with two- or three-wheeled motor vehicle in traffic accident**

● ■ **V22.9   Unspecified motorcycle rider injured in collision with two- or three-wheeled motor vehicle in traffic accident**

● **V23   Motorcycle rider injured in collision with car, pick-up truck or van**
    The appropriate 7th character is to be added to each code
    from category V23

    A   initial encounter
    D   subsequent encounter
    S   sequela

● **V23.0   Motorcycle driver injured in collision with car, pick-up truck or van in nontraffic accident**

● **V23.1   Motorcycle passenger injured in collision with car, pick-up truck or van in nontraffic accident**

● ■ **V23.2   Unspecified motorcycle rider injured in collision with car, pick-up truck or van in nontraffic accident**

● **V23.3   Person boarding or alighting a motorcycle injured in collision with car, pick-up truck or van**

● **V23.4   Motorcycle driver injured in collision with car, pick-up truck or van in traffic accident**

● **V23.5   Motorcycle passenger injured in collision with car, pick-up truck or van in traffic accident**

● ■ **V23.9   Unspecified motorcycle rider injured in collision with car, pick-up truck or van in traffic accident**

● **V24   Motorcycle rider injured in collision with heavy transport vehicle or bus**

    Excludes1   motorcycle rider injured in collision with military vehicle (V29.81)

    The appropriate 7th character is to be added to each code
    from category V24

    A   initial encounter
    D   subsequent encounter
    S   sequela

● **V24.0   Motorcycle driver injured in collision with heavy transport vehicle or bus in nontraffic accident**

● **V24.1   Motorcycle passenger injured in collision with heavy transport vehicle or bus in nontraffic accident**

● ■ **V24.2   Unspecified motorcycle rider injured in collision with heavy transport vehicle or bus in nontraffic accident**

● **V24.3   Person boarding or alighting a motorcycle injured in collision with heavy transport vehicle or bus**

● **V24.4   Motorcycle driver injured in collision with heavy transport vehicle or bus in traffic accident**

● **V24.5   Motorcycle passenger injured in collision with heavy transport vehicle or bus in traffic accident**

● ■ **V24.9   Unspecified motorcycle rider injured in collision with heavy transport vehicle or bus in traffic accident**

● **V25   Motorcycle rider injured in collision with railway train or railway vehicle**
    The appropriate 7th character is to be added to each code
    from category V25

    A   initial encounter
    D   subsequent encounter
    S   sequela

● **V25.0   Motorcycle driver injured in collision with railway train or railway vehicle in nontraffic accident**

● **V25.1   Motorcycle passenger injured in collision with railway train or railway vehicle in nontraffic accident**

● ■ **V25.2   Unspecified motorcycle rider injured in collision with railway train or railway vehicle in nontraffic accident**

● **V25.3   Person boarding or alighting a motorcycle injured in collision with railway train or railway vehicle**

● **V25.4   Motorcycle driver injured in collision with railway train or railway vehicle in traffic accident**

● **V25.5   Motorcycle passenger injured in collision with railway train or railway vehicle in traffic accident**

● ■ **V25.9   Unspecified motorcycle rider injured in collision with railway train or railway vehicle in traffic accident**

● **V26   Motorcycle rider injured in collision with other nonmotor vehicle**

    Includes   collision with animal-drawn vehicle, animal being ridden, streetcar

    The appropriate 7th character is to be added to each code
    from category V26

    A   initial encounter
    D   subsequent encounter
    S   sequela

● **V26.0   Motorcycle driver injured in collision with other nonmotor vehicle in nontraffic accident**

● Unacceptable First-Listed Diagnosis   ● Use Additional Character(s)   ■ Unspecified   **OGCR** Official Guidelines for Coding and Reporting
🝔 Complication\Comorbidity   🝔 Major C\C   Excludes 1   Excludes 2   Includes   Use additional   Code first   Code also

- **V26.1** Motorcycle passenger injured in collision with other nonmotor vehicle in nontraffic accident
- ◼ **V26.2** Unspecified motorcycle rider injured in collision with other nonmotor vehicle in nontraffic accident
- **V26.3** Person boarding or alighting a motorcycle injured in collision with other nonmotor vehicle
- **V26.4** Motorcycle driver injured in collision with other nonmotor vehicle in traffic accident
- **V26.5** Motorcycle passenger injured in collision with other nonmotor vehicle in traffic accident
- ◼ **V26.9** Unspecified motorcycle rider injured in collision with other nonmotor vehicle in traffic accident

- **V27** Motorcycle rider injured in collision with fixed or stationary object

  The appropriate 7th character is to be added to each code from category V27

A	initial encounter
D	subsequent encounter
S	sequela

  - **V27.0** Motorcycle driver injured in collision with fixed or stationary object in nontraffic accident
  - **V27.1** Motorcycle passenger injured in collision with fixed or stationary object in nontraffic accident
  - ◼ **V27.2** Unspecified motorcycle rider injured in collision with fixed or stationary object in nontraffic accident
  - **V27.3** Person boarding or alighting a motorcycle injured in collision with fixed or stationary object
  - **V27.4** Motorcycle driver injured in collision with fixed or stationary object in traffic accident
  - **V27.5** Motorcycle passenger injured in collision with fixed or stationary object in traffic accident
  - ◼ **V27.9** Unspecified motorcycle rider injured in collision with fixed or stationary object in traffic accident

- **V28** Motorcycle rider injured in noncollision transport accident

  Includes   fall or thrown from motorcycle (without antecedent collision)
  overturning motorcycle NOS
  overturning motorcycle without collision

  The appropriate 7th character is to be added to each code from category V28

A	initial encounter
D	subsequent encounter
S	sequela

  - **V28.0** Motorcycle driver injured in noncollision transport accident in nontraffic accident
  - **V28.1** Motorcycle passenger injured in noncollision transport accident in nontraffic accident
  - ◼ **V28.2** Unspecified motorcycle rider injured in noncollision transport accident in nontraffic accident
  - **V28.3** Person boarding or alighting a motorcycle injured in noncollision transport accident
  - **V28.4** Motorcycle driver injured in noncollision transport accident in traffic accident
  - **V28.5** Motorcycle passenger injured in noncollision transport accident in traffic accident
  - ◼ **V28.9** Unspecified motorcycle rider injured in noncollision transport accident in traffic accident

- **V29** Motorcycle rider injured in other and unspecified transport accidents

  The appropriate 7th character is to be added to each code from category V29

A	initial encounter
D	subsequent encounter
S	sequela

  - **V29.0** Motorcycle driver injured in collision with other and unspecified motor vehicles in nontraffic accident
    - ◼ **V29.00** Motorcycle driver injured in collision with unspecified motor vehicles in nontraffic accident
    - **V29.09** Motorcycle driver injured in collision with other motor vehicles in nontraffic accident
  - **V29.1** Motorcycle passenger injured in collision with other and unspecified motor vehicles in nontraffic accident
    - ◼ **V29.10** Motorcycle passenger injured in collision with unspecified motor vehicles in nontraffic accident
    - **V29.19** Motorcycle passenger injured in collision with other motor vehicles in nontraffic accident
  - **V29.2** Unspecified motorcycle rider injured in collision with other and unspecified motor vehicles in nontraffic accident
    - ◼ **V29.20** Unspecified motorcycle rider injured in collision with unspecified motor vehicles in nontraffic accident
      Motorcycle collision NOS, nontraffic
    - ◼ **V29.29** Unspecified motorcycle rider injured in collision with other motor vehicles in nontraffic accident
  - ◼ **V29.3** Motorcycle rider (driver) (passenger) injured in unspecified nontraffic accident
    Motorcycle accident NOS, nontraffic
    Motorcycle rider injured in nontraffic accident NOS
  - **V29.4** Motorcycle driver injured in collision with other and unspecified motor vehicles in traffic accident
    - ◼ **V29.40** Motorcycle driver injured in collision with unspecified motor vehicles in traffic accident
    - **V29.49** Motorcycle driver injured in collision with other motor vehicles in traffic accident
  - **V29.5** Motorcycle passenger injured in collision with other and unspecified motor vehicles in traffic accident
    - ◼ **V29.50** Motorcycle passenger injured in collision with unspecified motor vehicles in traffic accident
    - **V29.59** Motorcycle passenger injured in collision with other motor vehicles in traffic accident
  - **V29.6** Unspecified motorcycle rider injured in collision with other and unspecified motor vehicles in traffic accident
    - ◼ **V29.60** Unspecified motorcycle rider injured in collision with unspecified motor vehicles in traffic accident
      Motorcycle collision NOS (traffic)
    - ◼ **V29.69** Unspecified motorcycle rider injured in collision with other motor vehicles in traffic accident

● Unacceptable First-Listed Diagnosis   ● Use Additional Character(s)   ◼ Unspecified   **OGCR** Official Guidelines for Coding and Reporting
 Complication\Comorbidity   Major C\C   Excludes 1   Excludes 2   Includes   Use additional   Code first   Code also   1637

CHAPTER 20 (V01-Y99)

● **V29.8** **Motorcycle rider (driver) (passenger) injured in other specified transport accidents**

   ● **V29.81** **Motorcycle rider (driver) (passenger) injured in transport accident with military vehicle**

   ● **V29.88** **Motorcycle rider (driver) (passenger) injured in other specified transport accidents**

● ■ **V29.9** **Motorcycle rider (driver) (passenger) injured in unspecified traffic accident**
       Motorcycle accident NOS

OCCUPANT OF THREE-WHEELED MOTOR VEHICLE INJURED IN TRANSPORT ACCIDENT (V30-V39)

Includes	motorized tricycle
	motorized rickshaw
	three-wheeled motor car

Excludes1	all-terrain vehicles (V86.-)
	motorcycle with sidecar (V20-V29)
	vehicle designed primarily for off-road use (V86.-)

● **V30** **Occupant of three-wheeled motor vehicle injured in collision with pedestrian or animal**

Excludes1	three-wheeled motor vehicle collision with animal-drawn vehicle or animal being ridden (V36.-)

The appropriate 7th character is to be added to each code from category V30

A	initial encounter
D	subsequent encounter
S	sequela

● **V30.0** **Driver of three-wheeled motor vehicle injured in collision with pedestrian or animal in nontraffic accident**

● **V30.1** **Passenger in three-wheeled motor vehicle injured in collision with pedestrian or animal in nontraffic accident**

● **V30.2** **Person on outside of three-wheeled motor vehicle injured in collision with pedestrian or animal in nontraffic accident**

● ■ **V30.3** **Unspecified occupant of three-wheeled motor vehicle injured in collision with pedestrian or animal in nontraffic accident**

● **V30.4** **Person boarding or alighting a three-wheeled motor vehicle injured in collision with pedestrian or animal**

● **V30.5** **Driver of three-wheeled motor vehicle injured in collision with pedestrian or animal in traffic accident**

● **V30.6** **Passenger in three-wheeled motor vehicle injured in collision with pedestrian or animal in traffic accident**

● **V30.7** **Person on outside of three-wheeled motor vehicle injured in collision with pedestrian or animal in traffic accident**

● ■ **V30.9** **Unspecified occupant of three-wheeled motor vehicle injured in collision with pedestrian or animal in traffic accident**

● **V31** **Occupant of three-wheeled motor vehicle injured in collision with pedal cycle**

The appropriate 7th character is to be added to each code from category V31

A	initial encounter
D	subsequent encounter
S	sequela

● **V31.0** **Driver of three-wheeled motor vehicle injured in collision with pedal cycle in nontraffic accident**

● **V31.1** **Passenger in three-wheeled motor vehicle injured in collision with pedal cycle in nontraffic accident**

● **V31.2** **Person on outside of three-wheeled motor vehicle injured in collision with pedal cycle in nontraffic accident**

● ■ **V31.3** **Unspecified occupant of three-wheeled motor vehicle injured in collision with pedal cycle in nontraffic accident**

● **V31.4** **Person boarding or alighting a three-wheeled motor vehicle injured in collision with pedal cycle**

● **V31.5** **Driver of three-wheeled motor vehicle injured in collision with pedal cycle in traffic accident**

● **V31.6** **Passenger in three-wheeled motor vehicle injured in collision with pedal cycle in traffic accident**

● **V31.7** **Person on outside of three-wheeled motor vehicle injured in collision with pedal cycle in traffic accident**

● ■ **V31.9** **Unspecified occupant of three-wheeled motor vehicle injured in collision with pedal cycle in traffic accident**

● **V32** **Occupant of three-wheeled motor vehicle injured in collision with two- or three-wheeled motor vehicle**

The appropriate 7th character is to be added to each code from category V32

A	initial encounter
D	subsequent encounter
S	sequela

● **V32.0** **Driver of three-wheeled motor vehicle injured in collision with two- or three-wheeled motor vehicle in nontraffic accident**

● **V32.1** **Passenger in three-wheeled motor vehicle injured in collision with two- or three-wheeled motor vehicle in nontraffic accident**

● **V32.2** **Person on outside of three-wheeled motor vehicle injured in collision with two- or three-wheeled motor vehicle in nontraffic accident**

● ■ **V32.3** **Unspecified occupant of three-wheeled motor vehicle injured in collision with two- or three-wheeled motor vehicle in nontraffic accident**

● **V32.4** **Person boarding or alighting a three-wheeled motor vehicle injured in collision with two- or three-wheeled motor vehicle**

● **V32.5** **Driver of three-wheeled motor vehicle injured in collision with two- or three-wheeled motor vehicle in traffic accident**

● **V32.6** **Passenger in three-wheeled motor vehicle injured in collision with two- or three-wheeled motor vehicle in traffic accident**

● **V32.7** **Person on outside of three-wheeled motor vehicle injured in collision with two- or three-wheeled motor vehicle in traffic accident**

● ■ **V32.9** **Unspecified occupant of three-wheeled motor vehicle injured in collision with two- or three-wheeled motor vehicle in traffic accident**

● **V33** **Occupant of three-wheeled motor vehicle injured in collision with car, pick-up truck or van**

The appropriate 7th character is to be added to each code from category V33

A	initial encounter
D	subsequent encounter
S	sequela

● **V33.0** **Driver of three-wheeled motor vehicle injured in collision with car, pick-up truck or van in nontraffic accident**

● V33.1　Passenger in three-wheeled motor vehicle injured in collision with car, pick-up truck or van in nontraffic accident

● V33.2　Person on outside of three-wheeled motor vehicle injured in collision with car, pick-up truck or van in nontraffic accident

● ▣ V33.3　Unspecified occupant of three-wheeled motor vehicle injured in collision with car, pick-up truck or van in nontraffic accident

● V33.4　Person boarding or alighting a three-wheeled motor vehicle injured in collision with car, pick-up truck or van

● V33.5　Driver of three-wheeled motor vehicle injured in collision with car, pick-up truck or van in traffic accident

● V33.6　Passenger in three-wheeled motor vehicle injured in collision with car, pick-up truck or van in traffic accident

● V33.7　Person on outside of three-wheeled motor vehicle injured in collision with car, pick-up truck or van in traffic accident

● ▣ V33.9　Unspecified occupant of three-wheeled motor vehicle injured in collision with car, pick-up truck or van in traffic accident

● V34　Occupant of three-wheeled motor vehicle injured in collision with heavy transport vehicle or bus

　　Excludes1　occupant of three-wheeled motor vehicle injured in collision with military vehicle (V39.81)

　　The appropriate 7th character is to be added to each code from category V34

A	initial encounter
D	subsequent encounter
S	sequela

● V34.0　Driver of three-wheeled motor vehicle injured in collision with heavy transport vehicle or bus in nontraffic accident

● V34.1　Passenger in three-wheeled motor vehicle injured in collision with heavy transport vehicle or bus in nontraffic accident

● V34.2　Person on outside of three-wheeled motor vehicle injured in collision with heavy transport vehicle or bus in nontraffic accident

● ▣ V34.3　Unspecified occupant of three-wheeled motor vehicle injured in collision with heavy transport vehicle or bus in nontraffic accident

● V34.4　Person boarding or alighting a three-wheeled motor vehicle injured in collision with heavy transport vehicle or bus

● V34.5　Driver of three-wheeled motor vehicle injured in collision with heavy transport vehicle or bus in traffic accident

● V34.6　Passenger in three-wheeled motor vehicle injured in collision with heavy transport vehicle or bus in traffic accident

● V34.7　Person on outside of three-wheeled motor vehicle injured in collision with heavy transport vehicle or bus in traffic accident

● ▣ V34.9　Unspecified occupant of three-wheeled motor vehicle injured in collision with heavy transport vehicle or bus in traffic accident

● V35　Occupant of three-wheeled motor vehicle injured in collision with railway train or railway vehicle

　　The appropriate 7th character is to be added to each code from category V35

A	initial encounter
D	subsequent encounter
S	sequela

● V35.0　Driver of three-wheeled motor vehicle injured in collision with railway train or railway vehicle in nontraffic accident

● V35.1　Passenger in three-wheeled motor vehicle injured in collision with railway train or railway vehicle in nontraffic accident

● V35.2　Person on outside of three-wheeled motor vehicle injured in collision with railway train or railway vehicle in nontraffic accident

● ▣ V35.3　Unspecified occupant of three-wheeled motor vehicle injured in collision with railway train or railway vehicle in nontraffic accident

● V35.4　Person boarding or alighting a three-wheeled motor vehicle injured in collision with railway train or railway vehicle

● V35.5　Driver of three-wheeled motor vehicle injured in collision with railway train or railway vehicle in traffic accident

● V35.6　Passenger in three-wheeled motor vehicle injured in collision with railway train or railway vehicle in traffic accident

● V35.7　Person on outside of three-wheeled motor vehicle injured in collision with railway train or railway vehicle in traffic accident

● ▣ V35.9　Unspecified occupant of three-wheeled motor vehicle injured in collision with railway train or railway vehicle in traffic accident

● V36　Occupant of three-wheeled motor vehicle injured in collision with other nonmotor vehicle

　　Includes　collision with animal-drawn vehicle, animal being ridden, streetcar

　　The appropriate 7th character is to be added to each code from category V36

A	initial encounter
D	subsequent encounter
S	sequela

● V36.0　Driver of three-wheeled motor vehicle injured in collision with other nonmotor vehicle in nontraffic accident

● V36.1　Passenger in three-wheeled motor vehicle injured in collision with other nonmotor vehicle in nontraffic accident

● V36.2　Person on outside of three-wheeled motor vehicle injured in collision with other nonmotor vehicle in nontraffic accident

● ▣ V36.3　Unspecified occupant of three-wheeled motor vehicle injured in collision with other nonmotor vehicle in nontraffic accident

● V36.4　Person boarding or alighting a three-wheeled motor vehicle injured in collision with other nonmotor vehicle

● V36.5　Driver of three-wheeled motor vehicle injured in collision with other nonmotor vehicle in traffic accident

● V36.6　Passenger in three-wheeled motor vehicle injured in collision with other nonmotor vehicle in traffic accident

● V36.7　Person on outside of three-wheeled motor vehicle injured in collision with other nonmotor vehicle in traffic accident

● Unacceptable First-Listed Diagnosis　　● Use Additional Character(s)　　▣ Unspecified　　OGCR Official Guidelines for Coding and Reporting

🦠 Complication\Comorbidity　　🦠 Major C\C　　Excludes 1　　Excludes 2　　Includes　　Use additional　　Code first　　Code also

CHAPTER 20 (V01–Y99)

1639

● ■ **V36.9** Unspecified occupant of three-wheeled motor vehicle injured in collision with other nonmotor vehicle in traffic accident

● **V37** Occupant of three-wheeled motor vehicle injured in collision with fixed or stationary object

The appropriate 7th character is to be added to each code from category V37

A	initial encounter
D	subsequent encounter
S	sequela

● **V37.0** Driver of three-wheeled motor vehicle injured in collision with fixed or stationary object in nontraffic accident

● **V37.1** Passenger in three-wheeled motor vehicle injured in collision with fixed or stationary object in nontraffic accident

● **V37.2** Person on outside of three-wheeled motor vehicle injured in collision with fixed or stationary object in nontraffic accident

● ■ **V37.3** Unspecified occupant of three-wheeled motor vehicle injured in collision with fixed or stationary object in nontraffic accident

● **V37.4** Person boarding or alighting a three-wheeled motor vehicle injured in collision with fixed or stationary object

● **V37.5** Driver of three-wheeled motor vehicle injured in collision with fixed or stationary object in traffic accident

● **V37.6** Passenger in three-wheeled motor vehicle injured in collision with fixed or stationary object in traffic accident

● **V37.7** Person on outside of three-wheeled motor vehicle injured in collision with fixed or stationary object in traffic accident

● ■ **V37.9** Unspecified occupant of three-wheeled motor vehicle injured in collision with fixed or stationary object in traffic accident

● **V38** Occupant of three-wheeled motor vehicle injured in noncollision transport accident

> **Includes**   fall or thrown from three-wheeled motor vehicle
> overturning of three-wheeled motor vehicle NOS
> overturning of three-wheeled motor vehicle without collision

The appropriate 7th character is to be added to each code from category V38

A	initial encounter
D	subsequent encounter
S	sequela

● **V38.0** Driver of three-wheeled motor vehicle injured in noncollision transport accident in nontraffic accident

● **V38.1** Passenger in three-wheeled motor vehicle injured in noncollision transport accident in nontraffic accident

● **V38.2** Person on outside of three-wheeled motor vehicle injured in noncollision transport accident in nontraffic accident

● ■ **V38.3** Unspecified occupant of three-wheeled motor vehicle injured in noncollision transport accident in nontraffic accident

● **V38.4** Person boarding or alighting a three-wheeled motor vehicle injured in noncollision transport accident

● **V38.5** Driver of three-wheeled motor vehicle injured in noncollision transport accident in traffic accident

● **V38.6** Passenger in three-wheeled motor vehicle injured in noncollision transport accident in traffic accident

● **V38.7** Person on outside of three-wheeled motor vehicle injured in noncollision transport accident in traffic accident

● ■ **V38.9** Unspecified occupant of three-wheeled motor vehicle injured in noncollision transport accident in traffic accident

● **V39** Occupant of three-wheeled motor vehicle injured in other and unspecified transport accidents

The appropriate 7th character is to be added to each code from category V39

A	initial encounter
D	subsequent encounter
S	sequela

● **V39.0** Driver of three-wheeled motor vehicle injured in collision with other and unspecified motor vehicles in nontraffic accident

● ■ **V39.00** Driver of three-wheeled motor vehicle injured in collision with unspecified motor vehicles in nontraffic accident

● **V39.09** Driver of three-wheeled motor vehicle injured in collision with other motor vehicles in nontraffic accident

● **V39.1** Passenger in three-wheeled motor vehicle injured in collision with other and unspecified motor vehicles in nontraffic accident

● ■ **V39.10** Passenger in three-wheeled motor vehicle injured in collision with unspecified motor vehicles in nontraffic accident

● **V39.19** Passenger in three-wheeled motor vehicle injured in collision with other motor vehicles in nontraffic accident

● **V39.2** Unspecified occupant of three-wheeled motor vehicle injured in collision with other and unspecified motor vehicles in nontraffic accident

● ■ **V39.20** Unspecified occupant of three-wheeled motor vehicle injured in collision with unspecified motor vehicles in nontraffic accident
> Collision NOS involving three-wheeled motor vehicle, nontraffic

● ■ **V39.29** Unspecified occupant of three-wheeled motor vehicle injured in collision with other motor vehicles in nontraffic accident

● ■ **V39.3** Occupant (driver) (passenger) of three-wheeled motor vehicle injured in unspecified nontraffic accident
> Accident NOS involving three-wheeled motor vehicle, nontraffic
> Occupant of three-wheeled motor vehicle injured in nontraffic accident NOS

● **V39.4** Driver of three-wheeled motor vehicle injured in collision with other and unspecified motor vehicles in traffic accident

● ■ **V39.40** Driver of three-wheeled motor vehicle injured in collision with unspecified motor vehicles in traffic accident

● **V39.49** Driver of three-wheeled motor vehicle injured in collision with other motor vehicles in traffic accident

● **V39.5** Passenger in three-wheeled motor vehicle injured in collision with other and unspecified motor vehicles in traffic accident

● ■ **V39.50** Passenger in three-wheeled motor vehicle injured in collision with unspecified motor vehicles in traffic accident

● V39.59 Passenger in three-wheeled motor vehicle injured in collision with other motor vehicles in traffic accident

● V39.6 Unspecified occupant of three-wheeled motor vehicle injured in collision with other and unspecified motor vehicles in traffic accident

● ▣ V39.60 Unspecified occupant of three-wheeled motor vehicle injured in collision with unspecified motor vehicles in traffic accident
Collision NOS involving three-wheeled motor vehicle (traffic)

● ▣ V39.69 Unspecified occupant of three-wheeled motor vehicle injured in collision with other motor vehicles in traffic accident

● V39.8 Occupant (driver) (passenger) of three-wheeled motor vehicle injured in other specified transport accidents

● V39.81 Occupant (driver) (passenger) of three-wheeled motor vehicle injured in transport accident with military vehicle

● V39.89 Occupant (driver) (passenger) of three-wheeled motor vehicle injured in other specified transport accidents

● ▣ V39.9 Occupant (driver) (passenger) of three-wheeled motor vehicle injured in unspecified traffic accident
Accident NOS involving three-wheeled motor vehicle

CAR OCCUPANT INJURED IN TRANSPORT ACCIDENT (V40-V49)

Includes a four-wheeled motor vehicle designed primarily for carrying passengers
automobile (pulling a trailer or camper)

Excludes1 bus (V50-V59)
minibus (V50-V59)
minivan (V50-V59)
motorcoach (V70-V79)
pick-up truck (V50-V59)
sport utility vehicle (SUV) (V50-V59)

● V40 Car occupant injured in collision with pedestrian or animal

Excludes1 car collision with animal-drawn vehicle or animal being ridden (V46.-)

The appropriate 7th character is to be added to each code from category V40

A	initial encounter
D	subsequent encounter
S	sequela

● V40.0 Car driver injured in collision with pedestrian or animal in nontraffic accident

● V40.1 Car passenger injured in collision with pedestrian or animal in nontraffic accident

● V40.2 Person on outside of car injured in collision with pedestrian or animal in nontraffic accident

● ▣ V40.3 Unspecified car occupant injured in collision with pedestrian or animal in nontraffic accident

● V40.4 Person boarding or alighting a car injured in collision with pedestrian or animal

● V40.5 Car driver injured in collision with pedestrian or animal in traffic accident

● V40.6 Car passenger injured in collision with pedestrian or animal in traffic accident

● V40.7 Person on outside of car injured in collision with pedestrian or animal in traffic accident

● ▣ V40.9 Unspecified car occupant injured in collision with pedestrian or animal in traffic accident

● V41 Car occupant injured in collision with pedal cycle

The appropriate 7th character is to be added to each code from category V41

A	initial encounter
D	subsequent encounter
S	sequela

● V41.0 Car driver injured in collision with pedal cycle in nontraffic accident

● V41.1 Car passenger injured in collision with pedal cycle in nontraffic accident

● V41.2 Person on outside of car injured in collision with pedal cycle in nontraffic accident

● ▣ V41.3 Unspecified car occupant injured in collision with pedal cycle in nontraffic accident

● V41.4 Person boarding or alighting a car injured in collision with pedal cycle

● V41.5 Car driver injured in collision with pedal cycle in traffic accident

● V41.6 Car passenger injured in collision with pedal cycle in traffic accident

● V41.7 Person on outside of car injured in collision with pedal cycle in traffic accident

● ▣ V41.9 Unspecified car occupant injured in collision with pedal cycle in traffic accident

● V42 Car occupant injured in collision with two- or three-wheeled motor vehicle

The appropriate 7th character is to be added to each code from category V42

A	initial encounter
D	subsequent encounter
S	sequela

● V42.0 Car driver injured in collision with two- or three-wheeled motor vehicle in nontraffic accident

● V42.1 Car passenger injured in collision with two- or three-wheeled motor vehicle in nontraffic accident

● V42.2 Person on outside of car injured in collision with two- or three-wheeled motor vehicle in nontraffic accident

● ▣ V42.3 Unspecified car occupant injured in collision with two- or three-wheeled motor vehicle in nontraffic accident

● V42.4 Person boarding or alighting a car injured in collision with two- or three- wheeled motor vehicle

● V42.5 Car driver injured in collision with two- or three-wheeled motor vehicle in traffic accident

● V42.6 Car passenger injured in collision with two- or three-wheeled motor vehicle in traffic accident

● V42.7 Person on outside of car injured in collision with two- or three-wheeled motor vehicle in traffic accident

● ▣ V42.9 Unspecified car occupant injured in collision with two- or three-wheeled motor vehicle in traffic accident

● V43 Car occupant injured in collision with car, pick-up truck or van

The appropriate 7th character is to be added to each code from category V43

A	initial encounter
D	subsequent encounter
S	sequela

● V43.0 Car driver injured in collision with car, pick-up truck or van in nontraffic accident

● V43.01 Car driver injured in collision with sport utility vehicle in nontraffic accident

● V43.02 Car driver injured in collision with other type car in nontraffic accident

● Unacceptable First-Listed Diagnosis   ● Use Additional Character(s)   ▣ Unspecified   **OGCR** Official Guidelines for Coding and Reporting
🕭 Complication\Comorbidity   🕭 Major C\C   Excludes 1   Excludes 2   Includes   Use additional   Code first   Code also

1641

- ● V43.03   Car driver injured in collision with pick-up truck in nontraffic accident
- ● V43.04   Car driver injured in collision with van in nontraffic accident
- ● V43.1   Car passenger injured in collision with car, pick-up truck or van in nontraffic accident
  - ● V43.11   Car passenger injured in collision with sport utility vehicle in nontraffic accident
  - ● V43.12   Car passenger injured in collision with other type car in nontraffic accident
  - ● V43.13   Car passenger injured in collision with pick-up in nontraffic accident
  - ● V43.14   Car passenger injured in collision with van in nontraffic accident
- ● V43.2   Person on outside of car injured in collision with car, pick-up truck or van in nontraffic accident
  - ● V43.21   Person on outside of car injured in collision with sport utility vehicle in nontraffic accident
  - ● V43.22   Person on outside of car injured in collision with other type car in nontraffic accident
  - ● V43.23   Person on outside of car injured in collision with pick-up truck in nontraffic accident
  - ● V43.24   Person on outside of car injured in collision with van in nontraffic accident
- ● V43.3   Unspecified car occupant injured in collision with car, pick-up truck or van in nontraffic accident
  - ● ◼ V43.31   Unspecified car occupant injured in collision with sport utility vehicle in nontraffic accident
  - ● ◼ V43.32   Unspecified car occupant injured in collision with other type car in nontraffic accident
  - ● ◼ V43.33   Unspecified car occupant injured in collision with pick-up truck in nontraffic accident
  - ● ◼ V43.34   Unspecified car occupant injured in collision with van in nontraffic accident
- ● V43.4   Person boarding or alighting a car injured in collision with car, pick-up truck or van
  - ● V43.41   Person boarding or alighting a car injured in collision with sport utility vehicle
  - ● V43.42   Person boarding or alighting a car injured in collision with other type car
  - ● V43.43   Person boarding or alighting a car injured in collision with pick-up truck
  - ● V43.44   Person boarding or alighting a car injured in collision with van
- ● V43.5   Car driver injured in collision with car, pick-up truck or van in traffic accident
  - ● V43.51   Car driver injured in collision with sport utility vehicle in traffic accident
  - ● V43.52   Car driver injured in collision with other type car in traffic accident
  - ● V43.53   Car driver injured in collision with pick-up truck in traffic accident
  - ● V43.54   Car driver injured in collision with van in traffic accident
- ● V43.6   Car passenger injured in collision with car, pick-up truck or van in traffic accident
  - ● V43.61   Car passenger injured in collision with sport utility vehicle in traffic accident
  - ● V43.62   Car passenger injured in collision with other type car in traffic accident

- ● V43.63   Car passenger injured in collision with pick-up truck in traffic accident
- ● V43.64   Car passenger injured in collision with van in traffic accident
- ● V43.7   Person on outside of car injured in collision with car, pick-up truck or van in traffic accident
  - ● V43.71   Person on outside of car injured in collision with sport utility vehicle in traffic accident
  - ● V43.72   Person on outside of car injured in collision with other type car in traffic accident
  - ● V43.73   Person on outside of car injured in collision with pick-up truck in traffic accident
  - ● V43.74   Person on outside of car injured in collision with van in traffic accident
- ● V43.9   Unspecified car occupant injured in collision with car, pick-up truck or van in traffic accident
  - ● ◼ V43.91   Unspecified car occupant injured in collision with sport utility vehicle in traffic accident
  - ● ◼ V43.92   Unspecified car occupant injured in collision with other type car in traffic accident
  - ● ◼ V43.93   Unspecified car occupant injured in collision with pick-up truck in traffic accident
  - ● ◼ V43.94   Unspecified car occupant injured in collision with van in traffic accident
- ● V44   Car occupant injured in collision with heavy transport vehicle or bus

  > **Excludes1**   car occupant injured in collision with military vehicle (V49.81)

  The appropriate 7th character is to be added to each code from category V44

A	initial encounter
D	subsequent encounter
S	sequela

  - ● V44.0   Car driver injured in collision with heavy transport vehicle or bus in nontraffic accident
  - ● V44.1   Car passenger injured in collision with heavy transport vehicle or bus in nontraffic accident
  - ● V44.2   Person on outside of car injured in collision with heavy transport vehicle or bus in nontraffic accident
  - ● ◼ V44.3   Unspecified car occupant injured in collision with heavy transport vehicle or bus in nontraffic accident
  - ● V44.4   Person boarding or alighting a car injured in collision with heavy transport vehicle or bus
  - ● V44.5   Car driver injured in collision with heavy transport vehicle or bus in traffic accident
  - ● V44.6   Car passenger injured in collision with heavy transport vehicle or bus in traffic accident
  - ● V44.7   Person on outside of car injured in collision with heavy transport vehicle or bus in traffic accident
  - ● ◼ V44.9   Unspecified car occupant injured in collision with heavy transport vehicle or bus in traffic accident
- ● V45   Car occupant injured in collision with railway train or railway vehicle

  The appropriate 7th character is to be added to each code from category V45

A	initial encounter
D	subsequent encounter
S	sequela

  - ● V45.0   Car driver injured in collision with railway train or railway vehicle in nontraffic accident

- ● V45.1   Car passenger injured in collision with railway train or railway vehicle in nontraffic accident
- ● V45.2   Person on outside of car injured in collision with railway train or railway vehicle in nontraffic accident
- ● ▨ V45.3   Unspecified car occupant injured in collision with railway train or railway vehicle in nontraffic accident
- ● V45.4   Person boarding or alighting a car injured in collision with railway train or railway vehicle
- ● V45.5   Car driver injured in collision with railway train or railway vehicle in traffic accident
- ● V45.6   Car passenger injured in collision with railway train or railway vehicle in traffic accident
- ● V45.7   Person on outside of car injured in collision with railway train or railway vehicle in traffic accident
- ● ▨ V45.9   Unspecified car occupant injured in collision with railway train or railway vehicle in traffic accident

- ● V46   Car occupant injured in collision with other nonmotor vehicle

  | **Includes** | collision with animal-drawn vehicle, animal being ridden, streetcar |

  The appropriate 7th character is to be added to each code from category V46

A	initial encounter
D	subsequent encounter
S	sequela

  - ● V46.0   Car driver injured in collision with other nonmotor vehicle in nontraffic accident
  - ● V46.1   Car passenger injured in collision with other nonmotor vehicle in nontraffic accident
  - ● V46.2   Person on outside of car injured in collision with other nonmotor vehicle in nontraffic accident
  - ● ▨ V46.3   Unspecified car occupant injured in collision with other nonmotor vehicle in nontraffic accident
  - ● V46.4   Person boarding or alighting a car injured in collision with other nonmotor vehicle
  - ● V46.5   Car driver injured in collision with other nonmotor vehicle in traffic accident
  - ● V46.6   Car passenger injured in collision with other nonmotor vehicle in traffic accident
  - ● V46.7   Person on outside of car injured in collision with other nonmotor vehicle in traffic accident
  - ● ▨ V46.9   Unspecified car occupant injured in collision with other nonmotor vehicle in traffic accident

- ● V47   Car occupant injured in collision with fixed or stationary object

  The appropriate 7th character is to be added to each code from category V47

A	initial encounter
D	subsequent encounter
S	sequela

  - ● V47.0   Car driver injured in collision with fixed or stationary object in nontraffic accident
    - ● V47.01   Driver of sport utility vehicle injured in collision with fixed or stationary object in nontraffic accident
    - ● V47.02   Driver of other type car injured in collision with fixed or stationary object in nontraffic accident
  - ● V47.1   Car passenger injured in collision with fixed or stationary object in nontraffic accident
    - ● V47.11   Passenger of sport utility vehicle injured in collision with fixed or stationary object in nontraffic accident

- ● V47.12   Passenger of other type car injured in collision with fixed or stationary object in nontraffic accident
- ● V47.2   Person on outside of car injured in collision with fixed or stationary object in nontraffic accident
- ● V47.3   Unspecified car occupant injured in collision with fixed or stationary object in nontraffic accident
  - ● ▨ V47.31   Unspecified occupant of sport utility vehicle injured in collision with fixed or stationary object in nontraffic accident
  - ● ▨ V47.32   Unspecified occupant of other type car injured in collision with fixed or stationary object in nontraffic accident
- ● V47.4   Person boarding or alighting a car injured in collision with fixed or stationary object
- ● V47.5   Car driver injured in collision with fixed or stationary object in traffic accident
  - ● V47.51   Driver of sport utility vehicle injured in collision with fixed or stationary object in traffic accident
  - ● V47.52   Driver of other type car injured in collision with fixed or stationary object in traffic accident
- ● V47.6   Car passenger injured in collision with fixed or stationary object in traffic accident
  - ● V47.61   Passenger of sport utility vehicle injured in collision with fixed or stationary object in traffic accident
  - ● V47.62   Passenger of other type car injured in collision with fixed or stationary object in traffic accident
- ● V47.7   Person on outside of car injured in collision with fixed or stationary object in traffic accident
- ● V47.9   Unspecified car occupant injured in collision with fixed or stationary object in traffic accident
  - ● ▨ V47.91   Unspecified occupant of sport utility vehicle injured in collision with fixed or stationary object in traffic accident
  - ● ▨ V47.92   Unspecified occupant of other type car injured in collision with fixed or stationary object in traffic accident

- ● V48   Car occupant injured in noncollision transport accident

  | **Includes** | overturning car NOS |
  | | overturning car without collision |

  The appropriate 7th character is to be added to each code from category V48

A	initial encounter
D	subsequent encounter
S	sequela

  - ● V48.0   Car driver injured in noncollision transport accident in nontraffic accident
  - ● V48.1   Car passenger injured in noncollision transport accident in nontraffic accident
  - ● V48.2   Person on outside of car injured in noncollision transport accident in nontraffic accident
  - ● ▨ V48.3   Unspecified car occupant injured in noncollision transport accident in nontraffic accident
  - ● V48.4   Person boarding or alighting a car injured in noncollision transport accident
  - ● V48.5   Car driver injured in noncollision transport accident in traffic accident
  - ● V48.6   Car passenger injured in noncollision transport accident in traffic accident

● Unacceptable First-Listed Diagnosis   ● Use Additional Character(s)   ▨ Unspecified   **OGCR** Official Guidelines for Coding and Reporting

🅒 Complication\Comorbidity   🅒 Major C\C   Excludes 1   Excludes 2   Includes   Use additional   Code first   Code also   1643

CHAPTER 20 (V01–Y99)

- **V48.7** Person on outside of car injured in noncollision transport accident in traffic accident
- ■ **V48.9** Unspecified car occupant injured in noncollision transport accident in traffic accident

- **V49** Car occupant injured in other and unspecified transport accidents

    The appropriate 7th character is to be added to each code from category V49

    > A   initial encounter
    > D   subsequent encounter
    > S   sequela

- **V49.0** Driver injured in collision with other and unspecified motor vehicles in nontraffic accident
    - ■ **V49.00** Driver injured in collision with unspecified motor vehicles in nontraffic accident
    - **V49.09** Driver injured in collision with other motor vehicles in nontraffic accident
- **V49.1** Passenger injured in collision with other and unspecified motor vehicles in nontraffic accident
    - ■ **V49.10** Passenger injured in collision with unspecified motor vehicles in nontraffic accident
    - **V49.19** Passenger injured in collision with other motor vehicles in nontraffic accident
- **V49.2** Unspecified car occupant injured in collision with other and unspecified motor vehicles in nontraffic accident
    - ■ **V49.20** Unspecified car occupant injured in collision with unspecified motor vehicles in nontraffic accident
      Car collision NOS, nontraffic
    - ■ **V49.29** Unspecified car occupant injured in collision with other motor vehicles in nontraffic accident
- **V49.3** Car occupant (driver) (passenger) injured in unspecified nontraffic accident
      Car accident NOS, nontraffic
      Car occupant injured in nontraffic accident NOS
- **V49.4** Driver injured in collision with other and unspecified motor vehicles in traffic accident
    - ■ **V49.40** Driver injured in collision with unspecified motor vehicles in traffic accident
    - **V49.49** Driver injured in collision with other motor vehicles in traffic accident
- **V49.5** Passenger injured in collision with other and unspecified motor vehicles in traffic accident
    - ■ **V49.50** Passenger injured in collision with unspecified motor vehicles in traffic accident
    - **V49.59** Passenger injured in collision with other motor vehicles in traffic accident
- **V49.6** Unspecified car occupant injured in collision with other and unspecified motor vehicles in traffic accident
    - ■ **V49.60** Unspecified car occupant injured in collision with unspecified motor vehicles in traffic accident
      Car collision NOS (traffic)
    - ■ **V49.69** Unspecified car occupant injured in collision with other motor vehicles in traffic accident
- **V49.8** Car occupant (driver) (passenger) injured in other specified transport accidents

- **V49.81** Car occupant (driver) (passenger) injured in transport accident with military vehicle
- **V49.88** Car occupant (driver) (passenger) injured in other specified transport accidents
- ■ **V49.9** Car occupant (driver) (passenger) injured in unspecified traffic accident
      Car accident NOS

OCCUPANT OF PICK-UP TRUCK OR VAN INJURED IN TRANSPORT ACCIDENT (V50-V59)

> **Includes**   a four- or six-wheel motor vehicle designed primarily for carrying passengers and property but weighing less than the local limit for classification as a heavy goods vehicle
> minibus
> minivan
> sport utility vehicle (SUV)
> truck
> van

> **Excludes1**   heavy transport vehicle (V60-V69)

- **V50** Occupant of pick-up truck or van injured in collision with pedestrian or animal

    > **Excludes1**   pick-up truck or van collision with animal-drawn vehicle or animal being ridden (V56.-)

    The appropriate 7th character is to be added to each code from category V50

    > A   initial encounter
    > D   subsequent encounter
    > S   sequela

- **V50.0** Driver of pick-up truck or van injured in collision with pedestrian or animal in nontraffic accident
- **V50.1** Passenger in pick-up truck or van injured in collision with pedestrian or animal in nontraffic accident
- **V50.2** Person on outside of pick-up truck or van injured in collision with pedestrian or animal in nontraffic accident
- ■ **V50.3** Unspecified occupant of pick-up truck or van injured in collision with pedestrian or animal in nontraffic accident
- **V50.4** Person boarding or alighting a pick-up truck or van injured in collision with pedestrian or animal
- **V50.5** Driver of pick-up truck or van injured in collision with pedestrian or animal in traffic accident
- **V50.6** Passenger in pick-up truck or van injured in collision with pedestrian or animal in traffic accident
- **V50.7** Person on outside of pick-up truck or van injured in collision with pedestrian or animal in traffic accident
- ■ **V50.9** Unspecified occupant of pick-up truck or van injured in collision with pedestrian or animal in traffic accident

- **V51** Occupant of pick-up truck or van injured in collision with pedal cycle

    The appropriate 7th character is to be added to each code from category V51

    > A   initial encounter
    > D   subsequent encounter
    > S   sequela

- **V51.0** Driver of pick-up truck or van injured in collision with pedal cycle in nontraffic accident
- **V51.1** Passenger in pick-up truck or van injured in collision with pedal cycle in nontraffic accident

● Unacceptable First-Listed Diagnosis   ● Use Additional Character(s)   ■ Unspecified   **OGCR** Official Guidelines for Coding and Reporting
🔖 Complication\Comorbidity   🔖 Major C\C   Excludes 1   Excludes 2   Includes   Use additional   Code first   Code also

● V51.2   Person on outside of pick-up truck or van injured in collision with pedal cycle in nontraffic accident

● ■ V51.3   Unspecified occupant of pick-up truck or van injured in collision with pedal cycle in nontraffic accident

● V51.4   Person boarding or alighting a pick-up truck or van injured in collision with pedal cycle

● V51.5   Driver of pick-up truck or van injured in collision with pedal cycle in traffic accident

● V51.6   Passenger in pick-up truck or van injured in collision with pedal cycle in traffic accident

● V51.7   Person on outside of pick-up truck or van injured in collision with pedal cycle in traffic accident

● ■ V51.9   Unspecified occupant of pick-up truck or van injured in collision with pedal cycle in traffic accident

● V52   Occupant of pick-up truck or van injured in collision with two- or three-wheeled motor vehicle

The appropriate 7th character is to be added to each code from category V52

A	initial encounter
D	subsequent encounter
S	sequela

● V52.0   Driver of pick-up truck or van injured in collision with two- or three-wheeled motor vehicle in nontraffic accident

● V52.1   Passenger in pick-up truck or van injured in collision with two- or three-wheeled motor vehicle in nontraffic accident

● V52.2   Person on outside of pick-up truck or van injured in collision with two- or three-wheeled motor vehicle in nontraffic accident

● ■ V52.3   Unspecified occupant of pick-up truck or van injured in collision with two- or three-wheeled motor vehicle in nontraffic accident

● V52.4   Person boarding or alighting a pick-up truck or van injured in collision with two- or three-wheeled motor vehicle

● V52.5   Driver of pick-up truck or van injured in collision with two- or three-wheeled motor vehicle in traffic accident

● V52.6   Passenger in pick-up truck or van injured in collision with two- or three-wheeled motor vehicle in traffic accident

● V52.7   Person on outside of pick-up truck or van injured in collision with two- or three-wheeled motor vehicle in traffic accident

● ■ V52.9   Unspecified occupant of pick-up truck or van injured in collision with two- or three-wheeled motor vehicle in traffic accident

● V53   Occupant of pick-up truck or van injured in collision with car, pick-up truck or van

The appropriate 7th character is to be added to each code from category V53

A	initial encounter
D	subsequent encounter
S	sequela

● V53.0   Driver of pick-up truck or van injured in collision with car, pick-up truck or van in nontraffic accident

● V53.1   Passenger in pick-up truck or van injured in collision with car, pick-up truck or van in nontraffic accident

● V53.2   Person on outside of pick-up truck or van injured in collision with car, pick-up truck or van in nontraffic accident

● ■ V53.3   Unspecified occupant of pick-up truck or van injured in collision with car, pick-up truck or van in nontraffic accident

● V53.4   Person boarding or alighting a pick-up truck or van injured in collision with car, pick-up truck or van

● V53.5   Driver of pick-up truck or van injured in collision with car, pick-up truck or van in traffic accident

● V53.6   Passenger in pick-up truck or van injured in collision with car, pick-up truck or van in traffic accident

● V53.7   Person on outside of pick-up truck or van injured in collision with car, pick-up truck or van in traffic accident

● ■ V53.9   Unspecified occupant of pick-up truck or van injured in collision with car, pick-up truck or van in traffic accident

● V54   Occupant of pick-up truck or van injured in collision with heavy transport vehicle or bus

> **Excludes1**   occupant of pick-up truck or van injured in collision with military vehicle (V59.81)

The appropriate 7th character is to be added to each code from category V54

A	initial encounter
D	subsequent encounter
S	sequela

● V54.0   Driver of pick-up truck or van injured in collision with heavy transport vehicle or bus in nontraffic accident

● V54.1   Passenger in pick-up truck or van injured in collision with heavy transport vehicle or bus in nontraffic accident

● V54.2   Person on outside of pick-up truck or van injured in collision with heavy transport vehicle or bus in nontraffic accident

● ■ V54.3   Unspecified occupant of pick-up truck or van injured in collision with heavy transport vehicle or bus in nontraffic accident

● V54.4   Person boarding or alighting a pick-up truck or van injured in collision with heavy transport vehicle or bus

● V54.5   Driver of pick-up truck or van injured in collision with heavy transport vehicle or bus in traffic accident

● V54.6   Passenger in pick-up truck or van injured in collision with heavy transport vehicle or bus in traffic accident

● V54.7   Person on outside of pick-up truck or van injured in collision with heavy transport vehicle or bus in traffic accident

● ■ V54.9   Unspecified occupant of pick-up truck or van injured in collision with heavy transport vehicle or bus in traffic accident

● V55   Occupant of pick-up truck or van injured in collision with railway train or railway vehicle

The appropriate 7th character is to be added to each code from category V55

A	initial encounter
D	subsequent encounter
S	sequela

● V55.0   Driver of pick-up truck or van injured in collision with railway train or railway vehicle in nontraffic accident

● V55.1   Passenger in pick-up truck or van injured in collision with railway train or railway vehicle in nontraffic accident

---

● Unacceptable First-Listed Diagnosis   ● Use Additional Character(s)   ■ Unspecified   OGCR Official Guidelines for Coding and Reporting

🍎 Complication\Comorbidity   🍎 Major C\C   Excludes 1   Excludes 2   Includes   Use additional   Code first   Code also

● V55.2 Person on outside of pick-up truck or van injured in collision with railway train or railway vehicle in nontraffic accident

● ■ V55.3 Unspecified occupant of pick-up truck or van injured in collision with railway train or railway vehicle in nontraffic accident

● V55.4 Person boarding or alighting a pick-up truck or van injured in collision with railway train or railway vehicle

● V55.5 Driver of pick-up truck or van injured in collision with railway train or railway vehicle in traffic accident

● V55.6 Passenger in pick-up truck or van injured in collision with railway train or railway vehicle in traffic accident

● V55.7 Person on outside of pick-up truck or van injured in collision with railway train or railway vehicle in traffic accident

● ■ V55.9 Unspecified occupant of pick-up truck or van injured in collision with railway train or railway vehicle in traffic accident

● V56 Occupant of pick-up truck or van injured in collision with other nonmotor vehicle

> **Includes** collision with animal-drawn vehicle, animal being ridden, streetcar

The appropriate 7th character is to be added to each code from category V56

A	initial encounter
D	subsequent encounter
S	sequela

● V56.0 Driver of pick-up truck or van injured in collision with other nonmotor vehicle in nontraffic accident

● V56.1 Passenger in pick-up truck or van injured in collision with other nonmotor vehicle in nontraffic accident

● V56.2 Person on outside of pick-up truck or van injured in collision with other nonmotor vehicle in nontraffic accident

● ■ V56.3 Unspecified occupant of pick-up truck or van injured in collision with other nonmotor vehicle in nontraffic accident

● V56.4 Person boarding or alighting a pick-up truck or van injured in collision with other nonmotor vehicle

● V56.5 Driver of pick-up truck or van injured in collision with other nonmotor vehicle in traffic accident

● V56.6 Passenger in pick-up truck or van injured in collision with other nonmotor vehicle in traffic accident

● V56.7 Person on outside of pick-up truck or van injured in collision with other nonmotor vehicle in traffic accident

● ■ V56.9 Unspecified occupant of pick-up truck or van injured in collision with other nonmotor vehicle in traffic accident

● V57 Occupant of pick-up truck or van injured in collision with fixed or stationary object

The appropriate 7th character is to be added to each code from category V57

A	initial encounter
D	subsequent encounter
S	sequela

● V57.0 Driver of pick-up truck or van injured in collision with fixed or stationary object in nontraffic accident

● V57.1 Passenger in pick-up truck or van injured in collision with fixed or stationary object in nontraffic accident

● V57.2 Person on outside of pick-up truck or van injured in collision with fixed or stationary object in nontraffic accident

● ■ V57.3 Unspecified occupant of pick-up truck or van injured in collision with fixed or stationary object in nontraffic accident

● V57.4 Person boarding or alighting a pick-up truck or van injured in collision with fixed or stationary object

● V57.5 Driver of pick-up truck or van injured in collision with fixed or stationary object in traffic accident

● V57.6 Passenger in pick-up truck or van injured in collision with fixed or stationary object in traffic accident

● V57.7 Person on outside of pick-up truck or van injured in collision with fixed or stationary object in traffic accident

● ■ V57.9 Unspecified occupant of pick-up truck or van injured in collision with fixed or stationary object in traffic accident

● V58 Occupant of pick-up truck or van injured in noncollision transport accident

> **Includes** overturning pick-up truck or van NOS
> overturning pick-up truck or van without collision

The appropriate 7th character is to be added to each code from category V58

A	initial encounter
D	subsequent encounter
S	sequela

● V58.0 Driver of pick-up truck or van injured in noncollision transport accident in nontraffic accident

● V58.1 Passenger in pick-up truck or van injured in noncollision transport accident in nontraffic accident

● V58.2 Person on outside of pick-up truck or van injured in noncollision transport accident in nontraffic accident

● ■ V58.3 Unspecified occupant of pick-up truck or van injured in noncollision transport accident in nontraffic accident

● V58.4 Person boarding or alighting a pick-up truck or van injured in noncollision transport accident

● V58.5 Driver of pick-up truck or van injured in noncollision transport accident in traffic accident

● V58.6 Passenger in pick-up truck or van injured in noncollision transport accident in traffic accident

● V58.7 Person on outside of pick-up truck or van injured in noncollision transport accident in traffic accident

● ■ V58.9 Unspecified occupant of pick-up truck or van injured in noncollision transport accident in traffic accident

● V59 Occupant of pick-up truck or van injured in other and unspecified transport accidents

The appropriate 7th character is to be added to each code from category V59

A	initial encounter
D	subsequent encounter
S	sequela

● V59.0 Driver of pick-up truck or van injured in collision with other and unspecified motor vehicles in nontraffic accident

CHAPTER 20 (V01-Y99)

● Unacceptable First-Listed Diagnosis   ● Use Additional Character(s)   ■ Unspecified   **OGCR** Official Guidelines for Coding and Reporting
🞮 Complication\Comorbidity   🞮 Major C\C   Excludes 1   Excludes 2   Includes   Use additional   Code first   Code also

● ◾ **V59.00** Driver of pick-up truck or van injured in collision with unspecified motor vehicles in nontraffic accident

● **V59.09** Driver of pick-up truck or van injured in collision with other motor vehicles in nontraffic accident

● **V59.1** Passenger in pick-up truck or van injured in collision with other and unspecified motor vehicles in nontraffic accident

     ● ◾ **V59.10** Passenger in pick-up truck or van injured in collision with unspecified motor vehicles in nontraffic accident

     ● **V59.11** Passenger in pick-up truck or van injured in collision with other motor vehicles in nontraffic accident

● **V59.2** Unspecified occupant of pick-up truck or van injured in collision with other and unspecified motor vehicles in nontraffic accident

     ● ◾ **V59.20** Unspecified occupant of pick-up truck or van injured in collision with unspecified motor vehicles in nontraffic accident

         Collision NOS involving pick-up truck or van, nontraffic

     ● ◾ **V59.21** Unspecified occupant of pick-up truck or van injured in collision with other motor vehicles in nontraffic accident

● ◾ **V59.3** Occupant (driver) (passenger) of pick-up truck or van injured in unspecified nontraffic accident

     Accident NOS involving pick-up truck or van, nontraffic

     Occupant of pick-up truck or van injured in nontraffic accident NOS

● **V59.4** Driver of pick-up truck or van injured in collision with other and unspecified motor vehicles in traffic accident

     ● ◾ **V59.40** Driver of pick-up truck or van injured in collision with unspecified motor vehicles in traffic accident

     ● **V59.49** Driver of pick-up truck or van injured in collision with other motor vehicles in traffic accident

● **V59.5** Passenger in pick-up truck or van injured in collision with other and unspecified motor vehicles in traffic accident

     ● ◾ **V59.50** Passenger in pick-up truck or van injured in collision with unspecified motor vehicles in traffic accident

     ● **V59.59** Passenger in pick-up truck or van injured in collision with other motor vehicles in traffic accident

● **V59.6** Unspecified occupant of pick-up truck or van injured in collision with other and unspecified motor vehicles in traffic accident

     ● ◾ **V59.60** Unspecified occupant of pick-up truck or van injured in collision with unspecified motor vehicles in traffic accident

         Collision NOS involving pick-up truck or van (traffic)

     ● ◾ **V59.69** Unspecified occupant of pick-up truck or van injured in collision with other motor vehicles in traffic accident

● **V59.8** Occupant (driver) (passenger) of pick-up truck or van injured in other specified transport accidents

     ● **V59.81** Occupant (driver) (passenger) of pick-up truck or van injured in transport accident with military vehicle

● **V59.88** Occupant (driver) (passenger) of pick-up truck or van injured in other specified transport accidents

● ◾ **V59.9** Occupant (driver) (passenger) of pick-up truck or van injured in unspecified traffic accident

     Accident NOS involving pick-up truck or van

OCCUPANT OF HEAVY TRANSPORT VEHICLE INJURED IN TRANSPORT ACCIDENT (V60-V69)

Includes   armored car
            panel truck
            18 wheeler

Excludes1   bus
            motorcoach

● **V60** Occupant of heavy transport vehicle injured in collision with pedestrian or animal

     Excludes1   heavy transport vehicle collision with animal-drawn vehicle or animal being ridden (V66.-)

     The appropriate 7th character is to be added to each code from category V60

     A   initial encounter
     D   subsequent encounter
     S   sequela

     ● **V60.0** Driver of heavy transport vehicle injured in collision with pedestrian or animal in nontraffic accident

     ● **V60.1** Passenger in heavy transport vehicle injured in collision with pedestrian or animal in nontraffic accident

     ● **V60.2** Person on outside of heavy transport vehicle injured in collision with pedestrian or animal in nontraffic accident

     ● ◾ **V60.3** Unspecified occupant of heavy transport vehicle injured in collision with pedestrian or animal in nontraffic accident

     ● **V60.4** Person boarding or alighting a heavy transport vehicle injured in collision with pedestrian or animal

     ● **V60.5** Driver of heavy transport vehicle injured in collision with pedestrian or animal in traffic accident

     ● **V60.6** Passenger in heavy transport vehicle injured in collision with pedestrian or animal in traffic accident

     ● **V60.7** Person on outside of heavy transport vehicle injured in collision with pedestrian or animal in traffic accident

     ● ◾ **V60.9** Unspecified occupant of heavy transport vehicle injured in collision with pedestrian or animal in traffic accident

● **V61** Occupant of heavy transport vehicle injured in collision with pedal cycle

     The appropriate 7th character is to be added to each code from category V61

     A   initial encounter
     D   subsequent encounter
     S   sequela

     ● **V61.0** Driver of heavy transport vehicle injured in collision with pedal cycle in nontraffic accident

     ● **V61.1** Passenger in heavy transport vehicle injured in collision with pedal cycle in nontraffic accident

     ● **V61.2** Person on outside of heavy transport vehicle injured in collision with pedal cycle in nontraffic accident

● Unacceptable First-Listed Diagnosis   ● Use Additional Character(s)   ◾ Unspecified   **OGCR** Official Guidelines for Coding and Reporting

◐ Complication\Comorbidity   ◓ Major C\C   Excludes 1   Excludes 2   Includes   Use additional   Code first   Code also   1647

CHAPTER 20 (V01-Y99)

● ■ **V61.3** **Unspecified occupant of heavy transport vehicle injured in collision with pedal cycle in nontraffic accident**

● **V61.4** **Person boarding or alighting a heavy transport vehicle injured in collision with pedal cycle while boarding or alighting**

● **V61.5** **Driver of heavy transport vehicle injured in collision with pedal cycle in traffic accident**

● **V61.6** **Passenger in heavy transport vehicle injured in collision with pedal cycle in traffic accident**

● **V61.7** **Person on outside of heavy transport vehicle injured in collision with pedal cycle in traffic accident**

● ■ **V61.9** **Unspecified occupant of heavy transport vehicle injured in collision with pedal cycle in traffic accident**

● **V62** **Occupant of heavy transport vehicle injured in collision with two- or three-wheeled motor vehicle**

The appropriate 7th character is to be added to each code from category V62

A	initial encounter
D	subsequent encounter
S	sequela

● **V62.0** **Driver of heavy transport vehicle injured in collision with two- or three-wheeled motor vehicle in nontraffic accident**

● **V62.1** **Passenger in heavy transport vehicle injured in collision with two- or three-wheeled motor vehicle in nontraffic accident**

● **V62.2** **Person on outside of heavy transport vehicle injured in collision with two- or three-wheeled motor vehicle in nontraffic accident**

● ■ **V62.3** **Unspecified occupant of heavy transport vehicle injured in collision with two- or three-wheeled motor vehicle in nontraffic accident**

● **V62.4** **Person boarding or alighting a heavy transport vehicle injured in collision with two- or three-wheeled motor vehicle**

● **V62.5** **Driver of heavy transport vehicle injured in collision with two- or three-wheeled motor vehicle in traffic accident**

● **V62.6** **Passenger in heavy transport vehicle injured in collision with two- or three-wheeled motor vehicle in traffic accident**

● **V62.7** **Person on outside of heavy transport vehicle injured in collision with two- or three-wheeled motor vehicle in traffic accident**

● ■ **V62.9** **Unspecified occupant of heavy transport vehicle injured in collision with two- or three-wheeled motor vehicle in traffic accident**

● **V63** **Occupant of heavy transport vehicle injured in collision with car, pick-up truck or van**

The appropriate 7th character is to be added to each code from category V63

A	initial encounter
D	subsequent encounter
S	sequela

● **V63.0** **Driver of heavy transport vehicle injured in collision with car, pick-up truck or van in nontraffic accident**

● **V63.1** **Passenger in heavy transport vehicle injured in collision with car, pick-up truck or van in nontraffic accident**

● **V63.2** **Person on outside of heavy transport vehicle injured in collision with car, pick-up truck or van in nontraffic accident**

● ■ **V63.3** **Unspecified occupant of heavy transport vehicle injured in collision with car, pick-up truck or van in nontraffic accident**

● **V63.4** **Person boarding or alighting a heavy transport vehicle injured in collision with car, pick-up truck or van**

● **V63.5** **Driver of heavy transport vehicle injured in collision with car, pick-up truck or van in traffic accident**

● **V63.6** **Passenger in heavy transport vehicle injured in collision with car, pick-up truck or van in traffic accident**

● **V63.7** **Person on outside of heavy transport vehicle injured in collision with car, pick-up truck or van in traffic accident**

● ■ **V63.9** **Unspecified occupant of heavy transport vehicle injured in collision with car, pick-up truck or van in traffic accident**

● **V64** **Occupant of heavy transport vehicle injured in collision with heavy transport vehicle or bus**

Excludes1	occupant of heavy transport vehicle injured in collision with military vehicle (V69.81)

The appropriate 7th character is to be added to each code from category V64

A	initial encounter
D	subsequent encounter
S	sequela

● **V64.0** **Driver of heavy transport vehicle injured in collision with heavy transport vehicle or bus in nontraffic accident**

● **V64.1** **Passenger in heavy transport vehicle injured in collision with heavy transport vehicle or bus in nontraffic accident**

● **V64.2** **Person on outside of heavy transport vehicle injured in collision with heavy transport vehicle or bus in nontraffic accident**

● ■ **V64.3** **Unspecified occupant of heavy transport vehicle injured in collision with heavy transport vehicle or bus in nontraffic accident**

● **V64.4** **Person boarding or alighting a heavy transport vehicle injured in collision with heavy transport vehicle or bus while boarding or alighting**

● **V64.5** **Driver of heavy transport vehicle injured in collision with heavy transport vehicle or bus in traffic accident**

● **V64.6** **Passenger in heavy transport vehicle injured in collision with heavy transport vehicle or bus in traffic accident**

● **V64.7** **Person on outside of heavy transport vehicle injured in collision with heavy transport vehicle or bus in traffic accident**

● ■ **V64.9** **Unspecified occupant of heavy transport vehicle injured in collision with heavy transport vehicle or bus in traffic accident**

● **V65** **Occupant of heavy transport vehicle injured in collision with railway train or railway vehicle**

The appropriate 7th character is to be added to each code from category V65

A	initial encounter
D	subsequent encounter
S	sequela

● **V65.0** **Driver of heavy transport vehicle injured in collision with railway train or railway vehicle in nontraffic accident**

● Unacceptable First-Listed Diagnosis   ● Use Additional Character(s)   ■ Unspecified   **OGCR** Official Guidelines for Coding and Reporting
🔹 Complication\Comorbidity   🔹 Major C\C   Excludes 1   Excludes 2   Includes   Use additional   Code first   Code also

● V65.1 Passenger in heavy transport vehicle injured in collision with railway train or railway vehicle in nontraffic accident

● V65.2 Person on outside of heavy transport vehicle injured in collision with railway train or railway vehicle in nontraffic accident

● ▪ V65.3 Unspecified occupant of heavy transport vehicle injured in collision with railway train or railway vehicle in nontraffic accident

● V65.4 Person boarding or alighting a heavy transport vehicle injured in collision with railway train or railway vehicle

● V65.5 Driver of heavy transport vehicle injured in collision with railway train or railway vehicle in traffic accident

● V65.6 Passenger in heavy transport vehicle injured in collision with railway train or railway vehicle in traffic accident

● V65.7 Person on outside of heavy transport vehicle injured in collision with railway train or railway vehicle in traffic accident

● ▪ V65.9 Unspecified occupant of heavy transport vehicle injured in collision with railway train or railway vehicle in traffic accident

● V66 Occupant of heavy transport vehicle injured in collision with other nonmotor vehicle

> **Includes** collision with animal-drawn vehicle, animal being ridden, streetcar

The appropriate 7th character is to be added to each code from category V66

A	initial encounter
D	subsequent encounter
S	sequela

● V66.0 Driver of heavy transport vehicle injured in collision with other nonmotor vehicle in nontraffic accident

● V66.1 Passenger in heavy transport vehicle injured in collision with other nonmotor vehicle in nontraffic accident

● V66.2 Person on outside of heavy transport vehicle injured in collision with other nonmotor vehicle in nontraffic accident

● ▪ V66.3 Unspecified occupant of heavy transport vehicle injured in collision with other nonmotor vehicle in nontraffic accident

● V66.4 Person boarding or alighting a heavy transport vehicle injured in collision with other nonmotor vehicle

● V66.5 Driver of heavy transport vehicle injured in collision with other nonmotor vehicle in traffic accident

● V66.6 Passenger in heavy transport vehicle injured in collision with other nonmotor vehicle in traffic accident

● V66.7 Person on outside of heavy transport vehicle injured in collision with other nonmotor vehicle in traffic accident

● ▪ V66.9 Unspecified occupant of heavy transport vehicle injured in collision with other nonmotor vehicle in traffic accident

● V67 Occupant of heavy transport vehicle injured in collision with fixed or stationary object

The appropriate 7th character is to be added to each code from category V67

A	initial encounter
D	subsequent encounter
S	sequela

● V67.0 Driver of heavy transport vehicle injured in collision with fixed or stationary object in nontraffic accident

● V67.1 Passenger in heavy transport vehicle injured in collision with fixed or stationary object in nontraffic accident

● V67.2 Person on outside of heavy transport vehicle injured in collision with fixed or stationary object in nontraffic accident

● ▪ V67.3 Unspecified occupant of heavy transport vehicle injured in collision with fixed or stationary object in nontraffic accident

● V67.4 Person boarding or alighting a heavy transport vehicle injured in collision with fixed or stationary object

● V67.5 Driver of heavy transport vehicle injured in collision with fixed or stationary object in traffic accident

● V67.6 Passenger in heavy transport vehicle injured in collision with fixed or stationary object in traffic accident

● V67.7 Person on outside of heavy transport vehicle injured in collision with fixed or stationary object in traffic accident

● ▪ V67.9 Unspecified occupant of heavy transport vehicle injured in collision with fixed or stationary object in traffic accident

● V68 Occupant of heavy transport vehicle injured in noncollision transport accident

> **Includes** overturning heavy transport vehicle NOS overturning heavy transport vehicle without collision

The appropriate 7th character is to be added to each code from category V68

A	initial encounter
D	subsequent encounter
S	sequela

● V68.0 Driver of heavy transport vehicle injured in noncollision transport accident in nontraffic accident

● V68.1 Passenger in heavy transport vehicle injured in noncollision transport accident in nontraffic accident

● V68.2 Person on outside of heavy transport vehicle injured in noncollision transport accident in nontraffic accident

● ▪ V68.3 Unspecified occupant of heavy transport vehicle injured in noncollision transport accident in nontraffic accident

● V68.4 Person boarding or alighting a heavy transport vehicle injured in noncollision transport accident

● V68.5 Driver of heavy transport vehicle injured in noncollision transport accident in traffic accident

● V68.6 Passenger in heavy transport vehicle injured in noncollision transport accident in traffic accident

● V68.7 Person on outside of heavy transport vehicle injured in noncollision transport accident in traffic accident

● Unacceptable First-Listed Diagnosis   ● Use Additional Character(s)   ▪ Unspecified   **OGCR** Official Guidelines for Coding and Reporting

 Complication\Comorbidity   Major C\C   Excludes 1   Excludes 2   Includes   Use additional   Code first   Code also

1649

CHAPTER 20 (V01-Y99)

● ■ **V68.9**   Unspecified occupant of heavy transport vehicle injured in noncollision transport accident in traffic accident

● **V69**   Occupant of heavy transport vehicle injured in other and unspecified transport accidents

> The appropriate 7th character is to be added to each code from category V69

> | | |
> |---|---|
> | A | initial encounter |
> | D | subsequent encounter |
> | S | sequela |

● **V69.0**   Driver of heavy transport vehicle injured in collision with other and unspecified motor vehicles in nontraffic accident

    ● ■ **V69.00**   Driver of heavy transport vehicle injured in collision with unspecified motor vehicles in nontraffic accident

    ● **V69.09**   Driver of heavy transport vehicle injured in collision with other motor vehicles in nontraffic accident

● **V69.1**   Passenger in heavy transport vehicle injured in collision with other and unspecified motor vehicles in nontraffic accident

    ● ■ **V69.10**   Passenger in heavy transport vehicle injured in collision with unspecified motor vehicles in nontraffic accident

    ● **V69.19**   Passenger in heavy transport vehicle injured in collision with other motor vehicles in nontraffic accident

● **V69.2**   Unspecified occupant of heavy transport vehicle injured in collision with other and unspecified motor vehicles in nontraffic accident

    ● ■ **V69.20**   Unspecified occupant of heavy transport vehicle injured in collision with unspecified motor vehicles in nontraffic accident

> Collision NOS involving heavy transport vehicle, nontraffic

    ● ■ **V69.29**   Unspecified occupant of heavy transport vehicle injured in collision with other motor vehicles in nontraffic accident

● **V69.3**   Occupant (driver) (passenger) of heavy transport vehicle injured in unspecified nontraffic accident

> Accident NOS involving heavy transport vehicle, nontraffic
> Occupant of heavy transport vehicle injured in nontraffic accident NOS

● **V69.4**   Driver of heavy transport vehicle injured in collision with other and unspecified motor vehicles in traffic accident

    ● ■ **V69.40**   Driver of heavy transport vehicle injured in collision with unspecified motor vehicles in traffic accident

    ● **V69.49**   Driver of heavy transport vehicle injured in collision with other motor vehicles in traffic accident

● **V69.5**   Passenger in heavy transport vehicle injured in collision with other and unspecified motor vehicles in traffic accident

    ● ■ **V69.50**   Passenger in heavy transport vehicle injured in collision with unspecified motor vehicles in traffic accident

    ● **V69.59**   Passenger in heavy transport vehicle injured in collision with other motor vehicles in traffic accident

● **V69.6**   Unspecified occupant of heavy transport vehicle injured in collision with other and unspecified motor vehicles in traffic accident

● ■ **V69.60**   Unspecified occupant of heavy transport vehicle injured in collision with unspecified motor vehicles in traffic accident

> Collision NOS involving heavy transport vehicle (traffic)

● ■ **V69.69**   Unspecified occupant of heavy transport vehicle injured in collision with other motor vehicles in traffic accident

● **V69.8**   Occupant (driver) (passenger) of heavy transport vehicle injured in other specified transport accidents

    ● **V69.81**   Occupant (driver) (passenger) of heavy transport vehicle injured in transport accidents with military vehicle

    ● **V69.88**   Occupant (driver) (passenger) of heavy transport vehicle injured in other specified transport accidents

● ■ **V69.9**   Occupant (driver) (passenger) of heavy transport vehicle injured in unspecified traffic accident

> Accident NOS involving heavy transport vehicle

BUS OCCUPANT INJURED IN TRANSPORT ACCIDENT (V70-V79)

> **Includes**   motorcoach
> **Excludes1**   minibus (V50-V59)

● **V70**   Bus occupant injured in collision with pedestrian or animal

> The appropriate 7th character is to be added to each code from category V70

> | | |
> |---|---|
> | A | initial encounter |
> | D | subsequent encounter |
> | S | sequela |

> **Excludes1**   bus collision with animal-drawn vehicle or animal being ridden (V76.-)

● **V70.0**   Driver of bus injured in collision with pedestrian or animal in nontraffic accident

● **V70.1**   Passenger on bus injured in collision with pedestrian or animal in nontraffic accident

● **V70.2**   Person on outside of bus injured in collision with pedestrian or animal in nontraffic accident

● ■ **V70.3**   Unspecified occupant of bus injured in collision with pedestrian or animal in nontraffic accident

● **V70.4**   Person boarding or alighting from bus injured in collision with pedestrian or animal

● **V70.5**   Driver of bus injured in collision with pedestrian or animal in traffic accident

● **V70.6**   Passenger on bus injured in collision with pedestrian or animal in traffic accident

● **V70.7**   Person on outside of bus injured in collision with pedestrian or animal in traffic accident

● ■ **V70.9**   Unspecified occupant of bus injured in collision with pedestrian or animal in traffic accident

● **V71**   Bus occupant injured in collision with pedal cycle

> The appropriate 7th character is to be added to each code from category V71

> | | |
> |---|---|
> | A | initial encounter |
> | D | subsequent encounter |
> | S | sequela |

● **V71.0**   Driver of bus injured in collision with pedal cycle in nontraffic accident

● **V71.1**   Passenger on bus injured in collision with pedal cycle in nontraffic accident

● **V71.2**   Person on outside of bus injured in collision with pedal cycle in nontraffic accident

● ■ **V71.3**   Unspecified occupant of bus injured in collision with pedal cycle in nontraffic accident

CHAPTER 20 (V01-Y99)

● V71.4 **Person boarding or alighting from bus injured in collision with pedal cycle**

● V71.5 **Driver of bus injured in collision with pedal cycle in traffic accident**

● V71.6 **Passenger on bus injured in collision with pedal cycle in traffic accident**

● V71.7 **Person on outside of bus injured in collision with pedal cycle in traffic accident**

● ■ V71.9 **Unspecified occupant of bus injured in collision with pedal cycle in traffic accident**

● V72 **Bus occupant injured in collision with two- or three-wheeled motor vehicle**

The appropriate 7th character is to be added to each code from category V72

A	initial encounter
D	subsequent encounter
S	sequela

● V72.0 **Driver of bus injured in collision with two- or three-wheeled motor vehicle in nontraffic accident**

● V72.1 **Passenger on bus injured in collision with two- or three-wheeled motor vehicle in nontraffic accident**

● V72.2 **Person on outside of bus injured in collision with two- or three-wheeled motor vehicle in nontraffic accident**

● ■ V72.3 **Unspecified occupant of bus injured in collision with two- or three-wheeled motor vehicle in nontraffic accident**

● V72.4 **Person boarding or alighting from bus injured in collision with two- or three-wheeled motor vehicle**

● V72.5 **Driver of bus injured in collision with two- or three-wheeled motor vehicle in traffic accident**

● V72.6 **Passenger on bus injured in collision with two- or three-wheeled motor vehicle in traffic accident**

● V72.7 **Person on outside of bus injured in collision with two- or three-wheeled motor vehicle in traffic accident**

● ■ V72.9 **Unspecified occupant of bus injured in collision with two- or three-wheeled motor vehicle in traffic accident**

● V73 **Bus occupant injured in collision with car, pick-up truck or van**

The appropriate 7th character is to be added to each code from category V73

A	initial encounter
D	subsequent encounter
S	sequela

● V73.0 **Driver of bus injured in collision with car, pick-up truck or van in nontraffic accident**

● V73.1 **Passenger on bus injured in collision with car, pick-up truck or van in nontraffic accident**

● V73.2 **Person on outside of bus injured in collision with car, pick-up truck or van in nontraffic accident**

● ■ V73.3 **Unspecified occupant of bus injured in collision with car, pick-up truck or van in nontraffic accident**

● V73.4 **Person boarding or alighting from bus injured in collision with car, pick-up truck or van**

● V73.5 **Driver of bus injured in collision with car, pick-up truck or van in traffic accident**

● V73.6 **Passenger on bus injured in collision with car, pick-up truck or van in traffic accident**

● V73.7 **Person on outside of bus injured in collision with car, pick-up truck or van in traffic accident**

● ■ V73.9 **Unspecified occupant of bus injured in collision with car, pick-up truck or van in traffic accident**

● V74 **Bus occupant injured in collision with heavy transport vehicle or bus**

Excludes1 bus occupant injured in collision with military vehicle (V79.81)

The appropriate 7th character is to be added to each code from category V74

A	initial encounter
D	subsequent encounter
S	sequela

● V74.0 **Driver of bus injured in collision with heavy transport vehicle or bus in nontraffic accident**

● V74.1 **Passenger on bus injured in collision with heavy transport vehicle or bus in nontraffic accident**

● V74.2 **Person on outside of bus injured in collision with heavy transport vehicle or bus in nontraffic accident**

● ■ V74.3 **Unspecified occupant of bus injured in collision with heavy transport vehicle or bus in nontraffic accident**

● V74.4 **Person boarding or alighting from bus injured in collision with heavy transport vehicle or bus**

● V74.5 **Driver of bus injured in collision with heavy transport vehicle or bus in traffic accident**

● V74.6 **Passenger on bus injured in collision with heavy transport vehicle or bus in traffic accident**

● V74.7 **Person on outside of bus injured in collision with heavy transport vehicle or bus in traffic accident**

● ■ V74.9 **Unspecified occupant of bus injured in collision with heavy transport vehicle or bus in traffic accident**

● V75 **Bus occupant injured in collision with railway train or railway vehicle**

The appropriate 7th character is to be added to each code from category V75

A	initial encunter
D	subsequent encounter
S	sequela

● V75.0 **Driver of bus injured in collision with railway train or railway vehicle in nontraffic accident**

● V75.1 **Passenger on bus injured in collision with railway train or railway vehicle in nontraffic accident**

● V75.2 **Person on outside of bus injured in collision with railway train or railway vehicle in nontraffic accident**

● ■ V75.3 **Unspecified occupant of bus injured in collision with railway train or railway vehicle in nontraffic accident**

● V75.4 **Person boarding or alighting from bus injured in collision with railway train or railway vehicle**

● V75.5 **Driver of bus injured in collision with railway train or railway vehicle in traffic accident**

● V75.6 **Passenger on bus injured in collision with railway train or railway vehicle in traffic accident**

● V75.7 **Person on outside of bus injured in collision with railway train or railway vehicle in traffic accident**

● ■ V75.9 **Unspecified occupant of bus injured in collision with railway train or railway vehicle in traffic accident**

CHAPTER 20 (V01–Y99)

● Unacceptable First-Listed Diagnosis   ● Use Additional Character(s)   ■ Unspecified   **OGCR** Official Guidelines for Coding and Reporting

 Complication\Comorbidity    Major C\C | Excludes 1 | | Excludes 2 | Includes   Use additional   Code first   Code also

1651

● **V76** **Bus occupant injured in collision with other nonmotor vehicle**

> **Includes**   collision with animal-drawn vehicle, animal being ridden, streetcar

> The appropriate 7th character is to be added to each code from category V76

> | A | initial encounter |
> |---|---|
> | D | subsequent encounter |
> | S | sequela |

● V76.0   Driver of bus injured in collision with other nonmotor vehicle in nontraffic accident

● V76.1   Passenger on bus injured in collision with other nonmotor vehicle in nontraffic accident

● V76.2   Person on outside of bus injured in collision with other nonmotor vehicle in nontraffic accident

● ■ V76.3   Unspecified occupant of bus injured in collision with other nonmotor vehicle in nontraffic accident

● V76.4   Person boarding or alighting from bus injured in collision with other nonmotor vehicle

● V76.5   Driver of bus injured in collision with other nonmotor vehicle in traffic accident

● V76.6   Passenger on bus injured in collision with other nonmotor vehicle in traffic accident

● V76.7   Person on outside of bus injured in collision with other nonmotor vehicle in traffic accident

● ■ V76.9   Unspecified occupant of bus injured in collision with other nonmotor vehicle in traffic accident

● **V77** **Bus occupant injured in collision with fixed or stationary object**

> The appropriate 7th character is to be added to each code from category V77

> | A | initial encounter |
> |---|---|
> | D | subsequent encounter |
> | S | sequela |

● V77.0   Driver of bus injured in collision with fixed or stationary object in nontraffic accident

● V77.1   Passenger on bus injured in collision with fixed or stationary object in nontraffic accident

● V77.2   Person on outside of bus injured in collision with fixed or stationary object in nontraffic accident

● ■ V77.3   Unspecified occupant of bus injured in collision with fixed or stationary object in nontraffic accident

● V77.4   Person boarding or alighting from bus injured in collision with fixed or stationary object

● V77.5   Driver of bus injured in collision with fixed or stationary object in traffic accident

● V77.6   Passenger on bus injured in collision with fixed or stationary object in traffic accident

● V77.7   Person on outside of bus injured in collision with fixed or stationary object in traffic accident

● ■ V77.9   Unspecified occupant of bus injured in collision with fixed or stationary object in traffic accident

● **V78** **Bus occupant injured in noncollision transport accident**

> **Includes**   overturning bus NOS
> overturning bus without collision

> The appropriate 7th character is to be added to each code from category V78

> | A | initial encounter |
> |---|---|
> | D | subsequent encounter |
> | S | sequela |

● V78.0   Driver of bus injured in noncollision transport accident in nontraffic accident

● V78.1   Passenger on bus injured in noncollision transport accident in nontraffic accident

● V78.2   Person on outside of bus injured in noncollision transport accident in nontraffic accident

● ■ V78.3   Unspecified occupant of bus injured in noncollision transport accident in nontraffic accident

● V78.4   Person boarding or alighting from bus injured in noncollision transport accident

● V78.5   Driver of bus injured in noncollision transport accident in traffic accident

● V78.6   Passenger on bus injured in noncollision transport accident in traffic accident

● V78.7   Person on outside of bus injured in noncollision transport accident in traffic accident

● ■ V78.9   Unspecified occupant of bus injured in noncollision transport accident in traffic accident

● **V79** **Bus occupant injured in other and unspecified transport accidents**

> The appropriate 7th character is to be added to each code from category V79

> | A | initial encounter |
> |---|---|
> | D | subsequent encounter |
> | S | sequela |

● V79.0   Driver of bus injured in collision with other and unspecified motor vehicles in nontraffic accident

   ● ■ V79.00   Driver of bus injured in collision with unspecified motor vehicles in nontraffic accident

   ● V79.09   Driver of bus injured in collision with other motor vehicles in nontraffic accident

● V79.1   Passenger on bus injured in collision with other and unspecified motor vehicles in nontraffic accident

   ● ■ V79.10   Passenger on bus injured in collision with unspecified motor vehicles in nontraffic accident

   ● V79.19   Passenger on bus injured in collision with other motor vehicles in nontraffic accident

● V79.2   Unspecified bus occupant injured in collision with other and unspecified motor vehicles in nontraffic accident

   ● ■ V79.20   Unspecified bus occupant injured in collision with unspecified motor vehicles in nontraffic accident
        Bus collision NOS, nontraffic

   ● ■ V79.29   Unspecified bus occupant injured in collision with other motor vehicles in nontraffic accident

● ■ V79.3   Bus occupant (driver) (passenger) injured in unspecified nontraffic accident
     Bus accident NOS, nontraffic
     Bus occupant injured in nontraffic accident NOS

● V79.4   Driver of bus injured in collision with other and unspecified motor vehicles in traffic accident

   ● ■ V79.40   Driver of bus injured in collision with unspecified motor vehicles in traffic accident

   ● V79.49   Driver of bus injured in collision with other motor vehicles in traffic accident

● V79.5   Passenger on bus injured in collision with other and unspecified motor vehicles in traffic accident

   ● ■ V79.50   Passenger on bus injured in collision with unspecified motor vehicles in traffic accident

   ● V79.59   Passenger on bus injured in collision with other motor vehicles in traffic accident

● V79.6   Unspecified bus occupant injured in collision with other and unspecified motor vehicles in traffic accident

● Unacceptable First-Listed Diagnosis   ● Use Additional Character(s)   ■ Unspecified   **OGCR** Official Guidelines for Coding and Reporting
🔖 Complication\Comorbidity   🔖 Major C\C   Excludes 1   Excludes 2   Includes   Use additional   Code first   Code also

● ■ V79.60   Unspecified bus occupant injured in collision with unspecified motor vehicles in traffic accident
     Bus collision NOS (traffic)

● ■ V79.69   Unspecified bus occupant injured in collision with other motor vehicles in traffic accident

● V79.8   Bus occupant (driver) (passenger) injured in other specified transport accidents

     ● V79.81   Bus occupant (driver) (passenger) injured in transport accidents with military vehicle

     ● V79.88   Bus occupant (driver) (passenger) injured in other specified transport accidents

● ■ V79.9   Bus occupant (driver) (passenger) injured in unspecified traffic accident
     Bus accident NOS

OTHER LAND TRANSPORT ACCIDENTS (V80–V89)

● V80   Animal-rider or occupant of animal-drawn vehicle injured in transport accident
     The appropriate 7th character is to be added to each code from category V80

> A   initial encounter
> D   subsequent encounter
> S   sequela

● V80.0   Animal-rider or occupant of animal drawn vehicle injured by fall from or being thrown from animal or animal-drawn vehicle in noncollision accident

     ● V80.01   Animal-rider injured by fall from or being thrown from animal in noncollision accident

         ● V80.010   Animal-rider injured by fall from or being thrown from horse in noncollision accident

         ● V80.018   Animal-rider injured by fall from or being thrown from other animal in noncollision accident

     ● V80.02   Occupant of animal-drawn vehicle injured by fall from or being thrown from animal-drawn vehicle in noncollision accident
         Overturning animal-drawn vehicle NOS
         Overturning animal-drawn vehicle without collision

● V80.1   Animal-rider or occupant of animal-drawn vehicle injured in collision with pedestrian or animal

> **Excludes1**   animal-rider or animal-drawn vehicle collision with animal-drawn vehicle or animal being ridden (V80.7)

     ● V80.11   Animal-rider injured in collision with pedestrian or animal

     ● V80.12   Occupant of animal-drawn vehicle injured in collision with pedestrian or animal

● V80.2   Animal-rider or occupant of animal-drawn vehicle injured in collision with pedal cycle

     ● V80.21   Animal-rider injured in collision with pedal cycle

     ● V80.22   Occupant of animal-drawn vehicle injured in collision with pedal cycle

● V80.3   Animal-rider or occupant of animal-drawn vehicle injured in collision with two- or three-wheeled motor vehicle

     ● V80.31   Animal-rider injured in collision with two- or three-wheeled motor vehicle

     ● V80.32   Occupant of animal-drawn vehicle injured in collision with two- or three-wheeled motor vehicle

● V80.4   Animal-rider or occupant of animal-drawn vehicle injured in collision with car, pick-up truck, van, heavy transport vehicle or bus

> **Excludes1**   animal-rider injured in collision with military vehicle (V80.910)
> occupant of animal-drawn vehicle injured in collision with military vehicle (V80.920)

     ● V80.41   Animal-rider injured in collision with car, pick-up truck, van, heavy transport vehicle or bus

     ● V80.42   Occupant of animal-drawn vehicle injured in collision with car, pick-up truck, van, heavy transport vehicle or bus

● V80.5   Animal-rider or occupant of animal-drawn vehicle injured in collision with other specified motor vehicle

     ● V80.51   Animal-rider injured in collision with other specified motor vehicle

     ● V80.52   Occupant of animal-drawn vehicle injured in collision with other specified motor vehicle

● V80.6   Animal-rider or occupant of animal-drawn vehicle injured in collision with railway train or railway vehicle

     ● V80.61   Animal-rider injured in collision with railway train or railway vehicle

     ● V80.62   Occupant of animal-drawn vehicle injured in collision with railway train or railway vehicle

● V80.7   Animal-rider or occupant of animal-drawn vehicle injured in collision with other nonmotor vehicles

     ● V80.71   Animal-rider or occupant of animal-drawn vehicle injured in collision with animal being ridden

         ● V80.710   Animal-rider injured in collision with other animal being ridden

         ● V80.711   Occupant of animal-drawn vehicle injured in collision with animal being ridden

     ● V80.72   Animal-rider or occupant of animal-drawn vehicle injured in collision with other animal-drawn vehicle

         ● V80.720   Animal-rider injured in collision with animal-drawn vehicle

         ● V80.721   Occupant of animal-drawn vehicle injured in collision with other animal-drawn vehicle

     ● V80.73   Animal-rider or occupant of animal-drawn vehicle injured in collision with streetcar

         ● V80.730   Animal-rider injured in collision with streetcar

         ● V80.731   Occupant of animal-drawn vehicle injured in collision with streetcar

     ● V80.79   Animal-rider or occupant of animal-drawn vehicle injured in collision with other nonmotor vehicles

         ● V80.790   Animal-rider injured in collision with other nonmotor vehicles

         ● V80.791   Occupant of animal-drawn vehicle injured in collision with other nonmotor vehicles

● V80.8   Animal-rider or occupant of animal-drawn vehicle injured in collision with fixed or stationary object

● Unacceptable First-Listed Diagnosis   ● Use Additional Character(s)   ■ Unspecified   **OGCR** Official Guidelines for Coding and Reporting

 Complication\Comorbidity   Major C\C   Excludes 1   Excludes 2   Includes   Use additional   Code first   Code also

1653

CHAPTER 20 (V01–Y99)

- **V80.81** **Animal-rider injured in collision with fixed or stationary object**
- **V80.82** **Occupant of animal-drawn vehicle injured in collision with fixed or stationary object**
- **V80.9** **Animal-rider or occupant of animal-drawn vehicle injured in other and unspecified transport accidents**
  - **V80.91** **Animal-rider injured in other and unspecified transport accidents**
    - **V80.910** **Animal-rider injured in transport accident with military vehicle**
    - **V80.918** **Animal-rider injured in other transport accident**
    - **V80.919** **Animal-rider injured in unspecified transport accident**
      Animal rider accident NOS
  - **V80.92** **Occupant of animal-drawn vehicle injured in other and unspecified transport accidents**
    - **V80.920** **Occupant of animal-drawn vehicle injured in transport accident with military vehicle**
    - **V80.928** **Occupant of animal-drawn vehicle injured in other transport accident**
    - **V80.929** **Occupant of animal-drawn vehicle injured in unspecified transport accident**
      Animal-drawn vehicle accident NOS

- **V81** **Occupant of railway train or railway vehicle injured in transport accident**

  | **Includes** | derailment of railway train or railway vehicle
  person on outside of train |

  | **Excludes1** | streetcar (V82.-) |

  The appropriate 7th character is to be added to each code from category V81

  > A   initial encounter
  > D   subsequent encounter
  > S   sequela

  - **V81.0** **Occupant of railway train or railway vehicle injured in collision with motor vehicle in nontraffic accident**

    | **Excludes1** | occupant of railway train or railway vehicle injured due to collision with military vehicle (V81.83) |

  - **V81.1** **Occupant of railway train or railway vehicle injured in collision with motor vehicle in traffic accident**

    | **Excludes1** | occupant of railway train or railway vehicle injured due to collision with military vehicle (V81.83) |

  - **V81.2** **Occupant of railway train or railway vehicle injured in collision with or hit by rolling stock**
  - **V81.3** **Occupant of railway train or railway vehicle injured in collision with other object**
    Railway collision NOS
  - **V81.4** **Person injured while boarding or alighting from railway train or railway vehicle**
  - **V81.5** **Occupant of railway train or railway vehicle injured by fall in railway train or railway vehicle**
  - **V81.6** **Occupant of railway train or railway vehicle injured by fall from railway train or railway vehicle**
  - **V81.7** **Occupant of railway train or railway vehicle injured in derailment without antecedent collision**

- **V81.8** **Occupant of railway train or railway vehicle injured in other specified railway accidents**
  - **V81.81** **Occupant of railway train or railway vehicle injured due to explosion or fire on train**
  - **V81.82** **Occupant of railway train or railway vehicle injured due to object falling onto train**
    Occupant of railway train or railway vehicle injured due to falling earth onto train
    Occupant of railway train or railway vehicle injured due to falling rocks onto train
    Occupant of railway train or railway vehicle injured due to falling snow onto train
    Occupant of railway train or railway vehicle injured due to falling trees onto train
  - **V81.83** **Occupant of railway train or railway vehicle injured due to collision with military vehicle**
  - **V81.89** **Occupant of railway train or railway vehicle injured due to other specified railway accident**
- **V81.9** **Occupant of railway train or railway vehicle injured in unspecified railway accident**
  Railway accident NOS

- **V82** **Occupant of powered streetcar injured in transport accident**

  | **Includes** | interurban electric car
  person on outside of streetcar
  tram (car)
  trolley (car) |

  | **Excludes1** | bus (V70-V79)
  motorcoach (V70-V79)
  nonpowered streetcar (V76.-)
  train (V81.-) |

  The appropriate 7th character is to be added to each code from category V82

  > A   initial encounter
  > D   subsequent encounter
  > S   sequela

  - **V82.0** **Occupant of streetcar injured in collision with motor vehicle in nontraffic accident**
  - **V82.1** **Occupant of streetcar injured in collision with motor vehicle in traffic accident**
  - **V82.2** **Occupant of streetcar injured in collision with or hit by rolling stock**
  - **V82.3** **Occupant of streetcar injured in collision with other object**

    | **Excludes1** | collision with animal-drawn vehicle or animal being ridden (V82.8) |

  - **V82.4** **Person injured while boarding or alighting from streetcar**
  - **V82.5** **Occupant of streetcar injured by fall in streetcar**

    | **Excludes1** | fall in streetcar:
    while boarding or alighting (V82.4)
    with antecedent collision (V82.0-V82.3) |

  - **V82.6** **Occupant of streetcar injured by fall from streetcar**

    | **Excludes1** | fall from streetcar:
    while boarding or alighting (V82.4)
    with antecedent collision (V82.0-V82.3) |

● Unacceptable First-Listed Diagnosis   ● Use Additional Character(s)   ■ Unspecified   **OGCR** Official Guidelines for Coding and Reporting
🐾 Complication\Comorbity   ✎ Major C\C   Excludes 1   Excludes 2   Includes   Use additional   Code first   Code also

● V82.7 **Occupant of streetcar injured in derailment without antecedent collision**

> Excludes1   occupant of streetcar injured in derailment with antecedent collision (V82.0-V82.3)

● V82.8 **Occupant of streetcar injured in other specified transport accidents**
> Streetcar collision with military vehicle
> Streetcar collision with train or nonmotor vehicles

● ◻ V82.9 **Occupant of streetcar injured in unspecified traffic accident**
> Streetcar accident NOS

● V83 **Occupant of special vehicle mainly used on industrial premises injured in transport accident**

> Includes   battery-powered airport passenger vehicle
> battery-powered truck (baggage) (mail)
> coal-car in mine
> forklift (truck)
> logging car
> self-propelled industrial truck
> station baggage truck (powered)
> tram, truck, or tub (powered) in mine or quarry

> Excludes1   special construction vehicles (V85.-)
> special industrial vehicle in stationary use or maintenance (W31.-)

The appropriate 7th character is to be added to each code from category V83

A	initial encounter
D	subsequent encounter
S	sequela

● V83.0 **Driver of special industrial vehicle injured in traffic accident**

● V83.1 **Passenger of special industrial vehicle injured in traffic accident**

● V83.2 **Person on outside of special industrial vehicle injured in traffic accident**

● ◻ V83.3 **Unspecified occupant of special industrial vehicle injured in traffic accident**

● V83.4 **Person injured while boarding or alighting from special industrial vehicle**

● V83.5 **Driver of special industrial vehicle injured in nontraffic accident**

● V83.6 **Passenger of special industrial vehicle injured in nontraffic accident**

● V83.7 **Person on outside of special industrial vehicle injured in nontraffic accident**

● ◻ V83.9 **Unspecified occupant of special industrial vehicle injured in nontraffic accident**
> Special-industrial-vehicle accident NOS

● V84 **Occupant of special vehicle mainly used in agriculture injured in transport accident**

> Includes   self-propelled farm machinery
> tractor (and trailer)

> Excludes1   animal-powered farm machinery accident (W30.8-)
> contact with combine harvester (W30.0)
> special agricultural vehicle in stationary use or maintenance (W30.-)

The appropriate 7th character is to be added to each code from category V84

A	initial encounter
D	subsequent encounter
S	sequela

● V84.0 **Driver of special agricultural vehicle injured in traffic accident**

● V84.1 **Passenger of special agricultural vehicle injured in traffic accident**

● V84.2 **Person on outside of special agricultural vehicle injured in traffic accident**

● ◻ V84.3 **Unspecified occupant of special agricultural vehicle injured in traffic accident**

● V84.4 **Person injured while boarding or alighting from special agricultural vehicle**

● V84.5 **Driver of special agricultural vehicle injured in nontraffic accident**

● V84.6 **Passenger of special agricultural vehicle injured in nontraffic accident**

● V84.7 **Person on outside of special agricultural vehicle injured in nontraffic accident**

● ◻ V84.9 **Unspecified occupant of special agricultural vehicle injured in nontraffic accident**
> Special-agricultural vehicle accident NOS

● V85 **Occupant of special construction vehicle injured in transport accident**

> Includes   bulldozer
> digger
> dump truck
> earth-leveller
> mechanical shovel
> road-roller

> Excludes1   special industrial vehicle (V83.-)
> special construction vehicle in stationary use or maintenance (W31.-)

The appropriate 7th character is to be added to each code from category V85

A	initial encounter
D	subsequent encounter
S	sequela

● V85.0 **Driver of special construction vehicle injured in traffic accident**

● V85.1 **Passenger of special construction vehicle injured in traffic accident**

● V85.2 **Person on outside of special construction vehicle injured in traffic accident**

● ◻ V85.3 **Unspecified occupant of special construction vehicle injured in traffic accident**

● V85.4 **Person injured while boarding or alighting from special construction vehicle**

● V85.5 **Driver of special construction vehicle injured in nontraffic accident**

● V85.6 **Passenger of special construction vehicle injured in nontraffic accident**

● V85.7 **Person on outside of special construction vehicle injured in nontraffic accident**

● ◻ V85.9 **Unspecified occupant of special construction vehicle injured in nontraffic accident**
> Special-construction-vehicle accident NOS

● Unacceptable First-Listed Diagnosis   ● Use Additional Character(s)   ◻ Unspecified   **OGCR** Official Guidelines for Coding and Reporting

🗈 Complication\Comorbidity   🗈 Major C\C   Excludes 1   Excludes 2   Includes   Use additional   Code first   Code also

CHAPTER 20 (V01-Y99)

1655

● **V86 Occupant of special all-terrain or other motor vehicle, injured in transport accident**

> **Excludes1** special all-terrain vehicle in stationary use or maintenance (W31.-)
> sport-utility vehicle (V50-V59)
> three-wheeled motor vehicle designed for on-road use (V30-V39)

> The appropriate 7th character is to be added to each code from category V86

> | | |
> |---|---|
> | A | initial encounter |
> | D | subsequent encounter |
> | S | sequela |

● **V86.0 Driver of special all-terrain or other motor vehicle injured in traffic accident**

   ● **V86.01 Driver of ambulance or fire engine injured in traffic accident**

   ● **V86.02 Driver of snowmobile injured in traffic accident**

   ● **V86.03 Driver of dune buggy injured in traffic accident**

   ● **V86.04 Driver of military vehicle injured in traffic accident**

   ● **V86.09 Driver of other special all-terrain or other vehicle injured in traffic accident**
      Driver of dirt bike injured in traffic accident
      Driver of go cart injured in traffic accident
      Driver of golf cart injured in traffic accident

● **V86.1 Passenger of special all-terrain or other motor vehicle injured in traffic accident**

   ● **V86.11 Passenger of ambulance or fire engine injured in traffic accident**

   ● **V86.12 Passenger of snowmobile injured in traffic accident**

   ● **V86.13 Passenger of dune buggy injured in traffic accident**

   ● **V86.14 Passenger of military vehicle injured in traffic accident**

   ● **V86.19 Passenger of other special all-terrain or other off-road motor vehicle injured in traffic accident**
      Passenger of dirt bike injured in traffic accident
      Passenger of go cart injured in traffic accident
      Passenger of golf cart injured in traffic accident

● **V86.2 Person on outside of special all-terrain or other motor vehicle injured in traffic accident**

   ● **V86.21 Person on outside of ambulance or fire engine injured in traffic accident**

   ● **V86.22 Person on outside of snowmobile injured in traffic accident**

   ● **V86.23 Person on outside of dune buggy injured in traffic accident**

   ● **V86.24 Person on outside of military vehicle injured in traffic accident**

   ● **V86.29 Person on outside of other special all-terrain or other motor vehicle injured in traffic accident**
      Person on outside of dirt bike injured in traffic accident
      Person on outside of go cart in traffic accident
      Person on outside of golf cart injured in traffic accident

● **V86.3 Unspecified occupant of special all-terrain or other motor vehicle injured in traffic accident**

   ● ■ **V86.31 Unspecified occupant of ambulance or fire engine injured in traffic accident**

   ● ■ **V86.32 Unspecified occupant of snowmobile injured in traffic accident**

   ● ■ **V86.33 Unspecified occupant of dune buggy injured in traffic accident**

   ● ■ **V86.34 Unspecified occupant of military vehicle injured in traffic accident**

   ● ■ **V86.39 Unspecified occupant of other all-terrain or other motor vehicle injured in traffic accident**
      Unspecified occupant of dirt bike injured in traffic accident
      Unspecified occupant of go cart injured in traffic accident
      Unspecified occupant of golf cart injured in traffic accident

● **V86.4 Person injured while boarding or alighting from special all-terrain or other motor vehicle**

   ● **V86.41 Person injured while boarding or alighting from ambulance or fire engine**

   ● **V86.42 Person injured while boarding or alighting from snowmobile**

   ● **V86.43 Person injured while boarding or alighting from dune buggy**

   ● **V86.44 Person injured while boarding or alighting from military vehicle**

   ● **V86.49 Person injured while boarding or alighting from other special all-terrain or other motor vehicle**
      Person injured while boarding or alighting from dirt bike
      Person injured while boarding or alighting from go cart
      Person injured while boarding or alighting from golf cart

● **V86.5 Driver of special all-terrain or other motor vehicle injured in nontraffic accident**

   ● **V86.51 Driver of ambulance or fire engine injured in nontraffic accident**

   ● **V86.52 Driver of snowmobile injured in nontraffic accident**

   ● **V86.53 Driver of dune buggy injured in nontraffic accident**

   ● **V86.54 Driver of military vehicle injured in nontraffic accident**

   ● **V86.59 Driver of other special all-terrain or other motor vehicle injured in nontraffic accident**
      Driver of dirt bike injured in nontraffic accident
      Driver of go cart injured in nontraffic accident
      Driver of golf cart injured in nontraffic accident
      Driver of race car injured in nontraffic accident

● **V86.6 Passenger of special all-terrain or other motor vehicle injured in nontraffic accident**

   ● **V86.61 Passenger of ambulance or fire engine injured in nontraffic accident**

   ● **V86.62 Passenger of snowmobile injured in nontraffic accident**

   ● **V86.63 Passenger of dune buggy injured in nontraffic accident**

● Unacceptable First-Listed Diagnosis   ● Use Additional Character(s)   ■ Unspecified   **OGCR** Official Guidelines for Coding and Reporting
🔃 Complication\Comorbidity   🔃 Major C\C   Excludes 1   Excludes 2   Includes   Use additional   Code first   Code also

● V86.64 Passenger of military vehicle injured in nontraffic accident

● V86.69 Passenger of other special all-terrain or other vehicle injured in nontraffic accident
    Passenger of dirt bike injured in nontraffic accident
    Passenger of go cart injured in nontraffic accident
    Passenger of golf cart injured in nontraffic accident
    Passenger of race car injured in nontraffic accident

● V86.7 Person on outside of special all-terrain or other motor vehicles injured in nontraffic accident

  ● V86.71 Person on outside of ambulance or fire engine injured in nontraffic accident

  ● V86.72 Person on outside of snowmobile injured in nontraffic accident

  ● V86.73 Person on outside of dune buggy injured in nontraffic accident

  ● V86.74 Person on outside of military vehicle injured in nontraffic accident

  ● V86.79 Person on outside of other special all-terrain or other motor vehicles injured in nontraffic accident
    Person on outside of dirt bike injured in nontraffic accident
    Person on outside of go cart injured in nontraffic accident
    Person on outside of golf cart injured in nontraffic accident
    Person on outside of race car injured in nontraffic accident

● V86.9 Unspecified occupant of special all-terrain or other motor vehicle injured in nontraffic accident

  ● ▣ V86.91 Unspecified occupant of ambulance or fire engine injured in nontraffic accident

  ● ▣ V86.92 Unspecified occupant of snowmobile injured in nontraffic accident

  ● ▣ V86.93 Unspecified occupant of dune buggy injured in nontraffic accident

  ● ▣ V86.94 Unspecified occupant of military vehicle injured in nontraffic accident

  ● ▣ V86.99 Unspecified occupant of other special all-terrain or other motor vehicle injured in nontraffic accident
    All-terrain motor-vehicle accident NOS
    Off-road motor-vehicle accident NOS
    Other motor-vehicle accident NOS
    Unspecified occupant of dirt bike injured in nontraffic accident
    Unspecified occupant of go cart injured in nontraffic accident
    Unspecified occupant of golf cart injured in nontraffic accident
    Unspecified occupant of race car injured in nontraffic accident

● V87 Traffic accident of specified type but victim's mode of transport unknown

  Excludes1 collision involving:
    pedal cycle (V10-V19)
    pedestrian (V01-V09)

The appropriate 7th character is to be added to each code from category V87

A	initial encounter
D	subsequent encounter
S	sequela

● V87.0 Person injured in collision between car and two- or three-wheeled powered vehicle (traffic)

● V87.1 Person injured in collision between other motor vehicle and two- or three-wheeled motor vehicle (traffic)

● V87.2 Person injured in collision between car and pick-up truck or van (traffic)

● V87.3 Person injured in collision between car and bus (traffic)

● V87.4 Person injured in collision between car and heavy transport vehicle (traffic)

● V87.5 Person injured in collision between heavy transport vehicle and bus (traffic)

● V87.6 Person injured in collision between railway train or railway vehicle and car (traffic)

● V87.7 Person injured in collision between other specified motor vehicles (traffic)

● V87.8 Person injured in other specified noncollision transport accidents involving motor vehicle (traffic)

● V87.9 Person injured in other specified (collision) (noncollision) transport accidents involving nonmotor vehicle (traffic)

● V88 Nontraffic accident of specified type but victim's mode of transport unknown

  Excludes1 collision involving:
    pedal cycle (V10-V19)
    pedestrian (V01-V09)

The appropriate 7th character is to be added to each code from category V88

A	initial encounter
D	subsequent encounter
S	sequela

● V88.0 Person injured in collision between car and two- or three-wheeled motor vehicle, nontraffic

● V88.1 Person injured in collision between other motor vehicle and two- or three-wheeled motor vehicle, nontraffic

● V88.2 Person injured in collision between car and pick-up truck or van, nontraffic

● V88.3 Person injured in collision between car and bus, nontraffic

● V88.4 Person injured in collision between car and heavy transport vehicle, nontraffic

● V88.5 Person injured in collision between heavy transport vehicle and bus, nontraffic

● V88.6 Person injured in collision between railway train or railway vehicle and car, nontraffic

● V88.7 Person injured in collision between other specified motor vehicle, nontraffic

● V88.8 Person injured in other specified noncollision transport accidents involving motor vehicle, nontraffic

● V88.9 Person injured in other specified (collision) (noncollision) transport accidents involving nonmotor vehicle, nontraffic

● V89 Motor- or nonmotor-vehicle accident, type of vehicle unspecified

The appropriate 7th character is to be added to each code from category V89

A	initial encounter
D	subsequent encounter
S	sequela

  ● ▣ V89.0 Person injured in unspecified motor-vehicle accident, nontraffic
    Motor-vehicle accident NOS, nontraffic

● Unacceptable First-Listed Diagnosis   ● Use Additional Character(s)   ▣ Unspecified   OGCR Official Guidelines for Coding and Reporting
🔗 Complication\Comorbidity   🔗 Major C\C   Excludes 1   Excludes 2   Includes   Use additional   Code first   Code also

● ■ **V89.1** **Person injured in unspecified nonmotor-vehicle accident, nontraffic**
Nonmotor-vehicle accident NOS (nontraffic)

● ■ **V89.2** **Person injured in unspecified motor-vehicle accident, traffic**
Motor-vehicle accident [MVA] NOS
Road (traffic) accident [RTA] NOS

● ■ **V89.3** **Person injured in unspecified nonmotor-vehicle accident, traffic**
Nonmotor-vehicle traffic accident NOS

● ■ **V89.9** **Person injured in unspecified vehicle accident**
Collision NOS

WATER TRANSPORT ACCIDENTS (V90-V94)

● **V90** **Drowning and submersion due to accident to watercraft**

> **Excludes1**   civilian water transport accident involving military watercraft (V94.81-)
> fall into water not from watercraft (W16.-)
> military watercraft accident in military or war operations (Y36.0-, Y37.0-)
> water-transport–related drowning or submersion without accident to watercraft (V92.-)

The appropriate 7th character is to be added to each code from category V90

> A   initial encounter
> D   subsequent encounter
> S   sequela

● **V90.0** **Drowning and submersion due to watercraft overturning**

   ● **V90.00** **Drowning and submersion due to merchant ship overturning**

   ● **V90.01** **Drowning and submersion due to passenger ship overturning**
Drowning and submersion due to ferry-boat overturning
Drowning and submersion due to liner overturning

   ● **V90.02** **Drowning and submersion due to fishing boat overturning**

   ● **V90.03** **Drowning and submersion due to other powered watercraft overturning**
Drowning and submersion due to hovercraft (on open water) overturning
Drowning and submersion due to jet ski overturning

   ● **V90.04** **Drowning and submersion due to sailboat overturning**

   ● **V90.05** **Drowning and submersion due to canoe or kayak overturning**

   ● **V90.06** **Drowning and submersion due to (nonpowered) inflatable craft overturning**

   ● **V90.08** **Drowning and submersion due to other unpowered watercraft overturning**
Drowning and submersion due to windsurfer overturning

   ● ■ **V90.09** **Drowning and submersion due to unspecified watercraft overturning**
Drowning and submersion due to boat NOS overturning
Drowning and submersion due to ship NOS overturning
Drowning and submersion due to watercraft NOS overturning

● **V90.1** **Drowning and submersion due to watercraft sinking**

   ● **V90.10** **Drowning and submersion due to merchant ship sinking**

   ● **V90.11** **Drowning and submersion due to passenger ship sinking**
Drowning and submersion due to ferry-boat overturning
Drowning and submersion due to liiner overturning

   ● **V90.12** **Drowning and submersion due to fishing boat sinking**

   ● **V90.13** **Drowning and submersion due to other powered watercraft sinking**
Drowning and submersion due to hovercraft (on open water) sinking
Drowning and submersion due to jet ski sinking

   ● **V90.14** **Drowning and submersion due to sailboat sinking**

   ● **V90.15** **Drowning and submersion due to canoe or kayak sinking**

   ● **V90.16** **Drowning and submersion due to (nonpowered) inflatable craft sinking**

   ● **V90.18** **Drowning and submersion due to other unpowered watercraft sinking**

   ● ■ **V90.19** **Drowning and submersion due to unspecified watercraft sinking**
Drowning and submersion due to boat NOS sinking
Drowning and submersion due to ship NOS sinking
Drowning and submersion due to watercraft NOS sinking

● **V90.2** **Drowning and submersion due to falling or jumping from burning watercraft**

   ● **V90.20** **Drowning and submersion due to falling or jumping from burning merchant ship**

   ● **V90.21** **Drowning and submersion due to falling or jumping from burning passenger ship**
Drowning and submersion due to falling or jumping from burning ferry-boat
Drowning and submersion due to falling or jumping from burning liner

   ● **V90.22** **Drowning and submersion due to falling or jumping from burning fishing boat**

   ● **V90.23** **Drowning and submersion due to falling or jumping from other burning powered watercraft**
Drowning and submersion due to falling and jumping from burning hovercraft (on open water)
Drowning and submersion due to falling and jumping from burning jet ski

   ● **V90.24** **Drowning and submersion due to falling or jumping from burning sailboat**

   ● **V90.25** **Drowning and submersion due to falling or jumping from burning canoe or kayak**

   ● **V90.26** **Drowning and submersion due to falling or jumping from burning (nonpowered) inflatable craft**

   ● **V90.27** **Drowning and submersion due to falling or jumping from burning water-skis**

   ● **V90.28** **Drowning and submersion due to falling or jumping from other burning unpowered watercraft**
Drowning and submersion due to falling and jumping from burning surf-board
Drowning and submersion due to falling and jumping from burning windsurfer

● Unacceptable First-Listed Diagnosis   ● Use Additional Character(s)   ■ Unspecified   **OGCR** Official Guidelines for Coding and Reporting
🔖 Complication\Comorbidity   🔖 Major C\C   Excludes 1   Excludes 2   Includes   Use additional   Code first   Code also

● ▣ **V90.29** **Drowning and submersion due to falling or jumping from unspecified burning watercraft**
> Drowning and submersion due to falling or jumping from burning boat NOS
> Drowning and submersion due to falling or jumping from burning ship NOS
> Drowning and submersion due to falling or jumping from burning watercraft NOS

● **V90.3** **Drowning and submersion due to falling or jumping from crushed watercraft**

● **V90.30** **Drowning and submersion due to falling or jumping from crushed merchant ship**

● **V90.31** **Drowning and submersion due to falling or jumping from crushed passenger ship**
> Drowning and submersion due to falling and jumping from crushed ferry-boat
> Drowning and submersion due to falling and jumping from crushed liner

● **V90.32** **Drowning and submersion due to falling or jumping from crushed fishing boat**

● **V90.33** **Drowning and submersion due to falling or jumping from other crushed powered watercraft**
> Drowning and submersion due to falling and jumping from crushed hovercraft
> Drowning and submersion due to falling and jumping from crushed jet ski

● **V90.34** **Drowning and submersion due to falling or jumping from crushed sailboat**

● **V90.35** **Drowning and submersion due to falling or jumping from crushed canoe or kayak**

● **V90.36** **Drowning and submersion due to falling or jumping from crushed (nonpowered) inflatable craft**

● **V90.37** **Drowning and submersion due to falling or jumping from crushed water-skis**

● **V90.38** **Drowning and submersion due to falling or jumping from other crushed unpowered watercraft**
> Drowning and submersion due to falling and jumping from crushed surf-board
> Drowning and submersion due to falling and jumping from crushed windsurfer

● ▣ **V90.39** **Drowning and submersion due to falling or jumping from crushed unspecified watercraft**
> Drowning and submersion due to falling and jumping from crushed boat NOS
> Drowning and submersion due to falling and jumping from crushed ship NOS
> Drowning and submersion due to falling and jumping from crushed watercraft NOS

● **V90.8** **Drowning and submersion due to other accident to watercraft**

● **V90.80** **Drowning and submersion due to other accident to merchant ship**

● **V90.81** **Drowning and submersion due to other accident to passenger ship**
> Drowning and submersion due to other accident to ferry-boat
> Drowning and submersion due to other accident to liner

● **V90.82** **Drowning and submersion due to other accident to fishing boat**

● **V90.83** **Drowning and submersion due to other accident to other powered watercraft**
> Drowning and submersion due to other accident to hovercraft (on open water)
> Drowning and submersion due to other accident to jet ski

● **V90.84** **Drowning and submersion due to other accident to sailboat**

● **V90.85** **Drowning and submersion due to other accident to canoe or kayak**

● **V90.86** **Drowning and submersion due to other accident to (nonpowered) inflatable craft**

● **V90.87** **Drowning and submersion due to other accident to water-skis**

● **V90.88** **Drowning and submersion due to other accident to other unpowered watercraft**
> Drowning and submersion due to other accident to surf-board
> Drowning and submersion due to other accident to windsurfer

● ▣ **V90.89** **Drowning and submersion due to other accident to unspecified watercraft**
> Drowning and submersion due to other accident to boat NOS
> Drowning and submersion due to other accident to ship NOS
> Drowning and submersion due to other accident to watercraft NOS

● **V91** **Other injury due to accident to watercraft**

> | **Includes** | any injury except drowning and submersion as a result of an accident to watercraft |

> | **Excludes1** | civilian water transport accident involving military watercraft (V94.81-) |
> | | military watercraft accident in military or war operations (Y36, Y37-) |

> | **Excludes2** | drowning and submersion due to accident to watercraft (V90.-) |

The appropriate 7th character is to be added to each code from category V91

> A   initial encounter
> D   subsequent encounter
> S   sequela

● **V91.0** **Burn due to watercraft on fire**

> | **Excludes1** | burn from localized fire or explosion on board ship without accident to watercraft (V93.-) |

● **V91.00** **Burn due to merchant ship on fire**

● **V91.01** **Burn due to passenger ship on fire**
> Burn due to ferry-boat on fire
> Burn due to liner on fire

● **V91.02** **Burn due to fishing boat on fire**

● **V91.03** **Burn due to other powered watercraft on fire**
> Burn due to hovercraft (on open water) on fire
> Burn due to jet ski on fire

● **V91.04** **Burn due to sailboat on fire**

● **V91.05** **Burn due to canoe or kayak on fire**

● **V91.06** **Burn due to (nonpowered) inflatable craft on fire**

● **V91.07** **Burn due to water-skis on fire**

● **V91.08** **Burn due to other unpowered watercraft on fire**

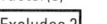
● Unacceptable First-Listed Diagnosis   ● Use Additional Character(s)   ▣ Unspecified   **OGCR** Official Guidelines for Coding and Reporting

🗪 Complication\Comorbidity   🗪 Major C\C   Excludes 1   Excludes 2   Includes   Use additional   Code first   Code also

1659

CHAPTER 20 (V01-Y99)

● ■ **V91.09   Burn due to unspecified watercraft on fire**
Burn due to boat NOS on fire
Burn due to ship NOS on fire
Burn due to watercraft NOS on fire

● **V91.1   Crushed between watercraft and other watercraft or other object due to collision**
Crushed by lifeboat after abandoning ship in a collision

> **Note:** Select the specified type of watercraft that the victim was on at the time of the collision.

● **V91.10   Crushed between merchant ship and other watercraft or other object due to collision**

● **V91.11   Crushed between passenger ship and other watercraft or other object due to collision**
Crushed between ferry-boat and other watercraft or other object due to collision
Crushed between liner and other watercraft or other object due to collision

● **V91.12   Crushed between fishing boat and other watercraft or other object due to collision**

● **V91.13   Crushed between other powered watercraft and other watercraft or other object due to collision**
Crushed between hovercraft (on open water) and other watercraft or other object due to collision
Crushed between jet ski and other watercraft or other object due to collision

● **V91.14   Crushed between sailboat and other watercraft or other object due to collision**

● **V91.15   Crushed between canoe or kayak and other watercraft or other object due to collision**

● **V91.16   Crushed between (nonpowered) inflatable craft and other watercraft or other object due to collision**

● **V91.18   Crushed between other unpowered watercraft and other watercraft or other object due to collision**
Crushed between surfboard and other watercraft or other object due to collision
Crushed between windsurfer and other watercraft or other object due to collision

● ■ **V91.19   Crushed between unspecified watercraft and other watercraft or other object due to collision**
Crushed between boat NOS and other watercraft or other object due to collision
Crushed between ship NOS and other watercraft or other object due to collision
Crushed between watercraft NOS and other watercraft or other object due to collision

● **V91.2   Fall due to collision between watercraft and other watercraft or other object**
Fall while remaining on watercraft after collision

> **Note:** Select the specified type of watercraft that the victim was on at the time of the collision.

> | **Excludes1** | crushed between watercraft and other watercraft and other object due to collision (V91.1-)
drowning and submersion due to falling from crushed watercraft (V90.3-) |

● **V91.20   Fall due to collision between merchant ship and other watercraft or other object**

● **V91.21   Fall due to collision between passenger ship and other watercraft or other object**
Fall due to collision between ferry-boat and other watercraft or other object
Fall due to collision between liner and other watercraft or other object

● **V91.22   Fall due to collision between fishing boat and other watercraft or other object**

● **V91.23   Fall due to collision between other powered watercraft and other watercraft or other object**
Fall due to collision between hovercraft (on open water) and other watercraft or other object
Fall due to collision between jet ski and other watercraft or other object

● **V91.24   Fall due to collision between sailboat and other watercraft or other object**

● **V91.25   Fall due to collision between canoe or kayak and other watercraft or other object**

● **V91.26   Fall due to collision between (nonpowered) inflatable craft and other watercraft or other object**

● ■ **V91.29   Fall due to collision between unspecified watercraft and other watercraft or other object**
Fall due to collision between boat NOS and other watercraft or other object
Fall due to collision between ship NOS and other watercraft or other object
Fall due to collision between watercraft NOS and other watercraft or other object

● **V91.3   Hit or struck by falling object due to accident to watercraft**
Hit or struck by falling object (part of damaged watercraft or other object) after falling or jumping from damaged watercraft

> | **Excludes2** | drowning or submersion due to fall or jumping from damaged watercraft (V90.2-, V90.3-) |

● **V91.30   Hit or struck by falling object due to accident to merchant ship**

● **V91.31   Hit or struck by falling object due to accident to passenger ship**
Hit or struck by falling object due to accident to ferry-boat
Hit or struck by falling object due to accident to liner

● **V91.32   Hit or struck by falling object due to accident to fishing boat**

● **V91.33   Hit or struck by falling object due to accident to other powered watercraft**
Hit or struck by falling object due to accident to hovercraft (on open water)
Hit or struck by falling object due to accident to jet ski

● Unacceptable First-Listed Diagnosis   ● Use Additional Character(s)   ■ Unspecified   **OGCR** Official Guidelines for Coding and Reporting

1660   🅠 Complication\Comorbidity   🅠 Major C\C   Excludes 1   Excludes 2   Includes   Use additional   Code first   Code also

CHAPTER 20 (V01-Y99)

- **V91.34**   **Hit or struck by falling object due to accident to sailboat**
- **V91.35**   **Hit or struck by falling object due to accident to canoe or kayak**
- **V91.36**   **Hit or struck by falling object due to accident to (nonpowered) inflatable craft**
- **V91.37**   **Hit or struck by falling object due to accident to water-skis**
  Hit by water-skis after jumping off of waterskis
- **V91.38**   **Hit or struck by falling object due to accident to other unpowered watercraft**
  Hit or struck by surf-board after falling off damaged surf-board
  Hit or struck by object after falling off damaged windsurfer
- **V91.39**   **Hit or struck by falling object due to accident to unspecified watercraft**
  Hit or struck by falling object due to accident to boat NOS
  Hit or struck by falling object due to accident to ship NOS
  Hit or struck by falling object due to accident to watercraft NOS

- **V91.8**   **Other injury due to other accident to watercraft**
  - **V91.80**   **Other injury due to other accident to merchant ship**
  - **V91.81**   **Other injury due to other accident to passenger ship**
    Other injury due to other accident to ferry-boat
    Other injury due to other accident to liner
  - **V91.82**   **Other injury due to other accident to fishing boat**
  - **V91.83**   **Other injury due to other accident to other powered watercraft**
    Other injury due to other accident to hovercraft (on open water)
    Other injury due to other accident to jet ski
  - **V91.84**   **Other injury due to other accident to sailboat**
  - **V91.85**   **Other injury due to other accident to canoe or kayak**
  - **V91.86**   **Other injury due to other accident to (nonpowered) inflatable craft**
  - **V91.87**   **Other injury due to other accident to water-skis**
  - **V91.88**   **Other injury due to other accident to other unpowered watercraft**
    Other injury due to other accident to surf-board
    Other injury due to other accident to windsurfer
  - **V91.89**   **Other injury due to other accident to unspecified watercraft**
    Other injury due to other accident to boat NOS
    Other injury due to other accident to ship NOS
    Other injury due to other accident to watercraft NOS

- **V92**   **Drowning and submersion due to accident on board watercraft, without accident to watercraft**

  Excludes1   civilian water transport accident involving military watercraft (V94.81-)
  drowning or submersion due to accident to watercraft (V90-V91)
  drowning or submersion of diver who voluntarily jumps from boat not involved in an accident (W16.711, W16.721)
  fall into water without watercraft (W16.-)
  military watercraft accident in military or war operations (Y36, Y37)

  The appropriate 7th character is to be added to each code from category V92

A	initial encounter
D	subsequent encounter
S	sequela

  - **V92.0**   **Drowning and submersion due to fall off watercraft**
    Drowning and submersion due to fall from gangplank of watercraft
    Drowning and submersion due to fall overboard watercraft

    Excludes2   hitting head on object or bottom of body of water due to fall from watercraft (V94.0-)

    - **V92.00**   **Drowning and submersion due to fall off merchant ship**
    - **V92.01**   **Drowning and submersion due to fall off passenger ship**
      Drowning and submersion due to fall off ferry-boat
      Drowning and submersion due to fall off liner
    - **V92.02**   **Drowning and submersion due to fall off fishing boat**
    - **V92.03**   **Drowning and submersion due to fall off other powered watercraft**
      Drowning and submersion due to fall off hovercraft (on open water)
      Drowning and submersion due to fall off jet ski
    - **V92.04**   **Drowning and submersion due to fall off sailboat**
    - **V92.05**   **Drowning and submersion due to fall off canoe or kayak**
    - **V92.06**   **Drowning and submersion due to fall off (nonpowered) inflatable craft**
    - **V92.07**   **Drowning and submersion due to fall off water-skis**

      Excludes1   drowning and submersion due to falling off burning water-skis (V90.27)
      drowning and submersion due to falling off crushed water-skis (V90.37)
      hit by boat while water-skiing NOS (V94.x)

● Unacceptable First-Listed Diagnosis   ● Use Additional Character(s)   ▪ Unspecified   **OGCR** Official Guidelines for Coding and Reporting

🗞 Complication\Comorbidity   🗞 Major C\C   Excludes 1   Excludes 2   Includes   Use additional   Code first   Code also

1661

CHAPTER 20 (V01-Y99)

● **V92.08 Drowning and submersion due to fall off other unpowered watercraft**
     Drowning and submersion due to fall off surf-board
     Drowning and submersion due to fall off windsurfer

     | Excludes1 | drowning and submersion due to fall off burning unpowered watercraft (V90.28)
            drowning and submersion due to fall off crushed unpowered watercraft (V90.38)
            drowning and submersion due to fall off damaged unpowered watercraft (V90.88)
            drowning and submersion due to rider of nonpowered watercraft being hit by other watercraft (V94...)
            other injury due to rider of nonpowered watercraft being hit by other watercraft (V94...)

● ■ **V92.09 Drowning and submersion due to fall off unspecified watercraft**
     Drowning and submersion due to fall off boat NOS
     Drowning and submersion due to fall off ship
     Drowning and submersion due to fall off watercraft NOS

● **V92.1 Drowning and submersion due to being thrown overboard by motion of watercraft**

     | Excludes1 | drowning and submersion due to fall off surf-board (V92.08)
            drowning and submersion due to fall off water-skis (V92.07)
            drowning and submersion due to fall off windsurfer (V92.08)

● **V92.10 Drowning and submersion due to being thrown overboard by motion of merchant ship**

● **V92.11 Drowning and submersion due to being thrown overboard by motion of passenger ship**
     Drowning and submersion due to being thrown overboard by motion of ferry-boat
     Drowning and submersion due to being thrown overboard by motion of liner

● **V92.12 Drowning and submersion due to being thrown overboard by motion of fishing boat**

● **V92.13 Drowning and submersion due to being thrown overboard by motion of other powered watercraft**
     Drowning and submersion due to being thrown overboard by motion of hovercraft

● **V92.14 Drowning and submersion due to being thrown overboard by motion of sailboat**

● **V92.15 Drowning and submersion due to being thrown overboard by motion of canoe or kayak**

● **V92.16 Drowning and submersion due to being thrown overboard by motion of (nonpowered) inflatable craft**

● ■ **V92.19 Drowning and submersion due to being thrown overboard by motion of unspecified watercraft**
     Drowning and submersion due to being thrown overboard by motion of boat NOS
     Drowning and submersion due to being thrown overboard by motion of ship NOS
     Drowning and submersion due to being thrown overboard by motion of watercraft NOS

● **V92.2 Drowning and submersion due to being washed overboard from watercraft**
     Code first any associated cataclysm (X37.0-)

● **V92.20 Drowning and submersion due to being washed overboard from merchant ship**

● **V92.21 Drowning and submersion due to being washed overboard from passenger ship**
     Drowning and submersion due to being washed overboard from ferry-boat
     Drowning and submersion due to being washed overboard from liner

● **V92.22 Drowning and submersion due to being washed overboard from fishing boat**

● **V92.23 Drowning and submersion due to being washed overboard from other powered watercraft**
     Drowning and submersion due to being washed overboard from hovercraft (on open water)
     Drowning and submersion due to being washed overboard from jet ski

● **V92.24 Drowning and submersion due to being washed overboard from sailboat**

● **V92.25 Drowning and submersion due to being washed overboard from canoe or kayak**

● **V92.26 Drowning and submersion due to being washed overboard from (nonpowered) inflatable craft**

● **V92.27 Drowning and submersion due to being washed overboard from water-skis**

     | Excludes1 | drowning and submersion due to fall off water-skis (V92.07)

● **V92.28 Drowning and submersion due to being washed overboard from other unpowered watercraft**
     Drowning and submersion due to being washed overboard from surf-board
     Drowning and submersion due to being washed overboard from windsurfer

● ■ **V92.29 Drowning and submersion due to being washed overboard from unspecified watercraft**
     Drowning and submersion due to being washed overboard from boat NOS
     Drowning and submersion due to being washed overboard from ship NOS
     Drowning and submersion due to being washed overboard from watercraft NOS

● Unacceptable First-Listed Diagnosis   ● Use Additional Character(s)   ■ Unspecified   OGCR Official Guidelines for Coding and Reporting
🅒 Complication\Comorbidity   🅒 Major C\C | Excludes 1 | | Excludes 2 | Includes   Use additional   Code first   Code also

V93 **Other injury due to accident on board watercraft, without accident to watercraft**

> **Excludes1**   civilian water transport accident involving military watercraft (V94.81-)
> other injury due to accident to watercraft (V91.-)
> military watercraft accident in military or war operations (Y36, Y37-)

> **Excludes2**   drowning and submersion due to accident on board watercraft, without accident to watercraft (V92.-)

The appropriate 7th character is to be added to each code from category V93

> A   initial encounter
> D   subsequent encounter
> S   sequela

● **V93.0   Burn due to localized fire on board watercraft**

> **Excludes1**   burn due to watercraft on fire (V91.0-)

● **V93.00   Burn due to localized fire on board merchant vessel**

● **V93.01   Burn due to localized fire on board passenger vessel**
Burn due to localized Fire on board ferry-boat
Burn due to localized fire on board liner

● **V93.02   Burn due to localized fire on board fishing boat**

● **V93.03   Burn due to localized fire on board other powered watercraft**
Burn due to localized fire on board hovercraft
Burn due to localized fire on board jet ski

● **V93.04   Burn due to localized fire on board sailboat**

●■ **V93.09   Burn due to localized fire on board unspecified watercraft**
Burn due to localized fire on board boat NOS
Burn due to localized fire on board ship NOS
Burn due to localized fire on board watercraft NOS

● **V93.1   Other burn on board watercraft**
Burn due to source other than fire on board watercraft

> **Excludes1**   burn due to watercraft on fire (V91.0-)

● **V93.10   Other burn on board merchant vessel**

● **V93.11   Other burn on board passenger vessel**
Other burn on board ferry-boat
Other burn on board liner

● **V93.12   Other burn on board fishing boat**

● **V93.13   Other burn on board other powered watercraft**
Other burn on board hovercraft
Other burn on board jet ski

● **V93.14   Other burn on board sailboat**

●■ **V93.19   Other burn on board unspecified watercraft**
Other burn on board boat NOS
Other burn on board ship NOS
Other burn on board watercraft NOS

● **V93.2   Heat exposure on board watercraft**

> **Excludes1**   exposure to man-made heat not aboard watercraft (W92)
> exposure to natural heat while on board watercraft (X30)
> exposure to sunlight while on board watercraft (X32)

> **Excludes2**   burn due to fire on board watercraft (V93.0-)

● **V93.20   Heat exposure on board merchant ship**

● **V93.21   Heat exposure on board passenger ship**
Heat exposure on board ferry-boat
Heat exposure on board liner

● **V93.22   Heat exposure on board fishing boat**

● **V93.23   Heat exposure on board other powered watercraft**
Heat exposure on board hovercraft

● **V93.24   Heat exposure on board sailboat**

●■ **V93.29   Heat exposure on board unspecified watercraft**
Heat exposure on board boat NOS
Heat exposure on board ship NOS
Heat exposure on board watercraft NOS

● **V93.3   Fall on board watercraft**

> **Excludes1**   fall due to collision of watercraft (V91.2-)

● **V93.30   Fall on board merchant ship**

● **V93.31   Fall on board passenger ship**
Fall on board ferry-boat
Fall on board liner

● **V93.32   Fall on board fishing boat**

● **V93.33   Fall on board other powered watercraft**
Fall on board hovercraft (on open water)
Fall on board jet ski

● **V93.34   Fall on board sailboat**

● **V93.35   Fall on board canoe or kayak**

● **V93.36   Fall on board (nonpowered) inflatable craft**

● **V93.38   Fall on board other unpowered watercraft**

●■ **V93.39   Fall on board unspecified watercraft**
Fall on board boat NOS
Fall on board ship NOS
Fall on board watercraft NOS

● **V93.4   Struck by falling object on board watercraft**
Hit by falling object on board watercraft

> **Excludes1**   struck by falling object due to accident to watercraft (V91.3-)

● **V93.40   Struck by falling object on merchant ship**

● **V93.41   Struck by falling object on passenger ship**
Struck by falling object on ferry-boat
Struck by falling object on liner

● **V93.42   Struck by falling object on fishing boat**

● **V93.43   Struck by falling object on other powered watercraft**
Struck by falling object on hovercraft

● **V93.44   Struck by falling object on sailboat**

● **V93.48   Struck by falling object on other unpowered watercraft**

●■ **V93.49   Struck by falling object on unspecified watercraft**

● Unacceptable First-Listed Diagnosis   ● Use Additional Character(s)   ■ Unspecified   OGCR Official Guidelines for Coding and Reporting

 Complication\Comorbidity   Major C\C   Excludes 1   Excludes 2   Includes   Use additional   Code first   Code also

1663

CHAPTER 20 (V01-Y99)

● **V93.5 Explosion on board watercraft**
Boiler explosion on steamship

Excludes2   fire on board watercraft (V93.0-)

● **V93.50 Explosion on board merchant ship**

● **V93.51 Explosion on board passenger ship**
Explosion on board ferry-boat
Explosion on board liner

● **V93.52 Explosion on board fishing boat**

● **V93.53 Explosion on board other powered watercraft**
Explosion on board hovercraft
Explosion on board jet ski

● **V93.54 Explosion on board sailboat**

● ■ **V93.59 Explosion on board unspecified watercraft**
Explosion on board boat NOS
Explosion on board ship NOS
Explosion on board watercraft NOS

● **V93.6 Machinery accident on board watercraft**

Excludes1   machinery explosion on board watercraft (V93.4-)
machinery fire on board watercraft (V93.0-)

● **V93.60 Machinery accident on board merchant ship**

● **V93.61 Machinery accident on board passenger ship**
Machinery accident on board ferry-boat
Machinery accident on board liner

● **V93.62 Machinery accident on board fishing boat**

● **V93.63 Machinery accident on board other powered watercraft**
Machinery accident on board hovercraft

● **V93.64 Machinery accident on board sailboat**

● ■ **V93.69 Machinery accident on board unspecified watercraft**
Machinery accident on board boat NOS
Machinery accident on board ship NOS
Machinery accident on board watercraft NOS

● **V93.8 Other injury due to other accident on board watercraft**
Accidental poisoning by gases or fumes on watercraft

● **V93.80 Other injury due to other accident on board merchant ship**

● **V93.81 Other injury due to other accident on board passenger ship**
Other injury due to other accident on board ferry-boat
Other injury due to other accident on board liner

● **V93.82 Other injury due to other accident on board fishing boat**

● **V93.83 Other injury due to other accident on board other powered watercraft**
Other injury due to other accident on board hovercraft
Other injury due to other accident on board jet ski

● **V93.84 Other injury due to other accident on board sailboat**

● **V93.85 Other injury due to other accident on board canoe or kayak**

● **V93.86 Other injury due to other accident on board (nonpowered) inflatable craft**

● **V93.87 Other injury due to other accident on board water-skis**
Hit or struck by object while waterskiing

● **V93.88 Other injury due to other accident on board other unpowered watercraft**
Hit or struck by object while surfing
Hit or struck by object while on board windsurfer

● ■ **V93.89 Other injury due to other accident on board unspecified watercraft**
Other injury due to other accident on board boat NOS
Other injury due to other accident on board ship NOS
Other injury due to other accident on board watercraft NOS

● **V94 Other and unspecified water transport accidents**

Excludes1   military watercraft accidents in military or war operations (Y36, Y37)

The appropriate 7th character is to be added to each code from category V94

A	initial encounter
D	subsequent encounter
S	sequela

● **V94.0 Hitting object or bottom of body of water due to fall from watercraft**

Excludes2   drowning and submersion due to fall from watercraft (V92.0-)

● **V94.1 Bather struck by watercraft**
Swimmer hit by watercraft

● **V94.11 Bather struck by powered watercraft**

● **V94.12 Bather struck by nonpowered watercraft**

● **V94.2 Rider of nonpowered watercraft struck by other watercraft**

● **V94.21 Rider of nonpowered watercraft struck by other nonpowered watercraft**
Canoer hit by other nonpowered watercraft
Surfer hit by other nonpowered watercraft
Windsurfer hit by other nonpowered watercraft

● **V94.22 Rider of nonpowered watercraft struck by powered watercraft**
Canoer hit by motorboat
Surfer hit by motorboat
Windsurfer hit by motorboat

● **V94.3 Injury to rider of (inflatable) watercraft being pulled behind other watercraft**

● **V94.31 Injury to rider of (inflatable) recreational watercraft being pulled behind other watercraft**
Injury to rider of inner-tube pulled behind motor boat

● **V94.32 Injury to rider of non-recreational watercraft being pulled behind other watercraft**
Injury to occupant of dingy being pulled behind boat or ship
Injury to occupant of life-raft being pulled behind boat or ship

● **V94.4 Injury to barefoot water-skier**
Injury to person being pulled behind boat or ship

● Unacceptable First-Listed Diagnosis   ● Use Additional Character(s)   ■ Unspecified   **OGCR** Official Guidelines for Coding and Reporting
🅒 Complication\Comorbidity   🅒 Major C\C   Excludes 1   Excludes 2   Includes   Use additional   Code first   Code also

- **V94.8 Other water transport accident**
  - **V94.81 Water transport accident involving military watercraft**
    - **V94.810 Civilian watercraft involved in water transport accident with military watercraft**
      Passenger on civilian watercraft injured due to accident with military watercraft
    - **V94.811 Civilian in water injured by military watercraft**
      Civilian in water injured by military marine weapon
    - **V94.818 Other water transport accident involving military watercraft**
  - **V94.89 Other water transport accident**
- **■ V94.9 Unspecified water transport accident**
  Water transport accident NOS

AIR AND SPACE TRANSPORT ACCIDENTS (V95-V97)

> **Excludes1**   military aircraft accidents in military or war operations (Y36, Y37)

- **V95 Accident to powered aircraft causing injury to occupant**
  The appropriate 7th character is to be added to each code from category V95

A	initial encounter
D	subsequent encounter
S	sequela

  - **V95.0 Helicopter accident injuring occupant**
    - **■ V95.00 Unspecified helicopter accident injuring occupant**
    - **V95.01 Helicopter crash injuring occupant**
    - **V95.02 Forced landing of helicopter injuring occupant**
    - **V95.03 Helicopter collision injuring occupant**
      Helicopter collision with any object, fixed, movable or moving
    - **V95.04 Helicopter fire injuring occupant**
    - **V95.05 Helicopter explosion injuring occupant**
    - **V95.09 Other helicopter accident injuring occupant**
  - **V95.1 Ultralight, microlight or powered-glider accident injuring occupant**
    - **■ V95.10 Unspecified ultralight, microlight or powered-glider accident injuring occupant**
    - **V95.11 Ultralight, microlight or powered-glider crash injuring occupant**
    - **V95.12 Forced landing of ultralight, microlight or powered-glider injuring occupant**
    - **V95.13 Ultralight, microlight or powered-glider collision injuring occupant**
      Ultralight, microlight or powered-glider collision with any object, fixed, movable or moving
    - **V95.14 Ultralight, microlight or powered-glider fire injuring occupant**
    - **V95.15 Ultralight, microlight or powered-glider explosion injuring occupant**
    - **V95.19 Other ultralight, microlight or powered-glider accident injuring occupant**
  - **V95.2 Other private fixed-wing aircraft accident injuring occupant**
    - **■ V95.20 Unspecified accident to other private fixed-wing aircraft, injuring occupant**
    - **V95.21 Other private fixed-wing aircraft crash injuring occupant**

- **V95.22 Forced landing of other private fixed-wing aircraft injuring occupant**
- **V95.23 Other private fixed-wing aircraft collision injuring occupant**
  Other private fixed-wing aircraft collision with any object, fixed, movable or moving
- **V95.24 Other private fixed-wing aircraft fire injuring occupant**
- **V95.25 Other private fixed-wing aircraft explosion injuring occupant**
- **V95.29 Other accident to other private fixed-wing aircraft injuring occupant**
- **V95.3 Commercial fixed-wing aircraft accident injuring occupant**
  - **■ V95.30 Unspecified accident to commercial fixed-wing aircraft injuring occupant**
  - **V95.31 Commercial fixed-wing aircraft crash injuring occupant**
  - **V95.32 Forced landing of commercial fixed-wing aircraft injuring occupant**
  - **V95.33 Commercial fixed-wing aircraft collision injuring occupant**
    Commercial fixed-wing aircraft collision with any object, fixed, movable or moving
  - **V95.34 Commercial fixed-wing aircraft fire injuring occupant**
  - **V95.35 Commercial fixed-wing aircraft explosion injuring occupant**
  - **V95.39 Other accident to commercial fixed-wing aircraft injuring occupant**
- **V95.4 Spacecraft accident injuring occupant**
  - **■ V95.40 Unspecified spacecraft accident injuring occupant**
  - **V95.41 Spacecraft crash injuring occupant**
  - **V95.42 Forced landing of spacecraft injuring occupant**
  - **V95.43 Spacecraft collision injuring occupant**
    Spacecraft collision with any object, fixed, moveable or moving
  - **V95.44 Spacecraft fire injuring occupant**
  - **V95.45 Spacecraft explosion injuring occupant**
  - **V95.49 Other spacecraft accident injuring occupant**
- **V95.8 Other powered aircraft accidents injuring occupant**
- **■ V95.9 Unspecified aircraft accident injuring occupant**
  Aircraft accident NOS
  Air transport accident NOS

- **V96 Accident to nonpowered aircraft causing injury to occupant**
  The appropriate 7th character is to be added to each code from category V96

A	initial encounter
D	subsequent encounter
S	sequela

  - **V96.0 Balloon accident injuring occupant**
    - **■ V96.00 Unspecified balloon accident injuring occupant**
    - **V96.01 Balloon crash injuring occupant**
    - **V96.02 Forced landing of balloon injuring occupant**
    - **V96.03 Balloon collision injuring occupant**
      Balloon collision with any object, fixed, moveable or moving

---

● Unacceptable First-Listed Diagnosis   ● Use Additional Character(s)   ■ Unspecified   **OGCR** Official Guidelines for Coding and Reporting

🔾 Complication\Comorbidity   🔾 Major C\C   Excludes 1   Excludes 2   Includes   Use additional   Code first   Code also

1665

- V96.04   Balloon fire injuring occupant
- V96.05   Balloon explosion injuring occupant
- V96.09   Other balloon accident injuring occupant
- V96.1   Hang-glider accident injuring occupant
  - V96.10   Unspecified hang-glider accident injuring occupant
  - V96.11   Hang-glider crash injuring occupant
  - V96.12   Forced landing of hang-glider injuring occupant
  - V96.13   Hang-glider collision injuring occupant
    Hang-glider collision with any object, fixed, moveable or moving
  - V96.14   Hang-glider fire injuring occupant
  - V96.15   Hang-glider explosion injuring occupant
  - V96.19   Other hang-glider accident injuring occupant
- V96.2   Glider (nonpowered) accident injuring occupant
  - V96.20   Unspecified glider (nonpowered) accident injuring occupant
  - V96.21   Glider (nonpowered) crash injuring occupant
  - V96.22   Forced landing of glider (nonpowered) injuring occupant
  - V96.23   Glider (nonpowered) collision injuring occupant
    Glider (nonpowered) collision with any object, fixed, moveable or moving
  - V96.24   Glider (nonpowered) fire injuring occupant
  - V96.25   Glider (nonpowered) explosion injuring occupant
  - V96.29   Other glider (nonpowered) accident injuring occupant
- V96.8   Other nonpowered-aircraft accidents injuring occupant
  Kite carrying a person accident injuring occupant
- V96.9   Unspecified nonpowered-aircraft accident injuring occupant
  Nonpowered-aircraft accident NOS

- V97   Other specified air transport accidents
  The appropriate 7th character is to be added to each code from category V97

A	initial encounter
D	subsequent encounter
S	sequela

  - V97.0   Occupant of aircraft injured in other specified air transport accidents
    Fall in, on or from aircraft in air transport accident
    | Excludes1 | accident while boarding or alighting aircraft (V97.1) |
  - V97.1   Person injured while boarding or alighting from aircraft
  - V97.2   Parachutist accident
    - V97.21   Parachutist entangled in object
      Parachutist landing in tree
    - V97.22   Parachutist injured on landing
    - V97.29   Other parachutist accident

- V97.3   Person on ground injured in air transport accident
  - V97.31   Hit by object falling from aircraft
    Hit by crashing aircraft
    Injured by aircraft hitting house
    Injured by aircraft hitting car
  - V97.32   Injured by rotating propeller
  - V97.33   Sucked into jet engine
  - V97.39   Other injury to person on ground due to air transport accident
- V97.8   Other air transport accidents, not elsewhere classified
  | Excludes1 | aircraft accident NOS (V95.9)
 exposure to changes in air pressure during ascent or descent (W94.-) |
  - V97.81   Air transport accident involving military aircraft
    - V97.810   Civilian aircraft involved in air transport accident with military aircraft
      Passenger in civilian aircraft injured due to accident with military aircraft
    - V97.811   Civilian injured by military aircraft
    - V97.818   Other air transport accident involving military aircraft
  - V97.89   Other air transport accidents, not elsewhere classified
    Injury from machinery on aircraft

OTHER AND UNSPECIFIED TRANSPORT ACCIDENTS (V98-V99)

| Excludes1 | vehicle accident, type of vehicle unspecified (V89.-) |

- V98   Other specified transport accidents
  The appropriate 7th character is to be added to each code from category V98

A	initial encounter
D	subsequent encounter
S	sequela

  - V98.0   Accident to, on or involving cable-car, not on rails
    Caught or dragged by cable-car, not on rails
    Fall or jump from cable-car, not on rails
    Object thrown from or in cable-car, not on rails
  - V98.1   Accident to, on or involving land-yacht
  - V98.2   Accident to, on or involving ice yacht
  - V98.3   Accident to, on or involving ski lift
    Accident to, on or involving ski chair-lift
    Accident to, on or involving ski-lift with gondola
  - V98.8   Other specified transport accidents

- V99   Unspecified transport accident
  The appropriate 7th character is to be added to code V99

A	initial encounter
D	subsequent encounter
S	sequela

OTHER EXTERNAL CAUSES OF ACCIDENTAL INJURY (W00-X58)

SLIPPING, TRIPPING, STUMBLING AND FALLS (W00-W19)

Excludes1   assault involving a fall (Y01-Y02)
fall (in) (from):
     animal (V80.-)
     machinery (in operation) (W28-W31)
     transport vehicle (V01-V99)
intentional self-harm involving a fall (X80-X81)

Excludes2   at risk for fall (history of fall) Z91.81
fall (in) (from):
     burning building (X00.-)
     into fire (X00-X04, X08-X09)

● **W00   Fall due to ice and snow**

     Includes   pedestrian on foot falling (slipping) on ice and snow

     Excludes1   fall on (from) ice and snow involving pedestrian conveyance (V00.-)
          fall from stairs and steps not due to ice and snow (W10.-)

     The appropriate 7th character is to be added to each code from category W00

       A   initial encounter
       D   subsequent encounter
       S   sequela

   ● **W00.0   Fall on same level due to ice and snow**

   ● **W00.1   Fall from stairs and steps due to ice and snow**

   ● **W00.2   Other fall from one level to another due to ice and snow**

   ● ▨ **W00.9   Unspecified fall due to ice and snow**

● **W01   Fall on same level from slipping, tripping and stumbling**

     Includes   fall on moving sidewalk

     Excludes1   fall due to bumping (striking) against object (W18.0-)
          fall in shower or bathtub (W18.2-)
          fall on same level NOS (W18.30)
          fall on same level from slipping, tripping and stumbling due to ice or snow (W00.0)
          fall off or from toilet (W18.1-)
          slipping, tripping and stumbling NOS (W18.40)
          slipping, tripping and stumbling without falling (W18.4-)

     The appropriate 7th character is to be added to each code from category W01

       A   initial encounter
       D   subsequent encounter
       S   sequela

   ● **W01.0   Fall on same level from slipping, tripping and stumbling without subsequent striking against object**
       Falling over animal

   ● **W01.1   Fall on same level from slipping, tripping and stumbling with subsequent striking against object**

     ● ▨ **W01.10   Fall on same level from slipping, tripping and stumbling with subsequent striking against unspecified object**

       ● **W01.11   Fall on same level from slipping, tripping and stumbling with subsequent striking against sharp object**

         ● **W01.110   Fall on same level from slipping, tripping and stumbling with subsequent striking against sharp glass**

         ● **W01.111   Fall on same level from slipping, tripping and stumbling with subsequent striking against power tool or machine**

         ● **W01.118   Fall on same level from slipping, tripping and stumbling with subsequent striking against other sharp object**

         ● ▨ **W01.119   Fall on same level from slipping, tripping and stumbling with subsequent striking against unspecified sharp object**

       ● **W01.19   Fall on same level from slipping, tripping and stumbling with subsequent striking against other object**

         ● **W01.190   Fall on same level from slipping, tripping and stumbling with subsequent striking against furniture**

         ● **W01.198   Fall on same level from slipping, tripping and stumbling with subsequent striking against other object**

Category W02 deactivated. See category V00

● **W03   Other fall on same level due to collision with another person**

     Includes   fall due to non-transport collision with other person

     Excludes1   collision with another person without fall (W51)
          crushed or pushed by a crowd or human stampede (W52)
          fall involving pedestrian conveyance (V00-V09)
          fall due to ice or snow (W00)
          fall on same level NOS (W18.30)

     The appropriate 7th character is to be added to code W03

       A   initial encounter
       D   subsequent encounter
       S   sequela

● **W04   Fall while being carried or supported by other persons**

     Includes   accidentally dropped while being carried

     The appropriate 7th character is to be added to code W04

       A   initial encounter
       D   subsequent encounter
       S   sequel

● **W05   Fall from non-moving wheelchair**

     Excludes1   fall from moving wheelchair (V00.811)

     The appropriate 7th character is to be added to code W05

       A   initial encounter
       D   subsequent encounter
       S   sequela

● **W06   Fall from bed**

     The appropriate 7th character is to be added to code W06

       A   initial encounter
       D   subsequent encounter
       S   sequela

● **W07   Fall from chair**

     The appropriate 7th character is to be added to code W07

       A   initial encounter
       D   subsequent encounter
       S   sequela

● Unacceptable First-Listed Diagnosis   ● Use Additional Character(s)   ▨ Unspecified   **OGCR** Official Guidelines for Coding and Reporting
🗱 Complication\Comorbidity   🗱 Major C\C   Excludes 1   Excludes 2   Includes   Use additional   Code first   Code also   **1667**

CHAPTER 20 (V01-Y99)

● **W08 Fall from other furniture**

    The appropriate 7th character is to be added to code W08

A	initial encounter
D	subsequent encounter
S	sequela

● **W09 Fall on and from playground equipment**

    Excludes1   fall involving recreational machinery (W31)

    The appropriate 7th character is to be added to each code from category W09

A	initial encounter
D	subsequent encounter
S	sequela

   ● **W09.0 Fall on or from playground slide**

   ● **W09.1 Fall from playground swing**

   ● **W09.2 Fall on or from jungle gym**

   ● **W09.8 Fall on or from other playground equipment**

● **W10 Fall on and from stairs and steps**

    Excludes1   fall from stairs and steps due to ice and snow (W00.1)

    The appropriate 7th character is to be added to each code from category W10

A	initial encounter
D	subsequent encounter
S	sequela

   ● **W10.0 Fall (on) (from) escalator**

   ● **W10.1 Fall (on) (from) sidewalk curb**

   ● **W10.3 Fall (on) (from) incline**

       Fall (on) (from) ramp

   ● **W10.8 Fall (on) (from) other stairs and steps**

   ● ■ **W10.9 Fall (on) (from) unspecified stairs and steps**

● **W11 Fall on and from ladder**

    The appropriate 7th character is to be added to code W11

A	initial encounter
D	subsequent encounter
S	sequela

● **W12 Fall on and from scaffolding**

    The appropriate 7th character is to be added to code W12

A	initial encounter
D	subsequent encounter
S	sequela

● **W13 Fall from, out of or through building or structure**

    The appropriate 7th character is to be added to each code from category W13

A	initial encounter
D	subsequent encounter
S	sequela

   ● **W13.0 Fall from, out of or through balcony**

       Fall from, out of or through railing

   ● **W13.1 Fall from, out of or through bridge**

   ● **W13.2 Fall from, out of or through roof**

   ● **W13.3 Fall through floor**

   ● **W13.4 Fall from, out of or through window**

       Excludes2   fall with subsequent striking against sharp glass (W01.110)

   ● **W13.8 Fall from, out of or through other building or structure**

       Fall from, out of or through viaduct

       Fall from, out of or through wall

       Fall from, out of or through flag-pole

● **W13.9 Fall from, out of or through building, not otherwise specified**

    Excludes1   collapse of a building or structure (W20.-)

               fall or jump from burning building or structure (X00.-)

● **W14 Fall from tree**

    The appropriate 7th character is to be added to code W14

A	initial encounter
D	subsequent encounter
S	sequela

● **W15 Fall from cliff**

    The appropriate 7th character is to be added to code W15

A	initial encounter
D	subsequent encounter
S	sequela

● **W16 Fall, jump or diving into water**

    Excludes1   accidental non-watercraft drowning and submersion not involving fall (W65-W74)

               effects of air pressure from diving (W94.-)

               fall into water from watercraft (V90-V94)

               hitting an object or against bottom when falling from watercraft (V94.0)

    Excludes2   striking or hitting diving board (W21.3)

    The appropriate 7th character is to be added to each code from category W16

A	initial encounter
D	subsequent encounter
S	sequela

● **W16.0 Fall into swimming pool**

    Fall into swimming pool NOS

    Excludes1   fall into empty swimming pool (W17.3)

   ● **W16.01 Fall into swimming pool striking water surface**

     ● **W16.011 Fall into swimming pool striking water surface causing drowning and submersion**

       Excludes1   drowning and submersion while in swimming pool without fall (W67)

     ● **W16.012 Fall into swimming pool striking water surface causing other injury**

   ● **W16.02 Fall into swimming pool striking bottom**

     ● **W16.021 Fall into swimming pool striking bottom causing drowning and submersion**

       Excludes1   drowning and submersion while in swimming pool without fall (W67)

     ● **W16.022 Fall into swimming pool striking bottom causing other injury**

● Unacceptable First-Listed Diagnosis   ● Use Additional Character(s)   ■ Unspecified   **OGCR** Official Guidelines for Coding and Reporting

🔖 Complication\Comorbidity   🔖 Major C\C | Excludes 1 | | Excludes 2 | Includes   Use additional   Code first   Code also

● W16.03   Fall into swimming pool striking wall

    ● W16.031   Fall into swimming pool striking wall causing drowning and submersion

       Excludes1   drowning and submersion while in swimming pool without fall (W67)

    ● W16.032   Fall into swimming pool striking wall causing other injury

● W16.1   Fall into natural body of water

       Fall into lake
       Fall into open sea
       Fall into river
       Fall into stream

    ● W16.11   Fall into natural body of water striking water surface

       ● W16.111   Fall into natural body of water striking water surface causing drowning and submersion

          Excludes1   drowning and submersion while in natural body of water without fall (W69)

       ● W16.112   Fall into natural body of water striking water surface causing other injury

    ● W16.12   Fall into natural body of water striking bottom

       ● W16.121   Fall into natural body of water striking bottom causing drowning and submersion

          Excludes1   drowning and submersion while in natural body of water without fall (W69)

       ● W16.122   Fall into natural body of water striking bottom causing other injury

    ● W16.13   Fall into natural body of water striking side

       ● W16.131   Fall into natural body of water striking side causing drowning and submersion

          Excludes1   drowning and submersion while in natural body of water without fall (W69)

       ● W16.132   Fall into natural body of water striking side causing other injury

● W16.2   Fall in (into) filled bathtub or bucket of water

    ● W16.21   Fall in (into) filled bathtub

       Excludes1   fall into empty bathtub (W18.2)

● W16.211   Fall in (into) filled bathtub causing drowning and submersion

    Excludes1   drowning and submersion while in filled bathtub without fall (W65)

● W16.212   Fall in (into) filled bathtub causing other injury

● W16.22   Fall in (into) bucket of water

    ● W16.221   Fall in (into) bucket of water causing drowning and submersion

    ● W16.222   Fall in (into) bucket of water causing other injury

● W16.3   Fall into other water

       Fall into fountain
       Fall into reservoir

    ● W16.31   Fall into other water striking water surface

       ● W16.311   Fall into other water striking water surface causing drowning and submersion

          Excludes1   drowning and submersion while in other water without fall (W73)

       ● W16.312   Fall into other water striking water surface causing other injury

    ● W16.32   Fall into other water striking bottom

       ● W16.321   Fall into other water striking bottom causing drowning and submersion

          Excludes1   drowning and submersion while in other water without fall (W73)

       ● W16.322   Fall into other water striking bottom causing other injury

    ● W16.33   Fall into other water striking wall

       ● W16.331   Fall into other water striking wall causing drowning and submersion

          Excludes1   drowning and submersion while in other water without fall (W73)

       ● W16.332   Fall into other water striking wall causing other injury

● W16.4   Fall into unspecified water

    ● ▣ W16.41   Fall into unspecified water causing drowning and submersion

    ● ▣ W16.42   Fall into unspecified water causing other injury

● W16.5   Jumping or diving into swimming pool

    ● W16.51   Jumping or diving into swimming pool striking water surface

● W16.511 Jumping or diving into swimming pool striking water surface causing drowning and submersion

> Excludes1   drowning and submersion while in swimming pool without jumping or diving (W67)

● W16.512 Jumping or diving into swimming pool striking water surface causing other injury

● W16.52 Jumping or diving into swimming pool striking bottom

● W16.521 Jumping or diving into swimming pool striking bottom causing drowning and submersion

> Excludes1   drowning and submersion while in swimming pool without jumping or diving (W67)

● W16.522 Jumping or diving into swimming pool striking bottom causing other injury

● W16.53 Jumping or diving into swimming pool striking wall

● W16.531 Jumping or diving into swimming pool striking wall causing drowning and submersion

> Excludes1   drowning and submersion while in swimming pool without jumping or diving (W67)

● W16.532 Jumping or diving into swimming pool striking wall causing other injury

● W16.6 Jumping or diving into natural body of water
Jumping or diving into lake
Jumping or diving into open sea
Jumping or diving into river
Jumping or diving into stream

● W16.61 Jumping or diving into natural body of water striking water surface

● W16.611 Jumping or diving into natural body of water striking water surface causing drowning and submersion

> Excludes1   drowning and submersion while in natural body of water without jumping or diving (W69)

● W16.612 Jumping or diving into natural body of water striking water surface causing other injury

● W16.62 Jumping or diving into natural body of water striking bottom

● W16.621 Jumping or diving into natural body of water striking bottom causing drowning and submersion

> Excludes1   drowning and submersion while in natural body of water without jumping or diving (W69)

● W16.622 Jumping or diving into natural body of water striking bottom causing other injury

● W16.7 Jumping or diving from boat

> Excludes1   fall from boat into water - see watercraft accident (V90-V94)

● W16.71 Jumping or diving from boat striking water surface

● W16.711 Jumping or diving from boat striking water surface causing drowning and submersion

● W16.712 Jumping or diving from boat striking water surface causing other injury

● W16.72 Jumping or diving from boat striking bottom

● W16.721 Jumping or diving from boat striking bottom causing drowning and submersion

● W16.722 Jumping or diving from boat striking bottom causing other injury

● W16.8 Jumping or diving into other water
Jumping or diving into fountain
Jumping or diving into reservoir

● W16.81 Jumping or diving into other water striking water surface

● W16.811 Jumping or diving into other water striking water surface causing drowning and submersion

> Excludes1   drowning and submersion while in other water without jumping or diving (W73)

● W16.812 Jumping or diving into other water striking water surface causing other injury

● W16.82 Jumping or diving into other water striking bottom

● W16.821 Jumping or diving into other water striking bottom causing drowning and submersion

> Excludes1   drowning and submersion while in other water without jumping or diving (W73)

● W16.822 Jumping or diving into other water striking bottom causing other injury

● Unacceptable First-Listed Diagnosis   ● Use Additional Character(s)   ■ Unspecified   OGCR Official Guidelines for Coding and Reporting
🦠 Complication\Comorbidity   🦠 Major C\C   Excludes 1   Excludes 2   Includes   Use additional   Code first   Code also

- ● W16.83 Jumping or diving into other water striking wall
  - ● W16.831 Jumping or diving into other water striking wall causing drowning and submersion
    - **Excludes1**   drowning and submersion while in other water without jumping or diving (W73)
  - ● W16.832 Jumping or diving into other water striking wall causing other injury
- ● W16.9 Jumping or diving into unspecified water
  - ● ◼ W16.91 Jumping or diving into unspecified water causing drowning and submersion
  - ● ◼ W16.92 Jumping or diving into unspecified water causing other injury

- ● W17 Other fall from one level to another
  - The appropriate 7th character is to be added to each code from category W17

A	initial encounter
D	subsequent encounter
S	sequela

  - ● W17.0 Fall into well
  - ● W17.1 Fall into storm drain or manhole
  - ● W17.2 Fall into hole
    - Fall into pit
  - ● W17.3 Fall into empty swimming pool
    - **Excludes1**   fall into filled swimming pool (W16.0-)
  - ● W17.4 Fall from dock
  - ● W17.8 Other fall from one level to another
    - ● W17.81 Fall down embankment (hill)
    - ● W17.82 Fall from (out of) grocery cart
      - Fall due to grocery cart tipping over
    - ● W17.89 Other fall from one level to another

- ● W18 Other slipping, tripping and stumbling and falls
  - The appropriate 7th character is to be added to each code from category W18

A	initial encounter
D	subsequent encounter
S	sequela

  - ● W18.0 Fall due to bumping against object
    - Striking against object with subsequent fall
    - **Excludes1**   fall on same level due to slipping, tripping, or stumbling with subsequent striking against object (W01.1-)
    - ● ◼ W18.00 Striking against unspecified object with subsequent fall
    - ● W18.01 Striking against sports equipment with subsequent fall
    - ● W18.02 Striking against glass with subsequent fall
    - ● W18.09 Striking against other object with subsequent fall
  - ● W18.1 Fall from or off toilet
    - ● W18.11 Fall from or off toilet without subsequent striking against object
      - Fall from (off) toilet NOS

- ● W18.12 Fall from or off toilet with subsequent striking against object
- ● W18.2 Fall in (into) shower or empty bathtub
  - **Excludes1**   fall in full bathtub (W16.21-)
- ● W18.3 Other and unspecified fall on same level
  - ● ◼ W18.30 Fall on same level, unspecified
  - ● W18.31 Fall on same level due to stepping on an object
    - Fall on same level due to stepping on an animal
    - **Excludes1**   slipping, tripping and stumbling without fall due to stepping on animal (W18.41)
  - ● W18.39 Other fall on same level
- ● W18.4 Slipping, tripping and stumbling without falling
  - **Excludes1**   collision with another person without fall (W51)
  - ● ◼ W18.40 Slipping, tripping and stumbling without falling, unspecified
  - ● W18.41 Slipping, tripping and stumbling without falling due to stepping on object
    - Slipping, tripping and stumbling without falling due to stepping on animal
    - **Excludes1**   slipping, tripping and stumbling with fall due to stepping on animal (W18.31)
  - ● W18.42 Slipping, tripping and stumbling without falling due to stepping into hole or opening
  - ● W18.43 Slipping, tripping and stumbling without falling due to stepping from one level to another
  - ● W18.49 Other slipping, tripping and stumbling without falling

- ● ◼ W19 Unspecified fall
  - **Includes**   accidental fall NOS
  - The appropriate 7th character is to be added to code W19

A	initial encounter
D	subsequent encounter
S	sequela

EXPOSURE TO INANIMATE MECHANICAL FORCES (W20-W49)

Excludes1   assault (X91-Y08)
contact or collision with animals or persons (W50-W64)
exposure to inanimate mechanical forces involving military or war operations (Y36.-, Y37.-)
intentional self-harm (X70-X83)

● Unacceptable First-Listed Diagnosis   ● Use Additional Character(s)   ◼ Unspecified   **OGCR** Official Guidelines for Coding and Reporting

🅒 Complication\Comorbidity   🅒 Major C\C   Excludes 1   Excludes 2   Includes   Use additional   Code first   Code also

CHAPTER 20 (V01-Y99)

1671

● **W20 Struck by thrown, projected or falling object**

> *Code first any associated:*
> cataclysm (X34-X39)
> lightning strike (T75.0)

> **Excludes1** falling object in:
>   machinery accident (W24, W28-W31)
>   transport accident (V01-V99)
>   object set in motion by:
>   explosion (W35-W40)
>   firearm (W32-W34)
>   struck by thrown sports equipment
>   (W21.-)

> The appropriate 7th character is to be added to each code from category W20
>
> | | |
> |---|---|
> | A | initial encounter |
> | D | subsequent encounter |
> | S | sequela |

● **W20.0 Struck by falling object in cave-in**
> **Excludes2** asphyxiation due to cave-in (T71.21)

● **W20.1 Struck by object due to collapse of building**
> **Excludes1** struck by object due to collapse of burning building (X00.2, X02.2)

● **W20.8 Other cause of strike by thrown, projected or falling object**
> **Excludes1** struck by thrown sports equipment (W21.-)

● **W21 Striking against or struck by sports equipment**

> **Excludes1** assault with sports equipment (Y08.1-)
> striking against or struck by sports equipment with subsequent fall (W18.01)

> The appropriate 7th character is to be added to each code from category W21
>
> | | |
> |---|---|
> | A | initial encounter |
> | D | subsequent encounter |
> | S | sequela |

● **W21.0 Struck by hit or thrown ball**
  ● ■**W21.00 Struck by hit or thrown ball, unspecified type**
  ● **W21.01 Struck by football**
  ● **W21.02 Struck by soccer ball**
  ● **W21.03 Struck by baseball**
  ● **W21.04 Struck by golf ball**
  ● **W21.05 Struck by basketball**
  ● **W21.06 Struck by volleyball**
  ● **W21.07 Struck by softball**
  ● **W21.09 Struck by other hit or thrown ball**

● **W21.1 Struck by bat, racquet or club**
  ● **W21.11 Struck by baseball bat**
  ● **W21.12 Struck by tennis racquet**
  ● **W21.13 Struck by golf club**
  ● **W21.19 Struck by other bat, racquet or club**

● **W21.2 Struck by hockey stick or puck**
  ● **W21.21 Struck by hockey stick**
    ● **W21.210 Struck by ice hockey stick**
    ● **W21.211 Struck by field hockey stick**
  ● **W21.22 Struck by hockey puck**
    ● **W21.220 Struck by ice hockey puck**
    ● **W21.221 Struck by field hockey puck**

● **W21.3 Struck by sports foot wear**
  ● **W21.31 Struck by shoe cleats**
    Stepped on by shoe cleats
  ● **W21.32 Struck by skate blades**
    Skated over by skate blades
  ● **W21.39 Struck by other sports foot wear**

● **W21.4 Striking against diving board**
> Use additional code for subsequent falling into water, if applicable (W16.-)

● **W21.8 Striking against or struck by other sports equipment**
  ● **W21.81 Striking against or struck by football helmet**
  ● **W21.89 Striking against or struck by other sports equipment**

● ■ **W21.9 Striking against or struck by unspecified sports equipment**

● **W22 Striking against or struck by other objects**

> **Excludes1** striking against or struck by object with subsequent fall (W18.09)

> The appropriate 7th character is to be added to each code from category W22
>
> | | |
> |---|---|
> | A | initial encounter |
> | D | subsequent encounter |
> | S | sequela |

● **W22.0 Striking against stationary object**
> **Excludes1** striking against stationary sports equipment (W21.8)
  ● **W22.01 Walked into wall**
  ● **W22.02 Walked into lamppost**
  ● **W22.03 Walked into furniture**
  ● **W22.04 Striking against wall of swimming pool**
    ● **W22.041 Striking against wall of swimming pool causing drowning and submersion**
    > **Excludes1** drowning and submersion while swimming without striking against wall (W67)
    ● **W22.042 Striking against wall of swimming pool causing other injury**
  ● **W22.09 Striking against other stationary object**

● **W22.1 Striking against or struck by automobile airbag**
  ● ■ **W22.10 Striking against or struck by unspecified automobile airbag**
  ● **W22.11 Striking against or struck by driver side automobile airbag**
  ● **W22.12 Striking against or struck by front passenger side automobile airbag**
  ● **W22.19 Striking against or struck by other automobile airbag**

● **W22.8 Striking against or struck by other objects**
  Striking against or struck by object NOS
> **Excludes1** struck by thrown, projected or falling object (W20.-)

● Unacceptable First-Listed Diagnosis   ● Use Additional Character(s)   ■ Unspecified   **OGCR** Official Guidelines for Coding and Reporting
🔹 Complication\Comorbidity 🔹 Major C\C   Includes   Use additional   Code first   Code also

● **W23 Caught, crushed, jammed or pinched in or between objects**

> **Excludes1**   injury caused by cutting or piercing instruments (W25-W27)
> injury caused by firearms malfunction (W32.1, W33.1-, W34.1-)
> injury caused by lifting and transmission devices (W24.-)
> injury caused by machinery (W28-W31)
> injury caused by nonpowered hand tools (W27.-)
> injury caused by transport vehicle being used as a means of transportation (V01-V99)
> injury caused by struck by thrown, projected or falling object (W20.-)

> The appropriate 7th character is to be added to each code from category W23

A	initial encounter
D	subsequent encounter
S	sequela

● **W23.0 Caught, crushed, jammed, or pinched between moving objects**

● **W23.1 Caught, crushed, jammed, or pinched between stationary objects**

● **W24 Contact with lifting and transmission devices, not elsewhere classified**

> **Excludes1**   transport accidents (V01-V99)

> The appropriate 7th character is to be added to each code from category W24

A	initial encounter
D	subsequent encounter
S	sequela

● **W24.0 Contact with lifting devices, not elsewhere classified**
> Contact with chain hoist
> Contact with drive belt
> Contact with pulley (block)

● **W24.1 Contact with transmission devices, not elsewhere classified**
> Contact with transmission belt or cable

● **W25 Contact with sharp glass**

> *Code first any associated:*
> injury due to flying glass from explosion or firearm discharge (W32-W40)
> transport accident (V00-V99)

> **Excludes1**   fall on same level due to slipping, tripping and stumbling with subsequent striking against sharp glass (W01.10)
> striking against sharp glass with subsequent fall (W18.02)

> The appropriate 7th character is to be added to code W25

A	initial encounter
D	subsequent encounter
S	sequela

● **W26 Contact with knife, sword or dagger**

> The appropriate 7th character is to be added to each code from category W26

A	initial encounter
D	subsequent encounter
S	sequela

● **W26.0 Contact with knife**
> **Excludes1**   contact with electric knife (W29.1)

● **W26.1 Contact with sword or dagger**

● **W27 Contact with nonpowered hand tool**

> The appropriate 7th character is to be added to each code from category W27

A	initial encounter
D	subsequent encounter
S	sequela

● **W27.0 Contact with workbench tool**
> Contact with auger
> Contact with axe
> Contact with chisel
> Contact with handsaw
> Contact with screwdriver

● **W27.1 Contact with garden tool**
> Contact with hoe
> Contact with nonpowered lawn mower
> Contact with pitchfork
> Contact with rake

● **W27.2 Contact with scissors**

● **W27.3 Contact with needle (sewing)**
> **Excludes1**   contact with hypodermic needle (W46.-)

● **W27.4 Contact with kitchen utensil**
> Contact with fork
> Contact with ice-pick
> Contact with can-opener NOS

● **W27.5 Contact with paper-cutter**

● **W27.8 Contact with other nonpowered hand tool**
> Contact with nonpowered sewing machine
> Contact with shovel

● **W28 Contact with powered lawn mower**

> **Includes**   powered lawn mower (commercial) (residential)

> **Excludes1**   contact with nonpowered lawn mower (W27.1)

> **Excludes2**   exposure to electric current (W86.-)

> The appropriate 7th character is to be added to code W28

A	initial encounter
D	subsequent encounter
S	sequela

● **W29 Contact with other powered hand tools and household machinery**

> **Excludes1**   contact with commercial machinery (W31.82)
> contact with hot household appliance (X15)
> contact with nonpowered hand tool (W27.-)
> exposure to electric current (W86)

> The appropriate 7th character is to be added to each code from category W29

A	initial encounter
D	subsequent encounter
S	sequela

● **W29.0 Contact with powered kitchen appliance**
> Contact with blender
> Contact with can-opener
> Contact with garbage disposal
> Contact with mixer

● **W29.1 Contact with electric knife**

● **W29.2 Contact with other powered household machinery**
> Contact with electric fan
> Contact with powered dryer (clothes) (powered) (spin)
> Contact with washing-machine
> Contact with sewing machine

● Unacceptable First-Listed Diagnosis   ● Use Additional Character(s)   ▢ Unspecified   **OGCR** Official Guidelines for Coding and Reporting

🪱 Complication\Comorbidity   🪱 Major C\C   Excludes 1   Excludes 2   Includes   Use additional   Code first   Code also   1673

CHAPTER 20 (V01-Y99)

● **W29.3 Contact with powered garden and outdoor hand tools and machinery**
     Contact with chainsaw
     Contact with edger
     Contact with garden cultivator (tiller)
     Contact with hedge trimmer
     Contact with other powered garden tool
     | Excludes 1 | contact with powered lawn mower (W28)

● **W29.4 Contact with nail gun**

● **W29.8 Contact with other powered powered hand tools and household machinery**
     Contact with do-it-yourself tool NOS

● **W30   Contact with agricultural machinery**
     | Includes | animal-powered farm machine
     | Excludes 1 | agricultural transport vehicle accident (V01-V99)
                   explosion of grain store (W40.8)
                   exposure to electric current (W86.-)

The appropriate 7th character is to be added to each code from category W30

A	initial encounter
D	subsequent encounter
S	sequela

● **W30.0 Contact with combine harvester**
     Contact with reaper
     Contact with thresher

● **W30.1 Contact with power take-off devices (PTO)**

● **W30.2 Contact with hay derrick**

● **W30.3 Contact with grain storage elevator**
     | Excludes 1 | explosion of grain store (W40.8)

● **W30.8 Contact with other specified agricultural machinery**
     ● **W30.81 Contact with agricultural transport vehicle in stationary use**
         Contact with agricultural transport vehicle under repair, not on public roadway
         | Excludes 1 | agricultural transport vehicle accident (V01-V99)
     ● **W30.89 Contact with other specified agricultural machinery**

● ■ **W30.9 Contact with unspecified agricultural machinery**
     Contact with farm machinery NOS

● **W31   Contact with other and unspecified machinery**
     | Excludes 1 | contact with agricultural machinery (W30.-)
                   contact with machinery in transport under own power or being towed by a vehicle (V01-V99)
                   exposure to electric current (W86)

The appropriate 7th character is to be added to each code from category W31

A	initial encounter
D	subsequent encounter
S	sequela

● **W31.0 Contact with mining and earth-drilling machinery**
     Contact with bore or drill (land) (seabed)
     Contact with shaft hoist
     Contact with shaft lift
     Contact with undercutter

● **W31.1 Contact with metalworking machines**
     Contact with abrasive wheel
     Contact with forging machine
     Contact with lathe
     Contact with mechanical shears
     Contact with metal drilling machine
     Contact with milling machine
     Contact with power press
     Contact with rolling-mill
     Contact with metal sawing machine

● **W31.2 Contact with powered woodworking and forming machines**
     Contact with band saw
     Contact with bench saw
     Contact with circular saw
     Contact with molding machine
     Contact with overhead plane
     Contact with powered saw
     Contact with radial saw
     Contact with sander
     | Excludes 1 | nonpowered woodworking tools (W27.0)

● **W31.3 Contact with prime movers**
     Contact with gas turbine
     Contact with internal combustion engine
     Contact with steam engine
     Contact with water driven turbine

● **W31.8 Contact with other specified machinery**
     ● **W31.81 Contact with recreational machinery**
         Contact with roller-coaster
     ● **W31.82 Contact with other commercial machinery**
         Contact with commercial electric fan
         Contact with commercial kitchen appliances
         Contact with commercial powered dryer (clothes) (powered) (spin)
         Contact with commercial washing-machine
         Contact with commercial sewing machine
         | Excludes 1 | contact with household machinery (W29.-)
                      contact with powered lawn mower (W28)
     ● **W31.83 Contact with special construction vehicle in stationary use**
         Contact with special construction vehicle under repair, not on public roadway
         | Excludes 1 | special construction vehicle accident (V01-V99)
     ● **W31.89 Contact with other specified machinery**

● ■ **W31.9 Contact with unspecified machinery**
     Contact with machinery NOS

● Unacceptable First-Listed Diagnosis   ● Use Additional Character(s)   ■ Unspecified   **OGCR** Official Guidelines for Coding and Reporting
🔃 Complication\Comorbidity   🔃 Major C\C | Excludes 1 | | Excludes 2 | Includes   Use additional   Code first   Code also

● **W32 Accidental handgun discharge and malfunction**

> | Includes | accidental discharge and malfunction of gun for single hand use
> accidental discharge and malfunction of pistol
> accidental discharge and malfunction of revolver
> handgun discharge and malfunction NOS

> | Excludes1 | accidental airgun discharge and malfunction (W34.010, W34.110)
> accidental BB gun discharge and malfunction (W34.010, W34.110)
> accidental pellet gun discharge and malfunction (W34.010, W34.110)
> accidental shotgun discharge and malfunction (W33.01, W33.11)
> assault by handgun discharge (X93)
> handgun discharge involving legal intervention (Y35.0-)
> handgun discharge involving military or war operations (Y36.4-)
> intentional self-harm by handgun discharge (X72)
> Very pistol discharge and malfunction (W34.09, W34.19)

The appropriate 7th character is to be added to code W32

> | A | initial encounter |
> | D | subsequent encounter |
> | S | sequela |

W32.0 Accidental handgun discharge

W32.1 Accidental handgun malfunction
> Injury due to explosion of handgun (parts)
> Injury due to malfunction of mechanism or component of handgun
> Injury due to recoil of handgun
> Powder burn from handgun

● **W33 Accidental rifle, shotgun and larger firearm discharge and malfunction**

> | Includes | rifle, shotgun and larger firearm discharge and malfunction NOS

> | Excludes1 | accidental airgun discharge and malfunction (W34.010, W34.110)
> accidental BB gun discharge and malfunction (W34.010, W34.110)
> accidental handgun discharge and malfunction (W32.-)
> accidental pellet gun discharge and malfunction (W34.010, W34.110)
> assault by rifle, shotgun and larger firearm discharge (X94)
> firearm discharge involving legal intervention (Y35.0-)
> firearm discharge involving military or war operations (Y36.4-)
> intentional self-harm by rifle, shotgun and larger firearm discharge (X73)

The appropriate 7th character is to be added to each code from category W33

> | A | initial encounter |
> | D | subsequent encounter |
> | S | sequela |

● **W33.0 Accidental rifle, shotgun and larger firearm discharge**

● **W33.00 Accidental discharge of unspecified larger firearm**
> Discharge of unspecified larger firearm NOS

● **W33.01 Accidental discharge of shotgun**
> Discharge of shotgun NOS

● **W33.02 Accidental discharge of hunting rifle**
> Discharge of hunting rifle NOS

● **W33.03 Accidental discharge of machine gun**
> Discharge of machine gun NOS

● **W33.09 Accidental discharge of other larger firearm**
> Discharge of other larger firearm NOS

● **W33.1 Accidental rifle, shotgun and larger firearm malfunction**
> Injury due to explosion of rifle, shotgun and larger firearm (parts)
> Injury due to malfunction of mechanism or component of rifle, shotgun and larger firearm
> Injury due to piercing, cutting, crushing or pinching due to (by) slide trigger mechanism, scope or other gun part
> Injury due to recoil of rifle, shotgun and larger firearm
> Powder burn from rifle, shotgun and larger firearm

● **W33.10 Accidental malfunction of unspecified larger firearm**
> Malfunction of unspecified larger firearm NOS

● **W33.11 Accidental malfunction of shotgun**
> Malfunction of shotgun NOS

● **W33.12 Accidental malfunction of hunting rifle**
> Malfunction of hunting rifle NOS

● **W33.13 Accidental malfunction of machine gun**
> Malfunction of machine gun NOS

● **W33.19 Accidental malfunction of other larger firearm**
> Malfunction of other larger firearm NOS

● **W34 Accidental discharge and malfunction from other and unspecified firearms and guns**
> The appropriate 7th character is to be added to each code from category W34

> | A | initial encounter |
> | D | subsequent encounter |
> | S | sequela |

● **W34.0 Accidental discharge from other and unspecified firearms and guns**

● **W34.00 Accidental discharge from unspecified firearms or gun**
> Discharge from firearm NOS
> Gunshot wound NOS
> Shot NOS

● **W34.01 Accidental discharge of gas, air or spring-operated guns**

● **W34.010 Accidental discharge of airgun**
> Accidental discharge of BB gun
> Accidental discharge of pellet gun

● **W34.011 Accidental discharge of paintball gun**
> Accidental injury due to paintball discharge

● **W34.018 Accidental discharge of other gas, air or spring-operated gun**

● **W34.09 Accidental discharge from other specified firearms**
> Accidental discharge from Very pistol [flare]

● **W34.1 Accidental malfunction from other and unspecified firearms and guns**

 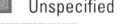
CHAPTER 20 (V01-Y99)

● ■ **W34.10   Accidental malfunction from unspecified firearms or gun**
     Firearm malfunction NOS

● **W34.11   Accidental malfunction of gas, air or spring-operated guns**

  ● **W34.110   Accidental malfunction of airgun**
       Accidental malfunction of BB gun
       Accidental malfunction of pellet gun

  ● **W34.111   Accidental malfunction of paintball gun**
       Accidental injury due to paintball gun malfunction

  ● **W34.118   Accidental malfunction of other gas, air or spring-operated gun**

● **W34.19   Accidental malfunction from other specified firearms**
     Accidental malfunction from Very pistol [flare]

● **W35   Explosion and rupture of boiler**

> **Excludes1**   explosion and rupture of boiler on watercraft (V93.4)

The appropriate 7th character is to be added to code W35

A	initial encounter
D	subsequent encounter
S	sequela

● **W36   Explosion and rupture of gas cylinder**
The appropriate 7th character is to be added to each code from category W36

A	initial encounter
D	subsequent encounter
S	sequela

  ● **W36.1   Explosion and rupture of aerosol can**

  ● **W36.2   Explosion and rupture of air tank**

  ● **W36.3   Explosion and rupture of pressurized-gas tank**

  ● **W36.8   Explosion and rupture of other gas cylinder**

  ● ■ **W36.9   Explosion and rupture of unspecified gas cylinder**

● **W37   Explosion and rupture of pressurized tire, pipe or hose**
The appropriate 7th character is to be added to each code from category W37

A	initial encounter
D	subsequent encounter
S	sequela

  ● **W37.0   Explosion of bicycle tire**

  ● **W37.8   Explosion and rupture of other pressurized tire, pipe or hose**

● **W38   Explosion and rupture of other specified pressurized devices**
The appropriate 7th character is to be added to code W38

A	initial encounter
D	subsequent encounter
S	sequela

● **W39   Discharge of firework**
The appropriate 7th character is to be added to code W39

A	initial encounter
D	subsequent encounter
S	sequela

● **W40   Explosion of other materials**

> **Excludes1**   assault by explosive material (X96)
> explosion involving legal intervention (Y35.1-)
> explosion involving military or war operations (Y36.0-, Y36.2-)
> intentional self-harm by explosive material (X75)

The appropriate 7th character is to be added to each code from category W40

A	initial encounter
D	subsequent encounter
S	sequela

● **W40.0   Explosion of blasting material**
     Explosion of blasting cap
     Explosion of detonator
     Explosion of dynamite
     Explosion of explosive (any) used in blasting operations

● **W40.1   Explosion of explosive gases**
     Explosion of acetylene
     Explosion of butane
     Explosion of coal gas
     Explosion in mine NOS
     Explosion of explosive gas
     Explosion of fire damp
     Explosion of gasoline fumes
     Explosion of methane
     Explosion of propane

● **W40.8   Explosion of other specified explosive materials**
     Explosion in dump NOS
     Explosion in factory NOS
     Explosion in grain store
     Explosion in munitions

> **Excludes1**   explosion involving legal intervention (Y35.1-)
> explosion involving military or war operations (Y36.0-, Y36.2-)

● ■ **W40.9   Explosion of unspecified explosive materials**
     Explosion NOS

Category W41 deactivated. See subcategory T70.4

● **W42   Exposure to noise**
The appropriate 7th character is to be added to each code from category W42

A	initial encounter
D	subsequent encounter
S	sequela

  ● **W42.0   Exposure to supersonic waves**

  ● **W42.9   Exposure to other noise**
     Exposure to sound waves NOS

Category W43 deactivated. See subcategory T75.2

Category W44 deactivated. See categories T15-T19

● **W45   Foreign body or object entering through skin**

> **Excludes2**   contact with hand tools (nonpowered) (powered) (W27-W29)
> contact with knife, sword or dagger (W26.-)
> contact with sharp glass (W25.-)
> struck by objects (W20-W22)

The appropriate 7th character is to be added to each code from category W45

A	initial encounter
D	subsequent encounter
S	sequela

● **W45.0   Nail entering through skin**

● **W45.1   Paper entering through skin**
     Paper cut

1676

● Unacceptable First-Listed Diagnosis   ● Use Additional Character(s)   ■ Unspecified   **OGCR** Official Guidelines for Coding and Reporting

🗣 Complication\Comorbidity   🗣 Major C\C   Excludes 1   Excludes 2   Includes   Use additional   Code first   Code also

CHAPTER 20 (V01-Y99)

● W45.2 **Lid of can entering through skin**

● W45.8 **Other foreign body or object entering through skin**
Splinter in skin NOS

● W46 **Contact with hypodermic needle**
The appropriate 7th character is to be added to each code from category W46

A	initial encounter
D	subsequent encounter
S	sequela

● W46.0 **Contact with hypodermic needle**
Hypodermic needle stick NOS

● W46.1 **Contact with contaminated hypodermic needle**

● W49 **Exposure to other inanimate mechanical forces**

    Includes   exposure to abnormal gravitational [G] forces exposure to inanimate mechanical forces NEC

    Excludes1   exposure to inanimate mechanical forces involving military or war operations (Y36.-, Y37.-)

The appropriate 7th character is to be added to each code from category W49

A	initial encounter
D	subsequent encounter
S	sequela

● W49.0 **Item causing external constriction**

    ● W49.01 **Hair causing external constriction**

    ● W49.02 **String or thread causing external constriction**

    ● W49.03 **Rubber band causing external constriction**

    ● W49.04 **Ring or other jewelry causing external constriction**

    ● W49.05 **Other item causing external constriction**

● W49.9 **Exposure to other inanimate mechanical forces**

EXPOSURE TO ANIMATE MECHANICAL FORCES (W50-W64)

    Excludes1   toxic effect of contact with venomous animals and plants (T63.-)

● W50 **Accidental hit, strike, kick, twist, bite or scratch by another person**

    Includes   Hit, strike, kick, twist, bite, or scratch by another person NOS

    Excludes1   assault by bodily force (Y04)
struck by objects (W20-W22)

The appropriate 7th character is to be added to each code from category W50

A	initial encounter
D	subsequent encounter
S	sequela

● W50.0 **Accidental hit or strike by another person**
Hit or strike by another person NOS

● W50.1 **Accidental kick by another person**
Kick by another person NOS

● W50.2 **Accidental twist by another person**
Twist by another person NOS

● W50.3 **Accidental bite by another person**
Human bite
Bite by another person NOS

● W50.4 **Accidental scratch by another person**
Scratch by another person NOS

● W51 **Accidental striking against or bumped into by another person**

    Excludes1   assault by striking against or bumping into by another person (Y08.2-)
fall due to collision with another person (W03)

The appropriate 7th character is to be added to code W51

A	initial encounter
D	subsequent encounter
S	sequela

● W52 **Crushed, pushed or stepped on by crowd or human stampede**
Crushed, pushed or stepped on by crowd or human stampede with or without fall

The appropriate 7th character is to be added to code W52

A	initial encounter
D	subsequent encounter
S	sequela

● W53 **Contact with rodent**
Contact with saliva, feces or urine of rodent

The appropriate 7th character is to be added to each code from category W53

A	initial encounter
D	subsequent encounter
S	sequela

    ● W53.0 **Contact with mouse**

       ● W53.01 **Bitten by mouse**

       ● W53.09 **Other contact with mouse**

    ● W53.1 **Contact with rat**

       ● W53.11 **Bitten by rat**

       ● W53.19 **Other contact with rat**

    ● W53.2 **Contact with squirrel**

       ● W53.21 **Bitten by squirrel**

       ● W53.29 **Other contact with squirrel**

    ● W53.8 **Contact with other rodent**

       ● W53.81 **Bitten by other rodent**

       ● W53.89 **Other contact with other rodent**

● W54 **Contact with dog**
Contact with saliva, feces or urine of dog

The appropriate 7th character is to be added to each code from category W54

A	initial encounter
D	subsequent encounter
S	sequela

● W54.0 **Bitten by dog**

● W54.1 **Struck by dog**
Knocked over by dog

● W54.8 **Other contact with dog**

● W55 **Contact with other mammals**
Contact with saliva, feces or urine of mammal

    Excludes1   animal being ridden - see transport accidents
bitten or struck by dog (W54)
bitten or struck by rodent (W53.-)
contact with marine mammals (W56.x-)

The appropriate 7th character is to be added to each code from category W55

A	initial encounter
D	subsequent encounter
S	sequela

    ● W55.0 **Contact with cat**

       ● W55.01 **Bitten by cat**

       ● W55.03 **Scratched by cat**

       ● W55.09 **Other contact with cat**

● Unacceptable First-Listed Diagnosis   ● Use Additional Character(s)   ▨ Unspecified   **OGCR** Official Guidelines for Coding and Reporting

🔖 Complication\Comorbidity   🔖 Major C\C   Excludes 1   Excludes 2   Includes   Use additional   Code first   Code also

1677

CHAPTER 20 (V01-Y99)

● W55.1 Contact with horse
- ● W55.11 Bitten by horse
- ● W55.12 Struck by horse
- ● W55.19 Other contact with horse

● W55.2 Contact with cow
Contact with bull
- ● W55.21 Bitten by cow
- ● W55.22 Struck by cow
Gored by bull
- ● W55.29 Other contact with cow

● W55.3 Contact with other hoof stock
Contact with goats
Contact with sheep
- ● W55.31 Bitten by other hoof stock
- ● W55.32 Struck by other hoof stock
Gored by goat
Gored by ram
- ● W55.39 Other contact with other hoof stock

● W55.4 Contact with pig
- ● W55.41 Bitten by pig
- ● W55.42 Struck by pig
- ● W55.49 Other contact with pig

● W55.5 Contact with raccoon
- ● W55.51 Bitten by raccoon
- ● W55.52 Struck by raccoon
- ● W55.59 Other contact with raccoon

● W55.8 Contact with other mammals
- ● W55.81 Bitten by other mammals
- ● W55.82 Struck by other mammals
- ● W55.89 Other contact with other mammals

● W56 Contact with nonvenomous marine animal

> **Excludes1** contact with venomous marine animal (T63.-)

The appropriate 7th character is to be added to each code from category W56

A	initial encounter
D	subsequent encounter
S	sequela

● W56.0 Contact with dolphin
- ● W56.01 Bitten by dolphin
- ● W56.02 Struck by dolphin
- ● W56.09 Other contact with dolphin

● W56.1 Contact with sea lion
- ● W56.11 Bitten by sea lion
- ● W56.12 Struck by sea lion
- ● W56.19 Other contact with sea lion

● W56.2 Contact with orca
Contact with killer whale
- ● W56.21 Bitten by orca
- ● W56.22 Struck by orca
- ● W56.29 Other contact with orca

● W56.3 Contact with other marine mammals
- ● W56.31 Bitten by other marine mammals
- ● W56.32 Struck by other marine mammals
- ● W56.39 Other contact with other marine mammals

● W56.4 Contact with shark
- ● W56.41 Bitten by shark
- ● W56.42 Struck by shark
- ● W56.49 Other contact with shark

● W56.5 Contact with other fish
- ● W56.51 Bitten by other fish
- ● W56.52 Struck by other fish
- ● W56.59 Other contact with other fish

● W56.8 Contact with other nonvenomous marine animals
- ● W56.81 Bitten by other nonvenomous marine animals
- ● W56.82 Struck by other nonvenomous marine animals
- ● W56.89 Other contact with other nonvenomous marine animals

● W57 Bitten or stung by nonvenomous insect and other nonvenomous arthropods

> **Excludes1** contact with venomous insects and arthropods (T63.2-, T63.3-, T63.4-)

The appropriate 7th character is to be added to code W57

A	initial encounter
D	subsequent encounter
S	sequela

● W58 Contact with crocodile or alligator
The appropriate 7th character is to be added to each code from category W58

A	initial encounter
D	subsequent encounter
S	sequela

● W58.0 Contact with alligator
- ● W58.01 Bitten by alligator
- ● W58.02 Struck by alligator
- ● W58.03 Crushed by alligator

● W58.1 Contact with crocodile
- ● W58.11 Bitten by crocodile
- ● W58.12 Struck by crocodile
- ● W58.13 Crushed by crocodile

● W59 Contact with other nonvenomous reptiles

> **Excludes1** contact with venomous reptile (T63.0-, T63.1-)

The appropriate 7th character is to be added to each code from category W59

A	initial encounter
D	subsequent encounter
S	sequela

● W59.0 Contact with nonvenomous lizards
- ● W59.01 Bitten by nonvenomous lizards
- ● W59.02 Struck by nonvenomous lizards
- ● W59.09 Other contact with nonvenomous lizards
Exposure to nonvenomous lizards

● W59.1 Contact with nonvenomous snakes
- ● W59.11 Bitten by nonvenomous snake
- ● W59.12 Struck by nonvenomous snake
- ● W59.13 Crushed by nonvenomous snake
- ● W59.19 Other contact with nonvenomous snake

● W59.2 Contact with turtles

> **Excludes1** contact with tortoises (W59.8-)

- ● W59.21 Bitten by turtle
- ● W59.22 Struck by turtle
- ● W59.29 Other contact with turtle
Exposure to turtles

● W59.8 Contact with other nonvenomous reptiles
- ● W59.81 Bitten by other nonvenomous reptiles
- ● W59.82 Struck by other nonvenomous reptiles

● Unacceptable First-Listed Diagnosis　　● Use Additional Character(s)　　■ Unspecified　　**OGCR** Official Guidelines for Coding and Reporting

🗝 Complication\Comorbidity　　🗝 Major C\C　　Excludes 1　　Excludes 2　　Includes　　Use additional　　Code first　　Code also

CHAPTER 20 (V01-Y99)

- W59.83 **Crushed by other nonvenomous reptiles**
- W59.89 **Other contact with other nonvenomous reptiles**

- W60 **Contact with nonvenomous plant thorns and spines and sharp leaves**

  | Excludes1 | contact with venomous plants (T63.x-) |

  The appropriate 7th character is to be added to code W60

A	initial encounter
D	subsequent encounter
S	sequela

- W61 **Contact with birds (domestic) (wild)**
  Contact with excreta of birds

  The appropriate 7th character is to be added to each code from category W61

A	initial encounter
D	subsequent encounter
S	sequela

  - W61.0 **Contact with parrot**
    - W61.01 **Bitten by parrot**
    - W61.02 **Struck by parrot**
    - W61.09 **Other contact with parrot**
      Exposure to parrots
  - W61.1 **Contact with macaw**
    - W61.11 **Bitten by macaw**
    - W61.12 **Struck by macaw**
    - W61.19 **Other contact with macaw**
      Exposure to macaws
  - W61.2 **Contact with other psittacines**
    - W61.21 **Bitten by other psittacines**
    - W61.22 **Struck by other psittacines**
    - W61.29 **Other contact with other psittacines**
      Exposure to other psittacines
  - W61.3 **Contact with chicken**
    - W61.32 **Struck by chicken**
    - W61.33 **Pecked by chicken**
    - W61.39 **Other contact with chicken**
      Exposure to chickens
  - W61.4 **Contact with turkey**
    - W61.42 **Struck by turkey**
    - W61.43 **Pecked by turkey**
    - W61.49 **Other contact with turkey**
  - W61.5 **Contact with goose**
    - W61.51 **Bitten by goose**
    - W61.52 **Struck by goose**
    - W61.59 **Other contact with goose**
  - W61.6 **Contact with duck**
    - W61.61 **Bitten by duck**
    - W61.62 **Struck by duck**
    - W61.69 **Other contact with duck**
  - W61.9 **Contact with other birds**
    - W61.91 **Bitten by other birds**
    - W61.92 **Struck by other birds**
    - W61.99 **Other contact with other birds**

- W62 **Contact with nonvenomous amphibians**

  | Excludes1 | contact with venomous amphibians (T63.81-R63.83) |

  The appropriate 7th character is to be added to each code from category W62

A	initial encounter
D	subsequent encounter
S	sequela

  - W62.0 **Contact with nonvenomous frogs**
  - W62.1 **Contact with nonvenomous toads**
  - W62.9 **Contact with other nonvenomous amphibians**

- W64 **Exposure to other animate mechanical forces**
  Exposure to nonvenomous animal NOS

  | Excludes1 | contact with venomous animal (T63.-) |

  The appropriate 7th character is to be added to code W64

A	initial encounter
D	subsequent encounter
S	sequela

ACCIDENTAL NON-TRANSPORT DROWNING AND SUBMERSION (W65-W74)

  | Excludes1 | accidental drowning and submersion due to fall into water (W16.-) |
  | | accidental drowning and submersion due to water transport accident (V90.-, V92.-) |

  | Excludes2 | accidental drowning and submersion due to cataclysm (X34-X39) |

- W65 **Accidental drowning and submersion while in bathtub**

  | Excludes1 | accidental drowning and submersion due to fall in (into) bathtub (W16.211) |

  The appropriate 7th character is to be added to code W65

A	initial encounter
D	subsequent encounter
S	sequela

  Category W66 deactivated. See category W16.

- W67 **Accidental drowning and submersion while in swimming pool**

  | Excludes1 | accidental drowning and submersion due to fall into swimming pool (W16.011, W16.021, W16.031) |
  | | accidental drowning and submersion due to striking into wall of swimming pool (W22.041) |

  The appropriate 7th character is to be added to code W67

A	initial encounter
D	subsequent encounter
S	sequela

  Category W68 deactivated. See category W16.

● Unacceptable First-Listed Diagnosis　　　● Use Additional Character(s)　　　　▥ Unspecified　　　**OGCR** Official Guidelines for Coding and Reporting

🔗 Complication\Comorbidity　　　⚔ Major C\C　　　Excludes 1　　　Excludes 2　　　Includes　　　Use additional　　　Code first　　　Code also

CHAPTER 20 (V01-Y99)

1679

● **W69 Accidental drowning and submersion while in natural water**

> **Includes** accidental drowning and submersion while in lake
> accidental drowning and submersion while in open sea
> accidental drowning and submersion while in river
> accidental drowning and submersion while in stream

> **Excludes1** accidental drowning and submersion due to fall into natural body of water (W16.111, W16.121, W16.131)

The appropriate 7th character is to be added to code W69

A	initial encounter
D	subsequent encounter
S	sequela

Category W70 deactivated. See category W16.

● **W73 Other specified cause of accidental non-transport drowning and submersion**

> **Includes** accidental drowning and submersion while in quenching tank
> accidental drowning and submersion while in reservoir

> **Excludes1** accidental drowning and submersion due to fall into other water (W16.311, W16.321, W16.331)

The appropriate 7th character is to be added to code W73

A	initial encounter
D	subsequent encounter
S	sequela

● ▪ **W74 Unspecified cause of accidental drowning and submersion**

> **Includes** drowning NOS

The appropriate 7th character is to be added to code W74

A	initial encounter
D	subsequent encounter
S	sequela

Categories W75-W77 deactivated. See category T71

Category W78 deactivated. See subcategory T17.81

Categories W79-W80 deactivated. See categories T17 and T18

Category W81 deactivated. See subcategory T71.2

Category W83 deactivated. See category T71

Category W84 deactivated. See subcategory T71.9

EXPOSURE TO ELECTRIC CURRENT, RADIATION AND EXTREME AMBIENT AIR TEMPERATURE AND PRESSURE (W85-W99)

> **Excludes1** exposure to:
> failure in dosage of radiation or temperature during surgical and medical care (Y63.2-Y63.5)
> lightning (T75.0-)
> natural cold (X31)
> natural heat (X30)
> natural radiation NOS (X39)
> radiological procedure and radiotherapy (Y84.2)
> sunlight (X32)

● **W85 Exposure to electric transmission lines**

> **Includes** Broken power line

The appropriate 7th character is to be added to code W85

A	initial encounter
D	subsequent encounter
S	sequela

● **W86 Exposure to other specified electric current**

The appropriate 7th character is to be added to each code from category W86

A	initial encounter
D	subsequent encounter
S	sequela

● **W86.0 Exposure to domestic wiring and appliances**

● **W86.1 Exposure to industrial wiring, appliances and electrical machinery**
> Exposure to conductors
> Exposure to control apparatus
> Exposure to electrical equipment and machinery
> Exposure to transformers

● **W86.8 Exposure to other electric current**
> Exposure to wiring and appliances in or on farm (not farmhouse)
> Exposure to wiring and appliances outdoors
> Exposure to wiring and appliances in or on public building
> Exposure to wiring and appliances in or on residential institutions
> Exposure to wiring and appliances in or on schools

Category W87 deactivated. See category W86

● **W88 Exposure to ionizing radiation**

> **Excludes1** exposure to sunlight (X32)

The appropriate 7th character is to be added to each code from category W88

A	initial encounter
D	subsequent encounter
S	sequela

● **W88.0 Exposure to X-rays**

● **W88.1 Exposure to radioactive isotopes**

● **W88.8 Exposure to other ionizing radiation**

● **W89 Exposure to man-made visible and ultraviolet light**

> **Includes** exposure to welding light (arc)
> **Excludes2** exposure to sunlight (X32)

The appropriate 7th character is to be added to each code from category W89

A	initial encounter
D	subsequent encounter
S	sequela

● **W89.0 Exposure to welding light (arc)**

● **W89.1 Exposure to tanning bed**

● **W89.8 Exposure to other man-made visible and ultraviolet light**

● ▪ **W89.9 Exposure to unspecified man-made visible and ultraviolet light**

● **W90 Exposure to other nonionizing radiation**

> **Excludes1** exposure to sunlight (X32)

The appropriate 7th character is to be added to each code from category W90

A	initial encounter
D	subsequent encounter
S	sequela

● **W90.0 Exposure to radiofrequency**

● **W90.1 Exposure to infrared radiation**

● Unacceptable First-Listed Diagnosis   ● Use Additional Character(s)   ▪ Unspecified   **OGCR** Official Guidelines for Coding and Reporting
🔖 Complication\Comorbidity   🔖 Major C\C   Excludes 1   Excludes 2   Includes   Use additional   Code first   Code also

● W90.2 **Exposure to laser radiation**

● W90.8 **Exposure to other nonionizing radiation**

Category W91 deactivated. See category W90

● W92 **Exposure to excessive heat of man-made origin**
The appropriate 7th character is to be added to code W92

A	initial encounter
D	subsequent encounter
S	sequela

● W93 **Exposure to excessive cold of man-made origin**
The appropriate 7th character is to be added to each code from category W93

A	initial encounter
D	subsequent encounter
S	sequela

● W93.0 **Contact with or inhalation of dry ice**

● W93.01 **Contact with dry ice**

● W93.02 **Inhalation of dry ice**

● W93.1 **Contact with or inhalation of liquid air**

● W93.11 **Contact with liquid air**
Contact with liquid hydrogen
Contact with liquid nitrogen

● W93.12 **Inhalation of liquid air**
Inhalation of liquid hydrogen
Inhalation of liquid nitrogen

● W93.2 **Prolonged exposure in deep freeze unit or refrigerator**

● W93.8 **Exposure to other excessive cold of man-made origin**

● W94 **Exposure to high and low air pressure and changes in air pressure**
The appropriate 7th character is to be added to each code from category W94

A	initial encounter
D	subsequent encounter
S	sequela

● W94.0 **Exposure to prolonged high air pressure**

● W94.1 **Exposure to prolonged low air pressure**

● W94.11 **Exposure to residence or prolonged visit at high altitude**

● W94.12 **Exposure to other prolonged low air pressure**

● W94.2 **Exposure to rapid changes in air pressure during ascent**

● W94.21 **Exposure to reduction in atmospheric pressure while surfacing from deep-water diving**

● W94.22 **Exposure to reduction in atmospheric pressure while surfacing from underground**

● W94.23 **Exposure to sudden change in air pressure in aircraft during ascent**

● W94.29 **Exposure to other rapid changes in air pressure during ascent**

● W94.3 **Exposure to rapid changes in air pressure during descent**

● W94.31 **Exposure to sudden change in air pressure in aircraft during ascent or descent**

● W94.32 **Exposure to high air pressure from rapid descent in water**

● W94.39 **Exposure to other rapid changes in air pressure during descent**

● W99 **Exposure to other man-made environmental factors**
The appropriate 7th character is to be added to code W99

A	initial encounter
D	subsequent encounter
S	sequela

EXPOSURE TO SMOKE, FIRE AND FLAMES (X00-X08)

Excludes1	arson (X97)

Excludes2	explosions (W35-W40)
	lightning (T75.0-)
	transport accident (V01-V99)

● X00 **Exposure to uncontrolled fire in building or structure**

Includes	conflagration in building or structure

Code first any associated cataclysm

Excludes2	exposure to ignition or melting of nightwear (X05)
	exposure to ignition or melting of other clothing and apparel (X06-)
	exposure to other specified smoke, fire and flames (X08.-)

The appropriate 7th character is to be added to each code from category X00

A	initial encounter
D	subsequent encounter
S	sequela

● X00.0 **Exposure to flames in uncontrolled fire in building or structure**

● X00.1 **Exposure to smoke in uncontrolled fire in building or structure**

● X00.2 **Injury due to collapse of burning building or structure in uncontrolled fire**

Excludes1	injury due to collapse of building not on fire (W20.1)

● X00.3 **Fall from burning building or structure in uncontrolled fire**

● X00.4 **Hit by object from burning building or structure in uncontrolled fire**

● X00.5 **Jump from burning building or structure in uncontrolled fire**

● X00.8 **Other exposure to uncontrolled fire in building or structure**

● X01 **Exposure to uncontrolled fire, not in building or structure**
Exposure to forest fire

The appropriate 7th character is to be added to each code from category X01

A	initial encounter
D	subsequent encounter
S	sequela

● X01.0 **Exposure to flames in uncontrolled fire, not in building or structure**

● X01.1 **Exposure to smoke in uncontrolled fire, not in building or structure**

● X01.3 **Fall due to uncontrolled fire, not in building or structure**

● X01.4 **Hit by object due to uncontrolled fire, not in building or structure**

● X01.8 **Other exposure to uncontrolled fire, not in building or structure**

● Unacceptable First-Listed Diagnosis   ● Use Additional Character(s)   ▪ Unspecified   **OGCR** Official Guidelines for Coding and Reporting

🅒 Complication\Comorbidity   🅜 Major C\C   Excludes 1   Excludes 2   Includes   Use additional   Code first   Code also

1681

● **X02   Exposure to controlled fire in building or structure**

    | **Includes** | exposure to fire in fireplace exposure to fire in stove |

    The appropriate 7th character is to be added to each code from category X02

    | A | initial encounter |
    | D | subsequent encounter |
    | S | sequela |

  ● **X02.0   Exposure to flames in controlled fire in building or structure**

  ● **X02.1   Exposure to smoke in controlled fire in building or structure**

  ● **X02.2   Injury due to collapse of burning building or structure in controlled fire**

     | **Excludes1** | injury due to collapse of building not on fire (W20.1) |

  ● **X02.3   Fall from burning building or structure in controlled fire**

  ● **X02.4   Hit by object from burning building or structure in controlled fire**

  ● **X02.5   Jump from burning building or structure in controlled fire**

  ● **X02.8   Other exposure to controlled fire in building or structure**

● **X03   Exposure to controlled fire, not in building or structure**

    | **Includes** | exposure to bon fire exposure to camp fire exposure to trash fire |

    The appropriate 7th character is to be added to each code from category X03

    | A | initial encounter |
    | D | subsequent encounter |
    | S | sequela |

  ● **X03.0   Exposure to flames in controlled fire, not in building or structure**

  ● **X03.1   Exposure to smoke in controlled fire, not in building or structure**

  ● **X03.3   Fall due to controlled fire, not in building or structure**

  ● **X03.4   Hit by object due to controlled fire, not in building or structure**

  ● **X03.8   Other exposure to controlled fire, not in building or structure**

● **X04   Exposure to ignition of highly flammable material**

    | **Includes** | exposure to ignition of gasoline exposure to ignition of kerosene exposure to ignition of petrol |

    | **Excludes2** | exposure to ignition or melting of nightwear (X05) exposure to ignition or melting of other clothing and apparel (X06) |

    The appropriate 7th character is to be added to code X04

    | A | initial encounter |
    | D | subsequent encounter |
    | S | sequela |

● **X05   Exposure to ignition or melting of nightwear**

    | **Excludes2** | exposure to uncontrolled fire in building or structure (X00.-) exposure to uncontrolled fire, not in building or structure (X01.-) exposure to controlled fire in building or structure (X02.-) exposure to controlled fire, not in building or structure (X03.-) exposure to ignition of highly flammable materials (X04.-) |

    The appropriate 7th character is to be added to code X05

    | A | initial encounter |
    | D | subsequent encounter |
    | S | sequela |

● **X06   Exposure to ignition or melting of other clothing and apparel**

    | **Excludes2** | exposure to uncontrolled fire in building or structure (X00.-) exposure to uncontrolled fire, not in building or structure (X01.-) exposure to controlled fire in building or structure (X02.-) exposure to controlled fire, not in building or structure (X03.-) exposure to ignition of highly flammable materials (X04.-) |

    The appropriate 7th character is to be added to each code from category X06

    | A | initial encounter |
    | D | subsequent encounter |
    | S | sequela |

  ● **X06.0   Exposure to ignition of plastic jewelry**

  ● **X06.1   Exposure to melting of plastic jewelry**

  ● **X06.2   Exposure to ignition of other clothing and apparel**

  ● **X06.3   Exposure to melting of other clothing and apparel**

● **X08   Exposure to other specified smoke, fire and flames**

    The appropriate 7th character is to be added to each code from category X08

    | A | initial encounter |
    | D | subsequent encounter |
    | S | sequela |

  ● **X08.0   Exposure to bed fire**
       Exposure to mattress fire

    ● ■ **X08.00   Exposure to bed fire due to unspecified burning material**

    ● **X08.01   Exposure to bed fire due to burning cigarette**

    ● **X08.09   Exposure to bed fire due to other burning material**

  ● **X08.1   Exposure to sofa fire**

    ● ■ **X08.10   Exposure to sofa fire due to unspecified burning material**

    ● **X08.11   Exposure to sofa fire due to burning cigarette**

    ● **X08.19   Exposure to sofa fire due to other burning material**

  ● **X08.2   Exposure to other furniture fire**

    ● ■ **X08.20   Exposure to other furniture fire due to unspecified burning material**

    ● **X08.21   Exposure to other furniture fire due to burning cigarette**

    ● **X08.29   Exposure to other furniture fire due to other burning material**

  ● **X08.8   Exposure to other specified smoke, fire and flames**

Category X09   deactivated. See category X08

● Unacceptable First-Listed Diagnosis   ● Use Additional Character(s)   ■ Unspecified   **OGCR** Official Guidelines for Coding and Reporting
   🏷 Complication\Comorbidity   🏷 Major C\C | Excludes 1 | | Excludes 2 | | Includes | Use additional   Code first   Code also

CHAPTER 20 (V01-Y99)

CONTACT WITH HEAT AND HOT SUBSTANCES (X10-X19)

Excludes1   exposure to excessive natural heat (X30)
exposure to fire and flames (X00-X09)

● **X10**   **Contact with hot drinks, food, fats and cooking oils**
The appropriate 7th character is to be added to each code
from category X10

A	initial encounter
D	subsequent encounter
S	sequela

● **X10.0**   **Contact with hot drinks**

● **X10.1**   **Contact with hot food**

● **X10.2**   **Contact with fats and cooking oils**

● **X11**   **Contact with hot tap-water**
Contact with boiling tap-water
Contact with boiling water NOS

Excludes1   contact with water heated on stove (X12)

The appropriate 7th character is to be added to each code
from category X11

A	initial encounter
D	subsequent encounter
S	sequela

● **X11.0**   **Contact with hot water in bath or tub**

Excludes1   contact with running hot water in
bath or tub (X11.1)

● **X11.1**   **Contact with running hot water**
Contact with hot water running out of hose
Contact with hot water running out of tap

● **X11.8**   **Contact with other hot tap-water**
Contact with hot water in bucket
Contact with hot tap-water NOS

● **X12**   **Contact with other hot fluids**

Includes   contact with water heated on stove

Excludes1   hot (liquid) metals (X18)

The appropriate 7th character is to be added to code X12

A	initial encounter
D	subsequent encounter
S	sequela

● **X13**   **Contact with steam and other hot vapors**
The appropriate 7th character is to be added to each code
from category X13

A	initial encounter
D	subsequent encounter
S	sequela

● **X13.0**   **Inhalation of steam and other hot vapors**

● **X13.1**   **Other contact with steam and other hot vapors**

● **X14**   **Contact with hot air and other hot gases**
The appropriate 7th character is to be added to each code
from category X14

A	initial encounter
D	subsequent encounter
S	sequela

● **X14.0**   **Inhalation of hot air and gases**

● **X14.1**   **Other contact with hot air and other hot gases**

● **X15**   **Contact with hot household appliances**

Excludes1   contact with heating appliances (X16)
contact with powered household appliances
(W29.-)
exposure to controlled fire in building or
structure due to household appliance
(X02.8)
exposure to household appliances electrical
current (W86.0)

The appropriate 7th character is to be added to each code
from category X15

A	initial encounter
D	subsequent encounter
S	sequela

● **X15.0**   **Contact with hot stove (kitchen)**

● **X15.1**   **Contact with hot toaster**

● **X15.2**   **Contact with hotplate**

● **X15.3**   **Contact with hot saucepan or skillet**

● **X15.8**   **Contact with other hot household appliances**
Contact with cooker
Contact with kettle
Contact with light bulbs

● **X16**   **Contact with hot heating appliances, radiators and pipes**

Excludes1   contact with powered appliances (W29.-)
exposure to controlled fire in building or
structure due to appliance (X02.8)
exposure to industrial appliances electrical
current (W86.1)

The appropriate 7th character is to be added to code X16

A	initial encounter
D	subsequent encounter
S	sequela

● **X17**   **Contact with hot engines, machinery and tools**

Excludes1   contact with hot heating appliances,
radiators and pipes (X16)
contact with hot household appliances (X15)

The appropriate 7th character is to be added to code X17

A	initial encounter
D	subsequent encounter
S	sequela

● **X18**   **Contact with other hot metals**

Includes   contact with liquid metal

The appropriate 7th character is to be added to code X18

A	initial encounter
D	subsequent encounter
S	sequela

● **X19**   **Contact with other heat and hot substances**

Excludes1   objects that are not normally hot, e.g., an
object made hot by a house fire (X00-
X09)

The appropriate 7th character is to be added to code X19

A	initial encounter
D	subsequent encounter
S	sequela

Categories X20-X29 deactivated. See category T63

● Unacceptable First-Listed Diagnosis   ● Use Additional Character(s)   ▨ Unspecified   **OGCR** Official Guidelines for Coding and Reporting

🗞 Complication\Comorbidity   🗞 Major C\C   Excludes 1   Excludes 2   Includes   Use additional   Code first   Code also

1683

EXPOSURE TO FORCES OF NATURE (X30-X39)

● **X30   Exposure to excessive natural heat**

> **Includes**   exposure to excessive heat as the cause of sunstroke
> exposure to heat NOS

> **Excludes1**   excessive heat of man-made origin (W92)
> exposure to man-made radiation (W89)
> exposure to sunlight (X32)
> exposure to tanning bed (W89)

> The appropriate 7th character is to be added to code X30

> | A | initial encounter |
> |---|---|
> | D | subsequent encounter |
> | S | sequela |

● **X31   Exposure to excessive natural cold**

> **Includes**   excessive cold as the cause of chilblains NOS
> excessive cold as the cause of immersion foot or hand
> exposure to cold NOS
> exposure to weather conditions

> **Excludes1**   cold of man-made origin (W93.-)
> contact with or inhalation of:
> dry ice (W93.-)
> liquefied gas (W93.-)

> The appropriate 7th character is to be added to code X31

> | A | initial encounter |
> |---|---|
> | D | subsequent encounter |
> | S | sequela |

● **X32   Exposure to sunlight**

> **Excludes1**   radiation-related disorders of the skin and subcutaneous tissue (L55-L59)
> man-made radiation (tanning bed) (W89)

> The appropriate 7th character is to be added to code X32

> | A | initial encounter |
> |---|---|
> | D | subsequent encounter |
> | S | sequela |

● **X34   Earthquake**

> **Excludes2**   tidal wave (tsunami) due to earthquake (X37.41)

> The appropriate 7th character is to be added to code X34

> | A | initial encounter |
> |---|---|
> | D | subsequent encounter |
> | S | sequela |

● **X35   Volcanic eruption**

> **Excludes2**   tidal wave (tsunami) due to earthquake (X37.41)

> The appropriate 7th character is to be added to code X35

> | A | initial encounter |
> |---|---|
> | D | subsequent encounter |
> | S | sequela |

● **X36   Avalanche, landslide and other earth movements**

> **Includes**   victim of mudslide of cataclysmic nature
> **Excludes1**   earthquake (X34)
> **Excludes2**   transport accident involving collision with avalanche or landslide not in motion (V01-V99)

> The appropriate 7th character is to be added to each code from category X36

> | A | initial encounter |
> |---|---|
> | D | subsequent encounter |
> | S | sequela |

● **X36.0   Collapse of dam or man-made structure causing earth movement**

● **X36.1   Avalanche, landslide, or mudslide**

● **X37   Cataclysmic storm**

> The appropriate 7th character is to be added to each code from category X37

> | A | initial encounter |
> |---|---|
> | D | subsequent encounter |
> | S | sequela |

● **X37.0   Hurricane**
> Storm surge   Typhoon

● **X37.1   Tornado**
> Cyclone   Twister

● **X37.2   Blizzard (snow) (ice)**

● **X37.3   Dust storm**

● **X37.4   Tidalwave**

> ● **X37.41   Tidal wave due to earthquake or volcanic eruption**
> > Tidal wave NOS
> > Tsunami

> ● **X37.42   Tidal wave due to storm**

> ● **X37.43   Tidal wave due to landslide**

● **X37.8   Other cataclysmic storms**
> Cloudburst
> Torrential rain
> > **Excludes2**   flood (X38)

● ■ **X37.9   Unspecified cataclysmic storm**
> Storm NOS
> > **Excludes1**   collapse of dam or man-made structure causing earth movement (X39.0)

● **X38   Flood**

> **Includes**   flood arising from remote storm
> flood of cataclysmic nature arising from melting snow
> flood resulting directly from storm

> **Excludes1**   collapse of dam or man-made structure causing earth movement (X39.0)
> tidal wave NOS (X39.2)
> tidal wave caused by storm (X37.2)

> The appropriate 7th character is to be added to code X38

> | A | initial encounter |
> |---|---|
> | D | subsequent encounter |
> | S | sequela |

● **X39   Exposure to other forces of nature**

> The appropriate 7th character is to be added to each code from category X39

> | A | initial encounter |
> |---|---|
> | D | subsequent encounter |
> | S | sequela |

> ● **X39.0   Exposure to natural radiation**

> > **Excludes1**   contact with and (suspected) exposure to radon and other naturally occuring radiation (Z77.122)
> > exposure to man-made radiation (W88-W90)
> > exposure to sunlight (X32)

> > ● **X39.01   Exposure to radon**

> > ● **X39.08   Exposure to other natural radiation**

> ● **X39.8   Other exposure to forces of nature**

> **Categories X40-X49 deactivated. See categories T36-T65 with fifth or sixth-character 1**

> **Categories X50-X51 deactivated. See category Y93**

● Unacceptable First-Listed Diagnosis   ● Use Additional Character(s)   ■ Unspecified   **OGCR** Official Guidelines for Coding and Reporting
🔧 Complication\Comorbidity   🔧 Major C\C   Excludes 1   Excludes 2   Includes   Use additional   Code first   Code also

CHAPTER 20 (V01-Y99)

ACCIDENTAL EXPOSURE TO OTHER SPECIFIED FACTORS (X52, X58)

● X52   **Prolonged stay in weightless environment**

     Includes   weightlessness in spacecraft (simulator)

     The appropriate 7th character is to be added to code X52

A	initial encounter
D	subsequent encounter
S	sequela

Category X53   deactivated. See subcategory T73.0

Category X54   deactivated. See subcategory T73.1

Category X57   deactivated. See subcategory T73.9

● X58   **Exposure to other specified factors**

     Includes   accident NOS exposure NOS

     The appropriate 7th character is to be added to code X58

A	initial encounter
D	subsequent encounter
S	sequela

INTENTIONAL SELF-HARM (X71-X83)

     Includes   purposely self-inflicted injury suicide (attempted)

Categories X60-X69   deactivated. See categories T36-T65 with fifth or sixth-character 2

Category X70   deactivated. See category T71

● X71   **Intentional self-harm by drowning and submersion**

     The appropriate 7th character is to be added to each code from category X71

A	initial encounter
D	subsequent encounter
S	sequela

● X71.0   **Intentional self-harm by drowning and submersion while in bathtub**

● X71.1   **Intentional self-harm by drowning and submersion while in swimming pool**

● X71.2   **Intentional self-harm by drowning and submersion after jump into swimming pool**

● X71.3   **Intentional self-harm by drowning and submersion in natural water**

● X71.8   **Other intentional self-harm by drowning and submersion**

● ■ X71.9   **Intentional self-harm by drowning and submersion, unspecified**

● X72   **Intentional self-harm by handgun discharge**

     Includes   intentional self-harm by gun for single hand use
           intentional self-harm by pistol
           intentional self-harm by revolver

     Excludes1   Very pistol (X74.8)

     The appropriate 7th character is to be added to code X72

A	initial encounter
D	subsequent encounter
S	sequela

● X73   **Intentional self-harm by rifle, shotgun and larger firearm discharge**

     Excludes1   airgun (X74.01)

     The appropriate 7th character is to be added to each code from category X73

A	initial encounter
D	subsequent encounter
S	sequela

● X73.0   **Intentional self-harm by shotgun discharge**

● X73.1   **Intentional self-harm by hunting rifle discharge**

● X73.2   **Intentional self-harm by machine gun discharge**

● X73.8   **Intentional self-harm by other larger firearm discharge**

● ■ X73.9   **Intentional self-harm by unspecified larger firearm discharge**

● X74   **Intentional self-harm by other and unspecified firearm and gun discharge**

     The appropriate 7th character is to be added to each code from category X74

A	initial encounter
D	subsequent encounter
S	sequela

● X74.0   **Intentional self-harm by gas, air or spring-operated guns**

● X74.01   **Intentional self-harm by airgun**
           Intentional self-harm by BB gun discharge
           Intentional self-harm by pellet gun discharge

● X74.02   **Intentional self-harm by paintball gun**

● ■ X74.09   **Intentional self-harm by other gas, air or spring-operated gun**

● X74.8   **Intentional self-harm by other firearm discharge**
           Intentional self-harm by Very pistol [flare] discharge

● X74.9   **Intentional self-harm by unspecified firearm discharge**

● X75   **Intentional self-harm by explosive material**

     The appropriate 7th character is to be added to code X75

A	initial encounter
D	subsequent encounter
S	sequela

● X76   **Intentional self-harm by smoke, fire and flames**

     The appropriate 7th character is to be added to code X76

A	initial encounter
D	subsequent encounter
S	sequela

● X77   **Intentional self-harm by steam, hot vapors and hot objects**

     The appropriate 7th character is to be added to each code from category X77

A	initial encounter
D	subsequent encounter
S	sequela

● X77.0   **Intentional self-harm by steam or hot vapors**

● X77.1   **Intentional self-harm by hot tap water**

● X77.2   **Intentional self-harm by other hot fluids**

● X77.3   **Intentional self-harm by hot household appliances**

● X77.8   **Intentional self-harm by other hot objects**

● ■ X77.9   **Intentional self-harm by unspecified hot objects**

● Unacceptable First-Listed Diagnosis   ● Use Additional Character(s)   ■ Unspecified   **OGCR** Official Guidelines for Coding and Reporting

🔹 Complication\Comorbidity   🔹 Major C\C   Excludes 1   Excludes 2   Includes   Use additional   Code first   Code also   1685

CHAPTER 20 (V01-Y99)

● **X78**   **Intentional self-harm by sharp object**
        The appropriate 7th character is to be added to each code from category X78

A	initial encounter
D	subsequent encounter
S	sequela

   ● **X78.0**   Intentional self-harm by sharp glass

   ● **X78.1**   Intentional self-harm by knife

   ● **X78.2**   Intentional self-harm by sword or dagger

   ● **X78.8**   Intentional self-harm by other sharp object

   ● ■ **X78.9**   Intentional self-harm by unspecified sharp object

● **X79**   **Intentional self-harm by blunt object**
        The appropriate 7th character is to be added to code X79

A	initial encounter
D	subsequent encounter
S	sequela

● **X80**   **Intentional self-harm by jumping from a high place**

     Includes   intentional fall from one level to another

        The appropriate 7th character is to be added to code X80

A	initial encounter
D	subsequent encounter
S	sequela

● **X81**   **Intentional self-harm by jumping or lying in front of moving object**
        The appropriate 7th character is to be added to each code from category X81

A	initial encounter
D	subsequent encounter
S	sequela

   ● **X81.0**   Intentional self-harm by jumping or lying in front of motor vehicle

   ● **X81.1**   Intentional self-harm by jumping or lying in front of (subway) train

   ● **X81.8**   Intentional self-harm by jumping or lying in front of other moving object

● **X82**   **Intentional self-harm by crashing of motor vehicle**
        The appropriate 7th character is to be added to each code from category X82

A	initial encounter
D	subsequent encounter
S	sequela

   ● **X82.0**   Intentional collision of motor vehicle with other motor vehicle

   ● **X82.1**   Intentional collision of motor vehicle with train

   ● **X82.2**   Intentional collision of motor vehicle with tree

   ● **X82.8**   Other intentional self-harm by crashing of motor vehicle

● **X83**   **Intentional self-harm by other specified means**

     Excludes1   intentional self-harm by poisoning or contact with toxic substance - see Table of Drugs and Chemicals

        The appropriate 7th character is to be added to each code from category X83

A	initial encounter
D	subsequent encounter
S	sequela

   ● **X83.0**   Intentional self-harm by crashing of aircraft

   ● **X83.1**   Intentional self-harm by electrocution

   ● **X83.2**   Intentional self-harm by exposure to extremes of cold

   ● **X83.8**   Intentional self-harm by other specified means

Category X84   deactivated. See category T14

ASSAULT (X92-Y08)

     Includes   homicide injuries inflicted by another person with intent to injure or kill, by any means

     Excludes1   injuries due to legal intervention (Y35.-)
                    injuries due to operations of war (Y36.-)
                    injuries due to terrorism (Y38.-)

Categories X85-X90 deactivated. See categories T36-T65 with fifth or sixth-character 3

Category X91 deactivated. See category T71

● **X92**   **Assault by drowning and submersion**
        The appropriate 7th character is to be added to each code from category X92

A	initial encounter
D	subsequent encounter
S	sequela

   ● **X92.0**   Assault by drowning and submersion while in bathtub

   ● **X92.1**   Assault by drowning and submersion while in swimming pool

   ● **X92.2**   Assault by drowning and submersion after push into swimming pool

   ● **X92.3**   Assault by drowning and submersion in natural water

   ● **X92.8**   Other assault by drowning and submersion

   ● ■ **X92.9**   Assault by drowning and submersion, unspecified

● **X93**   **Assault by handgun discharge**

     Includes   assault by discharge of gun for single hand use
                   assault by discharge of pistol
                   assault by discharge of revolver

     Excludes1   Very pistol (X95.8)

        The appropriate 7th character is to be added to code X93

A	initial encounter
D	subsequent encounter
S	sequela

● **X94**   **Assault by rifle, shotgun and larger firearm discharge**

     Excludes1   airgun (X95.01)

        The appropriate 7th character is to be added to each code from category X94

A	initial encounter
D	subsequent encounter
S	sequela

   ● **X94.0**   Assault by shotgun

   ● **X94.1**   Assault by hunting rifle

   ● **X94.2**   Assault by machine gun

   ● **X94.8**   Assault by other larger firearm discharge

   ● ■ **X94.9**   Assault by unspecified larger firearm discharge

● **X95**   **Assault by other and unspecified firearm and gun discharge**
        The appropriate 7th character is to be added to each code from category X95

A	initial encounter
D	subsequent encounter
S	sequela

●   Unacceptable First-Listed Diagnosis   ●   Use Additional Character(s)   ■   Unspecified   **OGCR**   Official Guidelines for Coding and Reporting

🍃 Complication\Comorbidity   🍃 Major C\C         Includes   Use additional   Code first   Code also

● **X95.0 Assault by gas, air or spring-operated guns**

   ● **X95.01 Assault by airgun discharge**
        Assault by BB gun discharge
        Assault by pellet gun discharge

   ● **X95.02 Assault by paintball gun discharge**

   ● **X95.09 Assault by other gas, air or spring-operated bun**

  ● **X95.8 Assault by other firearm discharge**
       Assault by very pistol [flare] discharge

● ■ **X95.9 Assault by unspecified firearm discharge**

● **X96 Assault by explosive material**

> **Excludes1**   incendiary device (X97)
>   terrorism involving explosive material (Y38.2-)

The appropriate 7th character is to be added to each code from category X96

A	initial encounter
D	subsequent encounter
S	sequela

  ● **X96.0 Assault by antipersonnel bomb**

> **Excludes1**   antipersonnel bomb use in military or war (Y36.2--)

  ● **X96.1 Assault by gasoline bomb**

  ● **X96.2 Assault by letter bomb**

  ● **X96.3 Assault by fertilizer bomb**

  ● **X96.4 Assault by pipe bomb**

  ● **X96.8 Assault by other specified explosive**

● ■ **X96.9 Assault by unspecified explosive**

● **X97 Assault by smoke, fire and flames**

> **Includes**   assault by arson
>   assault by cigarettes
>   assault by incendiary device

The appropriate 7th character is to be added to code X97

A	initial encounter
D	subsequent encounter
S	sequela

● **X98 Assault by steam, hot vapors and hot objects**
The appropriate 7th character is to be added to each code from category X98

A	initial encounter
D	subsequent encounter
S	sequela

  ● **X98.0 Assault by steam or hot vapors**

  ● **X98.1 Assault by hot tap water**

  ● **X98.2 Assault by hot fluids**

  ● **X98.3 Assault by hot household appliances**

  ● **X98.8 Assault by other hot objects**

● ■ **X98.9 Assault by unspecified hot objects**

● **X99 Assault by sharp object**

> **Excludes1**   assault by strike by sports equipment (Y08.0)

The appropriate 7th character is to be added to each code from category X99

A	initial encounter
D	subsequent encounter
S	sequela

  ● **X99.0 Assault by sharp glass**

  ● **X99.1 Assault by knife**

  ● **X99.2 Assault by sword or dagger**

  ● **X99.8 Assault by other sharp object**

● ■ **X99.9 Assault by unspecified sharp object**
       Assault by stabbing NOS

● **Y00 Assault by blunt object**

> **Excludes1**   assault by strike by sports equipment (Y08.0)

The appropriate 7th character is to be added to code Y00

A	initial encounter
D	subsequent encounter
S	sequela

● **Y01 Assault by pushing from high place**
The appropriate 7th character is to be added to code Y01

A	initial encounter
D	subsequent encounter
S	sequela

● **Y02 Assault by pushing or placing victim in front of moving object**
The appropriate 7th character is to be added to each code from category Y02

A	initial encounter
D	subsequent encounter
S	sequela

  ● **Y02.0 Assault by pushing or placing victim in front of motor vehicle**

  ● **Y02.1 Assault by pushing or placing victim in front of (subway) train**

  ● **Y02.8 Assault by pushing or placing victim in front of other moving object**

● **Y03 Assault by crashing of motor vehicle**
The appropriate 7th character is to be added to each code from category Y03

A	initial encounter
D	subsequent encounter
S	sequela

  ● **Y03.0 Assault by being hit or run over by motor vehicle**

  ● **Y03.8 Other assault by crashing of motor vehicle**

● **Y04 Assault by bodily force**

> **Excludes1**   assault by:
>   submersion (X92.-)
>   use of weapon (X93-X95, X99, Y00)

The appropriate 7th character is to be added to each code from category Y04

A	initial encounter
D	subsequent encounter
S	sequela

  ● **Y04.0 Assault by unarmed brawl or fight**

  ● **Y04.1 Assault by human bite**

  ● **Y04.2 Assault by strike against or bumped into by another person**

  ● **Y04.8 Assault by other bodily force**
       Assault by bodily force NOS

Category Y05 deactivated. See subcategories T74.0, T76.0

Category Y06 deactivated. See subcategories T74.0, T76.0

● Unacceptable First-Listed Diagnosis	● Use Additional Character(s) ■ Unspecified **OGCR** Official Guidelines for Coding and Reporting
⚕ Complication\Comorbidity ⚕ Major C\C Excludes 1 Excludes 2	Includes Use additional Code first Code also

CHAPTER 20 (V01-Y99)

1687

OGCR Section I.C.19.f.

Adult and child abuse, neglect and other maltreatment
Sequence first the appropriate code from categories T74.- or
T76.- for abuse, neglect and other maltreatment, followed by
any accompanying mental health or injury code(s).

If the documentation in the medical record states abuse or
neglect it is coded as confirmed. It is coded as suspected if it is
documented as suspected.

For cases of confirmed abuse or neglect an external cause code
from the assault section (X92-Y08) should be added to identify
the cause of any physical injuries. A perpetrator code (Y07)
should be added when the perpetrator of the abuse is known.
For suspected cases of abuse or neglect, do not report external
cause or perpetrator code.

If a suspected case of abuse, neglect or mistreatment is ruled
out during an encounter code Z04.71, Suspected adult physical
and sexual abuse, ruled out, or code Z04.72, Suspected child
physical and sexual abuse, ruled out, should be used, not a
code from T76.

● Y07   Perpetrator of assault, maltreatment and neglect
         Codes from this category are for use only in cases of
            confirmed abuse (T74.-)
         Selection of the correct perpetrator code is based on the
            relationship between the perpetrator and the victim

         Includes   perpetrator of abandonment
                         perpetrator of emotional neglect
                         perpetrator of mental cruelty
                         perpetrator of physical abuse
                         perpetrator of physical neglect
                         perpetrator of sexual abuse
                         perpetrator of torture

   ● Y07.0   Spouse or partner as perpetrator of maltreatment
             and neglect
               Spouse or partner as perpetrator of maltreatment
                 and neglect against spouse or partner
         Y07.01   Husband as perpetrator of maltreatment
                  and neglect
         Y07.02   Wife as perpetrator of maltreatment and
                  neglect
         Y07.03   Male partner as perpetrator of
                  maltreatment and neglect
         Y07.04   Female partner as perpetrator of
                  maltreatment and neglect

   ● Y07.1   Parent (adoptive) (biological) as perpetrator of
             maltreatment and neglect
         Y07.11   Biological father as perpetrator of
                  maltreatment and neglect
         Y07.12   Biological mother as perpetrator of
                  maltreatment and neglect
         Y07.13   Adoptive father as perpetrator of
                  maltreatment and neglect
         Y07.14   Adoptive mother as perpetrator of
                  maltreatment and neglect

   ● Y07.4   Other family member as perpetrator of
             maltreatment and neglect
      ● Y07.41   Sibling
            Y07.410   Brother as perpetrator of
                      maltreatment and neglect
            Y07.411   Sister as perpetrator of
                      maltreatment and neglect
      ● Y07.42   Foster parent
            Y07.420   Foster father as perpetrator of
                      maltreatment and neglect
            Y07.421   Foster mother as perpetrator of
                      maltreatment and neglect

   ● Y07.43   Stepparent or stepsibling as perpetrator of
             maltreatment and neglect
         Y07.430   Stepfather as perpetrator of
                   maltreatment and neglect
         Y07.432   Male friend of parent (co-
                   residing in household) as
                   perpetrator of maltreatment and
                   neglect
         Y07.433   Stepmother as perpetrator of
                   maltreatment and neglect
         Y07.434   Female friend of parent (co-
                   residing in household) as
                   perpetrator of maltreatment and
                   neglect
         Y07.435   Stepbrother as perpetrator or
                   maltreatment and neglect
         Y07.436   Stepsister as perpetrator of
                   maltreatment and neglect

   ● Y07.49   Other family member
         Y07.490   Male cousin as perpetrator of
                   maltreatment and neglect
         Y07.491   Female cousin as perpetrator of
                   maltreatment and neglect
         Y07.499   Other family member as
                   perpetrator of maltreatment and
                   neglect

   ● Y07.5   Non-family member
      ■ Y07.50   Unspecified non-family member as
                 perpetrator of maltreatment and neglect
      ● Y07.51   Daycare provider
            Y07.510   At-home childcare provider as
                      perpetrator of maltreatment and
                      neglect
            Y07.511   Daycare center childcare provider
                      as perpetrator of maltreatment
                      and neglect
            Y07.512   At-home adultcare provider as
                      perpetrator of maltreatment and
                      neglect
            Y07.513   Adultcare center provider as
                      perpetrator of maltreatment and
                      neglect
         ■ Y07.519   Unspecified daycare provider as
                      perpetrator of maltreatment and
                      neglect
      ● Y07.52   Healthcare provider
            Y07.521   Mental health provider as
                      perpetrator of maltreatment and
                      neglect
            Y07.528   Other therapist or healthcare
                      provider as perpetrator of
                      maltreatment and neglect
                        Nurse
                        Occupational therapist
                        Physical therapist
                        Speech therapist
         ■ Y07.529   Unspecified healthcare provider
                      as perpetrator of maltreatment
                      and neglect
         Y07.53   Teacher or instructor as perpetrator of
                  maltreatment and neglect
                    Coach as perpetrator of maltreatment and
                      neglect
         Y07.59   Other non-family member as perpetrator
                  of maltreatment and neglect

● Unacceptable First-Listed Diagnosis   ● Use Additional Character(s)   ■ Unspecified   OGCR Official Guidelines for Coding and Reporting
🔖 Complication\Comorbidity   🔖 Major C\C   [Excludes 1]   [Excludes 2]   Includes   Use additional   Code first   Code also

● **Y08   Assault by other specified means**
      The appropriate 7th character is to be added to each code
         from category Y08

A	initial encounter
D	subsequent encounter
S	sequela

   ● **Y08.0   Assault by strike by sport equipment**

      ● **Y08.01   Assault by strike by hockey stick**

      ● **Y08.02   Assault by strike by baseball bat**

      ● **Y08.09   Assault by strike other sport equipment**

   ● **Y08.8   Assault by other specified means**

      ● **Y08.81   Assault by crashing of aircraft**

      ● **Y08.89   Assault by other specified means**

EVENT OF UNDETERMINED INTENT (Y20-Y33)

Undetermined intent is only for use when there is
   specific documentation in the record that the
   intent of the injury cannot be determined. If no
   such documentation is present, code to accidental
   (unintentional)

Categories Y10-Y19 deactivated. See codes T36-T65 with fifth
   or sixth-character 4

Category Y20 deactivated. See category T71

● **Y21   Drowning and submersion, undetermined intent**
      The appropriate 7th character is to be added to each code
         from category Y21

A	initial encounter
D	subsequent encounter
S	sequela

   ● **Y21.0   Drowning and submersion while in bathtub,
            undetermined intent**

   ● **Y21.1   Drowning and submersion after fall into bathtub,
            undetermined intent**

   ● **Y21.2   Drowning and submersion while in swimming
            pool, undetermined intent**

   ● **Y21.3   Drowning and submersion after fall into
            swimming pool, undetermined intent**

   ● **Y21.4   Drowning and submersion in natural water,
            undetermined intent**

   ● **Y21.8   Other drowning and submersion, undetermined
            intent**

   ● ■ **Y21.9   Unspecified drowning and submersion,
            undetermined intent**

● **Y22   Handgun discharge, undetermined intent**

      | **Includes** | discharge of gun for single hand use,
         undetermined intent discharge of
         pistol, undetermined intent discharge
         of revolver, undetermined intent |
      |---|---|

Excludes:	Very pistol (Y24.8)

      The appropriate 7th character is to be added to code Y22

A	initial encounter
D	subsequent encounter
S	sequela

● **Y23   Rifle, shotgun and larger firearm discharge, undetermined
         intent**

Excludes:	airgun (Y24.0)

      The appropriate 7th character is to be added to each code
         from category Y23

A	initial encounter
D	subsequent encounter
S	sequela

● **Y23.0   Shotgun discharge, undetermined intent**

● **Y23.1   Hunting rifle discharge, undetermined intent**

● **Y23.2   Military firearm discharge, undetermined intent**

● **Y23.3   Machine gun discharge, undetermined intent**

● **Y23.8   Other larger firearm discharge, undetermined
         intent**

● ■ **Y23.9   Unspecified larger firearm discharge,
         undetermined intent**

● **Y24   Other and unspecified firearm discharge, undetermined
         intent**
      The appropriate 7th character is to be added to each code
         from category Y24

A	initial encounter
D	subsequent encounter
S	sequela

   ● **Y24.0   Airgun discharge, undetermined intent**
            BB gun discharge, undetermined intent
            Pellet gun discharge, undetermined intent

   ● **Y24.8   Other firearm discharge, undetermined intent**
            Paintball gun discharge, undetermined intent
            Very pistol [flare] discharge, undetermined intent

   ● ■ **Y24.9   Unspecified firearm discharge, undetermined
            intent**

● **Y25   Contact with explosive material, undetermined intent**
      The appropriate 7th character is to be added to code Y25

A	initial encounter
D	subsequent encounter
S	sequela

● **Y26   Exposure to smoke, fire and flames, undetermined intent**
      The appropriate 7th character is to be added to code Y26

A	initial encounter
D	subsequent encounter
S	sequela

● **Y27   Contact with steam, hot vapors and hot objects,
         undetermined intent**
      The appropriate 7th character is to be added to each code
         from category Y27

A	initial encounter
D	subsequent encounter
S	sequela

   ● **Y27.0   Contact with steam and hot vapors, undetermined
            intent**

   ● **Y27.1   Contact with hot tap water, undetermined intent**

   ● **Y27.2   Contact with hot fluids, undetermined intent**

   ● **Y27.3   Contact with hot household appliance,
            undetermined intent**

   ● **Y27.8   Contact with other hot objects, undetermined
            intent**

   ● ■ **Y27.9   Contact with unspecified hot objects,
            undetermined intent**

● **Y28   Contact with sharp object, undetermined intent**
      The appropriate 7th character is to be added to each code
         from category Y28

A	initial encounter
D	subsequent encounter
S	sequela

   ● **Y28.0   Contact with sharp glass, undetermined intent**

   ● **Y28.1   Contact with knife, undetermined intent**

   ● **Y28.2   Contact with sword or dagger, undetermined intent**

   ● **Y28.8   Contact with other sharp object, undetermined intent**

   ● ■ **Y28.9   Contact with unspecified sharp object,
            undetermined intent**

● Unacceptable First-Listed Diagnosis   ● Use Additional Character(s)   ■ Unspecified   **OGCR** Official Guidelines for Coding and Reporting

🔾 Complication\Comorbidity   🔾 Major C\C   Excludes 1   Excludes 2   Includes   Use additional   Code first   Code also

1689

CHAPTER 20 (V01-Y99)

● **Y29**   **Contact with blunt object, undetermined intent**
The appropriate 7th character is to be added to code Y29

A	initial encounter
D	subsequent encounter
S	sequela

● **Y30**   **Falling, jumping or pushed from a high place, undetermined intent**

Includes   victim falling from one level to another, undetermined intent

The appropriate 7th character is to be added to code Y30

A	initial encounter
D	subsequent encounter
S	sequela

● **Y31**   **Falling, lying or running before or into moving object, undetermined intent**
The appropriate 7th character is to be added to code Y31

A	initial encounter
D	subsequent encounter
S	sequela

● **Y32**   **Crashing of motor vehicle, undetermined intent**
The appropriate 7th character is to be added to code Y32

A	initial encounter
D	subsequent encounter
S	sequela

● **Y33**   **Other specified events, undetermined intent**
The appropriate 7th character is to be added to code Y33

A	initial encounter
D	subsequent encounter
S	sequela

LEGAL INTERVENTION, OPERATIONS OF WAR, MILITARY OPERATIONS, AND TERRORISM (Y35-Y38)

● **Y35**   **Legal intervention**

Includes   any injury sustained as a result of an encounter with any law enforcement official, serving in any capacity at the time of the encounter, whether on-duty or off-duty. Includes injury to law enforcement official, suspect and bystander

The appropriate 7th character is to be added to each code from category Y35

A	initial encounter
D	subsequent encounter
S	sequela

● **Y35.0**   **Legal intervention involving firearm discharge**

● **Y35.00**   **Legal intervention involving unspecified firearm discharge**
Legal intervention involving gunshot wound
Legal intervention involving shot NOS

● ■ **Y35.001**   **Legal intervention involving unspecified firearm discharge, law enforcement official injured**

● ■ **Y35.002**   **Legal intervention involving unspecified firearm discharge, bystander injured**

● ■ **Y35.003**   **Legal intervention involving unspecified firearm discharge, suspect injured**

● **Y35.01**   **Legal intervention involving injury by machine gun**

● **Y35.011**   **Legal intervention involving injury by machine gun, law enforcement official injured**

● **Y35.012**   **Legal intervention involving injury by machine gun, bystander injured**

● **Y35.013**   **Legal intervention involving injury by machine gun, suspect injured**

● **Y35.02**   **Legal intervention involving injury by handgun**

● **Y35.021**   **Legal intervention involving injury by handgun, law enforcement official injured**

● **Y35.022**   **Legal intervention involving injury by handgun, bystander injured**

● **Y35.023**   **Legal intervention involving injury by handgun, suspect injured**

● **Y35.03**   **Legal intervention involving injury by rifle pellet**

● **Y35.031**   **Legal intervention involving injury by rifle pellet, law enforcement official injured**

● **Y35.032**   **Legal intervention involving injury by rifle pellet, bystander injured**

● **Y35.033**   **Legal intervention involving injury by rifle pellet, suspect injured**

● **Y35.04**   **Legal intervention involving injury by rubber bullet**

● **Y35.041**   **Legal intervention involving injury by rubber bullet, law enforcement official injured**

● **Y35.042**   **Legal intervention involving injury by rubber bullet, bystander injured**

● **Y35.043**   **Legal intervention involving injury by rubber bullet, suspect injured**

● **Y35.09**   **Legal intervention involving other firearm discharge**

● **Y35.091**   **Legal intervention involving other firearm discharge, law enforcement official injured**

● **Y35.092**   **Legal intervention involving other firearm discharge, bystander injured**

● **Y35.093**   **Legal intervention involving other firearm discharge, suspect injured**

● **Y35.1**   **Legal intervention involving explosives**

● **Y35.10**   **Legal intervention involving unspecified explosives**

● ■ **Y35.101**   **Legal intervention involving unspecified explosives, law enforcement official injured**

● ■ **Y35.102**   **Legal intervention involving unspecified explosives, bystander injured**

● ■ **Y35.103**   **Legal intervention involving unspecified explosives, suspect injured**

● **Y35.11**   **Legal intervention involving injury by dynamite**

● **Y35.111**   **Legal intervention involving injury by dynamite, law enforcement official injured**

● Unacceptable First-Listed Diagnosis   ● Use Additional Character(s)   ■ Unspecified   **OGCR** Official Guidelines for Coding and Reporting
🅒 Complication\Comorbidity   🅜 Major C\C   Excludes 1   Excludes 2   Includes   Use additional   Code first   Code also

● Y35.112   Legal intervention involving injury by dynamite, bystander injured

● Y35.113   Legal intervention involving injury by dynamite, suspect injured

● Y35.12   Legal intervention involving injury by explosive shell

● Y35.121   Legal intervention involving injury by explosive shell, law enforcement official injured

● Y35.122   Legal intervention involving injury by explosive shell, bystander injured

● Y35.123   Legal intervention involving injury by explosive shell, suspect injured

● Y35.19   Legal intervention involving other explosives
Legal intervention involving injury by grenade
Legal intervention involving injury by mortar bomb

● Y35.191   Legal intervention involving other explosives, law enforcement official injured

● Y35.192   Legal intervention involving other explosives, bystander injured

● Y35.193   Legal intervention involving other explosives, suspect injured

● Y35.2   Legal intervention involving gas
Legal intervention involving asphyxiation by gas
Legal intervention involving poisoning by gas

● Y35.20   Legal intervention involving unspecified gas

● ■ Y35.201   Legal intervention involving unspecified gas, law enforcement official injured

● ■ Y35.202   Legal intervention involving unspecified gas, bystander injured

● ■ Y35.203   Legal intervention involving unspecified gas, suspect injured

● Y35.21   Legal intervention involving injury by tear gas

● Y35.211   Legal intervention involving injury by tear gas, law enforcement official injured

● Y35.212   Legal intervention involving injury by tear gas, bystander injured

● Y35.213   Legal intervention involving injury by tear gas, suspect injured

● Y35.29   Legal intervention involving other gas

● Y35.291   Legal intervention involving other gas, law enforcement official injured

● Y35.292   Legal intervention involving other gas, bystander injured

● Y35.293   Legal intervention involving other gas, suspect injured

● Y35.3   Legal intervention involving blunt objects
Legal intervention involving being hit or struck by blunt object

● Y35.30   Legal intervention involving unspecified blunt objects

● ■ Y35.301   Legal intervention involving unspecified blunt objects, law enforcement official injured

● ■ Y35.302   Legal intervention involving unspecified blunt objects, bystander injured

● ■ Y35.303   Legal intervention involving unspecified blunt objects, suspect injured

● Y35.31   Legal intervention involving baton

● Y35.311   Legal intervention involving baton, law enforcement official injured

● Y35.312   Legal intervention involving baton, bystander injured

● Y35.313   Legal intervention involving baton, suspect injured

● Y35.39   Legal intervention involving other blunt objects

● Y35.391   Legal intervention involving other blunt objects, law enforcement official injured

● Y35.392   Legal intervention involving other blunt objects, bystander injured

● Y35.393   Legal intervention involving other blunt objects, suspect injured

● Y35.4   Legal intervention involving sharp objects
Legal intervention involving being cut by sharp objects
Legal intervention involving being stabbed by sharp objects

● Y35.40   Legal intervention involving unspecified sharp objects

● ■ Y35.401   Legal intervention involving unspecified sharp objects, law enforcement official injured

● ■ Y35.402   Legal intervention involving unspecified sharp objects, bystander injured

● ■ Y35.403   Legal intervention involving unspecified sharp objects, suspect injured

● Y35.41   Legal intervention involving bayonet

● Y35.411   Legal intervention involving bayonet, law enforcement official injured

● Y35.412   Legal intervention involving bayonet, bystander injured

● Y35.413   Legal intervention involving bayonet, suspect injured

● Y35.49   Legal intervention involving other sharp objects

● Y35.491   Legal intervention involving other sharp objects, law enforcement official injured

● Y35.492   Legal intervention involving other sharp objects, bystander injured

● Y35.493   Legal intervention involving other sharp objects, suspect injured

● Unacceptable First-Listed Diagnosis   ● Use Additional Character(s)   ■ Unspecified   **OGCR** Official Guidelines for Coding and Reporting

🅒 Complication\Comorbidity   🅒 Major C\C   Excludes 1   Excludes 2   Includes   Use additional   Code first   Code also   1691

● Y35.8   Legal intervention involving other specified means

   ● Y35.81   Legal intervention involving manhandling

      ● Y35.811   Legal intervention involving manhandling, law enforcement official injured

      ● Y35.812   Legal intervention involving manhandling, bystander injured

      ● Y35.813   Legal intervention involving manhandling, suspect injured

   ● Y35.89   Legal intervention involving other specified means

      ● Y35.891   Legal intervention involving other specified means, law enforcement official injured

      ● Y35.892   Legal intervention involving other specified means, bystander injured

      ● Y35.893   Legal intervention involving other specified means, suspect injured

● Y35.9   Legal intervention, means unspecified

   ● ▪ Y35.91   Legal intervention, means unspecified, law enforcement official injured

   ● ▪ Y35.92   Legal intervention, means unspecified, bystander injured

   ● ▪ Y35.93   Legal intervention, means unspecified, suspect injured

● Y36   Operations of war

> **Includes**   injuries to military personnel and civilians caused by war, civil insurrection, and peacekeeping missions

> **Excludes1**   injury to military personnel occurring during peacetime military operations (Y37.-)
> military vehicles involved in transport accidents with non-military vehicle during peacetime (V09.01, V09.21, V19.81, V29.81, V39.81, V49.81, V59.81, V69.81, V79.81)

The appropriate 7th character is to be added to each code from category Y36

> A   initial encounter
> D   subsequent encounter
> S   sequela

● Y36.0   War operations involving explosion of marine weapons
         Weapons and military watercraft

   ● Y36.00   War operations involving explosion of unspecified marine weapons
           War operations involving underwater blast NOS

      ● ▪ Y36.000   War operations involving explosion of unspecified marine weapon, military personnel

      ● ▪ Y36.001   War operations involving explosion of unspecified marine weapon, civilian

● Y36.01   War operations involving explosion of depth-charge

   ● Y36.010   War operations involving explosion of depth-charge, military personnel

   ● Y36.011   War operations involving explosion of depth-charge, civilian

● Y36.02   War operations involving explosion of marine mine
         War operations involving explosion of marine mine, at sea or in harbor

   ● Y36.020   War operations involving explosion of marine mine, military personnel

   ● Y36.021   War operations involving explosion of marine mine, civilian

● Y36.03   War operations involving explosion of sea-based artillery shell

   ● Y36.030   War operations involving explosion of sea-based artillery shell, military personnel

   ● Y36.031   War operations involving explosion of sea-based artillery shell, civilian

● Y36.04   War operations involving explosion of torpedo

   ● Y36.040   War operations involving explosion of torpedo, military personnel

   ● Y36.041   War operations involving explosion of torpedo, civilian

● Y36.05   War operations involving accidental detonation of onboard marine weapons

   ● Y36.050   War operations involving accidental detonation of onboard marine weapons, military personnel

   ● Y36.051   War operations involving accidental detonation of onboard marine weapons, civilian

● Y36.09   War operations involving explosion of other marine weapons

   ● Y36.090   War operations involving explosion of other marine weapons, military personnel

   ● Y36.091   War operations involving explosion of other marine weapons, civilian

● Y36.1   War operations involving destruction of aircraft

   ● ▪ Y36.10   War operations involving unspecified destruction of aircraft

      ● ▪ Y36.100   War operations involving unspecified destruction of aircraft, military personnel

      ● ▪ Y36.101   War operations involving unspecified destruction of aircraft, civilian

- **Y36.11   War operations involving destruction of aircraft due to enemy fire or explosives**
    - War operations involving destruction of aircraft due to air to air missile
    - War operations involving destruction of aircraft due to explosive placed on aircraft
    - War operations involving destruction of aircraft due to rocket propelled grenade [RPG]
    - War operations involving destruction of aircraft due to small arms fire
    - War operations involving destruction of aircraft due to surface to air missile
    - **Y36.110   War operations involving destruction of aircraft due to enemy fire or explosives, military personnel**
    - **Y36.111   War operations involving destruction of aircraft due to enemy fire or explosives, civilian**
- **Y36.12   War operations involving destruction of aircraft due to collision with other aircraft**
    - **Y36.120   War operations involving destruction of aircraft due to collision with other aircraft, military personnel**
    - **Y36.121   War operations involving destruction of aircraft due to collision with other aircraft, civilian**
- **Y36.13   War operations involving destruction of aircraft due to onboard fire**
    - **Y36.130   War operations involving destruction of aircraft due to onboard fire, military personnel**
    - **Y36.131   War operations involving destruction of aircraft due to onboard fire, civilian**
- **Y36.14   War operations involving destruction of aircraft due to accidental detonation of onboard munitions and explosives**
    - **Y36.140   War operations involving destruction of aircraft due to accidental detonation of onboard munitions and explosives, military personnel**
    - **Y36.141   War operations involving destruction of aircraft due to accidental detonation of onboard munitions and explosives, civilian**
- **Y36.19   War operations involving other destruction of aircraft**
    - **Y36.190   War operations involving other destruction of aircraft, military personnel**
    - **Y36.191   War operations involving other destruction of aircraft, civilian**

- **Y36.2   War operations involving other explosions and fragments**
    - **Excludes1**   war operations involving explosion of aircraft (Y36.1-)
    - war operations involving explosion of marine weapons (Y36.0-)
    - war operations involving explosion of nuclear weapons (Y36.5-)
    - war operations involving explosion occurring after cessation of hostilities (Y36.8-)
    - **Y36.20   War operations involving unspecified explosion and fragments**
        - War operations involving air blast NOS
        - War operations involving blast NOS
        - War operations involving blast fragments NOS
        - War operations involving blast wave NOS
        - War operations involving blast wind NOS
        - War operations involving explosion NOS
        - War operations involving explosion of bomb NOS
        - **Y36.200   War operations involving unspecified explosion and fragments, military personnel**
        - **Y36.201   War operations involving unspecified explosion and fragments, civilian**
    - **Y36.21   War operations involving explosion of aerial bomb**
        - **Y36.210   War operations involving explosion of aerial bomb, military personnel**
        - **Y36.211   War operations involving explosion of aerial bomb, civilian**
    - **Y36.22   War operations involving explosion of guided missile**
        - **Y36.220   War operations involving explosion of guided missile, military personnel**
        - **Y36.221   War operations involving explosion of guided missile, civilian**
    - **Y36.23   War operations involving explosion of improvised explosive device [IED]**
        - War operations involving explosion of person-borne improvised explosive device [IED]
        - War operations involving explosion of vehicle-borne improvised explosive device [IED]
        - War operations involving explosion of roadside improvised explosive device [IED]
        - **Y36.230   War operations involving explosion of improvised explosive device [IED], military personnel**
        - **Y36.231   War operations involving explosion of improvised explosive device [IED], civilian**

●   Unacceptable First-Listed Diagnosis   ●   Use Additional Character(s)   ▨   Unspecified   **OGCR**   Official Guidelines for Coding and Reporting

🝝 Complication\Comorbidity   🝝 Major C\C   Excludes 1   Excludes 2   Includes   Use additional   Code first   Code also

1693

CHAPTER 20 (V01-Y99)

● Y36.24 War operations involving explosion due to accidental detonation and discharge of own munitions or munitions launch device

  ● Y36.240 War operations involving explosion due to accidental detonation and discharge of own munitions or munitions launch device, military personnel

  ● Y36.241 War operations involving explosion due to accidental detonation and discharge of own munitions or munitions launch device, civilian

● Y36.25 War operations involving fragments from munitions

  ● Y36.250 War operations involving fragments from munitions, military personnel

  ● Y36.251 War operations involving fragments from munitions, civilian

● Y36.26 War operations involving fragments of improvised explosive device [IED]
  War operations involving fragments of person-borne improvised explosive device [IED]
  War operations involving fragments of vehicle-borne improvised explosive device [IED]
  War operations involving fragments of roadside improvised explosive device [IED]

  ● Y36.260 War operations involving fragments of improvised explosive device [IED], military personnel

  ● Y36.261 War operations involving fragments of improvised explosive device [IED], civilian

● Y36.27 War operations involving fragments from weapons

  ● Y36.270 War operations involving fragments from weapons, military personnel

  ● Y36.271 War operations involving fragments from weapons, civilian

● Y36.29 War operations involving other explosions and fragments
  War operations involving explosion of grenade
  War operations involving explosions of land mine
  War operations involving shrapnel NOS

  ● Y36.290 War operations involving other explosions and fragments, military personnel

  ● Y36.291 War operations involving other explosions and fragments, civilian

● Y36.3 War operations involving fires, conflagrations and hot substances
  War operations involving smoke, fumes, and heat from fires, conflagrations and hot substances

  Excludes1 war operations involving fires and conflagrations aboard military aircraft (Y36.1-)
  war operations involving fires and conflagrations aboard military watercraft (Y36.0-)
  war operations involving fires and conflagrations caused indirectly by conventional weapons (Y36.2-)
  war operations involving fires and thermal effects of nuclear weapons (Y36.53-)

● Y36.30 War operations involving unspecified fire, conflagration and hot substance

  ● ▪ Y36.300 War operations involving unspecified fire, conflagration and hot substance, military personnel

  ● ▪ Y36.301 War operations involving unspecified fire, conflagration and hot substance, civilian

● Y36.31 War operations involving gasoline bomb
  War operations involving incendiary bomb
  War operations involving petrol bomb

  ● Y36.310 War operations involving gasoline bomb, military personnel

  ● Y36.311 War operations involving gasoline bomb, civilian

● Y36.32 War operations involving incendiary bullet

  ● Y36.320 War operations involving incendiary bullet, military personnel

  ● Y36.321 War operations involving incendiary bullet, civilian

● Y36.33 War operations involving flamethrower

  ● Y36.330 War operations involving flamethrower, military personnel

  ● Y36.331 War operations involving flamethrower, civilian

● Y36.39 War operations involving other fires, conflagrations and hot substances

  ● Y36.390 War operations involving other fires, conflagrations and hot substances, military personnel

  ● Y36.391 War operations involving other fires, conflagrations and hot substances, civilian

● Unacceptable First-Listed Diagnosis ● Use Additional Character(s) ▪ Unspecified OGCR Official Guidelines for Coding and Reporting
🗗 Complication\Comorbidity 🗗 Major C\C Excludes 1 Excludes 2 Includes Use additional Code first Code also

● **Y36.4 War operations involving firearm discharge and other forms of conventional warfare**

　● **Y36.41 War operations involving rubber bullets**

　　● **Y36.410 War operations involving rubber bullets, military personnel**

　　● **Y36.411 War operations involving rubber bullets, civilian**

　● **Y36.42 War operations involving firearms pellets**

　　● **Y36.420 War operations involving firearms pellets, military personnel**

　　● **Y36.421 War operations involving firearms pellets, civilian**

　● **Y36.43 War operations involving other firearms discharge**
　　　War operations involving bullets NOS

　　　Excludes1　war operations involving munitions fragments (Y36.25-)
　　　　　　war operations involving incendiary bullets (Y36.32-)

　　● **Y36.430 War operations involving other firearms discharge, military personnel**

　　● **Y36.431 War operations involving other firearms discharge, civilian**

　● **Y36.44 War operations involving unarmed hand to hand combat**

　　　Excludes1　war operations involving combat using blunt or piercing object (Y36.45-)
　　　　　　war operations involving intentional restriction of air and airway (Y36.46-)
　　　　　　war operations involving unintentional restriction of air and airway (Y36.47-)

　　● **Y36.440 War operations involving unarmed hand to hand combat, military personnel**

　　● **Y36.441 War operations involving unarmed hand to hand combat, civilian**

　● **Y36.45 War operations involving combat using blunt or piercing object**

　　● **Y36.450 War operations involving combat using blunt or piercing object, military personnel**

　　● **Y36.451 War operations involving combat using blunt or piercing object, civilian**

　● **Y36.46 War operations involving intentional restriction of air and airway**

　　● **Y36.460 War operations involving intentional restriction of air and airway, military personnel**

　　● **Y36.461 War operations involving intentional restriction of air and airway, civilian**

● **Y36.47 War operations involving unintentional restriction of air and airway**

　● **Y36.470 War operations involving unintentional restriction of air and airway, military personnel**

　● **Y36.471 War operations involving unintentional restriction of air and airway, civilian**

● **Y36.49 War operations involving other forms of conventional warfare**

　● **Y36.490 War operations involving other forms of conventional warfare, military personnel**

　● **Y36.491 War operations involving other forms of conventional warfare, civilian**

● **Y36.5 War operations involving nuclear weapons**
　　War operations involving dirty bomb NOS

　● **Y36.50 War operations involving unspecified effect of nuclear weapon**

　　● ■ **Y36.500 War operations involving unspecified effect of nuclear weapon, military personnel**

　　● ■ **Y36.501 War operations involving unspecified effect of nuclear weapon, civilian**

　● **Y36.51 War operations involving direct blast effect of nuclear weapon**
　　　War operations involving blast pressure of nuclear weapon

　　● **Y36.510 War operations involving direct blast effect of nuclear weapon, military personnel**

　　● **Y36.511 War operations involving direct blast effect of nuclear weapon, civilian**

　● **Y36.52 War operations involving indirect blast effect of nuclear weapon**
　　　War operations involving being thrown by blast of nuclear weapon
　　　War operations involving being struck or crushed by blast debris of nuclear weapon

　　● **Y36.520 War operations involving indirect blast effect of nuclear weapon, military personnel**

　　● **Y36.521 War operations involving indirect blast effect of nuclear weapon, civilian**

　● **Y36.53 War operations involving thermal radiation effect of nuclear weapon**
　　　War operations involving direct heat from nuclear weapon
　　　War operation involving fireball effects from nuclear weapon

　　● **Y36.530 War operations involving thermal radiation effect of nuclear weapon, military personnel**

　　● **Y36.531 War operations involving thermal radiation effect of nuclear weapon, civilian**

● Unacceptable First-Listed Diagnosis　　● Use Additional Character(s)　　■ Unspecified　　**OGCR** Official Guidelines for Coding and Reporting

🍏 Complication\Comorbidity　🍏 Major C\C　Excludes 1　Excludes 2　Includes　Use additional　Code first　Code also

1695

CHAPTER 20 (V01-Y99)

● **Y36.54 War operation involving nuclear radiation effects of nuclear weapon**
War operation involving acute radiation exposure from nuclear weapon
War operation involving exposure to immediate ionizing radiation from nuclear weapon
War operation involving fallout exposure from nuclear weapon
War operation involving secondary effects of nuclear weapons

   ● **Y36.540 War operation involving nuclear radiation effects of nuclear weapon, military personnel**

   ● **Y36.541 War operation involving nuclear radiation effects of nuclear weapon, civilian**

● **Y36.59 War operation involving other effects of nuclear weapons**

   ● **Y36.590 War operation involving other effects of nuclear weapons, military personnel**

   ● **Y36.591 War operation involving other effects of nuclear weapons, civilian**

● **Y36.6 War operations involving biological weapons**

   ● **Y36.6x War operations involving biological weapons**

      ● **Y36.6x0 War operations involving biological weapons, military personnel**

      ● **Y36.6x1 War operations involving biological weapons, civilian**

● **Y36.7 War operations involving chemical weapons and other forms of unconventional warfare**

   Excludes1   war operations involving incendiary devices (Y36.3-, Y36.5-)

   ● **Y36.7x War operations involving chemical weapons and other forms of unconventional warfare**

      ● **Y36.7x0 War operations involving chemical weapons and other forms of unconventional warfare, military personnel**

      ● **Y36.7x1 War operations involving chemical weapons and other forms of unconventional warfare, civilian**

● **Y36.8 War operations occurring after cessation of hostilities**
War operations classifiable to categories Y36.0-Y36.8 but occurring after cessation of hostilities

   ● **Y36.81 Explosion of mine placed during war operations but exploding after cessation of hostilities**

      ● **Y36.810 Explosion of mine placed during war operations but exploding after cessation of hostilities, military personnel**

      ● **Y36.811 Explosion of mine placed during war operations but exploding after cessation of hostilities, civilian**

● **Y36.82 Explosion of bomb placed during war operations but exploding after cessation of hostilities**

   ● **Y36.820 Explosion of bomb placed during war operations but exploding after cessation of hostilities, military personnel**

   ● **Y36.821 Explosion of bomb placed during war operations but exploding after cessation of hostilities, civilian**

● **Y36.88 Other war operations occurring after cessation of hostilities**

   ● **Y36.880 Other war operations occurring after cessation of hostilities, military personnel**

   ● **Y36.881 Other war operations occurring after cessation of hostilities, civilian**

● **Y36.89 Unspecified war operations occurring after cessation of hostilities**

   ● ■ **Y36.890 Unspecified war operations occurring after cessation of hostilities, military personnel**

   ● ■ **Y36.891 Unspecified war operations occurring after cessation of hostilities, civilian**

● **Y36.9 Other and unspecified war operations**

   ● ■ **Y36.90 War operations, unspecified**

   ● ■ **Y36.91 War operations involving unspecified weapon of mass destruction [WMD]**

   ● **Y36.92 War operations involving friendly fire**

● **Y37 Military operations**

   Includes   Injuries to military personnel and civilians occurring during peacetime on military property and during routine military exercises and operations

   Excludes1   military aircraft involved in aircraft accident with civilian aircraft (V97.81-)
military vehicles involved in transport accident with civilian vehicle (V09.01, V09.21, V19.81, V29.81, V39.81, V49.81, V59.81, V69.81, V79.81)
military watercraft involved in water transport accident with civilian watercraft (V94.81-)
war operations (Y36.-)

The appropriate 7th character is to be added to each code from category Y37

A	initial encounter
D	subsequent encounter
S	sequela

● **Y37.0 Military operations involving explosion of marine weapons**

   ● **Y37.00 Military operations involving explosion of unspecified marine weapon**
Military operations involving underwater blast NOS

      ● ■ **Y37.000 Military operations involving explosion of unspecified marine weapon, military personnel**

      ● ■ **Y37.001 Military operations involving explosion of unspecified marine weapon, civilian**

● Unacceptable First-Listed Diagnosis   ● Use Additional Character(s)   ■ Unspecified   **OGCR** Official Guidelines for Coding and Reporting
🗪 Complication\Comorbidity   🗪 Major C\C   Excludes 1   Excludes 2   Includes   Use additional   Code first   Code also

● Y37.01　Military operations involving explosion of depth-charge

　● Y37.010　Military operations involving explosion of depth-charge, military personnel

　● Y37.011　Military operations involving explosion of depth-charge, civilian

● Y37.02　Military operations involving explosion of marine mine

　　Military operations involving explosion of marine mine, at sea or in harbor

　● Y37.020　Military operations involving explosion of marine mine, military personnel

　● Y37.021　Military operations involving explosion of marine mine, civilian

● Y37.03　Military operations involving explosion of sea-based artillery shell

　● Y37.030　Military operations involving explosion of sea-based artillery shell, military personnel

　● Y37.031　Military operations involving explosion of sea-based artillery shell, civilian

● Y37.04　Military operations involving explosion of torpedo

　● Y37.040　Military operations involving explosion of torpedo, military personnel

　● Y37.041　Military operations involving explosion of torpedo, civilian

● Y37.05　Military operations involving accidental detonation of onboard marine weapons

　● Y37.050　Military operations involving accidental detonation of onboard marine weapons, military personnel

　● Y37.051　Military operations involving accidental detonation of onboard marine weapons, civilian

● Y37.09　Military operations involving explosion of other marine weapons

　● Y37.090　Military operations involving explosion of other marine weapons, military personnel

　● Y37.091　Military operations involving explosion of other marine weapons, civilian

● Y37.1　Military operations involving destruction of aircraft

　● Y37.10　Military operations involving unspecified destruction of aircraft

　● ▢ Y37.100　Military operations involving unspecified destruction of aircraft, military personnel

　● ▢ Y37.101　Military operations involving unspecified destruction of aircraft, civilian

● Y37.11　Military operations involving destruction of aircraft due to enemy fire or explosives

　　Military operations involving destruction of aircraft due to air to air missile

　　Military operations involving destruction of aircraft due to explosive placed on aircraft

　　Military operations involving destruction of aircraft due to rocket propelled grenade [RPG]

　　Military operations involving destruction of aircraft due to small arms fire

　　Military operations involving destruction of aircraft due to surface to air missile

　● Y37.110　Military operations involving destruction of aircraft due to enemy fire or explosives, military personnel

　● Y37.111　Military operations involving destruction of aircraft due to enemy fire or explosives, civilian

● Y37.12　Military operations involving destruction of aircraft due to collision with other aircraft

　● Y37.120　Military operations involving destruction of aircraft due to collision with other aircraft, military personnel

　● Y37.121　Military operations involving destruction of aircraft due to collision with other aircraft, civilian

● Y37.13　Military operations involving destruction of aircraft due to onboard fire

　● Y37.130　Military operations involving destruction of aircraft due to onboard fire, military personnel

　● Y37.131　Military operations involving destruction of aircraft due to onboard fire, civilian

● Y37.14　Military operations involving destruction of aircraft due to accidental detonation of onboard munitions and explosives

　● Y37.140　Military operations involving destruction of aircraft due to accidental detonation of onboard munitions and explosives, military personnel

　● Y37.141　Military operations involving destruction of aircraft due to accidental detonation of onboard munitions and explosives, civilian

● Y37.19　Military operations involving other destruction of aircraft

　● Y37.190　Military operations involving other destruction of aircraft, military personnel

　● Y37.191　Military operations involving other destruction of aircraft, civilian

● Unacceptable First-Listed Diagnosis　　　● Use Additional Character(s)　　　▢ Unspecified　　　**OGCR** Official Guidelines for Coding and Reporting

🗣 Complication\Comorbidity　　🗣 Major C\C　　Excludes 1　　Excludes 2　　Includes　　Use additional　　Code first　　Code also

CHAPTER 20 (V01-Y99)

1697

● **Y37.2 Military operations involving other explosions and fragments**

> Excludes1 | military operations involving explosion of aircraft (Y37.1-)
> military operations involving explosion of marine weapons (Y37.0-)
> military operations involving explosion of nuclear weapons (Y37.5-)

● **Y37.20 Military operations involving unspecified explosion and fragments**

> Military operations involving air blast NOS
> Military operations involving blast NOS
> Military operations involving blast fragments NOS
> Military operations involving blast wave NOS
> Military operations involving blast wind NOS
> Military operations involving explosion NOS
> Military operations involving explosion of bomb NOS

● ■ **Y37.200 Military operations involving unspecified explosion and fragments, military personnel**

● ■ **Y37.201 Military operations involving unspecified explosion and fragments, civilian**

● **Y37.21 Military operations involving explosion of aerial bomb**

● **Y37.210 Military operations involving explosion of aerial bomb, military personnel**

● **Y37.211 Military operations involving explosion of aerial bomb, civilian**

● **Y37.22 Military operations involving explosion of guided missile**

● **Y37.220 Military operations involving explosion of guided missile, military personnel**

● **Y37.221 Military operations involving explosion of guided missile, civilian**

● **Y37.23 Military operations involving explosion of improvised explosive device [IED]**

> Military operations involving explosion of person-borne improvised explosive device [IED]
> Military operations involving explosion of vehicle-borne improvised explosive device [IED]
> Military operations involving explosion of roadside improvised explosive device [IED]

● **Y37.230 Military operations involving explosion of improvised explosive device [IED], military personnel**

● **Y37.231 Military operations involving explosion of improvised explosive device [IED], civilian**

● **Y37.24 Military operations involving explosion due to accidental detonation and discharge of own munitions or munitions launch device**

● **Y37.240 Military operations involving explosion due to accidental detonation and discharge of own munitions or munitions launch device, military personnel**

● **Y37.241 Military operations involving explosion due to accidental detonation and discharge of own munitions or munitions launch device, civilian**

● **Y37.25 Military operations involving fragments from munitions**

● **Y37.250 Military operations involving fragments from munitions, military personnel**

● **Y37.251 Military operations involving fragments from munitions, civilian**

● **Y37.26 Military operations involving fragments of improvised explosive device [IED]**

> Military operations involving fragments of person-borne improvised explosive device [IED]
> Military operations involving fragments of vehicle-borne improvised explosive device [IED]
> Military operations involving fragments of roadside improvised explosive device [IED]

● **Y37.260 Military operations involving fragments of improvised explosive device [IED], military personnel**

● **Y37.261 Military operations involving fragments of improvised explosive device [IED], civilian**

● **Y37.27 Military operations involving fragments from weapons**

● **Y37.270 Military operations involving fragments from weapons, military personnel**

● **Y37.271 Military operations involving fragments from weapons, civilian**

● **Y37.29 Military operations involving other explosions and fragments**

> Military operations involving explosion of grenade
> Military operations involving explosions of land mine
> Military operations involving shrapnel NOS

● **Y37.290 Military operations involving other explosions and fragments, military personnel**

● **Y37.291 Military operations involving other explosions and fragments, civilian**

● Unacceptable First-Listed Diagnosis   ● Use Additional Character(s)   ■ Unspecified   **OGCR** Official Guidelines for Coding and Reporting
🚫 Complication\Comorbidity   🚫 Major C\C   Excludes 1   Excludes 2   Includes   Use additional   Code first   Code also

● **Y37.3**   **Military operations involving fires, conflagrations and hot substances**
> Military operations involving smoke, fumes, and heat from fires, conflagrations and hot substances
>> Excludes1   military operations involving fires and conflagrations aboard military aircraft (Y37.1-)
>> military operations involving fires and conflagrations aboard military watercraft (Y37.0-)
>> military operations involving fires and conflagrations caused indirectly by conventional weapons (Y37.2-)
>> military operations involving fires and thermal effects of nuclear weapons (Y36.53-)

  ● **Y37.30**   **Military operations involving unspecified fire, conflagration and hot substance**

    ● ▪ **Y37.300**   **Military operations involving unspecified fire, conflagration and hot substance, military personnel**

    ● ▪ **Y37.301**   **Military operations involving unspecified fire, conflagration and hot substance, civilian**

  ● **Y37.31**   **Military operations involving gasoline bomb**
> Military operations involving incendiary bomb
> Military operations involving petrol bomb

    ● **Y37.310**   **Military operations involving gasoline bomb, military personnel**

    ● **Y37.311**   **Military operations involving gasoline bomb, civilian**

  ● **Y37.32**   **Military operations involving incendiary bullet**

    ● **Y37.320**   **Military operations involving incendiary bullet, military personnel**

    ● **Y37.321**   **Military operations involving incendiary bullet, civilian**

  ● **Y37.33**   **Military operations involving flamethrower**

    ● **Y37.330**   **Military operations involving flamethrower, military personnel**

    ● **Y37.331**   **Military operations involving flamethrower, civilian**

  ● **Y37.39**   **Military operations involving other fires, conflagrations and hot substances**

    ● **Y37.390**   **Military operations involving other fires, conflagrations and hot substances, military personnel**

    ● **Y37.391**   **Military operations involving other fires, conflagrations and hot substances, civilian**

● **Y37.4**   **Military operations involving firearm discharge and other forms of conventional warfare**

  ● **Y37.41**   **Military operations involving rubber bullets**

    ● **Y37.410**   **Military operations involving rubber bullets, military personnel**

    ● **Y37.411**   **Military operations involving rubber bullets, civilian**

  ● **Y37.42**   **Military operations involving firearms pellets**

    ● **Y37.420**   **Military operations involving firearms pellets, military personnel**

    ● **Y37.421**   **Military operations involving firearms pellets, civilian**

  ● **Y37.43**   **Military operations involving other firearms discharge**
> Military operations involving bullets NOS
>> Excludes1   military operations involving munitions fragments (Y37.25-)
>> military operations involving incendiary bullets (Y37.32-)

    ● **Y37.430**   **Military operations involving other firearms discharge, military personnel**

    ● **Y37.431**   **Military operations involving other firearms discharge, civilian**

  ● **Y37.44**   **Military operations involving unarmed hand to hand combat**
>> Excludes1   military operations involving combat using blunt or piercing object (Y37.45-)
>> military operations involving intentional restriction of air and airway (Y37.46-)
>> military operations involving unintentional restriction of air and airway (Y37.47-)

    ● **Y37.440**   **Military operations involving unarmed hand to hand combat, military personnel**

    ● **Y37.441**   **Military operations involving unarmed hand to hand combat, civilian**

  ● **Y37.45**   **Military operations involving combat using blunt or piercing object**

    ● **Y37.450**   **Military operations involving combat using blunt or piercing object, military personnel**

    ● **Y37.451**   **Military operations involving combat using blunt or piercing object, civilian**

  ● **Y37.46**   **Military operations involving intentional restriction of air and airway**

    ● **Y37.460**   **Military operations involving intentional restriction of air and airway, military personnel**

    ● **Y37.461**   **Military operations involving intentional restriction of air and airway, civilian**

  ● **Y37.47**   **Military operations involving unintentional restriction of air and airway**

    ● **Y37.470**   **Military operations involving unintentional restriction of air and airway, military personnel**

    ● **Y37.471**   **Military operations involving unintentional restriction of air and airway, civilian**

● Unacceptable First-Listed Diagnosis   ● Use Additional Character(s)   ▪ Unspecified   OGCR Official Guidelines for Coding and Reporting

🝰 Complication\Comorbidity   🝰 Major C\C   Excludes 1   Excludes 2   Includes   Use additional   Code first   Code also

1699

CHAPTER 20 (V01-Y99)

● Y37.49   Military operations involving other forms of conventional warfare

  ● Y37.490   Military operations involving other forms of conventional warfare, military personnel

  ● Y37.491   Military operations involving other forms of conventional warfare, civilian

● Y37.5   Military operations involving nuclear weapons
         Military operation involving dirty bomb NOS

 ● Y37.50   Military operations involving unspecified effect of nuclear weapon

  ● ▢ Y37.500   Military operations involving unspecified effect of nuclear weapon, military personnel

  ● ▢ Y37.501   Military operations involving unspecified effect of nuclear weapon, civilian

 ● Y37.51   Military operations involving direct blast effect of nuclear weapon
         Military operations involving blast pressure of nuclear weapon

  ● Y37.510   Military operations involving direct blast effect of nuclear weapon, military personnel

  ● Y37.511   Military operations involving direct blast effect of nuclear weapon, civilian

 ● Y37.52   Military operations involving indirect blast effect of nuclear weapon
         Military operations involving being thrown by blast of nuclear weapon
         Military operations involving being struck or crushed by blast debris of nuclear weapon

  ● Y37.520   Military operations involving indirect blast effect of nuclear weapon, military personnel

  ● Y37.521   Military operations involving indirect blast effect of nuclear weapon, civilian

 ● Y37.53   Military operations involving thermal radiation effect of nuclear weapon
         Military operations involving direct heat from nuclear weapon
         Military operation involving fireball effects from nuclear weapon

  ● Y37.530   Military operations involving thermal radiation effect of nuclear weapon, military personnel

  ● Y37.531   Military operations involving thermal radiation effect of nuclear weapon, civilian

 ● Y37.54   Military operation involving nuclear radiation effects of nuclear weapon
         Military operation involving acute radiation exposure from nuclear weapon
         Military operation involving exposure to immediate ionizing radiation from nuclear weapon
         Military operation involving fallout exposure from nuclear weapon
         Military operation involving secondary effects of nuclear weapons

  ● Y37.540   Military operation involving nuclear radiation effects of nuclear weapon, military personnel

  ● Y37.541   Military operation involving nuclear radiation effects of nuclear weapon, civilian

 ● Y37.59   Military operation involving other effects of nuclear weapons

  ● Y37.590   Military operation involving other effects of nuclear weapons, military personnel

  ● Y37.591   Military operation involving other effects of nuclear weapons, civilian

● Y37.6   Military operations involving biological weapons

 ● Y37.6x   Military operations involving biological weapons

  ● Y37.6x0   Military operations involving biological weapons, military personnel

  ● Y37.6x1   Military operations involving biological weapons, civilian

● Y37.7   Military operations involving chemical weapons and other forms of unconventional warfare

    Excludes1   military operations involving incendiary devices (Y36.3-, Y36.5-)

 ● Y37.7x   Military operations involving chemical weapons and other forms of unconventional warfare

  ● Y37.7x0   Military operations involving chemical weapons and other forms of unconventional warfare, military personnel

  ● Y37.7x1   Military operations involving chemical weapons and other forms of unconventional warfare, civilian

● Y37.9   Other and unspecified military operations

 ● ▢ Y37.90   Military operations, unspecified

 ● ▢ Y37.91   Military operations involving unspecified weapon of mass destruction [WMD]

 ● Y37.92   Military operations involving friendly fire

● Y38   **Terrorism**
         These codes are for use to identify injuries resulting from the unlawful use of force or violence against persons or property to intimidate or coerce a government, the civilian population, or any segment thereof, in furtherance of political or social objective

         Use additional code for place of occurrence (Y92.-)

         The appropriate 7th character is to be added to each code from category Y38

         A   initial encounter
         D   subsequent encounter
         S   sequela

● Unacceptable First-Listed Diagnosis   ● Use Additional Character(s)   ▢ Unspecified   **OGCR** Official Guidelines for Coding and Reporting
🝢 Complication\Comorbidity   🝢 Major C\C   Excludes 1   Excludes 2   Includes   Use additional   Code first   Code also

● **Y38.0 Terrorism involving explosion of marine weapons**
Terrorism involving depth-charge
Terrorism involving marine mine
Terrorism involving mine NOS, at sea or in harbor
Terrorism involving sea-based artillery shell
Terrorism involving torpedo
Terrorism involving underwater blast

● **Y38.0x Terrorism involving explosion of marine weapons**

● **Y38.0x1 Terrorism involving explosion of marine weapons, public safety official injured**

● **Y38.0x2 Terrorism involving explosion of marine weapons, civilian injured**

● **Y38.0x3 Terrorism involving explosion of marine weapons, terrorist injured**

● **Y38.1 Terrorism involving destruction of aircraft**
Terrorism involving aircraft burned
Terrorism involving aircraft exploded
Terrorism involving aircraft being shot down
Terrorism involving aircraft used as a weapon

● **Y38.1x Terrorism involving destruction of aircraft**

● **Y38.1x1 Terrorism involving destruction of aircraft, public safety official injured**

● **Y38.1x2 Terrorism involving destruction of aircraft, civilian injured**

● **Y38.1x3 Terrorism involving destruction of aircraft, terrorist injured**

● **Y38.2 Terrorism involving other explosions and fragments**
Terrorism involving antipersonnel (fragments) bomb
Terrorism involving blast NOS
Terrorism involving explosion NOS
Terrorism involving explosion of breech block
Terrorism involving explosion of cannon block
Terrorism involving explosion (fragments) of artillery shell
Terrorism involving explosion (fragments) of bomb
Terrorism involving explosion (fragments) of grenade
Terrorism involving explosion (fragments) of guided missile
Terrorism involving explosion (fragments) of land mine
Terrorism involving explosion of mortar bomb
Terrorism involving explosion of munitions
Terrorism involving explosion (fragments) of rocket
Terrorism involving explosion (fragments) of shell
Terrorism involving shrapnel
Terrorism involving mine NOS, on land

Excludes1 terrorism involving explosion of nuclear weapon (Y38.5)
terrorism involving suicide bomber (Y38.81)

● **Y38.2x Terrorism involving other explosions and fragments**

● **Y38.2x1 Terrorism involving other explosions and fragments, public safety official injured**

● **Y38.2x2 Terrorism involving other explosions and fragments, civilian injured**

● **Y38.2x3 Terrorism involving other explosions and fragments, terrorist injured**

● **Y38.3 Terrorism involving fires, conflagration and hot substances**
Terrorism involving conflagration NOS
Terrorism involving fire NOS
Terrorism involving petrol bomb

Excludes1 terrorism involving fire or heat of nuclear weapon (Y38.5)

● **Y38.3x Terrorism involving fires, conflagration and hot substances**

● **Y38.3x1 Terrorism involving fires, conflagration and hot substances, public safety official injured**

● **Y38.3x2 Terrorism involving fires, conflagration and hot substances, civilian injured**

● **Y38.3x3 Terrorism involving fires, conflagration and hot substances, terrorist injured**

● **Y38.4 Terrorism involving firearms**
Terrorism involving carbine bullet
Terrorism involving machine gun bullet
Terrorism involving pellets (shotgun)
Terrorism involving pistol bullet
Terrorism involving rifle bullet
Terrorism involving rubber (rifle) bullet

● **Y38.4x Terrorism involving firearms**

● **Y38.4x1 Terrorism involving firearms, public safety official injured**

● **Y38.4x2 Terrorism involving firearms, civilian injured**

● **Y38.4x3 Terrorism involving firearms, terrorist injured**

● **Y38.5 Terrorism involving nuclear weapons**
Terrorism involving blast effects of nuclear weapon
Terrorism involving exposure to ionizing radiation from nuclear weapon
Terrorism involving fireball effect of nuclear weapon
Terrorism involving heat from nuclear weapon

● **Y38.5x Terrorism involving nuclear weapons**

● **Y38.5x1 Terrorism involving nuclear weapons, public safety official injured**

● **Y38.5x2 Terrorism involving nuclear weapons, civilian injured**

● **Y38.5x3 Terrorism involving nuclear weapons, terrorist injured**

● **Y38.6 Terrorism involving biological weapons**
Terrorism involving anthrax
Terrorism involving cholera
A serious, often deadly, infectious disease of small intestine
Terrorism involving smallpox

● **Y38.6x Terrorism involving biological weapons**

● **Y38.6x1 Terrorism involving biological weapons, public safety official injured**

● **Y38.6x2 Terrorism involving biological weapons, civilian injured**

● **Y38.6x3 Terrorism involving biological weapons, terrorist injured**

● Unacceptable First-Listed Diagnosis   ● Use Additional Character(s)   ■ Unspecified   **OGCR** Official Guidelines for Coding and Reporting

 Complication\Comorbidity   Major C\C   Excludes 1   Excludes 2   Includes   Use additional   Code first   Code also

1701

● **Y38.7**   **Terrorism involving chemical weapons**
      Terrorism involving gases, fumes, chemicals
      Terrorism involving hydrogen cyanide
      Terrorism involving phosgene
      Terrorism involving sarin

    ● **Y38.7x**   **Terrorism involving chemical weapons**

       ● **Y38.7x1**   **Terrorism involving chemical weapons, public safety official injured**

       ● **Y38.7x2**   **Terrorism involving chemical weapons, civilian injured**

       ● **Y38.7x3**   **Terrorism involving chemical weapons, terrorist injured**

● **Y38.8**   **Terrorism involving other and unspecified means**

    ● ▣ **Y38.80**   **Terrorism involving unspecified means**
         Terrorism NOS

    ● **Y38.81**   **Terrorism involving suicide bomber**

       ● **Y38.811**   **Terrorism involving suicide bomber, public safety official injured**

       ● **Y38.812**   **Terrorism involving suicide bomber, civilian injured**

    ● **Y38.89**   **Terrorism involving other means**
         Terrorism involving drowning and submersion
         Terrorism involving lasers
         Terrorism involving piercing or stabbing instruments

       ● **Y38.891**   **Terrorism involving other means, public safety official injured**

       ● **Y38.892**   **Terrorism involving other means, civilian injured**

       ● **Y38.893**   **Terrorism involving other means, terrorist injured**

● **Y38.9**   **Terrorism, secondary effects**
      This code is for use to identify injuries occurring subsequent to a terrorist attack, not due to the initial attack itself.

    ● **Y38.9x**   **Terrorism, secondary effects**

       ● **Y38.9x1**   **Terrorism, secondary effects, public safety official injured**

       ● **Y38.9x2**   **Terrorism, secondary effects, civilian injured categories**

Categories Y40-Y59 deactivated. See T36-T50 with fifth or sixth character 5

COMPLICATIONS OF MEDICAL AND SURGICAL CARE (Y62-Y84)

Includes   complications of medical devices surgical and medical procedures as the cause of abnormal reaction of the patient, or of later complication, without mention of misadventure at the time of the procedure

---

MISADVENTURES TO PATIENTS DURING SURGICAL AND MEDICAL CARE (Y62-Y69)

Excludes2   breakdown or malfunctioning of medical device (during procedure) (after implantation) (ongoing use) (Y70-Y82)
    surgical and medical procedures as the cause of abnormal reaction of the patient, without mention of misadventure at the time of the procedure (Y83-Y84)

Category Y60 deactivated. See complications within body system chapters

Category Y61 deactivated. See subcategory T81.5

● **Y62**   **Failure of sterile precautions during surgical and medical care**

    Y62.0   **Failure of sterile precautions during surgical operation**

    Y62.1   **Failure of sterile precautions during infusion or transfusion**

    Y62.2   **Failure of sterile precautions during kidney dialysis and other perfusion**

    Y62.3   **Failure of sterile precautions during injection or immunization**

    Y62.4   **Failure of sterile precautions during endoscopic examination**

    Y62.5   **Failure of sterile precautions during heart catheterization**

    Y62.6   **Failure of sterile precautions during aspiration, puncture and other catheterization**

    Y62.8   **Failure of sterile precautions during other surgical and medical care**

    ▣ **Y62.9**   **Failure of sterile precautions during unspecified surgical and medical care**

● **Y63**   **Failure in dosage during surgical and medical care**

    Excludes2   accidental overdose of drug or wrong drug given in error (T36-T50)

    Y63.0   **Excessive amount of blood or other fluid given during transfusion or infusion**

    Y63.1   **Incorrect dilution of fluid used during infusion**

    Y63.2   **Overdose of radiation given during therapy**

    Y63.3   **Inadvertent exposure of patient to radiation during medical care**

    Y63.4   **Failure in dosage in electroshock or insulin-shock therapy**

    Y63.5   **Inappropriate temperature in local application and packing**

    ● **Y63.6**   **Underdosing and nonadministration of necessary drug, medicament or biological substance**

       Y63.61   **Underdosing of necessary drug, medicament or biological substance**

       Y63.62   **Nonadministration of necessary drug, medicament or biological substance**

    Y63.8   **Failure in dosage during other surgical and medical care**

    ▣ **Y63.9**   **Failure in dosage during unspecified surgical and medical care**

● **Y64**   **Contaminated medical or biological substances**

    Y64.0   **Contaminated medical or biological substance, transfused or infused**

    Y64.1   **Contaminated medical or biological substance, injected or used for immunization**

    Y64.8   **Contaminated medical or biological substance administered by other means**

● Unacceptable First-Listed Diagnosis   ● Use Additional Character(s)   ▣ Unspecified   **OGCR** Official Guidelines for Coding and Reporting
🅒 Complication\Comorbidity   🅜 Major C\C   Excludes 1   Excludes 2   Includes   Use additional   Code first   Code also

■Y64.9　Contaminated medical or biological substance administered by unspecified means
　　　　Administered contaminated medical or biological substance NOS

●Y65　Other misadventures during surgical and medical care

Y65.0　Mismatched blood in transfusion

Y65.1　Wrong fluid used in infusion

Y65.2　Failure in suture or ligature during surgical operation

Y65.3　Endotracheal tube wrongly placed during anesthetic procedure

Y65.4　Failure to introduce or to remove other tube or instrument

●Y65.5　Performance of wrong procedure (operation)

●Y65.51　Performance of wrong procedure (operation) on correct patient
　　　　　　Wrong device implanted into correct surgical site

> **Excludes1**　performance of correct procedure (operation) on wrong side or body part (Y65.53)

●Y65.52　Performance of procedure (operation) on patient not scheduled for surgery
　　　　　　Performance of procedure (operation) intended for another patient
　　　　　　Performance of procedure (operation) on wrong patient

●Y65.53　Performance of correct procedure (operation) on wrong side or body part
　　　　　　Performance of correct procedure (operation) on wrong side
　　　　　　Performance of correct procedure (operation) on wrong site

Y65.8　Other specified misadventures during surgical and medical care

Y66　Nonadministration of surgical and medical care

> **Includes**　premature cessation of surgical and medical care

> **Excludes1**　DNR status (Z66)
> palliative care (Z51.5)

■Y69　Unspecified misadventure during surgical and medical care

---

MEDICAL DEVICES ASSOCIATED WITH ADVERSE INCIDENTS IN DIAGNOSTIC AND THERAPEUTIC USE (Y70-Y82)

> **Includes**　breakdown or malfunction of medical devices (during use) (after implantation) (ongoing use)

> **Excludes1**　misadventure to patients during surgical and medical care, classifiable to Y60-Y69 (Y60-Y69)
> later complications following use of medical devices without breakdown or malfunctioning of device (Y83-Y84)

●Y70　Anesthesiology devices associated with adverse incidents

Y70.0　Diagnostic and monitoring anesthesiology devices associated with adverse incidents

Y70.1　Therapeutic (nonsurgical) and rehabilitative anesthesiology devices associated with adverse incidents

Y70.2　Prosthetic and other implants, materials and accessory anesthesiology devices associated with adverse incidents

Y70.3　Surgical instruments, materials and anesthesiology devices (including sutures) associated with adverse incidents

Y70.8　Miscellaneous anesthesiology devices associated with adverse incidents, not elsewhere classified

●Y71　Cardiovascular devices associated with adverse incidents

Y71.0　Diagnostic and monitoring cardiovascular devices associated with adverse incidents

Y71.1　Therapeutic (nonsurgical) and rehabilitative cardiovascular devices associated with adverse incidents

Y71.2　Prosthetic and other implants, materials and accessory cardiovascular devices associated with adverse incidents

Y71.3　Surgical instruments, materials and cardiovascular devices (including sutures) associated with adverse incidents

Y71.8　Miscellaneous cardiovascular devices associated with adverse incidents, not elsewhere classified

●Y72　Otorhinolaryngological devices associated with adverse incidents

Y72.0　Diagnostic and monitoring otorhinolaryngological devices associated with adverse incidents

Y72.1　Therapeutic (nonsurgical) and rehabilitative otorhinolaryngological devices associated with adverse incidents

Y72.2　Prosthetic and other implants, materials and accessory otorhinolaryngological devices associated with adverse incidents

Y72.3　Surgical instruments, materials and otorhinolaryngological devices (including sutures) associated with adverse incidents

Y72.8　Miscellaneous otorhinolaryngological devices associated with adverse incidents, not elsewhere classified

●Y73　Gastroenterology and urology devices associated with adverse incidents

Y73.0　Diagnostic and monitoring gastroenterology and urology devices associated with adverse incidents

Y73.1　Therapeutic (nonsurgical) and rehabilitative gastroenterology and urology devices associated with adverse incidents

Y73.2　Prosthetic and other implants, materials and accessory gastroenterology and urology devices associated with adverse incidents

Y73.3　Surgical instruments, materials and gastroenterology and urology devices (including sutures) associated with adverse incidents

Y73.8　Miscellaneous gastroenterology and urology devices associated with adverse incidents, not elsewhere classified

●Y74　General hospital and personal-use devices associated with adverse incidents

Y74.0　Diagnostic and monitoring general hospital and personal-use devices associated with adverse incidents

Y74.1　Therapeutic (nonsurgical) and rehabilitative general hospital and personal-use devices associated with adverse incidents

Y74.2　Prosthetic and other implants, materials and accessory general hospital and personal-use devices associated with adverse incidents

Y74.3　Surgical instruments, materials and general hospital and personal-use devices (including sutures) associated with adverse incidents

---

● Unacceptable First-Listed Diagnosis　　● Use Additional Character(s)　　　■ Unspecified　　**OGCR** Official Guidelines for Coding and Reporting

🐾 Complication\Comorbidity　　🐾 Major C\C　　Excludes 1　　Excludes 2　　Includes　　Use additional　　Code first　　Code also

1703

CHAPTER 20 (V01-Y99)

Y74.8   Miscellaneous general hospital and personal-use devices associated with adverse incidents, not elsewhere classified

● Y75   Neurological devices associated with adverse incidents

Y75.0   Diagnostic and monitoring neurological devices associated with adverse incidents

Y75.1   Therapeutic (nonsurgical) and rehabilitative neurological devices associated with adverse incidents

Y75.2   Prosthetic and other implants, materials and neurological devices associated with adverse incidents

Y75.3   Surgical instruments, materials and neurological devices (including sutures) associated with adverse incidents

Y75.8   Miscellaneous neurological devices associated with adverse incidents, not elsewhere classified

● Y76   Obstetric and gynecological devices associated with adverse incidents

Y76.0   Diagnostic and monitoring obstetric and gynecological devices associated with adverse incidents

Y76.1   Therapeutic (nonsurgical) and rehabilitative obstetric and gynecological devices associated with adverse incidents

Y76.2   Prosthetic and other implants, materials and accessory obstetric and gynecological devices associated with adverse incidents

Y76.3   Surgical instruments, materials and obstetric and gynecological devices (including sutures) associated with adverse incidents

Y76.8   Miscellaneous obstetric and gynecological devices associated with adverse incidents, not elsewhere classified

● Y77   Ophthalmic devices associated with adverse incidents

Y77.0   Diagnostic and monitoring ophthalmic devices associated with adverse incidents

Y77.1   Therapeutic (nonsurgical) and rehabilitative ophthalmic devices associated with adverse incidents

Y77.2   Prosthetic and other implants, materials and accessory ophthalmic devices associated with adverse incidents

Y77.3   Surgical instruments, materials and ophthalmic devices (including sutures) associated with adverse incidents

Y77.8   Miscellaneous ophthalmic devices associated with adverse incidents, not elsewhere classified

● Y78   Radiological devices associated with adverse incidents

Y78.0   Diagnostic and monitoring radiological devices associated with adverse incidents

Y78.1   Therapeutic (nonsurgical) and rehabilitative radiological devices associated with adverse incidents

Y78.2   Prosthetic and other implants, materials and accessory radiological devices associated with adverse incidents

Y78.3   Surgical instruments, materials and radiological devices (including sutures) associated with adverse incidents

Y78.8   Miscellaneous radiological devices associated with adverse incidents, not elsewhere classified

● Y79   Orthopedic devices associated with adverse incidents

Y79.0   Diagnostic and monitoring orthopedic devices associated with adverse incidents

Y79.1   Therapeutic (nonsurgical) and rehabilitative orthopedic devices associated with adverse incidents

Y79.2   Prosthetic and other implants, materials and accessory orthopedic devices associated with adverse incidents

Y79.3   Surgical instruments, materials and orthopedic devices (including sutures) associated with adverse incidents

Y79.8   Miscellaneous orthopedic devices associated with adverse incidents, not elsewhere classified

● Y80   Physical medicine devices associated with adverse incidents

Y80.0   Diagnostic and monitoring physical medicine devices associated with adverse incidents

Y80.1   Therapeutic (nonsurgical) and rehabilitative physical medicine devices associated with adverse incidents

Y80.2   Prosthetic and other implants, materials and accessory physical medicine devices associated with adverse incidents

Y80.3   Surgical instruments, materials and physical medicine devices (including sutures) associated with adverse incidents

Y80.8   Miscellaneous physical medicine devices associated with adverse incidents, not elsewhere classified

● Y81   General- and plastic-surgery devices associated with adverse incidents

Y81.0   Diagnostic and monitoring general- and plastic-surgery devices associated with adverse incidents

Y81.1   Therapeutic (nonsurgical) and rehabilitative general- and plastic-surgery devices associated with adverse incidents

Y81.2   Prosthetic and other implants, materials and accessory general- and plastic-surgery devices associated with adverse incidents

Y81.3   Surgical instruments, materials and general- and plastic-surgery devices (including sutures) associated with adverse incidents

Y81.8   Miscellaneous general- and plastic-surgery devices associated with adverse incidents, not elsewhere classified

● Y82   Other and unspecified medical devices associated with adverse incidents

Y82.0   Other medical devices associated with adverse incidents

■ Y82.9   Unspecified medical devices associated with adverse incidents

SURGICAL AND OTHER MEDICAL PROCEDURES AS THE CAUSE OF ABNORMAL REACTION OF THE PATIENT, OR OF LATER COMPLICATION, WITHOUT MENTION OF MISADVENTURE AT THE TIME OF THE PROCEDURE (Y83-Y84)

Excludes1   misadventures to patients during surgical and medical care, classifiable to Y60-Y69 (Y60-Y69)

● Y83   Surgical operation and other surgical procedures as the cause of abnormal reaction of the patient, or of later complication, without mention of misadventure at the time of the procedure

● Unacceptable First-Listed Diagnosis   ● Use Additional Character(s)   ■ Unspecified   **OGCR** Official Guidelines for Coding and Reporting
🔹 Complication\Comorbidity   🔹 Major C\C   Excludes 1   Excludes 2   Includes   Use additional   Code first   Code also

Y83.0   Surgical operation with transplant of whole organ as the cause of abnormal reaction of the patient, or of later complication, without mention of misadventure at the time of the procedure

Y83.1   Surgical operation with implant of artificial internal device as the cause of abnormal reaction of the patient, or of later complication, without mention of misadventure at the time of the procedure

Y83.2   Surgical operation with anastomosis, bypass or graft as the cause of abnormal reaction of the patient, or of later complication, without mention of misadventure at the time of the procedure

Y83.3   Surgical operation with formation of external stoma as the cause of abnormal reaction of the patient, or of later complication, without mention of misadventure at the time of the procedure

Y83.4   Other reconstructive surgery as the cause of abnormal reaction of the patient, or of later complication, without mention of misadventure at the time of the procedure

Y83.5   Amputation of limb(s) as the cause of abnormal reaction of the patient, or of later complication, without mention of misadventure at the time of the procedure

Y83.6   Removal of other organ (partial) (total) as the cause of abnormal reaction of the patient, or of later complication, without mention of misadventure at the time of the procedure

Y83.8   Other surgical procedures as the cause of abnormal reaction of the patient, or of later complication, without mention of misadventure at the time of the procedure

Y83.9   Surgical procedure, unspecified as the cause of abnormal reaction of the patient, or of later complication, without mention of misadventure at the time of the procedure

Y84   Other medical procedures as the cause of abnormal reaction of the patient, or of later complication, without mention of misadventure at the time of the procedure

Y84.0   Cardiac catheterization as the cause of abnormal reaction of the patient, or of later complication, without mention of misadventure at the time of the procedure

Y84.1   Kidney dialysis as the cause of abnormal reaction of the patient, or of later complication, without mention of misadventure at the time of the procedure

Y84.2   Radiological procedure and radiotherapy as the cause of abnormal reaction of the patient, or of later complication, without mention of misadventure at the time of the procedure

Y84.3   Shock therapy as the cause of abnormal reaction of the patient, or of later complication, without mention of misadventure at the time of the procedure

Y84.4   Aspiration of fluid as the cause of abnormal reaction of the patient, or of later complication, without mention of misadventure at the time of the procedure

Y84.5   Insertion of gastric or duodenal sound as the cause of abnormal reaction of the patient, or of later complication, without mention of misadventure at the time of the procedure

Y84.6   Urinary catheterization as the cause of abnormal reaction of the patient, or of later complication, without mention of misadventure at the time of the procedure

Y84.7   Blood-sampling as the cause of abnormal reaction of the patient, or of later complication, without mention of misadventure at the time of the procedure

Y84.8   Other medical procedures as the cause of abnormal reaction of the patient, or of later complication, without mention of misadventure at the time of the procedure

Y84.9   Medical procedure, unspecified as the cause of abnormal reaction of the patient, or of later complication, without mention of misadventure at the time of the procedure

Categories Y85-Y89 deactivated. Replaced with 7th character S for categories V00-Y38

SUPPLEMENTARY FACTORS RELATED TO CAUSES OF MORBIDITY CLASSIFIED ELSEWHERE (Y90-Y99)

Note: These categories may be used to provide supplementary information concerning causes of morbidity. They are not to be used for single-condition coding.

Y90   Evidence of alcohol involvement determined by blood alcohol level

Code first any associated alcohol related disorders (F10)

Y90.0   Blood alcohol level of less than 20 mg/100 ml
Y90.1   Blood alcohol level of 20-39 mg/100 ml
Y90.2   Blood alcohol level of 40-59 mg/100 ml
Y90.3   Blood alcohol level of 60-79 mg/100 ml
Y90.4   Blood alcohol level of 80-99 mg/100 ml
Y90.5   Blood alcohol level of 100-119 mg/100 ml
Y90.6   Blood alcohol level of 120-199 mg/100 ml
Y90.7   Blood alcohol level of 200-239 mg/100 ml
Y90.8   Blood alcohol level of 240 mg/100 ml or more
Y90.9   Presence of alcohol in blood, level not specified

Category Y91 deactivated. See category F10

Y92   Place of occurrence of the external cause
The following category is for use, when relevant, to identify the place of occurrence of the external cause. Use in conjunction with an activity code.
Place of occurrence should be recorded only at the initial encounter for treatment

Y92.0   Non-institutional (private) residence as the place of occurrence of the external cause

Excludes1   abandoned or derelict house (Y92.89)
home under construction but not yet occupied (Y92.6-)
institutional place of residence (Y92.1-)

Y92.00   Unspecified non-institutional (private) residence as the place of occurrence of the external cause

OGCR Section I.C.20.b.

20.9 Place of Occurrence

Place of Occurrence Guideline

Codes from category Y92, Place of occurrence of the external cause, are secondary codes for use after other external cause codes to identify the location of the patient at the time of injury or other condition.

A place of occurrence code is used only once, at the initial encounter for treatment. No 7th characters are used for Y92. Only one code from Y92 should be recorded on a medical record. A place of occurrence code should be used in conjunction with an activity code, Y93.

Do not use place of occurrence code Y92.9 if the place is not stated or is not applicable.

● Unacceptable First-Listed Diagnosis   ● Use Additional Character(s)   ☐ Unspecified   OGCR Official Guidelines for Coding and Reporting
🅒 Complication\Comorbidity   🅒 Major C\C   Excludes 1   Excludes 2   Includes   Use additional   Code first   Code also   1705

CHAPTER 20 (V01-Y99)

● **Y92.01** **Single-family non-institutional (private) house as the place of occurrence of the external cause**
Farmhouse as the place of occurrence of the external cause

> **Excludes1**   barn (Y92.7x)
> chicken coop or hen house (Y92.7x)
> farm field (Y92.7x)
> orchard (Y92.7x)
> single family mobile home or trailer (Y92.02-)
> slaughter house (Y92.7x)

Y92.010   Kitchen of single-family (private) house as the place of occurrence of the external cause

Y92.011   Dining room of single-family (private) house as the place of occurrence of the external cause

Y92.012   Bathroom of single-family (private) house as the place of occurrence of the external cause

Y92.013   Bedroom of single-family (private) house as the place of occurrence of the external cause

Y92.014   Private driveway to single-family (private) house as the place of occurrence of the external cause

Y92.015   Private garage of single-family (private) house as the place of occurrence of the external cause

Y92.016   Swimming pool in single-family (private) house or garden as the place of occurrence of the external cause

Y92.017   Garden or yard in single-family (private) house as the place of occurrence of the external cause

Y92.018   Other place in single-family (private) house as the place of occurrence of the external cause

■ Y92.019   Unspecified place in single-family (private) house as the place of occurrence of the external cause

● **Y92.02** **Mobile home as the place of occurrence of the external cause**

Y92.020   Kitchen in mobile home as the place of occurrence of the external cause

Y92.021   Dining room in mobile home as the place of occurrence of the external cause

Y92.022   Bathroom in mobile home as the place of occurrence of the external cause

Y92.023   Bedroom in mobile home as the place of occurrence of the external cause

Y92.024   Driveway of mobile home as the place of occurrence of the external cause

Y92.025   Garage of mobile home as the place of occurrence of the external cause

Y92.026   Swimming pool of mobile home as the place of occurrence of the external cause

Y92.027   Garden or yard of mobile home as the place of occurrence of the external cause

Y92.028   Other place in mobile home as the place of occurrence of the external cause

■ Y92.029   Unspecified place in mobile home as the place of occurrence of the external cause

● **Y92.03** **Apartment as the place of occurrence of the external cause**
Condominium as the place of occurrence of the external cause
Co-op apartment as the place of occurrence of the external cause

> **Excludes1**   common areas and hallways of apartment building (Y92.xx)

Y92.030   Kitchen in apartment as the place of occurrence of the external cause

Y92.031   Bathroom in apartment as the place of occurrence of the external cause

Y92.032   Bedroom in apartment as the place of occurrence of the external cause

Y92.038   Other place in apartment as the place of occurrence of the external cause

■ Y92.039   Unspecified place in apartment as the place of occurrence of the external cause

● **Y92.04** **Boarding-house as the place of occurrence of the external cause**

Y92.040   Kitchen in boarding-house as the place of occurrence of the external cause

Y92.041   Bathroom in boarding-house as the place of occurrence of the external cause

Y92.042   Bedroom in boarding-house as the place of occurrence of the external cause

Y92.043   Driveway of boarding-house as the place of occurrence of the external cause

Y92.044   Garage of boarding-house as the place of occurrence of the external cause

Y92.045   Swimming pool of boarding-house as the place of occurrence of the external cause

Y92.046   Garden or yard of boarding-house as the place of occurrence of the external cause

Y92.048   Other place in boarding-house as the place of occurrence of the external cause

■ Y92.049   Unspecified place in boarding-house as the place of occurrence of the external cause

● **Y92.09** **Other non-institutional residence as the place of occurrence of the external cause**

Y92.090   Kitchen in other non-institutional residence as the place of occurrence of the external cause

CHAPTER 20 (V01-Y99)

Y92.091 Bathroom in other non-institutional residence as the place of occurrence of the external cause

Y92.092 Bedroom in other non-institutional residence as the place of occurrence of the external cause

Y92.093 Driveway of other non-institutional residence as the place of occurrence of the external cause

Y92.094 Garage of other non-institutional residence as the place of occurrence of the external cause

Y92.095 Swimming pool of other non-institutional residence as the place of occurrence of the external cause

Y92.096 Garden or yard of other non-institutional residence as the place of occurrence of the external cause

Y92.098 Other place in other non-institutional residence as the place of occurrence of the external cause

Y92.099 Unspecified place in other non-institutional residence as the place of occurrence of the external cause

● Y92.1 Institutional (nonprivate) residence as the place of occurrence of the external cause

Y92.10 Unspecified residential institution as the place of occurrence of the external cause

● Y92.11 Children's home and orphanage as the place of occurrence of the external cause

Y92.110 Kitchen in children's home and orphanage as the place of occurrence of the external cause

Y92.111 Bathroom in children's home and orphanage as the place of occurrence of the external cause

Y92.112 Bedroom in children's home and orphanage as the place of occurrence of the external cause

Y92.113 Driveway of children's home and orphanage as the place of occurrence of the external cause

Y92.114 Garage of children's home and orphanage as the place of occurrence of the external cause

Y92.115 Swimming pool of children's home and orphanage as the place of occurrence of the external cause

Y92.116 Garden or yard of children's home and orphanage as the place of occurrence of the external cause

Y92.118 Other place in children's home and orphanage as the place of occurrence of the external cause

Y92.119 Unspecified place in children's home and orphanage as the place of occurrence of the external cause

● Y92.12 Nursing home as the place of occurrence of the external cause
Home for the sick as the place of occurrence of the external cause
Hospice as the place of occurrence of the external cause

Y92.120 Kitchen in nursing home as the place of occurrence of the external cause

Y92.121 Bathroom in nursing home as the place of occurrence of the external cause

Y92.122 Bedroom in nursing home as the place of occurrence of the external cause

Y92.123 Driveway of nursing home as the place of occurrence of the external cause

Y92.124 Garage of nursing home as the place of occurrence of the external cause

Y92.125 Swimming pool of nursing home as the place of occurrence of the external cause

Y92.126 Garden or yard of nursing home as the place of occurrence of the external cause

Y92.128 Other place in nursing home as the place of occurrence of the external cause

Y92.129 Unspecified place in nursing home as the place of occurrence of the external cause

● Y92.13 Military base as the place of occurrence of the external cause

Excludes1 military training grounds (Y92.83)

Y92.130 Kitchen on military base as the place of occurrence of the external cause

Y92.131 Mess hall on military base as the place of occurrence of the external cause

Y92.133 Barracks on military base as the place of occurrence of the external cause

Y92.135 Garage on military base as the place of occurrence of the external cause

Y92.136 Swimming pool on military base as the place of occurrence of the external cause

Y92.137 Garden or yard on military base as the place of occurrence of the external cause

Y92.138 Other place military base as the place of occurrence of the external cause

Y92.139 Unspecified place military base as the place of occurrence of the external cause

● Y92.14 Prison as the place of occurrence of the external cause

Y92.140 Kitchen in prison as the place of occurrence of the external cause

Y92.141 Dining room in prison as the place of occurrence of the external cause

● Unacceptable First-Listed Diagnosis   ● Use Additional Character(s)   Unspecified   OGCR Official Guidelines for Coding and Reporting

🗞 Complication\Comorbidity   🗞 Major C\C   Excludes 1   Excludes 2   Includes   Use additional   Code first   Code also   1707

Y92.142   Bathroom in prison as the place of occurrence of the external cause

Y92.143   Cell of prison as the place of occurrence of the external cause

Y92.146   Swimming pool of prison as the place of occurrence of the external cause

Y92.147   Courtyard of prison as the place of occurrence of the external cause

Y92.148   Other place in prison as the place of occurrence of the external cause

Y92.149   Unspecified place in prison as the place of occurrence of the external cause

● Y92.15   Reform school as the place of occurrence of the external cause

Y92.150   Kitchen in reform school as the place of occurrence of the external cause

Y92.151   Dining room in reform school as the place of occurrence of the external cause

Y92.152   Bathroom in reform school as the place of occurrence of the external cause

Y92.153   Bedroom in reform school as the place of occurrence of the external cause

Y92.154   Driveway of reform school as the place of occurrence of the external cause

Y92.155   Garage of reform school as the place of occurrence of the external cause

Y92.156   Swimming pool of reform school as the place of occurrence of the external cause

Y92.157   Garden or yard of reform school as the place of occurrence of the external cause

Y92.158   Other place in reform school as the place of occurrence of the external cause

Y92.159   Unspecified place in reform school as the place of occurrence of the external cause

● Y92.16   School dormitory as the place of occurrence of the external cause

> **Excludes1**   reform school as the place of occurrence of the external cause (Y92.15-)
> school buildings and grounds as the place of occurrence of the external cause (Y92.2x)
> school sports and athletic areas as the place of occurrence of the external cause (Y92.3x)

Y92.160   Kitchen in school dormitory as the place of occurrence of the external cause

Y92.161   Dining room in school dormitory as the place of occurrence of the external cause

Y92.162   Bathroom in school dormitory as the place of occurrence of the external cause

Y92.163   Bedroom in school dormitory as the place of occurrence of the external cause

Y92.168   Other place in school dormitory as the place of occurrence of the external cause

Y92.169   Unspecified place in school dormitory as the place of occurrence of the external cause

● Y92.19   Other specified residential institution as the place of occurrence of the external cause

Y92.190   Kitchen in other specified residential institution as the place of occurrence of the external cause

Y92.191   Dining room in other specified residential institution as the place of occurrence of the external cause

Y92.192   Bathroom in other specified residential institution as the place of occurrence of the external cause

Y92.193   Bedroom in other specified residential institution as the place of occurrence of the external cause

Y92.194   Driveway of other specified residential institution as the place of occurrence of the external cause

Y92.195   Garage of other specified residential institution as the place of occurrence of the external cause

Y92.196   Pool of other specified residential institution as the place of occurrence of the external cause

Y92.197   Garden or yard of other specified residential institution as the place of occurrence of the external cause

Y92.198   Other place in other specified residential institution as the place of occurrence of the external cause

Y92.199   Unspecified place in other specified residential institution as the place of occurrence of the external cause

● Y92.2   School, other institution and public administrative area as the place of occurrence of the external cause

Building and adjacent grounds used by the general public or by a particular group of the public

> **Excludes1**   building under construction as the place of occurrence of the external cause (Y92.6)
> residential institution as the place of occurrence of the external cause (Y92.1)
> school dormitory as the place of occurrence of the external cause (Y92.16-)
> sports and athletics area of schools as the place of occurrence of the external cause (Y92.3x)

● Unacceptable First-Listed Diagnosis   ● Use Additional Character(s)   ■ Unspecified   **OGCR** Official Guidelines for Coding and Reporting

🅒 Complication\Comorbidity   🅒 Major C\C   Excludes 1   Excludes 2   Includes   Use additional   Code first   Code also

● Y92.21 School (private) (public) (state) as the place of occurrence of the external cause

Y92.210 Daycare center as the place of occurrence of the external cause

Y92.211 Elementary school as the place of occurrence of the external cause
Kindergarten as the place of occurrence of the external cause

Y92.212 Middle school as the place of occurrence of the external cause

Y92.213 High school as the place of occurrence of the external cause

Y92.214 College as the place of occurrence of the external cause
University as the place of occurrence of the external cause

Y92.215 Trade school as the place of occurrence of the external cause

Y92.218 Other school as the place of occurrence of the external cause

▪ Y92.219 Unspecified school as the place of occurrence of the external cause

Y92.22 Religious institution as the place of occurrence of the external cause
Church as the place of occurrence of the external cause
Mosque as the place of occurrence of the external cause
Synagogue as the place of occurrence of the external cause

● Y92.23 Hospital as the place of occurrence of the external cause

Excludes1   ambulatory (outpatient) health services establishments (Y92.53-)
home for the sick as the place of occurrence of the external cause (Y92.12-)
hospice as the place of occurrence of the external cause (Y92.12-)
nursing home as the place of occurrence of the external cause (Y92.12-)

Y92.230 Patient room in hospital as the place of occurrence of the external cause

Y92.231 Patient bathroom in hospital as the place of occurrence of the external cause

Y92.232 Corridor of hospital as the place of occurrence of the external cause

Y92.233 Cafeteria of hospital as the place of occurrence of the external cause

Y92.234 Operating room of hospital as the place of occurrence of the external cause

Y92.238 Other place in hospital as the place of occurrence of the external cause

▪ Y92.239 Unspecified place in hospital as the place of occurrence of the external cause

● Y92.24 Public administrative building as the place of occurrence of the external cause

Y92.240 Courthouse as the place of occurrence of the external cause

Y92.241 Library as the place of occurrence of the external cause

Y92.242 Post office as the place of occurrence of the external cause

Y92.243 City hall as the place of occurrence of the external cause

Y92.248 Other public administrative building as the place of occurrence of the external cause

● Y92.25 Cultural building as the place of occurrence of the external cause

Y92.250 Art gallery as the place of occurrence of the external cause

Y92.251 Museum as the place of occurrence of the external cause

Y92.252 Music hall as the place of occurrence of the external cause

Y92.253 Opera house as the place of occurrence of the external cause

Y92.254 Theater (live) as the place of occurrence of the external cause

Y92.258 Other cultural public building as the place of occurrence of the external cause

Y92.26 Movie house or cinema as the place of occurrence of the external cause

Y92.29 Other specified public building as the place of occurrence of the external cause
Assembly hall as the place of occurrence of the external cause
Clubhouse as the place of occurrence of the external cause

● Y92.3 Sports and athletics area as the place of occurrence of the external cause

● Y92.31 Athletic court as the place of occurrence of the external cause

Excludes1   tennis court in private home or garden (Y92.09)

Y92.310 Basketball court as the place of occurrence of the external cause

Y92.311 Squash court as the place of occurrence of the external cause

Y92.312 Tennis court as the place of occurrence of the external cause

Y92.318 Other athletic court as the place of occurrence of the external cause

● Y92.32 Athletic field as the place of occurrence of the external cause

Y92.320 Baseball field as the place of occurrence of the external cause

Y92.321 Football field as the place of occurrence of the external cause

Y92.322 Soccer field as the place of occurrence of the external cause

Y92.328 Other athletic field as the place of occurrence of the external cause
Cricket field as the place of occurrence of the external cause
Hockey field as the place of occurrence of the external cause

● Unacceptable First-Listed Diagnosis   ● Use Additional Character(s)   ▪ Unspecified   OGCR Official Guidelines for Coding and Reporting
🅒 Complication\Comorbidity   🅒 Major C\C   Includes   Use additional   Code first   Code also

- **Y92.33 Skating rink as the place of occurrence of the external cause**
  - Y92.330 Ice skating rink (indoor) (outdoor) as the place of occurrence of the external cause
  - Y92.331 Roller skating rink as the place of occurrence of the external cause
  - Y92.34 Swimming pool (public) as the place of occurrence of the external cause
    - **Excludes1** swimming pool in private home or garden (Y92.06)
  - Y92.39 Other specified sports and athletic area as the place of occurrence of the external cause
    - Golf-course as the place of occurrence of the external cause
    - Gymnasium as the place of occurrence of the external cause
    - Riding-school as the place of occurrence of the external cause
    - Stadium as the place of occurrence of the external cause
- **Y92.4 Street , highway and other paved roadways as the place of occurrence of the external cause**
  - **Excludes1** private driveway of residence (Y92.0x4, Y92.1x3)
  - **Y92.41 Street and highway as the place of occurrence of the external cause**
    - Y92.410 Unspecified street and highway as the place of occurrence of the external cause
      - Road NOS as the place of occurrence of the external cause
    - Y92.411 Interstate highway as the place of occurrence of the external cause
      - Freeway as the place of occurrence of the external cause
      - Motorway as the place of occurrence of the external cause
    - Y92.412 Parkway as the place of occurrence of the external cause
    - Y92.413 State road as the place of occurrence of the external cause
    - Y92.414 Local residential or business street as the place of occurrence of the external cause
    - Y92.415 Exit ramp or entrance ramp of street or highway as the place of occurrence of the external cause
  - **Y92.48 Other paved roadways as the place of occurrence of the external cause**
    - Y92.480 Sidewalk as the place of occurrence of the external cause
    - Y92.481 Parking lot as the place of occurrence of the external cause
    - Y92.482 Bike path as the place of occurrence of the external cause
    - Y92.488 Other paved roadways as the place of occurrence of the external cause

- **Y92.5 Trade and service area as the place of occurrence of the external cause**
  - **Excludes1** garage in private home (Y92.05) schools and other public administration buildings (Y92.2-)
  - **Y92.51 Private commercial establishments as the place of occurrence of the external cause**
    - Y92.510 Bank as the place of occurrence of the external cause
    - Y92.511 Restaurant or café as the place of occurrence of the external cause
    - Y92.512 Supermarket, store or market as the place of occurrence of the external cause
    - Y92.513 Shop (commercial) as the place of occurrence of the external cause
  - **Y92.52 Service areas as the place of occurrence of the external cause**
    - Y92.520 Airport as the place of occurrence of the external cause
    - Y92.521 Bus station as the place of occurrence of the external cause
    - Y92.522 Railway station as the place of occurrence of the external cause
    - Y92.523 Highway rest stop as the place of occurrence of the external cause
    - Y92.524 Gas station as the place of occurrence of the external cause
      - Petroleum station as the place of occurrence of the external cause
      - Service station as the place of occurrence of the external cause
  - **Y92.53 Ambulatory health services establishments as the place of occurrence of the external cause**
    - Y92.530 Ambulatory surgery center as the place of occurrence of the external cause
      - Outpatient surgery center, including that connected with a hospital as the place of occurrence of the external cause
      - Same day surgery center, including that connected with a hospital as the place of occurrence of the external cause
    - Y92.531 Health care provider office as the place of occurrence of the external cause
      - Physician office as the place of occurrence of the external cause
    - Y92.532 Urgent care center as the place of occurrence of the external cause
    - Y92.538 Other ambulatory health services establishments as the place of occurrence of the external cause

● Unacceptable First-Listed Diagnosis   ● Use Additional Character(s)   ■ Unspecified   **OGCR** Official Guidelines for Coding and Reporting
Complication\Comorbidity   Major C\C   Excludes 1   Excludes 2   Includes   Use additional   Code first   Code also

Y92.59 **Other trade areas as the place of occurrence of the external cause**
    Office building as the place of occurrence of the external cause
    Casino as the place of occurrence of the external cause
    Garage (commercial) as the place of occurrence of the external cause
    Hotel as the place of occurrence of the external cause
    Radio or television station as the place of occurrence of the external cause
    Shopping mall as the place of occurrence of the external cause
    Warehouse as the place of occurrence of the external cause

● Y92.6 **Industrial and construction area as the place of occurrence of the external cause**

Y92.61 **Building [any] under construction as the place of occurrence of the external cause**

Y92.62 **Dock or shipyard as the place of occurrence of the external cause**
    Dockyard as the place of occurrence of the external cause
    Dry dock as the place of occurrence of the external cause
    Shipyard as the place of occurrence of the external cause

Y92.63 **Factory as the place of occurrence of the external cause**
    Factory building as the place of occurrence of the external cause
    Factory premises as the place of occurrence of the external cause
    Industrial yard as the place of occurrence of the external cause

Y92.64 **Mine or pit as the place of occurrence of the external cause**
    Mine as the place of occurrence of the external cause

Y92.65 **Oil rig as the place of occurrence of the external cause**
    Pit (coal) (gravel) (sand) as the place of occurrence of the external cause

Y92.69 **Other specified industrial and construction area as the place of occurrence of the external cause**
    Gasworks as the place of occurrence of the external cause
    Power-station (coal) (nuclear) (oil) as the place of occurrence of the external cause
    Tunnel under construction as the place of occurrence of the external cause
    Workshop as the place of occurrence of the external cause

● Y92.7 **Farm as the place of occurrence of the external cause**
    Ranch as the place of occurrence of the external cause
    Excludes1 farmhouse and home premises of farm (Y92.01-)

Y92.71 **Barn as the place of occurrence of the external cause**

Y92.72 **Chicken coop as the place of occurrence of the external cause**
    Hen house as the place of occurrence of the external cause

Y92.73 **Farm field as the place of occurrence of the external cause**

Y92.74 **Orchard as the place of occurrence of the external cause**

Y92.79 **Other farm location as the place of occurrence of the external cause**

● Y92.8 **Other places as the place of occurrence of the external cause**

● Y92.81 **Transport vehicle as the place of occurrence of the external cause**
    Excludes1 transport accidents (V00-V99)

Y92.810 **Car as the place of occurrence of the external cause**

Y92.811 **Bus as the place of occurrence of the external cause**

Y92.812 **Truck as the place of occurrence of the external cause**

Y92.813 **Airplane as the place of occurrence of the external cause**

Y92.814 **Boat as the place of occurrence of the external cause**

Y92.815 **Train as the place of occurrence of the external cause**

Y92.816 **Subway car as the place of occurrence of the external cause**

Y92.818 **Other transport vehicle as the place of occurrence of the external cause**

● Y92.82 **Wilderness area**

Y92.820 **Desert as the place of occurrence of the external cause**

Y92.821 **Forest as the place of occurrence of the external cause**

Y92.828 **Other wilderness area as the place of occurrence of the external cause**
    Swamp as the place of occurrence of the external cause
    Mountain as the place of occurrence of the external cause
    Marsh as the place of occurrence of the external cause
    Prairie as the place of occurrence of the external cause

● Y92.83 **Recreation area as the place of occurrence of the external cause**

Y92.830 **Public park as the place of occurrence of the external cause**

Y92.831 **Amusement park as the place of occurrence of the external cause**

Y92.832 **Beach as the place of occurrence of the external cause**
    Seashore as the place of occurrence of the external cause

Y92.833 **Campsite as the place of occurrence of the external cause**

Y92.834 **Zoological garden (zoo) as the place of occurrence of the external cause**

Y92.838 **Other recreation area as the place of occurrence of the external cause**

Y92.84 **Military training ground as the place of occurrence of the external cause**

● Unacceptable First-Listed Diagnosis   ● Use Additional Character(s)   ■ Unspecified   **OGCR** Official Guidelines for Coding and Reporting
Complication\Comorbidity   Major C\C   Excludes 1   Excludes 2   Includes   Use additional   Code first   Code also

1711

CHAPTER 20 (V01-Y99)

Y92.85 Railroad track as the place of occurrence of the external cause

Y92.86 Slaughter house as the place of occurrence of the external cause

Y92.89 Other specified places as the place of occurrence of the external cause
Derelict house as the place of occurrence of the external cause

■ Y92.9 Unspecified place or not applicable
OGCR See Section I.C.20.c.
20.10 Activity code

● Y93 Activity code
Note: Category Y93 is provided for use to indicate the activity of the person seeking healthcare for an injury or health condition, such as a heart attack while shoveling snow, which resulted from, or was contributed to, by the activity. These codes are appropriate for use for both acute injuries, such as those from chapter 19, and conditions that are due to the long-term, cumulative effects of an activity, such as those from chapter 13. They are also appropriate for use with external cause codes for cause and intent if identifying the activity provides additional information on the event. These codes should be used in conjunction with codes for external cause status (Y99) and place of occurrence (Y92).

This section contains the following broad activity categories:

Y93.0 Activities involving walking and running

Y93.1 Activities involving water and water craft

Y93.2 Activities involving ice and snow

Y93.3 Activities involving climbing, rappelling, and jumping off

Y93.4 Activities involving dancing and other rhythmic movement

Y93.5 Activities involving other sports and athletics played individually

Y93.6 Activities involving other sports and athletics played as a team or group

Y93.7 Activities involving other specified sports and athletics

Y93.a Activity involving other cardiorespiratory exercise

Y93.b Activity involving other muscle strengthening exercises

Y93.c Activities involving computer technology and electronic devices

Y93.d Activities involving arts and handcrafts

Y93.e Activities involving personal hygiene and household maintenance

Y93.f Activities involving person providing caregiving

Y93.g Activities involving food preparation, cooking and grilling

Y93.h Activities involving property and land maintenance, building and construction

Y93.i Activities involving roller coasters and other types of external motion

Y93.j Activities involving playing musical instrument

Y93.k Activities involving animal care

Y93.8 Other activity

Y93.9 Unspecified activity

● Y93.0 Activities involving walking and running
[Excludes1] walking an animal (Y93.k1)
walking or running on a treadmill (Y93.a1)

Y93.01 Walking, marching and hiking
Walking, marching and hiking on level or elevated terrain
[Excludes1] mountain climbing (Y93.31)

Y93.02 Running

● Y93.1 Activities involving water and water craft
[Excludes1] activities involving ice (Y93.2-)

Y93.11 Swimming

Y93.12 Springboard and platform diving

Y93.13 Water polo

Y93.14 Water aerobics and water exercise

Y93.15 Underwater diving and snorkeling
SCUBA diving

Y93.16 Rowing, canoeing, kayaking, rafting and tubing
Canoeing, kayaking, rafting and tubing in calm and turbulent water

Y93.17 Water skiing and wake boarding

Y93.18 Surfing, windsurfing and boogie boarding
Water sliding

Y93.19 Other activity involving water and watercraft
Activity involving water NOS
Parasailing
Water survival training and testing

● Y93.2 Activities involving ice and snow
[Excludes1] shoveling ice and snow (Y93.h1)

Y93.21 Ice skating
Figure skating (singles) (pairs)
Ice dancing
[Excludes1] ice hockey (Y93.22)

Y93.22 Ice hockey

Y93.23 Snow (alpine) (downhill) skiing, snow boarding, sledding, tobogganing and snow tubing
[Excludes1] cross country skiing (Y93.24)

Y93.24 Cross country skiing
Nordic skiing

Y93.29 Other activity involving ice and snow
Activity involving ice and snow NOS

● Y93.3 Activities involving climbing, rappelling and jumping off
[Excludes1] hiking on level or elevated terrain (Y93.01)
jumping rope (Y93.56)
trampoline jumping (Y93.44)

Y93.31 Mountain climbing, rock climbing and wall climbing

Y93.32 Rappelling

Y93.33 BASE jumping
Building, Antenna, Span, Earth jumping

Y93.34 Bungee jumping

Y93.35 Hang gliding

Y93.39 Other activity involving climbing, rappelling and jumping off

● Y93.4   **Activities involving dancing and other rhythmic movement**
  | Excludes1 | martial arts (Y93.75)

  Y93.41 **Dancing**

  Y93.42 **Yoga**

  Y93.43 **Gymnastics**
      Rhythmic gymnastics
      | Excludes1 | trampolining (Y93.44)

  Y93.44 **Trampolining**

  Y93.45 **Cheerleading**

  Y93.49 **Other activity involving dancing and other rhythmic movements**

● Y93.5   **Activities involving other sports and athletics played individually**
  | Excludes1 | dancing (Y93.41)
          gymnastic (Y93.43)
          trampolining (Y93.44)
          yoga (Y93.42)

  Y93.51 **Roller skating (inline) and skateboarding**

  Y93.52 **Horseback riding**

  Y93.53 **Golf**

  Y93.54 **Bowling**

  Y93.55 **Bike riding**

  Y93.56 **Jumping rope**

  Y93.57 **Non-running track and field events**
      | Excludes1 | running (any form) (Y93.02)

  Y93.59 **Other activity involving other sports and athletics played individually**
      | Excludes1 | activities involving climbing, rappelling, and jumping (Y93.3-)
              activities involving ice and snow (Y93.2-)
              activities involving walking and running (Y93.0-)
              activities involving water and watercraft (Y93.1-)

● Y93.6   **Activities involving other sports and athletics played as a team or group**
  | Excludes1 | ice hockey (Y93.22)
          water polo (Y93.13)

  Y93.61 **American tackle football**
      Football NOS

  Y93.62 **American flag or touch football**

  Y93.63 **Rugby**

  Y93.64 **Baseball**
      Softball

  Y93.65 **Lacrosse and field hockey**

  Y93.66 **Soccer**

  Y93.67 **Basketball**

  Y93.68 **Volleyball (beach) (court)**

  Y93.6a **Physical games generally associated with school recess, summer camp and children**
      Capture the flag
      Dodge ball
      Four square
      Kickball

  Y93.69 **Other activity involving other sports and athletics played as a team or group**
      Cricket

● Y93.7   **Activities involving other specified sports and athletics**

  Y93.71 **Boxing**

  Y93.72 **Wrestling**

  Y93.73 **Racquet and hand sports**
      Handball
      Racquetball
      Squash
      Tennis

  Y93.74 **Frisbee**
      Ultimate frisbee

  Y93.75 **Martial arts**
      Combatives

  Y93.79 **Other specified sports and athletics activity**
      | Excludes1 | sports and athletics activities specified in categories Y93.0-Y93.6

● Y93.a   **Activity involving other cardiorespiratory exercise**
      Activity involving physical training

  Y93.a1 **Exercise machines primarily for cardiorespiratory conditioning**
      Elliptical and stepper machines
      Stationary bike
      Treadmill

  Y93.a2 **Calisthenics**
      Jumping jacks
      Warm up and cool down

  Y93.a3 **Aerobic and step exercise**

  Y93.a4 **Circuit training**

  Y93.a5 **Obstacle course**
      Challenge course
      Confidence course

  Y93.a6 **Grass drills**
      Guerilla drills

  Y93.a9 **Other activity involving other cardiorespiratory exercise**
      | Excludes1 | activities involving cardiorespiratory exercise specified in categories Y93.0-Y93.7

● Y93.b   **Activity involving other muscle strengthening exercises**

  Y93.b1 **Exercise machines primarily for muscle strengthening**

  Y93.b2 **Push-ups, pull-ups, sit-ups**

  Y93.b3 **Free weights**
      Barbells
      Dumbbells

  Y93.b4 **Pilates**

  Y93.b9 **Other activity involving other muscle strengthening exercises**
      | Excludes1 | activities involving muscle strengthening specified in categories Y93.0-Y93.a

● Y93.c   **Activities involving computer technology and electronic devices**
      | Excludes1 | electronic musical keyboard or instruments (Y93.j-)

  Y93.c1 **Computer keyboarding**
      Electronic game playing using keyboard or other stationary device

● Unacceptable First-Listed Diagnosis   ● Use Additional Character(s)   ▪ Unspecified   **OGCR** Official Guidelines for Coding and Reporting

🔖 Complication\Comorbidity   🔖 Major C\C | Excludes 1 | | Excludes 2 | Includes   Use additional   Code first   Code also   1713

Y93.c2   **Hand held interactive electronic device**
Cellular telephone and communication device
Electronic game playing using interactive device

Excludes1   electronic game playing using keyboard or other stationary device (Y93.c1)

Y93.c9   **Other activity involving computer technology and electronic devices**

● Y93.d   **Activities involving arts and handcrafts**

Excludes1   activities involving playing musical instrument (Y93.j-)

Y93.d1   **Knitting and crocheting**

Y93.d2   **Sewing**

Y93.d3   **Furniture building and finishing**
Furniture repair

Y93.d9   **Activity involving other arts and handcrafts**

● Y93.e   **Activities involving personal hygiene and household maintenance**

Excludes1   activities involving cooking and grilling (Y93.g-)
activities involving property and land maintenance, building and construction (Y93.h-)
activity involving persons providing caregiving (Y93.f-)
dishwashing (Y93.g1)
food preparation (Y93.g1)
gardening (Y93.h2)

Y93.e1   **Personal bathing and showering**

Y93.e2   **Laundry**

Y93.e3   **Vacuuming**

Y93.e4   **Ironing**

Y93.e5   **Floor mopping and cleaning**

Y93.e6   **Residential relocation**
Packing up and unpacking involved in moving to a new residence

Y93.e8   **Other personal hygiene activity**

Y93.e9   **Other household maintenance**

● Y93.f   **Activities involving person providing caregiving**

Y93.f1   **Caregiving involving bathing**

Y93.f2   **Caregiving involving lifting**

Y93.f9   **Other activity involving person providing caregiving**

● Y93.g   **Activities involving food preparation, cooking and grilling**

Y93.g1   **Food preparation and clean up**
Dishwashing

Y93.g2   **Grilling and smoking food**

Y93.g3   **Cooking and baking**
Use of stove, oven and microwave oven

Y93.g9   **Other activity involving cooking and grilling**

● Y93.h   **Activities involving property and land maintenance, building and construction**

Y93.h1   **Digging, shoveling and raking**
Dirt digging
Raking leaves
Snow shoveling

Y93.h2   **Gardening and landscaping**
Pruning, trimming shrubs, weeding

Y93.h3   **Building and construction**

Y93.h9   **Other activity involving property and land maintenance, building and construction**

● Y93.i   **Activities involving roller coasters and other types of external motion**

Y93.i1   **Rollercoaster riding**

Y93.i9   **Other activity involving external motion**

● Y93.j   **Activities involving playing musical instrument**
Activity involving playing electric musical instrument

Y93.j1   **Piano playing**
Musical keyboard (electronic) playing

Y93.j2   **Drum and other percussion instrument playing**

Y93.j3   **String instrument playing**

Y93.j4   **Winds and brass instrument playing**

● Y93.k   **Activities involving animal care**

Excludes1   horseback riding (Y93.52)

Y93.k1   **Walking an animal**

Y93.k2   **Milking an animal**

Y93.k3   **Grooming and shearing an animal**

Y93.k9   **Other activity involving animal care**

● Y93.8   **Other activity**

Y93.81   **Refereeing a sports activity**

Y93.82   **Spectator at an event**

Y93.83   **Rough housing and horseplay**

Y93.84   **Sleeping**

Y93.89   **Other activity**

● Y93.9   **Unspecified activity**

Y95   **Nosocomial condition**

Category Y96   deactivated- use code Y99.0

Category Y97   deactivated- See categories Z57, Z77

Category Y98   deactivated. See categories Z72, Z73

● Y99   **External cause status**

Note: A single code from category Y99 should be used in conjunction with the external cause code(s) assigned to a record to indicate the status of the person at the time the event occurred.

Y99.0   **Civilian activity done for income or pay**
Civilian activity done for financial or other compensation

Excludes1   military activity (Y99.1)

Y99.1   **Military activity**

Excludes1   activity of off duty military personnel (Y99.8)

Y99.8   **Other external cause status**
Activity NEC
Hobby not done for income
Leisure activity
Off-duty activity of military personnel
Recreation or sport not for income or while a student
Student activity
Volunteer activity

Excludes1   civilian activity done for income or compensation (Y99.0)
military activity (Y99.1)

■ Y99.9   **Unspecified external cause status**

● Unacceptable First-Listed Diagnosis   ● Use Additional Character(s)   ■ Unspecified   **OGCR** Official Guidelines for Coding and Reporting
🗬 Complication\Comorbidity   🗬 Major C\C   Excludes 1   Excludes 2   Includes   Use additional   Code first   Code also

OGCR See Guidelines, **Section II.C.21.**

CHAPTER 21

FACTORS INFLUENCING HEALTH STATUS AND CONTACT WITH HEALTH SERVICES (Z00-Z99)

Note: Z codes represent reasons for encounters. A corresponding procedure code must accompany a Z code if a procedure is performed. Categories Z00-Z99 are provided for occasions when circumstances other than a disease, injury or external cause classifiable to categories A00-Y89 are recorded as "diagnoses" or "problems." This can arise in two main ways:

(a) When a person who may or may not be sick encounters the health services for some specific purpose, such as to receive limited care or service for a current condition, to donate an organ or tissue, to receive prophylactic vaccination (immunization), or to discuss a problem which is in itself not a disease or injury.

(b) When some circumstance or problem is present which influences the person's health status but is not in itself a current illness or injury.

This chapter contains the following blocks:

Z00-Z13	Persons encountering health services for examination and investigation
Z14-Z15	Genetic carrier and genetic susceptibility to disease
Z16	Infection with drug resistant microorganisms
Z17	Estrogen receptor status
Z20-Z28	Persons with potential health hazards related to communicable diseases
Z30-Z39	Persons encountering health services in circumstances related to reproduction
Z40-Z53	Persons encountering health services for specific procedures and health care
Z55-Z65	Persons with potential health hazards related to socioeconomic and psychosocial circumstances
Z66	Do not resuscitate [DNR] status
Z67	Blood type
Z68	Body mass index (BMI)
Z69-Z76	Persons encountering health services in other circumstances
Z77-Z99	Persons with potential health hazards related to family and personal history and certain conditions influencing health status

PERSONS ENCOUNTERING HEALTH SERVICES FOR EXAMINATIONS (Z00-Z13)

Note: Nonspecific abnormal findings disclosed at the time of these examinations are classified to categories R70-R94.

Excludes1 examinations related to pregnancy and reproduction (Z30-Z36, Z39.-)

● **Z00**   **Encounter for general examination without complaint, suspected or reported diagnosis**

     Excludes1 encounter for examination for administrative purposes (Z02.-)

     Excludes2 encounter for pre-procedural examinations (Z01.81-)

           special screening examinations (Z11-Z13)

● **Z00.0**   **Encounter for general adult medical examination**

     Encounter for adult periodic examination (annual) (physical) and any associated laboratory and radiologic examinations

     Excludes1 encounter for examination of sign or symptom - code to sign or symptom

           general health check-up of infant or child (Z00.12.-)

❶ **Z00.00**   **Encounter for general adult medical examination without abnormal findings**

     Encounter for adult health check-up NOS

❶ **Z00.01**   **Encounter for general adult medical examination with abnormal findings**

     Use additional code to identify abnormal findings

● **Z00.1**   **Encounter for newborn, infant and child health examinations**

● **Z00.11**   **Newborn health examination**

     Health check for child under 29 days old

     Use additional code to identify any abnormal findings

     Excludes1 health check for child over 28 days old (Z00.12-)

❶ **Z00.110**   **Health examination for newborn under 8 days old**

     Health check for newborn under 8 days old

❶ **Z00.111**   **Health examination for newborn 8 to 28 days old**

     Health check for newborn 8 to 28 days old

     Newborn weight check

● **Z00.12**   **Encounter for routine child health examination**

     Encounter for development testing of infant or child

     Health check (routine) for child over 28 days old

     Excludes1 health check for child under 29 days old (Z0.11-)

           health supervision of foundling or other healthy infant or child (Z76.1-Z76.2)

           newborn health examination (Z00.11-)

❶ **Z00.121**   **Encounter for routine child health examination with abnormal findings**

     Use additional code to identify abnormal findings

❶ **Z00.129**   **Encounter for routine child health examination without abnormal findings**

     Encounter for routine child health examination NOS

❶ **Z00.2**   **Encounter for examination for period of rapid growth in childhood**

❶ **Z00.3**   **Encounter for examination for adolescent development state**

     Encounter for puberty development state

❶ **Z00.5**   **Encounter for examination of potential donor of organ and tissue**

❶ **Z00.6**   **Encounter for examination for normal comparison and control in clinical research program**

● Unacceptable First-Listed Diagnosis   ● Use Additional Character(s)   ❶ First Listed   ❶/❷ First Listed or Secondary

🅒 Complication\Comorbidity   🅜 Major C\C   ❷ Secondary Only   ⬛ Unspecified   **OGCR** Official Guidelines for Coding and Reporting

Excludes 1   Excludes 2   Includes   Use additional   Code first   Code also

- **Z00.7 Encounter for examination for period of delayed growth in childhood**
  - **Z00.70 Encounter for examination for period of delayed growth in childhood without abnormal findings**
  - **Z00.71 Encounter for examination for period of delayed growth in childhood with abnormal findings**

    Use additional code to identify abnormal findings

- **Z00.8 Encounter for other general examination**

  Encounter for health examination in population surveys

- **Z01 Encounter for other special examination without complaint, suspected or reported diagnosis**

  Includes   routine examination of specific system

  Note: Codes from category Z01 represent the reason for the encounter. A separate procedure code is required to identify any examinations or procedures performed.

  Excludes1   encounter for examination for administrative purposes (Z02.-)

  encounter for examination for suspected conditions, proven not to exist (Z03.-)

  encounter for laboratory and radiologic examinations as a component of general medical examinations (Z00.0-)

  encounter for laboratory, radiologic and imaging examinations for sign(s) and symptom(s) - code to the sign(s) or symptom(s)

  Excludes2   screening examinations (Z11-Z13)

  - **Z01.0 Encounter for examination of eyes and vision**

    Excludes1   examination for driving license (Z02.4)

    - **Z01.00 Encounter for examination of eyes and vision without abnormal findings**

      Encounter for examination of eyes and vision NOS

    - **Z01.01 Encounter for examination of eyes and vision with abnormal findings**

      Use additional code to identify abnormal findings

  - **Z01.1 Encounter for examination of ears and hearing**

    - **Z01.10 Encounter for examination of ears and hearing without abnormal findings**

      Encounter for examination of ears and hearing NOS

    - **Z01.11 Encounter for examination of ears and hearing with abnormal findings**

      - **Z01.110 Encounter for hearing examination following failed hearing screening**

      - **Z01.118 Encounter for examination of ears and hearing with other abnormal findings**

        Use additional code to identify abnormal findings

    - **Z01.12 Encounter for hearing conservation and treatment**

  - **Z01.2 Encounter for dental examination and cleaning**

    - **Z01.20 Encounter for dental examination and cleaning without abnormal findings**

      Encounter for dental examination and cleaning NOS

    - **Z01.21 Encounter for dental examination and cleaning with abnormal findings**

      Use additional code to identify abnormal findings

- **Z01.3 Encounter for examination of blood pressure**

  - **Z01.30 Encounter for examination of blood pressure without abnormal findings**

    Encounter for examination of blood pressure NOS

  - **Z01.31 Encounter for examination of blood pressure with abnormal findings**

    Use additional code to identify abnormal findings

- **Z01.4 Encounter for gynecological examination**

  Excludes2   pregnancy examination or test (Z32.0-)

  routine examination for contraceptive maintenance (Z30.4)

  - **Z01.41 Encounter for routine gynecological examination**

    Encounter for general gynecological examination with or without cervical smear

    Encounter for gynecological examination (general) (routine) NOS

    Encounter for pelvic examination (annual) (periodic)

    Use additional code:

    for screening for human papillomavirus, if applicable (Z11.51)

    for screening vaginal pap smear, if applicable (Z12.72)

    to identify acquired absence of uterus, if applicable (Z90.71-)

    Excludes1   gynecologic examination status-post hysterectomy for malignant condition (Z08)

    screening cervical pap smear not a part of a routine gynecological examination (Z12.4)

    - **Z01.411 Encounter for gynecological examination (general) (routine) with abnormal findings**

    - **Z01.419 Encounter for gynecological examination (general) (routine) without abnormal findings**

      Use additional code to identify abnormal findings

  - **Z01.42 Encounter for cervical smear to confirm findings of recent normal smear following initial abnormal smear**

- **Z01.8 Encounter for other specified special examinations**

  - **Z01.81 Encounter for preprocedural examinations**

    Encounter for preoperative examinations

    Encounter for radiological and imaging examinations as part of preprocedural examination

    - **Z01.810 Encounter for preprocedural cardiovascular examination**

    - **Z01.811 Encounter for preprocedural respiratory examination**

    - **Z01.812 Encounter for preprocedural laboratory examination**

      Blood and urine tests prior to treatment or procedure

● Unacceptable First-Listed Diagnosis   ● Use Additional Character(s)   ❶ First Listed   ⑫ First Listed or Secondary
🅒 Complication\Comorbidity   🅜 Major C\C   ❷ Secondary Only   ■ Unspecified   **OGCR** Official Guidelines for Coding and Reporting

Excludes 1   Excludes 2   Includes   Use additional   Code first   Code also

❶ **Z01.818 Encounter for other preprocedural examination**
Encounter for preprocedural examination NOS
Encounter for examinations prior to antineoplastic chemotherapy

❶ **Z01.82 Encounter for allergy testing**
Excludes1 encounter for antibody response examination (Z01.84)

❶ **Z01.83 Encounter for blood typing**
Encounter for Rh typing

❶ **Z01.84 Encounter for antibody response examination**
Encounter for immunity status testing
Excludes1 encounter for allergy testing (Z01.82)

❶ **Z01.89 Encounter for other specified special examinations**

● **Z02 Encounter for administrative examination**

❶ **Z02.0 Encounter for examination for admission to educational institution**
Encounter for examination for admission to preschool (education)
Encounter for examination for re-admission to school following illness or medical treatment

❶ **Z02.1 Encounter for pre-employment examination**

❶ **Z02.2 Encounter for examination for admission to residential institution**
Excludes1 examination for admission to prison (Z02.8)

❶ **Z02.3 Encounter for examination for recruitment to armed forces**

❶ **Z02.4 Encounter for examination for driving license**

❶ **Z02.5 Encounter for examination for participation in sport**
Excludes1 blood-alcohol and blood-drug test (Z02.83)

❶ **Z02.6 Encounter for examination for insurance purposes**

● **Z02.7 Encounter for issue of medical certificate**
Excludes1 encounter for general medical examination (Z00-Z01, Z02.0-Z02.6, Z02.8-Z02.9)

❶ **Z02.71 Encounter for disability determination**
Encounter for issue of medical certificate of incapacity
Encounter for issue of medical certificate of invalidity

❶ **Z02.79 Encounter for issue of other medical certificate**

● **Z02.8 Encounter for other administrative examinations**

❶ **Z02.81 Encounter for paternity testing**

❶ **Z02.82 Encounter for adoption services**

❶ **Z02.83 Encounter for blood-alcohol and blood-drug test**
Use additional code for findings of alcohol or drugs in blood (R78.-)

❶ **Z02.89 Encounter for other administrative examinations**
Encounter for examination for admission to prison
Encounter for examination for admission to summer camp
Encounter for immigration examination
Encounter for naturalization examination
Encounter for premarital examination
Excludes1 health supervision of foundling or other healthy infant or child (Z76.1-Z76.2)

❶ ▦ **Z02.9 Encounter for administrative examinations, unspecified**

OGCR Section II.C.21.c.6.

21.2.2. Observation

There are two observation Z code categories. They are for use in very limited circumstances when a person is being observed for a suspected condition that is ruled out. The observation codes are not for use if an injury or illnesses or any signs or symptoms related to the suspected condition are present. In such cases the diagnosis/symptom code is used with the corresponding external cause code.

The observation codes are to be used as principal diagnosis only. Additional codes may be used in addition to the observation code but only if they are unrelated to the suspected condition being observed.

Codes from subcategory Z03.7 Encounter for suspected maternal and fetal conditions ruled out, may either be used as a first listed or as an additional code assignment depending on the case. They are for use in very limited circumstances on a maternal record when an encounter is for a suspected maternal or fetal condition that is ruled out during that encounter (for example, a maternal or fetal condition may be suspected due to an abnormal test result). These codes should not be used when the condition is confirmed. In those cases, the confirmed condition should be coded. In addition, these codes are not for use if an illness or any signs or symptoms related to the suspected condition or problem are present. In such cases the diagnosis/symptom code is used.

Additional codes may be used in addition to the code from subcategory Z03.7, but only if they are unrelated to the suspected condition being evaluated.

Codes from subcategory Z03.7 may not be used for encounters for antenatal screening of mother. *See Section I.C.21.c.5, Screening.*

For encounters for suspected fetal condition that are inconclusive following testing and evaluation, assign the appropriate code from category O35, O36, O40 or O41.

The observation Z code categories:
Z03   Encounter for medical observation for suspected diseases and conditions ruled out
Z04   Encounter for examination and observation for other reasons
Except: Z04.9, Encounter for examination and observation for unspecified reason

● Unacceptable First-Listed Diagnosis ● Use Additional Character(s) ❶ First Listed ▦ First Listed or Secondary
Complication\Comorbidity Major C\C ❷ Secondary Only ▦ Unspecified **OGCR** Official Guidelines for Coding and Reporting
Excludes 1 Excludes 2 Includes Use additional Code first Code also

1717

CHAPTER 21 (Z00-Z99)

● **Z03 Encounter for medical observation for suspected diseases and conditions ruled out**

This category is to be used when a person without a diagnosis is suspected of having an abnormal condition, without signs or symptoms, which requires study, but after examination and observation, is ruled out. This category is also for use for administrative and legal observation status.

> **Excludes1**   contact with and (suspected) exposures hazardous to health (Z77.-)
> newborn observation for suspected condition, ruled out (P00-P04)
> person with feared complaint in whom no diagnosis is made (Z71.1)
> signs or symptoms under study - code to signs or symptoms

❶ **Z03.6 Encounter for observation for suspected toxic effect from ingested substance ruled out**
Encounter for observation for suspected adverse effect from drug
Encounter for observation for suspected poisoning

● **Z03.7 Encounter for suspected maternal and fetal conditions ruled out**
Encounter for suspected maternal and fetal conditions not found

> **Excludes1**   known or suspected fetal anomalies affecting management of mother, not ruled out (O26.-, O35.-, O36.-, O40.-, O41.-)

     ❶ **Z03.71 Encounter for suspected problem with amniotic cavity and membrane ruled out**
Encounter for suspected oligohydramnios ruled out
Encounter for suspected polyhydramnios ruled out

     ❶ **Z03.72 Encounter for suspected placental problem ruled out**

     ❶ **Z03.73 Encounter for suspected fetal anomaly ruled out**

     ❶ **Z03.74 Encounter for suspected problem with fetal growth ruled out**

     ❶ **Z03.75 Encounter for suspected cervical shortening ruled out**

     ❶ **Z03.79 Encounter for other suspected maternal and fetal conditions ruled out**

● **Z03.8 Encounter for observation for other suspected diseases and conditions ruled out**

     ● **Z03.81 Encounter for observation for suspected exposure to biological agents ruled out**

         ❶ **Z03.810 Encounter for observation for suspected exposure to anthrax ruled out**

         ❶ **Z03.818 Encounter for observation for suspected exposure to other biological agents ruled out**

     ❶ **Z03.89 Encounter for observation for other suspected diseases and conditions ruled out**

● **Z04 Encounter for examination and observation for other reasons**

> **Includes**   encounter for examination for medicolegal reasons

This category is to be used when a person without a diagnosis is suspected of having an abnormal condition, without signs or symptoms, which requires study, but after examination and observation, is ruled-out. This category is also for use for administrative and legal observation status.

❶ **Z04.1 Encounter for examination and observation following transport accident**

> **Excludes1**   encounter for examination and observation following work accident (Z04.2)

❶ **Z04.2 Encounter for examination and observation following work accident**

❶ **Z04.3 Encounter for examination and observation following other accident**

● **Z04.4 Encounter for examination and observation following alleged rape**
Encounter for examination and observation of victim following alleged rape
Encounter for examination and observation of victim following alleged sexual abuse

     ❶ **Z04.41 Encounter for examination and observation following alleged adult rape**
Suspected adult rape, ruled out
Suspected adult sexual abuse, ruled out

     ❶ **Z04.42 Encounter for examination and observation following alleged child rape**
Suspected child rape, ruled out
Suspected child sexual abuse, ruled out

❶ **Z04.6 Encounter for general psychiatric examination, requested by authority**

● **Z04.7 Encounter for examination and observation following alleged physical abuse**

     ❶ **Z04.71 Encounter for examination and observation following alleged adult physical abuse**
Suspected adult physical abuse, ruled out

> **Excludes1**   confirmed case of adult physical abuse (T74.-)
> encounter for examination and observation following alleged adult sexual abuse (Z04.41)
> suspected case of adult physical abuse, not ruled out (T76.-)

     ❶ **Z04.72 Encounter for examination and observation following alleged child physical abuse**
Suspected child physical abuse, ruled out

> **Excludes1**   confirmed case of child physical abuse (T74.-)
> encounter for examination and observation following alleged child sexual abuse (Z04.42)
> suspected case of child physical abuse, not ruled out (T76.-)

❶ **Z04.8 Encounter for examination and observation for other specified reasons**
Encounter for examination and observation for request for expert evidence

● Unacceptable First-Listed Diagnosis		● Use Additional Character(s)	❶ First Listed	🔢 First Listed or Secondary
🅒 Complication\Comorbidity	🅒 Major C\C	❷ Secondary Only	▦ Unspecified	**OGCR** Official Guidelines for Coding and Reporting
	Excludes 1	Excludes 2	Includes	Use additional	Code first	Code also

OGCR See Section II.C.21.c.7.

The follow-up codes are used to explain continuing surveillance following completed treatment of a disease, condition, or injury. They imply that the condition has been fully treated and no longer exists. They should not be confused with aftercare codes, or injury codes with 7th character "D," that explain ongoing care of a healing condition or its sequelae. Follow-up codes may be used in conjunction with history codes to provide the full picture of the healed condition and its treatment. The follow-up code is sequenced first, followed by the history code.

A follow-up code may be used to explain multiple visits. Should a condition be found to have recurred on the follow-up visit, then the code for the condition should be assigned as an additional diagnosis.

The follow-up Z code categories:
Z08   Encounter for follow-up examination after completed treatment for malignant neoplasm
Z09   Encounter for follow-up examination after completed treatment for conditions other than malignant neoplasm
Z39   Encounter for maternal postpartum care and examination

1/2 ☒ **Z04.9 Encounter for examination and observation for unspecified reason**

> Encounter for observation NOS

1/2 **Z08 Encounter for follow-up examination after completed treatment for malignant neoplasm**

> **Includes**   medical surveillance following completed treatment

> Use additional code to identify any acquired absence of organs (Z90.-)

> Use additional code to identify the personal history of malignant neoplasm (Z85.-)

> **Excludes1**   aftercare following medical care (Z43-Z49, Z51)

1/2 **Z09 Encounter for follow-up examination after completed treatment for conditions other than malignant neoplasm**

> **Includes**   medical surveillance following completed treatment

> Use additional code to identify any applicable history of disease code (Z86.-. Z87.-)

> **Excludes1**   aftercare following medical care (Z43-Z49, Z51)
> surveillance of contraception (Z30.4-)
> surveillance of prosthetic and other medical devices (Z44-Z46)

● **Z11 Encounter for screening for infectious and parasitic diseases**

> Screening is the testing for disease or disease precursors in asymptomatic individuals so that early detection and treatment can be provided for those who test positive for the disease.

> **Excludes1**   encounter for diagnostic examination - code to sign or symptom

1/2 **Z11.0 Encounter for screening for intestinal infectious diseases**

OGCR Section II.C.21.c.5.

Screening

Screening is the testing for disease or disease precursors in seemingly well individuals so that early detection and treatment can be provided for those who test positive for the disease (e.g., screening mammogram).

The testing of a person to rule out or confirm a suspected diagnosis because the patient has some sign or symptom is a diagnostic examination, not a screening. In these cases, the sign or symptom is used to explain the reason for the test.

A screening code may be a first listed code if the reason for the visit is specifically the screening exam. It may also be used as an additional code if the screening is done during an office visit for other health problems. A screening code is not necessary if the screening is inherent to a routine examination, such as a pap smear done during a routine pelvic examination.

Should a condition be discovered during the screening then the code for the condition may be assigned as an additional diagnosis.

The Z code indicates that a screening exam is planned. A procedure code is required to confirm that the screening was performed.

The screening Z codes /categories:
Z11   Encounter for screening for infectious and parasitic diseases
Z12   Encounter for screening for malignant neoplasms
Z13   Encounter for screening for other diseases and disorders
   Except:Z13.9, Encounter for screening, unspecified
Z36   Encounter for antenatal screening for mother

1/2 **Z11.1 Encounter for screening for respiratory tuberculosis**

1/2 **Z11.2 Encounter for screening for other bacterial diseases**

1/2 **Z11.3 Encounter for screening for infections with a predominantly sexual mode of transmission**

> **Excludes2**   encounter for screening for human immunodeficiency virus [HIV] (Z11.4)
> encounter for screening for human papillomavirus (Z11.51)

1/2 **Z11.4 Encounter for screening for human immunodeficiency virus [HIV]**

● **Z11.5 Encounter for screening for other viral diseases**

> **Excludes2**   encounter for screening for viral intestinal disease (Z11.0)

1/2 **Z11.51 Encounter for screening for human papillomavirus (HPV)**

1/2 **Z11.59 Encounter for screening for other viral diseases**

1/2 **Z11.6 Encounter for screening for other protozoal diseases and helminthiases**
> *Diseases or infestations caused by parasitic worms*

> **Excludes2**   encounter for screening for protozoal intestinal disease (Z11.0)

1/2 **Z11.8 Encounter for screening for other infectious and parasitic diseases**
> Encounter for screening for chlamydia
> Encounter for screening for rickettsial
> Encounter for screening for spirochetal
> Encounter for screening for mycoses

1/2 ☒ **Z11.9 Encounter for screening for infectious and parasitic diseases, unspecified**

CHAPTER 21 (Z00-Z99)

● Unacceptable First-Listed Diagnosis   ● Use Additional Character(s)   ❶ First Listed   1/2 First Listed or Secondary
C&C Complication\Comorbidity   Major C\C   ❷ Secondary Only   ☒ Unspecified   OGCR Official Guidelines for Coding and Reporting
Excludes 1   Excludes 2   Includes   Use additional   Code first   Code also

1719

● Z12   **Encounter for screening for malignant neoplasms**

Screening is the testing for disease or disease precursors in asymptomatic individuals so that early detection and treatment can be provided for those who test positive for the disease.

Use additional code to identify any family history of malignant neoplasm (Z80.-)

| Excludes1 | encounter for diagnostic examination - code to sign or symptom |

ⱱ²Z12.0   **Encounter for screening for malignant neoplasm of stomach**

● Z12.1   **Encounter for screening for malignant neoplasm of intestinal tract**

ⱱ² ■ Z12.10   **Encounter for screening for malignant neoplasm of intestinal tract, unspecified**

ⱱ²Z12.11   **Encounter for screening for malignant neoplasm of colon**

ⱱ²Z12.12   **Encounter for screening for malignant neoplasm of rectum**

ⱱ²Z12.13   **Encounter for screening for malignant neoplasm of small intestine**

ⱱ²Z12.2   **Encounter for screening for malignant neoplasm of respiratory organs**

● Z12.3   **Encounter for screening for malignant neoplasm of breast**

ⱱ²Z12.31   **Encounter for screening mammogram for malignant neoplasm of breast**

| Excludes1 | inconclusive mammogram (R92.2) |

ⱱ²Z12.39   **Encounter for other screening for malignant neoplasm of breast**

ⱱ²Z12.4   **Encounter for screening for malignant neoplasm of cervix**

Encounter for screening pap smear for malignant neoplasm of cervix

| Excludes1 | encounter for screening for human papillomavirus (Z11.51) when screening is part of general gynecological examination (Z01.4-) |

ⱱ²Z12.5   **Encounter for screening for malignant neoplasm of prostate**

ⱱ²Z12.6   **Encounter for screening for malignant neoplasm of bladder**

● Z12.7   **Encounter for screening for malignant neoplasm of other genitourinary organs**

ⱱ²Z12.71   **Encounter for screening for malignant neoplasm of testis**

ⱱ²Z12.72   **Encounter for screening for malignant neoplasm of vagina**

Vaginal pap smear status - post hysterectomy for non-malignant condition

Use additional code to identify acquired absence of uterus (Z90.71-)

| Excludes1 | vaginal pap smear status - post hysterectomy for malignant conditions (Z08) |

ⱱ²Z12.73   **Encounter for screening for malignant neoplasm of ovary**

ⱱ²Z12.79   **Encounter for screening for malignant neoplasm of other genitourinary organs**

● Z12.8   **Encounter for screening for malignant neoplasm of other sites**

ⱱ²Z12.81   **Encounter for screening for malignant neoplasm of oral cavity**

ⱱ²Z12.82   **Encounter for screening for malignant neoplasm of nervous system**

ⱱ²Z12.83   **Encounter for screening for malignant neoplasm of skin**

ⱱ²Z12.89   **Encounter for screening for malignant neoplasm of other sites**

ⱱ² ■ Z12.9   **Encounter for screening for malignant neoplasm, site unspecified**

● Z13   **Encounter for screening for other diseases and disorders**

Screening is the testing for disease or disease precursors in asymptomatic individuals so that early detection and treatment can be provided for those who test positive for the disease.

| Excludes1 | encounter for diagnostic examination - code to sign or symptom |

ⱱ²Z13.0   **Encounter for screening for diseases of the blood and blood-forming organs and certain disorders involving the immune mechanism**

ⱱ²Z13.1   **Encounter for screening for diabetes mellitus**

● Z13.2   **Encounter for screening for nutritional, metabolic and other endocrine disorders**

ⱱ²Z13.21   **Encounter for screening for nutritional disorder**

● Z13.22   **Encounter for screening for metabolic disorder**

ⱱ²Z13.220   **Encounter for screening for lipoid disorders**

Encounter for screening for cholesterol level
Encounter for screening for hypercholesterolemia
Encounter for screening for hyperlipidemia

ⱱ²Z13.228   **Encounter for screening for other metabolic disorders**

ⱱ²Z13.29   **Encounter for screening for other suspected endocrine disorder**

| Excludes1 | encounter for screening for diabetes mellitus (Z13.1) |

ⱱ²Z13.4   **Encounter for screening for certain developmental disorders in childhood**

Encounter for screening for developmental handicaps in early childhood

| Excludes1 | routine development testing of infant or child (Z00.1-) |

ⱱ²Z13.5   **Encounter for screening for eye and ear disorders**

| Excludes2 | encounter for general hearing examination (Z01.1-) encounter for general vision examination (Z01.0-) |

ⱱ²Z13.6   **Encounter for screening for cardiovascular disorders**

● Z13.7   **Encounter for screening for genetic and chromosomal anomalies**

| Excludes1 | genetic testing for procreative management (Z31.4-) |

ⱱ²Z13.71   **Encounter for nonprocreative screening for genetic disease carrier status**

ⱱ²Z13.79   **Encounter for other screening for genetic and chromosomal anomalies**

● Unacceptable First-Listed Diagnosis   ● Use Additional Character(s)   ❶ First Listed   ⱱ² First Listed or Secondary

🩺 Complication\Comorbidity   🩺 Major C\C   ❷ Secondary Only   ■ Unspecified   **OGCR** Official Guidelines for Coding and Reporting

| Excludes 1 | | Excludes 2 | | Includes | | Use additional | | Code first | | Code also |

● Z13.8 **Encounter for screening for other specified diseases and disorders**
　Excludes2　screening for malignant neoplasms (Z12.-)

● Z13.81 **Encounter for screening for digestive system disorders**

⑦Z13.810 **Encounter for screening for upper gastrointestinal disorder**

⑦Z13.811 **Encounter for screening for lower gastrointestinal disorder**
　Excludes1　encounter for screening for intestinal infectious disease (Z11.0)

⑦Z13.818 **Encounter for screening for other digestive system disorders**

● Z13.82 **Encounter for screening for musculoskeletal disorder**

⑦Z13.820 **Encounter for screening for osteoporosis**

⑦Z13.828 **Encounter for screening for other musculoskeletal disorder**

⑦Z13.83 **Encounter for screening for respiratory disorder NEC**
　Excludes1　encounter for screening for respiratory tuberculosis (Z11.1)

⑦Z13.84 **Encounter for screening for dental disorders**

● Z13.85 **Encounter for screening for nervous system disorders**

⑦Z13.850 **Encounter for screening for traumatic brain injury**

⑦Z13.858 **Encounter for screening for other nervous system disorders**

⑦Z13.88 **Encounter for screening for disorder due to exposure to contaminants**
　Excludes1　those exposed to contaminants without suspected disorders (Z57-Z58)

⑦Z13.89 **Encounter for screening for other disorder**
Encounter for screening for genitourinary disorders

❷ ▪ Z13.9 **Encounter for screening, unspecified**

GENETIC CARRIER AND GENETIC SUSCEPTIBILITY TO DISEASE (Z14-Z15)

● Z14 **Genetic carrier**

● Z14.0 **Hemophilia A carrier**

⑦Z14.01 **Asymptomatic hemophilia A carrier**

⑦Z14.02 **Symptomatic hemophilia A carrier**

⑦Z14.1 **Cystic fibrosis carrier**

⑦Z14.8 **Genetic carrier of other disease**

● Z15 **Genetic susceptibility to disease**
　Includes　confirmed abnormal gene
Use additional code, if applicable, for any associated family history of the disease (Z80-Z84)

● Z15.0 **Genetic susceptibility to malignant neoplasm**
Code first if applicable, any current malignant neoplasm (C00-C75, C81-C96)
Use additional code, if applicable, for any personal history of malignant neoplasm (Z85.-)

❷Z15.01 **Genetic susceptibility to malignant neoplasm of breast**

❷Z15.02 **Genetic susceptibility to malignant neoplasm of ovary**

❷Z15.03 **Genetic susceptibility to malignant neoplasm of prostate**

❷Z15.04 **Genetic susceptibility to malignant neoplasm of endometrium**

❷Z15.09 **Genetic susceptibility to other malignant neoplasm**

● Z15.8 **Genetic susceptibility to other disease**

❷Z15.81 **Genetic susceptibility to multiple endocrine neoplasia [MEN]**

❷Z15.89 **Genetic susceptibility to other disease**

INFECTION WITH DRUG RESISTANT MICROORGANISMS (Z16)

⑦Z16 **Infection with drug resistant microorganisms**
This category is intended for use as an additional code for infectious conditions classified elsewhere to indicate the presence of drug-resistance of the infectious organism
Code first the infection

ESTROGEN RECEPTOR STATUS (Z17)

● Z17 **Estrogen receptor status**
Code first malignant neoplasm of breast (C50.-)

⑦Z17.0 **Estrogen receptor positive status [ER+]**

⑦Z17.1 **Estrogen receptor negative status [ER-]**

PERSONS WITH POTENTIAL HEALTH HAZARDS RELATED TO COMMUNICABLE DISEASES (Z20-Z28)

● Z20 **Contact with and (suspected) exposure to communicable diseases**
　Excludes1　carrier of infectious disease (Z22.-) diagnosed current infectious or parasitic disease - see Alphabetic Index
　Excludes2　personal history of infectious and parasitic diseases (Z86.1-)

● Z20.0 **Contact with and (suspected) exposure to intestinal infectious diseases**

⑦Z20.01 **Contact with and (suspected) exposure to intestinal infectious diseases due to Escherichia coli (E. coli)**

⑦Z20.09 **Contact with and (suspected) exposure to other intestinal infectious diseases**

⑦Z20.1 **Contact with and (suspected) exposure to tuberculosis**

⑦Z20.2 **Contact with and (suspected) exposure to infections with a predominantly sexual mode of transmission**

⑦Z20.3 **Contact with and (suspected) exposure to rabies**

⑦Z20.4 **Contact with and (suspected) exposure to rubella**

⑦Z20.5 **Contact with and (suspected) exposure to viral hepatitis**

⑦Z20.6 **Contact with and (suspected) exposure to human immunodeficiency virus [HIV]**
　Excludes1　asymptomatic human immunodeficiency virus [HIV] infection status (Z21)

● Unacceptable First-Listed Diagnosis　　◆ Use Additional Character(s)　　❶ First Listed　　⑦ First Listed or Secondary
◆ Complication\Comorbidity　　◆ Major C\C　　❷ Secondary Only　　▪ Unspecified　　OGCR Official Guidelines for Coding and Reporting
Excludes 1　　Excludes 2　　Includes　　Use additional　　Code first　　Code also
1721
CHAPTER 21 (Z00-Z99)

Z20.7 Contact with and (suspected) exposure to pediculosis, acariasis and other infestations

● Z20.8 Contact with and (suspected) exposure to other communicable diseases

  ● Z20.81 Contact with and (suspected) exposure to other bacterial communicable diseases

    Z20.810 Contact with and (suspected) exposure to anthrax

    Z20.811 Contact with and (suspected) exposure to meningococcus

    Z20.818 Contact with and (suspected) exposure to other bacterial communicable diseases

  ● Z20.82 Contact with and (suspected) exposure to other viral communicable diseases

    Z20.820 Contact with and (suspected) exposure to varicella

    Z20.828 Contact with and (suspected) exposure to other viral communicable diseases

  Z20.89 Contact with and (suspected) exposure to other communicable diseases

Z20.9 Contact with and (suspected) exposure to unspecified communicable disease

Z21 Asymptomatic human immunodeficiency virus [HIV] infection status

  Includes   HIV positive NOS

  Code first Human immunodeficiency [HIV] disease complicating pregnancy, childbirth and the puerperium, if applicable (O98.7-)

  Excludes1 acquired immunodeficiency syndrome (B20)
      contact with human immunodeficiency virus [HIV] (Z20.6)
      exposure to human immunodeficiency virus [HIV] (Z20.6)
      human immunodeficiency virus [HIV] disease (B20)
      inconclusive laboratory evidence of human immunodeficiency virus [HIV] (R75)

● Z22 Carrier of infectious disease

  Includes   colonization status
           suspected carrier

Z22.0 Carrier of typhoid

Z22.1 Carrier of other intestinal infectious diseases

Z22.2 Carrier of diphtheria

● Z22.3 Carrier of other specified bacterial diseases

  Z22.31 Carrier of bacterial disease due to meningococci

  Z22.32 Carrier of bacterial disease due to staphylococci

  Z22.33 Carrier of bacterial disease due to streptococci

    Z22.330 Carrier of Group B streptococcus

    Z22.338 Carrier of other streptococcus

  Z22.39 Carrier of other specified bacterial diseases

Z22.4 Carrier of infections with a predominantly sexual mode of transmission

● Z22.5 Carrier of viral hepatitis

  Z22.50 Carrier of unspecified viral hepatitis

  Z22.51 Carrier of viral hepatitis B
      Hepatitis B surface antigen [HBsAg] carrier

Z22.52 Carrier of viral hepatitis C

Z22.59 Carrier of other viral hepatitis

Z22.6 Carrier of human T-lymphotropic virus type-1 [HTLV-1] infection

Z22.8 Carrier of other infectious diseases

Z22.9 Carrier of infectious disease, unspecified

Z23 Encounter for immunization

  Code first any routine childhood examination

  Note: Procedure codes are required to identify the types of immunizations given.

● Z28 Immunization not carried out and underimmunization status
  Vaccination not carried out

  ● Z28.0 Immunization not carried out because of contraindication

    Z28.01 Immunization not carried out because of acute illness of patient

    Z28.02 Immunization not carried out because of chronic illness or condition of patient

    Z28.03 Immunization not carried out because of immune compromised state of patient

    Z28.04 Immunization not carried out because of patient allergy to vaccine or component

    Z28.09 Immunization not carried out because of other contraindication

  Z28.1 Immunization not carried out because of patient decision for reasons of belief or group pressure
    Immunization not carried out because of religious belief

  ● Z28.2 Immunization not carried out because of patient decision for other and unspecified reason

    Z28.20 Immunization not carried out because of patient decision for unspecified reason

    Z28.21 Immunization not carried out because of patient refusal

    Z28.29 Immunization not carried out because of patient decision for other reason

  Z28.3 Underimmunization status
    Delinquent immunization status
    Lapsed immunization schedule status

  ● Z28.8 Immunization not carried out for other reason

    Z28.81 Immunization not carried out due to patient having had the disease

    Z28.82 Immunization not carried out because of caregiver refusal
      Immunization not carried out because of guardian refusal
      Immunization not carried out because of parent refusal

      Excludes2 immunization not carried out because of caregiver refusal because of religious belief (Z28.1)

    Z28.89 Immunization not carried out for other reason

  Z28.9 Immunization not carried out for unspecified reason

PERSONS ENCOUNTERING HEALTH SERVICES IN CIRCUMSTANCES RELATED TO REPRODUCTION (Z30-Z39)

● **Z30　Encounter for contraceptive management**

　● **Z30.0　Encounter for general counseling and advice on contraception**

　　● **Z30.01　Encounter for initial prescription of contraceptives**

　　　Ⓜ**Z30.011　Encounter for initial prescription of contraceptive pills**

　　　Ⓜ**Z30.012　Encounter for prescription of emergency contraception**
　　　　　　Encounter for postcoital contraception

　　　Ⓜ**Z30.013　Encounter for initial prescription of injectable contraceptive**

　　　Ⓜ**Z30.014　Encounter for initial prescription of intrauterine contraceptive device**

　　　Ⓜ**Z30.018　Encounter for initial prescription of other contraceptives**

　　　Ⓜ▨ **Z30.019　Encounter for initial prescription of contraceptives, unspecified**

　　Ⓜ**Z30.02　Counseling and instruction in natural family planning to avoid pregnancy**

　　Ⓜ**Z30.09　Encounter for other general counseling and advice on contraception**
　　　　　Encounter for family planning advice NOS

　Ⓜ**Z30.2　Encounter for sterilization**

　● **Z30.4　Encounter for surveillance of contraceptives**

　　Ⓜ▨ **Z30.40　Encounter for surveillance of contraceptives, unspecified**

　　Ⓜ**Z30.41　Encounter for surveillance of contraceptive pills**
　　　　　Encounter for repeat prescription for contraceptive pill

　　Ⓜ**Z30.42　Encounter for surveillance of injectable contraceptive**

　　Ⓜ**Z30.43　Encounter for surveillance of intrauterine contraceptive device**
　　　　　Encounter for checking, reinsertion or removal of intrauterine contraceptive device

　　Ⓜ**Z30.49　Encounter for surveillance of other contraceptives**

　Ⓜ**Z30.8　Encounter for other contraceptive management**
　　　Encounter for postvasectomy sperm count
　　　Encounter for routine examination for contraceptive maintenance

> **Excludes1**　sperm count following sterilization reversal (Z31.42)
> 　　sperm count for fertility testing (Z31.41)

　Ⓜ▨ **Z30.9　Encounter for contraceptive management, unspecified**

● **Z31　Encounter for procreative management**

> **Excludes1**　complications associated with artificial fertilization (N98.-)
> 　　female infertility (N97.-)
> 　　male infertility (N46.-)

　Ⓜ**Z31.0　Encounter for reversal of previous sterilization**

● **Z31.4　Encounter for procreative investigation and testing**

> **Excludes1**　postvasectomy sperm count (Z30.8)

　Ⓜ**Z31.41　Encounter for fertility testing**
　　　Encounter for fallopian tube patency testing
　　　Encounter for sperm count for fertility testing

　Ⓜ**Z31.42　Aftercare following sterilization reversal**
　　　Sperm count following sterilization reversal

　● **Z31.43　Encounter for genetic testing of female for procreative management**
　　　Use additional code for habitual aborter, if applicable (N96, O26.2-)

> **Excludes1**　nonprocreative genetic testing (Z13.7-)

　　Ⓜ**Z31.430　Encounter of female for testing for genetic disease carrier status for procreative management**

　　Ⓜ**Z31.438　Encounter for other genetic testing of female for procreative managment**

　● **Z31.44　Encounter for genetic testing of male for procreative management**

> **Excludes1**　nonprocreative genetic testing (Z13.7-)

　　Ⓜ**Z31.440　Encounter of male for testing for genetic disease carrier status for procreative management**

　　Ⓜ**Z31.441　Encounter for testing of male partner of habitual aborter**

　　Ⓜ**Z31.448　Encounter for other genetic testing of male for procreative management**

　Ⓜ**Z31.49　Encounter for other procreative investigation and testing**

Ⓜ**Z31.5　Encounter for genetic counseling**

● **Z31.6　Encounter for general counseling and advice on procreation**

　Ⓜ**Z31.61　Procreative counseling and advice using natural family planning**

　Ⓜ**Z31.62　Encounter for fertility preservation counseling**
　　　Encounter for fertility preservation counseling prior to cancer therapy
　　　Encounter for fertility preservation counseling prior to surgical removal of gonads

　Ⓜ**Z31.69　Encounter for other general counseling and advice on procreation**

● **Z31.8　Encounter for other procreative management**

　❶ **Z31.81　Encounter for male factor infertility in female patient**

　❶ **Z31.82　Encounter for Rh incompatibility status**

　❶ **Z31.83　Encounter for assisted reproductive fertility procedure cycle**
　　　Patient undergoing in vitro fertilization cycle
　　　Use additional code to identify the type of infertility

> **Excludes1**　pre-cycle diagnosis and testing - code to reason for encounter

● Unacceptable First-Listed Diagnosis　　● Use Additional Character(s)　❶ First Listed　Ⓜ First Listed or Secondary
🦠 Complication\Comorbidity　　🦠 Major C\C　　❷ Secondary Only　　▨ Unspecified　　OGCR Official Guidelines for Coding and Reporting
Excludes 1　　Excludes 2　　Includes　　Use additional　　Code first　　Code also

1723

❶ Z31.84 Encounter for fertility preservation procedure
> Encounter for fertility preservation procedure prior to cancer therapy
> Encounter for fertility preservation procedure prior to surgical removal of gonads

⑫ Z31.89 Encounter for other procreative management

⑫ ◼ Z31.9 Encounter for procreative management, unspecified

● **Z32 Encounter for pregnancy test and childbirth and childcare instruction**

  ● **Z32.0 Encounter for pregnancy test**

    ⑫ Z32.00 Encounter for pregnancy test, result unknown
> Encounter for pregnancy test NOS

    ⑫ Z32.01 Encounter for pregnancy test, result positive

    ⑫ Z32.02 Encounter for pregnancy test, result negative

  ⑫ Z32.2 Encounter for childbirth instruction

  ⑫ Z32.3 Encounter for childcare instruction
> Encounter for prenatal or postpartum childcare instruction

● **Z33 Pregnant state**

  ❷ Z33.1 Pregnant state, incidental
> Pregnant state NOS

> **Excludes1**   complications of pregnancy (O00-O99)

  ❶ Z33.2 Encounter for elective termination of pregnancy

> **Excludes1**   early fetal death with retention of dead fetus (O02.1)
> late fetal death (O36.4)
> spontaneous abortion (O03)

● **Z34 Encounter for supervision of normal pregnancy**

> **Excludes1**   any complication of pregnancy (O00-O99)
> encounter for pregnancy test (Z32.0-)
> encounter for supervision of high risk pregnancy (O09.-)

  ● **Z34.0 Encounter for supervision of normal first pregnancy**

    ❶ ◼ Z34.00 Encounter for supervision of normal first pregnancy, unspecified trimester

    ❶ Z34.01 Encounter for supervision of normal first pregnancy, first trimester

    ❶ Z34.02 Encounter for supervision of normal first pregnancy, second trimester

    ❶ Z34.03 Encounter for supervision of normal first pregnancy, third trimester

  ● **Z34.8 Encounter for supervision of other normal pregnancy**

    ❶ ◼ Z34.80 Encounter for supervision of other normal pregnancy, unspecified trimester

    ❶ Z34.81 Encounter for supervision of other normal pregnancy, first trimester

    ❶ Z34.82 Encounter for supervision of other normal pregnancy, second trimester

    ❶ Z34.83 Encounter for supervision of other normal pregnancy, third trimester

❶ Z34.9 Encounter for supervision of normal pregnancy, unspecified

  ❶ ◼ Z34.90 Encounter for supervision of normal pregnancy, unspecified, unspecified trimester

  ❶ ◼ Z34.91 Encounter for supervision of normal pregnancy, unspecified, first trimester

  ❶ ◼ Z34.92 Encounter for supervision of normal pregnancy, unspecified, second trimester

  ❶ ◼ Z34.93 Encounter for supervision of normal pregnancy, unspecified, third trimester

⑫ Z36 Encounter for antenatal screening of mother

> **Excludes1**   abnormal findings on antenatal screening of mother (O28.-)
> diagnostic examination - code to sign or symptom
> encounter for suspected maternal and fetal conditions ruled out (Z03.7-)
> suspected fetal condition affecting management of pregnancy - code to condition in Chapter 15

> **Excludes2**   genetic counseling and testing (Z31.43-, Z31.5)
> routine prenatal care (Z34)

● **Z37 Outcome of delivery**
> This category is intended for use as an additional code to identify the outcome of delivery on the mother's record. It is not for use on the newborn record.

> **Excludes1**   stillbirth (P95)

  ❷ Z37.0 Single live birth

  ❷ Z37.1 Single stillbirth

  ❷ Z37.2 Twins, both liveborn

  ❷ Z37.3 Twins, one liveborn and one stillborn

  ❷ Z37.4 Twins, both stillborn

  ● **Z37.5 Other multiple births, all liveborn**

    ❷ ◼ Z37.50 Multiple births, unspecified, all liveborn

    ❷ Z37.51 Triplets, all liveborn

    ❷ Z37.52 Quadruplets, all liveborn

    ❷ Z37.53 Quintuplets, all liveborn

    ❷ Z37.54 Sextuplets, all liveborn

    ❷ Z37.59 Other multiple births, all liveborn

  ● **Z37.6 Other multiple births, some liveborn**

    ❷ ◼ Z37.60 Multiple births, unspecified, some liveborn

    ❷ Z37.61 Triplets, some liveborn

    ❷ Z37.62 Quadruplets, some liveborn

    ❷ Z37.63 Quintuplets, some liveborn

    ❷ Z37.64 Sextuplets, some liveborn

    ❷ Z37.69 Other multiple births, some liveborn

  ❷ Z37.7 Other multiple births, all stillborn

  ❷ ◼ Z37.9 Outcome of delivery, unspecified
> Multiple birth NOS
> Single birth NOS

● **Z38 Liveborn infants according to place of birth and type of delivery**
> This category is for use as the principal code on the initial record of a newborn baby. It is to be used for the initial birth record only. It is not to be used on the mother's record.

  ● **Z38.0 Single liveborn infant, born in hospital**
> Single liveborn infant, born in birthing center or other health care facility

    ❶ Z38.00 Single liveborn infant, delivered vaginally

    ❶ Z38.01 Single liveborn infant, delivered by cesarean

❶ Z38.1 Single liveborn infant, born outside hospital

❶ ☐ Z38.2 Single liveborn infant, unspecified as to place of birth
Single liveborn infant NOS

● Z38.3 Twin liveborn infant, born in hospital

    ❶ Z38.30 Twin liveborn infant, delivered vaginally

    ❶ Z38.31 Twin liveborn infant, delivered by cesarean

❶ Z38.4 Twin liveborn infant, born outside hospital

❶ ☐ Z38.5 Twin liveborn infant, unspecified as to place of birth

● Z38.6 Other multiple liveborn infant, born in hospital

    ❶ Z38.61 Triplet liveborn infant, delivered vaginally

    ❶ Z38.62 Triplet liveborn infant, delivered by cesarean

    ❶ Z38.63 Quadruplet liveborn infant, delivered vaginally

    ❶ Z38.64 Quadruplet liveborn infant, delivered by cesarean

    ❶ Z38.65 Quintuplet liveborn infant, delivered vaginally

    ❶ Z38.66 Quintuplet liveborn infant, delivered by cesarean

    ❶ Z38.68 Other multiple liveborn infant, delivered vaginally

    ❶ Z38.69 Other multiple liveborn infant, delivered by cesarean

❶ Z38.7 Other multiple liveborn infant, born outside hospital

❶ ☐ Z38.8 Other multiple liveborn infant, unspecified as to place of birth

● Z39 Encounter for maternal postpartum care and examination

❶ Z39.0 Encounter for care and examination of mother immediately after delivery
Care and observation in uncomplicated cases when the delivery occurs outside a healthcare facility

    Excludes1 care for postpartum complication - see Alphabetic index

❶ Z39.1 Encounter for care and examination of lactating mother
Encounter for supervision of lactation

    Excludes1 disorders of lactation (O92.-)

❶ Z39.2 Encounter for routine postpartum follow-up

ENCOUNTERS FOR OTHER SPECIFIC HEALTH CARE (Z40-Z53)

Categories Z40-Z53 are intended for use to indicate a reason for care. They may be used for patients who have already been treated for a disease or injury, but who are receiving aftercare or prophylactic care, or care to consolidate the treatment, or to deal with a residual state

    Excludes2 follow-up examination for medical surveillance after treatment (Z08-Z09)

● Z40 Encounter for prophylactic surgery

    Excludes1 organ donations (Z52.-)
therapeutic organ removal - code to condition

● Z40.0 Encounter for prophylactic surgery for risk factors related to malignant neoplasms
Admission for prophylactic organ removal
Use additional code to identify risk factor

    🔢 ☐ Z40.00 Encounter for prophylactic removal of unspecified organ

🔢 Z40.01 Encounter for prophylactic removal of breast

🔢 Z40.02 Encounter for prophylactic removal of ovary

🔢 Z40.09 Encounter for prophylactic removal of other organ

🔢 Z40.8 Encounter for other prophylactic surgery

🔢 ☐ Z40.9 Encounter for prophylactic surgery, unspecified

● Z41 Encounter for procedures for purposes other than remedying health state

🔢 Z41.1 Encounter for cosmetic surgery
Encounter for cosmetic breast implant
Encounter for cosmetic procedure

    Excludes1 encounter for breast reduction (N62)
encounter for plastic and reconstructive surgery following medical procedure or healed injury (Z42.-)
encounter for post-mastectomy breast implantation (Z42.1)

🔢 Z41.2 Encounter for routine and ritual male circumcision

🔢 Z41.3 Encounter for ear piercing

🔢 Z41.8 Encounter for other procedures for purposes other than remedying health state

🔢 ☐ Z41.9 Encounter for procedure for purposes other than remedying health state, unspecified

● Z42 Encounter for plastic and reconstructive surgery following medical procedure or healed injury

    Excludes1 encounter for cosmetic plastic surgery (Z41.1)
encounter for plastic surgery for treatment of current injury - code to relevent injury

❶ Z42.1 Encounter for breast reconstruction following mastectomy

    Excludes1 deformity and disproportion of reconstructed breast (N65.1-)

❶ Z42.8 Encounter for other plastic and reconstructive surgery following medical procedure or healed injury

● Z43 Encounter for attention to artificial openings

    Includes closure of artificial openings
passage of sounds or bougies through artificial openings
reforming artificial openings
removal of catheter from artificial openings
toilet or cleansing of artificial openings

    Excludes1 artificial opening status only, without need for care (Z93.-)
complications of external stoma (J95.0-, K91.4-, K91.7-, N99.5-)

    Excludes2 fitting and adjustment of prosthetic and other devices (Z44-Z46)

🔢 Z43.0 Encounter for attention to tracheostomy 🔗

🔢 Z43.1 Encounter for attention to gastrostomy

🔢 Z43.2 Encounter for attention to ileostomy

🔢 Z43.3 Encounter for attention to colostomy

🔢 Z43.4 Encounter for attention to other artificial openings of digestive tract

● Unacceptable First-Listed Diagnosis   ● Use Additional Character(s)   ❶ First Listed   🔢 First Listed or Secondary
🔗 Complication\Comorbidity   🔗 Major C\C   ② Secondary Only   ☐ Unspecified   **OGCR** Official Guidelines for Coding and Reporting
Excludes 1   Excludes 2   Includes   Use additional   Code first   Code also

1725

CHAPTER 21 (Z00-Z99)

🔢Z43.5   Encounter for attention to cystostomy

🔢Z43.6   Encounter for attention to other artificial openings of urinary tract
Encounter for attention to nephrostomy
Encounter for attention to ureterostomy
Encounter for attention to urethrostomy

🔢Z43.7   Encounter for attention to artificial vagina

🔢Z43.8   Encounter for attention to other artificial openings

🔢 ⬛ Z43.9   Encounter for attention to unspecified artificial opening

● Z44   Encounter for fitting and adjustment of external prosthetic device

> **Includes**   removal or replacement of external prosthetic device
>
> **Excludes1**   malfunction or other complications of device - see Alphabetical Index
> presence of prosthetic device (Z97.-)

● Z44.0   Encounter for fitting and adjustment of artificial arm

● Z44.00   Encounter for fitting and adjustment of unspecified artificial arm

🔢⬛ Z44.001   Encounter for fitting and adjustment of unspecified right artificial arm

🔢⬛ Z44.002   Encounter for fitting and adjustment of unspecified left artificial arm

🔢⬛ Z44.009   Encounter for fitting and adjustment of unspecified artificial arm, unspecified arm

● Z44.01   Encounter for fitting and adjustment of complete artificial arm

🔢Z44.011   Encounter for fitting and adjustment of complete right artificial arm

🔢Z44.012   Encounter for fitting and adjustment of complete left artificial arm

🔢 ⬛ Z44.019   Encounter for fitting and adjustment of complete artificial arm, unspecified arm

● Z44.02   Encounter for fitting and adjustment of partial artificial arm

🔢Z44.021   Encounter for fitting and adjustment of partial artificial right arm

🔢Z44.022   Encounter for fitting and adjustment of partial artificial left arm

🔢 ⬛ Z44.029   Encounter for fitting and adjustment of partial artificial arm, unspecified arm

● Z44.1   Encounter for fitting and adjustment of artificial leg

● Z44.10   Encounter for fitting and adjustment of unspecified artificial leg

🔢 ⬛ Z44.101   Encounter for fitting and adjustment of unspecified right artificial leg

🔢 ⬛ Z44.102   Encounter for fitting and adjustment of unspecified left artificial leg

🔢 ⬛ Z44.109   Encounter for fitting and adjustment of unspecified artificial leg, unspecified leg

● Z44.11   Encounter for fitting and adjustment of complete artificial leg

🔢Z44.111   Encounter for fitting and adjustment of complete right artificial leg

🔢Z44.112   Encounter for fitting and adjustment of complete left artificial leg

🔢 ⬛ Z44.119   Encounter for fitting and adjustment of complete artificial leg, unspecified leg

● Z44.12   Encounter for fitting and adjustment of partial artificial leg

🔢Z44.121   Encounter for fitting and adjustment of partial artificial right leg

🔢Z44.122   Encounter for fitting and adjustment of partial artificial left leg

🔢 ⬛ Z44.129   Encounter for fitting and adjustment of partial artificial leg, unspecified leg

● Z44.2   Encounter for fitting and adjustment of artificial eye

> **Excludes1**   mechanical complication of ocular prosthesis (T85.3)

🔢 ⬛ Z44.20   Encounter for fitting and adjustment of artificial eye, unspecified

🔢Z44.21   Encounter for fitting and adjustment of artificial right eye

🔢Z44.22   Encounter for fitting and adjustment of artificial left eye

● Z44.3   Encounter for fitting and adjustment of external breast prosthesis

> **Excludes1**   complications of breast implant (T85.4-)
> encounter for adjustment or removal of breast implant (Z45.81-)
> encounter for initial breast implant insertion for cosmetic breast augmentation (Z41.1)
> encounter for breast reconstruction following mastectomy (Z42.1)

🔢 ⬛ Z44.30   Encounter for fitting and adjustment of external breast prosthesis, unspecified breast

🔢Z44.31   Encounter for fitting and adjustment of external right breast prosthesis

🔢Z44.32   Encounter for fitting and adjustment of external left breast prosthesis

🔢Z44.8   Encounter for fitting and adjustment of other external prosthetic devices

🔢 ⬛ Z44.9   Encounter for fitting and adjustment of unspecified external prosthetic device

CHAPTER 21 (Z00-Z99)

● Unacceptable First-Listed Diagnosis   ● Use Additional Character(s)   ❶ First Listed   🔢 First Listed or Secondary
🩺 Complication\Comorbidity   🩺 Major C\C   ❷ Secondary Only   ⬛ Unspecified   **OGCR** Official Guidelines for Coding and Reporting

| Excludes 1 | Excludes 2 | Includes | Use additional | Code first | Code also |

● **Z45**   **Encounter for adjustment and management of implanted device**

> **Includes**   removal or replacement of implanted device
>
> **Excludes1**   malfunction or other complications of device - see Alphabetical Index
>
> **Excludes2**   encounter for fitting and adjustment of non-implanted device (Z46.-)
> presence of prosthetic and other devices (Z95-Z97)

● **Z45.0**   **Encounter for adjustment and management of cardiac device**

   ● **Z45.01**   **Encounter for adjustment and management of cardiac pacemaker**

     ⑫ **Z45.010**   Encounter for checking and testing of cardiac pacemaker pulse generator [battery]

         Encounter for replacing cardiac pacemaker pulse generator [battery]

     ⑫ **Z45.018**   Encounter for adjustment and management of other part of cardiac pacemaker

   ⑫ **Z45.02**   Encounter for adjustment and management of automatic implantable cardiac defibrillator

   ⑫ **Z45.09**   Encounter for adjustment and management of other cardiac device

⑫ **Z45.1**   **Encounter for adjustment and management of infusion pump**

⑫ **Z45.2**   **Encounter for adjustment and management of vascular access device**

     Encounter for adjustment and management of vascular catheters

> **Excludes1**   encounter for adjustment and management of renal dialysis catheter (Z49.01)

● **Z45.3**   **Encounter for adjustment and management of implanted devices of the special senses**

   ⑫ **Z45.31**   **Encounter for adjustment and management of implanted visual substitution device**

   ● **Z45.32**   **Encounter for adjustment and management of implanted hearing device**

> **Excludes1**   encounter for fitting and adjustment of hearing aide (Z46.1)

     ⑫ **Z45.320**   Encounter for adjustment and management of bone conduction device

     ⑫ **Z45.321**   Encounter for adjustment and management of cochlear device

     ⑫ **Z45.328**   Encounter for adjustment and management of other implanted hearing device

● **Z45.4**   **Encounter for adjustment and management of implanted nervous system device**

   ⑫ **Z45.41**   **Encounter for adjustment and management of cerebrospinal fluid drainage device**

     Encounter for adjustment and management of cerebral ventricular (communicating) shunt

   ⑫ **Z45.42**   **Encounter for adjustment and management of neuropacemaker (brain) (peripheral nerve) (spinal cord)**

   ⑫ **Z45.49**   Encounter for adjustment and management of other implanted nervous system device

● **Z45.8**   **Encounter for adjustment and management of other implanted devices**

   ● **Z45.81**   **Encounter for adjustment or removal of breast implant**

     Encounter for elective implant exchange (different material) (different size)

     Encounter removal of tissue expander without synchronous insertion of permanent implant

> **Excludes1**   complications of breast implant (T85.4-)
> encounter for initial breast implant insertion for cosmetic breast augmentation (Z41.1)
> encounter for breast reconstruction following mastectomy (Z42.1)

     ⑫ **Z45.811**   Encounter for adjustment or removal of right breast implant

     ⑫ **Z45.812**   Encounter for adjustment or removal of left breast implant

     ⑫ ▨ **Z45.819**   Encounter for adjustment or removal of unspecified breast implant

   ⑫ **Z45.82**   Encounter for adjustment or removal of myringotomy device (stent) (tube)

   ⑫ **Z45.89**   Encounter for adjustment and management of other implanted devices

⑫ ▨ **Z45.9**   **Encounter for adjustment and management of unspecified implanted device**

● **Z46**   **Encounter for fitting and adjustment of other devices**

> **Includes**   removal or replacement of other device
>
> **Excludes1**   malfunction or other complications of device - see Alphabetical Index
>
> **Excludes2**   encounter for fitting and management of implanted devices (Z45.-)
> issue of repeat prescription only (Z76.0)
> presence of prosthetic and other devices (Z95-Z97)

⑫ **Z46.0**   **Encounter for fitting and adjustment of spectacles and contact lenses**

⑫ **Z46.1**   **Encounter for fitting and adjustment of hearing aid**

> **Excludes1**   encounter for adjustment and management of implanted hearing device (Z45.32-)

⑫ **Z46.2**   **Encounter for fitting and adjustment of other devices related to nervous system and special senses**

> **Excludes2**   encounter for adjustment and management of implanted nervous system device (Z45.4-)
> encounter for adjustment and management of implanted visual substitution device (Z45.31)

⑫ **Z46.3**   **Encounter for fitting and adjustment of dental prosthetic device**

     Encounter for fitting and adjustment of dentures

⑫ **Z46.4**   **Encounter for fitting and adjustment of orthodontic device**

● Unacceptable First-Listed Diagnosis   ● Use Additional Character(s)   ❶ First Listed   ⑫ First Listed or Secondary

🎗 Complication\Comorbidity   🎗 Major C\C   ❷ Secondary Only   ▨ Unspecified   **OGCR** Official Guidelines for Coding and Reporting

Excludes 1   Excludes 2   Includes   Use additional   Code first   Code also

● **Z46.5 Encounter for fitting and adjustment of other gastrointestinal appliance and device**

> **Excludes1** encounter for attention to artificial openings of digestive tract (Z43.1-Z43.4)

🔢 **Z46.51 Encounter for fitting and adjustment of gastric lap band**

🔢 **Z46.59 Encounter for fitting and adjustment of other gastrointestinal appliance and device**

🔢 **Z46.6 Encounter for fitting and adjustment of urinary device**

> **Excludes2** attention to artificial openings of urinary tract (Z43.5, Z43.6)

● **Z46.8 Encounter for fitting and adjustment of other specified devices**

🔢 **Z46.81 Encounter for fitting and adjustment of insulin pump**
> Encounter for insulin pump instruction and training
> Encounter for insulin pump titration

🔢 **Z46.82 Encounter for fitting and adjustment of non-vascular catheter**

🔢 **Z46.89 Encounter for fitting and adjustment of other specified devices**
> Encounter for fitting and adjustment of wheelchair

🔢 ▣ **Z46.9 Encounter for fitting and adjustment of unspecified device**

● **Z47 Orthopedic aftercare**

> **Excludes1** aftercare for healing fracture - code to fracture with 7th character D

🔢 **Z47.1 Aftercare following joint replacement surgery**
> Use additional code to identify the joint (Z96.6-)

🔢 **Z47.2 Encounter for removal of internal fixation device**

> **Excludes1** encounter for adjustment of internal fixation device for fracture treatment - code to fracture with appropriate 7th character
> encounter for removal of external fixation device - code to fracture with 7th character D
> infection or inflammatory reaction to internal fixation device (T84.6-)
> mechanical complication of internal fixation device (T84.1-)

● **Z47.8 Encounter for other orthopedic aftercare**

🔢 **Z47.81 Encounter for orthopedic aftercare following surgical amputation**
> Use additional code to identify the limb amputated (Z89.-)

🔢 **Z47.82 Encounter for orthopedic aftercare following scoliosis surgery**

🔢 **Z47.89 Encounter for other orthopedic aftercare**

● **Z48 Encounter for other postprocedural aftercare**

> **Excludes1** encounter for follow-up examination after completed treatment (Z08-Z09)

> **Excludes2** encounter for attention to artificial openings (Z43.-)
> encounter for fitting and adjustment of prosthetic and other devices (Z44-Z46)

● **Z48.0 Encounter for attention to dressings, sutures and drains**

> **Excludes1** encounter for planned postprocedural wound closure (Z48.1)

🔢 **Z48.00 Encounter for change or removal of nonsurgical wound dressing**
> Encounter for change or removal of wound dressing NOS

🔢 **Z48.01 Encounter for change or removal of surgical wound dressing**

🔢 **Z48.02 Encounter for removal of sutures**
> Encounter for removal of staples

🔢 **Z48.03 Encounter for change or removal of drains**

🔢 **Z48.1 Encounter for planned postprocedural wound closure**

> **Excludes1** encounter for attention to dressings and sutures (Z48.0-)

● **Z48.2 Encounter for aftercare following organ transplant**

🔢 **Z48.21 Encounter for aftercare following heart transplant**

🔢 **Z48.22 Encounter for aftercare following kidney transplant**

🔢 **Z48.23 Encounter for aftercare following liver transplant**

🔢 **Z48.24 Encounter for aftercare following lung transplant**

● **Z48.28 Encounter for aftercare following multiple organ transplant**

🔢 **Z48.280 Encounter for aftercare following heart-lung transplant**

🔢 **Z48.288 Encounter for aftercare following multiple organ transplant**

● **Z48.29 Encounter for aftercare following other organ transplant**

🔢 **Z48.290 Encounter for aftercare following bone marrow transplant**

🔢 **Z48.298 Encounter for aftercare following other organ transplant**

🔢 **Z48.3 Aftercare following surgery for neoplasm**
> Use additional code to identify the neoplasm

● **Z48.8 Encounter for other specified postprocedural aftercare**

● **Z48.81 Encounter for surgical aftercare following surgery on specified body systems**
> These codes identify the body system requiring aftercare. They are for use in conjunction with other aftercare codes to fully explain the aftercare encounter. The condition treated should also be coded if still present.

> **Excludes1** aftercare for injury - code the injury with 7th character D

> **Excludes2** aftercare following organ transplant (Z48.2-)
> aftercare following surgery for neoplasm (Z48.3)
> orthopedic aftercare (Z47.-)

🔢 **Z48.810 Encounter for surgical aftercare following surgery on the sense organs**

🔢 **Z48.811 Encounter for surgical aftercare following surgery on the nervous system**

> **Excludes2** encounter for surgical aftercare following surgery on the sense organs (Z48.810)

Z48.812 Encounter for surgical aftercare following surgery on the circulatory system

Z48.813 Encounter for surgical aftercare following surgery on the respiratory system

Z48.814 Encounter for surgical aftercare following surgery on the teeth or oral cavity

Z48.815 Encounter for surgical aftercare following surgery on the digestive system

Z48.816 Encounter for surgical aftercare following surgery on the genitourinary system

> **Excludes1**   encounter for aftercare following sterilization reversal (Z31.42)

Z48.817 Encounter for surgical aftercare following surgery on the skin and subcutaneous tissue

Z48.89 Encounter for other specified surgical aftercare

● **Z49** Encounter for care involving renal dialysis
Code also associated end stage renal disease (N18.6)

● **Z49.0** Preparatory care for renal dialysis
Encounter for dialysis instruction and training

Z49.01 Encounter for fitting and adjustment of extracorporeal dialysis catheter
Removal or replacement of renal dialysis catheter
Toilet or cleansing of renal dialysis catheter

Z49.02 Encounter for fitting and adjustment of peritoneal dialysis catheter

● **Z49.3** Encounter for adequacy testing for dialysis

Z49.31 Encounter for adequacy testing for hemodialysis

Z49.32 Encounter for adequacy testing for peritoneal dialysis
Encounter for peritoneal equilibration test

● **Z51** Encounter for other aftercare
Code also condition requiring care

> **Excludes1**   follow-up examination after treatment (Z08-Z09)

❶ **Z51.0** Encounter for antineoplastic radiation therapy

● **Z51.1** Encounter for antineoplastic chemotherapy and immunotherapy

> **Excludes2**   encounter for chemotherapy and immunotherapy for nonneoplastic condition--code to condition

❶ **Z51.11** Encounter for antineoplastic chemotherapy

❶ **Z51.12** Encounter for antineoplastic immunotherapy

Z51.5 Encounter for palliative care

● **Z51.8** Encounter for other specified aftercare

> **Excludes1**   holiday relief care (Z75.5)

Z51.81 Encounter for therapeutic drug level monitoring
Code also any long-term (current) drug therapy (Z79.-)

> **Excludes1**   encounter for blood-drug test for administrative or medicolegal reasons (Z02.83)

Z51.89 Encounter for other specified aftercare

● **Z52** Donors of organs and tissues

> **Includes**   autologous and other living donors

> **Excludes1**   cadaveric donor - omit code examination of potential donor (Z00.5)

● **Z52.0** Blood donor

● **Z52.00** Unspecified blood donor

❶ Z52.000 Unspecified donor, whole blood

❶ Z52.001 Unspecified donor, stem cells

❶ Z52.008 Unspecified donor, other blood

● **Z52.01** Autologous blood donor

❶ Z52.010 Autologous donor, whole blood

❶ Z52.011 Autologous donor, stem cells

❶ Z52.018 Autologous donor, other blood

● **Z52.09** Other blood donor
Volunteer donor

❶ Z52.090 Other blood donor, whole blood

❶ Z52.091 Other blood donor, stem cells

❶ Z52.098 Other blood donor, other blood

● **Z52.1** Skin donor

❶ Z52.10 Skin donor, unspecified

❶ Z52.11 Skin donor, autologous

❶ Z52.19 Skin donor, other

● **Z52.2** Bone donor

❶ Z52.20 Bone donor, unspecified

❶ Z52.21 Bone donor, autologous

❶ Z52.29 Bone donor, other

❶ **Z52.3** Bone marrow donor

❶ **Z52.4** Kidney donor

❶ **Z52.5** Cornea donor

❶ **Z52.6** Liver donor

● **Z52.8** Donor of other specified organs or tissues

● **Z52.81** Egg (Oocyte) donor

❶ Z52.810 Egg (Oocyte) donor under age 35, anonymous recipient
Egg donor under age 35 NOS

❶ Z52.811 Egg (Oocyte) donor under age 35, designated recipient

❶ Z52.812 Egg (Oocyte) donor age 35 and over, anonymous recipient
Egg donor age 35 and over NOS

❶ Z52.813 Egg (Oocyte) donor age 35 and over, designated recipient

❶ Z52.819 Egg (Oocyte) donor, unspecified

❶ **Z52.89** Donor of other specified organs or tissues

❶ **Z52.9** Donor of unspecified organ or tissue
Donor NOS

● Unacceptable First-Listed Diagnosis   ● Use Additional Character(s)   ❶ First Listed   *V/2* First Listed or Secondary

🏥 Complication\Comorbidity   🩺 Major C\C   ❷ Secondary Only   ▪ Unspecified   **OGCR** Official Guidelines for Coding and Reporting

Excludes 1   Excludes 2   Includes   Use additional   Code first   Code also

1729

CHAPTER 21 (Z00-Z99)

● Z53   **Persons encountering health services for specific procedures and treatment, not carried out**

   ● Z53.0   **Procedure and treatment not carried out because of contraindication**

     ⑫Z53.01   **Procedure and treatment not carried out due to patient smoking**

     ⑫Z53.09   **Procedure and treatment not carried out because of other contraindication**

   ⑫Z53.1   **Procedure and treatment not carried out because of patient's decision for reasons of belief and group pressure**

   ● Z53.2   **Procedure and treatment not carried out because of patient's decision for other and unspecified reasons**

     ⑫■ Z53.20   **Procedure and treatment not carried out because of patient's decision for unspecified reasons**

     ⑫Z53.21   **Procedure and treatment not carried out due to patient leaving prior to being seen by health care provider**

     ⑫Z53.29   **Procedure and treatment not carried out because of patient's decision for other reasons**

   ⑫Z53.8   **Procedure and treatment not carried out for other reasons**

   ⑫■ Z53.9   **Procedure and treatment not carried out, unspecified reason**

PERSONS WITH POTENTIAL HEALTH HAZARDS RELATED TO SOCIOECONOMIC AND PSYCHOSOCIAL CIRCUMSTANCES (Z55-Z65)

● Z55   **Problems related to education and literacy**

   | Excludes1 | disorders of psychological development (F80-F89)

   ⑫Z55.0   **Illiteracy and low-level literacy**

   ⑫Z55.1   **Schooling unavailable and unattainable**

   ⑫Z55.2   **Failed school examinations**

   ⑫Z55.3   **Underachievement in school**

   ⑫Z55.4   **Educational maladjustment and discord with teachers and classmates**

   ⑫Z55.8   **Other problems related to education and literacy**
     Problems related to inadequate teaching

   ⑫■ Z55.9   **Problems related to education and literacy, unspecified**
     Academic problems NOS

● Z56   **Problems related to employment and unemployment**

   | Excludes2 | occupational exposure to risk factors (Z57.-)
     problems related to housing and economic circumstances (Z59.-)

   ⑫■ Z56.0   **Unemployment, unspecified**

   ⑫Z56.1   **Change of job**

   ⑫Z56.2   **Threat of job loss**

   ⑫Z56.3   **Stressful work schedule**

   ⑫Z56.4   **Discord with boss and workmates**

   ⑫Z56.5   **Uncongenial work environment**
     Difficult conditions at work

   ⑫Z56.6   **Other physical and mental strain related to work**

   ● Z56.8   **Other problems related to employment**

     ⑫Z56.81   **Sexual harassment on the job**

     ⑫Z56.82   **Military deployment status**
       Individual (civilian or military) currently deployed in theater or in support of military war, peacekeeping and humanitarian operations

     ⑫Z56.89   **Other problems related to employment**

   ⑫■ Z56.9   **Unspecified problems related to employment**
     Occupational problems NOS

● Z57   **Occupational exposure to risk factors**

   ⑫Z57.0   **Occupational exposure to noise**

   ⑫Z57.1   **Occupational exposure to radiation**

   ⑫Z57.2   **Occupational exposure to dust**

   ● Z57.3   **Occupational exposure to other air contaminants**

     ⑫Z57.31   **Occupational exposure to environmental tobacco smoke**

       | Excludes2 | exposure to environmental tobacco smoke (Z77.22)

     ⑫Z57.39   **Occupational exposure to other air contaminants**

   ⑫Z57.4   **Occupational exposure to toxic agents in agriculture**
     Occupational exposure to solids, liquids, gases or vapors in agriculture

   ⑫Z57.5   **Occupational exposure to toxic agents in other industries**
     Occupational exposure to solids, liquids, gases or vapors in other industries

   ⑫Z57.6   **Occupational exposure to extreme temperature**

   ⑫Z57.7   **Occupational exposure to vibration**

   ⑫Z57.8   **Occupational exposure to other risk factors**

   ⑫■ Z57.9   **Occupational exposure to unspecified risk factor**

● Z59   **Problems related to housing and economic circumstances**

   | Excludes2 | problems related to upbringing (Z62.-)

   ⑫Z59.0   **Homelessness**

   ⑫Z59.1   **Inadequate housing**
     Lack of heating
     Restriction of space
     Technical defects in home preventing adequate care
     Unsatisfactory surroundings

     | Excludes1 | problems related to the natural and physical environment (Z77.1-)

   ⑫Z59.2   **Discord with neighbors, lodgers and landlord**

   ⑫Z59.3   **Problems related to living in residential institution**
     Boarding-school resident

     | Excludes1 | institutional upbringing (Z62.2)

   ⑫Z59.4   **Lack of adequate food and safe drinking water**
     Inadequate drinking water supply

     | Excludes1 | effects of hunger (T73.0)
       inappropriate diet or eating habits (Z72.4)
       malnutrition (E40-E46)

   ⑫Z59.5   **Extreme poverty**

   ⑫Z59.6   **Low income**

   ⑫Z59.7   **Insufficient social insurance and welfare support**

   ⑫Z59.8   **Other problems related to housing and economic circumstances**
     Foreclosure on loan
     Isolated dwelling
     Problems with creditors

   ⑫■ Z59.9   **Problem related to housing and economic circumstances, unspecified**

● Z60   **Problems related to social environment**

   ⑫Z60.0   **Problems of adjustment to life-cycle transitions**
     Empty nest syndrome
     Phase of life problem
     Problem with adjustment to retirement [pension]

   ⑫Z60.2   **Problems related to living alone**

CHAPTER 21 (Z00-Z99)

● Unacceptable First-Listed Diagnosis   ● Use Additional Character(s)   ❶ First Listed   ⑫ First Listed or Secondary
🩺 Complication\Comorbidity   🩺 Major C\C   ❷ Secondary Only   ■ Unspecified   OGCR Official Guidelines for Coding and Reporting

| Excludes 1 | | Excludes 2 | Includes   Use additional   Code first   Code also

▣Z60.3　Acculturation difficulty
　　　　Problem with migration
　　　　Problem with social transplantation

▣Z60.4　Social exclusion and rejection
　　　　Exclusion and rejection on the basis of personal
　　　　　characteristics, such as unusual physical
　　　　　appearance, illness or behavior.
　　　　Excludes1　target of adverse discrimination such
　　　　　　　　　　as for racial or religious reasons
　　　　　　　　　　(Z60.5)

▣Z60.5　Target of (perceived) adverse discrimination and
　　　　persecution
　　　　Excludes1　social exclusion and rejection (Z60.4)

▣Z60.8　Other problems related to social environment

▣ ▢ Z60.9　Problem related to social environment, unspecified

● Z61　Problems related to negative life events in childhood
　　　　Excludes2　maltreatment syndromes (T74.-)

▣Z61.0　Loss of love relationship in childhood

▣Z61.1　Removal from home in childhood

▣Z61.2　Altered pattern of family relationships in
　　　　childhood

▣Z61.3　Events resulting in loss of self-esteem in childhood

▣Z61.7　Personal frightening experience in childhood

● Z61.8　Other negative life events in childhood

　　● Z61.81　Personal history of abuse in childhood
　　　　　　Excludes2　personal history of adult
　　　　　　　　　　　　abuse (Z91.41-)

　　▣Z61.810 Personal history of physical and
　　　　　　sexual abuse in childhood
　　　　　　Excludes1　current child
　　　　　　　　　　　　physical
　　　　　　　　　　　　abuse (T74.12,
　　　　　　　　　　　　T76.12)
　　　　　　　　　　　　current child
　　　　　　　　　　　　sexual abuse
　　　　　　　　　　　　(T74. 12,
　　　　　　　　　　　　T76.12)

　　▣Z61.811 Personal history of psychological
　　　　　　abuse in childhood
　　　　　　Excludes1　current child
　　　　　　　　　　　　psychological
　　　　　　　　　　　　abuse (T74.32,
　　　　　　　　　　　　T76.32)

　　▣Z61.812 Personal history of neglect in
　　　　　　childhood
　　　　　　Excludes1　current child
　　　　　　　　　　　　neglect
　　　　　　　　　　　　(T74.02,
　　　　　　　　　　　　T76.02)

　　▣ ▢ Z61.819 Personal history of unspecified
　　　　　　abuse in childhood
　　　　　　Excludes1　current child abuse
　　　　　　　　　　　　NOS (T74.92,
　　　　　　　　　　　　T76.92)

　　▣Z61.88　Other negative life events in childhood

▣ ▢ Z61.9　Negative life event in childhood, unspecified

● Z62　Problems related to upbringing
　　　　Current and past negative life events in childhood
　　　　Current and past problems of a child related to
　　　　　upbringing
　　　　Excludes2　maltreatment syndrome (T74.-)
　　　　　　　　　problems related to housing and economic
　　　　　　　　　　circumstances (Z59.-)

▣ Z62.0　Inadequate parental supervision and control

▣ Z62.1　Parental overprotection

● Z62.2　Upbringing away from parents
　　　　Excludes1　problems with boarding school
　　　　　　　　　　(Z59.3)

　　▣ Z62.21　Child in welfare custody
　　　　　　Child in care of non-parental family
　　　　　　　member
　　　　　　Child in foster care
　　　　　　Excludes2　problem for parent due to
　　　　　　　　　　　　child in welfare custody
　　　　　　　　　　　　(Z63.5)

　　▣ Z62.22　Institutional upbringing
　　　　　　Child living in orphanage or group home

　　▣ Z62.29　Other upbringing away from parents

▣ Z62.3　Hostility towards and scapegoating of child

▣ Z62.6　Inappropriate (excessive) parental pressure

● Z62.8　Other specified problems related to upbringing

　　● Z62.81　Personal history of abuse in childhood

　　　　▣ Z62.810　Personal history of physical and
　　　　　　　　sexual abuse in childhood
　　　　　　　　Excludes1　current child
　　　　　　　　　　　　　physical
　　　　　　　　　　　　　abuse (T74.12,
　　　　　　　　　　　　　T76.12)
　　　　　　　　　　　　　current child
　　　　　　　　　　　　　sexual abuse
　　　　　　　　　　　　　(T74. 12,
　　　　　　　　　　　　　T76.12)

　　　　▣ Z62.811　Personal history of psychological
　　　　　　　　abuse in childhood
　　　　　　　　Excludes1　current child
　　　　　　　　　　　　　psychological
　　　　　　　　　　　　　abuse (T74.32,
　　　　　　　　　　　　　T76.32)

　　　　▣ Z62.812　Personal history of neglect in
　　　　　　　　childhood
　　　　　　　　Excludes1　current child
　　　　　　　　　　　　　neglect
　　　　　　　　　　　　　(T74.02,
　　　　　　　　　　　　　T76.02)

　　　　▣ ▢ Z62.819　Personal history of unspecified
　　　　　　　　abuse in childhood
　　　　　　　　Excludes1　current child abuse
　　　　　　　　　　　　　NOS (T74.92,
　　　　　　　　　　　　　T76.92)

　　● Z62.82　Parent-child conflict
　　　　▣Z62.820　Parent-biological child conflict
　　　　　　　　Parent-child problem NOS

　　　　▣Z62.821　Parent-adopted child conflict

　　　　▣Z62.822　Parent-foster child conflict

　　● Z62.89　Other specified problems related to
　　　　　　upbringing
　　　　▣Z62.890　Parent-child estrangement NEC

　　　　▣Z62.891　Sibling rivalry

　　　　▣Z62.898　Other specified problems related
　　　　　　　　to upbringing

▣ ▢ Z62.9　Problem related to upbringing, unspecified

● Z63　Other problems related to primary support group,
　　　　including family circumstances
　　　　Excludes2　maltreatment syndrome (T74.-, T76)
　　　　　　　　　parent-child problems (Z62.-)
　　　　　　　　　problems related to negative life events in
　　　　　　　　　　childhood (Z62.-)
　　　　　　　　　problems related to upbringing (Z62.-)

● Unacceptable First-Listed Diagnosis　　　● Use Additional Character(s)　　❶ First Listed　　▣ First Listed or Secondary
🖾 Complication\Comorbidity　　　🖾 Major C\C　　❷ Secondary Only　　▢ Unspecified　　**OGCR** Official Guidelines for Coding and Reporting
Excludes 1　　Excludes 2　　Includes　　Use additional　　Code first　　Code also

1731

CHAPTER 21 (Z00-Z99)

●Z63.0　Problems in relationship with spouse or partner
　　Excludes1　counseling for spousal or partner abuse problems (Z69.1)
　　　　　　counseling related to sexual attitude, behavior, and orientation (Z70.-)

●Z63.1　Problems in relationship with in-laws

●Z63.3　Absence of family member
　　Excludes1　absence of family member due to disappearance and death (Z63.4)
　　　　　　absence of family member due to separation and divorce (Z63.5)

●Z63.31　Absence of family member due to military deployment
　　Individual or family affected by other family member being on military deployment
　　Excludes1　family disruption due to return of family member from military deployment (Z63.71)

●Z63.32　Other absence of family member

●Z63.4　Disappearance and death of family member
　　Assumed death of family member
　　Bereavement

●Z63.5　Disruption of family by separation and divorce
　　Marital estrangement

●Z63.6　Dependent relative needing care at home

●Z63.7　Other stressful life events affecting family and household

●Z63.71　Stress on family due to return of family member from military deployment
　　Individual or family affected by family member having returned from military deployment (current or past conflict)

●Z63.72　Alcoholism and drug addiction in family

●Z63.79　Other stressful life events affecting family and household
　　Anxiety (normal) about sick person in family
　　Health problems within family
　　Ill or disturbed family member
　　Isolated family

●Z63.8　Other specified problems related to primary support group
　　Family discord NOS
　　Family estrangement NOS
　　High expressed emotional level within family
　　Inadequate family support NOS
　　Inadequate or distorted communication within family

●Z63.9　Problem related to primary support group, unspecified
　　Relationship disorder NOS

●Z64　Problems related to certain psychosocial circumstances

●Z64.0　Problems related to unwanted pregnancy

●Z64.1　Problems related to multiparity

●Z64.4　Discord with counselors
　　Discord with probation officer
　　Discord with social worker

●Z65　Problems related to other psychosocial circumstances

●Z65.0　Conviction in civil and criminal proceedings without imprisonment

●Z65.1　Imprisonment and other incarceration

●Z65.2　Problems related to release from prison

●Z65.3　Problems related to other legal circumstances
　　Arrest
　　Child custody or support proceedings
　　Litigation
　　Prosecution

●Z65.4　Victim of crime and terrorism
　　Victim of torture

●Z65.5　Exposure to disaster, war and other hostilities
　　Excludes1　target of perceived discrimination or persecution (Z60.5)

●Z65.8　Other specified problems related to psychosocial circumstances

●Z65.9　Problem related to unspecified psychosocial circumstances

DO NOT RESUSCITATE STATUS (Z66)

❷ Z66　Do not resuscitate
　　Includes　DNR status

BLOOD TYPE (Z67)

●Z67　Blood type

●Z67.1　Type A blood
　　❷ Z67.10　Type A blood, Rh positive
　　❷ Z67.11　Type A blood, Rh negative

●Z67.2　Type B blood
　　❷ Z67.20　Type B blood, Rh positive
　　❷ Z67.21　Type B blood, Rh negative

●Z67.3　Type AB blood
　　❷ Z67.30　Type AB blood, Rh positive
　　❷ Z67.31　Type AB blood, Rh negative

●Z67.4　Type O blood
　　❷ Z67.40　Type O blood, Rh positive
　　❷ Z67.41　Type O blood, Rh negative

●Z67.9　Unspecified blood type
　　❷ Z67.90　Unspecified blood type, Rh positive
　　❷ Z67.91　Unspecified blood type, Rh negative

BODY MASS INDEX (BMI) (Z68)

●Z68　Body mass index (BMI)
　　Kilograms per meters squared
　　Note: BMI adult codes are for use for persons 21 years of age or older.
　　BMI pediatric codes are for use for persons 2-20 years of age. These percentiles are based on the growth charts published by the Centers for Disease Control and Prevention (CDC)

❷ Z68.1　Body mass index (BMI) 19 or less, adult

❷ Z68.2　Body mass index (BMI) 20-29, adult
　　❷ Z68.20　Body mass index (BMI) 20.0-20.9, adult
　　❷ Z68.21　Body mass index (BMI) 21.0-21.9, adult
　　❷ Z68.22　Body mass index (BMI) 22.0-22.9, adult
　　❷ Z68.23　Body mass index (BMI) 23.0-23.9, adult
　　❷ Z68.24　Body mass index (BMI) 24.0-24.9, adult
　　❷ Z68.25　Body mass index (BMI) 25.0-25.9, adult
　　❷ Z68.26　Body mass index (BMI) 26.0-26.9, adult
　　❷ Z68.27　Body mass index (BMI) 27.0-27.9, adult
　　❷ Z68.28　Body mass index (BMI) 28.0-28.9, adult
　　❷ Z68.29　Body mass index (BMI) 29.0-29.9, adult

● Unacceptable First-Listed Diagnosis　　● Use Additional Character(s)　　❶ First Listed　　⑫ First Listed or Secondary
🅒 Complication\Comorbidity　　🅜 Major C\C　　❷ Secondary Only　　■ Unspecified　　OGCR Official Guidelines for Coding and Reporting
Excludes 1　　Excludes 2　　Includes　　Use additional　　Code first　　Code also

● **Z68.3**   Body mass index (BMI) 30-39, adult
   ❷ Z68.30   Body mass index (BMI) 30.0-30.9, adult
   ❷ Z68.31   Body mass index (BMI) 31.0-31.9, adult
   ❷ Z68.32   Body mass index (BMI) 32.0-32.9, adult
   ❷ Z68.33   Body mass index (BMI) 33.0-33.9, adult
   ❷ Z68.34   Body mass index (BMI) 34.0-34.9, adult
   ❷ Z68.35   Body mass index (BMI) 35.0-35.9, adult
   ❷ Z68.36   Body mass index (BMI) 36.0-36.9, adult
   ❷ Z68.37   Body mass index (BMI) 37.0-37.9, adult
   ❷ Z68.38   Body mass index (BMI) 38.0-38.9, adult
   ❷ Z68.39   Body mass index (BMI) 39.0-39.9, adult

❷ **Z68.4**   Body mass index (BMI) 40 or greater, adult 🔒

● **Z68.5**   Body mass index (BMI) pediatric
   ❷ Z68.51   Body mass index (BMI) pediatric, less than 5th percentile for age
   ❷ Z68.52   Body mass index (BMI) pediatric, 5th percentile to less than 85th percentile for age
   ❷ Z68.53   Body mass index (BMI) pediatric, 85th percentile to less than 95th percentile for age
   ❷ Z68.54   Body mass index (BMI) pediatric, greater than or equal to 95th percentile for age

PERSONS ENCOUNTERING HEALTH SERVICES IN OTHER CIRCUMSTANCES (Z69-Z76)

● **Z69**   Encounter for mental health services for victim and perpetrator of abuse
   Counseling for victims and perpetrators of abuse

   ● **Z69.0**   Encounter for mental health services for child abuse problems

     ● **Z69.01**   Encounter for mental health services for parental child abuse

       ⑫ Z69.010 Encounter for mental health services for victim of parental child abuse

       ⑫ Z69.011 Encounter for mental health services for perpetrator of parental child abuse
         | Excludes1 | encounter for mental health services for non-parental child abuse (Z69.02-)

     ● **Z69.02**   Encounter for mental health services for non-parental child abuse

       ⑫ Z69.020 Encounter for mental health services for victim of non-parental child abuse

       ⑫ Z69.021 Encounter for mental health services for perpetrator of non-parental child abuse

   ● **Z69.1**   Encounter for mental health services for spousal or partner abuse problems

     ⑫ Z69.11   Encounter for mental health services for victim of spousal or partner abuse

     ⑫ Z69.12   Encounter for mental health services for perpetrator of spousal or partner abuse

   ● **Z69.8**   Encounter for mental health services for victim or perpetrator of other abuse

     ⑫ Z69.81   Encounter for mental health services for victim of other abuse
       Encounter for rape victim counseling

     ⑫ Z69.82   Encounter for mental health services for perpetrator of other abuse

● **Z70**   Counseling related to sexual attitude, behavior and orientation
   Encounter for mental health services for sexual attitude, behavior and orientation
   | Excludes2 | contraceptive or procreative counseling (Z30-Z31)

   ⑫ **Z70.0**   Counseling related to sexual attitude

   ⑫ **Z70.1**   Counseling related to patient's sexual behavior and orientation
     Patient concerned regarding impotence
     Patient concerned regarding non-responsiveness
     Patient concerned regarding promiscuity
     Patient concerned regarding sexual orientation

   ⑫ **Z70.2**   Counseling related to sexual behavior and orientation of third party
     Advice sought regarding sexual behavior and orientation of child
     Advice sought regarding sexual behavior and orientation of partner
     Advice sought regarding sexual behavior and orientation of spouse

   ⑫ **Z70.3**   Counseling related to combined concerns regarding sexual attitude, behavior and orientation

   ⑫ **Z70.8**   Other sex counseling
     Encounter for sex education

   ⑫ ▪ **Z70.9**   Sex counseling, unspecified

● **Z71**   Persons encountering health services for other counseling and medical advice, not elsewhere classified
   | Excludes2 | contraceptive or procreation counseling (Z30-Z31)
     sex counseling (Z70.-)

   ⑫ **Z71.0**   Person encountering health services to consult on behalf of another person
     Person encountering health services to seek advice or treatment for non-attending third party
     | Excludes2 | anxiety (normal) about sick person in family (Z63.7)
       expectant (adoptive) parent(s) pre-birth pediatrician visit (Z76.81)

   ⑫ **Z71.1**   Person with feared health complaint in whom no diagnosis is made
     Person encountering health services with feared condition which was not demonstrated
     Person encountering health services in which problem was normal state
     "Worried well"
     | Excludes1 | medical observation for suspected diseases and conditions proven not to exist (Z03.-)

   ⑫ **Z71.2**   Person consulting for explanation of examination or test findings

   ⑫ **Z71.3**   Dietary counseling and surveillance
     Use additional code for any associated underlying medical condition
     Use additional code to identify body mass index (BMI), if known (Z68.-)

   ● **Z71.4**   Alcohol abuse counseling and surveillance
     Use additional code for alcohol abuse or dependence (F10.-)

     ⑫ **Z71.41**   Alcohol abuse counseling and surveillance of alcoholic

     ⑫ **Z71.42**   Counseling for family member of alcoholic
       Counseling for significant other, partner, or friend of alcoholic

● Unacceptable First-Listed Diagnosis   ● Use Additional Character(s)   ❶ First Listed   ⑫ First Listed or Secondary
🔒 Complication\Comorbidity   🔒 Major C\C   ❷ Secondary Only   ▪ Unspecified   **OGCR** Official Guidelines for Coding and Reporting
| Excludes 1 | | Excludes 2 | Includes   Use additional   Code first   Code also

1733

Z71.5   Drug abuse counseling and surveillance

Use additional code for drug abuse or dependence (F11-F16, F18-F19)

Z71.51   Drug abuse counseling and surveillance of drug abuser

Z71.52   Counseling for family member of drug abuser

Counseling for significant other, partner, or friend of drug abuser

Z71.6   Tobacco abuse counseling

Use additional code for nicotine dependence (F17.-)

Z71.7   Human immunodeficiency virus [HIV] counseling

Z71.8   Other specified counseling

Excludes2   counseling for contraception (Z30.0-)
counseling for genetics (Z31.5)
counseling for procreative management (Z31.6-)

Z71.81   Spiritual or religious counseling

Z71.89   Other specified counseling

Z71.9   Counseling, unspecified

Encounter for medical advice NOS

Z72   Problems related to lifestyle

Excludes2   problems related to life-management difficulty (Z73.-)
problems related to socioeconomic and psychosocial circumstances (Z55-Z65)

Z72.0   Tobacco use

Tobacco use NOS

Excludes1   history of tobacco dependence (Z87.891)
nicotine dependence (F17.2-)
tobacco dependence (F17.2-)
tobacco use during pregnancy (O99.33-)

Z72.3   Lack of physical exercise

Z72.4   Inappropriate diet and eating habits

Excludes1   behavioral eating disorders of infancy or childhood (F98.2-F98.3)
eating disorders (F50.-)
lack of adequate food (Z59.4)
malnutrition and other nutritional deficiencies (E40-E64)

Z72.5   High risk sexual behavior

Promiscuity

Excludes1   paraphilias (F65)

Z72.51   High risk heterosexual behavior

Z72.52   High risk homosexual behavior

Z72.53   High risk bisexual behavior

Z72.6   Gambling and betting

Excludes1   compulsive or pathological gambling (F63.0)

Z72.8   Other problems related to lifestyle

Z72.81   Antisocial behavior

Excludes1   conduct disorders (F91.-)

Z72.810   Child and adolescent antisocial behavior

Antisocial behavior (child) (adolescent) without manifest psychiatric disorder
Delinquency NOS
Group delinquency
Offenses in the context of gang membership
Stealing in company with others
Truancy from school

Z72.811   Adult antisocial behavior

Adult antisocial behavior without manifest psychiatric disorder

Z72.82   Problems related to sleep

Z72.820   Sleep deprivation

Lack of adequate sleep

Excludes1   insomnia (G47.0-)

Z72.821   Inadequate sleep hygiene

Bad sleep habits
Irregular sleep habits
Unhealthy sleep wake schedule

Excludes1   insomnia (F51.0-, G47.0-)

Z72.89   Other problems related to lifestyle

Self-damaging behavior

Z72.9   Problem related to lifestyle, unspecified

Z73   Problems related to life management difficulty

Excludes2   problems related to socioeconomic and psychosocial circumstances (Z55-Z65)

Z73.0   Burn-out

Z73.1   Type A behavior pattern

Z73.2   Lack of relaxation and leisure

Z73.3   Stress, not elsewhere classified

Physical and mental strain NOS

Excludes1   stress related to employment or unemployment (Z56.-)

Z73.4   Inadequate social skills, not elsewhere classified

Z73.5   Social role conflict, not elsewhere classified

Z73.6   Limitation of activities due to disability

Excludes1   care-provider dependency (Z74.-)

Z73.8   Other problems related to life management difficulty

Z73.81   Behavioral insomnia of childhood

Z73.810   Behavioral insomnia of childhood, sleep-onset association type

Z73.811   Behavioral insomnia of childhood, limit setting type

Z73.812   Behavioral insomnia of childhood, combined type

Z73.819   Behavioral insomnia of childhood, unspecified type

Z73.82   Dual sensory impairment

Z73.89   Other problems related to life management difficulty

Z73.9   Problem related to life management difficulty, unspecified

● **Z74   Problems related to care provider dependency**

> **Excludes2**   dependence on enabling machines or
> devices NEC (Z99.-)

● **Z74.0   Reduced mobility**

🔢**Z74.01   Bed confinement status**
Bedridden

🔢**Z74.09   Other reduced mobility**
Chairridden
Reduced mobility NOS

> **Excludes2**   wheelchair dependence
> (Z99.3)

🔢**Z74.1   Need for assistance with personal care**

🔢**Z74.2   Need for assistance at home and no other
household member able to render care**

🔢**Z74.3   Need for continuous supervision**

🔢**Z74.8   Other problems related to care provider
dependency**

🔢 ▨ **Z74.9   Problem related to care provider dependency,
unspecified**

● **Z75   Problems related to medical facilities and other health
care**

🔢**Z75.0   Medical services not available in home**

> **Excludes1**   no other household member able to
> render care (Z74.2)

🔢**Z75.1   Person awaiting admission to adequate facility
elsewhere**

🔢**Z75.2   Other waiting period for investigation and
treatment**

🔢**Z75.3   Unavailability and inaccessibility of health care
facilities**

> **Excludes1**   bed unavailable (Z75.1)

🔢**Z75.4   Unavailability and inaccessibility of other helping
agencies**

🔢**Z75.5   Holiday relief care**

🔢**Z75.8   Other problems related to medical facilities and
other health care**

🔢 ▨ **Z75.9   Unspecified problem related to medical facilities
and other health care**

● **Z76   Persons encountering health services in other
circumstances**

🔢**Z76.0   Encounter for issue of repeat prescription**
Encounter for issue of repeat prescription for
appliance
Encounter for issue of repeat prescription for
medicaments
Encounter for issue of repeat prescription for
spectacles

> **Excludes2**   issue of medical certificate (Z02.7)
> repeat prescription for contraceptive
> (Z30.4-)

❶ **Z76.1   Encounter for health supervision and care of
foundling**

❶ **Z76.2   Encounter for health supervision and care of other
healthy infant and child**
Encounter for medical or nursing care or
supervision of healthy infant under
circumstances such as adverse socioeconomic
conditions at home
Encounter for medical or nursing care or
supervision of healthy infant under
circumstances such as awaiting foster or
adoptive placement
Encounter for medical or nursing care or
supervision of healthy infant under
circumstances such as maternal illness
Encounter for medical or nursing care or
supervision of healthy infant under
circumstances such as number of children at
home preventing or interfering with normal
care

🔢**Z76.3   Healthy person accompanying sick person**

🔢**Z76.4   Other boarder to healthcare facility**

> **Excludes1**   homelessness (Z59.0)

🔢**Z76.5   Malingerer [conscious simulation]**
Person feigning illness (with obvious motivation)

> **Excludes1**   factitious disorder (F68.1-)
> peregrinating patient (F68.1-)

● **Z76.8   Persons encountering health services in other
specified circumstances**

🔢**Z76.81   Expectant parent(s) prebirth pediatrician
visit**
Pre-adoption pediatrician visit for
adoptive parent(s)

🔢**Z76.82   Awaiting organ transplant status**
Patient waiting for organ availability

🔢**Z76.89   Persons encountering health services in
other specified circumstances**
Persons encountering health services
NOS

**PERSONS WITH POTENTIAL HEALTH HAZARDS RELATED TO FAMILY AND PERSONAL
HISTORY AND CERTAIN CONDITIONS INFLUENCING HEALTH STATUS (Z77-Z99)**

> Code also any follow-up examination (Z08-Z09)

● **Z77   Other contact with and (suspected) exposures hazardous
to health**

> **Includes**   contact with and (suspected) exposures to
> potential hazards to health

> **Excludes2**   contact with and (suspected) exposure to
> communicable diseases (Z20.-)
> exposure to (parental) (environmental)
> tobacco smoke in the perinatal period
> (P96.81)
> newborn (suspected to be) affected by
> noxious substances transmitted via
> placenta or breast milk (P04.-)
> occupational exposure to risk factors (Z57.-)
> toxic effects of substances chiefly
> nonmedicinal as to source (T51-T65)

● **Z77.0   Contact with and (suspected) exposure to
hazardous, chiefly nonmedicinal, chemicals**

● **Z77.01   Contact with and (suspected) exposure to
hazardous metals**

🔢**Z77.010   Contact with and (suspected)
exposure to arsenic**

🔢**Z77.011   Contact with and (suspected)
exposure to lead**

● Unacceptable First-Listed Diagnosis   ● Use Additional Character(s)   ❶ First Listed   🔢 First Listed or Secondary
�️ Complication\Comorbidity   �️ Major C\C   ❷ Secondary Only   ▨ Unspecified   **OGCR** Official Guidelines for Coding and Reporting   1735
[Excludes 1]   [Excludes 2]   Includes   Use additional   Code first   Code also

⑫Z77.018 Contact with and (suspected) exposure to other hazardous metals
Contact with and (suspected) exposure to chromium compounds
Contact with and (suspected) exposure to nickel dust

● Z77.02 Contact with and (suspected) exposure to hazardous aromatic compounds

⑫Z77.020 Contact with and (suspected) exposure to aromatic amines

⑫Z77.021 Contact with and (suspected) exposure to benzene

⑫Z77.028 Contact with and (suspected) exposure to other hazardous aromatic compounds
Aromatic dyes NOS
Polycyclic aromatic hydrocarbons

● Z77.09 Contact with and (suspected) exposure to other hazardous, chiefly nonmedicinal, chemicals

⑫Z77.090 Contact with and (suspected) exposure to asbestos

⑫Z77.098 Contact with and (suspected) exposure to other hazardous, chiefly nonmedicinal, chemicals
Dyes NOS

● Z77.1 Contact with and (suspected) exposure to environmental pollution and hazards in the physical environment

● Z77.11 Contact with and (suspected) exposure to environmental pollution

⑫Z77.110 Contact with and (suspected) exposure to air pollution

⑫Z77.111 Contact with and (suspected) exposure to water pollution

⑫Z77.112 Contact with and (suspected) exposure to soil pollution

⑫Z77.118 Contact with and (suspected) exposure to other environmental pollution

● Z77.12 Contact with and (suspected) exposure to hazards in the physical environment

⑫Z77.120 Contact with and (suspected) exposure to mold (toxic)

⑫Z77.121 Contact with and (suspected) exposure to harmful algae and algae toxins
Contact with and (suspected) exposure to (harmful) algae bloom NOS
Contact with and (suspected) exposure to blue-green algae bloom
Contact with and (suspected) exposure to brown tide
Contact with and (suspected) exposure to cyanobacteria bloom
Contact with and (suspected) exposure to Florida red tide
Contact with and (suspected) exposure to pfiesteria piscicida
Contact with and (suspected) exposure to red tide

⑫Z77.122 Contact with and (suspected) exposure to noise

⑫Z77.123 Contact with and (suspected) exposure to radon and other naturally occuring radiation

Excludes2 radiation exposure as the cause of a confirmed condition (W88-W90, X39.0-)
radiation sickness NOS (T66)

⑫Z77.128 Contact with and (suspected) exposure to other hazards in the physical environment

● Z77.2 Contact with and (suspected) exposure to other hazardous substances

⑫Z77.21 Contact with and (suspected) exposure to potentially hazardous body fluids

⑫Z77.22 Contact with and (suspected) exposure to environmental tobacco smoke (acute) (chronic)
Exposure to second hand tobacco smoke (acute) (chronic)
Passive smoking (acute) (chronic)

Excludes1 nicotine dependence (F17.-) tobacco use (Z72.0)

Excludes2 occupational exposure to environmental tobacco smoke (Z57.31)

⑫Z77.29 Contact with and (suspected) exposure to other hazardous substances

● Z77.9 Other contact with and (suspected) exposures hazardous to health

● Z78 Other specified health status

Excludes2 asymptomatic human immunodeficiency virus [HIV] infection status (Z21)
postprocedural status (Z93- Z99)
sex reassignment status (Z87.890)

⑫Z78.0 Asymptomatic menopausal state
Menopausal state NOS
Postmenopausal status NOS

Excludes2 symptomatic menopausal state (N95.1)

⑫Z78.9 Other specified health status

● Z79 Long term (current) drug therapy

Includes long term (current) drug use for prophylactic purposes

Code also any therapeutic drug level monitoring (Z51.81)

Excludes2 drug abuse and dependence (F11-F19)
drug use complicating pregnancy, childbirth, and the puerperium (O99.32-)

● Z79.0 Long term (current) use of anticoagulants and antithrombotics/antiplatelets

Excludes2 long term (current) use of aspirin (Z79.83)

⑫Z79.01 Long term (current) use of anticoagulants

⑫Z79.02 Long term (current) use of antithrombotics/antiplatelets

Z79.1 Long term (current) use of non-steroidal anti-inflammatories (NSAID)

Excludes2 long term (current) use of aspirin (Z79.82)

Z79.2 Long term (current) use of antibiotics

Z79.3 Long term (current) use of hormonal contraceptives
> Long term (current) use of birth control pill or patch

Z79.4 Long term (current) use of insulin

● **Z79.5 Long term (current) use of steroids**

    🔢**Z79.51 Long term (current) use of inhaled steroids**

    🔢**Z79.52 Long term (current) use of systemic steroids**

● **Z79.8 Other long term (current) drug therapy**

  ● **Z79.81 Long term (current) use of agents affecting estrogen receptors and estrogen levels**
> *Code first, if applicable:*
> malignant neoplasm of breast (C50.-)
> malignant neoplasm of prostate (C61)
>
> Use additional code, if applicable, to identify:
> estrogen receptor positive status (Z17.0)
> family history of breast cancer (Z80.3)
> genetic susceptibility to malignant neoplasm (cancer) (Z15.0-)
> personal history of breast cancer (Z85.3)
> personal history of prostate cancer (Z85.46)
> postmenopausal status (Z78.0)
>
> | Excludes1 | hormone replacement therapy (postmenopausal) (Z79.890) |

    🔢**Z79.810 Long term (current) use of selective estrogen receptor modulators (SERMs)**
> Long term (current) use of raloxifene (Evista)
> Long term (current) use of tamoxifen (Nolvadex)
> Long term (current) use of toremifene (Fareston)

    🔢**Z79.811 Long term (current) use of aromatase inhibitors**
> Long term (current) use of anastrozole (Arimidex)
> Long term (current) use of exemestane (Aromasin)
> Long term (current) use of letrozole (Femara)

    🔢**Z79.818 Long term (current) use of other agents affecting estrogen receptors and estrogen levels**
> Long term (current) use of estrogen receptor downregulators
> Long term (current) use of fulvestrant (Faslodex)
> Long term (current) use of gonadotropin-releasing hormone (GnRH) agonist
> Long term (current) use of goserelin acetate (Zoladex)
> Long term (current) use of leuprolide acetate (leuprorelin) (Lupron)
> Long term (current) use of megestrol acetate (Megace)

  🔢**Z79.82 Long term (current) use of aspirin**

  ● **Z79.89 Other long term (current) drug therapy**

    🔢**Z79.890 Hormone replacement therapy (postmenopausal)**

    🔢**Z79.891 Long term (current) use of opiate analgesic**
> Long term (current) use of methadone for pain management
>
> | Excludes1 | methadone use NOS (F11.2-) use of methadone for treatment of heroin addiction (F11.2-) |

    🔢**Z79.899 Other long term (current) drug therapy**

● **Z80 Family history of primary malignant neoplasm**

  🔢**Z80.0 Family history of malignant neoplasm of digestive organs**
> Conditions classifiable to C15-C26

  🔢**Z80.1 Family history of malignant neoplasm of trachea, bronchus and lung**
> Conditions classifiable to C33-C34

  🔢**Z80.2 Family history of malignant neoplasm of other respiratory and intrathoracic organs**
> Conditions classifiable to C30-C32, C37-C39

  🔢**Z80.3 Family history of malignant neoplasm of breast**
> Conditions classifiable to C50.-

  ● **Z80.4 Family history of malignant neoplasm of genital organs**
> Conditions classifiable to C51-C63

    🔢**Z80.41 Family history of malignant neoplasm of ovary**

    🔢**Z80.42 Family history of malignant neoplasm of prostate**

    🔢**Z80.43 Family history of malignant neoplasm of testis**

    🔢**Z80.49 Family history of malignant neoplasm of other genital organs**

  ● **Z80.5 Family history of malignant neoplasm of urinary tract**
> Conditions classifiable to C64-C68

    🔢**Z80.51 Family history of malignant neoplasm of kidney**

    🔢**Z80.52 Family history of malignant neoplasm of bladder**

    🔢**Z80.59 Family history of malignant neoplasm of other urinary tract organ**

  🔢**Z80.6 Family history of leukemia**
> Conditions classifiable to C91-C95

  🔢**Z80.7 Family history of other malignant neoplasms of lymphoid, hematopoietic and related tissues**
> Conditions classifiable to C81-C90, C96.-

  🔢**Z80.8 Family history of malignant neoplasm of other organs or systems**
> Conditions classifiable to C00-C14, C40-C49, C69-C79

  🔢 ■ **Z80.9 Family history of malignant neoplasm, unspecified**
> Conditions classifiable to C80.1

● **Z81 Family history of mental and behavioral disorders**

  🔢**Z81.0 Family history of mental retardation**
> Conditions classifiable to F70-F79

  🔢**Z81.1 Family history of alcohol abuse and dependence**
> Conditions classifiable to F10.-

  🔢**Z81.2 Family history of tobacco abuse and dependence**
> Conditions classifiable to F17.-

● Unacceptable First-Listed Diagnosis   ◆ Use Additional Character(s)   ❶ First Listed   🔢 First Listed or Secondary

🔗 Complication\Comorbidity   🔗 Major C\C   ❷ Secondary Only   ■ Unspecified   **OGCR** Official Guidelines for Coding and Reporting

| Excludes 1 | | Excludes 2 | | Includes | Use additional | Code first | Code also |

Z81.3 Family history of other psychoactive substance abuse and dependence
Conditions classifiable to F11-F16, F18-F19

Z81.4 Family history of other substance abuse and dependence
Conditions classifiable to F55

Z81.8 Family history of other mental and behavioral disorders
Conditions classifiable elsewhere in F01-F99

● **Z82 Family history of certain disabilities and chronic diseases (leading to disablement)**

Z82.0 Family history of epilepsy and other diseases of the nervous system
Conditions classifiable to G00-G99

Z82.1 Family history of blindness and visual loss
Conditions classifiable to H54.-

Z82.2 Family history of deafness and hearing loss
Conditions classifiable to H90-H91

Z82.3 Family history of stroke
Conditions classifiable to I60-I64

● **Z82.4 Family history of ischemic heart disease and other diseases of the circulatory system**
Conditions classifiable to I00-I52, I65-I99

Z82.41 Family history of sudden cardiac death

Z82.49 Family history of ischemic heart disease and other diseases of the circulatory system

Z82.5 Family history of asthma and other chronic lower respiratory diseases
Conditions classifiable to J40-J47

Excludes2 family history of other diseases of the respiratory system (Z83.6)

● **Z82.6 Family history of arthritis and other diseases of the musculoskeletal system and connective tissue**
Conditions classifiable to M00-M99

Z82.61 Family history of arthritis

Z82.62 Family history of osteoporosis

Z82.69 Family history of other diseases of the musculoskeletal system and connective tissue

● **Z82.7 Family history of congenital malformations, deformations and chromosomal abnormalities**
Conditions classifiable to Q00-Q99

Z82.71 Family history of polycystic kidney

Z82.79 Family history of other congenital malformations, deformations and chromosomal abnormalities

Z82.8 Family history of other disabilities and chronic diseases leading to disablement, not elsewhere classified

● **Z83 Family history of other specific disorders**

Excludes2 contact with and (suspected) exposure to communicable disease in the family (Z20.-)

Z83.0 Family history of human immunodeficiency virus [HIV] disease
Conditions classifiable to B20

Z83.1 Family history of other infectious and parasitic diseases
Conditions classifiable to A00-B19, B25-B94, B99

Z83.2 Family history of diseases of the blood and blood-forming organs and certain disorders involving the immune mechanism
Conditions classifiable to D50-D89

Z83.3 Family history of diabetes mellitus
Conditions classifiable to E09-E13

● **Z83.4 Family history of other endocrine, nutritional and metabolic diseases**
Conditions classifiable to E00-E07, E15-E90

Z83.41 Family history of multiple endocrine neoplasia [MEN] syndrome

Z83.49 Family history of other endocrine, nutritional and metabolic diseases

Z83.5 Family history of eye and ear disorders
Conditions classifiable to H00-H53, H55-H83, H92-H95

Excludes2 family history of blindness and visual loss (Z82.1)
family history of deafness and hearing loss (Z82.2)

Z83.6 Family history of other diseases of the respiratory system
Conditions classifiable to J00-J39, J60-J99

Excludes2 family history of asthma and other chronic lower respiratory diseases (Z82.5)

● **Z83.7 Family history of diseases of the digestive system**
Conditions classifiable to K00-K93

Z83.71 Family history of colonic polyps

Excludes1 family history of malignant neoplasm of digestive organs (Z80.0)

Z83.79 Family history of other diseases of the digestive system

● **Z84 Family history of other conditions**

Z84.0 Family history of diseases of the skin and subcutaneous tissue
Conditions classifiable to L00-L99

Z84.1 Family history of disorders of kidney and ureter
Conditions classifiable to N00-N29

Z84.2 Family history of other diseases of the genitourinary system
Conditions classifiable to N30-N99

Z84.3 Family history of consanguinity

● **Z84.8 Family history of other specified conditions**

Z84.81 Family history of carrier of genetic disease

Z84.89 Family history of other specified conditions

● **Z85 Personal history of malignant neoplasm**

Code first any follow-up examination after treatment of malignant neoplasm (Z08)

Use additional code to identify:
alcohol use and dependence (F10.0-)
exposure to environmental tobacco smoke (Z77.22)
history of tobacco use (Z87.891)
occupational exposure to environmental tobacco smoke (Z57.31)
tobacco dependence (F17.-)
tobacco use (Z72.0)

Excludes2 personal history of benign neoplasm (Z86.01-)
personal history of carcinoma-in-situ (Z86.00-)

● **Z85.0 Personal history of malignant neoplasm of digestive organs**

Z85.00 Personal history of malignant neoplasm of unspecified digestive organ

Z85.01 Personal history of malignant neoplasm of esophagus
Conditions classifiable to C15

● Unacceptable First-Listed Diagnosis   ● Use Additional Character(s)   ❶ First Listed   First Listed or Secondary
Complication\Comorbidity   Major C\C   ❷ Secondary Only   Unspecified   **OGCR** Official Guidelines for Coding and Reporting
Excludes 1   Excludes 2   Includes   Use additional   Code first   Code also

● **Z85.02　Personal history of malignant neoplasm of stomach**

　　🄥Z85.020　Personal history of malignant carcinoid tumor of stomach
　　　　　　　Conditions classifiable to C7a.092

　　🄥Z85.028　Personal history of other malignant neoplasm of stomach
　　　　　　　Conditions classifiable to C16

● **Z85.03　Personal history of malignant neoplasm of large intestine**

　　🄥Z85.030　Personal history of malignant carcinoid tumor of large intestine
　　　　　　　Conditions classifiable to C7a.022-C7a.025, C7a.029

　　🄥Z85.038　Personal history of other malignant neoplasm of large intestine
　　　　　　　Conditions classifiable to C18

● **Z85.04　Personal history of malignant neoplasm of rectum, rectosigmoid junction, and anus**

　　🄥Z85.040　Personal history of malignant carcinoid tumor of rectum
　　　　　　　Conditions classifiable to C7a.026

　　🄥Z85.048　Personal history of other malignant neoplasm of rectum, rectosigmoid junction, and anus
　　　　　　　Conditions classifiable to C19-C21

● **Z85.05　Personal history of malignant neoplasm of liver**
　　　　Conditions classifiable to C22

● **Z85.06　Personal history of malignant neoplasm of small intestine**

　　🄥Z85.060　Personal history of malignant carcinoid tumor of small intestine
　　　　　　　Conditions classifiable to C7a.01-

　　🄥Z85.068　Personal history of other malignant neoplasm of small intestine
　　　　　　　Conditions classifiable to C17

　🄥Z85.07　Personal history of malignant neoplasm of pancreas
　　　　Conditions classifiable to C25

● **Z85.09　Personal history of malignant neoplasm of other digestive organs**

● **Z85.1　Personal history of malignant neoplasm of trachea, bronchus and lung**

　● **Z85.11　Personal history of malignant neoplasm of bronchus and lung**

　　🄥Z85.110　Personal history of malignant carcinoid tumor of bronchus and lung
　　　　　　　Conditions classifiable to C7a.090

　　🄥Z85.118　Personal history of other malignant neoplasm of bronchus and lung
　　　　　　　Conditions classifiable to C34

　🄥Z85.12　Personal history of malignant neoplasm of trachea
　　　　Conditions classifiable to C33

● **Z85.2　Personal history of malignant neoplasm of other respiratory and intrathoracic organs**

　🄥🔲 Z85.20　Personal history of malignant neoplasm of unspecified respiratory organ

　　🄥Z85.21　Personal history of malignant neoplasm of larynx
　　　　　　Conditions classifiable to C32

　　🄥Z85.22　Personal history of malignant neoplasm of nasal cavities, middle ear, and accessory sinuses
　　　　　　Conditions classifiable to C30-C31

　● **Z85.23　Personal history of malignant neoplasm of thymus**

　　🄥Z85.230　Personal history of malignant carcinoid tumor of thymus
　　　　　　　Conditions classifiable to C7a.091

　　🄥Z85.238　Personal history of malignant neoplasm of thymus
　　　　　　　Conditions classifiable to C37

　　🄥Z85.29　Personal history of malignant neoplasm of other respiratory and intrathoracic organs

● **Z85.3　Personal history of malignant neoplasm of breast**
　　　　Conditions classifiable to C50.-

● **Z85.4　Personal history of malignant neoplasm of genital organs**
　　　　Conditions classifiable to C51-C63

　🄥🔲 Z85.40　Personal history of malignant neoplasm of unspecified female genital organ

　　🄥Z85.41　Personal history of malignant neoplasm of cervix uteri

　　🄥Z85.42　Personal history of malignant neoplasm of other parts of uterus

　　🄥Z85.43　Personal history of malignant neoplasm of ovary

　　🄥Z85.44　Personal history of malignant neoplasm of other female genital organs

　🄥🔲 Z85.45　Personal history of malignant neoplasm of unspecified male genital organ

　　🄥Z85.46　Personal history of malignant neoplasm of prostate

　　🄥Z85.47　Personal history of malignant neoplasm of testis

　　🄥Z85.48　Personal history of malignant neoplasm of epididymis

　　🄥Z85.49　Personal history of malignant neoplasm of other male genital organs

● **Z85.5　Personal history of malignant neoplasm of urinary tract**
　　　　Conditions classifiable to C64-C68

　🄥🔲 Z85.50　Personal history of malignant neoplasm of unspecified urinary tract organ

　　🄥Z85.51　Personal history of malignant neoplasm of bladder

　● **Z85.52　Personal history of malignant neoplasm of kidney**

　　　　┌──────────┐
　　　　│ Excludes1 │　personal history of malignant neoplasm of renal pelvis (Z85.53)
　　　　└──────────┘

　　🄥Z85.520　Personal history of malignant carcinoid tumor of kidney
　　　　　　　Conditions classifiable to C7a.093

　　🄥Z85.528　Personal history of other malignant neoplasm of kidney
　　　　　　　Conditions classifiable to C64

● Unacceptable First-Listed Diagnosis　　　🔲 Use Additional Character(s)　　❶ First Listed　　🄥 First Listed or Secondary

🗝 Complication\Comorbidity　　🗝 Major C\C　　❷ Secondary Only　　🔲 Unspecified　　OGCR Official Guidelines for Coding and Reporting

┌─────────┐　　┌─────────┐　　┌─────────┐
│Excludes 1│　│Excludes 2│　│ Includes │　Use additional　　Code first　　Code also
└─────────┘　　└─────────┘　　└─────────┘

1739

CHAPTER 21 (Z00-Z99)

⑫Z85.53   **Personal history of malignant neoplasm of renal pelvis**

⑫Z85.59   **Personal history of malignant neoplasm of other urinary tract organ**

⑫Z85.6   **Personal history of leukemia**
Conditions classifiable to C91-C95

> **Excludes1**   leukemia in remission C91.0-C95.9 with 5th character 1

● **Z85.7**   **Personal history of other malignant neoplasms of lymphoid, hematopoietic and related tissues**

⑫Z85.71   **Personal history of Hodgkin lymphoma**
Conditions classifiable to C81

⑫Z85.72   **Personal history of non-Hodgkin lymphomas**
Conditions classifiable to C82-C85

⑫Z85.79   **Personal history of other malignant neoplasms of lymphoid, hematopoietic and related tissues**
Conditions classifiable to C88-C90, C96

> **Excludes1**   multiple myeloma in remission (C90.01)
> plasma cell leukemia in remission (C90.11)
> plasmacytoma in remission (C90.21)

● **Z85.8**   **Personal history of malignant neoplasms of other organs and systems**
Conditions classifiable to C00-C14, C40-C49, C69-C79, C7a.098

● **Z85.81**   **Personal history of malignant neoplasm of lip, oral cavity, and pharynx**

⑫Z85.810   **Personal history of malignant neoplasm of tongue**

⑫Z85.818   **Personal history of malignant neoplasm of other sites of lip, oral cavity, and pharynx**

⑫■Z85.819   **Personal history of malignant neoplasm of unspecified site of lip, oral cavity, and pharynx**

● **Z85.82**   **Personal history of malignant neoplasm of skin**

⑫Z85.820   **Personal history of malignant melanoma of skin**
Conditions classifiable to C43

⑫●Z85.821   **Personal history of Merkel cell carcinoma**
Conditions classifiable to C4a

⑫●Z85.828   **Personal history of other malignant neoplasm of skin**
Conditions classifiable to C44

● **Z85.83**   **Personal history of malignant neoplasm of bone and soft tissue**

⑫●Z85.830   **Personal history of malignant neoplasm of bone**

⑫●Z85.831   **Personal history of malignant neoplasm of soft tissue**

> **Excludes2**   personal history of malignant neoplasm of skin (Z85.82-)

● **Z85.84**   **Personal history of malignant neoplasm of eye and nervous tissue**

⑫●Z85.840   **Personal history of malignant neoplasm of eye**

⑫●Z85.841   **Personal history of malignant neoplasm of brain**

⑫●Z85.848   **Personal history of malignant neoplasm of other parts of nervous tissue**

● **Z85.85**   **Personal history of malignant neoplasm of endocrine glands**

⑫●Z85.850   **Personal history of malignant neoplasm of thyroid**

⑫●Z85.858   **Personal history of malignant neoplasm of other endocrine glands**

⑫●Z85.89   **Personal history of malignant neoplasm of other organs and systems**

⑫■Z85.9   **Personal history of malignant neoplasm, unspecified**
Conditions classifiable to C7a.00, C80.1

● **Z86**   **Personal history of certain other diseases**
Code first any follow-up examination after treatment (Z09)

● **Z86.0**   **Personal history of in-situ and benign neoplasms and neoplasms of uncertain behavior**

> **Excludes2**   personal history of malignant neoplasms (Z85.-)

● **Z86.00**   **Personal history of in-situ neoplasm**

⑫Z86.000   **Personal history of in-situ neoplasm of breast**

⑫Z86.001   **Personal history of in-situ neoplasm of cervix uteri**

⑫Z86.008   **Personal history of in-situ neoplasm of other site**

● **Z86.01**   **Personal history of benign neoplasm**

⑫Z86.010   **Personal history of colonic polyps**

⑫Z86.011   **Personal history of benign neoplasm of the brain**

⑫Z86.012   **Personal history of benign carcinoid tumor**

⑫Z86.018   **Personal history of other benign neoplasm**

⑫Z86.03   **Personal history of neoplasm of uncertain behavior**

● **Z86.1**   **Personal history of infectious and parasitic diseases**
Conditions classifiable to A00-B89, B99

> **Excludes1**   personal history of infectious diseases specific to a body system sequelae of infectious and parasitic diseases (B90-B94)

⑫Z86.11   **Personal history of tuberculosis**

⑫Z86.12   **Personal history of poliomyelitis**

⑫Z86.13   **Personal history of malaria**

⑫Z86.19   **Personal history of other infectious and parasitic diseases**

⑫Z86.2   **Personal history of diseases of the blood and blood-forming organs and certain disorders involving the immune mechanism**
Conditions classifiable to D50-D89

● **Z86.3 Personal history of endocrine, nutritional and metabolic diseases**
Conditions classifiable to E00-E90

🄵🄻 **Z86.31 Personal history of diabetic foot ulcer**
> Excludes2   current diabetic foot ulcer (E09.640, E10.640, E11.640, E13.640)

🄵🄻 **Z86.39 Personal history of other endocrine, nutritional and metabolic disease**

● **Z86.6 Personal history of diseases of the nervous system and sense organs**
Conditions classifiable to G00-G99, H00-H95

🄵🄻 **Z86.61 Personal history of infections of the central nervous system**
Personal history of encephalitis
Personal history of meningitis

🄵🄻 **Z86.69 Personal history of other diseases of the nervous system and sense organs**

● **Z86.7 Personal history of diseases of the circulatory system**
Conditions classifiable to I00-I99
> Excludes2   old myocardial infarction (I25.2) postmyocardial infarction syndrome (I24.1)

🄵🄻 **Z86.71 Personal history of venous thrombosis and embolism**

🄵🄻 **Z86.72 Personal history of thrombophlebitis**

🄵🄻 **Z86.73 Personal history of transient ischemic attack (TIA), and cerebral infarction without residual deficits**
Personal history of prolonged reversible ischemic neurological deficit (PRIND)
Personal history of stroke NOS without residual deficits
> Excludes1   personal history of traumatic brain injury (Z87.820) sequelae of cerebrovascular disease (I69.-)

🄵🄻 **Z86.74 Personal history of sudden cardiac arrest**
Personal history of sudden cardiac death sucessfully resuscitated

🄵🄻 **Z86.79 Personal history of other diseases of the circulatory system**

● **Z87 Personal history of other diseases and conditions**
Code first any follow-up examination after treatment (Z09)

● **Z87.0 Personal history of diseases of the respiratory system**
Conditions classifiable to J00-J99

🄵🄻 **Z87.01 Personal history of pneumonia (recurrent)**

🄵🄻 **Z87.09 Personal history of other diseases of the respiratory system**

● **Z87.1 Personal history of diseases of the digestive system**
Conditions classifiable to K00-K93

🄵🄻 **Z87.11 Personal history of peptic ulcer disease**

🄵🄻 **Z87.19 Personal history of other diseases of the digestive system**

🄵🄻 **Z87.2 Personal history of diseases of the skin and subcutaneous tissue**
Conditions classifiable to L00-L99
> Excludes2   personal history of diabetic foot ulcer (Z86.31)

● **Z87.3 Personal history of diseases of the musculoskeletal system and connective tissue**
Conditions classifiable to M00-M99
> Excludes2   personal history of (healed) traumatic fracture (Z87.81)

●**Z87.31 Personal history of (healed) nontraumatic fracture**

🄵🄻 **Z87.310 Personal history of (healed) osteoporosis fracture**
Personal history of (healed) fragility fracture
Personal history of (healed) collapsed vertebra due to osteoporosis

🄵🄻 **Z87.311 Personal history of (healed) other pathological fracture**
Personal history of (healed) collapsed vertebra NOS
> Excludes2   personal history of osteoporosis fracture (Z87.310)

🄵🄻 **Z87.312 Personal history of (healed) stress fracture**
Personal history of (healed) fatigue fracture

🄵🄻 **Z87.39 Personal history of other diseases of the musculoskeletal system and connective tissue**

● **Z87.4 Personal history of diseases of the genitourinary system**
Conditions classifiable to N00-N99

🄵🄻 **Z87.41 Personal history of urinary (tract) infection(s)**

🄵🄻 **Z87.42 Personal history of nephrotic syndrome**

🄵🄻 **Z87.43 Personal history of urinary calculi**

🄵🄻 **Z87.44 Personal history of cervical dysplasia**
> Excludes1   personal history of malignant neoplasm of cervix uteri (Z85.41)

🄵🄻 **Z87.49 Personal history of other diseases of the genitourinary system**

● **Z87.5 Personal history of complications of pregnancy, childbirth and the puerperium**
Conditions classifiable to O00-O99
> Excludes2   habitual aborter (N96)

🄵🄻 **Z87.51 Personal history of pre-term labor**
> Excludes1   current pregnancy with history of pre-term labor (O09.21-)

🄵🄻 **Z87.59 Personal history of other complications of pregnancy, childbirth and the puerperium**
Personal history of trophoblastic disease

● **Z87.7 Personal history of congenital malformations and deformations**
Conditions classifiable to Q00-Q89 that have been repaired or corrected

🄵🄻 **Z87.71 Personal history of hypospadias**

🄵🄻 **Z87.79 Personal history of other congenital malformations and deformations**

● **Z87.8 Personal history of other specified conditions**
> Excludes2   personal history of self harm (Z91.5)

🄵🄻 **Z87.81 Personal history of (healed) traumatic fracture**
> Excludes2   personal history of (healed) nontraumatic fracture (Z87.31-)

● **Z87.82 Personal history of other (healed) physical injury and trauma**
> Conditions classifiable to S00-T98, except traumatic fractures

⑫ **Z87.820 Personal history of traumatic brain injury**
> | Excludes1 | personal history of transient ischemic attack (TIA), and cerebral infarction without residual deficits (Z86.73)

⑫ **Z87.828 Personal history of other (healed) physical injury and trauma**

⑫ **Z87.89 Personal history of other specified conditions**

● **Z88 Allergy status to drugs, medicaments and biological substances**
> | Excludes2 | allergy status, other than to drugs and biological substances (Z91.0-)

⑫ **Z88.0 Allergy status to penicillin**

⑫ **Z88.1 Allergy status to other antibiotic agents status**

⑫ **Z88.2 Allergy status to sulfonamides status**

⑫ **Z88.3 Allergy status to other anti-infective agents status**

⑫ **Z88.4 Allergy status to anesthetic agent status**

⑫ **Z88.5 Allergy status to narcotic agent status**

⑫ **Z88.6 Allergy status to analgesic agent status**

⑫ **Z88.7 Allergy status to serum and vaccine status**

⑫ **Z88.8 Allergy status to other drugs, medicaments and biological substances status**

⑫ ☐ **Z88.9 Allergy status to unspecified drugs, medicaments and biological substances status**

● **Z89 Acquired absence of limb**
> | Includes | amputation status
> postprocedural loss of limb
> post-traumatic loss of limb
> | Excludes1 | acquired deformities of limbs (M20-M21)
> congenital absence of limbs (Q71-Q73)

● **Z89.0 Acquired absence of thumb and other finger(s)**

● **Z89.01 Acquired absence of thumb**

⑫ **Z89.011 Acquired absence of right thumb**

⑫ **Z89.012 Acquired absence of left thumb**

⑫ ☐ **Z89.019 Acquired absence of unspecified thumb**

● **Z89.02 Acquired absence of other finger(s)**
> | Excludes2 | acquired absence of thumb (Z89.01-)

⑫ **Z89.021 Acquired absence of right finger(s)**

⑫ **Z89.022 Acquired absence of left finger(s)**

⑫ ☐ **Z89.029 Acquired absence of unspecified finger(s)**

● **Z89.1 Acquired absence of hand and wrist**

● **Z89.11 Acquired absence of hand**

⑫ **Z89.111 Acquired absence of right hand**

⑫ **Z89.112 Acquired absence of left hand**

⑫ ☐ **Z89.119 Acquired absence of unspecified hand**

● **Z89.12 Acquired absence of wrist**
> Disarticulation at wrist

⑫ **Z89.121 Acquired absence of right wrist**

⑫ **Z89.122 Acquired absence of left wrist**

⑫ ☐ **Z89.129 Acquired absence of unspecified wrist**

● **Z89.2 Acquired absence of upper limb above wrist**

● **Z89.20 Acquired absence of upper limb, unspecified level**

⑫ ☐ **Z89.201 Acquired absence of right upper limb, unspecified level**

⑫ ☐ **Z89.202 Acquired absence of left upper limb, unspecified level**

⑫ ☐ **Z89.209 Acquired absence of unspecified upper limb, unspecified level**
> Acquired absence of arm NOS

● **Z89.21 Acquired absence of upper limb below elbow**

⑫ **Z89.211 Acquired absence of right upper limb below elbow**

⑫ **Z89.212 Acquired absence of left upper limb below elbow**

⑫ ☐ **Z89.219 Acquired absence of unspecified upper limb below elbow**

● **Z89.22 Acquired absence of upper limb above elbow**
> Disarticulation at elbow

⑫ **Z89.221 Acquired absence of right upper limb above elbow**

⑫ **Z89.222 Acquired absence of left upper limb above elbow**

⑫ ☐ **Z89.229 Acquired absence of unspecified upper limb above elbow**

● **Z89.23 Acquired absence of shoulder**

⑫ **Z89.231 Acquired absence of right shoulder**

⑫ **Z89.232 Acquired absence of left shoulder**

⑫ ☐ **Z89.239 Acquired absence of unspecified shoulder**

● **Z89.4 Acquired absence of toe(s), foot, and ankle**

● **Z89.41 Acquired absence of great toe**

⑫ **Z89.411 Acquired absence of right great toe**

⑫ **Z89.412 Acquired absence of left great toe**

⑫ ☐ **Z89.419 Acquired absence of unspecified great toe**

● **Z89.42 Acquired absence of other toe(s)**
> | Excludes2 | acquired absence of great toe (Z89.41-)

⑫ **Z89.421 Acquired absence of other right toe(s)**

⑫ **Z89.422 Acquired absence of other left toe(s)**

⑫ ☐ **Z89.429 Acquired absence of other toe(s), unspecified side**

● **Z89.43 Acquired absence of foot**

⑫ **Z89.431 Acquired absence of right foot**

⑫ **Z89.432 Acquired absence of left foot**

⑫ ☐ **Z89.439 Acquired absence of unspecified foot**

1742

● Unacceptable First-Listed Diagnosis   ● Use Additional Character(s)   ❶ First Listed   ⑫ First Listed or Secondary

🔖 Complication\Comorbidity   🔖 Major C\C   ❷ Secondary Only   ☐ Unspecified   **OGCR** Official Guidelines for Coding and Reporting

| Excludes 1 | | Excludes 2 | | Includes | | Use additional | | Code first | | Code also |

● **Z89.44   Acquired absence of ankle**
     Disarticulation of ankle

     🔢 Z89.441   Acquired absence of right ankle

     🔢 Z89.442   Acquired absence of left ankle

     🔢 ■ Z89.449   Acquired absence of unspecified ankle

● **Z89.5   Acquired absence of leg below knee**

     🔢 ■ Z89.50   Acquired absence of leg knee, unspecified side

     🔢 Z89.51   Acquired absence of right leg below knee

     🔢 Z89.52   Acquired absence of left leg below knee

● **Z89.6   Acquired absence of leg above knee**

     ● **Z89.61   Acquired absence of leg above knee**
         Acquired absence of leg NOS
         Disarticulation at knee

         🔢 Z89.611   Acquired absence of right leg above knee

         🔢 Z89.612   Acquired absence of left leg above knee

         🔢 ■ Z89.619   Acquired absence of unspecified leg above knee

     ● **Z89.62   Acquired absence of hip**
         Disarticulation at hip

         🔢 Z89.621   Acquired absence of right hip

         🔢 Z89.622   Acquired absence of left hip

         🔢 ■ Z89.629   Acquired absence of unspecified hip

🔢 ■ **Z89.9   Acquired absence of limb, unspecified**

● **Z90   Acquired absence of organs, not elsewhere classified**

     Includes   postprocedural or post-traumatic loss of body part NEC

     Excludes1   congenital absence - see Alphabetical Index

     Excludes2   postprocedural absence of endocrine glands (E89.-)

     ● **Z90.0   Acquired absence of part of head and neck**

         🔢 Z90.01   Acquired absence of eye

         🔢 Z90.02   Acquired absence of larynx

         🔢 Z90.09   Acquired absence of other part of head and neck
             Acquired absence of nose

             Excludes2   teeth (K08.1)

     ● **Z90.1   Acquired absence of breast and nipple**

         🔢 Z90.10   Acquired absence of unspecified breast and nipple

         🔢 Z90.11   Acquired absence of right breast and nipple

         🔢 Z90.12   Acquired absence of left breast and nipple

         🔢 Z90.13   Acquired absence of bilateral breasts and nipples

     🔢 **Z90.2   Acquired absence of lung [part of]**

     🔢 **Z90.3   Acquired absence of stomach [part of]**

     🔢 **Z90.4   Acquired absence of other parts of digestive tract**

     🔢 **Z90.5   Acquired absence of kidney**

     🔢 **Z90.6   Acquired absence of other parts of urinary tract**
         Acquired absence of bladder

     ● **Z90.7   Acquired absence of genital organ(s)**

         Excludes1   personal history of sex reassignment (Z87.890)

         Excludes2   female genital mutilation status (N90.81-)

● **Z90.71   Acquired absence of cervix and uterus**

     🔢 Z90.710   Acquired absence of both cervix and uterus
         Acquired absence of uterus NOS
         Status post total hysterectomy

     🔢 Z90.711   Acquired absence of uterus with remaining cervical stump
         Status post partial hysterectomy with remaining cervical stump

     🔢 Z90.712   Acquired absence of cervix with remaining uterus

● **Z90.72   Acquired absence of ovaries**

     🔢 Z90.721   Acquired absence of ovaries, unilateral

     🔢 Z90.722   Acquired absence of ovaries, bilateral

🔢 **Z90.79   Acquired absence of other genital organ(s)**

● **Z90.8   Acquired absence of other organs**

     🔢 Z90.81   Acquired absence of spleen

     🔢 Z90.89   Acquired absence of other organs

● **Z91   Personal risk factors, not elsewhere classified**

     Excludes2   contact with and (suspected) exposures hazardous to health (Z77.-)
         exposure to pollution and other problems related to physical environment (Z77.1-)
         occupational exposure to risk factors (Z57.-)
         personal history of physical injury and trauma (Z87.81, Z87.82-)

● **Z91.0   Allergy status, other than to drugs and biological substances**

     Excludes2   allergy status to drugs, medicaments, and biological substances (Z88.-)

     ● **Z91.01   Food allergy status**

         Excludes2   food additives allergy status (Z91.02)

         🔢 Z91.010   Allergy to peanuts

         🔢 Z91.011   Allergy to milk products

             Excludes1   lactose intolerance (E73.-)

         🔢 Z91.012   Allergy to eggs

         🔢 Z91.013   Allergy to seafood
             Allergy to shellfish
             Allergy to octopus or squid ink

         🔢 Z91.018   Allergy to other foods
             Allergy to nuts other than peanuts

     🔢 **Z91.02   Food additives allergy status**

     ● **Z91.03   Insect allergy status**

         🔢 Z91.030   Bee allergy status

         🔢 Z91.038   Other insect allergy status

     ● **Z91.04   Nonmedicinal substance allergy status**

         🔢 Z91.040   Latex allergy status
             Latex sensitivity status

         🔢 Z91.041   Radiographic dye allergy status
             Allergy status to contrast media used for diagnostic x-ray procedure

         🔢 Z91.048   Other nonmedicinal substance allergy status

     🔢 **Z91.09   Other allergy status, other than to drugs and biological substances**

● Unacceptable First-Listed Diagnosis   ● Use Additional Character(s)   ❶ First Listed   🔢 First Listed or Secondary

🦠 Complication\Comorbidity   🦠 Major C\C   ❷ Secondary Only   ■ Unspecified   **OGCR** Official Guidelines for Coding and Reporting

Excludes 1   Excludes 2   Includes   Use additional   Code first   Code also

1743

CHAPTER 21 (Z00-Z99)

● Z91.1   Patient's noncompliance with medical treatment and regimen

❷ Z91.11   Patient's noncompliance with dietary regimen

● Z91.12   Patient's intentional underdosing of medication regimen

Code first underdosing of medication (T36-T50) with fifth or sixth character 6

| Excludes1 | adverse effect of prescribed drug taken as directed - code to adverse effect poisoning (overdose) - code to poisoning |

❷ Z91.120   Patient's intentional underdosing of medication regimen due to financial hardship

❷ Z91.128   Patient's intentional underdosing of medication regimen for other reason

● Z91.13   Patient's unintentional underdosing of medication regimen

Code first underdosing of medication (T36-T50) with fifth or sixth character 6

| Excludes1 | adverse effect of prescribed drug taken as directed - code to adverse effect poisoning (overdose) - code to poisoning |

❷ Z91.130   Patient's unintentional underdosing of medication regimen due to age-related debility

❷ Z91.138   Patient's unintentional underdosing of medication regimen for other reason

❷ Z91.14   Patient's other noncompliance with medication regimen
Patient's underdosing of medication NOS

⑫Z91.15   Patient's noncompliance with renal dialysis

❷ Z91.19   Patient's noncompliance with other medical treatment and regimen

● Z91.4   Personal history of psychological trauma, not elsewhere classified

● Z91.41   Personal history of adult abuse

| Excludes2 | personal history of abuse in childhood (Z62.81-) |

❷ Z91.410   Personal history of adult physical and sexual abuse

| Excludes1 | current adult physical abuse (T74.11, T76.11) current adult sexual abuse (T74. 21, T76.11) |

❷ Z91.411   Personal history of adult psychological abuse

❷ Z91.412   Personal history of adult neglect

| Excludes1 | current adult neglect (T74.01, T76.01) |

❷ ◼Z91.419   Personal history of unspecified adult abuse

❷ Z91.49   Other personal history of psychological trauma, not elsewhere classified

❷ Z91.5   Personal history of self-harm
Personal history of parasuicide
Personal history of self-poisoning
Personal history of suicide attempt

● Z91.8   Other specified personal risk factors, not elsewhere classified

❷ Z91.81   History of falling
At risk for falling

⑫Z91.82   Personal history of military deployment
Individual (civilian or military) with past history of military war, peacekeeping and humanitarian deployment (current or past conflict)
Returned from military deployment

❷ Z91.89   Other specified personal risk factors, not elsewhere classified

● Z92   Personal history of medical treatment

| Excludes2 | postprocedural states (Z98.-) |

❷ Z92.0   Personal history of contraception

| Excludes1 | counseling or management of current contraceptive practices (Z30.-) long term (current) use of contraception (Z79.3) presence of (intrauterine) contraceptive device (Z97.5) |

● Z92.2   Personal history of drug therapy

| Excludes2 | long term (current) drug therapy (Z79.-) |

⑫Z92.21   Personal history of antineoplastic chemotherapy

⑫Z92.22   Personal history of monoclonal drug therapy

⑫Z92.23   Personal history of estrogen therapy

● Z92.24   Personal history of steroid therapy

⑫Z92.240   Personal history of inhaled steroid therapy

⑫Z92.241   Personal history of systemic steroid therapy
Personal history of steroid therapy NOS

⑫Z92.25   Personal history of immunosupression therapy

| Excludes2 | personal history of steroid therapy (Z92.24) |

⑫Z92.29   Personal history of other drug therapy

❷ Z92.3   Personal history of irradiation
Personal history of exposure to therapeutic radiation

| Excludes1 | exposure to radiation in the physical environment (Z77.12) occupational exposure to radiation (Z57.1) |

● Z92.8   Personal history of other medical treatment

❷ Z92.81   Personal history of extracorporeal membrane oxygenation

⑫Z92.82   Status post administration of tPA (rtPA) in a different facility within the last 24 hours prior to admission to current facility

Code first condition requiring tPA administration, such as:
acute cerebral infarction (I63.-)
acute myocardial infarction (I21.-, I22.-)

● Unacceptable First-Listed Diagnosis   ● Use Additional Character(s)   ❶ First Listed   ⑫ First Listed or Secondary
🔖 Complication\Comorbidity   🔖 Major C\C   ❷ Secondary Only   ◼ Unspecified   **OGCR** Official Guidelines for Coding and Reporting

| Excludes 1 | | Excludes 2 | | Includes | | Use additional | | Code first | | Code also |

Ⅶ Z92.83 Personal history of failed moderate sedation
Personal history of failed conscious sedation

> **Excludes2**   failed moderate sedation during procedure (T88.52)

❷ Z92.89 Personal history of other medical treatment

● **Z93   Artificial opening status**

> **Excludes1**   artificial openings requiring attention or management (Z43.-)
> complications of external stoma (J95.0-, K91.4-, K91.7-, N99.5-)

❷ Z93.0 Tracheostomy status

❷ Z93.1 Gastrostomy status

❷ Z93.2 Ileostomy status

❷ Z93.3 Colostomy status

❷ Z93.4 Other artificial openings of gastrointestinal tract status

● **Z93.5 Cystostomy status**

   ❷ ▣ Z93.50 Unspecified cystostomy status

   ❷ Z93.51 Cutaneous-vesicostomy status

   ❷ Z93.52 Appendico-vesicostomy status

   ❷ Z93.59 Other cystostomy status

❷ Z93.6 Other artificial openings of urinary tract status
Nephrostomy status
Ureterostomy status
Urethrostomy status

❷ Z93.8 Other artificial opening status

❷ ▣ Z93.9 Artificial opening status, unspecified

● **Z94   Transplanted organ and tissue status**

> **Includes**   organ or tissue replaced by heterogenous or homogenous transplant

> **Excludes1**   complications of transplanted organ or tissue -
> see Alphabetical Index

> **Excludes2**   presence of vascular grafts (Z95.-)

❷ Z94.0 Kidney transplant status ✪

❷ Z94.1 Heart transplant status ✪

> **Excludes1**   artificial heart status (Z95.811)
> heart-valve replacement status (Z95.2-Z95.4)

❷ Z94.2 Lung transplant status ✪

❷ Z94.3 Heart and lungs transplant status ✪

❷ Z94.4 Liver transplant status ✪

❷ Z94.5 Skin transplant status
Autogenous skin transplant status

❷ Z94.6 Bone transplant status

❷ Z94.7 Corneal transplant status

● **Z94.8 Other transplanted organ and tissue status**

   ❷ Z94.81 Bone marrow transplant status ✪

   ❷ Z94.82 Intestine transplant status ✪

   ❷ Z94.83 Pancreas transplant status ✪

   ❷ Z94.84 Stem cells transplant status ✪

   ❷ Z94.89 Other transplanted organ and tissue status

❷ ▣ Z94.9 Transplanted organ and tissue status, unspecified

● **Z95   Presence of cardiac and vascular implants and grafts**

> **Excludes1**   complications of cardiac and vascular devices, implants and grafts (T82.-)

❷ Z95.0 Presence of cardiac pacemaker

> **Excludes1**   adjustment or management of cardiac pacemaker (Z45.0)

❷ Z95.1 Presence of aortocoronary bypass graft

❷ Z95.2 Presence of prosthetic heart valve
Presence of heart valve NOS

❷ Z95.3 Presence of xenogenic heart valve

❷ Z95.4 Presence of other heart-valve replacement

❷ Z95.5 Presence of coronary angioplasty implant and graft

> **Excludes1**   coronary angioplasty status without implant and graft (Z98.61)

● **Z95.8 Presence of other cardiac and vascular implants and grafts**

   ● **Z95.81 Presence of other cardiac implants and grafts**

    ❷ Z95.810 Presence of automatic (implantable) cardiac defibrillator

    ❷ Z95.811 Presence of heart assist device ✪

    ❷ Z95.812 Presence of fully implantable artificial heart

    ❷ Z95.818 Presence of other cardiac implants and grafts

   ● **Z95.82 Presence of other vascular implants and grafts**

    ❷ Z95.820 Peripheral vascular angioplasty status with implants and grafts

> **Excludes1**   peripheral vascular angioplasty without implant and graft (Z98.62)

    ❷ Z95.828 Presence of other vascular implants and grafts
Presence of intravascular prosthesis NEC

❷ ▣ Z95.9 Presence of cardiac and vascular implant and graft, unspecified

● **Z96   Presence of other functional implants**

> **Excludes1**   complications of internal prosthetic devices, implants and grafts (T82-T85)
> fitting and adjustment of prosthetic and other devices (Z44-Z46)

❷ Z96.0 Presence of urogenital implants

❷ Z96.1 Presence of intraocular lens
Presence of pseudophakia

● **Z96.2 Presence of otological and audiological implants**

   ❷ ▣ Z96.20 Presence of otological and audiological implant, unspecified

   ❷ Z96.21 Cochlear implant status

   ❷ Z96.22 Myringotomy tube(s) status

   ❷ Z96.29 Presence of other otological and audiological implants
Presence of bone-conduction hearing device
Presence of eustachian tube stent
Stapes replacement

❷ Z96.3 Presence of artificial larynx

● **Z96.4 Presence of endocrine implants**

   ❷ Z96.41 Presence of insulin pump (external) (internal)

   ❷ Z96.49 Presence of other endocrine implants

● Unacceptable First-Listed Diagnosis   ● Use Additional Character(s)   ❶ First Listed   Ⅶ First Listed or Secondary

✪ Complication\Comorbidity   ✪ Major C\C   ❷ Secondary Only   ▣ Unspecified   **OGCR** Official Guidelines for Coding and Reporting

| Excludes 1 | Excludes 2 | Includes | Use additional | Code first | Code also |

1745

CHAPTER 21 (Z00-Z99)

● **Z96.5**   Presence of tooth-root and mandibular implants

● **Z96.6**   Presence of orthopedic joint implants

   ❷ ▪ **Z96.60**   Presence of unspecified orthopedic joint implant

   ● **Z96.61**   Presence of artificial shoulder joint

     ❷ **Z96.611**   Presence of right artificial shoulder joint

     ❷ **Z96.612**   Presence of left artificial shoulder joint

     ❷ ▪**Z96.619**   Presence of unspecified artificial shoulder joint

   ● **Z96.62**   Presence of artificial elbow joint

     ❷ **Z96.621**   Presence of right artificial elbow joint

     ❷ **Z96.622**   Presence of left artificial elbow joint

     ❷ ▪**Z96.629**   Presence of unspecified artificial elbow joint

   ● **Z96.63**   Presence of artificial wrist joint

     ❷ **Z96.631**   Presence of right artificial wrist joint

     ❷ **Z96.632**   Presence of left artificial wrist joint

     ❷ ▪**Z96.639**   Presence of unspecified artificial wrist joint

   ● **Z96.64**   Presence of artificial hip joint

       Hip-joint replacement (partial) (total)

     ❷ **Z96.641**   Presence of right artificial hip joint

     ❷ **Z96.642**   Presence of left artificial hip joint

     ❷ **Z96.643**   Presence of artificial hip joint, bilateral

     ❷ ▪**Z96.649**   Presence of unspecified artificial hip joint

   ● **Z96.65**   Presence of artificial knee joint

     ❷ **Z96.651**   Presence of right artificial knee joint

     ❷ **Z96.652**   Presence of left artificial knee joint

     ❷ **Z96.653**   Presence of artificial knee joint, bilateral

     ❷ ▪**Z96.659**   Presence of unspecified artificial knee joint

   ● **Z96.66**   Presence of artificial ankle joint

     ❷ **Z96.661**   Presence of right artificial ankle joint

     ❷ **Z96.662**   Presence of left artificial ankle joint

     ❷ ▪**Z96.669**   Presence of unspecified artificial ankle joint

   ● **Z96.69**   Presence of other orthopedic joint implants

     ❷ **Z96.691**   Finger-joint replacement of right hand

     ❷ **Z96.692**   Finger-joint replacement of left hand

     ❷ **Z96.693**   Finger-joint replacement, bilateral

     ❷ **Z96.698**   Presence of other orthopedic joint implants

❷ **Z96.7**   Presence of other bone and tendon implants

       Presence of skull plate

● **Z96.8**   Presence of other specified functional implants

   ❷ **Z96.81**   Presence of artificial skin

   ❷ **Z96.89**   Presence of other specified functional implants

❷ ▪ **Z96.9**   Presence of functional implant, unspecified

● **Z97**   Presence of other devices

   | Excludes1 | complications of internal prosthetic devices, implants and grafts (T82-T85)

                 fitting and adjustment of prosthetic and other devices (Z44-Z46)

   | Excludes2 | presence of cerebrospinal fluid drainage device (Z98.2)

   ❷**Z97.0**   Presence of artificial eye

   ● **Z97.1**   Presence of artificial limb (complete) (partial)

     ❷ ▪ **Z97.10**   Presence of artificial limb (complete) (partial), unspecified

     ❷ **Z97.11**   Presence of artificial right arm (complete) (partial)

     ❷ **Z97.12**   Presence of artificial left arm (complete) (partial)

     ❷ **Z97.13**   Presence of artificial right leg (complete) (partial)

     ❷ **Z97.14**   Presence of artificial left leg (complete) (partial)

     ❷ **Z97.15**   Presence of artificial arms, bilateral (complete) (partial)

     ❷ **Z97.16**   Presence of artificial legs, bilateral (complete) (partial)

   ❷ **Z97.2**   Presence of dental prosthetic device (complete) (partial)

       Presence of dentures (complete) (partial)

   ❷ **Z97.3**   Presence of spectacles and contact lenses

   ❷ **Z97.4**   Presence of external hearing-aid

   ❷ **Z97.5**   Presence of (intrauterine) contraceptive device

     | Excludes1 | checking, reinsertion or removal of contraceptive device (Z30.44)

   ❷ **Z97.8**   Presence of other specified devices

● **Z98**   Other postprocedural states

   | Excludes2 | aftercare (Z43-Z49, Z51)

                 follow-up medical care (Z08-Z09)

                 postprocedural complication - see Alphabetical Index

   ❷ **Z98.0**   Intestinal bypass and anastomosis status

     | Excludes2 | bariatric surgery status (Z98.84)

                 gastric bypass status (Z98.84)

                 obesity surgery status (Z98.84)

   ❷ **Z98.1**   Arthrodesis status

   ❷ **Z98.2**   Presence of cerebrospinal fluid drainage device

       Presence of CSF shunt

● ❷ **Z98.3**   Post therapeutic collapse of lung status

       Code first underlying disease

● **Z98.4**   Cataract extraction status

       Use additional code to identify intraocular lens implant status (Z96.1)

     | Excludes1 | aphakia (H27.0)

● Unacceptable First-Listed Diagnosis   ● Use Additional Character(s)   ❶ First Listed   🔢 First Listed or Secondary

🅒 Complication\Comorbidity   🅜 Major C\C   ❷ Secondary Only   ▪ Unspecified   **OGCR** Official Guidelines for Coding and Reporting

| Excludes 1 | | Excludes 2 | Includes   Use additional   Code first   Code also

❷ **Z98.41**   Cataract extraction status, right eye

❷ **Z98.42**   Cataract extraction status, left eye

❷ ▪**Z98.49**   Cataract extraction status, unspecified eye

● **Z98.5**   Sterilization status

> **Excludes1**   female infertility (N97.-)
> male infertility (N46.-)

❷ **Z98.51**   Tubal ligation status

❷ **Z98.52**   Vasectomy status

● **Z98.6**   Angioplasty status

❷ **Z98.61**   Coronary angioplasty status

> **Excludes1**   coronary angioplasty status with implant and graft (Z95.5)

❷ **Z98.62**   Peripheral vascular angioplasty status

> **Excludes1**   peripheral vascular angioplasty status with implant and graft (Z95.820)

● **Z98.8**   Other specified postprocedural states

● **Z98.81**   Dental procedure status

❷ **Z98.810**   Dental sealant status

❷ **Z98.811**   Dental restoration status
Dental crown status
Dental fillings status

❷ **Z98.818**   Other dental procedure status

❷ **Z98.82**   Breast implant status

> **Excludes1**   breast implant removal status (Z98.86)

❷ **Z98.83**   Filtering (vitreous) bleb after glaucoma surgery status

> **Excludes1**   inflammation (infection) of postprocedural bleb (H59.4-)

❷ **Z98.84**   Bariatric surgery status
Gastric banding status
Gastric bypass status for obesity
Obesity surgery status

> **Excludes1**   bariatric surgery status complicating pregnancy, childbirth, or the puerperium (O99.84)

> **Excludes2**   intestinal bypass and anastomosis status (Z98.0)

❷ **Z98.85**   Transplanted organ removal status
Transplanted organ previously removed due to complication, failure, rejection or infection

> **Excludes1**   encounter for removal of transplanted organ -code to complication of transplanted organ (T86.-)

❷ **Z98.86**   Personal history of breast implant removal

● **Z98.87**   Personal history of in utero procedure

❷ **Z98.870**   Personal history of in utero procedure during pregnancy

> **Excludes2**   complications from in utero procedure for current pregnancy (O35.7)
> supervision of current pregnancy with history of in utero procedure during previous pregnancy (O09.82-)

❷ **Z98.871**   Personal history of in utero procedure while a fetus

❷ **Z98.89**   Other specified postprocedural states
Personal history of surgery, not elsewhere classified

● **Z99**   Dependence on enabling machines and devices, not elsewhere classified

> **Excludes1**   cardiac pacemaker status (Z95.0)

❷ **Z99.0**   Dependence on aspirator

● **Z99.1**   Dependence on respirator
Dependence on ventilator

❷ **Z99.11**   Dependence on respirator [ventilator] status 🅒

❶ **Z99.12**   Encounter for respirator [ventilator] dependence during power failure 🅒

> **Excludes1**   mechanical complication of respirator [ventilator] (J95.850)

❷ **Z99.2**   Dependence on renal dialysis
Hemodialysis status
Peritoneal dialysis status
Presence of arteriovenous shunt for dialysis
Renal dialysis status NOS

> **Excludes1**   encounter for fitting and adjustment of dialysis catheter (Z49.0-)
> noncompliance with renal dialysis (Z91.15)

❷ **Z99.3**   Dependence on wheelchair
Wheelchair confinement status

> *Code first cause of dependence, such as:*
> muscular dystrophy (G71.0)
> obesity (E66.-)

● **Z99.8**   Dependence on other enabling machines and devices

❷ **Z99.81**   Dependence on supplemental oxygen
Dependence on long-term oxygen

❷ **Z99.89**   Dependence on other enabling machines and devices
Dependence on machine or device NOS

● Unacceptable First-Listed Diagnosis   ● Use Additional Character(s)   ❶ First Listed   🄑 First Listed or Secondary
🅒 Complication\Comorbidity   🅜 Major C\C   ❷ Secondary Only   ▪ Unspecified   **OGCR** Official Guidelines for Coding and Reporting
Excludes 1   Excludes 2   Includes   Use additional   Code first   Code also   **1747**

CHAPTER 21 (Z00-Z99)

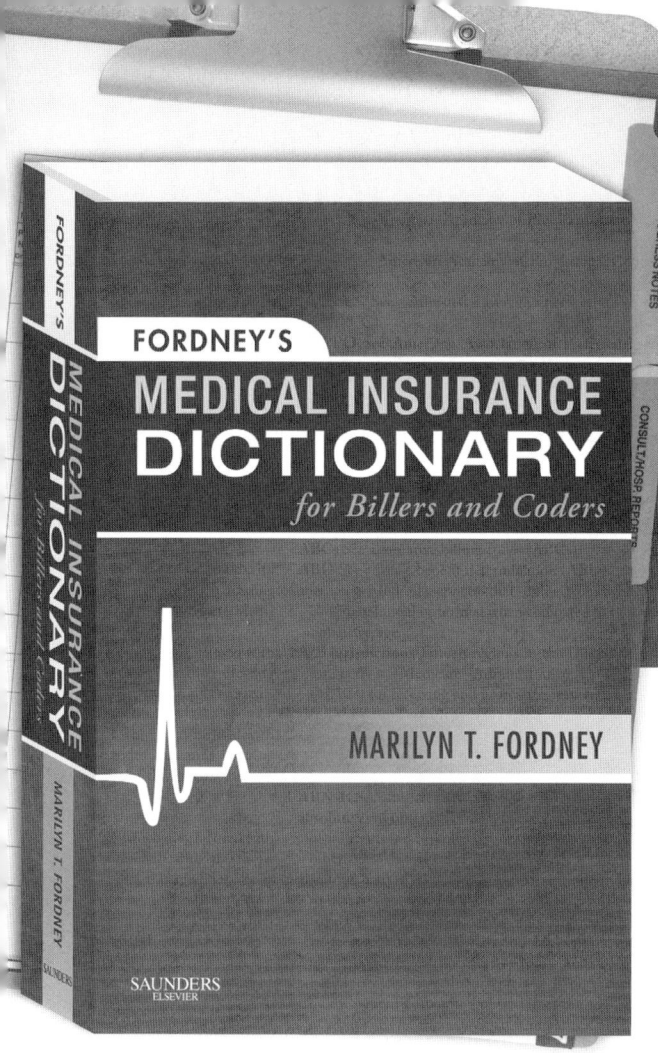

Trust Carol J. Buck and Elsevier for the

resources you need at *each step* of your coding career!

Track your progress toward complete coding success!

Step 1: Learn

- ☐ Step-by-Step Medical Coding 2010 Edition • ISBN: 978-1-4160-6836-5
- ☐ Workbook for Step-by-Step Medical Coding 2010 Edition • ISBN: 978-1-4377-0218-7
- ☐ Medical Coding Online for Step-by-Step Medical Coding 2010 • ISBN: 978-1-4377-0369-6
- ☐ Virtual Medical Office for Step-by-Step Medical Coding 2010 Edition • ISBN: 978-1-4377-1505-7

Step 2: Practice

- ☐ The Next Step: Advanced Medical Coding 2010 Edition • ISBN: 978-1-4377-0441-9
- ☐ Workbook for The Next Step: Advanced Medical Coding 2010 Edition • ISBN: 978-1-4377-0675-8
- ☐ Advanced Medical Coding Online for The Next Step 2010 Edition • ISBN: 978-1-4377-0442-6
- ☐ Online Internship for Medical Coding 2010 Edition • ISBN: 978-1-4377-0819-6

Step 3: Certify

- ☐ CPC® Coding Exam Review 2010: The Certification Step • ISBN: 978-1-4377-0817-2
- ☐ CCS Coding Exam Review 2010: The Certification Step • ISBN: 978-1-4377-0815-8
- ☐ The Extra Step: Facility-Based Coding Practice 2010 Edition • ISBN: 978-1-4377-1365-7
- ☐ The Extra Step: Physician-Based Coding Practice 2010 Edition • ISBN: 978-1-4377-0767-0

Step 4: Specialize

- ☐ Evaluation and Management Step: An Auditing Tool • ISBN: 978-1-4160-6724-5

Coding References

- ☐ 2010 ICD-9-CM for Physicians, Volumes 1 & 2, Professional Edition • ISBN: 978-1-4377-0208-8
- ☐ 2010 ICD-9-CM for Hospitals, Volumes 1, 2 & 3, Professional Edition • ISBN: 978-1-4377-0207-1
- ☐ 2010 ICD-9-CM for Physicians, Volumes 1 & 2, Standard Edition • ISBN: 978-1-4377-0748-9
- ☐ 2010 ICD-9-CM for Hospitals, Volumes 1, 2 & 3, Standard Edition • ISBN: 978-1-4377-0747-2
- ☐ 2010 ICD-9-CM for Physicians, Volumes 1 & 2, Professional Softcover Edition • ISBN: 978-1-4377-1434-0
- ☐ 2010 ICD-9-CM for Physicians, Volumes 1 & 2, Professional Compact Edition • ISBN: 978-1-4377-1433-3
- ☐ 2010 ICD-9-CM for Hospitals, Volumes 1, 2 & 3, Professional Compact Edition • ISBN: 978-1-4377-1432-6
- ☐ 2010 HCPCS Level II Professional Edition • ISBN: 978-1-4377-0211-8
- ☐ 2010 HCPCS Level II Standard Edition • ISBN: 978-1-4377-0818-9
- ☐ 2010 ICD-10-CM Standard Edition Draft Manual • ISBN: 978-1-4160-2567-2
- ☐ 2010 ICD-10-PCS Standard Edition Draft Manual • ISBN: 978-1-4160-6412-1

Author and
Educator
Carol J. Buck,
MS, CPC-I, CPC,
CPC-H, CCS-P

Get the next resources on your list today!

- Order securely at **www.elsevierhealth.com**
- Call toll-free **1-800-545-2522**
- Visit your local bookstore

ELSEVIER